’ アポストロフィ apostrophe

1 **短縮形で文字が省略された部分につける。**
I’m = I am / don’t = do not
wouldn’t = would not

2 **所有格を作るとき。**
my mother’s name (私の母
a girls’ school (女子校)

[ ] ブラケット bracket

引用 ... などを加えるときにつける。
... morrow [meaning today].”
... ことですが]それをする」と

“ ” ダブルクオーテーションマーク(二重引用符) double quotation marks

1 **人の発言などを引用するときにつける。**
He said, “I have to go home.”
(彼は「家に帰らなくちゃ」と言いました。)

2 **詩・短編小説・歌・記事などの題名に。**
The song they selected was “Bohemian Rhapsody” by Queen.
(彼らが選んだ歌はクイーンの『ボヘミアン・ラプソディ』でした。)

( ) 丸かっこ parentheses

文中で説明や省略可能な部分を補足するときにつける。
She decided to get the blue dress. (I also liked it a lot.) (彼女は青いドレスを買うことに決めました。(私もそれがとても気に入りました。))

... and/orの代わりに使う。
He talked to/with May in English.
(彼はメイと英語で話しました。)

2 **perの意味でつける。**
80 km/h (時速80キロメートル)

3 **年月日やインターネットのアドレスで。**
《米》5/3/2021, 《英》3/5/2021
(2021年5月3日)
https://www.gakken.co.jp/

— ダッシュ dash

1 **文中で説明や語句を挿入するときにつける。**
We have three tests today—science, Japanese(,) and math.
(今日は3つのテストがあります—理科と国語と数学です。)

2 **人名などが不明のときや明示を避けるときに。**
Mr. — was found guilty of murder.
(—氏は殺人で有罪判決を受けた。)

- ハイフン hyphen

1 **21から99までの数詞や複合語につける。**
twenty-one (21)
up-to-date information on Covid-19
(新型コロナウイルスの最新の情報)

2 **行末で単語が2行にまたがるときに，単語の音節の区切り目のあとに。**
..., but I didn’t find the book interesting at all. (…，しかし私はその本がまったくおもしろくなかった。)

大文字とイタリック体 capital letters and *italics*

1 **文，固有名詞，書名・題名などの最初の文字は大文字にする。**

2 **強調したい語句，外来語，書名・新聞名・小説名・学名などはイタリック体を使う。**
Over 100 years ago, Natsume Soseki wrote *Botchan*.
(100年以上前に，夏目漱石は『坊っちゃん』を書きました。)
I asked Dad to get me a new bike, and he *really* bought one last week.
(私は父に新しい自転車を買ってくれるように頼んだら，先週本当に買ってくれました。)

THE SUPER ANCHOR

JAPANESE-ENGLISH DICTIONARY

FOURTH EDITION

スーパー・アンカー和英辞典

編集主幹
明海大学名誉教授 応用言語学博士
山岸勝榮

Gakken

スーパー・アンカー
和英辞典

SA

THE SUPER
ANCHOR
JAPANESE-ENGLISH
DICTIONARY
FOURTH EDITION

ANCHORは「いかり」,
「頼みの綱」. ずっしり
重い信頼のマークです.

初版
2000年
第2版
2004年
第3版
2012年
第4版
2021年

本書は, 下記辞典を
ベースにした
全面改訂新版である.

ニュー・アンカー
和英辞典
初版
1991年

編集主幹
山岸勝榮(明海大学名誉教授・応用言語学博士)

編集委員
Edwin L. Carty
Eve N. Okawa

日本語監修
浅田秀子(日本語コスモス代表)

執筆者
山岸勝榮, Edwin L. Carty, 今井淳二
Evan Kirby, 大石五雄, 小林酉子, 塩沢 正, 杉浦正好
関根紳太郎, 高瀬 博, 多田裕吾, David A. Thayne
西出公之, 山崎千秋, Rie Kirby, 脇山 怜

執筆協力
田久保千之, Joseph R. Tabolt
浅田秀子, 浅見明博, 中山梅太郎
西田 稔, Nobu Yamada, 平野靖雄, 水沢敏寛

編集協力
今居美月, 内山典子, 上保匡代
英検出版㈱, ㈲エートゥーゼット, オプティマ企画編集室
小縣宏行, Kathryn A. Craft, 小森里美
佐藤美穂, Scott D. Silvey, 祖父江雅子
高山春花, 滝本信一, 田中裕子, Daniel Kern
David Telke, 長尾和夫, 中久喜泉, 濵田啓太
Peter MacMillan, Benjamin Marceau
森田桂子, 山口富美子, 吉岡光子
Rocky N. Bergen, 渡辺泰葉

編集部
小野史子, 阿部武志, 堀江朋子

デザイン
高橋コウイチ(WF)
イラスト
たむらかずみ
DTP協力
株式会社四国写研
組版・印刷
共同印刷株式会社

[第4版まえがき]

「自前の英語」(English of our own)を求めて

編集主幹　山岸勝榮

1970年(昭和45年)の春から数年間、私は某社の英語雑誌で、英文添削の助手を務めた。その時、当時発行されていた学習和英辞典の主だったものをつぶさに検討する機会に恵まれた。そして愕然とする日が続いた。はっきりと言えば、肝心なところで「役立たず」だと感じられることが頻繁だったのである。具体的に言えば、以下の諸点である。

見出し語と訳語の問題 —

[1] 多数の見出語について、訳語だけを羅列したものが多く、意味の違いが分からない。
例)公務員 a public employee, an official, a civil servant, a government employee、たぶん probably, likely, perhaps。

[2] 日本的な語彙の場合、その意味分析が不十分なものが多く、使いものにならない。
例)甘え、因縁、縁起、遠慮、親孝行、親不孝、恩、義理。

[3] 日本的な事物を表す語彙の訳出が不十分で、日本語とその訳語との間に相当なイメージの異なりが生じている。 例)一寸法師 a dwarf、うす a mortar、縁側 a veranda(h), a porch、押入れ a closet、おにぎり a rice ball。

[4] 訳語が英語文化の中に求められているために、日本語の実体を正しく伝えていない場合が多い。 例)おかず a side dish、神 God、先輩 a senior、後輩 a junior、名づけ親 a godparent, a godfather, a godmother。

[5] 見出語と訳語との間のスピーチレベルのズレが多い。 例)解雇とクビ、証拠とネタ、
とのっぽ、留置場と豚箱。

表示が旧態依然としていて、現実語法を反映していない。 例)ガソリン《米》gasoline,
《米》a can,《英》a tin、トラック《米》a truck,《英》a lorry、
iew mirror,《英》a driving mirror。

ある。

の時代的意識に後れを取っている。

going Dutch、風疹 German measles。

のズレが考慮されていない。 例)アイドル an idol、

alance。

例)いまいち、うんこ、おしっこ、かっこいい、

えないような訳語がきわめて多い。

cises、子煩悩 a doting father [mother]、

［11］　人称代名詞の場合、日本語と英語との間に慣用法上のズレがあることがほとんど無視されており、その結果、きわめて不自然な日本語文例が使用されている。例）彼≠he、彼女≠she、彼ら≠they、あなた［きみ／おまえ］≠you。

ℬ 用例について —

［1］　受験英語に見られるような、生硬で直訳調の用例、不自然な日本語がきわめて多い。
［2］　日本的な文例が少ない。例）いただきます、ごちそうさま、行ってきます、行って(い)らっしゃい、お帰り(なさい)、おかげさまで。
［3］　用例に登場する人名・地名・国名等には必要以上に英語国のものが多い。
［4］　非日本的な迷信・言い伝え・風習などに言及した用例が多く、和英辞典にもかかわらず日本的なものが少ない。例）はしごの下を歩くと悪いことがあるという迷信がある。
［5］　日常的に頻用される口語表現が極端に少ない。例）当たり！、危ない！、さすがぁ！、残念！、ショック！、そうこなくっちゃ！。

上記のような様々な問題点について、「私ならこのように解決する」、「このような処理の仕方をしたい」などと、具体的に考えながら、手元の学習和英辞典の余白や自作のノートにその解決法を書き留[illegible]ていった。また、某英語雑誌の特集として、「和英辞典を考える」といった題名の記事を数年に[illegible]公表した。それが、後日、本辞典の初版である『ニューアンカー和英辞典』（1991年）とし[illegible]の「本辞典のねらい」の最終頁に、私は、「これからの日本人に真に必要となる[illegible]《English of our own》である」と書いた。そして、その考え方は今に至[illegible]

詳細は同辞典のその「本辞典のねらい」に譲るが、そこに書い[illegible]が、その後、他社の学習和英辞典編纂にさまざまな影響を与え[illegible]なら、私が初めて指摘した上記の諸点が、その後のそうした[illegible]れてきているからである。『ニューアンカー和英辞典』[illegible]ないかといささか自負している。

その後も、「和英辞典とは何か」、「和英辞典はど[illegible]英辞典編纂論とその実践』（2001、こびあん書[illegible]和英辞典（Japanese-English dictionary fo[illegible]英語に直す際に必要となると思われる言語・[illegible]編纂された学習辞典である」と、学習和英辞[illegible]

さて、このたび、上掲書の具体的実践として、『スーパー・アンカー和英辞典』の第４版を世に問うことにした。本辞典は、「理想的な和英辞典」を求め続けてきた私の第３版以降の研究成果を紙面の許す限り盛り込んだものである。もちろん、これで満足というつもりはない。これからも「より望ましい和英辞典」を求めて、命のある限り、同様の努力を欠かさないつもりである。

本辞典の特長を述べておく。

[１] 基本的な特色は旧版をそのまま引き継いでいる（他辞典の真似をしないという方針も本辞典の特色の１つ）。

[２] 今回は第３版と比較して、情報量を大幅に増やし、結果的に48,000項目を収録できた。日常的な事柄を英訳するのに不自由はないはずである。

[３] 最近の語句を追加した。 例）歩きスマホ、オレオレ詐欺、オフ会、オワコン、コロナウィルス、終活、体幹、タッチパネル、テレワーク、バズる、リモート。

[４] 巻末付録「数・数式の英語表現」を新たに設けて、類書初ともいえる、数学の主な公式の英語での読み方を、まとめて示した。

学習和英辞典は良き学習国語辞典でありたい、言葉を愛する学習者を育てるのに役立つ辞典でありたい、自国と自国文化をよく知る学習者を育てるのに役立つ辞典でありたい、そうした想いで本辞典を編纂した。その際、私は本辞典の全ての頁に目を通し、自らが大量の用例・解説を書いた。もちろん、私一人で可能となったものではない。本辞典の完成に欠かせなかったのは、誰よりもEdwin. L. Carty氏と今井淳二氏（前々編集長）の二人の友人である。日本語と日本文化に通じたCarty氏のひた向きな献身がなければ、本辞典は実現しなかった。今井氏も退職後の全ての時間を本辞典のために費やしてくださった。阿部武志氏（前編集長）も同じく本辞典の改良のために多くの時間を費やしてくださった.

また、Joseph R. Tabolt氏には日英語の微妙な違いを多数ご指摘いただいた。また小野史子・編集長を初め、学研プラス・辞典編集室の諸氏には大変なご苦労をおかけし、ご配慮をいただいた。心から感謝の意を表する。

２０２１年（令和３年）１２月

この辞典の使い方

Ⅰ 見出語

収録語数 本辞典には日常生活で用いられる基本語を中心に新語や俗語，ＳＮＳや医学関係等の専門語も加え，約48,000項目を収録した.

重要語指示 全見出語を次の３段階に分類した.

①特別重要語……特に頻度の高いと考えられる重要語は２行見出しとし，赤で印刷した（約1,300語).

②準重要語……①に準じる語．１行見出しのまま，赤で印刷した.

③その他の一般語

配列 **1** 見出語の配列は五十音順とした.

同一のかなの中では，

①清音→濁音→半濁音の順

（例）**ハーフ** → **ハーブ** → **ハープ**

きかい 機会 → **きがい** 危害 → **ぎかい** 議会

②直音→促音→拗音の順

（例）**めつき** 目つき → **めっき**

きよう 器用な → **きょう** 今日

③独立語→接頭語→接尾語の順

（例）**こ** 子 → **こ-** 故- → **-こ** -個

④ひらがな→カタカナの順

（例）**てんぽ** 店舗 → **テンポ**

2 長音記号（ー）を含む見出語は，それぞれ「ア」行の音に置き換えた位置に配列した.

（例）**カード** →**カァド**

リード →**リィド**

フード →**フゥド**

デート →**デェト**

コード →**コォド**

3 読み方が同じになる語の場合は，別の見出語とし，左肩に1, 2, 3の小数字をつけて区別した．配列は原則として名詞を先にし，動詞や形容詞はその後にした.

（例）**1ちかい** 地階

2ちかい 誓い

3ちかい 近い

複合名詞 名詞の見出語に他の名詞が結合してできた複合名詞は，その見出語の末尾に‖をつけて置いた．ただし，複合名詞は本文中に例文として扱われているものも多いし，独立の別見出語として扱われているものも多数ある.

II 訳語

品詞 見出語そのものの訳語を出す場合は，そのまま対応する英語を出した．見出語の品詞と異なる訳語を出す場合は，原則として動詞ならば見出語のあとの漢字に「する」をつけ，形容詞ならば「な」や「の」をつけて示した．

(例) **かいがん** **海岸** a **beach**（浜辺，砂浜）; **the seashore**（水に接する陸地，岸辺）;

かいめい **解明する** **solve**+㊐; **clarify**+㊐（明らかにする）;

げんかく **厳格な** **strict**（好ましい意味で）;

さらに，派生的な訳語を示す場合は **一動** や **一形** **一副** を冠した．

なお，主に形容詞として用いるカタカナ語は見出語のすぐあとに，形容詞の英語を示した．

(例) **スマート** **slender**, **slim**（ほっそりした）

配列 訳語が2つ以上ある場合は，見出語の訳語としてより適当なもの，あるいは使用度の高いものから順に出した．2つ（または3つ）の訳語の意味・用法にあまり差がないときはコンマ（，）で区切った．意味または用法上の差がある場合は，セミコロン（；）で区切り，違いをカッコ内に示した．

発音記号 訳語のうち，読み方に注意を要する語や必要と思われる語にはそのあとに/ /で発音記号をつけた．‖で区切られたものは，前者が米音，後者が英音である．

(例) **ずつう** **頭痛** a **headache** /hédeɪk/

スケジュール a **schedule** /skédʒuːl ‖ ʃédjuːl/

解説 **語法** 意味・用法差などを（ ）では簡単に示せないような重要語については，解説のためのコラムを特別に設けて，詳しく説明した．主なコラムについては，p.［10］の索引を参照．

a と the 名詞の訳語の場合，数えられる名詞（可算名詞）には a または an をつけて示した．可算・不可算の両用法がある名詞については（a）または（an）のようにかっこに入れて示した．また，通例 the をつけて用いる名詞には，**the** ～の形で示した．

イタリック体 イタリック体で示した訳語は，原則として日本語をそのままローマ字化して訳語として採用したものである．完全に英語化した語や，*Oxford English Dictionary* など英米の大辞典に日本語起源の語として収録されている語は，英語とみなし，立体で示した．

(例) **てんぷら** **天麩羅** **tempura**（➤英語化している）

なっとう **納豆** ***natto***

結びつき 訳語に対して特定の結びつきを示す語（主に前置詞，副詞）は，訳語のあとに《 》で包んで示した．

(例) **ねらう** **狙う** **1**【射撃で】**aim**《at》,

目的語 通例目的語を必要とする動詞（他動詞）には，+㊐ をそのあとにつけた．

(例) **一動** **議論する** **discuss** +㊐

訳語メニュー 語義区分が多数にわたるような多義語については，検索の便を図るために，主な訳語とその語義番号をかこみにして示した．

（例）「**出る**」の項

> 📖 **訳語メニュー**
> **外へ出る** →go out of **1**
> **出発する** →leave **2**
> **卒業する** →graduate from **3**
> **到達する** →come to **4**
> **出席する** →be present at **5**
> **出演する** →appear **6**

つ づ り　訳語のつづりはアメリカ式を原則としたが，必要に応じて英米両方のつづりを併記した．なお，例文中では米つづりで統一した．

（例）**ライセンス** 《米》a **license**,《英》a **licence**

Ⅲ 用 例

配　　列　**1** 原則として句用例→文用例の順に配列した．訳語を出してある場合は，原則としてその訳語を使った句または文を優先的に出した．

2 用例が多数にわたる場合は，読みやすさを考え，適宜改行した．

3 1つの日本文に対して2つ以上の訳例が考えられる場合は／で区切って並べた．

文　　体　英訳上の文体は基本的には自然で平易な現代口語文を目ざしたが，特に留意したのは日本語と英語のスピーチレベルの一致である．すなわち，改まった日本語に対しては改まった英語を，くだけた日本語にはくだけた英語を与えるよう努めた．また，2文ある場合は，必要に応じて（➤後者のほうがよりインフォーマル）のような補注を加えた．

太字とイタリック体の対応　求める表現を検索しやすいように，日本文中の見出語相当部分を太字で示し，英文中の対応部分をイタリック体で示した．これはあくまで便宜であって，日本文の太字が動詞であっても，英文のイタリック体は名詞であるようなケースも多い．

文　　型　動詞を中心にした語句のきまった結びつきを，広く「文型」ととらえて，その基本となるものを【文型】として示した．

①S + Vは「主語 + 動詞」の文が続くことを表す．

② 一般動詞は do で代表させた．過去形は did とした．

（例）「**仮定**」の項

> 【文型】
> **～と仮定する**
> **suppose that** S + V
> **～と仮定すると**
> **if** S + V
> **supposing**［**suppose**］(**that**) S + V
> **解説** 事実と反する，あるいは，まず起こりえない仮定をいうときにはVは仮定法になる．

(例)「**必ず**」の項

> **【文型】**
> **人・物(A)が必ず…する**
> A **is certain to** do.
> A **is sure to** do.
> **I'm sure［certain］A will** do.
>
> **◀解説▶** sure が話し手の「希望」を含めた主観的な判断を暗示するのに対して，certain はより根拠のある客観的な判断を表すのに使われる．いちばん下は話者の確信であることをいう．

英訳する際の手順や考え方，また注意すべき点を「英訳のツボ」としてマークのあとに解説した．

✉ Eメールや文通などで使える例文を ✉ のマークをつけて提示した．

ことわざ 日本のことわざの前につけた．「１日１個のリンゴで医者いらず」のような英語国のことわざは（➤…）でその旨を記した．

Ⅳ　記　号

（ ）と［ ］　用例中における（ ）は，その部分が省略可能であることを示す．また［ ］は前の語（句）と置き換え可能であることを示す．

(例)「**言う**」の項

今，何か**言った**？ *Did* you *say* something (to me) just now?

➡ to me は省略して Did you say something just now? としてもよいことを示す．

「**委員会**」の項

彼女はいくつかの**委員会**の委員だ She is［serves］on several *committees.*（➤serveは堅い語）.

➡ She is on several committees. としても，She serves on several committees. としてもよいことを示す．

《米また》《英また》　《米また》は「米用法ではまた」の意で，前に出した訳語のほかに，アメリカではこの語も用いられる，の意である．《英また》も同様．

(例) **フライパン**　a **frying**［**fry**］**pan**，《米また》a **skillet**

➡ frying［fry］pan のほかに《米》では skillet も用いられる，の意．

かんづめ　a **can**，《英また》a **tin**

➡ can のほかに《英》では tin も用いられる，の意．

《参考》　ここでは主に，英語国の文化的背景に関する情報や，日英文化の違いなどについて記述した．

（➤ ）　語法上の注意や，英文のニュアンスなどを示す．

⇀　他項目参照．⇀のあとの見出語を引けばさらに詳しい情報が得られることを示す．

☛**不案内**（⇀見出語）　例えば「案内」の項の末尾に置かれた ☛**不案内** は，その語が独立した見出語として別にあることを示す．

コラム索引

「解説」と「語法」

タイトルのついた解説と語法をリストアップした．本文には，このほかにも多数の解説と語法が収録されている．

コラム索引

あなたの英語はどう響く？

日本人がつい何げなく使ってしまう表現がネイティブ・スピーカーには奇妙に響いたり，不自然な英語と受けとられたりすることがある．この種の表現をコラムとしてまとめたのが「あなたの英語はどう響く?」である．国際コミュニケーション時代の常識として覚えておこう．

(例)

あなたの英語はどう響く?
日本人はとかく「おもしろい」= interesting と考えて interesting を使い過ぎる傾向があるが，例えば「サーフィンはおもしろい」を Surfing is *interesting*. と訳すのは不自然. interesting は「(知的好奇心をかきたてるので)おもしろい」という意味だからである. Surfing is *a lot of fun*. ／Surfing is *enjoyable*. ／I *like to* surf. などのように言うのが適切.

(p.234)

コラム索引

日本紹介

コラム索引

～のいろいろ

アイスクリームや犬などの種類，また，園芸やスポーツなどに関連のある語をコラム「～のいろいろ」としてまとめた．

コラム索引

逆引き熟語

熟語を逆引きでまとめることで，語頭からの検索だけでは見えづらい日英の言葉比較ができる．語彙力や表現力を広げるのにも役立ててほしい．

ページ

ページ

コラム索引

直訳の落とし穴

日本語の発想で英訳した際に生じるミスを採り上げ，正用法を解説した

コラム索引

危ないカタカナ語

発音記号表

母音		子音	
記号	例	記号	例
/iː イー/	peel /piːl/	/p プ/	pot /pɑːt‖pɔt/
/i イ/	happy /hǽpi/	/b ブ/	bat /bæt/
/ɪ イ/	hit /hɪt/	/t ト, トゥ/	top /tɑːp‖tɔp/
/e エ/	egg /eg/	/ţ ト, トゥ/*	city /síţi/
/æ ア/	apple /ǽpəl/	/d ド, ドゥ/	door /dɔːʳ/
/æ ア‖ɑː アー/	ask /æsk‖ɑːsk/	/k ク/	kid /kɪd/
/ɑː アー/	father /fɑ́ːðəʳ/	/g グ/	go /goʊ/
/ɑː アー‖ɔ オ/	top /tɑːp‖tɔp/	/f フ/	fruit /fruːt/
/ɔː オー/	all /ɔːl/	/v ヴ/	very /véri/
/uː ウー/	rude /ruːd/	/θ ス/	thick /θɪk/
/u ウ/	actual /ǽktʃuəl/	/ð ズ/	that /ðæt/
/ʊ ウ/	put /pʊt/	/s ス/	sit /sɪt/
/ʌ ア/	cup /kʌp/	/z ズ/	zone /zoʊn/
/əːʳ アー/	bird /bəːʳd/	/ʃ シ/	shrine /ʃraɪn/
/əʳ ア/	over /óʊvəʳ/	/ʒ ジ/	measure /méʒəʳ/
/ə ア/	about /əbáʊt/	/h フ/	heart /hɑːʳt/
/ɑːʳ アー/	car /kɑːʳ/	/tʃ チ/	church /tʃəːʳtʃ/
/ɔːʳ オー/	store /stɔːʳ/	/dʒ ヂ/	jewel /dʒúːəl/
/eɪ エイ/	ache /eɪk/	/m ム, ン/	month /mʌnθ/
/aɪ アイ/	like /laɪk/	/n ヌ, ン/	nut /nʌt/
/ɔɪ オイ/	oil /ɔɪl/	/ŋ ング/	singer /síŋəʳ/
/aʊ アウ/	cow /kaʊ/	/l ル/	little /líţl/
/oʊ オウ/	most /moʊst/	/r ル/	rope /roʊp/
/ɪəʳ イア/	gear /gɪəʳ/	/w ウ/	way /weɪ/
/eəʳ エア/	care /keəʳ/	/j イ/	yes /jes/
/ʊəʳ ウア/	tour /tʊəʳ/	/*h*w (フ)ウ/	wheel /*h*wiːl/
		*《米》で/d/に似た音になる.	

あ

あ・ア

あ **Oh** ▶あ，そうだ *Oh*, yeah !‖あ，わかった *Oh*, I see.‖あ，流れ星だ！ *Look !* There goes a shooting star.‖あ，木村先生だ *Hey* [*Why*], here comes Mr. Kimura.‖あ，ごめん *Oops* [*Whoops*]! Sorry. (➤ oops /ʊps/, whoops /*h*wʊps/ は失敗などをしたときに言う). ⇀あっ.

[1]**ああ** **so, that**(そんなに)；**like that**(あのように) ▶彼のお母さんがああ若いとは思わなかった I never expected his mother to be *so* [*that*] young. (➤ この that は「そんなに」の意のインフォーマルな副詞)‖彼がああ(＝あのように)言っているんだからそれは本当だろう It is probably true since he says *so*.‖彼女はああ言っているが実現は無理だよ *Despite what* she *says*, it can't be done.‖学生はああでなくてはいけないね I'd like all students to be *like that*.／I wish all students were *like that*.‖あの博物館はああ見えても新しい *It may not look it*, *but* that museum is new. (➤「そうは見えないかもしれないが」の意).
▶《慣用表現》この子はいつもああ言えばこう言うだ He [She] *is* always *talking back*. (➤ talk back は「口答えする」)‖あまり他人のことについてああだこうだ言わないでほしい You should mind your own business. (➤「あなたの知ったことではない」の意)‖2人は長いことああでもないこうでもないと議論し合った The two guys discussed [argued about] *this or that* endlessly.

[2]**ああ** **1【感嘆】wow**(喜びを表す)；**ugh** /ʊx, ʌg, jʌx/(疲労・嫌悪などを表して) ▶ああ，うれしい *Wow*, I'm so happy !‖ああ，へとへとだ *Ugh*, I'm exhausted !‖ああ，さっぱりした I feel *so* refreshed !‖ああ，嫌だ嫌だ I'm (*really*) sick and tired of this.
2【応答】Sure ▶ **対話**「ちょっとこのかばん，見ていてくれる？」「ああ，いいよ」"Could you watch this bag for a while ?" "*Sure.*"‖**対話**「あす，お休みをいただいてもいいでしょうか」「ああ，いいよ」"Can I have a day off tomorrow ?" "*Sure.*／*No problem.*"
▶ああ，そうですか *Oh ?* Is that so ? (➤ Is that so ? のイントネーションを上げて驚きの気持ちを表すか，下げて相づちを打つ).
3【願望】▶ああ，いつまでも若かったらいいのになあ *I wish* I could stay young forever.
4【その他】▶ああ，思い出した *Now* I remember.‖ああ，やっぱり *Aha !* Just as I thought. (➤ 多少皮肉っぽい表現).

ああいう **like that**(あのような) ▶ああいう失礼なことを言っちゃいけない You shouldn't say impolite things *like that*.‖ああいう大人になってはいけない Don't become a grown-up *like him* [*her*].／Don't be *like him* [*her*] when you grow up.‖ああいうふうにのびのびと歌えたらなあ I wish I could sing effortlessly (and naturally) *like that*.

アーカイブ an **archive** ▶オンラインで検索可能なアーカイブ a searchable online *archive*‖映画や写真の電子化されたアーカイブを構築する create a digital *archive* of movies and photos.

アーカンソー **Arkansas** /ɑ́:ʳkənsɔ:/ (アメリカ中南部の州；略 AR, Ark.).

アーケード an **arcade** /ɑ:ʳkéɪd/
‖アーケード街 a shopping arcade [mall].

アース 《米》(a) **ground**,《英》(an) **earth**.

アーチ an **arch** ▶アーチ型の橋 an *arched* bridge‖その強打者は特大のアーチ(＝ホームラン)を放った The slugger blasted a powerful *home run* [*homer*].

アーチェリー **archery** ▶アーチェリーをする practice *archery*. ⇀弓道.

アーティスティックスイミング **artistic swimming** /ɑ:ʳtístɪk swímɪŋ/ (➤ 旧名はシンクロナイズドスイミング). ▶アーティスティックスイミングをする perform *artistic swimming*.

アーティスト an **artist**.

アート (an) **art**
‖アートワーク (an) artwork‖現代アート contemporary art.

アームチェア an **armchair**.

アーメン **Amen !** /èmén/ ▶アーメンと唱える say *amen*.

アーモンド an **almond** /ɑ́:mənd/.

アール an **are** /eəʳ/ (➤ 面積の単位).

あーん **1【大きく口を開ける様子】**▶歯医者は女の子に「ほら，あーんして」と言った The dentist said to the little girl, "Open (your mouth) wide. Say '*Ahh.*'" 《参考》イギリスでは医者が患者に "Open (your mouth) wide and say ninety-nine." と言うことがある. イギリス英語の発音では数字の99を発音するときに口が大きく開くからである.
2【子供が大口を開けて泣く様子】▶その迷子は母親の顔を見たとたんにアーンと泣き出した As soon as the lost child saw his [her] mother's face, he [she] *burst out crying*.

[1]**あい 愛** **love**(愛情)；**affection**(穏やかな情愛)
▶人類愛 *love for humanity*‖子供に対する母親の愛 *a mother's love* for her children‖生徒たちへの教師の愛 a teacher's *affection* for his [her] students‖真実の愛って何だろう What is *true love* ?‖いじめっ子は親の愛に飢えていることが多い Bullies are often hungry for *parental love*.‖2人の友情が愛に発展した Their friendship developed into *love*.‖愛さえあればほかには何もいらない *As long as there's love* (*between us*), we don't need anything else.‖彼らは強い愛で結び付いている They're bonded by (a) strong *love*.‖私はついに彼の愛を勝ち得た I *have* finally *won his heart*.
✉ **菜々子より愛を込めて** *Love*, Nanako ➤ (1) 結びの文句として，恋人・家族・親しい同性の友人への手紙の中で，特に女性が使う. With (much) love, とするとやや改まった感じになる. (2) 異性の親しい友人には Yours, Nanako とする.
☛ **愛する，愛情** (⇀見出語)

[2]**あい 藍** **indigo** /índɪgoʊ/ (染料)；**indigo (blue)**, **deep blue**(藍色).

あいあいがさ 相合い傘 ▶その若い2人は雨の中を相合い傘で歩いた The young couple walked together in the rain *under one umbrella*.

あいいれない 相容れない **incompatible**(両立しない) ▶資本主義と共産主義は相いれない概念だ Capitalism is *incompatible* with communism.‖彼の考えは時

あ

流とは相いれない His ideas *are out of step with* the times. (英語では「…と歩調を乱している」と考えて be out of step with を用いる).

アイウエア **eyewear**(➤ 眼鏡・サングラス・ゴーグルなど).

あいうえお **A-I-U-E-O** ▶あいうえお順では私の名前は最初に来る My name comes first *according to the order of the Japanese kana syllabary*. (➤ the Japanese *kana* syllabary は「日本語の50音図」).

アイエイチちょうりき IH 調理器 an **induction cooker**; 《米》an **induction range**, 《英》an **induction range cooker**(大型のもの) (➤ 《米》では an induction cooktop /kóktɑ:p/ ともいうが小型のものを指すこともある) 《参考》IH は induction heating (誘導加熱)の略だが英語では一般的ではない.

アイエムエフ the **IMF**(➤ International Monetary Fund (国際通貨基金)の略).

あいえんか 愛煙家 a **smoker**.

アイオーシー the **IOC** (➤ International Olympic Committee (国際オリンピック委員会)の略).

アイオワ **Iowa**(アメリカの州; 略 IA, Ia.).

あいかぎ 合鍵 a **duplicate** /djú:plɪkət/ **key**, a **spare key** (複製した鍵); a **master key**, a **passkey** (どの錠にも合う親鍵).

あいかた 相方 one's **partner** ▶漫才の相方 one's *partner* in manzai.

あいかわらず 相変わらず (as ...) as ever; as usual (いつものように)

【文型】
相変わらず…だ
as ... as ever
as ... as before
➤ …は形容詞・副詞

《解説》as ever は「ずっと変わらず」, as before は「以前と同じように」というニュアンス.

▶きみの姉さん, 相変わらず美人だね Your sister is (*as*) beautiful *as ever* [*before*]. ‖ 彼は相変わらず頑固だ He is (*as*) stubborn *as ever*.

▶この商品は相変わらず需要がある This product *continues* to be in (good) demand. ‖ 何だ, おまえ. 相変わらずの遅刻か Hey, I see you're late *as usual*! (日本語の「何だ, おまえ」につられて Hey, you とするのは英語では極めて乱暴に響くので, 英訳に反映させないほうがよい) ‖ 彼はまたカラオケかい? 相変わらずだなあ Is he going to karaoke again? *He never changes*. ‖ 対話「やあ, ポール. どうしてた?」「相変わらずだね. 君は?」"Hi, Paul! How (have) you been?" "*The same as usual*. / *Nothing new*. / *Same old* (*same old*). How (have) you been?" (➤ くだけた会話中では How have you been? の have が省略されることがある).

1**あいがん 哀願する** **beg** +目 (恥も外聞もなく); **plead with** (必死に) ▶彼は妻に別れないでくれと哀願した He *begged* [*pleaded with*] his wife not to leave him.

2**あいがん 愛玩**
‖愛玩犬 a pet dog ‖ 愛玩動物 a pet (animal).

あいきどう 合気道 **aikido**(➤ 英語化している) ▶合気道をする practice *aikido* ‖ 彼と合気道の試合をする have an *aikido* bout with him.

アイキュー (an) **IQ** /àɪkjú:/ ▶アイキューの高い生徒たち students with high *IQs*.

あいきょう 愛敬 **charm** ▶愛きょうのある娘 a *charming* [*lovable*] girl(➤ lovable は「愛すべき」) ‖ 彼女は忘年会で愛きょうを振りまいた At the year-end party, she did her best to *charm* everyone present. ‖ 猿は動物園の愛きょう者だ Monkeys are *popular animals* at the zoo.

あいきょうしん 愛郷心 **love of** [**for**] one's **hometown** ▶その県の出身者は愛郷心が強いといわれる People from that prefecture are said to have a strong *love* for it [a strong *attachment* to it]. (➤ attachment は「愛着」).

あいくるしい 愛くるしい **lovely**(抱き締めたくなるような); **cute** (かわいらしい) ▶愛くるしいつぶらな目をした赤ん坊 a baby with *lovely* round eyes ‖ 何て愛くるしい女の子なんだろう What a *cute* little girl!

あいけん 愛犬 one's (**pet**) **dog**
‖愛犬家 a dog lover.

1**あいこ** ▶A 高校とは 3 勝 3 敗か. これであいこだ We have 3 wins and 3 losses with A High. Now we're *even*. (➤ even は「貸し借りなしの, 五分五分の」の意の形容詞. tied としてもよい) ‖ じゃんけんぽん, あいこ(=引き分け)でしょ Rock-paper-scissors, go! (➤ あいこになった場合は, 繰り返して言う).

2**あいこ 愛顧** **patronage** /pǽtrənɪdʒ/
✉ 今後ともご愛顧のほどよろしくお願い申し上げます We hope you will honor us with your continuing *patronage*. (英語では「A (人)に B という栄誉を与える」と考えて honor A with B の形を用いる).

あいご 愛護 ▶動物愛護の精神 kindness to animals.
‖動物愛護協会 a humane society; the Japan Animal Welfare Society(日本の); the Society for the Prevention of Cruelty to Animals(英米の) ‖ 動物愛護週間 Animals Week ‖ 目の愛護デー a special day for eye care.

あいこう 愛好する **love** +目 ▶スポーツを愛好する *love* sports ‖ 音楽愛好家 a music *lover*.

あいこうしん 愛校心 **love of** [**for**] one's **school**, an **attachment for** [**to**] one's **school** 《参考》母校に対する卒業生の愛校心なら love for one's alma mater /ǽlmə mɑ́:tər/ という.

あいこく 愛国 ▶愛国的な演説 a *patriotic* speech.
‖愛国者 a patriot /péɪtriət/ ‖ 愛国心 patriotism, nationalism(➤ 後者はしばしば排他的な愛国心を指す); chauvinism /ʃóʊvənɪ̀zəm/ (極端な愛国心).

> 日↔英比較 第二次大戦後の日本では戦前・戦中の反動で, 「愛国的」「愛国者」などに過敏に反応しやすいが, 多民族から成るアメリカでは patriotic, patriot は国家を成り立たせるうえで必要なこととして積極的に受け止められている. America, love it or leave it. (アメリカを愛せ, さもなくば去れ)という表現まである.

あいことば 合い言葉 a **password**(味方どうしの); a **motto**(標語) ▶我々は「安全第一」を合いことばにしている "Safety first" is our *motto*.

アイコン an **icon** ▶ (パソコンの)アイコンをクリックする click on *an icon*.

アイコンタクト **eye contact** ▶打席に入りかけたジーターがイチローにアイコンタクトをとった Jeter *made eye contact* with Ichiro just before he stepped up to the plate.

あいさい 愛妻 one's (**loving** / **beloved**) **wife** (➤ loving は「愛情豊かな」, beloved は「いとしい」) ▶彼は愛妻家だ He *really loves* his *wife*. (英語ではこの例

のような訳し方がふつう. He is a loving husband. は堅い言い方で日常的ではない) ‖ 課長は毎日**愛妻弁当**を持って来る Every day, the section chief brings *a lunch* (*lovingly*) *made by* his *wife*.

あいさつ 挨拶 **1【会ったり別れたりするときの言動】** a **greeting**; **greetings** (挨拶のことば) **一動 挨拶する greet** +㊐ ▶**挨拶**を交わす exchange *greetings* ‖ 彼女はにっこり笑ってぼくに**挨拶**した She *greeted* me with a big smile. ‖ 今どきの若者の多くはきちんと**挨拶**もできない Many young people today can't even *greet* others properly. ‖ あの男は**挨拶**もせずに先に帰ってしまった That man left *without so much as saying goodbye*. ‖ 知っている人に会ったらちゃんと**挨拶をする**んですよ When you meet (the) people you know, be sure to *greet* them properly. ‖ お互いに忙しい身だから, **堅苦しい挨拶**は抜きでいきましょう Let's skip *the formalities*. We're both very busy people.

✉ **正月には親戚の家へ挨拶回りをします** During the New Year holidays, we pay visits to our relatives to *greet* them and wish them well.

日⇔英比較 日本人は病院・鉄道駅・空港などの待合室やエレベーターで見知らぬ人と一緒になった場合でも, 挨拶を交わすことはあまりない. これに対して, 英語圏では, そういう場合, Hello. とか Hi. などと声を出して挨拶するか, 最低でも目礼することが多い. これは多民族から成る英語圏の場合, 「私はあなたに敵意を持つ者ではありません」というメッセージに代わる社交的マナーの1つだからである. したがって, そういった場所で何も言わない日本人と居合わせた場合, 彼らはそこでの居心地の悪さを感じるであろう.

2【スピーチ】 an **address** /ədrés/; a **few words** (➤「二言三言」ではなく, 3分～5分程度の短い話で, お祝いや歓迎あるいは感謝などの「ことば」や「挨拶」に当たる) **一動 挨拶する give an address, say a few words** ▶開会[閉会]にあたって宇野氏が**挨拶した** Mr. Uno *gave an* opening [*a* closing] *address*. ‖ **ひと言歓迎のご挨拶**を申し上げます Allow me to say *a few words of welcome*. ‖ これより新婦のお母様が皆さまに**ご挨拶申し上げます** The mother of the bride will now *say a few words*.

3【返答・わび・礼など】 ▶大いに助けてやったのに彼からまだひと言の**挨拶**もない I helped him a lot, but I haven't heard [gotten] *a word of thanks* from him.

4【確認】 ▶アパートの部屋を改造するときは大家にひと言**挨拶**しておいたほうがいい You should (always) *check with* your landlord before doing any work on your apartment. (● 英語では「(大丈夫かと) A(人)に確かめる」と考えて, check with A の形を用いる).

‖**挨拶状** a greeting card (クリスマスなどの).

あいじ 愛児 one's (**beloved**) **child** ▶彼はがんでたった1人の**愛児**を失った He lost *his* (*beloved*) only *child* to cancer.

アイシーユー an **ICU** (intensive care unit の略).

1**あいしゃ 愛車** one's (**treasured**) **car** ▶彼は**愛車**を駆って横浜へ行った He drove *his car* to Yokohama. →**マイカー**.

2**あいしゃ 愛社** ▶日本企業の社員は一般に**愛社精神**に富む Generally speaking, Japanese corporate workers *are very loyal to their companies*.

‖**愛社精神** spirit of devotion to one's company.

アイシャドー eye shadow ▶まぶたにアイシャドーをつける apply *eye shadow* (to the eyelids).

あいしゅう 哀愁 melancholy /mélənkɑːli/ (もの悲しさ); **pathos** /péiθɑːs/ (哀感); **sadness** (寂しさ) ▶小樽は**哀愁**の漂う町だ Otaru is the kind of town that brings on feelings of *sadness*.

1**あいしょう 愛唱** ▶これは人々に**愛唱されている**古い民謡の1つです This is one of the old folk songs people *love to sing*. ‖ 社長の**愛唱歌**は『マイ・ウェイ』です "My Way" is one of the president's *favorite songs*.

2**あいしょう 相性 compatibility** ▶さいころで**相性占い**をする *foretell compatibility* with dice ‖ 彼女は新しい同僚と**相性がいい** She *gets along well with* her new co-worker. / She *hits it off* (*well*) *with* her new co-worker. (➤ 後者のほうがよりインフォーマルな言い方) ‖ 小田君を嫌うやつが多いけれど, ぼくは彼とは**相性がいい** Though a lot of guys don't like Oda, *there's good chemistry* between him and me. (➤ chemistry は愛情や友情の通い合いをいうインフォーマルな語;「化学反応」の意から) ‖ 2人は**相性が悪い**ということで離婚した They divorced each other on the grounds of *incompatibility*. (➤ incompatibility は「性格の不一致」) ‖ あのカップルは明らかに**相性がよくない** That couple is obviously *incompatible*.

3**あいしょう 愛称** a **pet name** (親しみを込めてつける名); a **nickname** (あだ名)
▶エリザベス女王の**愛称**はリリベットだ Queen Elizabeth II's *pet name* is "Lilibet." (➤ Elizabeth の伝統的な nicknames には "Betty" "Beth" "Liz" などがある. それに対して pet name は自由につけたかわいらしい名) ‖ JRの寝台特急列車はブルートレインの**愛称で親しまれた** JR's (overnight) express sleeper trains *were familiarly called* BLUE TRAINs. ‖ 「ボブ」はロバートの**愛称**だ 'Bob' is the *nickname* for Robert. →**あだ名**.

あいじょう 愛情 love; **affection** (穏やかな愛) ▶**愛情のこもった手紙** an *affectionate* letter ‖ 母の手紙にはいつも**愛情**があふれていた My mother's letters were always full of *love*. ‖ 2人の間に**愛情**が芽生えた *Affection* sprang up between the two.

あいじん 愛人 a **lover** (➤ 以前は男性を指すことが多かったが, 現在は女性にも用いる; しばしば性的関係があることを暗示する); a **love** (通例女性); a **mistress** (めかけ; 古風な語); **the other woman** (不倫の相手).

アイス ice; (an) **ice cream** (アイスクリーム).

あいず 合図 a **sign** /saɪn/ (身ぶりなどによる); a **signal** (光・音・手旗などによる) **一動 合図する signal** (+㊐), **make a sign** ▶うなずくことはふつう同意の**合図**である Nodding (of the head) is generally *a sign* of approval. ‖ **ピストルの合図**で競走が始まった *At the sound of the pistol*, the race began. ‖ 私たちの工場では始業のベルを**合図**に一斉に仕事を始めます At our factory, we start work all at the same time *at* the sound of the starting bell.

【文型】
人(A)に…せよと合図する
signal (**to**) A **to** do

▶彼はその娘に逃げろと**合図した** He *signaled* (*to*) the girl *to* escape.

アイスキャンデー 《米》 a **Popsicle** (➤ 商標名), 《英》 **ice(d) lolly.**

アイスクリーム (an) **ice cream**, 《英また》 an **ice**; an

ice cream cone (コーンつきの) ▶ 対話「アイスクリーム 2 つください」「何味になさいますか」「バニラにしてください」"Two *ice creams*, please." "What flavor ?" "Vanilla, please." (➤ flavor は「味」).

「アイスクリーム」のいろいろ アーモンド almond／小倉 ground red bean／ココナッツ coconut／ストロベリー strawberry／チョコレート chocolate／パイン pineapple／バニラ vanilla／パンプキン pumpkin／ピーチ peach／ブルーベリー blueberry／ペパーミント peppermint／マスカット muscat／抹茶 powdered green tea／マロン chestnut／メロン melon／モカ mocha／ヨーグルト yog(h)urt／ラムレーズン rum raisin／レモン lemon

‖アイスクリーム店 an ice cream parlor.

アイスコーヒー ice(d) coffee.

アイススケート ice skating 一動 アイススケートをする ice-skate, skate ▶河口湖にアイススケートに行った We *went skating* on Lake Kawaguchi. (➤ (×) to Lake Kawaguchi とはしない).

アイスティー ice(d) tea (➤ iced tea がふつう).

アイスバーン an icy slope.

あいすべき 愛すべき lovable (人好きのする, 愛きょうのある) ; agreeable (感じのよい) ▶彼は愛すべき男だ He is a *lovable* person. ／He is *lovable*.

アイスホッケー ice hockey, 《米》 hockey (➤ 《英》では単に hockey といえば陸上ホッケー(field hockey)を指す).

アイスランド Iceland.

あいする 愛する love +目 ; fall in love 《with》 (好きになる) ▶人を愛する *love* a person ‖ 自分の国を愛する *love* one's country ‖ 平和を愛する人々 *peace-loving* people ‖ 愛する人 a *loved* one ‖ 彼は愛する息子を亡くした He lost his *beloved* son. ‖ 私は日本を深く愛している I *have a* deep *love for* Japan. ／I *am* deeply *attached to* Japan. ‖ 大石先生は母親のように生徒たちを愛した Miss Oishi *loved* her students as if they were her own children [*had* a mother's *affection for* her students]. (➤ affection は「穏やかで持続的な愛情」) ‖ ミッキー・マウスは子供たちみんなに愛されている Mickey Mouse *is loved* by all children. ‖ 若い2人はすぐに愛し合うようになった The young couple soon *fell in love with each other*. ‖ 弘子とたけしは愛し合っている Hiroko and Takeshi *love each other* [*are in love*]. ‖ 対話「私のこと, 愛してる?」「うん, 愛してるよ」"Do you *love* me ?" "Yes, I do."

✉ あなたを心から愛しています I *love* you with all my heart. (● love は「状態」を表す動詞なので進行形にはならない).

☛ 愛すべき (→見出語)

あいせき 相席 ▶相席させていただいてよろしいですか May I *share your table* ? (➤ share は「…を共同で使う」) ‖ 対話 《レストランで》「ご相席になりますがよろしいでしょうか」「結構です」"Would you mind *sharing a table* ?" "No, not at all."

アイゼン (a pair of) crampons (雪山を登降する際に靴底に取り付ける, 滑り止めのための金具).

あいそ(う) 愛想 ▶愛想のない人 an *unsociable* [an *unfriendly*／a *reserved*] person (➤ unsociable は「非社交的な」, unfriendly は「気さくでない」, reserved は「内気な, 打ち解けない」) ‖ あの娘は誰にでも愛想がいい That girl *is friendly* with everyone. ‖ 老人は愛想よく質問に答えてくれた The old man answered my question *amiably*.

▶ 《慣用表現》 きみにはほとほと愛想が尽きたよ I *am* completely *fed up with* you. ‖ 彼女は夫のあまりの嫉妬深さに愛想を尽かして出ていった She *became sick and tired of* her husband's excessive jealousy and finally walked out on him. ‖ 店員はもみ手をしながら愛想笑いを浮かべた The salesclerk gave *a phony smile* and rubbed his hands together. (➤ phony は「偽りの」).

☛ お愛想, 無愛想 (→見出語)

あいぞう 愛憎 love and hate.

あいた 開いた・空いた **1** 【ひらいている】 open ▶開いた窓からその家に忍び込む sneak into the house through an *open* window ‖ 窓は開いたままだった The windows *were still open*. (➤ 閉めてあるはずが開いたままの場合. 意図的に開けてある場合は were left open となる).

2 【ふさがっていない】 vacant (席が) ; free (時間が) ▶前列に空いた席が3つある There are three *vacant* [*unoccupied*] seats in the front row. ‖ 空いた時間にはどんなことをしますか How do you spend your *free time* ?

あいだ 間

訳語メニュー
- 時・場所の間 →between **1, 2**
- 期間 →during, for **1**
- …している間 →while **1**
- …まで(の間) →until **1**
- 関係 →between, among **3**

1 【時間】 between ; during ; for, throughout

語法 「…の間」と「…の間に」の表し方

(1)「A の間ずっと」の意味では **throughout** A, **all through** A を用いる. A が a month や two weeks など具体的な長さを表す語のときには **for** A という.
(2) **the whole** A のような言い方もある.
(3)「A(期間)にわたって」と全体に及ぶ意識では **over** A を用いる.
(4)「…している間」のように文が続くときは **while** を用いる.
(5)「A の間に」と期間中の一部を指すときには **during** A を用いる.「A から B の間に」は **between** A **and** B とする.

▶夜の間に雨が降った It rained *during the night*. (➤「夜じゅう」は throughout [all through] the night, または the whole night) ‖ 彼女から何か月もの間 [長い間] 便りがない She hasn't written me *for months* [*for a long time*] now. ‖ ここ半年の間に弟はとても背が高くなった My younger brother has grown quite tall *over* the last six months. ‖ 勉強をしている間はラジオを切っておきなさい Keep the radio off *while* (you're) studying. ‖ 大阪に着くまでの間, ずっとその本を読み続けた I continued reading the book *until* I got to Osaka. (➤ until は「…までずっと」) ‖ 彼は順番を待つ間携帯で電話をしていた He talked on his cellphone *while* waiting (for) his turn. ‖ 夏休みの間に北海道を旅行するつもりです I'm planning to take a trip to Hokkaido *during* (the) summer vacation. ‖ きょうの午後2時半から3時までの間に私の事務所に来てください Come to see me at my office *between* 2 : 30 and 3 : 00 p.m.

this afternoon.

2【場所】**between** ▶ここからそこへ行く間にとても静かな自然教育園があります There is a very quiet nature study park *between* here and there. ‖ 四つ葉のクローバーが中学時代の教科書の間に挟まっていた I found a four-leaf clover (pressed) *between* the pages of my junior high school textbook. ‖ 課長は部長の隣に間を空けて座った The section manager sat down next to the department manager, *giving* him *a wide berth*. (➤ berth は「(船が停泊する際の)他船との距離」が原義).

3【関係, 間柄】**between, among** ▶親しい友だちの間でも挨拶は必要だ Proper greetings are necessary *between* even the closest friends. ‖ その先生は生徒の間で人気がある That teacher is popular *among* [*with*] his students. ‖ 何でも言ってくれよ. きみとぼくの間じゃないか Whatever it is, tell me! *Aren't we friends*?

▶彼女はオランダ人の父と日本人の母との間に生まれた She was born *to* a Dutch father *and* a Japanese mother. ‖ これら一連の強盗事件の間には共通点がある There is a common feature *in* this series of robberies. ‖ 日本とアメリカの間で新しい貿易協定が結ばれた A new trade agreement has been reached *by* [concluded *between*] Japan *and* the U.S. ‖ 母と言い合いをしたが, 兄が間に入ってくれた My (older) brother managed to *make peace between* my mother and me after we had a heated argument.

あいだがら 間柄 **relationship**(関係) ; **terms**(仲) ▶森田さんと私は会ってもことばを交わす間柄ではありません Mr. Morita and I *are* not *on speaking terms*. (➤ be on ... terms で「…の仲だ」; …には good, friendly, speaking などがくる) ‖ あの方と私は師弟の間柄です He and I are *teacher and student* [*master and pupil*]. ‖ 対話「きみは和子といったいどういう間柄なんだ」「ただの友だちですよ」"*What's your relationship* with Kazuko ?" "We're just friends, that's all."

アイダホ **Idaho** /áɪdəhoʊ/ (アメリカの州 ; 略 ID, Id., Ida.).

あいちゃく 愛着 (an) **attachment** ▶この古いギターには愛着がある I *have an attachment for* this old guitar. / I *am attached to* this old guitar.

[1]**あいちょう 愛鳥**
‖愛鳥家 a bird lover ‖ 愛鳥週間 Bird Week.

[2]**あいちょう 哀調** ▶哀調を帯びたメロディー a *sad* [*plaintive*] melody (➤ 後者のほうが堅い言い方).

あいつ **that guy** ▶あいつはいいやつだ *He*'s a good guy [fellow]. (➤ 男性の場合) / *She*'s a good girl. (➤ 女性の場合) ‖ あいつめ! *Damn him* [*her*]!

あいついで 相次いで **one after another** (1つまた1つと) ▶彼の小説が相次いで刊行された His novels were published *one after another*.

あいつぐ 相次ぐ ▶彼は相次ぐ不幸に見舞われた He had *a run* [*a spell*] *of* bad luck. ‖ 警察は相次ぐ難事件にお手上げのていだった The police threw up their hands in despair over the *series of* difficult cases.

あいづち 相づち ▶彼はときどき相づちを打ちながら(=うなずきながら)私の話を聞いた He listened to what I had to say, *nodding his head* occasionally.
解説 (1)日本人は相手の話を聞きながら半ば無意識に相づちを打つが, 英米人は黙って相手の目を見つめながら話を聞き, 相手の言っていることがひとまとまりの意味を成したり, 相手が話し終えたりしたところで, Uh-huh /ʌhʌ́/, I see., Really ? などと相づちを打つ. (2)日本人の相づちは英米人には Yes と答えていると誤解される可能性が高い.

あいて 相手 **1**【相棒, 仲間】a **partner** ▶ダンスの相手 a dancing *partner* ‖ 結婚相手 a marriage *partner* ‖ 相談相手 *someone to talk with* [*turn to*] *about one's concerns* ‖ 話し相手が欲しい I'd like *someone to talk with*. ‖ 主演男優の相手役を選ぶためのオーディション a cast audition for a suitable *actress to play opposite* the leading actor ‖ あの女の子には遊び相手がいない That girl *has no one to play with*.

▶もうあんたなんか相手にしたくない I'*m not going to have anything to do with* you from now on. / *I'm through with* you. (● 後者は「あんたとは終わった」と考えた場合) ‖ あいつなんか相手にするな Don't *bother with* him. ‖ うそばかりついていると, 今に誰も相手にしてくれなくなるよ If you keep lying all the time, *no one is going to take you seriously* [*no one will believe anything you say*]. (➤ take a person seriously は「人の言うことをまともに受け止める」). ‖ 山本君は相手かまわず議論を吹っかける癖がある Yamamoto has a habit of starting arguments with *anyone present*. (●「居合わせた誰とでも」と考える).

2【対抗して争う人】an **opponent** /əpóʊnənt/ (対戦相手) ; a **match**(好敵手), an **equal**(同等の人) ; a **rival**(ライバル) ▶きょうの(柔道の)相手はいろいろな技を持っているに違いない No doubt my *opponent* in today's (judo) match will have all sorts of moves ready. ‖ 高木君ならば相手として不足はない Takagi is a good *match* for me. ‖ 彼ならきみの相手になれるだろう You'll meet your *match* [*equal*] in him. / He'll be a good *rival* for you. ‖ 相手チームにはすばらしいピッチャーがいる *Our rival* (*baseball*) *team* has an excellent pitcher. (➤ opposing team でもよい) ‖ 相手方の言い分も聞く必要がある We need to hear what *the other party* has to say.

3【対象】▶若者相手の店 a shop *for* young people ‖ うちは外国人相手に商売をしている Our shop *caters to* [《英》*for*] foreigners.

アイデア an **idea** /aɪdíːə/ ▶いいアイデアがあります I've got a good *idea*. ‖ それはいいアイデアだ That's a good *idea*. ‖ アイデアはいいが実現不可能だ That's a good *idea*, but it's unfeasible [it's not feasible]. ‖アイデア商品 novelties(➤ 通例複数形で) ‖ アイデアマン an idea man, a man of ideas.

アイティー **IT**(情報技術)(➤ information technology の略)
‖IT革命 the IT revolution ‖ IT企業 an IT company ‖ IT産業 the IT industry.

アイディー **ID** (➤ identification (身分証明)の略)
‖IDカード an ID card.

あいて(いる) 空いて(いる) →空く.

あいてどる 相手どる ▶彼女は国を相手どって訴訟を起こした She filed a suit *against* the Government. ‖ 県を相手どって裁判を起こす *sue* the prefectural government / *take* the prefectural government *to court*.

アイデンティティー **identity** ▶アイデンティティーを確立する[失う] establish [lose] one's *identity*.

あいとう 哀悼 **condolences**(哀悼のことば)
✉ **ご尊父のご逝去に対し心から哀悼の意を表します** Please accept my very sincere *condolences* on the death of your father. →お悔やみ.

あ

あいどく 愛読 ▶この本は若者たちに愛読されている This book *is popular* among [with] young people. ‖私は夏目漱石を愛読している I *like* Natsume Soseki's works. ／Natsume Soseki is my *favorite* author. ‖彼は『タイム』の愛読者だ He is *a regular reader* of "Time." ／He reads "Time" faithfully. ‖これは私の愛読書の１つです This is one of my *favorite books*. ／This book is one of my *favorites*.

アイドリング idling ▶車のエンジン音はアイドリングしているときはとても静かだ The car engine is very quiet when it *is idling*. ‖《掲示》アイドリングストップ No Idling ／Do Not Idle.

アイドル an idol ; a hero（英雄）▶映画［テニス］界のアイドル a movie [tennis] *idol* ‖彼女は昔アイドル歌手だった She was once *a singing idol* [*a pop idol*].

> **危ないカタカナ語✸ アイドル**
> **1**「アイドル」は「偶像」の意の idol からきており,「若者たちのアイドル」は young people's idol のようにいえるが, スポーツ選手などの場合は hero(英雄)を使ってもよい.
> **2**「アイドル歌手」は idolized singer(偶像化された歌手)とか singing idol(歌うアイドル)のようにいうが, idol singer とはいわない.

あいにく 生憎 unfortunately(運悪く) ; to one's disappointment（失望したことには）▶あいにく店は閉まっていた *To my disappointment*, the shop was closed. ‖あいにくのお天気だ *It's too bad* that the weather is so lousy. ／*It's a pity* that the weather is so bad.（➤後者は《主に英》）‖ 対話「今度の日曜日, 映画に行かないか」「おあいにくさま. ほかにやることがあるの」"How about going to a movie this Sunday ?" "*I'm sorry but* I have something else to do." ‖ 対話「コンサートのチケット, 完売で手に入らなかったよ」「それはあいにくだったわね」"All the tickets for the concert had been sold out and I couldn't get one." "*That's too bad.* ／*That was a shame.*"

✉ **ご招待いただきましたが, あいにく伺うことができません** Thank you for your kind invitation, but *unfortunately* I won't be able to come.

アイヌ ‖アイヌ語 Ainu ‖アイヌ民族(の人) an Ainu ; the Ainu(s)（➤全体）.

あいのて 合いの手 ▶彼女の歌を聴きながら聴衆は手拍子で合いの手を入れた The audience *clapped along with the beat* as they listened to her song.

あいのり 相乗り ▶《タクシー乗り場で》相乗りで行きましょう Let's *share* a cab.

アイバンク an eye bank.

あいはんする 相反する ▶両者の主張は相反する(＝矛盾する) The claims of both parties *are contradictory*.

あいびき 合い挽き a mixture of ground beef and ground pork.

あいびょう 愛猫 one's (pet) cat.

あいぶ 愛撫 a caress /kərés/ ; petting（いちゃつき）一動 愛撫する caress /kərés/ ＋目 ▶彼女のうなじを愛撫する *caress* the back of her neck.

あいべや 相部屋 ▶彼女となら相部屋でもかまいません I don't mind *sharing a room* with her.

あいぼう 相棒 an associate, a partner（事業などの）; a buddy, a mate（仲間）▶運よく仕事のいい相棒を見つけた Happily, I found a good *business associate* [*partner*]. ‖あいつは俺の相棒だよ He's my *buddy*.

アイボリー ivory /áɪvəri/（象牙）; ivory-color, creamy white（象牙色）.

あいま 合間 ▶仕事の合間に歌の練習をする practice singing *in one's time off* [*in one's spare time*] ‖長雨の合間をぬって先祖の墓参りに行った We visited our ancestors' grave *during a short letup* in the middle of a rainy spell.

あいまい 曖昧な ambiguous /æmbígjuəs/（いろいろな意味に解釈できる）; vague /veɪg/（ことば・形などがはっきりしない）; ambivalent /æmbívələnt/（どっちつかずの）; equivocal（語句などが両方の意味に取れる）; noncommittal /nà:nkəmítl/（本気で関わろうとしない）; uncertain（ぐらついている）; obscure /əbskjóə^r/（理解しにくい）; evasive /ɪvéɪsɪv/（のらりくらりした）▶彼の説明は曖昧だった His explanation was *ambiguous*. ‖彼女はぼくの質問に対して曖昧な返事［答え方］をした She gave a *vague* answer [*evasive* answers] to my question. ‖ここのこの句の意味がまだ曖昧なんです The meaning of this phrase here is still *obscure* to me. ‖教師はいじめの問題に対して曖昧な態度は許されない No teacher is permitted to take an *ambivalent* [*ambiguous*] attitude toward the problem of bullying. ‖事件の真相は曖昧模糊(もこ)としている The truth about the incident is still *rather vague* [is still *uncertain*].

あいまって 相俟って ▶コーチのよい指導と選手自身の努力が相まってこのたびの好成績につながった It was the coach's superior guidance *combined* with the athlete's own efforts that resulted in this striking achievement.

あいよう 愛用 ▶愛用の(＝自分用の)自転車 a bicycle *for one's personal use* ‖これは私の愛用の辞書です This is my *favorite* dictionary. ‖父は新しく買ったデジタルカメラを愛用している My father *loves using* his new digital camera.

アイライン a line drawn around one's eyes to emphasize the size（➤「アイライナー」は eyeliner だが, eyeline は「視線」).

あいらしい 愛らしい sweet ; adorable /ədɔ́:rəbəl/（主に子供・動物がかわいい）; cute（かわいい）▶愛らしいほほえみ a *sweet* smile ‖愛らしい子 an *adorable* child ‖その女の子は小さな愛らしい口元をしている The girl has a *cute*, small mouth.

アイランド an island.

アイルランド Ireland /áɪə^rlənd/ 一形 アイルランドの Irish ▶アイルランド(人)の少年 an *Irish* boy. ‖アイルランド人 an Irishman(男), an Irishwoman(女) ; the Irish(全体).

アイロニー (an) irony. →皮肉.

アイロン an iron /áɪə^rn/ ▶このワイシャツにアイロンをかけてくれますか Could you *iron* this shirt (for me) ? ‖毎日アイロンがけが山ほどある I have piles of *ironing* (to do) every day. ‖彼女はドレスのしわをアイロンで伸ばした She *ironed out* the wrinkles in her dress. ‖アイロン台 an ironing board.

[1]あう 合う

> **訳語メニュー**
> 寸法などが体に合う →fit **1**
> 色などが合う →match **2**
> 意見などが合う →agree **3**
> 体質・好みに合う →suit **6**

1【寸法・型などが】 fit(＋目), sit ▶この靴は私の足にぴったり合う These shoes *fit* me perfectly. ／These shoes are a perfect *fit*. ‖その上着，肩のところがうまく合ってないわよ That jacket *does not sit* [*fit*] properly on your shoulders.

2【色・釣り合いなどが】match(+目), **go well**《with》▶カーテンに合ったカーペットを選ぶべきだ I advise you to choose a carpet that *matches* your curtains. ‖この背広に合いそうなネクタイを何本か見せてください Please show me some ties that would *go well with* this suit. ‖赤ワインは肉と，白ワインは魚と合う Red wine *goes well with* meat, and white (wine) *goes well with* fish. ‖青はきみに合うよ You *look good* in blue. ／Blue *looks great* [*good*] on you.

3【意見などで】agree《with》▶彼とは多くの点で意見が合わない I don't *agree with* him in many respects. ‖絵の趣味がおありなら，うちの部長と話が合うことでしょう You'll probably *get along well with* our department head if you have a taste for art. (➤ get along well with A は「A(人)と仲よくやっていく」の意).

4【時計・答えなどが】▶きみの時計合ってるかい？ *Is* your watch *on time* [*right* ／*correct*]？‖あなたの答えは合っています Your answer *is right* [*correct*].

5【音程・調子などが】▶ドラムのテンポは曲とあまりよく合っていなかった The drummer's tempo *was out of beat with* the music. ‖誰か音程の合ってない人がいるね Somebody's *out of tune*.

6【体質・好みなどに】suit +目 ▶ここの気候は私に合っているので老後はここで暮らしたい The weather here *suits* [*agrees with*] me, so I'd like to live here when I'm old. ‖ロックは私の好みに合わない Rock (music) *does not suit* my taste. ／I *don't care much for* rock music. ‖お口に合いますか？ Well, (how) do you *like* it？／Well, how does it *taste* to you？‖うなぎは私の口に合わない I *don't care much for* eel. ／I'*m not* very *big on* eel. (➤ 後者はよりくだけた言い方) ‖たいていの果物は誰の口にも合う Most fruits *have an agreeable taste*.

7【「…し合う」の形で】▶水を掛け合う *splash* water *on each other* ‖私たちはいつもクリスマスカードを出し合っています We always *exchange* Christmas cards. ‖クラブの会員は常に連絡をとり合っている The club members always *keep in touch with each other*.

☛ **合わせる，合わない** (→見出語)

²あう 会う・遭う **1【人と】meet**(+目)(知り合いになる，日時を決めて会う，会ってことばを交わす)；**see**(+目)(姿を見かける，会ってことばを交わす)；**run into** [**across**](偶然出会う)；**get together**(集まる)▶初めて林さんにお会いになったのはいつ頃ですか When did you *meet* Mr. Hayashi for the first time？‖今晩コンサートで典子さんにお会いになったらよろしくお伝えください If you *see* Noriko tonight at the concert, say hello (to her) for me. ‖今晩7時頃に渋谷で[ハチ公のところで]会おう *Let's meet* in Shibuya [at Hachiko] tonight at around seven. ‖土曜日に石田君と会うことに(＝手はずに)なっています I'*ve arranged to meet* Ishida on Saturday. ‖県民の代表5名が知事と会った Five representatives of the prefecture's citizens *met* (*with*) the governor. (➤「会見する，会談する」の意で with をつけるのは主に《米》用法) ‖会うは別れの初め *Meeting* is the beginning of parting.

▶じゃあ，あとで会いましょう *See you* (*later*). (🏺 See you again. と訳すと「(いつ会えるかわからないが)また会いましょう」の意になるので注意) ‖また近いうちに会いましょうよ(＝集まろう) *Let's get together* soon. ‖(路上などで)また会ったね Hello, again. ‖今週はよく会うね We've been *running into* each other a lot this week. (➤ run into は「人にひょっこり出くわす」) ‖ねえ，以前どこかで会ったことない？ Say, *haven*'t we *met* before somewhere？‖最近よくお会いしますね *Our paths seem to cross* very often these days, don't they？(🏺 英語では「お互いの道が(よく)交差するようだ」と考える) ‖ここできみに会おう(＝きみを見かける)とは夢にも思わなかった I never thought I'd *see* [*run into*] you here. ‖先日ある友人と銀座でばったり会った I *ran into* [*across*] a friend of mine in Ginza the other day. ／I *happened* [*chanced*] *to meet* a friend of mine in Ginza the other day. ‖最近秀明君とはあまり会っていない I *haven't seen much of* Hideaki lately.

✉ **シドニーで会えるのを楽しみにしています** I am looking forward to *seeing* you in Sydney.

✉ **しばらくお会いしていませんが，お元気ですか** I *haven't seen* you for a while, but I hope you are well.

2【雨・災難などに】get caught《in》(にわか雨などに)；**meet with**(事故・不幸などに)▶いつにわか雨にあうかわからないので，いつも折り畳みの傘を持ち歩いています I always carry a folding umbrella because I never know when I'll *get caught in* a shower. (🏺「大嵐にあう」のような場合は have を用いて have a big storm のようにいう) ‖空港へ行く途中彼らは交通事故にあった On the way to the airport, they *got into* [*had* ／*met with*] a traffic accident. ‖私の計画は家族全員の猛反対にあった My plan *ran up against the strong opposition* of my whole family. ‖万一スキー中に事故にあわれた場合この保険が費用をカバーします This insurance covers all expenses if you should *have an accident* while skiing. ‖教授は学生たちの質問攻めにあった The professor *faced a barrage of questions* from the students. ／The professor *was bombarded with questions* from the students. (➤ barrage は「(質問・打撃などの)連発」, be bombarded with は「(質問・不平などを)浴びせられる」).

☛ **会わせる** (→見出語)

アウト an out ▶《野球》打者[走者]をアウトにする *get* the batter [runner] *out* (➤ out は省いてもよい) ‖佐藤はサードゴロ[フライ]でアウトになった Sato *grounded* [*flied*] *out* to third. ‖中日の攻撃は今ツーアウトフルベースだ The Dragons now have the bases loaded and *two outs*.

▶《比喩的》昔の恋人の写真を持ってることが彼女にばれたらアウトだ You're going to be *in hot water* if your girlfriend finds out that you still have a picture of your old flame. (➤ in hot water は「まずいことになる」の意のインフォーマルな表現；old flame は「昔心を燃やした人」の意味).

アウトコース the outside lane [**track**](トラック競技の)；**the outside course (of the plate)**(野球の球筋)▶アウトコースの球 an *outside* pitch ‖斎藤投手はアウトコースいっぱいにストレートを投げた Saito pitched a straight ball just over *the far side of the plate* (from the batter).

アウトサイダー an **outsider**.

アウトソーシング outsourcing.

アウトドア outdoor

‖アウトドアスポーツ outdoor sports ‖アウトド

あ

ア用品 outdoor goods.

「アウトドア活動」のいろいろ ウォーキング walking／オートキャンプ recreational vehicle (RV) camping／オリエンテーリング orienteering／カヌー canoeing／カヤック kayaking／キャンプ (tent) camping／クロスカントリースキー cross-country skiing／サイクリング cycling／スキューバダイビング scuba diving／スノーボード snow-boarding／釣り fishing／登山 mountain climbing／トレッキング trekking／バードウォッチング bird-watching／ハイキング hiking／パラグライダー paragliding／ハンググライダー hang gliding／マウンテンバイク mountain biking

アウトプット output 一動 アウトプットする output +目 ▶必要なデータをアウトプットする *output* needed data ‖ 顧客データから名前と電話番号だけをアウトプットする *output* only names and phone numbers from the customers' data.

アウトライン an outline(大筋)；a summary (要約, 大意) ▶とりあえず計画のアウトラインだけでも説明してくれよ Just give [tell] me the *outline* of the plan for now.

アウトレット an outlet
‖ アウトレットモール an outlet mall.

アウトロー an outlaw(無法者).

あうんのこきゅう 阿吽の呼吸 ▶2人の刀鍛冶はあうんの呼吸で交互に鉄を打った The two swordmakers took turns striking the iron *with perfect timing.*

あえぐ 喘ぐ 1【息を切らす】breathe hard(苦しそうに大きく深い息をする)；pant(激しい運動などのあと, 浅く小刻みに)；gasp(苦しさ·恐怖·驚きなどで) ▶そのマラソン選手はゴールインした後, 盛んにあえいでいた The marathoner *breathed hard* [*panted*] after he reached the finish. ‖ 警察犬は長時間の追跡であえいでいた The police dog *was panting* after the long chase. (➤ 犬が舌を出してあえぐは pant) ‖ 彼はあえぎあえぎ急な坂道を上った He went up the steep slope *gasping and panting*. (➤ 同義語を重ねることで強調される. いずれか1語でも可).

2【苦しむ】▶人々は重税にあえいだ The people *groaned* under the burden of heavy taxes. (➤ groan は「うめく」) ‖ 出版界は今不況にあえいでいる The publishing world *is suffering from* a slump (in sales).

あえて 敢えて ▶知事の提案に対してあえて反対の意見を言う人は1人もいなかった No one *was willing to* [No one *dared to*] speak (out) against the governor's proposal. ‖ あえて言わせてもらえば, あの映画は駄作だ That movie is trash, *if I may say so* [*if you ask my opinion*].

▶あえて(＝わざわざ)書き直すほどのことでもありません You need not *bother* [*take the trouble*] *to* write it all over again.

あえない 敢えない tragic /trǽdʒɪk/ (悲劇的な)；miserable (惨めな) ▶その武将の最期はあえないものであった That warrior's end was *very sudden and tragic*. ‖ うち(の学校)のチームはあえなく1回戦で敗退した Our (school's) team was *miserably* defeated in the first round.

あえもの 和え物 *aemono*；chopped fish, shell-fish and vegetables that are mixed and dressed in miso and vinegar(➤ 説明的な訳).

あえる 和える dress +目 ▶ワカメとキュウリを酢であえる *dress* wakame (seaweed) and cucumber with vinegar.

あえん 亜鉛 zinc ▶鉄板を亜鉛でめっきする plate steel with *zinc*.

あお 青 blue(➤ 通例 blue color とはいわない) ▶薄い[濃い]青 light [dark] *blue* ‖ 信号が青になってから道路を渡りなさい Cross the street after the traffic light turns *green*. 《参考》日本語の「あお」には blue (青), green (緑), indigo (藍色), azure (空色)が含まれるが, 信号の「青」は英語では green.
‖ 青リンゴ an green apple.
☞ 青い, 青信号 (→見出語)

あおあお 青々 ▶青々とした芝生 a *green* lawn ‖ 海が青々と広がっていた The *blue* sea spread out before us. ‖ 公園の草木が青々と茂っている The grass and trees in the park are *lush and green*. (➤ lush は「みずみずしく茂った」).

あおい 青い 1【色が青い】blue；green(緑の) ▶青い海 the *blue* sea [ocean] ‖ 青い芝生 *green* grass ‖ 青い目の男の子 a *blue-eyed* boy (➤《英·インフォーマル》ではこの表現は「お気に入り」の意味で用いられる) ‖ 青いリンゴ a *green* apple ‖ 柿はまだ青い The persimmons on the tree(s) are still *green*.

▶青い(＝青ざめた)顔してどうしたの？ You look *pale*. What's the matter?

2【未熟な】green ▶きみのやることはまだ青いね You are still *green*. ／You're still *wet behind the ears*. (👂 後者は文字どおりには「まだ耳の後ろがぬれている」ということであるが, これは体を洗ったあと子供は耳の後ろをよく拭かないところから出た比喩表現で, 一般には「(人が)経験不足の」の意味で用いる).

日↔英比較 日本語の「青」は「青春」「青二才」などの表現に見られるように, 未経験だが明るい未来があることを感じさせる. これに対して, 英語の blue には blue chip (優良株), blue ribbon (最高賞, 最優秀)などのようなプラスイメージもあるが, feel blue (気がめいる), look blue (しょげている), blue Monday (憂鬱な月曜日)などの場合のようにマイナスイメージも強い.

あおいきといき 青息吐息 ▶金欠で青息吐息だ I'm *having a hard time* financially.

あおいろしんこく 青色申告 a blue tax return (➤ 青色は日本独自のもの) ▶青色申告を提出する file a *blue tax return*.

¹あおぐ 扇ぐ fan +目 ▶あおいで火をおこす *fan* the fire to get it started ‖ 彼女は扇子で襟元をあおいだ She *fanned* her neck. (➤「扇子」の意は言外に含まれる).

²あおぐ 仰ぐ 1【見上げる】look up《at》▶彼は祈るかのように天を仰いだ He *looked up at the sky* as if to pray.

2【尊敬する】look up《to》▶私はパーキンス氏を師と仰いでいる I *look up to* Mr. Perkins *as my teacher*.

3【頼る】▶日本は原油の供給を他国に仰いでいる Japan *is dependent on* foreign countries for its supply of crude oil.

あおくさい 青臭い ▶この野菜ジュースは青臭くない This vegetable juice doesn't *smell of raw greens*. (➤ greens は「青物」. 英米人には「青臭くて嫌だ」という感じ方はない).

▶青臭い意見 a *half-baked* opinion ‖ 青臭い(＝子供っぽい)ことを言うな Don't say such *childish* things. ‖ あいつはまだ青臭い男だよ That guy's still *green*. ⇀青い.

あおざめる 青ざめる turn [go] pale ▶彼女は恐怖に青ざめた She *turned* [*went*] *pale* with fear. (➤ pale 以外に green, white も使える) ‖ 彼女は青ざめた顔で私を見た She turned a *pale* [*pallid*] face to me. (➤ pallid は病気などで病的に青い場合).

あおじゃしん 青写真 a blueprint ▶その計画はまだ青写真の段階だ The plan has only reached *the blueprint stage* so far.

あおじる 青汁 *aojiru*; a green vegetable drink (typically made of kale or young barley leaves) (➤ 説明的な訳).

あおじろい 青白い pale ▶彼は青白い疲れた顔をしている He is *pale* and tired-looking.

あおしんごう 青信号 a green light (➤ blue は用いない) ▶青信号で進む go on *green* ‖ 彼は青信号になるとアクセルをぐいと踏み込んだ He stomped on the gas pedal when the *green light* came on.

あおすじ 青筋 ▶彼は青筋を立てて怒った He was so angry that *the veins on his temples stood out*. (● 日本語の意味は「こめかみの血管(静脈)が浮き出るほど怒った」ということだが, 英語的発想では「血管が破裂しそうなほど怒った」(He was so angry he nearly burst a blood vessel.) と表現することが多い).

あおぞら 青空 a blue sky ▶ほんとに久しぶりの青空だ We have *a blue sky* for the first time in ages. ▶青空駐車する park (a car) outdoors / leave a car parked in the open air.

‖青空市(場) an open-air market ‖ 青空教室 an open-air classroom ‖ 青空コンサート an open-air concert.

あおだいしょう 青大将 《動 物》 a Japanese rat snake.

あおたがい 青田買い *aota-gai*; recruiting the brightest college graduates long before other companies do (➤ 説明的な訳).

あおにさい 青二才 a greenhorn (未熟者) ▶黙れ, この青二才! Keep your mouth shut, (*you*) *greenhorn*! ‖ 青二才のくせにずいぶん大きな口をきくんだな, え? That's big talk for *someone wet behind the ears* [*a whippersnapper*] like you, eh? (● この「青二才」には someone wet behind the ears (「青い」2 の「英訳のツボ」を参照) を用いるとよい; whippersnapper は「若造」の古風な言い方).

あおば 青葉 green leaves ▶青葉の季節 the season of *green leaves*.

✉ **青葉の目にしみる候となりましたが, お変わりありませんか** Summer has set in and the leaves on the trees are deep green. I hope this change in seasons finds you well [in good health]. ➤ 英米では手紙の書き始めにこのような挨拶文は書かない.

あおむけ 仰向け ▶あおむけに寝てください Lie down *on your back*. ‖ 彼女は滑ってあおむけに倒れた She slipped and *fell on her back*. ‖ ぼくたちは芝生の上にあおむけになって寝転んだ We lay on the lawn *face up* [*on our backs*].

あおむし 青虫 a (green) caterpillar.

あおもの 青物 greens (青野菜), vegetables (野菜類); blue-skinned fish (サバ・イワシなど背の青い魚)

‖青物市場 a vegetable market.

あおり 煽り ▶交通ストのあおりを食ってこの辺りはどの道路も混雑している Every street around here is congested *as a result of* the transit workers' strike. ‖ 不況のあおりを受けて倒産する会社が急増した *Influenced by* the recession, the number of corporate bankruptcies has increased sharply. ▶突風のあおりで立ち木が倒れた The tree was knocked down *by* the sudden gust of wind.

あおりうんてん 煽り運転 (malicious) tailgating ((悪意ある)後方からの異常接近).

《参考》 tailgate は衝突事故が起こりそうなほど他の車のすぐ後ろに接近して運転することで, 「あおる」に当たる. 「あおり運転」は他にいくつもの行為を含むが, 「(悪意をもって)急ブレーキをかける」は brake test, または brake check で, 動詞としては brake-test, brake-check とつづる. 「幅寄せする」は人を主語にして drive too close to a vehicle in an adjacent lane, 車を主語にして get [move] too close to the side of another vehicle, swerve into a vehicle (in an adjacent lane) などと表現できる. 全てを含めて provocative driving (挑発的な運転)としてもよい. なお, 「運転中の突然の怒り爆発」は road rage と呼ぶ.

¹**あおる 煽る** fan +㊐ (火を); kindle +㊐, stir up (怒りなどを); inflame +㊐ (感情を) ▶折からの突風にあおられて火の手は南へ広がった *Fanned* by the gusty wind, the fire spread to the south. ‖ 警察の行動は群衆の怒りをあおった The police action *kindled* [*stirred up*] the anger of the crowd. ‖ 恐怖心をあおる *inflame* fears ‖ 後ろの車が私をひどくあおって, 私をもっと速く走らせようとした The car behind me aggressively *tailgated* me and tried to make me go faster. (➤ tailgate は「(前の車に)異常に接近して運転する」).

²**あおる 呷る** gulp down ▶ウオツカは一気にあおらないでちびりちびり飲むんだよ Don't *drink* your vodka *in one gulp*; sip it.

¹**あか 赤** red (➤ 通例 red color とはいわない); crimson (深紅色); scarlet (緋(ひ)色) ▶まだ道路を渡っている間に信号が赤になってしまった The traffic light *turned red* while I was still crossing the street. ‖ 校正刷りに赤を入れる *red-pen* [*red-ink*] a proof 《参考》 英米ではよく青鉛筆を使うので「(原稿などを)訂正・削除する」の意味で blue-pencil を用いることも多い.

▶《慣用表現》あの女性は赤の他人だよ (= 全く面識がない) That woman is *a total* [*complete*] *stranger* to me.

☛ 赤い, 赤信号 (⇀見出語)

²**あか 垢** dirt ▶体のあかを落とす *wash* oneself / *wash off the dirt* ‖ ワイシャツの襟があかだらけだ The shirt collar *is badly soiled*.

あかあか 赤々・明々 ▶キャンプファイアの火が赤々と燃えた The campfire burned *brightly*.

▶通りには明々とネオンが輝いている The streets are *brightly* lit [lighted] by neon signs.

あかい 赤い

red; crimson (深紅色の) ▶赤い靴を履いた少女 a little girl wearing *red* shoes / a little girl with *red* shoes on ‖ 彼女は赤い服を着ていた She *was dressed in red*. ‖ 屋根は赤い色に塗ってください Please paint the roof *red*. (➤ 通例 red color とはしない) ‖ 髪を赤く染める dye one's hair *red* [*brown* / *auburn*] (➤ brown は「栗毛色の」, auburn /ɔ́:bərn/ は「赤褐色の」).

▶興奮のあまり彼の顔は赤くなった His face *became* [*turned*] *red* with excitement. (➤ with は from でもよい) / His face *flushed* with excitement. ‖ 恥ずかしくて顔が赤くなった I *blushed* (with embarrassment). (➤ 恥ずかしさに「赤面する」は blush で, 熱や感情が高ぶって顔が「紅潮する」は flush, 「紅潮している」は形容詞 flushed を使って be flushed) ‖ 父は

あ

顔を赤くして怒った Father *flushed* with rage. ‖ 彼女はビールをコップ 1 杯飲んだだけで顔を赤くした Her face *was flushed* after one glass of beer. ‖ 夕日が雲を赤く染めた The sunset *reddened* the clouds. ‖ 柿の実が赤くなり始めた The persimmons have begun to *change color* [*turn red*].

✉ **私たちは（運命の）赤い糸で結ばれているんですね** We must be destined for each other.

● 日本的な表現なので「お互いのために存在する運命にある」と考える.

あかいはね 赤い羽根 a **Red Feather** ▶赤い羽根運動に協力する donate to *the Red Feather campaign* [*a Red Feather community chest drive*].

‖**赤い羽根（共同）募金** the Red Feather community chest.

アカウンタビリティー **accountability**（説明責任）.

アカウント an **account**（コンピュータ用の）▶グーグルのアカウントを作る create *a* Google *account*.

あがき 足掻き a **struggle** ▶あれが彼の最後のあがきだよ That's his *last struggle*.

☛ **悪あがき**（⇀見出語）

あかぎれ **chapped skin**（あかぎれた皮膚）; **chaps**（あかぎれ）▶あかぎれは痛い *Chaps* are painful. ‖ 寒さで手にあかぎれが切れた My hands *were chapped* from the cold.

あがく 足掻く **struggle** ▶あがけばあがくほどロープが手に食い込んだ *The more I struggled*, the deeper the rope bit into my arms. ‖ 彼女は借金から抜け出そうとあがいた She *struggled* to get out of debt.

あかげ 赤毛 **red hair** ▶赤毛の子 a child with *red hair* ／a *red-headed* child（➤『赤毛のアン』の原題は "Anne of Green Gables"）.

あかご 赤子 a **baby** ▶《慣用表現》チャンピオンにとってその挑戦者を退けるのは赤子の手をひねるようなものだった Beating that challenger was *child's play* to the champ.（➤ child's play は「たやすいこと」）.

あかし 証し **evidence, proof**（➤ 証拠；後者のほうが確証性が高い）; (a) **token**（しるし, 象徴）▶生きた証しに何かを残したいと考える人は多い Many people want to leave something behind (after death) *as proof that they have lived* [*to prove that their lives had meaning*]. ‖ 身の証しを立てる *prove one's innocence*.

あかじ 赤字 **the red**（マイナス分）; a **deficit**（欠損）▶わが社は赤字に転落した Our company *went* [*fell*] *into the red*. ‖ わが社は赤字経営だ Our company *is operating in the red*. ‖ 友人から借金して一時赤字を埋めておいた I borrowed some money from my friend to *cover* [*make up for*] *the deficit*.

‖**赤字予算** a deficit budget ‖ **赤字路線** a deficit-ridden [money-losing] line ‖ **貿易赤字** a trade deficit.

アカシア《植物》a **(false) acacia** /əkéɪʃə/,《米》a **locust (tree)**《参考》ともに日本でふつうにアカシアと呼んでいる木で, 正式名は「ニセアカシア」.

あかしお 赤潮 a **red tide**（➤ Ⓤ 扱いもある）▶ことしはたびたび赤潮が発生した There have been many occurrences of *red tide(s)* this year.

あかしんごう 赤信号 a **red light** ▶赤信号で止まる stop at the *red light* ‖ その子は赤信号を無視して道路を渡った The kid crossed the street *on the red light* [*against the light*].

▶《比喩的》高血圧の人で手足が震えるようになると赤信号だ Trembling of the hands and feet is *a warning sign* for people with high blood pressure.

あかす 明かす **1**【明らかにする】**reveal** ＋㊀ ▶こっそり寄付した人物は全く正体を明かしていない The secret donor has never *revealed his or her identity*. ‖ 種を明かせばこのとおり This is the way it works. ／This is the trick of it. ‖ 隼人は笑理に胸のうちを明かした Hayato *opened his heart* to Emiri.

2【夜を】▶彼らは海岸で一夜を明かした They *spent* [*passed*] *the night* on the beach. ‖ 私たちは一晩中語り明かした We *sat up* all night *talking*.

あかせて 飽かせて ▶その実業家は金に飽かせて名画を買い込んだ That industrialist *spent mountains of* [*tons of*] *money on* famous paintings.

あかだし 赤だし ***akadashi*** ; **red** [**dark brown**] **miso soup**.

あかちゃける 赤茶ける ▶何度も毛染めを繰り返したら髪が赤茶けてきた My hair has started to *turn reddish brown* after dying it repeatedly.

あかちゃん 赤ちゃん a **baby** ▶男 [女] の赤ちゃん *a baby boy* [*girl*]（➤ 語順に注意）‖ 早く赤ちゃんが欲しいわね I hope we'll have *a baby* soon. ‖ 中村さん夫婦に赤ちゃんが生まれた *A baby* was born to the Nakamuras. ‖ ほら, ライオンの赤ちゃんよ Look, there's a *baby* lion.

✉ **《カードで》赤ちゃんのお誕生おめでとう** Congratulations on *your new baby*. ／Congratulations on *the birth of your daughter* [*son*].

あかちょうちん 赤提灯 an ***akachochin*** ; an inexpensive [a cheap] drinking place marked by a red lantern（➤ 説明的な訳）▶赤ちょうちんの常連 a regular at *an akachochin* (*drinking place*).

あかつき 暁 **dawn** /dɔːn/, **daybreak** ▶暁の空に金星が見えている The morning star is out in the *dawn sky*.

▶《慣用表現》当選の暁には（＝当選したときには）必ず公約を果たします *Once* elected, I will never fail to carry out my campaign pledges.

あがったり 上がったり ▶こんなに客が少なくては商売あがったりだ Our *business will be ruined* if we keep having so few customers.

あかつち 赤土 **red earth** ; **red clay**（粘土質の土）.

アカデミーしょう アカデミー賞 an **Academy Award**.

アカデミック **academic** /æ̀kədémɪk/ ▶この大学にはアカデミックな雰囲気がない This university does not have an *academic* atmosphere. ‖ 彼の講演はアカデミックすぎて理解しにくかった His lecture [talk] was too *academic* for me to understand.

‖（大学の）**アカデミックアドバイザー** an academic advisor ‖ **アカデミックハラスメント** (an) abuse of power and position on campus（➤「アカデミックハラスメント」は和製語）.

あかてん 赤点 a **failing grade** [**mark**] ▶赤点をもらう receive *a failing grade*.

あかとんぼ 赤とんぼ a **red dragonfly** ▶赤トンボの群れ a flight of *red dragonflies* ⇀とんぼ.

あかぬけ 垢抜けした **refined, polished**（洗練された）; **sophisticated**（教養がある, 知的な）▶あか抜けした話し方 a *refined* way of speaking ‖ 彼はあか抜けしている He's *polished*. ‖ 最近陽子はとてもあか抜けしてきた Recently, Yoko *has become* very *sophisticated*. ‖ 彼女はあか抜けしない田舎娘だった She was just an *unpolished* country girl.

あかねいろ 茜色 **ruby (red)**（ルビー色）; **madder (red)**（植物のアカネに由来する色）▶あかね色の空 a *ruby-*

colored sky ‖ 夕焼け空があかね色に染まった The sky at sunset turned *ruby-red* [*russet*]. (➤ russet は「赤褐色」).

あかはじ 赤恥 ▶あなたのせいで, お母さんは先生の前で赤恥をかいたわよ Thanks to you, I *was totally humiliated* in front of the teacher.

アカハラ →アカデミックハラスメント.

あかふだ 赤札
‖赤札セール a sacrifice sale, a (bargain) sale.

アカペラ a cappella /àː kəpélə/ ▶アカペラで歌う sing *a cappella*.

あかぼう 赤帽 a porter, a redcap.

1**あかみ 赤み** redness ; flush (紅潮) ▶まもなく女の子の青白い顔に赤みがさしてきた A slight *flush* soon came to the girl's pale cheeks. ‖栗毛とは赤みを帯びた茶色をいう Chestnut is a *reddish*-brown color.

2**あかみ 赤身** ▶赤身の魚 a *red-fleshed* fish / a *dark-fleshed* fish.

あがめる 崇める worship +㊐ (崇拝する) ; venerate +㊐ (敬う) ; revere /rɪvíəʳ/ +㊐ (深い敬意を払う) ▶あんな教祖をあがめる気にはとてもなれない I'd never *worship* a cult leader like him. ‖カトリック信者は聖母マリアをあがめる Catholics *venerate* the Virgin Mary.

あからがお 赤ら顔 a ruddy /rʌ́di/ face ▶赤ら顔の男 a man *with a ruddy face* / a *ruddy-faced* man.

あからさま ▶あからさまなうそ a *downright* lie ‖あからさまの(=公然とした)敵意に直面する face *overt* hostility ‖重役たちは会長の独断をあからさまに非難した The executives *openly* [*frankly*] criticized the chairman's arbitrary decision.

あからめる 赤らめる blush (赤面する) ▶人間は顔を赤らめる唯一の動物である Humans are [Man is] the only animal that *blushes*. ‖「一緒に歌ってくれませんか」と頼んだら, 彼女は恥ずかしそうに顔を赤らめた She *blushed* [Her *face turned red*] with embarrassment when I asked her to sing with me.

あかり 明かり 1【光】light ▶彼女は窓のカーテンを開けて明かりを入れた She opened the window curtain(s) to let in *light*.
‖明かりとり a window (窓), a skylight (天窓).
2【灯火】a light ▶彼は自分の部屋の明かりをつけた [消した] He *turned on* [*off*] *the light* in his room.

あがり 上がり 1【上昇】▶階段を上がり降りする *go up and down* the stairs ‖最近は物価の上がり下がりが激しい *Price movements* are sharp these days. / Recently, *price fluctuations* have been extreme.
2【終わり, 完了】▶きょうはこれで上がりにしよう *Let's call it a day*. (● 英語では「1日の仕事を切り上げよう」と発想して, その意の慣用句 call it a day を用いる) ‖《料理店などで》一丁上がり! *One up!*
3【収益】a profit (利益) ; proceeds (売り上げ) ▶彼らはバザーの上がりを慈善事業に寄付した They donated the *proceeds* of the bazaar to charity.

-あがり -上がり 1【直後】▶雨上がりの道 a road *just after rain* ‖康夫は病み上がりだ Yasuo *has just recovered from his sickness*. ‖風呂上がりのビールほどうまいものはないと父は言う My father says nothing tastes as good as a beer (*just*) *after* a hot bath.
2【出身】▶役人上がり(の人) an *ex*-government official (➤ ex- は「前…だった」) / a *former* government official ‖学者上がりの政治家 a scholar-*turned*-politician (➤ turned は「変更[転職]した」).

あがりこむ 上がり込む ▶あの人は話し好きで, いったん上がり込んだらなかなか帰らない He is really talkative, so once he *gets his foot in the door*, he just doesn't leave.

あがる 上がる・挙がる・揚がる

> 📖 訳語メニュー
> 高い方へ行く →rise, go up 1, 2
> 落ち着きを失う →be [get] nervous 3
> 向上する →improve 4
> 数値が大きくなる →go up, rise 5
> 終わる →finish, stop 7

1【物が高い方へ行く】rise, go up ▶《劇場で》まもなく幕が上がります. お席へお着きください The curtain will *rise* momentarily. Please take your seats. ‖風を受けてたこが空高く揚がっていった Catching the wind, the kite *climbed* higher and higher. ‖左の腕が痛くて上がらない(=上げられない) My left arm hurts so bad that I *can't raise* it. ‖先生が質問すると, 教室のあちこちから手が挙がった When the teacher asked a question, many students *raised* their hands. ‖夏の夜空に花火が揚がった The fireworks *shot up* [*were fired*] into the summer night (sky). (➤ shot は shoot(放つ) の過去形).
▶銚子港にサンマが大量に揚がった(=陸揚げされた) A large catch of Pacific saury *was landed* at Choshi Harbor.

2【人が高い方へ行く】go [walk] up ▶2階に[上の階に]上がる *go upstairs* ‖父はぼくのフリスビーを取ろうと屋根に上がった My father *climbed onto* [*went up on*] the roof to get my Frisbee. ‖彼女は靴を脱いで祭壇に上がっていった She took off her shoes and *stepped up* [*walked up*] to the altar. ‖彼女は3歳のときから舞台に上がっている She*'s been on stage* since she was three. ‖早くプールから上がりなさい Hurry and *get out* of the pool.
▶どうぞお上がりください(=中へ入ってください) Please *come in*. / *Come on in*, please. ‖上の子は来年小学校へ上がる The older child *starts* elementary school next year.
▶《敬語》あす大事なことでご相談にあがってもよろしいですか May I *come to see you* about an important matter tomorrow? ‖あすの午後それをいただきにあがります I'll *come* to pick it up tomorrow afternoon. ‖どうぞ(ケーキを)おあがりください *Help yourself* (to a piece of cake). ‖どうぞスイカでもあがってください *Have* some watermelon.

3【冷静さ・平静を失う】be [get] nervous ▶大勢の前で話すときは多くの人があがるものだ Many people *get nervous* [*have stage fright*] when they have to give a speech in front of a large audience. ‖ぼくは女の子の前に出るとすぐあがってしまう I'*m* very *nervous* around girls. / I *get tongue-tied* around girls. (➤ tongue-tied は「(舌がもつれて)うまくしゃべれない」).

4【状態が向上する】improve ▶2学期は英語の成績が上がった My English grades *improved* [*went up*] in the second term. ‖父はだいぶゴルフの腕が上がったようだ I hear that my father has really *improved* his golf game. ‖彼の名声は一気に上がった All of a sudden, his reputation *soared*. ‖彼は最近地位が上がった He *moved* [*was promoted*] *to a higher position* recently.

5【数値が上昇する】go up, rise ▶4月にJRの運賃が上がるそうです They say that the JR fares are going to *go up* [*be raised*] in April. ‖ 気温は28度に上がった The temperature *rose* [*went up*] to 28℃.

6【出現する，はっきりと認められる】▶証拠が挙がったからあの男を逮捕できる Now that we *have* evidence, we can arrest him. ‖ 容疑者の１人として彼の名が挙がっていた His name was *on the list* of suspects. ‖ 強盗犯人がけさあがった（＝捕まった） The robber *was caught* [*was picked up*] this morning. ‖ ４月の販売実績が統計として挙がっている April's sales results *are available* in statistical form.

7【終了する，完了する】**finish** ＋㊐，**wrap up**（仕事などが）；**stop**，**let up**（雨などが）▶この仕事は３日もあれば上がるよ We can *finish* [*wrap up*] this job in three days. ‖ ゲームはぼくが１番に上がった I *finished* the game first. ‖ 雨が上がったら散歩に行こう When the rain *stops* [*lets up*], let's go for a walk. ‖（クリーニング店などで）いつ上がりますか When will it *be ready?*

▶このカメラの修理は思いのほか安く上がった I *was able to get* this camera repaired *for less* than I (had) expected. ／ The repair cost for this camera was *unexpectedly low*.

▶車のバッテリーが上がった（＝切れた） My car battery *died*.

8【望ましい結果・収入を得る】▶うちのアパートから月々家賃が50万円ずつ上がる I *make* half a million yen a month in rent from my apartment house.

9【揚げ物ができる】▶天ぷらが揚がった The tempura *is done* [*is finished*]. ‖ このフライドチキンはからっと揚がっている This fried chicken *is nice and crisp*.

☛ あがったり（→見出語）

あかるい 明るい

📖 訳語メニュー
場所が明るい →light 1
性格が明るい →cheerful 2
見通しが明るい →bright 4

1【明るさが】**light**（光が十分さして）；**well-lit**（照明が十分で）；**bright**（輝いて）▶明るい風通しのよい部屋 a *light*, airy room ‖ 月の明るい夜だった It was a *bright* moonlit night. ‖ 明るいうちに帰って来るのよ．わかった？ Come home *before dark*. OK? ‖ 新校舎の教室は明るくてとても気分がよい The classrooms in the new building are *bright* [*well-lit*] and very pleasant. ‖ 明るいグリーン *bright* [*light*] green（➤色の場合 light は「薄い」）.

2【性格・状態が】**cheerful**，**sunny**（快活な）；**upbeat**（陽気な）▶にこにこした明るい女の子 a smiling, *cheerful* girl ‖ 彼女は生まれつき性格が明るいのでみんなに人気がある She has a *sunny* disposition, so she is popular with everybody. ／She is naturally *cheerful*, so everyone likes her. ‖ ごく明るいタイプの人 an extremely *upbeat* sort of person ‖ その知らせを聞いて彼女の顔は明るくなった Her face *lit up* when she heard the news.（➤ lit は light（明るくなる）の過去形）‖ 花を生けたら玄関が明るくなった The flowers I arranged *brightened* (*up*) the entrance hall.

▶不正のない明るい社会を作ろう Let's build a just and *harmonious society*. ‖ 物事の明るい面を見るようにしなさい Try to look on [at] the *bright side* of things.

3【詳しい】▶彼は京都の地理に明るい He *really knows* Kyoto. ／ He *knows every nook and cranny of* Kyoto.（➤ every nook and cranny は「隅々まで」の意のインフォーマルな言い方）‖ おじはコンピュータに明るい My uncle *knows all about* computers. ／My uncle *knows* computers *inside (and) out*.

4【見通し・将来が】**bright** ▶ことしの国際貿易の見通しは明るい The prospects *look bright* for international trade this year. ‖ 彼の外科医としての将来はとても明るい His prospects as a surgeon are very *bright*.

あかるさ 明るさ **brightness**（輝き）；**cheerfulness**（快活さ）▶満月の光は１ルクスの明るさだ The *brightness* of a full moon is equal to one lux.

▶明るさが彼のとりえだ His strong point is his *cheerfulness*.

あかるみ 明るみ ▶また１つ政界の不祥事が明るみに出た Yet another political scandal *came to light* [*was made public*].

あかんべ ▶あの子，ぼくにあかんべしたよ！ That kid *made faces at* me!（➤ make faces は「しかめっ面をする」）.

▶ 対話「その梨一口かじらせてよ」「あかんべーだ！」"Give me a bite of your pear." "*No way!* ／ *Fat chance!*"（➤ No way! は「嫌だ，だめだ」，Fat chance! は「まさか！，ありえない！」）.

あかんぼう 赤ん坊 a **baby**（乳飲み子）；an **infant**（➤《英》では通例７歳未満の小児を指すが，《米》では一般的には２歳くらいまでの乳幼児をいう）▶男［女］の赤ん坊 a *baby* boy [girl] ‖ 彼女はまるで大きな赤ん坊だ She is like *a big child*. ／She is *a big baby*. ‖ 赤ん坊のようなまねはよせ Don't act *like a baby*. →赤ちゃん．

[1]あき 秋

fall，**autumn**（➤《米》では前者がふつう）▶秋は読書にもスポーツにもいちばんよい季節だ *Fall* [*Autumn*] is the best season for both reading and outdoor sports. ‖ 春は暖かく，秋は涼しい It is warm in (the) spring, but (it is) cool in (*the*) *fall* [*autumn*]. ‖ 祖父母はこの秋中国を旅行する My grandparents are taking a trip to China *this fall* [*autumn*]. ‖ 日ごとに秋めいてきた It's *getting more fall-like* [*autumn-like*] each day. ‖ めっきり秋めいてきた *Fall* [*Autumn*] is now *at its peak* [*best*]. ／Now we are *at the height of autumn*. ‖ 秋の夜長に草むらの虫が鳴いている *In the long autumn night*, insects are chirping in the grass. ‖ 実りの秋を迎え農家は忙しくなった The farmers became very busy with the arrival of *the fall* [*autumn*] *harvest season*.

ことわざ 女心［男心］と秋の空 Changeable things: a woman's [man's] mind and the fall [autumn] sky.

ことわざ 秋の日はつるべ落とし Fall days turn quickly into night. ／The autumn sun sinks fast.

✉ 当地長野は秋で，爽やかなお天気です *It's fall* here in Nagano and we are enjoying the crisp fall [autumn] air. ➤ (1)crisp は「身の引き締まるような」の意．(2)「お天気」の部分は weather でもよいが，「秋の空気(を)」と考えて fall [autumn] air とするほうが英語として自然．

✉ 日本の秋は木々が紅葉し，食欲が増し，私のいちばん好きな季節です In Japan, *fall* [*autumn*] is the season when the leaves of the trees turn

●は英訳の手順や注意点を解説した「訳のつぼ」
red and yellow and
It's my favorite seas
解説「秋」は
「秋」には,《英》
るのが一般的
tumn が好
(1) sun,
続く場合
(秋の
に a
(2

r appetite increases.

n? fall?
mn,《米》では fall を用い
下の場合は《米》でも au-
とに短母音のある単音節語が
が悪く, the autumn sun
n wind (秋の風) などのよう
月) は full moon と, fall
en leaves と聞き違えやすいた
oon, autumn leaves を用い
of autumn (秋たけなわ), the
autumn (秋の七草) など, やや
utumn を用いる.

ith, by)
する) ▶
at his
の汚い
her
(ア
e

n wind [breeze] ‖ **秋口** the [autumn] ‖ **秋の七草** the seven … utumn.
出語)
ancy (空き部屋, 欠員) ; an **opening** の) ▶このアパートには**空き部屋**が2つある …artment has two *vacancies.* ‖《掲示》空…あります *Vacancy* (ホテルの) ／ (Rooms) For …t,《英また》(Rooms) To Let (貸し間の ; ⇀空き…) ‖ こちらの保育園には職員の**空き**がありますか Are there any teaching positions *open* at this nursery school? ‖ うちの販売部に**空き**がある We have an *opening* in our sales department. ‖《切符売場などで》まだ座席に**空き**はありますか Are there any seats *available* [*left*]? ‖ きょうは忙しくて**空き時間**がない I am so busy today (that) I have no *time to spare.*
‖**空き缶** an empty can [《英また》tin] ‖ **空き瓶** an empty bottle.

[3]**あき 飽き** ▶私はその仕事に**飽き**がきてやめた I *got bored with* the job and quit. ‖ 順子はどうやら広志に**飽き**がきたようだ Evidently Junko *has lost interest in* Hiroshi. ‖ ことしは上品で**飽き**のこないデザインが流行している Elegant and *conservative* designs are in (fashion) this year. (➤ conservative は「地味な」).

あきあき 飽き飽きする be fed up《with》▶ぼくは母の小言には**飽き飽きしている** I *am fed up with* my mother's nagging. ‖ あの先生のお説教には**飽き飽きした** That teacher's preaching *bored* me *to death.* ／ I*'ve had quite enough of* that teacher's preaching.

あきさせる 飽きさせる bore +目 (退屈させる) ▶彼の話は聴衆を**飽きさせない** His talks do*n't bore* his audience.

あきさめ 秋雨 (a) **fall rain,** (an) **autumn rain**
‖**秋雨前線** an autumnal rain front.

あきす 空き巣 a **sneak thief** (鍵のかかっていないドアや窓から入るこそ泥), a **cat burglar** (塀・壁・電柱などから入る), a **prowler** /práʊləʳ/ (うろつき回って, 様子をうかがって入る) ▶あの男は**空き巣**ねらい専門だ That guy is a specialist in (*cat*) *burglary.* ‖ うちに**空き巣**が入った Our house *was burglarized* [*was broken into*] *during our absence.* ‖《標語》**空き巣**にご用心! Beware of prowlers!

あきたりない 飽き足りない ▶彼の仕事ぶりはどこか**飽き足りない** I'*m not completely satisfied* [*happy*] *with* his work. ‖ 今の生活には**飽き足りない** My present life *leaves a lot to be desired.*

あきち 空き地 a **vacant lot** ; an **open space** (広場) ▶子供たちが**空き地**でキャッチボールをしている Children are playing catch in the *vacant lot.*

あきっぽい 飽きっぽい ▶彼女は何をやっても**飽きっぽい** She *doesn't stick to anything.* (●「何事も長続きしない」と考える) ‖ あなたって**飽きっぽい**人ね You *easily get tired of* [*get bored by*] things, don't you?

あきない 商い (a) **trade, business** ▶このところ**商い**が芳しくない *Business* is slow these days.

あきなう 商う **deal in** ; **sell** (売る) ▶うちは茶やのりを**商っている** We *deal in* [*sell*] green teas and nori (laver).

あきなす 秋茄子 a **fall eggplant** ▶ [ことわざ] **秋なすは嫁に食わすな** Don't feed fall eggplants to your daughter-in-law. (●このままの訳例では誤解を招くおそれがあるので, 例えば「嫁に食わすにはうますぎるから」(because they are too delicious to feed her) のような何らかの説明を付け加えるとよい ; また, このことわざの解釈には諸説ある).

あきばれ 秋晴れ ▶陸上競技大会は**秋晴れ**の空のもとで行われた The track meet was held *under a clear fall* [*autumn*] *sky.* ‖ ピクニックには絶好の**秋晴れ**ですね It's *a perfect fall* [*autumn*] *day* for a picnic, isn't it?

あきびより 秋日和 a **clear fall** [**autumn**] **day, crisp fall** [**autumn**] **weather** ▶行楽には絶好の**秋日和**です It's *a perfect fall* [*autumn*] *day* for taking a pleasure trip.

あきや 空き家 a **vacant** [**an unoccupied**] **house** (人の住んでいない家) ; a **house for rent** [《英》**to let**] (貸し家) ▶その家は長いこと**空き家**になっている The house has been left *vacant* for a long time. (➤ いつもは人がいるはずの場所が現在からになっていることを表すのが vacant であるから, ここでは「がらんとして何もない」の意の empty は使えない) ‖ 彼は**空き家** [**部屋**] を探している He is looking for *a house* [*an apartment*] *to rent.* ／He is house [apartment] hunting.

あきらか 明らか

一形 明らかな clear, obvious, evident, plain, apparent
一副 明らかに clearly, obviously, plainly

> **語法** (1) **clear** が最も一般的な語で,「曖昧さがない」の意. **obvious** と **evident** はともに「議論の余地がないほど明らかな」の意だが, 前者のほうが明白さの度合いが強い. **plain** は「単純明快な」の意.
> (2) **apparent** は「見た目に明らかな」の意で, 目に見えるような場合に好まれる.

▶**明らかな証拠** *clear* evidence ‖ **明らかな間違い** an *obvious* mistake ‖ 彼が自分でこの絵を描いたのでないことは**明らかだ** *It is clear* [*obvious* ／ *evident*] *that* he did not draw the picture himself. ‖ 彼女が健康を損ねていることは**明らかだ** *It's apparent* [*clear*] *that* she has ruined her health. ／*Clearly* she has ruined her health. ‖ その文句の意味は**明らかだ** The meaning of that phrase *is* quite *plain.*
▶息子は**明らかに**天才だ My son is *definitely* a genius. ‖ きみは**明らかに**間違っているよ You are *obviously* [*plainly*] wrong. ‖ 彼女はその事故で**明らかに**気が動転していた She was *clearly* upset by the accident.
▶計画の細かい点はまだ**明らかにされていない** The details of the plan *are not* yet *known* [*made public*]. ‖

警察は事件の原因を明らかにしなかった The police did not *make* the cause of the accident *public*. (➤ make public は「公表する」) ‖ 市長はこの件で態度を明らかにすべきだ The mayor should *make* his position *clear* [should *clarify* his position] on this issue.

▶彼の落選は火を見るより明らかだ His defeat in the election is *a foregone conclusion*. (➤ a foregone conclusion は「初めからわかっている結末」).

あきらめ 諦め resignation /rèzɪgnéɪʃən/ ▶去年新しいカメラをなくしたが, なかなか諦めがつかなかった I lost my new camera last year, and *couldn't resign myself to* the loss easily. ‖ 何事も諦めが肝心だ *Resignation* is the first lesson of life. ‖ 敗戦続きで選手たちはすっかり諦めムードになった A streak of losses has *undermined the players' morale*. (➤「選手の士気がすっかり失われた」の意). 《参考》潔く負けを認める人のことを good loser という. 反対は bad loser.

あきらめる 諦める give up, abandon +目 (➤ 後者は「断念する」に相当する堅い語) ▶諦めるのはまだ早い It's too early to *give up*. ‖ その鍵はなくなった [その犬は死んだ] ものと諦めたほうがいいよ You'd better *give up* the key for lost [the dog for dead]. (➤ for は as でもよい).

▶おまえはかなわぬ恋をしている. あの娘のことは諦めなさい This love of yours is hopeless. *Forget* about her [*Give* her *up*]. ‖ 夢を諦めるな *Don't give up* your dream. (「夢を持ち続けよ」と考えた場合の訳. Don't give up on your dream. のように on をつけた場合の give up は実現不能と考えたり, 自信をなくしたりして「見切りをつける」の意).

【文型】
…するのを諦める
give up doing
give up on doing
《解説》give up は単に「(中途で)やめる」に対し, give up on は能力不足・自信喪失などで「見込みなしとさじを投げる」.

▶老人は車の運転を諦めた The old man *gave up* driv*ing*. (➤「運転をやめた」の意) ‖ 若者は職探しを諦めるところだった The young man nearly *gave up* look*ing* for work. ‖ 息子はピアノを習うのを諦めた My son *gave up on* learn*ing* how to play the piano. (これ以上やっても無駄, というような場合の訳. gave up learning は, 例えば, ほかの習い事や勉強で忙しくなったのでというような場合) ‖ (これから)運転免許取るの諦めたわ I've *given up* (*on*) try*ing* to get a driver's license. (give up (on) trying to do は「…しようとするのを諦める」の意. これに対して give up doing は「今…していることを(もうできないと)やめる」の意だから, ここではこの形は使えない).

▶彼らはその計画を諦めなければならなかった They had to *abandon* the project. ‖ 北海道へのスキー旅行は諦めた I *decided not to* take a ski trip to Hokkaido. (➤「…しないことに決めた」の意) ‖ 父のがんは治らないものと諦めねばならなかった We had to *come to terms with* our father's cancer. (➤ come to terms with は「(困難を)諦めて受け入れる」) ‖ 祖父は加齢による視力の低下を諦めて受け入れた My grandfather *resigned* him*self to* the deteriorating eyesight caused by aging. (➤ resign oneself to は「…を諦めて受け入れる」) ‖ (何事も)諦めることなかれ Never say die. (➤ 英語のことわざ) ‖ 対話「この問題, 解けないや」「諦めちゃだめだよ」"I can't sol his problem." "Don't *give up* (*on it*)."

あきる 飽きる get tired [s ay] of

【文型】
…するのに飽きる
get tired [sick] of doing

▶勉強に飽きてきた. 気分転換にう *getting tired of* study*ing*. I break by watch*ing* TV. ‖ 学 *tired* [*am sick*] *of* eat*ing* at the ria. (➤ sick は「うんざり」に近く強意 聴いても飽きない I *never get tired* jazz.

▶いくらラーメンが好きでも毎日じゃ食べ飽 though I do like ramen a lot, I'd them if I ate them every day.

☛ 飽きっぽい (→見出語)

あきれかえる 呆れ返る be disgusted 《at, w (うんざりする) ; be appalled 《by, at》(がく然と 彼のいいかげんさにはあきれ返る I *am disgusted* irresponsibility. ‖ 彼女はあきれ返った顔で息子 部屋を見つめた She looked *disgustedly* at son's messy room. ‖ あきれかえった聴衆は講演者 ーイングした The *appalled* audience booed t speaker.

アキレスけん アキレス腱 Achilles (') /əkíliːz/ tendon ▶彼はサッカーの試合中にアキレスけんを切った He cut [tore] his *Achilles' tendon* while playing soccer.

▶《比喩的》サードの不安定な守備がそのチームのアキレスけん(＝弱点)だ The uncertain fielding of the third baseman is *the Achilles' heel* [*the weak point*] of that team.

あきれる 呆れる be amazed 《at, by》(驚いている) ; be disgusted 《by, with》(うんざりしている) ▶きみの軽率なのにはあきれるよ Your carelessness *amazes* me. ／I *am amazed at* your carelessness. ‖ 教科書も持って来なかったの? あきれた子ね! You didn't even bring your textbook? *You're just unbelievable!* ‖ みんなあきれて顔を見合わせた We all looked at each other *with disgust*. ‖ 対話「DNAって何?」「あきれたね. DNA も知らないのかい」"What's DNA?" "*What?* You don't even know what DNA is?" (➤ イタリック体の what は「何だって? まさか」の意の間投詞).

¹あく 悪 (a) vice (悪徳) ; (an) evil, wickedness (邪悪) ; (a) wrongdoing (不正) ▶悪の道に入る *sink into vice* ／*fall into evil ways* ‖ 幼児は世の中の善と悪とがまだ見分けられない Little children are unable to discriminate between *good and evil*. ‖ 死刑は必要悪だと主張する人もいる Some people claim that capital punishment is *a necessary evil*.

²あく 灰汁 harshness (渋さ・苦さなど) ; bitterness (苦さ) ; harsh [bitter] taste (野菜のもつ渋味など) ; scum (肉などを煮たときに出る泡状のもの) ▶ゴボウのあくを抜く remove the *harshness* [*bitterness*] of burdock ‖ スープのあくをすくい取る skim (off) *the scum* from the soup.

▶《比喩的》彼はあく(＝個性)が強い He *has a strong personality*.

³あく 開く・空く・明く 1【閉じていたものがひらく】open ; be open (開いている) ▶車のドアがひとりでに開いた The car door *opened* by itself. ‖ その鍵でドアが開いた The key opened the door. ‖ **鏡台の引き出しがどうしても開かない** The drawer of the dressing table *won't open* [*come out*].

▶**デパートは10時にならないと開かない** Department stores *don't open* till ten. ‖ **ホテルのバーは午後4時に開きます** The hotel bar *opens* at 4 p.m. ‖《店員に》**おたくは何時まで開いてますか** How late *are* you *open* ? ‖ **その店は土曜日の夜は遅くまで開いている** That store *stays open* late on Saturday nights. ‖ (芝居の)**幕は午後5時に開きます** The curtain *rises* at 5 p.m.

2【空間や空白ができる】▶**子犬は生後2週間め頃に目があく** A puppy first *opens* its eyes about two weeks after birth. ‖ **競泳用の水着は大きく背中があいている** Competitive swimsuits are *cut* very *low* in the back. ‖ **ジャムの瓶が1つ空いた** I'*ve finished* one of the jars of jam. ‖ **水道管の破裂で道路に大穴があいた** The water pipe burst *made a large hole* in the road.

3【使われていない】▶**今頃の電車は空いている席が多い** There are many *empty* [*vacant*] seats on the train at this time of the day. ‖ **運良く,駐車スペースが1つ空いていた** Luckily, I found an *empty* [*available*] parking space. ‖《ホテルで》**今晩空いてませんか** *Do you have a room* for tonight ? ‖ 対話 「この席,空いてますか」「ええ,空いてます」"Is this seat taken ?" "No, it isn't." (● (1)問いの文を(×)Is this seat empty ? と訳さないこと. 人がいるかいないかは見ればわかるので,わざわざこんな聞き方はしない. 英語では「誰かにとられているか」と発想する. (2)質問は「この席はふさがっていますか」の意なので,「空いている」は No で答える).

▶**事務職員の席が1つ空いている** *There is an opening* for an office worker. ‖ **来年の春,准教授のポストが1つ空く** One post for an associate professor will *be available* next spring.

▶**その週刊誌,あいたら(=済んだら)貸してください** Please lend me the weekly magazine *when you are through with* it. ‖ **おーい,手があいたらちょっと手伝ってくれ** Hey, *when you have a minute*, give me a hand. ‖ **今晩,あいてますか** *Are you free* this evening ? ‖ **年末に時間のあいている人は少ない** Few people *have time to spare* at the end of the year.

☛ **開いた・空いた** (→見出語)

アクアラング an **aqualung** /ɑ́:kwəlʌŋ/, **scuba gear** 《参考》aqualung はフランスで開発された scuba の商品名. ▶**アクアラングをつけて潜る** dive with *scuba gear* / *scuba*-dive.

あくい 悪意 **ill will** ; **malice** /mǽlɪs/ (敵意) ▶**悪意のある中傷** *malicious* slander / slander *with ill intention* ‖ **彼は私のことばを悪意にとった** He *read ill intention* into my words (where there was none). ‖ **きみには悪意は抱いていない** I don't harbor any *ill will* [*malice*] toward you. ‖ **彼は悪意があって言ったのではない** He didn't mean any *harm*. ‖ **悪意があったかなかったかはわからないが,誰かが上空を飛んでいる飛行機にレーザー光線を向けた** Someone, *either innocently or maliciously*, pointed a laser beam at the airplane flying above.

あくうん 悪運 ▶**最近は悪運続きだ** I've had a run of *bad luck* lately. ‖ **いよいよやつらの悪運も尽きたな** It's time for them to *get their just deserts*. (➤ get one's just deserts は「悪業の報いを受ける」の意) ‖ **あいつは全く悪運が強い** He *has the luck to get away with every bad thing he does*.

あくえいきょう 悪影響 a **bad influence** ▶**喫煙は健康に悪影響がある** Smoking *is bad for* the health. ‖ **こういうテレビドラマは子供たちに悪影響を及ぼすと思います** I'm afraid this kind of TV drama will *have a bad influence on* children.

あくぎょう 悪行 (a) **wrongdoing**.

あくさい 悪妻 (a) **bad** [(an) **evil**] **wife**(悪い妻) ; an **awful wife**(ひどい妻).

あくじ 悪事 an **evil** [a **wicked**] **deed** ; a **crime** (犯罪) ▶**悪事を働く** commit [do] *a crime*.

ことわざ **悪事千里を走る** Bad news travels fast. (➤「悪い知らせは素早く伝わる」の意の英語のことわざだが,日本語のほうが「悪い行いや悪い評判はすぐに世間に知れ渡る」という意味である点で,両者にはずれがある).

あくしつ 悪質な **outrageous** /aʊtréɪdʒəs/ (けしからぬ) ; **vicious** (凶悪な) ; **malicious** (悪意のある) ▶**最近,悪質な犯罪が増えている** The number of *outrageous* [*vicious*] crimes has increased recently. ‖ **先生の教務手帳を破るなんて悪質ないたずらだ** Tearing the teacher's record book into pieces is nothing but a *malicious* prank.

アクシデント an **accident** (➤日英語ともに事故・不慮の出来事という意味があるが,英語には日本語にない「偶然・運(chance)」の意味もある).

あくしゅ 握手 a **handshake** 一動 (…と)**握手する** **shake hands**《with》▶**選手たちは試合の前に握手を交わした** The players *shook hands* (*with* each other) before the game.

1あくしゅう 悪臭 a **bad** [**nasty**] **smell** ; a **stink** (極めて強い) ▶**腐りかけた肉の悪臭がぷーんと鼻をついた** The *stink* [*putrid smell*] of the stale meat hit my nose. (➤ putrid /pjú:trɪd/ は「腐敗した」) ‖ **生ごみは悪臭を放つ** Garbage *smells* (*bad*). / Garbage *stinks*. / Garbage *gives off* [*out*] *a bad smell*.

2あくしゅう 悪習 a **bad habit** ▶**深酒という悪習** the *bad habit* of excessive drinking ‖ **選挙に金がかかり過ぎるという悪習は改められなければならない** We have to reform the *bad practices* of overly expensive election campaigns.

あくしゅみ 悪趣味 **bad taste** ; **vulgar taste** (低級・低俗な) ; **poor taste** (つまらない) ▶**悪趣味な冗談** a *sick* joke / a joke *in bad taste* ‖ **彼の服装はいつも悪趣味だ** He always dresses in *very poor taste*.

あくじゅんかん 悪循環 a **vicious circle** [**cycle**] ▶**サラ金に借金を返そうとして別のサラ金から借金していれば,結局は悪循環を繰り返すことになる** Borrowing money from a loan shark to pay another only results in *a vicious circle*.

あくじょ 悪女 **1【悪い女】** a **wicked** /wɪ́kɪd/ **woman** (邪悪な女) ; a **man-eater** (「男殺し」).

2【醜い女】 an **ugly woman**.

あくじょうけん 悪条件 **bad conditions** ; **unfavorable conditions** (不利な) ; a **handicap** (ハンディキャップ) ▶**炭鉱労働者たちは悪条件のもとで働かなくてはならなかった** Miners had to work *under bad conditions*. ‖ **ヨットが遭難したのは乗員が初心者だったうえに台風という悪条件が重なったからだ** The yacht's distress was caused by the *combination* of the typhoon and the crew's inexperience.

アクション an **action**

‖**アクション映画** an action film [movie] ‖ **アクションスター** an action hero.

1あくせい 悪政 **bad government** (悪い政治) ; **misrule**, **misgovernment** (失政) ▶**悪政で苦しむのはいつも一般市民だ** It is always the ordinary people that suffer

あ

from *bad government* [*misrule*].

²**あくせい 悪性の** **malignant** /məlígnənt/ ▶**がんは悪性の腫瘍だ** A cancer is a *malignant* tumor. ‖ **悪性の**(＝ひどい)かぜがはやっている A *bad* cold is going around.

あくせく ▶あくせく働く *work like a slave* [*a dog*] ‖ 毎日家事で**あくせくしています** Day after day I *slave* (*away*) around the house. (➤ slave (away) は「(奴隷のように)あくせく働く」の意で，おどけて用いたり軽蔑的に用いたりする) ‖ 父は年中**あくせく働いている** Dad *keeps his nose to the grindstone* all year round. (英語では「砥石(といし)に鼻をくっつける(ようにして一生懸命働く)」が原義の keep one's nose to the grindstone を用いて表現する) ‖ **あくせく働く**だけが人生じゃない There's more to life than just *work*, *work*, *work*.

アクセサリー an **accessory** /əksésəri/ ; **jewelry**(宝石類) ▶**アクセサリー**を身に着ける put on *jewelry* ‖ 車の**アクセサリー** an auto [a car] *accessory*.

> 危ないカタカナ語 **アクセサリー**
> **1** 日本語では装身具のことを「アクセサリー」といっているが，英語の accessory は帽子・ハンドバッグ・手袋・スカーフ・ハンカチなどを指し，「アクセサリー」とは意味の範囲が異なる.
> **2** イアリング・ネックレスなど宝石をあしらった装身具は，英語では jewelry と呼ぶのがふつう.

アクセス (an) **access** /ǽkses/ ; **transportation** (交通機関) ▶インターネットでホワイトハウスに**アクセスする** *access* the White House through the Internet ‖ その競技場は交通の**アクセス**がよくない The stadium *doesn't have good transportation*.

アクセル an **accelerator** /əksélərèɪṭə^r/ ; a **gas pedal** (アクセルペダル) ▶**アクセル**を踏む step on *the accelerator* ／step on the gas (➤ 後者はインフォーマルな表現).

あくせん 悪銭 ▶ ことわざ **悪銭身につかず** Ill got, ill spent. ／Easy come, easy go. (➤ 後者は単に「得やすいものは失いやすい」という意味で用いることが多い. したがって日本語のことわざの意味とはずれる).

あくせんくとう 悪戦苦闘 ▶その若夫婦は育児に**悪戦苦闘**している That young couple *is struggling with* child-rearing. ‖ 数年間は大した金もなく**悪戦苦闘**の生活だった We *struggled along* for some years without much money.

アクセント 1【強勢】 an **accent**, a **stress** ▶hotel は e に**アクセント**がある There's *an accent* on the 'e' in 'hotel.'
2【なまり】 an **accent** ▶彼はおかしな**アクセント**で話す He speaks with *a* strange *accent*.
3【強調点】 ▶このドレスは胸元のリボンが**アクセント**になっている The ribbon on the chest *highlights* this dress. ‖ この水着は胸に**アクセント**を置いている This swimsuit *accents* the bosom. ／This swimsuit draws attention to the breasts.

あくたい 悪態 **abusive language** ▶彼は悔し紛れにぼくに**悪態をついた** In his frustration he *used abusive language* against me. ‖ 子供は母親に向かって「ばか!」「とんま!」と**悪態をついた** The kid *called* his mother *names*, shouting things like "You idiot!" and "Blockhead!" (➤ call ... names で「いろいろな呼び方で(人を)あしざまに言う」).

あくだま 悪玉 a **bad guy**, a **baddie**.

あくてんこう 悪天候 **bad weather** ▶**悪天候**のため運動会は延期になった The sports day was postponed due to *bad weather*. ‖ **悪天候**で船は横浜を出港できなかった *Bad weather* prevented the boat from leaving Yokohama. ‖ 遭難者の捜索活動は**悪天候**をついて終日行われた Search activities for the missing victims continued all day long *in spite of* (*the*) *bad weather*.

あくどい ▶あくどい詐欺 a *vicious* deception ‖ あの商社は**あくどい**商法で金をもうけた That trading company earned money by *crooked* [*fraudulent* ／ *unscrupulous*] business practices. (➤ crooked /krókɪd/ は「いんちきの」，fraudulent /frɔ́:dʒələnt/ は「人をだます」，unscrupulous /ʌnskrú:pjələs/ は「悪質な」).

あくとう 悪党 a **scoundrel** /skáʊndrəl/, a **rascal** (➤ ともに古風な語).

あくとく 悪徳 (a) **vice** ▶裏切りは卑しむべき**悪徳**である Betrayal is a hateful *vice*. ‖ **悪徳**不動産業者 a *dishonest* [an *unscrupulous*] real estate agent (➤ unscrupulous /ʌnskrú:pjələs/ は「良心的でない」の意).
‖**悪徳商法** unscrupulous [fraudulent] business practices.

あくなき 飽くなき **insatiable** /ɪnséɪʃəbəl/ (貪欲な) ; **persistent** /pəˈsístənt/ (ひるむことのない) ▶**飽くなき**知識欲 an *insatiable* desire for knowledge ‖ 刑事の**飽くなき**執念がついに実を結んだ The detective's *persistence* finally bore fruit.

あくにん 悪人 a **bad person**, a **wicked** /wíkɪd/ **person**.

-あぐねる ▶卒業後，どうするか思い**あぐねて**両親に相談した I *was at a loss* what to do after graduation, so I asked my parents for advice. ‖ 赤ん坊の名前をどれにするか決め**あぐねている** We're *having trouble deciding* what to name our baby. →-あぐむ.

あくび 欠伸 a **yawn** /jɔ:n/ 一動 **あくびをする** **yawn** ▶**あくび**をかみ殺す stifle [suppress] *a yawn* ‖ 手で**あくび**を隠す hide *a yawn* with one's hand ‖ **あくび**の出るような(＝退屈な)講義 a *boring* [*dull*] lecture ‖ **あくび**は行儀は悪いが正直な批判である *Yawning* is bad manners but an honest opinion.
☞ **生あくび** (→見出語)

あくひつ 悪筆 **bad handwriting** ▶何て**悪筆**だ. 読めやしない What *awful handwriting*! I can't make out a thing.

あくひょう 悪評 a **bad reputation** ; **notoriety** /nòʊṭəráɪəṭi/ (悪名) ▶彼は近所で**悪評**が立っている He has *a bad reputation* in his neighborhood.

あくびょうどう 悪平等 (a) **false** [(an) **inappropriate**] **equality** (➤ false, inappropriate はそれぞれ「間違った」「不適当な」) ▶できる生徒とできない生徒を同じ教室で同時に教えるのは**悪平等**であると言う人もいる Some people say that teaching quick students and slow ones in the same room at the same time is a case of *false* [*inappropriate*] *equality*.

あくぶん 悪文 **poor writing** (下手な文章) ; a **bad style** (まずい文体) ▶**悪文**を書く *write badly* ‖ この取扱説明書の文章は**悪文**だ *The writing* in this manual *is terrible*. ／*The way* this manual is written *is awful*.

あくへい 悪弊 a **bad practice** ▶談合などという**悪弊**は一掃すべきだ We should eliminate *bad practices* such as rigging bids.

あくへき 悪癖 a **bad habit** ▶ぼくは爪をかむ**悪癖**がいまだに抜けないでいる Even now, I can't stop that *bad habit* of biting my nails.

あ

あくま 悪魔 an **evil spirit**, a **devil**; **the Devil**, **Satan** /séɪtn/ (魔王) ▶それは悪魔の仕業に違いない It must be the work of *the Devil*. ‖ 彼女は悪魔的な魅力をもっている She has a *seductive* [*devilish*] charm.
‖**悪魔ばらい** exorcism /éksɔːˌsìzəm/.

> **日↔英比較 悪魔と devil**
> ほとんどの日本人にとって,「悪魔」と言われても具体的なイメージは湧かないであろう. この点, 英語の devil はキリスト教など一神教を信奉する人にとっては, 全能の神に反逆を試みて天界から地獄に落とされた悪の化身であり, 具体的なイメージの湧く存在である. その一般的イメージは, 足はひづめが割れていて, 体は黒く毛むくじゃらで目は皿のように大きく, 鼻から火を噴き, ヤギのような角があったり, 尾があったり, コウモリのような翼があったりするものである.

あくまで(も) 飽くまで(も) ▶彼女はその提案にあくまでも反対した She opposed the proposal *stubbornly*. (➤ stubbornly は「頑固に」) ‖ 彼女は自分の意見にあくまでも固執した She persisted in her opinion *no matter what*. ‖ これはあくまでも私の個人的な感想で公式見解ではありません This is *strictly* my personal view, not an official statement. (➤ strictly は「もっぱら…だけ」) ‖ これはあくまでも私の臆測です This is a pure guess on my part (*for what it's worth*). (➤ for what it's worth は「取り立てて言うほどのことではないかもしれないが」) ‖ 安曇野の空はあくまでも青かった The sky over the Azumino Plain was *as* blue *as* (it) *could be* [was *impossibly* blue].

あくむ 悪夢 a **bad dream**; a **nightmare** (恐ろしいうなされるような夢) ▶悪夢にうなされる [悩まされる] *have* [*be troubled with*] *a nightmare* ‖ あの交通事故は生涯うなされる悪夢のような出来事だった That traffic accident was *a nightmare* from which I'll suffer forever.

-あぐむ ▶考えあぐんだ末, ご相談に参りました I *was at a complete loss as to what to do*, and so I came to ask you for advice. ‖ 挑戦者は終始攻めあぐんだ The challenger kept *attacking futilely*. (➤ futilely は「無駄に」の意).

あくめい 悪名 a **bad name**; a **bad reputation** (悪評); **notoriety** /nòʊt̬əráɪət̬i/ (悪名の高さ) ▶悪名の高い会社 a *notorious* company ‖ その政治家は賄賂を取ることで悪名が高い The politician is *notorious* [*infamous*] *for* accepting bribes. (➤それぞれ /noʊtɔ́ːriəs/, /ínfəməs/ と発音する) ‖ やくざはアメリカでも悪名をとどろかせている Yakuza have *a bad name* [have achieved *notoriety*] even in America.

あくやく 悪役 a **villain** /vílən/, 《主に米・インフォーマル》 a **bad guy**, a **baddie** (➤後者はよりくだけた語) ▶あの俳優は悪役を演じることが多い That actor usually plays (the part of) a *villain*.

あくゆう 悪友 **bad company** (➤ company は集合的に「仲間」の意) ▶悪友と交わる *keep bad company*. ▶《反語的に》悪友たちと飲む drink with one's *cronies* (➤ crony には次例の3語と異なり, 軽蔑的響きがあることも多い) ‖ 木村君は学生時代からの悪友でしてね Kimura has been *an old pal* [*buddy* / 《英》 *chum*] *of mine* since school days.

あくよう 悪用 **abuse** /əbjúːs/ 一動 **悪用する** **abuse** /əbjúːz/ +目, **misuse** +目 ▶あの役人は地位を悪用して金をもうけた That government official earned money by *abusing* [*misusing*] his position. ‖ 彼は一度社名を悪用したことがあった He *had* once *used* the company's name *for a bad purpose*.

あぐら ▶床にあぐらをかく *sit cross-legged* [*sit Indian style*] on the floor ‖ 鼻があぐらをかいた男 a *pug-nosed* man.
▶《比喩的》彼は過去の栄光の上にあぐらをかいている He *is resting on his laurels*. (➤「過去の成功に満足してさらなる努力をしない」の意).

あくらつ 悪辣 ▶悪辣な行為 *villainous* conduct ‖ その周旋屋は悪辣な手段で私をだまそうとした That broker tried to play a *dirty* [*mean* / *nasty*] trick on me.

あくりょう 悪霊 an **evil spirit** ▶悪霊を追い払う drive out [away] *an evil spirit*.

あくりょく 握力 a **grip** ▶その力士は桁外れに握力が強い The sumo wrestler has an extraordinarily strong *grip*.
‖**握力計** a hand dynamometer, a grip meter.

アクリル **acrylic** /əkrílɪk/ **resin (s)** (アクリル樹脂); **acrylic fiber(s)** (アクリル繊維)
‖**アクリルセーター** an acrylic sweater.

あくる 明くる ▶明くる3月10日に on the *following* day, the 10th of March ‖ 少年は前の晩は体の具合が悪かったが, 明くる日はまた元気になったようだ The boy was sick in the evening, but *on the following* [*next*] *day* he seemed well again. ‖ 明くる年先生は結婚した Our teacher got married *the next year*. (➤「翌年」の場合は the が必要).

あくろ 悪路 a **rough road** ▶四輪駆動車は泥沼のような悪路を物ともせずに突っ走った The four-wheeler easily drove through the *terribly* [*horribly*] *muddy road*.

アクロバット **acrobatics** /ækrəbǽt̬ɪks/ (曲芸); an **acrobat** /ǽkrəbæt/ (曲芸師) ▶アクロバットを演じる perform *acrobatics* ‖ アクロバット的な演技 *acrobatic* acting ‖**アクロバット飛行** stunt flying.

-あけ -明け **1**【終わること, 終わったばかり】▶ことしは梅雨明けが遅かった The rainy season lasted longer than usual this year. / *The end of the rainy season* came later than usual this year. ‖ 連休明けに英語の小試験がある We'll have a quiz in English *after the* (*consecutive*) *holidays*.
2【始まったばかり】▶シーズン明けはまだ調子の出ない選手が多い Many players are still out of shape *at the beginning of the season*.

あげあし 揚げ足 ▶生徒たちは新米の先生の揚げ足を取った The students *tripped up* the new teacher *on his* [*her*] *wording*. (➤ trip up は「(人を)つまずかせる」) ‖ 彼はいつも人の揚げ足を取るので同僚たちに嫌われている The people he works with don't like him because he *pounces on every slip of the tongue*. (➤「言い間違いを攻撃する」の意) ‖ その批評家はていのいい揚げ足取りだ That critic is nothing but a pretentious *faultfinder*. (➤ pretentious は「格好をつけただけの」).

あけがた 明け方 **dawn** /dɔːn/, **daybreak** ▶明け方になってやっととろとろ眠った I finally managed to doze off around *dawn* [*daybreak*]. ‖ 明け方まで4人でマージャンをした The four of us played mah-jongg till *the crack of dawn*. (➤ the crack of dawn は「夜明け」).

あげく 挙げ句 ▶彼は長いこと入院したあげく死んだ *After* a long stay in the hospital, he finally died. ‖ さんざん考えたあげく, 車を手放すことにした *After a lot of thinking*, I decided to give up my car. ‖

彼は家が全焼し，車を盗まれ，あげくの果てに仕事まで失った His house burned down, his car was stolen, and *on top of that*, he lost his job.

あけくれ 明け暮れ day and night（昼も夜も）▶母は戦場で戦っている息子の無事を明け暮れ祈った The mother prayed *day and night* for the safety of her son, who was fighting on the battlefield. ‖ 最近私は受験勉強の明け暮れです These days I'm cramming for entrance exams *from morning till night* [*day in, day out*].（➤ cram for は「…の詰め込み勉強をする」の意のインフォーマルな言い方）.

あけくれる 明け暮れる ▶仕事仕事で明け暮れるのはもうたくさんだ I can't stand this working *from dawn to dusk* any longer. ‖ 息子はサッカーに明け暮れている My son *lives and breathes* soccer.（➤ live and breathe は「（特定の事柄・活動など）に没頭する」の意のインフォーマルな言い方）.

あげしお 上げ潮 the rising tide ▶上げ潮だ *The tide is in.*
▶（比喩的）わが党は今回の選挙戦では上げ潮ムードだ *Things are looking up* for our party in this election campaign.

あけしめ 開け閉め ▶ドアの開け閉めは静かにしてほしい I wish you would *open and close* the door quietly.

あけすけ 明け透け ▶あけすけな冗談 a *crude* joke（➤ crude は「露骨な」）‖ 彼はあけすけに物を言うね He *says what he thinks straight out* [*point-blank*], doesn't he？／He's *too outspoken*, isn't he？（➤ outspoken は「ことばが無遠慮な」）.

あげぜんすえぜん 上げ膳据え膳 ▶毎日上げ膳据え膳で，私って，何て幸せなんでしょう！How lucky I am to *be waited on hand and foot* every day！（英語では「まめまめしく（食事の）世話をされて」と考えて，be waited on hand and foot という慣用句を用いて表す）.

あげぞこ 上げ底 a raised [false] bottom ▶この焼きのりの箱は上げ底なので，実際は中身が少ない This box doesn't actually contain much toasted nori because it has *a raised* [*false*] *bottom*.

あけっぱなし 開けっ放し ▶ドアを開けっ放しにしないでください Please don't *leave* [*keep*] the door *open*.（➤ keep ... open は意図的に「開けたままにする」）‖ 窓は開けっ放しになっていた The window *was left* [*was kept*] *open*.

あけっぴろげ 開けっ広げ ▶開けっ広げな性格 a *frank* personality ‖ 開けっ広げな人 an *open-hearted* person ‖ 彼は誰に対しても開けっ広げだ He *is free and open with* everybody.

あげつらう ▶自分の欠点を棚に上げて，人の欠点をあげつらうのはやめよ Don't *draw attention to* other people's shortcomings while ignoring your own faults.

あけてもくれても 明けても暮れても day in and day out ▶彼は夏休みになると天候におかまいなく明けても暮れても魚釣りに出かける During summer vacation, he goes fishing, *day in and day out*, no matter what the weather is like.
✉ 明けても暮れても思うはきみのことばかりだよ I think only of you *day and night*.

あけのみょうじょう 明けの明星 the morning star（➤「金星」は Venus）.

あげは（ちょう） 揚羽蝶（虫）a swallowtail.

あけはなつ 開け放つ ▶窓を開け放つ *open* the window(s) *all the way*.

あけぼの 曙 **1**【明け方】dawn /dɔːn/, daybreak ▶春はあけぼの Spring is most beautiful *at dawn*.
2【始まり】the dawn ▶文明のあけぼの *the dawn* of civilization.

あげもの 揚げ物 fried food, a fried dish（➤ fry はいため物も指すので，特に揚げ物をいうときは deep-fried food, a deep-fried dish という）.

[1]**あける 開ける・空ける** **1**【閉じていたものをひらく】open ▶戸を押して［手前に引いて／横に引いて］開ける *push* [pull／slide] a door *open* ‖ ドアは開けたままにしておきますか Should I *leave* the door *open*？‖ 35ページを開けると答えが出ています If you *open* your book to [（英）at] page 35 [If you *turn to* page 35], you will find the answer. ‖ 包装紙がまた使えるよう小包を開けるときは注意してください Be careful when you *unwrap* [*undo*／*open*] the package so (that) we can use the paper again.
▶手紙の封を開ける *open* a letter ‖ 今晩は取って置きのカニ缶を開けよう I'll *open* one of my precious [special] cans of crab meat tonight. ‖ まぶしくて目を開けていられないよ It's so bright out (that) I can't *keep* my eyes *open*. ‖ 口を大きく開けて「あー」と言ってください *Open* your mouth *wide* and say "Ahh."（→あーん，あんぐり）.
▶表門は夜中の12時まで開けてあります The front entrance *is open* until midnight. ‖ 店は毎日10時に開けます Our store *opens* at ten every day.
2【空間や空白をつくる】▶穴をあける *make* a hole ‖ この板にきりで穴を２つあけてください Could you *drill* a couple of *holes* in this board for me？‖ 彼は一気にグラスを空けた He *emptied* the glass in one gulp. ‖ バケツの水を表に空けてきてくれ Could you go outside and *empty* the water from the bucket？
3【使わないでおく】▶あとからもう１人来ますので，席を１つ空けておいてください There will be another person coming later, so please *reserve* a seat for him [*save* him a seat]. ‖ 先生は生徒たちに１行ずつ空けて書くように言った The instructor told the students to write on *every other* [*every second*] *line*. ‖ 忘年会をやろうと思ってるんだけど，来月の最初の土曜日，空けておいてくれる？I'm organizing a year-end party. Can you *keep* the first Saturday next month *open* [*free*]？‖ 筋肉を大きくしたければ筋トレは中２日空けてやるとよい If you want to make your muscles bigger, you should *rest* (*for*) *two days* between workouts.
▶ゴールデンウイークはいつも家を空けています I'*m* always *out* [*away from home*] during the 'Golden Week' holidays. ‖（いつまでも終わらない会議に次の予定の人が）すみませんが会議室を空けて（＝退室して）いただけますか Excuse me, but could I ask you to *leave* the conference room？‖ 近づいてくる救急車には道を空けることが法律で定められている The law requires that you *yield to* [*make way for*] an oncoming ambulance.

[2]**あける 明ける** **1**【夜が】▶目を覚ましたら夜が明けるところだった When I woke up, *the day* [*dawn*] *was breaking*.（➤ night を主語にしないことに注意）.
2【年が】▶新年は静かに明けた The new year *dawned* quietly. ‖ 明けましておめでとう *Happy New Year！*（→おめでとう）.
3【終わる】▶やっと梅雨が明けてみんなほっとしている Everybody is relieved because the rainy season *has ended* [*has passed*] at last.

あげる 上げる・挙げる・揚げる

📖 訳語メニュー
高い方へ動かす →put up, raise **1**
与える →give **2**
向上させる →improve **3**

1【高い方へ動かす】put up ; raise /reɪz/ ＋目 (一時的に持ち上げる) ; **lift** ＋目 (重い物を手で) ▶その箱を屋根裏部屋に**上げなさい** *Put* the box *up* in the attic. ‖ 彼女は名前を呼ばれて**顔を上げた** She *looked up* when her name was called. ‖ 答えがわかった人は手を**挙げなさい** *Put* your hand *up* [*Raise* your hand] if you know the answer. ‖ 数人の子供たちが校庭でたこを**揚げていた** Some children *were flying* kites on the playground. ‖ 地元では**花火を揚げて**その選手の優勝を祝った The player's hometown celebrated his victory *with fireworks display*.
▶仏壇にお線香を**あげる** *offer* incense (sticks) on a household Buddhist altar.

2【与える】give ＋目 ▶卒業祝いにこのカメラを**あげよう** I'*m giving you* this camera as a graduation gift. ‖ この本, きみに**あげる** This book *is for you*. ／*I'm giving* this book *to you*. You can keep it. (➤「返さずに持っていていい」の意).
▶庭の芝生を刈って**あげましょう** *I'll* mow the lawn *for you*. ‖ 手紙を読んで**あげましょうか** *Shall I* read the letter *for you*? ／*Do you want me to* read the letter *for you*?

3【状態を向上させる】improve ▶きみもだいぶ囲碁の**腕を上げたね** I notice that you have really *improved* in *Go*. ‖ 我々の会社は**能率を上げる**ためにフレックスタイム制を導入した Our company has adopted flextime (in order) to *increase efficiency*.

4【数値などを上昇させる】raise ＋目 ▶部屋の温度を20度まで**上げる** *raise* the room temperature to 20° Celsius ‖ 物価がどんどん上がるのに, 給料はなかなか**上げてもらえない** Though prices are rising steadily, it's almost impossible to *get a raise* [《英》*rise*] (in salary). ‖ 彼らは給料を3パーセント**上げるよう**要求した They demanded that wages *be raised* by 3 percent. ／They demanded a 3 percent wage *hike*. (➤ wage hike は「賃上げ」) ‖ **スピードを上げて**よ *Speed up*. ／*Faster*, please. (➤ 反対は Slow down. ／Slower, please.) ‖ もっと**スピードを上げて**仕事したらどうかね I suggest you work a little *faster*. ‖ ラジオのボリュームをもうちょっと**上げて**くれないかな Could you turn *up* (the volume on) the radio? (➤「下げる」は turn down).

5【目立つように現す】▶海岸で子供たちが波しぶきを**上げて**遊んでいる At the beach, children are having fun *splashing around* in the water. ‖ 彼女は苦痛のあまり**悲鳴を上げた** She *let out* a yelp of pain. ‖ 人々はどっと**歓声を上げた** The crowd *gave a loud cheer* all at once. ／Suddenly the crowd *gave a loud cheer* [*cheered loudly*].
▶**例を挙げる** *cite* [*give*] *an example* ‖ 私がうそをついていると疑うんなら, **証拠を挙げてみろ** If you think I'm lying, *try to prove it*. ‖ 彼は役に立ちそうな本の題名を1つ**挙げた** He *mentioned* a book that might be useful. ‖ 中国地方の5つの県名を**挙げてごらん** *Name* the five prefectures in the Chugoku district.
▶**結婚式**はいつ**挙げた**のですか When *was* the wedding ceremony *held*? ‖ 刑事は3年の苦労の末やっと**容疑者を挙げた** The detective finally *arrested* the suspect after three years of painstaking investigation.
▶**全力を挙げて**財政改革を行う決意であります I will *do everything in my power* to achieve financial reform. ‖ オリンピックは**国を挙げて**盛大に行われた The Olympic Games *received nationwide support* and were held on a large scale. ‖ わが町は**町を挙げて**観光客集めに取り組んでいる *Our whole town* is working [making an effort] to attract tourists. ／*Our town is making an all-out effort* to attract tourists. (➤ 後者は「総力で取り組んでいる」ことを強調する場合).

6【終了させる, 完了させる】get ... done ; finish ＋目 (終える) ▶この仕事をあすの朝までに**上げなくてはならない** I've got to *get* this job *done* by tomorrow morning. ‖ 誕生パーティーを1万円**以内で上げたい** I'd like to *do* the birthday party *for less than* 10,000 yen.

7【望ましい結果・収入を得る】▶期待した成果を**上げる**ことができなかった I did not *obtain* the desired results. ‖ 彼は経理部長として**良い成績を上げた** He *has done well* as head of the accounting department. ‖《野球で》3回に7点を**上げる** *score* seven runs in the third inning ‖ 会社は順調に**利益を上げている** Our company is *making* steady *profits*.

8【揚げ物を作る】fry ＋目 →**揚げ物** ▶**魚を揚げる** *fry* fish ‖ 夕食にエビのフライを**揚げましょうか** Do you want me to *make* deep-fried prawns for supper?

9【吐く】throw up ▶お母さん, 大二郎がまた**あげちゃった**よ! Mom, Daijiro *threw up* again!

-あげる -上げる ▶赤ん坊を**抱き上げる** *take* a baby *into one's arms* ‖ レポートを**書き上げる** *finish writing* one's (term) paper.

あけわたす 明け渡す ▶彼は借金が返済できず, サラ金業者に家を**明け渡す**はめになった He couldn't pay back the money he had borrowed from a loan shark and was forced to *give up* [*vacate*] his house. ‖ そのボクサーはわずかひと月でチャンピオンの座を**明け渡した** That boxer *lost* his championship crown after only one month.

あご 顎

a jaw (口の中の上下の骨 ; ふつうは下顎) ; **the chin** (下顎の先) ▶上[下]**顎** the upper [lower] *jaw* ‖ 二重**顎** a double *chin* ‖ とがった**顎** a pointed *chin* ‖ 彼の**顎**に一発かましてやった I punched him hard on *the chin* ‖ 笑い過ぎて**顎**が外れるほどだった I almost laughed my *jaw* out of joint.
▶《慣用表現》あの店の主人は店員を**顎で使う** The storekeeper *orders* the clerks *around* [*leads* the clerks *by the nose*]. (➤ order around は「あれこれと指図する」, lead ... by the nose は「人の鼻面をとって引き回す」が原義) ‖ 彼は威勢よくその事業を引き受けたが, 3か月もたたないうちに**顎を出した** He undertook the project with enthusiasm, but by the time three months had passed he *was* already *worn out*. (➤ be worn out は「へたばる」).

アコーディオン an **accordion** ▶アコーディオンを弾く play the *accordion*.
‖アコーディオンドア a folding door.

あこがれ 憧れ (a) **longing, yearning** ; a **dream** (夢) ▶同時通訳が彼女の**憧れ**の職業だ Simultaneous interpretation is the job *of her dreams*. ／Her *dream* is to become a simultaneous inter-

あ

preter. ‖ その作家は若者たちの**憧れの的だ** That author is an *object of admiration* for young people. (➤ admiration は「賞賛」) ／That author is *admired* by young people. ‖ あの俳優は多くの十代の女の子たちの**憧れの的だ** That actor is *a heartthrob* for millions of teenage girls. (➤ heartthrob は「胸をときめかす男性有名人」) ‖ 恭子は学生時代ぼくらの**憧れの的だった** All the boys *had a crush on* Kyoko when we were in school (together). (➤ have a crush on は「…に熱を上げる」の意のインフォーマルな言い方).

あこがれる 憧れる ▶その女優に**憧れている** I *admire* that actress. ‖ 私はスイスに**憧れている**(＝一度は行ってみたい) I *long to visit* Switzerland *once*. (➤ long to do は「…することを切望する」の意) ‖ 子供の頃プロ野球選手に**憧れた**ものです When I was a little boy [girl], I *dreamed of becoming* a professional baseball player. ‖ 若者は都会生活に**憧れる**ものだ Young people *are attracted by* city life.

あこぎな **greedy and heartless**.

あごひげ 顎髭 a **beard** /bɪəʳd/ ▶顎ひげを生やした男 a *bearded* man. →ひげ.

¹**あさ 朝** **morning**(➤ 夜が明けてから正午または昼食時までの「午前中」を指す) ▶朝から晩まで *from morning till* [*to*] *night* ‖ **朝早く** *early in the morning*(➤「けさ早く」は early this morning) ‖ 日曜日の**朝に** *on Sunday morning* (➤ 特定の日の朝は in ではなく on ; この表現は直近の日曜日で, 何日のことかがわかるとき. 「たまたま日曜日である朝」は on a Sunday morning のように a が必要) ‖ 7月のある**朝に** *one morning* in July ‖ 起きて, 朝よ Wake up. It's *morning*. ‖ **朝**のうちに宿題をやってしまおう I'll finish up my homework *during* [*in*] *the morning*. ‖ とても寒い**朝**だった It was such a chilly *morning*. ‖ 初夏の**朝**はすがすがしい Early summer *mornings* are refreshing. ‖ 式は4月5日の**朝**だ The ceremony will be held on the *morning* of April 5. ‖ うちの祖母は**朝が早い** My grandmother is *an early bird*. (➤ 文字どおりには「早起き鳥」).

▶日曜の**朝**は寝坊をする I sleep late *on Sunday morning*(*s*). ‖ きょうは**朝**雨が降った It rained *this morning*. ‖ きょうは**朝から**雨だ It's been raining *since* (*this*) *morning*. (➤ 現在完了形とともに用いる起点を表す語は since) ‖ 天気予報ではあすは**朝から**雨だ The weather forecast calls for rain *from tomorrow morning*. ‖ 彼はきのうの**朝**ホノルルへたった He left for Honolulu *yesterday morning*. ‖ うちでは**毎朝**みんな一緒に食事をする In my family we all eat breakfast together *every morning*. (➤ this, yesterday, every などがついて副詞句となる場合は in などの前置詞をつけない) ‖ **翌朝**は雪だった It snowed (*the*) *next* [*following*] *morning*.

²**あさ 麻** **hemp**(植物, 繊維) ; **linen** /lɪ́nɪn/ (麻製品) ▶麻のシャツ a *linen* shirt ‖ **麻糸** hemp thread ‖ **麻布** hemp cloth ‖ **麻袋** a hemp sack.

あざ 痣 a **birthmark**(生まれつきの) ; a **bruise** /bruːz/ (打ち身による) ▶その男の子は足じゅうあざだらけにしている The boy has *bruises* all over his legs. ‖ 廊下で転んで肘に**あざができた** I fell over in the corridor and *bruised* [*got a bruise on*] my elbow. ‖ 彼女はすぐに**あざができる** She *bruises* easily. ‖ 彼はけんかで殴られて目の周りに**あざができた** He *got a black eye* in the fight. 《参考》 black eye は「(打たれてできた)目の周りの黒あざ」. なお, 日本人などの「黒い目」は 通例 dark eyes という.

あさい 浅い **1**【深さが】**shallow** ▶底の浅い鍋 a *shallow* pan ‖ 川上に行くにしたがって流れは**浅くなる** The stream *becomes shallower* as you move upriver. ‖ この木は**根が浅い** This tree *has shallow roots* [*has its roots in shallow soil*].

2【時間・月日などが】**short** ▶この会社に勤めてまだ**日が浅い** *It's only been a short time* since I started working for this company. ‖ この国は10年前独立したばかりで, まだ**歴史が浅い** This country became independent just ten years ago, so it still *has a short history*. ‖ **春はまだ浅い** It is still *early* spring. ／Spring *has just begun*.

3【知識・経験などが】**shallow, superficial** ▶**経験の浅い**登山者 an *inexperienced* mountain climber ‖ 彼女は**考えが浅い** She *is shallow-minded*. ／She *is a shallow* [*superficial*] *thinker*. ‖ 彼の**知識の浅い**のにはがっかりした I am disappointed with the *shallowness* of his knowledge.

4【傷・眠りが】▶**浅い傷** a *slight* injury ‖ 近頃**眠りが浅い** I *sleep lightly* these days.

¹**あさいち 朝市** a **morning open-air market** ▶朝市で野菜を買った I bought vegetables at the *morning open-air market*.

²**あさいち 朝いち** ▶あす**朝いち**で打ち合わせしよう Let's meet and make arrangements *first thing tomorrow morning*.

あさがえり 朝帰り ▶父はきょう**朝帰り**した My father *came home this morning after staying out all night*.

あさがお 朝顔 (植物) a **morning glory**.

¹**あさがた 朝方** ▶きのうの**朝方**, この先でぼやがあったらしい I hear there was a small fire around here (*early*) *yesterday morning*.

²**あさがた 朝型** ▶私はどちらかと言うと**朝型人間**です I'm more of a *morning person*.

あさぎいろ 浅葱色 **light blue-green**.

あさぐろい 浅黒い **swarthy** /swɔ́ːʳði/ ▶**浅黒い顔の人** a *swarthy* person ／a person *with a dark complexion* ‖ 彼女は**肌が浅黒い** She *is dark-complexioned*.

あざける 嘲る **ridicule** /rɪ́dɪkjuːl/ ＋㊐ (笑い物にする, 冷やかす) ; **make fun of** (おもしろがって) ; **scoff** 《at》 (強く公然と) ▶クラスメートたちは足の遅い彼女を**嘲った** The plodding girl's classmates *made fun of* [*ridiculed*] her. ‖ 彼の妻は禁煙しようという彼の努力を**嘲った** His wife *scoffed at* his efforts to stop smoking. ‖ なまりがあるからといって転校生を**嘲ってはいけない** You mustn't *make fun of* transfer students who have accents different from your own.

あさごはん 朝御飯 **breakfast** →**朝食** ▶おじいちゃんは**朝ごはん前**に少なくとも一仕事は済ませてしまう My grandfather gets at least one task [chore] done *before breakfast*.

あさせ 浅瀬 a **shoal** /ʃoʊl/, **the shallows** ; a **ford** (歩いて[車で]渡れる所) ▶**浅瀬**でカニを捕る hunt for crabs *in the shallows* ‖ 川の**浅瀬**を渡る cross a stream at the *ford* ‖ その船は**浅瀬に乗り上げた** The ship *ran aground* (*on a shoal*). ／The ship *ran ashore*. ／The ship *was driven ashore*.

あさって 明後日 **(the) day after tomorrow** ▶あさっての朝[晩] the morning [evening] *after next* ‖ **あさって**ロンドンに出発します I'm going to London *the day after tomorrow*. ‖ **対話**「あすかあさってはどう？」「どちらでもかまわないよ」"How about tomorrow or *the day after*?" "Either is fine with me."

あさっぱら 朝っぱら ▶朝っぱらからご機嫌だね You're awfully chipper *for so early in the morning*. ‖ なんでこんな朝っぱらからやかましい工事を始めるんだろう Why must they start the noisy construction work *so early* (*in the morning*)?

あさつゆ 朝露 **morning dew.**

あざとい **vicious** /víʃəs/ (悪徳の); **dirty** (ずるい); **unscrupulous** /ʌnskrúːpjələs/ (破廉恥な) ▶おじはあざとい商売でひともうけしたらしい I hear that my uncle made a killing with some *dirty* [*unscrupulous*] business. (➤ make a killing は「大もうけする」).

あさね 朝寝する **sleep late (in the morning)** ▶日曜日は家じゅうで朝寝をします My family *sleeps late* [*sleeps in*] on Sundays. ／My family *rises* [*gets up*] *late* on Sundays. ‖ けさも朝寝坊した I *got up late* again this morning. ‖ 彼はよく朝寝坊して学校に遅刻して来る He often *oversleeps* and comes late to school.

あさはか 浅はかな **shallow** (浅薄な); **superficial** (表面的な); **foolish** (常識や分別を欠いた); **silly** (態度や動作がおかしくてばかばかしい); **thoughtless** (思慮のない) ▶浅はかな考え方[人] *shallow* [*superficial*] thinking [person] ‖ 浅はかな行い a *thoughtless* act ‖ 私って何て浅はかなんでしょう How *silly* [*foolish*] I am! ‖ 私は浅はかにもセールスマンの口車に乗ってしまった *It was silly* [*foolish*] *of me* to be taken in by that salesman's smooth talk. (➤ be taken in は「だまされる」).

あさばん 朝晩 **1【朝と晩】morning and evening** ▶朝晩めっきり涼しくなった It is quite cool these days (*in the*) *mornings and evenings*. ／We have much cooler *mornings and evenings* these days. ‖ 朝晩のラッシュ時に電車に乗るのは嫌いだ I don't like to take the train during the *morning and evening* rush hours. ‖ 父は毎日朝晩(1時間)ジョギングをする My father jogs (for an hour) *every morning and evening*.

2【いつも】day and night ▶私は戦場にいる恋人の無事を朝晩祈っている I pray *day and night* that my sweetheart will be safe on the battlefield.

あさひ 朝日 **the morning [rising] sun** ▶私の書斎には朝日が入る My study *gets the sun in the morning*. ‖ 2人の若者が朝日を浴びてテニスをしていた I saw two young men playing tennis *in the morning sunshine*.

あさましい 浅ましい **base** (下劣な) ▶あさましい考え[動機] a *base* idea [motive] ‖ 報酬が目当てで友人を裏切るとはあさましい(＝卑劣な)やつだ It was *mean* [*despicable*] of him to betray a friend for a reward.

あざみ 薊 《植物》 a **thistle** /θísəl/.

あざむく 欺く **deceive** ＋㊐ (思い違いをさせたり, 本当のことを知らせなかったりする); **cheat** ＋㊐ (不正やいんちきをする); **trick** ＋㊐, **fool** ＋㊐ (必ずしも悪意はないが計略を使って) ▶ギリシャ軍はトロイ人を欺くために木馬を用いた The Greek army used a wooden horse to *deceive* [*trick*] the Trojans.

あさめしまえ 朝飯前 ▶そんなの朝飯前だ *There's nothing to it*. ／I could *do* that *in my sleep* [*with one hand tied behind my back*]. ‖ あんな運転試験は朝飯前だったよ The driving test was *a breeze* [*a piece of cake* ／ *a cinch* ／ *a walk in the park*]. (➤ いずれも「たやすいこと」の意のインフォーマルな言い方).

あさもや 朝靄 (a) **morning mist** (薄霧); (a) **morning haze** (かすみ) ▶山頂は朝もやに覆われていた The mountaintop was covered with *morning mist*.

あざやか 鮮やか **1【鮮明な】bright; vivid** (生き生きした) ▶鮮やかな赤 *bright* red ‖ 月は鮮やかに輝いていた The moon was shining *brightly*. ‖ その懐かしい思い出は今も私の心に鮮やかに残っている That fond memory is still *vivid* in my mind.

2【見事な】excellent (同類の中でひときわ優れた); **splendid** (印象的ですばらしい) ▶《手品などを見て》鮮やかなお手並みを拝見しましたよ I saw your *excellent* [*splendid*] performance. ‖ 監督はわがままな選手たちを鮮やかにさばいてみせた The manager handled the selfish players *with brilliant skill*. ‖ 白鵬は鮮やかに上手投げを決めた Hakuho pulled off a *beautiful* overarm throw.

あさやけ 朝焼け **the morning glow** ▶東の空が朝焼けに染まっていた The eastern sky was touched with [by] *the morning glow* [*light*].

あさゆう 朝夕 **morning and evening**

✉ **朝夕はめっきり冷え込むようになって参りました** It has begun to be noticeably chilly *in the mornings and evenings*.

あざらし 《動物》 a **seal** ▶アザラシの毛皮のコート a *sealskin* coat.

あさり 《貝》 a **short-necked clam** ▶アサリを掘る dig for (*short-necked*) *clams*.

あさる 漁る **scavenge** /skǽvɪndʒ/ ＋㊐ (ごみの中を); **forage** /fɔ́ːrɪdʒ/ ＋㊐ (特に食料を) ▶野良犬が餌をあさっている A homeless dog *is scavenging* for food. ‖ 空き巣は冷蔵庫の中をあさった The burglar *foraged* in the refrigerator.

あされん 朝練 **morning practice** ▶あすはサッカーの朝練がある We have soccer *practice* tomorrow *morning*.

あざわらう 嘲笑う **scoff** 《at》, **ridicule** ＋㊐ (➤ 後者は「冷やかす」というユーモラスな気持ちで使うこともある) ▶上司は私の計画をあざ笑った My boss *scoffed at* [*ridiculed*] my plan. ‖ 同僚たちは彼の無知を心の中であざ笑った His colleagues *laughed up their sleeves at* his ignorance. (➤ laugh up one's sleeve は「(人の無知などを)ひそかにあざ笑う」).

1 **あし 足・脚** **1【足部】**a **foot** [複 **feet**], a **leg**; a **paw** (猫などの); a **hoof** (ひづめを持つ動物の)

> **《解説》「足」と「脚」**
> 日本語では足と脚の区別をあまりしないが, 英語では足首から先を foot, ももの付け根から足首までを leg と区別する. また leg は机や椅子の「脚」にも使う.

▶畳の上に1時間も座っていたので足がしびれた After sitting on the tatami floor for an hour, my *feet* [*legs*] were asleep. (➤ しびれた部分により foot を使うか leg を使うかが決まる) ‖ 彼はスキーをしていて足を折った He *broke his leg* while skiing. ／He *got a broken leg* (while) skiing. ‖ 彼女は足をくじいた She *sprained her ankle*. (➤ ankle は「足首」. この場合 foot は使えない) ‖ 彼は足を組んで椅子に腰掛けていた He was sitting on a chair *with his legs crossed*. (➤ 電車の中でよく見られるような足の組み方; →あぐら; 「足を開いて」は with his legs apart).

▶久美子はとてもすらりとした長い足をしている Kumiko has *such long, slender legs*. ／Kumiko is *very leggy*. ‖ 電車に乗り込もうとしたとき足を踏まれた Somebody stepped on my *foot* just as I was getting on the train. ‖ 彼は階段を下りる途中足を踏み外した He *missed his step* (as he was) going down the

stairs.
▶あの古い**机の脚**が1本折れた One of *the legs on* that old *desk* is broken.
‖**足の裏** a sole ‖ **足の指** a toe.
2【歩行，進行】▶彼は**足が**(＝走るのが)**速い**［**遅い**］ He *runs fast* ［*slowly*］. ／He *is a fast* ［*slow*］ *runner*. (➤「歩くのが速い」なら He walks fast.／He is a fast walker.) ‖ 私は何かに心を引かれ，その店の前で**足を止めた** Something made me *stop* in front of the store.
3【交通手段】▶**足の便のよい**温泉地 a hot spring resort that *is easily accessible* ‖ きょうの交通ストで約9万人の通勤客が**足を奪われた** Due to today's transit strike, about 90,000 people *were deprived of* (*their means of*) *transportation*. ‖ その山奥の温泉には車で行く以外**足がない** *There are no means of transportation* other than cars to reach that remote mountain hot spring. ／The only way you can get to that remote mountain hot spring is by car.
4【慣用表現】 足が地に着く▶渡辺君はまだ若いが，地に足が着いた考え方をしている Even though Watanabe is still young, his way of thinking is very *realistic* ［he's *down-to-earth*］. **足が付く**▶その男は盗んだ品物から足が付いた He *was traced* through the stolen goods. **足が出る**▶今月も家計に足が出た We've *gone* ［*run*］ *over* our budget again this month. ‖ 忘年会をやるのに1人あたま5000円じゃ足が出るよ Five thousand yen per person *will not cover expenses* for the year-end party. **足が遠のく**▶友人たちの足は哲也から遠のき始めた Tetsuya's friends began to *keep away from* him. **足が早い**▶サバは足が早い Mackerel *spoil* ［*go bad*］ *quickly*. **足が棒になる**▶一日中歩き回ったので足が棒になった After walking all day, *my legs feel like logs* ［*are as stiff as boards*］. ‖ 彼は足を棒にして，いなくなった愛犬を捜し回った He *walked his legs off* searching for the missing dog. **足の踏み場もない**▶彼女の部屋は足の踏み場もないほど散らかっている Her room is so cluttered (up) that you *can't even walk in it without stepping on something*. **足の向くまま**▶足の向くまま気の向くまま浅草界わいを探検した I explored the Asakusa area *wherever my feet* and fancy *took me*. **足を洗う**▶彼はようやくギャンブルから足を洗った He *has* finally *kicked* the gambling *habit*. (➤ kick the habit は「(悪習などを)きっぱりやめる」の意のインフォーマルな表現). **足を取られる**▶その選手はちょっとした起伏に足を取られて転倒した The player *tripped over* a slight bump in the ground. **足を延ばす**▶九州旅行では足を延ばして屋久島まで行った When I went to Kyushu, I *took a side trip to* Yakushima. 《参考》「足を伸ばす」は stretch one's legs. **足を運ぶ**▶先日は個展に足をお運びくださりありがとうございました It was very kind of you to *take the trouble of visiting* my solo exhibition the other day. **足を引っ張る**▶彼らは互いに足を引っ張り合ってばかりいる They *are* always *trying to trip* each other *up*. (➤ trip up は「(人を)つまずかせる」の意) ‖ 野手がエラーをして投手の足を引っ張った A fielder's error *cramped* the pitcher*'s style*. (➤ cramp A's style は「A(人)の調子を狂わせて本領を発揮させない」の意). **その足で**▶彼女は銀行で少し金を下ろし，その足でドレスを買いに行った She withdrew some money at the bank *and went* (*right*) *on to* buy a dress.

²あし 葦《植物》a **reed** ▶沼には**アシ**が生い茂っていた *Reeds* were growing thickly in the marsh.
▶《比喩的》人間は考える**アシ**である Man is a thinking *reed*. (➤ 哲学者パスカルの言葉).

¹あじ 味 **1【飲食物の】taste；flavor**（香り，風味）▶苦い**味** a bitter *taste* ‖ 母の作ってくれたみそ汁の**味**が忘れられない I can't forget the *taste* of my mother's homemade miso soup. ‖ だんだん刺身の**味がわかる**ようになってきた I'm gradually acquiring *a taste* for sashimi.

【文型】
A **な味がする**
taste A ➤ A は形容詞
B **の味がする**
taste like ［**of**］ B ➤ B は名詞

解説 (1)A には bad（まずい），bitter（苦い），bland（はっきりしない，味の薄い），delicious（とてもおいしい）；good, nice（おいしい），salty（しょっぱい），sour（酸っぱい），sweet（甘い）などの味を表す形容詞がくる.
(2)taste like は B が当然予想される基本的な味のときに使い，taste of は副次的な(かすかな)風味や，しばしば好ましくない予想外の味のときに使う. taste of の代わりに have a taste of ... ともいう.

▶このさつまいもは**味がいい**（＝おいしい）This sweet potato *tastes* good. (→**おいしい**) ‖ あのホテルで食べた朝食は**ひどい味だった** The breakfast (I had) at that hotel *tasted* awful ［terrible］. ‖ あのラーメン屋のラーメンはあっさりした［こってりした］**味だ** The ramen at that ramen shop has a light ［rich］ broth. (➤「スープがあっさり［こってり］している」の意) ‖ このスープは**味が薄い** This soup *tastes bland* ［does*n't have much flavor*］. (➤ bland は「味が薄くておいしくない」) ‖ このチーズはすっかり**味が落ちている** This cheese *tastes* quite stale. (➤ stale は「古くなった」) ‖ ワニの肉は鶏肉**のような味**だそうだ I hear crocodile meat *tastes like* chicken. ‖ このスープはニンニク**の味がする** This soup *tastes of* garlic.
▶近頃の学生食堂は概して食事の**味がいい** Food at college cafeterias is generally *good* these days. (➤「すばらしい」なら wonderful や excellent,「最高」なら great) ‖ **対話**「**お味はいかがでしょうか**」「とてもおいしいです」"*How does it taste ?*" "Very good. ／Delicious."
▶かぜをひいているので**味がわからない** I *can't taste* since I have a cold. ‖ シェフは料理を作りながら何度も**味を見る** A chef *tastes* a dish several times while preparing it. ‖ シチューに**もう少し塩味をつけなさい** *Add a little more salt* to the stew.
2【魅力，趣】▶ぜいたくの**味は忘れがたい** It is hard to forget the *taste* of the good life. ‖ 彼女はたばこ［酒］**の味を覚えた** She *has taken to smoking* ［*drink*(*ing*)］. (➤ take to は「…が好きになってふける」) ‖ 彼の文章には何とも言えない**味がある** There is an inexpressible *flair* in his style of writing. (➤ flair は「(自分流の)スタイル，センス」) ‖ あの俳優は**味のある**演技をする That actor gives a performance *full of character*.
▶《慣用表現》最初の小説の**成功に味を占めて**彼は2作目を書く決心をした *The taste of success* from his first novel *encouraged* him to begin a second (one). ‖ 彼は**味なことをする** He *does things with style*. (→**味な**) ‖ 彼女は**貧乏の味をよく知っている** She

is no stranger to poverty. (● 英語では「…に無縁の人ではない」と発想する) ‖ 彼女は**味もそっけもない**返事をした She made a *curt* reply.

☛ **味付け, 味な, 味見** (→見出語)

2**あじ 鰺** 《魚》 a **horse mackerel** ▶アジの開き *a horse mackerel* cut open then dried.

アジア **Asia** /éɪʒə ‖ éɪʃə/ 一形 **アジアの** **Asian** ▶日本は**アジアの**一国である Japan is an *Asian* nation [country].

‖**アジア人** an Asian 《参考》《米》では日本人も Asian (または East Asian)だが,《英》では Asian は主として,パキスタン人,インド人,スリランカ人などを指す.日本人,中国人,韓国人などは通例 Asian には含まれず, Oriental で表されるが,この総称には軽蔑的な響きもあるので,最近では Japanese, Chinese, Koreans など具体的民族名で表されることが多い. ‖**アジア大陸** the Asian Continent ‖**アジア民族** Asian peoples [nations].

あしあと 足跡 a **footprint**(個々の足跡); a **track**(通った跡; 複数形で用いることが多い) ▶クマの**足跡** bear *tracks* / *footprints* of a bear ‖ 雪の中に残されたウサギの**足跡**をつける follow the rabbit *tracks* in the snow ‖ 我々は**足跡**を頼りに彼らの行方を追った We followed their *footprints* to see which way they had gone.

あしおと 足音 a **footstep**(1度の) ▶隣の部屋で**足音**がした I heard *a footstep* [*footsteps*] in the next room.

▶《比喩的》**春の足音**は着実に近づいて来ている You can hear *the footsteps of spring* approaching slowly but steadily. (➤ 極めて文語的な言い方).

あしか 《動物》 a **sea lion**.

あしがかり 足掛かり ▶彼女はついに映画女優になる**足がかりをつかんだ** At last she *got her foot into* the door of the movie world.

▶その絶壁には**足がかり**(=足場)がなかった The cliff gave me no *footing*.

あしかけ 足掛け ▶東京に来て**足かけ5年になる** *This is my fifth year* in Tokyo.

あしかせ 足枷 **shackles**(手かせ, 足かせ; 拘束) ▶《比喩的》彼女の場合, 病気の両親が**足かせになっている** In her case, her sick parents are *shackling* her freedom. (➤ 文語的表現).

あしがため 足固め ▶ヨーロッパ市場で**足固めをする** *secure* [*establish*] *a foothold* in the European market ‖「ことしは**足固め**の年だと思っています」とそのルーキーは語った "I think this is the year for me to *consolidate my basic skills*," said the rookie. (➤ consolidate は「強固にする」).

あしからず 悪しからず ▶お手伝いできませんけれど**あしからず** *I am sorry* I cannot be of help (to you). ‖ いかなる場合にも返金はいたしませんので, **あしからずご了承ください** Please understand that we can't make refunds under any circumstances. (●「あしからず」は特に表現しない).

あしくび 足首 an **ankle** ▶**足首**のきゅっと締まった女の子 a girl with slender [well-turned] *ankles* ‖ 祖父は階段を下りるとき足を踏み外し, 片方の**足首**をひどく捻挫した My grandfather sprained his *ankle* badly when he missed a step on the stairs.

あしげ 足蹴 ▶そのフットボール選手は怒ってレフェリーを**足蹴にした** The angry footballer *kicked* the referee [*gave* the referee *a kick*].

▶《比喩的》彼からこんなに**足蹴にされる**(=ひどい仕打ちを受ける)とは思わなかった I didn't expect such *harsh treatment* from him.

あじけない 味気ない **dull**(変化がなくて退屈な); **boring**(倦怠(けんたい)感を覚えるような); **tedious**(飽き飽きする); **uninteresting**(興味がもてない) ▶**味気ない**スピーチ a *dull* speech ‖ たった独りでする食事ほど**味気ない**ものはない Nothing is as *boring* [*tedious*] as eating alone.

あしこし 足腰 ▶父はランニングをして**足腰**(=下半身の力)を鍛えている My father is building his *lower body strength* by running. ‖ **足腰が立たなくなる**くらい痛めつけてやるぞ I'm going to beat you up so bad *you won't* (*even*) *be able to stand*. ‖ 祖父はいつも**足腰の立つうちは**働きたいと言っている My grandfather always says that he wants to work *as long as he can still get around* [*about*]. (➤ get around [about] は「元気に動き回る」).

あじさい 《植物》 a **hydrangea** /haɪdréɪndʒə/.

あししげく 足繁く **frequently**(頻繁に); **very often** (しょっちゅう) ▶そのレポートをまとめるまで図書館に**足しげく通った** I *visited* the library *frequently* until I finished writing the paper.

アシスタント an **assistant**(助手); a **helper** (手伝い人)(➤ 日本語の「アシスタント」は後者の意で用いることも多い).

あした 明日 **tomorrow** →あす ▶じゃ, また**あした** See you *tomorrow*. ‖ **あした**天気になあれ I hope the weather is nice *tomorrow*. ‖ **あしたの午後2時に**私のオフィスに来てください Please come to my office *at 2 p.m. tomorrow*. ‖ **あしたの**ミーティングはどこでやるの? Where are we going to have *tomorrow's* meeting [the meeting *tomorrow*]?

ことわざ **あしたはあしたの風が吹く** Tomorrow will take care of itself. / Tomorrow is another day. (➤ 後者は「きょうを最後と思うな. あしたという日もあるのだから」という積極的な意味で用いることが多い).

あしだい 足代 a **fare**(交通費); **traveling expenses**(特に旅行の);《米》 a **carfare**(バス代・電車賃など).

あじつけ 味付け **seasoning** ▶このスープは**味付けがいい** [**悪い**] This soup *is well* [*poorly* / *badly*] *seasoned*. ‖ コックは肉にこしょうをたくさん振りかけて**味付けをした** The cook *seasoned* [*flavored*] the meat with plenty of pepper.

‖**味付けのり** seasoned *nori* [laver].

あしでまとい 足手まとい a **drag**(足を引っ張るもの); a **burden**(重荷) ▶彼は出世のためには愛人が**足手まとい**に思えた He felt that his lover was *a drag* on his career. ‖ 若い人の**足手まとい**になりたくないと考える老人が多い Many old people don't want to become *a burden* on young people.

アジト a **hideout** /háɪdaʊt/ (犯人などの); a **safe house** (隠れ家).

あしどめ 足止め ▶我々は嵐のために3日間その島で**足止めを食った** We *were stranded* [*were held up*] on the island for three days during the storm.

あしどり 足取り **1**【**歩き方**】▶その老人は**重い足取り**で通りを歩いて行った The elderly man walked along the street *with heavy steps*. / The elderly man *trudged* along the street. ‖ 彼女の夫は酔っ払って**危なっかしい足取りで**帰宅した Her husband came *staggering* home, drunk. (➤ stagger は「よろめく」) ‖ 彼女は**足取りも軽く**恋人と映画に行った She went to the movies with her boyfriend *in high spirits* [*with her heart singing*].

2【**歩いた道筋**】▶警察はその男の**足取りを追った**結果, 静岡にいることを突き止めた The police *traced* the

あ

man's movements and found him in Shizuoka.

あじな 味な ▶彼もなかなか味なことをするじゃないか He *plays it smart*!

あしなみ 足並み ▶足並みを乱して歩く walk *out of step* ‖ 選手たちは足並みをそろえて体育館に入場した The athletes entered the gym *marching in step*.

あしならし 足慣らし ▶我々は富士登山の足慣らしに近くの山でハイキングした We went hiking in the nearby hills (*as a warm-up*) *to get in shape* before climbing Mt. Fuji.

あしば 足場 a **foothold** (崖などを登るときの); a **scaffold**, (a) **scaffolding** (建築現場などの) ▶(建築現場で)足場を組む[外す] set up [take down] (*a*) *scaffolding* ‖ 足場を確保する gain *a foothold* (➤ 比喩的にも用いる; ⇀足固め).

▶建設現場はゆうべの雨で足場が悪くなっていた The construction site *had become slippery and muddy* from last night's rain.

あしばや 足早 ▶彼女はチョコレートの入った箱をぼくに手渡すと足早に立ち去った She handed me a box of chocolates and walked away *quickly*.

あしぶみ 足踏み ▶大尉は兵士たちに足踏みをさせた The captain *made* the soldiers *mark time*. (➤ 軍隊用語などの「足踏み始め!」の号令は "Mark time!").

▶《比喩的》交渉は足踏み状態にある(=行き詰まっている) The negotiations *have reached a stalemate*. / The negotiations *are at a standstill*.

あじみ 味見する **taste** +㊐ ▶彼はスープの味見をして塩を加えた He *tasted* the soup, then added salt.

あしもと 足元 ▶その老人は足元がおぼつかなかった The old man was not steady on *his feet*. ‖ 暗いですから足元に気をつけてください It's dark around here. *Watch your step!*

▶《慣用表現》ぼくはスキーでは彼の足元にも及ばない I'*m no match for* him as far as skiing is concerned. ‖ 商人は買い手の足元を見て法外な値段を吹っかけた When the seller *caught a glimpse of the buyer's weakness*, he inflated the price outrageously. (➤ outrageously は「法外に」) ‖ 足元の明るいうちにとっととうせろ! Get out of here *while you still have legs*! ‖ 独り暮らしの老人の足元につけ込む悪徳業者が大勢いる There are many dishonest salesmen who *take advantage of* elderly people living alone.

あしゆ 足湯 a (**hot-spring**) **foot bath**.

あしらう **1【扱う】 treat** +㊐ (待遇する), **deal with** (対応する) ▶人を冷たくあしらう *treat* [*deal with*] a person coldly.

▶《慣用表現》彼女は私の提案を鼻であしらった She *turned up her nose at* my proposal.

2【取り合わせる】▶パセリはサラダにあしらうのによく使われる Parsley is often used to *garnish* salads. (➤ garnish は「(料理に)添える」).

あじわい 味わい ▶味わい深いことば *significant* remarks ‖ 彼の演技には一種独特の味わいがある There is a unique *charm* about his acting.

あじわう 味わう **taste** +㊐ (試食する, 味を楽しむ); **appreciate** +㊐ (良さがわかる); **experience** +㊐ (体験する) ▶日本料理を味わう *taste* [*enjoy*] Japanese food ‖ そんなに急いで食べないで, よく味わって食べなさい Don't eat so fast! Take time to *taste* the food. ‖ 詩を味わうためには声に出して読むべきだ In order to *appreciate* a poem, you should read it aloud. ‖ ひどい胃けいれんで死の苦しみを味わった I had severe stomach cramps and *suffered* [*experienced*] excruciating pain.

あす 明日 **1【きょうの次の日】 tomorrow** ⇀あした ▶あすは日曜日です *Tomorrow* is Sunday. ‖ じゃあ, あすの朝[夜]また See you *tomorrow morning* [*night*]. ‖ あすの3時に上野で会おう Let's meet at Ueno *at three tomorrow*. ‖ あすから大学1年生だ I'll be a freshman *starting tomorrow*. ‖ 「あすお電話ください」と彼女は言った She said, "Please call me *tomorrow*." / She asked me to call her *the next day*.

▶《慣用表現》前線の兵士はあすをも知れぬ命だ The *lives* of soldiers on the front *hang by a thread*. (➤「生命が糸1本でぶら下がっている」の意).

ことわざ あすはわが身 Others' misfortune today may fall upon us tomorrow. (➤ 日本語からの意訳).

2【将来】 the future ▶この町のあすのために働く人を議員に選ぶべきだ We must elect members to the town assembly who are willing to work for *the future* (*prosperity*) of this town.

1**あずかる 預かる** **1【保管する】 keep** +㊐ ▶この荷物をしばらく預かってください Would you please *keep* this luggage for a while? ‖ 銀行は人から預かった金を貸しつけることによって利潤を得る Banks make a profit by lending out *their depositors' money*. (➤ depositor は「預金者」).

‖預かり金 a deposit (内金) ‖ 預かり証 a claim tag (手荷物の引換証).

2【世話する, 管理する】 take care of (責任をもって面倒を見る); **look after** (見守る) ▶この子は私が預かっている子です This is the child I'm *taking care of*. ‖ ベビーシッターが子供たちを預かってくれている A babysitter is *looking after* my children. ‖ 私は留守を預かっている者です I'm just *looking after the house* during the owner's absence. ‖ パイロットは乗客の命を預かっている A pilot *is responsible for the safety* of his [her] passengers. (➤「安全に対して責任がある」の意).

2**あずかる 与かる** ▶お招きにあずかりありがとうございます Thank you very much *for your kind invitation*. ‖ この件は私の全くあずかり知らぬことです I *have nothing to do with* this matter. / This matter is *not my business* [*concern*].

あずき 小豆 an ***azuki*** [***adzuki***] **bean** ▶小豆を煮て潰したものがあんこです *Azuki beans* that have been boiled and crushed are called anko.

あずけもの 預け物 ▶フロントに預け物をする *leave* [*check*] *something* at the front desk ‖ 預け物(=預けたもの)を取りに行く go and get *the item one has checked*.

あずける 預ける **1【保管を頼む】 leave** +㊐; **deposit** +㊐ (預金する); 《米》 **check** +㊐ (一時預かりに預ける) ▶荷物はクロークに預けるようにと言われた We were told to *leave* [*check*] our baggage in the cloakroom. ‖ 銀行にお金を預けるのが嫌いな人もいる Some people do not like to *deposit* [*put*] their money in banks. ‖ 彼は車を私に預けた He *left* his car *in my care*. / He *asked* me *to take care of* his car (for him). ‖ この銀行に500万円預けてある I *have* five million yen *deposited* in this bank. / I *have* five million yen *on deposit* in this bank. ‖ 入り口でコートを預けた I *checked* my coat at the door.

2【世話を頼む】 leave +㊐; **entrust** +㊐ (任せる) ▶

休暇で出かけている間, 犬を彼女［ペットホテル］に預けておかなければならない While we are on vacation, we'll have to *leave* the dog *with* her [*at* the kennel]. ‖兄は入院中３人の子供を私たちに預けた My brother *entrusted* his three children *to* us while he was in the hospital.

アスパラガス《植物》**asparagus** /əspǽrəgəs/ ▶アスパラガス１本 a stalk [piece] of *asparagus*.

アスピリン (an) **aspirin** /ǽsprın/ (➤「アスピリン錠剤」の意味では an を付ける).

アスファルト **asphalt** /ǽsfɔːlt/ ▶道路をアスファルトで舗装する pave a road with *asphalt*.

アスベスト **asbestos** /æsbéstəs/.

あずまや 東屋 a **bower**(木陰の) ; a **gazebo**(庭園を見渡せる).

アスリート an **athlete** /ǽθliːt/.

アスレチック an **obstacle course** (障害物コース)

‖**アスレチッククラブ** an athletic club, a fitness [sports] club.

あせ 汗 **sweat** /swet/, **perspiration** (➤後者のほうが上品な語で, 女性に好まれる傾向がある) ━動 **汗をかく** **sweat**

▶私はすぐ［よく］汗をかく I *sweat* easily [a lot]. ‖彼らは汗をだらだら流して働いている They are *streaming with sweat* as they work. ‖大久保君は汗かきだ Okubo *sweats* [*perspires*] *heavily*. ‖このシャツは汗臭い This shirt *smells of sweat*. ‖彼は汗びっしょりだ He'*s dripping with sweat*. ／He'*s sweating all over*. ‖何か月ぶりかのテニスでいい汗をかいた I played tennis for the first time in months and *worked up a good sweat*. ‖彼は額に玉のような汗を浮かべて土を掘った He dug until *beads of sweat* broke out on his forehead.

▶《慣用表現》手に汗を握るような試合 a *breathtaking* game ‖私たちは飛行機が木の上すれすれに飛び立つのを手に汗を握って見つめた We watched *breathlessly* as the plane took off, just missing the treetops. ‖額に汗して働く者の努力が報われるべきだ The effort of the workers living *by the sweat of their brows* should be rewarded.

アセスメント (an) **assessment** ‖**環境アセスメント** an environmental assessment.

あせだく 汗だく ▶配達人は汗だくになってトラックから荷物を下ろしていた *Dripping with sweat*, the deliverer was unloading the truck.

▶私たちは客の応対に汗だくになった We *knocked ourselves out* [*worked like crazy*] taking care of the customers. (➤ knock oneself out は「全力でがんばる」の意のインフォーマルな表現).

あせばむ 汗ばむ ▶きょうは汗ばむような陽気だ It's warm enough today to *bring out a slight sweat*.

あせみず 汗水 ▶汗水たらして稼いだ金 the money I earned *by the sweat of my brow* (➤「額に汗して」の意 ;「苦労して稼いだ金」を hard-earned money という) ‖１か月汗水たらして働いた給料がこれっぽっちか Is this all the salary I get for my month's *hard work*?

あぜみち 畦道 a **footpath between rice paddies** [**fields**].

あせも 汗疹 **prickly heat**, (a) **heat rash** ▶うちの子はあせもがひどい My baby has terrible *prickly heat*.

あせり 焦り **impatience** ▶秘密を知りたいという彼の焦りが身の破滅のもととなった His *impatience* to find out the secret was his ruin. ‖思うように仕事がはかどらないので焦りを感じています My work isn't going as planned, so I'*m beginning to panic*. ‖結婚には焦りは禁物 You *shouldn't rush* into marriage.

[1]**あせる 焦る** **panic**(うろたえる) ; **be impatient**(待ち切れない) ▶締め切りが迫っているので, 気ばかり焦っています Since the deadline is approaching, I'm starting to *panic* (*a bit*). ‖彼らは勝ちを焦っているようだ They seem to *be impatient* for a win. ‖彼女は仕事の遅れを取り戻そうと焦って(＝あわてて)いる She *is in a hurry* to catch up with her work. ‖焦らずにやりなさい *Take it easy!* ／*Take your time!* ‖功を焦るな Don't *be too eager for* success. ‖焦って結婚, ゆっくり後悔 *Marry in haste, repent at leisure*. (➤英語のことわざ).

✉《お見舞い状で》**焦らずにゆっくり休養なさってください** Take it easy and get a good rest. ➤ take it easy は「のんびりする」の意.

[2]**あせる 褪せる** **fade**(＋目) ; **discolor**(＋目)(変色する) ▶色のあせたジーンズ *faded* jeans ‖日に当たって麦わら帽子の色があせた The sun *has faded* my straw hat. (●英語では「太陽が変色させた」と考える).

あぜん 唖然とする **be speechless** (絶句する) ; **be dumbfounded** (びっくり仰天する) ▶彼の奇行にみんなあぜんとした His strange behavior *left* everybody *speechless*. ‖彼は彼女の派手な格好を見て, あぜんとしてその場に立ち尽くした He stood there, *dumbfounded* by his girlfriend's flashy outfit.

あそこ **there**(そこに) ; **over there**(遠くを指して「あそこに」)

語法 下の方を指して言えば down there, 上を指して言えば up there となる. また外を指して言えば out there, 内を指して言えば in there となる.

▶ほら, 彼はあそこにいるよ Look, *there* he is. ‖あそこにその石碑が見える You see the stone monument *over there*.

▶彼もあそこまで言うことはないのに He shouldn't have said *so much*. ／He didn't need to say *that*. ‖彼があそこまで落ち込んでいるとは思わなかった I didn't think he was *that* [*so*] depressed.

あそばせる 遊ばせる ▶子供を公園に連れていって遊ばせる take a child out in the park to *play*.

▶我々は機械［土地］を遊ばせておくわけにはいかない We can't *have* the machines [our land] *lying idle*. (●「使わないまま, ほったらかしておく」と考えて have ... lie idle と表現する) ‖遊ばせておくような金はないよ I don't have any *money to spare*.

あそび 遊び **1**【遊戯】**play** (子供の) ; a **game** (ゲーム) ▶遊びに夢中になって時間を忘れてしまう子がいる Some children get so deeply absorbed in *play* that they forget the time of day. ‖ママ, 外に遊びに行ってもいい？ Can I *go out and play*, Mom? ‖２人の少女はままごと［人形］遊びをしていた The two girls *were playing house* [*dolls*]. ‖あの子には遊び相手がいない That child has no *one to play with*. ／That child has no *playmates*. ‖ジョンソンさんの家を訪ねたときに伝統的なクリスマスの遊びをいくつか覚えた While visiting Mr. Johnson's home, I learned how to play several traditional *Christmas games*.

▶うちの隣には遊び盛りの子供が３人いる Our next-door neighbors have three *active* children.

2【娯楽, 行楽】a **pastime** (気晴らし) ▶スノーボードは私の好きな遊びの１つです Snowboarding is one of my favorite *pastimes*. ‖きのうの夜, 友だちと遊びに行った I *went out* with my friends last night. ‖来春私はカナダへ遊びに行く Next spring I'm going to *take a pleasure trip* to Canada. ‖ きょうの午後家へ**遊びにいらっしゃい** *Come (on) over* this afternoon. ／Why don't you *come (on) over* this afternoon? ‖ おいは東京に滞在中，ほとんど毎日曜日わが家へ**遊びに来た** During his stay in Tokyo, my nephew *came to see me* almost every Sunday.

3【真面目でないこと】▶あの女の子とは単に**遊びだった** I *was* just *playing around* with that girl. ‖ テニスは**遊び半分**で習ってもうまくならないよ You cannot become a good tennis player if you*'re not serious* about it.

4【ハンドルやロープのゆとり】play ▶このハンドルは**遊びが多すぎる** This steering wheel has too much *play*.

‖**遊び着** playclothes ; a playsuit（特に子供用）; rompers（上着とズボンが続きになった幼児用遊び着）‖ **遊び時間** playtime ‖ **遊び道具** a plaything ‖ **遊び場** a playground.

あそびあるく 遊び歩く go out（外出する）▶彼は毎晩**遊び歩いている** He *goes out* (*to have fun* [*enjoy himself*]) every night.（🔊 大人の場合には play ではなく have fun や enjoy oneself を用いる．なお play around とすると「軽い気持ちで異性と付き合う」の意となる；→遊び **3**）.

あそびごころ 遊び心 ▶**遊び心**のある製品 a product which appeals to the *imagination* ‖ あの博物館は機能を重視しているが，**遊び心**もあって楽しい The museum values functionality, but it also has *playful touches* that make it fun to visit. ‖ 彼は真面目一方で**遊び心を忘れている** He is too serious and *doesn't know how to enjoy himself*.

あそびほうける 遊び呆ける ▶最近の子供は夢中になって**遊びほうける**ということがない Children nowadays *are* not so *absorbed in playing*.

あそぶ 遊ぶ

1【勉強・仕事以外の好きなことをして】play（子供が）; **enjoy** [**amuse**] **oneself**（楽しむ）

▶子供は戸外で**遊ぶ**べきだ Children should *play* outside. ‖ きのうは友だちと野球をして**遊んだ** Yesterday I *enjoyed myself* playing baseball with friends. ‖ 彼らは飲んだり食べたりして**楽しく遊んだ** They *had a good time* eating and drinking. ‖ **遊んでばかりいないで**勉強しなさい！ Stop *fooling* [*goofing*] *around* and get down to studying!（➤ fool [goof] around は「ずるける，サボる」の意のインフォーマルな言い方）‖ 彼は**遊ぶ金**欲しさにアルバイトをしている He is working part-time to get *spending money*. ‖ 六本木は**遊ぶ**場所が多い Roppongi has a lot of places where you can *enjoy yourself* [*have fun*]. ‖ かわいい子犬がじゃれ合って**遊んでいる** Some cute puppies *are playing friskily with each other*.（➤ friskily は「跳ね回って」）.

> **あなたの英語はどう響く?**
> 「今度の日曜日，うちに遊びにおいでよ」と言うつもりで Come to play [Come and play] at my house next Sunday. と言わないこと．play は「(子供が)おもちゃ・ゲームなどで遊ぶ」とか「エッチな遊びをする」の意味で用いるのがふつう．上記の意味では Come and visit me next Sunday. ／Come and see me next Sunday. ／Drop by my place next Sunday. などの言い方がよい．

2【定職をもたずぶらぶらする】idle away ▶彼は(仕事がなくて)**遊んでいる** He *is out of work* now.（🔊「今は仕事がない」のほうを英訳し，「遊んでいる」は無視してよい）‖ 退職後彼はずっと**遊んでいる** Since retirement he has been *idling away his time*. ‖ 私のような薄給の労働者には**遊んで暮らせる**余裕などはない A poorly-paid worker like me cannot afford to *be idle*.

3【酒や女遊びにふける】▶彼は若いときはずいぶん**遊んだ**ものだ When young, he *played around* a lot.

☞ **遊ばせる**（→見出語）

あだ 仇・徒 1【かたき，仕返し】▶彼は恩を**あだで返す**ようなやつなんだ He is the kind of person who will *bite the hand that feeds him*.（🔊 英語では「食べさせてくれる人の手をかむ」と発想し，それに相当する bite the hand that feeds him [her] を用いる）‖ 今どき**あだ討ち**ははやらない *Vendettas* are no longer fashionable.（➤ vendetta /vendétə/ は「憎み合いによるあだ討ち」）.

2【害】▶彼女にはぼくの好意がかえって**あだになった**ようだ It seems that what I had done with good intentions *turned out to be harmful* to her.

3【無駄】▶彼女の親切な忠告も彼には**あだになった** Her kind advice was *wasted* [*lost*] *on* him.

あたい 値《数学》**a value**.

あたいする 値する deserve +目（賞罰などに）; **be worth**（価値がある）▶そのミュージカルは確かに**一見に値する** The musical *is* well *worth seeing*. ‖ 彼らの努力は**賞賛に値する** Their efforts *deserve* to be praised. ／Their efforts *are worthy of* praise [praise*worthy*]. ‖ O 氏が果たしてノーベル賞に**値する**だろうか After all, does Mr. O *deserve to receive* the Nobel Prize? ‖ 彼の行動は**軽蔑にも値しない** His conduct *is beneath contempt*.

あたえる 与える

give +目 ; **award** +目（賞を）; **present** /prɪzént/ +目（贈り物を；堅い語）▶もう一度チャンスを**与えて**くださいませんか Would you please *give* me one more chance? ‖ 今月は彼の売り上げがいちばん良かったので，ABC 社は彼に**賞を与えた** ABC Company *awarded* him a prize [*gave* him an award] for being the top salesman for this month. ‖ トーナメントの優勝者には賞金1000万円が**与えられた** The winner of the tournament *was presented with* a cash award of ten million yen. ‖ 試験の時間は 1 時間**与えられている** You *have* one hour to complete the examination. ‖ パヴァロッティの歌は聴衆に**大きな感銘を与えた** Pavarotti's songs *deeply moved* [*impressed*] the audience. ‖ 求めよ，さらば**与えられん** Ask, and it shall *be given* you.（➤ 新約聖書の一節）.

▶この前の台風は作物に大打撃を**与えた** The latest typhoon *caused* a great deal of damage to (the) crops. ‖ 長い日照りは米の収穫に**被害を与えた** The long dry spell *damaged* [*hurt*] the rice crop. ‖ 子供の急死は家族にひどく**ショックを与えた** The child's sudden death *shocked* the family deeply. ／The family *was* deeply *shocked* by the child's sudden death.

あたかも as if, as though（➤ これらは同義で，どちらを用いるかはリズムや個人の好みなどによるが，後者をやや堅い言い方と見る人もいる）▶彼は**あたかも**ぼくたちの計画について何もかも知っているかのような口ぶりだ He speaks *as if* [*as though*] he knew all about our plans.（➤ 事実と異なる場合は as if 節中はふつう仮定法となる）.

あたたかい 暖かい・温かい

1【温度が】warm（ちょうど気持ちがよいくらいに暑い）; **hot**（熱い，暑い）; **mild**（気候が温和な）

▶暖かい手袋 *warm* gloves ‖ 温かい料理 *hot* dishes ‖ ことしの冬は暖かい We're having a *mild* [*warm*] winter. ‖ だんだん暖かくなってきた It's *getting warmer*.

2【気持ち・態度などが】**warm**；**cordial**（心からの）▶気持ちの温かい人 a *warm-hearted* person ‖ 私たちはタイで温かい歓迎を受けた We received a *cordial* [*warm*] reception in Thailand. ‖ 彼女は温かい（＝愛があふれる）家庭に恵まれている She is blessed with a *loving* home.

✉ **あなたの温かい励ましのことばは私に力を与えてくれました** Your *warm* words of encouragement gave me strength.

あたたかみ 暖かみ・温かみ warmth ▶その男には人間的な温かみが感じられなかった There was no sense of (any) *human warmth* in him. ‖ 植村さんは温かみのある人だった Mr. Uemura had *a warm heart*. ‖ 温かみのない人ね！You *cold-hearted* man！

あたたまる 暖まる・温まる get warm ▶セントラルヒーティングの部屋はじきに暖まる Rooms with central heating *warm up* quickly. ‖ お風呂に入って温まってください Please take a bath and *get warm*. ‖ 老夫婦のもてなしに身も心も温まった The kind hospitality of the elderly couple *warmed* [*comforted*] me (both) physically and emotionally. (➤ comfort は「慰める」).

あたためる 暖める・温める warm (up) ▶こっちへ来て火で体を温めたらどう？Why not come and *warm yourself* by [before] the fire？‖ ぼくは冷めたコーヒーを温めた I *warmed* [*heated*] *up* the cold coffee. ‖ 彼女はごはんを電子レンジで温め直した She *reheated* the rice in the microwave oven. ‖ めんどりは21日間卵を温める A hen *incubates* its eggs for 21 days. (➤ incubate /íŋkjəbeɪt/ は「(鳥が卵を) 抱く」).

▶私には長い間温めている計画がある I have a plan *I've been mulling over* (*in my mind*) for a long time.

アタック attack（攻撃）**一動 アタックする try (and do), have a go**《at》（やってみる；後者はインフォーマルな言い方）▶アイガー北壁にアタックする *try and climb* the north face of the Eiger ／*make an assault on* the Eiger from its north wall (➤ make an assault on はジャーナリズムで多用される) ‖ 彼女が好きならアタックしてみろよ If you like her, why don't you *have a go at* her？

> **あなたの英語はどう響く?**
> 「挑戦する」の意味で「アタックする」と言うことがあるが，この意味で attack はほとんど使えない. attack は主に人に暴力を振るうことだからである. したがって,「彼女が好きならアタックしてみろよ」のような文で attack を使ったら大変なことになる. 彼女をレイプすることになってしまう.

アタッシェケース an **attaché** /æ̀təʃéɪ/ **case.**

-あたって ▶委員を引き受けるにあたっては条件があります *Before* I agree to assume a position on the committee, I have some conditions (that must be met). (➤ カッコ内は「満たされるべき」の意).

あだな 渾名 a nickname /níkneɪm/ ▶私たちの先生のあだ名はパンダです Our teacher's *nickname* is 'Panda.' ‖ 彼らは体重の重いヒロシに「横綱」というあだ名をつけた They *nicknamed* Hiroshi [Hiroshi *was nicknamed*] 'Yokozuna' because of his weight.

あたふた ▶あたふたするんじゃないよ Don't *panic*.／Don't *get rattled*. (➤ rattle は「慌てさせる」の意のインフォーマルな語) ‖ 彼は試験開始直前にあたふたと教室に駆け込んで来た He came [rushed] into the classroom *hurriedly* [*in a hurry*] just before the exam began.

アダプター an **adapter**, an **adaptor.**

あたま 頭

> **訳語メニュー**
> 頭部 →the head **1**
> 頭髪 →one's hair **2**
> 頭脳 →mind **3**
> 最初 →the beginning **4**

> **解説 「頭」と head**
> (1) 日本語の「頭」はふつう頭髪（hair）のある部分をいうのに対して，英語の head は首から上の部分をいう. したがって,「頭を洗う」は wash one's *hair* である. → 顔, 首.
> (2)「頭」を含んだ表現は必ずしも head を使って英訳できない. 例えば,「きみのことが頭に浮かんだ」は You came across my mind.,「頭の痛い問題」は a tricky problem,「頭の悪い学生」は students without any brains などとなる.

1【頭部, 先端部】**the head** ▶人間［動物］の頭 a human [an animal] *head* ‖ 彼はドアに頭をぶつけた He hit his *head* on the door. ‖ 彼はぼくの頭を殴った He *hit* [*struck*] me *on the head*. ‖ 彼はきまり悪そうに頭をかいた He *scratched his head* in embarrassment. (➤ これは日本人のしぐさで, 英米人はいらだったときなどに頭をかく) ‖ 彼は頭を深く［軽く］下げた He *bowed* (*his head*) deeply [slightly]. ‖（ぶつからないよう）頭に気をつけて *Watch* [《英》*Mind*] *your head*. ‖ その少年は頭のてっぺんからつま先まで泥まみれになっていた The boy was covered with mud *from head to toe*. ‖ たかしはほかの生徒より頭ひとつ背が高い Takashi is *a head taller* than the other students. ‖ 蛇は獲物を頭から飲み込んだ The snake swallowed the prey *headfirst* [*headlong*]. (➤ ともに「頭から先に」の意の副詞).

▶ゆうべ徹夜だったので頭が重い I was up all last night and my *head feels heavy* [*dull*]. ‖ かぜで頭がひどく痛い Because of this cold I *have a* terrible [bad] *headache*. ‖ 頭がくらくらする I *feel dizzy*.

▶《比喩的》くぎの頭 the *head* of a nail.

ことわざ 頭隠して尻隠さず It is almost like sticking your head in the sand like an ostrich [like a stupid ostrich].

2【頭髪】one's **hair** ▶よく頭を洗いなさい Wash your *hair* well. ‖ 母は美容院で頭を洗ってもらった My mother *had her hair washed* at the beauty parlor. ‖ ぼくは１か月に１回頭を刈ってもらう I *have* [*get*] *my hair cut* [I *get a haircut*] once a month. ／I *go to the barber* [《英また》*the barber's*] once a month.

> **逆引き熟語 ○○頭**
> おかっぱ頭 a bob, bobbed hairstyle ／白髪頭 a head of gray [white] hair ／白髪交じりの頭 gray-streaked hair, salt-and-pepper hair, grizzled hair ／はげ頭 a bald head；a bald-head（人）

あ

3【頭脳，考え方】mind, a head, brains

❨解説❩ **mind** は「知力」および「思考」や「意思」をつかさどる頭や心の働きを表す．**head** は「頭部」の意味からその働きにまで意味が広がったもの．**brains** も「脳」が頭脳を表す使い方．

▶彼女はとても**頭がいい** She is very *bright* [*smart* / *sharp*]. / She *has a sharp* [*brilliant*] *mind*. ‖ 彼は**頭が悪い** He's *stupid* [*dumb*]. ‖ その母親は子供が死んでから悲しみのあまり**頭がおかしくなった** After her child's death, the mother *went crazy* [*was deranged*] with grief. ‖ 彼は少し**頭が変だ** He's *not* quite *all there*. / He's a little *crazy*. / He *isn't* quite *normal*.

▶長時間読書をしたので**頭が疲れた** Because I was reading books for many hours, I *was mentally exhausted*. / All that reading (I did) *wore* me *out*. ‖ 今は仕事のことで**頭がいっぱいです** My *head is full of* work now. / I *can't think about anything except* work now. / I'*m preoccupied with* work now. ‖ こんなにやかましくては**頭が変になる** All this noise is going to *drive me out of my mind*. ‖ 真由美のことが**頭から離れない** I *can't get* Mayumi *out of* my *mind* [*head*]. ‖ 我々の人生には限りがあることは**頭ではわかっている** We know *in the abstract* that life is limited. (「抽象的には」「実感は持てないが」と考える).

▶大学時代はドイツ語を一生懸命に勉強したのだが，今は**何も頭に残っていない** I studied German hard in college, but do*n't remember a thing*. ‖ **頭の体操**にクイズをやろう Let's work on some quizzes to *exercise our brains*. ‖ もう少し**頭を使いなさい** *Use your head* a little more. ‖ 彼を説得するにはどうしたものかと**頭をひねった**(＝知恵を絞った) I *racked my brain thinking* of ways to persuade him.

4【最初】the beginning, the first part ▶この小説の**頭の部分**はおもしろくない *The first part* of this novel is not interesting. →頭から.

5【慣用表現】**頭が上がらない** ▶奥さんのほうが会社でも先輩だし，給料も多いので，彼は家でも奥さんに**頭が上がらない** His wife has joined the company earlier and earns more, so he *has no choice but to defer to* her even at home. (➤ defer to は「敬意を払って人の言うことに従う」). **頭が痛い** ▶どうやって借金を返そうかと考えると**頭が痛い** I always *get a headache* when I think about how to pay back my loan. **頭が下がる** ▶ →下がる. **頭が古い** [**固い**] ▶部長は**頭が古い** [**固い**] から新しいものにはついていけない Our department manager is so *old-fashioned* [*inflexible* / *stubborn*] that he cannot keep up with the current trends. **頭がやわらかい** ▶佐藤教授は学者にしては**頭がやわらかい** Professor Sato is *flexible* for a scholar. **頭にくる** ▶**頭にきた**なあ．あいつまたすっぽかしやがった *I've had it* (*up to here*) [*I'm up to here*] with him. He's stood me up again! (英語ではふつう手で頭を指しながら，「ここまできている」(be up to here) と表現する) ‖ あいつにはしょっちゅう**頭にきている** He's always *driving* me *nuts*. (英語では「…の気を変にさせる，いらいらさせる」の意のインフォーマルな表現である drive ... nuts を用いる) ‖ あいつ彼女の肩ばかり持って，ほんとに**頭にくる**よ *I'm sick and tired of* him taking her side. **頭を痛める** ▶社長は資金繰りに**頭を痛めている** The president *is worried about* how to raise the necessary funds. **頭を抱える** ▶彼はあまりの難問に**頭を抱えた** He *racked his brain*(*s*) for an answer to that difficult question. **頭を下げる** ▶彼にはもう絶対に**頭を下げたくない** I won't *bow* (*down*) *and scrape* to him [*be submissive* to him] any more. (➤ bow (down) and scrape は「ぺこぺこする」). **頭を冷やす** ▶**頭を冷やせよ**(＝落ち着けよ) *Calm down*. ‖ 2人とも**頭を冷やして**からもう一度話し合ってみたらどうだ Why don't both of you resume your discussion after you *calm* [*cool*] *down* a bit. **頭を丸める** ▶彼[彼女]は**頭を丸めて**僧[尼僧]になった He [She] *shaved his* [*her*] *head* and became a priest [nun]. **頭をもたげる** ▶彼の中でさいぎ心が**頭をもたげた** Suspicion *raised its* (*ugly*) *head* in him.

-あたま -頭 per ▶1人**あたま**5000円の予算でパーティーを開く hold a party with a budget of five thousand yen *per person*.

あたまうち 頭打ち ▶このところわが社の業績は**頭打ちの状態だ** Our sales *have reached a plateau* [*have plateaued*]. (➤ plateau /plætóʊ/ は「停滞状態」).

あたまかず 頭数 ▶**頭数**を数える count *heads* ‖ マージャンをするには**頭数**が1人足りない We're short one *player* for mah-jongg.

あたまから 頭から from the first(最初から) ; flatly (きっぱりと) ▶警察は**頭から**(＝最初から)私が犯人だと決めつけていた The police had decided [concluded] *from the beginning* that I was the culprit. ‖ もう一度**頭から**やろうよ Let's do it (all over) again *from the beginning*. / Let's start *from scratch*. (➤ from scratch は「ゼロから」に近いインフォーマルな言い方) ‖ 彼は**頭から**それを否定した He denied it *flatly* [*strongly*]. (➤ strongly は「強く」).

あたまきん 頭金 a down payment ▶郊外に家を買うので**頭金**として500万円払った We paid five million yen *down* [*as a down payment*] on our house in a suburb.

あたまごし 頭越し ▶彼は私の**頭越し**に課長に話を持っていった He went *over my head* to the section chief and had a talk with him. / He took the matter *over my head* to the section chief.

あたまごなし 頭ごなし ▶母親は息子を**頭ごなし**に叱りつけた The mother scolded her son *without giving him a chance to explain*. (➤「釈明する機会も与えずに」の意).

あたまだし 頭出し ▶CD は曲の**頭出し**が簡単だ With a CD, you can *easily switch* [*get*] *to the beginning of any song*.

あたまでっかち 頭でっかち ▶あのビルは**頭でっかち**だから，台風のときが心配だ I worry about that building during the typhoon season because it is so *top-heavy*. ‖ うちの会社は少し**頭でっかち**だ(＝幹部が多過ぎる) Our company is a bit *top-heavy*. ‖ 口先ばかりで行動力の伴わない**頭でっかちな**学生が多いようだ Many students seem to be *all talk and no action*.

あたまわり 頭割り ▶ガソリン代は**頭割り**にしよう Let's *split* the gas costs (*equally* [*evenly*]).

あだやおろそか 徒や疎か ▶あの人のことは**あだやおろそか**に思ってはいけないよ You should not treat him *without proper respect*. ‖ ご恩は決して**あだやおろそか**にはいたしません I *will never forget* [*I will always appreciate*] your kindness.

あたらしい 新しい

1【新規の】new ▶きみの**新しい**住所を教えてくれる? Could you tell me your *new* address? ‖ この車が

わが社の**最も新しい型**です This car is our company's *newest* model. ‖ 知津子は**真新しい**スーツを着て式に出た Chizuko attended the ceremony in her *brand-new* suit. (➤ brand-new は「新品の」) ‖ 私は**新しく**入社したばかりです I am a *new* employee at this company.
▶この条約は両国友好の歴史に**新しい** 1 ページを加えた This treaty added a *new* page of friendship to the history of the two nations.
▶**新しく**オープンした店 a *newly*-opened store ‖ 窓枠を**新しくする** *renew* a window frame ‖ パスポート[運転免許証]を**新しくしてもらった** I *got* my passport [driver's license] *renewed*.
2【新鮮な】fresh ▶魚が**新しい**かどうかは目を見ればわかる You can judge whether (or not) a fish is *fresh* by looking at its eyes. ‖ あの店の野菜はとても**新しい** The vegetables at that store are very *fresh*.
3【斬新な, 現代的な】up-to-date ▶会長はもう70歳だが, 考えがとても**新しい** Even though our chairman is already 70 years old, his ideas are very *up-to-date*. ‖ 時代に合った**新しい**感覚(の持ち主)が求められている People who *are in step with the times* are in demand.

あたらしものずき 新し物好き a **faddist**(一時的流行を追う人); an **early adopter**(新しいものに飛びつく人); a **novelty seeker**(新奇なものを追い求める人) ▶彼は**新し物好き**で, 何でも新しいものに飛びつく He is very *fond of new things* [*novelty*] and jumps at anything new. ‖ 要するにきみは**新し物好き**なのさ You're just *a faddist* [*a novelty seeker*]. That's all.

あたらずさわらず 当たらず障らず ▶あのニュース解説者は**当たらず障らず**のことしか言わない That news commentator *never says anything original or daring*. (➤「斬新で思い切ったことは何も言わない」の意).

あたらずといえども 当たらずといえども ▶きみの言っていることは**当たらずといえども**遠からずというところだね You're *close to the mark but not on the money*. / *Nice try* [*Close*], *but no cigar*. (● 前者は「的に近いが, 賞金というところまではいかない」と考え, 後者は「いい線まで行っているが, (賞品の)葉巻を手に入れるまでには至らない」と考えて英訳したもの).

[1]**あたり 当たり** **1【命中, 的中】**▶**当たり**! *You hit it*! / *You've got it*. / *Right*! / *Bingo*! (➤ 最後の言い方はビンゴゲームから) ‖ たったの 1 発で**当たりだ** *A bull's-eye* with only one shot! (➤ bull's-eye は「ダーツなどの的の中心」, 転じて「命中」) ‖ 対話「このTシャツい
…と思う?」「1500円」「**当たり**!」"How much
…k this T-shirt was?" "1,500 yen."
…*right*! / *Bull's-eye*! / *Bingo*!" ‖
…取った(= 大ヒットした) That movie
…寅さんは渥美清の**当たり役**だった
…mi Kiyoshi's *most successful*
…
…[winning] number (当選番
…(当たり券).
…丸山さんは**当たり**がやわらかい
…*mild manner*. / Mr. Mar-
…*a friendly*] *person*. (➤
…よく話しやすい」).
…ロ[ライナー] a *sharp*
…
…ている I *can guess*

[2]**あたり 辺り** ▶**辺り**に人はいなかった There was not a soul *around* [*about*]. ‖ あの**辺り**に知り合いはいるのかい? Do you know anybody *around there*? ‖ この**辺り**は静かでいい It is nice and quiet *around here*. ‖ やっとそこに着いたとき, **辺り**は真っ暗だった When I finally arrived, *the vicinity* [*neighborhood*] was pitch-dark. (➤ vicinity はやや堅い語) ‖ 彼は**辺りかまわず**大声でしゃべる He talks loud(ly), *paying no attention to other people around him*. ‖ 彼はその女性が誰に向かってほほえんだのかと思い, **辺りを見回した** He *looked around* to see who the woman could have smiled at. →-辺り.

[1]**-あたり -当たり** **per** ▶日本人**1人当たり**の国民所得 Japanese *per capita* income (➤ per capita は「1人当たり」の意の堅い言い方) ‖ わが家は毎月**1人当たり**2キロの米を消費する Every month our family consumes two kilograms of rice *per person* [*per head*].
▶このレンタカーは**1日当たり**50ドルです This rental car costs 50 dollars *a* [*per*] *day*.

[2]**-あたり -辺り** ▶伊豆**辺り**なら住んでもいい I wouldn't mind living (*somewhere*) *around* Izu. ‖ あした**あたり**おやじが顔を出すかもしれないよ Maybe Dad will come to see us *sometime* tomorrow.
▶さりげなく花を飾っておく**あたり**, いかにも中田さんらしいね It is typical of Miss Nakata to decorate by using flowers in such a casual way.

あたりさわり 当たり障り ▶そのスポークスマンは**当たり障りのない**返答をした The spokesman gave a *non-committal* reply. ‖ 見合いの席では皆**当たり障りのない**話題で**当たり障りのない**話をする At the *miai* arranged meeting, we *make small talk on innocuous topics*. (➤ small talk は「世間話」, innocuous /mɑ́:kjuəs/ は「害のない」).

あたりちらす 当たり散らす ▶猫に**当たり散らす**のはよせ Don't *take it out on* the cat.

あたりどし 当たり年 ▶ことしはリンゴの**当たり年**だった We had *a bumper crop* of apples this year. (➤ bumper crop は「大豊作」) ‖ ことしは新人の**当たり年**だ(= 優秀な新人がたくさん入った) This year *many excellent people have joined us* [*our company*].

あたりはずれ 当たり外れ ▶**当たり外れのない**商売 a business *without risks* ‖ 以前はテレビやテープレコーダーなどの機器には**当たり外れ**があって, 実際に使用してみないといいかどうかわからなかった Appliances such as TVs and tape recorders used to *be like a lottery ticket*. You didn't know till you used them whether they were any good. (➤「宝くじのようだった」の意).

あたりまえ 当たり前 **1【当然だ】be natural**

> **【文型】**
> **〜であるのは当たり前である**
> **It's (only) natural that** S + V [S **should** do].
> ➤ would do も使う. should はやや堅い
> **人(A)が…するのは当たり前だ**
> **It's natural for** A **to** do.

▶うそをついたのだから, お父さんが怒るのは**当たり前**よ You lied, so *it's only natural that* your father *should* get angry [*that* your father got angry]. / You lied, so *it's* (*only*) *natural for* your father *to* get angry. ‖ 冬になれば寒いのは**当たり前だ** *It's only natural that* it is [《英また》 it *should* be] cold in the winter. / *Naturally*, it's cold in the winter.

あ

【文型】
A があるのを当たり前だと思う
take A for granted

▶現代の若者はたいがい自由があるのを当たり前だと思っている Most young people today *take* freedom *for granted*. ‖ 我々は電気があるのをごく当たり前に思っている We *take* electricity *for granted*.
▶彼は大手術をしたばかりなので弱っているのは当たり前だ He just had a major operation, so it*'s no wonder* [*only natural*] that he feels weak. (➤ no wonder は「不思議でも何でもない」) ‖ 彼女がきみのことを冷たい男だと言うのは当たり前だ She *has every right* [*reason*] *to* say you are cold-hearted. (➤ right は「権利」).
▶私は当たり前のことをしただけです I only did *what I had to do* [*what had to be done*]. ‖ 彼の要求は当たり前(＝もっとも)のように思われる His demand seems *reasonable*. ‖ 対話「この仕事, あしたやったらまずいかな」「当たり前だろ. マネージャーにきょう中に終わらせるって約束したのはきみじゃないか」"Do you think it would be a problem if I did this work tomorrow?" "*Obviously*. You're the one who promised the manager to get it done today."
2【ふつうの】ordinary(平凡な); **standard**(標準の); **regular**(決まった) ▶世界には平和で穏やかな, ごく当たり前の暮らしさえできない人が大勢いる There are a lot of people in the world who can't even lead peaceful, serene, *quite ordinary* lives. ‖ うちでは昔ながらのごく当たり前のやり方で豆腐を作り続けています We keep making tofu in a conventional and *quite ordinary* [*standard*] way.

あたりや 当たり屋 1【車や歩行者にわざとぶつかって金をゆする人】a **fake (car-)accident extortionist.**
2【賭け事で運の良い人】a **lucky person in betting** [**gambling**].

あたる 当たる

訳語メニュー
ぶつかる →hit **1**
的中する →guess right **3**
当たり散らす →take it out on **5**
指名される →be called on **6**
相当する →be equal **7**

1【ぶつかる】hit ▶バドミントンの羽根が先生の頭に当たった The shuttlecock *hit* the teacher *on* the head. ‖ 模型飛行機が窓に当たってガラスが割れた The model airplane *hit* the windowpane and broke it. ‖ あられが窓ガラスに強く当たっている Snow pellets *are beating* [*battering*] *against* the windowpane. ‖ 波が岸辺の岩に当たっては砕けた The waves *dashed* [*broke*] *against* the rocks on the shore.
ことわざ 当たって砕けろ Go for broke. / Take a chance. / Go ahead and try. / Have a go (at it). (➤ 最後の表現は主に《英》).
2【さらされる】get ▶私の書斎は南向きなので日がよく当たる My study faces (the) south, so it *gets* plenty of sunshine. ‖ コンピュータは直射日光の当たる所には置かないでください Please avoid placing the computer *in* direct sunlight. ‖ 山腹には日がよく当たっていた The hillside *was bathed in* sunlight. ‖ 早朝の日の光がポーチに当たっている The early morning sun *is shining down* on the porch. ‖ 日光に当たり過ぎるのは危険だ It is dangerous to *expose* your body to *too much* sunlight.
▶3年生の教室はいつも北風が当たる The third-grade classroom is always *exposed to* northerly winds. ‖ 花が咲いたら雨に当たらないように屋根を作ったほうがいい You'd better build a roof over the flowers *to protect* them *from* the rain after they bloom. ‖ たき火 [ストーブ] に当たる(＝体を温める) *warm oneself* at a fire [a stove].
3【的中する】guess right(正しく推測する); **turn out right**(予報などが) ▶私の予想が当たった I *guessed* (*it*) *right*. ‖ きょうの天気予報は当たった Today's weather forecast *was accurate*. / Today's weather forecast *turned out right*. ‖ 最近の天気予報は当たらないね The weather forecast is often *wrong* these days, isn't it? ‖ 彼の予想は全く当たらなかった His guess was *way off*. (➤「大きく外れた」の意) ‖ 宝くじで100万円当たった I *won* a million yen in the public lottery. / I *drew the winning number* for a million yen in the public lottery. ‖ 対話「私の推測は当たってますか」「いいえ, でもいい線いってますよ」"*Have I guessed it right?*" "No, but you're on the right track."
4【成功する, うまくいく】▶『アバター』という映画はすごく当たった The movie "Avatar" *was a big hit* [*a smash*]. ‖ 甘い! このミカンは当たったね Very sweet! I *picked out* a delicious mikan. (➤「おいしいミカンを選んだ」の意). ‖ 《野球》青木は今当たっている [いない] Aoki *is in good* [*is out of*] *form* now. (🏺「調子がいい [悪い]」と考える).
5【中毒する, 害をなす】▶きのう食べたものの何かにあたった I *got food poisoning* from something I ate yesterday. ‖ 夏の暑さに当たったのか少年はげんなりしていた The boy looked groggy. He might have *been affected* by summer heat.
▶靴の中に何か入っていて足にあたる Something has gotten in my shoe and it's *bothering* me. (➤ bother は「痛みで悩ます」).
▶父は会社でおもしろくないことがあったらしく, 家に帰って来て私たちに当たった My father seemed to have had a bad day at the office and when he got home he *took it out on* us. (➤ take it out on は「…に当たり散らす」) ‖ まま母はシンデレラにつらく当たった Cinderella's stepmother *was hard on* her. / Cinderella's stepmother *treated* her *badly* [*like dirt*]. (➤ like dirt は「ちりあくたのように」).
6【指名される】be called on ▶なぜか数学の時間にはよく当たる For some reason I'*m* often *called on* in math class. ‖ きょうは英語の予習を全然し… たりませんように! I haven't prepare… day's English class. *I hope I u*…
7【相当する】be equal 《to》 ▶… に当たる One meter *is equa*… meter *equals* 3.3 feet. ‖ E… る約7000万人が1万平方キロ… る About seventy millio… sixty percent of Japa… live in a densely-pop… sand square kilomet… る One dollar *is wort*…
▶日本の国会はイギリス… Japanese Diet *co*… liament. ‖「片思… the English w… はことしは日曜日… Sunday this…

▶《慣用表現》彼[illegible]たらない *It is no w*[illegible]
8【立ち向か[illegible]2回戦でSチ[illegible]n the secon[illegible] ‖私は政治生命[illegible]I am determine[illegible]-cult situation, [illegible]my political career a[illegible]火に当たった The fire fig[illegible]mmedi-ately to put out the [illegible]事件の捜査に当たった Twenty d[illegible]*ked on* the case.
▶年頭にあたりことしの抱負を発[illegible]る announce the year's goals *at the beginni*[illegible]*f the year* ‖会長就任にあたりひと言ご挨拶申し上げます I would like to say a few words *on* my appointment to chairperson. (➤ on は「…に際して」).
9【調査する】▶ほかの所を当たってみてくれませんか *Try* somewhere else, please. ‖別の店に当たってみましょう I'*ll check* another store. ‖難しい単語は大辞典に当たって調べなさい *Consult* a large dictionary for the meaning of difficult words. ‖引用は元の出典に当たったほうがいい You should *trace* quotations *back* to their original sources.

アダルト ▶アダルトムービー an *adult* movie ‖アダルトな(＝大人の)雰囲気のバー a bar with a *sophisticated* atmosphere.

アチーブメントテスト **an achievement test.**

あちこち **here and there**(そこここ)；**from place to place, from one place to another** (場所から場所へ)；**all over** (いたる所) ▶スズメが数羽庭の木の間をあちこち飛び回っていた Some sparrows were flitting *here and there* among the trees in our garden. ‖私たちは津和野をあちこち歩き回った We walked *all over* Tsuwano. ‖営業職はあちこち旅をしなければならない Salespeople have to travel *all around* [*from place to place* / *from one place to another*]. ‖子供たちは校庭をあちこち走り回っている The children are running around *this way and that* on the playground. ‖博覧会を見に人が世界のあちこちからやって来た People came *from all over* the world to see the exposition.

あちら ▶あちらに見えるのが沢田先生のお宅です The house you see *over there* is Mr. Sawada's. ‖あちらのご婦人はどなたでしょう Who is *that* lady? ‖あちらへどうぞ Go *that way*, please. →あっち.
▶子供たちは長い間あちらに(＝海外に)いましたので日本語がうまく話せません My children can't speak Japanese well because they have lived *overseas* for a long time.
▶ ことわざ あちら立てればこちらが立たぬ You can't side with both parties. (➤side with は「…に味方する」).

あちらこちら **here and there.** →あちこち.

あっ **Oh !, Ah !** ▶あっ, そうか. わかった *Oh*, I see. ‖あっ, 鍵を忘れちゃった *Oh dear !* I've forgotten my key. (➤ Oh dear ! は主に女性が用いる) ‖あっ, 大変だ. 急がなくっちゃ *Oh, no !* I've got to hurry.

あつあげ 厚揚げ ***atsuage*, a thick deep-fried tofu.**

あつあつ 熱々 ▶ピザは熱々を食べるのがおいしい Pizza tastes best when it is *piping hot*. (➤ piping hot は「ジュージュー音がするほど熱い」).
▶結婚して5年になるのに2人はまだ熱々だ They have been married for five years, but they *are* still *passionately in love*.

[1]**あつい 暑い・熱い** **1【気温などが高く感じる】** **hot, very warm** ▶きょうは暑いですね *It's hot* today, isn't it ? ‖京都の夏は暑い *It's hot* in the summer in Kyoto. / Kyoto *is hot* in the summer. ‖夏の間は2階は暑い *It's very warm* upstairs in the summer. ‖私は暑くならないうちに宿題をやってしまった I finished my homework *before it got hot*. ‖きのうよりきょうのほうがもっと暑い *It's even hotter* today than yesterday. / Today *is even hotter* than yesterday (was).
▶そんなに着込んで暑くないの? Aren't you *hot* bundled up like that ? (➤ bundle up は「着込む」) ‖暑い夏がやっと終わった At (long) last the *hot* summer is over. ‖あー, 暑い暑い! Boy, *is it hot* [*am I hot*]! (➤ am I hot は「俺ってカッコいいじゃん!」というような意味にもなる).
✉ **だんだん暑くなって参りました** It's been getting *hotter and hotter* [*gradually hotter*].
2【水・物の温度が高く感じる】 **hot** ▶熱い湯に入る take [have] a *hot* bath ‖お茶は熱いのが好きだ I like my tea *hot*. ‖熱い! *Ouch !* (➤ 発音は /aʊtʃ/).
3【情熱的】▶2人は熱い仲だ The two *are passionately in love*. ‖彼女はその男性歌手に熱い視線を送った She cast *yearning glances* at the male vocalist. ‖そう熱くなるなよ(＝落ちつけよ) Don't get [be] so *worked up*. / Calm down.

[2]**あつい 厚い** **1【厚みがある】** **thick** ; **heavy** (厚くて重い) ▶厚い辞書 [ステーキ] a *thick* dictionary [steak] ‖厚いオーバー a *heavy* overcoat ‖厚い雲に覆われた空 the sky covered with *thick* [*heavy*] clouds ‖その氷は人が歩けるほど厚かった The ice *was thick* enough to walk on. ‖アメリカの水泳陣は選手層が厚い The American swimming team consists of *numerous* excellent swimmers.
2【度合いが強い】 **warm** (もてなしなどが) ▶私たちは友人の厚いもてなしに感激した We were deeply moved by the *warm* hospitality of our friends. ‖彼は友情に厚い His friendship (with me) is *deep* [*warm*]. ‖彼は上司に厚く信頼されている He enjoys the *strong* confidence of his boss. ‖彼女はキリスト教をあつく信仰している She *deeply* [*firmly* / *strongly*] believes in Christianity. (➤ She's a devout Christian. と表現するのが普通).
✉ **お心尽くしの贈り物をいただき厚くお礼申し上げます** I am *deeply* grateful for your thoughtful gift.

あっか 悪化する **get worse, worsen, deteriorate** /dɪtíəriəreɪt/ (➤ 最後の語がいちばん堅い)；**悪化させる** **make ... worse, deteriorate** +目 (➤ 後者は堅い語)；**aggravate** /ǽgrəveɪt/ +目 (すでに悪いものをさらに)；**exacerbate** /ɪgzǽsəˈbeɪt/ +目 (病気・怒り・状況などを) ▶天候は次第に悪化している The weather *is getting worse*. ‖彼女の病状は急に悪化した Her condition *took a* sudden *turn for the worse*. / Her condition *worsened* [*deteriorated*] suddenly. ‖かぜを放っておくと悪化することがある A cold may *be aggravated* by neglect. ‖両国の関係は悪化の一途をたどっている The relations between the two countries *are getting worse and worse* [*are deteriorating*]. ‖誰もこれ以上の状況悪化を望んでいない Nobody wants to further *aggravate* [*exacerbate*] the situation.

あつかい 扱い **handling** ▶瀬戸物の扱いには気をつけてください Please *handle* the china *with care*. ‖彼女は

あ

小さい子供の**扱いがうまい** She *is good at dealing with* small children. / She *has a way with* small children. (➤ 後者はインフォーマルな言い方).

–あつかい –扱い ▶警察は私を犯人扱いした The police *treated* me *as* [*like*] *a criminal*. ‖ じゃあ, きみは出席扱いにしよう OK. I'll *think of* you *as present*.

あつかう 扱う **1【人を】treat** +⊞ (待遇する) ; **deal with** (対応する) ; **handle** +⊞ (うまく接する) ▶彼女は客を丁寧に**扱う** She *treats* her guests politely. ‖ 彼は人を**扱うのがうまい** He *is good at dealing with* people. / He *has a way with* people. (➤ 後者はインフォーマルな言い方) ‖ 私は小さい子供を**扱う**のに慣れていない I am not used to *handling* small children. ‖ 小山田夫人は**扱いにくい** Mrs. Oyamada *is hard to please*. (➤「喜ばせるのが難しい」の意) / Mrs. Oyamada is a *difficult* person. ‖ あの人はどんな**扱いにくい**客でもうまく応対する He can manage the most *difficult* clients.

2【物・問題などを】handle +⊞ ▶この箱は注意して**扱う**必要がある This box needs careful *handling*. ‖ 国連は国際問題を**扱う**ことになっている The United Nations *handles* [*deals with*] international problems. (🔘「…ことになっている」に引かれて be supposed to ... とすると批判めいた響きが出ることが少なくないので, 訳例のように言い切る形がよい) ‖ この窓口は書留だけを**扱う** (=受け付ける) This window *accepts* only registered mail. / This window *is* just *for* registered mail. ‖ その本の書評は文化欄で**大きく扱われた** The review of that book *took up* quite *a lot of space* in the culture column. ‖ 当店では輸入品は**扱っておりません** We don't *deal in* imported goods at this store. (➤ deal in は「商う」) / Our store doesn't *carry* [*sell*] imported products.

あつかましい 厚かましい **nervy** (ずうずうしい) ; **pushy** (押しの強い) ▶**厚かましい**頼み a *nervy* request ‖ **厚かましい**男 a *pushy* man ‖ おいが**厚かましく**もまた金の無心にやって来た My nephew *had the* [*a*] *nerve to* come and ask me for money again. ‖ 黙って上がり込むとは**何て厚かましいんだろう** Barging into the house without a word—*what nerve*! (🔘 what a nerve! と a を入れるのは一般的ではない).

✉ **厚かましいお願いですが, 空港まで迎えに来てくださいませんか** Perhaps it is *too much to ask*, but I wonder if you could possibly pick me up at the airport. ➤ 前半は I am afraid I may be asking too much, としてもよい.

あつかましさ 厚かましさ **impudence ; nerve, cheek** (➤ ともにインフォーマル ; cheek は主に《英》).

あつがみ 厚紙 **thick paper** (厚い紙) ; **cardboard** (ボール紙).

あつがり 暑がり ▶彼女は大変な**暑がり**で, 夏は毎年軽井沢で避暑をする Since she *is* very *sensitive* [*susceptible*] *to the heat*, she spends the summer at Karuizawa every year.

あつかん 熱燗 ***atsukan*, hot sake** ▶お銚子(ちょうし) 1本, 熱かんで頼むよ (I'll have) *a bottle of hot sake*, please.

1**あっかん 悪漢** a **villain** /vílən/ ; a **criminal** (犯罪者).

2**あっかん 圧巻** **the highlight** (山場) ; **the best scene** (いちばんよい場面) ▶その映画の戦闘シーンは**圧巻**だった The battle scene was *the highlight* of the movie.

あつぎ 厚着 ▶寒かったので彼女は**厚着をした** She *wore* [*put on*] *warm clothes* to keep out the cold. (➤ wear は着ている状態を, put on は着る動作をいう) ‖ 子供にはあまり**厚着をさせない**ほうがいい It's better not to *clothe* your children too *heavily*.

あつぎり 厚切り a **thick slice** ▶**厚切り**のハム *a thick slice* of ham / *thickly sliced* ham.

あつくるしい 暑苦しい **stuffy ; close** /kloʊs/ (風通しが悪い) ▶この部屋, **暑苦しい**わね It's *stuffy* in this room, isn't it? ‖ **暑苦しい**から窓を開けてください *It's* very *hot and stuffy* [*close*] in here. Could you open the window? ‖ その**暑苦しい**髪型, 何とかならない? Isn't there anything you can do with that *stuffy* hairstyle?

あっけ 呆気 ▶彼の無作法には**あっけにとられた** I *was taken aback* by his rudeness. ‖ 彼の突拍子もない返事を聞いて**あっけにとられて**しまった When I heard his astonishing answer, I *was dumbfounded*.

あつげしょう 厚化粧 **heavy make-up** ▶**厚化粧**の女性 a woman *with heavy make-up*.

あっけない 呆気ない **disappointing** (期待外れの) ▶花火大会は短くて**あっけなかった** The firework(s) display *was disappointingly short*. ‖ 会議は**あっけなく**済んだ The meeting was over *all too soon* [*all too quickly*]. (➤ all は強調) ‖ そのテニス選手は対戦相手に**あっけなく**敗れた That tennis player was beaten by his [her] opponent *all too easily*.

あっけらかん ▶彼はカンニングを見つけられても**あっけらかんと** (=平然と) していた He behaved *as if nothing had happened* when he got caught cheating on the test.

あっこう 悪口 **abuse** /əbjúːs/ ▶彼女は夫に**悪口**雑言の限りを尽くした She *called* her husband *names*. (➤ call ... names は「…をばかだの畜生だのとののしる」の意) / She *let out a torrent of abuse* on her husband. ‖ 人の**悪口を言わない**ほうがよい You should*n't speak ill of* others. (🔘 日本人学習者は speak ill of をよく用いるが, これはここに示したように「あっこうを言う」に相当する堅い言い方).

1**あつさ 暑さ・熱さ** **(the) heat** ▶ぼくは沖縄出身なので**暑さ**は平気です I am from Okinawa, so I do not mind *the heat*. ‖ **この暑さでは**眠れない I can't sleep (at all) in *this heat*. ‖ 梅雨が明けて, 富山はこれから**暑さに向かう** With the rainy season over, the weather in Toyama *will become hotter* day by day. ‖ ことわざ **暑さ寒さも彼岸まで** Both heat and cold last until the equinox days.

▶私は風呂のあまりの**熱さ**に飛び上がった The bath was *so hot* I jumped up.

✉ **暑さ厳しき折からご自愛ください** I hope you will take good care of yourself in this *heat*.

2**あつさ 厚さ** **thickness** ▶**厚さ** 8 センチのれんが an eight-centimeter *thick* brick / a brick with a *thickness* of eight centimeters ‖ 対話「その板, **厚さ**はどのくらい?」「そうね, 5 センチくらいだね」"*How thick* is that board?" "Hmm, about five centimeters."

あっさく 圧搾 **compression** 一動 **圧搾する** **compress** +⊞ ‖ **圧搾空気** compressed air ‖ **圧搾器** a compressor.

あっさり ▶**あっさりした**食べ物 *light* [*plain*] food / *lightly seasoned* food (➤ 後者は「味付けがあっさりした」) ‖ **あっさりした**食事をとる have a *light* meal ‖ 母は**あっさりした**服が似合う Mom looks good in *simple* clothes. ‖ 父は金や名誉には**あっさりしている** My father *doesn't care much about* money or honor.

▶彼は万引きしたことを**あっさり**認めた He *readily* admitted having shoplifted. ‖ 彼に丁重な手紙を出して頼んだが, **あっさり**断られてしまった I sent him a very polite letter of request, but I got a *flat* refusal. ‖ 彼はあっさり首を切られてしまった He was let go *just like that*. (➤ just like that は「いとも簡単に」).

あっし 圧死 ▶その地震では多くの人が倒れた家の下敷きになって圧死した In that earthquake many people *were crushed to death under* the collapsed houses.

あっしゅく 圧縮 compression 一動 圧縮する compress +目 (圧力を加えて) ; condense +目 (文章などを短縮する) ▶プロパンガスを圧縮してボンベに詰める *compress* propane gas and put it into a cylinder ‖ 段落を1つの文章に圧縮する *condense* [*shorten*] a paragraph into one sentence ‖ データ [ファイル] を圧縮する *compress* data [a file] (➤「解凍する」は decompress ; インフォーマルな言い方では zip (反意語は unzip)). ‖ 圧縮空気 compressed air.

あっしょう 圧勝 an overwhelming victory ; a landslide victory (特に選挙の) ▶中日が巨人に9対1で圧勝した The Dragons *won an overwhelming victory over* the Giants by (a score of) 9 to 1. ‖ 保守党が選挙で圧勝した The Conservative Party *won by a landslide*.

あっせい 圧制・圧政 oppression (抑圧) ; tyranny /tírəni/ (専制) ▶圧制に苦しむ groan under *oppression*.

あっせん 斡旋 ▶彼に就職をあっせんする *help* him *find* a job ‖ 友人のあっせんである出版社に勤めることができた *Through* [*By*] *the good offices of* a friend of mine, I was able to get a job at a publishing company. (● good offices は「あっせん」に近い堅い言い方で, 日常的には I used my connections to get me a job at a publishing company. のような言い方が好まれる).

あつぞこぐつ 厚底靴 platform shoes.

あっち ▶あっちへ行け Go *over there!* ／Go *away!* (➤ 後者は「立ち去れ!」の意) ‖ 《子供に》(うるさいから) あっちへ行きなさい *Run along now!* ／*Get lost!* ／*Beat it!* (➤ あとの二者のほうがより乱暴な言い方) ‖ あっちこっち捜したが眼鏡は見つからなかった I searched *here and there*, but I could not find my glasses.

あつで 厚手の thick ▶厚手のノート a *thick* notebook ‖ 冬物は厚手の生地で作る Winter wear is made of *heavy* cloth.

-あっての ▶サポーターあってのプロサッカーだぞ. そのことを忘れるな *Without supporters*, professional soccer would never exist. Don't forget that.

あっというま あっと言う間 ▶男は金を奪うとあっと言う間に姿を消した The man took the money and disappeared *in no time*. ‖ カップにお湯を注げばあっと言う間に出来上がり If you pour hot water into the cup, it will be ready *in an instant*. ‖ 1時間の休憩はあっと言う間に過ぎた The hour-long break passed by *before I knew it*.

あっといわせる あっと言わせる surprise +目 (思いがけないことで驚かせる) ; astonish +目 (仰天させる) ▶太郎は美人のガールフレンドを連れてきてみんなをあっと言わせた Taro *surprised* all of us when he brought his beautiful girlfriend with him. ‖ みんなをあっと言わせるような新企画を考えているんだ I'm working on a new plan which will *astonish* everybody.

あっとう 圧倒する overwhelm +目 ; overpower +目 (打ち勝つ) 一形 圧倒的な overwhelming ▶彼女の意気込みにはただもう圧倒された I *was* simply *overwhelmed* with her enthusiasm. ‖ わがチームは相手チームを圧倒した Our team *overpowered* our opponents. ‖ その政治家は選挙で圧倒的勝利を収めた The politician *won by a landslide*. ‖ 彼の動議は圧倒的多数で可決された His motion was passed *by an overwhelming* [*a sweeping*] *majority*.

アットホーム ▶アットホームな雰囲気のペンション a resort inn with a *homelike* [an *at-home*] atmosphere.

アットマーク an at sign [symbol] 《略@》(➤「アットマーク」は和製語 ; なお, 日本ではEメールアドレスを伝えるとき@を「アットマーク」と読むが英語では at とだけ言えばよい.「アットマーク」と発音すると@mark と受け止められる).

アッパーカット an uppercut ▶アッパーカットを食らってダウンする be knocked down by *an uppercut*.

あっぱく 圧迫 pressure (押さえつける [つけられる] こと) ; oppression (圧制, 弾圧) ; suppression (抑圧, 鎮圧) 一動 圧迫する press +目, oppress +目, suppress +目 ▶満員電車で胸が圧迫されて苦しかった I felt an oppressive pain in the chest due to the *press* of people on the packed train. (➤ この場合の press は「押すこと」という行為) ‖ 《医者が》胸に圧迫感を感じることはありますか? Do you feel any *pressure* on your chest? ‖ 言論の自由を圧迫する *suppress* the freedom of speech.

あっぱれ ▶あっぱれ, あっぱれ *Well done!* ／*Bravo!* ／*Good show!* ‖ あっぱれな行為 an *admirable* deed ‖ 敵ながらあっぱれだ That's an enemy *you have to admire*.

アップ ▶アップの写真 a *close-up* picture (➤ 発音は /klóʊsʌ̀p/) ‖ 彼女は髪をアップにしている She wears her hair *up* [*upswept*]. (➤「アップの髪型」は upswept hairstyle) ‖ 彼は上司に給料をアップしてくれと頼んだ He asked his boss for *a raise* [《英》*a rise*].

> **危ないカタカナ語✹ アップ**
> **1** 英語の up と日本語の「アップ」は用法がかなり異なる. 英語の up にも動詞用法はあるが, 基本的に動詞と一緒に使う副詞または前置詞.「料金をアップする」は raise the fare,「イメージをアップする」は improve the image のように別の動詞を使うのがふつう.
> **2**「ベースアップ」「グレードアップ」「イメージアップ」など〈名詞+アップ〉の語は多くが和製語である.

あっぷあっぷ ▶子供たちは水に落ちてあっぷあっぷしている友だちを助けようとした The children tried to save their friend who had fallen into the water and *was struggling for air*.
▶《比喩的》物価が高すぎてわが家はいつもあっぷあっぷだ We are always *on the verge of going under* [*struggling to keep our heads above water*] because of the high cost of living. (➤ go under は「沈む」「破産する」).

アップデート an update /ʌ̀pdéɪt/ 一動 アップデートする update +目.

アップテンポの up-tempo ▶アップテンポの曲 an *up-tempo* number.

アップリケ (an) appliqué /æ̀pləkéɪ/ ▶大きなアップリケのついた子供服 children's wear with large *appliqué* decoration.

アップルパイ (an) apple pie.

アップロード 《コンピュータ》an upload 一動 アップロードする upload +目 ▶動画をユーチューブにアップロードする *upload* a video to YouTube.

あつぼったい 厚ぼったい ▶厚ぼったい唇 *thick* [*full*] lips.

あ

あつまり 集まり a **gathering**(同じ目的をもった人たちによる内輪の)；a **meeting** (会議・打ち合わせのための)；a **get-together** (非公式な, または懇親のための) →**会合** ▶そのコンサートは客の**集まり**がよかった［悪かった］The concert *was well* [*poorly*] *attended*. ‖あすPTAの**集まり**があります A PTA [parent-teacher] *meeting* will be held tomorrow. ‖星雲は星の**集まり**(＝集団)だ Nebulae are *clusters* of stars.

あつまる 集まる

1【寄り集まる】gather；**meet** (時間・場所を決めて)；**get together** (パーティーなどで；インフォーマルな語)；**attend** (＋目)(出席する)；**assemble** (ある目的で)；**swarm** (昆虫などが) ▶火事があると必ず人が**集まる** People always *gather* when there is a fire. ／Whenever there is a fire, a crowd always *gathers*. ‖将棋クラブは毎週金曜日に**集まる** The shogi club *meets* every Friday. ‖10時30分に京都駅に**集まろう** *Let's meet* at Kyoto Station at 10：30. ‖ミツバチが花の周りに**集まっていた** Bees *were swarming* [*buzzing*] around the flowers.

▶演奏会に**集まった人々**は優に2000人を超えていた The total *attendance* at the concert was well over 2,000. ‖その問題を討議するために世界各地から科学者たちが**集まった** Scientists from all over the world *assembled* to discuss the problem. ‖元日は私たちの家族全員が**集まる**日です New Year's Day is when my whole family *gets together*. ‖きのうの晩, みんなが何となくうちに**集まった** There was an impromptu *get-together* last evening at my house. (➤ impromptu /ɪmprɑ́ːmptjuː/ は「準備なしの」).

✉《パーティーの招待カードで》**集まろうよ**！*Let's get together*！

▶みんなが**集まったら**すぐに始めよう As soon as everyone *gets here* [*shows up*], let's get started. (➤ show up は「姿を現す」の意のインフォーマルな表現) ‖交番の前に**大勢の人が集まっていた** *There was a crowd of people* in front of the police box. ‖**集まれ**！*Gather around*！／*Line up*！(➤ 後者は「整列！」の意) ‖みんな, ここに**集まって並び**なさい Everyone, *line up* here.

2【集中する】focus《on》▶みんなの目が私に**集まった** All eyes *focused on* me. ‖世間の関心は都市の防災問題に**集まった** Public attention *became focused on* (the need for) preparations for natural disasters in urban areas. ‖世間の同情はその孤児に**集まった** The orphan *attracted* much public sympathy. ／Everybody felt sympathy for the orphan. ‖主な官庁は千代田区を中心に**集まっている** (The) major government office buildings *are concentrated* in Chiyoda Ward.

あつみ 厚み thickness ▶彼の**厚みのある**胸 that *thick* chest of his ‖本の価値は**厚み**だけでは判断できない The value of a book cannot be judged by its *thickness* alone. ‖そのオーケストラの**厚みのある**音 the orchestra's *rich* sound.

あつめる 集める

📖 **訳語メニュー**
寄せ集める →gather **1**
収集する, 集金する →collect **1**
注目などを集める →draw, attract **2**

1【寄せ合わせる】gather ＋目 (散らばっているものを1か所に)；**collect** ＋目 (目的をもって) ▶答案用紙を**集める** *collect* answer sheets ‖女の子は浜辺で貝殻を**集めた** The little girl *gathered* seashells on the beach. ‖私の趣味はいろいろな国の切手を**集めること**です My hobby is *collecting* stamps from different countries. ‖弟は模型自動車をたくさん**集めている** My younger brother *has a* large *collection* of model cars. ‖この本はロシアの民話を**集めたもの**です This is *a collection* of Russian folktales.

▶校長先生は生徒たちを講堂に**集めた** The principal *had* the students *assemble* in the auditorium. ‖総理大臣は主だった側近を**集めた**(＝招集した) The prime minister *summoned* his chief aides.

▶私たちは交通遺児を援助するためにお金を**集めています** We're *collecting* [*taking up*] money to help children orphaned by traffic accidents. (➤ take up はインフォーマルな言い方) ‖今月末までに10万円**集めなければならない** We must *raise* 100,000 yen by the end of this month. (➤ raise は「(金を)調達する」).

2【集中させる】draw ＋目 (注意・関心を)；**attract** ＋目 (注目させる, 人を引きつける) ▶サリン事件は世間の非常な**注目を集めた** The sarin incident *drew* [*attracted*] much public *attention*. (➤ drew は draw の過去形) ‖そのサーカスは多数の観客を**集めた** The circus *attracted* [*drew*] a large number of spectators. ‖孤児の哀れな姿はみんなの同情を**集めた** The miserable appearance of the orphan *captured* the sympathy of many people. (➤ capture は「(人の心・注意などを)捉える」).

あつもの 羹 ▶〔ことわざ〕**あつものに懲りてなますを吹く** Having been hurt by eating food that was too hot, the cautious person even blows on cold food.

あつやき 厚焼き
‖**厚焼き卵** *atsuyaki*, a thick Japanese omelet.

あつらえ 誂え ▶このスーツは**あつらえ**です This suit was *custom* [*tailor*]*-made*.

あつらえむき 誂え向き →**おあつらえ向き**.

あつらえる 誂える order ▶背広を15万円で**あつらえた** I *ordered* myself a new suit for [at] 150,000 yen.

あつりょく 圧力 pressure ▶大気の**圧力** (the) atmospheric *pressure*.

▶財界はその法律を変えるよう政府に**圧力をかけた** Business circles *put pressure on* [*pressured*] the government to change the law. ‖彼は**圧力をかけられて**その本の出版を断念した He *was pressured into* giving up on publishing the book.

‖**圧力団体** a pressure group；a lobby (議会への) ‖**圧力鍋**［**釜**］a pressure cooker.

あつれき 軋轢 friction (摩擦)；**conflict** /kɑ́ːnflɪkt/ (衝突)；**discord** /dískɔːʳd/ (不一致) ▶親子(父と息子)の**あつれき** *friction* between father and son ‖領土問題で日中両国の間に**あつれき**が生じている A territorial issue has caused *friction* between Japan and China.

あて 当て 1【目的, 目指すところ】a **purpose**；an **aim** (狙い)；an **object** (目的) ▶**あて**のない旅 a trip with no *particular object* [*destination*] in mind (➤ destination は「目的地」) ‖**あて**もなく外国へ行くのはばかげている It is foolish to go abroad *with no plan*. ‖彼にはどこへも行く**あて**がなかった He *was uncertain* where to go. →**あてど**.

2【信用, 頼み】一動 あてにする count on (援助などを)；**rely on** (過去の経験から判断して大丈夫だと)；**de-**

pend on（援助が必要なので）▶彼の援助をあてにする *count on* his help ‖ ぼくをあてにしていいよ You *can count on* me. ‖ あの人はあてにできる That person *is reliable* [*trustworthy*].（➤ ともに「信頼できる」の意だが，後者のほうがより強意的）／That person *can be depended upon*. ‖ 彼の約束はあまりあてにしないほうがいい You shouldn't *put* much *faith in* his promises. ‖ あまり人をあてにしてはいけない You shouldn't *expect* too much of others.

▶田沼の言うことはあてにならない We *cannot rely upon* Tanuma's words. ／We *cannot believe* Tanuma. ‖ 外見はあてにならないことが多い *Appearances are* often *deceptive*.

3【見込み，期待】▶昇給を期待していたのにあてが外れた I'd been expecting a pay raise, but I *was disappointed*. ‖ 交通渋滞があるのでバスはあてにならない You *can't depend* [*count*] *on* buses because of traffic jams. ‖ 当分結婚のあてはない I have no *prospect* of getting married for the time being. ‖ あいつは報酬をあてにして警察に垂れ込んだんだ He tipped off the police *in expectation of* a reward. ‖ 就職のことなら，私にあてがあるから頼んであげよう If you are looking for a job, I *know* a company I can introduce you to.

-あて -宛て ▶私宛ての手紙はありますか Is there a letter *for* me? ／Is there any mail *addressed to* me?

✉ **会社宛てに請求書をお送りください** Send the bill to me *c/o* [(*in*) *care of*] my office.

あてがう 1【ぴったりつける】apply +目；**put** +目 ▶目に双眼鏡をあてがう *put* [*hold*] the field glasses *to* one's eyes ‖ 机の寸法を聞かれたので，物差しをあてがってみた I was asked about the length of the desk, so I *used* a ruler to measure it.

2【割り当てる】allot +目，**assign** +目，**give** +目（➤ 順に語の改まり度が減少するが，assign からは行為者の恣意が感じられる）▶私たちは民宿で狭苦しい部屋をあてがわれた We *were allotted* [*were assigned* ／ *were given*] a cramped room at the tourist home. ‖ その新入社員は退屈な仕事をあてがわれた The new employee *was assigned* boring tasks.

3【与える】give +目 ▶親は子供によいおもちゃをあてがうべきだ Parents should *give* beneficial toys *to* their young children.

あてこすり 当てこすり a **dig** ▶彼は遅刻常習者に触れた上司のことばが自分への当てこすりだと気づいた He realized that the boss's remarks about habitual latecomers were *a dig* at him. ‖ 彼のことばは明らかに私への当てこすりだった Evidently his words *were meant* [*were intended*] *for* me.

あてこむ 当て込む expect +目（期待する）▶昇給を当て込んで彼は車を買った *In expectation* [*In hopes*] *of* a pay raise [《英》rise], he bought a car.

あてさき 宛先 an **address**（住所）▶封筒に宛先を書く write the *receiver's address* on an envelope.

あてじ 当て字 *kanji* used for their sound without regard for their meaning（➤「お目出度（めでと）う」のような場合）; *kanji* used for their meaning without regard for their original meaning（➤「煙草（たばこ）」のような場合）.

あてずいりょう 当て推量 a **wild** [**rough**] **guess**; a **conjecture**（➤ 改まった語）.

あてずっぽう 当てずっぽう a (**wild**) **guess, guesswork** ▶彼の答えは全くの当てずっぽうだった His answer was just *a shot in the dark*. ‖ 対話「彼女の年，いくつかな」「当てずっぽうで言ってみろよ」"I wonder how old she is." "Just *take a* (*wild*) *guess*."

あてつけがましい 当てつけがましい ▶彼女は一郎の当てつけがましい態度に気を悪くした She was offended by Ichiro's *snide* [*insinuating*] manner.（➤ snide は「意地の悪い」，insinuating は「（何かを）ほのめかすような」）.

あてつける 当てつける ▶私の言ったことはきみに当てつけたのではない My remarks were not *aimed at* you.

あてど 当て所 ▶（俳人の）山頭火はあてどのない旅に出た Santoka went on a journey *with no particular destination in mind*. ‖ 失業者たちがあてどなく通りをうろついていた The jobless people wandered *aimlessly* in the streets. →あて.

あてな 宛名 an **addressee** /ædresíː/（人）; an **address**（住所）《参考》「住所氏名」をはっきり表すには name and address とする ▶この小包の宛名は間違っている This package has the wrong *address*. ／This package is incorrectly addressed. ‖ 手紙の宛名ははっきり書いてください Please *address* the letter clearly. →-宛て.

あてにげ 当て逃げ a **hit-and-run accident** ▶車を当て逃げされたんだって？ I heard *another car crashed into your car and the driver just drove off*.

アテネ Athens /ǽθɪnz/（ギリシャの首都）.

あてはずれ 当て外れ a **disappointment**, a **letdown**（➤ 後者はインフォーマル）▶競艇での彼の敗退はとんだ当て外れだった His defeat in the speedboat race was quite *a disappointment* to me. ‖ おじさんのお年玉は少なくて当て外れだった The New Year's gift of money from my uncle was *disappointingly* small [was smaller than *I* (*had*) *expected* ／ was smaller than *I was hoping for*].（➤ expected は予想や期待より，hoping for は希望していたものより少なかった場合）.

あてはまる 当てはまる apply《to》, **fit** +目 ▶同じことが彼にも当てはまる The same *applies to* him. ／That *is* also *true of* him. ／That *is* also *the case with* him. ‖ 空所に最もよく当てはまる語句を次の中から選びなさい Fill in the blanks with *the most suitable* words or phrases from the following.

あてはめる 当てはめる apply +目 ▶この主人公の生き方を自分自身の場合に当てはめてみなさい Try *applying* the hero's way of life to your own case. ‖ 公式を当てはめて，この計算式を解きなさい *Apply* the formula to solve this calculating problem.

あでやか 艶やかな gorgeous ▶パーティーにはあでやかに着飾った若い女性が大勢出席していた Many *gorgeously dressed* young women attended the party.

あてられる 当てられる ▶私は新婚夫婦の仲の良さにさんざん当てられた I *felt* greatly *embarrassed by* the newlyweds' display of affection.（➤「きまりの悪い思いをした」の意）.

[1]あてる 当てる

📖 **訳語メニュー**
ぶつける →hit **1**
さらす →expose **2**
あてがう →put **3**
推測する →guess **4**
指名する →call on **5**

1【ぶつける，的中させる】hit +目 ▶バットの中心にボールを当てる *hit* the ball with the center of the bat

あ

‖彼は1発で的に矢を当てた He *hit* the target (with his arrow) on the first try.
▶《(くじなどを)福引きで1等賞を当てた(＝引いた)I *drew* the first prize ticket in the lottery. ‖株で当てて大もうけをした I *hit the jackpot* on the stock market. (➤ hit the jackpot は「(ポーカーなどで)積み立てられた掛け金を得る」が原義).
2【さらす】expose +目 ▶布団を外気に当てる *air* (*out*) the futon／*expose* the futon *to the air* ‖この鉢植えの植物は日に当てる必要がある This potted plant *needs* (*some*) *sunlight*.
3【あてがう】put +目 ; **direct** +目 (向ける) ▶看護師は熱をみるため私の額に手を当てた The nurse *put* her hand *on* my forehead to check my temperature. ‖ヒロインが登場すると, 照明係はさっとスポットライトを当てた When the heroine appeared on the stage, the lighting technician immediately *put* a spotlight on her.
4【推測する】guess +目 ▶この箱の中に何が入っているか当ててごらんなさい Try to *guess* what I have inside this box. ‖私が誰だか当ててごらん *Guess* who I am. (➤ 単に Guess who? ともいう).
5【指名する】call on ▶鈴木先生は教室でよく私を当てる Mr. Suzuki often *calls on* me in class. ‖きょうは国語の時間に2回当てられた Today I *was called on* twice in Japanese class.
6【充当する】devote +目, **allot** +目 ▶彼は暇な時間は残らずシナリオ書きに当てている He *devotes* all his spare time *to* writing screenplays. (➤ devote A to B で「A(時間など)をB(仕事・目的・人など)にささげる」) ‖彼は1日1時間を歌の練習に当てている He *allots* an hour a day *to* practicing singing. (➤ allot A to [for] B で「A(時間など)をB(目的など)に割り当てる」).
▶英単語に適切な訳語を当てる *supply* a suitable Japanese equivalent *for* an English word.
☛ 当てられる (→見出語)

2あてる 宛てる address /ədrés/ +目 ▶吉田という人に宛てた手紙がきのうここに配達された A letter *addressed to* a Mr. Yoshida was delivered here yesterday. (➤ address A to B の形で「A(手紙)をB(人)宛てにする」) ‖これは誰に宛てた手紙かしら? I wonder who this letter is *for*.

あてレコ dubbing. →アフレコ, 吹き替え.

あと 後・跡 1【時間】一副 あとで later ▶あとでもう一度やり直そう Let's try it again *later*. ‖あとで後悔するよ You'll be sorry *later*. ‖夕食のあとでトランプをしよう Let's play cards *after* dinner. ‖秘密は口外しないでくれと彼女の家に頼みに行ったときには, 彼女はもう何もかもしゃべったあとだった She *had already* blurted out everything by the time I got to her home to ask her not to leak the secret. ‖あとから行きます *I'll follow you*.
▶彼女は35歳の若さで亡くなり, あと(＝死後)には3人の子供が残された She died at the young age of 35 and left *behind* three children.
2【将来, 結末】▶あとは任せたよ *I'll leave the rest to you*. (●「あとはよろしく」のような単なる挨拶は See you tomorrow [Monday]. などでよい) ‖あとはどうなろうと知ったこっちゃない *Beyond that* I don't know. ／I don't know *the rest* of the story.
ことわざ あとは野となれ山となれ After me the deluge. (●「我々が死んだあとは大洪水が来たって関係ない」という英語のことわざを当てる).
3【順序】▶あとについて言ってください Repeat *after me*, please. ‖生徒会の会議に到着したのは私がいちばんあとだった I was *the last one* to get to the student council meeting.
4【後方】▶子供はひと言も言わずに母親のあとについて行った The child *followed* his mother without saying a word. ‖子犬は子猫のあとを追いかけた The puppy *ran after* [*chased* (*after*)] the kitten. ‖彼女は失意の果てに故郷をあとにした She *left* her hometown with a broken heart.
5【残り】the rest ▶あとはみんなきみにあげるよ You can have *the rest*. ／*The rest* is yours. ‖水着が1枚あればあとは何もいらないよ If you have a bathing suit, you don't need anything *else*. ‖ここまで言えば, あと(＝残り)は言わなくてもわかるでしょう After saying this much, you can guess *the rest*, right?

【文型】
あと時間・日数(A)で
in A

▶あと5分で終わります We will finish *in* five minutes. (● five minutes later は不可. 現在が起点のときは in を用いる) ／Five minutes *more*, and we will be finished. ‖あとひと月で卒業だ We're graduating [We (will) graduate] *in a month*. ／We have *one month to go* before we graduate. (➤ 後者は「卒業するまでひと月ある」).
▶あと3日で夏休みが始まる (The) summer vacation begins three days *from now*. ‖列車が発車するまであと(＝まだ)10分ある We *still* have ten minutes before the train leaves. ‖あと3人座れます There's room for three *more* people. ‖パンと牛乳と, あと(＝それから)お肉を買って来てくれる? Can you pick up some bread, milk, *and* meat for me?
▶下書きはできた. あとは清書するだけだ The draft is finished. *Now all I have to do is* to make a clean copy.
6【後継者, 後任】▶彼は父親の会社の跡を継いだ He *took over* his father's company. ／He *succeeded to* the presidency of his father's company. (➤ 後者は堅い言い方) ‖田中家の跡は次男の茂が継ぐことになった It has been decided that the second son, Shigeru will *become heir to* the Tanaka family. (➤ heir /eəʳ/ は「跡取り」) ‖その家は13代であとが絶えた The family line *ended* with the 13th generation.
7【痕跡, 形跡】a track (通った跡) ; **a mark** (汚れなどの) ; **a trace** (痕跡) ▶車輪の跡 wheel *tracks* ／the *track* of wheels ‖キツネが通った跡 fox *tracks* ／*footprints* of a fox ‖テーブルに指の跡をつけてはいけません Don't leave [make] *finger marks* on the table. ‖彼は右腕に傷の跡がある He has *a scar* on his right arm. ‖寝室には泥棒が入った跡があった There was *evidence* in the bedroom that a burglar had broken in.
▶彼は頑張ったと言っているが, 努力の跡が全然見られない He said he worked very hard, but I couldn't see any *results from his efforts*. ‖君の作る最近の陶器はずっと良くなっている. 努力の跡 (＝いかに努力したか)が見られるよ Your pottery has gotten much better recently. I can see *how much effort you've put into it*.
8【同じ行動をとること】▶誰かが私たちの跡をつけている Someone *is shadowing* us. ‖駐車違反が跡を絶たない *There is no end to* illegal parking. ／Illegal parking *is an unending problem*.

9【遺跡】remains, ruins（廃虚）▶水田の下から古代の住居の**跡**が発見された The *remains* of ancient dwellings were discovered beneath the rice field. ‖ ポンペイの**跡**を訪ねてみたい I would like to visit the *ruins* of Pompeii.

10【慣用表現】あとへ引けない ▶ことここに至ってはあとへは引けない Since things have come to this, we *can't retreat* [*yield*] *an inch*. (➤「後戻りできない」というニュアンスならば,there's no turning back now という). **あとを引く** ▶ポテトチップスはあとを引く Once you begin eating potato chips, *it's hard to stop*. ／If you eat one potato chip, *you'll eat the whole bag*.

☛ 後から後から（⇀見出語）

あとあし 後足 a **hind** /haɪnd/ **leg** ▶馬が驚いて**後足で立った** The horse *rose up on its hind legs* in fright. ／The horse *reared up* in fright.

▶《慣用表現》あんなに面倒を見てやったのに, あの女は私に後足で**砂を掛けるようなことをした** Although I've done so much for her, she *knifed* me *in the back* [she *did some ungrateful thing to* me] *when* she *left*.

あとあじ 後味 an **aftertaste** ▶このケーキは何だか**後味が悪い** This cake leaves somewhat of *an* unpleasant *aftertaste*. (➤ aftertaste だけで後味の悪さを表すことも多い).

▶《比喩的》その事件は**後味が悪かった** The event *left a bad taste in my mouth*. ‖ 弟と口げんかをして**後味の悪い思いをした** I *felt bad* after I argued with my brother.

あとあと 後々 in the long run（長い目で見れば）; **in the future**（将来は）; **later**（あとで）▶正直に話したほうが**あとあと**のためにいい Telling the truth will be better for you *in the long run*. ‖ 今生命保険に入っておけば**あとあと**安心です If you take out life insurance now, you'll be able to feel [rest] easy *later*.

あとおい 後追い ▶その歌手が死んで, **後追い自殺**が何件かあった Several people *committed suicide immediately after* the death of the singer.

あとおし 後押し backing ▶彼には政界の**後押し**がある He has *backing* from political circles.

あとがき 後書き an **afterword**（書物の）; a **postscript**（手紙の追伸; 通例 P.S. と略す）.

あとかたづけ 後片付け ▶部屋の**後片づけをする** *put* a room *in order* ／*straighten up* a room ‖ **食事の後片づけをする** *clear the table and wash the dishes* ‖ 仕事を終えると彼女はきちんと**後片づけ**して帰った After she finished her job, she *put everything back in its proper place* and went home.

あとかたもなく 跡形もなく ▶テーブルの上に魚を置いたが, 次に見たときは**跡形もなく**消えていた I put the fish on the table, but when I looked a moment later, it had disappeared *without a trace* [*into thin air*].

あとがま 後釜 a **successor**（後継者）▶社長の**後釜**には誰が座るのだろうか Who will *succeed* [*replace*] the president? ／Who will *step into* the president's *shoes*?

あとからあとから 後から後から one after another（次々に）▶**後から後から**やっかいなことが出てきて, 全く嫌になってしまう Problems have cropped up *one after another*. I feel really frustrated. (➤ crop up は「(問題などが) 不意に持ち上がる」の意のインフォーマルな表現).

あとくされ 後腐れ ▶割り勘にして**後腐れのないようにしよう** Let's split the bill to *avoid future trouble* [to *keep our good relationship*]. (➤ 後者は「良い関係を続ける」の意).

あとくち 後口 an **aftertaste**. ⇀後味.

あどけない innocent ▶子供の**あどけない**寝顔 the *innocent* face of a sleeping child ‖ その青年にはまだ**あどけない**ところがあった There was still something *innocent* about the young man.

あとさき 後先 ▶彼はいつも**後先のことも考えずに**突っ走る He always pushes ahead *without considering the consequences*. (➤「結果を考えずに」の意).

▶**話が後先になりましたが**… I should have told you this first, but ...

あとしまつ 後始末 ▶借金の**後始末をする** *settle* (all) one's debts ‖ 社員全員で宴会場の**後始末をした** All the employees pitched in to *straighten up* [*clean up*] after the banquet. ‖ 彼は家庭内のごたごたの**後始末をしている** He *is* now *dealing with* [*taking care of*] his family trouble(s).

あとずさり 後ずさりする step back; shrink back（尻込みする）▶1, 2 歩**後ずさりする** *step back* a pace or two ‖ **後ずさりして**犬の足を踏む *step back* on a dog's paw ‖ その幼い女の子は犬にほえられて**後ずさりした** The little girl *shrank back* from the barking dog. (➤ shrank は shrink の過去形).

あとち 跡地 a **former site** ▶基地の**跡地**利用を巡って市議会は紛糾した The members of the city council were at loggerheads over (the issue of) how to use the *site of the former army base*. (➤ at loggerheads は「対立して」).

あとぢえ 後知恵 hindsight /háɪndsaɪt/ ▶**後知恵**でそんなことを言ってみてもしかたがない It is no use saying that *in hindsight*.

《参考》英語には Hindsight is 20 /20. (後知恵の視力は完璧; 後知恵で言うことには狂いがない) という言い方がある. ⇀[1]しりょく.

あとつぎ 跡継ぎ・後継ぎ an **heir** /eəʳ/, an **inheritor**（相続人）; a **successor**（後継者）▶彼の家には**跡継ぎ**がいない There is no *successor* in his family.

あとで 後で ⇀あと.

あととり 跡取り ⇀跡継ぎ.

あとのまつり 後の祭り ▶今さら後悔しても**後の祭り**だ *It is too late* now to regret what you did. ／The damage is (already) done. (● 後者は already が省略可能だが, これを付けるほうが「手遅れだ」という感じをよりよく出せる) ‖ **対話**「鼻の整形, しなきゃよかった」「今さら遅すぎるわよ. **後の祭りね**」"I shouldn't have had a nose job." "It's too late now. You *can't change what's been done* [*change the past*]."

アドバイザー an **adviser**, an **advisor** ▶**アドバイザー**に意見を求める consult *an adviser*.

アドバイス advice /ədváɪs/ **一動 アドバイスする advise** /ədváɪz/ ＋目 (➤ つづりと発音に注意) ▶私は彼に気楽にやれと**アドバイスした** I *advised* him to take it easy.

▶ぼくは彼に **1 つアドバイスをした** I *gave* him *a piece of advice*. (● an advice とするのは不可.「いくつかのアドバイス」なら some pieces of advice となる).

あとばらい 後払い ▶テレビを**後払いで**(＝クレジットで)買った I bought a TV (set) *on credit*. ‖ (バスの運転手が) **料金は後払いです** *Please pay the fare when you get off the bus*.

アドバルーン an **advertising balloon** (➤ ad-balloon とはしない) ▶デパートの上空に**アドバルーン**が 2 個浮かんでいる There are two *advertising balloons* over the department store.

アドバンテージ《テニス》**advantage.**

アトピー **atopy** /ǽtəpi/ (➤医学用語；英米では日本語ほど一般化した用語ではなく，eczema（湿疹）を使うことが多い) ▶娘はひどいアトピーに悩まされています My daughter suffers from severe *eczema*.

‖**アトピー性皮膚炎** atopic dermatitis, (atopic) eczema.

あとまわし 後回し ▶試験ではやさしい問題から答えて，難問は**後回し**にするほうがよい In exams, it's better to answer the easy questions first and *leave* the hard problems *for later*. ‖それは**後回し**してよい *That can wait*.

▶そのプロジェクトは3年間**後回しにされた** The project *was put on the back burner* for three years. (● 英語では「(仕事・問題などを)後回しにする」の意のインフォーマルな表現である put ... on the back burner を用いる).

あともどり 後戻りする **turn back** ▶川に橋が架かっていなかったので，私たちはしかたなく**後戻りした** There was no bridge over the river, so we had to *turn back*. ‖計画がここまで進んでしまったら，今さら**後戻り**はできない We can't *turn back* [It's too late to *turn back*] after coming this far in the plan.

アトラクション ▶卒業パーティーの呼び物は数名の教師による凝った**アトラクション**だった The highlight of the graduation party was the elaborate *stage show* put on by some of the teachers. ‖「プーさんのハニーハント」は東京ディズニーランドで最も人気のある**アトラクション**の1つだ "Pooh's Hunny Hunt" is one of the most popular *attractions* at Tokyo Disneyland.

> **危ないカタカナ語✸ アトラクション**
> **1** 英語の attraction は第1例が示すように,「引きつけるもの，魅力」の意で，イベントなどの中心になる呼び物をいうが，日本語の「アトラクション」は添え物的な余興を指すことも多い. したがって，後者の意味をはっきりさせるには entertainment（総称としての「演芸」), stage show（ステージショー), side show（付け足しの出し物の余興）を用いるほうがよい.
> **2** また最近では，日本語の「アトラクション」から東京ディズニーランドや大規模遊園地などにある乗り物（ジェットコースター，メリーゴーラウンドなど）を連想する人も多くなっているが，このイメージは英語の attraction にもある.

アトランタ **Atlanta**（アメリカ，ジョージア州の州都).

アトランダム **at random** ▶**アトランダム**に選んだ50名 fifty people chosen *at random*.

アトリエ a **studio**, an **atelier** /æ̀tljéɪ/.

アドリブ an **ad lib** /æ̀d líb/ ▶絶妙な**アドリブ** an exquisite *ad lib* ‖彼の演技は全くの**アドリブ**だった His performance was entirely *ad-lib*. ／He performed entirely *ad lib*. (➤前者は形容詞用法，後者は副詞用法) ‖その女優はせりふを忘れて**アドリブ**をした The actress forgot her lines and *ad-libbed*.

アドレス an **address** /ǽdres/ ▶きみのメール**アドレス**を書くのを忘れないでね Don't forget to write your *e-mail address*.

アドレナリン **adrenaline** /ədrénəlɪn/.

あな 穴 **1**【くぼみ，空所】a **hole**; an **opening**（割れ目，隙間); a **pothole**（道路などの); a **hollow**（中が空洞の); a **cavity**（虫歯などの); a **cave**（洞穴) ▶ウサギの**穴** a rabbit *hole* [*burrow*] ‖壁の**穴** *an opening* in the wall ‖針の**穴** the *eye* of a needle ‖**穴をあける** make *a hole* ‖**穴をふさぐ** stop up [fill] *a hole*.

▶このジャケットには**穴があいている** There's *a hole* in this jacket. ‖靴下に**穴があいてしまった** I've *got a hole* in my sock. ‖その木には大きな**穴があいていた** I found *a* large *hollow* (*place*) in the tree. ‖この道路には真ん中に大きな**穴があいている** There is *a* big *pothole* right in the middle of this road.

▶大工はドリルで材木に**穴をあけた** The carpenter *drilled a hole* in the wood. ‖ネズミが食器戸棚をかじって**穴をあけた** A mouse has *gnawed a hole* in the cupboard. ‖犬は骨を埋めるため地面に**穴を掘った** The dog *dug a hole* in the ground to bury his bone. ‖猫が生け垣の**穴**をくぐって庭に入って来た A cat came into the garden *through an opening* in the hedge.

2【欠点】a **defect**; a **hole**（不備の意の「穴」) ▶あなたの計画には**穴がある** There is *a defect* in your plan. ‖その主張は**穴だらけだ** That argument *is full of holes*.

3【欠損】a **loss** ▶ずさんな経理で帳簿に**穴があいた** Slipshod accounting caused the books to show *a loss*. ‖借金の**穴**は早く埋めたほうがいい You should pay off your *debt* as soon as possible. ‖主演俳優の突然の病気で，舞台に**穴があいた** A role in the play *opened up* due to the sudden illness of the leading actor.

4【慣用表現】▶彼は**穴があく**ほどじっと私の顔を見つめた He stared me *hard* in the face. (➤あまり一般的ではないが I felt like he was staring a hole in my head. とすることも可能) ‖恥ずかしくて**穴があったら入りたい気持ちだった** I was so embarrassed that *I could have dropped* [*sunk*] *through the floor*. (● 日本語に似た crawl into a hole という言い方もあるが，英語では用例に示したように「床の下に沈む」と発想した表現のほうがふつう).

アナ(ー)キスト an **anarchist.**

あなうめ 穴埋め ▶この**穴埋め**はきっとするから I'll *make up for* this, I promise. ‖その会社は赤字の**穴埋め**に躍起になっている That company is trying hard to *cover* [to *make up*] *its deficit*.

‖**穴埋め記事** a filler ‖**穴埋め問題** a fill-in-the-blank(s) question, a cloze question.

アナウンサー an **announcer** /ənáʊnsəʳ/; a **newscaster**（ニュース原稿を読む); an **anchorperson**（ニュース番組の総合司会をする); a **sportscaster**（スポーツ番組の).

アナウンス an **announcement** 一動 **アナウンスする** **announce** ＋㊐ ▶停車駅［停留所］を**アナウンスする** *announce* the stops ‖電車が遅れているという駅の**アナウンスがあった** There was *an announcement* at the station saying that the train would be delayed. ／The train delay *was announced* at the station.

> **危ないカタカナ語✸ アナウンス**
> **1** 日本語では「駅のアナウンスによれば…」のようにいうが，英語の announce は動詞なので，正しくは according to the announcement of the train station ... のように名詞形を使っていう必要がある.
> **2** また英語の announce は「(結婚・死亡などを新聞などに)公表する」が第一義で，「放送」とは限らない.

あながち ▶彼の言うことも**あながち**(＝完全に)間違いではない What he says is *not altogether* wrong. ‖労働条件の劣悪さを考えると，組合の要求も**あながち**不当とは言い切れない Taking the very poor working conditions into account, I cannot conclude that the labor union's requests are *all that* unreasonable. (➤ all that は「それほど」).

アナクロ an **anachronism** /ənǽkrənìzəm/ (時代錯誤) ▶**門限が8時だなんて, おまえのところのおやじはアナクロもいいところだ** Setting a curfew at eight shows your dad is completely *behind the times*. (➤ behind the times は「時代遅れの」の意).

あなご 穴子 《魚》a **conger** /kɑ́:ŋgəʳ/ **(eel)**.

あなた **you**(主格, 目的格), **your** (所有格) ; **yours** (あなたの物) ; **yourself** (あなた自身)

> **《解説》「あなた」と you**
> (1)この語に相当するのは you で, 男女に関係なく相手を指すのに用いる. ただし, 日本語では目上の人に面と向かって「あなた」は使えないが, 英語の you は使える. →**あんた**.
> (2)英米の年配の夫婦はお互いを (my) dear, honey, sweetheart, darling などと呼ぶが, 若い人たちはファーストネームで呼び合うことが多くなってきている.

▶**あなたの言うとおりだ** *You*'re right. ‖ **あなた, 用意はできたの?** Are you ready, *dear* ?

✉ **あなたのことを教えてください** Please tell me about *yourself*.

あなたまかせ あなた任せ ▶**何事もあなた任せでは成功しないよ** You cannot succeed if you *depend too much on others*.

あなどる 侮る **look down (up) on** (対等視しない); **make light of** (軽視する); **underestimate** +📖 (低く評価する) ▶**侮りがたい相手** an opponent *to be reckoned with* (➤「(強敵として)考慮に入れるべき相手」の意) ‖ **若いからといって彼女を侮ってはいけない** Don't *look down upon* her just because she's young. ‖ **彼らはその少年の実力を侮っているようだ** They seem to *be making light of* the boy's ability. ‖ **敵を侮ってはいけない** Don't *underestimate* your opponent.

あなば 穴場 a **good out-of-the-way spot**, a **good little-known place** ▶**釣りの穴場を知らない?** Do you happen to know any *good out-of-the-way* fishing *spots* ? ‖ **プラネタリウムはデートの穴場だ** A planetarium is *a great place for a date that few people think about*.

アナリスト an **analyst** ▶**証券アナリスト** a securities *analyst*.

アナログ **analog(ue)** /ǽnəlɔ:g/

‖**アナログ時計** an analog(ue) clock [watch].

あに 兄 an **older** [**elder**] **brother**, 《インフォーマル》a **big brother** →**兄さん, 兄貴**.

> **《解説》**(1)英米では長幼の順をあまり問題にせず, 単に brother ということが多い.
> (2)older brother は《米》で, big brother は年少者の間でそれぞれ好まれる傾向がある.

▶**いちばん上の兄** one's oldest [eldest] *brother* ‖ **2番目の兄** one's second oldest *brother* ‖ **私には兄はいません** I don't have any *older brothers*.

‖**兄弟子** an elder disciple.

あにき 兄貴 one's **big brother** (➤ 親代わりの兄といったイメージがある).

アニメ an **animated cartoon** (動画) (➤ 単に cartoon ということも多い. また anime も英語化しつつあるが, 日本のアニメまたはそれをまねしたものをさす) ; (an) **animation** (主に動画の製作)

‖**アニメ作家** an animator, an animation cartoonist.

あによめ 兄嫁 one's **brother's wife**, one's **sister-in-law** 《参考》older, elder などの形容詞をつけない限り, 「弟の嫁」も one's brother's wife または one's sister-in-law となる.

あね 姉 an **older** [**elder**] **sister**, 《インフォーマル》a **big sister** →**姉さん, 姉貴**.

> **《解説》**(1)英米では長幼の順をあまり問題にせず, 単に sister ということが多い.
> (2)older sister は《米》で, big sister は年少者の間でそれぞれ好まれる傾向がある.

▶**いちばん上の姉** one's oldest [eldest] *sister* ‖ **義理の姉** one's *sister*-in-law.

‖**姉さん女房** a wife older than her husband.

あねき 姉貴 one's **big sister** (➤ 親代わりの姉といったイメージがある) ▶**姉貴, 給料日まで1万円貸してよ** Could you loan me ten thousand yen till payday, *sis* ? (➤ 英米では名前で呼ぶのがふつう).

あねったい 亜熱帯 **the subtropics** 一形 **亜熱帯の** **subtropic(al)**

‖**亜熱帯気候** a subtropical climate ‖ **亜熱帯植物** a subtropical plant ‖ **亜熱帯地方** the subtropics, the subtropical zones.

アネモネ 《植物》an **anemone** /ənéməni/, a **windflower**.

あの **that** [複 **those**] ▶**あの塔** *that* tower ‖ **あの人** *that* person / *that* man (あの男) / *that* woman (あの女) ‖ **あの人は誰ですか** Who is *that* man [woman] ? (● 知らない人をいきなり Who is he [she] ? とは言わない. 逆に知っている人を that man [woman] というときはしばしばマイナスの意味合いを伴う. 例えば, 夫を指して That man drives me crazy. (あの男は頭に来る) とすると, He drives me crazy. よりもいらだちが強い) ‖ **あの人たち** *those* people ‖ **あなたのあの笑顔** *that* smile of yours (➤ your that smile としない) ‖ **あの辺の原っぱでお弁当にしようよ** Why don't we have lunch in *that open field* ? ‖ **彼はあの手この手で契約を迫った** He employed *one ploy after another* to persuade the other party to sign the contract. (➤「さまざまな手」を強調して, tried everything としてもよい).

あのう ▶**あのう, それぼくの靴なんですけど** *Excuse me*, I think those might be my shoes. ‖ **(電話で) あのう, もしもし, サリーさんですか** *Er* [*Uh*]... Hello, is this Sally ? →**あのね**.

あのころ あの頃 **those days** 一副 **あの頃は** **in those days** ▶**あの頃日本人は皆貧しかった** All the Japanese were poor *in those days*. ‖ **あの頃はよかった** *Those were the days*. ‖ **あの頃に戻れたら!** I wish I could return to *those days*.

あのね ▶**あのね, ちょっと話したいことがあるんだけど** *Say*, I've got something to talk to you about. 《参考》(1)この say は「あのう」という気持ちでも用いられる. (2)おもしろい話題などを持ち出すときには, Do you know what ? とか I'll tell you what. などと言うこともある.

▶**《注意を促して》あのね, 人の本を使うときは断るもんだよ** *Look*, you should ask me first if you want to use my book. ‖ **あのねえ, ぼくはきみの言ってることは間違ってると思うんだ** *Well*, I think you're wrong.

あのよ あの世 **the next** [**other**] **world**, **the afterlife** ▶**あの世へ行く** *go to Heaven* / *leave this world*.

アノラック an **anorak** /ǽnəræk/ (➤ anorak の一種

に parka があるが，日常語としては両者は区別なく用いられることが多い．ただし後者は主に《米》)．

アパート 《米》an **apartment house**, 《英》a **block of flats** ▶彼はそのアパートを2年契約で借りている He has the *apartment* on a two-year lease.

> **危ないカタカナ語✸ アパート**
> **1**「アパートメント」を省略した形だが，英語の apart は「離れて」の意味にしかならない．アパートの建物全体は apartment house [building]，一世帯分は apartment という．ただし，建物全体を apartment ということもある．
> **2** 日本語の「アパート」は賃貸式のものをいうが，英語の apartment は集合住宅一般をいう．したがってマンションも apartment の一種である．→**マンション**．

アバウト ▶アバウトな人 an *easy-going* [a *sloppy*] person(➤ sloppy は「いいかげんな」の意)．→**大体**．

あばく 暴く **expose** +⽬ (人の正体・悪事などを)；**reveal** +⽬ (秘密などを)；**disclose** +⽬ (発表・公表されていなかったことを)；**violate** +⽬ (神聖な場所を)
▶陰謀を暴く *expose* a plot ‖ 秘密を暴く *reveal* [*disclose*] a secret ‖ 墓を暴く *violate* a grave ‖ 真相を暴く *bring* the truth *to light* ‖ おまえの正体をいつか暴いてみせる Someday I'll *reveal* your true colors.

あばた a **pockmark**, a **pit** ▶月面はあばただ The moon has a *pockmarked* surface.
ことわざ あばたもえくぼ Even pockmarks are dimples (to a lover). (➤日本語からの直訳) ／Love is blind. (➤「愛は盲目」の意の英語のことわざ) ／Love covers many infirmities. (➤「愛は多くの欠点を覆い隠す」の意)．

あばらぼね 肋骨 a **rib**(骨1本)；**the ribs** (全体) ▶あばら骨を折る break *a rib* ‖ 彼はあばら骨が見えるくらい痩せている He is so thin that his *ribs* stand out.

あばらや あばら家 a **shabby house**, a **rickety house**, a **hovel** 《参考》謙遜して自宅を「あばら家ですが…」というときは，英語でも one's humble cottage などを使う．

アパルトヘイト **apartheit** /əpɑ́ːʳteɪt/.

あばれうま 暴れ馬 a **runaway horse**.

あばれる 暴れる **1【激しく体を動かす】** **get violent** (狂暴になる)；**get unruly** (手に負えなくなる)；**struggle** (もがく) ▶あの入院患者は夜中に暴れることがある That inpatient sometimes *becomes violent* [*unruly*] in the middle of the night. ‖ 看護師が注射をしようとすると嫌がってその男の子は暴れた The boy *threw* [*had*] *a tantrum* when the nurse tried to give him a shot. (➤ throw a tantrum は子供が「かんしゃくを起こす」) ‖ 暴れないようにこの男をしっかり押さえていろ Hold this guy tight so that he can't *struggle*. ‖ その黒馬は自由になろうとして暴れた The black horse *struggled* to break free.
2【思うままに活動する】 **rage** ▶台風は九州地方で暴れている The typhoon *is raging* in Kyushu. ‖ 若いころはずいぶん暴れたもんだよ I *was* quite *wild* in my youth.

あばれんぼう 暴れん坊 a **wild guy**；a **rowdy** /ráʊdi/, a **roughneck** (乱暴者)；a **hooligan** (暴力を振るうちんぴら)．

アピール an **appeal**(呼びかけ)；a **petition** (請願) 一 動 (…に)アピールする **appeal** 《to》 ▶国連へのアピール *a petition* to the United Nations ‖ キャッチャーは(打者の)バットが回ったと審判にアピールした The catcher *appealed to* the umpire, saying the batter had swung.
▶この詩には私の心にアピールする何かがある There is something in this poem that *appeals to* me. ／There is something *appealing* about this poem. ‖ メーカーは常にテレビの視聴者にアピールする宣伝を考える Manufacturers are always trying to come up with commercials that *appeal to* TV viewers.
▶彼女は彼氏に料理の腕前をアピールした She *tried to impress* her boyfriend with her cooking ability. (● この場合，英語では「感心させようとした」と発想し用例のように表現する．appeal は使えない)．

あびせる 浴びせる **pour** +⽬；**shower** +⽬ (雨のように)；**fire** +⽬ (質問・非難などを矢継ぎ早に) ▶彼は私に水を浴びせた He *poured* [*showered*] water *over* me. ‖ 米軍は敵の要塞目がけて集中砲火を浴びせた The U.S. Army *showered* concentrated fire *on* the enemy's fortress. ‖ ボブは恋人の顔じゅうにキスを浴びせた Bob *showered* kisses all over his girlfriend's face. ‖ 記者たちはその政治家に質問を浴びせた The reporters *fired* questions *at* the politician.

あひる 家鴨 a (**domestic**) **duck**；a **drake**(雄の) ▶アヒルの子 *a duckling* ‖ 池でアヒルがガーガーいっている Some *ducks* are quacking in the pond.

あびる 浴びる **1【風呂などを】** **take** +⽬, **have** +⽬ ▶ひと風呂浴びてくるよ I'll *take* [《英また》*have*] *a bath*. ‖ 私は朝起きるとすぐシャワーを浴びます I *take a shower* right after I get up in the morning.
2【光など，好ましいものを】 **get** +⽬ ▶日の光を十分に浴びる *get* enough sun.
▶デビュー曲のヒットでその新人歌手は一躍脚光を浴びた The new singer *was* suddenly *in the limelight* because his [her] first song was a big hit. ‖ 彼女のスピーチは大きな拍手を浴びた Her speech *received* great applause.
3【ほこりなど，好ましくないものを】 **be covered** 《with》；**be exposed** 《to》(さらされる) ▶放射能を浴びる *be exposed to* radioactivity ‖ 長時間紫外線を浴びるのはよくない It is not good to *expose yourself to* UV rays for a long time. ‖ 書棚の整理をしたら体じゅうにほこりを浴びてしまった I *was completely covered* with dust after (re)organizing the bookshelf.
▶おやじは昔は毎晩浴びるように酒を飲んでいた Dad used to *drink like a fish* every evening.
▶首相の弁明は多くの非難を浴びた The prime minister's explanation *came in for* a lot of criticism. (➤ come in for は「(非難などの)的になる」)．

あぶ 虻 《虫》a **horsefly**, a **gadfly**.
☛ あぶはち取らず (→見出語)

アフィリエイター an **affiliator**, a **marketing affiliator** (自分のホームページなどに広告主の商品広告などを掲載して成功報酬を得る人)．

アフィリエイト ▶アフィリエイトでお金をもうける earn [make] money *from affiliate marketing*.

アフガニスタン **Afghanistan** /æfgǽnəstæn/.

あぶく **foam** /foʊm/；a **bubble**(泡の1つ) ▶あぶくが立っている *Bubbles* are forming.
‖ あぶく銭 easy money.

アフターケア **aftercare**(病後の健康管理) ▶アフターケアの施設 an *aftercare* institution.

アフターサービス **after-sale(s) service** (販売後の)；**after-purchase service** (購入後の) ▶B社はアフターサービスが行き届いている B Company has a good *after-*

sales service system. ／B Company offers a good *warranty* on [for] its products.

アフターファイブ after work, after hours (➤ after five は「5時過ぎに」と時間を表すだけ) ▶アフターファイブに同僚と飲みに行く go for a drink with one's colleague(s) *after work* [*after hours*].

あぶない 危ない 1【危険な】dangerous ; unsafe (安全でない) ▶流れの急な川で泳ぐのは危ない Swimming in a rapid river is *dangerous*. ‖夜, 鍵をかけないのは危ない It *isn't safe* to leave your house unlocked at night. ‖警官は任務遂行に当たってはときに命が危ないことがある Police officers sometimes *put their lives in danger* [*risk their lives*] in the performance of (their) duty. ‖人質たちは命が危ないと感じていた The hostages felt that their *lives were in danger*. ‖患者は危ない状況だ The patient is *in critical condition* [*critically ill*].

▶危ないところだったね. もう少しであのトラックにはねられるところだったよ *That was a close call* [*shave*]. The truck nearly ran you over. (➤ close /kloʊs/ call [shave] は「危機一髪」に相当).

▶《慣用表現》彼はこれまでに何度も危ない橋を渡ってきた He *has engaged in* a lot of *activities that border on crime* [*that are borderline criminal*]. (➤「犯罪と紙一重のことをしてきた」の意).

▶《駅のアナウンス》電車が参ります. 危ないですから白線の内側までお下がりください Please *watch out for* the approaching train and stand behind the white line. (➤ watch out for は「…に注意する」) ‖《注意を促して》危ない! *Look out!* ／ *Watch out!* ／ *Be careful!* (● 行動を促すので Danger! (危険)ではなく動詞を使って表すのがふつう) ‖危ない! 穴があるぞ *Look out for* that hole!

2【疑わしい】doubtful /dáʊtfəl/ (疑問である) ; unlikely (可能性がなさそう) ▶彼女がフランス語の最終試験にパスできるかどうか危ないものだ It *is doubtful* [*unlikely*] that she will pass the final examination in French. ‖だいぶ雲が出てきたから, 夕方まで天気がもつかどうか危ないものだ With these clouds, it's *unlikely* the weather will hold (up) until evening. ‖予選で3敗した日本チームは決勝進出が危なくなった The Japanese team's chance of advancing to the finals *is slim* seeing that they lost three games in the preliminaries. (➤「見込みが薄い」の意).

▶売り上げが好転しないと会社が危ない The company *may go bankrupt* if sales do not improve. (➤「破産するかもしれない」の意) ‖早く手を打たないと地球が危ない Unless prompt countermeasures are taken, the earth *will be in danger*. ‖彼は自分の首が危なくなっているのに気がつかない He hasn't noticed that he *could be fired* any moment.

3【不安定な】unreliable (当てにならない) ▶あのセールスマンの約束は危ない That salesman's promises are *not reliable*.

あぶなく 危なく →危うく.

あぶなげない 危なげない reliable, trustworthy (➤ 後者がより強意) ▶彼の守備はいつも危なげない His fielding is always *reliable*. ‖横綱は危なげなく勝った The yokozuna won *comfortably* [*without much effort*]. (➤ comfortably は「余裕で」).

あぶなっかしい 危なっかしい dangerous (危ない) ; awkward, clumsy (不器用な) ▶彼は危なっかしい手つきで赤ん坊を抱いた He took the baby in his arms *awkwardly*.

アブノーマルな abnormal.

あぶはちとらず 虻蜂取らず ▶彼は英語とロシア語を同時にマスターしようとしたが, あぶはち取らずに終わった He tried to master both English and Russian, but *couldn't master either of them* [but he *ended up mastering neither of them*].

あぶら 油・脂 1【あぶら】oil (液体の) ; fat (固形の脂肪) ; grease (獣脂) ▶ジャガイモを油で揚げる fry the potato (in *oil*) ‖きみの車は油が切れているよ Your car is *out of oil*. ‖シェーバーの調子が悪くなったので油をさした Something was wrong with my shaver, so I *oiled* it. ‖脂のとり過ぎは体によくない Consuming too much *fat* is not good for your health.

▶妹は脂性で1日に何回も顔を洗う Since my (younger) sister *has oily skin*, she washes her face many times a day. ‖中華料理は油いためが多い Many Chinese dishes are *stir-fried* [*pan-fried*] *in oil*. (➤ stir-fry は中華料理の場合によく使われる) ‖私の髪はぱさぱさで油気が全然ない My hair is very dry and not at all *oily*.

2【慣用表現】**脂が乗る** ▶サンマは秋には脂が乗ってきてぐんとおいしくなる In autumn, Pacific saury *put on fat* and become much more delicious. ‖彼は今いちばん脂の乗っている時だ He is *at his peak* now. ／ He is *in the prime of life*.

油を売る ▶こんなに遅くなって. どこで油を売ってたんだい? You sure are late — where've you *been wasting time* [*goofing off*]? **油を絞る** ▶ぼくは先生にこってり油を絞られた My teacher *gave* me *a good talking-to*. (➤ give … a good talking-to は「…をうんと叱る」の意のインフォーマルな言い方) ‖彼は学校をサボって油を絞られた He *was chewed out* [*got a severe talking-to* ／ *was hauled over the coals*] for cutting school. (➤ いずれも「叱られた」の意のインフォーマルな表現). **油を注ぐ** ▶そのひと言は彼の怒りに油を注ぐ結果になった That one word only *added fuel to* his anger.

あぶらあげ 油揚げ *aburaage*, *aburage* ; a thin slice of deep-fried tofu or a tofu pouch (➤ 説明的な訳).

あぶらあせ 脂汗 greasy sweat /swet/ ▶トイレを我慢して脂汗が出た Desperate for a toilet, I *broke out in a clammy sweat*.

あぶらえ 油絵 (an) oil painting, a painting in oils ▶油絵を描く *paint in oils*.

‖**油絵画家** an oil painter ‖**油絵の具** oils, oil paints, oil colors.

あぶらぎる 脂ぎる ▶脂ぎった男 an *oily-faced* man.

あぶらげ 油揚げ →油揚げ(あぶらあげ)

あぶらっこい 油[脂]っこい greasy ▶油っこい食べ物 *greasy* [oily] food(s).

あぶらとりがみ 脂取り紙 facial oil blotting [absorbing] paper.

あぶらむし 油虫 《虫》a cockroach (ゴキブリ) ; an aphid, a plant louse (アリマキ).

アプリ an app [複 apps] (➤ application としてもよい ; 日本語のような省略のしかた, (×) appli は用いない) ▶スマートフォンアプリ a smartphone *app* ／ an *app* for smartphones ‖無料の携帯アプリ a free mobile (phone) *app* ‖キラーアプリ a killer *app*.

アフリカ Africa 一形 アフリカの African ▶アフリカの砂漠 the *African* deserts ／ the deserts *of Africa*.

‖**アフリカ人** an African ‖**アフリカ大陸** the Afri-

あ

can Continent (➤ 単に Africa と言うのがふつう).

アプリケーション 《コンピュータ》 an **application (program), application software.**

あぶる 焙る **roast, broil, grill** (魚や肉を); **warm** (温める) ▶するめを弱火であぶる *grill* dried squid over a low flame ‖ のりを軽くあぶる *pass* nori *lightly over a flame* ‖ ヒーターで手をあぶる *warm* one's hands over a heater.

アフレコ **dubbing** /dʌ́bɪŋ/, **postrecording** /pòʊstrɪkɔ́ːˈdɪŋ/ ▶アニメ映画のアフレコをする *dub* an animated film.

あふれる 溢れる **overflow**(+目) (液体・人などが); **run over** (液体が); **brim** (縁までいっぱいになる) ▶大雨で川があふれた The river *overflowed* [*flooded*] (*its banks*) because of the heavy rain. ‖ 湯船からあふれないうちにお湯を止めなさい Turn off the water before the bathtub *overflows*. ‖ 彼女の目には涙があふれていた Her eyes *were brimming* [*were filled*] *with tears*. (➤「涙のあふれそうな目」なら eyes brimful of tears) ‖ カップからあふれそうなホットミルク a *brimming* cup of hot milk.

▶ホームは乗客であふれていた(=大混雑していた) The platform *was overcrowded with* passengers. ‖ メール受信箱は迷惑メールであふれている(=氾濫している) My inbox *is flooded with* spam.

▶彼は自信にあふれている He *is full of* [*is overflowing with*] *confidence*. / He *is brimming over with confidence*. ‖ その新人歌手は若さにあふれていた The new singer *was radiant with youthful energy*. ‖ 豊漁で港は活気にあふれていた The harbor *was bustling* [*was alive*] *with activity* due to the big catch.

あぶれる ▶今は不況のため仕事にあぶれている者が多い Due to the recession, many people *are without jobs* [*are jobless*]. / The current recession has put a lot of people *out of work*.

アプローチ an **approach** ▶《ゴルフ》アプローチの練習をもっとしなくちゃ I need more practice in *approach shots*.

▶先方へどうアプローチすればいいかわからない I don't know how to *approach* them.

アフロ(ヘア) an **Afro** [複 **Afros**].

あべこべ ▶サリーは靴を左右あべこべに履いている Sally is wearing her shoes *on the wrong feet*. ‖ きみの言うこととさみの弟さんの言うことは全くあべこべだね You and your (younger) brother are saying completely *opposite things*. / What you say flatly *contradicts* your brother's statement. ‖ ぼくは間違えてあべこべの方向へ行ってしまった I went *the other way* [in *the opposite direction*] by mistake. ‖ 感謝されると思ったのにあべこべに(=それどころか)ぶつぶつ文句を言われちゃったよ I expected to be thanked, and got grumbled at *instead*.

アベック a **couple.** →カップル.

アベレージ an **average** /ǽvərɪdʒ/ ▶バッティングアベレージ(=打率) a batting *average* ‖ アベレージを出す take *an average*.

あへん 阿片 **opium** /óʊpiəm/ ▶あへん中毒になる become addicted to *opium*.

アポイント(メント) an **appointment** 《参考》日本語では「アポイント」「アポ」というが, いずれも和製語. ▶アポイントはおありですか Do you have *an appointment*? ‖ ブラウンさんにアポイントをとりたいのですが I'd like to *make an appointment* with Mr. Brown.

あほ(う) 阿呆 a **fool**, a **stupid person** ▶あほなことを言うな Don't talk *nonsense*! ‖ 対話「おさい銭に10万円あげちゃった」「あほか!」"I gave a hundred thousand yen at a shrine." "*Are you crazy?*" 《参考》阿波(あわ)踊りのはやし歌として知られる「踊るあほうに見るあほう, 同じあほなら踊らにゃ損々」は, 例えば Some fools watch while some fools dance; if we're all to be fools, then let's all dance! のように英訳できる.

あほうどり 《鳥》 an **albatross** /ǽlbətrɑːs/.

アボカド 《植物》 an **avocado** /æ̀vəkɑ́ːdoʊ/.

アポストロフィ an **apostrophe** /əpɑ́ːstrəfi/.

あほらしい 阿呆らしい **absurd** (ばかばかしい) ▶あんなやつに金をやってしまったかと思うとあほらしい気がする When I think that I gave that money to that kind of man, *I could just kick myself!* (➤ I could just kick myself. は自分の不用意 [浅はか] な言動を悔やむときに使う決まり文句).

アボリジニー an **Aborigine** /æ̀bərídʒəni/.

[1]**あま 尼** a **(Buddhist) nun** /nʌn/ (➤ Buddhist /búːdɪst/ は「仏教の」) ▶尼になる become *a nun* / enter a convent.

[2]**あま 海女** an ***ama***; a **female [woman] sea diver.**

アマ →アマチュア.

あまあし 雨足 ▶雨足が激しくなってきた It has started to *rain hard* [*heavily*].

あまい 甘い **1【味が】sweet** ▶私の家族は皆甘いものが好きだ All of my family like *sweet things*. / All of my family *have a sweet tooth*. (➤ 後者は決まった言い方) ‖ このケーキは甘すぎる This cake *tastes* [*is*] *too sweet*. ‖ 甘いワイン *sweet* wine (➤「辛口」は dry) ‖ このみそ汁は甘い(=塩気が足りない) This miso soup *needs salt*.

▶《慣用表現》彼がいちばん甘い汁を吸った He *skimmed the cream off*. (➤ cream は「最良の部分」) / He *took the lion's share*. (➤ the lion's share は「いちばん大きい[良い]分け前」).

2【音声・香り・雰囲気が快い】sweet ▶甘い声 a *sweet* voice ‖ 甘いマスクの男優 a male actor with a *handsome* [*sweet*] face ‖ バラの甘い香りが部屋中に漂っている The room is filled with the *sweet* smell of roses. ‖ バーには甘いメロディーの音楽が流れていた *Sweet* music was being played in the bar. ‖ 甘いことばには気をつけなさい Beware of *honeyed words*.

3【態度・考えなどが厳しくない】soft ▶一人娘に甘い父親 a father who *is indulgent to* his only daughter (➤ be indulgent to は「…を甘やかす」) ‖ 彼は若い女の子に甘い He *has a soft spot for* young girls. ‖ あの先生は点が甘い That teacher is *an easy* [*a lenient*] *grader*. ‖ 親は子供に甘いものだ Parents often *indulge* their children. (➤ indulge は「甘やかす」).

▶人がすぐに助けに来てくれると思ってるのならそれは考えが甘いよ Your idea that people are going to rush to help you *is wishful thinking* [*overly optimistic*]. (➤ wishful thinking は「こうなったらいいのに」という叶いそうもない願望を持つこと) / You'*re kidding yourself* if you think people are going to rush in to help you. (➤ be kidding yourself は「思い違いをしている」).

▶ジムの両親は甘すぎる Jim's parents are *too permissive*. (➤ permissive は「自由放任の」) ‖ 私は判断が甘かった I was (*too*) *optimistic* in my judgement. / My judgement was *overly optimistic* [*too simplistic*]. (➤ simplistic は「単純な」) ‖ 世の

中そんなに甘くないよ Things aren't that *easy* in the world. (→甘く見る)

▶ 対話「こんな仕事なら3時までにできるよ」「甘いんじゃないの」"If it's just this job, I'll get it done by three o'clock." "I'm afraid you're being *too optimistic*." (●「見方が甘い」ということなので「楽観的」と考え, optimistic を用いる).

4【程度が低くて不十分；ゆるい】▶甘いねじ a *loose* screw ‖ 3割バッターに対して甘い球は禁物だ You shouldn't throw *easy* balls to a .300 batter. (➤.300は three hundred とよむ) ‖ この写真はピントが甘い This picture is slightly *out of focus*.

あまえ 甘え ⚠「甘え」に相当する英語はないので, ***amae***, **(emotional) dependence**（心情的依存）などを適宜用いる.

▶きみにはいつも甘えがあるようだね You seem to *be too dependent on others*. ／You seem to *be* always *seeking favors from other people*.

‖『甘えの構造』"The Anatomy of Dependence" (➤書名).

あまえる 甘える ▶人の親切に甘える *take advantage of* a person's kind offer (➤ take advantage of は「…に便乗する」) ‖ トミーはいくつになっても赤ん坊みたいに私に甘えるのよ No matter how old he gets, Tommy *acts like a baby*. ‖ 甘えるんじゃないよ Don't expect me to go easy on you! ／Don't expect special treatment! ‖ 対話「ぜひ, うちでお昼をご一緒に」「ではおことばに甘えて」"We'd love to have you for lunch. Do come." "Then I'll *take you at your word*." (➤「ことばどおりに受け取る」の意).

あまえんぼう 甘えん坊 ▶うちの息子は甘えん坊でしょうがありません My son is impossible! He's *so spoiled* [*so dependent on me* ／ *such a mama's boy*]. ‖ この猫, 甘えん坊なのよ This cat *likes a lot of affection*. →甘ったれ.

あまがえる 雨蛙《動物》a **tree frog**.

あまがさ 雨傘 an **umbrella**. →傘.

あまから 甘辛 ▶魚を甘辛に煮る boil fish *with sugar and soy* (*sauce*) ‖ 甘辛の煮付け flavoring *with sugar and soy* (*sauce*) ／ *salty-sweet* flavoring (●日本語で「(魚を)甘辛に煮る」といった場合, 甘いのは砂糖で辛いのはしょうゆだが, 英語圏で「肉を甘辛に煮る」といった場合の「辛い」はふつう塩辛いということであるから注意して訳す必要がある).

あまぐ 雨具 **rain gear, rainwear** ▶雨具持参のこと Be sure to bring your *rain gear*. (● umbrella（傘）, raincoat（レインコート）などと具体的にいうのがふつう).

あまくだり 天下り ⚠ぴったりの対応語はないので, ***amakudari*** とローマ字で表記するか, 用例のように日本語の意味を解釈して訳すしかない.

▶今度の専務は財務省からの天下りだ The new managing director joined our company as an executive after retiring from a high position in the Ministry of Finance.

‖天下り人事 the appointment of a former government official to a responsible position in a private corporation.

あまくち 甘口 ▶甘口のカレー *mild* curry ‖ 甘口のワイン *sweet* wine (➤「辛口」は dry).

あまぐつ 雨靴 **rain boots** [**shoes**],《英また》**wellington boots, wellingtons**（長靴）; **rubber overshoes**（靴の上に履くゴム製のもの）; **galoshes** /gəlɑ́ːʃɪz/（長いオーバーシューズ）.

あまくみる 甘く見る ▶俺を甘く見るんじゃあないぞ Don't *underestimate* me. (●英語では「低く評価する」と発想する) ‖ あいつは人生を甘く見過ぎている He's *too optimistic*. (➤「楽観的すぎる」の意) ‖ 相手チームを甘く見ているとやられるぞ You'll lose if you *underestimate* your opponent.

あまぐも 雨雲 a **rain cloud** ▶雨雲はみるみるうちに広がった *Rain clouds* spread in the blink of an eye (over the horizon).

あまごい 雨乞いする **pray for rain.**

あまざけ 甘酒 ***amazake***

日本紹介 ✉ **甘酒は米で作った甘い酒です. 白くてどろっとしています. ふつうの酒と違って子供も飲みます. 体が暖まるので, 冬に家庭で作ったり, 正月に神社で参詣者にふるまったりします** *Amazake* is a sweet alcoholic drink made from rice. It is a thick, white liquid. Unlike ordinary Japanese sake, it is low in alcohol and is even drunk by children. Since it is a warming drink, people sometimes make *amazake* at home during wintertime. It is also served to visitors at shrines during the New Year.

あまざらし 雨曝し ▶自転車を雨ざらしにする *leave* a bicycle *out in the rain* ‖ 商品が雨ざらしにされてだめになった *Exposure to the rain* ruined the goods. ／The merchandise was rain-damaged.

あます 余す ▶その写真集は古い町並みの美しさを余すところなく伝えている That collection of photos *fully* shows the beauty of the town's old buildings. ‖ 開幕戦まで余すところ2日となりました We have *just two days left* before the opening game.

あまずっぱい 甘酸っぱい **sweet and sour** (➤ ふつうは料理の味についていう) ▶甘酸っぱいイチゴ a *sweet and sour* strawberry ‖ 甘酸っぱい初恋の思い出に浸る indulge in the *bitter-sweet* memories of one's first love.

アマゾン アマゾン川 **the Amazon** ▶アマゾンの奥地 the deep interior of *the Amazon*.

あまだれ 雨垂れ a **raindrop**（1滴）.

アマチュア an **amateur** /ǽmətʃʊəʳ ‖ ǽmətə/ ▶アマチュアのゴルフ選手 an *amateur* golfer ‖ アマチュアの無線家 an *amateur* radio operator ／a (radio) ham.

▶ヨーロッパのサッカー選手はアマチュアが多い Many soccer players in Europe are *nonprofessional*.

あまったるい 甘ったるい **too sweet**; **sugary**（砂糖のような）; **saccharine** /sǽkəriːn/（ひどく感傷的な）; **mushy** /mʌ́ʃi/, **sentimental**（感傷的な；前者はインフォーマル）

▶甘ったるい歌詞 *saccharine* lyrics ‖ このケーキ, いやに甘ったるいね This cake is a little *too sweet*. ‖ 彼女は甘ったるい声をしている She has a *sugary* [*saccharine*] voice. ‖ 私は甘ったるいことばは嫌いだ I don't like *honeyed* words. ‖ その映画はひどく甘ったるい(＝感傷的な)ものだった The movie was too *mushy* [*sentimental*].

あまったれ 甘ったれ ▶この甘ったれ! *You spoiled child*! ／*Old fool*! ／*Silly thing*! →甘えん坊.

あまったれる 甘ったれる **act like a baby** ▶甘ったれた態度 a *self-indulgent* attitude ‖ 甘ったれるんじゃないよ! Stop *kidding* [*coddling*] *yourself*!

あまっちょろい 甘っちょろい ▶甘っちょろい考え方 an *easygoing* way of thinking ‖ うちのおやじとおふくろなんて甘っちょろいもんだ My dad and mom are (*real*) *pushovers*. (➤ pushover は「扱いやすい相手, すぐに負ける人」の意の俗語) ‖ 父親の七光りで出世しようなんて甘っちょろい考えは通らないよ If you think

あ

you'll get promotions through the influence of your father, *you're too optimistic* [*naive*].

あまど 雨戸 an ***amado***; a **rain shutter.**

あまとう 甘党 ▶父はどちらかと言うと甘党です(＝酒よりも甘いものが好きだ) My father does*n't care for drinking. He'd rather have sweets*. (「甘党である」ことを have a sweet tooth とか like sweet things とする学習者が多いが, これはあくまでも「甘いものが好き」という意味であって, 日本語の「甘党」(酒よりも甘いものが好き)という意味にはならない. したがって訳例のように表現するのがよい).

あまなっとう 甘納豆 ***amanatto***; sugar-glazed beans (➤ 説明的な訳).

あまのがわ 天の川 the Milky Way, the Galaxy /gǽləksi/ ▶ほら, あれが天の川よ Look! That's *the Milky Way*.

あまのじゃく 天の邪鬼 a **perverse person** (つむじ曲がり); a **contrary person** (人の逆を行って喜ぶ人) ▶みんながその計画に乗り気なのにあなただけ反対だなんて, あまのじゃくね How *perverse* of you to oppose the plan even though everyone else is ready to go with it.

あまみ 甘み sweetness ▶ちょっと甘みのあるカレー curry with a tint of *sweetness* ‖ このスイカはちょっと甘みが足りないね This watermelon *isn't sweet enough*.

あまみず 雨水 rainwater ▶雨水を飲料水に利用する make use of *rainwater* for drinking (water).

あまもり 雨漏り ▶2か所雨漏りするところがある There are two *leaky* places. ‖ 対話「この屋根はいつも雨漏りするのかい」「いや, 雨の日だけだ」"Does this roof always *leak*?" "No, only on rainy days."

あまやかす 甘やかす indulge +目 (気ままにさせる); **pamper** +目 (過保護にする); **spoil** +目 (甘やかしてだめにする) ▶最近は子供を甘やかす親が多い Nowadays many parents *indulge* [*pamper*] their children. ‖ 新入社員を甘やかすな Don't *baby* our new employees. (➤ baby は「赤ん坊のように大切に扱う」の意).

▶その子は甘やかされて育った That child was raised *leniently*. ／That child had a *permissive* upbringing. (➤ leniently /líːniəntli/ は「寛大に」, permissive upbringing は「自由放任の養育」).

あまやどり 雨宿りする take shelter (from the rain) ▶子供たちは近くの公園の藤棚の下で雨宿りした The children *took shelter from the rain* under the wisteria trellis in the nearby park. ‖ あの店の軒下で雨宿りしよう Let's go (stand) under the eaves of that store to *get out of the rain*.

[1]**あまり 余り 1【残り】(the) remainder** (割り算の); **leftovers** (食べ物の) ▶16割る5は3で余り1だ 16 divided by 5 is 3 with *a remainder* of 1. ‖ 食べ物の余りを犬にやった We gave the *leftovers* [*leftover food*] to our dog.

ことわざ 余り物には福がある There's good luck in what is left behind.

2【以上】over, more than ▶彼は2年余り東京に住んでいる He has been living in Tokyo (for) *over* [*more than*] two years. ‖ 日本列島は3700余りの島から成る The Japanese archipelago consists of *more than* 3,700 islands.

3【余りある】遺族の悲しみは察するに余りある We *cannot imagine* the grief [sorrow] of the bereaved family. ‖ 彼のその後の活躍は最初の失敗を補ってなお余りあるものだった His later achievements *more than made up for* his initial mistakes.

[2]**あまり 余り 1【「あまり…ない」の形で】not ... very, not ... much; seldom, rarely** (めったにない) ▶ことしはあまり雨が降らない We *aren't* getting *much* rain this year. ／We *didn't* have *much* rain this year. (➤ 後者はその年の後半, あるいは年が押し詰まった頃に用いる) ‖ パパイヤはあまり好きではありません I *don't* like papayas *very much*. ‖ 弟はあまり勉強しない My brother does*n't* study *very hard*.

▶出発まで時間があまりない There is*n't much* time before we have to leave. ‖ あした雨が降る可能性はあまりない It's *not very likely* that it will rain tomorrow. ／*There is only a slim chance* of rain tomorrow. (➤ slim chance は「わずかな見込み」).

▶父は小説家で, あまり外出しない My father is a novelist, so he *seldom* [*rarely*] goes out. ‖ 夫は娘の婚約をあまり喜んではいないんですよ My husband is *not too* [*very*] happy about our daughter's engagement.

2【あまりに…(過ぎる)】too ...; so ..., such (a [an]) ... ▶彼のやり方はあまりに強引すぎる His way of doing things is *too* high-handed. ‖ あまりたばこを吸い過ぎないように Don't smoke *too much*.

> **【文型】**
> **あまりに A なので (B は) …できない**
> **too A (for B) to do**
> **so A (that) B can't do**
> ➤ A は形容詞・副詞; so A (that) … や次の such a … (that) の文型は A が原因となって, 必然的に B 以下の結果が生じたときに用いる. 逆に言えば, 必然的に B 以下の結果につながるほどに A が原因として重要であることを強調する. →ので; too … to do の文型で主語が同じ B の場合は for B は省略される.
> **such a [an] A (that) B can't do**
> ➤ A は名詞

▶私はあまりに疲れていたので宿題をできなかった I was *too* tired *to* do my homework. ／I was *so* tired (*that*) I *couldn't* do my homework. (➤ 宿題をやれないほど疲れていた) ‖ その数学の問題はあまりに難しくて, 誰も解くことができなかった The math problem was *so* difficult *that* no one *could* solve it. ／It was *such a* difficult math problem *that* no one *could* solve it. (➤ この2つは誰も解けないほどの難しさを強調する) ／The math problem was *too* difficult *for* anyone *to* solve. (➤ この表現は, 他の人にとってはどうかわからないが, 私には解けない難しさであったことをいう).

▶その箱はあまりに重くて, 私には持ち上げられなかった The box was *so* heavy (*that*) I *couldn't* lift it. (➤ 異常なほど [予想外] の重さを強調して, 私にはとても無理であるし, 誰でも簡単には持ち上げられないだろうというニュアンスになる) ／The box was *too* heavy *for* me *to* lift. (➤ 絶対的に重いのではなく,「私には持ち上げられない重さであった」を表す. 例えば, 自分が非力で, あるいは, 腰痛やそのときの体力では自分には持ち上げられなかったことをいう. 屈強の者には大したことのない重さかもしれない場合に用いる) ‖ 私はあまりに眠くてほとんど目を開けていられなかった I was *so* sleepy (*that*) I *could barely* keep my eyes open. ／I was *extremely* sleepy and could barely keep my eyes open. (➤ barely は否定的意味あいで「あまり [ほとんど] …ない」の意).

▶あまりにのどが渇いていたので, 水を1リットルも飲まずにはいられなかった I was *so* thirsty *that* I *couldn't* help drinking a liter of water. (➤ 後半が I drank a glass of water の場合は so ... that を使うのは不自然. I was very thirsty, so I drank a glass of water. (のどがとても渇いていたので, 水を1杯飲んだ) なら問題ない.so ... that は I couldn't help drinking a liter of water (水を1リットル飲まざるをえなかった) に近い因果関係の必然性を表す).

▶あまりにくだらない番組だったのでチャンネルを変えた It was *such a* stupid program (*that*) I switched to another channel. ‖ あまりにすばらしい天気だったので仕事を中止して散歩に出かけた It was *such a* wonderful day (*that*) I stopped working and went out for a walk.

▶その毛皮のコートはあまりにも高すぎて誰も手が出なかった Nobody could afford the fur coat because of its *absurd* [*exorbitant*] price. (➤ absurd, exorbitant はそれぞれ「ばかげた」「法外な」).

3【…するあまり, …のあまり】▶ショックのあまり彼女は床にへなへなと座り込んでしまった She was *so* shocked (*that*) she sank weakly to the floor. ‖ 急ぐあまりコピーをとるのを忘れた *In my haste*, I forgot to make a photocopy. ‖ 優勝者はうれしさのあまり跳び上がった The winner jumped *for joy*. ‖ 息子を亡くして, 悲嘆のあまり彼女は寝込んでしまった She took to her bed *from excessive grief* over the loss of her son.

アマリリス 《植物》 an **amaryllis** /æ̀mərfílɪs/.

あまる 余る **1**【残る】**leave** ▶7を3で割ると1が余る Seven divided by three *leaves* one. ‖ 彼には余るほど金がある He's got money *to spare* [*to burn*]. ‖ まだ食べ物が余っている There *is* still some food *left*. ‖ **対話**「問題用紙が余っていませんか」「はい, ここにあります」"Are there any *extra* question sheets ?" "Yes, they're right here."

2【慣用表現】▶この仕事はきみの手に余るよ This job is *too much* [*too hard*] for you. ‖ 身に余る光栄です The honor is *more than I deserve*. ‖ 彼の態度は目に余る(=許せない) His attitude is *intolerable*.

アマルガム 《化学》 **amalgam** /əmǽlgəm/.

あまんじる 甘んじる **be content with** (現状で満足する); **be reconciled to** (諦める); **settle for** (不本意ながら受け入れる) ▶彼は17年間も助手の地位に甘んじている He *has been content with* his post as an assistant for 17 years. ‖ 彼は自分の運命に甘んじている He *is reconciled* [*resigned*] *to* his fate. (➤ 後者がより堅い言い方) ‖ 彼は3位に甘んじた He *settled for* third place. ‖ 現状に甘んじているうちは進歩はない If you keep *being complacent with* [*taking it easy in*] *your present situation*, there's no way you'll ever get ahead.

あみ 網 a **net**; **netting, network** (網製品, 細工) ▶網で昆虫を捕まえる catch insects with *a net* / net insects ‖ 網を打つ throw [cast] *a net* ‖ 網を引く draw (in) *a net* ‖ 網にかかった魚 *netted* fish.

▶《比喩的》法律の網にかかる *get caught in the clutches* of the law ‖ 彼はうまく法の網をかいくぐった He cunningly evaded *the clutches of the law*.

あみき 編み機 a **knitting machine**.

あみだ 阿弥陀 **Amitabha** /ʌ̀mɪtáːbə/ (阿弥陀仏); **Amida** /áːmɪdə/ (日本の) ▶彼は帽子を少しあみだにかぶる He wears his cap *pushed back* a little.

▶誰がいくら払うかを決めるためみんなであみだくじを引いた We all drew *lots* to decide who should pay how much.

あみだす 編み出す **work** [**think**] **out** (考え出す); **invent** +㊐ (発明する); **devise** +㊐ (考案する)

▶戸田教授がその問題を解く方法を編み出した Professor Toda *worked out* a way to solve the problem.

あみだな 網棚 a **rack**, 《英また》 a **luggage rack** ▶バッグを網棚に載せる put one's bag on the *rack* ‖ 網棚からバッグを下ろす lift down one's bag from the *rack*.

あみど 網戸 a **screen door**; a **window screen** (窓の).

アミノさん アミノ酸 an **amino acid**.

あみのめ 網の目 ▶全国に鉄道が網の目のように走っている *A network* of railroads covers the whole country. ‖ 容疑者は捜査の網の目をかいくぐって逃走した The suspect managed to escape *a dragnet* [escape from *the police dragnet*].

あみばり 編み針 a **knitting needle** (➤ 通例複数形で); a **crochet** /kroʊʃéɪ/ **needle** (かぎ針).

あみぼう 編み棒 a **knitting needle**.

あみめ 網目 (a) **mesh** ▶網目のストッキング *meshed* [*netted*] stockings.

あみもの 編み物 **knitting** /nítɪŋ/ (編むこと) ▶編み物をする do *knitting* / knit.

あむ 編む **knit** /nɪt/ (毛糸を); **braid** (髪を); **plait** /pleɪt ‖ plæt/ (髪・ひもなどを) ▶手袋を編む *knit* (a pair of) gloves ‖ 髪を編む *braid* [*plait*] one's hair ‖ 姉は髪を三つ編み[お下げ]に編んでいる My sister *wears* her hair *in braids*.

▶彼は四季折々の短歌を集めて歌集を編んだ(=編集した) He collected seasonal tanka (s) and *compiled* (them into) an anthology.

アムステルダム **Amsterdam** /ǽmstəˈdæm/ (オランダの首都).

[1]**あめ 雨** **1**【空から降る水滴】**rain**; a **rainfall** (降雨) ▶雨のひと滴 a drop of *rain* / a *raindrop* ‖ けさ雨が降った *It rained* this morning. ‖ 今週は3日雨が降った *It rained* three days this week. ‖ この夏は2日雨が降っただけだ *We've had* only two *rainy days* this summer. ‖ きょうは一日中雨が降ったりやんだりしている *It's been raining on and off* [*off and on*] all day today.

▶あした雨が降らないといいな I hope *it doesn't rain* tomorrow. ‖ 雨が降り始めた It has begun to *rain*. / It's started *raining*. ‖ 雨が降りそうだ *It looks like rain*. / *It's threatening* (*to*) *rain*. / *It looks as if it's going to rain*. (➤ as if の代わりに like でもよい) ‖ ふつう6月にはよく雨が降る Usually *we get a lot of rain* in June.

▶「雨が降るといけないから傘を持って行ったほうがいいわよ」と母が言った My mother told me, "You'd better take an umbrella with you *in case it rains* [*just in case*]." ‖ ちょっと前に雨がやんだ *The rain stopped* [*let up*] a few minutes ago. / *It stopped raining* a few minutes ago.

▶子供たちは傘を持っていなくて雨に降られた The children *were caught in the rain* without umbrellas. ‖ ことしの運動会は雨のため中止[延期]になった Our sports day *was rained out* this year. (➤ be rained out は「(競技などが)雨で中止または延期になる」) ‖ こんな雨の日に出かけるの? Are you going out on such a *rainy day* ? ‖ この夏は雨降りの日が長く続いている We've been having a long *wet* spell this summer. (➤ spell は「(天候などの)ひと続き」) ‖ **対話**「午後から雨だって」「こんな青空なのに?」"They say it will *rain* this afternoon." "Even with this blue sky ?"

ことわざ 雨降って地固まる The ground becomes

あ

firm after rain.(➤日本語からの直訳)／After a storm comes a calm. (➤英語のことわざ).

2【比喩的】▶戦場では砲弾が雨あられと降ってくる Shells are *raining* all over the battlefield.

「雨」のいろいろ **大雨** heavy rain ／**おやみなく降る雨** steady rain ／**霧雨** drizzle, misty rain ／**豪雨** torrential rain ／**小雨** light rain, drizzle ／**小ぬか雨** fine rain ／**五月雨(さみだれ)** early summer rain ／**しとしと降る雨** drizzle ／**たたきつけるような雨** lashing rain ／**断続的な雨** intermittent rain ／**天気雨** sun shower ／**通り雨** (passing) shower ／**どしゃ降り** downpour, drencher ／**長雨** long rain ／**にわか雨** shower ／**氷雨(ひさめ)** freezing rain ／**夕立** shower ／**横殴りの雨** driving rain ／**夜通し降る雨** overnight rain ／**雷雨** thunderstorm

☛ **雨上がり, 雨男, 雨模様, 大雨** (→見出語)

²あめ 飴 《米》 (a) **(hard) candy,** 《英》 a **sweet**； a **lollipop** (棒付きのペロペロキャンデー) ▶あめをなめる suck (on) *a candy* ／lick *a lollipop*.

▶《慣用表現》あめとむちの政策をとる adopt *a carrot-and-stick policy*.

‖**あめ玉** (a piece of) hard candy, a hard candy ball.

あめあがり 雨上がり ▶雨上がりで道がひどくぬかった The road was muddy *after the rainfall*. ‖雨上がりのあとは緑がいっそう濃くなった *After the rain stopped* [*let up*], the leaves looked greener.

アメーバ 《動物》 an **amoeba** /əmíːbə/.

あめおとこ 雨男 ▶靖夫はいわゆる「雨男」で彼と旅行すると必ず雨だ Yasuo is what we call "*a rain man* [*a rain-bringer*]." Every time I travel with him, it rains. ‖きのうまで晴れていたのにきみが来たら雨になった. 雨男だね, きみは It was sunny till yesterday ; *you must have brought the rain*. (➤「きみが雨を連れてきたに違いない」の意).

アメニティー an **amenity** ▶プールやフィットネスセンターといったアメニティー *amenities* like a pool and a fitness center.

‖(ホテルの)**アメニティー(グッズ)** bath [bathroom] amenities, (hotel) toiletries(➤「アメニティーグッズ」は和製語).

あめもよう 雨模様 ▶雨模様の(＝降りだしそうな)空 a *threatening* sky ‖きょうは雨模様です *It looks like rain* today. ／*It's going to rain* today. 《参考》どちらの文も「雨が降りだしそう」であることを表す.「現実に雨が降っている」ことを表して, 例えば「京都は雨模様です」と言うときは, It is raining in Kyoto., There are rainy skies over Kyoto. のようにいう.

アメリカ

America ; the United States (of America) (アメリカ合衆国; 略称は the U.S.(A.)) **一形 アメリカの American** ▶アメリカに住む live in *America* [*the U.S.*] ‖ジュディーさんはアメリカ人です Judy is *American*. (➤(×) Judy is an American. とはふつうはいわない) ‖(私が会った)アメリカの人たちはみんなとても陽気で親切でした The *Americans* (I met) were all very cheerful and kind. ‖アメリカの大学に留学したい I'd like to study at an *American* college. [a college *in the U.S.*]

‖**アメリカ英語** American English, the American language ‖**アメリカ人** an American ‖**アメリカ政府** the U.S. Government ‖**アメリカ文学** American literature ‖**北[南／中央]アメリカ** North [South ／Central] America.

アメリカナイズ アメリカナイズする Americanize ▶日本は第二次世界大戦後に大いにアメリカナイズされた Japan *was Americanized* to a large extent after World War Ⅱ. ‖カリフォルニア巻きはアメリカナイズされた日本食の一例だ The California roll is an example of *Americanized* Japanese food. ‖麻里はアメリカで勉強してからアメリカナイズされている Mari *has been acting like an American* ever since she studied in the U.S.

アメリカン American 《参考》アメリカ風の薄いコーヒーを「アメリカン」というが, これをアメリカで American coffee といっても通じない. アメリカでは薄いコーヒー(weak coffee)が一般的だからである. 単に coffee とだけいえばよい.

アメリカンフットボール American football 《参考》football は《米》では常にアメリカンフットボールを指すが, 《英》ではサッカーやラグビーをいう. したがって, 誤解を生みそうな場合には American をつける. ▶アメリカンフットボールの選手 [試合] a *football* player [game].

あめんぼ 《動物》 a **water strider,** a **pond skater.**

あやうい 危うい ▶私たちは危ういところで助かった We *had a narrow escape*. ‖彼女はこのゴルフトーナメントで勝ち抜けるかどうか危うい *It is doubtful* that she will manage to win this golf tournament.

あやうく 危うく almost, nearly (あと少しで)； **(only) just** (まさにもう少しというところで)； **barely** (際どいところで, ぎりぎりのところで)； **narrowly** (やっと) ▶その少年は危うく溺れるところだった The boy *almost* [*nearly*] drowned. (➤ almost は死に至らなかった点を強調し, nearly は死に至るほどだったにもかかわらずよく助かったという点を強調する) ‖その老人は危うく車にひかれるところだった The old man (*only*) *just* escaped being run over by a car.

あやかる ▶きみの幸運にあやかりたいね I'*d like a piece of your luck*. ‖あの男, 宝くじで500万円当てたんだって. あやかりたいものだね Someone told me that guy won five million yen in the lottery. I'*d* sure *like to be in his shoes*. (➤ be in ~'s shoes で「~の立場になる」) ‖彼らは亡きＦ１レーサーのセナにあやかって, 男の子に瀬奈と名づけた They named their baby boy Sena *after* the late F 1 racing driver Senna.

あやしい 怪しい・妖しい

📖 **訳語メニュー**
不審な →suspicious **1**
神秘的な →mysterious **2**
疑わしい →doubtful **3**

1【異様な, 不審な】suspicious, strange ▶私は怪しい者ではありません I'm not a *suspicious* character. ‖あの男が怪しい I *suspect* that man. (➤ suspect は「(犯人ではないかと)疑う, 嫌疑をかける」) ‖裏口で怪しい物音がした I heard a *strange* noise at the back door.

▶《恋愛関係》あの２人の仲はどうも怪しい It looks like *there's something going on* between those two. (➤「２人の間で何かが起こっている」の意).

2【神秘的な】mysterious ▶その女優には妖しい魅力がある That actress has a *mysterious* charm.

3【疑わしい, 信頼できない】doubtful ▶そのニュースの出どころは怪しい The source of the news is *unreliable*. ‖あいつの言うことなど怪しいものだ I *can hardly believe* what he says. ‖彼の誠実さなんて怪しいものよ I *doubt* his sincerity. (➤ doubt は「…を信用しない」) ‖彼の英語はかなり怪しい His English (ability) is rather *poor* [*shaky*].

【文型】
～かどうか怪しい
It is doubtful whether ～.
I doubt whether [if] ～.

《解説》(1)ともに whether 以下のことが「疑問で確信がもてない」ということを表すが, It is doubtful は「誰が見ても疑問だ」のような客観性をもつのに対し, I doubt は, 個人の主観的な意見を表す.
(2) that 節を続けると「～でないと思う」という意味になる.

▶選挙公約など守られるかどうか怪しいものだ *It is doubtful* [*I doubt*] *whether* their campaign pledges will be kept. ‖ 彼女が約束どおり来るかどうか怪しいものだ I *doubt whether* [*if*] she will show up as promised. ／*You never know if* she will show up as promised.

あやしげ 怪しげ ▶怪しげな男 a *suspicious looking* man ‖ 怪しげな話 a *fishy* story (➤ fishy は「ありそうもない」の意のインフォーマルな語).

あやしむ 怪しむ **suspect** +㊀ (…だろうと思う) ; **doubt** +㊀ (…ではないらしいと思う) ▶先生は彼がカンニングをしたのではないかと怪しんだ The teacher *suspected* him *of* cheating.
▶彼は誰にも怪しまれずに(＝気づかれずに)受付を素通りした He passed by the reception desk *without being noticed* by anybody.

あやす **amuse** +㊀ (おもしろがらせる) ; **lull** /lʌl/ +㊀ (寝かしつけるために) ▶赤ん坊をあやすのは容易でない It's not easy to *keep* a baby *amused*. ‖ 彼女は泣いている赤ん坊をあやして寝かしつけた She *lulled* the crying baby *to sleep*.

あやつりにんぎょう 操り人形 a **puppet** ; a **marionette** /mæriənét/ (糸で操るもの) ▶《比喩的》その政治家は財界の操り人形だ That politician is *a puppet* of [*in the pockets of*] the moneyed interests. (➤ be in the pocket of A または be in A's pocket は「Aの言いなりである」).

あやつる 操る **1【物を動かす】** **manipulate** /mənípjəleɪt/ +㊀ (いいように[巧みに]操作する) ; **use** +㊀ (使用する) ▶人形を操る *manipulate* a puppet ‖ 首相は世論をうまく操った The prime minister deftly *manipulated* public opinion. ‖ 彼はパソコンを自由自在に操ることができる He can *use* a personal computer *with ease* [*skillfully*].
2【言語を使いこなす】 ▶彼女はフランス語と英語を自由に操る She *has a good command of* French and English. ／She *speaks* French and English *fluently*.
3【陰で動かす】 **pull the strings** ▶知事は実権を握っていなかった. 陰で操っている者がいた The governor wasn't in control. Someone *was pulling the strings*. [He was being manipulated.]

あやとり 綾取り **cat's cradle** ▶あや取りをする play *cat's cradle*.

あやぶむ 危ぶむ **doubt** +㊀ (疑う) ▶私はその情報の信ぴょう性を危ぶんでいる I *doubt* the credibility of that (piece of) information. ‖ あすの天気が危ぶまれる Tomorrow's weather *looks doubtful*. ／The weather might be bad tomorrow. ‖ このままでは入賞が危ぶまれる成績だ Your current record *may not be good enough* to win a prize.

あやふや ▶あやふやな返事 a *vague* answer ‖ あやふやなことを言うな Don't *speak ambiguously*. ／Don't *use ambiguous expressions*. (➤ ambiguous /æmbígjuəs/ は「曖昧な」).

あやまち 過ち an **error**, a **mistake** (間違い) ; a **fault** (過失) ▶過ちを犯す commit *an error* ／make *a mistake* ‖ 自分の過ちを認める admit one's *mistake* ‖ それは私の過ちです It is my *fault*. ‖ 誰にも過ちはあるものだ Everyone makes *mistakes*. ／To *err* is human. (➤「過ちを犯すのが人間だ」の意) ‖ 彼は若気(わかげ)の過ちでガールフレンドを妊娠させてしまった *Due to a youthful indiscretion*, he got his girlfriend pregnant.

あやまり 誤り an **error**, a **mistake** (➤ 両者の違いに関しては「間違い」の項を参照) ▶判断の誤り *an error* of judgment ‖ ネイティブスピーカーでも英語を書いたり話したりするときに文法的な誤りをするものだ Even native English speakers make grammatical *mistakes* [*errors*] when writing or speaking English. ‖ 誤りがあったら直しなさい Correct any *errors* you may find. ／If there are any *errors*, correct them. ／Correct *errors*, if any.

[1]**あやまる 誤る** **make a mistake** 一副 **誤って** **by mistake** (間違えて) ; **mistakenly** (思い違いして) ▶進路の選択を誤る *make a mistake* in choosing one's career ‖ 人物の判断を誤る *misjudge* a person's character ‖ きみのその副詞の使い方は誤っている The way you use that adverb is *wrong* [*mistaken*]. ‖ 彼はギャンブルで人生を誤った He *ruined his life* by gambling.
▶その男の子は誤って私を母親だと思った The boy *took* [*mistook*] me *for* his mother. (➤ take [mistake] A for B で「誤ってAをBと思う」) ‖ 私は誤って人を傷つけてしまった I hurt a person *by mistake*. ‖ その運転手は滑りやすくなった道路で運転を誤り, 石塀に衝突した The driver *lost control* on the slippery road and smashed into a stone wall.
▶学校はいつやめてもいいんだなどという誤った考えは捨てなさい You should forget this *erroneous* [*false* ／ *misguided*] notion that you can quit school any time you like. (●「誤った」を「正確ではない」と考えれば erroneous /ɪróʊniəs/ を,「真実ではない」と考えれば false を,「心得違いの」と考えれば misguided を用いることができる).

[2]**あやまる 謝る** **apologize** /əpɑ́ːlədʒaɪz/ ▶きみが謝る必要はないよ You don't have to *apologize*. ／There's no need for you to *apologize*. ‖ 私が悪かった. 謝るよ I was wrong. *I'm sorry*. ‖ 謝って済むことではない This is not something you can be excused for by *apologizing*.

【文型】
人 (A) に B のことで謝る
apologize to A **for** B
➤ B は名詞・動名詞. to A や for B が省略されることもある

▶娘が失礼な態度をとったことを謝ります I *apologize to* you *for* my daughter's rude behavior.
▶ 対話「良夫君に謝りなさい」「やだ, ぼく悪くないもん」"*Apologize* to Yoshio. ／ *Tell* Yoshio *you're sorry*." "No way. I didn't do anything wrong." ‖ 彼は彼女に心から謝った He sincerely *apologized to* her. ／He *made a* sincere *apology to* her.

あやめ 《植物》a **Japanese iris**, a **blue flag**.

あゆ 鮎 《魚》an *ayu* , a **sweetfish** ▶アユ釣りを楽しむ enjoy *ayu fishing* ‖ 若アユのような(＝ぴちぴちした)娘

a *sprightly* young girl.

あゆみ 歩み ▶そのフィルムはわが社の50年の歩み(＝歴史)を記録したものだ The film is a record of the 50-year *history* of our company.

あゆみより 歩み寄り (a) **compromise** /kɑ́:mprəmaɪz/ (妥協); **mutual concessions** (互譲) ▶歩み寄りで紛争を解決する settle a dispute *by compromise* [*mutual concessions*] ‖ その労働争議には歩み寄りの余地はなかった The labor dispute allowed no room for *compromise*.

あゆみよる 歩み寄る (…に)**walk up** 《to》 ▶その子は母親の方に歩み寄った The child *walked up to* his [her] mother.

▶《比喩的》両者は契約条件で歩み寄った The two (sides) *met* each other *halfway* [*compromised*] on the terms of the contract.

あゆむ 歩む walk ▶苦難の道を歩む *tread* a thorny path ‖ その画家の歩んだ人生は苦難の連続であった *The life that* the painter *lived* was filled with hardship. ／The painter *lived a life* filled with hardship. ‖ 彼は演劇の道を歩む決心をした He made up his mind to *pursue an* acting *career*.

1**あら 粗** a **fault**(欠点); **shortcomings**(ささいな短所) ▶きみはいつも彼の仕事のあらを見つけようとしているね You're always trying to *find fault with* his work, aren't you? ‖ 彼女の処女作はあらばかりが目につく Her maiden work is full of *shortcomings* [*flaws*]. ‖ 人のあらを探すのはやめなさい Stop *nitpicking* others. (→あら探し).

2**あら Oh!** ▶あら, いらっしゃい *Oh*, good to see you! Come in! ‖ あら, そうですか *Oh, is that so?* ／*Really?* ‖ あら, まあ *Oh!* ／*Oh, my!* ／*Dear me!* (➤ 最後の例は高齢の女性に多い言い方) ‖ あら嫌だ. 道間違えちゃったわ *Oh, no!* I took the wrong road. ‖ 《子供に》あらあら, こんな所で寝ちゃだめよ *Oh dear*, you shouldn't be sleeping here. 《参考》日本語の「あら」は女性用語だが, 対応する Oh は男女とも使う. ただし, my や dear はやや古風な女性用語.

アラー Allah /ǽlə/ (イスラム教の神).

アラーム an **alarm (clock)** (時計).

あらあらしい 荒々しい rough /rʌf/ (乱暴な), **coarse, harsh** (粗野な); **violent** (激しい); **rude** (無作法な) ▶彼は態度が荒々しい He has a *rough* manner. ‖ 彼はノブをつかんで鍵のかかっているドアを荒々しく揺さぶった He grabbed the knob of the locked door and shook it *violently*.

1**あらい 荒い rough** (波などが) ▶きょうは波が荒い The ocean is *rough* today. ‖ 紀州犬は気性が荒い Kishu dogs are *rough-natured*. ‖ 男は息遣いが荒かった The man was breathing *hard*.

▶うちの課長は(全く)人使いが荒い Our section manager is a (real) *slave driver*. (➤「こき使う上司」の意) ‖ 息子は金遣いが荒くて困る The trouble with my son is he *is too free with money* [he *spends money too carelessly*]. →荒っぽい.

2**あらい 粗い** **1【隙間がある, 滑らかでない】coarse** (織物の目・粒などが); **rough** (手触りが) ▶目の粗い網 *coarse* meshes ‖ 粗いしま模様のセーターを編む knit a sweater with *large* stripes ‖ このスーツの生地は手触りが粗い This suit material *feels rough*. ‖ コーヒーは粗くひいてドリップでいれるとうまい Coffee tastes good when it is ground *coarsely* for dripping.

2【大ざっぱな】rough ▶このロッキングチェアは仕上げが粗い This rocking chair has a *rough* finish. ‖ 彼女の仕事はまだまだ粗い Her work *leaves a lot to be desired*. (➤「遺憾な点が多い」の意).

あらいぐま 洗い熊 《動物》 a **raccoon.**

あらいざらい 洗いざらい ▶容疑者は犯行を洗いざらい白状した The suspect told the *whole* story. ／The suspect confessed *everything*.

あらいざらし 洗いざらし ▶その若者は洗いざらしのジーンズをはいていた The young man wore *washed-out* jeans.

あらいだす 洗い出す ▶盗難車の持ち主を洗い出せ *Search out* the owner of the stolen car. ‖ まず最初に問題点を洗い出す必要がある First we need to *bring* any problems *to light*.

あらいなおす 洗い直す wash again (もう一度洗う); **reconsider** +目 (再検討する) ▶その計画はもう一度洗い直す必要がある The plan needs to *be reconsidered*. ‖ 刑事は容疑者一人一人の身元をもう一度洗い直した(＝再調査した) The detective *looked into* each suspect's background *once again*.

あらいながす 洗い流す wash away [**off**]; **rinse away** [**off**] (水で軽くすすいで) ▶汚れを洗い流す *wash away* the dirt ‖ 自転車の土ぼこりを洗い流した I *rinsed* the dust *off* (of) my bicycle.

あらいもの 洗い物 washing (洗濯物) ▶うちでは毎日洗い物が山ほどある We have a lot of *washing* to do every day. ‖ 姉は今食後の洗い物で忙しい My sister is busy *doing* [*washing*] *the dishes* now. ／《英》My sister is busy *washing up* now. (➤ wash up は《米》では「手や顔を洗う」の意).

あらう 洗う wash +目; **shampoo** /ʃæmpúː/ +目 (髪を) ▶夕食の前に手を洗う *wash* one's hands before dinner ‖ 野菜を水で洗う *wash* the vegetables (*off*) in water ‖ 体を洗う *wash oneself* (➤ (×)wash one's body とはしない) ‖ 雨靴の泥を洗い落とす *wash* the mud *off* one's rain boots.

▶私は1日おきに髪を洗います I *shampoo my hair* every other day. ‖ うちでは食器を洗うのは子供たちの仕事の1つです In our home, *doing* [*washing*] *the dishes* is one of the children's chores. ‖ 彼の純粋さに私は心が洗われるように思った It felt like *my soul was cleansed* by his purity (of heart). (➤ cleanse は /klenz/ と発音).

▶《比喩的》私立探偵がおまえの過去を洗って(＝調べて)いるらしいぞ I hear a private detective *is checking into your past*.

あらうみ 荒海 rough seas; **raging seas** (荒れ狂う海).

あらかじめ 予め in advance, beforehand (➤ 前者が「あらかじめ」により近い堅い言い方) ▶おいでになるときはあらかじめお電話ください When you come, please phone (me) *beforehand* [*ahead of time*]. (➤ 後者は《米》に多い言い方) ‖ 一度お買い求めいただいたチケットはお取り替えできませんので, あらかじめご了承ください We would like to notify you *in advance* that once a ticket has been purchased, it cannot be refunded [be exchanged].

あらかせぎ 荒稼ぎ ▶彼は闇ブローカーと手を組んで荒稼ぎをした He *made* [*raked in*] *a bundle of money* by teaming up with an under-the-table broker.

あらかた almost (ほとんど) ▶工事はあらかた終わった The construction is *almost* completed. ‖ 村上春樹の本はあらかた読んでしまった I have read *most* of Murakami Haruki's books.

アラカルト a la carte /ɑ̀: lɑ: kɑ́:ʳt/.

あらけずり 粗削り ▶あの作家は粗削りだが素質はあるよ That author is *unrefined* but talented. ／That author is *a diamond in the rough*. (➤ a diamond in the rough は「磨いていないダイヤモンド」の意で, 比喩的に「粗削りだが優れた素質をもった人」をいう).

アラサー around thirty (30歳前後).

あらさがし 粗探し faultfinding, 《インフォーマル》 nitpicking ▶他人のあら探しをする *find fault with* a person ‖ 彼女は私の仕事のあら探しをしようとした She tried to *find flaws* in my work. (➤ flaw は「欠陥, 不備」). →粗.

あらし 嵐 a storm ▶嵐の海 a *stormy* sea ‖ 大嵐に遭う get caught in *a heavy storm* ‖ 昨夜は嵐だった *It stormed* last night. ‖ 嵐になりそうだ *It is getting stormy*. / *A storm threatens*. ‖ 嵐のあとにはなぎが来る *After a storm comes a calm*. (➤ 英語のことわざ).
▶歌手が入場すると嵐のような拍手が起こった *A storm of applause* arose when the singer entered the auditorium.
▶ 対話 「おやじ, 最近ずいぶんおとなしいね」「そうね, 嵐の前の静けさでなけりゃいいんだけど」"Dad's been very quiet lately." "Yes, but I'm afraid it's only *the calm* [*lull*] *before the storm*." (➤ lull は「(嵐・活動などの)小休止」の意).

あらす 荒らす **1**【荒れた状態にする】 damage +目 ▶野生の動物たちが作物を荒らした Wild animals *damaged* the crops. ‖ イノシシに田畑を荒らされた The fields *were damaged* by wild boars.
2【盗んで害を与える】 ▶2人の男がそのスーパーを荒らして500万円を奪った Two men *robbed* the supermarket *of* five million yen. (➤ rob A of B で「A からBを奪う」).
▶都内の宝石店を荒らし回っていた3人組の泥棒が, ついに昨夜捕まった The three robbers who had *broken into* many jewelry stores in Tokyo were finally arrested last night.

アラスカ Alaska (アメリカの州 ; 略 AK, Alas.).

あらすじ 粗筋 a plot, an outline (➤ 前者はフィクションの, 後者はノンフィクションの大意 [要旨] を指す傾向がある) ; a summary (要約) ▶小説のあらすじ the *plot* [*outline*] of a novel.

あらそい 争い a quarrel (口論) ; (a) dispute (論争) ; a battle (争い) ; a struggle (奮闘・闘争) ; competition (競り合い)
▶法廷での争い a court *battle* ‖ 遺産相続を巡って骨肉の争いが起きた There was *a family quarrel* over the inheritance. ‖ 2人は土地の権利のことで争いになった The two *got into a dispute* over the land rights. ‖ 労使の争いは解決した The *dispute* [*struggle*] between management and labor has been settled.
▶巨人と中日が首位争いをしている The Giants and the Dragons are *struggling* [*competing*] *for first place*.

あらそう 争う

quarrel, argue (ともに「口論する」ことをいうが, 前者はしばしば後者が高じた結果生じる争いをいう) ; fight (敵などと戦う) ; compete (競争する) ▶兄弟どうしで争うべきではない Brothers should not *quarrel* (with each other). ‖ 隣の夫婦はいつも争っている The couple nextdoor *are* always *quarreling* [*arguing*]. ‖ 身内が父親の遺産を争っている The family members *are fighting over* the father's legacy. (➤ fight over は「…を巡って争う」) ‖ 彼らは先を争って電車に乗った They *scrambled* [*struggled* (*with one another*)] to get onto the train.

【文型】
A を目指して争う
fight for A
compete for A

▶彼らは社長の椅子を争った They *fought for* the post of president. (➤ fought は fight の過去形) ‖ 20組以上のチームが優勝を争った More than twenty teams *competed for* the championship. ‖《慣用表現》母の容体は一刻を争う危険な状態だった My mother was in such critical condition that *there was not a moment to lose* in trying to save her life.

あらそえない 争えない ▶最近は新聞の字が見えにくくなってね. 年は争えないよ These days I can't read a newspaper as easily as I used to do because of my poor eyesight. *You can't escape* (*the effects of*) *aging* [《英》 *ageing*]. [*I can't deny age is catching up with me*.] (● 英語では最後の言い方のように「年が私を追いかけてくる」と発想することも多い) ‖ 彼の息子も音楽家になったそうだ. 血は争えないものだね I hear his son has also become a musician. It must *run in the family*. (➤ run in the family は「家系に受け継がれている」).

あらた 新たな new ▶私の胸に新たな希望が湧いてきた *New* [*Fresh*] hope welled up in my heart. ‖ 当店は来春, 装いも新たにオープンいたします Our store will *be remodeled* and open again next spring. ‖ 業務拡張に伴って新たに社員を5人雇った We hired five *new* employees in conjunction with (our) business expansion.

あらだてる 荒だてる ▶何も今になって事を荒だてることはない There's no need to *make matters worse* [*stir up trouble*] now. ‖ 先ほどはつい声を荒だてたりして, すみませんでした I'm sorry that I *yelled at* you a little while ago. (➤ yell は「どなる」).

¹あらたまる 改まる **1**【変わる】 change ▶年が改まった The *new* year has come. ‖ 1989年に年号が昭和から平成へと改まった In 1989 the name of the era *was changed* from Showa to Heisei.
2【良くなる】 ▶あれだけ注意しても彼の行いは少しも改まらない His behavior has*n't improved* at all, even though I have repeatedly warned him.
3【儀式ばる】 become formal ▶彼は急に改まった態度をとった He suddenly *became* very *formal*. / He suddenly put on a *solemn* face. (➤ solemn は「しかつめらしい」) ‖ 改まった服装をすると肩が凝る I always get stiff shoulders when I have to wear *formal* clothing. ‖ ぼくは改まった席は苦手なんだ I just hate *formal* gatherings. ‖ 対話 「折り入ってお話があるんですが」「急に改まって何だい?」"I would like to have a private talk with you." "Why are you being so *formal*?" ‖「申し訳ありません」は「すみません」の改まった言い方だ "Moushiwake-arimasen" is a *formal* way of saying "Sumimasen (I'm sorry)."

²あらたまる 革まる ▶老人は病があらたまって昨夜亡くなった The old man *suddenly got worse* and passed away last night.

あらためて 改めて again (もう一度) ; later (あとで) ▶ではまた改めて伺います I'll try *again later* [*another time*]. (➤ ふつう, I'll come again. とは言わない) ‖ その件についてはいずれ改めて話し合いましょう Let's talk about the matter *some other time*. ‖ 病気をして健康のありがたさを改めて痛感した After getting sick the preciousness of (good) health was brought home to me *anew*. ‖ **席を改めて**飲み直しましょう Why don't we *go to another bar* to have some more drinks? ‖ **改めて**注意するまでもないが，お得意様には失礼のないように *Needless to say*, we should be careful not to be rude to our customers.

あらためる 改める 1【新しく変える】**change** +㊐ ▶彼は芸名を「ヒロミ」から「ヒロ」に**改めた** He *changed* his stage name from 'Hiromi' to 'Hiro.' ‖ 彼女はいったん帰宅すると，服装を**改めて**パーティーに出た She came back home briefly, *changed* clothes, and went out to a party.

2【良くする】**correct** +㊐（訂正する）; **improve** +㊐（改善する）; **revise** +㊐（改訂する）; **modify** +㊐（部分的に修正する）; **mend** +㊐（行いなどを）

▶過ちを**改める** *correct* one's mistake ‖ 息子は今後素行を**改める**と言っている My son promises to *improve* his conduct [*mend* his ways] in the future. ‖ あの法律の不備な点は**改めなければならない** That law *should be revised* to eliminate loopholes. ‖ きみは考えを**改めたほうがいいね** You had better *modify* your ideas.

3【調べる】**verify** +㊐ ▶（封筒などの）中身を**あらためてください** Please *verify* the contents.

あらっぽい 荒っぽい rough /rʌf/ ▶**荒っぽい**態度 *rough* manners ‖ 息子は**荒っぽい**運転をする My son drives *recklessly*. ／My son is a *reckless* driver. ‖ 彼はことばづかいが**荒っぽい** He *uses bad* [*coarse*] *language*.

あらて 新手の new ▶**新手の**ねずみ講 *a new type of* pyramid investment scheme.

あらなみ 荒波 rough [**high**] **waves** ▶船は太平洋の**荒波**に飲み込まれた The boat was swallowed by the *high waves* of the Pacific.

▶私たちは世間の**荒波**にもまれてきた We have gone through *the hardships of life*. ／We have been tossed about in *the storms of life*.

あらぬ ▶講演者の話が続いているのに彼は**あらぬ方**を眺めていた Though the speaker was still talking, he was staring off in *another direction*. ‖ 私はその事件で**あらぬ疑い**をかけられた I was *unjustly* [*wrongly*] suspected in that incident.

アラバマ Alabama（アメリカの州；略 AL, Ala.）.

アラビア Arabia

‖**アラビア海** the Arabian Sea ‖ **アラビア語** Arabic ‖ **アラビア人** an Arab ‖ **アラビア数字** Arabic numerals ‖ **アラビア半島** the Arabian Peninsula.

アラブ Arab

‖**アラブ首長国連邦** the United Arab Emirates /émərəts/ ‖ **アラブ諸国** the Arab nations ‖ **アラブ人** an Arab.

アラフォー around forty（40歳前後）.

あらまし an **outline**（大筋）; a **summary**（内容の要約）▶計画の**あらまし**をご説明いたします I'll explain the *outline* of the plan.

▶きみの言いたいことぐらい，**あらまし**見当がつくさ I can *roughly* guess [I have a *rough* idea] what you are going to say. →**あらかた**.

あらゆる all（すべての）; **every**（いずれも）▶世界の**あらゆる国** *all* the countries [*every* country] in the world ‖ 医師たちはその少女の命を救うために**あらゆる手**を尽くした The doctors tried *every possible* means to save the little girl. →**ありとあらゆる**.

あらりえき 粗利益 a **gross profit**.

あらりょうじ 荒療治 drastic treatment（思い切った治療）; a **drastic measure**（思い切った処置）▶事態を収拾するには**荒療治**が必要だ *Drastic measures* will be necessary to remedy the situation.

あられ 霰 ice pellets（➤ 通例複数形）▶けさ早く**あられが降った** *Ice pellets* fell early this morning.

あられもない ▶シェリーは**あられもない**パジャマ姿で現れた Cherie appeared in pajamas *that were not fit to be seen*.

あらわ ▶彼女は肌も**あらわ**だった She was dressed *scantily*. ‖ 彼は嫌悪の情を**あらわにした** He *showed* his hatred *openly*. ／He *showed* an *open* hatred.

あらわす 現す・表す・著す

📖 **訳語メニュー**
出現する →appear **1**
表現する →express **2**
記号などで示す →represent **3**
本を書く →write **4**

1【見えなかったものが見えるようになる】**appear**（出現する）; **show** +㊐（見せる）; **exhibit** +㊐（示す）▶背の高い男が突然表玄関に**姿を現した** A tall man suddenly *appeared* at the front door. ‖ 3時間川岸で粘っていると，カワセミはようやく**姿を現した** I waited patiently at the riverside for three hours. Then the kingfisher finally *appeared*.

▶彼はこのミュージカルで真の**才能を現した** He *exhibited* real talent in this musical. ‖ その男は追い詰められて**本性を現した** That man *showed his true colors* when he was forced into a corner. ‖ 彼は地球物理学の分野で**名をあらわした** He *made a name for himself* in the field of geophysics.

2【見えないものを見えるようにする】**express** +㊐（表現する）▶私は贈り物をすることで，彼女に感謝の気持ちを**表した** I *expressed* my gratitude to her by giving her a gift. ‖ 彼女は絵を通して自分の悲しみを**表した** She *gave expression to* her grief through (her) painting. ‖ その島の美しさはことばでは**表せなかった** The beauty of the island *was beyond description*.

3【意味する】**mean** +㊐; **represent** +㊐（絵・記号などで示す）; **stand for**（…の象徴［略］である）▶この印は何を**表していますか** What does this mark *represent* [*mean*]? ‖ フランスの三色旗は，自由・平等・博愛を**表している** The tricolor of France *stands for* liberty, equality, and fraternity. ‖ IMF は International Monetary Fund（国際通貨基金）を**表している** The letters 'IMF' *stand for* 'International Monetary Fund.' ‖ 十字架はイエス・キリストの死と復活を**表す**（＝象徴する）The cross *symbolizes* the death and resurrection of Jesus Christ.

4【本を書く】**write** +㊐ ▶その教授は歴史の本を数冊**著している** The professor *has written* several books on history. ‖ 前首相の**著した**回顧録 a memoir *written by* the former prime minister.

あらわれ 表れ (an) **expression**（表現）; (a) **manifestation**（発露）▶彼らの行為は熱烈な愛国心の**表れである** Their actions are *a manifestation* [*an expression*] of their ardent patriotism.

あらわれる 現れる・表れる 1【見えなかったものが見えるようになる】**appear** ▶暗闇の中から急に父が**現れた**のでぎくっとした I was startled when my father suddenly *appeared* out of nowhere from the darkness. ‖ 太陽が雲の間から**現れた** The sun *broke* through the clouds. ‖ 霧が晴れて港が**現れた** The fog lifted and *revealed* the harbor. (➤ reveal は「(見えなかったもの)を見せる, 現す」) ‖ パトカーが**現れる**や泥棒は逃げ出した The thief took off as soon as the police car *arrived* (on the scene). ‖ 捜査を続けるうちに事件の全貌が**現れてきた** The details of the case *were uncovered* as the investigation proceeded.

2【人がやって来る】show up（到着する）▶彼女は会議の定刻前に**現れた**ためしがない She *has* never *shown up* early at a meeting. ／She *has* never *come* early to a meeting. (➤ この意味では appear は用いないことに注意).

3【なかったものができる】▶最近, 女性だけのリサイクル会社が**現れた** Recently, a recycling company run only by women *appeared*. ‖ がんの特効薬が**現れる**(＝発見される)日が来るだろうか I wonder if the day will come when a specific cure for cancer *is discovered*.

4【感じられるようになる】work（効く）; **show**（＋目）（表情に出る）▶アスピリンの効果がすぐに**表れた** The aspirin began to *work* (on me) right away. ‖ 病人の顔にはすでに死相が**表れていた** The shadow of death already *appeared* on the sick person's face. ‖ 驚きの様子がその男の顔に**表れていた** The man's expression *showed* surprise. ／The man had a look of surprise on his face. ‖ 友情の真価はまさかのときに**現れる**ものである The true worth of friendship will *be revealed* when you are in need.

あらんかぎり あらん限り ▶少年は顔を真っ赤にして**あらん限りの力**で岩を持ち上げようとしていた Flushed (red) with the effort, the boy was trying to lift the rock *with all his might*.

あり 蟻《虫》an **ant** ▶**アリ**が1列になって行進している The *ants* are marching in a line.

▶《慣用表現》大使公邸は**アリのはい出る隙もないほど**の警戒ぶりだった The official residence of the ambassador was *very closely* guarded.

アリア《音楽》an **aria** /ɑ́ːriə/ ▶**アリアを歌う** sing *an aria*.

‖**G線上のアリア** the air on the G-string (➤ air /eəʳ/ は「素朴な調べ」).

ありあまる 有り余る ▶暇なら**有り余るほど**ある As for free time, I have *more than enough* (*of it*). ‖ 兄は体力が**有り余ってる**みたいだ It seems my brother *has more* energy *than* he *knows what to do with*. ‖ **有り余る**才能に恵まれた作曲家 a *highly* gifted composer.

ありありと vividly（生き生きと）; **clearly**（はっきりと）▶私はその交通事故を今でもきのうのことのように**ありありと**覚えている I still remember the car accident as *vividly* as if it happened only yesterday. ‖ 彼の顔には焦りが**ありありと**見てとれた Panic [Irritation] *clearly* showed on his face.

ありあわせ 有り合わせ ▶私たちは**有り合わせのもの**で食事を済ませた We ate *whatever we could find*.

アリーナ an **arena**.

ありうる 有り得る ▶彼が願書を出し忘れたというのは**ありうる**[**大いにありうる**]ことだ It is *possible* [(*very*) *probable*] that he forgot to send in his application. (➤ possible は「10中1〜3」, probable は「10中8〜9」の意で後者に very をつければさらに強意になる).

ありえない 有り得ない ▶彼が我々の提案を拒絶するということは**ありえない** *It is impossible that* he will reject our proposal. ／He *cannot possibly* reject our proposal. ‖ それはまず**ありえない**ケースだ That is an *improbable* case.

ありか 在りか ▶宝物の**在りか**を探り出す find out *where* the treasure *is* (*kept*).

ありかた 在り方 ▶私たちは政治の**在り方**について話し合った We talked about *how* politics *should be conducted*. ‖ 英語教育の**在り方**についてはいろいろの意見がある There are many different opinions as to the *ideal way* of teaching English. (➤「理想的な教授法」の意).

ありがたい 有り難い 1【感謝したい】

> **【文型】**
> **…していただけるとありがたいのですが**
> **I'd appreciate it if you would** do.
> **I would be grateful [obliged] if you would** do.
>
> **《解説》**(1)obliged のほうが grateful よりも改まった言い方.
> (2)I would は I'd とも短縮される.
> (3)if you would do は if you could do の形も使われる.

▶お願いを聞いていただけると**ありがたいのですが** *I'd appreciate it if you would* do me a favor. ／*I wonder if I could ask you to* do me a favor. ‖ (男性に対して)すみませんが席を代わっていただけると**ありがたいのですが** Sir, *I would be* very *grateful if you would* change seats with me. (➤ 女性には Ma'am を使う).

✉ **同書を1部お送りくだされば大変ありがたいのですが** I *would be very grateful* [(*much*) *obliged*] if you could send me a copy of that book. ➤ 改まった表現.

▶私は彼の申し出を**ありがたく**受けた I accepted his offer *with thanks* [*gratefully*]. ‖ 彼女の心遣いは涙が出るほど**ありがたかった** Her consideration *almost made me cry with joy*. ‖ **ありがたい**(＝よかった), 雨がやんだ *Thank goodness* it has stopped raining. ‖ **対話**「今度の土曜日に夕食にお誘いしたいのですが」「**ありがたいのですが**, 先約がありまして」"May I invite you to dinner next Saturday?" "*That's very kind* [*nice*] *of you*, but I'm afraid I have an engagement."

2【尊い】sacred（神聖な）; **precious**（貴重な）▶仏の**ありがたい**教えを守る observe the *sacred* [*precious*] teachings of Buddha ‖ 天皇陛下から**ありがたい**おことばを賜った I received a *gracious* message from His Majesty the Emperor.

3【都合がよい】▶年寄りには暖かい冬ほど**ありがたい**ものはない Nothing is so *great a blessing* to old people as a mild winter. ‖ 昇給はいつだって**ありがたい**(＝歓迎だ) A pay raise *is* always *welcome*. ‖ **ありがたいことに**(＝幸運にも), 社内のみんなはぼくの失敗に気づいていないらしかった *Luckily*, nobody in the office seemed to have noticed my mistake.

ありがたなみだ 有り難涙 ▶老夫婦は彼女の親切に**ありがた涙**に暮れた The elderly couple *cried tears of gratitude* for her kindness.

ありがたみ 有り難み (a) **value**（値打ち）; a **blessing**（恩恵）▶人は病気になって初めて**健康のありがたみ**がわかる People don't know *the value* [*blessing*] *of health* until they get sick. ／People realize *how*

あ

valuable health is only when they get sick. ‖ 親のありがたみは親がいなくなって初めてわかるものだ You never realize *how much* you *owe* (*to*) *your parents* until you lose them. (➤「親を亡くすまで自分(たち)がどれだけ親に世話になっていたかはわからない」の意).

ありがためいわく 有り難迷惑 ▶彼が手伝ってくれたが，邪魔になるだけでありがた迷惑だった He offered to help me, but it *turned out to be more trouble than it was worth.* ／He offered to help me, but he *proved to be more of a hindrance.* ‖ そんなに大きくて高価な贈り物は彼にとってはありがた迷惑だった Such a large, expensive gift was nothing but *a white elephant* to him. (➤ white elephant (白い象)は「金ばかりかかって始末に困る物」) ‖ 入院しているときに見舞いを受けるとかえってありがた迷惑なこともある When one is in the hospital, visitors can be *more an annoyance than a consolation.* (➤「慰めになるよりも迷惑なことも多い」の意).

ありがち 有りがち ▶いたずらは子供にはありがちだ Children *tend* [*are apt*] *to* get into mischief [trouble]. ‖ その種の日本語の間違いは外国人にはありがちだ Those kinds of errors in Japanese *are common to* foreigners.

ありがとう 有り難う **Thank you (very much).**

《解説》「ありがとう」の言い方
軽い「ありがとう」には **Thanks.** ／**Thank you.** ／《英・インフォーマル》**Ta.** などが，「どうもありがとう」には **Thanks a million.** ／**Thanks a lot.** ／**Many thanks.** などが，また「どうもありがとうございます」には **Thank you very much.** ／**Thank you so much.** などがそれぞれ相当することが多い.

【文型】
A をありがとう
Thank you [Thanks] for A.
…してくれてありがとう
Thank you [Thanks] for doing.

▶手伝ってくれてありがとう *Thank you for* your help. ‖ いろいろとありがとう *Thank you for everything.* ‖ 来てくれてありがとう *Thanks for* coming. ‖ (子供に向かって) ありがとうは？ What about your "*thank you*"? ／What do you say when people give you something? ‖ ご親切ありがとうございました *Thank you very* [*so*] *much for* your kindness. ／I really *appreciate* your kindness. (➤ 後者は改まった表現；⇀感謝)
‖ **対話**「きのうはどうもありがとうございました」「いえ，どういたしまして」"*Thank you very much* for yesterday." "You are welcome. ／Don't mention it. ／It was my pleasure." (➤ 英米人はふつうきのうのことで改めて謝意を表すことはしない) ‖ **対話**「(車に)乗せていただいてありがとうございました」「こちらこそありがとう. おかげで道に迷わずに済みました」"*Thank you for* the ride." "No, *I should be thanking you.* [No, *it is I that* [*who*] *should be thanking you.*] You kept me from getting lost." (➤ (1)後者のほうがより改まった表現で，手紙などでもよく使う. (2)会話では相手の Thánk you. に対して，Thank yóu. と you を強めて発音すれば「こちらこそ」の意になる).
▶ご披露宴にお招きくださいましてありがとうございます *It's very kind* [*nice*] *of you* to invite us to your (wedding) reception. ‖ 彼女はありがとうと言ってその本を返した She returned the book to me *with thanks.*
✉ **いろいろとお骨折りくださいまして誠にありがとう存じます** *I am really grateful* [*I am much obliged* ／*I am deeply indebted*] to you for all the trouble you have taken for me. ➤ 主として書きことばで使う改まった表現で，I am much obliged はどちらかといえば男性が好む.

あなたの英語はどう響く?
親しくなった外国人から If you have any problems, don't hesitate to call me. (何かお困りのときは，ご遠慮なくお電話ください)と言われたときに，「ありがとうございます. そうさせていただきます」のつもりで Thank you. I *will*. と答えないこと. 相手は *don't* hesitate to ... と言っているのだから，これだと「遠慮しておきます」の意味になってしまう. 一般的には Thank you. I'll keep that in mind. (ありがとう. 覚えておきます)のように答えるのがよい.

ありがね 有り金 ▶私は有り金をはたいてこの時計を手に入れた I spent *all the money I had* to obtain this watch.

ありきたり ▶ありきたりの品 an *ordinary* article ‖ ありきたりの(＝従来の)やり方ではうまくいくまい The *conventional* method will not work any more.

ありさま 有り様 a **condition,** a **state** ▶きみのおやじさんはきみのことが心配で仕事も手につかないありさまだよ Your dad has been so worried about you he's in no *condition* to get any work done. ‖ うちの会社の財政状態はひどいありさまだ Our company's finances are in *a terrible state* [in *a mess*]. (➤ 後者はインフォーマル) ‖ 飲み会が終わったあとの私の部屋のありさまはひどいものだった My apartment was *a sight* after the party. (➤ この sight は「ひどいありさま」の意のインフォーマルな語) ‖ 何だ，このありさまは！ What on earth has happened?

ありじごく 蟻地獄 《虫》an **ant lion larva** /lɑ́ːˈvə/ (ウスバカゲロウの幼虫).

ありそう ▶彼の話はありそうな話だ What he said is *likely to be true* [is *plausible*]. (➤ likely は起こる可能性が10中5〜7程度の場合) ‖ 彼女は何かいいことがありそうな気がした She *had the feeling* something good *was going to happen.* ‖ もっとサッカーを練習する必要がありそうだ You *may need to* practice soccer more.
▶社長が我々の要求を受け入れることはまずありそうもない It *seems very unlikely* that the president will accept our demands. (➤ probable は起こる可能性が10中8〜9の場合) ‖ 修がひろみさんと結婚することなどまずありそうもなかった It *was highly improbable* that Osamu would marry Hiromi. ‖ 今までありそうでなかった商品 a product that *surprisingly didn't exist* until now.

アリゾナ Arizona /æ̀rɪzóʊnə/ (アメリカの州；略 AZ, Ariz.).

ありつく ▶彼はうまく職にありついた(＝見つけた) He was lucky (enough) to *get* [*find*] a job. ‖ やたら忙しくて2時まで昼飯にありつけなかった I was so busy I *couldn't* (*find time to*) *have* lunch until 2 p.m.

ありったけ ▶彼女はありったけの声で助けを求めた She screamed [shouted] for help *at the top of her voice* [*lungs*]. ‖ ありったけの力で綱を引っ張った I pulled the rope *with all my strength.*

ありとあらゆる every (possible) ▶ありとあらゆる手段を講じてみたが，無駄だった I tried *every possible* means, but in vain. ‖ 近年日本人はありとあらゆる国で暮らすようになった These days there are Japanese people living in (*just about*) *every* country. (➤ just about は「ほとんど」).

ありのまま ▶ありのままに言いますが，あなたの息子さんはいじめをしているとして訴えられています *To tell you the truth* [*To be quite frank with you*], your son has been accused of bullying. ‖ ありのままを言いなさい Tell *the plain truth*. ／Tell it *as* [*like*] *it is*. ‖ ありのままのきみが好きだよ I love you *as you are*.

アリバイ an alibi /ǽləbaɪ/ ▶アリバイをでっちあげる set up *an alibi* ‖ ぼくにはアリバイがある I have *an alibi*. ‖ 容疑者のアリバイが崩れた The suspect's *alibi* fell through. ‖ 彼女のアリバイはまだ立証されていない Her *alibi* has not been established [proven].

ありふれた common (ふつうの) ; ordinary (平凡な) ▶ありふれた病気 a *common* disease ‖ ありふれた服 an *ordinary* dress ‖ 昔はわらぶき屋根の家はありふれた光景だった In the old days, houses with thatched roofs were a *common* sight. ‖ 停電などその国じゃありふれたことだよ Power failures are *common* in that country.

ありもしない ▶ありもしない話 a *made-up* story (➤「作り話」の意) ‖ ありもしないことを言わないでよ Don't *make up stories*.

ありゅう 亜流 ▶その作家は漱石の亜流といわれる The author is said to *have imitated* (the style of) Soseki.

ありゅうさんガス 亜硫酸ガス sulfurous /sʌ́lfərəs/ acid gas.

[1]ある 有る·在る

> 📖 **訳語メニュー**
> 存在する →there is [are] **1**
> 所有する →have **3**
> 起こる，行われる →happen, take place **5**

1【物が存在する】there is [are] ▶うちの庭には何本かの桜の木がある *There are* several cherry trees in our garden. (➤ Our garden *has* several cherry trees. とか We *have* several cherry trees in our garden. のように，所有を表す have を用いて表現することもできる).

▶浦安は東京より東にある Urayasu *is* (to the) east of Tokyo. ‖ そこには池がある *There's* a pond there. (➤ 最後の there を落とさないこと) ‖ 松の木は日本中どこへ行ってもある Pine trees *can be found* everywhere in Japan. (➤ be found は「見られる」) ／We [You ／One] *can find* pine trees anywhere in Japan.

▶ドレスにはいろいろなサイズがある Dresses *come in* many sizes. ‖ 金はある所にはあるもんだ Money *gathers where* money *is*. ‖ **対話**「スイス製の時計はありますか」「はい，ございます」"Do you *have* [*sell* ／*carry*] any Swiss watches?" "Yes, we do." (➤ (1) Are [Is] there ...? とはいわない. (2) carry は「取り扱っている」の意).

▶《位置する》私たちの新キャンパスは海抜150メートルの所にある Our new campus *is* 150 meters above sea level. ‖ 皇居は東京の中心にある The Imperial Palace *is situated* [*is located*] in the heart of Tokyo. (➤ situated または located を略しても意味は同じ) ‖ その教会は市を見下ろす丘の上にある The church *is* [*stands*] on the top of a hill overlooking the city.

▶《存する》成功の鍵は努力するか否かにある The key to success *depends on* whether you work hard or not. ‖ ラベルによるこの編曲の魅力は卓越した管弦楽法にある The charm of this arrangement by Ravel *consists in* its excellent orchestration.

▶《慣用表現》彼女はおしゃべりで，あることないこと言い触らす She is a blabbermouth, and what she tells everybody is a mixture of *fact and fiction* [*truth and untruth*].

2【人が地位·境遇などにいる】 ▶彼は長く学長の要職にある He *has held* the important position of president of the university for a long time. ‖ その頃彼は委員長の地位にあった At that time, he *was* chairman. ／At that time, he *held* the position of chairman. ‖ 人は逆境にあるときその真価が現れる People show their true worth *in adversity*.

3【所有する，備える】have +㊐ ▶私には妻子がある I *have* a wife and children. (➤ 子供が1人のときは I have a wife and child. となる. child に a をつけない) ‖ お話ししたいことがあります I *have* something to talk to you about. ‖ 質問のある人は手を挙げてください Raise your hand if you *have* a question. ‖ ちょっとご相談があるんですが I would like to *have* a word with you. ‖ 何か知っておきたいことはあるかい？ *Is there* anything you want to know?

▶その事務室には南向きに窓がある The office *has* a window facing south. ‖ 彼は鼻のてっぺんに小さなほくろがある He *has* [*There is*] a small mole on the tip of his nose.

▶それぞれの民族には固有の文化がある Each people *has* its own culture. ‖ 恭子には男を夢中にさせる魅力がある Kyoko *has* a charm about her which can drive a man crazy.

4【数量を示す】 ▶その蛇は体長が2メートルある That snake *measures* two meters in length. ‖ ここから博多まであとどのくらいありますか *How far is it* from here to Hakata? (➤ 距離を聞く場合) ／*How long does it take* from here to Hakata? (➤ 時間を聞く場合) ‖ オリンピックまでまだ2か月ある The Olympic Games are *still two months away*. ／*There are still two months before* the Olympic Games begin. ‖ **対話**「あなたの家，まだなの？」「まだまだずいぶんあるよ」"Is your house very far from here?" "Yes, we still *have a long way to go*."

5【起こる】happen (偶然に) ; **take place** (予定の行事などが) ▶きょうサッカーの試合がある *There'll be* a soccer game today. ‖ あす息子の学校で運動会がある Tomorrow they *are having* sports day at my son's school. ‖ 運動会は本当にあるんですか *Is* our sports day definitely *on*? ‖ そのジャズコンサートはあすある The jazz concert *will be held* [*will take place*] tomorrow. ‖ きょう健康診断があった We *had* a physical examination today. ‖ 彼女がぼくをだましてるだなんて，そんなことあるもんか *There's no way* she could be cheating on me.

ことわざ 二度あることは三度ある What happens twice happens three times. (→二度).

6【「…ことがある」「…こともある」の形で】 ▶たまには外で夕食をとることもあります We *occasionally* eat out.

▶私は奈良を3回訪れたことがあります I *have visited* Nara three times. ‖ 富士山に登ったことはありません I*'ve never climbed* Mt. Fuji.

あ

【文型】
…することがありますか
Do you ever do？
…したことがありますか
Have you ever done？

▶あなたは孤独を感じることがありますか *Do you ever feel* lonely？‖歌舞伎を見たことがありますか *Have you ever seen* Kabuki？‖対話「北海道へ行ったことがありますか」「はい，あります」"*Have you ever been* to Hokkaido？" "Yes, I *have*."
7【「…とある」の形で】▶このマイクからの手紙には，彼は来月渡米するとある（＝と書いてある）In this letter Mike *wrote that* he's going to the States next month.
8【「…である」の形で】▶吾輩(わがはい)は猫である I *am* a cat.‖3＋5は8である Three plus five *is* eight.／Three and five *make* eight.
☛ ありうる，ありえない，ありがち，ありそう，あるべき，あるまじき（⇀見出語）

2**ある** 或る ▶ある女性 a *certain* woman（➤誰かわかっているが言及するのを避けるときの言い方）‖あるときあの男が突然やって来た That man suddenly showed up here *once before*.‖あるときは彼が来，あるときは彼の弟が来た *Sometimes* he came, and *at other times* his brother came [did].‖ある日涼子に道で出会った *One day* I ran into Ryoko on the street.‖ある意味であなたは正しい You are right *in a* [*one*] *sense*.‖次郎の言うこともある程度はわかる I can understand what Jiro says *to some extent*.‖対話「私が清さんとお付き合いしてるってどうしてわかったの？」「ある人が教えてくれたのよ」"How did you find out I have been going out with Kiyoshi？" "Ah, *a little bird told me*."（日本人が「ある人が教えてくれた，小耳に挟んだ」と考えるところを英語では A little bird told me.（小鳥が教えてくれた）と考える．秘密などの出どころを明らかにしないときの言い方．Ah, I have my sources. とか，Ah, I have my ways. のようにも言える）．
▶ある人たちは UFO を見たと言うし，ある人たちはそんなものはないと言う *Some people* claim that they have seen UFOs, and *others* say that there is no such thing.‖昔，ある所に貧しい漁師が妻と2人の娘と一緒に住んでいました *Once there lived* a poor fisherman with his wife and two daughters.

あるいは 或いは **1**【または】or ▶きみかあるいは小西君が行かなければならない *Either* you *or* Konishi has to go.（➤動詞の形は or のあとの主語に一致させる）．
2【ひょっとすると】▶あるいはあす雪が降るかもしれない *It is possible that* it may snow tomorrow.／*It just might* snow tomorrow.（➤後者のほうがインフォーマルな表現）‖あるいは事実かもしれない It *may* be a fact [what really happened].

アルカイダ Al Qaeda /æl káɪdə/（➤イスラム原理主義の過激派組織）．

あるがまま ▶あるがままの私を見てください Please try to see me *as I really am*.（➤実際に言うときは Look！It's me. とすることが多い）‖彼は厳しい現実をあるがまま受け入れた He accepted the harsh realities *as they were*.‖私は事実をあるがままに（＝あるがままの事実を）話した I told the *plain* truth.

アルカリ alkali /ǽlkəlaɪ/ ━形 アルカリの alkaline /ǽlkəlaɪn/ ▶この溶液はリトマスを青くするからアルカリ性だ This solution is *alkaline* because it turns litmus blue.
‖アルカリ性 alkalinity‖アルカリ性食品 alkaline food‖アルカリ性反応 alkaline reaction‖アルカリ電池 an alkaline battery [cell].

あるきスマホ 歩きスマホ using a smartphone [texting] while walking ▶歩きスマホは危険です It's dangerous to *use a smartphone while walking*.

あるきまわる 歩き回る walk around [about]；walk up and down（室内などを行ったり来たりする）；wander（当てもなく）▶公園周辺を歩き回る *walk around* (in) the park‖夜の街を歩き回る *wander* the streets at night‖部屋の中をそんなにのそのそ歩き回るなよ Don't *walk up and down* the room like that.
▶この休みに私はイングランドの田舎を歩き回った I *hiked around* the English countryside during the vacation.

あるく 歩く **1**【徒歩で行く】walk, go on foot（➤後者は堅い言い方で，徒歩で行くことを強調する）▶私は運動のために毎日2時間歩く I *walk* two hours a day for exercise.‖私はふつう歩いて学校[会社]へ行きます I usually *walk to school* [*work*].（➤「自転車で行く」「走って行く」なら動詞はそれぞれ cycle, run とする）‖きょうは1日歩き疲れた *I'm tired from walking* all day today.‖歩き方ですぐ彼とわかった I recognized him at once by his *walk*.
▶学校まで歩いて10分かかる It takes ten minutes to *go* to school *on* [*by*] *foot*.／It's a ten-minute *walk* to school.（➤後者のほうが日常的）‖ぼくのアパートは駅から歩いてほんの4分のところです My apartment is just a four-minute *walk* from the station.‖海岸を歩く *take a walk* along the beach.
▶ビルにはエレベーターがないので4階まで歩いて上がるしかない Since the building doesn't have an elevator, we have no choice but to *walk up to* the fourth floor.
2【比喩的】▶彼は長い間政界を歩いてきた人だ He *has been involved in* politics for years.（➤be involved in は「…に関わる」）‖父は20年技術畑を歩いてきた My father *has pursued a career as* an engineer for 20 years.‖父はこれまで真面目に人生を歩いてきた My father *has lived honestly* all his life [*has* always *lived honestly*].
▶投手は2人の打者を四球で歩かせた The pitcher *walked* two batters.

> 「歩く」のいろいろ 大股で歩く stride／軽やかに歩く walk lightly／すたすた歩く walk briskly／つま先で歩く tiptoe／どしんどしんと歩く stomp／とぼとぼ歩く plod／ふらふら歩く stagger／ぶらぶら歩く stroll／ふんぞり返って歩く swagger／よちよち歩く toddle

アルコール alcohol /ǽlkəhɔːl/；liquor, spirits（酒）▶今晩のパーティーはアルコール抜きだそうだ I hear that no *alcoholic drinks* will be served at the party tonight.
‖アルコール依存症 alcoholism‖アルコール使用障害 alcohol use disorder‖アルコールランプ a spirit lamp‖消毒用アルコール rubbing alcohol,《英》surgical spirit.

アルゴリズム《数学》an **algorithm**.

あるじ 主 a **master**（一般的に主人；女性は mistress）；a **landlord**（宿の主人・大家；女性は landlady）；a **host**（客をもてなす人；女性は hostess）▶ぼくもいつかは一国一城の主になってみせる I'll *be my own boss* some day.

アルジェリア Algeria /ældʒíəriə/.

アルゼンチン **Argentina** /ɑ̀ːʳdʒəntíːnə/
‖**アルゼンチン人** an Argentine /ɑ́ːʳdʒəntiːn/.

アルツハイマー アルツハイマー病 **Alzheimer's** /ɑ́ːltshaɪməʳz/ **(disease)** ▶アルツハイマー病になる develop *Alzheimer's* ‖その老人はアルツハイマーだった The elderly man had *Alzheimer's* (*disease*).

アルト《音楽》**alto**
‖**アルト歌手** an alto (singer) ‖**アルトサックス** an alto saxophone.

アルバイト a **part-time job**（仕事）; a **part-time worker**（人）▶パン屋でのアルバイトを見つける find *a part-time job* at a bakery ‖アルバイトをして（＝アルバイトで学資を稼いで）大学を出る *work one's way* through college ‖ことしの夏，中学生に英語を教えるアルバイトをした This summer I *found a job* teaching English to a junior high school student. ‖彼は毎土曜の夜，水泳のコーチのアルバイトをしている Every Saturday night he *moonlights* as a swimming coach.（➤ moonlight は「（本業のほかに）バイトをする」の意のインフォーマルな語）.
✉ **私は週２日ファーストフード店でアルバイトをしています** I *work part-time* at a fast-food restaurant twice a week.
‖**アルバイト学生** a working student.

> **危ないカタカナ語✹ アルバイト**
> **1** ドイツ語の *Arbeit*（仕事，研究）からきているが，英語としては使えない．
> **2** 日本語の「アルバイト」に近いのは part-time job や side job だが，日本語の「アルバイト」が「学生や勤め人が本業の勉強や勤めのかたわらする仕事」とか「臨時の仕事」といった意味で用いるのに対し，英語の part-time job や side job は「（正社員・店員の正規の労働時間が１日８時間・週５日制だとして）例えば１日４時間，週２日の割合で働くようなこと」をいうので，学生が夏休みや冬休みを利用して１か月間通して終日働くような場合に用いるのは不自然となる．したがって，そのような場合は，用例のようにさまざまな表現を併用するとよい．

ディベートルーム「**高校生は積極的にアルバイトをすべきだ**」

アルバニア **Albania** /ælbéɪmiə/
‖**アルバニア人** an Albanian.

アルバム an **album**, a **photo album** ▶その写真はアルバムに貼っておきなさい Stick [Paste] those pictures in the *album*.
▶ビヨンセのニューアルバムが出た Beyoncé's new *album* is out.
‖**記念アルバム** a commemorative album ‖**卒業アルバム** a yearbook.

アルファベット **the alphabet** /ǽlfəbet/（A から Z までの全体．A, B, C などの文字，1つ1つは alphabet でなく，letter という）▶英語のアルファベットはいくつあるか知ってる？ Do you know how many letters there are in the English *alphabet*?（➤ アルファベットは文字（letter）の集合体だから，how many alphabets とはしない）‖この棚の本はアルファベット順に並べてあります The arrangement of books on these shelves is *alphabetical*. ‖このパソコンは入力した単語をアルファベット順に並べ替える機能をもっている This computer has a function that arranges entered words *alphabetically* [*in alphabetical order*]. ／This computer has a function that *alphabetize* entered words.
《参考》alphabet には英語のそれの元になった，Roman [Latin] alphabet の他に，ギリシャ（Greek），キリル（Cyrillic），ヘブライ（Hebrew）などいくつかある．日本語のかなの50音図のような，１音節１文字の文字体系は syllabary という．

アルプス **the Alps** ▶冬のアルプスは特に美しい *The Alps* in winter are especially beautiful.
‖**日本アルプス** the Japan Alps.

あるべき ▶これが教育のあるべき姿なのです This is *as* education *should be*.

アルペン **Alpine** /ǽlpaɪn/
‖**アルペン種目** the Alpine events ‖**アルペンスキー** Alpine skiing（競技）; Alpine skis（スキー板）.

あるまじき ▶紳士にあるまじき態度 *ungentlemanly* behavior ‖それは学生にあるまじき行為だ Such conduct is *highly inappropriate* [*improper*] for students. ‖酒酔い運転などは警察官にあるまじき行為だ Drinking and driving is something a police officer *should never do*.

アルミ（ニウム）《米》**aluminum** /əlúːmɪnəm/,《英》**aluminium**
‖**アルミ缶** an aluminum can ‖**アルミサッシ** an aluminum sash ‖**アルミ製品** aluminum ware ‖**アルミホイル** aluminum foil.

1**あれ** **1**【遠くの物を指して】**that**［複 **those**］▶あれが私の家です *That* is my house. ‖あそこにあるあれは何ですか What's *that* over there? ‖あれをご覧なさい Look at *that* (*one*). ‖これが私の，あれがトムの絵です These are my drawings and *those* are Tom's.（➤ それぞれの絵は複数ある）.
▶《過去の時》あれから２か月して赤ん坊が生まれた A baby was born two months *after that*. ‖あれ以来，彼からは音沙汰がない *Since then* we haven't heard anything from him.
2【ぼかして】▶クルミを割るあれどこにある？ Where's *the thing* for cracking nutshells? ‖こんな所であれですけど，これ，今回のお礼です *This may not be the proper place*, but please accept this as a token of our appreciation. ‖あれぐらいのことで騒ぐんじゃない Don't make a fuss about a trivial thing *like that!*
☛ **あれで，あれでは，あれでも，あれほど，あれよあれよ**（→見出語）

2**あれ** ▶あれ，ぼくの傘がない (*Good*) *heavens!* My umbrella's gone.

あれきり ▶彼女からはあれきり何の音沙汰もない I haven't heard from her *since*.

あれくるう 荒れ狂う **rage, go on a rampage** ▶嵐は一日中荒れ狂った The storm *raged* all day. ‖彼は希望を失って荒れ狂った Losing all hope, he *went on a rampage*.

アレグロ《音楽》**allegro** /əlégroʊ/.

あれこれ ▶あれこれ考えてみたがそれがいちばんいい解決策だ I *considered a few options*, but that's the best solution. ‖あれこれやってみたけどだめだった I *tried one thing and another* but it was no good. ‖決まったことをあとになってあれこれ言うな Don't *grumble over* what's decided.

あれしき ▶あれしきのことで怒るなよ Don't get angry over *an unimportant thing like that*.

あれしょう 荒れ性 ▶彼女の肌は荒れ性だ She has *dry* skin.

あれだけ ▶あれだけ勉強したのに不合格だなんて After studying *so hard*, I never dreamed I'd fail.

あれち 荒れ地 **wasteland**;《英》**moors**（ヒースの茂る原

野）.

あれで ▶あれでよく社長が務まるね I wonder how he ever got to be a company president, *the way he acts.* ／(*Judging from the way he acts,*) I wonder how he ever got to be a company president. (➤発音するときは how のあとの he にアクセントを置き，あとは下降調) ‖ 彼はあれでなかなか味にうるさいんだ *Despite appearances* (*to the contrary*), he's pretty fussy about how food tastes. (➤「一見そんな風には見えないが」の意) ‖ あれで大卒かねえ *It's hard to believe* he's really a college graduate.

あれでは ▶健太郎が勉強をしているのは見たことがない．あれでは大学は受からないよ I don't think I've ever seen Kentaro studying. *At this rate*, he'll never make it to college.

あれでも ▶彼女は若く見えるけど，あれでも40歳なんだ She may look young, but she's *actually* 40.

あれの 荒れ野 a［the］**wilderness, the wilds.**

あれはてる 荒れ果てる go［**grow**］**wild ; fall into disrepair**（手の施しようがなくなる）▶庭は荒れ果てている The garden *has gone wild.* ‖ 持ち主が死んでからその家は荒れ果ててしまった Since the owner died, the house *has fallen into disrepair*［*has become dilapidated*］.

あれほど ▶ダイビングにあれほど（多く）金がかかるとは知らなかった I didn't think diving would cost *so*［*that*］*much.* ‖ 彼があれほど（うまく）英語が話せるとは思わなかった I didn't know he could speak English *so well.* ‖ あれほどの美人は見たことがないね I've never seen *such* a beautiful woman before. ‖ 対話「お母さん，私定期券なくしちゃった」「また？あれほど注意したのに」"Mom, I lost my commuter ticket." "Again? *You can't say I haven't warned you* (many times)." (🔴英語では「注意しなかったなんて言わないでよ」と発想する).

あれもよう 荒れ模様 stormy［**rough**］**weather** ▶その日は荒れ模様だったので我々は出発を延期した As *the weather was stormy*［*rough*］on that day, we put off our departure.

▶《比喩的》彼女はけさから荒れ模様だから気をつけたほうがいいぞ Watch out for her. She has been *in a nasty mood* since this morning.

あれやこれや one thing or another, this and that（➤語順に注意）▶あれやこれやで忙しくて彼と連絡をとる暇もなかった I was so busy *with one thing or another* that I had no time to contact him.

あれよあれよ ▶筑波は小さな村だったのがあれよあれよという間に近代都市へと様変わりしていった Tsukuba used to be a small village, but it grew into a modern city *overnight* [it became a modern city *in no time*]. (➤ overnight は「一夜にして」, in no time は「すぐに」の意).

あれる 荒れる

1【天候などが厳しい】be stormy ▶今夜は荒れるだろう It will *be stormy* tonight. ‖ 冬山は荒れることが多い There are frequent *storms* in the mountains in winter. ‖ 漁師は海が荒れても出かけなければならないことがある There are times when fishermen must go out in *stormy*［*rough*］*seas.*

2【行動が乱暴になる】go violent［**rowdy**］▶彼は酒を飲むと荒れる He *gets violent*［*rowdy*］when he drinks. ‖ 親の愛が欠けると青少年は荒れることが多くなる Young people often *misbehave* due to a lack of parental love. (➤ misbehave は「悪い行いをする」).

3【生活・精神などがすさむ】▶彼は妻に家出されてから生活が荒れた His life *became disordered*［*unsettled*］after his wife left him. ‖ この前の国会は相当荒れた The last session of the Diet *got out of control*［*got out of order*］.

4【土地・建物などが傷む】go to ruin ▶あの建物は荒れるに任せてある That building has been left to (*go to*) *ruin.* ‖ 庭が荒れている The garden *has run wild.* ／The garden *is ill kept*［*poorly maintained*］. (➤後者はいずれも「手入れが不十分だ」の意).

5【がさがさになる】become［**get**］**chapped** ▶唇が荒れている My lips *are chapped.* ‖ 冬は乾燥するので，すぐ肌が荒れる The winter is dry, so my skin is prone to *getting chapped.*

アレルギー (an) **allergy** /ǽlərdʒi/ 一形 **アレルギーの allergic** /əlɚ́ːrdʒɪk/ ▶何かアレルギーはありますか Do you have any *allergies*? ‖ 卵アレルギーの人は多い Lots of people are *allergic to eggs.* ‖ 母はアレルギー体質だ My mother has (*a tendency toward*) *allergies.*

▶《比喩的》核アレルギーは世界的な風潮だ *Nuclear allergy*［*Dislike of nuclear weapons*］is spreading throughout the world. ‖ あの人たちは警察アレルギーだ Those people have got *a police phobia.* (➤ phobia /fóʊbiə/ は「恐怖症」).

‖**アレルギー性疾患** an allergic disease ‖ **アレルギー反応** allergic reaction.

アレンジ (an) **arrangement** ▶次の会合の日程と場所のアレンジは私がやります I'll take care of *arranging* the date and place of the next meeting. ‖ このレシピは日本人の味覚に合うようにアレンジされています This recipe *has been adapted* to suit Japanese tastes. (➤ adapt は「…するように変える」).

アロエ an **aloe.**

アロハシャツ an **aloha shirt,** a **Hawaiian print**［**sport**］**shirt.**

[1]**あわ 泡 foam** /foʊm/（小さな泡の白い集まり）; **froth**（foam と交換可能な場合もあるが，特にビールや口元に生じる泡をいい，「はかなく消える」という比喩的イメージもある）; a **bubble**（大きな泡の１つ）; **lather** /lǽðər/, **suds**（特にせっけん［洗剤］の細かい泡；後者がより細かい）▶波頭にできる白い泡 white *foam* on the crest of a wave ‖ せっけんの泡 a soap *bubble* (➤シャボン玉；白い細かな泡の塊は lather または suds) ‖ このシャンプーはよく泡が立つ This shampoo makes a lot of *lather.* ‖ ビールの泡がコップからあふれた *The head on the beer* overflowed the glass. (➤ head はビールなどを注いだときコップの上にできる泡をいう).

▶《慣用表現》ぼくらは「あした試験だ」と言われて泡を食った We *were thrown into confusion*［We *got flustered*］when (we were) told, "There will be an exam tomorrow." ‖ 今にあいつに一泡吹かせてやるぞ I'll *get even with* him someday. (➤ get even with A は「A(人)に仕返しをする」).

☛ 泡立つ，泡立てる，水の泡（→見出語）

[2]**あわ 粟 millet.**

あわい 淡い light, pale（色が；後者がより薄い）; **faint**（かすかな）▶淡いブルー *light* blue ‖ ラベンダーは淡い紫色だ Lavender is (a) *pale* purple.

▶淡い期待を抱く cherish a *faint* hope ‖ それは私の淡い初恋でした It was my first, *fleeting* love. (➤ fleeting は「つかの間の」).

あわせ 袷 *awase* (**lined kimono**).

あわせて 合わせて・併せて 1【合計で】**in all, altogether**（みんなで）; **all told**（合計で）▶合わせて7000円になります It's 7,000 yen *altogether*. ‖ 学生数は3クラス合わせて100人だ The number of students in the three classes *totals* 100.（➤この total は「合計で…となる」の意の動詞）.
2【一緒に】▶ご家族のご健康と併せて事業の繁栄を心よりお祈りいたします I sincerely wish your family good health *and* wish you success in your business.

[1]あわせる 合わせる・併せる

訳語メニュー
ぴったり付ける →put ... together 1
合計する →add up 2
混ぜる →mix 3
調整する →adjust 4

1【ぴったり付ける】**put ... together** ▶両手を合わせる *put* one's hands *together*（➤「祈る」の意の「手を合わせる」は put one's hands [palms] together (in prayer)）‖ 紙の継ぎ目と継ぎ目を合わせてのりで貼る *align* the edges of the two sheets of paper and glue them together（➤ align /əláin/ は「まっすぐにそろえて並べる」）.
2【一緒にする】**add up**（合計する）; **work together**（協力する）▶上半期の売り上げと下半期の売り上げを合わせる *add up* the sales of the first and the second half of the year ‖ うちは夫婦の収入を合わせても月50万に満たない Even *combining* our incomes, my wife and I still do not make half a million yen a month.
▶洪水のあと, 何百人もの人が被災者を助けるために力を合わせた After the flood, hundreds of people *worked together* [*pitched in*] to help the victims.（➤ pitch in は「協力する」の意のインフォーマルな表現）‖ 力を合わせてこの問題の解決に当たりましょう Let's *work together* [*join forces*] to solve this problem. ‖ 私たちは声を合わせて歌った We sang *in chorus*. ‖《演奏家が》一度合わせてみましょう Let's *play it together* and see how it sounds.
3【混ぜる】**mix** +目 ▶黄色と青を合わせると緑になる If you *mix* yellow and blue, you'll get green.
4【一致させる】**fit** +目（ぴったり）; **set** +目, **adjust** +目（調整する）; **time** +目（タイミングを）; **check** +目（突き合わせる）▶ 対話「いつがいいですか」「私のほうはそちらのご都合に合わせますから, いつでも結構です」"When is it convenient for you?" "I can *adjust my schedule to yours* [I can *work around your schedule*], so any day will be fine with me."
▶目覚まし時計を6時に合わせる *set* an alarm clock for 6 o'clock ‖ きみの答えと本の後ろに出ている答えとを合わせてみなさい *Check* your answers *against* the answers in the back of the book.
5【適合させる】**fit** +目（ぴったり）; **match** +目（色・柄などを）▶カメラの焦点を合わせる *focus* a camera ‖ スーツは体型に合わせて買い換える必要がある You need to buy a new suit that *fits* your body shape. ‖ 彼女はいつもドレスに合わせて靴も買う Whenever she buys a dress, she buys shoes to *match* (the dress).
▶ピアノの曲に合わせて踊りなさい Dance *to* the music of the piano. ‖ あいつには適当に調子を合わせておけばいいんだよ Don't take him seriously. Just *play* [*go*] *along with* him. ‖ 来週もチャンネルを合わせてください Please *tune in* again next week.
6【慣用表現】▶こんな失敗をして彼に合わせる顔がない I'm (too) *ashamed to look* him *in the face* [*eye*] after such a big mistake.

[2]あわせる 会わせる・遭わせる 1【人に】▶きみのお姉さんに会わせてくれよ I'd like to *meet* your sister. ／Could you *introduce* me to your sister? ‖ 私は2人を会わせてやった I *brought* them *together*. ／I *arranged a meeting* between them.
2【災難に】▶覚えてろ, 今にひどい目に遭わせてやるから I'll *get even with* you. ／You *won't get away with this*.

あわただしい 慌ただしい **busy**（忙しい）; **hurried**（せきたてられた）▶きょうは慌ただしい一日だった I've had a *busy* day today. ‖ 階下で慌ただしい足音がするのが聞こえた I heard *hurried* footsteps downstairs. ‖ こんな慌ただしい東京暮らしなどもう飽き飽きだ I'm tired of the *fast* pace of life in Tokyo. ‖ 岩崎先生が慌ただしく教室へ入って来た Mr. Iwasaki *rushed* (*noisily*) *into* the classroom.

あわだつ 泡立つ **bubble**（ぶくぶくと）; **foam**（小気泡が集まる）; **lather**（せっけんが）▶このせっけんはよく泡立つ This soap *lathers* well. ‖ 泡立つ波が岸に寄せていた The *foaming* waves lapped (at) the shore. → 泡.

あわたてき 泡立て器 an (**egg**) **beater**（回転式の）, a **whisk**（針金を膨らませた形の）.

あわだてる 泡立てる **whip**（クリームや卵の白身などを急激に）; **beat**（卵などを勢いよくかき混ぜて）▶卵白を泡立てるにはふつう泡立て器を使う We usually use a whisk to *whip* egg whites (into froth).

あわてふためく 慌てふためく **panic** ▶火事のときは慌てふためいてはいけない In case of fire, don't *panic*. ‖ あんな小さな地震で慌てふためくんじゃなかった I shouldn't have *lost my head* over such a small earth tremor.（➤ lose one's head は「うろたえる」）.

あわてもの 慌て者 a **hasty person**（せっかちな人）; a **careless person**（不注意な人）; a **scatterbrain**（おっちょこちょい）▶サザエさんは慌て者の代表だ Sazae-san is a typical *scatterbrain*.

あわてる 慌てる

rush（急ぐ）; **panic, get into a panic**（慌てふためく）; **be confused**（まごつく）; **be upset**（落ち着きを失う）▶慌てるな *Don't rush*. ／*Don't get flustered*. ／*Take it easy*. ‖ 地震のときは慌てるな Don't *panic* in an earthquake. ‖ 先生が突然現れたのでぼくらは慌てた We *panicked* when our teacher suddenly showed up. ‖ 彼は定期券をなくして慌てた He *was upset* when he lost his commuter ticket.
▶慌てて昼食をとる eat lunch *on the run*（➤ on the run は「そそくさと」）‖ 財布を忘れたことに気づいて, 彼は慌てて家に引き返した He noticed that he had left his wallet at home, and went back for it *in a hurry*.（➤ in a hurry は「急いで」）‖ 私は慌てていて弁当を持って来るのを忘れた I *was in a hurry* and forgot to bring my lunch with me. ‖ 何を慌ててるの? *What's the rush?*
☞ 慌てふためく, 大慌て（→見出語）

あわてんぼう 慌てん坊 a **hasty** [**careless**] **person** ▶もう少しお待ちなさい. みんな慌てん坊ね! Just a minute! What *a hasty* [*careless*] *bunch* you are!（➤ bunch は「連中, 仲間」）.

あわない 合わない ▶役者なんて合わない商売ですよ You see, show business *doesn't pay*.（➤ pay は

金銭的に得になる場合にも, 精神的に報われる場合にも使える) ‖ 1時間働いて500円では**割に合わない** *It isn't worth it* to work for five hundred yen an hour. ‖ 手助けして文句を言われたのでは**合わない** *It's not worth* giving you a hand if you're going to complain.

あわび 鮑 《貝》 an **abalone** /æbəlóʊni/, an **ear shell** 《参考》 英米ではふつう生では食べず, ステーキ(abalone steak)にすることが多い.

あわや ▶イチローの当たりはあわやホームランかという大飛球だった Ichiro hit such a big fly ball that he *almost* made a home run. ‖ 彼女はあわやというときに助け出された She was (just) rescued *at the last moment*. ⇀危うく.

あわゆき 淡雪 ▶春の淡雪 *short-lived* [*-lasting*] *snow* in the spring.

あわよくば ▶あわよくば我々は優勝できるかもしれない We may win the championship *if all goes well*. (➤「万事順調にいけば」の意) ‖ 表向きの目標はメダル1個だが, あわよくば全種目入賞を狙っている The official goal of the team is to win one medal, but they*'re hoping* to win a prize in all the events.

あわれ 哀れな **sad** (悲しい) ; **miserable** (惨めな) ▶哀れな話 a *sad* story ‖ 哀れな死に方をする die a *miserable* death ‖ その男の人生は全く哀れなものであった That man's life has been sheer *misery*. ‖ 彼女はその老婆を哀れに思った She *felt compassion* [*sorry*] *for* the old woman. (➤ compassion は「助けてあげたいという同情の気持ち」).

あわれっぽい 哀れっぽい ▶その犬は子供たちに石を投げつけられ, 哀れっぽい声で鳴いた The dog *whined* [*yelped*] as the children threw stones at it.

あわれみ 哀れみ **pity** (哀れむこと) ; **compassion** (同情) ; **mercy** (慈悲の心) ▶哀れみ深い人 a *compassionate* [*merciful*] person ‖ 私は哀れみなどいらない I don't want *pity* [*compassion*]. ‖ その光景を見て哀れみの情が込み上げてきた Looking at the scene, I felt a rush of *pity*.

あわれむ 哀れむ **pity** +㊐, **take** [**have**] **pity** 《on》, **feel pity** 《for》 (かわいそうに思う) ; **sympathize** 《with》 (同情する) ; **have mercy** 《on》 (慈悲をかける) ▶漁師はカメを哀れんで海へ放してやった The fisherman *took pity on* the turtle and released it in the ocean. (➤ take pity on はかわいそうに思って行動を起こすときに用いる) ‖ 私は彼女の悲惨な境遇を哀れんだ I *felt pity for* her miserable situation.

▶《反語的に》 彼女が世の中は金がすべてだと本当に考えているのなら, 私は彼女を哀れむね I *pity* [*feel pity for*] her if she really thinks money is all that counts.

[1]**あん 案** **1** 【意見, 考え】 an **idea** ▶プレゼン能力を改善したいのですが, いい案はありませんか I want to improve my presentation skills. Do you have any good *ideas* [*suggestions*]?

2 【計画, 提案】 a **plan** (計画) ; a **proposal** (提案) ▶改革案 a reform *plan* ‖ 企画案 a project *proposal*, a *plan* ‖ 予算案 a budget *proposal* [*plan*] ‖ 案を具体化する give shape to *a plan* ‖ 案はできた. さあ実行だ We've made our *plans*. Now it's time to carry them out. ‖ 新しい公共図書館を造ろうという案が出された *A proposal* was advanced that a new public library should be built.

[2]**あん 餡** *an* ; **sweet bean paste**

日本紹介 ✉ **あんは小豆から作る甘いペースト状の食べ物で, 西洋のジャムに似たところがあります.「あんこ」ともいいます. 小豆を軟らかくなるまで煮て, 砂糖で甘く味付けします. この甘いペースト状のものは多くの和菓子に使われています** *An* is a sweet bean paste made from *azuki* beans, somewhat similar to jam in the West. Sometimes it is called '*anko*.' After being boiled until they are very soft, the beans are sweetened with sugar. This sweet paste is used in many Japanese sweets.

‖**あんパン** a bun stuffed with sweet bean paste.

あんい 安易な **easy** ▶安易な生活を送る lead an *easy* life ‖ 人生はきみが思うほど安易なものではないよ Life is not as *easy* as you think. ‖ 一部の若い人たちは安易に結婚をするようだ Some young people of today seem to marry *without thinking it over carefully* [*on impulse*]. (➤ think over は「…を熟考する」, on impulse は「衝動的に」) ‖ 海外留学を安易に考えてはいけない You shouldn't *take* studying overseas *lightly*. ‖ きみの考え方は安易すぎるよ Your (way of) thinking is *too easygoing*. (➤ easygoing は「のんきな」).

あんうん 暗雲 **dark clouds** ▶空に暗雲が垂れこめている *Dark clouds* hang low over the sky.

[1]**あんか 安価** a **low price** 一㊒ **安価な** **cheap** ; **inexpensive** (安い) ▶安価な模造品 a *cheap* imitation.

[2]**あんか 行火** a **foot warmer** (**used in bed**)

‖**電気あんか** an electric foot warmer.

アンカー an **anchor** /ǽŋkə^r/ (リレーの最終走者 ; ニュース番組の総合司会者) (➤ 性を区別して anchorman, anchorwoman ということもある) ▶アンカーにバトンを渡す pass the baton to the *anchor*.

あんがい 案外 **unexpectedly** (意外に) ; **surprisingly** (驚いたことに) ; **beyond** one's **expectation(s)** (予想以上に) ; **contrary to** one's **expectations** (予想に反して) ▶中間試験の結果は案外よかった The results of my midterm exams were *unexpectedly* [*surprisingly*] *good*. ／The results of the midterm exams were *better than* [were *not as bad as*] *I* (*had*) *expected*.

▶この本は案外(＝結構)おもしろかった This book was *fairly* interesting.

あんかん 安閑 ▶入試が1年後に迫ってきた. もう安閑としてはいられない The entrance exam is only a year away. I *cannot afford to just sit back and relax*.

あんき 暗記 **memorization** 一㊍ **暗記する** **memorize** +㊐, **learn ... by heart** ▶詩を暗記する *memorize* a poem ／*learn* a poem *by heart* ‖ 先生は私たちに教科書に出てくる各課のメーンの対話文を暗記させるのが好きだ Our teacher likes to *have* us *learn* the main dialogue of every lesson in the textbook *by heart*.

▶私は啄木の詩はほとんど暗記している I *know* most of Takuboku's poems *by heart*. ／I *have* most of Takuboku's poems *down* [《英》 *off*] *pat*. ‖ 彼の暗記力はすごい He has an extraordinary *memory*.

☛ 丸暗記 (⇀見出語)

あんぎゃ 行脚 **traveling on foot** ▶選挙応援で首相はまさに全国行脚だ The prime minister, who is campaigning for his party's candidates, is literally *going all over the country*.

あんぐり ▶彼女は口をあんぐり開けたまま突っ立っていた She stood *open-mouthed*. ／She stood *with her mouth agape*.

アングル an **angle**(角度)；a **point of view**(視点) ▶カメラアングル a camera *angle* ‖ この写真はアングルが悪い This photo was taken from the wrong *angle*. ‖ その事件はアングルを変えて見る必要がある That case needs to be examined *from a different angle*.

アングロサクソン an **Anglo-Saxon**(1人)；**the Anglo-Saxons**(全体).

アンケート a **questionnaire** /kwèstʃənéəʳ/

> **危ないカタカナ語✸ アンケート**
> 1 フランス語の *enquête* からきている.「調査」とか「質問」の意味で, 英語の inquiry と同類.
> 2「アンケート」に当たる英語は questionnaire で, 質問がリストになった調査用紙を指す.「世論調査」の意味なら opinion poll を使ってもよい.

▶アンケートに答える answer [fill in] *a questionnaire* (➤ fill in は「書き込む」) ‖ 我々は防衛問題について1000人の人にアンケートを求めた We sent out *questionnaires* on the defense issue to a thousand people.

あんけん 案件 an **issue**(問題)；an **item**(項目) ▶討議項目中の重要案件 an important *item* on the agenda.

あんこ 餡こ →餡(あん).

あんこう 鮟鱇《魚》an **angler(fish)**.

あんごう 暗号 a **code**, a **cipher** /sáɪfəʳ/；a **cryptogram** /kríptəgræm/(暗号文) ▶暗号電報を打つ send *a coded telegram* / telegram in code ‖ 暗号文を解読する decode *a cryptogram* / decipher (*a code*) ‖ その通信文は暗号で書かれていた The message was written *in code* [*cipher*].
‖暗号資産 cryptocurrency.

アンコール an **encore** /ɑ́ːnkɔːʳ ‖ ɔ́ŋkɔː/ ▶会場は「アンコール!」の声で満ちた The hall was filled with shouts of "*Encore!*" ‖ アンコールに応えて彼女は3曲歌った She sang three *encores*. ‖ 聴衆は何度もアンコールを求めた The audience called for *encores* over and over.

あんこく 暗黒 **dark, darkness**
‖暗黒街 the underworld；gangland ‖ 暗黒時代 a dark age.

あんさつ 暗殺 (an) **assassination** /əsæ̀sɪnéɪʃən/ 一動 **暗殺する assassinate** +目 ▶彼らは大統領を暗殺しようとたくらんだ They plotted to *assassinate* the President. / They planned an attempt on the President's life. (➤ attempt on ~'s life は「~(人)の暗殺計画」).
▶犬養毅は1932年に暗殺された Inukai Tsuyoshi *was assassinated* in 1932.
‖暗殺者 an assassin /əsǽsn/.

1**あんざん 安産** an **easy delivery** ▶彼女は安産で男の子を産んだ She had *an easy delivery*, giving birth to a (baby) boy. / Her son's birth was easy.

2**あんざん 暗算** **mental arithmetic** [**calculation**] ▶暗算をする do *mental arithmetic* / calculate in one's head ‖ 私は暗算で答えを出した I got the answer *using mental calculation* [*arithmetic*]. / I worked out the answer *in my head*.

アンサンブル 1【そろいの婦人服】an **ensemble** /ɑːnsɑ́ːmbəl/.
2【合奏・合唱(団)】an **ensemble**.

あんじ 暗示 a **hint**, (a) **suggestion** 一動 **暗示する hint** +目, **suggest** +目 ▶悲劇的結末を暗示する出来事 an incident that *suggests* a tragic ending ‖ 母は暗示にかかりやすい My mother is easily influenced by *suggestion*. / My mother is very suggestible.

あんしつ 暗室 a **darkroom**.

あんじゅう 安住する **settle down**(定住する)；**live in peace**(安心して住む) ▶ここを安住の地に決めました I chose this *place to settle down in*.

1**あんしょう 暗唱** **recitation** 一動 **暗唱する recite** +目；**memorize** +目(暗記する) ▶誰か「ゲティスバーグの演説」を暗唱できますか Can anyone *recite* the Gettysburg Address?

2**あんしょう 暗礁** a **(sunken) rock**(岩礁)；(a) **deadlock**(行き詰まり) ▶船は濃霧のため暗礁に乗り上げ真っ二つに割れた The ship *struck a (sunken) rock* [*a reef*] in a thick fog and broke in half.
▶《比喩的》交渉は暗礁に乗り上げた The negotiations *have come to* [*have reached*] *a deadlock*.

あんしょうばんごう 暗証番号 a **code number**, a **personal identification number**(➤ 略は PIN だが PIN number ともいう) ▶暗証番号を入力する enter one's *PIN* (*number*) ‖ 暗証番号を押してください Please enter [key in / input] your *PIN* (*number*).

あんじる 案じる 1【心配する】**worry**；**be concerned**(気がかりだ) ▶太郎君, お母さんがきみのことを案じておられるよ Your mother *is worried about* you, Taro. ‖ 父の健康状態を案じています *I'm concerned about* my father's health. ‖ ことわざ 案ずるより産むがやすし It's easier to tackle a task [to start working on solving a problem] (without delay) than worry about it.
✉ お母さまは手術後いかがお過ごしかと案じております I *am wondering* [*am anxious about*] how your mother is doing after the operation.
2【考える】▶彼女を招待するのに一計を案じた I *worked out a plan* to invite her.

あんしん 安心

security(安全が確保されていること)；**relief**(ほっとすること) ▶食の安全・安心を確保する ensure food safety and *security* (➤ relief (安ど)は用いない) ‖ 津波の危険が去ったことを知って大いに安心した I *was greatly relieved* to know that the danger of a tsunami had passed. / I learned *to my great relief* that the danger of a tsunami had passed. ‖ 老後の安心のために, 十分な貯金をしておきたいと思っています I'd like to save enough money for (financial) *security* after retirement [for my old age]. ‖ ここにいる限り安心していいよ You can *feel secure* [*feel safe*] as long as you stay here. ‖ 当ホームは24時間看護態勢をとっておりますので, 夜間も安心です Since we provide 24-hour nursing care, you can *feel secure* even during the night.
▶安心して(=信頼して)その仕事を私に任せなさい You can *trust* me to do the job. ‖ 末娘を結婚させるまでは安心できない I *can't afford to relax* until my youngest daughter is happily married off. ‖ そんなに安心してはだめだぞ. まだ試験に合格したわけではないのだから You *can't rest* [*take it easy*]. You haven't passed your exam(s) yet. ‖ 患者さんはもう安心ですよ(=危機を脱した) The patient *is now out of danger*.
✉ 報告書は年内に仕上げますのでどうぞご安心ください Please *rest assured* that I will finish the report this year. ➤ rest assured は堅い言い方.
☛ 一安心(→見出語)

あ

あんず 杏《植物》an **apricot** /éɪprɪkɑːt/ ▶アンズを砂糖漬けにする preserve *apricots* with sugar.
‖干しアンズ a dried apricot.

あんせい 安静 **rest** ▶安静にする *rest* [*lie*] *quietly* ‖医者は私に**絶対安静**を命じた The doctor has ordered me to have *complete* [*absolute*] *rest*.

あんぜん 安全 **safety**；**security**（危険から守られている状態）一形 **安全な safe**, **secure** ▶安全な旅 a *safe* trip ‖安全策をとる take *precautions* ‖列車で行くほうが安全だろう It would *be safer* to go by train. ‖東京は世界でも最も安全な大都会の１つだ Tokyo is one of *the safest* large cities in the world. ‖歩道橋は人が道路を安全に渡るためのものだ Pedestrian bridges are there so that you can cross the street *safely*. ‖警察には市民の身の安全を守る責任がある The police are responsible for the *security* of citizens. ‖安全装置が作動しなかった The *safety device* didn't work [function].
‖**安全委員会** a safety [security] committee ‖**安全運転** safe driving（➤標語として用いる場合は "Drive safely."）‖**安全衛生管理者** a safety and health supervisor ‖**安全かみそり** a safety razor ‖**安全規則** safety regulations；road safety rules（道路の）‖**安全週間** Safety Week ‖**安全装置** a safety device；a safety catch（銃の）‖**安全地帯** a safety zone；a safety island（道路中央の一段高くなった所）‖**安全ピン** a safety pin ‖**安全ベルト** a safety belt；a seat belt（座席の）‖**安全弁** a safety valve ‖**安全保障条約** a security treaty [pact].

あんそく 安息 ▶魂の安息 *the repose* of a soul.
‖**安息日** the Sabbath /sǽbəθ/（キリスト教・ユダヤ教の）；a [the] day of rest（休息日）.

あんた **you** ▶あんた, だあれ？Who are *you*? ‖あんたの知ったことじゃない It's none of your business. ／Mind your own business.

あんだ 安打 a **single**, a **base hit** ▶イチローは５打数３安打だった Ichiro *went three for five* (at the plate). ‖浅尾が好投して広島を４安打に抑えた Asao hurled a four-*hitter* against the Carp.

アンダーシャツ an **undershirt**,《英また》a **vest**.

アンダースロー an **underhand throw**（送球）；an **underhand pitch**（投手の）▶アンダースローで投げる throw [pitch] *underhand*（➤ pitch は投手の場合）‖アンダースローの投手 an *underhand* pitcher [hurler] ／a *submarine* pitcher.

アンダーライン an **underline** ▶私は特に大切な文章にはいつもアンダーラインを引きます I always *underline* particularly important passages. ‖アンダーラインの箇所を訳しなさい Translate the *underlined* parts.

あんたい 安泰 **peace**（平和）；**security** /sɪkjʊ́ərəṭi/（安全）▶社業が順調なので森氏の社長の座は安泰だ Business is smooth, so Mr. Mori's seat as company president is *secure*.

あんたん 暗澹たる **dark**；**gloomy**（悲観的な）▶わが社の将来は暗たんたるものだ The future of our company looks *gloomy*.

アンダンテ《音楽》**andante** /ɑːndɑ́ːnteɪ/.

あんち 安置 ▶仏像を本堂に安置する *place* a Buddhist statue in the main hall of a temple.

アンチ- ▶私はアンチジャイアンツです I always *root against the Giants*.

あんちゅうもさく 暗中模索 ▶ホテルの経営は初めてなので, いまだに暗中模索の状態です I am still *groping in the dark* since this is my first time running a hotel.

あんちょく 安直な **cheap**（安い）；**sloppy**, **lazy**（いい加減な）；**easy**（手間のかからない）▶パチンコは安直な娯楽だ Pachinko is a *cheap* pastime.（➤英語ではしばしば a mindless pastime（頭を使わない暇つぶし）と表現する）‖そんな安直なやり方を認めるわけにはいかない I cannot approve of such a *sloppy* [*lazy*] way of doing things.

あんちょこ a **crib**, a **pony**（虎の巻）▶あまりあんちょこに頼ってはいけない You shouldn't depend too much on *cribs*.

アンツーカー **all-weather**（➤日本語はフランス語の en-tout-cas /ɑ̀ːŋtuːkɑ́ː/（晴雨兼用の傘）から）▶アンツーカーのテニスコート an *all-weather* tennis court.

あんてい 安定 **stability**；**steadiness**（不変であること）一形 **安定した stable** /stéɪbəl/ 一動 **安定する stabilize** /stéɪbəlaɪz/ ▶このテーブルは安定していない This table is *unstable*. ‖彼は生活が安定している He *is leading a stable life*. ‖患者の病状は安定している The patient is in *stable* condition.
▶物価はかなり安定してきた Prices *have* pretty much *stabilized*. ‖雷雨のあとは天気は安定する（＝落ち着く）でしょう The weather should *settle* after the thunderstorm. ‖あの子は精神の安定を欠いているから興奮しやすい Since that child is mentally [emotionally] *unstable*, he [she] is easily excited.
☛ 不安定（→見出語）

アンティーク **antique** /æntíːk/ ▶アンティークのテーブル an *antique* table ‖アンティークの店 an *antique* shop.

アンデス **the Andes** /ǽndiːz/.

アンテナ《米》an **antenna**,《英》an **aerial**
‖**アンテナショップ** a pilot shop（➤「アンテナショップ」は和製語）‖**パラボラアンテナ** a parabolic antenna, a dish（➤後者はその形状に由来する日常語）.

あんど 安堵 **relief** /rɪlíːf/；**peace of mind**（心の平穏）一動 **安どする feel relieved** ▶安どのため息をつく give *a sigh of relief* ‖母はいかにも安どしたようにため息をついた My mother sighed *as though a great weight had been lifted* from her [from her shoulders].

あんどん 行灯 a **wood-framed paper lantern**.

あんな **like that**（あのように；あのような）▶あんな思いはもう二度としたくないね I don't ever want to have an experience *like that* again. ‖ぼくはあんなきれいな人は見たことがない I have never seen *such* a beautiful woman before.
▶私, あんな（タイプの）人たち嫌いだわ I don't like *that kind* [*sort*] *of* people. ／I don't like people *of that kind*. ‖あんなに驚いたことはない I have never been *so* surprised (before).

あんない 案内 **1**【導くこと】**guidance** /gáɪdns/ 一動 **案内する show** ＋目；**lead** ＋目（先に立って連れて行く）；**guide** ＋目（自分のよく知っている場所へ）

> **【文型】**
> 人(A)を場所(B)へ案内する
> show A to B
> 人(A)を(場所(B)の中を)案内する
> show A around (B)

▶この方を職員室へご案内してください Please *show* this gentleman (the way) *to* the teachers' room. ／Please *take* this gentleman *to* the

teachers' room.
▶博覧会場の中をご案内いたします Let me *show* you *around* the exhibition. ‖ キャンパス［家の中］を案内するよ I'll *show* you *around* the campus［the house］. ／I'll *give* you *a tour of* the campus［the house］. (➤ give ... a tour of の場合, 個人の家なら大邸宅を連想させる).
▶《レストランで店員が客に》ご案内するまでお待ちください Please wait *while we find you a table*. (➤ 掲示なら Please wait to be seated.) ‖ 係の人が私を席まで案内してくれた The usher *led* me to my seat. (➤ led は lead の過去形).
✉ **日本にいらっしゃったときは松江の町をご案内いたします** When you come to Japan, I'll *show you around* the city of Matsue.
2【招待】
✉ **令和３年11月23日, 娘昌子の結婚式にご参列くださいますようご案内申し上げます** We request your presence at the marriage of our daughter Masako on November 23, 2021. ➤ 英語で書くときには年号は西暦に書き換えるのがふつう.
3【通知】▶《店内アナウンス》お客さまにご案内申し上げます May I have your attention, please?
4【取り次ぎ】▶受付で案内を請うた I asked the receptionist to *show me the way*.
‖**案内係** a guide ; a bellhop (ホテルのボーイ) ; an usher /ʌ́ʃəʳ/ (劇場・教会・映画館の) ‖ **案内書** a guide(手引) ; a guidebook(ガイドブック) ; a handbook(職業教育用などの) ‖ **案内所** an information desk (デパートの ; 屋外にあるものは information booth という) ‖ **案内状** an invitation, an invitation card［letter］ ‖ **案内図** a guide map ; a guideboard (特に案内板) ‖ **案内人** a guide.
☛ **不案内** (→見出語)

あんに 暗に ▶彼は暗に(＝間接的に)賄賂を要求した He *indirectly* asked for a bribe. ‖ その閣僚は暗に辞意をにおわせた The cabinet minister *hinted at* his resignation. ‖ 条約には相互防衛が暗に含まれている Mutual defense is *implicit* in the treaty. (➤ implicit は「…に暗に含まれる」の意の形容詞).

あんにんどうふ 杏仁豆腐 almond jelly, almond pudding.

あんのじょう 案の定 as one expected［feared］(● よくないことが起こったことを明確にしたいときは feared を用いるほうがよい) ▶案の定ホテルは満員で泊まれなかった *As we had feared*, the hotel was fully booked and we couldn't get a room. ‖ 案の定あいつも伸子さんの誕生日パーティーにやって来た *Sure enough*, he showed up at Nobuko's birthday party. (➤ sure enough はインフォーマルな言い方) ‖ 案の定(＝予想通り), 彼はきょうも遅刻して出社して来た *As I expected*, he came to the office late today, too.

あんば 鞍馬 a side horse, 《英》 a pommel horse (器具) ; the side horse, 《英》 the pommel horse (競技種目).

あんばい 塩梅 ▶いいあんばいにバスが来てコンサートに間に合った *Luckily*［*As luck would have it*］, a bus came and I was just in time for the concert.

アンパイア an umpire /ʌ́mpaɪəʳ/ ▶野球の試合のアンパイアをする *umpire* a baseball game.

アンバランス (an) imbalance ▶貿易のアンバランス a trade *imbalance* ‖ まもなく人口と食糧のアンバランスが生じるだろう An *imbalance* between population and food will soon arise.

> **危ないカタカナ語✸ アンバランス**
> 英語の unbalance は名詞の形で用いることは少なく, unbalanced mind(取り乱した心)のように形容詞として用いることが多い. 名詞としてはimbalanceがふつう.

あんぴ 安否 safety(安全) ▶乗組員の安否が気遣われます There is great anxiety about the *safety* of the crew members.

あんぷ 暗譜する memorize a piece of music ▶暗譜でソナタを弾く play a sonata *from memory*.

アンプ an amplifier.

あんぶん 案分 ▶働きに応じて, もうけを案分する *divide* the profit (s) *in proportion* to each person's contribution.

アンペア an ampere /ǽmpɪəʳ/ ▶30アンペアの電流 a current of 30 *amperes*.

あんまり ▶あんまりスピードを出さないでくれ Don't drive *too* fast. →余(あま)り.
▶そりゃあんまりだ(＝ひどすぎる)! *That's too much!* ／ *That's going too far!*

あんみつ 餡蜜 *anmitsu* ; a fruit cocktail with gelatin cubes and sweet azuki［adzuki］paste (➤ 説明的な訳).

あんみん 安眠 a sound sleep ▶私は部屋が暗くないと安眠できない I *can't sleep well* if the room isn't dark. ‖ 兄のいびきは安眠妨害だ My (older) brother's snoring *disturbs my sleep*.

あんもく 暗黙の tacit /tǽsɪt/ (ことばに表さない, 無言の) ; implicit(暗に意味された) ▶彼は彼女が何も言わないのを暗黙の同意だと誤解した He mistook her silence for *tacit* consent. ‖ 2人の間には何か暗黙の了解があったに違いない There must have been some *tacit* understanding［agreement］between the two. ‖ 彼の提案は暗黙のうちに委員会に受け入れられた His proposal was *implicitly* accepted by the committee.

アンモニア ammonia /əmóʊniə/
‖**アンモニア水** ammonia water, ammonia solution.

あんやく 暗躍する act behind the scenes ▶(会社の)乗っ取りにX氏が暗躍したと言われている Mr. X is said to *have been behind the scenes* of the takeover.

あんよ ▶あらあら, あんよが汚くなったわよ Look, your *feet* have gotten all dirty! ‖ あんよが上手! Now you can *walk* quite well!

あんらく 安楽 comfort ━ 形 **安楽な** comfortable /kʌ́mfəʳṭəbəl/ ▶人生は安楽なことばかりではない Life is not *a bed of roses*. ／Life is not *all roses*. (➤ ともに「人生は楽しいことばかりではない」の意の決まり文句) ‖ 祖父母は田舎で安楽な日々を送っている My grandparents live *in comfort* in the country.
‖**安楽椅子** an easy chair.

あんらくし 安楽死 euthanasia /jùːθənéɪʒə/, mercy killing 《参考》「医師が患者に死に至る薬を与えて, 手助けする自殺」という意味で doctor-［physician-］assisted suicide とも呼ばれる. ▶彼は傷ついたその犬を獣医に頼んで安楽死させてやった He got a vet to *put* the injured dog *painlessly to sleep*［*put* the injured dog *out of his misery*］. (➤ put the dog down と言ってもよい) ‖ 安楽死も植物状態で生きるのも嫌だ. 自然な死に方がいい I don't want either *euthanasia* or to be kept alive in a vegetative state. I want to die naturally.
ディベートルーム 「安楽死は人間の正当な権利である」

い・イ

[1]い 胃 **the stomach** /stʌ́mək/ ▶胃が痛い I *have a pain in my* [*the*] *stomach*. ／I *have* (*a*) *stomachache*. (➤ a を省略するのは主に《英》) ‖ 昼に食べた物がまだ胃にもたれている The food I had for lunch still lies heavy on my *stomach*. ‖ しばらく胃の具合が悪かった I *have had stomach trouble* for some time. ‖ 私は胃が丈夫だ［弱い］ I *have strong* [*poor*] *digestion*. ／I *have a strong* [*poor*] *digestive system*. (➤「消化力が強い［弱い］」と表現する. a strong stomach とすると「血などグロテスクなものを平気で見聞きできる, 肝がすわっている」の意になる).

☛ 胃炎, 胃潰瘍, 胃カメラ (→見出語)

[2]い 意 ▶今度の部長は何でも自分の意のままになると思っている Our new general manager thinks he *can have everything his own way*. (●「意のままになる」は「思いどおりになる」ということだから, その相当句 can have everything one's own way を用いるとよい) ‖ 彼女は人の言うことなど意に介さない She does*n't care* [does*n't pay attention to* ／ does*n't worry about*] what people say (about her). ／She *disregards* what people say (about her). ‖ 社長の意を受けて(＝要請で), 我々はその会社の買収に乗り出した *As requested by* our company president, we launched an attempt to buy out the company. ‖ 私は意を決して受診した I *made up my mind* and saw a doctor. ‖ 先生のことばに私は意を強くした(＝励まされた) I *was encouraged by* my teacher's words. ‖ 陶芸家は, 意にかなう作品はなかなかできません, と言った The ceramist told me that he could rarely produce *a piece that satisfied him*. ‖ 彼女は意に染まぬ結婚を強いられた She was forced to marry *against her will*. ‖ 私は意に反することはしたくない I don't want to do anything *against my will*. ‖ 教祖は信者を意のままに操った The cult leader manipulated his believers *as he pleased*. ‖ この論文を読みながら「わが意を得たり」と感じた As I read this thesis, I thought *it expressed exactly how I feel*. ことわざ 読書百遍意おのずから通ず Reading something a hundred times makes the meaning understood. (➤直訳) ／ Repeated reading makes the meaning clearer.

[3]い 異 ▶理事長の決定に異を唱える者など誰もいない Nobody will *raise an objection* to what the chairman of the board of trustees decides.

[4]い 井 a well(井戸) ▶ ことわざ 井の中のかわず大海を知らず A frog in the well doesn't know the ocean. (➤日本語からの直訳. 英語には「井の中のかわず(カエル)」に当たる言い方に a big fish in a small pond (小池の大魚；小さな組織で大物ぶっている人)がある).

☛ 井の中のかわず (→見出語)

[5]い 医 **medicine** ▶ ことわざ 医は仁術 Medicine is a benevolent art.

-い -位 **1**【順位】▶第 1 位になる take [win] *first* (*place*) ／rank *first* ‖ 第 2 位に上がる［下がる］ go [drop] to *second* (*place*) ／move up [down] to *second* ‖ ぼくは1500メートル競走で第 2 位になった I finished the 1,500-meter race in *second place*. ‖ ぼくたちのチームはそのレースで 3 位だった Our team came in *third* in that race.

2【位取り】▶小数第 3 位まで計算しなさい Calculate to *three decimal places*.

いあつ 威圧 **coercion** /koʊə́ːʃən/ 一動 威圧する **coerce** ＋目 ▶威圧的な態度をとる assume a *coercive* [*overbearing*] attitude ‖ 大学の講堂は何となく威圧感があって, 私はあまり好きではない I don't like university auditoriums so much because they have a somewhat *intimidating atmosphere*.

いあわせる 居合わせる ▶私たちは犯行［事故］の現場に居合わせた We *happened to be at* the scene of the crime [the accident]. ‖ 居合わせた人々は皆協力して椅子を図書室に運び込んだ *Everyone there* [*present*] helped to carry the chairs into the library.

いあん 慰安 ‖(会社の) 慰安旅行 a company-sponsored trip for employees《参考》英米では主に販売員や目標を達成した優秀な人を対象に行われる.

いい →よい

> 訳語メニュー
> 良い →good, nice **1, 2, 3**
> 適当な →right **4**
> 善良な →good-natured **5**
> すばらしい →wonderful **6**
> 十分な →enough **7**

1【程度が優れている】**good, nice** ▶テストでいい点を取る get a *good* grade [a *high* score] on the test ／ do well on the test ‖ 井上先生はいい先生だ Mr. Inoue is a *good* [*nice*] teacher. (● 力量[技量]の良さをいう場合は good を, 人格の良さをいう場合は nice をそれぞれ用いることが多い) ‖ ドラゴンズにはいいピッチャーがそろっている The Dragons have *strong* pitchers. ‖ 彼は本当に頭がいい He is really *smart*. ‖ 山本医師は腕がいいと評判だ Dr. Yamamoto is known for *his skill*. ‖ 彼女は目がいいから遠くの看板でもよく読める She has *good eyesight*, so she can read signs from far away.

2【好ましい】**good** ▶そこが市川君のいいところだ That's the *good* thing about Ichikawa. ‖ 彼女にもやはりいいところはある There's some *good* in her after all. (➤この good は「美点」の意の名詞) ‖ 温泉でのんびりするのは本当にいい気分だ I really *enjoy* relaxing at a hot spring. ／It *feels great* to take it easy at a hot spring. ‖ 対話「いい天気ですねえ」「ほんとに」 "*Nice* day, isn't it ?" "Yes, isn't it." (➤応答は Yes, it's beautiful ! ／It really [sure] is ! などでもよい. Yes, it is. と答えるより温かみが感じられる).

3【有益な】**good** ▶ジョギングは健康にいい Jogging is *good* for the health. ‖ 試験の前には 2, 3 回深呼吸するといいよ. 落ち着くから It is *good* to take a couple of deep breaths before taking an exam. It helps you calm down. ‖ 地下鉄でロンドン市内の観光をするなら路線図を手に入れるといい If you're going to go sightseeing in London by subway, it will be *helpful* to get a route map. ‖ 酢は高血圧にいい(＝効く)という人もいる Some people say vinegar is

effective against high blood pressure.
4【適当な】right ▶いい人が見つかったら早く結婚しなさいよ If you find the *right* man, marry him quickly.（●「いい人」が女性なら man を woman に，him を her にする；→いい人）‖きみはちょうどいい時に来てくれた You came just at the *right* time. ‖高尾山は初心者にはいい山だ Mt. Takao is *good* for beginner mountaineers. ‖このカフェテリアは高校生にちょうどいい This cafeteria is (really) *ideal* for high school students. ‖ここから新宿へ出るにはタクシーがいい To get to Shinjuku from here, it's *best* to take a taxi. ‖私は今こんなことをしていていいのだろうか I wonder if it's *okay* for me to be doing (something like) this (right) now. ‖対話「お城へ行くにはこのバスでいいですか」「いや，10番のバスです」"Does this bus go to the castle ?" "No, you should take the No. 10 bus." ‖対話「東北新幹線に乗るには何番線へ行けばいいですか」「22番または23番線です」"Which track *should* I go to to get on the Tohoku Shinkansen ?" "That will be track 22 or 23."
5【善良な，優しい】good-natured ▶正雄君はとてもいい(＝優しい)人よ Masao is really *good-natured*.／Masao is a really *nice* guy. ‖由美子はいい(＝親切な)子だ Yumiko is a *kind-hearted* girl.
6【すてきだ，すばらしい】wonderful ▶富士山頂からの眺めはとてもいい The view from the top of Mt. Fuji is *wonderful*. ‖このユリは香りがいい This lily *smells good*. ‖この自動車は乗り心地がいい This car *is comfortable*. ‖姉は声がいい My (older) sister has a *good* voice. ‖真吾っていい男(＝美男子)だね Shingo is really *handsome*, isn't he ?（➤ 性格や感じがいいならば nice）‖課長の奥さんはいい所のお嬢さんだったそうだ I hear that the section chief's wife came from *a good family*.
▶ 対話「生まれて初めて京都に行くんだ」「それはいいね」"I'm going to Kyoto for the first time in my life." "*That sounds great*." ‖対話「あしたプールに泳ぎに行こう」「いいね」"Let's go for a swim in the pool tomorrow." "*OK.*／*Yeah, let's*." ‖対話「あのレストランで昼食をとろう」「いいね」"How about having lunch at that restaurant ?" "*Why not ?*" ‖対話「この時計20万もしたんだよ」「ずいぶんいい値段ね」"This watch cost me 200,000 yen." "Really ? That's *quite a price to pay* (for a watch)."
7【十分な】enough ▶それだけ言えばもういいじゃないですか Don't you think you've (already) said *enough* ? ‖《レストランで》ハムだけでいいです．卵はいりません *Just* ham, please. I don't want an egg [eggs]. ‖対話《隠れんぼで》「もういいかい？」「まあだだよ！」"*Ready* (*or not*) ?" "No ! Not yet !"（➤「もういいよ」は "Ready !"）.
8【いらない，不必要】 ▶コーヒーには砂糖を入れてくれ．クリームはいい I'd like sugar in my coffee but *no* cream. ‖きみはもういい．クビだ We do*n't need* you *any more*. You are fired. ‖《飲み屋で勘定を払うとき》いいから，いいから．ここはぼくが持つよ *Don't worry about it*. Let me pick this up. ‖対話「この本，貸してあげようか」「いいよ，持ってるもの」"Would you like to borrow this book ?" "*No, thanks*. I have my own copy."

【文型】
…しなくていい
don't have to do
don't need to do
➤ don't have to は拘束力に，don't need to は必要性に力点がある

▶（ここは）靴を脱がなくていい You do*n't have to* [do*n't need to*] take your shoes off. ‖きみは謝らなくていい You do*n't have to* apologize. ‖きょうは傘を持っていかなくていい I do*n't need to* bring my umbrella today.
9【許可，許容，承諾】
▶今度の英語のテストでは辞書を使ってもいいことにする You *can* use your dictionaries during the next English quiz. ‖何ならきみの代わりに会議に出てもいいですよ Well, I *could* go to the meeting in your place [for you].

【文型】
…してもいいですか
May I do … ?
Can I do … ?

《解説》(1) may は「…してもよろしいですか」に当たる，目上の人などに許可を得るときの改まった言い方．返事も，Yes, you may. は「よろしい」という感じ．
(2) can は「…してもいい」に当たる，よりくだけた日常的な言い方．家族や友人との間では主にこちらを用いる．返事の「いいよ」は Sure. や Go ahead.
(3)「…してもかまわないですか」に当たる言い方には Do you mind if … ? や I wonder if … . がある．

▶クレジットカードで支払っていいですか *Can I* pay by credit (card) ? ‖対話「あなたの車，運転していい？」「いいわよ」"*May I* [*Is it all right if I*] drive your car ?" "*Sure*."（➤ Is it … ? の形には疑念の気持ちがある）‖対話「お母さん，冷蔵庫のビール飲んでいい？」「何言ってるの．あんたまだ高校生よ」"Mom, *can I* have some of the beer in the refrigerator ?" "Of course not. You're still a high school student."
▶ 対話「この花瓶に触ってもいいでしょうか」「いいですよ」"*I wonder if I could* touch this vase." "*Certainly*." ‖対話「たばこ吸ってもいいですか」「かまいません」"*Do you mind if* I smoke ?" "Not at all."（➤ 遠慮してもらいたいときには I'd rather you didn't. という）‖対話「ひとつ頼みを聞いてくれないか」「いいよ，何だい」"Could you do me a favor ?" "*Sure*. What is it ?" ‖対話「来週ぼくんちへ来てくれるかい？」「いいとも！」"Can you come over next week ?" "*Sure thing !*／*Sounds great !*"（➤ Sure thing！は All right！の意のインフォーマルな言い方）‖対話「この手紙を投かんしてください」「いいですとも」"Would you mind mailing this letter ?" "*No, of course not.*／*No problem*." ‖対話「手を貸してくれませんか」「いいですよ」"I wonder if you could lend me a hand." "*With pleasure.*／*Certainly*." ‖対話「どんなはさみが必要ですか」「どんなのでもいいよ」"What kind of scissors would you like to use ?" "*Any* (scissors) *will do*."（➤ will do は「用が足りる」）‖対話「お礼の申しようもありません」「いいんですよ」"I don't know how to thank you." "*Don't worry about it*."
10【願望，羨む】

【文型】
～だといいのだが
I hope (**that**) S + V.
I wish (**that**) S + V.

《解説》(1)I hope は実現可能なことを「そうなるとい

い

いと思う」の意．あとの動詞は未来形または現在形．
(2)I wish は実現の難しい，または現実とは逆の状況を「…だといいのに」という気持ちで表す．あとの動詞は仮定法になり，現在と未来のことは過去形で，「…だとよかったのに」は過去完了形で表す．

▶阪神が勝てば**いいなあ** *I hope* the Tigers (will) win. ‖ 両親がいつまでも元気でいてくれる**といいのだが** *I hope* my parents stay healthy for a long time. (➤ (×)I wish my parents stay healthy. としないこと) ‖ 少しでもお役に立てる**といいのですが** *I hope* I can be of some help for you. ‖ おやじが新車を買ってくれる**といいんだけど** *I wish* my father *would* buy me a new car. (💰 実現しそうもない願望を表す場合，仮定法(この場合は would)を伴った I wish を用いる) ‖ あの歌手と握手ができ**たらいいのになあ**！*How I wish* I could shake hands with that singer！‖ 対話「雨は上がると思いますか」「**そうだといいですね**」“Do you think it'll stop raining？” “*I sure hope so*.”

▶入試なんてなければ**いいのに** *If only* we had no entrance exams！(➤ If only ... は通例あとに仮定法がくる) ‖ きみは友だちがたくさんいて**いいなあ**（＝羨ましい）*I envy you* because you have so many friends. ‖ 対話「うちの会社は有給休暇が年間40日もあるんだよ」「**いいなあ**」“Our company gives us 40 days of paid vacation a year.” “*Lucky you！／Wow, you're lucky！／I envy you*.”

11【好む】▶飲み物は何が**いい**ですか *What would you like* to drink？‖ ドレッシングはブルーチーズよりサウザンドアイランドが**いい** As for (salad) dressing, I *prefer* Thousand Island *to* blue cheese. (➤ prefer A to B で「B よりAを好む」) ‖ ぼくは週末はサーフィンに行くより家でごろごろしている**ほうがいい** I'*d rather* lie around at home on the weekend *than* go surfing. (➤ would rather A than B で「B よりもむしろ A をしたい」) ‖ 対話「どのネクタイになさいますか」「これが**いいな**」“Which tie would you like？” “I *like* [I'll *take*] this one.” (➤ take は「買う」の意).

12【忠告，勧め】

【文型】
(あなたは)…するほうがいい
You **should** do.
It's better (for you) **to** do.
You **had better** do.

【解説】(1)should do は1つの提案として，「…するのがよい」「…すべきだ」と勧めるのに用いる．ことばの感じがやわらかく，年上の人や目上の人に用いても失礼にならない．
(2)It's better to do はもう1つの選択肢と比較して，「…するほうがよりよい」を意味する．It **would be** better for you to do とすると相手に助言するときに用いられる丁寧な表現になる．
(3)had better do は「…しないと困った事態になるよ」の意味で，軽い命令や忠告を表す．ときには脅迫の含みをもつこともある．

▶医者に診てもらった**ほうがいい** You *should* see a doctor. ‖ 気をつけた**ほうがいい** You *should* be careful. (➤ You'd better be careful. は「さもないと困ったことになるよ」の含み) ‖ どうしたら**いい**かおわかりでしょう You know what you *should* do. ‖ たばこは吸わない**ほうがいい** You *shouldn't* smoke. ‖ 買うより借りる**ほうがいい** *It's better to* rent than buy. ‖ このまま放っておく**ほうがたぶんいい** *It's* probably *better to* leave it as it is. ‖ きみたちはまだ18歳だろ？ 結婚は2，3年待った**ほうがいいよ** You're both still eighteen, right？ *It would be better* for you *to* wait a couple of years before getting married. ‖ 急いだ**ほうがいい** You'*d better* hurry. (➤「急がないと間に合わないよ」の意) ‖ きみは行かない**ほうがいいよ** You'*d better not* go. (➤ (×)You'd not better ... としない).

13【当然】▶長い日照りが続いたのだからもう雨が降っても**いい頃だ** After such a long dry spell, *it is* (*about*) *time* it rained. (➤ It is (about) time のあとの文中の動詞は通例過去形) ‖ きみは6年間も英語を学んでいるのだから，簡単な英語の手紙くらい書けても**いいはずだ** You've been studying English for six years, so you *ought to* be able to write a simple letter in English by now.

14【念を押す】▶**いいか**，これが最後だぞ *Look now*, this is (going to be) the last time. ‖ **いいか**，覚えてろよ *Now* get that into your head！‖ 金を貸すのはこれっきりだよ．**いいね** This will be the last time that I ever lend you (any) money. *Is that clear？* (➤「はっきりわかっているか」の意).

☛ **いい気，いい気味，いい子，いいことに，いい線，いい年，いい人，いい目**（→見出語）

いいあい 言い合い an **argument**, a **quarrel** (➤ ともに「口論」のことだが，しばしば前者が高じて後者に発展する)；a **spat**, a **tiff**（夫婦・友人間などのささいな）
▶どのテレビ番組を見るかで弟と**言い合い**をした I *had an argument* with my (younger) brother over which TV program to watch. ‖ ゆうべ2人はちょっとした**言い合い**をした Last night they *had a* small *fight* [*argument*／*quarrel*].

いいあう 言い合う **argue**《with》, **quarrel**《with》▶**言い合う**のはやめてお願いしてることやってよ Stop *arguing* and do as I ask. ‖ 私の大学進学のことで両親は毎晩のように**言い合っている** My parents *quarrel* almost every evening over whether I should go to college. (➤「行くか行かないかで」の意．「どこの大学へ行くか」なら whether を where にする).

いいあてる 言い当てる **guess right** ▶彼はそのスーツケースの重量を見当をつけてうまく**言い当てた** He guessed the weight of the suitcase, and he *guessed right*.／He *correctly guessed* the weight of the suitcase. ‖ 一郎はすぐさま答えを**言い当てた** Ichiro promptly *guessed the right answer*.

いいあらそい 言い争い an **argument**, a **quarrel**
▶何で**言い争い**になったの？ What started the *argument* [*quarrel*]？‖ もう**言い争い**はやめよう Let's stop *arguing*. ‖ 2人の**言い争い**はその女性を巡ってのものだった The *quarrel* between the two (men) was over the woman. ‖ あの2人はよく**言い争い**をする Those two men often *exchange sharp words* (*with* each other).／Those two *are* always *snapping at each other*.

いいあらそう 言い争う **argue**, **quarrel** ▶**言い争い**たくはない．議論したいだけだ I don't want to *argue*. I just want to discuss it. ‖ 2人は土地の所有権を巡って**言い争った** The two (people) *quarreled* [*had a quarrel*] over the ownership of the property.

いいあらわす 言い表す **express** ▶思うことを外国語で自由に**言い表す**のは難しい It is hard to *express* your thoughts [*express* yourself] freely in a foreign language. ‖ この悔しさはことばでは**言い表せない** I can't *express* my bitter disappointment in [by] words.

いいえ

語法「いいえ」と No
「はい」は yes,「いいえ」は no と機械的に訳さないこと. 英語では返事が肯定文のときは yes, 否定文のときは no で答える. したがって否定疑問文に答えるときは特に注意が必要.

1【疑問内容と対立する返事】▶対話「おすしはお好きですか」「いいえ, あまり好きではありません」"Do you like sushi ?" "*No*, I don't like it very much." ‖ 対話「きみは泳げますか」「いいえ, 泳げません」"Can you swim ?" "*No*, I can't." ‖ 対話「たばこを吸ってもいいですか」「いいえ, 困ります」"Do you mind if I smoke ?" "*Yes*, I do mind." (➤ ふつうは角が立たないように I'd rather you didn't. / I wish you wouldn't. のように控えめな答え方をする) ‖ 対話「甘い物はお好きではないのですか」「いいえ, 好きです」"Don't you like sweets ?" "*Yes*, I do." (➤ "No, I don't." とすると「はい, 好きではありません」の意になる) ‖ 対話「車の運転はできないんですか」「いいえ, できますよ」"Can't you drive a car ?" "*Yes*, I can."
2【応答・相づち・強調】▶対話「大変ごちそうになりました」「いいえ, どういたしまして」"Thank you very much for such a delicious dinner." "*You're* (*very*) *welcome*. I'm glad you enjoyed it."

いいおとす 言い落とす forget to mention ▶大事なことを言い落とした I *forgot to mention* something important. ‖ 何か私が言い落としたことはありますか Is there anything I (have) *left unsaid* ? (● 英語では「言わずにおいたことはありますか」と発想して訳例のように言う. leave ... unsaid は「…を言わずにおく」の意).

いいかえす 言い返す talk back ; retort +目 (少し憤慨して)
▶上役に言い返す *talk* [*answer*] *back* to one's boss ‖「悪いのはあなたのほうよ」と彼女は言い返した "It was your fault," she *retorted*. ‖ 言いなりになってばかりいないで, たまには奥さんに言い返してやんなさいよ Don't always give in to your wife—*tell* her *a thing or two* (*in return*) once in a while.

いいかえる 言い換える ▶「規格化」を易しいことばに言い換える *say* 'standardization' *in* simpler *words* ‖ その熟語を言い換えることができますか Can you *put* that idiomatic phrase *in other words* ? ‖ 言い換えれば, 私たちの成功は彼らのおかげである *In other words*, we owe our present success to them.

いいがかり 言い掛かり a false accusation ▶電車の中で足を踏んだと言いがかりをつけられた (＝けんかを吹っかけられた) Someone *picked an argument with* me in the train, claiming I'd stepped on his foot.

いいかける 言いかける ▶「ばかやろう！」と言いかけたがやめた I *was going* [*was about*] *to say* "You idiot !" but I stopped myself.

いいかげん いい加減 1【適度】▶風呂はちょうどいいかげんだ The bath temperature *is just right*. ‖ ギャンブルはいいかげんにやめたほうがいいよ *It is* (*about*) *time that* you gave up gambling. (● この日本語には非難の響きが感じられるが, 英語では「…していてよい頃なのに(…していない)」の意を表す慣用句 It is (about) time にその響きが感じられる. この句のあとの文は訳例が示すように過去の形が続く) ‖ そんなばかなこと (言う [する] の), いいかげんにしなさいよ *Enough of* that nonsense ! ‖ テレビを見るのはいいかげんにして, 勉強しなさい *Stop* watching TV *so much* and do some studying. ‖ もういいかげんにしなさい *Knock it off !* (➤ 騒いでいる子供などに向かって言うインフォーマルな表現) ‖ 対話「宿題を手伝ってくれる？」「いいかげんにしてちょうだい. たまには自分一人でやったら」"Would you help me with my homework ?" "*Give me a break* and do it by yourself for a change." (➤ Give me a break. は「勘弁してくれ, いらつくことを言うのはよしてくれ」の意).
2【無責任】▶いいかげんな人間 an *irresponsible* [*unreliable*] person (➤ 後者は「信頼できない」) ‖ いいかげんなことを言うな No *nonsense*, please ! ‖ 彼はいつもいいかげんな仕事をする He never does his work properly. ‖ 彼は何をやらせてもいいかげん (＝中途半端) だ He leaves everything *half-done*. ‖ 質問の意味がわからなかったので, いいかげんに返事をしてごまかした I didn't understand the question, so I gave a *vague* answer.
3【かなり】▶もうその話を聞くのはいいかげん嫌になった I've gotten *really* [*pretty*] sick and tired of hearing about it.

いいかた 言い方 ▶相手に謝罪するときの言い方を教えてください *What should I say* when I want to apologize ? ‖ 正雄は「なかなかうまい言い方をするね」とアメリカ人に褒められた An American praised Masao by telling him he *expressed himself very well*. ‖ 彼はいつも丁寧な言い方 (＝話し方) をする He always *speaks politely*. ‖ 君はもっと丁寧な言い方 (＝表現) をすべきだったんだよ You should have used a more polite *expression*.
▶きみの言い方が悪かったんじゃないの？ Maybe your *choice of words* wasn't appropriate. ‖ ほかに言い方はないのかね You might *put* it another way. ‖ そんな言い方はないだろう？ How dare you *speak* to me like that ? ‖ ひどい言い方をするね What *an awful thing to say* ! (● この日本文は「ひどいことを言うね」と言い換えられるから, 訳例のように awful thing を用いればよい. 《英》では What a nasty thing ... と言う).

いいき いい気 ▶不二夫は入試が間近なのに漫画ばかり読んでいい気な (＝のんきな) もんだ Fujio is quite *happy-go-lucky* [so *nonchalant*], reading nothing but comic books when the entrance exam is near at hand. (➤ nonchalant は「無頓着な」) ‖ あの子, 美人だと思っていい気になっているんだわ She thinks that she is so beautiful ! (➤ so を強調して伸ばして発音する) ‖ 人が黙っていればいい気になって, 彼はあることないこと言い触らした He spread rumors about me that blended truth with fiction, *taking advantage of* the fact that I never say anything to defend myself.

いいきかせる 言い聞かせる persuade +目 (説得する) ; **advise** +目 (助言・忠告する) ; **tell** +目 (命じる) ; **convince** +目 (納得させる) ; **lecture** +目 (お説教する)
▶私は娘にもっと慎重になるよう言い聞かせた I *tried to convince* my daughter to be more cautious. / I *lectured* my daughter about being more cautious. ‖ そんな高価なハンドバッグを買ってはだめと自分に言い聞かせた I *talked myself out of* buying such an expensive purse. (➤ talk ... out of doing は「話して聞かせてやめさせる」).

いいきみ いい気味 ▶あの政治家が逮捕されたって？(そいつは) いい気味だ That politician was arrested ? (*It*) *serves him right*. (● 英語では「(それは) 彼に正しく報いている」と発想する. him は相手によって her, them などに換える) ‖ 対話「試験, 失敗しちゃったよ」「いい気味だ！全然勉強しなかっただろ？」"I failed the exam." "*It serves you right !* You didn't study at all, right ?"

いいきる 言い切る declare +目 (断言する) ; **con-**

clude +目（結論を下す）▶幸司は現役でT大に合格してみせると**言い切った** Koji *declared* that he would pass the (entrance) exams for T University on his first try. ‖ 彼はその事件とは無関係だときっぱり**言い切った** He flatly *denied* having anything to do with the incident.（➤ deny は「否定する」）‖ 今の時点ではまだ彼が犯人だとは**言い切れない** At this stage, we *cannot conclude* that he is the culprit. ／It's *too early to conclude* that he is the culprit.

いいぐさ 言い草・言い種 ▶母親に向かって何て**言いぐさ**なの？ *How dare you talk like that* to your own mother?

いいくるめる 言いくるめる smooth-talk +目（うまいことを言って丸め込む）▶あの販売員に**言いくるめられて**無駄な物を買ってしまった That salesperson *smooth-talked* me *into* buying something I didn't need. ▶《慣用表現》あの政治家は**黒を白と言いくるめる**のがうまい That politician is good at deceptive talk. He *tries to make people believe that black is white* (*and white is black*).

いいこ いい子 a good boy［girl］▶**いい子**だからおとなしくしていてね Be quiet. *That's a good boy*［*girl*］. ‖ **いい子**だから, あれ取って来て *Be a sweetie*［*lamb*］and fetch that for me.（● 訳例が示すように英語にも sweetie という語がある. 後者の lamb /læm/ は文字どおりには「子羊」, 転じて「従順な人」）‖ みんなで規則を破ったのに彼は自分だけ**いい子になろう**としている He's trying to *play the good boy*［*pretend to be innocent*］even though all the others have admitted breaking the regulations.

いいことに ▶上司の留守を**いいことに**彼は万事を思いどおりにした *Taking advantage of* the boss' absence, he did everything his own way.（➤ take advantage of は「…を利用する, …につけ込む」）.

いいこめる 言い込める ▶広中君は理論家だから, 私はあっさり**言い込められてしまった** Since Hironaka is such a logician, I *lost the argument hands down*.

イージー easy

> **危ないカタカナ語✹ イージー**
> **1** easy は「容易な」「気楽な」「手軽な」の意. 安易な方法をとることを非難して「イージーゴーイング」とか「イージーな」というが, 英語の easygoing は「こせこせしない」の意で, 悪い意味はない. easygoing teacher は「（うるさいことを言わない）おおらかな先生」である.
> **2** 洋服の「イージーオーダー」は easy と order(注文)から作った和製語. イージーオーダーそのものが日本独特の方法で, 英語で表すなら tailoring a suit without a fitting(仮縫いなしの仕立て)となる.

いいしれぬ 言い知れぬ unspeakable（ことばで表せない）▶続く異常気象に住民たちは**言い知れぬ**不安を覚えた When the abnormal weather continued, the inhabitants felt *unspeakable* fear.

いいすぎ 言い過ぎ ▶そりゃあちょっと**言い過ぎ**だよ You *went* a bit *too far* when you said that.（➤ go too far は「やり過ぎる」）／You *put it* a bit *too strongly*. ‖ Y博士はわが大学の宝と言っても**言い過ぎではない** *It is not too much to say*［*It is no exaggeration to say*］*that* Dr. Y is the treasure of our university. →過言.

イースター Easter ▶**イースター**は3月または4月にあるキリスト教徒たちのお祭りです *Easter* is a Christian festival in March or April.

イースト yeast /jiːst/
‖**イースト菌** a yeast fungus /fʌ́ŋɡəs/.

いいせん いい線 ▶彼女, **いい線いってる**じゃないか She's *not bad*. ／She's *really cute*［*cool*］, isn't she? ‖ 初めて作ったミートパイにしては, 我ながら**いい線いっている**と思う Considering this is the first time I made meat pies, *they're not bad*, if I say so myself. ‖ 彼から電話があったって？ **いい線いってる**じゃない You got a call from him? Looks like *you are on the way up*.（➤ on the way up は「上り調子で」）.

いいそこなう 言い損なう ▶彼女にあんな風に言うつもりはなかったんだ. **言い損なった**だけなんだよ I didn't mean to say things like that to her. It was only *a slip of the tongue*.（● 英語では「失言だった」と考えて訳例のように a slip of the tongue を用いる）‖ 急いでいて彼女にいちばん大事なことを**言い損なった**（＝言い忘れた）I was in such a hurry I *forgot to tell* her the most important thing.

いいそびれる 言いそびれる ▶私は「ありがとう」のひと言を彼に**言いそびれた** I *failed to say* "Thanks" to him. ‖ 父が退院をとても喜んでいたので, 本当の病名をつい**言いそびれた** I *missed the chance to tell* my father (about) the real name［the true nature］of his disease because he was so glad to leave the hospital.

いいだくだく 唯々諾々と obediently（従順に）; unquestioningly（批判の余地なく）▶軍隊では上官の命令に**唯々諾々と**従うしかない In the army you have no choice but to obey your superior's orders *unquestioningly*.

いいだしっぺ 言い出しっぺ ▶**言い出しっぺ**はきみだよ（だからきみが最初にやれ）You *said it first*(, so you have to do it first).

いいだす 言い出す suggest +目（控えめに提案する）; propose +目（積極的に提案する）▶授業をサボろうなんて誰が**言い出した**んだ？ Who *suggested* that you (should) cut classes?（➤《米》では通例 should のない原形を用いる）‖ このプランは誰が**言い出した**の？ Who *proposed* this plan *first*?
▶彼女は社員旅行の前日になって「私は行きません」と**言い出した** It was only the day before the company trip that she *came out and said* she would not go with us.（● 何のためらいもなくずばっと言ったというニュアンスは英語では come out and say を用いて表現できる）‖ 彼は頑固で**一度言い出したら聞かない** He's stubborn. *Once he has expressed his opinion*, he won't listen to anyone else's.

いいつくす 言い尽くす ▶私は言いたいことはすでに**言い尽くしました** I *have* already *said everything* I want to. ‖ その風景はことばで**言い尽くせない**ほど美しいものだった The landscape was *more* beautiful *than words could describe*. ／The beauty of the landscape was *beyond description*［*indescribable*］.
✉ **私の感謝の気持ちはことばでは到底言い尽くせません** I cannot thank you enough. ➤「いくら感謝をしてもし足りない」の意.

いいつけ 言い付け an order（命令）▶人の**言いつけ**を守る obey a person's *order*(*s*) ‖ **言いつけどおりに**しなさい Do *as I tell you*［*as you are told*］.

いいつける 言い付ける **1**【命じる】tell ▶新入社員に用事を**言いつける** *tell*［*order*］a new employee to do an errand［some errands］.
2【告げ口する】tell on ▶石井先生が戻って来たらおまえのことを**言いつけて**やるからな I'll *tell on* you when Mrs. Ishii gets back. ／I'll *tell* Mrs. Ishii all

about you when she gets back. ‖ きっと誰かがぼくのことを先生に言いつけたんだ I'm sure someone *has snitched* [《英》*has sneaked*] *on* me to the teacher. (➤ snitch [sneak] on は特に年少者が用いる) ‖ あの子, すぐ人に言いつけるんだから She's [He's] *a sneak*.

いいつたえ 言い伝え a **legend** (伝説) ▶この山には天狗(てんぐ)が住んでいたという言い伝えがある *The legend says* [*Legend has it that*] there was a 'tengu' living in this mountain.

いいつたえる 言い伝える ▶私の田舎の村には昔から言い伝えられてきた悲しい話がいくつもある In my home village, there are lots of sad tales that *have been handed* [*have come*] *down* from ancient times.

イーティーシー ETC (Electronic Toll Collection の略) ▶ETC利用者は料金所で停止することなくETCレーンを通過することができる *ETC users* can travel through *ETC lanes* without stopping at tollgates. ‖ ETCカード an ETC card.

いいとこどり いいとこ取り cherry-picking, the cream of the crop ▶この料理は和洋のいいとこ取りだ This dish is a *cherry-picking* of Japanese cuisine and western cuisine.

いいとし いい年 ▶きみもいい年をして子供みたいなまねはよせよ You *are old enough to know better*, so you should stop behaving like a child. (● 英語では「分別がつく [ばかなことをしない] 年齢なのだから」と発想して訳例のように表現する) ‖ おやじが病気になるのも無理ないよ. いい年をして働き過ぎたからね With all the overwork *at his age*, it's hardly surprising that Dad got sick. (● 英語では「あの年で」と考えて, 訳例のように at his age を用いる).

いいなおす 言い直す correct oneself (訂正する) ▶もう少しわかりやすく言い直してください Please *tell* me *again*, more simply. ‖ 彼女はフィアンセの名前を間違えて慌てて言い直した She gave her fiancé's name incorrectly and (then) hurriedly *corrected herself* [*said it right*].

いいなずけ 許嫁・許婚 a **fiancé** /fiːɑːnséɪ ‖ fiɔ́nseɪ/ (男); a **fiancée** /fiːɑːnséɪ ‖ fiɔ́nseɪ/ (女).

いいなり 言いなり ▶あいつは母親の言いなりだ He's completely *under* his mother's *thumb*. (● 英語では「A(人)の支配下にある」の意のインフォーマルな慣用句 under A's thumb を用いる) ‖ 最近では子供の言いなりになる親が多い Nowadays, many parents *let* their children *have their own way*. (➤ let A have A's own way で「A(人)の好きなようにさせる」) ‖ きみは彼の言いなりになる必要はないのだ You don't have to *do just as he tells you*.

いいにくい 言いにくい ▶きみは言いにくいことをずいぶんはっきり言うね You talk about *awkward things* [*delicate subjects*] in a really straightforward way. ‖ 彼は言いにくそうに50万貸してほしいと言った He *hesitantly* asked for a loan of 500 thousand yen.

[1]**いいね 言い値** an **asking price, the price asked** [**named**] ▶彼女はその茶わんを言い値で買った She bought the tea bowl *for the asking price*.

[2]**いいね** 《インターネットの》 a **like** ▶その動画は100万以上の「いいね」を獲得した The video earned [garnered] more than one million *likes*.

いいのがれ 言い逃れ an **excuse** /ɪkskjúːs/ (言い訳); an **evasion** (曖昧な返答) ▶言い逃れをするつもりかい Do you intend to *make excuses*? ‖ 彼女はうまい言い逃れを思いついた She invented [cooked up] *a good excuse*. (➤ cook up は「でっち上げる」の意でくだけた言い方) ‖ 彼の返事は単なる言い逃れだった His answer was *a* mere *evasion*.

いいのこす 言い残す ▶何か言い残したことはありませんか Is there *anything you forgot to mention*? / Is there *anything else you want to say*? ‖ 「元気でね」と言い残して (= 言って) 彼は去って行った He left *saying* "Stay well."

いいはる 言い張る insist 《on, that》 ▶彼女は独りで中国に行くと言い張っている She *insists on* going to China alone. ‖ 息子はどうしても大学に行かないと言い張っている My son *insists on* not going to college. ‖ 彼はその盗難事件については何も知らないと言い張っている He *insists that* he knows nothing about the robbery.

いいひと いい人 a **nice person** (感じのいい人) ▶彼はいい人だけど少しおっちょこちょいだ He is *a nice person*, but something of a scatterbrain.
▶最近彼女にいい人 (= 恋人) ができたらしい Apparently, she *is seeing somebody* [*some guy*] these days.

いいふくめる 言い含める ▶彼は自分の娘に言い含めて五郎と結婚させた He *talked* his daughter *into* marrying Goro.

いいふらす 言い触らす ▶彼らはその候補者についてでたらめなことを言い触らした They *spread* [*circulated*] false stories about the candidate. ‖ 彼は曽根さんがうそつきだと言い触らしている He *is telling everybody* that Mr. Sone is a liar.

いいふるされた 言い古された stale (新味のない); **worn-out** (使い古した); **hackneyed** (陳腐な) ▶言い古された冗談 a *stale* joke ‖ 言い古されたことばですが, 「初心忘るべからず」を肝に銘じています It may sound *stale* [*corny*], but I try to remember not to forget the eagerness [enthusiasm] I started with. 《参考》言い古された陳腐な表現を cliche /kliːʃéɪ/ という. → 決まり文句.

いいぶん 言い分 an **excuse** (過失・欠席などの); a **claim** (主張) ▶言い分を述べる give *an excuse* ‖ 彼の言い分を確かめてみよう Let's check up on his *claim*. ‖ 彼の言い分も聞いてやらなければならない We must hear *what he has to say*. ‖ 彼女の言い分も聞こうじゃないか Let her have *her say*. (➤ her say で「彼女の言いたいこと」) ‖ 両者とも大いに言い分があるようだ There seems much *to be said* on both sides. ‖ 私にも言い分 (= 不満) はある I*'ve got a bone to pick with* you, too. (● 英語では「A(人)に文句 [不満] がある」の意のインフォーマルな慣用句 have (got) a bone to pick with を用いる).

いいまかす 言い負かす ▶徹子は口が達者なので誰も彼女を言い負かせない Tetsuko is such a clever talker (that) nobody can *win an argument with* her. ‖ 悔しいが言い負かされてしまった I felt upset to *lose the argument* [*to be argued down*].

いいまちがい 言い間違い a **slip of the tongue** [**the lip**] ▶言い間違いは誰にでもある Anyone can make *a slip of the tongue*. / Anyone can make *a mistake when speaking*.

いいまわし 言い回し ▶おもしろい言い回し an interesting *turn of phrase* ‖ うまい言い回し a clever *way of putting it* ‖ 日本語特有の言い回し a uniquely Japanese *figure of speech* (➤ figure of speech は「比喩的表現」の意).

いいめ いい目 ▶あいつういい目を見たなあ He is quite

い

lucky. ‖ 彼は今まであまりいい目に遭わなかった So far *things have gone rather badly for* him. ‖ おまえはいい目にばかり遭ってきたから他人の心が読めないのだ You cannot understand how others feel because you have *led such a lucky life*.

イーメール Eメール (an) **email**, (an) **e-mail** (➤「郵便物」の mail は不可算名詞だが, email, e-mail は可算名詞として使うこともある) →メール ▶信子に E メールを送った I *sent an email* to Nobuko. ／I *emailed* Nobuko. ‖ E メールを(送ったけど)読んでくれた? Have you read my *email*? ‖ 毎日50通以上の E メールが来る I get more than fifty *emails* every day.

ディベートルーム「手紙より E メールや携帯メールのほうが優れたコミュニケーション手段だ」

いいよう 言い様 ▶言いようのない悲しさに胸を打たれた I was struck with an *indescribable* feeling of sorrow. ‖ お母さんの病状については, 今は何とも言いようがありません We *can't say anything definite* about the condition of your mother's disease now.

ことわざ 物は言いよう[物も言いようで角が立つ] The way you express things may cause either good feelings or bad [bitter] feelings. ／Harsh words lead to confrontation and sweet words make things go smoothly.

いいよる 言い寄る ▶彼は会社の受付嬢に言い寄っている He has been *propositioning* [*making advances to*] a receptionist in his firm. (➤ 前者がややくだけた言い方. 《米・インフォーマル》では put the make on ともいう).

いいわけ 言い訳 an **excuse** /ɪkskjúːs/ **一動 言い訳をする make an excuse** ▶うまい[下手な]言い訳 a good [poor] *excuse* ‖ 遅刻の言い訳をする *make an excuse* for being late ‖ 言い訳は聞きたくない I don't want to hear (your) *excuses*. ‖ 言い訳ばかりするのは男らしくない It's not manly to *make excuses* all the time. (➤ 英米では make an excuse ができないようでは成人として恥ずべきと考える傾向にある).

いいわすれる 言い忘れる forget to say [**tell**] ▶「きみを愛している」と言い忘れた I *forgot to say* "I love you." ‖ 彼女は翌日留守にすることをボーイフレンドに言い忘れた She *forgot to tell* her boyfriend that she would be away the following day. ‖ そうだ, 言い忘れるところだった Oh, I almost *forgot to tell* you (something).

いいわたす 言い渡す sentence +目 (刑を宣告する); **order** +目 (命じる) ▶裁判長は被告人に死刑の判決を言い渡した The presiding judge *sentenced* the accused to death. ‖ 市当局はそのビルの不法居住者に立ち退きを言い渡した The city authorities *ordered* the squatters to vacate the building.

1いいん 医院 《米》a **doctor's office**, 《英》a **surgery**; a **clinic** (診療所) ▶山根(歯科)医院 Yamane (Dental) *Clinic*.

2いいん 委員 a **member of a committee**, a **committee member** (1人); a **committee** (全員) ▶クラブ[クラス]の委員に選ばれて光栄です I'm honored to be chosen as *a member* of this club's *committee* [a class *representative* ／a class *monitor*]. ‖ きみは何の委員をしていますか What *committee* are you *on*? (➤ on は「…に所属して」).

いいんかい 委員会 a **committee** (機関); a **committee meeting** (committee による会議); a **commission** (特に権限などをほかから委任された); a **board** (特に学校・企業などを管理・運営する) ▶運営[常任]委員会 a steering [standing] *committee* ‖ 教育委員会 the *Board* of Education ‖ 原子力委員会 the Atomic Energy *Commission* ‖ 委員会を設置する form [organize] *a committee* ‖ 委員会を開く[招集する] hold [summon] *a committee meeting* (➤ この場合, 単に committee では不可) ‖ 彼女はいくつかの委員会の委員だ She is [serves] on several *committees*. (➤ serve は堅い語).

いいんちょう 委員長 a **chairman**, a **chairwoman**, a **chairperson** (➤ 最後は男女兼用語. 単に the chair ということもある) ▶彼は委員全員によって委員長に選ばれた He was elected *chairman* by all the members of the committee. (➤ 役職が1名に限られている場合は名詞には a や the はつかない).

いう 言う

訳語メニュー
口に出す →say **1, 4**
しゃべる →speak **1**
…と呼ぶ →call **3**
相手に伝える →tell **4, 5**

1【人間が音声を発する】say; speak (話す) ▶「はい」と言う *say* "Yes" ‖ 彼女は私におはようと言った She *said*, "Good morning" to me. ‖ 蛇を見せたら彼は「ギャッ!」と言って後ずさりした When I showed him a snake, he *said*, "Yikes!" and stepped back. ‖ 今, 何か言った? *Did* you *say* something (to me) just now?

▶もっと大きい声で言ってください *Speak up*, please. ‖ 彼女はぼくの言うことなすことが気に入らない She doesn't like anything I *say or do*. ‖ こう言っては何ですが, 彼女はちょっと変わってますね *If you'll excuse the expression*, I think she's a bit strange. ‖ 《飲み物をついでいて》よかったらいいって言ってよ *Say when!* (➤「あ, それでいい」は OK. ／Fine! ／That's enough! など).

> **語法「…と二郎が言った」の訳し方**
> (1)この言い方は, Jiro said, "…." または "…," Jiro said. のような前置と後置による英訳が可能であるが, 後置の場合は said Jiro とすることもできる. また文章が二分できる場合には, "…," said Jiro, "…." のようにも表現できる. ただし, he, she などの代名詞の場合は, said he の語順にしないのがふつう.
> (2)このような相手のことばを直接引用する文は英語では主に文章体で, 会話では間接話法で表すのがふつう. 例えば「『頭が痛い』と恵子は私に言った」は Keiko said (to me), "I have a headache." ではなく, Keiko told me she had a headache. とする. 代名詞の使い方に注意. ただし, 劇的効果を狙って直接話法を用いることもある.

2【書いてある】say ▶新聞の社説では次のように言っている The newspaper editorial *says* as follows [the following]: (➤: のあとに文が続く).

3【…と呼ぶ】say; call +目 (名付ける) ▶ 対話「英語でゴキブリは何といいますか」「コックローチといいます」"*How do you say* 'gokiburi' in English?" "Cockroach." ‖ 対話「この花, 英語で何といいますか」「ピオニー(=ボタン)といいます」"*What do you call* this flower in English?" "Peony." ‖ 対話「きのうここに来た少年の名は何といいますか」「友一です」"*What is the name* of the boy who came here yesterday?" "Yuichi."

4【告げる, 訴える】say; tell +目 (人にあることを知らせる) ▶意見を聞かれたら何か言うことが大切です You must *say* something when asked for an opinion. ‖ 言いたいことがあったら言えよ *Say* what you *have to say*. ‖ それは言わないでおいたほうがよかったのに It would have been better if you *had left* it *unsaid*. ‖ 一体きみは何を言いたいのだ Just *what are you trying to say* ? ／Just *what do you mean* ? ／Just *what are you driving at* ? ‖ 筆者のいちばん言いたいことを把握することが大切だ It is very important to understand what the writer *wants to say* [*convey*] most.

▶この頃は多くの日本人が英語で自分の考えを言うことができる Many Japanese can *express themselves* in English these days. ‖ 容疑者は２日間の取り調べの後, ついに自分が殺したと言った(＝白状した) The suspect *confessed to* the murder after a two-day interrogation. ‖ 対話「正直に言ってごらん. 本当にカンニングしたの？」「いいえ, してません」"*Be honest*. Did you really cheat during the exam ?" "No, I didn't."

5【知らせる, 伝える】tell ＋㊐ ▶俺に彼女ができたっておやじに言ってくれ *Tell* Dad that I've got a girlfriend. ‖ 英語のテストが30点だったこと, お母さんに言わないでよ *Don't let* Mom *know* that I got only 30 on the English exam. (➤ 前文の tell が「一方的に伝える」の意であるのに対して, let ... know は「(相手の希望などに従って)知らせる」の意) ‖ お父さんによろしく言ってください *Say hello to* your father (for me). ／*Give* your father *my best regards*. (➤ 後者は堅い言い方).

6【うわさする, 批評する】say ▶進と洋子は結婚するだろうってみんなが言っている *Everyone says* Susumu and Yoko are going to get married. ‖ 今度の社長は優柔不断だと社員が言っている The employees *say* that their new president is indecisive. ‖ その教授のことは多くの学生が悪く言っている A lot of students *say bad things* about that professor. ‖ 評論家の言うことなどいちいち気にしてはいられない I can't bother with what the critics have to *say* about me.

7【命令する】tell ＋㊐

> 【文型】
> **人(A)に…するように言う**
> **tell** A **to** do
>
> 《解説》この tell は「…しなさいと言いつける, 命じる」の意.「…してねと言う」の場合は ask (頼む)を用いる. →頼む.

▶先生は生徒たちにその文章を書き換えなさいと言った The teacher *told* the students *to* rewrite the sentences. ／The teacher *said* for the students *to* rewrite the sentences. (➤ 後者の構文は《米・インフォーマル》で好まれる).

▶盲導犬はとてもよく言うことを聞く A guide dog always *obeys* its master's *orders*. ‖ あまりにも疲れて体が言うことを聞かなかった I was so tired that I *couldn't move* my body.

▶言ってくれれば(＝…してと言えば)手伝ったのに I would have helped you *if you had asked me*.

8【物音がする】▶扉が風でガタガタいっている The door *is rattling* in the wind.

9【「…でいうと」の形で】▶うちの犬は10歳で, 人間でいうと60代です Our dog is ten years old—in her [his] sixties *in human years* [*terms*]. ‖ 日本語の「おはようございます」は英語でいうと"Good morning."だ The Japanese phrase "Ohayogozaimasu" is *an equivalent of* [*for*] *the English* "Good morning."

10【「…といわれる」「…といわれている」の形で】▶山下清は日本のゴッホといわれた Yamashita Kiyoshi *was called* the van Gogh of Japan. ‖ 私は人からサッカーが上手だといわれている People *tell* me I'm good at soccer. ／I *am told* I am a good soccer player. (● I am said to be a good soccer player. なら「そういううわさがある」というニュアンス. なお, (×)I am said a good soccer player. はよくある間違いの文) ‖ アイザック・ニュートンはリンゴが地上に落ちるのを見て引力を発見したといわれている Isaac Newton *is said* to have discovered gravity when he watched an apple fall to the ground.

11【「…という」の形で】→-という ▶資本主義という制度 a system *called* capitalism ‖ 鈴木という投手が今度野球部に入った A pitcher *named* Suzuki has joined the baseball club. ‖ 和歌山県にはアメリカ村という所がある There is a place *called* 'American Village' in Wakayama Prefecture.

▶うわさによると２人は近々結婚するという *Rumor has it that* [*According to the rumor*,] they are going to get married soon. ‖ アメリカにいるビルから来月日本に来るという手紙が来た I got a letter from Bill in America. He *says* he is coming to Japan next month. ‖「正直は最善の策」ということわざがある There is a proverb, "Honesty is the best policy." ‖ 当地には昔老婆が山に捨てられたという伝説が伝わっております There is a legend here *that* in ancient times elderly women were abandoned in the mountains.

12【「…という…」の形で】▶北海道では５月になると花という花が一斉に咲く In Hokkaido, *very many* (*kinds of*) *flowers* go into full bloom in May. ‖ 今度という今度はただじゃおかないからな You're going to pay dearly for it *this time* for sure.

13【「…といい～といい」の形で】▶彼女の評論は文体といい内容といい申し分ないね Her critique is perfect *both* in style *and* content.

14【「…というもの」「…ということ」の形で】▶山国育ちの彼は海というものを見たことがない He was raised in the mountains and has never seen the sea. (● この「というもの」は訳出不要) ‖ オリンピックに出るということは大変なことだ *To* participate in the Olympic Games is a great accomplishment.

15【「…といってよい」の形で】▶武満は最も偉大な日本人作曲家だったといってよい Takemitsu was *arguably* [*may well* have been] the greatest Japanese composer ever. (➤ arguably を使うほうが主張の確信度が高い).

16【「…といえば」の形で】▶テニスといえば僕は最近凝っていてね *Talking about* [《英》 *of*] tennis, I'm really into it these days. ‖ クリント・イーストウッドといえば, 彼の新作を見た？ *Speaking of* Clint Eastwood, have you seen his new movie ?

17【慣用表現】▶そら言わないこっちゃない. やっぱりすっぽかされたでしょ *Don't bother to tell me*. You got stood up, right ? ‖ 彼は早く帰れと言わんばかりの態度だった He was so rude. He *might as well have said*, "Get lost." (● 英語では「(ひどく無礼で)…と言ったとしてもおかしくなかっただろう」と発想して, 訳例のように might as well have said と表現する) ‖ この試作機の完成までには言うに言われぬ苦労があった Producing this sample machine required *indescribable*

い

effort. ‖ 彼女は料理が上手で，和食と言わず洋食と言わず何でもお手の物だ She's an excellent cook who excels at *both* Japanese *and* Western cuisine. ‖ 日本では言わず語らずのうちに思いが相手に伝わるのをよしとする風潮がある There is a tendency in Japan to consider it desirable to get your ideas across [to convey your ideas] *without saying anything*. ‖ 石川五右衛門は言わずと知れた大泥棒だ Ishikawa Goemon was a great robber, so notorious *that everybody knows* him [his name].

ことわざ 言わぬが花 Some things are better left unsaid. ／It's better to leave some things unsaid.

ことわざ 言うは易(やす)く行うは難(かた)し Easier said than done.

いうことなし 言うこと無し ▶この作文は言うことなしだ This composition is *perfect*. ／This composition *leaves nothing to be desired*. (➤ leave nothing to be desired は文字どおりには「遺憾な点が全くない」) ‖ お風呂はいいし，料理はおいしいし，この旅館言うことなしね Good bath and good food. This inn is *just perfect*. ‖ きみの仕事については言うことなしだ I *am perfectly satisfied with* your work.

いうまでもない 言うまでもない

> 【文型】
> ～であるのは言うまでもない
> Needless to say, ～.
> It goes without saying that ～.
> 《解説》後者は that 節を強調する場合に好まれるが，冗長としてこれを不必要とみなす人も多く，一般には前者のほうが好まれる.

▶健康が富に勝ることは言うまでもない *Needless to say*, health is more important than wealth. ／*It goes without saying that* health is above wealth.

> 【文型】
> A は言うまでもなく
> not to mention A
> to say nothing of A

▶彼はアジア諸国は言うまでもなくヨーロッパでもよく知られている He is well known in Europe, *not to mention* [*to say nothing of*] Asian countries. (➤ 前者の言い方のほうがふつう).

▶モルディブは言うまでもなく沖縄に行く余裕さえない I cannot afford to take a trip to Okinawa, *let alone* [*much less*] the Maldives. (➤ let alone ..., much less ... は「…などとんでもない」の意. 前文と対比する語句が続き，このように否定文のあとに用いるのがふつう).

いえ 家 1【家屋】a house, a home

> 《解説》**home と house**
> house は「一軒家」に対し，home はアパートやマンションでもよい. home は「家族の生活が営まれる所」という意味では Ⓤ 扱いだが，不動産関連ではこの単語がもつ「ぬくもり」を生かして house の代用語とすることがある. その場合は Ⓒ 扱いになる.

▶家を建てる build *a house* (➤ 自分で建てる場合にも，建築業者に依頼して建てる場合にも使える) ‖ 私たちは月15万円でこの家を借りています We rent this *house* for 150,000 yen a month. ‖ 家を失った何十万というアフリカ人が難民キャンプに住んでいます The hundreds of thousands of Africans who lost their *homes* are now living in refugee camps.

2【家庭，自宅】home →うち ▶会社でのつらい一日の仕事のあと家に帰るとくつろげる After a rough day at the office, I feel relaxed at *home*. ‖ アメリカ留学中の彼女は週に一度は家に電話します She is now studying in the United States and calls *home* once a week. (➤ この例と次例の home は「家へ」の意の副詞) ‖ 家まで車で送ろうか Do you want me to drive you *home*? ‖ 私は高校を卒業するとすぐ家を出ました I *left home* right after graduating from high school. ‖ 父はきょうは家にいます My dad *is at home* today. ‖ 家では秋田犬を飼っている We have an Akita dog *at home*. ‖ おかげさまで家の者（＝家族）は全員元気にしております *My family* are *all* well [*Everyone in my family* is well], thank you. ‖ 兄は結婚して家をもった My elder brother got married and had *a family* of his own. ‖ 彼は毎朝7時に家を出る He *leaves the* [*his*] *house* at seven every morning.

> **あなたの英語はどう響く?**
> 「朝何時に家を出ますか」を What time do you *leave home* in the morning? と訳す人が多いが，leave home は「家出をする」というニュアンスが強いので，この場合の「家を出る」には不適切. leave だけにするか，leave your house または leave for school [for work] のような言い方がよい.

▶ 対話「きみの家はどこですか」「このマンションの12階です」 "Where is your *home*? ／Where do you live?" "It's on the twelfth floor of this condo. ／I live on the twelfth floor of this condo." (➤ 一軒家の場合は，Where is your house? ともいう).

3【家系，商売】a family ▶岡田さんの家は代々学者だ Scholarship runs in the Okada *family*. ‖ 佐藤君ちでは次男が家を継ぐようだ It seems the Sato's second son will take over the *family* business.

いえい 遺影 a picture [photo] of the departed person.

いえがら 家柄 ▶家柄の良い人 a person *from a good family* ‖ 彼は家柄がいい He *comes from a good family*. ／He *is of good birth*. (➤ 後者は堅い言い方).

いえき 胃液 gastric juices.

いえじ 家路 ▶家路に就く *start* [*set out*] *on the road home* ‖ ホームは家路を急ぐ人々で混雑していた The platform was crowded with people *hurrying home*.

イエス yes ▶きみからイエスかノーか，はっきりした返事をもらいたいんだ I want a (clear) *yes or no* (answer) from you.

‖**イエスマン**（上司の言うことに何でも賛成する人）a yes-man.

いえで 家出する run away from home, leave home

‖**家出人** a home leaver, a runaway (➤ 後者は主に年少者) ‖ **家出少年[少女]** a runaway boy [girl].

いえてる 言えてる ▶ 対話「あの子最近，生意気じゃない?」「言えてる」 "She's cocky these days, don't you think?" "*You said it*."

いえども ▶いかに秀才といえども勉強なくしては成功は望めない (*Even*) the most brilliant person cannot hope to succeed without hard work. (➤ even

がなくても最上級だけで「どんなに…といえども」の意を表すことができる). →当たらずといえども.

いえもと 家元 ▶裏千家の家元を継ぐ succeed *the head* [*the headmaster*] of the Ura-Senke school of tea ceremony.

‖**家元制度** the *iemoto* system ; the hereditary headmaster system in a traditional Japanese art(➤ 説明的な訳).

イエローカード《サッカー》a **yellow card.**

イエローストーン **Yellowstone**

‖**イエローストーン国立公園** Yellowstone National Park.

いえん 胃炎 **gastritis** /gæstráɪṭɪs/, **inflammation of the stomach.**

いおう 硫黄《米》**sulfur** /sʌ́lfəʳ/,《英》**sulphur.**

イオン an **ion** /áɪən/

‖**陰イオン** a negative ion, an anion /ǽnàɪən/ ‖ **水素イオン** a hydrogen ion ‖ **陽イオン** a positive ion, a cation /kǽtàɪən/.

¹**いか**《動物》a **cuttlefish** (コウイカ) ; a **squid** (ヤリイカ).

²**いか 以下** **1【数量, 程度】less than, below ; up to** (…まで)

> **解説 「…以下」の言い方**
> (1) 日本語で「100以下」という場合, 100を含めてそれより小さい数をいう. したがってこれを英語で表現する場合, 厳密には 100 or less のように100を明示しなくてはならない. less than 100 では100を含まないからである. しかし厳密な数字にこだわらない場合には, less than か below を用いて表現してよい.
> (2)「10万円以下の罰金」のように, 上限を示す場合は up to を用いる.

▶この種の修繕は10万円**以下**でできます This kind of repair can be done for *less than* one hundred yen. ‖お申し込みが10人**以下**の場合は催行いたしません If the applicants are *less than* 10, the trip will be cancelled. ‖ 誤差は 5 パーセント**以下**です The margin of error is 5 percent *or less*. ‖ 目下, 預金金利は大概0.2パーセント**以下**である At present, interest rates on most bank accounts are 0.2 percent *or less*.

▶この部屋の温度は25度**以下**に保たねばなりません The temperature of this room must be kept *below* 25 degrees Celsius. ‖ 100万円**以下**(=まで)のお金ならお貸しできます I can lend you money if you need *up to* one million yen. ‖この法律に違反すると10万円**以下**の罰金だ If you violate this law, you will be fined *up to* 100,000 yen. ‖ 私の息子は**10歳以下**の子供たちのサッカーの試合に出場した My son participated in a soccer game for children (of) *ten and under* [*ten or younger*]. (➤ 年齢については below でなく under を用いる) ‖《掲示》**小学生以下**は入場無料 Admittance free for *children in elementary school or younger*.

▶ **対話**「生物のテストどうだった？」「**平均以下**だったよ」 "How did you do on the biology test ?" "My grade was *below average*."

▶このマンションの**3階以下**には事務所や商店が入っている *The first three floors* of this apartment building are occupied by offices and stores. ‖ 老婆の金を奪うなんて, あの男はけだもの**以下**だ That man stole money from an old woman. He's *worse than* an animal.

2【ほか】▶校長**以下**, 先生方は全員参加した All the teachers participated, *from* the principal *on down*. ‖ 船長**以下**300人がその船に乗っていた A total of 300 crew members, *including* the captain, were on board the ship.

3【続き, 下記】▶**以下**次号(に続く) *To be continued*. ‖ **以下**315ページに続く *Continued* on page 315.

▶**以下**は優勝者のスピーチの全文です *The following* is the full text of the winning speech. ‖ 首相の演説の要旨は**以下のとおり**です The gist of the Prime Minister's address is *as follows*. (➤ 実際はピリオドでなく, コロン(:)を置いて要旨を続ける).

³**いか 医科**

‖**医科大学** a medical school [college].

いが 毬 a **bur(r)** ▶クリのいがが割れた The chestnut *bur* split.

¹**いがい 遺骸** a (**dead**) **body** (死体) ; one's **remains** (時間・年月が経過したという含みがあることが多い).

²**いがい 意外な** **unexpected** ▶**意外**な結果 an *unexpected* result ‖ それは全く**意外**な出来事だった The incident was totally *unexpected*. ‖ **対話**「テスト, どうだった？」「うん, **意外と**(=予期していたより)簡単だったよ」 "How did you do on your test ?" "Well, it was easier *than I* (*had*) *expected*."

▶モロッコできみに出会うとは全く**意外だった** It *was* quite *a surprise* [*I never expected*] to see you in Morocco. ‖ きみが彼の意見を支持するとは**意外**だね(=驚いた) I *was surprised* to learn [hear／find out] that you support his opinion. ‖ **意外にも**(=思いがけないことに)美佐子にラブレターを書いたのは担任の教師だった *Unexpectedly* [*To our surprise*], the homeroom teacher turned out to be the one who wrote the love letter to Misako. ‖ **意外や意外**！ *What a surprise*！

▶推理小説は**意外性**がないとおもしろくない Detective stories are worthless without an *element of surprise* [*unpredictability*].

³**いがい 以外** **1【…以外は】except, but** (➤ 前者が一般的で, かつ, 除外の含みが強い) ; **other than** (…のほかに[の]) ▶邦子**以外**はみんな英語が好きだ Everybody *except* Kuniko likes English. ‖ 月曜日**以外は**毎日うちにいます I am at home every day *except* (on) Mondays.

▶山頂には雪**以外**何も見えなかった Up on the mountain peak, there was *only* snow [*nothing but* snow]. ‖ 軍関係者**以外**立入禁止 Off limits *except for* military personnel. (➤ except for は「…を除いてほかの人は」の意).

▶巨人**以外の**チームに優勝してもらいたい I want any team *other than* the Giants to win the pennant. ‖ 費用の問題**以外は**アメリカ生活は快適でした *Apart from* the cost, my stay in America was pleasant. (➤ apart from は「…を除いては」).

▶私はみずえ**以外に**友だちはいない I have no friends *besides* Mizue. ／Mizue is the only friend I have. ‖ その詩人は自国**以外では**ほとんど知られていない That poet is little known *outside* his own country. ‖ 私はもう靖子に頼む**以外にない**んだ I *have no choice but* to ask Yasuko. ‖ 練習**以外に**上達の道はない There's no way to improve *without* practice. ‖ 許可された車両**以外の**駐車を禁じます No parking *without* permit. ／ Authorized vehicles only.

い

2【…に加えて】in addition《to》▶うちのおじはベンツ以外にアウディも持っている My uncle has an Audi *in addition to* a Mercedes(-Benz). ‖ 山本教授は中国語以外にインドネシア語も話します Professor Yamamoto speaks Indonesian *as well as* Chinese. ‖ 彼女は給料以外の収入が多い She has a good income *on top of* her salary. (➤ on top of は「…に加えて」).

いかいよう 胃潰瘍 a stomach ulcer, a gastric ulcer /ʌ́lsəʳ/.

いかが 如何 →どう 1【様子を聞いて】how

> 【文型】
> A はいかがですか
> How is [are] A?
> How do you like A? ➤ A は名詞・動名詞など
> What do you think of [about] A?
>
> 《解説》(1)How do you like A? は経験・体験に基づいた感想を聞き，気に入りぐあいや好みなどを質問している．
> (2)What do you think of [about] A? は「Aをどう思いますか」と意見や感想を聞く．実際に経験や体験があるかどうかは問わない．

▶ 対話「ご機嫌いかが？」「元気でやってます．あなたは？」"*How are you doing?*" "Pretty good. How about you?" ‖ 対話「お母さんの具合はいかがですか」「快方に向かっています」"*How is* your mother?" "She is getting better, thank you." ‖ 対話「景気はいかがですか」「まあ何とかやっております」"*How's* (your) business?" "We are doing all right." ‖ 対話「バリ島(旅行)はいかがでしたか」「とてもよかったです」"*How was* (the trip to) Bali?" "It was just fantastic." (◉「バリはいかがでしたか」のつもりで How about Bali? としないこと．これだと「(旅行先として)バリはいかがですか」の意味になる．旅行から帰った人に「バリはいかがでしたか」と聞くには How did you like Bali? で，旅行中の人に「バリはいかがですか」は How do you like Bali? という).

▶新居でのお暮らしはいかがですか *How do you like* (living in) your new home? ／*How is* (*it*) living in your new home? (➤ 前者は総合評価や全体的感想を，後者はより細かな具体的な状況を聞く．前者には It's great. (すばらしいですよ)や It's better than I expected. (思っていた以上です)で十分だが，後者には I enjoy the more spacious living room. (リビングが広くなっていいですよ)などと具体的に応じる) ‖ 新しい仕事はいかがですか *How do you like* your new job? (➤ 総合的な感想を聞く) ／*How is* your new job? (➤ より具体的な返事を求めている) ‖ 今年の新入社員たちはいかがですか *What do you think of* the new employees this year?

▶ 対話「野球の試合，いかがでしたか」「シーソーゲームでおもしろかったわ」"*How did you enjoy* the ball game?" "It was an exciting seesaw game."

✉ **いかがお過ごしですか** *How have you been*? ➤ しばらくご無沙汰したときの表現．「ご機嫌いかが？」「その後いかが？」のようなややくだけた言い方に相当するのは How's everything?, How are you getting along? など．

✉ **新しい学校はいかがですか** *How do you like* your new school?

2【勧めて・誘って】How about ...?, What about ...? (➤ 後者のほうが少し改まった感じの言い方)

> 【文型】
> A はいかがですか
> How about A? ➤ A は名詞・動名詞など
> Would you like A?
> How would you like A?
>
> 《解説》(1)Would you like A? ／How would you like A? は改まった丁寧な聞き方．to do がきて「…するのはいかがですか」と誘う言い方にも用いる．
> (2)Would you like A? が Yes か No かを聞くのに対して，How would you like A? は同意を前提としたより積極的な誘いになる．

▶コーヒーを1杯いかが(ですか) *How about* a cup of coffee? ／*Would you like* [*care for*] a cup of coffee? ‖ お菓子はいかが(ですか) *How about* a piece of cake? ‖ 対話「このブルーのネクタイはいかがですか」「いいですねえ．いただきましょう」"*How about* this blue tie?" "It's (quite) nice. I'll take it." ‖ 対話「ウーロン茶はいかがですか」「お願いします」"*Would you like* a cup [glass] of oolong tea?" "Yes, thank you." ‖ もう少しいかがですか *Would you like* some more? (➤ 勧めるときは some を用いて，Yes を言いやすくする．→少し) ‖ こちらのスマートフォンはいかがですか *How about* this smartphone? (➤ 選択に迷っている人などに言う．いきなり勧めては言わない) ／*How do you like* this smartphone? ／*What do you think of* this smartphone? (➤ 後者2つは感想を聞く場合もある．→いかが 1; How would you like ...? というと売り込みの最終段階のニュアンスになる) ‖ 今晩は外で食事というのはいかがですか *How about* going out for dinner this evening? ／*How would you like to* go out for dinner this evening? ‖ 対話「今度その店に行くときはご一緒にいかがですか」「ありがとうございます．ぜひお願いします」"*Would you like to* [*How would you like to*] come with me when I visit the restaurant next time?" "Thank you. I'd like that [I'd like to] very much."

> **直訳の落とし穴「いかがですか」「いかがでしたか」**
> (1)「いかが」＝ How about? と思い込んでいる人が多く，「夏休みはいかがでしたか」を(×)How about your summer vacation? と言ってしまう間違いが多い．様子を聞くのであるから，How was your summer vacation? としなければならない．
> (2)食事ですし屋に誘って「すしはいかがですか」もいきなり，(△)How about (going for) sushi? とは言わない．Would you like (to go for) sushi? (すしがいいですか)が正しい．How about (going for) sushi? はどこに行こうか話が出たあとで，1つの提案として言うときには用いられる．また，すし屋で食事中に「ここのすしはいかがですか」と聞くには How do you like the sushi here? あるいは What do you think of the sushi here? という．さらに，店を出てから感想を聞いて「(今召し上がった)すしはいかがでしたか」は How did you like the sushi?, Did you enjoy the sushi?, How was the sushi? などという．

3【疑問視する】▶公共工事の大幅削減はいかがなものかと思います I wonder *if* [*whether*] it's a good thing to drastically cut public works projects.

いかがわしい dubious /djúːbiəs/ (怪しげな); obscene /əbsíːn/ (淫らな) ▶いかがわしい写真[本] an *obscene* picture [book] ‖ いかがわしい(＝まっとうでない)商売 a *shady* business ‖ 彼はかなりいかがわしい手段で財を成したらしい I've heard he earned his fortune by rather *dubious* means. ‖ あんないかがわしい(＝えたいが知れず信用できない)男に娘はやれないね I won't let such a *questionable* [an *untrustworthy*] man like him marry my daughter. ‖ あんないかがわしい(＝評判のよくない)場所に近づいてはいけない Keep away from that *disreputable* place.

いかく 威嚇 a **threat** /θret/ 一動 **威嚇する threaten** ＋目 ▶威嚇的な態度に出る take a *threatening* attitude ‖ 威嚇射撃 *warning* shots ‖ 空砲を撃って暴徒を威嚇する *warn off* the rioters by firing blank shots ‖ 犬は怪しい侵入者を威嚇してほえた The dog barked to *threaten* the suspicious intruder.

いがく 医学 medicine 一形 **医学の medical** ▶医学を学ぶ study *medicine* ‖ 私には多少医学の知識がある I have some *medical* knowledge.
‖医学界 the medical field, the medical community ‖ 医学(部学)生 a medical [《インフォーマル》med] student ‖ 医学博士 a doctor of medicine (➤ 学位は Doctor of Medicine と書き, M. D. ときに D. M. と略す) ‖ 医学部 the school [college] of medicine, the medical school [college] ; 《英》 the faculty of medicine.

いがぐり 毬栗 ▶いがぐり頭 *close-cropped* hair (→坊主, 丸坊主).

いかさま 一動 **いかさまをする cheat** ▶今の勝負はいかさまだ! You *cheated* (to win)! ‖いかさま師 a crook /krʊk/ ; a fraud /frɔːd/ (詐欺師).

いかす 生かす **1【生存させる】**▶清流にすむ魚を水槽で長く生かしておくのは難しい It is difficult to *keep* fish that used to live in a clear stream *alive* in a fish tank for a long time. ‖ 誘拐犯たちは人質を身代金欲しさに生かしておく(＝殺さない)だろう The kidnappers will *spare* the hostage's *life* [*keep* the hostage *alive*] in hopes of (getting) ransom (money). ‖ 材料の味を生かすも殺すも料理人の腕次第だ The skill of a chef may be judged by whether he [she] *brings out* the flavors of the ingredients (in each dish) or smothers them. ‖ 花瓶の花一輪が床の間を生かしも殺しもする A single flower in a vase often *enhances or detracts from* [*makes or mars*] the *tokonoma*.
2【発揮する】▶与えられたチャンスを最大限に生かす *make the most of* every given chance [opportunity] ‖ 語学力を生かせる仕事に就きたい I'd like to get a job where I can *make good use of* [*make the most of*] my language ability. ‖ 作者のフランスでの体験が彼の小説に生かされている The writer *utilizes* his experiences in France in his novels. ‖ 彼女は才能を生かすことができた She was able to *put* her talent(s) *to work* [*to good use*].

いかすい 胃下垂 gastroptosis /gæstrɑːptóʊsɪs/ (➤ 医学用語) ; a **downward displacement of the stomach.**

いかだ 筏 a **raft** (➤ いかだで川下りをするスポーツを rafting という) ▶いかだで川を下る go down (a) stream on *a raft*.

いがた 鋳型 a **mold**(➤《英》では mould) ; a **cast** ▶鉄を鋳型に流し込む pour melted iron into *a mold* [*a cast*]. ‖《比喩的》生徒を鋳型にはめるような教育に対する批判が高まっている Criticism of an education system that squeezes [forces] students into *the same mold* is growing. (➤「画一的教育」は one-size-fits-all education).

いかつい stern(いかめしい) ; **square**(角張った) ▶いかつい顎 a *square* jaw ‖ 校長先生はいかつい顔をしている The principal of our school has a *stern* face.

いかなる 如何なる ▶いかなる苦難に遭おうとも, 私は自由を得るために戦う *No matter what* difficulties come my way, I will never give up the fight to be free. ‖ いついかなるときにも希望だけは捨てるな *No matter what* happens, never give up hope. ‖ いかなる状況でも全力を尽くすことが重要だ It's important to do your best *under any circumstances*.

いかに 如何に **1【疑問】**▶日本の国際貢献がいかにあるべきか真剣に論議された (The question of) *what form* Japan's international aid should take was seriously debated.
2【程度の強調】▶その事業がいかに(＝どれほど)大変であるか, 誰にも予測できなかった No one really realized *how* difficult the project would prove to be. ‖ この危機をいかに(＝どのようにして)乗り切るかが問題だ The problem is *how to* get over this crisis.
3【譲歩】▶いかに多忙でも電話をくれるくらいの時間はあるはずだ *No matter how* busy you are, you must have time to call me.

いかにも 如何にも ▶それはいかにも(＝確かに)ありそうなことだ It is *most* likely. ‖ やることなすことみんなうまくいって, 彼はいかにも(＝本当に)うれしそうだった He looked *quite* satisfied that everything he tried went well. ‖ 正雄君のデートの誘いをすげなく断ったって? いかにも彼女らしいね She gave Masao a quick brush-off when he asked her out? That's *just like* her. ‖ そんなことをするなんていかにも太田君らしい That's (*just*) the sort of thing you'd expect Ota to do. (● It's characteristic of Ota to do. としがちだが, 訳例のように「それこそ太田君がやるだろうと思ってよいことだ」と発想するのが英語的) ‖ こたつはいかにも日本的なすばらしい暖房器具だ The kotatsu is a wonderful heater that is *typically* Japanese.
▶彼はいかにもその秘密を知っているかのような話し方をする He talks *as if* he knew [knows] the secret. ‖ 由美子の態度はいかにも自分は美人だと言わんばかりだ Yumiko's attitude *shows* that she thinks she's a beauty.

いかばかり ▶ご両親の悲嘆はいかばかりかとお察しいたします I can imagine *how* heartbroken his [her] parents *must be* (and I sympathize with them).

いかほど →どのくらい.

いがみあう いがみ合う quarrel(口げんかする) ▶彼らはどうしていつもいがみ合ってばかりいるのだろう I wonder why they *are* always *quarreling* [*at odds*] *with each other*. (➤ be at odds with で「…と不和である, 争っている」).

いかめしい 厳めしい stern(厳しい) ; **grave** (重々しい) ▶あの人は顔は見るからにいかめしいが, 実際は実にくだけた人だ He looks quite *stern* but in fact he is very easy to talk with. ‖「子供はここに入ってはいけない」と守衛がいかめしい声で言った The guard said in a *grave* voice, "Children aren't permitted to enter here." ‖ いかめしい肩書き a *high-sounding* title ‖ いかめしい警備 *tight* security.

いカメラ 胃カメラ a **gastric camera**, a **gastrocamera** ▶先月, 胃カメラの検査を受けた Last month I had *a gastric camera examination*. / Last month I underwent *an endoscopic examination of my stomach*. (➤ endoscopic /èndəskɑ́ːpɪk/ examination は「内視鏡検査」).

いがらっぽい ▶喉がいがらっぽい I have an *irritated*

[a *scratchy*] throat. ／My throat *feels scratchy*.

[1]**いかり 怒り** **anger, rage, fury** (➤ この順に怒りが激しくなる)；**wrath**《文語》▶彼の言い訳を聞いているうちに**怒り**が込み上げてきた As I was listening to him make excuses, I was filled with *anger*. ／When I heard him make excuses, *anger* rose within me. ‖ 彼女の不注意なことばが彼の**怒り**を招いた Her careless words aroused his *anger*. ‖ ウエーターの言動は客の**怒り**を買った The waiter's behavior invited the customer's *fury*. ‖ (一神教での) 神の怒り the *wrath* of God ‖『怒りの葡萄(ぶどう)』"The Grapes of *Wrath*" (➤ John Steinbeck の小説名).

[2]**いかり 錨** an **anchor** /ǽŋkəʳ/ ▶いかりを上げろ[下ろせ]！*Weigh* [*Drop*] *anchor !* (➤ 決まった言い方で a や the は不要).

いかる 怒る ⇀おこる.

いかれる 1【だめになる】▶この扇風機少しいかれてきたようだ This fan is *on the blink*. (➤ on the blink は「(機械などが) 修理が必要な状態で」) ‖ 友子はあんないかれたやつがいいって言うのかい？Do you mean that Tomoko loves a *crazy* guy like him ? ‖ あいつ，ちょっと頭がいかれてるよ He's *missing a few screws*. (➤ He has a screw loose. などとも言う) ／《英》He is a little *barmy*.

2【ほれ込む】▶やつがあの子にいかれてるのは確かだ You can see (that) he *is crazy about* her [he's *lost his head over* her].

[1]**いかん 遺憾** ▶私たちの意図が通じなかったのは**遺憾だ** *It is to be regretted* [*It is regrettable*] *that* our intentions were not well taken. ‖ 今回の不祥事は**誠に遺憾です** This current scandal is *deeply regrettable*. ‖ 大臣はその事故に**遺憾の意**を表した The Minister expressed his *regret* over the accident.

▶彼はそのレースで**遺憾なく**実力を発揮した He showed his *full* strength in the race.

✉ **あなたのご要望に応えられないことを遺憾に存じます** *I regret that* I cannot comply with your request. ➤ I am sorry ... より堅い表現.

[2]**いかん 移管する** (…に) **transfer**《to》▶その件は刑事局に**移管される**予定です That case is going to *be transferred to* the Criminal Investigation Bureau.

[3]**いかん 如何** ▶問題がここまでこじれたら，**いかんともしがたい** Seeing that the problem has gotten this complicated, *nothing can be done about it*. ‖ 天候の**いかんにかかわらず**(そちらへ)参ります *No matter what* the weather is, we will definitely come.

▶今度のテストの結果**いかんで**進路が決まる My future direction in life *depends on* the results of the next test(s).

いがん 胃癌 **stomach cancer** ▶胃がんになる get *stomach cancer*.

[1]**いき 息** **1【呼吸，呼気】**(a) **breath** /breθ/ **一動** **息をする** **breathe** /briːð/ ▶深く[軽く]息をする *take a* deep [shallow] *breath* ／*breathe* deeply [lightly] ‖ **息を吐く**[**吸う**] *breathe out* [*in*] ‖ **息が苦しい** I *can hardly breathe*. ‖ 患者はすでに**息がなかった** The patient had already *stopped breathing*.

▶**息が臭くてすみません** I'm sorry for my *bad breath*. ‖ 鼻が詰まって**息ができません** My nose is stuffed up and I *can't breathe*. ‖ 口で**息をしてはいけません**．**鼻でしなさい** Don't *breathe* through your mouth. Use your nose. ‖ 大きく**息を吸って**，止めて *Take a* deep *breath* and hold it. (➤ X 線技師などの指示) ‖ 救助された少年は手当てのかいもなくまもなく**息絶えた** Despite our attempts to save him, it wasn't long before the rescued boy *breathed his last*. ‖ 被害者は**息も絶え絶え**の状態です The victim is *breathing faintly*. ‖ **対話**「満員電車には慣れましたか」「だめです．**息が詰まり**そうになります」"Have you gotten accustomed to jam-packed trains ?" "No. I always feel like I'm *suffocating* on them."

2【慣用表現】 **息が合う** ▶校長と教頭は息が合っているようだ The principal and the vice-principal seem to *get along well with* each other [*make a good team*]. **息が切れる** ▶階段を駆け上がったら息が切れた I *was winded* [*out of breath*] after running up the stairs. ／After running up the stairs I *was breathless*. **息が長い** ▶トンネル工事は息の長い仕事だ Tunneling work *takes a long time*. ／It *takes a long time* to cut [dig] a tunnel. ‖ あの小説家は息が長い That novelist *has been writing for a long time*. ／He [She] *has been a novelist for a long time*. (● 前者は「あの小説家は長い年月執筆活動をしている」と発想し，後者は「彼[彼女]は長い年月小説家をしている」と発想したもの) **息つく暇もない** ▶次から次へと講演を頼まれて息つく暇もないよ I've been being asked to do one lecture after another and *don't have time to breathe* [*have no time to catch my breath*]. **息を凝らす** ▶群衆は息を凝らして処刑を見つめた The crowd watched the execution of the criminal *breathlessly* [*with bated breath*]. **息を殺す** ▶刑事は息を殺してドアの陰に隠れていた The detective hid behind a door *holding his breath*. **息をのむ** ▶息をのむような美人 a *breathtaking* beauty ‖ グランドキャニオンの美しさに思わず息をのんだ The majestic view of the Grand Canyon *took my breath away*. **息を弾ませる** ▶父は石段を上り切ると息を弾ませていた My father *was panting* when he reached the top of the stone steps. **息を引き取る** ▶午後11時 2 分，その財界の巨頭はついに息を引き取った At 11 : 02 p.m. the business tycoon *breathed his last*. ‖ 祖母は入院して 3 日後，静かに息を引き取った My grandmother was taken to (the) hospital and *passed away* peacefully three days later. **息を吹き返す** ▶ 30分の人工呼吸の結果，彼女は息を吹き返した She *came to* (*life*) [*was revived*] after thirty minutes of artificial respiration.

☛ **息苦しい，息せき切って，息遣い** (⇀見出語)

[2]**いき 意気** ▶私たちは初めて会ったときから**意気投合した** We *hit it off* right from the start. ‖ 彼らは試合に勝って**意気揚々**としていた They were *riding high* [*in high spirits*] on winning the match. ‖ 祖父は老いてなお**意気盛ん**だ My grandfather is *hale and hearty* in his old age. ‖ 彼は期待が外れて**意気消沈した** He *was despondent* [*depressed*] when his expectations were not met. ‖ **その意気，その意気** That's the way ! ／That's the spirit !

[3]**いき 域** ▶彼のそば打ちの技術は**名人の域に達している** His skill at making soba noodles *has reached a master's level*. ／He *has achieved mastery* in making soba noodles. ‖ 英語も彼の**域**にまで達するには長年の修練がいる It takes many years of training to have as good a command of English as he does. (➤「彼と同程度に上手に英語を使いこなすには」と考える).

[4]**いき 粋な** **smart, stylish** (➤ 後者には「一時的で移ろいや

すい」という含みがあることが多い) ▶彼のお父さんはいつも粋な格好をしている His father is always *smartly* dressed. ‖ 粋な帽子をかぶってるね That's a *stylish* hat you're wearing. ‖ それは粋な計らいだね That's a *smart* way to deal with it. ‖ 都心の粋な老舗(しにせ) a *refined* [*quietly elegant*] old shop in downtown Tokyo.

☞ 粋がる (→見出語)

5**いき 生き** ▶生きのいい魚 a *fresh* fish ‖ 生きのいい若者 a *lively* young person.

6**いき 行き** ▶行きは雨だったが帰りは晴れた *On my way there* it was raining, but on my way back the skies were clear. ‖ 行きはバスを利用したが帰りはタクシーで帰って来た I *went there* by bus but took a taxi home.

▶鹿児島中央行きの新幹線 a Shinkansen (super-express) train (*bound*) *for* Kagoshima-Chuo ‖ 羽田行きのバスに乗る take the bus *to* [*for*] Haneda / take the Haneda bus (🏺 羽田行きのバスが何台も通っているのなら the を a にする) ‖ 対話「この電車はどこ行きですか」「大宮行きです」"*Where* does this train *go*?" "Omiya."

7**いき 遺棄する** **abandon** +目, **desert** +目 ▶ペットを遺棄する *abandon* one's pet.

1**いぎ 意義** **significance** (重大な影響力を持つ); (a) **meaning** (意味, 目的) ▶大いに意義のあること a matter of great *significance* ‖ それは地域の人々にとって意義ある事業だ It is a *significant* project for the people in the community. ‖ 私は意義ある人生を送りたいと思う I would like to lead a *meaningful* life.

2**いぎ 異議** an **objection** ▶私に異議はありません I have no *objection*. ‖ この提案に対して異議はありませんか Is there any *objection* to this proposal? ‖ 異議なしと認めます I see no *objection*. ‖ 異議あり! *Objection!* ‖ 異議なし! *No objection!*

いきあたりばったり 行き当たりばったり ▶彼のやることは行き当たりばったりで, 計画性がない The way he does things is *hit-or-miss* [*haphazard*] and he doesn't plan anything beforehand. ‖ 彼女は行き当たりばったりのやり方で店を経営している She is running her store in a *hit-or-miss* manner. ‖ 私は行き当たりばったりの旅が好きだ I like traveling *without any plans*.

いきいき 生き生きした **lively** /láɪvli/ (活発な); **vivid** (鮮やかな) ▶生き生きした若者 a *lively* young man ‖ この花は生き生きしている These flowers *are full of life*. ‖ この小説には逆境に負けない主人公のたくましさが生き生きと描かれている This novel *vividly* depicts its main character's strength in the face of adversity. ‖ 新婚の恵子は生き生きした表情をしていた Keiko, who had recently gotten married, was *radiant* [*glowing*]. (➤ radiant は「輝いて晴れやかな」, glowing は「健康的に」あるいは,「ほてって」「赤らんで」).

いきうつし 生き写し ▶きみはお父さんに生き写しだね You *look exactly like* your father. (➤「顔立ちがそっくりだ」の意) ‖ 彼女は母親に生き写しだ She is *a complete* [*the spitting*] *image* of her mother. (➤ the spitting image of は「～の口から吐き出されたような(よく似た)人」が原義で, spitting の代わりに living を用いることもある).

いきうま 生き馬 ▶ビジネスの世界は生き馬の目を抜くような所だ The business world is one of *cutthroat competition* [*dog-eat-dog competition*]. (➤ dog-eat-dog は「食うか食われるか」の意).

いきうめ 生き埋め ▶その山崩れで大勢の村人が生き埋めになった The landslide *buried* many villagers *alive*. (➤ bury /béri/ は「埋める」).

いきおい 勢い 1【動きの圧力】**power** (「力」の意の一般語); **force** (動作・動きなどが現れる) ▶川の水の勢い the *force* of the river water ‖ 水の流れは勢いを増した The water flow *grew stronger*. ‖ 嵐の勢いが静まったのでバスは動き始めた Since the storm had *died down*, the bus began to move. ‖ 白鵬は勢いよく相手を押し出した Hakuho shoved his opponent out of the ring *with a powerful push*. ‖ 消防士がボタンを押すとノズルから水が勢いよく噴き出した As soon as the firefighter pushed the button, water *gushed* out of the nozzle. (➤ gush は「噴出する」) ‖ 彼は勢い余ってつんのめった His *own force drove* him onto the ground. ‖ 日本チームは破竹の勢いで勝ち進んだ The Japanese team kept on winning *with crushing force*.

2【元気, 活力】**vigor** (活力) ▶勢いのいい(=よく育つ)植物 a *vigorous* plant ‖ 今の中日ドラゴンズには勢いがある The Dragons *are* currently *on a roll*. (🏺 英語では訳例のように,「勝ち[つき]まくっている」の意のインフォーマルな慣用句 on a roll を用いる) ‖ その横綱にかつての勢いはない The yokozuna doesn't have the *power* he used to have. ‖ 3昼夜経過して山火事の勢いはようやく衰え始めた The forest fire finally started to *subside* after three days and nights. ‖ 文壇にデビューしたての頃の彼は日の出の勢いだった When he made his debut in the world of literature, he was *an up-and-coming man* [*a rising star*].

3【はずみ, 調子】▶中年のサラリーマンが酔った勢いで外国人に近づいていって英語で話しかけた *Emboldened by alcohol*, a middle-aged office worker approached and spoke to a foreigner in English. (➤「酒を飲んで大胆になって」の意).

4【影響力】▶あいつは酒の勢いを借りないと何も言えない男さ *Without the courage gained from alcohol*, he cannot express his opinions.

5【自然の成り行き】▶子供を全員大学へやれば, いきおい生活は苦しくなる Life *naturally* becomes hard when you send all of your children to college.

いきがい 生き甲斐 ⚠ **1語でぴったり対応する語がないので, 文脈に応じて「生き(てい)ることの価値」「生きる目的」などと言い換えて英語に直す.**

▶生きがいのある人生とは何だろう What kind of life is *worth living*? / What (is it that) makes life *worth living*? (➤「生きがいのない人生」は an empty life) ‖ 妻に先立たれ, 私にはもう生きがいがない I lost my wife and now *have nothing to live for*. ‖ サッカーチームの指導は彼の生きがいだ Coaching the soccer team is his *reason for living*. ‖ 子供の成長を生きがいにする親もいる Some parents *live* to watch their children grow up. ‖ きみのおかげで生きがいを感じるよ You make me *feel life is worth living*. / You make *life worth living* for me. ‖ 何か生きがいを探しなさい Find *something to live for*. ‖ あなたの生きがいは何ですか What do you *live* [are you *living*] *for*?

いきかえり 行き帰り ▶学校への行き帰りに1時間かかる It takes me an hour to *get to school and back*.

いきかえる 生き返る **come back to life** ▶死者が生き返るなんてことがあるのだろうか Is it possible for a dead person to *come back to life*? ‖ 溺れた少年を人工

い

呼吸で**生き返らせる** *revive* [*resuscitate*] a drowned boy with artificial respiration(➤ resuscitate は「蘇生(そせい)させる」の意の堅い語).

▶《比喩的》久しぶりの雨で街路樹が**生き返った** The first rain in many days *has revived* the (street) trees. ‖ 風呂で温まって**生き返ったような気がする** I *feel like a new man* [*woman*] after taking a hot bath. ／I *feel totally* [*completely*] *refreshed* after taking a hot bath. (🏺日本人学習者は feel like refreshed と訳しがちだが, 訳例のように「生まれ変わった」と考えるほうが英語的).

いきがかり 行き掛かり ▶**行きがかり上**, その子犬をうちで飼うことになった *Circumstances forced me to* keep the puppy in my house.

いきかた 生き方 one's **way of life** ▶私は平凡な**生き方**が好きだ I prefer plain *living*. ‖ 彼女の**生き方**は理想的だ Her *lifestyle* [*way of life*] seems ideal.

いきがる 粋がる ▶**粋がる**んじゃないよ Don't *put on airs*. (➤「お高くとまるな」の意).

いきき 行き来 ▶母は一日に何度も台所とリビングを**行き来**(＝往復)する My mother *goes back and forth* between the kitchen and the living room many times every day. ‖ あの家の人たちとはしばらく**行き来**(＝交際)していません We haven't had any *contact* with the people in that house for a long time. ‖ ぼくたちは今でもよく**行き来している**(＝会う) We still *get together* often.

いきぎれ 息切れする **get out of breath** ▶数分走っただけで**息切れがした** I *got out of breath* after running for just a few minutes.

いきぐるしい 息苦しい ▶室内はたばこの煙で**息苦しい**ほどだった The cigarette smoke in the room was *suffocating*. ‖ 記者会見は**息苦しい**雰囲気の中で行われた The press conference was held in a *tense* [an *oppressive*] atmosphere. (🏺「息苦しい」を「張り詰めた」と考えれば tense,「抑圧的な」と考えれば oppressive を使うことができる) ‖ この部屋は狭くて**息苦しい**感じがする This room looks *oppressively small* to me.

いきごみ 意気込み **eagerness**(熱心さ, 熱意) ; **enthusiasm** /ɪnθjúːziæzəm/ (熱狂) ▶最初の**意気込み**はどこへやら, 彼はしょんぼりして帰って来た He went out full of *eagerness* [*enthusiasm*] but came back dejected.

いきごむ 意気込む ▶彼女は金メダルを取ると**意気込んでいる** She *is eager to* win a gold medal. ‖ 彼は1年でフランス語をマスターすると**意気込んでいる** He *is intent on* learning French in a year. ‖ **意気込んで**アメリカに来たものの, 奨学金が少なくてがっかりしてしまった I came to the U. S. *with great expectations*, but I was disappointed to have only a small scholarship.

いきさき 行き先 one's **destination**(目的地) ▶私たちの**行き先**は浅虫温泉だった Our *destination* was Asamushi Hot Spring. ‖ 私は妻に必ず**行き先**を言う I never fail to tell my wife *where I'm going*. ‖ 彼は**行き先**を言っていきましたか Did he say *where he was going*? ‖《タクシーの運転手が客に》お客さん, **行き先**は? *Where to*, sir [ma'am]? ‖ **行き先**の電話番号をここに置いておくわね Here's the phone number *where I'll* [*we'll*] *be*. ／Here's (the phone number) *where you can reach me* [*us*]. (➤ reach は「電話で人と連絡を取る」).

いきさつ 経緯 ▶いつ, どのような**いきさつ**でその事件のことを知ったのですか When and *how* did you *come to* know about the incident? ‖ どういう**いきさつ**で生け花に興味をもたれるようになったのですか, タイラーさん *What is it that* got you interested [*How did you* become interested] in ikebana, Miss Tyler? (🏺「あなたを生け花に興味をもたせるようにしたのは何ですか」と考えて, 前者のように表すこともできる) ‖ **いきさつは知らない**が, 山田君は退学するそうだ I hear Yamada's going to quit school, but I *don't know why* [I *don't know the details*]. ‖ 彼女にほれ込んだ**いきさつ**を話してくれよ Could you tell me *what has made* you fall for her? (➤ fall for は「人に引かれて好きになる」).

いきじびき 生き字引 a **walking dictionary** ▶彼はとても多くのことばを知っていて, まるで**生き字引**だ He has such a large vocabulary that he's (like) *a walking dictionary*.

いきすぎ 行き過ぎ ▶それはちょっと**行き過ぎ**だ That's *going* a little *too far*. ／You *have gone* a little *too far* there. ‖ この警備は**行き過ぎ**だ Security here is *excessive*.

いきすぎる 行き過ぎる **1【通り越す】** →通り越す, 通り過ぎる.
2【やり過ぎる】 →やり過ぎ.

いきせききって 息せき切って ▶「お母さん, ぼく算数で100点取った」と息子が**息せき切って**帰って来た My son came home *panting* and said, "Mom, I got a perfect score on my arithmetic test."

いきた 生きた **live** /laɪv/ (生きている) ▶**生きた**魚 a *live* fish ‖ **生きた**知識 *practical* knowledge (➤「実際的な」の意) ‖ **生きた**表現 an *up-to-date* expression (➤「現代に即応した」の意) ‖ **生きた**英語を学ぶためにイギリスへ行く go to Britain to learn *everyday* English ‖ 地震が起きたときは**生きた心地がしなかった** I *was scared to death* when the earthquake hit.

いきちがい 行き違い ▶私たちの手紙は**行き違い**になったらしい Our letters seem to *have passed each other* [*have crossed in the mail*].
▶国と国の間の**行き違い**(＝誤解)が戦争を引き起こすこともある *Misunderstandings* between nations may lead to war.

いきちがう 行き違う →行き違い.

いきづかい 息遣い **breathing** /bríːðɪŋ/ ▶患者の**息遣い**が荒くなってきた The patient began to have difficulty (in) *breathing*.

いきつけ 行きつけの **favorite**(ひいきにしている) ▶私の**行きつけ**のレストラン my *favorite* restaurant ‖ ジムの**行きつけ**のパブ a pub *where* Jim *is a regular customer* ‖ 母の**行きつけ**の美容院をのぞくと母はそこにいた I glanced into the beauty shop my mother *always goes to*, and there she was.

いきづまり 行き詰まり (a) **deadlock**, a **dead end** (交渉などの ; 後者は「行き止まり」に近い) ▶両国の和平会談の**行き詰まり**を打開する方法は見当たらない There is no way to break the *deadlock* in peace talks between the two nations.

[1]**いきづまる 行き詰まる** **stall** (一時的に止まる) ; **be** [**get**] **bogged down** (動きが取れなくなる) ; **be** [**get**] **stalemated** (手詰まりになる) ▶人生に**行き詰まったら**できるだけいろいろな人に会うとよい When you *reach an impasse* in life, it is helpful to meet as many different kinds of people as possible. (➤ impasse /ímpæs ‖ æmpɑ́ːs/ は「行き詰まり, 難局」) ‖ ダム建設計画は数か月前に**行き詰まった** The dam construction project *stalled* a few months ago. ‖ そのプロジェクトは開始後まもなく**行き詰まった** The project

got bogged down soon after it started. ‖ 仕事に行き詰まるようなことがあれば私に相談しなさい In case you *get bogged down* [*stuck*] in your work, just come and ask me for advice. ‖ 経営者側との話し合いは完全に行き詰まった The talks with the management *have reached a complete deadlock* [*stalemate*]. (➤ deadlock は「膠着(こうちゃく)状態」, stalemate は「手詰まり」の意のチェス用語) ‖ 中田氏は資金的に行き詰まっている Mr. Nakata *is stuck* for lack of funds. (➤ be stuck は「動きが取れなくなっている」).

2**いきづまる 息詰まる** ▶息詰まる熱戦 a *thrilling* game ‖ 息詰まるような沈黙 an *oppressive* silence ‖ 今度は何が起きるかと彼は息詰まるような思いで見つめていた He was watching with *breathless* interest to see what was going to happen next.

いきつもどりつ 行きつ戻りつ ▶老人は通りを行きつ戻りつしていた The elderly man was walking *backward*(*s*) *and forward*(*s*) along the street. ／The elderly man was walking *up and down* the street. →行ったり来たり.

いきていく 生きて行く →生きる.

いきどおり 憤り anger ; indignation (不正などに対する) ; resentment(人・言動に対する) ▶彼女は不公平な待遇に憤りを感じた She *felt indignant* [*indignation*] at the unfair treatment (that she had received).

いきどおる (…に)**憤る** get indignant《about, at》(公正・公平でないことに怒りを覚える) ; get offended《by, at》(傷つく) ; resent (ひどく嫌う) ▶不平等な扱いに憤る *get indignant about* [*at*] the unfair treatment (one has received) ‖ 彼女は上司の性差別発言に憤っていた She *was indignant at* her boss's sexist remark.

いきとどく 行き届く ▶サービスの行き届いた旅館 an inn where the service is *excellent* [*impeccable*] ‖ 誠に行き届いたおもてなしで恐縮です Thank you for your *gracious* hospitality.

✉ **初めての仕事で行き届きませんが, 全力で頑張りますのでよろしくお願いいたします** I'll do my best but since I don't have any experience in this type of work, I hope you'll help me out once in a while. (● これは日本的表現で, 英語では I may not have any experience in this type of work, but I'll do my best. のような言い方が好まれる).

いきどまり 行き止まり a dead end, the end of a road ▶ 500メートルも行くとこの道路は行き止まりになります After about five hundred meters, this road comes to *a dead end*.

いきながらえる 生き長らえる live long(長生きする) ▶寝たきりになってまで生き長らえようとは思わない I don't want to *live* so *long* that I become bed-ridden.

いきなり suddenly(突然) ; abruptly(出し抜けに ; suddenlyよりさらに予想外でショックが大きい) ▶角からいきなり猫が飛び出した A cat *suddenly* dashed out from around the corner. ‖ 彼はいきなり私に殴りかかってきた He *abruptly* swung (his fist) at me. ‖ 新人がいきなりアカデミー賞を獲得した A new face *unexpectedly* won an Academy Award. ‖ いきなり何を言い出すの？ What did you just *blurt out*?

いきぬき 息抜き ▶息抜きに散歩しましょう Let's take a walk *for a change* (*of pace*). ‖ 毎日毎日仕事ばかりじゃ体に悪いよ. たまには息抜きしなくっちゃあ All work and no play will damage your health, so you'd better *take a rest* once in a while.

いきぬく 生き抜く survive /sәʳváɪv/ ▶祖父母は戦中戦後を生き抜いた My grandparents *lived through* [*survived*] the war and post-war period. (➤ live through は「苦難のときを経験する」の意味. survive は「(死なずに)生き延びる」の意味で, ときに命に関わるような深刻な状況を乗り切ったというニュアンス).

いきのこる 生き残る survive /sәʳváɪv/ (+目) ▶核戦争に生き残る *survive* a nuclear war ‖ 新人が芸能界で生き残るのは大変だ It is hard for a new face to *survive* in show business.

いきのね 息の根 ▶あいつの息の根を止めてやる I will *finish* [*destroy*] him.

いきのびる 生き延びる survive /sәʳváɪv/ (+目) ▶漂流した漁船の船長は島で何日くらい生き延びたのですか How long did the skipper of the drifting fishing boat manage to *survive* on the island? (➤ manage to は「何とかして…する」の意).

いきまく 息巻く ▶きみとは絶交だと彼は息巻いた He *said furiously* [*in great anger*] that he would have nothing more to do with me. ‖ そのボクサーは全試合に勝ってやると息巻いた The boxer *bragged* that he would win all the fights. (●「…と自慢して言った」と考えて訳例のように bragged (現在形は brag) を用いる).

いきもの 生き物 a living thing(生命を持つもの), life (全生物) ; a (living) creature (特に植物以外の) ▶海の生き物 marine *life* ‖ あらゆる生き物の中でことばを話せるのは人間だけだ Of all *living things*, humans alone can use language. ／Humans are the only *creatures* that can use language. ‖ 生き物(＝動物)をいじめてはいけません Don't ever tease or mistreat *animals*.

いきょう 異郷 a foreign land ▶異郷に骨をうずめる die *in a foreign land* [*far from home*] ‖ 異郷にありて故郷を偲(しの)ぶ get homesick in *a foreign* [*strange*] *land*.

いぎょう 偉業 a great achievement ▶彼の仕事は歴史に残る偉業だ His work is *a great achievement* which will go down in history.

いきょうと 異教徒 a pagan /péɪgәn/, a heathen /híːðәn/ (➤ どちらもかつて用いられた語 ; 現在は差別用語とみなされる ; 「違う宗教の信者」は a believer in another faith という).

いきょく 医局 a medical office
‖医局員 a member of the medical staff (1人 ; 全体は the medical staff) ‖ 医局長 the senior member of the medical staff.

イギリス Britain, the United Kingdom (連合王国 ; 略 U.K.) ━形 イギリスの British

> **解説 Britain と England**
> (1)Britain は Great Britain の略称として用いられ, England, Wales, Scotland から成る.
> (2)the United Kingdom は上記の Great Britain に Northern Ireland を含めたもの.
> (3)England, English をそれぞれ Britain, British の意で用いるのは正式ではない. →イングランド.

▶イギリスに行く go to *Britain* ‖ イギリス首相 a *British* prime minister ／the prime minister of *Britain* ‖ 5月のイギリスの田園風景は最高に美しい The landscape of *the British countryside* in May is as beautiful as it can be. ‖ 彼はイギリス人だ He is *British* [is *from Britain*]. ‖ サッカー, ゴルフ, テニスはイ

ギリス発祥のスポーツだ Soccer, golf and tennis originate from *Britain*.
‖**イギリス英語** British English ‖ **イギリス海峡** the (English) Channel ‖ **イギリス連邦** the Commonwealth (of Nations).

いきりたつ いきり立つ ▶そんなささいなことでいきりたつなよ Don't *fume over* such a trivial matter.

いきる 生きる **1【生存する】live ; be alive**(生きている) ▶**生きる**ために食うのであって,食うために**生きる**のではない We eat to *live*, not *live* to eat. ‖ 80までは**生き**たいと思う I want to *live* to be eighty. ‖ 近頃では90歳代まで**生きる**人も多い These days many people *live* into their nineties. ‖ パンダはササの葉を食べて**生きている** (Giant) Pandas *live on* bamboo leaves. (➤ live on は「…を常食とする」) ‖ **生きているうちに**万里の長城を見たいものです I want to see the Great Wall of China *before I die*. (「生きているうちに」を直訳すれば while I'm alive だが,英語では before I die (死ぬ前に)というほうがふつう. ただし,さらにふつうの言い方をすれば Someday I want to see ～. (いつか～を見てみたい)となる) ‖ このイカ,まだ**生きている**よ,ピクピクしてる This squid *is* still *alive* and twitching. ‖ もし祖父が**生きていれば**90歳になる If my grandfather *were alive* now, he would be ninety years old. ‖ 死んだと思われた3人の漁師が**生きて**帰って来た The three fishermen who were thought to be dead returned *alive*.
▶彼は限りある命を精いっぱい**生きた** He *lived his few remaining days* to the full.
2【生活する】live ▶独りで**生きてゆく** *live* alone / *lead a* single *life* ‖ この不況に失業して,これからどうやって**生きていけばいい**かわからない I lost my job in this recession, and don't know how I'll *make a living* from now on. ‖ 残業手当が出るかどうかは基本給の安いわが家にとっては,**生きるか死ぬかの問題**だ Since my base pay is low, getting overtime pay (or not) is *a life or death matter* [*a matter of life and death*] for my family.
3【生きがいをもって生活する】 ▶**生きる**とは何と楽しいことだろう How exciting it is to *be alive*! ‖ あなたにとって**生きる**とは何ですか What does *life* mean to you? ‖ どんなことがあっても,希望をもって**生きよう** Let's *live* with hope no matter what happens.
▶彼は仕事一筋に**生きている** He is *living only for his work* now. / He *concentrates solely on his work* now. ‖ 国王は**愛に生きるため**王位を捨てた The king gave up the throne *for love*. ‖ 植村さんは山に**生き**,山に死んだ Mr. Uemura *lived* and died in the mountains.
4【機能・効力や影響力がある】 ▶その国では19世紀の終わり頃できた法律が今なお**生きている** In that country, laws made toward the end of the nineteenth century are still *in force* [*in effect*] today. ‖ モンゴル語の知識が今になって**生きてきた** My knowledge of Mongolian *has* finally *turned out to be useful*. ‖ バックを少し暗めにしたほうが人物は**生きる** The human figure will *come alive* if you make the background a little darker. ‖ 内野手のエラーでランナーが**生きた** The runner *was safe* due to the infielder's error.
☛ **生きた** (→見出語)

いきわかれ 生き別れ ▶彼女は戦争で両親と**生き別れ**になった During the war, she *was* [*became*] *separated from* her parents, *never to see* them *again*.

いきわたる 行き渡る ▶皆に**行き渡る**だけの食糧はある There is enough food to *go around* [*round*]. ‖ 喫煙の危険に対する認識は全国に**行き渡り**つつある Awareness of the dangers of smoking is *spreading* throughout the country.

[1]**いく 行く** **1【ある場所へ】go, come ; visit** +⑪ (観光・見学などで訪れる)

> **語法 go と come**
> (1) go は自分を中心にして自分がいる場所からよそへ行く動作を表し, come は相手のいる[行く]場所などへ自分が近づいて行く動作を表す. したがって,日本文に「行く」とあっても come を用いる場合があるので要注意.
> (2)「(場所に)着く」の意では get to や reach を用いる.

▶私はこの冬休みにラスベガスに**行く**予定だ I'm planning to *go* to Las Vegas during this winter vacation. ‖ あす,きみのうちに**行く**よ I'll *come* over (to your house) tomorrow. ‖ 《呼ばれて》すぐ**行く**よ (*I'm*) *coming!* (I'm going. と言うと相手から離れてよそへ行くという意味になる) ‖ 私もそのパーティーに**行く**わ I'*m coming* [*going*] to the party, too. ‖ 嵐山へはどう**行く**んですか How do I *get to* Arashiyama? ‖ 駅へ(**行く**に)はどう行ったらいちばん速いですか What's the quickest way (to *get*) *to* the station? (➤ 以上2例の get は「着く」の意 ; go だと不自然) ‖ そちらへは11月3日に**行きます** I'm going to *be* [*arrive*] there on November 3. ‖ **対話**「すまない,俺もう**行か**なくちゃ」「あら,もう?」"Sorry, I'd better be *going*." "Oh, so soon?" ‖ **対話**「会社へはふだん何時に**行きますか**」「7時です」"What time do you usually *go to* [*leave* (*home*) *for*] the office?" "At seven." ‖ **対話**「シンガポールへはいつ**行きますか**」「6月2日です」"When are you *leaving for* Singapore?" "On June 2." (➤ (1) leave は「出発する」. (2)「東京をたってシンガポールに行く」という場合は leave Tokyo for Singapore となる) ‖ **対話**「この電車は芦屋へ**行きますか**」「はい,ここから5つ目です」"Does this train *go* to Ashiya?" "Yes. It's the fifth stop from here." ‖ **対話**「ニュージーランドへ**行ったことがありますか**」「一度あります」"*Have you ever been* [《米また》*gone*] to New Zealand?" "Yes, once."
▶三浦半島は東京から簡単に**行ける** The Miura Peninsula *is* easily *accessible* from Tokyo. ‖ さあ**行こう** Let's *go*. / Let's *get going*. ‖ さあさあ,子供はあっちへ**行った**. 忙しいんだから *Run along* now, children. I'm busy. ‖ 今までどこに**行ってた**の? Where *have* you *been* all this while? ‖ 急行電車は**今行ったばかり**です The express train *has just left*. ‖ 息子は今ムンバイに**行っています** My son *is in* Mumbai now. ‖ 《タクシーを拾って地図などを見せながら》ここに**行ってください** Can you *take* me here?
✉ **いつかあなたの国に行きたいと思っています** I would like to *visit* your country someday.
2【通う】 ▶歩いて学校へ**行く** *walk* to school / *go* to school *on* [*by*] *foot* (➤ walk to school のほうが日常的) ‖ バス[電車]で会社へ**行く** *go* to work by bus [train] ‖ 弟は3か月間学校に**行っていない** My younger brother hasn't *been* [hasn't *gone*] to school for three months. ‖ **対話**「どこの大学へ**行ってる**の?」「C大学」"Where do you *go* to college?" "(I go to) C University." ‖ **対話**《同窓生

どうしの会話》「今どこの会社へ行ってるの？」「D電器だよ」"What company do you *work for* now?" "(I work for) D Electric."

3【…しに行く】

【文型】
…しに行く
go doing

【解説】(1)この形は go fishing (釣りに行く), go skiing (スキーに行く), go shopping (買い物に行く), go sightseeing (見物に行く)など, 活動がレクリエーション性のある決まった表現で用いられる.
(2)あとの前置詞は活動の場所を表す at や in になる. go に引かれて to としない.
(3)「人を出迎えに行く」など目的を表す一般的な言い方は go to meet a person のような,「…するために」に当たる言い方を用いる. ⇀ため.

▶ママは渋谷[スーパー]に買い物に行ったよ Mom *went shopping* in Shibuya [at the supermarket]. (➤「(場所に)行く」に重点を置いて go to Shibuya to shop という言い方は可能) ‖ 対話「大磯にサーフィンしに行こうよ」「うん, 行こう」"Let's *go surfing* at Oiso." "OK, let's."
▶散歩に行く *go for a walk*. ‖ 対話「そのうち遊びに行ってもいいですか」「いつでもどうぞ」"Can I *come to see* you [*come over*] some day?" "Sure. Anytime."

4【選ぶ, 通り過ぎる】▶いちばん近い道を行く *take* the shortest way ‖ 国道246号線を行こう Let's *take* Route 246. (➤この take は「行く道として選ぶ, 利用する」) ‖ この道を行けば村に行けます This road *takes* you to the village. (➤この take は「人を連れて行く」) ‖ 沖を大型客船が行く A cruise ship *is passing* off the coast. ‖ 手を挙げたけれどバスは行ってしまった I put up my hand, but the bus *didn't stop*.

5【進行する】▶さあいくぞ *Here we go*. (➤何かを始めるとき) ‖ 今夜はすき焼きでいこう *Let's* have sukiyaki this evening. ‖ くじ引きでいこう *Let's* draw lots. ‖ 物事は思いどおりにいくとは限らない Things don't always *go the way we want them to*. ‖ 学園祭は万事うまくいった Everything *went well* with our school festival. ‖ 国の経済は経済学者の言うとおりにはいかないことが多い A nation's economy often *turns out different* from what the economists say.
▶対話「計画はうまくいったの？」「そう思いますけど」"*Has* your plan *worked out*?" "I think so." ‖ 対話「同僚とはうまくいってる？」「まあまあです」"*Are* you *getting along well* with your colleagues?" "Yes, I'm doing all right."

6【届く】▶近いうちにおいからお願いのメールが行くと思いますからよろしく Just to let you know, you should *be getting* an email from my nephew with a request. Any help you can give him will be appreciated. (➤just to let you know は「お知らせしておきますが」) ‖ 当選の場合には通知が行きます If you win a prize, you will *be notified*.

7【到達する】▶いい線いっているぜ *Good for you*! ‖ 私は最後まで彼の説明には納得がいかなかった I *remained unconvinced* by his explanation till the end.

8【「…ていく」の形で】▶《移動》遠慮しないで, 上がってお茶でも飲んでいきなさい Don't hesitate. Just come on in and *have some tea* with us. ‖ 駅まで送っていってあげよう I'll *drive you* to the train station. ‖ 販売員は試供品を置いていった The salesman *left* a free sample before he left.
▶《進行》これからも勉強を続けていくつもりです I intend to *continue* studying. ‖ 事態はどんどん悪化していった The situation *went from bad to worse* [*deteriorated*] rapidly.
☛ 行ける, 行ってきます, 行ってらっしゃい (⇀見出語)

²いく 逝く pass away (➤die の婉曲(えんきょく)的な言い方) ▶そのヒロインは18歳の若さで逝ってしまう The heroine *passes away* at the young age of eighteen.

イグアナ 《動物》 an **iguana** /ɪgwáːnə/.

いくきゅう 育休 ⇀育児.

¹いくじ 育児 childcare, child-rearing, child-raising ▶姉は育児に追われている My sister is busy *taking care of her baby*. ‖ 育児の終わった女性がたくさんこの講座を受講している A lot of women who have finished *child-rearing* [*child-raising*] are attending this class.
▶3か月間の育児休暇を取る take *childcare* [*parental*] *leave* for three months (➤「育児休暇中である」は be on childcare [parental] leave; 女性の場合は maternity leave (産休)ともいい, 男性, あるいは性別に関係ない場合には parental leave を用いる; 有給の育児休暇の場合は前に paid, 無給の場合には unpaid をつければ違いがはっきりする).

²いくじ 意気地 ▶あいつは意気地がない He *has no backbone*. (➤backbone は「気骨, 勇気」) ／He's *spineless*. ‖ そんな意気地のないことでどうするの! Don't be such *a coward*! (➤coward は「臆病者」) ‖ この意気地なし! You *coward*!

いくせい 育成する grow +目 ▶農業試験場ではあらゆるタイプの稲の苗を育成している They *grow* all types of rice plants at the agricultural experiment station. ‖ 中国では国家が優秀なスポーツ選手の育成に積極的に当たっている In China, the government is aggressively trying to *develop* superior athletes.

いくた 幾多の many ▶社会人になれば幾多の困難に出合うことでしょう When you go out into the world, you will probably meet with *many* [*numerous*] difficulties.

いくつ 幾つ

1【個数】how many (➤あとに名詞が続く場合は複数形になる)
▶この家にはいくつ和室がありますか *How many* Japanese-style rooms are there in this house? ‖ (電車などで) 銀座はいくつ先ですか *How many* stops until Ginza? ‖ これほど貴重な宝は世界にいくつもない There are*n't many* precious treasures like this in the world. ／Precious treasures like this are *few and far between* in the world. (➤be few and far between は「きわめてまれである」) ‖ 同じハンドバッグをそんなにいくつも買ってどうするの? Why did you buy *so many* of the same handbag? ‖ いくつでも好きなだけ持っていってください Take *as many as* you like. ‖ もういくつ寝るとお正月 *How many* nights (are there) before New Year?

2【年齢】how old ▶アカリちゃん, 今度いくつになるの? *How old* will you be on your next birthday, Akari? ‖ お兄さんとはいくつ違いですか *How much older* is your brother than you? ‖ 子供はいくつで小学校へ上がりますか *At what age* do children enter elementary school? ‖ 彼女はいくつになっても変わらない She doesn't change *no matter how old she* *gets.* ／She hasn't changed a bit. (➤「全然変わらない」と考える) ‖ 彼はいくつになってもばかをやる He *never learns.* (➤「(経験などから)学ぶことがない」の意).

あなたの英語はどう響く?
日本人はよく「おいくつですか」という質問をするが, これに相当する How old are you ? は失礼に響くことが多い. 子供に対してならばさほど問題はないが, 自分より年長の大人や女性に対しては避けるべきである. アメリカなどでは就職の面接で年齢を聞くことは法律で禁じられている. どうしても聞く必要があるときは May I ask your age ? とか Would you mind if I asked your age ? のような丁寧な言い方をすること.

いくつか **幾つか** **some ; a few ; several**

語法 「いくつか」の言い方
(1)数をあまり意識せず「いくつか」というときは some を用いる. 少し意識して 2, 3 ～ 4, 5 くらいの気持ちのときは a few を, それより少し多めの場合には several を用いる.
(2)ほかに漠然とした数を表す some に近い意味の a number of がある.

▶これをいくつか差し上げましょう I'll give you *some* of these. ‖ 箱の中にリンゴがいくつか残っている There are *some* apples left in the box.
▶きみの英作文にはいくつか間違いがある There are *a few* mistakes in your English composition. ‖ 私のほうが彼女よりいくつか年下です I am *a few* years younger than her.

いくつも **a lot of, many, any number of** (たくさんの) ; **numerous** (数多くの) ; **a number of** (いくつかの) ▶犯人はいくつもの偽名を使った The culprit used *many* [*a number of*] aliases. ‖ その映画はいくつもの賞を取った The movie won *numerous* awards. ‖ 日本には女子ラグビー部はいくつもない *There aren't so many* women's rugby teams in Japan. ‖ このタイプのオルゴールは世界にもういくつも残っていない *Not many* [*Few*] music boxes of this type *remain* in the world. ／*There aren't* (*very*) *many* music boxes of this type *left* in the world.

いくど **幾度** →何度.

いくどうおん **異口同音** ▶人々は異口同音に彼の勇気を褒めたたえた People praised his courage *with one voice* [*unanimously*].

イグニッション an **ignition** (点火装置)
‖イグニッションキー (エンジンスイッチ) an ignition key.

いくぶん **幾分** ▶彼女の顔はいくぶん痩せて見えた Her face looked *somewhat* thin. ‖ いくぶん日が伸びてきた The days have gotten *a little* longer. ‖ 私の英語はいくぶんかは上達したと思う I think my English has improved *to some degree* [*extent*].

イクメン **ikumen** (father taking an active role in child-rearing) (➤ 日本独特の表現なので説明的な訳にするしかない ; 日本語は単数・複数を区別しないが, 英語は -men なので複数と取られかねない). ▶彼は「イクメン」だ He's a so-called *ikumen who takes an active role in child-rearing* in his family.

いくもうざい **育毛剤** a **hair growth formula**, a **hair restorer.**

いくら **幾ら** **1【値段】how much**

【文型】
A はいくらですか
How much is A ?
How much [What] does A cost ?
What's the price of A ?

▶ 対話「このTシャツはいくらですか」「3000円です」"*How much is* this T-shirt ? ／*How much does* this T-shirt *cost* ? ／*What's the price of* this T-shirt ?" "(It's) 3,000 yen." (➤ does の代わりに would を用いると響きが柔らかくなる) ‖ 対話「東京から名古屋までの運賃はいくらですか」「新幹線なら1万円くらいですね」"*What's* [*How much is*] *the fare* from Tokyo to Nagoya ?" "It's about 10,000 yen by Shinkansen." ‖ 対話「ヘアカット, いくら取られた?」「5000円さ」"*How much* did they charge for your haircut ?" "5,000 yen." ‖ 彼らは1日いくらで給料をもらっている They are paid *by the day.* ‖ 彼女は1週間いくらで働く She works *for so much a week.* (➤ so much は「いくら(いくら)」の意の名詞) ‖ 彼女は10万円で買った指輪をたったの1万いくらで手放した She sold her 100,000 yen ring for only *a little over 10,000 yen.* ‖ チケットはいくらからあるんですか What do (the) tickets *start at* ?

2【譲歩】

【文型】
いくら A でも [しても]
no matter how A
however A
➤ A は形容詞・副詞

解説 以下用例の no matter how は however に置き換えられ, またその逆も可能だが, no matter how のほうがくだけた表現でやや強調した印象も与えるので, 会話で多く用いられる傾向がある. 一方簡潔な印象を与える however は書きことばやスピーチなどで用いられる傾向がある. また, however は《米》よりも《英》で好まれる.

▶いくら食べても太らないなんて羨ましいね I envy you. You don't gain weight *no matter how much* you eat. ‖ いくら頑張っても500メートルも泳げない I can't swim 500 meters, *however hard* I (may) try. ‖ いくら夜遅くなっても今晩電話ちょうだい Please give me a call tonight, *no matter how late* it is. ‖ いくら短時間でもいいからきょう会いたい I'd like to see you today, *no matter how briefly.*
▶健康にはいくら注意しても注意し過ぎることはない You *can't be too* careful about your health. (➤ can't [cannot] be too ... で「いくら…しても…し過ぎることはない」の意 ; …には形容詞がくる) ‖ こんな簡単なことはいくら子供でもわかるだろう *Even a child* can understand such a simple thing. ‖ この食事で1万円とはいくら何でも高すぎる There is *no way* (*in the world*) that this meal is worth ten thousand yen.
▶いくら何でもそれはひどい *Whatever the reason is,* that is too cruel [horrible]. ‖ こういうものはいくらあっても助かります You can *never have too many* of these. (➤ 洗剤・タオルなどの日用品をもらったときの挨拶) ‖ いくら友達どうしだからと言っても, 貸した金をいつまでも返さないのはおかしい *Even though* we are friends, it's (just) not right that he [she] still hasn't returned the money I lent him [her] (long ago).

イクラ **salmon roe** /sǽmən ròʊ/ (➤「イクラ」はロシア

語の *ikra* から. 英米人はふつうは食べない).

いくらか 幾らか **1【数量】**▶いくらかでもあるのはないよりましだ *Something* is better than nothing. ‖ きみはフランス語をいくらかでも知ってるの？ Do you know *any* French？ ‖ 対話「お父さん, お金いくらか貸してよ」「ああ, いいよ」"Dad, could you lend me *some* money？" "Sure."

2【程度】▶彼はいくらか疲れているようだ He looks *a little* [*a bit*] tired. ‖ 彼の言ったことはいくらか(＝ある程度まで)当たっている What he said is true *to some extent*.

いくらでも 幾らでも ▶おなかがぺこぺこでいくらでも入りそうだ I'm so hungry that I could eat *any amount* [*a horse*]. (● 英語では「(おなかがぺこぺこで)馬一頭でも食べられそうだ」と発想して could eat a horse を用いる. 極めて日常的な言い方) ‖ きみの代わりはいくらでもいるんだ There are *lots of* people who could replace you. ‖ そのダリの絵を売ってくれるんでしたらいくらでも出します I'll pay *whatever you ask* if you sell me the Dali. ‖ 当図書館は本はいくらでも必要なだけ貸し出しいたします Here, you can check out *as many* books *as* you need. ‖ (寄付は)いくらでも結構です *Any sum* will be appreciated.

いくらも 幾らも ▶グアム島旅行ならいくらもお金はかからないわよ A trip to Guam would*n't* cost that *much* (money). ‖ 締め切りまで日にちはもういくらもない There are*n't many* days left before the deadline. ‖ 大きな問題点はほぼ解決したが, 細かい点はまだいくらも残っている The main problem is almost solved, but there are still *more than a few* minor details left (to be dealt with).

いけ 池 a **pond**; a **lake** (pond より大きいもの); a **pool** (小池) ▶子供たちははだしで池に入って遊んでいる The children are playing barefooted in the *pond*. ‖ ぼくは池のコイに毎日餌をやる I feed the carp in the *pond* [*pool*] every day. 《参考》英米の一般家庭の庭には日本のような池はない.

いけい 畏敬 **awe** /ɔː/; **reverence** (崇敬) ▶Y先生には畏敬の念を抱いています I *hold* Mr. Y *in awe*. ／I *revere* Mr. Y.

いけがき 生け垣 a **hedge** ▶私の家には生け垣が巡らしてある My house is surrounded by *a hedge*.

いけしゃあしゃあ ▶あの男, 俺にいけしゃあしゃあとうそをついた That man *had the nerve* [*was brazen enough*] *to* lie to me.

いけす 生けす a **fish tank**; a **fishpond** (池).

いけすかない いけ好かない ▶上役におべっかばかり使っていけ好かない男だ That man is *disgusting* [I *can't stand* that man]. He flatters the boss all the time. (➤ stand は「我慢する」).

いけづくり 生け作り a **sliced live fish.**

イケてる **cool, awesome.**

いけどり 生け捕り ▶子グマを生け捕りにする *catch* a bear cub *alive* ‖ 私たちは網で大きな魚を生け捕りにした We *netted* a big fish. ‖ カウボーイは野生馬を投げ縄で生け捕りにした The cowboy *lassoed* a wild horse.

いけない **1【良くない】** **bad** (悪い); **wrong** (間違った) ▶いけないことをする do something *wrong* ‖ いけない子ね！ You're a *bad* boy [girl]! ／You're being *naughty*. (➤ naughty /nɔ́ːṭi/ は「悪さをする」の意) ‖ 約束を破るなんていけない父さんだ It was *wrong* for Dad to break his promise to you. ‖ いけないのはきみの口の利き方だよ *What's wrong with you is* the way you talk. ‖ 無免許で運転したのだからきみがいけない You are *at fault* [It's your *fault*] because you drove a car without a driver's license. ‖ どうもこの部屋はじめじめしていけない(＝困る) *The trouble* [*The problem*] *is*, this room is too damp. ‖ いけない, 財布に1円も入ってない！ *Oh, no!* I don't have any money in my wallet. ‖ 対話「けさはせきがひどかったんです」「それはいけませんね」"I had a terrible cough this morning." "Oh, *that's too bad*."

2【禁止】 **Don't, must not, shouldn't**

> **【文型】**
> **…してはいけない**
> **Don't** do … .
> **must not** do … .
> **shouldn't** do … .

▶ばかなことをしてはいけない *Don't* be stupid. ‖ 文子ちゃん, 隆君とデートしてはいけませんよ Fumiko, you *mustn't* go out with Takashi. ‖ 人の携帯メールを読むなんていけないことだよ You *shouldn't* be reading someone else's text messages. (● 他人の携帯メールを現に読んでいる人に向かって言うのならこの訳例にあるように進行形を用いる. 一般論としての注意なら You shouldn't read … . とする). ‖ 次回は遅刻してはいけないよ You *had better not* be late the next time. (➤ had better は, そうしないと困ったことになるよ, と伝えるとき) ‖ 芝生へ入ってはいけません *Keep off* the grass. ‖ 授業中に私語はいけません Talking *isn't allowed* in class. ‖ 対話「オートバイで登校してもいいですか」「いけません」"May I ride a motorcycle to school？" "No, *you may not*." ‖ 対話「レポートは鉛筆で書いてはいけませんか」「いけません」"*Can* I write the term paper in pencil？" "No, *you can't*."

> **語法「…してはいけない」の言い方**
> (1) **Do not** … は否定の命令文を作るとき, You **must not** … は改まって強い禁止を伝えるとき, You **ought not to** … は「(道義上・責任上)当然…してはならない」の意を改まって伝えるとき, You **should not** … は「(私の考えでは)…しないほうがよい」の意で穏やかに禁止を伝えるとき. ほかに, You **may not** … は不許可・軽い禁止を表すとき, You **cannot** … は禁止に近い言い方で「…できない」の意を伝えるときにそれぞれ用いられる.
> (2) 日常的には Don't, You mustn't, You shouldn't, You can't のように, 短縮形を用いることが多い. 短縮形を用いると禁止の強さの程度が弱くなる.

3【義務, 必要】 **must, have (got) to** →-ならない

> **語法 must と have (got) to**
> (1) must は義務や道徳的な事柄について, あるいは命令的に強く言う場合に, have got to はすぐにも行動しなければならないような事柄について, have to は習慣的に繰り返されるような事柄について, それぞれ用いる.
> (2) 周囲の事情からそうせざるをえないというときは have (got) to を用いることが多い.

▶次の水曜日までにこの論文を仕上げなくちゃいけない I *must* finish this paper by next Wednesday. ‖ 車を修理に出さなくちゃいけない I*'ve got to* have my car repaired. ‖ 対話「あした暇かい？」「いや, うちの犬を動物病院へ連れていかなきゃいけないんだよ」"Are you free tomorrow？" "No. I *have to* take my dog to the vet." ‖ 対話「そろそろ帰らなくてはいけません」「あら, お急ぎにならなくてもいいでしょう」"I*'d better* be going." "There's no need to hurry off."

4【危ぶむ気持ち】

【文型】
〜するといけないから
in case S + V

▶雨が降るといけないから傘を持っていきなさいよ Take your umbrella (with you) *in case* it rains. (➤未来のことでも it will rain とせず現在形を用いる；in case it should rain とすると「万が一雨が降るといけないから」となり，should によってあまり起こりそうにないことを表せる. in case it rains の代わりに just in case でもよい) ‖ 寒くなるといけないからセーターを持ってきた I ('ve) brought a sweater (with me) *in case* it gets cold. (この英文は，今もセーターを持っていることを暗に表しているが，I brought a sweater (with me) in case it got cold. とすると単に過去の事実を述べた文になる).

▶雪でスリップするといけないからタイヤにチェーンを巻きなさい Put snow chains on the tires *so* (*that*) you [your car] *won't* skid. ‖ 肺がんになるといけないからたばこはやめたほうがいいよ You'd better stop smoking. *Otherwise* you might get lung cancer. (➤ otherwise は「さもないと」) ‖ 彼女は会議に遅れるといけないと思って駅まで急いだ She hurried to the train station *so* (*that*) she *wouldn't* be late for the meeting. ‖ 雨が入るといけないので窓を閉めた I closed the window *for fear of* rain coming in. (➤ for fear of は堅い言い方).

あなたの英語はどう響く?

「雨が降るといけないから傘を持っていきなさい」を Take an umbrella (with you) *lest* it should rain. と訳す人が少なくないが，これは Take an umbrella *lest* you (*should*) get wet. (ぬれないように傘を持っていきなさい) が正しい. ただし，これも古風で堅い言い方で，日常的には Take an umbrella (with you) *just in case*. とか Take an umbrella (with you) *in case* it rains. などのようにいう.

いけにえ 生贄 a sacrifice /sǽkrɪfaɪs/ ▶動物のいけにえをささげる offer an animal as a *sacrifice*.

いけばな 生け花 ikebana (➤英語化している)；(the art of) flower arrangement《参考》arrangement は出来上がった作品を指すことが多いので，「生け花クラブ」「華道部」を英訳する場合は flower arranging club がよい.

日本紹介 ✉ **生け花は花や枝を美しく花器に挿す伝統的な技芸で，華道ともいいます. いくつかの流派があります** Ikebana is the traditional art of arranging flowers and twigs aesthetically in a vase. It is also called *kado* (the way of flowers). There are several different schools of ikebana. ‖ 彼女は先生について生け花を習っている She is taking formal lessons in *ikebana* [*flower arrangement*].

イケメン イケ面 a good-looking [handsome] guy.

¹いける 生ける arrange ▶野の花を花瓶に生ける *arrange* wild flowers in a vase ／ *put* a wild flower in a vase (➤後者は一輪挿しの場合).

²いける 行ける 1【到達できる】▶その山へは車で行ける You *can get to* that mountain by car. ‖ 日光へは東武鉄道で2時間ほどで行ける Nikko *can be reached* in about two hours on the Tobu line. ‖ まあちゃんは独りでおしっこに行けるでしょ Ma-chan, you *can go* to the potty alone, can't you? ‖ この子は独りでお使いに行ける This boy *can go* on an errand by himself.

2【水準に達している，うまい】▶このつまみ，なかなかいけるね This snack is really *good*. ‖ これはいける This is *good* [*not bad*]. ‖ 彼の英語はなかなかいける He speaks pretty *good* English. ‖ 今度入ったピッチャー，いけるね Our new pitcher *is good* [*will do well*].

3【酒がたくさん飲める】▶彼はいける口だ He is a drinker. ／ He can hold his liquor. (➤ hold one's liquor は「酒を飲んでもくずれない」).

¹いけん 意見 1【考え】an opinion；a comment (論評，批評)；a view (ものの見方，見解) ▶きょうの会議では彼と私は少し意見が分かれた He and I had a small [slight] difference of *opinion* at today's meeting. ‖ 私はあなたとは意見が違う I have a different *opinion* from yours. ／ My *opinion* differs from yours. ‖ この点では私たちの意見は違う Our *opinions* differ on this. ‖ この件に関して皆さんの意見をお聞かせいただきたい I'd like to hear everybody's *opinion* [I'd like you to express your *opinion*] on this matter. ‖ 皆さん，遠慮なく意見を述べてください Everybody, please don't hesitate to express your *opinions* [to say *what you think*]. ‖ 生徒委員会は制服は廃止すべしということで意見がまとまった The student council *reached an agreement* that the school uniform should be abolished.

▶私の意見では，多くの日本の学校は1学級の人数が多すぎる *In my opinion*, the class sizes at many Japanese schools are too large. ‖ ストライキをするかどうかについて意見はまちまちだった *Opinions varied* on whether or not they would go on (a) strike. ‖ この頃の学生は政治について特に意見はないと答えることが多い Students today often say they have no particular *opinion* about politics. ‖ 日本の大学教育について意見を聞かせてください What is your *opinion* about college education in Japan? (opinion を使った質問は形式ばったところがあるので，ふつうは次の例文のように What do you think of ... を用いる) ‖ 対話「クローニングについてどういう意見を持って (＝どういうふうに考えて) いますか」「それに関しては意見が言えるほどよくは知らないんです」"*What do you think of* cloning?" "I don't know enough about it to form *an opinion*." ‖ 佐藤先生，何かご意見 (＝批評) はございますか Mr. Sato, do you have any *comments*? ‖ 死刑については反対意見だけでなく賛成意見もある There are affirmative as well as negative *views* on capital punishment. ‖ 民主主義では少数意見も尊重される Even a *minority opinion* is respected in a democracy.

あなたの英語はどう響く?

日本人にとって，「(特に) 意見はありません」と言うのはふつうであるが，そのつもりで I have no (particular) opinion. と言うと，「(あなたの話はばかばかしくて) 意見など言えない」と，相手を非難しているように響いたり，意見も言えない優柔不断な人間だと思われたりするおそれがあるので要注意. 自己主張を当然とする英語社会では，意見を持たない人は軽蔑，あるいは軽視される傾向さえある.

2【忠告】advice ▶きみはお父さんの意見に従ったほうがいい You should take [follow] your father's *advice*. ‖ 母が意見し (＝説教し) てから弟は反抗的になった

After my mother *admonished* my brother, he became rebellious.

2**いけん 違憲の** **unconstitutional** ▶この新しい法律は明らかに**違憲**だ This new law is clearly *unconstitutional*.

いげん 威厳 **dignity** ▶**威厳のある**人 a *dignified* person ‖あの人にはどこか**威厳がある** There is something *dignified* about him [her]. ‖あの校長先生は**威厳がない** That principal lacks *dignity*.

1**いご 囲碁** →碁.

2**いご 以後** ▶午後11時**以後**は外出してはならない You must not go out *after* 11 : 00 p.m. ‖彼とは**それ以後**会っていない I have not seen him *since then*. ‖うちでは**それ以後**あのデパートとは取り引きをやめた We stopped doing business with that department store *from then* [*from that time*] *on*.
▶**以後**気をつけなさい Be careful *from now on* [*in the future*]. →以降.

いこい 憩い ▶あの公園は市民の**憩いの場**です That park is *a place of recreation and relaxation* for the people of the city. ‖夕食後の**憩いのひととき**をクイズ番組でお楽しみください We'll have a quiz show for you while you *relax* after dinner, so sit back and enjoy.

1**いこう 意向** **wishes** (願い), (an) **intention** (意図) ▶この件について先方の**意向**を尋ねてほしい I'd like you to ask their *wishes* in this matter.
✉ **残念ながらご意向には添えません** We are sorry to inform you that we cannot comply with your *wishes*.

2**いこう 移行** ▶日本の6-3-3制の教育制度は6-6制へ**移行するかもしれない** The Japanese six-three-three school education system may *be changed to* a six-six one.
‖**移行期間** a transitional period ‖**移行措置** transitional measures.

3**いこう 威光** **prestige** /prestíːʒ/ ▶彼は父親の**威光**で当選した He won the election owing to his father's *prestige*.

4**いこう 遺稿** a **posthumous** /páːstʃəməs/ **manuscript** (死後に発見された)
‖**遺稿集** a collection of unpublished works.

5**いこう 以降** ▶日本の近代文学はふつう明治**以降**の作品を指す Modern literature in Japan usually refers to works written during the Meiji era *or later*. →以後.

6**いこう 遺構** **structural remains.**

7**いこう 衣桁** a **kimono** [**clothes**] **rack.**

イコール **equal** /íːkwəl/ ▶ 3 マイナス 1 **イコール** 2 Three minus one *equals* [*is*] two. ／Three minus one *leave*(*s*) two. ‖ 4 プラス 2 **イコール** 6 Four and two *make*(*s*) six. 《参考》「イコール」は英語の equal からきているが, 英語では訳例のように equal のほかに is, leave, make などを用いることもできる.
▶貧乏**イコール**不幸という図式は必ずしも正しくない *The equation of* poverty *with* unhappiness is not always true.

いこく 異国 a **foreign country** ▶**異国**で暮らす live in *a foreign country* ‖マレーシアの音楽は**異国情緒**があふれている Malaysian music is filled with *exotic emotion*.

いごこち 居心地 ▶友人の家は**居心地がよかった**[**悪かった**] My friend's house *was comfortable* [*uncomfortable*]. ‖知らない人の前で話をするのはあまり**居心地のいいものではない** I feel uncomfortable speaking in front of strangers. ‖ホームステイ先での**居心地**はどうでした？ How did you enjoy *staying* [*being*] *with* your host family ?

いこじ 意固地な **obstinate** /áːbstɪnət/ (意見を変えない) ; **stubborn** (強情な) ▶**いこじな**態度をとる take an *obstinate* attitude ‖そう**いこじになる**なよ Don't be so *stubborn*. ‖父は私が歌手になるのを**いこじになって**反対した My father *stubbornly* objected to my becoming a singer.

いこつ 遺骨 one's **ashes** (火葬にした) ; one's **remains** (➤ 婉曲(えんきょく)語. 時間・年月が経過したという含みがあることが多い) ; a **holy** [**sacred**] **relic** (釈迦(しゃか)・聖人などの保存されている聖遺骨) ▶戦没者の**遺骨**を収集する gather the *remains* [*bones*] of the war dead ‖彼の**遺骨**は先祖代々の墓に葬られた His *remains* were laid in the family grave.

いざ ▶**いざ**戦いとなると彼は全くの小心者であった *When it came to* actual combat, he proved to be a coward. ‖**いざ**旅行に出かける**という段になって**彼女はやめると言い出した *Just when* we were ready to leave on the trip, she said she wasn't going. ‖**いざというとき**彼は頼りになる男だよ You can count on him *when the chips are down*. (➤「せっぱ詰まったら」の意のインフォーマルな表現).
▶**いざというときは**いつでも遠慮なく相談にいらっしゃい *If you should run into trouble* [*should have a problem*], feel free to come to me for advice. (➤ if 節の should は可能性が小さいときや改まった口調にするときに用いる).
▶**いざというときのために**少しは貯金をしておきなさい You should save some money *for a rainy day*. (➤ for a rainy day は「万一に備えて」) ‖**いざとなったら**私も力になるわよ *If something should happen*, you can count on me.

1**いさい 委細** **details, particulars** ▶**委細**面談 *Particulars* to be arranged in person (➤ 広告文) ‖彼は**委細かまわず**(＝結果を考えずに)計画を推し進めた He went on with his plan *without giving any thought to the consequences*.

2**いさい 異彩** ▶これらの絵の中でも彼の作品は真の傑作として**異彩を放っている** Among these paintings, his work *stands out* as a real masterpiece.

いさかい a **spat** (けんか).

いざかや 居酒屋 a **tavern.** →赤ちょうちん.

いさぎよい 潔い ▶**潔い**最期を遂げる die a *noble* death ‖**潔く**敗北を認める accept (one's) defeat *gracefully* ‖彼女に 3 度も誘いを断られたからには**潔く**諦めるとするか She's turned me down three times now, so (I guess) I'll *admit defeat and give up on* dating her. ‖大臣は**潔く**辞任した The minister *had the grace to* resign his position. ‖負けを認めないとは**潔くない**ぞ It *isn't sportsmanlike* to refuse to admit defeat. 《参考》「潔く負けを認めない人」を a bad [poor] loser という. ‖彼はそのことでうそをつくことを**潔しとしなかった** He *was too proud to* lie about it. ‖部長は接待を受けることを**潔しとしない** Our general manager *is above* being wined and dined. (●「(高潔ゆえに)…を恥とする」に相当する be above ... を用いた訳例).

いさく 遺作 a **posthumous** /páːstʃəməs/ **work** ▶ショパンの20番嬰(えい)ハ短調ノクターン(**遺作**) Chopin's nocturne # 20 in C sharp minor (*posthumous*) ‖年末に刊行された小説がその作家の**遺作**となった The novel that was published at the end of the year was done so *posthumously*. ‖松本清**遺作展** *a* *commemorative exhibition* of Matsumoto Kiyoshi's art works.

いざこざ (a) **trouble** ▶うちではいざこざが絶えないんだ I have a lot of family *trouble(s)*. ／There is no end of *trouble* in my family.

いささか **a little**（少し）; **somewhat**（いくぶん）; **rather**（かなり）▶その知らせを聞いていささか驚きました I was *a little* surprised to hear the news. ‖柔道のほうはいささか心得があるのですが，剣道のほうはからっきしだめです Though I've done *some* judo, I'm a complete stranger to kendo.

▶先生に褒められていささか鼻が高かった I felt *rather* proud when I was praised by my teacher. ‖電子時計はいささかも狂いがない Electronic clocks do*n't* gain or lose time *at all*.

いざしらず いざ知らず ▶アマチュアならいざ知らず，プロならもっといい演技をすべきだ I *don't know about* amateurs, *but* professionals should give a better performance.

いさましい 勇ましい **brave** ▶勇ましい行為 a *brave* [*courageous*] act(➤ courageous は brave よりも精神的な強さの含みがある) ‖彼らは勇ましく戦った They fought *bravely*. ／They fought a *brave* battle. ‖勇ましい行進曲 a *stirring* march ‖こんな寒い日に海に飛び込むなんて勇ましいね How *daring* of you to take a dive into the sea on such a cold day (as this).

いさみあし 勇み足 ▶《相撲》栃煌山は勇み足で負けた Tochiozan lost a bout *by stepping out of the ring unintentionally*.

▶《比喩的》そこまで言ったのは勇み足だったね You *went a little too far* in saying that.

いさめる (…を)**諌める** **remonstrate** /rɪmɑ́:nstreɪt ‖ rémən-/《with》(人を) ▶ごみを捨てたことについて彼をいさめる *remonstrate with* him about littering.

いさん 遺産 an **inheritance**（相続するもの）; a [**the**] **heritage**（祖先から受け継いだもの）; a **legacy**（遺言状によって残すもの）; a **fortune**(財産) ▶遺産争い a quarrel over *an inheritance* ‖父の遺産を継ぐ inherit my father's *fortune* ／ take over my father's *inheritance* ‖父は私に遺産を残さずに死んだ My father left me no *legacy*. ／My father had nothing to leave me.

▶《比喩的》能や歌舞伎は日本の大事な文化遺産である Noh and kabuki are part of the important *cultural heritage* of Japan. ‖厳島神社は世界遺産に指定されている Itsukushima Shinto Shrine is designated as *a World Heritage site*. (⇀世界).

[1]**いし 石** (a) **stone**, (a) **rock**; a **pebble**（小石）
語法 (1)stone の場合，「石材」の意では不可算名詞だが，「石ころ」の意では可算名詞で a をつける. (2)《米》では rock(本来は「岩」)を stone と同義に用いる.

▶石づくりの塀 a *stone* wall ‖この建物は石でできている This house is made of *stone*. ‖山道は石がごろごろしていた *Stones and rocks* were scattered all over along the mountain path.

▶《慣用表現》この研究は石にかじりついてもやり抜くぞ I'll complete this research *at any cost* [*no matter what*]. (● 英語では「どんな犠牲を払ってでも」や「どんなことがあっても」のような発想をする) ‖私は目標達成までは石にかじりついてでもやるつもりだ I will *stick to it* until I reach my goal. (➤ stick to it で「最後までやり通す」).

ことわざ 石の上にも３年 Even a (cold) rock will get warm if you keep sitting on it for three years. ／Persevere for three years.

[2]**いし 意志** (a) **will** ▶彼は意志の強い[弱い]男だ He is a man of strong [weak] *will*. ‖彼女は意志薄弱だ She *has a weak will*. ／She is *weak-willed*.

[3]**いし 意思** (an) **intention**(意向); a **resolution**(決意) ▶市長には来たる選挙に出馬の意思はない The mayor has no *intention* of running in the coming election. ‖彼の辞職の意思は固いようだ His *resolution* [*resolve*] to quit the company seems very firm. ‖きみたちクラブのメンバーは意思の疎通ができていないみたいだね It looks as though you club members *aren't communicating*. ‖はっきり意思表示をしてください Please *express your intention(s)* clearly.

‖意思決定 decision-making.

[4]**いし 遺志** a **dying wish** ▶故人の遺志を尊重して葬儀は行わないことにいたしました Respecting the *wishes* of the deceased, it has been decided that a funeral will not be held.

[5]**いし 医師** a **doctor** ▶医師の診断を仰ぐ request [seek] *a doctor's diagnosis*.

[6]**いし 縊死** a **suicide by hanging**.

[1]**いじ 意地** **1【根性・気立てなど】**▶意地の悪い人 a *mean* [《主に英》*nasty*] person ／an *ill-natured* person ‖後藤さん，そんな意地の悪いことはやめなさいよ！ Don't be so *mean*, Goto! ／Be nice, Goto! ‖彼は先生に意地の悪い質問をした He asked his teacher an *embarrassing* [a *malicious*] question.

2【我(が)・強情など】▶きみは少し意地を張り過ぎる You're a little too *obstinate* [*stubborn*]. ‖この計画は意地でも成功させてみせる I will make this project a success *at any cost*. ‖意地でもあのチームには負けられない Our pride will not allow us to be beaten by that team. (● 英語では「我々の誇りが負けることを許さない」と発想して訳例のように表現する) ‖横綱は千秋楽結びの一番に勝って意地を見せた The yokozuna won the last bout of the grand tournament and *kept his pride intact*.

3【物を欲しがる気持ち】▶おまえは何て意地が汚いんだ You're really *greedy*!

☛ 意地汚い，意地っ張り（⇀見出語）

[2]**いじ 維持** **maintenance**; **upkeep** /ʌ́pki:p/（建物・車などの）一動 **維持する** **maintain** +㊐ ▶世界の平和を維持する *maintain* world peace ‖健康を維持する *maintain* good health ‖当教会は献金によって維持されています This church *is maintained* by donations. ‖自民党は40年近く政権を維持していた The Liberal Democratic Party *had retained* power for nearly forty years. ‖車の維持費は月にいくらぐらい？ What does the *upkeep* of your car cost a month? ／How much do you spend a month on car maintenance?

‖生命維持装置 a life-support system, life-sustaining equipment.

[3]**いじ 遺児** a **child whose parents have died**

‖交通遺児 children orphaned in traffic accidents.

いしあたま 石頭 ▶あいつは石頭で自分の誤りを認めないんだ He is too *hardheaded* [*stubborn* ／ *pigheaded*] to admit that he's wrong. 《参考》(1) stubborn は「頑固な」，pigheaded は「どうしようもないほど頑固な」の意. (2)文字どおり「頑丈で硬い頭」の意なら His head is hard. がふつう.

いじいじ ▶あの女の子はいじいじした感じで好きになれない She's so *timid and indecisive* I just can't take to her.

いしうす 石臼 a **stone mortar.**

いしがき 石垣 a **stone wall** ▶石垣を築く put up *a stone wall.*

いしき 意識 **1【感覚があること】consciousness** ▶犯人は重傷を負ったが意識ははっきりしている The culprit was critically injured, but his *mind* is (still) clear [but he's still fully *conscious*]. ‖ そのボクサーはノックアウトされて意識を失った The boxer *lost consciousness* when he was knocked out. ‖ 心肺蘇生法を行ったところ，彼女は意識を回復した She *regained consciousness* [*came to*] after I gave her CPR (➤ CPR は cardiopulmonary resuscitation の略). ‖ 彼はまだ意識不明だ He *is* still *unconscious*.

2【認識】awareness, consciousness (➤ 問題などに対する認識の意では前者がふつう) ▶あの大震災のあと節電意識が高まった After that great earthquake, our *awareness of the importance of* saving electricity increased. ‖ その事故は原子力発電の危険性に対する人々の意識を高める結果になった The accident resulted in raising *public awareness* of the risks of nuclear power generation.

【文型】
Aを意識している
be aware of A
be conscious of A
➤ of A でなく，that (…ということを)の節が続くことも多い．

▶衛兵は写真を撮られているのを意識していた The guard *was conscious of* being photographed [*was aware that* he was being photographed]. ‖ 食事をするときは総カロリーを意識するようにしています I try to *be conscious* [*aware*] *of* the total calories when I have a meal. ‖ その19歳の少女にはまだ母親としての意識がなかった The nineteen-year-old girl *was* still *not fully aware* [*conscious*] *of* what it meant to be a mother.

▶あなたは男子を意識し過ぎるのよ You*'re too conscious of* boys [*too* boy *conscious*].

▶何の罪もない人々を殺してもゲリラたちは罪の意識が全くなかった Although they killed innocent people, the guerillas had no *feeling of guilt* at all. ‖ 住民は被害者意識が強い The residents *feel strongly* that they have been victimized. ‖ うちの野球チームは優勝を意識して(＝勝たねばならないと思って)硬くなってしまった *Thinking that* they had to win, our baseball players became too nervous. ‖ 一般に学生の政治意識は低い Students *are* generally *apathetic* toward politics.

▶まず英語教師の意識改革が必要だ What we need first is *a revolution in* English teachers' (*way of*) *thinking*. ‖ 彼女は意識過剰だ She's *too self-conscious*. (→自意識) ‖ 教授は意識的に鹿児島弁を使った The professor *intentionally* spoke with a Kagoshima accent.

いじきたない 意地汚い **greedy** ▶意地汚い食べ方をしてはいけません You mustn't eat *greedily*. ‖ あの意地汚い男はひとりでパーティーの食べ物を平らげてしまった That *glutton* ate all of the food at the party.

いしく 石工 a **stonemason.**

いじくりまわす いじくり回す **fiddle around** [《英また》**about**]《with》(指でもてあそぶ); **tamper**《with》(勝手に［不法に］手を加える); **tinker**《with》((…を直そうと)下手な修理をする) ▶コンピュータをいじくり回す *fiddle* (*around*) *with* a computer ‖ 弟は自分のラジオをいじくり回していた My brother was *tinkering with* his radio. ‖ 時計の内側をいじくり回して壊す *mess around with* the insides [inside] of one's watch and ruin it (➤ mess around with は《インフォーマル》).

いじくる **finger** +㊐ (指で); **play with** (もてあそぶ) ▶彼女は落ち着かない様子でボタンをいじくっていた She was nervously *fingering* a button. ‖ 耳をいじくってはいけません Don't *play with* your ear. →いじる.

いしけり 石蹴り **hopscotch** ▶石蹴りをして遊ぶ play *hopscotch*.

いじける ⚠自分をだめなものと思い込んで弱気になったり，卑屈になったりすることをいうが，英語にはこの含みを適切に表現する語はない．したがって **become timid** (おどおどする), **sulk** (すねる)などを用いて近似の表現をするしかない．
▶うちの末っ子は知らない人に会うといじけてしまう My youngest son [daughter] *becomes timid* when he [she] meets strangers. ‖ そんな隅っこでいじけていないで，こっちへいらっしゃい Stop *sulking* in the corner and come join us. ‖ いじけた心の持ち主 a person with *a warped mind* (➤ warped は「ひねくれた」).

いじげん 異次元の ▶異次元の金融緩和政策 an *unconventional* money easing policy.

いしころ 石ころ a **pebble.**

いしずえ 礎 a **foundation**(基礎); a **basis** /béisis/ (基準) ▶民俗学の礎を築く *lay the foundation* for folklore studies.

いしだたみ 石畳 a **stone pavement** ▶石畳の道を歩く walk along *a stone-paved road*. 《参考》(1) stone は一般に「石」のことで形状は問題にしない．(2) 板状の石の石畳であれば a pavement [road／street] paved with flagstones となり，丸石・四角石であれば cobblestones となる．

いしだん 石段 (a **flight of**) **stone steps** ▶おばあさんが神社の石段を上がっていくのが見えた I saw an elderly woman walking up the *stone steps* to the shrine.

いしつ 異質の **different**(違った) ▶あのグループでは彼だけが異質だ He is the only *different type* of person in that group. ‖ 若いうちに異質の文化に触れておくのは大事なことです It is important to experience *different* cultures while you are young.

いじっぱり 意地っ張り ▶あの娘は意地っ張りで私の手に負えない I can't handle that girl as she is too *obstinate* [*stubborn*]. (➤ obstinate は「頑固で自分の意見を変えない」, stubborn は「生まれつき強情な」の意).

いしつぶつ 遺失物 a **lost item** [**article**]
‖遺失物取扱所 a lost-and-found office (➤ 掲示では Lost and Found が多い).

いしばし 石橋 a **stone bridge** ▶《慣用表現》彼は石橋をたたいて渡るような男だ He *knocks on a stone bridge before crossing it*. ／He is an *extremely cautious* man.

いじましい **petty**(心の狭い); **stingy, tight**(**-fisted**) (けちな).

いじめ **bullying** /búliŋ/ ▶いじめはなかなか表面化しにくい，あるいは時すでに遅しとなるところが問題だ The problem is, *bullying* rarely comes to the surface or does so too late. ‖ 学校でのいじめは大きな社会問題である *Bullying* at school [School *bullying*] is a big social problem. ‖ 弱い者いじめをするな Don't *be a bully*. ／Don't *play the bully*.

✉ **あなたの学校にはいじめはありますか** Is there any *bullying* [Are there any *bullying incidents*] at your school? ➤「いじめの事例」の意.

いじめっこ いじめっ子 a **bully** /bóli/ ▶あのいじめっ子, 自分よりできる子ばかりいじめるんだよ The *bully* only picks on children who are smarter than he is.

いじめられっこ いじめられっ子 a **bullied child.**

いじめる **bully** /bóli/ +⊜ (精神的・肉体的苦痛を与える); **pick on** (ちょっと嫌がらせをする, からかう); **be hard on** (つらく当たる) ▶下級生をいじめるな Don't *bully* younger students. ‖ 彼は自分より小さな子をいじめてばかりいる He always *picks on* [He *is* always *hard on*] children who are smaller than him. ‖ 彼女は男の子たちにいじめられた She *was bullied* [*was picked on*] by the boys. ‖ みんなからいじめられるから学校に行きたくないんだ I don't want to go to school because everybody *picks on me* there. ‖ 動物をいじめてはいけません Don't *be cruel to* animals.

いしゃ 医者 a **doctor**, a **physician** (➤ 一般語. ただし歯科医や精神科医は含まない); a **surgeon** /sə́:ʳdʒən/ (外科医); a **general practitioner** (一般総合医; 内科診療と簡単な外科手術その他全科を担当)

「医者」のいろいろ **眼科医** ophthalmologist /ɑ̀:fθælmɑ́:lədʒɪst/, eye doctor ／**形成外科医** plastic surgeon ／**外科医** surgeon ／**産科医** obstetrician /ɑ̀:bstətríʃən/ ／**歯科医** dentist ／**耳鼻咽喉科医** ENT (ear-nose-throat) doctor ／**小児科医** pediatrician /pì:diətríʃən/ ／**神経科医** neurologist /njurɑ́:lədʒɪst/ ／**整形外科医** orthop (a) edist /ɔ̀:ʳθəpí:dɪst/ ／**精神科医** psychiatrist /saɪkáɪətrɪst/ ／**内科医** internist /íntəːʳnɪst, ɪntə́:ʳnɪst/ ／**脳外科医** brain surgeon ／**泌尿器科医** urologist /jʊrɑ́:lədʒɪst/ ／**皮膚科医** dermatologist /də̀:ʳmətɑ́:lədʒɪst/, skin doctor ／**美容整形外科医** cosmetic surgeon ／**婦人科医** gyn (a) ecologist /gàɪnəkɑ́:lədʒɪst/ ／**放射線科医** radiologist /rèɪdiɑ́:lədʒɪst/ ／**麻酔科医** 《主に米》 anesthesiologist /ænəsθì:ziɑ́:lədʒɪst/, 《主に英》 an (a) esthetist /ənésθəṭəst ‖ əní:sθətɪst/

▶私は生まれてこのかた医者にかかったことがない I have never been to *a doctor* in my life. ‖ 医者を呼びましょうか Do you want me to *call* (*in*) *a doctor*? ／Shall I *call* (*in*) *a doctor* for you? ‖ 医者にすぐ診てもらったほうがいいよ You should see *a doctor* right away. ‖ かかりつけの医者はいますか Do you have *a primary care physician* [*a family doctor*]? (➤ primary care physician は病気になったとき最初に診てもらう医師のことで, family doctor は家庭医療を専門にする医師のこと) ‖ 私は今[まだ]医者にかかっている I am now [still] *under medical treatment*.

いしやきいも 石焼き芋 ***ishiyakiimo***; a sweet potato baked in [on] hot pebbles (➤ 説明的な訳).

いじゃく 胃弱 ▶私は胃弱です I *have a weak stomach*. (➤ a strong stomach は「ずぶとい神経, 度胸」の意).

いしゃりょう 慰謝料 **compensation** (**money**), **consolation money** (➤ 離婚の際の慰謝料は後者がよい) ▶事故の犠牲者の遺族に慰謝料を支払う *compensate* an accident victim's family.

いしゅう 異臭 an **offensive smell** (胸が悪くなるような) ▶異臭を放つ give off *an offensive smell* ‖ 彼の実験室には異臭が立ちこめていた His laboratory was filled with *bad* [*foul*] *smells*.

いじゅう 移住 **move** (転居); **immigration** (外国からの); **emigration** (外国への) **一動 移住する** **move**; **immigrate** 《to》 (外国から…へ), **emigrate** 《from》 (…から外国へ) ▶彼の一家は昨年東京からオーストラリアへ移住した His family *moved* from Tokyo to Australia last year. ‖ 彼らは海外移住を考えている They are considering *emigrating to a foreign country*. →移民.

いしゅがえし 意趣返し **retaliation 一動 意趣返しをする** **retaliate** 《against, for》 (人に, 行為に).

いしゅく 萎縮する・畏縮する **shrink** (縮む); **be intimidated** (びびる); **hang back** (尻込みする) ▶使わない筋肉は萎縮する Unused muscles *shrink*. ／Muscles that aren't used tend to *atrophy*. (➤ atrophy /ætrəfi/ は医学用語).

▶相手がお偉いさんだからといって畏縮する(＝尻込みする)必要はない There's no need (for you) to *feel intimidated* [*hang back*], just because someone is a big shot. ‖ 日本選手の中には大きな国際大会になると萎縮して(＝硬くなって)実力が出せなくなる者がいる Some Japanese athletes *get nervous* and can't show their ability in big international competitions.

いしょ 遺書 a **will** ▶その資産家は財産のすべてを一人娘に譲る旨の遺書を作成した The wealthy man drew up *a will* in which he left all he had to his only daughter. (➤ 自殺者が残す遺書は suicide note という).

1**いしょう 衣装** **clothes**; a **dress** (女性のドレス); (a) **costume** (民族・時代に特有の; 舞台用の); **dress** (ある地域・時代に特有の) ▶花嫁衣装 *a wedding dress* ‖ オランダの伝統衣装 traditional Dutch *dress* ‖ 民族衣装を着けた彼女は息をのむほど美しかった She was breathtaking in her *national* [*folk*] *costume*. ‖ 彼女は衣装持ちだ She *has a large wardrobe*. (➤ wardrobe は「衣装だんす」から「持ち衣装全体」の意).

ことわざ **馬子にも衣装** Fine clothes make the man. (➤ 英語のことわざ) ／Fine feathers make fine birds. (➤「立派な羽毛は鳥まで立派に見せる」の意の英語のことわざ).

2**いしょう 意匠** an **elaborate** /ɪlǽbərət/ **design** ▶意匠を凝らす work out *an elaborate design*.

‖**意匠登録** registration of designs.

1**いじょう 以上** **1** **[…より上] more than, over**

《解説》「…以上」の言い方
日本語で「100以上」というと100を含むから, 英訳する場合, 厳密には one hundred or more のようにいう必要がある. しかし厳密さが求められない場合には more than [over] one hundred (100は含まれない)でよい.

▶京都には1500以上の寺院がある Kyoto has *more than* [*over*] 1,500 Buddhist temples. ‖ 高速道路では時速50キロ以上の速度で走行しなくてはならない You have to go *more than* fifty kilometers per hour on expressways. ‖ 靴を2足以上お買い上げのお客様にはスニーカーを1足サービスします If you buy two *or more* pairs of shoes, we will throw in a pair of sneakers. ‖ 両議院はおのおのその総議員の３分の１**以上**の出席がなければ議事を開き議決することができない Business cannot be transacted in either House unless one-third *or more* of the total membership is present. (➤ 日本国憲法第56条) ‖ 日本の法律は**20歳以上**の人にのみ飲酒や喫煙を認めている Japanese laws permit only those *who are twenty or older* to drink and smoke. ‖ うちの高校には**60歳以上**の先生が２人いる There are two teachers *who are sixty or over* at our high school. (➤ above sixty とすると61, 62, 63…を指す).

▶このビルの４階**以上**(＝より上)はアパートです In this building, all floors *from* the fourth *on up* are occupied by apartments.

▶子供は**必要以上**の金を持つべきでない Children should not have *more* money *than necessary* [*needed*]. ‖ 康夫, おまえ**平均点以上**の成績は取るんだよ Yasuo, your grades (had) better be at least *above average*. ‖ 阪神が**予想以上**に善戦している The Tigers are doing *better than we expected*. ‖ その国の反日感情は**予想以上**に強かった The country's anti-Japanese feelings were stronger *than I had thought*. ‖ **それ以上**は何も知りません I don't know any *more than that*. ／That's all I know. ‖ 疲れているのでもうこれ**以上**歩けません I'm so tired I can't walk *any further*. ‖ **これ以上**きみに説明しても無駄だね There's no use explaining it to you *any longer*. ‖ **これ以上**のことは私にはできません *This is the best* I *can do*.

2【…するからには】▶大学を卒業した**以上**独立しなくてはいけませんね *Now that* you have graduated from college, you have to be independent. ‖ 日本に住んでいる**以上**日本の法律に従うべきです *Since* [*As long as*] you live in Japan, you are obliged to obey Japanese laws.

3【その他】▶《話を締めくくって》**以上です** Well, *that's about all*. ‖ **以上**で会議を終わります The meeting is *now* adjourned. ‖ **以上**に示した事件は決して珍しいものではありません The *above-mentioned* cases are not at all uncommon.

2いじょう 異常な **abnormal**(正常でない) ; **unusual** (ふつうでない) ; **extraordinary**(並外れた) ; **exceptional**(例外的な) ▶**異常な**人間 an *abnormal* person ‖ **異常な**ふるまい *extraordinary* behavior ‖ 農家は長期にわたる**異常な**干ばつの被害を受けた Farmers suffered from the *abnormally* long dry spell. ‖ 辺りは**異常**な雰囲気に包まれていた An *unusual* atmosphere pervaded the surrounding area. ‖ この夏は**異常に**暑かった It has been *unusually* [*exceptionally*] hot this summer.

‖**異常乾燥注意報** a dry-weather alert ‖ **異常心理(学)** abnormal psychology.

3いじょう 異状 **trouble**(故障) ; (a) **disorder**(心身の不調) ▶彼は倒れる３日前から**腹部の異状**を訴えていた He started complaining of *stomach trouble* [*a stomach disorder*] three days before he collapsed. ‖ 体に**異状**を感じたらすぐ医者に診てもらったほうがいい If you *feel anything wrong* (*physically*), you had better go and see the doctor right away. ‖ エンジンにどこか**異状**がある *Something is wrong with* the engine. (➤「エンジンの故障」は engine trouble) ‖ 医学的な検査では何の**異状**も認められなかった The medical examination showed that nothing *was wrong*. ‖ 留守中に何か**異状**はなかったかい？ *Was everything all right* while I was out？

4いじょう 委譲 (a) **transfer** /trǽnsfəːʳ/ **一動 委譲する** **transfer** /trænsfə́ːʳ/ +㊐ ▶Ｘ氏に権限を**委譲する** *transfer* my rights to Mr. X.

1いしょく 移植 **transplantation**(移植すること) ; a **transplant**(移植手術) **一動 移植する** **transplant** +㊐ ▶松の木を校庭に**移植する** *transplant* a pine tree to a schoolyard.

▶**臓器移植** an organ *transplant* ‖ 肝臓［腎臓］**移植** a liver [kidney] *transplant* ‖ 骨髄**移植**を受ける［行う］receive [perform] a bone marrow *transplant*.

‖**心臓移植手術** a heart transplant operation.

2いしょく 異色の **unique** ▶その学者は学界では**異色の**存在だ That scholar has a *unique* position in academic circles.

3いしょく 衣食 ▶**衣食住** *food, clothing and housing* [*shelter*] ／*food, shelter and clothing* ／*shelter, clothing and food*(➤ 最初の言い方が最もふつう).

4いしょく 委嘱 **commission** /kəmíʃən/ (作品の制作依頼, 仕事の依頼) ; **appointment** (役職への任命) **一動 委嘱する** **commission** +㊐ , **appoint** +㊐ ▶**委嘱**作品 a *commissioned* work [piece] ‖ 彼は市から環境調査を**委嘱された** He *was commissioned* by the city to carry out an environmental survey. ‖ 彼は編集委員を**委嘱された** He *was appointed* to the editorial committee.

いじらしい ⚠**日本語では女性や幼い子供がその年齢や弱さにも似合わず懸命に何かをしたり, 耐えたりしている場合にこの語を用いるが, 英語にはこの含みを適切に表現する語はない.**

▶たった１人の肉親を失ったのに, じっと涙をこらえているこの少女が**いじらしい** I *find* the girl who is trying to hold back her tears after she lost her only relative *so touching*. (➤ touching は「心を揺さぶる, 哀れをそそる」).

いじる **1**【もてあそぶ】**play**《with》; **finger** +㊐ , **fiddle**《with》(指で) ; **tinker**《with》(下手に直そうとする) ⇀いじくる ▶おもちゃを**いじる** *play with* a toy ‖ ラジオを**いじる** *fiddle with* a radio(➤「選局してあちこち回す」の意) ‖ 彼女は髪の毛をよく無意識に**いじる** She often *plays with* [*fingers*] her hair without realizing it. ‖ 誰かがこの DVD レコーダーを**いじった**らしい Someone seems to *have tinkered with* this DVD recorder.

2【不必要に手を加える】**tamper**《with》▶細かい規則を**いじって**も根本的な解決にはつながらない *Making minor changes* in the rules [*Tampering with* the rules] won't lead to a fundamental solution.

3【道楽で手入れをする】▶父は庭を**いじる**のが好きです My father likes *gardening*.

いしわた 石綿 **asbestos** /æsbéstəs/.

いじわる 意地悪 a **mean** [**nasty**] **person**, 《インフォーマル》a **meanie** (人) **一形 意地悪な** **mean, nasty, ill-natured** (➤ 最後は堅い語) ▶由紀江の**意地悪**！How *mean* you are, Yukie！‖ 浩は**意地悪**だと思われているが, 本当はなかなか親切だ People say Hiroshi is *mean*, but actually he is quite kind. ／Hiroshi is thought to be *ill-natured*, but in reality he is very kind. ‖ 愛子は**意地悪**をして佐知子に消しゴムを貸さなかった Aiko *acted mean* [*stingy*] and refused to let Sachiko use her eraser. ‖ **意地悪**してごめんなさいね I'm sorry for *being* so *mean* to you. ‖ 先生

は私に意地悪な質問をした The teacher asked me an *embarrassing* [a *malicious*] question. (「意地悪な」を「人をまごつかせる(ような)」と考えれば前者,「悪意のある」と考えれば後者のように言うことができる) ‖ その委員は意地悪く人の弱みを突いてきた That committeeman *maliciously* sniped at my weak points.

1**いしん 威信** prestige /prestíːʒ/ ▶警察の威信に関わる大失態 a grave blunder which might jeopardize the *prestige* of the police.

2**いしん 維新**
‖明治維新 the Meiji Restoration.

いじん 偉人 a great person ▶歴史上の偉人たち *the great names* of history ‖ 鷗外は近代文学における偉人の1人だ Ogai is one of *the greats* of modern literature.
‖偉人伝 the biography [life] of a great person.

いしんでんしん 以心伝心 silent communication
▶あの2人は以心伝心の間柄のようだ The two seem to *understand each other telepathically* [*without the use of language*]. ‖ 妻とはお互い何も言わなくても以心伝心で考えていることはすぐわかる Even if we say nothing, my wife and I *can read each other's mind*.

いす 椅子 1【腰掛け】 a chair

> ◀解説▶ (1)**chair** は椅子の総称としても用いられるが,通例背もたれのある1人用の椅子を指す. (2)背もたれのない椅子は **stool** といい, 2人以上が掛けられる横長の椅子は **bench** または **sofa** という.

▶椅子から立ち上がる rise from *a chair* ‖ 椅子に座る sit (down) on [in] *a chair* (➤ in は「肘掛け椅子」など中に入るイメージの場合) ‖ この椅子にお掛けください Please take [sit on] this *chair*. ‖ 彼女はゆったりと椅子の背にもたれた She settled back in her *chair*. (➤ 深々と座る場合は on でなく in を用いる) ‖ 私は椅子を引き寄せた I pulled [drew] up the *chair*.
‖椅子取りゲーム musical chairs.
2【地位】▶現在6人の候補者が市長の椅子を目指して選挙運動中です Six candidates are campaigning for *the mayorship*. ‖ 前任者の急死で社長の椅子が彼のところに転がり込んできた The sudden death of his predecessor brought him (to) *the presidency*.

> **逆引き熟語 ○○椅子**
> 安楽椅子 an easy chair / 折り畳み椅子 a folding chair / 回転椅子 a swivel chair / 車椅子 a wheelchair / 社長の椅子 the presidency / 電気椅子 an electric chair / 肘掛け椅子 an armchair / 揺り椅子 a rocking chair

イスタンブール Istanbul (トルコの都市).

いずまい 居住まい ▶居ずまいを正す *sit up straight* / *straighten* one's (*sitting*) *posture*.

いずみ 泉 a spring (自然の) ; a fountain (人工の) ▶湧き出る泉 a gushing *spring*.
▶《比喩的》図書館は知識の泉だ A library is *a fountain of knowledge*.

イスラエル Israel /ízriəl/
‖イスラエル人 an Israeli /ɪzréɪli/ [複 Israelis, Israeli].

イスラム(きょう) イスラム(教) Islam /ízlɑːm, ís-/
▶イスラム(教)にはいくつかの宗派がある *Islam* has several sects. ‖ イスラム教徒はアラーを唯一神としてあがめている *Muslims* worship Allah as the only God.
‖イスラム教徒 a Muslim /mʌ́zləm/ ‖ イスラム教国 an Islamic country.

いずれ 1【どちらか】 either /íːðəʳ ‖ áɪðə/ ▶今場所は白鵬か琴欧洲のいずれかが優勝するだろう *Either* Hakuho *or* Kotooshu will win the championship (in) this tournament. ‖ 甲子園に整列した高校野球チームはいずれも強そうだった *All* the high school baseball teams which lined up at Koshien looked very strong. ‖ どのバレーボールチームもいずれ劣らぬ強豪だ *Each* of the volleyball teams is very strong.
ことわざ いずれがあやめかかきつばた Who can choose between ayame irises and kakitsubata irises (since both are equally beautiful)? / Who can decide which woman is more beautiful? (➤ 意訳).
▶いずれにしても, 試合には出なくてはならない *Either way* [*In either case*], I've got to take part in the game. ‖ いずれにせよ, あしたきみに電話をするよ *In any case* [*In any event*], I'll call you tomorrow.
2【結局は】 in the end ▶いずれ先方が折れるだろう I think the other party will give in *in the end* [*sooner or later*]. (「結局」と考えれば in the end を,「遅かれ早かれ」と考えれば sooner or later を使うことができる).
3【近いうち, いつか】▶いずれそのうち1杯やろう Let's go for a drink *one of these days*. ‖ いずれまた会いましょう I'll see you *later*. (I'll be seeing you soon. とすると「近いうちに会いましょう」の意味になる) ‖ いずれ(=いつか)次郎は私のもとに戻ってくると信じています I believe Jiro will come back to me *some day*.

いすわる 居座る ▶山川氏は来月で80歳だがまだ会長の椅子に居座るつもりだ Mr. Yamakawa will be 80 next month, but he intends to *stay on* as chairman. ‖ 梅雨前線が日本列島の上に居座っている The seasonal rain front *has settled in* over the Japanese Islands.

1**いせい 威勢** ▶威勢のいい若者 a *dashing* young man ‖ 店員の威勢のいい声 the store clerk's *high-spirited* voice ‖ 太郎君, きょうはずいぶん威勢がいいじゃないか Taro, you are quite *lively* today, aren't you?

2**いせい 異性** the opposite [other] sex (➤ 男性から見た場合の女性, あるいは女性から見た場合の男性)
▶彼は異性に優しい He is kind to *the opposite sex*. ‖ 彼女は常に異性を意識している She's always got *boys* on her mind.

3**いせい 以西** ▶私の兄弟は皆, 岡山以西に住んでいる All my brothers live *west of* Okayama.

いせいしゃ 為政者 a statesman (男の政治家), a stateswoman (女の政治家) (➤ statesperson, political leader が性差のない語) ; a ruler (統治者).

いせいじん 異星人 a creature from another world [outer space] ; an alien /éɪliən/, an E.T. (SF などで地球人に対して).

いせえび 伊勢海老 a (spiny) lobster (➤「身」を指すときには a をつけない) ▶伊勢エビ料理 a *lobster* dish.

1**いせき 遺跡** ruins (大規模な廃虚) ; remains (過去から残された物・建物) ▶古代ギリシャの遺跡 the *remains* [*ruins*] of ancient Greece ‖ 三内丸山遺跡 the San'nai Maruyama *archeological site* (➤「考古学的な場所」の意) ‖ 遺跡を発掘調査する excavate the *ruins*.

2**いせき 移籍** (a) **transfer** /trǽnsfəːʳ/ **一動 移籍する transfer** /trænsfə́ːʳ/ (＋自) ▶その選手が阪神に**移籍する**ことが正式に発表された They formally announced that the player *would be transferred* to the Tigers.

1**いぜん 以前 before**(前に) ; **formerly** (昔は) ▶1980年**以前**に生まれた人たち those people who were born *before 1980* (➤ 1980年を含む場合は in 1980 or [and] before とする).

▶明治**以前**の文学作品はことばが難しくて読みにくい Literary works *before the Meiji era* are difficult to read because of their difficult wording. (● 日本語の「…以後」がその時点・時期を含むのに対して,「…以前」では含む場合と含まない場合がある. 訳例は含まない場合(つまり江戸時代から前)を表しており, 明治時代も含める場合は Literary works of the Meiji era and before ... とする).

▶彼らは**以前**(＝昔)私が教えた生徒たちだ They are my *former* students. ／They are students I taught *before* [*in the past*]. ‖ この映画は**以前**(＝前に)見たことがある I have seen this film *before*. ‖ この路線は**以前**にも増して混むようになった This route is more crowded than *ever* [*before*]. ‖ 彼の小説は**以前**は人気があった His novels were *once* popular. ‖ あの教授は**以前**はテレビのニュースキャスターをしていた That professor was *formerly* a TV newscaster. ‖ あなたのお母さんのことはずっと**以前**から存じ上げていますよ I know your mother *from way back*. (➤ from way back は「ずっと昔から」) ‖ 科学者になることが彼の**以前からの**(＝長い間抱いている)念願だった His *long-cherished* wish was to become a scientist. ‖ 父は**以前**ほど元気ではない My father is not *as* strong *as he used to be*.

▶きみ, それは常識**以前**の問題じゃないか Come on! That's *even more basic than common sense*.

2**いぜん 依然 still** ▶容疑者は**依然**逃走中だ The suspect is *still* at large. ‖ 彼の容体は**依然として**目が離せない状態にある His condition *still* requires constant monitoring. ／His condition *continues to* require constant monitoring. (➤「依然」の意味は continue に含まれる). ‖ **依然として**これが最良の方法と信じている I *still* believe this is the best way.

いそ 磯 a **rocky beach** [**seashore**] ▶**磯**で小魚を捕まえる catch small fish at *a* (*rocky*) *seashore* ‖ **磯釣りをする** *fish on the rocky beach* ／*fish from shore rocks* (➤「磯釣り」は surf casting という).

いそいそ ▶私のルームメートは**いそいそと**デートに出かけていった My roommate was *excited and happy* when she went out on her date. (➤「興奮してうれしそうだった」の意).

1**いそう 移送する transfer** ＋自 ; **transport** ＋自 (輸送する) ▶患者を大学病院に**移送する** *transfer* a patient to a university hospital.

2**いそう 位相** a **phase.**

いそうろう 居候 a **freeloader** ; a **hanger-on**(やっかい者 ; 複数形は hangers-on) ▶私はいちばん上の兄の家に**居候している** I'm *living off* my oldest brother. ‖ うちの**居候**はよく食べるよ That *freeloader* at our house eats a lot.

いそがしい 忙しい

1【暇がない】be busy ; **be engaged**(予定がある ; 堅い語) ▶**忙しい**人 a *busy* person ‖ きょうは**忙しい**1日だった I had a *busy* day today. ‖ **忙しくて**新聞も読めない I'*m* too *busy* even to read the newspaper. ／I'*m* so *busy* (that) I can't read even the newspaper.

▶今仕事で目が回るほど**忙しい** I'*m up to my ears* in work at the moment. (➤ 文字どおりには「耳まで仕事に埋まっている」の意) ／*Things are hectic* at work [at the office] right now.

▶ 対話「相変わらずテニスはやってますか?」「いや, **忙しく**ってね」"Are you still playing tennis?" "No. I'*m* too *busy*."

✉ **お忙しいところ, 街を案内してくださいましてありがとうございました** Thank you very much *for taking time from your busy schedule* to show me around the city. ➤「多忙なスケジュールから時間を割いてくださって感謝します」の意.

【文型】
作業(A)で忙しい
be busy with A
…するのに忙しい
be busy doing

▶父はいつも仕事で**忙しい** My father *is* always *busy with* his work. ‖ 試験の準備で今週は**忙しかった** I *have been busy* prepar*ing* for the examinations this week. ‖ 太郎は報告書作りで**忙しい** Taro *is busy* writ*ing* a report.

直訳の落とし穴「…するのに忙しい」
「…するのに」を「…するために」に置き換えるのか, 学習者はすぐ to do を思い浮かべるようで,「…するのに忙しい」を(×)be busy to do とする間違いが極めて多い. 正しい英語は, 例えば「彼は家の引っ越しの手伝いをして忙しい」ならば He's busy helping his family move. である. これを to help とすると, ネイティブには too busy to help と言おうとしているように響き,「忙しくて手伝えない」の意と捉えられてしまう. to do は未来志向型といわれ, まだ着手していない行為を表してしまうのである. 何かをしていて忙しいは現在進行中の行為を表す doing と結びついて, busy doing である.「父は仕事で忙しすぎる」は My father is too busy working. で (×)to work ではない.

2【よく動き回る】▶ミツバチが**忙しく**巣穴に出たり入ったりしている The honeybees are *busy* entering and leaving their hive.

いそがせる 急がせる hurry ▶「早く, 早く」って**急がせないで**よ Would you quit saying, "Hurry up, hurry up"? ‖ 《レストランでウエーターが》もう少々お待ちください. **急がせます**から I'll *rush* your order, so please be patient for a few more minutes.

いそぎ 急ぎの urgent(至急の) ▶**急ぎの**注文 a *rush* order ‖ **急ぎの**メール an *urgent* email ‖ **急ぎの**用がありますのできょうはこれで失礼します I have to say good-by for now since I have *urgent* business.

☛ **大急ぎ** (→見出語)

いそぎあし 急ぎ足 ▶遅れそうだ. **急ぎ足**で行こう Better *step on it*, or we'll be late. (➤ Better は We had better の略. step on it は「急ぐ」の意のインフォーマルな言い方 ;「アクセルを踏む」が原義) ‖ 自宅から駅までは**急ぎ足**で 5 分ほどです The station is (a) five minutes' *brisk walk* from my house.

いそぎんちゃく 磯巾着 a **sea anemone.**

いそぐ 急ぐ

hurry /hə́ːri ‖ hʌ́ri/ **一副 急いで in a hurry** ; **hastily**(慌てて) ; **quickly**(素早く) ▶目的地に向かって**急ぐ** *hurry* to one's destination ‖ **急げ**. でないと学校に遅刻するぞ *Hurry up*, or you'll be late for school. (➤ hurry up は「(今よ

り）もっと急ぐ」）‖急ぐ必要はありません There is no need *to hurry*. ‖急ごう．雨になりそうだ *Let's hurry*. It looks like rain.

▶暗くなってきたので帰り道を急いだ It was getting dark, so we *hurried* home. ‖急いでいたので傘をタクシーの中に忘れた *In my hurry* [*haste*], I left my umbrella in the taxi. ‖そんなに急いで食べてはだめよ You shouldn't eat so *quickly*. ‖この報告書は急いで書いたらしい．間違いだらけだ This report must have been written *in a hurry*. There are lots of mistakes in it.

▶運転手さん，急いでください Driver, *step on the gas*, please.（➤ 訳例の step on the gas は「アクセルを踏む」が原義で，インフォーマルな表現）‖空港まで，急いで頼むよ To the airport, and *be quick about it*. ／To the airport, and *make it quick*.

▶結論を急ぐな Don't *jump* [*leap*] *to conclusions*.

ことわざ 急がば回れ If you're in a hurry, take a roundabout way (rather than a risky one). ／Slow and steady wins the race. ／More haste, less speed.（第 1 例は日本語からの直訳．第 2 例は「ゆっくり着実にすることが競走に勝つことになる」，第 3 例は「慌てるとかえって遅くなる」の意の英語のことわざ．Haste makes waste. ともいう）．

✉ **急いでおりますので，今月末までにお返事をいただけるとありがたいのですが** *As this matter is urgent*, I hope to hear from you by the end of the month.

いぞく 遺族 **the bereaved family, the bereaved**
▶今ご遺族を弔問してきたところです I've just called on *the bereaved family* to offer [express] my condolences.
‖遺族年金 a survivor's pension [annuity].

いそしむ 勤しむ ▶仕事にいそしむ *work hard* [*diligently*] ‖彼は日夜勉学にいそしんだ He *was occupied* with his studies [in studying] day and night.

いそん 依存 **dependence** 一動（…に）**依存する** **depend**《on》▶日本は天然資源を諸外国に大きく依存している Japan *depends* heavily *on* foreign countries for natural resources.

いぞん 異存 an **objection** ▶私の提案に何かご異存がおありですか Do you have any *objection* to my proposal? ‖きみが工学部を選ぶことには異存はない I have no *objection* if you decide on the engineering school.

いた 板 a **board**（縦長の薄い）; a **plank**（厚板）; a **sheet**（ガラス・金属などの薄板）▶（開かないように）戸に板を打ちつける *board up* a door ‖その板にくぎを打ってはいけない Don't nail the *board*.
▶《慣用表現》あいつのスピーチもだいぶ板についてきた He's *getting* more *confident* about speaking in public.（➤「自信がついてきた」の意）‖きみの英語もすっかり板についてきたね You're now quite *at home* in English.（➤ at home は「十分慣れて，精通して」）．
‖板戸 a wooden door ‖板の間 a room with a wooden floor ‖板塀 a board fence.

[1]**いたい 遺体** **the body (of a dead person)**, a **corpse** /kɔːˈps/（➤ the [a] body だけで表すことが多い；後者は死体を物体として見るという含みがあることが多い）; one's **remains**（➤ 遺体が損壊していたり，死後長い時間［年月］が経過したりという含みがあることが多い）▶遺体を埋葬する bury *the body of a deceased person* ‖遺体はとうとう発見されなかった The *body* was never found. ‖彼女の遺体は飛行機で彼女の国へ送り返された Her *remains* were flown back to her country.
‖遺体安置所 a morgue /mɔːˈg/.

[2]**いたい 痛い** **1【肉体的に苦痛がある】** **hurt** →痛み，痛む ▶足が痛い My feet *hurt* (me). ／My feet *are killing* me.（➤ be killing は hurt よりも痛みがかなり強い場合）‖胃が痛い I *have* (*a*) *pain* [*have pains*] in my stomach. ／I *have* a stomach*ache*.（➤ a を省略するのは主に《英》．次例も同じ．→胃痛）．
▶歯［耳］が痛い I *have* a tooth*ache* [an ear*ache*]. ‖頭が（割れそうに）痛い I *have* a (splitting) head*ache*.（➤ headache の場合は《英》でも a を伴うのが一般的）‖喉［目］が痛い I *have* a *sore* throat [*sore* eyes]. ‖ママ，痛いよ！ Mom, *it hurts*! ‖誰かに足を踏まれて思わず「痛い！」と叫んだ Someone stepped on my foot and I reflexively cried out, "*Ouch!*"（➤ ouch は /autʃ/ と発音する）‖右手のひっかき傷がまだひりひりと痛い The scratch on my right hand still *smarts*.（➤ smart は「ずきずき［ひりひり］痛む」の意の動詞）‖ 対話「どこが痛いんですか」「体じゅうです」"Where does it *hurt*?" "All over."
2【比喩的】 ▶きみのつらい気持ちは痛いほどよくわかるよ I *really do* feel for you. ‖彼女の忠告はいつも耳が痛い Her advice always *hits a sore spot* [*hits where it hurts*]. ‖全く二郎の受験には頭が痛いよ It *gives* me *a headache* just to think how Jiro will do on the entrance exam. ‖そんなことをすると痛い目に遭うよ You'll *get into trouble* if you do that. ‖あいつを痛い目に遭わせてやろう *I'll give* him *a hard time*. ／*I'll teach* him *a lesson*.（➤ 前者は「つらい思いをさせる」，後者は「おきゅうを据える」）．
▶きみに悪口を言われたって痛くもかゆくもないさ You can say bad things about me. It *won't hurt me at all*. ／Sticks and stones may break my bones, but *words will never hurt me*.（➤ 後者は「口で何と言われてもへっちゃらだ」の意で，子供がけんかのときに言う文句）‖小川君と言い合って痛いところを突かれた When I argued with Ogawa, he *hit a sore spot* [*a raw nerve*]. ‖彼はいつも自分の自慢話ばかりで人の話を聞かない痛い人だ．He's *pathetic* [*cringeworthy*／*painful to watch*] as he's always bragging about himself and never listens to others.
3【被害・失敗がつらい】 ▶1000円の損だってぼくにはとても痛い Even losing one thousand yen *hurts* me very much. ‖英語の試験に失敗したのが痛かった Failing the English exam *was a real blow*.（➤ blow は「打撃」）‖きのうの試合は大事なところで痛いミスが出て負けた We lost the game yesterday because of *a costly error* at a crucial moment.

[1]**いだい 偉大な** **great** ▶偉大な発見 a *great* discovery ‖パブロ・カザルスは偉大なチェリストだった Pablo Casals was a *great* cellist.

[2]**いだい 医大** (a) **medical school** [**college**]（➤ 教育の場として Ⓤ 扱いが多い）．▶医大に行く［を卒業する］go to [graduate from] *medical school*.

いたいけ ⚠ **幼くてかわいらしい様子や，弱々しくて痛々しい様子を表すこの語にぴったりの英語はないので，very young and touching（かわいそう）; very young and endearing（かわいい）などを適宜用いる．**

いたいじ 異体字 a **kanji variant.**

いたいたしい 痛々しい **painful**（苦痛を覚える）; **pitiful**（見る者が哀れを催す，同情する）▶彼が松葉づえを突いて歩く姿は実に痛々しかった It was very *painful* to see him walk on crutches. ‖傲慢な大統領の末路は見るも痛々しい光景であった The downfall of the once arrogant president was a *pitiful* sight to watch. ‖誘拐された少年は痛々しいほどやつれていた The kidnapped boy was *painfully* [*pitifully*] emaciated.

いたがる 痛がる ▶あの子は甘えて大げさに痛がっているのよ That child pretends to *be in great pain* just to get attention. (●「注意を引こうとしてうわべだけ痛がって泣いている」と考える).

いたく 委託する **commission** +目 (正式に依頼する); **entrust** +目 (人に任せる); **outsource** +目 (外注する) ▶この契約の交渉は私が御社の社長より委託されております I *have been entrusted* by the president of your company to take care of the contract negotiations.

▶彼は自然食品の委託販売をやっている He *sells* natural foods *on commission*. (➤ on commission は「(委託による)歩合制で」).

‖(業務の)外部委託 outsourcing.

いだく 抱く **hold** +目 (しっかりと); **bear** +目 (ある感情を); **cherish** +目 (心に大切に); **foster** +目 (育み育てるように); **harbor** +目 (心にずっと隠し持って)

▶彼女に恨みを抱く *bear* [*hold*] a grudge against her (➤ bear のほうが日本語に近い堅い語) ‖希望を抱く *entertain* [*cherish*] a hope (➤ 日常的な表現は have hope) ‖私は子供の頃からジェット機のパイロットになる夢を抱いてきた I *have fostered* [*have harbored*] a dream of becoming a jet pilot since (my) childhood. ‖その山村は深い森に抱かれている That mountain village *is surrounded* by a thick forest.

いたけだか 居丈高な **overbearing** ▶そんなものはいらないと言うと, セールスマンは急に居丈高になった When I said I didn't want to buy it, the salesman suddenly *took an overbearing attitude* [*came on strong*].

いたしかた 致し方 ▶ご同意いただけないのであれば致し方ありません *It can't be helped* if you can't agree. →しかたない, やむをえない.

いたしかゆし 痛し痒し ▶うちの両親は子供の面倒をよく見てくれるのはいいんだけど, 甘やかし過ぎるから痛しかゆしってところなのよね It's nice that my parents often look after the children for me, but *it's a sort of mixed blessing* because they spoil the children. (➤ mixed blessing は「ありがたいようなありがたくないようなもの[こと]」).

いたす 致す ▶ご案内いたします *Please follow me.* / *Let me show the way* [*usher you*]. (➤ usher は「席まで案内する」).

いたずら 悪戯

1【悪さ】 a **prank** (からかって楽しむ); a **trick** (人をだます); **mischief** /místʃɪf/ (子供っぽい, 実害のない悪ふざけ); a **practical joke** (相手を驚かせたり, 困らせたりする仕掛け) ▶悪質ないたずら a malicious *prank* ‖悪意のないいたずら a harmless *prank* ‖あの子たちにいたずらをさせないようにしてください Please keep those children out of *mischief*. ‖あの子たち, きみにいたずらしようとしてるよ Those kids are going to *play a prank* [*trick*] on you. (➤ 動詞は pull でもよい) ‖そのライターをいたずらしちゃあだめだ! Don't *play with* that lighter! ‖子供たちがとても静かだが, 何かいたずらをしているに違いない The children are very quiet — they must be doing something *naughty*. (● They must be up to something [to some mischief / to no good]. とも訳せる).

▶このいたずら小僧め, 何してるんだ! You *little rascal* [*monkey*], what're you doing? ‖ここにいたずら書きをしてはいけません Don't *write graffiti* here. ‖私はゆうべいたずら電話で起こされた Last night I was wakened by *a crank* [*prank*] *call*. (➤「卑わいな電話」を明確にするには an obscene call) ‖この絵はいたずら半分に描いたものだ I painted this picture *just for fun*. (➤「おもしろ半分に」の意) ‖そのアメリカ人の少女は私に向かっていたずらっぽくウインクした That American girl winked at me *slyly*.

▶《比喩的》ちょっとした運命のいたずらでその2人は再会できなかった By some *quirk of fate*, the two were never able to meet again.

2【淫らなふるまい】 ▶女子生徒にいたずらをした中年の男が昨晩逮捕された A middle-aged man who had *molested* a schoolgirl was arrested last evening. (➤ molest は「(女性・子供に)淫らなことをする」の意. 「いたずらをする人」は molester).

いたずらに 徒に ▶青春の貴重な時間をいたずらに過ごすな Don't *waste* [*idle away*] your precious youth. ‖いたずらに(=不必要に)彼を刺激しないでほっときなさい It's better to leave him alone than provoke him *needlessly*. ‖私は賄賂など受け取ってはいない. いたずらに騒ぎ立てるのはやめてくれ I have not taken a bribe or anything of the sort. You *have no good reason to create such a fuss*, so please stop.

いただき 頂 **the top**, **the summit** (山頂; 後者は堅い語); **the peak** (とがった山頂) ▶鳥海山の頂 *the top* of Mt. Chokai ‖富士山の頂は11月にはすでに雪で覆われていた *The peak* [*summit*] of Mt. Fuji was already covered in snow in November.

いただきます

> **解説 「いただきます」について**
> (1) 食前の「いただきます」に対応する英語表現はないが, キリスト教徒の中には食前[食後]の祈り(grace)をする人はいる.
> (2)「いただきます」をあえて英訳するならば, 例えば I take [receive] this meal with thanks. (この食事をありがたくいただきます) とか, Thank you for this meal. (この食事をありがとうございます) などと表現するしかない. →ごちそうさま, 頂く.

▶ **対話** 「どうぞ召し上がれ」「はい, いただきます」"Please help yourself." "Oh, thank you (very much)." (➤「はい, ありがとうございます」の意. これに It looks good [delicious]. (おいしそうですね)のようなことばを付け加えてもよい).

いただく 頂く

1【もらう, 食べる】 ▶このパンフレット頂いてよろしいですか Can [May] I *have* this brochure? ‖名刺を頂けますか Could I *ask for* your business card [name card]? ‖山田さんからリンゴを頂いた *I've received* some apples from Mr. Yamada. / Mr. Yamada *gave* me some apples. ‖お返事をできるだけ早く頂きたいのです *Please let me have* your answer as soon as possible. ‖冷たい水を1杯頂きたいのですが *May I* [*Could I*] *have* a glass of cold water, please? ‖ **対話** 「サラダをもう少しいかがですか」「はい, 頂きます」"Won't you have some more salad?" "Yes, *please*." (➤「いえ, 十分頂きました」なら "No, thank you. I've had enough [I'm full]." などと答える; →十分) ‖《店で》じゃ, それ頂くわ OK, I'll *take* it.

▶よし, この試合は頂きだな OK. This game *is ours* [*is in* the bag]. (➤ be in the bag は「(勝利などが)確実である」).

い

2【…してもらう】

【文型】
…していただけますか
Could you (please) do?
Would you (please) do?
Would you mind doing?

【解説】(1) Could you …? はもともと可能性を, Would you …? は相手の意思を尋ねるが, 前者はややインフォーマルでふだんよく使われ, 後者はより改まっていて押しが強いという受け止め方が一般的.
(2) Would you mind doing? は「頼み事を嫌[迷惑]と思わないか」の意. 進行中の行為に言及するときは口調にもよるが, 皮肉や批判が込められることもあるので注意.

▶トイレはどこか教えていただけますか *Could you* (*please*) tell me where the restroom is? ‖ もう少し詳しく説明していただきたいのですが *Could you* explain a little more about that? (➤ I'd like you to explain a little more about that. とすると「…してほしい」と上司が部下に指示するような口調になる. また, 学習者がしばしば間違える I wish you would … は現状への不満を言うときの言い方) ‖ 帰るときに電気を消していただけますか *Would you* turn off the lights when you leave? / *Would you mind* turn*ing* off the lights when you leave?

直訳の落とし穴「…していただけませんか」
「…していただけますか」や「…していただけませんか」に, Would you mind doing? を使うときには要注意. この表現は, 特に目の前で進行中の行為に言及するときは口調にもよるが, 往々にして, 皮肉や批判が伴う. 例えば, 例文の「靴を脱いでいただけますか[いただけませんか]」を Would you mind taking off your shoes? とすると, そのくらいの気を遣ってくれてもいいのでは, というニュアンスを込めたいらだちを表す表現となる. Could you please …? とするのがよい. 「たばこを吸わないでくれますか」も Would you mind not smoking? はきつい表現で適当ではない. I'd appreciate it if you didn't smoke. が相手に配慮した丁寧な表現である.

▶靴を脱いでいただけますか(日本ではそれが習慣ですから) *Could I ask you to* take off your shoes? (It's the custom here in Japan.) ‖ 写真を撮っていただけますか *Could I ask you to* take a picture of me? ‖ 対話「ちょっと辞書を貸していただけますか」「ええ, どうぞ」"*May* [*Could*] *I* borrow your dictionary a moment?" "Certainly." (➤ May I …? はかしこまった頼み方) ‖ 打ち合わせを金曜日に変更していただけますか *Would it be possible to* change our meeting to Friday? (➤ やや頼みにくいことを切り出すときの言い方).

【文型】
…していただきたいのですが
I was wondering if you could do.
…していただけるとありがたいのですが
I would appreciate it if you did [could do / would do].

【解説】(1) 前者はやや頼みにくいことを頼むときの丁寧な表現. (2) 後者はビジネスレターなどの書面でよく用いる改まった丁寧な頼み方. (3) if の文は過去形を用いる. 後者では if の文の内容を受ける it を落とさないこと.

▶宿題を手伝っていただきたいのですけど *I was wondering if you could* help me with my homework. (➤ 例えば, 相手が忙しそうにしていて, 少し頼みにくいときなどに使う表現) ‖ 二度とメールを送らないでいただきたいのですが *I would appreciate it if* you *would*n't send me any more emails [*if* you *would* stop sending me emails].

3【「…させていただきます」の形で】▶ぜひ伺わせていただきます *I'll be very happy to* call on you. ‖ その件についてはもう少し考えさせていただきます *I'll have to* think the matter over a little more.

4【上に置く】▶富士山は雪を頂いて(=かぶって)いる Mt. Fuji *is crowned* with snow.

いただけない 頂けない ▶きみの欠席理由は頂けないね I *don't buy* your excuse for being absent. (➤ この buy はあまり合理的でない説明などを「受け入れる」) ‖ 売り上げが去年より5%落ちてる? そいつは頂けないな Sales are down 5% from last year—*I can't say I like it*. ‖ これはあんまり頂けないね This is*n't so good*.

いたたまれない 居たたまれない ▶自分の愚かさに気づき私は恥ずかしさで居たたまれない気持ちになった When I realized how stupid I had been, I was so filled with shame I *wanted to run away* [*I felt that I had to leave*]. ‖ あまりにも下品な彼の態度に友人たちはその場に居たたまれなくなった His excessively crude behavior made it *uncomfortable* for his friends *to stay any longer*. ‖ しゅうとめの嫁いびりのひどさに彼女は居たたまれなくなって(=我慢できなくなって)実家へ逃げ帰った She ran home because she *couldn't stand* the cruel treatment by her mother-in-law.

いたち 《動物》**a weasel** ▶《慣用表現》戦いが憎しみを生み, 憎しみが再び戦争を引き起こす—これはいたちごっこだ War breeds hate, and hate leads to war again. It's *a vicious circle*. (➤ vicious circle は「悪循環」) ‖ 物価と賃金はいたちごっこを続けている Prices and wages keep *chasing each other like a dog after his own tail*.

いたチョコ 板チョコ **a chocolate bar.**

いたって 至って ▶うちの子は至って気が小さい Our son [daughter] is *very* shy. ‖ おふくろは至って元気だよ My mother is in *extremely* good health.

いたで 痛手 **a great [heavy] blow** (打撃) ▶彼の欠場はわがチームには大きな痛手だった His absence was *a great blow* to our team. / Our team suffered *a great blow* by his absence.
▶痛手を負う get *severely wounded* (深手を負う); suffer *a heavy blow* (大打撃を受ける).

いたばさみ 板挟み ▶義理と人情の板挟みになる *be torn between giri*-obligation *and* compassion (➤ compassion は「(他人に対する)同情」) ‖ 母親には大学へ行けと言われ, 父親には就職しろと言われ, 私は板挟みになっている I'm *being pulled in two directions*. My mother tells me to go to college, while my father advises me to get a job. (➤ 英語の dilemma (ジレンマ) はどちらを選んでも本人にとって困ったことになる状況, どちらも受け入れ難い状況をいうので, このような単に選択に困っていることには使わない).

いたまえ 板前 a **(trained) cook of Japanese cooking** (➤ … in a Japanese restaurant としてもよい); a **(trained) sushi chef** (すし屋の) ▶板前の修業をする undergo training to become *a chef of Japanese cooking* [*a sushi chef*].

いたましい 痛ましい **sad** (悲しい); **tragic** (悲劇的な); **pitiful** (哀れな); **painful** (つらい) ▶痛ましい事故 a *sad* [*tragic*] accident ‖ 一家心中という痛ましい事件 a *sad* [*tragic*] case of a family suicide ‖ 18歳で

死ぬとは何と痛ましい How *pitiful* [*sad* / *heartbreaking*] it is that he died at the age of 18!

[1]**いたみ 痛み** (a) **pain**, an **ache** /eɪk/
語法 (1)pain は継続して起こる慢性的な痛みを, an ache は1回ごとの一時的な痛みをいうことが多い. (2) ache は head*ache* (頭痛), stomach*ache* (胃痛, 腹痛)のように複合語になる場合が多い.
▶痛みに耐える bear [endure] the *pain* ‖ 慢性的な腰の痛みに苦しむ suffer from chronic back *pain* (➤ pain は Ⓤ 扱いのことも多い) ‖ 脇腹にひどい[鈍い]痛みを感じる feel a bad [dull] *pain* in one's side ‖ 膝に少し痛みがある I have a little *pain* in my knee(s). ‖ きょうは腰に痛みがある I have a back*ache* today. ‖ ひどい胃の痛みに苦しむ suffer from severe *stomach pain* [a severe *stomachache*] (➤ 前者は慢性的なもの. 後者は一時的なもの) ‖ 体じゅうに激しい痛みがある I have severe *aches and pains* all over.
▶《医者が》痛みはありますか? Do you feel any *pain*? ‖ この薬が激しい胃の痛みをとってくれた This medicine relieved the sharp *pain* in my stomach. ‖ しばらく横になったら痛みがだいぶ和らいだ The *pain* eased considerably after lying down for a while. ‖ 《比喩的》恋人を失った心の痛みから立ち直る recover from a *broken heart*.
‖痛み止め a pain reliever, a painkiller.

[2]**いたみ 傷み** **damage** (損傷); a **bruise** /bruːz/ (果実などの) ▶その家は思ったより傷みがひどかった The house was *damaged* more badly than I expected.

いたみいる 痛み入る ▶お心遣い, 痛み入ります *I'm so grateful* for your thoughtfulness.

いたみわけ 痛み分け a **draw due to injury**, a **draw in which both sides suffered damage.**

[1]**いたむ 痛む** **1【肉体的に】hurt** →痛い ▶傷, 痛む? Does the cut *hurt*? ‖ どこ[足のどこ]が痛むの? Where does it [your foot] *hurt*? ‖ 頭が少し痛む I *have* a slight head*ache*. ‖ かぜのせいで節々が痛む I have a cold and *feel pain* in my joints. ‖ ときどきこめかみが痛む I *have* occasional *pains* in my temples. ‖ ゆうべは歯がひどく痛んだ I *had* a bad tooth*ache* last night.
2【心が】▶飛行機事故で一人娘を亡くした親御さんのことを思うと胸が痛む I *feel very sad* when I think of [*My heart goes out to*] those parents who lost their only daughter in the plane crash. ‖ そのかわいそうな少女の姿を見ると心が痛む It *makes my heart ache* to see that poor girl. / *My heart aches* when I see that poor girl.

[2]**いたむ 傷む** **go bad**((飲食物が)悪くなる); **suffer**(損傷を受ける) ▶暑いときには魚や肉はすぐに傷む Fish and meat soon *go bad* in hot weather. (➤《英》では go off ともいう) ‖ このトマト傷んでるわ. 捨ててちょうだい This tomato has *gone bad*. Throw it out. ‖ 少し痛んだ果物 slightly *spoiled* [*bruised*] fruit (➤ spoiled は悪くなってはいるが rotten (完全に腐った) ではなく, 悪いところを取り除けば食べられる可能性はある状態; bruised は「傷のある」).
▶このケーキ, 傷んでるかしら Is this cake *stale*? (➤ パン・ケーキ・クッキーなどが「日にちがたっておかしな味になる」は stale). ‖ その道路は大型ダンプが頻繁に通行するので, かなり傷んでいる Large dump trucks pass frequently over that road, so it *has suffered* quite a lot of *damage* [it *has been damaged* quite a bit]. ‖ 私たちの学校は古くてあちこち傷んでいる Our school is an old one, and it *needs repairs* here and there. (●「修理の必要がある」と考えて訳例のように表現する).

[3]**いたむ 悼む** **mourn** +目 ▶友の死を悼む *mourn* [*grieve over*] the death of one's friend ‖ 人気スターの死を悼んで追悼番組が放映された A memorial program was broadcast to *show respect for* the deceased star.
✉ **お父さまのご逝去を悼み, お花を送らせていただきます** We will be sending flowers to *express* our *condolences on* your father's passing. (●「…に哀悼の意を表すために」と考えて訳例のように表現する. その際, 「逝去」と同じく婉曲(えんきょく)語の passing を用いる).

いためつける 痛めつける ▶学生の頃彼にはよく痛めつけられたものだ He used to *pick on* me [*bully* me *around*] a lot (back) during our school days. (➤ ともに「いじめる」の意) ‖ あいつを少し痛めつけてやれ *Let's make* him *suffer* a little.

[1]**いためる 痛める** **hurt** +目 ▶転んで右手を痛めたため字が書けません I can't write since I fell and *hurt* my right hand. ‖ 私は(かぜなどで)喉を痛めている I have a *sore* throat.
▶《比喩的》彼は資金集めに頭を痛めている He is *worrying about* [*racking* his *brain over*] how to get together enough money. ‖ 妹は根も葉もないそのうわさにひどく心を痛めている My sister *is* deeply *troubled by* the groundless rumor. ‖ その悲しい知らせに少女は小さな胸を痛めた The sad news *made* the girl's little *heart ache*.

[2]**いためる 炒める** **fry** +目; **sauté** /soʊtéɪ/ +目 (さっと) ▶お昼にはソーセージと野菜をいためましょうか Shall I *fry* some sausages and vegetables for lunch? 《参考》「肉野菜いため」は stir-fried vegetables with beef [pork] のようにいえばよい.

[3]**いためる 傷める** **damage** +目.

いたらない 至らない ▶太郎がぐれたのは私が至らなかったせいです It's *my fault* Taro became a delinquent. ‖ 至らぬところがありましたらどうか注意してください Please let me know if I'm *not being attentive enough*.

いたり 至り ▶市長よりお祝いのおことばを頂けるとは光栄の至りです It is *a great honor* to be congratulated by the mayor. ‖ 今回の件は若気の至りと思って許してやろう I'll forgive you for this incident, considering it as *due to youthful impulsiveness* [*impetuosity*] (➤ impulsiveness は「衝動的行為」, impetuosity は「性急な言動」).

イタリア **Italy** /ɪ́ṭəli/ ━形 **イタリアの Italian** /ɪtǽljən/ ‖**イタリア語** Italian ‖ **イタリア人** an Italian.

イタリック **italics**(斜体字) ▶本の題名をイタリックで表す *italicize* a book's title / *put* [*type*] a book's title *in italics*(➤ type はパソコンなどの場合).

いたる 至る **1【達する】lead** 《to》 ▶この道は奥多摩を経て甲府に至る This road *leads to* Kofu via Okutama. ‖ 尾道から今治に至るしまなみ海道が1999年に開通した The Shimanami-Kaido Expressway from Onomichi *to* Imabari was opened to traffic in 1999. ‖ 現在に至るまで彼の消息は不明だ *Up to now* nothing has been heard of him.
2【事態が…になる】▶新図書館はまだ完成に至っていない Our new library *has not yet* been completed. ‖ 火災は大事に至る前に消し止められた The fire was put out *before* it got serious. ‖ 事ここに至っては社長の私が責任を取るほかはない *Now that the situation has come to this*, as president I have

no choice but to take responsibility.

いたるところ 至る所 ▶彼はボストンの至る所を知っている He knows *every part* [*every corner*] of Boston. ／He knows Boston *like the back of his hand*. (後者の like the back of one's hand は文字どおりには「自分の手の甲のように」の意で,「(場所など)を隅々まで知っている」というときに動詞の know とともに用いる慣用句) ‖松は日本国中至る所にある Pine trees can be found *all over* Japan. ‖新横綱は至る所で大歓迎された The new yokozuna was welcomed *wherever he went*. (➤「行く先々で」の意).

いたれりつくせり 至れり尽くせり ▶至れり尽くせりの歓迎ぶり a welcome that *left nothing to be desired* ‖あのホテルのサービスは至れり尽くせりだった The service at the hotel was *perfect*.

いたわり 労わり **caring** (いたわること) ; **consideration** (思いやり) ▶障害者へのいたわりの心 *caring* for people with disabilities ‖あの男には年老いた自分の両親に対するいたわりなどみじんもない That man doesn't have the slightest bit of *consideration* for his elderly parents.

いたわる 労わる **take good care** 《of》 (しっかり世話をする) ▶両親をいたわる *take good care of* one's parents ‖「少しは年寄りをいたわるものだ」とそのじいさんは言った "You should *show* some *consideration for* [*show* some *kindness to*] elderly people," said the old man. ‖彼はけがをした足をいたわりながら歩いた He walked *nursing* his injured leg.

▶監督は全力を尽くして負けた選手たちをいたわった The coach *comforted* [*said kind words to*] the players who had done their best but lost the game.

いたん 異端 **heresy** /hérəsi/ ▶異端的な意見 a *heretical* view ‖当時その映画監督は異端者扱いされた At that time, the film director was treated as *a heretic*. ‖彼の作品は最初は異端視された His works *were* initially *regarded as heretical* [*unorthodox*].

[1]いち 一 **one** ; **the first** (1番目) ▶1＋1は2 *One* and *one* makes [is] two. ‖2分の1 *one half* ‖5分の1 *one fifth* (⇀分数) ‖《トランプ》ハート[クラブ]の1 the *ace* of hearts [clubs].

▶山下君はクラス一の優秀な生徒だ Yamashita is *the brightest* student *in our class*. ‖富士山は高さでは日本一だ Mt. Fuji is *number one* in height *among all* the mountains *of Japan*. ‖日本は東洋一の工業国だ Japan is *the greatest* industrial nation *in the East*. ‖この船は世界一の大型タンカーだ This ship is *the largest* tanker *in the world*.

▶私は一音楽家にすぎない I am *only a musician*.

▶《慣用表現》また一から出直すさ I have to *go back to square one* (and start all over). ／ I'll *start from scratch* again. (前者は「振り出しに戻る」の意の go back to square one (原義は「最初のます目に戻る」)を, また後者は「ゼロ[最初]からやり直す」の意の start from scratch をそれぞれ当てて訳したもの) ‖彼は我々の計画に一も二もなく賛成した He *readily* agreed to our plan. ／He gave *ready* consent to our plan. ‖一に努力, 二に努力 *First*, hard work. After that, more hard work. ‖彼女の言うことは一から十までうそだ *Every* word of hers [*Whatever* she says] is false. ‖冴子は一を聞いて十を知る人だ Saeko is *very quick to understand*. ‖西田さんは英語[数学]ではクラスで一, 二を争う Nishida is *one of the best* English [math] students in her class. ‖ハワイは人気で一, 二を争う旅行先です Hawaii is *the most, or the second most*, popular tourist destination.

☛ 一か八か (⇀見出語)

[2]いち 位置 a **position** (相対的な) ; a **location** (地理的な) ; a **situation** (環境的な) ▶このテーブルの位置を変えたほうがよい We'd better change the *position* of this table. ‖日比谷公園は東京の中央に位置している Hibiya Park *is located* [*is situated* ／*lies*] in the center of Tokyo. ‖千葉県の北に位置するのは何県ですか What prefecture *is* north of Chiba Prefecture? ‖彼は地図でその町の位置を示した He *located* the town on a map. ‖彼は今会社で重要な位置に就いている He is now in an important *position* in the company.

▶《競技の合図》位置について! *Ready!* ／*On your mark(s)!* 《参考》前者を使って「位置について, 用意, ドン」と言う場合は Ready, steady, go! となり, 後者の場合は On your mark(s), get set, go! となる.

☛ 位置づける (⇀見出語)

[3]いち 市 a **market** (市場) ; a **fair** (祭りと関連したような) ▶次の市は30日に開かれます The next *market* is on the 30th. ‖ここら辺りは日曜の朝ごとに青空市が立つ *An outdoor market* is held every Sunday morning in this neighborhood.

‖国際見本市 an international trade fair ‖ノミの市 a flea market.

[1]いちい 一位 ▶100メートル競走で1位になる take [win] *first* (*place*) in a 100-meter race ／finish *first* in a 100-meter race ‖彼女は声楽のコンクールで全国第1位になった She won (*the*) *first prize* at the national vocal music contest [competition]. ‖小数点以下第1位を四捨五入しなさい Round (off) to whole numbers. (➤ whole number は「整数」).

[2]いちい 櫟 《植物》 a **yew** /juː/.

いちいせんしん 一意専心 ▶一意専心, 書道に精進します I will devote [apply] myself *single-mindedly* to the art of calligraphy.

いちいち 一々 ▶矢野先生は私のすることにいちいちけちをつける Mr. Yano, our teacher, finds fault with *everything* I do. ‖細かいことをいちいち覚えていられないよ I can't be bothered to keep *every* detail in mind.

▶彼の言うことはいちいちもっともだ *Everything* he has said is completely reasonable [《英また》 is spot-on].

[1]いちいん 一因 a **cause** ▶その事故の一因として運転士の過重労働が指摘された The fact that the driver had been overworked has been raised as *one of the possible causes* of the accident. ‖そのスキャンダルは彼の落選の一因となった The scandal *contributed* to his loss in the election. (➤ contribute は「一因[一助]となる」).

[2]いちいん 一員 a **member** ▶その政治家は保守党の一員だ That politician is *a member* of the Conservative Party. ／That politician belongs to the Conservative Party.

いちえん 一円 ▶北関東一円にひょうが降った There was a hailstorm *throughout* [*all over*] the North Kanto district.

いちおう 一応 ⚠**この語は「(不十分ながら)最低限の基準を満たしている」と話し手が考えたときに用いる語だが, 実際の用法はさまざまで, ときにはほとんど意味もなく, 相づち的に用いることさえある. したがって, この語**

にぴったりの英語はなく，文脈によって適宜訳語を考える必要がある．

▶きみの言うことは一応（＝ある点では）もっともだ What you say is reasonable *in a* [*one*] *way*. ‖ 一応（＝さしあたり）これで結構です This will do *for the moment* [*for the present* / *for the time being*]. ‖ 彼らは一応（＝仮の）合意に達した They reached a *tentative* agreement. ‖ 一応（＝一とおり）全ページに目を通しました I've *looked over* [I've *glanced through*] all the pages.

▶一応（＝非公式に）彼の意見を聞いてみます I'll ask his opinion *informally*. ‖ 一応（＝念のため）傘は持っていったほうがいいよ You'd better take an umbrella with you *just in case*. ‖ ぼく，一応大学卒なんですよ *After all*, I'm a college graduate.（➤ 大卒者にふさわしい学力などを示せるとき）‖ 一応（＝なんとか），大学は卒業しました Well, *somehow or other* I managed to graduate from college.

▶ 対話「きみのお父さん，東大教授なんだって？」「ええ，まあ，一応（＝そういうことです）」"I hear that your father is a professor at the University of Tokyo." "Yeah, *that's right*."

いちおし 一押し ▶新作スイーツの中ではこれが一押しです Of all the new sweets this is my *first recommendation*.

いちがいに 一概に ▶塾が一概に悪いとは言えない Japanese cram schools, called *juku*, are *not altogether* bad. ‖ 大卒だから「できる」とは一概には言えない Being a college graduate does*n't necessarily* mean that one is capable.

いちがつ 一月 **January**《略 Ja., Jan.》▶1月は晴れ着姿の若い女性をよく見かける We often see girls in colorful kimono *in January*. ‖ 私たちは1月2日に神社に初詣をした *On January 2*, we paid our first visit of the year to a shrine.

いちかばちか 一か八か ▶ここは一か八か（＝危険を冒してでも）三塁への盗塁を狙おう I'll *take a chance* and try to steal third. ‖ 一か八かやってみろ *Go for broke*.

いちがん 一丸 ▶わが校では教師が一丸となって校内暴力を一掃した We teachers *united as one* to eliminate school violence. ‖ 国民全体が一丸となってオリンピックを成功させた The whole nation *united* to make a success of the Olympic Games.

いちがんレフ 一眼レフ
‖一眼レフカメラ a single-lens reflex camera.

いちぐう 一隅 a **corner** ▶庭の一隅にひっそりと咲く野草 wild flowers that bloom quietly in *a corner* of a garden.

1 **いちぐん 一群** ▶村がオオカミの一群に襲われた The village was attacked by *a pack of* wolves. ‖ その囲いの中には一群の牛がいた I saw *a herd of* cattle in the pen. →群れ.

2 **いちぐん 一軍**《野球》**the first team,**《米》a **major league** [**club**] ▶一軍入りをする *make the majors*. →二軍.

いちげい 一芸 ▶一芸に秀でた人 *a master of an art* ‖ 一芸を窮めるのは容易なことではない It is no easy task to *master an art*.

いちげき 一撃 a **blow**（体の一部への）; a **punch**（げんこつによる）; a **stroke**（意図的に加える，または武器などによる）▶そのボクサーは顎に一撃を食らってマットに沈んだ Getting *a blow* [*a punch*] on his jaw, the boxer sank onto the mat. ‖ マイクは彼を一撃で倒した Mike knocked him down *with a single blow* [*punch*].

いちげん 一見 ▶一見さんお断り No *first-time customers*.

いちげんか 一元化する **unify** ＋目; **integrate** ＋目（統合する，一体化する）▶年金制度を一元化する *unify* pension systems ‖ 情報処理を一元化する *unify* [*integrate*] data processing.

いちげんこじ 一言居士 ▶あの人は一言居士だ That man *has something to say about everything*.

いちご 苺《植物》a **strawberry** ▶イチゴを摘む pick *strawberries* ‖ イチゴ農園 a *strawberry* farm ‖ イチゴのショートケーキ *strawberry* shortcake ‖ イチゴ畑 a *strawberry* field.

いちごいちえ 一期一会 **Every encounter (, even with a person we have known for a long time,) is a precious once-in-a-lifetime experience. / Each encounter is a unique experience that will never be repeated.**

いちころ 一ころ ▶この殺虫剤をまけば害虫はいちころですよ This insecticide will *kill* pests *easily*. ‖ ちょっと親切にしてやれば彼なんかいちころよ All you have to do is be a little nice to him and he'll *be in the palm of* your *hand*.

いちごん 一言 ▶弟子たちは師匠のことばを一言半句も聞き漏らすまいとした The disciples listened to their master, trying not to miss even *a single word*.

いちざ 一座 a **troupe** /truːp/ ▶勘三郎一座はヨーロッパ巡業を行った Kanzaburo and his *troupe* made [went on] a tour of Europe.

1 **いちじ 一時** **1【ある時，かつて】for a time, for a while**（しばらくの間）; **at one time**（一時期）; **once**（かつて）

▶私は一時釣りに凝っていた *For a time* [*For a while*], I was deeply interested in fishing. / *Once* I was crazy about fishing. ‖ その会社には一時1000人近い従業員がいた The company employed nearly 1,000 workers *at one time*. ‖ あの横綱は一時ほどの元気がない That yokozuna is not as energetic as he *once* was. ‖ 一時はどうなることかと思ったが，せきの発作が治まってよかった *At one point*, I was really worried, but I'm glad that my fit of coughing stopped.

2【しばらく】▶《天気予報》曇り，一時雨 cloudy with *intermittent* showers（➤ intermittent は「断続的な」）‖ 野球の試合は雨で一時中断した The baseball game was interrupted *for a while* by (the) rain.

▶荷物を一時預かりに預ける leave one's baggage temporarily at a *baggage check* ‖ 洪水の被災者は一時しのぎのプレハブ住宅で不自由な生活を送っている The flood victims are living an inconvenient life in *makeshift* prefabricated houses. ‖ 一時逃れの（＝時間稼ぎの）うそをつく lie to *buy time* ‖《掲示》一時停止 Stop / Halt.

‖一時金 a one-time allowance /əláuəns/ ‖ 一時払い spot payment ‖ 一時避難所 a temporary refuge [shelter]《参考》飼い主のいない犬・猫などを一時的に収容する場所，駐車違反の車を一時的に留め置く場所を pound と呼ぶ.

☞ 一時的（→見出語）

2 **いちじ 一次** ▶一次試験はうまくいったが二次は自信がない I was lucky enough to pass *the primary examination* but I'm not sure about the secondary one. ‖ 第一次世界大戦が始まったのは1914年だった It was in 1914 that *World War I* [*the First World War*] broke out.（➤ 前者には the をつけな

い).

いちじいっく 一字一句 ▶一字一句漏らさずに訳す translate *word for word* (➤ word for word は「単語を1つも漏らさず」).

いちじがばんじ 一事が万事 ▶彼女は一事が万事そんな調子だ She always does things like that. ／ That is just one example of how she always does things [how she always is].

いちじく (植物) a fig.

いちじつせんしゅう 一日千秋 →いちにちせんしゅう.

いちじつのちょう 一日の長 ▶車の運転にかけては妻より私のほうに一日の長がある I'*m just a bit better* than my wife at driving.

いちじてき 一時的な temporary (短期間の) ; transitory (すぐ変わる) ▶一時的な現象 a *transitory* phenomenon ‖ 一時的な寒さ[暖かさ] a cold [warm] *spell* (➤ spell は「短い期間」) ‖ 最近の自動車の売れ行き不振は一時的な現象だ The recent decrease in car sales is *temporary*.

▶我々は不発弾処理のため一時的に避難した We were *temporarily* evacuated while a bomb was being defused.

いちじゅういっさい 一汁一菜 ▶一汁一菜の質素な夕食 a simple supper consisting of *one side dish and one bowl of soup*.

いちじゅん 一巡する make a round ▶放課後に構内を一巡する *make the rounds* of the campus after classes are out (➤ 場所を「巡回する」の意では make rounds と複数形を用いる).

▶わがチームは3回打者一巡の猛攻で5点をあげた Our team scored five runs in a fierce offensive where we *went through the batting lineup* in the third inning. ／ Our team *batted around* and scored five runs in the third inning. ‖ 5チームがドラフト一巡目でその投手を選んだ Five teams selected the pitcher *in the first round* of the draft.

いちじょ 一助 ▶我々の活動が地域発展の一助となれば幸いです We hope our activities will *contribute to* the development of the area.

いちじるしい 著しい striking (印象的な) ; remarkable (注目に値する) ; sharp, marked (くっきりした, 顕著な) ; dramatic (急激で驚くほどの) ; pronounced (はっきりした) ▶彼のテニスの上達ぶりは著しい His improvement in tennis is *striking*. ‖ 遺伝子工学は近年著しい進歩を遂げた The field of genetic engineering has seen *remarkable* progress in recent years. ‖ 新政権は前政権と著しい対照をなしている The new administration is in *sharp* [*marked*] contrast to the previous one. ‖ 最近株価が著しく上がった Stock prices have risen *remarkably* [*sharply*] recently.

▶著しい天候の変化 a *dramatic* [*(clearly) noticeable*] change in the weather ‖ その薬は著しい効果があった The medicine had a *pronounced* effect.

いちず 一途 ▶子供たちのいちずな気持ち(＝熱意)に動かされてその犬を飼うことにした I was so touched by my children's *enthusiasm* that I decided to keep the dog.

▶彼女はいちずにきみのことを思っているよ She loves you *wholeheartedly*. ‖ 父は仕事いちずだ *Work is* my Dad's *whole life*.

いちぞく 一族 an entire family ; a clan (氏族) ▶最上一族は伊達の軍勢に滅ぼされた *The entire* Mogami *family* was destroyed by the Date soldiers. ‖ あの人たちは平家一族の子孫だと言っている They claim that they are descendants of the Heike *clan*.

いちぞん 一存 ▶この件は私の一存では決められません This matter cannot be decided *by me alone*. ‖ この問題はきみの一存では決められないのだ This matter is not one that can be settled *by your decision alone*. ／ You can't decide this matter *on your own*. (➤ on one's own は「ひとりで」).

いちだい 一代 **1** 【一生】▶彼は一代で財産を築き上げた He made a fortune *in his lifetime*.

ことわざ 人は一代, 名は末代 A man dies, but his name remains.

2 【その時代】▶勝新太郎は一代の名優だった Katsu Shintaro was one of the greatest actors *of the age*.

いちたいいち 一対一の one-to-one, 《米また》 one-on-one ▶一対一の話し合いをする have a *one-to-one* talk ‖ 一対一で勝負しようじゃないか Let's *fight one-on-one*.

いちだいじ 一大事 ▶国家の一大事 *a matter of* national *concern* ‖ これが先生に知れたら一大事だ *What if* the teacher found out about this! (● 英語では「…したらどうなるだろう(大変だ)」(What if ...) のように発想する) ‖ 彼が会議に出てこなかったら一大事だ If he doesn't come to the meeting, it will be *one big problem*. (➤ one と big に強勢を置く).

いちだん 一団 a group (群れ, かたまり) ; a party (ある行動に参加する人々) ; a convoy (軍隊・戦隊・トラックなどの行動を共にする) ▶観光客の一団 a *group* [*party*] of tourists ‖ トラックの一団 *a convoy* of trucks [《英》 lorries].

▶陳情者たちは国会まで一団となって進み, 法務大臣に面会を求めた The petitioners marched as *a group* [*in a body*] to the Diet Building and demanded to see the Minister of Justice.

いちだんと 一段と ▶花嫁姿の彼女は一段と(＝いつもよりさらに)美しかった She was *all the more* beautiful in her wedding dress. ‖ きのうの雨で秋が一段と深まった Fall *has certainly deepened* [Fall *has advanced a step*] since yesterday's rain. ／ (Fall *has deepened* and) we're *a step closer to winter* since yesterday's rain. ‖ このカメラはこれまで私が使ったものよりも一段とよくできている This camera *is a cut above* all the others I have used. (➤ a cut above は「(人・物が)…より一段上で」の意のインフォーマルな表現).

いちだんらく 一段落 ▶仕事が一段落してほっと一息ついているところです I'm just now taking a break *after completing the first big part* of the job. ‖ ここらで一段落としましょう I think this is *a good place to stop*.

▶これで一段落だ I've [We've] solved the problem for the time being. ／ Now I've [we've] come to the end of the first stage. (➤ 前者は「ひとまず問題は解決できた」, 後者は「第一段階が終わった」の意).

いちづける 位置づける ▶彼は文壇ではどう位置づけられているのだろう Where does he *stand* in the literary world?

いちど 一度

1 【1回】 once ▶ボストンへは一度行ったことがある I have been to Boston *once*. (➤「1回」でなく「前に」の意味ならば, I've been to Boston (before). という. →直訳の落とし

穴)‖ 対話 「『ガリバー旅行記』を読んだことがありますか」「ええ, 一度あります」 "Have you ever read 'Gulliver's Travels'?" "Yes, (I've read it) *once*." ‖ 祭りは年に一度秋に行われる The festival is held *once a year* in autumn.

▶私は彼女が笑ったのを一度も見たことがない I have *never* seen her smile. ‖ オリンピックは4年に一度行われる The Olympic Games are held *every four years*. ‖ 一生に一度でいいからあんな車に乗ってみたいものだ I wish I could drive a fine car like that just *once in my life*.

▶たった一度の失敗でくじけてはいけない You must not be discouraged by a *single* failure. ‖ もう一度説明しましょう I'll explain it to you *once more*. ‖ もう一度おっしゃってください I beg your pardon? ／Pardon? (➤ いずれも上昇調で言う).

2【1回でも】▶《商品の宣伝で》ぜひ一度お試しください Have a try. ／Give it a try. ‖ 一度(＝いつか)原作者に会いたいと思う I would like to meet the author *sometime*.

直訳の落とし穴 一度…したことがある[…したい]

(1)学習者には「一度」＝once がすぐ頭に浮かぶので, 回数を特に意識しない「かつて, 一度」の意味にも once を使いすぎる傾向がある.once は,「複数回でなく, 1回」の含みが強いので注意.「漱石の『こころ』は一度読んだことがある」(回数というより「前に」や「かつて」の意味に近い場合)は, 現在完了形を使って I have read Soseki's Kokoro (before). とするがよい. once を用いると,「2回(以上)でなく1回」の含みとなる. ただし,once には「かつて, 一度」の意味もあり, 過去形とともに,I *once* read Soseki's Kokoro. や I read Soseki's Kokoro *once* when I was in high school. と言うと「かつて読んだことがある」の意味になる.

(2)「(近いうちに)一度会いましょう」「一度パリへ行ってみたい」は Let's get together sometime (soon)., I'd like to visit Paris sometime [someday]. などがよく, ここに once を用いると, 1回限りです, 2回以上は考えていません, というニュアンスになる. そのため, 前者の例文ではせっかくの提案が冷たい印象を与えてしまう.

【文型】
一度～すると, …
Once S + V, … .
➤ V は未来のことでも現在形・現在完了形を用いる

▶一度こつをつかめば何度でも楽にできるようになる *Once* you get the knack of it, you'll be able to do it easily many times. ‖ 一度悪い癖がつくとなかなか直らないものだ *Once* you have formed a bad habit, it is not easy to get rid of it.

☛ 一度に (→見出語)

[1]いちどう 一同 ▶クラス一同を代表してぼくが意見を述べます I would like to express some opinions on behalf of *the entire class*.

✉ **みどりさん, 早く元気になってください―クラス一同より** Dear Midori, we hope you get well soon. *―From all your classmates* [*From everyone in the class*].

[2]いちどう 一堂 ▶世界中から多くの若き有能なピアニストたちが一堂に会して競い合った Many young and gifted pianists *got together* (*in one place* ／*in the hall*) from all over the world to compete.

いちどく 一読 ▶一読すればこの本のおもしろさがわかります *A brief look* at this book will tell you how interesting it is.

▶一読してこの本が子供向きでないことがわかった *Looking over* the book, I found it not suitable for children. ‖ この小説は一読の価値がある This novel *is worth reading*.

いちどに 一度に at a [one] time (一時に) ; **at the same time** (同時に) ▶一度にそんなにたくさんのチョコレートを食べちゃだめ! You mustn't eat so much chocolate *at a time* [*at one time*]. ‖ 盆と正月が一度に来たようだ I feel as if the Bon festival and New Year came *at the same time*.

いちなん 一難 ▶ ことわざ 一難去ってまた一難 A misfortune goes, a misfortune comes. (➤ 日本語からの意訳) ／Misfortunes never come singly. (➤ 英語での対応表現).

いちにち 一日 1【一昼夜, 終日】a day ; one day (特に「一」の意味を強調する場合) ▶1日は24時間です There are twenty-four hours in *a day*. ‖ 私ならこの本は一日で読める I can read this book *in a day*. (➤ I に強勢を置く) ‖ 彼女は一日置きに買い物に出かける She goes shopping *every other day*. ‖ その仕事をやるのに丸一日かかった It took me *a whole day* to finish the task. ‖ きのうは一日中忙しかった I was busy *all day* (*long*) yesterday. (➤ 会話では long を省略することが多い) ‖ 大変な一日だったね You've had *quite a day*. ‖ 春の一日を公園で遊ぶ spend *a spring day* playing in the park.

▶一日一善をする do a good deed *each day* ‖ 私たちは一日に2度動物に餌をやります We feed the animals twice *a day*. ‖ 彼らはたっぷり一日分の仕事をやった They have done [put in] *a good day's work*. ‖ 一日ごとに寒くなる It is getting colder *day by day*.

▶あと一日待ってください Could you wait *another day*? ‖ 交通事故のない日は一日もない *Not a day passes without* a traffic accident.

ことわざ ローマは一日にして成らず Rome was not built in a day.

‖一日乗車券 a one-day pass.

2【慣用表現】▶一日も早くきみに会いたい I hope to see you *as soon as possible*. ‖ 一日二日休みを取って休養したら? How about taking *a day or two* off to rest? ‖ 一日二日ではこのせりふは覚えられない I can't memorize the lines *in a day or two*. ‖ 彼は東京駅の一日駅長を務めた He served as Tokyo Station's *one-day stationmaster*.

いちにちせんしゅう 一日千秋 ▶姉は会社から採用決定の知らせが来るのを一日千秋の思いで待っている *One day seems* [*feels*] *like a thousand years* for my sister who is waiting to hear if the company will hire her.

いちにん 一任する entrust +㊐ ; **leave** +㊐ (任せる) ▶私はその仕事を彼に一任した I *entrusted* him with the task. ／I *entrusted* the task to him. (➤ entrust A with B, entrust B to A は「A(人)にB(仕事など)を託す」) ‖ 支配人はそのホテルの運営を一任されている The manager *is entrusted with full responsibility* for running the hotel. ‖ 切符の手配は彼に一任しよう I'll *leave* it *up to* him to buy the tickets. ／I'll *leave* buying the tickets *to* him. (➤ leave A (up) to B は「A(仕事など)をB(人)に

任せる」).

いちにんまえ 一人前 1【1人分】▶このすしは1人前1000円です This sushi is 1,000 yen *a head* [*per person*].

2【成熟した】▶一人前になる(=成人する) come of age ‖ 彼はもう一人前の男だ He is now a *self-supporting* man. ‖ 彼女は今や一人前のデザイナーだ She's a *full-fledged* designer now. ‖ あの子ももう一人前の口を利きますよ He [She] talks *like a grown-up*. (➤「大人のように」の意).

▶この子は体だけは一人前だ(がやることは子供だ) He's got the body of *a man* (, but he still acts like a child).

1**いちねん 一年** a **year** ▶1年は365日ある *A year* has 365 days. ／There are 365 days in *a year*. ‖ ベゴニアは一年中咲く Begonias bloom *all year round* [*throughout the year*].

▶彼が渡米して早1年になる He's been in America (for) *a year* now. ‖ 会費は1年につき3000円です The membership fee is 3,000 yen *per year* [*per annum*]. (➤ per は「…につき」の意. annum /ǽnəm/ は year と同義).

▶1年に一度の会合 an *annual* meeting ‖ 息子は1年ごとに背が伸びる My son grows taller *year by year*. ‖ この柿の木は1年置きに実をつける This kaki tree bears fruit *every other year* [*every two years*].

2**いちねん 一念** ▶何としても交渉を成功させてみせるという彼の一念が先方に通じたらしい The other party must have sensed his *determination* to make the negotiation successful despite any obstacles. (➤ determination は「決意」) ‖ 彼は一念発起して韓国語の勉強を始めた He *made a sudden resolution* to begin studying Korean. ／He *gathered up his resolve* and decided to begin learning Korean.

いちねんせい 一年生 a **first-year student**

> **《解説》「1年生」の言い方**
> (1)《米》では小学校から中学校, ときには高校までの学年を通算で数えるので, 小学校1年生は first grader, 中学校1年生は seventh grader, 高校1年生は tenth grader となる.
> (2) 大学1年生(ときに《米》で高校1年生)は freshman で, 最近では freshperson ともいう. 《英・インフォーマル》では fresher という.
> (3) 日本の小学校1年生は first-year pupil [student] か,《米》式に first grader で, 中学校1年生は first-year student か,《米》式に seventh grader で, また高校1年生は first-year student か,《米》式に tenth grader で表せばよい.

▶中学1年生のクラス a *seventh-grade* class ‖ 高校1年生の女の子 a *tenth-grade* girl ／a (female) *high school freshman* (➤ female は言わないことが多い) ‖ H大学1年生 *a freshman* at H University ／*a first-year student* at H University ／a student who is in his [her] freshman year at H University.

▶《比喩的》一年生議員 a *first-year* Diet member.

✉ 私は小野田高校[中学校]の1年生です I am *a first-year student* at Onoda Senior [Junior] High School.

✉ 私は金沢小学校で1年生を教えています I teach *first graders* [I am a *Year One* teacher] at Kanazawa Elementary School. ➤ 児童が「…(小学校)の1年生です」という場合は I'm in the first grade [I am a first grader] at … ; 一般的な「1年生の担任の先生」は a first grade teacher.

‖ 一年生植物 an annual (plant).

いちば 市場 a **market** ▶市場に買い物に行く go to (the) *market*.

‖ 青物市場 a vegetable market ‖ 魚市場 a fish market.

いちばつひゃっかい 一罰百戒 **punish one person as a lesson for a hundred (people).**

いちはやく いち早く ▶その事件をいち早く知った記者たちが彼の家に殺到した Reporters who were (among) *the first to* get the news rushed to his house.

いちばん 一番 1【順位や序列の最初】**first place, number one** (➤ ともに通例 the をつけずに用いる) ▶マラソンは雄二が1番だった Yuji *won first place* in the marathon. ‖ プロなら1番を目指せ You should aim to become *number one* as long as you are a pro player. ／Pros should aim to be *number one* [aim for *the top*]. ‖ 島田君はクラスで1番だ Shimada is *at the top of* his *class*.

▶あすの朝一番にお電話をください Please call me *first thing tomorrow morning*. (➤ 決まった言い方) ‖ その場所へは彼が一番乗りをした He was *the first* (*person*) to arrive there.

‖ 一番弟子 a senior apprentice, one's best pupil ‖ 一番星 the first star of evening ‖ 一番列車 the first train.

2【最高, 最も】(➤ 形容詞・副詞の最上級を用いる) ▶かぜには休養がいちばんだ Rest is *the best thing* for a cold. ‖ アイススケートには軽井沢がいちばんだ Karuizawa is *the best place* [*the number one place*] for ice skating. ／You can't beat Karuizawa for ice skating.

▶ゆう子はクラスでいちばん英語が話せる Yuko is *the best* English speaker in her class. ‖ これは今まで読んだうちでいちばんおもしろいSFです This is *the most* interesting science fiction novel that I have ever read.

▶花の中ではバラがいちばん好きだ I like roses (*the*) *best* of all flowers. (➤《米》では副詞の best に the をつけることも多い) ‖ **対話**「果物は何がいちばん好きですか」「パイナップルです」"What fruit do you like *best*?" "Pineapples."

▶日光は秋がいちばん美しい Nikko is *most* beautiful in the fall. (➤ この most beautiful はほかの場所との比較ではなく, あとに続く名詞がないため, the を用いない) ‖ 頂上に登れなかったのがいちばんの心残りだ What I regret *most* is that I didn't make it to the top of that mountain peak. (➤ make it は「(目的地などに)たどり着く」).

▶私は妹に誕生日のお祝いに何がいちばん欲しいかと聞いた I asked my sister what she wanted *most* for her birthday. ‖ そのホテルへ行くには地下鉄がいちばん早い The subway is *the fastest* way to get to the hotel.

3【試合】a **game**; a **bout** /baʊt/ (相撲の).

いちびょうそくさい 一病息災 a person with a minor illness can often live a healthier and longer life (than one with none) (➤ 説明的な訳).

いちぶ 一部 **1【一部分】**(a) **part**

【文型】
A の一部
(a) **part of** A
➤ A は単数形の名詞
【解説】(1) Aが数えられない名詞または単数形の名詞のときに用いる. aはつけないのがふつうだが, つけることもある. (2) 複数名詞がくるときは part の代わりに some を用いる.

▶彼の説明には一部わからないところがある I don't understand *part of* his explanation. ‖ 多くの外国語の単語が今は日本語の一部になっている Many foreign words are now *part of* Japanese. ‖ これはぼくの宿題の一部です This is (*a*) *part of* my homework. (「ある限られた一部分」という含みを出したい場合には a をつける) ‖ 彼女はそのケーキのほんの一部を食べただけだった She ate only *a small part of* the cake. (➤ この例のように small を用いると a をつける. 用いなければ a は省略可). →部分.
▶この学校の一部の生徒は帰国子女です *Some* students at this school are returnees (from abroad). ‖ 昔はほんの一部の人しか字が書けなかった In ancient times, only *a few* people knew how to write. ‖ ごく一部の人の意見に流されてはいけない Don't be swayed by the opinions of *a very few*.

直訳の落とし穴「一部の住民」「住民の一部」
「一部」= (a) part であるが,「一部の住民」「住民の一部」を(×) (a) part of the residents などとは言えない. (a) part of のあとにくるのは part of his job (彼の仕事の一部), part of a plan (計画の一部) など単数の名詞である. 数えられる複数の名詞の場合は some を用いる. したがって,「一部の住民はダム建設に反対している」は Some residents are opposed to the construction of the dam. とし,「その作家の名前は一部の人にしか知られていない」の場合は限定されていることを明確にして, The author's name is only known to a limited number of people. とする.

2【1冊】 a **copy** ▶別便で近著を1部お送りいたしました I have sent you *a copy* of my recent book under separate cover. ‖ このパンフレットは1部 200 円です This brochure costs 200 yen (*a copy*). (➤ 英語ではふつうカッコ内は言わない).

いちぶしじゅう 一部始終 ▶被告はその事件の一部始終を語った The defendant gave *a full account* [stated *all the details*] of the case.

いちぶぶん 一部分 (a) **part** ▶わが社の新しいビルは一部分だけ完成している Our company's new office building is only *partly* [*partially*] completed.

いちべつ 一瞥 a **glance** ▶彼は記者団にいちべつもくれなかった He didn't even cast *a glance* at the reporters.

いちぼう 一望 ▶この丘から湖が一望のもとに見渡せる You *can see clear across* the lake from this hill. ‖ このビルの屋上に上ると町全体を一望できる If you go up on the roof of this building, you *can get a good view* of the entire town.

いちまい 一枚 a **slice** (パン・肉・ハムなどの) ; a **sheet** (紙・板・ガラスなどの) ▶パン1枚 *a slice* of bread ‖ 紙1枚 *a sheet* of paper ‖ トーストをもう1枚ください I'd like *another slice* of toast, please.
▶《慣用表現》その計画に私も一枚加わらせてください Let me *join* the project, too. ／Let me *get in on the act*. (➤ 後者は「(もうけ話などに)一口乗る」の意の熟語) ‖ このわなに引っかからないとはキツネのほうが人間より一枚うわてだな Seeing that this trap hasn't worked at all (yet), I guess foxes are *cleverer* [*more clever*] than human beings. ‖ 彼女のほうがあなたより一枚うわてね She *has a slight edge on* you, it seems. (➤ edge は「優位」).

いちまいいわ 一枚岩 a **monolith** /mɑ́ːnəlɪθ/ (1本の巨石) ▶一枚岩の組織 a *monolithic* organization.

[1]**いちまつ 一抹** a **touch** ▶転職は決めたものの, 一抹の不安は残る Although I decided to change jobs, I still feel *a little* [*a touch* ／*a tad*] uneasy.

[2]**いちまつ 市松** ▶市松模様 a *checkered* pattern ／*checks*.

いちみ 一味 a **gang**(悪者) ; a **ring** (犯罪者などのグループ) ▶密売人の一味 *a ring* of traffickers ‖ 強盗の一味は残らず検挙された The entire *gang* of robbers was arrested. ‖ あとになって彼が陰謀団の一味に加わっていたことが明らかになった It was later revealed that he had *taken part in* the conspiracy.

いちみゃく 一脈 ▶2つの学説には一脈相通じるものがある You can *draw a parallel* between the two theories.

いちめい 一命 one's **life** ▶この注射で私は一命を取り留めたのです This injection *saved my life*. ‖ 素早い手当てによってその男の子は一命を取り留めた The boy's *life was saved* by quick treatment.

いちめん 一面 **1【全面】** ▶河口湖は一面に氷が張っていた Lake Kawaguchi was *completely* frozen *over*. ‖ 辺り一面に霧が立ちこめていた It was foggy *all around*. ‖ 野山は一面の雪景色だった The fields and hills were *covered* (*all over*) with snow.
2【半面, 側面】 a **side**, an **aspect** /ǽspekt/ ▶彼にはひょうきんな一面がある His humor is *one side* of his character [personality]. ‖ これは彼の性格の一面を示している This shows *one aspect* [*facet*] of his character.
▶森先生は優しいが厳しい一面もある Mr. Mori is generally very kind, but he also has *a* strict *side*. ‖ 彼の言うことには一面の真理がある There is *some* truth in what he says.
3【新聞の第1ページ】the front [first] page.

いちめんしき 一面識 ▶一面識もない人から手紙が来た I got a letter from *a total stranger*.

いちもうだじん 一網打尽 ▶警察はその地区のすりたちを一網打尽にした The police *made a clean sweep of* the pickpockets in the area.

いちもく 一目 ▶ぼくはリリーフ投手としての彼には一目置いている I would *give* him *the edge on* me as a relief pitcher. (英語では「BよりAを少し優れていると見る」(give A the edge on B) と発想する).

いちもくさん 一目散 ▶泥棒は警官に追われて一目散に逃げた The thief *took to his heels* to escape from the police officer chasing him. (➤ take to one's heels で「一目散に逃げる」).

いちもくりょうぜん 一目瞭然 ▶グラフにすれば温度の変化が一目瞭然だ If the temperature changes are charted on a graph, they will be clear *at a glance*.

[1]**いちもつ 一物** ▶あいつは腹に一物ある男だ That guy *has an ax to grind*. (「他人に斧(おの)を研がせようという腹のある」が原義の have an ax to grind が日本語の「腹に一物ある」に相当する).

い

[2]**いちもつ 逸物** a **superb item** [**work**] (優れた出来栄えの物).

いちもん 一文 ▶弟の宿題を手伝ってやっても一文にもならない *There is nothing to be gained* [*There is no profit*] in helping my younger brother with his homework.

▶財布をすられて一文無しになった I *was penniless* [*was broke*] after my pocket was picked. (➤ be broke は「無一文である」).

☛ **びた一文** (→見出語)

いちもんいっとう 一問一答 **a question and an answer** ▶首相は記者団と一問一答した The prime minister held a *question-and-answer* session with reporters.

いちや 一夜 **one** [**a**] **night** ▶私はその老人の家で一夜を過ごした I passed *a night* at the elderly man's house. ‖ 洪水の被災者たちは不安な一夜を過ごした The victims of the flood spent *an* uneasy *night*.

▶情勢は一夜のうちに変わった The whole situation has changed *overnight*. ‖ 一夜明けると, 前日とは打って変わってすばらしい青空が広がっていた *The next day* [*As day broke*], the weather changed completely and the sky was wonderfully blue.

☛ **一夜漬け** (→見出語)

いちゃいちゃ ▶電車の中で若い男女がいちゃいちゃするなど昔の日本では考えられなかった In the past, Japanese young men and women would never have thought of *hugging* (*and kissing*) on the train. (➤「抱き合ったりキスしたり」の意; →いちゃつく).

いちやく 一躍 ▶今までいつもびりだった沢田君が一躍トップに躍り出た Sawada, who had always been last, jumped to first *in one leap*. ‖ その体操選手は一躍人気者になった The gymnast turned into a star *overnight*.

いちゃつく ⚠ **英語国では人前で愛情を表現することを不自然とは考えないので, 英語にはこの語にぴったりの対応語はない. したがって訳例のような言い方で代用するしかない.**

▶人前でいちゃつくのはよせ Don't *hang all over* her [him] like that in public. (➤ hang all over は「…にぴったり寄り添う, 寄りかかる」) ‖ あのカップルはいつでもいちゃついている That couple *is lovey-dovey*. (➤ lovey-dovey は「ラブラブの」).

いちやづけ 一夜漬け ▶キュウリの一夜漬け cucumbers *pickled overnight*.

▶《比喩的》彼は歴史の試験はいつも一夜漬けだ He always *crams overnight for* (the) history exams. (➤ cram は「詰め込み勉強をする」) ‖ 一夜漬けだけじゃAの成績は取れないよ *Overnight cramming* isn't enough to get A's.

いちゃもん ▶俺にいちゃもんつける気かよ You want to *pick a fight* with me?

いちゅうのひと 意中の人 ▶きみの意中の人の名を明かしてくれないか Would you give me the name of *the person you have in mind* [*the person you love*]? (💡「心当たりの人, 心に決めた人」と考えれば前者のように, また「好きな人」と考えれば後者のように訳せる).

▶意中の人はいますか Do you have *anyone you've decided on*? (💡「好きな人」であることを明確にするには anyone you love のようにする).

いちよう 一様に **unanimously** /junǽnɪməsli/ (全員一致で); **uniformly** (同じように) ▶労働者は一様にもっと長い休暇を求めている The workers are *unanimous* in asking for longer vacations. ‖ 島民は一様に気さくで親切であった The islanders were *uniformly* friendly and kind.

▶これらの真珠の大きさは一様ではありません The sizes of these pearls are not *uniform*. ‖ 関係者は一様に驚きの表情を見せた *Everyone* concerned expressed surprise.

[1]**いちょう 銀杏** 《植物》 a **ginkgo** /gíŋkoʊ/, a **maidenhair tree** ▶イチョウの葉が散り始めた The *ginkgo* leaves began to fall.

[2]**いちょう 胃腸** **the stomach and intestines** ▶弟は胃腸が弱い [強い] My brother has weak [good] *digestion*. (➤ a weak [strong] digestion とすることもある).

‖**胃腸薬** stomach [digestive / gastrointestinal] medicine.

[3]**いちょう 移調** 《音楽》 (a) **transposition** 一動 **移調する** **transpose** ＋目 ▶曲をト長調からハ長調に移調する *transpose* a piece from G major to C major.

いちよく 一翼 ▶わが社の生産する車が輸出産業の一翼を担っている The cars we produce are *a large and significant part* of our nation's exports.

[1]**いちらんせい 一卵性**

‖**一卵性双生児** identical twins (➤ その1人は an identical twin).

[2]**いちらんせい 一覧性** **browsability** (閲覧可能性); **readability** (読みやすさ) ▶紙の辞書は一覧性に優れている A paper [print] dictionary has excellent *browsability*.

いちらんひょう 一覧表 a **list** (表); a **table** (表組みの) ▶ことし購入したい図書を一覧表にした We made a *list* of all the books we want to buy this year.

いちり 一理 ▶彼の言うことにも一理あるが, 私としては賛成しかねる There is *some truth* in what he says, but I still I can't agree.

[1]**いちりつ 一律** ▶全国一律(＝均一)料金の通話サービスを始める begin [offer] a phone service between any two points at a *single* rate ‖ 運賃は一律(＝均一に) 5パーセント値上げされた The fare was raised five percent *across the board*. ‖ 一律に(＝1人あたま) 100円集めることにしよう Let's collect 100 yen *per person*. ‖ それらの問題は一律には(＝同じようには)扱えない Those problems cannot be treated *in the same manner*.

[2]**いちりつ 市立** →しりつ.

いちりづか 一里塚 a **post to mark one "ri" in distance** (about 3.9 kilometers) (➤ 英語はマイル単位なので milepost や milestone がある).

いちりゅう 一流の **first-class**, **first-rate** (➤ 後者のほうがより慎重な評価によるというニュアンスが強い); **leading** (主要な); **top-ranking** (最高位の); **foremost** (第1位の); **exclusive** (高級な) ▶一流のデパート a *first-class* department store ‖ 一流の会社 a *leading* [*top-ranking*] company ‖ 一流の大学 a *prestigious* [*top-notch*] university (➤ top-notch は「トップクラスの」) ‖ 一流のレストラン an *exclusive* restaurant ‖ 彼は当代一流の作家だ He is a *first-rate* writer [one of the *foremost* writers] *of the day*.

▶彼一流の(＝独特の)皮肉 *his peculiar* sarcasm ‖ それは彼一流の考え方だよ It's *his* (*own*) *characteristic* way of thinking.

いちりょうじつ 一両日 **a day or two** ▶一両日中にご連絡します I'll contact you *in a day or two*.

いちりん 一輪 a (**single**) **flower** (花); a (**single**) **wheel** (車輪) ▶一輪の菊 *a* (*single*) chrysanthemum.

‖一輪挿し a single-flower vase.

いちりんしゃ 一輪車 a **monocycle**; a **unicycle**(特に曲芸用の) ▶一輪車に乗る ride *a unicycle*.

いちる 一縷 ▶家族は父親の意識回復にいちるの望みをかけていた The family held *a glimmer of hope* that their father would regain consciousness.

いちるい 一塁 **first (base)** →ファースト ▶吉田君が一塁を守っている Yoshida plays *first base*. ‖ランナー一塁で岡田君がホームランを打った With a runner on *first base*, Okada belted a home run.

‖一塁手 a first baseman.

1**いちれい 一礼** a **bow** /baʊ/ ▶その生徒は軽く一礼して職員室に入って来た The student *made a* slight *bow* [*bowed* slightly] as he entered the teachers' room.

2**いちれい 一例** an **example**(代表的・典型的な); an **instance**(実例) ▶この事件は最近の犯罪傾向を示す典型的な一例だ This case is a typical *example* showing recent trends in crime.

▶一例を挙げますと… To give *an example*, ... / *For example* [*instance*], ‖これはほんの一例に過ぎません This is only *one example* [*instance*] (among many).

いちれつ 一列 a **line**; a **row**(横列); a **rank**(横列; 兵隊・タクシーなどの); a **file**(縦列) ▶コンサートの前売り券を買う若者たちが大勢一列に並んでいた Many young people *lined up* [*made a line* /《英また》*queued up*] to buy advance tickets for the concert.

▶一列に並べ! *Line up!* / *Make a line!* ‖《掲示》一列にお並びください Form *a line*. ‖自転車は一列で走ろう Ride your bicycles *in (a) single file*.

いちれん 一連

> **語法** 「一連の…」の意味は a series of (同類のものが並ぶ場合), a chain of (論理的順序のある場合), a sequence of (時間的順序のある場合), a train of (事件・出来事などが並ぶ場合)などを用いて表す.

▶一連の出来事 *a chain* [*train*] *of* events ‖佐藤氏は理事会で会社の経営に関する一連の質問を行った At the directors' meeting, Mr. Sato asked *a series of* questions concerning company management.

▶この一連の地震活動が大規模地震につながらなければいいのだが I hope this *series of* earthquakes will not lead to one of great magnitude.

いちろ 一路 ▶犬ぞり隊は一路北極点を目指して進んだ The dog sleds headed *straight* for the North Pole.

いちろう 一浪 ▶私は一浪してK大学に入った I passed the entrance examination for K University *on my second try*. (➤「2回目の挑戦で」の意) ‖私はことしの大学受験に失敗して今は一浪中です I failed this year's college entrance exams for the first time and *am preparing for the next chance*.

いつ 何時

when; **what time**(何時に, どの時期に) ▶今度はいつ会える? *When* can we see each other [get together] *again*? / *How soon* can we meet [see each other] *again*? (➤後者には「早く会いたい」の含みがあることが多い) ‖花見はいつ頃がいちばんいいですか *What time* is best for seeing cherry blossoms? ‖それ, いつ頃送れる? *About when* can you send it? ‖いつがいい? *When's* [*What's*] a good day (for you)? (➤相手の都合を聞くときの決まり文句).

▶ **対話** 「いつ見本の品をお持ちしましょうか」「いつでも結構ですよ」"*When* shall I bring a sample to you?" "(Please) bring it *any time* you like." (➤When shall I ...? の型は《英》ではふつうだが,《米》では改まった場合以外あまり用いられない.《米》では親しい間柄の場合, When do you want me to ...? の型が好まれる) ‖彼がいつ来るのかはわからない I can't tell you *when* he's coming. ‖その男がいつここに来たか知っていますか Do you know *when* the man was here? ‖はっきりいつとは申せませんが, 近いうちにお邪魔します I cannot say exactly *when*, but I'll come and see you soon. ‖きみはいつ見てもきれいだね You get prettier *every time I see you*.

> **あなたの英語はどう響く?**
> We're planning a year-end party. (忘年会を計画してるんだけど)と言われて「いつ頃?」と聞く場合, When? とだけ言うのはぶっきらぼうすぎる.「いつなんだ?」という感じだからである. When is it going to be? のように言えば丁寧に聞こえる.

☛ いつか, いつかは, いつから, いつでも, いつ何時, いつになく, いつになったら, いつのまにか, いつまで, いつまでも (→見出語)

いつう 胃痛 (a) **stomachache**(一時的な); **stomach pain(s)**(慢性的な) ▶胃痛に苦しむ suffer from *(a) stomachache* (➤a を省略するのは主に《英》).

いつか 何時か

1【過去の】before(以前); **once**(かつて); **sometime**(あるとき) (➤sometime を some time と2語につづると「しばらくの間」の意にもなる) ▶彼女にはいつかパーティーで会いました I *once* met her at a party. ‖いつかの約束, 覚えている? Do you remember what you *once* promised (to do)? ‖この方がいつかお話しした松田さんです This is Miss Matsuda who(m) I *once* spoke to you about. ‖去年のいつか彼と電話で話した I talked on the phone with him *sometime last year*. ‖**対話** 「いつかどこかでお会いしませんでした?」「お会いしていないと思いますが」"Haven't I seen you somewhere *before*?" "I don't think so."

> **直訳の落とし穴「いつか…(した)ことがある」**
> 「いつか…したことがある」の「いつか」には sometime ではなく once, one time を用いる. この once は過去形の文で用いることにも注意.「いつか8歳か9歳のとき両親といっしょに香港に行ったことがある」は I visited Hong Kong with my parents once when I was eight or nine.,「いつか100メートルを12秒ちょっとで走ったことがある」は One time I ran the 100 meters in just over twelve seconds. となる.

2【未来の】some day, someday(ある日); **one of these days**(近いうちに); **sometime**(あるとき); **eventually**(いつかそのうちに) ▶彼はいつか(そのことを)後悔するだろう He will be sorry (for it) *some day*. ‖いつかお伺いします I'm coming to see you *one of these days*. ‖いつかパリへ行ってみよう Let's go to Paris *sometime* [*someday*]. ‖いつか一流の翻訳家になりたいと思う *Eventually*, I want to become a first-rate translator. ‖**対話** 「ねえ, ハワイに連れてってよ」「ああ, いつかね」"Honey, I'd like you to take me

い

to Hawaii." "Yeah, *someday*."

3【いつのまにか】▶いつか雨が雪になっていました The rain had changed to snow *before we* [*I*] *knew it*.

☛ いつかは (→見出語)

[1]**いっか 一家** a **family**(家族); a **home**, a **house** (家庭) ▶きのうわが家は一家そろって動物園へ行った *My whole family* went to the zoo yesterday. ‖ 一家団らんの夕食にお邪魔してすみません I'm sorry to disturb you while *you and your family are enjoying dinner*. ‖ 中野さん一家は神戸に住んでいる *The* Nakano *family* [*The* Nakanos] live in Kobe. ‖ 一家心中をする commit *a family suicide* (➤ 英語には本来「一家心中」という考え方はない).

▶和田氏は陶芸家として一家を成している Mr. Wada *has established himself* as a ceramic artist.

[2]**いっか 一過** ▶台風一過, 青空が広がった A blue sky stretched above *after the typhoon passed*. ‖ 熱は一過性のものでしょう The fever should be a *transient* one. (➤ transient は「一時の, つかの間の」).

[1]**いっかい 一階** 《米》**the first floor**, 《英》**the ground floor** ▶自動販売機は1階にある The vending machine is on *the first floor*. ‖ 1階に誰がいるか見て来てください Could you go and see who is *downstairs*? (➤ downstairs は2階建ての家の1階).

[2]**いっかい 一回** **once**, **one time** ▶わかったわよ. 1回だけよ All right, but just *one time*. ‖ もう1回言ってください Could you say that again [*one more time*]? ‖ 私は月に1回 ボウリングをする I go bowling *once a month*.

▶彼は1回で入試に合格した He passed the entrance examination *on his first try*. ‖ 《ゲームなどで》1回100円 100 yen *a try* [*a game*] / 100 yen *per play* ‖ (トーナメントの) 1回戦第2試合 the second of *the round-one games* / the *round-one* second game.

[3]**いっかい 一介** ▶私は一介のサラリーマンだ I'm a *mere* [*just* an] office worker.

いっかくじゅう 一角獣 a **unicorn**.

いっかくせんきん 一獲千金 ▶一獲千金を夢見る dream of *getting rich quick* [*making a fortune overnight*].

いっかげん 一家言 ▶井上氏は演劇に関しては一家言もつ Mr. Inoue *has strong opinions* about the theater. (➤ strong は「確固たる」).

[1]**いっかつ 一括** ▶家賃は3か月分を一括して(=ひとまとめにして)納めていただきます You are expected to pay three months' rent *in one lump sum*. ‖ 留学生の問題は一括して(=総括的に)私が処理しましょう I'll handle the non-Japanese students' problems *as a whole* [*all together*].

▶ボーナス時一括払いでパソコンを買った I bought a personal computer *on credit charged as a lump sum* against my bonus. (➤「一括払い」のことを one-time [once-only] payment ということもある).

[2]**いっかつ 一喝** ▶教師は隠れてたばこを吸っている生徒を見つけて一喝した The teacher *thundered* [*stormed*] at a student who was found smoking.

いつかは 何時かは **someday**(いつの日か); **sooner or later**(遅かれ早かれ) ▶人間皆いつかは死ぬのだ Everyone must die *someday*. ‖ 最強のチャンピオンでもいつかは負ける時が来る Even the strongest champion will lose *sooner or later*.

いつから 何時から

【文型】
いつから〜ですか
How long ＋現在完了形？
When 〜？

《解説》(1)これまでの期間を聞くときには **How long** ＋現在完了(進行)形？を用いる. 始まりの時を聞くときには, ふつう単に **When ...?** を用いる. From when ...? はあまり用いない.
(2) Since when ＋現在完了形？は非難・からかい・驚きのニュアンスで用いられることが多い.

▶ **対話** 「いつから日本にお住まいですか」「3年前[2019年]からです」"*How long have* you *been* in Japan?" "Three years [Since 2019]." ‖ 太郎君とはいつから付き合っているの？ *How long have* you *been* seeing Taro? ‖ いつから熱っぽいの？ *How long have* you *had* a temperature? ‖ 夏休みはいつから始まりますか *When* does your summer vacation begin [start]? / 《英》*When* do you break up for the summer holidays? ‖ あなた, いつからそんなに生意気な口を利くようになったの？ *Since when have* you *been* so cocky? / *When* did you start getting so cocky? (➤ 後者のほうが普通の言い方).

▶ **対話** 「冬休みはいつからいつまでですか」「12月21日から1月12日までです」"*How long* is your winter vacation?" "It's from December 21 to January 12." ‖ この池にいつからともなくカメがすみついている Tortoises have been living in this pond *since we don't know when*.

[1]**いっかん 一貫** ▶一貫した方針 a *consistent* policy ‖ 彼は言うこととすることが一貫していない His words are *not consistent with* his deeds. / He says *one thing and* does *another*. ‖ 広島市は一貫して原水爆禁止を訴えてきた The City of Hiroshima has *consistently* called for a ban on atomic and hydrogen bombs. ‖ きみの発言には一貫性がないね Your remarks lack *consistency*. ‖ 私は横浜にある中高一貫の学校に通っている I go to a *combined* junior and senior high school in Yokohama.

[2]**いっかん 一環** ▶文化祭の一環として模擬店を出すことになった It has been decided that refreshment stands will be set up *as* (*a*) *part of* the school festival.

[3]**いっかん 一巻** a **volume** ▶漱石全集の第1巻 *the first volume* of a set of Soseki's works

▶ 《慣用表現》きみのひと言でぼくと彼女の仲は一巻の終わりだよ Your remark has brought *an end* to my relationship with her.

[1]**いっき 一気** **1【途中休まずに】**▶私はきのうレポートを一気に書き上げた Yesterday I wrote the paper *in one sitting*. ‖ 私は200段の石段を一気に駆け上がった I ran up the 200 stone steps *in* [*at*] *a dash*. ‖ ビールをぐうっと一気に飲んだ I *chugged* [*chugalugged*] (a glass of) beer. (➤ chugalug /tʃʌ́gəlʌ̀g/ は「(酒を)一気に飲む」の意のインフォーマルな言い方) ‖ 一気飲みは危険だ *Chugging* [*Chugalugging*] is dangerous.

2【ひと息に】▶真犯人の自首でその難事件も一気に解決した The difficult case was resolved *in one stroke* [*swoop*] after the criminal gave himself [herself] up.

[2]**いっき 一期** a **term** ▶堀氏は市長を一期務め終えたところです Mr. Hori has just finished his *first term* as mayor.

3**いっき 一揆** an **uprising**（蜂起）; a **riot**（暴動）
▶百姓一揆 a peasant *uprising*.

いっきいちゆう 一喜一憂 ▶この春は野菜の値動きが激しく，農家の人たちは**一喜一憂した** This spring vegetable prices fluctuated wildly, causing farmers to *go back and forth between delight and dismay* [to *be alternately delighted and dismayed*]. ‖ 激しいシーソーゲームに観客は**一喜一憂した** The spectators *swung back and forth between hope and despair* as they watched the heated seesaw game.（➤ swung は swing（揺れ動く）の過去形；「希望と絶望の間を揺れ動いた」の意）.

いっきうち 一騎打ち ▶その選挙区では２人の候補者の**一騎打ち**となった In that election district, it turned out to be *a one-on-one battle* [*a head-to-head battle*] between the two candidates.

いっきゅう 一級 ▶彼は最近そろばんの**１級（の免状）**を取った Recently he got *a first-grade certificate* in abacus calculation.
▶彼女は**第一級**の生物学者だ She is a *first-rate* biologist. ‖ 彼の作品は誰が見ても**第一級**のものだ Everybody agrees his work is *first-rate*. →**一流**.

いっきょいちどう 一挙一動 ▶その歌手はその**一挙一動**が話題になる The singer's *every action* [*movement*] gets talked about.

いっきょに 一挙に ▶謎を**一挙に**解決する clear up a mystery *once* (*and*) *for all*（➤ once (and) for all は「きっぱりと，これを最後として」）‖ この回わがチームは**一挙に** 8 点を取った Our team picked up 8 runs *in* [*at*] *a single stroke* in this inning.

いっきょりょうとく 一挙両得 ▶このアルバイトは金にもなるし英語も覚えられるし，**一挙両得だ** This part-time job *serves two purposes*—I can earn money and learn English as well. →**一石二鳥**.

いつく 居着く ▶ホームレスの一団があの空き家に**居ついて**しまっている A band of homeless people has been *squatting* in that empty house.（➤ squat は「（他人の家屋や公有地などに）無断で居つく」）.
▶彼の一人息子は家に**居つかない** His only son *does not stay* at home *much*.

いつくしむ 慈しむ love tenderly（優しく愛する）; **be charitable**《to》（…に寛大である）▶祖母の**慈しむ**ようなまなざしが懐かしい I miss my grandmother's *tender, loving* glance.

1**いっけん 一見 1【一度見ること】**▶その史跡は（十分）**一見の価値がある** That historical sight *is* (well) *worth seeing*.
ことわざ **百聞は一見にしかず** Seeing a thing once is better than hearing about it a hundred times.（➤ 日本語からの直訳）.《**参考**》ぴったりの英語のことわざはないが，Seeing is believing.（見ることは信じることである，自分のこの目で見れば信じる），A picture is worth a thousand words.（一枚の絵は千語の価値がある，いろいろ説明されるより一枚の絵のほうが手っ取り早い）などが近い．
2【ちょっと見ること】▶２人は**一見**恋人風だった The two were *apparently* [*seemingly*] lovers.（➤ ともに「見かけは」の意）‖ 偽札は精巧にできていて**一見した**だけでは気づかない You can't tell *at a glance* that it's a fake bill because it was so skillfully made. ‖ それは**一見**たやすい仕事に思えた It seemed an easy task *at first glance* [*sight*].

2**いっけん 一軒** ▶刑事は**一軒一軒**殺人事件の聞き込みに歩いた The detective went *from door to door* asking questions about the murder case.
‖**一軒家** a house（一戸建ての家；→**一戸建て**）; an isolated [a solitary] house（ぽつんと１軒だけある家）.

3**いっけん 一件** ▶**一件落着** *Case solved* [*closed*].

いっこ 一個 →**一個**.

1**いっこう 一行** a **party**; a **group**（１集団）▶探検隊の**一行**は成田に着いたばかりだ The exploratory *party* has just arrived at Narita. ‖ 団体旅行の**一行**がバスを降りて金閣寺へ向かった *The members* of the tour group got off the bus and headed to Kinkakuji Temple. ‖ 私は母の病気のため**一行**に加わることができなかった I could not join the *group* because my mother was sick.

2**いっこう 一考** ▶タイトルは**一考を要する** We *need to give some thought* to the title. ‖ 我々の提案をよろしくご**一考**ください We hope you'll *carefully consider* [*give careful consideration to*] our proposal.

いっこうに 一向に ▶交渉は**一向に**進展しない The negotiations *aren't* making any progress *at all*. ‖ 彼女は**一向に**結婚する気配がない She *doesn't* seem to be interested in marriage *at all*. ‖ 彼の話は**一向に要領を得ない** I *can't make heads or tails of* what he is saying.（➤ can't make heads or tails of は「…がさっぱりわからない」の意のインフォーマルな言い方）‖ あんな卑劣なやつに何と言われようと，ぼくは**一向に平気だ** I *couldn't care less* what that mean guy says about me.（➤ couldn't care less は「全然気にしない」の意のインフォーマルな言い方）.

1**いっこく 一刻** ▶そのけが人は**一刻も早く**手術しなければならない *It is most urgent that* the injured person (should) be operated on.（➤ should は主に《英》用法で，省略可能）‖ **一刻も早く**彼女に会いたくてバスを使わずにタクシーに乗った I took a taxi instead of a bus because I wanted to see her *as soon as possible*. ‖ 大至急手術が必要だ．**一刻を争う** We have to perform an emergency operation as soon as possible. We *have no time to lose* [*cannot waste a second*].

2**いっこく 一国** a **country**, a **land**（➤ 後者は文学的な語）▶**一国一城**の主 a lord who *rules a domain and owns a castle*.

いっこだて 一戸建て a **house**（➤ a house だけで「一戸建て，独立家屋」の意であるから，an independent house などとしなくてもよい；ただし，ほかの建物から分離していることを強調する場合は detached house ということはふつう）▶お住まいは**一戸建て**ですか，それともマンションですか Do you live in *a house* or in an apartment?

いつごろ 何時頃 ▶インターネットが普及したのは**いつ頃**からですか *When* did the Internet come into widespread use? →**いつ**.

いっさい 一切 1【全部】▶（この件に関しては）あなたに**一切**お任せします (As far as this matter is concerned,) I leave *everything* to you. ‖ 彼はそのことについては**一切**自分に責任があると言っている He says he accepts *full* responsibility for it.
2【全然[少しも]…ない】▶私は彼の過去は**一切**知りません I know *nothing* about his past. ‖ 彼女はこの仕事に関しては**一切**責任がない She is *not* responsible for this work *in any way*. ／She has *no* responsibility *whatsoever* for this work. ‖ 彼はその事件とは**一切関係がなかった** He *had nothing to do with* the incident. ‖ 当店では掛け売りは**一切**いたしません We *never* sell on credit.

いつざい 逸材 a **talented person**（才能のある人）; an **outstanding person**（傑出した人）▶菊池選手は10年に1人の**逸材**だ Kikuchi is the kind of *talented* play-

い

er who comes around (only) once in a decade.

いっさいがっさい 一切合財 ▶老夫婦は一切合財を処分して老人ホームに入った The elderly couple disposed of *everything* [*all their possessions*] and entered a nursing home.

いっさくじつ 一昨日 the day before yesterday ▶一昨日お伺いしたのですがお留守でした I went to visit you *the day before yesterday*, but you were out. →おととい.

いっさくねん 一昨年 the year before last ▶一昨年の夏はバリ島へ旅行した I took a trip to Bali in the summer of *the year before last*. (➤ カッコ内は言わないほうがふつう). →おととし.

いっさんかたんそ 一酸化炭素 carbon monoxide /mənɑ́ːksaɪd/ ▶一酸化炭素中毒で死ぬ die of *carbon monoxide poisoning*.

いっさんに 一散に →一目散.

1**いっし 一糸** ▶彼女は一糸まとわぬ姿で私の部屋へ入って来た She came into my room *without a stitch on her* [*without a single piece of clothing*]. ‖ 生徒たちは一糸乱れず行進した The students marched *in perfect order*.

2**いっし 一矢** ▶5－0で負けていたジャイアンツは坂本のホームランで一矢を報いた Trailing 5 to 0, the Giants *rallied back* with Sakamoto's home run. (➤ rally back は「反撃する」).

いつしか ▶この作曲家の名前はいつしか忘れられた This composer's name was forgotten *somewhere along the line* [*as time passed*]. ‖ 父が亡くなっていつしか10年の歳月が流れた *Before I know it*, ten years has passed since my father died.

いっしき 一式 a (complete) set ▶ゴルフクラブ一式 *a set* of golf clubs ‖ 応接間の家具一式 a drawing-room *suite* (➤ suite は一式の家具やホテルなどの一続きの部屋を表す語で, /swiːt/ と発音する).

いっしそうでん 一子相伝 ▶一子相伝の奥義 esoteric art that has been *passed down from a parent to only one child* [*from father to son*] (➤ esoteric /èsətérɪk/ は「秘伝の」).

いっしゅ 一種 a kind, a sort(種類；後者はややくだけた語)；**a type**(型)；**a variety**(変種)；**a specimen**(生物分類上の「種(しゅ)」) ▶イルカは鯨の一種だ Dolphins are *a kind* [*a sort*] of whale. ‖ あの人は一種の(＝ある意味での)天才だよ He is a genius *in a sense*. ‖ この果物は一種独特の味がする This fruit has a *unique* flavor.

1**いっしゅう 一周 a round 一動 一周する go around** ▶校庭を一周する *go around* the school grounds ‖ この湖は一周どのくらいですか What is the *circumference* of this lake? (➤ circumference /səʳkʌ́mfrəns/ は「周囲, 円周」) ／ How far is it *around* this lake? ‖ この国は大変狭いので車で一周するのにたった1日しかかかりません This country is very small, so it takes no more than a day to *drive around* it. ‖ 血液は体内を1分間で一周する Blood *circulates* through the body in one minute. (➤ circulate は「循環する」).
▶世界一周旅行をする *take* [*go on*] *a trip around* the world (➤「世界一周旅行」は around-the-world trip) ‖ 北海道一周旅行をする travel *around* Hokkaido. ‖ あすで祖父の1周忌を迎える Tomorrow is *the first anniversary of* my grandfather's *death*. ‖ わが校は来月創立1周年を迎えます Our school will celebrate *the first anniversary of its founding* next month.

2**いっしゅう 一蹴** ▶ぼくたちのチームは大差で相手を一蹴した Our team *beat* them *easily* by a large margin. ‖ 父にこづかいの値上げを要求したが一蹴された My father *laughed off* my request for a larger allowance. (➤ laugh off は「…を笑って退ける」).

いっしゅうかん 一週間 →週, 週間.

いっしゅん 一瞬 a moment(何かが起きるとき, ごく短い時間)；an **instant**(瞬時性・即時性を強調する)
▶観衆は優勝者発表の一瞬を待った The whole audience waited for the *moment* when the champion would be announced. ‖ 衝突は一瞬の出来事だった The collision happened *in an instant*. ‖ 彼はプールに飛び込むのを一瞬ためらった He hesitated *a moment* before diving into the pool.

いっしょ 一緒 **1【1つにまとめる】**▶私の写真をチョコレートと一緒に彼に送った I sent him my photo *together with* a box of chocolates. ‖ あんな不真面目な連中と一緒にされては困る I don't like to *be lumped* (*together*) *with* those lazy guys. (➤ lump は「一様に扱う」) ‖ 彼らは大学を出たらすぐ一緒になろう(＝結婚しよう)と約束した They promised to *get married* right after graduating from college.

2【行動をともにする】一副 一緒に together ▶ぼくらは死ぬまで一緒だよ We will be *together* until death (do us part). ‖ 一緒に帰ろう Let's go home *together*. (➤ with me としない) ‖ この前の日曜日私たちは一緒にハイキングに行った We went hiking *together* last Sunday. ‖ ポーラとスージーは姉妹のようにいつも一緒に行動する Paula and Susie are always *doing things together* just like sisters.

【文型】
人・物(A)と一緒に
with A

▶一緒に行ってもいいですか Can I go *with you*? ‖ 子供と一日一緒になって遊ぶのは疲れる It's very tiring to play *with children* for an entire day.
▶あした魚釣りに行くけど, 一緒に行かないかい We're going fishing tomorrow. *Why don't you come along, too?* (➤ あとの文を Why don't you join us? としてもよい). ‖ 私と一緒に散歩に行きませんか How about going for [taking] a walk (*together*)? (➤ この together は省略可能).

> **直訳の落とし穴「一緒に行く」**
> 「一緒に」は together であるが, 使い方を間違える学習者が多い. together は主語が複数のときに用いる語であり, They went together. は可能であるが, (×) I went together. は不可である. したがって,「(私も)一緒に行ってもいいですか」を (×)Can I go together, too? などとしない.「あなたと一緒に」の省略と考えて, Can I go with you? とする. 逆に,「一緒に帰ろう」は Let's go home together. で, (×) Let's go home with me. とするのは間違い. 英語では Let's の us に一緒に行動する全員が含まれるために, with me では合わなくなってしまう. 日本語では「私と(＝with me) 一緒にやろう(＝Let's do it)」が可能であるために, ミスが絶えない. Let's do it together. とする.

▶彼と私は上京以来同じ部屋で一緒に暮らしている He and I have been *sharing a room* since I came to Tokyo. (➤ share は「共有する」; live together

はしばしば「同せいする」の意になるので注意)‖サンドイッチ, たくさん持って来たの. **一緒に食べない?** I've brought a lot of sandwiches. *Won't you have some?*‖《教室で先生が》さあ, **みんな一緒に** Now, *all together*.‖《来客が帰るとき》**その辺までご一緒しましょう**(=一緒に歩きましょう) I'll *walk you* part of the way home.
3【同一の】▶きのう田村さんと**一緒の電車に乗り合わせた** Yesterday I happened to be on *the same* train *as* Mr. Tamura.‖**我々は皆一緒のものを注文した** We all ordered *the same thing*.‖**私たちは小学校から中学校まで一緒だった** We went to *the same* elementary and junior high school.

[1]いっしょう 一生
1【生物としての存生期間】(one's) **life** ▶アゲハの**一生** the *life* of a swallowtail (butterfly)‖セミは羽化すると2週間ぐらいで**短い一生を終える** A cicada ends its short *life* (*span*) about two weeks after growing wings.‖**彼は一生独身を通した** He remained single *throughout his life*.
2【人生】(one's) **life**, one's [a] **lifetime**(生涯)
▶**一生に一度でいいから**, あんな大きな伊勢エビを食べてみたい I'd like to have a (spiny) lobster as big as that *once in my life*.‖**これは一生に一度の機会だ** This is *a once-in-a-lifetime opportunity*.‖**人の一生はしばしば航海にたとえられる** *Life* is often compared to a voyage.‖**人の一生は長いようで短い** Although *life* seems long, actually it's short.‖**彼は細菌の研究に一生をささげた** He *devoted* (*all*) *his life to* the study of bacteria.‖**その後2人は幸福な一生を送りました** They *led* [*lived*] a happy *life* ever after. / They *lived* happily ever after.(➤物語の結びの文句).
▶**彼は一生かけても読み切れないほどの本を持っている** He has more books than he can possibly read *in his whole life*.‖**ピアノコンクールの優勝は一生の思い出です** Winning the piano competition is a memory that will last my *lifetime*.(➤「私」に限定しないときは last a lifetime という)‖**現在の妻と結婚しないと一生後悔すると思った** I thought I would regret it *all my life* [*my entire life* / *for the rest of my life*] if I didn't marry my present wife.‖**私は陶芸を一生の仕事にしたいと思います** I would like to *make* ceramic art *my career*.(➤ choose ... for my career としてもよい).
✉《ラブレターで》**ぼくは一生きみを愛し, 大切にします** I will love and cherish you *as long as I live*.

> **あなたの英語はどう響く?**
> 「あなたのご親切は一生忘れません」を I'll never forget your kindness forever. と訳す人がいるが, これでは「あなたのご親切は一生忘れないわけではありません」の意味になってしまう. never と forever との結び付きが部分否定になるからである. I'll remember your kindness forever. とするか, I'll never forget your kindness. とするのが正しい.

3【強調して】▶**ドイツで音楽を勉強するのが私の一生の願いです** It is my *lifelong desire* to study music in Germany.‖**それちょうだい, 一生のお願い** Please let me have it! *I'll never ask for anything again*.(➤文頭の please を強く言う. 文末に「誓うから」という意味で I swear! をつけてもよい).
☛ **九死に一生**(→見出語)

[2]いっしょう 一笑 ▶**課長は私の提案を一笑に付した** The section chief *laughed off* [*at*] my proposal. / The section chief *dismissed* my proposal *with a laugh*.

いっしょうけんめい 一生懸命
very hard; **earnestly**(真剣に) ▶**一生懸命走ったが4着に終わった** I ran *as* fast *as* I *could*, but ended up in fourth place.‖**一生懸命頑張ります** I'll *do my very best*.‖**大学に行きたいんなら一生懸命に勉強しなきゃだめだ** If you want to go to college, you'll have to *work very hard*.‖**彼は一生懸命に働いた** He worked *very hard*. / He worked *like a dog* [*a horse*].(➤ work like a dog [a horse] はインフォーマルな表現で, 男性に好まれる)‖**一生懸命やってだめならしかたがない** If you *do your best* and it still doesn't turn out, then that's the way the cookie crumbles.(➤後半は, うまくいかないことがあったときに, 「世の中そういうものだから, どうしようもない」の意のことわざ).
▶**彼女は一生懸命にピアノの練習をしている** She is practicing the piano *earnestly* [*in earnest*].‖**学園祭で伸夫は一生懸命にギターを弾いた** In the school festival, Nobuo *put all his efforts into* his guitar playing.

いっしょく 一色 ▶**けさ戸を開けると外は雪で白一色になっていた** When I opened the door this morning, *everything* outside *was white* with snow.
▶《比喩的》**町は新横綱の歓迎ムード一色だった** A festive mood of welcome for the new yokozuna *pervaded* the town.(➤ pervade は「(場所に)充満する」).

いっしょくそくはつ 一触即発 ▶**2つの暴力団はお互いに一触即発の状態にある** It's *a touch-and-go situation* now with the two gangs squaring off.(➤ square off は「身構える」).

いっしょくた 一緒くた ▶**あんなひきょうなやつとぼくを一緒くたにしないでくれ** Don't *categorize* me *with* a coward like him. / Don't *put* me *in the same category as* a coward like him. / Don't *lump* me *together with* a coward like him.(➤ lump ... together は「…をひとまとめにする」の意).

[1]いっしん 一新 ▶**メンバーを一新する** *undergo a complete change* in membership‖**気分を一新してもう一度やり直しましょう** Let's *forget everything* and make a fresh start.

[2]いっしん 一身 ▶**芳江は両親の愛情を一身に受けて育った** Yoshie was raised *with* her parents' affections *centered on her*.‖**清一は女子学生たちの人気を一身に集めている** Seiichi *is the center of* the female students' attention. / Seiichi is extremely popular with the female students.‖**彼はすべての非難を一身に引き受けて辞職した** He *took all the blame on himself* and left his job.‖**私は一身上の都合で会社をやめた** I quit my job *for personal reasons*.

[3]いっしん 一心 ▶**彼はアメリカに行きたい一心で懸命に英語を勉強した** He studied English hard because he was so *eager* to go to America.‖**彼女は一心にジグソーパズルをしている** She *is lost* [*is absorbed*] *in* a jigsaw puzzle.‖**夫婦は一心同体であるとは言い古されたことばだ** It is proverbially said that husband and wife are *one flesh* [*as one*].

[4]いっしん 一審 **the first trial** ▶**二審では一審の有罪判決が覆った** The court reversed *the first* guilty *ver-*

い

dict in the second trial [judgment].

いっしんいったい 一進一退 ▶**一進一退**の試合 a *seesaw* match [game] ‖ 校長の病状は依然として**一進一退**だ The principal's condition is still *fluctuating between better and worse*.

いっしんきょう 一神教 **monotheism** /mɑ́:nəθìizəm/.

いっすい 一睡 ▶ゆうべは隣の犬がうるさくてほとんど**一睡**もできなかった Last night the neighbors' dog made so much noise that I *could hardly get any sleep*.

いっする 逸する **miss** +目 ((タイミングを)のがす), **lose** +目 (なくす) ▶得点の好機を**逸する** *miss* an opportunity to score ‖ ぼくは彼女にプロポーズするチャンスを**逸した** I *missed* my chance to propose to her. (➤ miss は自分が「捕まえ損ねる」で,「残念なことに」あるいは「惜しくも」というニュアンスがある. また, チャンスは再びあるかもしれない) ‖ ジャイアンツはペナントレース優勝のチャンスを**逸した** The Giants *lost* [*missed*] their chance to win the pennant. (➤ lose は責任が自分にあるとは限らず,「(チャンス) をなくす, つぶす」. ここで missed とするのは惜しくも僅差で負けた場合).

いっすん 一寸 ▶深い霧のため**一寸**先も見えなかった I *could not see even an inch ahead* due to the dense fog.

▶《慣用表現》ビジネスの世界は**一寸先は闇**だ In the business world, *everything beyond the immediate present is shrouded in mystery*. (英語では「現在ただ今より先のことはすべて謎に覆い隠されている」のように発想する).

ことわざ **一寸の虫にも五分の魂** Even an inch-long worm has a half an inch spirit. (➤ 日本語からの直訳) / Even a worm will turn. (➤「踏めば虫けらさえも向き直ってくる」が原義)

ことわざ **一寸の光陰軽んずべからず** Don't think even a fraction of passing time unimportant.

いっすんぼうし 一寸法師 a **dwarf**, a **midget** (小人); **Tom Thumb** (イギリスの昔話の主人公『親指トム』) 《参考》日本の『一寸法師』は "One-Inch Boy" と英訳されている.

いっせ 一世 ▶会社を興すというのは**一世一代**の大仕事だ Establishing a company is a *once-in-a-lifetime* undertaking. ‖ **一世一代の名演技** a superb performance given *once in a lifetime*.

いっせい 一世 ▶パウロ一世 Paul *I* (➤ I は the first と読む). →風靡.

‖日系一世 an issei, a first-generation Japanese-American (アメリカの; ブラジルなら Japanese-Brazilian).

いっせいに 一斉に **at the same time, simultaneously** (同時に; 前者には「一度に」の意もある. 後者は(意図的に)まさに同じ時刻に); **all at once** (いちどきに); **all together** (みんな一緒に); **in unison** /jú:nɪsən/, **in chorus** /kɔ́:rəs/ (声をそろえて) ▶子供たちは**一斉に**しゃべり始めた The children began talking *at the same time* [*all at once*]. ‖ 合図と同時に, みな**一斉に**綱を引いた The instant the signal sounded, everybody pulled the rope *all together*. ‖ 模擬試験が全国の会場で**一斉に**行われた The practice test was held *simultaneously* at test centers all over the nation. (➤「時刻を合わせて同時に」という場合は simultaneously を使う) ‖ 1匹の犬がほえだすとほかの犬も**一斉に**ほえ始めた When one dog started barking, other dogs also began to bark *in unison*.

1**いっせき 一席** ▶**一席ぶつ** *make a speech* ‖ T氏のために**一席設ける**ことにいたしましたのでお出かけください We are going to *give a little party* for Mr. T, so please join us.

2**いっせき 一石** ▶知事の発言は教育行政に**一石を投じた** The governor's comment *created a stir* in the (prefectural) educational administration.

いっせきにちょう 一石二鳥 ▶**一石二鳥**の好機だ. 逃すんじゃないぞ Don't miss it. It's *a chance to kill two birds with one stone*. ‖ **一石二鳥の名案** a good idea *that serves two purposes*. →一挙両得.

1**いっせつ 一節** a **paragraph** (1区切り); a **passage** (1かたまりの文章) ▶彼は『雪国』の**一節**を引用してみせた He quoted *a paragraph* from "Snow Country."

2**いっせつ 一説** ▶**一説によると**あの火事は放火だったそうだ *Some say that* the fire was a case of arson. (➤ この some は「一部の人」の意) / *According to one report*, that fire was a case of arson.

1**いっせん 一線** ▶公人であることと私人であることとの間に**一線を画する**ことは難しい It is hard to *draw a line* [*make a clear distinction*] *between* what one does as an officeholder *and* (what one does as) a private individual. ‖ **最後の一線を越える** *go over* [*beyond*] *the limit* ‖ **一線級の選手** a *top-notch* athlete [player] (➤ top-notch /tà:pnɑ́:tʃ/ は「一流の, 最上の」の意).

☛ 第一線 (→見出語)

2**いっせん 一戦** a **fight** (格闘); a **battle** (戦闘); a **game** (試合) ▶「**一戦一戦**を大切に戦っていきたい」と監督は語った "I want to fight to win *every game*," said the manager.

いっそ ▶あいつに頭を下げるくらいなら**いっそ**死んだほうがましだ I *would rather* [*would sooner*] die than bow down to him. ‖ いつまでもぐずぐずしているのなら**いっそ**のこと出かけるのをやめたら? If you're going to fiddle around for such a long time, you*'d better* [*why not*] just forget about going.

1**いっそう 一層** **still** (なおいっそう; 比較級を強調する); **even more, all the more** ▶これからは**いっそう**寒くなるでしょう It will get *still* colder from now on. ‖ 花嫁姿の高田さんはいつもより**いっそう**美しく見えた Miss Takada looked *even more* beautiful than ever in her wedding dress. ‖ とも子は末っ子だった**ので**父親は**いっそう**かわいがった Her father loved Tomoko *all the more because* she was his youngest child. ‖ 車の窓を開けたら**いっそう**暑くなった Opening the car windows made it *all the hotter*. ‖ 不況の折, 各人**いっそうの**努力を望む During this time of economic recession, I expect each of you to make *greater* efforts.

2**いっそう 一掃する** **wipe out** (良くないものを); **sweep away** (さっと払いのける) ▶政府は違法薬物の**一掃**に努めている The government is making a lot of effort to *wipe out* drug trafficking. (➤ trafficking は「密売」) ‖ その疑惑は今や**一掃された** The suspicion has now *been swept away*. (➤ swept は sweep の過去分詞形) ‖ この町から犯罪を**一掃しよう** Let's *clean up* the town. (➤ clean up は「浄化する」) / Let's *eradicate* crime from this town. (➤ eradicate は「根絶する」の意の堅い言い方).

いっそくとび 一足飛び ▶彼は課長から**一足飛びに**総務部長に昇進した He was promoted from section chief to head of the general affairs department *in one jump*.

いつぞや ▶**いつぞやは**お世話になりました Thank you for what you did *sometime ago*. (英米では過去のことで改めてお礼を言うのはふつうではない. また, 英語では

two months ago（２か月前）とか during the vacation（休暇中）のように具体的に言うのがふつう．しかし，曖昧さが持ち味の日本語を無理に明確な英語にすると，ときに滑稽なことになる）．

¹**いったい 一体** **1**【１つにまとまること】▶**我々は一体となって行動すべきだと彼は主張した** He insisted that we should act together *as one* (*body*). ‖ 山へ登ると自然と**一体になったような**気分になる Climbing a mountain makes you feel *at one with* (all) nature.

2【一体全体】**ever, on earth** ▶**彼女は一体何が欲しいのだろう** *Just what* [*What ever*] does she want? (➤《インフォーマル》では疑問詞を just で強める言い方がよく使われる) ‖ **一体きみはここで何をしてるんだい** What (*on earth*) are you doing here? (➤ on earth を省く場合は you に強勢を置く) ‖ **一体彼はどこにいるのだろう** Where *can* he be? (➤ can に強勢を置く) ‖ **一体どうしてそんなことが起きたのだろう** How *could* such a thing have happened? (➤ could は過去の推量を強く表す).

▶**今の老人たちは一体何を考えているのだろう** *I wonder* what elderly people nowadays are thinking about. ‖ **一体全体，このざまは何だ！** What *the hell* is this? (➤ 品のない乱暴な言い方．hell の婉曲（えんきょく）語である heck を用いた表現の What the heck や What in the world にすると穏やかになる).

²**いったい 一帯** ▶**この辺り一帯には野良猫が多いんです** There are many stray cats *in this neighborhood*. ‖ **ことし東北地方一帯は豪雪に見舞われた** This year heavy snow has fallen *all over* the Tohoku district.

いったいかん 一体感 **oneness**（切り離し難く，一つであること）; **a sense of connectedness**（結びついている感覚）; **a feeling of togetherness** [**unity**]（仲間としての一緒感，団結感）▶**練習を積むうちに，チームに一体感が生まれた** As practice went on, *a feeling of togetherness* [*unity*] grew in the team. ‖ **自然との一体感を覚える** feel *oneness* [*a sense of connectedness*] with nature.

いつだつ 逸脱 **deviation** /dìːviéɪʃən/; **departure**（従来の規準などからの）**—動**（…から）**逸脱する** **deviate** 《from》▶**彼の発言は会社の方針から逸脱している** His statement *deviates from* the company's policy.

いったりきたり 行ったり来たり ▶**彼はそわそわと廊下を行ったり来たりしていた** He nervously *walked up and down* the corridor. ‖ **ライオンはおりの中を行ったり来たりした** The lion *paced back and forth* in its cage. (➤ pace は「歩き回る」の意だが，それ自体に「そわそわしながら」という含みがある).

▶**彼女とは家族ぐるみで行ったり来たりする仲だ** I'm on such friendly terms with her that my family and her family *go around together* [*enjoy each other's company*]. →行きつ戻りつ．

いったん 一旦 ▶**いったん（＝ちょっと）車を止めて地図を調べてみよう** Let's stop the car *a minute* and study the road map. ‖ **踏切ではいったん停止せよ** Stop at railroad crossings. (●「いったん」に当たる語は訳出不要) ‖ **私はいったん（＝一度）決めたらどこまでもやる** *Once* I have made up my mind, I never give up. ‖ **いったん家に戻って着替えてから，また来ます** I'll go back home to change *first* and then come back. ‖ **紛争はいったん終息したように見えたがすぐ再燃した** The conflict seemed to come to an end *temporarily* [*for a short time*], but soon flared up again.

いっち 一致 **agreement, accordance**（➤ 後者は堅い語）

—動 一致する **agree**（２つの内容が）; **match** ＋㊐, **accord** 《with》, **coincide** 《with》（…にぴったり合う）
▶**うわさと事実は必ずしも一致しない** Rumors and facts do not always *agree*. ‖ **あなたの話は彼女が話してくれたことと一致しません** Your account (of what happened) doesn't *accord with* [doesn't *match*] what she has told us. ‖ **理論と実際は必ずしも一致しない** Theory and practice do not necessarily *go together* [*coincide*]. (➤ go together は「両立する」).

▶**彼女の記憶は私の記憶と完全には一致しなかった** Her recollections did not exactly *correspond with* mine. (➤ correspond with は「…に対応する」) ‖ **我々はもう一度やり直すことで意見が一致した** We *agreed to* start over. ／We *agreed that* we should start over. ／We *agreed on* starting over. ‖ **彼と私は意見が一致している** He and I are *of the same opinion*.

▶**ぼくたちは趣味が一致している（＝同じだ）** Our tastes are exactly *the same* [are *identical*]. ‖ **彼は言うこととすることが一致しない** He *says one thing and* does *another*. ‖ **現場に残された指紋は彼の指紋と一致した** The fingerprints left at the scene of the crime *matched* his.

▶**野生動物の絶滅を防ぐために一致協力する** *make a concerted effort* to prevent the disappearance of wild animals ‖ **私たちは演奏会を成功させるために一致協力した** We *worked together* [*cooperated* ／ *collaborated*] to make the concert a success. ‖ **全組合員が一致団結して交渉に当たる必要がある** All union members need to *be united* as we enter into negotiations.

☞ **全会一致，不一致**（→見出語）

いっちゃく 一着 **1**【競走の】**first (place)** ▶**100メートル競走の１着は誰だったの？** Who came in *first* in the 100-meter dash?

2【衣服の】a **suit** ▶**紺のスーツは１着しか持っていない** I have only *one* blue *suit*.

いっちゅうや 一昼夜 ▶**彼女は丸一昼夜高熱で苦しんだ** She suffered (from) a high fever *all day and night*. (➤ all day and night は高熱が始まったのが昼からという含みで，夜から始まった場合には all night and day がふつう).

いっちょう 一丁 ▶**豆腐一丁** *a block* of tofu ‖ **カレーライス一丁！** *One* (*order of* ／ *plate of*) curry and rice!

▶《仕事などを》**さあ，一丁やるか** Well, *shall we get to work* [*get started*]? (➤ get to は「…に取りかかる」).

いっちょういっせき 一朝一夕 ▶**正しい行儀作法は一朝一夕には身につかない** You can't master good manners *overnight* [*in a short period*].

いっちょういったん 一長一短 ▶**提出された企画にはどれも一長一短があった** Each plan that was presented had its own *advantages and disadvantages* [*merits and demerits*].

いっちょうら 一張羅 one's **best clothes,**《インフォーマル》one's **Sunday best** ▶**一張羅のブレザーをくぎに引っ掛けてだめにしてしまった** My *best* blazer was ruined when I snagged it on a nail.

いっちょくせん 一直線 **a straight line** ▶**彼の打球は一直線にレフトスタンドへ飛んでいった** The ball he hit went *straight* into the left stands.

い

いつつ 五つ five ▶五つ星ホテル a *five-star* hotel.
いっつい 一対 a pair ▶一対の湯飲み *a pair of* teacups.
いつつご 五つ子 quintuplets /kwɪntʌ́pləts ‖ kwɪ́ntjupləts/ (➤ そのうちの1人は a quintuplet) ▶五つ子が生まれた *Quintuplets* were born.
いって 一手 1【自分だけですること】 ▶彼が客の案内を一手に引き受けてくれたので助かった He was a great help as he *took full charge of* showing guests around. ‖ この辺のピーナツの商いは彼が一手に握っている He *monopolizes* the peanut business around here.
‖一手販売 exclusive sale.
2【1つの方法】 ▶それも一手だね That's *one way* to do it.
いってい 一定 ▶一定の場所 a *fixed* place ‖ 一定の間隔で at *regular* intervals ‖ 一定の速度を守る keep to a *steady* speed ‖ 音楽ファイルの音量を一定にする *standardize* the volume of music files ‖ 放水量を一定にする *keep* the volume of discharged water *constant*.
▶交渉には一定のルールがある There are *certain* rules for negotiations. ‖ 受講希望者が一定の人数に達しない場合，講座は開かれません If there aren't at least *a certain* number of applicants, the class won't be offered. ‖ 私は起きる時間が一定していない I don't get up at any *fixed* time. ‖ 今回の調査は一定の成果があった This time (our) research showed *some* (*concrete*) *results*. (➤ concrete は「明確な，具体的な」の意).
いってき 一滴 a drop ▶一滴残さず飲み干す drink *to the last drop* ‖ 一滴の水も大切に使いましょう Please don't waste even one *drop* of water.
いってきます 行って来ます ▶ 対話「行ってきます」「行ってらっしゃい，遅くなっちゃだめよ」"*I'm going now*." "All right, (but) don't stay out late !"

> **解説「行ってきます」について**
> 英語には「行ってきます」に当たる固定した表現はない. 英米人は例えば I'm going over to Mary's house. (ちょっとメアリーの家に行ってきます) とか, **I'm going now.** (じゃあ行ってくるね) のように言い，家の者は OK, see you later. (じゃあね) とか, Have a good time. (楽しんでいらっしゃい) などと答える. 人によっては簡単に **Good-bye**! とか **Bye (-bye)**! と言い，送るほうもそれと同じ表現を用いて答えたりする. →行ってらっしゃい.

いってつ 一徹 ▶老いの一徹 *obduracy* [*obstinacy*] of old age. (➤ obduracy /ɑ́:bdjərəsi/, obstinacy /ɑ́:bstɪnəsi/ はともに「がんこ，強情」の意).
いってみれば 言ってみれば so to speak ▶彼は言ってみれば大きな赤ん坊だ He is, *so to speak*, (just) a big baby. ‖ 幸福とは言ってみれば影のようなものです Happiness is, *in a way*, like a shadow. (➤ in a way は「見方によれば」) ‖ 人生は言ってみれば長い旅だ Life *may be likened* [*can be compared*] *to* a long journey. (➤ be likened [compared] to は「…にたとえられる」).
いつでも 何時でも any time (任意のときに) ; always (常に) ▶そのＤＶＤが見たければいつでも見せてあげるよ If you'd like to see the DVD, I'll be glad to let you see it *any time*. ‖ いつでも好きなときに遊びにいらっしゃい Come and see me *any time* [*whenever*] you like. ‖ 来週ならいつでもいいよ I'm available *any time* [*any day*] next week. ‖ 対話「辞書を貸してくれてありがとう」「いつでもどうぞ」"Thanks for lending me your dictionary." "*Anytime*." (➤「どういたしまして，またいつでもどうぞ」の意).
▶治の成績はいつでもクラスのびりだ Osamu is *always* at the bottom of his class. ‖ マージャンをするといつでも兄が勝つ *Whenever* we play mah-jong, my (older) brother wins. →いつも.
いってらっしゃい 行ってらっしゃい

> **解説「行ってらっしゃい」について**
> 英語には「行ってらっしゃい」に当たる固定した表現はなく, **See you later.** (じゃあね) とか, **Good-bye (for now)**!, **Bye (-bye)**! などと言う. また，会社に出かける夫に対して妻は **Have a good day**, honey. などと言い，パーティーや旅行に行く人には **Have fun.** とか **Have a good time.** と言う. いずれも「楽しんでいらっしゃい」の意. →行ってきます.

[1]**いってん 一転** ▶終盤の立て続けのゴールで，さえないゲームが一転してはらはらどきどきのゲームになった Back-to-back goals at the last moment *turned* a dull game *into* an exciting one. ‖ 彼は30歳になると優しい男から一転して厳しい男になった When he got to be thirty years old, he *changed abruptly* from a gentle, kind man to a tough, hard one.
[2]**いってん 一点** ▶ぼくたちの野球チームはその試合を1点差で落とした Our baseball team lost the game by *one run*. (➤ run は「(野球の) 得点」) ‖ 入試では1点に泣くケースもある Some students fail entrance exams by *a single point*. →点.
▶私たちは船が水平線上の一点になるまで見つめていた We watched the ship until it became *a* mere *dot* on the horizon.
▶彼女の潔白については一点の曇り (＝疑い) もなかった There was not *a shadow of* (*a*) *doubt* that she was innocent.
いってんばり 一点張り ▶その医者は自分の診断は間違ってはいないの一点張りだった The doctor *persisted in saying* that his diagnosis was not wrong. (➤ persist in ... は「(物事) をあくまでやり通そうとする」).
いっと 一途 ▶米の消費は近年減少の一途をたどっている Rice consumption has been *on the decline* [*on a steady decline*] in recent years. ‖ 母の容体は悪化の一途をたどっている My mother's condition *is deteriorating* [*worsening*] *steadily*.
いっとう 一等 (the) first place ; (the) first prize (賞品) ▶運動会で一等を取ったので父が自転車を買ってくれた Since I won (*the*) *first place* [*prize*] on field day, my father bought me a bicycle.
‖一等航海士 a first officer [mate] ‖ 一等星 a star of the first magnitude.
いっとうち 一等地 prime land ; a choice location (えり抜きの場所) ▶わが社は都心の一等地に本社がある Our company has its headquarters *in a prime location* in central Tokyo.
いっとうりょうだん 一刀両断 ▶複雑な問題を一刀両断に解決する solve a complicated problem *elegantly* [*neatly*] (➤ ともに「手際よく」) ‖ 政府の政策を一刀両断にする (＝批判する) *rip* the government policy *to pieces*.
いつなんどき いつ何時 ▶いつ何時大地震が関東地方を襲うかもしれない A big earthquake could hit the Kanto region *at any time* [*moment*].
いつになく 何時になく unusually ▶その日の彼女はい

つになくはしゃいでいた She was *unusually* exhilarated that day. ‖その日父はいつになく早起きしてジョギングに出かけた My father got up *unusually* early that day and went jogging.

いつになったら 何時になったら ▶一体いつになったら, バイク買ってくれるの? *When on earth* are you [*When* are you *ever*] going to buy me a motorcycle?

いつのまにか 何時の間にか ▶秋がいつのまにか忍び寄ってきた Autumn crept in *without our knowing it* [*before we were aware of it*]. ‖いつのまにか彼女は隣でうたた寝をしていた She dozed off beside me *before I knew* [*realized*] *it*.

いっぱ 一派 a **school**(流派, 学派); a **group**(一般的にグループ) ▶マネとその一派は印象派と呼ばれている Manet and his *school* are called Impressionists.

いっぱい 一杯 **1【分量】**▶大さじ1杯分の塩 *a tablespoonful of* salt ‖コップ1杯のミルク *a glass of* milk ‖籠1杯のサクランボ *a basketful of* cherries. ‖**対話**「お茶を1杯いかがですか」「頂きます」"How about *a cup of* tea?" "Thank you." ‖**対話**「コーヒーをもう1杯頂けますか」「どうぞ」"Can I have *another cup of* coffee?" "Certainly [Sure]."

2【酒を飲むこと】 a **drink** ▶1杯やりながら大いに語り合った We talked a lot *over a drink* [*over drinks*]. (➤この over は「…しながら」) ‖そのうち1杯やろう *Let's have a drink* sometime soon.

3【あふれるほど】▶母は姉の結婚式のことで頭がいっぱいで, ぼくのことなんかほとんどかまってくれない My mother's so *full of* plans for my sister's wedding that she hardly cares about me. ‖ホールは人でいっぱいだった The hall *was crowded* [*was packed*] *with* people.

▶すしを腹いっぱい食べてみたいなあ I want to eat sushi *till I've had my fill* [*till I'm stuffed*]. (➤ till I'm stuffed は少し下品な言い方) ‖もうおなかがいっぱいだ *I've had enough.* / *I'm full.* ‖ぼくたちはボートを力いっぱいこいだ We rowed the boat *as hard as we could*. ‖ロープを力いっぱい引っ張ってください Pull the rope *with all your might*. ‖新婚カップルは幸せいっぱいといった様子だった The newlyweds looked *as happy as* (*happy*) *could be*.

4【たくさん】▶バケツに水をいっぱい入れる *fill* a bucket with water ‖きょうの午後はやることがいっぱいある I have *a lot* to do this afternoon. ‖本多先生のアパートには本がいっぱいあった Mr. Honda's apartment *was filled with* books.

5【ぎりぎり】▶私たちは今月いっぱいロスにいます We will be in L.A. *all* [*throughout*] *this month*. ‖時間いっぱいまで粘ったがその問題は解けなかった I used up *all the allotted time*, but I still couldn't figure out the answer to the problem. ‖道路の左側いっぱいまで車を寄せる pull a car *all the way over to the left side* of the road.

6【慣用表現】▶彼にはまんまと一杯食わされた We *were* (nicely) *taken in* by him. (●この「一杯食わされた」は「だまされた」のインフォーマルな言い方だから, 英語の be (nicely) taken in が適当) ‖きみは一杯食わされたんだよ I think you'*ve been had*. (●この be had は「ぺてんにかかる」に相当するインフォーマルな慣用句で, 訳例のような用い方をする).

いっぱく 一泊 ▶弘前で1泊しよう Let's *stay one night* at Hirosaki. ‖彼らはサンフランシスコへ着きそこで1泊した They reached San Francisco, where they *stayed for the night*. ‖私が泊まったホテルの部屋は1泊2食付きで15000円だった The hotel charged me 15,000 yen *a night for a room and two meals*. ‖箱根へ一泊旅行をする[に出かける] make [go on] *an overnight trip* to Hakone.

いっぱし 一端 ▶あの子はまだ15歳だが, もういっぱしの悪(わる)だ Though he is only fifteen, he is already a *full-blown* hoodlum. (➤ full-blown は文字どおりには「満開の, 本格的な」) ‖娘ももういっぱしの大人のような口を利くようになった My daughter now talks just like a *full-fledged* adult. (➤ full-fledged は「一人前の」).

いっぱつ 一発 ▶猟師はキツネを狙って一発撃った The hunter fired *a shot* at a fox. ‖父はその鳥を一発でしとめた Father downed the bird *with a single shot*. ‖一発の銃声が聞こえた I heard *a gunshot*.

▶そのボクサーは顎に一発パンチを食らった The boxer *took a punch* on [to] the jaw. (➤ on のほうが多少直撃感が強い).

▶きょうの西武はここというときに一発(=タイムリーヒットなど)が出ない Today the Lions are not getting *a timely hit* (just) when they need one. ‖ジャイアンツは坂本の一発で試合を逆転した The Giants turned the tables with Sakamoto's *home run*.

▶運転試験なんか一発で受かってやるよ I'll pass the driving test *the first time around* [*on my first try*].

いっぱん 一般 **一形** 一般の **common**(よくある); **general**(多くの人に共通の) **一副** 一般に **commonly, generally** ▶一般の読者 *common* readers ‖一般の大学生 an *average* university student.

▶その女優に過去があることは一般に知られていた The fact that the actress had a past was *generally* known. ‖子供は一般に家の中にいたがらないものだ Children *usually* don't like to stay (at) home. ‖その名画はあすから一般公開される The famous picture will *be exhibited to the public* starting tomorrow. ‖その情報は一般大衆には明かされなかった The information wasn't revealed to *the general public*.

直訳の落とし穴「一般大衆」

「世間一般の」=general と覚えるために,「世間一般の人」や「一般大衆」を(×)general people と訳す人がいるが, このような言い方はない. the general public がよく使う言い方である. 富裕層でも知識階級でもない「庶民」という意味では the masses という堅い言い方もある.「一般」を「ふつうの」と捉えた ordinary people が最も多く用いられるが,「平均的な」と捉えた average people も用いられる. common people はマイナスイメージを与えることがある.

‖一般会計 the general account ‖一般教養科目 liberal arts ‖一般席 a general admission seat.

いっぱんてき 一般的な **common**(よくある); **general**(多くの人に共通の) **一副** 一般的に **generally, in general** ▶日本では現在子供が1人または2人の家庭が一般的だ These days families with one or two children are *very common* in Japan. ‖日本車は一般的に海外での人気が高い *Generally*, Japanese cars are popular overseas. ‖一般的に言って, 英語話者が日本語を使いこなすのは難しい *Generally speaking*, Japanese is difficult for English speakers to master.

い

いっぴきおおかみ 一匹狼 a **lone wolf** ▶彼は自分が一匹おおかみであることを誇りにしている He prides himself on being something of *a lone wolf* [*a maverick*]. (➤ maverick /mǽvərɪk/ は「徒党を組まず, 独自に行動する人」).

いっぴつ 一筆 a **line**, a **note**(➤ 前者がややインフォーマル) ▶シドニーに着いたら一筆お便りください *Drop me a line* when you get to Sydney.

✉ **失礼を顧みず一筆差し上げます** I am taking the liberty of *writing to* you.

いっぴん 逸品 a **superb piece.**

いっぷいっぷせい 一夫一婦制 **monogamy** /mənɑ́:gəmi/.

いっぷう 一風 ▶一風変わった人 an *eccentric* person / a *quirky* person [character] (➤ eccentric はしばしば変わっていることを好意的に受け止めている. また, quirky は「普通と違って興味深い」というニュアンス) ‖ 一風変わったフランス料理を出す店 a restaurant serving its *original* French cuisine (➤ original は「奇抜な, 斬新な」の意).

1**いっぷく 一服** a **dose** /doʊs/ 《of》(薬の) ▶薬を一服飲む take *a dose* of medicine ‖ この辺でちょっと一服(＝休憩)しよう Let's *take a breather* now. (➤「たばこを吸うための」を言うときには Let's take a smoke break.).

2**いっぷく 一幅の** a **roll (of)** (巻物の) ▶眺めは一幅の絵のようであった The view was *just like a picture* [*very picturesque*]. (➤ picturesque は /pɪ̀ktʃərésk/ と発音).

いっぷたさいせい 一夫多妻制 **polygamy** /pəlígəmi/.

1**いっぺん 一片** ▶空には一片の雲も見られなかった There was not *a cloud* in the sky. ‖ 誘拐犯には一片の良心も見られなかった The kidnapper did not show even *a trace of* conscience.

2**いっぺん 一変する** **change completely** ▶私の子供の頃から見るとこの辺りは一変した This neighborhood *has completely changed* since when I lived here as a child.

3**いっぺん 一遍** →一度, 一回.

いっぺんとう 一辺倒 ▶アメリカ一辺倒の政策 policies that *lean heavily toward* the U.S. ‖ 彼はロック一辺倒だ He's *an out-and-out fan* of rock music. ‖ 母は日本茶一辺倒だ My mother drinks *only* green tea.

いっぺんに 一遍に **at one time**(一度に) ; **at once** (すぐに) ▶いっぺんに全部はできないよ You cannot do them all *at one time*. ‖ その小説はおもしろくていっぺんに読んでしまった The novel was so interesting that I read it *in one sitting*. / The novel was so interesting I couldn't put it down. (◉ 英訳する場合, 前者のように「(おもしろくて)一気に(読んだ)」(in one sitting は文字どおりには「一座り」)と考えるか, 後者のように「(おもしろくて)本を下に置けなかった」と考える) ‖ 私が仲裁に入ったら2人はいっぺんに仲直りした They resolved their disputes *at once* as soon as I began to mediate. ‖ テレビドラマを見てその女優がいっぺんに好きになってしまった After I saw the TV drama, I *took an immediate liking to* the actress.

いっぽ 一歩 a **step** ▶一歩一歩進む go *step by step* ‖ 足が痛くてもう一歩も歩けないよ My feet hurt so much I *can't walk another step*. ‖ 日本語学習の第一歩は仮名を覚えることだ *The first step* in learning Japanese is to master the *kana*. ‖ 彼女は俳優としての第一歩を踏み出したところだ She is on *the first rung* of an acting career. (◉ 英語では「…のはしごの一段目(the first rung)にいる」と発想する) ‖ 一歩前進, 半歩後退を繰り返す repeat the pattern of *one step forward* and a half step backward ‖ これで目標に向かって一歩前進だ This means I*'ve advanced a step* toward my goal.

▶彼はその点に関しては一歩も譲ろうとしなかった He would not give (away) *an inch* on that point. (➤ give (away) は「譲歩する」) ‖ 彼はいつも友だちを一歩リードしている He *is* always *one-up on* his friends. (➤ one-up は「人より一歩先んじて」).

1**いっぽう 一方** **1**【片方】▶ボートは急に一方に傾いた Our boat suddenly listed *to one side*. ‖ この色鉛筆は一方が赤で, もう一方が青だ This colored pencil is red at *one end* and blue at *the other*.

▶一方では世界的に英語のネイティブスピーカーの割合は減りつつあり, もう一方では英語を第二言語として話している人の割合は増えつつある *On the one hand*, the proportion of English native speakers is decreasing worldwide, and *on the other* (*hand*), the proportion of people who speak English as a second language is increasing.

▶ここは一方通行だ This is *a one-way street*. (➤「一方通行」の標識は One Way).

2【「…する一方」の形で】▶地価は下がるどころか上がる一方だ Far from falling, land prices *keep on* rising. (◉「上がり続けている」と考えて, 訳例のように keep on rising とする) ‖ 海外で生活する日本人は毎年増える一方だ The number of Japanese who live overseas has been increasing *steadily* every year. ‖ 私の数学の成績は悪くなる一方だ My math grades *are getting worse and worse*.

3【話変わって・同時に】▶一方, アリはせっせと冬支度をしていました *In the meantime* [*Meanwhile*], the ant was busy (in) preparing for the winter. ‖ トムは勉強していた. 一方, スーはピアノを弾いていた Tom was studying. *Meanwhile*, Sue was playing the piano. (➤ meanwhile は同時に起きていることを並べる) ‖ カナダは天然資源が豊富だ. 一方, 日本は乏しい Canada has abundant natural resources. *By contrast*, Japan has few. (◉ この場合の「一方」は「(それとは)対照的に」という意味だから, by contrast を用いてそれに続く文全体に掛けるとよい).

2**いっぽう 一報** ▶向こうに着き次第ご一報ください *Please let me know* as soon as you get there. (◉「電話が欲しい」なら let me know を give me a call に,「手紙が欲しい」なら drop me a line に替える).

いっぽうてき 一方的な **one-sided** (一方が優勢な) ; **unilateral** /jù:nilǽt̬ərəl/ (相手方を顧みない) ▶一方的な決定 (a) *unilateral* decision ‖ 彼の意見は一方的だ His opinion is *one-sided*. ‖ 試合は我々のチームの一方的な勝利に終わった The game ended in a *one-sided* victory for our team. ‖ 彼らは一方的に会談の終結を宣言した They *unilaterally* declared an end to the talks.

いっぽん 一本 **1**【細長いもの1個】▶チョーク1本 *a piece of* chalk ‖ ビール1本 *a bottle of* beer ‖ ボールペンを1本貸してください Can you lend me *a* ballpoint pen ?

2【慣用表現】▶来た電車が混んでいたので一本あとのに乗った Because the train was very crowded, I waited and took *the next one*. ‖ 物書き一本で生活するのは難しい It's not easy to make a living *by* *writing alone* [*by only writing*]. ‖ こりゃ, **一本取られた** You *got me there*！(➤「参った」「降参した」の意).

▶《柔道などで》**一本**！ *Ippon*！(➤ a full throw, a clear, single throw などと説明的にしてもよい；「一本取る」は score an ippon) ／*Touché* /tuːʃéɪ/! (➤ フェンシングで,「(突きあり) 一本！」の意).

一本締め ▶*ipponjime*; clapping hands in unison at the cue of the person in charge by all present to conclude or celebrate a successful meeting or deal, etc., with a beat of da-da-da, da-da-da, da-da-da, and ending with one da.

一本立ち ▶早く息子に一本立ちしてほしいと思っている I want my son to *become an independent adult* soon. **一本調子** ▶校長先生の一本調子の式辞にはうんざりした We got bored with the principal's *monotonous* address. **一本やり** ▶彼は国立大学一本やりだ He is *only* trying for [aiming at] a national university.

いっぽんか 一本化 ▶両案を一本化する *combine* two plans into one.

いっぽんぎ 一本気 ▶一本気な性格の人 a *single-minded* person.

いつまで 何時まで ▶いつまでにお返事すればよろしいでしょうか *By when* should I give an answer？‖ 連絡はいつまでならいいですか *When is the latest* I can let you know？‖ **対話**「いつまでこの本をお借りできますか」「いつまででもいいですよ」"*How long* can I keep this book？" "You can keep it *as long as you like*." (➤ Until when ...？はほとんど用いられない).

▶いつまで待っても無駄だよ It's a waste of time to wait *endlessly*.

いつまでも 何時までも **forever** /fərévəʳ/; **endlessly** (絶え間なく) ▶いつまでも若く美しくが大半の女性の願いだ It's the wish of most women to stay young and beautiful *forever*. ‖ いつまでもこんなことをやってはいられない We can't keep on doing this *forever*！‖ やってしまったことをいつまでも悩んでいてはいけない You should not brood (*endlessly*) over what's been done. (➤ brood (くよくよ気にやむ) に「いつまでも」という含みがあるので, 特に強調するのでなければ endlessly, forever などは不要). ‖ きみのことはいつまでも忘れないよ I'll *never* forget you. (➤「私のこと, いつまでも忘れないでね」なら Please don't ever forget me. →**一生**) ‖ どうかお2人がいつまでもお幸せでありますように I hope both of you will be happy *for the rest of your lives*. (●「いつまでも」を「これからの人生をずっと」と考えた場合の訳) ‖ 私は彼の便りをいつまでも待っていた I *waited and waited* for a letter from him. (●同じ語を繰り返すことで,「いつまでも…する」という意味を表す).

ことわざ **いつまでもあると思うな親と金** There are two things you can't expect to be around forever with you—parents and money. (➤ 日本語からの直訳).

直訳の落とし穴 いつまでも

「いつまでも」= forever ではあるが,「いつまでも若く美しくいたい」を I want to be [stay] young and beautiful forever. とすると, これを聞いた英米人からはすぐ「それは不可能だよ」という反応が返ってきそうである. 日本語の意味するところは I want to be [stay] young and beautiful for as long as possible. が近いと思われる. あるいは, かなわぬ願いと捉えるならば I wish I could be [stay] young and beautiful forever. となり, これなら英米人にも通じる.「いつまでもお元気で」という挨拶も forever は不可能なので, I hope you'll stay well [healthy] for a long time [for many years]. とする. なお, 愛し合っている夫婦が「いつまでも一緒だよ」を We are and will be together forever. とするのは, 肉体が滅びたあとも来世や霊魂の不滅を信じるならば可能である.

いつも 何時も **1**【どんなときでも】**always**; **all the time** (年がら年中) ▶ぼくはいつも朝7時に起きる I *always* get up at seven in the morning. (●「(違う日もあるが) いつもは」なら usually を用いる) ‖ 彼はいつも約束の時間に遅れる He is *always* late for appointments. ‖ 彼はいつも不平ばかり言っている He's *always* grumbling. ／He grumbles *all the time*. (● 進行形と always または現在形と all the time を用いることで話者の腹立ちを表す).

▶土曜日の午後はいつもみんなでサッカーをする We play soccer *every* Saturday afternoon. ‖ 彼に何度電話をかけてもいつも留守だ No matter how often I try to call him, he's *always* out. ‖ 父はいつも「情けは人のためならず」と言っていた My father *used to* say, "One who is kind to others is sure to be rewarded." (● used to do は「よく…したものだ」という過去における継続的習慣を表す).

▶彼女はいつもはっきりと自分の意見を言わない She *never* says what she thinks. (●「いつも…でない」は never で表す；not always とすると「いつも…とは限らない」の意になる).

【文型】
〜するといつも…
Whenever S + V, … .
Every time S + V, … .

▶両親がけんかするといつも母さんが勝つ *Whenever* [*Every time*] my parents have an argument, my mother wins. ‖ 彼女と話をするといつもけんかになってしまう *Whenever* I talk to her, we end up quarreling.

2【ふつうの場合, ふだん】**usually** 一形 **いつもの usual** ▶いつものとおり自転車で登校した I went to school by bicycle *as usual*. ‖ その日私はいつもより1時間早く起きた On that day, I got up an hour earlier *than usual*. ‖ この夏はいつもの年より暑い It is hotter *than usual* this summer. ‖ 彼はいつもの場所で彼女を待った He waited for her at the *usual* place. ‖ けさはいつものバスに乗り遅れた I missed the *usual bus* [*my bus*] this morning. ‖ 森先生はいつもと違ってスーツを着込んでいた Mr. Mori was wearing a suit, *which was unusual for him*. ‖《行きつけの喫茶店などで》ぼく, いつもの *My usual*, please.

いづらい 居辛い ▶夫婦げんかが始まったので, 居づらくなって帰って来たよ I was *uncomfortable* when the couples started quarreling [fighting], so I came home. ‖ 彼は仕事で大きなミスをして, その会社に居づらくなった It *became uncomfortable* for him at his company after he made a big blunder in his work. (➤ blunder は「(仕事などの) 大失敗」の意).

いつわ 逸話 an **anecdote** /ǽnɪkdoʊt/ ▶彼についてはユーモラスな逸話がたくさんある There are many humorous *anecdotes* about him.

いつわり 偽り a **lie** (人をだまそうという意図をもった)；a **falsehood** (真実でないこと) ▶偽りを言う tell *a lie* ‖ 彼の証言は全くの偽りであることがわかった His testimony turned out to be *false*. ‖ 彼の偽りのない気持ちを聞いてやってほしい I would like you to hear him out on his *true feelings*. ‖ 彼の言うことにうそ偽りはない There is nothing *insincere* in what he says. (➤ insincere は「誠意のない」).

いつわる 偽る **lie**(うそをつく) ; **pretend**(ふりをする) ▶自分の持っている資格を偽る *lie* about one's qualifications ‖ 私は社長と偽って電話をかけた I made a call *pretending* to be the president. ‖ 男は医師と偽って患者を診察した The man saw patients *pretending* he was a doctor. ‖ 帰国してほっとしたというのが偽らざる気持ちです *To tell* (*you*) *the truth*, I feel relieved after coming back from abroad.

イデオロギー (an) **ideology** /àɪdiɑ́:lədʒi, ìdi-/ ▶イデオロギーの違い *ideological* differences.

いてざ 射手座 (a) **Sagittarius** /sæ̀dʒɪtéəriəs/ ▶射手座の女性 *a female Sagittarian*.

いでたち 出で立ち **clothes** /kloʊz/ (衣服) ; an **outfit** (装具[衣装]一式).

いてつく 凍てつく ▶いてつくような風 a *freezing* (*cold*) wind ‖ 今夜はやけにいてつく晩だ It is *freezing cold* tonight.

いてもたっても 居ても立っても ▶入試の結果がわかるまでは居ても立ってもいられなかった Until I got the result of the entrance examination, I *couldn't sit still*. (➤ still は「じっとして, 静止して」の意) ‖ 一人娘の帰宅がいつになく遅かったので, 私たちはその夜は居ても立ってもいられない気持ちだった We *were* (really) *anxious* [*on pins and needles*] that night because our only daughter was unusually late coming home.

いてん 移転 a **move** 一動 **移転する move** ▶C 大学は都心から郊外へ移転した C University *moved* from the center of the city to the suburbs. ‖ きみの移転先をまだ聞いていなかったね I haven't got your *new address* yet. ‖**移転通知** a notice of a change of address, 《英》a removal notice.

いでん 遺伝 **heredity** ▶遺伝する病気 a *hereditary* disease ‖ はげは遺伝するでしょうか Is baldness *hereditary*?
‖**遺伝学** genetics ‖ **遺伝学者** a geneticist.

いでんし 遺伝子 a **gene** /dʒi:n/ 一形 **遺伝子の genetic** /dʒənétɪk/ ▶遺伝子の仕組み *genetic* mechanism ‖ 遺伝子を受け継ぐ inherit *genes* ‖ 長寿遺伝子 a longevity *gene* (➤ longevity は /lɑ:ndʒévəti/ と発音).
‖**遺伝子組み換え** gene recombination ‖ **遺伝子組み換え食品** a genetically-modified food ‖ **遺伝子工学** genetic engineering ‖ **遺伝子操作** genetic manipulation ‖ **遺伝子療法** gene therapy.

[1]**いと 糸** (a) **thread**(縫い糸) ; (a) **yarn** (織り糸, 編み糸) ; (a) **string** (太い糸, 楽器の弦) ; a **line** (釣り糸) ; a **stitch** (傷口を縫う針の糸) ▶絹糸 silk *thread* ‖ クモの糸 *threads* of a spider (➤「クモの巣」は (cob)web) ‖ 針と糸で雑巾を縫う patch together a dustcloth with needle and *thread* (➤ needle and thread で「糸の通った針」) ‖ 針に糸を通す *thread* a needle ‖ 糸の先につけた風船 a balloon on *a string*.
▶糸はいちばん弱いところで切れる The *thread* breaks at its weakest point. ‖ 彼はたこの糸をぐんぐん伸ばした He let out more and more of the kite *string*. ‖ 納豆はよく糸を引く Natto *forms* (long) *threads*. ‖ (釣り)糸を垂れる drop one's (*fishing*) *line* (➤ drop A a line は「A(人)に一筆書く」).
▶《比喩的》やくざが陰で糸を引いていたことがわかった The yakuza proved to have been *pulling strings* [been *manipulating*] behind the scenes. ‖ 彼はその出来事を思い出そうとかすかな記憶の糸を手繰った He went back over his *faint memory* of the incident.

[2]**いと 意図** an **intention** (初めからの意思) ; a **purpose** (明確な目的) ▶彼は何を意図していたのだろうか What was his *intention*? / What was he *aiming at*? (➤ aim at は「…を狙う」) ‖ こんな雑誌を出す意図がわからない I can't understand *what they expect to accomplish* by publishing a magazine like this. ‖ 彼とすれ違うとき, 彼女は意図的かどうかわからないが, ハンカチを落とした She dropped her handkerchief, *intentionally or not*, when she passed by him. ‖ 彼女は意図的に典子の靴を隠した She hid Noriko's shoes *on purpose* [*deliberately*].

[1]**いど 井戸** a **well** ▶井戸を掘る dig [sink] *a well* ‖ 井戸の水をくむ draw water from *a well* ‖ その井戸はかれてしまった The *well* has dried up [has run dry].
‖**井戸水** well water.

[2]**いど 緯度** **latitude** ▶私はうっかりして緯度と経度を間違えてしまった I was so absent-minded that I mistook *latitude* for longitude. ‖ ロサンゼルスと東京はほぼ同じ緯度にある Los Angeles and Tokyo are approximately on the same *latitude*.
☞ **経度, 南緯, 北緯** (→見出語)

[1]**いとう 以東** ▶私は京都以東はずいぶん旅行した I have traveled a lot in Kyoto *and* in regions (*to the*) *east of* Kyoto.

[2]**いとう 厭う** **dislike** +目 (嫌う) ; **mind** +目 (気にする) ▶子供を幸せにするためなら親はどんな苦労もいとわない Parents *don't mind experiencing hardship*(*s*) [Parents *spare no efforts*] to make their children happy. (➤ spare no efforts は「努力を惜しまない」).

[1]**いどう 異動** a **change** ▶ことしはうちの課の人事に異動はない There will be no personnel *changes* [no staff *changes*] in my department this year. (➤ personnel は /pə̀:rsənél/ と発音).

[2]**いどう 移動** (a) **movement** 一動 **移動する[させる] move** (+目) ▶1人ではその車の移動は無理だ It will take more than one man to *move* that car.
‖**移動図書館** 《米》a bookmobile, 《英》a mobile library.

いとおしい ▶いとおしい自分 myself that *I cherish* ‖ 一人娘をいとおしく思う *hold* one's only daughter *dear*.

いとおしむ ▶命をいとおしむ *have reverence for* life ‖ 彼の作品には自然を深くいとおしむ気持ちが表れている His works show his deep *love* [*attachment*] for nature.

いときりば 糸切り歯 a **canine tooth** (犬歯 ; canine /kéɪnaɪn/ は堅い語または専門用語で「犬の」).

いとぐち 糸口 a **clue** /klu:/ ▶糸口をつかむ find *a clue* [*a lead*] ‖ その女性店員の証言が事件解決の糸口になった The saleswoman's testimony was *a clue* leading to the solution of the case.

いとこ 従兄弟・従姉妹 a **cousin** /kʌ́zən/ ▶敬子とぼくはいとこどうしです Keiko and I are *cousins*. (➤「またいとこ」は second cousin).

いどころ 居所 one's **address** (住所) ; one's **whereabouts** (行方, 所在) ▶彼の現在の居所を知ってますか Do you know *where he lives* now? ‖ 彼女の居所はまだわかっていない Her *whereabouts* are still unknown.

いとしい 愛しい **dear** ▶いとしいわが子 my *dear* child ‖ああ麗子！おまえがいとしいよ Oh, Reiko！You are such *a darling*！‖いとしいあなたのためならどんなことでもするわ For you, *my dear*, I would do anything. ‖わがいとしき人よ my *beloved one*.

いとすぎ 糸杉 《植物》a **cypress** /sáɪprəs/.

いとなみ 営み ▶日々の営み daily *life* ‖「愛の営み」とは性交のことである '*Lovemaking*' means having sexual intercourse.

いとなむ 営む **run** ＋目（事業を）▶パン屋［花屋］を営む *run* a bakery［a flower shop］‖農業を営みながら俳句を作る compose haiku (poems) while *engaged in* farming.

いとのこ 糸鋸 a **coping saw**, a **fret saw**（➤後者はより刃が細く，細かい細工・作業に向いている）；a **jigsaw**（電動の）.

いどばたかいぎ 井戸端会議 ▶井戸端会議も時には楽しいものだ It is sometimes fun to *stand around chatting with the neighbors*. ‖女房はいつも井戸端会議で新しい情報を仕入れてくる My wife is always picking up new information at *hen parties*.（●英語では「女性たちだけの集まり」の意の hen party を用いる．この語は日本語の「井戸端会議」に似てやや軽蔑的な響きがある）.

いとま 暇 ▶（人に）いとまを告げる bid *farewell* (to a person) ‖彼が急いで通り過ぎたので私は挨拶をするいとま(＝時間)もなかった He passed by me so quickly that I didn't even have *time* to say hello.

☛ おいとま（→見出語）

いどむ 挑む **challenge** ＋目（勇気を持って）；**try** ＋目（試しに）→挑戦 ▶不可能に挑む *challenge* the impossible（●他人には不可能でも自分には可能だということを立証したい場合に用いる）‖新記録に挑む *try to set* a new record ‖挑むような目つきで見返す stare back with a *challenging* look.

いとめ 糸目 ▶着物のことになると彼女は金に糸目をつけない She *spends money lavishly* on kimono(s).（➤lavishly は「惜しげなく」）／She *spares no expense* on kimono(s). ‖徹はいい車を手に入れるためなら金に糸目をつけない Toru will *pay any price* for a good car.

いとめる 射止める **shoot** ＋目（撃つ）；**win** ＋目（獲得する）▶ライフルでクマを射止める *shoot* a bear with a rifle ‖彼女のハートを射止めるのは至難の業だよ It will be extremely difficult for you to *win her heart*.

いとも ▶難題をいとも簡単に片づける solve a difficult problem *as if it were nothing*.

いな 否 ▶それが真実か否か私にはわからない I cannot say *whether* it is true *or not*. ／*Whether or not* it is true I do not know. →いや.

いない 居ない ▶今ぼくの父は東京には居ない My father *isn't* in Tokyo at the moment. ‖ばか言わないでよ．幽霊なんか居ないわよ Don't be silly—*there's no such thing as* ghosts. ‖《部屋に向かって》誰か居ないの？*Is* anyone in (there)？（➤だれかいるかなと思って「誰かいるの？」と確認するときは Is someone in (there)？）‖《迷子が》ママが居ないよ！I lost my mommy！‖この次，春が巡ってくるころには私はいない The next time spring rolls around, I'll *be gone*. →居なくなる.

-いない -以内 **within**；《インフォーマル》**inside** ▶30分以内に戻ります I'll be back *within*［*inside*／*in*］thirty minutes.（➤in は「それだけ時間がたてば」の意で，未来を表す文とともに用いる）‖1時間以内で学校へ行けますか Can you get to school *within*［*in less than*］an hour？‖1週間以内に返事をください Please give me your answer *within* a week. ‖ホテルは駅から車で5分以内のところにあった The hotel was situated *within* (a) five minutes' (taxi) ride of the train station.

いないいないばあ **peekaboo** /pìːkəbúː/ ▶母親はいないいないばあをして赤ん坊をあやした The mother soothed the baby by playing "*Peekaboo*！"（➤《英》では peepbo /píːpboʊ/ とも）.

いなおる 居直る ▶彼女は万引きをして捕まったのに居直った She *took a defiant attitude* when she was caught shoplifting.（●「挑戦的な態度をとった」と考える；defiant は /dɪfáɪənt/ と発音し，「挑戦的な，反抗的な」の意）‖スランプのときはいい意味の居直りが必要だ When you are in a slump, you need *to look on the bright side of things*.（●「いい意味の居直り」は「物事の明るい面を見ること」と考えて訳例のように表現するとよい）.

いなか 田舎

1【都会に対して】 a **rural area**［**region**］（都会と対比して，人口の少ない農村地帯，「地方」）；**a small town (in the country)**（田舎町）；**the country**（都会から（遠く）離れた，人家のまばらな農村地帯）；**the countryside**（田園風景が広がる自然豊かな場所）

▶田舎の自然 nature *in the countryside*［*country*］‖田舎の生活 *rural* life／life *in a small* (*rural*) *town*／life *in the country* ‖ぼくは田舎育ちだ I grew up in *the country*［*countryside*］.／I was raised in *a small* (*rural*) *town*［*in a small town* (*in the country*)］. ‖田舎暮らしに憧れる退職者は多い Many retirees long for *life in the countryside*.

▶私の両親は田舎町でのんびり暮らしています My parents are living peacefully in *a rural town*［*in a small town* (*in the country*)］. ‖あの人たちのことばには田舎なまりがある They speak with a *provincial*［*country*］*accent*. ‖あの子はぽっと出の田舎娘だ She *is fresh from the country*.（➤fresh from は「…から出てきたばかり」の意）. ‖うちはど田舎にあるんだよ My house is *in the middle of nowhere*. ／I live *in the back of* (*the*) *beyond*.（➤the は《主に米》）.

2【郷里】 (one's) **home(town)** ▶田舎の両親に便りを出す write to the folks *back home* ‖正月休みには田舎に帰ります I'm going *home*［going back to my *hometown*］for the New Year holidays. ‖**対話** 「きみの田舎はどこですか」「岐阜です」"*Where are you from*？" "I'm from Gifu."

いなかっぺ 田舎っぺ a (**country**) **bumpkin**, a (**country**) **yokel**, 《米また》a (**country**) **hick**（➤いずれも日本語の「田舎っぺ」同様，軽蔑的な響きがあるが，(country) yokel にはおどけた響きもある）.

いながらにして 居ながらにして ▶インターネットのおかげで居ながらにして世界の情報が入手できる Thanks to the Internet, we can get information from all over the world *even as we sit in our living room*.

いなくなる 居なくなる ▶この川には昔ほど魚が居なくなった *There aren't* as many fish in this river as there used to be［as there were in the past］. ‖その大学生，部屋代も払わないで居なくなっちゃったのよ That college student *cleared out* without paying his room rent.（➤clear out は「立ち去る」の意）‖彼女が居なくなったこの世にはもう未練はない Now that she's *gone*, I have no reason to go on living.

い

いなご (虫) a **locust** (➤ イナゴを含むバッタ科の昆虫の総称. イギリスでは繁殖しない) ▶イナゴの大群 a large swarm of *locusts*.

いなさく 稲作 **rice cultivation** (栽培すること) ; a **rice crop** (収穫) ▶稲作は東南アジアにその源流がある *Rice cultivation* has its roots in Southeast Asia. ‖ ひどい日照不足のため稲作は大損害を受けた Because of the severe shortage of sunlight, the *rice crop* suffered serious damage.

いなす **dodge** (+⊞) (身をかわす) ; **parry** +⊞ (質問を受け流す) ▶質問をいなす *parry* a question.

いなずま 稲妻 **lightning** ▶家を出たとたん空に稲妻が走った The moment I stepped out of my house, there was *a flash of lightning* in the sky.
☞ 雷(かみなり) (→見出語)

いななく **neigh** /neɪ/ (馬・ロバが) ; **bray** /breɪ/ (ロバが).

いなびかり 稲光 a (**flash of**) **lightning**.

いなほ 稲穂 an **ear of rice** ▶たわわに実った稲穂 heavily ripe *ears of rice*.

-いなや -否や

> **語法 「…するやいなや」の言い方**
> (1) **no sooner ... than, hardly ... when [before], scarcely ... when [before]** が日本語の「…するやいなや」に相当する堅い表現. いずれも前半部分が過去完了形になることが多い.
> (2)「…するとすぐ」の意味で最もふつうに用いられるのは as soon as ... だが, the moment や soon [immediately] after を用いてもよい. →すぐ.

▶子供は玄関にかばんを置くやいなや外に遊びに飛び出した *No sooner* had the child put his schoolbag inside the front door *than* he left home to play outside. ／The child had *hardly* [*scarcely*] put his schoolbag inside the front door *when* he left home to play outside. (➤ 前者は no sooner が文頭に出て主語と動詞が倒置されている) ‖ 彼は先生の姿を見るやいなや逃げ出した *The moment* he saw the teacher, he ran away.

いなり 稲荷 ***inari***
日本紹介 ✉ **稲荷は収穫をつかさどり, 商売繁盛のご利益もあるとされる神を祭った神社です. 商売をしている人が繁栄を願って多くお参りします. キツネがこの神様の使いとされ, 稲荷の入り口にはキツネをかたどった一対の石像と赤いのぼりが立っています** An *inari* is a shrine that is dedicated to a harvest god who is also believed to give success in business. Storekeepers and businesspeople visit this type of shrine to pray for prosperity. Foxes are thought to be the god's messengers and a pair of stone fox statues and an orange-red streamer stand at the entrance to the shrine.
‖**稲荷神社** an *inari* shrine ‖ **稲荷ずし** inarizushi ; sushi rice stuffed in an *abura-age* [deep-fried tofu] pouch seasoned with soy sauce and sugar (➤ 後者は説明的な訳).

いなん 以南 ▶種子島以南には数多くの小さな島がある There are many small islands *south of* Tanegashima.

イニシアチブ (**the**) **initiative** /ɪníʃəṭɪv/ ▶今回のサミットでは日本がイニシアチブを取った Japan took *the initiative* in this summit.

イニシャル **initials** /ɪníʃəlz/ (姓名の) ▶ぼくの昔のガールフレンドのイニシャルは Y.A. だ The *initials* of my ex-girlfriend were Y.A. (➤ YとAの2つだから initials と複数形にする) ‖ ここにあなたのイニシャルを書いてください Please *put* [*write*] *your initials* here. ／Please *initial* here.

いにん 委任する **entrust** +⊞ (人に託す) ; **delegate authority** (権限を委任する) 《**to**》 ▶私はこの問題の処理をすべて弁護士に委任した I *entrusted* the attorney with authority to deal with this problem. ／I *authorized* the attorney to deal with this problem. ‖**委任状** a power of attorney.

イニング (野球) an **inning**.

いぬ 犬 **1** 【**動物の**】 a **dog** 《参考》「猟犬」は hound /haʊnd/,「子犬」は puppy /pʌ́pi/ という. ▶犬の病気 a *dog's* disease ／a *canine* disease (➤ 後者の canine /kéɪnaɪn/ は堅い語または専門用語) ‖ 私は猫より犬が好きだ I like *dogs* better than cats. ‖ 犬はリードにつないでおかなくてはいけません *Dogs* must be kept on a leash [《英》 a lead]. ‖ お宅の犬は雄ですか雌ですか Is your *dog* a he or a she? (●「雌犬」は bitch というが, この語には「あばずれ」という意があるので, 訳例のような言い方をするのがよい) ‖ 私は犬を2匹飼っている I have two *dogs*. ‖ 犬を散歩させるのはぼくの役目です It's my duty to *walk the dog*.
ことわざ **夫婦げんかは犬も食わぬ** Marital squabbles are so trivial even a dog would know better than to care about them. (● 日本語からの意訳 ; squabble は「つまらないけんか」, know better than to do は「…するようなばかなことはしない」) ／One should not interfere in quarrels between a husband and wife.
ことわざ **犬も歩けば棒に当たる** The dog that roams will come across a stick. (➤ 日本語からの直訳) ／One who gets around will sometimes have a lucky break. (➤ lucky break は「幸運」).
‖**犬小屋** a doghouse, a kennel (➤ 前者がふつう) ‖ **犬猫病院** a pet(s') hospital.
2 【**スパイ**】 a **spy** ▶彼らは警察のイヌだということがわかった They turned out to be *police spies*. 《参考》俗語では「警察のイヌ」を nark または plant という. なお police dog とすると文字どおり「警察犬」の意になる.

> 「犬」のいろいろ **秋田犬** Akita (dog) ／**イングリッシュ・セッター** English setter ／**グレートデン** Great Dane ／**グレーハウンド** greyhound ／**ゴールデン・レトリーバー** golden retriever ／**コッカースパニエル** cocker spaniel ／**コリー** collie ／**シーズー** Shih Tzu ／**シェパード** German shepherd dog ／**柴犬** shiba (dog) ／**シベリアン・ハスキー** Siberian husky ／**スコッチ・テリア** Scottish terrier ／**スピッツ** spitz ／**セントバーナード** St. Bernard ／**ダックスフント** dachshund ／**ダルメシアン** Dalmatian ／**チャウチャウ** chow chow ／**チワワ** Chihuahua ／**チン** Japanese chin ／**ドーベルマン・ピンシェル** Doberman pinscher ／**パグ** pug ／**バセット・ハウンド** basset hound ／**ビーグル** beagle ／**プードル** poodle ／**ブルテリア** bull terrier ／**ブルドッグ** bulldog ／**ペキニーズ** Pekingese ／**ポインター** pointer ／**ボクサー** boxer ／**ポメラニアン** Pomeranian ／**ボルゾイ** Borzoi ／**マスチフ** mastiff ／**マルチーズ** Maltese ／**ヨークシャー・テリア** Yorkshire terrier ／**ラブラドル・レトリーバー** Labrador retriever

イヌイット an **Inuit** /ínjuɪt/.

いぬかき 犬掻き **dog paddle** ▶犬かきなら15メートルは泳げる I can *dog-paddle* (some) fifteen meters.

いぬき 居抜き ▶店舗を居抜きで買う *buy* a store

with all its furnishings.

いぬじに 犬死に ▶その戦いでは多くの若者たちが**犬死に**(＝無駄死に)した Many young men *lost their lives for nothing* [*died in vain*] in the battle. (➤ die like a dog とすると「惨めな死に方をする」の意になる).

いね 稲 **rice**; a **rice plant** (植物) ▶稲を刈る reap [harvest] *rice*(➤「稲刈り」は rice reaping).

いねむり 居眠り a **doze**; a **nap**(昼の) **一動 居眠りする** **doze**《off》, **nap** ▶テレビを見ながら[の前で]**居眠りする** *doze off* watching [in front of the] TV ‖ 祖父は肘掛け椅子に座って**居眠りしていた** My grandfather was *dozing* [*napping*] in the armchair. ‖ 彼は仕事中によく**居眠りする** He often *dozes* during work.

▶母は本を読んでいるうちに**居眠りを始めた** My mother *began to nod* over the book. ‖ 彼は**居眠り運転をしていて**前の車に追突した He rammed into the car ahead after *falling asleep at the wheel*. (➤ at the wheel は「運転中に」).

いのいちばん いの一番 ▶**いの一番に**早瀬さんがやって来た Hayase was *the first* to show (up). ‖ 大学に合格したら, **いの一番に**私に電話してほしい If you pass the entrance examination for the university, *the first thing* I'd like you to do is to give me a call.

いのこる 居残る ▶残業で会社に**居残る** *remain* in the office to work overtime ‖ 宿題を忘れて**居残りをさせられた** I *was forced to stay* [*I got detention*] *after school* because I'd forgotten my homework.

いのしし 猪《動物》a **wild boar**.

いのち 命 **1【生命】**(a) **life** ▶彼は交通事故で**命を落とした** He *lost his life* in a traffic accident. ‖ 彼女は絶望して自ら**命を絶った** Giving in to despair, she *took* her own *life*. ‖ ネルソン提督は祖国のために**命をささげた** Admiral Nelson *gave his life* for his country. ‖ そのワクチンのおかげで父は**命を取り留めた** That vaccine *saved* my father's *life*. / My father's *life was saved* by that vaccine. / My father *escaped death* thanks to that vaccine. ‖ 彼は溺れかかった少年の**命を救った** He *saved* the boy from drowning. (● save the boy だけで「少年の命を救う」の意) ‖ **命ばかりはお助けを！** Please just spare my *life*.

▶**命ある限り**あなたを愛します I will love you *as long as I live*. ‖ あの方は私にとって**命の恩人**です I *owe* that lady *my life*. ‖ その病気は**命に関わる**心配はなかった The disease didn't prove *fatal*. (⇀命取り) ‖ 動くと**命がないぞ** *You're dead* if you move. / Freeze, or *you're dead*! ‖ この母の形見は**命から2番目に大切**なものだ I treasure this keepsake of my mother *second only to my own life*.

2【最も大切なもの】▶音楽家にとっては耳が**命だ** Hearing is a musician's *most important asset*.

3【慣用表現】 **命あっての物種** ▶While there is life, there is hope. (➤ 英語のことわざ) **命に懸けて** ▶私は命に懸けてそれは事実でないと誓うことができる I can swear *on my life* that it is not true. **命の洗濯** ▶久しぶりに温泉に出かけて命の洗濯をした I went to a hot spring resort for the first time in a long time and *felt refreshed* (*in mind and body*). **命を懸ける** ▶彼はロボット研究に命を懸けてきた He has devoted *his whole life to* the study of robots.

いのちがけ 命懸け ▶昔は海外へ出かけるのも**命懸けだった** Traveling overseas used to involve *risking your life*. ‖ 私は**命懸けで**その川を泳ぎ渡った I swam across the river *at the risk of my life*. ‖ この仕事は**命懸けでやる**つもりです I intend to *devote all my efforts* to this job.

いのちからがら 命からがら ▶戦地から**命からがら**脱出する have a very narrow escape from a battle front ‖ 昨夜の大地震で**命からがら逃げ出した**人が大勢いた Many people had to *run for their lives* in the big earthquake last night.

いのちごい 命乞い ▶その男は何人も人を殺しておいて自分が死刑を宣告されると**命乞いをした** After killing so many people, the man *begged for his life* when he was sentenced to death.

いのちしらず 命知らず a **daredevil** ▶あの男は全くの**命知らずだ** That man is *a* real *daredevil*. ‖ この嵐に山へ登るなんて, あなたってほんとに**命知らずね** What *a daredevil* you are to be climbing a mountain in this storm!

いのちづな 命綱 a **lifeline** ▶潜水夫は**命綱**を引っ張って合図をする Deep-sea divers signal by tugging on the *lifeline*.

▶《比喩的》この連絡船が島民の**命綱だ** This ferry is the islanders' only *link* [*tie*] with the outside world.

いのちとり 命取り ▶**命取りになる**病気 a *fatal* disease ‖ 胸の傷が彼の**命取りになった** The wound in his chest *proved fatal* to him. / The wound in his chest *took his life*.

▶《比喩的》その失敗が小田氏の**命取りになるだろう** That failure will be *the end* of Mr. Oda. / That failure will *cost* Mr. Oda *his job*. (➤「失敗の代償として失職する」の意).

いのちびろい 命拾い ▶彼女はナイフを持った暴漢に襲われたが, 柔道の心得があったので**命拾いをした** Her judo experience *saved her life* when a hooligan attacked her with a knife.

いのなかのかわず 井の中の蛙 ▶ ことわざ **井の中のかわず大海を知らず** A frog in the well doesn't know the ocean. (➤日本語からの直訳) / He who stays in the valley shall never get over the hill. (➤「谷の中にとどまる者は決して山を越えることはない」の意の英語のことわざ) 《参考》このことわざを使った「あの男は井の中のかわずだ(＝世間知らずだ)」は That guy doesn't know much of the world. と表現すればよい.

☛ 井 (⇀見出語)

イノベーション (an) **innovation**.

いのり 祈り a **prayer** /preəʳ/; **grace** (食前食後の感謝の祈り) ▶平和を願って無言で**祈りをささげる** *offer a silent prayer for* peace ‖ マザー・テレサの一生は**祈りにささげられた** Mother Teresa's life was devoted to *prayer*.

▶彼女はいつも食前[就寝前]の**お祈りをします** She always *says grace* before meals [*says her prayers* before going to bed].

いのる 祈る **pray** /preɪ/ (神仏に); **wish**(幸運などを願う) ▶神の加護を**祈る** *pray for* divine protection ‖ 彼らは死者のために熱心に**祈った** They *prayed* earnestly for the dead. ‖ 彼女は夫の無事を神様に**祈った** She *prayed* to the *kami* for her husband's safety. ‖ 彼らは地球が平和でありますようにと**祈った** They *prayed* that peace might prevail on earth.

✉ **皆々様のご多幸をお祈り申し上げます** I wish you and your family every happiness. / Best

い

wishes to you and your family. ➤手紙文の末尾などに添える改まった言い方.

✉ **成功を祈る** May you succeed! ／I wish you success. ／Good luck! ➤最後の例はインフォーマルな表現で, 試合や仕事に出かける人に言う.

✉ **ご無事を祈っています** We're praying for your safety. ／Our prayers are with you. ／We wish you all the best. ➤最後の例は「ご多幸を祈っています」の意.

✉ **T大合格を祈る** I *sincerely hope* you will be accepted to [by] T University.

1**いはい 遺灰** (one's) **ashes** ▶死者の遺灰を収めたつぼ an urn containing the *ashes* of a deceased person ‖ 彼女は夫の遺灰を海にまいた She scattered her husband's *ashes* at sea.

2**いはい 位牌** an ***ihai***, a (Buddhist) memorial tablet (➤説明的な訳).

いばしょ 居場所 →居所.

いばら 茨 a **thorn** ▶《慣用表現》彼はいばらの道をたどって, ついには著名な画家となった He trod *a thorny path* [*road*] but finally became a famous painter.

いばりちらす 威張り散らす **dominate** 《over》(横暴に振る舞う)

▶部下に威張り散らす *dominate over* his [her] subordinates ／*lord it* [*run roughshod*] *over* his [her] subordinates (➤run roughshod はややインフォーマルな言い方).

いばる 威張る ▶彼は威張っている He *is acting bossy* [*self-important*]. (➤act は形容詞を従えて「…の風にふるまう」の意) ／He *is a snob*. (➤家柄や財産を鼻にかけている場合) ‖ 彼は金があるので威張っている His wealth makes him *arrogant*. (➤arrogant は「傲慢な」) ‖ おやじがここの市長だからって威張るんじゃないよ Don't *act* so *arrogant* just because your dad is the mayor of this city.

▶彼は威張った態度で話す He speaks in a *bossy* manner. ‖ あの教授の威張った態度が嫌いだ I don't like the *high-and-mighty* attitude of that professor. (➤high-and-mighty は「高慢ちきな」) ‖ 銅メダルを取ったのだから大威張りで日本に帰れるよ You won a bronze medal, so you can go back to Japan *with pride*.

いはん 違反

(a) **violation** (法律・協定などに対する積極的な) ; an **offense** (不法行為) ━ 動 **違反する** **violate** +目 ; **disobey** +目 (従わない)

▶刑法に違反する *violate* criminal law ‖ 校則に違反する *disobey* a school regulation ‖ それは法律違反だ That's *a violation* [*an offense*] against the law. ／That's *against* the law. ／You're *breaking* the law. ‖ きみの行為は協定違反だ What you did *is against* our agreement.

▶彼は交通[駐車]違反で罰金を取られた He was fined for *a traffic* [*parking*] *violation*. (➤「駐車違反」は illegal parking ともいう. 「スピード違反」は speeding) ‖ 彼らは公職選挙法違反の容疑で逮捕された They were arrested on charges of election law *violation(s)*.

‖**違反者** a violator, an offender.

いびき a **snore** ▶やかましいいびきをかく *snore* loudly ‖ ゆうべは父のいびきで一晩中眠れなかった I couldn't sleep at all last night because my father was *snoring* all night.

いびつ ▶いびつなやかん a *warped* kettle ‖ 人にけなされてばかりいると性格がいびつになる Constant criticism may *distort* the character.

いひょう 意表 ▶意表をついてバントする bunt *deceptively* ／hit a surprise bunt ‖ 彼はひょうきん者で人の意表をついて驚かせるのが好きだ He is a joker, so he likes to do *extraordinary* things to surprise people [to throw a curve].

いびょう 胃病 a **stomach disease** [**illness**].

いびる **pick on** (あら探しをする) ; **be hard on** (つらく当たる) ▶昔は嫁をいびるしゅうとめが多かったが, 最近では形勢が逆転しているらしい There once were a lot of mothers-in-law who *picked* [*were hard*] *on* their son's wives, but now it seems the tables have been turned.

いひん 遺品 ▶祖父の遺品 *things* my grandfather *left when he died* ‖ 墜落現場には遭難者の遺品が散乱していた The victims' *possessions* were scattered all around the crash site.

‖**遺品整理業者** a memento disposer.

いふ 畏怖 **awe** /ɔ:/ ▶神を畏怖する *stand in awe of* God ‖ 巨大な鯨を目の前で見て, 私は畏怖の念に打たれた I *was awe-struck* when I saw the huge whale right before my eyes.

イブ **Eve** (イベントの前夜) ▶クリスマスイブ Christmas *Eve*.

いぶかしい 訝しい ▶その知らせを聞いて彼女はいぶかしげな顔をした Her face showed that she was *doubtful* about the news.

いぶかる 訝る **doubt** +目 (違うのではないかと疑う) ; **suspect** +目 (怪しいのではないかと思う) ▶いぶかっておられるのなら, ご自分の目でお確かめください If you *doubt me*, take a look for yourself.

いぶき 息吹 ▶谷川に雪どけ水が流れ始め春の息吹が感じられる As water from melted snow begins to flow down into mountain streams, you can feel *the breath of spring*.

いふきょうだい 異父兄弟 [姉妹] a **half-brother** (男) ; **half-sister** (女) (➤明確にする必要があれば "by a different father" というがふつうは単に half-brother [-sister] という). →異母兄弟.

いふく 衣服 **clothes** /kloʊz/, **clothing** /klóʊðɪŋ/

> **《解説》** (1) clothes は「服」に当たる日常語で必要に応じて何枚かを重ね着したり, 脱いだりするものという意識がある. many [a lot of], a few, some をつけることはできるが, 数詞をつけて数えない.
> (2) clothing は「衣料品」に当たるより改まった語で, 商品として大量に生産したり販売したりする段階でよく用いる. 服以外に帽子, 靴下, 靴, 手袋など身に着けるものの総体を集合的に指す場合もある. 数えるときは an article [two articles] of clothing, または a piece [two pieces] of clothing のようにいう. clothing の代わりに, a garment, two garments という場合もある. なお, 企画・生産から販売の過程では apparel とも呼ばれる.
> (3) しばしば正式な衣服, あるいは豪華な衣服を指す語に **attire** があるが, 堅い語.

▶避難した人たちは十分な替えの衣服を持ち合わせていなかった The evacuees didn't have enough (*changes of*) *clothes*.

いぶくろ 胃袋 **the stomach** /stʌ́mək/ ▶おまえ, よくまあ, 胃袋に入るね! You can really *pack it away*! (➤pack away は「(食物などを)胃に入れる」の意のインフォーマルな表現).

いぶす 燻す **smoke** +目 (煙で曇らす ; くん製加工をする) ; **fumigate** /fjú:mɪgeɪt/ +目 (殺虫・消毒のために) ;

oxidize /ɑ́:ksɪdaɪz/ ＋目（金属を酸化させる）
▶炭は木をいぶして作る Charcoal is made by the *slow, airless burning* of wood.
‖いぶしガラス smoked glass ‖ いぶし銀 oxidized silver.

1いぶつ 異物 a **foreign body** [**substance**] ▶このオレンジジュースは変な味がする. 何か異物(＝変な物)が混じっているに違いない This orange juice tastes strange. *Something strange* must have gotten into it.

2いぶつ 遺物 a **relic**(遺品)；**remains**（遺跡）▶彼は前世紀の遺物のような男だ He looks like *a relic* of the last century.

イブニングドレス an **evening dress**.

いぶんか 異文化 a **foreign** [**different**] **culture**
▶異文化間コミュニケーション *intercultural* [*cross-cultural*] communication ‖ 異文化に接する come into contact with *a different culture* ‖ 異文化との接触は常にわが国の文化に活気を与えてきた Encounters with *foreign* [*different*] *cultures* have always (re)vitalized our own.

いぶんし 異分子 a **foreign element**；an **outsider**(部外者) ▶あいつはうちの部では異分子だ He's *an outsider* in our department. ／In our department he does*n't fit in*.

イベリア Iberia ▶イベリア半島 the *Iberian* Peninsula.

いへん 異変 something unusual [**abnormal**]（異常な出来事）；an **accident**（思わぬ出来事）；a **disaster**（災難）；a **calamity** /kəlǽməṭi/（大災害）
▶天候の異変 the *unusual* [*unseasonable*] weather ‖ 暖冬異変で各地のスキー場はがらがらだ Because of the *abnormally mild winter*, ski resorts in various regions are almost deserted.

イベント an **event**；a **show**(ショー)；a **festival**(祭り)
▶スポーツイベント a sporting *event* ‖ イベントを企画する plan [make plans for] an *event* ‖ 本日のメインイベント today's *main event*.

いぼ 疣 a **wart** /wɔ:ʳt/ ▶いぼができる get *a wart* ‖ 彼は右手にいぼがある He has *a wart* on his right hand.

いぼいぼ 疣々 ▶いぼいぼがいっぱいあるカエル a toad covered with *warts* ‖ いぼいぼのあるサンダル sandals with *nubby* [*knobby*] insoles (➤ nubby は /nʌ́bi/, knobby は /nɑ́:bi/ と発音).

いほう 違法の illegal /ɪlí:gəl/, **unlawful** ▶違法建築 an *illegally built* house ／an *illegal* construction ‖ 違法駐車 *illegal* parking (➤「違法駐車をする」は park (a car) illegally).
▶違法行為をする commit an *unlawful* [*illegal*] act ‖ 飲酒運転は違法だ Drinking and driving is *illegal*.

いほうじん 異邦人 a **foreigner**；an **alien** /éɪliən/ (➤後者は法律用語).

いぼきょうだい 異母兄弟 [**姉妹**] a **half-brother**（男）；a **half-sister**（女）(➤明確にする必要があれば "by a different mother" というがふつうは単に half-brother[-sister] という) ▶ぼくと弟は実は異母兄弟です The fact is that my younger brother and I are *half-brothers* (*by a different mother*). ／Actually, my younger brother is *my half-brother*. →異父兄弟.

いほく 以北 ▶私は仙台以北には行ったことがない I've never been *further north than* Sendai.

1**いま 今** 1【現在】**now** ▶今いちばん関心のあることは何ですか What are you most interested in *now*? ‖ 逃げるなら今だ If you're going to escape, *now is the time*. ‖ 今, 何時ですか What time is it? ／What's the time? (➤文末に now をつけるのは一般的ではない) ‖ これは今はやりの帽子です This hat is *the latest fashion craze*.
▶今から50年後の日本はどうなっているだろうか What will Japan be like fifty years *from now*? ‖ 今からでも遅くはない. 頑張りなさい It's *still* not too late. Keep at it. ‖ 今から思えばあのとき彼は死を決意していたのだ *Looking back now*, I can see that at that time he was ready to die. ‖ 私は今でも彼女を愛している I *still* love her.
▶今のイギリスの首相は誰か知ってるかい Do you know who the *present* British prime minister is? ‖ 今の若い者は手紙の書き方を知らない Young people *nowadays* [(*of*) *today*] don't know how to write letters.
▶今は春です It's spring *now*. ／We are *now* in spring. ‖ 今はナノテクノロジーの時代だ *This* is the age of nanotechnology. ‖ 今はちょうどひどく忙しい時なのです *Right now*, I'm terribly busy. ‖ 今は一年中トマトが食べられる *Today* [*Nowadays*] we can eat tomatoes all (the) year round. (➤ nowadays はやや堅い語).
2【近い未来】**right now**（今すぐに）；**right away**（すぐに；インフォーマルな言い方）▶今彼に電話をするところです *I'm just going to* give him a call. ‖《来客に》どうぞお上がりください. 今お茶を入れますから Please come in. I'll fix you some tea *right away*. (● right now とすると「今すぐに」のニュアンスが出る) ‖ 対話「朝ごはん, できたわよ」「今すぐ行くよ」"Breakfast's ready!" "*I'll be right there*!" (➤答えの文は "I'm coming!" でもよい. 相手の方へ行く場合 go は使わない).
3【近い過去】▶父はたった今帰宅しました My father's *just* come back. ／My father came back *just now*. (➤ just now は強調以外, 通例現在完了形とともには用いない) ‖ 今の人誰なの? Who was that man *just now*?
4【さらに】▶いましばらくの辛抱だ Have *a little more* patience. ／Be *a little more* patient.
☛ 今か今かと, 今頃, いまさら, いましがた, 今でこそ, 今どき, 今となっては, 今に, 今にも, 今のところ, いまひとつ, 今まで, 今や (→見出語)

2**いま 居間** a **living room**,《英また》a **sitting room**, a **lounge** /laʊndʒ/《参考》英米の家庭ではスペースの関係で居間が応接間に早変わりすることもあるため, 家族の者だけがくつろげる部屋を特に family room とか recreation room と呼ぶことがある.

いまいち ▶ 対話「このドレスどう?」「うーん, いまいちだなあ」"How do you like this dress?" "Well, *something seems to be missing*. ／Well, it *leaves something to be desired*." (➤ Well は音声としては聞き取れないくらい速く発音されることも多い). →いまひとつ.

いまいましい irritating /ɪ́rɪteɪṭɪŋ/（腹立たしい）
▶いまいましいやつ an *irritating* fellow ／a *disgusting* fellow (➤「全く嫌な」の意) ‖ あいつは本当にいまいましいやつだ He's *a* real *pain in the neck*. (➤ a pain in the neck は「いらいらさせる人[もの]」の意のインフォーマルな表現) ‖ 彼女の生意気な態度を父親はいまいましく思っている Her father *feels irritated* with her cocky attitude. ‖ 彼はいまいましげに若いカップルに目をやった He looked at the young couple *in irritation*.

いまかいまかと 今か今かと ▶初孫の誕生を今か今か

と待っています We *can hardly wait for* our first grandchild's birth. (🏺「待ち遠しくてたまらない」の意) ‖ 少年は雨の中で彼女の来るのを**今か今かと**待っていた The boy waited for her *impatiently* in the rain.／The boy waited in the rain, expecting her to show up *any minute*.

いまごろ 今頃 (about) this time
▶田辺君は**今頃**もう大阪に着いているだろう Tanabe should have arrived in Osaka *by now*. (🏺「今頃は大阪だろう」なら Tanabe should be in Osaka by now.) ‖ 毎年**今頃**は天気が変わりやすい The weather is always very changeable *about this time* of (the) year. ‖ **昨年の今頃**は水虫に悩まされていた I was suffering from athlete's foot *about this time last year*. ‖ あしたの**今頃**までには全部片づけられるでしょう By *this time tomorrow*, I will have settled everything.
▶**今頃**誰だろう Who could that be *at this hour*? ‖ **今頃**ありがとうもないもんだ It is too late for you to say, "Thank you." ‖ あきら, **今頃まで**どこに行っていたの？ Where have you been *all this time* [*all this while*], Akira?

いまさら 今更 ▶**いまさら**謝ってもだめだ It is too late *now* to apologize. (➤ now は文尾に置いてもよい) ‖ **いまさら**そんなことを言って何になる What's the use of all that *now*? ‖ 私は自分の愚かしさに**いまさらながら**あきれた I was *all the more* disgusted at my own foolishness.

いましがた 今しがた ▶彼なら**いましがた**部屋を出ていったばかりです He left the room *just a minute ago*. ‖ **いましがた**会社から帰ったところなんだ I've *just* come back from the office.

いましめ 戒め (a) warning(警告); a lesson(教訓) ▶あなたのことばを**戒め**とします I will take your words as *a warning*. ‖ その失敗は私にとってはよい**戒め**となった That failure was *a* valuable *lesson* for me.

いましめる 戒める admonish +目(諭す, 注意する); caution +目(警告する) ▶息子の不心得を**戒める** *admonish* my son for his misconduct.

いまだかつて 未だ曾て ▶アイスランドは**いまだかつて**外国に侵略されたことがない Iceland has *never* been invaded by a foreign country. ‖ ぼくは**いまだかつて**あんな美人に会ったことがない She is the most beautiful woman I (have) *ever* met.

いまだに 未だに still ▶彼は昔の恋人が忘れられず, **いまだに**独身だ He is *still* single because he cannot forget about the girl he was in love with before. ‖ 弟は**いまだに**指をしゃぶる癖が治らない My little brother *still* can't get out of a habit of sucking his fingers. ‖ その事故の原因は**いまだに**わからない The cause of the accident is *not* known *yet*.

いまでこそ 今でこそ ▶**今でこそ**笑い話だけど, あの時はどうなることかと思った We can laugh it away *now*, but at that time we were really worried about what would happen (to us).

いまどき 今どき ▶**今どき**パソコンも使えないの？ You can't even use a personal computer *in this day and age*? ‖ **今どきの**日本の子供たち *today's* Japanese children ‖ **今どき**はかまをはいて町を歩く人は少ない Few people wear hakama on the streets *nowadays*. (➤ nowadays は today より堅い語).

いまとなっては 今となっては ▶もう少し早く相談してくれればなあ. **今となっては**手遅れだ If only you had asked me for advice earlier. It's too late *now*.

いまに 今に someday(いつか); before long(そのうち)
▶**今に**私もオリンピック選手になってやる I'm going to become an Olympic athlete *someday*. ‖ **今にやつにも**天罰が下るさ He will receive proper punishment *before long*. ‖ **今に見てろよ！** *Someday* I'll show you! (➤ 文脈によっては「今に見ていろ, 俺だって」の意味になる) ‖ **今に見ろ**, きっとやってみせるから *Just wait and see*. I'll prove that I can do it. ‖ お笑い番組のくだらなさは**今に始まったことではないが**, それにしてもあきれ返る The absurdity of comedy programs *isn't something new*, yet it's really appalling.

いまにも 今にも ▶**今にも**雨が降りだしそうだ It's likely to rain *any minute now*. ‖ 彼女は**今にも**泣きだしそうだった She looked *on the verge of* tears. ‖ その老人は**今にも**倒れそうに見えた That elderly man appeared as if he *was about to* fall.

いまのところ 今のところ ▶**今のところ**(＝ちょうど今)わが社は多くの仕事を抱えている Our company has a lot of business *at the moment*. ‖ **今のところ**(＝まだ)この工場では事故は起きていない We *haven't had* any accidents at this plant *so far*. ‖ **今のところ**(＝さしあたり)会社勤めですが, 将来は教師になろうと思っています *For the time being* I am working for a company, but I want to be a teacher in the future. ‖ **今のところ**(＝これまでのところ)誰も解決策を見つけていない No one has found a solution *as yet*. (➤ as yet は通例否定文・疑問文で用いる).

いまひとつ 今一つ ▶彼の翻訳は**いまひとつ**十分でない His translation *is not quite good enough*.／His translation *leaves something to be desired*.

いまふう 今風 ▶**今風の**店 a *trendy* store ‖ **今風の**お嬢さん a young *with-it* woman.

いままで 今まで ▶**今まで**きみは何をしていたんだい？ What have you been doing *all this while* [*until now* / *so far*]? ‖ **今まで**そんな話は聞いたことがない I've *never* heard (of) such a thing *before* [*in the past*]. ‖ 富士山には**今まで**(＝過去に) 3 回登ったことがある I've climbed Mt. Fuji three times *before* [*in the past*]. (➤ 現在完了形の経験を表す肯定文では通例「今までに」の意味で ever は使えない. 次の訳例も同様) ‖ **今までに**(＝以前)何度かお会いしたことがあるかと思いますが I'm pretty sure we've met several times *before* [*in the past*]. ‖ これは**今まで**プレーした中でいちばんおもしろいゲームだ This is the most interesting game I have *ever* played. (➤ この訳例のように〈最上級＋名詞〉のあとに現在完了形の文が続く場合は「今までの」の意味で ever を使える).
▶**今までのところは**うまくいっている *So far*, so good. (➤ so far は「今までのところは」の意の副詞句) ‖ **今までのところ**何も起きていない Nothing has turned up *as yet*. (➤ as yet には「先のことはわからないが」という含みがある) ‖ **今までのところ**何も問題はなかった *Up to now* there has been no problem. (➤ up to は「…に至るまで」) ‖ **今までどおり**剣道の稽古をしてください Please practice [keep practicing] kendo *the way you always have* (*been practicing it*).

いまや 今や ▶**今や**地球上のすべての人が環境問題を真剣に考えるべき時だ *Now* is the time for every person on Earth to seriously think about environmental problems. ‖ **今や**ほとんどの会社にコンピュータが導入されている *Nowadays* almost all companies utilize computers. ‖ 観客は舞台の幕が開くのを**今や遅しと待っていた** The audience *waited impatiently* for the curtain to go up.

いまわ 今わ ▶**いまわの際に**言い残す leave words *in one's dying moments*.

いまわしい 忌まわしい ▶あんな忌まわしい事件など思い出したくもない I don't want to recall that *horrible* [*awful*] incident.

いみ 意味 1【意味内容】(a) **meaning**（伝えようとする）; a **sense**（語・句がもつ個々の）; an **implication**, a **connotation**（含み, ニュアンス; connotation は単語に関していう）一動 意味する **mean** +目, **imply** +目 ▶この語はどういう意味か教えてください Could you please tell me the *meaning* of this word？／Could you please tell me what this word *means*？‖ take という語にはたくさんの意味がある The word 'take' has many *meanings* [*senses*]. ‖ mistress という語には悪い意味がある The word 'mistress' has bad *connotations*. ‖ 意味がわからなければ辞書で調べなさい Look up the word in the dictionary if you don't understand *what it means*.

▶彼の手紙は意味が全くわからない I can't make out *what* his letter *says*.（➤ make out は「理解する」）‖ 対話「きみは21世紀型の美人だね」「それ, どういう意味ですか」"You're a 21st century type beauty." "*What do you mean* by that？"／"*What are you implying* by that？"（➤ 反発して「それ, どういう意味？」と言うときもこれでよい）.

▶ある意味では彼の言い分は正しいかもしれない He may be right *in a sense* [*in a way*]. ‖ そんな意味のことを彼に言ったかもしれない I may have said *something like that* [*to that effect*] to him.（➤ to that effect は「そんな趣旨の」）‖ 母は意味ありげに私を見た My mother gave me a *meaningful* look.

2【意義】(a) **meaning**, (a) **significance**; **point**（効用, 利益）; a **sense**（理由, 価値）▶私は50を過ぎて人生の意味がやっとわかってきた When I passed fifty, I came to understand the *meaning* of life. ‖ 彼の研究はがん治療にとって非常に重要な意味をもつ His research has great *significance* in cancer treatment.

▶健康でなければ金など意味がない Money *means nothing* if you are not healthy. ‖ 今さらこんな本を読んだって意味がないよ *There isn't much point* in reading these books now. ‖ ほんの数日の禁煙なんておよそ意味がないね It's *pointless* to give up smoking only for a few days. ‖ あなたが死んでしまったら生きてゆく意味がないわ My life will be *meaningless* if you die. ‖ これはこれで意味のある仕事だ This is, in itself, very *meaningful* work.

‖意味論 semantics.

☞ 無意味（→見出語）

いみあい 意味合い (a) **meaning**（意味）; (an) **implication**（含みの意味）; a **shade of meaning**（ニュアンス）▶"Strike while the iron is hot." と「鉄は熱いうちに打て」はだいぶ意味合いが違う "Strike while the iron is hot." and "Tetsu-wa-atsuiuchini-ute" have a considerable difference of *meaning*.

いみきらう 忌み嫌う **abhor** /əbhɔ́ːʳ/; **loathe** /loʊð/（嫌悪する）.

いみことば 忌みことば a **taboo** (**word**).

いみじくも ▶先ほどあなたがいみじくもおっしゃったとおり, … as you *aptly* said a short while ago, … .

いみしんちょう 意味深長 ▶彼が別れ際に私に言ったことばは意味深長だった His parting words to me were *full of meaning*. →いわく.

イミテーション (an) **imitation** ▶イミテーションのルビー an *imitation* ruby ‖ このダイヤ, 本物みたいだけど実はイミテーションなのよ This diamond seems genuine, but in fact it is *an imitation* [*a fake*].

いみょう 異名 ▶その実力者は「闇将軍」の異名をとった That kingpin *was dubbed* the 'Shadow Shogun.'（➤ dub は「…にあだ名をつける」）.

いみん 移民 an **immigrant** /ímɪgrənt/（外国からの）; an **emigrant** /émɪgrənt/（外国への）一動 移民する **emigrate**《from》（…から外国へ）; **immigrate**《to》（外国から…へ）

▶日本からカナダへ移民した人たちの歴史はあまり知られていない Few people know about the history of those who *emigrated from* Japan to Canada.

‖不法移民 an illegal [undocumented] immigrant（➤ undocumented は「有効な書類を所持していない」の意で, 主に移民に同情的な立場の人が用いる; 他国への移民は emigrant）.

いむしつ 医務室 a **doctor's** [**medical**] **room**; a **sick bay**（船などの）▶医務室に行っていいですか Can I *go to the doctor's room*？

イメージ 1【心に思い浮かべる姿・形など】an **image** /ímɪdʒ/ ▶アトリエで目を閉じると美しい古城のイメージが浮かんできた When I closed my eyes in my studio, *an image* of a beautiful old castle came into my mind.

2【印象】an **image**; an **impression**（印象）▶その歌手に対する私のイメージと伸子さんのそれとは少し違う My *image* of that singer is a bit different from Nobuko's. ‖ 彼には教師というイメージは全くない He does not give the slightest *impression* of being a teacher.

▶父の会社はイメージアップを図っている My father's company is trying to *improve its image*. ‖ 社名のロゴの変更は会社のイメージアップにつながった The change in the corporate logo *improved* the company's *image*. ‖ スキャンダルはその女優のイメージダウンにつながった The scandal *hurt* the actress's *reputation*. ／The scandal *tarnished* the actress's *image*.（➤ tarnish は「(光沢・つやのある物)を曇らせる」の意で, ここではその比喩的用法として用いている）

▶彼女は髪をショートボブにしてイメージチェンジした She cut her hair into a short bob to *change her look*(*s*).（➤「見た感じを変える」の意; 人・企業・ブランドなどのイメージの作り替えは an image makeover, あるいは単に a makeover）.

‖イメージガール a poster girl.

> **危ないカタカナ語✹ イメージ**
> 1 日本語では「人に与える印象」の意味で使うことが多いので, image のほかに impression も使える.
> 2「イメージを良くする」の意味で「イメージアップ」というが, これは和製語. improve one's image とか polish one's image のようにいう必要がある. また,「イメージダウン」「イメージチェンジ」も同様で, 前者は damage one's image, 後者は change one's look(s) などとする.

いも 芋 a **potato**（ジャガイモ）; a **sweet potato**（サツマイモ）; a **taro**（サトイモ）▶芋掘りに行く go out to *dig for potatoes*.

▶《慣用表現》その日の三浦海岸は芋を洗うような混雑だった On that day, Miura Beach *was packed with people*. ‖ すりの一味は芋づる式に捕まった A band of pickpockets were arrested *one after another*.（➤ one after another は「次々と」）.

いもうと 妹 a **younger sister**

い

◀解説▶ 英語では younger sister の younger はやや改まった場合以外は省くのがふつう. 改まらない日常会話では little sister ともいう. いちばん下の妹は youngest sister のほか, baby sister, kid sister などともいう.

▶いちばん下の妹 my youngest *sister* ‖きみの妹さん, 何歳なの？ How old is your *sister*?

いもの 鋳物 a **casting**
‖**鋳物工場** a foundry ‖**鋳物製品** castings.

いもむし 芋虫 a **caterpillar** /kǽṭəʳpɪləʳ/.

いもり《動物》a **newt**; an **eft**（未成熟の）.

いもん 慰問 ▶私たちは火事で焼け出された人々を**慰問する**ために公民館を訪れた We visited the public hall to *console* the people who had lost their homes in the fire. ‖子供たちは被災地の人々に**慰問の手紙**を出した Those children sent *letters of sympathy* to the people of the disaster area.

[1]**いや 1【否定】no** ▶あの映画は 5 回, いや 6 回は見た I have seen that film five, *no*, six times at least. ‖ 対話 「おけがはありませんでしたか」「いや全然. どうもありがとう」“Did you hurt yourself?” “*No*, not at all, thanks.” ‖ 対話 「英語が上手ですね」「いやいや」“You speak good English.” “*Not* good enough.”（➤英語では謙遜せず “Thank you.” と答えるのがふつう）‖ 対話 「どこへ行くんだい」「いや別に」“Where are you going?” “*Well*, nowhere in particular.”

2【感嘆して】▶いや, 驚いたね！ *Now*, that's a surprise! ‖いやあ, 彼女, きれいだね！ *Gee*, she is so pretty!（➤ gee /dʒiː/ は感嘆・驚きなどを表すが Jesus の略と考えられており, これを好まない人も多い）‖いやあ, きょうは寒いね！ *Boy*［*Man*］, is it cold today!（➤ is it と語順を逆にして感嘆を強めている）.

[2]**いや 嫌 1【不愉快だ】**▶下宿生活なんて**嫌だ** I *don't like* living in boardinghouses.（「好きではない」の意の一般的な言い方. 次例の hate はこれより強い嫌悪感を表し, 敵意や悪意が含まれる）‖あいつの顔は見るのも**嫌だ** I *hate* the very sight of him. ／The very sight of him *makes me sick*. ‖こんな寒い日に散歩に出るのは**嫌だ**（＝出たくない）I *don't want* to go out for a walk on a cold day like this. ‖そんな悲しい話は思い出すのも**嫌だ**（＝耐えられない）I *can't bear* even to think of that sad story.

▶ああいう持って回った言い方って**いやーね** That roundabout way of talking *turns me off*.（➤ turn off は「うんざりさせる」）‖彼は**嫌な顔ひとつせず**私の言うことを聞いてくれた He listened to me *without showing the least sign of annoyance*［*unwillingness*］. ‖何て**嫌な男なんだ** What an *awful* man (he is)! ‖あいつは本当に**嫌なやつだ** He's an absolute *pest*.（➤子供について言うことが多い；インフォーマル）.

▶他人の陰口を聞くことほど**嫌なことはない** Nothing is as *disgusting*［*unpleasant*］as hearing someone talk about others behind their backs.（➤ disgusting は「むかむかするような」）‖**嫌な奴が来た** *Look what the cat dragged in!*（➤「猫が引きずって来た（あの薄汚い）ものをご覧」の意だが, 仲間うちで, 当人に聞こえないように言う）‖ 対話 「ねえ, お茶でも飲まない?」「**嫌よ!**」“How about a cup of tea?” “*No, thanks!*”

2【悪い】▶彼はそれを聞いて**嫌な笑い方**をした (On) hearing it, he laughed in an *ugly* way. ‖この**嫌な**臭い何？ What's this *unpleasant*［*bad* ／*awful* ／ *horrible*］smell? ‖家を出るとき**嫌な予感**がした When I left home, I felt like something *bad* would happen［I felt a foreboding］.（➤ foreboding は「胸騒ぎ」）.

3【「嫌になる」の形で】▶考えれば考えるほど転校が**嫌になった** The more I thought of my transfer, *the less* I *liked* it. ‖勉強なんか本当に**嫌になった** I'*m* so *sick and tired of* studying. ‖あなた, もう私が**嫌になった**ようね You seem to have *lost interest in* me. ‖なぜだかあの人と結婚するのが**嫌になった** I don't know why, but I *have become reluctant to* marry him.

いやいや 嫌嫌 unwillingly（不満ながら）; **reluctantly**（気乗りはしないが）▶彼は**いやいや**歯医者へ行った He went to the dentist's *unwillingly*［*reluctantly*］. ‖私はきみに**いやいや**仕事をやってもらおうとは思わない I won't force you to work (*if you don't want to*).

▶知らない人に抱かれて, その赤ん坊は**いやいやをした** The baby *showed unwillingness* to be held by a stranger. ／The baby *was afraid* to be held by a stranger.

いやおうなしに 否応なしに ▶彼女は**いやおうなしに**その仕事を毎日しなければならない *Whether she likes it or not*, she has to do the job every day. ‖父親は**いやおうなしに**息子を医学部へ進ませた The father forced his son to go to medical school (*whether he wanted to or not*).（「A（人）に…することを強制する」と考えて force A to do の構文を用いるとよい; force 自体が「いやおうなしに」の含みをもっている）.

いやがうえにも いやが上にも ▶聖火の到着でオリンピックムードは**いやが上にも**盛り上がった With the arrival of the Olympic Torch, the expectant atmosphere for the Olympics has become *all the more* intense.

いやがらせ 嫌がらせ harassment /hərǽsmənt/
▶性的な**嫌がらせ** sexual *harassment* ‖**嫌がらせの手紙** *hate* mail ‖それは明らかに**嫌がらせ**だよ That's evidently *harassment*. ‖わざわざ家の前で大声で話すとは**嫌がらせ**としか思えない They must be *trying to harass*［*annoy*］us by talking in such a loud voice in front of our house, of all places.（➤ annoy は「（つまらないことで）人を不愉快にさせる」）‖きょうも**嫌がらせの電話**がきた I got *a nuisance*［*prank*］(*telephone*) *call* today again.（➤ nuisance /njúːsəns/ は「迷惑」の意）.

いやがる 嫌がる don't like +㊐, **dislike** +㊐, **hate** +㊐（➤ dislike は not like よりも強く, hate よりも弱い）▶彼は他人のために働くのを**嫌がる** He *does not like* to work for other people. ／He *dislikes* working for other people. ‖彼女は人前でスピーチをするのをとても**嫌がる** She *hates* to make speeches in public. ‖彼女は情報の提供を**嫌がった** She *was unwilling*［*reluctant*］to give any information. ‖母親は**嫌がる**子供を無理やり幼稚園へ連れていった The mother dragged her *unwilling* child to kindergarten.

いやく 意訳 (a) **free translation** ▶この翻訳は**意訳し過ぎ**て原文とは意味がずれているよ This *translation was done too freely* and deviates in meaning from the original. ‖これは**意訳し過ぎ**だ This *translation is too free*.

いやくきん 違約金 a **penalty** /pénlti/ (**fee**) ▶ご都合で解約される場合は**違約金**を頂きます Should you choose to cancel the contract, *a penalty fee* will be charged.

いやくひん 医薬品 **pharmaceuticals** /fɑːˈməsjúːṭɪkəls/, **medical supplies** ▶難民キャンプに医薬品を送る send *medical supplies* to a refugee camp.

いやけ 嫌気 ▶彼女はその会社に嫌気がさして辞めた She quit the company because she *got sick of* [*disgusted with*] it.

いやし 癒やし **healing**; **comfort**(安らぎ) ▶音楽の癒やしの力 the *healing power* of music ‖ 我々はつらいときには癒やしを必要とする We need *comfort* at difficult times. ‖ 癒やしの音楽 *soothing* music.

いやしい 卑しい **greedy**(食い意地の張った); **vulgar**(下品な); **mean**(けちな); **humble**(身分が低い) ▶品性の卑しい人 a *vulgar* person ‖ 岩崎弥太郎は卑しい身分の出であった Iwasaki Yataro came from *humble* beginnings. ‖ あいつは金に卑しいやつだ He is *mean* about money matters.

いやしくも ▶いやしくも教師ならそんなことはすべきではない No teacher *worthy of* the name should do that.

いやしむ 卑しむ **despise**(軽蔑する) ▶卑しむべき残酷な行為 a *despicable* act of cruelty.

いやす 癒やす **heal**(けがや心の傷を); **quench** /kwentʃ/(喉や心の渇きを); **cure**(病気を) ▶心を癒やしてくれる音楽 *soothing* music (➤ healing music は「治癒効果のある音楽」) ‖ 時は心の傷を癒やすという They say (that) time *heals* a broken heart. 《参考》Time heals all wounds. (時は傷を全て癒やす) や Time is a [the] great healer. (時は(悲しみの)大いなる癒やし手である) という英語のことわざがある. ‖ 彼女はアイスコーヒーを飲んで喉の渇きを癒やした She *quenched her thirst* with a glass of iced coffee.

いやでも 嫌でも ▶この仕事が片づくまでは嫌でもこの会社を辞められない *No matter what*, I can't quit this company until I get this project completed.

いやというほど 嫌と言う程 ▶机の角で嫌と言うほどかかとをぶつけた I banged my heel *really* hard against the corner of the desk. ‖ 母から同じ話を嫌と言うほど聞かされた My mother *forced* me *to* listen to the same story. / My mother *bent my ear* with the same story. (● 前者は「A (人)に無理やり…させる」と考えて force A to do の構文を, また後者は「(愚痴などを)A (人)がうんざりするほど話して聞かせる」の意の慣用句 bend A's ear をそれぞれ用いたもの).

いやに **extraordinarily** /ɪkstrɔ́ːˈdnèrəli/ (異常なほど); **unusually**(いつになく); **awfully**(ひどく) ▶手続きはいやに複雑だ The proceedings are *extraordinarily* complex. ‖ あの新転校生は女の子たちにいやにもてる That new transfer student is *extraordinarily* popular with the girls. ‖ 1月にしてはいやに暖かい It's *unusually* [*unpleasantly*] warm for January. ‖ いやに(=ばかに)暑いね It's *awfully* [*terribly*] hot, isn't it?

いやはや ▶いやはや(驚いた)! *Well, I never!* (➤ well と never に強勢を置く) ‖ あいつがP大学に受かったとは, いやはや驚いたね It's *really* surprising he got into P University.

イヤホーン an **earphone**; an **earbud**(耳に入れるより小型の) (➤ともに通例複数形) ▶イヤホーンで音楽を聴く listen to music with *earphones*.

いやみ 嫌味 a **sarcastic remark**(嫌みなことば); a **disagreeable remark**(不愉快なことば); a **snide remark**(遠回しにけなすようなことば) ▶上司に向かって嫌みを言う *make a sarcastic* [*disagreeable* / *snide*] *remark* to one's superior ‖ 彼女のことばは嫌みたっぷりだった Her remark *was full of sarcasm* [*snark*]. ‖ 私, あの人嫌い. いつも友だちに嫌み言ってるから I don't like that guy. He's always *making snarky* [*snide*] *comments* to his friends. ‖ 嫌みな上司にねちねちやられた I got chewed out by my *grouchy* boss. (➤ grouchy は「文句たらたらの」, chew out は「さんざんに絞る」).

いやらしい 嫌らしい **dirty** (下品な); **obscene** /əbsíːn/ (卑わいな); **disgusting** (むかつくような); **indecent** /ɪndíːsənt/ (汚らわしい) ▶上司は好んで嫌らしい冗談を言う My boss loves to crack *dirty* jokes. ‖ あのおじさん, エッチな雑誌を見てにたにた笑ってるわ. 何て嫌らしいんでしょう The man is smirking over a dirty magazine. How *disgusting*! ‖ その女優は嫌らしいほど(=出し過ぎなくらい)胸元を出したドレスを着ていた The actress was wearing a dress that showed her breasts *to an indecent extent*. ‖ その男は嫌らしい目つきで私を見た That man *leered at* [*ogled*] me. ▶あの先生は嫌らしい問題を出す That teacher always asks *trick* questions. (➤ trick question は「人を迷わせる問題」).

イヤリング an **earring**; a **pierced earring**(ピアス) (➤ともに通例複数形で) ▶イヤリングを着ける put on (a pair of) *earrings*.

いよいよ **1**【ますます】▶話はいよいよおもしろくなってきた The story got *more and more* interesting. ‖ 顔を赤らめたところを見るといよいよ怪しい Now that I've seen you blush, I'm getting *more* suspicious. ‖ 雪はいよいよ激しくなってきた It is snowing *harder and harder* [*harder than ever*]. ‖ 久美子はいよいよ美しくなった Kumiko has become *more* beautiful *than ever*.

2【ついに】**at last**(➤長い時間がかかって[待って]「とうとう」; よい結果に用いることが多い); **finally**(最終的に) ▶いよいよ入試の時がやって来た The entrance exam(ination) season has come *at last*. ‖ 合格発表はいよいよあすだ The results of the examination will *finally* be announced tomorrow. ‖ 次はいよいよ私の番のようだ It looks like it's *finally* my turn.

3【せっぱ詰まったとき】▶彼女はいよいよというときになってためらった *At the last moment* she hesitated. ‖ いよいよとならないと(=せきたてられないと)書き始めない作家が多い Many writers never start writing *unless* [*until*] *they are pressed*. (➤「せっぱ詰まったとき」を表す when push comes to shove という熟語を用いてもよい).

¹いよう 異様な **strange**(変わった); **weird** /wɪəˈd/ (気味の悪い) ▶会場は一種異様な雰囲気に包まれていた A *strange* [*weird*] atmosphere settled over the meeting hall.

²いよう 偉容 ▶新宿にはいくつもの高層ビルが偉容を誇っている In Shinjuku a number of high-rise buildings reach *grandly* [*magnificently*] into the sky.

いよく 意欲 (a) **will**(意志); (a) **desire** (欲望); (an) **eagerness**(…したい[を得たい]という熱意); (an) **enthusiasm**(…に対する熱意) ▶働く意欲を失う lose the *will* to work ‖ 勉強意欲旺盛な生徒 an *eager* student ‖ あの留学生たちは勉強意欲が旺盛だ Those students from overseas *are very eager* to study. ‖ 2学期になってようやく英語の勉強に対する意欲が湧いてきた It was during the second term that I finally found *a desire* to study English. ‖ 彼女は英語を身につけたいという生徒たちの意欲をかきたてるすべを知っている She knows how to increase her students'

eagerness to learn English.
▶荻野は3回目のオリンピックに**意欲満々**であった Hagino was *full of enthusiasm* for his third Olympics. ‖この企画には全員意欲的に取り組んでいるようです It seems that everybody *is working earnestly* on this project. ／It looks as if everyone *is fired up* about this project. (➤後者はインフォーマルな言い方).
‖**意欲作**(力作) an ambitious work ; a tour de force /tʊ̀əʳ də fɔ́ːʳs/.

1**いらい 依頼** 1【願い, 頼み】(a) **request** 一動 **依頼する ask** +目, **request** +目 (➤後者のほうが形式ばった語で, 丁寧に頼む感じが強い) ▶私は木田氏の**依頼**でその記事を書いた I wrote that article at Mr. Kida's *request* [at the *request* of Mr. Kida].

【文型】
人(A)に…するように依頼する
request A **to** do
request that A (**should**) do

▶我々は専門家にそのつぼの鑑定を**依頼した** We *requested* an expert *to* assess the value of the vase. ‖私は助手に代わりをしてくれるよう**依頼した** I *requested* [*asked*] my assistant *to* take my place.
▶ひとつご依頼申し上げたいことがあるのですが Could I ask you a favor? ／May I ask a favor of you? (➤後者は堅い表現で, 日本語により近い ; 「お願いがあるんだけど」に相当するのは Will you [Can you] do me a favor?).
‖**依頼状** a letter of request, a written request.
2【頼ること】▶きみは依頼心が強すぎる You *depend* [*rely*] *too much on others*. ／You *expect too much of others*. (➤「他人を当てにしすぎる」の意).

2**いらい 以来** **since, ever since** (➤後者は強調形) ▶私はそれ以来いとこに会っていない I haven't seen my cousin (*ever*) *since*. ‖私は昨年の夏以来祖父母に会っていない I have not seen my grandparents *since* last summer. ‖やあ健二君, 久しぶり. 大学以来会わなかったね Hello, Kenji. I haven't seen you *since* we were in college. ‖父の死以来5年になります It has been five years *since* my father died. (➤It is five years since ... は《米・インフォーマル》ではあまり用いられない) ／Five years have [has] passed *since* my father died. (➤前の文よりも堅い表現).

いらいら **irritation**(腹立たしさ) ; **nervousness** (神経過敏) ; **frustration** (欲求不満) 一動 **いらいらする get irritated, get nervous** ▶赤ん坊の泣きわめく声を聞くといらいらする That baby's crying irritates [annoys] me. ‖その男優は開演を前にしていらいらしていた The actor *was nervous* before the opening of the play. ‖一日中家に閉じこもっているといらいらする It's really *frustrating* being stuck in the house all day.
▶我々はバスの到着をいらいらしながら待った We waited *impatiently* for the arrival of the bus. ‖そんなにいらいらしないでよ Don't *be* so *nervous* [*edgy*]! (➤edgy は「(人・気分などが)ぴりぴりして」) ‖好きな音楽を聴いたらやっといらいらが治まった I was finally able to *calm down* after listening to my favorite music.

いらか 甍 a **roof tile**(瓦) ; a **tiled roof**(屋根).

イラク Iraq 一形 **イラクの Iraqi** /ɪrάːki/
‖**イラク人** an Iraqi [複 Iraqis].

イラスト an **illustration** /ìləstréɪʃən/ (➤説明図も含む) ; a **picture**(絵) ▶本にイラストを入れる *illustrate* a book (➤「イラストの入った本」は illustrated book ; illustrate は /ɪ́ləstreɪt/ と発音) ‖この本はイラストが多くてわかりやすい This book is full of *illustrations* and easy to understand.

イラストレーター an **illustrator** /ɪ́ləstreɪṭəʳ/ (➤プロであることを明確にするのなら professional illustrator とする).

いらだたしい 苛立たしい irritating ▶あいつは生返事ばかりで, 何ともいらだたしい He never really answers anything I ask him—it's really *irritating*! ‖私はその生徒のことをいらだたしく思った I *felt irritated* with the student.

いらだち 苛立ち irritation ; frustration(欲求不満).

いらだつ 苛立つ get irritated ; get worked up, work oneself up(徐々に興奮する) ▶彼は研究が計画どおりに進まないので次第にいらだってきている He's *getting irritated* because his research isn't progressing as planned. ‖彼はささいなことでいらだつ He *gets worked up* [*works himself up*] about trivial things.

いらっしゃい ▶こちらへいらっしゃい (*Come*) this way, please. ‖またいらっしゃいね Please *come* again. ‖《歓迎して》やあみんないらっしゃい *Welcome*, friends! ‖さあいらっしゃい. サバの大安売りだよ *Walk up, walk up*. Get your mackerel here cheap! (➤Walk up, walk up! は店での呼び込みの決まり文句).
▶《店で》いらっしゃいませ *Hello!* Can I help you, sir [ma'am ／madam]? (➤答えには Yes, I think so. とか, No, thank you, I'm just looking (around). (ちょっと見てるだけですから)などと言う) ‖《ホテルなどで》いらっしゃいませ *Good morning* [*afternoon*] (, *sir* [*ma'am* ／*madam*]).

いらっしゃる 1【「行く」「来る」の尊敬語】▶ようこそいらっしゃいました *Thanks for coming.* ／*It's really nice of you to come!* (➤この2つは誘いに応じて相手が来てくれた場合) ／*Welcome.* ／*Nice to see you!* ‖あなたもいらっしゃいますか *Are* you *going* [*coming*], too? ‖その映画へはいらっしゃいましたか *Have* you *been to* the movie? ‖《飲み屋などで》佐藤さんは近頃よくいらっしゃいますよ Mr. Sato often *drops in* these days. (➤「立ち寄る」の意).
2【「いる」「です」の尊敬語】▶田中さんはいらっしゃいますか *Is* Mr. Tanaka *at home* [*in* ／*home*]? (➤in, home はくだけた表現).
▶小野田さんでいらっしゃいますね (You *are*) Mr. [Mrs. ／Miss ／Ms.] Onoda, I believe.

いらぬ 要らぬ ▶いらぬお世話だ *None of your business.*

いられない ▶去年亡くなった妹のことを思わずにはいられない I *can't stop thinking of* my sister who passed away last year.

【文型】
…せずにはいられない
can't help doing
can't help but do
➤前者は「どうしても…してしまう」, 後者は「…してしまうほかない」のニュアンス

▶彼の滑稽な服装を見たら**笑わずにはいられなかった** I *couldn't help laughing* [*couldn't help but laugh*] at his funny outfit.
▶これだけ痛めつけられてはもう**黙ってはいられない** I *can't put up with* [*endure*] this kind of mistreatment any longer. (●「我慢できない」と考えて can't put up with を用いるか, その堅い言い方である can't en-

dure を用いる) ‖ 来年は入試だ. もうぐずぐずしてはいられない I *can't procrastinate any longer*. The entrance exams are coming up next year.

イラン **Iran** 一形 **イランの** **Iranian** /ɪréɪniən/
‖**イラン語** Iranian ‖ **イラン人** an Iranian.

いり **入り** ▶きょうは(観客の)入りがよい We have a good sized *audience* today. ‖ バーゲンの初日は特に客の入りがよい Stores get especially *big crowds of customers* on the opening day of sales.
▶日の入りは何時ですか When does *the sun set*? ‖ ことしは梅雨入りが遅い The rainy season is late *coming* this year.
▶ブランデー入りのチョコレート chocolates *with* brandy *filling*.
▶彼の父親は大学教授を辞めて政界入りした His father quit his job as a university professor and *entered the world of politics* [*the political world*].

いりえ **入り江** an **inlet**; a **cove** (小湾).

いりぐち (…の)**入り口** an **entrance** 《to》; a **door** 《to》 (戸口) ▶ホワイトハウスの入り口 the (main) *entrance to* the White House ‖ 診察室の入り口 the *door to* the doctor's office ‖ 入り口はどこですか Where is the *entrance*? ‖ アイスクリーム売りのおじさんが公園の入り口に居た The ice-cream man was at the *park gate*. ‖ 《掲示》入り口 Entrance / 《英まれ》Way In.

いりくむ **入り組む** ▶入り組んだ海岸線 a *rugged* coastline / a *ria* coastline (➤ rugged は /rʌ́ɡɪd/, ria は /ríːə/ と発音) ‖ 入り組んだ事情 *complicated* [*convoluted*] circumstances.

いりたまご **煎り卵** **scrambled eggs.**

イリノイ **Illinois** /ìlənɔ́i/ (アメリカ中部の州; 略 IL, Ill).

いりひ **入り日** **the setting sun.**

いりびたる **入り浸る** ▶美奈子は修に夢中で, 最近は彼のアパートに入り浸っている Minako is so crazy about Osamu that she *spends most of her time* at his apartment these days. ‖ 最近彼女の夫は新宿のあるバーに入り浸っている Recently, her husband *has been spending* his evenings at a bar in Shinjuku.

いりまじる **入り交じる** **mingle** ▶喜びと悲しみの入り交じった複雑な気持ちだった I had *mingled* feelings of joy and sorrow.

いりみだれる **入り乱れる** ▶敵味方入り乱れて激しく戦った Both sides fought *in great confusion*.

いりゅう **慰留** ▶A氏の辞任を慰留する (*try to*) *persuade* Mr. A *not to* resign from (his) position [post] (➤「慰留した」を persuaded とすると「慰留がうまくいった」の意になるので注意. →説得).

いりゅうひん **遺留品** **things left behind** ▶犯人の遺留品として小さなバッジが押収された The police seized a small badge *which* they thought might have *been left behind* by the suspect.

いりよう **入り用** ▶ほかに入り用なものがあればおっしゃってください Please let me know if there's anything else (that) you *need*.

1**いりょう** **衣料** **clothing** (衣料品); **clothes** (服; 日常語) →衣服 ▶春物[秋物]衣料 spring [fall] *clothes* ‖ 地震および津波被災地は食糧も衣料も不足していた The earthquake and tsunami-devastated areas were in need of food and *clothing*.
‖**衣料品店** a clothing store.

2**いりょう** **医療** **medical care** [**treatment**] ▶人は皆できるだけよい医療を受けようとする People try to get the best *medical care* possible.
‖**医療過誤** medical malpractice; a medical error (➤ 後者は「医療ミス」に相当する一般語) ‖ **医療機関** a medical institution ‖ **医療機器** a medical instrument ‖ **医療器具** medical apparatus; a medical tool [implement] ‖ **医療行為** (a) medical practice ‖ **医療従事者** a healthcare worker ‖ **医療センター** a medical [health] center ‖ **医療費** medical expenses ‖ **医療崩壊** the collapse of the medical care system ‖ **医療保険制度** a medical insurance system.

> **逆引き熟語 ○○医療**
> **緩和医療** palliative care / **救急医療** emergency medical care / (**高度**) **先進医療** (highly) advanced medical care [technology] (➤ 研究開発段階にあるようなものを含めていうのなら後者が適当) / **再生医療** regenerative medicine / **終末期医療** terminal care / **代替医療** alternative medicine

いりょく **威力** **power** ▶あのボクサーのパンチにはすごい威力がある That boxer's punches are very *powerful*. / That boxer's punches *pack a lot of power*. ‖ 津波の威力を思い知らされた It sank in (to me) *how strong* a tunami could be. ‖ 核兵器の威力は破壊的だ Nuclear weapons are *highly destructive*.

1**いる** **要る** **need** +目 (欠けているものを必要とする); **take** +目 (日数・人数・労力などを); **cost** +目 (金・費用などを) ▶私には手伝いが要る I *need* a helping hand. ‖ 要るだけ持っていきなさい Take all you *need*. ‖ それは要らないから好きなように処分してくれ I *don't need* it, so dispose of it as you like. ‖ 要らないものは捨てなさい Throw away *what you don't need* [*unnecessary things*].
▶その仕事には5人要る That job *takes* five people. ‖ 1冊の辞書を編むには大変な金が要る Compiling a dictionary *costs* a lot of money. ‖ コンピュータのプログラムを組むには忍耐力が要る Computer programming *requires* patience. (➤ require は need の堅い語だが, 話しことばでも用いられる) ‖ 外国に行くにはパスポートが要るよ You *need* a passport to go abroad. ‖ 大学の入学手続きに要る(=必要な)書類が全部整った I have gotten all the *necessary* papers ready for my college enrollment. ‖ 対話「お菓子食べる?」「要らない」"Would you like some cake?" "*No, thanks*."

2**いる** **居る** **1**【**存在する, 生存する**】**be** ▶鳥籠の中にオウムが1羽居る *There is* a parrot in the cage. ‖ あのおりの中に何が居るの? What'*s* in that cage? ‖ 昔々あるところにひとりの王様が居ました. そしてその王様には大変美しい娘が居ました Once upon a time, *there lived* a king whose daughter was very beautiful. ‖ うちの村には今でもキツネが居る Foxes *are* still *found* in our village. ‖ 校長先生の居るところでは, 先生たちは愛想がいい The teachers act nice when the principal *is around* [*present*]. ‖ 神様が居ることを信じますか Do you *believe in* God? (● 一般の欧米人にとっての神は唯一絶対神だから「神の存在を信じる」は believe in God (in がなければ「神のことばを信じる」)となるが, 日本を含め多神教の国では believe in the gods [the Kami] と訳すのが適当). →神.
2【**滞在する, 居住する**】**be**; **stay** (滞在する) ▶きょう

い

の夜うちに居る? Will you *be* [《英》*be* at] home tonight ? ‖ きのうはとても疲れていたので一日中家に居ました Since I was so tired yesterday, I *stayed* at home all day long. ‖ 会社に木村さんを訪ねたが居なかった I tried to meet with Mr. Kimura's office, but he *wasn't there* [*wasn't in*]. ‖ 公園には誰も居なかった *Nobody was* in the park. ／*There was no one* in the park. ‖ 毎年夏は宮城のおばのところに居ます I *stay* with my aunt in Miyagi every summer. ／I *spend* every summer at my aunt's house in Miyagi.

3【所有する】have ▶大輔にはガールフレンドが居る Daisuke *has* a girlfriend. ‖ あの家には猛犬が居る They *have* a fierce dog (at that house).

4【「…している」の形で】 ▶スケートをしていて, 転んで足を折った I fell and broke my leg *while* (I *was*) *skating*.

☛ 居ない, 居なくなる (→見出語)

³**いる 煎る・炒る roast** +⊜ ; **scramble** +⊜ (卵を) ▶コーヒー豆[ピーナツ]を煎る *roast* coffee beans [peanuts] ‖ 卵を煎る *scramble* eggs.

⁴**いる 射る shoot** +⊜ (矢・鳥を) ; **hit** +⊜ (的を) ▶男は飛んでいる鳥に矢を射た The man *shot* an arrow at a flying bird. (➤ 当たったかは不明) ‖ 与一の矢は扇を射た Yoichi's arrow *hit* the fan. (➤ 扇に当たった).

いるい 衣類 clothes, clothing →衣服 ▶そろそろ冬物の衣類を出さなくっちゃね It's about time we got our winter *clothes* ready.

いるか 海豚《動物》a **dolphin** ; a **porpoise** /pɔ́ːrpəs/ (ネズミイルカ) ▶イルカを調教する train *a dolphin*. →鯨.

いるす 居留守 ▶彼女に居留守を使われたような気がする I have the feeling she was just *pretending not to be in* [*pretended to be out*] *when I called*.

イルミネーション illumination ▶その船には美しいイルミネーションが施してあった The ship *was* beautifully *illuminated*.

¹**いれい 異例の exceptional** ▶ 30歳で社長になるとは異例の昇進だ To become president of a company at the age of thirty is an *exceptional* promotion.

²**いれい 慰霊** ▶慰霊碑を建てる build [erect] *a memorial* ‖ 慰霊祭を行う hold *a memorial service*.

いれかえ 入れ替え a **change** ▶打順の入れ替えをする *change* the batting order.

いれかえる 入れ替える change +⊜ ▶電池を入れ替える *change* the batteries ‖ 場所を入れ替える *change* places ‖ 部屋の空気を入れ替えたほうがいい You had better *air out* this room [*let some fresh air into* this room]. ‖ 彼女はお茶を入れ替えてくれた She *made fresh tea* for me.

▶《比喩的》彼は刑務所で勤めあげたあと, 心を入れ替え て真面目に働いた After completing his time in prison, he *turned over a new leaf* and led an honest life.

いれかわりたちかわり 入れ替わり立ち替わり ▶その店には入れ替わり立ち替わり客がやって来た Customers came to the shop *one after another*.

いれかわる 入れ替わる ▶弁当を開けてみたら, 中身がいつのまにか弟のと入れ替わっていた When I opened my lunch box, I found that it had *been switched with* my brother's.

イレギュラー イレギュラーの irregular ▶打球がイレギュラーしてヒットになった The hit ball bounced *irregularly* and became a hit.

いれぐい 入れ食い ▶入れ食い状態だった They were biting as soon as *I cast my line*.

いれこ 入れ子 ▶入れ子になっている箱 a *nest* of boxes.

いれこむ 入れ込む ▶あの子, 最近彼氏に入れ込み過ぎじゃないの *Is*n't she *too obsessed with* her boyfriend these days ? (➤ be obsessed with は「…のことしか頭にない」の意).

いれずみ 入れ墨 a **tattoo** /tætúː/ [複 **tattoos**] ▶彼は背中に竜の入れ墨をしている He has *a tattoo* of a dragon on his back. (➤「彼は背中に竜の入れ墨をしてもらった」は He had a dragon tattooed on his back.).

いれぢえ 入れ知恵 ▶これは遠藤が山内に入れ知恵したに違いない Endo must have *suggested the idea* to Yamauchi. ／Endo must have *dropped a hint* to Yamauchi.

いれちがい 入れ違い ▶きみが出て行くのと入れ違いに明子が帰って来たよ *Right after* [*Soon after*] you left, Akiko came home. (◉「…の直後に」といいたい場合は前者のように, またもう少し間を置いた感じを表したい場合は後者のように表現するとよい).

いれば 入れ歯 a **false tooth** ; **dentures** (総入れ歯) ▶彼は入れ歯だ He is wearing [He has] *false teeth*. ‖ 祖父は総入れ歯だ My grandfather wears *dentures*. ‖ おせんべいを食べていたら, 入れ歯がポロリと取れてしまった As I was eating a rice cracker, my *false tooth* fell out.

いれもの 入れ物 a **container** (木箱・ボール箱など) ; a **case** (ケース) ; a **vessel** (つぼ・鍋など) ▶壊れやすい物はこの入れ物に入れてください Put fragile items in this *container*. ／Fragile items go in this *container*.

いれる 入れる 1【中へ入らせる】put ... into ; let in ▶妹はそのおもちゃをポケットに入れた My little sister *put* the toy *into* her pocket. ‖ 新鮮な空気を入れるために窓を開けた I opened the window to *let in* some fresh air. ‖ 私を部屋の中に入れてください Please *let* me *into* the room. (➤ 文脈によっては Please let me in. でよい) ‖ その病人はすぐ病院に入れる必要がある That patient needs to *be put into the hospital* [*to be hospitalized*] at once. ‖ その箱を(家の)中に入れてくれ! *In with* that box ! ／*Put* that box *into* the house. ‖ この 2 語の間に to という単語を入れなさい *Put* the word 'to' *between* these two words.

▶計画に反対の人もいることを頭に入れておいてください Please *keep in mind* that some of us are against the plan.

2【力などを加える】 ▶新しい橋の開通式で市長がテープにはさみを入れた The mayor *cut* the tape at the opening ceremony of the bridge. ‖ 2 人は幸せそうにウエディングケーキにナイフを入れた The couple happily *cut* the [their] wedding cake.

3【良くしようと手を加える】 ▶草稿に手を入れる *revise* [*edit*] a draft ‖ 庭の木に手を入れる *trim* a garden tree.

4【機能させる】turn [switch] on ▶冷房を入れる *turn* the air conditioner *on* ‖ 炊飯器のスイッチを入れる *switch on* a rice cooker.

5【異質なものを混ぜる】put ... in [into] ▶コーヒーはたいていミルクを入れて飲みます I usually *put* milk *in* my coffee. ／I usually drink coffee *with* milk. ‖ 紅茶に砂糖を入れますか Would you like (to *put* some) sugar *in* your tea ?

6【参加させる, 加える】admit +⊜ (許可する) ; **join**

+目（人を仲間に入れる）▶以前は男性会員だけだったそのゴルフクラブは今は女性も**入れている** The formerly all-male golf club now *admits* women. ‖ 彼を我々のテニス部に**入れたい** I want to *get* him *on* our tennis team. ‖ 私も（そのゲームに）**入れてください** Let me *join in* (the game), please. ‖ 仲間に**入れてくれますか** Can I *join* you? ‖ 彼は娘を京都の大学に**入れた** He *sent* his daughter *to* a university in Kyoto. ▶彼女は毎月5万円家に**入れている** She *contributes* 50,000 yen to household expenses. ‖ 取引先を訪問する前に**電話を入れた** I *called* my customers [clients] before paying them a visit. ‖ 先方に**わびを入れて**おいたほうがいい You should *apologize* to the other party.

7【認める, 受け入れる】▶問題はゲリラが我々の**要求をいれる**かどうかだ The question is whether the guerillas will *comply with our request* (or not). ‖ 校長は私たちの**意見をいれる**人ではない The principal never *accepts our opinions*.

8【収容する】seat +目 ▶その劇場は1000人の人を**入れる**ことができる The theater *seats* one thousand persons. ‖ この講堂はどのくらいの人数を**入れられます**か What is *the seating capacity* of this hall?

9【含める】include +目 ▶一行は私を**入れて**15人です The party consists of fifteen persons *including* me [myself]. ‖ 沖縄旅行は雑費を**入れて**1人約5万円です The trip to Okinawa costs about fifty thousand yen per person, *including* miscellaneous [incidental] expenses. (➤ miscellaneous は「種々雑多な」, incidental は「付随的な」) ‖ 彼女は親切にも私を**傘に入れてくれた** She was kind enough to *let* me *share her umbrella*. (➤ share は「一緒に使う」).

10【お茶を】make +目 ▶私は自分でコーヒーを**入れた** I *made* myself a cup of coffee. ‖ お茶を**入れましょう**か Shall I *make* tea for you? ／Shall I *fix* you some tea?

11【投票する】vote《for》（候補者に）▶誰に**入れよう**か迷っています I haven't made up my mind who I'm going to *vote for*. ／I haven't made up my mind on who *vote for*.

いろ 色

> **《解説》色のイメージ**
> 色彩に関する表現は日本語と英語ではかなりのずれがある. 例えば「青信号」「青野菜」などの「青」は英語では常に green で表す. また, 日本語の「赤」は明るい暖色の総称として用いられており, 英語の red よりも意味が広い. さらに日本人は「ピンク(桃色)」を「わいせつ」と結び付けることがあるが, 英米人は blue をそれに結び付ける.

1【色彩】a color ▶明るい[暗い]**色** bright [dark] *colors* ‖ 私は**白い色**が好きだ I like *white*. ／I like *the color white*. (➤ I like (the) white color. とはいわない) ‖ 虹は赤, だいだい, 黄, 緑, 青, 藍, 紫の**7色**です A rainbow has seven *colors*: red, orange, yellow, green, blue, indigo, and violet. (➤ 英米では indigo を省いて6色と考える人も少なくない) ‖ ドアの**色は何色**にしようか *What color* should I paint the door?

▶動物の中には**色の識別**ができないものがいる Some animals can't *see colors*. ‖ この**色**はあなたには少し地味[派手]すぎる This *color* is a little too quiet [loud] for you. ‖ 山々はだいぶ**秋の色**が濃くなってきた The *autumn(al) colors* in the mountains have turned deeper. ‖《店で客が》このほかの**色**はありますか Does this come in *other colors*? ／Do you have this in *other colors*?

▶《慣用表現》テストの成績が上がったので, 母はおこづかいに**色をつけてくれた** My mother *added a little something to* my allowance because I got a better grade in the test than the last time. ‖ 客は**色をなして**ウエーターをどなりつけた The customer *flushed with anger* and yelled at the waiter.

2【皮膚の色】a complexion（顔の）▶芳子は**色が白い** Yoshiko *has a fair complexion*. (→**色白**) ‖ 彼は海水浴で**日に焼けて色が黒くなった** He *got a (sun)tan* at the beach. (➤ He became black ... とはいわない).

3【雰囲気】▶彼の顔には**疲労の色が見えた** *Fatigue* could be seen in his face. (➤ この場合の「色」は英語では表さないのがふつう) ‖ 救助隊員の顔に**苦悩の色**が浮かんだ The rescue team showed *signs of anxiety*.

いろあい 色合い light and shade, (a) hue (➤ 後者は主に文語) ▶この油絵は中間色の**色合い**がうまく出ている This oil painting uses *light and shade* effectively [to good effect].

いろあせる 色褪せる fade ▶鮮やかな色の生地は日に当たるとすぐ**色あせる** Brightly-colored materials *fade* easily in the sun.

▶《比喩的》真実の愛は**色あせる**ことがない True love never *fades*.

いろいろ 色々

一形 いろいろな a (wide) variety of, various (➤ various は「何種類かの」, あるいは, それより多少多い程度をいう ; 主に互いに違うことをいっており,「種類が多い」という意味はない. 多種多様であることをいうには a wide variety [range] of のようにいう必要がある) ; **a number of**（いくつかの）▶貝殻の**いろいろ** *a (wide) variety of* seashells ‖ **いろいろな**長さの針金 *a variety of* lengths of wire ‖ **いろいろな**仕事に就いて働く work at *a number of different* jobs.

▶田中さんは**いろいろな**理由をつけて私の申し出を断った Mr. Tanaka refused my offer for *various* reasons. ‖ 街頭の売店では**いろいろな**物を売っている They sell *all sorts* [*a wide variety*] *of* things at newsstands. ‖ 彼女は**いろいろな**草花の育て方を知っている She knows how to grow *all different kinds of* [*many different kinds of*] flowers. ‖ 世の中には**いろいろな**人がいる It takes *all kinds* [*sorts*] to make a world. (➤ 英語のことわざ ; 文字どおりには「世の中を構成するにはいろいろな人が必要だ」の意) ‖ 彼は**いろいろ**と(＝たくさん)忠告してくれた He gave me *a lot of* advice.

▶私は弟に留学を諦めさせようと**いろいろ**やってみたがだめだった I tried *many ways* to persuade my (younger) brother not to study abroad but it was in vain. ‖ 値段は500円から5万円まで**いろいろあります** Prices *range* from 500 yen to 50,000 yen. ‖ **いろいろ面倒をおかけしました** I'm afraid I caused you *a lot of* trouble. ‖ **いろいろ考えた**けど, 私は行かないことにした I *thought* it *over* and decided against going.

✉ **いろいろお世話になりました** You've been helpful to me [us] *in so many ways*.

1いろう 慰労 ▶退職する人を**慰労する会**が催された A party was held *in appreciation* [*recognition*] *of* the retiring person's *long years of service*. (➤「慰労会」に相当する英語はない).

い

‖慰労金 a bonus payment for special services.

2いろう 胃瘻《医学》a **gastric fistula** /fístʃələ ‖ -tjʊ-/ ‖胃ろう造設 gastronomy.

いろえんぴつ 色鉛筆 a **colored pencil.**

いろおとこ 色男 a **ladies' man,** a **lady-killer** (➤後者はやや古風な語).

いろか 色香 a **woman's charms** ▶色香に迷う be captivated by *a woman's charms.*

いろがみ 色紙 **colored paper** ▶色紙で帆掛け船を折る fold a piece of *colored paper* into the shape of a sailboat.

いろぐろ 色黒の **dark** ▶彼女は色黒だ She *is dark* (*-skinned*). ／ She *has a dark complexion.*

いろけ 色気 **sex appeal**(性的魅力) ▶恭子は色気がある Kyoko *is sexy* [*has sex appeal*]. ‖弟は近頃色気づいてきた My brother is *beginning to show interest in girls.* ／My brother is *beginning to be aware of the opposite sex.* (➤後者は「異性を意識し始めた」の意).
▶社長の座に色気を示す *show an interest* in [*a willingness* for] the seat of president.

いろこい 色恋 **love**(恋愛).

いろごと 色事 a **love affair.**

いろじろ 色白の **fair** ▶彼女は色白だ She *has a fair complexion.* ／She *has fair skin.*

いろちがい 色違い ▶《店で客が》このバッグの色違いはありますか Do you have this bag in *a different color* [*in different colors*]? ‖このシャツは色違いで2枚持っている I have two shirts of this kind *in different colors.*

いろづく 色づく **turn colors**; **turn yellow** [**red**] ▶木の葉が色づき始めた The (autumn) leaves are *turning yellow.* (➤モミジの葉なら yellow の代わりに crimson または red を用いる) ／The (autumn) leaves began to *turn* (*colors*).

いろつけ 色付け ▶下絵を色付けする *color* a rough sketch.

いろっぽい 色っぽい **sexy** ▶色っぽいしぐさ *sensual* movements ‖彼女は色っぽい目つきでちらりとぼくを見た She gave me a *come-hither* look. ‖ひろ子は最近すっかり色っぽくなったね Hiroko looks quite *sexy* these days, doesn't she? ‖研二の色っぽさは中年女性の心をくすぐる Kenji's *sex appeal* tickles the fancy of middle-aged women. ‖私には最近とんと色っぽい話がない Recently, I've had no *love life* to speak of.

いろつや 色艶 a **complexion**(顔の); **luster** (物の); **gloss**(物の表面の) ▶80歳の祖父は今でも色つやがよい My eighty-year-old grandfather still has a good and healthy *complexion.*

いろどり 彩り ▶この絵はあなたの部屋に彩りを添えるでしょう This picture will *make* your room *look more attractive* [*more pleasant*].

いろとりどり 色とりどり ▶子供たちは色とりどりの服を着ていた The children wore clothes *of various colors.*

いろどる 彩る **color** +目 ▶花火が夏の夜空を彩った Fireworks *colored* the summer night sky.

いろは **the ABC(s)**(初歩) ▶私も文化人類学のいろはぐらいは知っている I know *the ABCs* [*basics* ／*fundamentals*] of cultural anthropology. ‖竹田さんは育児のいろはも知らない Takeda doesn't know *the first thing* about child care.

いろむら 色むら ▶色むらのある染め物 a cloth dyed *unevenly.*

いろめ 色目 ▶男に色目を使う *make eyes at* a man ‖松田のやつ, 来る女来る女に片っ端から色目を使っているんだぜ Matsuda's been *making sheep's eyes at* every girl he meets. (日本語の「…に色目を使う」自体がやや古風な表現なので, それに近い make sheep's eyes at ... を用いるとよい).

いろめがね 色眼鏡 **sunglasses**(サングラス); (a) **prejudice**(偏見) ▶《慣用表現》最近は女の校長というだけで色眼鏡で見る人はいなくなった Today nobody would *be prejudiced against* a woman for being a school principal.

いろめきたつ 色めき立つ ▶その容疑者逮捕の報に報道局は色めき立った People in the news division *got excited* by the report of the arrest of the suspect.

いろよい 色好い ▶色よい(＝好ましい)返事を待ってるよ I hope to receive a *favorable* [*positive*] reply from you. (➤きっと色よい返事になる, という期待があるときは I look forward to receiving ... という).

いろり 囲炉裏 an ***irori***; a sunken fireplace in the middle of the room(➤説明的な訳).
‖いろり端 the fireplace.

いろわけ 色分け **color-coding** ▶このグラフは色分けされているからわかりやすい This graph is easy to understand because it *is color-coded.*

いろん 異論 a **different opinion**(異なる意見); an **objection**(反対意見) ▶それに対しては異論はない I have no *objection* to it. ‖校長の制服廃止案に対して一部の先生方は異論を唱えた Some teachers *raised an objection* to the principal's proposal to abolish the school uniform.

いろんな →いろいろ.

いわ 岩 (a) **rock** ▶岩の多い山 a *rocky* mountain ‖波は激しく岩にぶち当たった The waves lashed against the *rocks.*
‖岩登り rock climbing.

いわい 祝い a **celebration**(祝賀); **congratulations** (祝いのことば; 常に複数形); a **present,** a **gift**(祝いの品) ▶その晩私たちはささやかなお祝いをした That evening we had a little *celebration.* ‖彼は2人にお祝いを言った He offered the couple his *congratulations.* ‖友人たちは彼の成功に対してお祝いを述べた His friends *congratulated* him *on* his success. ‖私たちは彼女に合格祝いとして万年筆を贈った We gave her a fountain pen to *congratulate* her *on* [*for*] passing the exam. ‖この時計は高校の入学祝いにもらったものです I got this watch as *a gift for starting high school.*

逆引き熟語 ○○祝(い)
還暦の祝い one's sixtieth birthday celebration; a sixtieth birthday present [gift](贈り物) (➤sixtieth を seventieth にすれば「古稀の祝い」に, seventy-seventh にすれば「喜寿の祝い」に, eighty-eighth にすれば「米寿の祝い」になる) ／**結婚祝い** a wedding party(パーティー),a wedding reception(披露宴); a wedding present [gift](贈り物) ／**合格祝い** the celebration of one's passing the exam; a present [gift] for one's passing the exam(贈り物) ／**就職祝い** the celebration of one's getting a (new) job ／**新築祝い** the celebration of the completion of a person's new house; a housewarming present [gift](贈り物) ／**卒業祝い** the celebration of one's graduation from high school [col-

lege]; a graduation present [gift](贈り物)/**誕生祝い** a birthday party(パーティー); a birthday present [gift](贈り物)/**引っ越し祝い** a housewarming (party); a housewarming present [gift](贈り物)

いわう 祝う **celebrate** +目(記念日などを皆で); **congratulate** +目(人に祝辞を言う)

▶誕生日を**祝う** *celebrate* a person's birthday ‖ きのう, 会社の創立20周年を**祝った** Yesterday our company *celebrated* the twentieth anniversary of its founding.

【文型】
人(A)の成功など(B)を祝う
congratulate A **on** B
➤ Bは名詞・動名詞

▶家族の者みんなで私の大学卒業を**祝ってくれた** My family *congratulated* me *on* having graduated [my graduation] from college.

▶《披露宴で》お2人の前途を**祝って**乾杯! *Here's* to the happy future of the newly married couple!

✉ **ご卒業を心からお祝い申し上げます** I offer [send] you my warmest *congratulations* on your graduation. ➤ warmest の代わりに heartfelt でもよい.

いわかん 違和感 ▶肩に**違和感を覚える** *Something feels off* with my shoulders. ‖ コンタクトレンズは最初はちょっと**違和感があった** My contact lenses *felt* a little *strange* [*funny*] at first. ‖ 彼はその会社へ入ってからしばらくたっても**違和感が抜けなかった** He still *felt* a little *out of place* [*felt that he didn't fit in*] long after he joined the company.

いわく 曰く ▶いわくつきの男 a man *with a past* ‖ この話の裏にはいろいろ**いわくがある** There is *a long story* behind this. ‖ 彼が急にアメリカへ出発したのには何か**いわく**(=理由)**がありそうだ** There must be some *reason* for his sudden trip to the U.S. ‖ 彼女は何やら**いわくありげに**私をちらりと見た She gave me a *significant* [*meaningful*] glance. ‖ 彼女は**いわくつきの女**だ She *has a history*.

いわし 鰯 《魚》a **sardine** /sɑːˈdíːn/ ▶**イワシの缶詰** a can of *sardines*.

[ことわざ] **いわしの頭も信心から** Faith makes even the head of a sardine look holy. (➤ 日本語からの直訳).

‖**いわし雲** fleecy clouds (➤ fleecy は「羊毛状の」).

いわずもがな 言わずもがな ▶記者は遺族に「息子さんが犠牲になって悲しくなかったですか」と**言わずもがなの質問をした** The journalist asked the bereaved family the *unnecessary* question, "Did you feel sorrow when you lost your son?"

▶**言わずもがなのことを言ってしまった** I said something I *shouldn't have*. (➤ have のあとには said が略されている).

いわな 岩魚 《魚》a **char** /tʃɑːʳ/ (➤ カワマスもこの名で呼ぶ).

[1]**いわば 岩場** a **rocky area** ▶**岩場で足を滑らせる** slip in *a rocky area* [*spot*].

[2]**いわば 言わば** **so to speak, as it were**(➤ 後者がより堅い言い方) ▶私にとって東京は**いわば**第二の故郷だ To me Tokyo is, *so to speak*, a second hometown. ‖ ラクダは**いわば**砂漠の船だ The camel is, *as it were*, the ship of the desert. ⇀**言ってみれば**.

いわやま 岩山 a **rocky mountain**.

いわゆる **what you might call**; **so-called** (➤ しばしば「本当かどうか疑わしい」という含みをもつ) ▶**これらのいわゆる「進歩派」の政治家たち** these *so-called* progressive politicians.

▶彼はこの辺の**いわゆる「顔」**だよ He is *what you might call* a big man in this area. ‖ 兄は**いわゆる「独身貴族」**です My brother is a 'swinging bachelor.' (● 文字で書く場合は引用符で囲めば,「いわゆる, 世に言う」に相当する what you [they/we] (might) call などは省いてもよい).

いわれ ▶**いわれのない非難** *undeserved* criticism ‖ きみに文句をつけられる**いわれはない** You have no right to blame me. (➤「きみにはぼくを責める権利はない」の意) ‖ 何の**いわれ**(=理由)もなく首になるとは妙な話だ It is strange that he should be fired for no *reason*.

▶この川の名には何か**いわれ**(=言い伝え)があるのですか Is there some *story* behind the name of this river?

[1]**いん 陰** **yin**(陽に対して) ▶どこかの寺の鐘が**陰に籠もって**(=陰鬱に)ゴーンと鳴った There boomed the *melancholy* sound of a temple bell. ‖ あの学生は**陰に籠もる**(=喜怒をはっきり出さない)傾向がある That student tends to *hide his feelings* [*emotions*].

[2]**いん 韻** **rhyme** /raɪm/ ▶この詩は**韻を踏んでいる** This poem is *rhymes*. /This poem *is in rhyme*.

[3]**いん 印** a **seal**(印章); a **stamp** (スタンプ, 印章) ▶**印を押す** affix *a seal* ‖ ㊙の**印を押した書類** documents *stamped* 'Confidential.'

いんうつ 陰鬱な **gloomy** (暗い) ▶**陰鬱な天気** *gloomy* weather ‖ その悲報を聞いて誰もが**陰鬱な顔をしていた** All of them *looked depressed* when they heard the sad news.

いんえい 陰影 a **shadow**(影); (a) **shade** (部分的な陰) ▶**陰影に富んだ表現** a phrase *rich with nuance*.

いんか 引火する **catch fire** ▶たばこの火がガソリンに**引火して**自動車は火だるまになった The gasoline *caught fire* from a lighted cigarette and the car burst into flames.

インカ **Inca**

‖**インカ帝国** the Inca Empire.

いんが 因果 **cause and effect**(原因と結果); **karma**(業(ごう)) ▶**因果応報** As you sow, so shall you reap. /You reap what you sow. (➤「人は種をまいたとおり刈り入れをすることになる」の意の聖書のことば) ‖ 事故の**因果関係を調べる** find *the cause-and-effect relationships* in the accident ‖ **何の因果で**, 坊主になんかなったのだろう I wonder *by what fate* I became a Buddhist priest.

いんがし 印画紙 **photographic paper**.

いんかん 印鑑 an ***inkan***, a (**registered**) **seal**(印章); a **stamp**, a **seal impression**(印影) ⇀**判** ▶**印鑑を登録する** have one's *inkan* [*personal seal*] registered ‖ **印鑑証明をもらう** *have* one's *inkan* [*personal seal*] *notarized*.

いんき 陰気な **gloomy**, **melancholy** ▶**陰気な人** a *gloomy* person ‖ **陰気くさい部屋** a *gloomy* room ‖ この家は何となく**陰気だ** This house has something *gloomy* about it. ‖ 彼女は**陰気な性格だ** She has a *gloomy* [*melancholy*] disposition.

いんきょ 隠居 **retirement** 一動 **隠居する** **retire** ▶彼は**隠居して**年金生活をしている He *retired* (*from work*) and lives on a pension.

い

‖ご隠居 a retired man [woman], a retiree /rɪtàɪəríː/.

いんきょく 陰極《電気》the cathode.

いんぎん 慇懃な polite ▶いんぎんな態度 *polite* manner ‖いちばん嫌なのはいんぎん無礼なやつだ Nobody is more disgusting than someone who *masks his or her arrogance behind politeness*. (➤「丁重さの陰に横柄さを隠している」の意).

インク ink ▶インクで書く write *in ink*.

‖インク消し an ink eraser ‖インク瓶 an ink bottle.

イングランド England 《参考》この語を曖昧に (Great) Britain (イギリス) の意味で用いることもあるが, 狭義には England は (Great) Britain の一部である. →イギリス.

‖イングランド人 an Englishman (男), an Englishwoman (女), the English (➤ 総称).

いんけい 陰茎 the penis /píːnɪs/. →ペニス.

いんけん 陰険な sinister (邪悪な) ; crafty (悪賢い) ▶陰険な目つきをしている have a *sinister* look ‖陰険な手を使う use *crafty* means ‖ぼくたちのことを先生に告げ口するとは陰険なやつだ It was *sly* [*sneaky*] of him to tell the teacher on us.

いんげんまめ 隠元豆 a kidney bean ; 《米》a string bean, 《英》a runner bean (サヤインゲン).

いんこ 《鳥》a parakeet /pǽrəkìːt/ ; a parrot (オウム) 《参考》インコ・オウムの仲間は種類が多く, それぞれに固有の名がある. 例えば budgerigar /bʌ́dʒərigɑːʳ/, budgie (セキセイインコ), cockatoo (冠羽のあるバタンなどのオウム・インコの仲間), lovebird (ボタンインコ), macaw (コンゴウインコ) など.

いんご 隠語 jargon ▶やくざ世界の隠語 underworld *jargon* of the yakuza.

いんこう 咽喉 the throat.

インコース the inside lane [track], an inner lane [track] (陸上競技などで) ; the inside course (of the plate) (野球の球筋) ▶平井はインコースぎりぎりを突いた Hirai hurled *in the innermost course*. / Hirai threw an *innermost* strike.

いんさつ 印刷 printing 一動 印刷する print +目 ▶論文を印刷する *print* one's paper / *have* one's paper *printed* (➤ 後者は「(印刷所に)印刷してもらう」の意) ‖リストを(出力して)印刷する *print out* a list ‖この本は印刷がきれいだ This book is *neatly printed*. ‖カラー印刷の技術は飛躍的に進歩している Color *printing* technology is advancing by leaps and bounds.

‖印刷機 a press, a printing machine ‖印刷業者 a printer ‖印刷所 《米》a printshop, 《英》a printing office [shop] ‖印刷物 printed matter ; a handout (会議や授業で配られるプリント).

いんさん 陰惨な ghastly /gǽstli/ ▶陰惨な光景 a *ghastly* scene.

いんし 印紙 a stamp ▶契約書に印紙を貼る put *a stamp* on a contract.

‖収入印紙 a revenue stamp.

いんしつ 陰湿な insidious /ɪnsídiəs/ ▶近年のいじめは陰湿化しているらしい I hear that bullying has *gotten insidious* in recent years. ‖彼のいじめは陰湿だ His bullying is *furtive and malicious*. (➤ furtive は「こそこそと行われる」, malicious /məlíʃəs/ は「悪意のある」の意).

いんしゅ 飲酒 drinking ▶飲酒運転をしてはいけない Don't *drink and drive*. / Don't *drink-drive*. (➤ 名詞の「飲酒運転」は drunk [drunken] driving) ‖彼は飲酒癖をやめられなかった He couldn't break [overcome] his *drinking habit*.

‖飲酒検知器 an alcohol detector, a breathalyzer /bréθəlaɪzəʳ/ (➤ 後者は主に《英》で好まれる).

いんしゅう 因習 an old custom (社会的習慣) ; (a) convention (慣例) ▶因習を打破する break down *old customs*.

いんしょう 印象

(an) impression 一形 印象的な impressive ▶良い [悪い / 強い] 印象を与える *make a* good [bad / strong] *impression* (➤「強くしっかり刻まれる印象」の意味では make an impression がふつうで give は用いない. give an impression は「漠然とした, しばしば不正確な感じ」の意味になる) ‖鮮やかな印象を受ける *get a* vivid *impression*.

▶彼の演説は全聴衆に強烈な印象を与えた His speech *made* a strong *impression on* the entire audience. ‖私は彼女には良い印象をもたなかった I *got an unfavorable impression* of her. ‖その国を旅行していちばん私の印象に残ったのは空の青さです When I made a trip to that country, what most *impressed me* was the blueness of the sky.

▶彼はどうも印象が薄い He *has a* rather *colorless* [*bland*] *personality*. ‖エミリーの笑顔は中でも特に印象的だった Emily's smile was the most *impressive* of all.

▶長崎の第一印象はいかがでしたか What were your *first impressions* of Nagasaki ?

✉ **日本の印象はいかがでしたか** *What were your impressions* of Japan ? / *How did you like* Japan ?

✉ **しばらく台湾に住んでみて, 私が最初に受けたそこの印象は変わりました** My *impression* of Taiwan changed after I had been there for a while.

‖印象主義[派] Impressionism.

いんしょく 飲食 eating and drinking (➤ 日本語との語順の違いに注意)

‖飲食店 an eating and drinking establishment ; a restaurant (レストラン) ‖飲食物 food and drink.

いんすうぶんかい 因数分解 《米》factoring, 《英》factorization ▶x^2-y^2を因数分解せよ *Factor* [*Factorize*] x^2-y^2. (➤ x^2は x squared とか the square of x と読む).

インスタグラム Instagram (➤ 商標名) ▶動画をインスタグラムに載せる post a video on *Instagram*.

インスタばえ インスタ映えする instagrammable /ínstəgræ̀məbl/ ▶インスタ映えする料理 an *instagrammable* dish.

インスタント ▶最近のインスタント食品はなかなかうまい *Instant foods* nowadays taste quite good.

‖インスタントコーヒー[スープ] instant coffee [soup] ‖インスタントラーメン instant ramen, instant noodles in broth (➤ 後者は説明的).

インストール installation 一動 インストールする install +目 ▶このソフトをどうやってインストールするのか教えてよ Can you tell me how to *install* this software program ?

インストラクター an instructor ▶スキーのインストラクター a ski *instructor*.

インスピレーション (an) inspiration ▶インスピレーションで詩を書く write a poem with *inspiration* / be inspired to write a poem ‖私はインスピレーションが働いたことなど一度もない I've never *had any sudden* *inspirations*.

[1]**いんせい 陰性の** negative ▶ＨＩＶ検査の結果は陰性だった The result of the HIV test was *negative*.

[2]**いんせい 院政** rule by a retired emperor.

いんぜい 印税 a royalty /rɔ́iəlti/ ▶自分の書いた本の印税で生活する live on the *royalties* of one's books.

[1]**いんせき 隕石** a meteorite /míːt̬iəraɪt/.

[2]**いんせき 姻戚** ▶山内社長は元首相と姻戚関係にある Our company president, Mr. Yamanouchi, *is related to* a former prime minister *by marriage*.

[3]**いんせき 引責** ▶このたびの不祥事に際しまして社長が引責辞任することに決定いたしました It has been decided that the president will *accept responsibility* for the scandal *and resign*.

いんぜん 隠然 ▶その元首相はいまだに隠然たる勢力をもっているようだ That former prime minister still has influence *behind the scenes*.

いんそつ 引率する take +㊐ (連れていく) ; lead +㊐ (先導する) ; escort +㊐ (案内する) ; chaperon(e) +㊐ (同行して面倒を見る) ▶30人の生徒を引率して筑波山へキャンプに行った I *took* thirty students on a camping trip to Mt. Tsukuba. ‖子供たちは教師に引率されて九州を旅行した The children traveled around Kyushu, *led* by their teachers. ‖この生徒たちの引率者は誰ですか Who is the *chaperon(e)* of these students? ／Who *is chaperoning* these students?

インター ▶どこのインターで下りればいいの？ Which *interchange* do I get off on? →インターチェンジ.

インターチェンジ an interchange ▶厚木のインターチェンジから高速へ入る get onto the expressway from [at] the Atsugi *Interchange*.

インターネット the Internet

> 「インターネット用語」のいろいろ Ｅメール email ／Ｅメールアドレス email address ／ウェブ the Web (World Wide Web) ／サーバー server ／サイバースペース cyberspace ／ダウンロード download ／チャット chat ／ドメイン名 domain name ／ネットサーフィン net surfing ／バイト byte ／ハイパーテキスト hypertext ／ハッカー hacker ／ビット bit ／ブラウザー Internet [Web] browser ／プロバイダー Internet (service) provider ／ホームページ web page ／リンク link ／ログイン login, logging in

▶インターネットで博多のおいしいレストランを探す search for [look up] good restaurants in Hakata on *the Internet*.

▶インターネットでファイルを送る send a file *over* [*through*] *the Internet* ‖インターネットで首相官邸にアクセスする access *the Internet* site of the Prime Minister's Residence.

ディベートルーム 「インターネットは無制限に普及されるべきではない」

インターハイ an inter-high-school athletic competition ▶来月水泳のインターハイが当地で行われる *An inter-high-school* swimming *competition* is going to be held here next month.

インターフェース an interface ▶ユーザーに優しいインターフェースを開発する develop a user-friendly *interface*.

インターフェロン interferon /ìnt̬əʳfíərɑːn/.

インターホン an intercom /ínt̬əʳkɑːm/, an interphone (➤前者のほうがふつう) ▶インターホンで話す talk over the *intercom*.

インターン an intern, 《英また》a houseman (インターン生) ; internship (インターンの期間・地位).

いんたい 引退 retirement 一動 (…を)引退する retire 《from》 ▶そのテニス選手はついに引退を表明した The tennis player finally announced his *retirement*. ‖その野球選手は体力の衰えを感じて現役引退を決意した The baseball player decided to *retire from* active play(ing) because he felt his body growing weak. ‖政界を引退する *retire from* politics [political life].

‖引退生活 one's retired life ‖引退相撲 a sumo wrestling match in honor of a retiring wrestler.

インダス インダス川 the Indus (インド北西部の大河).

インタビュー (an) interview 一動 (人に)インタビューする interview +㊐ ▶市長はその件に関するインタビューを一切拒否した The mayor refused all *interviews* on the matter. ‖首相は記者団のインタビューを受けた The prime minister *had an interview* with the press.

▶その女性歌手は何十人もの記者にインタビューされた The female singer *was interviewed* by scores of reporters.

インチ an inch ▶60インチの大画面テレビ a TV set with a big 60″ screen／a 60″ TV set. (➤″ は inch を表す記号).

いんちき cheating (だますこと) ; a fake (偽物) 一形 いんちきな false (うその) ; fraudulent (人をだます)

▶いんちきな訳 a *false* translation ‖いんちき広告 *fraudulent* advertising ‖いんちきするな Don't be a cheat. ／Don't be dishonest.

▶彼女が出したこの出費報告書は実にいんちきくさい This account of her expenses is really *suspicious* [*fishy*].

‖いんちき医者 a quack (➤「偽医者」は phon(e)y doctor).

いんちょう 院長 ▶学院の院長 the *president* [*director*] of a school ‖病院の院長 the *director* of a hospital.

インディアナ Indiana /ìndiǽnə/ (アメリカの州 ; 略 IN, Ind.).

インディアン a Native American (➤アメリカの先住民を指す ; an (American) Indian という言い方は避けられる).

インテリ an intellectual, an educated person ▶彼はハーバード大出のインテリだ He is *a Harvard-educated man*.

▶ぼくはああいうインテリ連中は信用しない I don't trust those *eggheads*.

> **危ないカタカナ語✹ インテリ**
> **1** ロシア語の *intelligentsiya* (インテリゲンチャ)から英語になった intelligentsia がもと. the intelligentsia の形で集合的に知識階級を指す. インテリ個人は an intellectual という. また, an educated person も可.
> **2** 日本語の「インテリ」はときに軽蔑的に用いられるが, これに相当する英語には highbrow, egghead, longhair などがある.

インテリア the interior /ɪntíərɪəʳ/ (内部) ; interior decor [decoration], the decor (室内装飾)

‖インテリアデザイナー an interior designer, an interior decorator.

い

危ないカタカナ語 インテリア
(1) 日本語の「インテリア」は「室内装飾」の意で用いることが多いが，英語の interior には「室内(の)，内部(の)」の意味しかない．したがって日本語の意味を表すには interior decor または decoration という必要がある．
(2)「すてきなインテリア」というように家具や調度を指すときは furniture や furnishings を用いる．

インテリジェントビル an **intelligent building**.

インデント an **indent**.

インド India 一形 **インドの Indian**
‖**インド人** an Indian ‖**インド洋** the Indian Ocean.

インドア indoor(室内の).

いんどう 引導 ▶あいつに引導を渡してやれ *Finish* him *off*. (➤ finish ... off は「始末する，殺す」) ／*Tell* him *to give up on the plan*. (➤「計画をあきらめるように言え」の意). 《参考》僧侶が臨終者に言い渡すものは address final words to the dying person とすればよい.

インドシナ Indochina /ìndoʊtʃáɪnə/
‖**インドシナ半島** the Indochina Peninsula (➤通例単に Indochina という).

イントネーション intonation(声の抑揚，音調) ▶正しいイントネーションで英文を読む read a passage in English with correct *intonation*.

インドネシア Indonesia /ìndəníːʒə, -ziə/ 一形 **インドネシアの Indonesian**
‖**インドネシア語** Indonesian ‖**インドネシア人** an Indonesian.

いんとん 隠遁 seclusion ▶隠とん生活を送る *live in seclusion*.

いんないかんせん 院内感染 (an) **infection within the hospital**.

いんねん 因縁 1【因と縁】▶ここであなたに会えたのも何かの因縁でしょう It must be *God's will* that I met you here. ／It is our *destiny* [*karma*] that we should meet here. (➤ (1)前者はキリスト教的発想. (2)仏教用語の karma は「業(ごう)＝善業・悪業の結果」の意で英語化しており，インフォーマルでは「宿命」の意でも用いられる).
2【由来】▶この岩には何かいわく因縁がありそうだ This rock seems to have its own *tale to tell*. (→いわく).
3【言いがかり】▶車内でちんぴらに因縁をつけられ困ってしまった I got in trouble on the train when a punk *picked a fight* with me. (➤ pick a fight は「言いがかりをつける」) ‖おまえ俺に何か因縁つける気かよ，えっ? You've *got something to say* to me, eh?

いんのう 陰のう the scrotum /skróʊṭəm/.

インバウンド インバウンドの inbound (➤ inbound は「よそから元へ［本国へ］向かう」を表す言葉で，訪日観光客という意味はない) ▶インバウンド観光 *inbound* tourism.

インパクト impact /ímpækt/ ▶インパクトの強い広告文 copy that makes a strong *impact* ／ punchy copy.

いんぶ 陰部 the pubic [**genital**] **region, the private parts** (➤後者は婉曲(えんきょく)語).

インフォメーション information (➤数えられない名詞なので「1つの情報」というときは a piece of information とする)
‖**インフォメーションカウンター** an information counter.

インプット input ▶データをインプットする *input* [*enter*] data ‖このコンピュータには100万の用例がインプットしてある One million reference items have *been inputted* [*entered*] in this computer.

インフルエンザ influenza /ìnfluénzə/, 《インフォーマル》 **(the) flu** ▶インフルエンザにかかる get (*the*) *flu*.
‖**季節性インフルエンザ** seasonal influenza ‖**新型インフルエンザ** a new strain of influenza (➤いわゆる「豚インフルエンザ」は swine influenza [flu] または H1N1 influenza と呼ぶ) ‖**鳥インフルエンザ** avian influenza (➤俗に bird flu と言う).

インフレ inflation
‖**インフレ時代** the age of inflation.

いんぶん 韻文 verse(散文に対する) ; **poetry** (詩歌).

いんぺい 隠蔽する conceal +目 ▶事実を隠蔽する *conceal* a fact.

インポ impotence, impotency (➤形容詞はともに impotent ; 現在は ED (electile dysfunction)(勃起障害)というのがふつう).

いんぼう 陰謀 a **plot**(計画) ; a **conspiracy** (徒党を組んでの) ; an **intrigue** /íntriːg/ (陰険で手の込んだ) ▶彼らの陰謀は発覚した Their *plot* has been discovered. ‖政府転覆の陰謀が明るみに出た The *conspiracy* to overthrow the government was uncovered.

いんめつ 隠滅する ▶証拠を隠滅する *destroy* the evidence.

いんもう 陰毛 (a) **pubic** /pjúːbɪk/ **hair** ▶陰毛が生えてきた I've started to grow *public hair*.

いんゆ 隠喩 a **metaphor** /méṭəfɔːʳ/. →直喩.

1**いんよう 引用** (a) **quotation**(発言のままの) ; (a) **citation** (例証のための) 一動 **引用する quote** +目 ; **cite** +目 ▶彼の文章には鷗外の作品からの引用が多い His works are full of *quotations* from Ogai. ‖M先生はその本の一節を引用した Mr. M *quoted* [*cited*] a passage from the book.
▶彼は吉川英治の句を引用してスピーチを結んだ He concluded his speech *quoting* Yoshikawa Eiji's phrase.
‖**引用符** quotation marks, 《インフォーマル》 quotes (➤一重引用符 single quotation marks と二重引用符 double quotation marks とがある) ‖**引用文** a quotation.

2**いんよう 飲用** ▶この水は飲用に適する The water *is safe to drink* [*is potable*].

3**いんよう 陰陽 yin and yang**.

いんりつ 韻律 (a) **meter**, 《英》 **metre** (詩の) ; (a) **rhythm**(音のリズム).

いんりょう 飲料 ▶砂漠を旅するには飲料水が何より貴重だ Nothing is more valuable than *drinking water* when traveling across the desert.
‖**清涼飲料** soft drinks.

いんりょく 引力 gravitation ▶ニュートンは万有引力の法則を発見した Newton discovered *the law of universal gravitation* [*the Law of Gravity*].

いんれき 陰暦 the lunar calendar ▶陰暦の9月9日 September 9 as reckoned by *the lunar calendar*.

う・ウ

う 鵜《鳥》a **cormorant** /kɔ́ːʳmərənt/ ▶鵜匠は鵜を使って魚を捕る Cormorant fishermen use *cormorants* to catch fish. ☞ **鵜飼い**（→見出語）

ウイークエンド a **weekend**. →週末.

ウイークデー a **weekday** ▶ウイークデーは早起きします I get up early on *weekdays*.

ウイークポイント a **weak point** ▶いいキャッチャーがいないのがその野球チームの唯一のウイークポイントだ A lack of good catchers is that baseball team's only *weak point*.

ウィーン Vienna /viénə/（オーストリアの首都）.

ういういしい 初々しい pure and innocent（清純で好ましい）; **wide-eyed**（物事を新鮮に受け止めて驚異の目を見張る）, **unsophisticated**（世間ずれしていない）; **mentally fresh**（気持ちが新鮮な）▶初々しい新入生 an *wide-eyed* [*unsophisticated*] freshman ‖ 彼女は本当に初々しい She looks so *pure and innocent*. ‖ 真新しい制服姿の新入生は本当に初々しい The incoming students look *charmingly fresh* in their new uniforms.

ういざん 初産 one's **first childbirth**.

ういじん 初陣 ▶そのチームは甲子園で初陣を飾った The team successfully *won its first game* at Koshien.

ウイスキー whiskey, whisky（➤ スコッチウイスキーやカナディアンウイスキーでは後者のつづりが好まれる）▶ウイスキーを1杯ください. 水割りじゃなく, ストレートで A (glass of) *whiskey*, please. I'd like it straight, not with water.（➤「ウイスキーの水割り」は whiskey and water）.

ウィスコンシン Wisconsin（アメリカ中北部の州; 略 WI, Wis., Wisc.）.

ウイット wit ▶ウイットに富んだ表現 a *witty* expression ‖ 彼のスピーチはいつもウイットに富んでいる His speeches *are* always *witty* [*full of wit*].

ういてんぺん 有為転変 vicissitudes /vəsísətjuːd/.

ウイニングショット a **winning shot**（試合を決めるショット）; one's **best pitch**（投手の決め球）.

ウイニングボール a **ball caught to end a game**（➤ winning は a winning goal（決勝点となるゴール）のように「試合を決める」の意で用いる）.

ウイニングラン a **victory lap**（➤ 試合に勝った後グラウンドなどを一周すること; この意味での「ウイニングラン」は和製語; winning run は game-winning run ともいい, 野球の「決勝点」の意）.

ウイルス a **virus** /váɪrəs/ 一形 **ウイルス性の viral** ‖ **ウイルス性肝炎** viral hepatitis /hèpətáɪtɪs/ ‖ **コンピュータウイルス** a computer virus ‖ **ウイルス対策ソフト** anti-virus software.

ウインカー a **turn signal** [**indicator**]; 《米・インフォーマル》a **blinker**, 《英・インフォーマル》a **winker** ▶ウインカーを出す put on *a turn signal*.

ウインク a **wink** 一動（…に）**ウインクする wink** 《at》; **bat** one's **eyes** 《at》（誘うように）▶彼女はぼくに（色っぽい）ウインクをした She *batted her eyes at* me.

> **危ないカタカナ語✸ ウインク**
> wink は何かを合図したり, 秘密を分かち合っていることを示したり, からかったりなど, いろいろな目的で多用されるジェスチャーだが, 日本語の「ウインク」は「色目を使う」の意味で用いられることが多い. したがって, この意味では wink よりも bat one's eyes のほうが適切. →まばたき.

ウインタースポーツ winter sports（➤ 複数形で用いる）.

> 「ウインタースポーツ」のいろいろ アイススケート ice-skating ／アイスホッケー ice hockey ／カーリング curling ／スキー skiing ／スノーボード snowboarding ／スノーモービル snowmobiling ／バイアスロン biathlon ／ボブスレー bobsledding [《英》bobsleighing] ／モーグル moguls ／リュージュ luge, tobogganing

ウインドーショッピング window-shopping ▶私は昼休みにときどきウインドーショッピングをする I sometimes *window-shop* [*go window-shopping*] during my lunch hour.

ウインドサーフィン windsurfing, boardsailing（➤「ボード」は sailboard）▶ウインドサーフィンをする *windsurf* ／ *go windsurfing*.

ウインドブレーカー《米》a **windbreaker**, 《英》a **windcheater**, a **windjammer**.

ウインナソーセージ a **wiener** (**wurst**) /wíːnəʳ (wə̀ːʳst)/; a **Vienna sausage**（オードブル用の）.

ウィンブルドン Wimbledon（ロンドン郊外の地区. テニスの選手権試合が行われる）.

ウーマンリブ women's liberation ▶Ms. という敬称はウーマンリブ運動の結果生まれた The title 'Ms.' was created as a result of *the women's liberation movement*.

ウール wool /wʊl/ 一形 **ウールの wool, woolen** ▶ウールのセーター a *wool* [*woolen*] sweater ‖ このスーツはウールだ This suit is made of *wool*.

ウーロンちゃ ウーロン茶 oolong tea.

うーん hmm（考えながら）; **um**（考え込んで）; **well, ugh** /ʊx, ʌg/（つなぎ言葉）▶うーん, ちょっと考えさせてください *Well*, let me think about it. ‖ うーん, このパソコンは動きが実に遅い *Ugh!* This PC is really slow.

¹うえ 上

> **訳語メニュー**
> 表面に接して上に →on 1, 2
> 表面に接しないで上に →over, above 1
> 上の方へ →up 1
> 前の方に →above 3
> 上部 →the top 1, 4

1【空間的に基準より高い方（に）】on（表面に接して）; **over**（真上に）; **above**（上方に）; **up**（上の方へ）; **the top**（上部）▶その本, 机の上に置いといて Put that book *on* the desk. ‖ 多くの家の屋根の上にはテレビのアンテナがある There are TV antennas *on* the roofs of many houses. ‖ 母は冷蔵庫の上に花瓶を置いた My mother put a flower vase *on top of* the refrigerator.（➤ on top of は「…の上に」を強調する

表現).
▶大きなライトがテーブルの上にぶら下がっている A large light hangs *over* the table. ‖ テレビスタジオは頭の上にたくさんのライトがついていた There were a lot of lights *above* us in the TV studio. ‖ ジャンボジェット機は着陸待ちのためロサンゼルスの上を旋回した Our jumbo jet circled *over* Los Angeles waiting for permission to land. ‖ 飛行機は雲の上を飛ぶので下は見えませんよ The airplane will fly *above* the clouds, so you will be unable to see anything below.
▶《山登りなどで》もっと上へ行ってみようよ Let's go further *up*. ‖ 金子さんのお宅はこの上の階です The Kanekos live on the floor *above*. ‖ 飛行大会参加者たちは手製の翼を使って丘の上から飛んだ The participants in the flying contest flew from *the top* of the hill on handmade wings. ‖ このビルのいちばん上の階はレストランになる予定です There are plans for a restaurant to be built on *the top floor* of this building. ‖ 上から 6 行目を読みなさい Read the sixth line from *the top*. ‖ **対話**「高層アパートに住むとして,上の方の階と下の方の階ではどちらがいいですか」「上の方がいいね」"Suppose you lived in a highrise apartment building. Which would you prefer, to live on an *upper* (*floor*) or a lower floor ?" "I would prefer to live on an *upper floor*."
2【空間的に基準より外側の方に】on ▶表は寒いから上にオーバーを羽織ったほうがいいわね You should put on an overcoat since it is cold outside. ‖ 彼女はプレゼントをきれいな紙で包み,上に相手の名前を書いた She wrapped the present with beautiful paper and wrote the name of the recipient *on* it.
3【順序的に前の方】above ▶理由は上に書いてある The reason is written *above*. ‖ 上の住所にご連絡ください Please contact us at the *above* address.
4【地位が高い,能力が優れている】▶会社では地位が上になればなるほど責任が重くなる *The higher* you go in the company, the heavier your responsibilities (will) become. ‖ 日本の学校では,学年が上の学生は下の学生から「先輩」と呼ばれる At Japanese schools, students in lower grades call those *in upper grades* 'senpai.'
▶彼はクラスで上から 3 番目です He is (the) third *from the top* in his class. ‖ 英語の会話力では彼のほうが私より上だ He speaks English *better than* I do. ‖ 柔道に関する限り,斎藤君のほうがはるかに上だ As far as judo is concerned, Saito *is* much *stronger than* I am. ‖ ある民族が他民族より知力において上だとは言えない You can't say that one race is *superior to* others in intelligence. ‖ 上には上があるものだ There's always someone [something] better.
5【年齢】older(年上の) ▶いちばん上の兄は大学院生です My *oldest* [*eldest*] brother is a graduate student. ‖ 2 人の娘のうち上のほうは沖縄に住んでおります *The older* of my two daughters now lives in Okinawa. ‖ 主人は私より 3 つ上です My husband is three years *older* than I am. (➤ My husband is older than I by three years. はあまり使わない).
6【…の面では】▶年金をもらっているから生活の上では心配はない I don't have concerns *about living expenses* since I'm getting my pension. ‖ 酒の上の言動でもそれに対して責任を取らねばならない You are responsible for everything that you say or do even *when drunk* [even *while under the influence of alcohol*]. ‖ 暦の上ではもう秋なのに,まだまだ残暑が厳しい *According to the calendar*, it is already fall, but the heat still lingers.
7【…以上は】▶テストは英語も数学も振るわなかった,このうえは国語で頑張ってばん回するしかない I didn't do well on [《英》in] the English and math tests. *Such being the case* [*Since that's the case*], I have no choice but to do my best in Japanese to make up for my poor grades on them.
8【…に加えて】besides, on top of ▶彼女はきれいなうえに,頭がいい *Besides* being pretty, she is smart. ‖ さんざんごちそうになったうえ,お土産まで頂いてどうもすみません We cannot thank you enough for the wonderful present *on top of* [*coming after*] the delicious dinner.
9【…のあとで】▶コーチと相談したうえで退団するかどうか決めます I have to talk with the coach *before* I decide whether or not I will leave the team. ‖ その件に関しましては,十分検討したうえでなければお返事できかねます *Unless* we give due consideration to that matter, we cannot make any reply.
10【上を下への】▶突然の地震で場内は上を下への大騒ぎとなった A sudden earthquake threw the place *into total* [*utter*] *confusion*.
☞ 真上 (→見出語)

[2]**うえ 飢え hunger** (空腹) ; **starvation** (飢餓) ▶かわいそうに少年は飢えで死んだ The poor boy died of *hunger*. ‖ 今日依然として多くの人がひどい飢えに苦しんでいる Many people still suffer greatly from *starvation*.

ウエーター a waiter, (food) server(➤ 後者は性差がないのでウエートレスにも使える). →ボーイ.

ウエート weight(比重 ; 重量) ; **emphasis**(重点) ; **importance** (重要性) ▶もっと英語にウエートを置いて勉強しなさい You must put more *emphasis* on English. ‖ 最近日本の高校では創造性を伸ばすことにウエートを置いている These days Japanese high schools are *placing more importance* on developing creativity.
‖ **ウエートコントロール** weight control ‖ **ウエートリフティング** weight lifting.

ウエートレス a waitress (➤ 最近では性差のない (food) server を用いることがある) ▶ウエートレスにコーヒーを注文する order a cup of coffee from *a waitress* ‖ 彼女は現在神戸のレストランでウエートレスをしている She is now *waiting on tables* at a restaurant in Kobe. (➤ wait on tables は「給仕をする」).

ウエーブ a wave(波) ; **a Mexican wave** (応援の)
▶彼女の髪の毛はウエーブがかかっている Her hair is *wavy*. /She has *wavy* hair.
▶スタンドにウエーブが起こった *A Mexican wave* broke out in the stands.

ウェールズ Wales ▶ウェールズ人はケルト系の国民である *The Welsh* are a Celtic people. (➤ the Welsh は集合的な言い方 ; 1 人を指す場合は a Welshman, a Welshwoman, a Welsh boy [girl] などとなる).
‖ **ウェールズ語** Welsh, the Welsh language.

うえき 植木 a pot [potted] plant (鉢植えの) ; **a garden tree [plant]** (庭木) ▶彼は週に 1 回植木の手入れをする He looks after the *garden plants* once a week.
‖ **植木ばさみ** (a pair of) garden shears ‖ **植木鉢** a flowerpot ‖ **植木屋** a gardener(人).

うえこみ 植え込み shrubbery, shrubs(低木の) ▶植え込みに野球のボールが入った My baseball flew into the *shrubs in the garden*.

うえした 上下 **a top and a bottom**（上下に分かれた衣類の）▶その絵は上下逆に掛かっているよ That picture is hung *upside down*.

うえじに 飢え死に →餓死.

ウエスタン a **Western**［**western**］（西部劇）; **Western**［**western**］**music**（ウエスタンミュージック；ふつう country and western という）.

ウエスト a **waist** /weɪst/ ▶ズボンのウエストを詰める take in the *waist* of the trousers ‖ 妹はウエストがほっそりしている My (younger) sister has a slim *waist*. ‖ウエストに肉がついてきた I'm getting fat around *the middle*.（➤ the middle は漠然と「胴回り」の意）‖ ウエストはどのくらいありますか What is your *waist size*［*measurement*］?

> **危ないカタカナ語✸ ウエスト**
> **1** 胴回りの意の「ウエスト」は waist で発音は /weɪst/. 同じ発音の waste は「浪費する」の意. →腰.
> **2** 野球で投手が故意にストライクゾーンを外して投げるボールを「ウエストボール」というが, 英語では waste pitch という.

ウエストバージニア **West Virginia**（アメリカ東部の州；略 WV, W.Va.）.

ウエストポーチ a **waist pack**；《米また》a **fanny pack**,《英また》a **bum bag**（➤ ほかにも belt pack, belt bag, belly bag, hip pack などいろいろな名で呼ばれる）.

ウエストミンスター **Westminster**（ロンドンの一地区）‖ウエストミンスター寺院 Westminster Abbey.

うえつける 植え付ける **plant** +目（植物を）; **implant** +目（思想・菌などを）▶塀に沿って低木を植え付ける *plant* shrubs along the wall ‖ 大腸菌を寒天培養地に植え付ける *implant* colon bacilli on agar.
▶《比喩的》「金がすべてだ」という考え方を子供の心に植え付けるのは好ましくない It is not a good thing to *(im)plant* the idea in children's minds that money is everything.

ウエット **wet**（ぬれた）▶ウエットな性格の人 a *sentimental* person（➤ wet person は「ぬれた人」）.
‖ウエットティッシュ wet wipe.

ウエディング a **wedding**
‖ウエディングケーキ a wedding cake ‖ ウエディングドレス a wedding dress ‖ ウエディングベル a wedding bell.

ウエハース a **wafer** /wéɪfəʳ/.

ウェブ **the web**［**Web**］
‖ウェブサイト a website, a site ‖ ウェブデザイナー a web designer ‖ ウェブページ a web page.

ウエリントン **Wellington**（ニュージーランドの首都）.

1 **うえる 植える** **plant** +目 ▶庭にバラを植える *plant* roses in one's garden / *plant* one's garden *with* roses（➤ 後者は関心が rose よりも garden にある）.
▶熱帯の植物は日本に持ってきて植えてもたいていはよく育たない Most tropical plants do not grow well when they *are transplanted* to Japan.（➤ transplant は「移植する」）‖ 高速道路沿いの傾斜地にはツツジが植えてある Azaleas *are planted* on the slopes along the expressway.

2 **うえる 飢える** **be**［**go**］**hungry**; **starve**（ひどく飢える）▶ほかの人が飢えているときにぜいたくに暮らしている人が大勢いる Many live in luxury while others *are starving*. ‖ 愛に飢えた子供は非行に走りやすい Children who *are hungry for love*［*affection*］are prone to delinquent behavior. ‖ 血に飢えたオオカミ a *bloodthirsty* wolf.

ウエルターきゅう ウエルター級 **the welterweight class** ▶ウエルター級の選手 a welterweight.

うお 魚 a **fish**［複 **fish**］→さかな
‖魚市場 a fish market.
☞ 魚河岸, 魚座, 魚の目（→見出語）

うおうさおう 右往左往 ▶前方に巨大な氷山を見つけて, 船客は甲板を右往左往した Seeing a huge iceberg ahead, the passengers *ran back and forth* on the deck *in confusion*.（➤ in confusion は「うろたえて」）.

うおーっ ▶ジープが近づいて来るとライオンはウオーッとほえた The lion *roared* at the approaching jeep.
《参考》漫画などでは「ウオーッ」を Roooar! などとつづることもある.

ウォーミングアップ a **warm-up**（➤ warming-up は一般的ではない）▶5分間のウォーミングアップをする do a five-minute *warm-up* ‖ 前田をリリーフするため, 木村がウォーミングアップを始めた Kimura began to *warm up* to relieve Maeda.

ウォールがい ウォール街 **Wall Street**（ニューヨークの金融街）.

うおがし 魚河岸 a (**riverside** / **riverbank**) **fish market.**

うおざ 魚座 (a) **Pisces** /páɪsiːz/ ▶ 対話「あなたは何座?」「魚座よ」"What's your sign?" "(I'm *a*) *Pisces*."

ウオツカ **vodka** /vɑ́ːdkə/.

うおのめ 魚の目 a **corn** ▶左足の裏に魚の目ができちゃったよ I've got *a corn* on the sole of my left foot.

うか 羽化 **eclosion** /ɪklóʊʒən/ 一動 羽化する **eclose** /ɪklóʊz/.

1 **うかい 迂回する** **make**《米また **take**》**a detour** /díːtʊəʳ/ ▶本通りが通行止めになっていたので, 私たちはう回した Since the main street was closed, we *made*［*took*］*a detour*. ‖このう回路を利用してください Take this *detour*.《参考》「う回路」の掲示・看板では Detour,《英》Diversion と書く.

2 **うかい 鵜飼い** **cormorant** /kɔ́ːʳmərənt/ **fishing**（漁）; a **cormorant fisherman**（鵜匠）.

うがい **gargling**; a **gargle**（1回の）一動 うがいをする **gargle** ▶私は学校から帰ると必ずうがいをする I always *gargle* after I get home from school.
‖うがい薬 gargle（➤ 消臭用のものは mouthwash という）.

うかうか ▶青春をうかうかと過ごすな Don't *idle* your youth *away*. ‖ うかうかしてると子供たちにお肉をみんな食べられちゃいますよ Don't *dawdle*, or the kids will eat up all the meat.（➤ dawdle /dɔ́ːdl/ は「ぐずぐずする」）‖ うかうかしてると車にはねられるよ *If you're not careful*, you'll get hit by a car.（➤「気をつけなさい. さもないと」の意）.

うかがい 伺い ▶出張が必要かどうかは部長にお伺いを立てたほうがいい You should *ask* the general manager (*for instructions* as to) whether or not a business trip is necessary.（カッコ内は言わないほうが自然）.

1 **うかがう 伺う** **1**【聞く】**be told**（人から言われる）; **hear** +目（耳にする）▶橋本さんのお父さんは高名な数学者だと伺っております *I'm told* Ms. Hashimoto's father is a famous mathematician.
✉ おばあさまが回復に向かっていらっしゃると伺い, うれしく思います I am glad to *hear*

[*learn*] your grandmother is recovering. ➤ learn は「…ということを知る」の意.

2【質問する】ask +目 ▶１つ伺いたいことがあるのですが May I *ask* you a question? ‖ ちょっと伺いますが, 科学博物館はどこでしょうか *Excuse me, but* could you tell me the way to the Science Museum? (🔘 could you tell me の代わりに may I ask you としてもよい) ‖ その件について先生のご意見を伺いに参りました I came to *ask* your opinion about that matter (we were talking about).

3【訪問する】visit +目 →訪ねる ▶ 対話「次の日曜日にお宅に伺ってもよろしいでしょうか」「どうぞ」"Do you mind if I *visit* you next Sunday?" "Certainly not." ‖ 明朝お宅へ伺います I'll *pay a visit* to your home tomorrow morning.

²**うかがう 窺う 1【隙間などからのぞき見る】peep through** (➤ 部屋の中などをちょっとのぞく程度なら peep into) ▶彼女はカーテンの隙間から外の様子をうかがった She *peeped out* through the curtains. ‖ 少年は薄暗い台所の中をうかがった The boy *peeped into* the dimly-lit kitchen.

2【狙う】watch for ▶泥棒は家の中に忍び込む機会をうかがった The burglar *watched for* a chance to sneak into the house.

3【探る】 ▶課長は部長の顔色をうかがってばかりいる The section chief is always *studying* the department head's facial expressions (to gauge his mood). ／The section chief *is sensitive to* the department head's changes in mood.

うかされる 浮かされる ▶彼は熱に浮かされて何事かつぶやいている He'*s delirious with a fever* and is mumbling something.

うかす 浮かす ▶倹約すれば旅費を１万円浮かすことができるだろう If you economize, you will be able to *save* ten thousand yen on [*cut* ten thousand yen *off*] your traveling expenses.

うかつ 迂闊な careless ▶彼女の話をうのみにするなんて, きみもうかつだったね It was *stupid* of you to swallow her story. ‖ こんな所でうかつな話はできないよ We cannot speak *carelessly* around here. ‖ 彼女はうかつにもそれをしゃべってしまった She *thoughtlessly* blurted it out.

うがった 穿った penetrating /pénətreɪtɪŋ/ (洞察力のある) ▶なかなかうがった見方だね That is a quite *penetrating* insight. (➤ 誤用の「疑ってかかる」という意味で,「うがった見方をする」は view ... with suspicion).

うかぬかお 浮かぬ顔 ▶彼女は浮かぬ顔をして面接室から出てきた She came out of the interview room *looking gloomy* [*with a subdued look*]. (➤ subdued は「沈んだ」) ‖ 親族会議に集まった人たちは皆浮かぬ顔をしていた All those gathered at the family council *had long faces* [*appeared* (*to be*) *down in the dumps*]. (➤ be down in the dumps は「憂鬱だ」の意のインフォーマルな言い方).

うかばれる 浮かばれる ▶官僚の世界では一度大きなミスを犯せば一生浮かばれない In the bureaucracy, one big mistake will *ruin all your chances of promotion.* ‖ 無実が証明されれば亡くなった父も浮かばれ(＝成仏でき)ます My father's soul will *rest in peace* if he is exonerated. (🔘 英語では My father will rest in peace ... のようにいうほうがふつう).

うかびあがる 浮かび上がる ▶死んだ魚が水面に浮かび上がってきた A dead fish *came up* to the surface.

▶捜査線上に浮かび上がったのは田口という男だった In the course of investigations, a man named Taguchi *emerged as a suspect*.

うかぶ 浮かぶ 1【水面や空中に】float /floʊt/ ▶山中湖にはたくさんのボートが浮かんでいた Many boats *were floating* on Lake Yamanaka. ‖ ミジンコは水中に浮かんで上がったり下がったりしている Water fleas are *moving* up and down *in* the water. ‖ 青空に白い綿のような雲が浮かんでいる White fleecy clouds *are floating* in the blue sky.

2【表面に出る】appear ▶３連勝して監督の顔にはやっとほほえみが浮かんだ A smile finally *appeared on* the manager's face after the three consecutive wins. ‖ 虐待された子供の話を聞くと目に涙が浮かんできた The story about the abused children *brought tears to my eyes.* ‖ 彼女の話を聞くと, 父親の顔に不快そうな表情が浮かんだ When he heard what she said, her father *had* a displeased expression on his face. ‖ 前科のある男が有力な容疑者として捜査線上に浮かんできた As the investigation progressed, an ex-convict *emerged* as a prime suspect.

3【はっきりする】occur (to) ▶彼は突然いい考えが浮かんだ A good idea *occurred to* him suddenly. ／He *was struck with* a bright idea. ‖ すぐに浮かんだのがきみの名前なんだよ The name that immediately *came to my mind* was yours. ‖ すばらしい作戦が監督の頭に浮かんだ The manager *hit upon* a fantastic strategy. ‖ ワールドトレードセンター崩壊の情景が今も目に浮かぶ I still *vividly remember* the collapse of the World Trade Center.

うかべる 浮かべる float /floʊt/ +目 (水面などに) ▶湯船におもちゃの船を浮かべる *float* a toy boat in the bath.

▶彼女は目に涙[口元にほほえみ]を浮かべながらその話をした She told the story *with tears in her eyes* [*with a smile on her lips*]. ／*Tears were in her eyes* [*A smile was on her lips*] as she related the story.

うかる 受かる pass +目 ▶あの学校に受かるとはずいぶん勉強したんでしょうね You must have studied very hard to have *passed* the entrance examinations for that school. →合格.

うかれる 浮かれる ▶あの人たちは昼間から酒を飲んで浮かれている They *are* drinking and *having a good time* in the middle of the day.

うがん 右岸 ▶隅田川右岸 *the right bank* of the Sumida River.

ウガンダ Uganda(アフリカ中東部の国).

¹**うき 浮き a float, a bobber** (釣り用の); a **buoy** /búːi ‖ bɔi/ (浮標) ▶釣り糸に浮きをつける put *a float* on a fishing line.

²**うき 雨季・雨期 the rainy season** ▶この島では11月から雨季に入る On this island *the rainy season* sets in in November. (➤ set in は「(季節などが) 始まる」).

うきあがる 浮き上がる ▶彼は利根川に大量の魚が浮き上がっているのを発見した He spotted a large number of fish *floating on the surface* in the Tone River.

▶《比喩的》うちの会社の幹部は一般社員から浮き上がっている The executives at our company *have lost touch with* [*have lost the support of*] the rank and file. (➤「支持を失っている」の意).

うきあしだつ 浮き足立つ ▶国会議員たちは選挙が近いので浮き足だっている The members of the Diet are *restless* [*nervous*] because the election is near at hand.

うきうき 浮き浮き ▶理恵はうきうきとデートに出かけて行った Rie went out on her date *in a great mood*. ‖きょうはやけにうきうきしているじゃない You're awfully *cheerful* today, aren't you? ‖彼は生まれて初めてロンドンに出かけるのでうきうきしている He is *on cloud nine* since he is going to London for the first time in his life. (➤ on cloud nine は「とても幸福で」の意のインフォーマルな表現).

うきくさ 浮き草 a **floating weed** ▶《比喩的》浮き草の暮らしをする lead a *drifter's* life (➤ drifter は「流れ者の」の意).

うきぐも 浮き雲 a **floating cloud**.

うきしずみ 浮き沈み **ups and downs** ▶浮き沈みの多い人生を送る lead a life with many *ups and downs*.

うきしま 浮き島 a **floating island**.

うきたつ 浮き立つ ▶好結果を予期して気分が浮き立った I *was in a good mood* in anticipation of good results.

うきぶくろ 浮き袋 a **float** (水泳用, また魚の); a **swimming ring** [**belt**] (水泳用); a **life preserver** (救命用).

うきぼり 浮き彫り **relief** ▶浮き彫りの像 a figure *sculptured in relief*.
▶《比喩的》その小説は明治時代の世相を浮き彫りにしている The novel *depicts* the social aspects of the Meiji era *in full relief*.

うきめ 憂き目 ▶どうしてあんなに優しい寅さんがこんな憂き目に遭うのだろうか Why does *life have to be* so *tough* [*hard*] on a kindhearted man like Tora-san? (● 英語では「あんなに優しい男性に人生はなぜこれほど過酷なのか」と考える) ‖彼は２度目の選挙で落選の憂き目を見た He *had the bitter* [*miserable*] *experience* of losing in his second election.

うきよ 浮き世 **life** (人生); **the world** (世間) ▶浮き世の荒波にもまれる go through the whirlpools of *life* ‖それが浮き世の常だ That's the way of *the world*. / Such is *life* [*the world*]. ‖父は浮き世離れした学者だった My father was a scholar who didn't care about *worldly things*.

うきよえ 浮世絵 an ***ukiyoe***; a wood-block print depicting Edo-period scenes and customs (➤ 説明的な訳).

うきわ 浮き輪 a **float (ring)**, an **inner tube (used as a float)**.

うく 浮く **1【水面・空中に】** **float** /floʊt/ ▶木は水よりも軽いので水に浮く Wood *floats* because it is lighter than water. ‖ 対話 「泳げるようになった?」「いや, でもやっと浮くようになったよ」 "Have you learned to swim?" "No, but I've finally learned to *float*."
2【遊離する】 ▶あの男は歯の浮くようなお世辞を言う That man's flattery is *nauseating* [*disgusting*] to me. (→歯) ‖彼はクラスの中で１人だけ浮いている He *is isolated* [*alienated*] from his classmates.
3【感情的に高ぶる】 ▶ぼくは決して浮いた気持ちなんかじゃないんだ I'm not *being flippant*. I'm really serious. ‖「彼女に振られちゃった」と弘は浮かない声で言った "My girlfriend dumped me," said Hiroshi in a *depressed* voice.
4【使わずに済む】 ▶目的地まで歩いたので1000円浮いた I *saved* one thousand yen by walking to my destination.
☛ 浮かぬ顔 (→見出語)

うぐいす 鶯 《鳥》 a **bush warbler**
日本紹介 ✉ **ウグイスは春を告げる小鳥です. その鳴き声はのどかに晴れ渡った春の日を連想させます. 昔から「梅にウグイス」として絵の題材としてもよく描かれてきました** The *uguisu* (bush warbler) is a bird which announces spring [is symbolic of spring]. Its song is associated with clear (bright) spring days. 'An *uguisu* perching on an *ume* branch' is a traditional subject of paintings.
‖ウグイス色 sage green, olive green.

ウクライナ **Ukraine** /jukréɪn/ (ヨーロッパ東部の国).

ウクレレ a **ukulele** /jùːkəléɪli/.

¹うけ 受け **popularity** (人気); **reputation** (評判) ▶秋山先生はいい先生なのに生徒の受けがよくない Even though Mr. Akiyama is a good teacher, he *isn't popular with* [*among*] his students.

²うけ 有卦 ▶有卦に入(い)る *have a run of good luck* (➤「幸運続きである」の意).

うけあう 請け合う **assure** +目 (確かである[間違いない]と保証する); **guarantee** +目 /gæ̀rəntíː/ (品質などを保証する) ▶彼が任務を完璧に遂行できることは私が請け合います I *assure* you he'll carry out his duties perfectly. ‖この品物が上等なことは請け合います I *guarantee* the quality of this article.

うけい 右傾 ▶主流派の政治家が右傾化した Mainstream politicians *have shifted to the right*.

うけいれ 受け入れ ▶その国は難民の受け入れを拒否した That country refused to *accept* refugees.

うけいれる 受け入れる **accept** +目 (招待・申し出を承知する); **comply** 《with》 (願い・要望に応じる); **receive** +目 (差し出されたものを受け取る); **yield** 《to》 (要求に屈する) ▶彼は私の援助の申し出を受け入れようとしなかった He would not *accept* my offer to help. ‖私はきみの要求を絶対に受け入れることはできない I can by no means *yield to* your demand(s). ‖私たちの学校はまだ外国人留学生を受け入れる態勢が十分整っていない Our school is not yet ready to *accept* students from overseas [to *receive* foreign students]. ‖公の場での喫煙はますます受け入れられなくなっている Smoking in public places is becoming less *acceptable*. ‖原子力発電所を受け入れてくれる自治体を探すのは易しくはない It's not an easy matter to find a municipality that will *agree to host* a nuclear power plant. ‖私たちは新たな日常を受け入れていくしかない We have to *come to terms with* the new normal. (➤ come to terms with は困難な状況や人の死などを「徐々に受け止めていく, 慣れていく」) ‖彼女のことはありのままに受け入れるべきだと思う I think you should *accept* her *as* she *is*.

うけうり 受け売り ▶人の受け売りをする *echo* [*merely repeat*] what someone says (●「人の言うことを繰り返す」と考える) ‖彼の意見は先生の言われたことの受け売りだ His opinion is just *a rehash* of what his teacher said. (➤ rehash /rìːhǽʃ/ は「焼き直し」) ‖彼女はマネージャーの意見の受け売りをしているだけだ She is only *parroting* the manager's view. (➤ オウムが人間の口まねをするところから).

うけおい 請負 (a) **contract** /kɑ́ːntrækt/ (工事などの契約) ▶その工事は請負に出した We have put the construction work out to *contract*. ‖**請負仕事** a contract job ‖**請負人** a contractor.

うけおう 請け負う **contract** /kəntrǽkt/ +目 (契約する); **undertake** +目 (工事などを引き受ける) ▶うちの会社は新しい橋の建設を請け負っている Our company *has contracted* to build a new bridge.

うけこたえ 受け答え ▶受け答えがうまい be good at *answering questions* / *give* quick-witted *replies*

(➤ 後者は「とっさに気のきいた答え方をする」) ‖ 彼女は受け答えがしっかりしている She always gives *a* firm *answer*.

うけざら 受け皿 a **saucer**(コーヒーカップの受け皿)
▶受け皿付きのコーヒーカップ a cup and *saucer* (➤ /kʌ̀pənsɔ́:səʳ/ と発音).
▶《比喩的》わが国には多くの難民を受け入れる受け皿がない Our country *is not prepared to accept* many refugees.

うけたまわる 承る **1【受ける】**▶《レストランなどで》ご注文を承ります *May I take* your order now ? ‖《和菓子屋で》賃餅(ちんもち)承ります We *accept* orders for *mochi* [rice cake].
2【聞く】▶ご住所とお名前を承ります *May I have* your name and address ? ‖ 部長はあいにく外出しておりますので, 私が代わって承ります The manager is out of the office, so may I help you instead ?
3【承諾する】▶ご依頼の件は確かに承りました We will certainly *comply with* your request.

うけつぐ 受け継ぐ **take over**(事業・責任などを) ; **succeed** +㊀ (地位・身分・財産などを) ; **inherit** +㊀ (遺伝する ; 財産を相続する) ▶彼は父親の事業を受け継いだ He *took over* his father's business. ／He *succeeded* his father in his business. ‖ 彼女は母親の性質を受け継いでいる She *inherited* her mother's character [personality]. (➤ 英語は過去形になる) ‖ これらの伝統芸能は親から子へと受け継がれてきた These traditional performing arts *have been passed on* from generation to generation [from parents to children].

うけつけ 受付 **1【受け付ける所】** a **reception** [an **information**] **desk** ; a **receptionist** (受付係) ▶私は受付(の人)に名を告げた I gave my name to the *receptionist*.
2【受理】 **acceptance** ▶応募の受付は1月31日までです Applications will *be* [are *being*] *accepted* until January 31. ‖《掲示》予約受付中 Now Accepting Reservations.
‖**受付番号** a receipt /rɪsí:t/ number.

うけつける 受け付ける **accept** +㊀ ▶願書は本日から受け付けます Applications *are accepted* starting today.
▶社長は我々の抗議を受け付けなかった Our president did not *accept* our protest. ‖ その病人は衰弱がひどくて流動食さえ受け付けなかった The patient grew so weak that he [she] *could not keep* even liquid food *down*. (➤ keep down は「(食べた物を)戻さずにいる」).

うけとめる 受け止める **1【つかむ】** **catch** +㊀ ▶ボールをしっかりと受け止める *catch* a ball without fail.
2【対応する】 **take** +㊀ ▶首相は沖縄県民の思いをしっかりと受け止めると言った The prime minister said he would *take* the sentiments of the people of Okinawa seriously.

うけとり 受け取り **1【受け取ること】**▶私はルームメートに荷物の受け取りを頼んだ I asked my roommate to *receive* a parcel for me. ‖ その男は小包の受け取りを拒否した He refused to *accept* [*take*] the parcel. (➤ 単に配達されてものを「受け取る」は receive でよいが, この例では受領をOKするか否か, 意思を表す必要があるので, receive は不適切) ‖ 落し物の受け取りには本人を証明するものが必要です You need identification to *claim* a lost item. (➤「自分の所有物だと言う」は claim).
2【領収書】 a **receipt** /rɪsí:t/ ▶小包の受取にサインする sign *a receipt* for the package.

うけとる 受け取る **1【手に受ける】** **take** +㊀ ▶彼女は夫の手から赤ん坊を受け取った She *took* her baby from her husband's arms.
2【手に入れる】 **get** +㊀ ; **receive** +㊀ (受領する) ; **take** +㊀ (もらう) ; **accept** +㊀ (喜んで, または同意して) ▶きのう彼から礼状を受け取った I *got* [*received*] a letter of thanks from him yesterday. ‖ きみからの寄付は受け取れない I cannot *take* [*accept*] your donation.
3【解釈する】 **take** +㊀ ; **get** +㊀ (理解する) ▶先方はあなたのことばをどう受け取っただろう ? How did they *take* what you said ? ‖ きみは私の言ったことを間違って受け取ったようだ You seem to *have gotten* me *wrong*. (➤ get ... wrong で「…を誤解する」).

うけながす 受け流す ▶あの大臣はいつも記者の質問を受け流す That Minister always *evades* [*dodges*] questions from reporters.

うけみ 受け身 **passivity** (消極性) ; ***ukemi*** (柔道の ; 英語では a breakfall (technique) とか the art of falling などと説明されることもある) ; **the passive voice** (文法上の) ▶次郎はいつも受け身になっている Jiro *is* always *passive* [always *takes a passive attitude*].

うけもち 受け持ち ▶受け持ち(＝担任)の先生 one's *class* [《米また》*homeroom* ／《英また》*form*] *teacher* ‖ ことしのきみの受け持ちの先生, 誰 ? Who's your *homeroom teacher* this year ? ／Who's in charge of your class this year ?
‖**受け持ち区域** a district assigned to a person ; one's beat (警官や郵便配達の).

うけもつ 受け持つ **be in charge** 《of》, **take charge** 《of》 ▶吉川先生が私たちのクラスを受け持っている Mr. Yoshikawa *is in charge of* our class. ‖ きょうから1年4組を受け持つことになった平井です I'm Mr. Hirai and I'll *be in charge of* the fourth class of the first year starting today. (➤ 幼い子供たちに向かって話すときはこのように自分の名前に Mr. をつけることがある) ‖ 彼は皿洗いを受け持たされた He *was assigned to* wash the dishes.

うける 受ける

訳語メニュー
(手で)受け止める →catch **1**
受け入れる →accept **2**
受け取る →get, receive **3**
試験などを →take **4**

1【受け止める】 **catch** +㊀ ▶ボールを受ける *catch* a ball ‖ 雨漏りをバケツに受ける(＝集める) *catch* the leaking rain in a bucket.
2【受け入れる】 **accept** +㊀ ▶人の挑戦を受ける(＝受けて立つ) *accept* a person's challenge ‖ 喜んでご招待をお受けいたします I'm delighted to *accept* your invitation. ‖ マッキーバー氏がある仕事に付かないかと誘ってくれたので, 私はそれを受けようと思う Mr. McKeever offered me a job, and I think I'll *take* it *on*. (➤ take on は「任務・仕事を引き受ける」).
3【受け取る, 得る】 **get** +㊀ ; **receive** +㊀ (受領する) ▶生活保護を受ける *receive* welfare ‖ 開発途上国は先進工業国から多額の援助を受けている Developing countries *get* a lot of aid from the industrialized nations. ‖ ジャイアント・パンダは希少動物として手厚い保護を受けている As an endangered species, the giant panda *is protected* with great care. ‖

その件についてはまだ報告を受けていない I have *not been informed* of that matter. ‖ 対話「井上さんからの電話を受けたのは誰ですか」「私です」"Who *took* the phone call from Inoue?" "I did."

4【試験・検査などを】take +目 (試験などを) ; **have** +目 (苦楽・状況などを) ▶来年G大学を受けるつもりです I am going to *take* the entrance examination for [of] G University next year. ‖ 母は右足の手術を受けた My mother *had an operation on* her right leg. ／My mother's right leg *was operated on*. ‖ 血圧の検査を受けなさい *Have* your blood pressure *checked*. (➤ have ... checked で「…を検査してもらう」の意).

5【被る】▶その少年は父親からひどい扱いを受けた The boy *was abused* by his father. ‖ その町は敵の攻撃を受けた That town *was attacked* by the enemy. ‖ 彼は兄たちの影響を受けてサッカー部に入った He *was influenced* by his brothers to join the soccer team.

6【人気を得る】▶玉木先生のギャグは学生に受ける Mr. Tamaki's silly jokes *go over well with* his students. ‖ 山登りが中高年に受けている Mountain climbing *has caught on* with [among] middle-aged and elderly people.

うけわたし 受け渡し delivery
▶商品の受け渡しは代金と引き換えでお願いします Please pay for the goods on *delivery*. ／Please pay C.O.D. (➤ C.O.D. は cash on delivery (配達時現金払い), または collect on delivery (配達時代金回収) の略).

うげん 右舷 starboard (反 port).

うごかす 動かす

訳語メニュー
移動させる →move **1**
作動させる →run, operate **2**
使う →use **2**
心を動かす →move **3**

1【移動させる】move +目 ▶本棚が置けないから机を左側へ動かそう There's not enough room for the bookcase, so let's *move* the desk to the left. ‖ ブルドーザーでもその岩を簡単には動かせなかった Even the bulldozer couldn't *move* that big rock easily. ‖ この象はロープを引っ張ってダンプカーを動かすことができる This elephant can *pull* a dump truck on a rope.

2【作動させる】run +目 ; **operate** +目 (操作する) ; **use** +目 (使う) ▶この工場の機械はすべてロボットが動かしています All the machines in this factory *are operated* [*are run*] by robots. ‖ このパソコンの動かし方, 教えてくれる? Could you show me *how to use* this computer?

3【体・心を動かす】move +目 ▶小坂君は耳をぴくぴく動かすことができる Kosaka can *wiggle* his ears. ‖ 腕を前後に動かしてごらんなさい *Swing* your arms back and forth. ‖「体を動かさないでください」とX線技師が言った "Please don't *move*," said the X-ray technician. ‖ ごろごろしてばかりいないで少しは体を動かしたら? Stop lying around and *get* some *exercise*. ‖ 私は彼の障害者への奉仕に心を動かされ, 寄付することにした *Moved* by his devoted service to disabled people, I decided to donate some money.

▶《慣用表現》彼は友人の死の知らせを聞いても眉一つ動かさなかった He *didn't bat an eye* [*eyelid*] at the news of his friend's death. (●「まばたきもしない」が原義の not bat an eye [eyelid] を用いる).

4【働かせる】▶人を動かすには自分自身が勤勉でなくてはならない You have to be hardworking if you want to *get* other people *to work*. (➤ get ~ to do で「～に…させる」) ‖ 山中氏は50人の課員を動かしている Mr. Yamanaka *has* fifty people *working under* him in his section. ‖ 人々の民主化運動はやがて社会を動かす(＝変える)大きな力となった The people's democratization movement was a great force in *changing society*.

5【「動かせない」の形で】▶職場によって男女差別が残っているのは動かせない事実です It's *an undeniable* [*indisputable*] *fact* that gender discrimination still exists in some workplaces. (➤ undeniable は「否定できない」, indisputable は「議論の余地のない」).

うごき 動き 1【動作】movement (規則正しい動き) ; **a move** (ある意図をもった動き) ▶目の動き the *movement* of one's eye(s) ‖ 心の動き the *movement* of one's heart ‖ 敵の動きを読む anticipate the enemy's *move* ‖ ナマケモノは動きが鈍い A sloth *moves slowly*. ／A sloth is a *slow-moving* animal. ‖ このナンバリングは動きが悪い This numbering machine *doesn't work well*. ‖ 彼は年の割に動きが機敏だ He is *quick* for his age. (● quick は quick in action の省略) ‖ 人混みで動きがとれなかった I *could not budge* (*an inch*) in the crowd.

▶《慣用表現》きょうは忙しくて動きがとれません I'*m tied up* today. ‖ 今晩は出かけられないよ, 宿題が山のようにあって動きが取れないんだ I can't go out this evening because I'*m bogged down with* piles of homework. (➤ be bogged down with は「…で全く進めない」) ‖ 彼は借金で動きがとれない He *is up to* his *ears* in debt. (➤ be up to one's ears in は「…にはまり込んでいる」).

2【変動】(a) change ▶時代の動き *changes* in the times ‖ 世の中の動きが激しくてとてもついていけない The world is *moving* [is *changing*] so fast that I can hardly keep up with it. ‖ 新内閣の閣僚にだいぶ動きがあるようだ There will probably be a major *change* [*reshuffle* ／ *shakeup*] of ministers in the new cabinet. ‖ 《報道番組で》そちらに何か動きがあったら報告してください Please report to us *if things change*. ‖ 為替と株の動き *movements* [*trends*] in exchange rates and stocks ‖ 今週の株の動きは活発[不活発]だった The *stock market* was active [dull ／inactive] this week.

うごく 動く

訳語メニュー
位置を変える →move **1**
機能する →run, work **2**

1【位置を変える】move ▶カタツムリはゆっくり動く Snails *move* slowly. ‖ 動くな Don't *move*! ／Hold it! ／Freeze! (➤ freeze は特に強盗や警官などが用いる) ‖ 動くと撃つぞ I'll shoot if you *move*. ‖ 私は大阪から動きたくありません I don't want to *leave* Osaka. ‖ 天候が回復するまでここを動かないほうがいい We should *stay here* until the weather improves. ‖ 対話「あの人たちどうしてあんな所に座っているの?」「腹が減って動けない(＝歩けない)んだよ」"Why are they sitting there?" "Maybe they are too

う

hungry to *walk*."

2【機械などが】run（順調に運動を続ける）; **work**（機能する）▶SL は石炭で動く Steam locomotives *run* on coal. ‖この機械は24時間動いています This machine *operates* twenty-four hours a day. ‖おかしいわね, 洗濯機が動かない［動いていない］That's strange. The washing machine doesn't *work* [isn't *working*]. ‖台風で公共交通機関は大半が動いていない Most public transportation *isn't in operation* [*is out of operation*] because of the typhoon. ‖ 対話「東京では電車は朝何時に動き始めますか」「4 時半頃です」"What time in [of] the morning do the trains *start running* in Tokyo ?" "Around 4 : 30." ‖このボタンを押すとエアコンが動き始めます If you push this button, the air conditioner will *turn on*. ‖ 対話 (医者が)「どうしました?」「右腕が動かないんです」"What seems to be the trouble ?" "I *can't move* my right arm."
▶今度の選挙では大金が動いたらしい A large sum of money seems to *have changed hands* in the last election. (➤ change hands は「所有者が変わる」).

3【行動する】▶政治家の中には金で動く人もいるらしい It seems that some politicians can *be influenced by money*. ‖この法案を成立させるために多数の財界人が陰で動いた A lot of businesspeople *maneuvered behind the scenes* to see that the bill would be passed. (➤ maneuver behind the scenes は「舞台裏で策を巡らす」) ‖いくら私がこうしてはと言っても, 部下が思うように動いてくれないんだよ My subordinates don't *respond* as I would like, no matter what I say.

4【「動かない」の形で】▶彼の有罪は動かないだろう It isn't likely his conviction (of the crime) will be *reversed* [*overturned*]. ‖犯人の残した指紋が動かぬ証拠となった The criminal's fingerprints were *strong* [*hard*] *evidence* (in the case). ‖いくら言ってもオーストラリアに留学するという彼女の決意は動かないだろう Whatever you may say, you *can't shake her resolution* to study abroad in Australia.

うごのたけのこ 雨後の筍 ▶雨後のたけのこのようにパソコンショップが増えた Personal computer shops have appeared [have sprung up] *like mushrooms* (*after rain*). 《参考》mushroom は「キノコ」で, しばしば成長の早いものの代表と考えられる. タケノコは英米人にはあまりなじみがない.

うごめく squirm ▶巣箱ではミツバチの幼虫がうごめいている The hive is full of *squirming* bee larvae.

うざい ▶何度も同じことを言って, うざいんだよ You keep saying the same thing again and again. *It's really annoying* [*irritating*].

うさぎ 兎 a **rabbit**(穴ウサギ) ; a **hare**（野ウサギ）
▶うさぎ跳びをする hop in a squatting position.
‖ウサギ小屋 a rabbit hutch.

うさばらし 憂さ晴らし ▶憂さ晴らしに酒でも飲もうぜ How about a drink to *let off* some *steam* [*take our minds off things*] ?

うさんくさい 胡散臭い suspicious, 《インフォーマル》**fishy**（怪しげな）; **shady**（後ろ暗い）
▶うさんくさい話 a *suspicious* story ‖あのセールスマンはどこかうさんくさいところがある There's something *fishy* about that salesman. ‖うさんくさい男 a *suspicious-looking* man ‖うさんくさい仕事 *shady* business.

¹うし 牛 cattle ; a **bull**, a **cow**

《解説》**牛について**
(1)牛の総称は **cattle**（集合名詞で複数扱い）だが, 個別には **bull**（雄牛), **cow**（雌牛), **calf** /kæf ‖ kɑ:f/（子牛), **ox**（労役用·食用の去勢雄牛)のようにいう.
(2) cow は「雌牛」だが, 一般語としては「牛」の代表. ただし, 動物学的には ox で代表される.
(3)鳴き声を表す英語は moo /mu:/ が一般的. bellow は特に雄牛が大声で鳴くときに用いる.

▶彼は牛を60頭飼っている He raises [(英) rears] sixty head of *cattle*. (➤ 家畜を数える単位としての head は単複同形) ‖牛と羊が牧場で草を食べている *Cows* and sheep are grazing in the pasture.

²うし 丑（十二支の）**the Ox**
‖丑の日 the day of the Ox.

¹うじ 蛆 a **maggot**(ハエなどの幼虫) ; a **grub**（甲虫の幼虫）▶ごみ捨て場にうじが湧いた *Maggots* are breeding in the garbage dump.
▶ (比喩的) うじ虫みたいなやつ a *despicable* person／scum（人間のかす).
ことわざ 男やもめにうじが湧く Widowers are generally untidy. (➤ 日本語からの意訳).

²うじ 氏 a **family name**(姓) ; (a) **lineage** /líniidʒ/（家系）; **birth**(生まれ)
ことわざ 氏より育ち Breeding is more important than birth.

うじがみ 氏神 an **ancestral deity** /dí:əṭi/（祖先の）; a **local deity**(その土地の).

うじうじ ▶そんなにうじうじしてないではっきりしたらどうだ Stop being so *wishy-washy* and make up your mind.

うしなう 失う **1【なくす】lose** /lu:z/ +目 ▶命を失う *lose* one's life ‖バランスを失う *lose* balance ‖彼はギャンブルで全財産を失った He *lost* everything he owned by gambling. (➤ lost は lose の過去形) ‖彼女は幼いとき視力を失った She *lost* her eyesight in childhood. ‖私はそのテレビ番組に興味を失った I've *lost* interest in that TV program. ‖彼女は倒れた拍子に頭を強く打って気を失った She *lost consciousness* when she collapsed and hit her head. ‖地球上から緑がどんどん失われつつある Forests (and plants) *are* rapidly *disappearing* from the earth. ‖彼らはその大地震の間も冷静さを失わなかった They *remained composed* [*didn't lose their cool*] even during the great earthquake.

2【死に別れる】lose +目 ▶たった1人の妹を失う *lose* one's only sister ‖彼女は交通事故で両親を失った She *lost* her parents in a traffic accident.

3【取り逃がす】miss +目 ▶私は一生に一度の機会を失ったのかもしれない I may *have missed* the chance of a lifetime. ‖巨人はノーアウト満塁という絶好のチャンスを失った The Giants *missed* their best chance to score with the bases loaded and no outs.

4【点を取られる】▶森田は3回で6点を失い, マウンドを降りた Morita left the mound after *yielding* six runs in the first three innings.

5【わからなくなる】▶一行は深い霧のために方角を失った The party *lost their bearings* in the thick fog.

うじむし 蛆虫 →うじ.

うじゃうじゃ ▶桜の木の枝に毛虫がうじゃうじゃいるのを見て気持ちが悪くなった The *swarms of* hairy caterpillars on the branches of the cherry tree made me feel sick. (➤ swarm は「昆虫などの群れ」) ‖ 火事場にやじ馬がうじゃうじゃ集まってきた Many people began *crowding* [*swarming*] around the site of the fire.

うしろ 後ろ 1【物の背後に】**behind** ▶授業中私の後ろで私語している人が2，3人いた There were a couple of students whispering *behind* me in class. ‖ 家の後ろに(＝裏に)大きなリンゴの木がある There is a big apple tree *behind* [*at the back of* ／《米また》*in back of*] my house. ‖ 後ろへ下がってください *Step back*, please. ‖ 敵の後ろへ回れ Get *behind* the enemy.
▶後ろを振り向かないでまっすぐ行きなさい Go straight. Don't *look back*. ‖ 医者は私に後ろを向くように言った The doctor told me to *turn around*. ‖ リンカーンは劇場で後ろから銃で撃たれた Lincoln was shot *from behind* in a theater. ‖ 後ろから誰かついて来るのでとても怖かった I was scared because someone *was following* me.
✉《写真説明で》椅子の後ろに立っているのが私です I am the one standing *behind* the chair.
2【後部】**the back, the rear** (➤ 後者はやや堅い言い方，また特に車や建物の後部[裏手]をいう) ▶後ろの車輪 [バンパー] a *rear* wheel [bumper] ‖ 後ろ(の方)に聞こえるように大きな声で言ってください Speak up so that the people in *the back* can hear you. ‖ 学生の多くは教室の後ろの席に座るのが好きだ Most students prefer seats toward *the back* of the classroom. ‖ 我々はバスの後ろ(＝奥)へ移動した We moved to *the rear* of the bus. (➤「後ろへ移動してください」なら Move to the rear, please.) ‖ 電車はふつう後ろの方と前の方の車両がすいている There is usually more room in *the back* and front cars of the train. ‖ 列の後ろについて並んでください Please stand at [go to] *the back of the line*.
☞ 真後ろ (→見出語)

うしろあし 後ろ足 a **hind** /haɪnd/ **leg** ▶犬は後ろ足で立った The dog stood (up) *on its hind legs*.

うしろがみ 後ろ髪 ▶私は後ろ髪を引かれる思いでその子供たちと別れた I had to *drag myself away* from the children.

うしろぐらい 後ろ暗い ▶あの人はほとんど出歩かない．何か後ろ暗いところがあるに違いない He rarely goes out. There must be something *shady* about him.

うしろすがた 後ろ姿 ▶人の後ろ姿を見かける catch sight of a person's *back* ‖ 彼女は後ろ姿がきれいだ She has a lovely *appearance from the back*. ‖ 後ろ姿のしぐれてゆくか (➤ 山頭火の俳句) His back is disappearing [vanishing] in a cold drizzle of early winter.

うしろだて 後ろ盾 **support**(支援)；a **supporter**(支援者)；a **backer**(後援者) ▶あの人が勲章をもらったのは大物政治家の後ろ盾があったからだ It was because a major politician *backed* him that the man was decorated.

うしろで 後ろ手 ▶強盗は女性を後ろ手に縛って金を奪った The robber tied the woman's *hands behind* her *back* and took her money.

うしろまえ 後ろ前 ▶彼はセーターを後ろ前に着ているのに気づかない He hasn't noticed that he's got his sweater on *backward* [《主に英》*back to front*].

うしろむき 後ろ向き ▶後ろ向きに歩く walk *backward* ‖ 後ろ向きになってごらん *Face backwards*. ／*Turn around*. ／*Turn* your *back* (to us).
▶彼は私たちの計画に後ろ向きの(＝消極的な)態度をとった He took a *negative* attitude toward our project. ‖ きみの考えは後ろ向きだ Your ideas are *backward* [*retrogressive*].

うしろめたい 後ろめたい **feel guilty** ▶母にうそついて遊びに行ったから，ちょっと後ろめたかった I *felt* a bit *guilty* for lying to my mother and going out to enjoy myself. ‖ きみは友人を裏切って後ろめたくないのかい？ Doesn't it give you *a bad* [*guilty*] *conscience* to betray your friend？(➤ bad [guilty] conscience は「やましい気持ち」).

うしろゆび 後ろ指 ▶私は人に後ろ指をさされるようなことはしたくない I don't want to do anything to *make* people *talk* [*criticize* me] *behind my back*.

うす 臼 a **mortar**(つき臼)；a **hand mill**(ひき臼) ▶臼で餅をつく pound steamed rice for *mochi* in *a mortar* 《参考》英語国民は mortar から「すり鉢」の一種を連想してしまうので，日本の「臼」は a wooden mortar used for *mochi*-pounding とするのもよい．

うす- 薄- ▶薄茶色 *light* brown ‖ 薄緑 *light* green ‖ 薄塩の魚 fish with *little* salt ／fish *lightly* salted.

-うす -薄 ▶彼はこの計画には気乗り薄だ He is *not enthusiastic* about this plan. ‖ ホウレンソウが品薄になってきた We are *running short of* spinach. ‖ 彼の当選は見込み薄だ *There is little hope* of his getting elected.

うず 渦 a **whirlpool**(勢いのよい水の)；a **whirl**(回転の速い)；a **maelstrom** /méɪlstrəm/(大きな；文語的で比喩的に用いることが多い)；an **eddy**(水や風の小さな) ▶漁船は大きな渦に巻き込まれた The fishing boat was caught in the *whirlpool*. ‖ 風が渦を巻きながら少女の帽子を運んでいった The wind *whirled* the little girl's hat away. ‖ 風に木の葉は小さく渦を巻いた The wind *whirled* the leaves about. (➤ whirl は「くるくる回す」).
▶《比喩的》彼女は争いの渦に巻き込まれてしまった She got [was] drawn into *the maelstrom of the dispute*.
‖渦潮 an eddying current.

うすあかり 薄明かり **the twilight**(日の出・日没前の；夕方の薄明かりは the dusk ともいう).

うすあじ 薄味 ▶関西人は概して薄味を好む People in the Kansai district generally like their foods *lightly seasoned* [*salted*].

うすい 薄い

訳語メニュー
厚さ・濃度などが →thin 1, 2, 3
飲み物が →weak 2
色・味が →light 2

1【厚さが】**thin** ▶このノートは薄い This notebook is *thin*. ‖ けさ，池に薄い氷が一面に張った This morning the pond was covered with *thin* ice. ‖ パンは薄く切ってください Please cut the bread into *thin* slices. ／Please slice the bread *thinly*. ‖ 彼女の唇は母親に比べて薄い She has *thinner* lips than her mother.
2【濃度が】**weak, thin；light**(色・味が) ▶薄い紅茶[コーヒー] *weak* tea [coffee] ‖ 辺りは薄い霧に包まれた The neighborhood was veiled in a *thin* mist. ‖ 私は薄いピンクのブラウスが好きだ I like *light* pink blouses. ‖ 簡単に消せるように薄く書いてください Please write *lightly* so that you can erase

easily.

3【量・度合いが】▶私の父は頭のてっぺんが少し薄い My father's hair is a little *thin* on top. ‖ 彼は髪が薄くなってきた His hair is *getting thin*(*ner*). ／He is *becoming* [*growing*] *bald*. ‖ 彼の成功の可能性は薄い His chances of success are *slim*. ‖ 一般に都会は人情が薄いといわれる It is generally said that *social ties* [*relations*] *are weak* in cities. ‖ 彼は利益の薄い商売をしている He's running a business *with a small* [*slim*] *profit margin*. ‖ 今度の選挙は国民の関心が薄い This coming election is *not attracting much public attention*. ‖ 冬季オリンピックにはなじみの薄い競技がいくつかある The winter Olympic Games has [have] several events that are *relatively unfamiliar* (to us).

▶《慣用表現》北君は何となく影が薄い Somehow Kita is *not* the kind of person whose *presence is felt* [who *is noticed by other people*]. ／Kita just doesn*'t leave much of an impression* (on people).

うすうす 薄々 **vaguely** /véɪgli/ (ぼんやりと) ; **slightly** (わずかに) ▶私は彼の悪事にうすうす気づいていた I was *vaguely* aware of his wrongdoing. ‖ 彼は私の意図をうすうす知っていたようだ He seems to have been *slightly* aware of my intention. ／He seems to have had a *faint* idea of what I was up to. (➤ be up to は「…をしようとしている」).

うずうず ▶彼は昇進したことをみんなに言いたくてうずうずしている He *is dying* [*itching*] to tell them about his promotion. ‖ 免許を取ったばかりの息子は早く車を運転したくてうずうずしている My son just got his driver's license and *is raring* [*can't wait*] to drive.

うすがた 薄型 a **thin** [**slim**] **type** ▶薄型テレビ a *flat* (*-screen*) television.

うすぎ 薄着 ▶私は薄着を習慣にしている I make it a habit to *dress lightly*.

［ことわざ］だての薄着 A dandy usually dresses lightly. (➤ 日本語からの直訳).

うすぎたない 薄汚い **dirty** (汚れた) ; **untidy** (乱雑な) ▶彼女は薄汚いセーターを着ていた She wore a *dirty* sweater.

うすきみわるい 薄気味悪い **weird** /wɪəʳd/, **eerie** /ɪ́əri/ ▶あの人はどこか薄気味悪い He is a *weird* character. ‖ 屋根裏から薄気味悪い音が聞こえてくる *Eerie* noises are coming from the attic.

うすぎり 薄切り a (**thin**) **slice** ▶薄切りのハム *a thin slice of* ham ‖ 大根を薄切りにする cut a daikon into *thin slices*.

うずく 疼く **ache** /eɪk/ (鈍く継続的に痛む) ; **smart** (刺すように痛む) ▶歯がひどくうずいてよく寝られなかった I couldn't sleep well due to a *piercing* [*throbbing*] tooth*ache*. ‖ 腕の傷がうずく The cut in my arm *smarts*.

▶《比喩的》私を助けるために犠牲になったあの人のことを思うと心がうずく My heart *aches* each time I remember that he sacrificed his life to save me.

うすくち 薄口の **light** ▶薄口しょうゆ *light* soy sauce.

うずくまる **crouch** /kraʊtʃ/ (**down**) ▶気分が悪くなって彼はそこにうずくまった Feeling unwell, he *crouched down* there. ‖ 猫が塀の上にうずくまっている A cat *is crouching* on the wall. 《参考》crouch の類語に squat があるが, こちらは動物的な連想を伴うことが多い. 例えば The dog squatted. は排便の姿勢を思わせる.

うすぐもり 薄曇り ▶あすは薄曇りの天気でしょう It will be *slightly cloudy* tomorrow.

うすぐらい 薄暗い **dim** ▶薄暗い部屋 a *dim* [*dusky*] room ／a *dimly-lit* room (➤ 照明の薄暗さについていう場合は後者のほうが明瞭) ‖ 劇場の照明が薄暗くなった The lights in the theater *dimmed*. ‖ 冬は5時前に薄暗くなる In winter it *gets dark* before five.

うすくらがり 薄暗がり ▶薄暗がりでの読書は目に悪い Reading in *dim light* is bad for your eyes.

うすげしょう 薄化粧 ▶彼女はきょうは薄化粧をしている She *is wearing light makeup* [*isn't wearing a lot of makeup*] today.

▶《比喩的》薄化粧をした富士山の眺めはすばらしかった Mt. Fuji looked magnificent with a *light layer of snow* [*lightly covered with snow*].

うずしお 渦潮 an **eddying current**.

うずたかく ▶返品が廊下までうずたかく積んであった Even the corridor was *piled high* with returned goods. ‖ うずたかく積まれた報告書に目を通している暇がない I have no time to look through that *vast heap of* reports.

うすっぺら 薄っぺらな **thin** (薄い) ; **shallow** (深みのない) ▶薄っぺらな本 a *thin* book ‖ 薄っぺらな布 *flimsy* cloth ‖ 薄っぺらな知識 *shallow* [*superficial*] knowledge ‖ 薄っぺらな人間 a *shallow* [*superficial*] person.

うすで 薄手の **thin** ▶薄手の紙［生地］*thin* paper [cloth] ‖ 薄手のコート a *lightweight* coat.

うすのろ a **dimwit**, a **nitwit** (➤ 軽蔑の度合いは前者が強い) ▶このうすのろめ！You *dimwit*!

うすび 薄日 ▶雨が上がって薄日が差してきた After the rain let up, the sun began to *shine weakly*.

うすべったい 薄べったい **flat** (平べったい) ; **thin** (薄い) ▶薄べったい石 a *flat* stone.

うずまき 渦巻き a **whirl** ; a **whirlpool** (勢いのよい水の) ; an **eddy** (水や風の小さな) ▶砂ぼこりの渦巻きが次々と校庭を駆け抜けていった One *dust whirl* after another moved across the playground.

うずまく 渦巻く **whirl** ▶岩の上を渦巻く水の流れ a stream *swirling* [*whirling*] over rocks.

▶《比喩的》私の心の中では怒りが渦巻いていた Anger *surged* within me. (➤ surge は「(感情が)湧き上がる」).

うすまる 薄まる ▶氷がとけてウイスキーが薄まった As the ice melted, the whisky *became watered down*.

うすめ 薄目 **1【少し薄いこと】**▶私は薄めのお茶が好きだ I like my tea *weak*. ／I prefer *weak* tea. (● I like *weaker* tea. とすると「もっと薄いお茶が好きです」の意味になり, お茶を出してくれた相手に失礼に響く) ‖ 味は薄めにしてください Please season it *lightly*.

2【少し開いた目】▶彼は薄目を開けてぼくの方を見た He looked at me *with his eyes slightly open*.

うすめる 薄める **thin** ＋㊐, **dilute** /daɪlúːt/ ＋㊐ (➤ 後者は特に液体を別の液体で薄める場合) ▶ニスをシンナーで薄める *thin* varnish with thinner ‖ スープを水で薄める *thin* the soup by adding water ‖ そのうがい薬は水で薄めて使うんだったんだよ You should have *diluted* that gargle (*with water*) before using it. ‖ ロシア人の多くはウオツカを薄めずに(＝生(き)で)飲む Many Russians drink vodka *straight* [*neat*].

うずめる 埋める **bury** /béri/ ＋㊐ ▶宝物を木の下にうずめる *bury* a treasure under a tree. (→うめる).

▶観客がスタンドをうずめた(＝いっぱいにした) Spectators *filled* the stands. ‖ 彼女は恋人の胸に顔をうずめた

She *buried* her head in her boyfriend's chest.

うずもれる 埋もれる **be buried**《in, under》; **be covered**《with》(覆われる) ▶**雪にうずもれた町** a *snow-covered* [*snowed-under*] town ‖ **畑は雪に深くうずもれていた** The field *was buried* deep in snow. (→**うもれる**).
▶これだけの人材が今まで**うずもれていた**とは！ It's a shame such talent has *gone undiscovered*.

うすよごれた 薄汚れた **dingy** /díndʒi/ (場所が汚く陰気な); **scruffy** (手入れされずに汚れた) ▶**薄汚れた感じの**工場街 a *dingy* street of small factories ‖ **薄汚れた**トレンチコート a *scruffy* [*slightly soiled*] trench coat.

うずら 鶉《鳥》a **quail** /kweɪl/.

うすらぐ 薄らぐ **fade** (記憶などが); **ease** (痛みが) ▶息子のコンピュータゲーム熱はまもなく**薄らぐ**だろう My son will probably soon *lose* interest in computer games. ‖ 足にけがをしてから1週間が過ぎ, やっと痛みも**薄らいだ** A week has passed since I hurt my leg, and the pain *has eased* [*is almost gone*]. ‖ ロンドンの思い出はもう**薄らいでいる** My memories of London have already *faded*.
✉ **寒さも日ごとに薄らいできましたね** It is *getting warmer* [*less cold*] every day, isn't it?

うすらさむい 薄ら寒い ▶**薄ら寒い**部屋 a *chilly* room ‖ 何だか**薄ら寒く**なってきた It's become *somewhat* [*rather*] *cold*.

うすれる 薄れる **wane** (程度・勢力などが弱くなる); **fade** (色・記憶・感情などが) →**薄らぐ** ▶ぼくのプロ野球に対する興味は**薄れた** My interest in pro baseball *has waned*. ‖ 子供の頃の記憶は年とともに**薄れる** Childhood memories *fade* with age. ‖ 小学校時代の記憶はすでに**薄れて**しまった My memories of elementary school have already *faded*.

うすわらい 薄笑い a **faint smile** (かすかな笑い); a **sneer** (あざけりの笑い) ▶**薄笑いを浮かべる** wear *a faint smile* ‖ 彼は私の発言に対して**薄笑いで**応えた He responded to my remarks *with a sneer*.

うせつ 右折 a **right turn** 一動 **右折する** **go** [**turn**] **right, make a right turn** ▶次の曲がり角を**右折して**ください *Make a right turn* at the next corner. ‖《掲示》**右折禁止** No Right Turn.

うせる 失せる ▶あまり親がうるさく言うと, かえって子供のやる気は**うせる** Children may *lose* all desire to try if their parents nag them too much. ‖ **とっととうせろ！** *Get lost!* / *Beat it!* / *Out* [*Get out*] *of my sight!*

うそ 嘘 **1【事実・真実でないこと】** a **lie** (悪意を含んだ, または故意のうそ); 《インフォーマル》a **fib** (たわいのないうそ) 一動 (…に) **うそをつく** **lie**《to》, **tell a lie**《to》 ▶**真っ赤なうそ** *a barefaced* [*downright*] *lie* ‖ **悪意のないうそ** *a harmless* [*white*] *lie* ‖ 親に**うそをつくものではない** You must not *lie to* [*tell lies to*] your parents. ‖ あなたが**うそをつけば**すぐにわかる I can tell right away when you're *lying* [*telling lies*]. ‖ **うそはすぐにばれる** *A lie has no legs*. (➤ have no legs は「(真実であると) 証拠立ててくれるものがない」) ‖ あゆみちゃんはいつも学校で**うそついてる**んだよ Ayumi's always *telling fibs* at school. ‖ **うそついちゃあだめ！** *You shouldn't tell stories!* (➤この表現は主に子供どうしが, あるいは親が子供に向かって用いる).
▶**うそつけ** (＝ばかを言うな) *Don't be silly*. / *Come off it!* (➤後者はくだけた言い方). 《参考》lie は日本語の「うそ」よりもはるかに強い意味をもっているので, このような軽い意味の場合に用いてはならない.
▶そのうわさは**うそだ** (＝真実でない) The rumor is *false* [*untrue*]. / The rumor is *not true*. ‖ 上司のご機嫌をとるためにその社員は**うその** (＝偽りの) 報告書を提出した The employee submitted a *false* report to please his boss. ‖ 彼はぼくに**うそ** (＝誤った情報) を教えた He gave me *false information*.
▶《慣用表現》あら本当？ **うそでもうれしいわ** Really? *It's nice to hear that*. / Really? *Thank you for the compliment*. / Really? *Even if it's a lie*, I love to hear you say it. (➤1つ目は「それを聞いてうれしい」, 2つ目は「褒めてくれてありがとう」, 3つ目は「うそだとしてもあなたがそう言うのを聞くのが大好きだ」の意) ‖ 腹が立たないと**言えばうそになる**が, ここで怒りだすのはあまりにも大人気ないのでね *I'd be lying if I said* I am not offended at all, but it would be immature of me to get angry now. ‖ すべて順調と**言えばうそになる** I would *be dishonest* if I said everything is going well. (➤dishonest は「真実を語っていない」).
▶**そうこなくっちゃうそだよ** That's exactly what I wanted to hear. (➤「それこそぼくが聞きたいと思っていたことだ」の意) ‖ こんなに勉強したんだから合格しなけりゃ**うそだよ** After studying this hard, *I've just got to* pass. / After studying this hard, *there's no way* I won't pass. (➤There is no way ... は「…だなんてありえない」の意) ‖ その日は前日の雨が**うそのように**晴れた The day was so bright and clear I could *hardly believe* there'd been rain the day before.
ことわざ **うそも方便** Lying is sometimes expedient. / A lie is sometimes necessary. (➤日本語からの意訳).
‖ **うそ発見器** a lie detector.
2【信じられないこと】 ▶竹田さんがK大に入れたなんて**うそみたいね** It is *incredible* that Takeda was admitted to K University. ‖ 私が宝くじに当たったって本当？ **うそみたい** Did I really win the lottery? *I can't believe it*. ‖ 対話「ねえ, ねえ, 俊雄とあけみが婚約したんだって」「**うそー** [**ウッソー**]！」"Hey, you know what? Toshio and Akemi got engaged." "*No kidding!*" (➤I don't believe it! とか, 単に No! のようにも言う).

うそつき 嘘つき a **liar** ▶彼女は「**うそつき！**」と私をなじった She reproached me, saying "*You liar!*" 《参考》英語の liar には相手を道徳的に非難するような強い響きがあるので, 軽い気持ちで「うそつき(だ)ね」と言うときは No kidding! とか, You're not serious. / You must be joking! などと言う.

うそなき 嘘泣き ▶子供はよく**嘘泣きする** Kids often *shed false tears*.

うそはっぴゃく 嘘八百 ▶**嘘八百を並べる** tell *a* (*whole*) *pack of lies* / tell *all sorts of lies*.

うた 歌 a **song** ▶**歌を歌う** sing (*a song*) ‖ 彼は**歌がうまい** [**下手だ**] He *is a good* [*poor*] *singer*. ‖ その**歌の文句**は忘れてしまった I have forgotten *the words of the song*.

「歌」のいろいろ **演歌** *enka* / **数え歌** counting song / **歌謡曲** (Japanese) popular song / **カンツォーネ** canzone / **軍歌** war song, military song / **恋歌** love song / **校歌** school song / **黒人霊歌** (Negro) spiritual / **ゴスペル** gospel / **国歌** national anthem / **子守歌** lullaby, cradle song / **賛美歌** hymn / **シャンソン** chanson / **主題歌** theme song / **童謡** children's song, nursery rhyme / **バラード** ballad / **フォークソング**

う

folk song／**ポップス** pop song／**民謡** (traditional) folk song／**リート**(ドイツ歌曲) lied /liːd/／**流行歌** popular song

▶俵万智の**歌**(＝短歌)が好きだ I like Tawara Machi's tanka *poems*.

うたいもんく 謳い文句 a **catch phrase**, a **catchword** ▶ユニークなうたい文句を考え出す think up *a* unique *catch phrase*.

1 **うたう 歌う** **sing** +㊐ ; **hum** +㊐ (鼻歌を) ▶ビートルズの歌を歌う *sing* a Beatles song ‖ みんな一緒に歌おう *Let's sing* (*a song*) together. (➤「歌う」という行為に重点がある場合は通例 a song は省く) ‖ 彼は(ジョン・レノンの)『イマジン』をしっとりと歌った He *sang* "Imagine" with subdued emotion. ‖ 『北国の春』を歌って聞かせてよ *Sing* "Kitaguni-no-haru" for us. ‖ 彼女はよく歌を歌って赤ん坊を寝かしつけた She would often *sing* her baby *to sleep*.

2 **うたう 謳う** **extol** +㊐ (褒めたたえる) ; **state** +㊐ (述べる) ▶平和共存は共同声明の中にうたってある Peaceful coexistence *is extolled* in the joint communiqué. ‖ 平和の精神は憲法の前文にうたってある A commitment to peace *is* (clearly) *stated* in the preamble to the Constitution.

▶上杉鷹山は名君とうたわれている(＝名声が高い) Uesugi Yozan *is reputed* to have been an enlightened feudal lord.

うたがい 疑い **1**【嫌疑, 疑惑】(a) **suspicion** ▶その業者には恐喝の疑いがかけられている The dealer *is suspected of* blackmailing. ‖ 多くの兵士がスパイ活動の疑いで逮捕された Many soldiers were rounded up *on suspicion of* espionage activities. (➤ on suspicion of は「…の疑いで」) ‖ その青年は関西空港に着くとすぐコレラの疑いで近くの病院へ送られた The young man who *was suspected of* having cholera was rushed to a nearby hospital immediately upon his arrival at Kansai Airport. ‖ その社長は詐欺の疑いで逮捕された The company president was arrested *on a charge of* [*on charges of*] fraud. (➤ on a charge of [on charges of] は「…の罪で」).

▶政治家を疑いの目で見る人が多い Many people *are suspicious of* politicians. ‖ 大沢先生, そんな疑いの目で私たちを見ないでください Mr. Osawa, please don't look at us so *suspiciously*. ‖ 盗みをしたとして補導された生徒はまもなく疑いを晴らすことができた The student who had been put under police guidance on suspicion of theft was soon able to *clear his name*. ‖ きみは裁判官だから世間の疑いを招くようなことは決してしないように As you are a judge, you must not do anything that would *invite* people's *suspicions*.

2【疑問】(a) **doubt** /daʊt/ ▶最近の調査であの絵が本物のレンブラントかどうか疑いが出てきた Recent research has led to *doubt* as to whether (or not) that painting is really an original Rembrandt. ‖ 私はこの計画が実現できるかどうかに疑いをもっている I have my *doubts* about the feasibility of this project. ‖ カーリングがますます人気を呼ぶことは疑いない *I have no doubt that* curling will become [get] even more popular. ‖ その弁護士の正直さには疑いの余地がない *There's no doubt* that the lawyer is honest.

うたがいぶかい 疑い深い **suspicious** (人・性質など が) ; **skeptical** (人などを容易に信じない) ▶この前は本当に実家に泊まったんだって. もう, 疑い深いんだから I really did stay at my mother's the other day. Boy, you are so *suspicious*!

うたがう 疑う

📖 **訳語メニュー**
…ではないかと思う →suspect **1**
信用しない →doubt **2**

1【信じ込む, 嫌疑をかける】**suspect** +㊐

【文型】
～ではないかと疑う
suspect that S + V
人(A)の犯罪行為など(B)を疑う
suspect A **of** B
人(A)を疑っている
be suspicious of A

▶うちの花壇を踏み潰したのは隣の少年ではないかと疑っている I *suspect that* it was the boy next door who trampled on my flowerbed. ‖ 警官はその男が酒酔い運転をしたのではないかと疑った The police officer *suspected* the man *of* drunk driving. ‖ 男はその誘拐事件への関与を疑われている The man *is suspected of* involvement [being involved] in the kidnapping.

▶ (犯人はあなただと)疑ったりしてごめんね I'm sorry I *suspected* you. (➤ I was suspicious of you. は「あなたを信用できない［怪しい］人物と思い警戒した」の意. また, I doubted you. は「あなたの言ったことを信用しなかった」の意) ‖ 人をやたらに疑わないようにしよう Let's try not to *be too suspicious of* others. ‖ 祖母は人に疑われるようなことをするなと私に言った My grandmother told me not to do anything that would *invite suspicion*.

2【信じない, 疑問視する】**doubt** /daʊt/ +㊐

【文型】
～かどうかを疑う, ～かどうか疑わしい
doubt if [**whether**] S + V
➤ whether のほうが堅い言い方

▶私は彼が実業家として成功するかどうかを疑っている I *doubt if* [*whether* / *that*] he will become a successful businessman. (➤ that にすると「とてもじゃないが」という強い疑いを示すことになる. なお, 次例のように否定文のあとは接続詞は常に that).

▶今シーズンのジャイアンツの優勝を疑う人はいない Nobody *doubts that* the Giants will win the championship this season. ‖ 彼の無実は疑う余地がない His innocence *is beyond the shadow of a doubt*. ‖ 私は会社への彼の忠誠心を信じて疑わない I don't *doubt* his loyalty to the company. ‖ 合格者名の中に自分の名前を発見したときはわが目を疑った I *couldn't believe* my eyes [*couldn't believe it*] when I found my name in the list of successful applicants. ‖ 科学者は他人の理論を疑ってみる傾向がある Scientists tend to *doubt* other people's theories. ／Scientists tend to *take a critical view of* the theories of others. ‖ そんなことを言うと常識を疑われるよ People will *doubt your common sense* if you say things like that.

うたかた a **bubble** (泡) ▶うたかたの恋 *fleeting* [*ephemeral*] love.

うたがわしい 疑わしい **doubtful, dubious** (➤ 後者のほうが疑いの気持ちが強い) ▶疑わしい人物 a *dubious*

[*doubtful*] person ‖ 彼が音楽家として成功するかどうか疑わしい It *is doubtful* whether he will succeed as a musician. ／I *doubt* if [whether] he can become a great musician. ‖ そのうわさは疑わしいと思う I *doubt* the truth of the rumor. ／ I *am doubtful of* the rumor. ‖ 疑わしきは罰せず A person should be considered innocent unless proven otherwise. (➤「無実ではないと証明されない限り，無実と見なされるべき」の意).

うたげ 宴 a **banquet.**

うたごえ 歌声 a **singing voice** ▶子供たちの歌声が廊下から聞こえてくる I can hear the children *singing* from the hallway.

うたたね うたた寝 a **doze**(浅い眠り)；a **nap** (昼寝) **一動 うたた寝する have** [**take**] **a nap, doze** [**nod**] **off** ▶彼は仕事中にうたた寝した He *fell into a doze* while at work. ‖ ぼくはテレビの前でうたた寝してしまった I *dozed* [*nodded*] *off* in front of the television. ‖ 父は肘掛け椅子に座って30分ほどうたた寝をした My dad *took a* 30-minute *nap* in the armchair.

うだつ ▶あんな店長のもとではいつまでたってもうだつが上がらないだろうよ You'll *never move up to a better position* as long as that manager is around. ‖ あの男はどうもうだつが上がらないね That guy just ca*n't get ahead in the world.* (➤ get ahead in the world は「出世する」).

うたひめ 歌姫 a **diva** /díːvə/ (大歌手) ; a **female singer**(女性歌手).

うだる swelter ▶盆地にあるその町は夏の間うだるような暑さが続く That town is located in a basin and has *sweltering heat* throughout the summer. ‖ 連日の暑さにうだっています I'*m sweltering* because it's been so hot for days (on end).

うたれる 打たれる ▶その修験者は滝に打たれて修行していた The ascetic trained himself *by standing* [*sitting*] in the torrents of a waterfall. ‖ 彼女の優しさに深く心を打たれた I *was* deeply *touched* [*moved*] by her kindness. ‖ アジサイの花が雨に打たれていた The hydrangeas were *pelted* by the rain. ‖ 彼は打たれ強い He *thrives under adversity.* (●「逆境でも活躍する」と考える).

うち 内･家

📖 **訳語メニュー**
内部 →the inside **1**
時間的に…の間に →while, in **2**
…の中で →of **3**
身内の →my, our **5**
自分の家 →home, house **5, 6**

1【空間的に内部】the inside ▶このドアは内からは開かない This door doesn't open from *the inside.* ▶バレー選手たちは闘志を内に秘めていた The volleyball players harbored a great fighting spirit *inside themselves.* ‖ 胸の内を聞いてくれる友だちが欲しい I want to have friends who will listen to *me* [who I can open *my heart* to].

2【時間的にある範囲内】while, in ▶ヨーロッパにいるうちにユングフラウに登りたい I'd like to climb (up) the Jungfrau *while* I am in Europe. ‖ 暗くならないうちに出かけましょう Let's get started *before* it gets dark. ‖ 兄は慌てて家を出ていったが，2分もしないうちに戻って来た My (older) brother left the house in a hurry, but he was back *in less than* two minutes. ‖ 宿題はその日のうちにやってしまいました I finished my homework *before the day was over* [*was out*]. ‖ 一晩のうちに雪が1メートル積もった A meter of snow fell *overnight.* ‖ 2，3日のうちに公園の桜は満開になるでしょう The cherry trees in the park will be in full bloom *in* a couple of days.

3【限定された対象の範囲内】of ▶3人の息子のうちで1人だけがサラリーマンになった Only one *of* my three sons became a white-collar worker. ‖ 50人の生徒のうち45人がその制服は嫌いだと言っている Forty-five *out of* fifty students say that they dislike the school uniform. (➤「ある数の中のいくつ」の意の場合は out of) ‖ **対話**「シェークスピアの作品のうち，どれがいちばん好きですか」「『ベニスの商人』です」"Which *of* Shakespeare's works do you like best?" "'The Merchant of Venice' is my favorite."

4【ある状態の範囲内】 ▶退勤後の付き合いも仕事のうちだ，と言う人がいる Some people say that socializing with co-workers after office hours is *part of* their job. ‖ 「子育てなんて苦労のうちには入りませんわ」と彼女は言った "Child care [raising] is no trouble," she said.

5【自分が所属するところ】 ▶《自分の会社》うちは従業員20人の小さな会社です *Ours* is a small firm with twenty employees. ‖ うちの会社は今注文に追われててんてこまいです Things are hectic at *our* company with all the orders coming in. ‖ そんなに自分の会社が嫌なら，今度うちへ来いよ If you hate working for your company so much, why don't you join *us*?

▶《自分の家庭》日曜はうちでごろごろしているのがいちばんだ There is nothing like kicking back *at home* on Sundays. ‖ あっ，もう11時だ．うちに電話しなくちゃあ Oh, it's already eleven o'clock. I have to *call home.* (➤ この home は「家へ」の意の副詞) ‖ 今夜うちへ来いよ Why don't you *come over* [*come to my place*] tonight? →**家.**

▶《自分の家族》うちはみんなカレーが大好きです Everyone in *my family* loves curry and rice very much. ‖ 早く帰らないとおうちの人が心配するよ *Your family* [*parents*] will get worried if you don't get home early. ‖ うちの兄は日本電気に勤めています *My* (*older*) *brother* works for NEC. ‖ うちの人(＝夫)はサラリーマンです *My husband* is an office worker. ‖ おうちの方はお元気ですか How are *your folks*? (➤ one's folks は「家族，両親」の意のインフォーマルな表現).

✉ **うちは6人家族です** There are six *in my family.*

✉ **うちは八百屋をやっています** *My parents* run [have] a fruit and vegetable shop. ➤ run は「…を経営している」の意.

6【家屋】a **house** →**家** ▶通りの角に大きなうちがある There is a large *house* on the street corner. ‖ 彼女は大きな犬を2匹もうちの中で飼っている She keeps two large dogs *inside the house.*

うちあい 撃ち合い a **shoot-out.**

うちあげ 打ち上げ 1【高く上げること】a **display** (花火の)；a **launch(ing)** (ロケットの) ▶新しい人工衛星の打ち上げが8月に予定されている The *launching* of a new satellite is scheduled for August.

‖**打ち上げ花火** a (sky)rocket.

2【終了】a **closing** ▶1か月公演のショーはあす打ち上げとなる The one-month long show *closes* [*ends*] tomorrow. ／The *closing* of the one-month-long show is tomorrow. ‖ 文化祭の打ち上げをやろ

う *Let's have a party to celebrate the success of* the school festival.

うちあけばなし 打ち明け話 ▶私たちは互いに打ち明け話をした We *exchanged confidences.*／We *opened up* to each other. (➤ open up は「打ち明ける」の意のインフォーマルな表現).

うちあける 打ち明ける tell ＋目; confide /kənfáɪd/ 《in》(相手を信用して私事を) ▶人に秘密を打ち明ける *tell* [*confide*] one's secret to a person ‖ 彼になら何でも打ち明けられる I can *confide in* him. ／I can *confide* just about anything to him. ‖ 彼女は私にいろいろと打ち明けてくれた She *opened up* to me and told me a great many things. ‖ 妻は私に何でも打ち明ける My wife *keeps nothing from* me. (➤「隠し事をしない」の意).

うちあげる 打ち上げる **1【高く上げる】** set [shoot] off (花火などを); send up, launch ＋目 (ロケットなどを); loft ＋目 (フライなどを) ▶学園祭の朝は花火を打ち上げる予定だ On the morning of our school festival, we are going to *set off* fireworks. ‖ 世界最初の人工衛星は1957年に打ち上げられた The first artificial satellite *was launched* [*was sent up*] in 1957. ‖ 最初のバッターはセンターに高いフライを打ち上げてしまった The first batter *lofted* a fly ball into center field.

2【岸に】 wash up ▶難破船が海岸に打ち上げられた A wrecked boat *was washed up* on the beach.

3【公演などを終える】 finish, end ▶楽天は沖縄キャンプを打ち上げた Rakuten *finished* [*ended*] a training camp in Okinawa.

うちあわせ 打ち合わせ arrangement(s) (取り決め); a meeting (会議) ▶吉井さんと面会時間の打ち合わせをしておきなさい *Make arrangements with* Mr. Yoshii about the interview time. ‖ きょうは３時から打ち合わせがある We have *a meeting* at three today.

うちあわせる 打ち合わせる ▶旅行の日程について打ち合わせよう Let's *discuss* [*make*] *arrangements* for the trip.

うちいわい 内祝い a private [family] celebration.

うちうち 内々で in private, privately ▶内々でお話ししたいのです I would like to talk with you *in private* [*privately*].

うちうみ 内海 an inland sea.

うちおとす 撃ち落とす shoot down ▶ミサイルを撃ち落とす *shoot down* a missile.

うちかつ 打ち勝つ **1【克服する】** get over, overcome ＋目 ▶困難に打ち勝つ *get over* [*overcome*] a difficulty ‖ 病に打ち勝つ *get over* [*overcome*] one's illness.

2【野球】 outhit ▶巨人は広島に８対５で打ち勝った The Giants *outhit* the Carp 8-5.

うちがわ 内側 the inside ▶彼は寝室の内側から鍵を掛けた He locked the bedroom from *the inside.* ‖ 彼女は門の内側に立っていた She was standing *inside* the gate. ‖ 子供は道路の内側を歩かせなさい Make your children walk *on the inside* of the street.
▶戦争を内側から見たルポ an *inside* story on the war.

うちき 内気な shy /ʃaɪ/; bashful (はにかむ) ▶内気な少女 a *shy* girl ‖ うちの息子はとても内気です Our son is very *shy.* ‖ 静男はとても内気で女の子にデートの申し込みもできない Shizuo is too *bashful* to ask a girl for a date. 《参考》(1) 英語圏, とりわけ異民族から成る米国では, 積極性が大事で, 内気は高い評価を受けないことが多い. (2)《英》では「おとなしい, 臆病である」を意味する wouldn't say boo to a goose という決まったフレーズがある.

うちきる 打ち切る break off (急にやめる); cut off (供給を遮断する) ▶その国との関係を打ち切る *break off* relations with the country ‖ 経済援助を打ち切る *cut off* economic aid ‖ 天候の悪化で遭難者の捜索はひとまず打ち切られた Bad weather forced the search for the victims to *be suspended* for the time being. (➤ suspend は「中断する」) ‖ きょうの仕事はこれで打ち切ろう *Let's call it a day.* (➤ 決まった言い方).

うちきん 内金 (a) partial [part] payment; (a) deposit (手付金) ▶マンションを買うのに内金として200万円払った I made a two million yen *down payment* [*partial payment*] on a condominium. ‖ この車はいくら内金を入れればいいんですか How much *money* [*deposit*] should I *put down* on this car?

うちくずす 打ち崩す knock out ▶相手チームの先発投手を打ち崩す *knock out* a starting pitcher of the opposing team.

うちくだく 打ち砕く smash ＋目 (投げつけるなどして粉々に); crush ＋目 (押し潰したりして細かく) ▶彼はハンマーで岩を粉々に打ち砕いた He *smashed* the rock into small pieces with a hammer. ‖ ドイツチームはデンマークチームを破りワールドカップ進出の望みを打ち砕いた The German team beat the Danish team and *crushed* [*dashed*] their hopes of making it to the World Cup.

うちけす 打ち消す deny /dɪnáɪ/ ＋目 ▶彼は離婚のうわさを打ち消した He *denied* the rumor that he was going to divorce his wife.

うちこむ 打ち込む **1【打って中に入れる】** ▶金づちで板にくぎを打ち込む *drive* a nail *into* the board with a hammer ‖ 《テニスなどで》相手側のコートにボールを打ち込む *smash* a ball *into* the opponent's court
▶この数字を(コンピュータに)打ち込んでおいてくれ Please *enter* [*input*／*key in*] these numbers.

2【専心する】 throw oneself 《into》; devote oneself 《to》 (専念する) ▶彼はその研究プロジェクトに打ち込んだ He *threw himself into* the research project. ‖ 父は長年翻訳の仕事に打ち込んできた My father *has devoted himself to* his translation work for many years. ‖ 私は全身全霊を打ち込める仕事がしたい I would like to have a job that I *can put my heart and soul into.*

うちじに 討ち死にする be killed in battle.

うちぜい 内税 tax included in the price.

うちだす 打ち出す ▶パソコンのデータをプリンターで打ち出す *print out* data from a (personal) computer ‖ 内閣は新政策を打ち出した The cabinet *has set out* a new policy.

うちたてる 打ち立てる establish ＋目 ▶新記録を打ち立てる *establish* [*set*] a new record. (➤「記録を出す」には set を用いるのがふつう)

うちつける 打ちつける ▶柱に頭をしたたか打ちつけた I *struck* [*hit*] my head hard *against* a post.
▶彼は壁に棚をくぎで打ちつけた(＝打って留めた) He *nailed* a shelf *to* the wall.

うちづら 内面 ▶彼は外づらはいいが, 内づらはよくない He is all smiles outside the house, but bad-tempered at home. (➤ 個人を家族との関係で見た場合)／He is all smiles when talking to customers, but bad-tempered with the people he works with. (➤ 個人を会社などの内側から見た場

合).

うちでし 内弟子 an **apprentice living with his** [**her**] **master** ▶落語家の内弟子になる *become apprenticed* to a rakugo comedian.

うちでのこづち 打ち出の小槌 a **magic mallet** ; **Aladdin's lamp**（望みをかなえてくれる魔法のランプ).

うちとける 打ち解ける become friendly ; **unbend**（くつろぐ）▶子供たちは互いにすぐ打ち解けた The children soon *became friendly* with each other. ‖彼にはどこか打ち解けないところがある There is something *reserved* about him. ‖しばらくすると彼女は打ち解けて私たちの仲間に加わった After a little while, she *unbent* [*loosened up*] and joined us.

うちどころ 打ち所 ▶彼は打ち所が悪かったのか, 病院に運ばれてすぐ死んだ Perhaps he *was hit in a vital spot* ; he died soon after he was taken to the hospital. (➤ vital spot は「急所」).

▶《慣用表現》この報告書は非の打ちどころがない This report *leaves no room for criticism*.

うちとる 打ち取る ▶《野球》田中は内川をセンターへの凡フライに打ち取った Tanaka *got* Uchikawa on a pop to center. ‖前田は坂本を三振に打ち取った Maeda *struck* Sakamoto *out*. ／Maeda *fanned* Sakamoto. (➤ strike out がふつうの言い方. fan はインフォーマルな語).

うちならす 打ち鳴らす ▶1776年7月8日,（アメリカの）独立宣言書採択を告げるため自由の鐘が打ち鳴らされた On July 8, 1776, the Liberty Bell *was rung* to announce the adoption of the Declaration of Independence.

うちぬく 打ち抜く・撃ち抜く penetrate /pénətrèit/ ＋ⓔ（貫通する）; **shoot through**（撃ち抜く）▶弾は車のドアを撃ち抜いた The bullet *shot through* the car door.

うちのめす 打ちのめす beat up ▶彼はいじめっ子を打ちのめしてやりたかった He wanted to *beat up* the bully. (➤「めちゃくちゃに打ちのめす」なら beat the bully to (a) pulp のようにいう) ‖そのボクサーは相手を一発で打ちのめした The boxer *floored* his opponent with one blow.

▶《比喩的》大黒柱を失った遺族は悲しみに打ちのめされた Having lost the pillar of the family, they *were overwhelmed* with grief.

うちひしがれる 打ちひしがれる ▶被害者の母親は悲しみに打ちひしがれた表情だった The victim's mother had a *grief-stricken* look [expression] on her face.

うちべんけい 内弁慶 ▶うちの息子は内弁慶で困ります My son is *a little devil* [*a terror*] *at home but meek when outside*. (➤「うちではいたずらっ子ですが, 外では意気地がないんですよ」の意).

《参考》英語には A lion at home, a mouse abroad.（内ではライオン, 外ではネズミ）という表現がある.

うちポケット 内ポケット an **inside** [**inner**] **pocket** ▶背広の内ポケット *an inside* [*inner*] *pocket* of a suit jacket.

うちまく 内幕 a **secret**（秘密）; **inside information**（内部の情報）▶内幕を暴く expose *a secret* ‖彼は我々に政界の内幕を語った He told us *what was going on behind the scenes* in the political world. (➤「舞台裏で行われていること」の意).

‖（新聞などの）**内幕物** the inside story.

うちまご 内孫 a **child of** one's **heir** [**successor**].

うちまた 内股の pigeon-toed ▶子供のころぼくはひどい内股だった As a child I was very *pigeon-toed*. ‖彼女はちょっと内股で歩く She walks slightly *pigeon-toed*. ‖着物を着たときはもう少し内股で歩くものよ When you wear a kimono, you should walk *with your feet pointing slightly inward*.

うちみ 打ち身 a **bruise** /bru:z/ ▶テーブルに足をぶつけて打ち身をつくった I've got *a bruise* on my leg from bumping into the table.

うちみず 打ち水 ▶庭に打ち水する *sprinkle* the garden (*with water*) ／*water* the garden ‖通りに打ち水をする *sprinkle* [*splash*] *water* on the street (to reduce summer heat).

うちむき 内向きの introverted ▶内向きな性格 an *introverted* personality (➤「内向きな性格の人」は introvert という. 逆の「外向きな人」は extrovert).

‖**内向き思考** introverted thinking ‖**内向き志向の** inward-looking.

うちやぶる 打ち破る break down（壊す）; **defeat** ＋ⓔ（負かす）▶彼らは門を打ち破って中へ入った They *broke down* the gate and marched in.

▶敵を打ち破った英雄も反対派の議論を打ち破ることはできなかった Even the hero who had *defeated* the enemy could do nothing to *break down* the arguments of the opposition.

うちゅう 宇宙 the universe（天体を含めた総体）; **the cosmos** /kɑ́:zməs/（秩序をもった統一体としての）; (**outer**) **space**（大気圏外の空間）▶宇宙は膨張し続けている *The universe* keeps on expanding. ‖宇宙は150億年ほど前に誕生した *The universe* came into existence some 15 billion years ago. ‖いつか宇宙からこの目で地球を見てみたい Some day I'd like to see the earth *from outer space* with my own eyes. ‖宇宙ロケットの打ち上げをテレビで見た I saw *a space rocket* launched on TV.

‖**宇宙衛星** a space satellite ‖**宇宙科学** space science ‖**宇宙時代** the space age ‖**宇宙人** a creature [visitor] from outer space ; an alien /éɪliən/（異星人）‖**宇宙ステーション** a space station ‖**宇宙船** a spacecraft, a spaceship ‖**宇宙飛行士** an astronaut /ǽstrənɔ̀:t/, a cosmonaut（ロシアの）‖**宇宙服** a space suit ‖**宇宙遊泳** a spacewalk ‖**宇宙旅行** space travel.

☛ 小宇宙（→見出語）

うちょうてん 有頂天 ▶地元民は彼の優勝に有頂天になった The local people *went into raptures* [*were euphoric*] over his victory. ‖輝雄から結婚を申し込まれて私は有頂天になった When Teruo asked me to marry him, I *was on cloud nine* [*in seventh heaven*]. (➤ ともに「とても幸福で」の意のインフォーマルな言い方) ‖ちょっといい点を取ったくらいで有頂天になるんじゃないよ Don't let the fact you did pretty well on the test *go to your head*. (➤ go to one's head は「いい気にさせる, うぬぼれさせる」).

うちよせる 打ち寄せる ▶波が岸に打ち寄せている Waves are *breaking* [*beating*] on the beach.

¹うちわ 内輪 1【内々】▶内輪の集まり a *private* meeting ‖これは内輪の話です This is a *family* matter. ／This (matter) is *between ourselves*. ‖誰でも内輪の恥はさらしたくないものだ Nobody wants to have their dirty linen washed in public. (➤ 文字どおりには「汚れた（リンネル製の）下着を人前で洗われたくない」の意) ‖あの野球チームの選手たちは内輪もめしている The baseball team members *are squabbling among themselves*. ‖内輪もめはみっともない *Infighting* is [*Family feuds* are] shameful. (➤ カッコ内は

う

「家族間の」; feud は /fjuːd/ と発音).

2【控えめ】▶費用は内輪に見積もっても200万円かかる The cost is *conservatively* estimated at two million yen.

²**うちわ 団扇** a **(round) fan** ▶うちわを使う *use a fan* / *fan oneself* ‖ うちわであおぐ fan oneself *with a fan*.

☞ 左うちわ (→見出語)

うちわけ 内訳 a **breakdown**, a **detail** (明細); an **item**(細目)

▶経費の内訳が欲しいのですが I'd like *an itemized statement* [*a breakdown*] of these expenses. / Could you please itemize these expenses? (➤ itemize /áɪṭəmaɪz/ は「箇条書きにする」).

¹**うつ 打つ・撃つ・討つ**

📖 訳語メニュー
たたく →strike, hit **1**
ヒットを打つ →hit **4**
心を打つ →move, touch **5**
銃を撃つ →shoot **13**

1【物理的にたたく】 **strike** +㊐, **hit** +㊐ (狙いをつけて; 後者のほうがよりくだけた語); **beat** +㊐ (続けざまに); **tap** +㊐ (軽く); **slap** +㊐ (平手で); **swat** +㊐ (ぴしゃりと); **clap** +㊐ (手を) →たたく ▶金づちでくぎを打つ *strike* a nail with a hammer ‖ 丸めた新聞でハエをぴしゃりと打つ *swat* a fly with a rolled up newspaper ‖ 少年はその犬を棒で何度も打った The boy *beat* the dog with a stick. ‖ 子供たちは手を打って喜んだ The children *clapped their hands* with joy. ‖ 雨が窓ガラスを激しく打っていた Rain *was beating* against the windowpanes.

2【たたいて音を出す】▶太鼓を打つ *beat* a drum ‖ 時計が7時を打った The clock *struck* seven.

▶《慣用表現》打てば響くような答え a *quick response* ‖ ひろしは打てば響くような子だ Hiroshi is *smart as a whip* [*quick on the uptake*].

3【ぶつける】▶息子はバスケットボールの試合中に転んで頭を打った My son fell and *struck* his head during a basketball game. ‖ 彼は屋根から転落し全身を強く打って死亡した He fell from the roof and died from *contusions* to his entire body. (➤ contusion /kəntjúːʒən/ は「打撲傷」).

4【たたいて飛ばす】 **hit** +㊐ ▶ヒットを打つ *hit* a single ‖ 高橋は5回に二塁打を打って3点を入れた Takahashi *belted* a three-run double in the fifth. (➤ belt のほかに bang, clout, slam, slug などもよく使われる) ‖ 今度はぼくたちが打つ番だ It's our *turn at bat*.

5【感動させる】 **move** +㊐ (人の心を動かす); **touch** +㊐ (人を感傷的な気持ちにさせる) →打たれる ▶ノックス師の演説は人々の心を打った The Reverend Knox's speeches *moved* [*touched*] people's *hearts*. ‖ 彼女の歌は聴衆の胸を打った Her songs *moved* the audience.

6【感覚を刺激する】▶すさまじい轟(ごう)音が耳を打った The roaring sound *struck* my ear. ‖ 亜硫酸ガスの強烈な臭いが鼻を打った The pungent smell of sulfurous acid gas *assailed* our nostrils.

7【はり・注射を】▶予防注射を打つ *get* [*receive*] a vaccination ‖ 肩凝りははりを打つと楽になりますよ You can relieve stiff shoulders *with acupuncture*.

8【キーボードなどを】▶パソコンのキーボードのキーを打つ *type* on a computer keyboard ‖ 受験生に合格電報を打つ *telegraph* the news of success to applicants for admission (to a university) ‖ 文章の終わりに句点を打つ *put* a period at the end of a sentence ‖ その箱に1から10まで番号を打ってください *Number* the boxes (from) 1 to 10.

9【ゲーム・ばくち・興行などを】▶私の趣味は碁を打つことです My hobby is *playing* 'Go.' ‖ 私も若いときはばくちを打った I also *gambled* when I was young.

10【手立て・技などを】▶問題が起こる前に早めに手を打つことが必要だ You need to *take action* early before any problem arises. ‖ 会社が倒産したから打つ手がないよ The company has gone bankrupt so *there's nothing we can do* [*we have no more cards to play*].

11【水・コンクリート・網を】▶庭に水を打つと涼しく感じる It feels cooler if you *sprinkle water* in the yard.

▶《慣用表現》会場は水を打ったように静まり返っていた *A hush fell over* the audience in the hall. ‖ 漁師たちは投網を打ってウグイを捕った The fishermen *cast* [*threw*] *a net* to catch Japanese dace.

12【麺類を】▶そばを打つ *make* buckwheat noodles.

13【弓矢・銃弾などで襲う】 **shoot** ▶銃を撃つ *shoot* [*fire*] a gun ‖ 撃つな! 警察だ! Don't *shoot*! We're police officers! ‖ 猟師はクマの頭を撃った The hunter *shot* the bear in the head. (👉 命中したのはクマなので, the head of a bear とはいわず, まず「全体」をいい, 次に前置詞を用いて「部分」を示す) ‖ 彼はその大蛇を撃った He *shot* (at) the big snake. (➤ at がなければ弾丸[矢]は大蛇に命中したことを意味し, at があれば大蛇を狙って撃ったことを強調する) ‖ その若者は誤って銃で撃たれて死んだ The young man *was accidentally shot* and killed [*was fatally shot* by accident].

14【人を殺す】▶敵を討つ *defeat* an enemy ‖ 父親のあだを討つ *avenge* one's father.

☞ 打って変わって, 打って出る (→見出語)

²**うつ 鬱** **depression** →うつ病 ▶彼はうつ状態に陥っている He's suffering from *depression*. / He's *depressed*.

うつうつ ▶ここ数日何となくうつうつしている I've *been depressed* for days for no apparent reason.

うっかり **carelessly**(不注意で), **inadvertently**(気づかずに, 思わず); **absent-mindedly**(ぼんやりして) ▶うっかりミスをする make a *careless* mistake ‖ 秘密をうっかりしゃべってしまう *blurt out* a secret ‖ うっかりしてかばんをタクシーに忘れてきた I *carelessly* left my bag in the taxi. ‖ そのメールをうっかり別の人に送ってしまった I sent the email to the wrong person *by mistake*. (➤「まちがって」の意) / I *inadvertently* sent the email to the wrong person. (➤「無意識に」) ‖ うっかりして切手を貼らずに彼に手紙を出してしまった I was so *absent-minded* (that) I mailed an unstamped letter to him. ‖ きょうが久美子の誕生日であることをうっかり忘れていた It *slipped my mind* that today was Kumiko's birthday. ‖ また電車を乗り過ごしたの? あなたって本当にうっかり者ね You missed your station again? You really *are absent-minded*.

うつぎ 空木 《植物》 a **deutzia** /djúːtsiə/.

うつくしい 美しい **beautiful**; **lovely** (魅力的な); **pretty** (かわいく美しい)

▶美しい顔[女性] a *beautiful* face [woman] ‖ 美しい旋律 a *lovely* melody ‖ 花が咲き鳥が歌う美しい季節になった The *beautiful* season when flowers bloom and birds sing has arrived. ‖ 佐和子は美しく着飾っていた Sawako was *beautifully* dressed.

‖踊りのお師匠さんの立ち居振る舞いが美しい Our dance teacher carries herself *beautifully* [*gracefully*]. ‖あなたが羨ましいわ. いつまでもお美しくて I envy you. You're taking your years well. (➤ take one's years well は「上手な年の取り方をする」) ‖彼は美しい字を書く He has *beautiful* handwriting.

▶美しい話 a *beautiful* [*moving*] story (➤ moving は「感動的な」) ‖美しい友情 *beautiful* friendship ‖美しい心の持ち主 a person *with a heart of gold* ‖美しい生き方をする have a *beautiful* way of life ‖美しく生きる[死ぬ] live [die] *beautifully*.

うつくしさ 美しさ beauty ; purity (純粋さ) ▶私たちはその庭園の美しさに感嘆した We were struck by the garden's *beauty*. ‖人によって美しさの規準は異なる *Beauty* is in the eye of the beholder. (● 訳例に示した「美は見る者の中にある」の意のことわざがこれに相当する) ‖美しさはうわべだけのもの *Beauty* is only skin-deep. (➤ 英語のことわざ) ‖彼女の心の美しさ(＝内面の美しさ) her inner *beauty*.

うっくつ 鬱屈 depression ; pessimism (悲観) ▶彼の鬱屈した気持ちがあの事件を起こしたのだろうか Did his *depression* cause that incident?

うっけつ 鬱血 congestion ▶左手の小指が鬱血している My left little finger *is congested*.

うつし 写し a copy(手・機械による) ; a duplicate (正副 2 通作成したうちの副) →コピー ▶契約書の写しが 2 通いります We need two (*photo*) *copies* of the contract.

1 うつす 写す・映す

1【文字などを】 copy +㊐ ; duplicate /djúːplɪkeɪt/ +㊐ (複写する) ▶テストで人の解答を写す *copy* answers on a test ‖生徒たちは先生の板書をノートに写すのに忙しい Students are busy *copying* what their teacher has written on the blackboard into their own notebooks. ‖江戸時代の医学生たちはオランダ語の医学書を写して勉強した Medical students in the Edo period *copied* Dutch medical texts and studied them.

2【鏡や水面に】▶鏡に自分の顔を映してみて, にきびの多いのに驚いた When I *looked* at myself *in the mirror*, I was surprised to find so many pimples on my face. ‖山中湖は湖面に富士山を映していた Mt. Fuji *was reflected* in Lake Yamanaka.

3【スクリーンに】 project /prədʒékt/ +㊐ ▶スクリーンにスライド[映画]を映す *project* a slide [a film] on (to) a screen ‖彼はコンピュータの画面に会社の組織図を映し(出し)た He *got* the company's organization chart on the computer screen.

4【写真を】 take +㊐ ▶日本人は旅行に行くと写真をたくさん写す Japanese people *take* lots of *pictures* when they travel.

2 うつす 移す

1【別の場所に】 move +㊐ (動かす) ; shift +㊐ (位置などを変える) ; transfer +㊐ (職場などを) ▶このソファーを隣の部屋に移したい I want to *move* this sofa to the next room. ‖当社はこのたび本社を熊本に移しました We have *moved* our head office to Kumamoto. ‖手品師は野球のボールを左手から右手に素早く移した The magician *shifted* a baseball from his left hand to his right quickly. ‖カレーを別の鍋に移してください Please *put* the curry in another pot. ‖私は本籍を群馬県前橋市に移しました I have *transferred* my permanent legal residence to the city of Maebashi, Gunma Prefecture. ‖オールスター第 2 戦は舞台を千葉マリンスタジアムに移して行われた The second all-star game was held *at a different venue*: the Chiba Marine Stadium. (➤ venue /vénjuː/ は「会場」).

2【別の状態に】▶部長は計画を早速実行に移した The manager *implemented* the plan immediately.

3【感染させる】 give +㊐ ▶おたふくかぜを友だちにうつさないように注意してね Be careful not to *give* the mumps to your friends. ‖父にインフルエンザをうつされてしまった I *caught* the flu from Dad.

うっすらと slightly (わずかに) ; thinly (薄く) ; lightly (軽く) ▶うっすらと雪の積もった庭 a garden *slightly* covered with snow ‖彼女はうっすらと目を開けて私の方を見た She looked at me through *slightly* opened eyes. ‖子供の頃死別した父のことはうっすらと記憶に残っています I have a *dim* memory of my father who died when I was a child. ‖ひん死の病人の顔にうっすらと赤みがさした The face of the critically ill patient *regained a bit of color*.

うっせき 鬱積した pent-up ▶鬱積した怒り *pent-up* anger ‖彼女の心には不満が鬱積していた Discontent *smoldered* in her heart. ‖社員の間に不平が鬱積している There is *smoldering* discontent among the company's employees.

うっそう 鬱蒼 ▶うっそうとした森 a *dense* forest ‖富士山ろくには樹木がうっそうと茂っている Trees grow *thickly* at the foot of Mt. Fuji.

うったえ 訴え a suit, a lawsuit (主に訴訟行為) ; an action (主に訴訟手続き) ; a charge(告発) ; an appeal (懇願) ; (a) complaint(痛みや苦しみの) ▶訴えを取り下げる drop [withdraw] a *charge* ‖高い税金に対する人々の訴え people's *complaint* about high taxes ‖彼は医者に対して損害賠償の訴えを起こした He *brought a suit* [*a lawsuit*] for damages against the doctor. ／He *sued* the doctor for damages.

うったえる 訴える

📖 **訳語メニュー**
裁判所に →sue **1**
心に →appeal (to) **2**
痛みなどを →complain (of) **3**
手段を使う →resort (to) **4**

1【告訴する】 sue /suː ‖ sjuː/ +㊐, take ... to court (裁判所に ; 後者はおもに話しことばで用いる)

【文型】
人(A)を罪状(B)で訴える
sue A for B
take A to court for B

▶父親は子供に対する暴力行為で先生を訴えた The father *sued* the teacher *for* beating his child. ‖早く金を返さないと詐欺で訴えるぞ If you don't pay me back the money soon, I will *take* you *to court for* fraud.

▶被害者の家族たちは製薬会社を訴えた The families of the victims *brought a lawsuit against* the pharmaceutical company. (➤ lawsuit は「訴訟」) ‖立ち退かないと警察に訴え(＝通報し)ますよ If you don't leave, I'll *report* you *to* the police.

2【心に働きかける】 appeal (to) ▶世論に訴える *appeal to* public opinion ‖(世界の指導者に)核廃絶を訴える *appeal* (*to* world leaders) for nuclear disarmament ／ *appeal* (*to* world leaders) to abolish nuclear weapons ‖ 罪を償うように犯人の良心に**訴えたい** I want to *appeal to* the culprit's conscience to atone for his or her crime. ‖ それは心に強く**訴える**映画だった It was a deeply *moving* film. ／That film deeply *moved* me [strongly *appealed to* me].

3【痛みなどを】complain《of》▶胃の痛みを**訴える** *complain of* pains in the stomach ／*complain of* a stomachache.

4【手段を使う】resort《to》▶暴力に**訴えて**物事を解決しようとする人もいる Some people try to settle matters by *resorting to* violence.

うっちゃる ▶私は家事を長い間**うっちゃって**(＝放って)おいた I *have been neglecting* the housework [*letting* the housework *slide*] for a long time.

▶《相撲で》正代は佐田の海を**うっちゃった** Shodai *threw* Sadanoumi *backward by pivoting on his heels*. (➤ pivot on one's heels は「かかとで回る」の意).

うつつ 現 ▶夢か**うつつ**か Am I dreaming or is this *reality*? ‖ 彼はマージャンに**うつつを抜かしている** He *is addicted to* mah-jongg. ‖ どうして兄があんな女に**うつつを抜かしている**のか, ぼくにはわからない I can't understand (the reason) why my brother *is crazy* [*mad*] *about* a woman like that. ／I can't see why my brother's so *besotted with* that kind of woman. (➤ be besotted with は「…にぼうっとなる」).

うってかわって 打って変わって ▶パーティーに現れた彼女は, ふだんと**打って変わって**華やかなドレスを着ていた She showed up at the party, wearing a gorgeous dress *quite different from* her usual attire. ‖ 彼女はその後, 夫に対して以前とは**打って変わって**冷たくなった After that, she *suddenly changed* and became cold toward her husband.

うってつけ 打ってつけ ▶彼は営業に**うってつけだ** He is *just the* man *for* the sales department. ／He *is made to* be a sales representative. ‖ きみに**うってつけ**の仕事があるよ I've got *just the right* job *for* you. ‖ 警備員は元警官には**うってつけ**の職だ A security guard is an *ideal* job *for* an ex-policeman.

うってでる 打って出る ▶彼は今度の選挙に**打って出る**そうだ He is reportedly *putting himself forward* as a candidate in the coming election. ‖ 彼は20代早々で文壇に**打って出た**(＝デビューした) He *made his* literary *debut* in his early twenties.

うっとうしい ▶きのうは**うっとうしい**天気だった We had *gloomy* [*dull*] weather yesterday. ‖ 前髪が伸びて**うっとうしい** My bangs have grown long and *bother* me. (➤ bother は「うるさがらせる」) ‖ 初めてコンタクトを入れたときは何だか**うっとうしかった**わ When I first got my contact lenses, they kind of *bothered* me. (➤ kind of は「何だか, ちょっと」の意のインフォーマルな表現).

うっとり ▶夕焼けの美しさに**うっとりした** I *was enchanted by* the magnificent evening glow. ‖ 彼女は**うっとり**とその音楽に聞きほれていた She *was spellbound* [*entranced* ／ *enraptured*] as she listened to the music. ‖ 花嫁姿の京子はただただ**うっとり**するほどの美しさだった Kyoko in her wedding dress was just *ravishing*.

うつびょう 鬱病 (**psychotic** /saɪkɑ́ːṭɪk/) **depression** ▶**うつ病になる** *get* [*become*] *depressed*.

‖**うつ病患者** a depressive.

うつぶす lie face down ▶子供たちは床に**うつぶした**まま寝てしまった The children fell asleep *lying face down* on the floor.

うつぶせ うつ伏せ ▶**うつ伏せ**になってください Lie down *on your stomach*. ／Lie *face down*. ‖ 我々は彼が深い雪にうずもれて**うつ伏せ**に倒れているのを発見した We found him lying *face down* deep in the snow.

うっぷん 鬱憤 pent-up anger(鬱積した怒り) ; **temper**(不機嫌) ▶彼女はいつも**鬱憤**を縫いぐるみのクマにぶちまけた She always vented her *temper* on her teddy bear. ／She always took out her *frustrations* [*anger*] on her teddy bear. (➤ 第 2 文がインフォーマルな言い方) ‖ 彼は妻をどなりつけて**鬱憤を晴らした** He *gave vent to his* (*pent-up*) *anger* by yelling at his wife. (➤ give vent to は「(怒りなどを)発散させる」) ／He *blew off steam* by yelling at his wife. (➤ blow off steam は「鬱憤を晴らす」の意のインフォーマルな表現).

うつむく hang one's **head** (うなだれる) ; **look down** (下を向く) ▶褒められると少年は恥ずかしそうに**うつむいて**しまった The boy *looked down* bashfully when he was praised. ‖ その子は**うつむいた**ままじっと黙っていた The boy kept silent *with his head down*.

うつらうつら →うとうと.

うつり 写り・映り ▶このテレビは**映りがいい** We *get a clear* [*sharp*] *picture* on this TV. (➤「映りが悪い」なら形容詞を dim, fuzzy などに変える) ‖ あなたって, **写真写りがいい**のね You're so *photogenic*. ／You *photograph well*.

うつりかわり 移り変わり a change ▶日本庭園には季節の**移り変わり**を楽しめるものが多い There are many Japanese gardens where you can enjoy *the changes of the seasons*. ‖ IT 業界は**移り変わりが激しい** The IT industry is *changing rapidly*.

うつりかわる 移り変わる change ▶時代とともにことばも**移り変わる** Languages *change* with the times. ‖ 流行はどんどん**移り変わる** Fashions *change* rapidly.

うつりぎ 移り気な fickle(愛情などが) ▶**移り気な**恋人 a *fickle* lover ‖ あいつは**移り気な**男だから信用できない I can't trust him because he *often changes his mind* [because he *can't stick to anything*]. (➤ stick to は「やり抜く, 頑張る」の意のインフォーマルな表現).

1**うつる 移る** **1【場所が移転・移動する】move**《to》; **transfer**《to》(所属などが) ▶私たちは 7 月 1 日に新居に**移る**予定です We plan to *move to* our new home on July 1. ‖ 皆さん, 前の方の席へ**移って**ください Everyone, please *move to* the front seats. ‖ 私は法学部へ**移って**刑法の勉強がしたい I'd like to *transfer to* the school of law and study criminal law. ‖ 山下氏は大阪の本社に**移った** Mr. Yamashita *was transferred to* the head office in Osaka. (➤ 社命による転勤なので動詞が受け身形になっている).

2【状態が変わる】change《to》, **shift**《to》▶話題が貿易摩擦に**移る**と学生たちは黙ってしまった The students fell silent when the topic of discussion *changed to* trade friction. ‖ スカウトの関心は大学野球の選手から高校野球の選手に**移った** The interest of baseball scouts *has shifted* from college *to* high school (baseball) players. ‖ では次の項目に**移ります** Now, let's *move on to* the next item (on the agenda). ‖ 彼は行動に**移る**までに時間がかかる He takes his time before *making his move*. ‖ 犬の嫌

いな人でもしばらく飼うと**情が移る**ものだ Even those who don't like dogs may *become attached to* them after raising them for a while.

3【感染する】catch +目 (➤主語は病名でなく「人」) ▶姉のおたふくかぜが**うつった** I *caught* the mumps from my sister. / My sister *gave* me her mumps. ‖いとこのはしかが息子に**うつった** My son *caught* his cousin's measles. ‖ぼくのかぜがきみに**うつら**なけりゃあいいんだけど I hope you don't *catch* my cold. ‖性感染症は肉体的接触によって**うつる** Sexually transmitted diseases [STDs] *are contracted* through physical contact.

2 **うつる 写る・映る** **1【写真に】**▶この写真, とてもよく**写ってる**ね These pictures *are taken very well*, aren't they? ‖この写真は弘美がよく**写っている** Hiromi *looks nice* in this picture. / This picture *flatters* Hiromi. (➤ flatter は「実物よりよく見せる」) ‖きみはどの写真にも**写っていない**じゃないか You'*re not in* any of these pictures, are you?

2【反射する】be reflected ▶月が池の面に**映っていた** The moon *was reflected on* the surface of the pond. ‖その犬は水に**映った自分の姿**を見てほえ立てた The dog barked at *his own reflection* in the water.

3【映像が現れる】▶最近のテレビはよく**映る** Today's TV sets *have* [*get*] *a good picture*. ‖うちのテレビは4チャンネルがよく**映らない** Our TV doesn't *get* Channel 4 very well. ‖けさのテレビにきみんちの近くの神社が**映ってた**よ The shrine near your house *was on* TV this morning.

4【人に感じられる】▶西洋人の目に**映った**明治の日本 Meiji-era Japan as *viewed* by a Westerner ‖彼の行為は社内の人間の目にはよく**映らなかった** His behavior *was not viewed favorably* at the office.

うつろ 空ろ・虚ろ ▶**うつろな**(=力のない)声 a *hollow* voice ‖**うつろな**表情 a *vacant* look ‖彼女は**うつろな**目で事故現場を見ていた She *vacantly* looked [gazed] at the scene of the accident.

うつわ 器 **1【容器】**a **container**; a **vessel**, a **receptacle** (➤両語とも堅い語) ▶気密性の高い**器** an airtight *container* ‖素焼きの**器** an earthenware *vessel* ‖電子レンジ[オーブン]で使える**器** a microwavable [an ovenproof] *dish* ‖果物をガラスの**器**に盛る serve fruit(s) in a glass *bowl*.

2【力量】caliber /kǽləbəʳ/; **ability** (才能); **capacity** (潜在能力) ▶**器**の大きな人 a person of large [high] *caliber* ‖彼は指導者の**器**ではない He is not executive [management] *material*.

うで 腕 **1【肩と手の間の部分】**an **arm** ▶右**腕**に注射をする get an injection in the right *arm* ‖**腕が上がりません** I can't raise my *arm(s)*. ‖**腕を組んで歩く** walk *arm in* [*and*] *arm* ‖彼は柔道の練習中に**腕**を折った He broke his *arm* in judo practice. ‖**腕を組んで**(=腕組みして)講義を聴くのは失礼な感じがする It seems rude to listen to a lecture *with folded arms*. ‖**腕を伸ばして**, はい曲げて *Stretch your arms*. Now bend them. ‖(シャツの)**腕をまくり上げ**なさい *Roll up* your *sleeves*.

2【腕前】skill (習得した技能・技術) ▶この頃チェス[奇術]の**腕が上がった** My chess game *has* [My magic *skills have*] *improved* recently. ‖最近あまりゴルフをしないので**腕が鈍った** Since I haven't been playing much golf recently, I've *lost my touch* [I've *gotten rusty*]. (➤前者は「勘が鈍った」, 後者は「腕が錆びついた」の意) ‖シェフは**腕によりをかけて**首相の口に合う料理を作った The chef *exerted his utmost skill* to create a dish suitable for the prime minister. ‖石井さんは**腕のいい**職人だ Ishii is a *skilled* craftsman. ‖ここがきみの**腕の見せどころ**だ This is your *chance to show your skill*. ‖町の理容師コンテストで私たちは**腕を競った** We *competed* in the city-sponsored barbers' contest. ‖ぼくはパリへ行ってコックとしての**腕を磨きたい** I want to *polish* [*hone*] my cooking *skills* in Paris. ‖待ちに待った競技会に**腕が鳴る**なあ I *can't wait to show you what I can do* at the competition. ‖龍馬は**剣の腕に覚えがあった** Ryoma was confident of his *skill in sword fighting*.

うできき 腕利きの **able** (有能な); **skilled** (腕のいい) ▶**腕利きの**新聞記者 an *able* newspaper reporter ‖**腕利きの**大工 a *skilled* carpenter.

うでぐみ 腕組み ▶先生は難問に**腕組みをして**考え込んだ When asked a difficult question, our teacher *folded his arms* and lost himself in thought.
《参考》(1) 日本人は考え込む場合によく腕組みをするが, 英米人にはこれは拒絶や反抗の動作と映ることが多い. (2) 英米人もひとりで考え込むときにはこの動作をすることがある.

うでくらべ 腕比べ ▶いつか彼女とテニスの**腕比べ**をしたい I'd like to *compete* with her at tennis some day. ‖兄とトランプ手品の**腕比べ**をしたが残念ながら勝てなかった I *tried myself* [*my skills*] *against* my brother at card tricks, but unfortunately I lost.

うでじまん 腕自慢 ▶**腕自慢**の菓子職人たちが全国から集まった Confectioners (who are) *confident in their skills* gathered from across the country.

うでずく 腕ずく ▶その少年は私から**腕ずくで**カメラを奪った The boy took my camera *by force*. / My camera was *forcibly taken* by the boy.

うでずもう 腕相撲 **arm wrestling** ▶彼は**腕相撲**がめっぽう強い He is second to none in *arm wrestling*. (➤ be second to none は「誰にも劣らない」) ‖ぼくは弟と**腕相撲をした** I *arm-wrestled* with my brother.

うでたてふせ 腕立て伏せ 《米》a **push-up**, 《英》a **press-up** ▶私は毎朝**腕立て伏せ**を30回する I do 30 *push-ups* every morning.

うでだめし 腕試し ▶私は**腕試し**にスノーボード大会に出場した I took part in a snowboarding contest to *test* [*try*] *my ability* [*skill(s)*]. / I *tried my luck* in a snowboarding contest.

うでっぷし 腕っ節 ▶**腕っぷしの強い**男 a man *of great strength* / a *strong* man ‖彼は**腕っぷし**を強くするためにいろいろなことをやった He did everything to *build up his muscles*.

うでどけい 腕時計 a **wristwatch**, a **watch** ▶デジタルの**腕時計** a digital *watch* ‖アナログの**腕時計** an analog *watch* ‖電波**腕時計** a radio-controlled *watch*.

うでまえ 腕前 **skill** (習得した技術・技能); **workmanship** (出来栄) ▶手術が成功するかどうかは外科医の**腕前**にかかっている The success of an operation depends on the surgeon's *skill*. ‖彼は器用で日曜大工で机を作るほどの**腕前**だ He is so *skillful with his hands*, he's able to make a desk although he's just a do-it-yourselfer. ‖きみの手品の**腕前**を見せてよ Let me see *how well* you can do magic tricks.

うでまくら 腕枕 ▶父は**腕枕**してうたた寝している My father is dozing *with his head on his arm*.

うでまくり 腕まくり ▶彼は**腕まくり**をして日曜大工を始めた He *rolled* [*turned*] *up his sleeves* and began his do-it-yourself project.

う

うでわ 腕輪 a **bracelet**; a **bangle**(輪の形が固定したもの).

うてん 雨天 ▶あすのデモ行進は雨天でも決行される Our protest march will be carried out tomorrow *even if it rains* [*even in case of rain* / *rain or shine*]. ‖体育祭は雨天順延の予定だ *In case of rain*, the athletic meet *will be put off until the first fine day*. ‖その試合は雨天中止となった The game *was rained out*.

うとい 疎い ▶学者は世事に疎いと言われる It is said that scholars *know little of the real world*. ‖私はコンピュータに疎い I *know nothing about* computers. / I'm computer-illiterate. (➤ 後者は「コンピュータ音痴」に当たる) ‖ ことわざ 去る者は日々に疎し Out of sight, out of mind.

うとうと ▶書類を読みながら私はついうとうとしてしまった I *fell* [*dropped*] *into a doze* while reading the documents. ‖母はテレビを見ながらよくうとうとする Mother often *nods* [*dozes*] *off* while watching TV.

うどのたいぼく うどの大木 a **big useless person**, 《インフォーマル》 a **big oaf** (➤ oaf /oʊf/ は通例男についていう) ▶あの新人はまるでうどの大木だ. 何の役にも立たない That new employee is just *a big oaf*. He's good for nothing.

うとましい 疎ましい ▶先生は私を疎ましく思っているようだ My teacher seems to have *taken a dislike* to me.

うどん ***udon***

日本紹介 ✉ **うどんは小麦粉を原料にした太い麺です. 比較的安価な食べ物で, 多くは昼食として食べます. ふつうゆでて, 天ぷら, 油揚げ, 鶏肉などの具を入れた熱いつゆと一緒に丼に入れて食べます** *Udon* are thick noodles made from wheat. It is a relatively cheap food that is often eaten at lunch. *Udon* are usually boiled and served in a large bowl with hot broth, and tempura, *aburaage* (fried tofu) or chicken.

▶腰のあるうどん (slightly) chewy [firm] *udon*.

‖うどん粉 wheat flour ‖うどん屋 an *udon* (noodle) restaurant ‖手打ちうどん handmade [home-made] *udon* (noodles).

うとんじる 疎んじる ▶うちの主人は近頃会社で疎んじられているみたい It seems that my husband is *being kept at arm's length* by the people in his office.

うながす 促す **1【催促する】urge** 《to do》((人に)…するよう強く催促する); **press** +㊐ (急がせる); **(strongly) suggest that** (…と(強い調子で) 提案する); **promote** +㊐ (促進する); **facilitate** +㊐ (容易にする) ▶彼に返答を促す *press* him for an answer ‖私は早く行こうと父を促した I *urged* my father *to* go soon [early]. / I (*strongly*) *suggested* to my father *that* we leave quickly. ‖ソフトウェアのアップデートを促すメッセージが出た A message appeared (on the screen) that *urged* me *to* update the software. ‖中国は北朝鮮に自制を促した China *urged* self-control on North Korea. ‖先生はその2つの文法構文の違いについて私たちの注意を促した Our teacher *called our attention* to the difference between the two grammatical structures. ‖よい教師は生徒の学習を促す Good teachers *facilitate* their students' learning.

2【促進する】promote +㊐ ▶テストステロンは筋肉の発育を促す Testosterone *promotes* muscular development [the development of muscles]. ‖肥料は草花の成長を促す Fertilizers *promote* the growth of flowering plants.

うなぎ 鰻 an **eel**

日本紹介 ✉ **ウナギは淡水魚で, 栄養価に富む食べ物として知られています. 夏ばてしないように夏の最も暑い頃に食べる習慣があります. ふつうはかば焼きにして食べます** *Unagi*, fresh-water eel, is known as a very nutritious food. It is customary to eat it during the hottest days of summer to combat summer fatigue. The most common way to eat it is grilled and basted with a sweetened soy-based sauce. This method of preparing eel is called '*kabayaki*.'

▶《慣用表現》ぼくの家はうなぎの寝床だ My house is *long and narrow*. ‖物価[ウォーキングシューズの売り上げ]はうなぎ登りだ Prices [Sales of walking shoes] *are skyrocketing*. (➤ skyrocket は「(物価などが)急上昇する」).

うなされる ▶私はよく悪夢にうなされる I often *have nightmares*.

うなじ 項 **the back** [**nape**] **of the neck**.

うなじゅう 鰻重 ***unaju***; broiled eel and rice in a lacquered box [tiered lacquered boxes] (➤ 説明的な訳).

うなずく nod ▶彼はひと言も言わずにうなずいた He *nodded* without saying a word. ‖「もううそはつかないね」と言うとその男の子はこっくりとうなずいた When I said, "You won't lie again, will you?" the boy *gave* me *a nod*. ‖彼女はうなずいて賛意を表した She *nodded* (*her*) *approval*.

▶彼女の美貌を見れば彼が夢中になるのもうなずける If you see her beautiful face, *you'll understand* why he is crazy about her. ‖悪いがきみの説明はどうもうなずけない Sorry, but I just *can't accept* your explanation.

うなだれる bow [**hang**] one's **head** ▶容疑者は犯行を認めて深くうなだれた The suspect *hung his head* deeply in admission of his crime.

うなどん 鰻丼 ***unadon***; a bowl of rice topped with broiled eel (➤ 説明的な訳).

うなりごえ 唸り声 ▶おりの中のクマは私が近づくと低いうなり声を上げた The bear in the cage gave *a* low *growl* as I approached.

うなる 唸る **growl** /graʊl/ (動物が); **groan** (うめく) ▶その犬はぼくを見てうなった The dog *growled* at me. ‖病人は一日中苦しんでうなっていた The sick man *groaned* with pain all day. ‖その彫刻の見事さに審査員は皆うなった(=感銘を受けた) Every judge *was* greatly *impressed* by the excellence of the sculpture.

▶《比喩的》あいつのおやじはうなるほど金を持っているんだぜ His father *is rolling in money*. / His father *has money to burn*. (➤ ともにインフォーマルな表現).

うに 雲丹 a **sea urchin** /ə́ːʳtʃɪn/; **seasoned sea-urchin eggs** [**roe**] (食品).

うぬぼれ 自惚れ **(self-) conceit, conceitedness** /kənsíːtədnəs/; **arrogance** (ごう慢); **pride** (自尊心) ▶彼はうぬぼれが強い[うぬぼれ屋だ] He *is full of himself*. / He *is swell-headed*. / He *thinks too highly of himself*. ‖私は彼女のうぬぼれの強さに我慢できなかった I couldn't stand her overwhelming *conceit*. ‖彼のあのうぬぼれが身の破滅になるよ His *pride* will be his ruin.

うぬぼれる 自惚れる **be conceited** ▶彼はうぬぼれが強い He*'s very conceited*. ‖こんなことでうぬぼれるんじゃな

いよ Don't let this *go to your head*. ‖ 優子は自分が美人だとうぬぼれている Yuko *thinks that* she's [she *fancies herself* (to be)] a real beauty. (➤ 後者は《英》) ‖ 恵美は自分に音楽の才能があるとうぬぼれている Emi *flatters herself* on her musical talent.

うね 畝 a **ridge**(畑の) ; a **rib**(織物・編み物の).

うねうね ▶道は麓までうねうねと下っている The road *winds down* to the foot (of the hill).

うねり **undulation** /ʌ̀ndʒəléɪʃən/ (山などの起伏 ; 文語的な語) ; a **swell**(波の) ▶丘の緩やかなうねり gentle *undulation* of the hill ‖ 船は大波のうねりに木の葉のように揺れた The ship was tossed like a leaf in the *heavy* [*big*] *swell*. (➤ swell は Ⓤ 扱いが多いが swells にもなる). ‖ きょうはうねりが高いから出航は見合わせよう Today *the sea is rough*, so let's put off taking the boat out.

うねる **undulate** /ʌ́ndʒəleɪt/ (土地に起伏がある ; 文語的な語) ; **swell**(波が) ; **meander** /miǽndəʳ/ (川が蛇行する) ; **wind** /waɪnd/ (道が) ▶飛行機からうねって流れる川がよく見えた The *meandering* river was clearly visible from the plane. ‖ 私たちはうねった道をたどって行った We followed the *winding* road.

うのう 右脳 **the right brain, the right hemisphere of the brain** ▶右脳思考 *right-brain* thinking.

うのみ 鵜呑み 一動 うのみにする **swallow** +目 ▶彼の話をうのみにするな Don't *swallow* his story. / Don't *fall for* what he says. (➤ fall for は「…を真に受ける」) / Don't *take* him *at his word*. ‖ 私たちはテレビで耳にする大量の情報のすべてをうのみにしないように注意しなければならない We must be careful not to *swallow whole* [*blindly believe*] everything we hear on TV. ‖ 彼は詐欺師の言うことをうのみにしてしまった He *swallowed* the swindler's story *hook, line and sinker*. (➤ hook, line and sinker は「すっかり」の意のインフォーマルな表現 ; 「釣り針・糸・おもりまで丸ごと」が原義).

うのめたかのめ 鵜の目鷹の目 ▶うの目たかの目で探す search *with sharp* [*keen*] *eyes* ‖ 会社は首を切れそうな社員をうの目たかの目で探している The company is *keeping a sharp eye out for* any excuses to fire employees.

うは 右派 **the right wing**(グループ) ; a **right winger**, a **rightist** (右派の人).

うば 乳母 a (**wet**) **nurse**.

うばいあう 奪い合う ▶犬たちは骨を奪い合った The dogs *fought* over the bone. ‖ 乗客はよい席を奪い合った Passengers *scrambled* to get good seats.

うばいとる 奪い取る **rob**(強奪する ; rob A of B (A (人) の B (金品) を奪う) の形で用いる) ; **grab** +目 (強引につかむ) ▶その女性はダイヤの指輪を奪い取られた The woman *was robbed of* her diamond ring. ‖ 博は良子のおもちゃを奪い取った Hiroshi *grabbed* Yoshiko's toy from her (by force). (➤ by force は「力ずくで」だが grab に含意されているので, 強調する場合を除いては言わない).

うばう 奪う

1【無理やり取る】 **rob** +目 ; **snatch** +目 (引ったくる)

> **【文型】**
> 人(A)から金品など(B)を奪う
> **rob** A **of** B

▶その男は老婦人からハンドバッグを奪った The man *robbed* an old woman *of* her purse. ‖ ギャングがQ銀行から5000万円を奪った Gangsters *robbed* Q Bank *of* fifty million yen. ‖ 暴走族は住民から眠りを奪った The hot rodders *robbed* the residents *of* their sleep. ‖ 彼は商売の帰り道で(強盗に)大金を奪われた He *was robbed of* a large sum of money [A mugger snatched a large sum of money from him] on his way home from his shop.

2【なくさせる】 **rob**《of》, **deprive** /dɪpráɪv/《of》(➤ 前者は後者よりややくだけた語) ▶汗は蒸発するとき体から熱を奪う When it evaporates, perspiration *robs* the body *of* heat. ‖ 鉄道のストライキで約200万人の通勤客と学生が足を奪われた An estimated two million commuters and students *were deprived of transportation* [*were inconvenienced*] by the railroad strike.

▶50人の人命を奪った事故から丸1年がたつ A full year has passed since that accident which *took* [*claimed*] 50 *lives*. (➤ claim は「(事故などが人命を)奪う」の意).

3【注意などを】 ▶彼女の奇抜な服装はぼくたちの目を奪った Her bizarre clothing *attracted our attention* [*drew all eyes*].

4【点などを取る】 ▶阪神タイガースは3回に近本のホームランで3点を奪った The Tigers *grabbed* three runs when Chikamoto hit a home run in the third inning.

うばぐるま 乳母車 《米》a **baby carriage**, a **baby buggy**,《英》a **perambulator** /pəræ̀mbjəleɪṭəʳ/,《英・インフォーマル》a **pram** 《参考》折り畳み式のものは《米》では stroller,《英》では pushchair という.

うぶ 初な **innocent, naive** /naɪíːv/ ▶うぶな少女 an *innocent* young girl ‖ 広告に書いてあることを信じるなんてきみもうぶだね It is *naive* of you to believe what advertisements say! (➤ naive には好ましくないイメージがある).

うぶげ 産毛 **fine soft hair, down** ▶産毛の生えた腕 *downy* arms.

うぶごえ 産声 ▶母親は赤ん坊の産声を聞くと感動するものだ Mothers are deeply moved when they hear their baby's *first cry*.

▶《比喩的》その会社は戦後の焼け野原の中で産声を上げた The company *was built from scratch* in the burned area after the war.

うぶゆ 産湯 ▶赤ん坊に産湯を使わせる give a newborn baby its *first bath* ‖ 《映画『男はつらいよ』での寅(とら)さんのせりふ》わたくし, 柴又帝釈天で産湯を使い I *was blessed* at Taishakuten Temple in Shibamata. (➤ bless は「(宗教的儀式によって身を)清める」の意).

うへっ **Yuck!** /jʌk/ (飲食物がまずいとき) ; **Ugh!** /ʊx/ (嫌悪・軽蔑・恐怖などの感情を表して) ▶うへっ, まずい! *Yuck*, terrible! ‖ うへっ, 何, この写真! 気持ちわるーい *Ugh!* What's this picture? It's gross [disgusting]. ‖ 口臭はうへっという感じになる Bad breath is a *turnoff*. (●「つや消し[興味をそぐもの]」だと考えて, その意のインフォーマルな語 turnoff を用いる).

うま 馬 **1【動物】** a **horse**

> **《解説》馬について**
> (1) **horse** は一般語で, 狭義には成長した雄馬を指す. (2) 区別すれば, **mare**(特に雌馬), **colt**(雄の子馬), **filly**(雌の子馬), **foal**(幼馬), **stallion**(種馬), **gelding**(去勢馬), **pony**(ふつうより小型の品種の馬)など. (3) 鳴き声を表す英語は neigh /neɪ/.

▶馬から降りてください Please get off the *horse*. ‖ 馬に乗ったことがありますか Have you ever ridden (on)

う

a horse？‖コロラドの山の中を馬に乗って歩き回ったのは本当に楽しかった I really enjoyed riding around *on horseback* in the Colorado mountains. ‖では馬に乗ってください Now please *mount the horse*.
‖馬小屋 a stable, 《米》 a barn.
2【慣用表現】▶高野氏とは馬が合わない Mr. Takano and I *are not on the same wavelength*. (☞「波長が合わない」の意から) ‖監督は選手たちに説教したが馬の耳に念仏だった The manager lectured the players but *it went in one ear and out the other* [but *it was like talking to a brick wall*]. ‖どこの馬の骨かわからない男 a man of *unknown origin(s)*.

うまい 旨い・上手い **1【おいしい】good, nice** (➤味や香りに具体的に言及する場合は前者がふつう) ; **delicious** (とてもおいしい) ▶うん, これはうまい Great ! This is really *good* [*delicious*]. 《参考》くだけた(特に子供の)会話では Yum-yum ! /jʌ̀mjʌ́m/ とか Yummy ! と言うことが多い. ‖このスパゲッティは実にうまい This spaghetti *tastes* really *good*. ‖今夜は何かうまいものを食いたいなあ I want (to have) *something good* for dinner tonight. ‖あの刺身はうまかった The sashimi was *good*. ‖牧場の朝の空気は実にうまい The morning air on the ranch is *crisp and cool*.
2【上手な, 巧みな】good ▶あのアメリカ人は日本語がうまい That American speaks *good* Japanese. ／That American is a *good* speaker of Japanese. ‖リアーナは歌がうまい Rihanna is a *good* singer. ‖三郎は字がうまい Saburo has *good* handwriting. ／Saburo's handwriting is *beautiful*. ‖美佐子は習字がうまい Misako is a *skilled* calligrapher. ‖俺の母よりきみのお母さんのほうが料理がうまいよ Your mother is *better* at cooking than my mother. ‖秀夫は言い訳をするのがうまい Hideo *is good* [*clever*] *at* making excuses.
▶うまいうまい, よくやった *Great !* You did it. ‖それはうまい考えだ That's *a good idea*. ‖きみもなかなかうまいことを言うね You certainly have a way of putting things. ／That's a good way of putting it [to put it].
3【好都合な】▶うまい具合に話［交渉］がとんとん拍子に進んだ I'm happy that things [the negotiations] went very *smoothly*. ‖うまいこと予約がとれた *Luckily* [*Fortunately*], I was able to make a reservation. ‖やあ, うまいときにタクシーが来たね Oh, here comes a taxi *at just the right time*. ‖加藤のやつ, いつでもうまい汁を吸ってるぜ Kato always *skims off the top*. ／Kato always *takes the lion's share*. (➤ともに「最良の部分を取る」の意) ‖10万円投資すれば来年100万円もらえるとおっしゃるんですか？ちょっと話がうますぎますね Do you mean to say that I can get a million yen next year if I invest one hundred thousand yen now? That sounds *too good to be true*. (➤「よすぎて本当とは思えない」の意) ‖うますぎる話には用心しなさい *If it seems too good to be true, it probably is*. (➤「話がうますぎると思えるようなら, 多分その通りなのだ」の意の慣用句).

うまく **1【上手に】well ; successfully** (首尾よく) ▶森さんはネパール語をうまく話す Mr. Mori speaks Nepalese *well*. ‖彼女は『マイ・フェア・レディ』のイライザ役をうまくこなした She *skillfully* played the part of Eliza in "My Fair Lady." ‖箸を使うのは最初はとても難しかったが少しずつうまくなってきた At first it was very difficult to use chopsticks, but I have gradually *become better* at it. ‖もっとうまく英語が話せるようになりたい I hope I (can) get *better* at speaking English.
▶テニスがうまくなりたい I want to be a *good* tennis player. ‖このチキンはうまく焼けている This chicken is cooked *to perfection*. ‖彼女は誰ともうまくやっていくことができなかった She didn't *get along well with* anyone. ‖新しい同僚とはうまくやっていますか How *are you getting along with* your new co-worker? ‖うまく言えないが, あの演奏は心に響いてこなかった *I can't explain why*, but that performance failed to speak to me.
2【運よく, 都合よく】▶数学の試験はうまくいったが, 英語の試験はうまくいかなかった I *did well* on the math test, but *not* on the English test. ‖うまくいけばきみが次期社長だよ *With (any) luck* [*If things go well*], you will be the next president. ‖その合弁事業はうまくいかなかった The joint venture didn't *work out* [*pay off*].
▶うまくいけばわが家は12月までには出来上がります *Hopefully*, our house will be finished by December. (➤ hopefully は「うまくいけば」の意の文修飾語としてインフォーマルで多用される) ‖万事うまくいっている Everything *is going (just) fine*. ／So far so good. ‖うまくいったね！ *Good job !* ／*Way to go !* ‖ **対話**「先週の物理の試験どうだったの？」「うまくいったよ」"How did you do on the physics exam last week?" "I think I *aced it*." (➤ ace は《インフォーマル》で「試験で高得点を取る」).

うまづら 馬面 ▶彼は馬面だ He's *horse-faced*.

うまとび 馬跳び leapfrog ▶馬跳びをする play *leapfrog*.

うまのり 馬乗り ▶その少年は弟に馬乗りになっていた I found the boy *sitting astride* his brother.

うまみ 旨み **1【おいしさ】umami (flavor), savoriness ; flavor** (味) ▶素材のうまみを引き出す bring out the *savoriness* [*the (umami) flavor*] of the ingredients ‖この汁は昆布のうまみが効いている This soup has a lot of (savory) kombu *flavor* [kombu *umami*]. ／There's a lot of (savory) kombu *flavor* in this soup. ‖このつみれはイワシのうまみをよく引き出している The *savory taste* of sardines is brought out well in this tsumire (fish meatball).
2【利点】advantage ▶それはなかなかうまみのある商売だ That's quite a *profitable* business.

うまや 馬屋 a **stable**, 《米》 a **barn**.

うまる 埋まる be buried /bérid/ (埋められる) ; **be filled** (いっぱいになる) ▶土砂に埋まった家 a house *buried* under earth and rocks ‖次々に流れ下る溶岩で谷はすっかり埋まってしまった The valley *was* [*got*] completely *filled up* by the lava which flowed in continuously.
▶今度のコンサート, 席が埋まるかしら I wonder if the seats will *(all) be filled* at the coming concert. ‖欠員は埋まった The vacancy *was filled*.

うまれ 生まれ ▶彼女はドイツ生まれだ She *was born* in Germany. ‖彼は3月［4月1日］生まれだ He *was born* in March [on April 1]. ‖《映画『男はつらいよ』での寅(とら)さんのせりふ》わたくし生まれも育ちも葛飾柴又です I *was born and brought up* [*born and raised*] in Shibamata, Katsushika. ‖祖父は大阪生まれの商人だった My grandfather was an *Osaka-born* merchant.
▶ **対話**「きみは何年生まれですか」「2005年生まれです」"When *were* you *born*?" "I *was born* in 2005."

‖ 対話 「どちらのお生まれですか（＝ご出身はどちらですか）」「長崎生まれです」"*Where are you from*?" "I'm *from* Nagasaki."
‖**生まれ故郷** one's home, one's hometown, one's birthplace.

うまれかわり 生まれ変わり (a) **reincarnation** /rìːɪnkɑːˈnéɪʃən/ ▶北の湖はかつて谷風の生まれ変わりと言われた Kitanoumi was once said to be a *second* Tanikaze [Tanikaze *reincarnated*].

うまれかわる 生まれ変わる ▶もし生まれ変わったら何になりたいですか *If* you *could be born again*, what would you want to be? ‖ 彼は妻と別れてから生まれ変わったように明るくなった Since he separated from his wife, he has been so cheerful (that) he's *like a different person*.

うまれそだつ 生まれ育つ ▶人は誰でも生まれ育った町には愛着があるものだ It's (only) natural to feel attached to the place where you *were born and raised*.

うまれつき 生まれつき **by nature, naturally** ▶彼は生まれつき臆病だ He is timid *by nature*. ‖ あの子は生まれつき頭のいい子だ That child *was born* smart. ‖ 生まれつきの悪人はいない No one *is born* bad. ／We are not *naturally* bad. ‖ 彼女は生まれつき気持ちが優し[体が弱]かった She *was born with* a gentle disposition [a weak constitution]. ‖ 対話 「その髪染めたの？」「ううん，茶色いのは生まれつきなの」"Did you dye your hair?" "No, the brown hair is *natural*."

うまれつく 生まれつく ▶たぶん彼は詩人に生まれついていたのだろう Perhaps he *was meant to* be a poet.

うまれながらの 生まれながらの **born** ▶彼女は生まれながらのミュージシャンだ She is a *born* musician. ／She *was born* a musician. ‖ 彼女は生まれながらの器量よしだ She *was born* beautiful.

うまれる 生まれる **be born** ▶父は昭和45年3月25日に東京で生まれた My father *was born* in Tokyo on March 25 in the 45th year of Showa [in 1970]. ‖ 彼女は金持ちの家に生まれた She *was born* into a rich family.
▶きょう彼女に男の子が生まれた She *had* a (baby) boy today. ／A (baby) boy *was born* to her today. (➤ 後者は堅い言い方) ‖ 生まれたのはかわいい女の子だった The *new arrival* was a cute baby girl. (➤ arrival は「生まれてきた子」) ‖ 彼女は来月子供が生まれる予定だ She is going to *have* a baby next month. ‖ 彼は生まれたときの体重が2600グラムだった He weighed 2,600 grams *at birth*.
▶私は生まれてこの方病気をしたことがない I have never been sick *since the day I was born*. ‖ きのう，生まれて初めてナマズを食べた Yesterday I ate a catfish *for the first time* (*in my life*). ‖ イチローは野球選手になるために生まれてきたような人だ Ichiro is a *born* baseball player. ‖ 生まれたばかりの子猫 a *newborn* kitten.
▶国連がどのように生まれたか知っていますか Do you know how the United Nations *was born* [*came into existence*]? ‖ そのオリンピックではたくさんの世界新記録が生まれた Many world records *were set* [*were established*] at the Olympics. ‖ 傑作は数奇な体験から生まれることが多い Many masterpieces *are born* from adverse experiences.
▶生まれたままの姿で泳ぐ[日光浴をする] swim [sunbathe] *au naturel* (➤ au naturel /oʊ nàːtʃərél/ はフランス語起源の慣用句で，日本語の場合のようにややユーモラスな響きがある).

1**うみ 海** **the sea; the ocean** (➤「大洋」の意味だが，《米・インフォーマル》では the sea と同意に用いる) ▶海は地球の表面の約4分の3を覆っている *The sea* covers about three-fourths of the earth's surface. ‖ 子供たちが海で泳いでいる Children are swimming *in the sea* [*ocean*]. ‖ 彼らは甲板から次々に海に飛び込んだ One after another they leaped from the deck *into the sea*. ‖ 日本は四方を海に囲まれている Japan is surrounded *by the sea* [*the ocean*] on all sides.
▶海の生物 *marine* life ‖ この夏は海の近くの別荘で休暇を過ごす予定です I'm going to spend my summer vacation at a cottage *by the sea*. ‖ 彼の別荘は海の近くにある His (summer) cottage is situated *near the sea*. ‖ あした海へ泳ぎに行こうよ Let's go for a swim [go swimming] *in the sea* tomorrow. ‖ 去年の夏，おじ夫婦と海へ行った Last summer I *went to the beach* [《英》*went to the seaside*] with my uncle and his wife. 《参考》「海へ行く」は go to the seashore でもよいが，遊びで行く場合は《米》では go to the beach が一般的.
▶《比喩的》事件現場はまるで血の海であった The crime spot was just like *a pool of blood*. ‖ 飛行機が墜落して辺り一面火の海となった An airplane crashed and turned the area into *a sea of flames*.
▶《慣用表現》彼が今取り組んでいる発明品は海の物とも山の物ともつかない *Nobody knows what* the invention he's working on now *will turn out to be*.
‖**海の男** a sailor, a seafaring man(船乗り); a fisherman(漁師) ‖ **海の幸** products of the sea, seafood ‖ **海の日** Marine Day.

2**うみ 膿** **pus** /pʌs/, **(infected) matter** ▶彼の足の傷にはうみがたまっている The wound in his leg is filled with *pus*. →うむ.

うみがめ 海亀 a **(sea) turtle** (➤《英》では通例 a turtle).

うみせんやません 海千山千 ▶あのセールスマンは海千山千のしたたか者だ That salesman is *a sly* [*crafty*] *old fox*. (● 英語では「ずる賢いキツネ」と表現するのでそれを当てる).

うみだす 生み出す **produce** ＋目; **generate** ＋目 (アイデアなどを) ▶アイデアを生み出す *generate* ideas ‖ その会社はまだ利益を生み出すには至っていない The company *has* not yet *produced* [*turned*] a profit. ／The company *has* so far *made* no profits.

うみなり 海鳴り **the roar of the sea** ▶海鳴り(の音)が聞こえる I can hear *the roar of the sea*.

うみねこ 海猫 《鳥》a **black-tailed gull**.

うみのおや 生みの親 **1**【実の親】one's **biological** [**natural**] **parent(s)**, one's **birth parent(s)** (➤「生みの母」は birth mother または natural [biological] mother).
2【創設者】**the founder** ▶この大学の生みの親は歯科医師だった *The founder* of this university was a dentist.

うみのくるしみ 産みの苦しみ **the pain of childbirth, labor pains**(陣痛); **growing pains, birth pangs** (創業時・拡大期の苦難).

うみびらき 海開き ▶江の島海岸はあしたが海開きだ Tomorrow marks *the start of the swimming season* at Enoshima beach. (●「海開き」に当たる英語はないので，「海水浴の季節の始まり」と考える).

うみべ 海辺 《米》 **the beach,** 《英》 **the seaside** ▶海辺をぶらぶら歩く stroll down *the beach* ‖ 海辺の小さな村 a small village *by the sea*.

1 **うむ 生む・産む** **1**【卵や子供を】**lay** +㊐ (卵を) ; **give birth to, have** +㊐ (子を) →出産 ▶卵を産む *lay* an egg ‖ 洋子は女の子を産んだ Yoko *had* a baby girl. ／Yoko *gave birth to* a baby girl. ／Yoko has become the mother of a baby girl. ‖ 私は(子供を)産もうかおろそうか悩んでいます I'm troubled about whether to *give birth* (*to* the baby) or have an abortion. ‖ サケは卵を産むために自分が生まれた川に戻ってくる Salmon return to the river where they were born in order to *spawn* eggs. (➤ spawn は「(魚などが卵を)産む」) ‖ 牛が子供を産むところを見たことがありますか Have you ever seen a cow *give birth to* a calf?
2【作り出す】**produce** +㊐ ; **yield** +㊐ (利益などを) ▶無知は偏見を生む Ignorance *breeds* prejudice. ‖ 銀行にその金を預けておいても大した利子を生まないだろう Even if you deposit the money in a bank, it won't *yield* much interest. ‖ 長嶋は日本が生んだ最高の打者の1人である Nagashima is one of the greatest batters that Japan *has* (ever) *produced*.

2 **うむ 膿む** **fester ; become infected** (傷口が菌に感染する) ▶右足の傷がうみ始めた The wound on my right leg began to *fester* [*form pus*]. ‖ 手の傷口がうんだ The cut on my hand *has become infected*. ‖ おできがうんできた The boil *has swollen* [*has gathered*]. (➤この gather は「うんで腫れる」).

3 **うむ 有無** ▶欠席者の有無を調べる check and see if anyone is absent ‖ 我々はその品の在庫の有無をメーカーに問い合わせた We checked with the manufacturer whether they had the item in stock or not. ▶有無を言わせずあいつにやらせろ Make him do it *whether* he *is willing or not*.

うめ 梅 an **ume tree** (木) ; a **Japanese apricot** /éɪprɪkɑ:t/
日本紹介 ✉ **梅は早春, 桜に先立って花をつける木です. plum と訳されることもありますが, apricot の一種です. 梅の花は桜のような華やかさはありませんが, よい香りを放ちます. 昔から絵画や焼き物の題材とされてきました** *Ume* trees bloom in early spring before cherry trees. *Ume* is usually translated as 'plum,' but it is actually a type of apricot. While not as luxuriant in appearance as cherry blossoms, the flower of the *ume* has a lovely scent. The *ume* has long been a popular subject in painting and pottery decoration.
▶私たちは熱海へ梅を見に行った We went to Atami to view the *ume blossoms*.

うめあわせ 埋め合わせ **compensation** ▶損失の埋め合わせ the *compensation* for the loss ‖ 超過勤務の埋め合わせということで特別手当をもらった I was given a bonus to *make up for* the extra time spent at work. (➤ make up for で「…の埋め合わせをする」) ‖ きみにはずいぶん世話になったね. いつかこの埋め合わせをするよ You've been so kind. Someday I hope to *return* the favor.

うめあわせる 埋め合わせる **make up** 《for》; **offset** +㊐ (相殺する) ▶損失を埋め合わせる *make up for* a loss ‖ 失った時間を金で埋め合わせることはできない Money cannot *make up for* lost time. ‖ 多くの会社が売り上げ減を埋め合わせるために経費削減をしている Many companies are cutting costs to *offset* a decline in sales.

うめきごえ 呻き声 a **groan** (短く重い) ; a **moan** (やや長い) ▶地震で倒壊した建物の下からうめき声が聞こえてきた I heard *a groan* from under the building that had collapsed in the earthquake. ‖ けがをした男は痛さでうめき声を上げていた The injured man *was groaning* [*moaning*] with pain.

うめく 呻く **groan** (短く重く) ; **moan** (やや長く) ▶病院では多くの負傷者が苦痛でうめいていた At the hospital many of the injured were *groaning* [*moaning*] with pain.

うめくさ 埋め草 a **filler.**

うめしゅ 梅酒 ***umeshu*, *ume* liquor, plum wine.**

うめたて 埋め立て **reclamation** (干拓による) ; **landfilling** (ごみによる) ▶羽田沖ではまだ埋め立て工事が進んでいる *Reclamation work* is still in progress off Haneda. ‖ 埋め立て地に家が建ち始めた Houses began to be built on the *reclaimed land*.
‖ (ごみ利用による)埋め立て地 a landfill site.

うめたてる 埋め立てる **reclaim** +㊐ (海を) ; **fill up** (池・川などを) ; **fill in** (穴・溝などを) ▶湾を埋め立てて新空港が建設されている A new airport is being built on land *reclaimed* from the bay. ‖ その湖全体を埋め立てる *fill in* [*up*] the whole lake.

うめづけ 梅漬け **pickled *ume*.**

うめぼし 梅干し (an) ***umeboshi***
日本紹介 ✉ **梅干しは梅の実を塩漬けにし, 天日で乾燥させた後, さらに漬け込んだ食品です. 体によいとされ, 雑菌の繁殖を防ぐ効果もあるので, おにぎりやお弁当には欠かせません** *Umeboshi* (often called 'salted plums') are pickled *ume* which have been sun-dried and then further pickled. They are considered to be healthful and prevent the propagation of bacteria, which make them an essential ingredient in *onigiri* and *bentos* [box lunches].

うめる 埋める **1**【うずめる】**bury** +㊐ /béri/ ▶犬はよく骨を土の中に埋める Dogs often *bury* bones (in the ground). (●「土の中に」は訳さなくてもわかる場合が多い) ‖ その人の遺骨は家代々の墓に埋められた His ashes *were buried* in the family plot.
2【ふさぐ ; 満たす】**fill in ; fill** +㊐ ▶地面にできた穴を埋める *fill in* a hole in the ground ‖ 《試験問題の指示》空所を埋めなさい *Fill in* the blanks. ‖ 群衆が広場を埋めた A crowd *filled* the square.
3【補う】**make up** ▶損失を埋める *make up* a loss ‖ レジ係は5000円足りないのを発見し, 自分の金で穴を埋めなくてはならなかった The cashier found 5,000 yen missing, and had to *make it up* from her own pocket.

うもう 羽毛 a **feather** (1本1本の羽) ; **plumage** /plú:mɪdʒ/ (feather が集まったもの) ; **down** (綿毛)
‖ 羽毛布団 a down quilt.

うもれる 埋もれる **be buried** /bérid/ ▶その温泉へ行くには雪に埋もれた道を1時間も歩かねばならない To get to the hot spring, we have to walk for an hour down a road *buried under snow*. ‖ 小道は落ち葉に埋もれて(＝覆われて)いた The path *was covered* with dead leaves.
▶埋もれた人材を発掘する discover a *hidden* talent ‖ (歴史に)埋もれた作品を発掘し, 紹介する discover works that have *been forgotten or lost* and introduce them to the public.

うやうやしい 恭しい **respectful** (尊敬の念を示す) ;

polite (丁寧な) ▶恭しい態度 a *respectful* [*polite*] manner ‖ その学生は校長の姿を見ると恭しく一礼した The student made a *respectful* bow when he saw the principal.

うやまう 敬う respect +㊐ ; worship +㊐ (神を) ▶年寄りを敬う *show* [*pay*] *respect to* elderly people ／ *have respect for* senior citizens ‖ その校長は全生徒に敬われた That principal *was respected* by all the pupils.

うやむや ▶彼はうやむやな(＝曖昧な)返事をした He gave a *vague* answer. ‖ この問題をうやむやにするな Don't *leave* the question *undecided* [(*up*) *in the air*]. (➤ up in the air は「未解決で」の意のインフォーマルな表現) ‖ その汚職事件はうやむやになってしまった The bribery scandal *was* (*hushed up and*) *finally forgotten*.

うようよ ▶地面には蛇が何匹もうようよしていた The ground was *crawling with* snakes. (➤ crawl with は「(場所に)(蛇・虫などが)うじゃうじゃいる」の意) ‖ その池にはオタマジャクシがうようよしていた The pond was *alive with* tadpoles. (➤ alive with は「(魚・ボートなどで)いっぱいで」).

うよきょくせつ 紆余曲折 ▶幾多の紆余曲折を経て2人は仲直りした After many *twists and turns* [*complications*] they have become friends again.

うよく 右翼 the right wing (イデオロギーの) ; a rightist (人) ; (the) right field (野球の) ▶彼は極端な右翼思想の持ち主だ He is an ultra-*rightist*. ／ He is an extreme *right-winger*.
‖右翼団体 a right-wing organization.

¹うら 裏

📖 訳語メニュー
裏面 →the back 1
後ろ →the back, behind 2
衣服の裏地 →lining 3
野球の →the bottom 5

1【裏面】 the back ; the reverse [flip] side (レコードなどの) ; tails (硬貨の) ▶答案の裏 *the back* of an answer sheet ‖ 《表示》裏を見よ《米》*Over*. ／《英》*Please turn over*. (➤ P.T.O. と略す) ‖ 赤ちゃんの足の裏をくすぐっちゃだめよ Don't tickle the baby's *feet*. (➤「足の裏」は the sole だが, ここでは不要) ‖ コインの表か裏かを当てる遊びをする play heads or *tails* ‖ 用紙の裏に書く write on *the wrong side* of the paper (➤ the wrong side は本来「表」を使う物の「誤った側」の意).

> **あなたの英語はどう響く?**
> 「取り扱い説明は裏に印刷してあります」の意味で, The instructions are printed on the *backside*. のようにいわないこと. backside は「尻, 臀(でん)部」の意味のくだけた語である. ... are printed on the *back* とか ... are printed on the *reverse side* などの言い方が正しい.

2【後ろ】 the back, the rear →うしろ ▶私の家は裏に花壇がある There is a flower bed at *the back* of my home. ／My home has a garden in *back*. ‖ 車庫は家の裏にあります Our garage is *behind* [*at the rear of*] the house. ‖ 玄関は鍵が掛かっている. 裏へ回ろう The front door is locked. Let's go around *back*. ‖ 小さい頃はよく裏の林でセミ捕りをしたものだ When I was little, I often went to catch cicadas *in the woods behind our house*.

3【衣服の裏地】 (a) lining. →裏地.

4【隠された面】 ▶政治には裏があるものだ Politics has *a dark side*. ‖ 私はその英文の裏の意味がつかめなかった I couldn't get the *hidden meaning* [*implication*] of that English sentence. ‖ 彼は汚職で訴えられたが, 裏から手を回して告訴を取り下げさせた He was charged with bribery, but he *pulled some strings* (*behind the scenes*) and had it dropped. (➤ pull (the) strings は「陰で糸を引く」) ‖ 裏メニュー a *secret menu* (➤ 1品だけであれば a secret dish).

5【野球】 the bottom (➤「表」は the top) ▶日本ハムファイターズは1回の裏に7点を入れて試合を決めてしまった The Fighters scored seven runs in *the bottom* of the first inning to sew up the game.

6【慣用表現】 ▶アリバイの裏を取る(＝確かめる) *confirm* an alibi ／*check out* an alibi ‖ 起訴に必要な十分な裏を取る(＝証拠を集める) *collect* enough *evidence* to indict a person ‖ やつらの裏をかいて遠回りして行こう Let's *outwit* them and take a roundabout route. ‖ 裏には裏がある There are *wheels within wheels*. (➤ wheels within wheels は「複雑な事情, 込み入った事情」) ‖ 彼は何事にも慎重だが, 裏を返せば決めるのが遅いということだ He's cautious in everything, but *to put it the other way*, he's slow in making decisions.

²うら 浦 a cove (入り江).

うらうち 裏打ち lining (衣服の) ; backing (絵などの) 一動 **裏打ちする** line +㊐, back +㊐ ▶《比喩的》彼の名声は実力に裏打ちされている His fame *is backed* (up) by his ability.

うらおもて 裏表 both sides ▶彼氏からの手紙は裏表にびっしり「好きだ」と書いてあった The letter from my boyfriend was filled with the words "I love you" *on both sides*.
▶《比喩的》裏表のない人 an honest person ／《米・インフォーマル》a straight shooter ‖ 裏表のある人 a double-faced [two-faced] person ／《インフォーマル》a double-dealer ／ a hypocrite /hípəkrɪt/ (偽善者) ‖ 彼は政界の裏表に通じている He *knows all the ins and outs* of the political world.

うらがえし 裏返し ▶強風で傘が裏返しになった The strong wind blew my umbrella *inside out*. ‖ まあ嫌だ, あなたったら靴下を裏返しに履いてるじゃない Oh my goodness, you've got your socks on *inside out*. ‖ 皆さん, 解答用紙を裏返しにしてください Everyone, *turn* your answer sheet *face down*.
▶彼の高慢な態度はコンプレックスの裏返しだ His arrogant attitude is the *flip side* of his inferiority complex. (➤ flip side は「レコードのB面」が原義).

うらがえす 裏返す turn over (引っくり返す) ; turn inside out (内側を外に出す) ▶肉を裏返して焼く *turn* the meat *over* to cook the other side ‖ 彼女はコートを裏返した She *turned* her coat *inside out*.

うらがき 裏書き endorsement 一動 **裏書きする** endorse +㊐ ▶手形に裏書きしてください Please *endorse* the bill [draft].
▶《比喩的》その論文は筆者の無能を裏書きしている The thesis only *confirms* the author's incompetence. (➤ confirm は「裏付ける」).

うらかた 裏方 a sceneshifter, a stagehand (➤ ともに「舞台係」の意) ▶今度の計画では私は裏方を務める I'll take *a behind-the-scenes role* in the coming project. (➤ behind-the-scenes role は「舞台裏の

役割」).

うらがなしい うら悲しい rather [somewhat] melancholy (どことなく人の心を重くするような); rather [somewhat] mournful (どことなく悲しげな) ▶夕暮れの港はどこかうら悲しい雰囲気がある The port at dusk has a *rather melancholy* atmosphere.

うらがね 裏金 off-the-book money; a slush fund (不正資金); a bribe (賄賂).

うらがわ 裏側 the back ▶封筒の裏側に名前を書く write one's name on *the back* of an envelope ‖ 月の裏側 the *back side* [the *other side*] of the moon ‖ (家の)裏側へ回ってみよう Let's go around *back*. ／Let's go around *to the back* (of the house).

うらぎり 裏切り (a) betrayal (信頼・約束などに対する); (a) treachery /trétʃəri/ (反逆); 《インフォーマル》 a double-cross (共謀者への) ▶私は彼の裏切り行為を責めた I condemned his *act of treachery*. ‖ 彼は妻が自分に対して裏切りを働いていることを知らなかった He did not know that his wife *was unfaithful* to him. ‖**裏切り者** a traitor ／《インフォーマル》 a double-crosser.

うらぎる 裏切る **1【信頼に背く, 約束などを破る】** betray +目; cheat 《on》, two-time +目 (➤ともに「(配偶者・恋人を)裏切る」の意) ▶友人を裏切る *betray* one's friend ‖ 恋人が私を裏切っていることがわかった I found out my boyfriend *was cheating on* [*was two-timing*] me. ‖ おまえ, 裏切ったな You *double-crossed* me, didn't you? (➤ double-cross はもともとギャングや窃盗団などが多く用いたくだけた語).

2【期待に反する】 disappoint +目 ▶そのコンサートは私の期待を裏切った The concert *disappointed* me. ／The concert *didn't live up to my expectations*. (➤ live up to は「(期待に)応える」) ‖ あの新人選手の活躍はいい意味で期待を裏切った (＝期待以上だった) That newcomer played very well, which *exceeded my expectations* [*was more than I had expected*].

うらぐち 裏口 a back door ▶裏口から入る enter by [through] the *back door* ‖ 裏口へ回ってください Please come to the *back door*.

うらぐちにゅうがく 裏口入学 a back-door admission, an admission fraud (➤ fraud は「不正行為」) ▶大学の理事を買収して子供を裏口入学させる bribe a college trustee to *get* one's child *admitted through the back door* ‖ 彼の息子は大学に裏口入学したらしいよ They say his son *bought his way into college*. (➤ buy one's way into は「金を使って…へ入る」).

うらこうさく 裏工作 behind-the-scenes maneuvering.

うらごえ 裏声 falsetto /fɔːlsét̬oʊ/ ▶裏声で歌う sing *in falsetto*.

うらごし 裏ごしする sieve +目 ▶ゆでたじゃがいもを裏ごしする *mash* boiled potatoes *and sieve* them.

うらサイト 裏サイト an unofficial clandestine website (➤ clandestine /klændéstɪn/ は「秘密の」).

うらさく 裏作 second cropping.

うらさびしい うら寂しい (somewhat) forlorn /fərlɔ́ːrn/ (打ち捨てられた感じのする); (somewhat) lonely (孤立した感じのする) ▶うら寂しい田舎町 a *(somewhat) forlorn* country town.

うらじ 裏地 (a) lining ▶裏地がチェックのジャケットだなんて, おしゃれね A jacket with checked *lining*? That's really stylish!

うらづけ 裏付け ▶私は彼の有罪の裏付けとなる証拠を持っている I have evidence that will *prove* him guilty. ‖ 事実の裏付けのない議論はしてもしかたがない There is no point in having a discussion (that is) *not based on* facts. ‖ 警察は現在その男の有罪を立証するために裏付け捜査をしている The police are now conducting *an investigation to establish evidence* of the man's guilt.

うらづける 裏付ける prove +目 (証明する) ▶彼は自分の仮説を裏付ける資料を集めている He is collecting data to *prove* his hypothesis. ‖ 昔からの生活の知恵は科学的にも裏付けられるものが多い Much of the traditional wisdom about how to live our daily lives can *be backed up* scientifically.

うらて 裏手 the back (後ろ); the rear (後部) ▶そのビルは郵便局の裏手にあります The building is located *at the back of* [*in the rear of*] the post office. ／The building is *behind* the post office.

うらどおり 裏通り a back street; an alley /æli/ (狭い) ▶銀座の裏通りにはバーがひしめいている The *back streets* of Ginza are crowded with bars.

うらない 占い fortune(-)telling ▶母は占ってもらった My mother *had her fortune told*. ‖**占い師** a fortune-teller; a palmist /pάːmɪst/ (手相見).

うらなう 占う tell one's fortune ▶私は占い師にボーイフレンドとの相性を占ってもらった I *had* a fortuneteller *tell* whether or not my boyfriend and I are compatible. ‖ トランプで運勢を占ってくれませんか Could you *tell* [*read*] *my fortune* with the cards? ▶藤田さんに今年のセ・リーグの優勝チームを占って (＝予測して) いただきましょう Let's ask Mr. Fujita to *predict* which team will win the Central League pennant this year.

ウラニウム →ウラン.

うらにわ 裏庭 a backyard, a back garden ▶裏庭には花が植えてある There are flowers planted in the *backyard*.

うらばなし 裏話 an inside story ▶政界の裏話 *an inside story* of the political world.

うらはら 裏腹 ▶うちの父は言うこととすることが裏腹だ What my father does *is contrary to* what he says (he will do). ‖ 親の期待とは裏腹に彼女は大学へ進まなかった *Contrary to* her parents' expectations, she didn't go to college.

うらばんぐみ 裏番組 a program on another [a different] channel ▶私は紅白歌合戦が見たかったのに, 弟は裏番組の映画を見たがった I wanted to watch the "Kohaku Uta Gassen" singing contest, but my little brother wanted to watch a movie on *another channel*.

うらぶれる ▶うらぶれた港町 a *desolate* port town ‖ 彼女はうらぶれたなりをしていた She was dressed *shabbily*.

うらぼん うら盆 →盆.

うらみ 恨み a grudge /grʌdʒ/; hard feelings (悪感情); (an) enmity (敵意) ▶彼には恨みがある I have *a grudge* against him. ／I bear him *a grudge*. ‖ 彼女はその恨みを一生忘れないでしょう She will probably carry those *hard feelings* to the grave. ‖ そんなことをしたら彼女の恨みを買うよ You will *earn* her *enmity* if you do that.

▶彼らは長い間お互いに恨みを抱いてきた They have long *had it in for* each other. (➤ have it in for

は「…に恨みを抱く」の意のインフォーマルな表現；「折さえあれば仕返しをする」という含みがある）‖ 男はようやく昔の恨みを晴らすことができた The man finally managed to *pay off some old scores*. ▶この薬はよく効くが値が張るのをうらみとする This medicine is very effective, but *to our regret*, it's rather expensive. (➤ to our regret は「残念ながら」).

うらみち 裏道 a **back lane** [**street**]（裏通り）; a **byway**（間道）.

うらみっこなし 恨みっこなし ▶どっちが勝っても恨みっこなしだぞ. いいな! No matter who wins, *no hard feelings*, OK? (➤「感情を害さずにいよう」の意) ‖ これで恨みっこなしよ Now we*'re even*. ／Let's *call it quits*. (➤ともに「五分五分だ, あいこだ」の意；この quits は形容詞).

うらみつらみ 恨みつらみ grudges（恨み）; **grievances**（苦情）▶男は前の雇用主に対する恨みつらみを並べ立てた The man voiced *one grievance after another* against his former employer.

うらむ 恨む feel bitter（人を）; **have** [**hold** ／ **bear**] **a grudge**《against》（人から受けた侮辱などを）▶俺を恨むなよ Don't *feel bitter* toward me! ‖ 彼女は担任の先生をひそかに恨んでいた She *had a* secret *grudge against* her teacher. ‖ もう恨んでなんかいないよ I *have no hard feelings* toward you anymore.
▶今さら自分の怠慢を恨んでも（＝後悔しても）過ぎてしまった時間は取り返せない No matter how much you *regret* your laziness, you can't turn the clock back.

うらめ 裏目 ▶我々の計画は裏目に出た Our plan *backfired* on us. (➤ backfire は「（計画などが）期待を裏切る結果になる」) ‖ 彼の行動はすべて裏目に出た Everything he did *worked against* him.

うらめしい 恨めしい ▶彼女は何も言わなかったが, 恨めしそうな目つきで私を見た She said nothing, but stared at me *reproachfully* [*resentfully*]. (➤ reproachfully は「非難するように」, resentfully は「憤慨して」) ‖ 子供たちは恨めしげに雨空を見上げた The kids *ruefully* looked up at the rainy sky. ‖《幽霊が》恨めしや〜 *Curses on* [*upon*] *you* ... .

うらやま 裏山 a **hill behind** one's **house.**

うらやましい 羨ましい

envy +㊀, **be envious of**（羨む）; **begrudge** /bɪɡrʌ́dʒ/ +㊀（妬む）

【文型】
人・人の境遇など(A)が羨ましい, を羨む
envy A
be envious of A
人(A)の境遇など(B)が羨ましい, を羨む
envy A B

▶私は彼女の境遇が羨ましい I *envy* (her) her situation [position]. ‖ 彼女の音楽的才能が羨ましい I *envy* (her) her musical talent. ／*I'm envious of* her musical talent. (➤ envy がしばしば単に羨ましいだけなのに対し, 同じ意味の be envious of はときに「…を妬んでいる」という負の感情を伴うことがある) ‖ きみは流ちょうに英語がしゃべれて羨ましいよ You speak English so fluently—I *envy* you! ‖ 私はあの人の名声を羨ましいとは思いません. 名声に値する人ですから I don*'t envy* [*begrudge*] him his fame. He deserves it. (➤ begrudge は否定文で用いることが多い).
▶彼の新車を友人たちは皆羨ましがった His new car *was the envy of* all his friends. (➤この envy は「羨望の的」) ‖ 彼らは羨ましそうにちらりと私の服を見た They glanced *enviously* at my dress.

うらやむ 羨む envy, be envious of →羨ましい
▶人の成功を羨むのはみっともない It is shameful to *envy* another person's success. ‖ 山本さん夫妻は人も羨む夫婦仲だ Everyone *is envious of* Mr. and Mrs. Yamamoto because they get along so well. ‖ 誰もが彼女の美貌を羨んだ Everyone *envied* [*was envious of*] her beauty.

うららか 麗らか ▶うららかな日和 *serene* weather (➤イギリス人はこの語から夏を連想することが多い) ‖ このうららかな春の日はいつまで続くのだろうか How long will these *lovely* [*beautiful*] spring days last?

うらわざ 裏技 a **secret** [**clever**] **technique** [**trick**]; a **tip.**

ウラン uranium /juréɪniəm/ ▶濃縮ウラン enriched *uranium*.

[1]うり 瓜《植物》a (**vegetable**) **marrow**,《米》a **squash.**
☛ うりニつ（→見出語）

[2]うり 売り ▶この家は売りに出されている This house is *for sale* [*on the market*].

逆引き熟語 ○○売り
押し売り a high-pressure sales ／卸売り wholesale (➤卸値は a wholesale price) ／空売り short selling ／たたき売り discount sales ／投げ売り a sacrifice sale ／（…を）ばら売りする sell ... by the piece, sell ... separately ／安売り a bargain (sale), a sale

うりあげ 売り上げ sales(➤常に複数形で) ▶先月はスマートフォンの売り上げが上がった[下がった] The *sales* of smartphones were up [were down] last month. ‖**売上金** the takings（店の）; the proceeds（興行などの）‖**売上高** a turnover ‖**売上伝票** a sales slip.

うりあるく 売り歩く peddle +㊀（行商する）▶彼は田舎を回って小物を売り歩いた He traveled about the countryside *peddling* small goods.

うりおしみ 売り惜しみ ▶宅地を売り惜しみする *be unwilling to sell* housing plots *in anticipation of better prices*.

うりかけ 売り掛け credit ‖**売掛金** accounts receivable.

うりきれ 売り切れ ▶申し訳ありません, チーズバーガーは全部売り切れなんですよ Sorry, we're *out of* cheeseburgers. ‖《掲示》売り切れ Sold Out.

うりきれる 売り切れる sell out; go out of stock（在庫がなくなる）▶創刊号はすぐに売り切れてしまった The first issue *has sold out* quickly.

うりこ 売り子 a **salesclerk**, a **salesperson**,《英》a **shop assistant**; a **salesgirl**（女）, a **salesman**（男）.

うりことば 売り言葉 ▶ 対話「どうして友里にあんなこと言ったの？」「彼女が私にひどいこと言ったからよ. 売りことばに買いことばって言うじゃない」"Why did you say that to Yuri?" "She said awful things to me, so I did the same thing to her. It was (*verbal*) *tit-for-tat*, you know." (➤ tit-for-tat は「しっぺ返し」).

うりこみ 売り込み ▶新製品の売り込みをする conduct *a sales campaign* for a new product ‖ あのセールスマンは売り込みがうまい That salesman *has got good salesmanship* [*has got a good sales pitch*].

うりこむ 売り込む sell +㊀; **promote** +㊀（宣伝して販売を促進する）▶新しい化粧品を女性に売り込む *sell* new cosmetics to women ‖ 新人歌手を売り込む *promote* a new singer ‖ その政治家は大衆の中に溶

け込んで**自分を売り込もう**とした The politician attempted to *sell himself* (to the public) by mingling with the people.

うりさばく 売り捌く sell +㊀ ▶盗品を売りさばく *sell* stolen goods.

うりだし 売り出し ▶年賀はがきの売り出しは11月1日からです New Year's postal cards (will) *go on sale* (on) November 1. ▶彼女は今売り出し中の作家だ She is an *up-and-coming* writer.

☛ 大売り出し (→見出語)

うりだす 売り出す put ... on the market (市場に出す) ▶この新製品は来月**売り出す**予定です These new products are to *be put on the market* next month. ‖ あの子は最近テレビで**売り出して**(＝人気が出始めて)いる歌手だ That young singer is now *gaining popularity* on television.

うりつける 売りつける ▶彼は私にその品物を高値で**売りつけた** He *talked* me *into buying* the product at a high price. ‖ あの宝石商は私に偽のダイヤを**売りつけた** That jeweller *hustled* me *into buying* a fake diamond.

うりて 売り手 a seller ▶**売り手**が多いのに買い手が少なく, その株は値下がりした The stock price dropped because there were so many *sellers* and very few buyers.

‖**売り手市場** a seller's [sellers'] market.

うりとばす 売り飛ばす sell off ▶お母さん, こんな古い家具**売り飛ばし**ちゃったら？ Mom, why don't we *sell off* these old pieces of furniture? ‖ 彼は兄のオートバイをただ同然で**売り飛ばしてしまった** He *sold* his brother's motorcycle for next to nothing.

うりぬける 売り抜ける ▶株を高値で**売り抜ける**(＝売る) *sell* stocks at a high price ‖ 暴落する前に株を**売り抜ける** *sell off* one's stock just before it crashes.

うりぬし 売り主 a seller.

うりね 売り値 the selling price ; the asking price (売り主の言い値).

うりば 売り場 a department (デパートの) ; a counter (売り台) ▶食品**売り場** the food *department* ‖ **売り場**の女子店員 a girl at the *counter* ／a salesgirl ‖ あのデパートは**売り場面積**日本一を誇っている That department store boasts the largest *floor space* in Japan.

うりはらう 売り払う sell off ; dispose of (処分する ; 堅い語) ▶私は古本を1000冊以上も**売り払った** I *sold off* more than one thousand used books. ‖ あの一家は家財を**売り払って**引っ越した That family has moved after *disposing of* their household goods.

うりふたつ 瓜二つ ▶彼らは**うり二つ**だ They *are exactly alike.* ／They *are like two peas (in a pod)*. ‖ 彼女は妹と**うり二つ**だ She *looks just like* her sister.

うりもの 売り物 ▶この置物は**売り物**ですか *Is* this ornament *for sale*? ‖ この車は**売り物ではない** This car *is not for sale*. ‖ この桃は傷だらけで**売り物にならない** These peaches are covered with bruises and *are unfit for sale*.

▶あの店は安さが**売り物**だ That store's low prices are its *major attraction*. ／That store *boasts of* its low prices.

▶《比喩的》野茂投手はフォークボールが**売り物**だった Pitching forkballs was Nomo's *claim to fame*. (➤ claim to fame は「自慢の種」).

うりや 売り家 a house for sale ▶**売り家**の広告 an advertisement for *a house for sale* ／a house ad [《英また》advert] ‖《掲示》**売り家** House for Sale (➤ 家そのものに掲示されたときは house は省略可能).

うりょう 雨量 rainfall, precipitation (➤ 後者は雪などを含む「降水量」に当たる専門用語) ▶きのうの東京の**雨量**は5ミリだった In Tokyo, we had 5 millimeters of *rain* yesterday. ‖ 東京の年間**雨量**はロンドンのそれよりもはるかに多い The annual *rainfall* [*precipitation*] in Tokyo is much higher than that in London.

うりわたす 売り渡す sell +㊀ ▶家屋敷を**売り渡す** *sell* a house.

[1]**うる 売る** **1【販売する】** sell +㊀ ▶ (人が)路上でリンゴを**売る** *sell* apples on the street ‖ ボルドーワインを1本5000円で**売る** *sell* a Bordeaux wine *at* 5,000 yen a bottle (➤ 単価は at, 合計の売価は for を用いることが多い) ‖ 自宅マンションを2000万円で**売る** *sell* one's condo *for* twenty million yen ‖ あの店はイタリアワインを**売っている** That store *sells* [*carries*] Italian wines. ／They *sell* Italian wines at that store. (➤ they は店の人を指す) ‖ お宅で電池は**売って**ますか Do you *sell* batteries here? ‖ 切手はどこで**売って**いますか Where can I get some postage stamps? (➤「どこで買えるか」の意) ‖ **対話** 「アメリカでは新聞はどこで**売って**いますか」「街頭の新聞売店で**売って**います」"Where do they *sell* newspapers in the United States?" "At newsstands on the street."

▶《掲示》この家**売ります**. 1234-5678 にお電話ください *For Sale.* Call 1234-5678.

2【仕掛ける】 ▶彼女は声優として**名を売った** She *built up a reputation* [*made a name for herself*] as a voice actress. ‖ おまえ, ぼくに**けんかを売る**気か？ Are you trying to *pick a fight* with me? ‖ 彼にはだいぶ**恩を売った** I *did* him *a* great *favor*. ／I *did a* great *favor* for him.

3【裏切る】 betray +㊀ ▶祖国を**売る** *sell out* [*betray*] one's country (➤ 前者が日本語により近い).

[2]**うる 得る** →える.

うるうどし 閏年 (a) leap year ▶**うるう年**は4年に一度ある There is *a leap year* every four years. ‖ 彼は**うるう年**生まれだ He was born during a *leap year*.

うるうる ▶サラ・ブライトマンの歌声を聴いているうちに(目が)**うるうる**してきた As I was listening to Sara Brightman singing, I got *teary-eyed*.

うるおい 潤い ▶**潤い**のある声 a *sweet and soft* voice ‖ **潤い**のある肌 *moist* skin ‖ もっと**潤いのある生活**がしたい I want to have *a richer, more enjoyable* [*more varied*] *life*. ‖ クリームを塗って肌の**潤いを保ちなさい** *Keep* your skin *moist* by applying some cream.

うるおう 潤う ▶夕立で庭の木々が**潤った** The trees in the garden *were moistened* by the shower.

▶その臨時収入でしばらくは家計が**潤った** The extra income *eased the pressure* on our family budget for a while. ‖ ショッピングセンターの建設で我々の地域全体が**潤った** The construction of the shopping center *has benefited* our whole community.

うるおす 潤す moisten /mɔ́ɪsən/ +㊀, wet +㊀ (湿らす) ; profit +㊀ (役に立つ) ; enrich +㊀ (豊かにする) ▶喉を**潤す** *quench* [*satisfy*] one's *thirst* ／ *wet* one's *whistle* ‖ 人の心を**潤す**優しい調べ a sweet melody that *soothes* your heart ‖ 久しぶりの雨が大

地を潤した The rain that fell for the first time in weeks *moistened* the earth. ‖その発明は会社を大いに潤した The invention *profited* [*enriched*] the company a great deal.

ウルグアイ **Uruguay**(南米南東部の国).

うるさい **1【音・声が】noisy ; loud** (大きい) ▶うるさい犬 a *noisy* dog ‖うるさい！Don't be noisy！／Be quiet！／Shut up！(➤最後がいちばん強い言い方) ‖ここは車の音がうるさすぎて住み心地が悪い I feel uncomfortable living here because there's *too much noise* from passing cars.

2【口やかましい】particular (こだわりがある)；**fussy** /fʌ́si/, **choosy** (えり好みする) ▶うちの娘は食べ物にうるさい My daughter is *fussy* [*choosy* ／*picky*] about food. ‖彼はラーメンにかけては少々うるさい He's a bit *particular* about ramen. (➤ particular は fussy, choosy, picky より堅い語) ‖彼女はクラシック音楽にかけては少々うるさい She's *something of a connoisseur of* classical music. ‖彼は服装の好みがうるさい He is *finicky* about his clothes. ／He is a *finicky* dresser.

▶今度の先生, 校則破るとうるさいぞ Our new teacher will really *get on your case* [is *a real pain* (*in the neck*)] if you break school regulations. (➤ pain は「嫌な人物」) ‖父があまりうるさく言うものだから大学に行くことにしました My father *harped* (*on*) *about* going to college so much that I finally decided to go. (➤ harp は「くどくど言う」) ‖息子がパソコンを買ってくれとうるさくてしようがない My son *keeps bugging* me to buy him a personal computer. (➤ bug は「困らせる」) ‖うるさくするのやめてよ！私が忙しいのがわからないの？*Be quiet！* Can't you see I'm busy？‖母親は息子に一日中うるさく小言を言った The mother *nagged* her son all day. (➤ nag は「がみがみ言う」) ‖《子が親に》いちいちうるせーんだよ Quit nagging me. (➤「がみがみ言うのをやめろ」の意).

うるさがた **うるさ型** a **fussy** [**picky**] **person** (こだわる人)；a **faultfinder** (あら探しをする人).

うるし **漆** (**Japanese**) **lacquer** /lǽkəʳ/, **japan** ▶漆塗りのお盆 a *lacquered* tray ‖漆細工はこの地方の名産だ *Lacquer ware* [*Lacquerware*] is the chief product of this region.

うるむ **潤む** ▶祖母の苦労話を聞いているうちに母の目が涙で潤んできた As she listened to the story of my grandmother's hard times, my mother's eyes *teared up* [*became moist with tears*]. ‖彼女の潤んだ瞳が好きだ I like her *misty* eyes.

うるわしい **麗しい** **1【美しい】beautiful** ▶見目麗しい乙女 a *beautiful* young girl.

2【心温まる】▶小さな男の子が妹の手を引く姿は麗しい情景だった The little boy leading his sister by the hand was a *heart-warming* scene.

うれい **憂い, 愁い** **sorrow** (癒やしがたく長引く)；**melancholy** (訳もない) ▶彼女の心の深い愁い the *grief* [*deep sorrow*] in her heart ‖彼女の愁いを帯びた表情がたまらない I can't resist her *melancholy* look [her *pensive* air]. ‖私は二胡(にこ)の愁いを帯びた音色が好きだ I like to listen to the *melancholy* [*plaintive*] sound(s) of the erhu. ‖彼には将来の憂いはない He has no *anxiety* [*worries*] *about the future*.

うれえる **憂える, 愁える** ▶若者たちが皆都会に出てしまい, 村人たちは村の行く末を憂えている With all the young people leaving to live in cities, the villagers *feel concerned about* the future of the village.

うれしい **嬉しい** **be glad, be happy, be pleased, be delighted** (➤ glad と happy はくだけた表現で, pleased と delighted は改まった語. この順にうれしさの程度が強くなる) ▶お会いできてとてもうれしいです (I'*m* very) *glad* to meet you. ／(*It's*) *nice* to meet you. (➤初対面の挨拶) ‖お越しいただいてとてもうれしいわ I *am* very *glad* you could come. (➤客が来たときだけでなく, 帰るときにも使える) ‖きみに会えてうれしかったよ I'*m very glad* [*happy*] to have met you. (➤別れ際の挨拶) ‖本日皆さまに社会福祉についてお話しするのは大変うれしいことです Today it gives me *a* great *pleasure* to talk to you about social welfare.

▶恭子がぼくのプロポーズを受けてくれたときはほんとにうれしかったよ I *was* really *happy* [*glad*] when Kyoko accepted my proposal (of marriage). (➤ glad がしばしば一時的な喜びを表すのに対し, happy は持続的でより深い満足度を表す) ‖うれしいことに就職が決まった I'*m glad* [*happy*] I found a job. ／*To my delight*, I found a job. (➤後者は文章で用いる堅い言い方) ‖少しでもあなたのお役に立てばうれしく思います I *would be very happy* if I could be of any help to you.

▶うれしい知らせが届いた I received *good* news. ‖彼女はうれしそうなほほえみを浮かべた She smiled *gladly*. ‖父は還暦祝いをしてもらいうれしそうだった Father *looked happy* when we celebrated his sixtieth birthday. ‖親にとって子供たちのうれしそうな顔を見ることくらい幸せなことはない Nothing gives greater pleasure to parents than to see the *happy* faces of their children. ‖補欠選手の活躍はうれしい誤算だった The good performance of the reserve player was *a happy miscalculation*.

✉ **あなたが私のペンパルになってくださるとのこと, とてもうれしいです** I *am* very *glad* [very *happy* ／ very *pleased* ／ *delighted*] that you have agreed to be my pen pal.

✉ **またお便りいただいてうれしかったです** It *was so good* to hear from you again.

✉ **ご婚約のお知らせ, うれしいやら驚くやらでした** The news of your engagement came as *a pleasant surprise*. ／It was *a pleasant surprise* to hear about your engagement. ➤ a pleasant surprise (うれしい驚き)は手紙の慣用表現.

✉ **うれしいことに息子は無事に大学入試に合格しました** *What* (*really*) *made us happy was* (that) my son passed his college entrance exams.

☛ うれしい悲鳴 (→悲鳴)

うれしがる **嬉しがる** ▶彼女はぼくのプレゼントを見てうれしがった She *was pleased with* my present. ／She *was glad* to get my present. (● 前者はプレゼントの品物を, 後者は行為を喜んだの意を表す場合の訳例) ‖母は姉の合格を聞いてとてもうれしがっていた Mother *looked very happy* when she heard about my sister's success in the entrance exam.

うれしさ **嬉しさ** **joy, delight** (➤前者が意味が強い) ▶うれしさのあまり飛び上がる jump for *joy*.

うれしなき **嬉し泣き** ▶息子が無事発見されたと聞いて彼女はうれし泣きした She *cried for joy* at the news that her son had been found safe.

うれしなみだ **嬉し涙** **tears of joy** ▶息子と10年ぶりに再会して母親はうれし涙を流した The mother *cried for joy* [*shed tears of joy*] when she met her

son for the first time in ten years.
うれすじ 売れ筋 ▶この店は売れ筋の商品をそろえている This store is stocked with *good sellers*.
ウレタン **urethane** /jʊ́ərəθeɪn/
‖ウレタンフォーム urethane foam.
うれっこ 売れっ子の **sought-after**(引っ張りだこの) ▶いちばんの売れっ子歌手 the most *sought-after* singer ‖ 彼は売れっ子の作家だ He is a *popular* writer. ／He is one of the *most popular* writers. ‖ 彼女は売れっ子の漫画家になった She has become a *successful* cartoonist.
うれのこる 売れ残る **remain unsold** ; **be on the shelf** (➤ 比喩的に「(女性が婚期を逃して)売れ残る」の意味でも用いる) ▶その冷蔵庫は売れ残った That refrigerator *remained unsold*.
うれゆき 売れ行き ▶新製品の売れ行きはどうかね How is our new product *selling*? ‖ スマートフォンは売れ行きがよい Smartphones *are selling well*. ／ Smartphones *are good sellers*. ‖ 値下げされたにもかかわらず車の売れ行きは落ちた (*The pace of*) car *sales* dropped even though prices were cut.
1**うれる 売れる** **sell** ▶そのアルバムは100万部以上売れた The album *sold* more than a million copies. ‖ うちではこの品がよく売れているんですよ These goods *are selling well* at our store. ‖ ゴッホの「ひまわり」が約50億円で売れた Van Gogh's 'Sunflowers' *was sold* for about five billion yen.
▶《比喩的》彼はコピーライターとして名が売れている He *is well-known* as a copywriter. ‖ 今いちばん売れているテレビタレントは誰? Who is *the most popular* [*sought-after*] TV personality?
2**うれる 熟れる** **be ripe** ▶そのアボカドは熟れて食べ頃だ The avocados *are ripe* enough to eat. ‖ そのメロンはまだよく熟れていない The melons *are not ripe* yet.
うろ a **hollow** ▶木のうろ a tree *hollow* ／the *hollow* of a tree.
うろうろ ▶うちの父はよくリビングの中を下着でうろうろする My father often *walks about* [*walks up and down*] the living room in his underwear.
うろおぼえ うろ覚え ▶子供の頃よくそこへ行ったらしいが, うろ覚えにしか覚えていない When I was a child I often went there, but I have only *a faint memory* now. ‖ うろ覚えだが, たしか値段は3000円ぐらいだったと思う *Though I can't remember the exact* price, I believe it was somewhere around 3,000 yen.
うろこ 鱗 a **scale** ▶魚のうろこを取る *scale* a fish ／ remove the *scales* from a fish (➤ 前者の言い方がより日常的).
▶《慣用表現》先生のお話を伺って目からうろこが落ちる思いがしました As I listened to your lecture, I felt *the scales fall from my eyes*. (➤ 聖書の話から).
‖うろこ雲 (a) cirrocumulus /sìroʊkjú:mjələs/ ‖ うろこ取り a fish scaler.
うろたえる **lose** one's **head** (慌てる) ; **be upset** (気が転倒する) ▶何を聞いてもうろたえるな Whatever you hear, don't *lose your head*. ‖ 父が急死したという知らせを聞いて私はうろたえた I *was upset* at the news of my father's sudden death. ‖ 彼は火事が起きたときもうろたえなかった He *kept calm* when the fire broke out.
うろちょろ ▶用もないのに人の前をうろちょろするな If you don't have any business with me, *get out of my way*. (➤「邪魔にならないようにどけ」の意).

うろつく **wander**(さまよう) ; **hang around** [**about**] (ぶらぶらする) ▶森の中をうろつく *wander about* in the forest ‖ 今までどこをうろついていたんだ Where have you been *hanging around* all this while?
うわあご 上顎 **the upper jaw**.
うわーん ▶弟はいじめっ子に顔を殴られてうわーんと泣き出した My brother *burst out crying* when the bully punched him in the face. 《参考》漫画などでの泣き声は Boohoo(-hoo)! のようにつづる.
うわき 浮気する **have an affair** 《with》 ▶彼の奥さん, 浮気をした[している]らしいよ His wife *had* [*is having*] *an affair with another man*, I hear. (➤ affair は「情事」) ‖ 夫は決して浮気しないと約束しました My husband promised to *be faithful to* me. ‖「浮気しないでね」と彼女は言った She said, "Please don't *cheat on* me." (➤ cheat on は「…を裏切る」の意のインフォーマルな表現).
うわぎ 上着 a **jacket**, a **coat**

> **《解説》jacket** は背広の上着, 女性用スーツの上着, レジャー用の替え上着などを指す. **coat** も同義に用いられるが, これはレインコート, オーバーコート, モーニングコートなども指す.

▶彼は上着を脱いで仕事をしていた He was working *in his shirt sleeves*. (➤ in one's shirt sleeves は「ワイシャツ姿で」).
うわぐすり 釉薬 (a) **glaze** ▶うわぐすりを塗った陶器 *glazed* earthenware.
うわくちびる 上唇 **the upper lip**.
うわぐつ 上靴 **indoor shoes**. →上履き.
うわごと 譫言 **delirious words** ▶うわごとを言う *talk in delirium*.
うわさ 噂 **1【世間で言い触らされている話】** (a) **rumor**, **word**, 《インフォーマル》**talk** ▶根も葉もないうわさ *a groundless* [*an unfounded*] *rumor* ‖ そのうわさはたちまち学園中に広がった The *rumor* [*talk*] spread across the campus in a flash. ‖ その会社についての悪いうわさが本当とわかった The *bad rumor* about the firm has turned out to be true. ‖ また授業料が上がるといううわさだ *There's a rumor* (*going around*) *that* (the) tuition is going up again. ‖ うわさによると将来ここにスーパーができるそうです *There is a rumor* [*Rumor has it*] *that* a supermarket will be built here.
2【他人についての話題】 **gossip** /gɑ́:səp/ ▶人はみんな他人のうわさをするのが好きだ Everybody likes to *gossip*. ‖ あの人ほんとにうわさ話が好きな人ね He's *a* real *gossip*(*monger*). ‖ おうわさはかねがね細川君から伺っております *I've heard a lot about you* from Hosokawa. 《参考》これに対する応答としては, 例えば, I hope it's not all bad. (悪いことばかりでなければいいのですが)のような言い方がある. ‖ きのうあなたのおうわさをしたばかりですよ We *were talking about* you only yesterday.
▶話題にしていた健がリビングに入ると, 桂子が「あら, うわさをすれば何とかね」と言った "Well, *speaking of the devil*!" Keiko said when Ken, who she had been talking about, entered the living room. (➤「うわさをすれば影(が差す)」は Speak [Talk] of the devil and he is sure to appear. となるが, 日常会話では例文のように前半部だけしか言わない).
ことわざ 人のうわさも75日 People's gossip lasts only seventy-five days. (➤ 日本語からの直訳) ／A wonder lasts but nine days. (➤「不思議がるのも

9日しか続かない」の意の英語のことわざ).
うわずみ 上澄み a **clear upper layer of a liquid**.
うわずる 上ずる ▶上ずった声で叫ぶ cry in *a shrill voice* ‖ 初めてカラオケで歌ったときは緊張のあまり声が上ずってしまった The first time I sang karaoke, I was so nervous that my voice *cracked*.
うわぜい 上背 **height, stature** (➤ 後者は「身の丈(たけ)」に相当する堅い語) ▶リンカーンは上背があった Abraham Lincoln was *quite tall*. ／Abraham Lincoln was a man *of great stature*. (➤ 後者は比喩的に「偉大な男」の意にもなる).
うわついた 浮ついた ▶浮ついた気持ちで孝君と付き合っているのなら, 会うのはよしなさい Stop seeing Takashi if you're going about with him *just for fun* [if you're *not serious* about him]. (➤ 前者は「おもしろ半分で」, 後者は「本気でない」の意).
うわっつら 上っ面 a **surface**(表面) ; an **appearance** (外観) ▶上っ面(＝外観)で人を判断してはいけない Do not judge a person by his or her *appearance*. ‖ フランス語は1年間学んだが上っ面をなでただけだ I studied French for one year, but only *skimmed the surface*.
うわっぱり 上っ張り a **smock** ▶白い上っ張りを着た画家 a painter in a white *smock*.
うわて 上手 ▶テニスでは彼のほうがぼくよりうわてだ He *is better* at tennis than I am. ‖ きみのほうが彼より一枚うわてだったな You *were a cut above* him, weren't you ? (➤ a cut above は「…より一枚うわて」の意のインフォーマルな表現).
‖**上手投げ**《相撲》*uwate-nage*, an over-arm throw ;《野球》an overhand throw.
うわぬり 上塗り **top coating** ; (a) **top coat**(仕上げ塗り). →恥.
うわのせ 上乗せ ▶経営者側は協定した賃金に5パーセント上乗せすることを約束した The management promised to *add* an extra 5 percent to the wages already agreed upon.
うわのそら 上の空 ▶彼女は私が話しかけたのにうわの空といった様子だった I spoke to her, but she looked as if *her mind were somewhere else* [*her mind were on other things*]. ‖ テレビを見ていたのでうわの空で返事をした I was watching television and answered *in an absent way* [*absent-mindedly*]. (➤ ともに「注意散漫の状態で」).
うわばき 上履き (a **pair of**) **indoor shoes**, (a **pair of**) **slippers** ▶日本では校舎内で生徒に上履きを履かせることが多い In many Japanese schools, students are made to wear *indoor shoes*.
うわばみ a **heavy drinker** (大酒飲み).
うわべ a **surface**(表面) ; an **appearance** (外観) ▶うわべを飾る keep up *appearances* ‖ うわべを繕う save *appearances* ‖ 彼の丁重さはうわべだけ(＝表面的)だった His politeness was only *superficial*.
うわまえ 上前 a **rake-off** ; a **kickback** (脅し・密約などによるリベート) ▶上前をはねる get *a rake-off* ‖ ボスはもうけの半分を上前としてはねた Our boss pocketed half of our profit as *a kickback*.
うわまわる 上回る **exceed** ＋目, **surpass** ＋目 (➤「数量を超える」にはどちらも用いるが, exceed がふつう ; limit を越えるには exceed を用いる ; surpass は「優れる」の意で用いる) ▶この製品の売れ行きは目標を上回った The sales of this product *exceeded* [*surpassed*] *our target*. ‖ わが社のことしの収益は予想を上回った Our company's profit this year has *exceeded* [*surpassed*] *our expectations*. ‖ そのゴルフ選手は従来のベストスコアを上回った The golfer *surpassed* his previous best score. ‖ 工費は10億円を上回りそうだ The construction cost is likely to *exceed* one billion yen. ／The construction work will likely *cost more than* one billion yen. ‖ 請求額は私の予想をはるかに上回った The amount claimed *was much larger than I had expected*. ‖ 彼の収入は全国平均を上回っている His income *is above* [*exceeds*] *the national average*.
うわむき 上向き ▶景気は上向きだ Business *is looking* [*turning*] *up*.
うわむく 上向く **turn upward** ▶市況が上向いてきた The market is *picking up*. ‖ 会社の業績は上向いてきている Our company's sales figures are *on the upturn* [*on a rising trend*].
うわめづかい 上目使い ▶容疑者は上目使いで刑事を見た The suspect *cast an upward glance at* the detective. ／The suspect *cast* the detective *an upward glance*.
うわやく 上役 →上司.
うわる 植わる ▶庭に1本ナツメの木が植わっていた A jujube tree *was planted* in the garden.
うわん 右腕 **the right arm** ‖**右腕投手** a right-handed pitcher ／a right hander.
1**うん 運** **1【巡り合わせ】chance ; luck, fortune** (➤ 善悪両方の運をいう ; fortune は堅い語) ▶あいつは運がいい[悪い]やつだ He is a *lucky* [an *unlucky*] guy. ‖ 運よくいいアパートが見つかった *Fortunately*, I found a good apartment. ‖ 運よく大統領に会うことができた I was *lucky enough to* meet the president. ‖ 運悪くそのコンサートは聞き逃した *Unfortunately*, I missed the concert. ‖ 私って, お天気運が悪いのよね I *have no luck when it comes to weather*, it seems. ‖ 勝負は時の運 Victory *depends on chance*. ‖ 運を天に任せてやってごらん *Take a chance*. (➤「一か八かやってごらん」の意) ‖ 対話「宿題忘れて行ったけど, きょうは先生休みだったよ」「運がいいね」"I forgot my homework, but our teacher was absent today." "*You were lucky*."
2【幸運】luck, fortune ▶その詐欺師にだまされたのが運の尽きだった *My luck ran out* when I was taken in by the fraud. ‖ 運はいつも彼女に味方する *Fortune* always favors her.
2**うん** **yes, sure ; yeah** /jeə/, **uh-huh** /ʌ́hʌ/ (➤ あとの2つはぞんざいな答え方)《参考》《米・インフォーマル》では yep とも yup とも言い, 同じくぞんざいな答え方. →はい ▶ 対話「その本貸してくれない?」「うん, いいとも」"Will you lend me the book ?" "*Yes*, of course. ／*Sure*. ／*Uh-huh*."
▶うん, やっと思い出したよ *Ah*, now I remember it. ‖ 黙ってうんと言え! *Just nod !* ‖ 彼にうんと言わせるのは難しいだろう You will find it hard to *get* his *OK*.
☛ うんともすんとも (→見出語)
うんうん ▶病気の妹がうんうん苦しみ始めたので救急車を呼んだ My sick sister began *groaning in pain* so we called (for) an ambulance. ‖ お父さんはお母さんの話にうんうんうなずくだけでちゃんと聞いていない Dad *nods to* Mom when she is talking to him but he isn't really listening.
うんえい 運営 **management** 一動 **運営する** **manage** ＋目 ▶日野氏が会社の運営を引き継いだ Mr. Hino took over the *management* of the company. ‖ ことしの運動会は生徒会が運営することになった It has been decided that the athletic meet this year will *be managed* [*staged*] by the student coun-

う

cil. ‖運営委員 a member of the steering committee ‖運営資金 operating funds.

うんが 運河 a **canal** /kənǽl/ ▶運河を開く dig [build] *a canal* ‖ベニスには多数の運河が巡らされている Venice has a network of *canals*. ‖我々の船はパナマ運河を通過した Our ship passed through *the Panama Canal*.

うんかい 雲海 a **sea of cloud(s)**.

うんきゅう 運休する be canceled(取り消しになる); **be suspended** (中断される) ▶霧のために列車が運休している Because of the fog, trains *have been canceled*. ‖沼津・静岡間のバスは運休になっている Bus service between Numazu and Shizuoka *has been suspended*.

うんこ →うんち, くそ, 大便, 便.

1**うんこう 運行 service**(乗り物などの); **movement** (天体の) ▶昨夜の地滑りで列車の運行が止まっている *Train service* has been suspended due to the landslide which occurred last night. ‖バスは15分ごとに運行しています The buses *run* every fifteen minutes.
▶天体の運行 the *movement* of heavenly bodies.

2**うんこう 運航 service**(乗り物の便); a **flight** (飛行便) ▶当社は熊本へは毎日4便運航しています We *have* four *flights* to Kumamoto daily.

うんざり 一動 うんざりする get sick and tired 《of》, **be fed up** 《with》 ▶永井君の長話にはうんざりしたよ I *got sick and tired of* Nagai's long-windedness. ‖おまえにはもううんざりだ I'*m fed up with* you! (➤「…に飽き飽きしている」の意) ‖試験のことを考えただけでうんざりする The mere idea of exams *makes me sick*. (➤ make ... sick は「…の気分を悪くさせる」) ‖こう毎日雨じゃあ, 全くうんざりするね All this rain every day is really *getting me down*. (➤ get down は「憂鬱にする」の意のインフォーマルな表現) ‖渡辺の下品なことばづかいには全くうんざりするよ I'*m up to here with* Watanabe's vulgar language. (➤ be up to here with は「…に耐えられない」の意のインフォーマルな表現; これを用いるとき右手を広げて下に向け鼻のすぐ下に持って来る動作をすることもある) ‖勉強, 勉強って, もううんざりだよ *I'm sick of* you nagging me about studying!

うんさんむしょう 雲散霧消 ▶疑念が雲散霧消した All my suspicions *vanished into thin air*.

うんすい 雲水 a **wandering Buddhist monk**(諸国を巡る); a **novice monk** [**priest**] **who is undergoing zen training**(禅宗の).

うんせい 運勢 fortune ▶友人の運勢を見る tell a friend's *fortune* (➤「自分の運勢を見てもらう」なら have one's fortune told) ‖彼はことしは運勢が悪い His *horoscope is unfavorable* this year.

うんそう 運送 《米》 **transportation**, 《英》 **transport** 一動 **運送する transport** +⊞ ▶かつては新鮮な魚や野菜を遠隔地へ運送するのは不可能だった It was impossible to *transport* fresh fish and vegetables great distances in former times.
‖運送会社 a transportation company ‖運送業 the transport(ation) industry [business] (貨物輸送, 航空・海上輸送); the passenger transport(ation) industry (タクシー, バス, 電鉄など) ‖運送業者 a carrier; a mover (引っ越しの) ‖運送店 a forwarding agency ‖運送料 transport [transportation] fees.

うんだめし 運試し a **trial** [**test**] **of one's luck** ▶運試しのつもりで試験を気楽に受けたのがよかったみたい I took the exam just to *try* [*test*] *my luck*. I guess I did well on it because I was relaxed about it.

うんち poop, poo-poo /púːpuː/, **doodoo** ▶うんちに行く go *poop* [*poo-poo* / *doodoo*] ‖うんちする *make poo-poo* [*doodoo*] ‖ママ, うんち! Mommy, *poo-poo*! ‖犬のうんち踏んづけちゃあだめよ Don't step in the dog's *doodoo*. ‖タマが台所にうんちしたよ Tama *did number two* in the kitchen. (➤ number two は number one (おしっこ)に対応する表現).

うんちく 蘊蓄 profound knowledge ▶エスニック料理のうんちくを傾ける display one's *profound knowledge* of ethnic food(s).

うんちん 運賃 a **fare**(旅客の); **freight rates** (貨物の) ▶東京・秋田間の新幹線の子供運賃はいくらですか What is the Shinkansen train *fare* for a child from Tokyo to Akita?
‖航空運賃 an airfare ‖鉄道運賃 a railroad [《英》 railway] fare ‖割引運賃 a reduced fare.

うんでいのさ 雲泥の差 ▶聞くと見るとでは雲泥の差だった What I actually saw was something *very different from* what I had heard. ‖2人とも学者だといっても, その知識には雲泥の差がある Both of them may be scholars, but when it comes to knowledge there is *a world of difference* between the two.

うんてん 運転

driving(自動車などの); **operation** (機械の) 一動 **運転する drive** +⊞; **operate** +⊞ ▶アメリカの高校では車の運転が1つの科目になっている In American high schools, *driving* is offered as a subject. ‖彼女は車の運転が上手だ She is *a good* [*safe*] *driver*. (● (×)She is a safety driver. とはしないこと) ‖少しでもアルコールを飲んだら運転してはいけません Don't *drive* if you have drunk even a bit (of alcohol). ‖運転中はよそ見をしないようにしなさい Do not take your eyes off the road while you are *at the wheel*. (➤ at the wheel は「ハンドルを握って」) ‖**対話**「アメリカでは運転免許を取りに教習所へ行きますか」「いいえ, ふつうは家の周りで練習します」"In the States, do you have to go to driving school to get *a driver's license*?" "No, we usually practice driving near our homes." (➤《英》では「運転免許」は driving licence という).
▶エレベーターは運転中です The elevator is *working* [*is in operation*]. ‖会社をやっていこうにも運転資金さえない We don't even have *operating capital* to run a company.
‖運転席 a driver's seat (車の); a traindriver's seat (電車の) ‖(トラックなどの)運転台 a cab.

> **逆引き熟語 ○○運転**
> 安全運転 safe driving / 折り返し運転 (a) shuttle service / 酒酔い [酔っ払い] 運転 drinking and driving; drunk driving (➤ 後者は泥酔状態を連想させる) / 試運転 a test [trial] run / 正常運転 regular [normal] operation / 無人運転 unstaffed operation / 無謀運転 reckless driving / 無免許運転 driving without a license / 脇見運転 inattentive driving

うんてんしゅ 運転手 a **driver** ▶バスの運転手 a bus driver ‖タクシーの運転手 a taxi driver / a cabdriver ‖トラックの運転手 a truck [《英また》 lorry] driver ‖機関車の運転手 a train driver, 《米また》 a locomotive engineer ‖電車の運転手 a train driver ‖お抱えの運転手 a chauffeur /ʃoʊfə́ːr ‖

ʃóʊfə/.

うんと ▶うんと酒を飲む[たばこを吸う] drink [smoke] *heavily* ‖ うんと勉強する study *hard* ‖ 人をうんと待たせる keep a person waiting *for a long time*.
▶子供を私立校にやるにはうんとお金がかかる It costs *a lot of* money to send a child to a private school. ‖ この子をうんと叱ってやってください Please give him [her] a *good* scolding.

うんどう 運動 **1【身体の】exercise** /éksəˈsaɪz/ (体を動かすこと); **sports**, (a) **sport** (スポーツ) ⇀スポーツ
一動 **運動する get** [**take** / **do**] **exercise** ▶水泳はよい運動になる Swimming is good *exercise*. ‖ 私の同僚は運動のために埼玉から東京まで自転車で通勤している One of my colleagues commutes by bicycle to Tokyo from Saitama just for the *exercise*. ‖ 弟は運動(=スポーツ)がよくできる My (younger) brother is good at *sport(s)*. ‖ 健康のために何か運動をしたほうがいいですよ You should *take up some sport* to stay in shape. (➤ take up は「始める」) ‖ ポチを運動させに公園へ行ってくるよ, お母さん Mom, I am going to take Pochi to *get some exercise* in the park.
▶この頃運動不足のため気分がすっきりしません I don't feel my best these days because I *haven't been getting enough exercise*. (➤「運動不足」に相当する名詞は lack of exercise または inactivity) ‖ 対話 「どんな運動をしていますか」「ボウリングを時々やります」 "What (kind of) *sports* [What *sport*] do you do?" "I bowl once in a while."
‖運動具 sporting goods [gear] ‖ 運動靴 gym shoes; running shoes (マラソン・ジョギング用の) ‖ 運動場 a playground, an athletic field ‖ 運動神経 (⇀見出語) ‖ 運動選手 an athlete /ǽθli:t/ ‖ 運動部 an athletic club.
2【活動, 働きかけること】a **movement** (集団による); a **campaign** (組織的活動) ▶学生運動の指導者 a leader in the *student movement* ‖ 覚醒剤追放運動 *a campaign against* stimulant drugs ‖ 騒々しい選挙運動はこりごりだ I'm sick and tired of noisy *election campaigns*. ‖運動員 a campaigner (ある目的のための); a canvasser (選挙・寄付などの).
3【物体の動き】(a) **motion**
‖運動エネルギー kinetic energy.

> **逆引き熟語 ○○運動**
> ◆軽い運動 light exercise / 屈伸運動 a knee-bend / 準備運動 (a) warm-up exercise; a warm-up / 激しい運動 strenuous [hard / vigorous] exercise / 腹筋運動 a sit-up / 無酸素運動 anaerobic /ænəróʊbɪk/ exercise / 有酸素運動 aerobic exercise
> ◆学生運動 a student movement / 芸術運動 an art movement / 市民運動 a citizens' movement / 住民運動 a residents' movement / 選挙運動 an election campaign / 反戦運動 an antiwar movement / …反対運動 a protest movement against … / 不買運動 a consumer strike [boycott] / 労働運動 a labor movement
> ◆永久運動 perpetual motion / 円運動 circular motion [movement] / 回転運動 rotary motion [movement]; rotation / 上下運動 up-and-down motion / ピストン運動 piston action

うんどうかい 運動会

> **解説** (1)学校の運動会(の日)は **(school) field day** または **(school) sports day** がよい. 前者は《米》で, 後者は《英》で好まれる.
> (2)**athletic meet** [《英》**meeting**] には公式タイムを計ったり, 2つ以上の学校 [会社など] が競い合ったりするという響きがある.
> (3)**track meet** は「陸上競技(大)会」.

▶きょうは私たちの運動会です This is our *Sports Day*. ‖ (今度の)日曜日に幼稚園の運動会がある The kindergarten *field day* is scheduled for Sunday.

うんどうしんけい 運動神経 a **motor nerve**; **reflexes** /rí:fleksiz/ (反射神経) ▶彼は運動神経が発達している[鈍い] He *has quick* [*slow*] *reflexes*. / He *has good* [*bad*] *coordination*.

うんともすんとも ▶計画に賛成かと何度聞かれても, 彼女はうんともすんとも言わなかった Even though she was asked many times whether she was in favor of the plan, she did*n't say a word* [she wold*n't give an answer*].

うんぬん ▶今さら結果をうんぬんしてもしかたがない It is no use *commenting* [*saying this and that*] about the result now.

うんぱん 運搬 《米》**transportation**, 《英》**transport** 一動 **運搬する transport** +目 ▶石油をタンカーで運搬する *transport* [*ship*] oil by tanker.

うんめい 運命 **fate** (しばしば不運や死を暗示する); **destiny** (良い意味でも用いる) ▶運命が2人を会わせてしまった *Fate* has brought the two together. ‖ それは起こる運命だったのだ It *was destined* [*was fated*] to happen.
▶その俳優は全身まひになったとわかったとき運命として潔く受け入れた When the actor discovered that he was completely paralyzed, he *accepted his fate* bravely.
▶その独裁者は暗殺される運命にあった. 彼自身が多くの人を殺したのだから The dictator *was destined to* be assassinated because he himself killed a lot of people. (➤ destine は「運命づける」) ‖ ユヅルはフィギュアスケーターになる運命だった I think Yuzuru *was meant to be* a figure skater. ‖ 運命論者は, すべてのことは運命に左右されると信じている *A fatalist* believes that all things are subject to *fate*.
▶運命のいたずらで私たちは再会できなかった By *an irony* [*a quirk*] *of fate*, we were never to meet again. ‖ 今度は運命の女神がきみにほほえむことを祈る May *Fortune* smile on you this time. (➤ 大文字で始まる Fortune は「人の運命をつかさどる女神」の意) ‖ 来年はわが社の運命を左右する年になるだろう Next year will *decide* our company's *fate*. ‖ 彼は二度と再び故郷に帰れない運命にあった He *was* never *to* return to his home again. (➤ この be to do は「…する運命である」の意).
‖運命論 fatalism.

うんも 雲母 **mica** /máɪkə/.

うんゆ 運輸
‖運輸会社 a transportation [an express] company ‖ 運輸機関 a means of transportation.

うんよう 運用 ▶資金を運用する *employ* funds ‖ 規則を作るのは簡単だが適正な運用は難しいことがある It is easy to make a rule, but it can be hard to *apply* it appropriately.

え・エ

[1]**え 絵** a **picture**(絵画)；a **painting** (絵の具による)；a **drawing** (鉛筆・ペン・チョークなどによる)；an **illustration** (挿し絵) ▶馬の絵を描く paint [draw] (*a picture* of) a horse ‖浅間山の絵 *a picture* [*a painting*] of Mt. Asama ‖ピカソの(＝ピカソが描いた)絵 *a picture* (painted) by Picasso.
▶《慣用表現》絵のような光景 a *picturesque* scene ‖点々と小舟の浮かぶ海は絵のような眺めだった With small boats dotting the sea, the scene was *like something out of a picture*. ‖長嶋さんは何をやらせても絵になるね Mr. Nagashima *looks impressive*, no matter what he does. ‖ 3年でわが社の売り上げを倍にするなど絵に描いた餅だ Doubling our sales in the next three years is *pie in the sky* [(*completely*) *unrealistic*]. (➤ pie in the sky は「当てにならない甘い約束」の意).

「絵」のいろいろ **油絵** oil painting ／**細密画** miniature ／**挿し絵** illustration ／**写生画** sketch ／**肖像画** portrait ／**水彩画** watercolor ／**静物画** still life ／**石版画** lithograph ／**銅版画** copperplate print ／**日本画** Japanese painting ／**風景画** landscape ／**フレスコ画** fresco ／**木炭画** charcoal

[2]**え 柄** a **handle**(持つところ) ▶包丁 [傘] の柄 the *handle* of a knife [an umbrella] ‖ほうきの柄 a broom*stick* ‖金づちの柄が取れてしまった The *handle* came off the hammer.

[3]**え** →えっ.

[4]**え 餌** →えさ.

エアーズロック **Ayers Rock**(オーストラリアの巨大な岩で，正式名は Uluru /ùːlərúː/).

エアコン an **air conditioner**(装置) ▶部屋にエアコンをつける install *an air conditioner* in one's room ‖エアコンをつけて[切って]いい？ Can I turn on [turn off] *the air conditioner*? ‖この部屋，エアコンが効いてないんじゃないの？ *The air conditioner* in this room *isn't working well*, is it?

危ないカタカナ語✹ エアコン
「エアコン」は air conditioning(空気調節)の日本式省略形．「エアコン装置」は air conditioner という．日本では「クーラー」ともいうが，英語の cooler は主に冷却器を指す．したがって「ルームクーラー」は room air conditioner，「カークーラー」は car air conditioner というのが正しい．→クーラー．

エアターミナル an **air terminal**.

エアバス an **airbus**(➤ もとは商標).

エアバッグ an **airbag**.

エアポケット an **air pocket** ▶飛行機はエアポケットに入ってひどく揺れた Our plane hit *an air pocket* and was violently shaken.

エアメール **airmail**(航空便；航空便で送る手紙類) ▶この小包，エアメールでお願いします I'd like to send this parcel *by airmail*.

エアロビクス **aerobics** /eəróʊbɪks/ (➤ 単数扱い) ▶シェイプアップのためにエアロビクスをする *do aerobics* (in order) to get in shape.
《参考》「有酸素運動」のことを aerobic exercise といい，「無酸素運動」のことは anaerobic /ænəróʊbɪc/ exercise という.

[1]**えい《魚》** a **ray**；a **skate** (ガンギエイ)；a **stingray** (アカエイ)；a **manta ray** (イトマキエイ).

[2]**えい** ▶「えい」とばかりに彼はその荷物を持ち上げた He lifted the load *with all his might*. ‖えい，こん畜生め！ *Damn* (*it*)!

[3]**えい 嬰《音楽》sharp**
‖嬰ハ短調 C sharp minor.

えいい 鋭意 ▶ソフトウェアの改良版を鋭意開発中です We're *devoting ourselves* (*singlemindedly*) *to* the development of an improved version of the software program.

えいえい 英英
‖英英辞典 an English-English dictionary.
《参考》英語国では英英は通常の形式なので，単に English dictionary [dictionary of English] (英語辞典)としか言わない．学習者用の英英辞典は a learner's English dictionary [dictionary of English] と呼ぶのでこれを当ててもよい.

えいえん 永遠 **eternity** 一形 永遠の **eternal** (始まりも終わりもない，時間を超越した)；**everlasting** (朽ち果てることのない；やや文学的な語)；**permanent** (限りなく続く) 一副 永遠に **forever, eternally, everlastingly**
▶永遠の愛 [真理 ／眠り] *eternal* love [truth ／ sleep] ‖永遠の平和 *everlasting* [*permanent*] peace ‖彼の名は永遠に歴史に残るだろう His name will *be remembered forever*. ／His name will *go down in history*. ‖その日は永遠に続くように思われた The day seemed *never-ending*. →永久.

[1]**えいが 映画** a **movie**, a **film**(個々の)；**the movies**, 《英》**the cinema**(ともに総称) ▶スピルバーグ監督の映画 *a movie* directed by Spielberg ／a Spielberg *movie* ‖映画に出る *appear on the screen* ‖映画界に入る enter *the movie world* [*the film world*].
▶きみは1年に何回映画館で映画を見ますか How often in a year do you *go to the movies* [*the cinema*]? (◉「映画を見に行く」の意味では，ほかに go to a movie, go to see a movie も可能) ‖ゆうべテレビで古い映画を見た I *saw* [*watched*] an old *movie* on television last night. ‖『源氏物語』はこれまでに何度か映画化された "The Tale of Genji" *has been made into* several *movies*.
‖映画音楽 screen music ‖映画館 a movie theater, a cinema ‖映画監督 a movie director ‖映画スタジオ a movie studio ‖映画俳優[スター] a movie star, a film star (➤ 男女を区別する場合は a movie [film] actor (男優)，a movie [film] actress (女優)としてもよい) ‖映画ファン a movie fan [buff], a film fan [buff].

逆引き熟語 ○○映画
アクション映画 an action film [movie] ／**アニメ映画** an animated movie ／**ＳＦ映画** a sci-fi movie ／**家族向け映画** a family-oriented mov-

ie／**子供向け映画** a child-oriented movie, a children's film／**字幕入り映画** a subtitled film／**白黒映画** a black-and-white [monochrome] movie／**3-D映画** a 3-D movie／**成人映画** an adult film [movie]／**戦争映画** a war movie／**チャンバラ映画** a samurai movie／**ディズニー映画** a Disney movie／**ノーカット映画** an uncut movie／**ピンク映画** a blue film [movie]／**ホラー映画** a horror movie／**ポルノ映画** a pornographic film,《俗》a skin flick／**漫画映画** a cartoon

2**えいが 栄華** **prosperity**（繁栄）; **glory**（栄光）▶清盛の時代，平氏は**栄華を極めた** In Kiyomori's times the Heishi clan was at the height of its *prosperity* [*glory*]. ‖ **栄華を極めた**ソロモンさえ，この花の1つほどには着飾っていなかった Not even Solomon in all his *glory* [*splendor*] was dressed like one of these (lilies).

えいかいわ 英会話 ⚠**日本では「英会話」に English conversation を当てるが，English conversation（英語の会話）という発想は本来，英米にはない．日本人に「日本語の会話」(Japanese conversation) という発想がないのと同様である．したがって「英会話」という日本語を用いた表現は以下のように英訳するのがよい．**
▶**英会話**（＝会話英語）の講習を受ける take lessons in *conversational English* ‖ 彼は**英会話が得意だ**（＝英語を上手に［自由に］話す）He *speaks very good English* [*speaks English fluently*]. ／He *is a good speaker of English*. ／He *is good at speaking English*. (● He is good at English conversation. も間違いではないが，「英会話術にたけている」といった響きがある).
▶きちんと練習すれば半年で日常的な**英会話**はできるようになりますよ Regular practice will enable you to carry on everyday *conversation in English* in six months.
‖**英会話学校** an English language school.

えいかく 鋭角 an **acute** /əkjúːt/ **angle** ▶**鋭角**的なフォークボール a forkball that drops at *an acute angle*.

えいかん 栄冠 **the crown** ▶果たしてどなたの頭上に**勝利の栄冠**が輝くことでしょうか Which one of these people will wear *the crown of victory*? ‖ このレースで**勝利の栄冠を勝ち取る**のは篠沢だろう Shinozawa will be the one to *win the laurels* (*of victory*) in this race. (➤ laurel（月桂(けい)樹）は古代ギリシャで勝者に月桂樹の冠を与えたことから).

えいき 英気 ▶きみはゆっくり休養して**英気を養う**ことが大切だ It is important (for you) to rest and *replenish your energy*. (➤ replenish /rɪplénɪʃ/ は「補充する」; recharge your batteries（充電する）を用いてもよい).

えいきゅう 永久の **permanent** 一副 **永久に** **permanently, forever**（➤ 後者はやや文学的な語）▶右頬のその傷跡は**永久に残る**でしょう The scar on the right cheek will be *permanent*. ‖ 2人は**永久に別れた** The two broke up *permanently* [*for good*]. ‖ ぼくはきみを**永久に忘れない**だろう I will remember you *forever*. ／I will never forget you. ‖ 彼は**永久に故国を去った** He left his homeland *for good*.
‖**永久歯** a permanent tooth.

えいきょう 影響 (an) **influence** /ínfluəns/; (an) **effect**（効果）; (an) **impact**（強烈な）▶考古学に興味をもつようになったのはおじの**影響**だった It was through my uncle's *influence* that I became interested in archaeology. ‖ そのテレビ番組は青少年に**悪い影響を与えた** That TV program *had a bad influence* on [*adversely influenced*] young people. (➤ adversely は「逆効果で」) ‖ 親の離婚はしばしば子供に**悪い影響を与える** Divorce often *has an adverse* [*a negative*] *effect on* children. ‖ ビートルズは多くのミュージシャンに**大きな影響を与えた** The Beatles *had a great effect on* a lot of musicians. ‖ インターネットは社会に**多大な影響を与えた** The Internet *has made an enormous impact on* society.
▶彼女は人に**影響されやすい** She *is* easily *influenced* (by other people). ‖ おかしなことにその汚職議員は今でもわが国の政界に**大きな影響力をもっている** Strangely, that corrupt Dietman still *carries great weight* [*has a great influence*] in the political world of this country.
☞ **悪影響**（→見出語）

えいぎょう 営業 **business**（業務）; **sales**（販売）▶その店は10時から7時まで**営業している**（＝店を開いている）The store *is open* from ten till seven. ‖ お宅は何時まで**営業していますか** How late *are* you *open*? ‖ その新しい店は来週から**営業を開始する** The new store *opens up* next week.
▶《掲示》**営業時間**は午前9時より午後5時まで *Business hours*: 9 a.m. – 5 p.m. ／*Open* from 9 a.m. to 5 p.m. ‖ その店は3か月の**営業停止**を命じられた The shop was ordered to *suspend its business* for three months.
▶先月は**営業不振だった** *Business was slow* [*down*] last month. ‖ 対話「お仕事は？」「出版社の**営業**（＝販売）です」"What do you do (for a living)?" "I'm in the *sales department* of a publishing company."
‖**営業案内** a business guide ‖**営業所** a sales office（営業活動のための事務所）; a branch office（支所，支店）‖**営業費** business expenses ‖**営業日** a business day ‖**営業部** a sales department [division] ‖**営業部長** a sales manager ‖**営業妨害** obstruction of business ‖**営業方針** a business policy.

えいご 英語 **English, the English language**（➤ 後者には通例 the が必要; 堅い言い方）▶**英語**を外国語として学ぶ study *English* as a foreign language ‖ 対話「きみ，**英語**は話せる？」「ええ少し」"Can you speak *English*?" "Yes, a little." (➤ Can you ...? は相手の言語能力について尋ねているように響くので使用を避けるべきであると解説されることがあるが，実際の会話ではふつうに使われる．しかし，相手に配慮して「ふつうに英語を使っていますか」の意で，Do you speak English? と尋ねるほうが好ましい).
▶彼は**流ちょうな英語で**挨拶した He gave a speech *in* fluent *English*. ‖「タヌキ」は**英語で何と言いますか** How do you say 'tanuki' *in English*? ／What is *the English* (*word*) *for* 'tanuki'? ‖ この小説は**英語に翻訳されている** This novel has been translated *into English*.
▶何か**英語の雑誌**はありますか Do you have any *English language magazines*? ‖ あした**英語の試験**がある We have *an English exam* [*an exam in English*] tomorrow. ‖ スミス夫人は**英語の先生**です Mrs. Smith is *a teacher of English*.
語法 an English teacher とすると「イングランド出身の先生」とも「英語の先生」とも解釈できるので，「英語の

え

先生」と言いたい場合は English に強勢を置いて発音する。

▶仕事で**英語**を使いますか Do you use *English* at work? ‖ **英語を生かせる職業**に就きたい I want to get *a job where I can use my English*. ‖ 今学期はトンプソン先生の**英語(科目)**をとるつもりです I am going to take Mrs. Thompson's *English course* this semester.

▶大学入試が中学・高校の**英語教育**に大きな影響を与えている College entrance examinations have a great impact on *English-language education* in junior and senior high schools. ‖ その生徒は**英語嫌い**になってしまった That student *has lost interest in English*. ‖ 彼女は自分の**英語力**を知るためにそのテストを受けた She took that test to find out her *English (proficiency) level*.

‖**英語学** English linguistics [philology] ‖ **英語圏** English-speaking world ‖ **英語国** an English-speaking country ‖ **英語話者** an English speaker ‖ **アメリカ英語** American English ‖ **イギリス英語** British English ‖ **現代英語** present-day [contemporary] English ‖ **工業英語** technical English ‖ **実用英語** practical English ‖ **商業英語** commercial English ‖ **標準英語** standard English ‖ **和製英語** (→見出語).

ディベートルーム **「英語の教育は小学生から始めるべきである」**

[1]**えいこう 栄光** **glory** ▶勝利の**栄光**はそのいちばん若い泳者の上に輝いた The *glory* of victory went to the youngest swimmer. ‖ ワールドカップで優勝したチームは**栄光**に包まれていた The team that won the World Cup basked in *glory*.

[2]**えいこう 曳航** a **tow** /toʊ/ 一動 **曳航する tow** +目.

えいこく 英国 →イギリス.

えいこせいすい 栄枯盛衰 **rise and fall** ▶この本にはローマ帝国の**栄枯盛衰**が描かれている This book describes the *rise and fall* of the Roman Empire. ‖ **栄枯盛衰**は世の習い[常] *Ups and downs* are the way of the world. / Life is full of *vicissitudes* [*advances and reversals of fortune* / *ups and downs*]. (➤ vicissitude /vəsísətjuːd/ は「栄枯盛衰, 浮き沈み」).

えいさい 英才 **brilliant intellect** (才能); a **gifted person** (人) ‖**英才教育** special education for gifted children.

えいさくぶん 英作文 (an) **English composition** ▶「日本の秋」という題で**英作文**を書きなさい Write *an English composition* [*essay*] under the title of "Autumn in Japan." ‖ 彼は**英作文**がうまい He is good at *English composition*.

えいじしんぶん 英字新聞 an **English-language (news)paper**.

えいしゃ 映写 **projection** 一動 **映写する project** /prədʒékt/ +目

‖**映写機** a (movie / slide) projector ‖ **映写室** a projection booth [room].

えいじゅう 永住する **settle down** ▶オーストラリアに**永住する** *live* [*settle*] *permanently* in Australia / *make a permanent home* in Australia ‖ 彼はスペインに渡って**永住**しようと決心した He resolved to move to Spain and *settle down* there.

‖**永住許可証** a permanent residence permit.

えいしん 栄進 (a) **promotion** (昇進) 一動 **栄進する get promoted, get a promotion** ▶このたびのご**栄進**おめでとうございます Congratulations on your recent *promotion*.

エイズ AIDS (➤ acquired immune deficiency [immunodeficiency] syndrome (後天性免疫不全症候群)の頭文字をとったもの) ▶今や HIV から**エイズ**への発症を予防する薬がある There are now drugs that prevent HIV from developing into *AIDS*. (➤「エイズを発症する」は develop AIDS) ‖ **エイズ**で亡くなる die of *AIDS*.

‖**エイズ患者** an AIDS patient [victim], a patient with AIDS (➤「エイズの人たち」は people (living) with AIDS と表現することが多い) ‖ **エイズ感染者** an HIV carrier (エイズの原因となるウイルスは HIV なので,「エイズ」ではなく「ＨＩＶに感染する」と表現する. → HIV).

[1]**えいせい 衛生** **sanitation** (環境[衛生]設備の状態), **hygiene** /háɪdʒiːn/ (衛生状態, 衛生学) 一形 **衛生的な sanitary**

▶赤ちゃんの世話をするときは**衛生**に気をつけなければいけない When you look after babies, you have to pay attention to *hygiene*. ‖ この容器は**衛生的でない** This container *is unsanitary*. ‖ この水を飲むのは**衛生上**好ましくない It would be *hygienically* unwise to drink this water.

‖**衛生室** a medical room.

☛ **非衛生, 不衛生** (→見出語)

[2]**えいせい 衛星** a **satellite** /sǽṭlaɪt/, a **moon** ▶土星の最大の**衛星**はタイタンである The biggest *satellite* of Saturn is Titan. ‖ **衛星放送**でマスターズゴルフの試合を見た We watched *a satellite broadcast* of the Masters Golf Tournament on TV.

▶**気象衛星**からの写真に台風の目が写っていた The picture from *the weather satellite* showed the eye of the typhoon. ‖ この番組は**通信衛星**を通じてロンドンから生中継されています This program is being relayed live via *communications satellite* from London.

‖**衛星国** a satellite state [nation], a satellite ‖ **衛星都市** a satellite town.

☛ **人工衛星** (→見出語)

えいせいちゅうりつ 永世中立 **permanent neutrality**

‖**永世中立国** a permanently neutral state [nation].

えいぜん 営繕 **building and repairs** (建設と修理)

‖**営繕課** a building and repairs section.

えいぞう 映像 a **picture**, an **image**

▶テレビの**映像** *a* TV *picture* / *an image* on a TV screen ‖ このテレビは**映像**が鮮明だ This TV set gives a clear *picture*. ‖ 現代は**映像**の時代と言われる The present age is said to be the age of *visual images*.

‖**映像周波数** video frequency (略 VF).

えいぞく 永続する **last** ▶その地に**永続的**な平和が訪れるのはいつの日のことだろう I wonder when people in that region will be able to enjoy (a) *lasting* peace.

えいたいくよう 永代供養 Buddhist services performed in perpetuity for the repose of someone's soul (➤ 説明的な訳).

えいたつ 栄達 **promotion** (昇進) 一動 **栄達する win promotion**.

えいだん 英断 a **wise decision** ▶社長が東南アジア市場からの撤退を決めたのは今にして思えば**英断**だった In retrospect, our company president's decision to withdraw from the Southeast Asian market was *a wise one*. (➤ one は decision を指す).

え

えいち 英知 wisdom ▶英知を持った人 a person of *intellect* [*wisdom*] ／a wise person ‖ 人類の英知は地球を破滅から救うであろうか Will *human genius* save the Earth from destruction?

エイチアイブイ HIV (➤「ヒト免疫不全ウイルス」(human immunodeficiency virus)の頭文字から. エイズの原因となるウイルス) ▶HIV 感染 *HIV* infection ‖ HIV に感染する get infected with *HIV* ／get *HIV* ／contract *HIV* (➤ 最後は堅い言い方) ‖ 彼は HIV 検査で陽性であった He tested positive for *HIV*.

えいてん 栄転 promotion ―動 (…に) 栄転する be promoted and transferred《to》▶おめでとう. きみ, 本社の部長に栄転するんだってね Congratulations! I heard you would *be promoted and transferred* [*be transferred with a promotion*] to the head office as general manager.

えいねん 永年 long years
‖ 永年勤続 long years of service.

えいのう 営農 farming.

えいびん 鋭敏な keen, sharp ▶犬は鋭敏な鼻をしている Dogs have a *keen* [*sharp*] nose. ／Dogs have a *keen* sense of smell. ‖ 彼は鋭敏な頭脳の持ち主だ He has *a keen intellect*.

えいぶん 英文 English ; an English sentence (1文) ▶英文の手紙 an *English* letter ／a letter (*written*) *in English* ‖ 彼女は英文を書くのがうまい She writes *English* well. ／She writes good *English*. ‖ この英文を和訳しなさい Translate [Put] this *English sentence* into Japanese.

えいぶんか 英文科 the English literature department, the department of English literature.

えいぶんがく 英文学 English literature (英語を使った) ; British literature (イギリスの).

えいへい 衛兵 a guard ▶バッキンガム宮殿の衛兵 the *guards* at Buckingham Palace.

えいべい 英米 Britain and America ▶英米の文化 *British and American* culture.
‖ 英米語学科 the British and American English department ／the department of British and American English ‖ 英米人 the British and Americans.

えいまい 英邁な wise ▶英まいな君主 a *wise* monarch.

えいみん 永眠する pass away (➤ die の婉曲(えんきょく)的な言い方) ▶元大統領は昨夜遅く永眠されました The former president *passed away* late last night.

えいめい 英名 1【英語の呼称】an English name.
2【高い評判】an excellent reputation ▶英名をはせる enjoy *an excellent reputation*.

えいやく 英訳 (an) English translation ▶この日本文を英訳しなさい *Translate* [*Put*] this Japanese sentence *into English*. ‖ これは三島由紀夫の『金閣寺』の英訳です This is *an English translation* of Mishima Yukio's "The Temple of the Golden Pavilion."

えいゆう 英雄 a hero /híːroʊ, híəroʊ/ ▶英雄的行為 a *heroic* deed ‖ 人を英雄視する *make a hero of* a person ‖ リンカーンとワシントンはアメリカの国民的英雄だ Lincoln and Washington are *national heroes* of the United States.

えいよ 栄誉 honor /ɑ́ːnəʳ ‖ ɔ́nə/ ; glory (栄光) ▶彼が表彰されたことはわが校の栄誉だ His receiving official commendation is a great *honor* for our school. ‖ 彼女は水泳で金メダルの栄誉に輝いた She *was honored* by winning the gold medal in [for] swimming. ／She *basked in glory* after winning the gold medal in [for] swimming. (➤ bask は「(恩恵などに)浴する」).
‖ 国民栄誉賞 the People's Honor Award.

えいよう 栄養 nourishment /nə́ːrɪʃmənt ‖ nʌ́r-/ (栄養物), nutrition /njutríʃən/ (栄養摂取) ▶栄養をとる take *nourishment* ‖ 栄養のある食物 (a) *nourishing* [*nutritious*] food ／*nourishment* ‖ 子供たちの栄養には十分留意する必要がある You should give sufficient thought to your children's *nutrition*. ‖ 母乳には赤ちゃんに必要なあらゆる栄養が入っている Mother's milk contains all the *nourishment* babies need.
▶バナナは栄養が豊富だ Bananas are *highly nutritious* [*nutritionally rich*]. ‖ その国では多くの人々がひどい栄養失調にかかっている In that country lots of people are suffering from severe *malnutrition*. ‖ 最近は栄養不足で病気になる人は少ない These days few people get sick due to *a nutritional deficiency* [*malnutrition*].
‖ 栄養価 nutritional value ‖ 栄養学 nutrition ‖ 栄養過多 overnutrition ‖ 栄養士 a dietitian /dàiətíʃən/ ‖ 栄養素 a nutrient ‖ 管理栄養士 a nutrition manager ; a clinical nutrition manager (病院の).

1**えいり 営利** (making a) profit ▶企業は営利を第一の目的とする The prime objective of a company is (*making a*) *profit*.
‖ 営利事業 a profit-making [commercial] enterprise ‖ 非営利団体 a nonprofit organization.

2**えいり 鋭利な** sharp ▶カーテンは鋭利な刃物で切り裂かれていた The curtain was slit with a *sharp* knife. ‖ 鋭利な洞察力を持つ have *sharp* powers of observation.

えいりん 営林 forestry
‖ 営林所 a forestry office.

えいれい 英霊 spirits of the war dead ▶この神社は英霊を祭ってある This shrine is dedicated to *the spirits of the war dead*.

えいわ 英和
‖ 英和辞典 an English-Japanese dictionary.

ええ 1【承認を表したり, 相づちとしたりして】▶ええ (そうです, いいですよ) *Uh-huh*. ／*Mm*. (➤ uh-huh は /ʌhʌ́/ と発音し, mm は口を閉じて uh-huh と言っているような気持ちで鼻孔から音を抜く) ‖ ええ (なるほどね, そうですよね) *Yeah*. ／*Yes*. (➤ 前者はくだけた返事). ⇀う ん.
2【驚き・疑問を表して】▶ええっ？ (本当ですか？) *Really?* ／*Is that so?*

エーイーディー AED (= automated external defibrillator /diːfíbrɪleɪţəʳ/ (自動体外式除細動器) の頭文字)
▶エーイーディーを使用する use an *AED*.

エーエム AM (= amplitude modulation の頭文字)
‖ AM 放送 an AM broadcast.

エーカー an acre《略 a., A.》.

エークラス Aクラス a top group ▶ヤクルト・スワローズは辛うじてAクラスを維持した The Yakult Swallows barely maintained their *top-group status*.

エーゲかい エーゲ海 the Aegean /ɪdʒíːən/ Sea.

エージェント an agent.

エース 1【野球】an ace (pitcher)
‖ リリーフエース a relief ace, a bullpen ace.
2【トランプ】an ace ▶ハートのエース the *ace* of hearts.

え

エーティーエム ATM (= automated [automatic] teller machine(現金自動預け払い機)の略);《英また》a **cashpoint** ▶エーティーエムでお金を引き出す withdraw money from *an ATM* ‖ エーティーエムに現金を預ける deposit cash into *an ATM* ‖ エーティーエムカードを挿入する insert *an ATM card*.

ええと **let me see, let's see**; **well** (ところで) ▶ええと, きみの用事は何だったかな *Well*, what did you come to see me about? ‖ 対話「この曲わかりますか」「ええと, サティだと思います」"Do you recognize this music?" "*Let me see* ... My guess is that it's by Satie."

エープリルフール **April Fools' [Fool's] Day, All Fools' Day** (日).

> **危ないカタカナ語 エープリルフール**
> **1** 日本では4月1日を指して「エープリルフール」と言っているが, 英語の April fool はこの日にだまされた人, またはその日のうそ, いたずらをいう.
> **2** その日は April Fools' [Fool's] Day または All Fools' Day(万愚(ばんぐ)節)という.

エール a **yell** /jel/ ▶ハーフタイムには両校のエールの交換があります The supporters of both schools exchange *yells* during half time. ‖ オリンピックに参加する日本選手たちにエールを送りたい We'd like to *give three cheers* [*wish good luck*] to the Japanese athletes who will compete in the Olympic Games.

えがお 笑顔 a **smile** ▶笑顔で彼らを迎える greet them with *a smile* ‖ 泣かないで. ほら, 笑顔を見せて Stop crying now and give me *a smile*. ‖ 絵美は笑顔がすてきだ Emi has a charming [winning] *smile*.

えかき 絵描き a **painter**; an **artist** (美術家, 画家).

えがく 描く **1**【絵にする】**draw** +⾃ (線で絵や図を); **paint** +⾃ (彩色して) ▶先生は黒板に歯車の図を描いた The teacher *drew* a gear on the blackboard. ‖ その墓の壁には4種の動物が描かれていた Four kinds of animals *were painted* on the walls of the grave.
▶《比喩的》その少女は歌手になった自分を心に描いた The young girl *pictured herself* as a singer.
2【表現する】**describe** +⾃ ▶その小説は当時のイギリスの社会を生き生きと描いている The novel vividly *describes* British society in those days. ‖ ブルーインパルスの編隊が弧を描いて飛んだ The Blue Impulse Squadron *formed* [*described*] an arc as they flew in formation.

えがたい 得難い ▶得難い人材 a person *of rare* [*extraordinary*] talent ‖ 得難い経験をする have a *rare* experience ‖ これは二度と得難いチャンスだ This is *a one-in-a-million opportunity* [*a once-in-a-lifetime chance*].

えがら 絵柄 a **design** (柄); a **pattern** (繰り返しの模様).

[1]**えき 駅** a **station** (➤ 鉄道の駅であることをはっきりさせるには train station または railroad [(英) railway] station とする) ▶大阪駅で5時に待ち合わせしよう Let's meet at *Osaka Station* at five o'clock. (➤ 駅名には通例 the をつけない) ‖ 駅へはどう行けばいいですか How do I get to *the train station*? ‖ わが社は駅から歩いて5分です Our company office is a five-minute walk from *the train station*. ‖ 神戸まであと1駅です Kobe is *the next station* [*stop*]. ‖ 次の駅はどこですか Where do we stop *next*?
☞ 駅員, 駅長, 駅ビル, 駅弁, 駅前 (→見出語)

[2]**えき 液** (a) **liquid** (液体); a **solution** (溶液) ▶私はその液にリトマス試験紙を浸してみた I dipped the litmus paper into the *solution*.

[3]**えき 益** **good** (良いこと); **use** /juːs/ (役に立つこと); **benefit** (利益) ▶子供をぶって何の益があるのか What *good* is it to beat a child? ‖ 今さら悔やんでも益はない It is *useless* to regret it now.
▶紫外線の浴び過ぎは害はあっても益はない Too much exposure to ultraviolet rays is *harmful and not beneficial*. ‖ この本は読者に益するところが大きい This book *is of* much *benefit* [is very *useful*] to its readers. (➤ of benefit は形容詞の beneficial と同義).

えきいん 駅員 a **station attendant** [**employee**]; **the station staff** (全員).

えきか 液化
‖液化天然ガス liquefied natural gas《略 LNG》.

えきがく 疫学 **epidemiology** /èpɪdìːmiɑ́ːlədʒi/
‖疫学者 an epidemiologist.

エキサイト ▶相手チームの反則で選手全員がエキサイトした The entire team *was furious* [*enraged*] at their opponents' foul play.

> **直訳の落とし穴「エキサイトする」**
> (1)「エキサイト」は excite がもとだが, 使い方はだいぶ異なる. excited, exciting は基本的に「わくわくする」「はらはらする, 手に汗握る」などプラスイメージのことばである. get excited は「興奮する」でも, 試合などがおもしろくて興奮するのである. それに対して「エキサイトする」は選手どうしがつかみ合いをしそうな危険な状態をイメージする. したがって,「相手チームの反則で選手全員がエキサイトした」は(×) The entire team got excited ... とは言えず,「怒った」「かっかした」に当たる語を使って, 上の用例のように訳す.
> (2) excited するのは観客など人であって, 試合ではない. したがって,「エキサイトした試合」のつもりで, (×) an excited game などとは言えない. an exciting game は「手に汗握るようなおもしろい試合」である. 荒れてラフプレーが目立つという意味では an ugly game があり,「試合はエキサイトした」は The game got ugly. と言える.
> (3) 下の例のように「エキサイト」と excited が同じような意味で使われることもある.

▶応援する球団がホームランを打ったとき, ファンはおおいにエキサイトした The fans *were* really *excited* when their team scored a homerun.

エキシビション an **exhibition** /èksɪbíʃən/.

えきしゃ 易者 a **fortune-teller** (➤ 英米ではふつうは女性) ▶易者に運勢を見てもらう have one's fortune told by *a fortune-teller*.

えきしょう 液晶 **liquid crystal** ▶私の時計は液晶表示だ My watch uses [has] *a liquid crystal display*.
‖液晶テレビ a liquid crystal display TV, an LCD TV (➤ a flat-screen TV (薄型テレビ) というほうが理解が早い).

えきじょうか 液状化 **liquefaction** /lìkwɪfǽkʃən/ ━動 液状化する **liquefy** ▶この一帯は大地震で液状化が見られた The ground in this area *liquefied* during the big earthquake.
‖液状化現象 (the phenomenon of) liquefaction.

エキス (an) **extract** /ékstrækt/ ▶はちみつエキス入りドリ

ンク剤 a health drink that contains *a honey extract*.

エキストラ an **extra** /ékstrə/ ▶映画にエキストラで出演する be *an extra* in a film.

エキスパート an **expert** /ékspəːrt/ ▶あの先生は幼児教育のエキスパートだ He is (*an*) *expert* on teaching preschool children. (➤ an をつけなければ形容詞としての用法になる；前置詞は on 以外に at, in が可能).

エキスパンダー an **expander**, a **chest pull**.

エキセントリック エキセントリックな **eccentric** /ɪkséntrɪk/ 《参考》皆と違うことをあまり好ましく思わない日本では「エキセントリック」は芳しくないニュアンスがあるが，個性を尊重する英米では eccentric は好意的に受け止められることがある.

▶あの映画監督にはちょっとエキセントリックなところがある That film director is something of *an eccentric*.

エキゾチック エキゾチックな **exotic** /ɪɡzáːṭɪk/ ▶熱帯のエキゾチックな果物[花] an *exotic* tropical fruit [flower] ‖ エキゾチックな顔立ちの女性 a woman with *exotic* features.

《参考》何をエキゾチックと感じるかは民族によって異なる．日本人ならば，中近東や南アジアの事物や人たちを連想することが多いと思われる．アメリカ人にとっては，東アジアの人の中では，感情をストレートに表すことの少ない(本心の知れない)日本人は，中国人や韓国人よりも exotic と結び付きやすい．また，歌舞伎，能，芸者，着物，茶の湯などの比較的よく知られた日本の伝統もそれぞれ exotic なイメージに一役買っている．

えきたい 液体 (a) **liquid**；**fluid** (流動体)

‖**液体酸素** liquid oxygen ‖ **液体洗剤** cleaning fluid, a liquid detergent ‖ **液体燃料** liquid fuel.

えきちゅう 益虫 a **useful insect**.

1**えきちょう 益鳥** a **useful bird**.

2**えきちょう 駅長** a **stationmaster**

‖**駅長室** a stationmaster's office.

えきでん 駅伝 a **road relay**, a **long-distance relay**, an **ekiden** (➤ 英語化している) ▶高校[大学]駅伝 an inter-high school [intercollegiate] *road relay* ‖ 駅伝競走に出場する compete in *a long-distance relay*.

えきなか 駅ナカ **the premises of a railroad station** ▶駅ナカショップ an *in-station* shop [store] ‖ 品川駅の駅ナカの店で弁当を買った I bought a box lunch at *a shop in Shinagawa Station*.

えきびょう 疫病 an **epidemic** /èpɪdémɪk/ (流行病)；(a) **plague** /pleɪɡ/ (悪疫) ▶疫病を撲滅する wipe out *an epidemic*.

えきビル 駅ビル a **railroad station building**, a **building built above a railroad station** [**terminal**].

えきべん 駅弁 an ***ekiben***；a **box lunch sold at a railroad station (or on a train)** ▶鉄道の旅では駅弁を買うのが楽しみだ When traveling by train, I enjoy buying *box lunches at a train station or on a train*.

えきまえ 駅前 ▶交番は駅前にありますよ The police box is *in front of the railroad station*. ‖ 今，駅前(＝駅の外)の人混みの中で金田さんを見かけた I just saw Kaneda in the crowd *outside the station*.

‖**駅前通り** the street in front of the train station ‖ **駅前広場** a station square [plaza].

えきり 疫痢 **children's** [**childhood**] **dysentery** /dísənteri/.

エクアドル **Ecuador**(南米，赤道直下の国).

えぐい **(sharp and) bitter** ▶このたけのこ，あく抜きが足りないからまだえぐいな You haven't blanched these bamboo shoots enough. They still *have a bitter taste*. ‖ 私の上司のモラハラは，まじでエグい The moral harassment by my boss is really *cruel*.

エクササイズ an **exercise** (練習問題)；**exercise** (運動).

エクステリア **the exterior** (➤ 英語は主に建物の「外側」や「外装，外観」を指す).

えくぼ a **dimple** ▶彼女は笑うとえくぼができる She has *dimples* when she smiles. (➤ 片方だけなら a dimple) ‖ 真由美はえくぼがかわいい Mayumi's *dimples* are cute.

えぐる **hollow out** ▶丸太をえぐって丸木舟を作る *hollow out* a log to make a canoe ‖ 川の両岸は流水でえぐられている Both riverbanks have *been hollowed out* by water.

▶《比喩的》彼に別れを告げるのは胸をえぐられる思いだった It *almost broke my heart* to say good bye to him.

エクレア an **éclair** /eɪkléər/.

えげつない ▶あんなえげつない人とは商売しないほうがいいですよ You shouldn't do business with him；he is really *greedy* [is *unscrupulous*]. (➤ unscrupulous /ʌnskrúːpjələs/ は「あくどいことも平気でやる」の意).

エコ ▶エコ製品 an *eco-friendly* product, a *green* product ‖ エコに配慮した住宅を建てる build an *eco-friendly* house ‖ エコ意識の高い消費者 an *eco-conscious* consumer.

‖**エコカー** an eco(-friendly) car, a fuel-efficient car ‖ **エコテロリスト** an eco-terrorist ‖ **エコテロリズム** eco-terrorism ‖ **エコバッグ** a reusable shopping bag, an eco(-friendly) bag.

エゴ **egotism**；**selfishness** (利己心) ▶彼はエゴの塊だ He is *an egotist* to the core. (➤ to the core は「心の底まで」) ／He is the personification of *selfishness*. (➤ personification は「権化，化身」).

エゴイスト a **self-centered person**, an **egotist** [**egoist**] ▶あいつは自分のことしか考えないエゴイストだ He *is self-centered* [*egotistical*] and he doesn't think of anyone but himself.

エゴイズム **egotism, egoism**；**selfishness** (わがまま) ▶そりゃあ，エゴイズムってものだよ Well, that's *egotism* for you.

> **危ないカタカナ語✹ エゴイズム**
> **1** egoism でも egotism でもよいが，前者は倫理学や哲学で用いることが多い．
> **2**「エゴイスト」は自己中心的な人のことだから self-centered person と言ってもよい．

エコー an **echo** /ékoʊ/ (こだま，反響)；an **echo effect** (カラオケなどの音響効果).

えごころ 絵心 ▶彼には絵心がある He has *a talent for painting*. ／*He's good at painting*. (➤「絵が得意だ」の意；「絵を見る目がある」の意では He has an eye for art. という).

えこじ →いこじ.

エコノミー **economy**

‖**エコノミークラス** economy class.

エコノミスト an **economist**.

えこひいき ▶彼だけ褒めてはえこひいき(＝不公平)になる It would be *unfair* to praise only him. ‖ 私は誰にもえこひいきしない I am *partial to no one*. (➤ be partial to で「…にえこひいきをする」の意) ／I am *fair with everybody*. ‖ 教師は特定の生徒にえこひいきするべ

え

きではない A teacher should not *favor* a particular student [should be impartial].

エコロジー **ecology**.

えさ 餌 **bait** /beɪt/ (釣りなどの) ; **food** (食物) ▶**餌**で誘う lure with *bait* ‖ 釣り針に**餌をつける** *bait* a fishhook ‖ この魚の**餌**は何ですか What does this fish *feed on*? ‖ ウサギに**餌やった**? Did you *feed* [*give food to*] the rabbits?

▶《比喩的》彼は結婚を**餌**に女に金を貢がせた He used marriage as *a lure* to swindle women out of their money. (➤ lure は「にせ餌(ぇ)」).

えし 壊死 (a) **necrosis** /nekróʊsɪs/.

えじき 餌食 (a) **prey** ▶ウサギやネズミはよくフクロウの**餌食**になる Rabbits and mice *are* often *preyed on* by owls. ‖ ライオンはシマウマやキリンを**餌食にする** Lions *prey on* zebras and giraffes.

▶《比喩的》10人の人がその悪徳商法の**餌食になった** Ten people *fell victim* [*prey*] *to* the scam.

エジプト **Egypt** /íːdʒɪpt/

‖**エジプト人** an Egyptian.

えしゃく 会釈する **make a bow** /baʊ/ ▶人に軽く**会釈をする** *make a* slight *bow* to a person / *nod* to a person. 《参考》アメリカ人は会釈をしないで手を振る (wave at) ことが多い.

エシャロット 《植物》a **shallot** (➤「エシャロット」はフランス語の échalote から).

エジンバラ **Edinburgh** /édɪnbə̀ːrə ‖ -bərə/ (イギリスの都市).

エスエフ **SF, science fiction**

‖**ＳＦ映画** a science-fiction [an SF / a sci-fi] movie (➤ sci-fi はインフォーマルな語で /sàifái/ と発音) ‖ **ＳＦ作家** a science-fiction [an SF] writer ‖ **ＳＦ小説** a science-fiction [an SF] novel.

エスエル a **steam locomotive** /lòʊkəmóʊṭɪv/ (➤ SL は日本式略語) ▶そのローカル線に**ＳＬファン**が詰めかけた *Steam locomotive* [*train*] *enthusiasts* flocked to the local line.

エスオーエス an **SOS**, a **mayday (signal)** ▶**ＳＯＳ**を発する send out *an SOS* [*a mayday signal*].

エスカルゴ **escargots** /èskɑːʳgóʊz/ (➤ フランス語).

エスカレーター an **escalator** /éskəleɪṭəʳ/ ▶**エスカレーター**で上[下]に行く go up [go down] on *an escalator* ‖ **エスカレーターに乗る** get on *an escalator* ‖ 彼女は**エスカレーター**でまっすぐ6階へ行った She took the *escalator* straight to the sixth floor. ‖ **下り[上り]のエスカレーター**はどこですか Where's the *down* [*up*] *escalator*?

▶《比喩的》あの中学へ入れば**エスカレーター式**に大学まで行ける Once you get into that junior high school, you're assured of steady advancement *all the way up* through college.

エスカレート 一動 **エスカレートする** **escalate** /éskəleɪt/ ▶彼女の要求は次第に**エスカレートしてきた** Her demands gradually *escalated* [*mounted*]. (➤ mount は「増大する」の意).

エスキモー an **Eskimo** /éskɪmoʊ/, an **Innuit** /ínjuɪt/ 《参考》Eskimo は「生肉を食べる人」が原義で, 民族的蔑称になることがある.「エスキモー」と呼ばれる人たちは自分たちのことを Innuit または Inuit (カナダ系), Yupik または Yupik Eskimo (西南アラスカ系) などと呼ぶ.

エスコート 一動 **エスコートする** **escort** +目 ▶彼女は野球部のキャプテンに**エスコートされて**ご機嫌だった She was very pleased to *be escorted* by the captain of the baseball team.

エスサイズ Ｓサイズ a **small size** ▶**Ｓサイズの**手袋 *small-size* (*d*) gloves ‖ **Ｓサイズの**コーラ a *small-size* (*d*) coke.

エスタ **ESTA** (➤ electronic system for travel authorization (電子渡航認証システム) の頭文字をとったもの) ▶アメリカ旅行に先立って**エスタに申請する** *apply for an ESTA* in advance to travel to the US.

エステ a **spa** [**cosmetic**] **treatment**

‖**エステサロン** a day spa.

エスディージーズ **SDGs** (➤ Sustainable Development Goals (持続可能な開発目標) の略) ▶**SDGs** を推進する propel the *SDGs*.

エスニック **ethnic** ▶**エスニック料理** *ethnic* cuisine (➤ cuisine /kwɪzíːn/ は「料理」の意の堅い語) ‖ **エスニックな**雰囲気のレストラン a restaurant with an *ethnic* atmosphere.

エスプリ **esprit** /esprí:/ (➤ フランス語) ▶**エスプリの利いた**文章 *witty* writing.

エスペラント **Esperanto**.

えせ- **pseudo-** /sjúːdoʊ/ (偽の) ; **would-be** (自称) ▶**えせ**芸術家 a *would-be* artist ‖ **えせ文化人** a *pseudo*-highbrow.

えそらごと 絵空事 a **pipe dream**.

えだ 枝 a **branch** ; a **bough** /baʊ/ (大枝) ; a **twig** (細い小枝) ; a **shoot** (若枝) ▶**枝の張った**カシの木 a *spreading* oak ‖ 木の**枝を切り落とす** cut *a branch* off a tree.

えたい 得体 ▶**えたいの知れない** (=不思議な) 物体 a *strange* [*mysterious*] object ‖ **えたいの知れない**不安 *unaccountable* anxiety.

えだげ 枝毛 a **split hair end** ▶髪が傷んで**枝毛**ができちゃった My hair is damaged and I have *split ends*. ‖ **枝毛を防ぐ**トリートメント a treatment that *prevents hair ends from splitting*.

えだまめ 枝豆 **edamame** /èdəmáːmiː, -meɪ/, **green soybeans**.

えだわかれ 枝分かれする **branch off** ▶本線から**枝分かれした**線 a line that *branches off* the main line ‖ 英語とオランダ語は祖語である西ゲルマン語から**枝分かれした**ものだ English and Dutch *branched off* from an older parent, West Germanic.

‖《言語学》**枝分かれ図** a tree diagram.

エチオピア **Ethiopia** /ìːθióʊpiə/ (アフリカ東部の国)

‖**エチオピア人** an Ethiopian.

エチケット **etiquette** ; **manners** (行儀作法) (→マナー) ▶贈り物を受け取ったら礼状を書くのが**エチケット**にかなっています It is good *etiquette* to write a thank-you note when you receive a gift.

▶最近の親は昔ほど**エチケット**をうるさく言わない Parents today are not as strict about *manners* as they used to be.

> **危ないカタカナ語✹ エチケット**
> 礼儀作法のことを「エチケット」というが, この語はフランス語から来ていて, 英語では manners ほどは使われていない. 特に人の行儀の良さ[悪さ]をいうときは etiquette を使わず, He has good [bad] manners. のようにいうのがふつう.

えつ 悦 ▶彼は珍本を手に入れて**悦に入(い)っている** He *is immensely pleased with* the rare volume he found.

えっ ▶《疑問》**えっ**? *Huh*? / *Ha*! / *Eh*? ‖ **えっ? 何とおっしゃいましたか** *What*? / (*I beg your*) *pardon*? (➤ (I beg your) pardon? は尻上がりに発音する. 尻下がりだと「すみません」「ごめんなさい」の意になる).

▶《驚き》えっ？ それは本当かい *What !* Is it true ? ‖ えっ！そいつは驚いた *Well now ! ／Well,* (*my*) *goodness* ! ／*Well, what do you know* ?

えっきょう 越境 ▶越境して逃げる escape *over the border* ‖ そのメキシコ人たちは越境してアメリカへ入った The Mexicans *crossed the border* into America. ▶越境入学する *enter a school outside the school district*.

エックスせん エックス線 X-rays ▶《医者が患者に》胃のＸ線写真を撮ったほうがいいですね We'd better take *an X-ray* of your stomach. ‖ 私は胸部のＸ線写真を撮ってもらった I *had* my chest *X-rayed*. (➤動詞は x-ray と小文字にしてもよい).

‖エックス線検査 an X-ray examination.

えづけ 餌付け ▶タンチョウヅルの餌付けに成功する succeed in *getting* Tancho cranes *to accept food*.

1**えっけん 越権** ▶反対派を封じるなんて議長の越権行為だ Putting down objectors is *an abuse of* a chairperson's *authority*. ／The chairperson is clearly *overstepping his authority* by putting down objections.

2**えっけん 謁見** an audience ▶女王［教皇］に謁見する *have an audience* with the Queen［the Pope］.

エッセー an essay /éseɪ/ ▶将来の夢について200語程度で英語のエッセーを書いてください Write *an essay* in English of approximately 200 words on your future dream(s).

‖エッセイスト an essayist.

エッセンス essence /ésəns/ ▶バニラエッセンス vanilla *essence* ‖ 彼女の音楽のエッセンスが集約されたようなＣＤ a CD that has captured the *essence* of her music.

エッチ ▶エッチな冗談言わないで！ Don't tell *dirty*［*blue*］jokes. ‖ あいつエッチだから近づかないほうがいいよ You'd better stay away from that man—he's *got a dirty*［*filthy*］*mind*. ‖ 変なところに触らないでよ, エッチねえ Keep your hands off me, *you pervert*［*creep*］! (➤ pervert は「変質者」, creep は「嫌なやつ」) ‖ エッチをする *have sex*.

エッチアイブイ HIV ⇀エイチアイブイ.

エッチビー HB (➤ hard black の略) ▶HBの鉛筆 an *HB* pencil.

えっちらおっちら ▶えっちらおっちら山道を登る *trudge up* a mountain path (➤ trudge は「重い足取りで歩く」の意).

エッチング (an) etching ▶銅板にエッチングをする *etch* on a copper plate.

えっとう 越冬 ▶彼は観測隊に加わって南極で越冬した He joined an expedition (party) and *spent the winter* in Antarctica.

‖越冬隊 a wintering party［team］.

エッフェルとう エッフェル塔 the Eiffel /áɪfəl/ Tower.

えつらん 閲覧 ▶図書館で参考図書を閲覧する *read* reference books in the library.

‖閲覧室 a reading room ‖ インターネット閲覧ソフト Internet browser software.

えて 得手 one's forte, one's strong point ▶人には皆それぞれ得手不得手があるものだ Everyone has *his*［*her*］*strong and weak points*.

えてして 得てして ▶人はえてして他人の不幸には鈍感なものだ People *tend to* be insensitive to other people's misfortunes. ‖ 人はえてして自分には甘い People *generally tend to* be easy on themselves.

エデン

‖エデンの園 Eden /íːdn/, the Garden of Eden.

えと 干支 *eto*

日本紹介 ✉ **干支は伝統的な中国の暦で周期的に用いられる12種の動物のことです．１年ごとにネズミ, 牛, トラ, ウサギ, タツ, 蛇, 馬, 羊, 猿, 鶏, 犬, イノシシの12の動物が当てられています．「ことしはねずみ年だ」「私はうし年生まれです」のような言い方をします．また, 年賀状にその年の干支がよく描かれます** *Eto* are the twelve animals used cyclically in the traditional Chinese calendar. Each year there is a different animal ; rat, ox, tiger, rabbit, dragon, snake, horse, sheep, monkey, rooster, dog, boar. People say things like "This is the year of the Rat." "I was born in the year of the Ox." Also, the *eto* of the year is often depicted on New Year's greeting cards. ⇀**十二支**.

▶ 対話「あなたのえとは何？」「申(さる)よ」"What's the animal for the year you were born in? ／What's your *Chinese zodiacal sign*［*symbol*］?" "Monkey." (➤ zodiacal sign［symbol］は「十二宮」のこと).

えど 江戸 Edo ▶ちゃきちゃきの江戸っ子 a real *Tokyoite* ／*a Tokyoite* born and bred (➤ Tokyoite の -ite /-aɪt/ は「…の人」の意).

‖江戸時代 the Edo period［era］‖ 江戸幕府 the Edo shogunate /ʃóʊgənert/.

えとく 会得する learn ＋㊐ ▶ゴルフのこつを会得するには時間がかかる It takes time to *learn how to* play golf［*get the knack of* golf］. (➤ knack /næk/ は「こつ」).

エナメル enamel /ɪnǽməl/ 《参考》この語は塗料, (マニキュア用)エナメル剤, 歯のエナメル質をいう場合に用い, 革靴には用いない.

‖エナメル靴 patent-leather shoes ‖ エナメル質 tooth enamel.

えにし 縁 ▶私は小川さんとは不思議なえにしを感じている I feel an uncanny［a mysterious］*bond* with Mr. Ogawa.

エニシダ 《植物》a genista /dʒənístə/.

エヌジー NG (➤ no good の略とされるが英語では通じない) ▶その俳優はエヌジーを連発した The actor *spoiled*［*ruined*］*one scene after another*.

エネルギー energy /énərdʒi/ (➤「エネルギー」はドイツ語の *Energie* から) ▶太陽［核］エネルギー solar［nuclear］*energy* ‖ 位置エネルギー potential *energy* ‖ 運動エネルギー kinetic *energy* ‖ エネルギー保存の法則 the law of the conservation of *energy* ‖ エネルギーを節約する conserve *energy* (➤「エネルギーの節約」なら energy conservation) ‖ エネルギー問題を解決する solve *the energy problem* ‖ 日本のエネルギー資源は限られている Japan's *energy resources* are limited.

▶仕事にエネルギー(＝精力)を傾ける apply［devote］one's *energy* to one's work.

エネルギッシュ energetic /ènərdʒétɪk/ ▶エネルギッシュな教師 an *energetic* teacher ‖ エネルギッシュに働く work *energetically* ‖ 候補者はエネルギッシュに全国を遊説して歩いた The candidate stumped the entire country on an *energetic* speaking tour.

えのき 榎 《植物》a (Japanese) hackberry

‖えのきだけ enoki mushrooms.

えのぐ 絵の具 paints, colors 《参考》チューブ入りの１

本は a paint tube といい,「油絵の具」は oils, oil paints または oil colors,「水彩絵の具」は water-paints, watercolors という.
▶赤い絵の具を貸して Could you lend me your *red* (*tube*)? ‖ 彼女は油絵の具で[水彩絵の具で]その町の美しい風景を描いた She painted a lovely view of the town *in oils* [*in watercolors*].
‖絵の具箱 a paintbox.

えはがき 絵葉書 a **picture postcard**, a **postcard**
✉ 衛兵交替の絵はがきありがとう Thank you for your *postcard* showing the changing of the guards.

えび 海老 a **spiny** [**rock**] **lobster**(伊勢エビ); a **prawn**(車エビなど); a **shrimp**(小エビ・芝エビの類い) ▶《慣用表現》えびで鯛(たい)を釣る throw a sprat to catch a mackerel(➤ 英語では「サバをとるためにイワシを投げる」という).
‖エビフライ a fried prawn.

エピソード an **interesting story**; an **episode**(歴史上の人物・有名人の); an **anecdote** /ǽnɪkdoʊt/(逸話) ▶ひとつ彼の学生時代の傑作なエピソードを聞かせよう Let me tell you *an interesting story* about something that happened when he was a student.

エフエム FM(➤ frequency modulation(周波数変調)の略) ▶私はＦＭでよくクラシック音楽を聴く I often listen to classical music on *FM*.
‖ＦＭ放送局 an FM station.

エプロン an **apron** /éɪprən/; a **pinafore** /pínəfɔːʳ/(胸当てのついた) ▶佐知子はエプロン姿で玄関に出てきた Sachiko came to the door (*still*) *wearing an apron*.

エフワン F1(➤ Formula 1 の略)
‖エフワンカー an F1 car ‖ エフワンレース an F1 race.

エベレスト Mount [**Mt.**] **Everest** 《参考》チベット名は Chomolungma(チョモランマ)という.

えへん ahem /mhm, əhém/(➤ せき払いを表す擬音語) ▶父は私たちの注意を引こうとエヘンとせき払いをした My father *hemmed* [*cleared his throat*] to attract our attention.

えほん 絵本 a **picture book**; an **illustrated book**(挿し絵入りの本)
‖絵本作家 a picture-book writer.

えま 絵馬 an ***ema***
日本紹介 ✉ **絵馬は主に馬の絵が描かれた木の札です. 願い事や感謝のことばを書いて神社や寺の専用の棚に掛けます.** *Ema* are small wooden plaques that mostly have horses painted on them. People write their wishes or thanks to the gods on them and hang them on special racks at Shinto shrines and Buddhist temples.

えまき 絵巻 a **picture scroll.**

えみ 笑み a **smile** ▶老人の顔に笑みが浮かんだ *A smile* came to the old man's face. ‖ 祖母は満面に笑みを浮かべて私を迎えてくれた *A broad smile* broke out on [across] my grandmother's face as she came to greet me.

エムサイズ Mサイズ a **medium size** ▶MサイズのＴシャツ[ピザ] a *medium-size*(*d*) T-shirt [pizza].

エムブイピー an **MVP**(➤ most valuable player の略).

エメラルド (an) **emerald.**

えもいわれぬ 得も言われぬ indescribable ▶得も言われぬよい香り a fragrance *that can hardly be put into words* ‖ モーリシャス島の夜明けは得も言われぬ美しさだった The dawn on Mauritius was beautiful *beyond description*.

えもじ 絵文字 an ***emoji***, an ***emoji* pictograph** [**pictogram**]; an **emoticon**(顔文字) ▶絵文字を使ってメールを送る send a text message with *emoji pictographs* [*emoticons*].

エモティコン an **emoticon.**

えもの 獲物 game
語法「獲物」の意味の game は集合名詞扱いで a はつかない.「20匹の獲物」は twenty head of game のように言う.
▶大きな獲物 big *game*(➤ 特にライオンや象など) ‖ 狩りに行ったが獲物は全くなかった I went hunting but *bagged nothing* [*did not get any game*]. (➤ bag は「(獲物を)しとめる」の意) ‖ きょうはたくさんの獲物があった I have gotten *a lot of game* today. / I have made *a good bag* [*a good catch*] today. (➤ 名詞の catch は魚について用いることが多い).

えもんかけ 衣紋掛け a **kimono hanger**(和服); a **dress hanger**(洋服).

えら 鰓 a **gill** /gɪl/(魚の) ▶魚はえらで呼吸する Fish breathe through their *gills*.
▶その俳優はえら(＝顎)が張っている That actor *has a square jaw*.

エラー an **error** ▶《野球》手痛いエラーをする commit *a costly error* ‖ 凡フライをエラーする *drop* a pop fly *for an error* ‖ 坂本は凡ゴロをエラーした Sakamoto *muffed* an easy grounder *for an error*. (➤ muff は「取り損なう」; 第２, 第３例のように状況を表す別の動詞を使うのがふつう).

えらい 偉い **1**【偉大な】**great**; **distinguished**(有名な) ▶偉い学者 a *great* [*distinguished*] scholar ‖ そこが彼の偉いところだ That's where his *greatness* lies. ‖ 彼女は自分を偉い人物だと思っている She thinks that she is (*a*) *somebody*. / She thinks (*too*) *highly* of herself. ‖ 山田はいつも自分を実際よりも偉く見せようとする Yamada always tries to *make* himself *out to be more than* he *is*. (➤ make out は真実ではないことを「…かのように言う[見せる]」).
▶そんな偉そうなことを言うんじゃないよ Don't *be* so *conceited*. ‖ お母さんの手伝いか, えらいね You're helping your mother? That's *great*. / *I'm proud of you*. ‖ えらい! よく頑張った *Good for you*! You did a great job.
2【重要な, 地位の高い】**important** ▶きょうは会社の偉い人に会うのでとても緊張している I'm very nervous because I have to meet with someone *important* in the company today. ‖ ここに業界のお偉いさんたちが集まっている *Leading figures* in the industry are here. ‖ 対話「松田君は最近どうしてるかな?」「ああ, あいつ, 偉くなったよ」"I wonder how Matsuda is getting along?" "He'*s a big shot* now." (➤「お偉方」のことをインフォーマルで big shot や bigwig という).
3【重大だ】▶会長を怒らせるとはまたえらいことをしてくれたもんだ I can't believe you *went and* angered the chair. (➤ go and do は人が「困った[ばかげた]ことをする」) ‖ きょうはえらい目に遭ったよ I *had a hard time* today.
4【程度が甚だしい】**terrible** ▶きょうはえらい暑さだ It's *terribly* [*awfully*] hot today.
☛ どえらい (→見出語)

えらく very, awfully, terribly(➤ あとの２語は very のくだけた語); **really**(実に)

▶きょうはえらく張り切ってるじゃない You're *really* going at it [full of vim and vigor] today! (➤ go at は「(仕事などに)懸命に取り組む」) ／You're *awfully* peppy today!

えらぶ 選ぶ

📖 **訳語メニュー**
選択する →choose, select **1, 3**
取る →take **1**
選出する →elect **2**

1【選択する】choose +㊐; **select** +㊐ (比較・検討して慎重に); **pick out** (選び出す; インフォーマルな言い方); **single out** (1人[1つ]だけ選ぶ); **take** +㊐ (取る) ▶候補者を選ぶ *choose* a candidate ‖ 進路を選ぶ *choose* a career ‖ 証人は慎重にことばを選んだ The witness *chose* his [her] words carefully. ‖ 彼女はぼくにネクタイを選んでくれた She *selected* a tie for me.

▶彼女はその店でドレスを選ぶのに1時間もかかった She spent an hour in the shop *selecting* a dress. ‖ どうぞお好きなものをお選びください Please *pick out* anything you like. ‖ 第2外国語としてドイツ語を選ぶつもりです I'm going to *take* German as a second foreign language.

【文型】
A から B を選ぶ
choose B **from** [**from among**] A
➤ Aは複数の名詞
among A とすることもある
A と B から(どちらかを)選ぶ
choose between A **and** B

▶テーブルの上の本の中から1冊を選ぶ *choose* a book *from among* those on the table ‖ この名前の挙がった5人の中から視聴者が優勝者を選びます Viewers will *choose* the winner *from among* the five nominees. ‖ 健康と富のどちらかを選ぶとすれば私は健康のほうを選ぶ If I had to *choose between* health *and* wealth, I would *take* health.

▶どのカメラが欲しいの? 好きなのを選びなさい Which camera do you want? *Take your pick*. (➤ この pick は「選択」の意の名詞) ‖ 彼は私の選んだ人よ He is the man *of my choice*. ‖ 国会のがなり合いは子供のけんかと選ぶところがない(=差がない) Shouting matches in the Diet are *no different* from children's quarrels.

2【選出する】elect +㊐ ▶加藤シズエは国会議員に選ばれた最初の女性の1人であった Kato Shizue was one of the first women (to *be*) *elected* to the Diet. ‖ 私たちは佐藤さんをクラス委員に選んだ We *elected* Sato (as) class secretary. (➤ 役職が1名に限られるときは a や the をつけない).

3【選抜する】select ▶彼女は50,000人の応募者の中から主役に選ばれた She *was selected* as the leading actress from among 50,000 applicants.

えらぶる 偉ぶる ▶あいつは偉ぶってるから嫌いだ I don't like him because he *has an attitude* [he's *arrogant*]. (➤ have an attitude は「威張った態度をとる」の意の 俗語) ‖ キーン教授は高名な学者なのに少しも偉ぶったところがない Professor Keene does*n't brag about himself* in spite of his great fame as a scholar.

えり 襟 a **collar**; a **lapel** /ləpél/ (背広などの襟の折り返し) ▶コートの襟を立てる turn up one's coat *collar* ‖ 上着の襟にバッジをつける wear a badge on [in] the *lapel* of one's jacket.

▶《慣用表現》二度とこんなことが起きないよう襟を正していきたい We're going to *straighten up our acts* so this doesn't happen again.

えりあし 襟足 the nape of one's **neck** ▶ぼくは彼女の襟足の美しさに引き付けられた I was attracted by the beauty of *the hairline along her neck* [*her nape*]. 《参考》欧米では襟足は女性のチャームポイントとは考えられていない.

エリート the elite (エリートたち) ▶彼女はエリート意識が強いようだね She really *believes she's one of the elite*, doesn't she? ‖ 彼はエリートコースを歩んでいる He's on *the fast track* [*the elite path*]. (➤ the fast track は「出世街道」) ‖ 彼女のお兄さんは外務省のエリート中のエリートだ Her brother is *among the best and the brightest* at the Ministry of Foreign Affairs.

‖エリート社員 an elite employee ‖ エリート主義 elitism.

> **危ないカタカナ語✹ エリート**
> **1** 英語の elite は集合的に「エリートたち」の意味で用いられる. したがって1人を指す場合は one of the elite とするか, a member of the elite とする必要がある.
> **2**「選ばれた」が元の意味なので, 日本語の「エリート」よりもさらに限定された特権階級のニュアンスが強く, しばしば軽蔑的な響きがある.

エリカ 《植物》an **erica**.

えりくび 襟首 ▶髪を襟首にかかるくらいまでカットしてください Please cut my hair so that it will just touch my *collar*.

えりごのみ 選り好み ▶彼は食べ物をえり好みする(=食べ物にうるさい) He *is fussy about* what he eats. ‖ 彼女は洋服のえり好みが激しい She *is very choosy* [*picky*] *about* her clothes.

えりすぐり 選りすぐり ▶当店はえりすぐりのワインをそろえております We offer a wide range of *select wines*.

▶M大学にはえりすぐりのラグビー選手が入学する The *very top* rugby players enter M University.

えりすぐる 選りすぐる select +㊐ (比較・検討して); **pick** (**out**) (選び出す; インフォーマルな言い方)

▶彼らはその神社を再建するのに腕利きの宮大工をえりすぐった They *selected* [*picked*] the most skillful of all the (shrine) carpenters to rebuild the shrine.

えりぬき 選り抜きの select (最高のものと判断された); **choice** (多くの中から1つ良いものとして選ばれた) ▶昔はえり抜きのごく少数の者だけしか大学へ行かなかった Formerly only a *select* few went to college. ‖ 当店はえり抜きのワインを取りそろえております We have a large assortment of *choice* wines.

えりまき 襟巻き a **scarf**, a **muffler**; 《英また》a **comforter** (長い毛織りの) ▶襟巻きをする[外す] put on [take off] *a scarf* (➤「襟巻きをしている」は wear a scarf). →マフラー.

えりわける 選り分ける pick out (選ぶ); **sort out** (分ける) ▶ホームレスの男はゴミの中から使えるものをえり分けていた The homeless man was *picking out* [*sorting out*] any usable items from the trash.

エリンギ a **king oyster** [**king trumpet**] **mushroom**, an ***eringi* mushroom**.

え

える 得る **get** +目（「手に入れる」の意の一般語）; **gain** +目（有利なもの, ためになるものを首尾よく）; **obtain** +目（目的のものを努力して）; **acquire** +目（目的のものを時間をかけて）; **win** +目（勝ち取る）; **earn** +目（働いて得る）▶金を得る *get* money ‖ 当局の許可を得る *obtain* permission from the authorities ‖ 学習によって知識を得る *obtain* [*acquire*] knowledge from study（➤（×）learn knowledge とは言わない）‖ 一等賞を得る *win* first prize ‖ 生活費を得る *earn* [*gain*] one's living.
▶彼はその発明で富と名声を得た He *gained* fame and wealth through the invention. ／The invention brought him fame and fortune. ‖ 努力なしには何も得られない Nothing can *be gained* without effort. ‖ こんなチャンスは二度と得られないよ You'll never *get* this kind of chance again. ‖ そのセミナーに出席したが, 得るところはあまりなかった I attended the seminar, but I didn't *get* much out of it.
☛ -せざるをえない（⇀見出語）

エルエル 1 **LL**（➤ language laboratory の日本式略称）.
2 an **extra-large size**.

エルサイズ Lサイズ a **large size** ▶Lサイズのソックス *large-size*(*d*) socks ‖ フライドポテトのLサイズ *large* French fries.

エルサレム **Jerusalem** /dʒərúːsələm/（イスラエルの首都）.

エルディーケー ⚠ **LDK は Living, Dining, Kitchen の頭文字から作った和製略語で, 英語では通じない.**
▶4LDKのマンションに住む live in a condominium *with a living room, a combined dining room /kitchen* [*an eat-in kitchen*] *and four other rooms*.

エルニーニョ **El Niño** /el níːnjoʊ/（➤ スペイン語で「神の子」の意）.

エレガント **elegant** ▶エレガントな装い [女性] an *elegant* dress [lady] ‖ エレガントにふるまう behave *elegantly*.

エレキギター an **electric guitar**.

エレクトーン an **electronic organ** [**piano**]（➤ Electone は商標名）.

エレクトロニクス **electronics** /ɪlèktrɑ́ːnɪks/.

エレジー an **elegy**.

エレベーター 《米》an **elevator** /élɪvèɪtəʳ/, 《英》a **lift**
▶エレベーターを降りる get out of [step off] the *elevator* ‖ 私たちはエレベーターで1階まで下りた We took the *elevator* down to the first floor. ／《英》We took the *lift* down to the ground floor.（➤「エレベーターに乗る」は take an elevator [a lift]）.
《参考》混んだエレベーターを降りる場合,「すみません, ちょっと通してください」などと言うが, 英語ではそれを Excuse me, may I get through? ／Please let me pass (through). ／Can I get by, please? などと言う.

エロチック **erotic** ▶エロチックな絵 an *erotic* picture.

エロほん エロ本 a **dirty book**（わいせつな本）; **pornography, porn, porno**（➤ 三者とも集合的に「ポルノ」の意）.

[1]**えん 円** 1【円形】a **circle** ▶円の中心 the center of *a circle* ‖ 円を3つ描きなさい Draw three *circles*. ‖ 子供たちは火の周りに円を作って座った The children sat *in a circle* around the fire.
2【日本の貨幣単位】**yen** /jen/（➤ 複数でも s をつけない）▶1000円の紙幣 a 1,000-*yen* bill [《英》note] ‖ あいにく500円玉しかありません Sorry, I have only a five hundred-*yen* coin on me.
▶そのノートは200円です That notebook costs two hundred *yen*. ‖ 今1ドルは何円ですか How much is a dollar *in yen* now? ／*How many yen* is a dollar now? ‖ 1000ドルは日本円にするといくらですか How much is 1,000 dollars in *Japanese yen*? ‖ 円が値上がり[値下がり]している *The yen* is rising [falling].
☛ 円高, 円安（⇀見出語）

[2]**えん 縁** 1【巡り合わせ】a **karmic connection** [**relation**] ▶こうして知り合いになれたご縁（＝関係）を大切にしていきたい Now that we've gotten to know each other, I'd like to keep up our *relationship* (in the future). ‖ 縁があったらまた会おう I hope we can meet again someday.（英語では「いつかまた会えることを期待する」のように考える）‖ ぼくは明美と一緒になりたかったが縁がなかった I had hoped to marry Akemi, but it *didn't work out*.（「成就しなかった」と考える）‖ これをご縁によろしく I hope we can have a good relationship [can be good partners] (in the future). ‖ 不思議な縁でまた信夫に会った *By a curious coincidence*, I ran into Nobuo again.（➤「縁」を「偶然」に置き換える）‖ 彼女はなぜか縁遠い Somehow, she has *little prospect of getting married*. ‖ パソコンはうちのおばあちゃんには縁遠い Computers are *alien to* my grandmother.
ことわざ 袖触れ合うも他生の縁 Even a chance encounter is predestined (by the karma of a previous life).
ことわざ 縁は異なもの味なもの You can't predict or know how a man and a woman will meet.
2【人と人とのつながり; 血縁】▶飲んだくれの亭主とはじきに縁が切れると思うわ I think I'll *divorce* my alcoholic husband soon.（➤ divorce は「離婚する」）‖ 私はあの女性とは縁もゆかりもない I *have nothing to do with* that woman.（➤ have nothing to do with は「…と無関係である」の意.「あの女性とは縁が深い」なら I have a deep connection with that woman. とする）.
▶息子とはとっくの昔に親子の縁を切っている We *disowned* our son a long time ago.（➤ disown は「勘当する」）‖ あの人は皇室と縁続きにあるそうだ He is said to *be related to* the royal family.
ことわざ 金の切れ目が縁の切れ目 When money goes, so do friends. ／Out of money, out of friends.
3【つながり, 関係】▶この仕事とはまだ縁が切れない It seems I *am* still *stuck with* this job. ‖ これまでスポーツとはほとんど縁のなかった私だが, この年になってテニスに熱中している I *had little interest in* sports before, but now at this age, I have suddenly become crazy about tennis.
☛ 縁結び（⇀見出語）

えんいん 遠因 a **distant** [**remote**] **cause**.

えんえい 遠泳 a **long-distance swim** ▶全校生徒で遠泳を行った The entire school took *a long-distance swim*.
‖遠泳大会 a long-distance swim meet.

えんえきほう 演繹法 **deduction**.

えんえん 延々 ▶試験は延々5時間に及んだ The examination lasted five *long* hours. ‖ その政治家は延々と話し続けた That politician just *kept on* talking.
▶綿花畑が延々と続いている The cotton field stretches *as far as the eye can see* [*reach*].（➤

「見渡す限り」の意).

1**えんか 演歌** (an) ***enka***
日本紹介 ✉ **演歌は恋愛に絡む恨みつらみや人の定めなどを歌った日本の歌です. 第二次大戦後よく作られるようになりました. 若い人より年配者が好みます.「こぶし」と呼ばれる節回しは演歌独特のものです** *Enka* are Japanese-style ballads about subjects such as the grudges and bitterness accompanying love and personal tragedy. Many *enka* were composed after World War Ⅱ. They are more popular with older people than with the younger generation. '*Kobushi*,' which is something like a tremolo, is a unique characteristic of *enka*.

2**えんか 塩化**
‖**塩化水素** hydrogen chloride /klɔ́:raɪd/ ‖**塩化ナトリウム** sodium chloride ‖**塩化ビニール** vinyl /váınl/ chloride ‖**塩化物** a chloride.

1**えんかい 宴会** an ***enkai*(-party)**; a **banquet** (改まった, または多人数の) ▶**宴会を開く** throw *an enkai (-party)* /hold *a banquet*.
‖**宴会場** a room for an *enkai* (-party), a banquet hall.

2**えんかい 沿海** a **coast**
‖**沿海漁業** coastal fishery.

えんがい 塩害 **damage from salt water.**

えんかく 沿革 **history** ▶**当社の沿革** our (company's) *history*.

えんかくいりょう 遠隔医療 **remote medical care.**

えんかくがくしゅう 遠隔学習 **distance learning.**

えんかくそうさ 遠隔操作 **remote control.**

えんかつ 円滑な **smooth** /smu:ð/ ▶経営陣の切り替えはあまり**円滑に**いっていない The changeover in management is not going very *smoothly*.

えんがわ 縁側 an ***engawa***
日本紹介 ✉ **縁側は家の1階の内側, 和室との間に庭に面して取り付けられた板敷きの間(ま)です. 部屋とは障子で, 庭とはガラス戸で仕切られているのがふつうです. 都会では縁側のある家は珍しくなってきています** An *engawa* is a wooden deck or veranda(h) outside a Japanese-style room facing the garden on the first floor. It is partitioned from the room by sliding screens and is sometimes enclosed by sliding glass doors (that open out to the garden). Houses with *engawa* have become rare in cities.

えんがん 沿岸 **the coast** ▶私の町は瀬戸内海**沿岸**にある My town is on *the coast* of the Seto Inland Sea. ‖船は日本海**沿岸**を航行した The ship sailed along *the coast* of the Japan Sea.
‖**沿岸漁業** coastal [inshore] fishery.

1**えんき 延期** (a) **postponement** /poʊstpóʊnmənt/, (a) **deferment** (➤ 後者はより堅い語) **━動 延期する** **postpone** +目, **put off** (➤ 後者は「延ばす」という日本語に近い); **defer** /dɪfə́:r/ (➤ 前の2つよりも堅い語) ▶試合を**延期する** *postpone* [*put off*] a game ‖支払いを**延期する** *postpone* [*defer*] payment.
▶学園祭の**延期**に生徒たちはブーブー言った The students complained about the *postponement* of the school festival. ‖天気が悪かったので運動会は次の日曜日まで**延期された** Our athletic meet *was postponed* [*was put off*] till next Sunday due to bad weather.

2**えんき 塩基** 《化学》 a **base**
‖**塩基配列** a base sequence.

1**えんぎ 演技** (a) **performance ━動 演技する perform**
▶秀吉を演じた彼の**演技**はすばらしかった His *performance* in acting the part of Hideyoshi was excellent. ‖彼 [彼女] は**演技がうまい** He [She] is *a good actor* [*actress*].
▶《比喩的》芳美が失恋したって泣いてたけど, あれは絶対**演技**よ Yoshimi was crying, saying she had had her heart broken, but I'm sure she was putting on *an act*.

2**えんぎ 縁起** ▶こいつぁあ朝から**縁起がいい**わ This is *a good sign* for the rest of the day! ‖西洋では鏡が割れるのは**縁起が悪い** (=凶事の前兆) とされる In the West, to break a mirror is considered *a bad* [*an ill*] *omen*. ‖彼は**縁起を担ぐ** He is *superstitious*. (➤「迷信深い」の意) ‖**縁起でもないことを言わないでくれ** Don't say that—you'll bring (on) *bad luck*.
《参考》日本人は災難よけのつもりで「縁起でもない!」と言うが, 英語国民は Knock (on) wood. とか《英》では Touch wood! などと言いながら, 身近にある木(製品)に触れたり, Keep your fingers crossed. と言いながら, 2本の指(人さし指と中指)を組んだりしてこの意を表す.
▶招き猫は商売人にとっては**縁起物**です 'Beckoning cat' statues are believed to *bring good luck* to merchants. ‖ 対話 「けさ茶柱が立ってたよ」「それは**縁起がいいじゃない**」"I saw a tea stem floating upright in my tea this morning." "That's *a good sign* [*omen*]."

えんきょく 婉曲な **euphemistic** /jù:fəmístɪk/ ▶「開発途上国」は「低開発国」の**婉曲表現**だ 'Developing country' is *a euphemism* for 'underdeveloped country.' (➤ euphemism は「婉曲語法」) ‖彼はぼくの申し出を**婉曲に**断った He turned down my offer *in a roundabout way*. (➤ roundabout は「遠回しの, 間接の, 婉曲の」の意).

えんきょり 遠距離 a **long distance** ▶**遠距離**恋愛 *long-distance* love ‖毎日の**遠距離**通学 [通勤] は楽じゃない Going such *a long way to school* [*work*] every day is no fun at all.

えんきん 遠近 ▶**遠近法**で風景画を描く paint a landscape in *perspective* ‖**遠近両用の眼鏡**をかける wear *bifocals* ‖眼帯をすると**遠近感**が狂うね When you wear an eye patch, your *sense of distance* is distorted, isn't it?

えんぐみ 縁組み **marriage** (結婚); **adoption** (養子縁組み) ▶両家は去年**縁組み**をした The two families were united by *marriage* last year. ‖その夫婦は孤児と**養子縁組みをした** The couple *adopted* the orphan.

えんぐん 援軍 **reinforcements** /rì:ɪnfɔ́:rsmənts/ (➤ 複数形で用いる).

1**えんけい 円形** a **circle**; a **round shape**
‖**円形劇場** an amphitheater /ǽmfəθi:əṭər/.

2**えんけい 遠景** a **distant view** (遠い景色); **the background** (背景).

1**えんげい 園芸** **gardening, horticulture** /hɔ́:rṭəkʌ̀ltʃər/
‖**園芸家** a gardener ‖**園芸植物** garden plants ‖**園芸センター** a garden center, a nursery ‖**園芸展示会** a gardening exhibition, a horticultural exhibition [show].

「**園芸用語」のいろいろ** **移植ごて** trowel /**植木ばさみ** shears, clippers /**植木鉢** flowerpot /**刈り込み** pruning, trimming /**刈り込みばさみ** pruner, pruning shears /**熊手** rake /**鍬(くわ)** hoe

え

／殺虫剤 insecticide／シャベル shovel／じょうろ watering can／除草剤 weed-killer, herbicide／鋤(すき) spade／スコップ scoop, shovel／堆肥 compost／接ぎ木 graft／トピアリー topiary／苗 seedling／肥料 fertilizer／プランター planter／水やり watering

2えんげい 演芸 **entertainment**
‖演芸会 a variety show ‖演芸場 a variety hall ‖大衆演芸 mass entertainment.

エンゲージリング an **engagement ring** (➤ (×) engage ring とはしない).

えんげき 演劇 (a) **drama, the theater** ; a **play** (芝居) ▶演劇を勉強する study *drama* ‖演劇の道を志す pursue a career in *the theater* ‖大学生時代は演劇に熱中した When I was a college student I was into *drama*.
‖演劇部 a drama [theatrical] club.

エンゲルけいすう エンゲル係数 an **Engel's coefficient** ▶わが家はエンゲル係数が高い *The Engel's coefficient* of our family is high.

1えんこ 縁故 **connections** (➤この意味では通例複数形) ▶縁故を頼って上京する go [come] to Tokyo trusting in one's *connections* ‖彼は縁故でこの会社に入った He joined this company *through personal connections*.

2えんこ ▶雪の中で車がえんこした My car *conked out* [*got stuck*] in the snow. (➤前者は「故障した」の意のくだけた言い方, 後者は「動けなくなった」の意).

3えんこ 円弧 an **arc of a circle.**

えんご 援護 **support** (支援・支持) ; **help, assistance** (手伝い・助力 ; 後者は堅い語) ▶その団体は貧しい人々を援護している The organization *gives support* [*assistance*] *to* poor people. ‖地震の被災者に援護の手を差し伸べる *give a helping hand* to the victims of an earthquake.

えんこん 怨恨 a **grudge** /grʌdʒ/ (恨み) ▶えん恨による犯行 a crime committed by someone with a *grudge*.

えんざい 冤罪 a **false charge** [**accusation**] ▶彼はえん罪に20年間苦しんだ He has suffered twenty years for *a crime he didn't commit*. ‖彼女はやっとえん罪を晴らすことができた At last she was able to *clear herself of the false charge*.

えんさん 塩酸 **hydrochloric** /hàɪdrəklɔ́ːrɪk/ **acid.**

えんざん 演算 (a) **calculation,** (an) **operation** ▶算術の四則演算 *the four operations* of arithmetic.
‖演算子 an operator ‖演算能力 computing power.

えんし 遠視 《米》 **farsightedness, hyperopia** /hàɪpəróʊpiə/, 《英》 **longsightedness**
▶父はひどい遠視だ My father is terribly *farsighted* [*longsighted*].

1えんじ 園児 a **kindergarten child,** a **kindergartener.**

2えんじ 臙脂 **deep red** ▶えんじ色のブラウス a *cochineal* blouse (➤ cochineal /kátʃɪniːl/ はエンジムシから採取した赤色).

エンジニア an **engineer** /èndʒɪníəʳ/.

1えんしゅう 円周 (a) **circumference** /səʳkʌ́mfərəns/ ▶この円の円周は 3 メートルある This circle has *a circumference* of three meters. ／This circle is three meters *in circumference*.
‖円周率 pi /paɪ/, the ratio of the circumference of a circle to its diameter, 《記号》 π.

2えんしゅう 演習 **1**【大学の】an **exercise** ; a **seminar** /sémɪnɑːʳ/ (ゼミナール) ▶英文法の演習 *exercises* in English grammar ‖英文学演習に出席する attend *a seminar* in English literature.
2【軍隊の】a **military exercise, maneuvers,** a **drill** ▶自衛隊は大演習を行った The SDF carried out major *maneuvers*.

えんじゅく 円熟 **maturity** ▶円熟した歌手 a *mature* singer ‖彼はこの 5 年間で大いに円熟した He *has* greatly *matured* during the past five years. ‖彼の芸は円熟の域に達している His performance has attained *maturity*.

えんしゅつ 演出 **direction** 一動 演出する **direct** +目 (➤イギリスの演劇界では produce ということもある) ▶この劇はA氏が演出した This play *was directed* by Mr. A.
‖演出家 a director, 《英また》 a producer.

えんじょ 援助 **help, assistance** (手伝い・助力 ; 後者は堅い語) ; **aid** (困っている人への積極的な ; 堅い語) 一動 援助する **help** +目, **assist** +目, **aid** +目
▶援助を申し出る offer *help* ‖家を失った人々に援助の手を差し伸べる give *aid* [lend *a helping hand*] to homeless people.
▶弟が大学を卒業するまでずっと援助する *see* one's brother *through* college ‖私はおじから学費の援助を受けている I am getting *help* from my uncle [My uncle is *helping* me (*out*)] with school expenses. ‖私は彼の事業を援助した I *aided* [*assisted*] him in his business.
▶おじ夫婦は父の会社が倒産しかけたとき多大な援助をしてくれた My uncle and aunt *helped* my father *out* a lot when his company was on the verge of bankruptcy.
‖援助交際 (schoolgirl prostitution disguised as) compensated dating (➤「報酬をもらうデート (に見せかけた女子学生の売春)」の意 ; カッコ内は売春であることを明確にする場合).

エンジョイ ▶仕事ばかりしていないでもっと人生をエンジョイしたら？ Instead of just working all the time, how about *enjoying* your life more？

1えんしょう 炎症 (an) **inflammation** (赤く腫れること) ; a **cold sore** (口唇ヘルペス) ▶傷口が炎症を起こしている. すぐに医者へ行ったほうがいい The wound *is inflamed* [*is infected*]. You had better go to a doctor right away. (➤ be infected は「化膿(かのう)している」の意).

2えんしょう 延焼 ▶延焼を免れる escape *catching fire* ‖石油コンビナートへの延焼は何としても食い止めなくては We must by all means stop the fire from *spreading* to the petrochemical complex.

えんじょう 炎上 **1**【火事で燃え上がる】▶鹿児島沖で漁船が炎上した A shipping boat *went up in flames* off the coast of Kagoshima.
2【インターネットで】▶私のブログが炎上した My blog *was flamed* [*was swarmed*]. (➤ flame は「中傷メールで攻撃する」, swarm は「たくさんのものであふれ返る」).

えんじる 演じる **play** +目, **act** +目 (➤後者はやや堅い語) ; **perform** +目 (演技をする) ▶彼はテレビドラマで将軍を演じた He *played* a shogun in a TV drama. ‖私はハムレットを演じた I *acted* (the part of) Hamlet. ／I *played* Hamlet.
▶彼の演じた織田信長はひどかった His *performance* as Oda Nobunaga was terrible. (➤ performance は「演技」).
▶彼女は人前では貞淑な妻を演じている (＝ふりをしている)

She *pretends* to be a virtuous wife in public. ▶震災からの復興にはボランティアが重要な役割を演じた Volunteers *played* an important role in (the area's) recovery from the earthquake. ‖ 彼はゆうべの宴会で醜態を演じた He *disgraced himself* at the banquet last night.

えんじん 円陣 a **circle** ▶ナインはダッグアウトの前で円陣を組んだ The nine players *stood in a circle* in front of the dugout.

エンジン an **engine** ▶きのうまたエンジンが故障した Yesterday we had some *engine* trouble again. ‖ 彼はオートバイのペダルを蹴ってエンジンをかけた He kick-started the motorcycle *engine*. ‖ (車の)エンジンをかけておいてくれ Will you *start the engine* for me? (➤「切る」なら動詞は cut, kill, turn off など) ‖ 彼はオートバイのエンジンを吹かした He *gunned* the motorcycle *engine* (into life). (➤ gun は「エンジンを吹かす」の意のインフォーマルな言い方) ‖ エンジンブレーキを使う use *low gear*.
▶《慣用表現》ぼくはどうも午前中はエンジンがかからない It's hard for me to *get* (*myself*) *going* in the morning.

えんしんぶんりき 遠心分離機 a **centrifuge** /séntrɪfjuːdʒ/.

えんしんりょく 遠心力 **centrifugal** /sentrífjəgəl/ **force** ▶洗濯機の脱水機は遠心力を利用したものである The spin dryer in a washing machine utilizes *centrifugal force*.

えんすい 円錐 a **cone** ▶円すい形の塔のある城 a castle with a *conical* tower.

エンスト **engine failure** [**stall**] ▶エンストが起こったら合図をして車を安全な場所まで惰力運転しなさい When you have *engine failure*, signal and try to coast to a safe place.
▶どうもエンジンがおかしくなったみたいだ. よくエンストする There must be something wrong with the engine because it often *stalls*.

> **危ないカタカナ語✹ エンスト**
> エンジンがストップすることから「エンスト」というが, (×)engine stop という英語はない. 英語では engine failure または engine stall という.「エンストした」は The engine stopped [died]. のようにも言うことはできるが, これも stall を動詞に使って The engine stalled. のように表現するほうがよい.

えんせい 遠征 an **expedition**(探検旅行) ; a **visit** (運動選手の) ▶私たちのチームはこの秋アメリカに海外遠征する Our team will *make a* (*playing*) *tour* of the U.S. this fall.
‖遠征隊 an expeditionary force (軍) ; a visiting team (選手団).

えんせいかん 厭世観 **pessimism** /pésəmìzəm/.

えんせき 遠戚 a **distant relative**.

えんぜつ 演説 a **speech** 一動 **演説する** **make** [**give**] **a speech** ▶その会議で彼は環境汚染について演説した At that meeting, he *made* [*gave*] *a speech* on environmental pollution.
‖選挙演説 a campaign speech.

エンゼルフィッシュ 《魚》an **angelfish**.

えんせん 沿線 ▶私の家は山の手線沿線にある My house is *on* the Yamanote Line. ‖ この沿線にはまだ緑が残っている There is still a lot of greenery *along* this railway line.

えんそ 塩素 **chlorine** /klɔ́ːriːn/ ▶このプールは塩素が強すぎて目が痛い The *chlorine* in this pool is too strong and is making my eyes hurt. ‖ このフィルターは水道水の塩素を取り除いてくれる This water filter removes *chlorine* from tap water. ‖ この水道水は塩素で消毒済みだ The tap water here has been disinfected with *chlorine*.
‖塩素ガス chlorine gas.

えんそう 演奏 a (**musical**) **performance** 一動 **演奏する** **play** +目, **perform** +目 ▶バイオリンの生演奏を聴く listen to a *live* violin *performance* ‖ ボストン交響楽団の演奏によるブラームスの第四交響曲 Brahms' Fourth Symphony *played* [*performed*] by the Boston Symphony Orchestra ‖ 彼女は生まれて初めて大観衆の前でピアノの演奏をした For the first time in her life, she *played* [*performed* at] the piano before a large audience.
▶演奏会はあすの午後5時です The *concert* will be held [will be given] at 5 p.m. tomorrow. (➤「独奏会」であれば recital) ‖ 一流演奏家による室内楽コンサート a chamber music concert by first-rate *performers*.
‖演奏曲目 a program (全体) ; a piece on the program (1曲) ‖ 演奏家 a player, a performer, an artist (➤ 最近では artist が好まれる).

えんそく 遠足 an **outing** /áʊṭɪŋ/, an **excursion** /ɪkskɔ́ːʳʒən/ (➤ ともに短い団体旅行を指し, 後者は堅い語. 日帰りであることを明確にしたい場合は前に day をつけるとよい) ; a **hike** (ハイキング) ; a **picnic** (ピクニック) ; a **field trip** (実地見学) ▶日帰りの遠足 a day [day's] *outing*.
▶私たちは学校の遠足で鎌倉へ行った We went to Kamakura on our school *outing* [*excursion*].

えんたい 延滞 ▶彼は家賃を延滞している He's *in arrears* [He's *behind*] with his rent.
‖延滞金 arrears /əríəʳz/.

1**えんだい 遠大な** **grand** ▶遠大な志 a *great* ambition ‖ その独裁者は隣国すべてを征服しようという遠大な計画を立てていた The dictator had concocted a *grand* [*far-reaching*] scheme to conquer all the neighboring countries.

2**えんだい 縁台** an ***endai***, a wooden or bamboo bench for enjoying the evening cool in the summer (➤ 説明的な訳).

えんだか 円高 **appreciation of the yen**(円の騰貴) ; **the strong(er) yen**(強い円) ▶ここ2, 3週間為替相場はやや円高だった *The yen has strengthened* somewhat on the exchange market during the last few weeks.
▶最近は円高ドル安だ Recently, *the yen has strengthened against the dollar*.
‖円高差益 a profit from the strong yen.

1**えんだん 演壇** a **platform** ; a **podium** (講演者・指揮者などが立つ台) ; a **lectern**(原稿を置く台) ▶私は演壇に立つのは苦手なんです I am not good at public speaking.

2**えんだん 縁談** an **offer** [a **proposal**] **of marriage**(結婚の申し込み) ; a **match**(縁組み) ▶その娘には現在3つの縁談がある The girl has three *offers* [*proposals*] *of marriage* at present. ‖ 両親はこの縁談に反対した My parents objected to the *match*.

えんちゃく 延着 ▶列車は事故で40分延着した The train *was delayed* forty minutes because of the accident.

えんちゅう 円柱 a **cylinder** /sílɪndəʳ/ (円筒) ; a **pillar**, a **column**(柱).

え

[1]**えんちょう 延長** **1【長さ・期間の】** (an) **extension** **一動 延長する** **extend** +目(先へ延ばす) ; **prolong** +目(引き延ばす) ▶ビザの延長を申請する apply for *an extension* to one's visa ‖契約期間を延長する *extend* the contract period.
▶予約購読を延長する(=更新する) *renew* one's subscription ‖滞在期間を延長したいのですが I'd like to *extend* my stay. / I want to stay longer. ‖地下鉄は埼玉まで延長された The subway line *was extended* to Saitama.
▶集会は夕刻まで延長された The meeting *was prolonged* into the evening.
‖延長コード an extension cord ‖延長料金 overtime [extension] charge.
2【スポーツの】 ▶延長戦に入る go into *extra innings* (➤野球で;「延長戦になった試合」は an extra-inning game という) / go (into) *overtime* (➤サッカーなどで).
▶巨人は延長11回に3点を入れた The Giants scored three runs in the *11th inning*. (➤この場合 extra をつける必要はない).

[2]**えんちょう 園長** ▶保育園の園長 *the head* of a nursery school ‖動物園の園長 *the head* [*director*] of a zoo (➤ director は大規模な動物園の場合).

エンデミック an **endemic** /endémɪk/ (地方病, 風土病). →パンデミック.

えんでん 塩田 a **saltern**, a **salt pan**.

えんてんか 炎天下 ▶炎天下の甲子園で両チームの熱戦が繰り広げられた A thrilling game between the two teams was fought *under the blazing sun* at Koshien Stadium.

えんとう 円筒 a **cylinder** /sɪ́lɪndəʳ/ ▶こけしは円筒形の胴に球形の頭のものが最も一般的だ *Kokeshi* dolls usually consist of a round head on a *cylindrical* body.

[1]**えんどう 豌豆** a **pea** ▶エンドウの豆をむく take *peas* out of their pods / shell *peas*.

[2]**えんどう 沿道** a **route**(道筋) ▶人々は横綱の優勝パレードを一目見ようと沿道に並んでいた People lined the *route* [*road*] to catch a glimpse of the yokozuna's victory parade.
▶沿道の群衆はそのランナーに声援を送った The crowd *along the street* shouted encouragement to the runner.

えんとつ 煙突 a **chimney**(主に家庭の) ; a **smokestack** (工場・機関車などの) ▶晴れた日には工場の煙突から煙が立ち上るのがよく見える On a clear day you can easily see the smoke pouring out of the factory *smokestacks*.

エンドラン →ヒットエンドラン.

エントリー an **entry** ▶トーナメントにエントリーしているのは今のところ30か国です At present, the number of countries that have *entered* this tournament is thirty. / So far, thirty countries have *entered* this tournament. ‖エントリーナンバー3番 the *entry number* 3.

えんにち 縁日 a **festival day** ▶縁日にはこの通りにいろんな屋台が出る The street is lined with stalls selling various foods on *festival days*.

えんのう 延納 ▶私は家庭の事情で授業料を延納した I *got a tuition deferral* [*deferment*] for family reasons. (➤ deferral /dɪfə́ːrəl/, deferment はともに「延期」の意だが, その動詞 defer に対応する名詞としては後者が好ましいとする見方がある ;「延納を頼む」なら ask for a deferral [deferment]).
▶彼は税務署に税金の延納の申請をした He petitioned the taxation office for *a deferral* [*deferment*] *of payment*.

えんのした 縁の下 ▶野良猫が縁の下に住みついてしまった Homeless cats are living in *the space under the floor* [in *the crawl space*]. (➤ crawl space は「(天井裏や床下などの)狭い空間」).
▶《慣用表現》照明係は舞台劇での縁の下の力持ちだ Lighting technicians are the *unsung heroes* of stage plays. (➤ unsung hero は「詩歌で歌われなかった英雄」が原義で,「報われない功労者」の意).

エンパイアステートビル **the Empire State Building** (ニューヨークにある高層ビル).

えんばく 燕麦 **oats**.

えんばん 円盤 《米》a **disk**, 《英》a **disc** ; a **discus** (競技用の) 《参考》《米》でもレコードやコンパクトディスクは disc とつづる.
‖空飛ぶ円盤 a flying saucer, a UFO (→ユーフォー) ‖円盤投げ the discus throw.

えんぴつ 鉛筆 a **pencil** ▶HBの鉛筆 an HB *pencil* ‖鉛筆の芯 the lead of *a pencil* (➤ lead の発音は /led/ で,「黒鉛」の意) ‖鉛筆で書く write *with a pencil* [*in pencil*].
《参考》アメリカでは鉛筆の硬さを番号で表す. #1 (number one と読む)は日本の鉛筆の B, #2 は HB, #3 は H, #4 は 2 H に当たる. #2 が最も一般的に用いられる.
‖鉛筆削り a pencil sharpener ‖赤鉛筆 a red pencil ‖色鉛筆 a colored pencil.

えんびふく 燕尾服 a **swallow-tailed coat** (➤正式な言い方), a **tailcoat**, **tails**.

えんぶきょく 円舞曲 a **waltz**.

えんぶん 塩分 **salt** ▶このあたりの海水は塩分が多い The seawater in this area has a high *salt* content. ‖彼は腎臓が悪いので塩分を控えた食事をとらなくてはいけない He is on *a low salt diet* because he has kidney trouble.

えんぽう 遠方 ▶遠方に阿蘇山が見える Mt. Aso can be seen *in the distance*. ‖旧友が遠方から訪ねてきた An old friend of mine has come *a long way* [*from far away*] to see me.

えんまく 煙幕 a **smokescreen**.

えんまちょう 閻魔帳 a **teacher's mark** [**grade**] **book** ▶きみの名前をえんま帳につけておこう Your name is going into my *black book*. (➤ black book は「要注意人物をメモしたリスト」).

えんまん 円満な **well-rounded** (バランスよくできた) ; **peaceful** (平和的な) ▶夫婦円満 *a happy married life* ‖彼は円満な人柄だ He has a *well-rounded* personality. ‖できるだけ円満な解決法を見つけてください Find as *peaceful* a solution as possible. / Find as *satisfactory* a settlement as possible. ‖その問題は円満に解決した The problem has been solved *peacefully*.
▶私たち夫婦はいたって円満に暮らしています We are living *in* perfect *harmony*. ‖このたび会社を円満に(=支障なく)退職しました I left the company *without any trouble*.

えんむすび 縁結び **match-making** ▶縁結びの神様にお参りする pay a visit to the shrine of the *matchmaking* god [of the god who *helps to arrange marriages*].

えんめい 延命 ▶私ががんになっても延命措置はとらないでほしい I don't want *life-prolonging measures* to be taken if I get cancer.

‖**延命医療** life-prolonging treatment ‖ **延命装置** a life-prolonging device 《参考》延命装置を外すことをくだけた言い方で pull the plug と言う.

えんもく 演目

‖**演目表** a program (➤ 項目の1つは an item).

えんやす 円安 **depreciation of the yen**(円の下落) ; **the weak(er) yen**(弱い円) ▶最近相場は**円安**続きだった Recent tendencies in the exchange market have been for a continued *weakening of the yen.* ‖ここ2, 3週間, **円安ドル高**だ *The yen has weakened against the dollar* in the last few weeks.

えんゆうかい 園遊会 a **garden party.**

えんよう 遠洋 an **ocean** ▶**遠洋**航海に出る set out on *an ocean voyage.*

‖**遠洋漁業** deep-sea fishery.

えんりょ 遠慮

> **《解説》遠慮と reserve**
> (1)自分の意見をはっきり言うことが美徳とされる西洋では「遠慮」という考え方は日本と比べると希薄. したがって「遠慮しないで」は「ちゅうちょしないで」,「遠慮なく」は「自由に, 率直に」と考えて訳す.
> (2)「遠慮」に近い英語に reserve があるが, これは自分の気持ちや態度を抑制することをいう. 日本語の「遠慮」にはほかの人への配慮のニュアンスがあるので, この意味ではむしろ consideration が近い.

1【気兼ね, 控えめ】▶質問があったら**遠慮しないで**先生に聞きなさい If you have any questions, *don't hesitate to* ask your teacher. ‖何か困ったことがあったら**遠慮しないで**いつでも私のところに相談にいらっしゃい If you should have a problem, *feel free to* come to me (for advice). (➤ feel free to do は don't hesitate to do とほぼ同意で,「気軽に…する, 自由に…する」の意).

▶私は言いたいことを**遠慮なく**言った I said *frankly* what I wanted to say. ／I spoke my mind. (➤ speak one's mind は「言おうと思っていたことを言う」の意のインフォーマルな表現) ‖(おすしを)**遠慮なく**召し上がってください Please *help yourself* (*to* sushi). (➤ help oneself は「自分で取って食べる」の意) ／Please have *all* the sushi *you want.* ‖最近は家族に**遠慮して**家ではカラオケをやらないことにしている *Considering* [*Taking into consideration*] *the feelings* of my family, I've recently given up singing karaoke songs at home.

▶ **対話**「このローストチキン, 頂いていいですか」「どうぞ**遠慮なく**(召し上がれ)」"Can I have some of this roast chicken?" "*Please go ahead.* ／*Please help yourself.*"

▶私に**遠慮は**いらないから何日でも泊まっていってよ It's no problem for me, so you'*re free to* stay here as long as you wish. ‖入ってよ, ポール. **遠慮しないで** Come in, Paul. *Don't be shy.* (● この場合の「遠慮しないで」は訳例のように「恥ずかしがらないで」と考えて Don't be shy. とするのが英語的. Don't stand on ceremony. という言い方もあるが, これは「ご遠慮なさらないでください」に近い堅い言い方).

▶武のホストファミリーは**遠慮しない**(＝くつろぐ)よう促した Takeshi's host family urged him to *make himself at home.* ‖彼はいつも私に**遠慮のない**批評をしてくれる He always gives me an *honest* [a *frank*] opinion. ‖彼女はしゅうとめにいつも**遠慮しながら**暮らしている She always behaves *with constraint* toward her mother-in-law. (➤ constraint は「窮屈さ, 気兼ね」) ‖彼女は**遠慮がちに**「私も仲間に入れて」と言った She *shyly* asked, "May I join you?" ／ She *shyly* asked if she could join us. ‖日本人は**遠慮深い**国民だとよく言われる It is often said that the Japanese are a *reserved* people. ‖彼は他人の仕事をいつも**遠慮会釈なく**批判する He criticizes others' work *without restraint.*

2【差し控えること, 辞退すること】▶彼女の気持ちを傷つけたくなかったので, 真実を告げることを**遠慮した** I *held back from* speaking the truth because I didn't want to hurt her feelings. (➤ hold back from で「…を控える」) ‖車内での携帯電話のご使用は**ご遠慮ください** *Kindly refrain from* using cellphones on the train.

✉ **かぜ気味で気分がよくありませんので, このご招待は遠慮させていただきます** *I'd like to decline* this invitation since I have a slight cold and don't feel well. (➤ decline は「(丁寧に)断る」の意).

▶ **対話**「すみませんが, ここではたばこは**ご遠慮願います**」「あ, すみません」"Excuse me, but *would you mind not* smoking here?" "I'm sorry."

☞ **無遠慮** (→見出語)

えんろ 遠路 ▶**遠路**はるばるお越しいただき恐縮でございます Thank you very much for coming such *a long way.* (●「恐縮する」は英語では「感謝する」と考える) ‖彼女は**遠路**はるばる出迎えに来てくれた She's come *from quite a distance* just to meet me.

お・オ

お 尾 a **tail** ▶クロは私に気づいて尾を振った Kuro recognized me and *wagged his tail.*
▶《慣用表現》日本経済は世界金融危機の影響が尾を引いて, まだ完全には立ち直れていない The Japanese economy has not yet fully recovered due to the *lingering* effects from the global financial crisis.

おあいそ お愛想 ▶彼女はお愛想(＝お世辞)を言っているだけだよ She is simply paying you a *compliment.* ／She's just being polite. (➤「社交辞令で言っているだけ」)／She's just saying that.
▶《料理店などで客が》おあいそ(＝勘定)をお願いします *Check* [*Bill*], *please!* (➤ bill は主に《英》).

おあいにくさま お生憎様 ▶《皮肉で》おあいにくさま! *Sorry about that!* ‖ おあいにくさま, その手には乗りませんよ *Too bad for you!* I won't fall for that!

オアシス an **oasis** /ouéɪsɪs/ [複 **oases** /ouéɪsiːz/] ▶ベシャールはサハラ砂漠のオアシスだ Béchar is *an oasis* in the Sahara Desert.
▶《比喩的》その喫茶店はサラリーマンのオアシスになっている That coffee shop is *a sort of haven* for office workers. (➤ haven /héɪvən/ は「避難所」).

おあずけ お預け ▶《犬などに向かって》「お預け」"*Stay!*" (➤「よし」は "O.K.").
▶父がかぜをひいたため旅行は来週の日曜までお預けになった Because of Dad's cold, the trip *was put off* till next Sunday. (➤「延期された」の意) ‖ 宿題が終わるまでこのケーキはお預けよ *You can't have* this piece of cake until you finish your homework.

おあつらえむき お誂え向き ▶このアパートは独身者にはおあつらえ向きだ This apartment would be *ideal* for a single person. ‖ ハイキングにはおあつらえ向きの天気だ This is *ideal* hiking weather.

1**おい 甥** a **nephew** /néfjuː, név-/ ▶私にはおいは3人いるが, めいはいない I have three *nephews* but no nieces.

2**おい 老い** **old age**(老齢) ▶祖母はとても元気で老いを知らないようだ My grandmother is so healthy she doesn't seem to feel her *age* at all. ‖ 老いは足からとよく言われる It's often said that *getting old* [*aging*] starts from your legs. ‖ 祖父は老いの一徹で80歳の今も現場で働き続けている Even now at eighty, my grandfather, *with the stubbornness* [*obstinacy*] *of age*, keeps working on site. ‖ 老いも若きもその祭りを待ちわびている *Both young and old* are looking forward to the festival. (➤ 語順に注意).

3**おい** ▶おい, おまえ聞いてるのか? *Hey!* Are you listening to me? ‖ おい, きみ. 待てよ! *Hey*, you! Wait! (● この日本文は見知らぬ他人に声をかける場面を想定しているが,「きみ」が友人・知人であれば英語では you とは言わず, 相手の名(例えば John など)を言うのがふつう).

> **直訳の落とし穴「おい!」**
> 日本人の夫婦間であれば,「おい[おーい], ビールを持ってきてくれ!」というような言い方は珍しくないが, これを直訳して (×)Hey, bring me a beer! と言うのはたとえ夫婦間であっても横暴な命令になる. 英語では例えば, Mary [Honey], could you bring me a beer? というように, 相手の名(訳例では Mary)や愛情を示す呼びかけ語(訳例では honey)を用いるのがふつう.

おいあげる 追い上げる **catch up** 《with》(追いつく); **close in** 《on》(迫る) ▶もっとスピードを出したら? ほかの車がどんどん追い上げてくるよ You'd better drive faster. The other cars are *catching up* fast. ‖ ゴール近くで2位の選手がぐんぐん追い上げた Coming toward the finish, the second runner *closed in on* the first.

おいうち 追い討ち ▶次々とまるで追い討ちをかけるように不幸が彼らを襲った *As though to heap misfortune on misery*, a run of bad luck befell them. (➤ befell は befall(悪いことが降りかかる)の過去形).

おいえげい お家芸 one's **specialty** ▶かつて柔道は日本のお家芸だった Judo used to be one sport that Japanese athletes *were especially good at.*

おいえそうどう お家騒動 a **family disturbance**; **family strife.**

1**おいおい 追々** **gradually**(だんだんに); **in (due) time** (そのうち) ▶おいおい仕事にも慣れますよ You will *gradually* get used to the job. ‖ 詳細についてはおいおいお話しいたします I'll tell you about the details *in time.*

2**おいおい** ▶母親は無事救助された息子を抱き締めながら, おいおい泣いた The mother hugged her son, who had been rescued safely, and *cried her eyes* [*her heart*] *out.*

おいおとす 追い落とす ▶フセインは政敵を追い落として大統領の座に就いた Hussein *drove* his political enemy *away* [*out*] and assumed the presidency.

おいかえす 追い返す **send back** ▶犬が駅までついてきたので追い返さなければならなかった Our dog followed me to the station, so I had to *send* him *back.*

おいかける 追いかける **run after**(あとを追う); **chase** +(目)(捕まえようと激しく追う) ▶犬は子猫を追いかけた The dog *ran after* the kitten. ‖ 彼はオートバイに乗って全速力でその車を追いかけた He *chased* the car on his motorcycle at top speed.
▶彼は女の子の尻ばかり追いかけている He's always *chasing* girls. ‖ 先に出発してくれ. すぐ追いかける(＝追いつく)から Go on ahead. We'll soon *catch up with* you.
▶彼女はいつも流行を追いかけている She always *follows* [*keeps up with*] the latest fashions. (➤ 後者は「遅れないようにする」).

おいかぜ 追い風 a **fair** [**favorable**] **wind**, (a) **tail wind** ▶追い風に乗って帆走する *sail before the wind* ‖ 風は追い風だ The wind is *favorable.* ‖ 追い風で飛行機は30分早く着いた Because there was *a tail wind*, the airplane arrived 30 minutes ahead of schedule. (➤ tail wind は通例船や飛行機についていう).
▶景気回復が追い風となって与党が圧勝した The recovering economy *contributed to* the ruling party's overwhelming victory. (➤ contribute

to は「…に貢献する」).

おいこし 追い越し ▶《標識》追い越し禁止 No Passing／《英また》No Overtaking.

‖追い越し車線 a fast lane, a passing lane,《英また》an overtaking lane.

おいこす 追い越す **1【追いついて先に出る】pass** +㊀, **overtake** +㊀ ▶登校の途中早川先生を追い越した I *passed* Mr. Hayakawa on my way to school.

▶彼の車はバスを追い越した His car *passed* [*overtook*] the bus. (➤ overtake はまれに「追いつく」の意になる場合もある)／His car *got past* [*got ahead of*] the bus.

2【能力・業績などで】outstrip +㊀ (…を上回る) ; **surpass** /səˈpǽs/ +㊀ (…をしのぐ) ▶彼はライバルたちに追い越されてしまった He *was outstripped* by his rivals. ‖姉は母の身長を追い越した My older sister is *taller* than my mother *now*. ‖彼は数学で友だちを追い越した He *surpassed* [*beat*] his friends in mathematics. (➤ beat は「打ち負かす」の意のインフォーマルな語) ‖「X 社に追いつき, 追い越せ」がわが社のスローガンだ Our company's slogan is "*Catch up with* X Company and *pass* [*get ahead of*] them!"

おいこみ 追い込み ▶選挙戦はいよいよ追い込みに入った The election campaign *has entered its final stage*.

おいこむ 追い込む **drive** +㊀ ▶牛を囲いに追い込む *drive* the cows *into* the enclosure.

▶私の発言が彼を窮地に追い込むことになってしまった I *drove* him *into a corner* with my remarks.／My remarks *had* him *in a corner*. ‖あの失敗で彼は窮地に追い込まれている That one failure *has driven* him *into great difficulties*.

おいさき 老い先 ▶「わたしゃもう老い先短いんだから, 大事にしてちょうだいよ」とおばあちゃんはよくぼくに言う "I *haven't got much longer to live*, so you'd better be nice to me!" my grandmother often says to me.

おいしい **good** (味・香りなどがよい; ふつう, … tastes [is] good. (…はおいしい) の形で用い, 名詞の前ではあまり使わない) ; **tasty** (味覚を楽しませてくれる) ; **delicious** (とてもおいしい)

▶おいしいリンゴ a *delicious* apple (➤ a good apple は「傷んでいないリンゴ」) ‖このアップルパイはおいしい [とてもおいしい] The apple pie *tastes good* [*tastes great*]. (➤ (×) The apple pie has a good taste. としない) ‖おいしい水 *sweet* water (➤この sweet は「悪臭・塩分・苦味などのない」の意) ‖おいしそうなごちそう *appetizing* dishes (➤ appetizing は「(色や香りなどで)食欲をそそる」の意の形容詞) ‖山のおいしい空気を胸いっぱいに吸い込む breathe in the *fresh, crisp mountain air* (➤ crisp は「すがすがしい」).

▶うーん, (これは)おいしいね Mmm ... this *tastes good* [*nice*]. (➤「いい味がする」の意で nice のほうがよりくだけた語; Yummy! /jʌ́mi/ と言うこともあるが子供っぽい言い方) ‖このケーキ, 本当においしいわ This cake *is* [*tastes*] really *good*. ‖たまには何か(本当に)おいしいものを食べに行きたいわね How about going out for something (really) *good* for a change? (➤ delicious を用いてもよい).

▶あのレストランはおいしい中華料理を出す They serve *good* Chinese food [dishes] at that restaurant. ‖どこかおいしいラーメン屋さん知らない? Do you know (of) any *good* ramen shops? ‖体調が悪いと何を食べてもおいしくない *Nothing tastes good* when you don't feel well.

✉ **(ホストファミリーに) あなたの焼いてくれたチェリーパイはとてもおいしかったです. マーブルケーキもおいしかったです** The cherry pie you baked for me was *really good* [*delicious*／*scrumptious*]. Your marble cake was *good*, too. (➤ scrumptious は「とてもおいしい」の意のくだけた言い方).

▶《比喩的》おいしい話には気をつけたほうがいいよ You should beware of *tempting* [*enticing*] *offers*. (➤ enticing は /ɪntáɪsɪŋ/ と発音).

> **直訳の落とし穴「おいしい」「おいしく頂く」**
>
> (1)「おいしい」= delicious と思い込んでいる学習者がいるが, ふだん使う「おいしい」は good である. delicious は「(感心するほど)美味な」に相当するやや改まった語で, 料理を作ってくれた人への褒めことばとしてはよく用いる. また, 食べながら, あるいは今食べたものを「おいしい」のつもりで, (×) (It's) good taste. と言う日本人が多いが, これは「いい趣味です」の意味にしかならない. (It) tastes good. が正しい.
>
> (2)「食事をおいしく頂く」を (×)eat a meal deliciously とは言わない. enjoy a meal がふつうで,「ゆっくり味わう」の意では savor a meal とすることもできる. eat [have] a good meal を用いる場合もある.
>
> (3) 料理を運んできた店員が客に言う「どうぞ, ごゆっくり」は "Enjoy your meal." あるいは, 単に, "Enjoy."
>
> (4)「おいしく頂きました」「ごちそうさま」はふだん言わないので決まった表現はないが, 作ってくれた人に感謝して, I really enjoyed the meal. あるいは That was very good [delicious]. とはよく言う.

おいしげる 生い茂る ▶城壁のすぐ外側に木々が生い茂っていた Trees *grew thick* just outside the castle wall. ‖庭には雑草が生い茂っている The garden *is overgrown with* weeds.

おいしさ **(good) flavor, deliciousness** ▶味付けが濃すぎると料理はおいしさがわからなくなってしまう If you overseason a dish, some of its *deliciousness* [*good flavor*] will be lost. ‖一家団らんで食べると食事もおいしさが増す When your family gets together for a meal, you can *enjoy* it *more*. (➤「より楽しめる」の意).

おいすがる 追い縋る ▶大臣は追いすがる報道陣を振り切るように車に乗り込んだ The minister got into a car, shaking off the reporters who *dogged* his *footsteps*. (➤ dog は「しつこく追跡する」の意).

オイスター an **oyster**

‖オイスターソース oyster sauce.

おいそれと ▶そんな仕事をおいそれと引き受けるな Don't take on that kind of job *lightly*. ‖彼女の電話番号をおいそれとは教えられないよ I'm afraid I can't give you her phone number *so easily* [*just like that*].

おいだき 追い焚き reheating the bath water (➤説明的な訳).

おいだす 追い出す **drive out (of)** (大きいものを) ; **shoo** /ʃuː/ **away** [**off**] (「しっ!」と言うように) ▶農夫は牛を庭から追い出した The farmhand *drove* the cows *out of* the garden. ‖彼は猫を部屋から追い出した He *shooed* the cat *from* the room. ‖彼, 家を追い出されたんだって He told me he had *gotten kicked out* *of* his house. ‖ 会長一派が社長を追い出そうとしたんですよ The chairman's group tried to *boot* the president *out of* office. (➤ boot ... out (of) は「無理やり追い出す［首にする］」の意のインフォーマルな言い方).

‖追い出しコンパ a send-off party.

おいたち 生い立ち one's **early life** ▶誰もその女優の生い立ちを知らない No one knows anything about the actress's *early life*. ‖ 彼は不幸な生い立ちである His *early life* was quite unhappy. ／He had an unhappy *childhood*.

おいたて 追い立て ▶彼は家主から追い立てを食っている He has been given (*a*) *notice to move out* by the landlord. (➤ a のない形がふつう)《参考》「立ち退(の)き命令」は正式には an eviction notice という.

おいたてる 追い立てる ▶追い立てるようですみませんねえ I'm sorry to *rush* you (like this). ‖ きょうは仕事に追い立てられていて話をしている暇がないんだ I'm afraid I'*m snowed under* (*with work*) today and can't talk. (● 英語ではこういう場合,「雪で埋まった」が原義の be snowed under を用いて表すとよい).

おいつおわれつ 追いつ追われつ ▶追いつ追われつの試合 a *seesaw* game ／a *close* game.

おいつく 追いつく catch up with ▶ぼくは彼女に追いつこうと思って走った I ran to *catch up with* her. ‖ 人に追いついて追い越す *catch up with* and overtake [surpass] a person.

▶クラスのみんなに追いつくために頑張る work hard to *catch up with* the rest of the class(➤ the rest は「(自分を除く)ほかの人たち」).

おいつめる 追い詰める hunt down；**chase** +目 (捕らえるために素早い動きで) ▶少年たちはウサギを追い詰めた The boys *hunted down* a rabbit. ‖ 警察は犯人を路地に追い詰めた The police *chased* the criminal *into* a narrow alley. ‖ 追い詰められて泥棒は自殺を図った *Hunted into a corner*, the thief tried to kill himself.

-おいて -於いて at, in (➤ 場所を点としてとらえた場合は前者を, 広がりをもってとらえた場合は後者を用いる) ▶あす3時, 音楽室においてカラオケ大会を開きます. 奮ってご参加ください Tomorrow at 3 : 00 p.m. there will be a karaoke competition *in* the music room. Be sure to come！

おいで 1【来る, 行く】▶またおいでください *Please come* again. ‖ ようこそおいでくださいました I'm very glad you could come. (➤「来てくださってとてもうれしい」の意) ／I am very glad to meet you. (➤「お会いできてとてもうれしい」の意；初対面の挨拶) ‖ きょうはあなたにおいでいただいてとてもうれしく思います We're very happy to *have* you *with us* today.

▶マミちゃん, おじいちゃんがおいでおいでをしているよ Mami, Grandpa'*s calling* [*beckoning*] you to him. (➤ beckon は「手招きする」).

✉ **こちらにおいでの節はぜひお立ち寄りください** Please drop by [in] when you *come* this way. ／Be sure to drop by [in] when you *are in* the area. ➤「この付近に来たら」の意.

2【在宅, 滞在】▶お父さまはおいでですか Is your father (*at*) *home*？ (➤ at をつけないときの home は「在宅して」の意の副詞) ‖ いつまでこちらにおいでですか How long are you going to *stay* here？

3【「…しておいで」の形で】▶ぼく, おじさんについておいで You *come with me*, son. ‖ お金をあげるから映画でも見ておいで I'll give you some money, so *go* (*and*) see a movie or something. (➤ and は言わないことが多い).

おいてけぼり 置いてけぼり ▶彼はのろまなのでしょっちゅう置いてけぼりを食っている He is such a slowpoke that he *is* always being *left behind*. (➤ leave behind は「置き去りにする」).

おいとま お暇 ▶そろそろおいとましなければなりません *I think I should be going* [*be on my way*] *now*. 《参考》これに対して招いた側は Don't leave so soon！(まだいいじゃないですか), Must you go so soon？(こんなに早くですか), We're sorry you have to leave. (それは残念ですね)などと答える.

おいぬく 追い抜く pass +目 (…の前に出る)；**excel** /ɪksél/ +目 (…より優れる) ▶彼はゴール直前で先頭走者を追い抜いた He *passed* the front-runner just before the finish line.

▶中国はＧＮＰで日本を追い抜いた China has *surpassed* Japan in GNP. (➤ surpass は「…に勝る」).

おいはぎ 追い剝ぎ a **highwayman**(かつて街道に出た馬に乗った強盗)；a **robber**(暴力・脅しで物を奪う強盗).

おいはらう 追い払う drive away [**off**]；**chase away** [**off**] (追いかけて) ▶警察は群衆を追い払った The police *drove* the crowds *away* [*off*]. ‖ あの犬まだついて来るわ. ねえ追い払ってよ That dog is still following me. Will you *chase* him *off* (for me)？

おいぼれ 老いぼれ an **old man** [**woman**]；a **dotard** (もうろくした人).

おいぼれる 老いぼれる ▶俺も老いぼれちまったなあ I'*m getting old*, it seems. ‖ おじいちゃんは老いぼれちゃったね. 最近物忘れがひどいよ Grandpa *is getting senile*. He's so forgetful these days.

おいまくられる 追いまくられる ▶父は仕事に追いまくられて休む暇もない My father *is* so *loaded with work* he does not have any time to relax.

おいまわす 追い回す ▶若い男がかわいい女の子を追い回すのはごく自然なことだ It is quite natural for young men to *run* [*chase*] *after* pretty girls. ‖ 子供は一日中母親を追い回す(＝母親に付きまとう)ものだ A child will *follow* her [his] mother *around* [*about*] all day long.

おいめ 負い目 ▶あいつには負い目があるから悪口は言えない I *am indebted to* him so I can't say anything bad about him. (➤ be indebted は「感謝すべき恩義がある」の意の堅い表現).

おいもとめる 追い求める pursue /pərsjúː/ +目；**chase** +目 (追いかける)；**seek after** (追求する)

▶快楽を追い求める *pursue* pleasure ‖ 彼女は夢ばかり追い求めている She is always *chasing* some dream. ／She always *chases rainbows*. (● 後者は「虹を追い求める」と発想する英語的慣用句の chase rainbows を用いたもの).

▶コロンブスは富と名声を追い求めた Columbus *sought* (*after*) fame and fortune.

おいやる 追いやる drive +目 (追い払う；駆り立てる) ▶母親はうるさそうに子供を外へ追いやった The mother *kicked* [*drove*] her son *out* (*of the house*) with an annoyed look. ‖ 何が彼女を自殺に追いやったのだろう What was it that *drove* her *to* suicide？

おいる 老いる get old；**age**(年を取る) ▶節子はぼけたり卒中になったりせず, いかに老いるかを常に考えている Setsuko is always thinking how she can *age* without getting senile or having physical problems like strokes.

▶うちのおやじは老いてますます盛んだ My dad is *getting more active as he ages*. ‖ 老いらくの恋 a love affair *in old age*.

ことわざ 老いては子に従え Obey your child when you get old. (➤ 日本語からの直訳).

オイル **oil**(油・石油) ▶むらなく焼けるよう体にオイルを塗る apply [rub] *oil* on the body to tan evenly ‖ オイルとバッテリーの点検をお願いします Please check the *oil* and battery. ‖ オイルを調べてみましょうか Shall I check the *oil*?

‖**オイルフェンス** an oil [a containment] boom (➤「オイルフェンス」は和製語) ‖ **エンジンオイル** engine oil ‖ **オリーブオイル** olive oil ‖ **サラダオイル** salad oil (➤ 植物由来の油を表す vegetable oil というほうが通じる. また, 実際には具体的に corn oil, olive oil, sesame oil などというのが普通).

おいろなおし お色直し ***oironaoshi***; the bride's changes of dress during a wedding reception (➤ 説明的な訳).

1**おう 王** a **king** ▶アーサー王 *King* Arthur ‖ ライオンは百獣の王だ The lion is *the king of beasts*. ‖ ベーブ・ルースは生涯に714本のホームランを打ち, ホームラン王として有名だ Babe Ruth is famous as *the home-run king*, with 714 home runs during his career. ‖ 発明王エジソンの名は誰でも知っている Edison, *the great inventor*, is well known to everybody. (➤「偉大なる発明家エジソン」の意で決まった言い方).

2おう 追う

訳語メニュー
追いかける →run after **1**
ついて行く →follow **1**
追い払う →drive away **2**

1【追いかける】 **chase** +目, **chase after, pursue** +目 (追跡する, 追求する); **run after**(走って追う); **hunt** +目 (犯人などを); **follow** +目(ついて行く) ▶泥棒を追う *chase* [*pursue*] a thief ‖ 2人の警官が泥棒を追った Two police officer *chased after* [*ran after*] the thief. (➤ 前者のほうがスピード感がある. chase が結果的に追いつく, chase after がなかなか追いつかない, という含みをもつことがある) ‖ 生徒たちは先生のあとを追った The students *chased after* their teacher. ‖ 警察は誘拐犯を追った The police *hunted* the kidnapper. ‖ 犬は主人のあとを追って家に帰った The dog *followed* his master home.

▶理想を追うのもいいが, 現実を見失ったらおしまいだ It is fine to *pursue* ideals, but once you lose sight of reality, it's (all) over for you. ‖ 若者は流行を追うのに熱心だ Young people are eager to *follow* (the latest) trends. ‖ 彼女は交通事故で死んだ恋人のあとを追って自殺した She killed herself to *follow* her boyfriend, who died in a traffic accident, in death.

▶あの企業は利益を追い過ぎると非難されている That company is criticized for *pursuing* profit *too aggressively*.

2【追い払う】 **drive away** ▶この犬は追っても追ってもついてくる This dog insistently follows me, no matter how often I try to *drive* it *away*. ‖ 彼は犯罪を犯して故郷を追われた He *was driven out* from his hometown because he committed a crime. / He had to leave his hometown for committing a crime. (➤ 自ら去った場合).

3【「追われる」の形で】 ▶弟は勉強に追われている My brother *is* always *busy with* his studies. ‖ 兄はいつも時間に追われている My big brother *is* always *pressed for* time. ‖ 彼女は生活に追われている She *is struggling* to make ends meet. (➤ make ends meet は「家計をやりくりする」の意) ‖ きょうは雑用に追われっぱなしだった I *was swamped with* odd jobs today. (➤ be swamped with は「…に忙殺される」).

4【たどる】 ▶順を追って事の次第を話しなさい Tell me how it happened *step by step*. ‖ 日を追って寒く[暖かく]なってくる It's getting colder [warmer] *day by day*. ‖ がん患者は年を追うごとに増加の一途をたどっている The number of cancer patients is increasing *every year* [*year by year*]. ‖ 彼女は点字を指で追いながらすらすらと読んだ *Running her fingers* over the dots, she read the Braille book with ease.

3おう 負う

訳語メニュー
背負う →carry **1**
責任などを負う →take **2**
恩恵を被る →owe **4**

1【背負う】 **carry ... on** one's **back** ▶背中に大きな荷を負った行商人 a peddler *carrying* a big bundle *on his* [*her*] *back* ‖ 人生は重荷を負うて遠き道を行くがごとし Life is like a long journey *with* a heavy burden *on your back*.

2【自分の身に受ける】 **take** +目 ▶この問題の責任は私が負います I will *take* [*assume*] responsibility for this problem. ‖ 国民は納税の義務を負っている The citizens *are under obligation* [*have an obligation*] *to* pay their taxes. ‖ 曽祖父は無実の罪を負って服役した My great-grandfather served time *under the shadow of* a false accusation. ‖ おじは死んだ弟の借金を負わされた My uncle *was saddled with* his late brother's debts. ‖ 彼はその失火の罪を負わされた (*The*) *blame* for that fire *was placed on* him [*on* his *shoulder*]. (➤「ひょっとすると無罪かもしれない」の含み).

3【痛手を被る】 **get wounded** /wúːndɪd/ (刃物・弾丸などによって傷を); **get injured**(主に事故によって傷を) ▶頭部に傷を負う *get* [*be*] *wounded* in the head ‖ 彼は自動車事故で重傷を負った He *got* [*was*] *seriously injured* in an automobile accident.

4【恩恵を被る】 **owe** 《to》 ▶現代社会はハイテクの発達に負うところが多い Modern society *owes* a great deal *to* high technology.

▶あなたに負うところが多い I *am* greatly *indebted to* you. (➤ be indebted to は「…から恩恵を受けている」の意で堅い表現).

おうい 王位 **the throne** ▶王位につく mount [take] *the throne* ‖ 皇太子は王位を捨てて平民の娘と結婚した The crown prince gave up *the throne* in order to marry a commoner's daughter.

おういん 押印 ▶文書に署名押印する write one's signature and *put* [*affix*] one's *seal* [*hanko*] on a document.

おうえん 応援 **1【声援】** **cheering** 一動 (…を)応援する **cheer** 《on, up》, 《米》 **root** 《for》 ▶地元のチームを応援する *cheer* (*on*) [*root for*] one's home team ‖ 私, きょう100メートル競走に出るの. 応援してね I am taking part in the 100-meter dash today. So please *cheer* me (*on*) [*root for* me].

‖**応援歌** a fight song; 《米》 a rooters' song; 《英》 a supporters' song ‖ **応援団** a cheering squad [party], 《米》 cheerleaders ‖ **応援団員** a member of a cheering squad [party] ; 《米》 a cheerleader (主に女子) ‖ **応援団長** the leader of a cheering squad.

2 【支持】 support ; backup (後援) **一動 応援する support** +目, **back (up)** ▶学生運動を応援する *support* [*back*] a student movement ‖ 父は私を全面的に応援してくれた My father *gave* me *all the backup* I needed.

‖ **応援演説** a campaign speech ; 《インフォーマル》 a pep talk.

おうおう 往々 ▶日本人でさえ往々にして敬語の使い方を間違える Even Japanese misuse Japanese honorific expressions *often*.

おうか 謳歌 ▶あの若者たちは今青春を謳歌しているんですよ. だからあまりがみがみ言わないでやってください Those youngsters *are* now *enjoying the golden days of their youth* [*the best days of their lives*], so try not to get on their case too much. (➤ get on someone's case は「(人)にうるさく干渉する」).

おうかくまく 横隔膜 the diaphragm /dáɪəfræ̀m/.

おうかん 王冠 a **crown** ▶頭に王冠を頂く have *a crown* on one's head.

▶ビールの王冠を集める collect beer bottle *caps*.

1**おうぎ 扇** a **(folding) fan** ▶扇形をした砂糖菓子 a *fan-shaped* candy (➤ 幾何でいう扇形は a sector).

2**おうぎ 奥義 esoteric knowledge, the secrets** 《of》.

1**おうきゅう 応急の first-aid** ▶私はその場で応急処置 [手当て] をしてもらった I got *first-aid treatment* on the spot. ‖ すぐ応急策を講じるつもりだ We'll take *emergency measures* at once.

2**おうきゅう 王宮** a **royal palace**.

おうけ 王家 the royal family.

おうけん 王権 royal power, the power of the king.

おうこう 横行 ▶高級官僚による不正が横行している Corruption among high-ranking officials *is rampant*.

おうこく 王国 a **kingdom** ▶オランダはヨーロッパの北西部にある王国だ The Netherlands is *a kingdom* in northwestern Europe.

▶《比喩的》ラスベガスはギャンブル王国だ Las Vegas is *a paradise for gamblers*.

おうごん 黄金 gold 一形 黄金の gold (金製の) ; **golden** (金色の)

‖ **黄金時代** a golden age ‖ **黄金の国** the country of gold ‖ **黄金の茶室** a tea ceremony room made of gold ‖ **黄金比** the golden ratio ‖ **黄金分割** the golden section ‖ **黄金律** a golden rule.

おうざ 王座 the throne (王の席, 地位) →王位 ▶ (イギリスの) ビクトリア女王は約64年間王座についていた [在位した] Queen Victoria *occupied the throne* [*reigned*] for about sixty-four years.

▶彼はフライ級の王座についた [王座を明け渡した] He won [lost] the flyweight boxing *championship*.

おうさま 王様 a **king** (王) (➤ 直接呼びかけるときは King Arthur ! などと名も言う) ▶ポップスの王様, マイケル・ジャクソン Michael Jackson, *the king of pop*.

1**おうし 雄牛** an **ox** (去勢した), a **bull** (去勢しない).

2**おうし 横死** an **accidental** [**unexpected**] **death**

▶横死する *meet an accidental* [*unexpected*] *death*.

1**おうじ 王子** a **prince** ▶ウィリアム王子 *Prince* William.

2**おうじ 往時 long ago**.

おうしざ 牡牛座 (a) **Taurus** /tɔ́ːrəs/ ▶今週の牡牛座の運勢は良い This week is a good week for *Taureans*. (➤ Taurean は「牡牛座生まれの人」).

おうしつ 王室 a **royal family** ▶王室に関する記事を読む [書く] read [write] about *the royal family*.

おうじゃ 王者 a **king** (王) ; a **monarch** /mɑ́nəᶦk/ (君主) ; **the champion** (優勝者).

1**おうしゅう 欧州 Europe** /jʊ́ərəp/

‖ **欧州市場** European markets ‖ **欧州大陸** the European Continent ‖ **欧州連合** the European Union, EU.

2**おうしゅう 応酬** (an) **exchange** ▶やじ [パンチ] の応酬 *exchanges* of heckling [punching] ‖ 彼女が最初にその提案をすると彼は怒った口調で応酬した When she first suggested the idea, he *retorted* hotly. (➤ retort は「言い返す」).

3**おうしゅう 押収 seizure** /síːʒəᶦ/ **一動 押収する seize** /siːz/ +目 ; **confiscate** /kɑ́ːnfɪskèɪt/ +目 (没収する) ▶密輸品を押収する *seize* smuggled goods ‖ その俳優の家から覚醒剤が押収された Illegal stimulants *were confiscated by police* at the home of that actor.

おうじょ 王女 a **princess** /prɪ́nsəs ‖ prɪ̀nsés/ ▶アン王女 *Princess* Anne (➤ 称号として用いるときは /prɪ́nsəs/).

おうじょう 往生 ▶あいつは実に往生際の悪いやつだった He was really *a bad loser*. (➤「負けてぐずぐず言う人」の意).

▶そこからの帰り道がわからなくて往生した I *had great difficulty* [*trouble*] finding the way back from there. ‖ ここのところ腰痛で往生しています I'*m troubled* with (lower) back pain these days.

☛ **大往生** (→見出語)

おうしょくじんしゅ 黄色人種 a **yellow race** 《参考》最近では皮膚の色をあからさまにいうことを避け, Asians, East Asians などを用いたり, 民族名・国籍で表現したりすることが多い.

おうじる 応じる

1 【こたえる】 meet +目, **comply** /kəmpláɪ/ 《with》 (要求や希望などに ; 後者は堅い語) ; **accept** +目 (受け入れる) ; **answer** (質問などに) ▶注文に応じる *accept* [*take*] an order ‖ 学習者のニーズに応じる *meet* the learners' needs ‖ 要求に応じる *comply with* a request ‖ 先約があって招待には応じられなかった Due to a previous engagement, I was unable to *accept* their (kind) invitation. ‖ 質問にはいつでも応じますよ I'll *answer* your questions anytime. ‖ 大臣は記者たちの問いかけに応じなかった The minister *made no response* to the reporters' questions. ‖ 間取りはご希望に応じて変更いたします The layout (of the house) will be changed *according to* your request.

2 【応募する】 apply for ▶私は水泳部の部員募集に応じた I *applied for* membership in the swimming club.

3 【ふさわしい】 ▶収入に応じた生活をする lead a life *suited to* one's income ‖ あの商社は社員の実力に応じた待遇をしている That trading company pays its employees *according to* their ability. ‖ この中学校は能力に応じた教育をすることで知られる This junior high school is known for educating students *in accordance with* their abilities.

おうしん 往診 a **house call 一動 往診する make a house call** [**visit**] ▶先生は午前中は宅診で, 往診は午後です The doctor sees patients at the clinic in the morning and *makes house calls* in the

afternoon.
‖往診料 a house-call fee ; a fee for a doctor's visit.

1おうせい 王政 **monarchy** /mɑ́:nəʳki/
‖王政復古 the Restoration.

2おうせい 旺盛 ▶赤ん坊は好奇心が旺盛だ Babies *are intensely curious* about everything around them. ‖祖父は今70歳だが元気旺盛だ My grandfather is seventy now, but he's still *full of vigor*. ‖香川君はいつも食欲旺盛だ Kagawa always *has a hearty* [*good*] *appetite*.

おうせつ 応接 reception
‖応接室(会社などの) a reception room ‖応接間(家庭の) a drawing room.

おうせん 応戦する counter(ことばや行動で) ; **return fire**(撃ち返す) ; **fight back**(反撃する) ▶暴徒たちが投石を始めると機動隊は放水銃で応戦した When the mob began to throw stones, the riot squad *countered* with water cannons.

おうぞく 王族 a **royal family**.

おうだ 殴打 a **blow**.

おうたい 応対 reception 一動 **応対する receive** ＋目 ▶部長はその部屋で客に応対した The manager *received* visitors in that room. ‖きょうは一日中電話の応対に忙しかった Today I was busy *answering* the telephone [telephone calls]. ‖彼女は知らない人にでも親切に応対する She *treats* even people she doesn't know kindly.

1おうだん 横断 **crossing** 一動 **横断する cross** (＋目), **go across**(➤ 後者はややインフォーマル) ▶通りを横断する *cross* [*walk across*] a street ‖大西洋を飛行機[船]で横断する *cross* the Atlantic Ocean *by plane* [*ship*] ／ *fly* [*sail*] *across* the Atlantic Ocean(➤ go across the Atlantic Ocean は単に「大西洋を横断する」の意) ‖そこは横断禁止ですよ *You can't cross the street* there. (➤「横断禁止」の掲示は No Crossing).
✉ **アメリカを1か月かけてバイクで横断する計画です** We plan to take a month to *cross* the U.S. by motorcycle.
‖横断歩道 a pedestrian crossing, 《米また》 a crosswalk, 《英また》 a zebra crossing ‖横断幕 a banner ‖横断面 a cross section.

2おうだん 黄疸 **jaundice** /dʒɔ́:ndɪs/ ▶おうだんにかかる be affected with *jaundice* ‖おうだんは肝臓病のサインだ *Jaundice* is a sign of liver disease.

おうちゃく 横着 ▶息子は横着をして寝る前に歯を磨かない My son is *lazy* about brushing his teeth before going to bed. ‖足でドアを閉めようなんて横着だよ Closing the door with your foot is a *sloppy* thing to do. 《参考》英米人は両手がふさがっている場合, よく足や, (特に女性は)尻でドアを閉める.

おうちょう 王朝 a **dynasty** /dáɪnəsti/ ▶この花瓶は明(みん)王朝期のものだ This is a vase made during *the Ming dynasty*. ／This is a *Ming dynasty* vase.

おうて 王手 ▶(将棋で)王手! *Check* [*Checkmate*]! (➤ checkmate は「(勝ったときの)王手詰み」の意) ‖その将棋名人は相手に王手をかけた That shogi master *checked* his opponent's king.
▶《比喩的》(日本シリーズで)西武は対戦成績を3勝2敗とし, 巨人に王手をかけた The Lions improved their record against the Giants to three wins and two losses, *putting* the Giants *in check*.

おうてん 横転 ▶車は氷の上でスリップし横転したが, 全員無事だった The car skidded on ice and *turned over on its side*, but no one was hurt. (➤「ゆっくり横転する」は topple over という).

おうと 嘔吐 vomit /vɑ́:mɪt/ ▶私はその事故現場を見ておう吐を催した Looking at the scene of the accident, I *almost vomited* [I *was nauseous*].
《参考》(1)駅のプラットホームのおう吐物をおどけて platform pizza ということがあるが, これはその内容物がしばしばピザであるため. 内容物にしたがって, platform cookies, platform biscuits, platform doughnuts, platform tacos ということもある. (2)このことから, lose one's pizza といえば, 「おう吐する」の意味になる. →げろ.

おうどいろ 黄土色 ocher /óʊkəʳ/.

おうとう 応答 a **response** ; an **answer**(返事) 一動 **応答する respond, answer** ▶何度もドアのベルを押してみたが応答がなかった I rang the doorbell over and over again but nobody *responded*. ‖《無線で》応答願います Come in, please. ／Do you read me? Over. (➤ read は「聞き取る」の意).

おうどう 王道 ▶ (…への)王道 *the royal road* 《to》 ‖ [ことわざ] 学問に王道なし There is no royal road to learning.

おうとつ 凹凸 ▶凹凸のある方を上にしてください Turn the *uneven* side up. ‖この道には凹凸があって車がよく揺れる The car is jolting a lot because of this *bumpy* road.

おうねつびょう 黄熱病 yellow fever.

おうねん 往年 ▶江夏は往年の名投手だ Enatsu was a great pitcher *in years past*. ‖祖父は往年のような元気がない My grandfather is not as energetic *as he used to be*.

おうばんぶるまい 椀飯振る舞い →大盤振る舞い.

おうひ 王妃 a **queen** 《参考》queen は「女王」の意にもなるので, 正確には queen consort という. consort /kɑ́:nsɔ:ʳt/ は「配偶者」の意.

おうふう 欧風の European-style, western-style.

おうふく 往復

一動 **往復する go back and forth** ▶父は会社の往復に3時間かかる It takes my father three hours to *go to* the office *and back*. ‖今は東京から博多まで1日で往復できる Now we are able to *get* from Tokyo *to* Hakata *and back* in a day. ‖このフェリーは島と本土の間を往復している This ferry *makes round trips* between the island and the mainland. ‖やがて青森・博多間を(列車で)日帰りで往復できるときが来るだろう The time will come when we'll be able to *make a round trip* [*go back and forth*] between Aomori and Hakata in a day.
▶盛岡までの往復運賃はいくらですか How much [What] is the *round-trip fare* to Morioka? (➤ round-trip は《英》では周遊旅行をいうことが多い) ‖長崎までの往復切符を2枚ください (I'd like) two *round-trip* [《英》 *return*] *tickets* to Nagasaki, please.
▶この番組への参加希望者は往復はがきでお申し込みください Those wishing to appear on this program are requested to write to us by *reply* [*double*] *postal card*. (➤ 英米には往復はがきはない).

おうへい 横柄な arrogant(偉そうにふるまって相手のことなど気にかけない) ; **haughty** (家柄・地位を鼻にかけて) ; **overbearing** (威圧するような) ; **insolent** (上の者に対して) ▶あの政治家は横柄だ That politician is *arrogant*. ‖彼は従業員に対して横柄だ He is *overbearing* to his employees. ‖ぼくは彼女の横柄な態度には我慢できない I can't stand her *haughty* attitude.

お

おうべい 欧米 **Europe and America** ▶欧米では圧倒的に多くの人々がキリスト教徒だ In *Europe and America*, the vast majority of the people are Christians.
‖欧米諸国 European and American countries ‖欧米人 Europeans and Americans.

おうぼ 応募 (an) **application**(志願すること)；(an) **entry** (懸賞などへの) 一動 **応募する** **apply** 《for》, **enter** (＋目) ▶会社の社員募集に応募する *apply for* a job [position] with a company ‖新聞の懸賞に多くの人が応募した A lot of people *entered* the newspaper's prize contest. ‖私はそのクイズにはがきで応募(＝回答)した I *replied* to the quiz by postcard.
‖応募者 an applicant ‖応募用紙 an application (form).

おうぼう 横暴な **tyrannical** /tɪrǽnɪkəl/ ▶彼女は夫の横暴なふるまいにたまりかねて家を出た She couldn't stand her husband's *tyrannical* behavior and (so she) left him.

おうむ 《鳥》 a **parrot**；a **cockatoo** /kɑ́ːkətuː ‖ kɔ̀kətúː/ (バタン，冠羽のあるオウム) 《参考》オウムに Polly とか Poll という名前をつけることが少なくない.
▶《慣用表現》「悪い子なんだから」と母親が叱ると，「悪い子なんだから」と女の子はおうむ返しに言った "You're being naughty," said the mother and the girl *echoed* "You're being naughty." (➤ echo は「(人のことばの)まねをする」の意).

おうめんきょう 凹面鏡 a **concave mirror.**

1**おうよう 鷹揚** ▶おうような人 a *generous* [*liberal*] person ‖軽井沢の別荘を夏の合宿に使わせてくれと頼んだら，おじはおうようにうなずいた When I asked my uncle if we could use his Karuizawa villa for our club's summer camp, he *generously* [*magnanimously*] gave his consent.

2**おうよう 応用** **application**；**practice** (実用) 一動 (…に)**応用する** **apply** 《to》 ▶理論の応用 the *application* of a theory ‖ハイテクの知識を自分の仕事に応用する *apply* one's knowledge of high technology *to* one's own work.
▶その方法は広く応用が利く The method *has a wide range of applications*. ‖クルミ割りはてこの原理を応用して(＝利用して)いる Nutcrackers *make use of* the principle of the lever.
‖応用言語学 [物理学／科学／心理学] applied linguistics [physics／science／psychology] ‖応用問題 an applied problem.

おうらい 往来 **1** 【行き来】**traffic** ▶ここは夜は車の往来が少ない There is little *traffic* here at night. ‖この通りはいつも人の往来が激しい There is usually a lot of pedestrian *traffic* on this street. ‖江戸時代の日本は海外との往来を固く禁じていた In the Edo period, *entering and leaving* Japan was entirely prohibited.
2 【通り】a **street** ▶往来で遊んではいけません Don't play *on* [《英》 *in*] *the street*.

おうりつ 王立の **royal** ▶デンマーク王立バレエ the *Royal* Danish Ballet.

おうりょう 横領 **embezzlement** /ɪmbézlmənt/
一動 **横領する** **embezzle** ＋目 ▶彼は会社の金を500万円横領した He *embezzled* five million yen from the company. ‖彼は公金横領の疑いをもたれている He is suspected of having *embezzled* public money.

おうレンズ 凹レンズ a **concave lens.**

おえつ 嗚咽 **sobbing**(すすり泣き)；a **sob**(すすり泣く声)
一動 **おえつする** **sob** ▶おえつをこらえる suppress *a sob*.

おえらがた お偉方 an **important person,** 《インフォーマル》 a **big shot,** a **bigwig**；《インフォーマル》 **the higher-ups**(全体) ▶きょうはお偉方が顔をそろえている All the *big shots* are present today.

おえる 終える **finish** ＋目 (始めたことを最後までやる)；**end** ＋目, **close** ＋目 (➤ 前者は単に「終える」という事実をいうだけだが，後者は時間を制限して終わらせるという含みがある) ▶一生を終える *finish* [*end*] one's life ‖きょうの仕事を終える *finish* today's work ‖大学を終える(＝卒業する) *graduate from* (a) university ‖彼は中学を終えるとすぐ働き始めた He started working just after *finishing* junior high school. ‖彼女はジョークでスピーチを終えた She *ended* [*closed*] her speech with a joke.
▶彼女は『風と共に去りぬ』を読み終えた She *finished reading* [*got through with*] "Gone with the Wind." (➤ get through with は「(仕事などを)し終わる」の意のインフォーマルな言い方.「…し終える」は finish doing で (×)finish to do とはしないこと. →終わる) ‖これは時間までには終えられそうもない It looks like I can't *get* this *done* [*finished*] on time. (➤ get ... done は「…を終える」の意のインフォーマルな言い方).

おおあじ 大味 ▶この種の魚は大味だ This kind of fish *is tasteless*. ‖そのレストランのステーキは高いが大味だ The steak they serve at the restaurant is expensive, but it *doesn't have much flavor*.

おおあたり 大当たり a **great** [**big**] **hit**；a **great success**(大成功) ▶大当たりの事業 a *bonanza* enterprise (➤ bonanza /bənǽnzə/ は「(思いがけない)幸運」の意のインフォーマルな言い方) ‖あの映画は大当たりだった That film was *a great hit* [*success*]. ‖その監督は『アバター』で大当たりをとった The director *hit the jackpot* with "Avatar." (➤ hit the jackpot はポーカーで「積み立てかけ金を取る」が原義) ‖ことしはミカンが大当たり(＝豊作)だ We had *a good harvest* [*a bumper crop*] of mikan this year. ‖きょうのイチローは5打数4安打の大当たりだった Ichiro *was really hot* today, going four for five.

おおあな 大穴 ▶父は競馬でよく大穴を当てる My father often *makes a big hit* at the horse races. ／My father often *hits on a dark horse*.

おおあめ 大雨 (a) **heavy rain** ▶ゆうべは大雨だった It *rained very hard* last night. ／We *had a heavy rain* last night. ‖大雨が降っている It is *raining heavily*. ‖大雨が降りだした The *rain* began *pouring down*.
▶彼女は大雨の中を出かけた She went out in the *pouring rain* [*the downpour*]. ‖川は大雨のあと水かさが増す The river rises after *a heavy rainfall* [*heavy rainfalls*]. (➤ rainfall は「(降)雨量」) ‖近畿ならびに中部地方に大雨洪水注意報が出ています *Rain and flood warnings* have been issued for the Kinki and Chubu regions.

おおあり 大有り ▶広島の逆転優勝の可能性は大ありだ *There is a good chance* [*every possibility*] of the Carp's come-from-behind winning of the championship.

おおあれ 大荒れの **stormy**(➤ 天候にも比喩的にも用いる) ▶きょうは海は大荒れだ The sea is *very rough* today. ‖山はきのう大荒れだった Yesterday *a storm raged* in the mountains.
▶《比喩的》きょうの会議は大荒れだった Today's con-

ference was *stormy*.

おおあわて 大慌て ▶彼は大慌てで出て行った He went out *in a big hurry* [*in great haste*].（➤後者はかなり固い言い方）‖ぼくは朝はいつも大慌てで家を飛び出します Every morning I dash out of the house *completely disorganized*.（●「ひどく散らかしたままで」「大混乱のうちに」と考えて，訳例のように表現するとよい）‖財布をなくしたと気がついたときは大慌てした I *was in a complete panic* when I found my wallet was missing.

[1]**おおい 覆い** a **cover** ▶彼女はその皿に覆いをした She *put a cover on* the dish. ／She *covered* the dish.

[2]**おおい 多い** **1【数が】a lot of, many** ▶彼女の悪口を言う人が多い *A lot of* people complain about her. ／*Many* people complain about her.（➤後者は堅い言い方）‖前田教授は蔵書が多い Professor Maeda has *a large number of* books.（➤堅い言い方）‖その渓流にはニジマスが多い That mountain stream *is full of* rainbow trout. ／That mountain stream *abounds with* [*in*] rainbow trout. ‖はしかは子供に多い病気だ *Lots of* children catch measles.

▶東京はニューヨーク市より人口が多い The population of Tokyo is *larger than* that of New York City.（➤「人口が多い」というときの「多い」は通例 large で表す）‖日本は山が多い Japan *has a lot of mountains*. ／Japan is a *mountainous* country. ‖うちは家族が多い I *have a large family*. ／My family is *large*. ‖ぼくたちのチームは1人多いのに，相手のチームは1人足りないんだ Our team has *one* player *too many* and the other side has one too few. ‖私たちの学校は男子生徒より女子生徒のほうがずっと多い There are *many* [*a lot*] *more* girls than boys in our school. ‖新しい医療保険制度は問題が多い The new health care system *has a lot of problems* [*is problematic*].

> **語法「多い」の使い分け**
> (1)数や量の多さを表す場合，インフォーマルな言い方では **a lot of, lots of, plenty of, full of** などが用いられる．このうち plenty of は「必要以上の数［量］の；たっぷりの」，full of は「(…で)いっぱいの；満ちた」の意味．
> (2) **many, much** もそれぞれ数，量を表すが，多くは文の主語か疑問文・否定文に用いられる．
> (3)頻度や回数の多さを表す副詞には **often, frequently** があるが，後者は堅い語．

2【量が】a lot of, much ▶6月は雨が多い We have *a lot of* [*lots of*] rain in June. ／It rains *a great deal* in June.（➤後者は堅い言い方）‖《フランス人に》フランスでは冬は雪が多いですか Do you have *much* snow in winter in France? ‖サウジアラビアは石油だけでなく鉱物資源も多い Saudi Arabia *is* not only *rich in* oil, but also in mineral resources. ‖彼は文句が多い He complains *a lot*. ／He's *always complaining*.（➤後者は頻度を言っている）‖お釣りが50円多いですよ You gave me *50 yen too much* change [in change].

3【頻度が】be frequent ▶日本は地震が多い Earthquakes *are frequent* in Japan. ／We have *frequent* earthquakes in Japan. ‖この頃彼女とのデートの回数が多いじゃないか You've gone out with her *a lot* [*many times*] recently, haven't you? ‖ぼくは日曜日は家でごろごろしていることが多い I *often* loaf around doing nothing at home on Sunday(s).

☞ 多く（→見出語）

[3]**おおい** **hey** ▶おおい，堀田君 *Hey*, Hotta! ‖人混みの中に私を見つけた父は「おおい！」と叫んだ When Dad found me in the crowd, he yelled "*Hey!*"

おおいかくす 覆い隠す **conceal** ＋㊐ ▶真実を覆い隠す *conceal* [*cover up*] the truth（➤cover up はややインフォーマル）．

おおいそぎ 大急ぎ ▶大急ぎの用 *urgent* business ‖大急ぎでこの仕事を終わらせます I will finish this job *right away* [*as quickly as possible*]. ‖彼は朝ごはんも食べずに大急ぎで出かけた He *hurried out* without (eating) breakfast. ‖大急ぎで（＝今すぐ）救急車を呼んで！おばあちゃんの喉にお餅がつかえちゃったの Call an ambulance *right now* [*immediately*]! Grandma is choking on a rice cake!

おおいなる 大いなる **great; total**（完全な）▶新社長のもと，わが社の大いなる躍進を願っています We hope to make *great* progress under the new president. ‖それは向こうの大いなる誤解だよ That's a *total* misunderstanding on the other party's side.

おおいに 大いに ▶私たちは箱根で休日を大いに楽しみました We enjoyed our vacation in Hakone *very much*. ‖彼の小説は批評家から大いに賞賛された His novel was *highly* [*greatly*] praised by the critics.

▶この案内図は大いに役立つ This guide map is *very* useful. ‖大いに勉強しなさい Study *very hard*. ‖彼女の独り善がりは大いに迷惑だ Her self-righteousness is *extremely* annoying.（➤extremely は「とても」の意のインフォーマルな語）‖ゆうべは大いに語り合った We talked *a lot* last night. ‖大いによろしい *Very well done!*

おおいちばん 大一番 a **big game** [**bout**]（➤bout はボクシング・相撲などの試合）．

おおいばり 大威張り ▶和夫は英語で満点を取って大威張りだった Kazuo *was all puffed up* because he had gotten a perfect score in English.

おおいり 大入り ▶その芝居は連日大入りだ The play has been *a big hit* day after day. ‖ゆうべの巨人・阪神戦は大入りだった The Giants-Tigers game last night *had a big crowd*. ‖《掲示》大入り満員 House Full.

‖**大入り袋** a full-house bonus.

おおう 覆う **cover** ＋㊐; **carpet** ＋㊐（一面に覆う）; **wrap** /rǽp/ ＋㊐（包む）

> **【文型】**
> A で B を覆う
> **cover** B **with** A

▶恥ずかしさに彼女は両手で顔を覆った She *covered* her face *with* both hands in embarrassment. ‖湖は氷で覆われていた The lake *was covered with* ice.

▶落ち葉が中庭を覆っていた Dead leaves *carpeted* the courtyard. ‖死体は毛布で覆われていた The dead body *was wrapped in* a blanket. ‖夜7時を過ぎると夜の闇がすっかり辺りを覆ってしまう After 7:00 in the evening, the darkness of night *covers* everything.

▶災害現場は目を覆いたくなるような光景だった I could *hardly bear to look at* the disaster site.（➤「ほとんど見るに忍びない」の意）．

おおうつし 大写し a **close-up** /klóʊsʌp/ ▶顔を大写

お

しにしないで Don't take *a close-up* of my face.

おおうりだし 大売り出し a **sale** ▶冬物大売り出し a winter *sale* ‖(掲示)大売り出し中 (Now on) Sale ‖10階で大売り出しをやっています We're *having a sale* on the tenth floor.

‖**歳末大売り出し** a great [big] year-end sale.

オーエス **OS**(➤ an operating system の略).

オーエル a **(woman) office worker** ▶昼休みにはこの喫茶店は近くの会社の若いＯＬでいっぱいになる During lunch time, this coffee shop is filled with *young women working in* nearby *offices*. ‖妹は東京の商社でＯＬをしています My younger sister *works for* a trading company in Tokyo.

> **危ないカタカナ語✹ オーエル**
> OL は office lady の頭文字をとったものであるが, office lady という英語は存在しない. (woman) office worker とするか, 訳例のように説明的に表す. office girl を当てる場合もあるが, これは事務所などで手伝い仕事をする使い走りのような女性を指す.

おおおく 大奥 *ooku*; the inner palace of Edo Castle, the Shogun's harem (➤説明的な訳).

おおおじ 大伯父・大叔父 a **great uncle**, a **granduncle**.

おおおとこ 大男 a **giant**(巨人); a **big** [**tall**] **man**(大きな男) ▶ ことわざ 大男総身に知恵が回りかね Intelligence cannot circulate through the whole body of a big man. (➤日本語からの直訳) ／He has more brawn than brains. (➤英語のことわざ).

おおおば 大伯母・大叔母 a **great aunt**, a **grand-aunt**.

おおがかり 大掛かりな **large-scale** ▶大がかりな実験 a *large-scale* experiment.

オーガズム (an) **orgasm** ▶オーガズムに達する achieve [reach] *orgasm* ／have [get] *an orgasm*.

おおかた 大方 **1**【ほとんど】▶仕事はおおかた終わった The work is *almost* [*nearly*] done. ‖大方の予想に反して[予想どおり]日本は韓国に負けた Contrary to [In line with] *most people's expectations*, Japan lost to South Korea.

2【おそらく】**probably** ▶あすはおおかた雨だろう It will *probably* rain tomorrow. ‖おおかたそんなことだろうと思っていた *I thought as much*.

おおがた 大型の **large-scale, large-sized** ▶大型の台風 a *big* [*large-scale*] typhoon ‖大型のダンプカー a *large-sized* dump truck ‖都の予算は年々大型化している The budget of Tokyo Metropolis *gets larger* year by year.

‖**大型車** a full-size(d) car ‖**大型バス** a motor-coach, a coach /koʊtʃ/.

オーガニックの **organic**

‖**オーガニックフード** organic food.

おおがねもち 大金持ち a **very rich person**, a **filthy rich person**(➤後者はくだけた表現).

おおかみ 狼 a **wolf** /wʊlf/ [複 **wolves**] ▶(比喩的)男はみんなオオカミよ All men are *wolves*.

☞ 一匹おおかみ, 送りおおかみ (→見出語)

おおがら 大柄 ▶大柄な模様のドレス a *bold-patterned* dress.

▶大柄な人 a person *of large build*.

おおかれすくなかれ 多かれ少なかれ ▶たいていの人は多かれ少なかれ利己的だ Most people are selfish *to some degree*.

▶誰にも多かれ少なかれ悩みはある Everybody has worries, *to a greater or lesser degree* [*to one degree or another*]. ／All of us have problems *to some degree or other*.

おおきい 大きい **1**【サイズなどが】**big, large**; **vast**(面積が); **loud**(声が); **tall**(背が)

> 語法 (1)物についていうときは **big** は重量・かさの大きさに, **large** は面積・広さに重点がある.
> (2)数・量については **large** が一般的. **big** はインフォーマルな語で, 話し手の感情が込められていることが多い.

▶大きい犬 a *big* dog ‖何て大きい石なんだろう What a *big* [*huge*] stone! (➤ huge は大きいことを誇張していう場合) ‖東京は世界でいちばん大きい都市の１つだ Tokyo is one of the *largest* cities in the world. ‖彼女は年の割に大きい She is *tall* [*big*] for her age. (➤ big には太っているという含みが伴う) ‖大きな荷物があるので駅まで迎えに来てくれない？ I have some *heavy* luggage, so can you come and pick me up at the station? ‖(買い物で)これの大きいのありませんか Do you have it in *a bigger size*? ‖このセーターは私には大きすぎる This sweater is *too large* for me. ‖すみません. 今大きいお札しか持ってないんです I'm sorry but I have only *large bills* [*notes*] with me.

▶彼は声が大きい He has a *powerful* voice. ‖シーッ, 声が大きい! Shh, *don't talk so loud*. ‖もっと大きな声でおっしゃってください Could you speak a little *louder*?

▶彼は人物が大きい He *is a man of great character*.

2【程度が甚だしい】**big, great, serious** ▶大きな間違い a *big* [*great*] mistake ‖大きな地震 a *big* [*strong* ／*severe*] earthquake (➤ severe は「猛烈な」) ‖大きな発見 a *major* discovery(➤ major は「重要な」) ‖大きな損失 a *big* loss ／a *heavy* loss (➤どちらも比喩的にも用いる).

▶これは我々の命取りになりかねないほど大きな(＝重大な)問題だ This is a *serious* problem that might prove fatal to us. ‖その台風で私たちの学校は大きな被害を受けた The typhoon did *great* [*serious*] damage to our school. ‖子供にあまり大きな期待をかけてはいけない Don't expect *too much* of your children. ‖彼女には歌手になりたいという大きな夢がある She has a *great* ambition to become a singer. ‖彼の死は日米関係に大きな影響を与えるだろう His death will have (a) *great* impact on Japan-U.S. relations.

3【慣用表現】▶今度の監督は大きなことばかり言っている Our new manager is always *talking big* [*boasting*]. (➤ talk big は「大口をたたく, ほらを吹く」に相当するくだけた言い方) ‖子供のくせに大きな口たたくな You'*ve got a big mouth* for a kid. ‖失敗したくせにあまり大きな顔をするな You failed. You have nothing to *brag about*.

おおきく 大きく ▶口を大きく開けなさい Open your mouth *wide*. (➤「もっと大きく」なら wider) ‖駅前のスーパーは最近店を大きくした The supermarket in front of the train station *has been enlarged* [*been extended*] lately. ‖テレビ[ラジオ]の音を大きくしてちょうだい Could you *turn up the volume* on the TV [radio], please? (➤「小さくする」は turn down).

▶もう大きくなったのだから自分のことは自分でしなさい You are now *old enough* to take care of yourself. ‖しばらく見ない間にずいぶん大きくなったわねえ You'*ve gotten* a lot *bigger* [You'*ve grown a lot*] since I last saw you. ‖大きくなったら何になりたいの？ What are you going to be [to do] when you *grow up*? ‖ この町はここ2，3年で**大きくなった** This town *has grown* (*larger*) during the past few years.

▶周りが騒いだので，余計に問題が**大きくなった**(＝重大化した) The problem *has become serious* [*gotten worse*] because people made a fuss. ‖ 彼は横浜で**大きく**商売をやっている He is doing business *on a large scale* in Yokohama. ‖ その中学生の自殺が**大きく**報道された The suicide of the junior high school student was *widely* taken up by the media.

▶中日は巨人に15勝8敗と**大きく**勝ち越している The Dragons are *way* ahead of the Giants with 15 wins and 8 losses this year.

▶「世界初」とは，またずいぶん**大きく出た**な *What an exaggeration* for them to claim 'First ever in the world'! ‖ 兄は酔うと気が**大きくなって**人に物をやってしまう When my big brother gets drunk, he *becomes generous* and starts giving things away.

おおきさ 大きさ size ▶あなたの帽子の**大きさ**はどのくらいですか What *size* hat do you wear? ／What is your hat *size*?

▶ジャイアントパンダはクマくらいの**大きさ**の，体の大きな白黒の動物です A giant panda is a large black and white animal *the size* of a bear. ‖ きのう捕まえた魚はどのくらいの**大きさ**でしたか *How big* was the fish you caught yesterday?

▶カードの**大きさ**は横3センチ縦5センチです The card *measures* 3 by 5 centimeters. (➤ measure は「寸法がある」).

おおきな 大きな →大きい.

おおきめ 大きめ ▶この学生帽はぼくには少し**大きめ**だ This school cap is a bit *on the large side* (for me). (➤ on the ... side は「いくぶん…気味」の意) ‖ もう少し**大きめ**のかばんを見せてください Please show me a little *larger* bag. ‖ 私は少々**大きめ**のシャツが好きだ I like my shirts slightly *big* [*loose*]. (➤ loose は「ゆったりした」).

おおく 多く 一形 **多くの** many, a lot of (数が)；much, a lot of (量が) →多い ▶桜の花の季節になると公園に**多く**の人が集まる When the cherry blossom season comes around, *many* people flock to parks. ‖ そのお年寄りは子供たちには**多く**の金を残さなかった The elderly man didn't leave *much* money to his children. ‖ あのレストランで1000円**多く**支払ってしまった I paid *1,000 yen too much* at that restaurant.

▶私たちの**多く**がその事実に気づいていました *Many* of us were aware of the fact. ‖ この大学の卒業生の**多く**(＝大部分)は実業界へ行く *Most* (of the) graduates of this college go into business. ‖ 彼が言ったことの**多く**は真実だとわかった *Much* of what he said proved to be true. ‖ その映画スターは過去について**多く**を語りたがらなかった That film star didn't care to talk about his past *much*.

▶電車は1時間に**多くて**(＝せいぜい) 5本だ There are, *at most*, five trains in an hour.

おおぐい 大食い ▶あいつはいわゆる「痩せの**大食い**」なんだ He's one of those *people who never get fat no matter how much they eat*.

オークション (an) auction /ɔ́:kʃən/ ▶**オークション**を催す hold *an auction* ‖ 宝石を**オークション**で売る sell jewels *at* [*by*] *auction*.

▶彼は**オークション**でゴーギャンの絵を競り落とした He obtained [made a successful bid for] a Gauguin *at* (*an*) *auction*.

おおぐち 大口 **1**【大きな口】▶彼はいつも**大口**を開けて笑う He always laughs *with his mouth wide open*. ▶《慣用表現》**大口**をたたくな Don't *talk big*. ／Don't *boast*.

2【大量】▶**大口**の注文[取り引き] a *big* order [deal] ‖ **大口**の買い物 a *large* purchase.

おおぐまざ 大熊座 the Great Bear; Ursa /ə́ːrsə/ Major.

オーケー OK, O.K., okay, all right ▶両親から旅行に行ってもいいという**オーケー**(＝承認)をもらった I got *an O.K.* from my parents on my travel plans. ‖ 彼は私の計画に**オーケー**した He *okayed* [*OK'd*] my project. (➤この OK は動詞).

▶ 対話「どんな具合ですか」「万事**オーケー**です」"How is everything with you?" "Everything is *all right* [*okay*]."

> **直訳の落とし穴「あなたはオーケーですか」**
> 「午後いちばんに打ち合わせをしたいのですが，あなたはオーケー(＝都合がいい)ですか」というとき，I'd like to have a meeting first thing in the afternoon. (×)Are you OK? などとしない. Are you OK? は具合が悪そうな人や手助けが要りそうな人に対して聞くときの「大丈夫ですか」に当たる. 都合を聞くときには人を主語にしないで，that や it を主語にして Is that OK [all right] (with you)? とする. また，Are you OK with that? (それでかまわないか，それで異存[問題]はないか)という言い方は，場合によっては，相手にとって不都合かもしれないことや相手の判断基準・信条などに照らして「(そういうことで，そういう条件や受け止め方で)大丈夫か」などと聞く場合に用いる.

おおげさ 大袈裟な exaggerated /ɪɡzǽdʒəreɪṭɪd/ ▶その話はちょっと**大げさ**だ The story is a bit *exaggerated*. ‖ あいつの話はいつも**大げさ**だから割り引いて聞いたほうがいい He always *exaggerates*. You should take what he says with a grain of salt. (●「A(人の話など)を割り引いて聞く」という場合，英語では「1粒の塩と食べる」が原義の take A with a grain of salt を訳例のように用いる).

▶彼は物事を**大げさに言う**癖がある He always *stretches* the truth. ‖ 私たちは結婚披露宴をあまり**大げさ**にしたくありません We don't want to make *a big production* of our wedding reception.

オーケストラ an orchestra /ɔ́:ʳkɪstrə/ (管弦楽団) ▶私は学校の**オーケストラ**部員です I am in the *school orchestra*.

おおごえ 大声 a loud voice ▶あいつの**大声**は生まれつきだ His *loud voice* is something he was born with. ‖ 弟は**大声**でぼくを呼んだ My younger brother called (*out to*) me *in a loud voice*. ‖ ぼくたちは皆**大声**で笑った We all laughed *loudly*. ‖ そのお年寄りは**大声**を上げて助けを求めた That elderly man *screamed* [*cried*] for help. ‖ **大声**を出さないでちょうだい. ちゃんと聞こえてます Don't *shout* [*holler*]. I can hear you.

おおごしょ 大御所 a leading [an influential] figure, an outstanding figure ▶文壇の**大御所** *a* (*senior*) *leading figure* in the literary world.

おおごと 大事 ▶あなたの高血圧は早く手を打たないと**大事**になるかもよ If you don't do something about your high blood pressure right away, it could turn into *a serious problem*. ‖ これがおやじにばれたら

大事だ If my dad finds out about this, I'm (*going to be*) *in trouble*.

おおざけのみ 大酒飲み a **heavy drinker**, a **hard drinker** ▶おやじは大酒飲みだ My dad is *a heavy drinker*. ／My dad *drinks a lot*. 《参考》キリスト教文化では大酒飲みは「社会的落後者」と見なされることが多い.

おおさじ 大匙 a **tablespoon** ▶ここでお酒を大さじ1杯加えます Now add *a tablespoon* [*tablespoonful*] of sake.

おおざっぱ 大雑把 ▶彼らは大ざっぱな試合運びで結局負けた They played *carelessly* [*sloppily*] and, as a result, lost. ‖やつの考え方は元来大ざっぱだから行き詰まるんだよ The reason he always gets bogged down is that he *never has a clear idea* of what he wants to do. →大まか.

▶大ざっぱに言って日本はイギリスの1.5倍の面積がある *Roughly speaking*, Japan is fifty percent larger than Great Britain in area. ‖大ざっぱに見積もって費用はいくらくらいになりますか Could you give me *a rough estimate* of how much this will be [cost]?

おおさわぎ 大騒ぎ **1【ひどく騒ぐこと】**a **fuss** /fʌs/ ▶何でもないことに大騒ぎするな Don't *make a fuss* over nothing! ‖ゆうべは飲み会で大騒ぎをした Last night we *whooped it up* at the drinking party. (➤ whoop it up は「大声を上げて［飲んで］浮かれ騒ぐ」の意のインフォーマルな言い方).

2【混乱】confusion ▶市長の汚職で市議会は大騒ぎだ The mayor's scandal has thrown the city council into *confusion*.

▶人々は産業廃棄物処理施設建設計画を巡って大騒ぎしている People *are up in arms* about the plan to construct a treatment facility for industrial waste. (➤ be up in arms は「怒って激しく抗議している」の意).

おおしい 雄々しい **brave**(勇ましい)；**manly**(男らしい) ▶難局に雄々しく立ち向かう deal with a difficult situation *bravely*.

オージー an **Aussie** /ɔ́:si ‖ ɔ́zi/
‖オージービーフ Aussie beef.

おおしお 大潮 a **spring tide**.

おおじだい 大時代な **antiquated and pompous**(古めかしく大げさな).

おおすじ 大筋 an **outline** ▶きのうの会議で計画の大筋が決まった We decided the *outline* of the plan at yesterday's meeting. ‖大筋ではきみの案に賛成だ I agree with your plans *in general*.

オーストラリア **Australia** /ɔ:stréɪliə/ 一形 オーストラリアの **Australian** ▶オーストラリア(人)の学生 an *Australian* student.
‖オーストラリア人 an Australian, 《インフォーマル》an Aussie /ɔ́:si ‖ ɔ́zi/.

オーストリア **Austria** /ɔ́:striə/ 一形 オーストリアの **Austrian** ‖オーストリア人 an Austrian.

おおずもう 大相撲 a **grand sumo tournament** ▶大相撲九州場所 the Kyushu *Grand Sumo Tournament*. →相撲.

おおせ 仰せ ▶仰せのとおりに *as you say* ‖まさに仰せのとおりです You'*re completely correct* [*right*].

おおぜい 大勢 ▶山開き当日，富士山には大勢の登山客が押しかけた *A great number of* [*A lot of*] climbers came to Mt. Fuji on the official opening day. ‖子供たちは大勢海水浴に繰り出した Children turned out *in great numbers* to swim at the beach. ‖彼は大勢の前で歌を歌った He sang *in public*.

おおぜき 大関 an *ozeki*; a sumo wrestler of the second-highest rank (➤ 説明的な訳).

おおそうじ 大掃除 (a) **general cleaning** ▶日本では家の大掃除は年の暮れにするが，アメリカでは春にする In Japan people do (a) *house cleaning* [*clean the whole house*] at the end of the year; in the U.S. people do it in spring.

オーソドックス **orthodox** /ɔ́:ʳθədɑ:ks/ ▶オーソドックスな戦法 *orthodox* tactics [strategies].

おおぞら 大空 **the (blue) sky**
語法 (×)the big sky とは言わない. 形容詞を前につける言い方は，その反意表現(この場合は「小さな空」)が想定できないものは英語では通例しない.「美しい自然」「広大な宇宙」なども同様.《参考》Big Sky Country はアメリカのモンタナ州の愛称の1つ.
▶トキが再び大空を自由に舞う日が来るといいな I hope the day will come when Japanese crested ibises fly freely *in the sky*.

オーソリティー an **authority** /əθɔ́:rəṭi/ ▶経済学のオーソリティー *an authority* on economics.

おおぞん 大損 a **heavy loss** ▶株で大損をした I *suffered a heavy* [*great*] *loss* on the stock market.

オーダー an **order**(注文)
‖ラストオーダー the last order ‖オーダーストップ the last order.

オーダーメイド ▶オーダーメイドの靴 *custom-made* shoes ‖このスーツはオーダーメイドです This suit is *custom-made*. ／This suit is *made-to-order*.

> **危ないカタカナ語✹ オーダーメイド**
> 注文による製品を「オーダーメイド」というが英語では custom-made あるいは made-to-order といい，いずれも形容詞として用いる.「レディーメイド」は ready-made でよい. →イージー.

おおだい 大台 ▶1日の売り上げが100万円の大台に乗った Sales for the day *topped* [*exceeded*] the one million yen *mark*. (➤ top は「…を上回る」) ‖昨年のわが家のリンゴの収穫は100トンの大台を超えた Last year our apple harvest *surpassed* [*topped*] the one hundred ton *mark*.

おおだいこ 大太鼓 a **bass** /beɪs/ **drum**.

おおだすかり 大助かり ▶彼に荷物を運んでもらって大助かりだった He was *a great help* [was *very helpful*] to me in carrying my baggage. ‖あなたが子供の面倒を見てくれるので大助かりだわ You'*re really helping me* by taking care of our child.

おおだてもの 大立者 ▶政界の大立者 *a big figure* in politics.

おおちがい 大違い ▶見ると聞くとでは大違いだ What we see *is quite* [*very*] *different from* what we hear. ‖彼の言ったことは事実と大違いだ What he said *is far from* the truth.

おおづかみ 大づかみ ▶全文を一度通し読みして，骨子を大づかみする read through the whole text once and *get a rough grasp of* the main points [*get* the gist].

おおっぴら ▶息子は20歳になったとたんおおっぴらに酒を飲むようになった As soon as my son turned 20, he began to drink *openly*.

おおつぶ 大粒 ▶大粒の涙 a *large* tear ‖大粒の汗 a *large bead of* sweat ‖突然大粒の雨が降りだした All of a sudden, *huge drops* of rain began to fall.

おおづめ 大詰め **the final stage [phase]** ▶労働組合との折衝は大詰めに入った Negotiations with the labor union have entered *the final stage*.

おおて 大手 ▶私の兄は東京の大手の建設会社に勤務している My (older) brother works for a *large* [*major*] construction company in Tokyo. ‖ わが社はおもちゃ業界の最大手だ Our company is *number one* in the toy industry.

おおで 大手 ▶嫌疑が晴れて, これで大手を振って歩けます I've been cleared of all suspicion. Now, I can *look people in the eye*. (➤ look ... in the eye は「(やましいところがないので)…の目[顔]をまともに見る」の意 ; I can walk with my head up [held high]. という表現もある).

オーディオ **audio** ▶彼はオーディオに詳しい He is an expert on *audio and stereo systems*.
‖**オーディオショップ** an audio equipment shop ‖ **オーディオ製品** audio gear ‖ **オーディオマニア** an audiophile /ɔ́:dioʊfaɪl/.

オーディション an **audition** /ɔ:díʃən/ ▶オーディションに合格する[落ちる] pass [fail] *an audition* ‖ 彼はフィガロ役のオーディションを受けた He had *an audition* [*auditioned*] for the part of Figaro. (➤「…のオーディションを受ける」は have an audition for のほか, 動詞用法で audition for ともいう).

オーデコロン **(eau de) Cologne** /(òʊ də) kəlóʊn/ ▶首筋にオーデコロンをつける put (*eau de*) *Cologne* on the nape of one's neck.

おおどうぐ 大道具 a **stage set**.

おおどおり 大通り a **main street** ; an **avenue**(一般に南北に走る) ; a **boulevard**(並木のある) ▶この道を行くと大通りに出ますか Does this road lead to the *main street*?

オートキャンプ **auto-camping**
‖**オートキャンプ場** an auto-camping site.

オートクチュール **haute couture** /òʊt kuʃʊ́əʳ/ (➤ フランス語から. 英語訳の high fashion も用いる).

オートバイ a **motorcycle**, 《英また》 a **motorbike**
▶ぼくはオートバイで登校している I go to school *on my motorcycle*.

> **危ないカタカナ語** ✱ **オートバイ**
> **1** オート (auto) とバイシクル (bicycle) を組み合わせて作った和製語で, 英語では motorcycle がふつう. 《英》では motorbike とも言うが, 《米》ではこれは特に小型のものを指す.「オートバイに乗る人」は motorcyclist.
> **2** 日本語では「バイク」とも言い, 《英》の bike も同義で用いられることもあるが, 《米》の bike は通例, 自転車(bicycle)を指す.

オートパイロット (an) **autopilot**, (an) **automatic pilot** ▶オートパイロットで飛行する fly *on autopilot*.

オートフォーカス an **autofocus**.

オードブル an **hors d'oeuvre** /ɔ̀:ʳ dɔ́:ʳv/ ▶オードブルは何がいい? What would you like for *an hors d'oeuvre*?

オートマチック **automatic** ▶オートマチック車 a car with *an automatic transmission* / an automatic.

オートミール **oatmeal** ; 《英》 **porridge**.

オートメーション **automation** ▶工場をオートメーション化する *automate* a factory ‖ この製品はオートメーションで作られる This product is made *through an automated process*.

オートレース a **car race**.

おおとろ 大とろ *otoro*, **very fatty tuna meat**.

オートロック ▶このドアはオートロックだ This is a *self-locking* door.

オーナー an **owner** /óʊnəʳ/ ▶別荘のオーナー the *owner* of a resort home ‖ ホテルのオーナー a hotel *owner* ‖ 西武ライオンズのオーナー the *owner* of the Seibu Lions ‖ イタリア料理店のオーナーシェフ *the chef and owner* of an Italian restaurant (➤ owner and chef の語順もある ; owner-chef も用いる) ‖ **オーナードライバー** *the owner and driver* of a car (➤ 車は所有者＝ドライバーのことが多いので, car owner で済ますことが多い).

おおなた 大なた a **big hatchet** ▶公共事業に大なたを振るう *make drastic cuts* in [*drastically slash*] public works projects.

オーバー **1【越える, 超える】**▶センターオーバーの二塁打 a two-base hit *over* center field ‖ 九州旅行は予算を少しオーバーした The expense of the trip to Kyushu slightly *exceeded* the estimate.
▶これ以上乗ると定員オーバーになります No more people can get in, or we'll be *over the limit for passengers*.
2【大げさ】▶オーバーな演技 *exaggerated* acting ‖ あの子, 自分で言ってるほど具合は悪くないと思うわ. きっとオーバーに言ってるのよ I don't believe she's as sick as she says ; she'*s exaggerating* [she'*s playacting*].
3【がいとう】an **overcoat**, a **coat**.

オーバーオール **overalls**.

オーバーコート an **overcoat**.

オーバースロー 《野球》 an **overhand throw** (野手の送球) ; (an) **overhand pitch** (投手が打者に投げる投球) 《参考》 overthrow は「エラーとなる高い悪送球, 暴投」の意. ▶小池はオーバースローだ Koike *pitches overhand*.

オーバーヒート **overheat** 一動 **オーバーヒートする** **overheat** (＋自) ▶エンジンがオーバーヒートした The engine *overheated*.

オーバーホール an **overhaul** 一動 **オーバーホールする** **overhaul** ＋自 ▶車の調子が悪いのでオーバーホールしてもらう必要がある Something is wrong with my car. I need to have it *overhauled*.

オーバーラン 《野球》 an **overrun** ▶彼は三塁をオーバーランしてタッチアウトとなった He *overran* third base and was tagged out. (➤ ベースを滑り越した場合は overslide).

おおはば 大幅 ▶ことしは大幅な賃上げは望めない No *substantial* pay raises are expected this year. ‖ 大幅な人事異動があった There were *drastic* changes in personnel.
▶工事は大幅に遅れた The construction was *considerably* delayed. ‖ 冬物が大幅に値下げになった There have been *sharp* reductions in the prices of winter clothes.

おおばんぶるまい 大盤振る舞い a **(huge) feast** ▶客たちに大盤ぶるまいをする *lay out a* (*huge*) *feast* for one's guests.
▶きょうは給料日なので家族にすてきなレストランで大盤ぶるまいした Today was payday, so I *treated* my family *to dinner* at a nice restaurant. (● この場合,「家族にすてきなレストランでディナーをごちそうした」と考えて, (huge) feast などを用いないで訳出するほうが英語として自然).

オービー ▶ＯＢとの合同演奏会 a joint concert

with *the alumni* ‖ 我々はＫ大のＯＢです We are *graduates* of K University. ／We are K University *alumni*. ／We went to K University.

危ないカタカナ語✹ オービー
1 男子の卒業生を指す OB は old boy の頭文字をとったと考えられるが, 英語ではこの略語はほとんど用いられない.
2 日本語の「オービー」には「卒業生」という意味で graduate /grǽdʒuət/ や alumnus /əlʌ́mnəs/ [複 alumni /əlʌ́mnaɪ/] を当てる. また訳例のように went to を用いてその意を表すこともできる.

おおひろま 大広間 a **great hall**.

おおぶね 大船 ▶大船に乗ったつもりで, 万事私に任せておきなさい You *can rest at ease*. Leave everything to me.

1**おおぶり 大振り**
1【手・物を大きく振ること】 a **big** [**long**] **swing** ▶バット[ラケット]を大振りする *swing* a bat [racket] *hard* ／*take a big swing*.
2【物・人の体がふつうより大きめ】 ▶やや大ぶりな鍋 a somewhat *large* pot.
‖**大振り袖** a long outdoor *furisode* kimono worn by young women.

2**おおぶり 大降り** **heavy rain** [**snow**]. →本降り.

おおぶろしき 大風呂敷 ▶あの男は大風呂敷を広げるのが好きだ That guy loves to *talk big*. ‖ 釣りの話となると彼はすぐに大風呂敷を広げる When it comes to fishing, he's got more *tall tales* than anyone. (➤ tall tale は「ほら話」; 釣り人がしがちな「ほら話」は fish story ともいう).
▶またあいつの大風呂敷が始まったな He started *bragging* again.

オーブン an **oven** /ʌ́vən/ ; a **microwave** (**oven**) (電子レンジ) ▶オーブンでケーキを焼く bake a cake in *the oven*.
‖**オーブントースター** a toaster oven.

オープン 1【開店】 ▶近くにスーパーが新しくオープンした A new supermarket *opened* around the corner. ‖《掲示》本日オープン Open Today.
2【隠さないこと】 ▶とても気さくでオープンな人 a very friendly, *open* person.
▶お互いにオープンでいこう Let's *be open with* each other. ‖ オープンに話してくれないか Will you *be frank with* me?
3【テニス】 ▶全米オープン the U.S. *Open* Tennis Championships.

オープンカー a **convertible** (畳み込み式のほろのついた) ▶野球部員は地元の町をオープンカーでパレードした The school baseball team paraded through their hometown in *convertibles*.

オープンせん オープン戦 an **exhibition game** (➤ open game とはしない).

オーボエ an **oboe** /óʊboʊ/ ▶オーボエを吹く play the *oboe*.

おおまか 大まか ▶おおまかな(＝大ざっぱな)性格の人 a person of *generous* disposition ‖ おおまかな数字でいいですから教えてもらえますか Could you just give me a *rough* estimate? ‖『ロミオとジュリエット』のおおまかな筋を教えて Tell me the *general* plot of "Romeo and Juliet."

おおまじめ 大真面目 ▶ふざけてなんかいないよ. 大真面目だよ I'm not joking. *I'm dead serious*.

おおまた 大股 ▶大股で歩く walk *with long strides* ‖ 彼は大股だからついていくのに苦労する He has *a long stride*, so I have to struggle to keep up with him.

おおまちがい 大間違い ▶何でも買ってもらえると思ったら大間違いよ You'*re making a big mistake* [You'*ve got another think coming*] if you think I'll buy you anything you ask for!

おおみえ 大見得 ▶彼は「いつか社長になってみせる」と大見得を切った He *declared dramatically* [*theatrically*] that he would be company president someday. (➤ theatrically は「芝居がかって」の意).

おおみず 大水 a **flood** /flʌd/ ▶大水(＝洪水)ですべて流された The *flood* washed everything away. ‖ ゆうべの雨でうちの前が大水になった Last night's heavy rainstorm left *a huge pool* in front of our house.

おおみそか 大晦日 **the last day of the year, New Year's Eve.**

おおみだし 大見出し a **banner headline** 《参考》事件・人物が大見出しで新聞に「でかでかと載る」ことを make headlines という.

オーム (電気) **Ohm** (➤ 記号はΩ).

おおむかし 大昔 **ancient times** ▶大昔この辺にマンモスがすんでいたという Mammoths are said to have lived here *long, long ago*. ‖ あの岩は大昔からあそこにある The rock has been there *from time immemorial*. ‖ 昔, 昔, 大昔… *Long, long ago and far away* ....

おおむぎ 大麦 **barley.**

おおむこう 大向こう **the gallery** ▶大向こうをうならせるすばらしい演技 a superb performance that captures the hearts of *the audience in the gallery*.

おおむね 大旨・概ね **generally** (一般に) ; **on the whole** (全体から見て) ; **in the main** ▶患者の術後の経過はおおむね良好である *On the whole*, the patient is making good progress after the operation. ‖ あすは一日中おおむね晴天です Tomorrow we'll *mostly* have clear skies all day. ‖ 彼の言うことはおおむね正しい What he says is *about* right.

オオムラサキ (虫) **great purple emperor** (**butterfly**).

1**おおめ 多め** ▶彼は大食漢だからご飯は多めに炊いておきなさい He's a big eater, so you should cook *extra* rice.
▶《ホットドッグ店で》からしは多めにしてください *Heavy* on the mustard, please. (➤ 逆に「少なめ」のときは heavy を light または easy にする) ‖ お菓子は多めに買っておこう Let's buy *plenty of* snacks just in case. (➤ just in case は「万一に備えて」).

2**おおめ 大目** ▶今回は大目に見てあげるけど次からはそうはいかないわよ This time I'll *overlook* it [*let* it *go*], but next time around you are going to get it. (➤ get it は「罰を受ける」の意のくだけた言い方).

おおめだま 大目玉 ▶おやじのカメラを壊して大目玉を食った I broke Dad's camera and really *got chewed out* [*got a good scolding*]. ／I really *caught it* for breaking Dad's camera. (➤ get chewed out, catch it とも「(ひどく)叱られる」の意のくだけた言い方).

おおもうけ 大儲けする **make a pile** (**of money**), **make a killing** (➤ pile は《インフォーマル》で「大金」).

おおもじ 大文字 a **capital letter** ; 《印刷》 **upper case** ▶大文字で書く write in *capital letters*.

おおもて 大もて ▶(…の間で)大もてである *be extremely popular* with [among] ... ‖ そのお笑い芸人は若い女性たちに大もてだ That comedian *is very* *popular with* [*among*] young women.

おおもの 大物 a **big shot** ▶彼は将来きっと**大物**になるだろう He'll probably be *an important person* [*a big shot*] someday. (➤ big shot はしばしば牛耳っている人というようなマイナスイメージを伴う) ‖ カラヤンはクラシック音楽界の**大物**だった Karajan was *a big name* in the classical music world. (➤ big name は「名士, 有名人」の意のインフォーマルな語).

▶おやじは**大物**(＝大きい獲物)を狙って釣りに行った Dad went fishing, hoping to catch *a big one*.

おおもめ 大もめ ▶基地建設問題で議会は**大もめ**になった The assembly *was in a heated dispute* over the base construction issue.

おおもり 大盛り ▶**大盛り**のご飯 an *extra big serving* of rice ‖ ポテトサラダをお皿に**大盛り**にして出す serve a *heaping* bowl of potato salad ‖ カレーライスの**大盛り** 1 つお願いします I'll have *a large serving* of the curry and rice.

おおや 大家 a **landlord** ; a **landlady** (女性) ▶私は月末に**大家**さんに家賃を払っている I pay the rent to the *landlord* at the end of the month.

おおやいし 大谷石 **Oya stone** ▶**大谷石**の塀 an *Oya stone* wall.

おおやけ 公 **1**【国, 政府】一形 **公の public** (公的な) ; **official** (公式の) ▶**公**の費用で外国へ行く go abroad at *public* expense ‖ **公**の数字はまだ公表されていない *Official* statistics have not been issued yet.

2【社会, 世間】▶その件は**公**にするな Don't *make* the matter *public* [*known*]. ‖ きみは**公**の席でその事実を話したほうがいい You should speak about that fact *in public*.

おおやすうり 大安売り a **big sale** ▶その店では今夏物を**大安売り**している That store is having *a big sale* on summer clothes.

おおゆき 大雪 (a) **heavy snowfall** ▶今夜は**大雪**になりそうだ We're expecting *a heavy snowfall* tonight. ‖ **大雪**のため列車は立ち往生した The train was stalled in the *heavy snowfall*. ‖ 関東地方に**大雪注意報**が出された *Heavy snowfall warnings* were issued for the Kanto region.

おおよそ ▶行方不明者の**おおよそ**の数 *an estimate* of (the number of) missing people ‖ 彼女がなぜそう言ったのか**おおよそ**の見当はついている I can make a *rough* guess at why she said that. ‖ **おおよそ**の旅費を知りたいのです We would like *a general idea* of what travel (ing) costs will be. (➤ general idea は「見当」).

▶きみの勘は**おおよそ**のところ当たってるね Your guess is *basically* correct. → おおよそ.

オーラ an **aura** ▶そのカリスマ美容師には独特の**オーラ**がある That charismatic beautician has a unique *aura* about him.

オーライ **all right, O.K.** ▶発車, **オーライ** *All right*. Let's start ! ‖ バック, **オーライ**…ストップ ! *All right*, come on back—back—back—stop !

おおらか 大らか ▶**おおらか**な心の持ち主 a person *with a big heart* / a *big-hearted* [*generous-natured* / *easygoing*] person (➤ generous-natured は「寛大な」, easygoing は「のんびりした」) ‖ あんな不公平な扱いに黙っていられるなんてきみも**おおらか**な人だね It's *magnanimous* of you to put up with such unfair treatment. (➤ magnanimous /mægnǽnɪməs/ は「度量の大きい」).

オーラル **oral** ▶**オーラル**コミュニケーション *oral* communication ‖ **オーラル**セックス *oral* sex.

¹オール an **oar** /ɔːʳ/ (船のかい) ▶**オール**でボートをこぐ *oar* a boat.

²オール《全部》▶私は小学校時代は**オール 5** だった I got *straight 5's* all through elementary school. (➤ 英語国では straight A's がふつう. なお, 's は数字・アルファベットなどの複数形の書き方).

オールスターゲーム an **All-Star game.**

オールドミス an **old maid.**

オールナイト **all-night** ▶**オールナイト**の映画館 an *all-night* movie theater ‖ **オールナイト**で踊り明かそう Let's dance together *all through the night* [*all night long*].

オールバック ▶髪を**オールバック**にする comb one's hair *straight back* (➤ all back とはしない).

オールマイティー an **all-rounder** (なんでもこなす人) 一形 **オールマイティーな almighty** (➤ 英語では通例神に関連して用いる語) ; **unbeatable** (無敵の).

> **危ないカタカナ語✸ オールマイティー**
> 英語の almighty が元だが, この形容詞はふつう the Almighty (God), Almighty God, God Almighty (全能の神, 全能者である神)の形で使い, また, 全能の神を連想させる力を持った存在に用いる.「オールマイティー」はなんでもこなす器用な人を言うので all-rounder がぴったり. He's [She's] able to do anything. (なんでもできる) と表すこともできる.

オールラウンド 《主に米》**all-around,** 《主に英》**all-round** ▶彼は**オールラウンド**の運動選手だ He is an *all-around* athlete. ‖ 彼女は冬のスポーツにかけては**オールラウンド**だ She excels in *all* winter sport.

オーロラ an **aurora** /ərɔ́ːrə/ 《参考》英語ではふつう南北を区別して, 南極のオーロラは the aurora australis /ɔːstréɪləs/ または the southern lights, 北極のオーロラは the aurora borealis /bɔːriǽləs/ または the northern lights という.

おおわらい 大笑い a **good laugh** ▶父の海外での珍体験にみんな**大笑い**した Everybody *had a good laugh* over Dad's strange experiences abroad.

おおわらわ 大わらわ ▶みんな姉の結婚式の準備で**大わらわ**だった *Things were really hectic* with everyone getting ready for my sister's wedding.

おか 丘 a **hill** ; a **hillock** (小丘) ▶**丘**を上る [下る] go up [go down] *a hill* ‖ 百合が**丘** *Hill* of Lilies (➤ Yurigaoka のようにローマ字表記でもよい) ‖ 私たちの高校は坂を上りきった**丘**の上にある Our high school is situated on top of *a hill*.

おかあさん お母さん a **mother** (母親) ; **Mother, Mom, Mommy** (➤ あとの 3 語は家庭内での呼びかけにも用いられる) → ママ ▶**お母さん**はご在宅? Is *your mother* (at) home ? ‖ 彼女は来春, **お母さん**(＝母親)になる She will be *a mother* next spring. / She is expecting a baby next spring. ‖《母の日のカードで》**お母さん, ありがとう** Happy Mother's Day ! (➤「母の日おめでとう」の意).

▶**お母さん**, 何を作ってるの? What are you cooking, *Mom* ?

おかえし お返し a **return gift** 《参考》(1) 英語圏には物をもらって, それにただちに物を返礼として贈るという習慣はない. (招かれたら, 招き返すというように, あとで何らかのかたちで返礼に当たることをするというのはよく行われる.) (2) したがって, return gift を贈り主に向かって用いるのは普通ではない. ▶日本には物をもらったら**お返し**をするという習慣がある In Japan, we have a custom of *sending*

お

something in return when we receive a gift.
▶《比喩的》一郎が授業中に消しゴムを投げつけたので，ぼくもお返しをしてやった Ichiro threw an eraser at me during class, so I *gave* him *the same in return*.
▶いいか，このお返しはきっとさせてもらうからな I'll *pay* you *back for* this.
✉ **ロンドンではあなたが私の勉強を手伝ってくれたんだから，今度は私がお返しをしましょう** In London, you helped me with my studies, so I'll *return the favor* this time.

おかえりなさい お帰りなさい

> **《解説》「お帰りなさい」について**
> (1)「お帰り(なさい)」に相当する表現は英語にはない．ふつうは，Hello！(やあ) とか，Hi！(ハーイ) とか，Did you have a good time？(楽しかった？) のような言い方をする(Hello！と Hi！は「ただいま！」にも相当).
> (2)海外から帰国した人に対しては Welcome home [back]！とか，I'm glad to see you back home. と言う．後者は特に長い間留守をしていた人に対する言い方.

おかかえ お抱え ▶お抱え医者 a *personal* physician ‖ お抱え運転手 *a chauffeur* /ʃoufə́ːr: ‖ ʃóufə/ ‖ 彼女はうちのプロダクションのお抱え(＝専属)女優だ She is an actress *attached to* our agency.

おがくず 大鋸屑 sawdust.

おかげ お陰

1【力添え】

> **【文型】**
> A のおかげで
> thanks to A
> ➤ 好ましくないことの原因を皮肉を込めて言うのにも用いる →2
> A は B のおかげである
> owe A to B
> owe B A

▶近代科学技術のおかげで私たちの生活はずいぶん便利になった *Thanks to* modern technology, our lives have become much more convenient (than before). ／Modern technology has brought us many conveniences. (➤「近代科学技術が…をもたらした」の意) ‖ その奨学金のおかげで妹はカナダに留学できた *Thanks to* the scholarship my younger sister was able to go to Canada to study. ／The scholarship *enabled* my younger sister to study in Canada. ‖ 何から何まで彼のおかげです I *owe* him everything. ‖ そのドラマの人気はかなりのところ，優れた脚本のおかげである The drama *owes* much of its popularity *to* the excellent screenplay. ‖ 彼が今日あるのは奥さんのおかげだ He *owes* what he is today *to* his wife.
▶私はあの方には多大なおかげを被っている I *am* greatly *indebted to* that gentleman. (➤ 堅い言い方).

> **あなたの英語はどう響く？**
> 外国人教師などから You are making very good progress in English. (きみの英語の上達ぶりはたいしたものだ) と言われた場合に，「ありがとうございます．先生のおかげです」のつもりで Thank you. *I owe it all to you*. と答えないこと．owe ～ to ... は「人に恩恵を被っている」という意味であるが，英語を教えることを仕事にしている人に使うにはおおげさで不自然．Thank you. *It's all thanks to you*. のように答えるほうがよい．

2【せい】▶朝寝坊したおかげでバスに乗り遅れた I missed the bus this morning *because* I overslept. ‖ きみのおかげで失敗しちゃったよ I *have* you *to thank for* my failure. (➤ have A to thank for B で「B は A の責任だ」の意).
▶道路工事のおかげで水道が止まってしまった *Thanks to* [*Because of*] the road repair work, the water (supply) has been cut off. (➤ thanks to はこのように皮肉な意味でも用いる).

3【「おかげさまで」の形で】⚠ 日本的発想に基づく表現だが，英語では相手が気遣ってくれたことに感謝する表現形式をとったり，「幸運にも，運がよかったから」のように言ったりすることが多い．
▶おかげさまで息子は F 大に受かりました *Fortunately*, my son got into F University. ‖ 対話「お元気ですか」「はい，おかげさまで(元気です)」"How are you doing？" "I'm fine, *thank you*." ‖ 対話「正彦君のおけがはいかがですか？」「おかげさまですっかりよくなりました」"How is Masahiko's injury？" "*Thanks for your concern*. He has recovered completely." (➤ Thanks for your concern. はけがや病気を気遣ってくれた人に対して言う).
✉ **3 年間あなたとメールの交換をしたことがとても役立ちました．おかげさまで留学のための奨学金の試験に合格することができました** Exchanging emails with you for three years really helped me. *Thanks to you*, I passed the exam for a scholarship for overseas study.
✉ **おかげさまで熊本の両親はとても元気でおります** *I'm glad to say* my parents in Kumamoto are very healthy. (● Thanks to you. とはしない．この言い方は実際に何かをしてくれた人への挨拶．ただし，Thanks to everyone. は使用可).

おかしい

1【滑稽な】funny；amusing (ユーモラスな) ▶何がそんなにおかしいの？ What's so *funny*？‖ 彼の話がおかしくてみんな大笑いした His story was so *amusing* that all of us burst out laughing. →おもしろい.

2【変な，不適切な】strange (変な)；**unusual** (ふつうでない)；**suspicious** (不審な)；**false** (人を迷わす)；《米・インフォーマル》**flaky** (変わった言動をする) ▶彼女がその事実を否定するのはおかしい It is *strange* that she should deny the fact.
▶お母さん，ポチの様子がおかしいよ Mother！*Something is wrong* [*is the matter*] with Pochi！‖ 車のエンジンの調子がおかしい *There is something wrong with* the car engine. ‖ きょうは体の調子がおかしい *I'm in bad condition* [*shape*] today. ／I *don't feel well* [*so good*] today.
▶夏なのにこんなに涼しいのはおかしいですね *Isn't it strange* for the weather to be so cool in summer？‖ 親の口から言うのもおかしいが，息子はとても他人に思いやりがある My son is very considerate of others, *if I do say so myself*. (➤「あえて私が自分で言うとすれば」の意) ‖ スピーチのことを考えたら胃がおかしくなった My stomach *churned* at the thought of making a speech. (➤ churn は「(胃が)むかつく」の意のインフォーマルな語).
▶教師のきみがそんな所へ出かけてはおかしい(＝よくない)よ

It would be *improper* for you, as a teacher, to go to such a place. ‖ おかしなことを言うな Don't talk such *nonsense*. ‖ おかしな話だが，ぼくは同じ夢を３晩続けて見た *Strange to say*, I had the same dream three nights in a row.

▶おかしなまねをしたら命はないぞ One *false* move, and you'll be a dead man. ‖ おかしいな．明かりがついているのに誰も出て来ない That's *strange*. Nobody is answering the door, even though the lights are on in the house.

▶どうもあの人の行動はおかしい His conduct seems a bit *suspicious*.

おかしな →おかしい.

おかしらつき 尾頭付き a **whole fish**, a **fish complete with head and tail** ▶息子の入試合格をタイの尾頭付きで祝った We celebrated my son's passing the entrance examination with *a whole sea bream*. (●「タイの尾頭付き」が縁起物であることを知らない外国人には，with 以下を例えば by serving a whole sea bream, a fish eaten on festive occasions (おめでたいときに食べる魚のタイを尾頭付きで出して) とするとよい).

1**おかす 犯す** **commit** +目 (罪を) ; **break** +目 (法を) ▶過ちを犯す *commit* an error ‖ 殺人を犯す *commit* murder ‖ ミスを犯す *make* a mistake ‖ 校則を犯す *break* a school regulation ‖ 女性を犯す *violate* a woman (*sexually*) (➤ violate は rape の婉曲(えんきょく)語) ‖ 私は絶対に殺人は犯していない I *am* completely *innocent of* the murder. (➤ innocent は「潔白な」).

2**おかす 侵す** **infringe (on)** (侵害する) ; **invade** (侵入する) ▶他人の権利を侵す *infringe* (*on*) the rights of others ‖ 日本の領空を侵す *invade* [*violate*] Japanese airspace.

3**おかす 冒す** ▶彼は肺を冒されている His lungs *are affected*. ／He is suffering from lung trouble.

▶危険を冒す *run* a risk ‖ 風雨を冒して我々は出港した We sailed out *in the face of* a severe storm. (➤ in the face of は「…を物ともせず」).

おかず ***okazu***

日本紹介 ✉ **おかずはご飯と一緒に食べる，肉や魚や野菜などの副食をいいます．日本人のふつうの食事は，ご飯，みそ汁，２～３品のおかずで成り立っています** *Okazu* refers to side dishes (such as meat, fish, or vegetables) that are served with rice. A typical Japanese meal consists of rice, miso soup and two or three *okazu* dishes.

おかっぱ a **bob (haircut)**, **bobbed hair** (➤ bob よりも長いものが lob ; bob と lob の中間が mob). ▶おかっぱ(頭)にする wear one's hair in *a bob*.

おかどちがい お門違い ▶妻に文句を言ったら，妻はお門違いだとかんかんになって怒った When I complained to my wife, she got mad and shot back that I was *barking up the wrong tree*. (➤ bark up the wrong tree は「見当違いなことをする」の意).

おかぶ お株 ▶私は自分がカラオケがうまいと思っていたが，ゆうべばかりは細川君にお株を奪われた I thought I was a good karaoke singer, but last evening Hosokawa *beat* me *at my own game* [*stole* my *thunder*]. (➤ steal A's thunder は「A (人) を出し抜いて注目される」).

おかま a **queen**, a **fruit**.

おかまい お構い ▶何のお構いもできませんが (＝特別なものは何もありませんが) 一緒に夕食でも食べていってください *We're not having anything special*, but please stay and have dinner with us.

▶《客が帰るときに》何のお構いもできませんで I'm glad you could come. (➤ 英語では「おいでいただけてよかった」と肯定的に言うが，次例のように謙遜のことばを付け加えることもある) ／ (It was so nice of you to come.) I only wish we'd treated you to something better. (➤「もっとよいおもてなしができればよかったのですが」の意).

▶ 対話「どうぞ，お上がりください．今お茶でも入れますから」「いえ，どうぞお構いなく」 "Please come in. I'll make you some tea." "No, please *don't bother* [*don't go to any trouble*]."

おかまいなし お構いなし ▶彼らは病人が寝ているのにお構いなしに大声でしゃべっている They are talking loud *with no regard for* the fact that there are sick people here.

▶彼女は身なりのことにはお構いなしだ She *doesn't care about* her appearance.

1**おかみ お上** **the government** (政府) ; **the authorities** /əθɔ́ːrəṭiz/ (当局) ; one's **wife** (他人の妻).

2**おかみ 女将** an ***okami*** ; a **proprietor**.

おがみたおす 拝み倒す ▶拝み倒されてしかたなく PTA の役員を引き受けた They *begged and pleaded* me into taking on an executive position in the P.T.A.

おがむ 拝む **pray** (祈る) ; **worship** (+目) (あがめる) ▶ひざまずいて拝む *pray* on one's knees ‖ イスラム教徒はアラーを拝む Muslims *worship* Allah. ‖ うちの両親は毎日神棚を拝む My parents *pray before* the Shinto family altar every day. ‖ 彼に拝むようにして (＝必死に) 金を貸してくれと頼んだ I *desperately* begged him to lend me money.

おかめはちもく 岡［傍］目八目 ▶ ことわざ 岡目八目 Lookers-on can see eight moves ahead. ／ Onlookers see more than the players. (➤ 前者は日本語からの直訳，後者はその意訳).

おかゆ お粥 ***okayu*** ; **rice porridge**. →かゆ.

おから ***okara*** ; a byproduct of making tofu (➤ 説明的な訳).

オカリナ an **ocarina** /ɑ̀kəríːnə/ ▶オカリナを吹く play the *ocarina*.

オカルト **(the) occult** /əkʌ́lt ‖ ɔ́kʌlt/ ▶オカルト映画［小説］ an *occult movie* [*novel*].

おがわ 小川 a **(small) stream**, a **brook** (➤ 後者はやや文語的) ▶小川のせせらぎ the murmur of *a stream* ‖ 夏になるとよく家の近くの小川で泳いだものだ In summer, I used to go swimming in *a stream* near my house.

おかわり お代わり **another helping** ▶お代わりをください *Another helping*, please. ‖ お代わりしてもいいですか May I have *seconds*? ／May I ask for *another helping*? ‖ お茶のお代わりはいかが？ Would you care for *another* cup (of tea)? ／Would you like *a refill*? (➤「ご飯」の場合は第１文の cup (of tea) を bowl (of rice) に変える) ‖ 対話「コーヒーのお代わりはいかがですか」「お願いします」 "Would you like *more* coffee?" "Please." (➤「もう結構です」なら No, thank you. と答えるか，これに続けて I've had enough. と言う).

おかん 悪寒 a **chill** ▶かぜをひいたらしく，家に帰ると悪寒を覚えた (I think) probably I had caught a cold, since I *had chills* after coming home.

おかんむり ▶結婚記念日を忘れていたので妻はおかんむりだった My wife was *upset* [*in a sour mood*], since I'd forgotten about our wedding anniversary.

おき 沖 ▶彼らは３キロ沖まで泳いだ They swam as far

as three kilometers *offshore*. ‖ 今頃船は九十九里沖にいるはずだ The ship must now be somewhere *off* (the coast of) Kujukuri. ‖ 沖合に釣り船やヨットが見える I can see fishing boats and sailboats *offshore*.

-おき -置き

語法「-置き」は「…ごとに」を意味する every ... を利用する. 注意しなければならないのは, 例えば every three years は「3年ごと」なので「2年置き」になることである.「1つ置き」は every two ... または〈every other + 単数名詞〉で表す. 例えば「1週間置き」は every two weeks または every other week となる. ただし,「1時間置き」は every two hours で, every other hour は「ひっきりなしに」のニュアンスがあり, いらだちやせわしなさを表す ; She sends text messages to her boyfriend every other hour. (彼女は彼氏にひっきりなしに携帯メールを送る). ただし下の用例の「5時間置きに」「15分置きに」のように「…ごと」と同じような意味で使われることもあるので文意から適切に訳す必要がある.

▶父は1日置きに東京の大学で教えている My father teaches at a college in Tokyo *every other day* [(*once*) *every two days*]. ‖ この薬を5時間置き [2日置き] に飲んでください Take this medicine *every five hours* [*every three days*]. ‖ 作文は1行置きに書きなさい Compositions should be written *on every other line*.

▶ 対話「このバスは何分置きに出ますか」「15分置きです」"*How often* does the bus run?" "It runs *every* fifteen minutes [*at* fifteen-minute *intervals*].

おきあがる 起き上がる get up ▶その子は石につまずいて転んだがすぐに起き上がった The child tripped on a stone and fell, but *got up* immediately. ‖ 《患者が医者に》ベッドに起き上がってもいいですか Can I *sit up* in bed?

オキアミ 《動物》krill.

おきかえる 置き換える rearrange +目 (並べ換える) ; replace +目 (取り替える) ▶テーブルの上の花瓶を別のに置き換える *replace* the vase on the table *with* another one.

おきがけ 起きがけ ▶起きがけに電話が鳴った The telephone rang *right after I woke up* [*as soon as I got out of bed*].

おきざり 置き去り ▶人を置き去りにする *leave* a person *behind* ‖ 別荘地に置き去りにされた猟犬が危険な野犬となった The hounds *abandoned* in the summer resort became dangerous feral dogs.

オキシダント an oxidant ▶都市部ではオキシダント濃度が年々上昇している Every year the concentration of *oxidants* in city air is increasing.

おきて 掟 a rule (規則, 約束事) ; a law (法律 ; 自然界などの法則) ▶おきてを守る keep *a rule* [*a law*] (➤「破る」の場合の動詞は break).

▶強いものだけが生き残る. それが自然界のおきてだ It is *a law of nature* that only the strong survive. / Only the strong survive. That is *the way nature works*.

おきてがみ 置き手紙 a note (メモ) ; a message (伝言) ▶置き手紙をして家出してきちゃった I *left a note* and ran away from home.

おきどけい 置き時計 a table clock, a desk clock.

おぎなう 補う make up (for), compensate 《for》(埋め合わせる) ; supplement +目 (補充する) ▶損失を補う *make up* (*for*) a loss ‖ 家計を補う *supplement* the household budget ‖ 勉強はしばしば才能の不足を補う Hard work often *compensates for* lack of ability.

▶空所に適当な語を補え *Fill in* the blanks with suitable words. ‖ できるだけ早く欠員を補わねばならない We must *fill* the vacancy as soon as possible.

おきにいり お気に入り a favorite (人, 物) ▶お気に入りのセーター one's *favorite* sweater ‖ 彼は先生のお気に入りだ He is his teacher's *favorite*. (➤ teacher's pet ということもあるが, ときに軽蔑的なニュアンスを伴う).

おきにめす お気に召す ▶お気に召しましたか *Is it to your liking?*

おきぬけ 起き抜け →起きがけ.

おきば 置き場 ▶この駅の近くには自転車置き場がない There is no good *place to leave* a bicycle near this station. ‖ 百科事典はいいが, わが家には置き場がない Encyclopedias are fine, but there's simply no *room* for one in my house. (➤ この room は「空間, 余裕」).

おきびき 置き引き a (baggage / luggage) thief (人) ; (a) baggage [luggage] theft (行為) ▶荷物の置き引きを防ぐ prevent *baggage* [*luggage*] *theft* ‖ ちょっと目を離した隙に, かばんを置き引きされた When I looked away for just a second, my briefcase *was stolen*.

おきまり お決まり ▶試合のあとはお決まりの監督のお小言だった After the game the manager gave his *usual* lecture.

おきみやげ 置き土産 a parting gift (せん別) ; a memento /məméntoʊ/ (思い出となる物) ▶卒業生はこのモザイクを置き土産とした The graduates left this mosaic as *a parting gift*. ‖ ジョーンズ氏は1冊のスケッチブックを私への置き土産として帰国して行った Mr. Jones went home, leaving me a sketchbook as *a memento* [*keepsake*].

おきもの 置物 an ornament (飾り物) ; a statuette /stætʃuét/ (小立像) ▶ウサギの置物 a rabbit-shaped *ornament*.

おきゃく お客 →客.

おきゅう お灸 ▶背中におきゅうを据える *cauterize* the back *with moxa* (➤ cauterize /kɔ́:ṭəraɪz/ は「(傷口などを)焼く」, moxa /mά:ksə/ は「もぐさ」の意) (➤ 治療法の1つとしてのおきゅうを知らない人には残酷な行為と映るおそれがある).

▶《比喩的》弱い者いじめをして父におきゅうを据えられた I *was* lectured [*told off*] by my father for bullying someone weaker than me. (➤ tell off は「ひどく叱る」の意のインフォーマルな言い方).

おきる 起きる

📖 訳語メニュー
起床する →get up **1**
目を覚ます →wake up **2**
遅くまで起きている →stay up **4**
事件などが →happen, break out **5**

1 【起床する】 get up ▶私は朝6時に起き, 夜は11時に寝る I *get up* at six in the morning and go to bed at eleven at night. ‖ ぼくが起きたときには, 母はもう起きていた My mother *was* already *up* when I *got up*. ‖ 起きなさい *Get up!* ‖ けさは遅く起きた I *got up* late this morning.

2 【目を覚ます】 wake up, awake (➤ 後者は比喩的な意味で用いられることが多い) ▶赤ん坊が起きるから静かにしなさい Be quiet or the baby will *wake up*. ‖ 《教室でぼーっとしている生徒に》きみ，**起きてる**の？ Are you *up*？（➤ Are you awake？は朝の起床時に用いる）‖最近夜眠れなくて，夜中に何度も**起きて**しまう I'm not sleeping well these days, and often *wake up* in the middle of the night.

3【起き上がる】▶彼は少なくとも1週間は**起きられない**だろう He won't *be up and about* for at least a week.（➤ up and about は「(病人が)床を離れて」）‖母はようやく**起きられる**ようになった My mother is finally well enough to *leave her bed*.

4【寝ないでいる】stay up ▶ゆうべ何時まで**起きていた**の？ How late did you *stay up* last night？‖今夜は遅くなるから**起きて待っている**ことはないよ You don't have to *wait up* [*stay up*／*sit up*] *for* me, since I'll be coming back late tonight.‖何，まだ**起きてる**の？ What, you'*re* still *up*？

5【発生する】happen, occur（偶然に；後者は前者より堅い語）；**break out**（突発的に）⇀**起こる** ▶困ったことが**起きた** Something distressing *has happened*.‖その大火は私が5歳のときに**起きた** The big fire *broke out* when I was five years old.‖世界で**起きつつある**すべてのことを知ることはできない We can't know everything that *is happening* [that *is going on*] in the world.

▶同じことは**誰にでも起きる**可能性がある The same thing can *happen to anybody*.‖この小冊子を読んでいて**疑問が起きたら**教室へ(疑問点を)持って来なさい If you *have any questions* while reading this booklet, bring them to class.

6【火が盛んになる】▶炭火が**真っ赤におきている** The charcoal *is scarlet-red* in the fire.

おきわすれる 置き忘れる leave +目；**misplace** +目（…を置いた場所がわからなくなる）▶私は電車の中に傘を**置き忘れた** I *left* my umbrella on [《英》in] the train.（➤ 場所を示す語句があるときはふつう forget でなく leave を用いる；⇀**忘れる**）‖誰かが眼鏡を**置き忘れていった** Someone *has forgotten* his [her] glasses.

▶それはどこかに**置き忘れた**ようだ I seem to *have misplaced* it.

[1]**おく 億** a [one] **hundred million** ⇀**万**

《参考》(1)英語国では数字を3桁に区切ることからもわかるように，3桁(0が3つ)ごとに単位が変わる.

1,000… a thousand(千)
1,000,000… a million(100万)
1,000,000,000… a billion(10億)
1,000,000,000,000… a trillion(1兆)
1,000,000,000,000,000… a quadrillion(1000兆)

一方，日本語は4桁(0が4つ)ごとに単位が変わる. 兆は0が12個なので日英語でそろうが，それ以外の万，億，そして京は英語では千を10個，百万を100個，千兆を10個と数えることになる.

10,000… ten thousand(万)
100,000,000… a hundred million(億)
10,000,000,000,000,000… ten quadrillion(京)

(2)2億，3億，…と言う場合も two hundred million, three hundred million, … とし，hundred や million に複数語尾の s はつけないのがふつう.

▶ABC銀行で**3億円**が強奪された ABC Bank was robbed of *three hundred million yen*.‖世界の人口は約**70億**だ The world's population is about *seven billion*.

[2]**おく 奥 1【入り込んだ所】**▶森の奥 *the depths* of a forest‖森の**奥**に小屋を見つけた I found a lodge *deep* in the forest.‖喉の**奥**が痛い *The back* of my throat hurts.

2【家屋などの】▶庭の奥 *the end* [《英》*the bottom*] of a garden‖弟は**奥の部屋**で遊んでいる My little brother is playing in the *back room*.‖《バスで運転手が》もう少し**奥に詰めて**ください *Move in* a bit, please！

3【心などの】▶私は**心の奥**では息子を許している *Deep in my heart*, I forgive my son.‖**心の奥**では私たちの関係はうまくいかないだろうとわかっていた I knew *deep in my heart* that our relationship wasn't going to go well.

[3]**おく 置く**

訳語メニュー
物の上に置く ⇀put, place **1**
(店が)扱う ⇀carry, have **3**
残しておく ⇀leave **4**
そのままにしておく ⇀leave **7**

1【据える，載せる】put +目；**place** +目（置き方・置く場所が正確である場合）；**set** +目（ある特定の場所に）；**lay** +目（注意深く水平に）▶机の上に本を**置く** *put* a book on the desk‖テレビはどこに**置く**の？ Where are you going to *place* the TV set？‖彼女はテーブルの上に花瓶を**置いた** She *set* a flower vase on the table.

▶車はどこに**置いて**(＝駐車して)もいいの？ Can I *park* the car anywhere？‖ぼくは彼女の肩にそっと手を**置いた** I *laid* my hand on her shoulder lightly.‖彼はいつも辞書をそばに**置いている** He always *keeps* a dictionary at hand.（➤ at hand は handy でもよい）‖**対話**「この箱どこに**置く**の？」「そこに**置いて**ちょうだい」"Where do you want this box？" "Over there, please."（➤「置く」という動詞を訳出する必要のない例）.

2【配置する】put +目，**allocate** /ǽləkeɪt/ +目（➤ 後者は堅い語）；**station** +目（人を駐在させる）▶若い人を数人営業部に**置く**つもりだ We plan to *put* a few young people in the sales department.／We're planning to *assign* several young employees to the sales department.‖わが社は今度大阪に支店を**置く**ことにした We have decided to *open* a branch office in Osaka in the near future.

▶近辺が物騒になってきたからガードマンを常時**置く**ことにした Since the neighborhood is getting dangerous, we decided to *station* (security) guards 24 hours a day.

▶わが社は現在非常に困難な状況に**置かれている** Our company *is* now *faced with* a very difficult situation.（➤「直面している」の意）‖目標をどこに**置く**かで方法が変わってくる The approach we should take depends on where we *set* our goals [how high we *set* our goals].

3【商店で扱う】carry +目（在庫がある）；**have** +目（持っている）▶あの店はほとんどあらゆる銘柄のハムを**置いている** They *carry* [*have*] almost every brand of ham in that store.‖**対話**「乾電池ありますか」「あいにくうちには**置いてません**」"Do you have any batteries？" "Sorry, we don't *carry* them here."

4【あとに残してくる】leave +目 ▶子供を家に**置いてき**ましたので，これで失礼いたします I must excuse myself now as I *left* my children at home.（➤ left は

お

leave の過去形) ‖ 大きな荷物はホテルへ置いて出かけた I *left* my heavy things [luggage] at the hotel and went out.
▶あっ, 傘を電車の中に置いてきちゃった Oh, I *left* [*forgot*] my umbrella on the train. ‖ 彼は妻子を置いて家出した He walked out on his wife and children. (➤ walk out on は「…を見捨てて出て行く」の意のくだけた言い方).
▶ぐずぐずしていると置いてっちゃうよ Hurry up, or *we'll go without you*. (🏺 英語では「あなたを連れない[伴わない]で行く」と考える).
5【放置する】▶お湯を注いで 3 分間置きなさい Pour hot water and *let* it *stand* for three minutes.
6【隔てる】▶お隣の生け垣から 3 メートル置いてうちの塀がある The wall of our house is 3 meters *away from* our neighbor's hedge. ‖ 写真前列の右端が父, **1 人置いて**隣がおじです In the picture, my father is at the right end in the front row, and my uncle is *the second from* him. ‖ 次に薬を飲むのは **3 日置いて**ください Please take this medicine again *four days from now* [*in four days*]. (➤ どちらも「きょうから 4 日後に」の意). (→–置き).
7【「…(のままに)しておく」の形で】 **leave** +⑪ ▶真っ暗は怖いから電気はつけておいてね It's scary when it's dark, so *leave* the light *on*, okay? ‖ 皿洗いはあとでしますから, **そのままにしておいてください** Please *leave* the dishes *where they are*. I'll wash them later.
▶**言わせておけば**いい気になりやがって I'*ve been letting* you *say* whatever you want, but now you're going too far. (🏺 英語では「言いたいことを言わせてきたが, もう程度をはるかに超えてきている」と発想して, 訳例のように表現する) ‖ **言わせておくさ** *Let him say what he wants*. ‖ 母が夕食を**作っておいてくれた** Mom *had* dinner *ready* for me.
8【「…ことにしておく」の形で】▶電話がかかってきたら, ぼくは**いないことにしておいてくれ** If there's a phone call for me, *say that* I'm not in. ‖ その女の子をきみの恋人**ということにしておこう** *Let's leave it as a given* [*Let's say*] for now that she's your girl(-friend). (➤ この given は「既定の事実」の意の名詞).

おくがい 屋外 ▶こういう天気のいい日には**屋外で**運動しなさい You should go out and exercise *in the open air* [*out of doors*] on fine days like this.

おくさま 奥様 **1【呼びかけ】** **madam** ▶ **対話** (女主人が使用人に)「窓を閉めなさい」「はい, 奥さま」"Close the window." "Yes, *ma'am*." (➤ ma'am はインフォーマルで madam の略. ただし《英》では madam がふつう).
2【夫人】▶**奥さま**によろしく Say hello to *your wife* for me. (➤ Mrs. ～ とするほうが丁寧) ‖ 山田さんの**奥さま**は高校の先生をしていらっしゃいます *Mrs.* Yamada is a high school teacher.

おくさん 奥さん a **wife** ▶**奥さん**はお元気? How is *your wife*? ‖ お隣の**奥さん**はよく銀座へ買い物に出かける The *lady* next door often goes out shopping in Ginza. ‖ **佐藤さんの奥さん**は昨日退院した *Mrs. Sato* left hospital yesterday.

おくじょう 屋上 a **rooftop**, a **roof** ▶お天気の日には**屋上**から富士山が見えます On a clear day, you can see Mt. Fuji from the *rooftop*. ‖ **屋上**にはプールがあります There is a swimming pool on the *rooftop*. ‖ **屋上にある**レストラン a *rooftop* restaurant. ‖ ことわざ **屋上屋を架す** build a roof on top of a roof (➤ 直訳) ; That's like gilding the lily. ／《英》Don't carry coals to Newcastle. (➤ ともに「余計なことをする」の意の慣用表現).
‖**屋上庭園** a roof [rooftop] garden ‖ **屋上緑化** roof [rooftop] greening.

おくする 臆する **become timid** ▶お偉いさんたちの前でも**臆することなく**意見が言えるようにならなければだめだ You should *be bold enough to* express your opinion even in front of the higher ups. ／ You *shouldn't be afraid to* [*hesitate to*] speak your mind even in front of the big shots.

おくそく 臆測 (a) **speculation** ; (a) **conjecture** (証拠もなしに推測で結論を出すこと ; 堅い語) ; a **guess, guesswork** (推測 ; 後者は数えられない名詞) ▶彼の後継者に関して盛んな**臆測**がなされていた A lot of *speculation* went around regarding his successor. ‖ **臆測で**物を言ってはいけない You shouldn't say things that are just your own *speculation* [*unfounded guesswork*].
▶それは単なる**臆測**にすぎない It is pure *conjecture*. ‖ きみの**臆測**は外れていたよ You *guessed* wrong. ／ Your *guess* was wrong.

おくそこ 奥底 **the depth(s)** (深い所) ; **the bottom** (底) ▶**心の奥底から**彼を愛しているとは言えないわね I can't say I love him *from the bottom of my heart*.

オクターブ an **octave** /ɑ́:ktəv/ ▶彼女は**2 オクターブ**の声が出せる She has a singing range of *two octaves*.

おくち 奥地 **the depths** ; **the interior** (内陸部) ▶アマゾンの**奥地**を探検する explore *the interior* of the Amazon.

おくづけ 奥付 **the publisher's inscription** (at [added to] the end of a book).

おくて 奥手 ▶うちの子は**おくて**でしてね. まだガールフレンドもいないんですよ My son is *a late developer* [*a late bloomer*]. He doesn't have a girlfriend yet.

おくない 屋内の **indoor** /índɔ̀:ʳ/ **一副 屋内で** **indoors** /ìndɔ́:ʳz/ ▶雨だったので体育の授業は**屋内で**やった We had the PE class *indoors* since it was raining outside. (➤ PE は physical education (体育) の頭文字).
‖**屋内スポーツ** an indoor sport ‖ **屋内プール** an indoor swimming pool ‖ **屋内練習場** a gymnasium /dʒɪmnéɪziəm/, a gym.

おくに お国 ▶**お国**はどちらですか Where are you from? ／Where do you come from? (➤ 両例とも国内の出身地を聞く場合にも使える) ‖ 彼は私の家に来るといつも**お国自慢をする** Every time he comes to see us, he *talks proudly about his own home* [*country*].
‖**お国なまり** the dialect of one's hometown (故郷の方言) ; a provincial accent (地方なまり).

おくのて 奥の手 ▶この計画がだめでも, ぼくらには**奥の手**がある Even if this plan doesn't work, we still *have one up our sleeve* [*have our secret weapon*]. (➤ have ... up one's sleeve は「…を袖の中に隠してある」が原義).

おくば 奥歯 a **back tooth** ; a **molar** (臼歯) ▶**奥歯**を 1 本抜いてもらった I had *a molar* pulled out.
▶《慣用表現》**奥歯に物が挟まったような**言い方はしないでください Would you please stop beating around [about] the bush? (➤ beat around [about] the bush は「茂みの周りをたたいて獲物の鳥を追い出す」の意から「要点を言わない」).

おくび ▶《慣用表現》彼はそんなことは**おくびにも出さない**

だろう He probably will *not so much as hint* such a thing. (➤ not so much as do で「…すらしない」の意).

おくびょう 臆病 cowardice /káʊərdɪs/ (意気地なし) ; timidity (内気) 一形 臆病な timid, cowardly ▶臆病な人 a *timid* person ／a coward ‖ 概して日本人は外国語を話す場合**臆病**すぎる Generally speaking, Japanese are too *timid* when they speak a foreign language. ‖ 今頃になって**臆病風に吹かれた**か Are you going to *chicken out* now? ／It's too late to *chicken out*. (● 前者は「今になっておじけづき出したか」, 後者は「今頃おじけづくのでは遅すぎる」と発想して英訳したもの).

おくふかい 奥深い deep ; profound (比喩的な意味で) ▶奥深い森 a *deep* forest ‖ 聖書の中の話は易しいようだが, **奥深い**真理がある The stories in the Bible, though they seem (to be) simple, have *deep* [*profound*] truth in them.

おくまった 奥まった ▶奥まった(＝奥の)部屋 a *back* room ‖ 通りから少し**奥まった**所にある家 a house standing a little *back* from the street ‖ その店は**奥まった**所にあるので見つけにくい The shop is not easy to spot since it *is* a little *tucked away*. (➤ be tucked away は「人目につかない所にある」).

おくまんちょうじゃ 億万長者 a multimillionaire, a billionaire.

おくめんもなく 臆面も無く ▶うちの娘むこは**臆面もなく**金の無心をする My son-in-law *has the nerve* [*the impudence*] *to* tap us for money. (➤「ずうずうしくも…する」の意 ; tap A for B は「A (人)にB (物)をせびる, ねだる」).

▶**臆面もなく**よくそんなことが言えるものだ *How dare* you say such a thing!

おくやみ お悔やみ condolence ; condolences /kəndóʊlənsiz/ (お悔やみのことば) ▶彼の家へ**お悔やみ**に行った I visited him to offer my *condolences*.

✉ **お父さまご逝去の由, 誠にご愁傷さまに存じます. 謹んでお悔やみ申し上げます** I am very sorry [I was deeply grieved] to hear of your father's death. Please accept my *heartfelt sympathy* [my *sincere condolences*] on your great loss. (➤ sympathy は「同情」が転じて「お悔やみ」の意. condolences のほうが形式ばった語).

✉ 《お供えの花に添えるカードで》**心からお悔やみ申し上げます** With (love and) *deepest sympathy* ／*Deepest sympathy* from Mari and Mamoru Hayashi ➤ 贈り主の名は例示のような書き方をする.

‖ **お悔やみ状** a letter of condolence.

おくゆかしい 奥床しい ⚠ **日本的な表現で, これにぴったりの英語はない. refined (洗練された), graceful (しとやかな, 上品な), modest (謙遜した), demure ((女性が)慎み深い) などの形容詞を適宜用いる.**

▶女官たちの**奥ゆかしい**ことばづかい the *refined* language of court ladies ‖ **奥ゆかしい**女性 a *graceful* woman ‖ 人を助けて名前も言わずに立ち去るとは何て**奥ゆかしい**人だろう How *modest* of him to rescue someone and leave without even giving his name!

おくゆき 奥行き depth (深さ) ▶金庫の**奥行き** the *depth* of a safe ‖ その建物は間口が10メートル, **奥行き**が20メートルある The building is 10 meters wide, and *extends* back 20 meters. ‖ その家は**奥行きがある** The house *extends far back*.

オクラ 《植物》 okra.

おくらいり お蔵入り ▶その映画は不評で**お蔵入り**になった The movie *was put in storage* [*was suspended*] because it received unfavorable criticism.

おくらせる 遅らせる delay ▶吹雪のため出発を**遅らせる**ことにした Because of the snowstorm, we've decided to *delay* our departure. ‖ もうこれ以上計画を**遅らせる**ことはできない The plan cannot *be delayed* any more [any further].

オクラホマ Oklahoma /òʊkləhóʊmə/ (アメリカの中南部の州 ; 略 OK, Okla.).

おくりおおかみ 送り狼 ▶家まで乗せていってほしいけど, **送りおおかみ**はごめんだわ I need someone to give me a ride home, but no *wolves* (*in sheep's clothing*), please. (➤「羊の皮を着たオオカミ」とは親切を装った危険人物のこと).

おくりかえす 送り返す send back ▶この花瓶はひびが入っているからすぐに**送り返して**くれ This vase is cracked, so *send* it *back* immediately.

おくりがな 送り仮名 *okurigana* ; an inflectional ending added in *kana* after a *kanji*(➤ 説明的な訳).

おくりこむ 送り込む send 《to, into》 ▶その男はスパイとして日本に**送り込まれた** The man *was sent into* Japan as a spy.

おくりさき 送り先 ▶この荷物の**送り先**(＝受取人)はどなたにしますか Who will be *the recipient* of this package?

▶**送り先**(＝場所)をきちんと書いてください Please write down *the destination* precisely.

おくりじょう 送り状 an invoice.

おくりだす 送り出す **1【外へ】** send off ▶朝は主人と子供たちを**送り出す**まではてんてこまいなの I'm terribly busy in the morning till I *send* [*pack*] my husband and children *off*. (➤ pack off は「…をせかして(ほかの場所へ)行かせる」の意のインフォーマルな表現).

2【相撲で】 ▶白鵬は把瑠都を**送り出した** Hakuho *shoved* Baruto out of the ring *from the rear*.

3【世の中へ】 ▶私たちの高校は数多くの音楽家を世に**送り出している** Our high school *has produced* many professional musicians.

おくりとどける 送り届ける ▶彼女を家まで**送り届けて**やってくれるかい? Will you *take* [*drive* ／*see* ／*walk*] her *home*? (➤ drive は車で, walk は徒歩のとき. see は改まった語). →送る.

おくりぬし 送り主 a sender.

おくりバント 送りバント 《野球》 a sacrifice bunt ▶ヤクルトは**送りバント**でランナーを二塁に進めようとした The Swallows attempted to *sacrifice* the runner to second. (➤ sacrifice は「送り [犠牲] バントで進塁させる」).

おくりび 送り火 *okuribi* ; a bonfire built to send off the spirits of ancestors on the last day of the Bon Festival(➤ 説明的な訳).

おくりむかえ 送り迎え ▶彼女は毎日夫を駅まで車で**送り迎え**している She *drives* her husband *to and from* the train station every day.

おくりもの 贈り物 a present, a gift (➤ 日常語としては前者が好まれる) ▶**贈り物**を交換する exchange *presents* ‖ 息子への誕生日 [クリスマス] の**贈り物**に自転車を買った I bought my son a bicycle for his birthday [for Christmas]. (➤ この文では present は不要. ただし for 以下を as a birthday [Christmas] present とするのは可).

お

▶美穂への**贈り物**は赤いバラにしよう My *present* to Miho will be red roses. ／I am going to give Miho red roses. ‖ この時計は我々が結婚したときに**贈り物**としてもらったものです This clock was given to us as a wedding *gift*.

[1]おくる 送る

訳語メニュー
発送する →send **1**
行かせる →send **2**
車で送っていく →give ... a ride **4**
見送る →see ... off **5**
時を過ごす →lead, spend **6**

1【移す，発送する】send +目；**ship** +目（客に商品を）▶クリスマスカードを航空便で**送る** *send* a Christmas card by airmail ‖ 品物を台湾に**送る** *send* [*ship*] the merchandise to Taiwan ‖ ご両親からは毎月いくら**送ってくる**のですか How much (money) do your parents *send* to you each month ? ‖ 私は彼に**郵便で**小包を**送った** I *mailed* him a parcel. ‖ 私はコンサートに遅れると裕子に**ケータイメールを送った** I *sent a text message* to Yuko [I *texted* Yuko] to tell her I'd be late for the concert. ‖ 画像ファイルをメールで**送って**ください Please *send* [*transmit*] the image files by email.

✉ **卒業祝いにネクタイをお送りします** I'*m sending* you a tie as a graduation gift. ➤ 同封でも別便でも，今送りますというときは進行形を使うのが最も一般的. これから送るときは I'll be sending ... や I'll send ... でもよいが，後者は「あとで送る」の意を強調する.

✉ **ネクタイをお送りくださってありがとう** Thank you very much for the tie you *sent* me.

✉ **私の写真を同封します. あなたの写真を送ってくれますか** I'm enclosing a photo of myself. Will you please *send* me a picture of yours ?

> **直訳の落とし穴「家まで送るよ」**
> send =「送る」と覚えているために，「(きみを)家まで送るよ」を (×)I'll send you home. などと間違える人がいる. send は荷物などを先方に「送る」で，人の場合は「用があって差し向ける」「行かせる」に用いる. 客などを「見送っていく」はやや改まっては I'll see you home. で，ふつうに「一緒に歩いていく」場合は I'll walk you home. という. 車で送る場合は I'll drive you home. がふつうで，ときに，I'll take you home in my car.（例えば，「あなた」の車が急な故障で使えないような場合. この言い方で by car は不自然）も用いる. さらに，「乗せていく」の意では I'll give you a ride [lift] home. とすることができる. →**4**

2【行かせる】send +目 ▶国際会議に特使を**送る** *send* a special envoy to an international conference ‖ 心臓は全身に血液を**送る**ポンプである The heart is a pump which *sends* blood throughout the body. ‖ 応援団は彼女に盛んな声援を**送った** The cheerleaders *gave* her a shout of encouragement.

3【順に移動させる】▶（野球で）ランナーをバントで二塁へ**送る** *sacrifice* a runner to second.（→送りバント）.

4【目的地まで一緒に行く】take +目；**give ... a ride, drive** +目（車で）▶家まで**お送りしましょう** I'll *take* [*walk*] you *home*.（➤ take は車で送る場合にも使える. walk は徒歩のときのみ）‖ お客さんを門まで**お送りしな**さい Will you *see* our visitors *to* the gate ? ‖ お宅まで私の**車で送らせましょう** I'll *send* you home in my car.（➤ 使用人やお抱え運転手に送らせるときの決まり文句）.

▶ **対話**「東京駅まで**車で送っていただけませんか**」「いいですよ」"Would you mind *giving* me *a ride* to Tokyo Station ?" "No, not at all."（➤ もっとくだけて言う場合は "Can you drive me to Tokyo Station ?" と言う）.

5【別れを見届ける】see ... off ▶私はいとこを成田まで**送りに行った** I went to *see* my cousin *off* [to *see off* my cousin] at Narita Airport.

6【時を過ごす】lead +目；**spend** +目 ▶平穏な生活を**送る** *lead* a peaceful life [existence]（➤ このように lead は lead a ... life の形になることが多い）‖ 彼女は音楽家として幸せな一生を**送った** She *lived* happily as a musician.

▶彼は退職して田舎で静かに余生を**送っている** He is *spending* his retirement (years) quietly in the country.

[2]おくる 贈る

give +目；**present** /prɪzént/ +目（➤ 式典を行って「贈呈する」に当たる堅い語で，日常の贈り物には使わない）；**award** +目（賞などを）

【文型】
人(A)に物(B)を贈る
give A B ＝**give** B **to** A
present A **with** B ＝**present** B **to** A
award A B ＝**award** B **to** A
➤ いずれも to A は「誰に」を強調する言い方

▶私は彼女に赤いバラ [真珠のネックレス] を**贈った** I *gave* my girlfriend a red rose [a pearl necklace]. ‖ スウェーデン国王は川端康成にノーベル（文学）賞を**贈った** The King of Sweden *presented* the Nobel Prize (for Literature) *to* Kawabata Yasunari [*presented* Kawabata Yasunari *with* the Nobel Prize (for Literature)].

▶父は退職時に置き時計を**贈られた** My father *was presented with* a table clock when he retired. ‖ 彼女は絵画で一等賞 [特別賞] を**贈られた** She *was awarded* first prize [a special prize] for her painting.

▶横浜市はその芸術家に名誉市民の称号を**贈った** Yokohama City *conferred* the title of Honorary Citizen *on* the artist.（➤ confer は「(称号などを）授ける」）.

おくれ 遅れ・後れ (a) **delay** ▶上越新幹線は雪のため２時間の**遅れが出ている** Service on the Joetsu Shinkansen Line *has been delayed* for two hours due to snow. ‖ 飛行機は**定刻より30分遅れで**成田に到着した Our plane arrived at Narita *30 minutes behind schedule*. ‖ 病気で長いこと学校を休んだので夏休みに**後れを取り戻さねばならない** I was sick and absent from school for a long time, so I have to *make up for* (*the*) *lost time* [*catch up on my work*] during summer vacation.（➤ 前者は「失った時間分を取り戻す」，後者は「たまった仕事 [勉強] の埋め合わせをする」）.

▶仲間に**後れを取る** *lag behind* the group（➤ lag behind は「…より遅れる」）‖ テニスばっかりやっていると勉強で人に**後れを取る**よ You will *fall behind* in your studies if you play tennis so often.

おくればせながら 後ればせながら ▶**後ればせながら**心よりお祝いを申し上げます I offer you my sincere *though belated* congratulations.（➤ belated は「遅くなった」の意の堅い語）.

✉ **後ればせながらお誕生日おめでとうございます** A Belated Happy Birthday!

おくれる 遅れる・後れる

1【約束の時間などに】be late《for》（遅くなる）; **be delayed**（事故などはっきりした原因によって遅延する）▶**遅れてすみません** I'm sorry I'm *late*. ／I'm sorry to be *late*.（➤ 前者のほうがふつう）‖ 私たち, もう20分も**遅れているよ** We'*re* already 20 minutes *late*.

> 【文型】
> 授業・待ち合わせなど(A)に遅れる
> be late for [to] A

▶彼は職場に**遅れて来る**ことはめったにない He's rarely *late for* [*to*] work.（➤ party, class など場所の含みがあるときは to が多く, an appointment（約束）は for がふつう）.

▶私は約束の時間に**遅れる**のが大嫌いです I hate *being late for* appointments. ‖ メグは約束の時間に**遅れて**来た Meg came *late for* the appointment. ‖ 学校に**遅れない**ようにしなさいよ Try not to *be late for* [*to*] school.

▶大雪のために列車は30分**遅れた** The train *was* 30 minutes *late* [*was delayed* 30 minutes] because of the heavy snow.

▶そのプロジェクトは資金不足で2年**遅れた** The project *was delayed* by two years because of the shortage of funds. ‖ 会議は予定より30分**遅れて**始まった The meeting started thirty minutes *behind schedule*. ‖ 卒業式は進行が15分**遅れていた** The graduation ceremony was *running* 15 minutes *behind schedule*.

2【時計が】lose ▶ぼくのクオーツ時計は年に10秒ほど**遅れる** My quartz watch *loses* about ten seconds a year.（➤「進む」は gain）‖ この柱時計は5分**遅れている** This clock *is* five minutes *slow*.（➤「進んでいる」は be fast）‖ このデジタル時計は時報より2秒**遅れている** This digital watch *is* two seconds *behind* the correct time.

3【進み方が遅い】fall behind（後れる）; **lag behind**（後れている）▶ぼくは学校を4か月間も休んだので勉強が**後れてしまった** I *fell behind* in my studies because of a four-month absence from school. ‖ 彼は同級生より学校の勉強が**後れている** He *is behind* his classmates in his schoolwork. ‖ 彼はほかのランナーよりも**後れた** He *lagged behind* the other runners in the race. ‖ 学園祭の準備が**遅れている**（＝準備ができていない）We *are not ready for* our school festival. ‖ えっ, この歌知らないの？ **後れてるわね**！ What! You don't know this song? You'*re behind the times*!

▶流行のスタイルに**後れないようについていく** *keep up with* the latest styles.

おけ 桶 a **tub**; a **(wooden) bucket**（取っ手のついた;《米》では pail ともいう）▶おけ1杯の水 *a tub of* water ‖ 風呂おけ a *bathtub*（➤「湯船」も bathtub という）.

おける 於ける ▶世界における中国の役割はますます重要になってきている China's role *in* the world is becoming increasingly important.

おこがましい ▶自分のこともろくにできないくせに, 他人の世話を焼きたがるなんて**おこがましい**（＝生意気だ）ね It is *presumptuous* of him to advise others when he can't even handle his own affairs. ‖ **おこがましい**ようですが, 私の意見を申し上げてよろしいでしょうか It may be *presumptuous* of me, but may I tell you what I think?

おこげ お焦げ scorched rice ▶少しお焦げのところがおいしい Partly *scorched rice* tastes good.

おこさまランチ お子様ランチ a **kid's** [**kids'**] **meal.**

おこさん お子さん a **child** [複 **children**] ▶**お子さんは**いらっしゃいますか Do you have any *children*?（➤ 日本人がよくしがちな, このようなプライベートな質問は要注意で, 避けるのが賢明. ただし, 気さくなアメリカ人は聞かれる前に, 本人が進んで話してくれることも多い）.

> **直訳の落とし穴「お子さんは元気？」**
> 日本語でもくだけた言い方として, また, いくぶん親しみを込めて「キッズ」をしばしば用いるが, 英語の kids はかなりくだけた言い方. 改まったときは children を用いるほうがよい. 特に単数形 kid は丁寧さに欠ける品のない響きがある.「お子さんは元気？」のつもりで,（×）How is your kid (getting along)? としないこと. 性別がわかっていれば,（×）How is your child? も不自然. 男の子なら son を, 女の子なら daughter を用いる. ごく幼い子供であれば, boy, girl を用いることもある. 複数形の How are your kids? は割合問題なく使えるが, 改まっては How are your children? がよい.

おこし お越し ▶ようこそ**お越し**くださいました We are glad to *have the honor of your presence here*.

おこす 起こす・興す

> 📖 **訳語メニュー**
> 眠りから →wake (up) **1**
> 体を起こす →raise **2**
> 生じさせる →cause **3**
> 開始する →start **4**

1【眠りを覚ます】wake (up), awaken ＋目（➤ 後者は堅い語で, 比喩的にも用いられる）▶ 10時頃までは私を**起こさないでね** Please don't *wake* me (*up*) till about ten. ‖ そんな大きな声を出したら, 赤ちゃんを**起こしちゃう**でしょ You'll *wake* the baby *up* with your loud voice. ‖ あすの朝6時半に**起こしてね** *Wake* me (*up*) at six thirty tomorrow.《参考》この訳例はホテルなどで電話をかけて起こしてもらうときにも使えるが, Can you give me [Can I have] a wake-up call at six thirty tomorrow morning? とか I'd like a wake-up call at six thirty tomorrow morning. のような言い方がよい.

▶**起こさないでください** Do Not Disturb（➤ ホテルで部屋のドアに掛ける掲示）.

2【立てる】raise ＋目 ▶床にごろっと横になってください. 今度は上体を**起こして** First stretch yourself out on the floor. Now *raise* your upper body. ‖ 彼女は病人をベッドの上に**起こして**食事をさせた She *helped* the patient *sit up* in bed to eat.（➤ sit up は「上半身を起こす」）.

▶手を貸して**起こしてちょうだい** Give me a hand *up*. ‖ 庭師は洪水で倒れた庭石を**起こした** The gardener *righted* [*set up*] the garden rock knocked down by the flood.

▶リンカーンは貧困から**身を起こした** Lincoln *lifted himself* out of poverty.

3【生じさせる】cause ＋目（問題・事故などを）; **bring about**（変化・結果などを）▶奇跡を**起こす** *bring about* a miracle ‖ あいつはどこに行っても問題を**起こす** He

お

causes trouble wherever he goes. ‖ そんなにスピードを出すと事故を起こすよ If you drive so fast, you may *have* an accident. ‖ あのドライバーはよく事故を起こす That driver *is prone to accidents*.／That driver *is accident-prone*. (➤ prone は「(好ましくないことを)しがちな」の意) ‖ 彼は運転中に心臓発作を起こした He *had* [*suffered*] a heart attack while (he was) driving. ‖ 傷口を消毒しなかったら炎症を起こしてしまった Since I didn't disinfect the wound, it *became* [*got*] *infected*. (➤ got のほうがインフォーマル).

▶太陽のエネルギーで電気を起こす *generate* electricity by solar energy.

4【開始する】start ▶新しく事業を興す *start* [*set up*] a new enterprise ‖ 仏陀(ぶっだ)は仏教という偉大な宗教を興した Buddha *started* [*founded*] a great religion called Buddhism. ‖ 津田梅子は女子教育を興した人として有名だ Tsuda Umeko is famous for *establishing* advanced education for women. ‖ 訴訟を起こすのは金がかかるよ It costs a great deal of money to *file a suit*. (➤ file は「(書類などを)提出する」の意).

5【書く】▶録音機から会見内容を起こす *transcribe* an interview from a recorder(➤「録音したものを起こす」は transcribe a recording).

6【火の勢いを盛んにする】▶火鉢に火をおこす *build a fire* in a hibachi.

おごそか 厳かな stately(壮麗な)；**grave**(重々しい) ▶厳かな行列 a *stately* procession ‖ 神主さんは厳かな顔で祝詞をあげた The Shinto priest looked *grave* when he offered a prayer.

▶落成式は厳かに行われた The (building) completion ceremony was conducted *solemnly* [*with dignity*].

おこたる 怠る neglect +目 ▶彼は父親としての義務を怠った He *neglected* his duty as a father. ‖ 日頃の鍛錬を怠るな Don't *neglect* your daily discipline. ‖ 私は日記をつけることを2，3日怠った I *failed to* write in my diary for a few days.

おこない 行い behavior(ふるまい)；**conduct**(品行)；a **deed**(行為；特にその是非に言及するような場合に用いる) ▶今後行いを改めなさい Try to *reform your conduct* [*mend your ways*] from now on. ‖ 対話「やあ，ついてるね」「日頃の行いが物を言うのさ」"Lucky you!" "It looks like *my* (*good*) *behavior* has paid off." (➤ pay off は「報われる」) ‖ 晴れたね．これも私の日頃の行いがいいからよ The sky has cleared up. This must be because *my* (*everyday*) *behavior* is good.

おこなう 行う do +目(する)；**conduct** +目(調査・実験などを；堅い語)；**hold** +目(催す) ▶実験を行う *do* [*conduct*] an experiment ‖ 会合を行う *hold* a meeting ‖ 試合を行う *play* a game／*have* a match.

▶あす英語のテストを行います *There will be* an English test tomorrow. ‖ 卒業式は来月行われる The graduation ceremony will *be held* next month. ‖ 冬季オリンピックは4年ごとに行われる The Winter Olympic Games *take place* every four years. (➤ take place は通例「予定されていたことが行われる」の意).

▶七夕は一年に一度7月7日の晩に行われる Tanabata *is observed* on the night of July 7th every year. (➤ observe は「(儀式などを)行う，(記念日などを)祝う」).

おこのみやき お好み焼き *okonomiyaki*

日本紹介 ✉ お好み焼きは水で溶いた小麦粉を鉄板で焼くパンケーキのような料理です．中には小さく切った肉，エビ，キャベツなどを混ぜます．焼き上がったら特製ソースと青のりなどをかけて切り分けて食べます An *okonomiyaki* is a kind of flour pancake cooked on a griddle. In the batter are mixed pieces of meat, shrimp, cabbage, etc. When it is done, a special sauce is put on it and *aonori* (green laver) flakes are sprinkled on it. People cut *okonomiyaki* into small pieces before eating.

おこり 起こり the origin(起源)；**the beginning**(始まり) ▶キリスト教の起こり *the origin* of Christianity ‖ オリンピック競技の起こりは紀元前776年にさかのぼる The Olympic Games trace their origins to 776 B.C. ‖ 事の起こりは何だったのか How did it all *begin* [*start*]?

1おごり 奢り a **treat** ▶これ，私のおごりよ This is my *treat*.／This is *on* me. (➤この on は「…の費用で」の意．「店のおごり」は on the house).

2おごり 驕り・傲り arrogance, pride.

おこりっぽい 怒りっぽい ▶あいつは怒りっぽい(＝短気だ) He is *quick-tempered*. ‖ 怒りっぽい人は嫌いです I don't like people who *get offended easily*.

おこりんぼう 怒りん坊 a **hothead**；a **grouch** /graʊtʃ/ (不平ばかり言う人) ▶何が気に入らないの？ 怒りん坊さん What's bothering you, *grouch* [*hothead*]?

1おこる 怒る 1【腹を立てる】get angry, get mad (➤後者のほうがインフォーマル)；**get upset**(立腹する)

> **【文型】**
> 人(A)のことを怒る
> get angry with [at] A
> get mad at A
> 物事(B)のことで怒る
> get angry about [at／over] B
> get mad about B
> 物事(B)のことで人(A)を怒る
> get angry with [at] A for [about] B
> get mad at A for [about] B
>
> **解説** (1)「怒る」という行為は get angry というが，「怒っている」という継続的状態は be angry と be 動詞を使う．
> (2)この get はあとに形容詞が来て「(ある状態に)なる」の意．→なる．

▶あなたはまだ私のことを怒っているのですか *Are* you still *angry with* me? ‖ 彼は何を怒っているのですか What *is* he *angry about*? ‖ そんなつまらないことで怒るな Don't *get mad about* such a small thing. ‖ 僕がデートに遅刻したことに彼女はかんかんに怒った My girlfriend *got very angry* with me for being late for the date.／My girlfriend *got very angry* about my being late [that I was late] for the date. (➤前者は「私」が直接怒られ，後者の2つは彼女が怒っていることを間接的に知ったというニュアンスがある).

▶先生は怒って教室から出ていった The teacher went out of the classroom *angrily* [*in anger*]. ‖ これ以上，しらを切ってると怒るよ If you play innocent any longer, I'll *lose my temper*. ‖ もう一度言ったら本気で怒るよ If you say that again, I'll *blow up*. (➤ blow up は「かんかんに怒る」).

▶ 対話「どうしてそんなに怒ってるの？」「弟なんて大嫌い. もう口を利いてやるもんか」"Why *are* you so *upset*?" "I hate my brother! I'll never talk to him again!" (➤ be upset は「(怒って)気を取り乱している」の意) ‖ あなたは思いどおりにならないと, すぐ**怒る**んだから You *get upset* easily when you don't get your way.

2【叱る】 ▶おやじは真っ赤になって**怒った** My dad *was red with anger*. ／My dad *saw red*. ‖ 彼女はぷんぷん**怒って**帰ってしまった She went home *in a huff*. ‖ 恵子が帰って来たら**怒ってやらなきゃあ** I'll *talk to* Keiko when she gets back! (➤ talk to は「(人を)叱る, 意見をする」の意のくだけた言い方).

▶遅く帰ったら父に**怒られちゃうわ** I'll *catch it* from Dad if I'm home late. (➤ catch it は「叱られる」の意のくだけた言い方) ‖ 彼女は彼が遅刻したので**怒った** She *was upset* [*annoyed*] that he was late. (● 「気を悪くする, 気分を損ねる」の意の be upset や「むっとする」の意の be annoyed が適当. 遅れたぐらいで angry を使うのは大げさ).

²**おこる 起こる** **happen, occur** (➤ 後者は「いつ」「どこで」などを伝えるときに用いることが多い)；**break out** (戦争・火災などが突発的に)

▶多くの事故は不注意によって**起こる** Many accidents *happen* due to carelessness. ‖ そういうことは毎日**起こっている**ことだ That kind of thing *happens* every day. ／That is an everyday *occurrence*. (➤ 後者は堅い言い方).

▶事件は月曜の朝早くに**起きた** The incident *occurred* early Monday morning. ‖ 第三次世界大戦は**起こる**と思いますか Do you think that World War III will *break out*?

¹**おごる 奢る** **1【ごちそうする】** **treat** +目；**buy** +目 (買ってやる)

> **【文型】**
> **人(A)に食事(B)をおごる**
> **treat** A **to** B
> **buy** A B

▶今夜きみに夕食を**おごる**よ I'll *treat* you *to* dinner tonight.

▶昼食はぼくが**おごる**よ Lunch is *on* me. (➤ この on は「…の費用で」).

2【ぜいたくをする】 ▶彼らは**おごった**暮らしをしている They live *luxuriously* [*in luxury*]. ／They *live high on the hog*. (➤ live high on the hog は「ぜいたくな暮らしをする」の意で《主に米》) ‖ 彼女は**口がおごっている**(＝おいしい物を食べつけている) She *is particular about her food*.

²**おごる 驕る・傲る** ▶たとえすべてが思いどおりに行っても**おごって**はいけません It's not good to *swagger* [Don't *get a swell(ed) head*] even when everything goes just as you hope.

おさえ 押さえ・抑え ▶その子供たちは母親の**抑えが利かない** That mother *cannot control* her children.

おさえこむ 押さえ込む・抑え込む ▶兄とけんかをして**押さえ込まれた** I had a fight with my big brother and I *was held down* by him. ‖ その柔道家は**押さえ込み**で勝った The judoka won the game on *a mat hold*.

おさえつける 押さえつける・抑えつける **hold down** (動けないように) ▶彼女は薬を飲ませるために嫌がる子を**押さえつけた** She *held down* her unwilling child in order to give him [her] some medicine. ‖ 人々の自由は軍国主義によって**抑えつけられていた** The people's freedom *was suppressed* [*was oppressed*] by militarism.

おさえる 押さえる・抑える **1【力を加えて動かないようにする】** **hold** +目 ▶この段ボール箱を中に入れるまでドアを**押さえて**て! Please *hold* the door open until I've got this cardboard box in! ‖ はしごをしっかり**押さえていてくれ**. 上っていくから *Hold* the ladder *steady*. I'm going (to climb) up.

▶彼女は犬が飛びつかないように**押さえていてくれた** She *held* the dog *down* so that it wouldn't jump at me. ‖ うめき声がしたので振り返ると, 隆夫が腹を**押さえて**うずくまっていた I heard a groan and turned around to find Takao crouching down *holding* his stomach.

2【抑制する】 **hold** [**keep**] **back** ▶その悲惨な光景を見て私は涙を**抑えることができなかった** When I saw that tragic sight, I could not *hold* [*keep*] *back* my tears. ‖ 私はやっとのことで**怒りを抑えた** I somehow managed to *swallow my anger*. (➤ swallow は「(怒りなどを)我慢する」) ／I *controlled my anger* [*myself*] with difficulty. ‖ **抑えて抑えて**(＝冷静に) *Cool down*. ／*Hold your horses*. (➤ はやる気持ちを).

▶わがチームはひしめく強豪を**抑えて**優勝した Our team won the championship by *beating* so many strong teams.

3【ある範囲内に収める】 ▶田中はロッテを３安打１点に**抑えた** Tanaka *held* [*kept*] the Marines to one run on three hits. ‖ 今月は支出を**抑えなければならない** We have to *keep down* our expenses this month. ‖ 給料はここ数年**抑えられたまま**なんです Our salary *has been frozen* for the last few years. (➤ freeze は「(給料・物価などを)凍結する」) ‖ スープの塩分を**抑えてくれますか**? Don't put too much salt in my soup.

4【支配下に置く】 ▶我々は彼がやったという証拠を**押さえている** We *have* proof of his guilt. ‖ ５人分のチケットを**押さえてあります** I've *secured* [*booked*] tickets for five people. (➤ secure は「確保する」, book は「予約する」) ‖ その生徒は万引きの現場を**押さえられた**(＝捕らえられた) The student *was caught* in the act of shoplifting. ‖ 今どきの若い人は他人に**頭から押さえられる**のを嫌がる Today's young people don't like to *be under anyone's thumb*. (➤ be under ~'s thumb は「～の言いなりになる」の意のインフォーマルな言い方).

5【把握する】 **grasp** +目 ▶文章の要点をしっかり**押さえなければいけない** You have to *grasp* the gist of the text.

おさがり お下がり **hand-me-downs,**《英 また》**reach-me-downs** ▶美樹はいつも姉さんの**お下がり**ばかり着るのを恥ずかしがっている Miki is embarrassed by always having to wear *hand-me-downs* from her (older) sister.

おさき お先 ▶**お先に**どうぞ(行ってください) After you, please. ／Go ahead, please. (➤ 後者は「(話の続きを促して)その先をどうぞ」,「遠慮しないで[好きなように]どうぞ」などの意にも解釈されるおそれがあって曖昧) ‖ それでは**お先に失礼します** Well, *I must be running along* [*be going*] *now*. ／Well, *I'd better be on my way*. 《参考》退社するときの「お先に(失礼します)」に対しては Good-bye. ／Good night. ／See you tomorrow. ／Have a nice weekend. などを適宜用いる.

▶会社は首になるし，部屋は追い出されるし，これじゃお先真っ暗だ I got fired and got kicked out of my apartment, too. *My future is bleak.*

おさきぼう お先棒 ▶お先棒を担ぐ *be a willing tool* [*cat's paw*] (for someone)（➤「進んで働く手先」の意).

おさげ お下げ **pigtails**；《米》 a **braid,**《英》 a **plait** /pleɪt ‖ plæt/（➤ pigtails は髪を編んでいる編んでいないにかかわらず耳の後ろで２つに分けてたらしたもの；braid [plait] は束ねて編みあげたもの）▶髪を長いお下げにする wear one's hair in (two) long *braids* ‖ お下げの少女 a *pigtailed* little girl.

おさつ お札 《米》 a **bill,**《英》 a (**bank**) **note.**

おさと お里 ▶そんなにがつがつするとお里が知れるよ Don't guzzle like that. It will *reveal* [*show*] *your upbringing*.

おさない 幼い **very young**；**little**（小さい）▶幼い男の子 a *very young* boy ‖ 幼い頃よくこの木の下で遊んだものだ I used to play under this tree *when I was a child* [*when I was little*].
▶彼女の考えは幼い（＝幼稚だ）Her idea is *childish.*

おさなごころ 幼心 ▶幼心にも友だちとの別れはとても悲しかった (*Even*) *though I was a* (*small*) *child*, I felt very sad at parting from my friends.（➤「(まだ)子供だったが」と考える).

おさななじみ 幼馴染み a **childhood friend** ▶10年ぶりに幼なじみに会った I met one of my *childhood friends* for the first time in ten years. ‖ 彼とは幼なじみだ He was my *childhood playmate.* ／He and I were *boyhood chums.*（➤ chum は「(通例男の子どうしの）仲よし」の意のインフォーマルな語).

おざなりな **perfunctory** /pəˈfʌ́ŋktəri/（通りいっぺんの）；**sloppy**（いいかげんな）；**careless**（不注意な）
▶おざなりな講義 a *perfunctory* lecture ‖ おざなりな仕事をする do a *sloppy* [*careless*] job.

おさまる 収まる・納まる・治まる・修まる

1【枠内にきちんと入る】 **fit** ▶これだけの本がこの本棚に収まると思うかい？ Are you sure that all of these books will *fit* on this bookshelf？‖ 答案の枠に収まるように書いてください Write *within* the boxes [frames] in the answer sheet.
▶原稿が長すぎて１ページに収まらない The text is too long to *fit into* one page. ‖ 旅行の費用はどうやら予算内に収まった The cost of the trip somehow *fell within* the budget.

2【ふさわしい所に落ち着く】 ▶偶然見つかったその名画はさる美術館に収まることになった It was decided that the famous drawing which was accidentally discovered would *be kept* in a certain art museum. ‖ 龍馬は土佐に収まりきらないくらいの大人物だった Ryoma was too great a figure to *be contained within* the Tosa clan.
▶《慣用表現》あの２人は結局元のさやに収まったらしい I've heard that the couple *is back together again.*

3【静まる】 **subside**（次第に）；**die down**（風雨が）
▶風が収まった The wind *has died down.* ‖ まもなく嵐は収まった The storm soon *subsided* [*calmed*].（➤ calmed down とはしない）‖ 火事が収まった The fire *was put under* (*control*). ‖ 痛みはやがて治まりますよ The pain will *go away* [*subside*] soon.
▶きみが行けばけんかも収まるだろう If you go, their quarrel will *subside.* ‖ その暴動は収まったが，新しい不穏な動きが起こりかけている The riot *has been suppressed* [*quelled*], but new unrest is brewing again.

4【「おさまらない」の形で】 ▶そんな説明では彼は納まらない（＝納得しない）よ He *won't be satisfied with* your explanation. ／Your explanation will not satisfy him. ‖ このお礼を受け取ってもらわなければ，私の気持ちが治まりません Unless you accept this money, *I'll feel like I owe you* (*something*) [*I'll feel indebted* (*to you*)].

5【平和になる】 ▶新国王が即位してから，国はうまく治まっている Since the new king came to the throne, the country *has been at peace.*

6【行動が模範的になる】 ▶彼は30にもなってまだ素行が修まらない He *cannot conduct himself properly*, though he is already thirty.

おさむい お寒い ▶わが国の社会福祉政策の現状はお寒い限りだ The present condition of our social welfare system is extremely *poor* [*unsatisfactory*].

おさめる 収める・納める・治める・修める

📖 訳語メニュー
枠内に入れる →keep, put **1**
しまう →put ... back《in》**2**
納付する →pay **2**
混乱を静める →settle **4**
統治する →rule **5**

1【枠内に入れる】 **keep** ＋㊐；**put** ＋㊐（置く）▶本を書棚に収める *put* [*keep*] the books on the shelves ‖ パーティーの予算は３万円以内に収めよう I'll try to *keep* the budget for the party *within* 30,000 yen.

2【ふさわしい所に落ち着かせる】 **put ... back**《in》（しまう）；**pay** ＋㊐（納付する）▶おひなさまを来年まで納戸に収めましょう Let us *put* the *hina*-dolls *back in* the closet until next year. ‖ 我々は野鳥の鳴き声をテープに収めた We *captured* the wild birds' calls [songs] on tape.
▶同窓会費を納める *pay* the alumni association dues ‖ 今月末までに授業料を指定の口座に納めてください Please *pay* your tuition into the designated bank account by the end of this month. ‖ 税金を納めるのはすべての国民の義務だ *Paying* taxes is an obligation of every citizen.

3【自分の物にする，手に入れる】 ▶ほんの感謝の気持ちですがお納めください Please *accept* this (gift) as a small token of my gratitude. ‖ わが校はその野球の試合で勝利を収めた We *won* (*a victory* in) the baseball game. ‖ その積極的な宣伝活動が成功を収めた The aggressive advertising campaign *ended in success* [*ended successfully*]. ‖ 彼はその商売で多くの利益を収めた He *made* large *profits* in that venture. ‖ 信長は権力を手中に収めた Nobunaga *seized* power.

4【混乱を静める】 **settle** ＋㊐ ▶この事態を治められるのは彼しかいない He is the only person that can *settle* this situation. ‖ ２人のけんかを収めてくださいよ Please *patch up* the quarrel between the two.

5【国家を統治する】 **administer** ＋㊐（行政管理する）；**govern** ＋㊐（政治組織を通して支配する）；**rule**《over》（権力で統治する）▶中国へ返還される前はイギリスが香港を治めていた The United Kingdom *administered* [*governed*] Hong Kong before its return to Chinese jurisdiction.（➤ jurisdiction

は「管理権」) ‖江戸時代には将軍が日本を治めていた During the Edo period, the shoguns *ruled* (*over*) Japan.

6【学問・技芸を身につける】acquire +目 ▶ひととおり茶の湯を修めるには5年はかかる It takes at least five years to *acquire* an in-depth knowledge of the art of (the) tea ceremony.

▶彼は大学では法律を修めた He *studied* law at the university.

おさらい a review ▶《先生が教室で》きのうの授業のおさらいをしましょう Let's *review* yesterday's lesson. ‖各自,きょうの要点をもう一度家でおさらいしておいてください I ask each of you to *go over* the main points of today's lesson at home.

おさらば ▶友人におさらばする *bid farewell to* one's friend ‖きょうで独身生活ともおさらばだ Today, I must *say good-bye to* [*bid farewell to*] my single life.

おさん お産 childbirth, delivery (出産) ▶お産の苦しみ the pain of *childbirth* ‖妻はお産が軽かった[重かった] My wife had an easy [a difficult] *delivery*.

おさんどん ▶家では妻と交替でおさんどんをします My wife and I take turns *doing the cooking* at home.

おし 押し 1【押すこと】a push ▶横綱は一押しで相手の力士を土俵の外へ突き出した The yokozuna shoved his opponent out of the ring with *one push*. ‖もう一押しすればその木は倒れます *One more push*, and the tree will fall to the ground.

▶彼は押しの一手で久美子をものにした He won Kumiko's heart by *going after* her *with dogged persistence*. (➤「飽くなき執ようさで彼女を追いかけて」の意).

2【主張を通すこと】▶よい販売員は押しが強くなければならないが,強引ではいけない You've got to be *aggressive* but not pushy to be a good salesperson. (➤ aggressive は客には嫌われるが,セールスする側にとっては「積極性のある」というよい意味).

おじ 伯父・叔父 an uncle 《参考》日本語では父母の兄には「伯父」,弟には「叔父」を用いるが,英語にはその区別はない. ▶きのう名古屋のおじが上京して来た My *uncle* in Nagoya came to Tokyo yesterday. ‖信男おじさんは秋田に住んでいる *Uncle* Nobuo lives in Akita. →おじさん.

おしあいへしあい 押し合いへし合い ▶みんな花嫁の姿を一目見ようと押し合いへし合いになった Everybody *pushed and shoved* to get a look at the bride.

おしあける 押し開ける push open ▶うちの犬はドアを鼻で押し開けることができる Our dog can *push open* the door with its nose.

おしあげる 押し上げる boost +目 ▶出生率を押し上げる *boost* the birthrate ‖物価を押し上げる *push up* prices.

おしあてる 押し当てる ▶彼女はハンカチを目頭に押し当てた She *dabbed at* her eyes with a handkerchief. (➤ dab は「軽くたたく」).

おしい 惜しい 1【なくすことが】⚠「惜しい」に相当するぴったりの英語はないので,「よすぎてもったいない」の意味では too good,「残念だ」の意味では a shame などを使って訳す.

▶そのコートはリサイクルに出すには惜しい That overcoat *is too good* to bring to a thrift shop. ‖まだ使える扇風機を捨てるのは惜しいよ *It's a shame* to throw away a fan when you can still use it. ‖命が惜しいのなら警察になんか駆け込むなよ Don't go to the police *if you value your life*. ‖《ドライブの話をしていて》彼女が運転するのなら,私行かないわよ.命が惜しいから If she's driving, count me out. I'm *too young to die*. (➤「死ぬには若すぎる」と考える; count me out は「私は除外してね」の意) ‖この仕事が終わるまでは1時間でも時間が惜しい I *can't spare* [*can't afford to lose*] *even one hour* until this job is done. ‖歌手になれるのならどんな犠牲を払っても惜しくありません I *would give anything* to be a singer. (➤「(…できるのなら)何でも与える」の意).

2【残念な】▶惜しいことに1等賞を逃してしまった *To my regret*, I missed first prize. ‖おじさんからもらったカメラをなくして惜しいことをした I *feel bad* about having lost the camera my uncle gave me. ‖惜しいね,もう少しで正解だったのに! *So close!* You almost guessed right. ‖得点する惜しいチャンスを逃した It's too bad we missed [wasted] a *good* chance to score.

☞ 惜しくも,惜しげもなく(→見出語)

おじいさん,おじいちゃん a grandfather (祖父); Granddad(dy), Grandpa (あとの2者は「おじいちゃん」に相当する; また,《米・インフォーマル》では「おじいちゃん」と呼びかけるのに Gramps を用いることがある); an elderly man, an elderly gentleman (お年寄り; 後者のほうがより丁寧) ▶ぼくのおじいさんは1950年生まれだ My *grandfather* was born in 1950. ‖あのおじいさんとは毎朝公園で会う I see that *elderly man* in the park every morning.

おしいる 押し入る break 《into》(侵入する); rob +目 (銀行などを暴力的に襲う) ▶泥棒が昨夜あの家に押し入った A burglar *broke into* that house last night.

▶3人の男がきのう神戸の銀行に押し入った Three men *robbed* a bank in Kobe yesterday.

おしいれ 押し入れ an *oshi-ire*

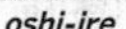

oshi-ire closet

日本紹介 ✉ **押し入れは日本独特の作りつけの戸棚です. closet と異なり,布団などの寝具を収納するのが本来の目的です.畳の部屋にはたいてい押し入れがついていて,前面はふすまという紙を張った引き戸になっています** An *oshi-ire* is a kind of typical (built-in) Japanese storage cabinet. Unlike a Western closet, its original purpose is to store futon(s) and other bedding. Most tatami rooms contain an *oshi-ire* with sliding paper-covered screens called '*fusuma*.'

▶布団を押し入れにしまう put the futon (away) in the *oshi-ire*.

おしうり 押し売り high-pressure selling,《インフォーマル》(a) hard sell; a high-pressure salesperson (人) ▶それじゃまるで押し売りじゃないか That seems to be *a hard sell*. ‖販売員に時計を押し売りされそうになったが買わなかった The watch *was pushed on* me by the salesperson, but I didn't buy it. (➤ pushed の代わりに forced を使えば結果的に買わされた意を含む) ‖ (掲示) 押し売りお断り No Soliciting (➤ solicit は「せがむ」) ／We don't buy from salespeople.

▶《比喩的》親切の**押し売り** *unwanted* kindness ‖ 彼は彼女に親切の**押し売りをした** He *forced* his attentions *on* her. (➤ attentions は「心遣い」) ‖ 忠告の**押し売り**はよくないよ You should not *force* your well-meant advice *on* others.

おしえ 教え **teaching** (知識・技術をつけさせるための) ; (a) **precept** (道徳的な) ; **instruction** (系統的指導による)
▶教授の**教えを請う** ask the professor for *instruction* ‖ 私はあの先生に大学院で**教えを受けた** That professor *taught* me in graduate school.
▶マザーテレサはキリストの**教え**を説きかつ実行した Mother Teresa both preached and practiced the *precepts* of Christianity [the *teachings* of Christ].

おしえご 教え子 one's **student** ▶うちの父は**教え子**のことを自分の子のことのように自慢する My father boasts about *his students* as if they were his own children.

おしえこむ 教え込む **teach** +⊟ (知識を) ; **train** +⊟ (技術・技能を) ▶猿に芸を**教え込む**のは短時間にできることではない *Training* a monkey to do tricks is not something you can do in (such) a short time.

おしえる 教える

📖 訳語メニュー
学科・教訓などを教える →teach **1**, **2**
道順などを告げる →tell, show **3**

1【学科・技術・考え方などを】 **teach** +⊟ ; **tutor** +⊟ (家庭教師として) ; **instruct** +⊟ (指導する)

【文型】
人(A)に学科(B)を教える
teach A B
teach B **to** A

▶母は高校で生物を**教えている** My mother *teaches* biology at high school. ‖ 私は外国人学生に日本語を**教えています** I *teach* Japanese *to* foreign students. ‖ 彼女は私にトルコ語を**教えてくれた** She *taught* me Turkish. (➤ この文は「私はトルコ語をものにした」という含みがある. She taught Turkish to me. とすると, 単に「彼女にトルコ語を教えてもらった」の意).
▶彼はアルバイトで中学生を**教えている** He *tutors* a junior-high school student as a part-time job. ‖ 彼女は私の娘にピアノを**教えてくれている** She *gives piano lessons to* my daughter. (➤ give lessons は「(音楽などの) レッスンをする」で, この場合の動詞に teach は使えない) ‖ ここのところはどういう意味か**教えて** (＝説明して) ください Please *explain* what this (part ／section) means.

【文型】
人(A)に…のやり方を教える
teach A **how to** do
➤ teach A to do とすることもある

▶テニスを**教えてくださいますか** Could you please *teach* [*show*] me *how to* play tennis? ‖ 学生たちにノートのとり方をきちんと**教えなければならない** We should *teach* [*show*] the students *how to* take notes. (➤ teach は技術や技能を「系統だって教える」, show は「実際にやって見せる」→**3**) ‖ 母は私に料理のしかたを**教えてくれた** My mother *taught* me (*how*) *to* cook. ‖ 彼女は子供たちに読み書きを**教えている** She *teaches* children *to* read and write [reading and writing].
▶ (人に) **教えた経験**はおありですか Do you have any *teaching experience*? ‖ 戦後日本人は, 民主主義こそ正しいと**教えられた** Japanese people *were taught* to believe in democracy after the war. (➤ believe in は「…が価値あるものだと信じる」).

2【教訓などを】 **teach** +⊟ ▶彼は息子に正直の大切さを**教えた** He *taught* his son the importance of honesty. ‖『ロビンソン・クルーソー』は逆境でいかに生きるべきかを**教えてくれる**本だ "Robinson Crusoe" is a book that *teaches* us *how to live* under adversity.
▶彼女の生き方には**教えられることが多い** We can *learn a lot* [*draw many lessons*] from her (way of) life. ‖ あなたのお話を聞いて**教えられることばかり**でした I *learned a lot* from what you told us. ／I found your talk *very instructive*.

3【こつ・道順などを】 **tell** +⊟, **show** +⊟, **direct** +⊟

> **語法** **tell** はことばだけで教えることを, **show** は図を描いたり指で差したり案内したりして教えることをいう. **direct** は show の堅い語.

【文型】
人(A)に物(B)を教える
tell A B
show A B
人(A)に…のやり方を教える
tell [**show**] A **how to** do

▶その少年は駅へ行く道を**教えてくれた** The boy *told* [*showed*] me the way to the train station. ‖ お名前をどう発音するか**教えていただけますか** Could you please *tell* me *how to* pronounce your name? ‖ 妹に『エクセル』の使い方を**教えてやった** I *showed* my (younger) sister *how to* use Microsoft Excel.
▶彼女がいつ帰宅するか**教えて** (＝知らせて) ください Please *let* me *know* when she will be home. ‖ きみの携帯番号を**教えてくれよ** Please *give* [*tell*] me your cellphone number. ‖ ヤンキースタジアムに行きたいのですが, 道順を**教えていただけますか** Could you *direct* me [*tell* me *the way*] to Yankee Stadium? ‖ (謎などが) わからない, **教えて**! I give up. *Give* [*Tell*] me the answer.
✉ **あなたの国のポップミュージックについて教えてください** Please *tell* me about pop music in your country.

おしおき お仕置き ▶悪さをしたら**お仕置きするぞ** I'll *punish* you if you misbehave.

おしかえす 押し返す **push back** ▶車内でよろけたら隣の女性に**押し返された** When I staggered on the train, I *was pushed back* by the woman next to me.

おしかける 押しかける **crowd** 《into》 (大勢で) ▶記者たちは情報を求めて警察に**押しかけた** Reporters *crowded into* (the) police headquarters, seeking information.
▶来週の日曜日にみんなできみの所に**押しかけるからね** We'll *come and visit* you together next Sunday. (➤ 話し相手の所に行く場合は come を用い, go としないことに注意) ‖《パーティーなどで》急に**押しかけてすみません** I'm sorry to come *uninvited*.

おじぎ お辞儀 a **bow** /baʊ/ ▶おじぎは東洋の挨拶の習慣である *Bowing* is a customary form of greeting in the Orient. ‖ 校長先生に会ったらおじぎするのよ You must *bow* to the principal when you meet him [her].
▶その紳士は私に丁寧に[軽く]おじぎした The gentleman *made a* polite [slight] *bow* to me. ／The gentleman *bowed* politely [slightly] to me. ‖ その大使は天皇(陛下)に恭しくおじぎをした The ambassador *bowed* respectfully to (His Majesty) the Emperor.

おしきせ お仕着せ ▶お仕着せの修学旅行なんか参加したくない I don't want to go on one of those school trips *where the teachers decide everything ahead of time*. (➤「先生たちが前もって何もかも決める」の意).

おじぎそう 《植物》 a **sensitive plant.**

おしきる 押し切る ▶あの2人は親の反対を押し切って結婚した They got married *despite* their parents' opposition.

おしくも 惜しくも ▶日本のマラソン選手は惜しくも(＝僅かの差で)2位に終わった The Japanese marathon runner came in second *by a narrow margin*.

おしくらまんじゅう 押しくら饅頭 ▶通勤電車の押しくらまんじゅう(＝押し合いへし合い)は私の年齢では体にこたえる *Pushing and shoving* [《英また》*Hustling and jostling*] in commuter trains is exhausting at my age. ‖ 押しくらまんじゅう, 押されて泣くな *Push and shove, push and shove*. Don't cry if you are pushed hard.

おじけづく 怖じ気づく **be frightened** ▶その大きな犬を見て, 弟はおじけづいてしまった My younger brother *was frightened* [*was terrified*] when he saw the large dog.
▶彼女はスピーチコンテストが始まる前からすっかりおじけづいてしまった She *got cold feet* [*chickened out*] even before the speech contest had started. (➤ get cold feet も chicken out も「尻込みする」の意のインフォーマルな表現).

おしげもなく 惜しげもなく ▶困っている人々に惜しげもなく金を与える give money *freely* [*generously*] to the needy ‖ そのお年寄りは惜しげもなく(＝進んで)弁当を猫にやった The elderly man *willingly* gave his lunch to the cat.

おしこむ 押し込む ▶彼女はスーツケースに衣類を押し込んだ She *stuffed* her clothes into the suitcase. (➤ stuff は「ぎゅうぎゅうに詰め込む」) ‖ 人々はエレベーターに押し込まれた People *were squeezed* [*were jammed*] into the elevator.

おしこめる 押し込める ▶大勢の人質が大使公邸に押し込められていた Lots of hostages *were crammed* into the official residence of the ambassador. ‖ あいつらを裏の部屋に押し込めておけ *Lock* them *up* in the back room.

おしころす 押し殺す ▶そのアナウンサーはニュースを読みながら必死に笑いを押し殺していた The announcer struggled to *suppress laughter* [*keep from laughing*] as he read the news item. ‖ 暗闇から「おい!」と押し殺した声がして, どきっとした I felt my heart stop when I suddenly heard *a tense whisper*, "Hey!" out of the dark.

おしさげる 押し下げる ▶石油価格を押し下げる *drive down* oil prices.

おじさん an **uncle, Uncle** (血縁関係の; 後者は主に呼びかけで); a **man** (よその); **Sir, Mister** (他人に対する呼びかけ; 後者はややインフォーマル) ▶敬三おじさんは大きなクマの縫いぐるみをくれた *Uncle* Keizo gave me a big teddy bear.
▶よそのおじさん(＝知らない人)について行っちゃだめだよ Don't go off with *strangers*!

おしずし 押し寿司 ***oshizushi*, pressed sushi**; sushi rice topped with various ingredients that is pressed in a mold (➤ 説明的な訳).

おしすすめる (…を)**推し進める** **push forward** [**ahead**] 《with》 ▶環境保護対策を推し進める *push forward with* environmental protection measures.

おしたおす 押し倒す **push down** [**over**] ▶いじめっ子がその子を押し倒した The bully *pushed* the boy *over*.

おしだし 押し出し **1**【相撲】▶稀勢の里が押し出しで勝った Kisenosato won by *pushing* his opponent *out of the ring*.
2【野球】▶押し出しの四球 a *bases-loaded* walk ‖ 藤川投手は9回裏満塁で, 阿部を歩かせてジャイアンツに押し出しの1点を与えた Fujikawa walked Abe with the bases loaded in the bottom of the ninth to *force* (*in*) a run for the Giants.
3【人前での見かけ】**presence** ▶社長は押し出しが立派だ Our boss has a commanding *presence*.

おしだす 押し出す **push out** ▶稀勢の里は白鵬を押し出した Kisenosato *pushed* Hakuho *out of the ring*.
▶私は列の先頭に押し出された I *was shoved* to the front of the line.

おしだまる 押し黙る ▶妻が愚痴をこぼしている間, 彼は押し黙っていた He *remained silent* while his wife grumbled about something.

おしつけがましい 押しつけがましい **pushy** ▶ママの忠告はいつも押しつけがましい My mother *is* always *so pushy* with her advice.

おしつける 押しつける **press** 《against》(押す); **force** 《on》(無理強いする) ▶窓ガラスに鼻を押しつけるとブタの顔になる *Press* your nose *against* the windowpane and you'll end up with a pig-like face.
▶彼はいつも他人に自分の意見を押しつける He always *forces* [*imposes*] his opinion *on* others. ‖ ぼくに責任を押しつけないでくれ Don't try to *put* your responsibility *on* me. ／Don't try to *place* [*put*] the blame *on* me. (➤ 後者は「私のせいにしないでくれ」).
▶姉は皿洗いを私に押しつけた My (older) sister *forced* me *to* do the dishes (in her place). ‖ 女房は赤ん坊をぼくに押しつけて遊びに出かけた My wife *stuck* me *with* the baby and went out to enjoy herself. (➤ stick A with B は「A(人)に B(やっかいな人・物)を押しつける」の意).

おしっこ (a) **pee** ▶おしっこに行く go for *a pee* [*a wee* (*-wee*)] (➤ 幼児の言い方) ／go to the bathroom [restroom] (➤ 小さな子でもこちらを用いるのがふつう) ‖ おしっこ! I *have to pee* [*wee*]. ／I *have to go number one*. (➤ 後者は子供が学校などで; また, number one は number two (うんち)に対する語) ‖ 夜起きておしっこに行きますか Do you get up to *urinate* at night?
▶またおしっこ漏らしちゃったのね You *wet your pants* again. →うんち, 小便, 尿.

おしつぶす 押し潰す **crush** ＋目 ▶女性が倒れてきた石塀に押し潰されて死んだ A woman *was crushed to*

お

death by a collapsing stone wall. ‖ 卵は袋の中で押し潰された The eggs *broke* in the bag. ‖ 数軒の家が雪の重みで押し潰された Several houses *collapsed* under the weight of snow. (➤ collapse は「(建築物が)崩壊する」).
▶《比喩的》その戦争は少年の夢を無残に押し潰した The war mercilessly *destroyed* the boy's dreams.

おしつまる 押し詰まる ▶ことしも押し詰まってきた We are *getting close to the end* of the year. ‖ ことしもあと1週間と押し詰まった *There is only* a week *to go* until the end of the year.

おしてしるべし 推して知るべし ▶この問題が解けないようじゃ, あとは推して知るべしだね If you can't solve this problem, *it's easy to guess* your (limited) ability.

おしとおす 押し通す ▶彼は自分の考えを押し通した He *insisted on* his opinion. (➤ insist on は「…を強く主張する」) ‖ 彼は知らぬ存ぜぬで押し通した He *persisted in* denying his knowledge of it. (➤ persist in は「…に固執する」の意で, 非難の響きがある) ‖ 彼女はいつもわがままを押し通そうとする She always wants to *have her own way*.
▶妻は冬の下着を出してくれたが, 私は冬中薄着で押し通した Although my wife took out my winter underwear, I *made it through* the winter lightly dressed.

おしとやか →しとやか.

おしどり 《鳥》 a **mandarin duck** ▶《慣用表現》2人はおしどり夫婦だ They *are very happily married*. 《参考》この言い方がふつうだが, a close /klous/ couple, an inseparable couple [pair], a couple of lovebirds を「おしどり夫婦」に当てることもある.

おしながす 押し流す **wash away** ▶洪水で橋が押し流された The bridge *was washed* [*was swept*] *away* by the flood. ‖ ボートは沖へ押し流された The boat *was carried away* to the open sea.
▶《比喩的》私は時流に押し流されたくない I don't want to *get swept away* by current trends.

おしなべて 押しなべて **on the whole** (全体的に見て); **by and large** (おおむね) ▶日本の製品はおしなべて品質がよい *On the whole*, Japanese products are of high quality.

おしのける 押しのける ▶子供が大人を押しのけて先に電車に乗り込んだ A child *pushed his way through* the adults to get on the train first. ‖ 彼は多くのライバルを押しのけてそのポストを勝ち取った He *elbowed* his rivals *out of the way* and got the position. (➤ elbow は「肘で押す」が原義).

おしのび お忍び ▶王女さまはお忍びでクラブに現れた The princess showed up at the club *incognito*. (➤ /ìnkɑːgníːtou/ と発音する).

おしはかる 推し量る **guess** +㊐ ▶この手紙からは彼女の本心を推し量ることはできない I can't *guess* from this letter what she really means.

おしばな 押し花 a **pressed (and dried) flower** ▶本に挟んで朝顔の押し花を作る press a morning glory petal in a book.

おしべ 雄蕊 a **stamen** /stéɪmen/ (➤ 雌しべは pistil) ▶子供の頃お母さんから「雄しべと雌しべ」の話, 聞かなかったの? Didn't your mother tell you about *the birds and the bees* when you were little? (➤ 英米では子供に性について教えるのに鳥やミツバチの交尾を例に使う).

おしボタン 押しボタン a **push button** ▶押しボタン式の歩行者用信号 a *push-button* pedestrian-controlled lights.

おしぼり お絞り a **steamed** [**hot**] **hand towel** (蒸した[熱い]手拭き用タオル) 《参考》英語国ではおしぼりを出す習慣はない.

おしまい ▶《子供にお菓子などを与えるとき》これでおしまいよ This is [will be] *the last one*. (➤ will be は残っていてもそれで最後にしたいとき) ‖ 話はそれでおしまい(=終わり)だ That's *the end* of the story. ‖ こんな議論はもうおしまいにしようよ Let's *have no more of* [Let's *put an end to*] this arguing. ‖ きょうはこれでおしまいにしよう Let's *call it a day*. / *That's all* for today. (➤ 前者は主に仕事を切り上げるときの決まり文句) ‖ おしまいまで言わせてよ Let me finish what I have to say. / (Please) hear me out. (➤ 後者は「おしまいまで聞いてよ」の意) ‖ あんなスキャンダルを起こしては彼ももうおしまいだ He's *finished* now that he's gotten involved in a scandal like that. ‖ それではきみはおしまいだよ It'll *be curtains for* you. (➤ be curtains for A は「A は終わりを迎える, 破産する, クビになる, 即死する」の意). →終わり.

おしまれる 惜しまれる ▶その選手は皆に惜しまれながら引退した When the player retired, everyone *was sad to* see him go. ‖ 彼の死は国家のためにも惜しまれる His death *is a loss* to our country. (➤「損失だ」の意).

おしみない 惜しみない ▶聴衆はそのピアニストの演奏に惜しみない拍手を送った The audience gave the pianist *unstinting* [*lavish*] applause.

おしむ 惜しむ

1【残念に思う】 **regret** +㊐, **feel sorry** (for) ▶先生との別れを惜しんでお茶の会を催した We were *sorry* to see our teacher go, and held a tea party (for him). ‖ その名優の葬儀には彼の死を惜しむ(=哀悼する)ファンが多数参列した Many fans who *were mourning* the passing of the great actor attended his funeral.
▶彼女が会社を辞めたら皆が惜しむだろう Everyone will *miss* her when she quits the company. (➤ miss は「(人が)いなくなるのを惜しむ」の意) ‖ 行く春を惜しんで宴を開く hold a banquet to *lament* the passing of spring.

2【大事にする】 ▶彼女は寸暇を惜しんで読書している She *devotes every spare moment* to reading.

3【けちけちする】 ▶彼は食事の時間も惜しんで勉強している He studies all the time and *hardly takes time* to have meals. ‖ 彼女は骨身を惜しまず働く She works hard *without sparing herself* [*grudging no pains*]. ‖ きみが本当にキャプテンになる気があるのならぼくは協力を惜しまないよ If you really want to be captain, I *am more than ready to* give you (all) my cooperation.

おしむらく 惜しむらくは ▶ギョーム・ルクーは才能と前途のある作曲家であったが, 惜しむらくはようせつして作品が少ない Guillaume Lekeu was a talented and promising composer. *It is to be regretted that* he died young and left behind few works.

おしめ 《米》 a **diaper** /dáɪəpəʳ/, 《英》 a **nappy** ▶赤ん坊のおしめを替える *change a baby* (➤ 決まった言い方) ‖ あなた, 徹のおしめ取り替えてくださる? Will you change Toru's *diaper*? ‖ おしめがびちょびちょよ The *diaper* is soaked. ‖ 息子はまだおしめをしている[おしめが取れたばかりです] My son still *wears diapers* [*is barely out of diapers*].

おしめり お湿り ▶結構なお湿りですこと It's a welcome *sprinkling of rain*.

おしもおされもせぬ 押しも押されもせぬ ▶あの人は今や押しも押されもせぬ学者になっている He is now an *established* scholar. ／He is now a scholar with *an established reputation*. ‖ 吉永小百合は押しも押されもせぬ大女優だ Yoshinaga Sayuri is a great actress of *established standing*.

おしもんどう 押し問答 ▶怒った客が店員としばらくの間押し問答した The angry shopper *argued back and forth* with the clerk for some time.

おじや →雑炊.

おしゃか お釈迦 ▶携帯を水の中に落としておしゃかにしてしまった I dropped my cellphone in the water and *ruined* it.

おしゃく お酌 →酌 ▶若い子のお酌で飲めるとはうれしいね How happy [lucky] I am to have a young woman *pour sake for me*! (➤ 欧米では人に酌をするのは一般的でない).

おしゃぶり 《米》 a **pacifier** /pǽsɪfaɪəʳ/, 《英》 a **dummy**; a **teething ring** (輪形の).

おしゃべり お喋り ▶母は隣のおばさんとおしゃべりしていた My mother *was having a chat* [*was chatting*] with the next-door woman. (➤ was chattering と言うとくだらないおしゃべりのニュアンスになる) ‖ 授業中におしゃべりするな *Be quiet* during class.

▶あなたおしゃべりね You *talk too much*. ／You're a real *chatterbox*. (➤ chatterbox は「おしゃべりな人」の意のインフォーマルな語) ‖ あのじいさんのおしゃべりには参ったよ I was annoyed by the *talkative* old man. (➤ talkative は「話し好きな」の意. 口数が少ないことをよしとする日本と違って, 英米では talkative であることは「おしゃべり」ほどのマイナスイメージはない).

▶伸子には話さないでね. 彼女, おしゃべり(＝言い触らし屋)だから Don't tell anything to Nobuko. She *has a big mouth*.

おしゃま ▶うちの孫娘は時々おしゃまなことを言うんですよ My granddaughter sometimes talks *just like a grown-up*. (➤「大人のような口を利く」の意) ‖ ミカちゃんはおしゃまだね You're *quite the little lady*, aren't you, Mika-chan?

おじゃま お邪魔 ▶《場所をふさいだりして》お邪魔でしょうか Am I *in your way*? (→邪魔).

▶《人の部屋などを訪れて》ちょっとお邪魔してもいいですか May I *take a few minutes of your time*? ／Do you mind if I *come in for a moment*? ‖ お邪魔じゃないでしょうか I hope I'm not *disturbing* you. (➤「邪魔をしていなければいいのですが」の意) ‖ 突然お邪魔してごめんなさい I'm sorry to *visit* you without making an appointment. (➤「約束もしていないのに」の意) ‖ そちらさえよければあすお邪魔します I'll *come to see you* tomorrow if it's O.K. with you. (➤「あなたに会いにいく」の意; 相手の所に行くときは go でなく come を用いることに注意).

▶どうもお邪魔しました Thank you for your time. ／I'm sorry I've taken so much of your time. 《参考》日本人は相手に時間を割かせて悪かったという気持ちから後者を使うことが多いが, 英語国民はこの気持ちが特別に強い場合以外は前者のような言い方で感謝の気持ちを表す.

おしゃれ お洒落 ▶おしゃれな(＝洗練された)紳士 a *refined* [*fine*] gentleman ‖ おばはとてもおしゃれだ My aunt *is a* very *good dresser*. ／My aunt *dresses tastefully* [*has good taste in clothes*]. ‖ あなた, きょうはどうしておしゃれしてるの? How come you *are* all *dressed up* today? ‖ 最近はおしゃれなスイーツがよく売れる *Fancy-looking* sweets sell very well these days.

おじゃん ▶あいつのおかげでぼくの計画はおじゃんになった My plan *has fallen through* [*has gone up in smoke*], thanks to him. (➤ fall through, go up in smoke はともに「実現されない」の意のくだけた言い方) ‖ これで何もかもおじゃんだ Everything'*s ruined*.

おしょう 和尚 a **Buddhist priest**.

おじょうさん お嬢さん ⚠「お嬢さま」を含め, ぴったりの語は英語にはないので, refined young lady (洗練された若い女性), demure young lady (しとやかな[慎み深い]若い女性), upper-class young lady (上流社会に属する若い女性)などを適宜用いる.

▶お嬢さん, 何を差し上げましょうか What can I get you, *young lady* [*Miss*]? ‖ お宅のお嬢さんはおいくつですか How old is *your daughter*, may I ask?

▶きみはいくつになってもお嬢さん(＝苦労知らず)だね You still *don't know anything* (*about hardship*), do you? ／You *never grow up*, do you? ‖ あそこはお嬢さん学校だ That's *a young ladies' school*. ／That's *a school for upper-class girls*.

おしょく 汚職 **corruption**, 《米また》 **graft** (➤ ともに「不正利得」の意で, 後者は主に新聞用語); a **scandal** (汚職事件) ▶政界の汚職事件 a political *scandal* ‖ 政府の汚職を根絶せよ Eradicate [Root out] *corruption* in the government!

▶市の汚職追放に市民が立ち上がった The citizens banded together to wipe out *corruption* in the city government.

おしよせる 押し寄せる **surge** (波・群衆などが); **advance** (軍隊などが) ▶見ろ, 大波が押し寄せてくるぞ! Look! Huge waves are *surging upon* us. ‖ 敵がその町に押し寄せ, ついにそこを征服した The enemy *advanced on* [*toward*] the city and finally conquered it.

▶やじ馬が押し寄せ, 辺りは大混乱になった The crowds *flocked* [*swarmed*] to the scene causing great confusion. (➤ 前者は「鳥のように集まる」, 後者は「ハチのように集まる」の意).

おしろい 白粉 **powder** ▶おしろいをつける apply [put on] *powder* ／powder one's face.

おしろいばな 《植物》 a **four-o'clock**.

オジロワシ 《鳥》 a **white-tailed eagle**.

おしわける 押し分ける **push** one's **way through** ▶そのアイドル歌手はファンを押し分けるようにして進んだ The pop idol *pushed his way through* his fans.

おしんこ お新香 **pickled vegetables** (**especially Chinese cabbage**).

¹おす →おっす.

²おす 雄 a **male** ▶雄猫 a *male cat* ‖ 雄の鳥はふつう雌の鳥よりきれいな羽をしている *Male* birds usually have brighter plumage than female birds. ‖ お宅の犬は雄ですか雌ですか Is your dog *a he* or a she?

³おす 押す・推す

訳語メニュー
力を加えて動かす →push **1**
押しつける →press **2**
推薦する →recommend **5**
推測する →guess **6**

1【力を加えて動かす】 **push** ＋ⓔ ▶机をもっと壁際の方へ押してください *Push* the desk nearer to the wall, please. ‖ 押さないでよ! *Don't push* (against me)! ‖ 全くこの石は押しても引いてもびくともしないんだから This rock will never budge *whether we push it or pull it*. (➤ budge は「ちょっとでも動く」).

2【圧力を加える】press +㊐ ▶ご用の方はボタンを押してください When you want me, please *press* [*push*] the button. ‖ オリエンテーリングでは途中数か所でカードにスタンプを押さなければならない You must *stamp* your card at several spots along the way during orienteering. ‖ きのうぶつけた所が押すと痛い The bruise I got yesterday hurts whenever it's *touched*.

3【勢いで相手を上回る】 ▶小田氏の威厳に押されて一郎は一言も反論できなかった *Overwhelmed* by Mr. Oda's stern dignity, Ichiro couldn't say a word in reply.

4【強行する】 ▶彼女は病気を押して(＝にもかかわらず)学校へ行った She went to school *in spite of* her sickness [*though* she was sick]. ‖ その計画は住民の反対を押して実行された The plan was carried out *against* the residents' objections.

5【推薦する】recommend +㊐ ; **nominate** +㊐ (指名する) ▶私たちは野田さんを生徒会長に推した We *recommended* Noda [*put up* Noda] as president of our Students' Association. (➤ put up はインフォーマルな表現) ‖ 私の父は市長に推された My father *was nominated* [*was put up*] for mayor.

6【推測する】guess +㊐ ▶ことばのなまりから推して彼は大阪の出身だろう From his accent, I'd *guess* he is from Osaka.

おすい 汚水 polluted water (汚染された水) ; **sewage** /súːɪdʒ/ (下水) ; **waste water** (廃水) ▶あの工場は汚水を垂れ流している That factory is discharging *polluted water*.

‖ **汚水浄化槽** a *septic tank*.

おずおず timidly (おどおどと) ; **nervously** (臆病そうに) ; **hesitantly** (ためらいながら) ▶子供はおずおずとドアの後ろからこちらをのぞき込んだ The child *nervously* peeked in from behind the door.

オスカー 《映画》 an **Oscar** (➤ アカデミー賞受賞者に与えられる金の像).

おすすめ お勧め ▶イタリア料理を食べたいんだけど, どこかお勧めの店ない？ I feel like (eating) Italian food. *Do you know* (*of*) *a good place* [*any good places*]? / *What place would you recommend*? ‖ こちらのお勧め料理は何ですか What is *the specialty of the house*? (➤ What would you recommend? と言ってもよい).

▶このテレビはお勧め品ですよ This television set is *a bargain* at this price. (➤ bargain は「買い得品」) / This is a good television set which I can highly recommend.

おすそわけ お裾分け ▶これはほんのお裾分けです. 母が箱いっぱいリンゴを送ってくれたものですから My mother sent me a box of apples and *I'd like you to have some*. (➤ 英語では「少し食べていただきたい」と考える).

おすなおすな 押すな押すな ▶見本市は押すな押すなの盛況だった The trade fair was *filled with jostling visitors*. / There was *a large crowd* at the trade fair.

おすまし お澄まし ▶(写真の)真ん中でお澄まししている女の子はだあれ Who is this girl in the middle who is trying to *look so prim and proper*?

おすみつき お墨付き ▶二郎は必ずT大に受かると受け持ちの先生からお墨付きを頂いたわ Jiro's homeroom teacher *assured* me that Jiro would pass the entrance examination for T University. (➤ assure は「保証する」).

オスロ Oslo /ɑ́ːzloʊ/ (ノルウェーの首都).

オセアニア Oceania.

おせいぼ お歳暮 →歳暮.

おせおせ 押せ押せ ▶連続シュートを決めて相手チームは押せ押せムードになってきた After getting successful back-to-back shots, the opponent team only *intensified* their *offense*. ‖ 進行が押せ押せになってきている Things are *falling behind schedule*. (➤ (式典などが)予定どおり進まず遅れ遅れで時間が足りなくなっていることを表す).

おせじ お世辞 a **compliment** (褒めことば ; この語自体には悪い意味はない) ; **flattery** (人をうれしがらせることば, おべっか) ; **ass-kissing** (ごますり) ▶宮田さんったら, お世辞がお上手ね You're so good with *compliments*, Miyata. ‖ あの男はよく心にもないお世辞を言う That guy often makes *empty compliments*. ‖ お世辞を言ったってだめだよ *Flattery* will get you nowhere. ‖ あなたのお世辞はもうたくさん I've had enough of your *flattery*. ‖ 彼は上司にお世辞ばっかり言っている He *always flatters* his boss.

▶彼女はお世辞にも英語がうまいとは言えない I can't say that she speaks good English *even to be polite*.

おせち お節 ***osechi***

日本紹介 ✉ **お節(料理)は正月三が日用の特別料理です. 年末に, 重箱と呼ばれる何段も重ねた箱に黒豆, 数の子, かまぼこ, エビ, 野菜の煮しめなどを美しく詰めて新しい年を迎える準備をします. 近年では家庭で作るよりも, スーパーで出来合いのものを買ったり, 特別に注文しておいたりすることが多くなっています** *Osechi* is food eaten only on the first three days of the New Year. It is served in '*j ū bako*' (tiered lacquerware boxes). *Osechi* includes beautifully arranged items such as black beans, herring roe, steamed fish cakes, shrimp and vegetables simmered in soy sauce prepared to welcome the new year. In recent years, fewer people make it at home and it has become common to buy ready-made *osechi* at supermarkets or to order specially made *osechi*.

おせっかい お節介 ▶私のやることにおせっかいを焼かないでいただきたい I wish you wouldn't *meddle in* my affairs. (➤ meddle in のあとには「人」ではなく「事」がくる) ‖ 彼女って, すごくおせっかいな人よ She's *a* very *nosy person*. (➤ nosey ともつづる).

▶ **対話**「たまには机の上を片づけたほうがいいよ」「余計なおせっかいだよ」"You should clean up your desk once in a while." "*Mind your own business*. / *Don't stick your nose in my business*." (➤ 前者は「自分のことを気づかったらどうだい」の意 ; 後者は「私のことなどに口を出さないでくれ」の意で, かなり強い言い方).

‖ **おせっかい焼き** a busybody, 《英・インフォーマル》 a nosy parker.

おせっきょう お説教 →説教.

おせん 汚染 pollution ; **contamination** (毒物・放射能などによる) **一動 汚染する pollute** +㊐ (自然環境を), **contaminate** +㊐ (汚染物質で不純にする) ▶環境[大気]汚染は人類にとって深刻な問題である *Environmental* [*Air*] *pollution* is a serious problem for humanity. ‖ 多くの川はもはや飲料水には適さないくらい汚染されている Many rivers have *become* so *polluted* that they can no longer be used for drinking water. ‖ 人々は危険とは知らずに汚染された水を飲んでいる People drink *contaminated* water without knowing the danger. ‖その地域はダイオキシンによって**汚染された** The area *was contaminated* by dioxin.

‖**汚染物質** a pollutant, polluting matter.

おぜんだて お膳立て ▶これで会議の**お膳立て**ができた All the *arrangements* for the meeting have been made. ‖俊雄に和美とデートできるよう**お膳立て**を頼まれた Toshio asked me to *fix* him *up with* Kazumi. (➤ fix up with は「…とのデートを取り持つ」の意のくだけた言い方).

おそい 遅い

> 📖 訳語メニュー
> 時刻が遅い →late 1
> 速度が遅い →slow 2

1【時刻・時機が】late ▶**遅い**朝食をとる have a *late* breakfast (→遅れる) ‖後悔してももう**遅い** It is too *late* for regrets. ‖もう**遅い**から帰ります I must be going as it's *getting late*. ‖ことしは春の来るのが**遅い**ようだ Spring seems to *be late* this year.

> 【文型】
> …するのが遅くなる
> be late (in) doing
> ➤ インフォーマルでは in を省略することが多い

▶母親は子供の学校からの**帰りが遅い**ので, 心配し始めた The mother began to worry when her child *was late* coming *home* from school.

▶ゆうべ寝るのが**遅かった**からきょうは眠い I am sleepy today because I went to bed *late* last night. ‖私は**遅く**結婚したので子供たちはまだ小さい I got married *late* [*at a late age*], so my children are still young.

▶急いで! **遅くなっちゃった**わよ Hurry up! It's *getting late*. ‖伺うのが**遅くなって**すみません I apologize for *not coming* (*here*) *sooner*. ‖きょうから学校の始まるのが30分**遅くなる** Beginning today, school starts thirty minutes *later*. ‖ 対話 「**遅くなって**ごめん」「いえ, 大丈夫よ」"*I'm sorry I'm late*." "It's OK." ‖ 対話 「**遅かった**じゃないか, もう3時半だよ」「ごめん, 道路が混んでたんだよ」"*You're late*! It's already three thirty." "I'm sorry. Traffic was heavy."

▶駅前の店は**夜遅くまで**開いている The stores in front of the station are open *until* [*till*] *late* (*hours*). ‖あいつは**朝早くから夜遅くまで**働くのがいいと思っているんだ He believes in working *early and late*. (➤ early and late は「朝早くから夜遅くまで」の意の決まり文句).

▶こんなに**遅くまで**勉強しているの? You're still studying *this late*? (➤ Yes か No かを聞く質問でなく, 状況を見ての確認のようなものなので, 平叙文の語順で, 尻上がりに発音する) ‖急を聞いて駆けつけたが, 病院に着いたときは**遅かった** After getting the emergency call, I rushed to the hospital, but it *was too late*.

✉ **お返事が遅くなってすみません** I am sorry I didn't write you back sooner. / Sorry it took me so long to sit down and answer your letter. ➤ 後者は「机の前に座って返事を書くのに時間がかかった」の意.

2【速度が】slow ▶あのバスは**遅い** That bus is *slow*. ‖彼は英語の**進歩が遅い** He is *making little* [*slow*] *progress* in [with] English. ‖彼は決断が**遅い** He *is slow in* making decisions. ‖私足が**遅い**から30分ぐらいかかると思うわ I'm *a slow walker*. So it'll probably take me thirty minutes or so. ‖**頭の回転の遅い人**とは付き合えないな I have no patience with *slow-witted* people.

☛ 遅くとも (→見出語)

おそいかかる 襲いかかる attack +目 ▶目の前でライオンがシマウマに**襲いかかる**のを見た Right before my very eyes, I saw a lion *attack* a zebra. ‖彼らは敵兵に背後から**襲いかかった** They *attacked* the enemy from behind.

おそう 襲う 1【人が】attack +目 (襲撃する) ; **assault** /əsɔ́:lt/ +目 (激しく襲う) ▶侵略者がその城を**襲った** The invaders *attacked* the castle. ‖昔はこの辺りでよく旅人が山賊に**襲われた**ものだ In former times travelers *were* often *assaulted* by bandits near here. ‖3人組の男が銀行を**襲った** A group of three men *held up* a bank. (➤ hold up は「(店などに)強盗に入る」の意).

2【災難などが】strike +目, **hit** +目 (➤ 後者はややくだけた語) ▶大嵐がその都市を**襲った** A heavy storm *struck* the city. (➤ struck は strike の過去形) ‖私の故郷はよく台風に**襲われる** My hometown *is* often *hit* by typhoons. ‖大きな地震がその町を**襲った** A big earthquake *hit* the city. ‖私は20歳のとき病魔に**襲われた** When I was twenty, I *was stricken* by a disease. ‖突然言いようのない恐怖感に**襲われた** All of a sudden, I *was overcome with* indescribable fear. (➤ be overcome with は「(恐怖などのために)どうにもならなくなる」の意).

おそうまれ 遅生まれ ⚠ **4月から始まる日本の学制から生まれた表現なので, 訳例のように表す.** ▶**遅生まれ**の子 a child *born between April 2 and December 31* [*born on or after April 2*].

おそかれはやかれ 遅かれ早かれ sooner or later ▶彼は**遅かれ早かれ**横綱になるよ He will reach the rank of yokozuna *sooner or later*. / His rise to yokozuna is only a matter of time. (➤ 後者は「横綱への昇格はただ時間の問題だ」の意).

おそくとも 遅くとも at (the) latest ▶今夜は**遅くとも**10時には帰ります I'll be back by ten o'clock *at* (*the*) *latest* tonight.

おそざき 遅咲きの ▶**遅咲き**の桜 a *late-blooming* [*late-blossoming*] cherry tree ‖**遅咲き**の人 *a late bloomer*.

おそじも 遅霜 a late frost.

おそなえ お供え an offering ▶仏壇にご飯を**お供えする** *offer* a bowl of rice to the family altar.

‖**お供え餅** a rice cake for a ritual offering.

おそばん 遅番 a late shift ▶今週は**遅番だ** I'm *on the late shift* this week.

おそまきながら 遅まきながら ▶還暦を迎えて**遅まきながら**韓国語の勉強を始めた *Though 60 is a little late*, I have started studying Korean.

おぞましい hideous (醜悪な) ; horrifying (ぞっとするほど恐ろしい) ; nauseating (吐き気を催すほどの) ▶戦争の**おぞましい**光景 a *horrifying* war scene.

おそまつ お粗末な poor (劣る) ; lousy /láʊzi/ (ひどい) ▶**お粗末な**演技 *poor* [*lousy*] acting ‖その劇の結末は何とも**お粗末だった** The ending to that play was really *poorly acted*. ‖ 対話 「ごちそうさま」「**お粗末さまでした**」"Thank you very much for the wonderful meal." "*I'm glad you enjoyed it*." (➤「お気に召していただいてうれしく思います」の意).

おそらく 恐らく probably →たぶん ▶雲が真っ黒だから, **恐らく**雨になるだろう The clouds are very dark, so it will *probably* rain. ‖**恐らく**彼はまだ家に帰ってい

ないだろう He *probably* hasn't gone home yet. ‖ 対話「彼女，うんと言ってくれるかな」「恐らくだめだろうね」"I wonder if she will say yes." "*Probably* not."

おそるおそる 恐る恐る timidly（おどおどしながら）; nervously（びくびくしながら）; fearfully（怖がりながら）▶彼は恐る恐る校長室のドアをノックした He knocked at the principal's door *timidly* [*nervously*]. ‖ 男の子は恐る恐るその犬に近づいていった The boy approached the dog *fearfully* [*gingerly*]. (➤ gingerly は「用心しながらゆっくりと」の意).
▶子供たちはそのつり橋を恐る恐る渡っていた The children were *walking on eggs* as they crossed the hanging bridge. (➤ walk on eggs は「気をつけて歩く」の意).

おそるべき 恐るべき ▶調査の結果，恐るべき事実が明るみに出た The investigation turned up some *horrifying* facts. ‖ 彼女は恐るべき才能の持ち主だ She has a *marvelous* talent. ／She is a person of *marvelous* talent.

おそれ 恐れ・畏れ・虞 **1**【恐怖】(a) fear（おびえ）; horror（ぞっとするような恐ろしさ）▶神に対して畏れを抱く have *a fear* of God ‖ その男は全く恐れを知らなかった The man *was* utterly *fearless*.
2【心配】(a) fear; danger（危険）; (a) suspicion（疑い）▶このままでは日本はさらに治安が悪くなるおそれがある If things go on like this, *I fear* that public safety in Japan will deteriorate even more. ‖ その船は沈没のおそれがあった The ship *was in danger of* sinking. ‖ 父はがんのおそれがある My father *is suspected of* having cancer. ／*There is suspicion* that my father has cancer. ‖《天気予報》今夜半から大雨のおそれ（＝可能性）があります There is *a chance* [*possibility*] of heavy rain (s) starting late tonight.

おそれいる 恐れ入る **1**【恐縮する】▶いろいろご面倒をおかけしまして恐れ入ります *I'm very sorry* to have given you so much trouble. ‖ ご親切恐れ入ります It's very kind of you.
▶恐れ入りますが山下公園へ行く道を教えていただけませんか *Excuse me, but* could [would] you tell me the way to Yamashita Park? (➤ could のほうが would よりもやや丁寧) ‖ 対話「きみの推薦状，書いておいたよ」「誠に恐れ入ります」"I finished writing your recommendation." "*I'm much obliged to you.*" ‖ 対話「どうだ，参ったか」「恐れ入りました」"Take that! (Have you) had enough yet?" "*OK, you win. I give up!*" (➤ Take that! は攻撃などを加えて「受けてみよ」「これでどうだ」).
2【驚く，閉口する】▶佐藤さんの記憶力がいいのにはただただ恐れ入った I *was amazed* [*astonished*] at Mr. Sato's good memory. ‖ 彼女の身勝手な要求には全く恐れ入ったよ I *was* completely *taken aback* by her self-centered demands. (➤ be taken aback は「あっけにとられる」).

おそれおおい 恐れ多い・畏れ多い awe-inspiring ▶皇居のような恐れ多い場所へは行ったことがありません I've never been to such an *awe-inspiring* place as the Imperial Palace. ‖ このような場所にお招きいただくことは誠に恐れ多いことでございます I'*m very honored* to be invited here.
▶畏れ多くも陛下からじきじきにおことばを賜った His Majesty the Emperor *graciously* spoke to me in person.

おそれる 恐れる

1【怖がる】be afraid of; fear +目（恐怖を感じる；前者よりも堅い語）

> **【文型】**
> 人・物(A)を恐れる
> be afraid of A
> …することを恐れる
> be afraid of doing

▶臆病者は自分の影をも恐れる A coward *is afraid of* his own shadow. ‖ 私たちは皆職を失うことを恐れています We'*re* all *afraid of* losing our jobs. ‖ 私は死[死ぬこと]を恐れてはいません I'*m not afraid of* death [*of* dying]. ‖ 間違いを恐れていては外国語は上達しない If you *are afraid of* making mistakes, you won't get any better at speaking a foreign language.
▶私は父に本当のことが知れるのを恐れた I *feared* that my father would find out the truth. ‖ その蛇は全くの無害だから恐れることはない That snake is completely harmless, so you have nothing to *fear*. ‖ 人々は軍が政権を握る可能性があるのではないかと恐れた People *dreaded* the possibility that the military might seize power. (➤ dread は fear よりも強意).
2【心配する】▶最も恐れていたことが実際に起きてしまった *What I had feared most* actually happened. ‖ 彼は留年するのを恐れて（＝留年しないように）一生懸命勉強した He studied hard *for* [*out of*] *fear of* having to repeat the same year.
3【畏まり敬う】▶日本では人々は自然をおそれてきた People have *been humbled* by nature in Japan.

おそろい お揃い ▶あの姉妹はいつもおそろいの服を着ている Those sisters always wear *matching* dresses. ‖ 私は彼とおそろいのセーターを買った I bought *his-and-her* [*matching*] sweaters for my boyfriend and myself. (➤ his-and-her は「男女ペアの」の意).
▶皆さんおそろいでどちらへ? Where are you *all* going? ‖ 彼女は日曜日は決まってご主人とおそろいで外出する She goes out *with* her husband every Sunday.

おそろしい 恐ろしい

1【怖い】horrible; terrible（恐怖感を抱かせる）; frightening（人を脅かす）; dreadful（身震いするような；悪いことを予感させる語）▶恐ろしい光景 a *horrible* [*dreadful*] sight ‖ 恐ろしい事件が次々に起きた *Dreadful* incidents happened one after another. ‖ 飢えほど恐ろしいものはない Nothing is more *terrible* than hunger. ‖ ゆうべ恐ろしい夢を見た I had a *terrible* dream last night. ‖ 私は高い所が恐ろしい I *am afraid of* high places. ‖ 私は手術を受けるのが恐ろしかった I *was afraid of* undergoing the operation.
2【非常な】▶そのスポーツカーは恐ろしいスピードで走り去った The sports car sped away at an *extremely* [a *terribly*] *high* speed.

おそろしく 恐ろしく terribly ▶東京の物価は恐ろしく高い In Tokyo, prices are *terribly* [*awfully*] high. (➤ awfully /ɔ́:fli/ は女性が使うことが多い) ‖ 今度の相手は恐ろしく手ごわい Our opponent this time is *terribly* tough. ‖ 父は恐ろしくけちん坊だ My father is an *awful* miser.

おそろしさ 恐ろしさ fear, terror (➤ 後者のほうが意味が強い) ▶空襲の恐ろしさは体験した者でなければわかるまい The *terror* of an air raid cannot be understood by a person who has never experienced one.

おそわる 教わる ▶私は週1回山野先生にピアノを教わ

った I *took* piano *lessons* from Miss Yamano once a week. ‖ 誰に英語を教わったの？ Who *taught* you English？‖ 教わった(＝言われた)とおりに書きなさい Write *as you were told* (*to*).

オゾン ozone /óʊzoʊn/ ▶フロンガスなどの化合物によるオゾン層の破壊がますます進んでいる Destruction of *the ozone layer* due to compounds like CFC is accelerating.

‖オゾンホール an ozone hole.

おだい お代 a fee ▶お代はいくら？ *How much is it*？‖ お代は見てのお帰り *See first, pay later*.

おたおた ▶おたおたする *get flustered*.

おたがい お互い each other, one another. →互い.

> **直訳の落とし穴「お互いに頑張ろう」**
> 日本語の「お互い」は「それぞれ」「ともに」と同じ目標に向かって行動するときにも用いるが，この場合 each other, one another は使えない. each other も one another も「相互に」影響し合うときに用いる表現である. したがって,「お互いに頑張ろう」は (×)Let's work hard each other. でなく, Let's both [all] work hard [do our best]. で，２人の場合は both, ３人以上の場合は all とする.

▶お互い，力を合わせてこの仕事を完成させよう Let's help *each other* [*one another*] to finish this job.(➤ ３者以上ではどちらも区別なく用いるが，２者では each other が一般的) ／Let's work *together* to finish this job. (➤「お互い」より「力を合わせて，協力して」をポイントにして，後者のように表現するのが普通) ‖ お互いにいつまでも元気でいよう We hope *both* [*all*] *of us* stay healthy for as long as possible.

▶お互いにもっとよく話し合うべきではないですか You should talk more frankly to *each other*. (➤「お互い(に)」は副詞用法が多いが，each other, one another ともに代名詞扱いなので，前に前置詞が必要になることがある) ‖ お互いが相手を尊重し合うことが大切だ It's important for *us* to respect *each other*. ／*Mutual* respect is important. (➤ mutual は「相互の」の意).

おたがいさま お互い様 ▶困ったときはお互いさまですからどうか気になさらないでください Don't thank me. We *are all in the same boat*. (➤「同じ境遇にある」の意) ／You don't have to thank me for this. I think people *should help each other* when the chips are down. (➤ when the chips are down は「いざというときに」の意のインフォーマルな表現) ‖ 対話「ずいぶん白髪が増えたね」「お互いさまだよ」"You've gotten a lot more gray (hair), I see." "*I'm not the only one*. ／*Join the club*!"

おたかくとまる お高く止まる ▶お高く止まるなよ Don't *be stuck up*. ／Don't *play hard to get*. (➤ 後者は「(主に女性が)簡単には落ちませんよという顔をする」の意のくだけた言い方).

おたから お宝 one's treasure, a treasured item

おたく お宅 ▶お宅(＝住まい)はどちらですか Where do you live？‖ ご立派なお宅(＝家)ですね You have quite *a home*. ／What a lovely *home*！(➤ 後者は主に女性が言う) ‖ あすお宅へ伺います I think I'll pay a visit to *your place* tomorrow. ‖ お宅からお電話です You have a call from *home*.

▶お宅(＝あなた)だあれ？ Who are *you*？(➤ ぞんざいな言い方) ‖ お宅はどちらのご出身ですか Where are *you* from？‖ お宅のご主人，今し方お出かけになったわよ *Your husband* left (just) a moment ago. ‖ このサンプルは，この間お宅の若い人が置いていったものですよ This sample is something the young man *from your company* left here the other day.

オタク a geek /giːk/, an otaku [複 otaku] (➤ 英語では geek, nerd, freak などを当てるが，otaku も英語に入っており，この語を知っている人も多い；geek のほうが nerd より「かっこいい」ニュアンスがある) ▶アニメオタク an anime *geek* [*nerd*] ／an anime *otaku* ‖ 科学オタク a science *geek* [*nerd*] ‖ ゲームオタク a game *geek* ／a *hard-core* gamer ‖ 健康オタク a health *freak*.

▶コンピュータオタク a computer *nerd* [*geek*] ‖ 数学オタク a math *geek* ‖ 鉄道オタク a railroad *geek* [*freak*].

‖オタク文化 otaku [geek] culture.

おだく 汚濁 ▶河川の水質汚濁を調べる investigate the *deterioration of river water quality*.

おたけび 雄叫び a battle cry, a triumphant shout.

おたずねもの お尋ね者 ▶あいつはお尋ね者だ That guy *is wanted by the police*. ／He is *a wanted suspect*. (➤ suspect /sʌ́spekt/ は「容疑者」).

おだて flattery ▶そんなおだてになんか乗るものですか！I'm not going to fall for that kind of *flattery*. (➤ fall for は「…にだまされる」) ‖ 妻はセールスマンのおだてに乗って化粧品を買った My wife *was sweet-talked* [*was flattered*] by a salesman into buying cosmetics.

おだてる flatter ＋目，《インフォーマル》sweet-talk ＋目 ▶おだてるなよ Don't *flatter* me. ‖ 彼をおだてると何でもしてくれるよ You can *flatter* him into doing anything. ‖ 敬太は妹をおだてて自分の部屋を掃除させた Keita *sweet-talked* his little sister into cleaning his room.

おたふくかぜ お多福風邪 mumps (➤ 通例単数扱い) ▶メグはおたふくかぜで寝ている Meg is in bed with *mumps*. ‖ その男の子はいとこからおたふくかぜをうつされた That boy caught *mumps* from his cousin.

おだぶつ お陀仏 ▶車がこの崖から下の海に落ちでもしたらぼくたちはおだぶつだね We'll *be dead ducks* if you steer this car over the cliff into the ocean. (➤ dead duck は「自ら災いを招くようなことをする人」の意のインフォーマルな言い方).

▶カンニングしてるところを先生に見つかったらおだぶつだぞ If you get caught cheating, you'll *be a goner* [you'll *be dead for sure*]. (➤ goner は「死んだ人」の意のインフォーマルな語).

おたま お玉 a ladle ▶おたまでみそ汁をよそう serve miso soup with *a ladle*.

おだまき 《植物》a columbine.

おたまじゃくし a tadpole (カエルの子) ▶オタマジャクシはやがてカエルになる *A tadpole* grows into a frog.

▶俺，おたまじゃくし(＝音符)が読めないんだ I can't read *music*. (➤ read music は「楽譜を読む」).

おためごかし お為ごかし an "it's for your own good" tactic [approach] (➤ 説明的な訳) ▶おためごかしの親切 *pretended* kindness.

おだやか 穏やか **1【人柄が】** mild (生来の性質として)；gentle (動きや態度が) ▶穏やかな人 a *mild* person ‖ 彼は穏やかな人柄だ He is a *gentle-natured* man. ／He is *gentle by nature*. ／He is a (man of) *gentle nature*.

2【気候や海が】 mild, gentle；calm (静かな) ▶穏やかな気候 a *mild* climate ‖ 穏やかな春の日ざし the *gentle* sunshine of spring ‖ けさは海がとても穏やかだ The sea is very *calm* this morning.

3【話しぶりなどが】calm, quiet ▶そう興奮するな, もっと穏やかに話そう Don't get so excited. Let's talk more *calmly*.

おたんこなす ▶このおたんこなす！ *You nincompoop* [*goof*]！(➤ nincompoop は /nínkəmpu:p/ と発音).

オタワ Ottawa(カナダの首都).

おち 落ち 1【漏れ, 抜け】an **omission** ▶申込書類に落ちがないか, もう一度確認してください Please check the application forms again to make sure there are no *omissions*. ‖ 彼女の仕事には落ちがない There are no *oversights* [*mistakes*] in her work. (➤ oversight は「見落とし」).

2【結末】▶振られるのが落ちよ You will *end up with* a broken heart. ‖ そんな親切は迷惑がられるのが落ちだ Such consideration will surely *end up* being seen as a bother (by the recipient). (➤ recipient は「受け手, 相手」).

3【聞かせどころ】a **point** ▶ジョークの落ちがわかった？ Did you see the *point* of the joke？‖ 彼の話にはたいてい落ちがついている His stories usually have *a punch line*. (➤ punch line は「あっと言わせる箇所」).

おちあう 落ち合う meet ▶落ち合う場所を決めておこう Let's decide where we are going to *meet*. ‖ 2本の川はそこで落ち合う The two rivers *meet* there.

おちいる 陥る fall《into》▶患者は危篤状態に陥った The patient *fell into* critical condition. ‖ 彼は二者択一を迫られ, ジレンマに陥った Being forced to choose between the two, he *fell into* [*was in*] a serious dilemma. ‖ その市は財政難に陥っている The city *is in* financial difficulties.

おちおち ▶彼女は息子のことが心配で夜もおちおち眠れないと言っている She complains that she cannot sleep *in peace* [cannot have a good (night's) sleep] because of anxiety about her son. ‖ ここはうるさくておちおち本も読めない I cannot read *quietly* in this noisy place.

おちかづき お近づき ▶お近づきになる *become acquainted with* someone／*get to know* someone (➤ 前者が日本語により近い) ‖ お近づきのしるしに１杯やりましょう Let's have a drink *to celebrate our* (*new*) *friendship*. ‖ お近づきになれてうれしく思います I'm (very) pleased *to make your acquaintance*. 《参考》初対面の人への別れ際の挨拶としては I'm very happy to have met you. とか Nice meeting you. のように言う.

おちこぼれ 落ちこぼれ a **dropout**(中途退学者)
▶高校［大学］の落ちこぼれ a high school [college] *dropout*／a high school [college] *student who has fallen behind in his* [*her*] *studies* ‖ 社会の落ちこぼれになるなよ I don't want you to end up *a dropout* from society.

おちこみ 落ち込み a **slide**, a **decline**；a **slump**(不振, 急落) ▶販売の急激な落ち込み a steep *slide* [*decline*] in sales.

おちこむ 落ち込む 1【低い所に】▶トラは仕掛けておいた穴にまんまと落ち込んだ The tiger *fell into* the trap as we had planned. ‖ 不景気で消費が落ち込んでいる Consumption *has fallen off* [*declined*] due to the recession.

2【落胆する】▶彼は離婚したあとひどく落ち込んでいた He *was despondent* [*very depressed*] after his divorce. ‖ 何だか落ち込んでいるようだけど, どうかしたの？ You look a little *depressed* [*down*]. What's the matter？‖ 落ち込むなよ Don't *let it get you down*. (➤ この it は状況を表す).

おちつき 落ち着き calmness；composure(平静)
▶落ち着きのある［落ち着きのない］子 a *calm* [*restless*] child ‖ 彼女は何が起ころうと落ち着きを失わない She *keeps her composure* [*keeps her cool*] no matter what happens. ‖ 自殺志願男は警察の根気強い説得でようやく落ち着きを取り戻した The man who was trying to kill himself finally *regained his presence of mind* [*pulled himself together*] after the persistent persuasion of the police.
▶今のところ病人は落ち着きを見せて(＝安定して)いる The patient is *in stable condition* for now.

おちつきはらう 落ち着き払う ▶彼はインタビューの間落ち着き払っていた He was *very cool* while being interviewed. ‖ 対戦相手は憎らしいほど落ち着き払っていた My opponent looked so *calm and collected* I felt jealous of him. (➤ collected は「心を落ち着かせている」の意).

おちつく 落ち着く

> 📖 訳語メニュー
> 心が →feel at ease **1**
> 情勢などが →relax, stabilize **2**
> 生活などが →get settled **3**

1【心・動作などが】feel at ease [**at home**] ▶落ち着いた人 a *calm* [*self-possessed*／《インフォーマル》*together*] person ‖ きみと一緒だといつも気持ちが落ち着くんだ I always *feel at ease* when I'm with you. ‖ このインテリアは落ち着く I *feel at home* with this decor.
▶ここは静かだから落ち着いて勉強ができる I can *settle down* and study because it is (so) quiet here. ‖ 彼は落ち着いて話を続けた He kept on talking *in an easy manner* [*in a relaxed manner*]. ‖ 落ち着いて！ *Calm down*！／*Take it easy*！‖ 落ち着いた雰囲気のレストラン a restaurant with a *relaxed* [*homey*] atmosphere.
▶試験の直前なので気持ちが落ち着かない I *feel nervous* [*uneasy*] since the examination is around the corner. ‖ 彼はそわそわして落ち着かない様子だった He appeared restless and *unsettled*. ‖ スピーチをしなければならなくなると, 私は決まって落ち着かなくなる Whenever I have to make a speech, I *get the jitters*.／I always *have butterflies in my stomach* when I have to make a speech. (🏺 前者は「どきどき［そわそわ］する」の意のインフォーマルな慣用句を用いた訳例で, 後者は「どきどき［そわそわ］する」(「胃の中にチョウがいる」が原義)の意の慣用句を用いた訳例. 後者には胃(の辺り)がおかしくなるという含みがある).

2【情勢・天候などが】relax(緩む)；**stabilize**(安定する) ▶両国間の緊迫した情勢はやや落ち着いた The tense situation between the two countries has *eased* [*relaxed*] somewhat. ‖ 物価は近頃落ち着いている Prices *have stabilized* recently.
▶母の容体はようやく落ち着いた My mother's condition *has* finally *stabilized*. ‖ このところ天気が落ち着かない The weather is *unsettled* [*changeable*] these days.

3【生活・住所などが】get settled ▶落ち着いたらきっと便りをくれよ Be sure to drop me a line when you *get settled*.
✉ **ここへ来て半年, ようやく私たちもこの家に落ち着きました** It has been six months since

we moved here, and at last we *feel settled* in our new home.

4【色・服装などが】 一形 **落ち着いた quiet, subdued** ▶落ち着いた色 a *quiet* color ‖ 落ち着いた服装を心がけなさい You should try to wear *quiet* [*subdued*] colors and styles.

5【話・結果などが】 ▶話し合いは結局制服を変えるべきだということに落ち着いた We finally *reached* [*came to*] *the conclusion that* the (school) uniform should be changed.

おちつける 落ち着ける ▶家に帰ると落ち着ける I *feel relaxed* [*at ease*] when I'm home. ‖ 気を落ち着けなさい *Calm yourself*. ／*Calm down*. ／Try to *compose yourself*. ‖ 気を落ち着けてから話をしなさい *Calm yourself* before you speak.

▶ことしは腰を落ち着けて翻訳の仕事をしたい I'd like to *settle down* to work on a translation project this year.

おちど 落ち度 (a) **fault** ▶自分の落ち度を認める admit one's *fault* [*error*] ‖ こちらの落ち度です. 申し訳ありません It is our *fault* and we are very sorry (about it). ‖ きみに落ち度はない You *are not to blame*.

おちのびる 落ち延びる ▶当地には義経が落ち延びたという伝説がある Legend has it that Yoshitsune *escaped and reached here safely after losing the battle*.

おちば 落ち葉 fallen leaves (➤ その 1 枚は a fallen leaf) ▶落ち葉を掃く rake up *fallen leaves* ‖ 道は落ち葉に埋まっていた The road was buried under *fallen leaves*.

おちぶれる 落ちぶれる ▶あの人は昔は金持ちだったが, 今は落ちぶれてしまっている He was once a rich man, but he *has come down in the world*. ‖ 世間の人は落ちぶれた人間には目もくれない People turn their backs upon a *down-and-out* person.

おちめ 落ち目 ▶あの会社も落ち目だ The company *is on the decline*. ‖ 彼も落ち目だなあ His fortune is *on the wane*. (➤ on the wane は「(力が)衰えかけて」) ‖ あの歌手の人気も落ち目になってきた That singer is *losing his* [*her*] *popularity*.

おちゃ お茶 Japanese (green) tea

日本紹介 ✉ **日本人が昔から飲んでいるお茶は緑茶です.「お茶」と言えば, ふつうは緑茶を指します. 原料は紅茶と同じ茶の葉ですが, 発酵させていないのでビタミンCが豊富です. 飲むときに砂糖やミルク, レモンなどを加えることはありません. 多くの人が特に時間に関係なくいつでも飲みます** In Japanese, '*ocha*,' which means "tea," usually refers to green tea because it is the type of tea traditionally drunk in Japan. Although it is made from the same tea leaves as black tea, it doesn't go through a fermentation process and is therefore rich in vitamin C. When drinking it, people do not add milk, sugar or lemon slices. It is drunk anytime of the day by many people.

▶彼女は私にお茶を入れてくれた She *made* [*prepared*] *Japanese* (*green*) *tea* for me. ／She *fixed* me *Japanese* (*green*) *tea*. ‖ お茶していかない？ How about (stopping in for) a cup of *tea*? (➤ stop in は「立ち寄る」の意).

▶彼女はお茶(＝茶道)とお花を習っている She is taking lessons in *tea ceremony* and flower arrangement.

▶《慣用表現》その場はそう言って何とかお茶を濁しておいた I said it just to *save* [*keep up*] *appearances* for the moment. (➤save [keep up] appearances は「その場［体裁］を取り繕う」の意).

おちゃくみ お茶汲み ▶お茶くみをする *serve tea*.

おちゃづけ お茶漬け →茶漬け.

おちゃっぴい a **talkative and sprightly girl.**

おちゃのこ お茶の子 ▶そんなことはお茶の子さいさいだ It's *a piece of cake* [*a walk in the park*].

おちゅうげん お中元 →中元.

おちょうしもの お調子者 ▶彼女はお調子者だ She *is easily flattered*. ／She often *gets carried away*. (➤ 前者は「すぐおだてに乗る」, 後者は「調子に乗ってはめを外す」の意).

おちょくる make fan《of》(からかう) ; **make a fool**《of》(ばかにする).

おちょこ お猪口 a small *sake* cup ▶《慣用表現》傘がおちょこになった My umbrella *was blown inside out*.

おちょぼぐち おちょぼ口 ▶妹はおちょぼ口だ My sister has *a cute little mouth*.

おちる 落ちる

📖 **訳語メニュー**
低い所へ →fall, drop **1**
抜ける →come out, come off **2**
程度が下がる →drop, decline **3**
失敗する →fail **4**

1【物が低い所へ移動する】fall ; drop (落下する, 滴る) ; **give way** (重みなどに耐えられなくなって落下する) ▶網棚から私の荷物が落ちた My suitcase *fell* off the rack. ‖ 強風でたくさんのリンゴが落ちた Many apples *fell* due to the strong wind. ‖ ボールは池に落ちた The ball *dropped* into the pond. ‖ 突然石がぼくの頭上に落ちてきた Suddenly a stone *tumbled down* onto my head from above. (➤ tumble は「転げ落ちる」) ‖ 飛行機は海に落ちた The airplane *crashed into* the ocean. ‖ 廊下にごみが落ちている Some rubbish *is* (*lying*) in the corridor.

▶その橋は車の重みで落ちた The bridge *gave way* under the weight of the car. ‖ 地震で壁が落ちた(＝崩れた) The wall *collapsed* [*crumbled*] in the earthquake. ‖《木馬に乗っている子供などに》しっかりつかまっていないと落ちるよ Hold (on) tight or you'll *fall*. ‖ 小さな男の子が公園の池に落ちた A small boy *fell into* the pond in the park. ‖ 子供が階段から落ちてけがをした The child was injured when he *fell down* the stairs. (➤ fall from the stairs とはいわない) ‖ その小さな男の子は三輪車から落ちた The little boy *fell off* the tricycle. (➤ fell down としないこと. down はある程度上方から下方への距離がある場合に用いる).

▶雨がぽつぽつ落ちてきた It is beginning to rain lightly. ／The first drops of rain have started to *fall*. ‖ 空から白いものがちらほら落ちてきた It started to snow lightly. ‖ 向こうのけやきの木に雷が落ちたそうだ I hear that *lightning hit* a zelkova tree over there.

▶砂漠に日が落ちた The sun *has gone down* below the horizon in the desert.

2【本体から離れる, 抜ける】come out [**off**] (染みが落ちる, 色が抜ける) ▶この染みはせっけんでは落ちない The stains will *not come out* [*cannot be removed*] with soap. ‖ この洗剤は油汚れがよく落ちる This detergent *removes* oil very well. (➤ remove は「取り除く」).

▶この洋服は洗濯したら色が落ちたみたい The dress seems to *have faded* after washing. (➤ fade は「色があせる」) ‖ この生地は色が落ちない This cloth *holds dye well.*

▶お名前が落ちて(＝漏れて)いたそうで, 申し訳ありません I'm sorry that your name *is missing* (from the list).

3【程度が下がる】drop ; decline(レベルなどが低下する) ▶成績がクラスの真ん中くらいまで落ちた My class ranking *has dropped* to about the middle (of the class). ‖ 売り上げが急激に落ちた Sales *dropped* sharply. ‖ 彼女も人気が落ちてきた Her popularity is *declining.* ‖ そんなことをすると信用が落ちるよ You'll *lose* your credibility if you do such a thing.

▶年を取ってさしもの名人の腕も落ちた That great master craftsman has *lost his skill* [*lost his touch*] due to age. ‖ 国産のコートは英国製よりだいぶ落ちると思う I think that domestic coats are far *inferior to* those made in Britain.

▶彼も落ちるところまで落ちた He *went as low as he could go.* ‖ 落ちるところまで落ちてそのアルコール依存患者はようやく酒を断った *After* he (*had*) *hit rock bottom,* the alcoholic finally stopped drinking. (「どん底に落ちる」の意の慣用句 hit rock bottom を用いると日本語の感じが出せる) ‖ あいつがいるといつも話が落ちる(＝卑わいになる) Whenever he's around, the conversation always *deteriorates* [*gets dirty*].

▶新幹線は風が強いとスピードが落ちる The Shinkansen *reduces* [*drops*] its speed when winds are strong. ‖ 鮮度の落ちた魚は売れなくて当然だ It's quite natural that fish which have *lost* their freshness do not sell well.

4【失敗する】fail ▶私の兄は入試に落ちた My (older) brother *failed* (in) the entrance examination. (➤ in をつけるのは古風) ‖ あの人はこの前の選挙に落ちた He *lost* the last election.

5【ある状態にはまる】▶眠りに落ちる *drop off to sleep* / *fall asleep* ‖ 2人は出会ってまもなく恋に落ちた The two *fell in love* soon after they met each other. ‖ 彼はまんまと我々が仕掛けたわなに落ちた He easily *fell into the trap* we had set.

6【持ちこたえられなくなる】▶大坂城は何か月囲まれても落ちなかった Osaka Castle *did not fall* despite being surrounded by the enemy for months. ‖ (刑事が)ホシはゆうべ落ちた(＝自白した)ぜ Last night I got the suspect to *cave in and admit* he did it. (➤ cave in は「降参する」の意のインフォーマルな言い方).

7【人手に渡る】▶その名画は1億円で, あるドイツ人の手に落ちた That famous painting *has gone* [*has been knocked down*] to a German for a hundred million yen. (➤ knock down は「競り落とす」).

おちんちん a **dick,** 《英また》a **willie,** 《英また》a **peter** 《参考》penis /píːnɪs/ は医学用語で無難な言い方. dick, willie, peter は男どうしで使う.

おつ 乙 ▶甲と乙 the former and *the latter* / the one and *the other* ‖ 両者甲乙つけがたい Both are so good *it is difficult to tell which is better.*

▶これはなかなかおつな味だね This dish *has a subtle and delicate flavor.*

おつかい お使い an **errand** ▶5歳の息子をお使いにやった I *sent* my five-year-old son *on an errand.* ‖ (食料品の)お使いに行ってきてくれる? Would you *go* [*run*] *and pick up* some groceries for me?

おっかけ 追っかけ a **groupie** /grúːpi/ (➤スターを追いかけ回す主に女性ファン) ▶母は韓流映画スターの追っかけをやっている My mother *is an enthusiastic fan* of South Korean movie stars and *regularly follows them around.*

おっかない ▶そんなおっかない顔しないでちょうだい Don't look so *fierce,* please. / Will you stop being so *serious*? (➤ serious は「真剣な」) ‖ あの先生, おっかないぞ That teacher's quite *strict,* I tell you.

おっかなびっくり ▶彼女はおっかなびっくり(＝こわごわ)車を運転した She drove the car *extremely nervously.* ‖ 女の子はおっかなびっくり馬のたてがみに触った The little girl touched the horse on the mane *timidly.*

おつかれさま お疲れ様 ▶ 対話 (仕事などを終えて)「お先に失礼します」「お疲れさま」 "Good night." "*See you.*" (➤「じゃあまた」の意).

解説 英語にはこれに対応する1語はない. 対話例のほかには, 例えば, 相手に手数をかけた場合などの「お疲れさま」には Thank you very much. や Thank you for your trouble. がよく, 勤めから帰った夫や妻などに言う「お疲れさま」には How was work today? や How was your day today? などが適当. また,「きょうはいい仕事をしたね」の意の You did a good job today. を「お疲れさま」の代わりに使うこともできる.

おっくう 億劫 ▶雨の日は駅まで行くのもおっくうでね I *don't* even *feel like* going to the train station on a rainy day.

▶私は出かけるのがおっくうで家に居た I *felt* too *weary* to go out and stayed at home.

オックスフォード Oxford(イギリスの都市 ; オックスフォード大学がある).

おつくり お作り →刺身.

おっこちる 落っこちる fall ▶彼女は階段から落っこちて足の骨を折った She *fell down* the stairs and broke her leg. ▶兄貴はT大を受けたけど落っこちた My (older) brother tried to get into T University, but he *failed* the exam.

おっことす 落っことす drop +目 ▶瓶を落っことす *drop* a bottle ‖ 買い物に行く途中で財布を落っことした(＝なくした) I *lost* my purse on the way to go shopping.

おっさん ▶おい, おっさん! そこで何やってんだよ! Hey, *Pop*! What are you doing there? ‖ 公園で変なおっさんに絡まれた Some strange *middle-aged man* tried to pick a fight with me in the park.

おっしゃる ▶あなたのおっしゃることはよくわかりますが… I understand what you *are saying,* but ... . ‖ うそおっしゃい! No! (I don't believe it.) ‖ 何とおっしゃいました? I beg your pardon? (➤ 尻上がりに言う) / Could you say that again? / 《英また》Sorry? ‖ 何かございましたらおっしゃってください *Let me* [*us*] *know* if you need any help.

▶お名前は何とおっしゃいます? May I have your name (, please)? ‖ 市川さんとおっしゃる方がご面会です *A* Mr. Ichikawa is here to see you. (➤ この a は固有名詞につけて「…という人」の意).

おっす ▶おっす, 元気でやってるかい? *Hi* [*Hey* / *Yo*]! How are you doing? ‖ おっす, 何かおもしろいことでもあるかい? *Howdy,* what's new? (➤ howdy /háʊdi/ は主に《米》で, くだけた語).

おっちょこちょい a **scatterbrain**(注意散漫な人) ; a **butterfingers**(よく物を落としたり壊したりする人) ▶うちの

家内はおっちょこちょいでね My wife is *a scatterbrain*. ‖おっちょこちょいだね, きみは！ What *a scatterbrain*! ／What *a butterfingers*!（➤両者ともユーモラスな言い方).

[1]**おって 追っ手** a **pursuer** ▶追っ手をまく dodge *a pursuer*.

[2]**おって 追って** ▶詳細は追ってお知らせいたします We will notify [inform] you of the details *later on*. ／You shall have details *in due time*.

[1]**おっと 夫** a **husband** ▶うちの夫は, 夫は家事に口を出すもんじゃないって言ってるわ My *husband* says (that) *a husband* shouldn't interfere with household matters.（➤husband を短縮した hubby があるが, 現代英語ではほとんど使われない).

[2]**おっと** ▶おっと！もう少しで花瓶を引っくり返すところだった *Oops* [*Oh/Uh-oh*]! I almost overturned the vase.（➤Oops は /ʊps/ と発音）‖おっと, 危ない！ *Watch out!*／*Be careful!*

おっとせい《動物》a **fur seal**; a **seal**（アザラシ・オットセイ・アシカなどの総称）▶オットセイに芸を仕込む teach tricks to *a fur seal*.

おつとめひん お勤め品 a **bargain**.

おっとり ▶育ちがいいせいか彼女はおっとりしている She is *very easygoing* [is *quiet and composed*] probably because of her good upbringing.

おっぱい **1【乳】**▶（赤ん坊に）今おっぱいを飲ませたところです I just finished *breast-feeding* her [him]. ‖赤ん坊はおっぱいを飲みたがっている The baby wants to *be fed*. ／The baby wants to *have its milk*.

2【乳房】 **breasts**（➤通例複数形で用いる）▶彼女, いいおっぱいしてるね She has nice *breasts* [a nice set of *boobs*].（➤boobs は俗語で, 女性に不快感を与えるおそれがある. boobies ともいう).

おつまみ → つまみ.

おつり お釣り **change** ▶3ドル50セント？ 20ドルからだとお釣りはいくらだっけ？ $3.50 out of $20? How much should the *change* be?（➤$3.50 の読み方は three (dollars) fifty または three dollars and fifty cents).

▶おつりが間違っているようですが I'm afraid this isn't the right *change*. ‖まだおつりをもらっていませんが I haven't gotten my *change* yet. ‖**対話**「1万円でお釣りもらえますか」「はいどうぞ」"Can you give me *change* for a ten-thousand-yen bill?" "Yes, here is your change."

☛ 釣り(銭)（→見出語）

おて お手 ▶《犬に》お手！*Shake* (*hands*)!

おてあげ お手上げ ▶彼は物理は得意だが生物のほうはお手上げのようだ He is good at physics, but seems *out of his depth* at biology.（➤out of one's depth は「理解できない, 手に負えない」）‖その少年には先生たちもお手上げだった The teachers *gave up on* the boy. ／The teachers *threw up their hands* (at the boy's behavior). ‖もうお手上げだ I *give up*. ／I wash my hands of it.（➤「手を引く」の意).

おてあらい お手洗い a **bathroom**,《主に英》a **toilet** →トイレ ▶お手洗いはどちらでしょうか Where's the *bathroom* [*toilet*]?（➤ホテル・デパート・劇場などでなら Where's the restroom? とか Where's the men's [ladies'] room? と聞くことが多い）‖お手洗いをお借りしていいですか *May I use your bathroom* [*toilet*], please?

おでい 汚泥 **sludge**.

おでき a **boil**; a **swelling**（できもの）▶背中におできができた I've got *a boil* on my back.

おでこ **the forehead** /fɔ́(ː)rɪd, fɔ́ːrhed/（額）▶秀子ちゃんはおでこちゃんね Hideko *has a high forehead*, doesn't she?

おてだま お手玉 a **beanbag** ▶彼女はお手玉を5つ使って遊べる She can juggle five *beanbags*. **《参考》** 英語の beanbag は野球ボール大で, 主に的に投げつけて遊ぶ.

おてつき お手付き ▶《カード遊びで》今のお手付きじゃない？ Didn't you *touch the wrong card* just now?

おてつだいさん お手伝いさん《英》a **home help**（通いの家政婦）; a **resident** [**live-in**] **help**（住み込みの）; a **housekeeper**（家事全般をこなす人）.

おてのもの お手の物 ▶料理は私にとってお手の物だ I'*m good at* cooking. ／Cooking *is my forte* [*my strong suit*].（➤forte は「得意のもの」）‖弟は暗算はお手のものです My brother *can* do mental arithmetic *in his sleep*.（➤can do in one's sleep は「難なくできる」).

おでまし お出座し ▶ほら, 大女優のおでましだ *Here comes* the great actress in all her glory. ／The great actress *is* now *making her appearance*.

おてもり お手盛り ▶お手盛りの役員報酬 *self-serving* [*self-decided*／*self-approved*] executive compensation.

おてやわらかに お手柔らかに ▶どうかお手柔らかにお願いします I hope you'll go easy on me. ／I hope you won't be too hard on me.（➤be hard on は「…につらく当たる」）‖お手柔らかにね！ Take it easy on me [us]!

おてん 汚点 a **stain**; a **blot**（➤比喩的意味では両者は同義だが, もともと前者は「液体によるしみ」, 後者は「インクやペンキの汚れ」の意）▶今回の事件は彼の経歴に拭うことのできない汚点を残すだろう The recent incident will leave an indelible *stain* [*blot*] on his career.

おでん *oden*

日本紹介 ✉ **おでんはちくわ, 豆腐, ゆで卵, 大根, こんにゃくなどを材料にした一種の煮込み料理で, かつお節やしょうゆで味付けしたつゆに浸してあります. 体が温まるので特に寒い季節に食べます. 材料が串に刺してあることもあります** *Oden* is a hodgepodge dish made of *chikuwa* (cylinder-shaped steamed fish cake), tofu, hard-boiled eggs, vegetables such as *daikon*, and *konnyaku* (*konnyaku* jelly) in a broth flavored with *katsuobushi* (bonito flakes) and soy sauce. It is a very warming food eaten especially in winter. Sometimes the ingredients are on skewers.

おてんきや お天気屋 ▶彼はお天気屋だから扱いにくい He is *moody* [*fickle*], so he is hard to deal with.

おてんとさま お天道様 ▶悪いことをしたらおてんとさまはちゃんとお見通しだよ *God* will know if you do anything bad. ‖**対話**「お兄ちゃん, 今度はいつ帰るの？」「さあな, おてんとさまに聞いてくれ」"Brother, when are you coming back?" "Well, *that's something you'd better ask the wind*."（➤映画『男はつらいよ』でのさくらと寅さんの対話; 英語では「風に聞いてくれ」と表現する).

おてんば お転婆 a **tomboy**.

おと 音 (a) **sound**; (a) **noise**（騒音）▶大きい音 a loud [big] *sound*（➤big は「でかい」に相

当する) ‖小さい音 a low *sound* ‖鈍い音 a dull *sound* ‖岩に砕ける波の音 the *sound* of waves breaking on rocks ‖大砲の音 the *roar* of a cannon ‖ベルの音 the *ring* of a bell.
▶外で妙な音がした I heard a strange *sound* outside. ‖聞こえるのは時計がかすかに時を刻む音だけだった All I could hear was the faint *sound* of a ticking clock. ‖あの鐘はひびが入ったような音がする That bell *sounds* like it has a crack in it. ‖テレビの音が出ないよ There's no *sound* from the TV. ／The TV's *sound* is dead. ‖雷の音が遠くで聞こえる I can hear *thunder rolling* in the distance. (➤「雷がゴロゴロ鳴っているのが聞こえる」の意) ‖タイヤがパンクする音がした I *heard* a tire blow out. (➤ hear は「…の音が聞こえる」の意だから sound という語を使う必要はない).
▶大木が大きな音を立てて倒れた A great tree fell (over) *with a crash*. ‖バイオリンは高い音を出し, コントラバスは低い音を出す The violin produces *high-pitched sounds* and the contrabass low ones. ‖音を立てるな *Don't make a sound*. ／*Be quiet*. ‖勉強中だからうるさい音を立てないでください I'm studying now, so please don't make any *noise*. ‖ステレオの音(＝音量)を小さくしてください Please lower the *volume* of the stereo. ／Please turn down the stereo.

おとうさん お父さん a **father**(父親) ; **Father, Dad, Daddy** (➤ あとの３語は家庭内での呼びかけにも用いられる. Daddy は小児語) ▶お父さんが私にカメラを買ってくれた *My father* bought me a camera. ‖お父さん, どこへ行くの? Where're you going, *Dad* [*Daddy*] ? ‖《母親が子供に》お父さん, また遅いのかしら I wonder if *Dad* will be late (coming home) again. ‖《父の日のカードで》お父さん ありがとう! Happy Father's Day! ⇀おやじ.

おとうと 弟 a **younger brother**, a **little brother**, 《米・インフォーマル》a **kid brother**
語法 (1)最後の語は, 年齢差があって親代わりになっている兄や姉から見ていう場合に用いる. (2)日本語は「兄」と「弟」を区別するが, 英語ではふつうは区別をせず, 単に brother で済ませる.
▶大学生の弟は北海道にいます My (*younger*) *brother* is a college student, and lives in Hokkaido. ‖《小学生が》私の弟は３歳[１歳]です My *little* [*baby*] *brother* is three years [one year] old. (➤ baby brother はいちばん年下の弟を指していう).
‖弟弟子 a junior pupil [disciple] (➤ 欧米ではふつう, 兄, 弟を区別せず, 単に弟子と考える).

おとおし お通し an **appetizer**, a **small dish of hors d'oeuvres**.

おどおど ▶警官に行き先を聞かれて男はおどおどした The man *looked nervous* when the police officer inquired where he was going. ‖面接を受けるときはおどおどしてはだめだ Don't *be shy* during an interview.

おどかす 脅かす **1**【脅す】**threaten** ＋目 (脅迫する) ▶その男は彼女の万引きを告げ口すると言って脅かした The man *threatened* to snitch on her shoplifting.
2【びっくりさせる】**scare** ＋目 ; **startle** ＋目 (飛び上がらせるほど) ▶弟は後ろから「わっ」と言って私を脅かした My brother *scared* [*startled*] me by yelling from behind. ‖対話「そのせきは肺がんかもしれないよ」「脅かすなよ」“That cough could be a sign of lung cancer.” “Don't *scare* me!”

おとぎばなし おとぎ話 a **fairy tale** ; a **bedtime story** (子供に就寝時に聞かせる) ▶幼い頃父はよくおとぎ話をしてくれた Dad used to tell me *fairy tales* [*bedtime stories*] when I was a kid.

おどけもの おどけ者 a **joker**(冗談やいたずらをして人を笑わせる人) ; a **clown**(道化師).

おどける ▶おどけた顔をする put on a *funny* expression ‖ちょっとおどけて(＝冗談を言って)みただけさ I was only *joking*.

おとこ 男

> 語法 (1)一般的に「(１人の)男」は a man, くだけた言い方では a guy, 性別を強調したい場合は a male という. (2)「(いったいに)男というものは」と総称的にいう場合は men.

1【男性】a **man** [複 **men**] ▶男物のシャツ a *man's* shirt ‖ふつうの男 an average *man* ‖女は男より強いと思うかい Do you think women are stronger than *men*? ‖やっぱいい(＝好感のもてる)男ですよ He's quite *a guy*. ‖あら, いい(＝ハンサムな)男ね What *a handsome man* (he is)! ‖赤ちゃんは男のお子さんでしたか, 女のお子さんでしたか Is the baby *a boy* or a girl? ‖利香は男と暮らしている Rika lives with *a man* [*her lover*]. (➤ man には日本語の場合に似て露骨な響きがある. her boyfriend とするのが無難).
‖男親 a male parent, a father ‖男友だち a male [man ／gentleman] friend ; a boyfriend (➤ 日本語の「ボーイフレンド」よりも意味が狭く, 通例親密な間柄の友を指す) ‖男やもめ a widower.
2【慣用表現】▶西郷は男の中の男だ Saigo is *a man among men*. ‖北野氏はその映画の成功で男を上げた Mr. Kitano *earned a high reputation* with the success of the film. ／The success of the film *earned* Mr. Kitano *a high reputation*. (➤ earn a high reputation は「(自分の)評判を上げる」の意) ‖きみを男と見込んで頼みがあるんだ I'm asking you (to do this) because *I consider you a man*. ‖ここで引き下がったんでは男が廃る I will *lose face* [*my honor*] if I back down now. ‖あいつを男にしてやろう I'll *make a man of* him.
☛ 大男 (⇀見出語)

> **逆引き熟語 〇〇男**
> 雨男 a rain man [bringer] (➤ 後者は女性にもいえる) ／いい男 a handsome man, a good-looking guy ／押しの強い男 a pushy man ／堅い男 a law-and-order guy ／家庭的な[家庭を大事にする]男 a family man ／口のうまい[口先だけの]男 a smooth [smooth-spoken] man ／軽薄な男 a shallow guy, a flip [flippant] man ／独身男 a bachelor ／向こう見ずな男 a reckless man ／女々しい男 an effeminate man, a sissy

おとこうん 男運 ▶幸子は男運がない Sachiko *has no luck with men*.

おとこぎ 男気 ▶私は徹雄の男気にほれた I admire Tetsuo's *manly spirit* [*manliness*].

おとこざかり 男盛り ▶彼は今男盛りだ He's *in the prime of life*. (➤ the prime of life は「人生の盛り, 全盛期」の意で, 主語を she に変えればそのまま「女盛り」に適用できる) ‖40代は男盛りだ A man is *in his prime* in his forties.

おとこしゃかい 男社会 a **man's world** ; a **male-oriented world**(男中心の社会).

おとこで 男手 ▶引っ越しするから男手が必要だ I need some *men to help* with moving. ‖ 奥さん亡きあと彼は男手一つで2人の娘を育てた He raised two daughters *all by himself* after his wife passed away.

おとこなき 男泣き ▶引退セレモニーで大打者は感極まって男泣きした At his retiring ceremony, the great batter was overwhelmed with emotion and *wept in spite of himself*.

おとこのこ 男の子 a **boy** ▶その赤ちゃんは男の子だった The baby was *a boy*. (➤「男の赤ちゃん」は a baby boy という).

おとこまえ 男前 a **handsome** /hǽnsəm/ **man** ▶お宅の息子さん, なかなかの男前ね Your son is quite *a handsome* (*young*) *man*.

おとこまさり 男勝り

> 《解説》「男勝り」にぴったりの英語はない. manly は「(男性の容姿・声・外見などが)男らしい」, mannish は「(女性の容姿・外見などが)男っぽい」の意でそれぞれ用いられる.

▶森さんは男勝りの活躍をしている Ms. Mori's performance *overshadows that of any man* [*puts men to shame*]. (➤ overshadow は「…を見劣りさせる」. 後者は文字どおりには「男性を恥じ入らせる」の意).

おとこらしい 男らしい **manly** ; **masculine** ▶男らしくしろ Be (like) a man ! ／Act like a man !

おとさた 音沙汰 ▶息子からは去年の夏以来まるで音沙汰がない I *have heard nothing from* my son since last summer. ‖ 彼は3年前に家出をしてその後何の音沙汰もない He left home three years ago and *has not been heard of* since.

おどし 脅し a **threat** /θret/ ▶「タイムズに投書するぞ」というのがイギリス人の好きな脅し文句である "I will write to *The Times*" is *a* favorite *threat* of the British.

おとしあな 落とし穴 a **pit(fall)** ▶まぬけな忍者め. 落とし穴に落ちたぞ What a dumb ninja ! He's fallen into the *pit*.
▶契約をする際には落とし穴に注意すべきだ When you sign a contract, watch out for *loopholes*. (➤ loophole は「抜け穴」) ‖ あの問題やけに易しかったけど, どこかに落とし穴があったのかなあ The questions on the test seemed awful easy. I wonder if there were any *trick questions* [if they had *catches*].

おとしいれる 陥れる ▶周りのやつらはいつもぼくを陥れようとしている The guys around me are always *setting* [*laying*] *traps for* me.

おとしこむ 落とし込む ▶文書をファイルに落とし込む *drag and drop* a document into a folder ‖ 防波堤に沿って仕掛けを(海に)落とし込む *drop* fishing traps along the edge of a surf breaker.

おとしだま お年玉 *otoshidama* ; a **New Year's monetary gift**, a **New Year's gift of money**
日本紹介 ✉ **お年玉は正月に子供たちが両親や親戚からもらうお金です. 特別の小さな紙の袋に入れてあります. 年賀の挨拶をしたあと手渡されるのがふつうです** *Otoshidama* is money that children receive from parents and relatives during the New Year holiday. The money is put in a small envelope. Usually it is handed to the children in person after they have said their New Year's greetings.
▶おばさんはお年玉に5000円くれた My aunt gave me five thousand yen as *a New Year's gift*.
‖**お年玉つき年賀はがき** a New Year's lottery postcard.

おとしどころ 落とし所 **common ground**, a **meeting point**.

おとしぬし 落とし主 ▶この品物の落とし主は誰だろう Who is *the person who lost* this ? ／Who lost this ?

おとしもの 落とし物 a **lost article** ▶落とし物をする *lose* something ‖ 落とし物は何ですか What did you *lose* ? ‖ 落とし物は守衛室に保管してあります *Lost articles* are kept at the security guard's office.

おとす 落とす

> 📖 訳語メニュー
> 低い所へ落とす →drop **1**
> なくす →lose **2**
> 汚れなどを取る →take out **3**
> 学科を落とす →fail **4**

1【物を低い方へ】**drop** +㊐ ▶洗っていた皿を落として割った I *dropped* and broke a plate [dish] while washing it. ‖ 子供たちが橋の上から水面に石を落として遊んでいた The children on the bridge were amusing themselves by *dropping* rocks into the river below. ‖ あいつがボールを落とさなかったら勝っていたのに If he hadn't *dropped* the ball, we would have won the game. ‖ 阿部は何でもないフライを落とした Abe *muffed* an easy fly (ball). (➤ muff は「捕り損なう」) ‖ 母はよく物を落とす My mother often *lets things slip through* her *fingers*. ／My mother has butterfingers. (➤「バターがべったりとついた指」の意 ; よく物を落とす人に向かって "Butterfingers !" とユーモラスに言うことがある).

2【なくす】**lose** /luːz/ +㊐ ▶私は慌てていて定期券をどこかで落とした In my hurry, I *lost* my commuter pass somewhere. ‖ どうやら財布を落としたらしい I think I might *have lost* my wallet somewhere. ‖ 公園の木々は大半がすでに葉を落としている Most trees in the park *have* already *shed* their leaves.
▶肝臓がんで命を落とす *die* of liver cancer ‖ 接戦の末我々はその試合を落とした(＝負けた) It was a seesaw game and we (unfortunately) *lost*. ／It was a close game which we (unfortunately) *lost*. ‖ 彼はコーチとしての信用を落とした He *has lost* his credibility as a coach.
▶富田先生は出席をとるとき, なぜか私の名前を落とした(＝漏らした) For some reason, Mr. Tomita *skipped* my name when he called the roll. ‖ 番号と名前を落とした(＝書き忘れた)人がいるよ Someone *forgot to write* their name and number. ‖ 誰でもときにはミスをするんですから, どうか気を落とさないように Everybody makes mistakes from time to time. So *don't let it get you down* [*don't get discouraged*].

3【抜く, 剝ぎ取る】**take out** ▶この染みを落とすにはどうしたらいいですか ? Please tell me how to *take* these stains *out*. ‖ 風呂に入って1日のあかを落とした I got in the bath and *washed off* the grime of a day's work. ‖ 洗顔して化粧を落とすとほっとする It's always a relief when I wash my face and *remove* my make-up.

4【学科・生徒・学生を】**fail** +㊐, **flunk** +㊐ (➤ 後者はインフォーマル) ▶今学期は英語を落としそうだ I'm afraid I'm going to *fail* [*flunk*] English this

お

semester. ‖ 山本先生は試験で 3 人の学生を落とした Mr. Yamamoto *failed* [*flunked*] three students in the exam. ‖ 数学の試験でクラスの 3 分の 1 が落とされた One third of the class *failed* [*flunked*] the mathematics exam.

5【程度を下げる】▶明かりを落とす *turn* the lights *down* ‖ 舞台の照明を落とす *turn down* [*turn off*] the stage lights (➤ turn off は「完全に消す」の意) ‖ ダイエットをして体重を落とす *lose* weight by dieting.

▶品質を落とす *lower* the quality ‖ うちは商品の値段は下げても品質は絶対に落とさない We may lower the prices of our products but will *never cut down on* their quality. ‖ あんまり話を落とすなよ Don't *lower the level of our conversation* (by such dirty language).

▶駅に近づくにつれて電車はスピードを落とした The train *slowed* (*down*) as it approached the station.

6【自分の思いに従わせる】▶見てろ. いつか恵子を落としてみせるからな You wait and see. Someday I'm going to *win* Keiko's *heart* [*make* Keiko *mine*].

7【伝票の処理をする】▶タクシー代は必要経費で落とせる Taxi fares may *be claimed* as a deductible expense. (➤ claim は「請求する」).

おどす 脅す **threaten** /θrétn/ +㊐; **intimidate** +㊐ (脅迫する; 堅い語)

> **【文型】**
> …するぞと脅す
> **threaten to** do
> 人(A)に行動(B)を起こすと脅す
> **threaten** A **with** B

▶患者はその医師を裁判に訴えると脅した The patient *threatened to* sue the doctor [bring a lawsuit against the doctor]. ／The patient *threatened* the doctor *with* a lawsuit. ‖ いじめっこが殺すぞと彼を脅した The bully *threatened to* kill him. ／The bully *threatened* him *with* death.

▶その男はピストルで行員を脅して金を奪った The man *threatened* the bank teller with a gun and grabbed the money. ‖ 兄は私を脅して両親に金をねだらせた My (older) brother *intimidated* me into weaseling money out of my parents.

おとずれ 訪れ ▶春の訪れは近い Spring *is near at hand*. ／Spring *is just around the corner*. ／Spring will *soon be here*.

おとずれる 訪れる **visit** +㊐; **call on** (人を) ▶私は日比野氏を事務所に訪れた I *visited* [*called on*] Mr. Hibino at his office. ‖ 彼の家には誰も訪れる者がない No one ever *goes to* his house. ‖ 父は毎年仕事で何回かインドを訪れる My father *makes* several business *trips to* India every year. →訪ねる.

▶高原では秋が平地より一足早く訪れる Autumn *arrives* earlier in the highlands than (it does) in the plains. ‖ ジャイアンツに願ってもないチャンスが訪れた An unexpectedly lucky opportunity *has come up* for the Giants.

おととい 一昨日 **the day before yesterday** ▶おととい帰国いたしました I came home *the day before yesterday*. (➤《米》では the を省略することもある) ‖ それはおとといの朝の出来事だ It happened *two days ago in the morning*. (➤ 英語では, 話しているときが例えば水曜日なら It happened (on) Monday morning. (それは月曜日の朝起こった)のように言うことが多い).

▶《慣用表現》おととい来い(＝もう来るな) I don't want to see your face here ever again! ／Never come here again!

おととし 一昨年 **the year before last** ▶おととしのことはもうよく覚えていない I don't remember very well what happened *two years ago* [*the year before last*].

おとな 大人 a **grown-up** (➤ 子供が大人を指すのに用いることが多い); an **adult** /ədʌ́lt ‖ ǽdʌlt/ (成人); a **man** (男の); a **woman** (女の) ▶大人はいつもぼくたちにもっと勉強しなさいと言う The *grown-ups* always tell us to study harder. ‖ この映画は大人向け(＝成人向け)よ. 高校生は見ちゃだめ This movie is *for adults* only. High school students may not see it. ‖ 大人 2 人と子供 1 人の予約を取りたいんですが I would like to make a reservation for two *adults* and one child. ‖ 大人になったら医者になりたいです I want to be a doctor *when* I *grow up*.

▶きみももう少し大人になったらどうかね Why don't you behave a little more like *an adult*? ／You should think and act like *a grown-up*. ‖ 娘は年の割に大人びている My daughter *looks quite grown-up*. ／My daughter *looks mature* for her age.

おとながい 大人買い **going on a spending spree**(買いまくり) ▶漫画『ワンピース』全巻を大人買いしたい I want to *buy a complete set of* the comic book series "ONE PIECE." (➤「全巻を買う」の意).

おとなげない 大人げない ▶大人げない議論 a *childish* argument ‖ チャンネル争いするなんてお父さんも大人げないわね You*'re no better than a child* yourself to argue over which channel to watch on TV. (➤「子供同然だ」の意).

おとなしい **quiet** /kwáɪət/ (もの静かな); **obedient** /oʊbíːdiənt/ (従順な) 《参考》obedient は大人に対して使うと「独立心の欠如した」という否定的な含みが出るのがふつう. ▶彼女の夫はおとなしい人だ Her husband is a *quiet* man. ‖ 彼女はおとなしく(＝従順に)親の言うことを聞いた She followed her parents' advice *obediently*. ‖ その子は劇の間中おとなしくしていた The child *kept quiet* throughout the play. ‖ おばさんの家に行ったらおとなしくしないといけませんよ When you go to your aunt's house, you must *behave yourself*. (➤ behave oneself は「行儀よくする」).

▶おとなしくしなさい Be quiet. ／Be a good boy [girl]. (➤ 前者は「静かにしなさい」, 後者は「いい子でいなさい」の意) ‖ お宅の犬はおとなしいね Your dog is *gentle* [*well-behaved* ／*quiet*], isn't he [she]? (➤ gentle は動物が「従順な」, well-behaved は「お行儀のよい」, quiet は「物静かな, 吠えない」) ‖ おとなしい感じの帽子をかぶる wear a *sensible* hat (➤「派手な飾りなどついていない」の意).

おとなびる 大人びる ▶息子は大人びた顔立ちだ My son *looks grown-up*.

おとぼけ ▶彼はおとぼけがうまい He *puts on a good show of being ignorant*. ／He *is good at playing dumb*. (➤ play dumb /dʌm/ は「ばかのふりをする」の意).

おとめ 乙女 **a maiden** (➤ 文語); **a (young) girl** (少女) ▶きみは乙女心が全くわかっていない You don't understand at all *how young girls feel*.

おとめざ 乙女座 (a) **Virgo** /vɚ́ːɡoʊ/ ▶乙女座の女性は牡牛(おうし)座の男性と相性がいい *Virgo* women and Taurus men are very compatible.

おとも お供 ▶よろしかったら途中までお供しましょう I'll *go* part of the way *with you* if you like. ‖ 母のお

供で京都へ行ってきた I went to Kyoto *with* my mother. ‖ 彼女はお供を3人連れていた She was accompanied by three *attendants*. (➤ attendant は「お供の人」).

おとらず 劣らず ▶きょうもきのうに劣らず寒い It is *just as* cold today *as* (it was) yesterday. ‖ あの娘は母親に劣らず背が高い The daughter is *no less* tall *than* her mother. ‖ 運動は健康上大切だが, 栄養もそれに劣らず大切だ Exercise is important for good health, but proper nutrition is *no less* important. ‖ 兄は父に劣らずテニスがうまい My brother plays tennis *just as well as* my father (does).

おどらす 躍らす ▶初めての飛行機に子供たちは胸を躍らせている Since this is the first time to fly, the kids' hearts *are filled with anticipation* [*expectation*].

おとり 囮 a **decoy** /díːkɔɪ/, 《インフォーマル》 a **stool pigeon** ▶警察は犯人を捕まえるために彼をおとりとして使った The police used him as *a decoy* [*a stool pigeon*] to apprehend the criminal. ‖ 近頃景品をおとりにして商品を売るやり方が目につく A kind of sales approach often seen lately is to offer "free gifts" as *a lure* to customers. ／Offering free gifts to tempt customers is a sales approach often seen lately.

‖(客寄せ用の)**おとり商品** a loss leader ‖ **おとり捜査** a sting operation, an undercover investigation.

おどり 踊り a **dance**; **dancing** (踊ること) ▶私, 火曜の夜は踊りのお稽古があるの I take *dance lessons* every Tuesday night.

おどりあがる 躍り上がる ▶ジャイアンツに勝って広島ファンは躍り上がって喜んだ The Carp fans *jumped with joy* when their team beat the Giants.

おどりこ 踊り子 a **dancer**; a **dancing girl** (プロの).

おどりば 踊り場 a **landing** ▶お年寄りは踊り場でひと休みした The elderly man took a rest on the *landing*.

おとる 劣る **be inferior** /ɪnfíəriəʳ/ 《to》 ▶この商品は見本より劣る These articles *are inferior to* the samples. ‖ 次郎はテニスの腕では父親に劣る(＝父親ほどではない) Jiro is*n't as* skilled a tennis player *as* his father. ‖ あいつは犬畜生にも劣る(＝犬畜生並みの)やつだ He is *no better than* a beast.

▶母の手料理はたいていのレストランの料理にも決して劣らない My mother's cooking *is just as good*, *if not better than* that of most restaurants. ‖ この望遠鏡は型は古いが, 性能は新型に劣らない The design of this telescope may be a little out-of-date, but as far as performance goes, it's every bit *as good as* the newest models. ‖ 数学にかけては彼は誰にも劣らない He *is second to none* in mathematics.

☛ 劣らず (→見出語)

おどる 踊る・躍る **1【舞踊をする】dance** ▶踊りましょう Let's *dance*! ‖ 彼女はギターとカスタネットに合わせてフラメンコを踊った She *danced* [*stepped*] a flamenco to a guitar and castanets. ‖ 一緒に踊ってもらえますか Will you *dance* with me?

2【操られる】 ▶結局総理といえども黒幕に踊らされているだけじゃないか After all, even the Prime Minister *dances to the tune of* the leader behind the scenes.

3【興奮する】 ▶あす彼女に会えると思うと胸が躍る *My heart dances with joy* [*My heart jumps* ／ *My heart goes pitter-patter*] at the very thought that I'll see her tomorrow. (➤ go pitter-patter は「ドキドキ鳴る」).

おとろえ 衰え **decline** ▶この頃彼は体力の衰えが気になっている These days he is concerned about the *decline* in his physical strength. ‖ 祖父はまもなく80歳だが記憶力は衰えを見せない Though nearly eighty, my grandfather's memory shows no signs of *failing*.

おとろえる 衰える **decline** (衰弱する); **fail** (弱まる); **become weak(er)** (次第に弱くなる) ▶大病をして体力が衰えた My strength *declined* because of a major illness. ‖ 悲しいかな, あの女優の容色はかなり衰えた Sadly, that actress's beauty and charm *have declined* considerably. ‖ 祖母の視力は急速に衰えてきている My grandmother's eyesight is rapidly *failing*. ‖ 祖父は日増しに衰え, とうとう帰らぬ人となった My grandfather *became weaker* day by day and finally passed away. ‖ 一雨降れば火勢はじきに衰えるだろう If it rains, the fire will soon *die down*.

おどろおどろしい ▶水木しげるのおどろおどろしい妖怪たち Mizuki Shigeru's *flesh-creeping* specters.

おどろかす 驚かす **surprise** +㊀; **astonish** +㊀ (ひどく); **startle** +㊀ (どきっとさせる) ▶彼の突然の来訪はみんなを驚かせた His unexpected visit *surprised* them all. ‖ その少年は世界を驚かすような大発見をした The boy made a great discovery that *astonished* the world. ‖ 後ろからわっと言ってあいつを驚かしてやろう I'm going to make a big yell from behind and *startle* him.

おどろき 驚き (a) **surprise, astonishment, amazement** (➤ この順に驚きの程度が大きくなる); a **shock** (精神的な強いショック) ▶知人が殺人容疑で逮捕されたと知った彼女の驚きは, たとえようもなかった When she found that her acquaintance had been arrested on suspicion of murder, her *surprise* [*shock*] was beyond description. ‖ 彼は驚きのあまりその場にくぎづけになった *Astonishment* [*Amazement* ／ *Shock*] nailed him to the spot. ／He was rooted to the spot with *astonishment* [*amazement* ／ *shock*]. (●その場にくぎづけになるほどの驚きであるから surprise では弱すぎて不適当).

▶あの有名子役がもう40歳だとは驚きです It *comes as a surprise* to know that the once famous child actor is already forty years old. (➤「驚くべきこと」の意なので a がつく) ‖ 彼女がたばこをやめていないのは私には驚きだった *It was a* (*big*) *surprise* to me (*to* find out) she hasn't stopped smoking. ／*It was surprising* [*amazing*] to me *that* she hasn't stopped smoking.

おどろく 驚く

1【びっくりする】be surprised (思いがけないことに); **be astonished** (びっくり仰天する); **be amazed** (驚きのあまり当惑する) →びっくり

【文型】
A に驚く
be surprised by [at] A
…して驚く
be surprised to do
〜ということに驚く
be surprised that S + V

▶私の本がこんなに注目されて驚いています I'*m surprised at* [*by*] all the attention my book has gotten. ‖

その知らせには**驚いた** I *was surprised by* [*at*] the news. (➤ by は直接驚きの原因を表し, at は「…に接して, 触れて」と多少の距離感がある) ‖ お年寄りたちがいとも簡単にだまされるのには**驚く** *I'm surprised by* [*at*] how easily elderly people are swindled. ‖ 中国の変貌の速さを見て**驚きました** I *was surprised to* see how swiftly China was changing. ‖ 三郎君が退学したとは**驚いた** I *was surprised that* Saburo quit school.

▶彼が事故に遭ったと聞いて**驚いている** I *was amazed* [*was astonished*] *to* hear about his accident. (➤ ともに be surprised よりも驚きの程度が大きい) ‖ その女性の大胆さにはみんな**驚いてしまった** That woman's boldness *astonished* us all. ‖ 父は**驚いて**ぼくの顔を見た My father looked at me *in surprise*.

▶ここできみに会うとは**驚いたね** *What a surprise* to run into you here! ‖ きみの変わりようには**驚いた** I *can't get over* how different you've become. (➤「その事実を受け入れられないほどだ」の意で, 良くなったか悪くなったかは文脈による) ‖ 私の好きな俳優が自殺したというニュースを読んで**ひどく驚いた** *It came as a great shock* to read that my favorite actor had committed suicide. ‖ **驚いたことに**真犯人は被害者の妻だった *To my surprise* [*Surprisingly* / *What surprised me was*], the murderer turned out to be the victim's own wife. (➤ この順にフォーマル度が下がる) ‖ 彼が試験に落ちたからって**何も驚くことはない**よ *No* [*Little* / *Small*] *wonder* he failed the exam. ‖ **驚いたなあ.** 知らなかったよ *Well, that's* (*sure*) *a surprise* [*that* (*sure*) *is a surprise*]! I didn't know that.

2【感心する・驚嘆する】be amazed 《at》; **marvel** 《at》(ふつうとは思えないすばらしさに驚く) ▶彼の博識には**驚く** I *am amazed at* his profound knowledge. ‖ 彼女にいじめっ子に立ち向かう勇気があったとは**驚いた** I *marveled at* her courage in standing up to the bully. (➤ marvel は wonder よりも強意) ‖ パソコンの性能の向上は**驚くばかりだ** The advance in personal computer performance is simply *amazing*.

おどろくべき 驚くべき amazing (驚異的な, すばらしい, すごい); **astonishing** (びっくり仰天するような); **surprising** (予想もしなかったほどの); **remarkable** (注目すべき) ▶最近のその国の発展ぶりにはまさに**驚くべきものがある** Recent development in that country has been simply *amazing* [*astonishing*]. ‖ スティーヴィー・ワンダーは**驚くべき**天才だ Stevie Wonder is an *amazing* genius. ‖ 子供たちは**驚くべき**速さで逃げていった The children ran away with *surprising* speed. ‖ 彼女のタミル語は短期間に**驚くべき**進歩を遂げた She has made *remarkable* progress in Tamil within a short period.

おどろくほど 驚くほど amazingly, astonishingly (驚嘆するほど, すばらしく); **surprisingly** (意外でびっくりするほど); **remarkably** (著しく) ▶大聖堂の天井は**驚くほど**高かった The ceiling of the cathedral was *amazingly* [*astonishingly*] high. ‖ 薬は**驚くほど**よく効いた The medicine worked *amazingly* [*surprisingly*] well. (➤ amazingly が「すばらしさに目を見張る」に対して surprisingly は「それほどと思っていなかったが, びっくりするくらい」というニュアンス) ‖ この2つの論文は**驚くほど**似ている These two papers are *remarkably* similar. ‖ その力士は小兵ながら**驚くほどの**力を見せた The sumo wrestler showed *surprising* strength for his small stature.

おないどし 同い年 ▶母は私たちの先生と**同い年**です My mother is *the same age as* our teacher (is). ‖ 我々はみんな**同い年**だ We are all *the same age*.

おなか the stomach /stʌ́mək/, one's **belly** (胃; 腹部の婉曲(えんきょく)語として用いる); **the insides** (胃と腸); a **womb** (子宮) ▶(少し)**おなかがすいた** I *am* (a little) *hungry*. ‖ **おなかがぺこぺこだ** *I'm starving* [*famished*]. ‖ **おなかがいっぱいだ** I *am full*. / *I'm stuffed*. (➤ 後者はインフォーマルな言い方) ‖ **おなかが痛い** I *have a pain in my stomach* [*belly*]. / I *have a stomachache*. ‖ **おなかの調子が悪い** I have an upset *stomach*. (➤ 胃をいう場合) / I have an upset *tummy*. (➤ やや漠然と胃や腸をいう場合; tummy は本来幼児語だが, 《インフォーマル》では大人にもよく使われる) ‖ **おなかに脂肪がついてきた** I'm getting fat around *the middle*. ‖ 父はだいぶ**おなかが出てきた** My father *is developing a beer belly*.

▶妻は今**おなかが大きい** My wife *is expecting*. ‖ 彼女の**おなか**には赤ちゃんがいる She is carrying a baby (in her *womb*). ‖ (妊娠している人に)**おなかが大きくなってきた**ね Your *belly* has gotten big (and round).

おなが 尾長 《鳥》an **azure-winged magpie**.

おながれ お流れ ▶雨で遠足は**お流れになった** The school trip *was called off* because of rain. / The school trip *was rained out*.

おなさけ お情け pity (哀れみ, 同情); **charity** (慈悲) ▶他人の**お情け**にすがりたくない I don't want to be dependent on the *charity* of others. / I won't take *charity*. (➤ 後者は「施しは受けない」の意で, 貧しくても毅然(きぜん)たる態度をとるときの表現) ‖ 先生は**お情けで**いい点をくれた My teacher gave me a good grade *as a special favor*. / My teacher *took* [*had*] *pity on* me and gave me a good grade. ‖ 彼は**お情けで**その仕事をやらせてもらっていた He was allowed to keep his job *on sufferance*. (➤ sufferance は「黙許」).

おなじ 同じ 1【同一・同種・同等・同様の】the same 《as, that》; **identical** (そっくりの); **similar** (同じような) (➤ identical は見分けがつかないくらい「そっくり」で, similar は見かけ・傾向が似ている「同じような」) ▶《同一の》ぼくたちは毎日**同じ**電車で学校に通う We take *the same* train to school every day. ‖ 合宿中は150人の部員が**同じ**屋根の下で暮らす During the training camp, all 150 club members live under *the same* roof. ‖ シェークスピアとセルバンテスは**同じ**年の**同じ**日に死んだ Shakespeare and Cervantes died on *the same* day of *the same* year. ‖ **同じ**間違いを繰り返すな Don't repeat *the same* mistake. ‖ 全員が**同じ**目標に向かって努力することが大切だ It's important that all members be working toward *the same* goal. ‖ 私たちは**同じような**携帯電話を持っている We have *identical* cellphones. ‖ どの学校も**同じような**問題を抱えている Every school has *similar* problems. ‖ [ことわざ] **同じ穴のむじな** They [We / You] are just the same. / They [We / You] are all alike. (➤ 日本語からの意訳).

> **【文型】**
> A **と同じ** B
> **the same** B **as** A
> **the same** B **that** [**as**] S + V
> ➤ B は名詞

▶これは以前聞いた話と**同じ**話だ This is *the same* story *that* I heard before. ‖ ぼくはきみと**同じ**辞書を持っている I have *the same* dictionary *as* you (do). / My dictionary is *the same as* yours. ‖

私は多くの人とだいたい**同じような**理由で毎週プールに行く，つまり体調維持のために I go to the pool every week for much *the same* reason *that* many people do—to keep fit. ‖ジェニーは少しも変わっていない．10年前と**同じだ** Jenny hasn't changed a bit. She looks (*just*) *the same as* (she did) ten years ago. ‖《書類で》上記に**同じ** *The same as* (mentioned) above.／See above.／Ditto.（➤最後は do. と略される）．

▶ 対話「チーズバーガー１つとコーヒーをください」「私にも**同じものを**」"A cheeseburger and a coffee, please." "*Same here, please.*／*I'll have the same, please.*"

【文型】
A **と同じくらい**…
as … as A
➤…は形容詞・副詞

▶非言語コミュニケーションは言語コミュニケーションと**同じくらい**重要である Nonverbal communication is *as* important *as* verbal communication. ‖彼女は私の姉と**同じくらいの年**だと思う I suppose she *is about as old as* [*about the same age as*] my sister.

▶その２人の教師は**同じ数**の生徒を抱えている The two teachers have *an equal* number of students. ‖国語も英語も**同じくらい**大切な教科だ Japanese and English are *about equally* important as academic subjects.

▶その件に関してはきみと**同じ意見だ** I am of *the same* opinion *as* you on that matter.／I agree with you on that matter. ‖幸福で健康な暮らしをしたいのはみんな**同じだ** Everyone *shares the same* desire to lead a happy and healthy life.（➤ share は「共有する」）‖彼が来ようと来まいと**同じだ** Whether he comes or not is *all the same* (to me). ‖あなたのすることもほかの人たちと**同じね** You act *just like* all the others. ‖１つのサイズが万人に合うわけではない．教育も**同じことが言える** One size does not fit all. *The same can be said* about education.

▶台本が俳優にとって大切なのと**同じように**，スコア（総譜）は音楽家にとって大切だ Scores *are to* musicians *what* scripts *are to* actors or actresses.（➤ A is to B what X is to Y. の形で「AのBに対する関係はXのYに対する関係と同じだ」の意を表す）．

▶**同じ**盛り場でも，新宿と銀座では全く雰囲気が違う *Although they're both considered* downtown hot spots, Shinjuku and Ginza have entirely different atmospheres.

直訳の落とし穴「同じ人間だから」
日本語では「皆同じ人間だから」とか「同じ日本人として」という言い方をするので，「同じ」につられて，英語で言うときも the same を使いがち．しかし（×）We're the same human beings. では意味が通らない．日本語の意味するところは We're all human beings.（私たちは皆人間です）である．「Aさんの国際コンクール優勝を同じ日本人として誇りに思います」も（×）We're the same Japanese. ではどういう人たちと（別人でなく）同一の日本人かを言わないと意味が通らない．As a (fellow) Japanese, I'm proud of Miss A's winning the international competition. とする．fellow は「仲間の，同胞の」の意．

2【どうせ】▶**同じ**やるならうまくやりなさい If you do it *at all*, do it well. ‖**同じ**金を使うなら生きた金の使い方をしなさい If you're going to spend the money *anyway*, you should get the best value for it.

おなじく 同じく ▶彼女は母親と**同じく**体が弱い She has a weak constitution *like* her mother. ‖２年A組，山田君．**同じく**，鈴木君 Yamada, 2nd grade A class, Suzuki, (*the*) *same class*.

おなじみ お馴染み ▶それでは皆さま**おなじみ**の曲をおかけいたしましょう Now, here's a *familiar* old number.／Now, here's one of your old favorites.

オナニー masturbation ▶**オナニーをする** *masturbate*／*play with oneself*（➤俗語では jerk off, beat off, toss off などがあり，男性について使う）《参考》「オナニー」はドイツ語の *Onanie* からきており，英語でいえば onanism だが，専門的な語で一般にはほとんど用いない．

おなみだちょうだい お涙頂戴 ▶**お涙頂戴の**（＝感傷的な）歌 a *sentimental* song ‖それは**お涙頂戴の**映画だった The movie was *a tearjerker*.（➤ tearjerker /tíəʳdʒə̀ːʳkəʳ/ は「お涙頂戴式のもの」の意．映画にも劇にも用いる）‖卒業式の挨拶は**お涙頂戴**になることが多いから嫌いだ I don't like graduation speeches, because they often deteriorate into *sentimental mush*.（➤ mush は「ふにゃふにゃしたもの；感傷的なこと」）．

おなら gas ▶**おならをする** pass *gas*／fart（➤後者は「へ」に近いが日常的には多用される）；break wind（➤婉曲(えんきょく)表現）‖**おならが出て**困る I am troubled with *gas* [*flatulence*].（➤ flatulence /flǽtʃələns/ は「ガスでおなかが張ること，膨満感」）‖サツマイモを食べると**おならがよく出る** Sweet potatoes cause *gas*. 《参考》英語圏ではおならは豆（beans）と結び付いており，子供たちがよく知っている歌に，Beans, beans, the musical fruit. The more you eat, the more you toot ...（豆は音楽を奏でる実，食べれば食べるほどおならがよく出る；beans は fruit ではないが，toot（プップッと鳴る）と韻を踏むためにおどけて用いたもの）というのがある．

▶誰かがエレベーターの中で**おならをした** Somebody *passed gas* [*farted*] in the elevator.《参考》(1) おならは生理現象なので欧米では大目に見てもらえる場合もある．(2) 音のしない，ひどく臭いおならをすることを do an S.B.D. という.silent but deadly（音なしだが耐え難い）の頭文字語で,Somebody just did an S.B.D.（だれかがこっそりひどく臭いやつを放ったな）のように使う．→屁，げっぷ．

おに 鬼 **1**【想像上の】an ***oni***（日本の）；an **ogre** /óʊgəʳ/（西洋の人食い鬼）

oni

ogre

日本紹介 ✉ **鬼は民話などに出てくる ogre のような恐ろしい存在です．全身，赤または緑色で，頭に角を生やし，牙をむき出しています．裸で腰にトラの毛皮のふんどしを巻き，手には金属の大きな棒を持っています．キリスト教の devil のような宗教的なイメージはありません** An '*oni*' is a dreadful creature similar to an ogre that appears in folk stories. Its body is red or green and it has horns on its head. Fangs jut out of its mouth.

It is often naked except for a tiger-skin breechcloth and it usually carries a large metal club. It does not typically carry a religious association like the Christian devil.
▶桃太郎は鬼が島の**鬼**退治に出かけました Momotaro went to Onigashima to rid the island of the *oni*. ‖ あの山には**鬼**が住んでいるという言い伝えがある There is an old legend that says there is *an ogre* living on that mountain. ‖ **鬼は外, 福は内** Out with the devil! In with luck!／In with happiness, out with misfortune!
▶《比喩的》**仕事の鬼** *a work fiend*／*a workaholic* ‖ あの人は**鬼のような人**(＝残忍な人)だ He is *a fiend* [*demon*／*devil*].／He is *a devil of a man*.
2【**鬼ごっこの**】**it**, a **tagger** ▶きみが**鬼**だぞ You're *it* now. ‖ 今度はぼくが**鬼**だ It's my turn to be *it*. ‖《手を打ちながら》**鬼さんこちら, 手の鳴る方へ** Catch me if you can. (➤「捕まえられるなら捕まえてごらん」の意).
3【**慣用表現**】 **鬼に金棒** ▶きみが加勢してくれれば鬼に金棒だ If you'll join us, *no one will be able to beat* us [we'*ll be unbeatable*]. **鬼の居ぬ間に洗濯** ▶When [While] the cat is away, the mice will play. (➤「猫が居ない間はネズミたちが遊ぶものだ」の意の英語のことわざ) **鬼のかくらん** ▶あの小林先生が病気だって? 鬼のかくらんとはこのことだね Dr. Kobayashi is sick? Well, that goes to show that *even the devil can get heatstroke*. (➤日本語からの直訳で「悪魔でも日射病になることがある」の意) **鬼の首を取ったよう** ▶隆夫はK大に現役で入って鬼の首でも取ったように得意がっている After getting into K University on the first try, Takao is acting as pleased *as if he'd won a Nobel Prize* [Takao is as pleased with himself *as if he'd accomplished something* (*truly*) *great*.]. **鬼の目にも涙** ▶tears in the eyes of a cruel person (like an ogre)／Even an ogre-like person sheds tears. **鬼も十八, 番茶も出花** ▶Even an *oni* is sweet at eighteen, and low-grade green tea is good when freshly brewed. (➤日本語からの直訳) **心を鬼にする** ▶彼女は心を鬼にして厳しく子供を叱った She *steeled* [*hardened*] *herself* and scolded her child severely. (➤「心を冷酷にした」の意) ‖ 私は心を鬼にしてきょう2人を首にした I had to *play the ogre* and fire two men today. **来年のことを言うと鬼が笑う** ▶The *oni* are sure to laugh when you predict [talk of] the next year. (➤日本語からの直訳)／There is no telling what will happen next year. (➤「来年は何が起こるかわからない」の意) **渡る世間に鬼はない** ▶There is kindness to be found everywhere. (➤「どこへ行っても人の親切はあるものだ」の意).

おにいさん お兄さん →兄さん.

おにぎり お握り an ***onigiri***
日本紹介 ✉ **おにぎりは塩味を効かせたご飯を三角形や丸形に握ったもので,「おむすび」とも言います. 中には梅干し, サケ, コンブのつくだ煮などを入れ, ふつう黒い海苔(のり)を巻きます. ハイキングなどのときの弁当として人気があります** *Onigiri* are 'handfuls' of boiled rice pressed into the shape of a triangle or a ball, and often seasoned with a sprinkle of salt. They are also called '*omusubi*.' They usually have an *umeboshi* (salted plum), salmon flakes or kelp that has been boiled in sweet soy sauce or other ingredients at the center and are usually wrapped in *nori* (laver). They are popular lunch box items for outings.

おにごっこ 鬼ごっこ tag; **blindman's buff** (目隠しの) ▶表で**鬼ごっこしよう** Let's *play tag* [*blindman's buff*] outside.

おにもつ お荷物 a **burden** (重荷) ▶お年寄りたちは一般に自分が家族の**お荷物**になるのではないかと心配している Elderly people generally fear that they might become *a burden* to [on] their families.

おね 尾根 a **ridge** ▶**尾根**伝いに歩けば必ずあの山の頂上に着くはずだ If we follow the *ridge*, it should take us to the mountain top.

おねえさん お姉さん →姉さん.

おねがい お願い ▶**お願い**があるんですが Can I ask a favor of you?／Will [Can] you do me a favor? (➤後者の文のほうがややくだけた言い方) ‖ **お願い**だから, 鼻にピアスをするのだけはやめてくれ *I'm begging you*—please don't pierce your nose. ‖ ほかに**お願い**できる人がいません You are the only person I *can ask* this *of*. →願い, 願う.
▶ 対話「車で家まで送りましょうか」「**お願いできます?**」"Do you want me to drive you home?" "*Would you?*"
✉ **貴校の交換留学生計画についての情報をお送りいただきたく, よろしくお願い申し上げます** I am sending this letter to request [I am writing to request] information about your exchange program.

おねしょ bed-wetting ▶**おねしょ**をする子 a *bed-wetting* child／a bed-wetter ‖ うちの息子は6年生になってもまだ**おねしょをしている** My son is in the sixth grade and he still *wets the bed*.

おねつ お熱 ▶彼女は英語の先生に**お熱だ** She *has a crush on* her English teacher. (➤ crush は賞賛を伴った「一時的なのぼせ上がり」).

おの 斧 an **ax(e)**; a **hatchet** (手おの) ▶**おの**で木を切り倒す chop down a tree with *an ax*.

おのおの 各々 each ▶**おのおの**2枚ずつ用紙を取ってください Please take two forms *each*. (➤この each は副詞) ‖ 生徒は木切れを使って**おのおの**好きな物を作った *Each* student made an object of his [her] choice from a piece of wood. (➤この each は代名詞).
▶弁当は**おのおの**持参してください Everyone is expected to bring *their own* lunch. (➤ his にするのが文法的には正しいが, インフォーマルな言い方では their にするのがふつう).

おのずから 自ずから ▶事実は**おのずから明らかになるだろう** The fact will *speak for itself*.

おのずと 自ずと ▶自分を信じて励めば道は**おのずと開かれる** Trust yourself and work hard. The road will open *by itself*. [You'll find a way *in due course*.] →自ずから.

おののく 戦く・慄く shudder (激しく身震いする); **tremble** (恐怖などで小刻みに震える); **shiver** (ぶるっと震える) ▶恐怖に**おののく** *tremble* with fear.

おのぼりさん お上りさん a **rubberneck** (➤首を伸ばして珍しそうに見るところから) ▶はとバスはいつも**お上りさん**でいっぱいだ *Hato* buses are always filled with *rubbernecks* [*tourists*]. 《参考》都会の人が tourist と言うときは一般に軽蔑的なニュアンスがある.

オノマトペ onomatopoeia /ɑ̀:nəmæt̬əpí:ə/.

おのれ 己 oneself ▶**己の欲するところを人に施せ** *Do unto others as you would have them do unto you*. (➤新約聖書から出た英語のことわざ).

おば 伯母・叔母 an **aunt** 《参考》日本語では父母の姉には「伯母」，妹には「叔母」を用いるが，英語にはその区別はない．▶母方のおば *an aunt* on one's maternal side ‖ 私は毎夏九州のおばの所へ出かける I visit my *aunt* in Kyushu every summer. →おばさん.

おばあさん, おばあちゃん a **grandmother**（祖母）; **Grandma, Granny**（あとの 2 者は「おばあちゃん」に相当する）; an **old woman**, an **old lady**（老婦人；後者のほうが前者より丁寧）▶ぼくのおばあさんは70歳ですがとても元気です My *grandma* is very healthy at the age of seventy. ‖ 母は自分のことを孫に「おばあちゃん」と呼ばせないで「ママ」と呼ばせている My mother tells her grandchild(ren) to call her "Mama" instead of "*Grandma.*" ‖ 《電車の車内で若者が》おばあさん，ここに座りませんか *Ma'am*, would you like my seat ?（➤ old lady を呼びかけに用いるのは侮辱的でよくない．英語には呼びかけとして使える「おばあさん」に当たることばはない）．

オパール (an) **opal** /óʊpəl/.

オハイオ **Ohio** /oʊháɪoʊ/（アメリカ北東部の州；略 OH, O.）.

おはぎ *ohagi*. →ぼた餅.

おはぐろ お歯黒・鉄漿 *ohaguro*, **tooth blacking.**

おばけ お化け an *obake* (**demon** /díːmən/)

> 《解説》(1)「お化け」は一般には一つ目小僧，唐傘のお化け，ちょうちんのお化けなど，ユーモラスなものを指すことが多いが，これにぴったりの英語はない．
> (2) monster は「怪物」. ghost や bogey(man)，あるいは《インフォーマル》の spook は「幽霊」に相当する．

▶一つ目小僧はよく知られたお化けだ *Hitotsume-kozo*, the one-eyed kid, is a well-known *obake*. ‖ お化けみたいな犬だった．あんな大きな犬，見たことがないよ That dog was *a real monster*; I have never seen such a big dog. ‖ 《子供を脅かして》お～ば～け～ *Boo!*

‖**お化け屋敷** a haunted [spook] house.

おはこ 十八番 one's **specialty** ▶五木ひろしの『千曲川』が父のおはこだ Itsuki Hiroshi's "Chikuma-gawa" is my father's *specialty* [*favorite song*].

おばさん an **aunt, Auntie**（血縁関係の；後者は主に呼びかけで）; a **woman**（よその）; **Ma'am**（他人に対する呼びかけで）▶長野にいるおばさんが訪ねて来た *My aunt* in Nagano came to visit me. ‖ 万智子おばさんは若いときヨーロッパに住んでいた *Aunt* Machiko lived in Europe when she was young. ‖ お母さんは外で山本さんのおばさんと話をしている Mother is talking with *Mrs. Yamamoto* outside.

▶どうせ，私はもうおばさんですよ I know I'm *a middle-aged woman*. ／I'm *not young anymore*.

おはじき (an) *ohajiki*; small glass or shell discs used in the children's game of *ohajiki*（➤ 説明的な訳）.

おはち お鉢 ▶忘年会でとうとう歌［余興］のお鉢（＝順番）が回ってきた My *turn* to sing [perform] at the year-end party finally came round.

おはつ お初 ▶お初にお目にかかります *I'm glad to meet you.* ／*How do you do?*

おばな 雄花 a **male flower.**

おはなばたけ お花畑 a **field of alpine flowers**（高山の）.

おはよう お早う **Good morning.** ▶お父さんにおはよう言った？ Did you say *good morning* to your father? ‖ 対話「先生，おはようございます」「やあ，みんなおはよう」"*Good morning*, sir!" "*Morning*, everybody!"（➤ 若い人たちは友だちどうしでは Good morning. よりも Hello! とか Hi! と声を掛け合うことが多い）. →おっす.

おはらい 御祓い a (**Shinto**) **purification ceremony** ▶最近，不幸が続いたので，神社へ行って神主さんにおはらいをしてもらった Because I (have) had a run of bad luck recently, I went to a Shinto shrine and *had the priest conduct a purification ceremony* (*to ward off evil spirits*).（➤ ward off negative influences としてもよい）.

おはらいばこ お払い箱 ▶20年使っていたビデオレコーダーをお払い箱にした（＝捨てた）I finally *threw out* the VCR which I had been using for the last twenty years.

▶マネージャーはその怠け者の会計係をお払い箱にした The manager *gave* the lazy cashier *the ax* [《英また》*the* (*frozen*) *mitten*].（➤ give A the ax で「A を首にする」）‖ そんなことをするとお払い箱（＝首）になるぞ Do that and you will *get fired*.

おび 帯 an **obi**; a **broad sash**（➤ 前者は英語化しているが，あまり一般的ではない）▶帯を締めるのを手伝ってくださらない？ Could you help me tie the *obi*?

▶《慣用表現》「帯に短し，たすきに長し」で適任者は見当たらない It's *a case of too much or too little*, with no one just right for the job.

おびえる 怯える **be frightened** ▶少女はおびえたような目で私を見つめた The little girl stared at me with *frightened* eyes. ‖ 人々は新たな山崩れの不安におびえながら一夜を過ごした The people spent the night *in fear of* another landslide.

おびきだす おびき出す ▶警察は乗っ取り犯人を飛行機からおびき出した The police *lured* the hijackers *away from* the plane.

おびきよせる おびき寄せる **lure** ＋㊐ ▶腹をすかせたライオンは肉におびき寄せられて，おりの中に入った The hungry lion *was lured* with meat into a cage.

おひたし お浸し *ohitashi*; boiled green vegetables especially spinach sprinkled with soy sauce（➤ 説明的な訳）.

おびただしい ▶その紛争での犠牲者はおびただしい数に上った *A great many* [*A large number of*] people were killed in that conflict. ‖ 兄の部屋は汚いことおびただしい My (older) brother's room is a *terrible* mess [is *very* messy]. ‖ 手作業集計は効率が悪いことおびただしい Counting by hand is *extremely* [*wildly*] inefficient.

おひつ an *ohitsu*; a tub [container] for cooked rice（➤ 説明的な訳）.

おひつじざ 牡羊座 (an) **Aries** /éəriːz/.

おひとよし お人好し a **good-natured person** ▶おやじはお人よしでだまされてばかりいる My father is too *good-natured man* and he is always getting cheated. ‖ 私はそんな話を信じるほどのお人よしではありません I'm not so *simple* as to believe that kind of story. ／I'm not such *a fool* [*a dupe*] as to believe that kind of story.（➤ dupe は「だまされやすい人」の意）. ‖ 寅さんはお人好しの心優しい物売りである Tora-san is a *simple*, *good-natured* peddler.（➤ simple には「頭が良くなく，騙されやすい」の意味もある）.

オピニオン・リーダー an **opinion leader.**

おひや お冷や (**cold**) **water**（水）▶お冷やを 1 杯頂けますか Could I have *a glass of* (*cold*) *water*, please?

おびやかす 脅かす threaten /θrétn/ +㊀ ▶村の安全を脅かすような凶悪な犯罪が起こった A vicious crime was committed that *threatened* the peace and safety of the whole village. ‖ 放射性物質は人間の生命を脅かす Radioactive substances *are a threat* to human life. (➤ threat は「脅威」) ‖ スキャンダルでその政治家は地位を脅かされている The scandal *has put* the politician's position *in jeopardy*. (➤ put ... in jeopardy で「…を危うくする」).

おひゃくど お百度 ▶祖母は私が重い病気にかかったとき, その寺にお百度参りをしてくれた When I was seriously ill, my grandmother *visited* that temple and *prayed* for my recovery by walking a fixed route *one hundred times*.

おひょう 《魚》 a **Pacific halibut** /hǽlɪbət/.

おひらき お開き ▶今夜の忘年会はこの辺でお開きにしましょう Well, it's about time to *break up* tonight's year-end party.

おひる お昼 →昼, 昼食.

おびる 帯びる **1【含む, もつ】**▶彼の演説は次第に熱を帯びてきた His speech gradually *grew passionate*. ‖ 西の空が赤みを帯びている The sky in the west *is tinged* [*is streaked*] *with red*. (➤ be streaked は「しまになっている」の意).
2【引き受ける】▶そのスパイは重要な使命を帯びてイギリスへ渡った The spy went to Britain *on* an important mission.

おひれ 尾鰭 ▶彼女の話はいつも尾ひれが付くからぼくは信用しない She always *exaggerates*, so I don't believe what she says. (➤ exaggerate は「大げさに言う」).

おびれ 尾びれ a **caudal** /kɔ́ːdl/ **fin**.

おひろめ お披露目 an **unveiling ceremony**.

オフ **off** ▶スイッチをオフにする *turn* the switch *off* ‖ 彼女は今日はオフ(＝休み)だ She*'s off* today. ‖ スラックスはすべて20パーセントオフになっております All slacks are 20 percent *off*.

オフィス an **office** ▶原さんのオフィスにこれを持っていってください Take this to Mr. Hara's *office*.
‖オフィス街 a street lined with office buildings.

オフェンス **offense**.

オフかい オフ会 an **offline gathering** (３人以上の) ; an **offline meetup** (２人以上の).

おふくろ お袋 《米》one's **mom** [《英》**mum**] ▶おふくろの味が懐かしい I miss *my mom's home cooking*. ‖ おふくろさんに苦労をかけるなよ Don't give *your mom* any trouble. ／Don't cause *your mom* any trouble.

オブザーバー an **observer** ▶彼は会議にオブザーバーとして出席した He attended the meeting as *an observer*.

オフサイド 《競技》 **offside** /ɔ̀ːfsáɪd/.

おぶさる 負ぶさる **ride on ~'s back** ▶子供の頃, よく父の背におぶさったのを覚えている I remember *riding on my father's back* often when I was a kid.

オブジェ an **objet d'art** /àːbʒeɪ dáːʳ/, an **art object** ▶公園に置かれたオブジェ *an objet d'art* placed in the park.

オプション an **option** ▶工場見学はオプションです The visit to the factory is *optional*. ‖ パソコンのオプションのソフト *optional* software for a personal computer.

おふせ お布施 an **offering (to a priest)** ; a **donation**(寄付金).

おふだ お札 a **talisman** /tǽlɪsmən/ (お守り). →お守り.

オフタイム **off time**.

おぶつ 汚物 **filth** (汚い物) ; **excretions, bodily waste** (排せつ物)
▶川に流れ込んだ汚物が原因で魚が死んだ The *filth* [*polluted waste*] that was released into the river killed the fish. (➤ 後者は「汚染された廃棄物」の意).

おぶついれ 汚物入れ a **disposal box (for feminine sanitary products)**.

オフライン **offline** ▶オフラインの会 an *offline* meeting [party] ‖ これらの商品はオンラインでもオフライン(実店舗)でも購入できます These items are available both online and *offline*.

おふる お古 →お下がり.

オフレコ ▶オフレコだけど, 女房と別れようと思ってるんだ This is *off the record* [*a secret*], but I'm thinking of getting a divorce.

オフロード オフロードの **off-road**
‖オフロード車 an off-road vehicle.

おべっか **flattery** ; **ass-kissing**(➤ 文字通りには「おしりにキスをすること」) ▶おべっかを使う *use flattery* ／*flatter* ‖ あいつはおべっか使いだ He is a *flatterer* [an *ass-kisser* ／a *brown-noser*].
▶彼は上役におべっかばかり使っている He's always *kissing up to* his seniors. (➤ flatter は「相手を喜ばせることを言う」で, 必ずしも悪い意味ではないのに対して, kiss up to は魂胆があって力のある人に「媚びへつらって取り入ろうとする」. ass-kiss や suck up to も同じように用いる). →お世辞, へつらい.

オペック **OPEC** /óʊpek/ (石油輸出国機構) (➤ the Organization of Petroleum Exporting Countries の略).

オペラ an **opera** ▶オペラを見にいく go to the *opera*.

オベリスク an **obelisk**(先端がピラミッドの形をした方尖(ほうせん)塔) ▶ワシントン記念塔はオベリスクの１例だ Washington Monument is an example of *an obelisk*.

オペレーター an **operator**(➤ 電話交換手, 機械の操作者をいう).

おべんちゃら **flattery** ▶おべんちゃらを言うのはやめてくれ Don't *butter* me *up*. (➤くだけた言い方) ／Don't *flatter* me.

おぼえ 覚え **1【記憶, 習得】**▶彼は仕事の覚えが早い[遅い] He *is quick* [*slow*] *to learn* his job. ‖ 彼女は覚えが早い[遅い] She *is a quick* [*slow*] *learner*. ／She is *a quick* [*slow*] *study*.
2【経験】▶私にも同じような目に遭った覚えがありますよ I've *had a* similar *experience*. ‖ この母の写真は見た覚えがない I *don't remember* seeing this picture of my mother. ‖ そんなことを言った[した]覚えはない I *don't remember* [*recall*] having ever said [done] anything like that. ‖ カンニングなど身に覚えのないことです I *had nothing to do with* the cheating.
3【自信】▶料理なら腕に多少の覚えがあります I *am* fairly *confident of* my cooking ability.
4【上司の引き立て】 **favor** ▶あの新入りは社長の覚えがめでたい That newcomer is *in favor with* the boss [*in the* boss's *good books*].

おぼえがき 覚書 a **memorandum** ▶覚書を作る make *a memorandum*.

おぼえる 覚える

📖 **訳語メニュー**
記憶する →learn ... by heart **1**
記憶している →remember **1**
習得する →learn **2**
感じる →feel **3**

1【記憶する】learn ... by heart, memorize +㊐（暗記する）; **remember** +㊐（覚えている；思い出す）▶ぼくはボブ・ディランの歌は全部**覚えた** I *learned* all (of) Bob Dylan's songs *by heart*. ‖１日に英語の単語を10語**覚える**のは難しい It is hard to *memorize* ten English words a day. ‖私は人の名前をなかなか**覚えられない** I *am not good at remembering* names. ／I *have a poor memory for* names.

▶あの夜のことは全く**覚えていない** I *don't remember* at all what happened that evening. ‖以前あの人に会ったことがあるが，いつどこでだったか**覚えていない**（＝思い出せない）I'm sure I met him before but I *can't remember* when or where. ‖メロディーは**覚えている**けど歌詞が思い出せない I *know* the melody but can't recall the words. ‖あの映画のラストシーンは今でもよく**覚えている** Even today, I can still vividly *recall* the last scene of that movie.（➤ recall は「思い起こす」）‖初めてデートしたときのことを**覚えてる**？ Do you *remember* our first date [the first time we went on a date]?

【文型】
(人(A)が)…したことを覚えている
remember (A) **doing** ➤ A's とすることもある
～ということを覚えている
remember that S + V

▶そのホテルに一度泊まったことは**覚えている** I *remember* stay*ing* at that hotel once.（➤「…したことを覚えている」は remember doing の形をとる. remember to do は「忘れずに…する」の意）‖その映画をテレビで見たのを**覚えている** I *remember seeing* that movie on TV. ‖私は彼が恥ずかしがり屋でおとなしい子であったことを**覚えている** I *remember that* he was a shy and quiet boy. ／I *remember* him *as* being shy and quiet. ‖あなたの言ったことをよく**覚えておきます** I'll *keep* [*bear*] what you said *in mind*. ‖畜生，**覚えてやがれ**！ Damn it! *I'm going to remember this* [*get even with you for this*]!

2【習得する，経験する】learn +㊐ ▶技術を**覚える** *learn* a skill ‖子供はことばを**覚える**のが早い Children can *learn* [*pick up*] a language quickly. ‖早く仕事を**覚えたい** I want to *learn* the job [the ropes] quickly. ‖彼は教わりもしないのに，たちまち車の運転を**覚えた** He *learned* to drive by himself in no time. ‖彼女は最近酒の味を**覚えてしまった** She has *acquired a taste for alcohol* recently.

3【感じる】feel +㊐ ▶しばらくして手に痛みを**覚えた** After a while, I *felt* a pain in my hand. ‖私は近頃夜になるとどっと疲れを**覚える** I *feel* very tired at night these days. ‖『戦争と平和』を読んで体の震えるような感動を**覚えた** When I read "War and Peace," I *felt a certain thrill* all through my body.（➤ この certain は「(ちょっと特殊で) 表現しようのない，なんとも言えない」）.

オホーツク **オホーツク海 the Sea of Okhotsk**/oʊká:tsk/.

おぼしい ▶高校生と**おぼしき**連中が大勢電車に乗り込んできた A group that *appeared to* be high school students boarded the train. →思われる.

おぼつかない **覚束ない** **1【頼りない】**▶お年寄りは**おぼつかない**足取りで歩き始めた The elderly man began to walk on *unsteady* legs. ‖彼女は**おぼつかない**手つきでピアノを弾く She plays the piano *awkwardly*.（➤「不器用に」の意）‖久美の英語はまだまだ**おぼつかない** Kumi's English is still *very basic*.

2【見込みのない】▶エラーばかりしていたのでは，我々が勝つことなど**おぼつかない** We *have very little chance of* winning since we've done nothing but make errors. ‖彼の今の成績ではＴ大はおろか，Ｍ大だって**おぼつかない** It is *very doubtful* that he will pass the entrance exam for M University, much less for T University.

おぼっちゃん **お坊ちゃん** ▶何てかわいい**お坊ちゃん**だこと What *a* cute *little boy*!

▶彼は**お坊ちゃん**だ He *knows nothing about the world*.（➤「世事に疎い」の意）／He is the *pampered son of a good* [*rich*] *family*.（➤「良家の甘やかされた息子」の意）‖彼は**お坊ちゃん育ち**で経済観念がない He *was brought up* (*as*) *a rich boy*, so he has no sense of the value of money. →坊ちゃん.

おぼれる 溺れる

1【水に】drown /draʊn/, **be drowned** ▶**溺れている**子供を助ける save a *drowning* child ‖彼女はプールで**溺れる**ところだった She (*was*) almost *drowned* in the swimming pool.（➤ drown, be drowned とも「溺れ死ぬ」の意なので，助かった場合には almost をつける必要がある）‖泳ぎのうまい人が**溺れる**ことは多い Good swimmers *are* often *drowned*. ‖彼は木更津海岸で遊泳中に**溺れて死んだ** He *was* [*got*] *drowned* while swimming at Kisarazu Beach.

ことわざ **溺れる者はわらをもつかむ** A drowning man will grasp [clutch] at a straw.

2【比喩的】▶麻薬に**溺れる** *get hooked on* drugs（➤ get hooked on は「病みつきになる」の意のくだけた言い方）‖彼は事業に失敗してから酒に**溺れた** He *indulged* (*himself*) *in drinking* [*took to drinking*] after failing to make the project a success. ‖彼女は四十男との愛に**溺れていた** She *was infatuated with* a man in his 40s.（➤ be infatuated with は「…にのぼせている」の意）.

おぼろげ ▶教会の尖(せん)塔が深い霧の中で**おぼろげ**に見えた The church steeple looked *indistinct* in the dense fog. ‖その男性のことは**おぼろげ**に記憶しています I have a *vague* memory of that gentleman. ‖祖父のことは**おぼろげ**にしか覚えていない I have only *hazy* memories of my grandfather.（➤ hazy は「(もやがかかったように) 不明確な」）.

おぼろづき **朧月** a **hazy** [**misty**] **moon** ‖**おぼろ月夜** a night with a hazy moon.

おぼん **お盆** →盆.

おまいり **お参り** ▶入試に合格できるよう神社に**お参り**に行った I *visited a shrine to pray* to pass the entrance examinations.

おまえ **お前** **you**

> **【解説】** 日本人は相手に直接呼びかける場合，自分と相手との長幼・社会的身分関係などによって「きみ」や「あなた」と言ったり，「おまえ」と言ったりするが，英語ではすべて you である.

▶**おまえ**はうそつきの名人だな *You* are a good storyteller [a great liar]. ‖おい，**おまえ**！ Hey, *you*!（➤ ぞんざいな言い方；hey と you をともに強く発音すると，怒って人に注意するときなどの表現となる）‖《愛する人などに呼びかけて》ねえ，**おまえ** My dear! ／Darling! ／

Honey！（➤ 前の２つは年長者に多い言い方；Honey！は若い人たちも用いるがファーストネームで呼びかけることが多くなってきている）．

おまけ お負け ▶これはおまけ（＝ただ）です This is included *free* (*of charge*) [as *a free gift*]. ‖ チョコレートを２枚買ったら10円おまけしてくれた I got *a* ten-yen *discount* [got ten yen *off*] when I bought two bars of chocolate. ‖ ＤＶＤレコーダーをお買い上げの方にはＤＶＤ－Ｒを３枚おまけに差し上げます If you buy a DVD recorder, we'll *throw in* three DVD-R's. (➤ throw in は「…をおまけとして添える」).

おまけに ▶日が暮れて，おまけに雨まで降りだした It got dark and *to make matters worse* [*what was worse*], it began to rain. (➤ ともに「もっと悪いことには」の意) ‖ このネクタイは色が気に入らない．おまけに値段が高すぎる I don't like the color of this tie. *Besides*, [*What's more,*] it's too expensive.

おませな precocious ▶おませな子供 a *precocious* child ‖ おませなことを言うものじゃありません Don't *talk like a grown-up*. (➤「大人のような口を利くな」の意) ‖ あの女の子は年の割にはおませね That girl is too *grown-up* for her age. ⇀**おしゃま.**

おまちかね お待ちかね ▶お客様がさっきからお待ちかねですよ The guests have been *waiting for* you for some time.

おまちどおさま お待ち遠さま ▶お待ちどおさま，ごはんですよ！Dinner *is ready* at last. (Sorry for the long wait.) ‖《出前を届けて》お待ちどおさま Thank you for waiting.

おまつりきぶん お祭り気分 ▶文化祭は終わったのに，生徒たちはまだお祭り気分で勉強に身が入らない Although the school festival is over, the students are still *in a festive mood* and can't get back into their studies.

おまつりさわぎ お祭り騒ぎ merrymaking（浮かれ騒ぐこと）；**festivities**（祝いの行事・催し）▶日本人は一般にお祭り騒ぎが好きだ Generally, Japanese people love *merrymaking* [*festivities*]. ‖ 地元の高校が優勝して町はお祭り騒ぎだ The local high school team won the tournament, so the entire town *joined in* (*the*) *celebration*. (➤ celebration は「祝賀」).

おまもり お守り an **amulet**, a **charm**（災いから身を守ってくれる；後者には「幸運をもたらしてくれるお守り」の意もある）；a **talisman**（不思議な魔力を持つ）▶交通安全のお守り *a lucky charm* for safe driving ‖ 災難よけのお守りを身に着ける wear *a charm* against bad luck.

おまる a **potty(-chair)**（幼児用の）；a **bedpan**（病人用の）▶おまるに座る sit on *a potty* ‖ 母親は赤ん坊をおまるに載せた The mother put her baby on the *potty-chair*. 《参考》子供の排便訓練用のおまるの改まった言い方は toilet training chair [seat].

おまわりさん お巡りさん a **police officer**

語法 (1)特に男女を区別する必要がある場合は policeman, policewoman を用いる. (2)cop は「お巡り，サツ」に近い少しぞんざいな言い方.

▶《呼びかけて》お巡りさん，すみませんが… Excuse me, *officer* ... (➤ ふつう Policeman [-woman]！とは呼びかけない) ‖ お巡りさんが親切に駅へ行く道を教えてくれた The *police officer* kindly showed me the way to the station.

おまんま ▶こう暇じゃ，おまんまの食い上げだ If business stays this slow, we *won't be able to make a living*.

おみき お神酒 ***omiki***; sake offered to the Shinto gods; sacred sake (➤ 説明的な訳).

おみくじ お神籤 an ***omikuji***; a fortune written on a slip of paper (➤ 説明的な訳)

日本紹介 ✉ **おみくじは神社や寺で手に入る運勢を書いた紙切れです．少額の金を払ってくじを引くか機械から買います．吉が出ると持って帰りますが，凶が出るとよく境内の木に結び付けて残します** *Omikuji* are slips of paper which people get at Shinto shrines or Buddhist temples on which fortunes are written. People pay a small amount of money to draw one or buy one from a machine. If the fortune is good, people take it home. If it is bad, however, they often tie it to a tree at the shrine or temple and leave it behind.

▶おみくじを引く pick *an omikuji* ‖ 神社でおみくじを引いたら大吉が出た The *omikuji* I got at the shrine said "Great fortune."

おみこし お神輿 an ***omikoshi***. ⇀**みこし.**

おみそれ お見逸れ ▶永井さん，ヨットに乗れるの？お見それしました You can sail a yacht, Mr. Nagai? I *underestimated you*!

おみやまいり お宮参り a **baby's first visit to a shrine**

日本紹介 ✉ **お宮参りは新しく生まれた子の健やかな成長を願って，神社にお参りすることです．男の子の場合は32日目に，女の子の場合には33日目に地元の神社に参るのがふつうです** *Omiyamairi* means going to a Shinto shrine to pray for a new baby's healthy growth. Japanese parents usually visit their local shrine 32 days after a boy is born, or 33 days after a girl is born.

おむすび お結び ⇀**おにぎり.**

おむつ a **diaper** /dáɪəpəʳ/ ‖ **大人用おむつ** an adult diaper ‖ **紙おむつ** a paper diaper ‖ **使い捨ておむつ** a disposable diaper. ⇀**おしめ.**

オムライス *omuraisu*; an omelet topped with ketchup or demi-glace sauce with a filling consisting of pan-fried rice mixed with ketchup, chicken, onions and other vegetables (➤ 説明的な訳).

オムレツ an **omelet(te)** /ɑ́ːmlət/ ▶フライパンでオムレツを作る cook *an omelet* in a frying pan.

おめい 汚名 disgrace（不名誉）；a **bad reputation**（悪評）；a **stigma**（恥辱・不面目の印）▶彼が裏切り者の汚名をすすぐには時間がかかるだろう It will take time for him to *live down* his reputation as a traitor. (➤ live down は「（汚名などを）あとの生活態度で償う」；「汚名をすすぐ」だけなら clear one's name) ‖ 彼は怠け者の汚名を返上しようと猛烈に勉強を始めた He began studying furiously to *overturn his previous reputation* as a slacker. ‖ 前科者の汚名を着て暮らす live with the *stigma* of being a person with a criminal record.

おめおめ shamelessly（恥知らずにも）；**unashamedly**（恥じている様子もなく）▶このままおめおめと故郷には帰れない I can't go back home *in this shameful state*.

おめかし 一動 おめかしする dress (oneself) up ▶彼女は鏡の前でかなり長い間おめかし（＝化粧）していた She spent quite a long time in front of the mirror *putting on make-up*. ‖ おめかししちゃって，きょうはデートなの？You'*re all dressed up* [*spruced up*]. Are you going on a date today?

おめだま お目玉 ▶そんなことをしたらお目玉を食うよ If you do that, you'll *get a good scolding* [*talking-*

to]. (➤ talking-to は「小言」の意のインフォーマルな語).

おめつけやく お目付け役 a **watchdog** (➤本来は「番犬」の意).

おめでた ▶前田さんの奥さん, またおめでただそうですね I hear Mrs. Maeda is *expecting* (*a baby*) again. ‖ おめでたはいつなの? When is *the happy event*? (➤ happy event は「めでたい事」の意で, 特に出産を指す).

おめでたい **1【喜ばしい】**▶きょうはおめでたい日だ Today is a *joyful* [*happy*] day. ‖ ことしわが家におめでたいことが続いた This year we have had many *causes for celebration*.

2【お人よし】▶あいつを信じるなんてきみもおめでたいね What *a simpleton* [*How naive*] you are to trust him!

おめでとう

【解説】 (1) 日本語の「おめでとう」はめでたいことなら何にでも用いられるが, 英語では事柄によって表現を変える. 入学・卒業・婚約・結婚・昇進・成功など本人の努力によって達成し, ともにたたえるべきことには **Congratulations**! が一般的 (-s をつけることに注意). →結婚.
(2) 毎年巡ってくる祝い事, 祝日や記念日などの挨拶には Congratulations! ではなく, **Happy ...**! を用いる.

【文型】
あなたの A, おめでとう
Congratulations on your A!
➤ A は名詞・動名詞, -s を落とさないこと

▶入試合格おめでとう *Congratulations on* passing the entrance exam. ‖ R 大学に合格したんだってね. おめでとう! I heard you've been accepted by R University. *Congratulations!*

▶信子さんから聞いたけど, きみのお姉さん結婚なさったんだってね. おめでとう Nobuko told me your sister got married. *Give her my congratulations* [*my best regards*]!

▶ **対話** 「明けましておめでとうございます」「やあ, おめでとう」*"Happy New Year."* "Oh. *Happy New Year* [*(The) same to you*]." (➤ (A) Happy New Year! は「良いお年を(お迎えください)」の意味で, 年末から使うことができる. また日本語と異なり, 1月2日以降には通例この挨拶をしない. なお, 口で言うときは a は省略する) ‖ **対話** 「お誕生日おめでとう」「ありがとう」*"Happy birthday (to you)!"* "Thanks."

✉ **ご卒業[結婚/昇進]おめでとうございます. ますますのご発展を祈ります** *Congratulations on* your graduation [marriage / promotion]. I wish you success in the future. (➤結婚の場合は success に代えて happiness を用いる).

おめにかかる お目にかかる ▶校長[スミス]先生にお目にかかりたいのですが I would like to *see* the principal [Mr. Smith]. / I am here to *see* the principal [Mr. Smith]. (➤後者は面会の予約がある場合; 英語では職位名より個人名で言うのがふつう) ‖ 初めてお目にかかります *How do you do?* ‖ お目にかかれて光栄です *It is a real pleasure* [*an honor*] *to meet you.* (→はじめまして) ‖ では明日お目にかかります Then, *see* you tomorrow.

▶お目にかけたいものがございます I have something I'd like to *show* you. ‖ これはめったにお目にかかれない逸品です This is an excellent item you *can rarely get a chance to see*.

おめみえ お目見得 ▶新型の燃料電池車が展示場にお目見えした A newly designed fuel cell car *was exhibited for the first time* [*made its debut at the exhibition*]. (➤前者は「展示された」の意).

[1]おもい 重い

📖 訳語メニュー
重さが →heavy **1**
責任が →heavy, important **2**
病気が →serious **3**

1【重さが】heavy ▶重い箱 a *heavy* box ‖ プロパンガスは空気よりも重い Propane gas is *heavier* than air. ‖ この石は重くて運べない This stone is too *heavy* for me to carry. ‖ この戸は重くて開かない This door is too *heavy* for me to open. ‖ ぼくは父より5キロ重い I *weigh* 5 kilograms *more* than my father. / I am 5 kilograms *heavier* than my father. ▶ (データの)重いファイル a *heavy* file.

2【責任などが】heavy, weighty (➤後者は堅い語); **important** (重要な) ▶責任の重い仕事 a job with *heavy* [*weighty*] responsibility ‖ 父は会社で重い地位に就いている My father holds an *important* position in his company. ‖ 政府はこの事態を重く見ている The government considers this situation an *important* issue.

3【病気が】serious ▶重い病気にかかる suffer from a *serious* [*grave*] illness ‖ 母の病気は重い My mother *is seriously ill* [*very sick*].

4【気分などが】▶きょうはかぜ気味で頭が重い I have a cold, so my head *feels heavy* [*dull*] today. ‖ きのう10キロ走ったのできょうは体が重い I ran ten kilometers yesterday so today my body *feels like lead*. (➤「体が鉛のようだ」の意; lead の発音は /led/) ‖ あすから期末テストだと思うと学校へ行くのも気が重い When I think of final exams coming up tomorrow, I *feel* so *depressed* I don't even want to go to school. ‖ 彼は口が重い He *is a man of few words*.

5【罰が】severe (厳しい) ▶彼は業務上過失致死罪で重い罰を受けた He received a *severe* sentence for manslaughter due to professional negligence.

[2]おもい 思い

1【考え, 予想】(a) **thought** ▶彼は腕組みをして何か思いにふけっていた He folded his arms, *deep in thought* about something. ‖ そんなことになるとは思いもしなかった It's *the very last thing I expected*. (➤「それは最も予期しなかったことだ」の意) / *Little* did I *expect* that things would turn out that way. (→思いのほか, 思いも寄らない).

2【願い, 望み】one's **dream**, one's **wish** ▶私は長い間の思いがかなってうれしい I'm glad my long cherished *dream* has come true. ‖ 彼はいつも思いのままにふるまう He always does *whatever he wants*.

3【恋心, 愛情】love ▶きっときみの思いは彼女に通じるよ I'm sure you can get your *feelings* across [convey your *love*] to her. (➤ get ... across は「(考えなどを)わからせる」の意) ‖ 雄太は明子に思いを寄せている Yuta *cares* (*a lot*) [*has deep feelings*] *for* Akiko. ‖ うちの息子たちは祖父母思いだ (=祖父母に優しい) Our sons are *very kind to* [*very thoughtful of*] their grandparents.

4【経験】an **experience** ▶おかげで楽しい思いをさせても

らったよ You have given me *a delightful experience*. ／I *enjoyed myself* [*had a very good time*] thanks to you. ‖ 子供に悲しい思いをさせてはいけない You must not *make* your children (*feel*) *sad* [*unhappy*]. ‖ 初めてフランスに行ったときは，ことばがわからずつらい思いをした I *had a hard time* during my first stay in France because I couldn't understand the language.

おもいあがる 思い上がる ▶思い上がった若者 an *arrogant* young man (➤ arrogant は「尊大な，傲慢な」の意) ‖ あの人は思い上がっている That man *thinks too highly of himself*. (➤ think highly of は「…を高く評価する」) ‖ 思い上がるのもいいかげんにしろ Don't *think so highly of yourself*. ／Don't *be so arrogant* [*stuck-up*].

おもいあたる 思い当たる ▶彼女にそう言われてみると思い当たる節があった What she said *reminded* me *of* something in myself. (➤ remind A of B は「A(人)に B を思い出させる」) ‖ 彼女，ぼくのこと怒ってるみたいだけど，思い当たることは何もないんだよね She looks like she's mad at me, but there's nothing I can *put my finger on*. (➤ put one's finger on は「(原因などを)的確に指摘する」の意のインフォーマルな表現).

おもいあまる 思い余る ▶思い余って父に相談してみた *At a loss for* [*Not knowing*] *what to do*, I talked over the matter with my father. (➤ 前半を Since I couldn't decide what to do, としてもよい).

おもいいれ 思い入れ ▶作者の最も思い入れのある作品 the author's most *cherished* work ‖ この小説が私の処女作品なのでいちばん思い入れが深いです Since this novel is my first work, I'm most *deeply attached to it* [it's *dearest to my heart*].

おもいうかぶ 思い浮かぶ ▶その先生の名前がどうしても思い浮かばない(＝思い出せない) I just *can't remember* the teacher's name.

おもいうかべる 思い浮かべる **remember** ＋㊐；**come to mind**(心頭に浮かぶ) ▶子供の頃を思い浮かべる *remember* one's childhood days ‖ イタリアというと私はすぐ長靴を思い浮かべる When I hear "Italy," I'*m* always *reminded of* a boot [I always *think of* a boot]. (➤ be reminded of … は「…を思い出す」).
▶「ふるさと」と聞いてまず思い浮かべるものは何ですか What is the first thing that *comes to mind* when you hear the word "hometown"? ／What first *comes to* your *mind* when you hear the word "hometown"?

おもいえがく 思い描く **imagine** ＋㊐ (想像する)；**visualize** ＋㊐ (心に描く) ▶彼女は新婚生活をあれこれと思い描いてみた She *imagined* [*pictured to herself*] this and that aspect of her future married life. ‖ ぼくは彼女がラブレターを読んでくれているところを思い描いた I *visualized* her reading my love letter.

おもいおこす 思い起こす **remember** ＋㊐，**recall** ＋㊐，**recollect** ＋㊐ ⇀思い出す ▶古き良き時代を思い起こす *recollect* the good old days ‖ 思い起こせば20年前，おやじと大げんかをして「もう一生帰ってきてやらないぞ」とわが家を飛び出したのでした *Now that I think of it*, it was just 20 years ago when I had a big fight with my father and ran out, swearing never to return for the rest of my life.

おもいおもい 思い思い ▶子供たちは思い思いに絵を描いた The children drew pictures *after their own fancy*. ／The children drew pictures, *each in his or her* [*each in their*] *own way*. (➤ their を使うのはインフォーマルな言い方) ‖ 兄弟は思い思いの(＝別々の)道に進んだ The brothers went their *separate* ways.

おもいかえす 思い返す **look back** (振り返る)；**change** one's **mind**(考え直す) ▶思い返してみればあっという間の3年間でした *Looking back now*, it was a quick three years. ‖ 冷蔵庫を買い換えるつもりだったが，思い返してもう少し我慢することにした I was going to replace the fridge with a new one, but *changed my mind* [*had second thoughts* ／ *thought better of it*] and decided to keep it for a little longer.

おもいがけず 思いがけず **unexpectedly** ▶思いがけず私の絵が美術展に入選した My picture was *unexpectedly* accepted for the art exhibition. ‖ 仙台で思いがけず旧友に会った I *unexpectedly* met [ran into] an old friend (of mine) in Sendai.

おもいがけない 思いがけない **unexpected** (予期しない)；**surprising** (驚くべき) ▶思いがけない客 an *unexpected* visitor ‖ 思いがけない出来事 a *surprising* event ‖ あなたにここで会うとは思いがけないことでした I *didn't expect* to see you here.

おもいきった 思い切った **daring** /déərɪŋ/；**drastic** (抜本的な)；**bold** (行動などが大胆な) ▶きみはずいぶん思い切ったことを言うんだね You really *say daring things*, don't you? ／You're really *outspoken*, aren't you? ‖ 何か思い切った手段をとってみたらどうだい Why not take some *drastic* [*bold*] action?

おもいきって 思い切って ▶その外国人が困った様子だったので私は思い切って声をかけてみた The foreigner looked troubled, so I *mustered* (*up*) *my courage* and spoke to him. (➤ muster (up) は「(勇気を)奮い起こす」) ‖ 思い切ってその試験を受けてみたら？ Just *make up your mind* and take the examination. ‖ 彼は思い切って会社を興した He *took the plunge* and started a company. (➤ take the plunge は「覚悟を決めて踏み切る」).

おもいきや 思いきや ▶午後は晴れると思いきや，また怪しい空模様になってきた *I thought* it was going to clear up in the afternoon, *but* the sky began to darken again.

おもいきり 思い切り **1【決断，諦め】**▶彼女は思い切りよくロングヘアをショートにした She *just made up* her *mind* and cut her long hair short. ‖ 祖父母は思い切りよく家財の多くを処分した My grandparents *resolutely* disposed of most of their household goods. ‖ 済んでしまったことをいつまでもぐずぐず言うとは，彼も思い切りの悪いやつだ He's such an *indecisive* guy, harping on and on about what's done. (➤ harp on は「くどくど言う」).
2【存分に】▶独身のうちに思い切り遊びなさい Enjoy yourself *all you can* while you're single. ‖ 思い切り遊んでいらっしゃい Go ahead and have a great time. (➤ 遊園地などで親が子供に向かって言う場合) ‖ ぼくはボールを思い切り蹴飛ばした I kicked the ball *with all my strength*.

おもいきる 思い切る ▶今の彼とは別れるべきと思うんだけど，なかなか思い切れない I think I should break up with my current boyfriend, but I *can't seem to gather up the courage* [*set my mind to it* ／ *take the plunge*].

おもいこみ 思い込み a **preconceived idea** [**notion**] (前もって抱いている考え)；an **assumption**(証拠はないが当然と思っていること) ▶彼は思い込みが激しく，人の話に耳を貸さない He *has a lot of preconceived ideas* [*notions*] and doesn't listen to anyone. ／He *tends to be opinionated* and doesn't listen to anyone. ‖ 年を取ると記憶力が落ちるというのは，単なる**思い込み**だ The idea that your memory declines as you age is nothing more than *an assumption*.

おもいこむ 思い込む ▶別の大学も受けておけばよかったよ．K大なら受かると**思い込んでいた**（＝確信していた）ぼくが間違ってた I should have applied to other universities as well. It was my fault because I *was so sure* that I would be admitted to K University. ‖ うちの娘はいったんこうと**思い込んだら**（＝心に決めたら）周りの者がいくら言っても聞かない Once my daughter *makes up her mind* (about something), nobody (around her) can convince her otherwise.

おもいしらせる 思い知らせる ▶彼にこのことを**思い知らせて**やらなければいけない I have to *teach* him *a lesson* about this.

おもいしる 思い知る ▶私にはどうすることもできないのだということを**思い知った** I *learned the hard way* that there's nothing I could do about it. (➤ the hard way は「苦い経験を通して」の意) ‖ どうだ，**思い知ったか** Take that! Have you learned your lesson now?

▶津波の威力を**思い知らされた** I'*m shocked to learn* how strong a tsunami can be. ／It *sank in* (*to* me) how strong a tsunami could be. (➤ sink in は「実感としてわかる」).

おもいすごし 思い過ごし ▶それはきみの**思い過ごし**だよ It's all in your *imagination*. ／You're imagining things.

おもいだしわらい 思い出し笑い ▶何を**思い出し笑い**してるの？ What *has brought that smile to your face*? (● 英語では「何がその笑いをもたらしたのか」と発想するので訳例のようになる) ‖ 彼女は**思い出し笑いをした** She *laughed* [*chuckled*] *to herself*. (➤ chuckle は「含み笑いをする」).

おもいだす 思い出す **remember**＋㊐, **recall**＋㊐, **recollect** ＋㊐

> **語法** (1) **remember** が「思い出す」の意の一般語．思い出そうと意識的に努力する場合にも，ふと思い出す場合にも用いる．
> (2) **recall** と **recollect** はともに「意識的に思い出す」の意のやや堅い語．
> (3)「思い出す」はこれらの語のほかに，**call up (memories of)**, **think of** などを用いて表すこともできる．

▶その男の名前を**思い出す**ことができなかった I couldn't *remember* his name. ‖ 松尾君に電話をかけなければいけないことをふと**思い出した** I just *remembered* that I had to call Matsuo. ‖ 息子の遊んでいる姿を見て自分の子供時代を**思い出した** Seeing my son playing *called up memories* of my own childhood. (➤ call up は「(物事が記憶を)呼び起こす」の意).

▶私は5年前に起こったある事件を，まるできのうのことのように**思い出す** I *recall* an incident that occurred five years ago as vividly as if it had happened yesterday. ‖ きみを見ていると学校時代の友だちを**思い出す**よ You *remind* me *of* a friend I went to school with. (➤ remind A of B で「A(人)にBを思い出させる」の意) ‖ このアルバムを見るたびに楽しかった学生時代を**思い出す** I can never look at this album without *being reminded of* my happy school days. ‖ 彼のことは今でも時折**思い出す**ことがある He still *comes to my mind* now and then. ‖ その歌は古き良き時代を**思い出させる** The song *brings back* the good old days.

▶どうしても彼女の名前が**思い出せません** I just can't *recollect* her name. ‖「ちゅうちょ」にあたる英語が**思い出せない**んだ I just can't *think of* the English word for 'chucho.'

✉ **ご一緒に過ごした楽しい日々をよく思い出します** I often *think of* the happy days we spent together.

✉ **湖にウォータースキーに行ったことをよく思い出します** I often *remember* the time we went water-skiing on the lake.

おもいたつ 思い立つ ▶彼は**思い立ったら**すぐにやらないと気が済まないタイプだ He is the type that must do at once whatever *comes to* him [*enters his mind*]. ‖ 彼女は急に旅行を**思い立って**出かけた *The idea of* traveling *came to her mind* and she set off immediately.

ことわざ **思い立ったが吉日** The day you've made up your mind is the lucky day you should act. ／Strike while the iron is hot. (➤「好機を逃すな」の意のことわざ).

おもいちがい 思い違い (a) **misunderstanding** ▶それはあなたの**思い違い**だ That is *a misunderstanding* on your part. ‖ あなたは信頼できる人だと思ったけど，とんだ**思い違い**だったわね I thought you were reliable, but I *was terribly mistaken*.

おもいつき 思いつき an **idea** ▶それはいい**思いつき**だ That's a good *idea*. ‖ ほんの**思いつき**ですけど夏の合宿に野尻湖はどうでしょうか I'd say, just *off the top of my head*, that Lake Nojiri would be a good place for our summer camp. (➤ off the top of one's head は「よく考えたわけではないが」の意のインフォーマルな言い方).

おもいつく 思いつく **strike** [**hit**]《on》(名案などがふと浮かぶ)；**think**《of》(考えつく) ▶名案を**思いついた** I *struck* [*hit*] *on* a good plan. ／I'*ve* just *had a brainstorm*. (➤ brainstorm は「突然の思いつき」の意のインフォーマルな語) ‖ うまいことばが**思いつかない** I cannot *think of* the right words. ／The right words do not *come to mind*.

おもいつめる 思い詰める ▶次郎はその女の子のことを**思い詰めている** Jiro *has his heart* [*mind*] *set on* that girl. ‖ そんなに**思い詰める**と体によくないよ It's bad for your health to *brood* (*over* things) like that. ‖ 失恋したからって，あんまり**思い詰めない**ほうがいいよ I understand you've had your heart broken, but you shouldn't *think too much about* it. ‖ さっき美穂を見かけたけど，何か**思い詰めた**様子だったよ I saw Miho a little while ago. She looked like she *was brooding* [*worrying*] *about* something.

おもいで 思い出 a **memory**（心に浮かぶ）；**recollections**（意識的に記憶の糸をたどった結果としての思い出；通例複数形で）；(a) **remembrance**（忘れていたことが自然によみがえるような場合）

▶アルバムを開けると幼い頃の**思い出**がよみがえってきた When I opened the album, *memories* of my childhood came back to me. ‖ イタリア旅行はいい**思い出**です I have *happy* [*pleasant*] *memories* of my trip to Italy.

▶この旅行はいい**思い出**になります We will have *good memories* of this trip. ／This will be a memorable trip. ‖ フィラデルフィアには楽しい**思い出**がたくさんある Philadelphia holds many pleasant *memories* for me. ‖ その小説は作者の高校生時代の**思い出**を土台にしている The novel is based on the author's *recollections* of his high school days. ‖ 私たちにはともに過ごした日々の楽しい**思い出**がたくさんある We have many happy *remembrances* of our days together.

▶亡き妻の**思い出**(＝形見)にこのオルゴールをとってある I keep this music box as *a remembrance* [*a memento*] of my wife who passed away. (➤ともに「思い出の品」の意) ‖ 彼らは大学時代の**思い出話**に花を咲かせた They exchanged lively *reminiscences* of college days. (➤ reminiscences /rèmɪnísənsɪz/ は「懐かしい昔の話」) ‖ 高校時代, 林先生に叱られたのも今では**懐かしい思い出だ** I *feel nostalgic* now *to remember* how Mr. Hayashi in high school reprimanded me.

✉ **いろいろありがとう. トロントからたくさんの楽しい思い出を持ち帰りました** Thank you for everything. I have brought home many happy *memories* from Toronto.

おもいどおり 思い通り ▶子供の**思いどおりに**させなさい Let the children do *as they wish*. ‖ 彼は何でも自分の**思いどおりに**しようとする He wants to *do* [*have*] everything *his own way*.

おもいとどまる 思い止まる **deter** +目; **discourage** +目 (意欲をくじかれて) ▶悪天候のため彼は飛行を**思いとどまった** Bad weather *deterred* him from flying. ‖ 両親は彼が海外留学するのを**思いとどまらせ**ようとした His parents tried to *discourage* him from studying overseas. ‖ 彼にちょっと文句を言おうとして**思いとどまった** I was going to tell him a thing or two, but I *held myself back* [*checked myself*].

おもいなおす 思い直す →考え直す.

おもいなし 思いなし ▶**思いなしか**, きょうは彼女はいつもの元気がないようだ *It may be my imagination*, but she doesn't look her usual self today.

おもいなやむ 思い悩む **worry** (**about**) ▶そんなささいなことで**思い悩んで**いたらきりがないよ You shouldn't spend all your time *worrying about* such a small thing. ‖ 先のことをあまり**思い悩むな** Do not *think too much about* the future.

おもいのこす 思い残す ▶この世に**思い残す**ことは何もない I have no unfinished business left to take care of before I die.

おもいのほか 思いの外 ▶**思いのほか**よく釣れた I caught an *unexpectedly* large number of fish. ／*Much to my surprise*, I caught a lot of fish. ‖ 入院中の友人を見舞ったら彼は**思いのほか元気だった** When I visited my friend in the hospital, he was *better than I expected*.

おもいもよらない 思いも寄らない ▶あの堤防が決壊するなんて**思いも寄らなかった** I'*ve never dreamed* [*imagined*] that that embankment would collapse. ‖ **思いも寄らない人**からラブレターをもらった I got a love letter from *the last person I could have imagined*.

おもいやられる 思いやられる ▶今からそんな弱気じゃあ先が**思いやられる**ね I *can't help worrying about* your future when I see you being so weak-kneed.

おもいやり 思いやり **thoughtfulness, consideration, sensitivity**

《解説》 (1)「思いやり」に対応する英語で, 日本人学習者の多くがきちんと区別していないと思われるのが thoughtfulness と consideration である. 前者は「相手に幸福(感)をもたらそうとあれこれ気遣うこと」を意味し, 後者は「相手の要求や気持ちを察し, その人の気持ちを害さないように気遣うこと」を意味する. 例えば, 身内・友人など親しい人の誕生日などを記憶しておいてカードやプレゼントを贈ることは前者の思いやりであり, 電車などで音楽を楽しむ場合, イヤホンから音が外に漏れないように周囲に気を配るのは後者の思いやりである.

(2) thoughtfulness はまた,「相手に選択権を与えること」という含みがあるから, 日本人が考えがちな思いやりは, 英語国民から見ると, 少なからずお節介な行為だと思われてしまう. 例えば, すし屋で同僚などのしょうゆ皿に無言でしょうゆを注ぐ行為を, 日本人なら相手への思いやりだと考えるだろうが, 英語国では, この行為は相手の選択権を奪った行為だと解釈されがちである.

(3)「感受性(の豊かさ)」の意の sensitivity も日本語の「思いやり」を表すのに適当な語の1つである.

▶彼は隣人に対する**思いやりがない** He *has no consideration for* his neighbors. ‖ あの先生は学生にとても**思いやりがある** That teacher *is* very *thoughtful of* [*kind to*] his students. (➤前置詞に注意) ‖ **思いやりのない人ね**! How *inconsiderate* you are! ／You're really *inconsiderate*. ‖ 彼のコメントは**思いやりを欠いていた** His comment lacked *sensitivity*. ‖ **思いやりのある人**になってほしい I want you to become *a person who cares about* (*the feelings of*) *others*.

▶さらに**思いやりのある**社会を目指して頑張ろう Let's work together to build a more *caring* society. ‖ ひとりにしてあげることが今は彼女へのいちばんの**思いやり**です Let her be alone ... that's the best thing you can do for her now. (➤「彼女にしてあげられる最良のことです」の意).

おもいやる 思いやる ▶娘には人を**思いやる**ことができる子に育ってほしいと思います I'd like my daughter to grow up to be a person who *is considerate* [*thoughtful*] *of* others. ‖ 少しは彼女の気持ちを**思いやりなさい** *Have some consideration* for her feelings. ‖ 彼は母親の気持ちを**思いやって**その計画を諦めた He gave up the plan *out of consideration* for his mother.

おもいわずらう 思い煩う **worry, be worried** [**concerned**] ▶将来をあまり**思い煩うな** Don't *be* too *concerned* about your future. ／Don't let the future *worry* you too much. ‖ あすのことを**思い煩うことなかれ** Don't *worry* about tomorrow. (➤聖書のことば).

おもう 思う・想う

📖 **訳語メニュー**
- 考える →think **1**
- 望む →want, hope **2**
- 意図する →be going to **3**
- 予期する →expect **4**
- みなす →consider, take **5**
- 感じる →feel **6**
- いぶかる →doubt, suspect **7**

1【考える, 推測する】 **think** +目; **believe** +目 (推量の確かさにある程度の自信がある場合); **suppose** +目 (推量の域を出ない場合) ▶きみの自転車は盗まれたのだとぼくは**思う** I *think* [*believe*／*suppose*] (that) your bicycle has been stolen. ‖ きみはあの人を誰だと**思う**? Who do you *think* he is? ‖ あなた, 私の兄さん

をどう思う？ *What do you think of* my big brother？（➤ How …? としない）‖自分が正しいと思うことをやりなさい Do what you *believe* is right. ‖ 対話「日本のテレビはくだらない番組が多すぎると思う」「私もそう思います」"I *think* there are too many lowbrow programs on TV in Japan." "*I agree.* ／*I think so, too.*"

▶ 対話「彼女，間に合うと思う？」「間に合わないと思うね」"Do you *think* she can make it？" "(No,) I don't *think* so. ／I'm *afraid* she can't. ／I'm *afraid* not."（➤ afraid を使うほうが響きがやわらかい）‖ 対話「あなた，パーティーに出られる？」「うん，行けると思うよ［いや，行けないと思う］」"Are you coming to the party？" "Yes, I *suppose* so [No, I *suppose* not]." ‖ 対話「あしたは雨が降ると思う？」「降らないと思うわ」"Do you *think* it will rain tomorrow？" "No, I don't *think* so."

あなたの英語はどう響く？
「あしたは雨が降らないと思う」「彼は天才ではないと思う」のような文を，それぞれ *I think* it will not rain tomorrow. や *I think* he is not a genius. のように言うと不自然に響く．英語では *I don't think* it will rain tomorrow. や *I don't think* he is a genius. のように「…だとは思わない」と考えるのがふつう．

2【望む，願う】want（＋目）；**hope**（＋目）（実現可能と感じられることについて）；**wish**（＋目）（実現不可能または可能性の少ないことについて）▶私はちゃんとした英語を話せるようになりたいと思います I *want to* learn how to speak proper English. ‖私は小さいとき看護師になりたいと思っていた I *wanted to* be a nurse when I was small. ‖母がすぐによくなればよいと思う I *hope* my mother will get well soon. ‖物事は自分の思うとおりにはいかないものだ Things do not always go *as one would wish.*

▶スノーボードがうまくできたらなあと思う *I wish I could* snowboard well. ‖英語がすらすら話せるようになりたいと思ったことはありませんか *Have you ever wished* you could speak English fluently？‖もっと若かったらと思ったことはありませんか *Have you ever wished* you were younger？

3【意図する，志す】be going to do ▶私はこの夏沖縄へ行こうと思う I'*m going to* (go to) Okinawa this summer. ／I'*m thinking of* going to Okinawa this summer.（➤ be thinking of には「はっきりとは言えないが」「できないかもしれないが」という含みがある）‖ビルは外科医になろうと思っている Bill *intends to* become a surgeon. ‖やろうと思ったことは即実行すべきだ Once you've *made up your mind to* do something, you should carry it out immediately.

4【予期する，予想する】expect ＋目；**think** ＋目（考える）；**suppose** ＋目（➤ think よりも根拠が薄弱な場合）；**dream** ＋目（➤ 主に否定文・疑問文で）

▶試験は思ったより易しかった The examination was easier *than* I (*had*) *expected.* ‖今場所も横綱が優勝すると思う I *think* [*suppose*] the yokozuna will win this tournament again.（➤ think は絶好調とか強力な相手が見つからないなどの明確な根拠がある場合）‖こんな所であなたに会おうとは思わなかった I *never expected* [*thought*] I'd meet you here. ‖彼女がR社に入社するなんて夢にも思わなかった I *never dreamed* she would be accepted by R Company.

5【みなす，評価する】consider A (**to be**) B [A **as** B], **look upon** A **as** B, **regard** A **as** B（➤ いずれも「AをBと考える」の意）▶私は彼女は歌が上手だと思う I *consider* her (*to be*) a good singer.（➤ 堅い言い方；to be は通例つけない）‖あの学生は右翼だと思われている That student *is considered* (*as*) a rightist. ／That student *is looked upon* [*is regarded*] *as* a rightist. ‖彼は自分のことを天才だと思っている He *thinks of* himself *as* a genius.

▶きみはぼくをばかだと思っているのか Do you *take* me *for* a fool？（➤ take A for B は「A（人）をBとみなす」）‖彼の話し方を聞いて中国人だと思った I *took* him *to be* Chinese from his way of speaking. ‖その刀は本物の正宗だと思われていた The sword *was taken for* a genuine Masamune.（➤ この場合の take A for B は mistake A for B と同じで，「誤ってAをBとみなす」の意）‖多くの人が私を批判したが，自分では正しいと思ったことをした Many people criticized me, but I did *what I thought was right.*

6【感じる，気持ちを抱く】feel（＋目）▶きみの考えがいちばんいいように思う I *feel* that your idea is the best one. ‖ドアにぶつかったときあまり痛いとは思わなかった I didn't *feel* much pain when I bumped into the door. ‖今度の首相，どう思う？ *How do you feel about* our new prime minister？‖負けて悔しいと思わないのか *Don't you feel discouraged* [*frustrated*] by the fact you lost the game？

7【いぶかる】doubt ＋目（…ではないかと思う，…かどうか疑問に思う）；**suspect** ＋目（…ではないかと思う）；**wonder** ＋目（…だろうかと思う）▶日本チームが近い将来ワールドカップを取る見込みはないと思う I *doubt that* the Japanese team will have a chance to win the World Cup in the near future.（➤ I doubt では「望んでも見込みは多分ない」というニュアンスだが，I don't think にすると「見込みは全くないと思う」になる）‖彼は本気でそう言ったと思う I *don't doubt that* he meant it. ‖事態がそれほど大きく変わるかどうか疑問に思う I *doubt if* [*whether*] things will change that much. ‖彼はその事について何もかも知っているのではないかと思う I *suspect* (*that*) he knows everything about it.（➤ suspect は think よりも当たっている確率が低いことを暗示する）.

▶彼は彼女がなぜパーティーに来ないのかと思った He *wondered why* she didn't come to the party. ‖その悪い知らせをどう切り出そうかと思っていた I *was wondering how* to break the bad news.

8【回想する】▶アルバムを見ながら過ぎし日を思う *reminisce* while looking at pictures in an album.

9【気遣う，配慮する】▶母はいつでもぼくのことを思ってくれている My mother *is* always *thinking of* me. ‖子を思う親の心に勝るものはない Nothing can compare with the *love* of parents *for* their children.

10【愛情を寄せる，恋う】▶浩は今でも芳恵を思っている Hiroshi still *loves* [*cares for*] Yoshie. ‖外国暮らしが長いと，故郷の山河を思うことも多い Since I've lived overseas for a long time, I often *long for* the mountains and rivers [the natural surroundings] of my hometown.

✉ **いつもあなたのことを思っています** I am always *thinking of* you.

おもうぞんぶん 思う存分 to the full, to one's **heart's content**（➤ 後者はやや古風）▶思う存分楽しんだ I have enjoyed myself *to the full.* ‖思う存分旅行を楽しんでいらっしゃい Enjoy your trip *to the full.* ‖彼は実力にふさわしいポストに就いて思う存分の働きをした

お

Having been placed in a position appropriate to his ability, he demonstrated his abilities *to the fullest*. (➤ あとに extent が省略されている) ‖ 冬休みになったら**思う存分**スキーをしたい I want to spend the winter vacation skiing *to my heart's content*.

おもうつぼ 思う壺 ▶今じたばたしたらそれこそ彼の思うつぼさ If you make a fuss now, you'll be *playing* (*right*) *into his hands*. (➤「(敵などの)思うつぼにはまる」の意).

おもおもしい 重々しい **dignified** (威厳に満ちた) ; **solemn** /sɑ́:ləm/ (荘厳な) ▶**重々しい**口調で話す speak in a *dignified* tone ‖ 行列は**重々しい**足取りで進んだ The procession advanced at a *solemn* pace.

おもかげ 面影 ⚠「面影」にぴったり当たる英語はないので, 人の場合は **resemblance** (類似) などを用いるか, 文意をくみ取って意訳する. 場所の場合は **trace** (痕跡) などを用いる.

▶その少年には父親の**面影**がある That boy *has some resemblance to* his father. ‖ 修にはどこか子供の頃の**面影**が残っている Osamu still *retains some of his boyish looks*. ‖ 彼女には昔の**面影**はなかった She *was a shadow of her former self*. (➤「(衰弱して)かつての彼女の幻にすぎなかった」の意) ／She looked *quite different* [*another person*] *from* what she once was.

▶金沢はひっそりした町だが, 華やかだった頃の**面影**を今もとどめている Kanazawa is a quiet city but still retains *some traces* of its former glory [splendor].

おもき 重き ▶私たちの学校では英語に**重きを置いている** Our school *puts stress on* (the study of) English. ／Our school *lays emphasis on* (the study of) English. ‖ 彼は金よりも地位に**重きを置く** He *values* social status above money [wages].

おもくるしい 重苦しい **heavy** ; **oppressive** (息苦しい) ▶空には灰色の雲が**重苦しく**垂れこめていた Gray clouds hung *heavily* in the sky. ‖ 部屋には**重苦しい**雰囲気が漂っていた There was an *oppressive* atmosphere in the room. ‖ 食べ過ぎて胃が**重苦しい** I ate too much and my stomach feels *heavy*.

おもさ 重さ **weight** ▶このスーツケースの**重さ**を当ててごらん Guess the *weight* of this suitcase. ／Guess how much this suitcase weighs. ‖ この包みは**重さ**が5キロある This package *weighs* five kilograms. ‖ オリンピックの日本代表に選ばれて責任の**重さ**を痛感しています Now that I have been chosen as an Olympic athlete representing Japan, I keenly feel *the weight of my responsibility*.

おもし 重し a **weight** ▶母は漬物に**重し**をした Mother laid *a weight* on top of the salted vegetables.

おもしろい 面白い **1【興味深い】** **interesting** (知的な興味をそそる) ; **amusing** (愉快な, 楽しい) ; **enjoyable**, **entertaining** (演劇・音楽などが楽しめる) ; **intriguing** (興味をそそる) ▶**おもしろい**話 an *interesting* [*amusing*] story ‖ この推理小説はとても**おもしろい** This detective story is very *interesting*. ‖ 何か楽器を演奏できるようになれば, 音楽がもっと**おもしろくなる**でしょう If you learn to play a musical instrument, music will *become more interesting* to you. ‖ 何て**おもしろい**芝居なんだろう What an *enjoyable* play ! ‖ のみの市で**おもしろい**ものを見つけた I found something *interesting* [*intriguing*] at a flea market.

▶バドミントンよりテニスのほうが**おもしろい**と思わない？ Don't you think tennis is more *fun* than badminton ? (➤ fun は「おもしろいこと, 楽しくさせるもの」の意の名詞) ‖ 私はスケートはあまり**おもしろい**とは思わない For me, ice skating is no great *fun*. ‖ 旅行でいろいろな人と話をするのは**おもしろい** *It is fun* to talk with a lot of different people during a trip. ‖ 遠足はとても**おもしろかった** We *had lots of fun* on the outing.

▶きみの新著, **おもしろく**読んだよ Your new book was *interesting* to read. ‖ このDVDはとても**おもしろかった** I *enjoyed* this DVD very much. (➤「楽しんだ」の意) ‖ ビデオゲームのどこが**おもしろい**のかわからない I can't see the *fascination* of video games. ／I can't see *what people find so fascinating* about video games.

▶独りで旅をしてもちっとも**おもしろくない** Traveling alone is*n't fun* [*enjoyable*] at all. ‖ あの先生の授業は**おもしろくない** (＝退屈だ) That teacher's lessons *are boring*. ‖ きみは**おもしろい人**だね You're *quite a character*. (➤「おもしろい人」を a delightful person のようにもいう. この delightful は「周囲の人を楽しくさせる」) ‖ **対話**「沖縄へダイビングに行こうよ」「ええ, **おもしろそう**ね」"How about going diving in Okinawa ?" "*Sounds like fun*." (➤ 文頭に that が省略されている).

> **あなたの英語はどう響く?**
> 日本人はとかく「おもしろい」＝interesting と考えて interesting を使い過ぎる傾向があるが, 例えば「サーフィンはおもしろい」を Surfing is *interesting*. と訳すのは不自然. interesting は「(知的好奇心をかきたてるので)おもしろい」という意味だからである. Surfing is *a lot of fun*. ／Surfing is *enjoyable*. ／I *like to* surf. などのように言うのが適切.

2【滑稽だ】 **funny** /fʌ́ni/ ▶**おもしろい人** a funny person ／a joker (➤ 後者は「冗談を言う人」) ‖ あのピエロの帽子は何て**おもしろい**んだろう What a *funny* hat that clown is wearing ! ‖ 武はよく**おもしろいこと**を言ってみんなを笑わせようとする Takeshi often tries to make people laugh by saying something *funny*. ‖ そのジョーク, どこが**おもしろい**の？ What's *funny* about that joke ?

3【好ましい】 ▶あいつにくそみそに言われて**おもしろくない** *It's no fun at all* the way he puts me down. ‖ けさは**おもしろい**ように魚が釣れた This morning I caught *almost as many* fish *as I had wanted* [*hoped*] *to*.

おもしろおかしく 面白おかしく ▶彼はアフリカ旅行での失敗談を**おもしろおかしく**話してくれた He told us quite *comically* [*humorously*] about the blunders he made during his trip in Africa.

おもしろがる 面白がる ▶少年は漫画を読んで**おもしろがった** The boy *amused himself* by reading the comic books. ／The boy *enjoyed* reading the comic books.

おもしろさ 面白さ **interest** (興味) ; **fun** (楽しさ) ▶一通り操作できるようになってパソコンの**おもしろさ**がわかってきた I'm beginning to *see why people enjoy* PCs now that I can use mine quite well.

おもしろはんぶん 面白半分に **for fun** ▶子供たちは**おもしろ半分に**いたずらをするものだ Children play tricks *for fun*. ‖ 私は**おもしろ半分に**言っただけです I *was* only *kidding*.

おもしろみ 面白味 ▶**おもしろみのない**人 an *uninteresting* [*insipid*] person ‖ 学問の**おもしろみ**がわかってきた I am coming to understand [appreciate] the *pleasure* of learning.

おもたい 重たい →重い.

おもだった 主立った・重立った **main, principal** ▶石川県のおもだった産物は何ですか What are the *principal* products of Ishikawa Prefecture? ‖ 先生は私に日本のおもだった川をいくつか挙げてごらんと言った The teacher told me to give the names of several of the *main* [*chief*] rivers of Japan. →主な, 主要な.

おもちゃ 玩具 a **toy** ▶おもちゃのピアノ a *toy* piano ‖ 子供はおもちゃで遊ぶのが好きだ Children like playing with *toys*. ‖ スプーンをおもちゃにしてはいけません Don't *play with* your spoon. ‖ おもちゃとばかにしてはいけません. ちゃんとパンが焼けます You shouldn't dismiss this as *a toy*. You can bake bread with it.

▶《比喩的》彼はあなたのことをおもちゃにしている(=もてあそんでいる)んじゃないの? I think he's just *playing* [*toying*] *with* you. ‖ 私は(あなたの)おもちゃじゃないわよ I'm not *a toy*, you know!

‖**おもちゃ箱** a toy box / a toy chest ‖ **おもちゃ屋** a toyshop.

おもて 表

訳語メニュー
裏に対して →the front **1, 2**
戸外 →the outside **3**
野球の →the top **4**

1【薄いものの表面】the front, a **face** ▶その封筒の表に宛名を書きなさい Write your address on *the front* of the envelope. ‖ この紙はどちらが表ですか Which side of this piece of paper goes *up*? ‖ この生地の表と裏の区別ができますか? Can you tell *the right* (*side*) from the wrong side of this piece of cloth? ‖ 表を上にしてトランプを並べなさい Place the cards *face up* in a row. ‖《コインを投げて》さあ, 表か裏か? *Heads or tails*? (➤ heads (人の像が彫られている面) が「表」, tails が「裏」).

2【建物などの前面】the front ▶わが家は表から見ると大邸宅だが, 裏へ回るとそれほどでもない Our house looks huge from *the front*, but when you go around in back you can see that it's not all that big. ‖ 裏口へこそこそ回らずに, 表から堂々と入って来い Don't sneak in the back door. Come in openly *through the front door*. ‖ 表の通りで交通事故があった There was a traffic accident in *the street out front*.

3【戸外】the outside ▶表で遊びなさい Go play *outside*. (➤ インフォーマルでは Go and play ... よりも Go play のほうがふつう) ‖ 表はもう暗い It is dark now *outside*. (➤ 以上2例の outside は副詞) ‖ 突然の地震に驚いて表へ飛び出した Startled at the sudden earthquake, I dashed out *into the street*. ‖ 表へ出るときは帽子をかぶりなさい Put your hat on before you *go out*. ‖《けんかで》やるんなら表へ出ろ! You want a [to] fight? *Step outside!* (➤ 話し手だけがすでに表にいるのなら Come outside! と言う).

4【野球】the top, the first half ▶西武の1回表の攻撃は三者凡退に終わった Three Lions batters in a row were retired in *the top* of the first inning.

おもてざた 表沙汰 ▶秘密にしておいたことが表沙汰になった A matter which I had been keeping secret *was made public*. ‖ 誰でも子供の不始末は表沙汰にしたくないものだ People don't want to *make* their children's misconduct *public knowledge*. ‖ 汚職が表沙汰になった The corruption *was brought to light*.

おもてだつ 表立つ ▶捜査員が1時間前に中に入りましたが, その後表立った動きは何もありません The investigators went inside an hour ago, and since then, there has been no *visible* change (from outside).

おもてどおり 表通り a **main street** ▶彼の店は表通りに面しているので, 繁盛している His shop *is on the main street*, so it does (a) good business.

おもてむき 表向き ▶建て前とはある個人が属している集団の表向きの見解である 'Tatemae' is the *official* viewpoint [position] of the group to which a person belongs. ‖ その夫婦は表向きはなかなか円満そうに見えた *Outwardly*, the couple seemed to be very happy. ‖ 私は表向きは病気ということにして学校を休んでスケートに行った I played hooky *on the pretext of* illness and went skating. (➤ pretext /príːtekst/ は「口実」).

おもと 万年青 《植物》a **Rohdea japonica.**

おもな 主な

main (同種の人や物の中で最重要の; 主要部を成す); **chief** (勢力・重要度などがほかより勝った); **principal** (勢力・重要度などの順位が第1位の; 最も中心的な, 代表的な) ▶主な登場人物 the *main* [*principal*] characters ‖ これがサッカー部の主なメンバーです These are the *main* members of the soccer team. ‖ そのサーカスの主な呼び物は空中ぶらんこと綱渡りである The *chief* [*principal*] attractions of the circus are the trapeze and tightrope walking.

おもなが 面長 ▶彼女は面長だ She *has an oval face*. (➤ oval は「だ円の」) 《参考》a long face は「浮かない顔」の意になる.

¹おもに 重荷 1【重い荷物】a **heavy load** ▶重荷を背負って山を登る climb the mountain with *a heavy load* on one's back.

2【負担】a **burden** ▶子供は親にとって重荷になることがある Children can be *a* (*heavy*) *burden* to their parents. ‖ 私には両親の期待に添うのが重荷だ Coming up to my parents' expectations is *a burden* (for me).

²おもに 主に **mainly, chiefly** (主として); **mostly** (大部分は) ▶この辞書は主に高校生を対象にしている This dictionary is *mainly* [*chiefly*] intended for senior high school students. ‖ 黒のフォーマルスーツは主にお葬式のときに着ます We wear black formal suits *mainly* for funerals.

▶生け花クラブのメンバーは主に女性です The members of the flower arranging club are *mostly* women. ‖ 負傷者は主に子供だった The injured were *mostly* children. / *Most of* the injured were children.

おもねる 阿る **fawn** 《upon, on》; **flatter** +㊐ (へつらう); **play up** 《to》(機嫌をとる) ▶権力者におもねる *fawn upon* [*flatter* / *play up to* / *curry favor with*] those in power.

おもはゆい 面映ゆい **feel embarrassed** ▶受賞おめでとうと会社のみんなに言われて面はゆくてたまりませんでした Everybody in the office congratulated me on winning the prize. I *felt both pleased and embarrassed*.

おもみ 重み **weight** ▶雪の重みで屋根が潰れた The roof gave way *under the weight of* the snow.

▶彼女の発言には重みがある Her words *carry weight*. ‖ この町を歩くと歴史の重みを感じる Walking

お

through the town makes one feel *the weight* of its (long) history.

おもむき 趣 **1【味わい】**▶趣のある庭 a garden built *with good taste* ／a garden *with a quiet charm* [*a quiet sophistication*].

2【様子】▶この辺りにはまだ田園の趣が残っている This area still retains a rural *touch* [*feeling*].

おもむく 赴く ▶その外交官は新しい任地に赴いた(＝向かった) The diplomat *proceeded to* [*left for*] his [her] new post.

▶欲望の赴くままに行動してはならない You must not act *just as you please* [purely *in accordance with* your desires].

おもむろに 徐に **slowly**(ゆっくり)；**quietly**(静かに)；**calmly**(落ち着いて) ▶おもむろに立ち上がる stand up *slowly* [*calmly*].

おももち 面持ち a **facial expression** ▶住民たちは不安な面持ちで増水する川を見つめた The residents watched the river rising with worried *expressions on their faces*.

おもや 母屋 **the main house.**

おもゆ 重湯 **(thin) rice gruel** [**porridge**]. →かゆ.

おもらし お漏らし ▶またお漏らしをしたのね You'*ve wet your diaper* [*your bed*] again！(➤ 前者は「おしめ」, 後者は「ベッド」の場合) ‖ お漏らししちゃだめよ Don't *pee in your pants*！(➤ pee は「おしっこする」) ‖ 赤ちゃんがまたお漏らしをしたみたい I think the baby'*s* just *wet himself* [*herself*] again.

[1]**おもり 重り** a **weight**；a **sinker** (釣り用の) ▶釣り糸に重りをつける *weight* a (fishing) line.

[2]**おもり お守り** **babysitting** ▶私, 妹のお守りをしないといけないから遊びに行けないの I can't go out to play with you, because I have to *sit with* [*look after*] my baby sister.

おもわく 思惑 ▶人の思わくを気にしていては何もできない You won't be able to do a thing if you worry about *what other people think*. ‖ 事はなかなか思わくどおりには運ばないものだ Things do not always go *as one would want*. ▶株を思惑買いする(＝株に投機する) *speculate* (in stock).

おもわしくない 思わしくない ▶就職の面接の手応えは彼には思わしくなかった He did*n't feel that* his job interview *had gone as well as he had hoped* (it would). ‖ 体の具合が思わしくない I'm *not in good shape*.

おもわず 思わず **unconsciously**(無意識に)；**involuntarily**(無意識のうちに, 意図せず；不本意にも)；**in spite of** oneself (我知らず) ▶彼女はラブシーンを見ていて思わずため息をついた She sighed *unconsciously* [*without realizing it*] at the love scene. ‖ 映画のラストシーンに感動して思わず拍手をしてしまった I was so deeply moved by the last scene of the movie that I *involuntarily* applauded. ‖ その漫画を読んでいて思わず吹き出した While reading the comic book, I burst out laughing *in spite of myself*. ‖ 彼女のジョークに思わず笑ってしまった I *couldn't help* laugh*ing* at her joke.

おもわせぶり 思わせぶり ▶その男は彼女に思わせぶりな視線を向けた That man gave her a *significant* look.

おもわぬ 思わぬ ▶白鵬は思わぬ不覚を取って悔しがった Hakuho met with an *unexpected* defeat that caused him bitter disappointment. ‖ 思わぬときに彼がやって来た He came *when least expected*.

おもわれる 思われる **seem**(主観的に判断して)；**appear** (少なくとも外見では) ▶彼の言ったことは私にはおかしく思われる What he said *seems* strange to me. ‖ 彼はきみに何かを隠しているように思われる He *seems* to be hiding something from you. ／*It seems that* he is keeping something from you. ‖ 高そうな毛皮のコートを着ているところから見るとあの女性は金持ちと思われる Judging from the expensive fur coat she is wearing, that woman *appears* (*to be*) rich.

▶私はみんなに秀才だと思われている I *am thought of* as a bright student by everyone. ／ Everyone thinks of me as a bright student.

おもんじる 重んじる **value** ＋㊐ (評価する)；**respect** ＋㊐ (尊重する) ▶私は勝つことよりもフェアプレーを重んじる I *value* fair play above winning. ‖ 彼は女性の意見を重んじる He *respects* women's opinions. ‖ 日本の封建社会では家柄が重んじられた In feudal times in Japan, one's family's social standing *carried great weight*. (➤ carry weight は「重要視される」の意).

[1]**おや 親** **parents**(両親)；a **parent** (父または母) ▶親の愛 *parental* love ‖ 子供を育てるのは親の責任だ *Parents* have a responsibility to raise [bring up] their children. ‖ きみは親の言うことを聞くべきだ You should obey your *parents*. ‖ 生みの親より育ての親とよく言われる It is often said that *one's foster parents are better than one's natural parents*.

▶まったくどんな育て方をしたのだろう. 親の顔が見てみたいよ I wonder how his [her] parents brought him [her] up. I'*d like to see their faces*. ‖ 息子は職にも就かないで, いつまで家でぶらぶらしているんだろう. 親の心子知らずだね I wonder how long my son will keep loafing around the house without getting a job. Really, *children don't understand their parents' feelings* [*how their parents feel*].

ことわざ 親は無くとも子は育つ Children grow up even without their parents. ／Nature is a good mother. ‖ この親にしてこの子あり Like father, like son. ／ Like mother, like daughter.

▶《トランプで》今度はきみが親(＝配る番)だよ It's your *deal*.

‖ **親会社** a parent company.

☛ **生みの親, 育ての親** (→見出語)

直訳の落とし穴「私の親」

(1)「親に相談して決めます」「親が迎えに来てくれます」などを日本人学習者はそのまま(×)I'll talk with my parent before I decide., (×) My parent is coming to pick me up. と単数形で使いがち. 英語ではどちらか 1 人の場合は, my father または my mother とはっきり言う. my や your など所有格をつけて parent を使うのは「両親」を表す my [your] parents に限るのがよい.

(2)同様に,「日曜日に親戚の所に遊びに行ってきた」は, 英語では relative としないで, uncle(おじ), aunt (おば), cousin(いとこ), nephew(おい)などと具体的に言うことが多い. さらには名前まで言って I went to see my uncle Bob on Sunday. とすることもふつう.

[2]**おや** **Oh！**(驚きなどを表して)；**Oh, boy！**(➤ 単に Oh！または Boy！とだけ言うよりも強意) ▶おや！もうこんな時間だ *Oh* [*Oh, God*] *!* It's quite late already. (➤ キリスト教徒の中には Oh, God！を神の名をみだりに口にする不敬として嫌悪する人もいる) ‖ おやまあ！*Oh, boy！*／

My goodness!（➤ 後者は主に女性が用いる）‖おや，どなたかと思いました（あなたでしたか）*Why!* It's you.（➤ 主に《米》で用いられる；《英》では古風）／Look at you.（➤ いつもと違って着飾っているときなどにいう）‖おや，これ何だろう？ *Well*, what's this?（➤ ちゅうちょを表す）．

おやおもい 親思い **be devoted to** one's **parents** ▶息子は親思いの優しい子です My son is kindhearted and *considerate of his parents*.

おやおや ▶おやおや，これは何の騒ぎなの？ *Oh dear* [*Oh my*]! What's going on here?（➤ 両者とも主に女性が用いる）‖おやおや，元気な赤ちゃんだこと *Well, well*, what a lively baby he [she] is!（➤ 古風な言い方）‖おやおや，ひどい成績を取ったもんだね *Oh, no* ... your grades are horrible.（➤「こんなのないよ；何ということだ」という気持ち）．

おやがかり 親掛かり ▶私はまだ親がかりの身なので，ぜいたくはできません I still *depend on my parents economically*, so I can't spend money on luxuries. ‖彼は35歳にもなって親がかりの結婚式を挙げた Although he was 35, he got married *at his parents' expense*.

おやかた 親方 a **master**（職人などの）；a **foreman**（作業員を監督する人）；a **boss**（親分）▶相撲の親方 a stable *master* ‖大工の親方 a *master* carpenter. ▶親方日の丸の考え方を捨てなければうちは行き詰まってしまう If we don't give up *the idea that the government will foot the bill*, we will go under.（●「政府が費用の面倒を見る」と考えた英文）．

おやがわり 親代わり ▶母親を亡くしてからは，彼女がずっと兄弟の親代わりをしてきた After her mother died, she *acted like a mother* to her brothers.

おやくしょしごと お役所仕事 →役所．

おやこ 親子 **parent(s) and child(ren)** ▶キリンの親子 a giraffe with [and] its baby ‖ライオンの親子 a lion and its cub ‖あの2人は親子だ They are *father* [*mother*] *and son* [*daughter*].（➤ They are parent and child. は堅い表現）．
▶日曜日の動物園は親子連れでごった返していた On Sunday the zoo was packed with *families with young children*. ‖最近親子のきずなが薄くなっていると思う I think that *the emotional ties between parents and children* have gotten weaker recently. ‖彼女は親子ほども年の違う男性と結婚した She married a man who was *old enough to be her father*.
‖**親子電話** a telephone and its extension(s) ‖**親子丼** a bowl of rice topped with chicken and eggs.

おやこうこう 親孝行

> **解説** (1)「親孝行」は儒教に影響された東洋的概念で，ぴったりの対応語はない．filial piety という語はあるが，これは「(親に対する)子としての敬愛(の気持ち)」の意で，日本語とはずれがある．
> (2)「あいつは親孝行な息子です」は He's a good son. または He's good [considerate] to us. とするのがよい．なお，やや改まった言い方には a dutiful son がある．

▶今まで面倒をかけてきたのだから，これからは親孝行をしなくっちゃ Since I've lived off my parents for many years, I'll have to *take good care of* them from now on.（➤「世話をする，大事にする」の意）．
ことわざ 親孝行したい頃には親はなし We rarely realize the debt we owe our parents until they are gone.（➤ 日本語からの意訳；「親が死ぬまでは親の恩になかなか気がつかないものだ」の意）．

おやごころ 親心 ▶それが親心というものですよ That is what *parental love* is all about.

おやごさん 親御さん **parents** ▶親御さんはお元気でしょうか How are *your parents* doing?

おやじ 親父 one's **dad** ▶おやじ，オートバイ買ってくれる？ *Dad*, will you buy me a motorcycle? ‖ラーメン屋のおやじさん（＝所有者）*the proprietor* of a ramen shop.
‖**おやじギャグ** a middle-aged man's corny joke（中年男の使い古された冗談）．

おやしお 親潮 **the Oyashio Current, the Kurile Current**（千島海流）．

おやしらず 親知らず a **wisdom tooth** ▶親知らずを抜いてもらう have *a wisdom tooth* [one of one's *wisdom teeth*] pulled (out).

おやすい お安い ▶ 対話「テーブル運ぶの手伝ってくれる？」「お安いご用さ」"Please give me a hand with this table." "Sure. *No problem.*"

おやすくない お安くない ▶きみたち，真っ昼間からデートかい．お安くないね You two are seeing each other all day? Looks like *you're (getting) pretty serious about each other*.

おやすみ お休み ▶お休みなさい *Good night*.／*Sleep well*.（➤ 家族・同居人などに）／*Sleep tight*.（➤ 家族などごく親しい人に）‖おじいちゃんにお休みなさいを言ってらっしゃい Go and *say good night* to your grandpa. ‖お母さまはもうお休みになられましたか Has your mother *gone to bed* yet?

おやだま 親玉 a **ringleader**（悪者の一味の）；a **mastermind**（陰謀の主謀者）▶その陰謀の親玉は誰だったのか Who was the *mastermind* of that plot?

おやつ お八つ an **afternoon snack**, a **snack**（食間の軽食）；《英》**(afternoon) tea**（午後の軽食）▶おやつですよ *Teatime!* ‖ぼくは学校から帰っておやつを食べた I ate [had] *a snack* after I came home from school.

おやばか 親馬鹿 a parent who lavishly praises his [her] children（➤ 説明的な訳）▶息子にあんな高い車を買ってやるなんて，あいつもいいかげん親ばかだよ He's what I'd call *a* real *doting parent* to have bought his son an expensive car like that.（➤ doting parent は「(子供を)溺愛する親」）．

おやばなれ 親離れ ▶あの人もいい年をして親離れができてないよ He hasn't *left the nest* at his age.／Despite his age, he still hasn't been able to *become independent of his parents*.

おやふこう 親不孝

> **解説**「親孝行」と同様，英語にはこれの対応表現はない．したがって，「あいつは親不孝な息子 [娘] です」は He's a bad son. とか She's a bad daughter. のように言う．→親孝行．

おやぶん 親分 a **boss** ▶親分，あっしに任せてくだせえ *Boss*, leave it to me. ‖あんまり親分風を吹かせるんじゃあない Don't *be so bossy*. ‖彼には親分肌のところがある He's *a big-brother type*.

おやまのたいしょう お山の大将 ▶彼はお山の大将俺一人というような顔をしている He acts as if he thinks he's *the cock of the walk* [*(the) king of the castle*]. →井の中のかわず．

おやもと 親元 ▶私は親元から月々9万円の仕送りを受けています I get a monthly allowance of 90,000 yen *from* (*my parents back*) *home*. ‖ 彼女は仙台の大学に進学するので, まもなく**親元を離れる** Since she will be attending a university in Sendai, she will soon be *leaving her parents* [*the nest*].

おやゆずり 親譲り ▶**親譲り**の財産でもなければ今どきあんないい生活はできないよ He would not be able to live as well as he does if he hadn't *inherited* property *from his parents*. ‖ 不器用なのは**親譲りだ** I *got* my clumsiness *from my father* [*mother*]. ／Clumsiness *runs in my family*. (➤ run は「(性格などが家系に)伝わる」).

おやゆび 親指 a **thumb** /θʌm/ (手の) ; a **big toe** (足の) ▶**親指**にとげが刺さった I got a splinter in my *thumb*. →**指**.

おゆ お湯 →**湯**.

およぎ 泳ぎ **swimming**(水泳) ; a **swim** (一泳ぎ)
▶弟は**泳ぎ**がうまい My brother *is good at swimming*. ／My brother *is a good swimmer*. ‖ 私は**泳ぎ**ができない I *can't swim*. ／I *don't know how to swim*. ‖ プールに**泳ぎに行こう** *Let's go for a swim* [*go swimming*] in the pool. ‖ この川で**一泳ぎしよう** Let's *have a swim* in the river. ‖ あの島までは**一泳ぎだ** It's *just a short swim* (over) to that island.

およぐ 泳ぐ **swim** ▶長良川で**泳ぐ** *swim* in the Nagara River ‖ 川を**泳いで渡る** *swim across* a river ‖ どのくらい(遠くまで)**泳げる**? How far (out) can you *swim*? ‖ この辺りの海で**泳ぐ**のは危険だ It is dangerous to *swim* in the sea around here. ／The sea around here is dangerous to *swim* in. ‖ きみは**クロール**[**背泳ぎ**]で**泳ぐ**ことができますか Can you *swim the crawl* [*the backstroke*]? (➤ swim の代わりに do も可) ‖ やっと25メートル**泳げる**ようになった Finally, I *got to be able to swim* 25 meters.
▶5月の空にこいのぼりが**泳いでいた** Carp streamers *were billowing* [*swimming*] in the May sky. ‖ 確かな証拠が挙がるまで, もう少しホシを**泳がせておこう** Shall we *leave* the culprit *at large* [*let* the culprit *remain free*] a while longer till we have definite proof? (➤ at large は「(犯人などが)逃走中で」).

およそ **1** 【**だいたい**】 **about, around** (➤《米》では後者もふつう) ; **approximately** (概算で) →**約** ▶彼は**およそ**1時間前に家へ帰った He went home *about* one hour ago. ‖ あの絵は**およそ**100万円の価値がある That painting is valued at *approximately* [*around*] one million yen.
▶この車の修理費は**およそ**どのくらいですか Can you give (me) a *rough estimate* (*of*) how much it will cost to repair this car?
2 【**全然**】 **quite** ▶その小説は**およそ**つまらなかった The novel was *quite* boring. ‖ ぼくは**およそ**金とは縁がない Money and I are complete strangers. ‖ 小森氏は**およそ**学者といった風体ではない Mr. Komori does*n't* come across as [does*n't* look and act like] a scholar *in the least*.

およばずながら 及ばずながら ▶**及ばずながら**お手伝いしましょう I will help you *all I can*. (➤ all one can は「できる限り」) ‖ 対話「先日話した翻訳の仕事だけど, きみの力を借りられないかね」「**及ばずながら**お手伝いするよ」"Can you help me with the translation I told you about the other day?" "*I'm not very good at* translation, but I'll help (all I can)."

およばない 及ばない ▶わがチームの力では彼らの**足元にも及ばない** Our team's ability *is nowhere near* theirs. ‖ 社長としてはX氏はその前任者たちには**遠く及ばない** Mr. X *cannot measure up to* his predecessors as (company) president.
▶今さら後悔してももう**及ばない**よ It's no use crying over spilt milk. (➤「こぼれたミルクのことを嘆いても始まらない」の意の英語のことわざ) ‖ きみが来るには**及ばない**よ You *don't have to* come.

およばれ お呼ばれ ▶今夜はお友だちの家へ**お呼ばれ**なの I *am invited to* dinner at my friend's house this evening.

[1]および お呼び ▶奥さま, **お呼び**でございますか Did you *call* [*want*] me, madam? ‖ あんたなんか**お呼びじゃない**(＝用はない)よ *None of your business*. ／*You're not wanted* here.

[2]および 及び **and** ▶東京・大阪**および**京都の知事が顔を合わせた The governors of Tokyo, Osaka *and* Kyoto met. ‖ 教科書はA書店, B書店**および**C書店でも購入できます Your textbooks are available at Bookstores A, B *and* C.

およびごし 及び腰 **half-hearted, wishy-washy.**

およびたて お呼び立て ▶**お呼び立て**して申し訳ありません I'm very sorry to have *asked* you *to come*. ／I'm very sorry to have *made* you *come*. 《**参考**》日本人は電話でもこう言うが, 英米人は一般に電話でこうは言わない. ただし,「夜遅く**お呼び立て**して申し訳ありません」に相当する言い方として I'm very sorry for calling you up so late at night [at such a late hour]. がある.

およぶ 及ぶ **1** 【**広い範囲に広がる**】 **reach** (＋目) (達する) ; **extend** (＋目) (広がる)
▶その年の冷害は東北地方全域に**及んだ** Damage from the cold wave *extended* across the entire Tohoku district that year. ‖ 光害は大都市の郊外にまで**及んでいる**(＝広がっている) Light pollution *has spread to* [*has reached*] the outskirts of large cities. ‖ きみにまでとばっちりが**及ぶ**とは思ってもみなかったよ I never thought you would *be involved* in such a mess.
2 【**行き着く**】 ▶会議はしばしば深夜に**及んだ** Conferences often *lasted until late at night* [*stretched deep into the night*]. ‖ **この期**(ご)**に及んで**逃げるとはひきょうだ Shame on you for trying to escape *at this stage of the game*. ‖ 話が小学校時代のことに**及んだ** The conversation *extended* to our elementary school days. ‖ 私の**力の及ぶ限り**お手伝いしましょう Let me help you *as much as I can*. ／Let me do *everything I can* to help you.
3 【**数値が達する**】 ▶建築費は総額1000億円に**及んだ** The total cost of construction *amounted* [*came*] *to* one hundred billion yen. (➤「総計…になった」の意) ‖ デモの参加者は10万人に**及んだ** *As many as* 100,000 people took part in the demonstration.
4 【**匹敵する**】 ▶日本史では彼に**及ぶ**者はいない No one can *equal* [*match*] him in Japanese history. (➤ equal は「…と同等である」, match は「…と互角である」の意) ‖ 幹子さんの英語に比べたら, 私なんか**及びもつきません**よ My English *is no match for* Mikiko's.
☛ **及ばない** (→見出語)

およぼす 及ぼす ▶その教師は教え子たちに大きな**影響を及ぼした** The teacher *had* [*exerted*] *a* great *influence on* his students. (➤ exert は堅い語) ‖ その台風は九州に大きな**被害を及ぼした** The typhoon seriously *damaged* the island of Kyushu. ‖ 麻薬は青

少年に大きな害を及ぼしている Drugs *do* a lot of *harm to* young people.

オランウータン《動物》an **orangutan(g)** /əræ̃ŋətæn ‖ ɔːr-/.

オランダ **the Netherlands** /néðəˀləndz/, **Holland** (➤後者は通称) ━形 **オランダの** Dutch

‖**オランダ語** Dutch ‖**オランダ人** a Dutchman (男), a Dutchwoman(女).

1 **おり 檻** a **cage**(鳥獣用の); an **aviary** /éɪvieri/ (動物園などで鳥を入れる大型の); a **hutch**(小動物・ペット用の); a **pen** (市場・品評会などで一時的に家畜を入れる).

2 **おり 折** **1**【時】▶私は折に触れて(＝時々)彼女のことを思う I think of her *at times*. ‖私は3日間長崎に滞在した折に原爆記念館を訪れた *While* I was staying in Nagasaki for three days, I visited the Atomic Bomb Memorial Hall.

✉ **ご上京の折にはぜひお立ち寄りください** Please visit me [drop in] *if you have a chance* to come to Tokyo. ／Come and see me *when* you are in Tokyo.

2【機会】an **opportunity** ▶折があったら彼女にそう伝えます I'll tell her so *at the first opportunity*. ／I'll tell her so *the next time I see her*. (➤後者は「今度会ったら」の意).

☛ 折から (→見出語)

3 **おり 織り** a **weave** ▶平織り *a plain weave* ‖手織りの着物地 *hand-woven* kimono fabric.

4 **おり 澱** **dregs** ▶ワインのおり *the dregs* of wine.

おりあい 折り合い ▶彼女はおしゅうとめさんと折り合いが悪い She *is on bad terms with* her mother-in-law. ／She and her mother-in-law *do not get along* [*on*] *well*. ‖彼とは折り合いがついたの? Did you *come to an understanding* [*agreement*] *with* him?

おりあう 折り合う **come to an agreement**(話がまとまる) ▶我々は利益を山分けにするという条件で折り合った We *came to an agreement* on condition that we should divide the profit equally. →妥協.

おりあしく 折悪しく ▶折あしく接近中の台風のため連絡船は欠航となった *Unluckily*, the ferryboat service was cancelled due to the approaching typhoon.

おりいって 折り入って ▶折り入ってご相談があるのですが *I'm sorry to trouble you*, but I have something I'd like to talk to you about. ‖折り入って頼みがあるのですが I'd like to ask you *a special favor*.

オリーブ《植物》an **olive** ▶オリーブの枝 an *olive* branch (➤平和の象徴) ‖オリーブ色のドレス an *olive* dress ‖**オリーブ油** olive oil.

オリエンテーション (an) **orientation** ▶オリエンテーションの期間 a *orientation* period ‖ 3日間のオリエンテーションを受ける receive three days of *orientation* ‖新入生のためのオリエンテーションを行う hold *an orientation session* for freshmen.

オリエンテーリング **orienteering** /ɔ̀ːriəntíərɪŋ/.

おりおり 折々 ▶ 折々の歌 *occasional* verse [tanka], *seasonal* verse ‖この高原では四季折々の花を楽しむことができる In these highlands, you can enjoy the flowers *of each of the four seasons*.

おりかえし 折り返し **1**【衣服の】a **cuff** /kʌf/,《英》a **turn-up**(ズボンの裾の); a **lapel** /ləpél/ (襟の) ▶このズボンには折り返しがない These trousers have no *cuffs*.

2【引き返し】▶ただ今事故のため品川・横浜間の折り返し運転をいたしております Due to an accident, we can only provide *shuttle train service* between Shinagawa and Yokohama.

‖(マラソンの) **折り返し地点** the halfway stage [point ／mark].

3【すぐに】▶折り返しお電話します I'll *call* you *back* (with an answer) right away. ‖担当者に折り返しお電話をさせます I'll *have* the person in charge *call you back*.

✉ **折り返しお返事ください** Please reply *by return mail*.

おりかえす 折り返す ▶袖を折り返す *turn up* [*fold back*] one's sleeve ‖走者はここで折り返して残り半分を走ります The runners will *make a turn* here and run the remaining half back.

おりかさなる 折り重なる ▶電車が急停止したので乗客は折り重なって倒れた The train stopped abruptly, so the passengers *fell over each other*.

おりかさねる 折り重ねる ▶古新聞を折り重ねておく *fold and pile up* old newspapers.

おりがみ 折り紙 **origami**(➤英語化している)

日本紹介 ✉ **折り紙は色鮮やかな正方形の紙を鳥, 動物, 花などの形に折っていく伝統的な紙の芸術です. のりやはさみは使いません. 小さな子は幼稚園で習いますが, 大人の中にはアートとして本格的に作る人もいます. 代表的な形は鶴で, できたものは「折り鶴」と呼ばれます** Origami is the traditional art of folding square pieces of brightly colored paper into forms such as birds, animals, and flowers. No glue, paste or scissors are used. Little children do origami in kindergarten, but it is also an art form that some adults engage in seriously. The most famous shape is the crane which is called *orizuru* (literally : folded crane).

▶《慣用表現》彼の人物はぼくが折り紙をつけます(＝保証します)よ I *stand guarantee for* him. ‖このつぼは折り紙つきだ This is a *certified* vase. (➤certified は「保証書付きの」) ／This is a vase (that has been) *certified for authenticity*.

おりから 折から ▶折からの強風にあおられて火はたちまち広がった Fanned by the strong wind, the fire spread quickly. (➤「折からの」はこの文では the で示されている).

✉ **寒さ厳しき折から御身大切に** Please take care of yourself *in this cold weather* [*at this very cold time of the year*].

おりぐち 降り口 **the way out**.

おりこみ 折り込み ▶折り込み広告を見て買い物に出かけた I felt like going shopping when I saw the *ad insert*.

‖(雑誌の) **折り込みページ** a foldout, a gatefold ; a centerfold(特に大型の).

おりこむ 織り込む ▶金糸銀糸を織り込んだ豪華な帯 a gorgeous obi *interwoven with* gold and silver threads ‖その小説には彼女のバリ島での体験が織り込まれている Her experiences in Bali *are woven* [*incorporated*] *into* the novel.

オリジナリティー **originality** ▶そのデザインはオリジナリティーに欠ける[富む] The design is lacking [rich] in *originality*.

オリジナル **the original** ▶オリジナルな企画 an *original* plan ‖これは私が日本語に翻訳した小説のオリジナル(＝原本)です This is the *original novel* that I translated into Japanese. ‖当店オリジナルの特製ラーメン

special house ramen ‖ 歌手はオリジナル曲を10曲歌った The singer sang ten of her [his] *original songs*.

‖オリジナルグッズ official merchandize (➤ original goods は「ユニークな品(物)」の意).

おりたたみ 折り畳み ▶折り畳み式の椅子 a *folding* [*foldaway*] chair ‖ 折り畳み式の傘 a *folding* umbrella / a *portable* umbrella / a *collapsible* umbrella / a *pocket* umbrella (➤最後の言い方が最も小型のものを指す) ‖ 折り畳み式のナイフ a *clasp* knife ‖ このベッドは折り畳み式になっていますか Is this a *folding* bed [cot]?

おりたたむ 折り畳む **fold** +◉ ▶(封筒に入れる前に)手紙を折り畳む *fold* a letter ‖ 彼女はその紙を半分に折り畳んだ She *folded* the paper *in half*. ‖ 椅子を折り畳んでから退室しなさい Please *fold* the chairs before leaving the room.

おりづる 折り鶴 a **folded** (**paper**) **crane.** ➝折り紙.

おりまげる 折り曲げる **bend** +◉ (曲げる); **fold** +◉ (紙や布を折り畳む) ▶この柳の枝,折り曲げられる? Can you *bend* this willow branch? ‖ この書類はコンピュータで処理しますので折り曲げないでください The form will be processed by computer, so do not *fold* it.

おりめ 折り目 a **crease**(ズボンの) ▶(アイロンをかけて)ズボンに折り目をつける *put a neat crease* in one's pants ‖ あの人のズボンは折り目がついていない(=プレスが効いていない) His pants *are not well-pressed*. ‖ 他人の本のページに折り目をつけてはいけない Do not *dog-ear* the pages of other people's books. (➤ dog-ear は「(目印に)ページの隅を折り曲げる」).

▶折り目正しい青年 a young man *with good manners* / a *well-mannered* young man.

[1]おりもの 織物 (**woven**) **cloth**; **textile goods** (繊維製品) ▶(京都の)西陣は織物で有名だ Nishijin is famous for its *woven cloth*.

‖織物業者 a textile manufacturer ‖ 織物産業 the textile industry ‖ 絹[毛]織物 silk [woolen] fabrics.

[2]おりもの 下り物 (a) **vaginal discharge.**

おりよく 折よく **fortunately, luckily** (➤後者は前者よりややインフォーマル) ▶彼は折よく近くを通りかかった漁船に救助された He was saved by a fishing boat which *fortunately* happened to be passing by.

おりる 下りる・降りる

> 📖 訳語メニュー
> 下へ移動する ➝go [come] down **1**
> 乗り物から出る ➝get off **2**
> 途中でやめる ➝quit **3**

1【下方へ移動する】 **go** [**come**] **down** (➤話し手・聞き手から離れた方へ移動する場合は go を,話し手・聞き手のいる方へ移動する場合は come を用いる); **descend** (➤堅い語) ▶階段を1段ずつ下りる *go down* the stairs step by step ‖ 彼らは川の所まで下りていった They *went down* to the river. ‖ すぐに(2階から)下りて来なさい *Come downstairs* right now. ‖ 飛行機がだんだん降りてきた The airplane gradually *descended*.

▶幕が下りる The curtain *falls* [*drops*]. (➤ト書きでは Curtain falls.) ‖ その金庫は厳重に錠が下りていた The safe *was* securely *locked*. ‖ やっと探し当てた店はシャッターが下りていた The shop I took great trouble to find *was closed* with its shutters down.

▶アポロ宇宙飛行計画によって人類は初めて月の表面に降りた(=着地した) Humans *landed* on the surface of the moon for the first time during the Apollo mission.

▶《慣用表現》言いたいことを全部言ったら胸のつかえが下りた After I said all I wanted to say, I *felt relieved*. ‖ 大仕事を成し遂げて肩の荷が下りた Now that I have completed the big job, *I feel a load* [*a burden*] *has been lifted off my shoulders*.

2【乗り物から外へ出る】 **get off** (電車・列車・バスなどから); **get** [**climb**] **out of**(車などから; climb は車体の特定部分に手をかけながらゆっくりと) ▶バスから降りる *get off* a bus (➤「ひょいと飛び降りる」なら hop out of a bus) ‖ 彼女は駅前でタクシーを降りた She *got* [*climbed*] *out of* the taxi in front of the station. ‖ 次の駅で降りますからどうぞお座りください I'*m getting off* at the next stop, so please take this seat. ‖ 豪華船からたくさんの人が降りてきた A lot of people *got off* [*disembarked from*] the luxury liner. (➤ disembark は「(船・飛行機から)降りる」の意の堅い語).

3【仕事などを途中でやめる】 **quit** +◉; **drop out**(抜ける) ▶テレビの番組を降りる *quit* [*leave*] a TV program ‖ 私は主役を降りる気はない I'm not going to *give up* the leading role. ‖《マージャンなどで》きょうはついてない,降りた! Luck is not with me today. *I think I'll drop out*. ‖ 会長を降りる潮時だな It's about time (for me) to *step down* [*resign*] as chairman.

4【許可などが出る】 ▶学部新設の許可が下りた The establishment of a new department *has been approved*. ‖ 毎月年金が10万円ずつ下りる I *receive* a pension of 100,000 yen every month.

5【霜ができる】 ▶庭じゅう真っ白に初霜が降りていた The entire garden *was covered with* brilliant white frost for the first time this season.

オリンピック **the Olympic Games, the Olympics, the Olympiad** ▶第1回のオリンピックは1896年にアテネで開かれた *The* first *Olympic Games* were held in Athens in 1896. ‖ すばらしいオリンピックだった It was a great *Olympics*. (➤ Olympics は通例複数扱いだが,どんなオリンピックかを言って単数扱いにすることもある) ‖ リオデジャネイロオリンピックに出るのが夢です It's my dream to compete in *the Rio de Janeiro Olympics*. ‖ 彼は冬季オリンピックで新記録を出した He set a new record in *the Winter Olympic* [*the Olympic Winter*] *Games*.

‖オリンピック選手 an Olympic athlete (➤体操選手は gymnast), an Olympian ‖ オリンピック村 an Olympic village.

[1]おる 折る **1【折り畳む】** **fold** +◉ ▶用紙を2つ[半分]に折る *fold* a form in two [in half] (➤「3つに折る」は fold ... in thirds) ‖ 目印に本のページの端を折る人がいる Some people *fold* the corner of the page *down* to mark their place. (➝折り目) ‖ この報告書は折らないでください Please don't *fold* these reports. ‖ 点線のところを内側に折りなさい *Fold* inward along the dotted line. ‖ 彼女はその紙で鶴を折った She *folded* the sheet of paper *into a crane*.

2【曲げて壊す】 **break** +◉ ▶桜の枝を折る *break off* a branch from a cherry tree ‖ 彼女は腕を折っている She *has a broken arm*. ‖ **対話**「どうしてスキーをしないの」「足を折るのが怖いんだ」"Why don't you go skiing?" "Because I'm afraid I might *break* my leg."

2**おる 織る** weave +目 ▶織機で布を織る *weave* cloth on a loom ‖ 糸を織って布を作る *weave* thread into cloth.

オルガン an organ, a pipe organ (パイプオルガン); a harmonium, a reed organ (教室などにある小型の) ▶オルガンを弾く play the *organ*
‖オルガン奏者 an organist.

オルゴール a music (al) box (➤《英》では musical box が好まれる) ▶オルゴールを鳴らす play *a music box*.

おれ 俺 I ⚠ 英語には「俺」に相当する語はない. 「俺」も「わた(く)し」も「ぼく」も, 一人称はすべて I で表す; →私.
▶俺とおまえの熱い友情 the warm friendship between *you and me*(➤ 語順に注意. 礼儀上, 一人称は最後にくる) ‖ 山下とは俺とおまえの仲だ Yamashita and I are so *close (that) we call each other by our nicknames*. (●「俺とおまえの仲」にぴったりの英語表現はないが, 極めて親しい間柄ということなので,「お互いをニックネームで呼び合うくらい親しい」と考えて英訳する).

おれい お礼 thanks(感謝); a reward (謝礼) ▶お礼のことばを述べる express a word of *thanks* ‖ お礼のことばもございません I don't know how to thank you. / I can't thank you enough. ‖ これはほんのお礼のしるしです This is just a small token of my *thanks* [*gratitude*].

おれいまいり お礼参り ▶やくざのお礼参り(=報復)が怖い I fear *retaliation* by [from] gangsters.

オレオレさぎ オレオレ詐欺 an "it's-me" scam; a telephone scam involving calls from pretended relatives in distress(➤ 説明的な表現で,「困惑している親戚を装った電話による電話詐欺」という意味).

おれきれき お歴々 bigwigs.

オレゴン Oregon(アメリカ北西部の州; 略 OR, Oreg., Ore.).

おれせんグラフ 折れ線グラフ a line graph.

おれまがる 折れ曲がる bend(曲がる) ▶折れ曲がったくぎ a *bent* nail.

おれる 折れる **1【折り畳んである】** be folded ▶ページの角が折れている The corner of the page *is folded*. / The page *is dog-eared*. ‖ コリーは耳の先端が少し前方に折れている The ends of a collie's ears *are folded* forward a little.
2【曲げて壊れる】 break ▶この鉛筆の芯は折れやすい This pencil lead *breaks* easily. (➤ lead の発音は /led/) ‖ 台風でたくさんの街路樹が折れた Many of the trees along the street *were broken in two* by the typhoon. ‖ 松の枝が雪の重みで折れた A branch of the pine (tree) *broke* [*gave way*] under the weight of the snow.
▶菊の茎がポキンと折れた The chrysanthemum [mum] stalk *snapped*. ‖《レントゲン写真を見て》薬指の骨が折れていますね The bone of your ring finger *is broken*. ‖《比喩的》心が折れそうになった I felt *crushed*. / I felt really *disheartened*. / I felt *as if I had hit a wall*.
3【進行方向に曲がる】 turn ▶その先の信号を右に折れると地下鉄の駅はすぐです If you *turn* right at the next signal, you'll find the subway station straight ahead.
4【譲歩する】 give in ▶学校当局もついに折れた The school authorities *gave in* at last. ‖ 両親もついに折れて娘の願いを聞き入れた The parents finally *gave in* to their daughter's request.

オレンジ an orange(果物); orange (色) ▶デザートにオレンジを食べる have *an orange* for dessert ‖ 東京タワーはオレンジ色にライトアップされていた Tokyo Tower was lit up in *orange*.
‖オレンジジュース orange juice, orange fruit drink, 《英また》orange squash 《《参考》》英語の orange juice は100パーセントのオレンジ果汁をいう.

おろおろ ▶おろおろした声 a *faltering* voice (➤ faltering は「しどろもどろの, 口ごもった」) ‖ 地震のときはたいていの人がおろおろする Most people *panic* [*are thrown into panic*] when an earthquake hits.

おろか 愚かな foolish ▶あんな怪しげな事業に手を出すなんてきみも愚かだったね It was *foolish* of you to get involved in such a suspicious undertaking. ‖ そんな愚かなことをするな Don't do such a *foolish* thing.
▶彼は愚かにも金を全部賭け事に使い果たしてしまった He was *foolish enough to* use up all his money (in) gambling.

-おろか ▶彼は詩はおろか小説も読まない He does not read novels, *let alone* poetry. ‖ 私は(アメリカの)西海岸はおろか, ハワイにも行ったことがない I haven't even been to Hawaii, *much less* the West Coast.
語法 let alone, much less はともに通例否定文[語]のあとで用いるが, 前者のほうがインフォーマル.

1**おろし 卸** wholesale(卸売り) ▶それは卸で買ってあげられると思います I think I can get them for you *wholesale*. (➤ この例と次例の wholesale は副詞用法) ‖ あの店は卸売りをしている That store *sells* (things) *wholesale*. ‖ 4月の卸売り物価は前月より3パーセント上がった *Wholesale prices* are three percent higher in April than in the previous month.
‖卸売り業者 a wholesaler, a wholesale dealer ‖ 卸売り店 a wholesale store ‖ 卸値 a wholesale price.

2**おろし 下ろし・卸し**
‖下ろし金 a grater ‖ 大根下ろし grated daikon (下ろした大根).

おろしたて 下ろしたて ▶この靴は下ろしたてです I'm *wearing* these shoes *for the first time*. ‖ 彼は下ろしたての靴で出社した He came to the office wearing *brand-new* shoes. (➤ brand-new は「まっさらの, 新品の」).

おろす 下ろす・降ろす・卸す **1【下方へ移動させる】** take down; bring down(上へ行って持って来る) ▶網棚からかばんを下ろす *take down* one's bag from the rack ‖ 2階からベッドを階下へ下ろす *bring* a bed *down* from upstairs ‖ 30分たったら鍋を火から下ろしなさい *Take* the pot *off* (the burner) in thirty minutes. ‖ 社長はソファーにどっかりと腰を下ろした The company president *sank* heavily *into* the sofa.
▶ブラインドを下ろしてください Could you *pull down* the shades [《英》blinds], please? (➤ pull down は「引っ張って下ろす」) ‖《教室で生徒たちに》手を下ろしなさい *Put* your hands *down*. (➤ Hands down. だけでもよい).
▶船の帆を下ろす *lower* the sails ‖ 屋根の雪を下ろす *shovel the snow off* the roof ‖ 船は港にいかりを下ろした The ship *dropped* [*cast*] *anchor* in the harbor. ‖ 店の戸はことごとく錠が下ろされている All the doors of the store *are locked* without exception.
2【乗り物から出す】 drop off; let off(出させる)
▶次の交差点の手前で降ろしてください Please *drop*

me *off* just before the next intersection. ‖ スクールバスは生徒たちを降ろすために止まった The school bus stopped to *let off* students. ‖ 親切な女の子が手を貸してバスから降ろしてくれた A young girl kindly helped me *get off* the bus. (➤「私が降りるのを助けた」と考える) ‖ 貨車から積み荷を降ろす *unload* the cargo from a freight car.

3【本体から外す】 ▶瀬戸内晴美は髪を下ろして寂聴と名乗った Setouchi Harumi *shaved her head* (to become a nun) and called herself Jakucho. ‖ 彼女は妊娠 3 か月のときに子供をおろした She *had an abortion* when she was two months pregnant. (→妊娠).

▶プロデューサーはそのテレビタレントを主役から降ろした The producer *dropped* the TV personality from the lead role.

4【口座から金を引き出す】 withdraw +目, **take out** (➤ 前者は後者より堅い語) ▶銀行口座から 2 万円下ろした I *have withdrawn* twenty thousand yen from my bank account. ‖ 銀行で少しお金を下ろさないといけないわ I have to *take* some money *out* of the bank.

5【新しく使い始める】 ▶きょうスーツを下ろした I *wore* my new suit today *for the first time*. (➤「初めて着た」の意).

6【問屋から売る】 wholesale ▶その店は小売業者に品物を卸している The store *wholesales* (the) goods to retailers.

7【さばいて処理する】 ▶大根を下ろす *grate* daikon ‖ 魚を三枚に下ろす *fillet* a fish / *slice* a fish lengthwise.

おろそか 疎か 一動 おろそかにする neglect +目 ▶絵描きになりたいのならデッサンをおろそかにしてはいけない If you want to become an artist, you must not *neglect* sketching. ‖ あなた, 最近勉強のほうがおろそかになっているわよ. もっと努力しなくっちゃあ Your (school) work *has been slipping* recently. You've got to make more effort. (➤ slip は「(成績などが)下がる」の意).

おわかれかい お別れ会 a **farewell party** (退職者・旅行へ行く人のための) ; a **going-away party** (主に旅行へ行く人のための).

オワコン ▶あのアニメはもうオワコンだ That anime is*n't popular anymore*.

おわせる 負わせる injure +目, **hurt** +目 (傷などを ; 後者はややくだけた語) ; **wound** +目 (銃や刃物などで傷を) ; **shuffle off** (責任などを転嫁する) ▶彼の心に傷を負わせる *injure* [*hurt*] his feelings ‖ 男は青年にナイフで傷を負わせた The man *wounded* the young man with a knife. ‖ 彼は自分の責任を同僚の 1 人に負わせた He *shifted* his responsibility onto one of his co-workers.

おわらい お笑い ▶あいつが友子にプロポーズしたって？とんだお笑い(ぐさ)だね He proposed to Tomoko? That's *a joke* [*a laugh*]!

‖**お笑いタレント** an entertainer who gets a lot of laughs, a comedian ‖ **お笑い番組** a comedy program.

おわり 終わり an **end**, a **close** /klous/ ; an **ending** (結末) ▶年の終わり the *end* of the year ‖ 初めから終わりまで *from beginning to end* ‖ 前期も終わりに近づいた The first semester *has drawn to a close*. ‖ 今月もきょうで終わりだ This month *is over* today. / Today *marks the end of* the month. ‖ テロとの戦いに終わりは見えない The war on terrorism has no *end* in sight.

▶じゃあ, きょうの授業はここで終わりにしよう All right! *That's all for* today. ‖ その話, 終わりはどうなるの？ What is *the ending* of the story going to be? / How does the story end?

▶コンサートはおもしろくなかったけど, それでも私たちは終わりまで座っていた We didn't enjoy the concert, but we *sat* it *out* anyway. (➤ sit ... out は「…の終わりまで退席しないでいる」) ‖ 終わりまで聞きなさい *Hear* me *out*.

▶本は終わりまで読まないとよさはわからない You can't appreciate a book unless you *read* it *through* [*to the end*]. ‖ 私はこの本を初めから終わりまで読んだ I read this book *from cover to cover* [*from beginning to end*].

▶ここで足を滑らせて落ちたら終わりだよ If you slip and fall down from here, that will be *the end of your life*. ‖ ここで諦めたら終わりだ If you give up now, you'll be *a goner*. (➤ goner は「助からない人, 見込みのない人」).

▶彼と付き合ってはいけないよ. 終わり. You can't go out with him, *period*. (➤ period は「以上, きっとだよ」の意の間投詞).

ことわざ 終わりよければすべてよし All's well that ends well. (➤ 英語のことわざ ; シェークスピアの喜劇の題名としても有名).

おわる 終わる 1【終了する】 end, be over (➤ 後者はインフォーマルな言い方で, 完了後の状態を強調する) ▶野球の試合は午後 9 時に終わった The ball game *ended* at 9 p.m. ‖ 学校は 3 時に終わる School *is over* [*lets out*] at three. (➤ let out は《米・インフォーマル》) ‖ 学校の図書館は土曜日は正午で終わる(＝閉まる) Our school library *closes* at noon on Saturday.

▶仕事は 6 時に終わるから待っていてくれ Please wait for me until I *get off* at six [until I *get through with* work at six]. (I want you to wait ... . とするとやや命令口調になるので避けたい.「待ってくれる？」と聞くのであれば Could you wait ...? とする) ‖ 長い夏休みも終わってしまった The long summer vacation *has come to an end*.

▶宿題は終わったの？ *Have* you *finished* your homework? (➤ Is your homework finished? としない) ‖ 工事が終わった Construction work *has been completed*. ‖ 事件は未解決に終わった The case *ended* unsolved. ‖ 石川選手は 7 位に終わった Ishikawa *finished* 7th [in 7th place].

> 【文型】
> …し終わる
> **finish doing**

▶彼は夕食を食べ終わった He *finished* (*eating*) supper. (➤ eating は省略するのがふつう) ‖ 私たちは住宅ローンを払い終わった We (have) *finished* pay*ing* off our mortgage. ‖ 証人は話し終わった The witness *finished* speak*ing*.

▶きょう中にこの報告書を終わらせます I'll *get* this report *done* (sometime) today [by tonight]. ‖ これで報告を終わります With this I *conclude* my report.

2【…という結果になる】 ▶彼女の試みは失敗に終わった Her attempt *resulted* [*ended*] *in* failure. ‖ 彼のしたことは結局無駄に終わった All his efforts *were in vain*.

おわれる 追われる →追う.

おん 恩

〘解説〙他人，特に目上の人から受けた親切や好意を「(いつかは返さなくてはならない)恩」と解釈する考え方は欧米ではふつうではないので，これに対応する英語もない．したがって，やや日本語とはずれるが kindness(親切)，favor(好意)，gratitude(感謝の念)などの語を使って表現する．

▶ご恩は決して忘れません I will never forget *your kindness*. ‖ いつかはあの方のご恩に報いなければならない I must *return his kindness* [*favor*] some day. ➡ 恩義.

▶《慣用表現》Aさんの希望に添わなければ，私は恩をあだで返すことになってしまう If I go against Mr. A's wishes, I'll be *biting the hand that feeds me*. (➤ 文字どおりには「自分を養ってくれる人の手をかむ」の意)《参考》「恩をあだで返す」はほかに return ~'s kindness with ingratitude (~の親切に忘恩で報いる) とか, return evil for good (悪をもって善に報いる) などのようにも言うが，いずれも堅い表現．

▶いろいろ教えていただきありがとうございました．恩に着ます Thank you for all the things you've taught me. I *owe you a lot*. ‖ あの人には頼み事をしたくない．すぐ恩に着せるから I don't want to ask him a favor because he always tries to *make me feel indebted* to him.

オン on ▶オン・オフ(＝入／切)スイッチ an *on*-off switch ‖ パソコンをオンにしたままにする leave one's PC *on* all the time ‖ プリンターをオンにするには電源ボタンを押してください Press the power button to *turn on* the printer.

おんいき 音域 ▶バイオリンの音域は$3\frac{1}{2}$オクターブだ *The range of the violin* is $3\frac{1}{2}$ octaves.

オンエア on the air ▶番組がオンエアされるのはいつですか When will the program *go on the air* [*be broadcast*]?

おんかい 音階 a (musical) scale
‖長[短]音階 a major [minor] scale ‖ 半音階 a chromatic scale ‖ 全音階 a diatonic scale.

おんがえし 恩返し ▶私はあの方にいつか恩返しをしなくてはならない I must *repay his kindness* [*favor*] some day. ／I must *repay* him *for his kindness* [*favor*] some day. ‖ 鶴はその男から命を助けられた恩返しに厚い錦の反物を織った The crane wove a thick roll of brocade *to show her gratitude* to that man for saving her life.

おんがく 音楽 music ▶音楽を聴く listen to *music* ‖ 音楽の先生 a *music teacher* ‖ 音楽の才能 *musical talent* ‖ 父はまるで音楽を解さない My father *doesn't appreciate music* [*has no ear for music*]. ‖ 〔対話〕「音楽はどのジャンルが好き？」「クラシック以外なら何でも好き」"What genre [type] of *music* do you like?" "I like anything so long as it's not classical."
‖音楽家 a musician ‖ 音楽会 a concert ‖ 音楽学校 a music school.

「音楽」のいろいろ オペラ opera ／カントリーウエスタン country and western ／器楽 instrumental music ／クラシック classical music ／軽音楽 light music ／ゴスペル gospel (music) ／サルサ salsa ／室内楽 chamber music ／ジャズ jazz ／声楽 vocal music ／ソウル soul ／タンゴ tango ／ディスコ disco ／電子音楽 electronic music ／バレエ ballet ／フュージョン fusion ／ブルース blues ／ポピュラー popular music ／民族音楽 ethnic music ／ラップ rap (music) ／ラテン Latin (American) ／リズムアンドブルース rhythm and blues ／レゲエ reggae ／ロック rock

おんかん 音感 sense of pitch ▶音感がいい[悪い] have a good [bad] *sense of pitch* (➤ have a good ear for music は「音楽に対するセンスがある」の意).
‖音感教育 auditory training ‖ 絶対音感 absolute [perfect] pitch.

おんぎ 恩義 a debt of gratitude (他人に負うているもの，借り) ▶S先生には恩義を感じています I *am indebted* [*have a debt of gratitude*] to Mr. S. ‖ いつかY先生の恩義に報いる所存です I'm determined to *repay my debt of gratitude* to Mr. Y some day.

おんきせがましい 恩着せがましい ▶彼の恩着せがましい態度が嫌いだ I don't like his [him] taking a *patronizing* attitude. ‖ 彼女は私の仕事を手伝ってくれたけど，実に恩着せがましい態度なんだ She helped me with my work but she clearly *expect* something *in return*. (➤「見返りに何かを期待する」の意).

おんきゅう 恩給 a pension ▶軍人恩給 a soldier's *pension*.

おんきょう 音響 ▶ビルは大音響とともに一瞬のうちに崩れ落ちた The building collapsed in an instant *with a terrific boom*. ‖ このホールは音響効果がよい The *acoustics* of this hall are good.
‖音響効果 sound effects (効果音)；the acoustics (音の響き方).

おんけい 恩恵 (a) benefit ▶医学の発達は人類に多くの恩恵を与えた The development of medical science has given humankind many *benefits*. (➤「具体的にいろいろな恩恵」という意味で複数形になっている) ‖ この辞書からはずいぶんと恩恵を受けた I got a lot of *benefit* from this dictionary. ‖ 日本人は中国文化から多大の恩恵を受けている The Japanese *have benefited* greatly from Chinese culture.

おんけん 穏健な moderate /mɑ́ːdərət/ (極端に走らない)；sound (堅実な) ▶穏健な考え方 a *moderate* view ‖ 彼の思想は穏健だ His views are *moderate* [*sound*].
‖穏健派 the moderates (➤ 個人なら a moderate person).

おんこう 温厚な gentle ▶温厚な人 a *gentle* [*an affable*] person (➤ 後者は「人当たりのよい」) ‖ 彼は性格が温厚で，誰からも好かれている He *has a gentle nature* and is loved by everybody.

おんこちしん 温故知新 study the old and seek the new (➤ 説明的な訳).

おんさ 音叉 a tuning fork.

オンザロック ▶ジンをオンザロックで飲む drink gin *on the rocks* ‖ スコッチのオンザロックをください I'll have a Scotch *on the rocks*, please.

おんし 恩師 one's (former) teacher ⚠ 英語では教師を「習った恩のある人」とは捉えないので，「恩師」は「昔の先生」，「小学校時代の先生」のように表現するしかない．
▶私は小学校時代の恩師には必ず年賀状を出す Every year, I send New Year's cards to the *teachers* I had in elementary school.

¹おんしつ 温室 a greenhouse, a hothouse ▶温室でランの花を育てる grow orchids in the *greenhouse*.
▶《比喩的》彼女は温室育ちだ She *has had a sheltered upbringing*. (➤「大事に養育された」の意)

《参考》「温室育ちの人」をインフォーマルな英語では hothouse plant と言う.

‖温室効果 the greenhouse effect.

2おんしつ 音質 **sound** [**acoustic**] **quality**.

おんしゃ 恩赦 a **pardon**(個人に対する); (an) **amnesty** /ǽmnəsti/ (複数の人に対する) ▶政治犯たちは恩赦に浴した Political offenders *were granted an amnesty*.

おんしょう 温床 a **hotbed**; a **breeding ground**(➤「野生動物の繁殖地」の意から出た比喩表現) ▶《比喩的》悪の温床 *a hotbed* of vice ‖スラム街は犯罪の温床だ Slums are *the breeding ground* of crime.

おんじょう 温情 **kindness** (優しさ); **leniency** /líːniənsi/ (寛大さ, 哀れみ) ▶ゲームで活躍して監督の温情に応えたい I want to perform well in the game(s), and repay the manager for all his *kindness*. ‖その事件で温情判決が下った *A lenient judgment* was handed down in that case.

おんしらず 恩知らずな **ungrateful** ▶恩知らずな人 an *ungrateful* person ‖あれほど世話をしてやったのに今もって何の挨拶もないとは何て恩知らずなやつだ I've done so much for him, but I haven't heard a word of thanks (from him). What an *ungrateful* man! ‖あの男は恩知らずだ That guy *has no sense of gratitude*. (➤「感謝の気持ちをもたない」).

おんしん 音信 **news** ▶それ以来彼女との音信が途絶えてしまった I *haven't had any news from* her since then. ‖彼とは10年前に別れたきり音信不通です I *have heard nothing from* him since we parted ten years ago. (➤ hear from は当人から「便り・電話などがある」).

おんじん 恩人 a **benefactor** /bénɪfæktəʳ/ ▶M教授は私の一生の恩人である Professor M is my lifelong *benefactor*. ‖あなたは私の命の恩人です I *owe my life* to you. / I *owe* you *my life*.

オンス an **ounce** /aʊns/ 《略 oz.》 ▶16オンスは1ポンドに相当する Sixteen *ounces* is equivalent to one pound.

おんすい 温水 **warm water**

‖温水プール a heated pool.

おんせい 音声 (a) **sound**(音); (a) **voice** (声) ▶テレビの音声がどうも不明瞭だ The *sound* on the TV is rather unclear.

‖音声学 phonetics ‖音声合成 voice [speech] synthesis ‖音声合成装置 a voice [speech] synthesizer ‖音声多重放送 multichannel [multiplex] broadcasting ‖音声入力 voice data entry ‖音声認識 voice recognition.

おんせつ 音節 a **syllable** ▶3音節の単語 a word which has three *syllables* / a word with three *syllables* ‖この単語は第1音節にアクセントがあります You should stress *the first syllable* of this word.

おんせん 温泉 a **hot spring**(湯の沸き出る所); a **spa** (温泉地); a **hot-spring resort** (温泉のある保養地) ▶温泉につかる soak in *a hot spring* ‖日本には温泉が多い There are many *hot springs* in Japan. ‖別府は日本の有名な温泉地だ Beppu is *a* well-known *hot-spring resort* [*spa*] in Japan.

日本紹介 ✉ **日本は火山国なので各地に温泉が湧いています. 昔から温泉地に長期間滞在して湯につかるのが, 病気を治し, 心身をリラックスさせる最上の方法とされてきました. 観光地として開発された大きな温泉場もありますが, 山奥のひなびた温泉を好む人もいます** As there are many volcanos in Japan, there are many *onsen* (hot springs) bubbling up in various places. Since ancient times, staying for an extended period and taking baths at a hot spring has been considered the best way to relax and cure various illnesses. There are large hot spring resorts that have been commercially developed, but some people prefer rustic and isolated ones deep in the mountains.

‖温泉宿 an inn at a hot-spring resort.

おんぞうし 御曹子 a **scion** /sáɪən/ ▶資産家の御曹子 a *scion* [*an heir*] of a wealthy family.

おんそく 音速 **the speed of sound** ▶マッハは飛行機と音速との関係を表す 'Mach' indicates the speed of an aircraft in relation to *the speed of sound*. ‖このジェット機は音速の3倍で飛ぶ This jet flies at speeds of up to *Mach 3*.

‖超音速ジェット機 a supersonic jet (plane).

おんぞん 温存する **preserve** +目 (大事に保護する); **save** +目 (取っておく) ▶頂上アタックに備えて体力を温存する *preserve* one's strength for scaling a mountain summit.

1おんたい 温帯 **the Temperate Zone** (➤ 小文字でも書く) ‖温帯植物[動物] the flora [fauna] of the temperate zone ‖温帯地方 the temperate regions [latitudes] ‖温帯低気圧 an extratropical cyclone.

2おんたい 御大 a **kingpin**, a **boss**.

おんだん 温暖な **mild**, **warm** ▶日本の温暖な気候 Japan's *mild* climate ‖地球の温暖化がますます進んでいる *Global warming* is increasing [proceeding] at an accelerating rate.

‖温暖前線 a warm front.

おんち 音痴 **tone-deafness**; a **tone-deaf person** (人) ▶ぼくに歌わせないでくれよ. 音痴なんだ Don't ask me to sing—I'm *tone-deaf*. [I'm a terrible singer.] ▶《比喩的》父は方向音痴でよく道に迷う My father *has a poor sense of direction* and often gets lost. (➤「方向音痴」を geography illiterate と言うこともある) ‖私は語学音痴で, 英語もろくに話せません I'*m no good at languages*, and I can hardly speak a word of English.

おんちゅう 御中 ▶S社営業部御中 To the Sales Division, S Company.

おんちょう 恩寵 **grace** ▶神の恩寵 the *grace* of God / God's *grace*.

おんてい 音程 an **interval** ▶正しい音程で歌う sing *in tune* ‖このギターは音程が狂っている[合っている] This guitar *is out of* [*is in*] *tune*.

オンデマンド **on demand**.

おんてん 恩典 (a) **privilege**.

1おんど 温度 (a) **temperature** ▶高い[低い]温度 *a* high [low] *temperature* ‖午後になって温度がやや上がった[下がった] The *temperature* rose [fell] a little in the afternoon. / It (has) warmed up [cooled down] a little in the afternoon. ‖ 対話 「この温室の温度は何度ですか」「35度です」 "What's the *temperature* in this greenhouse?" "Thirty-five degrees (Celsius)."

‖温度計 a thermometer /θəʳmɑ́ːmət̬əʳ/ ‖温度差 (a) temperature difference; (やる気の違い) a difference in motivation.

2おんど 音頭 ▶木村さんに乾杯の音頭を取っていただきましょう Let me ask Mr. Kimura to *propose* [*make*] *a toast*. (➤ propose は「呼びかける」) ‖教頭が音頭を取って応援団が結成された The vice-principal *took* the reins and formed a cheering squad. (➤ take the reins は「仕切る」).

おんとう 穏当な reasonable (理にかなった); moderate (穏健な) ▶その考えは極めて**穏当**だ That is quite a *reasonable* idea. ‖ 彼女は**穏当な**考え方をする She is *moderate* in her views.

おんどく 音読 ▶私は英語の復習をするときには必ず教科書を**音読する**ことにしている I always *read* the textbook *aloud* when I review my English.

おんどり 雄鶏 a rooster,《英また》a cock《参考》cock には俗語で「ペニス」の意があるので《米》では rooster が好まれる.

おんな 女

> **語法** (1)一般に成人した女性は **woman** で, 成人前の若い娘は **girl** (大学生は young woman がよい). 性別を強調したい場合は **female.** (2) **lady** は目前の女性を指したり, old lady (老婦人) のような言い方をする場合に用いる.

1【女性】 a woman [複 women /wímɪn/] ▶**女物の傘** a *woman's* umbrella ‖ 私の学校には男の先生より**女の先生**のほうが多い Our school has more *female* teachers than male ones. ‖ 吉田さんとご一緒のあの**女の方**はどなたですか Who's that *lady* over there with Mr. Yoshida? ‖ **女心**の何たるかを解さない男が多い There are lots of men who do not understand the workings of *a woman's mind* [how *a woman's mind* works].

‖**女親** a female parent, a mother ‖ **女形** a female-role player ‖ **女嫌い** a woman-hater, a misogynist /mɪsɑ́:dʒənɪst ‖ -sɔ́dʒ-/ (➤ 後者は「女性嫌悪症の人」に相当する堅い語) ‖ **女友だち** a female [woman] friend; a girlfriend (➤ 日本語の「ガールフレンド」よりも意味が狭く, 通例親密な間柄の友を指す).

2【慣用表現】 ▶彼女はエステに通って**女磨き**に励んでいる She frequents a day spa and tries hard to *enhance her feminine charm*. ‖ **事件の陰に女あり** There's a woman behind every case. / Cherchez la femme. (➤「女を探せ」の意のフランス語).

ことわざ **女三人寄れば姦**(かしま)**しい** Three women get together and there's a racket. / Three women make a market.

☛ 女の子 (→見出語)

おんなざかり 女盛り ▶彼女は今**女盛り**だ She's *in the prime of life*. →男盛り.

おんなたらし 女たらし a womanizer; a smooth operator (女をくどくのがうまい人); a woman chaser (女性の尻を追いかける男)《参考》(1) lady-killer は「女性を引きつける魅力を生来備えている男性」の意で,「女たらし」とは違う. (2)「女癖の悪い男」を俗に skirt chaser と言う. →プレーボーイ.

おんなで 女手 ▶彼女は**女手ひとつ**で4人の子供を育てあげた She raised four children *all by herself* [*all on her own*]. (➤「自分だけで」の意).

おんなのこ 女の子 a girl ▶公園で**女の子**が2人で縄跳びをしていた I saw two *girls* skipping rope in the park. ‖ 彼女の最初の子は**女の子**だった Her first child was *a girl*.

おんならしい 女らしい feminine, ladylike

おんねん 怨念 a grudge.

おんのじ 御の字 ▶この仕事で1万円なら**御の字**ですよ Ten thousand yen is *more than enough* for this job. (➤ more than enough は「十二分で」).

おんぱ 音波 a sound [sonic] wave ▶**音波**は摂氏零度では空気中を毎秒約331メートルの速さで伝わる At zero degrees Celsius, *sound waves* travel through the air at a speed of about 331 meters per second.

おんびん 穏便 ▶そのトラブルを**穏便**に処理する deal with that trouble *leniently* / take a *lenient* attitude to the trouble.

おんぶ ▶赤ちゃんを**おんぶする** *carry* a baby *on* one's *back* (➤ おんぶひもを使用している状態を連想させる) ‖ 赤ちゃんを**おんぶした**お母さん a mother *with* her baby *strapped to her back* ‖ パパ, **おんぶして**! Give me *a piggyback ride*, Daddy! (➤ 背負う場合, おんぶひもは用いない) ‖ あの子ったらおじいちゃんに**おんぶされて**大喜びなの He loves to *be carried piggyback* by his grandpa.

▶《比喩的》何から何まであの人に**おんぶして** (＝頼って) しまった I've *been dependent on* him all the way. / I *owe* everything *to* him.

‖**おんぶひも** a baby strap (➤ 登山用リュックを応用したような頑丈な形状のものを特に baby carrier と呼ぶ).

おんぷ 音符 a (musical) note ▶この曲は**16分音符**が多くて私には難しい This music is hard for me because it has so many *16th notes*.

‖**四分音符** a quarter note,《英》a crotchet /krɔ́tʃɪt/ ‖ **16分音符** a sixteenth note,《英》semiquaver /sémikwèɪvəʳ/ ‖ **全音符** a whole note,《英》a semibreve /sémibri:v/ ‖ **二分音符** a half note,《英》a minim /mínɪm/ ‖ **八分音符** an eighth note,《英》a quaver /kwéɪvəʳ/ ‖ **付点音符** a dotted note.

おんぷう 温風 a warm current of air ▶**電気温風ヒーター** an electric *fan heater*.

オンブズマン an ombudsman.

おんぼろ ▶**おんぼろシャツ** a *worn-out* shirt ‖ そんな**おんぼろ**もう二度と着たくないよ I hope I don't have to wear these *rags* again. ‖ **おんぼろの車** a rattletrap,《米・インフォーマル》a clunker, a jalopy,《英・インフォーマル》a banger ‖ **おんぼろの机** a *rickety* desk.

おんみつ 隠密 ▶**隠密に**事を運ぶ do things *in secret* [*secretly*] / proceed *in utter secrecy*.

おんめい 音名 a pitch name.

おんやさい 温野菜 a warm [steamed] vegetable (➤ steamed は「蒸した」).

オンライン online, on-line ▶すべての図書館を**オンライン**で結ぶ link all libraries through an *online system* [*network*] ‖ 学校を**オンライン化する** *get* schools *online*.

▶利用者ガイドは**オンライン**で入手可能だ The user's guide is available *online*. ‖ その会議はズームを使って**オンライン**で行われる The conference will be held *online* via Zoom.

‖**オンライン英会話レッスン** online English conversation lessons ‖ **オンライン会議** an online meeting ‖ **オンライン授業** an online class ‖ **オンライン・ショッピング** online shopping (➤「オンライン・ショッピングをする」は shop online) ‖ **オンライン飲み会** an online drinking party.

おんりょう 音量 volume /vɑ́:ljəm/ ▶テレビの**音量を下げて** [**上げて**] くれる? Will you *turn down* [*up*] *the volume* on the TV, please?

おんわ 温和な mild (気候が); gentle (性格が) ▶**温和な**気候 a *mild* [*temperate*] climate ‖ 彼は大変**温和な**人だ He is a very *gentle* person.

か・カ

か

[1]か 可《学業成績》**satisfactory, fair, average**, a **C**; a **D** (一応の可) ▶英語は優, 国語は良, 地理は可だったが, 数学は不可だった I got an A in English, a B in Japanese, and *a C* in geography, but I failed [flunked] mathematics. (➤ flunk は fail よりインフォーマル) 《参考》アメリカの多くの学校では成績をA, B, C, D, Fで評価し, 可はCまたはDに当たる. 大学ではA, B, Cを, 大学院ではA, Bを卒業の単位に認める. →秀.
▶彼の仕事は可も無く不可も無い His work is *not particularly good or bad*. / His work is *mediocre* [(just) *so-so*].
▶分割払い可 *payable in installments*.

[2]か 科 a **department** (学校・病院などの); a **course** (課程, コース); a **family** (動植物分類の) ▶高校の普通[英語]科の生徒 a student in the general [English] *course* of a senior high school ‖ 彼女は大学の仏文科で教えている She teaches in *the department of French literature* at a university.
▶ライオンやトラはネコ科に属する Lions and tigers belong to *the cat family*.

[3]か 課 a **lesson** (教科書の); a **section** (会社などの) ▶あすは第10課を習う Tomorrow we will do *Lesson 10*.
▶彼女は庶務課に配置替えになった She has been transferred to the general affairs *section* (of the company).

[4]か 蚊《虫》a **mosquito** /məskíːt̬oʊ/ ▶蚊に刺された I was bitten by *a mosquito*.
▶《慣用表現》彼女はいつも蚊の鳴くような声で話す She always speaks *in a very faint voice*. / She always whispers. (➤「ささやく」の意).
‖蚊取り線香 a pyrethrum coil (➤ pyrethrum /paɪríːθrəm/ は「除虫菊」).

[1]-か -化 ▶地域を活性化する *revitalize* the region ‖ 工業化する *industrialize* ‖ 工業化 *industrialization* ‖ 経営の合理化 the *streamlining* [《英また》*rationalization*] of management ‖ 過密化した都市 an *overpopulated* city ‖ 製造工程を機械化する *mechanize* the production process ‖ サーチエンジンを最適化する *optimize* a search engine ‖ 日本では人口の高齢化が進んでいる In Japan, the population is steadily *ag(e)ing*.

[2]-か 1【疑問や不確かな気持ちを示して】▶《直接質問する場合》東京はこれが初めてですか? Is this your first visit to Tokyo? ‖ 大丈夫ですか? Are you all right?
▶《間接的に質問する場合》先生にいつ伺ったらいいか聞いておいてほしい Could you ask your teacher *when* I should visit him? / I'd like you to ask your teacher *when* I should see him.
▶《反語を示す場合》きみはどうしてそんなに冷たいことができるのか How can you be so unkind? ‖ そんなことぼくが知るか(=無関係だ) It's none of my business. / I have nothing to do with it.
▶《不確実な気持ちを示す場合》彼女は来るだろうか *I wonder if* she will come. / Will she come, *I wonder*? ‖ あの人は佐山とかいう名前だ His name is Sayama, *or something like that*.

2【勧誘・依頼の気持ちを示して】▶休憩にしませんか? *How about* taking a break? / *What do you say to* having a break? ‖ この本, とてもいい本なんだけど, 読んでみないか This is a really good book. *Why not* give it a read? ‖ そろそろ出発しようか *Shall we* get going? ‖ コーヒーを2つくれませんか? Two coffees, *please*. ‖ ちょっと静かにしてくれませんか? *Could you* be a little quieter, please? ‖ 前が見えないので, 帽子を脱いでいただけませんか? *Would you mind* taking off your hat? It's blocking my view. / Excuse me, but your hat is blocking my view. *Could you* take it off? →-しませんか, [1]くれる.

3【驚きや感動を示して】▶そういう訳だったのか Now I see what has caused all this. ‖ あ, そうか Oh, *I see*. ‖ 今度の絵, いいじゃないか! This (latest) painting is terrific!

4【並立や選択を示して】▶生きるか死ぬかの問題 a matter of life *or* death ‖ あの人には2度か3度会ったことがある I (have) met him two *or* three times. ‖ 彼はイギリス人かアメリカ人です He is (*either*) British *or* American. ‖ 家を出るか出ないかというときに雨が降りだした *I had hardly left my house when* it began to rain.

[1]が 我 ▶彼は我が強い He is *stubborn* [*obstinate* / (*overly*) *self-assertive*]. (➤ self-assertive は《米》では「自分の考えや立場をきちんと主張する」の意のプラスイメージで解釈されることも多い. したがって, 副詞の overly を添えるほうが日本語の含みにより近くなる) ‖ 彼はついに我を折って我々に同意した He *has* finally *given in* and agreed with us. (➤ give in は「降参する」) ‖ 彼は何にでも我を通そうとする He tries to *have* [*get*] *his own way* in everything. (➤ have one's own way は「思いどおりにする」) ‖ あんまり我を張るんじゃないよ Don't *assert yourself* too much. / Don't *be* too *pushy*. (➤ 後者のほうがインフォーマルな言い方).

[2]が 蛾《虫》a **moth**.

-が 1【動作・状態を表すものを示して】▶こちらが田中さんです This is Mr. Tanaka. ‖ 誰がガラスを割ったんだい *Who* broke the glass? ‖ 象は鼻が長い Elephants have long trunks. ‖ 祖父は耳が遠い My grandfather is hard of hearing.

2【動作・作用を受けるものを示して】▶向こうに山が見えます You can see a mountain over there. ‖ 彼は水泳がうまい He is good at swimming. / He is a good swimmer.

3【順当に続く事柄を結び付けて】▶先月北海道へ旅行したが, なかなか愉快だった I took a trip to Hokkaido last month *and* had a very good time. (➤ この場合の「が」は前文の内容を否定しているわけではないので but は使えない).

4【相反する事柄を結び付けて】▶手帳を家じゅう捜したが, 見つからなかった I looked for my pocket diary all over the house, *but* I couldn't find it. ‖ 一生懸命勉強したが, 成績は思わしくなかった I studied very hard, *but* my grades were not as good as I had hoped (they would be).

5【譲歩を示して】▶人がぼくのことを何と言おうが, ぼく

はぼくの道を行く *Whatever* (other) people may say of me, I'll go my own way. ‖ 降ろうが照ろうが, 彼はサーフィンに行く He goes surfing rain *or* shine.

6【叙述を和らげて】▶来週お目にかかりたいのですが I *wonder* [*I am wondering*] *if* I could possibly see you next week. ‖ できればご一緒したいのですが I *would* like to go with you if possible. (➤「ご一緒してもいいですか」の含み) ／I *would* go with you if I could. (➤「残念ながらご一緒できません」の含み) ‖ 終電に間に合えばいいがな. ちょっと無理かな *I hope* I can catch the last train, but it's not looking very likely.

カー a **car** 《参考》car は主に乗用車を指し, バスやトラックは含まない.

‖ **カークーラー** a car air-conditioner ‖ **カーステレオ** a car stereo (set) ‖ **カーナンバー** a car's (license plate) number ‖ **カーヒーター** a car heater ‖ **カーフェリー** a car ferry ‖ **カーマニア** a car fanatic／a car enthusiast ‖ **カー用品** car accessories ‖ **カーラジオ** a car radio ‖ **カーレース** a car race.

がーがー ▶アヒルの親子が池でガーガー鳴いている The mother duck and her ducklings are *quacking* in the pond.

カーキいろ カーキ色の **khaki.**

かあさん 母さん →お母さん.

カースト **caste, the caste system.**

ガーゼ **gauze** /gɔːz/ ▶ガーゼのマスク a *gauze* mask ‖ ガーゼを傷口に当てる apply *gauze* to the wound.

カーソル a **cursor** /kə́ːʳsəʳ/ ▶次の行へカーソルを移動しなさい Move the *cursor* down to the next line. ‖ カーソルが動かなくなった The *cursor* froze.

カーディガン a **cardigan** ▶カーディガンを着る[脱ぐ] put on [take off] *a cardigan*.

ガーデニング **gardening** ▶母は最近ガーデニングに凝っています My mother is into *gardening* these days.

カーテン a **curtain**; **drapes** (厚地の) ▶寝室の窓にカーテンをつるす hang *curtains* in [at] the bedroom window ‖ 暗くなってきたのでカーテンを閉めなさい Could you draw [close] the *curtains*? It's getting dark. 《参考》draw the curtains は文脈によっては「カーテンを開ける」の意にもなるので close (反対は open) のほうが好まれる.

カーテンコール a **curtain call** ▶カーテンコールを受ける take *a curtain call*.

カート a **cart**(手押し車).

カード 1【厚紙の紙片】 a **card** ▶英語の用例をカードに写す copy an English example sentence onto *a card*.

‖ **グリーティングカード** a greeting card ‖ **クリスマスカード** a Christmas card ‖ **図書館カード** a library card.

2【クレジットカードなど】 a **card** ▶カードで買い物をする use *a* (*credit*) *card* for shopping(➤ 文脈からわかる場合は credit は省略可能) ‖ カードは使えますか? Do you accept *credit cards*? →キャッシュカード.

3【トランプ遊び, またはその札】 **cards** (遊び); a **card** (その1枚) ▶彼らはカードをしてその夜を過ごした They spent the evening *playing cards*. (➤ play cards で「トランプ遊びをする」) ‖ 兄は慣れた手つきでカードを切った My brother shuffled the *cards* expertly.

4【試合の組み合わせ】 a **card**; a **matchup** ▶ボクシングの好カードが今度の土曜日に組まれている There is a really good boxing *card* scheduled for next Saturday.

[1]**ガード** 《陸橋》《米》 a **railroad overpass**, 《英》 an **elevated railway bridge** (➤ 日常的には単に overpass や (railway) bridge がふつう; この意味では guard は使えない) ▶あのガードをくぐって行きなさい Go under that *railroad overpass*.

[2]**ガード** 《防御》 **guard** ▶ガードを固める keep up one's *guard*／be on one's *guard*.

▶《慣用表現》彼女はいつもガードが固くてなかなかどけない I can't get anywhere with her because she's always *on her guard* [because *her guard is* always *up*].

ガードマン a (**security**) **guard** (➤guardmanとはしない).

カートリッジ a **cartridge**(プレーヤーや万年筆の) ▶プリンターのカートリッジ an ink *cartridge* (インクジェットプリンター用); a toner *cartridge* (レーザープリンター用) ‖ 万年筆のカートリッジを新しいものに取り替える replace a pen's *cartridge*.

ガードル a **girdle.**

ガードレール a **guardrail** ▶彼はカーブでハンドルを切り損ねてガードレールにぶつかった He failed to negotiate the curve, and crashed into the *guardrail*.

カートン a **carton.**

ガーナ **Ghana** /gɑ́ːnə/ 一 形 ガーナの **Ghanaian** /gɑːnéɪən/ ‖ **ガーナ人** a Ghanaian.

カーナビ a (**GPS**) **navigation system**, a **car GPS system**, a **car navigator.** ▶目的地まではカーナビを使って順調に行けた Guided by my *navigation system*, I reached my destination without any problem.

カーニバル a **carnival** ▶リオのカーニバル the *carnival* in Rio de Janeiro.

カーネーション a **carnation** ▶カーネーションの花束 a bouquet of *carnations*.

カーネギーホール **Carnegie Hall**(ニューヨークのコンサートホール).

カーブ 1【道などの曲がり】 a **curve** /kəːʳv/, a **bend** (➤ 後者のほうが曲がり方の程度が大きい; bend よりさらに曲がりくねった所を twist と呼ぶ) ▶カーブを曲がる go around *a curve*／take *a curve*(➤ 後者は車で) ‖ カーブで減速する slow down for *a curve* [*bend*] ‖ カーブした[カーブの多い]道 a *curved* [*curvy*] road ‖ 見通しの利かないカーブ *a blind curve* ‖ この道路は急カーブが多い There are many *sharp curves* on this road. ‖ **S字カーブ** an S bend ‖ **ヘアピンカーブ** a hair-pin bend.

2【野球】 a **curve**, a **curveball** ▶大きなカーブ *a roundhouse* (*curve*) ‖ 甘いカーブを投げる pitch *an easy curve*.

カーペット a **carpet** ▶床にカーペットを敷く cover a floor with *a carpet*／carpet a floor ‖ カーペットを敷いた部屋 a *carpeted* room.

ガーベラ 《植物》 a **gerbera.**

カーボン **carbon.**

カーラー a **curler.**

ガーリック **garlic** ▶ガーリック3片 3 cloves of *garlic*／3 *garlic* cloves ‖ ガーリック味のポテトチップス *garlic*-flavored potato chips.

カーリング **curling.**

カール a **curl** /kəːʳl/ ▶髪をカールさせる *curl* one's hair ‖ 彼女は髪をカールさせている She *wears* her hair *curly*. ‖ 私の髪はカールしやすい My hair *curls easily*.

ガールスカウト 《米》 **the Girl Scouts**, 《英》 **the Girl Guides**(➤ 一員は a girl scout または a girl guide という).

ガールフレンド a **girlfriend** ▶彼にはガールフレンドがたく

さんいる He has a lot of (*female*) *friends*. ‖ 今度ガールフレンドを連れてらっしゃいよ How about bringing your *girlfriend* next time ?

か

危ないカタカナ語✸ ガールフレンド
英語の girlfriend は「恋愛関係にある特定の若い女性, 恋人, 彼女」の意味で用いる. 女性どうしでは英語でも,「女友だち」の意味で girlfriend を用いることもあるが, 日常英語では friend だけで十分. 特に女性であることを示したいときは female friend とする.

かーん ▶カーンという音とともにボールはスタンドへ飛んでいった The *crack* of the bat could be heard as the ball went sailing out into the stands.

がーん ▶えっ? あの子転校しちゃうの? ガーン. ショックだよ Oh? She's going to transfer to another school? *Oh no!* That's a shock.

¹かい 会 **1【会合】** a **meeting**; a **conference** (公的または大規模な); a **party** (パーティー); a **gathering**, a **get-together** (集まり) ▶会はすぐ終わります The *meeting* will end soon. ‖ 転勤する山下先生のためにお別れ会を開いた We had *a going-away party* for Mr. Yamashita who is being transferred to another school.

2【団体】 an **association**, a **society**
《参考》society は association と同様にも使われるが, 目的がより限定され, 会員が積極的に活動する団体をいう. どちらの語を使用するかは各団体によって異なる.
▶日本医師会 *the Japan Medical Association* ‖ 映画友の会 *the Movie Buffs Association* (➤ buff は「熱狂的愛好者, ファン」の意).

²かい 貝 a **shellfish** (生物の); a **shell** (貝殻) ▶貝のように口を閉ざす shut up *like a clam* / clam up (➤ clam はハマグリの類いを指す語).
‖貝細工 shellwork.

³かい 櫂 an **oar** /ɔːr/ (ボートなどの; 通例複数形で); a **paddle** (カヌーなどの) ▶(舟を)かいでこぐ *oar* [*row*] a boat.

⁴かい 階 a **floor**; 《米》a **story**, 《英》a **storey** (➤ 建物のそれぞれの階をいうときは floor を,「…階建て」のように高さをいうときは story, storey を用いる)

語法「…階」の言い方
1階, 2階, 3階をアメリカでは the first floor, the second floor, the third floor というが, イギリスでは the ground floor, the first floor, the second floor となり, 日本語や《米》と1階ずれることに注意. また, 中2階は the mezzanine /mézənìːn/ という.

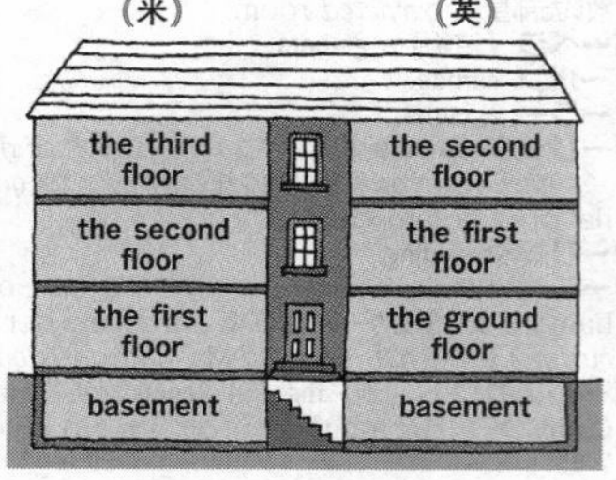

▶このエレベーターは30階まで直通です This elevator goes straight up to *the thirtieth floor*. ‖ 彼女は私と同じ階に住んでいる She lives *on our floor*. (➤ live on my floor とか live on the same floor とはふつういわない) ‖ 母さんは2階 [1階] にいます Mom is *upstairs* [*downstairs*]. (➤ upstairs, downstairs は2階建ての家屋の場合, それぞれ2階, 1階の意味になる) ‖ 地下1階ではバーゲンセールをやっています There's a sale on *the first basement level*. (➤ 地階の呼び方は英米共通) ‖ 対話「おもちゃ売り場はどこですか」「3階です」"Where is the toy department?" "It's on *the third* [《英》*second*] *floor*." ‖ 対話「あなたのアパートは何階にあるの?」「5階です」"*What floor* is your apartment on?" "It's on *the 5th* [《英》*4th*] *floor*." ‖ 対話「このビルは何階建てですか」「50階建てです」"*How many floors* [*stories*] does this building have?" "It has fifty *floors* [*stories*]." / "*How high* [*tall*] is this building?" "It's fifty *stories* high." (➤ (×)50 floors high とはいわない;「3階建ての家」は a three-story [《英》three-storey] house または a three-storied [《英》three-storeyed] house という).
‖最上階 the uppermost [top] floor; a penthouse (最上階の高級な部屋).

⁵かい 甲斐 **1【報い】** ▶努力のかいがあった [無かった] My efforts *have been rewarded* [*have gone for nothing* / *were in vain*]. ‖ 一生懸命勉強したかいがあって大学の入試に合格した I passed the university entrance examinations *thanks to* hard work. (➤ thanks to は「…のおかげで」) ‖ 《入試合格者などに》頑張ったかいがあったね Your hard work really *paid off*, didn't it? ‖ すばらしい映画だった. 見にいったかいがあったよ That was a great movie. *I'm glad I went to see it*. [*It was worth* going to see.] ‖ 猫は手当てのかいもなく死んだ The cat died *despite* the effort(s) to treat it.

2【「…がい」の形で】 ▶彼は頼りがいがある He is a person you *can depend on*. (➤「当てにできる」の意) / He is *very reliable* [*trustworthy*]. (➤ ともに「大いに信用できる」の意) ‖ 私の今の仕事はやりがいがある My present job is very *rewarding* [*challenging*]. (「報いられる, やるだけの価値のある」の意なら前者,「やる気を起こさせる, 実力を試される」の意なら後者がそれぞれ適当) ‖ もっと働きがいのある職場を探しているが, 私の年齢では簡単ではないだろう I'm doing my best to find another workplace with more *job satisfaction*, but it won't be easy at my age. ‖ 山田君は全く友だちがいの無いやつだ Yamada is *not what a friend should be*.
☛ 甲斐性 (→見出語)

⁶かい 下位 ▶下位の人 a person *of low rank* ‖ ヤクルトは現在最下位だ The Swallows are now in *last place*.
‖下位打線 the bottom of the line-up [the batting order].

¹-かい -回 **1【回数】** ... **times**; the **-th time** (…回目) ▶第136回ケンタッキーダービー *the 136th* Kentucky Derby ‖ 私は富士山に5回登りました I have climbed Mount Fuji *five times*. ‖ お母さんに何回同じことを言わせるの? *How many times* do I have to tell you that? ‖ もう1回やってごらんよ Try it *once again*. / Give it *one more* try.

2【スポーツ】 an **inning**, a **frame** (野球の; 後者はインフォーマル); a **round** (ボクシングの) ▶3回の表 [裏] に in the top [bottom] of the third *inning* ‖ 世界へ

ビー級選手権試合12回戦が始まるところです The 12-*round bout* of the world boxing heavyweight championship is about to begin.

2**-かい -界** a world, circles ▶スポーツ界 the *world* of sports ／sporting *circles* ‖ 実業界に入る enter *the business world* ／go into *business* ‖ 弱肉強食は自然界のおきてだ The stronger preying on the weaker is the rule in *the natural world*. ‖ 芸能界は浮き沈みが激しい *The world of show business* is full of ups and downs.

がい 害 harm (悪い結果や影響) ; damage (程度が計測できる損害や損傷)

【文型】
A に害がある, A に害を与える [及ぼす]
be harmful to A
harm A ／do [cause] harm to A
damage A ／do [cause] damage to A

▶薬は飲み過ぎると害を及ぼすことがある If you take too much (of a) medicine, it can *be harmful*. ‖ 喫煙は健康に害がある Smoking *is harmful to* health. ‖ 太陽光は皮膚に害を及ぼすことがある Sunlight can *be harmful to* the skin. ／Sunlight can *harm* [*damage*] the skin. ／Sunlight can *cause damage to* the skin. (➤ damage は深刻な皮膚への害を連想させる) ‖ どのくらいの大気中の放射線レベルが子供たちに害があるのですか What levels of radiation in the air can *be harmful to* [*do harm to*] children? ‖ 干ばつは作物に大きな害を与えた The drought *caused* a lot of *damage to* the crops. ‖ 子供が誤って洗剤を飲んでしまったんですが, 害はありませんか My child accidentally drank some dishwashing liquid. Will it *harm* him [her]? ‖ 酒の飲み過ぎは胃, 肝臓, 腎臓などに害を及ぼす Excessive drinking *causes* stomach, liver, and kidney *damage*.

▶《慣用表現》過度のジョギングは百害あって一利なしだ Excessive jogging *does you no good and much harm*.

☞ 害する (→見出語)

1**-がい -街** ▶商店街 a shopping *arcade* [*street*] (アーケードのある) ; a shopping district (地区) ‖ 繁華街 a busy *street* ‖ 電気街 an appliance and electronics *district* ‖ 中国人街 a China*town*. →歓楽街.

2**-がい -外** ▶時間外労働 *overtime* work ‖ それは全く問題外だ It's completely *out of the question*. ‖ エースの不調は想定外だった The ace pitcher's poor performance was *something we hadn't expected*.

3**-がい -甲斐** →5かい 2.

かいあく 改悪 a change for the worse ▶憲法を改悪する *revise* [*change*] the constitution *for the worse* ‖ それは改善でなく改悪だ That's no improvement; it's *a change for the worse*.

がいあく 害悪 (an) evil (悪) ; a harmful influence (悪影響) ▶都会の害悪 *evils* of the big city ‖ インターネットのサイトの中には社会に害悪を流すような内容のものもある The contents of some Internet sites have *a harmful influence* on society.

かいあげる 買い上げる buy up ▶政府は余剰米を買い上げた The government *bought up* the surplus rice. (➤ bought は buy の過去形) ‖ 1万円以上お買い上げのお客様には粗品を差し上げます Customers who *make a purchase* (of) over 10,000 yen will receive a small gift.

かいあさる 買い漁る hunt 《for》 (探し回る) ; go fishing 《for》 (得ようと躍起になる) ▶海外でブランド品を買いあさる *hunt* [*go fishing*] *for* name-brand products overseas.

がいあつ 外圧 foreign pressure ▶日本は外圧に弱い Japan easily gives in to *foreign pressure*.

かいいき 海域 a sea area ; waters (領海) ▶対馬海域 the *waters* [*sea area*] surrounding Tsushima Island.

かいいぬ 飼い犬 one's (own) dog ; a house dog (番犬) ; a pet dog (愛玩犬) ▶その社長は腹心の部下に裏切られた. 飼い犬に手をかまれたようなものだ That company president was betrayed by the man he had trusted most. *It was as if he was* [*were*] *bitten by his own dog*.

かいいれる 買い入れる buy +㊐ ▶サウジアラビアから原油を買い入れる *buy* crude oil from Saudi Arabia.

かいいん 会員 a member ▶パソコンクラブの会員になる *join* the PC Club ／*become a member of* the Computer Club ‖ その学会は会員が多い [少ない] The academic society *has a large* [*small*] *membership*. ‖ この会の会員は現在のところ1530名です The present *membership* of this society totals 1, 530. ‖ このテニスクラブは会員制だ This tennis club *is for members only*. ‖ 会員募集中です We are now accepting applications for *membership*.

‖会員証 a membership card (➤「会員券」もこの言い方でよい) ‖ 会員名簿 a membership directory [list] ‖ 終身 [名誉／正／準／賛助] 会員 a life [an honorary ／a regular [full] ／an associate ／a supporting] member 《参考》ふつうは a member だけで「正会員」を指す.

1**かいうん 海運** shipping, marine transportation

‖海運会社 a shipping company ‖ 海運業 a shipping business.

2**かいうん 開運** improvement of one's fortune [luck] ▶開運のお守り a *good-luck* charm.

かいえん 開演 ▶開演は午後6時半だ *The curtain rises* [*goes up*] at 6:30 p.m. (➤ 幕のある場合) ‖ 演奏会は午後7時開演, 9時終演の予定だ The concert is scheduled to *start* at 7 p.m. and end at 9 p.m. (➤ 幕のない場合) ‖ 《掲示》開演中入場お断り No Admittance during (the) Performance.

がいえん 外苑 an outer garden.

かいおうせい 海王星 Neptune.

かいおき 買い置き ▶買い置きの缶詰 *a back stock* of canned goods ‖ ティッシュペーパーの買い置きあったかしら Do we have *a stock* of tissue, I wonder?

1**かいか 階下** the downstairs /dàʊnstéəʳz/ ▶階下の部屋 a *downstairs* room ‖ 書斎は2階に, 居間は階下にある The study is upstairs and the living room is *downstairs*. (➤ この文の upstairs, downstairs はともに副詞用法) ‖ 階下は薄暗かった *The downstairs* was poorly lit [lighted].

2**かいか 開花する** bloom, come out (➤ 後者はややインフォーマル) ▶うちのバラはことしは早く開花した Our roses *bloomed* early this year. ‖ この地方の桜の開花はたいてい4月中旬だ In this region, the cherry blossoms usually *come out* in mid April.

▶《比喩的》彼女の才能は10代前半に開花した Her genius *flowered* in her early teens.

かいが 絵画 a picture ; a painting (絵の具で描いた) ; a drawing (鉛筆・クレヨン・ペンなどで描いた) ▶絵画を展示する exhibit *paintings* [*drawings*] ‖ 絵画を鑑賞する enjoy [view] *paintings* ‖ 蕪村の俳句には絵画的なも

のが多い Many haiku by Buson have a highly *visual* quality.
‖絵画館 an art gallery ‖絵画展 an art exhibition.

[1]がいか 外貨 foreign currency [money] ▶その国は外貨を獲得しようと躍起になっている That country is eager to obtain *foreign currency* [*money*].

[2]がいか 凱歌 ▶きのうの中日・巨人戦では中日にがい歌が上がった The Dragons *celebrated a victory* over the Giants in yesterday's game.

ガイガーカウンター a Geiger counter.

かいかい 開会 the opening of a meeting 一動 開会する open ▶開会の辞を述べる deliver *an opening address* ‖衆議院はきのう開会した The session of the House of Representatives *opened* yesterday. ‖国会が開会中だ The Diet *is* now *in session*.
‖開会式 an opening ceremony.

かいがい 海外 一形 海外の overseas /óʊvəˈsìːz/ 一副 海外に[へ] overseas /òʊvəˈsíːz/, abroad →外国 ▶海外に住む live *overseas* [*abroad*] ‖海外からの学生たち students *from overseas* / *overseas* students (➤ students overseas は「海外に行っている[行く]学生たち」の意).
▶近頃ハネムーンで海外へ行く新婚夫婦が多い Many newlyweds *go abroad* on their honeymoon these days. (➤ go abroad は「観光目的などで」, go overseas は「(仕事目的で)相当期間滞在するために」といった含みがあることが多い) ‖父は海外出張が多い My father often *travels overseas* [*abroad*] *on business*. ‖私は海外旅行がしたい I want to *travel overseas* [*abroad*]. / I want to take *an overseas trip*. ‖海外留学は学生時代に1度はやってみる価値がある *Studying overseas* [*abroad*] is worth experiencing once while you are a student. ‖池上氏は海外の事情に詳しい Mr. Ikegami knows all about *foreign affairs*. / Mr. Ikegami is well informed on *conditions in foreign countries*.
‖海外市場 an overseas market ‖海外ニュース foreign news ‖海外貿易 foreign trade ‖海外放送 overseas broadcasting ; an overseas broadcast (1回の).

[1]がいかい 外界 the outside world ▶刑務所は外界との接触が絶たれた世界だ A prison is a world cut off from *the outside*. / A prison is cut off from *the outside world*.

[2]がいかい 外海 the open sea ; the high seas (公海) ; the ocean (大洋).

かいがいしい 甲斐甲斐しい ▶しゅうとめにかいがいしく仕える wait on one's mother-in-law *hand and foot*.

かいかえる 買い替える ▶多くの電化製品は修理してもらうより買い替えるほうが経済的だ With many electrical appliances, it's more economical to *buy a new one* than to have them repaired.

かいかく 改革 (a) reform ; reformation (主に宗教上の) 一動 改革する reform +目 ▶現在行政改革が進行している *Administrative reform* is now being carried out. ‖彼は税制改革を提唱した He proposed *a tax reform*. ‖その首相は郵政事業の改革を断行した That prime minister resolutely carried out *a reform* of the postal service [system]. ‖選挙制度の改革(=改善)には時間がかかるだろう *Improving* the election system will take a lot of time.
‖医療保険制度改革 health care reform ‖宗教改革 (a) religious reformation ; the Reformation (16世紀ヨーロッパの) ‖農地改革 (an) agrarian reform.

がいかく 外角 (野球) outside /àʊtsáɪd/ (➤ outcourse とはしない) ▶外角低目のストライクだった It was a strike, *low and outside* [*away*].
‖外角球 an outside pitch.

がいかくだんたい 外郭団体 an affiliated organization (➤ 正式な言い方) ; an extra-governmental organization (政府組織の外にある団体).

かいかつ 快活な cheerful (陽気な) ; outgoing (外向的な) ▶快活な青年 a *cheerful* young man ‖雅夫は快活な性格なのでみんなに好かれる Everyone likes Masao because he has *a sunny disposition*. (➤「陽気な気質だ」の意) ‖彼女はとても快活だ She is very *outgoing*.

がいかつする 概括する summarize +目 ▶教授は過去3年間に行った研究を概括した The professor *summarized* the research he [she] had conducted over the past three years.

かいかぶる 買いかぶる overrate +目, overestimate +目 (➤ 共に「過大評価する」; 前者は overrated の形で受身形, または形容詞として用いることも多い ; 後者は ability など目的語が必要なことが多く, また,「多大に見積もる」の意もある) ▶正直なところ, 私は買いかぶられている[自分の能力を買いかぶりすぎていた]ような気がする Frankly, I feel I'*m overrated* [I *overestimated* my ability]. (➤ (×) I'm overestimated. はふつう言わない) ‖きみは彼の能力を買いかぶっていると思うよ I think you're *overestimating* his ability.

かいがら 貝殻 a shell ▶貝殻を拾う gather *shells*.
‖貝殻細工 shellwork.

[1]かいかん 会館 a hall
‖学生会館 a students' hall ‖市民会館 a community center ‖文化会館 a culture hall.

[2]かいかん 快感 a pleasant sensation ▶ハンググライダーで空を飛ぶたびに快感を覚える I feel *a pleasant sensation* [I feel good] whenever I fly in a hang glider. ‖性的快感を得る get *sexual pleasure*.

[3]かいかん 開館する open ▶図書館は9時開館です The library *opens* at nine. ‖午前10時から午後6時まで開館しています We *are open* from 10 a.m. to 6 p.m.

[1]かいがん 海岸 a beach (浜辺, 砂浜) ; the seashore (水に接する陸地, 岸辺) ; the seaside (娯楽施設などのある海岸地帯) ; a coast (沿岸 ; 地図・天気予報などに多く用いる) ▶海岸で貝を拾う gather seashells at [along] the *beach* ‖茅ヶ崎海岸はサーファーでいっぱいだった The Chigasaki *Beach* was crowded with surfers. ‖海岸には巨大なボウリング場があった There was a huge bowling alley at *the seashore* [by the *beach*]. ‖彼女は海岸のマンションに住んでいる She lives in an apartment house at *the seaside* [along the *beach*]. ‖白浜は海岸の保養地だ Shirahama is *a seaside resort*. ‖サンフランシスコはアメリカ西海岸にある San Francisco is on *the West Coast* of the United States. ‖この島は海岸線が長い This island has a long *coastline* [*shoreline*]. ‖海岸通りを散歩しよう Let's walk along *the waterfront*.

[2]かいがん 開眼 ▶文学に開眼する *come to understand* [*appreciate*] literature ‖彼はやっとバッティングに開眼したようだ It looks like he has finally *gotten the knack of* batting. (➤「こつをつかんだ」の意).
‖開眼手術 an operation to restore one's vision. →開眼(かいげん).

[1]がいかん 外観 an (outward) appearance ; an exterior

（建物の外面）▶家の**外観** the *exterior* of a house ‖ **外観**が洋風の家 a house with a Western-style *exterior* ‖ それは**外観**が金属のように見える It has the *appearance* of metal.

²**がいかん 概観** a general look［view］, a (general) survey /sɔ́ːˊveɪ/ ; an overview(大要) 一動 **概観する** survey /səˊvéɪ/ ＋目 ▶18世紀の世界史を**概観する** *make a general survey*［*take a general view*］*of* 18th-century world history ‖ これはわが校の創立から今日までを**概観した**パンフレットです This brochure *gives an overview of* our school's history, from its founding to the present.

¹**かいき 会期** a session ▶**会期**を20日間延長する extend the *session* for twenty days ‖ 国会は**会期中**である The Diet is now *in session*.

²**かいき 怪奇** a mystery ▶**怪奇**な犯罪 a *mysterious* crime ‖ 日本の政治の裏面は**複雑怪奇**だ The backstage of Japanese politics *is complicated and mysterious*. ‖**怪奇映画** a horror movie ‖ **怪奇物語** a horror story.

-かいき -回忌 ▶父の三［七］回忌 the second［sixth］*anniversary of* my father's *death* 《参考》法要は満2年目(英語では second)を三回忌, 満6年目(sixth)を七回忌と数えるので日英で数字がずれる.

かいぎ 会議 a meeting ; a conference →会合 ▶家族**会議** a family *meeting* ‖ 和平**会議** a peace *conference* ‖ **会議**を開く hold *a meeting* ‖ **会議**は私のオフィスで2時から行います The *meeting* will take place at 2 o'clock in my office. ‖ 私は3時まで**会議**があります I'll be in［at］*a meeting* until 3 o'clock. ‖ 出席しなければならない重要な**会議**がある I have an important *meeting* to attend. ‖ その計画は**会議**にかけなくてはならない We have to *present*［*submit*］the plan *at a meeting*. ／The plan has to *be reviewed at*［*in*］*a meeting*. ‖ ただ今より生徒会の**会議を始めます** I'd like to *call the meeting* of the student council *to order*. (➤開会を告げるときの決まり文句) ‖ これで**会議を終わります** The *meeting* is adjourned. (➤閉会を告げるときの決まり文句) ‖ 多くの**国際会議**では英語が使われます English is the official language of many *international conferences*.

▶《電話で》佐野はただ今**会議中**でございます Mr.Sano is *in*［*at*］*a meeting* (right) now. 《参考》日本の会社などでは対外的に同僚には敬称を付けないが, 英語圏の場合, この例のように付けるのがふつう ‖《掲示》**会議中** Meeting in Progress／Now in Session (➤Do Not Disturb(邪魔しないでください)を添えてもよい).

‖**会議室** a conference［meeting］room ‖ **テレビ会議** a teleconference.

がいき 外気 the (outside) air (➤通例カッコ内は言わない).

かいきいわい 快気祝い ▶友人たちに心ばかりの**快気祝い**を贈った I gave small *presents* to my friends *to thank them for their concern they showed while I was sick in the hospital*. (➤「入院中に自分を気遣ってくれたことに感謝して」の意 ; 快気祝いを贈る習慣は英米にはない).

かいきしょく 皆既食 a total eclipse of the sun［moon］(➤前者は太陽の, 後者は月の).

かいきせん 回帰線 ‖**北回帰線** the Tropic of Cancer ‖ **南回帰線** the Tropic of Capricorn.

かいぎてき 懐疑的な skeptical, 《英》 sceptical /sképtɪkəl/ ; suspicious(疑い深い) ▶私は早期英語教育については**懐疑的**だ I *am skeptical of* English (language) education for small children.

かいきゅう 階級 a class (社会の) ; rank (軍隊などの) ; a walk of［in］life (社会的地位) ▶日本人の多くは自分たちを**中流階級**だと思っている The majority of the Japanese think (that) they belong to *the middle class*. ‖ あらゆる**階級**の人々がその集会に出た *People from all walks of life* attended the rally. ‖ イギリスは今でも**階級社会**だ Britain is still *a class (-based) society*.

‖**階級制度** the class system ‖ **階級闘争** a class struggle／class warfare ‖ **下層階級** the lower class ‖ **支配階級** the ruling class ‖ **上流階級** the upper class ‖ **知識階級** the educated class／intellectuals ‖ **労働者階級** the working class.

かいきょ 快挙 ▶その選手は3年連続ホームラン王になるという**快挙**を成し遂げた The player achieved the *feat* of winning the home-run king title for three years in a row.

¹**かいきょう 海峡** a strait (➤固有名詞の場合はしばしば複数形で単数扱い) ; a channel /tʃǽnl/ (➤しばしば strait よりも大きい) ▶津軽**海峡**を渡る cross the Tsugaru *Straits*／cross the *Straits* of Tsugaru ‖ イギリス**海峡** the (English) *Channel*.

²**かいきょう 回教** Islam. →イスラム(教).

¹**かいぎょう 開業** the opening (of a business) 一動 **開業する** open［start］a business ▶新店舗の**開業** *the opening* of a new shop ‖ 東海道新幹線は**開業**以来大きな事故はほとんどない There have been few major accidents on the Tokaido Shinkansen Line since *the start of its operation*. ‖ 彼女は弁護士を**開業した** She *has opened* a law office. ／She *has hung out her shingle* as a lawyer. (➤hang out one's shingle は「看板を出す」の意の《米・インフォーマル》で, 医者や弁護士が開業することをいう) ‖ 彼は内科を**開業している** He *practices* internal medicine.

‖**開業医** a doctor in private practice／a private［an independent］physician.

²**かいぎょう 改行する** break a line(行を切る), start a new line(新しい行を起こす) 《参考》英語では記述が1文字単位ではなく, 1単語単位なので, 単語が行末に来たときはそれをどう処理するかに注意がいく. 行末での改行を a soft line break, 強制改行を a forced line break と呼ぶ. 入らない単語を次の行へ送るワープロソフトの処理は wordwrap という.

がいきょう 概況 general conditions (➤複数形で用いる) ▶天気**概況** the *general* weather *conditions* ‖ 販売促進の**概況**を報告する report *the general state* of sale promotions.

¹**かいきん 皆勤** perfect attendance ▶小学校の6年間は**皆勤**だった I *didn't miss a single day* of school in six years of elementary school. (➤「1日も休まなかった」の意).

‖**皆勤賞** a prize for perfect attendance.

²**かいきん 解禁** the opening of the fishing［hunting］season (➤前者は漁の, 後者は猟の) ▶錦川のアユの**解禁**は6月1日だ *The ayu season opens* on June 1st on the Nishiki River.

³**かいきん 開襟** ▶**開襟**シャツ an *open-necked* shirt.

がいきん 外勤 ▶今週は私は**外勤**です I'*m working outside the office*［*on outside duty*］this week.

がいく 街区 a block.

かいぐい 買い食い ▶塾の帰りにコンビニで**買い食い**した After my juku class(es), I *bought some snacks*［*food*］at a convenience store *and ate* them on my way home. 《参考》日本語の「買い食い」には今でも行儀が悪いという含みが残っているが, 英語の対応表現にはそれがないのがふつう.

かいくぐる ▶人混みをかいくぐる *slip* [*weave*] *through* the crowd ‖法の網をかいくぐる *slip through* loopholes in the law.

かいぐん 海軍 the navy, the naval forces ▶ジョンは20年前海軍に入った John joined *the navy* twenty years ago. ‖海軍将校［士官］a naval officer.

かいけい 会計 accounting(経理) ▶来週会計報告をします I will present the *treasurer's report* next week. (➤ treasurer は「(団体の)会計係」).
▶会計をお願いします Could you give us the *check* [*bill*], please?／*Check* [*Bill*], please. (➤ check も bill も「勘定書」の意で, 前者は《米》).
‖会計課 an accounting section ‖会計係 a treasurer(団体の会計担当者) ; a cashier /kæʃíəʳ/(レジ係) ‖会計学 accounting ‖会計監査 an account audit(➤「会社の会計監査をする」は audit a company で,「会社の帳簿を調べる」も audit a company's books と audit を用いる) ‖会計検査院 the Board of Audit ‖会計事務所 an accounting firm ‖会計年度《米》a fiscal year(10月に始まる) ; 《英》a financial year(4月に始まる) ‖公認会計士《米》a certified public accountant (➤ C.P.A. と略す) ; 《英》a chartered accountant (➤ C.A. と略す).

がいけい 外径 an outside diameter ▶外径10センチのパイプ a pipe measuring 10 centimeters *in outside diameter*.

かいけつ 解決 (a) solution ; (a) settlement (決着) 一動 解決する solve +㊐, resolve +㊐, settle +㊐ ▶その問題［紛争］の平和的解決法を見つける find a peaceful *solution* to the problem [conflict] ‖元大統領は国境紛争の解決に貢献した The former president contributed to *the settlement* of the border dispute. ‖この問題は直ちに解決しなくてはならない We must *solve* [*work out a solution* to] this problem immediately. ‖その殺人事件はまだ解決されていない The murder case *has not* yet *been solved*. ‖誘拐された少女が無事救出されて事件は解決した The case *was resolved* when the kidnapped girl was rescued unharmed.
☛ 未解決 (→見出語)

かいけつびょう 壊血病 scurvy.

[1]**かいけん 会見** an interview 一動 会見する have an interview《with》▶監督は新聞記者との会見に応じた The manager granted *an interview* to the newspaper reporters. ‖報道記者たちは帰ってきた探検家に会見を申し込んだ Reporters asked the returning explorer for *an interview*. ‖首相は記者団と会見した The Prime Minister *held a* press *conference* [*interview*]. ／The Prime Minister *had an interview with* the press corps.

[2]**かいけん 改憲** an amendment to the constitution, a constitutional amendment 一動 改憲する amend the constitution.

[1]**かいげん 開眼** ▶大仏開眼 *the consecration* of a Great Buddha *by painting its eyes*.

[2]**かいげん 改元** a change in [of] era name, an era name change.

がいけん 外見 an appearance ▶外見だけで人を判断すべきでない You should not judge people by *appearances* only. ‖その書物は外見は豪華だが内容は貧弱だ That book *looks* fancy, but it's lacking in content [substance]. ‖彼女は外見は(＝うわべは)おとなしそうだけど, 知り合ってみると全く違うわよ She seems quiet *on the surface*, but she is very different when you get to know her.

かいげんれい 戒厳令 martial /mɑ́ːʳʃəl/ law ▶その地区は今戒厳令下にある That district *is* now *under martial law*.

[1]**かいこ 蚕** a silkworm ▶蚕を飼う raise *silkworms*.

[2]**かいこ 回顧** ▶1990年代を回顧する *review* the 1990's／*see* the 1990's *in retrospect*.
‖回顧展 a retrospective exhibition ‖回顧録 memoirs /mémwɑːʳz/.

[3]**かいこ 解雇** dismissal, discharge ; (a) layoff (一時的な) 一動 解雇する dismiss +㊐, lay off ▶秘書を解雇する *dismiss* one's secretary ‖彼は人員整理で解雇された He *was dismissed* [*was discharged*] as a result of a staff cutback. ‖私は会社が赤字のため一時解雇された I *was laid off* because my company was (operating) in the red. (➤ laid は lay の過去分詞形). →首.
‖解雇通知 a dismissal notice ‖解雇手当 severance pay.

[4]**かいこ 懐古** ‖懐古趣味 nostalgia for the good old days.

かいご 介護 (nursing) care ▶寝たきり老人の介護をする *take care of* a bedridden elderly person ‖介護の仕事に就きたい I'd like to find *a nursing care job*.
‖介護支援専門員 a care manager ‖介護施設 a nursing care facility, a nursing home ‖介護保険 nursing care insurance ‖在宅介護 (in-)home care ‖老人介護 nursing care for the elderly ‖老老介護 elderly-to-elderly (nursing) care／(nursing) care of an elderly person by an elderly person.

[1]**かいこう 開校** the opening of a school ; foundation(創立) ▶この学校は明治20年に開校した This school *was founded* in 1887 [in the 20th year of the Meiji era]. (➤ found /faʊnd/ は「創立する」).
‖開校記念日 an anniversary of the school's founding／Founder's Day (➤後者は「創立者の日」の意で, 学校以外にも使える).

[2]**かいこう 開港** ▶江戸時代には出島だけが開港されていた Dejima was the only port *open to foreign ships* during the Edo period.

[3]**かいこう 海溝** a trench ▶マリアナ海溝 the Mariána *Trench*.

[4]**かいこう 開口** ▶彼女は開口一番,「元気そうじゃない」と言った *The first thing* she *said* was, "You look fine."

[5]**かいこう 開講** ▶4月5日開講 *The course will start* on April 5th.

かいごう 会合 a gathering(同じ目標をもった人たちによる内輪の) ; a meeting(会議・打ち合わせのための) ; an assembly(学校・教会・政治などの定期的討議のための) ; a get-together(気楽な集まり) ; a convention(代表者による大規模な) ; a conference(専門職者による) ▶私たちは昨日会合を開いてその予算について話し合った We *got together* yesterday and talked about the budget.

がいこう 外交 diplomacy /dɪplóʊməsi/ ▶武力外交 armed *diplomacy* ‖1941年日本はアメリカと外交関係を断った Japan broke off *diplomatic relations* with the United States in 1941.
‖(保険の)外交員 an insurance salesperson ‖外

交官 a diplomat /dípləmæt/, a diplomatic official ‖ **外交官試験** the Diplomatic Service Examination ‖ **外交政策** a foreign policy ‖ **外交問題** foreign affairs.

がいこうじれい 外交辞令 diplomatic language ▶彼の**外交辞令**を真に受けてはいけないよ Don't take his *diplomatic language* at face value.

がいこうてき 外向的な outgoing ▶**外向的な人** an extrovert /ékstrəvəːʳt/ ‖ 彼は**外向的な**性格の男だ He is an *extroverted* man [is *an extrovert*]. ／He has an *outgoing* personality.

1**かいこく 開国** ▶江戸幕府は1854年に**開国**した The Edo shogunate *opened Japan to the outside world* in 1854.

2**かいこく 戒告** (a) reprimand 一動 **戒告する** reprimand +目 ▶彼は職務怠慢で**戒告**処分を受けた He *was reprimanded* for neglect of duty.

がいこく 外国 a foreign country 一形 **外国の** foreign /fɔ́ːrən/ 一副 **外国へ**［に／で］abroad ; overseas（海外へ）▶**外国**に行く go *abroad* [*overseas*]（➤（×）go to abroad とはしない）.

> **解説** (1) go abroad と go overseas は同義であるが，日本のような島国から海外に行く場合は後者を用いるのがよい．(2) go abroad は「観光目的などで」，go overseas は「（仕事で）相当期間滞在するために」といった含みがあることが多い．(3)《米》では go to England, go to Australia のように行き先を具体的に言うことが多い．

▶**外国の習慣** *foreign* customs ‖ **外国**で生活する live in *a foreign country* ‖ **外国**で休暇を過ごす日本人が増えてきた More and more Japanese are spending their vacations *abroad* [*overseas*]. ‖ **外国**へ行ったことがありますか Have you ever been *abroad* [*to foreign countries*]? ‖ **外国**へ旅行すると日本のことがよくわかる When you travel *abroad* [*overseas*], you can understand Japan better. ‖ **外国**から来た人たちに対しては親切にしてあげなければいけない You should be kind to visitors *from abroad* [*from overseas* ／*from foreign countries*]. ‖ 彼女は**外国**生まれの**外国**育ちだ She *was born and raised* [*brought up*] *abroad*. ‖ 日本と**外国**との関係は常に満足すべきものであったわけではない Japan's relations with *other countries* [with *the rest of the world*] have not always been satisfactory.

▶大学生は少なくとも２つの**外国語**を履習することが要求される College students are required to study at least two (*foreign*) *languages*.（➤ 前後関係などから languages が「外国語」を指すことが明白な場合は foreign をつけないで languages だけで済ませることが多い）‖ このスマートフォンは**外国製**だ This is a *foreign-made* smartphone.（➤ Chinese-made（中国製の）のように具体的に国名をいうのがふつう）‖ **外国製品**の中には粗悪なものもある Some *foreign* [*imported*] *goods* are poor in quality. ‖ 彼の日本語にはやや**外国**なまりがある He speaks Japanese with a slight *foreign accent*.

‖ **外国為替** foreign exchange ‖ **外国語学部** the school [college] of foreign languages ‖ **外国語大学** a university of foreign studies ‖ **外国人** a foreigner /fɔ́ːrənəʳ/, an alien /éɪliən/（➤ 後者は法律用語）（⇀外人）‖ **第２外国語** a second foreign language.

> **あなたの英語はどう響く?**
> 学習者の中には，「外国の方ですか」のつもりで Are you a foreigner? と聞く人がいるが，外国人の多くがこの聞かれ方に不快感を示す．foreigner には「(異国からの)よそ者」の響きがあるからである．May I ask where you are from?（どちらから来られたのですか）ならそのような否定的な響きはないが，このように質問されること自体を好まない人もいるので注意が必要．

がいこつ 骸骨 a skeleton /skélətn/ ▶彼は**骸骨**のようにがりがりだ He is as thin [skinny] as *a skeleton*. ／He's nothing but skin and bones.

かいこむ 買い込む buy +目 ; lay in（集めて蓄える）▶食糧を**買い込む** *lay in* provisions.

1**かいこん 開墾** reclamation 一動 **開墾する** reclaim +目 ; clear +目（切り開く）; cultivate +目（耕す）▶森林を**開墾する** *clear* the woods ‖ 荒れ地を**開墾する** *reclaim* [*cultivate*] wasteland ／*bring* wasteland *under cultivation*.

‖ **開墾地** cultivated land.

2**かいこん 悔恨** remorse /rɪmɔ́ːʳs/ ▶彼は自分の行為に**悔恨**の念を表した He expressed *remorse* for his actions.

かいさい 開催する hold +目 ; host +目（主催する）▶第１回オリンピックはアテネで**開催**された The first Olympic Games *were held* [*took place*] in Athens.（➤ held は hold の過去分詞形）‖ マチス展は上野で**開催中**だ A Matisse exhibition *is* now *being held* in Ueno. ‖ その国際会議は今東京で**開催中**である That international conference *is* now *meeting* [*is* now *in session*] in Tokyo. ‖ 今度のオリンピックの**開催地**はどこですか? Where will the next Olympic Games *be held*? ／Which country [city] *is hosting* the next Olympic Games? ‖ 2016年のオリンピック**開催地**としてリオデジャネイロが選ばれた Rio de Janeiro has been chosen as the *venue* for the 2016 Olympic Games.（➤ 開催地を１語で言えば，この訳例のように venue がよい）.

‖ **開催国**［**都市**］the host country [city].

かいさく 改作 adaption 一動 **改作する** adapt +目 ▶その小説は映画に**改作**された The novel *was adapted* to a film.

かいさつ 改札 ▶定期券で**改札**（口）を通る pass *the ticket gate* [《英》*the* (*ticket*) *barrier*] by using one's commuter pass [《英》season ticket] ‖ **改札口**を出た所で待ってるよ I'll wait right outside *the ticket gate*.

‖ **改札係** a ticket man [woman] ‖ **自動改札機** an automatic ticket gate [barrier].

かいさん 解散 **1**【**終わって別れること**】a breakup, (a) dismissal（➤ 後者は堅い語）一動 **解散させる**［**する**］break up, dismiss +目 ▶クラス（の生徒）を**解散させる** *dismiss* a class（➤ クラス全体に向かって「解散してよし!」と言う場合は "Class dismissed!"）‖ 午前９時集合，午後４時**解散** To meet at 9 a.m.; to *break up* at 4 p.m. ‖ 会議は５時に**解散**した The meeting *broke up* [*was dismissed* ／*was adjourned*] at five.（➤ 最後の was adjourned は「散会した」に近い）‖ 機動隊はデモ隊を**解散**させた The riot police *broke up* [*dispersed*] the demonstrators.（➤ 後者は「分散させた」の意）.

2【**組織を無くすこと**】a breakup（グループの）; dissolution（議会の）一動 **解散させる**［**する**］break up ; dissolve /dɪzɑ́ːlv/ +目 ▶そのロックグループは最近**解散**し

た That rock group *has split up* [*has broken up*] recently. ‖ 国会が**解散**したからまもなく総選挙が行われるはずだ A general election will be held now that the Diet *has been dissolved.* ‖ 総理大臣は衆議院を**解散させる**権限をもつ The prime minister has the authority to *dissolve* the House of Representatives.

かいざん 改竄 一動 改ざんする falsify ＋目 ▶文書を**改ざんする** *falsify* a document ‖ データを**改ざんする** *falsify* data.

がいさん 概算 a **rough estimate** ▶彼女は**概算**で私の２倍は稼いでいる *At a rough estimate*, she earns twice as much as I do. ‖ **概算**で約１万円の赤字が出る Our losses are *roughly* estimated at ten thousand yen.

かいさんぶつ 海産物 marine products
‖ **海産物問屋** a wholesaler of seafood.

[1]**かいし 開始** a **start**; a **beginning** (何かの動作の第一歩) **一動 開始する start, begin** ▶工事の**開始**は来月からだ Construction work will *start* next month. ‖ 雷雨のため野球の試合**開始**が40分遅れた The ball game was 40 minutes late in *starting* due to a thundershower. ／Due to a thundershower, the ball game *started* [*began*] 40 minutes late. ‖ 戦闘が**開始された** A battle *has begun.*

[2]**かいし 怪死** a **mysterious death** (謎の死); a **suspicious death** (不審死).

かいじ 開示 disclosure 一動 開示する disclose ＋目 ▶情報の**開示** *the disclosure* of information ‖ 建築契約に関する情報を**開示する** *disclose* information about construction contracts.

がいし 碍子 《電気》 an **insulator.**

がいじ 外耳 the outer ear.

がいしけい 外資系 ▶**外資系**の会社で働く work for a *foreign-affiliated* firm.

がいして 概して generally (speaking) (一般論として; 通例文頭に置き, インフォーマルでは speaking を省略することも多い;「たいてい」の意の generally は文中でも用いる); **in general** (一般に); **on the whole** (全体として, 総合的には); **as a (general) rule** (通例, たいていは) ▶若い人は**概して**楽天的だ *On the whole*, young people are optimistic. ／Young people are *generally* optimistic. ‖ 交通事情はよくなるどころか, **概して**悪くなっている *In general* [*Generally* (*speaking*)], traffic conditions are getting worse, not better. ‖ ことしの作物の出来は**概して**良好である *On the whole*, this year's crops are excellent. ‖ **概して**日本の気候は温和であると言える It may be said, *as a* (*general*) *rule*, that the climate of Japan is mild. ‖ この大学は**概して**設備はいい *By and large*, the facilities are good at this university. (➤ by and large は generally, on the whole の意で用いられるが, 話しことばで用いられることが多い).

かいしめる 買い占める buy up; **corner** ＋目 (商品・株などを) ▶テニスの試合の切符を**買い占める** *buy up* all the tickets for a tennis match ‖ 小麦を**買い占める** *corner* the wheat market.

[1]**かいしゃ 会社** a **company**, a **firm**, a **corporation**; an **office** (仕事場としての)

> **《解説》会社の種類**
> (1) 会社の組織として, 株式会社や有限会社には《米》では **corporation** を用い, 《英》では **company** を用いる.
> (2) 《米》では company は合資会社に用いるが, 会社によっては株式会社の意で用いる.
> (3) **firm** は２人以上で構成される合資会社, 商会, 商店などに用いるが, インフォーマルでは company と同義に用いることも多い. →**株式会社**.

▶兄は横浜にある**会社**で働いている My big brother works in *a company* [*a firm*] in Yokohama. ‖ 中井氏は「年輪」という名前の**会社**を経営している Mr. Nakai runs *a company* called 'Nenrin.' ‖ 彼女は**石油会社**に入社した She was hired by *an oil company.* ‖ 父は典型的な**会社人間**だ My father is a real *corporate type.* ／My father is a typical *company man.*

▶東証一部上場**会社** *a company* listed on the first section of the Tokyo Stock Exchange ‖ 私は週に５日**会社**に行く I *go to work* [*go to the office*] five days a week. (➤「勤めに行く」の意では go to the company としない) ‖ **対話**「きみのお父さんはどちらの**会社**にお勤めですか」「ICM に勤めています」"What *company* does your father work for?" "He works for ICM." ‖ **対話**「お父さんは?」「**会社**です」"Where's your father?" "He'*s at the office* [*at work*]." (➤ 会社を「職場」の意味で使う場合は office とする).

‖ **会社説明会** a company explanatory meeting.
☛ **会社員** (→見出語)

[2]**かいしゃ 膾炙** ▶芭蕉の人口にかいしゃした俳句 a *well-known* haiku by Basho [one of Basho's *well-known* haiku].

がいしゃ 外車 a **foreign car**; an **imported car** (輸入車) ▶**外車**を乗り回す ride around in *a foreign car* ‖ この**外車**は右ハンドルだ This *foreign-made car* steers on the right.

> 「外車」のいろいろ **アウディ** Audi ／**アルファ・ロメオ** Alfa-Romeo ／**キャデラック** Cadillac ／**サーブ** Saab ／**シトロエン** Citroën ／**シボレー** Chevrolet ／**ジャガー** Jaguar ／**ビュイック** Buick ／**フィアット** Fiat ／**フェラーリ** Ferrari ／**フォード** Ford ／**フォルクスワーゲン** Volkswagen ／**プジョー** Peugeot ／**ベーエムベー** BMW ／**ベンツ** Mercedes(-Benz) ／**ポルシェ** Porsche ／**ボルボ** Volvo ／**ポンティアック** Pontiac ／**ルノー** Renault ／**ロールスロイス** Rolls-Royce

かいしゃいん 会社員 an **office worker**
✉ **父は鉄鋼関係の会社員です** My father is *an office worker* [*a company employee*]. He works for a steel company. ➤ company employee は事務職だけでなく, もっと範囲が広い.

▶ **対話**「ご職業は?」「**会社員**です」"What (kind of work) do you do?" "I work at an office [a company]. ／I'm *an office worker.*" (➤ 英米人は I'm an electrical engineer. (電気技師です) のように具体的に職業を言ったり, I work at a computer company. とか I work for X Electronics. のように業種や会社名を言ったりするほうがふつう).

かいしゃく 解釈 an **interpretation 一動 解釈する interpret** ＋目 ▶その句は一とおりの**解釈**しかできない That phrase admits (of) only one *interpretation.* ‖ この単語はいろいろに**解釈できる** This word *can be interpreted* in many ways. ／This word permits various *interpretations.* ‖ 彼は私の言ったことを好意的に**解釈した** He *interpreted* what I said favorably. ‖ あの人はいつも物事を自分の都合のいいように**解釈する**傾向がある He always *interprets* things in the way that is best for him. ‖次の論文の傍線部をわかりやすく**解釈しなさい** *Write* a simple *explanation* of each underlined portion in the following essay. ‖憲法についての誤った**解釈**ほど危険なものはない Nothing is more dangerous than a *misinterpretation* of the Constitution.

がいじゅ 外需 foreign demand.

1**かいしゅう 回収** (a) collection(集めること); (a) recall (欠陥品の); (a) repossession, 《インフォーマル》(a) repo(ローン返済不履行による家・車などの). ━動 **回収する** collect +目, recall +目; repossess +目 (ローン不払いのものを) ▶空き缶を**回収して**リサイクルする *collect* empty cans and recycle them ‖廃品を**回収する** *collect* junk ‖(代金不払いなので) 彼の車を**回収する** *repossess* his car ‖大掛かりな製品**回収** a major *product recall* ‖融資 [債権] を**回収する** *collect* credit [debt]. ‖先生は生徒からアンケートを**回収した** The teacher *collected* the questionnaires from the students. ‖メーカーは欠陥製品の大部分を**回収した** The manufacturer has *recalled* most of the defective products.

2**かいしゅう 改修** repair(➤「改修作業」の意味では通例複数形) ━動 **改修する** repair +目 (比較的大きな, または複雑なものを); renovate(古い建物などを); improve +目 (欠陥箇所などを); 《インフォーマル》do over (家などを) ▶古い野球場を**改修する** *renovate* an old ball park ‖わが家を**改修する**時期だ It's time to *do over* our house. ‖その橋は**改修工事**が行われている *Repairs* are (now) being made on the bridge. ／The bridge is *under repair*. ‖家を数か所**改修した** I *have made* several *improvements* to the house.

3**かいしゅう 改宗** (a) (religious) conversion ━動 **改宗する** convert /kənvɚ́ːʳt/ ▶仏教からイスラム教に**改宗する** *convert* from Buddhism to Islam.
‖**改宗者** a convert /kɑ́ːnvəːʳt/.

4**かいしゅう 会衆** a congregation(教会の); an audience(聴衆).

1**かいじゅう 怪獣** a monster
‖**怪獣映画** a monster movie.

2**かいじゅう 晦渋な** abstruse, obscure ▶かいじゅうな現代音楽 *abstruse* contemporary music.

3**かいじゅう 懐柔する** conciliate +目; placate +目 ▶**懐柔策をとる** take *a conciliatory approach*.

がいじゅう 害獣 a harmful animal; vermin(害を与える小動物や害虫の総称).

がいしゅつ 外出する go out ▶**外出して**もいい? May I *go out* now? ‖あしたは**外出しません**(=うちに居ます) I will *be* (*at*) *home* tomorrow. ／I'm going to *stay* (*at*) *home* tomorrow. ‖彼に電話したら**外出中**だった When I called, he was *out*. ‖(電話で) 木村はただ今**外出しております** Mr. Kimura *is out of the office* right now. 《参考》日本の会社などでは対外的に同僚には敬称を付けないが, 英語圏の場合, この例のように付けるのがふつう.

1**かいしゅん 買春する** buy [pay for] sex, pay for someone's sexual favors ▶高校生の少女と**買春する** *pay for sex* with a high school girl.
‖**児童買春** child prostitution.

2**かいしゅん 改悛** repentance.

かいしょ 楷書 ▶住所氏名は**楷書**で書いてください Please write your name and address *in block style kanji*.

1**かいじょ 解除** cancellation(取り消し) ━動 **解除する** lift +目 (禁止令・制裁・制限・規制・警報などの終了を発表する); cancel +目 (取り消す); remove +目 (取り除く); turn off, deactivate(作動しないように切る) ▶契約を**解除する** *cancel* a contract ‖マナーモードを**解除する** *turn off* [*deactivate*] silent mode ‖津波警報は今し方**解除された** The tsunami warning has just *been lifted* [*canceled*]. ‖厚生労働省はその新薬の販売禁止令を**解除した** The Ministry of Health, Labour and Welfare has *lifted* the ban on the sale of that new medicine. ‖一方通行の制限が**解除された** The restriction limiting this street to one-way traffic has *been lifted* [*removed*].

2**かいじょ 介助** help, aid
☛ **介助犬** (→見出語)

1**かいしょう 改称する** rename +目 ▶社名を『ジャイアント』と**改称する** *rename* the company 'Giant' ／ *change* the company name to 'Giant' ‖江戸は1868年に東京と**改称された** Edo *was renamed* Tokyo in 1868.

2**かいしょう 解消** (a) dissolution ━動 **解消する** dissolve /dɪzɑ́ːlv/ +目; break off (突然取り消す); reduce +目 (減らす) ▶そのアナウンサーは NBC との(専属)契約を**解消した** The announcer *dissolved* his (exclusive) contract with NBC. ‖三郎はすみ子との婚約を**解消した** Saburo *has broken off* his engagement to Sumiko. ‖ウォーキングはストレス**解消**に役立つ Walking helps *reduce stress*.

3**かいしょう 快勝する** win [gain] a clean-cut victory ▶きのうの野球の試合は6対0で私たちのチームが**快勝した** Yesterday our baseball team *had a clean-cut victory* with a score of six to zero.

4**かいしょう 甲斐性** ▶かい性のある男 a man *of substance* (➤「資力のある男」の意) ／a *dependable* man(➤「頼れる男」の意) 《参考》a good provider (しっかり稼いできちんと家族を養ってくれる人) という言い方もある. ‖このかい性なし! You *lazy bum*! ／ You're a *lazy good-for-nothing*! (➤ a bad provider も「かい性なし」の意).

1**かいじょう 会場** the grounds(用地; 野外の場合); a venu(会合・競技の行われる場所・施設) ▶オリンピックの**会場** an Olympic *venue* ‖コンサート**会場**は10代の聴衆でいっぱいだった The concert *venue* [*grounds*] were packed with teenagers. (➤ 会場が「ホール」の場合は The concert hall was ... となる) ‖彼は車で家族を万博**会場**に連れていった He drove his family to the Expo *grounds*.

2**かいじょう 海上** ▶静かな**海上**をヨットが走っていた Yachts were sailing *on the* calm *sea*.
‖**海上自衛隊** Japan Maritime Self-Defense Force ‖**海上保安庁** Japan Coast Guard ‖**海上保険** marine insurance.

3**かいじょう 階上** the upstairs /ʌ̀pstéəʳz/ ▶当ビルは**階上**の部屋はすべて賃貸になっております The *upstairs* rooms of this building are all rented.

4**かいじょう 開場** opening ▶ロイヤルシェークスピア劇場は夜7時30分に**開場する** The Royal Shakespeare Theatre *opens* at 7:30 p.m.

1**がいしょう 外相** the Foreign Minister. →外務(大臣).

2**がいしょう 外傷** an external injury [wound] ▶死体には**外傷**は無かった There was no *external injury* on the body.

かいしょく 会食 ▶友人たちと**会食する** *have a meal with* one's friends.

がいしょく 外食する eat out ▶私たちは週に1度**外食する** We *eat out* [*dine out*] once a week. (➤ カッコ内は堅い言い方) ‖ 対話 「食事は?」「全部**外食**です」

"What do you do for meals [food]?" "I (always) *eat out*."

かいじょけん 介助犬 a service [a helper／an assistance] dog ▶介助犬は障害者のためにさまざまな役目をこなすことができる *Service dogs* perform a variety of tasks for disabled people.

1**かいしん 会心** ▶勝者は会心の笑みを浮かべた The winner gave *a smile of great satisfaction*.‖この小説は彼女の会心の作だ She put her heart into this novel (and is extremely proud of it). (➤英文は「…に打ち込み, それを誇りにしている」の意).

2**かいしん 改心** reformation 一動 改心する reform oneself ▶改心して勉学に励むつもりです I'm going to *change my attitude* and study hard [diligently].

3**かいしん 回診** a doctor's rounds ▶1日1回, 医師が回診に来る The doctor *makes his rounds* [*visits his patients in the hospital*] once a day. (➤女性の場合は his を her にする).

4**かいしん 改新** (a) reform; reformation (政治・宗教などの) ▶大化の改新 the Taika *Reforms*.

1**かいじん 灰燼** ▶昨夜の火事で, 貴重な仏像が灰じんに帰した In last night's fire, a precious Buddhist statue *was reduced to ashes*.

2**かいじん 海神** the sea god ▶海神ネプチューン Neptune *the sea god*.

がいしん 外信 foreign news
‖外信部 the foreign news desk.

がいじん 外人 a foreigner /fɔ́:rənəʳ/; a foreign national (在留外国人)
《参考》foreigner には「よそ者」のニュアンスがあるので, 相手に面と向かっては使わないほうが無難. できれば国籍を表すことばを使う. なお, 'gaijin' は日本に来た外国人が最初に覚える日本語の1つで, また, そう言われると最もショックを受けることばでもある.

かいず 海図 a chart ▶日本海の海図を作る *chart* the Sea of Japan.

かいすい 海水 seawater
‖海水魚 a saltwater fish ‖海水パンツ swimming trunks ‖海水プール a seawater swimming pool.

かいすいよく 海水浴 swimming in the sea [ocean], 《英また》sea bathing /béiðɪŋ/ ▶私たちは九十九里浜に海水浴に行った We *went swimming* at Kujukurihama. (➤at を to としないこと)／We *went* to Kujukurihama *to swim in the ocean*.
‖海水浴客 a sea [an ocean] bather／a swimmer ‖海水浴場 a swimming [bathing] beach／a bathing resort.

かいすう 回数 ▶白石君は最近欠勤の回数が多い Shiraishi's been missing *a lot of* days of work lately. ‖優勝回数の最も多い横綱は誰ですか Which yokozuna has won the championship *most often*?／Which yokozuna has won the *most* tournaments?
‖回数券 a commutation [commuter] coupon ticket (通勤・通学の) (➤commutation (通勤・通学), commuter (通勤・通学者) を省略すれば, その他の目的のための回数券にも使える).

がいすう 概数 an approximate /əprɑ́:ksɪmət/ number ▶負傷者の概数は100人です The *approximate number* of injured people is 100.

1**かいする 介する** ▶番組の司会者は通訳を介してフランス人ピアニストと話した The program's host talked to the French pianist *through* an interpreter. ‖彼は世間の評判を少しも意に介さない He *doesn't care* at all about what people say (about him).

2**かいする 解する** appreciate +目 (わかる) ▶彼は詩を全く解さない He does not *appreciate* poetry in the least.／He has no appreciation whatsoever of poetry. ‖彼女はユーモアを解する人間だ She is *a person with* a *sense of* humor.

がいする 害する injure /índʒəʳ/ +目; damage +目 (損じる); offend +目 (人の感情を) ▶喫煙は健康をひどく害することがあります Smoking may [can] seriously *injure* [*damage*] your health. ‖そんなこと言われて気分を害したから, もう手伝わない I'm not going to help you any more because I'*m offended by* your remark.

1**かいせい 改正** (a) revision (より良くすること); (an) amendment (憲法・法律などの) 一動 改正する revise +目, amend +目 ▶時刻表を改正する *revise* the timetable ‖憲法を改正する *amend* the Constitution ‖健康保険制度が改正された The health insurance system *has been revised*.

2**かいせい 快晴** clear weather ▶きょうは雲1つない快晴だ Today is (*a*) *clear* (*day*) without a trace of cloud(s) in the sky. ‖ハイキングの日は快晴に恵まれた Luckily, it was *bright and sunny* on the day of the hike.

3**かいせい 改姓** ▶改姓届を出す *register a new name* ‖結婚して(妻ではなく)ぼくのほうが改姓しました It was I (not my wife) who *changed my last name* when I got married.

かいせき 解析 analysis [複 analyses] 一動 解析する analyze +目 ▶データ解析 data *analysis*.

かいせきりょうり 懐石料理 *kaiseki-ryori*
日本紹介 ✉ **懐石料理は, もともと茶道で茶を味わう前に食べる簡素な食事をいいましたが, 現在では高級料理店で出す日本料理のコースを指します. 1品ずつ吟味された旬の素材を使い, 美しい器に盛りつけられており, 高価です** *Kaiseki-ryori* originated as a light meal eaten before having tea at a tea ceremony. Now, however, it refers to a course of Japanese cuisine served at a high-class restaurant. Since each dish is made from carefully selected seasonal ingredients and served on beautiful plates, *kaiseki-ryori* is rather expensive.

1**かいせつ 解説** (an) explanation (説明); a commentary /kɑ́:mənteri/ (論評) 一動 解説する explain +目, comment 《on》 ▶音楽評論家はその作品についてわかりやすく解説した The music critic *provided* a clear *explanation* of the work. ‖新聞の解説によれば日本経済はしばらくは振るわないようだ According to *the newspaper commentary* [*a commentary in the newspaper*], the Japanese economy will continue to stagnate for some time. ‖そのニュース解説はサウジアラビアとエジプトとの外交問題を扱っていた The *news commentary* dealt with Saudi Arabia's diplomatic problems with Egypt. ‖きょうの新聞には地球温暖化についての解説記事が出ている There is *an interpretative* [*interpretive*] *article* on global warming in today's newspaper. (➤interpretative, interpretive はともに「解説的な」の意; 専門家による「論説[論評]記事」は an op-ed article という).
▶乱気流がどのようにして起きるかを解説する *explain* how turbulence occurs ‖今の取組について解説していただけますか Could you please *explain* how the

bout was fought？‖彼は事の次第をかいつまんで解説してくれた He *gave* me a brief *explanation* [*rundown*] of what (had) happened.（➤ rundown は「概要の説明」).

‖解説者 a commentator ‖解説書 an instruction manual（電気製品などの).

2**かいせつ 開設** establishment 一動 開設する establish ＋目 ▶へき地にようやく診療所が開設された At long last, a medical facility *was established* in the remote area.

がいせつ 概説 an outline ▶世界史概説 *an outline* of world history.

1**かいせん 改選** reelection 一動 改選する reelect ＋目 ▶この秋に委員の半数が改選される予定だ We are going to *reelect* half of the committee seats this fall.

2**かいせん 回線** a circuit /sə́ːʳkɪt/；a line（線）▶回線の接続が悪いのか，雑音が入る I guess something may be wrong with the *circuit* connection. There's noise (on it).

‖通信回線 a communication(s) line ‖電話回線 a (tele)phone line.

3**かいせん 海戦** a naval [sea] battle, a sea fight.

4**かいせん 開戦** an outbreak of war ▶日米開戦の日は1941年12月8日だ *The war between Japan and the U.S. began* on December 8, 1941.

5**かいせん 疥癬**《医学》scabies.

かいせんりょうり 海鮮料理 seafood cuisine.

かいぜん 改善 (an) improvement；(a) reform [reformation]（改革）一動 改善する improve（＋目）▶生活改善 (a) lifestyle *improvement* ‖食生活を改善する *improve* one's diet ‖北朝鮮との関係を改善する *improve* relations with North Korea ‖顧客サービスを改善する *improve* customer service ‖市当局はその保育所に施設の改善を勧告した The city authorities have advised the day-care center to *improve* its facilities. ‖労使の話し合いは賃金と勤務条件の改善を目指している The labor-management talks aim at obtaining a wage hike and *better* working conditions.

1**がいせん 外線** an outside line ▶外線は最初に0を押してください Please press zero for *an outside line*.

2**がいせん 凱旋する** make a triumphant [victorious] return ▶地元で優勝チームの凱旋パレードが行われた The champion team held *a triumphal parade* in their hometown. ‖凱旋門 a triumphal arch；an arch of triumph（➤パリの「凱旋門」は the Arch of Triumph という).

がいせんしゃ 街宣車 a sound truck.

がいぜんせい 蓋然性 probability.

1**かいそう 回想** recollection；(a) reminiscence /rèmənísəns/（追憶）一動 回想する recollect ＋目 ▶学生時代を回想する *recollect* one's school days ‖若者は未来に目を向け，老人は過去を回想するものだ The young look to the future, while the old *look to the past*.（➤ look to は「…の方を向く」）‖彼女はしばらく回想にふけっていた She was lost in *reminiscences* for some time.

‖回想シーン (a) flashback ‖回想録 memoirs /mémwɑːʳz/.

2**かいそう 回送** forwarding（転送）一動 回送する forward ＋目，send on（➤後者はややインフォーマル）▶引っ越すときに郵便物は新住所に回送してくれるよう郵便局に頼んだ When we moved, we asked the post office to *forward* [*send on*] all our mail to the new address.

‖回送電車 an out-of-service train.

3**かいそう 改装** refurbishment；remodeling（改築）；renovation（古い建物などの）一動 改装する refurbish ＋目；remodel ＋目，renovate ＋目 ▶店舗を改装する *refurbish* [*redecorate* / *renovate*] a store ‖地下室を改装して遊び部屋にする *remodel* the basement into a playroom.

4**かいそう 海草・海藻** seaweed, a sea vegetable ▶海藻は食品から肥料まで用途が広い *Seaweed* has a wide range of uses, from food to fertilizer.

5**かいそう 階層** ▶この団体はあらゆる階層の人々から成り立っている This organization is made up of *people from all walks of life*.（➤ a walk of life は「社会的地位，職業」).

6**かいそう 会葬** ▶本日はご多忙にもかかわらずご会葬いただきありがとうございました Thank you very much for *attending the funeral* despite your busy schedule. ‖会葬者 a mourner；a person who attends a funeral.

1**かいぞう 改造** (a) conversion（部屋や家の）；a reshuffle（内閣・人事の）一動 改造する convert ＋目；rework ＋目（手直しする）；reshuffle ＋目 ▶小野さんは車庫を工房に改造した Mr. Ono *has converted* his garage into a workshop. ‖犯罪に使われた拳銃はモデルガンを改造したものだった The gun used in the crime *was reworked* from a model gun. ‖食事ができるようにキッチンを改造する *remodel* the kitchen so that we can have meals there（➤ remodel は「リフォームする」).

▶内閣を改造する *reshuffle* the Cabinet.

2**かいぞう 解像** ‖（テレビなどの）解像度 definition ‖高解像度写真[画像] a high-definition photograph [image].

がいそう 外装 ▶この車は外装がよい This car has a good *paint job*. ‖そのビルは現在外装工事中だ The building is now receiving its *exterior* finish.

かいぞえ 介添え a helper（補助者，手伝いの人）；an assistant（助手）；a bridesmaid（新婦の），a best man（新郎の）▶花嫁[花婿]の介添え役を務める serve as *a bridesmaid* [*a best man*].

1**かいそく 快速** ▶この駅には快速（電車）は止まらない *Rapid-service* [*Fast*] *trains* do not stop at this station. ‖快速艇 a speedboat.

2**かいそく 会則** the regulations [rules] of a society.

かいぞく 海賊 a pirate /páɪrət/

‖海賊行為 piracy（➤「ソフトウェアの海賊行為（＝違法コピー）を防ぐ」は prevent software piracy）‖海賊船 a pirate ship [galleon] ‖海賊版 a pirated [bootleg] edition.

かいそっきゅう 快速球 a fastball, a fireball

‖快速球投手 a fastballer, a fireballer.

かいたい 解体 (a) demolition（建物の）一動 解体する demolish ＋目，pull down（建物を；前者が堅い語で日本語により近い）；take ... apart（ばらばらにする）；dismantle ＋目（機械などを分解する）；disband ＋目（組織などを）；dissect ＋目（解剖する）▶古いビルを解体する *demolish* [*pull down*] an old building ‖マグロを解体する *cut up* a tuna / *fillet* a tuna（➤骨を除いた切り身にする場合；発音は /fɪléɪ ‖ fílɪt/）‖自動車修理工はトラブルの原因を探るためにエンジン全体を解体した The car mechanic *took* the whole engine *apart* [*dismantled* the whole engine] to find the cause of the trouble. ‖彼らはリーダーに，彼が結成した政治組織の解体を迫った They pressed the leader to *disband* the political group he had formed.

かいたく 開拓 **reclamation**（荒れ地などの開墾）**—動** **開拓する** **reclaim** +目；**pioneer** /pàɪəníəʳ/ +目（先駆けとなる）；**open up**（開発する）▶北海道の荒れ地は本州の人々によって**開拓された** The Hokkaido wilderness *was pioneered* [*was opened up*] by people from Honshu. ‖ オレゴンはニューイングランドから来た人々によって**開拓された** Oregon *was settled* by New Englanders.（➤ settle は「植民する」の意）‖ 清教徒はアメリカ初期の**開拓者**だった Puritans were early *settlers* of America.

▶福沢諭吉は西洋文明研究の**開拓者**だった Fukuzawa Yukichi was *a pioneer* in the study of Western civilization. ‖ 新製品の販路を**開拓せよ** *Develop* [*Create*] a market for our new products.

‖**開拓者精神** frontier /frʌntíəʳ/ spirit ‖**開拓地** cleared land（切り開いた農地）；reclaimed land（干拓地）.

☛ **未開拓**（→見出語）

かいだく 快諾 ▶彼女は私の申し出を**快諾してくれた** She *readily accepted* my offer. ／She *readily consented to* my request.

かいだし 買い出し ▶父は魚河岸へ**買い出しに行った** My father *went shopping* at the fish market.

かいたたく 買い叩く **haggle** +目 ▶そんなに**買いたたかないでください** Please don't *haggle over the price* so much.

かいだめ 買いだめ ▶トイレットペーパーを**買いだめする** *stock up on* toilet paper ‖ 自然災害に備えて食料品を**買いだめしておく** *hoard* food against a natural disaster（➤ hoard は「ひそかに貯蔵する」；物不足を心配するあまり，群集心理を起こして多くの人がいっせいに買いに走ることを panic buying という）‖ 食料は**十分に買いだめしてある** We *have a good stock of* food.

がいため 外為 **foreign exchange**

‖**外為法** the Foreign Exchange and Foreign Trade Control Law.

1**かいだん 階段** **stairs**；**steps**（屋外の）；a **step**（1段）《参考》手すりや踊り場などを含む一続きの階段は staircase とか flight of stairs といい，通路としての階段に重点を置いた場合は stairway という ▶**階段**のいちばん上の段 the top step of the *stairs* ‖ **階段を上がる**［上る］go up [climb] *the stairs*（➤ climb は1段1段進むというイメージがある）‖ **階段を下りる** go down the *stairway* [*stairs* ／ *staircase*]（➤「歩いて下りる」は walk down,「走って下りる」は run down）‖ **階段から落ちる** fall down *the stairs* ‖ 金刀比羅宮へ行くには785段の**階段を上らねばならない** You have to go up 785 *steps* to reach the Kotohiragu Shrine. ‖ 私はいつも**階段を利用することにしている** I always take *the stairs*.

▶近藤君は入社後，**出世階段**を着実に上っている Since Mr. Kondo started working for the company, he has been steadily climbing *the ladder of success*.（➤ the corporate ladder ともいう）‖**階段教室** a (lecture) theater ‖ **非常階段** emergency stairs ／an emergency stairway [staircase] ‖ **らせん階段** a spiral staircase.

2**かいだん 会談** a **talk**；**talks**（通例正式な）**—動** **会談する** **talk with** [**to**]（➤《英》では to が好まれる）；**meet with**（会って話し合う）▶**会談は物別れに終わった** The *talks* were broken off. ‖ 米国とロシアの**軍縮会談**がウィーンで行われる The U.S. -Russia *talks on arms control* will be held in Vienna. ‖ 首相は今日の午後，フランス大統領と**会談した** The Prime Minister *met with* French President this afternoon. ‖ 外相は今朝，アメリカの国務長官と**電話会談をした** The Foreign Minister *had a telephone conversation* with the American Secretary of State this morning.

‖**首脳会談** a summit meeting ／summit talks.

3**かいだん 怪談** a **ghost story**.

ガイダンス **guidance** ▶就職の**ガイダンスがあった** We received *guidance* about job-hunting. ‖ 新入生は単位取得について**ガイダンスを受けた** The new students were given *guidance* [*an orientation*] on how to earn credits.（➤ orientation は「方向づけ指導，オリエンテーション」）.

かいちく 改築 **rebuilding, reconstruction**（➤後者には「複雑な設計に従って何かを建てる」というニュアンスがある）；a **home improvement, remodeling**（リフォーム）**—動** **改築する** **rebuild** +目，**reconstruct** +目；**remodel** +目 ▶校舎の**改築** the *rebuilding* [*reconstruction*] of a school building ‖ 家を**改築する** *rebuild* [*remodel*] one's house ‖ 家をアパートに**改築する** *convert* a house into apartments（➤ convert は「別の物へ改造する」）.

1**かいちゅう 海中** ▶**海中に飛び込む** dive *into the sea*

‖**海中公園** a marine park.

2**かいちゅう 懐中** ‖**懐中電灯** a flashlight,《英また》an electric torch ／a torch ‖ **懐中時計** a pocket watch.

3**かいちゅう 回虫** a **roundworm**.

1**がいちゅう 害虫** an **insect pest**, a **harmful insect**；**vermin**（➤害虫・害鳥・害獣などの総称）▶**害虫を駆除する** exterminate *insect pests* ‖ 麻薬の売人はいわば**社会の害虫だ** Drug dealers are what you might call the *vermin of society*.

2**がいちゅう 外注** **outsourcing** **—動** **外注する** **outsource** +目，**farm out, contract out**；**subcontract** +目（下請けに出す）▶日本の会社の多くが生産を中国やベトナムに**外注している** Many Japanese companies *outsource* production to China and Vietnam.

1**かいちょう 快調** ▶体はとても**快調だ** I'*m in good condition* [*shape*].（➤ shape はややインフォーマルな語）‖ 私の車のエンジンは**快調だ** My car's engine *is in good* [*top*] *condition*. ‖ そのマラソン走者は初めは**快調に飛ばした** At the start, the marathon runner ran *fast* (*and in good form*).（➤ in good form は「（競技者が）コンディションがよく」）.

2**かいちょう 会長** **the president**（協会などの）；**the chairperson**（会社などの）；**the head**（最高責任者）▶**生徒会会長** the *president* of the student council ‖ 彼は日本シェークスピア学会の**会長に選出された** He was elected *president* of the Shakespeare Society of Japan.（➤この場合，人ではなく役職を表すので，a や the はつけない）.

がいちょう 害鳥 a **harmful bird**.

かいつう 開通 (an) **opening** **—動** **開通する** **open, be opened** ▶高速道路の新しい区間の**開通** the *opening* of a new stretch of superhighway ‖ そのバス路線［トンネル］は先月**開通した** That bus route [tunnel] (*was*) *opened* last month.

‖**開通式** an opening ceremony.

かいづか 貝塚 a **shell mound, (kitchen) midden**（➤後者は考古学用語）.

かいつぶり《鳥》a **grebe**.

かいつまんで ▶**かいつまんで言えば**，「ノー」さ（*To put it*) *in a nutshell*, no. ‖ 報告書をかいつまんで話してくれ

Please give me a summary [*the gist*] of the report. (➤ gist は「要点」).

かいて 買い手 **a buyer, a purchaser** (➤ 後者は「購買者」に近い) ▶私の家はすぐに買い手がついた I found *a buyer* for my house right away.

‖**買い手市場** a buyer's market.

1**かいてい 海底** **the bottom of the ocean** [**sea**] ▶イギリスとフランスをつなぐ海底トンネル工事が1994年に完成した Construction of the *undersea tunnel* connecting Britain and France was completed in 1994. ‖**海底火山** a submarine volcano ‖**海底油田** a submarine oil field.

2**かいてい 改訂** **(a) revision** /rɪvíʒən/ **一動 改訂する** **revise** /rɪváɪz/ ＋⑬ ▶この地図帳は最近改訂された This atlas *has* recently *been revised*. ‖この辞書の改訂版は秋に出る The *revised edition* of this dictionary will be published in the fall.

3**かいてい 改定** **(a) revision** **一動 改定する** **revise** ＋⑬ ▶運賃[規則]の改定 *a revision* of fares [rules] ‖料金[規則]を改定する *revise* a price [rule].

4**かいてい 開廷** ▶ただ今より開廷します The court is now *in session*. (➤ The court is in session. は「開廷中」).

かいてき 快適な **comfortable** /kʌ́mfəˈṭəbəl/ (心地よい) ; **pleasant** (楽しめる) ; **congenial** (性に合った) ▶部屋を快適な温度に保つ keep the room at a *comfortable* temperature ‖これはあまり快適なベッドではない This is not a very *comfortable* bed. ‖快適な空の旅をお楽しみください We hope you enjoy a *pleasant* flight. ‖働くのに快適な環境を提供する provide a *congenial* atmosphere for work ‖アメリカ西海岸は空気が乾燥していて, 一年中快適だ Because of its low humidity, the climate of the U.S. West Coast is *pleasant* [*agreeable*] all year round. ‖その新車は快適だ The new car *drives* [*rides*] very *comfortably*. / The new car *is comfortable to drive* [*ride in*]. (➤ いずれも前者は「運転しやすい」, 後者は「乗り心地がよい」の意).

1**がいてき 外的な** **external** ▶外的な要因 an *external* factor ‖外的条件 an *external* condition ‖外的圧力 (an) *external* pressure.

2**がいてき 外敵** **a foreign enemy** (外国から来る敵) ; **a predator** (ほかの動物を襲うもの).

1**かいてん 回転** **(a) revolution** ; **(a) rotation** (自転) ; **a roll** (転がること) ; **(a) turnover** (客や商品の入れ替わり) **一動 回転する** **revolve, rotate** ▶地球は太陽の周りを回転する The earth *revolves* [*moves* / *goes*] *around* the sun. ‖こまはくるくると回転している The top *is spinning*.

▶資本をうまく回転させる *rotate* [*employ* / *circulate*] capital profitably ‖あのラーメン屋は(客の)回転が速い *Customer turnover* is high at that ramen shop.

▶《慣用表現》妹は頭の回転が速い My younger sister *has a quick mind*. / My younger sister *is quick-minded* [*is quick on the uptake*].

‖**回転競技** (スキーの) the slalom /slɑ́ːləm/ ‖**回転資金** a revolving fund ‖**回転寿司** a conveyor-belt sushi bar [restaurant] ‖**回転ドア[椅子]** a revolving door [chair] (➤「回転椅子」は swivel chair ともいう) ‖**回転木馬** a merry-go-round, 《米また》a carousel /kæ̀rəsél/.

2**かいてん 開店** **1【開業する】** **open** ＋⑬ ▶彼女は美容院を開店した She *has opened* a beauty parlor. ‖うちの店は開店休業の状態です Our store *is open, but business is slow*. (➤ この open は「開いている」の意の形容詞) ‖《掲示》本日(10時)開店 *Grand opening* today (at ten a.m.). (→オープン) ‖《掲示》近日開店 *Coming Soon*.

2【店を開ける】 **open** ▶開店は何時ですか What time [When] do you *open*? ‖そのスーパーは10時から7時まで開店している The supermarket *is open* from 10 a.m. to 7 p.m. ‖その花屋さんは午前9時に開店する The flower shop *opens* at 9 : 00 a.m.

がいでん 外電 an **overseas** [**international**] **telex, news from overseas**.

ガイド a **guide** (人, 案内書) ; a **guidebook** (ガイドブック) ▶その城はガイドが案内してくれる *A guide* will show you around the castle.

1**かいとう 解答** an **answer** (質問に対する) ; a **solution** (問題やパズルに対する) (➤ どちらも「…の解答」の「の」に当たる語には of でなく, to を用いる) **一動 解答する** **answer** (＋⑬), **solve** (＋⑬) (➤ 通例 question には answer を, problem には solve を用いる) ▶その問題に対する彼の解答は間違っている His *answer* to the question is wrong. ‖時には質問に対して教師がすぐに解答できないこともある Teachers sometimes are unable to *answer* questions immediately. ‖第2問に正しい解答をした人は32人中6人だけだった Only six out of thirty-two *gave the correct answer* to question two. ‖その物理の問題の解答を得るのに30分かかった It took me thirty minutes to *solve* the physics problem. ‖このパズルの解答は50ページに出ています The *solution* to the puzzle is given on page 50.

‖**解答者** a panelist (クイズ番組などの) ‖**解答用紙** an answer sheet [paper] ‖**解答欄** an answer column.

2**かいとう 回答** an **answer** (答え) ; a **response** (反応) ; a **reply** (返答) **一動 回答する** **answer** (＋⑬), **respond** (＋⑬), **reply** (＋⑬) ▶そのアンケート調査に対して多数の回答が寄せられた There were numerous *responses* to the survey.

‖**回答者** a respondent (アンケートなどの).

3**かいとう 怪盗** a **mysterious burglar** ▶怪盗紳士アルセーヌ・ルパン Arsène Lupin, *Gentleman Burglar*.

4**かいとう 解凍する** **thaw** /θɔː/ **(out), defrost** ＋⑬ ; **decompress** ＋⑬, **unzip** ＋⑬ (圧縮したファイルなどを ; 後者はインフォーマル) ▶冷凍食品を解凍する *thaw* (*out*) [*defrost*] frozen food ‖ファイルを解凍する *decompress* [*unzip*] a file.

1**かいどう 街道** 《米》a **highway**, 《英》a **highroad** ▶《比喩的》彼は出世街道まっしぐらだ He is on *the road to success*. 《参考》「青梅街道」のような固有名は the Oume Highway とするより, そのまま Oume-kaido とすることが多い.

2**かいどう 海棠** 《植物》a **Hall's crabapple**.

1**がいとう 街灯** a **streetlight** ▶街灯がついた The *streetlights* went on [came on].

2**がいとう 街頭** **the street** ▶街頭でちらしを配る distribute [hand out] fliers *on the street*.

‖**街頭演説** soapbox oratory / a speech made on a street corner ‖**街頭募金** street [on-the-street] fund raising.

3**がいとう 該当** ▶日本語の「おてんば」は英語の tomboy に該当する The word 'otenba' in Japanese *corresponds to* the English 'tomboy.' ‖手元にこの件に該当する資料があります I have some material(s) that *are pertinent* [*relevant*] *to* this matter on hand. ‖該当者は今月中に更新の手続きをしてくだ

さい *All concerned parties* are to make an application for renewal within the month. (➤ この party は「当事者」).

[4]**がいとう 外套** an **overcoat.**

[1]**かいどく 解読する** **decode** +目 (暗号などを); **decipher** +目 (文字などを) ▶探偵はその暗号を解読した The detective *decoded* the secret message. ‖ ロゼッタストーンはエジプト象形文字解読の鍵を与えた The Rosetta stone provided the key to the *deciphering* of Egyptian hieroglyphics.

[2]**かいどく 買い得** ▶このソファーは本当に買い得だった This sofa was a real *good buy* [a real *bargain* / *a good deal*]. (➤ この buy は名詞で「お買い得品」の意のくだけた語).

がいどく 害毒 **harm**; (an) **evil** (悪) ▶社会に害毒を流すウェブサイトが多い There are many websites that are *harmful* to society.

ガイドブック a **guidebook.**

ガイドライン a **guideline** ▶政府のガイドラインに合わせる meet [comply with] government *guidelines*.

かいとり 買い取り **buying, purchasing.**

かいとる 買い取る **buy** +目 ▶売れ残った自分の著書を全部買い取る *buy* (*up*) all one's unsold books.

かいならす 飼い慣らす **tame** +目, **domesticate** +目 (➤ 後者には「家畜化する」の意味もある) ▶野生の動物を飼い慣らすのは難しい It is difficult to *domesticate* wild animals. ‖ エルザは飼い慣らされたライオンだった Elsa was a *tame* lion. (➤ この tame は形容詞).

かいなん 海難 a **shipwreck**; a **disaster at sea** (航海中の事故) ▶海難救助に当たる be one of the people involved in *a rescue at sea* / assist in *a sea rescue* ‖ バーミューダ三角海域は海難事故が多いことで知られる The Bermuda Triangle is famous as a site of many *shipwrecks*.

かいにゅう 介入 **intervention**; **involvement** (掛かり合うこと) 一動 (…に)介入する **intervene** 《in》 ▶アメリカはソマリアに軍事介入した The United States *intervened militarily in* Somalia. ‖ アメリカのベトナムへの軍事介入は失敗に終わった America's *military involvement in* Vietnam ended in failure.

[1]**かいにん 解任** **dismissal, discharge** (➤ 両者は交換可能だが, 軍務からの解任には後者を用いることが多い) 一動 解任する **dismiss** +目, **discharge** +目 ▶事件後, 大使は解任された The ambassador *was dismissed* [*was relieved of his responsibilities*] after the incident.

[2]**かいにん 懐妊** **pregnancy** (妊娠); **conception** (受精).

かいぬし 飼い主 an **owner** (所有者); a **keeper** (世話係); a **master** (主人) ▶飼い主のいない犬 an *ownerless* dog / a *stray* dog (➤ 後者は「迷い犬, はぐれ犬」) ‖ 犬は飼い主に似ると言われる It is said that dogs come to resemble their *owners* [*masters*].

かいね 買い値 a **purchase price.**

がいねん 概念 a **concept**; an **idea** (考え方) ▶美の概念は民族によって異なる *Concepts* of beauty differ according to culture. / Each nationality has its own *ideas* of beauty. ‖ 彼の演説は概念的で具体性に乏しかった His speech was too *conceptual* and lacked specific details.

‖概念図 a conceptual diagram.

[1]**がいはく 外泊** ▶無断で外泊してはいけません Don't *stay out all night* without permission. ‖ 2週間友だちの家に外泊した I *stayed at* a friend's house for two weeks.

[2]**がいはく 該博** ▶日本の民間伝承に関する該博な知識 (*an*) *extensive* knowledge of Japanese folklore.

かいばしら 貝柱 an **adductor muscle** /mʌ́səl/.

かいはつ 開発 **development** 一動 開発する **develop** +目 ▶宇宙開発計画 a space *development* plan [project] ‖ 新しい交通システムを開発する *develop* a new public transport system ‖ この島は開発が後れている This island *is underdeveloped*. ‖ これはG社によって開発された新薬だ This is a new medicine *developed* by G Company. ‖ 開発中の薬 a drug *under* [*in*] *development* ‖ 能力開発のために自由な時間を有効に利用すべきです You should use your free time effectively to *develop your skills*.

‖開発途上国 a developing country.

☛ 再開発, 未開発, 乱開発 (→見出語)

かいばつ 海抜 (an) **elevation** ▶月山は海抜1980メートルある Mt. Gassan is 1,980 meters *above sea level*. ‖ アテネは海抜はどのくらいですか *How high* is Athens *above sea level*? / *What* is *the elevation* of Athens?

がいはんぼし 外反拇趾 《解剖学》 **hallux valgus** /hǽləks vǽlgəs/, a **bunion** /bʌ́njən/ (➤ 前者は医学用語, 後者は俗に使われる名).

[1]**かいひ 会費** **membership dues** [**fees**]; **dues** (分担金) ▶PTAの会費を納める pay PTA *dues* ‖ こちらのクラブの年会費は1万円です The *membership dues* [*fees*] of this club are 10,000 yen *a year*. ‖ 今晩のパーティーに出席される方は会費として1人1万円お支払いください Those who will attend the party tonight are kindly requested to pay 10,000 yen each to *cover expenses*.

[2]**かいひ 回避** **avoidance** (危険・害などの); **evasion** (義務などの巧みな) 一動 回避する **avoid** +目, **evade** +目 ▶危険[混乱]を回避する *avoid* danger [confusion] ‖ 彼女は明らかに責任を回避しようとしている She is obviously trying to *evade* her (own) responsibility. ‖ 交通ストは回避される模様だ It looks like the transportation strike will *be called off*. (➤ call off は「中止する」).

かいびかえ 買い控え ▶不景気でぜいたく品の買い控えが起きている People *are holding off* (*on*) *buying* [*deferring the purchase of*] luxury items because of the recession.

かいひょう 開票 **ballot** [**vote**] **counting** ▶開票の結果は今晩10時にラジオとテレビで放送されます The *election results* [*returns*] will be broadcast at 10 p.m. on radio and TV. (➤ 小規模な開票結果は a vote tally という).

‖開票所 a ballot [vote] counting office ‖ 開票速報 early [up-to-the-minute] returns ‖ 開票立会人 a ballot [vote] counting witness.

かいひん 海浜 a **beach** (水泳・日光浴などに適した); **the seashore** (水に接する陸地) ▶海浜(＝海辺の)公園 *a seaside park*.

がいぶ 外部 **the outside** (外側); **the outside world** (外界) ▶外部からの圧力 *outside* [*external*] pressures / pressure(s) *from outside* ‖ その被災地は外部との交通が遮断されている The disaster area is cut off from *the outside world*. ‖ 秘密が外部に漏れた The secret *leaked out* [*got out*].

かいふう 開封する **open** (**an envelope**) ▶手紙を開封する *open* a letter ‖ 書籍を開封で送る send [mail] a book *unsealed* (➤ 外国に送る場合, 封をしたときより安い料金で送ることができる).

かいふく 回復 **recovery** 一動 **回復する** **recover** ⦅from⦆; **restore**(元どおりにする)
▶彼は若いので疲労の回復が早い He is young, so he *recovers* quickly *from* fatigue. ‖ 病気のときは寝ていると回復が早い Staying in bed [Bed rest] when you are sick *helps restore your health* [*helps you recover*] *quickly*. ‖ 彼は急速に回復しつつある He's quickly *recovering from* his illness [*getting better*]. ‖ 母の健康は徐々に回復している My mother's health is *improving* little by little.
✉ ⦅病気見舞いで⦆ **1日も早いご回復をお祈りしております** I'm praying [hoping] for your speedy *recovery*.
▶一度失った信用を回復する(=取り戻す)のは難しい It's hard to *restore* trust once it is lost. ‖ 景気が回復してきた Business is *looking up*. ‖ 午後には天気も回復した The weather *took a turn for the better* in the afternoon.
▶大雪でまひした首都圏の交通機関は翌日回復した Tokyo area mass-transit systems, which had been paralyzed by a heavy snow, *resumed* (*full*) *operations* [*were restored to* (*full*) *operation*] on the following day.

かいぶつ 怪物 a **monster** ▶ゴジラは映画に出てくる人気者の怪物だ Godzilla is a popular movie *monster*. ‖ ダルビッシュ有は怪物だ Darvish Yu is *a* (*pitching*) *phenomenon* [*a pitching prodigy*].

> **直訳の落とし穴「ダルビッシュは怪物だ」**
> 常人には及びもつかない, ずば抜けた能力を持つスポーツ選手など, 人を指して「ダルビッシュは怪物だ」のようにいうことがあるが, ここに monster を使うことはできない. 人間について monster が使えるのは, 殺人鬼やヒトラーのような途方もない悪人の場合である.「人間離れした者」を表すのは a freak of nature であるが, この語にはマイナスイメージもあるので, 意味するところをとって,「類いまれな才能や能力の持ち主」を指す phenomenon を用いて, a (pitching) phenomenon ということもできる. wonder (驚異の人)や prodigy (神童)がふさわしい場合もある.

かいぶん 回文 a **palindrome** /pǽlɪndroʊm/ (➤ 前から読んでも後ろから読んでも同じ読み方になる文など; 日本語では「たけやぶやけた」, 英語では Madam, I'm Adam. の類い).

がいぶん 外聞 ▶外聞を気にするな Don't worry about *what other people think of you*. ‖ 先日, 社内で外聞をはばかる事件が起こった The other day something *scandalous* happened within the company.

かいへい 開閉 ▶冷蔵庫のドアの開閉は素早くしなさい Please *open and close* the refrigerator door quickly.

かいへいたい 海兵隊 ⦅米⦆ **the Marine Corps** /mərí:n kɔ̀:ʳz/, **the Marines**; ⦅英⦆ **the Royal Marines** ‖ **海兵隊員** a marine.

がいへき 外壁 an **outer** [**outside**] **wall**.

かいへん 改編 ▶組織を改編する *make a structural change* in an organization ‖ 会社を改編する *reorganize* a company (➤ 全面的に組み替えることを意味する).

かいべん 快便 ▶快食快便 a good appetite and *regular bowel movements*.

[1]**かいほう 解放** **liberation**, (a) **release** (➤ 後者は必ずしも長時間[期間]の自由を保証しない) 一動 **解放する** **liberate** +目, **release** +目 ▶人質を解放する *liberate* [*release*] a hostage ‖ あと1年で受験勉強から解放される In one year, I'll *be free from* having to study for college entrance exams. ‖ あと数年は子育てから解放されないでしょう I won't *be released from* the responsibilities of child-rearing for another several years. ‖ エイブラハム・リンカーンは南北戦争のさなかに奴隷解放宣言を布告して奴隷を解放した During the Civil War, Abraham Lincoln issued *the Emancipation Proclamation freeing* slaves [*setting* slaves *free*].
‖ **女性解放運動** the women's liberation movement, women's liberation [lib].

[2]**かいほう 開放する** **open**(開ける); **leave ... open**(開けたままにする) ▶窓を開放する *leave* the windows *open* ‖ ⦅掲示⦆ **開放厳禁** Shut [Close] the Door after You Leave / Keep Gate Closed (➤ 前者はドアの, 後者はゲートの場合).
▶その小学校は日曜日には校庭を一般の人に開放する The playground of that elementary school *is open to* the public on Sundays. ‖ 彼女は開放的な家庭に育った She grew up in a very *open* [*permissive*] family. (➤ permissive は「自由放任の」でマイナスイメージ).

[3]**かいほう 介抱する** **look after, care for** (➤ 後者のほうが堅い言い方) ▶父は病気の妹を寝ずに介抱した My father *looked after* [*cared for* / *sat up with*] my sick sister all night. (➤ sit up with は「寝ずに看病する」) ‖ 鈴木, だいぶ酔っ払ってるぜ. 介抱してやれよ Suzuki is pretty drunk. *Take care of* him, will you?

[4]**かいほう 快方** ▶母の病気は快方に向かった My mother's illness *has taken a turn for the better*. ‖ その患者は快方に向かっている The patient *is getting better* [*is improving* / *is recovering*].

[5]**かいほう 会報** a **bulletin** /bʊ́lətn/ (会員のための定期的な); **transactions** (学会などの); a **newsletter**(会社・団体などの).

かいぼう 解剖 **dissection**(研究・実験などのための); an **autopsy** /ɔ́:tɑ:psi/ (死因究明のための) 一動 **解剖する** **dissect** +目 ▶カエルを解剖する *dissect* a frog ‖ **死体解剖の結果, 被害者は毒殺されたものと判明した** The *autopsy* proved the victim had been poisoned.

がいまい 外米 **foreign rice**.

かいまく 開幕 **the opening**(開始) ▶舞台の開幕までまだ30分ある There are still thirty minutes left before *the curtain rises* [*goes up*].
▶いよいよ野球シーズンが開幕した The baseball season *has* finally *opened* [*started*].
‖ **開幕試合** an opening game, ⦅インフォーマル⦆ an opener ‖ **開幕投手** an opening game starter.

かいまみる 垣間見る **get a glimpse** ⦅of⦆ ▶ビデオにより彼のストックホルムでの生活がかいま見られた We *caught a glimpse of* what his life in Stockholm was like by watching the video.

かいみょう 戒名 a **posthumous** /pɑ́:stʃəməs/ **Buddhist name** ▶生前戒名 *a pre-death Buddhist name*.

かいむ 皆無 ▶彼女が歌手になれる見込みは皆無だ She has *no* chance *whatever* of becoming a singer. (➤ whatever は否定を強調し,「少しの…も」の意) ‖ 彼の車に対する知識ときたら皆無といってよい He knows little or *nothing* about cars.

がいむ 外務 **foreign affairs** ‖ **外務省** the Ministry of Foreign Affairs ⟪参考⟫ アメリカでは the Department of State が, イギリスでは the Foreign and Commonwealth Office が, それぞれ外務担当省. ‖ **外務大臣** the Minister of Foreign Affairs／the Foreign Minister(➤ 前者が正式名称) 《参考》アメリカでは the Secretary of State が, イギリスでは the Foreign Secretary が外務担当大臣.

か

[1]**かいめい 解明する** **solve** +㊐ ; **clarify** +㊐ (明らかにする) ; **investigate** +㊐ (詳細に調べる) ▶問題を解明する *solve* a problem ‖ 世の中にはまだ**解明されない**謎が数多くある There are so many *unsolved* mysteries in the world. ‖ 彼らはその飛行機事故の原因の**解明**に乗り出した They started to *investigate* the cause(s) of the plane crash.

[2]**かいめい 改名** one's **change of name** ▶日本では**改名**するのは難しい It is difficult to *change your name* in Japan. ‖ **改名届**を市役所に出した I reported *my change of name* to the city office.

[3]**かいめい 階名**《音楽》a **solfège syllable,** a **sol-fa syllable.**

かいめつ 壊滅する **be devastated** /dévəsteɪṭɪd/ ▶その町は爆撃で**壊滅的打撃を受けた** The town *suffered devastating damage* in the bombing attack.／The town *was devastated* in the bombing raid.

[1]**かいめん 海面** **the surface of the sea** ▶**海面**は鏡のように滑らかだった The *sea* was as smooth as glass.(➤「面」は考えなくてよい) ‖ 潜水艦が**海面**に姿を現した The submarine rose to *the surface*.／The submarine *surfaced*.

[2]**かいめん 海綿** a **sponge** /spʌndʒ/.

がいめん 外面 **the exterior** /ekstíəriəʳ/, **the outside**(➤ 前者が日本語により近い) ; an **appearance**(うわべ) ▶建物の**外面** *the exterior* [*outside*] of a building. ▶**外面**を飾る keep up *appearances* ‖ 彼女は**外面**は平静を装っていたが, 心中は全く穏やかではなかった She *appeared* calm, but inwardly she was quite uneasy. ‖ **外面的な美しさ** *outward* [*external*] beauty.

かいもく 皆目 ▶この車のエンジンのどこが悪いのか**皆目わからない** I *don't have the slightest* [*I have no*] *idea* what's wrong with this car engine. ‖ 私にはその講義は**皆目わからなかった** I *was unable to make head(s) or tail(s) of* the lecture. (➤ make head(s) or tail(s) of は「…を理解する」の意のくだけた表現 ; 通例否定文・疑問文で用いる ;《米》では複数形,《英》では単数形を用いることが多い).

かいもどす 買い戻す **buy back** ; **redeem** +㊐ (質ぐさなどを).

かいもとめる 買い求める **buy** +㊐, **purchase** +㊐. →買う.

かいもの 買い物

訳語メニュー
買うこと →shopping **1**
買ったもの →a buy **2**

1【行為】shopping ▶元町に**買い物に行く** *go shopping* in Motomachi(➤ この場合 (×)to Motomachi としない)／*go* to Motomachi *to shop* ‖ 母は街に**買い物に行った** My mother *went shopping* in town.／My mother *went* to town *to shop*. ‖ 近頃は多くの人がインターネットでたくさんの**買い物をする** Many people *do* a great deal of *shopping* [*shop* a lot] online [on the Internet] these days. ‖ 今月はたくさん**買い物がある**から, 家計が大変だ This month our family budget will be very tight because we *have to buy many things*. ‖ パパ, 帰りに**買い物してきてね** Honey, could you *do some shopping* on your way home?

▶スーパーマーケットの**買い物客**は**買い物籠**を提げているか, ショッピングカートを押している *Shoppers* at a supermarket either carry *shopping baskets* or push carts.

‖ **買い物袋** a shopping bag.

2【品物】 a **buy,** a **bargain** (➤ ともに「掘り出し物」の意で, 前者は通例 good, bad などを伴う) ▶この単車は**いい買い物だぜ** This motorcycle is *a good buy* [*a (good) bargain*].

がいや 外野 1【野球】the outfield ▶**外野**を守る play *(the) outfield*

‖ **外野手** an outfielder ‖ **外野席** the bleachers.

2【第三者】 ▶**外野**がうるさい *Bystanders* make all sorts of comments.

かいやく 解約 (a) **cancellation**(契約などの) 一動 **解約する** **cancel** +㊐ ▶今借りている部屋を**解約したい** I want to *cancel* [*break*] *the lease on* my apartment. ‖ 彼女は宝石類の盗難保険を**解約した** She *canceled* the theft insurance on her jewelry. ‖ 銀行の口座を**解約する** *close* one's account with a bank(➤「口座を閉じる」と表現する).

かいゆう 回遊 **migration** 一動 **回遊する** **migrate** ▶マグロは**回遊する** Tuna *migrate*.

‖ **回遊魚** a migratory fish.

がいゆう 外遊する **travel abroad** [**overseas**] ▶久保田夫妻は現在**外遊中**です Mr. and Mrs. Kubota *are* now *traveling abroad*.

[1]**かいよう 海洋** **the ocean, the sea**

‖ **海洋国** a maritime nation [country] ‖ **海洋小説** a sea story ‖ **海洋深層水** deep ocean water ‖ **海洋生物学** marine biology ‖ **海洋博覧会** a marine exposition.

「海洋」のいろいろ 注 すべて the をつける.
インド洋 Indian Ocean／**オホーツク海** Sea of Okhotsk／**カリブ海** Caribbean Sea／**黄海** Yellow Sea／**紅海** Red Sea／**黒海** Black Sea／**大西洋** Atlantic Ocean／**太平洋** Pacific Ocean／**地中海** Mediterranean Sea／**南極海** Southern Ocean／**日本海** Sea of Japan／**バルト海** Baltic Sea／**東シナ海** East China Sea／**ベーリング海** Bering Sea／**北海** North Sea／**北極海** Arctic Ocean／**南シナ海** South China Sea

[2]**かいよう 潰瘍** an **ulcer** /ʌ́lsəʳ/ ▶胃に**潰瘍**ができていると医者に言われた My doctor told me I had a stomach *ulcer*.

[1]**がいよう 概要** an **outline**(あらまし) ; a **summary** (まとめ) ▶事件の**概要**を述べる give *an outline* of an event ‖ 報告書の**概要**を記す make *a summary* of a report.

[2]**がいよう 外洋** **the open sea, the high seas.**

かいらい 傀儡 a **puppet** /pʌ́pɪt/ ▶あの**かいらい政権**は将軍たちに支配されている That *puppet government* is controlled by the generals.

がいらい 外来 ▶この科では**外来**(患者)しか扱いません This department only accepts *outpatients*. (➤「入院患者」は inpatient).

がいらいご 外来語 a **loanword,** a **borrowed word.**
ディベートルーム「外来語は積極的に日本語にとり入れるべきである」

がいらいしゅ 外来種 an **introduced** [**alien**] **species.**

かいらく 快楽 (a) **pleasure** ; (a) **joy** (歓喜) ▶つかの

間の快楽にふける give oneself up to passing *pleasure* ‖ 彼は人生の快楽を知らずに若くして死んだ He died young, without knowing *the joys of life*.

かいらん 回覧 ▶彼らはその雑誌を回覧した They *passed* the magazine *around*.
‖回覧板 a notice.

かいり 海里 a **nautical mile.**

かいりき 怪力 ▶怪力のレスラー a wrestler with *incomparable power* ‖ 怪力を発揮する exhibit *miraculous strength* [*power*].

かいりつ 戒律 a **religious precept** /príːsept/ ▶戒律を守る[破る] follow [break] *a religious precept* ‖ イスラム教は戒律が厳しいことで知られる Islam is well known for the strictness of its *precepts*.

がいりゃく 概略 a **summary**(要約, まとめ); an **outline**(あらまし) ▶彼の演説の概略が新聞に載った *A summary* of his speech was printed in the newspaper. ‖ 事件の概略は次のとおりです The following is *a general summary* of the incident.

かいりゅう 海流 an **ocean current** ▶黒潮とも呼ばれる日本海流は暖流である *The Japan Current*, also called the Black Stream, is a warm current.

かいりょう 改良 (an) **improvement** 一動 **改良する improve** +目 ▶品質改良 quality *improvement* ‖ 牛の品種を改良する *improve* a breed of cattle ‖ パソコンのソフトは常に改良されている Computer software is always *being improved*. ‖ 日本の教育制度はまだまだ改良の余地がある Japan's education system still has much room for *improvement*.

1**かいろ 回路** a **circuit** /sə́ːˈkɪt/
‖集積回路 an integrated circuit《略 IC》‖電気回路 an electric circuit.

2**かいろ 海路** ▶首相は鹿児島から海路沖縄入りした The Prime Minister went from Kagoshima to Okinawa *by sea*.
ことわざ 待てば海路の日和あり Ideal weather for sea travel will come to those who wait. (➤ 日本語からの直訳) ／All storms blow over eventually. (➤ 意訳).

3**かいろ 懐炉** a **portable body** [**hand**] **warmer.**

カイロ Cairo(エジプトの首都).

がいろ 街路 a **street**, an **avenue** 《参考》アメリカの都市では南北に走る縦の大通りを Avenue, それに交差して東西に走る横の通りを Street と呼ぶことがある. ▶街路樹の緑が美しい The *trees along the street* are beautiful and green.

かいろう 回廊 a **cloister**(中庭を囲むもの); a **corridor**(廊下).

カイロプラクティック chiropractic /káɪrəpræ̀ktɪk/(脊椎矯正法, 整体療法) ▶カイロプラクティックに行く *go to see the chiropractor*(➤ chiropractor は「脊椎矯正師, 整体師」).

がいろん 概論 a **survey** /sə́ːˈveɪ/ (概説, 概観); an **outline**(あらまし); an **introduction** (入門, 手引き) ▶この本のタイトルは『英詩概論』である This book is (en)titled "*A Survey* of English Poetry."

かいわ 会話 a **conversation** ▶インドの人と英語で会話する *speak with* [*talk to*] a person from India in English ‖ 彼女は英語の会話が上手だ She *speaks* English *well*. ‖ 仲よしが何年かぶりに集まったので会話が弾んだ When the good friends got together after some years, the *talk flowed freely*. ‖ 対話「バンクーバーではカナダ人と英語で会話したのですか」「いやいや, いつも通訳に頼っていました」"When you were in Vancouver, did you *talk with* Canadians in English?" "No, I always relied on an interpreter."
☛ 英会話 (→見出語)

かいわい 界隈 a **neighborhood**; **vicinity**(近隣一帯) ▶この界わいはお寺が多い There are many temples in this *neighborhood* [*vicinity*]. ‖ お花見シーズンには上野界わいは大変な人出になる A great many people go to *the area around Ueno* [*the Ueno vicinity*] when the cherry trees are in full bloom there.

かいわれだいこん 貝割れ大根 daikon sprouts.

かいん 下院 the Lower House(各国共通); **the House of Representatives** (アメリカの); **the House of Commons** (イギリスの)
‖下院議員《米》a member of the House of Representatives (➤ a Representative ともいう), a Congressman [-woman] ／《英》a member of the House of Commons, a Member of Parliament (➤ MP と略す).

1かう 買う

> 訳語メニュー
> 物を買う →buy **1**
> 正しく評価する →appreciate **3**
> 買って出る →volunteer **4**

1【物を】buy +目

> 【文型】
> **人(A)に物(B)を買ってやる**
> **buy** A B
> **buy** B **for** A
> ➤ for A の形は「誰に」に重点がある.
> **物(A)を金額(B)で買う**
> **buy** A **for** [**at**] B
> ➤ 総額には for を, 単価には at を用いる
> **物(A)を(店で)買う**
> **shop for** A
> ➤「…を買いに店に行く, 店で…を探す」の意.

▶おまえにいいものを買ってやろう I'll *buy* [*get*] you something nice. ／I'll *buy* [*get*] something nice for you. (➤ get はインフォーマルな語) ‖ 欲しいものは何でも買ってやるというわけにはいかないよ There's no way (that) I'm going to *buy* you everything you want. ‖ 彼は6歳の息子に自転車を買ってやった He *bought* a bicycle *for* his six-year-old son. (➤ bought は buy の過去形) ‖ この店ならそのデジタルカメラはもっと安く買えるよ You can *buy* [*get*] that digital camera cheaper at this store. ‖ この万年筆は2000円で買った I *bought* this fountain pen *for* two thousand yen ‖ そのリンゴは1個150円で買った I *bought* the apples *at* one hundred (and) fifty yen apiece. ‖ うちでは週に2度近くのスーパーに食料品を買いに行く We go to a nearby supermarket twice a week to *shop for* groceries. ‖ 私は放課後新しいＣＤを買いに行った I *went shopping for* a new CD after school. →購入.

▶これいくらで買ったんだい？ *How much did you pay for* this? ‖ 金で愛を買うことはできない Money can't *buy* (you) love. ‖ (店で客が) じゃあ, これ買うわ All right, *I'll take this* (*one*). (➤「特定の品物に決める」という場合は take を用いる) ‖ 対話「お父さん, オートバイ買ってよ」「だめだね. そんなの買う余裕はないよ」"Dad, will you *buy* me a motorcycle?" "No, I *can't afford to buy* you one."

2【招く】▶彼女のことばが彼の怒りを買った Her words

made him *angry*. ‖ 人の**恨みを買う**ようなことをした覚えはありません I don't remember doing anything that would *cause* people *to hold a grudge against* me.

3【認める, 評価する】appreciate +㊐ ▶きみの熱意は**買う**が, 計画は認められない I *appreciate* your enthusiasm, but I can't approve your plan. ‖ 部長は田中さんの語学力を**高く買っている** The department head *prizes* Mr. Tanaka's linguistic ability.

4【進んで引き受ける】volunteer /vὰ:ləntíəʳ/ ▶彼はその役を**買って出た** He *volunteered* to play that role. ‖ 彼は売られたけんかを**買った** He *took up* the challenge. ‖ 若いうちの苦労は**買ってでも**しろ Hardship is so good for young people that they should *pay for* [*buy*] it. (➤ 日本語からの直訳) ／ You shouldn't be afraid to take on hardship while young. (➤ 意訳).

2**かう 飼う** **have** +㊐ (ペットなどを所有する) ; **keep** +㊐ (飼って世話をする ; 場所を表す語句とともに用いることが多い) ; **raise** +㊐, **rear** +㊐ (飼育する ; 《英》では後者が一般的) ▶彼の農場では牛60頭と豚80頭を**飼っている** He's *raising* [He *has*] 60 cows and 80 hogs on his farm. (頭数は変化するので進行形で表すのがふつう. 頭数が示されていなければ, He raises cows and hogs on his farm. とする) ‖ **対話** 「どんなペットを**飼っていますか**」「犬と小鳥を**飼っています**」 "What kind of pets do you *have*?" "I *have* a dog and some birds."

カウボーイ a **cowboy**
‖**カウボーイハット** a cowboy hat ‖ **カウボーイブーツ** cowboy boots.

ガウン a **gown** ; a **dressing gown**, a **robe** (部屋着).

カウンセラー a **counselor** ▶結婚**カウンセラー** a marriage *counselor* ‖ 心(＝精神衛生)のケアをする**カウンセラー** a mental health *counselor* ‖ その件について**カウンセラー**に相談する consult *a counselor* about the matter.

カウンセリング **counseling** ▶私は問題児に**カウンセリング**している I *counsel* children who have [children with] problems. ‖ 家庭内のいざこざについて専門家から**カウンセリングを受けた** I *received* [*got*] *counseling* from a professional about our family problems.

カウンター a **counter** (テーブル ; 計算器) ▶《店で》お勘定は**カウンター**(＝レジ)でお願いします Please pay at the *checkout counter*. ‖ 私はすし屋ではテーブルより**カウンター**で食べるのが好きだ In sushi shops, I prefer eating at the *counter* rather than at the table.

> **危ないカタカナ語✹ カウンター**
> **1** 日本語の「カウンター」はバーやスナックなどを連想させるが, 英語の counter は銀行の窓口, デパートなどの売り台, 台所の調理台など広い意味をもつ.
> **2** ホテルや空港などの受付を「カウンター」ということがあるが, 英語では front desk (フロント), check-in desk (搭乗手続き所) のように desk を用いることが多い.

カウンターテナー 《音楽》 a **countertenor**.

カウント **1【野球】a count** (➤ ball count とはいわない) ▶阿部は 3－0 の**カウント**から左中間に三塁打を放った Abe slammed a triple to left center on a 3-0 *count*. (➤ ボール→ストライクの順に数えるアメリカ方式が日本でも導入されつつある).
‖**フルカウント** a full count ／a 3-2 count.

2【ボクシング】a count ▶挑戦者は**カウント** 8 で立ち上がった The challenger got to his feet at the *count* of eight.

カウントダウン a **countdown** ▶ロケット発射の**カウントダウン**が始まった The *countdown* for the rocket take-off has started.

かえ 替え ▶《文房具店で》シャープペンシルの**替え芯**, ありますか? Do you have mechanical pencil *refills*? ‖ 服の**替え**は持ってきましたか Did you bring *a change* of clothes?
‖**替えズボン** spare pants [trousers ／slacks].

かえうた 替え歌 a **parody** ▶『森のくまさん』の**替え歌** *a parody* of the song "Mori-no-kuma-san"

かえぎ 替え着 a **change of clothes**. →着替え.

1**かえす 返す** **1【物を元の場所へ戻す】return** +㊐, **give back**

> **【文型】**
> 人(A)に物(B)を返す
> **give** B **back to** A
> **return** B **to** A
> **give** A **back** B
> **【解説】** (1) B が it, that など代名詞のときは **give** B **back to** A の語順にするが, 名詞のときは give back B to A ともいう.
> (2) A の人が me, him など代名詞のときは **give** A **back** B の文型を使う.

▶図書館に本を**返さないといけない** I must *return* the [my] books *to* the library. (➤ my books とすると「私が借り出していた本」の意) ‖ 先日お貸ししたCDを**返してください** Please *return* (me) the CD (that) I lent you the other day. (➤ 《米》では me を付けない. return me は《英》) ‖ 忘れ物は持ち主に**返しなさい** *Give* the things (that have been) left behind *back to* their rightful owners. ‖ 審査官はすぐ私にパスポートを**返してくれた** The inspector immediately *gave* me *back* my passport [*returned* my passport *to* me]. (➤ 《英》では returned me my passport という) ‖ 《プラカードで》平和な生活を**返せ** *Give* us *back* our peaceful life.

▶読み終わったらその本は棚に[元の所に]**返しておきなさい** *Put* the book *back* on the shelf [where it was] when you are through (with it). ‖ 私の鏡, 用が済んだら**返してくれる**? When you're done with my mirror, could I *have* it *back* please?

▶波は寄せては**返す** The waves surge and *recede*. ‖ 一度損なわれた環境を元の状態に**返す**(＝復元する)ことは難しい It is difficult to *restore* the environment to its original condition once it has been damaged.

2【金を貸し手に戻す】 ▶先日貸した金を**返してもらいたい** I want you to *pay back* the money I lent you the other day. ‖ 彼は借金を全部**返した** Now he has *paid off* (all) his debts.

3【受けた行為と同様の, または逆の行為をする】 ▶恩をあだで**返す** *return evil for good* ／*requite kindness with ingratitude* (➤ requite /rɪkwáɪt/ は「…に報いる」の意の堅い語) ‖ おことばを**返すようですが**, 彼を当てにしないほうがいいですよ *I'm sorry to contradict you*, but you'd better not rely on him. ‖ **返すことば**も無かった I was at a loss for *an answer*. ／I did not know *how to answer* (him). ‖ 中日は 2 回に 3 点取られたあと, 7 回にようやく 1 点**返した** The Dragons, after giving up three runs in the second

inning, at (long) last *scored* one run in the seventh inning.
4【なかったことにする】▶一切を白紙に返そう *Let's forget* all about it. ‖ 白紙に返してやり直そう Let's start (all) over again.

2**かえす 帰す** ▶我々を故郷に帰してくれ *Allow* us *to return to* our hometown. ／*Let us go back to* our hometown. (● 後者は「故郷に帰ろう!」の意にもなるので, 英訳としては前者が明確) ‖ 先生はその生徒を厳しく注意して帰した The teacher *dismissed* the boy [*sent* the boy *home*] after admonishing him. ‖ 父は釣り上げた魚を川に帰してやった My father *returned* the fish he had caught to the river. ‖ 中村は犠牲フライを打って三塁ランナーを帰した Nakamura's sacrifice fly *returned* the base runner on third to score one run.

3**かえす 孵す** **hatch** +⊞ (➤ ふ化する前の「卵を抱く」ことを incubate /íŋkjəbeɪt/ という) ▶卵をかえす *hatch* an egg ‖ 軒先でツバメがひなをかえした Swallows *hatched* their young under the eaves.

-かえす -返す ▶ボールを打ち返す *hit* a ball *back* ‖ 母親に言い返す *talk back* to one's mother ‖ 殴られたら殴り返せ If he hits you, *hit* him *back*.
▶同じ文章を何度も読み返す *read* the same sentences *over and over again*.

かえすがえすも 返す返すも ▶その力士が再び土俵に立てないのは返す返すも残念だ *It is a great pity* (that) that sumo wrestler will never again stand in the ring (for a bout).

かえだま 替え玉 one's **double** ▶暗殺された将軍は実は替え玉だった The general who was assassinated was actually *his double* [turned out to be *his double*]. ‖ 替え玉受験 use of *a substitute* in taking an (entrance) examination.

かえって 却って ▶彼は黙っていたのでかえって我々の注意を引いた His silence actually attracted our attention (*all the*) *more*. (➤ all the more は「かえって, ますます」) ‖ 薬を飲めば飲むほどかえって気分が悪くなった *The* more medicine I took, *the* worse I felt. (➤「the ＋比較級, the ＋比較級」で「…すればするほどそれだけ…になる」).
▶ジョギングはやり過ぎるとかえって害になる Too much jogging can do (you) *more* harm *than good*. ‖ あなたに手伝ってもらうとかえって余計手間がかかるから, 黙って見ていてちょうだい Having you help me *just makes more needless work* for me. So just sit over there and watch me do it. ‖ 痩せようと思ってダイエットを始めたのに, かえって太ってしまった I started going on a diet to lose weight, *but in fact* I ended up gaining (weight).

かえで 楓 《植物》a **maple (tree)** ▶カエデの葉 a *maple* leaf.

かえば 替え刃 a **spare blade** ▶かみそりの替え刃 *a spare* razor *blade*.

かえり 帰り ▶野球部の生徒は毎日帰りが遅い Baseball club members *go home late* every day. (➤ 家の者からいえば come home となる) ‖ 下関へは電車で行ったが, 帰りはバスを利用した I went to Shimonoseki by train and *returned* by bus. ‖ 帰りの列車は混み合っていた The train was crowded *on my way home*. ‖ 学校からの帰りに道で100円玉を拾った I picked up a one hundred yen coin on the street *on my way* (*home*) from school. ‖ 対話 「お帰りは何時ですか」「6時頃だね」"What time will you *be back*?" "Around six, I suppose."

☞ お帰りなさい (→見出語)

かえりうち 返り討ち ▶返り討ちに遭う *be killed in a fight where one is trying to seek revenge*.

かえりがけ 帰りがけ ▶父は会社の帰りがけに(＝帰宅途中)よく飲み屋に立ち寄る My father often drops in at a pub *on his way home* from work. ‖ 彼は帰りがけに(＝帰り際に)私を映画に誘った *As we were going home*, he asked me to go to a movie with him.

かえりざく 返り咲く **make a comeback** ▶その力士は大関に返り咲いた The sumo wrestler *made a great comeback*, becoming ozeki.

かえりじたく 帰り支度 ▶日本への帰り支度をする *get ready to return* to Japan ‖ 帰り支度はできています I'*m* (*all*) *ready to go* (*back*). (➤ go home とすると子供っぽく響く).

かえりみち 帰り道 ▶学校からの帰り道, いとこに会った I met my cousin *on my way* (*home*) from school.

かえりみる 顧みる・省みる **look back** 《on》(振り返る) ▶自分の過去を顧みる *look back on* one's past.
▶若者は子供を救うために, 身の危険を顧みず火の中へ飛び込んだ The young man plunged into the flames to rescue the child *with no thought for* his own safety. ‖ 父は家庭を顧みない人でした My father was the kind of person who *paid no attention* to his family [who *took* his family *for granted*]. (●「注意を払わない」と考えれば前者,「ありがたみを感じない」と考えれば後者のように訳すとよい).
▶私は寝る前に一日の行いを省みることにしている Before going to bed, I always *think over* what I've done during the day.

1**かえる 蛙** a **frog**; a **toad** (ヒキガエル) ▶田んぼでカエルが盛んに鳴いている *Frogs* are croaking loudly in the rice paddies.
▶《慣用表現》彼女に説教しても無駄だよ. 何を言ったってかえるの面に水なんだから It is no use giving her advice. Anything you say will be *like water* (*rolling*) *off a duck's back*. (➤「アヒルの背を流れ落ちる水のようだ」が原義; Anything you say will go in one ear and out the other. (片方の耳からもう一方の耳に抜けてしまう)を使ってもよい).
ことわざ かえるの子はかえる The child of a frog is a frog. (➤ 日本語からの直訳) ／Like father, like son. (➤ 英語のことわざ).

2**かえる 帰る** **come [go] home, get back, return**

> **語法** (1) come home は「(外から)家へ帰って来る」, go home は「家へ帰って行く」の意. get back と return はどちらの意味にもなる(前者はインフォーマルな言い方).
> (2) 英語は動作そのものよりも, その結果を中心に表現する傾向があり,「帰る」の場合 come home [back] と言う代わりに be back (帰宅している) という結果的な表現をすることもしばしばある.

▶学校が終わるとすぐ家に帰ります I *go home* as soon as school is over. ‖《外で遊んでいる子供に》きみたち, もう遅いから家へ帰りなさい It's getting late, children! You'd better *go* (*on*) *home*. ‖《出がけに》暗くならないうちに[いつもの時間に]帰ります I'll *come back* before dark [(at) the usual time]. ／I'll *be back* before dark [the usual time]. ‖ そろそろ帰らなければなりません I *must be going* (*home*) now. (→

おいとま）‖家まで10分で**帰れます** I *can get home* in ten minutes.（➤ I can go home in ten minutes. とすると「10分したら退出できます」の意になる）‖彼女はゆうべ**帰って来る**のがとても遅かった She *came* [*got back*] *home* very late last night. ‖ **対話**「彼，いつ**帰って来る**の？」「さあ，わからないね」“When will he *be back*? ／ When is he expected *back*?” “Who knows?” ‖ **対話**「早く**帰って来**なさいよ」「うん，すぐ**帰る**よ」“Don't be long.” “I won't (be).”
▶彼はヨーロッパ旅行から**帰って来た**ばかりだ He *is just back* [*has just returned home*] from his trip to Europe. ‖ママが呼んでるからもう**帰らなくちゃあ** I guess I have to *leave*. I hear my mother calling. ‖《昼食を外でとったあとなどに》そろそろ会社に**帰るか** It's time to *head back to* the office. ‖**急いで家に帰った** I *hurried* home. ‖彼は久しぶりに**故郷へ帰った** He *went back to his hometown* for the first time in a long time. ‖サケは４年後に生まれ育った川に**帰って来る** Salmon *return* to the river where they were born when they are four years old. ‖彼女はヨーロッパへ（執筆）取材に行ったまま**帰らぬ人となった** She *passed away* (*unexpectedly*) in Europe, where she had gone to gather material (for her writing).

[3]**かえる** 返る **return** ▶貸した金はまず**返ってこない** Money once lent never *returns*. ‖長いこと貸してあった「漱石全集」がやっと**返ってきた** At last, my set of the complete works of Natsume Soseki I had loaned out *were returned*. ‖無くなった腕時計が**返ってきて**うれしい I am happy (that) I *got back* the watch I lost. ‖「ヤッホー」と呼ぶと「ヤッホー」とこだまが**返ってきた** When I shouted, “Ya-ho,” ya-ho echoed *back*.（→ヤッホー）‖あの駅の自動券売機の１つが壊れていて，お釣りが**返ってこない** One of the ticket vending machines at that station is broken and doesn't *give* change.
▶彼は名前を呼ばれて**我に返った** He *was brought back to reality* when his name was called. ‖遊園地で息子と一緒に**童心に返って**遊んだ Playing with my son at the amusement park, I *felt as if I were a kid again*. ‖若い時は二度と**返らない** You're only young once.（➤「若い時は一度しかない」の意）.

[4]**かえる** 変える・替［換］える・代える **1**【形・性質・状態を異なるものにする】**change** ＋目；**turn** ＋目（変化させる）▶考え［意見］を**変える** *change* one's mind [opinion] ‖妻が髪形を**変えた** My wife *changed* [*altered*] her hairstyle.（➤ alter は「部分的に変える」の意）‖カメレオンは周囲に合わせて体の色を**変える** A chameleon *changes* its color to match the environment. ‖父親の死が彼女の人生を大きく**変えた** The death of her father *changed* her life greatly. ‖あすは予定を**変えて**庭の草むしりでもしよう Let's *change* our plans [*have a change of* plans] and do some weeding in the garden or something tomorrow.

> **【文型】**
> A **を** B **に変える**
> **change** A **into** [**to**] B
> **turn** A **into** [**to**] B

▶熱は氷を水に**変える** Heat *turns* ice *into* water. ‖松下は社名をパナソニックに**変えた** Matsushita *changed* its company name *to* Panasonic. ‖彼は屋根裏を息子の部屋に**変えた** He *turned* [*converted*] the attic *into* a room for his son.
▶《慣用表現》その選手は**目の色を変えて**（＝非常に興奮して）アンパイアの判定に抗議した The player *got very excited* and protested the umpire's decision.
2【別のものと取り替える】**replace** ＋目；**change** ＋目（全部を入れ替える）

> **【文型】**
> **古い物（A）を新しい物（B）に替える**
> **replace** A **with** B

▶古くなったタイヤを（新品に）**替える** *replace* a worn tire (*with* a new one) ‖そのコンビニは店内の照明をＬＥＤに**換えた** The convenience store *replaced* its indoor lights *with* LED ones. ／The convenience store switched its indoor lights to LED ones. ‖彼はベンツをプリウスに**換えた** He *replaced* his Mercedes *with* a Prius.
▶**円をドルに替える** *change* yen into dollars ‖この100円玉を10円玉に**替えてください** Could you *give* me ten-yen coins *for* this 100-yen coin? ‖彼女のことはもういいよ．**話題を変えよう** Enough of her. Let's *change* the subject. ‖あいつ，また**仕事を替えた**んだってさ I hear that he has *changed jobs* again.（➤ jobs と複数形にすることに注意；change places（場所を変える；席を変わる）も同様）‖彼女はバスに酔いやすいので，前の方の席に**換えてもらった** Because she gets motion sickness easily on buses, she *had* her seat *changed* to one in the front. ‖下着は毎日**替えなさい** *Change* your underwear every day. ‖もっと大きな部屋に**換えてください** Could you *move* me *to* [*upgrade* me *to*] a bigger room? ／Could I get a bigger room?
▶小切手を**現金に換える** *cash* a check ‖株券を**現金に換える** *cash* in one's stock.
▶金魚鉢の水を**換えて**ちょうだい *Change* the water in the goldfish bowl. ‖たまには机の位置を**変えて**気分転換を図ろう How about *moving* the desk now and then for a change (of pace)? ‖当選は賞品の発送をもって発表に**代えさせていただきます** Prizes will be sent to prize-winners without prior notification.
3【別の人に務めさせる】**replace** ＋目 ▶監督は佐藤を古田に**代えた** The coach *replaced* Sato *with* Furuta [*subbed* Furuta *for* Sato].（➤ replace A with B, sub B for A はともに「AをBに取り替える」の意で，後者は中継放送などで使われるくだけた語）‖あの係の人は不親切だから担当者を**代えてほしい** The man at that counter is not helpful. You should *have* him *replaced*.

[5]**かえる** 孵る **hatch** ▶卵はいつかえるの？ When will the eggs *hatch*? ‖ツバメのひなが３羽かえった Three swallows *have hatched* (*out*).

かえんびん 火炎瓶 a **Molotov** /mɑ́ːlətɔːf/ **cocktail**, 《英また》a **petrol bomb**.

かお 顔

> **訳語メニュー**
> 顔面 →the face **1**
> 頭部 →the head **1**
> 目鼻だち →features **1**
> 表情 →look **2**
> 面目 →face **3**

1【顔面，頭部】**the face**；**the head** ▶うれしそうな［にこ

にこした] 顔 a happy [smiling] *face* ‖ 美しい顔 a beautiful *face* ‖ 立派な顔 a handsome *face* (➤ handsome /hǽnsəm/ は「りりしく整った美しさ」を表す語で, 主に男性の顔について用いる) ‖ 四角い顔 a square *face* ‖ 醜い顔 an ugly *face*.

▶彼女はとても愛らしい顔をしている She has such a lovely *face*. ‖ 彼はいい顔をしている He has *handsome* [*good*] *features*. (➤ features は「目鼻だち」) ／He is *handsome* [*good-looking*]. ‖ 私は毎朝起きるとすぐ顔を洗う I *wash my face* as soon as I get up every morning.

▶私たちは顔を見合わせた We *looked at each other*. ‖ 私は恥ずかしくて彼の顔を見ることもできなかった I was so ashamed (that) I couldn't *look him in the face*. (➤ この場合 (×)look at his face とはしない) ‖ 彼女の顔を見ればきみを愛していることがわかるよ One look at her *face* tells me (that) she loves you. ／Her *face* says [shows] that she loves you. ‖ 赤ん坊は母親の顔を見るとにっこり笑った The baby smiled when he saw his mother. (➤ he saw his mother's face としなくてよい) ‖ あいつの顔は見るのも嫌だ The very sight of him disgusts me. ／I can't bear the sight of him. ‖ ぼくはそのむごい光景から思わず顔を背けた I could not help *turning my face away* from that tragic scene. ‖ ぼくが話しかけると彼女は顔を赤くした She *blushed* when I spoke to her. ‖ 彼の顔を知っていますか Do you *know* his *face* [him *by sight*]?

▶窓から顔を出してはいけない Don't *stick your head* out (of) the window. (➤ この場合の「顔」は「頭部」のことだから face は使えない) ‖ 彼女は両手で顔を覆った She *covered her face* in her hands. ‖ 彼は本から顔を上げた He *looked up* from the book he was reading.

2【表情, 顔つき】a **look**

> 【文型】
> 顔(つき)が A である
> **look** A
> ➤ A は形容詞

▶彼女はうれしそうな[がっかりしたような／ばつの悪そうな]顔をしていた She *looked* happy [disappointed／embarrassed].

▶彼女は驚いた[ほっとした]ような顔をして私の方を振り向いた She turned to me *with a look of* surprise [relief] *on her face*. ‖ 彼女は朝から浮かぬ顔をしている She has had *a long face* since this morning. ／She has been *looking gloomy* [*glum*] since this morning. (●「浮かぬ顔をしている」は have a long face でよいが, 「憂鬱そうな」「ふさぎ込んだ」という感じを出すなら訳例のように, それぞれ gloomy, glum を用いるとよい) ‖ 私たちの先生は真面目な顔をしてよく冗談を言う Our teacher often makes jokes *with a straight face*. ‖ 彼は通りで会ってもよく知らん顔をする He often *looks through* me when we meet on the street. (➤ look through は「…を通り越して先を見る」の意味から転じて「…の存在を無視する」).

▶翌日彼は何食わぬ顔をして学校に出た The next day he attended school *as if nothing had happened*. ‖ その知らせを聞くと彼女は顔を曇らせた When she heard the news, *a cloud came over her face*. ‖ 彼はめったに感情を顔に出さない He seldom *shows* his emotions. ／His (facial) expressions rarely *betray* his emotions. ‖ おまえはうそを言ってるね. ちゃんと顔に書いてあるよ You're lying. *It is written* [*I can see it*] *all over on your face*.

3【面目】**face** (➤ この意味では Ⓤ 扱い) ▶それでは私の顔が潰れる That would *make* me *lose face*. ‖ きみのおかげで私の顔が潰れたよ You've *put* me *in a very embarrassing position*. ‖ 彼の顔を潰すようなことはするな Don't *let* him *lose face*. ‖ それでぼくの顔も立つ That will *save face* for me, too. ‖ ここはひとつ, 俺の顔を立てて言うことを聞いてくれよ Do as I say just this once so (that) I do*n't lose face*. ‖ 借り物の高価な花瓶を割ってしまって彼に合わせる顔がない I *can't bear to face* [*show my face to*] him because I broke a very expensive vase (which) I had borrowed from him.

4【姿】▶彼は遅くなって会に顔を見せた He *showed up* late for the meeting. ‖ たまには顔を出せよ *Look* me [us] *up* once in a while. ‖ 近頃あまり志村君の顔を見ない I *haven't seen* much of Shimura lately. ‖ 彼とは数回顔を合わせたことがある I have *met* him briefly several times. ‖ パーティーには財界の有名人が顔をそろえていた Many famous business people and financiers *were present* [*showed up*] at the party.

5【慣用表現】 **嫌な顔** ▶嫌な顔をする *make a face* ‖ 文子にお使いを頼んだら嫌な顔ひとつしないで行ってくれた When I asked Fumiko to run an errand for me, she did it *without showing the least sign of unwillingness* [*reluctance*]. **大きな顔** ▶あいつはいつも大きな顔をしているので嫌いだ I don't like him because he always *acts big*. (➤ act big は「偉そうにふるまう」). **顔が売れている** ▶彼は博多では顔が売れている *Everyone knows* him in Hakata. ‖ 彼女は日本で一番顔の売れた知事の一人だ She is one of the most *visible* governors in Japan. **顔が利く** ▶彼は警察に顔が利く He *has pull* with the police. (➤ pull は「コネ」の意のインフォーマルな語) ‖ 彼女の父親は実業界に顔が利く Her father *has influence* in the business world. **顔が広い** ▶彼は顔が広い He *knows a lot of people*. **顔から火が出る** ▶(恥ずかしくて)顔から火が出た I *was flushed* with shame. ／I *turned red as a beet* (with embarrassment). (➤ ともに「真っ赤になった」の意). **顔を貸す** ▶おい, ちょっと顔貸せよ Hey you, *get over here*.

> **逆引き熟語 ○○顔**
> ◆**いかつい顔** a craggy [rough-hewn] face／**浮かない顔** a long face／**うりざね[面長の]顔** an oval face／**えらの張った顔** a heavy-jowled face／**かわいい顔** a pretty [cute／sweet] face／**四角い顔** a square face／**にきび顔** a pimply face; a crater face(にきび跡のある顔)／**ひきつった顔** a drawn face／**細い顔[細おもて]** a narrow face／**丸顔** a round [moon] face／**むくんだ顔** a puffy face, a bloated face／**やつれ顔** a haggard [pinched] face
> ◆**あきれ顔** an amazed look／**陰気くさい顔** a gloomy expression, a melancholy face／**きつい顔** a stern look, a hard-featured face／**さえない顔** a depressed look

かおあわせ 顔合わせ ▶新会員はあす顔合わせをする New members will *get together* [will *be introduced to one another*] tomorrow.

かおいろ 顔色 **1**【顔の色】a **complexion** ▶彼は顔色がいい He has a good [healthy] *complexion*. ‖ その写真を見ると彼女は顔色を変えた She *turned pale* when she saw the photograph. ／She *changed* *color* at the sight of the photograph. (➤ turn pale は「青くなる」の意；change color は赤くなることを含む) ‖ 彼は顔色ひとつ変えずに重大決定を行った He made a weighty decision *with an impassive face*. ‖ 対話「顔色が悪いよ, どうしたの？」「めまいがするんです」"What's the matter (with you)? You *look pale*." "I feel dizzy."

2【表情】 an **expression** ▶私は父の顔色をうかがった I studied my father's *expression*. ‖ 組員たちは常に親分の顔色をうかがっている(＝怒らせないようにしている) Gang members *are* always *eager to avoid displeasing* the big boss. ‖ 父が同意していないことは顔色でわかった I could tell by my father's *face* that he disagreed.

かおく 家屋 a **house**(家)；a **building**(建物)；**premises** /prémɪsɪz/ (土地を含めた正式な言い方).

カオス **chaos** /kéɪɑːs/.

かおだし 顔出し ▶平井さんの所に顔出しに行ってくる I'm just going to *drop by* [*drop in at*] Mr. Hirai's place.

かおだち 顔立ち **features**(目鼻だち) ▶繊細な[整った]顔だちの青年 a young man of delicate [regular] *features* ‖ 木村君は上品な顔だちをしている Kimura has *a refined-looking face*. ‖ きみはぼくのおじに顔だちが似ている You *look like* my uncle. ‖ 顔だちのはっきりした青年 a young man *with clear-cut features*.

かおつき 顔付き a **look** ▶彼の顔つきからそれが気に入らないことがわかった I could tell by *the look on his face* that he didn't like it. ‖ 健は不安げな顔つきをしていた Ken wore an uneasy *look* on his face. ‖ 彼女はいつも憂鬱そうな[幸せそうな]顔つきをしている She always has a long [happy] *face*. ／She always looks gloomy [happy].

かおつなぎ 顔つなぎ ▶顔つなぎに久しぶりに会に出席した I attended the meeting for the first time in a long time so that *people wouldn't forget my face* [*to maintain useful contacts*].

かおなじみ 顔馴染み a **familiar face**；an **acquaintance** /əkwéɪntəns/ (知人) ▶パーティーでたくさんの顔なじみに会った I met plenty of *familiar faces* at the party. ‖ 彼女とは昔からの顔なじみだ She is *an old friend* [*an old acquaintance*] of mine. ／I've known her since way back (when). (➤ 後者はくだけた表現).

かおパス 顔パス ▶俺はあの映画館は顔パスだ I can get in that movie theater (*for*) *free*.

かおぶれ 顔ぶれ a **lineup**；a **member**(メンバー) ▶今晩のショーに登場する歌手たちの豪華な顔ぶれ a spectacular *lineup* of singers who will appear on tonight's show ‖ いつもの顔ぶれが会議室にそろった *The regular* [*usual*] *members* gathered in the conference room. ‖ ニュージーランド遠征隊の顔ぶれはまだ全部は決まっていない Not all the *members* of the New Zealand expedition have been chosen yet.

かおまけ 顔負け ▶彼女はプロの歌手顔負けの歌を歌う She sings so well (that) she *puts* even professional singers *to shame*. (➤ put ... to shame は「…を恥じ入らせる」).

かおみしり 顔見知り an **acquaintance** /əkwéɪntəns/ ▶彼女は私の友人ではありません. ただの顔見知りです I wouldn't say that she's a friend of mine. She's just *an acquaintance*. ‖ 浅野氏とは顔見知りだが親友ではない I *know* Mr. Asano *by sight*, but we're not close (friends). ‖ その殺人は顔見知りの犯行に違いない Whoever committed the murder must *have known* the victim *personally*.

かおみせ 顔見せ ▶きょうの会議はお互いの顔見せが主な目的だ The purpose of today's meeting is mainly to *meet each other for the first time* [*to make acquaintances with each other*].

かおむけ 顔向け ▶あんなことをしておいてよくも我々に顔向けができるね *How can you face* [*show your face to*] us after you've done that? ‖ あんなばかなことをしてとても世間に顔向けができない I *can't face people* after doing such a stupid thing.

かおもじ 顔文字 an **emoticon** (➤ emotion と icon の合成語)；a **smiley**(笑顔の).

かおやく 顔役 a **big boss**(盛り場・暗黒街などの) ▶あの男は新宿辺りの顔役らしい I hear he's *a big boss* around the Shinjuku area.

かおり 香り・薫り **fragrance** /fréɪɡrəns/ (主に花の)；**aroma**(コーヒーやたばこの)；**perfume**(芳香)；(a) **smell** (一般に匂い) ▶応接室はラベンダーの香りに満ちていた The reception room was filled with the *fragrance* of lavender. ‖ 庭のジンチョウゲはよい香りがする The daphnes in our garden give [have] *a sweet smell*.

▶どこからかクチナシの香りがする I don't know where it is coming from, but *I smell* a gardenia [but *there is the scent* of gardenia]. ‖ バラの香りがする香水が好きです I love perfumes that *smell like roses*. ‖ 海藻は海の香りがするので大好きです I love seaweed because it *smells of the sea* [it *has a nice sea scent*]. ‖ このワインは香りがよい This wine has a nice *bouquet*. (➤ bouquet /boʊkéɪ/ は特にワインの香り). →におい.

▶《比喩的》その作品はロマン派文学 [音楽] の薫りが高い The work is rich in romantic literary [music] *flavor*. (➤ flavor は「趣」).

かおる 香る・薫る **be fragrant**(主に花が)；**smell**(匂いがする) ▶ジンチョウゲの香る庭 a garden *fragrant* with daphne blossoms.

✉ **風薫る5月となりました** With the arrival of May, the air seems sweeter and fresher. ➤「5月の到来とともに空気はいっそう甘くすがすがしくなってきたようです」の意. 英語国民は手紙の初めにこういう時候の挨拶は書かないのがふつう. ただし, 文中で季節を話題にすることはある.

がか 画家 a **painter**, an **artist** ▶彼は画家です He's *a painter*. (➤ painter には「ペンキ屋」の意もあるが, 家を塗装するペンキ屋は house painter, 看板を描く人は sign painter というのがふつう).

‖ **油絵画家** an oil painter ‖ **現代画家** a contemporary painter [artist] ‖ **肖像画家** a portrait painter ‖ **抽象画家** an abstract painter ‖ **日曜画家** a Sunday [an amateur] painter ‖ **日本[洋]画家** a painter in the Japanese [Western] style ／a Japanese-style [Western-style] painter ‖ **風景画家** a landscape painter.

かかあでんか かかあ天下 ▶彼の家はかかあ天下でね, 何をするにもまずかみさんに相談してからなんだ He's *a* real *henpecked husband*. He never does anything without asking his wife first. (➤ henpecked husband は「恐妻家」)《参考》「彼の家はかかあ天下だ」は His wife wears the pants [《英》trousers] in his family. ／His wife is the boss [the dominant figure] in his family. ということも多い.

かがい 課外 ‖ **課外活動** extracurricular /èkstrəkəríkjələʳ/ activities (➤「課外活動に参加す

る」は participate in extracurricular activities) ‖ 課外授業 an extracurricular lesson.

かがいしゃ 加害者 a perpetrator (犯罪を犯した者) ; an assailant (暴行事件の) ▶事故の被害者のような顔をしていた男が実は加害者だった That man who was acting like a victim turned out to be *the one who caused the accident*.

かかえこむ 抱え込む 1【しっかり抱く】▶弟はおもちゃの自動車を抱え込んで放そうとしなかった My little brother *hugged* the toy car *tightly* and refused to let go (of it).
2【引き受ける】▶やっかいな仕事を抱え込んでしまった I *have taken on* a troublesome job.

かかえる 抱える 1【手・腕などで】hold +㊀ (しっかり持つ) ; carry +㊀ (運ぶ) ▶人形を腕に抱える *carry* [*hold*] a doll in one's arms ‖ 本を小脇に抱える *have* [*carry*] a book under one's arm.
2【負担になるものを】have +㊀ (持つ) ; be burdened (のしかかっている) ▶家に病人を抱える *have* a sick person at home to take care of ‖ 大家族を抱える *have* a large family to support ‖ うちでは従業員を5人抱えている We *employ* five people. ‖ 彼女は今大きな悩みを抱えている She *is burdened* by a big worry now. ‖ その銀行は多額の不良債権を抱えている That bank *is burdened* with bad loans amounting to a large sum. ‖ インドは人口過剰という問題を抱えている India *faces* [*is confronted with*] the problem of overpopulation. (➤「直面している」の意).
3【慣用表現】▶政府は相次ぐ不祥事に頭を抱えている The government *is reeling* under a series of corruption scandals. (➤ reel は「動揺する」) ‖ そのコメディアンの熱演に我々は腹を抱えて笑った The comedian's inspired performance *had* us all *holding our sides* [*rolling in the aisles*] *with laughter*. (➤ roll in the aisles /aɪlz/ は「(観客が)笑い転げる」の意のインフォーマルな表現).

カカオ (a) cacao /kəkáʊ, -kɑ́:oʊ/.

かかく 価格 a price ▶米の価格を下げる lower the *price* of rice ‖ デジカメを割引価格で買う buy a digital camera at *a reduced price* [at *a discount*]. ‖ 全品表示価格の3割引きで販売いたします We sell all items at a 30 percent discount off the *list prices*.
‖価格表 a price list ‖ お手ごろ価格 a reasonable price (適正な) ; an affordable price (買いやすい) ‖ 卸売価格 a wholesale price ‖ カタログ価格 a list price ‖ 公定価格 an official price ‖ 小売価格 a retail price ‖ 再販価格 a resale price ‖ 市場価格 a market price ‖ 消費者価格 a consumer price ‖ 二重価格 a dual [two-tier] price ‖ 末端価格 (麻薬の) a street price.
☛ 価格破壊 (→見出語)

[1]**かがく 科学** science 一形 科学の, 科学的な scientific ▶科学に興味をもつ子供たちが減っている The number of children interested in *science* is shrinking. ‖ 最近はマラソンの練習にも科学的な方法が取り入れられている A *scientific* approach is now used in marathon training. ‖ その説はまだ科学的に証明されていない The theory hasn't been *scientifically* proven yet. ‖ 科学技術の進歩 *technological* progress.
‖科学技術 science and technology (科学と技術) ; technology (技術) ‖ 科学雑誌 a science magazine ‖ 科学者 a scientist ‖ 科学捜査 forensics /fərénsɪks/, forensic science ‖ 科学博物館 a science museum ‖ 応用科学 applied sciences ‖ 自然科学 natural sciences ‖ 社会科学 social sciences ‖ 人文科学 the humanities.

[2]**かがく 化学** chemistry 一形 化学の chemical ▶化学の実験をする conduct *chemistry experiments* ‖ 銀は硫黄に触れると化学変化を起こす Silver undergoes *a chemical change* when it is immersed in sulfur.
‖化学記号 a chemical symbol ‖ 化学工業 the chemical industry ‖ 化学工場 a chemical plant ‖ 化学式 a chemical formula ‖ 化学者 a chemist ‖ 化学繊維 (a) chemical fiber (➤ synthetic /sɪnθétɪk/ fiber (合成繊維) というのがふつう) ‖ 化学調味料 monosodium glutamate /glúːṭəmeɪt/ 《略 MSG》(グルタミン酸ナトリウム) ‖ 化学反応 a chemical reaction ‖ 化学肥料 (a) chemical fertilizer /fə́ːʳṭəlaɪzəʳ/ ‖ 化学兵器 a chemical weapon ‖ 化学療法 chemotherapy /kìːmoʊθérəpi/.

ががく 雅楽 *Gagaku* ; the traditional music of the Japanese Imperial Court (➤ 説明的な訳).

ががくせい 画学生 an art student.

かかくはかい 価格破壊 price slashing ▶航空各社は航空券の価格破壊を始めた Airlines have started to *slash* air *fares* [flight *prices*].

かかげる 掲げる hang up (高い所につるす) ; fly +㊀ (旗を) ▶玄関には「売り家」という掲示が掲げてある *There is* a 'For Sale' sign (*hanging*) on the front door. ‖ その軍艦はマストの上に星条旗を掲げていた The warship was *flying* the Stars and Stripes on its masthead. (→掲揚).
▶青年は理想を高く掲げるべきだ Young people should *set* lofty ideals. ‖ 模範解答は巻末に掲げてあります Model answers *are shown* at the end of this book. ‖ 巻頭には編者のモットーが掲げてある The editor's motto *appears* [*is proclaimed*] at the beginning of the book. (➤ proclaim は「宣言する」の書きことばで, やや大げさに響く).

かかし a scarecrow 《参考》(1)「crow (カラス) を scare (脅かす)」という2つの意味が結び付いてできた語. (2) 英米のかかしは2本足でズボンをはき, シャツに帽子といった格好のものが多い.

かかす 欠かす ▶私はそのテレビの連続番組が好きで欠かさず見ている I like that TV series and *never miss* an episode. (➤ episode /épɪsoʊd/ は「(連続物の) 1話, 1回分」) ‖ 私は重要な会議には欠かさず出席する I *never fail to* [*always*] attend important meetings.
▶十分な睡眠は健康に欠かすことができない (＝不可欠だ) Good sleep *is essential to* good health. ‖ この辞書は英作文には欠かせない This dictionary *is a must* for English composition. (➤ この must は「不可欠のもの」の意の名詞) ‖ 我々の事業を成功させるには彼の協力は欠かせない We cannot succeed in business *without* his cooperation. ‖ あの人はその組織に欠かせない存在となっている That person has *established* his [her] *presence* in the organization. ／That person has become *indispensable* to the organization.

かかと 踵 a heel ▶ (片方の) ストッキングのかかとに穴があいている There is a hole in *the heel* of one of my stockings. ‖ 彼女はいつもかかとの高い靴を履く She always wears *high heels* [*high-heeled shoes* ／ *shoes with high heels*]. ‖ 彼の靴のかかとはすり減っている His shoes are worn down at (*the*) *heel*(*s*).

[1]**かがみ 鏡** a mirror ; a full-length mirror (姿見) ▶彼女は正装してから自分の姿を鏡に映してみた She dressed

up and looked at herself in *a mirror* [*glass*]. ‖ 合わせ鏡をする arrange two *mirrors* at such an angle that you can see your own back ‖ 航海中, 海は鏡のようだった During our voyage, the sea was *as smooth as glass* [*as calm as a mirror*].

[2]**かがみ 鑑** a **paragon**(体現した人); an **example**(手本, 模範) ▶美徳のかがみ *a paragon* of virtue ‖ ほら見ろ, あの練習ぶりを. あいつは野球選手のかがみだ Look (at) how hard he's practicing! He's *an example* for all of the baseball players. ‖ 母は主婦のかがみです My mother is *an ideal* [*a model*] *homemaker*.

かがみこむ 屈み込む ▶彼は腹を殴られて苦痛のあまりかがみ込んだ Hit in the stomach, he *doubled up* in pain.

かがみもち 鏡餅 ***kagamimochi***; a two-tier round mochi (rice cake) offered to the Kami [Shinto gods] (➤ 説明的な訳).

かがむ 屈む **stoop**(前かがみになる); **crouch** /kraʊtʃ/ (うずくまるように); **duck**(ひょいと頭を下げる) ▶戸口がとても低いから入るときはかがまないといけない The doorway is so low that you must *stoop* (*down*) to go through it. ‖ 前の列の人はかがんでください People in the front row, please *crouch down*. ‖《物が飛んで来るような場合に》かがめ! *Duck!* ⇀しゃがむ.

かがめる 屈める **bend**(上体を曲げる); **stoop** (前かがみになる) ▶ほら, 体をかがめないとかもいにぶつかるよ Watch out! You will bump into the door frame unless you *bend over* [*stoop down*]. ‖ 少年は身をかがめて硬貨を拾った The boy *bent over* [*stooped down*] and picked up the coin. (➤ bent は bend の過去形).

かがやかしい 輝かしい **bright**(明るい); **brilliant** (立派な); **glorious**(栄光ある); **glittering**(人が羨むような) ▶輝かしい前途 a *bright* future ‖ 輝かしい業績 *brilliant* achievements ‖ 輝かしい勝利 a *glorious* victory ‖ 輝かしい賞 a *glittering* prize(➤「輝かしい成功」の意でも用いる).

かがやかす 輝かす ▶彼は期待に目を輝かせた His eyes *shone* with hope. ‖ 彼女は目を輝かせて和男の計画に耳を傾けた She listened to Kazuo's plan(s) *with sparkling eyes*.

かがやき 輝き **brilliance**(光などの); **radiance** (目・顔色などの) ▶初夏の太陽の輝き the *brilliance* of the early summer sun ‖ 今日子の目の輝きは彼女が幸せであることを物語っていた The *radiance* of [*sparkle* in] Kyoko's eyes showed her happiness. ‖ ジュリア・ロバーツは女優としてますます輝きを増している Julia Roberts *is shining more brightly* than ever as an actress.

かがやく 輝く **shine**; **twinkle** (きらきら光る); **glitter** (断続的にきらきらする); **sparkle** (火花のようにせん光を発する); **beam**(光を放つ) ▶太陽は昼間輝き, 月は夜輝く The sun *shines* by day, the moon by night. ‖ 夜空に星が輝いている The stars *are twinkling* in the night sky. ‖ 彼女の耳にはダイヤのイヤリングが輝いていた Diamond earrings *sparkled* [*glittered*] in her ears. (➤ on her ears も可).

▶新入生たちの顔は期待に輝いていた The faces of the new students *were alight* with expectation. ‖ 彼の顔は喜びに輝いた His face *beamed* [*shone* / *shined*] with joy. (➤ shone は shined とともに shine の過去形) ‖ 入試合格の知らせを聞いて, 彼女の顔はぱっと輝いた Her face *lit up* when she heard of her success in the entrance exam. (➤ light up は「(顔・目・空などが)明るくなる」) ‖ 勝利の栄冠は田中選手の頭上に輝いた The crown of victory *shone* on (the player) Tanaka's head.

かかり 係 ⚠**「係」を表す英語の1語の単語はない.** ▶係の人(＝担当者)はどなたですか Who is *the person in charge*? / Who is responsible for this? ‖ 彼はホテルのフロント係をしている He is *a front desk clerk* [《英》*receptionist*] at a hotel.

‖**係官** an officer.

-がかり -掛かり ▶ピアノを運ぶのは5人がかりだ *Five people are needed* to carry the piano. ‖ その仕事は1週間がかりだった It *took me a whole week* to get that done. ‖ 彼の論文は3年がかりの研究の成果だ His thesis is the fruit of his *three years of* research.

☛ 親がかり, 通りがかり (⇀見出語)

かかりあい 掛かり合い **implication** 《in》(関与, 連座); **involvement**(巻き込むこと; 関係させること) ▶彼はその事件にかかり合いがある He *is implicated* [*is involved*] *in* the incident.

かかりあう 掛かり合う ▶そんなつまらない論争にかかり合いたくない I don't want to *get involved* in such a trivial dispute. ⇀関わり合う.

かかりいん 係員 an **attendant**; **the person in charge** (担当者) ▶駐車場の係員 a parking (lot) *attendant* ‖ 詳しいことは係員にお尋ねください For further details, please ask *the person in charge*.

かかりきり 掛かり切り ▶彼はこの3年間新しい地図帳の編さんに掛かりきりだ For the past three years he *has been devoted to* [*has been wrapped up in*] the task of compiling a new atlas. (➤ 後者はインフォーマルな言い方で, 日本語により近い) ‖ 今週いっぱいは答案の採点に掛かりきりです I'll *be busy* grading exam papers all this week. ‖ 彼女は子供に掛かりきりだ She *has her hands full* looking after her children.

かかりちょう 係長 ⚠**会社の組織が日・英・米で少しずつ異なるので, 係長にぴったりの英語はない. 日本の係長は subsection chief がよい.** ⇀課長.

かかりつけ 掛かり付け ▶掛かりつけの医者 a family doctor.

かがりび 篝火 a **bonfire**(野外における祝賀などのための); a **campfire** (野営の) ▶かがり火をたく build *a bonfire* [*a campfire*].

[1]かかる 掛かる・架かる・懸かる・係る

1【固定して支えられている】hang ▶壁に地図が掛かっている A map *is hanging* on the wall. / There is a map (*hanging*) on the wall. ‖ 入り口の上に看板が掛かっている *There is* a signboard *hanging* over the door. ‖ きみのコートはハンガーに掛かってるよ Your coat *is on* the hanger. ‖ シチューの鍋が火に掛かっていた The stew pot *was put over* the fire.

2【つながる, 結ばれる】▶多摩川に新しい橋が架かった A new bridge *was built* [*was constructed*] over the Tama River. ‖ 隅田川には10以上の橋が架かっている *There are* more than ten bridges *across* [*over* / *spanning*] the Sumida River. ‖ 腕が痛くて背中のボタンが掛からない I *cannot button up* the back because my arm hurts so much. ‖ クリスマスプレゼントには赤いリボンが掛かっていた The Christmas present *had* a red ribbon *on it*. ‖ サムから電話が掛かってきた *There was a phone call* from Sam. / *I got* [*had*] *a phone call* from Sam. ‖ その投手には3チームから声[誘い]がかかった That pitcher *got of-*

fers from three teams.

3【作用する】▶鍵が掛かった The lock *has* (*clicked*) *shut*. ‖ **鍵が掛からない** The lock *doesn't work* [*catch*]. ‖ **裏口のドアはいつも鍵が掛かっている** The back door *is* always *locked*. ‖ **ブレーキ[鍵]が掛からない** The brake [key] *doesn't work*.

▶けさはエンジンがなかなか掛からなかった This morning I had a hard time *starting* the engine [getting the engine to *start*].

▶キツネがわなに掛かった A fox *was caught* in a trap. ‖ **彼女は簡単に催眠術に掛かる** She can *be hypnotized* easily.

4【表面を覆う；被る】▶山には霧が低く掛かっている A fog *hangs* low over the mountain. ／The mountain *is shrouded* by fog. ‖ **雨上がりの空にきれいな虹が架かった** A beautiful rainbow *spanned* [*appeared* in] the clear sky after the rain. ‖ **食堂のテーブルには青いテーブルクロスが掛かっている** *There is* a blue tablecloth *on* the dining table.

▶ズボンに泥水が掛かった My pants *got splashed* with muddy water. ‖ **隣人の1人に疑いがかかった** Suspicion *fell on* one of my neighbors. ‖ **彼のしたことでいろいろな人に大変な迷惑がかかった** What he did *caused* many people *a lot of trouble* [*caused a lot of trouble* for [to] a lot of people].

5【時間や費用が必要である】take +㊐（時間が）; **cost** +㊐（費用が）**▶この仕事は時間がかかる** This work *takes* (*up*) *a lot of time*. ／This is *time-consuming* work. ‖ **まだしばらくかかりそうですか** Is it going to *take a while longer*?

> **【文型】**
> **A が…するのに時間(B)がかかる**
> **It takes** A B **to** do.
> **It takes** B **for** A **to** do.

▶学校までは歩いて20分かかる *It takes* (me) twenty minutes *to* walk to school. ‖ **景気回復には今しばらくかかる** *It will take a while for* the economy *to* recover. ／*It will be a while* before the economy recovers. ‖ **香港までは飛行機で何時間[どのくらい]かかりますか** How many hours [How long] does *it take to* fly to Hong Kong? ‖ **彼はその絵を完成するのに5年かかった** *It took* him five years *to* complete the painting.

▶一生かかってもこれだけの本は読めない It would *take more than a lifetime* to read all these books. ／A lifetime is not long enough to read all these books. ‖ **彼が全快するまでには数週間かかるだろう** It will be several weeks before he gets well. (➤ take は「(ある行為を)するのに時間がかかる」の意なので, この文では使えない).

> **【文型】**
> **人(A)に費用(B)がかかる**
> **cost** A B
> **人(A)が…するのに費用(B)がかかる**
> **It costs** A B **to** do.
> **It costs** B **for** A **to** do.

▶世界一周の船旅は数百万円かかる A cruise around the world *costs* several million yen. ‖ **この家を建てるのに500万円かかった** *It cost* us fifty million yen *to* build this house. ‖ **時計の電池交換にいくらかかりましたか** *How much did it cost to* have the battery in your watch replaced?

▶裁判は金もかかるし, 時間もかかる Lawsuits *require both time and money*. (➤ 英語では time and money の語順がふつう).

▶たばこ1箱には税金がいくらかかるんですか How much *tax* do you *pay* on a pack of cigarettes? ‖ **これらの品物にはどれも税金がかかりません** These articles are all *tax-free*.

6【医者に見せる】▶きみは医者に掛かる必要がある You should *see* [*consult*] *a doctor*. ‖ **彼は胃潰瘍で医者に掛かっている** He is now *under medical treatment* [*under the care of a doctor*] for a stomach ulcer /ʌ́lsəʳ/.

7【…次第である】depend on ▶それはきみたちが次に何をするかに係っている It *depends on* what you do next. ‖ **これの決定はきみに係っている** This decision *is up to you*. (➤ up to は「…次第で」) ‖ **今度の仕事が成功するか否かはきみたちの努力に係っている** Whether this job succeeds or not all *depends on* your effort(s).

8【託される】▶きょうの試合には全国大会出場が懸かっている Today's game will *decide* who will qualify to participate in the national (baseball) tournament. ‖ **《相撲で》この一番には優勝が懸かっている** The championship *rests* [*depends*] *on* this bout. ‖ **このつぼには保険が掛かっている** This vase *is insured*.

9【立ち向かう】▶さあ仕事にかかろう Now, *let's get to work*. ／Now, *let's get going*. ‖ **さあ, かかってこい** Come on! *Put 'em up!* (➤ 'em は them の略で「げんこつ」を指す).

[2]かかる 罹る ▶はしかにかかる *get* [*catch* ／*pick up*] measles (➤「かかっている」なら動詞は have) ‖ **結核にかかる** *contract* tuberculosis (➤ contract /kəntrǽkt/ は重い病気の場合) ‖ **彼女は先月原因不明の病気にかかった** Last month she *became* sick with an unknown disease.

-かかる ▶私はその川で溺れかかった I *was almost drowned* in that river. ‖ **地震でその家は壊れかかった** An earthquake *nearly* [*almost*] *destroyed* the house. ‖ **通りかかったからちょっとお寄りしたの** I *happened to pass by* your house so I dropped in. ‖ **電話が鳴ったとき私は家を出かかっていた** I *was about to leave* when the phone rang. ‖ **この魚は腐りかかっている** This fish *is beginning to* go bad. ‖ **うちの犬は老衰で死にかかっている** Our dog *is dying* of old age.

かがる sew /soʊ/ **up**（縫い合わす）; **mend** +㊐（繕う）**▶シャツの穴をかがる** *sew up* a hole in the shirt ‖ **ボタンの穴をかがる** *make* buttonholes.

-がかる ▶緑がかった黄色 *greenish* yellow ‖ **芝居がかった行動** *dramatic* [*theatrical*] behavior ‖ **その団体は左がかっている** That group *leans to the left*.

かかわらず 1【関係なく】regardless of ▶国籍・性別・年齢にかかわらず入会できます Membership is open to all, *regardless of* nationality, sex, or [and] age. ‖ **好むと好まざるとにかかわらずきみは働かねばならない** You must work *whether you like it or not*.

2【であるのに】(even) though, although (➤ 文が続く; 後者がより堅い; even though は though の強調形で, 対比が際立つ場合); **despite, in spite of** (➤ 名詞・動名詞が続く; despite は簡潔なため新聞などで多用される) **▶高齢にもかかわらず, 三浦さんは今も世界の最高峰の登頂をめざしている** *Although* [*Though*] advanced in years, Mr. Miura is aiming to scale high peaks of the world. (➤ この場合, although や though は省略できるが, 省略するとやや文学的な表現になる) ‖ **彼は三振したにもかかわらず平気な顔をしていた** He looked cool as a cucumber, *although* [*even though*] he had just struck out. ‖ 父は雨にもかかわらず散歩に出かけた Dad went for a walk *even though* it was raining. ‖ 達彦は足首をくじいたにもかかわらずジョギングを続けた Tatsuhiko continued jogging *in spite of* his twisted ankle. ‖ 関係者が最大限努力したにもかかわらず合意には至らなかった *Despite* the best efforts of all parties, an agreement could not be reached.

かかわり 関わり involvement(関与) ▶そのことにかかわりをもつのはやめなさい Don't *get involved* in the matter. (➤「将来的にかかわるな」と忠告する場合) ／Put an end to your *involvement in* the matter. (➤「(現在の)かかわりを断て」と忠告する場合) ‖ それは私には関わりのないことだ It's *none of my business.* ／I *have nothing to do with* it. ‖ ラグビーの試合は天候に関わりなく行われます The rugby match will take place *regardless of* the weather.

かかわりあう 関わり合う ▶その2つの事件は密接に関わり合っている Those two cases *are* closely *related to each other*. ‖ そんなつまらないことに関わり合っている暇はない I'm too busy to *be concerned about* such a trivial matter.

かかわる 関わる **1【関係を持つ】**▶多くの会社がその汚職事件に関わっていた Many companies *were involved in* the scandal. ‖ 私はそれには関わりたくない I'd rather not *get involved in* it. ‖ わが社の相談役は名誉職で直接経営には関わっていない The position of senior advisor at our company is an honorary post and isn't directly *involved in* the management. ‖ マザー・テレサは貧しい人々への奉仕に真剣に関わった Mother Teresa *committed herself to* serving the poor.

2【影響を与える】▶きみの行動はきみの家族の名誉に関わるだろう Your actions will *affect* the honor of your family. ‖ 彼を早く病院に運ばないと命に関わる Unless we take him to a hospital right now, *his life will be in danger* [*he may die*].

かかん 果敢な bold (思い切りのよい); courageous, brave(勇敢な) ▶吉田は果敢に3塁盗塁をした Yoshida *boldly* stole third (base). ‖ 兵士たちは果敢に戦った The soldiers fought *courageously* [*bravely*].

1かき 柿 a ***kaki***, a persimmon /pərsímən/

《参考》 persimmon は北アメリカ原産の柿に似た果物で, 大きさはスモモ大. 日本の柿は kaki または Japanese persimmon と呼ばれ, アメリカでも栽培され, 一般的になっている.

2かき 牡蠣 《貝》 an oyster /ɔ́istər/

‖カキフライ a fried oyster.

3かき 下記 ▶下記の者たちがあすの試合の出場者に選ばれた The *following* members have been chosen to play in tomorrow's game : (➤ :(コロン)のあとに出場者の氏名が並ぶ) ‖ 結果は下記のとおりです The results are *as follows* : (➤ as follows は「次のとおり」の意で, 通例 :(コロン)を打つ).

✉ 例会を下記のごとく開催します The regular meeting will be held *as described* [*detailed*] *below*.

4かき 夏期・夏季 summer, summertime ▶(予備校などの)夏期講習を受ける take *a summer course*.

‖夏期休暇 the summer vacation [《英》 holidays].

5かき 火気 fire ▶(掲示)火気厳禁 No Fire／Caution : Flammables.

6かき 花器 a flower vase.

1かぎ 鍵 **1【ドアなどの】** a key ; a lock(錠) ; a latch (掛け金) ▶鍵の束 a bunch of *keys* ‖ 金庫の鍵 *a key* to the safe (➤「…の鍵」の「の」には of ではなく, to を用いることに注意) ‖ 車の鍵 a car *key* ‖ 鍵穴に鍵を差し込む put *a key* in the *keyhole* ‖ ドアに鍵を掛ける[開ける] *lock* [*unlock*] the door.

▶201号室の鍵をください May I have the *key* to Room 201 ? ‖ ホテルのドアは閉めると自動的に鍵が掛かる Hotel doors *lock* automatically when you close them. ‖ 《ホテルで》鍵を部屋に忘れてきてしまいました I left my *key* in my room. (➤ I'm locked out of my room. と言ってもよい).

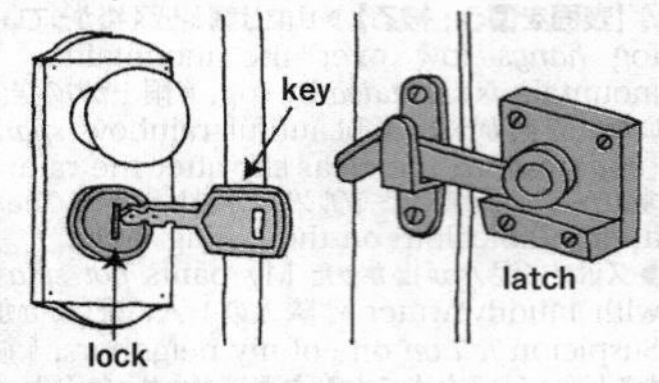

2【重要な点】 a key ▶夢をもち続けることが成功への鍵だ Keeping your dream alive is *the key* to success. ‖ 殺人事件の鍵を握る人物が現れた They found a person who *held the key* to the murder mystery.

☞ 鍵っ子 (→見出語)

2かぎ 鉤 a hook ▶その武器は棒の先にかぎがついている That weapon has *a hook* on the end. ‖ オウムはかぎ状のくちばしをしている Parrots have *hooked* beaks.

がき 餓鬼 a brat(手に負えない子供).

☞ がき大将 (→見出語)

かきあげ a ***kakiage*** ; tempura ; a deep-fried mixture of small shrimp(s) and strips of vegetables in tempura batter(➤ 説明的な訳).

かきあげる 書き上げる ▶締め切りの1週間前に卒論を書き上げた I *finished writing* my graduation paper a week before the deadline.

かきあつめる 掻き集める rake up (熊手で); scrape up (金を) ▶庭の枯れ葉をかき集める *rake up* the dead leaves in the garden.

▶彼はスポーツカーを買う金をかき集めた He *scraped up* enough money to buy a sports car.

かぎあな 鍵穴 a keyhole.

かきあらわす 書き表す express +㊐ ▶彼女は喜びや悲しみを詩に書き表した She *expressed* her joys and sorrows in poetry. ‖ 自分の考えを文章に書き表しなさい *Put* your ideas *down in writing*.

かきいれどき 書き入れ時 ▶暮れは商店の書き入れ時だ The year-end is (*the busiest and*) *the most prosperous season* for stores. ‖ 雨の日はタクシー運転手の書き入れ時だ Rainy days are (*the*) *busiest* (*days*) for taxi drivers.

かきいれる 書き入れる enter +㊐, put in(項目に) ; fill out, complete +㊐ (申込書などに) ; fill in(空所に) ▶きのうの売り上げを帳簿に書き入れた I *entered* yesterday's sales figures in the book. ‖ 申込書に(必要事項を)書き入れて送り返してください Please *fill out* [*complete*] the application form and return it to us. ‖ ここにあなたのお名前と生年月日を書き入れてください *Fill in* your name and birth date here, please.

かきうつす 書き写す copy +㊐ ▶私は朔太郎の詩を ノ

ートに書き写した I *copied* Sakutaro's poem into my notebook.

かきおき 書き置き a **note**, a **message** ▶彼の机の上に「急用のため会えない」という書き置きがあった He left *a note* [*a message*] on his desk, saying that he could not meet me due to urgent business. ‖ 彼女は書き置きを残して家出した She ran away from home, leaving *a note* behind. (➤ 自殺者が残す「書き置き」は a suicide note [letter] という).

かきおろす 書き下ろす ▶この小説は当文庫のために書き下ろされたものです This novel *was specially written* for the library.

かきかえる 書き換える **rewrite** +㊐ (別の表現で書き直す) ; **paraphrase** +㊐ (別の表現に言い換える) ; **renew** +㊐ (更新する)

▶次の英文を that 節を使って書き換えなさい *Rewrite* the following English sentence using a "that"-clause. ‖ 彼の論文は有名な学者の論文を部分的に書き換えたものだ His thesis is just a partially *rewritten* version of that of a famous scholar. ‖ 彼女はその古い英語の詩を現代英語で書き換えた She *paraphrased* the old English poem in modern English.

▶彼女は運転免許証を書き換えるのを忘れてしまった She forgot to *renew* her driver's license.

かきかた 書き方 ▶彼は論文の書き方がわかっていない He doesn't know *how to write* a paper.

▶この書き方(＝言い回し)では誤解を招く This *expression* is misleading.

かきくもる 掻き曇る ▶一天にわかにかき曇った All of a sudden the sky *clouded over*.

かきくわえる 書き加える **add** +㊐ ▶著者は改訂版を出す際に新たに 1 章を書き加えた The author *added* a new chapter to her book while revising it for the new edition.

かきけす 掻き消す ▶議長の声は怒号にかき消されてほとんど聞き取れなかった The chairperson's voice *was* almost *drowned* (*out*) by the angry roar. ／We could hardly hear the chairperson's voice over the angry roar.

かきごおり 欠き氷 **shaved ice with syrup over it**
《参考》日本の喫茶店などでは「フラッペ」と称しているところもあるが, 英語の frappé はかき氷の上にリキュールを注いだデザートの一種.

かきことば 書き言葉 **written language.**

かきこみ 書き込み **notes** (覚え書き) ; **writing** (電子掲示板・フォーラムの) ; a **message** (電子掲示板・フォーラムに掲載された情報) ▶教科書には書き込みをしないほうがよい You should not *make notes in* your textbook. ‖ 図書館から借りた本にはどのページにも欄外に書き込みがしてあった The book I borrowed from the library had *notes* scribbled in the margin of every page. (➤ scribble は「書き散らす」) ‖ ブログに(コメントの)書き込みをする *post a comment* on a blog.

‖書き込み [換え] 可能なＣＤ a rewritable CD, a CD-RW.

かきこむ 書き込む **write** +㊐ (書く) ; **fill in** (空所に記入する) ; **fill out** (全部記入する) ▶この用紙に書き込みなさい *Fill out* [*in*] this form. ‖ (インターネットの)フォーラムに書き込む *write* in a forum.

かぎざき 鉤裂き a **tear** /teəʳ/ ▶コートをくぎに引っかけて袖にかぎ裂きができた I *tore* my coat sleeve on a nail. (➤ tore は tear(裂く)の過去形).

かきしるす 書き記す ▶日記に日々の雑感を書き記す *write* one's daily thoughts in a diary.

かきそえる 書き添える ▶追伸として 1 行書き添える *write* [*add*] a line as a postscript.

かきそこない 書き損ない a **mistake in writing**, a **slip of the pen** (➤ 後者はボールペン・万年筆などによる ; 毛筆なら the calligraphy brush).

かきそこなう 書き損なう **make a mistake in writing, make a slip of the pen** (➤ 後者はボールペン・万年筆などによる ; 毛筆なら the calligraphy brush) ▶誰でも書き損なうことはある Anyone can *make a mistake when writing*. ／Anyone can *make a slip of the pen*.

かきぞめ 書き初め ***kakizome***
日本紹介 ✉ **書き初めは新年の最初に筆で字を書く伝統的な行事です. ふつう, 1月2日に行われます** *Kakizome* is a traditional event of doing calligraphy with a brush for the first time in the New Year. It is usually conducted on January 2.

がきだいしょう 餓鬼大将 **the boss of all the neighborhood kids** ▶少年は子供の頃近所のがき大将だった The boy was *the leader of all the neighborhood kids* when he was a child. ／When he was a child, the boy *bossed* all the other kids in the neighborhood.

かきだし 書き出し an **opening sentence** (初めの文) ; **opening lines** (初めの数行) ▶手紙の書き出しにはいつも気を遣う I always write the *opening lines* of a letter with great care.

かきだす 書き出す **make a list** 《of》 (リストを作る) ; **open** +㊐ (手紙などを書き始める) ▶ロンドン滞在中に訪れる博物館を書き出す *make a list of* museums to visit while I'm in London ‖ スーパーで買って来てほしい物を書き出してちょうだい Please *list* all the things you want me to buy at the supermarket. ‖ 彼女はその手紙を「こんにちは」で書き出した She *opened* the letter with "Hello."

かぎだす 嗅ぎ出す ▶秘密を嗅ぎ出す *ferret out* a secret ‖ 被災地ではがれきの下に埋まっている人を嗅ぎ出す救助犬が活躍した The rescue dogs played an important role in the stricken area by *sniffing out* buried people under the rubble.

[1]**かきたてる 掻き立てる** ▶その事件は私の好奇心をかきたてた The incident *aroused* [*excited*] my curiosity. ‖ その本を読んで私は歴史への興味をかきたてられた Reading that book *stirred* my interest in history. ‖ 監督のげきが選手たちの闘志をかきたてた The coach's pep talk *stirred up* the players' fighting spirit.

[2]**かきたてる 書き立てる** ▶新聞はそのスキャンダルを盛んに書きたてた Newspapers *wrote up* the scandal [*gave* the scandal *a lot of space*].

かきつけ 書き付け a **note.**

かきつける 書き付ける **write down** ▶買い物が多かったので紙に書きつけた I had a lot of things to buy so I *wrote* them all *down* on a piece of paper. (➤ wrote 以下を made a shopping list としてもよい).

かぎつける 嗅ぎつける **sniff out** (主に犬が匂いで ; 比喩的に「探り当てる」にも用いる) ; **discover** +㊐ (発見する) ; **find out** (見つけ出す) ▶犬 [警察] は犯人の居場所を嗅ぎつけた The dog [The police] *sniffed out* the criminal in his hideout. ‖ 秘密を嗅ぎつける *sniff out* a secret ‖ 警察はテロリストグループの怪しい動きを嗅ぎつけた The police *sniffed out* the suspicious activities of a terrorist group. ‖ メディアはまもなく彼らの贈賄を嗅ぎつけた The media soon *got* *wind of* their bribery. (➤ get wind of は「(悪事などの)うわさを嗅ぎつける」の意のインフォーマルな表現) ‖ トムは盗み聞きをして彼女の秘密を嗅ぎつけた Tom *discovered* [*found out*] her secret by eavesdropping.

かぎっこ 鍵っ子 a **latchkey child.**

かぎって 限って ▶誠に限ってうそは言わない Other people may lie, *but not* Makoto [*but* Makoto *never* would]. ‖ その試合に限って南野が欠場した Minamino didn't play in [sat out] that *particular* game. ‖ 大人は自分の子供に限って他人をいじめることなどないと思いがちだ Adults tend to believe that their *own* children could not possibly be bullying others. (➤ さらに強調して言うなら Adults tend to believe that, *of all children*, their own (children) could not ... とする; →よりによって) ‖ その日に限って私は家に居ませんでした It *just so happened* that I was not at home that day.

カキツバタ 《植物》 an **iris.**

かきとめ 書留 **registered mail** ▶彼女はその小包を書留で送った She sent the parcel *by registered mail*. ‖ 大切な物を郵送するときは書留にしたほうがよい When mailing something important, it's better to send it (as) *registered mail*.

‖書留速達 a registered special delivery letter.

かきとめる 書き留める **write** [**take** / **put**] **down**; **jot down** (ちょっとメモする) ▶先生の言うことを書き留める *write down* what the teacher says / *make a note of* the teacher's words ‖ 彼女の電話番号, ちょっと書き留めておいてくれる? Will you please *jot down* her telephone number?

かきとり 書き取り (a) **dictation** (読まれたことを書き取ること) 《参考》 (1) 日本の小学校で行う「(漢字の)書き取り」は dictation ではないので, 第3用例のように「ひらがな[かたかな]を漢字に直す(こと)」と考える. (2) また, 「(漢字の)書き取りテスト」は a (hiragana [katakana] to) kanji conversion test のようにいえる. ▶さあこれから書き取りテストをします Now, I'll *give* you *a dictation test*. ‖ 三田君はクラスでいちばん書き取りができる Mita does the best in the class on *putting hiragana* [*katakana*] *into kanji*. (➤ putting は changing でもよい) / Mita is the best *speller* in my class. (➤前者は漢字の書き取り, 後者は英語の場合).

かきとる 書き取る ▶学生たちは講義をノートに書き取った The students *took* [*made*] *notes of* the lecture. (➤ of は on でもよい).

かきなおす 書き直す **rewrite** +⑪ (文章を書き換える); **write ... over again** (もう一度書く); **correct** +⑪ (訂正する) ▶次の文を分詞構文を用いて[カッコ内に指示されたように]書き直しなさい *Rewrite* the following sentences using participial constructions [as directed in the parentheses]. ‖ きみの報告書は不正確だから書き直す必要がある Your report is inaccurate, so you should *correct* it [*make corrections*]. ‖ 私は申込書を書き直しさせられた I was made to *write* the application *over again*. (➤ 英語では, させた人を主語にして, He [She / They] made me write ... とするほうが自然).

かきなぐる 書きなぐる **scribble** +⑪ ▶書きなぐった手紙 a *scribbled* letter.

かきぬく 書き抜く **copy** +⑪ ▶教科書の大事な点をノートに書き抜いた I *copied* some of the important parts of the textbook into my notebook.

かきね 垣根 a **fence**; a **hedge** (生け垣) ▶池の周りには子供が落ちないように垣根が巡らされていた *A fence* was erected (all) around the pond to keep children from falling in. ‖ 彼らは家の周りを高い垣根で囲った They planted [laid] *a* high *hedge* around their house. ‖ 母は垣根越しに田島さんのおばさんと話していた My mother was talking to Mrs. Tajima *over the hedge*.

▶党派の垣根を越えて協力する *cross* party and faction *boundaries* and cooperate.

かきのける 掻き退ける **shove** +⑪ ▶買い物客たちが, 人を押しのけかきのけ特売品売り場に殺到した Shoppers were pushing and *shoving their way* to the bargain counter.

かきのこす 書き残す **leave a note** ▶自殺した少女は遺書を書き残した The girl *left a* suicide *note* before she killed herself. (➤left は leave の過去形).

かきまぜる 掻き混ぜる **stir** +⑪ (コーヒーやスープなどを); **beat** +⑪ (卵などを勢いよく); **whip** +⑪ (クリームや卵の白身などを泡状に) ▶砂糖がよく混ざるようにコーヒーをかき混ぜた I *stirred* the coffee to mix in the sugar well. ‖ 卵を泡立て器でかき混ぜなさい *Beat* the eggs with an eggbeater.

かきまわす 掻き回す **1【混ぜる】** **stir** +⑪ ▶彼女はコーヒーに砂糖とクリームを入れ, スプーンでかき回した She put sugar and cream in her coffee and *stirred* it.

2【めちゃくちゃにする】 **rummage** /rʌ́mɪdʒ/ **through**; **go through** (いじる) ▶私の引き出しかき回してたの誰? Who was *rummaging* [*going*] *through* my drawer? ‖ あの1年坊主はわがままなことをしてはよくクラスの中をかき回す(=混乱させる) That first-grader always behaves selfishly and often *disrupts* the class.

かきむしる 掻きむしる **scratch at ... hard** (ひどくかく); **tear at** (髪の毛を抜こうとする) ▶男の子はかゆいところをかきむしって, 血を出していた The boy *scratched at* his itchy skin so *hard* that he bled. ‖ 彼は怒りのあまり髪をかきむしった He *tore at* his hair with rage. (➤ tear one's hair は「激しく引き抜く」ととられかねない).

▶《慣用表現》いたいけな戦争孤児の姿を見ると胸がかきむしられる思いだ To see those innocent war orphans *wrings my heart*. (➤ wring one's heart は「精神的苦痛を与える」).

かきゅうせい 下級生 a **underclass student.**

[1]**かきょう 佳境** **the best part** (最良の部分) ▶連続ドラマも終盤に入り, いよいよ佳境を迎えた The serial drama is approaching the end and has finally gotten to *the best* [*the good*] *part*.

[2]**かきょう 華僑** a **Chinese (merchant) abroad**, an **overseas Chinese.**

かぎょう 家業・稼業 a **family business** (家の商売); a **job** (職業) ▶父は魚屋ですが, ぼくは家業を継ぎません My father runs a fish store, but I won't take over the *business*.

▶刑事なんて因果な稼業さ Being a detective is a rotten [lousy] *job*. (➤ rotten は「嫌な, つらい」, lousy は「お粗末な, ひどい」の意で, ともにくだけた語).

かきょく 歌曲 a **song**; a **lied** /liːd/ (ドイツ歌曲; 複数形は lieder).

かぎらない 限らない **not necessarily** [**always**] ▶旅行がいつも楽しいとは限らない Traveling is *not always* fun. ‖ 金持ちが必ずしも幸福とは限らないと人は言う People say (that) the rich are *not necessarily* happy. (➤ not necessarily は論理的な必然性がないことをいう) ‖ 早めに行かないと, 席が取れるとは限らないよ

Unless you arrive early, you *can't be sure* of getting a seat.

かぎり 限り a **limit** ▶限りある資源を大切に使いましょう Let's use our *limited* resources carefully. ‖ 私の忍耐にも限りがある There are *limits* to my patience. ／My patience has *a limit*. ‖ 紙面に限りがあるのであなたの投書は丸ごと掲載できません We are sorry we cannot print your whole letter *as space is limited* [*for want of space*]. ‖ 欲には限りがない Desire *knows no limits*. ‖ 子に対する親の限りない愛 *limitless* parental love for one's child (ren).

▶我々は力の限り戦った We fought *with all our strength* [*might*]. ‖ 彼は声を限りに助けを求めた He cried for help *at the top of his lungs* [*as loudly as he could* ／ *at the top of his voice*].

▶あなたがご援助くださるのは心強い限りです Your assistance is *most* encouraging to us. ‖ 祖母が亡くなって寂しい限りだ I am *extremely* sad because my grandmother has passed away.

-かぎり -限り **1【限度, 限界】**▶できる限りお手伝いしましょう I'll help you *as much as I can*. ／I'll *do all* [*everything*] *I can* to help you. ‖ できる限り早く仕事を済ませなさい Finish your work *as quickly as possible*.

2【制限, 最後】▶特売品は1人1点限りでお願いします Specially discounted items *are limited to one per person*. ‖ その庭園は今月の5日限りで閉園される That garden will be closed to the public *after the 5th* of this month. ‖ きょう限りきみとは絶交だ *After today* [*From today on*], I want nothing more to do with you. ‖ 展覧会はきょう限りだ The exhibition *closes today*. ‖ 彼に援助を頼むのも今回限りだ *This is the last time* I'll ask for his help.

3【範囲, 間】▶私の知る限り彼は海外へ行ったことはない *As far as I know* [*To the best of my knowledge*], he has never been overseas. ‖「生きている限り歌い続けます」とそのロック歌手は言った "I'll keep on singing *as long as I live*," said the rock singer. ‖ 見渡す限り砂ばかりだった *As far as the eye could reach*, nothing was to be seen but sand. ‖ 彼に関する限り, すべてがうまくいっている *As far as he is concerned*, everything is going all right. ‖ 謝らない限り家には入れてあげないわよ I won't let you in *unless* you apologize. (➤ unless は「…でなければ」).

かぎる 限る **1【制限する】** **limit** +⑬ (限界を設ける) ; **restrict** +⑬ (制限・条件をつける) ▶スピーチは1人10分に限ります Speeches *are limited to* ten minutes each. ／Each speaker has a maximum of ten minutes. ‖ 会員は女子学生に限る Membership *is restricted to* girl students. ‖ 男子に限り入場を許す Admission to *men only*.

2【最良である】▶夏の暑い日は冷たい麦茶に限る *Nothing beats* cold barley tea on hot summer days. (➤ beat は「…に勝る」) ‖ 休みの日はごろ寝に限ると父は言う My dad says there's *nothing he likes doing more* on his day off *than laying around* (*the house*).

☛ 限って, 限らない (→見出語)

かきわける 掻き分ける ▶私は人混みをかき分けて前に出た I *elbowed my way through the crowd* to stand in front. ‖ 10分ほどやぶをかき分けて進むと空き地に出た Ten minutes of *struggling through* the bushes brought me to a clearing.

かぎわける 嗅ぎ分ける **sniff out** (嗅いで見つける) ; **smell** +⑬ (嗅ぐ) ▶犬は不審な者を嗅ぎ分ける Dogs can *sniff out* suspicious people. ‖ シャネル5番とマダムロシャスを嗅ぎ分けられますか Can you *smell the difference* between Chanel No.5 and Madame Rochas?

かきわり 書き割り a **painted background** ▶銭湯の書き割りといえば富士山だ Most of the *painted scenery* at sento (public baths) depict Mt. Fuji.

¹かきん 課金する **charge a fee** ▶その新聞社は無料だった電子版に課金することを決めた The newspaper company has decided to *charge a fee* for its electronic version that has been offered for free.

²かきん 家禽 a **fowl** /faʊl/ ; **poultry** (➤ 集合的な言い方).

¹かく 角 **an angle** ▶ 30度の角 a thirty-degree *angle* ‖ 三角形の内角の和は180度である The sum of the *interior angles* of *a triangle* is 180 degrees.

²かく 格 **status** /stéɪṭəs/ (格式) ; **rank** (地位) ; a **class** (等級) ▶格の同じ人々 people of equal *status* ‖ 格が上がる［下がる］rise [fall] in *rank* ‖ このホテルはこの地区ではいちばん格が高いホテルです This is *the classiest* hotel in the area. (➤ classy は「高級な」の意のインフォーマルな語) ‖ うちの会社は彼の会社とは格が違うよ Our company is *not in the same league* as his. (➤「同類ではない」の意) ／Our company *doesn't compare* with his. (➤「うちの会社が劣っている」の意) ‖ 父は大阪に転勤して営業部長に格上げになった My father *was* transferred to Osaka and *promoted to* sales manager. (➤「格下げになる」は be demoted).

³かく 核 **1【原子核】** a **nucleus** /njúːkliəs/ **一形** 核の **nuclear** /njúːkliəʳ/ ▶核の拡散 *nuclear* proliferation /prəlìfəréɪʃən/ (➤「核の不拡散」は nuclear nonproliferation) ‖ その原発事故は核の安全性に対する不安を募らせた The nuclear reactor accident heightened concern about *nuclear safety*.

‖核開発計画 a nuclear program ‖ 核軍縮 nuclear disarmament ‖ 核戦争 a nuclear war ‖ 核廃棄物 nuclear waste ‖ 核分裂 nuclear fission ‖ 核保有国 a nuclear power ‖ 核ミサイル a nuclear missile ‖ 核融合 nuclear fusion.

2【大事な部分】 **the nucleus** ; **the core** (最も奥深い部分・芯) ▶家庭の主婦たちがその市民運動の核になった Housewives were *the core* [formed *the core*] of the grass-roots movement.

☛ 核家族, 核実験, 核兵器 (→見出語)

⁴かく 書く・描く

> **訳語メニュー**
> 文字や文章を書く →write **1**
> 絵などを描く →draw, paint **2**

1【文字などを】 **write** +⑬ ; **write** [**put**] **down** (書き留める) ▶友人に手紙を書く *write* (a letter) to one's friend ‖ 答えをボールペン［インク］で書く *write* one's answers with a ball-point pen [in ink] ‖ 雑誌に随筆を書く *write* an essay for a magazine.

▶彼女はとても上手にイタリア語の文章を書く She *writes* very good Italian. ／She *writes* Italian very well. ‖ 弟は字を書くのが上手［下手］だ My younger brother *has good* [*poor*] *handwriting*. ‖ 彼女は文章を書くのが上手［下手］だ She is *a good* [*poor*] *writer*. ‖ 私は故郷の家に長い手紙を書いた I *wrote* a long letter home. ‖ 彼は最近新しい本を書いた He

has written a new book recently.
✉ **送っていただいた写真を見ながらこの手紙を書いています** I'*m writing* this letter while looking at the pictures you sent me.
▶きみの住所を**書いて**(おいて)くれ *Write* [*Put*] *down* your address, please. ‖ 答案用紙には「優」と**書いて**あった The paper *was marked* 'Excellent.' ‖ 近く内閣改造があるだろうと新聞には**書いてある** The papers *say* it is probable (that) there will soon be a cabinet reshuffle. ‖ この本は易しい英語で**書かれている** This book *is written* in simple English. ‖ その物語は子供向けに**書かれている** That story *is intended for* children. (➤ be intended for は「…向けにできている」) ‖「マクドナルド」という語は英語ではどう**書き**(＝つづり)ますか How do you *spell* the word 'Makudonarudo' in English? ‖ 日本の城について**書いた**本をお持ちですか Do you have any books *on* Japanese castles? (➤ on は「…に関する」).
2【描く】draw +㊐ (鉛筆・クレヨンなどで); **paint** +㊐ (彩色して) (→**絵**) ▶壁に絵を**描く** *draw* a picture on the wall ‖ 駅から自宅までの略図を**描く** *draw* a rough (street / road) map from the station to one's home ‖ 肖像画を**描く** *paint* a portrait.

5かく 欠く 1【一部を壊す】chip +㊐ ▶誤ってコーヒー茶わんを**欠いて**しまいました I *chipped* the coffee cup by accident.
2【あるべきものがない】lack +㊐ ▶オリックスの攻撃は決め手を**欠いた** The Buffaloes' batters *lacked* decisive hits. ‖ あの先生は時々良識を**欠く**ような行動をとる That teacher sometimes behaves in a way that shows *a lack* of common sense. ‖ 日本では義理を**欠く**ことは恥とされている In Japan, *neglecting* to carry out social obligations is considered shameful. ‖ 野菜は人間の健康にとって**欠くことのできない**食物だ Vegetables are *indispensable* to human health.

6かく 掻く scratch +㊐ ▶虫に刺された所を**かく**な Don't *scratch* insect bites. ‖ 工藤君は答えを間違えて**頭をかいた** Kudo *scratched his head* in embarrassment when he gave a wrong answer. 《参考》scratch one's head は英米では「恥ずかしさ」ではなく,「当惑」のしぐさである.

かく- 各- each(おのおのの); **every**(どれも皆) ▶**各**クラスから1名ずつ代表を選んでください Please pick a representative for *each* class. ‖ わが校には**各**教室にテレビがある At our school there is a TV in *every* classroom. ‖ **各界**の名士がその会に集まった Prominent people from *various fields* attended the party. ‖ **各界**で活躍する人が叙勲を受けた People who have played active roles in *various sectors* were decorated. ‖ その声明に対して**各方面**から抗議が起こった The statement aroused protests from *all quarters*. ‖ (社会の)**各方面の人** people from *every walk of life* (➤ a walk of life は「職業,身分」) ‖ 欧州連合の**各国** the European Union *countries* ‖ 英連邦の**各国** the Commonwealth *nations*.

1かぐ 家具 furniture (➤ 集合名詞なので数えられない. したがって, 1個の家具は a piece [an article] of furniture という; furniture は部屋や家の家具全体を指す語で, 1点1点は table, desk, bed のように具体的にいうことが多い) ▶ぼくのうちには**家具**がたくさんある[あまり無い] There is a lot of [little] *furniture* in our house. ‖ 対話「**家具付きのアパート**をお探しですか」「いいえ, **家具無し**です」"Are you looking for *a furnished apartment*?" "No, I'm looking for an *unfurnished* one." (➤ 英米, 特にイギリスでは, 家具付きのアパートの場合, 日常生活に必要なものは備え付けになっている).
‖**家具店** a furniture store ‖**家具メーカー** a furniture maker ‖**北欧家具** Scandinavian furniture.

2かぐ 嗅ぐ smell ▶バラの匂いを**嗅ぐ** *smell* [*sniff at*] the roses ‖ 犬はその見知らぬ人の匂いをくんくん**嗅いだ** The dog *sniffed at* the stranger.

1がく 額 1【金額】a sum; an **amount**(量) ▶少しの**額**のお金 *a small sum* [*amount*] *of* money ‖ 不況の影響でボーナスの**額**が減った Our *bonus was reduced* [*was cut back*] because of the recession.
2【額縁】a (picture) frame ▶**額**に入った絵 a *framed* picture ‖ 絵を**額**に入れる put a picture into *a frame* / frame a picture ‖ 父の肖像画を**額に入れて**もらった We *had* our father's portrait *framed*.

2がく 学 ▶**学**のある女性 a *learned* woman (➤ 発音は /lə́ːrnɪd/) / a woman *of learning* ‖ **学**のあるところを見せる (try to) show off one's *knowledge* ‖ あんた,なかなか**学**があるね You're quite *a scholar*.
ことわざ **少年老いやすく学成り難し** Life is half spent before we learn what it [life] is all about.

3がく 萼 a **calyx** /kéɪlɪks, kǽl-/ (花の).

かくい 各位 ▶**会員各位** *To our members* (➤ To each of our members とするよりも複数がふつう).
‖**関係各位** To whom it may concern.

がくい 学位 an **academic degree** ▶経営学修士の**学位** *a degree* of Master of Business Administration [an M. B. A.] ‖ 心理学で**学位**を取る get [take] *a degree* in psychology ‖ どこで博士[修士]の**学位**を受けられたのですか Where did you get your doctor's [master's] *degree*?
‖**学位授与式** a degree (conferring) ceremony ‖**学位論文** a doctoral dissertation (博士); a master's thesis (修士).

かくいつか 画一化 standardization; **regimentation** (規格化).

かくいつてき 画一的な standardized(規格化された); **uniform**(一様な); **regimental**(統制的な) ▶**画一的な**商品 *standardized* goods ‖ **画一的な**教え方 a *regimental* style of teaching ‖ **画一的教育**の1つの欠陥は個性的人間が生まれにくいことである One defect of *uniform education* is that it produces few men and women with distinctive personalities.

がくいん 楽員 ▶オーケストラの**楽員** an orchestra *member* / *a member* of an orchestra.

かくう 架空の imaginary (想像上の); **fictitious** /fɪktíʃəs/ (フィクションの) ▶**架空の**動物 an *imaginary* animal ‖ このドラマの登場人物はすべて**架空のもの**です All the characters in this drama are *fictitious* [*imaginary*].

かくえき 各駅 ▶《新幹線のアナウンス》この列車は新大阪から先, **各駅**に止まります This train stops at *all stations* [at *every station*] beyond Shin-osaka. ‖ この電車は**各駅停車**の多治見行きです This train is *a local* (*train*) for Tajimi. (➤ local (train) は「普通電車」の意. 《米》では way train, 《英》では stopping [slow] train ともいう).

がくえん 学園 a school ▶娘はひばり**学園**高等学校に通っている My daughter goes to Hibari (*Gakuen*) Senior High School. ‖ 1人の学生を退学させたことから**学園紛争**に発展した The expulsion of a student led to *a disturbance on campus* [*campus un-*

rest].

‖**学園祭** a school [campus] festival ‖**つくば研究学園都市** Tsukuba Science City.

かくかい 角界 **the sumo world, the world of sumo.**

がくがい 学外 ▶**学外**から教授を招く invite a professor from *outside the college* ‖(大学の)**学外**で *off campus*.

がくがく ▶急な石段を上ったので足が**がくがく**した My legs *were shaking* after I climbed the steep flight of stone steps. ‖テーブルの脚が**がくがく**している The table is *wobbly*. ‖ブリッジが**がくがく**する My (dental) bridge *is loose*.

かくかくしかじか ▶君は**かくかくしかじか**の理由で遅れたと説明すべきだ You should explain that you're late for *such and such* a reason.

かくかぞく 核家族 **a nuclear family** ▶あの国では**核家族**化がますます進んでいる *The trend towards nuclear families* is advancing in that country.

かくがり 角刈り **a crew cut,**《米・インフォーマル》**a flat-top** ▶頭を**角刈り**にする get *a crew cut*.

かくぎ 閣議 **a Cabinet meeting** [**council**](➤ cabinet は特定の内閣を指すとき以外でもしばしば大文字で始める) ▶緊急**閣議**が明朝開かれることになっている *An urgent* [*emergency*] *Cabinet meeting* will be held tomorrow morning. ‖総理大臣が定例**閣議**を招集した The Prime Minister convened [called] *a regular Cabinet meeting*.

がくぎょう 学業 **studies**(勉強); **schoolwork**(学校の) ▶**学業**に励む throw oneself into *studies* ‖彼女は**学業**優秀だ She is *doing very well in her schoolwork*. ‖彼は家庭の事情で**学業**を放棄(=退学)しなければならなかった He was obliged to *leave school* for family reasons.

がくげい 学芸 **arts and sciences**(学問と芸術); **cultural attainments**(素養) ▶新聞の**学芸**欄 *the arts and sciences column* of a newspaper.

がくげいかい 学芸会 **the (students') musical and theatrical performances**(➤ 英米には日本の学芸会と同様の形式のものはない).

がくげき 楽劇 **a musical** [**music**] **drama.**

1**かくげつ 隔月** ▶その雑誌は**隔月**に刊行される The magazine is published *every other month*. (➤「隔月刊の雑誌」は a bimonthly /bàɪmʌ́nθli/ (magazine) という).

2**かくげつ 各月** **each month.**

かくげん 格言 **a saying, a proverb**(ことわざ); **a maxim**(処世訓).

かくご 覚悟する **make up** one's **mind**(決心する); **be prepared** [**ready**](心の準備ができている) ▶彼はようやく自宅を売る**覚悟**を決めた He finally *made up his mind* to sell his house. ‖ケントは日本語をマスターするためにはどんなことでもする**覚悟**だった Kent *made up his mind* to do whatever it took to master Japanese.

▶父に怒られるのは**覚悟**している I'*m prepared* to get a lecture from my father. ‖その殺人犯は「死は**覚悟**している」と言った The murderer said, "I'*m ready* [*prepared*] to die." ‖**対話**「入試に失敗したときの**覚悟**はできてるの?」「うん, そのときはコックになるつもりだよ」"*Are you prepared* [*ready*] *for* the possibility of failing the entrance exam?" "Yeah, in that case I plan to be a cook."

かくさ 格差 **a gap**(隔たり); **a difference**(差異); (a) **disparity**(不均衡) ▶両国間の生活水準の**格差**は大きい There is a wide [large] *gap* in the standard of living between the two countries. ‖男女の賃金**格差**は依然として存在する There is still *a wage difference* between male and female workers [a gender *gap in wages*]. ‖広がりつつある貧富の収入**格差** a widening *income disparity* between (the) rich and (the) poor ‖情報**格差**を縮める close *the digital divide*.

‖**格差社会** a society with a large gap between the rich and poor / a society with severe economic disparities.

かくざい 角材 **squared lumber** [《英》**timber**].

がくさいてきな 学際的な **interdisciplinary** /ìnṭəᵣdísəplənèri/ ▶**学際的な**研究 *interdisciplinary* studies [research].

かくさく 画策する **hatch** +目(企てる); **maneuver** /mənúːvəᵣ/ +目(陰で策動する) ▶社長の追放を**画策**する *hatch a plot* [*plan*] to expel the president from the company ‖裏で**画策する** *maneuver* behind the scenes.

かくさげ 格下げ (a) **demotion** ▶伍長は兵卒に**格下げ**になった The corporal *was demoted to* private.

かくざとう 角砂糖 **a cube** [**lump**] **of sugar, a sugar cube** ▶紅茶に**角砂糖**をいくつ入れますか How many *cubes* [*lumps*] *of sugar* do you take in your tea?

1**かくさん 拡散** **the spread**(四方に広がること); **proliferation**(細胞などの増殖, 核兵器の拡散) **一動 拡散する** **spread** +目, **proliferate** /prəlífərèɪt/ +目; **go viral**(ネット上で動画・画像などが瞬く間に)

▶核の**拡散**防止に努める make efforts to prevent nuclear *proliferation* [the *proliferation* of nuclear weapons].

2**かくさん 核酸** (a) **nucleic** /njuklíːɪk/ **acid** ▶デオキシリボ**核酸** deoxyribo nucleic acid《略 DNA》.

かくし 客死する **die abroad** ▶画家佐伯祐三は1928年パリで**客死した** The painter Saeki Yuzo *died in Paris* in 1928. (➤ "in Paris" とあるので, abroad は言うまでもない).

かくじ 各自 ▶**各自**行動には責任をもつように *Each individual* [*Everyone*] is requested to be responsible for his or her own actions. ‖現地までの費用は**各自**で負担しよう Let us *all* bear *our* [Let us *each* bear *his*] *own* share of the expenses until we get there.

1**がくし 学資** **school expenses** ▶彼はアルバイトをして**学資**を稼いでいる He works part-time to pay for his *school expenses*.

2**がくし 学士** **a bachelor's degree**(称号); **a university** [**college**] **graduate**(人) ▶教育学部に**学士**入学する *enter* a university's school [department] of education *with a B.A. from a different four-year college or university*.

‖(日本)**学士院** the Japan Academy ‖(日本)**学士院会員** a member of the Japan Academy ‖**学士力** graduate ability / scholastic ability upon graduation.

3**がくし 楽師** **a musician.**

かくしあじ 隠し味 **a secret ingredient to enhance the flavor.**

かくしカメラ 隠しカメラ **a hidden camera.**

かくしき 格式 **formality** ▶**格式**の高い旅館 an inn high in *social standing* ‖祖父は**格式**を重んじる昔かたぎの人だった My grandfather was an old-fashioned man who was *particular about formalities*.

がくしき 学識 **learning** ▶学識豊かな人 a *learned* person (➤ 発音は /lə́ːʳnɪd/) ／a person of *profound* [*great*] *learning* ‖ 学識経験者 a person of learning and experience, a literate /lítərət/ (学問[教育]のある人) ／a scholar (学者).

か

かくしげい 隠し芸 **hidden talent** (秘密の能力) ; a **parlor trick** (手品のような芸) ▶誰か隠し芸でもやりませんか Can anyone volunteer some *entertainment* now? (➤ entertainment は「余興」. 実際にはもっと具体的に Let's hear one of your songs. とか Let's see some of your magic tricks. などと言うほうが英語らしい).

かくしごと 隠し事 a **secret** ▶隠し事はやめなさい Stop *doing things behind my back*. (Don't hide anything from me. とすると「やめる」のニュアンスが出せないので, 訳例のように stop を用いる) ‖ 何か隠し事をしてるんじゃないの? Are you *keeping* something (*secret*) *from* me? ／Are you *hiding* something *from* me? (➤ 日本語が「じゃないの」なので, Aren't you ... としたくなるが, 否定形で言うと, お互いに知っていることを確認する, あるいは, 思い出させるニュアンスの質問になる. →-ない).

かくしだて 隠し立て ▶隠し立てをすると身のためにならないぞ It won't do you any good to *be* so *secretive*. ／It will do you no good to *keep secrets*.

かくしつ 確執 a **feud** /fjuːd/ (長期間の反目) ; (a) **discord** (意見の相違, 不和) ; (a) **conflict** (意見・利害などの衝突) ▶親子の確執 *a conflict* between father [mother] and son [daughter].

[1]**かくじつ 確実** 一形 **確実な** **certain** (客観的に) ; **sure** (主観的に) ; **positive** (自信がある) ; **reliable** (信用できる) ▶うちの新製品がヒットすることは確実だ *It is certain that* our new product will be a hit. ‖ その弁護士が総選挙で当選するのは確実だ *It is certain that* the lawyer will win the general election. ／The lawyer's success in the general election *is a certainty* [*is assured*]. ‖ その法案はほぼ確実に通る The bill *is almost certain to* pass. →確か.

▶確実な情報 *reliable* information (certain information とすると「ある(特定)の情報」の意になるのがふつう) ‖ 確実な証拠 *positive* proof ‖ たぶん行けると思うけど, 確実な返事はあすまで待ってよ I think I'll be able to go, but I'm not sure. Wait till tomorrow and I'll give you a *definite* answer.

☞ 不確実 (→見出語)

[2]**かくじつ 隔日** ▶その患者は隔日に注射を打たねばならない The patient must get an injection *every other* [*second*] *day*. ‖ 彼らは隔日勤務だ They *work on alternate days*. (➤ alternate /ɔ́ːltəʳnət ‖ ɔːltə́ːnət/ は「1つ置きの」).

かくじっけん 核実験 a **nuclear test** ▶核実験反対のデモ a demonstration against *nuclear tests* ‖ ネバダ州で地下核実験が行われた *Underground nuclear tests* were conducted in the state of Nevada.

かくしどり 隠し撮り ▶この写真は隠し撮りしたものだ This picture *was taken with a hidden camera*.

かくしマイク 隠しマイク a **hidden microphone**, a **bug** (➤ 後者はインフォーマル).

がくしゃ 学者 a **scholar** /skɑ́ːləʳ/ ▶偉い学者 a great *scholar* ‖ 学者肌の人 a *bookish* person (➤「本ばかり読んでいる人」,「学者ぶった人」の意になることもある) ‖ あのうちは学者一家です That is *an academic family*.

> 「学者」のいろいろ 海洋学者 oceanographer ／化学者 chemist ／気象学者 meteorologist ／経済学者 economist ／言語学者 linguist ／考古学者 arch(a)eologist ／昆虫学者 entomologist ／地震学者 seismologist ／社会学者 sociologist ／植物学者 botanist ／心理学者 psychologist ／人類学者 anthropologist ／数学者 mathematician ／政治学者 political scientist ／生物学者 biologist ／生理学者 physiologist ／地質学者 geologist ／哲学者 philosopher ／天文学者 astronomer ／動物学者 zoologist ／物理学者 physicist ／法律学者 jurist

かくしゃく 矍鑠 ▶祖父は来年卒寿を迎えるが, なおかくしゃくとしている My grandfather will be 90 next year, but he is still *hale and hearty* [*vigorous* ／ *in robust health*].

かくしゅ 各種 ▶ドラッグストアには薬以外にも各種の品がそろっている Drugstores stock *various kinds of* goods in addition to medicines.

かくしゅう 隔週 ▶その小冊子は隔週に出る That pamphlet is published *biweekly* [*every other week*]. ‖ 私は隔週の土曜日が休みです I have *every other* Saturday [*alternate* Saturdays] off. (➤ alternate /ɔ́ːltəʳnət ‖ ɔːltə́ːnət/ は「1つ置きの」).

かくじゅう 拡充する **expand** +目 (広げる) ▶図書館を拡充する *expand* a library ‖ 工場の施設を拡充する *expand and improve* on factory facilities.

がくしゅう 学習 **study** (勉強) ; **learning** (習得) 一動 **学習する** **study** +目, **learn** +目 ▶英語を学習する *study* English (➤ learn と異なり,「努力して勉強する」ことに重点がある) ‖ イルカが芸を覚えるのは学習の成果である The tricks that dolphins do are *learned* behavior. ‖ 日本には英語の学習者が大勢いるが, 完全にマスターする人は少ない There are many English *learners* in Japan, but only a few of them master the language.

▶彼女に英語の学習法を聞いたら,「できるだけ頻繁に使うことね」と言った When I asked her *how to learn* English, she answered, "Use it as often as possible."

‖ 学習参考書 a study-aid (book) ／a study guide ‖ 学習指導要領 official guidelines for school teaching ／the course of study ‖ 学習塾 (→塾) ‖ 遠隔学習 distance learning ‖ 生涯学習 lifelong learning ‖ 早期学習 early(-childhood) learning.

かくしゅがっこう 各種学校 a **specialty school** ; a **vocational school** (職業学校).

がくじゅつ 学術 **science and art** (科学と芸術) 一形 **学術的な** **scientific, academic** ▶学術の振興を図る promote *science and art*.

‖ 学術機関 an academic institution ‖ 学術研究 scientific [academic] research ‖ 学術誌 an academic journal ‖ 学術書 a scientific book ／an academic book ‖ 学術調査 academic research ‖ 学術用語 a technical [scientific] term ‖ 学術論文 a paper, a treatise (➤ 後者は堅い語) ‖ 日本学術会議 Science Council of Japan.

かくしょう 確証 **hard** [**sure**] **evidence, sure proof** ▶殺しの犯人が女性だという確証でもあるのですか Do you have any *hard evidence* that the killer was a woman?

がくしょう 楽章 a **movement** ▶第3楽章 the third *movement* ‖ 緩徐楽章 a slow *movement* ‖ 終楽章

the last *movement*.

がくしょく 学食 a school cafeteria.

1**かくしん 確信** conviction(固い信念); confidence(自信) 一動 **確信する** be sure, be certain(➤ sure のほうが主観的) ▶私は彼が正直な人だと**確信している** I'*m sure* [*certain*] that he is an honest man. ‖ 私は彼女の成功を**確信している** I *am sure* of her success. ‖ キリスト教徒はキリストが再び地上に戻ってくると**確信している** Christians *firmly believe* that Christ will come back to (the) earth. ‖ 彼は自分が正しかったので**確信をもって**話をした He told his story *with conviction* because he was right. ‖ 野球部の監督はことしはわが校が優勝すると**確信をもって**言った The manager of the baseball team said *confidently* [*with confidence*] that our school would win the championship this year.

‖**確信犯** a crime of conscience(宗教的・政治的に正当だと信じて行う犯罪); a person who commits a crime of conscience(宗教的・政治的に正当だと信じて犯罪を行う人)《参考》日本語で日常的に用いる「確信犯」はむしろ「故意犯」(a crime of intention; a person who commits a crime intentionally).

2**かくしん 革新** innovation(技術の); (a) reform(社会の) 一形 **革新的な** progressive(進歩的な); innovative(斬新な) ▶**革新的な技術** (an) *innovative* technology ‖ **革新的な考えをもつ候補者** a candidate with *progressive* ideas.

▶政治の**革新**を唱える propose a political *reform* ‖ 技術**革新**はいろいろな分野で生産性を向上させた *Technological innovation* increased productivity in various fields.

▶保守系の候補が**革新系**の候補を抑えて知事に当選した The conservative candidate defeated the *progressive* candidate in the election and was elected governor.

‖**革新政党** a reformist [progressive] party ‖ **革新団体** a reformist organization.

3**かくしん 核心** the core, the heart ▶問題の**核心**に迫る get to *the core* [*the very heart*] of a problem ‖ その報告書は事件の**核心**に触れていない The report does not touch on *the most important part* [*the main points*] of the case.

かくじん 各人 each (person), every one ▶(その件に関しては)**各人**各様の考えがある *Each person* has their [his or her] own opinion (on the matter).

かくす 隠す

訳語メニュー
見られないようにする →hide **1**
知られないようにする →keep secret **2**

1【見られないようにする】hide +⑪; **stash** +⑪(お金・貴重品を; インフォーマルな語) ▶彼はその箱を床下に**隠した** He *hid* that box under the floor. (➤ hid は hide の過去形) ‖ 彼女はそのお金をカーペットの下に**隠した** She *stashed* the money under the carpet. ‖ 彼女は戸の陰に**身を隠した** She *hid* (*herself*) behind the door. ‖ 彼女はハンカチで顔を**隠した** She *hid* her face in her handkerchief. ‖ 彼女は手で顔を**隠した** She *covered* her face with her hands. / She *buried* [*hid*] her face in her hands. (➤ bury /béri/ や hide は cover よりも「見えないように深く隠す」の意味合いが強く, 前置詞は in を使う) ‖ 彼はワイシャツについた染みを**隠す**ため急いでセーターを着た He hurriedly put on a sweater to *cover up* a stain on his shirt.

▶私はケーキを弟に**見えない所に隠した** I *put* the cake *out of* my little brother's *sight*.

2【知られないようにする】keep ... secret(秘密にしておく) ▶彼らは婚約したことを人に**隠しておいた** They *kept* their engagement *secret*. / They *kept* their engagement *to themselves*. ‖ 部長は計画を部下に**隠していた** The manager *kept* [*concealed*] his plan *from* his staff. (➤ keep [conceal] A from B で「A(物・事)をB(人)に隠しておく」の意; conceal は堅い語) ‖ ぼくは母には**何も隠さない** I *keep nothing from* my mother. / I *am completely open with* my mother.

▶きみの言うことはつじつまが合わない. 私に何か**隠してる**ね What you've told me doesn't hold water—you must *be keeping* something *from* me [*holding out on* me]. (➤ hold out on は「(秘密などを)隠す」の意のインフォーマルな言い方) ‖ **隠さずに全部話しなさい** Tell me *everything* you know about it. ‖ **何を隠そう**(=実を言うと), この手紙を書いたのはぼくなんだよ *To be frank with you* [*To tell you the truth*], I am the one who wrote the letter.

かくすう 画数 the number of strokes in [the stroke count of] a kanji character.

かくする 画する ▶これは従来のものとは**一線を画する**製品です This product *is in a different league* from conventional ones. (➤ in a different league は「格が違う」) ‖ **一時代を画する**傑出した人物 an *outstanding and revolutionary* figure.

かくせい 隔世 ▶当時を思うと**隔世の感がある** When I think of those days, *I feel I am living in a completely different age* [*world*].

‖**隔世遺伝** atavism /ǽṭəvìzəm/.

1がくせい 学生 a student

《解説》(1)《米》では小学生から大学生まですべてに **student** を,《英》では大学生には **student** を, 中等学校生(日本の高校生・中学生)には **student** または **pupil** を, 小学生にはふつう **pupil** を用いる.
(2)日常的には小学生から大学生までを **student** と呼ぶことも少なくない.

▶彼は平成大学の**学生**だ He is *a student* at Heisei University. (➤ 所属大学を表すのに(×)student *of* とはしない. of は何を勉強しているかをいうのに用いて, student of economics(経済学を勉強している学生)のように用いる) / He is a Heisei *student*. (➤ この言い方は「平成高校[中学校]の生徒」の意でも用いる) ‖ この大学の**学生数**は3000だ This university has *an enrollment* of 3,000. / The *student enrollment* of this university is 3,000. (➤ enrollment は「登録者数」) ‖ **学生時代**にはずいぶん旅行しました I traveled a great deal *when* [*while*] *I was a student*. ‖ 彼らは**学生結婚**だ They got married when they were students [at college]. (➤「学生結婚」に相当する英語はない).

‖**学生運動** a student movement ‖ **学生証** a student ID card ‖ **学生食堂** a student(s') dining hall, a school cafeteria ‖ **学生新聞** a student newspaper ‖ **学生生活** student life ‖ **学生部** a student affairs office [section] ‖ **学生服** a school [college] uniform (➤ 後者は大学生の) ‖ **学生部長** a director of a student affairs office [section], a dean of students(➤ 最後の言い方は

アメリカなどで使われるが，日本のそれと異なり，学生の生活指導や学習カウンセリング以外に，入学・入試に関しても発言権を持つ）‖**女子学生** a female [girl] student, a college woman（➤ 後者は大学の）‖**男子学生** a male [boy] student, a college man（➤ 後者は大学の）.

か

2**がくせい 学制** an **education(al) system.**

3**がくせい 楽聖** ▶楽聖ベートーベン Beethoven, *the maestro*.

かくせいき 拡声器 a **loud speaker**；《米》a **bullhorn**,《英》a **loudhailer**（ハンドマイク）；a **megaphone**（メガホン）.

かくせいざい 覚醒剤 a **stimulant drug, pep pills, speed**（➤ 後者2つはインフォーマルな言い方）▶彼は覚醒剤中毒だ He *is addicted to stimulant drugs*. 《参考》英米人は実際には He is addicted to (meth)amphetamines.（彼はアンフェタミン中毒だ）のように覚醒剤の具体名を挙げるか，または He is a speed addict [a drug freak]. のようにいうことが多い.

がくせき 学籍 a **(student's) enrollment record**
‖**学籍番号** a [one's] student (ID) number ‖**学籍簿** a school [college] register.

かくぜつ 隔絶 ▶ロビンソン・クルーソーは世間から隔絶された島に住んでいた Robinson Crusoe lived on an island *isolated* from the (rest of the) world.‖彼の考えは現実から隔絶している His ideas *are far removed* from reality.

がくせつ 学説 a **theory** ▶生命の起源に関する新しい学説 *a* new *theory* about the origin of life.

がくぜん 愕然 ▶先生たちはカンニングをしたのが生徒会長だと知ってがく然とした All the teachers *were shocked* to find that the student who had cheated on the exam was the president of the student council.

がくそう 楽想 a **musical idea** ▶楽想を練る develop *a musical idea* [*theme*／*motif*].

がくそつ 学卒 a **college** [**university**] **graduate.**

かくだい 拡大 **expansion**（広げること）**一動 拡大する** **enlarge** +目（大きくする）；**magnify** +目（物体を大きく見せる）；**expand** +目，**extend** +目（拡張する；前者は「四方八方に」という含みをもつ）▶地図を拡大する *enlarge* a map ‖拡大器で図面を2倍に拡大する *magnify* a plan twice under *a magnifier* ‖日本の国際貿易を拡大する *expand* Japan's international trade ‖わが社は輸出を中南米諸国にまで拡大した We *have extended* [*expanded*] our exports to Latin America.‖国境紛争が全面戦争に拡大した The border disputes *have escalated* into (a) total war.（➤ escalate は「段階的に拡大する」）‖インフルエンザ感染の拡大を防ぐ prevent *the spread* of influenza.
‖**拡大鏡** a magnifying glass, a magnifier；a reading glass（読書用の）‖**拡大コピー** an enlargement.

がくたい 楽隊 a **band** ‖**軍楽隊** a military band.

かくたる 確たる **definite**（はっきりした）；**positive**（強く確信できる）▶確たる証拠 *definite* proof.

かくだん 格段 ▶両者の実力には格段の差がある There is a *marked* [*distinct*／*great*] difference in ability between the two (persons).

がくだん 楽団 a **band**, an **orchestra**（➤ 前者はポピュラー音楽の楽団にしばしば用いられる）
‖**交響楽団** a symphony orchestra ‖**室内楽団** a chamber orchestra ‖**吹奏楽団** a brass band.

かくだんとう 核弾頭 a **nuclear warhead.**

かくち 各地 ▶世界各地から来た人々 people from *every part* [*every corner*] of the world／people from *all over* the world ‖この店では日本各地の名産を売っている This store sells specialties of *various regions* in Japan.‖全国高校野球大会の予選が各地で始まった The elimination rounds for the National Senior High School Baseball Tournament have started *nationwide* [*across the country*／*across the nation*].

1**かくちょう 拡張** **expansion** **一動 拡張する** **extend** +目，**expand** +目（➤ 後者には「四方八方に広げる」の含みがある）；**widen** +目（道路などの幅を広げる）▶販路[事業]を拡張する *extend* one's market [business]‖校舎を拡張する *expand* a school building ‖うちの近くで道路の拡張工事が進行している The street near my house is now *being widened*.
‖《コンピュータ》**拡張子** an extension（➤ 正式には a file extension；ファイル名の末尾につけられる .doc, .pdf などの種類識別の符号）.

2**かくちょう 格調** ▶格調のある家具 furniture *with class* [*style*]‖鷗外の格調高い文体 Ogai's *lofty* (*writing*) style ‖格調高い英語 *polished* English ‖安い進物もXデパートの包み紙に包むと格調高く見える Even an inexpensive gift looks more *impressive* when wrapped with X Department Store's (wrapping) paper.

がくちょう 学長 a **president** 《参考》(1)アメリカの一部の大規模大学では分校の学長を chancellor と呼ぶ. (2)イギリスでは大学によっては provost, principal, warden などを用いる.

かくづけ 格付け (a) **rating**（評価分け）；(a) **grading**（ランク付け）**一動 格付けする** **rate** +目（評価する）；**grade** +目（等級をつける）▶大学の格付け a university *ranking* [*rating*／*grading*]‖大学を塾が算出した偏差値によって格付けするのは無意味だ It is meaningless to *rate* colleges and universities according to cram schools' T-score calculations of the difficulty of their entrance examinations.‖ミシュランが三ツ星に格付けしたレストラン a Michelin-*rated* three-star restaurant ‖債権格付け機関 a bond-*rating*(*s*) agency ‖信用格付け (a) credit *rating*.

がくっ(と) ▶入試に失敗してがくっと来た *My heart fell* [*plummeted*] *to my feet* when I failed the entrance examinations.‖**対話**「旅行は中止だ」「がくっ！」"We're canceling the trip." "*That's too bad.*／*Oh, what a shame !*"（➤ この shame は「残念なこと」の意）.

かくてい 確定する **be decided**（決められる）；**be finalized**（最終的に決まる）▶その男は死刑が確定している The death sentence *has been decided* for that man.‖セ・リーグのチーム順位が確定した The ranking of the baseball teams in the Central League *has been finalized*.‖マジックナンバーが2となり西武の優勝がほぼ確定した A Lions victory seems *almost certain* now that their magic number is down to two.
▶（所得税の）確定申告はもう済ませましたか Have you already filed your (*final*) *income tax return*?
☛ **不確定**（→見出語）

カクテル a **cocktail**（酒にもオードブルにもいう）▶バーテンはジンとベルモットでカクテルを作った The bartender made *a cocktail* with gin and vermouth.
‖**カクテルパーティー** a cocktail party.

かくど 角度 **1**【角の大きさ】an **angle** ▶2本の線が45

度の角度で交差する The two lines meet at a 45° *angle* [*an angle* of 45°]. (➤°は degree(s) と読む).

2【観点】 an **angle**, a **point of view** ▶この問題はいろいろな角度から検討する必要がある This problem should be studied *from several* (*different*) *angles*.

1**かくとう 格闘** a **fight** 一動 (…と) 格闘する **fight** 《with》, **wrestle** 《with》 (➤後者はレスリングのような組み打ちを連想させる) ▶私は泥棒と格闘して取り押さえた I *fought* [*wrestled*] *with* the burglar and overcame him. (➤ fought は fight の過去形) ‖ サンボは柔道に似たロシアの格闘技だ Sambo is a Russian *combative sport* that resembles judo.

▶彼女は2時間近くも数学の難問と格闘した末, やっと解いた After *grappling* [*wrestling*] *with* a difficult math problem for nearly two hours, she finally managed to solve it.

2**かくとう 確答** a **definite answer** ▶政治家はしばしば確答を避ける Politicians often avoid giving *definite* [*clear*] *answers*.

がくどう 学童 a **schoolchild**; a **schoolboy** (男の), a **schoolgirl** (女の) ‖学童保育 after-school care for schoolchildren.

かくとく 獲得 acquisition 一動 獲得する **acquire** +目; **gain** +目 (大きな努力の末, 望みのものを); **obtain** +目 (苦労して; やや堅い語); **win** +目 (競争に勝って) ▶永住権を獲得する *acquire* the right of permanent residence ‖ 父は宝くじの特賞に当たり1000万円を獲得した My father hit the jackpot in the lottery and *won* ten million yen. (➤ won /wʌn/ は win の過去形) ‖ その国は戦争による大きな犠牲を払って自由を獲得した The nation *obtained* liberty at the sacrifice of many lives (lost) in war. ‖ 彼女は長い下積み生活のあとスターの座を獲得した She *attained* stardom after long years of obscurity. (➤ attain は「到達する」).

かくない 閣内 ▶閣内で within *the cabinet*.

がくない 学内 ▶学内に立ち入る enter the *school premises* [(*college*) *campus*].

かくにん 確認 confirmation 一動 確認する **confirm** +目; **check** +目 (調べる); **make sure** (本当かどうかを確かめる); **identify** +目 (身元を) ▶私はホテルの予約を確認した I *confirmed* my hotel reservation. ‖ ドアの鍵が全部かかっているか確認して *Make sure* that all the doors are locked. ‖ ほかの車が来ていないかバックミラーで確認しなさい *Check* the rearview mirror for other vehicles. ‖ もう一度彼女に確認します I'll *check* again with her. ‖ 踏切は左右を確認してから渡りなさい At railroad crossings, *look right and left* before crossing.

▶日本人のルーツはまだはっきりとは確認されていない The origins [roots] of the Japanese have still not *been* clearly *identified*. ‖ その事故では遺体の損傷がひどく, 身元の確認に手間取った The body was so badly mangled in the accident that it was difficult to *establish identity*.

☛ 再確認, 未確認 (→見出語)

かくねん 隔年 ▶その同人誌は隔年に発行されている The club magazine is published *every other year* [*every second year* / *every two years* / *in alternate years*].

がくねん 学年 **1【学年度】** a **school year**; an **academic year** (主に大学の) ‖学年末試験 a final examination, 《インフォーマル》 a final ‖ 学年暦 an academic calendar.

2【学生の年次】 《米》 a **grade**, 《英》 a **form**

> **《解説》学制と年次**
> (1)アメリカでは最近は elementary school (5年制), middle school (3年制), high school (4年制) へと進む 5-3-4制をとる学校が多く, 6-3-3制は少ない.
> (2)5-3-4制をとる学校ではふつう, 小学校から高校までを一続きの **grade** で表し, いちばん下は the first grade (小学校1学年), いちばん上は the twelfth grade(ハイスクール12学年)となる. したがって日本の中学校2学年は the eighth grade, 高校1学年は the tenth grade に相当する.
> (3)しかし, ハイスクールの学年については grade のほかに大学の学年と同じ表現も用いられる. すなわち, 4年制高校では9年生(日本の中3)が **freshman**, 10年生(高1)が **sophomore**, 11年生(高2)が **junior**, 12年生(高3)が **senior** となる. 3年制高校は1年生が sophomore, 2年生が junior, 3年生が senior となる. 日本の高校はふつう3年制だから, アメリカ流にいえば1年生は sophomore, 2年生は junior, 3年生は senior となる. ただし, 1年生は first-year high school student とするほうが誤解がない.
> (4)大学の学年は1年生が freshman, 2年生が sophomore, 3年生が junior, 4年生が senior である.

▶木村先生は高校3年の学年主任である Mrs.Kimura is *the head* of the twelfth *grade* homeroom teachers. ‖ 私たちは同じ学年です We're in *the same grade*.

☛ 高学年, 低学年 (→見出語)

かくのうこ 格納庫 a **hangar** ▶飛行機を格納庫に入れる put an airplane into *a hangar*.

がくは 学派 a **school (of thought)** ▶シカゴ学派 the Chicago *School*.

がくばつ 学閥 an **academic clique** [**faction**]; an **old-boy** [**old-girl**] **network** (卒業生どうしのきずな) ▶あの会社は学閥が強いそうだ I am told that company has *a strong faction of people from the same school*. / I am told that company is dominated by *an old-boy network*. 《参考》日本通の外国人の間では *gakubatsu* をそのまま用いる人もいる.

かくばった 角張った ▶清は角張った顎をしている Kiyoshi has a *square* chin.

がくひ 学費 **school** [**schooling**] **expenses** ▶学費は両親に出してもらっている I depend on my parents for my *school expenses*. / My parents are paying my *tuition*. (➤ tuition は「授業料」) ‖ 彼女はアルバイトで学費を稼ぎ大学を卒業した She *worked her way* through college. (➤ work one's way は「(働いて)稼ぎながら進む」).

1**がくふ 楽譜** (a **sheet of**) **music**; a **score** (総譜) ▶提示部を楽譜どおりに繰り返す repeat the exposition as written in the *score* ‖ 彼は楽譜が読めない He can't read *music*. ‖ そのピアニストは楽譜なしで演奏した The pianist played *entirely from memory*.

2**がくふ 学府** an **educational institution**; a **graduate school** (大学院) ‖ 最高学府 the highest *institution of learning* (➤「最高学府に学ぶ」は study at a university でよい).

がくぶ 学部 a **college** (総合大学の); a **school** (主に専門学部の); 《主に英》 a **faculty**

〘解説〙「学部」の言い方
(1)英米の大学では「学部」は college, school, faculty などで表され, どれを用いるかは大学によって異なるが, 一般に school が多く用いられている. faculty はアメリカではあまり用いられない.
(2)同じ大学でも学部によって異なった名称を用いることがある. 例えばボストン大学の場合, 教育学部は School of Education だが, 工学部は College of Engineering である.
(3)特定大学の学部・学科を述べる場合は最初の文字を大文字で書くことが多い.

▶K大医学部 *the School of Medicine* at K University(➤アメリカでは医学部は medical school と呼ばれ, 大学院課程に設けられる) ‖ 私たちの**文学部**には英米文学科と日本文学科がある Our *School of Humanities* [*Literature*] has a Department of American and British Literature and a Department of Japanese Literature. (➤日本の大学の「学科」は department で表す) ‖ 斎藤教授は農**学部**長です Professor Saito is *dean* of the College [School] of Agriculture. (➤be 動詞のあとで役職を表す語にはふつう the をつけない).
✉ **ぼくはM大学政治経済学部で経済を学んでいます. きみは学部はどこですか** I study economics at *the School of Political Science and Economics* of M University. What *school* [*college*] are you in?
‖**学部学生** an undergraduate (student).

がくぶち 額縁 a **(picture) frame.** →額.

かくへいき 核兵器 a **nuclear weapon,** 《インフォーマル》 a **nuke** /njuːk/ ▶地球上から**核兵器**を廃絶する eliminate [eradicate] all *nuclear weapons* from the face of the earth ‖ **核兵器**反対! No (more) *nukes*!
‖**核兵器保有国** a nuclear power.

かくべつ 格別な **exceptional** (類を見ない) ▶ことしの冬は**格別**暖かい This winter has been *exceptionally* mild. ‖ 彼女の手作りジャムの味は**格別**だ(=格別にうまい) Her homemade jam tastes *especially* good. ‖ 〘対話〙「香港旅行はいかがでした?」「まずまずで**格別**どうということもなかったよ」 "How was your trip to Hong Kong?" "It was okay, but nothing *special*."

かくほ 確保する **secure** +㊐ ; **save** +㊐ (取っておく) ▶優秀な人材を**確保する** *secure* talented people ‖ 泊まる所を**確保する** *secure* accommodations ‖ 我々は10日分の食糧と水を**確保した** We *had a* ten-day *supply* of food and water. ‖ 《学校で》食堂の椅子, **確保して**おいてね Could you *save* me a seat in the cafeteria? ‖ 列車は混んでいたが, 何とか席を2つ**確保**できた Though the train was crowded, we somehow *managed to get hold of* two seats. (➤get hold of は「…を見つける, 手に入れる」).

かくぼう 角帽 a **square** [**peaked**] **college cap** ; a **mortarboard** (大学の卒業式に教員や卒業生がかぶる房飾りのついたもの).

かくまう 匿う **harbor** +㊐ , **shelter** +㊐ (➤前者は特に犯罪者についていうときに用いる) ▶犯人を**かくまう**と罪になる It is illegal to *harbor* criminals. / *Harboring* [*Sheltering*] criminals is against the law. ‖ 2, 3日ここに**かくまって**くれないか Could you *let me hide out* here for a couple of days?

かくまく 角膜 《解剖学》 a **cornea** /kɔ́ːʳniə/
‖**角膜移植** a corneal transplant.

かくめい 革命 a **revolution** ▶**革命**を起こす start *a revolution* ‖ フランス[ロシア]**革命** *the French* [*Russian*] *Revolution* ‖ 産業**革命**は18世紀にイングランドで始まった *The Industrial Revolution* originated in England in the eighteenth century.
▶コンピュータは我々の日常生活に**革命をもたらした** The computer *has revolutionized* our daily life. ‖ 新しい時代に対応するにはまず上層部の**意識革命**(=姿勢の転換)が必要だ In order to meet the challenges of the new age, there must first be *a change in the attitudes* of the upper echelons of society.
‖**革命運動** a revolutionary movement ‖ **革命家** a revolutionary ‖ **革命軍** a revolutionary army ‖ **革命政府** a revolutionary government [regime].

がくめい 学名 a **scientific name** ▶ヒトの**学名**はホモサピエンスだ The *scientific name* for human beings is "Homo sapiens."

がくめん 額面 **face value** ▶**額面**1千万円の小切手 a check *for* [*in the amount of*] ten million yen ‖ 《比喩的》彼の言うことは**額面**どおりには受け取れないよ You shouldn't accept what he says *at face value*.
‖**額面価格** par (value) ‖ **額面割れの債権** a bond that has dropped below par / a subpar bond.

がくもん 学問 **learning** ; **study** (研究) ; **education** (教育) ; **knowledge** (知識) ▶**学問**を奨励する encourage *learning* ‖ **学問**のある人 an *educated* person ‖ **学問**に精を出す apply [devote] oneself to one's *studies* (➤studies にはふつう「勉強」の意のほか,「個人が行う特定の研究」の意もある) ‖ **学問的業績** *academic* achievement(s) ‖ **学問的著作** a *scholarly* work.
▶大学とは**学問をする**所であって, 遊ぶ所ではない College is a place to *study and learn*, not to play around. ‖ 応用言語学は比較的新しい**学問**だ Applied linguistics is a comparatively new *science* [*discipline*]. ‖ 私の**学問**は本からの学問ではなく耳学問です My *knowledge* has been *obtained by listening to other people* rather than by reading. ‖ 祖父は**学問**はなかったが, 物知りだった My grandfather received no formal *education*, but he was very knowledgeable.
〘ことわざ〙 **学問に王道なし** There is no royal road to learning.

がくや 楽屋 a **dressing room,** an **offstage waiting room** ; **backstage** (舞台裏).

かくやく 確約 a **definite promise** ▶彼女から**確約**を取りつける get *a definite promise* from her ‖ 秘密は口外しないと**確約する**よ I *give* you *my word of honor* (that) I will keep your secret. (➤one's word of honor は「誓言」) ‖ あすまでにこのレポートを終えるという**確約**はできない I cannot *promise* to finish this report by tomorrow.

かくやす 格安 ▶このカーペットは全く**格安**だった This carpet was *a* real *bargain* [*a* good *buy*]. (➤bargain, buy は「買い得品, 格安品」の意のインフォーマルな語) ‖ この携帯音楽プレーヤーは**格安の値段**で買った I bought this portable music player *at a bargain price*.

がくゆう 学友 a **schoolfellow,** a **schoolmate.**

かくゆうごう 核融合 **nuclear fusion.**

がくようひん 学用品 **school supplies, things for school** ▶**学用品**を買いそろえる buy all the necessary *school supplies*.

かぐら 神楽 ***kagura***; Shinto music and dancing performed at shrines(➤ 説明的な訳).

がくラン 学ラン a male student's uniform with a stand-up collar(➤ 説明的な訳).

かくり 隔離 **isolation** (分離); **quarantine** /kwɔ́:r-ənti:n/ (病気予防のための) **一動 隔離する isolate** +㊐, **quarantine** +㊐ ▶彼は手術後3日間集中治療室に**隔離された** He *was kept in isolation* in the intensive care unit for three days after surgery. ‖ その伝染病患者は2か月間**隔離された** The man carrying an infectious disease *was in quarantine* [*was quarantined*] for two months. ‖**隔離病棟** an isolation ward.

1**かくりつ 確立** **establishment 一動 確立する establish** +㊐ ▶世界平和の**確立** *establishment* of world peace ‖ その小説家は第2作で名声を**確立した** The novelist *established* a reputation with his [her] second novel. ‖ 経済面および文化面の交流にたゆまず努めれば, やがては両国の友好と理解を**確立する**ことができる Sustained efforts to promote exchanges in the economic and cultural fields will serve to *establish* friendship and understanding between our two countries.

2**かくりつ 確率** **probability**; (a) **chance**(公算, 見込み) ▶彼が逮捕される**確率**は50パーセントだ There is a fifty percent *probability* of his being arrested. ／The *probability* of his being arrested is fifty-fifty. ／He's got a 50-50 *chance* of being arrested. (➤ インフォーマルな英語では最後の例が最も一般的) ‖ 成功の**確率**はゼロに近い The *chances* of success are almost zero [nil]. ‖ 埼玉地方の降水**確率**は40%です There is a 40 percent *possibility* [*chance*] *of rain* in the Saitama area.

かくりょう 閣僚 a **Cabinet member** [**minister**]; a **member of the Cabinet** (➤ 特定の内閣を指す場合, cabinet はしばしば大文字で始める) ▶彼女は**閣僚の地位**にある She holds *a seat in the Cabinet*. ‖ 5か国の**閣僚**が集まって緊急会議をした *Cabinet ministers* from five nations gathered for an emergency meeting. ‖**閣僚会議** a Cabinet meeting ／a meeting of Cabinet ministers.

がくりょく 学力 **scholastic** [**academic**] **ability** ▶その新しいカリキュラムが導入されてから生徒の**学力水準**が向上したようだ Since the new curriculum was introduced, the *scholastic ability* [*level*] of students seems to have increased. ‖ 彼の英語の**学力**(＝知識)はあいつが自分で言うほどじゃないと思うよ I don't think his *knowledge* of English is as good as he claims. ‖ あす英語の**学力テスト**を行います We will have an English *proficiency test* tomorrow. (➤ proficiency は「熟達, 技能」).

かくれが 隠れ家・隠れ処 a **hideout**, a **hideaway** ▶警察は犯人の**隠れが**を見つけ出した The police found the criminal's *hideout*.

がくれき 学歴 one's **educational** [**academic**] **background**; **school education**(学校教育) ▶履歴書には**学歴**と職歴をそれぞれ項目ごとに書きなさい In your résumé, list your *educational background* and work experience separately. ‖ この地区の住民は概して**学歴が高い** People living in this area are generally known to *be highly educated*. ‖ 彼は(正規の)**学歴はほとんどない**が, 博識なジャーナリストだ He is a well-informed journalist, although he *has had little formal education*. ‖ 日本は**学歴社会**だと言われている Japan is said to be *a society that judges people by* their *educational background* [*where they went to school*]. (➤「受けた教育」および「どこの学校に行ったか」で人を判断する社会の意).

かくれみの 隠れ蓑 a **cloak**; a **cover** (覆う物); 《インフォーマル》 a **front** 《for》 (見せかけ) ▶マフィアは麻薬や銃の密輸をするために, その**隠れみの**として合法的なビジネスをしている The Mafia uses the *cloak* of legal business to carry out drug and gun smuggling. ‖ その会社は税金逃れのための**隠れみの**にすぎない That company is only *a front for* tax evasion.

かくれる 隠れる 1【見えなくなる】**hide** (oneself) ▶木立ちに**隠れる** *hide* among the trees ‖ 山の中に**隠れる** *hide out* in the hills ‖ ドアの陰に**隠れる** *hide* behind a door ‖ 車の陰にひょいと**隠れる** *duck* behind a car ‖ 月が雲に**隠れた** The moon *went* [*disappeared*] *behind* the clouds. ‖ 親には子供の**隠れた**才能を引き出してやる責任がある Parents have a responsibility to draw out their children's *hidden* abilities [talents].

2【人目につかないようにする】▶**隠れて**たばこを吸う smoke *on the sly*(➤ on the sly /slaɪ/ は「こそこそと」) ‖ 明は良枝と**隠れて**デートをしなければならなかった Akira had to date Yoshie *in secret*.

3【表面に出さない】▶**隠れた**意味 a *hidden* meaning ／ a subtext (➤ 後者は何かをする「隠された動機」の意味にも用いる).

4【口実とする】▶しつけの美名に**隠れて**子どもを虐待する abuse one's child(ren) *under the cloak of* discipline.

かくれんぼう 隠れん坊 **hide-and-seek** ▶子供たちは**かくれんぼう**をするのが好きだ Kids love to *play hide-and-seek*.

かくろん 各論 **specifics**(総論などに対して); **details**(詳細) ▶**各論**に入る go into [get down to] *specifics*.

かぐわしい 香しい **sweet**; **fragrant**(芳香のある) ▶バラのように**かぐわしい** *sweet* as a rose ‖ **かぐわしい**花園の中の小道をそぞろ歩きする take a stroll along a path in a *fragrant* flower garden.

がくわり 学割 a **special discount for students**, a **student discount** ▶当店では**学割**が利きます We allow *a special discount for students*. ／We give *a student discount*. ‖ **学割**は使えますか Is *a student discount* available? ／Do you have [give] *a student discount*?

かくん 家訓 a **family motto**.

がくん ▶彼のぼろ車は**がくんと**発進した His old car started *with a jerk*. (➤ jerk は「急な激しい動き」) ▶ことしはその大学の入学志願者数が**がくんと**(＝急激に)減った The number of the applicants (for entrance) to that university has decreased *sharply* this year.

かけ 賭け a **bet**; **gambling**(賭け事) ▶**賭け**で小遣いを全部無くした I lost all my spending money on *a bet*. ‖ マージャンで**賭けをして**私が勝った[負けた] I *made a bet* in mah-jongg and won [lost]. ▶結婚は一種の**賭け**だ Marriage is *a game of chance*. (➤「運任せの勝負事」の意) ‖ これは大きな**賭け**だ You're taking *a big chance*.

-かけ -掛け 1【掛けるもの】▶タオル**掛け** a towel *hanger* [*rack*] ‖ 帽子**掛け** a hat *rack* ／a hat tree (スタンド式の) ‖ 洋服**掛け** a clothes [coat] *hanger*.

2【やりかけ】▶吸い**かけ**のたばこ a *half-smoked* cigarette ‖ 食べ**かけ**のケーキ a *half-eaten* cake ‖ 仕事をやり**かけ**のままにする leave one's task *unfinished*. ‖ 使

いかけの生姜［シャンプー］a *partially used* ginger root［bottle of shampoo］.

1 **かげ 影** **1【影法師】**a **shadow**; a **silhouette** /sìluét/（シルエット）▶地面に映った木の影 a tree's *shadow* on the ground ‖ テレビ塔は地面に長い影を落とした The TV tower *cast a* long *shadow on* the ground. ‖ 日が傾いて影が長くなった As the sun dipped low, the *shadows* lengthened. ‖ テレビクイズの解答者たちはスクリーンに映った影だけを見てミッキーマウスを当てた The TV quiz show panelists recognized Mickey Mouse just by looking at his *silhouette* on the screen.

2【鏡などに映った姿】a **reflection** ▶鏡に映った彼女の影 her *reflection* in the mirror ‖ その臆病者は水に映った自分の影におびえた The coward was frightened by his own *reflection* in the water.

3【慣用表現】▶死の影におびえる tremble before *the shadow of death* ‖ 彼女に影のようにつきまとう follow her *like a shadow* ‖ ふるさとの生家は取り壊されて影も形も無い The house where I was born in my hometown was torn down, and *not even a trace remains.*（➤ trace は「痕跡」）‖ 5人兄弟のうち4男は無口で影が薄い Among the five brothers, the fourth is so quiet you *hardly notice* him. ‖ あの派閥の領袖は影響力を失って，もはや見る影も無い That faction leader has lost his influence, and is now *a mere shadow of his former self.* ‖ そのスキャンダルは政治家のキャリアに暗い影を落としている The scandal *has left its mark* on the politician's career.（➤ mark は「影響の跡」）.

☛ 影踏み（→見出語）

2 **かげ 陰** **1【光の当たらない所】shade** ▶木の陰で一休みする take a rest in the *shade* of a tree ‖ この塀でいい具合に陰ができる This fence offers welcome *shade.* ‖ ことわざ 寄らば大樹の陰 A big tree is a good shelter.

2【見えない所】▶その少年は生け垣の陰に隠れた The boy *hid behind* the hedge. ‖ 陰で人の悪口を言うな Don't say bad things about other people *behind their backs.* ‖ 陰の実力者 a power broker *behind the scenes.*

3【暗さ，陰気さ】▶あの俳優にはどこか陰があるが，それが魅力だ *There is something sad and mysterious about* that actor. Therein lies his appeal.（● dark には「後ろ暗い」というニュアンスがあるので something dark は避ける）.

4【慣用表現】▶この事件では誰かが陰で糸を引いているに違いない I'm sure there's somebody *pulling strings behind the scenes* in this affair. ‖ 彼女は陰になりひなたになりして彼を助けた She helped him *both openly and secretly*［*in every possible way*］. ‖ 陰ながらあなたのお幸せをお祈りしております I am praying for your happiness.（●「陰ながら」は (I am praying) in my heart ... のように訳せなくはないが，英語では特に何も言わないのがふつう）.

がけ 崖 a **cliff**; a **precipice** /présəpɪs/（絶壁）▶崖から飛び降りる jump off *a cliff* ‖ その子供は崖から落ちて大けがをした The child *fell over the cliff* and was seriously hurt.

▶《比喩的》わが社は現在潰れるかどうかの崖っぷちに立たされている Our company *is on the verge*［*the brink*］*of* bankruptcy.

☛ 崖崩れ（→見出語）

-がけ -掛け **1【…人用】**▶この席は3人掛けです This seat is *for* three people.

2【割】▶当店では全商品定価の8掛けで売らせていただいております We are selling all products *at 20 percent off.*（➤「2割引きで」の意）.

3【途中で，すぐあとで】▶帰りがけにバーで飲む drink at a bar *on one's way home* ‖ 兄さんは起きがけによくコーヒーを飲む My brother often has a cup of coffee *just after he gets up.*

4【身に着けて】▶彼女はたすき掛けで大掃除を手伝った She *tied up her* (*kimono*) *sleeves* and helped out with the annual house cleaning. ‖ 浴衣掛けで夕涼みをする go out to enjoy the evening coolness *in*［*wearing a*］*yukata.*

かけあい 掛け合い (a) **negotiation**（交渉）▶商品を取り替えてくれるようにと店に掛け合い（＝頼み）に行く go back to the store to *ask* for an exchange.

かけあう 掛け合う **1【互いに掛ける】**▶園児たちはプールの中で水を掛け合っていた The kindergartners *were splashing each other* in the swimming pool.

2【交渉する】negotiate ▶家賃の支払いを1か月延ばしてくれと大家にかけ合ったが，だめだった I tried to *negotiate* with the landlord for a one-month rent deferral, but it was no go.（➤ I negotiated with the landlord ... とすると，交渉によって何かが決まった，あるいは，何らかの成果があったという印象を与えかねない．ここは tried to を付けないと，あとの文とちぐはぐになる）.

かけあがる 駆け上がる **run up**; **rush up**（非常に慌てて）▶階段を駆け上がる *run up* the stairs ‖ ファンがステージへ駆け上がった The fans *ran up to* the stage.

かけあし 駆け足 a **run**; a **gallop**（馬などの最も速い走り方）▶駆け足で行く go *at a run*［*gallop*］‖ 彼女は駆け足でやって来た She came *running.* ‖ 駆け足進め！ March *double time*! ／*On the double*! ‖ 放れ馬が丘を駆け足で下った The runaway horse *galloped*［*went at a gallop*］*down* the hill.

▶《比喩的》我々は駆け足でヨーロッパ旅行をした We *made a whirlwind tour* of Europe.（➤ whirlwind は「つむじ風，旋風」が原義で，比喩的な意味での形容詞としては「大急ぎの」の意）／We *made a hurried tour* of Europe.（➤ hurried は「慌ただしい」という否定的なニュアンス）.

かけあわせ 掛け合わせ a **cross** ▶イノブタはイノシシとブタの掛け合わせである An Inobuta is *a cross* between a wild boar and a pig.

かけあわせる 掛け合わせる **cross** ＋目（交配させる）.

1**かけい 家系** a **family**（家柄）; **lineage** /lɪ́niɪdʒ/（血統）▶スコット氏は貴族の家系だ Mr. Scott *comes from* an aristocratic *family.* ／Mr. Scott is *of* aristocratic *lineage.* ‖ わが家の家系図を調べてみたが，有名な人はいなかった I investigated my *family tree,* but I found no famous people.

2**かけい 家計** a **family budget** /bʌ́dʒɪt/（家庭の予算）; **living expenses**（生活費）▶パートに出て家計を助ける take on a part-time job to help out (with) one's *family budget* ‖ インフレがわが家の家計を圧迫している Inflation is putting pressure on［is squeezing］our *family budget.* ‖ うちは家計が苦しい We are *not well-off.* ‖ 家計を預かる私としては今度の運賃値上げは痛い Being the one who *manages the family budget,* this transit fare hike really hurts.

▶うちは家計費が増えてやりくりが難しい Our *living expenses* have gone up, so it's hard to make ends meet.（➤ make ends meet は「やりくりをする」）‖ 母は念入りに家計簿をつけている My mother *keeps the household accounts* carefully. (●訳例の keep the household accounts は習慣として家計簿をつけることを指すので,「その日の家計簿をつけた」なら updated the household accounts とする; 帳面としての家計簿は household [housekeeping] accounts book).

かけうり 掛け売り a **credit sale** ▶掛け売りはいたしません We don't *sell on credit*.

かげえ 影絵 a **shadow picture**(手による); a **shadow puppet**(紙などで作った) ▶(壁に)影絵でウサギを作る make a shadow rabbit with one's hands (on the wall).

かけおち 駆け落ち (an) **elopement** 一動 **駆け落ちする elope** ▶彼女は若い男と駆け落ちした She *eloped* [*ran away*] with a young man.
‖駆け落ち結婚 a runaway marriage.

かけおりる 駆け下りる run down; **rush down**(非常に慌てて) ▶階段を駆け下りる *run down* the stairs.

かけがえのない 掛け替えの無い precious(貴い); **irreplaceable** (代わるものの無い) ▶人間の命ほど掛けがえのないものはない Nothing is as *precious* as human life. ‖掛けがえのない地球を守ろう Save our *precious* earth. ‖日本画壇は掛けがえのない人を失った The Japanese art world has lost an *irreplaceable* master.

かけがね 掛け金 a **latch** ▶ドアには掛け金がか掛っている The door has *a latch* on it. ／The door is on the *latch*. (➤後者は《英》で好まれる表現) ‖彼女は門の掛け金を外して中に入って来た She *lifted the latch* on the gate [*unlatched* the gate] and walked in. →鍵.

[1]**かげき 過激な radical**(急進的な); **extreme** (極端な) ▶過激な意見 a *radical* [an *extreme*] opinion ‖過激派の学生 a *radical* student (➤「過激論者」は extremist) ‖病み上がりだから過激な運動は避けるべきだ After your recent illness, you should refrain from *strenuous* exercise. (➤ strenuous は「非常なエネルギーを必要とする」).

[2]**かげき 歌劇** an **opera** ▶歌劇を見にいく go to see *an opera* ／go to the *opera*.

[1]**かけきん 掛け金** a **premium**(保険の払い込み金).

[2]**かけきん 賭け金** a **stake** ▶高額の賭け金をかけて勝負する play for high *stakes* (➤この熟語は「大きな賭けに出る, 一か八かの大勝負をする」という比喩的な意味にも用いる).

がけくずれ 崖崩れ a **landslide** (崖崩れ, 山崩れ) 《参考》土砂が崩れる場合には mudslide, 岩石が崩れる場合には rockslide とか rockfall と具体的に言うことも多い. ▶崖崩れで5人が生き埋めになった Five people were buried alive in *a landslide*.

かげぐち 陰口 backbiting(人の陰口を言うこと) ▶彼女はいつも陰口を利いてばかりいる She's always *talking about* people *behind their backs*. ‖友だちが陰口されるのを聞くのは嫌なものだ It is unpleasant to *hear rumors* about friends.

かけごえ 掛け声 ▶森さんは猿之助が登場すると,「千両役者!」と掛け声を掛けた When Ennosuke appeared (on the stage), Mori *shouted* [*called out*], "The Great Ennosuke!" 《参考》英語国民には一般に「千両役者!」のような特定の掛け声を掛ける習慣はないが, 映画館などでシューという音(hiss)を立てたり, 口笛を吹いたりはする.
▶《比喩的》政治改革は掛け声ばかりだ Political reform is *only a slogan*.

かけごと 賭け事 gambling ▶賭け事をする gamble ／make a bet ‖彼は賭け事に溺れ, 会社を首になった He *became a compulsive gambler* and ended up losing his job. (➤ compulsive gambler は「賭け事をせずにはいられない人」).

かけことば 掛け詞 ***kakekotoba***; a word in waka poems which has a double meaning(➤説明的な訳).

かけこみ 駆け込み ▶駆け込み乗車をする dash [rush] onto a train just before it leaves ‖《駅のアナウンス》危険ですから駆け込み乗車はおやめください (*Please*) *do not run*. Board trains in an orderly manner. (➤英語国では, このような決まった表現は一般には聞かれない).
▶4月の値上げを前にたばこの駆け込み需要が起きている There's been *a last-minute rush* on cigarettes before the price hike in April.

かけこみでら 駆け込み寺 a temple where women who wanted a divorce took refuge in the past(➤説明的な訳).

かけこむ 駆け込む rush 《into》 ▶道で財布を落とし, 最寄りの交番に駆け込んだ I lost my wallet on the street and *rushed into* the nearest police box (to report it).

かけざん 掛け算 (a) **multiplication** ▶掛け算の練習問題 exercises in *multiplication* ‖娘は掛け算の九九を暗記しようとしている My daughter is now trying to memorize the *multiplication table*. (→九九).

かけじく 掛け軸 a ***kakejiku***; a **hanging scroll**
日本紹介 ✉ **掛け軸は床の間に掛ける縦長の巻物で, 絵や書が貼ってあります. しまっておくときは巻いて木箱などに入れます. 季節や持ち主の気分に応じて掛け替えます** *Kakejiku* are scrolls with a picture or calligraphic work pasted in the center that are hung on the *tokonoma* (alcove) wall. They can be rolled up and stored in a wooden box. The owner chooses one in accordance with the change of seasons or one that suits his mood.

カケス 《鳥》 a **jay**.

かけず 掛け図 a **wall chart** [**map**] (➤前者は「図表」, 後者は「地図」).

かけすて 掛け捨て ▶掛け捨ての保険 *term* insurance ／insurance *with no refund payment* [*no cash value*].

かけずりまわる 駆けずり回る ▶俊二は仕事でいつも駆けずり回っている Shunji *is* always *on the run* (with his work). ‖彼は金策に駆けずり回っている He's *frantically* scraping up money. (➤ frantically は「死に物狂いで」, scrape up は「(金などを)かき集める」).

かけだし 駆け出し a **novice** /náːvəs/ ▶彼はまだほんの駆け出しだ He is still *a novice*. ／He is still *young and inexperienced* at this work. ‖彼女は CNN に勤める駆け出しの記者だ She works for CNN as a *cub* reporter. (➤ cub は「新米の」の意のインフォーマルな語).

かけだす 駆け出す ▶急に駆け出さないでよ Don't *start running* all of a sudden (like that)! ‖彼女は突然泣きだし, 家の外に駆け出した She burst out crying and *ran* [*rushed*] *outside*. ‖その不審な男は尾行の刑事をまくため突然駆けだした The suspect suddenly *took off running* to give the detective following him the slip. (➤ give ... the slip で「…をまく」).

かけちがえる 掛け違える ▶(コートの)ボタンを掛け違

える *button* (one's coat) *wrong*.
▶初めからボタンを掛け違えているのだから話し合いは進まない We *have been* (*talking*) *at cross-purposes* from the start, so we can't get anywhere in our negotiations.

か

かけつ 可決 passing (通過) ; adoption (採択) 一動 可決する pass +目, carry +目 (通過させる) ; approve +目 (承認する) ; adopt +目 (採用する) ▶法案は200票対45票で原案どおり可決された The bill *was passed* as drafted by a vote of 200 to 45 [by 200 votes against 45]. ‖ 生徒会は圧倒的多数の得票をもって新しい校則を可決した The student council *approved* the new school regulations by an overwhelming vote. ‖ 緊急動議を可決する *adopt* [*carry*] an emergency motion.

かけつける 駆け付ける run 《to》(急いで) ; rush 《to》(大急ぎで) ▶現場に駆けつける *rush to* the scene / *arrive hurriedly on* the scene ‖ 病院に駆けつける *hurry* [*run*] *to* the hospital.

かけっこ 駆けっこ a race 一動 駆けっこする race (+目) ▶ぼくは双子の弟とよく駆けっこをした I often had *races* with my twin brother. ‖ あの角まで駆けっこしよう! I'll *race* you to the corner!

がけっぷち 崖っ縁 the brink ▶会社を倒産の崖っぷちから引き戻す pull a company back from *the brink* of bankruptcy.

かけて 1【…にわたって】▶巨人は1965年から73年にかけて9連覇した The Giants won the league pennant for nine consecutive years *from* 1965 *to* 1973. ‖ 京都から奈良にかけて交通渋滞がひどかった The traffic congestion *from* Kyoto *to* Nara was terrible. ‖ 週末にかけて伊豆に旅行してきます I'm taking a trip to Izu *over* the weekend.
2【…について】▶世界史にかけては和美はクラスで1番だ *When it comes to* world history, Kazumi is at the top of her class. (➤ when it comes to は「…のことになると」) ‖ アメリカ研究にかけてはS博士は最も権威ある学者である *As far as* American studies *go* [*are concerned*], Dr. S is the most authoritative scholar. (➤ as far as ... be concerned は「…に関する限り」).

かけどけい 掛け時計 a wall clock.

かけぬける 駆け抜ける run through ▶数名の生徒が廊下を駆け抜けていった Several students *ran through* the hall. ‖ 彼女らはロックに明け暮れて青春を駆け抜けた Those girls *went through* [*passed*] *their youth quickly*, immersed in rock music.

かけね 掛け値 ▶これは掛け値なしの値段(=正価)です This is *the fair asking price*.
▶《慣用表現》彼は掛け値なしに(=誇張でなく)大投手だ I'm *not exaggerating* when I say that he's a great pitcher [one of the greatest pitchers (of all time)].

かけはし 懸け橋 a bridge ▶私は両国の懸け橋となって働きたい I'd like to serve *as a bridge* between the two countries.
✉ **私たちの友情が両国をつなぐ懸け橋となりますように** May our friendship serve as *a bridge* between our two countries.

かけはなれる 懸け離れる ▶両者の主張はまるでかけ離れていた Their claims *differed widely*. ‖ 彼の考え方は現実とかけ離れていませんか His ideas are (*far*) *removed* from reality, aren't they? ‖ 姉とは年がかけ離れているので, 親子と間違われることもある Our ages *are separated* so *widely* that my sister and I are often mistaken for parent and child.

かけひ 筧 a bamboo water pipe.

かけひき 駆け引き bargaining (値段についての) ; tactics, maneuvering (策略) ▶政治的な駆け引きにおいて彼に勝る政治家はいない No other politician has his finesse in political *tactics* [*maneuvering*]. (➤ finesse /fɪnés/ は「手際のよさ, 手腕」;「政治的駆け引き」のことをゲームにたとえて a political game と呼ぶことがある) ‖ 野球では投手と打者の駆け引きが見ものだ In baseball, the *maneuvering* between pitcher and batter is one of the main attractions.

かげひなた 陰日向 ▶陰ひなたのない人 an *honest* person / 《米・インフォーマル》*a straight shooter* ‖ 陰ひなたのある人 a *dishonest* person / 《インフォーマル》*a double-dealer* ‖ 陰ひなたなく働く work *honestly*.

かけぶとん 掛け布団 a comforter ; a quilt /kwɪlt/ (キルティングの) ; an eiderdown /áɪdəˈdaʊn/ (羽毛入りの).

かげふみ 影踏み shadow tag ▶影踏みをする play *shadow tag*.

かげぼうし 影法師 a shadow.

かげぼし 陰干し ▶色物のシャツを陰干しする (*hang up to*) *dry* a colored shirt *in the shade*.

かけまわる 駆け回る run about, run around ▶わが家の犬は庭を元気に駆け回っていた Our dog *ran about* cheerfully [energetically] in the yard.
▶兄は加藤氏の選挙運動で駆け回っています My (older) brother *is busy* campaigning for Mr. Kato. (➤ be busy doing は「…で忙しい」) ‖ 母は老人ホーム建設の募金運動で駆け回っている My mother *is active* in a fund drive for building a nursing home. (➤ be active は「活動して」) ‖ きょうは朝から駆け回って忙しかった I*'ve been on the run* all day.

かげむしゃ 影武者 a double (替え玉) ; a fixer (黒幕).

かけめぐる 駆け巡る ▶その重大ニュースはまたたく間に世界中を駆け巡った The big news *traveled* around the world in an instant.

かけもち 掛け持ち ▶小川氏は英語の非常勤講師として3つの大学を掛け持ちで教えている Mr. Ogawa teaches at three *different* universities as a part-time instructor in English.

かけよる 駆け寄る run (up) 《to》(走って) ; rush 《to》(大急ぎで) ▶母親はけがをした息子のそばへ駆け寄った The mother *rushed to* the side of her injured son.

かけら 欠片 a (broken) piece ; a fragment (断片, 破片) ; crumbs /krʌmz/ (パンなどの) ▶息子はガラス瓶のかけらで指を切った My son cut his finger on *a piece* of broken glass. ‖《慣用表現》あいつは良心のかけらもない悪党だ He is a scoundrel *without a trace* [*a hint*] *of conscience*.

かげり 陰り ▶あの子はどこか表情に陰りがある There's something *gloomy* [*melancholy*] in that child's expression. ‖ 90年代に入ってから経済成長に陰りが見え始めた It was at the beginning of the nineties that *a slowdown* in economic growth began to be apparent.

[1]かける 掛ける・架ける・懸ける

訳語メニュー
ぶら下げる →hang **1**
電話をする →call **2**
座る →sit (down) **2**
かぶせる →cover **3**
金を使う →spend **6**

1【固定して支える】hang +目（下げる）▶玄関に表札を掛ける *hang* a nameplate at the entrance ‖ 彼は店の前に大きな看板を掛けた He *hung* (*up*) a big signboard in front of his shop. (➤ hung は hang の過去形) ‖ 壁には風景画が掛けてあった *There was* a landscape painting (*hanging*) on the wall.

▶ハンガーにコートを掛ける *hang* one's coat on a hanger ‖ 彼女は毛布をベランダの手すりに掛けた She *hung* the blanket over the railing of the balcony.

▶眼鏡を掛ける *put on* one's glasses (➤「眼鏡を掛けている」という状態は wear glasses) ‖ 眼鏡を掛けた学生 a student *wearing* glasses／a student *with* glasses *on* ‖ ちゃんとボタンを掛けなさい *Button up* (properly).

2【つなぐ，結ぶ，置く】▶隅田川に新しい橋が架けられた A new bridge *has been built* [*been constructed*] over the Sumida River. ‖ クモが巣を架けている A spider is *spinning* [*weaving*／*making*] its web. ‖ ソファーに腰を掛ける *sit on* a sofa ‖ どうぞお掛けください Please *sit down* [*have a seat*／*take a seat*]. (➤ 後者 2 つのほうが丁寧な言い方) ‖ チョコレートの箱にリボンを掛ける *put* [*tie*] a ribbon on a box of chocolates ‖ 彼はその古新聞にひもを掛けた He *bound* the old newspapers *with string*. ‖ 彼はぼくの肩に手を掛けた He *put* [*placed*] his hand on my shoulder. ‖ レンジにやかんを掛ける *put* a kettle *on* the stove.

▶《電話で》何番にお掛けですか What number *are* you *calling*? ‖ あすもう一度掛け直してください Please *call again* tomorrow. ‖《ダイヤルサービスで》お掛けになった電話番号は現在使われておりません The number you *have reached* is not in service. ‖ 手助けが必要な方は声をお掛けください If you need assistance, please *ask* a staff member.

▶たまにはおじいちゃんに優しいことばの 1 つも掛けてあげなさい You should *say* something nice to your grandfather once in a while. ‖ 先生は「回れ，右」と号令を掛けた The teacher *gave the command*, "About face!"

3【表面を覆う，かぶせる】cover +目 ▶母はテーブルに白い布を掛けた Mother *covered* the table with a white cloth. ‖ 布団をしっかり掛けて寝ないとかぜをひきますよ *Cover* yourself *up* well or you'll catch cold.

▶サラダに塩を掛ける *sprinkle* [*shake*] salt on a salad／salt a salad ‖ カツにソースを掛ける *pour* Worcestershire sauce *over* a fried cutlet (➤ pour ... over は「たっぷり」のニュアンス) ‖ 豆腐にしょうゆを掛ける *put* some soy sauce *on* tofu (➤ put ... on は「たっぷり」にも数滴にも使える) ‖ サラダにドレッシングを掛ける *put* dressing *on* a salad ‖ 彼女はしおれかかった花に水を掛けた She *watered* the drooping flowers. ‖ 火のついた油に水を掛けても無駄だ It is no use *throwing* water on burning oil.

4【とらえる，課す，任せる】▶彼をわなにかける *trap* him ‖ 彼女を計略にかけて秘密をしゃべらせる *trick* her into telling a secret.

▶若い頃は両親にずいぶん苦労をかけた When I was young, I *caused* my parents a lot of trouble. ‖ 他人に迷惑をかけてはいけないね You mustn't *bother* [*trouble*] other people. ‖ ぼくは万引きの疑いをかけられた I *was suspected of* shoplifting.

▶事件を裁判に掛ける *take* a matter *to court* ‖ その問題は調査委員会に掛けられた That matter *was submitted to* the investigative committee.

▶農産物に関税をかける *levy* [*impose*] a customs duty on agricultural products ‖ 母は息子の非行がやむように神社に願を懸けた She *prayed* at a shrine that her son would stop his delinquent behavior.

5【働かせる】▶ラジオを掛ける *turn* [*switch*] *on* a radio ‖ 目覚まし時計を掛ける *set* an alarm clock ‖ ブレーキを掛ける *put on* the brakes ‖ 銃の安全装置を掛ける *put* the safety catch *on* a gun／*put* a gun *on* safety ‖ ドアに鍵を掛ける *lock* a door ‖ CD を掛ける *play* a CD.

▶松本選手は再三背負い投げを掛けた Matsumoto *tried* [*used*] a seoi-nage shoulder throw over and over again. ‖ 彼は勢いよくオートバイのエンジンを掛けた He *started* the engine of his motorcycle forcefully.

▶ワイシャツにアイロンを掛ける *iron* one's shirt ‖ 床にワックスを掛ける *wax* the floor.

6【時間・労力・金を使う】spend +目（費やす）▶彼女はずいぶん時間をかけて化粧をする She *spends* a lot of time putting on make-up. ‖ 500万円かけて家のリフォームをした We *spent* five million yen to have our house remodeled. ‖ どうもお手数をおかけしました I'm sorry to *have bothered* [*troubled*] you.

7【危険にさらす】risk +目 ▶命を懸けてわが子を守る protect one's child *at the risk of* one's life ‖ 戦争中若者は国を守るために命を懸けなければならなかった During the war, young people had to *risk their lives* to protect their country. ‖ 名誉に懸けて秘密を守ることを約束します *On my honor* I promise to guard this secret. ‖ リーグ優勝を懸けてあす巨人と中日が激突する The Giants and the Dragons will play a crucial (ball) game tomorrow to *decide the league pennant*.

8【掛け算をする】multiply /mʌ́ltɪplaɪ/ +目（倍数にする）▶ 3 に 5 を掛けると15になる Three *times* five is [are] fifteen. (➤ 3 × 5 = 15 をこう読む)／Three *multiplied* by five is [are] fifteen.

²かける 賭ける bet +目 ▶マージャンで金を賭けるのは違法だ It is a crime to *bet* money in a mah-jongg game. ‖ 彼は先日の競輪で佐々木選手に10万円賭けた He *bet* 100,000 yen on Sasaki at the bicycle races the other day. ‖ 日本シリーズでは広島が勝つと思うよ. 1 万円賭けてもいい I'm sure the Carp will win the Japan Series. I'*ll bet you* 10,000 yen.

▶大関は今場所に相撲人生を賭けている The ozeki has *put* his sumo career *on the line* in this tournament. (➤ put ... on the line は「…を危険にさらす」).

³かける 欠ける 1【物の一部が壊れる】chip（陶器などが）; **break**（割れる）▶皿の縁が欠けた The rim of the plate *chipped* [*got chipped*]. ‖ すみません. このコーヒーカップ欠けてますけど Excuse me. This coffee cup *is chipped*.

▶ご飯の中に石が入っていて, かんだら歯が欠けてしまった My tooth *was broken* by a small stone in my rice. ／I broke my tooth on a small stone in my rice. (➤ 後者のほうが英語的) ‖ 注意してね. このナイフの刃欠けてるから Be careful. The blade of this knife *is nicked*.

2【不足する】lack ▶彼のスピーチはユーモアに欠ける His speech *lacks* humor. ‖ 今日の学校教育には何かとても大事なものが欠けている Today's school education *is lacking* in something very important. ／

Something very important *is lacking* in today's school education. (➤ この lacking は形容詞. 後者がインフォーマル) ‖ その本は 4 ページ**欠けています** That book has four pages *missing*.

[4]**かける 駆ける** **run** ; **dash**(突進する) ; **gallop**(馬などが全力疾走する) ▶そんなに速く**駆けちゃ**だめよ Don't *run* so fast. ‖ その馬は全速力で**駆けた** The horse *galloped* at full speed.

-かける **1【人に向かって…する】**▶見知らぬ人に話し**かける** *speak to* a stranger ‖ その少女は恥ずかしそうに私にほほえみ**かけた** The little girl *smiled* shyly *at* me.

2【…し始める·もう少しで…する】▶台所仕事をし**かけ**たら郵便屋が書留郵便を持って来た The postal carrier brought a registered mail just as I *started* [*begun*] working in the kitchen. ‖ 夕食が終わり**かけ**たところに緊急電話が入った I had *almost finished* eating dinner when I got an emergency phone call.

▶救急車が着いたときには彼はもう**死にかけていた** He *was near death* [*nearly dead*] when the ambulance arrived. ／He *was on the verge* [*brink*] *of death* when the ambulance arrived. (➤ on the verge [brink] of death は「死の瀬戸際で」) ‖ その老画家はがんで**死にかけていた** The old artist *was dying* of cancer. (➤ be dying は主語が単数の場合は瀕死の状態がある期間続いていることを, また, 主語が複数の場合は次々と死を迎えようとしていることを表す).

☛ **言いかける** (⇀見出語)

かげる 陰る ▶突然日が**陰った** The sun suddenly *went behind the clouds*. ‖ 月が**陰り**, 一瞬真っ暗闇になった The moon *was veiled* [*was obscured*] *by clouds*, and for a moment it became pitch-dark. ‖ 日が**陰ってきた**から, 布団を取り込もう *It has started to get cloudy*, so let's bring in the futon (s).

[1]**かげろう 陽炎** (a) **heat haze** ▶道路に**かげろう**が立っているのが見えた I saw *a heat haze* shimmering over the road. (➤ shimmer は「ちらちら光る」).

[2]**かげろう 蜉蝣** 《虫》 a **mayfly**, a **dayfly**.

かげん 加減 **1【程合い, 具合】**▶お湯**加減**はいかがですか How is (*the temperature of*) *the bath water*? ‖ 暖房の**加減**はいかがですか Is the heat adequate? ／Is it warm enough (in this room)? (➤ 後者はくだけた自然な言い方) ‖ 肉の塩**加減**はどうかな Is the meat *properly* salted? ／Does the meat have enough salt on it?

▶コックはスープの**味加減を見た** The cook *tasted* the soup. ‖ **陽気の加減か**頭が痛い I have a headache. Maybe it's *the weather*. ‖ おまえの**ばかさ加減**にはあきれるよ Your *stupidity* is beyond belief. ／You *are really stupid* [*dumb*]!

2【調整すること】▶彼の話は**加減して**(＝割り引いて)聞け You have to *discount* what he says. ‖ 相手は子供なんだから**加減してあげなさい** You have to *take into account* that he's only a child. (➤ take into account は「考慮する」).

▶胃が悪いときは**食事をかげんしなさい** *Don't eat too much* [You should *eat moderately*] when you have stomach trouble.

3【体の調子】▶父はここ 1 週間かぜをひいて**加減が悪い** My father *has been under the weather* [*indisposed*] for a week with a cold. (➤ under the weather は「健康がすぐれない」の意のインフォーマルな表現. indisposed は「少し気分がすぐれない」の意の堅い言い方) ‖ **お加減はいかが**? How are you feeling?

✉ **お加減が悪いとはお気の毒です** I'm sorry to hear (that) you *are not feeling well* [you *are under the weather*].

4【少し…である】▶ぼくたちの先生はいつも**うつむきかげん**に歩く Our teacher always walks along *with his head* (*slightly*) *hanging*.

5【足し算と引き算】

‖**加減乗除** addition, subtraction, multiplication, and division.

☛ **いいかげん** (⇀見出語)

かこ 過去 **1【過ぎ去った時】the past** ▶**過去の記録** one's *past* record ‖ **過去を振り返る** reflect on *the* [*one's*] *past* ‖ **過去から学ぶことは多い** We have a lot to learn from *the past*. ‖ 悲しい**過去は忘れるようにしなさい** Try to forget the sad *past*. ‖ 私は**過去 4 年間**病気をしたことがない I haven't been sick *for* [*in*] *the past four years*. (➤ 前置詞の for, in は省略可能) ‖ あの政治家は**過去の人だ** That politician is *a has-been* [*is history*]. (➤ be history は《インフォーマル》で「過去のものだ」の意) ‖ 彼には暗い**過去がある** He has a dark [murky] *past*. ‖ **過去がある人** a person *with a past* [*who has a past*] (➤ この past は日本語と同じく「好ましくない経歴」の意).

2【文法】the past ▶go の**過去形**は went だ The *past* tense *form* of 'go' is 'went.'

‖**過去完了** the past perfect ‖ **過去分詞** a past participle.

☛ **過去ログ** (⇀見出語)

[1]**かご 籠** a **basket** ; a **cage**(鳥籠) ▶ **1 籠の果物** *a basket of* fruit ‖ 果物用の**籠** *a basket* for fruit ‖ **籠の鳥** a bird in *a cage*.

[2]**かご 加護** ▶神のご**加護**がありますように May God *protect* you [us].

[3]**かご 駕籠** a **palanquin** /pælənkíːn/.

かこい 囲い a **fence** ; a **pen**(家畜などを入れる) ▶野菜畑に**囲いをする** *put a fence* round the vegetable garden ‖ 私は子供が落ちないように池の周りに**柵で囲いをした** I *fenced off* the pond so that children would not fall in.

[1]**かこう 火口** a **crater** ▶**火口**から溶岩が噴出している Lava is spewing from *the mouth of the volcano*. (➤ crater は活動していない火山のイメージがあるので, この例文では用いないほうがよい).

‖**火口原** a crater-basin ‖ **火口湖** a crater lake.

[2]**かこう 河口** **the mouth (of a river)** ▶ニューヨークはハドソン川の**河口**にある New York is at *the mouth* of the Hudson (River). ‖ この川は**河口**の幅が150メートルある This river is 150 meters wide at its *mouth*.

[3]**かこう 加工** **processing** 一動 **加工する** **process** ＋目 ▶その工場ではバターとチーズを**加工**している Cheese and butter *are processed* at that plant. ‖ 彼女は銀を**加工**して指輪を作った She *forged* a ring from silver. (➤ forge は「金属を熱して作る」).

‖**加工業** processing industries ‖ **加工食品** processed food ‖ (食品などの)**加工日** the processing date.

[4]**かこう 下降** ▶その歌手の人気は**下降気味**だ That singer's popularity is *on the wane*. (➤ on the wane は「落ち目になって」) ‖ その国の出生率は**下降線**をたどっている The birth rate in that country is *on the decline*.

[5]**かこう 囲う** **enclose** ＋目 ▶彼は自分の土地を有刺鉄線で**囲った** He *enclosed* his lot with a barbed-

wire fence. ‖警察は殺人現場をロープで囲った The police *roped off* the scene of the murder.

かごう 化合 (chemical) combination ▶酸素は水素と化合して水になる Oxygen *combines with* hydrogen to form water. ‖水は水素2対酸素1の化合物だ Water is *a compound* of two parts hydrogen to one part oxygen. (➤ compound は /kɑ́:mpaʊnd/ と発音).

かこうがん 花崗岩 granite /grǽnɪt/.

がごう 雅号 a nom de plume, a pseudonym /sjú:dənɪm/.

かこきゅう 過呼吸 《医学》 overbreathing, hyperventilation /hàɪpəʳvenṭɪléɪʃən/.

かこく 過酷な・苛酷な severe(厳しい); oppressive(不当なほど重荷の); harsh(環境が厳しい); cruel(残忍な); grueling, 《英》 gruelling (困難で疲労困憊する) ▶過酷な気象条件 *severe* [*harsh*] weather conditions ‖過酷な税金 *oppressive* taxes ‖過酷な労働 *hard* labor (➤ 主に刑罰としてのもの) ‖過酷な旅 a *grueling* journey ‖その少女は過酷な運命にもてあそばれた The young girl was left to the hands of a *cruel* [*merciless*] fate.

かこつ grumble(愚痴を言う) ▶身の不運をかこつ *grumble* about one's misfortune.

かこつける ▶先約にかこつけて彼は会合に来なかった He did not attend the meeting *on the pretext of* a previous engagement. (➤ pretext /prí:tekst/ は「口実」).

かこみ 囲み ▶関連事項は次ページの囲み記事を参照せよ For related accounts, see the *boxed section* on the following page.

かこむ 囲む enclose +目, fence +目 (柵などで); surround +目 (四方を); encircle +目 (丸く); circle +目 (丸で) ▶その古い小屋は鉄柵で囲まれていた That old cabin *was enclosed* [*was fenced (in)* / *was surrounded*] by iron railings. ‖その湖は白樺(しらかば)に囲まれている The lake *is encircled* by [with] silver birches. ‖正しい答えを丸で囲みなさい *Circle* the correct answer. ‖その夜はみんなでキャンプファイアを囲み, 歌を歌った That night, we *gathered around* the campfire and sang songs. ‖日曜日は家族全員で夕飯の食卓を囲む Every Sunday evening, our whole family *sits down together* [*joins around the dining table*] for dinner.

✉ 日本は周囲を海に囲まれた国です Japan is a country *surrounded* by the sea.

かこログ 過去ログ archived blogs; a blog archive(まとめてしまってあるもの) ▶過去ログを見てね Take a look at my *blog archive(s)*.

かこん 禍根 a potential source of trouble ▶問題の先送りは将来に禍根を残すだけだ Delaying the solution of the problem will only leave *a potential source of trouble* as it is.

かごん 過言 ▶米以外の日本の穀物供給は輸入に依存していると言っても過言ではない *It is no exaggeration to say* [*It is not too much to say*] that Japan is dependent on imports for its supply of all grains except rice.

1**かさ 傘** an umbrella; a sunshade(日傘) ▶折り畳み式の傘 a folding [collapsible] *umbrella* ‖ワンタッチ式の傘 a push-button [self-opening] *umbrella* ‖傘を差す open [put up] one's *umbrella* ‖傘を差して歩く walk *under an umbrella* ‖傘をすぼめる[畳む] close [fold] one's *umbrella* ‖私の傘に入りなさいよ Why don't you *share* my *umbrella*? (➤ share は「共用する」) ‖ 対話 「きみの傘に入れてよ」「いいよ」 "Will you let me *share your umbrella*?" "Sure."

▶《比喩的》日本はアメリカの核の傘の下にある Japan is under *the nuclear umbrella* of the United States.

‖傘立て an umbrella stand.

2**かさ 笠** ▶電灯のかさ *a shade* / a lamp*shade* ‖きのこのかさ a (mushroom) *cap*.

▶《慣用表現》彼女は父親の威光をかさに着て偉ぶっている She thinks she is somebody *just because her father is an important person*.

3**かさ 嵩** bulk /bʌlk/, volume(容積); quantity(量) ▶この小包はかさは大きいが軽い This parcel is *bulky* but light. ‖雪どけで川の水かさが増した The river *rose* [*swelled*] with the thaw. / The river *was high* with melting snow.

かさい 火災 a fire ▶ビルの屋上で火災が発生した *A fire* broke out on the rooftop of the building. ‖《掲示》火災発生の場合はガラスを壊してください In Case of *Fire* Break Glass (➤ 火災報知器の文句).

‖火災訓練 a fire drill ‖火災警報 a fire alarm [warning / alert] ‖火災報知器 a fire alarm ‖火災保険 fire insurance ‖火災予防週間 Fire Prevention Week.

かざい 家財 household effects [belongings / furniture] ▶バーンズさん一家は火事で家財(道具)のすべてを失った The Burns family lost all their *household belongings* in a fire.

がざい 画材 drawing [painting] materials.

かさいりゅう 火砕流 《地質学》 a pyroclastic /pàɪrəklǽstɪk/ flow.

かさかさ ▶荒れてかさかさになった手 a rough, *chapped* hand.

▶木の葉が風にそよいでカサカサ音を立てた The leaves *rustled* in the wind.

がさがさ ▶夜中に何をガサガサ捜しているの? What are you *rustling around* for at midnight?

▶手ががさがさです My hands are *dry and rough*.

かざかみ 風上 ▶風がとても強く, 風上に船を走らせることはできなかった The wind was so strong (that) we were unable to sail *upwind*.

▶《慣用表現》彼はしばしば他人の作品を盗作する. 作家の風上にも置けないやつだ He often plagiarizes the works of other writers. He *doesn't deserve* to be called a writer. (➤「作家の名に値しない」の意) ‖あいつは男[女]の風上にも置けないやつだ He [She] is *a disgrace* to his [her] sex. (➤「同性にとって不名誉なやつだ」と考える).

かさく 佳作 a beautiful [fine] piece of work (➤ a good work でもよいが, これは「慈善行為; 信心からしたこと」の意味に解釈されるおそれもあるので要注意) ▶エッセー・コンテストで私の作品が佳作に選ばれた My essay was awarded *a merit prize* in the essay contest. (➤ merit prize は「佳作に与えられる賞」の意).

かざぐるま 風車 a pinwheel, 《英》 a windmill(ともにおもちゃの). →ふうしゃ.

かざごえ 風邪声・風声 a nasal [hoarse] voice due to a cold ▶彼は少しかざ声だ He's a little *hoarse from a cold*.

カササギ 《鳥》 a magpie.

かざしも 風下 ▶火事のときに風下に居ると危険だ It is dangerous to stand *downwind* of a fire.

かざす 翳す cover +目 (覆いをする); shade +目 (笠(かさ)をつける, 遮る) ▶ヘッドライトがまぶしくて思わず両手をかざした I instinctively *covered* [*shaded*] my eyes with my hands against the bright headlight. ‖ 彼女は石油ストーブに両手をかざして温めた She warmed her hands *over* the oil heater.

がさつ ▶がさつなふるまい *boorish* [*wild* / *rough*] behavior ‖ あんながさつな人とは口を利きたくないわ I don't want to talk to a *coarse* [*vulgar*] person like him.

がさっと ▶庭でガサッという音がした There was *a* (*short*) *rustling noise* from the garden.

かさなる 重なる **1**【物の上に物が載る】▶雑誌が２冊重なっている One magazine *is* (*lying*) *on top* of the other. ‖ 先生の机の上には本が山のように重なっていた *There was* a mountain of books *piled on* our teacher's desk.

▶娘の花嫁姿を見ていると妻の花嫁姿が重なった When I looked at my daughter in her wedding dress, the image of my wife in her wedding dress *overlapped* (in my mind's eye).

2【かち合う】▶残念！野球の放送が２つ重なっちゃった Too bad! Two baseball games are on (TV) *at the same time*. ‖ 祝日と日曜が重なると次の月曜日が休日になる When a national holiday *falls on* a Sunday, the following Monday becomes a holiday. (➤ fall on は「(日付が)当たる」).

3【さらに加わる】▶雨のため中央高速道路で事故が重なった The rain caused *a series of* accidents on the Chuo Expressway. ‖ 食糧不足と干ばつが重なり, アフリカでは多くの人が餓死した *A combination of* lack of food and drought caused many people to starve to death in Africa. ‖ 不幸が重なって彼女は心身ともに参っていた *Misfortune upon misfortune* exhausted her physically and mentally.

かさねがさね 重ね重ね

✉ **重ね重ねのご厚意厚く御礼申し上げます** I don't know how to thank you for *all* you have done for me.

かさねる 重ねる **1**【積み上げる】**pile** (**up**) ▶れんがを重ねる *pile* bricks on top of each other ‖ そんなに本を重ねると崩れるよ If you *pile* (*up*) too many books, they will collapse.

2【繰り返す】**repeat** ＋㊐ ▶同じまちがいを重ねるな Don't *repeat* the same mistake.

✉ **よろしくご協力のほど重ねてお願い申し上げます** *Once again*, I would like to ask for your cooperation.

かさばる 嵩ばる **be bulky** ▶この荷物はかさばっていて持ちにくい This package is too *bulky* to carry. / This *bulky* package is hard to carry.

かさぶた a **scab** ▶かさぶたをひっかくと傷口が治らないよ The cut won't heal if you pick at the *scab*. ‖ 傷は１週間くらいしたらかさぶたができるでしょう The wound will *scab* (*over*) in about a week.

かざみ 風見 a (**weather**) **vane**

‖風見鶏 a weathercock (➤ 人に対して比喩的に用いられることも多い).

かさむ 嵩む ▶仕事がかさんでいるから, この１週間は残業続きになるだろう I have such *a backlog* of work [So much work has *piled up*] that I'll have to do overtime all this week. (➤ backlog は「残務」) ‖ 出費がかさんで家計は赤字だ Household expenses have gotten so *high* that we are now (running) in the red.

かざむき 風向き **1**【風の吹く方向】▶風向きを知る see *which way the wind blows* (➤「世の中の動向を知る」の意にもなる) ‖ 風向きが北に変わった *The wind* has shifted to the north.

2【機嫌】▶きょうは上司の風向きが悪かった Our boss *was in a bad mood* [*was out of sorts*] today. (➤ be out of sorts は「不機嫌である」).

かざり 飾り a **decoration** (特別な行事のための) ; an **ornament** (美しい装飾品) ▶クリスマスツリーに飾りをつけましょう Let's put the *decorations* on the Christmas tree. / Let's decorate the Christmas tree. ‖ このポケットはただの飾りです This pocket is only *ornamental*.

‖飾り窓 a show [display] window.

かざりけ 飾り気 **affectation** (気取り) ▶彼女は誠実で飾り気のない人だ She is sincere and *unaffected*.

かざりつけ 飾り付け (a) **decoration** ▶店の飾りつけ shop *decorations* / window *dressing* ‖ きのうみんなで学園祭の飾りつけをした Yesterday we (all) *decorated* for the school festival.

かざりつける 飾り付ける **decorate** ＋㊐ ▶クリスマスツリーを飾りつける *decorate* [*trim*] a Christmas tree (➤ trim は「装飾物をつける」) ‖ ショーウインドーに冬物を飾りつける (＝陳列する) *display* winter clothing in a shopwindow.

かざりもの 飾り物 **1**【飾るためのもの】a **decoration**; an **ornament** (置物) ▶飾り物の餅 a mochi rice-cake as *an offering* (➤ offering は「お供え物」).

2【見てくれだけのもの】▶飾り物の校長 a principal *in name only* ‖ 小田社長は飾り物で, 仕事の実権は奥さんが握っている Mr. Oda, president of our company, is only *a figurehead*. His wife actually controls the business.

かざる 飾る **1**【きれいにする】**decorate** ＋㊐, **ornament** ＋㊐ ; **adorn** ＋㊐ (美しいものをより美しくする) ; **garnish** ＋㊐ (料理をちょっとした付け合わせで)

> **語法** (1)decorate と ornament は通例人には用いず, 前者のほうが派手に飾り立てるというニュアンスが強い. また前者は比喩的にことばやうわべなどを飾るというような場合は通例用いない.
> (2)人形などを飾るというときの「飾る」は単に並べてきれいに見せることなので display や set out (陳列する)を用いる.

▶机上を花で飾る *decorate* [*ornament*] one's desk with flowers (➤ 前者は「華やかに飾る」の意なので花が１輪の場合には不適) ‖ ディナーテーブルを花で飾る *adorn* the dinner table with flowers ‖ 料理にレモンの薄切りを添えて飾る *garnish* the dish with slices of lemon ‖ 部屋にひな人形を飾る *set* hina dolls *out* in the room.

▶その女優は高価な宝石で身を飾り立ててパーティーに出席した The actress came to the party *adorned with* [*decked out in*] expensive jewelry. (➤ be decked out in は「…で美しく着飾る」の意で, やや古風な言い方) ‖ スーザンは自分の寝室をカラフルなポスターで飾り立てた Susan *jazzed up* her bedroom with colorful posters.

2【表面だけをよく見せる】▶うわべを飾る keep up appearances ‖ 政治家はよくことばを飾る Politicians often *use pretentious* [*flowery*] *words*. (➤ pretentious は「もったいぶった, 仰々しい」) ‖ 須田先生は飾らない人柄で, 学生たちに人望がある Mr. Suda is *a modest man* who is popular among his students.

かさん 加算 addition **—動 加算する** add +目 ▶本給に残業代を加算する *add* overtime pay to one's basic salary.

かざん 火山 a **volcano** /vɑːlkéɪnoʊ/ ▶火山の爆発でその村は壊滅した The village was destroyed when the *volcano* erupted. ‖ 日本は火山国だ Japan is *a volcanic country*.

‖**火山活動** volcanic activity ‖ **火山帯[脈]** a volcanic zone [chain] ‖ **火山灰** volcanic ash ‖ **死[休／活]火山** an extinct [a dormant ／ an active] volcano.

1**かし 樫** (an) **oak** ▶カシの実 an acorn /éɪkɔːʳn/ 《参考》日本のカシは常緑樹であるが，欧米の oak は落葉する，日本でいうナラのなかま.

2**かし 菓子** (a) **candy**,《英》**sweets** (あめ・チョコレート・プリンの類い)；(a) **cake** (ケーキ類)；a **cookie** (クッキー)

> **語法** 菓子類を指す confectionery という語があるが，これはふつう業界で用いられる堅い語．ふつうは (a) candy, (a) cake (丸ごと１個；１切れは a piece of cake), (a) pastry (パイ・タルトの類い) などのように具体的にいう.

▶お菓子ばかり食べているから，晩ごはんが食べられないのよ It's because you keep eating *sweets* that you can't eat your dinner.

‖**菓子職人** a confectioner ‖ **菓子パン** a sweet roll ‖ **菓子屋** 《米》a candy store,《英》a sweet shop.

☛ **洋菓子, 和菓子** (→見出語)

3**かし 仮死** うちの子は仮死状態 (＝呼吸が止まった状態) で生まれた My baby *wasn't breathing* when he was born. ／My baby was born *with asphyxia*. (➤ asphyxia /æsfíksiə/ は「仮死」「窒息」を表す医学用語).

4**かし 華氏** **Fahrenheit** /fǽrənhaɪt/《略 F》▶気温は華氏90度だ The temperature is 90 degrees *Fahrenheit*. ‖ 華氏では水の氷点は32度，沸点は212度である *On the Fahrenheit scale* the freezing point of water is 32° and the boiling point 212°.

‖**華氏温度計** a Fahrenheit thermometer /θəʳmɑ́ːməṭəʳ/.

5**かし 歌詞** **the words**；**the lyrics** (主にポップス・ミュージカルの) ▶『イエスタデイ』の歌詞が大好きです I love *the words* [*lyrics*] of the song "Yesterday." (➤ to the song ともできる).

‖**歌詞カード** a lyrics sheet.

6**かし 貸し** (a) **loan** /loʊn/；a **bill** (売掛金) ▶私は彼女に５万円貸しがある She *owes* me fifty thousand yen. (➤「彼女は私に５万円借りている」の意) ‖ 彼にはだいぶ貸しがある He's greatly *indebted* to me. (➤ 比喩的な意味でも用いる) ‖ 貸しをきれいに返してもらおうじゃないか I think it's about time you *paid up*. (➤ pay up は「すっかり払う」).

‖**貸し衣装** a costume for rent [《英》for hire] ‖ **貸し金庫** a safe(ty)-deposit box ‖ **貸し自転車** a rental bicycle ‖ **貸しビデオ店** a rental video store ‖ **貸し別荘** a cottage for rent ‖ **貸しボート** a boat for [on] hire.

7**かし 可視** ▶警察での取り調べを可視化する必要がある Police interrogations need to *be* (*recorded and*) *videotaped*. (➤ コンピュータで映像にするという「可視化」は visualization であるが，この例では実際に意味するものは「録音・録画」なのでこうする).

‖**可視光線** a visible ray.

8**かし 河岸** a **fish market** (魚市場)；a **river bank** (川岸).

1**かじ 火事** a **fire** ▶昨夜この近くで火事があった Last night there was *a fire* near by. ‖ 火事だ！*Fire!* ‖ 消防署が火事だ！The fire station*'s on fire*！／The fire station*'s burning*！‖ 彼女の家はゆうべの火事で全焼した Her house burned down in the *fire* last night. ‖ 1906年，サンフランシスコで大火事があった *A big fire* broke out [There was *a big fire*] in San Francisco in 1906. ‖ アパートの火事で３人が焼死した The *fire* in the apartment house claimed three lives. (➤ claim は「(人命を)奪う」) ‖ 消防士たちは数分で火事の現場に到着した The firefighters arrived at *the scene of the fire* in a matter of minutes.

‖**火事場** the scene of a fire ‖ **山火事** a mountain fire (➤ forest fire (森林火災) ということが多い).

2**かじ 家事** **housework**；**house chores** /tʃɔːʳz/ (日常の雑用；「つまらない仕事」という含みがある)；**housekeeping** (家計の切り盛り) ▶家事をおろそかにする neglect the *housework* ‖ 姉は赤ん坊の世話と家事に追われている My sister is busy with a baby and *housework* [*house chores*]. ‖ 夏休みに母から家事を習った I learned *how to keep house* [*how to manage a home*] from my mother during the summer vacation.

‖**家事見習い** a (young) woman who is learning housekeeping.

3**かじ 舵** a **tiller** (舵柄(だへい))；a **rudder** (舵板)；a **helm** (舵輪) ▶彼は上手にかじを取り，船を港に着けた He *took the tiller* [*helm*] and skillfully guided the ship into harbor. 《参考》be at the helm は比喩的に「組織のかじ取り役をしている」「組織を率いている」の意で使われる.

がし 餓死 **death from hunger**；**starvation** (飢餓) ▶現在でも世界では毎年何万人という人が餓死している Even today, many thousands of people *die from* [*of*] *starvation* each year.

カシオペアざ カシオペア座 《天文学》**Cassiopeia** /kæ̀siəpíːə/.

かじかむ **go numb** /nʌm/《with》▶手がかじかんでコートのボタンがかからなかった My fingers were so *numb with cold* (that) I could not button (up) my coat.

かしかり 貸し借り ▶兄弟間でも金の貸し借りはしないほうがいい It's better not to *lend or borrow* money, even between brothers. ‖ これでおまえとは貸し借りなしだ This *makes* us *even*.

カジキ 《魚》a **marlin** (マカジキ)；a **swordfish** (メカジキ).

かしきり 貸し切りの **chartered** ▶この劇場はきょうは一日中団体客に貸し切りになっている This theater *has been reserved* for the day by a private party.

‖**貸し切りバス** a charter(ed) bus.

かしげる **tilt** +目 (水平になっている物の一方を持ち上げて) ▶さち子はしゃべるとき首をちょっとかしげる癖がある Sachiko has the habit of *tilting* [*inclining*] her head to one side as she speaks.

かしこ →敬具.

かしこい 賢い **wise, clever**；**bright** ▶賢い人 a *wise* person ‖ 賢い犬 a *clever* dog ‖ 賢く立ち回る act *wisely* [*cleverly*] ‖ 礼子はクラスでいちばん賢い Reiko is the *brightest* girl in her class. ‖ あの男の子はとても賢そうな顔をしている That little boy looks very *bright* [*smart*].

直訳の落とし穴「賢い少年」
「賢い＝wise」と考えて,「賢い少年」「その少年は賢い」を(×)a wise boy, (×)That boy is wise. と訳しがちである. しかし, wise は「年齢を重ね, 経験を積んで正しい判断ができる」の意味なので, ふつう子供には使わない.「賢い」に相当する語にはほかに bright, smart, clever などがあるが,「頭のいい」という意味では bright と smart が適切. したがって, a bright [smart] boy, That boy is bright [smart]. とするのがよい.「賢い消費者」は a smart shopper [consumer] である. なお, clever には「ずるい, 抜け目のない」の意味もあるので注意が必要.

かしこまりました ▶ 対話「席の予約をしたいのですが」「かしこまりました」"I'd like to make a table reservation." "*Certainly, sir.*" (➤ 相手が女性なら sir の代わりに ma'am (《英》では madam)というが, この応答はかなり改まった表現. ふつうは電話なら Thank you for calling. と応じて, 具体的なスケジュールを聞き始めてしまう).
✉ **古田教授にあなたの紹介状を書く件, かしこまりました** *I'll be delighted to* write a letter of introduction to Prof. Furuta for you. ➤「喜んでお書きします」の意.

かしこまる **stand on ceremony** ▶そんなにかしこまらないでください Please *don't stand on ceremony*. (➤ stand on ceremony は主に《英》でこの場合のようにふつう否定文で使う.《米》では Make yourself at home. (どうぞ気楽になさってください)や You don't need to be so formal. (改まる必要はありません)などというのがふつう)／Let's *dispense with ceremony*. ‖面接試験のときはかしこまっていたのでどもってしまった During the interview, I *was so tense* (*and stiff*) that I stuttered. (➤ stiff は「こちこちになって」) ‖母はかしこまって座り, お客と話をした My mother sat *erect* [*stiffly*] and talked with the guest. (➤ sit erect は「背筋を伸ばして座る」).

かししぶり 貸し渋り **the reluctance of banks to lend** [**make loans**], a **credit crunch**.

かしだおれ 貸し倒れ a **loan default**(債務不履行).

かしだし 貸し出し **1【金銭の】lending**, a **loan** ▶貸し出し額 the amount of *a loan*.
2【図書などの】▶その本は貸し出し中です The book is *out on loan*. (➤ on loan で「貸し出して」の意. out で帯出されていることを表す).

かしだす 貸し出す **lend out** ▶公共の図書館は無料で本を貸し出す Public libraries *lend out* books without charge. ‖自転車を貸し出す *lend* a bicycle／*rent* [《英》*hire*] (*out*) a bicycle (➤ rent [hire] は有料の場合) ‖この百科事典, 貸し出していますか Do you *lend out* this encyclopedia?

かしつ 過失 an **error**, a **mistake**(誤り；前者には非難のニュアンスがある)；a **fault** (比較的軽度の誤り)；a **blunder** /blʌ́ndəʳ/ (大失敗) ▶過失を認める admit one's *error* [*mistake*] ‖重大な過失を犯す commit *a serious error*／make *a blunder* ‖学生たちに間違った指示をしたのは私の過失です *It's my fault* that [*I'm to blame* because] I gave my students (the) wrong directions. ‖その男は過失致死の疑いで逮捕された That man was arrested on suspicion of *manslaughter*. (➤「業務上過失致死」は professional negligence resulting in death と訳せる) **《参考》** manslaughter は「非計画的殺人」で, murder より罪が軽い.

1**かじつ 果実** (a) **fruit** ‖果実酒 fruit liquor.

2**かじつ 過日** **several days ago**(数日前).

がしつ 画質 **picture** [**image**] **quality** ▶高画質映像 a *high quality* [*resolution*] image.

かしつき 加湿機 a **humidifier** /hju(ː)mídɪfaɪəʳ/.

かしつけ 貸し付け **loaning** /lóʊnɪŋ/ ▶銀行は利子を取ってお金の貸し付けをする A bank *lends* [《米また》*loans*] money with interest.
‖貸付係 a loan teller／a loan clerk ‖貸付金 a loan ‖貸付信託 a loan trust.

かしつける 貸し付ける **loan** /loʊn/ ▶銀行はその農場経営者に500万円を貸し付けた The bank *loaned* five million yen to the farmer.

かして 貸し手 a **lender**.

かじとり 舵取り **steering** (行為)；a **helmsman**, a **helmsperson**(人)(➤ 後者が性差のない語).

カジノ a **casino** /kəsíːnoʊ/.

かしパン 菓子パン ⇀**菓子**.

かしビル 貸しビル 《米》a **building for rent** [《英》**to let**] ▶彼は貸しビルの中で小さな店をやっている He runs a small shop in *a rental office building*. (➤ rental は「賃貸できる」; building for rent [for lease] は「入居者待ちの空きビル」の意なので, この文では不適).

かしま 貸間 《米》a **room for rent** [《英》**to let**] ▶《掲示》貸間あり Room(s) For Rent／Room(s) To Let.

かしましい **noisy**(騒々しい) ▶ ことわざ 女三人寄ればかしましい When three women get together, noisy chatter begins.

カシミヤ **cashmere** /kǽʒmɪəʳ ‖ kǽʃ-/ ▶カシミヤのセーター a *cashmere* sweater.

かしや 貸家 《米》a **house for rent**, 《英》a **house to let**.

かしゃ 貨車 a **freight** /freɪt/ **car**, 《英また》a (**goods**) **wagon**.

かじや 鍛冶屋 a **blacksmith**(人).

1**かしゃく 呵責** a **pang** [**prick**] **of conscience** ▶万引きしておまえは良心のかしゃくを感じなかったのか Didn't you feel any *guilt* at all after you shoplifted those things? (➤ guilt は「罪悪感」).

2**かしゃく 仮借** ▶仮借なき批判 *scathing* [*unsparing*] criticism.

がしゃん ▶花瓶が床に落ちてガシャンと割れた The vase fell to the floor and broke *with a crash*.

1**かしゅ 歌手** a **singer**
‖オペラ歌手 an opera singer ‖男性 [女性] 歌手 a male [female] singer ‖人気歌手 a popular singer ‖流行歌手 a pop singer.

2**かしゅ 火酒** (a) **hard liquor**.

かじゅ 果樹 a **fruit tree** ▶何種類もの果樹を栽培する cultivate many kinds of *fruit trees*. ⇀**果樹園**.

カジュアル ▶パーティーにはカジュアルな服装でお出かけください Please come to our party in *casual* attire [dressed *casually*]. (➤ この意味では Please come as you are. (ふだん着でいらっしゃってください)とよく言う).
‖カジュアルウエア casual wear [clothes] ‖カジュアルシューズ casual shoes.

かしゅう 歌集 a **songbook**(歌唱集)；a **song anthology**(選歌集)；a **collection of poems**(詩集).

1**かじゅう 果汁** **fruit juice**(➤ 英語は100パーセントの天然果汁にのみ用いる) ▶果汁入り飲料 a *fruit* drink. ⇀**ジュース**.

2**かじゅう 過重** ▶私たちは過重な労働を強いられている We are forced to work *unbearably hard*.

3**かじゅう 荷重** **load** ‖荷重制限 a load limit.

がしゅう 画集 a **book of paintings** ; a **collection of paintings** [**pictures**] (特定の画家の画集) ▶ピカソの画集 *a collection of* Picasso *paintings*.

カシューナッツ a **cashew (nut)**.

かじゅえん 果樹園 an **orchard** /ɔ́ːʳtʃəʳd/

《解説》(1) orchard は主にリンゴ, ナシ, 桃, アンズ, サクランボなどの果樹園を指す. (2) かんきつ類の場合は grove を用い, orange grove のようにいう. また「ブドウ園」は vineyard /vínjəʳd/ という.

ガジュマル 《植物》 a **Chinese banyan**.

かしょ 箇所 a **place** (場所) ; a **spot** (地点) ▶けさ3か所でぼやがあった Small fires broke out at *three places* this morning. ‖ 高速道路の2か所で交通事故があった *Two* traffic accidents happened on the expressway. ‖ 私はこれからお使いで3, 4か所回らなければならない I have to run *three or four* errands today. ‖ (校正の) 見落としは何か所ありましたか *How many* proofreading errors did I make? ‖ この練習問題は何か所も間違えているから, やり直したほうがいいね Since you have made *a lot of* mistakes in these exercises, it would be a good idea to do them (all) over again. ‖ 同じ箇所を読みなさい Read the same *paragraph*. (➤ paragraph は「(文章の) 1つの段落」).

[1]**かしょう 過小** ▶人は自分が過小評価されていると思いがちだ People tend to think that they *are undervalued* [*underestimated*].

[2]**かしょう 仮称** a **tentative name**.

[1]**かじょう 過剰** (an) **excess** (多すぎること) ; a **surplus** (余り) ▶熱意過剰 *an excess* of enthusiasm ‖ 自信過剰 *over*confidence ‖ キャベツは生産過剰で値が崩れた The price of cabbage fell because of *overproduction*. ‖ 彼女はお色気過剰だよ She's *overdoing the sex appeal*. ‖ その警官の行為は過剰防衛と見なされた The policeman's action was regarded as *excessive self-defense*.

[2]**かじょう 箇条** an **article** ▶わが校の校則は10か条から成る Our school regulations consist of ten *articles*. ‖ 彼は経費の内容を箇条書きにした He *itemized* his expenses.

[1]**がしょう 賀正** (A) **Happy New Year** (➤ I wish you a Happy New Year. のほうが丁寧になる ; 「あけましておめでとう」「謹賀新年」「頌春(しょうしゅん)」などいろいろあるが, 英語はこれしかない).

[2]**がしょう 画商** an **art** [**a picture**] **dealer**.

がじょう 牙城 a **stronghold** ▶民主党 [共和党] の牙城 a Democratic [Republican] *stronghold*.

かしょくしょう 過食症 bulimia /bulímiə/ (食べて戻したりする) ; **binge eating syndrome** (ただたくさん食べる) ▶彼女は過食症になっている She has *bulimia*.

かしょくのてん 華燭の典 nuptials /nʌ́pʃəlz/ ▶華燭の典を挙げる hold *a wedding*.

かしら 頭 a **head** (頭部) ; a **leader**, a **chief** (長) ; a **boss** (親分) ▶彼はサーカス一座の頭だ He is the *leader* [*head*] of the circus troupe. ／He leads the circus troupe.

▶ 10歳の子を頭に4人の子供がいる I have four children : a ten-year-old and three younger ones.

-かしら I wonder ... ⚠「あした, 雨かしら」のような文における「かしら」は女性的表現であるが, これに対応する英語表現の "I wonder if it will rain tomorrow." には特に女性的響きはない.

▶財布をどこで無くしたのかしら *I wonder* where I lost my wallet. ‖ 彼, どうしたのかしら. またデートに遅れるなんて *I wonder* what happened. He is late for our date again. ‖ すみません, ちょっとファックスをお借りしてよろしいかしら Excuse me, but *may I* use the fax machine? ‖ さっきからずっと待ってるのよ. もうちょっと早くできないかしら I've been waiting for ages [a long time]. *Could you* hurry up a bit? [*Don't you think* you could hurry up a little?]

かしらもじ 頭文字 an **initial (letter)** (名前の) ; a **capital (letter)** (大文字) ▶彼女はハンカチに頭文字を刺しゅうした She embroidered her *initials* on her handkerchief.

かじりつく 齧り付く bite 《into》 (かじる) ▶少年はとてもおなかがすいていたので, 待ちきれずにロールパンにかじりついた The boy was so hungry, he couldn't resist *biting into* the roll without waiting.

▶ 2, 3歳頃の幼児は母親にかじりついて離れない Children aged two to three years *cling to* their mothers. ／Two-to-three-year-old children don't like to let go of their mothers. ‖ 中間試験があるので徹夜で机にかじりついた With mid-term exams ahead, I spent the night *glued to my desk*.

かじる 齧る 1【少しずつかみ取る】bite +⊜ ; **nibble** +⊜ ; **crunch** +⊜ ; **gnaw** /nɔː/ +⊜

《語法》ナシ・リンゴなどの果物をかじる場合は bite, ウサギのように少しずつかじる場合は nibble, 煎餅・クラッカーなどを音を立ててかじる場合は crunch, ネズミのように物をカリカリかじる場合は gnaw を用いる.

▶リンゴをかじる *bite* into an apple ‖ 煎餅をかじる *crunch* a rice cracker ‖ ポチがテーブルの脚をかじった Pochi *gnawed* (on) the table leg. ‖ そのナシ, ちょっとかじらせて! *Give me a bite* [*Let me have a bite*] of that pear, please!

2【一部分だけを知る】▶中国語は少しかじっただけだ I *have* only *a smattering of* Chinese. (➤ smattering は「なまかじりの知識」) ‖ ぼくはドイツ語を少しかじっている I *know a little* German.

かしわ 柏 《植物》 a **Daimyo oak**

‖柏餅 *kashiwamochi* ; rice cake stuffed with sweet adzuki paste and covered with an oak leaf (➤説明的な訳) ‖ かしわ手 clapping in prayer in front of a Shinto shrine.

[1]**かしん 過信** ▶自分の力を過信してはいけない You should not *be overconfident in* yourself. ／Don't *overestimate* your own ability.

[2]**かしん 家臣** a **vassal** ; a **retainer** (召し使い, 下僕).

[1]**かじん 歌人** a (*tanka*) **poet**.

[2]**かじん 佳人** a **beautiful woman** ▶佳人薄命 *Beautiful women die young*.

[3]**かじん 家人** one's **family**, a **member in** one's **family**.

[1]**かす** ▶机の上には消しゴムのかすが散らかっていた The desk top was littered with *eraser rubbings* [*bits of eraser*].

▶《比喩的》あいつは人間のかすだ He is *a dreg of*

humanity [*society*].

[2]**かす 貸す**

か

> **語法** (1) 日本語の「貸す」は有料・無料に関係なく用いるが, 英語の **lend, loan** にもその区別はない. ただし, **loan** は鉛筆や消しゴムなど安価なものを貸す場合にはあまり用いられない. **rent (out)** は有料の場合.
> (2) 同じ有料でも《英》では家を賃貸しする場合は **let**, アパート・部屋の場合は **let out**, ボート・自動車などを賃貸しする場合は **hire (out)** を用いる.
> (3) 不動産を賃貸しする場合は **lease**,《米また》**rent** を用いる.

1【物や金を人に使わせる】lend +㊐, **loan** /loʊn/ +㊐ ▶彼は自分のバイクをぼくに貸してくれた He *lent* [*loaned*] me his (own) motorcycle. ‖ 当社では50万円まででしたらすぐにお貸ししますからお電話ください We can *lend* [*loan*] you up to a half million yen on the spot, so please call us anytime. ‖ **対話**「少し金を貸してくれないか」「きょうはだめだ. 文無しなんだよ」"Will you *lend* me some money?／May I borrow some money?" "Not today. I'm broke." (➤ May I borrow ...? のほうが遠慮がちな言い方. borrow は「借りる」. 物を貸す場合は通常無料だが, お金を貸す場合には利子が必要かどうかは文脈や社会通念による) ‖ **対話**「電話 [トイレ] を貸してください」「どうぞ」"*Can* [*May*] *I use* your telephone [bathroom], please?" "Sure, go ahead." (➤ 備え付けのものや移動不可能なものを貸してもらう場合はふつう use を用いる).

2【賃貸しする】rent (out) ▶私どもはこの家を月10万円で貸しています We *rent* [*let*] this house for 100,000 yen a month. ‖ ロンドンに行っている間この部屋を人に貸したい I want to *rent* [*let*] *out* this room while I am away in London. ‖ スーツケースを貸してくれるところ, 知らない? Do you know where I can *rent* a suitcase? (➤ この rent は「借りる」).

3【慣用表現】▶私が抱えている問題のことでちょっと知恵を貸してよ Could you *give* me *your advice* [*opinion*] on a problem I'm having? ‖ この冷蔵庫を動かしたいから手を貸してよ *Help* me move this refrigerator. ／Can you *give* me *a hand*? I want to move this refrigerator. ‖ 息子は私の言うことなんか, 全然耳を貸そうとしません My son doesn't *listen to* me at all. ‖ おい, ちょっと顔を貸せよ Hey, *come* (*over*) *here* for a minute. ／Hey, I *want to talk to you* for a second.

[3]**かす 粕・糟 sake lees**(酒かす)
‖ **かす漬け** food preserved in sake lees.

かず 数 a **number**; a **figure** (0から9までの数字) ▶8という数 the *number* 8 ‖ 大きい[小さい]数 a large [small] *number* ／a high [low] *number* ‖ 2桁の数 a two-digit *number* ／double *figures* ‖ これらの数字を数の小さい順に並べなさい Arrange these numbers *in order from smallest to largest*. ‖ 彼らは数において我々に勝っている They *outnumbered* us. ‖ 特売品は数に限りがあります Sale items *are limited in number*. ‖ 籠の中のリンゴの数を数えてごらん *Count the* (*number of*) apples in the basket. ‖ その地震で数多くの人命が失われた *A large number of* lives were lost in that earthquake. ／The earthquake claimed *many* lives. (◉ 後者は「(事故・病気などが) (人命)を奪う」の意の claim を用いた英語的発想に基づく訳例).

ことわざ **下手な鉄砲も数打てば当たる** Even a bad shot hits the mark if he tries often enough.

ガス 1【気体】gas ▶ガスが漏れている There is a *gas* leak. ／The *gas* is leaking. ‖ ガスをつけ [止め] なさい Turn on [off] the *gas*. ‖ ガスの臭いがする I smell *gas*. ‖ 火口から有毒ガスが発生している *Toxic gas* is rising from the mouth of the volcano. ‖ ガス欠になりそうだからガソリンスタンドに寄ろう We'*re running out of gas*, so let's stop at a gas station. ‖ その男は先月ガス自殺した That man *gassed himself to death* last month. ‖ **対話**「今月ガス代いくらなの」「1万円です」"How much is the *gas bill* for this month?" "It's 10,000 yen."
‖ **ガス管** a gas pipe (金属製の); a gas hose /hoʊz/ (ゴム製の) ‖ **ガス器具** gas fittings ‖ **ガスこんろ** a gas (cooking) stove ‖ **ガスストーブ** a gas heater [stove] ‖ **ガスタンク** a gas tank ‖ **ガス中毒** gas poisoning ‖ **ガスボンベ** a gas cylinder ‖ **ガスマスク** a gas mask ‖ **ガス湯沸かし器** a gas water heater,《英また》a gas geyser ‖ **ガスライター** a gas lighter ‖ **ガスレンジ**《米》a gas range [《英》cooker].

2【濃霧】(a) **dense fog** (➤ この意味では gas は使えない) ▶山頂はガスっていて, 全く何も見えない We can't see the mountaintop at all because it *is covered with a dense fog*.

3【おなら】gas ▶サツマイモを食べ過ぎちゃあだめよ. ガスがたまるから Don't eat too much sweet potato, or you'll *get gas*.

かすか 幽か・微か 一㊆ **かすかな faint, weak** (音・光・力などが弱い); **dim** (ぼんやりした) **一**㊫ **かすかに faintly, dimly, slightly** ▶かすかな物音 a *faint* noise ‖ かすかに息をする breathe *weakly* ‖ 彼らが生存しているというかすかな望みも消えた Now even the *faintest* hope of their being alive is gone. ‖ 窓から浅間山がかすかに見える I can see Mt. Asama *dimly* through the window. ‖ 幼稚園時代のことはかすかに覚えている I have a *faint* [*dim*] recollection of my kindergarten days. ／I remember my kindergarten days *vaguely*. ‖ そよ風が吹いて, カーテンがかすかに揺れた The curtains stirred *slightly* in the breeze.

かすがい a cramp iron ▶ ことわざ **子はかすがい** Children strengthen [A child strengthens] the bond between their [his or her] parents.

かすかすの dry and tasteless, mealy ▶かすかすのリンゴ a *mealy* apple.

かずかず 数々の numerous, a lot of ▶キャンパスには数々の楽しい行事がある There are *a lot of* [*numerous*] exciting events on campus.

カスタード custard
‖ **カスタードクリーム** custard cream ‖ **カスタードプリン** (a) custard pudding.

カスタネット castanets /kæ̀stənéts/ (➤ 通例複数形で) ▶そのダンサーはカスタネットを鳴らしながらフラメンコを踊った The dancer danced a flamenco while playing the *castanets*.

カステラ (a) **sponge** /spʌndʒ/ **cake**.

かずのこ 数の子 herring roe /roʊ/ (➤「ニシンの卵」の意. 日本語のような縁起のいいイメージはない).

カスピかい カスピ海 the Caspian Sea.

かすみ 霞 (a) **haze**, (a) **spring mist** (➤ 前者のほうが薄く, 湿気が少ない) ▶山にはかすみが掛かっている *A haze* [*spring mist*] is hanging over the mountain. ／The mountain looks *hazy*.

かすむ 霞む be blurred, be dimmed ▶目が涙でかすんだ Tears *blurred* [*dimmed*] my eyes. ／My eyes *were blurred* [*were misted*] with tears. ‖遠くの山がもやでかすんでいる The distant mountains *are veiled in haze*.
▶大女優も売り出し中の若手女優のためにかすんでしまった The famous actress *was upstaged* by an up-and-coming starlet. (➤ upstage は「人気をさらう」).

かすめる 掠める **1**【盗む】cheat +目 (だまし取る); make off with (こっそりと) ▶彼は私の分け前を1割かすめた He *cheated* me out of 10% of my share. ‖親の目をかすめて金を持ち出すとは何事だ How dare you take your parents' [our] money *without permission*!
2【僅かに触れる】skim ▶トンボが池の水面をかすめて飛んでいった A dragonfly *skimmed over* the pond and flew away. ‖犯人は自分の息子ではないかという考えがちらっと彼女の頭をかすめた The thought that it might have been her own son who was the criminal *flitted across her mind*.

かすりきず かすり傷 a scratch ▶車の衝突事故に遭ったが顔にかすり傷を負っただけで［かすり傷ひとつせずに］助かった I escaped the car crash with only *a scratch* on my face [without *a scratch*]. ‖当地の台風の被害はほんのかすり傷程度だった There was only *slight* damage from the typhoon in this area. ／The area *was only slightly affected* by the typhoon.

1**かする** graze +目, scrape +目 (こする) ▶車は車庫のドアをかすった The car *grazed* [*scraped*] the garage door. ‖ 対話 「宝くじ当たった？」「だめ. かすったんだけどね」"Did you win the lottery?" "Nope, but I *came close*." (➤ come close /klous/ は「すぐ(当たりの)そばまで行く」の意).

2**かする 化する** ▶爆撃で町全体が焼け野原と化した The whole town *was reduced to* ashes in the bombing.

3**かする 科する・課する** fine +目 (罰金を); levy +目 (税金を); assign /əsáin/ (任務を)
▶彼はスピード違反で罰金を科せられた He *was fined* for speeding.
▶上司は彼女に苦情を処理する仕事を課した Her boss *assigned* her the task of dealing with complaints. ‖高額所得者は重い所得税を課せられる High income taxes *are levied* against people with large incomes.

かすれる ▶悪いかぜをひいて声がかすれた(＝かれた) A bad cold has made me *hoarse*.
▶このペンはかすれてうまく書けない It is hard to write with this pen because it *skips*. (➤ skip は「(文字が)途切れ途切れになる」).

1**かぜ 風** **1**【空気の流れ】(a) wind; a breeze (微風)
語法 wind は通例 the wind の形で用いられるが, 形容詞を伴って種類をいうときは a cold wind のように a (または an) がつく.
▶一晩中風が吹いた The *wind* blew all night. ／It blew all night. ‖きょうは風が無くてむしむしする There is no *breeze* so it feels muggy. ‖風が出てきたようだ The *wind* is rising. ／There's *a breeze* starting. ‖我々がその島に着くと風がやんだ *The wind died down* when we arrived at the island. ‖きょうは風が強い It's (really) *windy* today. (➤ It's blowing hard. は漁師や農民以外はあまり用いない) ‖台風が近づいて風が次第に強くなってきた It's *getting windier* as the typhoon approaches. ／The *wind* is increasing in strength with the approach of the typhoon.
▶風に木の葉がそよいでいる The tree leaves are rustling *in the wind*. ‖愛子の長い髪が風になびいた Aiko's long hair streamed *in the wind*.
▶あすは南寄りの風で晴れでしょう It will be fair tomorrow with *a southerly wind*. ‖彼のヨットは強い風で沖へ流された His yacht was blown far off the coast by *a strong wind*. ‖その日は身を切るような風が吹いていた There was *a biting wind* blowing that day.
2【慣用表現】▶くよくよするな. あしたはあしたの風が吹くさ Don't worry. *Tomorrow will take care of itself*. ／*Tomorrow is another day*. (●後者は「きょう, うまくいかなかったからといって悲観するな」「あすに希望をもて」とあすへの希望をもつことを促す場合に用いるとよい) ‖彼は肩で風を切って(＝わが物顔で)歩く He walks *as if he owned the world*. ‖風の便りに音次郎がパリで成功したと聞いた *A little bird told me* that Otojiro was successful in Paris. (➤ a little bird told me は「ある人から聞いた」の意のインフォーマルな表現) ‖きみがこんな所へ顔を出すなんて, どういう風の吹き回しだい？ *What on earth* [*What ever*] brings you here? (➤ 来た理由や用件を遠回しに聞く言い方) ‖息子はあすの試験なぞどこ吹く風とばかり(＝まるで試験が無いかのように)遊び歩いている My son is gallivanting about *as if there were no test* tomorrow. ‖母は大事な息子を世間の冷たい風に当てまいとした The mother tried to protect her precious son from *the hardships of everyday life*.
☛ 風当たり, 風通し (→見出語)

> **逆引き熟語 ○○風**
> いてつくような風 a freezing wind ／追い風 a tail wind ／空っ風 a dry blast ／北風 a north [northerly] wind ／爽やかな風 a cool [fresh] breeze ／そよ風 a gentle [light] breeze ／(肌を)突き刺すような風 a biting [cutting] wind ／つむじ風 a whirlwind ／冷たい風 a cold [chill] wind ／激しい風 a fierce [driving] wind ／向かい風 a head wind

2**かぜ 風邪** a cold (ふつうの); influenza /ìnfluénzə/, 《インフォーマル》(the) flu (インフルエンザ)
▶かぜをひく *catch* (*a*) *cold* (➤ この場合は a を省略することがある) ‖父はひどいかぜをひいている My father has *a bad cold*. (➤ cold に形容詞がつくときは必ず a [an] をつける) ‖私はまだかぜが治らない I still haven't gotten rid of my *cold*. ‖かぜがはやっている There is a lot of *flu* going around. ‖母はかぜで寝ています My mother is in bed [is down] *with a cold*. ‖弟にかぜをうつされた My brother *gave me his cold*. ‖とうとう先生もかぜでダウンした Finally our teacher *came down with a cold*. ‖ 対話 「木下君は来ていますか」「かぜで休んでいます」"Is Kinoshita in today?" "No, he is out (sick) *with a cold*."
▶坂本はかぜ気味だったにもかかわらずホームランを打った Sakamoto hit a home run though he *had a slight* [*a touch of*] *cold*. ‖妹は鼻かぜをひいて鼻をくすんくすんさせている My younger sister is sniffing because she has *a head cold*. (➤ nose cold とはいわない) ‖夏かぜは治りにくい *Summer colds* are hard to get over.
ことわざ かぜは万病の元 A cold can lead to all kinds of diseases.

‖かぜ薬 cold medicine.

かぜあたり 風当たり ▶高層住宅の上階は**風当たり**が強い *The wind is strong* on the upper floors of high-rise apartments.

▶《比喩的》その市長は賄賂を受け取ったことで**世間の風当たりが強くなった** The mayor came *under severe criticism from the public* for accepting bribes.

¹かせい 火星 Mars /mɑːʳz/ ▶**火星**は太陽系では7番目に大きい惑星である *Mars* is the seventh largest planet in the solar system.

‖**火星人** a Martian /mɑ́ːʳʃən, -ʃiən/.

²かせい 仮性 ▶**仮性**近視 *false* nearsightedness [《英》shortsightedness].

³かせい 加勢 (a) backup ▶味方は無勢だ. **加勢を頼もう** We are outnumbered. We need to call for *backup*.

かぜい 課税 taxation 一動 **課税する** tax ＋目 ▶たばこは**課税されている** Tobacco *is taxed*. ‖これらの品はいずれも**課税の対象になる** These goods are all *taxable*.

‖**課税所得** taxable income ‖**課税率** a tax rate.

かせいか 家政科 the home economics department.

かせいがん 火成岩《地質学》an igneous /ígniəs/ rock.

かせいソーダ 苛性ソーダ《化学》caustic soda, sodium hydroxide.

かせいふ 家政婦 a housekeeper, a household worker (➤最近では後者を好む人が少なくない).

かせき 化石 a fossil /fɑ́ːsəl/ ▶貝[植物]の**化石** *fossil* shells [plants] ‖カモノハシは**生きた化石**と言われる Platypuses are called *living fossils*. ‖**化石になった**古代の植物 *fossilized* ancient plants. 《参考》「時代遅れになった人」を軽蔑したりおどけたりして「化石」ということがあるが, 英語でも fossil とか old fossil という. 同じ意味で old fogy ということもある.

‖**化石燃料** (a) fossil fuel.

かせぎ 稼ぎ earnings ▶彼の**稼ぎ**では一家を養っていけない His *earnings* are insufficient to support his family. ‖うちの亭主は**稼ぎが悪いのよ** My husband's *income is never enough*. ／My husband *earns pennies*. ‖幸運にもいい**稼ぎ口**を見つけた Luckily, I found *a job* that pays well.

‖**稼ぎ手** a breadwinner.

かせぐ 稼ぐ **1【収入を得る】**earn ＋目, make money ▶月に30万円**稼ぐ** *earn* [*make*] 300,000 yen a month (➤この make は「金を手に入れる」の意) ‖生活費を**稼ぐ** *earn* one's living ‖私よりも妻のほうが**稼ぐ** My wife *makes* more *money* than I do. ‖姉は小遣いを**稼ぐ**ために喫茶店でバイトをしている My sister is working part-time at [in] a coffee shop to *earn* spending money. ‖多くのアメリカ企業の重役たちは**大金を稼ぐ** Many U.S. corporate executives *earn* [*pull in*] *big salaries*. (➤ pull in は「(金を)稼ぐ」の意のインフォーマルな言い方).

ことわざ **稼ぐに追いつく貧乏なし** As long as you keep earning, poverty never catches up with you.

2【努力して気に入られるようにする】▶今度のことであいつはだいぶ先生の**点数を稼いだな** This time, he really *scored some* (*brownie*) *points* with the teacher. →点数.

3【時間を引き延ばす】▶私は彼に即答は無理ですと言って, 少し**時間を稼ごうとした** I tried to *play for time* [*buy time*] by telling him I couldn't give him an answer right away. (➤ play for time は「時間を引き延ばす」の意).

¹かせつ 仮説 a hypothesis /haɪpɑ́ːθəsɪs/ (➤仮説の前段階の研究上の疑問を research question という) ▶**仮説を立てる** form [formulate] *a hypothesis* ‖彼女の立てた**仮説**に対して強い反論が起こった There were strong arguments against her *hypothesis*.

‖**作業仮説** a working hypothesis.

²かせつ 仮設の temporary(一時的な)

‖**仮設住宅** temporary housing ‖(野球場などの)**仮設スタンド** temporary bleachers ‖**仮設トイレ** a temporary toilet ; a porta potty(排泄物を薬品で固める方式の). ‖**仮設舞台** a temporary stage.

カセット a cassette (tape) ▶テープレコーダーに**カセットを入れる** put *a cassette* (*tape*) into the tape recorder ‖FM の音楽番組を**カセットに録音する** *tape* the FM radio music program *on a cassette*.

‖**カセット(テープ)レコーダー** a cassette (tape) recorder ‖**カセットデッキ** a cassette deck.

かぜとおし 風通し ventilation ▶この部屋は**風通しがよい** This room *is well-ventilated* [*is airy*]. (➤「風通しが悪い」なら be close または be stuffy).

▶社内の**風通しをよくする** improve [enhance] *the flow of information* within the company ‖**風通しのよい会社** a company which *is open and communicative*.

がせねた false information, bum steer(➤後者は俗語).

¹かせん 化繊 (a) synthetic /sɪnθéṭɪk/ [chemical] fiber (合成繊維) ; a synthetic textile [fabric] (織られたもの) ▶**化繊**は水洗いが利く *Synthetic fabrics* are washable.

²かせん 河川 a river ‖**河川敷** a river bed.

³かせん 下線 an underline ▶重要な箇所に赤で**下線を引きなさい** *Underline* the important parts in red. ‖**下線部分**を日本語に訳しなさい Translate [Put] the *underlined parts* into Japanese.

⁴かせん 寡占《ビジネス》an oligopoly /ɑ̀ːləgɑ́ːpəli ‖ ɔ̀lɪgɔ́p-/ ▶その国の経済は独占企業と**寡占企業**が支配している The economy of that country is controlled by monopolies and *oligopolies*.

がぜん 俄然 suddenly ▶一度満点を取ったら息子は**がぜん**張り切って勉強しだした After getting his first 100, he *suddenly* get motivated and started studying harder.

かそ 過疎 depopulation ▶**過疎の村** a *depopulated* village ‖その村は**過疎化が激しい** That village is very rapidly *decreasing in population*.

‖**過疎地帯** a depopulated area [region].

がそ 画素《コンピュータ》a pixel(➤「100万画素」は a megapixel).

¹かそう 下層 ▶(土の)**下層**から化石が発見された A fossil was discovered in *the lower layer*.

‖**下層階級** the lower class(es).

²かそう 火葬 cremation ▶祖父の遺体を**火葬にした** We *had* our grandfather *cremated*. ‖死んだら**火葬にしてほしい**と望むアメリカ人がますます増えてきた More and more Americans wish to *be cremated* when they die.

‖**火葬場**《米》a crematory /kríːmətɔːri ‖ krémətəri/,《英》a crematorium.

³かそう 仮装 (a) disguise 一動 **仮装する** be dressed《as》, disguise oneself《as》▶ハロウィーンの**仮装をした**子供たち children *in* Halloween *costumes* ‖**仮装行列**が街路を練り歩いた The *procession of people in fancy dress* paraded through the streets.

‖**仮装舞踏会** a fancy ball ; a masked ball ／ a masquerade /mæskəréɪd/ (仮面を着けた).

[4]**かそう 仮想** (an) **imagination**(想像); (a) **supposition**(仮定) ▶コンピュータで**仮想現実**を作り出す create *a virtual world* by computer.

‖(インターネット上の)**仮想ショッピングモール** a virtual shopping mall ‖ **仮想通貨** a virtual currency ‖ **仮想敵国** a potential enemy; an enemy country inside virtual reality(コンピュータゲームなどの) ‖ **仮想メモリー** virtual memory.

がぞう 画像 an **image**(画面上の絵); a **picture**(画面の写り具合, 映像) ▶衛星**画像** a satellite *image* ‖ ビデオ**画像** a video *image* ‖ テレビの**画像**をもう少しはっきりできますか Can you get the *picture* on the television a little clearer? ‖ 高品位テレビはとても鮮明なデジタル**画像**を映し出す High-definition televisions offer very sharp digital *pictures*.

‖**画像処理** image processing ‖ **画像データ** image data ‖ **画像ファイル** an image file.

かぞえ 数え ⚠ **英語には「数え」に当たる表現がないので「…番目の暦年(calendar year)に当たる」と考える.** → 満 ▶祖父は**数え**で90歳だ My grandfather is in his ninetieth *calendar year*.

かぞえあげる 数え上げる **enumerate** +㊐(列挙する) ▶彼は私が犯した間違いをいちいち**数え上げて**非難した He criticized me, *enumerating* every single mistake I had made. ‖ 彼女の欠点は**数え上げたらきりがない** I *couldn't begin to tell you all* that's wrong with her. (➤「とても口で言えるどころではない」の意).

かぞえうた 数え歌 a **counting song**.

かぞえる 数える

1【勘定する】count +㊐ ▶ 1から100まで**数える** *count* from one to one hundred ‖ 指を折って**数える** *count* on one's fingers ‖ テーブルの上にリンゴがいくつあるか, **数えてごらん** *Count* the apples on the table. ‖ 対話「きみはフランス語でいくつまで**数えられる**?」「10までです」"How far can you *count* in French?" "I can count as far as [up to] ten." ‖ 大声でどなる前に10まで**数えよ** *Count to ten* before you yell. (➤「行動を起こす前に気を落ち着けよ」を表す処世訓) ‖ 10**数える**とあなたは催眠状態から覚めます You'll come out of the (hypnotic) trance *at the count of* ten. ‖ 私の成績はびりから**数えて** 3 番目くらいだった My grades were somewhere around (the) third *from the bottom*.

▶長嶋は現役時代**数え切れないほど**(多く)の賞をもらった Nagashima won *countless* prizes when he was an active baseball player. ‖ この新製品を使った場合の利点は**数え切れない** There are *countless* [*innumerable*] advantages to using this new product. ‖ 私は年に**数えるほどしか**映画に行かない I go to the movies so few times a year that I can *count* them *on my fingers*.

2【ある数になる】number +㊐ ▶集まった人々は100人を**数えた** Those who gathered *numbered* (as many as) a hundred.

3【その中の1つとする】▶彼はトップクラスのゴルファーに**数えられる** He *ranks among* the top golfers. ‖ ロードス島のアポロン巨像は世界七不思議の 1 つに**数えられる** The Colossus of Rhodes *is numbered* among the Seven Wonders of the Ancient World. (➤ Rhodes の発音は /roʊdz/).

かそく 加速 **acceleration** ━**動 加速する** **accelerate** (+㊐), **speed up** (➤ 後者は「スピードを上げる[出す]」に近い) ▶運転手はほかの車を追い越すために**加速した** The driver *accelerated* [*sped up*] to pass the other cars.

▶中東の和平プロセスを**加速させる** *accelerate* the peace process in the Middle East.

☞ **加速度** (→見出語)

[1]かぞく 家族

a **family**; 《インフォーマル》one's **folks**(特に両親や子供たち)

> **日↔英比較 「家族」と family**
> 両者は共通する部分が多いが, 微妙に違うところもある. (狭い意味での) family は親と子から成る集団をイメージするので, ふつう, 夫婦だけでは family とは言わない. これは start a family (家族をスタートさせる, 家族を持つ)が「初めての子をもうける」と同義であることからもうかがえる. ただし, 子のない夫婦がペットを一員と見なして一家を family と呼ぶことはありうる. 祖父母は生活をともにしていれば family に含めるが, 特に白人の家庭では別々に暮らすことが多いので, ふつうは, 含めない. もちろん, 祖父母と親は別のくくりの family ではある.

▶私の**家族**は父と母と姉と弟と私の 5 人家族です There are five (people) in my *family*: my father, mother, sister, brother and myself. (➤ 英語国民は mother, father の順に言うことが多い) ‖ わが家は大[小]**家族**です Ours is *a large* [*small*] *family*. ‖ きのうわが家に**新しい家族**が生まれた *A new family member* was born yesterday. ／A baby was born into our family yesterday. ‖ このアパートには 8 **家族**が住んでいる There are eight *families* in this apartment house. ‖ 夏休みには**家族そろって**北欧旅行をした We took a *family* trip around northern Europe during summer vacation. ‖ 私の給料では**家族を養う**だけで精いっぱいだ My salary is just enough to *support my family*. ‖ 対話「ご**家族**は何人ですか」「4 人です」"How many (people) are there in your *family*?" "There are four (people in my family)." (➤「家族は 4 人です」を (×)I have four families. とはしない).

> **直訳の落とし穴「4人家族」**
> (1)family =「家族」であるが, family はあくまで親と子から成る集団を指すので, 注意が必要. 例えば,「うちは 4 人家族です」を (×) We are [have] four families. とするのは初歩的なミス. (×)My family is four people. も言わない. There are four people in my family. または, We're a family of four. とする.「ご家族は何人ですか」は How many (people) are there in your family? となる.
> (2)赤ちゃんが生まれて「新しい家族が増えました」または「新しく家族が加わりました」は第 2 子以降ならば, A new baby girl [boy] was born to our family. あるいは Our family has a new addition. などという. 第 1 子の場合は, そもそも夫婦だけではふつう family と言えないので, We recently welcomed our first baby girl [boy]. または, We (recently) became a family with the birth of our daughter [son]. などとなる.

▶**ご家族の皆さん**はお元気ですか How are *all your folks*? ‖ **家族の者**は皆元気でおります *My family* are all well. (➤ 家族を構成する個々の人々を意識しているから動詞は複数扱い) ／*Everyone in the family* is well. ‖ 遊園地は**家族連れ**でにぎわった The amusement park was crowded with *children and their parents*. ‖ あのレストランには**家族的雰囲気**がある That restaurant has *a homey atmosphere*. ‖ 山田さんちは**家族付き合いをしている**友だちです The Yamadas are *friends of our family* [(*our*) *family friends*]. ‖ これは北海道旅行で撮った**家族写真**です This is *a family photo* taken during a trip to Hokkaido.

‖**家族会議** a family meeting ‖ **家族手当** a family allowance /əláuəns/.

> **直訳の落とし穴「うちの家族全員が」**
> (1)「うちの家族全員が」は直訳すれば all my family であるが, 英語ではこの言い方はあまりしない. 例えば, 「家族全員があなたにまた会えるのを楽しみにしています」は (△) All my family is [are] looking forward to seeing you again. とはしないで, The whole family [Everyone in my family] is looking forward to seeing you again. とするのがふつう. My whole family ... としてもよい.
> (2) 日本語でも「家族はみんなA型ですが, 私だけAB型です」のように, 取り出した人だけ「家族」に含まれない言い方があるが, 英語でも my family に I が含まれないことがあるので注意. 例えば, 「家族で夏休みにハワイ旅行をしました」のつもりで, My family took a trip to Hawaii during the summer vacation. とすると, 私は行かなかったと解釈することが多い. 私を含めるには, My family and I ... (あまり好ましくないが, 若者のくだけた話しことばでは Me and my family ... という言い方もある) とするか, I took a trip ... with my family. としなければならない. all my family があまり使われないのは, この family のあいまいさのせいかもしれない.

2**かぞく 華族** **the nobility**; a **nobleman** (男性), a **noblewoman** (女性).

かそくど 加速度 **acceleration** ▶急な下り坂では自転車に**加速度がつく**ので乗るのは怖い It is scary to ride a bike on a steep downhill slope because of *acceleration* [because you *pick up speed* so quickly].

ガソリン **gasoline**, 《米・インフォーマル》 **gas**, 《英また》 **petrol** ▶この車は**ガソリンを食う** This car burns a lot of *gasoline*. (➤「ガソリンを食う車」を俗語で gas-guzzler という) ‖ そろそろ**ガソリンが切れそうだ** We're running out of *gas*. ‖ (この車に) **ガソリンを満タンにして**ください *Fill it up*, please. (➤ 男性は it の代わりに her と言うこともある).

ガソリンスタンド a **gas(oline) station**

> **危ないカタカナ語✹ ガソリンスタンド**
> **1**「ガソリンスタンド」は和製語.「露店, 売店」の意味の stand はこの場合使えない. 英語では gas(oline) station という. 《英》ではガソリンを petrol と呼ぶことから petrol station ともいう. このほか service station, filling station は英米に共通.
> **2** 給油だけでなく, 修理も行う所は特に garage という.

1**かた 肩** **1【体の部位】** a **shoulder** ▶左の**肩が痛い** My left *shoulder* hurts. ‖ **肩が凝っている** My *shoulders* feel stiff. / I have a stiff neck. / I feel stiff in the neck. (→**肩凝り**) ‖ みこしは**肩で担**ぎます We carry the portable shrine *on our shoulders*. ‖ ぼくはそっと彼女の**肩**に手を掛けた I put my hand gently *on her shoulder*.

▶ランニングのあと**肩で息をする** *pant* [*breathe hard*] after running ‖ 弟と**肩を並べて歩く** walk *side by side* with my younger brother ‖ アメリカ人はよく**肩をすくめる** Americans often *shrug their shoulders*. (➤ 無関心・軽蔑・疑問などを表すときの動作) ‖ 警官が私の**肩をたたいた** A policeman *tapped* me *on the shoulder*. ‖ おじいさんの**肩をもんであげた** I *gave* my grandpa *a shoulder massage*. ‖ 私は**肩幅が狭い** [広い] I have narrow [broad] *shoulders*. ‖ あの捕手は**肩がいい** That catcher *has a strong arm*.

‖**なで肩** sloping [round] shoulders.

2【慣用表現】 **肩に掛かる** ▶会社の命運はひとえに諸君の肩に掛かっているのであります The destiny of our company entirely *depends upon* you. **肩の凝らない** ▶私は肩の凝らない読み物が好きだ I prefer *light* reading. **肩の荷が下りる** ▶それを聞いて肩の荷が下りたよ Hearing that *took a load off my mind*. **肩を怒らせる** ▶社長はいつも肩を怒らせて (＝傲慢な感じで) 座る The president always sits *arrogantly*. **肩を落とす** ▶彼は志望校全部に落ちて肩を落としている He *looks depressed* [*downhearted*] after failing all the entrance examinations for the schools [colleges] of his choice. **肩を並べる** ▶彼と肩を並べる外科医はいないだろう There's probably no surgeon that can *compare with* him. **肩を持つ** ▶父と母が口げんかをしたとき私は母の肩を持った I *took sides with* Mom [*took* Mom's *part*] against Dad in their argument.

2**かた 型**

> **訳語メニュー**
> **様式** →type, style, model **1**
> **形** →shape **2**
> **もとになるやり方** →form **3**

1【特有の様式】 a **type** (タイプ); a **style** (スタイル); a **model** (電気器具・自動車などの) ▶この**型**のハンドバッグは流行遅れなのよ This *type* of purse is out of fashion. ‖ 今流行の靴の**型**はどんなのかしら I wonder what *type* of shoes are in fashion now. ‖ **型落ち**のノートパソコン a *discontinued* [*out-moded*] laptop computer (➤ discontinued は「もう生産されていない」, outmoded は「流行遅れの」の意). ‖ **対話**「きみ, 血液**型**は何**型**?」「O **型**よ」"What blood *type* are you?" "I'm O." 《参考》 英語圏では医療関係以外では血液型をあまり話題にしない. →**-がた**.

2【形状】 a **shape**; a **mold** (鋳型) ▶安物のスーツを買ったらもう**型が崩れて**しまった I bought a cheap suit, and now it has completely lost its *shape*.

3【もとになるやり方】 a **form** ▶クラブダンスは決まった**型**が無いから踊りやすい Club dancing is easy since there are no *fixed forms*. ‖ 柔道の先生がいくつかの**型**を教えてくれた The judo teacher showed us several judo *kata*. (➤ 日本語の「型」から) ‖ **型を破る**にはまず**型**にはまれ To *break the mold*, you must first fit it. (➤ break the mold は「古い型を破る」の意の決まった言い方).

4【しきたり, 傾向】 ▶毎日**型**にはまった仕事をするのはうんざりだ I'm fed up with this daily *routine* work. (➤ routine /ruːtíːn/ は「決まりきった」) ‖ 学生たちは会社に入ると**型にはまった人間**になる傾向がある Students tend to *fall into the mold* after they join the workforce. (➤「個性を失う」の意) ‖ 祖父は**古い型の人間**です My grandfather is an *old-fashioned* man.

☛ **型破り** (→見出語)

3**かた 片** ▶借金の**片をつける** *pay off* the debt ‖ まず仕事の**片をつけねばならない** First of all, we have to *finish with* our work [*get* our job *done*]. ‖ この問

題の**片をつける**には時間がかかる It will take time to *settle* this question. ‖ その問題はほぼ**片がついた** We've almost *got* the problem *solved*.

[4]**かた 過多** ▶現代は**情報過多**の時代だ The present age is characterized by *a glut of information*. ‖ **栄養過多** overnutrition ‖ **供給過多** oversupply ‖ **脂肪過多** an excess of fat ／excessive fat ‖ **人口過多** overpopulation.

-かた -方 **1【方法, しかた】how to** do ▶パソコンの**使い方**［トラクターの**運転のしかた**］を教えてください Please show me *how to use* a personal computer［*how to drive* a tractor］. ‖ 私はひろ子の**話し方**［**笑い方**］がそもそも気に入らない First of all, I don't like *the way* Hiroko *talks*［*laughs*］.

2【人】▶この**方**が先日お話しした竹田さんです *This* is Mr. Takeda, who (m) I told you about the other day. ‖ 入場券をお持ちでない**方**はこちらにお並びください *People* without an admission ticket, please form a line here. ‖ これをおうちの**方**に差し上げてください Please take this *home* with you. ‖ 対話「あのピンクの服の**方**はどなた?」「野村さんよ」 "Who is that *woman* dressed in pink?" "That's Ms. Nomura."

3【気付】
✉ **三木様方森様** Mr. Mori, *c/o* Mr. Miki ➤ c/o は care of の略で封筒の表に書く.

4【側】▶**母方**のおじ an uncle *on one's mother's side*.

がた ▶**がたのきた**テーブル a *rickety* table ‖ このテレビは**がたがきている** This TV set *is falling apart*. (➤ fall apart は「(機械などが)ぼろになる」)／This TV set *is on its last legs*［*leg*］. (➤ on one's last legs［leg］は「寿命がきている」の意のインフォーマルな表現) ‖ 父も最近は年でだいぶ**がたがきている**ようだ My father seems to be *feeling the effects* of his age lately.

-がた -型 ▶**ハート型**のチョコレート a heart-*shaped* chocolate.
▶当店の電気器具・電子機器は皆**最新型**です Our electrical and electronic appliances are all *the latest models*. ‖ 私の車は**最新型**プリウスです My car is the *latest*(*-model*) Prius. (➤「私の車は2012年型だ」なら My car is a 2012 *model*. と言う) ‖ あなたの**髪型**, すてきね Your *hairstyle* is wonderful. ‖ 対話「きみ, **血液型**は何型?」「**O型**よ」 "What *blood type* are you?" "I'm O."

かたあし 片足 one leg ▶**片足**に体重をかける put one's weight on *one leg* ‖ **片足**で立ってごらん Try to stand *on one foot*［*leg*］.

かたい 固い・堅い・硬い

📖 **訳語メニュー**
物がかたい →hard **1**
肉がかたい →tough **1**
こわばってかたい →stiff **2**
団結がかたい →tight, strong, firm **3**

1【物が変形しにくい】hard ; tough /tʌf/ (肉・野菜などが) ▶**硬い**パン *hard* bread (➤「古くなって」ということを強調する場合は stale) ‖ 一晩おいたらパンがかちかちに**硬くなった** The bread *became* (*rock*) *hard*［*dry and hard*］over night. ‖ このステーキは**硬い** This steak is *tough*. (➤ 肉に hard は用いない) ‖ ママ, この豚肉**硬くて**食べられないよ Mom, this pork is too *tough* to eat.
▶この冷凍サケはこちこちに**硬くなっている** This salmon is frozen *hard*［*stiff*］. ‖ セメントは乾燥すると**硬くなる** Cement *hardens* when it dries. ‖ 彼はいつも２Ｈの**硬い**鉛筆を使っている He always writes with a 2H pencil. (➤ ２ＨのＨが hardness(硬さ)の略なので「硬い」は訳出不要).

2【柔軟性がない】stiff ; serious (真面目な) ▶彼の文章は**硬い** He writes in a *stiff*［*bookish*］style.／His writing is *formal*. ‖ 漫画ばかり読んでないで, たまには**堅い**本も読みなさい Instead of reading comic books all the time, why don't you read some *serious* books once in a while? ‖ あんまり**堅い**(＝厳格な)こと言わないでよ Don't be so *rigid*. ‖ **堅いこと**は抜きにしましょう Let's skip the *formalities*.／Let's forget about *ceremony*. (➤ ともに「格式ばったこと」の意).
▶うちのおやじは**頭が固い**(＝頑固だ) My father is *stubborn*. ‖ 年を取ると**頭が固くなる**ね The older we get, the *less mental flexibility* we *have*.
▶彼は若い女性の前に出ると**硬くなる**(＝上がる) He *gets nervous* in the presence of young women. ‖ 初めて舞台に上がったので, つい**硬くなって**しまった I *got nervous*［*froze*］since it was my first time on stage.

3【結合が強い】tight ; strong (強固な) **; firm** (しっかりした) ▶この結び目は**固すぎる** This knot *is too tight*. ‖ この瓶は栓が**固くて**開かない The bottle-top is too *tight* for me to open.／The cork is too *tight*, so I cannot open the bottle.
▶労働者の団結は**固い** Worker unity is *strong*. ‖ 私たちは**固い**握手をした We gave each other a *firm* handshake.

4【意志が強くて屈しない】▶彼女は**口が堅い** She *can keep a secret*. ‖ 外国留学しようとする彼女の**決意は固かった** She *was* (*very*) *determined* to go abroad to study.／Her drive and *determination* to study abroad *were strong*. (➤ drive は「やる気」).

5【信頼できる, 可能性が高い】▶**堅い**商売 a *reputable* business ‖ あの会社は**堅い**(＝商売が安定している) That company has *steady* business. ‖ わがチームの守備は**堅い** Our team has a *strong* defense. ‖ 今シーズン, 巨人の優勝は**堅い** This season, the Giants *are sure to* win the pennant. ‖ 彼のＸ大合格は**堅い** He *has a good chance* of passing the entrance exams for X University.
☛ **固く** (→見出語)

[1]**かだい 課題** **1【宿題】**an **assignment** ▶夏休みの**課題** a summer *assignment*.

2【解決すべき問題】a **task**, a **problem** ▶エネルギーの節約は全人類の**課題**である Energy conservation is *a task*［*a problem*］for all humankind. ‖ 新内閣は**課題山積**だ The new cabinet *has a pile of problems to solve*.

[2]**かだい 仮題** a **working**［**tentative**］**title**.

[3]**かだい 過大** ▶子供に**過大な**期待をかけないほうがいい It is best not to expect *too much* of your children. ‖ きみは彼女の能力を**過大評価している**と思うよ I think you're *overestimating* her abilities.

-がたい -難い ▶**耐え難い**試練 an *unendurable* trial ‖ **忘れ難い**光景 an *unforgettable* scene ‖ **許し難い**ミス an *unforgivable*［*unacceptable*／*inexcusable*］mistake (➤ unacceptable は「受け入れがたい」, inexcusable は「言い訳の立たない」) ‖ **得難い**機会 a *rare* opportunity ‖ 彼が我々をだますなんて**信じ難い**ことだ It *is hard*［*difficult*］*to believe* that he would have deceived us. ‖ 彼の提案は実行し難い It *is almost impossible to carry out* his proposal.

がだい 画題 a subject of a painting（絵のテーマ）.

かたいじ 片意地 ▶あまり片意地を張ると誰からも相手にされなくなるよ If you are too *obstinate*, no one will pay (any) attention to you.

かたいっぽう 片一方 ▶ぼくの手袋，片一方はあるけど，もう片一方はどこだろう Here's *one* of my gloves, but where's *the other one*? ‖ 片一方の肩ばかり持つことをえこひいきと言う Always taking *one person's* side is called favoritism.

かたいなか 片田舎 an out-of-the-way place.

かたいれ 肩入れする support +㊐ ▶ぼくは弱いチームに肩入れするタイプだ I am the type who likes to *support* the weak team [the losing side].

がたおち がた落ち ▶先月は成績ががた落ちだった My grades *slumped* last month. ‖ その映画スターはスキャンダルに巻き込まれ，人気ががた落ちになった The film star's popularity *slumped* [*took a nose dive*], following his involvement in a scandal.

かたおもい 片思い unrequited /ʌ̀nrɪkwáɪṭɪd/ love, one-sided love ▶若者はよく片思いに悩む Young people often suffer [experience] the pain of *unrequited love*. ‖ 徹は芳美に片思いをしていた Toru was *carrying a torch for* Yoshimi. (➤ carry a torch for は「(振り向かない相手に)恋の炎を燃やす」の意).

かたおや 片親 a single parent ▶片親だけの家庭が増えている There are more *single-parent* families than ever.

かたがき 肩書き a title（称号）; a position（地位）▶肩書きだけで人を信じてはいけない You must not trust people only on the basis of their *titles* [*positions*]. ‖ 就職のときに父の肩書きが物を言った My father's *position* proved helpful when I was job-hunting.

かたかけ 肩掛け a shawl /ʃɔːl/（ショール）; a stole /stoʊl/（ストール）.

かたかた ▶機を織るカタカタという音が家の中から聞こえる From inside the house, I can hear the *clack clack* of someone weaving on a loom.

かたがた 旁 ▶上京かたがたお伺いします I'm coming to Tokyo and would like to *take the occasion to* visit you. ‖ お礼かたがたご挨拶まで I'd like to send my greetings and *also* express my gratitude.

がたがた 1【音】▶地震で窓がガタガタした The window *rattled* in the earthquake. ‖ そのおんぼろ車はガタガタと音を立てて走っていった The jalopy *clattered* along.

2【体の震え】▶男の子は事故の模様を話しながら恐怖でがたがたと震えた The boy *trembled* with fear as he told us about the accident he had seen.

3【壊れそう】▶この椅子はがたがただ This chair is *rickety* [*shaky*]. (➤ 前者は「今にも潰れそうな」, 後者は「ぐらぐらする」) ‖ 私の体はもうがたがたです My health is*n't* going to *hold up* much longer. (➤ hold up は「持ちこたえる」) / I'*m falling apart*. (➤ fall apart は「(健康・精神状態などが)崩れる」の意) ‖ 大地震後，その国の経済はがたがただ The economy of that country *is in a shambles* [*in tatters*] after the big earthquake. (➤ in tatters は「(経済・評判などが) めちゃくちゃで」) ‖ その政治家の評判はがたがただ The reputation of that politician *is in tatters*.

4【うるさく不平を言う様子】▶やれるもんならやってみろ．でなきゃあがたがた言うな！If you can do it, fine. Otherwise, *keep your mouth shut*. ‖ みんなで相談して決めたことを今さらがたがた言うな It's a decision we reached after thorough discussion as a group, so *don't start complaining* now. ‖ あとでがたがた言うなよ I don't want to hear *any complaints* about this later on.

かたかな 片仮名 *katakana*; a *katakana* character（1文字）

日本紹介 ✉ **かたかなは日本語の音を表記する2種の文字の1つです．漢字を簡略化して作ったひらがなとは対照的に漢字の一部を取って作ったもので，46文字の体系です．主に擬声語や外来語を書くときに使います** *Katakana* is one of the two (phonetic) syllabaries used to represent the sounds of the Japanese language. It is a system of 46 letters that were created from parts of *kanji* characters, in contrast to *hiragana* which were formed from the abbreviated versions of whole *kanji*. They are mainly used to write onomatopoetic words and loanwords.

かたがわ 片側 one side ▶消防士が通れるよう群衆に片側に寄っているように言いなさい Tell the crowd to keep to *one side* to let the fire fighters get through. ‖ その道路は新しい水道本管が敷設される間，片側通行になっている *Traffic is restricted to one side of the road* while the new water main is installed.

▶工事期間中は片側通行だ During construction, *only one lane is open to traffic*. (➤「1車線だけが通行可能である」の意) ‖ この先は片側交互通行です *One lane is alternately used for both directions of travel* a bit further up. (💰 看板などの文句としては Single-lane, two-directional traffic ahead. のような簡潔な書き方がよい).

かたがわり 肩代わり ▶私は弟の借金を肩代わりした I *took over* [*assumed*] my (younger) brother's debt(s). / I *took it upon myself* to pay my (younger) brother's debt(s).

かたき 敵 a rival（競争相手）; an enemy（敵）▶彼は大学時代からの友人だが商売敵だ He is my *rival in business* though he has been a friend of mine since we were in college. ‖ 赤穂浪士は主君の敵を討った The Ako ronin *avenged* [*took revenge for*] their master's death. (➤「復しゅうした」の意) ‖ あいつがうちの犬を蹴飛ばしたから敵をとってやったんだ I *got even with* him for kicking our dog. (➤ get even with は「…に仕返しをする」) ‖ 彼はいつも私を目の敵にしている He *hates the very sight* of me.

‖ (映画などの)敵役 a heavy ‖ 恋敵 a rival in love, a rival lover ‖ 敵討ち revenge（私憤を感じての個人的な）; vengeance（正当な［当然の］懲罰・正義に基づくもの）.

[1]かたぎ 気質 ▶あの大工さんは昔の職人かたぎを受け継いでいる That carpenter has the old-time *craftsman's spirit*. ‖ 彼は学者かたぎの人だ He is *a scholarly type*.

[2]かたぎ 堅気の honest（正直な）; decent（まともな）▶堅気の人 an *honest* person ‖ 堅気の仕事に就く get a *decent* job ‖ 堅気で暮らす *make an honest living*.

[1]かたく 家宅 a house; premises（家屋敷）▶警察は家宅捜索をして証拠品を何点か押収した The police *searched the house* and seized several pieces of evidence.

[2]かたく 固く・堅く・硬く **1【物が変形しにくく】** hard ▶卵を固くゆでる make a *hard-boiled* egg.

2【結合が強く, しっかりと】**tightly**（きつく）▶強盗は被害者の手をロープで固く縛った The burglar tied the victim's hands together *tightly* with a rope. ‖彼は扉を固く閉ざして引きこもっていた He hid himself behind the *closed* [*locked*] door. ‖徹は裕美子を固く抱き締めた Toru held Yumiko *tightly* in his arms.

3【意志が強く, 厳しく】**firmly**（揺るぎなく）; **strictly**（厳しく）▶イスラム教徒はアラーの神の存在を固く信じている Muslims *firmly* believe in Allah. ‖私たちは患者には尊厳死する権利があると固く（＝強固に）信じています We *strongly* believe that every patient has the right to die with dignity. ‖ひろしと幸子は固く結婚を誓い合った Hiroshi and Sachiko made a *firm* commitment to get married.

▶合宿中の外泊は固く禁じられている Staying out all night is *strictly* forbidden during training camp. ‖《貼り紙》無断駐車は固くお断りします Unauthorized parking is *strictly* prohibited.

☛ かたくなる →かたい（見出語）

かたくな 頑なな **obstinate** /ɑ́:bstɪnət/ ▶彼は優しい性格だが, 少しかたくななところがある He has a gentle nature, but he can be *obstinate* on certain points. ‖その男はかたくなに口を閉ざし, 自白を拒んだ He fell *obstinately* silent and refused to confess.

カタクリ《植物》a **dogtooth violet**

‖かたくり粉 potato starch（➤ 現在はカタクリからでなく, ジャガイモから作るのでこういう）.

かたくるしい 堅苦しい **formal** ▶堅苦しいパーティーは嫌いだ I don't like parties that are *too formal*. ‖堅苦しいことはやめてください Please skip the *formalities*. ‖堅苦しいことは抜きにしてくつろぎましょうよ Let's *be informal* and relax. ‖そんなに堅苦しく考えなくていいんですよ You don't have to *take* it so *seriously*.

かたぐるま 肩車 ▶子供は肩車されるのが好きだ Children love to *be carried piggyback*. ‖パパ, 肩車してくれる？ Daddy, will you *give* me *a piggyback ride*? ‖父はぼくを肩車しておみこしを見せてくれた Dad *carried* me [*let* me *ride*] *on his shoulders* so I could see the *mikoshi*.

かたごし 肩越し ▶和夫が後ろから肩越しにのぞき込んで「何を読んでるの？」と言った Kazuo peeked *over my shoulder* and said, "What's that you're reading?"

かたこと 片言 ▶うちの娘はこの頃片言が言えるようになった Recently, my little daughter has become able to say *a few words*. 《参考》babble はしばしば「片言を言う」と訳されるが, これは「意味のない音を口に出す, ぶつぶつ言う」の意で, 必ずしも赤ん坊の「片言」を意味しない. ‖ヘンリーさんは片言の日本語を使う Henry speaks *a few words of* Japanese. (➤ broken Japanese は「(文法的に正しくない)でたらめの日本語」の意).

かたこり 肩凝り ▶肩凝りがする feel stiff in the neck／have a stiff neck [shoulder] ‖肩凝りをもみほぐす massage the *stiffness* out of one's shoulders 《参考》英語国民は一般に肩凝りを「首筋のこわばり」ととらえる.

かたさ 固さ・堅さ・硬さ **hardness** ▶鉛筆の芯の硬さ the *hardness* of pencil lead /led/.

▶走者たちはレース前に体の硬さをほぐした The runners *loosened up* [*warmed up*] before the race. ‖パーティーの硬さをほぐそうと接待役はゲームを提案した The host introduced a game to *break the ice* at the party. (➤ break the ice は「緊張をほぐす」).

かたじけない ▶手伝っていただいてかたじけない I'*m very grateful* [*obliged*] for your help.

かたず 固唾 ▶そのボクシングの試合には固唾をのむようなシーンが10回くらいあった There were dozens of *breathtaking* moments during the boxing match. ‖その女の子は固唾をのんでそのアクロバット演技を見ていた The girl watched the acrobatic performance *with bated breath*.／The girl *held her breath* as she watched the acrobatic performance. (➤ hold one's breath は「息をつめる[止める]」).

かたすかし 肩透かし ▶その女優はレポーターが突っ込んだ質問をすると, 話題を変えて肩透かしを食わせた When the reporter asked an intrusive question, the actress *dodged* [*sidestepped*] it by changing the subject.

かたすみ 片隅 a **corner** ▶大都会の片隅に生きる人々 people living in *a corner* of a big city ‖女の子は部屋の片隅にうずくまった The girl crouched down in *a corner* of the room. ‖彼女は本を閉じる前に読んだ最後のページの片隅を折った Before she closed the book, she *dog-eared* the last page she was reading.

かたたたき 肩叩き **1**【凝りをほぐすこと】▶おばあちゃんに(凝りをほぐすために)肩たたきをしてあげた I *pounded* (*lightly*) *on* my grandmother's *shoulders to remove the stiffness* [*to loosen the* (*shoulder*) *muscles*].

2【退職などを勧告すること】▶リストラで肩たたきされた I *was persuaded to retire early* because of corporate restructuring.／I *was pressured to take early retirement* as a part of corporate restructuring.

かたち 形

1【ものの外形】(a) **shape**（個々のものが持つ特有の）; (a) **form**（ある種類のものに共通する）▶葉っぱの形 the *shape* of a leaf ‖星の形をしたクッキー star-*shaped* cookies ‖椅子をコの字の形に並べる arrange the chairs *in a U shape* ‖すらりとした形のよい足をした女の子 a girl with slim, *well-shaped* [*shapely*] legs ‖形のいいスイカ a *nicely-rounded* watermelon.

▶その電話はとても変わった形だった That telephone had an unusual *shape*. ‖イタリアは長靴の形をしている Italy *is shaped* like a boot.

▶ 対話「そのチョコレートはどんな形をしていましたか」「ハートの形でした」"What shape was the chocolate?" "It *was shaped* like a heart." ‖郊外には形の似た家が並んでいる *Similar* houses stand side by side in the suburbs.

2【あるべき姿, モデル】**shape** ▶新しい遊園地はようやく形ができてきた The new amusement park is finally beginning to *take shape*. ‖再三討論を繰り返して, ようやくみんなが納得できる形に落ち着いた We came to *a* (*mutual*) *agreement* after a series of discussions.

3【表面上の形式】**form** ▶形だけの夫婦 husband and wife *in name only* ‖彼の研究は書物の形で発表された His research was published in book *form*. ‖これは形ばかりですが, お礼のしるしです This is *a small token* of my gratitude to you. (➤「僅かな感謝のしるし」の意).

かたちづくる 形作る・形造る **make up**（作り上げる）; **mold** ＋目（手でこねて形にする）; **shape** ＋目（材料などをある形にする）▶これらの島や山脈は環太平洋造山帯を形

づくっている These islands and mountain ranges *make up* the circum- Pacific orogenic zone. ‖ 彼の粘り強い性格は幼年期に形づくられたものだ His tenacious character *was molded* by his early childhood experiences.

かたづく 片付く **1**【整頓される】▶私はよく片づいた部屋でないと勉強できない I can't study unless it's in a *neat and tidy* room.

2【解決する, 終了する】**be settled**（決着する）; **be finished**（終了する）▶その殺人事件はやっと片づいた The murder case *has been settled* at last. ‖ この仕事は, きみが手伝ってくれれば正午までに片づきます If you help me with this job, it will *be finished* by noon.

がたつく ▶この椅子, がたつくんだけど見てくれない？ This chair *is shaky*. Would you mind having a look at it？

かたづける 片付ける

> 📖 訳語メニュー
> 整理する →tidy［straighten］up **1**
> 元の所へしまう →put away **1**
> 始末する →get rid of **1**
> 終わらせる →finish **2**
> 決着をつける →settle **2**

1【整頓する】**straighten up, tidy up**（整理する）; **clean out**（すっかり掃除する）; **put away**（しまう）; **get rid of**（始末する）▶部屋を片づける *straighten up*［*tidy up* ／*clean out*］one's room ‖ さあ子供たちはおもちゃを片づけて寝る時間よ Children, it's time to *put away* your toys and go to bed. ‖ この本を全部片づけてしまおう Let's *get rid of* all these books. ‖ テーブルの上を片づけなさい *Clear* the table.（➤ clear は「(食器類などをテーブルから)片づける」).

2【終わらせる】**finish** ＋㊐; **settle** ＋㊐（決着をつける）▶問題を片づける *settle* a matter［problem］‖ 台所の洗い物を片づける *finish* the dishes in the kitchen ‖ 肉料理を片づけてから, サラダを食べた After *finishing*［*polishing off*］the meat dish, I ate the salad.（➤ polish off は「(飲食物などを)さっさと終わらせる」）‖ この仕事は 3 月までに片づけねばならない We must *get* this job *done* by March. ‖ 学校から帰るとすぐに宿題を片づけた As soon as I got home from school, I *did* all my homework.

▶その英文法の問題は簡単だったのでさっさと片づけてしまった The questions on English grammar were easy and I *made short*［*quick*］*work of* them.（➤ make short work of は「…を手際よく処理する」の意).

3【邪魔者を除く】▶あの男を片づけてしまえ *Put* that guy *out of the way*. ／*Get rid of*［*Eliminate*］that guy.

がたっと ▶ 2 年になってがたっと成績が落ちた My grades dropped *sharply* in my second year.

かたっぱし 片っ端 ▶彼は図書館の本を片っ端から読んだ He read the books in the library *one by one*［*one after another*］.

かたつむり 蝸牛《虫》a **snail** ▶ほら, 手すりにカタツムリがはってるよ Look at the *snail* crawling on the handrail！

かたて 片手 **one hand** ▶一塁手は片手でファウルフライをつかんだ The first baseman caught the foul fly *with one hand*［made a *one-handed* catch of the foul fly］.

▶伊藤先生は片手にブリーフケースを, 片手に教科書を持って教室に入って来た Mr. Ito came into the classroom holding a briefcase *in one hand* and a textbook *in the other*.

かたてま 片手間 ▶これは片手間ではできない仕事だ This is not the sort of job you can do *in your spare*［*free*］*time*.

▶彼女は高校で国語を教える片手間に小説を書いている She teaches Japanese at a senior high school while writing a novel *on the side*.（➤ on the side は「余技に」).

かたどおり 型通りの **stereotyped**（型にはまった）; **routine**/rù:tí:n/（いつも決まった）▶型どおりの挨拶 a *stereotyped*［*formal*］greeting ‖ 警官はいくつかの型どおりの質問をした The police officer asked a few *routine* questions.

かたとき 片時 ▶花田君は亡くなった父親の写真を片ときも離さない Hanada *always* carries his late father's picture on him.

✉ **あなたのご親切は片ときも忘れません** I'll never forget your kindness.（➤「片ときも」を for even a moment と訳して加えると滑稽なほど大げさに響く).

かたどる 象る ▶水差しの蓋の部分は竜をかたどっています The lid of this water jug *is* (*in*) *the shape* of［*is shaped like*］a dragon.

かたな 刀 a **sword** /sɔ:ʳd/ ▶刀を抜く［さやに収める］draw［sheathe］one's *sword* ‖ 刀を差した侍 a samurai who *is carrying a sword*.

かたなし 形無し ▶課長は会社じゃ威張ってるけど, 奥さんにかかっちゃ形なしだね Our section chief acts big at the company, but his wife can *twist him round her little finger*.（➤ twist ... round one's little finger は「…を自分の意のままにする」の意のインフォーマルな言い方).

カタバミ（植物）a **creeping wood sorrel** ‖**ムラサキカタバミ**（植物）a violet wood sorrel.

かたはらいたい 片腹痛い ▶新入社員が社長を批判するとは片腹痛い It's *ridiculous*［*laughable* ／*absurd*］that a new employee should criticize what the president is doing.

がたぴし ▶このドアはがたぴししている This door *creaks*.（➤ creak は「キーと音を立てる」).

かたぶつ 堅物 a **straitlaced person**, a **square**（➤ 後者はインフォーマルな語).

かたほう 片方の **one** ▶彼女は片方の手にハンドバッグを, もう片方の手に携帯電話を持っていた She was carrying a purse in *one* hand and a cellphone in *the other*.

▶片方の耳が聞こえなくなった I have lost my hearing in *one* ear. ‖ 靴が片方見つからない I can't find *the other* shoe. ‖ ボートが片方に傾いて子供が湖に落ちた The boat listed *to one side* and the child fell into the lake.

かたぼう 片棒 ▶《慣用表現》彼は学長解任の陰謀の片棒を担いだと言われている He is said to *have taken part in* the conspiracy to have the president dismissed.（➤ take part in は「…に加わる, 関与する」).

かたまり 塊・固まり a **lump** ▶土［砂糖］の塊 *a lump* of dirt［sugar］‖ 氷の塊 3 個 three *lumps*［*pieces*］of ice.

▶《比喩的》あの老人は欲の塊みたいな人だ That old man is *the embodiment of greed*. ‖ 彼はファイトのかたまりだ He is *full of* fighting spirit.

かたまる 固まる **1**【**固くなる**】**harden**; **set**(セメント・ゼリーなどが) ▶セメントが固まった The cement *hardened* [*set*]. ‖ ゼリーが冷えて固まった The jello cooled and *set* (*firm*). ‖ 赤ん坊の頭の骨は生後1年ぐらいまで固まらない A baby's skull *doesn't harden* until about one year after birth.

2【**安定する, 決着する**】▶大学進学の決心が固まった My resolve to go on to college *hardened* [*firmed* (*up*)]. ‖ 委員の意見が固まったので, 総会で発表した The committee *had reached a consensus*, so it made an announcement at the general meeting. / After the committee members' opinions *were consolidated*, we announced them at the general convention.

3【**集まる**】**gather** ▶暴走族が数人そこに固まっていた Several hot-rodders *gathered* over there. ‖ 女の子ばかりで固まってないで少しこっちのグループに入れよ Instead of all you girls *hanging out by yourselves*, why don't you come over and join us? ‖ 湖畔にスイセンが固まって咲いていた Narcissuses were blooming *in clusters* along the lakefront.

[1]**かたみ 形見** a **keepsake**; a **memento** (記念の品); a **legacy**(遺言による) ▶この辞書は亡き親友の形見です This dictionary is *a keepsake* of my late close friend. ‖ おじは形見だと言ってこの万年筆をくれた My uncle gave me this fountain pen telling me to *remember* him by it. ‖ この真珠のネックレスは祖母の形見です These pearl necklaces are *a legacy* from my grandmother.

[2]**かたみ 肩身** ▶あんな息子を持って肩身が狭い(=恥ずかしい) I *feel ashamed of* having such a son. ‖ 3人兄弟の中でぼくだけが大学を出ていないので肩身が狭い Since I'm the only one of us three brothers who didn't go to college, I *feel that I don't measure up* (to them). (➤「一段, 達成度が低く, 対等でない感じを持つ」の意. 単に「恥ずかしい」というのなら I feel ashamed. でよい) ‖ コンピュータが苦手で, 会社では肩身が狭い Since I have poor computer skills, I *can't hold my head high* at the office. (➤「胸を張れない」の意).

▶甲子園出場者ばかりのパーティーで, 僕は野球選手として肩身が狭かった As a baseball player, I *felt out of place* at the party where everyone had played at Koshien. (➤ out of place は「仲間はずれの, 場違いの」の意. このように周りの目を意識する表現は, 本来英語にはなじまないので注意が必要) ‖ グループの中で英語を話せないのは私だけだったので, 少し肩身の狭い思いをした I *felt* a little *out of place* [*felt* a little *small*] because I was the only one in the group who couldn't speak English.

かたみち 片道 **one way** ▶片道500円です It's 500 yen *one way*. ‖ ここから新潟まで車で片道3時間だ It is a three-hour drive *one way* from here to Niigata. ‖ 大阪から熊本まで片道約1万円だ The *one-way* fare from Osaka to Kumamoto is [A *one-way* ticket from Osaka to Kumamoto costs] about ten thousand yen. (➤ fare は「運賃」).

‖**片道乗車券** a one-way ticket, 《英また》a single (ticket).

かたむき 傾き →傾向, 傾斜.

かたむく 傾く **1**【**斜めになる**】**lean**; **tilt** (片方が持ち上がる); **list**(船が); **slant** (水平・垂直でない) ▶ピサには傾いた有名な塔があり, ピサの斜塔と呼ばれている There is a famous tower in Pisa, which *leans* and is called the Leaning Tower of Pisa. ‖ 電柱がひどく傾いている The utility pole *is leaning* badly. ‖ あの額縁は右に少し傾いている That picture frame *is tilted* a little to the right.

▶私がシーソーに座ると一方に傾いた The seesaw *tilted* when I sat on it. ‖ 船が傾いたときは怖かった I was scared when the boat *listed* to one side. ‖ 彼女が字を書くときは左に傾く Her handwriting *slants* to the left.

2【**一方に寄る**】**lean** ▶息子の希望は物理学のほうに傾いていたが, 私は医者になるよう勧めた My son *leaned toward* a career in physics, but I urged him to become a doctor. ‖ 人は誰でも楽なほうへ楽なほうへと傾く傾向がある People *have a tendency* to take the easiest path.

▶どうやら運がこちらへ傾いてきたらしいぞ It looks as though luck *is coming* our way. / It seems that luck *is* now *on our side*.

3【**衰える**】**decline** ▶1930年代, 日本の国運は傾いた Japan's fortunes *declined* during the 1930s. ‖ あの海運会社は傾いてきた That shipping company *is on the decline*.

4【**太陽が**】▶日が西に傾いた The sun is *going down* [is *setting* / is *sinking*] in the west.

かたむける 傾ける **1**【**斜めにする**】**lean** +㊐ (垂直の物を); **tilt** +㊐ (水平になっている物を; 一方を持ち上げて) ▶頭を右に傾ける *lean* one's head to the right ‖ この箱は傾けないでください Please do not *tilt* this box.

2【**集中する**】▶雨だれのリズムに耳を傾ける *listen to* the rhythm of the raindrops ‖ あの少年は親の言うことに一切耳を傾けない (=聞こうとしない) That boy *doesn't listen to a thing* his parents say. ‖ 彼は今就職試験に向けて全力を傾けている He *is* now *immersed in* studying for the employment examinations. (➤ be immersed in は「…に没頭している」).

かため 片目 **one eye** ▶うちの犬は片目が見えない Our dog is blind in *one eye*. (➤「片目の犬」は one-eyed dog) ‖ 画家は片目をつぶってその木をじっと見た The painter gazed at the tree with *one eye* closed.

かためる 固める **1**【**物を固くする**】**harden**; **set**(ゼリーなどを) ▶こうして混ぜたものを1時間ほど冷蔵庫に入れて固めてください Place this mixture in the refrigerator and let it *harden* [*set*] for about an hour.

2【**安定させる**】**consolidate** +㊐ (強固にする); **strengthen** +㊐ (強化する) ▶首相は実力者を閣僚に起用して政権を固めた The prime minister *consolidated* his power by picking influential politicians as cabinet ministers. ‖ 私は会社を辞める決意を固めた I *made up my mind* to quit the company. ‖ 中井さんは20代に事業の基礎を固めた Nakai *built up the foundations* of his business in his twenties. ‖ きみもそろそろ身を固める年だ It is time you started *thinking about marriage*. / You are old enough to *get married and settle down*.

▶ジャイアンツは9回の裏守備を固めた The Giants *strengthened* their defense in the bottom of the ninth.

3【**まとめる**】▶みんなの荷物は固めて1か所に置いておきなさい *Gather* your things *together* and put them in one place. ‖ その政治家の証言はうそで固めたものだ

った The politician's testimony was nothing but *a pack of lies*.

かたやぶり 型破り ▶柳田氏の行動は型破りだ Mr. Yanagida's behavior is *unconventional* [*out of the ordinary*]. ／Mr. Yanagida always *behaves differently from others*. ‖ 彼女の服装はちょっと型破りだ Her clothes are a bit *offbeat*.

かたよる 偏る 一形 偏った biased /báiəst/ (偏向した) ▶兄は偏った物の見方をする My brother's view is *biased* [*prejudiced*]. ‖ 日本に関するその雑誌の記事は少し偏っている That magazine's article on Japan *is* rather *slanted*. ‖ 偏らない記事 an *impartial* article ‖ 偏った食生活は体に悪い It's bad for your health to keep eating *an unbalanced diet*.

かたりあう 語り合う talk《with》▶ぼくは奈美子と2人の将来について語り合った I *talked with* Namiko about our future. ‖ 彼らはいじめについて一晩中語り合った They *talked* all night about bullying.

かたりぐさ 語り草・語り種 ▶彼のファインプレーは今でも語りぐさとなっている His spectacular play *is* still *talked about*.

かたりつぐ 語り継ぐ ▶この家訓は代々わが家に語り継がれている Our family motto has *been passed down* from generation to generation.

かたりつたえる 語り伝える ▶この美談は代々語り伝えられることだろう This beautiful [moving] story will *be handed down* from generation to generation.

かたりて 語り手 a narrator /nǽreɪtə^r/.

1**かたる 語る** tell +目 (伝える); talk (おしゃべりする) ▶娘は事の一部始終を私に語った My daughter *told* me the whole story. ‖ 語るに落ちるとはまさにこのことだ This is a typical case of *revealing the truth inadvertently when talking with your guard down*.
▶《比喩的》顔に刻まれた深いしわが彼の人生の苦労を語っていた The deep lines on his face *told of* the hardships he had experienced in life.

2**かたる 騙る** ▶男は有名人の息子をかたって詐欺を働いた The man committed fraud by *pretending* to be the son of a celebrity.

カタル 《医学》catarrh /kətáːr/.

カタルシス 《心理学》(a) catharsis /kəθáːrsɪs/.

カタログ a catalog(ue) (商品目録); a brochure /broʊʃóər/ (宣伝用パンフレット) ▶最新型クライスラーのカタログ *a catalog* of the latest (model) Chryslers ‖ カタログショッピングがはやっている *Mail order shopping* is popular now.

✉ **貴社の時計のカタログを1部お送りください** Please send me *a catalog* of your watches.

かたわら 傍ら 1【すぐそば】▶その男の子は母親の傍らに座って母親が読んでくれるお話に聞き入った The little boy sat *by* [*beside*] his mother and listened attentively to the story she read to him.
2【何かをしながら, その一方】▶彼は小学校で教えるかたわら週末にボランティアで町の観光ガイドもしている He acts as a volunteer tour guide for the town on weekends *while* teaching at an elementary school.

かたん 加担する・荷担する take part《in》▶彼は政府転覆の企てに加担した He *took part* [*was involved*] *in* the conspiracy to overthrow the government.

かだん 花壇 a flower bed, a flowerbed, a bed of flowers ▶花壇に水をやる water the *flowerbed* ‖ 花壇を作る make [build] *a flower bed* ‖ 中央公園は色とりどりの花壇があってきれいだ The central park is beautiful with its colorful *flowerbeds*.

がたん ▶電車がガタンゴトンと走っていった The train *clickety-clacked* along. (➤ clickety-clack は「ガタンゴトンと音を立てる」).
▶今月は収入ががたんと減って生活が苦しくなった My income *took a dive* this month and we can't make ends meet. (➤ take a dive は「急に低下する」).

1**かち 価値** value, worth
語法 value は実際的な有用性や金銭的価値を, worth は精神的・道徳的価値を意味するが, 同じ意味で用いることも多い. ▶円の価値が上がった The *value* of the yen has gone up. ‖ インフレでお金の価値が下がる一方だ Money keeps *losing its value* due to inflation. ‖ お金の価値は自分で稼いでみないとわからない You don't realize the real *value* of money unless you earn it yourself.

> **【文型】**
> 金額(A)の価値がある
> be worth A
> …する価値がある
> be worth doing
> It is worthwhile to do [doing]

▶この絵は100万円の価値がある This picture *is worth* one million yen. ‖ このソフトはお金を出して買う価値があります This software program *is worth your money* [*is good value (for money)*]. (➤ 後者は「お値打ちだ」に当たる) ‖ どんなことでもやってみる価値はある Anything *is worth a try* [*worth trying*]. ‖ ナイアガラの滝は一見の価値がある Niagara Falls *is worth seeing*. ‖ 外国留学はする価値のあることだろうか I wonder if *it's worthwhile to* go abroad to study.
▶その本は出版するだけの価値が無い That book *does not deserve* to be published. (➤ deserve は「…に値する」).
▶この銀貨は古銭を集めている人にはとても価値のあるものだ This silver coin *is of great value* to the collectors of old coins. ‖ この彫刻は大変な美術的価値がある This sculpture *has* great *artistic value*. ‖ この市役所の建物は歴史的価値がある This city hall building *is historically valuable*. (➤「価値が無い」なら valueless).
▶こんなおんぼろ机でもまだまだ利用価値がある This desk is rickety, but it *is* still *serviceable* [it *can* still *be of use*]. ‖ 若い世代の価値観は古い世代のそれとは異なる The younger generation's *values* differ from those of the older generations. (➤「価値観」は a set of values とも訳せる).

2**かち 勝ち** a win (ゲームや競技の); a victory (勝利) ▶きみの勝ちだ You'*ve won*. ／You *win*. ‖ ゲームは私たちの勝ちだった We *won* the game. ‖**勝ち投手** the winning pitcher, the winner.

☛ **勝ち負け** (→見出語)

> **逆引き熟語 ○○勝ち**
> 逆転勝ち a come-from-behind win ／ (バレーボールなどの) ストレート勝ち win in straight sets ／ノックアウト勝ち a knockout victory ／早い者勝ち First come, first served. ／判定勝ち a win by a decision [on points] ／ひとり勝ち a winner-take-all ／ぼろ勝ち a sweeping [one-sided] victory

-がち -勝ち

【文型】
…しがちである
be prone to doing [to do]
be apt to do
be liable to do
tend to do

《解説》(1)これらは重なる部分があって使い分けは難しい. **be prone to doing, be apt to** do は習慣的に, または性格上の特徴として, 好ましくない行動を「しがち, 起こりがち」と表す. どちらも, 普通, 現在の傾向を表し, 未来には用いない. be apt to do は本来的に備わった傾向を表すときに好まれる. **be liable to** do は好ましくない結果を招きそうであるという含みで使うことが多い. (2)「…しがち」から通例連想するような悪いニュアンスに限らず, 単に「…する傾向がある」を表すには **tend to** do, have a tendency to do や be inclined to do を使う. しかし, これらを使わず, 単に **often** do (しばしば…する) で済むこともある. →傾向

▶急ぐとミスをしがちだ When in a hurry, people *are prone to* making [make] mistakes. (➤ tend to または have a tendency to でもよい; 可能性が高いという場合は be likely to を用いる) ‖ (雨に) 濡れた道では車はスリップを起こしがちだ Cars *are liable* [*apt*] *to* skid on wet roads. ‖ 役人は横柄になりがちだ Public officials *are prone* [*apt*] *to* become overbearing. ‖ 自然災害の教訓は時が経つにつれて忘れられがちだ People *are apt to* [People *often*] forget the lessons of natural disasters as time passes. ‖ お年寄りは家に引きこもりがちだ Elderly people *tend to* [*have a tendency to*] stay home most of the time. ‖ 私たちは自分の失敗を他人のせいにしがちです We *tend to* blame [*often* blame] others for our own mistakes.

▶怠けがちな少年たち young boys (who are) *inclined to be* lazy ‖ この子は病気がちだ He [She] is a *sickly* child. / He [She] *often* gets sick. ‖ 彼は約束を忘れがちなのが玉にきずだ His only fault is that he *is forgetful of* appointments.

かちあう かち合う ▶姉の結婚式とぼくの卒業式がかち合った My sister's wedding *fell on* the same day as my commencement day. (➤ fall on は「(行事などのある日が) …の日に当たる」) / My sister's wedding *clashed with* my commencement day. (➤ clash with は「…にぶつかる」の意のインフォーマルな言い方).

かちいくさ 勝ち戦 a **victorious battle** (勝った戦い); a **winning battle** (勝っている戦い) ▶石田三成は勝ち戦に負けた Ishida Mitsunari lost *the battle he had been winning*.

かちえる 勝ち得る **win** ▶彼女の信頼 [愛] を勝ち得る *win* her trust [love].

かちかち **1【音の】**▶時計のカチカチという音 the *tick* [*ticking*] of a clock.
2【硬い様子】▶道がかちかちに凍って滑りやすくなっているので注意しなさい The road is *frozen hard*, so be careful not to slip (on it). ‖ シャツはかちかちに凍っていた My shirt was frozen *stiff*. (➤ もともと柔らかい物の場合は hard でなく stiff がふつう) ‖ 面接ではかちかちになっているのが自分でもわかった I could tell by myself that I was *stiff as a board* at the interview. (➤ stiff as a board は「板のように硬い」の意).

がちがち ▶ウラジオストックでは寒くて歯がガチガチ鳴った It was so cold in Vladivostok that my teeth *chattered*. ‖ 緊張でがちがちになった I was so nervous that my whole body *froze stiff*. (➤ froze は freeze (こわばる) の過去形).

かちき 勝ち気 ▶勝ち気な女性 a (*highly*) *competitive* [*a strong-willed*] woman ‖ 友子は勝ち気な性格で, 人に負けるのが大嫌いだ Tomoko is a *competitive* woman who doesn't like to lose to anyone. (➤ determined は「意志の強い」).

かちく 家畜 a **domestic animal**; **livestock** (➤ 総称) ▶家畜を飼う raise *livestock*.

かちぐみ 勝ち組 **the winning** [**victorious**] **side**.

かちこし 勝ち越し ▶《野球》勝ち越し点を上げる score *the tie-breaking* [*go-ahead*] *run* ‖ 2点勝ち越しの二塁打を放つ hit a *tie-breaking* two-run double (➤ 相撲の「勝ち越す」は have more wins than losses).

かちこす 勝ち越す ▶今場所その大関は何とか勝ち越した In this sumo tournament, the ozeki managed to *win a majority* of his bouts.

かちっと ▶ドアを閉めるとカチッと掛け金の音がした The door *clicked* when I shut it.

かちどき 勝ちどき a **shout of victory**, a **triumphant shout** ▶勝ちどきを上げる let out *a shout of victory* / give *a triumphant shout*.

かちとる 勝ち取る **win** +⑬, **gain** +⑬ ▶勝利 [栄冠] を勝ち取る *win* victory [the victor's laurels].

かちぬき 勝ち抜き ▶勝ち抜き歌合戦 a singing tournament ‖ そのチームは勝ち抜き戦で3位になった The team took third place in the *tournament*.

かちぬく 勝ち抜く ▶トーナメントで5人勝ち抜く *defeat* five opponents *one after another* in a tournament / *get* five *straight wins* in a tournament ‖ 伊達選手はウィンブルドンでベスト4まで勝ち抜いた Ms. Date *made it to* the semifinals in the Wimbledon tennis tournament. (➤ make it to で「…までたどりつく」; it は状況を指す).

かちのこる 勝ち残る ▶決勝まで勝ち残る *get through to* the finals ‖ 関東勢では2高校チームが勝ち残っている Two of the Kanto area high-school teams *are among the surviving competitors*.

かちほこる 勝ち誇る ▶そのボクサーは相手をマットに沈めて勝ち誇った顔をした The boxer wore a *triumphant* expression after he had knocked out his opponent.

かちぼし 勝ち星 a **win** (勝利) ▶ (相撲などで) 勝ち星をあげる *have a win* ‖ 松坂は3度目の登板でようやく勝ち星をあげた Matsuzaka has pitched three games and this is his first *win*.

かちまけ 勝ち負け **a win or a loss** ▶きみは勝ち負けにこだわり過ぎる You care too much about *winning*. ‖ 勝ち負けは問題ではない, いかに戦うかだ What matters is not *winning or losing*, but how you fight. / It's not about *winning or losing*. It's about how you fight.

かちめ 勝ち目 ▶まともに戦っては彼に勝ち目はない In a square fight he hasn't got *a chance of winning*. ‖ わがチームの勝ち目は10に1つだ Our *chances* [*odds*] *of winning* are 1 in 10. 《参考》「勝ち目のある人, 本命」を odds-on favorite という.

がちゃがちゃ ▶台所からガチャガチャと食器のぶつかり合う音が聞こえてきた The *clatter* of dishes could be heard from the kitchen. ‖ 彼はポケットに入れた鍵をガチャガチャ鳴らした He *rattled* [*jangled*] his keys in his pocket.

か

がちゃん ▶彼は怒って電話を**ガチャンと**切った He *slammed* the receiver *down* in anger. (➤ slam は「(物を)乱暴に置く」の意) ‖ ボールが隣の家に飛び込んで窓ガラスが**ガチャンと**割れた The ball flew into the neighbor's yard and *broke* a windowpane. ‖ 皿が床に**ガチャンと**落ちた A dish *crashed* to the floor.

1**かちょう 課長** ⚠ **会社組織が日・英・米で少しずつ異なるので，課長にぴったりの英語はない．日本の課長は section chief, section head, section leader, manager などがよい．**

‖**課長代理** a deputy /dépjəti/ section chief, a deputy manager ‖ **課長補佐** an assistant section chief, an assistant manager.

2**かちょう 科長** **the head of a department**, a **department head**(学科・研究科の).

がちょう 鵞鳥《鳥》a **goose** ［複 **geese**］; a **gander** (特に雄であることを明示する場合).

かちん ▶なぜかわからないが彼女の言い方に**かちんときた** I don't know why, but the way she said it *got on my nerves*.

ガチンコ ▶ガチンコ勝負 a *serious* match ／an *unfixed* ［*unrigged*］ match(八百長のない勝負).

1**かつ 活** ▶(やつはたるんでいるから)**活を入れてやろう** I'll *light a fire under* him. (➤ light a fire under は「…に点火する」が原義).

2**かつ 勝つ** **1【勝利を得る】** **win** +目 (試合などに勝つ); **beat** +目, **defeat** +目 (相手を打ち負かす) ▶試合［訴訟／戦い］に**勝つ** *win* a game ［a suit／a battle］‖ ベイスターズはカープに**勝った** The BayStars *won* the game *against* the Carp. (➤ win は game や race などを目的語とするので，(×)win the Carp とはできない)／The BayStars *beat* ［*defeated*］ the Carp. ‖ レガッタで一橋大が東大に 1 艇身差で**勝った** Hitotsubashi *won a victory over* Todai by one length in the boat race. ‖ ドラゴンズはタイガースに 6 対 2 で**勝った** The Dragons *beat* ［*defeated*］ the Tigers 6-2 ［by a score of 6 to 2］. (➤ 6-2 は six to two と読む) ‖ どっちが**勝ってる**の？ Which team *is ahead* now？ ‖ **赤勝て，白勝て！** Go Red！ Go White！

▶**人に勝つより己に勝て** You must overcome yourself before you can overcome others. ‖ **年には勝てない** My age is beginning to tell (on me). (➤ tell on は「…に響く，こたえる」).

ことわざ **勝てば官軍** If you win, you are in the right. ／Might makes ［《主に英》is］ right.

> **直訳の落とし穴「ライオンズに勝つ」**
> 「ファイターズはライオンズに勝った」を (×)The Fighters won the Lions. とはいわない. win は「勝つ」であるが，「勝ち取る」という意味(反意語は lose)なので，あとにくるのは試合(game)，レース(race)，戦争(war)，選挙(election)，その他の競い事(competition)，また，それに付随する賞や賞金(prize)，選手権(championship)，タイトル(title)，金メダル(the gold medal)などである．競争相手を目的語にする場合には「…を破る，負かす」に当たる beat や defeat を使って，The Fighters beat ［defeated］ the Lions. とする．

2【克服する】 **resist** +目 (抑える) ▶ぼくはたばこの誘惑に**勝つ**ことができなかった I could not *resist the temptation* to smoke. (➤ resist は通例否定文で用いる).

3**かつ 且つ** **besides**(その上); **moreover**(加えて); **at the same time**(同時に) ▶そのカルト教団は危険**かつ**残忍である That cult is cruel *as well as* dangerous. ／That cult is both cruel and dangerous.

カツ a **(deep-) fried cutlet** /kʌ́tlət/ ▶豚カツ a fried pork *cutlet*.

かつあい 割愛する **omit** +目 ▶時間の都合で芸能ニュースは**割愛します** We will have to *omit* entertainment news due to the lack of time. (➤ 英米のテレビニュースなどでは Unfortunately, we have no time left for the entertainment news tonight. などと表現する).

かつあげ ▶少年は 3 人のチンピラたちから**かつあげされた** The boy *got shaken down* by three punk kids.

かつお 鰹《魚》a **bonito** /bəníːṭoʊ/.

かつおぶし 鰹節 **dried bonito**(塊); **bonito shavings**(削ったもの)

日本紹介 ✉ **かつお節はカツオから作ります．カツオの身を煮て，何回かいぶし，乾燥させます．石のように堅くなっていて釘(くぎ)を打つことさえできます．これをかんなのような道具で削り，出し汁を取るのに使います** *Katsuobushi* is a food made from a bonito. Bonito meat is boiled and then smoked several times and dried. It is hard as a stone and you can hammer a nail with it. It is shaved with a tool that resembles a plane, and the shavings are used to make soup stock.

1**かっか 閣下** **His** ［**Her**］ **Excellency**(大臣・大使・知事など); **His** ［**Her**］ **Honor**(裁判長など); **His Lordship**(貴族・司教など) (➤ いずれも直接呼びかけるときは Your … となる) ▶《呼びかけて》**大統領閣下** *Mr. President* ‖ **ペルー大使閣下** *His* ［*Her*］ *Excellency the* Peruvian *Ambassador* ／*His* ［*Her*］ *Excellency the Ambassador* from Peru.

2**かっか** ▶私は侮辱されて**かっかした** The insult *made* me *mad*. ／I *got* all *worked up* over the insult. (➤ get all worked up は「すっかり興奮する」の意のくだけた言い方) ‖ ちょっと遅れたからって，そう**かっかしなさんな** Don't *fly off the handle* just because I was a little late. (➤ fly off the handle は「かっとなる」の意のインフォーマルな表現).

がっか 学科 **1【科目】** a **(school) subject** ▶どんな**学科**が好きですか What *subjects* do you like？

‖**学科試験** a written test.

> 「学科」のいろいろ **英語** English ／**音楽** music ／**化学** chemistry ／**家庭科** home economics, homemaking ／**漢文** Chinese classics ／**公民** civics ／**国語** Japanese ／**古文** Japanese classics ／**数学** mathematics ／**政治経済** politics & economics ／**生物** biology ／**世界史** world history ／**体育** physical education, P.E. ／**地学** earth science ／**地理** geography ／**日本史** Japanese history ／**美術** arts ／**物理** physics ／**倫理** ethics

2【大学の課程】 a **department** ▶私は政治**学科**から経営**学科**に転科した I have transferred from *the Department of Political Science* to *the Department of Business Administration*. ‖ 何**学科**にいるんですか What *department* are you in？ (→学部).

かっかい 各界 **various fields.**

1**がっかい 学会** a **learned** /lə́ːʳnɪd/ **society**; an **academic conference** (会議) ▶日本英文**学会** the English Literary *Society* of Japan ‖ アメリカ**学会** the Japanese *Association* for American Studies.

2**がっかい 学界** **the academic world, academic circles**

▶父は日本の**学界**では名を知られている My father is a well-known figure in *the academic world* of Japan. ‖ 彼は**医学界**の権威の１人だ He is an authority in *medical circles* [in *the medical world*].

かっかざん 活火山 an **active volcano.**

かつかつ ▶安月給でわが家は**かつかつの生活です** We're just *scraping by* [*barely making ends meet*] on my small salary. (➤ scrape by は「どうにか暮らしを立てる」).

がつがつ ▶**がつがつ**食べる eat *greedily* ／eat *like a pig* ‖ そんなに**がつがつ**しなくても，まだお代わりはたくさんできますよ You don't have to *wolf* [*gobble*] *your food down*. There is plenty left for seconds.

がっかり 一動 **がっかりする be disappointed** (that ; in, by, with, at) ; **be discouraged** (by ; that) (落胆する)

> 【文型】
> **… ということにがっかりする**
> **be disappointed that …**
> A **にがっかりする**
> **be disappointed in** [**by** ／**with** ／**at**] A
> ➤ A が人の場合は in または with がふつうで，「に失望する」に近い
> **…してがっかりする**
> **be disappointed to** do
> ➤ あとの動詞は find, learn, see, hear, discover など

▶我々は日本チームが負けて［負けたと知って］**がっかりした** We *were disappointed that* [*to* learn that] the Japanese team had lost. ‖ ぼくは彼女が学校を休んだので**がっかりした** I *was disappointed* by her absence from school. ／I *was disappointed that* she was absent from school. ‖ 彼には［彼の演奏には］**がっかりした** I *was disappointed in* him [his performance]. ‖ ぼくは彼女が学校を休んだので**がっかりした** I *was disappointed by* her absence from school. ／I *was disappointed at* not finding her at school. ／I *was disappointed that* she was absent from school. ‖ 期末試験の結果には**がっかりした** I *was disappointed with* the results of my final examinations. ‖ 彼女はそのパーティーに招待されなくて**がっかりした** She *was disappointed not to* be invited to the party.

▶**がっかりしたことに**，ホイットニー・ヒューストンのベスト盤（CD）は売り切れだった *To my disappointment*, the "Whitney Houston's Greatest Hits" CD was sold out. ‖ 数学の点がちょっと悪かったからって，そんなに**がっかりするな**よ Don't *be* so *discouraged* just because your math grade was a bit low.

▶きみが顔を見せなかったので**がっかりしたよ** You *let* me *down* when you didn't show up. (➤ let ... down で「…を失望させる」) ‖ 料理がおいしくなかったので**がっかりだった** *It was a big disappointment that* the food wasn't good. ‖ この推理小説の終わり方には**がっかりだね** The ending of this detective story *was a letdown*. (➤ letdown は「期待外れ」の意のインフォーマルな語).

かっき 活気 vitality ; **spirit** (元気) ; **life** (生気) ▶**活気にあふれた**男性 a man of great *vitality* [*vigor*] ‖ **活気の無い**会社 a *lifeless* [*lethargic*] company ‖ **活気のある**町 a town *full of life* ／a *bustling* [*lively*] town.

▶春季キャンプ中の日本ハムの選手たちは**活気に満ちていた** The Fighters were *full of* (*fighting*) *spirit* during their spring training camp. ‖ 魚市場は競り人たちで**活気があった** The fish market *was lively* [*bustling* ／*alive*] *with* bidders. (➤ be lively with は「…でにぎやかだ」) ‖ 古い商店街はシャッターを閉じた店ばかりで**活気が無い** The old shopping street looks *lifeless* [*dull* ／*sleepy*] with many shuttered stores. (●「活気が無い」は「生気が無い」「不活発な」「眠っているような」と考えられるので，訳例のように lifeless, dull, sleepy を使えばよい).

[1]**がっき 楽器** a **musical instrument**, an **instrument** ▶音楽は好きですが，**楽器**は全くだめです I am fond of music, but I cannot play any (*musical*) *instruments*. ‖ 対話「何か**楽器**をやりますか」「ギターとピアノが弾けます」"Do you play *an instrument*?" "Yes, I play the guitar and the piano."

‖ **楽器店** a music shop ‖ **古楽器** a period instrument ‖ **打［弦／木管／金管／鍵盤］楽器** a percussion [string(ed) ／woodwind ／brass ／keyboard] instrument.

> 「楽器」のいろいろ **アコーディオン** accordion ／**ウクレレ** ukulele ／**オーボエ** oboe ／**オカリナ** ocarina ／**オルガン** (pipe) organ ／**カスタネット** castanets ／**ギター** guitar ／**クラリネット** clarinet ／**コントラバス** contrabass, double bass ／**サキソフォン** saxophone ／**シンセサイザー** synthesizer ／**シンバル** cymbals ／**スーザフォン** sousaphone ／**ダブルベース** double bass ／**タンバリン** tambourine ／**チェロ** cello ／**チューバ** tuba ／**ティンパニー** kettledrums, timpani ／**電子オルガン** electronic organ ／**トライアングル** triangle ／**ドラム** drum ／**トランペット** trumpet ／**トロンボーン** trombone ／**ハープ** harp ／**ハーモニカ** harmonica, mouth organ ／**バイオリン** violin ／**バンジョー** banjo ／**ピアノ** piano ／**ビオラ** viola ／**ピッコロ** piccolo ／**ファゴット** bassoon ／**フルート** flute ／**ホルン** French horn ／**マンドリン** mandolin ／**木琴** xylophone ／**リードオルガン** reed organ ／**リコーダー** recorder

[2]**がっき 学期** a (**school**) **term** (３学期制の) ; a **semester** /səméstəʳ/ (２学期制の) ▶ **１学期** the first *term* ‖ 春［秋］**学期** the spring [fall] *semester* ‖ ２年の**３学期** the third *term* of the second year ‖ アメリカでは９月に**新学期**が始まる In America, the *school year* begins [starts] in September.

‖ **学期末試験** a final examination, a final.

かつぎあげる 担ぎ上げる lift up ▶彼はその箱を肩に**担ぎ上げた** He *lifted* the box *up* on his shoulder.

▶我々は彼を委員長に**担ぎ上げた** We *made* him committee chair [chairman].

かつぎこむ 担ぎ込む ▶けが人を病院に**担ぎ込む** *carry* an injured person *into* a hospital.

かつぎだす 担ぎ出す carry out ▶消防士たちはその家から老人を**担ぎ出した** The firefighters *carried* the old man *out of* the house.

▶ぼくたちは神主さんをソフトボールの審判に**担ぎ出した** We *coaxed* the Shinto priest *into* umpir*ing* our softball game. (➤ coax /kouks/ into doing は「(人を)…するよううまく説き伏せる」の意).

かっきてき 画期的な revolutionary, epoch-making /épəkmèɪkɪŋ ‖ íːpɔk-/ ; **groundbreaking** (革新的な，新領域を開くような) ▶**画期的な**研究 *groundbreaking* research ‖ 蒸気機関は文明史上**画期的な**発明だった The steam engine was a *revolutionary* invention in the history of civilization.

[1]**がっきゅう 学級** a class, a form(➤ 後者はイギリスの中等学校で用いる) ▶1 学級20人が望ましい Twenty students per *class* is a desirable size. ‖ 3年2組はインフルエンザで学級閉鎖になる The 3rd grade, homeroom 2 class will *be suspended temporarily* due to the flu.
‖**学級委員** a class representative, a class secretary ‖**学級担任** a class teacher, 《米また》 a homeroom teacher, 《英また》 a form teacher ‖**学級崩壊** classroom breakdown.

[2]**がっきゅう 学究** a scholar(学問を研究する人) ▶彼女は学究肌だ There is *something scholarly* about her.

かっきょう 活況 activity ▶東京株式市場にようやく活況が戻りつつある The Tokyo Stock Market is *becoming active again* at last.

がっきょく 楽曲 a musical piece, a piece of music
‖**管弦楽曲** orchestral music ‖**器楽曲** instrumental music ‖**声楽曲** vocal music.

かっきり exactly ▶彼女は2時かっきりに現れた She turned up at *exactly* 2 p.m. [at 2 p.m. *sharp* / at 2 p.m. *on the dot*]. ‖この机は10万円かっきりだった This desk cost me *exactly* 100,000 yen.

かつぐ 担ぐ **1【肩に載せて運ぶ】** carry +㊐ ▶日本では祭りのときよくみこしを担ぐ In Japan, we often *carry* portable shrines *on our shoulders* at festivals. ▶我々は山田君を委員長に担いで組合を作った We founded a labor union *under the chairmanship of* Mr. Yamada.
2【縁起を】 ▶スポーツ選手は時に縁起を担ぐ Athletes are sometimes *superstitious.* (➤ superstitious /sùːpəˈstɪʃəs/ は「迷信深い」).
3【ふざけてだます】 trick +㊐ ▶人を担ぐようなことをしてはならない Don't *trick* other people *for fun.* ‖ 4月1日はいたずらで人を担いでもよいことになっている April 1 is the one day when you can *play tricks on* others. (➤ play a trick on は「(人に)いたずらをする」) ‖まんまと担がれたよ I *was* nicely *taken in.*

がっく 学区 a school district.

かっくう 滑空する glide ▶一度でいいからグライダーに乗って大空を滑空してみたい I'd like to ride a glider and *glide* [*sail*] high in the sky just for once.

がっくり ▶がっくりと膝をつく *fall down on* one's *knees.*
▶彼は一人娘に死なれてがっくりきている He *is heartbroken* over the loss of his only daughter. ‖これからやらなきゃならない仕事を見るとがっくりくるよ *My spirits sag* when I see all the work I have to do. (➤ sag は「(気が)めいる」) ‖彼女に振られて由紀夫のやつがっくりきてるんだ Yukio *is down in the dumps* [*is depressed*] because his girlfriend broke up with him.
▶ 対話「入試またためだったの?」「そうなんだ. がっくりだよ」"You failed the entrance examination(s) again?" "Yeah. I'*m really disappointed.* / It was *a big letdown.*"

かっけ 脚気 《医学》 beriberi /bèribéri/ ▶ビタミン B_1 を十分に取らないとかっけになるよ You'll develop *beriberi* if you don't get enough vitamin B_1.

かっけつ 喀血 《医学》 hemoptysis /hɪmɑ́ːptɪsɪs/ 一動 **かっ血する** spit [cough up] blood.

[1]**かっこ 括弧** a parenthesis /pərénθəsɪs/ [複 parentheses] (丸かっこ); a (square) bracket (角かっこ); a brace (大かっこ) 《参考》かっこはふつう( ), [ ], { }のように対になるので複数形で用いる. ▶補足説明はしばしばかっこで示される Supplementary explanations are often given [put] *in parentheses.* ‖かっこの中の単語は省略可能です A word or words *in parentheses* can be omitted.

[2]**かっこ 確固たる** firm(固い); unshakable(揺るぎない) ▶父は人間は生来怠け者であるという確固たる信念を抱いている My father's *firm* [*unshakable*] belief is that human beings are lazy by nature. ‖三島由紀夫は若くして文壇で確固たる地位を築いた Mishima Yukio *established himself* [*established a firm standing*] in literary circles when he was (still) young.

かっこいい cool, neat, awesome (➤ 後者2つは主に《米》) ▶彼ってかっこいい! He's *cool*! (➤ 行動のかっこよさも含む) ‖きみんちの兄さん, かっこいい車持ってるなあ Your brother's got a *neat* [*an awesome*] car! ‖わー, かっこいい! Wow! *Neat!* [*Awesome!*] ‖かっこいい鼻 a *nice* nose ‖彼女, かっこいいね She *looks terrific* [*great*].
✉ (同封した写真を説明して)ぼくの彼女の明日香です. かっこいいでしょ This is my girlfriend, Asuka. Doesn't she *look great*?[!]

[1]**かっこう 格好・恰好** **1【形, 姿】** (a) shape ▶魚の格好をしたペーパーナイフ a paper knife *shaped like* a fish ‖きょうは髪の格好が違うね You have a different *hairstyle* today, don't you?
▶ソウル駅は東京駅に格好が似ている Seoul Station *looks* much *like* Tokyo Station. ‖私たちの学校の校舎はおもしろい格好をしている Our school buildings have an unusual *design.* ‖バッターはバントをする格好をした The batter *made as if* to bunt [*feigned* a bunt].
▶ (パジャマ姿などで) こんな格好ですみません Please excuse *the way I look.* ‖よそ行きの格好してどこへ行くの? Where are you going *all dressed up* (*like that*)? ‖彼女はジーンズのほうがスカートよりも格好がいいと思っている She believes jeans are more *stylish* than skirts. (→かっこいい).
2【体裁】 ▶床の間には掛け軸が無いと格好がつかない The tokonoma *won't look right* if you don't hang a scroll in it. ‖レポートは何とか格好をつけて提出した Somehow I *managed to write a minimally acceptable* paper and handed it in.
3【ちょうどいい】 ▶これはブログの格好のネタになりそうだ This should be *good* [*suitable*] material for my blog. ‖骨董屋で格好の花瓶を見つけた I found a *nice* vase at an antique store.
☛ かっこいい, かっこつける, かっこ悪い, 不格好 (→見出語)

[2]**かっこう 郭公** 《鳥》 a cuckoo /kúːkuː/.

[3]**かっこう 滑降** (a) descent ▶急斜面をスキーで滑降する *ski down* a steep slope.
‖**滑降競技** a downhill race.

がっこう 学校 (a) school
語法 建物や施設としての学校をいう場合は Ⓒ であるが, 授業や学校教育をいう場合は Ⓤ 扱い.
▶ 対話「学校は何時から始まりますか」「8時20分からです」"What time does *school* start?" "At 8:20." ‖ 対話「どこの学校へ行ってるの?」「盛岡の学校へ行ってます」"Where do you go to *school*?" "I go to *school* in Morioka." (➤ What [Which] school do you go to? と言ってもよい).
▶学校は午後3時に終わります *School* gets out

[ends] at three in the afternoon. ‖月曜日は**学校**は何時に終わりますか? When is *school* out on Monday? (➤ 高校以下の場合) / What time do you get out of *class(es)* on Monday? (➤ 大学・大学院の場合) ‖きょうは**学校**は休みです I don't have *school* today. / I have [There will be] no *school* today. ‖順子ちゃん, きょうは**学校で**どんなこと勉強したの? What did you learn *at school* today, Junko? ‖**学校**は楽しい? Do you enjoy *school*? ‖**学校**(に行っているはず)じゃないの? Shouldn't you be *in school*?

▶長男は4月から**学校**(=小学校)に**上がります** My oldest son will *start school* next April. ‖岸田は**学校をやめた** Kishida *dropped out of school*.

▶佐々木さんは**学校では**目立たない子だった Sasaki was an inconspicuous student *at school* [*in her school days*]. ‖小沢君はいじめに遭って**学校**が嫌いになった Ozawa began to hate *school* after being bullied.

✉ **私の学校は私立で, 女子校です** My *school* is a private high school for girls. / My *school* is a girls-only private high school.

✉ **あなたの学校生活について教えてください** Please tell me (something) about your *school life*.

‖**学校教育** school education ‖**学校新聞** a school paper.

☞ **各種学校** (→見出語)

かっこく 各国 ▶春になると**世界各国**から多くの観光客がこの小さな町を訪れる In spring, numerous tourists come to this little town from *various countries of* [*around*] *the world*.

かっこつける **put on airs** (気取る; かっこよくふるまう) ▶**かっこつけん**じゃないよ Don't *put on airs*. ‖しゃれたネクタイなんかして, いやに**かっこつけてる**じゃないか *Who are you trying to impress*, wearing that fancy tie? (➤「誰の目を引こうとしているのか」の意).

かっこわるい かっこ悪い **awful** (ぞっとするほどひどい); **uncool** (ださい) ▶そんな**かっこ悪い**かばん, 嫌だよ I don't like that *awful* bag. ‖子供たちは私のヘアスタイルは本当に**かっこ悪い**という My kids tell me my hairstyle is really *uncool*. ‖妹と学校へ行くなんて, **かっこ悪いよ** I *wouldn't be caught dead* taking my little sister to school. (➤「絶対に見られたくない」の意).

かっさい 喝采 **applause** (拍手); **cheers** (歓声・拍手による); an **ovation** (大喝采) ▶オペラは割れるような**喝采**のうちに幕を閉じた The opera closed amid *tremendous cheers and applause*. ‖プリマドンナが歌い終わった瞬間, 観客は**総立ちになって喝采した** The moment the prima donna finished singing, the audience *gave* her *a standing ovation*. ‖彼のアフリカでの体験談は**大喝采を博した** His talk about his personal experiences in Africa *brought the house down*. (➤ bring the house down は「満場をうならせる」の意のインフォーマルな表現).

がっさく 合作 (a) **collaboration**, (a) **co-production** (➤ 前者がより堅い語) ▶**日中合作の**テレビドラマ a television drama *produced jointly by Japan and China*.

かつじ 活字 (a) **type** ▶あの辞典は**活字が大きい**ので見やすい That dictionary is easy to read since it is *printed in large type* [is *in large print*]. ‖私の原稿は**活字になって**その雑誌に載った My manuscript *was printed* in the magazine. ‖名前は**活字体**で書きなさい Write your name in *block letters*.

かっしゃ 滑車 a **pulley** ▶彼らは**滑車**で大きな石を持ち上げた They lifted huge stones using *a pulley*.

がっしゅうこく 合衆国 **the United States**. →アメリカ.

がっしゅく 合宿 (a) ***gasshuku***; a **training camp** (訓練のための) ◖解説◗ (1)日本語の(特に文化系のクラブが用いる)「合宿」には学習[訓練]と親睦のための共同生活という含みがあるが, これにぴったりの対応語は英語にはない. (2)したがって訓練を目的とするものでない合宿は gasshuku を用いて説明することも可能. (3) 場合によっては「トレーニング時間, 研修会」の意の a training session を用いることもできる. ▶軽井沢で**夏の合宿をする** have [hold] *a summer camp* at Karuizawa ‖山中湖で2週間の**合宿をする** have [hold] a two-week *gasshuku* at Lake Yamanaka ‖ぼくたちサッカー部は夏休みの2週間長野で**合宿をした** Our soccer club held *a training camp* in Nagano for two weeks during the summer vacation.

✉ **今, テニスクラブの合宿で蓼科に来ています** I am now in Tateshina taking part in our tennis club's *training camp*. ➤「合宿に参加して蓼科に居る」の意.

1**がっしょう 合唱** a **chorus** ▶この歌を**合唱しよう** Let's *sing* this song *together*.

‖**合唱隊[団]** a chorus; a choir /kwáɪəʳ/ (教会の) ‖**混[男/女]声合唱** a mixed [male / female] chorus ‖**三部合唱** a chorus in three voices [parts].

2**がっしょう 合掌** ▶東南アジアには**合掌して**挨拶する人々がいる Some people in Southeast Asia greet other people by *joining* [*pressing*] *their palms together*. ‖(追悼文の最後などで)**合掌** *R.I.P.* (➤ May he [she] rest in peace. (安らかに眠れ)の意のラテン語の頭文字).

‖**合掌造りの家** a wooden house with a steep rafter roof.

かっしょく 褐色 **brown** ▶子供たちはすっかり日焼けして**褐色の肌**になった The children had *nice tans*. (● The children were brown from the sun. のようにも訳せるが, 訳例のように表現するほうが健康的に日焼けしていることをイメージさせ, 英語としても自然) ‖そのアイルランドの少女は**赤みがかった褐色の髪**をしていた That Irish girl had *reddish-brown* hair.

がっしり ▶青木君は体が**がっしりしている** Aoki is a *strongly-built* man. / Aoki is (quite) muscular. (➤ muscular /mʌ́skjələʳ/ は「筋肉の発達した」) ‖あの人の**がっしりした**胸に抱かれたい I would love it if he pulled me tight against his *broad, muscular* chest.

かっすい 渇水 a **water shortage** ▶**渇水**のため給水制限が行われた Water rationing was imposed due to *a water shortage* [*a shortage of water*].

‖**渇水期** the dry season, the drought /draʊt/ season.

かっせいか 活性化 **activation** 一動 **活性化する** **vitalize**, **enliven** /ɪnláɪvən/ +目 (活気づける) ▶観光客を呼んで市の経済を**活性化する** *vitalize* the city economy by attracting tourists.

かっせいたん 活性炭 **activated carbon** [**charcoal**].

かっせん 合戦 a **battle** (戦闘); a **contest** (競技会) ▶天下分け目の**合戦** a crucial *battle*.

‖**合戦場** an old battlefield [battleground].

-がっせん -合戦 ▶**応援合戦**は赤組の勝ちだね The Red Squad will win the *cheerleading contest*.

‖**歌合戦** a singing contest.

かっそう 滑走する **glide** ▶氷上を**滑走する** *glide* over

the ice ‖**滑走路** a runway.

がっそう 合奏 an **ensemble** /ɑːnsɑ́ːmbəl/ (合奏曲, 合奏団) ▶私たちは行進曲を**合奏した** We *played* a march *in concert*. ‖独奏よりも**合奏**のほうが何倍も楽しい *Playing together* is several times more fun than playing solo.
‖**合奏団** an ensemble ‖**弦楽合奏** a string ensemble ‖**古楽合奏団** an early-music ensemble.

カッター a (**box**) **cutter**(➤ (×)cutter knife とはいわない).

がったい 合体する **unite**, **combine** 《with》.

かったるい **1**【**だるい**】**listless** ▶寝不足で**体がかったるい** I *feel listless* due to lack of sleep. ‖きょうはずいぶん歩いたから足が**かったるい**(＝重い) My legs *feel heavy* because I've walked a lot today.
2【**じれったい**】▶今どきスマホも使えないなんて, **かったるい野郎だな** You're living in this day and age and you can't even use a smartphone. What *a dork* (you are)! (➤ dork は「あほう」の意の俗語だが,「(時代遅れで)いらいらさせる人」という含みがある).

かつだんそう 活断層 《地質学》 an **active fault**.

がっち 合致 ▶それらの指紋は容疑者のものと**合致した** Those fingerprints *were identical with* those of the suspect. (➤ identical は複数のものが「寸分たがわない, そっくりの」).

かっちゅう 甲冑 **armor** ▶**甲冑をまとった**武将 a samurai commander *in armor*.

がっちり ▶彼は若いときラグビーをやっていたから**体ががっちりしている** He's *built like a stone wall* because he was a rugby player in his youth. ‖選手は**がっちりとスクラムを組んだ** The players formed a *tight* scrum. ‖大統領は首相と**がっちり握手した** The President shook hands *firmly* with the Prime Minister.
▶うちの嫁はなかなか**がっちりしている** My son's wife is rather *tightfisted*.

ガッツ **guts** ▶**ガッツのある**男 a *gutsy* man ‖あいつは**ガッツがある** He has a lot of *guts*. ‖挑戦者を KO したチャンピオンは得意げに**ガッツポーズをした** The champion *raised his fists over his head* [*pumped the air with his fists*] in triumph after his knockout win. (➤「(勝ち誇って)両拳を頭上に突き上げた」の意).

> **危ないカタカナ語✸ ガッツ**
> **1** 英語の guts(根性, 勇気)からきているが, これはもともと「内臓」とか「はらわた」を表すあまり品のよくない語である.
> **2**「ガッツポーズ」は日本式の言い方で, 英語には対応表現はない. したがって, a victory pose と表現するか, 本文のように意訳するしかない.

がっつく ▶そんなに**がっつくな** Don't *gobble* [*wolf*] your food *down*.

かつて **once**, **formerly**(➤ 後者のほうが堅い語); **at one time**(ひところは) ▶ラフカディオ・ハーンは**かつて**松江に住んでいた Lafcadio Hearn *once* lived in Matsue. ‖彼女は**かつて**私の学生だった She was *formerly* a student of mine. ‖彼は**かつては**FM銀座の人気DJだった He *used to* be [was *once*] a popular disc jockey on FM Ginza. ‖あの国会議員は**かつては**力士でした That Dietman is a *former* professional sumo wrestler. ‖**かつて**私は彼女を愛した *At one time* I loved her ‖**かつてないほどの**脅威 an *unprecedented* threat ‖**かつての**同盟国 an *erstwhile* ally (➤ erstwhile は「かつての」の意だが「現在は状況が違う」という含み).

かって 勝手 **1**【**自由, 気まま**】▶大学へ行くか行かないかは全くおまえの**勝手だ** It's *up to you* whether or not you go to college. (➤ up to は「…次第で」の意のインフォーマルな言い方) ‖《自分本位な人に向かって》**勝手なことを言うな**! Don't be selfish! ‖新聞記者は時に**勝手な**(＝無責任な)批評を書くことがある Newspaper reporters sometimes make *irresponsible* comments. ‖あいつは**勝手な男でね** He does what he likes with no concern for (how he affects) others.
▶**勝手に**私のお気に入りのセーターを着ないでよ Don't go taking my favorite sweater *without asking*. (➤ go doing は「(好ましくないことを)する」の意で, 主に非難するときに用いるインフォーマルな言い方) ‖このテニスコートは私たちのものですから, **勝手に**(＝許可なく)使わないでください Please don't use this tennis court *without permission*. It's our private property. ‖きみはもう独立したのだから**勝手に**(＝好きなように)やっていい Now that you're on your own, you can do *as you please*. ‖《我を通そうとする人などに向かって》**勝手にしろ**! Suit yourself! ／Have it your own way!
▶**勝手ですが**(＝すみませんが)早退させてください *Excuse me, but* I'd like to go home early. ‖きみだけ出席しないなんて, そんな**勝手は許さないよ** If you think you are the only one to get out of attending, you'd better *think again*. (➤ think again は「考え直す」).
2【**様子**】▶**勝手知ったる**友の家 my friend's house where I *know my way around* ‖京都は初めてなので**勝手がわからない** I do*n't know my way around* in Kyoto since this is my first visit. ‖新入社員ですのでまだ**勝手がわかりません** I do*n't know what to do* because I'm a new employee.
3【**台所**】a **kitchen** ▶《掲示》**勝手口**につき, 玄関へお回りください *The kitchen door*. Please go around to the front.
4【**使い勝手**】▶私は左利きなので, 道具の大半は**勝手が悪い** Since I'm left-handed, most tools are *hard to use*. ‖彼の仕事場はきちんと整理されていて**勝手がいい** His workshop is well organized [neat and tidy] and *comfortable to work in*.

かってでる 買って出る **volunteer** /vɑ̀ːləntíəʳ/ ▶私は送別会の幹事を**買って出た** I *volunteered to* organize the farewell party.

カット **1**【**髪の**】a **haircut** ▶彼女は髪を短く**カット**してもらった She *had* her hair *cut* short.
2【**削除**】a **cut** ▶その映画はテレビ放映の際暴力シーンが数か所**カットされた** Several violent scenes *were cut* when the movie was shown on television. ‖彼の給料は半分に**カットされた** His salary *was cut* in half. (➤「賃金カット」は a cut in wages [in salary]).
3【**挿し絵**】a **cut**, an **illustration**; **art**(挿し絵・写真などの総称).

ガット **gut**(ラケットなどの) ▶**ガット弦**をつけたギター a guitar with *gut* strings ‖**ガットを強く張る** *string* a racket taut [tightly].

かっとう 葛藤 **trouble**(困ること, 面倒); (a) **conflict**(意見などの衝突) ▶そのことで友人間に**葛藤が生じた** The matter caused *trouble* between the friends. ‖彼女の日記には**心の葛藤**が生々しく記されている Her diary vividly records her *emotional conflict*(*s*).

かつどう 活動 (an) **activity** ▶**経済活動**に弾みをつける spur *economic activity* ‖**クラブ活動**をする take part in *club activities* ‖ 彼女は環境保護運動で活発に活動している She *is* very *active* in the environmental protection movement. ‖ 1年間休止していたそのロックグループは最近活動を再開した The rock group recently *became active again* after a one-year hiatus. ‖ 富士山が再び火山活動を始めるだろうという人もいる Some people say that Mt. Fuji will *become active* again. ‖ 父は政治活動に没頭していて，家にはほとんど居ない My father is too deeply involved in *political activities* to spend much time at home. ‖ 日本の着物は活動的ではない You *don't have much freedom of movement* in a (Japanese) kimono. (●「着物は一般の人にとって…だ」と解釈して，一般の人を指す代名詞 you を用いて訳す) ‖ **活動家** an activist ‖ **課外活動** extracurricular /èkstrəkəríkjələʳ/ activities (➤「クラブ活動」の意でも用いる).

カットグラス cut glass.

かっとなる get furious, fly into a rage (➤ 後者はやや堅い言い方) ▶私は彼の発言を聞いてかっとなった I *got furious* [*flew into a rage*] at his remarks. ‖ ぼくはかっとなって大声を上げた I *blew my top* and started shouting. (➤ blow one's top は「かんかんに怒る」の意のくだけた言い方) ‖ かっとなって怒りをコントロールできなかった *The blood rushed to my head* and I couldn't control my anger. (➤「頭に血が上って」の意) ‖ 私たちの担任はかっとなりやすい Our homeroom teacher is *short-tempered* [*quick-tempered* / *hot-tempered*].

かっとばす かっ飛ばす hit +⊞ (打つ); let fly (飛ばす) ▶かっ飛ばせ，イチロー Go, Ichiro, go. *Hit* a big one. ‖ チャンスに高橋がホームランをかっ飛ばした Takahashi *hit* [*belted*] a timely homer.

カツどん カツ丼 a *katsudon*; a bowl of rice with a deep-fried pork cutlet and semi-cooked egg on top (➤ 説明的な訳).

かっぱ 河童 a *kappa*

日本紹介 ✉ **かっぱは川や沼に住むとされる，動物と子供の中間のような想像上の動物です．頭にある皿のようなくぼみに水が無くなると超能力が失われるといいます** *Kappa* are imaginary creatures that are a cross between an animal and a child. *Kappa* are believed to live in rivers or ponds. If the water or liquid in the crater-like hollow on their heads is spilled, they lose their supernatural power.

▶ ことわざ かっぱの川流れ Even a kappa is sometimes carried away in the river. / Even Homer nods. (➤ 後者は「ホメロスのような大詩人でも居眠りを(して下手な詩作を)する」の意).

▶ (比喩的) 彼はかっぱだ (＝水泳がうまい) He swims like a fish.

かっぱつ 活発な active (積極的で活動的な); lively /láɪvli/ (活気に満ちた); vigorous (精力的な); brisk (きびきびした) ▶活発な子供 an *active* child ‖ 活発に跳ね回る skip around *actively* [*briskly*] ‖ 活発な議論をお願いします I hope you will have a *lively* discussion. ‖ 政府は世界の平和と繁栄のために活発に外交政策を推進している The government is *vigorously* pursuing its foreign policy to promote world peace and prosperity. ‖ 今株式市場は活発だ The stock market *is active* [*brisk* / *bullish*] now.

かっぱらい かっ払い stealing, filching (盗み) (➤ 人は filcher).

かっぱらう かっ払う rip off; swipe +⊞ (➤ おどけた響きがある) ▶そのカメラ，どこでかっ払ってきたんだよ？ Where did you *rip off* [*swipe*] that camera?

かっぷ 割賦 →分割払い.

カップ a cup ▶小麦粉カップ2杯 two *cups* of flour. ‖ **カップケーキ** a cupcake ‖ **カップ麺** [カップラーメン] cup noodles ‖ **コーヒー[ティー]カップ** a coffee [tea] cup ‖ **優勝カップ** a trophy /tróʊfi/.

かっぷく 恰幅 ▶福田先生はかっぷくがよく堂々としている Mr. Fukuda *has a portly* [*stout*] *build* and looks quite imposing. (➤ portly は「でっぷり太った」. stout /staʊt/ は「太っているが，がっしりとした」というよい意味として使うこともある).

カップル a couple ▶似合いのカップル a well-matched *couple* ‖ その映画の観客は中年のカップルが多かった A lot of middle-aged *couples* came to see the movie.

> **危ないカタカナ語✹ カップル**
> 日本語の「カップル」は，中学・高校生に対しても使うが，英語の couple は夫婦や恋人どうしなど，大人の男女を指すのがふつうで，newly-married couple (新婚のカップル), young couple (若いカップル), devoted couple (仲むつまじいカップル) などのように，形容詞とともに用いることが多い.

がっぺい 合併 (a) merger (会社などの); fusion (政党などの); absorption (吸収) ―動 (…と) **合併する** merge《with》▶3つの小型店がある大型店と合併した Three small shops *merged with* [*were absorbed by*] a larger one. ‖ この町は隣の町と合併して市になった This town *was merged* [*was combined*] *with* the neighboring town to become a city. ‖ **合併授業** joint classwork ‖ **合併症** complications.

かつぼう 渇望する thirst《for》▶名声を渇望する *have a thirst for* fame.

かっぽう 割烹 a traditional Japanese-style restaurant ‖ **かっぽう着** an apron with long loose sleeves.

がっぽがっぽ ▶パチンコ店主にはがっぽがっぽと金が入ってくる Money just *rolls into* the hands of pachinko parlor owners. ‖ 対話「金はもうかるかい？」「がっぽがっぽさ」"Are you making money?" "Yes, it's really *rolling in*."

がっぽり ▶彼はきのう競馬でがっぽりもうけたらしい I heard that he *made a killing* at a horse race yesterday. ‖ 新しいおもちゃがヒットしてその会社はがっぽりもうけた The new toy proved to be a hit and the company *raked in profits*.

かつやく 活躍 ▶活躍の目立つ[目立たない]俳優 a *high-profile* [*low-profile*] actor ‖ 彼は生徒会長として学園祭で活躍した As president of the student council, he *was active* [*played an active role*] in the school festival. ‖ 今度のオリンピックでは中国チームが大活躍する (＝目覚ましい成果を上げる) だろう The Chinese team should [will likely] *achieve remarkable results* in the next Olympic Games. ‖ 前川さんの新しい職場でのご活躍を期待しております *Best of luck* in your new job, Mr. Maekawa.

✉ **お元気でご活躍のことと存じます** I hope you are *doing very well*. ➤ 日英語ともに大した意味はないのがふつう.

✉ **ご昇進おめでとうございます．今後のますますのご活躍をお祈りいたします** Congratulations on your promotion. I wish you continued

か

success in the future.

かつよう 活用 **1【利用】use** /juːs/ **一動**（…を）**活用する make (good) use**《of》▶余暇を十分に活用する *make* good *use of* one's spare time ‖ 辞書をもっと活用しなさい *Make* more [better] *use of* your dictionary. ／Consult your dictionary more often [frequently]. (➤「もっと頻繁に辞書を引きなさい」の意) ‖ 私はこの機会を最大限に活用したい I want to *make the most of* this opportunity.

2【文法で】conjugation ▶動詞の speak を活用させなさい *Conjugate* [*Give the conjugation of*] the verb 'speak.' ‖ 活用形 a conjugated form.

1**かつら 鬘** a **toupee** /tuːpéɪ/, a **hairpiece**（はげなどを隠すための）; a **wig**（頭全体を覆う）▶あのアナウンサー, かつらだと思うわ I bet that announcer's *wearing a toupee* [*hairpiece*].

2**かつら 桂**《植物》a **katsura (tree)**.

かつらく 滑落する slip (down) ▶急斜面を滑落する *slip down* a steep slope.

かつりょく 活力 vitality ▶ニンニクが私の活力源です The secret of my *vitality* is garlic.

かつれい 割礼 circumcision 一動 割礼を施す circumcise +⊜.

カツレツ →カツ.

かつろ 活路 a **way out**（解決法）▶今は苦境にありますが, きっと活路が開けると思っています Although I am in a difficult situation (now), I am convinced that there will be *a way out* (of it).

がつん ▶あいつの鼻にガツンと一発たたき込んでやれ *Punch* him on [in] the nose. ‖ ガラスのドアに勢いよくガツンとぶつかってしまった I *banged into* the glass door.

かて 糧 ▶日々の糧を得る earn one's *daily bread* ‖ 書物は心の糧である Books are *food for the mind*. ／Reading is [provides] *mental* [*intellectual*] *nourishment*.

1**かてい 家庭** a **home**（暮らしのある場所）; a **family**（家族）▶ケネディ兄弟は裕福な家庭に育った The Kennedy brothers were raised in a rich *family*. ‖ ネパールの青年を家庭に招いて夕食をごちそうした We invited a young Nepalese man to dinner *at our home*. ‖ 家庭のしつけが足りないと子供が非行に走ることが多い Lack of *discipline at home* often causes children to be delinquent. ‖ 私ももう34歳だからそろそろ家庭を持ちたい Now that I'm thirty-four, I want to get married and *have a family of my own* [*start a family*]. (➤ 後者には「子供をもうける」という意味合いがある. →家族).

✉ **ご結婚おめでとうございます. 明るい家庭を築かれますように** Congratulations on your marriage. I hope you'll have a happy *home* [*family*]. ➤ ただし, 英米では結婚のお祝いに家庭に関するコメントはつけないのがふつう. 通例 My best wishes for your future happiness. とか May your lives be filled with happiness. と書き添える.

▶家庭的な男性 a *family*(-*oriented*) man《参考》掃除・洗濯・料理など家事が好きな男性を domesticated man という. これは「飼い慣らされた男性」の意であり, おどけた調子で用いられる. また, 家に居ることを好む男性は domestic man という. この domestic は女性にも用いられる. ‖ 日曜日はぼくが家庭サービスをする日なんだ Sunday is the day I *spend quality time with my family*. (➤ quality time は絆を深めるために, 家族などと楽しく過ごす「かけがえのない時間」) ‖ 彼女は編み物の好きな家庭的な女性だ She is the *domestic* sort of woman who likes knitting. (➤「家庭的な女性」を family(-oriented) woman といってもよい) ‖ 村田君は家庭の事情で学校をやめるそうだ (I hear) Murata has to quit school *for family reasons*. ‖ 最近家庭内暴力がよく話題になる *Domestic violence* is often in the news these days. ‖ 先進工業国に家庭崩壊が多いのはなぜだろうか I wonder why there are so many *broken families* in industrialized nations. ‖ きょうは家庭訪問で先生がいらっしゃる日だ Today my homeroom teacher is *coming to my home* to see my parents. (➤「家庭訪問」は a home visit by a teacher とか a teacher home visit).

‖ **家庭科**（学科の）home economics, homemaking, domestic science (➤ 後の2者はやや気取った言い方) ‖ **家庭ごみ** household refuse, domestic waste ‖ **家庭菜園** a kitchen garden ‖ **家庭裁判所** a domestic relations court, a family court ‖ **家庭用品** household articles ‖ **家庭欄**（新聞などの）a homemaker's column [page], a home life column [page] ‖ **家庭料理** home cooking.

☛ 家庭教師（→見出語）

> **逆引き熟語 ○○家庭**
> **一般家庭** an average [ordinary] family ／**円満な家庭** a good [happy] family ／**幸せな家庭** a happy family ／**上流家庭** an upper-class family ／**中流家庭** a middle-class family ／**共稼ぎの家庭** a two- [double-] income family ／**父子家庭** a single parent [motherless] family, a father-child family ／**母子家庭** a single parent [fatherless] family, a mother-child family ／**裕福な家庭** a rich [well-to-do, an affluent] family

2**かてい 過程** (a) **process** /prάːses ‖ próʊ-/ ▶結果よりも過程が大事だ Results are less important than the *process* (of reaching them). ‖ これらの品物は製造過程で損傷を受けた These goods were damaged in *the manufacturing process*. ‖ 3年のとき授業でカエルの成長過程を観察した In my third year at school, we studied the *growth processes* of frogs.

3**かてい 課程** a **course**,《米また》a **program**; a **curriculum** /kərɪ́kjələm/（全課）▶高校の課程を修了する finish (senior) high school ／complete the whole *course* [*program*] in a senior high school ／complete the senior high school *curriculum* ‖ 彼女は修士 [博士] 課程に在籍している She is enrolled in *the master's* [*doctoral*] *program*. 《参考》「博士課程」は Ph.D. program ともいう.

4**かてい 仮定** (an) **assumption**（しばしば, 根拠のない勝手な思い込み, 想定）; (a) **supposition**（知識・経験などに基づいた推測）; a **hypothesis** /haɪpάːθəsɪs/（仮説）**一動 仮定する suppose, assume** ▶きみの仮定は間違っている Your *assumption* is wrong.

> **【文型】**
> **～と仮定する**
> **suppose that** S + V
> **～と仮定すると**
> **if** S + V
> **supposing [suppose] (that)** S + V
> **《解説》** 事実と反する, あるいは, まず起こりえない仮定をいうときには V は仮定法になる.

▶地球温暖化が加速すると仮定しましょう Let us *sup-*

pose that the pace of global warming accelerates. ‖ 英単語を1日5語覚えると仮定すれば1年で1800語以上身につく *If* [*Supposing that*] you memorize five English words a day, you'll be able to learn more than 1,800 words in a year. ‖ 願いが1つかなうと仮定したら何を望みますか *Supposing* you were granted one wish, what would you wish for?
▶仮定の質問にはお答えしません I won't answer *hypothetical* [*if*] *questions*.
‖《文法》仮定法 the subjunctive mood. 《参考》「仮定法」と聞くと日本人学習者は, if を用いる if I won the lottery (もし宝くじが当たったら)のような, まずありえない仮想の文を思い浮かべるが, 英語では I wish I had a brother. (兄弟がいればなあ)や It is necessary that you be on time. (時間どおりに来る必要があります)も subjunctive に含まれる.

かていきょうし 家庭教師 a **tutor**, a **private teacher** ▶家庭教師について勉強する study with [under] *a private teacher* ‖ 数学の家庭教師の口を探す look for a job as *a tutor* in mathematics ‖ 私は中学生の英語の家庭教師をしている I am *an English tutor* for a junior high school student.

カテーテル《医学》a **catheter** /kǽθɪṭəʳ/.

カテキン《化学》**catechin** ▶緑茶にはカテキンが多く含まれる Green tea is high in *catechins*.

カテゴリー a **category**.

-がてら ▶犬と散歩がてら郵便局に寄って切手を買った I stopped by the post office for some stamps *while* I was walking my dog. ‖ 広島へ調査旅行がてら旧友を訪ねた I visited an old friend *when* I made a field trip to Hiroshima [*when* I was in Hiroshima on a field trip]. ‖ この夏休みには勉強がてらヨーロッパへ遊びに行ってきた I went to Europe during the summer vacation, *half for study and* half for pleasure.

かでん 家電 ‖家電製品 home electric appliances / household appliances (➤ 通例複数形) ‖ 家電メーカー a home [household] appliance manufacturer ‖ 白物家電 white goods ‖ デジタル家電 a digital appliance ‖ 家電量販店 a home appliance and electronics discounter [discount store].

がてん 合点 ▶彼女の説明でようやく(その問題の)合点がいった With her explanation, everything *fell* [*clicked*] *into place*. (➤ fall [click] into place は「(事実などが)はっきりしてくる」) ‖ そんな説明では合点がゆかない That is *no explanation* at all. / That *doesn't explain anything*.
☛ 早合点, ひとり合点 (→見出語)

がでんいんすい 我田引水 ▶彼の議論はいつも我田引水だ His arguments are *self-serving*. / He *turns* every argument *to his own advantage*.

カデンツァ《音楽》a **cadenza** /kədénzə/.

¹かど 角 **1【物の端のとがった部分】** a **corner** ▶机の角に頭をぶつけた I knocked my head against the *corner* of the desk.
2【道の曲がり角】 a **corner** ▶角にポストが在る There is a mailbox *on the corner*. ‖ 角の薬屋の店員, 美人だよ The salesgirl at the *corner* drugstore is really pretty. (➤ この corner は「角に在る」の意の形容詞) ‖ 郵便局は角を曲がった所に在ります The post office is *just around the corner*. ‖ その角を右へ曲がってください. 伊藤さんのお宅は角から3軒目です Turn right [Take a right turn] at the *corner*. Ito's home is the third *from the corner*.
3【慣用表現】 ▶年を取るにしたがって彼も角が取れてきた He has *mellowed* with age. ‖ ことばに注意しないと角が立つよ Watch your language so as not to *offend* anyone [not to *be offensive*]. (➤ offensive は「無礼な」の意).
ことわざ **物も言いようで角が立つ** The way you say something can make it offensive [create bitter feelings]. / It's not what you say, but how you say it. (➤ 後者は「いけないのは内容ではなく言い方だ」の意).

²かど 過度の **excessive** ▶過度の運動はかえって体に良くない *Excessive* [*Too much*] exercise will do more harm than good. ‖ 過度の労働で健康を損ねてしまった My health has been ruined by *overwork*.

³かど ▶殺人のかど(=罪科)でその男を逮捕する arrest the man *on a charge of* murder ‖ 彼女はスパイのかど(=容疑)で拘留された She was held *on suspicion of* being a spy.

かとう 下等な **low, lower** (➤ 進化の程度が低い; 後者は higher (高等の)に対する語); **coarse** (粗野な); **mean** (卑劣な); **of low** [**inferior**] **character** (品位を欠く) ▶品性の卑しい下等な人間 a vulgar and *coarse* person ‖ 下等動物 a lower animal.

かどう 華道 →生け花.

-かどうか **if, whether**
語法 (1)この意味では前者はインフォーマルな語. (2)名詞節を導く場合, 両者は交換可能.
▶会社が忙しいから8時までに帰宅できるかどうかわかりません I don't know *if* [*whether*] I will be able to make it home before eight since I am tied up in the office. ‖ 彼がパスタを好きかどうか私にはわからない I don't know *whether or not* he likes pasta. (➤ この場合は if or not とはいえない) ‖ 成功するかどうかはおまえの努力次第だと思うよ I believe (that) success will depend on your efforts.

かとうきょうそう 過当競争 **excessive** [**fierce**] **competition** ▶二大メーカーがシェアを伸ばそうと過当競争をしている The two major manufacturers are engaged in *excessive* [*fierce*] *competition* to expand their market share(s).

かとき 過渡期 an **age of transition**, a **transition (period)** ▶ディケンズはイギリスが農業国から工業国へ移行する過渡期に生きた Dickens lived in *the age of transition* from an agricultural to an industrial Britain. ‖ 親と口を利きたがらないのは思春期から大人への過渡期に見られる現象である Unwillingness to speak to parents is a phenomenon often seen in the *transition* from adolescence to adulthood.

かどち 角地 a **corner plot**.

かどで 門出 ▶新郎新婦の門出を祝って乾杯しましょう Let's drink a toast to the bride and bridegroom and *wish them every happiness in their new life* together.
✉ **あなたの社会人としての新しい門出をお祝いいたします** Good luck in your *new life* as a company employee.

かどまつ 門松 a ***kadomatsu***
日本紹介 ✉ **門松は松の枝に竹や梅を添えた正月用の飾りで, 一対で玄関の門に飾ります.「松飾り」ともいいます. 常緑の松は長寿と祝賀を表しています** *Kadomatsu* are New Year decorations made of pine branches, bamboo stalks and ume [Japanese apricot] twigs. They are placed at the front gate in pairs. They are also

called '*matsukazari*.' The evergreen pine symbolizes longevity and celebration.

カドミウム《化学》**cadmium** /kǽdmiəm/

‖カドミウム汚染 cadmium contamination.

かとりせんこう 蚊取り線香 a **mosquito coil** ▶蚊取り線香をたく burn *a mosquito coil*.

カトリック Catholicism /kəθɑ́:ləsìzəm/（カトリック教）; a (**Roman**) **Catholic** /kǽθəlɪk/（カトリック教徒）▶カトリックの大学 a *Catholic* university ‖ 私はカトリックで, プロテスタントではありません I am (*a*) *Catholic*, not (a) Protestant. ‖ カトリックの司祭 *a Catholic priest*.

‖カトリック教会 the (Roman) Catholic Church.

カトレア《植物》a **cattleya** /kǽtliə/.

かどわかす abduct +目（誘拐する）▶若い娘をかどわかす *abduct* a young woman.

かな 仮名 (a) ***kana*** ▶かなで書く write *in kana*.

‖かな表（五十音図）the kana syllabary. →かたかな, ひらがな.

かなあみ 金網 wire netting ▶犬が入らないように花壇を金網で囲った I screened the flowerbeds with *wire netting* to keep the dogs out.

かない 家内 ▶皆で家内安全を祈った We all prayed for the *well-being of our family*.

▶家内（＝妻）は今実家に帰っています *My wife* has gone back to her parents' (home).

‖家内工業 a home [cottage] industry.

[1]**かなう 叶う・適う 1【現実になる】come true ; realize** +目（実現する）▶私の留学の夢はやっとかなった My dream of studying abroad *has* finally *come true*. ‖ 宇宙飛行士になりたいという息子の夢がかないますように！ May my son's desire to become an astronaut *be realized*! ‖ M王女は新聞記者とかなわぬ恋をした Princess M *fell in love* with a newspaper reporter, but *was unable to marry* him.

2【当てはまる】▶井上さんは私の理想にかなった人です Mr. Inoue is my *ideal* type.

[2]**かなう 敵う** ▶記憶力では木村君にかなう者はいない As far as memory is concerned, *nobody can match* Kimura. →かなわない.

かなえる 叶える・適える grant +目 ▶残念ですがきみの要求をかなえることはできません I'm sorry to say I can't *grant* your request. ‖ 対話「もしも１つだけ願いがかなえられるなら, どんな願いがいい？」「もっと背が高くなりたい」"If you *were granted* one wish, what would it be?" "I'd wish to be taller."（➤ 答えは It would be to grow taller. でもよい）.

かなきりごえ 金切り声 a **shriek** /ʃri:k/, a **scream** ▶金切り声を上げる give *a shriek* ‖ 痴漢に路上で襲われた少女は金切り声で助けを求めた When the girl was assaulted by a pervert in the street, she *shrieked* for help.

かなぐ 金具 metal fittings（金属の付属品）; **metal** [**metallic**] **items**（金属類）.

かなぐりすてる かなぐり捨てる ▶彼の父親は地位も名誉もかなぐり捨ててその娘と結婚した His father *threw away* his position and honor to marry that girl.

かなしい 悲しい

sad, sorrowful（➤ 後者は強い悲しみに打ち沈んでいる状態を指す）▶悲しい話 a *sad* story ‖ 私たちは悲しいときに泣く We cry when we *are sad*. ‖ その知らせを聞いて彼女は悲しかった She *was sad* to hear the news. ‖ 彼の早死にを思うと実に悲しい It is very *sad* to think of his early death. ‖ フレディ・マーキュリーの死は今も私を悲しくさせる Thinking about Freddie Mercury's death still *makes* me *sad*. ‖ 悲しそうだけどどうしたの？ What's the matter? You *look sad*.

▶ぼくがそう言うと彼女は悲しそうな顔をした When I said that, her expression turned *sad*. ‖ 孤児たちの悲しそうな表情がテレビにクローズアップされた Close-up shots of the orphans' *sorrowful* expressions were shown on TV. ‖ 悲しいことに歌手の急病でその公演は中止になった *Sadly*, the performance was cancelled due to the singer's sudden illness.

かなしげ 悲しげな sorrowful ▶彼は悲しげな表情をした He put on a *sorrowful* look. ／He assumed a *sorrowful* expression. ‖ 少女は悲しげにうなだれてそこに立っていた The girl stood there, her head drooping *sadly*.

かなしみ 悲しみ sadness ; sorrow（強い悲しみ）; **grief**（人の死などによる激しい悲しみ）▶悲しみを隠す conceal one's *sorrow* ‖ 一人息子を交通事故で失ったその母親は悲しみに打ちひしがれていた Having lost her only son in a car accident, the mother was overwhelmed with *grief*. ‖ 恋人に捨てられた和雄は悲しみに暮れていた Kazuo *was heartbroken* after his girlfriend left him. ‖ 時が彼の悲しみを癒やすだろう Time will heal his *grief*.

かなしむ 悲しむ be [feel] sad ; grieve（深く）▶級友たちはいじめに遭って自殺したMの死をとても悲しんだ The classmates *were* very *sad* because M committed suicide after becoming a victim of bullying. ‖ 1997年ダイアナ妃が事故死したとき, 多くのイギリス人は深く悲しんだ Many British people *grieved* when Princess Diana was killed in a car accident in 1997. ／Many British people *mourned* Princess Diana's death in a car accident in 1997. ‖ 生徒が先生に暴力を振るうとは悲しむべき（＝嘆かわしい）ことだ It is *regrettable* that some students use violence against their teachers.

かなた 彼方 ▶そのジェット機はたちまち空のかなたに消えていった In seconds, the jet vanished *into the far reaches of the sky*.（➤ 詩的な表現）‖ はるかかなたに雪を頂いた山々が見える Snow-capped mountains can be seen *far in the distance*.

カナダ Canada 一形 **カナダの Canadian** ▶カナダにはフランス語系カナダ人と英語系カナダ人が住んでいる In *Canada* there are French speaking *Canadians* and English speaking *Canadians*.

かなづかい 仮名遣い ▶歴史的かなづかい historical *kana usage* ‖ 現代かなづかい contemporary *kana usage*／contemporary *Japanese syllabic writing*.

かなづち 金槌 a **hammer** ▶厚板に金づちでくぎを打ち込む *hammer* a nail into the plank（➤ この hammer は動詞）.

▶《比喩的》ぼくは全然泳げないんだ. いわゆる金づちでね I can't swim at all. I *sink like a rock* in water.

かなでる 奏でる ▶楽器を奏でる *play* an instrument.

かなめ 要 the vital [**key** ／**most important**] **point**（最重要点）; **the most important thing** [**person**]（最重要の物事[人]）▶キャプテンはチームの要だ The captain is *the key* to a team's success or failure.

かなもの 金物 hardware, ironware /áɪəʳnweəʳ/

‖金物屋 a hardware store.

かならず 必ず

1【きっと】certainly ; definitely（確実に）; **without** (a) **doubt**（疑いなく）

【文型】
人・物(A)が必ず…する
A **is certain to** do.
A **is sure to** do.
I'm sure [**certain**] A **will** do.

【解説】sure が話し手の「希望」を含めた主観的な判断を暗示するのに対して, certain はより根拠のある客観的な判断を表すのに使われる. いちばん下は話者の確信であることをいう.

▶彼は必ず大歌手になるだろう He *is sure to* become a great singer. ／He will *certainly* [*Without a doubt* he will] become a great singer. ／*It is certain that* he will become a great singer. ‖ 彼女は必ず来る *I'm sure* she'*ll* come. ／She'll *definitely* come. ‖ 今夜必ず電話してね *Be sure to* [*Don't forget to*] call me tonight. ‖ 彼はいつか必ず私の元に戻って来ます *I am sure* he *will* come back to me someday.

▶我々は必ず甲子園に行く We're going to make it to Koshien, *no matter what*. (➤ no matter what は「何が何でも, 絶対」) ／We're *definitely* going to make it to Koshien. (➤ definitely は強い決意だけでなく,「まちがいなく」という確かさを表す場合もある) ‖ あす必ずお伺いします I will visit you tomorrow *without fail*. (➤ 堅い言い方) ‖ 必ずもうかるという話には用心したほうがいい You should be careful when someone tells you that you *can't fail to make a lot of money*. ／You should be cautious about such *get-rich-quick* schemes.

2【いつも, 決まって】▶うちの犬は知らない人を見ると必ずほえる Our dog barks *whenever* [*every time*] he sees a stranger. ‖ 先生, 私はこの薬を飲むと必ず眠くなるんです Doctor, I *always* get sleepy after taking this medicine. ‖ 金持ちが必ず幸せだとは言えない The rich are *not always* happy. (→必ずしも).

✉ **私たちは玄関で必ず靴を脱ぎます** We *never fail to* take off [We *always* take off] our shoes inside the door. ➤ 前者のほうが堅い言い方.

かならずしも 必ずしも not always(いつも…とは限らない) ; **not necessarily** (必ずしも…ではない) ; **not all** (全部が…とは限らない) ▶独身の男性が必ずしもだらしないとは限らない *It isn't necessarily true that* all unmarried men are slobs. ‖ プロ野球の選手が必ずしも高給取りとは限らない You *can't* say that *all* professional baseball players are well-paid. ／*Not all* professional baseball players have high salaries.

かなり pretty, fairly, rather

【語法】**pretty** が最も一般的な語で, インフォーマルな語. いい意味で「なかなか」というときは **fairly** を用いる. **rather** は fairly よりも意味が強く, しばしば「好ましくない」というニュアンスがある.

▶きみの作文はかなりよく書けていたよ Your composition was *quite* well written [was *pretty* good]. ‖ 私の友だちはかなり大きい家に住んでいる A friend of mine lives in a *fairly* big house. ‖ その花瓶はかなり高いよ That vase is *rather* expensive. ‖ 先生に向かってそんな口を利くなんて, あなたもかなり生意気ね You've got *some* nerve to talk that way to the teacher. (➤ この some は「大した」の意のインフォーマルな語で, 発音するときは /sʌm/ と強く言う).

▶この頃はかなりの数の日本人が海外で生活している These days *quite a few* [*a considerable number of*] Japanese people are living overseas. (➤ quite a few は「相当数の」) ‖ 日本はかなりの額の援助を開発途上国に対して行っている Japan provides a *sizeable* [*sizable*] amount of aid to developing countries. (➤ sizeable は「かなり大きい」の意の堅い語).

カナリア《鳥》a **canary** /kənéəri/ ▶カナリアをつがいで飼う have [keep] a pair of *canaries*.

かなわない 敵わない 1【匹敵しない】be no match for ▶計算となると人間はコンピュータにはかなわない Humans *are no match for* computers when it comes to performing calculations. ‖ 車の運転では誰も広瀬君にはかなわない *Nobody is a better* driver than Hirose. ／As a driver, Hirose *is second to none* [*has no equal*].

▶将棋では誰も木村君にはかなわない *No one can hold a candle to* Kimura at shogi. (➤ can't hold a candle to A で「Aにとても太刀打ちできない」の意) ／*Nobody can beat* Kimura at shogi. (➤「負かすことができない」の意) ‖ またぼくに宿題やらせる気かい? きみにはかなわないよ You want me to do your homework again? You're *impossible*. (➤ impossible は「どうしようもない」).

2【我慢できない】can't stand ▶日本の暑さと湿気にはかなわない I *can't stand* the hot weather and high humidity in Japan.

かに 蟹 a crab ▶カニに指を挟まれた I got my finger caught in *a crab's* pincers. (➤ pincers は「はさみ」).

‖カニ缶 canned crab.

かにく 果肉 flesh(メロン, バナナなどの身の締まった) ; **pulp**(みかん, ぶどうなどの果汁の混ざった) ▶若いメロンの堅い果肉 the firm *flesh* of a young melon.

かにざ 蟹座 (a) **Cancer** ▶かに座の女性 *a Cancer woman*.

がにまた 蟹股 bandy legs ▶がに股の男 a man *with bandy legs* ／a *bowlegged* man 《参考》「がに股の人(特に男性)」を俗語ではその形から a rainbow という. ‖ 五郎はがに股で歩く Goro walks *bowlegged*.

かにゅう 加入する join +目 ▶ヨットクラブに加入する *join* [*become a member of*] a sailing club ‖ 地震保険に加入する *insure* one's house against an earthquake.

カヌー a canoe /kənúː/ ▶カヌーをこぐ paddle *a canoe* ‖ 私たちはカヌーで湖を渡った We crossed the lake *by* [*in a*] *canoe*.

[1]かね 金

1【お金】money ▶金をもうける[使う] make [spend] *money* ‖ 金をためる save *money* ‖ 金を借りる borrow *money* ‖ オートバイは欲しいが, 買う金が無い I want a motorcycle but I don't have the *money* to buy one. ‖ 友情は金では買えない You can't buy friendship *with money*. ‖ 金に困って家を売った I sold my house because I *needed money*. ‖ すみませんがこの小切手をお金に換えてください Excuse me, but could you *cash* these checks? ‖ 彼女は下着に金をかけている She *spends a lot of money* on underwear.

▶金は一銭も無い I'm broke. ／I haven't got a penny to my name. (➤ 後者は「びた一文持っていない」の意の決まった言い方) ‖ 社長がベンツの新車を買ったんだって? 金があるねえ The president bought a new Mercedes? He *must be loaded*. (➤ be loaded は「金がたんまりある」の意) ‖ この仕事は金になるよ You can *make* (*a lot of*) *money* out of this job. ／*There is* (*a lot of*) *money* in this job. ‖ 東京は世界でいちばん金のかかる街の1つだ Tokyo is one of the most *expensive* cities in the world.

▶《慣用表現》彼は金に糸目を付けずに高価な土産を買った He bought expensive souvenirs *without even bothering about the prices*. ‖ おまえは金のなる木でもあると思ってるのか Do you think *money grows on trees*? ‖ あーあ, 金のなる木でもあったらなあ How I wish I had *a money tree*! ‖ 万事金が物を言う世の中だ Money talks.

ことわざ 金は天下の回りもの Money doesn't belong to any particular person. It circulates from one person to another. (➤日本語からの意訳) ／ Money comes and goes.

ことわざ 金の切れ目が縁の切れ目 When the money is gone, so are the friends. (➤日本語からの意訳).

2【通貨】currency /kə́ːrənsi ‖ kʌ́r-/ ▶オーストラリアのお金はドルです The Australian *currency* is the dollar. ‖ この韓国のお金を日本円に換えたい I want to change this South Korean *currency* [*money*] into Japanese yen.

²かね 鐘 a **bell** (➤小さな鈴にも, 大きな鐘にも用いる) ; a **gong** (どら) ▶教会の鐘が鳴っている There go the *church bells*. (➤この go は「鳴る」の意) ／ The *church bells* are ringing. ‖ 作文を書き終わったとき終業の鐘が鳴った The *bell for the end of class* rang (just) as I was finishing the composition.

かねあい 兼ね合い ▶勉強と遊びの兼ね合いが難しい It is hard to *balance* work *with* play.

かねかし 金貸し a **money lender.**

かねがね ▶かねがね(＝長年)探していた本を先日手に入れました The other day I got a book that I had been looking for *for years*. ‖ おうわさはかねがねお伺いしております I have heard much [a lot] about you. (➤「かねがね」の意味は現在完了形で表されている).

かねじゃく 曲尺 a **carpenter's square.**

かねそなえる 兼ね備える ▶彼は知性と教養を兼ね備えている He *has both* intelligence *and* culture.

¹かねつ 加熱 heating 一動 **加熱する heat** ＋目 ▶フラスコに水を入れて加熱しなさい Pour water into the flask and *heat* it. ‖ **加熱装置** a heating apparatus /æpərǽṭəs ‖ -réɪt-/.

²かねつ 過熱 overheating 一動 **過熱する overheat** ▶エンジンが過熱した The engine *overheated*.

▶近頃バレンタイン商戦は過熱気味だ The competition for sales of Valentine's Day gifts is *a bit overheated* these days. ‖ その事件に関して報道は加熱ぎみになっている Media covering of the case *has reached* (*a*) *fever pitch*.

かねづかい 金遣い ▶金遣いの荒い人 *a spendthrift* /spéndθrɪft/ (浪費家) ／*a big spender* (大金を使う人 ; 必ずしも悪い意味ではない) ‖ おまえは金遣いが荒いなあ You *spend your money wastefully* [*recklessly*]. ／You *throw your money away*.

かねづまり 金詰まり ▶うちの店は今金詰まりだ Our shop *is* now *pressed for* [*short of*] *money*. ‖ 金詰まりで新しいショッピングモールの建設計画は中止になった The planning for a new shopping mall has come to a stop because of *financial difficulties*.

かねづる 金蔓 ▶いい金づるを見つける find a good *source of income*.

かねて ▶かねて(＝先に)お伝えしましたとおり, 卒業式は来週の月曜日に行われます Graduation exercises will take place next Monday as was *earlier* reported. ‖ かねてからうわさの2人が結ばれた The two, who *had been* the subject of much gossip *for some time*, at last got married.

-かねない ▶大きな余震があれば, この家は倒壊しかねない This house *could* collapse if there is a big aftershock. ‖ あいつならカンニングもやりかねないね He's the type that *could very well* be cheating on exams.

▶彼は自分の目的を遂げるためにはどんなことでもやりかねない男だ He *would do anything* to achieve his objectives. ‖ 彼女は親とけんかをして家出もしかねない様子だった She looked *ready to* leave home after arguing with her parents.

かねばなれ 金離れ ▶安田氏は金離れがいい Mr. Yasuda is *free* [*generous*] *with* (*his*) *money*.

かねまわり 金回り ▶金回りのいい不動産屋 a *well-heeled* realtor ‖ 彼女は昔より金回りがよくなった She *is better off* than she used to be. (➤be well off は「暮らし向きがよい」; 反対は be badly off) ‖ このところ金回りが悪いんだ I'm really *pressed* [*pushed*] *for money* these days. (➤後者は《英・インフォーマル》).

かねめ 金目 ▶(ホテルの)部屋には金目の物を残しておかないように Do not leave *valuables* in the room.

かねもうけ 金儲け moneymaking ▶いい金もうけの方法があるけど一緒にやらないか I know a good way to *make money*. Will you go in with me? ‖ 彼は金もうけのためならどんな危険なことでもする He is ready to risk any danger *for money* [*to get rich*].

かねもち 金持ち a **rich** [**wealthy**] **person** ; **the rich** (➤総称) ▶ロンドンのウエストエンドには金持ちがたくさん住んでいる Lots of *rich* [*wealthy*] *people* live in London's West End. ‖ **金持ちの住む地区** an *upscale* [*upmarket*] neighborhood (➤前者は《米》) ‖ 彼は金融市場への投資で金持ちになった He *became rich* [*made a fortune*] investing in the money market. ‖ おじは金持ちだ My uncle *has* (*lots of*) *money*. (➤lots of がないほうが金持ちの程度が大きい) ‖ 彼は親の遺産を相続して大金持ちになった He became *a millionaire* [*billionaire*] when he inherited a fortune from his parents. (➤millionaire, billionaire はそれぞれ百万ドル[ポンド], 十億ドル[ポンド]単位の資産を持つ「億万長者」).

かねる 兼ねる ▶首相の留守中は外相が首相代理を兼ねる During the prime minister's absence, the foreign minister *serves as* the acting prime minister. (➤serve as は「…の役目を果たす」) ‖ 仕事と観光を兼ねてインドに行く予定です I am going to India *for both* business *and* sightseeing. ‖ 仕事を兼ねて2週間イタリアを旅行する予定だ I plan to take a two-week trip to Italy, and *at the same time*, do some business.

ことわざ 大は小を兼ねる The greater serves for the lesser [smaller].

-かねる ▶急なご注文ですので残念ながら応じかねます We are sorry that we *cannot* comply with your order on such short notice. ‖ 行きたいけど, 金が無いので決めかねています I would like to go, but since I'm short on money, I really *can't make a decision* [*commit myself*] *yet*.

かねん 可燃 ▶可燃性の液体 a *flammable* liquid (➤inflammable も同じ意味で用いる). ‖ **可燃物** (a) flammable material ; flammables (総称).

[1]**かのう 可能な** **possible**
語法「A(人)が…するのは可能だ」は it is possible for A to do の形で表す. A is possible to do は不可.
▶一生懸命に勉強すれば英語を流暢に話せるようになることは**可能だ** *It is possible* (*for* you) *to* become a fluent English speaker if you study hard. ‖ それは**可能だ**が難しい仕事だ It is a *possible* but difficult task. ‖ 日本は**可能な限り**貿易を自由化すべきだ Japan should liberalize trade *as much as possible*. ‖ **可能なら**きみも参加してくれよ Join us *if you can*.
▶実行**可能な**計画を作ろう Let us come up with a *workable* [*feasible*] plan. (➤ 後者は堅い語).

[2]**かのう 化膿** ▶傷が化のうした The wound *has formed pus* [*has festered*].

かのうせい 可能性 (a) **possibility**, (a) **chance** (見込み); (a) **potential** (潜在力) ▶無限の**可能性**をもった若者たち young people with *unlimited* [*infinite*] *potential* ‖ **可能性は無限大だ** *The sky is the limit*. ‖ 年配のドライバーのほうがアクセルとブレーキを踏み間違える**可能性が高い** Elderly drivers are *more likely* to step on the gas pedal instead of the brake. ‖ 彼が当選する**可能性は無い** *There is no possibility of* his winning the election. ／*There is no possibility that* he will win the election. ‖ 彼はレギュラー選手になれる**可能性が十分ある** He *has a good chance* [*possibility*] *of* becoming a regular. ‖ 復職の**可能性を残しておきたい** I'd like to leave *open the possibility of* coming back to work. ‖ さらなる一時解雇が行われる**可能性がある** *There's a possibility of* further layoffs. ‖ テロ行為であった**可能性を排除できない** We *can't eliminate* [*rule out*] *the possibility* that it was a terrorist act.

かのじょ 彼女 **1【話し手・聞き手以外の女性を指して】** **she** (主格), **her** (所有格, 目的格); **herself** (彼女自身) ▶**彼女はいい子だね** *She*'s a nice girl, isn't she? ‖ **彼女の名前, 何ていうんだい?** What's *her* name? ‖ **彼女によろしく** Say hello to *her*.

> **あなたの英語はどう響く?**
> 日本語の「彼女」は,「彼女はアメリカから来た方で, メアリー・スミスさんとおっしゃいます」のように用いてもおかしくないが, これを *She* comes from America, and her name is Mary Smith. と直訳するのは非英語的で失礼に響く. 英語の she [he／they] は前に一度話題に上った人を指す人称代名詞なので, 名前を紹介したあとで用いるが, This is ... . と紹介する際は続く文でもう一度名前をくり返し, そのあと代名詞にする. 例えば, This is Mary Smith. Mary comes from America. She's a high school teacher. のような言い方をするのが自然で好ましい.

2【恋人】 one's **girlfriend** →ガールフレンド ▶ぼくの**彼女**はちょっと太めだ My *girlfriend* is a bit plump.

-かのように **as if** ▶彼女はその件についてすべてを知っている**かのように**話した She talked *as if* she knew everything about it. (➤「知らなかったくせに」という含みがある).

カノン 《音楽》 a **canon** ▶パッヘルベルのカノン Pachelbel's *canon*.

[1]**かば 河馬** a **hippopotamus** /hìpəpɑ́:t̬əməs/, 《インフォーマル》 a **hippo**.

[2]**かば 樺** 《植物》 a **birch tree**.

カバー **1【覆い】** a **cover** ▶ソファーに**カバーを掛ける** put *a cover* on a sofa ‖ テーブルに布の**カバーを掛ける** *cover* a table *with* a cloth ‖ 本が汚れないように**カバーを掛けた** I *covered* the book to keep it from getting dirty.
‖**カバーガール** a cover girl ‖ **おむつカバー** a diaper cover ‖ **座布団カバー** a cushion case [slip] ‖ **便座カバー** a (toilet) seat cover ‖ **枕カバー** a pillowcase.

> **危ないカタカナ語 カバー**
> 日本の書店では本を買うとカバーを掛けてくれるが, 英米には一般的にこの習慣はない. また英語の cover は「表紙」のことで, 日本でいう「ブックカバー」は (dust／book) jacket とか dust cover という(《英》では wrapper).

2【補助, 補足】 ▶パートに出て家計の**赤字をカバーする** work part-time to *help make ends meet* (➤ make ends meet は「赤字を出さないでやりくりする」) ‖ 学校を1学期間休んだから後れを**カバーしないといけない** I must *make up* the schoolwork I missed when I was out of school for one term. ‖ ピッチャーが一塁を**カバーした** The pitcher *covered* first base.

3【範囲に収める】 ▶当社の通話サービスは全国を**カバーしています** Our telephone service *covers* the whole nation.

かばう 庇う **speak up for** (弁護する); **protect** +⑪ (守る) ▶彼女を**かばう**者は誰ひとりいなかった No one *spoke up for* her. ‖ 体の弱い子は**かばって**あげなさい You should *protect* physically weak children. ‖ やくざ風の男が絡んできたので, ぼくは麗子を後ろに**かばった** Some hood started to harass us, so I pulled Reiko behind me to *protect* her. (➤「かばうために後ろに引き寄せた」の意).

がばがば ▶金が**がばがば**入ってくる I'm getting *bags of* money. ／I'm *making money hand over fist*.
▶このアンダーシャツは**がばがばだ** This undershirt *is baggy*. ‖ この靴は**がばがばだ** These shoes *are too loose* [*too big*].

かばやき 蒲焼き ▶ウナギの**かば焼き** (split and) broiled [grilled] eel seasoned with sweetened soy sauce.

かばり 蚊針・蚊鉤 a **fly**.

かばん 鞄

a **briefcase** (書類用の); a **schoolbag**, a **bookbag**, a **satchel** /sǽtʃəl/ (学校用; 最後の語は特に肩掛け式の); a **tote bag** (大型の手提げかばん); a **suitcase** (旅行用) 《参考》単に bag というと「袋」を連想させる. ▶**かばん**を提げて学校へ行く go to school swinging his [her] *bookbag* (➤ この場合の swing はかばんが前後に揺れ動くことを含みとした「ぶら下げる」の意) ‖ そのセールスマンは**かばん**からパンフレットを取り出した The salesperson took a brochure out of his [her] *briefcase*. ‖ 私は**かばん**に荷物を詰めて旅行の用意をした I have packed the *suitcase* [*traveling bag*] for our trip.
‖**かばん持ち** a private secretary (私設秘書); a hanger-on (取り巻き, 腰巾着).

がばん 画板 a **drawing board**.

かはんしん 下半身 **the lower half of the body** ▶彼は**下半身**にひどいやけどをした *The lower half of his body* was burned severely.

かはんすう 過半数 a [**the**] **majority**, **most** ▶**過半数**を得る get *a majority* ‖ 教師の**過半数**は生徒会の提案に難色を示した *The majority* [*Most*] of the teachers showed disapproval of the student council's proposal.

かひ 可否 **1【よしあし】** ▶我々はそのダム建設の**可否**に

ついて議論した We discussed whether (or not) it was *advisable* to build the dam. (➤ advisable は「(…すべきと)勧められる」).

2【賛否】pros and cons (賛成か反対か) ▶我々は婚前交渉の**可否**について議論した We discussed *the pros and cons* of premarital sexual relations.

1**かび 黴** 《米》**mold**, 《英》**mould** (食物の); **mildew** /míldjùː/ (本などの) ▶このトマトは**かびが生えている** This tomato has *mold* on it. ／There is *mold* on this tomato. ‖梅雨時には本や靴に**かびが生える** Books and shoes *get mildew* on them during the rainy season.

▶ほら, このお餅**かびだらけ**よ Look, this rice cake *is covered with mold.* ‖この押し入れ, 少し**かび臭い**よ It *smells* sort of *musty* inside this closet. (➤ mold の形容詞 moldy は「かびが生えた」の意なので「かび臭い」のときは musty を用いる).

▶あの先生の教授法は**かび臭い** (＝古臭い) That teacher's teaching method is *outdated* [*out-of-date*].

2**かび 華美な showy** (派手で目立つ); **gorgeous** (豪華で印象的) ▶**華美な**服装 *showy* clothes.

かひつ 加筆 correction to writing; **improvement** (改善, 改良) ▶詩人が私の詩に**加筆してくれた** The poet *corrected* [*improved*] my poem.

がびょう 画鋲 《米》a **thumbtack** /θʌ́mtæk/, 《英》a **drawing pin** ▶ポスターを壁に**画びょうで留める** *tack* a poster on the wall.

かびる 黴びる 《米》**mold**, 《英》**mould** ▶暖かくて湿気が多いとチーズはすぐに**かびる** Cheese *gets moldy* easily in warm, wet weather.

1**かびん 花瓶** a **vase** ▶**花瓶**に水仙を生ける arrange daffodils in *a vase*.

2**かびん 過敏な** (**very**) **sensitive** ▶私は肌が**過敏だ** I have *very sensitive* skin. ‖彼女は**神経過敏**なので扱いにくい She is so *high-strung* [*hyper*] and hard to deal with.

‖**過敏症** hypersensitivity.

かふ 寡婦 a **widow**.

1**かぶ 株 1【株式】stock** (1つの会社の株式全体); a **stock** (特定の銘柄); a **share** (1株) 《**参考**》《英》では stock は「公債」の意でも用いる. ▶父はその会社の**株**を1万**株**持っている My father has 10,000 *shares* (*of stock*) in that company. ‖彼女は時々**株**でもうける She sometimes makes money *on the stock market*. (➤ stock market は「株式市場」) ‖**鉄鋼株が上がった** *Steel stocks* have risen. ‖1929年, ウォール街で**株が大暴落した** There was a big crash in *stocks* on Wall Street in 1929. ‖ニューヨーク株式市場に日本企業として初めて**株を上場した**のはソニーだ The first Japanese firm to *get a listing* [*go public*] on the New York Stock Exchange was Sony.

2【評価】▶満塁ホームランで吉沢の**株が上がった** Yoshizawa's *stock* (*on the team*) *has improved* [*risen*] since he hit that grand slam. ‖彼は**成長株**だ He is a *promising* young man. (➤ promising は「将来性のある」).

3【根付きの植物】▶プランターにミニトマトを3**株**植える plant three cherry tomato *plants* [*seedlings*] in a planter ‖スズランを**株分けする** *divide the roots* of lilies of the valley.

☛ **お株, 株券, 株式, 株主** (⇀見出語)

2**かぶ 蕪** 《植物》a **turnip** /tə́ːˈnɪp/.

3**かぶ 下部 the lower part**

‖**下部構造** a substructure ‖**下部組織** a subordinate organization (従属する組織); a subsidiary (子会社).

かふう 家風 a **family tradition** [**custom**] ▶大塚君の家と私の家とでは**家風が異なる** Otsuka's family and my [our] family *do things* (*quite*) *differently*.

カフェ café (喫茶店)

‖**カフェオレ** café au lait /kæ̀feɪ oʊ léɪ/ (➤ coffee with milk の意味のフランス語から) ‖**カフェテラス** a sidewalk café ／an outdoor café ‖**カフェ・ラテ** a latte ／a caffè latte (➤ milk coffee の意味のイタリア語から).

カフェイン caffein(e) /kæfíːn/ ▶**カフェイン抜き**のコーヒー *decaffeinated* coffee ／decaf.

カフェテリア a **cafeteria** /kæ̀fətíəriə/.

かぶか 株価 a **stock price** ▶**株価**は政局を反映して上下する *Stock prices* rise and fall in response to the political situation.

がぶがぶ ▶彼はその酒を**がぶがぶ飲んだ** He *guzzled down* the sake. ‖冷たいものを**がぶがぶ飲む**と下痢をするよ If you *guzzle* cold drinks, you will get diarrhea.

かぶき 歌舞伎 kabuki (➤ 英語化している); a **kabuki drama**

日本紹介 ✉ **歌舞伎は江戸時代に盛んになった伝統舞台芸術で, 演劇・舞踊・音楽を合わせた総合芸術です. 女性の役もすべて男が演じます** Kabuki is a traditional performing art that synthesizes drama, dance and music and became popular during the Edo period. All roles, including female ones, are played by men.

‖**歌舞伎役者** a kabuki actor.

かふく 禍福 fortune and misfortune ▶ ことわざ **禍福は**あざなえる縄のごとし In life, fortune and misfortune come and go. ／Life is full of ups and downs.

かふくぶ 下腹部 the lower abdomen.

かぶけん 株券 a **stock certificate**; 《インフォーマル》a **stock**, a **share**.

かぶさる 被さる ▶布団が**かぶさって**乳児が窒息死した The baby suffocated when her [his] head *was covered by* the quilt.

▶彼がやり残した仕事が私に**かぶさってきた** I *got stuck with* the work he had left undone. (➤ get stuck with は「…を押しつけられる」).

かぶしき 株式 stock (1つの会社の株式全体); 《英》**stocks and shares** (いろいろな株をまとめて) ⇀**株, 株券, 株主** ▶**株式を発行する** issue *stock* ‖最近は**株式相場**の変動が激しい *Stock prices* fluctuate greatly nowadays. ‖当社は10年前に**株式を公開しました** We *went public* ten years ago.

‖**株式市場** the stock market ‖**株式取引所** a stock exchange.

かぶしきがいしゃ 株式会社

> **《解説》**(1)「株式会社」には《米》では corporation, incorporated company などが, 《英》では company limited by shares, limited liability company などが相当する.
>
> (2)「富士株式会社」のような社名は《米》では Fuji Corporation ／Fuji Corp. ／Fuji Incorporated ／Fuji Inc., 《英》では Fuji Co., Ltd. ／Fuji Limited ／Fuji Ltd. などのように表記する.

カフス(ボタン) cuff /kʌf/ **links** (➤ 通例複数形で; 単に links ともいう) ▶**カフスボタンを掛ける**[**外す**] fasten [remove] *cuff links*.

危ないカタカナ語✹ カフス
「カフス」は cuff (袖口) の複数形 cuffs からきたことば. ワイシャツの袖口を留めるアクセサリーの「カフスボタン」は和製語で, 英語では cuff links という. なお, 袖口に縫いつけた貝のボタンは cuff buttons または sleeve buttons という.

かぶせる 被せる cover +㊐ (隠すように覆う) ▶チューリップの球根を植えて土をかぶせる plant tulip bulbs and *cover* them *with* earth ‖ 鍋に蓋をかぶせる *put* a lid *on* the pot ‖ 車にシートをかぶせる *cover* the car *with* a (sheet of) tarpaulin.
▶彼らは事業失敗の責任を私にかぶせた They *put* [*laid*] the blame for the business failure *on* me.

カプセル a **capsule** /kǽpsəl ‖ -sjuːl/ ▶錠剤２錠とカプセル１錠を食後に服用のこと Take two of the tablets and one *capsule* after meals. ‖ **カプセルホテル** a capsule hotel (➤ カプセルは a sleeping module) ‖ **タイムカプセル** a time capsule.

かふそく 過不足 ▶母親は４人の子供にキャンデーを過不足なく分配した The mother distributed the candies *equally* among her four children.

カプチーノ (a) **cappuccino.**

かぶと 兜 a (war) **helmet** ▶《慣用表現》きみはほんとにテニスがうまいね. かぶとを脱ぐよ You're a really good tennis player! *I take off my hat to you.*
ことわざ 勝ってかぶとの緒を締めよ Fasten your helmet string tight after you win. (➤ 日本語からの直訳) / Keep your guard up even after a victory. (➤「勝っても油断するな」の意).

かぶとむし 甲虫・兜虫 a **beetle**
《参考》beetle は広く甲虫類の総称で, クワガタムシ (stag beetle), カミキリムシ (long-horned beetle), ハンミョウ (tiger beetle) などを含む. 日本のカブトムシと同じものは英米にはいない.

かぶぬし 株主 《主に米》 a **stockholder,** 《主に英》 a **shareholder** ‖ **株主総会** a stockholders' [shareholders'] meeting.

がぶのみ がぶ飲み ▶ビールをがぶ飲みする *guzzle* beer ‖ 旅人は水をがぶ飲みした The traveler *gulped* water *greedily* [*thirstily*].

がぶり ▶あの川では何人かの人がワニに足首をがぶりとやられた Several people *had* their ankles *snapped at* by crocodiles in that river. (➤ snap at は「ぱくんとかみつく」).

かぶりつき かぶり付き a **front-row seat** (最前列の席) ; 《英》 **the stalls** ; a **ringside seat** (相撲などの).

かぶりつく ▶その少年はスイカにかぶりついた The boy *bit into* [*sank his teeth into*] the watermelon.

かぶる 被る

1【頭を覆う】put on ; wear (かぶっている) ▶野球帽をかぶる *put on* a baseball cap ‖ ぼくたちは麦わら帽子をかぶってセミを捕りに行った We *put on* broad-brimmed straw hats and went off to catch cicadas. ‖ 多くの子供たちがかつて巨人軍のマークのついた野球帽をかぶっていた Many children used to *wear* Giants baseball caps. ‖ 父は陳列棚の帽子を２つ３つかぶってみた My father *tried on* several hats from the showcase. (➤ try on は「試しに身に着けてみる」の意) ‖ 妹は雷の音を聞くと頭から毛布をかぶった My little sister *pulled* a blanket *over* her head when she heard the thunder.
2【上から浴びる】▶漁船は大波をかぶって転覆しそうになった The fishing boat *was dashed* by a big wave and was almost overturned. ‖ その机はほこりをかぶっていた The desk *was covered with* dust.
3【引き受ける】▶その組員は親分の罪をかぶった The gangster *took the rap for a crime* his boss had committed. (➤ take the rap は「人の犯した罪を着る」の意のインフォーマルな表現).

-かぶれ ▶アメリカかぶれした英語の先生 an *excessively Americanized* teacher of English / a teacher of English who *tries to act just like an American* ‖ 西洋かぶれした人 an *excessively Westernized* person.

かぶれる 1【皮膚が】get an allergic reaction ▶妹は漆にかぶれた My little sister *had an allergic reaction* from lacquer. / My little sister *got a rash* from touching lacquer. (➤ rash は「発疹(ほっしん)」).
2【主義・思想などに】▶彼は原理主義にかぶれているようだ He seems to *have become infected* [*greatly influenced*] by fundamentalism.

かふん 花粉 pollen /pɑ́ːlən/ ▶私は春先になると花粉症に悩まされる I suffer from *hay fever* [*pollen allergy*] in early spring.
‖ (空気中の) **花粉数** a pollen count.

《解説》「花粉症」について
(1)「花粉症」は hay fever または pollen allergy (花粉アレルギー) という. アメリカでは ragweed (ブタクサ) の花粉によるものがいちばん多く, 多数の患者が出るのは夏の終わりから秋にかけてである. なお, 病名としての「花粉症」は医学用語で pollinosis という.
(2) 日本に多い「杉花粉症」は hay fever caused by cedar pollen または cedar pollen allergy といえばよい.

かべ 壁 1【仕切り】a wall ▶コンクリートの壁 a concrete *wall* ‖ 白い壁の家 a house with white *walls* / a white-*walled* house ‖ 壁に絵を掛ける hang a picture on the *wall* ‖ 壁にしっくいを塗る plaster the *wall* ‖ 壁の穴から隣の部屋をのぞいてみた I peeped into the next room through *a hole in the wall.*
ことわざ 壁に耳あり (障子に目あり) Walls have ears (and *shoji* have eyes). (➤ Walls have ears. は英語のことわざ).
‖ **壁掛け** a wall ornament ‖ **壁紙** wallpaper.
2【障害】▶ことばの壁 a language *barrier* ‖ 交渉は壁にぶつかった (= 行き詰まった) The negotiations *were deadlocked* [*were stalemated*]. (➤ 後者はチェスに由来する語で「手詰まりになる」の意) ‖ 彼は三段跳びで初めて18メートルの壁を破った He was the first man to break the 18-meter *barrier* in the triple jump.

かへい 貨幣 money (お金) ; **currency** (通貨) ; a **coin** (硬貨) ▶10万円をイギリス貨幣に交換してほしいのですが I would like 100,000 yen in *British currency.* / I would like to exchange 100,000 yen into *pounds.* ‖ 最近のインフレで貨幣価値が下がった *The value of money* has declined because of recent inflation. ‖ **貨幣経済** a monetary economy ‖ **貨幣制度** the monetary [currency] system ‖ **貨幣単位** a currency [monetary] unit.

かべん 花弁 a **petal.**

[1]かほう 家宝 a **family heirloom** /éəʳluːm/, an **heirloom** ▶このつぼは家宝だから大切に扱いなさい This vase is *a family heirloom,* so handle it with care.

[2]かほう 下方に below, downward ▶展望台からはるか下

方に諏訪湖を望むことができます From the observation deck, you can see Lake Suwa *far below*. ‖ その会社の業績見通しは**下方修正された** The company's earnings forecast *was revised downward*. ‖**下方修正** (a) downward revision.

か

3**かほう 果報** ▶ ことわざ **果報は寝て待て** Good luck comes to a person who waits. ／All good things come to those who wait. (➤ 後者は忍耐の重要性を述べたもの).

がぼがぼ ▶水を飲み過ぎておなかが**ガボガボいっている** My stomach *is gurgling* because I drank too much water.

かほご 過保護 overprotection ▶**過保護な母親** an *overprotective* mother ／a helicopter mother ‖ **過保護の**子供 an *overprotected* child ‖ 彼女は息子に対して**過保護すぎる** She *is excessively protective of* her son. ‖ その子は一人息子なので両親に**過保護に育てられた** Since he is an only son, his parents *have been overprotective of* him.

かぼそい か細い ▶**か細い**声 a *light, thin* voice ‖ 彼女は体つきは**か細い**けど力は強いんだ She is *slim* but strong.

かぼちゃ 《植物》 a **(kabocha) squash**, a **Japanese [kabocha] pumpkin** (➤ 日本で普通に食べているのは winter squash (冬かぼちゃ) の一種で, 日本語でそのまま kabocha と呼ぶこともある. pumpkin ですぐ連想するのは, ハロウィーンのときにカボチャちょうちん (jack-o'-lantern) を作って飾るのに用いるオレンジ色の皮の厚い大きなかぼちゃ).

カポック 《植物》 a **dwarf schefflera** (➤ kapok は別種の木).

1**かま 釜** an **iron pot** ▶ご飯を**釜で**炊く boil rice in *an iron pot*.
▶《慣用表現》中村氏とは大学時代に2年間**同じ釜の飯を食った**仲だ I *lived under the same roof* as Mr. Nakamura for two years during college. (➤「同じ寮などに住んだ」の意).

2**かま 窯** a **kiln** ‖**窯元** a pottery.

3**かま 鎌** a **sickle** (片手用の) ▶《慣用表現》あなたにそんな聞き方をして, 彼女は**鎌を掛けた**んじゃないの? By questioning you like that, she was probably trying to *trick you into telling the truth*.

1**がま** 《動物》 a **toad** (ヒキガエル).

2**がま** 《植物》 a **cattail**.

かまう 構う

📖 訳語メニュー
気配りする →pay attention to **1**
気にする →care, mind **2**
からかう →tease **3**

1 【世話をする】 pay attention 《to》 ▶主人はとても忙しくて子供たちを**構ってくれません** My husband is really busy and won't *pay attention to* the children. ‖ 彼女は息子のことを**構い過ぎる** (＝過保護だ) She *is too protective* toward [of] her son. ／She *is overprotective* [*overly protective*] *of* her son. ‖ その女の子はちょっと**構ってもらいたいだけだった** The girl just *wanted* some *attention*.

2 【気にする】 (「かまわない」の形で) **not mind** +㊐ (嫌でない, 気にしない) ; **not care** 《about》 (どうでもいい) ▶少しくらいの不便 [長時間労働] **はかまいません** I do*n't mind* a little inconvenience [the long hours]. ‖ 彼は身なりを**かまわない** He does*n't care about* [*is indifferent to*] his appearance. ／He does*n't care* what he looks like [wears]. (➤ what, how などの疑問詞が続くときは about は省略することが多い) ‖ 費用 [時間] はいくらかかっても**かまいません** I do*n't care* how much it costs [how long it takes]. ‖ ぼくはどちらが勝とうが別に**かまわない** I do*n't* particularly *care* who wins. ‖ そんなこと, **誰がかまうものか** *Who cares about that?* ‖ 思っていることを**かまわず言ってください** Please *speak your mind* (*without hesitation*). ‖ 遅れた人に**かまわず**, 先に行ってください Please go (on) ahead. You *don't have to wait for* [*worry about* ／ *be concerned about*] the latecomers.

【文型】
…してもかまわない
I don't mind doing
(たとえ)～でもかまわない
I don't care if S + V.
I don't mind if S + V.

▶私は真ん中の席で**もかまいません** *I don't mind* tak*ing* a center seat. ‖ 少し待って**もかまいません** I *don't mind* wait*ing* for a while. ‖ きみが茶髪にしようが赤く染めようが**かまわない** *I don't care if* you dye your hair brown or dye it red. ‖ 暖房を止めて**もかまいません** *I don't mind if* you turn off the heater.

【文型】
～してもかまいませんか
Do you mind if I do?
Would you mind if I did?

【解説】 (1)下の Would で聞くほうが丁寧. Would のあとでは if の文の動詞は過去形にする.
(2) if の文の代わりに my doing の形も使われる. I や my は誰がするかで変える.
(3)答え方に注意する.
(4)単に「…していいですか」という気持ちでは, May I ～?, Can I ～? と聞く.

▶ 対話 「たばこ吸って**もかまいませんか**」「どうぞ」 "*Do you mind if I* smoke?" "No. Please go ahead." (➤ (1) mind は「気にする」の意だから, Do you mind ...? で聞かれたら,「どうぞ」は「気にしません」の意の No. で答える. (2) 反対に「いえ, 困ります」は I'm afraid I do (mind). だが, ふつうは穏やかに I'd rather you didn't (smoke). (お控えいただければと存じます) という) ‖ 対話 「ご一緒させていただいて**かまいませんか**」「ええ, どうぞ」 "*Do you mind if* I join you? ／*Would you mind if* I joined you?" "(No.) Please do. ／No problem."
▶あなたの代わりに誰が式に出席して**もかまいません** *It doesn't matter* who attends the ceremony in your stead. (➤ matter は「問題である」) ‖ **何時でもかまわないから**, きょう中に電話をくれ *It doesn't matter when*, but please call me today. ‖ 子供さんを連れて来て**もかまいませんよ** *It's all right* [*okay*] *to* bring your children. ‖ 対話 「どんなラケットが欲しいですか」「どんなのでも**かまいません**」 "What type of racket do you want?" "Any kind *is okay*." ‖ 対話 「あすの夕方の5時ではどうでしょうか」「**私のほうはかまいません**」 "How about five o'clock tomorrow evening?" "*That's OK* [*fine*] *with me*."

3 【いじめる】 tease +㊐ ▶猫を**構ってはいけません** Don't *tease* the cat. (➤ tease は「からかう」).

☞ **お構い, お構いなし** (→見出語)

かまえ 構え ▶彼の新居はどっしりした**構え** (＝外観) の家だ His new house has an imposing *appearance*.

‖危険を感じてとっさに身を守る**構え**(＝姿勢)をした I sensed danger and instinctively took a defensive *stance*.

かまえる 構える **1【身構える】**▶刀を上段に**構える** *hold* a sword over one's head ‖キャッチャーは低く**構えた** The catcher *knelt down* for a low pitch. (➤ knelt /nelt/ は kneel (ひざまずく) の過去形) ‖すばらしい塔に感心して私はカメラを**構えた** Admiring the magnificent tower, I *aimed* [*pointed*] my camera at it. ‖2人の兵士が銃を**構えて**門の前に立っていた Two soldiers stood in front of the gate with their rifles *at the ready*. (➤ at the ready は「すぐ発射できる状態で」).

2【住居などを】▶彼は結婚して一家を**構えた** He got married and *set up house* [*established a family*]. ‖(アメリカの外交官)タウンゼンド・ハリスは1856年に下田に居を**構えた** Townsend Harris *took up residence* in Shimoda in 1856.

かまきり《虫》a (**praying**) **mantis** ▶雌のカマキリは交尾中あるいは交尾後に相手の雄を食うことがよくある The female *mantis* often eats its mate during or after copulation.

がまぐち 蝦蟇口 a (**coin** ／**change**) **purse** ▶がまぐちに小銭を入れる put some change in one's *coin purse*.

かまくら a ***kamakura***; snow hut dedicated to the water god where children have fun(➤説明的な訳).

かまける ▶仕事にかまけて家庭を顧みてこなかった *Most of my time has been taken up with* work and I haven't paid enough attention to my family.

かまど a ***kamado***; traditional earthen cooking stove(➤説明的な訳) ▶かまどで炊いたご飯はおいしい Rice cooked on *a kamado* tastes good.

かまとと ▶彼女はかまととぶっているのでみんなに嫌われている Everyone dislikes her because she *pretends to be innocent about sex* [because she *acts like a prude*]. (➤ prude は「セックスに関する話題を嫌ってお上品ぶる人」).

かまびすしい noisy(うるさい) ▶早朝からカラスがかまびすしい Crows *have been making a racket* from early morning. ‖外野がかまびすしい Outsiders *are making all sorts of* (*uncalled-for*) *comments*.

かまぼこ 蒲鉾 steamed fish paste ▶かまぼこ形の屋根 a *semicylindrical* roof.

かまもと 窯元 a **pottery**.

かまわない 構わない →構う.

がまん 我慢

patience /péiʃəns/ **一動 我慢する be patient** (不便・不幸などに沈着冷静でいる); **stand** +㊀ (自制心を働かせて); **bear** +㊀ (痛み・苦しみなどの重さに); **put up with** (不平を言わずに)

《解説》(1)日本語の「我慢」には苦しみ・悲しみなどを表に出さず，耐えて乗り越えるとか，意地でしのぎとおすという含みがあることが多いが，英語にはその含みを持った1語はない.
(2)近似の英語は patience だが，これは「不平を言わずに[沈着冷静に]苦痛や試練に耐えること」ということで，受け身的な面を強調し，「乗り越える」とか「意地でしのぐ」という点にまでは言及していない．したがって，その点を考慮に入れた上で，例示したような語句を用いて適宜表現するとよい.

▶**我慢しなさい** *Be patient*. (➤命令形ではこの語を使って言うのがふつう) ‖映画の上映中におしゃべりする人には**我慢できない** I *can't stand* people who talk during movies. ‖この騒音には**我慢できない** I *can't put up with* all this noise. ‖私はうそつきには**我慢できない** I *have no patience with* liars. ‖隣の家の人のピアノにはもう**我慢できない**わ I'*ve lost patience with* my neighbor's loud piano playing. ‖私ならあんな失礼なこと**我慢できない**わ I *wouldn't take* that kind of rudeness (from anyone). (➤この take は「受け入れる」) ‖あいつの身勝手さにはもう**我慢できん**！ *I've had enough of* his selfishness! (➤「もう十分だ，うんざりだ」の意).

▶腹が立ったけれど**我慢した** I *controlled* [*bottled up*] my anger. ‖コーヒー切らしてるの．紅茶で**我慢してください**る？ I'm sorry, I'm out of coffee now. Would tea be *all right* with you instead? ‖おなかが痛かったが歯を食いしばって**我慢した** My stomach hurt, but I gritted my teeth and *bore* it. (➤ bore は bear の過去形) ‖睡眠4時間で**我慢した** I *made do with* four hours' sleep. (➤ make do with A は「十分ではないがAで間に合わせる」) ‖笑いたいのを**我慢する**のは大変だった I had a hard time *holding back* my laughter [*keeping myself from* laugh*ing*]. ‖もっとポテトチップスを食べたいという気持ちを**我慢できなかった** I *couldn't restrain* [*keep*] *myself from* eating more potato chips. ／I *couldn't control* my urge to eat more potato chips. ‖**対話**「ママ，トイレに行きたいよ」「次の駅に着くまで**我慢しなさい**」"Mom, I want to go to the restroom." "*Wait* until we get to the next stop." ‖眠気を**我慢する** *fight* drowsiness.

▶日本人は騒音に対して実に**我慢強い**と思う Japanese people seem to *be* very *patient with* [*have a* high *tolerance for*] noise. (➤ tolerance は「寛容」) ‖豊かな社会の子供たちは**我慢強さに欠ける** Children in affluent societies lack (in) *patience*. ‖あなたって**我慢強い**のね！ You're so *patient*! ‖こうなったらお互い**我慢比べ**だ Now we'll see *who holds out the longer*. (➤ hold out は「持ちこたえる」).

[1]かみ 神

a ***kami***, a **god**, a **deity** /díːəṭi, déiəṭi/; **God**

《解説》「神」と God
(1)日本人の一般的な宗教意識にはキリスト教の場合のような唯一絶対の神 God は存在しないので，日本の「神」は小文字の god (「女神」は goddess) で表すか，*kami* (複数形も *kami*), divine being, higher power などを使って表現する. (2) deity は god の意のやや古風な語で，「神性をもつもの」の意でも用いる.

▶家庭に祭ってある**神さま** a household *god* ‖神道の**神** a Shinto *god* ‖農耕の**神** an agrarian *god* ‖縁結びの**神** the *god* of marriage ‖八百万(やおよろず)の**神** the eight million *kami* [*deities*] ／a myriad of *kami* ‖《キリスト教の》**全知全能の神** *the Almighty God* ／*God Almighty* ‖古代ギリシャ[ローマ]の**神々** the *gods* of ancient Greece [Rome].

▶**神**を信じる believe in the Shinto *gods* (➤キリスト教の神を信じる場合は believe in God) ‖**神**に懸けて誓う *swear* [*promise*] *to God* ‖大学入試の合格を**神**さまに祈る pray to *the kami* [*the Shinto gods*] for success in college entrance exams.

▶《比喩的》お客さまは**神さま**です The customer is the king. ／The customer is always right. (➤「客の言うことは常に正しい」の意のことわざ).

ことわざ **苦しい時の神頼み** People turn to the gods [religion] in times of distress.

か

☛ 神懸かる (→見出語)

2**かみ** 紙 **paper** ▶1枚の紙 a sheet of *paper* ‖ 大きい紙 a large piece of *paper* ‖ 紙2枚 two sheets of *paper* ‖ 手すきの紙 hand-made *paper* ‖ 紙の人形 a *paper* doll ‖ 紙切れ a slip [scrap] of *paper* ‖ 思いついたことを紙に書いた I put my ideas (down) on *paper*. ‖ この鶴は紙でできている This crane is made of *paper*. ‖ この紙は薄すぎて字が書けない This *paper* is too thin to write on. (➤「字」は訳出不要) ‖ 何かもっと厚い紙ない? Don't you have any thicker *paper*?

‖**紙おむつ** a paper diaper /dáɪəpəʳ/ ‖ **紙コップ** a paper cup ‖ **紙タオル** a paper towel /táʊəl/ ‖ **紙ナプキン** a paper napkin ‖ **紙ばさみ** a folder, a paper file ‖ **紙袋** a paper bag ‖ **紙やすり** sandpaper.

逆引き熟語 ○○紙
厚紙[段ボール紙] cardboard / **折り紙** *origami*, folding paper / **画用紙** drawing paper / **感熱紙** thermal paper / **光沢紙** coated paper / **コピー紙** photocopy [copying] paper / **再生紙** recycled paper / **台紙** a mount / **包装紙** wrapping paper / **和紙** Japanese paper

3**かみ** 髪 **hair**(➤ 1本の髪の毛は a hair) ▶ふさふさした髪 thick *hair* ‖ (1本1本の)太い[細い]髪 a coarse [fine] *hair* (➤ coarse は /kɔːʳs/ と発音する) ‖ 髪にブラシをかける brush one's *hair* ‖ 父は髪が薄くなってきた My father is losing his *hair*. ‖ 彼女は髪が長い She has long *hair*. (➤ Her hair is long. より好まれる) ‖ 強い風でせっかくセットした髪が乱れてしまった A strong wind came and ruined my carefully set *hairdo*. (➤ hairdo /héəʳdùː/ は「髪型」) ‖ 今日は髪型が決まらない Today I'm *having a bad hair day*. (➤「今日はうまくいかない日だ」のように比喩的にも用いられる; →テンション) ‖ ぼくのおじいちゃんは髪がちょっとしか無い My grandfather doesn't have much *hair*. ‖ 髪は女の命という It's said that a woman's *hair* is her main charm. 《参考》聖書には A woman's hair is her glory. (髪は女の誉れなり)ということばがある. 『コリント人への手紙』11:15. ‖ **対話** 「みっちゃん, 私の髪の形どう?」「とってもいいわよ」 "How do you like my *hair* this way, Mitchan?" "It looks nice."

▶美容院へ行って髪をカットしてきます I'm going to the beauty salon to *get my hair cut*. (◉「美容院で髪をカットしてもらう」の意なので, 訳例のようにする. cut my hair とすると自分で自分の髪をカットすることになる) ‖ 太郎ちゃん, あなた髪を刈らなきゃ You need *a haircut*, Taro. / You should *get a haircut*, Taro. ‖ 高校野球の選手たちは髪を短くしている High school baseball players *wear their hair close-cropped*. ‖ 日本の女性の中には正月に髪を日本髪に結う人もいる In Japan, there are some women who *do up their hair in Japanese style* on New Year's Day. ‖ 助手席に髪の毛が落ちていた I found *a hair* on the passenger seat.

‖**髪飾り** a hair ornament ‖ **髪型** a hairstyle, a hairdo [複 ~ s].

4**かみ** 加味 ▶成績には平常点を加味します Your class work will *affect* your grades.

かみ- 神- 《解説》最上級の素晴らしさをほめて「神-」, 「神ってる」などというが, これにぴったりの英語はない. 「すばらしい」に当たる awesome や「驚くほどすごい」の amazing を強めるのが一つの方法である. ▶神アプリ a *killer* app ‖ 店員の問題処理法はまさに神対応であった The salesclerk's way of dealing with the problem was *pretty* [*totally*] *awesome*.

かみあう 噛み合う **mesh, engage** (歯車が; 後者のほうが堅い) ▶この歯車の歯はかみ合わない The cogs in this machine do not *mesh* [*engage*]. ‖ 私の歯はよくかみ合わない My teeth don't *fit together* well. / I have a poor bite.

▶彼女と私の意見は平行線をたどってかみ合わなかった She and I argued on different planes, and *got nowhere*. (➤ get nowhere は「結論が出ない」).

かみあわせ 噛み合わせ a **bite**, 《医学》**occlusion** /əklúːʒən/ (➤ 後者は専門用語で「咬合(こう)」に相当) ▶私の歯はかみ合わせが悪い My *bite* is not good.

かみがかる 神懸かる ▶彼の言動は神懸かっている His words and actions are those of *a fanatic*. (➤ fanatic は「狂信者」).

がみがみ ▶こんな成績じゃあまたおふくろにがみがみ言われそうだ With these grades, my mom's going to *get on my back* again. (➤ get on ~'s back は「~に小言を言う」) ‖ 彼はたばこをやめるよう奥さんにしょっちゅうがみがみ言われている He is always *being nagged* by his wife to stop smoking.

かみき 上期 **the first half of the year.** →上半期.

かみきる 噛み切る **bite off** ▶この餅, 硬くてかみ切れないよ This mochi [rice cake] is so tough I can't *bite off* a piece. ‖ つながれていた犬は綱をかみ切った The tethered dog *bit* the rope *in two*.

かみきれ 紙切れ a **piece of paper** ▶会社の倒産で株券が紙切れ同然となった Owing to the company's bankruptcy, its stock *became worthless as so many pieces of paper*.

かみくず 紙屑 **wastepaper; litter** (道路などに散らかったごみや紙くず) ▶オフィスからは紙くずが多量に出る An office produces a great deal of *wastepaper*. ‖ 公園には紙くずがいっぱい散らばっていた The park was littered with *wastepaper*. / There was *litter* everywhere in the park. (➤ 後者は空き缶・瓶・ごみなども含む). ‖**紙くず籠** a wastebasket, a wastepaper basket.

かみくだく 噛み砕く **crunch** +Ⓔ (ガリガリと); **chew** +Ⓔ (軟らかくなるまで) ▶骨をガリガリかみ砕く *crunch* a bone. ▶その講演者は抽象的なテーマをかみ砕いて説明した The lecturer explained the abstract subject *in simple, clear words*.

かみころす 噛み殺す **1【かんで殺す】bite to death** ▶野犬が子供をかみ殺した A wild dog *bit* the child *to death*. (➤ bit は bite の過去形).

2【抑える】stifle /stáɪfəl/ +Ⓔ ▶あくびをかみ殺す *stifle* [*smother*] a yawn.

かみざ 上座 ▶誰が上座に座るかでもめた They made a fuss about who would take *the best seat* [sit at *the head of the table*]. (➤ 前者は部屋の上席, 後者は食卓の上座).

かみさま 神様 →神 ▶松下幸之助は「経営の神様」と呼ばれた Matsushita Konosuke was called "*the king* [*genius*] *of management*." (◉ 英語では「王」とか「天才」と表現し, god とはいわない).

かみさん a **wife** ▶魚屋のおかみさん a fish dealer's *wife* ‖ かみさん(=女房)に電話しとかなくっちゃ I've got to call home to my *wife*.

かみしばい 紙芝居 (a) **kamishibai** (➤ 英語になっている; a picture card show といってもよい. 絵1枚は story card と呼べばよい).

かみしめる 噛み締める ▶スルメはかみしめるほど味が出

る The more you *munch* [*chew*] on dried cuttlefish, the more intense its taste becomes. ‖ 彼は悔しさに**唇をかみしめた** He *bit his lip* in frustration.
▶その話から得た教訓をじっくり**かみしめた** I *meditated* [*ruminated*] *on* the moral of the story.

かみしも 裃 ***kamishimo***; a samurai's formal attire(➤ 説明的な訳).

かみそり 剃刀 a **razor** /réɪzəʳ/ ▶**かみそり負けする** *get razor rash* ‖ ぼくは毎朝**電気かみそり**でひげをそります I shave with *an electric razor* every morning. ‖ 彼の頭は**かみそりのように切れる** His mind is *razor-sharp* [*is as sharp as a razor*].

かみだな 神棚 a ***kamidana***
日本紹介 ✉ **神棚は家庭内に置かれた, 日本古来の宗教である神道の神を祭った棚で, ふつう鴨居(かもい)の上にあります. 以前はどこの家にもありましたが, 最近の家では作らないことも多くなっています** *Kamidana* are household altars dedicated to the gods of Shinto(ism), a religion indigenous to Japan. They are usually placed above the lintel. Every home used to have a *kamidana*, but many modern homes don't have one.

かみだのみ 神頼み ⇀**神**.

かみつ 過密な **tight**; **hectic** (大忙しの) ▶大都市の列車ダイヤは**過密だ** In big cities train schedules are *tight*. ‖ あのテレビタレントは**過密スケジュール**に追われている That TV personality is pressed by a *tight* [*hectic*] *schedule*. ‖ 東京は世界でも有数の**過密都市**だ Tokyo is one of the world's most *overpopulated* [*overcrowded*] *cities*.

かみつく 噛み付く **1【かむ】** **bite** +⊕ ▶その猛犬は私の左足に**かみついた** The fierce dog *bit* me on [in] the left leg. (➤ bit は bite の過去形.「bite ＋人＋体の部位」はまず, かみつく対象全体をいい, 続いてその具体的部位をいう形で, 部位よりも対象に焦点があり, bite my left leg より好まれる言い方).
2【食ってかかる】 ▶キャッチャーはアンパイアの「ボール」の判定に**かみついた** The catcher *bit* [*snapped*] the umpire's *head off* for calling it a ball. (➤ bite [snap] ~'s head off は「〜に食ってかかる」の意のインフォーマルな表現).

かみづつみ 紙包み a **thing wrapped in paper**, a **paper parcel**.

かみづまり 紙詰まり ▶このコピー機はよく**紙詰まり**を起こす *Paper* often *gets jammed* in this copy machine. ／This copy machine often *jams* (*up*).

かみて 上手 **the left side of the stage**(舞台の) (➤ 日本語では観客から見て右・左をそれぞれ上手, 下手というが, 英語では舞台上の俳優の位置から見るので, 日本語の上手・下手は, それぞれ the left side (of the stage), the right side (of the stage) となる) ▶団十郎は**舞台の上手から**登場した Danjuro came to the stage *from stage left*. (➤ この場合の stage left は舞台慣用句で, 反対は stage right).

かみなり 雷 **thunder**(雷鳴); a **thunderstorm** (激しい雷雨) (➤「鳴る」のは thunder で,「光る」のは lightning. また,「落ちる」のも lightning のほうである)
▶遠くで**雷が鳴っている** *There is thunder* in the distance. ／*Thunder* is rolling [rumbling] in the distance. (➤ rumble は遠くで低くゴロゴロ鳴る音をいう) ‖ 近くに**雷が落ちた**ようだ It looks like *lightning struck* nearby. ‖ 彼は農作業の最中に**雷に打たれて死んだ** He *was struck dead by lightning* while he was working on the farm. ‖《天気予報》今晩は大雨になり, 所によっては**雷が鳴る**でしょう There will be a downpour this evening with occasional *thunder* (*and lightning*).
▶《慣用表現》課長はその新入社員に**雷を落とした** The section chief *yelled* [*thundered*] *at* the new employee. (➤ 後者はやや文語的) ‖ あの**雷おやじ**め! That *grouchy old man*! (➤ grouchy /gráʊtʃi/ は「不機嫌な」の意).

かみねんど 紙粘土 **papier-mâché** /pèɪpəʳ məʃéɪ, pæpieɪmæʃeɪ/.

かみのけ 髪の毛 **hair**; a **hair**(1本). ⇀**髪**.

かみはんき 上半期 **the first half of the year** ▶2012年度**上半期**の営業成績 the sales record of *the first half* of fiscal 2012.

かみひとえ 紙一重 ▶入選作と落選作の差は**紙一重だった** There was only *a razor's edge of difference* between the works that won prizes and those that were rejected. ／The difference between the winning works and the rejected ones was *very slight*. ‖ 天才と狂気は**紙一重** There's *a fine line* between genius and insanity.

かみふぶき 紙吹雪 **confetti** /kənféṭi/ ▶**紙吹雪**が新婚の2人の頭上に舞った *Confetti* was fluttered over the newly married couple's heads.

かみやすり 紙やすり **sandpaper**.

かみよ 神代 **the age of the gods** ▶**神代の昔から** *from time immemorial*(➤ 太古から).

かみわける 噛み分ける ▶**酸いも甘いもかみ分けた人** *an experienced* [*a seasoned*] *person* ／*a man* [*woman*] *of the world*(➤ 後者は「世の中がよくわかっている人」の意).

かみわざ 神業 a **miracle** (奇跡); a **superhuman** [**spectacular**] **feat** (人間業とは思えない[目をみはるような]妙技) ▶これぞまさしく**神業だ** It's *a miracle*! ‖ 彼のヘディングシュートは**神業に近い** His header are practically *superhuman feats*.

かみん 仮眠 a **nap** ▶**仮眠をとる** take [have] *a nap*.

カミングアウト **coming out**(➤ 英語ではふつう「同性愛者であることを公言する」の意で, 日本語のように広く「知られたくないことを告白する」という使い方はしない).

[1]**かむ 噛む** **bite** (+⊕) (かみつく, かみ切る); **chew** (+⊕) (かみ砕く) ▶爪を**かむな** Don't *bite* your nails. ‖ 犬に手を**かまれた** My hand *was bitten* by a dog. (➤ bitten は bite の過去分詞形) ‖ 犬が人をかんでもニュースにならないが, 人が犬をかめばこれはニュースだ When a dog *bites* a man that is not news, but when a man *bites* a dog that is news. (➤ アメリカのジャーナリスト, デイナのことば).
▶この頃は食べ物が軟らかいから, よく**かまない**人が多い Since food is soft these days, many people don't *chew* well. ‖ 授業中にガムを**かむ**生徒がいる Some students *chew* gum in class.
▶《慣用表現》その家庭教師は**かんで含めるように**教えてくれる That tutor is good at explaining things *in an easy-to-understand manner*. ‖ その詐欺には裏でやくざが**一枚かんでいる**に違いない You can be sure that the yakuza criminals *are involved* behind the scenes in that scam.

[2]**かむ** ▶アキちゃん, はなが出てますよ. ちゃんと**かみなさい** Aki-chan, your nose's running. *Blow* it (and wipe it).

ガム **(chewing) gum** ▶レモン味の**ガム**2枚 two sticks of lemon-flavored (*chewing*) *gum* ‖ **ガムをかむ** chew *gum*.

がむしゃら ▶彼は凶器を持った男に**がむしゃらに**突進していった He made a *reckless* dash at the armed man. ‖ 安田さんはマイホームを手に入れるためにがむしゃらに働いている Mr. Yasuda has been working *like mad* [*frantically*] in order to buy a home of his own. (➤ like mad は「猛烈に」の意のくだけた言い方；やや品のない言い方だが working his butt off ともいう).

か

ガムシロップ **simple syrup** ; **sugar** [**gomme**] **syrup**.

ガムテープ (**adhesive** /ədhíːsɪv/) **tape** (➤英語では gummed tape とはあまりいわない；adhesive tape は「ばんそうこう」も指す) ▶**ガムテープ**で箱に封をする seal a box with (*adhesive*) *tape*.

カムバック a **comeback** ▶芸能界で**カムバック**するのは難しい It is hard to *make* [*stage*] *a comeback* in show business.

カムフラージュ (a) **camouflage** /kǽməflɑːʒ/ ▶**カムフラージュ**した戦車 a *camouflaged* tank ‖ 自分の弱さを虚勢で**カムフラージュする** *hide* one's weakness by bluffing.

ガムラン 《音楽》**gamelan** (➤インドネシアの打楽器中心の合奏, およびその音楽).

1**かめ 亀** a **tortoise** /tɔ́ːʳt̬əs/ (陸ガメ)；a **turtle** (海ガメ) 《参考》日常英語では両者を区別せず, turtle を用いることが多い. ▶東アジアでは**カメ**は長寿を象徴するめでたい動物とされる In East Asia, the *turtle* is considered an auspicious animal which symbolizes long life.

2**かめ 瓶** an **urn** /əːʳn/ 《参考》この語から「埋葬用のかめ」や「骨つぼ」を連想する人もいる. ▶大きな水**がめ** a large water *urn* [*pot* ／*jar*].

1**かめい 加盟する** **join** ▶IOC に**加盟する** *join* [*become a member of*] the International Olympic Committee ‖ 日本は国連の**加盟国**です Japan is *a member* of the United Nations. ‖ その国際機構の**加盟国**はことしの２月現在, 41か国である The international organization has *a membership* of 41 nations [has 41 *member nations* ／has 41 *signatories*] as of February this year. (➤ signatory /sígnətɔ̀ːri/ は「署名国」).

‖**加盟団体** a member organization ‖ **加盟店** a member store [shop].

2**かめい 家名** a **family name** ▶**家名**に傷をつけるようなことはするな Don't do anything that might disgrace [tarnish] *the family name*.

3**かめい 仮名** an **assumed name** ; a **pseudonym** /sjúːdənɪm/ (ペンネーム).

カメオ a **cameo** /kǽmioʊ/.

がめつい **grasping**, **greedy** ▶あいつは**がめつい**やつだ He is *mean* [*tightfisted*] *and grasping*. (🔊 mean, tightfisted は「けちな」の意で, これらの語を加えることにより日本語の「がめつい」というニュアンスがいっそうはっきりする).

カメラ a **camera** ▶**カメラ**に新しいフィルムを入れた I put a new roll of film in my *camera*. ／I loaded my *camera* with a new roll of film. ‖ 皆さん, **カメラ**の方を見てください Look at [into] *the camera*, everybody. ‖ 父は**カメラ**嫌いなんです My father is *camera-shy*. ‖ 彼女は**カメラ慣れしている**[**していない**] She is [*not*] *used to being photographed*. ‖ 恭子は**カメラ写りがいい**ねえ Kyoko's *photogenic*, isn't she? ‖ 出火直後の様子が**携帯のカメラ**で捉えられていた The scene of a fire shortly after it broke out was captured by *a cellphone camera*. ‖ 女優は**カメラ目線**でほほえんだ The actress *smiled at* [*into*] *the camera*. (➤「カメラに向かってポーズをとった」は The actress posed for the camera.).

‖**カメラマン** a photographer /fətɑ́ːɡrəfəʳ/ ; a camera operator (テレビ・映画の) →**かこみ記事** ‖ **カメラ屋** a camera store [shop] ‖ **胃カメラ** a gastrocamera ‖ **一眼レフカメラ** a single-lens reflex camera (➤「デジタル一眼レフ」は digital single-lens reflex camera だが,「ミラーレス一眼」と呼ばれるものは mirrorless interchangeable lens camera (MILC) という) ‖ **監視カメラ** a surveillance [security] camera ‖ **高速度カメラ** a high-speed camera ‖ **水中カメラ** an underwater camera ‖ **赤外線カメラ** an infrared camera ‖ **使い捨てカメラ** a single-use [disposable] camera ‖ **デジタルカメラ** a digital camera ‖ **テレビカメラ** a television camera ‖ **ポケットカメラ** a pocket camera.

> **危ないカタカナ語✹ カメラマン**
> 英語の cameraman は映画・テレビの撮影技師を指す. これは日本語でも「テレビ[映画]カメラマン」といって同じであるが, 写真家の「カメラマン」は cameraman ではなく photographer という. なお, cameraman は最近では性差のない cameraperson や camera operator というほうが好まれる.

カメレオン 《動物》a **chameleon** /kəmíːliən/.

かめん 仮面 a **mask** ▶**仮面**を着ける wear [put on] *a mask*.

▶《比喩的》警察はスパイの**仮面を剝いだ** The police *unmasked* the spy.

がめん 画面 a **screen** (スクリーン)；a **picture** (映像) ▶テレビの**画面**がぼやけている The *picture* on the TV screen is fuzzy.

‖**待ち受け画面** (call [message]) waiting display [screen].

かも 鴨 **1**【鳥】a (**wild**) **duck** ; a **duckling** (子ガモ)；a **mallard** /mǽlərʳd/ (マガモ) ▶**カモ**猟に行く go *ducking* ／go *duck-shooting*.

2【餌食】▶彼らはその老人をいい**カモ**にして有り金全部をだまし取った They *made a sucker of* the senior citizen, conning him out of all his money. (➤ make A of B は「B (人・物) を A にする」の意；sucker は「だまされやすい人, カモ」の意).

-かも →**かもしれない**.

かもい 鴨居 a **lintel**.

1**かもく 科目** a **subject** ▶大学入学後２年間は**一般教養科目**を習う Students study *liberal arts* [*general education*] *subjects* during the first two years of college.

✉ **日本史は私の好きな科目の１つです. あなたはどんな科目が好きですか** Japanese history is one of my favorite *subjects*. What *subjects* do you like? →**学科**.

‖**選択科目** an elective [《英》optional] subject ‖ **必修科目** a required [《英》compulsory] subject 《参考》学生間では「単位の取りやすい科目」を an easy course, an easy three credits, a gut course などといい,「取りにくい科目」を a tough course, a demanding course, a tough three credits などという. three credits (３単位) は「科目」のことで, １科目が週３単位 (３時間) であることに由来する.

2**かもく 寡黙な** **reticent** (口数の少ない)；**taciturn** /tǽsɪtəːʳn/ (無口の) ▶**寡黙な人** a person *of few words* ／a *reticent* person ‖ 国際会議での日本人の**寡黙さ**は有名だ Japanese people are notoriously *reticent* [*taciturn*] at international meetings (➤ notoriously は「芳しくないことでよく知られて」).

かもしか 羚羊・氈鹿《動物》an **antelope**（主にアジア・アフリカ産）; a **serow** /sərόʊ ‖ sérou/（カシミール・中国産；日本の山地にいるカモシカは Japanese serow という）▶**彼女はカモシカのような足をしている** She has *legs like a gazelle's*. 《参考》gazelle はレイヨウの一種で,「優雅」のイメージがある.

かもしだす 醸し出す **create** +⊞ ▶**ホールに飾られたたくさんの花が華やいだ雰囲気を醸し出した** The many flowers decorating the hall *created* a luxurious atmosphere.

-かもしれない **may, might**（➤ might は may より可能性が低い場合）→**たぶん** ▶**ことしはタイガースが優勝するかもしれない** The Tigers *may* win the championship this year. ‖ **ジェット旅客機はどこかに不時着したのかもしれない** The jetliner *may* have made an emergency landing somewhere. ‖ **ひょっとすると今夜は雪かもしれない** It *might* snow tonight. ‖ **彼の説明はひょっとすると間違いかもしれない** *There is a possibility* (that) his explanation *might* be wrong.
▶**もし彼が満塁ホーマーを打たなかったらオリックスは敗れていたかもしれない** If he had not belted a grand-slam homer, the Buffaloes *might* have lost the game.（➤ 事実とは異なることを仮定する言い方）‖ **第三次世界大戦は起きるかもしれないし, 起きないかもしれない** World War III *may or may not* break out [occur].
▶ **対話**「あの容疑者白状したかしら」「したかも(しれない)よ」"I wonder if the suspect confessed to his crime." "*Maybe* he did. ／He *may* have." ‖ **対話**「体がぞくぞくする. かぜかも」「そうかも(しれない)ね」"I feel shivery. It *may be* a cold." "*Could be*."

かもつ 貨物 **freight** /freɪt/,《英また》**goods**; **cargo**（船荷, 航空貨物）▶**貨物の輸送には主にトラックが使われている** Trucks are mostly used for transporting *freight*. ‖ **大きなクレーンが大量の貨物を船倉に積み込んでいた** A huge crane was putting [loading] a lot of *cargo* into the hold.
‖**貨物駅** a freight station ‖ **貨物船** a cargo ship, a freighter ‖ **貨物列車** a freight train,《英また》a goods train.

カモノハシ《動物》a **platypus** /plǽṭɪpəs/, a **duckbill**.

カモフラージュ **camouflage** /kǽməflɑ:ʒ/. →**カムフラージュ**.

かもめ 鷗《鳥》a **(sea)gull**.

かもん 家紋 a **family crest**.

かや 蚊帳 a **mosquito** /məskí:ṭoʊ/ **net** ▶**蚊帳をつる[外す]** put up [take down] *a mosquito net*.

がやがや ▶**そんなにがやがや騒がないで** Don't *make* such *a racket* [*so much noise*]. ／Don't *be* so *noisy*. ‖ **会場ががやがやしていたので演説が聞こえなかった** I couldn't hear the speech over the *clamor of voices* in the hall.

かやく 火薬 **gunpowder** ▶**火薬の爆発で5人が重傷を負った** Five people were seriously injured in *a gunpowder explosion*.
‖**火薬庫** a powder magazine.

カヤック a **kayak** /káɪæk/.

かやぶき 茅葺き・萱葺き **thatched** /θætʃt/ ▶**かやぶきの田舎家** a *thatched* cottage ‖ **かやぶき屋根** a *thatched* roof.

かゆ 粥 ***kayu***; **rice porridge, rice gruel** /grú:əl/ **《解説》** 英米には日本のような米で作るかゆはない. porridge はオートミールなどの穀類を水や牛乳でどろどろに煮たもの, gruel はそれの薄いものをいう. 日本のかゆは *kayu* とするか, 訳語のように rice をつけて表す.

かゆい 痒い **itchy** /ítʃi/ ▶**右の耳がかゆい** My right ear *itches*. ／I *feel itchy* in my right ear. ‖ **ああ, 体中がかゆいよ！** Oh, I just *itch* all over! ‖ **私は皮膚が弱いからウールの服を着るとかゆくなることがある** I have very sensitive skin, so woolen clothes tend to *make* me *itch* [*itchy*].
▶《慣用表現》**彼の中傷なんか痛くもかゆくもない** His slander *doesn't matter* [*doesn't bother me*] *at all*. ／I *couldn't care less* about his slander.（➤ couldn't care less は「全然無関心だ」の意で, アメリカ英語では couldn't の代わりに could を用いることもある）‖ **このソフトはかゆい所に手が届く便利な機能が満載だ** This software program has every convenient function *you could wish for*. ‖ **彼の妻はかゆい所に手が届くようによく世話をする** His wife waits on him *hand and foot*.（➤ hand and foot は「まめまめしく」）.

かゆみ 痒み an **itch, itching** ▶**かゆみ止めを塗る** apply *anti-itch ointment* ‖ **頭のかゆみがなかなか治まらない** I can't get this *itching* on my scalp to go away.

かよい 通い ▶**ご希望なら通いで結構です** You can *live out* if you wish.（➤「通いのお手伝いさん」は day helper. 反対の「住み込みをする」は live in）.

かよう 通う **1【行く】** **go, attend** +⊞（➤ 後者はやや堅い語で, 通例義務的に行く感じを伴う）; **commute**（通学・通勤する）▶**私は札幌の学校に通っています** I *go* to [*attend*] school in Sapporo. ‖ **彼は八王子まで電車で通っている** He *commutes* to Hachioji by train. ‖ **会社へ通うのに往復2時間かかります** It takes me two hours to *commute* to and from work.（→**通学, 通勤**）‖ **夏休み中は毎日図書館に通った** I *went* to the library every day during summer vacation. ‖ **対話**「川崎までどうやって通ってるの？」「車で通っています」"How do you *commute* to Kawasaki?" "I *drive*. ／*By car*."
2【連絡手段がある】 ▶**空港とターミナルの間はバスが通っています** *There is (a) bus service* between the airport and the terminal. ‖ **2つの小さな町の間をバスが通い始めた** Buses began to *run* [Bus service began] between the two small towns.
3【心が届く】 ▶**血の通った教育** education *with a heart* ‖ **教師と生徒の心が通ったとき教育は成功する** Education is successful when the teacher and his or her students *understand one another well*.

かようきょく 歌謡曲 (a) ***kayokyoku***; a **Japanese popular song**. →**演歌**.

がようし 画用紙 **drawing paper** ▶**画用紙10枚** ten sheets of *drawing paper*.

かよう(び) 火曜(日) **Tuesday**《略 Tu. または Tues.》▶**火曜日は塾で英語を勉強します** I have English lessons at a juku on *Tuesday(s)*. →**曜日**.

かよわい か弱い **feeble** ▶**近頃か弱いのは女ではなく男だ** It is not women, but men, who are *weak* [*fragile*] nowadays.

¹から 空の **empty** ▶**空の箱** an *empty* box ‖ **ビールを1瓶空にする** *empty* a bottle of beer ‖ **引き出しをすっかり空にする** *empty out* a drawer ‖ **たばこを1箱空にする** *finish up* a pack of cigarettes ‖ **その牛乳パックはもう空です** There is *no* more milk in the carton [pack].

²から 殻 a **husk**（穀粒・種子の）; a **shell**（卵・貝・ナッツ・カタツムリなどの）▶**小麦の殻** a wheat *husk* ‖ **卵の殻** an egg*shell* ‖ **ゆで卵の殻をむく** *shell* a boiled egg.
▶《慣用表現》**この頃直美は自分の殻に閉じ籠もってしま**

い, 人と話したがらない These days Naomi *has withdrawn into herself* [*has retired into her shell*], and does not want to speak to anyone.

-から

訳語メニュー
起点・出どころ →from 1, 2, 3, 4, 5
から外へ →out of 1
(ある時間)に →at, on, in 2
以来 →since 2
原料 →from, of 6
原因 →out of, because 7

1【ある場所について】from ; out of (…から外へ) ▶《起点を示して》ロンドンからローマへ飛ぶ fly *from* London to Rome ‖ 車から降りなさい Get *out of* the car. ‖ 野球選手がバスから降りてきた The baseball players *got off* the bus. ‖ 相模川は山中湖から流れ出る The Sagami River originates *in* Lake Yamanaka. ‖ 学校は私の家から歩いて20分です Our school is a twenty-minute walk *from* my home. ‖ 13ページから始めよう Let's begin *on* [*at*] page 13. ‖ モンシロチョウが花から花へと飛んでいる Cabbage butterflies are fluttering [flittering] *from* flower to flower.

▶《範囲を示して》来週の月曜までに教科書の50ページから100ページまでを読んできなさい Read *pages 50 to 100* in the textbook by next Monday. ‖ 彼女はいつも自分の部屋を隅から隅まで掃除する She always cleans her room *from top to bottom.* ‖ 台風の被害は紀伊半島から北陸にかけての広い地域に及んだ Damage from the typhoon was reported over a wide area *from* the Kii Peninsula *to* the Hokuriku region. / The typhoon caused damage over a wide area *covering* the Kii Peninsula *to* the Hokuriku region.

▶《経由点を示して》強盗は窓からその家に入った The burglar broke into the house *through* the window. ‖ 隙間から光がさし込んだ Light filtered in *through* a gap. ‖ ホテルの窓から京都の通りが見えた I could see the streets of Kyoto *from* the hotel window. ‖ バスの窓から顔を出さないでください Don't stick your head *out* (*of*) the bus window.

2【ある時間について】at, on, in (➤ いずれも「に」の意で, それぞれ「時刻」「日」「月・年」を表す語が続く) ; **from, since** ▶《起点を示して》社員たちは朝8時30分から(=8時30分に)仕事を始める Employees begin (to) work *at* 8 : 30 in the morning. ‖ 学校は4月から(=4月に)始まる School starts *in* April. ‖ 冬休みは12月25日から(=12月25日に)始まる Winter vacation starts *on* December 25.

▶うちの主人は朝早くから働きます My husband works *from* early in the morning. ‖ ゆうべから頭が痛い I have had a headache *since* last night. ‖ 福島へ越してきてから(=以来)7年になります It has been [《英また》It is] seven years *since* we moved to Fukushima. ‖ 私は首相が子供だった頃から知っています I have known the Prime Minister *from* childhood [*since* he was a child]. (「私は私が子供だった頃から…」というのであれば, he を I にかえる) ‖ 彼女は30分前から(=30分間)待っています She has been waiting *for* thirty minutes. ‖《店で》おたくは毎日何時からやってますか *When* [*What time*] do you open every day? / *How early* are [do] you open every day?

▶《続いて起こることを示して》学校が終わってからアルバイトに行った I went to work part-time *after* school. ‖ 夕食を食べてから外出しよう Let's go out *after* dinner. ‖ 浅井さんは65歳になってからジョギングを始めた Asai began jogging *after* he turned sixty-five. ‖ 昼寝してから水泳に行った *After* taking a nap, I went swimming.

▶《範囲を示して》9時から5時まで働く work *from* 9 *to* [*till*] 5 ‖ 会員の年齢は16歳から80歳にまで及んでいます The ages of the members range *from* sixteen *to* eighty.

3【時間・空間以外の物事について】from ▶《出どころや起点を示して》マドリードに居る息子から手紙が来た I got a letter *from* my son in Madrid. ‖ 会社から電話がありましたよ There was a telephone call *from* the company. ‖ 彼は銀行から1000万円借りた He borrowed ten million yen *from* a bank. ‖ 私たちは会社から給料をもらっています We receive a salary *from* [are paid *by*] the company. ‖ 父から毎月8万円の送金がある My father sends 80,000 yen to me every month. ‖ 当ホテルの宿泊料は8000円からです Our room rates *start at* 8,000 yen. ‖ 宴会は乾杯から(=で)始まった The party started *with* a toast. ‖ さて何から始めようか *What* should we start *with*?

▶《範囲を示して》10号車から12号車までは自由席です *Cars number 10 to 12* have non-reserved seats. ‖ 何から何まで人任せにしてはいけないよ You shouldn't leave *everything* up to others.

4【論拠を示して】from ▶アメリカ人の目から見ると, 日本の女子大生は無邪気に見える *In American eyes*, female college students in Japan look very innocent. ‖ 日本人の立場から見ると, アメリカ人は個人主義的すぎる *From the Japanese point of view*, Americans are too individualistic. ‖ 社説から判断すると, この新聞は少し左寄りである *Judging from* the editorial, this newspaper leans a little to the left.

5【受け身などの動作の出どころを示して】from ▶私は英語をアメリカ人牧師から学んだ I learned English *from* an American missionary. ‖ あなたのことは主人からよく聞いています I have heard a lot about you *from* my husband. ‖ 彼の証言は検察当局からはあまり重視されなかった His testimony was not taken very seriously *by* the prosecution.

6【原料や構成要素を示して】from, of (➤ of は素材の成分が変化しない場合) ▶この繊維は石油から作られる This fiber is made *from* petroleum. ‖ それは何からできているのですか What is it made *of*? ‖ この論文は序論・本論・結論から成る This thesis *consists of* an introduction, a main subject and a conclusion. (➤ consist of は「…から成る」の意で複数名詞または2つ以上の名詞が続く; 受け身形・進行形にはできない).

7【原因や理由を示して】out of ; due to (…のために) ; **because** (…だから) ▶彼女は好奇心からラム酒を飲んでみた She tried rum *out of* curiosity. ‖ そのサッカー選手は不注意から右足にけがをした That soccer player sustained an injury to his right leg *due to* carelessness [*through* his own carelessness]. (➤ through は「…のために」の意だが, due to と異なり行為者が示されるのがふつう) ‖ 今度の企画がうまくいったのは, 彼女の力があったからだ *Thanks to* her, this project went well. / This project was successful *due to* her.

▶学校へ行くと友だちに会えるから楽しい School is fun

because I can see my friends (there). ‖ 外が寒いからといって部屋に閉じ籠もっているのはよくない It is not good (for your health) to stay shut up inside *just because* it's cold outside. ‖ 本は有名な作家によって書かれたからといって常によい本とは言えない A book is *not always* good *just because* it is written by a famous author.

8【話者の意志を示して】▶彼女に先に行くからと伝えてください Please tell her *that* I'm going on ahead. ‖ あんまり意地悪ばかりすると, もう遊んであげないからね If you keep being mean to me, I *won't* play with you anymore.

☛ -からには (→見出語)

がら 柄 **1**【模様】a **design** ; a **pattern** (全体の柄の中の個別の) ▶ペルシャじゅうたんの柄 the *design* of a Persian rug ‖ このセーター, おもしろい柄ですね This sweater has an interesting *design*, doesn't it? ‖ あなたの着物のその花柄, ちょっと地味[派手]じゃない? I think the *flower patterns* on your kimono might be a bit too plain [loud].

2【状態】▶彼は場所柄もわきまえずに下品な冗談を言った He told a dirty joke without taking the *occasion* into consideration. ‖ このへんは, よそから来た人にも優しい土地柄だ The local people [The people living in this area] *are known for* their kindness to strangers.

3【体格】(a) **build** ▶相撲取りは柄が大きい Sumo wrestlers *have a large build*.

4【性質, 品位】▶あいつは柄が悪い He is *rude*. ‖ 親分は柄にもなく泣いた The big boss shed *unaccustomed* [*uncharacteristic*] tears. (➤ unaccustomed は「いつにない, ふつうでない」, uncharacteristic は「その人らしくない」の意) ‖ 柄にもないことを言うね It's so *unlike you* to say that. ‖ ぼくはエースと呼ばれるような柄じゃない I *don't deserve to* be called an ace pitcher.

☛ 大柄, 小柄 (→見出語)

1**カラー** 《色》 **color** /kʌ́ləʳ/ ▶その映画[テレビ番組]はカラーではなかった That movie [TV program] was not *in color*.

‖カラー印刷 color printing ‖ カラーコピー a color copy ‖ カラー写真[スライド] a color photograph [slide] ‖ カラーテレビ a color television ‖ カラーフィルム color film ‖ カラープリント a color print.

2**カラー** 《襟》 a **collar** /kɑ́:ləʳ/ ▶お母さん, このカラー痛いよ Mom, this *collar* hurts me.

がらあき がら空き ▶その映画館はがら空きだった The movie theater *was nearly* [*practically*] *empty*. (➤ practically は「ほとんど…も同然」の意).

からあげ 空揚げ・唐揚げ ▶鶏のから揚げ a *deep-fried* chicken nugget.

カラーリング coloring.

からい 辛い **1**【味が】**hot** (ピリリとした持続的な) ; **salty** /sɔ́:lti/ (塩辛い) ; **dry** (ワインなどが) ▶東南アジアの料理は概して辛い Southeast Asian food is generally *hot*. ‖ ここのすしはわさびが効いていて辛い The sushi served here *has a nice wasabi bite*. (➤ わさびのツンとくる瞬間的な刺激は bite という. トウガラシのやや持続的な「辛さ」は heat. →辛さ) ‖ このシチュー, 少し辛いんじゃないか? I think this stew is a little *salty*. →辛口.

2【採点が】▶今度来た先生, 点が辛いわねえ! Our new teacher is *a hard grader*, isn't she [he]?

からいばり 空威張り **bluff** /blʌf/ 一動 から威張りする **bluff** ▶から威張りしてもきみが怖がっているのはわかるよ You may *bluff* [*act brave*], but I know how afraid you are.

カラオケ (a) **karaoke** (➤ 英語化している) ▶カラオケで『雪国』を歌う sing "Yukiguni" with a *karaoke* machine / sing "Yukiguni" at a *karaoke* center ‖ カラオケをしにいこうよ Let's go (out) and sing *karaoke*.

‖カラオケバー a karaoke bar ‖ カラオケボックス a karaoke room [box] (➤ 英語では前者がふつう).

からかう tease +目, 《インフォーマル》 **kid** +目 ; **make fun of** (笑い物にする) ▶からかうのはやめて Stop *teasing* [*making fun of*] me! ‖ 先生をからかっちゃおうぜ Let's go *tease* [*kid*] the teacher! (➤ go tease [kid] は go to tease [kid] のくだけた言い方) ‖ 私が国語の教科書を読むといつも友だちが私のなまりをからかう When I read the Japanese textbook, my friends always *make fun of* my accent. ‖ 子供たちにとって先生をからかうのはいつだって楽しいことなのだ It always amuses children to *poke fun at* [*tease*] their teachers. ‖ 彼はいつも妹をからかっていた He was always *pulling* his little sister's *leg*. (➤ pull ~'s leg は「(人を)担ぐ」) ‖ 10歳で大学を卒業した男の子がいるって? 大人をからかうものじゃないよ You say there's a boy who graduated from college at ten? Don't *kid a grown-up* [*pull a grown up's leg*] like that.

▶初めのうちはからかい半分のデートでしたが, 今では彼が気に入りました I dated him *just for fun* at first, but now I find myself interested in him. (➤ for fun は「あそびで」).

からかさ 唐傘 a ***karakasa*** ; oiled paper umbrella with bamboo ribs (➤ 説明的な訳).

からかみ 唐紙 →ふすま.

からから ▶水をくれ. 喉がからからだ Give me some water. *My throat is* [*I'm*] *parched*. ‖ この1か月間雨が一滴も降らないので空気がからからに乾いている There has not been a drop of rain for the last four weeks, so the air is *extremely dry*.

がらがら **1**【音】a **rattle** (おもちゃ) ▶がらがらで赤ん坊をあやす amuse a baby with *a rattle*.

▶がらがら声で話す speak in *a raspy voice* (➤「がらがら声」を cement-mixer voice ということがある).

‖がらがら蛇 a rattlesnake.

2【すいている】▶けさの始発電車はがらがらだった The first train I got on this morning was *almost* (completely) *empty*.

からきし ▶あそこの息子は家では威張っているが, 外へ出るとからきし意気地がない Their son is a tyrant at home but he's a *complete* [*an utter*] coward when he goes out. ‖ 秋田君は野球はからきしだめだ Akita *can't* play baseball *at all*. ‖ ぼくは歌はからきしだめなんです I'm *hopeless* at singing. / I *can't* sing *at all*.

からくさもよう 唐草模様 an **arabesque**.

からくじ 空くじ a **blank** (**ticket**) ▶弥生町商店街福引き空くじなし There are no *blank tickets* in the Yayoi-cho Shopping Street lottery. ‖ ぼくはくじ引きではいつも空くじを引く I always draw *blanks* in the lottery.

がらくた odds and ends (半端もの) ; **junk** (どうにも使いようのないもの) ▶がらくたを箱に詰め込む pack a box with *odds and ends* ‖ こんながらくた, 早く始末してしまいなさい Do something about this *junk* right away.

‖がらくた市 a flea market, 《米また》a rummage sale, 《英また》a jumble sale.

からくち 辛口 ▶辛口のカレー *very hot* [*spicy*] curry (➤ spicy は「薬味がよく効いた」) ‖ このしょうゆは辛口だ This is *extra-salty* soy sauce. ‖ 私は辛口のワインが好きだ I like *dry* wine.
▶辛口の批評 *unsparing* [*harsh*] criticism ‖ 辛口のコメント a *sharp* comment ／a *scathing* remark.

からくも 辛くも **barely** ▶辛くも締め切りに間に合った I *just barely* met the deadline.

からくり ▶その女の子は人形がどういうからくりで(＝どのようにして)動くのか知りたがった The little girl was curious to know *how* her doll worked. ‖ 政治家のところには黙っていても金が集まってくるからくりになっているらしい Politicians seem to know *all the tricks* of making money without having to do any work (for it).
‖からくり人形 a mechanical doll, a *karakuri ningyo*.

ガラケー a [an **old-style**] **flip phone** (折り畳み式の)；a **feature phone.**

からげんき 空元気 ▶彼はから元気を出している He *is pretending to be cheerful* [*courageous*]. **《参考》** 酒の上のから元気を特に liquid courage という.

からさ 辛さ **heat** ▶このカレーは辛さが足りない This curry *isn't hot enough*. ／This curry *needs more heat*.

からさわぎ 空騒ぎ a **fuss about nothing** ▶名古屋オリンピックは結局実現せず，から騒ぎに終わった In the end, the Nagoya Olympics never materialized. It was *all a big fuss that came to nothing* [It was *much ado about nothing*].

からし 辛子 **mustard** /mʌ́stəʳd/ ▶からしの無いホットドッグなんておいしくない Hot dogs without *mustard* aren't tasty.

からじし 唐獅子 an artistic image of a mythical lion-inspired beast from ancient China (➤ 説明的な訳).

1**からす 烏** a **crow** ▶都心でも増え過ぎたカラスに困っている An influx of *crows* has reached as far as the city center, causing a problem.
▶《慣用表現》父はいつもからすの行水だ My father is in the habit of *taking a hurried bath*.
‖カラスの足跡(＝目尻のしわ) crow's-feet.

2**からす 枯らす** ▶水をやり忘れて部屋の鉢植えを全部枯らしてしまった All of the potted plants in the room *withered and died* because I forgot to water them.

3**からす 涸らす** ▶天然資源をからす *exhaust* [*use up*] natural resources ‖ あまりたくさんの水を一度にくみ上げたので井戸をからしてしまった They carelessly *ran* the well *dry* by pumping up too much water at one time.

4**からす 嗄らす** ▶彼は大声を上げ過ぎて声をからしてしまった He *became hoarse* from shouting too much. ／His voice *became hoarse* from too much shouting.

ガラス **glass** ▶(シンデレラの)ガラスの靴 *glass* slippers ‖ 曇りガラス *frosted glass* ‖ 窓ガラスを壊したので弁償した I paid for the *windowpane* that I had broken.
▶《比喩的》政治はガラス張り(＝公明正大)であってほしい The nation should be governed in an *open and aboveboard* manner.
‖ガラス細工 glasswork ‖ **ガラス製品** glassware ‖ **ガラス繊維** glass fiber.

からすむぎ 烏麦 **oats.**

からだ 体

📖 訳語メニュー
肉体 →body **1**
体格 →build, physique **1**
健康 →health **2**

1【身体】 a **body**(肉体)；(a) **physique** /fizíːk/ (体格) ▶体を鍛えたい I want to build up my *body*. ‖ 彼女，いい体してるね She's *got a great body*. (➤ 主に男性が女性について言う場合) ‖ あの青年，いい体してるね That young man *has a good build* [*physique*]. (➤ 主に男性が同性について言う場合) ‖ 人の体に触るなよ! Don't touch *me*! ‖ 体をよく洗うのよ *Wash yourself* well. ‖ 仕事が忙しくて体の休まる暇がない I am too busy to *take a rest*. ‖ 体中にじんましんが出た I broke out in a rash *all over*. ／A rash broke out *over my whole body*.
▶伊藤君は体が小さい Ito is *small*. ‖ あの子は小学生にしては体が大きい He's rather *big* for an elementary school boy. ‖ 妹は体がほっそりしている My sister is *slim*. ‖ 彼女は体に障害がある She is *physically disabled*. ‖ 彼は体つきが父親と似ている He *is built like* his father.

2【健康】 **health** ▶彼は体が弱い He *has a weak constitution*. ／He is a *sickly* boy. ‖ 父は体が丈夫だ My father is *very strong*. ‖ 体に悪いからたばこはやめました I quit smoking because it is *bad for the health*. ‖ ニンニクは体にいいそうだ I hear garlic is *good for the health*. ‖ 彼女は体を壊して入院しています She *got sick* and is in the hospital now. ‖ やっと体の調子がよくなりました I *got better* at last. (➤ become better とすると「善人になる」とか，「(勉強などが)よくできるようになる」の意になる) ‖ こんな生活を続けていてはとても体がもたないよ If I keep up my present lifestyle, *my health will suffer*.
✉ **お体に気をつけてください** *Take care of yourself*. ／*Take care*. ➤ 後者はよりくだけた言い方.

3【慣用表現】 ▶仕事は頭でなく，体で覚えなさい You should learn your job not with your head, but *by doing it*. ‖ 運転は体で覚えなさい You should practice driving *until it becomes automatic*. ‖ (女が)男に体を許す *go all the way* with a man ‖ 月末は目の回るような忙しさで体がいくつあっても足りない At the end of the month, I am so busy (that) I *wish there were two of me*. ‖ 土曜の午後なら体が空く I'll *be free* [*available*] on Saturday afternoon.

からだき 空だき ▶風呂を空だきする *heat an empty bathtub* (➤ 英米では水を入れてたくタイプでなく，湯を張る浴槽がふつう).

カラタチ 《植物》a **trifoliate** /traɪfóʊliət/ **orange.**

からっかぜ 空っ風 a **dry wind** ▶この地域では冬になると強い空っ風が吹く A strong *dry wind* blows in this region in winter.

からっと ▶あすからっと晴れたらピクニックに行こう If it *clears up* tomorrow, let's go on a picnic. ‖ この天ぷらはからっと揚がっていてとてもおいしい This tempura is deep-fried just right—*crisp* and delicious.

カラット a **carat** (宝石の重さの単位) ▶1カラットのダイヤの指輪 a one-*carat* diamond ring.

がらっと ▶うちの部長は社長に会うとがらっと態度を変える When our manager meets the president, his manner *changes* [he *changes his tune*] *just like that*. (➤ just like that は「急に」).

からっぽ 空っぽの empty ▶この箱は空っぽだ This box is *empty*. ‖財布が空っぽだ I'm *flat* [*completely*] *broke* right now. (➤どちらも「すっからかんだ」の意のくだけた表現) ／I *haven't got a penny on me* (right) now. ‖彼は頭の中が空っぽだ He's *empty-headed*. ／He's *an airhead*. ／He's *got nothing upstairs*. (➤最後はやや婉曲(えんきょく)な言い方).

からつゆ 空梅雨 a **dry rainy season.**

からて 空手 1 karate (➤英語化している) ▶空手の練習をする practice *karate*.
‖空手チョップ a karate chop.
2【手に何も持っていないこと】▶父は国語辞典を買いに行ったが, 空手で帰って来た My father went to buy a Japanese dictionary, but returned *empty-handed*.

からてがた 空手形 1【融通手形】 a **kite** (➤「融通手形」に相当する専門語は an accommodation bill [note]).
2【実行の伴わない約束】▶父さんの約束はいつも空手形だ My dad's promises are like *rubber checks*. (➤rubber check は《米》で「不渡り手形」の意).

からとう 辛党 ▶ウイスキーが安くなります―辛党にはうれしいニュースです Whisk(e)y prices are going down—good news for (whisk(e)y) *drinkers*!

-からには ▶約束したからにはちゃんと守らなければならない *Once* you've made a promise, you must keep it. ／*Now* (*that*) you have made a promise, you must stick to it. ‖やるからには徹底的にやれ *If you decide to do something*, do it the best you can.

からぶかし 空吹かしする **gun an engine.**

からぶき 乾拭き ▶テーブルをから拭きする *wipe* a table *with a dry cloth*.

からぶり 空振り ▶スライダーを空振りする *swing and miss* a slider ‖松井選手は空振りの三振をした Matsui *swung* [*fanned*] *three times to strike out*. (➤swung は swing の過去形；「空振りの三振」は strikeout) ‖《ボクシング》堀口選手の右フックは空振りになった Horiguchi's right hook *failed to connect*. ▶捜査は空振り(＝不成功)に終わった The investigation was *unsuccessful*.

カラフル ▶カラフルな民族衣装 *colorful* folk costume(s).

からまつ 落葉松 《植物》 a **larch.**

からまる 絡まる **get tangled** ▶たこ揚げの糸が電線に絡まったため5本の新幹線が遅れた Five Shinkansen trains were delayed due to a kite string *getting tangled* around the electric power lines.
▶この政治疑獄にはいくつもの怪しげな事情が絡まっている Various suspicious circumstances *are involved* [*are mixed up*] in this political scandal.

からまわり 空回り ▶エンジンを空回りさせる *idle* an engine ‖雪でタイヤが空回りした The tires *spun* in the snow. (➤spun は spin (くるくる回る)の過去形).
▶私たちの議論は空回りした Our discussion *got us nowhere* [*went around in circles*]. (➤get ... nowhere は「(…にとって)成果がない」).

からみあう 絡み合う **get tangled** ▶私のヘッドホンのコードはすぐに絡み合う My headphone cords *get tangled* easily.
▶その事故はいくつもの原因が複雑に絡み合って起きた The accident occurred as a result of many complexly *interrelated* factors.

からみつく 絡み付く ▶ツタが木に絡みついた The ivy *entwined itself around* the tree.

からむ 絡む 1【巻きつく】 **get tangled** ▶ロープが足に絡んだ The rope *got tangled* around my leg. ‖ロープが絡んでほどけなくなった The rope *was tangled up* and I couldn't get it undone.
2【関わりをもつ】▶今度の人事には金が絡んでいるといううわさだ It is rumored that money *was involved* in the new personnel appointments. ‖この事件の裏には女が絡んでいるらしい It looks like *there's a woman* behind [*involved in*] this affair.
3【うるさくする】 **annoy** ＋㊐；**pick a quarrel** (けんかを吹っかける) ▶彼は酔うと人に絡む癖がある When he gets drunk, he tends to *annoy* [*pick quarrels with*] people (around him). ‖道で酔っ払いに絡まれた I *was hassled* on the street by a drunk.

がらもの 柄物 **patterned clothes** (衣類) ▶柄物のワンピース a *patterned* dress.

からやくそく 空約束 ▶もう空約束はするんじゃないよ. 誰からも信用してもらえなくなるからね You can't make any more *empty promises*. No one will trust you.

がらりと ▶今まで親切だったおばの態度ががらりと変わった My aunt who had always been very kind to me *suddenly changed* her attitude *completely*. ‖彼は彼女が社長の一人娘だとわかるとがらりと態度を変えた He *changed his tune* when he learned that she was the only daughter of the company president. (➤change one's tune は「曲を変える」が原義).

かられる 駆られる ▶私は彼を殴りつけたい衝動に駆られた I *felt an impulse* to hit him. ‖好奇心に駆られてその雑誌を買った *Out of curiosity*, I bought a copy of that magazine.

がらんと ▶がらんとした部屋にテーブルが1つ置いてあるだけだった There was just a (single) table in the *big empty* room.

がらんどう ▶がらんどうの広間 an *empty* hall ‖自由の女神像の内部はがらんどうですか Is the Statue of Liberty *hollow* (inside)?

¹かり 仮 1【一時的な】 **temporary** (臨時の)；**tentative** (試験的な) ▶仮のプラン a *tentative* plan ‖現在当社は仮営業所で営業しております We are doing business from *a temporary office*. ‖私は今このアパートに仮住まいしています I *am living temporarily* in this apartment house.
2【仮定】▶仮の話だけど, あなたがT大に合格したら, 弁論部に入んなさいね *This is just in case*, but if you get into T University, you should join the debate club. (→仮に).
3【偽りの】 **false** ▶あの男は仮の名を使っている That man uses *a false* [*fictitious*] *name*.
☛ 仮に, 仮縫い, 仮免 (→見出語)

²かり 狩り **hunting**, a **hunt** ▶山へイノシシ狩りに行く *go hunting* (for) wild boars in the mountains.
‖キノコ狩り mushroom gathering [picking] ‖ブドウ狩り grape picking ‖紅葉狩り an excursion to view the autumn leaves [foliage].

³かり 借り a **debt** /det/ (借金) ▶彼は私に借りがある He *owes* me some money. ／He *owes a debt* to me. ‖借りはいくらだったっけ？ *How much do I owe* you? ‖あす借りを返すよ I will *pay* you *back* [*I'll pay back what I owe you*] tomorrow.
▶《慣用表現》この借りはきっと返すから覚えてろよ I'll *get even with you* for this! (➤get even with で「…に仕返しをする」).

⁴かり 雁 《鳥》 a **wild goose.**

がり *gari*, **pickled ginger.**

かりあげ 刈り上げ ▶刈り上げのヘアスタイル［頭］a *close-cropped* hairstyle［head］‖ぼくは髪を刈り上げにしてもらった I had my hair *cut short*［*close*］.

かりあつめる 駆り集める **get together** ▶引っ越しの手伝いに4，5人，駆り集めてくれないか Could you *get* a few people *together* to help me with my move？

かりいれ 刈り入れ **reaping**（穀物の）；(a) **harvest, harvesting**（収穫）▶家じゅう総出で小麦の刈り入れをした The entire family joined in *harvesting*［*reaping*］the wheat.

[1]**かりいれる 刈り入れる** **reap**；**harvest**（収穫する）▶作物を刈り入れる *reap*［*harvest*］a crop.

[2]**かりいれる 借り入れる** **borrow.** →借りる.

カリウム《化学》**potassium.**

かりかえる 借り換える **refinance** ＋目 ▶ローンを借り換える *refinance* a loan.

かりかた 借方 a **debit.**

カリカチュア a **caricature.**

かりかり ▶うちの犬は骨をカリカリかじるのが好きだ Our dog likes to *crunch on* bones.

▶最近，父の帰りが遅いので母はかりかりしている Recently, my dad has been coming home late, so my mom is *on edge*［*edgy*］.‖そうかりかりするなよ！Don't be so *touchy*！‖今日は何をかりかりしているんだよ What's *bugging*［*bothering*／《主に英》*biting*］you today？

がりがり ▶ネズミが柱をガリガリかじっているみたいだ It sounds like a mouse *is gnawing on* the post.‖その犬はドアをガリガリひっかいていた The dog was *scratching at* the door.

▶がりがりに痩せた子供たちが1列に並んでミルクをもらっている A line of *bone-thin* children are waiting for milk.

カリキュラム a **curriculum** /kəríkjələm/（➤複数形は curricula または curriculums）▶この短大では音楽はカリキュラムに入っていない At this junior college, music is not included in the *curriculum*.

かりきる 借り切る **charter** ＋目（バスなどを）；**rent** ＋目（借りる）▶バスを1台借り切る *charter* a bus‖宴会場を借り切る *rent*［《英》*hire*］a banquet hall.

かりこむ 刈り込む **clip** ＋目（髪・羊毛などを）；**prune** ＋目（樹木を）；**mow** ＋目（芝を）；**shear** ＋目（羊の毛を）▶バラの木を刈り込む *prune* the rosebushes‖羊飼いは羊の毛を刈り込んだ The shepherd *clipped*［*sheared*］the sheep.‖彼は芝生を刈り込んでいる He is *mowing* the lawn.

かりしゃくほう 仮釈放 **parole** ▶囚人は仮釈放された The prisoner *was released on parole*.《参考》アメリカでは死刑のない州で，それに代わるものとして a life sentence without parole（仮釈放のない終身刑）という刑罰がある.

カリスマ **charisma** /kərízmə/ ▶カリスマ性のある人がよき指導者とは限らない Not all *charismatic* people make good leaders.

かりそめ ▶かりそめの恋 *transient* love.

かりそめにも →仮にも.

かりだす 借り出す **take**［**check**］**out**（本を）▶図書館から本を3冊借り出す *take out* three books from the library‖《図書館で》この本を借り出したいんですけど I'd like to *check out* this book.‖銀行から50万円借り出した I *got a loan* of 500,000 yen from the bank.

かりたてる 駆り立てる **drive** ＋目 ▶何が彼をその犯罪に駆り立てたのだろうか I wonder what *drove* him to commit the crime.

かりちん 借り賃 (a) **rent,** a **rental.**

かりて 借り手 a **borrower**；a **tenant**（店やアパートの）→借り主 ▶借り手にも貸し手にもなるなかれ Never a borrower or lender be.（➤『ハムレット』の中のせりふ）.

かりとる 刈り取る **cut** ＋目（切る）；**harvest** ＋目（刈り入れる）▶実った稲を刈り取る *harvest* the ripened rice.

▶《比喩的》悪の芽は大きくならないうちに刈り取らねばならない Evil should *be nipped* in the bud before it spreads.（➤ in the bud は「つぼみのうちに」）.

かりに 仮に **1**【一時的に】▶その女性の名前を仮にB子としておこう Let's call this young woman Miss B *for the present*［*for the time being*］.（→仮名）.

2【仮定して】**if** →もし ▶仮にナチスドイツが第二次世界大戦に勝っていたら世界はどうなっただろう What would have become of the world *if* Nazi Germany had won World War II？‖仮に（＝たとえ）きみの犬がいくつかのことばを理解したとしてもそれで日本語がわかるとはいえない *Even if* your dog does understand a couple of words, you cannot say that he really understands Japanese.‖仮にその距離を10キロだとしよう *Let's just say* the distance is ten kilometers.／*Suppose* the distance to be ten kilometers.（➤ Suppose ... はある仮定に立つとどうなるかを考えるときの使い方）.

かりにも 仮にも ▶仮にも一家の主人たるもの，家族を守れないでどうする *If you're the head of the house*, how can you not protect your family？

▶仮にも（＝冗談にも）親を侮辱するようなことを言ってはいけない *Even as a joke*, you should not say things that might insult your parents.

かりぬい 仮縫い a **fitting** ▶洋服屋に仮縫いに行く go to the dressmaker's for *a fitting*‖背広の仮縫いをしてもらう *have* one's suit *fitted*.

かりぬし 借り主 a **borrower**（一般に物の借り手）；a **debtor** /détəʳ/（借金などの）；a **tenant**（建物・土地などの）.

ガリばん ガリ版 a **mimeograph (machine)** ▶ガリ版刷りの問題用紙 a *mimeographed* question sheet.

カリフォルニア **California** /kæ̀ləfɔ́ːʳnjə/（アメリカ太平洋岸の州；略 CA, Calif. Cal.）.

カリブかい カリブ海 **the Caribbean (Sea).**

カリフラワー《植物》(a) **cauliflower** /kɔ́ːliflàʊəʳ/.

がりべん がり勉《主に米》a **grind,**《英》a **swot**（➤ともに主に人を指す．よい意味で「勉強家」は a hard-working student）**一動** **がり勉する** **plug**［**grind**］**away**《at》,《英また》**swot**《for》▶あいつは本当にがり勉だ He's *a* real *grind*.‖試験に備えてがり勉する *cram*［*swot*］for a test‖彼はがり勉してオール優を取った He *plugged*［*ground*］*away at* his studies and got straight A's.（➤ ground は grind の過去形）.

かりめん 仮免 a **temporary license,**《米》a **learner's permit,**《英》a **provisional licence**

‖**仮免ドライバー** a driver with a temporary license［a learner's permit／a provisional licence］,《英》a learner-driver, an L-driver /éldràɪvəʳ/.

かりもの 借り物 ▶このネクタイは山本君からの借り物なんだ This tie is one I *borrowed* from Yamamoto.‖借り物の（＝他人の）意見でなく，きみ自身の意見を言ってくれ Give your own opinion, not *somebody else's*.

かりゅう 下流 **the lower reaches (of a river)**（川の）

一副 **下流に downstream, down the stream** ▶ニューオリンズはミシシッピー川の下流に位置する New Orleans is located on the *lower* Mississippi. ‖ 私たちは2キロ下流でそのボートを発見した We found the boat two kilometers *downstream* [*down the river*].

がりゅう 我流 ▶私のテニスは我流です I play tennis *in my own style*. ‖ 対話「明子さん，この料理どこで習ったの？」「全くの我流よ」"Where did you learn to make this, Akiko?" "I invented it. ／At the Akiko School of Cooking." (➤ 後者は「明子料理学校で」の意で，少々おどけた感じを伴う).

かりゅうど 狩人 a **hunter**.

かりょう 加療 medical treatment ▶《カルテ》1か月の入院加療を要す Requires one-month *hospitalization and medical treatment*.

がりょう 雅量 magnanimity /mæ̀gnəníməṭi/ ▶雅量のある人 a *magnanimous* person.

がりょうてんせい 画竜点睛 ▶画竜点睛を欠く *lack the finishing touches* (➤ finishing touches は「仕上げの筆」).

かりょく 火力 heating power ▶このガスレンジは火力が強い［弱い］This gas range *has a strong* [*weak*] *flame*. ‖ **火力発電所** a thermal /θə́ːrml/ power plant [station].

かりる 借りる

> 語法 (1) 日本語の「借りる」は有料・無料に関係なく用いるが，英語では無料の場合は **borrow**，有料の場合は **rent**，不動産などを契約を交わして賃借りする場合は **lease** を用いる.
> (2)《英》では家・アパートなどを賃借りする場合は **rent**，レンタカーの場合は **hire** または **rent**，貸衣装・貸しボートなどの場合は **hire** を用いる.
> (3) 人や銀行から「お金を借りる」には **borrow** も使う．利子有りか，利子無しかは文脈や社会通念による.

1【返すことを条件に使わせてもらう】borrow +⊕；**owe** +⊕（支払う義務がある）

【文型】
人(A)から物や金など(B)を借りる
borrow B from A
人(A)に金(B)を借りている
owe A B
owe B to A

▶私は姉からドレスを借りた I *borrowed* a dress *from* my (older) sister. ‖ 私はM銀行から500万円借りた I *borrowed* [*got a loan of*] five million yen *from* M Bank. ‖ きみにいくら借りてたっけ？ How much do I *owe* you? ‖ ぼくは妹に3000円借りている I *owe* three thousand yen *to* my (younger) sister. ‖ 対話「この本，借りていい？」「いいよ」"*Can I borrow* this book?" "O.K." ‖ 私は学校の図書館から数冊本を借りている I'*ve taken out* [*borrowed*] several books *from* the school library.

▶ 対話「電話［トイレ］を借りていいかい」「いいよ」"*Can I use* the telephone [bathroom]?" "Sure." (➤ 備え付けのものや移動不可能なものを借りる場合は use を用いるのが正しいが，くだけた日常会話では borrow を用いることもある).

2【賃借りする】rent +⊕, **hire** +⊕, **lease** +⊕ ▶私はサンフランシスコで家を借り，月400ドル払った I *rented* a house in San Francisco for 400 dollars a month. ‖ このアパートをお借りしたいのですが I'd like to *rent* this apartment. ‖ 京都へ行ったらレンタカーを借りよう Let's *rent* [*hire*] a car in Kyoto. ‖ その不動産屋は土地を借りてマンションを建てた That realtor *leased* the land and built a condominium on it. ‖ うちの学校［会社］では年300万円で大型コンピュータを借りている We *lease* a large computer for three million yen a year. ‖ 上野動物園はパンダを2頭中国から借りている The Ueno Zoo has two giant pandas *on loan* from China. (➤ on loan は「借りて」).

3【一時的に借用する】 ▶人手を借りる *get help from other people* ‖ 彼女の知恵を借りよう Let's *ask* her *for* some ideas. ‖ 先輩の胸を借りて，テニスの大会に備えた I *practiced* tennis *with* one of the older students to prepare for the tournament.

かりん 花梨《植物》a **Chinese quince**.

かりんとう ***karinto***; a deep-fried stick-shaped cookie covered with brown syrup (➤ 説明的な訳).

[1]かる 刈る cut +⊕（頭髪などを）；**mow** +⊕（草を）；**reap** +⊕（穀物を）▶稲を刈る *reap* [*harvest*] rice ‖ 髪を刈ってもらう *have* one's hair *cut* ／get a haircut ‖ 息子に芝生を刈ってもらった I had my son *mow* the lawn. ‖ おまえは3週間に1回は髪を刈らなきゃいかんよ You need *a haircut* every three weeks.

[2]かる 狩る hunt +⊕ ▶獲物を狩る *hunt* game.

-がる ▶祖母はよく寒がる My grandmother often *complains of the cold*. ‖ その話をしたら彼は不思議がっていた He *looked puzzled* when I told him the story. ‖ 強がるんじゃないよ Stop *bluffing*.

かるい 軽い

1【重さが】light ▶軽い上着 a *light* coat ‖ 木は鉄より軽い Wood is *lighter* than iron. ‖ リチウムは最も軽い金属元素である Lithium is *the lightest* metal element. ‖ 私は父より体重が10キロ軽い I *weigh* ten kilos *less* than my father. ／I am ten kilograms *lighter* than my father. (➤ 前者の言い方がよりふつう) ‖ 対話「スーツケースを運びましょうか」「ありがとう．軽いから大丈夫です」"Shall I carry your suitcase?" "Thanks for offering, but it's *not too heavy*."

2【気持ちが】 ▶先生にすべてを話したら気持ちが軽くなった I *felt relieved* when I told my teacher everything. ‖ 軽い気持ちで幹事なんか引き受けるんじゃなかった It was a mistake to accept the job of organizer *lightly*.

3【程度が】light；mild（主に病気が）；**slight**（程度が）▶軽い食事 a *light* meal ‖ お昼のひととき，軽い音楽でおくつろぎください Here is some *light* music for your enjoyment during lunchtime. ‖ 軽いかぜをひきました I have a *slight* cold. (➤ slight は「わずかの」) ‖ 佐藤さんは軽い肝炎にかかっている Sato is suffering from a *mild* case of hepatitis. ‖ 妹は軽いはしかにかかった My younger sister had a *mild* attack of measles. ‖ 彼は足に軽いけがをした He received *minor* [*slight*] injuries to his leg. (➤ minor は「ちょっとした」) ‖ 定年を過ぎたら軽い仕事がしたい I want to have an *easy* job once I retire. (➤ easy は「簡単な」) ‖ 対話「お昼はお済みですか」「ええ，軽く食べました」"Did you have lunch?" "Yes, I just ate something *light*." ‖ あんなやつ，軽くやっつけてやったよ I defeated him *with no trouble*. (➤「何の面倒もなく」の意) ‖ 最近の教師は生徒に軽く見られているようだ These days it seems that teachers *are not respected* by students. (● are not respected を are looked down on とすると「軽蔑されている」という

異なった含みになる）‖ 対話「この仕事，あすまでにできるかい？」「軽い，軽い」"Can you complete this job by tomorrow?" "Sure, (it's *a*) *piece of cake*. ／*No sweat*."（➤ともにインフォーマルな言い方）.

4【慣用表現】▶あの女は尻が軽い（＝誰とでも寝る）She *sleeps around*. ‖あいつは口が軽い He *can't keep a secret*.

かるいし 軽石 (a) **pumice (stone)**.

カルカッタ Calcutta（インド東部の都市；現在の正式名は Kolkata（コルカタ））.

カルガモ 軽鴨《鳥》a **spotbill**, a **spot-billed duck**.

かるがる 軽々と easily（やすやすと）▶その男は重い荷を軽々と持ち上げた The man *easily* lifted the heavy load.

▶その女の子はピアノで難曲を軽々と弾きこなした The girl played the difficult piece on the piano *effortlessly*.

かるがるしい 軽々しい thoughtless（思慮に欠ける）▶軽々しいふるまい *thoughtless* behavior ‖軽々しい行為をするな Be careful about [of] your behavior. ／Don't *behave carelessly* [*rashly*]. ‖彼に頼まれても軽々しく引き受けるな If he asks something of you, don't say yes *without thinking it over*.

カルキ《化学》**chloride** /klɔ́ːraɪd/ **of lime, bleaching powder**（さらし粉）▶水道の水がカルキ臭い The tap water *smells of chlorine*.（➤chlorine /klɔ́ːriːn/は「塩素」）.

カルシウム calcium /kǽlsiəm/ ▶牛乳はカルシウムが豊富だ Milk is rich in *calcium*.

カルスト《地質学》**karst** /kɑ́ːʳst/.

カルタ playing cards（札）; a **card game**（遊び）▶カルタ取りをする play (*Iroha*) *cards*.

カルチャー (a) **culture** ▶海外旅行をしてカルチャーショックを受ける experience [get] *culture shock* (while) on an overseas trip.

> **危ないカタカナ語✹カルチャー**
> **1** 英語の culture は「(個人の)教養」とか，「(社会の)文化」という意味で，「カルチャースクール」や「カルチャーセンター」はそこから生まれた和製語.
> **2** 英語には「カルチャースクール」や「カルチャーセンター」の対応語がないので，これらに言及する場合には "culture school", "culture center" のように引用符付きで用いるのがよい．また，規模が大きく組織だったものなら組織名を冠して，ABC Center for Cultural Studies とか ABC Studies Center のように表現することも可能.
> **3** なお，英語の culture center は「文化の中心[発祥地]」の意で，主に社会学用語として用いられる.

カルテ a **chart**, a **clinical** [**medical**] **record**, a (**patient's**) **record**《参考》「カルテ」はドイツ語の *Karte* から.

カルテット《音楽》a **quartet** /kwɔːʳtét/.

カルデラ《地質学》a **caldera** /kældéərə/ ‖**カルデラ湖** a crater lake.

カルテル《経済学》a **cartel** /kɑːʳtél/ ▶鉄鋼3社が価格カルテルを結んだ Three steel manufacturing firms created *a price cartel*.

カルト a **cult** ‖**カルト集団** a religious cult ‖**カルトムービー** a cult movie.

かるはずみ 軽はずみな rash（性急な）; **careless**（不注意な）▶軽はずみな発言[行動]は慎むべきだ You should avoid making *rash* remarks [taking *rash* action]. ‖別の職を見つけないうちに仕事を辞めたのは軽はずみだったね It was *rash* [*imprudent*] of you to leave your job without first finding another one.（➤imprudent は「無分別な」）.

かるわざ 軽業 acrobatic feats, acrobatics /ækrəbǽṭɪks/ ▶サーカスの団員は軽業をする Some members of a circus perform *acrobatic feats*. ‖最近の体操競技はほとんど軽業に近い The gymnastics seen in modern competitions are closer to *acrobatics*. ‖**軽業師** an acrobat /ǽkrəbæt/.

かれ 彼 1【話し手・聞き手以外の男性を指して】he（主格），**his**（所有格；彼のもの），**him**（目的格）; **himself**（彼自身）▶彼は毎日車で通勤している *He* drives to work every day. ‖これ，彼の辞書かい？ Is this *his* dictionary? ‖この本，彼に渡してくれ Give this book *to him*.《参考》(1)本人がそばに居る場合は he より名前を使うほうがよい．(2)「お父さんはどちら？」と聞かれた場合，日本語ではふつう「父は庭に居ます」というように答えるが，英語では *He* is in the garden. というように代名詞の he を用いるのがふつう．→**彼ら**.

2【恋人】one's **boyfriend** ▶由紀の彼ってどんな人？ What's Yuki's *boyfriend* like?

[1]**かれい 鰈**《魚》a **flatfish**（カレイ・ヒラメの類いの総称）; a **flounder**（カレイ類）.

[2]**かれい 華麗な gorgeous** /gɔ́ːʳdʒəs/ ; **dazzling**（目がくらむほどの）; **magnificent**（抜きん出てすばらしい）; **glamorous**（魅惑的な）▶華麗な衣装 *gorgeous* costume ‖華麗な演技 a *dazzling* [*magnificent*] performance ‖ダイアナ妃の華麗な生涯 Princess Diana's *glamorous* life.

[3]**かれい 加齢 ag(e)ing**（➤ageing は《英》つづり）. ‖**加齢現象** an ag(e)ing phenomenon. ‖**加齢臭** ag(e)ing odor（➤老人臭はしばしばmustyで表される）.

ガレージ a **garage** /gərɑ́ːdʒ ‖ gǽrɑːdʒ/ ▶車をガレージに入れる drive [pull] a car into the *garage* ‖車をガレージから出す drive a car out of the *garage* ／back a car out of the *garage*（➤後者はバックさせて）. ‖**ガレージセール** a garage sale.

> **危ないカタカナ語✹ガレージ**
> **1** 英語の garage からきているが，英語での発音は /gərɑ́ːdʒ/ /gǽrɑːdʒ/ /gǽrɪdʒ/ である．《米》では最初の発音が，《英》では後の2者が好まれる.
> **2** garage には「車庫」の意のほかに，「自動車修理工場」の意もあり，《英》では修理工場がしばしばガソリンスタンドを兼ねているところから，ガソリンスタンドのことを garage と呼ぶこともある.

かれえだ 枯れ枝 a **dead branch** [**twig**], a **withered branch** [**twig**].

カレーライス curry and rice, curry with rice, curry rice《参考》カレーライスは日本食と考えて差し支えないから curry rice と表記することも可能だが，英語としては前の２つの言い方がふつう．▶カレーライスを１つください *Curry and rice*, please. ／One plate of *curry with rice*, please.

かれき 枯れ木 a **dead** [**withered**] **tree** ▶ ことわざ 枯れ木も山のにぎわい Even dead trees decorate a hill.（➤直訳）／Something is better than nothing. ‖枯れ木に花 Blossoms on a dead tree.

がれき 瓦礫 debris /dəbríː ‖ débriː/（破壊されたものの山）; **rubble**（岩・れんがなどの破片）▶ビルは爆破され，一瞬のうちにがれきの山となった The building was blown up and in an instant turned into *a heap of debris* [*rubble*].

かれくさ 枯れ草 dead [**withered**] **grass**.

かれこれ about（およそ）▶父がシカゴに転勤してかれこれ

5年たった It's been *about* [*nearly* ／*almost*] five years since my father was transferred to Chicago. ‖ 祖父はもう**かれこれ**80になります My grandfather is *close to* eighty. (➤ close /klous/ to は「…に近い」の意).

かれさんすい 枯れ山水 ▶枯れ山水の庭 a *dry landscape* garden.

かれし 彼氏 one's **boyfriend** ▶あの人, 真知子の**彼氏**よ That man is Machiko's *boyfriend*.

カレッジ a **college** ▶カレッジライフを楽しむ enjoy one's *college days* (➤ college life は一般的ではない).

かれは 枯れ葉 a **dead leaf** ▶**枯れ葉**が地面を覆っている The ground is covered with *dead leaves*.

かれら 彼ら they(主格), **their** (所有格), **them** (目的格) ; **theirs** (彼らのもの) ; **themselves** (彼ら自身) ▶**彼ら**は皆同じクラブに入った *They* all joined the same club. ‖ 私は**彼ら**が禅に興味があるかどうか(**彼らに**)聞いてみた I asked *them* if *they* were interested in Zen. ‖ **彼らの**国籍はどこですか What are *their* nationalities？‖ その野球のグローブは**彼らのもの**だ The baseball gloves are *theirs*.

1**かれる 枯れる die** ; **wither** (しおれる) ▶**枯れた**葉 *dead* [*withered*] leaves ‖ 花は水をやらないとすぐに**枯れる** Without water, flowers soon *die* [*wither*]. ‖ 庭のクチナシが霜に遭って**枯れてしまった** Frost *killed* the gardenia in our garden. (➤ kill は「枯らす」).
▶近頃あの男優の芸は**枯れて**(＝円熟して)きた That actor's skills *have* greatly *matured* recently.

2**かれる 涸れる go** [**run**] **dry, dry up** ▶この川は乾季になると**かれる** This river *goes* [*runs*] *dry* in the dry season. ‖ 雨が降らなかったので池の水が**かれた** The pond *has dried up* after all these days of no rain.

3**かれる 嗄れる become hoarse** ▶しゃべり過ぎて**声がかれ**ちゃったわ I'*m hoarse* from talking too much. ‖ 彼はひどいかぜをひいて**声がかれている** He *is* [His *voice is*] *hoarse* from a bad cold. ／A bad cold has made his voice *hoarse*.

かれん 可憐な pretty ▶**かれんな**花 a *pretty little* flower ‖ **かれんな**乙女 a *sweet* maiden (➤ maiden /méidn/ は「乙女」に相当する古風な語で, 現代英語では young girl).

カレンダー a **calendar** /kǽləndəʳ/ ▶**カレンダー**をめくる leaf through the *calendar*.

1**かろう 過労 overwork** /òʊvəʳwə́ːʳk/ ▶父は**過労**が原因ですっかり健康を害してしまった My father's health has been greatly damaged by *overwork*. ‖ ぼくはこのところ**過労気味**だ I'm afraid I'*m working too hard* [I'*m overworking*] these days.
☛ **過労死** (→見出語)

2**かろう 家老** a ***karo*** ; highest-ranking official under a *daimyo* (feudal lord)(➤ 説明的な訳).

がろう 画廊 an **art gallery**, a **picture gallery**.

かろうし 過労死 death from overwork ▶部長は**過労死**した The general manager *died from overwork*. (➤ 日本通の外国人の中には「過労死」を *karōshi* とローマ字化して用いる人もいる).

かろうじて 辛うじて barely ; **narrowly** (際どいところで) ▶**辛うじて**死を免れる *barely* escape death ‖ 中田選手はキャッチャーのタッチを**辛うじて**免れ, ホームスチールに成功した Nakata stole home after *narrowly* escaping the catcher's tag. ‖ 巨人はヤクルトに**辛うじて勝った** The Giants *edged* [*nosed out*] the Swallows. (➤ ともにインフォーマルな言い方) ‖ 対話 「期末試験の英語, どうだった？」「**辛うじて**パスしたよ」 "How did you do on the English final？" "I *just barely* passed it."

カロチン 《化学》**carotene** /kǽrətiːn/.

かろやか 軽やかな light and bouncy /báʊnsi/ ▶彼女は幸せいっぱいで足取りも**軽やか**だ She is so happy (that) even her steps are *light and bouncy*. ‖ 彼は**軽やかな**足取りで階段を上っていった He went up the stairs with a *light*, *springy* step.

カロリー a **calorie** /kǽləri/, a **calory** ▶彼女は**カロリー**に気を配っているが体重はあまり減っていない She's watching her *calories* but hasn't lost much weight yet. ‖ ご飯1杯は約140(**キロ**)**カロリー**ある A bowl of cooked rice has about 140 *Calories*. ‖ ポテトチップスは**カロリー**が高い Potato chips are high in *calories*. ‖ このアイスクリームはあのアイスクリームよりも**カロリー**が低い This ice cream has fewer *calories* than that ice cream. ‖ メニューに**カロリー数**を載せる list *calorie counts* on a menu.
‖**カロリー制限** calorie restriction ‖ **低カロリー食品** (a) low-calorie food.

ガロン a **gallon** (➤《米》では3.785リットル,《英》では4.546リットルに当たる).

かろんじる 軽んじる make light [**little**] **of** ▶戦争ではいつも人間の命が**軽んじられる** Human life *is* always *made light of* in war. ／Life *is cheap* in war. ‖ この改定は前任者たちの貢献を**軽んじる**ものではありません This revision is not to *belittle* the contribution of our predecessors.

1**かわ 川・河** a **river**(比較的大きな川) ; a **stream**, a **brook** (小川 ; 後者はやや文語的で「渓流」に近い) ▶**川を歩いて渡る** ford [walk across] *a river* (➤ ford は「浅瀬を渡る」) ‖ この**川**で泳ぐな Don't swim in this *river*. ‖ 少年は**川**を飛び越えようとした The boy tried to jump over the *stream* [*brook*]. ‖ **天竜川**の**川下り**はとても楽しかった It was great fun boating [shooting] down *the Tenryu* (*River*).
✉ **私たちの町の真ん中には川が流れています** *A river runs* right through the center of our town.

語法 (1)「…川」は the ... River [river] を用い, the Tenryu River(天竜川), the Sumida River (隅田川), the Tone River(利根川)のようにいうが, the つきの場合は用例のように River [river] を省略してもよい.
(2)《英》用法では the River Tenryu, the River Sumida のような語順になることがある.

直訳の落とし穴「川を飛び越える」
「川」をすぐ river と訳しがちだが, 英語の river はかなり大きな川にしかふつうは用いない. したがって,「川を飛び越える」を jump over a river と訳すと相手はびっくりするだろう. 日本人が考えているのはせいぜい「小川」であるから, jump over a stream [brook] とする必要がある.

2**かわ 皮・革** 1【動物の皮膚】(a) **skin** ; (a) **hide**, (a) **pelt** (生皮 ; 前者は大きな動物の, 後者は小さな動物の) ; **leather** (なめし革) ▶**動物の皮**で作ったコート a coat made out of (*an*) *animal hide* ‖ ビーバーの**皮** a beaver *pelt* ‖ ヒョウ**皮** leopard *skin* ‖ 日に焼けて**皮**がむけてきた My *skin* is peeling from (a)

sunburn. ‖ 牛の皮はなめし革を作るのに使える *Cow skins* can be used to make *leather*.
▶《慣用表現》ひと皮むけばみんな欲の塊みたいな連中だ *When you get below the surface*, they are all a bunch of greedy louts. ‖ あいつの面の皮の厚いことったら What (*a*) *nerve* he *has*! ／What *a pushy guy* he is!
‖ **革靴** leather shoes ‖ **革細工** leatherwork ‖ **革ジャン** a leather jacket ‖ **革製品** leather goods [products].
2【果物や野菜の皮, 樹皮】(a) **skin**（薄い皮）; (a) **peel**（主にむいた皮）; (a) **rind** /raɪnd/（厚い皮）; (a) **bark**（木の皮）▶リンゴの皮をむく *peel* an apple ‖ 竹の子の皮をむく *strip* a bamboo shoot ‖ ジャガイモを皮ごとゆでる boil potatoes *with the skin on* ‖ トマトを皮ごと食べる eat a tomato *skin and all* ‖ スイカの皮は厚い Watermelons have thick *rinds*.

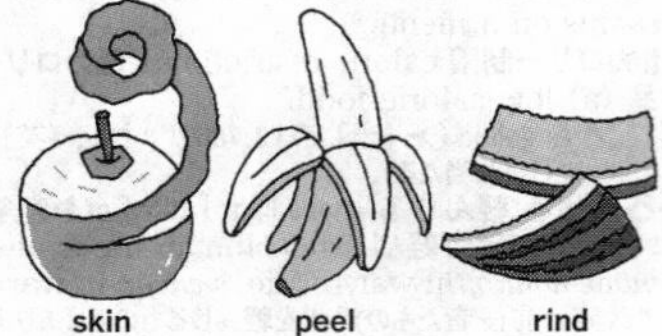

3【外側を包むもの】▶シュークリームの皮 a puff *shell* ‖ ギョーザの皮 a pot sticker *skin* ‖ パン[パイ]の皮 the *crust* of bread [a pie]（➤「パイの皮」は pie shell ともいう）.

逆引き熟語 ○○皮
◆**クマ皮** bearskin ／**サメ皮** sharkskin ／**ヘビ皮** snakeskin ／**ワニ皮** a crocodile [an alligator] skin
◆**オレンジの皮** an orange peel [rind] ／**ジャガイモの皮** a potato skin ／**スイカの皮** the rind of a watermelon, a watermelon rind ／**タマネギの皮** an onion skin ／**トウモロコシの皮** a cornhusk ／**バナナの皮** a banana peel [《英》skin] ／**ブドウの皮** a grape skin ／**リンゴの皮** an apple skin [peel]

がわ 側 **1【側面】** a **side** ▶川の向こう側に刑務所がある There is a prison on *the other side* of the river. ‖ 日本では車は**左側**の車線を走る In Japan, cars are driven on *the left*(*-hand*) *side* of the road [on *the left*]. ‖ シリコンバレーはサンフランシスコの**南側**にある Silicon Valley is *to the south of* San Francisco.
2【一方の側】 a **side** ▶その論争では彼は私の側についた He took *my side* in that controversy. ‖ その外交交渉においては**日本側**が大幅に譲歩した In the diplomatic negotiations, *the Japanese side* made a major concession.
▶労使の団体交渉で**労組側**の結束が崩れた The unity of *the labor side* collapsed in the course of collective bargaining.

かわいい 可愛い **1【愛らしい, 気に入っている】** **little**; **cute**（主に子供･動物が）; **pretty**（小さくて, 見て気持ちがよくて）▶かわいい小犬 a *little* dog（➤ small には「かわいい」のニュアンスはない）‖ まあ, **かわいい**, この赤ちゃん! Isn't this baby *cute*!（➤ この文は下降調で言う）‖ 風見君ってかわいくてすてき! Kazami is really *cute*! ‖ このバッグ, かわい〜い! Isn't this handbag *lovely*!（➤ lovely は「愛らしい, すてき」の意で, 主に女性用語）‖ あの女子大にはかわいい子がいっぱいいる There are a lot of *pretty* girls at that women's college.
▶ **対話**「うちの夫ったら, 会社から I love you. なんてメールを送ってくるのよ」「あら, **かわいいとこあるじゃない**」"My husband sends me text messages from work saying, 'I love you.'" "That's really *sweet* of him."（➤ sweet は「優しい」）‖ 彼女は私たちを見るとにこっとかわいらしく笑った She smiled *sweetly* when she saw us.
2【形が小さい】 **small** ▶このメーカーのバッグにはかわいいサイズもある This bag manufacturer offers [sells] a *smaller* size as well. ／Some bags from this manufacturer also come in a *cute*, *smaller* size.
3【いとしい, 愛情を感じる】▶人間誰だって, 自分のことがいちばんかわいい Everyone *loves* himself or herself the most. ‖ おじいちゃんたら孫がかわいくてしょうがないみたい Grandpa *treasures* his grandchildren. ／The grandchildren are *the apple of our grandpa's eye*.（➤ the apple of ~'s eye は「目に入れても痛くないもの」）.
ことわざ かわいい子には旅をさせよ Send your beloved child traveling.（➤ 日本語からの直訳）／The best education for an indulged child is being [to be] forced out into the world.

かわいがる 可愛がる **love** ＋目 ▶彼の祖父母は孫たちをとても**かわいがる** His grandparents *love* their grandchildren very much. ‖ **かわいがっていた孫娘に先立たれました** My *beloved* granddaughter died. ‖ 妻は息子をかわいがり過ぎる（＝甘やかす）My wife *pampers* our son *too much*. ／My wife *is spoiling* our son.（➤ spoil には「甘やかし過ぎてだめにする」というニュアンスがある）.
▶《比喩的》若造, **かわいがってやる**からかかってこい Now, come on young man! I'll *give you a real workout*!（➤ workout は本来「(スポーツの)練習」の意）.

かわいげ 可愛げ ▶あの男の子はかわいげがないので誰も付き合いたがらない That boy *has no endearing qualities*, so everybody avoids his company. ‖ 横柄なじいさんだね. 年寄りはもっとかわいげがなくちゃあ What an arrogant old man he is! Elderly people should *be* more *friendly*.

かわいこちゃん かわいい子ちゃん a **cutie** /kjúːṭi/ ▶おっす, かわい子ちゃん! 名前は何ていうの? Hello, *cutie*! What's your name?

かわいそう 可哀相･可哀想 一形 **かわいそうな** **poor**（哀れな）; **sad**（悲しむべき）; **pitiful**（ふびんな）▶かわいそうな孤児 a *poor* orphan ‖ **かわいそうな話** a *sad* story ‖ 足を折ったかわいそうな子猫 a *pitiful* kitten with a broken paw.
▶かわいそうに加藤君, 学校でいじめられてるのよ *Poor* Kato is being bullied at school. ／Poor Kato! *I feel sorry* for him. He is being bullied at school. ‖ 犬をそんなにいじめるなよ. **かわいそうじゃないか** Don't tease the *poor* dog like that.（➤ 英語では「かわいそうな犬をいじめるな」と考える）‖ **まあかわいそう!** このハトけがをしてるわ The pigeon is hurt—*poor thing*. ‖ **かわいそうに**. スワローズはまた負けたよ *Too bad!* The Swallows lost the game again.（➤ Too bad! は「残念だ, 気の毒だ」の意のくだけた言い方）‖ おしゅうとめさんと一緒に住んでいたときはおふくろは**かわいそうだった** My mother was *miserable* when she was living

with her mother-in-law. (➤ miserable は「惨めな」).

かわいらしい 可愛らしい →かわいい.

カワウソ 《動物》 an **otter**.

かわかす 乾かす dry +目 ▶洗濯物を乾燥機で乾かす *dry* washed clothes in a dryer.

▶服を火で乾かしなさい *Dry* the clothes by [in front of] the fire.

かわかみ 川上 the upper reaches (of a river) 一副 **川上に upstream, up the river** ▶この川の川上にダムがある There is a dam *up* this river. ‖ 川上でマスが釣れるよ You can catch trout *in the upper reaches of the river*.

1**かわき 乾き** ▶きょうはからっとしていて洗濯物の乾きが早いわ The air is dry today, so the laundry will *dry quickly*.

2**かわき 渇き** (a) **thirst**(喉の渇き) ▶喉の渇きを覚える *feel thirsty* / *have a thirst* ‖ この曲を聴いていると心の渇きが癒やされるようだ I feel as though *a thirst in my heart* were quenched when I listen to this music.

かわぎし 川岸 a **(river) bank** ▶川岸を歩く walk along the *bank* [*riverside*].

かわきり 皮切り ▶そのミュージシャンは東京を皮切りに各地で公演する The musician is to perform in various parts of Japan [nationwide], *starting with* Tokyo.

1**かわく 乾く dry** ▶洗濯物が乾いたら取り込んでおいてね Take in the laundry after it *dries*, will you? ‖ 天気が悪くて洗濯物がなかなか乾かない The laundry [washing] *doesn't dry* well in this bad weather.

▶空気が乾いていますから火の元には十分注意してください It [The air] is very *dry* now, so be careful with fire.

2**かわく 渇く get thirsty** ▶喉が渇いた I'*m* [I *feel*] *thirsty*. ‖ 炎天下をずっと歩いて来たので, 喉がからからに渇いている After walking so far under the blazing sun, my throat *is parched*. ‖ 湧き水で渇いた喉を潤した I *quenched my thirst* with some spring-water.

かわくだり 川下り ▶船で川下りをする *go down a river* in a boat [by boat] / *go downstream* in a boat / boat down a river.

かわざかな 川魚 a **river fish**.

かわざんよう 皮算用 →たぬき.

かわしも 川下 the lower reaches (of a river) 一副 **川下に downstream, down the river** ▶川下に行くほど川幅は広くなる The river gets wider as you go *downstream*. ‖ ボートが川下に流れた The boat drifted *downstream*.

1**かわす 交わす exchange** +目 ▶意見を交わす *exchange* opinions ‖ 近所の人とスーパーで出会い, 挨拶を交わした I came across my neighbor in the supermarket and *exchanged* greetings with her.

▶首相は大統領と握手を交わした The Prime Minister *shook hands with* the President. ‖ 服部君とはことばを交わしたことがない I've never *spoken to* [*with*] Hattori.

2**かわす dodge**(ひらりと体を; 比喩的にも用いる) ▶打者は悪球をひらりとかわした The batter nimbly *dodged* a bad pitch.

▶その政治家は答えにくい質問をかわすのが実にうまい That politician is very good at *dodging* difficult questions.

かわせ 為替 a **money order**; **exchange** (外国為替) ▶郵便為替で5000円送る send *a postal money order* for five thousand yen.

▶ユーロと円の為替レートが最近激しく変動している The euro-yen *exchange rate* has been fluctuating a lot recently.

‖**為替手形** a bill of exchange.

かわせみ 《鳥》 a **kingfisher** ▶カワセミは魚捕りの名人だ *Kingfishers* are expert fishers.

かわぞこ 川底 a **river bottom**; a **riverbed**(川床).

かわった 変わった

1【ふつうでない】strange; **odd** (とっぴな); **eccentric** /ɪkséntrɪk/ (常軌を逸した) ▶変わった男 a *strange* guy ‖ 彼女には別に変わったところはない There is nothing *strange* about her.

▶マミは変わった髪形をしている Mami has an *odd* hairstyle.

▶夫は真夜中に食事をするという変わった習慣をもっている My husband has an *eccentric* [*a peculiar*] habit of eating at midnight.

▶ 対話 (電話で)「もしもし, 紀香ちゃん? 佐賀の重子です. そちらは変わったことないですか」「あ, おばさん, お陰さまで皆元気です」"Hello, Norika? This is Shigeko in Saga. *Is everything O.K.* [*all right*] *there?*" "Oh, Aunt Shigeko. We're all fine, thanks." (➤ How are things there? や What's new? と言うことも多い).

2【違った】different; **new** (新しい) ▶アメリカへ行って何か変わったことを経験したい I hope to experience *something new and different* in the United States.

かわばた 川端 a **riverside**(川沿い); a **riverbank**(川岸) ▶川端の柳 a willow *on the riverbank*.

かわはば 川幅 the width of a river.

かわびらき 川開き a river festival marking the arrival of the summer season(➤ 説明的な訳).

かわむこう 川向こう the opposite side of a river ▶川向こうの町 a city *across the river*.

かわも 川面 the surface of a river.

かわや 厠 an **old-fashioned toilet**.

1**かわら 瓦** a **tile** ▶瓦屋根の家 a *tile-roofed* house.

2**かわら 川原・河原 the shores of a river** ▶きのうは多摩川の川原で1日過ごした Yesterday we spent the day in the *area along the Tama River*.

1かわり 代わり・替わり

1【代わりのもの】 一副 **代わりに instead** 《of》 ▶包帯が無かったので代わりにハンカチを使った Since we didn't have a bandage, we used a handkerchief *instead*. ‖ 鉛筆の代わりにボールペンを使ってもよろしい You can use a ball-point pen *instead of* a pencil.

▶このテーブルは机の代わりになる This table *serves as* a desk.

2【代理】 a **substitute** /sʌ́bstɪtjùːt/ (代理人); a **replacement**(入れ代わりのもの) ▶いつもの先生が病気なので, きょうは代わりの先生が教えています The regular teacher is ill, so *a substitute* is teaching today. ‖ うちの野球チームのコーチが辞めたので代わりの人を探しています The coach of our baseball team quit, so we are looking for *someone to take his place* [*for a replacement*]. ‖ 石井に彼女の代わりは務まらないよ Ishii can't *replace* her. / Ishii can't *fill her shoes*. (➤ fill ~'s shoes は「~の後釜に座る」) ‖ きょう私は柴田先生の代わりをした I *substituted for* Mr.

Shibata today.

【文型】
A の代わりに
instead of A
in place of A ／**in** A's **place**
《解説》「…の代わりのものとして，…の代理に」の意.
…する代わりに
instead of doing

▶地下鉄の代わりにタクシーに乗った We took a taxi *instead of* the subway. ‖首相の代わりにその秘書官がパーティーに出席した The secretary attended the party *in place of* [*for*] the Prime Minister. ‖新聞紙や雑誌は捨てる代わりに, リサイクルすべきです We should recycle newspapers and magazines *instead of* throwing them out.

3【交換, 代償】一副 代わりに in exchange (for) ▶中国人の女性から中国語を教えてもらう代わりに日本語を教えてあげた I taught Japanese to a Chinese woman *in exchange for* Chinese lessons. ‖彼の仕事は大失敗もない代わり大成功もない *Although* he has made no big mistakes, he has achieved no big successes.

☛ **お代わり, その代わり** (→見出語)

[2]**かわり 変わり** ▶最近はどこの大学も大して変わりがない *There's no real difference* between universities and colleges these days. ‖ちっともお変わりになりませんね *You haven't changed a bit.*

▶ 対話「お変わりありませんか」「はい, おかげさまで」"*How have you been?*" "I've been all right, thank you."

✉ **この前お会いして以来, お変わりないことと思います** I hope (that) *everything has been going well* for you since I saw you last.

かわりばえ 代わり映え ▶新内閣の顔ぶれは代わり映えがしない The new Cabinet lineup *is no better than* the last one. ／The new Cabinet *is none the better for the change* in members. (➤ none the better for は「…にもかかわらず一向によくない」の意).

かわりはてる 変わり果てる ▶竜巻で町の様子はすっかり変わり果てた The town *was changed beyond recognition* after the passage of the tornado. (➤ beyond recognition は「見分けがつかないほど」) ‖彼女はわが子の変わり果てた姿を見て泣いた She sobbed when she saw *the lifeless form* of her child.

かわりばんこ 代わり番こ ▶代わりばんこにしようよ Let's *take turns.* ‖ぼくたちは代わりばんこに運転して九州一周のドライブをした We *took turns driving* [*at the wheel*] while touring around Kyushu. (➤ at the wheel は「ハンドルを握って」).

かわりみ 変わり身 ▶変わり身の早い人 a person who *is quick to adapt to changing circumstances.*

かわりめ 変わり目 ▶私は季節の変わり目には体調を崩しやすい My health often worsens at *the turn* [*change*] *of the seasons.*

かわりもの 変わり者 an **odd fellow**, an **eccentric** (**person**), 《インフォーマル》 an **oddball** ▶あの人は有名な学者だが変わり者で通っている Though he is a famous scholar, he is also known as something of *an oddball.*

かわる 変わる・代わる・替わる・換わる

📖 **訳語メニュー**
変化する →change **1**
移動する →shift **2**
取って代わる →replace **4**
引き継ぐ →take over **4**

1【形や状態が異なるものになる】change(変化する)；**vary**(一様でない) ▶車のスタイルはしばしば変わる Car styles often *change.* ‖秋には木の葉の色が変わる In (the) fall, the leaves on (the) trees *change* color.

【文型】
A が B に変わる
A **changes into** [**to**] B.
A **turns into** [**to**] B.
《解説》into は変化に, to は変化後の結果に力点がある.

▶水が水蒸気に変わった Water *changed into* steam. ‖雨が雪に変わった Rain *turned to* snow. ‖毛虫はチョウに変わった The caterpillar *turned* [*transformed*] *into* a butterfly. ‖このポリープはがんに変わる可能性がある This polyp could *turn into* cancer. ‖城はホテルに変わった The castle *was turned* [*converted*] *into* a hotel. (● 自ら変わったのではなく, 変えられたのであるから受け身形にする).

▶アルプスの天気は急に変わる(＝変わりやすい) The weather in the Alps is very *changeable.* ‖あの店主は相手によってころりと態度が変わる That shopkeeper quickly *changes* his manner depending on the customer he is serving [is talking to]. ‖洪水で川の流れが変わった The flood caused the river to *change* its course. ／The river's course *was altered* due to the flood. ‖その事故以来, 彼女は人が変わった After the incident, she *was a changed woman.* ‖結婚してから彼はすっかり変わった He *became a new man* after getting married.

▶日本語では話す相手の社会的地位に応じて丁寧度が変わる In Japanese, the degree of politeness you use *varies* according to the social position of the person you are talking to.

2【移動する】shift ▶風が北風に変わった The wind *has shifted to* the north. ‖1868年, 日本の首都は京都から東京に変わった In 1868, Japan's capital *was moved* [*shifted*] from Kyoto to Tokyo. ‖今度, 仕事が変わりました I *moved into* a new job recently. ／My job *changed* recently. ‖陸上競技大会は19日から24日に変わった The date of the track meet *was changed* from the 19th to the 24th.

3【あるものをどけて別のものになる】 ▶すみませんが席を代わっていただけませんか Excuse me, would you mind *changing seats* with me? ‖最近, 窓ガラスはプラスチックに代わってきている Lately, the material used for windowpanes *has changed* from glass to plastic.

4【別の人が務める】replace ＋目 (取って代わる)；**take over** (引き継ぐ) ▶西田さんが病気になったので川野さんが代わって劇に出た Kawano *replaced* Nishida in the play when she became sick. ‖小田先生が病気なのできのうは森先生が代わって教えた Mr.Oda was sick, so Mr. Mori taught *in his place* yesterday. ‖だいぶ眠そうだから, 運転代わろうか You look awfully sleepy. Shall I *drive* [*take* the wheel]? (➤ wheel は「ハンドル」). ‖《電話で》ちょっとお待ちください. 父と代わります Hold the line, please. I'll *put* my father *on.* ‖ どなたか日本語のできる方と代わっていただけますか Could I *talk to* someone who speaks Japanese? ‖ 対話「先生が出席をとるとき，俺に代わって返事しておいてくれないか」「うん，いいよ」"Will you answer *for me* when the teacher calls the roll [takes attendance]?" "Okay. No problem."

かわるがわる 代わる代わる ▶余興に3人が代わる代わる歌を歌った Three people *took turns* singing (songs) to provide entertainment.

¹**かん 缶** a **can**,《英また》a **tin** ▶缶ビール *canned* beer／beer *in cans* ‖ 缶入りのオレンジジュースを2本ください Could I have two *cans of orange juice*, please?
☛ 缶切り，缶詰（→見出語）

²**かん 巻** a **volume** /vɑ́ːljəm/ ; a **reel**（映画フィルム）▶5巻物の作品 a work in five *volumes* ‖ その百科事典は全30巻だ The encyclopedia is made up of 30 *volumes*.

³**かん 感** ▶20年ぶりに再会した2人は感極まって号泣した When they met after 20 years, they *were so overcome with emotion* [*reached such a pitch of emotion*] that they burst into tears. ‖ 正義感の強い青年 a young man with a strong *sense of justice* ‖ その本の読後感はどんなものですか What was your *impression* of that book?

⁴**かん 勘** **intuition** /ìntjuíʃən/, **instincts** /ínstɪŋkts/（直観）; a **sixth sense**（第六感）; a **hunch** /hʌntʃ/（予感）▶息子は勘がいい My son *has good intuition.*／My son *catches on quickly*. (➤ catch on (to) は「(…に)すぐ感づく」) ‖ 父は勘が鈍い My father *is slow to catch on* (to things). ‖ 男性より女性のほうが概して勘が鋭い Generally, women are more *intuitive* than men. ‖ 事業で成功するには運だけでなく勘も必要だ To succeed in business, you need *business instincts* as well as (good) luck.
▶やっぱり雨だ．勘（＝予感）が当たったわ It's begun to rain. My *hunch was right*. ‖ 彼女は夫の浮気が勘でわかった She knew *by intuition* [*by a sixth sense*] that her husband was having an affair with another woman.

⁵**かん 癇・疳** ▶かんの強い子 a *temperamental* [*an irritable*] child ‖ 彼女のことばがかんに障った Her remarks *irritated* me.／I *was irritated* by her remarks. ‖ かんに障るやつだ He *gets on my nerves*.

⁶**かん 寒** **midwinter**（真冬）; **the coldest season**（最も寒い季節）▶寒の入り［明け］the beginning [end] of *the coldest season* ‖ 今週末には寒の戻りがありそうです It looks like *the cold weather will be back with us* for the weekend.

⁷**かん 燗** ▶燗をつける *warm sake* (*rice wine*).

¹**-かん -間** **1**【時間】**for** ▶私たちは廃校に抗議して2日間ストをした We went on a strike *for* two days in protest against closing down our school. ‖ ここで5分間の休憩を取ります We will *have a five-minute break* [*take five*] now.
2【場所】▶東京・ロサンゼルス間は飛行機で10時間です You can fly *from* Tokyo *to* Los Angeles in ten hours. ‖ 新宿・南小谷間を特急『あずさ』が走っている The special express "Azusa" runs *between* Shinjuku *and* Minami-Otari.
3【野球】▶二遊間を抜くヒットを放つ hit a single *up the middle* ‖ 岡田は三本間に挟まれた Okada was run down *between third and home*. ‖ 球は右中間を抜けた The ball went *through right and center*.
4【人・組織など】▶男女間の賃金格差を是正する rectify *gender-based* wage disparities (➤ gender-based は「性の違いを基準にした」).

²**-かん -観** ▶楽天的な人生観 an optimistic *outlook* [*view*] *of life* ‖ あの外国人の日本観はとてもユニークだ That foreigner's *view of Japan* is very unique.

¹**がん 雁**《鳥》a **wild goose**［複 **wild geese**］▶ガンは渡り鳥だ *Wild geese* are migratory birds.

²**がん 癌** (a) **cancer** /kǽnsəʳ/ ; a **malignant tumor**（悪性腫瘍）▶胃がん［肝臓がん］で死ぬ die of *stomach* [*liver*] *cancer* ‖ おばは乳がんに冒されとうとう亡くなった My aunt developed *breast cancer* and eventually died of [from] it. ‖ おじはがんにかかっていることがわかってから5年生きた My uncle lived five years after discovering he had *cancer*. ‖ 彼は末期がんと診断された He was diagnosed with *terminal cancer*. ‖ 彼女はがんとの長い闘いの末亡くなった She died after *a long battle with cancer*. ‖ 彼の肺がんはほかの臓器に転移している His *lung cancer* has spread to his other organs.
‖ **がん患者** a cancer patient ‖ **がん細胞** a cancer cell ‖ **がん治療** cancer treatment ‖ **抗がん剤** an anti-cancer drug(➤ 通常は cancer drug という).

> **「がん」のいろいろ** 胃がん stomach cancer／咽頭がん pharyngeal cancer／肝臓がん liver cancer／結腸がん colon cancer／口こうがん oral [mouth] cancer／甲状腺がん thyroid cancer／子宮がん uterine /júːṭərəm/ cancer／子宮頸(けい)がん cervical cancer／食道がん esophageal /ɪsɑ̀ːfədʒíːəl ‖ iːsɔ̀f-/ cancer／腎臓がん kidney cancer／すい臓がん pancreatic cancer／舌がん tongue cancer／前立腺がん prostate cancer／大腸がん cancer of the large intestine／直腸がん rectal cancer／乳がん breast cancer／肺がん lung cancer／皮膚がん skin cancer／ぼうこうがん bladder cancer／卵巣がん ovarian cancer ➤ なお，brain cancer は「悪性脳腫瘍」，bone cancer は「骨肉腫」に当たる

³**がん 願** a **prayer** /preəʳ/（祈り）; a **wish**（願い事）▶試験に受かるよう八幡(はちまん)様に願を懸けた I *offered prayers* at the Hachiman Shrine for (my) passing the examination.

かんい 簡易 ‖ **簡易書留** simplified registered mail [《英また》post] ‖ **簡易裁判所** a summary court ‖ **簡易宿泊所**《米》a (cheap) rooming house,《英》a (cheap) lodging house ;《米・インフォーマル》a flophouse,《英・インフォーマル》a dosshouse ‖ **簡易ベッド**《米》a cot,《英》a camp bed ‖ **簡易保険** postal [post-office] life insurance (➤ 英米にはない).

かんいっぱつ 間一髪 ▶間一髪のところで終電車に間に合った We (*just*) *barely* made the last train. ‖ 間一髪のところでトラックにひかれずに済んだ I *narrowly* missed being run over by a truck.／I avoided being run over by a truck *by a hairs breadth*.

かんえん 肝炎《医学》**hepatitis** /hèpətáɪṭɪs/
‖ **A型［B型］肝炎** hepatitis (type) A [B] ‖ **急性［慢性］肝炎** acute [chronic] hepatitis ‖ **血清肝炎** serum /síərəm/ hepatitis.

がんえん 岩塩 **rock salt.**

かんおけ 棺桶 a **coffin** ; a **casket**（➤ 婉曲(えんきょく)語）▶やっこさんはもう棺おけに片足を突っ込んでるよ He's got one foot in the *grave*. (➤ grave は「墓」).

¹**かんか 感化** **influence** ▶英文学に興味をもつようになったのは本田先生の感化によるものだ It was through Mr. Honda's *influence* that I became interested in

English literature. ‖ 友人から悪い感化を受けた My friend has been *a bad influence* on me.

²**かんか 看過** ▶これは看過できない問題だ This is a problem we *can't overlook* [*shouldn't leave unaddressed*].

¹**がんか 眼下** ▶眼下にグランドキャニオンが広がっていた I saw the Grand Canyon lying *far below me*.

²**がんか 眼科** 《医学》 **ophthalmology** /à:fθælmá:lədʒi/ ‖**眼科医** an eye doctor, an ophthalmologist.

¹**かんがい 灌漑** **irrigation** 一動 **かんがいする** **irrigate** +目 ▶乾燥した土地をかんがいする *irrigate* [*bring water to*] dry land ‖**かんがい池** an irrigation reservoir /rézəˈvwà:ˈ/ ‖ **かんがい用水** irrigation water.

²**かんがい 感慨** ▶ 対話「大関昇進おめでとうございます. 今のお気持ちはいかがですか」「感慨無量です」"Congratulations on your promotion to (the rank of) ozeki. How do you feel now ?" "*I'm overwhelmed with emotion.*" (➤ Thinking [Remembering] of how hard it was, I'm overwhelmed (with emotion). のように言ってもよい. →感無量).

³**かんがい 干害** **drought** /draʊt/ **damage**.

かんがえ 考え

📖 訳語メニュー
思考 →thought, idea **1**
意見 →opinion **2**
思いつき →idea **3**

1【考えること, 思考】**thought**, an **idea** (➤ 前者には「理性的に得られた」というニュアンスが強い) ▶新しい[古い]考え a new [an old] *idea* ‖ そこまでは考えが及ばなかった I *hadn't considered such a possibility*. ／I *hadn't thought such a thing would happen*. ‖ こんな重大な事故が起きるとは, 我々の考えが足りなかった The reason we had this kind of serious accident was because we *hadn't thought deeply* [*carefully*] *enough*.

▶息子は何とでも暮らしていけると思っているが, 考えが甘い My son thinks he'll be able to make a living somehow or other, but it's *just* (*his*) *wishful thinking*. ‖ 彼女は後先の考えもなく(＝結果を考えずに)高価な帯を買ってしまった She went out and bought an expensive obi *without thinking of the consequences* (*at all*).

2【意見】one's **opinion**; **ideas** (考え方); a **notion** (根拠のない, 漠然とした) ▶考えが進歩的な人 a person with progressive *ideas* ‖ 自分自身の考えをもちなさい Form your own *opinion*(*s*). ‖ ぼくの考えでは自動車の生産は制限されるべきだ *In my opinion*, the production of cars should be limited. (● (×) in my idea としないこと) ‖ 弟は地球に四隅があるというおかしな考えを持っている My younger brother has a strange *notion* that the earth has four corners.

▶私は彼女の考えがわからなかった I couldn't understand *what she was thinking* (*about*). ‖ きみの考えはもう古い Your *idea* is [*ideas* are] old-fashioned. ‖ 人それぞれに考えは違う No two people have exactly the same ideas.

3【思いつき】an **idea** ▶いい考えがある I've got a good *idea*. ／I've had *a brainstorm*. (➤ 《米》では後者のようにもいう) ‖ それはいい考えだ That's a good *idea*.

4【意図, 予定】(an) **intention** ▶私は辞任する考えはありません I have no *intention* of resigning. ‖ 卒業したらふるさとに帰って働く考えです I *am going to* go back to my hometown and find a job after graduation. ‖ そちらがその気なら私にも考えがある If you're going to be like that, *watch out for me*. ／Remember that two can play at that game. (● 後者は「そのゲームは2人でできることを忘れるな」と考える英語的発想に基づく訳例).

かんがえかた 考え方 one's **way of thinking**; one's **point of view** (観点) ▶考え方のしっかりした女性 a *sensible* woman ‖ ぼくは父とは考え方が違う My father and I *don't think alike*. ‖ あなたの考え方は間違っている You *are mistaken*. ／You *have the wrong idea*.

▶言語は人々のものの考え方を反映する Language reflects people's *ways of thinking*. ‖ 人生に対する現実的な考え方 a practical *outlook* on life (➤ outlook は「(人生などに対する) 変え方, 姿勢」).

かんがえごと 考え事 ▶彼女はいつも考え事にふけっている She *is* always *deep in thought*. ／She always *has her head in the clouds*. (➤ have one's head in the clouds は「ぼんやりして, 空想にふけって」の意) ‖ 対話「目を閉じて, どうかしたの？」「ちょっと考え事をしてただけだよ」"Sitting there with your eyes closed—is something the matter ?" "No. I *was just thinking about something*."

かんがえこむ 考え込む ▶健二, 何をそんなに考え込んでるの What seems to be *bothering* you, Kenji ? ／What's *on your mind*, Kenji ? ／What's *eating* you, Kenji ? (➤ あとになるほどくだけた言い方).

かんがえだす 考え出す **think up**, **devise** +目 (➤ 後者は堅い語) ▶一体誰がこんな計画を考え出したのか Who *thought up* [*devised*] this project ? ‖ この新製品は社長が自ら考え出したものだ This new product was the *brainchild* of our president. (➤ brainchild は「頭脳の産物, 発明品」の意のくだけた語).

かんがえちがい 考え違い a **misunderstanding** (誤解); a **mistake** (間違い) ▶きみは考え違いをしているよ You *have the wrong idea*. ／You*'re mistaken*.

かんがえつく 考えつく ▶きみ, うまいやり方を考えついたね Hey, that's a great idea you *came up with* !

かんがえなおす 考え直す **think over** (熟考する); **think again**, **reconsider** (もう一度考える; 後者はやや堅い語で「再考する」に相当) ▶S大を受験しようとしたら父が考え直せと言った When I was about to take the entrance exams for S University, my father advised me to *reconsider*. ‖ 大学は遊ぶ所だと思ってるんなら, 考え直すんだね If you think college is a place to play around, (then) *think again*. ‖ 毛皮のコートを買おうと思ったが考え直してやめた I thought of buying a fur coat, but *on second thought* decided against it. ／I had intended to buy a fur coat, but then *thought better of* it. (➤ think better of は「考え直してやめる」) ‖ 対話「いくら頼まれてもだめなものはだめだね」「そこを何とか考え直していただけませんか」"No matter how many times you ask me, no is no." "I understand, but *can't you try to reconsider ?*"

かんがえぬく 考え抜く **think through** [**out**] ▶考え抜いたうえでの結論 a *well thought out* conclusion ‖ 考え抜いた末, 結局医学部へは進学しないことにした After *thinking* it *through* [*out*], I decided not to go to medical school after all.

かんがえぶかい 考え深い **thoughtful**; **prudent** (慎重

な) ▶考え深い人 a *thoughtful* [*prudent*] person ‖ 彼は考え深い人だからそんな軽率なことを言うとは思えない He is too *thoughtful* to have made such a careless comment.

かんがえもの 考えもの ▶彼女があんな場所にひとりで行くのは考えものだ *I don't think it's sensible* of her to go to that kind of place alone. (➤ sensible は「分別のある」).

かんがえる 考える

訳語メニュー
思う →think **1**
想像する →imagine **2**
計画する →plan **3**

1【思う, 思考する】think ; consider (じっくりと) ▶考えてからしゃべりなさい *Think* before you speak.

【文型】
〜と(いうことを)考える
think (**that**) S + V
A について[のことを]考える
think of [**about**] A
➤ A は名詞・動名詞

【解説】(1)think のあとには that の文や wh- 疑問詞の文がよく続く. 前者の場合 that は省略されることが多い.
(2)「A のことを」では of と about が使われる. of は単に「頭に浮かんでくるままに考える, 思いつく」なのに対し, about はより意図的・積極的に「あれこれ考え, 検討する」というニュアンスの違いがある.

▶大半の日本人は日本はもう再び戦争をしないと考えている Most Japanese *think that* Japan will never again wage war. (➤ 今まさに考えている, でなく, 意見としてずっと持っているので, are thinking でなく, think を用いる) ‖ 失業しようとは考えもしなかった I *never thought that* I would lose a job. ‖ あなたのことばかり考えています *I am always thinking of you*. ‖ 私はまだ結婚のことを真面目に考えたことはありません I have never seriously *thought about* marriage.
✉ **もうすぐあなたにお会いできると考えただけで胸がわくわくします** I am thrilled *at just* the thought *of* seeing you soon.
▶そんなこと考えもしなかったよ I *never gave it a thought*. (➤ give ... a thought は「…について考えてみる」) ‖ そのことはもう一度考えてみましょう Let's *think* about that (matter) again. ／Let's *reconsider* that (matter). ／Let's *have another think* about that (matter). (➤ 最後の文は主に《英》) ‖ 考えてみると彼はきのうも居なかった *Come to think of it*, he was absent yesterday, too. (➤ come to think of it は前に When I が省略された形) ‖ 《ぼんやりしている人に》何考えてるの? *What are you thinking about*? ／A penny for your thoughts. (➤ 後者はインフォーマルな表現で,「考えていることを教えてくれれば1ペニーあげる」が原義) ‖ 外国語を学ぶことの本当の意味は何かをよく考えることが大切だ It is important to *consider* what the real significance of learning a foreign language is. ‖ ものは考えようだ It *all depends on how you look at it*. (➤「見方次第で事情は変わる」の意) ‖ 彼女はその問題を一晩寝て考えた She *slept on* the matter.

2【想像する】imagine +㊐ ▶父さんがどんなに怒るか考えてもごらんなさい Just *imagine* how angry Dad will be! ‖ 宇宙戦争とはどんなものか考えたこともない I've never *imagined* what war in space would be like. ‖ あのジェット旅客機が墜落したなんてとても考えられない I *can't believe* the passenger jet crashed.

3【計画する, 思いつく】plan +㊐

【文型】
…しようと考えている
be going to do
be planning to do
be thinking of doing

【解説】 **be going to** do は「…するつもり」という意思を, **be planning to** do は「…する計画」という予定をいう. **be thinking of** doing はあることに焦点を当てて考えている, だが, まだ, 実際の計画や準備開始に至らず, 実現しない[実行しない]可能性もある.

▶将来コンピュータのプログラマーになろうと考えています I *am going to* be a computer programmer in the future. ‖ ハイブリッド車を買おうと考えています I'*m planning to* buy a hybrid car. ‖ 恵まれない人々のために働きたいと考えています I *am thinking of* working for the underprivileged.
▶ **対話**「このタヒチ旅行は誰が考えたの?」「寺田さんです」"*Whose idea* was this Tahiti trip ?" "It was Mr. Terada's." ／"Who *came up with the idea of* going to Tahiti ?" "Mr. Terada did."

4【振り返る】look back《on》▶中学時代のことを考えてみてごらんなさい *Look back on* your junior high school days.

¹かんかく 間隔 an **interval** /íntə^r vəl/ (時間・距離の) ; (a) **space** (物と物との) ▶深夜に近づくほどバスの間隔は長くなる The closer it gets to midnight, the longer the *intervals* between buses become. ‖ 書くときは行の間隔を十分に[もっとゆったりと]取りなさい Leave enough *space* [a larger *space*] between lines when you write. ‖ 50センチの間隔をあけて並びなさい Line up with each person fifty centimeters *apart* from each other. ‖ **対話**「どのくらいの間隔でバスがありますか」「15分間隔です」"*How often* does the bus run ?" "It runs at fifteen-minute *intervals*. ／It runs *every* fifteen minutes."

²かんかく 感覚

1【五感の働き】(a) sense ; feeling (特に触覚) ▶犬は匂いに対する感覚がとても鋭い Dogs have a very keen *sense* of smell. ‖ 右腕の感覚が無くなった I've lost all *feeling* in my right arm. ‖ 寒さで指の感覚が無くなった My fingers *were numb* from [with] cold. ‖ 座布団を敷かないで座っていたら足の感覚が無くなった(＝しびれた) My legs *have gone to sleep* [*have become numb*] from sitting without a cushion.

2【感じ方, 趣味】(a) sense, (a) taste ▶現代感覚の建築 a building of *modern taste* ‖ 彼は新しい感覚のカメラマンとして知られている He is known as a photographer with *an original take* (on things). (➤ take は「…に対する受け止め方」の意の名詞) ‖ カンディンスキーは色彩感覚に優れていた Kandinsky had a marvelous *sense of* [*feel for*] *color*. ‖ 彼のビジネス感覚は経験から得られたものだ His *business sense* came from experience. ‖ 彼女には美的感覚というものが無い She has no *sense of beauty*. ‖ 彼女は音楽に対する優れた感覚(＝聞く耳)を持っている She has *a good ear for music*. ／She is very musical. ‖ あの人とは感覚的に合わないの He's not my kind of guy. ／I don*'t click with* him. ／He and I don*'t click* *with* each other. ‖ 新首相は庶民感覚に疎いようだ The new prime minister looks *out of touch with how ordinary people feel*.

‖ **感覚器官** a sense organ.

☛ **無感覚**（→見出語）

かんかつ 管轄 **jurisdiction**（管轄範囲, 管轄権）▶イギリスでは多くの交通犯罪は警察裁判所の**管轄**下にある In Britain, most driving offenses *come under the jurisdiction of* the police courts.

かんがっき 管楽器 a **wind instrument**

‖ **金管楽器** a brass instrument ‖ **木管楽器** a woodwind (instrument).

カンガルー a **kangaroo** /kæ̀ŋgərúː/ ▶**カンガルー**の雌には袋があって生まれた子をそこで育てる A female *kangaroo* has a pouch in which she raises her young.

かんかん **1【音】**▶時計台の鐘が**カンカン**と鳴る The clock tower bell *clangs*.

2【怒る様子】▶社長は今**かんかん**だから触らぬ神にたたり無しだよ The boss is *furious* about something right now, so you should leave him alone. ‖ 息子が大学に行くつもりはないと言うのを聞き彼は**かんかん**になって怒った He *hit the ceiling* when he heard that his son did not have any intention of going to college. (➤ hit the ceiling は「天井に頭をぶつける」が原義).

3【太陽が照る様子】▶海辺には真夏の太陽が**かんかん**と照りつけている The summer sun is *beating* [*blazing*] *down* on the beach. (➤ beat [blaze] down で「ぎらぎら照りつける」).

かんがん 宦官 a **eunuch** /júːnək/.

がんがん ▶頭が**がんがん**する I *have a throbbing headache*.

▶ガスストーブを**がんがん**たいてもちっとも暖かくならない The room hasn't gotten any warmer, even though we have the gas heater stove on *full blast*.

かんかんがくがく 侃々諤々 ▶彼の報告の結果, **かんかんがくがく**の議論が起こった His report caused *a heated debate*.

かんかんでり かんかん照り ▶**かんかん照り**の天気 *hot and dry* weather ‖ その日は**かんかん照り**だった That day *the sun was blazing down*. ／That day was *a scorcher*.

1**かんき 換気** **ventilation** /vènṭəléɪʃən/ ▶時々部屋の**換気**をしなさい *Ventilate* the room [(Open the window(s) and) *let in some fresh air*] from time to time. ‖ この部屋は**換気**が悪い[よい] This room *is poorly* [*well*] *ventilated*. ‖ **換気**のため書斎の窓が少し開けてある The study window is left slightly open *to let* (*some*) *fresh air in*.

‖ **換気扇** a ventilation [a vent ／an exhaust] fan, a ventilator ; a kitchen fan（台所の）(➤「換気扇を回す」は switch on the fan).

2**かんき 喚起する** **arouse** /əráʊz/ ＋㊐, **stir up** (➤ 前者が日本語により近い) ▶原発建設反対の世論を**喚起する** *arouse* [*stir up*] public opinion against the construction of a nuclear power plant.

3**かんき 歓喜** **joy**, **jubilation**（➤ 後者は堅い語で前者より強意的）; **ecstasy**（有頂天）▶彼は**歓喜**に我を忘れた He was beside himself [was ecstatic] with *joy*.

4**かんき 乾季** a **dry season**.

5**かんき 寒気** **cold air**.

かんきつるい 柑橘類 **citrus fruits**.

かんきゃく 観客 a **spectator**（スポーツなどの）; an **audience** /ɔ́ːdiəns/（コンサート・劇などの ; 集合的）▶巨人の試合はいつも**観客**が多い A Giants game always draws many *spectators* [a large *crowd*]. ‖ **観客**はそのショーにひどく興奮した The show greatly excited the *audience*. ／The *audience* was very excited by the show.

‖ **観客席** a seat ; the stands（スタンド）.

かんきゅう 緩急 ▶松坂は**緩急**をつけたピッチングでピンチを脱した Matsuzaka got out of the pinch with *a good combination of fast and slow pitches*.

がんきゅう 眼球 an **eyeball**.

かんきょう 環境

the environment /ɪnváɪərənmənt/（自然環境）, (an) **environment**（精神面に影響を及ぼす）; **circumstances**（生活環境, 暮らし向き）; **surroundings**（周囲の居住環境）; (an) **environment**（パソコンの）▶**環境**を守る[壊す] protect [destroy] *the environment* (➤「自然環境」は the natural environment ともいえるが, 日本語でも単に「環境」ということがあるのと同様に the environment で表すことが多い) ‖ 働くのに快適な**環境** a congenial work *environment* [*atmosphere*] (➤ 人が受けるその場の印象や感じを含む場合は atmosphere がふさわしい; 待遇を含めた「労働環境」は working conditions) ‖ 快適な**環境**で生活する[育つ] live [grow up] in comfortable *circumstances* ‖ 彼女は恵まれた**家庭環境**に育った She was raised in a well-to-do *family environment*. ‖ 真由はドイツ語が話されている**環境**で育ったので, ドイツ語が堪能だ Mayu is fluent in German because she grew up in a German-speaking *environment*. ‖ もっと**環境**のいい所に住みたい I'd like to live in better *surroundings*.

▶**環境に優しい**容器 an *eco-friendly* container (➤「生態系に優しい」の意. 「環境に優しい」は environment-friendly ／environmentally friendly ともいう) ‖ 松本は美しい**自然環境**にある Matsumoto has beautiful *natural surroundings*.

▶**環境汚染**はますます深刻な問題になってきている *Environmental pollution* is becoming an ever more serious problem. ‖ 我々はこれまであまり**環境保護**に関心を示さなかったというのが実情だ It is fact that we haven't shown much concern for *environmental protection* [for *the environment*] up until now. ‖ 私たちが一番関心をもっているのは**環境問題**です What we're most interested in is *environment problems*.

‖ **環境音楽** environmental music ‖ **環境省** the Ministry of the Environment《参考》アメリカには the Environmental Protection Agency（環境保護局）, イギリスには the Department of the Environment（環境省）がある ‖ **環境破壊** environmental disruption ‖ **環境保護論者** an environmentalist ‖ **環境ホルモン** an environmental hormone (➤ 正式には endocrine disruptor（内分泌かく乱物質）という).

がんきょう 頑強な **stubborn** /stʌ́bəʳn/（不屈の）▶その計画は彼らの**頑強な**反対に遭った The project met with their *stubborn* [*persistent*] opposition. ‖ 彼は私たちに謝ることを**頑強**に拒んだ He *stubbornly* [*obstinately*] refused to apologize to us.

かんきり 缶切り a **can opener**,《英また》a **tin opener** ▶**缶切り**で缶を開ける open a can with *a can opener* [with *an opener*].

1**かんきん 監禁** **confinement** ; **imprisonment**（投獄）— 動 **監禁する** **confine** ＋㊐, **imprison** ＋㊐ ▶一部の過激派学生たちが総長を一室に**監禁した** Some radical students *confined* the president to [*locked* the president in] a room. (➤ lock は「鍵を掛けて閉じ込める」の意).

[2]**かんきん 換金** cashing ▶小切手の換金には2, 3日かかる It takes two or three days to *cash* the check.

がんきん 元金 (a) principal ▶100万円の元金に1年で5千円の利子がついた *A principal* of one million yen yielded 5,000 yen in annual interest.

がんぐ 玩具 a toy, a plaything ▶木製玩具 a wooden *toy* ‖玩具店 a toy store.

かんぐる 勘繰る suspect +㊐ (怪しいと思う) ▶彼は同僚が自分を陥れようとしているのではないかと勘ぐった He *suspected* (that) a co-worker was setting traps for him.

[1]**かんけい 関係** 1【人と人との】(a) relationship, (a) relation (➤ relation が国と国, 組織と組織の協力関係などの公的な場合に用いることが多いのに対して(→3), relationship は個人どうしの行動上, あるいは心理的に親しく感じる断続的な関係を指すことが多い) ▶夫と妻の関係 *the relationship* between husband and wife ‖現代人の多くは複雑な人間関係でストレスを感じている Most people today feel stress caused by complicated *social relationships* [*relations*]. ‖両首脳は親密な関係を築いた The two leaders established *a close relationship* (*with each other*). ‖彼女はその重役と親戚関係にある She *is related to* the director. ‖私とゆかりとはおじとめいの関係です Yukari is my niece—that's our *relationship*. (➤ We are niece and uncle. と言えなくもないが, 個人主義の英語圏ではことさら「関係」を言わず, Yukari is my niece. と言うだけが普通) ‖ 対話「あなたは彼女とはどんな関係にあるのですか」「ただの教師と生徒です」"What's your *relationship* with her?" "Just teacher and student, nothing else [more]." ‖当社はそのセールスマンとは一切関係ございません We *have nothing to do with* that salesman.

2【人と物事との】▶私はその交通事故とは関係ありません I *have nothing to do with* that traffic accident. ‖次期社長に誰がなろうと私には何の関係もありません *It doesn't concern* me *at all* who becomes the next president. ‖あの人が汚職事件に関係していたとは驚いた I am surprised to hear that he *was involved in* political corruption. ‖きみには関係ないよ *None of your business!*

3【国と国との】relations, relationships ▶国際関係 *international relations* ‖その国はロシアと親密な関係にある The country has *close relations* with Russia. ‖その2国の関係が悪化した *Relations* between the two nations have worsened. ‖1941年日本はアメリカと外交関係を断絶した In 1941, Japan broke off *diplomatic relations* with the United States. ‖日朝関係の好転が望まれる It is hoped that *Japan-North Korea relations* will improve.

4【現象などとの関連性】a connection ▶犯罪と貧困との関係 the *connection* between crime and poverty ‖ストレスと胃潰瘍は大いに関係がある Stress *is closely linked to* stomach ulcers. /Stress *has a lot to do with* stomach ulcers. ‖米とアジア人との関係は小麦とヨーロッパ人との関係と同じであるとよく言われる It is often said that rice *is to* Asians *what* wheat *is to* Europeans. (➤ A is to B what X is to Y. は「AのBに対する関係はXのYに対する関係と同じである」の意) ‖水着の売れ行きは夏の暑さと切っても切れない関係にある Summer heat and swimsuit sales *are inseparably connected*.

5【理由, 都合】▶寒い気候の関係で北海道ではバナナができない *Due to* the cold weather in Hokkaido, bananas cannot be grown there. ‖時間の関係でスピーチは各人3分に限らせていただきます *In the interest of time*, each speech will be limited to three minutes. ‖父は仕事の関係でよく出張する My father often *goes on business trips*.

6【方面】▶ 対話「きみのお父さんはどんな関係のお仕事ですか?」「医療関係の仕事です」"What *type* [*line*] *of work* is your father in?" "He has *a healthcare-related* job." (➤ He's in health care. ともいう).

‖《文法》関係代名詞 a relative pronoun ‖《文法》関係副詞 a relative adverb.

☞ 関係者, 無関係 (→見出語)

逆引き熟語 ○○関係
医者と患者の関係 a patient-doctor relationship /因果関係 a casual relationship, cause-and-effect relationships /親子関係 a parent-child relationship /外交関係 diplomatic relations /血縁関係 a blood relationship /国際関係 international relations /婚姻関係 a marital relationship /(男女の)三角関係 a love triangle /信頼関係 a confidential relationship, a relationship of mutual trust /性的関係 a sexual relationship /対人関係 interpersonal relations /縦の(上下)関係 a vertical relationship /人間関係 human relations [relationships] /横の関係 horizontal relations /利害関係 an interest (in) /恋愛関係 a love [romantic] relationship /労使関係 an employer-employee relationship, labor-management relations

[2]**かんけい 奸計** an evil plan [plot].

かんげい 歓迎 a welcome 一動 歓迎する welcome +㊐ ▶歓迎の辞を述べる give *a welcoming address* ‖中国からの客[旅行客]を歓迎する *welcome* guests [tourists] from China ‖ソウルの友人を訪れたとき大歓迎を受けた I *received a warm welcome* when I visited a friend of mine in Seoul. ‖宮崎市の至る所に「歓迎巨人軍」の看板が見られた There were signs saying '*Welcome* Giants' everywhere in Miyazaki City.

▶《掲示》初心者歓迎 Beginners welcome. ‖5月14日に新入生歓迎コンパをする予定です We plan to have *a welcome party* for the new students on May 14. ‖恒例の新入生歓迎コンパ an annual *get-together to welcome* freshmen.

▶彼は歓迎されない客だった He was *an unwelcome guest*. ‖私の提案はあまり歓迎されなかった My proposal *was not well received*.

✉ **日本にいらっしゃったときはいつでもわが家で歓迎しますよ** When you're in Japan, *you are* always *welcome* in my home.

✉ **ぜひ日本へいらっしゃってください. 大歓迎します** Visit us in Japan. *I'll roll out the welcome mat for you*. [*I'll give you a big welcome.*] ➤ roll out the welcome mat は「玄関マットを広げて待っている」の意.

‖歓迎会 a welcome party.

かんげいこ 寒稽古 (a) winter practice ▶柔道の寒稽古 (a) judo *practice in the midst of winter*.

かんけいしゃ 関係者 ▶《手紙の文頭で》関係者各位

To whom it may concern (➤この英語は1人に対しても使える) ‖ その発明は**関係者**の間で話題になっている The invention has drawn much attention from *people in related fields*.

[1]かんげき 感激する **be moved ; be impressed** (感銘を受ける) ▶**感激的な**シーン a *moving* scene ‖ 田村選手が金メダルを受けるのを見たとき, 私はとても**感激した** I *was deeply moved* [*impressed*] when I saw Tamura receive a gold medal. ‖ **対話** 《映画を見たあとで》「おもしろかった？」「うん, **感激しちゃった**」 "How did you like the film [movie] ?" "I *was really moved*."

[2]かんげき 観劇 **theatergoing** ▶趣味は**観劇**です My (favorite) pastime is *going to the theater*.

[1]かんけつ 簡潔な **concise** /kənsáɪs/ ▶**簡潔な**説明 a *concise* explanation ‖ 彼の説明は**簡潔**で要領を得ていた His explanation was *concise* and to the point. ‖ 次の問いに**簡潔**に答えなさい Answer *briefly* the following questions. ‖ **簡潔は機知の精髄** Brevity is the soul of wit. (➤『ハムレット』の中のことばから).

[2]かんけつ 完結 (a) **conclusion** 一**動** **完結する** **conclude** ＋**自** ▶この小説は1年間新聞に連載されたが, ついに**完結した** This serial novel ran for a year in the newspaper, but has at last reached *a conclusion*. ‖ この記事は次号で**完結する**(予定だ) This article *is to be concluded* in the next issue.

かんけつせん 間欠泉 a **geyser** /gáɪzəʳ/.

[1]かんげん 換言 ▶「**換言すれば**」が彼の口癖だ "*In other words*" is his pet phrase.

[2]かんげん 還元 **reduction** (➤化学用語) ▶利益の一部を社会に**還元する** *return* part of the profits to society.

[3]かんげん 甘言 **flattery** (お世辞) ▶彼の**甘言**にだまされてはいけない Don't be deceived by his *flattery*. ‖ 多くの老人が**甘言**に釣られて土地を売らされた Many elderly people were coaxed into selling their property with *honeyed promises* [were sweet-talked into selling their property].

がんけん 頑健な **tough** /tʌf/ ▶さすがに**頑健な**彼もくたくたになったようだ *Strong* [*Tough*] as he is, he seemed (to be) dead tired. (➤「形容詞＋as A is」は「A は…であるにもかかわらず」の意).

かんげんがく 管弦楽 **orchestral music**
‖**管弦楽団** an orchestra /ɔ́:ʳkɪstrə/ 《**参考**》「交響楽団」(symphony orchestra) に対し, philharmonic のつく楽団名に「管弦楽団」の訳語を与えることが多い.

かんこ 歓呼 a **cheer** ▶日本チームが得点したとき観衆の間から**歓呼の声**が上がった When the Japanese team scored a goal, *a cheer* rose from the crowd.

[1]かんご 看護 **nursing ; care** (世話) 一**動** **看護する** **nurse** ＋**自** ; **look after, care for** (世話をする ; 後者のほうが堅い言い方) ▶姉は将来**看護**の仕事に就きたいと思っている My sister wants to make *nursing* her career. ‖ その母親は一晩中病気の子供の**看護をした** The mother *looked after* [*cared for*] her sick child all night.
‖**看護学生** a student nurse ‖ **看護学校** a nurses' school [college] ‖ **看護疲れ** nursing fatigue.
☛ **看護師** (→見出語)

[2]かんご 漢語 a **kanji** [**Chinese**] **word**.

がんこ 頑固 **stubbornness** /stʌ́bəʳnnəs/ (性格上の強情さ) ; **obstinacy** /ɑ́:bstɪnəsi/ (意見を変えないこと) 一**形** **頑固な** **stubborn, obstinate** ▶なんて**頑固な**ロバなんだ What a *stubborn* donkey ! (➤ロバやラバ (mule) は頑固な動物の代表とされる) ‖ そう**頑固な**(＝いこじな)ことを言わないでくれ Don't be so *obstinate*. ‖ この**頑固**おやじめ！ *Pigheaded* old man ! (➤ pigheaded は「石頭の」) ‖ その職人は**頑固**に自分の技を守り続けている That craftsman *tenaciously* safeguards and practices his traditional techniques. ▶この冬の初めは**頑固な**かぜに悩まされた Earlier this winter, I suffered from a *stubborn* [an *obstinate*] cold.

[1]かんこう 観光 **sightseeing** /sáɪtsì:ɪŋ/ (見物すること) ; **tourism** /tʊ́ərìzəm/ (事業としての) ▶**観光**は京都の主要産業である *Tourism* is the major industry of [in] Kyoto. ‖ パリの**市内観光をする** *see* [*do*] *the sights* of Paris ‖ 私たちは九州へ**観光旅行に行った** We *went* to Kyushu *and did some sightseeing*. (➤「観光旅行」は sightseeing tour) ‖ 秋は**観光シーズンだ** Fall is *the tourist season*. ‖ イタリアには**観光地が多い** Italy has a lot of *tourist* [*sightseeing*] *spots*. ‖ 日光は外国人**観光客**が多い There are many foreign *tourists* in Nikko. ‖ **対話** 《通関で》「カナダへ来られた目的は？」「**観光**です」 "What's the purpose of your visit to Canada?" "*Sightseeing*."
‖**観光案内所** a tourist information center ‖ **観光ガイド** a sightseeing [tour] guide ‖ **観光資源** tourist resources ‖ **観光施設** tourist facilities ‖ **観光バス** a sightseeing bus ‖ **観光ホテル** a tourist hotel ‖ **観光立国** a tourism nation.

[2]かんこう 刊行 **publication** 一**動** **刊行する** **publish** ＋**自** ▶今月末に彼の新著が**刊行される**予定だ His new book *is being published* [*is coming out*] at the end of this month. ‖ 近頃新しい漫画雑誌が次々に**刊行されている** These days new manga magazines *are appearing* one after another.
‖**刊行物** a publication ‖ **定期刊行物** a periodical /pɪəriɑ́:dɪkəl/.

[3]かんこう 敢行 ▶彼は冬のアラスカで登山を**敢行した** He *boldly carried out* his ascent of a mountain in Alaska in winter.

[4]かんこう 完工 ▶明春**完工**予定 Scheduled for *completion* next spring.

[5]かんこう 慣行 a (**common**) **practice** ▶談合は長いこと業界の**慣行**となっていた Bid rigging had been (*a*) *common practice* in the industry for a long time.

がんこう 眼光 ▶**眼光鋭い**刑事 an *eagle-eyed* [a *sharp-eyed*] detective.

かんこうちょう 官公庁 **government and municipal** /mjunɪ́sɪpəl/ **offices**.

かんこうへん 肝硬変 《医学》 **cirrhosis** /səróʊsɪs/ (**of the liver**).

かんこうれい 箝口令 a **gag order** ▶**箝口令を敷く** issue *a gag order*.

[1]かんこく 勧告 **advice** /ədváɪs/ (助言) ; **recommendation** (勧め) 一**動** **勧告する** **advise** /ədváɪz/ ＋**自** ▶医師の**勧告**でたばこをやめた I have stopped smoking on my doctor's *advice* [*recommendation*]. ‖ 父は早期退職の**勧告を受けた** My father *was urged* to retire early. ‖ その店は道路拡張のための立ち退き**勧告**に応じようとしない That store is refusing to comply with an official *recommendation* to vacate the premises in order to widen the street in front.

[2]かんこく 韓国 **South Korea** /kərí:ə/ ▶**韓国**は正式には大韓民国と呼ばれる *South Korea*'s official name is

the Republic of Korea.
‖韓国語 Korean /kərí:ən/ ‖ 韓国人 a South Korean. →朝鮮.
かんごく 監獄 a prison(刑務所); a jail(拘置所).
かんごし 看護師 a nurse
‖看護師長 a head nurse ‖ 準看護師 an assistant nurse ‖ 正看護師 a registered nurse ／an R.N.
かんこどり 閑古鳥 ▶《慣用表現》そのスーパーは最近は閑古鳥が鳴いている That supermarket *is nearly deserted* these days.
かんこんそうさい 冠婚葬祭 ceremonial occasions.
かんさ 監査 (an) inspection(調査, 視察); an audit (会社の会計などの) 一動 監査する inspect +㊐, audit +㊐ ▶会計を監査する *audit* accounts ‖ 財務諸表を監査する *audit* a financial statement.
‖監査役 an inspector, an auditor.
1**かんさい 完済** payment in full, full payment ▶借金を完済する *pay off* one's debt [loan] ‖ ローンを完済する *pay* one's loan *in full* ‖ ようやく借金を完済した I *cleared* all my debts at last.
2**かんさい 関西** the Kansai district [area]
‖関西弁 the Kansai dialect (方言); a Kansai accent (なまり) ‖ 関西(国際)空港 Kansai (International) Airport.
かんざいにん 管財人 a trustee,《英》a receiver.
がんさく 贋作 a forgery, a fake ▶そのピカソはがん作と判明した The Picasso was found to be *a forgery*.
かんざし 簪 a *kanzashi*, an ornamental hairpin ▶かんざしを挿す wear *a kanzashi* [*an ornamental hairpin*].
カンザス Kansas /kǽnzəs/ (アメリカ中部の州; 略 KS, Kan., Kans.).
1**かんさつ 観察** observation(研究目的での); watching (動きのあるものの) 一動 観察する observe +㊐, watch +㊐ ▶昆虫を観察する *observe* [*watch*] insects ‖ 野生の猿の生態を観察する *observe* the behavior of monkeys in the wild ‖ 自然観察に尾瀬に行く go on *a field trip* to Oze ‖ 私は朝顔の観察記録をつけた I kept *a record of my observations* on morning glories. ‖ 私の趣味は野鳥の観察です My hobby is *bird watching*. ／ I'm interested in *bird watching*.
2**かんさつ 監察** inspection 一動 監察する inspect +㊐
‖監察医 a medical examiner ‖ 監察官 an inspector.
3**かんさつ 鑑札** a license,《英》a licence.
1**かんさん 閑散** ▶新規開店のそのスーパーは閑散としていた That newly opened supermarket was *deserted*. ‖ この商店街は昼間は閑散としている This shopping center *has* [*draws*] *few customers* during the day.
2**かんさん 換算** conversion 一動 換算する convert /kənvə́:ʳt/ +㊐ ▶ヤードをメートルに換算する *convert* [*change*] yards into meters ‖ それ, 円に換算するといくらだい? How much is it *in* yen [*in* Japanese currency]? ‖換算表 a conversion table ‖ 換算率 an exchange rate.
1**かんし 監視** (a) watch 一動 監視する watch +㊐, keep (a) watch《on》(不都合がないように見張る); guard +㊐ (防衛目的で番をする) ▶その男の行動を監視する *watch* that man's movements ‖ 火山活動を監視する *keep watch on* the volcano's activities ‖ 国境[囚人たち]を監視する *guard* the border [prisoners] ‖ 2人は監視の目をくぐって屋敷に忍び込んだ The two men slipped into the premises *when the guards were not looking*. ‖ 上司に一日中監視されているのでストレスがたまる一方だ I have a lot of stress in my job because the boss *keeps a watch on* me all day long.
‖監視員 a guard; a lifeguard (特にプール・海水浴場の) ‖ (防犯目的の) 監視カメラ a surveillance /səʳvéiləns/ camera.
2**かんし 冠詞**《文法》an article
‖定冠詞 a definite article ‖ 不定冠詞 an indefinite article 《参考》『スーパー・アンカー英和辞典』では従来の「冠詞」をやめ, その役割を踏まえて, 学習者にわかりやすく「標識語」という用語を設け, 使用した. これは signal [signpost] word と訳せるが, 最近の英文法でよく使われる determiner(決定詞, 限定詞)と呼ばれるものと同じで, a, the のほか, some, all, each や my, your などの代名詞の所有格も含まれる. 詳しくは英和巻末の「[a]と[the]を見直す」を参照いただきたい.
3**かんし 漢詩** a Chinese poem(個々の詩); Chinese poetry (➤集合的に).
4**かんし 鉗子** a forceps /fɔ́:ʳsəps ‖ -seps/.
1**かんじ 漢字** (a) *kanji* ⚠「漢字」を Chinese character と訳すことが多いが, これは「中国の文字」「中国人的性格の人」などの意にもなるので, kanji を用いるほうがよい.
日本紹介 ✉ **漢字は中国で作られた表意文字です. 日常的に使うものだけでも何千字もあり, 読み方も複雑です. 日本文は漢字のほか, 日本で発達したひらがな, かたかなの3種を組み合わせて表記します** *Kanji* is an ideographic writing system created in China. There are several thousand characters [ideograms] in daily use and their pronunciations are complicated. In addition to *kanji*, Japanese is also written in *hiragana* and *katakana*, or in a combination of these three. *Hiragana* and *katakana* were developed in Japan.
▶名前を漢字で書きなさい Write your name in *kanji*. ‖ この漢字, 何て読むの? How do you read this *kanji*?
2**かんじ 幹事** a secretary, a manager; an organizer(一時的な集まりの) ▶忘年会の幹事 the *organizer* of a year-end party.
‖幹事長 the chief secretary.

3かんじ 感じ

訳語メニュー
印象 →impression **1**
感覚 →feeling **2**

1【印象】 an impression; a feeling(漠然とした) ▶お客さまにはいい感じを与えるように努めなさい Try to make a good *impression* on the customers. ‖ 阿部さんは感じがいい[悪い] Abe is a *pleasant* [*unpleasant*] person. (➤ friendly(気さくな) [unfriendly(無愛想な)]ともいえる) ／I *get good* [*bad*] *vibrations* from Abe. (➤ vibrations は「精神的電波, 雰囲気」の意で, 縮めて vibes というが今ではやや古風) ‖ 対話「あの人のことどう思う?」「感じいいじゃないの」"What do you think of him?" "He's *charming*." (➤ charming は「礼儀正しく, 社交的で, ユーモアがある」というニュアンス) ‖ 対話「今度来た先生, どんな感じ?」「嫌な感じ」"*What's* the new teacher *like*?" "*Bad news*." ／ "There's *something I don't like about him* [*her*]." ‖ 髪を切ったらずいぶん感じが変わったわね You *look* quite *different* with

your hair cut (shorter).
▶彼はいかにも強引な営業職といった**感じだ** He really *looks like* a hard-driving salesperson. ‖ このレポートは少し長すぎる**感じだ** This paper *seems* to be a little too long. ‖ 試験には受かりそうもない**感じがする** I *get the feeling* I won't be able to pass the examination. ‖ 彼女は我々の申し出を受けないような**感じがする** I'*ve got a feeling* she won't accept our offer. ／I don't *think* she'll accept our offer.

2【感覚, 感触】feeling

【文型】
感じが…である
feel A
➤ A は形容詞

▶早朝はすがすがしい**感じがする** We *feel* fresh early in the morning. ‖ この皮はすべすべ［ざらざら］した**感じだ** This leather *feels* smooth [rough]. ‖ 歯を抜いたので口の中が変な**感じだ** My mouth *feels* funny because I had a tooth pulled.
▶寒くて足の指の**感じが無い** My toes *are numb(ed)* from the cold. (➤ numb /nʌm/ は「感覚を失わせる」).

3【気分】▶グラススキーじゃ**感じ**(＝気分)が出ないよ. やっぱり雪の上でなくっちゃ It's impossible to get a *feel* for skiing on grass. You've got to do it on snow. ‖ 彼女の朗読はなかなか**感じがよく出ていた** Her reading was very *expressive*. ／She read aloud very *expressively*.

がんじがらめ ▶誘拐犯たちは彼を**がんじがらめに**縛り, 猿ぐつわをはめた The kidnappers bound [tied] him *hand and foot* and put a gag in his mouth.
▶規則規則で子供たちを**がんじがらめにしていた**のでは, 自主性は育たない If you *bind* [*tie*] kids *down* with rules and regulations, they will never learn any self-discipline.

かんしき 鑑識 judgment(判断, 鑑定); **identification**(犯罪捜査での同定).

ガンジスがわ ガンジス川 the Ganges /gǽndʒiːz/.

がんじつ 元日 New Year's Day
✉ **元日には大勢の日本人が(新年の健康や幸福を願って)神社や寺院にお参りに行きます** On *New Year's Day*, many Japanese people visit Shinto shrines and Buddhist temples (to pray for health and happiness in the new year).

かんして 関して →関する.

1**かんしゃ 感謝 thanks, gratitude** (➤ 後者はより堅い語) 一動 **感謝する thank** ＋目, **be grateful**《for》▶彼は支援者たちに**感謝**の気持ちを述べた He expressed his *thanks* [*gratitude*] to his supporters. ‖ **感謝**の気持ちでいっぱいです I *am* so *grateful*! ／I don't know how to *thank* you. (➤ 後者は「何とお礼を言ってよいかわかりません」の意の決まり文句).

【文型】
人(A)の行為(B)に感謝する
thank A **for** B
appreciate A's B
人(A)に B のことで感謝している
be grateful to A **for** B

▶私を応援してくれたクラスのみんなに**感謝します** I'd like to *thank* [*Thanks to*] all my classmates who rooted for me. ‖ ご協力に**感謝します** *Thank you for* your cooperation. ‖ お骨折りいただき**感謝します** I *appreciate* your efforts. (➤ appreciate /əpríːʃièɪt/ は「人」でなく「行為」を目的語にとることに注意) ‖ 妻が私の健康管理をうまくやってくれますので, とても**感謝しています** I *am very grateful to* my wife *for* looking out so carefully for my health.
✉ **いろいろお力添えいただき感謝いたします** I *appreciate* all the help you have given me.
‖**感謝祭** Thanksgiving Day (➤ アメリカの祝日で, 11月の第4木曜日) ‖**感謝状** a testimonial /tèstɪmóʊniəl/.

2**かんしゃ 官舎 housing for government employees** [**officials**](公務員の住まい); an **official residence**(首長の公邸).

かんじゃ 患者 a **patient**(医者にかかっている人); a **sufferer**(苦しんでいる人); a **case**(症例を持つ人) ▶がん**患者** a cancer *patient* [*sufferer*] ‖ 重病**患者** a seriously ill *patient*. ‖**外来患者** an outpatient /áʊtpèɪʃənt/ ‖**入院患者** an inpatient.

かんしゃく 癇癪 a **temper**(怒りっぽい気質); a **tantrum** /tǽntrəm/ (かんしゃくの発作; 子供に用いることが多い) ▶私の上司はすぐ**かんしゃくを起こす** My boss *loses his temper* [*flies into a temper* ／*blows his top*] easily. (➤ 最後の言い方はインフォーマル) ‖ 彼女は**かんしゃく持ち**なので扱いにくい She is hard to deal with because she *has* such *a hot temper*.
‖**かんしゃく玉** a firecracker.

かんじやすい 感じ易い sensitive ▶猫の目は非常に光を**感じやすい** Cats' eyes are very *sensitive* to light. ‖ **感じやすい**年頃の少年 a boy at a *sensitive* age.

かんしゅ 看守 a **guard**, a **jailer**.

かんじゅ 甘受 ▶運命を**甘受する** *passively* [*philosophically*] *accept* one's fate.

1**かんしゅう 観衆 spectators**; an **audience** (➤ 集合的) ▶彼のマジックショーの**観衆**のほとんどが若い女の子だ Most of the *spectators* at his magic shows are young girls. ‖ そのアメフトの試合は2万人の**観衆**を集めた The American football game drew 20,000 *spectators* [a *crowd* of 20,000].

2**かんしゅう 慣習** a **custom**, (a) **convention** (➤ ともに伝統的なしきたり; 後者はより堅い語); a **practice**(規則的に行う習慣) ▶**慣習**に従う follow *a custom* ‖ 古い**慣習**を破る break an old *custom* ‖ 地元の**慣習** a local *practice* ‖ その村ではまだ古い**慣習**を守っている They still keep their old *customs* in the village. ‖ **慣習**により大相撲の千秋楽には『君が代』が演奏される *By convention*, "Kimigayo" is played on the last day of the grand sumo tournament.

3**かんしゅう 監修** (**editorial**) **supervision** ▶この辞書は Y 教授の**監修**によって編さんされた This dictionary was compiled under the *supervision* of Professor Y.
‖**監修者** an editorial supervisor.

かんじゅく 完熟 ▶**完熟**トマト a *fully ripe* tomato.

かんじゅせい 感受性 sensitivity ▶一般に思春期の若者は**感受性が強い** In general, adolescents tend to be very *sensitive* [*impressionable*].

がんしょ 願書 an **application** ▶先週その学校に**願書**を提出した I sent in *an application* to that school last week. ‖ **願書**の受け付けは2月5日から20日までとする *Applications* will be accepted from February 5 through (the) 20. (●「願書の受け付けは2月5日からです」なら Applications will be accepted starting [beginning ／as of] February 5th).

1**かんしょう 干渉 interference**; **meddling** (自分に関係の無いことに首を突っ込んでおせっかいを焼くこと) 一動

(…に) **干渉する** interfere /ìntəʳfíəʳ/ ((in)), meddle ((in)) ▶内政に干渉する *interfere* [*meddle*] *in* internal affairs ‖ 他人の問題に干渉するな Don't *interfere in* the problems of others. (➤「他人」が話者以外の人たちを指す場合) / Mind your own business. (➤「他人」が話者自身を指す場合) ‖ 娘は近頃親の干渉をひどく嫌がる My daughter resents any sort of *interference* from us these days. ‖ もう子供じゃないんだからあんまり干渉しないでよ I'm not a child anymore, so why don't you just *stay out of it* [*butt out*]? (➤ stay out of it は「離れている, 関わり合わない」, butt out は((主に米・インフォーマル))で「差し出口をしない」) ‖ おばは事あるごとにわが家のことに干渉したがる My aunt is always *sticking her nose into* every aspect of our family affairs. (➤「口出しする」の意).
▶電波の干渉 radio wave *interference*.

2**かんしょう 感傷** sentimentality 一形 **感傷的な** sentimental ▶美樹は自分の部屋でひとり感傷に浸った Miki sat alone in her room, indulging in *sentimentality*. ‖ 感傷的な小説は嫌いだ I dislike *sentimental* [*saccharine*] novels. (➤ saccharine /sǽkəriːn, -raɪn/ は「甘ったるい」).

3**かんしょう 鑑賞** appreciation 一動 **鑑賞する** appreciate +目 (理解して味わう) ; enjoy +目 (楽しむ) ▶美術館で絵画を鑑賞する *appreciate* pictures at an art gallery ‖ バレエを鑑賞する *enjoy* ballet ‖ 私たちは音楽の時間に『フィガロの結婚』を観て, オペラの鑑賞のしかたを学んだ In the music class, we learned how to *appreciate* opera through "The Marriage of Figaro."
▶彼には文学を本当に鑑賞する力は無い He has no real *appreciation* of literature. ‖ 唯一の趣味は音楽[映画]鑑賞です My only pastime is *listening to music* [*seeing movies*].
‖ **名画鑑賞会** a special show of classic movies ‖ **名曲鑑賞会** a special concert of classic pieces of music.

4**かんしょう 観賞する** enjoy +目 (楽しむ) ▶菊を観賞する *enjoy looking* at the chrysanthemums ‖ 観賞用の植物 a *decorative* plant / an *ornamental* plant ‖ **観賞魚** an aquarium /əkwéəriəm/ fish.

5**かんしょう 完勝** a sweeping victory ▶ヤクルトは巨人に完勝した The Swallows *won a sweeping victory* over the Giants.

6**かんしょう 観照** ▶静かに自然を観照する *meditate on* [*contemplate*] nature quietly.

7**かんしょう 環礁** an atoll.

1**かんじょう 勘定 1【計算】** (a) calculation 一動 **勘定する** calculate /kǽlkjəleɪt/ (+目) (計算する) ; count (+目) (数える) ▶勘定を間違える make a mistake in *calculation* ‖ 生徒の人数を勘定してください Please *count* the students. ‖ うちのしゅうとめは勘定高くてすぐプレゼントの値踏みをする My mother-in-law is so *money-minded* that she always estimates the prices of the presents she gets. (➤ money-minded は「金銭に関心が強い」).

2【支払い】 ▶ ((レストランなどで)) お勘定お願いします Could I have the *check* [((英)) *bill*], please? (➤単に "Check [Bill], please!" と言うことも多い) ‖ 勘定はぼくがもつよ I'll pay the *bill*. / I'll pick up the *check* [*bill* / *tab*]. / This is on me. ‖ 勘定を済ませて10時にホテルを出た I *checked out* of the hotel at 10 o'clock.

3【考慮】 consideration ▶彼女が現れることまでは勘定に入れていなかった I hadn't *taken into consideration* [*account*] the possibility that she might show up.

2**かんじょう 感情** feeling(s) ; (an) emotion (強い感情) ▶彼女の感情を害する hurt her *feelings* / offend her ‖ 人間は感情の生き物である Human beings are creatures of *emotion*. / Man is an *emotional* creature. (➤ man は男性を連想させるので, 避けられる傾向がある) ‖ もっと感情を込めて歌いなさい Try to put more *feeling* into it when you sing. (➤ it は歌っている歌) ‖ ゆうべは感情が高ぶってよく眠れなかった I *was* too *agitated* to sleep well last night. ‖ 娘は感情の起伏が激しい My daughter *has violent swings of mood*. ‖ 彼は感情をすぐ顔に出す He *wears his heart on his sleeve*. (➤「心の中を露骨に [はっきりと] 表情に出す」の意の決まった言い方) ‖ あの政治家はすぐ感情的になる That politician easily *becomes emotional*.
▶当地では日ごとに対日感情が悪化している Anti-Japanese *sentiment* in the area is running high. (➤ sentiment は「(感情的な) 意見」).
‖ **感情移入** empathy.

3**かんじょう 環状の** circular
‖ **環状線** ((米)) a beltway [belt highway], ((英)) a ring road (道路) ; a belt [loop] line (鉄道).

がんじょう 頑丈な strong(強い) ; sturdy (がっしりした) ▶この机は頑丈にできている This desk is *strongly* [*firmly*] built. / This desk is *sturdy*. ‖ 岩田君は頑丈な体をしている Iwata has *a good physique*.

1**かんしょく 間食** a snack(軽食) 一動 **間食する** eat between meals ▶間食は肥満のもとです *Eating between meals* will make you fat. ‖ 間食しちゃあだめよ Don't *eat between meals*!

2**かんしょく 感触** a [the] feel, a [the] touch ▶絹の柔かい感触が好きだ I love the soft *feel* of silk.
▶ ((比喩的)) 我々の要求は満たされるだろうという感触を得た I got the *feeling* [*impression*] that our demand would be met.

3**かんしょく 寒色** a cool color.

4**かんしょく 閑職** a do-nothing job, a sinecure /sáɪnɪkjʊəʳ, síni-/ ▶人を閑職に追いやる *kick* a person *upstairs*.

5**かんしょく 官職** a government post.

6**かんしょく 完食** eat [finish] up ▶少年は大盛りのカレーライスを完食した The boy *ate up* his big plate of curry and rice.

がんしょく 顔色 ▶この数学の天才少年にかかっては大の大人も顔色なしだ Even grown-ups *pale* beside this boy math genius.

かんじる 感じる 1【感覚が生じる】 feel

【文型】
…を感じる
feel A
➤ A は名詞, または, 形容詞. pain または fear などの感情には名詞も用いるが, 五官で感じるものは形容詞がふつう

▶寒さを感じる *feel* cold ‖ 足にけがをした直後には痛みを感じなかった I did*n't feel any pain* in my foot at the time I was injured. ‖ 突然指にしびれを感じた I suddenly *felt numb* [lost all sensation] in my fingers.
▶電線に触ったらびりっと感じた I *got* [*received*] *an electric shock* when I touched the (electric) wire.

か

2【意識する, 心に思う】**feel** +目 ; **sense** +目 (感づく) ▶悲しみ[恐怖]を感じる *feel* sorrow [fear] ‖ 彼女は暗闇で危険を感じた She *sensed danger* in the dark. ‖ 横綱は何のプレッシャーも感じていないようであった The yokozuna looked as if he did*n't feel any pressure*. ‖ 生活スタイルを変える必要を感じていません I do*n't feel the need to* change my lifestyle. ‖ 授業をサボるたびに彼はやましさを感じる He *feels guilty* whenever he cuts classes. ‖ 彼には娘が誇らしく感じられた He *felt proud* of his daughter. ‖ 心に感じたままを表現しなさい Let your *feelings* flow (*naturally*). ‖ 天の川は宇宙の神秘を感じさせる Looking at the Milky Way *makes* us *feel the mystery and grandeur* of the heavens.

▶東南アジアへ行ってみて英語の国際語としての重要性を感じた(＝悟った) When I went to Southeast Asia, I *realized* how important English is as an international language.

☛ 感じやすい (→見出語)

1かんしん 感心 **admiration** 一動 感心する **admire** +目 ▶彼の勇気には感心した We *admired* him for his courage. ／We *admired* his courage. ‖ きみが北大に合格したのには感心したよ *It is wonderful that* you got into Hokkaido University. ‖ 感心しちゃった. うちの旦那, 意外と料理がうまいのよ *I was impressed!* My husband is a better cook than I expected! (➤ be impressed はすばらしさに「強く印象づけられる」) ‖ 娘のピアノの上達が早いのには全く感心する I*'m* really *struck with* how fast my daughter is improving on the piano. (➤ be struck with で「…に感心する」) ‖ 感心, 感心! Good for you! (➤「よくやった」の意のインフォーマルな表現).

▶隣の達夫君は今どき珍しい感心な子だ *A nice* [*wonderful*] *boy* like our neighbor's son Tatsuo is rare nowadays. ‖ お宅のお嬢ちゃん, 感心によくお手伝いすること! Your daughter is *wonderful* to be such a help around the house!

▶高校生がオートバイで登校するのは感心しない(＝賛成しない) I *don't approve of* high school students coming to school by motorcycle.

2かんしん 関心 (an) **interest** /íntrəst/ (興味); **concern** (気にすること) ▶彼の主な関心は好きな漫画家の漫画本を集めることだ His main *interest* is collecting the comic books by his favorite manga artist. ‖ 私はソウルミュージックに関心がある I*'m interested in* soul music. ‖ 保険のことに関心が無い人が多い Many people *have no interest in* insurance.

▶日本の親は子供の教育に対する関心が高い Japanese parents *are intensely interested in* matters concerning their children's education. ‖ クラスの中でカントリーミュージックへの関心が高まってきている My classmates are showing a growing *interest* in country music. ‖ 妹は最近, 碁に関心を示しだした Recently my sister has begun to show *an interest* in 'Go.'

▶地球の温暖化は世界中の人々の関心事(＝心配事)である Global warming is *a matter of concern* to people all over the world. ‖ 彼女の関心事は宝石と海外旅行だ Her *interests* are jewelry and overseas travel. ‖ 姉の目下の関心事は, いかにして少しでも美しくなるかということだ Right now, my sister *is preoccupied solely with* the problem of how to make herself look as beautiful as possible. (➤ be preoccupied with は「…で頭がいっぱいだ」).

☛ 無関心 (→見出語)

3かんしん 歓心 ▶彼女はいつも先生の歓心を買おうとしている She is always trying to *get in* her teacher's *good graces* [*get in* her teacher's *good books* ／ *win* her teacher'*s favor*].

かんじん 肝心な **important** (大切な) ; **crucial** (極めて重大な) ▶いちばん肝心なことを言い忘れるところだった I almost forgot to mention the most *important* thing. ‖ そこが肝心なところだ That's *the* (*main* ／ *important*) *point* [*the key*]. ／That's *the crux* of the problem.

▶株で肝心なのは先を読む目だ In the stock market, *the name of the game* is foresight. (➤ the name of the game は「肝心要なこと」の意のインフォーマルな言い方) ‖ 肝心なときに彼は気後れしてしまった *At the crucial moment* he lost his nerve. ‖ 光子ったら肝心なときに限って居ないんだから Mitsuko's never around *when you need* her.

1かんすい 完遂 **completion** 一動 完遂する **complete** +目 ▶任務を完遂する *complete* one's mission ‖ 私たちは計画を完遂した We *completed* our project. ／We *brought* the project *to completion*.

2かんすい 冠水 ▶大雨で道路が冠水した The heavy rain *flooded* the streets. ／ The streets *were flooded* by the heavy rain.

かんすう 関数 《数学》 a **function**

‖三角関数 a trigonometrical /trìgənəmétrɪkl/ function ‖関数方程式 a functional equation /ɪkwéɪʒən/.

かんすうじ 漢数字 a **kanji** [**Chinese**] **numeral**, a **kanji for a number**.

かんする 関する **about, on**

語法 about が最も一般的で, on は専門的な事柄について用いる傾向がある. ほかに with regard to, concerning があるが, ともに堅い言い方.

▶ファッションに関する情報 information *about* fashion ‖ 当店は東南アジアに関する書籍を専門に扱っております We specialize in books *on* Southeast Asia. ‖ その件に関してはすでに話し合いました We've already talked *about* the matter [*on* the subject]. ‖ 校内暴力に関しては, 校長先生は何も意見を言わなかった Our principal said nothing *concerning* school violence. (➤ concerning は主に書きことばで用いられる).

1かんせい 完成 **completion** /kəmplíːʃən/ 一動 完成する **complete** +目 ; **finish** +目 (終える) ▶その橋の完成は2015年の予定です The bridge is due to *be completed* in 2015. ‖ 論文を完成するのにどのくらい時間がかかりますか How long will it take you to *complete* [*finish*] your thesis [paper]? ‖ 今取りかかっている小説の翻訳は1か月で完成するはずです The translation of the novel I am working on should *be completed* [*be done*] in a month. ‖ この絵は完成度が高い This painting *is nearly* [*almost*] *perfect*.

‖完成品 a finished product.

2かんせい 閑静な **quiet** /kwáɪət/ ▶彼は閑静な住宅街に住んでいる He lives in a *quiet* residential area.

3かんせい 感性 (a) **sensibility** ▶彼女は洗練された美的感性の持ち主だ She has a refined *aesthetic sense* [*sensibilities*]. ‖ 若者のフレッシュな感性で商品開発をすることが大事だ It's important to develop products making use of young people's *fresh sensibilities*.

4かんせい 歓声 a **shout of joy** [**delight**] ; a **cheer** (声

援）▶彼らは自分たちのチームが点を入れるたびに**歓声を上げた** They *gave a shout of joy* each time their team earned a point. ‖ 彼が演壇に立つとどっと**歓声**が上がった The audience let out a big *cheer* when he took the podium.

5**かんせい 官製の government-made**
‖**官製はがき** a postal card（➤「私製はがき」は postcard だが，区別せずに postcard を用いることが多い）.

6**かんせい 慣性**《物理学》**inertia** /ɪnə́ːrʃə/ ▶**慣性の法則** *the law of inertia*.

7**かんせい 管制 control**
‖**航空管制** air traffic control ‖ **報道管制** a news blackout.

かんぜい 関税 tariff /tǽrɪf/（輸入品・輸出品にかけられる）; **customs duties**（輸入品にかけられる）▶政府は**関税を撤廃して**貿易を自由化しようとしている The Japanese government is in the process of *lifting all tariff barriers* and promoting free trade.（➤ tariff barriers は「関税障壁」）‖ わが国では一部の輸入品には**関税を課していない** Some imported goods are *duty-free* in Japan.

かんせいとう 管制塔 a **control tower.**

がんせいひろう 眼精疲労 eyestrain.

がんせき 岩石 (a) **rock.**

1**かんせつ 間接の indirect**; **secondhand**（また聞きの）**一副 間接的に indirectly** ▶私はその学者の**間接的な**影響を受けています I was *indirectly* influenced by that scholar's work. ‖ 井上夫妻の離婚については**間接に**聞いて知っています I heard about the Inoues' divorce *secondhand*.（➤この secondhand は副詞用法）‖ 彼女のことは**間接的には知っている**が，よくは知らない I *know of* her, but I don't know her.（➤ know of は「…のことは聞いて知っている」の意で，of をやや強めて言う）.
‖**間接[受動]喫煙** passive smoking ‖ **間接照明** indirect lighting ‖ **間接税** an indirect tax ‖ **間接選挙** indirect election ‖ **間接目的語**《文法》an indirect object ‖ **間接話法**《文法》indirect narration（➤《米》では indirect discourse,《英》では indirect speech ともいう）.

2**かんせつ 関節** a **joint** ▶肘[膝]の**関節** an elbow [a knee] *joint* ‖ **指の関節**をポキポキ鳴らす crack one's *knuckles* ‖ レフトの花田はダイビングキャッチをした際に**肩の関節を脱臼した** The left fielder, Hanada, *dislocated his shoulder* [*put his shoulder out of joint*] when he dived for the ball.
‖**関節炎** arthritis /ɑːrθráɪṭɪs/ ‖ **関節リューマチ** articular rheumatism /rúːmətìzəm/.

3**かんせつ 冠雪** ▶**冠雪した**山々 *snow-capped* mountains ‖ けさ富士山に**初冠雪があった** This morning, the summit of Mt. Fuji *was covered with snow for the first time this season*.

がんぜない 頑是無い ▶**がんぜない幼子** a young child who *can't tell right from wrong*.

1**かんせん 感染 infection**（主に空気伝染による）; **contagion**（接触伝染）**一動 感染する be infected**《with》（人が病気に）; **infect** +目（病気が人に）▶じんましんは**感染しない** Hives *is not infectious* [*contagious* ／ *catching*].（➤ catching はインフォーマルな語）‖ そのウイルスは人に**感染しない** The virus doesn't *infect* humans. ‖ ＨＩＶに**感染した**人が必ずエイズになるわけではない A person doesn't necessarily develop AIDS even if he or she *is infected with* HIV. ‖ ＨＩＶの**感染力**は弱く，**空気感染**や**飛まつ感染**はしない HIV has low *infectivity* and cannot be contracted as a result of *aerial* or *droplet infection*. ▶《比喩的》彼女のおっちょこちょいがみんなに**感染した** Her carelessness *infected* everyone.
‖**感染経路** a route of infection ‖ **感染源** a source of infection ‖ **感染症** an infectious disease.

2**かんせん 観戦する watch** ▶ぼくたちは阪神対中日の試合を**観戦した** We *watched* a baseball game between the Tigers and the Dragons.

3**かんせん 幹線** a **trunk line**
‖**幹線道路** a trunk [main] road.

4**かんせん 汗腺**《解剖学》a **sweat gland.**

5**かんせん 艦船 warships and other vessels.**

1**かんぜん 完全 perfection 一形 完全な perfect**（完璧な）; **complete**（必要なものが全部そろって）**一副 完全に perfectly**（完璧に）; **completely**（すっかり）▶彼には**完全**を期待しないほうがいい Don't expect *perfection* in [from] him.（➤ in は「彼という人物に」, from は「彼の仕事などから」）‖ 彼に仕事を任せたのは**完全な**失敗だった It was a *complete* mistake to have entrusted that job to him. ‖ 彼女は先生の言ったことを**完全に**誤解していた She *completely* misunderstood her teacher's remarks. ‖ 誰も英語を**完全に**マスターすることはできない Nobody can master English *perfectly* [*completely*]. ‖ 報告書は**完全に出来上がってはいなかった** The report *wasn't complete*.（➤ perfect にすると「出来栄えが完璧ではなかった」の意になる）.
▶水道，**完全に**止めた？ Did you turn off the water [turn the faucet off] *all the way*?（➤ all the way は「すっかり」）‖ 公共の場での喫煙は**完全に**禁止されるべきだと思っている I think smoking in public places should be *totally* banned. ／I think there should be a *total* ban on smoking in public places.
▶**完全雇用**がわが国の目標である *Full employment* is our nation's goal. ‖ 山田は**完全試合**を達成した Yamada pitched [hurled] *a perfect game*. ‖ **完全主義者**は外国語をマスターできない *A perfectionist* cannot master foreign languages.（➤「完全主義」は perfectionism）‖ その殺し屋は**完全犯罪**を狙った The hitman planned the *perfect crime*. ‖ 世の中に**完全無欠な**人はいない Nobody's *perfect*.
‖**完全燃焼** complete [perfect] combustion.
☛ **不完全**（→見出語）

2**かんぜん 敢然と bravely, courageously**（勇敢に）（➤前者は行動に力点があり，後者は精神的強さや決意の強さを強調する）; **resolutely**（決然と）▶住民は**敢然と**公害企業に立ち向かった The residents *courageously* stood firm against the company that was causing pollution.

がんぜん 眼前 ▶美しい田園風景が**眼前に**開けた Beautiful rural scenery unfolded *before our eyes*.

かんぜんちょうあく 勧善懲悪 ▶**勧善懲悪劇** a *morally didactic* /daɪdǽktɪk/ play.

かんそ 簡素 simplicity /sɪmplísəṭi/ **一形 簡素な simple** ▶**簡素な**結婚式 a *simple* wedding ceremony ‖ 業務を**簡素化する** *streamline* business practices ‖ 生活を**簡素化する** *simplify* one's life ‖ 彼は金持ちだが**簡素な**暮らしをしている Although he is rich, he lives *simply* [leads a *simple* life]. ‖ 彼の朝食はいつもトーストとコーヒーだけの**簡素な**ものだ Every day he eats a *simple* [*frugal*] breakfast of toast and coffee.

がんそ 元祖 the originator(創始者); the father (生みの親) ▶空手チョップの**元祖**は力道山だ The *originator* of the karate chop was Rikidozan.

か

1 **かんそう 感想** an impression (印象) 語法 物事に対する感想を聞くときはこの語を用いず, How did [do] you like ...? (…をどう思いました[思います]か)と表現することが多い.
▶新校舎の**感想はいかがですか** *How do you like* the new school building? ‖ 日本へ来られたご**感想はいかがですか** *How do you like* (being in) Japan? ‖ イギリスの家庭にホームステイした**感想はどうですか**? *What are your impressions of* your homestay with a British family? ‖ 私たちの計画についてのご**感想を**伺いたいんですが I'd like to hear *what you think of* our project. ‖ 夏目漱石の『坊っちゃん』を読んで**感想文**を書きなさい Read Natsume Soseki's "Botchan" and write *an essay* about it.

2 **かんそう 乾燥** dryness 一動 **乾燥する** dry (up) ▶このところ空気が**乾燥している** Recently, the air has been *dry*. ‖ 野菜を冷蔵庫に入れておいたら**乾燥してしまった** The vegetables in the refrigerator *have dried up*. ‖ 洗濯物を**乾燥機**で乾かしなさい Dry the clean clothes in the *dryer*.
‖**乾燥剤** a desiccant /désɪkənt/ ‖ **乾燥地帯** an arid zone.

3 **かんそう 完走** ▶そのランナーはふくらはぎの激痛にもかかわらず1万メートルを**完走した** Despite the sharp pain in his calves, the runner *ran the whole* [*entire*] 10,000-meter *race*.

1 **かんぞう 肝臓** the liver ▶父はかつての酒の飲み過ぎで**肝臓**を患っている My father has *liver* problems [is suffering from *liver* disease] because he used to drink too much.
‖**肝臓がん** liver cancer.

2 **かんぞう 甘草** 《植》licorice /líkərɪs, -rɪʃ/.

3 **かんぞう 萱草** 《植》a daylily.

かんそうかい 歓送会 a farewell party, a going-away party (➤ 前者は公式のものを指すことが多い) ▶私たちは大阪支店へ転勤する飯田さんの**歓送会**を開いた We held *a farewell party* for Mr. Iida, who is being transferred to the Osaka branch.

かんそうきょく 間奏曲 《音楽》an intermezzo /ɪ̀ntəʳmétsoʊ/, an interlude.

かんそく 観測 observation 一動 **観測する** observe ＋目 ▶気象衛星は気象の**観測をする** The weather satellite *makes* meteorological *observations* [*observes* weather conditions]. ‖ 富士山頂で初雪が例年より3日早く**観測された** The first snowfall on the summit of Mt. Fuji of the year *was recorded* three days earlier than average. (➤「記録された」と考える).
▶核兵器の廃絶は**希望的観測**にすぎないかもしれません The abolishment of nuclear weapons may be nothing but *wishful thinking*.
‖(**気象**)**観測所** a meteorological /mì:ṭiərəlá:dʒɪkəl/ station.

かんそん 寒村 a desolate village.

カンタータ 《音楽》a cantata.

カンタービレ 《音楽》cantabile.

1 **かんたい 歓待** ▶彼女は婚約者の家で**歓待された** She *was warmly welcomed* by her fiancé's family.
✉ **歓待してくださったことにお礼のことばもないほどです** I don't know how to thank you for your warm *hospitality*. ➤ hospitality は「親切なもてなし」の意.

2 **かんたい 寒帯** the Frigid Zone(➤ 小文字でも書く).

3 **かんたい 艦隊** a fleet ▶ドレーク率いる英国**艦隊**はスペインの無敵艦隊に大打撃を与えた The British *fleet* led by Drake did great damage to *the Invincible Armada*.

かんだい 寛大な broad-minded(心の広い); generous (おおまかな, こせこせしない); tolerant (他人の意見や態度に対して寛容な); lenient /lí:niənt/ (事を大目に見る) ▶**寛大な**人 a *broad-minded* [*generous*] person ‖ 彼にはもう少し**寛大**であってほしいと思う I wish he were a little more *generous*. ‖ 日本人は宗派を異にする人に対しても**寛大である** The Japanese are *tolerant* of those who belong to other religious sects. ‖ その警官は私の交通違反を**寛大に取り扱ってくれた** That policeman *was lenient with* me when he stopped me for a traffic violation.

がんたい 眼帯 an eye bandage, an eye patch ▶渡辺君は右目に**眼帯をしている** Watanabe *has* his right eye *bandaged*.

かんたいじ 簡体字 a simplified Chinese character.

かんたいへいよう 環太平洋 ‖**環太平洋地域** the Pacific Rim.

かんだかい 甲高い high-pitched; shrill (きんきんの) ▶**甲高い**叫び声を上げる let out a *shrill* cry ‖ 彼はいつも**甲高い声**で話す He always speaks in *a high voice*.

かんたく 干拓 land reclamation by drainage 一動 **干拓する** reclaim ＋目 ▶この耕作地は湖を**干拓した**ものだ This cultivated cropland *was reclaimed* from the lake. ‖**干拓工事** reclamation works ‖ **干拓地** reclaimed land.

1 **かんたん 簡単** 一形 **簡単な** easy (容易な); simple (内容的に単純な); brief (短時間の) 一副 **簡単に** easily (容易に); simply (単純に); briefly (手短に) ▶きょうの英語の試験はぼくにはとても**簡単**だった Today's English exam was very *easy* [*a piece of cake*] for me. ‖ アメリカでは大学に入ることは**簡単**だが出るのは難しい In the United States it is *easy* to get into college but hard to graduate. ‖ 貿易の自由化はきみが考えるほど**簡単な**問題ではない Liberalization of trade is not as *simple* as you think. ‖ 合唱クラブに入るには**簡単なテスト**を受けなくてはなりません You have to take *a brief test* to join the glee club.
▶ぼくらのチームは1回戦で**簡単に**負けてしまった Our team was *easily* beaten in the first round. ‖ このオートバイ, 時速150キロは**簡単に**出るぜ This motorcycle can do 150 kilometers per hour *with no trouble*. (➤ with no trouble は「いとも簡単に」) ‖ あの喫茶店で**簡単に**(＝軽く)食事を済まそうよ Let's have a *light* meal at that coffee shop. ‖ 契約書にはあまり**簡単に**はんこを押さないほうがいい You should never put your seal on a contract *without carefully reading and understanding it*.
▶**簡単に言えば**, 彼女がやつを振ったということさ *To put it simply* [*To put it in a nutshell*], she walked out on him. (➤ 後者は「要するに」の意のインフォーマルな言い方).

2 **かんたん 感嘆** admiration 一動 (…に)**感嘆する** marvel 《at》, admire ＋目 ▶先生はその生徒の英語力の上達ぶりに**感嘆した** The teacher *marvelled* [*was amazed*] *at* the student's progress in English. ‖ アクロバットの妙技に観客は**感嘆した** The spectators *were struck with wonder* at the acrobat's miraculous feats. ‖ 摩周湖の美しさに全員**感嘆の声を上げた** We all *cried out in admiration* of the beauty

of Lake Mashu.

‖感嘆符 an exclamation mark ‖感嘆文 an exclamatory sentence.

1**かんだん 寒暖** ▶ことしは例年になく**寒暖の差**が大きい There have been unusually great *changes in temperature* this year.

‖寒暖計 a thermometer.

2**かんだん 歓談** ▶オーストラリア代表団は首相と**歓談した** The Australian delegations *had a pleasant talk with* the Prime Minister.

3**かんだん 間断** ▶**間断なく**降る雨 *continuous* [*incessant*／*constant*] rain.

がんたん 元旦 (the morning of) New Year's Day ▶**元旦**に初日の出を拝んだ On *New Year's Day* I watched with reverence the first sunrise of the year. (➤ with reverence は「崇敬の念を抱いて」).

1**かんち 関知** ▶それは私の**関知するところではない** I *have nothing to do with* it. ／It is *none of my business*.

2**かんち 感知する** sense ＋目 (感じる)；become aware 《of》(気づく)；detect ＋目 (検知する) ▶煙を**感知して**火災報知器が鳴った The fire alarm sounded when it *detected* smoke.

‖火災感知器 a fire sensor.

3**かんち 完治** ▶水虫はなかなか**完治しない** Athlete's foot *is hard to completely heal*.

かんちがい 勘違い a mistake (間違い)；(a) misunderstanding (誤解) 一動 **勘違いする** mistake；misunderstand (誤解する) ▶その点はぼくの**勘違いでした** I *was mistaken* about that. ／It was my *mistake*. ‖電話でお嬢さんをあなたと**勘違いしました**よ I *mistook* [*took*] your daughter *for* you over the phone. (➤ mistake [take] A for B で「AをBと勘違いする」) ‖ぼくはそのことわざの意味を**勘違いしていた** I *had misunderstood* the meaning of that proverb. ‖日にちを**勘違いしていた** I *mixed up the dates*.

がんちく 含蓄 ▶ことわざの多くは**含蓄に富んでいる** Most proverbs are rich in *meaning* [*significance*].

かんちゅう 寒中 the coldest time of the year ▶何人かの友人に**寒中見舞い**を出した I sent *midwinter greetings* to a few friends.

✉ **寒中お見舞い申し上げます** I hope you're doing well despite *the cold weather*.

がんちゅう 眼中 ▶2人の店員はおしゃべりに夢中で私の存在など**眼中にない**ようだった The two salesclerks were deep in conversation and appeared to *take no notice of* me. ‖圭子はクラスの男子の中で靖雄のことしか**眼中にない** Keiko *has her eye on* Yasuo and *won't even look at any other* boy in her class. ‖あの会長の**眼中にあるのは**金もうけのことだけだ Moneymaking is that chairman's *one and only concern*. (➤「唯一の関心事だ」の意).

1**かんちょう 官庁** a government office ▶彼は**官庁街**の近くにある会社に勤めている He works for a company located near the *government office district* [*the civic center*].

2**かんちょう 干潮** a low tide ▶今は**干潮だ** *The tide is low* [*out*] now. ‖**干潮時**にはあの島まで歩いて行ける You can walk to that island *at low tide*.

3**かんちょう 館長** a curator /kjóreɪṭəʳ ‖ kjuréɪtə/ (博物館の)；a head [chief] librarian (図書館の).

4**かんちょう 艦長** a captain

‖艦長室 the captain's cabin.

5**かんちょう 浣腸・灌腸** 《医学》 an enema /énəmə/ ▶**かん腸**をしたら子供の熱は引いた After the child was given *an enema*, his [her] fever came down.

1**かんつう 貫通する** penetrate ＋目, go through (➤ 前者が日本語に近いやや堅い語) ▶弾丸が彼女の胸部を**貫通した** The bullet *penetrated* [*went through*] her chest.

▶そのトンネルはきょうついに**貫通した** The tunnel *was* finally *completed* today. (●「トンネルを掘る」は bore [dig] a tunnel であるが, 穴が通じたのであるから be completed で表す).

2**かんつう 姦通** adultery.

カンツォーネ 《音楽》 a canzone.

かんづく 感づく sense ＋目；be aware 《of》(気づいている) ▶彼女は何かおかしいと**感づいた** She *sensed* something (was) wrong. ‖彼女は娘がその男と親密な仲にあるということをすでに**感づいていた** She *was already aware of* the fact that her daughter was on intimate terms with that man. ‖彼がカンニングしたのを先生は**感づいた**ようだ The teacher seemed to *have caught on to* his cheating. (➤ catch on to は「…に気づく」).

かんづめ 缶詰 a can, 《英また》 a tin ▶**缶詰**を開ける open *a can* ‖マグロの**缶詰** *a can* of tuna ‖**缶詰のカニ** *canned* crab meat.

▶《比喩的》その作家はその小説を完成するためにホテルに3週間**缶詰めにされた** The writer *was confined* in a hotel room for three weeks to finish the novel.

‖缶詰食品 canned [tinned] foods.

1**かんてい 官邸** an official residence ▶ホワイトハウスはアメリカ大統領の**官邸**である The White House is the *official residence* of the President of the United States. ‖首相官邸 the Prime Minister's official residence.

2**かんてい 鑑定** ▶骨とう品を**鑑定する** *judge* a curio ‖筆跡を**鑑定する** *identify* [*analyze*] the handwriting ‖その焼き物を専門家に**鑑定してもらった** We *got* the piece of pottery *appraised* by an expert.

《参考》 美術品, 刀剣, ワインなどの鑑定家は connoisseur /kɑ̀ːnəsə́ːʳ/, 不動産など値段を査定する鑑定人は 《米》 appraiser, 《英》 valuer という.

がんてい 眼底 《解剖学》 the fundus of the eye, a fundus oculi.

かんてつ 貫徹 ▶彼女は初志を**貫徹した** She *carried out* her original intention. (➤ carry out は「成し遂げる」) ‖賃上げ要求を**貫徹する**ため従業員はストライキに入った The workers went on strike in order to *push through* their demand for higher wages.

1**かんてん 観点** a point of view, a viewpoint；a standpoint (立場)；an angle (角度) ▶基地問題は国の安全保障の**観点から**議論すべきだ The base issue should be discussed from the *standpoint* of national security. ‖いろいろな**観点から**計画の見直しをしよう Let's reconsider the project *from various angles* [*viewpoints*]. ‖**観点を変えて**考えよう Let's try looking at it *from a different angle*.

2**かんてん 寒天** agar /ɑ́ːgəʳ ‖ éɪgə/.

3**かんてん 干天** dry weather ▶**干天の慈雨** *beneficial rain after a spell of dry weather*.

かんでん 感電 ▶ぬれた手でアイロンのプラグをコンセントに差し込んだらびりっと**感電した** I plugged the iron in when my hands were wet and *got a mild electric shock*. ‖そのゴルファーは雷に打たれて**感電死した** The golfer *was electrocuted* when he was hit by lightning. (➤ electrocute /ɪléktrəkjuːt/ は「感電死させる；電気椅子で処刑する」).

かんでんち 乾電池 a dry battery [cell] ▶アルカリ[マン

ガン]乾電池 an alkaline [a manganese] *battery* ‖ 乾電池を交換する replace *a battery*.
《参考》乾電池は大きさによって Size D (単一), Size C (単二), Size AA (単三), Size AAA (単四), Size N (単五)に分かれる.

か

かんど 感度 sensitivity ▶このフィルムは感度がいい This film is *highly sensitive*. / This is *highly sensitive* film. ‖ BBC 放送がきちんと入る**高感度のラジオアンテナ**が欲しい I want *a high sensitivity radio antenna* to get good reception of BBC broadcasts.

1**かんとう 関東** the Kanto district [area]
‖**関東大震災** the Great Kanto Earthquake ‖ **関東平野** the Kanto plains.

2**かんとう 完投する** 《野球》 go the distance [length]; pitch a complete game ▶斎藤は完投で10勝目をあげた Saito chalked up his 10th win *by going the distance*.

3**かんとう 巻頭** the beginning of a book
‖**巻頭言** a preface(序文).

1**かんどう 感動** (deep) emotion; (an) impression (印象, 感銘) 一動 **感動する** be moved, be impressed ▶バリ島の美しい景色には深く感動した I *was* deeply *moved* [*impressed*] by the beautiful scenery of Bali. ‖ 私はその本を読んでとても感動した The book *moved* [*impressed*] me deeply. ‖ 私はその少年の真面目な態度に感動した The boy's sincere attitude *moved* [*touched*] me. (➤ touch は「(人の心に)触れる」) ‖ この映画のクライマックスは**感動的だ** The climax of this movie is *stirring* [*moving* / *touching*]. (➤ stirring は「(人の心を)揺り動かす」, moving は「感情や同情の念に影響を与える」, touching は「思いやりや同情を引き起こす」) ‖ そのミュージカルは世界中の人々に大きな感動を与えた The musical *stirred the hearts* of people across the globe.

2**かんどう 勘当する** disown +目 ▶おまえなんか勘当だ! You'*re disowned* [*cut off without a cent*]!

かんとうし 間投詞 《文法》 an interjection.

かんとうしょう 敢闘賞 a best-effort prize.

かんどうみゃく 冠動脈 《解剖学》 a coronary artery.

かんとく 監督 **1【取り締まる人】** a supervisor, a superintendent(一般の仕事の); a manager (野球・サッカーなどの); a coach(サッカーやバスケットボール, レスリングなどの); a director (映画などの); a proctor (試験の) ▶黒沢氏は世界的に有名な**映画監督**だった Mr. Kurosawa was *a* world-famous *film director*. ‖ 兄は道路工事の**現場監督**です My brother is *a supervisor* on a road construction crew.
2【取り締まり】 supervision, superintendence (人・仕事・事業などの; 後者はより堅い語) 一動 **監督する** supervise +目, superintend /sùːpərɪnténd/ +目; proctor +目 (試験を) ▶試験のときは監督を厳しくしないとカンニングをする学生がいる If you don't *supervise* [*proctor*] examinations strictly, some students might cheat.
▶日本の学校は文部科学省の**監督下にある** Japanese schools *are under the control of* the Ministry of Education, Culture, Sports, Science and Technology. (➤ control は「統制」) ‖ 陸上チームの**監督をする** *manage* a track team ‖ 映画の**監督をする** *direct* a film.

> **逆引き熟語 ○○監督**
> **映画監督** a film [movie] director / **音楽監督** a music director / **(工事)現場監督** a supervisor / **サッカーの監督** a soccer [football] coach / **試験監督** a proctor / **(映画などの)助監督** an assistant director / **舞台監督** a stage director [manager] / **野球の監督** a baseball manager

がんとして 頑として stubbornly, obstinately (➤ 後者は「頑迷に」に近く, マイナスイメージの強い語); adamantly(決心・考えを変えない); staunchly(断固として) ▶父は私が好きな人と結婚することに頑として反対している My father is *stubbornly* [*obstinately*] against my marrying the man I love. ‖ 会議で私は彼の提案に頑として反対した At the meeting, I was *adamantly* [*staunchly*] opposed to his proposal.

カントリー ‖**カントリークラブ** a country club ‖ **カントリーミュージック** country music.

かんな 鉋 a plane ▶目の粗い板にかんなを掛ける *plane* [*use a plane on*] a rough plank.
‖**かんなくず** wood shavings.

カンナ 《植物》 a canna /kǽnə/ (lily).

かんなん 艱難 adversity ▶ ことわざ 艱難汝(なんじ)を玉にす Adversity makes you a stronger person [makes a person wise].

かんにん 堪忍 patience ▶ ことわざ ならぬ堪忍するが堪忍 Patience is to bear the unbearable.

カンニング cheating, 《インフォーマル》 cribbing ▶物理のテストで**カンニングをする** *cheat* on [in] a physics test ‖ 英語の試験で彼のカンニングがばれてしまった He *got caught cheating* on [in] an English exam. (➤ in は《英》用法).

> **危ないカタカナ語✸ カンニング**
> **1**「カンニング」は「ずる賢い」の意の英語 cunning からきているが, この語に「試験での不正行為」の意味はない. 英語では cheating(いんちき行為)という.
> **2**「カンニングペーパー」は crib (sheet [note]) という. アメリカ俗語では a pony, a trot, a cheat sheet ともいう.

かんにんぶくろ 堪忍袋 ▶あいつには堪忍袋の緒が切れたよ I'm *out of patience* with him. / I'*ve lost* [*I've run out of*] *all patience* with him.

かんぬき a bar ▶戸にかんぬきを掛ける *bar* the door.

かんぬし 神主 a Shinto priest.

かんねん 観念 **1【考え】** an idea; a notion(根拠のない漠然とした); a concept(いろいろな事例からまとめ上げられた); a conception(ある事柄に関する個人的で漠然とした) ▶ロマンチックな観念 a romantic *notion* ‖ 彼女は教育について独特の観念を持っている She has her own unique *ideas* about education. ‖ あの政治家の政策は**観念的**すぎる That politician's policy is too *idealistic*. ‖ 彼の話は**観念的**(=抽象的)でわかりにくい He talks in *abstract* terms and it is difficult to understand him.
‖**観念論** idealism ‖ **強迫観念** an obsessive idea, an obsession ‖ **固定観念** a fixed idea.
2【意識】 sense ▶彼には時間の観念がないんじゃないか He has no *sense of time*, does he?
3【諦め】 ▶いい加減に観念しろよ *Give up* ... it's stupid to go on (insisting). ‖ 多くの証拠を突きつけられた殺人犯は**観念して**犯行を認めた Presented with a large amount of evidence, the murderer *gave up* and admitted his crime.

がんねん 元年 the first year ▶平成元年 *the first year* of Heisei [the Heisei era] ‖ ことしを市の福祉

元年にしたいものです We want to make this year *the first in an era* of comprehensive welfare services in our city.

かんのうてき 官能的な sensual /sénʃuəl/ ▶官能的なダンス a *sensual* dance ‖ 官能的なシーン a *sensual* scene.

かんのん 観音 *Kannon* ▶観音菩薩(ぼさつ) *the Kannon Bodhisattva* /boodəsʌ́tvə/.

かんぱ 寒波 a cold wave ▶東京はこの冬最大の寒波に見舞われた Tokyo was hit by the biggest *cold wave* of the winter.

カンパ a fund-raising campaign [drive] (募金運動); a contribution (公共目的などでの寄付金); a donation (慈善・宗教目的などでの寄付金) ▶地震被災者救援のためのカンパを行う launch *a fund-raising campaign* to help the victims of the earthquake ‖ アフリカの飢餓救済のため3万円カンパした I *contributed* [*donated*] 30,000 yen to a fund to relieve starvation in Africa.

> **危ないカタカナ語✹ カンパ**
> **1**「カンパ」は英語の campaign (運動) に相当するロシア語 *Kampanija* (闘争, 活動) が語源. ただし, 単に campaign では何の運動かわからないので, fund-raising (資金募集のための) をつける必要がある.
> **2**「カンパする」は「寄付する」の意味だから contribute や donate を用いる.

かんばい 完売 ▶あそこにできるマンション, 即日完売だったんだって All the units in the condominium that's under construction over there *were sold out on the first day they went on the market* [*on sale*]. ‖ そのコンサートチケットは完売いたしました Tickets for that concert *are sold out*.

[1]かんぱい 完敗 (a) complete defeat, (an) utter defeat (➤ 後者はややインフォーマルな言い方) ▶私たちのテニスチームはC高校チームに5対0で完敗した Our tennis team *was completely defeated* [*was soundly beaten* / *was thrashed*] by the C High School team 5-0. (➤ 5-0は five to zero と読む).

[2]かんぱい 乾杯 a toast 一動 (…に)乾杯する drink (a toast) 《to》 ▶乾杯! *Cheers!* / *Bottoms up!* / *Here's to you!* / *To your health!* (➤ 最後の例は「健康を祈って」の意) ‖ 岸さんの前途を祝して乾杯(しよう)! *Let's drink* (*a toast*) *to* Mr. Kishi! ‖ 宴会で小野氏が乾杯の音頭を取った Mr. Ono *proposed a toast* at the banquet.

かんばしい 芳しい 1【香りがよい】 fragrant ▶芳しいバラ a *fragrant* rose ‖ 芳しいラベンダーの香り the *fragrance* of lavender / a *sweet smell* of lavender.

2【「芳しくない」の形で】 ▶彼女の評判は芳しくない She has a *bad* reputation. / Her reputation is *not good*. ‖ 娘の1学期の成績はあまり芳しくなかった My daughter's grades *were not very good* during the first term. ‖ 父の病状は芳しくない My father's condition *is not good*.

カンバス a canvas /kǽnvəs/ ▶カンバスに向かう stand [sit down] before the *canvas*.

かんはつをいれず 間髪を容れず without a moment's hesitation; immediately (直ちに) ▶NATO軍は間髪をいれずに敵に空爆を加えた The NATO air force *immediately* made an air attack on the enemy.

[1]かんばつ 干魃 (a) drought /draʊt/ ▶干ばつのため稲が枯れた *A drought* killed the rice plants. / The rice plants died from *lack of rain*.

[2]かんばつ 間伐 forest thinning ‖ 間伐材 lumber from forest thinnings.

がんばり 頑張り perseverance (粘り強さ); persistence (しつこさ) ▶彼女の頑張りには感心する I admire her *perseverance*. ‖ 技術の習得には忍耐や頑張りが必要なことが多い It usually takes patience and *persistence* to acquire a skill. ‖ 年のせいか頑張りが利かなくなった Maybe it's my age, but I just don't have the *perseverance* [the *stick-to-itiveness*] that I used to have. (➤ stick-to-itiveness は「根気, ふんばり」).

がんばりや 頑張り屋 a hard worker; a go-getter (やり手) ▶頑張り屋の生徒 a *hard-working* student ‖ あの若者は実に頑張り屋だ That young man is *a* real *go-getter*.

がんばる 頑張る 1【努力する】

> **《解説》「頑張る」の言い方**
> (1)「頑張る」は多義なので, 使われる状況に合わせて英語を考える必要がある.「一生懸命働く[勉強する]」の意では **work [study] hard** や **do [try] one's best** とする.「諦めないで頑張る」の意では **stick with it** や **keep up one's effort(s)** などがよい.
> (2) 運動選手などに声援して言う「頑張れ!」は **Hang in there!** といい, 受験などに出かける人には「幸運を祈る」の意味で **Good luck!** が合う. また, いまひとつ調子が出ない人を励ますには「しっかりしろ」という意味で **Pull yourself together!** や「元気を出せ」の意味の **Cheer up!** などもよい.

▶希望の大学に入れるよう頑張れよ *Study hard* [*Try your best*] to get into the university of your choice. ‖ (諦めないで) 頑張れば, きっと夢を実現できるよ If you *stick with it* [*keep up your effort(s)*], I'm sure you can make your dream come true. ‖ きょう中に宿題をやっちゃおうと思って必死に頑張ったよ I *worked my butt off* [*broke my neck*] trying to finish my homework today. (➤ ともにインフォーマルな言い方) ‖ だめかもしれないけど, とにかく頑張れるだけ頑張るよ Maybe I can't make it, but I'll *bust a gut* anyway. (➤ do one's best より砕けた言い方) ‖ 対話「試験頑張れよ」「ありがとう. 頑張ってみるよ」"*Good luck on* your exam." "Thanks. *I'll do my best*." (➤ Good luck on … は「…の幸運を祈る」).

▶(ゴールまで)あと50メートルだ. 頑張れ! There's only fifty meters to the goal. *Hang in there!* ‖ ドラゴンズ頑張れ! *Come on* [*Let's go*], Dragons! (➤ 命令文で用いられた come on は「さあ行け」とか「元気を出せ」の意で, 今, 目前で何かをしている人に対して用いる).

▶《落ち込んでいる人を激励して》頑張れよ *Pull yourself together.* / *Cheer up!* / *Take heart* [*courage*]. (➤ 最後はやや改まった言い方).

▶いくら頑張ってもきみにはY大は無理だよ Y University is out of the question, *no matter how hard you try*. ‖ 徹夜で頑張ってもあすの締め切りには間に合いそうもない *Even if I work at it all night*, there is no way I am going to be able to meet tomorrow's deadline. ‖ 気合いを入れて頑張らないと月末までに仕事は終わらないぞ *Roll up your sleeves and get busy* [*get cracking*], or you won't be able to get your work finished by the end of the month. ‖ 頑張り過ぎるなよ Don't *push yourself too hard*.

2【その場を動かない】▶機動隊が正門前に頑張っていて，ぼくらは構内に入れなかった We couldn't enter the campus because the riot police *occupied* the area in front of the main gate.

かんばん 看板 1【宣伝・案内用の】a **sign**, a **signboard**（店の）; a **billboard**,《英また》a **hoarding**（道路やビルの広告板）; a **shingle**（医師・弁護士などの出す小看板）‖**ステ看板** an expendable [throwaway] signboard.

2【店などの信用】▶彼はうちの店の看板に傷をつけた He has hurt [has damaged] the *reputation* of our store.

▶《慣用表現》あの店は看板に偽りなしだ That store *lives up to its reputation*.

3【名目】▶うちの会社では副社長が実権を握っているので社長は看板にすぎない The vice president holds the real power and our president is *only a sort of figurehead*.（➤ figurehead は名目だけの「飾り物」）‖私たちの英語の先生は堂々としているように見えるけど看板倒れだね Our English teacher looks impressive, but *he is no good at all* [*is useless* (*at teaching*)].

4【閉店】▶《飲食店などで》もう看板なんですが It's closing time. ／We're closing now.

かんぱん 甲板 a **deck** ▶甲板に出て日光浴をしよう Let's go on *deck* and lie [bathe] in the sun.

かんパン 乾パン a **hard baked biscuit.**

がんばん 岩盤《地質学》**bedrock** ‖**岩盤浴** *ganban'yoku*; a hot stone spa.

1**かんび 完備** ▶アクセサリーの完備した新車 a brand-new car (*complete*) *with* all accessories ‖このキャンプ場は施設が完備している This camping ground *is fully equipped* [*has complete facilities*]. ／The facilities at this camping ground are complete. ‖あの大学は全教室が冷暖房完備だ At that college, all classrooms and lecture halls *are completely equipped with* heaters and air conditioners.

2**かんび 甘美な** **sweet** ▶甘美な果物 *sweet* [*luscious*] fruit ‖甘美なメロディー a *sweet* melody.

かんびょう 看病 **nursing**; **attendance**（付き添うこと）一動 **看病する** **nurse** +目; **look after**（世話をする）▶病気の祖母を看病してとても疲れた I am exhausted from *nursing* [*looking after* ／ *taking care of*] my sick grandmother. ‖子供の頃食中毒を起こしたとき，母が寝ずに看病してくれたことをまだ覚えています I still remember my mother *sitting up with* me when I had food poisoning in my childhood.（➤ sit up は「寝ないでいる」）.

かんぴょう 干瓢 ***kanpyo*, dried gourd shavings.**

がんびょう 眼病 an **eye disease**; **eye trouble**（➤婉曲(えんきょく)的な言い方）.

1**かんぶ 幹部** an **executive** /ɪgzékjəṭɪv/ ▶保険会社の幹部 *an executive* at an insurance company ‖労働組合の幹部たち union *leaders* ‖会社の最高幹部 the *top executives* of a company.

‖**幹部会** an executive board ‖**幹部会議** an executive meeting.

2**かんぶ 患部** an **affected part**; an **injured part**, a **wounded part**（負傷箇所）.

かんぷ 還付 **return**; **refund**（金銭の）▶税金の還付を受ける get a tax *refund* ‖**還付金** a refund.

カンフー **kung fu** /kʌ̀ŋ fúː, kʊ̀ŋ-/.

1**かんぷう 寒風** a **cold wind** ▶身を切るような寒風 *a* (*cold and*) *biting wind*.

2**かんぷう 完封** a **shutout** 一動 **完封する** **shut out**,《インフォーマル》**blank** +目 ▶渡辺投手は日本ハムを2安打に完封した Watanabe *shut out* the Fighters on two hits. ‖**完封勝ち** a shutout victory [win].

かんぷく 感服 ▶彼の知性には感服せざるをえない I have to *admire* his intelligence.

かんぶつ 乾物 **dried goods**（➤ dry goods は《米》で「織物類」）‖**乾物屋** a dried goods store.

かんぷまさつ 乾布摩擦 a **skin massage with a rough, dry towel** ▶乾布摩擦をしよう Let's *give ourselves a rubdown massage with a rough dry towel*.

かんぶん 漢文 **Chinese writing**; **Chinese classics**（漢文学）.

かんぺき 完璧 **perfection** 一形 **完璧な** **perfect** ▶完璧を期する aim at *perfection* ‖完璧な翻訳などまずありえない There is no such thing as a *perfect* translation. ／*Perfect* translation does not exist. ‖これで完璧だ Now it's *perfect*. ‖内村の床(ゆか)の演技は完璧だった Uchimura's performance in floor exercises was *sheer perfection*.

‖**完璧主義者** a perfectionist.

1**がんぺき 岸壁** a **wharf**（海・川の船着き場）; a **quay** /kiː/（主に荷役用のふ頭）.

2**がんぺき 岩壁** a **rock face.**

1**かんべん 勘弁する** **excuse** +目 ▶宿題を忘れたけれど先生は勘弁してくれた My teacher *excused* me [*let me off the hook*] for forgetting to do my homework. ‖この報告書をあすまでに提出しないといけないから，今晩のパーティーは勘弁してくれよ *I'm sorry I can't go to* tonight's party. I have to hand in this report by tomorrow.（➤何を勘弁してくれ（＝できない）というのかは状況に合わせて変える）‖また結婚[就職]の話かよ．勘弁してくれよ There you go again talking about my getting married [finding a job]. *Give me a break*.（➤ Give me a break. はいらだちを込めて，「いい加減にしてくれ」「よしてくれ」と言うときのインフォーマルな表現）. ‖おまえのやることはもう勘弁（＝我慢）できん I can no longer *stand* [*put up with* ／ *tolerate*] what you are doing.

2**かんべん 簡便** ▶簡便な方法 a *simple and easy* way ‖このデジタルカメラは簡便さが受けている This digital camera is popular because of its *ease of use* [*usability*].

1**かんぼう 感冒** a **cold**; **influenza**（インフルエンザ；日常的には flu という）.

2**かんぼう 官房** ‖**内閣官房長官** the Chief Cabinet Secretary.

かんぽう 漢方 **Chinese herbal medicine**

‖**漢方医** an [a] herb /əːʳb ‖ həːb/ doctor ‖**漢方薬** herbal medicine.

がんぼう 願望 a **hope**; a **wish**（すぐにはかなえられそうにない望み）▶長年の願望を果たす fulfill *a long-cherished hope* ‖私の最大の願望は司法試験に合格することです My greatest *hope* is to pass the bar examination.

かんぼく 灌木 a **bush**, a **shrub.**

カンボジア **Cambodia** /kæmbóʊdiə/ 一形 **カンボジアの** **Cambodian** ‖**カンボジア人** a Cambodian.

かんぼつ 陥没 (a) **subsidence** 一動 **陥没する** **subside, sink in, cave in** ▶地震のため道路が陥没した The road *sank* [*caved*] *in* because of the earthquake.

がんぽん 元本 **principal**（元金）; **capital**（資本金）▶元本保証 *Principal* guaranteed.

ガンマ **gamma** ‖**ガンマ線** a gamma ray.

かんまつ 巻末 **the back of a book** ▶巻末の索引を見て

ください Please see the index *at the back of the book*.

1**かんまん 干満** **ebb and flow** ▶干満の差 the range of *the tides* ‖ 潮の干満は赤ちゃんの誕生と関係があるといわれる It is said that the *ebb and flow* of the tide affects when babies are born.

2**かんまん 緩慢な** **slow** ▶うちの息子は動作が緩慢でいらいらする My son drives me crazy ; he is so *slow at* (*doing*) *everything*. ‖ 彼の緩慢な守備が巨人の敗因となった His *sluggish* fielding helped the Giants lose the game.

かんみりょう 甘味料 (a) **sweetener**
‖人工甘味料 an artificial sweetener.

かんみん 官民 **the public and private sectors** ▶景気回復には官民の協力が必要だ *The public and private sectors* need to collaborate to improve the economy.

かんむり 冠 a **crown** ▶冠をかぶる put on the *crown*.
☛ おかんむり (→見出語)

かんむりょう 感無量 ▶文化勲章を頂いて, 感無量です Receiving this Order of Cultural Merit—I'*m overwhelmed* (*with emotion*).

1**かんめい 感銘** ▶バッハの『マタイ受難曲』を聴いて深い感銘を受けた Bach's "St. Matthew's Passion" deeply *impressed* [*moved*] me. ‖ 校長の話は生徒たちに感銘を与えた The principal's story *gripped* the students. (➤ grip は「(人の)心をつかむ」).

2**かんめい 簡明な** **simple and clear** ▶私は簡明な説明を心がけたいと思っています I'd like to make my explanation *simple and clear*.

がんめい 頑迷な **bigoted** /bígəṱɪd/ (わからず屋の).

がんめん 顔面 **the face** ▶その知らせを聞いて彼は顔面そう白になった His *face* turned [went] pale when he heard the news. ‖顔面神経痛 facial neuralgia (➤ facial paralysis は「顔面神経まひ」).

がんもく 眼目 **the main point, the pith.**

がんもどき 雁擬き a ***ganmodoki*** ; deep-fried dumpling of crushed tofu and chopped vegetables(➤ 説明的な訳).

1**かんもん 関門** a **hurdle**(飛び越えなければならない障害物) ; a **barrier** (障壁) ; a **checkpoint** (検問所) ▶外交官試験にパスするための第一の関門は筆記試験である The written exam is the first *hurdle* to pass in the Diplomatic Service Examination.

2**かんもん 喚問** a **summons** /sʌ́mənz/ 一動 **喚問する** **summon** ＋㊐ ▶国会喚問 a Diet [Parliament] *summons* ‖ 喚問に応じる answer *a summons* to appear in court ‖ 前社長が証人として喚問されることに決定した They decided to *summon* the former company president as a witness.

かんやく 簡約する **abridge** ＋㊐
‖簡約版 an abridged edition.

かんゆ 肝油 **liver oil**(➤ 何からとるかによって, 前に cod (タラ), shark(サメ), whale(クジラ)などをつける).

かんゆう 勧誘 ▶あのセールスマンはしつこく生命保険の勧誘に来る That salesperson keeps coming back to *try to get me to buy* life insurance. ‖ 不動産屋が電話でワンルームマンションを買わないかと勧誘してきた A real estate agent called and *urged* me *to* buy a studio apartment. (➤ urge は「しきりに勧める」).
‖勧誘員 a (door-to-door) salesperson (注文取り) ; a canvasser (選挙の).

がんゆう 含有する **contain** ＋㊐ ▶鉱石の中にはウランを含有するものがある Some ores *contain* [*have*] uranium. ‖ オレンジはビタミンCの含有量が多い Oranges have a high vitamin C *content* [are high in vitamin C].

かんよ 関与 (an) **involvement** ▶その収賄事件には数人の政治家が関与しているようだ Several politicians seem to *have something to do with* [to *be involved in*] the bribery scandal. ‖ 兄は会社の重要な計画に関与している My older brother *is taking part in* an important company project.

1**かんよう 寛容** **tolerance**(心の広さ, 柔軟性) ; **generosity** (気前のよさ, 度量の大きさ) 一形 **寛容な** **tolerant** ; **generous** ▶父は寛容な人だ My father is a *tolerant* person. ／My father is *tolerant*. ‖ 人と付き合うには寛容の精神が必要だ When mixing with other people, you should be *broad-minded*. ‖ その男は息子が大金を使い込んだのを寛容にも許した The man *generously* forgave his son for squandering his money.

2**かんよう 慣用** **usage** ▶慣用がしばしばことばの意味を変化させる *Usage* often changes the meaning of words. ‖ 'a student at X University' (X大学の学生)を 'a student of X University' というのは英語の慣用に反する It is *not idiomatic* English to say 'a student of X University' instead of 'a student at X University.'
‖慣用句 an idiom ／an idiomatic [a common] expression ‖英語慣用法辞典 a dictionary of English usage.

3**かんよう 肝要** ▶成功には忍耐が肝要だ Patience *is vital* to success. (➤ vital は「基本的で欠くことができない」の意) ‖ いい成績を取るには勉強が肝要だ Studying *is essential* to getting good grades. (➤ essential は「絶対不可欠な」の意).

かんようしょくぶつ 観葉植物 a **foliage plant,** an **ornamental plant.**

がんらい 元来 **originally** /ərídʒənəli/ ▶茶は日本では元来薬用として飲まれていた Tea was *originally* drunk as a (kind of) medicine in Japan. ‖ うちの息子は元来(＝生まれつき)気が小さい My son is timid *by nature*. ／My son was born timid.

かんらく 陥落 a **fall** 一動 **陥落する** **fall** ▶ついにその都市も陥落した At last the city also *fell* to [*fell into the hands* of] the enemy.
▶《比喩的》おまえがいくらくどいても陽子は簡単には陥落しないぜ Yoko is not going to *fall into your arms*, no matter how much you sweet-talk her. ‖ オートバイが欲しかった健二はとうとう父親を陥落させた Kenji finally *talked* his father *into buying* him a motorcycle. ／Kenji finally *persuaded* his father *to buy* him a motorcycle.

かんらくがい 歓楽街 an **entertainment district,** a **red-light district.**

かんらん 観覧 ▶このワンマンショーを観覧ご希望の方はNHKへお問い合わせください Those who are interested in this one-man show, please contact NHK. ‖ 当寺院の宝物は現在観覧に供されております The treasures of the temple are *on display* now. ‖《掲示》観覧料500円 *Admission* : 500 yen
‖観覧車 a Ferris wheel ‖観覧席 a seat (劇場の) ; the stands, a seat (野球場の).

かんり 管理 **management** /mǽnɪdʒmənt/ (監督指導すること) ; **maintenance** (保全・維持) 一動 **管理する** **manage** ＋㊐, **maintain** ＋㊐ ▶家計を管理する *manage* the family budget ‖ この寮は学生が管理している This dormitory *is managed* by the students. ‖ このゴルフ場は市が管理(＝運営)している The city gov-

か

ernment *runs* [*operates*] this golf course. ‖ このマンションは管理が行き届いている This condominium *is very well maintained*.

▶管理職になる be promoted to *management* ‖ 管理職の人たちは毎日多くのストレスを感じている *People in managerial positions* [*People in management*] feel a lot of stress every day. (● are feeling を are under とすることもできる) ‖ 私は会社で人事管理の仕事をしています I'm working in *personnel management* at the company. ‖ 対話「あなたのアパートの管理費はいくら?」「月8000円よ」"How much is *the maintenance* on your apartment?" "Eight thousand yen a [per] month." (➤「維持費」の意味で upkeep を用いることもある).

‖管理教育 control-oriented education ‖ 管理社会 a managed [controlled] society ‖ 管理人 a manager, a superintendent (マンションなどの) ‖ 中間管理職 middle management ‖ 品質管理 quality control.

がんりき 眼力 **vision** (視力) ; **perceptiveness, discernment** (洞察力) ▶その老人は人の心を見抜く鋭い眼力を持っていた The elderly man had the *perceptiveness* [*discernment*] to see through to people's true motivations.

かんりゃく 簡略な **brief** ▶簡略なニュース記事 a *brief* news item ‖ 申請手続きを簡略化する *simplify* an application procedure ‖ 事務を簡略化する *simplify* [*streamline*] office work (➤ 後者は「能率化する」の意).

1 **かんりゅう 貫流する** **flow through** ▶淀川は大阪平野を貫流して大阪湾に注ぐ The Yodo River *flows through* the flatlands around Osaka and empties into Osaka Bay.

2 **かんりゅう 寒流** a **cold current**.

1 **かんりょう 完了** **completion** 一動 完了する **complete** +目 (課せられた仕事を), **finish** +目 (始めたことを) ; **finalize** +目 (最後の部分を終える ; 完了したものを公にする, という含みがあることが多い) ▶我々は計画を予定どおり完了した We *completed* our project as planned. ‖ 仕事はきょう中に完了します I will *finish* the task [job] by tonight. ‖ そのフィールドワークを完了する *finalize* the fieldwork ‖ 準備完了! (*We're*) *all set*! ‖ 任務完了! *Mission accomplished* [*completed*]! ‖完了形《文法》a perfect form ‖ 完了時制《文法》a perfect tense.

2 **かんりょう 官僚** a **government official** ; a **bureaucrat** /bjúərəkræt/ (➤ しばしば軽蔑的) ▶次官は官僚のトップである An undersecretary is a top-ranking *government official*. ‖ 官僚が日本の政治をだめにしている It's the *bureaucrats* who have destroyed [are destroying] the Japanese political system. ‖ 書類が不備だからといってそのまま突っ返してくるのはいかにも官僚的だ It's so *bureaucratic* when they refuse to do anything (and stick everything back into your hands) just because you didn't do the right paperwork.

‖官僚主義 bureaucratism ‖ 官僚政治 bureaucratic government ‖ 官僚政治家 a bureaucrat-turned-politician ‖ 官僚的形式主義 red-tapism, (the) red tape (➤ かつて公文書を赤いひも (red tape) で結んだところから) ‖ 高級官僚 a high-ranking bureaucrat [official].

がんりょう 顔料 (a) **pigment**.

かんれい 慣例 a **custom**, (a) **convention** (➤ 後者のほうがより堅い語) ▶慣例に従う follow *a custom* [*a convention*].

✉ 日本では人を訪問するときに手土産を持参するのが慣例です In Japan, we have *a custom* of taking a (small) gift with us when we visit others.

かんれいぜんせん 寒冷前線 a **cold front** ▶寒冷前線が日本列島の上にかかっている *A cold front* is lying across [over] Japan.

かんれいち 寒冷地 a **frigid** /frídʒɪd/ **zone** ▶寒冷地に転勤する be transferred to *a frigid zone*.

かんれき 還暦 one's **sixtieth birthday** ▶還暦を迎える reach *the age of sixty* ‖ 家じゅうで父の還暦を祝った All the family celebrated Father's *sixtieth birthday*.

かんれん 関連 **relation, connection** (➤ 後者のほうがつながりの強さを強調する) 一動 関連する **relate, connect** ▶彼の主張はきょうの議論のテーマとは何の関連も無い His assertion has no *relation* to the subject of today's discussion. / There is no *connection* between his assertion and the subject of today's discussion. ‖ そんなこと, 私が聞いてることと何の関連も無いじゃないの That *has nothing to do with* what I asked you. ‖ 地球温暖化に関連した話題は後ほどとり上げることにしよう Let's take up the topics *related to* global warming later. ‖ 今度の事件は昨年の汚職事件と関連がありそうだ It looks as if this incident *is tied in* [*is tied up*] *with* that bribery scandal last year. ‖ 喫煙と性的不能には関連性がある There is *a connection* between smoking and impotence.

‖関連会社 an affiliated [associated] company (➤ (1)前者は「子会社, 系列会社」, 後者は「合同会社」とも訳される. (2)「コンピュータ関連会社」は a computer-related company) ‖ 関連記事 a related article ‖ 関連産業 associated [ancillary /ǽnsəlèri/] industries, related industries ‖ (議会などでの)関連質問 a related question ‖ 関連団体 an affiliated organization, a member organization.

かんろく 貫禄 **presence** ; **dignity** (威厳) ▶今度の男の先生は貫禄がある The new teacher *is a man of presence* [*dignity*]. ‖ あの課長は貫禄が無い That section chief *lacks dignity*.

1 **かんわ 緩和する** **ease** +目 (束縛・渋滞などを) ; **relax** +目 (緊張などを) ; **alleviate** /əlíːvièɪt/ +目 (苦痛・悩みなどを) ▶交通渋滞を緩和する *ease* traffic congestion ‖ 日韓の緊張を緩和する *relax* tensions between Japan and South Korea ‖ 規制を緩和する *relax* [*liberalize*] a regulation (➤「規制緩和」は deregulation) ‖ 医師は患者の痛みを緩和しようとした The doctor tried to *alleviate* the patient's pain.

‖緩和医療 palliative medicine ‖ 緩和ケア palliative care.

2 **かんわ 漢和** ‖漢和辞典 a dictionary of Chinese characters used in Japanese (giving both original Chinese and Japanese meanings) as well as the on and kun readings of the characters (➤ 説明的にならざるを得ないが, 日本通の外国人の中には *kanji* dictionary, *kanwa* dictionary などと言う人もいる. Chinese-Japanese dictionary とすると「中日辞典」の意味になる).

3 **かんわ 閑話** ▶閑話休題 *Now let's get back to the subject at hand*. (➤ But I digress. とも言う).

き・キ

[1]**き 気** ⚠**「気」のつく表現をその意味によって「性質, 気質」,「気持ち, 気分」,「心配, 心遣い」,「意識, 正気」などのように分類することもある程度は可能であるが, そのほとんどは慣用表現としてとらえたほうが検索上便利なので, ここでは五十音順に配列した.**

1【慣用表現】

いい気 ▶ →見出語 **気が合う** ▶彼らは気が合う They *get along well.* ／They are *compatible.* ／They *have really good chemistry.* (➤この chemistry は「相性」の意) ‖ 原田君とはどうも気が合わないんだ I don't *get along well* with Harada. **気が荒い** ▶船乗りは概して気が荒い Generally, seamen are *rough-natured.* **気がある** ▶弘太郎は麻美に気がありそうだ It appears that Kotaro *likes* [*is interested in*] Asami. **気がいい** ▶ →気のいい. **気が多い** ▶ 対話「今度はカヌーをやってみたいと思っているんだ」「おまえも気が多いなあ」"I'm thinking of trying canoeing next time." "You sure *are interested in a lot of things*!" **気が大きい** ▶彼女は少しアルコールが入ると気が大きくなる She becomes *expansive* after a few drinks. **気が重い** ▶入試のことは考えるだけで気が重い I *feel depressed* just thinking about entrance exams. ‖ 私の計画に反対している両親を説得するのは気の重い仕事だ It's *depressing* to try to persuade my parents who are opposed to my plan. (➤気が滅入る原因となるものは depressing, 結果として気が滅入る状態になるのは depressed).

気が変わる ▶正樹さんはすぐ気が変わるから嫌いです I don't like Masaki because he *changes his mind* quickly [easily]. **気が利く** ▶鈴木さんの娘さんはよく気が利く人だ Mr. Suzuki's daughter is a *considerate* person. ‖ 近藤君は全く気が利かない Kondo is terribly *inconsiderate.* **気が気でない** ▶娘の車に乗ると事故を起こしはしないかと気が気でない Whenever I ride in the car with my daughter at the wheel, I'*m always afraid* she'll have an accident. ‖ 娘が11時になっても帰って来ないので気が気でなかった I *was beside myself with worry* when my daughter didn't come home even at eleven. **気が狂う** ▶その男は気が狂った That man *became crazy* [*went mad*]. ‖ 女の子は母親の姿を見失って気が狂ったように泣いた The little girl sobbed *hysterically* when she lost sight of her mother.

気が静まる ▶コーチは今興奮しているから気が静まるのを待とう The coach is highly agitated now. Let's wait for him to *calm down.* **気が知れない** ▶道夫と駆け落ちするなんて和子の気が知れない I *don't understand how* [*why*] Kazuko could have run away with Michio. (➤how は「正気でない」というニュアンス). **気が進まない** ▶浜田さんに助言を求めるなんて気が進まないわ I *don't feel comfortable* asking for Mr. Hamada's advice. ‖ 彼女は健二との結婚に気が進まなかった She *was reluctant* to marry Kenji. **気が済む** ▶試合に勝った夜, 彼らは気が済むまで飲んだ The night they won the game, they drank *to their heart's content* [drank *their fill*]. ‖ 俺を殴って気が済むんならいくらでも殴れよ If it will *make you feel better*, go ahead and hit me. ‖ あの生徒は完ぺきに理解しないと気が済まない That student *isn't satisfied* unless he understands (something) perfectly.

気がする ▶南極(大陸)へ行ってみたい気がする I *feel like* going [I'*d like to* go] to Antarctica. ‖ ことし中に日本に大地震が起こりそうな気がする I *have a feeling* that a major earthquake will hit Japan sometime this year. ‖ あなたとならうまくやっていけそうな気がするわ I *get the feeling* that you and I are going to get along just fine together. ‖ 彼女はその仕事には向いていないような気がする *It seems to me that* she isn't suitable for the job. ‖ お母さんが「だめ」と言うような気がした I *had a hunch* that my mom would say no. (➤hunch /hʌntʃ/ は「予感」) ‖ これっぽっちのお年玉じゃもらった気がしないな(＝もらわないも同じだ) If this is all I'm going to get for a New Year's present, then I *may as well* have not gotten anything at all. **気がせく** ▶この金曜日がレポート提出期限なので気がせく I *feel anxious* [*feel stressed out*] since I have a report due this Friday. **気がたつ** ▶今気がたっているのでひとりにしておいてくれ I'*m agitated* [*irritated*] now. So leave me alone.

気が小さい ▶息子は私に似て, 気が小さい My son is *timid* like me. **気が散る** ▶授業中私語している人がいると気が散ってしまう It always *distracts* me when other students talk in class. (➤distract は「(心・注意などを)そらせる」). **気がつく** ▶ →見出語 **気が強い** ▶気の強い娘 a *strong-minded* girl. **気が遠くなる** ▶年収 5 億円だなんて気の遠くなるような話だ It is quite *incredible* that he earns five hundred million yen a year. **気がとがめる** ▶彼にうそをついたので気がとがめる I *feel guilty* because I lied to him.

気が抜ける ▶ビールは缶を開けたら飲んでしまいなさい. 気が抜けてしまうよ Drink up the beer once you have opened the can. It'll go flat if you don't. (➤「気の抜けたビール」は flat beer) ‖ 入試が終わったら弟も気が抜けてしまうだろうな My brother's *enthusiasm will die down* after entrance exams are over.

気が早い ▶もう来年の夏休みの計画を話し合ってるの？気が早いわね Already making plans for next year's summer vacation? Aren't you *jumping the gun* a bit? (➤jump the gun は「先走ったことをする」の意のインフォーマルな表現). **気が張る** ▶試合中は気が張っていたから足の痛みを感じなかった I didn't feel any pain in my leg during the match because I *was so nervous* [*all keyed up*]. (➤be all keyed up は「すっかり興奮している」). **気が晴れる** ▶彼にいらいらをぶちまけたら気が晴れた I *felt better* after I vented my irritation on him. **気が引ける** ▶1脚しかない椅子に私だけ座るのは気が引けた I *felt quite uneasy* taking the only seat. ／I *felt uncomfortable* being the only one who could sit down.

気が変になる ▶車の騒音がひどいので気が変になりそうだ The noise from the traffic is so bad I think I'm *going crazy* [I feel about ready to *go crazy*].

気が短い ▶父は気が短いが母はとても気が長い My father is *quick-tempered* [*short-tempered*], but my mother is very patient. **気が向く** ▶気が向いたらパーティーに来てよ Come to the party *if you want to* [*if you feel like it*]. **気がめいる** ▶長い梅雨で気がめいってしまう I *feel gloomy* because of long rainy season. **気が優しい** ▶気が優しい少年 a *tenderhearted* [*kindhearted*] boy. **気が緩む** ▶試験が終わるとすっかり気が緩んだ I *got too relaxed* after exams are over. **気が弱い** ▶彼は気が弱いから指導者にはなれない He is too *timid* [*faint-hearted* / *chicken-hearted* / *wimpish*] to be a leader. **気が楽になる** ▶息子が大学に入ったので気が楽になった I *feel relieved that* my son got into college. (➤「(…ということに) ほっとしている」) / My son's getting into college *took a load off my mind*. (➤ 完全になくなったわけではないが,「心の重荷が減った」). **気が若い** ▶福田さんは年は取っているがまだ気が若い Mr. Fukuda is getting up there in years, but he's still *young at heart* [he still *feels young*].

気に入る ▶ ⇀見出語 **気にかかる** ▶故郷で独り暮らしをしている母のことがいつも気にかかっている The thought of my mother living alone back home always *weighs on my mind*. ‖ どうも彼の発言が気にかかる What he said *bothers* me a little. **気にかける** ▶彼はいつも家族のことを気にかけている He *is* always *anxious* [*concerned*] *about* his family. ‖ 彼は病弱な娘のことをひどく気にかけている He *is* very *worried about* his sickly daughter. **気に食わない** ▶俺に相談しないで決めてしまうなんて気に食わないね *It aggravates me* [*I can't get over the fact*] *that* you've decided the matter without asking for my opinion. **気に障る** ▶ぼくの意見が気に障ったら勘弁してほしい Please forgive me if what I said has *offended* you. **気にする** ▶ ⇀見出語 **気に染まない** ▶気に染まない仕事を引き受けることはないよ You shouldn't take on a job you'*re unwilling to do*. **気になる** ▶ ⇀見出語 **気に病む** ▶起きてしまったことは今さら気に病んでもしようがない It's useless to *worry about* something that has already happened. / It's useless to cry over spilt milk.

気のいい ▶高田君は気のいい男ですよ Mr. Takada is an *open-hearted and good-natured* man. **気の置けない** ▶健太郎は気の置けない友だちだ I *can relax* [I *feel at ease*] when I am with Kentaro. / I *don't have to be formal with* Kentaro. (➤ be formal with は人に対して「改まる」). **気の利いた** ▶気の利いたドレス[デザイン] a *cool* dress [design] ‖ 気の利いたアイデア a *smart* idea ‖ 気の利いた贈り物 a *thoughtfully* [*carefully*] *selected* gift. **気のせい** ▶気のせいか太ったみたい *Maybe it's just imagination*, but I seem to have gained a little weight. ‖ **対話**「誰かドアをノックしたみたいよ」「気のせいだろ」"I heard someone knock on the door." "It's your *imagination*. / You'*re hearing things*." (➤ 視覚的なことなら You're seeing things. という). ‖ クラスのだれもきみを嫌ってなどいない. それはきみの気のせいだよ Nobody in our class dislikes you. It'*s all in your head*. **気の長い** ▶それは気の長い(=長期にわたる)計画だ It is quite a *long-range* project. **気の抜けた** ▶気の抜けたビール *flat* beer.

気は心 ▶高価な品を彼女に送る必要はないよ. 気は心だから You don't have to send her such an expensive gift. *The thought is what counts* [*It's the thought that counts*]. (➤「大切なのは気持ちだ」の意. 後者は「気は心」に相当する英語のことわざ). **気は確か** ▶そのブランドものの財布に 7 万円も出すなんて, おまえ気は確かか? *Are* you *in your right mind* to buy a 70,000 yen designer wallet? ‖ きみ, 気は確かだろうね You *aren't crazy*, are you?

気を入れる ▶もっと気を入れて仕事をしなさい You should *put your heart* [*more effort*] into your work. **気を失う** ▶彼女は転んだ拍子に頭を打って気を失った She *lost consciousness* [*was knocked out*] when she fell and hit her head. **気を落ち着ける** ▶気を落ち着けて私の言うことをよく聞いてちょうだい *Calm down* and listen to me carefully. **気を落とす** ▶ **対話**「玲子に振られちゃったよ」「そうか. まあ, 気を落とすなよ」"Reiko dumped me!" "Did she? Well, *don't let it get you down*."

気を利かす ▶彼女のことだから気を利かしてみんなが食べる分を用意してくるわよ I'm sure she'll *put two and two together* and prepare enough food for everyone. / I'm sure she'll *have the sense* [*be thoughtful enough*] to get enough food ready for everyone. (➤ put two and two together は「事情を考え合わせて推測する」; 前の文と後者の最初は予測力を, 後者の言い換えは「思いやりがある」を表す). **気を配る** ▶客に気を配る *be attentive to* a guest ‖ お母さんは細かいところまで気を配ってくれる My mother *pays attention to* the smallest things.

気を確かにもつ ▶気を確かにもつんだ! *Keep a clear head*! **気を遣う** ▶ロンドン滞在中はいろいろ気を遣ってくれてありがとう Thank you for everything you *did for* me while I was in London. / Thank you for *looking after* me while I was in London. (➤ look after は身の回りの世話をしてくれたような場合) ‖ どうぞ気を遣わないでください Please *don't bother*. ‖ みどりは着る物にとても気を遣う Midori *pays* a lot of *attention* to what she wears. **気をつける** ▶ ⇀見出語. **気を強く持つ** ▶気を強く持て! *Stay strong*!

気を取られる ▶スマホにばかり気を取られて勉強がお留守になっているんじゃないの You'*re so wrapped up* in (using) your smartphone that studying is the last thing on your mind. **気を取り直す** ▶途中で数がわからなくなったが, 気を取り直して最初から数え直すことにした I got mixed up while counting, but I *took a breath* and decided to count again from the beginning.

気を抜く ▶相手が一瞬気を抜いたところを見て投げ飛ばした I caught my opponent *off guard* for an instant and threw him to the floor. **気を引く** ▶パーティーで明美の気を引こうとしたがうまくいかなかった I tried to *attract* Akemi's *attention* at the party, but it didn't work. ‖ 薫はあの手この手で静男の気を引こうとした Kaoru tried this way and that to *get* Shizuo *to notice* her. (➤ get A to do はこの場合, 説得でなく「人(A)が…するようにいろいろと工作して, その状態にもっていく」).

気を回す ▶うちのお母さんはぼくのガールフレンドに気を回し過ぎる My mother *pays too much attention* to my girlfriend. ‖ 太郎君は単なるいいお友だち, 変に気を回さないで Taro is just a good friend. Don't *go imagining things*. **気を持たせる** ▶長い間気を持たせておいて, 今になって断るとは For a long time, he *kept* me *hoping* [*kept leading* me *on*] and now he (turns around and) says, "No." (➤ 日本語の「…とは」は now 以下が現在形で表されていることで生々しく強調されている. また now も強く発音する). **気をもむ** ▶最初はどうなるかと気をもんだが万事うまくいった At

first I *was worried* (*about*) what would happen, but everything turned out all right.
気を緩める ▶ ⇀**気を抜く**. **気をよくする** ▶彼女は展覧会に絵が入選して気をよくしている Because her picture has been accepted for the art exhibition, she *is in a good mood*. **気を悪くする** ▶私のことで気を悪くしないでね Please don't *think badly of* me. ‖ こんなことを言っても気を悪くしないでください Please don't *be offended* by what I'm about to say. **その気** ▶ ⇀見出語 **やる気** ▶ ⇀見出語 **悪い気** ▶人から褒められれば誰だって悪い気はしない No one *feels displeased* when praised by others.
2【その他】 ▶ジャイアンツが負けると仕事をする気にもならない When the Giants lose a game, I *lose my will* to work. ‖ あなたのやり方に文句を言う**気はありません** I *have no intention of* finding [*I'm not trying to* find] fault with how you do it. ‖ ねえ, 部屋をこんなに散らかして**どうする気**? Say! *What's the big idea*, messing up the room like this? (➤ What's the big idea? は非難するときの言い方) ‖ **何の気無しに言った**ことが彼女の感情を害してしまった *Some casual words* [*remark* / *comment*] of mine hurt her feelings.

[2]**き 木** **1【樹木】** a **tree** (1本の) ; **wood** (木材) ▶**木**を植える plant *a tree* ‖ **木**をせんていする prune *a tree* ‖ **木**に登る climb *a tree* ‖ **木の無い山** a *bald* mountain ‖ **木の生い茂った山** a *wooded* [*tree-covered*] mountain.
▶この机は**木**でできている This desk is made of *wood*. (➤「木の机」は a desk made of wood または a wooden desk) ‖ 老人は**木の下**で休んだ The elderly man rested *under a tree*.
2【慣用表現】 ▶彼は私たちに**木で鼻をくくったような** (=そっけない) 返事をした He gave us a *curt* [*blunt*] reply. (➤ curt は「そっけない」, blunt は「デリカシーに欠ける」) ‖ **木に竹を接いだような文章** awkward stilted writing (➤「ぎこちなく気取った文章」の意) ‖ うちの社長は**木を見て森を見ず**だよ. 目先の利益にばかり気を取られて, 会社の将来を大局的に考えていないんだから Our president *can't see the forest* [*wood*] *for the trees*. He's too much swayed by the prospect of immediate profits, and doesn't think about the company's future in the long term.

> 「木」のいろいろ **アカシア** locust / **アジサイ** hydrangea / **イチョウ** ginkgo / **糸杉** cypress / **梅** *ume*, Japanese apricot / **カエデ** maple / **カキ** *kaki*, persimmon / **カシ** oak / **カラマツ** larch / **キリ** paulownia / **キンモクセイ** fragrant orange-colored olive / **クス** camphor / **クチナシ** gardenia / **クリ** chestnut / **クルミ** walnut / **ケヤキ** zelkova / **桜** cherry / **ザクロ** pomegranate / **サルスベリ** crape myrtle / **シラカバ** white [silver] birch / **ジンチョウゲ** daphne / **杉** Japanese cedar / **スズカケ(の木)** plane (tree), sycamore / **ソテツ** cycad / **ツゲ** box / **ツツジ** azalea / **ツバキ** camellia / **トチ** horse chestnut / **ニレ** elm / **ネコヤナギ** pussy willow / **ハギ** bush clover / **ハナミズキ** dogwood / **バラ** rose / **ヒイラギ** holly / **ヒノキ** Japanese cypress / **ヒマラヤスギ** cedar / **フジ** wisteria / **ブナ** beech / **ボケ** Japanese quince / **ポプラ** poplar / **松** pine / **モクレン** magnolia / **モミ** fir / **ヤシ** palm / **柳** willow / **ユーカリ** eucalyptus / **ユリノキ** tulip tree

[3]**き 機** **the time** (時機) ; a **chance** (機会) ▶**機は熟した** *The time* is ripe. ‖ きみが独立するにはまだ**機が熟していない** *The right time hasn't come yet* for you to become independent. ‖《慣用表現》あの男は**機を見るに敏**だ That man is *quick to seize an opportunity*. / That man *never misses a chance*.

[4]**き 奇** ▶**奇をてらった**服はすぐ廃れる *Eccentric* clothes soon go out of fashion. ‖ 彼は**奇をてらって**あんなことをやるんだよ He tries to *impress people by behaving in a deliberately strange way*.

[5]**き 黄** **yellow**. ⇀**黄色**.

[6]**き 生** ▶ウイスキーを**生**で飲む drink one's whiskey *straight* [*neat*].

-き 期 a **period** (期間) ; an **age** (時代) ; a **term** (任期) ; a **session** (会期) ▶ (病気の)潜伏**期** the *period* of incubation ‖ 第一氷河**期** the first Ice *Age* ‖ 私の父は市長を2**期**務めた My father served two *terms* as mayor.

ぎ 義 **justice, righteousness** /ráɪtʃəsnəs/ (➤ 後者は主に《文》) ▶**義を見てせざるは勇無きなり** *To see* [*know*] *what is right and not do it shows a lack of courage*.

ギア (a) **gear** (自動車・自転車の変速ギア ; 用具一式) ▶ 5段**ギア** [オートマチック**ギア**] の車 a car with five [automatic] *gears* ‖ **ギア**をトップ [ロー / セカンド] に入れる put the car in high [low / second] *gear* (➤《英》では high [low] gear を top [bottom] gear という) ‖ オートマチックの**ギア**をドライブに入れる put the automatic *gear lever* into Drive.

きあい 気合い **fight** (闘志) ; **spirit** (気迫) ▶きょうはうちのバスケットボール部は**気合いが入っている** Our basketball team *is full of fight* today. ‖ 試合に臨んで**気合いを入れた** I *psyched myself up* before the game. (➤「コーチはチームに気合いを入れた」は The coach psyched up the team.). ‖ きみのきょうの仕事ぶりは**気合いが入ってない**ぞ You'*re not concentrating on* your work today. (➤「集中していない」の意) ‖ 大学に行きたいんなら**気合いを入れて**勉強しなきゃあだめだ If you want to go to college, you'll have to *knuckle down* and study [*get cracking with* your studies]. (➤ knuckle down, get cracking はそれぞれ「本腰を入れてかかる」「ひと頑張りする」の意のインフォーマルな表現).

きあつ 気圧 **atmospheric** [**barometric**] **pressure** (大気の圧力) ; **air pressure** (空気圧) ▶ヘクトパスカルは**気圧**を表す単位である A hectopascal is a unit of *atmospheric pressure*. ‖ 上空へ行くほど**気圧**は低下する As you go higher, *the* (*air*) *pressure* drops. ‖ その地域は現在のところ**気圧の谷**に入っている The region is now in *a* (*low pressure*) *trough*. ‖ 冬型の**気圧配置** a winter-type *pressure pattern*. ‖ **気圧計** a barometer /bərɑ́ːmɪṭəʳ/ ‖ **気圧配置** a pressure pattern.
☛ **高気圧, 低気圧** (⇀見出語)

ぎあん 議案 a **proposal** ; a **bill, legislation** (ともに法案 ; 後者は集合名詞) ▶**議案**を提出する present [submit] *a proposal*, propose *legislation* [*a bill*].

きい 奇異な **strange** (変な) ; **odd** (常軌を逸した) ▶彼は最近**奇異な**行動が目立つ He often acts *strangely* [*oddly*] these days. ‖ 彼女の発言は私には**奇異に響いた** Her remark *sounded strange* [*odd*] to me.

キー a **key** ▶ピアノの**キー** the *keys* of a piano ‖ 車の**キー** a car *key* ‖ (コンピュータの) **キー**をたたく hit the *keyboard*.
▶**キー**を少し下げて私の声に合わせてくれますか Could you lower the *key* to match my voice, please?

きーきー ▶椅子の**キーキー**きしむ音がうるさくてたまらない

The *creaking* chair is getting on my nerves. ‖ 木の上で猿がキーキー鳴いている The monkey is *screeching* in the tree.

ぎーぎー ▶娘がバイオリンをギーギー弾いている My daughter is *sawing away* on the violin.

きいたふう 利いた風 ▶利いた風な口を利くな *Don't be fresh.* ／*Don't be a smart aleck.*

きいちご 木苺 《植物》 a **raspberry** /rǽzbèri/.

きいと 生糸 raw silk ▶生糸を紡ぐ spin *raw silk*.

キーパー 《サッカー》 a **goalkeeper,** 《インフォーマル》 a **goalie.**

キープ ▶ボールをキープする *keep possession of* the ball ‖ 開幕以来, 巨人は首位をキープしている The Giants *have stayed in first place* since the start of the pennant race.

キーボード a **keyboard** /kíːbɔːʳd/ (パソコンなどの) ; **the keyboards** (鍵盤楽器) ▶キーボードをたたく hit [tap (on)] *a keyboard* ‖ キーボードで1分間に何語打てますか How many words a minute can you type on the *keyboard*?

キーホルダー a **key ring,** a **key chain** (➤ key holder は一般的ではない ; 財布状のキーホルダーは特に key case という).

きいろ 黄色

yellow ; **amber** (交通信号の) ▶黄色いリボン a *yellow* ribbon ‖ 黄色っぽい帽子 a *yellowish* cap ‖ 彼女は黄色の服を着ていた She was (dressed) in *yellow*. ‖ 《慣用表現》 少女たちはひいきの歌手がステージに立つと黄色い声を上げた The girls *screamed in excitement* when their favorite singer appeared on the stage.

キーワード a **key word** ▶「保守的」という語はイギリスを理解するためのキーワードだ 'Conservative' is *a key word* you need to understand Britain.

きいん 起因 ▶職場の人間関係に起因するストレス stress *due to* poor human relationships in the workplace ‖ 少年非行は子供に対する両親の愛情の欠如に起因することがよくある Juvenile delinquency *is* often *caused* by parents' lack of love for their child(ren).

ぎいん 議員

> 《解説》 (1) 一般の議会などの議員は a **member of an assembly** で, 男女をいうときには assemblyman [-woman] という. 国会議員はアメリカでは a **member of Congress,** 下院議員を a **Congressman** [**-woman**], 上院議員を a **senator,** イギリスでは a **member of Parliament** 《略 MP》 という. (2) 日本の国会議員は a **Diet** [**Parliament**] **member** または a member of the Diet [Parliament] という.

▶県議会議員 a member of a prefectural assembly ‖ 衆議院議員 a member of the House of Representatives ‖ 参議院議員 a member of the House of Council(l)ors ‖ 神奈川県選出の国会議員 *a Diet member* for [representing] Kanagawa Prefecture ‖ 彼は当地区の市会議員だ He *represents* this area in the municipal assembly. (➤「市議会でこの地区を代表している」の意).

キウイ 《鳥》 《果物》 a **kiwi** /kíːwiː/.

きうん 気運 a **tendency,** a **trend** (風潮) ▶近頃二酸化炭素排出規制の気運が高まってきている These days there is a growing *tendency* to regulate [restrict] carbon dioxide emissions.

きえ 帰依 ▶仏教に帰依する *embrace* Buddhism ／*take refuge* in the Buddha.

1きえい 気鋭 ▶新進気鋭の映画評論家 a *smart, up-and-coming* movie critic.

2きえい 機影 ▶レーダーから機影が消えた The *airplane* disappeared [vanished] from the radar.

きえいる 消え入る ▶「私がやりました」と容疑者は消え入るような声で言った "I did it," the suspect said in a *faint* [*feeble*] voice. (➤ 後者は「か弱い」に近い).

きえうせる 消え失せる ▶とっとと消えうせろ！ *Get out of here!* ／*Get out of my sight!*

きえる 消える

> 訳語メニュー
> 火や明かりが →go out [off] 1
> 姿や形が →disappear, vanish 2
> うわさ・習慣などが →die out 3

1 【火・明かりが】 go out, go off (➤ 明かりの場合, 後者には「スイッチで」という含みがある) ▶息を吹きかけるとろうそくの火は消えた The candle *went out* when I blew on it. ‖ 家々の明かりが一斉に消えた The lights of the houses *went off* all at once. ‖ その島の大火はようやく消えた The big fire on that island *was* finally *put out*. (➤「消火された」の意) ‖ 街灯が消えている. 誰かが壊したのかもしれない The street lamps *are out*. Someone might have broken them. ‖ バーベキューグリルの炭火が消えかかっている The charcoal in the barbecue *is dying down*.

2 【姿・形が】 disappear ; **vanish** (突然視界から) ; **get erased** [《インフォーマル》 **trashed**] (パソコン内の文書などが) ▶機影がレーダーから消えた The plane *disappeared* [*vanished*] from the radar screen. ‖ 古い雪が消え (＝とけ) ないうちに新しい雪が降った Fresh snow fell before the old snow could *melt*.
▶金庫にしまってあった1000万円が煙のように消えていた The ten million yen in the safe *had vanished* without a trace. ‖ 暴走族なんか町から消えてしまえばいいのに I wish hot rodders would *disappear* from town. ‖ 繁華街は夜中の12時を過ぎても人影が消えない *There are people out and about* downtown even after midnight. ‖ 壁の落書きはなかなか消えない (＝消せない) It is hard to *get* the wall completely *clean of* graffiti. ‖ どういう訳かパソコンのその文書が消えてしまった Somehow the computer document *got erased*. ‖ とっとと消えろ (＝うせろ)！ *Out of my sight!* ／*Get lost!*

3 【なくなる・消滅する】 ▶時がたつにつれてそのうわさは消えた As time passed, the rumor *died out*. ‖ その薬を飲んだら背中の痛みがうそのように消えた The back pain *went away* like magic after I took the medicine. ‖ 雷の音は次第に遠ざかり, やがて消えた The thunder slowly grew more distant and finally *died away*. ‖ そういった習慣は次第に消えていっています Those customs are *fading away* now. ‖ 洗っても洗っても魚の臭いが手から消えない The fishy smell *lingers* no matter how hard [long] I wash my hands. (➤ linger は「しつこくとどまる」) ‖ そのアメリカの上院議員に対する疑惑はいまだに消えていない The suspicions about that U.S. senator have*n't been laid to rest*. (➤ be laid to rest は「(疑惑・不安などが) 解消する」) ‖ ダイアナ妃の名はいつまでも消えないだろう (The name of) Princess Diana will *be long remembered*.

きえん 気炎 ▶自分たちのチームが優勝したので彼らは気炎を上げている They *are in high* [*great*] *spirits* because their team (has) won the championship.

ぎえんきん 義捐金・義援金 a **contribution**, a **donation** /dounéiʃən/ →寄付 ▶地震の被害に遭われた方々のために義援金をよろしくお願いします Please make a generous *contribution* for the earthquake victims.

きおう 気負う ▶そんなに気負うなよ Don't *get so nerved up*. ‖社会福祉の問題は気負わず気長に取り組むことが大事だ Problems in social welfare are best approached with patience, *without being overly anxious for results*. (➤「結果を気にし過ぎないようにして」の意).

きおうしょう 既往症 **past illnesses** [**diseases**]; one's **medical history**(病歴).

きおく 記憶 (a) **memory** 一動 **記憶する** **memorize** +目(覚える); **remember** +目(覚えている, 思い出す) ▶記憶を失う lose one's *memory* ‖記憶すべき出来事 a *memorable* event ‖子供の頃の記憶は年を取るにつれて薄れる Childhood *memories* fade as one grows older. ‖英単語を記憶するだけでは十分ではない. 正しい使い方も身につけなければならない It's not enough to *memorize* English words. You also have to learn how to use them correctly. ‖このことはしっかり記憶して(＝心に留めて)おきなさい *Keep* [*Bear*] this (firmly) *in mind*.

▶私は少女の頃の景子に1度会った記憶がある I *remember* seeing Keiko once when she was a little girl. ‖そんなことを言った記憶はない I *don't remember* saying anything like that. (➤ 上の2例とも remember doing の形をとることに注意; →覚える) ‖私は小学生のときのことはあまり記憶にない I *can't remember* my elementary school days very well. ‖今生きている人々の記憶に残っている中で最酷寒の冬 the coldest winter *in* [*within*] *living memory* ‖祖母は記憶力がいい My grandmother *has a good memory*. (➤「記憶力が悪い」は have a poor memory) ‖私の記憶が正しければその名言はナポレオンが言ったのだと思う *If I remember correctly*, that famous remark was made by Napoleon. ‖その大地震は今なお記憶に新しい The big earthquake is still *fresh in our memories* [*minds*]. ‖8月15日が来るたびに日本人は太平洋戦争の記憶を新たにする Every year on August 15, Japanese *recall anew* [*afresh*] *the memories* of the Pacific War.

‖**記憶術** mnemonics /nɪmɑ́:nɪks/ ‖**記憶喪失症** amnesia /æmní:ʒə/ ‖(コンピュータの)**記憶装置** a memory, a storage device.

きおくれ 気後れ ▶大勢の人の前に出るとどうしても気後れしてしまう Every time I stand in front of a crowd, I *get stage fright* [*butterflies in my stomach*]. (➤ stage fright は「(聴衆や観客の前に出たとき興奮や不安のために)上がること」をいい, butterflies in one's stomach は文字どおりには「胃の中のちょう」の意で「ひどい不安, どきどき」の意のインフォーマルな言い方) ‖情報技術に気後れしてしまう人が多い Many people *are daunted* by information technology. (➤ daunt は「(人)をひるませる」).

キオスク a **kiosk** /kí:ɑsk, kí:ɔsk/; a **newsstand**(新聞・雑誌売り場)

> **危ないカタカナ語✹ キオスク**
> **1** 日本では専ら駅の売店のことを「キオスク」と呼んでいるが, この語はもともとトルコ語で, 「あずまや」の意.
> **2** 英語としてのkioskは駅に限らず, 街頭や広場の新聞売店, 電話ボックス(イギリスで), 広告塔などをも指す.

きおち 気落ちする **be disheartened** ▶彼は学年末試験の成績が悪かったので気落ちしてしまった He *was disheartened* [*discouraged*] because he got bad grades on his final exams.

きおん 気温 **temperature** ▶気温を測定する measure the *temperature* ‖気温の変化 a change in *temperature* ‖明け方に気温が急に下がった The *temperature* dropped suddenly at dawn. ‖午後になって気温がやや上がった The *temperature* rose [climbed／went up] a little in the afternoon. ‖この地方は年間を通して気温が高い[低い] The *temperature* is high [low] in this part of the country all year round. ‖**対話**「今, 気温は何度ですか?」「零下5度です」"*What's the temperature* now?" "Five degrees below freezing [below zero]." ‖きょうの東京の最高気温は(摂氏)34度だった Today's *high* (*temperature*) in Tokyo was 34 degrees (Celsius). (➤「最高気温」は the maximum temperature だが, 天気予報などでは訳例のようにいうことが多い. また Celsius は centigrade ともいう) ‖あすの最低気温は(摂氏)5度近くになるでしょう *The low* (*temperature*) for tomorrow will approach 5 degrees (Celsius). ‖前世紀, 地球の平均気温が1度上昇した Over the past century, *the average global temperature* rose 1 degree.

ぎおん 擬音 **sound effects**

‖**擬音語** onomatopoeia /ɑ̀:nəmæ̀təpí:ə/, an onomatopoeic [onomatopoetic] word.

[1]**きか 帰化** **naturalization** 一動 **帰化する** **be naturalized** ▶日本には帰化した中国人や韓国人が多数住んでいる There are many Chinese and Koreans in Japan who have *become naturalized* Japanese citizens. ‖**帰化植物**[**動物**] a naturalized plant [animal].

[2]**きか 幾何** **geometry** /dʒiɑ́:mətri/ ▶幾何学的な模様 a *geometric*(*al*) pattern. ‖**幾何級数** a geometrical series (➤「幾何級数的に」は exponentially).

[3]**きか 気化** **vaporization** 一動 **気化する** **vaporize** /véɪpəraɪz/ ▶この液体は体温で気化する This fluid *vaporizes* at body temperature.

‖**気化熱** the heat of vaporization.

きが 飢餓 **starvation**; **hunger**(空腹) ▶飢餓にあえいでいる人々が世界中に何百万人もいる Millions of people are suffering from *starvation* in the world. ‖世界中でたくさんの子供たちが飢餓で死んでいる A lot of children are dying of *hunger* throughout the world.

ギガー **giga-** ▶ギガバイト *a gigabyte*《略 GB》‖このノートパソコンのメモリーは2ギガバイトだ This notebook computer has a *2-gigabyte* memory.

[1]**きかい 機会** an **opportunity**(好機); a **chance**(偶然のチャンス); an **occasion**(ふさわしい時) ▶絶好の機会を逃す miss the best *chance* ‖祖父は正規の教育を受ける機会がなかった My grandfather had no *opportunity* to get a formal education. ‖新潟へ行く機会があったらおばのとこへ寄ってあげてよ If you ever have *a chance* to go to Niigata, look up my aunt. ‖機会があったらまた会おう Let's get together again *if we have a chance*. ‖機会があり次第伺います I'll visit you *at the first opportunity* [*as soon as I have a chance*]. ‖誕生日や祭りといった特別の機会によく赤飯を炊きます We often cook sekihan (red rice) *on special occasions* such as birthdays or festivals.

▶アメリカ人と会う機会があると彼は必ずいくつかの質問をす

る *Whenever* he *runs into* an American, he always tries to ask him [her] a question or two. ‖ その話は別の機会にしてくれませんか Could you *save* that topic *for some other time*? ‖ 結論は次の機会に譲りましょう Let's save the conclusion for *the next time*. ‖ 吉田君が熊本へ来るのを機会に(＝利用して)クラス会を開こう Let's *take advantage of* Yoshida's being in Kumamoto and have a class reunion.

²**きかい 機械** **a machine, machinery** (➤ 後者は集合的な言い方) ; a **gadget** /gǽdʒɪt/ (小道具) ▶機械を組み立てる assemble *a machine* ‖ 機械編みのセーター a *machine-knit* sweater ‖ このボタンを押すと機械が動き始めます Push this button and the *machine* will start. ‖ 秀夫は機械に弱い Hideo *is no good with anything mechanical*. ／Hideo *is not* (very) *mechanical*.
▶製造の全工程を機械化する *mechanize* [*automate*] the whole production process ‖《広告で》機械工3人至急求む Three *mechanics* urgently required. ‖ 当社は最新式の機械設備を大量に据え付ける計画です We plan to install a lot of up-to-date *machinery*. ‖ 英語の単語を機械的に覚えるのは退屈だ It's a bore to memorize English words *mechanically* [*by rote*]. ‖ **機械科** a course in mechanics ‖ **機械工学** mechanical engineering.

³**きかい 器械** an **instrument** ; (an) **apparatus** /æ̀pərǽṭəs ‖ -réɪt-/ (器具一式) ‖ **器械体操** apparatus gymnastics ‖ **医療器械** medical instruments.

⁴**きかい 奇怪な** **strange** (奇妙な) ; **weird** /wɪəʳd/ (気味の悪い) ▶一家が消え去るなんて奇怪な話だ It is *strange* that the whole family disappeared.

¹**きがい 危害** **harm** ▶このワニは人に危害を加えるようなことはしません This crocodile won't do anything to *harm* people. ／This crocodile won't bite. (➤ bite は「かみつく」).

²**きがい 気概** (a) **fighting spirit, grit** ▶わが社は気概のある人を求めています We are looking for [seeking to hire] *people with* (a) *fighting spirit* [*with grit*].

ぎかい 議会 an **assembly**(一般の) ; a **national assembly** (国会) ; a **legislature** (立法機関)《参考》日本の国会は the Diet または Parliament, アメリカの議会は Congress, イギリス・カナダ・オーストラリアなどの議会は Parliament という. →議員.
▶議会を招集 [解散] する convene [dissolve] *the assembly* ‖ あすから市 [県] 議会が開かれます The *municipal* [*prefectural*] *assembly* will meet tomorrow. ‖ **議会政治** parliamentary government ‖ **議会制民主主義** parliamentary democracy.

きがえ 着替え a **change of clothes** ▶2日の旅行だから着替えはいらないよ I don't need *a change of clothes* because it is only a two-day trip. ‖ 着替えはふたそろい持って来ている I've brought *two changes of clothes*.

きがえる 着替える **change** ▶パジャマ [ふだん着] に着替える *change into* one's pajamas [casual clothes] ‖ 着替える所が無くて困った I was in trouble as there was no place to *change clothes* in [at]. ‖ かぜをひくといけないから早く着替えなさい Hurry up and *change your clothes* [*get changed*] so (that) you don't catch (a) cold.

きがかり 気掛かり (a) **worry** (無用な心配, 心痛) ; (an) **anxiety** /æŋzáɪəṭi/ (不安な心境) ▶私は母の健康が気がかりだ I *feel anxious about* my mother's health. ‖ 娘の将来がひどく気がかりでね My daughter's future *is a big worry* to me. ‖ 接近している巨大な台風が気がかりだ I'*m concerned* about the approaching massive typhoon. ‖ あしたの英語の試験が気がかりだ I *have got* tomorrow's English exam *on my mind*. (➤ have (got) ... on one's mind で「…を心配している」).

¹**きかく 企画** **planning** (計画を立てること) ; a **plan**, a **project** (計画そのもの ; 後者は長期にわたる場合が多い)
一動 **企画する** **plan** ＋㊐ ▶企画には十分時間をかけるべきです We should spend enough time on [for] the *planning* stage. ‖ クラスの同窓会を企画しましたのでご出席のほどよろしくお願いします We have *arranged* a class reunion and hope you will be able to come. ‖ T社の企画部 [課] に勤めています I work in the *Planning Department* of T Corporation.

²**きかく 規格** a **standard** ▶国家規格 a national *standard* ‖ **規格品** a product made to the standard, a standardized product [article].

きがく 器楽 **instrumental music** ▶器楽合奏をする perform *instrumental music*.

きかげき 喜歌劇 a **comic opera**.

きかざる 着飾る **dress up, be dressed up** ▶着飾った女性たち women *dressed up in their best* ‖ 略式パーティーだからと招待状に書いたのに, 彼女は着飾ってきた I said in the invitation that it was an informal party, but she came *dressed* (*up*) *to the nines* [*dressed to kill*]. (➤ ともに「めかし込んで」の意のインフォーマルな表現).

きがする 気がする →気.

¹**きかせる 聞かせる** ▶あなたの将来の計画について聞かせてください *Tell me* something about your future plans. ‖ これは幼い子供たちには聞かせられない話だ This conversation is *not fit for the ears* of small children. ‖ この詩を読んで聞かせよう I'll *read* this poem *to* you. ‖ セレナーデを歌って聞かせてください Will you *sing me* a serenade?

²**きかせる 利かせる・効かせる** ▶彼女は気を利かせて席を外してくれた She *had the delicacy to* leave the room.
▶このサラダはもっと酢を効かせたほうがいいな This salad would taste better with more vinegar on it.

きがた 木型 a **wooden mold** (菓子作りなどに用いる ; cookie mold のように具体的にいうことが多い) ; a **wooden form** (靴の ; shoe form のように具体的にいうことが多い).

きがつく 気が付く **notice** ＋㊐ (目で見て, 耳で聞いて) ; **realize** ＋㊐ (状況などから判断して) ▶帳簿を調べていておかしな点があることに気がついた While examining the account book, I *noticed* [*became aware*] that there was something wrong. ‖ そんなに遅い時間だとは気がつかなかった I *didn't realize* how late it was. ‖ 気がつくと電車を間違えていた I *found myself* on the wrong train. ‖ 家に帰るまで財布をすられたのに気がつかなかった I *was not aware* that my wallet had been stolen until I got home. (→気づく). ‖《病人に》気がついた(＝意識を回復した)ようだね Looks like you've *come around*. ‖ 山本さんはよく気がつく人です Mr. Yamamoto is *thoughtful* [*sensitive*].

きがね 気兼ね **constraint** /kənstréɪnt/ ▶祖父は若夫婦の前では気兼ねしている My grandfather *is showing constraint* [*is ill at ease*] in the presence of the young couple. ‖ 気兼ねしないでできるだけ長く泊まっていってください Please *feel free to* stay with us as long as you like.

きがまえ 気構え ▶どんな事態が起きても大丈夫という気構えでいなくてはいけないよ You should *be prepared for* any situation.

きがる 気軽 ▶結婚を気軽に(＝軽く)考えられては困る I don't want you to take marriage *lightly*. ‖ 縄跳びは気軽に(＝簡単に)できる運動だ Jumping rope is an exercise that anyone can do *easily*. ‖ 彼は気軽に(＝快く)掃除を引き受けてくれた He *willingly* accepted the task of cleaning up. ‖ いつでもお気軽に(＝遠慮なく)お立ち寄りください *Feel free to* drop in anytime. ‖ このホールは誰でも気軽に利用できる This hall *is available for use by anyone*.

1**きかん 期間** a **period** ▶今試験期間中です We are now in the exam *period*. ‖ この薬は一定期間飲まないといけない You must take this medicine *for a certain period of time*. ‖《食品表示で》おいしく召し上がっていただける期間は2か月です Best if consumed within two months. ‖ この切符の有効期間は2日間限りだ This ticket is *valid* [*good*] *for* two days only.

逆引き熟語 ○○期間
一定期間 a certain period／**運転期間** an operating [operation] period／**謹慎期間** probation／**研修期間** a training period／**工事期間** a construction period／**在学期間** an attendance [enrollment] period／**在職期間** the period of one's service, one's tenure of office／**試験期間** a test [testing] period／**準備期間** a preparation period／**試用期間** a trial [probationary] period／**潜伏期間** an incubation period／**治療期間** a treatment period／**保証期間** the term of a guarantee [warranty], the guarantee [warranty] period／**有効期間** the period [term] of validity, the validity period／(**支払い**) **猶予期間** a grace period

2**きかん 機関** **1【エンジン】**an **engine** ‖ **機関士** 《米》an engineer /èndʒɪníəʳ/, 《英》a train [an engine] driver ‖ **機関車** a locomotive /lòʊkəmóʊṭɪv/.
2【手段】a **means** ▶この町ではバスが唯一の公共交通機関である In this town the bus is the only *means of public transportation*.
‖ **報道機関** news media /míːdiə/.
3【組織】an **institution**, an **organ**; an **agency**(政府の); an **organization**(組織)
‖ **医療機関** a medical institution ‖ **教育機関** an educational institution ‖ **行政機関** an administrative agency／an administration ‖ **金融機関** a financial institution ‖ **研究機関** a research institution ‖ **政府機関** a government institution [organ] ‖ **世界貿易機関** the World Trade Organization《略 WTO》‖ **世界保健機関** the World Health Organization《略 WHO》.

3**きかん 器官** an **organ** ‖ **消化器官** digestive organs ‖ **生殖器官** the genitals /dʒénəṭlz/／reproductive organs.

4**きかん 気管** **the windpipe**; **the trachea** /tréɪkiə ‖ trəkí(ː)ə/ (➤ 医学用語).

5**きかん 帰還** one's **return** (**home**); **repatriation** /riːpèɪtriéɪʃən/ (本国送還, 復員) ▶野口さんは宇宙から無事帰還した Mr. Noguchi *returned* (*home*) safely from outer space.

6**きかん 既刊** ▶ **既刊**(号) *previously published* (*back issue*).

7**きかん 旗艦** a **flagship** ‖ 旗艦店 a flagship store.

きがん 祈願 a **prayer** /preəʳ/ ▶入試の合格を祈願する *pray for* success in the entrance examinations.

ぎかん 技官 a **technical officer** [**official**].

ぎがん 義眼 an **artificial** [a **prosthetic**] **eye** (➤ prosthetic /prɑːsθéṭɪk/ は「人工補てつ物の」の意の医学用語); an **ocular prosthesis** /prɑːsθíːsɪs/.

きかんき 利かん気 ▶きかん気の子供 an *unyielding* child ‖ 由紀はなかなかのきかん気だ Yuki is rather *headstrong*. (➤ headstrong は「頑固な, わがままな」).

きかんさんぎょう 基幹産業 **main industries.**

1**きかんし 気管支** **bronchus** /brɑ́ːŋkəs/
‖ **気管支炎** bronchitis /brɑːŋkáɪṭɪs/ ‖ **気管支ぜんそく** asthma /ǽzmə ‖ ǽs-/.

2**きかんし 季刊誌** a **quarterly.**

きかんじゅう 機関銃 a **machine gun** ▶敵に向かって機関銃を乱射する fire at random at the enemy with *a machine gun* ‖ 徹子は機関銃のようにまくしたてた Tetsuko rattled on (and on) *like a machine gun*.／Tetsuko *aimed a stream of words at* her listeners. (➤ 英語では後者がふつう).

1**きき 危機** a **crisis** /kráɪsɪs/ [複 **crises** /kráɪsiːz/] ▶食糧危機 *a food crisis* ‖ その会社は重大な危機を乗り切った The company has gotten through a serious *crisis*. ‖ わが国は今や財政的危機に直面している Our country is now facing *a financial crisis*. ‖ ギリシャの財政は危機的状況にあった Greece was in *a critical financial situation*.
▶トキは絶滅の危機に瀕(ひん)している The Japanese crested ibis *is on the brink* [*verge*] *of* extinction.／The Japanese crested ibis is in imminent *danger* of extinction. ‖ 我々は危機一髪のところで交通事故を免れた We escaped having an auto accident *by a hair's breadth* [*by the skin of our teeth*]. ‖ ひゃあ, 危機一髪！もう少しででっかいトラックにはねられるところだったよ Wow, *did I have a close call*! I almost got hit by a huge truck. (➤ have a close /kloʊs/ call は「九死に一生を得る」の意のインフォーマルな表現).

2**きき 機器** (an) **apparatus** /æ̀pərǽṭəs ‖ -réɪt-/ (ある目的のための器具一式); an **instrument** (機器, 器具); **equipment** (設備, 備品; 集合的に用いるので equipments としない) ‖ **医療機器** medical equipment ‖ **オーディオ機器** audio equipment ‖ **教育機器** teaching machines ‖ **事務機器** office equipment ‖ **精密機器** precision instruments ‖ **通信機器** communications equipment ‖ **電子機器** electronic equipment.

ききあきる 聞き飽きる ▶母の小言は聞き飽きた I *am sick of hearing* my mother's nagging.

ききいる 聞き入る ▶生徒はみんな担任の先生の話に聞き入った All the students *listened intently* [*attentively*] to their homeroom teacher. ‖ 私たちは彼女のすばらしい歌に聞き入ってしまった We *listened entranced* by her splendid singing. (➤ entranced は「うっとりして」の意).

ききいれる 聞き入れる **grant** +㊂ ▶願いを聞き入れる *grant* [*listen to*] a request ‖ 退学しないよう説得したが, 彼女はどうしても聞き入れなかった She *wouldn't listen* no matter how (hard) I tried to persuade her not to quit school. ‖ 父に医者に診てもらうように言ってみたが, どうしても聞き入れなかった I tried to tell my father to see a doctor, but he *wouldn't* even *consider* it. ‖ 息子は私の助言を聞き入れようとしなかった My son *wouldn't heed* my advice. (➤ heed は「忠告などに従う」).

き

ききうで 利き腕 one's **dominant hand**［**arm**］▶私の利き腕は右［左］だ I *am right-handed*［*left-handed*］. →利き手.

ききおとす 聞き落とす **fail to catch** ▶私は彼の講演のいちばん重要な点を聞き落とした I did*n't catch* the most important point in his lecture.

ききおぼえ 聞き覚え ▶電話の声には聞き覚えがあった The voice on the telephone *sounded familiar* to me. ／I *had heard* that (caller's) voice somewhere *before*.

ききおぼえる 聞き覚える ▶オーストリアに居た間に少しドイツ語を聞き覚えた I *picked up* a little German while I was in Austria.

ききおよぶ 聞き及ぶ ▶すでにお聞き及びのこととは存じますが You may *have* already *heard* about this.

ききかいかい 奇々怪々 ▶奇々怪々な事件 a *truly bizarre*［*freaky*］incident.

ききかえす 聞き返す ▶質問をした男性の声が小さかったので私は聞き返した The man who asked the question spoke in a low voice, so I *asked* him *to repeat* (*what he had said*).

ききかじる 聞きかじる ▶ドイツ語は聞きかじった程度です I only have *a smattering of* German. (➤ smattering は「なまかじり」) ／I only have *a slight*［*small*］*knowledge of* German. ‖ 正夫はどこかで聞きかじってきた知識をもったいぶって話した Masao talked self-importantly about something he had *just heard and half-understood* somewhere or other.

ききぐるしい 聞き苦しい ▶マイクの調子が悪いので, お聞き苦しい点はお許しください The mike isn't working properly, so please excuse us if you *can't hear well*. ‖ かぜをひいて喉が痛いのです. どうかお聞き苦しい点をお許しください I caught a cold and have a sore throat. So please *excuse my voice*.

ききこみ 聞き込み ▶警察は現場周辺で聞き込みを行っている Police are trying to gather information by *questioning* people around the scene of the crime. ‖聞き込み捜査 legwork (足を使っての取材や調査).

ききこむ 聞き込む ▶聞き込むほどによさがわかる音楽がある You can appreciate some music better［Some music gets better］*the more you listen to it*.

ききざけ 利き酒・聞き酒 **sake** /sáːki/ **tasting** ▶利き酒をする *taste sake*.

ききしにまさる 聞きしに勝る ▶アブダビで泊まったホテルは聞きしに勝る豪華さだった The hotel I stayed at in Abu Dhabi was *more* luxurious *than I had expected*［*imagined*］*from what I had heard* about it.

ききじょうず 聞き上手 a **good listener**.

ききずて 聞き捨て ▶聞き捨てならないせりふ an *inexcusable* remark ／a remark that you *can't overlook*［*let pass*］‖ きみのその無礼なことばは聞き捨てならないね That's the kind of rude remark I *can't let pass*. (➤ let … pass は「見逃す, 聞き逃す」).

ききそこなう 聞き損なう ▶そこの部分は聞き損なった I *failed to hear*［*catch*］that part. ‖ きのうFMで放送されたレディー・ガガ特集を聞き損なった I *missed* an FM special on Lady Gaga yesterday.

ききだす 聞き出す ▶人から情報を聞き出す *draw*［*ferret*］*out* information from a person ／*get* information out of a person ‖ 私は彼女から少しずつ新型車の情報を聞き出した I gradually *pumped* the information *out of* her about the new-model car. (➤ pump は「(それとなく)尋ねる」の意のインフォーマルな語).

ききちがい 聞き違い ▶それはぼくの聞き違いだった I *heard* it *wrong*. ／I *misheard* it.

ききちがえる 聞き違える **mishear** (+目) ▶彼女は私の言ったことを聞き違えたに違いない She must have *misheard* me［*heard* me *wrong*］.

ききつける 聞きつける **hear** +目 (聞く) ▶私が大金を手に入れたことを聞きつけて, 最初に親戚連中がやって来た My relatives were the first to arrive on the scene when they *heard*［*got the news*］that I had come into a large sum of money. ‖ 彼女の悲鳴を聞きつけて生徒が全員駆けつけた When they *heard* her scream, all the other students ran to her.

ききづらい 聞きづらい ▶その講演は講演者の声が小さくて聞きづらかった The lecturer's voice was low and I found it *hard to hear* what he was saying. ‖ セックスのことは親には聞きづらい Sex is something I *hesitate to ask* my parents about.

1**ききて 聞き手** a **listener** ; an **audience** (聴衆) ▶聞き手には長く感じられた1時間だった To the *audience*, it was a long hour.
▶聞き手は後藤アナウンサーです The *interviewer* is Goto. (➤「アナウンサー」は訳さなくてもよい).

2**ききて 利き手** one's **dominant** /dάːmɪnənt/ **hand**. →利き腕.

ききとり 聞き取り ▶きょう英語の聞き取りテストがあった Today we had *a listening comprehension test* in English.

ききとる 聞き取る **hear** +目 (聞こえる) ; **catch** +目 (音声をとらえる) ; **follow** +目 (相手のことばなどについていく) ▶私は英語がほとんど聞き取れません I *can hardly understand* spoken English. ‖ 英語の映画のせりふは聞き取りにくい It is hard to *hear*［*catch*］the dialogue in English-language films. ‖ 彼は早口だから聞き取るのが大変だ He speaks fast, so I have difficulty *follow*ing him.

ききなおす 聞き直す **ask again** (もう一度尋ねる) ; **listen again** (もう一度聞く) ▶その女性の名前を聞き直す *ask* the woman her name *again*［*twice*］‖ 刑事は誘拐犯からの電話の録音を何度も聞き直した The detective *listened to* the recording of the telephone call(s) from the kidnapper *again and again*［*over and over*］.

ききながす 聞き流す ▶母親の小言を聞き流す *pay no attention to* the complaints of one's mother ‖ ママはしょっちゅうがみがみ言うけど, ぼくは聞き流してるんだ My mother is always nagging (at) me, but I *let it go in one ear and out the other*. (➤「片方の耳から入れて他方の耳から出す」の意).

ききにくい 聞きにくい →聞きづらい.

ききのがす 聞き逃す **miss** +目 ▶注意して聞きなさい. でないと要点を聞き逃しますよ Listen carefully. Otherwise you'll *miss* the point.

ききほれる 聞き惚れる ▶私たちはそのコーラスの美しいハーモニーに聞きほれた We *were charmed*［*were entranced*］by the beautiful harmony of the chorus.

ききみみ 聞き耳 ▶自分の名前が挙がったので, 私は聞き耳を立てた *My ears pricked* (*up*) when I heard my name mentioned. ‖ 里奈は社内に聞こえた地獄耳で, いつも聞き耳を立てている Rina is famous in our office for her sharp ears—she's always *got her ears pricked* (for rumors).

ききめ 効き目 (an) **effect** ▶この薬は効き目が速い This

medicine *works* [*takes effect*] *quickly*. ‖ この虫除けスプレーは効き目が長い This bug spray *lasts* (*for*) *a long time*. (➤ 否定文では not last long と言えるが, 肯定文では last (for) a long time がふつう) ‖ アスピリンは私には効き目がいまいちだ Aspirin does*n't work very well* for me. ‖ その治療は私にはほとんど効き目が無かった The treatment *did* me little *good*. ‖ あの子は叱っても効き目がない (＝無駄だ) *It is no use* telling him [her] off.

ききもの 聞き物 ▶次が今夜のコンサート1番の聞き物だ Next comes *the highlight* of tonight's concert.

ききもらす 聞き漏らす ▶大事なことを聞き漏らしたくない I don't want to *miss out on* anything important. (➤ miss out on は「もらい損なう, 見逃す, 聞き逃す」などの意) ‖ 彼の名を聞き漏らした I *failed to hear* [*catch*] his name.

ききやく 聞き役 ▶今回は専ら聞き役に回ろうと思う I think I'll assume *the role of* (*a*) *listener* [I'll just listen] this time.

ききゃく 棄却 (a) **dismissal** (訴訟の) ; (a) **rejection** (拒否) **一動 棄却する dismiss** +㊐, **reject** +㊐ ▶裁判所は彼らの損害賠償訴訟を棄却した The court *dismissed* their suit for damages.

1**ききゅう 気球** a **balloon** ▶気球を上げる fly *a balloon* ‖**観測気球** an observation balloon, a trial balloon ‖**熱気球** a hot-air balloon.

2**ききゅう 希求** ▶国際平和を希求する *wish* [*hope* ／ *long*] *for* world peace.

1**ききょう 桔梗** 《植物》 a **balloon flower.**

2**ききょう 帰郷** a **homecoming** ▶兄が3年ぶりに東京から帰郷します My brother is *coming home* from Tokyo for the first time in three years.

3**ききょう 帰京する return to Tokyo.**

1**きぎょう 企業** an **enterprise** /énṭəʳpràɪz/, (a) **business**, a **company**, a **corporation** ⇀会社 ▶多国籍企業 a multinational *corporation*.

‖**企業家** an entrepreneur /à:ntrəprənə́:ʳ ‖ ɔ̀n-/ ‖**企業診断士** a business consultant ‖**企業責任** corporate responsibility ‖**企業戦士** a corporate warrior ‖**企業年金** a company [corporate] pension ‖**企業文化** (a) corporate culture ‖**企業連合** a cartel corporation ‖**公共企業体** a public corporation ‖**民間企業** a private business [company ／ corporation].

☛ **大企業, 中小企業** (⇀見出語)

2**きぎょう 起業する start a business**

‖**起業家** an entrepreneur /à:ntrəprənə́:ʳ ‖ ɔ̀n-/.

ぎきょう(しん) 義侠(心) heroism.

ぎきょうだい 義兄弟 a **blood brother** (忠誠を誓い合った) ; a **brother-in-law** (義理の兄弟).

ぎきょく 戯曲 a **drama**, a **play** (➤ 後者はややインフォーマル) ▶戯曲を書く write *a drama* [*play*] ‖ 小説を戯曲化する *dramatize* a novel.

ききわけ 聞き分け ▶うちの子は聞き分けがなくて困ります My son *won't listen to reason* and always gives me trouble. (➤ listen to reason で「道理がわかる, 聞き分ける」の意) ‖ **聞き分けのないことを言わないで** *Don't be unreasonable*.

ききわける 聞き分ける ▶日本人はLとRを聞き分ける (＝区別する) のが苦手だ It is hard for Japanese to *distinguish* L from R.

ききわすれる 聞き忘れる forget to ask ▶しまった！ 彼女の電話番号を聞き忘れた Darn it ! I *forgot to ask* (her) her telephone number.

1**ききん 飢饉 famine** /fǽmɪn/ ▶天明の大飢きんでは数十万人が餓死したと言われる It is said that several hundred thousand people died in the *great famine* of the Tenmei era.

2**ききん 基金** a **fund** /fʌnd/ ▶年金基金 a pension *fund* ‖ **難民救済基金を募っています** We are raising *a refugee relief fund*.

3**ききん 寄金** a **donation** ▶慈善の寄金を集める collect charitable *donations*.

ききんぞく 貴金属 precious metals

‖**貴金属商** a dealer in precious metals ‖**貴金属店** a jewelry shop.

1**きく 菊** a **chrysanthemum** /krɪsǽnθɪməm/, 《インフォーマル》 a **mum** /mʌm/ (➤ 通例栽培されたものをいう ; 英米では主に葬儀用) ▶菊は10月がいちばん見頃だ *Chrysanthemums* are at their best in October. ‖**菊人形** figures formed from live chrysanthemums.

2**きく 聞く・聴く**

訳語メニュー
耳にする ⇀hear 1
注意して聞く ⇀listen to 2
聞いて知る ⇀hear, hear of, learn 3
聞き入れる ⇀listen to, obey 4
尋ねる ⇀ask 5

1【聞こえる, 耳にする】hear (+㊐) ▶ゆうべ9時頃女性の叫び声を聞いた I *heard* a woman's scream around nine o'clock last night. ‖ 私は彼が大声を上げるのを聞いたことがない I have never *heard* him shout. (➤ hear ～ do で「～が…するのを聞く」) ‖ ラジオで首相が演説するのを聞いた I *heard* the prime minister speak on the radio. ‖ ぼくたちは人に聞かれないように低い声で話した We spoke in a low voice so that we wouldn't *be overheard*.

ことわざ **聞いて極楽, 見て地獄** The place was like a paradise when I heard about it, but a hell when I (actually) saw it. (➤ 日本語からの直訳) ／Things always look better from a distance. (➤「物事は常に遠くから見たほうがよく見える」の意) ‖

ことわざ **聞くと見るとは大違い** There's a world of difference between hearing and seeing. ／ Hearing isn't anything like seeing. ‖ ことわざ **聞くは一時の恥, 聞かぬは一生の恥** To ask is a moment's embarrassment, but not to ask is a lifelong shame.

2【注意して聞く】listen to, hear (+㊐) ▶音楽を聴きながら勉強する study while *listening to* music ‖ 注意して聞きなさい *Listen* carefully. ‖ カウンセラーにとって最も大切なことは相談者の言うことをよく聞いてやることです The most important thing for a counselor is to *listen to* his clients attentively. ‖ ベートーベンの第九 (交響曲) は何回も聴きました I *have heard* Beethoven's Ninth Symphony many times. (➤ コンサートの場合は hear を用いる) ‖ 最後まで聞けよ *Hear me out !*

3【聞いて知る】hear +㊐, **hear of, learn** +㊐ ▶そのニュースはラジオで聞きました I *heard* the news on the radio. ‖ ある人から聞いたんだけど, 彼女は離婚したそうよ I *heard* (that) she got a divorce. ／ *Someone told me* that she got divorced. ‖ 真相は加藤さんから聞きました I *learned* the truth from Mr. Kato. ‖ 彼女は歌手の自殺の悲報を聞いてショックを受けた She was shocked *at* the sad news of the singer's suicide.

▶その後彼女のうわさは何も聞きません I *haven't heard*

of her since. (➤ hear of で「…のうわさを聞く」) ‖ 彼が1番だって？ 1番が聞いてあきれるね．こないだのテスト，あいつカンニングしたんだぜ He got the best grade? *I don't believe it!* You know, he cheated on the last exam.

き

4【聞き入れる，従う】listen to ; obey(従う) ▶彼女は私の忠告を聞かなかった She didn't *listen to* my advice. ‖ きみは先生方のおっしゃることを聞くべきだ You have to *listen to* your teachers. ‖ 彼はいつも父親の言うことを聞く He always *obeys* his father. ‖ 医師の言うことを聞いていたら，彼はもっと長生きできたのに If only he had *listened to* his doctor [If only he had *taken* his doctor's *advice*], he would have lived longer. ‖ 1つ頼みを聞いてよ Can you do me a favor? ‖ パパは私の言うことなら何でも聞いてくれるわ My dad *does anything* I say. ‖ 兄はカナダに留学すると言って聞かない My brother *is insistent on* going to Canada to study. ‖ 彼女は私のアドバイスに聞く耳を持たなかった She *turned a deaf ear* to my advice.

5【尋ねる】ask(+目) ▶犬を連れた女性に駅までの道を聞く *ask* a woman walking a dog *the way* [*for directions*] to the train station ‖ 母は私にどこが痛いのかと聞いた My mother *asked* me where I (was) hurt. ‖ わからなかったら遠慮せずに聞いてね If there is anything you don't understand, feel free to *ask*. ‖ 対話「1つ聞いていい？」「いいよ」"Can I *ask a question*?" "Sure."

[3]**きく 効く・利く** **1【効き目がある】be effective ; work** (うまく作用する) ▶この漢方薬は貧血症によく効く This herbal medicine *is* very *effective* against [*is* very *good for*] anemia. ‖ アスピリンが効いて頭痛が治った The aspirin *worked* [*took effect*] and my headache went away. ‖ 宣伝が効いて新製品がよく売れた The advertising *was effective* and the new product sold well. ‖ チャンピオンのアッパーカットが効いて挑戦者は倒れた The champion's uppercut *did the trick* and his opponent collapsed. (➤ do the trick は「効果を発揮する」) ‖ ウイスキーが利いてきた I'm *beginning to feel* the whisky. ‖ このすしはわさびが効いていない *There is not enough* wasabi on this sushi.

2【働く】▶彼女は機転が利く She is *quick-witted*. ‖ 犬は鼻がよく利く Dogs *have a keen sense of smell*. ‖ 神経痛で左手が利かない I *can't use* my left hand because of neuralgia. ‖ 年を取ったので体の自由が利かない I've gotten old and *can't get around easily*. (➤ get around は「(あちこち)動き回る」) ‖ この車はブレーキが利き過ぎる The brakes on this car *are too tight*. ‖ この部屋は冷房が効き過ぎている The air conditioning in this room is *too strong*. ‖ のりの効いたワイシャツ a *starched* shirt.

3【…ができる】▶この背広は寸法直しが利く This suit *can* (*easily*) *be altered*. ‖ きょうは霧が濃くて見通しが利かない Today the *visibility* is quite poor due to the thick fog. (➤ visibility は「視界」) ‖ コンピュータで作った原稿はあとでいくらでも直しが利く You can *go back and correct* a manuscript *as much as you like* if it has been typed on a computer. ‖ 彼は病み上がりだから無理は利かないよ He *mustn't overwork himself* because he has just recovered from a sickness.

[1]**きぐ 器具** an **instrument**, (an) **apparatus** /æ̀pərǽtəs/ (ともに特殊な仕事をするための精密器具をいう) ; a **utensil** /juténsəl/, an **appliance** (ともに家庭・家事用器具をいい，後者は特に電気製品に用いる) ▶手術用器具 surgical *instruments* [*supplies*].

‖**運動器具** exercise machines [equipment] ‖ **実験器具** an experimental instrument [apparatus] ‖ **暖房器具** a heating apparatus ‖ **調理器具** cooking utensils ‖ **電気器具** electrical appliances. →**農機具**.

[2]**きぐ 危惧** **apprehension** /æ̀prɪhénʃən/ ▶多くの人々が地球の将来に危惧の念を抱いている[を危惧している] Most people feel *apprehension* [*apprehensive*] about the future of the earth.

きぐう 奇遇 ▶ここできみに会うとは奇遇だね *What a coincidence*! I never expected to meet you here. (➤ coincidence /koʊɪ́nsɪdəns/ は「偶然の一致」の出来事) ／Fancy meeting you here! (➤ Fancy doing は「…するとは，…するなんて」の意 ; 主に《英》) ／*What a surprise to see* you here!

ぎくしゃく ▶ぎくしゃくした動作 *jerky* [*uneven*] movements ‖ 日米関係はこのところどうもぎくしゃくしている The relationship between Japan and the United States *is going through a rough patch* these days. ／Relations between Japan and the United States *have been awkward and strained* recently.

きくず 木くず **wood shavings.**

きくばり 気配り **consideration** (相手の気持ちを害さないようにしようとする心配り) ; **thoughtfulness** (相手に幸福感をもたらそうとする心配り) ; **attention** (気遣い) ▶彼女は気配りが行き届いている She's a *thoughtful* person. ‖ 彼は他人に対する気配りに欠ける He lacks *consideration* for others. ‖ 彼女のさりげない気配りがいつも本当にうれしい The way she is so *attentive* without being obtrusive is always really nice. (➤ obtrusive は「差し出がましい」)

きぐらい 気位 **pride** (自尊心) ▶彼は気位が高い He is *proud* [*conceited*]. ／He *has a high opinion of himself*. ‖ 愛さんは気位が高くてぼくたちとは付き合ってくれない Ai is too *proud* to mix with us.

ぎくり ▶その人は死んだ兄にそっくりだったのでぎくりとした His close resemblance to my late brother *shocked* [*stunned*] me.

きぐろう 気苦労 (a) **care** (相手への気遣いなど，よい意味での) ; (a) **worry** (無用な心配) ▶彼女は幸せで気苦労は何もなかった She was happy and didn't have *a care* in the world. ‖ 親は子供のことで気苦労が絶えない Parents are never free from *worry* about their children.

きけい 奇形 **deformity** /dɪfɔ́ːʳməṭi/ ▶ベトナム戦争終了後多くの奇形児が生まれた Many *deformed children* were born after the Vietnam War.

‖**奇形魚[植物]** a freak fish [plant].

ぎけい 義兄 a [an **older**] **brother-in-law** [複 **brothers-in-law**].

きげき 喜劇 (a) **comedy** ▶私は喜劇よりも悲劇のほうが好きだ I prefer tragedy to *comedy*.

‖**喜劇映画** a comic film [picture] ‖ **喜劇役者** a comedian ／a comic actor [actress].

[1]**きけつ 帰結** a **consequence** (結果) ; a **conclusion** (結論) ▶論理的な帰結 a logical *conclusion*.

[2]**きけつ 既決** ‖**既決囚** a convict /kɑ́ːnvɪkt/.

ぎけつ 議決 **decision** 一動 **議決する decide** ▶国会は国の議決機関である The Diet is the organ through which the nation *makes decisions*.

[1]**きけん 危険** **danger** /déɪndʒəʳ/ ; a **risk** (覚悟の上で冒す危険) 一形 **危険な dangerous, risky** (➤ 前者が危険そのものなのに対して，後者は「危険

があリそうな」の意）▶**危険な**投資 a *risky* investment ‖**危険な**賭け a *risky* bet ‖ 消防士の仕事は**危険**がいっぱいだ A firefighter's job is full of *danger*.（➤「危険な仕事」は a dangerous job）‖ その国はテロの**危険**に満ちている There is a *risk* of terrorism throughout the country. ／The *risk* of terrorism pervades the entire country. ‖ 長雨のため，崖崩れの**危険**があります There's *a danger* of landslides due to the long rain. ‖ ハンググライディングにはまだ**危険**が伴う Hang gliding still involves some *danger* [*risk*]. ‖ 平野さんは**身の危険を顧みず**（＝危険を冒して）強盗と戦った Hirano fought with the robber *at the risk of his life*. ／Hirano *risked his life* fighting with the robber. ‖ そんな**危険な**場所に近づいてはいけない Keep away from *dangerous* areas like that. ‖ この食物は発がん性の添加物が入っているので**危険だ** It *is dangerous* to eat this food because it contains carcinogenic additives. ‖ 彼は**危険人物**として警察からマークされている He has been singled out by the police as *a dangerous man*. ‖《掲示》**危険**！ Danger！／Caution！ ‖《掲示》**危険物持ち込み禁止** No Dangerous Objects ／Dangerous Objects Prohibited.

‖**危険信号** a danger signal.

²**きけん 棄権** **abstention** ━ 動 **棄権する** **abstain** 《from》（投票を）▶**投票を棄権する**のは政治に無関心ということだ *Abstention from voting* shows indifference to politics. ‖《マラソンで》中山選手は30キロ地点で**棄権した** The runner Nakayama *dropped out of the race* at the 30-kilometer mark.

¹**きげん 機嫌** a **mood** ▶きのう会ったときは彼女は**機嫌が良かった**［**悪かった**］She *was in a good* [*bad*] *mood* when I saw her yesterday. ‖ 政夫のやつ，けさはどうしたんだい？ えらく**機嫌が悪い**じゃないか What's wrong with Masao this morning？ He's really *grumpy*. ‖ **対話**「きょうの部長の**機嫌**はどうだい？」「苦虫をかみ潰したような顔をしてるよ」"*How's* our boss today？" "He seems to be in a bad mood."

▶店長の**機嫌を損なったら**大変なことになるぜ If you *rub* the manager *the wrong way*, you'll be in big trouble.（➤ rub ... the wrong way は「…を怒らせる」の意で，猫の毛を毛並みと逆方向になでると猫が怒ることに由来する表現）‖ あいつはいつも先生の**機嫌を取って**ばかりいる He's always *buttering up* his teacher.（➤ butter up は「（上司・先生など権限を持つ立場の人）におべっかを言う」の意のインフォーマルな言い方）‖ 悦子の**機嫌を取るのは難しい** Etsuko is *hard to please*. ‖ 妻は私とけんかしてから2，3日口を利いてくれなかったが，やっと**機嫌を直してくれた** After our fight, my wife would not speak to me for a few days, but she finally *came around*.（➤ この come around は「機嫌が直る」の意）.

☛ **ご機嫌，上機嫌，不機嫌**（→見出語）

²**きげん 期限** a **time limit**（時限）；a **deadline**（締め切り）；a **term**（特定の期間）▶**無期限の**ストライキ a *no-time-limit* [an *indefinite*] strike ‖ 支払い**期限を延ばす** extend the *term* of payment ‖ **期限を決める** set *a deadline* ‖ 彼は応募［申し込み］**期限に間に合わせられなかった** He missed the application *deadline*. ‖ この論文の提出**期限**は今月末だ The *deadline* for turning in this paper is the end of the month. ‖《生徒が先生に》**提出期限を延ばしてもらえますか** Do you think I could *get an extension*？（● extension 自体が「（提出期限などの）延長」の意だから「提出期限」は訳出不要）‖（図書館の）この本の返却はあすが**期限だ** This book *is due* tomorrow. ‖ このバスの定期券は5月10日で**期限が切れる** This bus pass *expires* on May 10. ‖ 家賃の**支払い期限が過ぎている** The rent is *overdue*.

> **逆引き熟語 ○○期限**
> **支払い期限** the term of payment, the due date ／**使用期限** an expiration date (for use) ／**賞味期限** "Best by" date, Best by [before]（日付）／**無期限** an indefinite period ／**申し込み期限** an application deadline ／**有効期限** an expiration date

³**きげん 起源** an **origin** ▶仏教の**起源** the *origin*(s) of Buddhism ‖ 多くの英単語はフランス語**起源だ** Many English words *originated* from French.（➤ originate は「由来する」）.

⁴**きげん 紀元**

> **語法**（1）西暦の年号を表す場合，「紀元…年」は AD で，「紀元前…年」は BC で表す.（2）AD は数字の前に置くのが正式だが，あとに置くこともある. BC は常に数字のあとに置く.

▶**紀元**1900年に in *AD* 1900（➤ AD は Anno Domini /ænoʊ dɑ́ːmənìː, -naɪ/（ラテン語で「主キリスト生誕の年に」の意）の略）‖ **紀元前**89年 89 *BC* [*BCE*]（➤ BC は Before Christ の略；BCE は before the common era の意で，キリスト教徒でない人に配慮した言い方）.

きご 季語 ***kigo***；a word [an expression] depicting a season（➤ 説明的な訳）▶俳句には通常**季語**が1つ入る Haiku usually contain one *seasonal word* [*expression*].（➤ 2語以上からなる季語は expression とする）.

¹**きこう 気候** (a) **climate**（ある地域のかなり長期にわたる気象）；**weather**（一時的な気象状況）▶アイスランドは冬の**気候**が厳しい Iceland has a harsh winter *climate*. ‖ ハワイは1年を通じてよい**気候だ** The *climate* of Hawaii is fine [mild] all (the) year round. ／Hawaii has a fine [mild] *climate* throughout the year. ‖ 将来は**暖かい気候の地**に住みたい I'd like to live in a warm *climate* in the future. ‖ 地球規模の**気候変動**によって多くの自然災害が起きている Global *climate change* has been causing a lot of natural disasters.（● 訳例の has been causing は気候変動が過去に始まり現在も続いている点を強調したものだが，現在進行中という点を強調して is causing とすることも，現在までの経過に焦点を当てて has caused とすることも可能）.

✉ **このところ気候が変わりやすいので体には十分気をつけてください** Take care of yourself as the *weather* is very changeable at this time of (the) year. ✉ **四季の区別がはっきりしているので，ぼくは日本の気候が気に入っています** I like the Japanese *climate* because the four seasons are so distinct.

> **逆引き熟語 ○○気候**
> **亜寒帯気候** a subarctic climate ／**亜熱帯気候** a subtropical climate ／**温帯湿潤気候** a humid temperate climate ／**サバンナ気候** a savanna(h) climate ／**ステップ気候** a steppe climate ／**大陸性気候** a continental climate ／**地中海性気候** a Mediterranean climate ／**ツンドラ気候** a tundra climate ／**内陸気候** an in-

land climate／熱帯雨林気候 a tropical rainforest climate

[2]きこう 機構 an **organization**(組織)；**structure**（構造）▶行政機構 an administrative *agency* [*organization*] ‖ 国連の機構を簡単に説明してください Give me a brief description of the *organization* of the United Nations.

[3]きこう 紀行 an **account of a trip** [**a journey**]（旅行記）；a **travelog(ue)**（紀行文・映画）▶彼の随筆『南米紀行』は好評だった His essay "*A Trip to South America*" was well received.

[4]きこう 寄稿 (a) **contribution** 一動 寄稿する **contribute** /kəntríbju:t/《to》▶彼女は毎月その雑誌に寄稿している She *contributes to* [*writes for*] that magazine every month.
‖寄稿者［家］a contributor /kəntríbjətəʳ/.

[5]きこう 寄港 ▶その船は長崎に行く途中で神戸に寄港する The ship *calls at* Kobe on its way to Nagasaki.

[6]きこう 起工 ▶きのう，新しい橋の起工式が行われた The *ground-breaking ceremony* of the new bridge was conducted yesterday.

[7]きこう 奇行 (an) **eccentricity** ▶グレン・グールドは奇行で有名だった Glenn Gould was famous for his *eccentricities*.

[8]きこう 気功 **qigong** /tʃì:gáŋ/, ***kiko*** ▶気功を行う practice *qigong*.

きごう 記号 a **sign**；a **mark**（文字・数字以外の）；a **symbol**（符号）；《音楽》a **clef**(音部記号）▶天文学の記号 astronomical *signs* ‖ 元素記号 the *symbol* of an element ‖ 化学記号 a chemical *symbol* ‖ これは何の記号ですか What does this *mark* stand for？‖ 私は発音記号の読み方がわからない I don't know how to read *phonetic symbols*. ‖ ト［へ］音記号 a G [an F] *clef*.

ぎこう 技巧 (a) **technique** /tekní:k/ ▶この小説は技巧が勝ち過ぎている This novel is *too technically elaborate*. ‖ リストのピアノ曲は高度に技巧的だ Liszt's piano compositions are highly *technical*.

きこうし 貴公子 a **young nobleman**.

ぎこうし 技工士 a **technician** ▶歯科技工士 a dental *technician*.

きこえ 聞こえ ▶「年配市民」と言えば聞こえはいいが，要するに老人のことだ 'Senior citizens' may *sound fine*, but the fact is, it means "old people." ‖ 伊藤君は小学校時代から秀才の聞こえが高かった Ito *has had a reputation for* being [*has been thought of as*] a genius since elementary school.

きこえよがし 聞こえよがし ▶彼女は聞こえよがしに私に皮肉を言った She made sarcastic remarks *in my hearing* [*earshot*]. (➤「私が聞いている所で」の意).

きこえる 聞こえる

1【耳に入る】**hear**(＋㊀) ▶（私の言うことが）聞こえてるの？*Do you hear* (me)？‖ 対話（電話で）「聞こえる？」「うん，よく聞こえるよ」"*Can you hear* me？" "Yeah, I *can hear* you quite clearly." (➤ 無線どうしでは Do [Can] you read me？という．また，電話で反応のない相手に「聞いているの？」と聞くときは Are you there？) ‖ 耳を傾けたが何も聞こえなかった I listened, but *heard* nothing. ‖ 遠くから波の音が聞こえてきた From afar, I *could hear* the sound of waves.／The sound of the waves *came to me* from a distance. ‖ 足音が聞こえなくなった I *could no longer hear* the footsteps. ‖ あの人たちは私に聞こえない所で何かひそひそ話している They are whispering something *where I can't hear them*. ‖ 祖父はほとんど耳が聞こえない My grandfather *is* almost *deaf* [*has* almost *no hearing* (*left*)].

> 【文型】
> A が…するのが聞こえる
> **hear** A do
> A が…しているのが聞こえる
> **hear** A doing

▶誰かが私の名を呼ぶのが聞こえた I *heard* someone call my name. ‖ きのうの朝庭先でウグイスの声が聞こえた Yesterday morning, I *heard* a bush warbler sing*ing* in my garden. ‖ 台所で妹が叫び声を上げているのが聞こえた I *heard* my sister scream*ing* in the kitchen. (➤ I heard my sister scream in the kitchen. は「台所から妹の叫び声がした」で，今は叫び声がしなくなっている．また，「台所で叫び声がした」は I heard my sister's scream from the kitchen.).

2【響く】**sound**；**carry**(届く)

> 【文型】
> A に聞こえる
> **sound** A
> ➤ A は形容詞
> A の［～である］ように聞こえる
> **sound like** A [**like** S + V]
> ➤ A は名詞

▶こんなことを言うと変に［皮肉に］聞こえますか Do you think it *sounds strange* [*sarcastic*] to say that？‖ 単純に聞こえるが実際は込み入っている That *sounds simple*, but in practice it's complicated. ‖ これはまぬけな質問のように聞こえるかもしれない This might *sound like* a dumb question. ‖ 冗談に聞こえるかもしれないが，私は本気だ It may *sound like* I'm joking, but I'm serious. ‖ テノール歌手の力強い声はホールの隅々まで聞こえた The tenor's powerful voice *carried* to every corner of the hall.

きこく 帰国する **return home, come** [**go**] **home, return** [**come back**／**go back**] **to one's country**
語法 (1)return が日本語に近く堅い語．(2)come と go の使い分けについては「行く」の項を参照．
▶父はきのうマレーシアから帰国した My father *returned* [*came*] *home* from Malaysia yesterday. ‖ ジョーンズ夫妻は先週（自分の国へ）帰国した Mr. and Mrs. Jones *returned home* [*went back to their country*] last week. ‖ あす日本に帰国します I'm *going back* to Japan tomorrow. (➤ 外国に居るときにその国の人とする会話；外国から日本へ電話する場合なら I'm coming ... とする) ‖ 首相はロシアへの公式訪問を終え，きょう帰国の途に就いた The Prime Minister *left for home* after his official visit to Russia today. ‖帰国子女 a child [a student] who has recently returned to Japan after living overseas《参考》(1) ここでは動詞は「最近帰国した」の意で現在完了形にしてあるが，文脈によって未来形などに変える必要がある．(2) 帰国子女を returnee child [student]，文脈から明らかであれば単に returnee ということもあるが，returnee /rɪtə̀:ʳní:/ には「復員兵，抑留からの帰還者」といったイメージがあるので避けたほうがよい．

きごこち 着心地 ▶和服は着心地がいい I *feel comfortable* wearing a kimono. ‖ タキシードは初めてなのでどうも着心地が悪い I have never worn a tuxedo before, so I *feel uncomfortable* (*in it*).

きごころ 気心 ▶我々は互いに気心が知れた者どうしだ Both of us *know what the other* [*each other*] *is thinking and feeling.*

ぎこちない **awkward** /ɔ́:kwərd/, **clumsy**(➤ 後者には軽蔑的な響きがあることが多い) ▶初めて親になったんだから赤ん坊の抱き方がぎこちないのも無理はないよ Since you are a new parent, it's quite natural that you should *be awkward* (in) holding a baby. ‖ 新横綱は動きがぎこちなかった The new yokozuna moved *awkwardly*.

きこつ 気骨 **grit, backbone**(➤ 後者は否定文で用いることが多い) ▶あの人は気骨がある He's got a lot of *grit*. ‖ 気骨の無い男は嫌いだ I don't like guys who *have no backbone* [who *are spineless*].

きこなし 着こなし ▶流行の服を着こなすにもセンスがいる You need fashion sense even in *wearing* trendy clothes *well*. ‖ 園子は着こなしが抜群にうまい Sonoko *dresses* very *well*. ／Sonoko is *a* very *good dresser*.

きこむ 着込む ▶きょうは寒いので私は着込んでいる Since it is cold today, I *am wearing layers of clothes* [*am warmly clothed*]. ／I *have bundled up* against the cold today. (➤ bundle up は「厚着をして温かくする」).

きこり 樵 a **woodcutter** ; a **lumberjack**(特にアメリカ・カナダの).

きこん 既婚の **married** ▶既婚の女性 a *married* woman ‖ 彼女は既婚か未婚かはっきりしない It's hard to tell whether she is *married or not*. ‖**既婚者** a married person ; the married (➤ 総称).

きざ 気障な **affected** (気取った) ; **snobbish** (俗物の) ▶きざな態度 an *affected* manner ‖ 母国語で言えるのにわざわざフランス語を使うのはきざだ You are being *snobbish* if you deliberately use French when you can express the same thing in your own language. ‖ 彼のしゃべり方はきざっぽい The way he talks is so *pretentious*. (➤ pretentious は「気取った, もったいぶった」) ／He sounds *affected*. ‖ 対話 「銀二のこと, どう思う?」「大嫌いよ, あんなキザ男!」 "What do you think of Ginji?" "Ugh! I can't stand that sort of *snob!*" (➤ snob は「通人気取り」の意).

1**きさい 記載する** **state** +目 (表明する) ; **mention** +目 (言及する) ; **enter** +目 (記入する) ▶《本などで》価格はケースに記載してあります The price *is stated* on the case. ‖ 記載漏れのないようにもう一度確認してください Please check again that there are no *omissions*.

2**きさい 起債する** **issue bonds.**

3**きさい 鬼才** a **genius**, a **wizard** ▶文学の鬼才 a literary *genius*.

きざい 機材 **equipment**(道具) ; **materials**(材料) ▶撮影機材 photography [filming] *equipment* ‖ 録音機材 recording *equipment* ‖ トラックに建設機材を積む load the truck with building *materials*.

きさき 后 a **queen**(王妃) ; an **empress** (皇后).

ぎざぎざ ▶縁にぎざぎざのある葉 a *serrated* leaf(➤「のこぎりの歯状をした」の意) ‖ 布を切るときは端がぎざぎざにならないように気をつけること Cut the cloth carefully so that the edges aren't *jagged*. (➤「ジグザグした」の意) ‖ 50円玉は縁にぎざぎざがある The 50-yen coin has a *milled* edge.

1**きさく 気さくな** **friendly**(友好的な) ; **frank**(率直な) ▶今度近所に来た人は気さくなのでよかった I am glad our new neighbor is [neighbors are] *easy to get along with*. (➤「付き合いやすい」の意) ‖ 日本人は知らない人に気さくに声をかけられない人が多い Many Japanese find it difficult to *be relaxed and open* when speaking to strangers.

2**きさく 奇策** a **clever plan that is used to outwit people** ; an **ingenious** /ɪndʒí:niəs/ **scheme.**

ぎさく 偽作 a **fake**, a **forgery.**

きざし 兆し a **sign** ; (an) **omen** (前兆となる現象) ▶景気が回復する兆しはまだ見えない There are no *signs* yet that business will recover. ‖ これは何か悪いことが起きる兆しではないだろうか This could be *an omen* that something bad will happen.

きさま 貴様 **you** ⇀きみ ▶貴様, そこをどけ! Get out of my way, *you son of a bitch*! (➤ 下品な言い方).

きざみ 刻み a **notch**(刻み目) ▶この板には5センチごとに刻みが入れてある There is *a notch* every 5 cm on this board. ‖ 3分刻みで列車が入って来る A train pulls in *every 3 minutes*.

きざむ 刻む **1【野菜などを】** **chop** +目, **mince** +目 (➤ 後者のほうが刻み方が細かい) ▶タマネギを刻む *chop up* an onion.

2【彫る】 **carve** +目 ; **engrave** +目 (金属・ガラスなど硬いものの表面を) ; **cut** +目 (細かく刻む) ▶彼はその木に自分のイニシャルを刻んだ He *carved* [*cut*] his initials on the tree. ‖ その事件は少年の記憶に刻まれた The incident *was engraved* in the boy's memory. (➤ engrave をこの場合のように比喩的に用いるのは《文》に多い) ‖ 老人の額には深いしわが刻まれていた The elderly man's forehead *was etched* [*scored*] *with deep wrinkles*. ‖ 大谷選手は野球の歴史にいくつも大記録を刻んだ Ohtani *notched* several great records in baseball history.

3【細かく分割する】 ▶時計の針が刻々と時を刻んでゆく Clocks mark the inexorable march of time. (➤「時計は止めようのない時の流れを表示する」の意).

1**きし 岸** a **bank**(川岸) ; a **shore** (水に接する陸地, 岸辺) ; a **coast** (大洋に接する広い範囲の海岸) ⇀海岸 ▶岸に向かって泳ぐ swim for the *shore* ‖ ボートを岸に引き上げる haul a boat *ashore*(➤ ashore は「岸に」の意の副詞).

☛ 向こう岸 (⇀見出語)

2**きし 騎士** a **knight** /naɪt/ ‖**騎士道** chivalry.

3**きし 棋士** a **Go player**(碁の) ; a **shogi player**(将棋の).

1**きじ 記事** an **article** ; a **story**(いろいろな事情を説明する) ▶第1面の記事 a front-page *article* ‖ その記事はまだ読んでいない I haven't read the *article* yet. ‖ その事故の記事は彼が言っていることとは違う The *story* about the car accident differs from his own. ‖ きみの発明はきっと記事(＝ニュース)になるよ I am sure your invention will *make news*. ‖**新聞[雑誌]記事** a newspaper [magazine] article.

☛ 三面記事 (⇀見出語)

2**きじ 生地** **fabric** (織物) ; **cloth** (布地) ; **material** (服地) ; **dough** /doʊ/ (パン生地) ▶あの生地屋さんでドレス用の生地を2着分買った I bought *material* for two dresses at the *fabric store*. ‖ クッキー[パン／ピザ]の生地 cookie [bread／pizza] *dough*.

3**きじ 雉**《鳥》a **green pheasant** /fézənt/ ▶キジは日本の国鳥だ The *green pheasant* is the national bird of Japan.

1**ぎし 技師** an **engineer** /èndʒɪníər/ ‖**X線技師** an X-ray technician ‖ **機械[電気／土木]技師** a mechanical [an electrical／a civil] engineer.

2**ぎし 義歯** a **false** [an **artificial**] **tooth** ; **(full) dentures** (総入れ歯) ; **partial dentures**(部分入れ歯) ; a **bridge** (架工義歯) ; a **dental prosthesis**(歯科補てつ物).

3**ぎし 義姉** a [an **older**] **sister-in-law** [複 **sisters-in-law**].

4**ぎし 義肢** a **prosthetic** [an **artificial**] **limb**(➤ prosthetic /prɑ̀:sθéṭɪk/ は「人工補てつ物の」の意の医学用語).

1**ぎじ 議事** **matters for discussion**(討議[審議]事項); an **agenda** /ədʒéndə/ (会議事項一覧) ▶これ以上議事の進行を遅らせるわけにはいかない We can't delay the *proceedings* any longer. ‖ これは重大な問題なので議事に取り上げていただきたい I would like this matter to be put on the *agenda* as it is of grave importance.
‖**議事録** the proceedings, the minutes.

2**ぎじ 疑似** ‖**疑似餌** a lure /lʊəʳ/ ‖ **疑似コレラ** paracholera, false cholera ‖ **疑似症状** a suspected case ‖ **疑似体験** a simulated experience.

きしかいせい 起死回生 ▶イチローは起死回生の二塁打を放った Ichiro hit a double which *brought a victory* to his team *when it was on the brink of defeat*.

ぎしき 儀式 a **ceremony**(華やかに, あるいは厳かに行われる); a **rite**(宗教上の儀式など); **ritual**(伝統的に決まった手順で行う儀式) ▶儀式を行う hold *a ceremony* ‖ 儀式ばるような会なら出席しないよ I won't attend the party if it is going to *be formal*.

ぎしぎし ▶その建物は古くて, 歩くと床がギシギシ鳴った The building was so old that the floor *creaked* when I walked on it.

きしつ 気質 a **disposition**; **nature** (生まれつきの性質, 天性) ▶陽気な気質 a cheerful *disposition* ‖ 彼女は父親から穏やかな気質を受け継いでいる She has inherited her father's mild *disposition*.

きじつ 期日 a **date**; a **deadline** (締め切りの) ▶工事着工の期日を決める fix the *date* for starting construction ‖ 期日が迫っている *The deadline* is approaching. ‖ 何が何でも期日に間に合わせろ You must meet *the deadline* no matter what. ‖ 報告書は期日に間に合わないだろう I don't think I can get the report done before *the deadline*.

ぎじどう 議事堂 **the Diet Building**(日本の) ⟪参考⟫アメリカの国会議事堂は the Capitol, イギリスの国会議事堂は the Houses of Parliament という.

キジバト ⟪鳥⟫ an **Eastern** [**Oriental**] **turtle dove**.

きしべ 岸辺 a **shore**(海・湖・大河などの); a **bank** (川岸); a **beach** (浜) ▶岸辺を散歩する take a walk along the *shore*.

きしむ 軋む **creak, squeak**(➤ ともに同じキーキーという音をいうが, 前者はやや長く高い音, 後者はネズミが発するような短く高い音) ▶ゆうべ階段のきしむ音が聞こえたけど, きみかい I heard the stairs *squeak* [*creak*] last night. Was that you?

1**きしゃ 汽車** →電車, 列車.

2**きしゃ 記者** a (**newspaper**) **reporter**(新聞記者); a **journalist** (報道関係者); a **correspondent** (特派員, 通信員) ⟪参考⟫newsman, newspaperman は女性に対する差別になるので避けられる傾向がある.
▶きのうの午後, 首相は官邸で緊急記者会見を行った The Prime Minister held an unscheduled *news* [*press*] conference at his official residence yesterday afternoon. (➤ 前者の方が一般的. conference は記者団との会見). ‖**記者団** a press corps /prés kɔ̀:ʳ/ ‖ **共同記者会見** a joint press conference ‖ **政治記者** a political correspondent.

きしゃく 希釈する **dilute** +㊐
‖**希釈液** a diluted solution.

1**きしゅ 機種** a **model** ▶電子書籍端末の新機種が発売された *New model* e-book readers went on sale.

2**きしゅ 騎手** a **rider**; a **jockey**(競馬の).

3**きしゅ 旗手** a **flag bearer**(旗持ち); a **standard-bearer** (先頭に立って引っ張っていく人) ▶日本チームの旗手 *a flag bearer* for the Japanese team ‖ 現代音楽の旗手 *a standard-bearer* for contemporary music.

4**きしゅ 気腫** ⟪医学⟫ **emphysema** /èmfɪsí:mə, -zí:mə/
‖**肺気腫** pulmonary emphysema, emphysema of the lungs.

5**きしゅ 期首** **the beginning of the term** [**year**].

6**きしゅ 機首** **the nose of a plane**.

ぎしゅ 義手 a **prosthetic arm** [**hand**] (➤ prosthetic /prɑ̀:sθéṭɪk/ (人工補てつ物の)の代わりに artificial も用いる).

きじゅ 喜寿 ▶祖父の喜寿を祝う celebrate one's grandfather's *77th birthday*.

きしゅう 奇襲 a **surprise attack** ▶小勢で多勢を破るには奇襲しかない The only way for a small troop to beat a big one is to make *a surprise attack*.

きじゅうき 起重機 a **crane**(クレーン); a **derrick** (船などの貨物をつり上げる).

きしゅくがっこう 寄宿学校 a **boarding school**.

きしゅくしゃ 寄宿舎 ⟪米⟫ a **dormitory**(➤⟪英⟫では寄宿舎内の一室を指す), ⟪米・インフォーマル⟫ a **dorm**, ⟪英⟫ a **hall of residence** ▶寄宿舎生活をする live in *a dormitory*.

1**きじゅつ 奇術** **magic** ▶奇術を使って帽子から小鳥を出す produce little birds out of one's hat by *magic* / use *magic* to pull little birds out of one's hat
‖**奇術師** a magician.

2**きじゅつ 記述** a **description** 一動 **記述する** **describe** +㊐; **write** +㊐ (書く) ▶事件の詳しい [正確な] 記述 a detailed [an accurate] *description* of what happened ‖ すべてこの報告書に記述されているとおりです Everything is exactly as *is described* in this report. ‖**記述式テスト** a written test.

3**きじゅつ 既述** ▶既述したとおり *as mentioned above* / *as previously mentioned* ‖ 既述した問題 the problem *mentioned above* / the *above-mentioned* problem.

ぎじゅつ 技術

(a) **technique** /tekní:k/ (専門的な技術・技能); (a) **technology** (科学技術); (a) **skill** (訓練などによって習得される技能) ▶クローン技術を開発する develop cloning *techniques* ‖ 外科技術を改良する improve surgical *techniques* ‖ 技術を要する仕事 a *skilled* job ‖ オーケストラを指揮するには大変な技術と経験を要する Conducting an orchestra requires a great deal of *skill* and experience. ‖ 光の速さで飛ぶことは技術的に不可能だ It is *technically* impossible to travel at the speed of light. ‖ 日本は開発途上国への技術援助を増やしている Japan is increasing its *technological assistance* to developing countries.
‖**技術革新** technical innovation, a technological revolution ‖ (学科の) **技術・家庭** technical arts and home economics ‖ **技術者** a technical expert, a technician; an engineer (技師).

きじゅん 基準 a **standard** (標準); a **criterion** /kraɪtíəriən/ [複 **criteria**] (判断基準); a **yardstick** (尺度); a **basis**(基礎, 目安) ▶客観的な基準に基づいて病気の診断をする diagnose a disease based on objective *criteria* ‖ 厳密な基準に基づいて人選する select a suitable person based on strict *criteria* ‖ どんな基準でその賞は授与されるのですか On what *criteria* is the prize awarded? ‖ あなたの決定は何を基準にしたものですか What was your decision *based* on? / On what *basis* did you make your decision ? ‖ **安全基準**を定める set *a safety standard* ‖ 家を建てるときは市の**建築基準**に合わせる必要がある You need to meet the city's *building standards* when you build a house.

1**きしょう 気象** (the) **weather** ━形 **気象の meteorological** /mì:ṭiərəlɑ́:dʒɪkəl/ (気象学の) ▶気象を観測する make *meteorological observations* ‖ 春先には**気象**の変化が生じやすい *The weather* is changeable in early spring. ‖ **気象条件**が悪く5便が欠航した Five flights were canceled due to bad *weather conditions*. ‖**気象衛星** a weather satellite ‖ **気象台** a meteorological observatory ‖ **気象庁** the Meteorological Agency ‖ **異常気象** extreme [abnormal / anomalous] weather.

2**きしょう 気性** (a) **disposition** (気質, 生まれもった性格) ; (a) **temper** (激しやすい性分) ▶気性の激しい男性 a man with *a fiery* [*violent*] *temper* [*temperament*] ‖ **気性の荒い**犬 an *aggressive* dog ‖ ぼくは自分で負けず嫌いな [さっぱりした] **気性**だと思う I would say I've got an unyielding [frank] *disposition*. ‖ きみはぼくの**気性**をよく知ってるだろ? You know my *temper* [*disposition*] well, don't you ? ‖ その女の子は**気性**が母親似だ *Temperamentally*, the girl takes after her mother.

3**きしょう 記章・徽章** a **badge** ▶私たちの学校では制服に**記章**をつけるのが規則です In our school we must wear the *school badge* on our uniform.

4**きしょう 起床する get up, rise from** one's **bed** ▶《日記で》朝6時**起床** *Got up* at six. (➤ 日記では主語のIは通例省略する) ‖**起床時間** the hour of rising / time to get up.

5**きしょう 希少 rare** ‖**希少動物** a rare animal.

1**きじょう 机上** ▶**机上版**の辞書 a *desk* dictionary. ▶《慣用表現》きみの言うことは**机上の空論**で全く非現実的だ What you say is *mere theory* and is quite impractical.

2**きじょう 気丈** ▶**気丈**な娘 a *courageous* girl ‖ **気丈**にふるまう behave *resolutely*.

3**きじょう 騎乗する ride (a horse)**.

1**ぎしょう 偽証 false testimony** [**witness**], (a) **perjury** ▶法廷で**偽証する** *give false testimony* [*bear false witness*] in a court of law ‖ **偽証罪**を犯す commit *perjury*.

2**ぎしょう 偽称** ▶肩書きを**偽称する** *misrepresent* one's title [position].

ぎじょう 議場 an **assembly hall** ; **the floor**(議員席).

きしょうかち 希少価値 scarcity value ▶この種の品物は**希少価値**が高い These kinds of items have high *scarcity value*.

きしょうてんけつ 起承転結 a **plot** (小説などの筋) ▶このドラマは**起承転結**がしっかりしている The *plot* of this drama *is* well *structured*. (➤ 各部は introduction, development, turn and conclusion といえる).

1**きしょく 気色** ▶台所でネズミの死骸を見て**気色が悪く**なった I *felt sick* when I saw a dead rat in the kitchen. ‖ **気色悪い**! *Ugh!* (➤ 発音は /ʊx, jʌx, ʌg/ など) / *Yuck!*

2**きしょく 喜色** ▶彼は**喜色満面**だった He *was all smiles* [He *was radiant*] *with joy*. / He *was beaming with satisfaction*.

きしる 軋る creak ▶引き戸が**きしる** The sliding door *creaks*.

1**きしん 寄進する donate** +目.

2**きしん 帰心** ▶**帰心矢のごとし** *Your mind hurries home more swiftly than you do*. ‖ **帰心**が募ってきた My *desire to return home* has grown intense.

きじん 奇人 an **eccentric (person)**, 《インフォーマル》 an **oddball**.

ぎじん 擬人 ━動 **擬人化する personify** +目 ‖**擬人法** personification.

ぎしんあんき 疑心暗鬼 ▶その伝染病の詳しい情報が入らなかったので我々は**疑心暗鬼**になった With no detailed information available about the contagious disease, we *were filled with fear and anxiety*.

きす 期す →期する.

キス a **kiss** ; a **peck**(おざなりの軽い) ; a **smack**(音を立ててする) ━動 **キスする kiss** +目 ▶熱い**キス** *a passionate* [*hot*] *kiss* ‖ 投げ**キスをする** *blow a kiss* ‖ 彼女におやすみの**キスをする** *kiss* her *good night*. ‖ ねえ, **キスして**よ Come on, *give me a kiss*. ‖ 頬に**キスして** *Kiss* me on the cheek. ‖ 2人は抱き合って**キスをした** The couple embraced and *kissed* each other. ‖ 母親は赤ん坊に**優しくキスをした** The mother *gave* her baby *a tender kiss*. ‖ 彼は子供たちの頬に**チュッとキス**をしてベッドの毛布を掛けてやった He *gave* the kids *a peck* on the cheek and tucked them in bed. ‖ レオはジュリアの頬に**チュッとキスをした** Leo *gave* Julia *a smack* on the cheek. ‖ せめて彼女に**別れのキス**ぐらいしてやれよ Why don't you *kiss* her *good-bye* at least ? ‖ 襟に**キスマーク** (=口紅) がついてるぞ There's *a lipstick mark* [There's *lipstick*] on your collar. 《参考》強く吸われてできるキスマークは hickey, lovebite, または俗語で monkey bite という.

☛ 投げキス (→見出語)

きず 傷

訳語メニュー
けが →injury, wound **1**
ひっかき傷 →scratch **1**, **2**
果物の傷 →bruise **2**
汚点 →stain **3**

1【けが】 an **injury** /índʒəri/ (事故などによる) ; a **wound** /wu:nd/ (武器・爆弾などの攻撃による) ; a **cut** (切り傷) ; a **bruise** /bru:z/ (打撲傷) →けが.

▶重い [軽い] **傷** a serious [slight] *injury* ‖ 銃で撃たれた**傷** a gunshot [bullet] *wound* ‖ 兵士は撃たれて**重い傷を負った** The soldier was shot and seriously [critically] *wounded*. (➤ 後者は命が危ない状況を表す) ‖ 祖父の左足には戦争で受けた**傷**がある My grandfather has an old battle *scar* on his left leg. (➤ scar は「傷痕」) ‖ 人さし指の**傷**がずきずき痛む The *cut* on my index finger hurts [smarts]. ‖ 外科医は**傷**に薬をつけ包帯を巻いた The surgeon applied medicine to the *wound* and put a bandage on it. ‖ そのレーサーは衝突事故で**頭に傷を負った** The race car driver *sustained head injuries* in the collision. ‖ これは石をぶつけられてできた**傷**です This is the *bruise* I got when I was hit by a stone. ‖ 顔のその**傷**どうしたの? How did you get those *scratches* on your face ? (➤ scratch は「ひっかき傷」). ‖**傷薬** (an) ointment.

2【傷んだ所】 a **bruise** /bru:z/ (果物の) ; a **flaw** /flɔ:/ (宝石などの) ; a **crack** (陶器の) ▶このリンゴは**傷**はあるがおいしい This apple has *bruises*, but it (still) tastes good. ‖ この皿, **傷**がある! This plate has *a crack* [*is cracked*] ! ‖ 私の新しい机に**傷をつけないで**よ Don't *scratch* [*damage*] my new desk ! ‖ このたん

すは傷があるので半値で売ります This chest of drawers *is scratched* [*damaged*], so you can have it at half price.

3【汚点】 a **stain** ▶この失敗で彼の経歴に傷がついた This failure has left *a stain* on his career.

4【心の傷】 ▶両親の離婚は少年時代の私にとって心の傷となった My parents' divorce was *a traumatic experience* in my childhood. (➤「心の傷となるような経験」の意).

「傷・けが」のいろいろ **打ち傷・打ち身** bruise／**切り傷** cut／**骨折** fracture／**刺し傷** stab／**霜焼け** frostbite, chilblains／**擦り傷** scrape／**擦りむけ** abrasion／**脱臼** dislocation／**打撲傷** bruise／**たんこぶ** bump／**肉離れ** pulled muscle／**捻挫** sprain／**腫れ** swelling／**ひっかき傷** scratch／**ひび(骨の)** crack, fissure／**むち打ち症** whiplash／**やけど** burn, scald／**裂傷** laceration

きずあと 傷痕・傷跡 a **scar** ▶彼は顎に傷痕がある There is *a scar* on his chin.
▶《比喩的》その村には戦争の傷痕が残っている The *scars* of war remain in that village. ‖ その出来事は私の心に傷痕を残した The incident left me with an emotional *scar*.

[1]**きすう 奇数** an **odd number** (➤「偶数」は even number) ‖**奇数日** an odd-numbered day.

[2]**きすう 基数** a **cardinal number**.

ぎすぎす ▶ぎすぎすした世の中 this *cold and inhuman* [*heartless*] world ‖ あの受付はどうしてあんなにぎすぎすしているのだろう Why is the receptionist so *surly* [*curt*]? (➤ それぞれ「つっけんどんな」「ぶっきらぼうな」).

きずく 築く build +目 ▶青葉城は伊達政宗が築いたものである Aoba Castle *was built* by Date Masamune. ‖ どうやって彼が巨富を築き上げたのかはいまだに謎だ It is still a mystery how he *made* such a huge fortune. ‖《結婚式のスピーチ》お幸せな2人には明るい家庭を築いていただきたいと思います I hope the happy couple will go on to *build* a warm and happy home [*create* a warm and happy family].

きずぐち 傷口 a **wound** /wuːnd/; a **cut**(切り傷) ▶傷口に包帯をする dress *a wound*.

きずつく 傷つく be [**get**] **hurt**(心・肉体が); **be** [**get**] **bruised**(果物などが); **be** [**get**] **cracked**(陶器などが); **be** [**get**] **scratched**(家具などが) ▶人はささいなことで心が傷つくものだ People *get hurt* by little [trivial] things. ‖ きみが器量のことを言うから彼女は傷ついたんだよ She *was offended* [Her feelings *were hurt*] by your comment on her looks. (➤ comment を主語にして,Your comment on her looks offended her [hurt her feelings]. ということもできる).

きずつける 傷つける hurt +目, **injure** /índʒəʳ/ +目 (事故・ことばなどが偶然に; 前者のほうが意味が軽くややインフォーマルな語); **wound** /wuːnd/ +目 (刃物・ことばなどで意図的に); **damage** /dǽmɪdʒ/ +目 (物の価値・機能を損なう) ▶手を傷つける *hurt* [*injure*／*wound*] one's hand ‖ 男は左肩をひどく傷つけられた That man *was* badly *wounded* on the left shoulder. ‖ 大事な花瓶だから傷つけないように注意してください This is a very precious vase, so please be careful not to *damage* it. ‖ 彼女のプライドを傷つけるようなことは言わないほうがいいよ It's best not to say anything to *hurt* her pride.

きずな 絆 a **bond**(愛情による永続的な); **ties**(義務・責任感などに基づく) ▶強い家族の絆 a strong family *bond*(➤ bond の代わりに tie でもよい) ‖ 友情のきずなは鉄よりも強い The *bonds* [*ties*] between good friends are stronger than iron. ‖ 2人は強い愛のきずなで結ばれていた The two *were united by a strong bond* of love. ‖ **対話**「私たちは見えないきずなで結ばれている気がしたわ」「ぼくもきみに初めて会ったときにそんなふうに感じたよ」"I felt like *it was meant* [*was fated*] for us *to be together*." "Me, too. That's just what I felt when I first met you." (➤ be meant /ment/ to be で「…になる運命にある」の意).

きする 期する ▶私たちは再会を期して別れた We parted, *promising* to meet again. ‖ 心中深く期するところがあります I have something *that I'm deeply determined to achieve*.

[1]**きせい 帰省** a **homecoming** 一動 **帰省する return** [**go**] **home** ▶8月中旬に帰省したいと思う I'd like to *return home* [*return to my hometown*] about the middle of August. ‖ 東京駅は帰省客であふれていた Tokyo Station was crowded with *people returning to their hometowns*.
‖**帰省バス** a bus for people returning to their (ancestral) hometowns.

[2]**きせい 既製の ready-made** ▶私は体が大きいので既製服ではだめなのです Since I am big, *ready-made clothes* won't fit me. ‖ これは既製品かね, それともあつらえかね? Is this *ready-made* or made-to-order?

[3]**きせい 既成** ▶既成の事実 *an established fact*／*a fait accompli*(➤ 後者はフランス語から) ‖ 既成の(=型にはまった)観念を若者に押しつけるのはよくない It is not good to impose *ready-made* [*stereotypical*] ideas on young people.

[4]**きせい 気勢** ▶初戦の勝利でわがチームの気勢は上がった The victory at the initial game *put* our team *in high spirits*. ‖ 警官の堂々たる貫禄(かん)に, ちんぴらは気勢をそがれてしまった The hooligan's *high spirits were dampened* by the police officer's commanding presence.

[5]**きせい 規制** (a) **regulation** 一動 **規制する regulate** +目 (規制に従って取り締まる); **restrict** +目, **put restrictions**《on》(制限する); **control** +目 (権限によって取り締まる) ▶規制を緩和[強化]する ease [tighten] *regulations* ‖ ストライキを厳重に規制する *regulate* strikes strictly ‖ 穀物の輸入を規制する *restrict* [*put restrictions on*] grain imports ‖ 今度の日曜日はマラソンが行われるので, この道路は午前10時から交通規制が行われる There will be a marathon on this street next Sunday, so *traffic will be restricted* after 10 a.m. ‖**規制緩和** a relaxation of regulations; deregulation (規制撤廃, 規制緩和) ‖ **環境規制** (an) environmental regulation ‖ **交通規制** traffic control, (a) traffic regulation ‖ **銃規制** gun control.

[6]**きせい 寄生 parasitism** /pǽrəsaɪtɪ̀zəm/ ▶ノミは猫や犬に寄生する Fleas *feed off* cats and dogs. ‖ ヤドリギはいろいろな木に寄生する Mistletoe *grows on* various trees.／The mistletoe is a plant which *grows as a parasite* on various trees. ‖**寄生虫** a parasite /pǽrəsaɪt/, a parasitic worm.

[7]**きせい 奇声** a **funny cry** ▶奇声を上げる let out *a funny cry*.

ぎせい 犠牲 (a) **sacrifice** ▶彼らの安全を守るために必要なあらゆる犠牲を払う *make* all the necessary *sacrifices* to keep them safe ‖ 彼は生命を犠牲にして少年を救った He saved the boy's life *at the sacrifice* [*cost*／*price*] *of his own life*. ‖ どんな犠牲を払ってもその絵を手に入れるつもりだ I'm going to

get that picture *at all costs* [*at any cost* / *no matter what it takes* / *whatever it takes*]. ‖ そんな機会が与えられるのならどんな犠牲でも払います I'*d give my eyeteeth* for a chance like that. (➤ would give one's eyeteeth for は「(…のためなら)どんな代償でも払う」) ‖ 多くの観光客が山崩れの**犠牲になった** Many tourists *became victims* of the landslide.
‖**犠牲者** a victim ‖**犠牲バント** a sacrifice (bunt) ‖**犠牲フライ** a sacrifice fly. (→**犠打**).

ぎせいご 擬声語 an **onomatopoeia** /à:nəmæṭəpí:ə/.

きせかえ 着せ替え ▶着せ替え人形 *a dress-up doll*.

1**きせき 奇跡** a **miracle** ▶**奇跡**を起こす work [perform] *a miracle* ‖ あなたは**奇跡**を信じますか Do you believe in *miracles*? ‖ その行方不明者が生還したのはまさに**奇跡**だった It was *a miracle* that the missing man came home safely. ‖ **奇跡**でも起こらぬ限り彼は回復しないだろう He won't recover unless *a miracle* occurs [without *a miracle*]. ‖ その男の子は5階から転落したが**奇跡的に**助かった The little boy *miraculously* escaped death after falling from the 5th floor.

2**きせき 軌跡** 《数学》 a **trajectory**, a **locus** [複 **loci** /lóʊsaɪ/] ▶同様の**軌跡**をたどる follow a similar *trajectory*.

ぎせき 議席 a **seat** ▶**議席**を獲得する win *a seat* ‖ **議席**を失う lose one's *seat* ‖ そのスキャンダルで彼は**議席**を失った The scandal deprived him of his *seat*. (➤「そのスキャンダルが彼から議席を奪った」の意) / The scandal cost him his (*Diet*) *seat*. ‖ 今度の選挙で自民党は何**議席**獲得するだろうか I wonder how many *seats* the LDP will capture in the next election.

きせずして 期せずして **unexpectedly** ▶期せずして彼と同じ列車に乗り合わせた I *unexpectedly* found myself on the same train he was on.

きせつ 季節 a **season** (四季の1つ); **the ... season** (…の最盛期) ▶春は私がいちばん好きな**季節**だ Spring is my favorite *season* [*time of year*]. ‖ **季節の変わり目には**体調を崩しやすい Our physical condition easily deteriorates *when the seasons change* [*at the turn*(*ing*) *of the seasons*]. ‖ **季節外れの**大雪で交通機関がまひした Transportation was paralyzed due to the *unseasonably* heavy snowfall.
▶梨は今が**季節**だ Pears *are* now *in season*. ‖ ショートパンツはもう**季節外れ**だ It is*n't the season* to wear shorts. ‖ 海水浴の**季節**がやって来た *The swimming season* has come. ‖ 日本人は**季節の変化**に敏感です The Japanese people are sensitive to *the change* [*changing*] *of the seasons*. ‖ キュウリやトマトが一年中出回って**季節感**が薄まった Our *sense of the seasons* has weakened now that cucumbers and tomatoes are on the market throughout the year. ‖**季節風** a seasonal [periodic] wind (➤インド洋の季節風は monsoon /mà:nsú:n/).

きぜつ 気絶 a **faint** 一動 **気絶する** **faint** (**away**), 《インフォーマル》 **pass out** ▶彼女は和夫の突然の死を知って**気絶**寸前だった She *nearly fainted* at the news of Kazuo's sudden death.

きせる 着せる **dress** +目 ▶子供に**服を着せる** *dress* one's child ‖ 私は彼女に着物を**着せて**やった I *helped* her *put on* the kimono. (➤「彼女が着るのを手伝った」と訳す) ‖ 卒業式の日には美容院で着物を**着せて**もらった On graduation day, I went to the beauty salon for *assistance in putting on* a kimono.
▶彼は私に罪を**着せた** He *laid* [*put*] the blame *on* me. (➤ laid は lay(負わせる)の過去形).

キセル ▶**キセル乗車**(=不正乗車) *ticket fraud* / *commuter pass fraud* ‖ **キセル**(=不正乗車)をする *cheat on the train fare* / steal a train ride (➤「キセルをする人」は a train ticket cheater).

きぜわしい 気ぜわしい ▶年の瀬が近づくと何となく気ぜわしくなる For some reason or other, I *feel restless* as the year's end draws near.

1**きせん 汽船** a **steamer**; a **steamship** (大型の); a **cruise ship** (観光用の); an **ocean liner** (遠洋定期船); a **steamboat** (河川・湖などの) ▶**汽船**氷川丸 the *S.S.* Hikawa-maru (➤ S.S. は steamship の略) ‖ 横浜港に豪華な**汽船**が停泊している There is a luxury *cruise ship* [*ocean liner*] at anchor in Yokohama Harbor.

2**きせん 機先** ▶**機先を制すれば**勝てる If you *forestall* [If you *get the jump on*] your opponent, you can beat him.

きぜん 毅然 ▶**きぜんたる**態度をとる assume a *resolute* attitude (➤ resolute は「決心の固い」) ‖ あんな不幸に遭ってもきぜんとしていられるとは龍馬は大した男だ What a great man Ryoma was to *remain steady* [*steadfast*] in the face of such misfortune! (➤ steady, steadfast はともに「ぐらつかない」の意で, 後者は堅い語) / Ryoma was quite a man to *keep a stiff upper lip* in the face of such misfortune. (➤「(耐えて)上唇を引き締めたままにする」が原義) ‖ そんな無理な注文は**きぜんとして**断るべきだ You should *firmly* refuse impossible demands like that.

ぎぜん 偽善 (a) **hypocrisy** /hɪpá:krəsi/ ▶この世には**偽善**が多くて時々嫌になる There is so much *hypocrisy* [There are so many *hypocrites*] in this world that it sometimes sickens me.
‖**偽善者** a hypocrite /hípəkrɪt/ (➤ two-faced person(裏表のある人)といういい方もある).

1**きそ 基礎** **1**【建物の土台】a **foundation** ▶彼の新築の家は**基礎**がしっかりしている His new house is built on a firm *foundation*.
‖**基礎工事** foundation work.
2【基本】(**the**) **basics**; (**the**) **fundamentals** (基礎的事項) ▶英語を**基礎**から学ぶ learn English from *the basics* [*the ABCs*] ‖ きみは数学の**基礎**ができていないね You haven't mastered *the basics* of mathematics. ‖ **基礎的な**日本語文法を勉強しなさい Study *basic* [*fundamental*] Japanese grammar. ‖ 彼にはコンピュータの**基礎知識**もない He lacks even *basic* computer *knowledge*. ‖**基礎控除** a basic deduction ‖**基礎体温** basal body temperature.

2**きそ 起訴** **prosecution** (刑事訴追); **indictment** /indáɪtmənt/ (陪審制を採用している国の) 一動 **起訴する** **prosecute** /prá:sɪkjù:t/ +目; **indict** /ɪndáɪt/ +目 (陪審制のもとでの) ▶彼は窃盗で**起訴された** He *was prosecuted* [*was indicted*] for theft.
‖**起訴状** a charging sheet (日本の); an indictment (陪審制を採用している国の).
☛ 不起訴 (→見出語)

1**きそう 競う** **compete** ▶18人の若い女性たちが美を**競った** Eighteen young women *competed* in the beauty contest. ‖ 人々は**競って**福袋を買った People *competed* to buy New Year's (lucky) grab bags.

2**きそう 起草する** **draft** +目 ▶憲法を**起草する** *draft* a constitution.

3**きそう 帰巣** ‖**帰巣本能** (a) homing instinct.

きぞう 寄贈する **give** +目, **present** /prɪzént/ +目

(➤ 後者が日本語に近い堅い語で，改まった儀式的な贈呈を連想させる)；**donate** +目 (寄付する) ▶多くの書籍がその学校に**寄贈された** Many books *were donated* [*were given*] to the school.
‖**寄贈雑誌** a gift periodical ‖ **寄贈者** a contributor ; a donator (慈善事業などの) ‖ **寄贈品** a gift.

き

ぎそう 偽装 (a) **camouflage** /kǽməflɑ̀:ʒ/ ▶**偽装**結婚 a *sham* marriage ‖ **耐震偽装マンション** *a killer condo* ‖ **食品偽装**は食の安全を脅かす *False food labeling* is a threat to food safety.
‖**偽装表示** a false label.

ぎぞう 偽造する **counterfeit** /káʊnṭəʳfɪt/ +目 ; **forge** +目 (文書などの) ▶公文書**偽造** official document *forgery* ‖ パスポートを**偽造する** *counterfeit* a passport (➤「偽造パスポート」は a counterfeit passport) ‖ 他人の署名を**偽造する** *forge* a person's signature. ‖**偽造紙幣** [**貨幣**] a counterfeit bill [coin] 《参考》自動販売機などに使用された偽造貨幣や貨幣状金属をインフォーマルでは slug という. ‖ **偽造品** a counterfeit. (→イミテーション).

きそうきょく 奇想曲 《音楽》 a **capriccio**.

きそうてんがい 奇想天外 ▶彼は**奇想天外**な行動に出て人を驚かすのが好きだった He liked to surprise people by doing *unexpected* things. ‖ 今回の企画はまさに**奇想天外**であった This new project comes as *a surprise* indeed. (➤ a surprise は「驚くべきこと」).

きそく 規則 a **rule**, a **regulation** (➤ 後者は強制力をもつものを含む場合がある) ▶**規則正しい**生活を送る keep *regular hours* ‖ わが社では社員は胸に名札をつけるのが**規則**になっている It is a company *rule* [*regulation*] that employees wear a name tag on their chest. ‖ **規則は守ら**なければいけない We must *observe* [*follow* / *obey*] the *rules*. ‖ 桜女子高は**規則がやかましい**ことで有名だ Sakura Girls' Senior High School is well known for its *strict rules* [*regulations*]. ‖ 二度と**規則違反**はいたしません I promise not to *break* [*violate*] *the rules* again. (➤ violate は堅い語) ‖ 通りには街灯が**規則的に**立っている The street lights stand *at regular intervals* along the street.
‖《文法》**規則動詞** a regular verb.
☛ **不規則** (→見出語)

きぞく 貴族 a **nobleman** (男), a **noblewoman** (女), an **aristocrat** /ərístəkræt/ (➤ 堅い語), 《英》 a **peer** (➤ 以上は1人) ; **the nobility, the aristocracy,** 《英》 **the peerage** (➤ あとの3者は総称) ▶アッシャーさんは**貴族の生まれ**だ Mr. Asher is *a nobleman*. / Mr. Asher is *of noble birth*. / Mr. Asher is *a blue blood*. (➤ blue blood は「高貴な血筋の人」) ‖ 森氏は**貴族的な**顔だちをした青年だ Mr. Mori is a young man with *noble* [*aristocratic*] features. ‖ 兄は**独身貴族**を楽しんでいる My brother is enjoying the advantages and pleasures of single life.

ぎそく 義足 a **prosthetic** [**an artificial**] **leg** (➤ prosthetic /prɑ̀:sθéṭɪk/ は「人工補てつ物の」の意の医学用語) ▶彼は事故で片足を失ったので**義足**を使っている Since he lost his leg in an accident, he wears [uses] *an artificial leg*.

きそん 既存の **existing** ▶**既存の**技術を用いる use *existing* technology.

きた 北 **the north** 一形 **北の** **northern** /nɔ́:ʳðəʳn/ ▶**北は**どっち？ Which way is *north*? ‖ ぼくの家は**北向き**だ My house *faces north*. (➤ この north は「北に」の意の副詞) ‖ 原子力潜水艦は**北に向かって**進んだ The nuclear submarine went (*toward the*) *north*. ‖ 北海道は本州の**北の方に**ある Hokkaido is (*to the*) *north of* Honshu. (➤ 接していない場合) ‖ 埼玉県は東京の**北に**ある Saitama Prefecture is *on the northern border of* Tokyo. (➤ 接している場合) ‖ 彼の学校は大阪駅の**北4キロの所に**ある His school is *four kilometers north of* Osaka Station.
☛ **北アメリカ, 北半球** (→見出語)

ぎだ 犠打 《野球》 a **sacrifice hit** ▶巨人は坂本の**犠打**で1点を追加した The Giants added a run on Sakamoto's *sacrifice fly* [*bunt*]. (➤ 実際はこのように「犠牲フライ」か「犠牲バント」かをはっきりさせるのがふつう).

ギター a **guitar** /gɪtɑ́:ʳ/ ▶**ギターを弾く** play the *guitar* ‖ **エアギターを弾く** play *air guitar*. ‖**ギター奏者** a guitarist /gɪtɑ́:rɪst/ ‖ **アコースティックギター** an acoustic guitar ‖ **エレキギター** an electric guitar.

きたアメリカ 北アメリカ **North America** (➤ North America は地理的には Mexico を含むが，文化的には通例，カナダと合衆国を指す) ▶当社は**北アメリカ**に500店舗を展開する予定です We plan to open 500 stores in *North America*.

1 **きたい 期待** **expectation(s)** ; **anticipation** (楽しみに待つこと) ; a **wish** (願い) ; (a) **hope** (希望) 一動 **期待する** **expect, hope** 《for》 ▶日本チームが敗れて大いなる**期待**が失望に終わった Great *expectations* [*anticipation*] ended in disappointment when the Japanese team lost the game. ‖ **ご期待に添え**なくて申し訳ありません I am sorry I wasn't able to *meet* [*come up to*] *your expectation(s)*. ‖ **ご期待に添える**かどうかわかりませんが，全力を尽くします I don't know if I will be able to *meet* [*live up to*] *your expectations*, but I'll do my best. ‖ 今度のオリンピック，頑張ってくださいね. 金メダルを**期待しています** Good luck in the coming Olympic Games. We*'re looking forward to* [We *expect*] a gold medal! ‖ あの新任の先生には大いに**期待しています** We *have high expectations* of our new teacher. ‖ 彼女の両親は彼女がもっと真剣に勉強することを**期待している** Her parents *expect* her to study harder. ‖ あなたは子供さんたちに**期待をかけ過ぎている** You *expect too much* of [from] your children.

> **直訳の落とし穴「皆さんに期待しています」**
> 「期待する」= expect であるが，「大いに皆さんに期待しています」を (×) I'm expecting all of you very much. とすることはできない.「人を expect」して，I'm expecting all of you. は「(来る予定がわかっているので) 皆さんをお待ちしています」という意味になる. 人に「期待をかけている」というときは I'm expecting a lot from [of] all of you. (➤ 即戦力として全力を尽くすことを期待) または，I have high expectations of you all. (➤ やがては見事に成長し，成功することを期待) とする.「息子にはあまり期待をかけていない」は I don't expect much from my son. (➤ 息子からは多くを望めない ; of my son は力を出して活躍しそうにない), I don't have high expectations of my son. (➤ 将来的に人生の成功者となりそうにない) となる.

▶ 対話「お土産買ってくるからね」「**期待しないで**待ってるわ」 "I'll bring you back a present." "*I won't hold my breath.*" (➤ hold one's breath は「(期待などで) 固唾をのむ」) ‖ 映画は**期待したほど**おもしろくはなかった The movie was not as interesting *as I had expected*. ‖ その小説は**期待外れ**だった The novel was *disappointing* [*a letdown*] to me. ‖ **期待を裏**

切ってわが校のバスケットボールチームは第１回戦で敗退した Our basketball team *let* everyone *down* by losing in the first round.

[2]**きたい 機体** the body of an airplane；a fuselage /fjúːsəlɑːʒ/（胴体）▶ジャンボ機が山腹に墜落し，**機体**が炎上した The jumbo jet crashed into the side of the mountain and burst into flames.

[3]**きたい 気体** (a) gas ▶空気はいろいろな**気体**の混合物である Air is a mixture of *gases*.

ぎだい 議題 a topic［a subject］for discussion；the agenda（協議事項；個別の協議事項は an item on［in］the agenda という）▶きょうの**議題**は何だったっけ？What was the *topic* for today？‖そんなつまらんことを**議題**に入れるべきじゃない Such an unimportant thing should not be on *the agenda*.‖その問題はきょうの会議で**議題に上る**と思います I think the problem will *be brought up* at today's conference.

ぎたいご 擬態語 a mimetic［an imitative］word.

きたえる 鍛える train ＋㊐（訓練して）；exercise ＋㊐（運動をして）；build up（作り上げる）；drill ＋㊐（繰り返し教え込むことで）▶選手たちを**鍛える** *train* athletes‖足腰を**鍛える** *exercise* one's legs‖精神を**鍛える** *build up*［*develop*］one's spirit‖毎朝10キロ走って**体を鍛える** *build up one's body* by running ten kilometers every morning‖先生は暗算ができるようクラス全体を**鍛えた** The teacher *drilled* the whole class in mental arithmetic.‖《剣道などで》かかって来い！**鍛えてやる** Come on, try me！*I'll teach you a thing or two！*

きだおれ 着倒れ ▶**京の着倒れ，大阪の食い倒れ** People in Kyoto *squander their money on clothes* and people in Osaka on food.

きたかぜ 北風 a north［northerly］wind ▶**北風**が吹いている The *north wind* is blowing.／The wind is blowing from the north.

きたきりすずめ 着た切り雀 ▶家へ帰る時間が無くて何日も**着た切り雀だ** I'*ve been wearing the same clothes* for days since I don't have time to go home.

きたく 帰宅する go home, come home ▶今田さんはもう**帰宅しました** Imada *has* already *gone home*.（➤話者は会社の同僚など）‖父はいつも**帰宅が遅い** My father always *comes home late*.（➤ come home は話者が自宅に居る場合）‖今**帰宅した**ばかりです I've just *come home*［*gotten home*］.‖**帰宅の途中**思いもかけず古沢君に出会った I happened to meet Mr. Furusawa *on my way home*.‖《災害時などの》**帰宅難民**［**困難者**］a stranded commuter.

きたぐに 北国 a northern district（地方）；a northern country（国）▶**北国**ノルウェー Norway, *a northern country*‖４月になっても**北国**では時折雪が降る In *northern districts* it sometimes snows even in April.

きたす 来す ▶携帯電話の使用は機内の計器に支障を**来す**恐れがある The use of your cellphone in the cabin may *cause* interference with flight instruments.

きたたいせいよう 北大西洋 ‖**北大西洋条約機構** North Atlantic Treaty Organization, NATO /néɪṭoʊ/.

きたちょうせん 北朝鮮 North Korea. →朝鮮.

きだて 気立て ▶**気立てが優しい** have *a sweet disposition*‖あの娘は**気立てがいい** She is an *amiable* girl［*sweet-tempered*］.‖嫁にするなら器量よしより**気立て**のいいのにしなよ When you choose your wife, you should pay more attention to *personality* than looks.

きたない 汚い

📖 訳語メニュー
不潔な →dirty, filthy **1**
品の無い →dirty **2**
ずるい →dirty, unfair **4**

1【汚れている】 dirty, filthy /fílθi/（➤後者のほうが汚れがひどい）；messy（散らかっていて）▶公衆トイレは大概**汚い**から使いたくない I don't like to use public restrooms because they are usually *dirty*.‖敏雄，そんな**汚い**下着を着ないでよ Toshio, don't wear such *dirty*［*filthy*］underwear.‖川の水はごみで**汚く**なっている The river is *foul* with rubbish.（➤ foul /faʊl/ は「悪臭がしてひどく不潔な」）‖イスラム教徒は左手は**汚い**と考えている Muslims regard the left hand as *unclean*.（➤この unclean は「(宗教的・道徳的に)不浄な」の意）.

▶林先生の机の上は散らかしっぱなしでいつも**汚い** Mr. Hayashi's desk *is* always *messy*.‖ロック・コンサートのあとの公園は**汚かった** The park *was a mess* after the rock concert.（➤ mess は「散らかった状態」）.

2【品の無い，不快な】 dirty；disgusting（胸の悪くなるような）；messy（だらしない）▶そういう**汚い**ことばを使ってはいけません Don't use *dirty* words like that.‖**汚い**話で恐縮ですが，最近痔(じ)で困ってるんです I know it is *not* a *nice* thing to talk about, but recently I have been suffering from hemorrhoids.（➤「話題にするのはふさわしくない」の意）.

3【整わない】 poor（字などが下手な）▶彼の字は**汚くて**読みづらい His handwriting is so *poor*［*messy*］that it is hard to read (it).（➤ messy は「乱雑な」）.

4【卑劣な】 dirty；unfair（公平・公正でない）▶彼の商売のやり方は**汚い** His business methods are *dirty*.‖２人がかりなんて**汚いぞ**．正々堂々と勝負しろよ！Two on one is *no fair*. Come on and play fair！‖あの市会議員は**汚い**手を使って票を集めた That assemblyman used *dirty* tactics to collect votes.‖あの男は金持ちだが金にとても**汚い** He is rich but very *miserly*［《英また》*mean*］*about money matters*.‖我々をだましたなんて(おまえ)**汚いよ** Tricking us was *a dirty thing* (for you) *to do*.

きたならしい 汚らしい dirty（汚い）；dirty-looking（汚く見える）▶**汚らしい**紙幣 a *dirty* (*-looking*) bill［note］.

きたはんきゅう 北半球 the Northern Hemisphere ▶**北半球**では今は夏だ It's summer now in *the Northern Hemisphere*.

きたまくら 北枕 ▶**北枕**は縁起が悪いので通常避けられる *Putting your head to the north when you sleep* is usually avoided because it's considered bad luck［it's said to bring (you) bad luck］.

きたる 来る coming

✉ **きたる６月３日土曜日の結婚式にぜひご出席くださいますようお願いいたします** We do hope you will come to our wedding to be held (on) the *coming* Saturday, June 3.

きたん 忌憚 ▶きたんのないご意見をお聞かせください We'd like to hear your *honest* opinions.／Please don't hesitate to express your *frank* opinions.

きだん 気団《気象》an air mass ‖**寒気団** a cold air mass.

1**きち 機知** wit ▶機知に富んだスピーチ a *witty* speech ‖ 彼は機知に富んでいる He is *full of wit*. ／He is *witty*.

2**きち 基地** a base ‖空軍［海軍］基地 an air [a naval] base ‖ 軍事基地 a military base.

3**きち 吉** good fortune.

-きち ▶ぼくの兄貴は釣りきちだ My big brother is *crazy about fishing*. ／My big brother is *a fishing nut* [*maniac*]. (➤ nut は「…狂」の意のくだけた語). ‖ 友だちはみんなぼくのことをカーきちという All my friends say I've got *the car bug*. (➤ bug は「熱狂」の意のくだけた語).

きちじつ 吉日 a lucky day

ことわざ 思い立ったが吉日 The day on which you resolve to do it is your lucky day. (➤ 日本語からの直訳)／There is no time like the present. (➤「今のようなよい時はない」の意).

きちゅう 忌中 ▶祖母が亡くなって忌中です I have *been in mourning* since the death of my grandmother. ‖《掲示》忌中 In Mourning.

1**きちょう 機長** a captain.

2**きちょう 貴重な** precious (金銭では得られない) ; valuable, invaluable (➤ ともに「金銭的価値がある, 大切な」の意で, 後者は前者の強意語) ; rare (珍しい) ▶貴重な写真 a *rare* photo(graph) ‖ 10代に外国暮らしができたのは私にとって貴重な経験でした Having lived in a foreign country when I was a teenager was a *precious* experience. ‖ 考古学は我々に古代の極めて貴重な情報を与えてくれる Archaeology gives us *invaluable* information about ancient times. ‖ 貴重品はこの袋に入れてください Please put your *valuables* in this bag. ‖ マツタケは今では貴重品だ Matsutake (mushrooms) *are a precious commodity* nowadays.

3**きちょう 基調** ▶黒を基調とした落ち着いたデザイン a quiet [subdued] design *utilizing* black *as its base* [*basic* ／*keynote*] *color*
‖ 基調演説 a keynote speech [address].

4**きちょう 記帳** a register (記録) ; an entry (記入) ▶《来賓などに》こちらにご記帳をお願いいたします May I trouble you to *sign the guest book*, please ? ‖ ATM で(通帳に)記帳する *update* one's *bankbook* on the ATM

《参考》ATM の「通帳記帳のキーを押す」ことを press the update bankbook key という。

ぎちょう 議長 the chairman, the chairperson, the chair ; the President (上院・参議院の) ; the Speaker (下院・衆議院の)

> 《解説》(1) chairman は男性にも女性にも用いられるが, 近年では性差のない chairperson や chair が好まれる傾向にある. (2) ただし, 呼びかけには Mr. Chairman (男性), Madam(e) Chairman (女性) を用いることが多い.

▶議長を務める serve as *chair*(*person*) ‖ 議長, 採決を求めます *Mr. Chairman* ! I call for a vote (on the matter) ! ‖ みんなが議長になりたがった Everyone wanted to *chair the meeting*.

きちょうめん 几帳面な methodical /məθάːdɪkəl/ ▶銀行の仕事はきちょうめんな人が向いている The people best suited for work in banking are those with *methodical* personalities. ‖ この仕事はそんなにきちょうめんにやらなくていいよ You don't have to be so *exact* in this job. (➤ exact は「正確な」).

きちんと 1【整った状態に】neatly ▶靴を脱いだらきちんとそろえておきなさい When you take off your shoes, make sure you line them up *neatly*. ‖ 彼の寝室はいつもきちんと片づいている His bedroom is always (kept) *neat and tidy*. ‖ 伊藤先生はいつもきちんとした服装をしている Mr. Ito *is* always *neatly dressed*. ‖ 彼女は何事によらずきちんとやる人だ Whatever she does, she does *with* (*scrupulous*) *care*. (➤「細心の注意を払って」の意) ‖ 泣いてないでお母さんにきちんと訳を話してごらん Don't cry—tell mommy *just* what the problem is.

2【間違いなく】▶全員きちんと 3 時に駅に来てください Everybody, *be sure to* come to the station at three. ‖ 彼は部屋代を毎月きちんと払う He pays his rent *on time* every month. (➤ on time は「期限通りに」)

きつい

> 📖 訳語メニュー
> 窮屈な →tight 1
> 厳しい, 苦しい →hard 2
> 強い →hard, strong 3

1【余裕がなくて窮屈な】tight ▶きつい帽子 a *tight* cap ‖ ジャムの瓶の蓋がきつくて開けられない The lid of this jam jar is (on) too *tight* and I can't open it. ／I can't open the lid of this jam jar. It's (on) too *tight*. ‖ このスケート靴はきつすぎて痛い These skates are on too *tight*, so they hurt. ‖ その新聞紙, もっときつく縛って Tie the newspaper more *tightly*.

2【厳しい, 苦しい】hard ; exhausting (心身を疲労させる) ▶きつい仕事 *hard* [*exacting*] work (➤ exacting は「骨の折れる」) ‖ チベット旅行はきつかった Our trip to Tibet *was exhausting*. ‖ 中村先生のピアノの練習はとてもきつい My piano teacher, Mr. Nakamura, is very *demanding* about practice. (➤ demanding は「要求が厳しい」) ‖ その仕事は肉体的にきつい The job is *physically demanding*. ‖ 我々はきついスケジュールをこなさなければならなかった We had to cope with a very *tight schedule*. ‖ 病み上がりでまだ体力がないので, 私には水泳はきつすぎます Swimming would *be too hard* for me because I am still weak after a recent illness. ‖ 200段の石段を上るのはきつい It's *tough* to climb 200 stone steps. ‖ 最もきついスポーツは何だと思う？ What do you think is *the toughest* sport ? ‖ 父親にきつく叱られてしまった I was scolded *severely* by my father.

3【強い】strong (酒などが) ; hard (目つきなどが) ; powerful (香水などが) ▶ウオツカなんてきつい酒は飲めないよ I can't drink anything *strong* like vodka. ‖ 美穂はきつい目をしている Miho has *hard* eyes. (➤ sharp eye は「よく利く目, 鋭い目」に相当) ‖ 陽子は性格がきつい Yoko is *strong-minded*. ‖ 順子, あなたちょっと香水がきついわよ That's some *powerful perfume* you've got on, Junko. ‖ ずいぶんきついことを言うのね Aren't you *critical* ! ／What *a critical thing to say* !

きつえん 喫煙 smoking ▶この部屋［ベッド］での喫煙はご遠慮ください Please refrain from *smoking* in this room [in bed]. ‖ 喫煙は指定の場所でお願いいたします *Smoking* is permitted only in designated areas. ‖ 間接［受動］喫煙は直接［能動］喫煙と同じくらい危険だ *Passive smoking* is almost as dangerous as *active smoking*. ‖ 喫煙室 a smoking room (➤「(ホテルなどの)喫煙できる部屋」の意でもある.

反対は a nonsmoking room) ‖ **喫煙者** a smoker ‖ **喫煙席** a smokers' section.

きつおん 吃音(症) **dysphemia.** ⇀どもり, どもる.

きづかい 気遣い ▶どうぞお気遣いなく *Please don't bother.*／*Please don't worry about me.*／*Please don't go to any special trouble for me.* (●いずれも決まった言い方だが, 第1例の場合, 文末に with me をつけるとかなりきつい響きになるので要注意) ‖ いろいろ**お気遣い**いただきまして心より感謝いたします I sincerely appreciate your *concern* (for me) [your *thoughtfulness* (toward me)]. ‖ ここに居れば誰にも見つかる**気遣い**(＝心配)はない As long as you are here, you don't have to *worry about* being found out by others.

きづかう 気遣う **be concerned**《about》 ▶孫たちは皆私たち夫婦の健康を**気遣ってくれる** All our grandchildren *are concerned about* our health. (➤ 高齢, あるいは, 高血圧や糖尿病などの病気が進んでいるというような明白な理由があって, 心配する場合は be worried about や be anxious about を用いる ; ⇀**心配**).

きっかけ (an) **impetus**(起動力, はずみ) ; an **opportunity**(チャンス) ▶行動の**きっかけ** an *impetus* to act [to action] ‖ せっかく彼女の名前がわかったのに話しかける**きっかけ**がつかめない I found out her name but I couldn't get *an opportunity* to talk to her. ‖ 彼と知り合うようになった**きっかけ**は何だったろうかと考えてみた I tried to recall *how* I first met him. ‖ **何がきっかけ**でこんな仕事をするようになったの? *What made* you take up this kind of work?

きっかり **sharp**, 《英また》 **prompt**(時刻が) ; **exactly**(正確に) ▶2時**きっかり**に私のオフィスに来てください Please come to my office at 2 o'clock *sharp*. ‖ 彼は時間にうるさいだけあって**きっかり**8時に到着した Being a punctual person, he arrived at eight o'clock *sharp* [at eight *on the dot*]. (➤ on the dot は「ぴったり目盛りの上に」が原義) ‖ 父親に180円くれと言ったら**きっかり**180円くれた When I asked my father to give me 180 yen, he gave me *exactly* 180 yen [gave me the *exact* amount]. ‖ その特急は**毎時きっかり**に新宿を出る The limited express leaves Shinjuku Station (*every hour*) *on the hour*.

きづかれ 気疲れ ▶立食パーティーは不慣れなので**気疲れ**してしまう I *get nervous and tired* at buffet parties since I am not used to them. (➤ get nervous は「神経質になる」) ‖ きみの場合は体の疲れではなく**気疲れ**というものだ In your case, you *are tired* not physically but *mentally*.

キック a **kick** 一動 **キックする** **kick** ＋目 ▶こっちにボールを**キック**してよ *Kick* the ball to me.
‖ **キックボクシング** kickboxing.

キックバック a **kickback** ▶建設会社から**キックバック**をもらう get *a kickback* from a construction company.

きづく 気付く **find** ＋目 (知る) ; **realize** ＋目 (考えて, 判断して) ; **notice** ＋目 (見て, 聞いて) ; **be aware**《of》(気づいている)
▶私はその金がなくなっているのに**気づいた** I *found* that the money was gone. ‖ 彼は今に自分の間違いに**気づく**だろう Some day he will *realize* that he was wrong. ‖ 鍵を引き出しに忘れてきたことに**気づいた** I *noticed* I had left the key in the drawer. ‖ 誰ひとりその危険に**気づいていなかった** No one *was aware of* the danger. ‖ きみのお母さんが待合室に居たのに**気づかなかった**よ I *wasn't aware* [I did*n't notice*] that your mother was in the waiting room. ‖ そのセールスマンにだまされたとは**全く気づかなかった** I *didn't have the faintest idea* [*I didn't realize at all*] that I had been tricked by the salesman. ‖ 私は家族に**気づかれずに**家を出た I left the house *without being noticed* by my family [without my family seeing me]. ‖ ほら, 彼**気づいた**みたいよ See! He's (finally) *noticed*. (➤「何かに気づいた」の意.「意識が戻った」は come to) ‖ 彼は私が居るのに**気づいて**うなずいて**挨拶した** He *acknowledged* my presence with a nod. (➤ acknowledge someone's presence は「人がいることに気づいて挨拶する[話しかける]」).

キックオフ a **kickoff** ▶**キックオフ**は7時です The game *kicks off* [*starts*] at seven. ‖ 7時ちょうどにレフェリーの**キックオフ**の笛が鳴った The referee's whistle *kicked off* the game at 7:00 sharp. (➤ kick off は「(ゲームを)開始する」).

ぎっくりごし ぎっくり腰 a **slipped disk** [**disc**] ▶彼は重たい箱を持ち上げようとして**ぎっくり腰**になった He *got a slipped disk* when he tried to lift a heavy box.

きつけ 着付け **dressing (and wearing)** (➤ wearing は着たあとの歩き方, 座り方などの所作も含む) ▶ひとりで**着付け**できない若い子が多い Most young women can't *put on a kimono* by themselves. ‖ **着付け教室** a kimono dressing (and wearing) class.

きづけ 気付 **care of**《略 c/o》 ▶アパートが見つかるまでおばの黒田方**気付**で手紙をください Write to me (*in*) *care of* Mrs. Kuroda, my aunt, till I find a new apartment. (➤《米》では in をつけることもある).

[1]**きっこう 拮抗** ▶両者は**勢力がきっ抗している** Both sides *are nearly equal in power* [*are evenly matched* (*in power*)].

[2]**きっこう 亀甲** (a) **tortoiseshell.**

きっさてん 喫茶店 a **coffee shop** ; a **tearoom**, a **café** (レストランなどの軽食もとれる喫茶室).

ぎっしり ▶公会堂は人で**ぎっしり**だった The public hall *was* (*jam-*)*packed* [*was jammed* ／《英》 *was chock-a-block*] *with* people. ‖ この箱には本が**ぎっしり詰まっている** This box *is cram-packed* [*closely packed*] *with* books. ‖ 私はスーツケースに衣類を**ぎっしり詰め込んだ** I *stuffed* the suitcase with clothes. ‖ 今月の私のスケジュールは**ぎっしり**です I have a *tight* schedule for this month.／My schedule is quite *tight* this month.

[1]**きっすい 生粋** ▶**生粋の**パリっ子 a Parisian *born and bred* [*raised*] ‖ 彼は**生粋の**江戸っ子です He is a *true* Tokyoite. (➤ -ite /-aɪt/ は「…の人」の意)／He's a Tokyoite to *the core*.

[2]**きっすい 喫水** **draft** ‖ **喫水線** the waterline.

きづち 木槌 a **wooden hammer**, a **mallet**(のみを叩くのに用いる ; 頭部がゴム製や金属製もある) ; a **gavel**(議長・競売人などが卓上を叩く).

ぎっちょ a **lefty**(➤《インフォーマル》で「左ききの人」) ▶彼は**ぎっちょ**だ He *is a lefty* [*a left-hander*].

きっちり ▶貸した金は**きっちり耳をそろえて**返してもらうよ I want you to pay back the money you owe me *in one lump sum*. ‖ こうした金の絡む問題は**きっちり**しておかないとあとで困るよ You'd better *settle* this money problem *squarely*, or you'll be sorry later.

キッチン a **kitchen.**

きつつき 《鳥》 a **(wood)pecker.**

きって 切手 a **(postage) stamp** ▶封筒に**切手**を貼る put *a stamp* on an envelope ‖ この手紙, いくら**切手**を貼ったらいい? What's the *postage* for this letter? (➤ postage は「郵便料金」) ‖ **80円切手**を5枚ください Five *eighty-yen stamps*, please. (● Give me five eighty-yen stamps. とすると「～をくれ」と言

っているように響いて不適当）‖趣味は切手収集です My hobby is *stamp collecting* [*collecting stamps*].

-きっての ▶彼は学校きっての俊足だ He is *the fastest runner in the whole school.*

き

[1]**きっと** sure(ly), certain(ly)（➤ 前者のほうが主観的で，よりインフォーマル）; be bound to do（きっと…する）→必ず ▶彼はきっと来るでしょう He *is sure* [*is bound*] *to* come. ／*I'm sure* he will come. ／He will *surely* [*certainly*] come. ／It's *certain* that he will come. ‖それはきっと本当のことだ It is *undoubtedly* true. ‖彼女はきっと昼前には家を出たはずだ She *must* have left home before noon. ‖心配しなくても，おばあちゃんはきっと今頃は天国で幸せに暮らしているわよ Don't worry—Grandma *must* be living happily in Heaven. ‖ぼくたちはきっと出会う運命だったんだよ *I believe* we were meant to meet.（➤ be meant /ment/ to do は「…する運命にある」）.
▶今夜きっと電話します I'll call you up this evening *for sure*. ‖きっと約束を忘れないでくれよ *Make sure* you don't forget your promise. ／*Be sure* not to forget your promise. ‖ 対話 「借りた金，あした返すよ」「きっとだぞ」"I'll pay you back tomorrow." "*You'd better.* ／*You better be sure* (*to*).

[2]**きっと** ▶先生は生徒たちがおしゃべりをやめないので，きっとにらんだ The teacher *glared at* the students because they wouldn't stop talking.

キット a kit ▶救急用具キット a first-aid *kit*.

きつね 狐 a fox ▶キツネの毛皮 *fox* fur.
▶《慣用表現》死んだはずの人がひょっこり姿を現したので，みんなきつねにつままれたような(＝めんくらった)顔をした Everybody *looked baffled* when the man, who was supposed to be dead, suddenly showed up. ‖**きつね色** light [golden] brown ‖**きつねそば** soba noodles with fried tofu and leek ‖**きつねの嫁入り** a sun shower（天気雨）‖**きつね火** a will-o'-the-wisp.

きっぱり flatly（断固として）; definitely（明確に）
▶「私は無関係よ」と彼女はきっぱりと言った She said *flatly*, "I have nothing to do with it." ‖そんな不当な要求はきっぱり断るべきだ You should refuse such unreasonable demands *point-blank*.（➤ point-blank は「あからさまに」の意）‖こんな頭の痛くなるようなごたごたはきっぱり片をつけたい I would like to put an end to such annoying hassles *once and for all*.（➤ once and for all は「これを最後に」）.

[1]**きっぷ 切符** a ticket ▶大阪までの切符 *a ticket* to Osaka ‖コンサートの切符 *a ticket* for the concert ‖切符を拝見します *Tickets*, please! ‖《掲示》切符の無い方は入場できません Admission by *Ticket* Only. ‖**切符売り場**《米》a ticket office,《英》a booking office ; a box office（劇場などの）‖**往復切符** a round-trip ticket,《英また》a return (ticket) ‖**片道切符** a one-way ticket,《英また》a single (ticket).

[2]**きっぷ 気っ風** ▶うちの部長はきっぷがいい Our manager is *frank and generous*.（➤「ざっくばらんで寛大だ」の意）.

きっぽう 吉報 good news ▶それは吉報だ That's *good news*.

きづまり 気詰まり ▶（話していて）気詰まりな人 a person who *is not easy* to talk to ‖みんな黙ってばかりで，何か気詰まりだなぁ I *feel ill at ease* with nobody talking.

きつもん 詰問 (a) cross-examination（➤ 法律用語としては「反対尋問」の意でもある）**一動** **詰問する** cross-examine ＋目 ▶彼女が遅く帰宅すると，父親は彼女に詰問した Her father *cross-examined* [*grilled* ／*interrogated*] her when she came home late.（➤ grill はくだけた語，interrogate は堅い語）.

[1]**きてい 規定・規程** a rule（規則）; a regulation（正式に決めた規則）▶倫理規定 [規程] ethics *rules* [*regulations*] ‖規定に従う observe the *rules* ‖規定の書式 (a) *prescribed* form ‖規定の(＝正規の)制服 a *regulation* uniform.
▶彼はキセル乗車が見つかり，規定の 3 倍の料金を取られた They caught him cheating on his fare, so (according to the rules,) he had to pay a fine amounting to *three times the regular fare*.

[2]**きてい 既定** ▶既定の(＝動かぬ)事実 an *established* fact ‖既定の(＝あらかじめ決められた)方針 a *prearranged* plan.

ぎてい 義弟 a (younger) brother-in-law [複 brothers-in-law].

ぎていしょ 議定書 a protocol.

きてき 汽笛 a (steam) whistle ▶船が汽笛を鳴らして港を出ていった The ship blew *a whistle* and left the port.

[1]**きてん 機転** quick wit(s) ; cleverness（巧妙さ）; tact（人を怒らせない）▶機転の利く [利かない] 人 a *quick-witted* [*slow-witted*] person ／a person who *has quick* [*slow*] *wits* ‖機転のきいた返事 a *tactful* reply ‖少年の機転でその女の子は溺れずに済んだ The boy's *quick action* saved the girl from drowning. ‖彼女はとっさの機転で浮気をうまくごまかした Her *cleverness* enabled her to cover up her affairs.

[2]**きてん 起点** the starting point ▶東北本線の起点は東京だ The Tohoku Main Line *starts from* Tokyo.

きと 帰途 ▶学校からの帰途ぼくは偶然その事故を見た I happened to see the accident *on my way home* from school. ‖2 週間の公式訪問の旅を終えて皇太子様は帰途に就いた The Crown Prince *is on his way home* after his two-week official visit.

きど 輝度 brightness.

きどあいらく 喜怒哀楽 ▶健太は喜怒哀楽(＝感情)を顔に出さない Kenta does not show his *emotions* (on his face).

きとう 祈禱 a prayer /preəʳ/
‖**祈とう師** a faith healer（信仰療法の）; a shaman（シャーマニズムの）; an exorcist /éksɔːʳsɪst/（悪魔ばらい師）‖**祈とう書** a prayer book.

[1]**きどう 軌道** an orbit ▶ロケットを軌道に乗せる put a rocket into *orbit* ‖《慣用表現》この仕事が軌道に乗るのに 2 年かかった It took me two years to *get* this business *on track* [*underway*]. ‖その計画は全く軌道に乗らなかった The plan *never got off the ground*.（➤ get off the ground は「離陸する」が原義）.

[2]**きどう 起動**《コンピュータ》boot, startup ▶コンピュータを起動する *boot up* [*start* (*up*)] a computer ‖コンピュータを再起動する *reboot* [*restart*] a computer（➤「再起動」は reboot または restart）.

[3]**きどう 気道** airways, the respiratory tract.

きどうたい 機動隊 (the) riot police, a riot squad.

きどうりょく 機動力 mobility ▶その会社は人数は少ないが機動力と若さを誇っている The company has only a small staff, but (it) takes pride in its *mobility* and youthfulness.

ぎとぎと ▶手が油でぎとぎとしている My hands *are slicked* [*are glistening*] *with oil*.

[1]**きとく 危篤** ▶おじが危篤だとの知らせが昨夜入った I

learned last night that my uncle *was in critical condition* [*was seriously ill*].

2**きとく 奇特** ▶道で拾った小銭入れを警察に届けるとは奇特な人もいるものだ What a *commendable* person he is to have handed over to the police the coin purse he found on the street!

きどく 既読 (already) read /red/ ▶彼女にメッセージを送ったが, 既読スルー[無視]された I sent a message to her, but she *ignored* it [me].

きとくけん 既得権 vested rights ▶どの国も領海に対しては既得権を有している Each country has *vested rights* to its territorial waters.

-きどり -気取り ▶あの2人は夫婦気取りだ They *act as if they were married.* / They *act like husband* [*man*] *and wife.* ‖ 彼は学者気取りだ He *poses as* [*pretends to be*] *a scholar.* ‖ 自分の詩が入選して妹はもう詩人気取りだ My sister *considers* [*fancies*] *herself* (*to be*) *a poet* now that her poem placed in the poetry contest.

きどる 気取る be affected; put on airs (お高く止まる) ▶彼は気取らない性格なのでみんなに好かれる Everyone likes him because he *doesn't put on airs.* ‖ 彼女はいつも気取った物の言い方をする She always speaks *affectedly* [*in an affected way*]. ‖ おまえは気取り過ぎるぞ You're *too prim and proper.* ‖ 彼はワイン通を気取っている He is a *wine snob.* ‖ たまに公園でスケッチするだけなのに, 彼はいっぱしの画家を気取っている He likes to *think of himself as* a full-fledged painter, though in fact, all he does is sometimes sketch in the park. (→かっこつける).

‖ 気取り屋 an affected person.

きない 機内 ▶機内での携帯電話のご使用はご遠慮ください Please refrain from using cellphones *on the plane* [*during the flight*]. ‖ 機内で昼食[軽食]が出ます A lunch [snack] will be served *in flight.* 《参考》機内で突然逆上して, 乗務員や他の乗客に対して暴力行為に及んだり, 暴言を吐いたりすることは air rage という. ‖ 機内映画 an in-flight movie ‖ 機内サービス in-flight service ‖ 機内食 an in-flight meal ‖ 機内販売 in-flight sales ‖ 機内持ち込み荷物 carry-on baggage (➤ 総称).

きなが 気長 ▶結婚はぴったりの相手が現れるまで気長に待ったほうがいい You'd better *be patient* and wait for the right person (to appear) when you marry. ‖ そんなに焦らずに気長に構えようよ Don't be so impatient; *take it easy.*

きなくさい きな臭い ▶家の中へ入ったとたん何かきな臭い臭いがした I smelled *something burning* (just) as I came into the house. ‖ また中東情勢がきな臭くなってきた The Middle East situation has become *touchy* [*liable to explode*] again.

きなこ きな粉 soy flour.

きにいる 気に入る like +目 (好きだ), be pleased 《with》(心にかなっている) ▶気に入っていただいてよかったわ I'm glad you *like* it. ‖ 私は彼のことがたちまち気に入った I *liked* him from the very first. ‖ 対話「小野さんたちは毎年夏に軽井沢に行くのよ」「よほどあちらが気に入っているんだね」"The Onos go to Karuizawa every summer." "They must *like it there* very much." ‖ きみの正直なところがとても気に入ったよ I *am* very *pleased with* your honesty. ‖ 彼の話し方が気に入らない I *don't like* the way he talks. ‖ 敬三は先生に気に入られようと努めた Keizo tried to *please* the teacher.

きにする 気にする worry 《about》(気に病む); mind +目, care +目 (➤ ともに主に否定文・疑問文で用いる; don't mind が「かまわない, 気にならない」に対し, don't care は「どうでもいい, 関心がない」) ▶彼の言ったことなんか気にするな Don't *worry about* [Don't *mind*] what he said. / Don't *be too concerned about* what he said. ‖ きみに何を言われても気にしないよ I *don't care* what you say about me. ‖ 対話「ゆうべは電話しないでごめんなさい」「気にしないで」"I'm sorry I didn't call you last night." "*That's OK.* / *No problem.*" (➤「お気になさらないでください」と丁寧に言うのなら "That's quite all right." となる) ‖ 対話「ご援助どうもありがとうございました」「なに, 気にしないでいいよ」"Thank you very much for your help." "Oh, *don't mention it.* / Oh, *think nothing of it.*" ‖ 彼に髪の毛の話をしたらだめだよ. とても気にしているから Don't mention his hair—he's very *sensitive* about it.

きになる 気になる care, mind (➤ ともに主に否定文・疑問文で用いる; →気にする); be concerned [worried] 《about》(心配している) ▶人が何と言おうとぼくは全然気にならないね People can say what they like. I *don't care at all.* (➤ I don't give a hoot. としてもよい) ‖ あすの天気が気になる I'*m concerned* [*worried*] *about* tomorrow's weather. ‖ ちえみのことでちょっと気になるうわさを聞いたわよ I heard a rather *disturbing* [*unsettling*] rumor about Chiemi. (「気になる」を「心をかき乱す(ような)」と考えれば前者を, 「人を不安にさせる(ような)」と考えれば後者をそれぞれ用いて訳すとよい) ‖ 今晩は食事を作る気にならない I do*n't feel like cooking* this evening.

きにゅう 記入 (an) entry 一動 記入する write down; enter +目 (宿帳や帳簿などに); fill out, fill in (用紙に必要事項を) ▶彼はすべての支出を手帳に記入した He *wrote down* all his expenses in his notebook. ‖ 訪問者名簿にお名前とご住所をご記入ください Please *enter* your name and address in the visitors' book. ‖ この用紙に必要事項を記入してください Please *fill in* [*fill out*] this form. ‖ この日記帳にはその日のことは何も記入されてない *There is no entry* for that day in this diary.

きぬ 絹 silk ▶絹のハンカチ a *silk* handkerchief.

‖ 絹糸 silk thread ‖ 絹織物 silk fabrics.

きぬけ 気抜け ▶いよいよとなって彼女が旅行に一緒に行かないと言いだしたので気抜けしてしまった I *felt* very *let down* when she said at the last moment she would not go on the trip with me. (➤ be let down で「がっかりする」).

きぬごし 絹ごし(豆腐) silken tofu.

きぬさや 絹さや young podded peas, young snow peas.

きね 杵 *kine*; a wooden mallet to pound steamed rice in an usu (mortar) (➤ 説明的な訳).

ギネスせかいきろく ギネス世界記録 the Guinness World Records (➤『ギネスブック』から改名).

きねん 記念

commemoration 一動 記念する commemorate +目 一形 記念の commemorative ▶学校の創立50周年記念日 the 50th *anniversary* of the founding of a school (➤ anniversary は「年ごとの記念日」) ‖ 我々は卒業記念に松の木を校庭に植えた We planted a pine tree on the campus *in commemoration of our graduation.* ‖ 3年2組全員で校庭に出て記念撮影をした Everyone in 3rd grade homeroom 2 gathered in the schoolyard to *take a class picture.*

▶退職する先生に記念の品を買う buy *a memento* for

き

a retiring teacher(➤ memento は「思い出となる品」) ‖記念にレストランの紙ナプキンをもらって帰った I brought home a paper napkin from the restaurant *as a souvenir*. ‖その詩人を記念して湖畔に像が建てられた A statue was erected by the lake *in memory* [*honor*] *of* the poet. ‖『羅生門』は日本映画史上記念すべき名作だ The movie "Rashomon" is *commemorated* [is *remembered*] as one of Japan's greatest films.

✉ **あなたがくださった人形はメキシコ旅行の良い記念です** The doll you gave me is *a* lovely *souvenir* [*memento* ／ *keepsake*] of my trip to Mexico. ‖**記念切手** a commemorative stamp ‖**記念コイン** a commemorative coin ‖**記念祭** a memorial festival, a commemoration, an anniversary ‖**記念写真** a souvenir picture [snapshot] (旅行などの) ‖**記念碑** a monument.

ぎねん 疑念 (a) **doubt**(不信)；(a) **suspicion**(…であるという疑い) ▶きみたちが自分たちのコーチの行動に疑念を抱くのは当然だ It is quite natural that you *have doubts* about your coach's behavior. ‖刑事は直感的に殺人事件ではないかという疑念をもった The detective *had* an instinctive *suspicion* [instinctively *suspected*] that it might have been a murder.

[1]**きのう 昨日** **yesterday** ▶きのうは 3 月11日だった *Yesterday* was March 11. ／It was March 11 *yesterday*. ‖きのう渋谷で夏子に会った I saw Natsuko in Shibuya *yesterday*. (➤ 時を表す副詞(句)は場所を表す副詞(句)よりあとにくる) ‖この展覧会はきのうから始まっているのよ. そのうち見にいきましょうよ This exhibition *started yesterday* [has been *open since yesterday*]. Why don't we go see it some time? ‖きのうの夕方は風が強かった It was very windy *last* [*yesterday*] *evening*. (「きのうの夜」の場合は last night であって, yesterday night とはいわないのがふつう. night の一部に today が含まれているからである) ‖きのうの朝彼は東京をたった He left Tokyo *yesterday morning*. ‖きのうの地震怖かったね *Yesterday's* earthquake was scary, wasn't it? ‖きのうの新聞でその事件を知った I learned of the event in *yesterday's newspaper*.

▶《スピーチで》勤続30年になりますが, 入社したのはついきのうのことのような気がします I have been working (here) for thirty years (now), but *it seems only yesterday* that I joined the company.

[2]**きのう 機能** a **function** 一動 **機能する function, work** ▶脳の機能 brain *function* ‖このツボを刺激すると肝臓の機能を高める効果があります Pressing these points will serve to enhance your liver *function*. ‖彼はバイクの事故で右腕の機能を失った He *lost the use of* his right arm in a motorcycle accident. (➤「身体の機能を失う」は lose the use of を用いるのがふつう) ‖今や苦情委員会は十分に機能していない The complaints committee *isn't functioning* [*working*] adequately now. ‖市全体が大停電のため機能不全に陥った The entire city *was crippled* by the massive power outage. ‖最近の分譲マンションは機能的にできている Condominiums nowadays are built *with function in mind*. (➤ with ... in mind は「…のことを考えて」)

‖**機能訓練指導員** a functional training instructor ‖**機能障害** (a) functional disorder ／dysfunction.

[3]**きのう 帰納** **induction**(➤「演繹(えんえき)」は deduction) 一形 **帰納的な inductive** 一動 **帰納する induce** +⑪ ‖**帰納法** induction, the inductive method.

ぎのう 技能 (a) **skill**(技術)；(a) **technique** /tekníːk/ (技巧) ▶技能を習得する[開発する／磨く] acquire [develop ／hone] *a skill* ‖英語の 4 技能を磨く improve one's four English *skills* (➤ speaking, listening, reading, writing のこと) ‖コンピュータの技能を生かせる職業に就きたい I'd like to get a job where I can utilize my computer *skills*. ‖その力士は技能賞を獲得した The sumo wrestler won *the Technical Prize*. ‖**技能オリンピック** an international vocational training competition ‖**技能検定**(**検査**) skill [proficiency] examination (➤ examination の代わりに test でもよい).

きのこ 茸 a **mushroom** /mʌ́ʃruːm/ ▶その木の根元にはキノコがびっしり生えていた *Mushrooms* clustered thickly at the base of the tree. ‖秋はキノコ狩りが楽しい Autumn is the time to enjoy *mushroom-gathering*. ‖**きのこ雲** a mushroom cloud.

きのどく 気の毒 **1【かわいそう】be sorry,**《インフォーマル》**be too bad**

【文型】
人(A)を気の毒に思う
be [feel] sorry for A
…して気の毒に思っている
be sorry to do
～とはお気の毒です
I'm sorry (that) S + V.
It's too bad (that) S + V.

▶ご病気とはお気の毒です *I am sorry* (*to hear*) *that* you are sick. (➤ to hear は人づてに聞いた場合) ‖この不景気で失業した人たちは本当にお気の毒です *I feel really sorry for* people who have lost their jobs in this recession. ‖途中で車がパンクしたとは気の毒だ *It's too bad* [*unfortunate*] *that* you got a flat tire on your way. ‖対話「昨年, 家が火事に遭いまして」「**それはお気の毒です**」"My house was burned down last year." "*I'm* (*very*) *sorry to hear that*. ／*That's really unfortunate*."

▶その選手がベンチに下げられたのは気の毒だよ *It's regrettable* [*a shame* ／*a pity*] *that* the player was benched. (➤ It's a pity は「…とはかわいそう」) ‖対話「今度の正月は休めないんだ」「何と気の毒な」"I can't take off anytime during the coming New Year holidays." "*What a bummer!*" (➤ bummer はインフォーマルで「まずいこと, 困ったこと」の意) ‖あんな前途有望な青年がそんなに若くして亡くなるとは気の毒だ *It's tragic that* such a promising young man should die so young. (深刻な内容なので, It's a pity や It's too bad では合わない) ‖彼女は本当に気の毒な人です I *feel* so *sorry for* her. ／She is indeed *an unfortunate* [*a pitiable*] woman.

▶私はその少年を気の毒に思い500円やった I gave the boy 500 yen *out of pity*. ‖我々は雨の中を 1 人で歩いている人を見て気の毒に思い, 最寄りの町まで車に乗せてあげた We *took pity on* a man walking alone in the rain and gave him a ride to the nearest town. ‖彼の娘は気の毒に交通事故で死んだ His *poor* daughter was killed in a traffic accident. (➤ この poor は「不運な」の意で, 日本語では「不運にも, かわいそうに, 気の毒に」などと副詞的な言い方になる).

✉ **おじいさまが亡くなられたとのこと, お気の毒に存じます** *I'm very sorry to hear that* your grandfather (has) passed away. (➤ くだけた言い

方）／I'd like to *express my condolences on* your grandfather's passing.（➤改まったときの決まり文句；→お悔やみ）.

2【すまない】be sorry ▶こんな寒い中を待ってもらって，気の毒なことをしたね *I'm really sorry to* have kept you waiting in this cold weather.

きのぼり 木登りをする climb a tree.

きのみきのまま 着のみ着のまま ▶突然の出火で我々は家から着のみ着のままで逃げ出した The sudden fire sent us out of the house *with nothing but the clothes on our backs*.

きのめ 木の芽 a **bud** ▶木の芽が顔を出す季節になった It is now the season when new *buds* appear.

きのり 気乗り ▶彼女は久米氏との結婚には気乗り薄らしい She seems to *be reluctant* to marry Mr. Kume.‖久美子は気乗りのしない返事をした Kumiko gave a *half-hearted* answer.（➤half-hearted は「不熱心な」）‖対話「ハイキングに参加しないの？」「うん，どうも気乗りがしなくて」"Aren't you going on the hike?" "No, I'*m not particularly interested in* going."

1**きば 牙** a **tusk**（象・イノシシなどの）; a **fang**（蛇・犬などの）▶牙をむき出す bare its *teeth* [*fangs*]‖セイウチは大きな牙を持っている Walruses have large *tusks*.

2**きば 騎馬 horseback riding** ‖騎馬警官 a mounted police officer‖騎馬戦 a mock chivalry battle‖騎馬民族 a horse-riding, nomadic people.

1**きはく 気迫 drive**（積極性）; **spirit**（気概）; **verve**（表現意欲）▶気迫に満ちたプレー *spirited* play‖きょうの明大チームには気迫が感じられなかった The players of the Meidai team seemed to be lacking (in) *drive* [*enthusiasm*] today.‖ゴッホの絵には気迫が籠もっている Van Gogh's paintings *are full of verve* [*energy*].／Van Gogh's paintings *are powerful* [*bold*].

2**きはく 希薄な thin** ▶その山の頂上は空気が希薄だった The air on the top of the mountain was *thin*.‖彼は自分の力でやろうという意欲が希薄だ He shows *little* enthusiasm for doing things by himself.

きばく 起爆 ‖起爆装置 a detonating device.

きはずかしい 気恥ずかしい ▶彼はひどく不作法なので付き合っていて気恥ずかしい思いをする He is so ill-mannered I *am embarrassed* to associate with him.

きはつ 揮発 ▶揮発性の高い油 a *highly volatile* /váːləṭl/ oil.

きばつ 奇抜な novel（目新しい）; **eccentric**（ひどく変わった）▶奇抜な思いつき a *novel* idea‖奇抜な衣装 *eccentric* clothes.

きばむ 黄ばむ turn yellow, yellow ▶黄ばんだパンツ *yellowed* underpants‖古いアルバムの写真が年月を経て黄ばんできた The photos in my old album *have yellowed* [*have become yellowish*] with age.

きばらし 気晴らし relaxation（息抜き）; a **change of pace**（何かを続けてやったあとの気分転換）; a **pastime**（慰み）; **recreation**（娯楽）▶ぼくは気晴らしによく旅に出かける I often go on trips *for relaxation* [*for a change*].（➤for a change は「ふだんと変えて，たまには」, for a change of pace は「何かを続けたので気分転換に」）‖私は気晴らしに漫画を読む I read comic books *to relax* [*for a change of pace*].‖絵を描くことはいい気晴らしになる Painting is a good *pastime*.‖きみは根を詰めて働き過ぎる. たまには気晴らしも必要だよ You are working too hard. You have to *relax and enjoy life* sometimes too.

きばる 気張る show off（かっこよく見せる）▶彼女の手前，気張って高価なランチを注文した I wanted to *show off* in front of my girlfriend, so I ordered an expensive lunch.

きはん 規範 a **standard**（標準）; a **model**（手本）▶若者にとって行動の規範が無いことは危険だ It is dangerous for young people to have no *standard(s) of behavior* to follow.

1**きばん 基盤 the basis**; a **foundation**（土台；「どっしりとした」というニュアンスが濃い）▶外国貿易がわが国の経済の基盤である Foreign trade forms *the basis* of our economy.‖会長がわが社の今日の基盤を作った Our chairman laid the *foundation* for what our company is today.（➤laid は lay（敷く）の過去形）‖上京して5年，青年はようやく生活の基盤を固めた Five years after he came to Tokyo, the young man is finally *making a stable* [*secure*] *living*.

2**きばん 機番** a **machine** [**an equipment**] **number.**

きひ 忌避する avoid ＋㊐ ▶徴兵を忌避する *avoid* [*dodge*] the draft ‖徴兵忌避者 a draft dodger.

1**きび 機微 subtleties** /sʌ́ṭltiz/（微妙な点）; **niceties** /náɪsəṭiz/（微細な点）▶これは人情の機微をうまくとらえた小説である This is a good novel which well describes the *subtleties of human nature*.

2**きび 黍 millet** ‖きびだんご a millet dumpling.

きびき 忌引 ▶（3日間の）忌引をとる *take* (three days of) *bereavement* [*compassionate*] *leave*‖彼女はきょうは忌引で欠席です She is *absent* today *on account of the death of a family member*.

きびきび ▶ぼくは彼女のきびきびした話し方が好きだ I like her *crisp* manner of speaking.（➤crisp は「歯切れのよい」）‖若い人がきびきび働く姿を見るのはいいものだ It is nice to see young people working so *briskly*.

きびしい 厳しい

1【厳格な】strict, severe /sɪvíəʳ/（➤後者は極めて強い意味の語で，人の性格についていう場合は前者が好まれる）; **stern**（妥協を許さない）; **harsh**（理不尽な，容赦のない）; **rigorous**（過酷で苦痛を感じるほど）; **grim**（不機嫌な，表情が深刻で近づきがたい）▶厳しい規則 *strict* [*draconian*] rules（➤draconian は法律やそれに基づく締め付けが「極めて厳しい，過酷な」）‖厳しい処罰 a *severe* punishment‖厳しい（顔の）裁判官 a *stern*(*-faced*) judge（➤stern はいささかも容赦しない厳しさをいう）‖厳しい顔で with a *grim* face‖亜紀の母はしつけが厳しい Aki's mother is very *strict* about manners.‖岸先生は大変厳しい先生です Mr. Kishi is a very *strict* [*demanding*／*harsh*] teacher.（➤strict はしばしば敬意を持たれる厳しさをいう. demanding は「要求することが厳しい」, harsh は「過度に厳しい」）‖父は子供に大変厳しかった My father *was* very *severe with* [*hard on*] his children.‖海兵隊の訓練は厳しい Training in the Marines is *rigorous*.
▶警察は選挙違反者に厳しい態度で臨むと言明した The police declared that they would *take a tough stance* toward election violators.‖対話「きみのこの写真，よく撮れてるけど，ちょっとアングルが悪いね」「キビシイなあ！」"This is a good picture, but I think you could have improved the angle of the shot." "Gee, you *always find something to criticize*."（➤「いつでも何かけちをつけるね」の意）.

2【ひどい，激しい】severe（被害・損害が予測される）; **harsh**（過酷な）; **brutal**（残酷なほど）▶北海道の冬は厳しい We have *severe* [*harsh*／*brutal*] winters in Hokkaido.（➤brutal は気候が「情け容赦なく痛めつける」）‖サボテンは厳しい環境に生きている Cactuses survive in a *harsh* environment. ‖ きょうは暑さが厳しい It's *very hot* today. ／Today is a *scorcher*. (➤ scorcher は「焼けつくように暑い日」).

3【困難である】difficult；《インフォーマル》**grim**(状況などが) ▶父が失業して生活が厳しくなった My father lost his job and we *were having a hard time making ends meet*. (➤ make ends meet は「何とか家計のやりくりをする」) ‖ 競争が激しいから来年の大学入試は厳しいぞ The competition is so tough that next year's college entrance examinations will be *very difficult*. ‖ 日本経済の見通しはますます厳しい The outlook for the Japanese economy *is becoming increasingly grim*.

きびす 踵 ▶きびすを返す *turn on* one's *heel* ／*turn back*.

キビタキ《鳥》a **narcissus flycatcher**.

きびょう 奇病 a **mysterious disease**(謎の病気).

きひん 気品 grace, class(➤ 後者はインフォーマルな語) ▶その女優にはもって生まれた気品がある That actress was born with *graceful* manners. ‖ 彼女のお母さんは本当に気品がある Her mother certainly has *class*. ‖ 彼にはどことなく気品がある There is *something refined* about him. (➤ refined は「洗練された」).

きびん 機敏な quick(反応が速い)；**prompt**(間を置かない) ▶機敏な行動 a *quick* action ‖ きみはもっと機敏な処置をとるべきだった You should have *acted* more *promptly*. ‖ 太ってはいるが彼は動作が機敏だ Even though he is overweight, he has *quick* [*good*] *reflexes*. (➤「反射神経がよい」の意).

きひんしつ 貴賓室 a **room for distinguished** [**honored**] **guests**；a **royal suite** /swiːt/ (➤ 後者は「王族[皇族]用特別室」).

きひんせき 貴賓席 a **royal box, seats for dignitaries** (➤ dignitary は「高位の人」).

きふ 寄付 (a) **contribution**；(a) **donation** (➤「寄付金」の意味ではともに a がつく) **一動 寄付する contribute** /kəntríbjuːt/ ＋㊐, **donate** ＋㊐

> **《解説》contribution** は「ほかの人たちと一緒に寄付すること, 献金などに一役買うこと」という含みで用いることが多く, ときに「持てる者が持たざる者にしてやること」という含みが生じることがある. これに対して, **donation** は「純粋に善意から出たもので見返りを求めないこと」という含みを持つ宗教色のある語.

▶資産家はその学校に100万円を寄付した The wealthy man *contributed* [*made a contribution of*] a million yen to the school. ‖ 彼は退職後, 学校の図書館に蔵書をすべて寄付した He *gave* all his books to the school library after his retirement. ‖ この体育館は町の有志の寄付金で維持されている The gymnasium is maintained by voluntary *contributions* from town residents. ‖ 彼らは被災者を救うために寄付金を募った They raised *contributions* [*donations*] to help the disaster victims.

ぎふ 義父 a **father-in-law** 《参考》「継父」は stepfather,「養父」は foster father という.

ギブアップ ギブアップする give up.

ギブアンドテイク

> **危ないカタカナ語✸ ギブアンドテイク**
> **1** 相手に利益を与え, 自分も相手から利益を得ることを「ギブアンドテイク」と言うが, 英語の give-and-take は双方が歩み寄って相手の希望［意見］をとり入れることを指し, 意味が異なる.
> **2** 日本語の「ギブアンドテイク」の意味を伝えるには, interdependence, mutual dependence (ともに「相互依存」の意)などを用いる.

きふう 気風 a (**character**) **trait** ▶関西人の気風 *character traits* of people in the Kansai district ‖ 土地の気風 the *distinctive atmosphere* of a place ／the *spirit of* a place.

きふく 起伏 ups and downs ▶起伏のある平原 a *rolling* plain ‖ 起伏に富む地形 *hilly* [*up-and-down*] terrain.

きぶくれ 着膨れ ▶上着を着ると着膨れして見える My jacket *makes* me *look fat*. ‖ 冬の電車は着膨れした人たちで混み合っている In winter, trains are crowded with people *bundled in heavy clothes* [*wearing heavy layers of clothes*].

きふじん 貴婦人 a **lady**.

ギプス a (**plaster**) **cast** ▶彼は右足を骨折し, 今ギプスをしている He broke his right leg and has it in *a cast*.

きぶつ 器物 ‖器物破損 property damage.

ギフト a **gift ‖ギフト券** [カード] 《米》a gift certificate, 《英》a gift token [voucher /váʊtʃəʳ/] ‖ **ギフトショップ** a gift shop.

きふるす 着古す wear out (**clothes**) ▶着古した衣服 *worn out* clothes.

きぶん 気分 1【体調からくる気持ち】

> **【文型】**
> 気分が…だ
> **feel** A
> ➤ A は形容詞(句)

▶きょうはとても[だいぶ]気分がいい I *feel great* [*much better*] today. ‖ かぜをひいて気分がすぐれない I have a cold and do*n't feel well*. ‖ **対話**《病人に》「けさはご気分はいかがですか」「とてもいいです」"*How are you feeling* this morning ?" "Pretty good, thanks." ‖ 気分が悪いので保健室で休ませてもらえますか I *feel sick*. Could I go lie down in the nurse's office ? ‖ 酒が入ると陽気な気分になる人がいる Some people *become cheerful* (*and talkative*) when they get tipsy. ‖ けさ電車に乗っていて気分が悪くなった I *got sick* on the train this morning. ‖ 猫の死体を見たら気分が悪くなった I *felt nauseous* when I saw the carcass of a cat. ‖ ゆうべ飲み過ぎちゃってけさはちょっと気分が悪いんだ I drank too much last night and *am feeling* a little *under the weather* this morning. (➤ under the weather は「体が本調子でない」).

2【心の状態】a mood ▶今は仕事をする気分にならない I am in no *mood* for work [to work]. ／I am not in the *mood* for work [to work]. ‖ **対話**「アイススケートに行かないか？」「だめだよ. そんな気分じゃないんだ」"Why don't we go ice-skating ?" "No, I'm really *not in the mood*." ‖ ひとりで居たい気分だった I *felt like* being alone. ‖ 阪神が優勝して最高の気分だ I *feel great* because the Hanshin Tigers won the pennant. ‖ 無視されたようで気分が悪い I *feel rather upset* because it seems that I have been ignored. ‖ 入試のことを考えると暗い気分になる Just the thought of entrance exams makes me *feel depressed*. ‖ 私は彼の気分を害さないよう気をつけた I was careful not to *hurt* his *feelings*.

▶気分転換にボウリングをしよう Let's go bowling *for a change* (*of pace*). (➤ for a change は「たまには, いつもと違えて」の意で, for a change of pace とすると

「(何かを続けてやったあとで)気晴らしに」の意になる) ‖ 野坂先生は**気分屋**だ Mr. Nosaka is *temperamental* [*a temperamental person*]. / Mr. Nosaka is *a moody person*. ‖ 仕事も半分を越えたから, **気分的にぐっと楽になった** Having finished more than half the job, I *feel much relieved*.

3【雰囲気, 感じ】▶スキーの練習は雪の上でないと**気分が出ない** I *don't feel like* I'm practicing skiing unless I'm actually on (the) snow. ‖ 心配事があると**気分が乗らない**ものだ It*'s hard to get into the mood* [*spirit*] when you have worries. ‖ 町はすっかりお祭り**気分**だった The entire town was in *a festive mood*.

ぎふん 義憤 (righteous) **indignation.**

きへい 騎兵 a **cavalry soldier** ; **the cavalry**(集合的に).

きべん 詭弁 **sophistry** /sá:fɪstri/ ▶核実験の再開は世界平和のためだったというのは全くの**詭弁**だ To say that the resumption of nuclear tests was for world peace was blatant *sophistry*.

きぼ 規模 a **scale** ▶**規模の大きな**計画 a *large-scale* project ‖ わが社は**規模**が小さい Ours is a small (*-scale* / *-size*) company. ‖ **事業規模**を拡大する expand [enlarge] one's *business*(➤「規模」は訳出不要).

☛ **小規模, 大規模** (→見出語)

ぎぼ 義母 a **mother-in-law** 《参考》「継母」は stepmother,「養母」は foster mother.

きほう 気泡 an **air bubble.**

きぼう 希望 **1【期待】**(a) **hope** 一動 **希望する hope** ▶**希望**に生きる live in *hope*(*s*) ‖ **希望**を捨てる give up *hope* ‖ **希望**を抱く cherish *a hope* ‖ 生きている限り**希望**はある While [Where] there is life, there is *hope*. (➤ 英語のことわざ) ‖ わがチームは現在4位だ. しかし優勝の**希望**を捨ててはならない We're in fourth place now, but we mustn't give up *hope* of winning the championship. (➤ hope to win としない) ‖ 由希子は**希望**を失って自殺した Yukiko lost all *hope* and killed herself. ‖ この治療は患者たちに新たな**希望**を与える This treatment offers [gives] renewed *hope* to patients. ‖ 当社は諸君のような**希望**に満ちた人を歓迎します We welcome *hope-filled* people like you.

2【要望】a **demand** ; a **wish**(願望) 一動 **希望する want** ▶オーストラリアに永住したいという**希望**をもっています I *want to* live in Australia permanently. ‖ 佐野君は父親の**希望**に反して音楽家になった Sano became a musician *against* his father's *wishes*. ‖ できるだけご**希望**に添いたいと思います We'd like to *meet* your *wishes* [*demands*] to the best of our ability. ‖ 彼は**希望**の大学に入った He got into the university *of his choice*. ‖ スピーチコンテストへの**参加希望者**はあすまでに申し出ること *Those wishing to participate in* the speech contest are requested to apply by tomorrow. (●「参加希望者」を applicants とすると後出の動詞 apply と意味的に重なるので不適当) ‖ **対話**「息子さんが将来どんな人になることを**希望**していますか」「国際的視野をもった人間になってくれるよう**希望**します」 "What kind of person do you *want* your son to become in the future ?" "I *hope* he'll be an internationally-minded person."

▶それは**希望的観測**にすぎない That's just *wishful thinking*. ‖ メーカーの**希望小売価格** the manufacturer's *recommended retail price*.

ぎほう 技法 a **technique.**

きぼり 木彫り **wood carving** ▶**木彫り**の面 a *wooden mask* / a mask *carved in wood*.

きほん 基本 a **basis** ; **(the) basics** (土台) ; **(the) fundamentals** (基礎的事項) 一形 **基本の basic, fundamental** ▶料理の**基本** *the fundamentals* of cooking ‖ **基本原理** a *basic* principle ‖ **基本原則** a *basic* rule ‖ **基本方針**を決める set [formulate] *basic policies* ‖ 観察が科学の**基本**だ Observation is *the basis* of science. ‖ もう一度**基本**から英語を始めよう Let's get back to *the basics* of English. / Let's learn English from *the basics* [*the ABCs*] again. ‖ まず学ぶべきは**基本**に忠実な演奏だ The first thing to learn is to give a performance *faithful to fundamentals*.

‖ **基本的人権** fundamental human rights ‖ **基本料金**(タクシー・ガス・電気などの) the basic rate.

ぎまい 義妹 a **(younger) sister-in-law** [複 **sisters-in-law**].

きまえ 気前 ▶**気前のいい**人 a *generous* person ‖ 祐二は**気前よく**仲間に夕食をごちそうしてやった Yuji *generously* treated his friends to dinner. ‖ 銀行家は母校に**気前よく**寄付した The banker donated *generously* to his alma mater. ‖ 兄は**気前よく**金を使い過ぎる My brother spends money *too freely* (on others). (➤ on others はおごったり, プレゼントしたりなど, ほかの人のことで金を使う場合).

きまぐれ 気まぐれ (a) **caprice** /kəprí:s/ ; (a) **whim** (出来心) 一形 **気まぐれな capricious** /kəprí∫əs/, **whimsical** /hwímzɪkəl/ ; **temperamental**(気分屋の) ▶**気まぐれな**男 a *capricious* [*whimsical*] man ‖ **気まぐれな**天気 *changeable* weather ‖ 偉大な芸術家はその多くが**気まぐれ**だ Many great artists are *temperamental*. ‖ 弟はほんの**気まぐれ**でその子犬をもらってきたのだ My little brother got that puppy *on a whim*. ‖ 彼女は一時の**気まぐれ**で辞めると言ったのではない She did not say that she would quit *on the spur of the moment*. (➤「時のはずみで, 深く考えもせずに」の意).

きまじめ 生真面目な **serious**(真剣・深刻に考える) ; **earnest**(ある目的のために熱心な) ▶**生真面目な**人 a *serious* [*an earnest*] person ‖ 彼は一見**生真面目**だがなかなかユーモアがある He looks *serious*, but he has a good sense of humor.

きまずい 気まずい **awkward** /ɔ́:kwəʳd/ ▶一瞬, 2人の間に**気まずい**空気が流れた There was a moment of *awkwardness* between the two. ‖ ちょっとした行き違いで2人の仲が**気まずくなった** Their relationship *has soured* [*gone sour*] due to a small misunderstanding. ‖ 会合は**気まずい**雰囲気で始まった The meeting began on *a sour note*. (➤ sour の代わりに high を用いると「盛り上がった」).

きまつ 期末 **the end of a term** [**semester**](➤ semester は2学期制の場合 ; term は数に関係なく「学期」)

‖ **期末試験** a term [an end of term] exam(ination) / a final exam(ination) (➤ 後者は学期に分かれていない試験の場合).

きまって 決まって ▶父は**決まって**5時に目を覚ます My father *always* wakes up at five. ‖ 私が金を持っているときに限って彼は**決まって**現れる *It never fails* – the minute I get some money he shows up, but I never see him otherwise. ‖ じゃんけんをすると**決まって**負ける I lose *whenever* I play rock-paper-scissors with someone.

きまま 気まま ▶**気ままな**人 a person who does *as he* [*she*] *pleases* / a *selfish* [*willful*] person(➤ selfish は「自分勝手な」, willful は「我を通す」) ‖ **気ままな**ライフスタイル one's *freewheeling* lifestyle ‖ 彼

き

女はいつも気ままにふるまう She always acts *as she pleases*. (➤「好きなように」の意) ‖ 一度でいいから気ままな旅をしてみたい I wish I could just once *travel wherever I please*. ／Just for once, I wish I could *take a trip to any place I please*. ‖ 息子がだめになったのは気ままに育てたせいだ My son became spoiled because I brought him up *letting* him *have his own way*. (➤「思いどおりにさせる」の意).

きまり 決まり **1【決着】**▶よし，それで話は決まりだ OK. *It's a deal*.

2【規則】 **a rule**；**a regulation**（公的規約）▶決まりに従う follow the *rules* ‖ 決まりを破る break the *rules* ‖ 学校へいくら寄付しなければならないという決まりはありません There is no *fixed rule* about how much you should donate to the school.

3【定例】▶来客にはまず抹茶を出すのがわが家の決まりだ It's *our family tradition* to serve guests powdered green tea before anything else.

☛ **お決まり**（→見出語）

きまりがわるい きまりが悪い **feel awkward**（落ち着かない，ぎこちなく感じる）；**be embarrassed**（困惑する）▶自分の妻に「愛している」なんて言うのはきまりが悪い I *would feel awkward* [*embarrassed*] saying "I love you" to my wife. ‖ 和雄は花束をもって電車に乗り込むときは少々きまりが悪かった Kazuo *felt* a little *embarrassed* when he got on the train with a bouquet in his hand.

きまりきった 決まり切った **routine** /rùːtíːn/ ▶決まり切った仕事 *routine* work ‖ 決まり切ったやり方 a *stereotyped* [*conventional*] way ‖ 会社では決まり切った仕事ばかりだ I do *the same old thing* every day at the office.

きまりもんく 決まり文句 **a set phrase** [**expression**]；**a cliché** /kliːʃéɪ/（陳腐な）▶彼のエッセーは陳腐な決まり文句でいっぱいだ His essay is full of *clichés*.

きまる 決まる **1【決定する】** **be decided** (**on**)；**be fixed** ▶彼の代わりに私が行くことに決まった It *has been decided* that I should go in his place. ‖ 新しい発電所の敷地はまだ決まっていない The site for the new power plant *has not* yet *been decided* (*on*). ‖ ダンスパーティーは土曜日の晩に決まった The date of the dance *has been fixed* [*scheduled*] for Saturday evening. ／The dance has *been* [*is*] *scheduled* for Saturday evening. ‖ 近藤君が今期の学級委員に決まった（＝選ばれた）Kondo *was chosen* as class representative for this term. ‖ 勝負はあっけなく決まった The game *ended* all too soon.

2【例外なくそうする】▶うちの娘はいつも決まった友だちとしか遊ばない Our daughter only plays with *particular* friends. ‖ 隣家のニワトリは毎朝決まった時刻に鳴く Our next-door neighbor's roosters crow at the *same* time every day.

▶こんなことをしたら父に叱られるに決まっている If I do this, I'm *sure* [I'm *bound*] *to* get a scolding from my father. ‖ 誰だって金は欲しいに決まっている *It goes without saying that* everybody wants money. ‖ そんなの決まってるじゃないか（＝誰でも知ってるさ）*Doesn't everybody know that?* ‖ **対話**「日本一の野球チームは？」「ドラゴンズに決まってるじゃないか」"What's the best baseball team in Japan?" "The Dragons, *of course*!"

3【びしりと落ち着く】▶松坂の150キロのストレートが内角へずばりと決まった Matsuzaka's 150 kph fast ball *hit* the inside of the home plate *precisely*. (➤ kph は kilometers per hour（時速…キロ）の頭文字) ‖ 福見選手の背負い投げが見事に決まった Fukumi *successfully* executed a shoulder throw.

▶彼のきょうの背広，きまってるわね The suit he's wearing today *looks sharp*. (➤ 女性について言うのなら chic でもよい).

☛ **決まって**（→見出語）

ぎまん 欺瞞 (a) **deceit** /dɪsíːt/（うそを真実と思わせること）；a **lie**（うそ）▶この報告は欺まんに満ちている This report is *fraudulent*.

[1]**きみ 君** **you**

> **【解説】** (1) 日本語の二人称は「きみ」「おまえ」「あなた」など多様であるが，標準英語にはただ1つ you があるのみ．しかし，言い方や前後の表現によってある程度のニュアンスを出すことはできる．(2) 英語の you は「きみたち，きみら」の意でもある．

▶きみの住所を教えてくれる Can you tell [give] me *your* address? ‖ きみにはきみの行く道がある *You* have *your* own path to follow. ‖ おいきみ，「立ち入り禁止」の掲示が見えないのか？ *Hey you*! Can't you see the sign, "Keep Out"? (➤ Hey you! はやや乱暴な言い方で，もう少し丁寧な言い方は Excuse me! とか Hello there!).

[2]**きみ 黄身** (a) **yolk** /jóʊk/, **egg yolk**, **yellow** ▶卵の黄身と白身とどちらが好き？ Which do you like better, the white of an egg or the *yolk*?

-ぎみ -気味 ▶彼女は美人コンテストでは上がり気味だった She was *a little nervous* during the beauty contest. ‖ 物価は最近上がり［下がり］気味だ Prices *tend to rise* [*fall*] these days. ‖ 私はかぜぎみだ I *have a bit of a cold*. ／I *have a slight cold*.

きみがよ 君が代 ***the Kimigayo*, the Japanese national anthem**（➤ His Majesty's Reign と訳されることもある）.

きみがわるい 気味が悪い **eerie** /íəri/（身の毛がよだつほど不気味な）；**uncanny**（説明できないほど不思議な）▶村外れに気味の悪い一軒家が立っていた On the outskirts of the village there was one house with an *eerie* look (to it). ‖ 彼女にはぼくの考えていることがすぐわかるようでとても気味が悪い It seems like she knows exactly what I'm thinking and it's very *scary* [*uncanny*]. ‖ 毎晩のように気味の悪い笑い声が聞こえてくるので，村人は決してその家に近づこうとしなかった The village people dared not go near the house because of the *evil* [*sinister*] laughter heard from there each night. (➤ それぞれ「不吉な，不快な」「薄気味悪い」の意) ‖ 課長はきょうは気味が悪いくらい（＝異常に）機嫌がいい Our section chief is *extraordinarily* cheerful [in an *exceedingly* good mood] today.

きみじか 気短な **short-** [**quick-**] **tempered** ▶父は気短です My father is *short-* [*quick-*] *tempered*. ／My father has *a short* [*quick*] *temper*.

[1]**きみつ 機密** **a secret** ▶国家の機密 a national *secret* ‖ これは最高機密であるから口外してはならない Since this is *a top-secret matter* [*highly confidential*], don't say a word about it to anyone else. ‖ 機密事項 classified information ‖ 機密書類 secret documents.

[2]**きみつ 気密** ▶気密性の高い容器 a *highly airtight* container ‖ 気密室 an airtight room.

きみどり 黄緑 **yellowish green.**

きみょう 奇妙な **strange**；**odd**（常識などから外れた）；《インフォーマル》**funny**（おかしな）▶彼は奇妙な帽子をか

ぶっている He has a *strange* hat on. ‖ 彼女は**奇妙な**歩き方をする She has a *strange* [*funny*] way of walking. ‖ 彼がそれを知らないとは**奇妙だ** *It is strange* [*odd*] *that* he doesn't know (about) it. ‖ **奇妙な**話だが英語の先生で英語を話せない人が多い *Strange* (*to say*), there are many English teachers who cannot speak English. (➤ strange (to say) の後に,「…だが」に相当する but をつけることも多い).

ぎむ 義務 (a) **duty**(良心・職責などから当然果たさなければならない長期の); (an) **obligation** (契約・法律などによって守るべき1回限りの) ▶**義務**を果たす do one's *duty* ／fulfill one's *obligations* ‖ 国民には納税の**義務**がある It is the *duty* of every citizen to pay taxes. ／ Every citizen has the *obligation* to pay taxes. ‖ あの人を幸せにするのがぼくの**義務**だと思う I feel it (is) my *duty* to make her happy. ‖ 我々には彼の命令に従う**義務はない** We *are under no obligation* to obey his order(s). ‖ シートベルトの着用が**義務づけられている** Wearing a seatbelt is *mandatory*. ‖ 消防法ですべての住宅に火災報知機の設置が**義務づけられている** The Fire Protection Law *mandates* that fire alarms be installed in every home.

‖**義務教育** compulsory [mandatory] education.

きむずかしい 気難しい **difficult** ▶**気難しい**男 a *difficult* man ‖ あの人は**気難しい**ので誰も話しかけない He's *grumpy*, so nobody talks to him. (➤ grumpy は「不機嫌で気難しい」).

きむすめ 生娘 an **innocent** [**pure**] **girl**; a **virgin**(処女).

キムチ **kimchi**, **kimchee**.

きめ 木目・肌理 **grain**; **texture** (手触り, 質感) ▶**きめの細かい**木材 wood of *fine grain* ／ *fine-grained* wood ‖ **きめの細かい肌**をしている be *smoothskinned* ／have a *fine complexion*. ‖ **きめ細かな**(＝入念な)準備をする make *elaborate* preparations ‖ 先生は**きめの細かい**(＝細心の, 丁寧な)指導をしてくださった The teacher gave us *careful* instructions.

きめい 記名 **signature** /sígnətʃəʳ/ (名前を書くこと); a **signature**, a **written name** (ともに「書かれた名前, 署名」) 一動 **記名する** **sign** ＋目, **put** one's **signature** 《on, to》 ‖**記名投票** a signed [an open] vote, a vote by signature.

ぎめい 偽名 a **false name**; an **alias** /éɪliəs/ (別名) ▶そのホテルに泊まったとき容疑者は佐藤という**偽名**を使っていた When the suspect stayed at the hotel, he [she] used the *alias* [registered under the *false name* of] Sato.

きめこむ 決め込む **1**【思い込む】**assume** ▶外国語を習得するのが不可能だと**決め込む**(＝結論する)のは正しくない It is not right to *jump to the conclusion* [*assume*] that it is impossible to master a foreign language. ‖ かつては家事は妻の仕事と**決め込んでいた**夫が多くいた Many husbands used to *take it granted* that it's wives who do household chores. (➤「当然のことと考える」の意). ‖ 妹は一生結婚しないと**決め込んでいる** My sister *is convinced* [*is sure*] that she will never get married. (➤「自分で納得している」「きっと…だと思っている」の意).

2【わざとする】▶話がまずいところへ来たので, ぼくはたぬき寝入りを**決め込む**ことにした They started talking about an embarrassing topic, so I decided to *pretend to be asleep*.

きめつける 決め付ける ▶まあ, そう**決めつけないで** Don't be so *judgmental*. (➤ judgmental は「すぐに悪く判断しがちな」). ‖ 警察は尋問しないうちから私を犯人と**決めつけていた** Even before they had interrogated me, the police *had already decided* [*had already come to the conclusion*] that I was the culprit. ‖ 人々は芸術家とはこういうものだと**決めつけがち**だ People tend to *stereotype* artists. (➤ stereotype は「型にはめて考える」の意).

きめて 決め手 **conclusive evidence**(決定的な証拠); a **clincher**(論争や試合に終止符を打つもの, 決定打) ▶残念ながら彼を犯人だとする**決め手**がない I am sorry, but there is no *conclusive evidence* that he committed the crime. ‖ デザインがこのスマホを選んだ**決め手**だった The design was the *clincher* that made me choose this smartphone.

きめる 決める

1【決定する, 決意する】**decide** 《on》; **fix** ＋目, **arrange** ＋目, **set** ＋目 (日時・定価などを; arrange は「手はずを整える, 段取りをする」, set は「設定する」の意で, fix はいずれの意にもなるくだけた語); **make up** one's **mind** (決心する) ▶くじ引きで順番を**決める** *decide* turns by lot ‖ 赤ん坊の名前を**決める** *decide on* a name for the baby ‖ 会議の時間と場所を**決める** *decide* [*fix*] the time and place for the meeting ‖ パーティーは次の木曜日に**決めました** We *set* [*fixed*] the date of the party for next Thursday. ‖ 付き合うんなら断然明美に**決めた** If I'm going to date anyone, it *has to* be Akemi. (➤ have to be … は「…でなければならない」) ‖ その案に賛成するかどうか彼は**態度を決めかねている** He *still doesn't know* whether or not he will support the plan. ‖ 投票で議長を**決めた**(＝選んだ) We *chose* the chairperson by vote.

▶結婚式はグアムの教会で行うことに**決めた** We *have decided* to have our wedding (ceremony) at a church in Guam. ‖ 私は毎朝6時に起きることに**決めた** I *decided* [*made up my mind*] (that) I would get up at six every morning. ‖ 何を買うか早く**決めてよ** Hurry up and *make up your mind* what you're going to buy! ‖ 《店内で》そのハンドバッグに**決めたら**? Why don't you *choose* that purse?

▶日本はデンマークを破ってワールドカップの決勝トーナメントへの**進出を決めた** Japan defeated Denmark and *advanced* [*won a ticket*] *to* the second round of the World Cup.

2【例外なく同じ結果にする】▶朝食はパンとコーヒーに**決めています** For breakfast, I *always* have coffee and toast. ‖ 毎朝ジョギングすることに**決めています** I jog every morning. ／I *make it a point to* jog every morning. (➤ 前者がふつうの言い方で, 後者は堅い表現). ‖ 先生は私が悪いと**決めてかかっている** My teacher just *assumes* I am (in the) wrong. ‖ 両親はニューヨークは危険だと**決めてかかっている** My parents *have a preconception* that New York City is dangerous. (➤ preconception は「先入観」).

3【びしりと落ち着かせる】▶彼はきょう三つぞろいの背広で**きめている** He *looks terrific* [*sharp*] today in his three-piece suit. (➤ terrific は「すてきな」の意のインフォーマルな語).

きも 肝 **the liver** (肝臓) ▶フグの**肝** the *liver* of a globefish. ‖ 《慣用表現》彼は**肝が小さい** He *is a coward* [*a wimp*]. ／He is *cowardly*. ‖ 章は**肝が太い** Akira *has pluck* [*guts* ／*grit*]. (➤ pluck, gut は元は「臓物」の意; grit はインフォーマルで「気骨」) ‖ 彼女は**肝が据わっている** She's *unflappable*. ／She *has steady nerves*. ‖ 女性政治家には男性政治家より**肝の据わった**人がいる Some female politicians are *made of sterner stuff* than male politicians. ‖ こ

の賢人のことばをよく肝に銘じておきなさい *Take* this wise man's words *to heart*. ／*Keep* this wise man's words *in mind*. ‖ 両親は息子の海外での体験談を聞いて肝を潰した The parents *were astounded* to hear of their son's experiences abroad.

☛ 肝っ玉（→見出語）

きもい キモい disgusting, creepy ▶キモいやつ a *disgusting* guy ‖ 彼はキモい He grosses people out.

きもいり 肝煎り ▶私たちはその政府高官の肝煎りで軍事施設を訪れることができた We were able to visit the military facilities *through the good offices of* the high government official.

きもだめし 肝試し a test of bravery [courage] ▶肝試しに幽霊屋敷に入ってごらんなさい Let's *see how brave* you are. Try going in that haunted house.

きもち 気持ち **1**【心の状態, 感情】feelings ▶あなたの本当の気持ちを知りたいのです I'd like to know your true *feelings*. ‖ 年寄りの気持ちを理解してあげなさい Try to understand *how* senior citizens *feel*. ‖ きみの気持ちはわかるよ I can understand *why you feel that way* [*how you feel*]. ／I understand *your feelings*. ‖ 人の気持ちのわかる人間になりたい I'd like to be the sort of person who can *empathize* [*sympathize*] with others. (➤ empathize は状況を理解して「気持ちを共有する」, sympathize は困難な状況にいる「相手を気づかう, 同情する」). ‖ 初戦に大勝しても気持ちを引き締めて次の試合に臨むことが大切だ Even though we did win the first game easily, we have to *brace ourselves* (*up*) [*steel ourselves*] for the next one. (➤ brace oneself (up) は「(困難に備えて)奮起する」, steel oneself は「覚悟を決めて立ち向かう」).
▶誰もぼくの気持ちなんかわかっちゃくれない No one understands *me*. (🍎「誰もぼくを理解してくれない」と考えて訳す. したがってこの場合の「気持ち」は訳さなくてもよい) ‖ ニューヨークで財布をなくしたときは泣きたい気持ちだった I *felt like crying* when I lost my wallet in New York City. (➤ feel like doing で「…したい気がする」の意) ‖ 対話「金メダルを取ったときはどんな気持ちでしたか」「やったあと思いました」"*How did you feel* when you won the gold medal ?" "I thought to myself, 'Wow ! I made [did] it.' "
▶きょうは負けたが, 気持ちを切り替えてあすの試合に臨みたい We lost today, but I'd like to *move on and focus on* tomorrow's game. (➤「気持ちを前向きにして, あすの試合に集中する」の意).
2【気分】▶気持ちのいい(＝快適な)部屋 a *comfortable* room ‖ ああ, いい天気だ! 気持ちがいいよ What a gorgeous day ! I *feel great*. (➤ great は「すばらしい」の意のインフォーマルな語) →気分 ‖ 何て気持ちのいい日だろう What a *wonderful* day ! ‖ きょうは二日酔いで気持ちが悪い I have a hangover and *feel lousy* today. (➤ lousy /láʊzi/ は「気分がひどく悪い」の意のインフォーマルな語) ‖ 対話「どうかしましたか」「気持ちが悪いんです」"What's wrong ?" "I *feel sick*."
▶愛子さんは気持ちのいい人だ Aiko is a *pleasant* [*good-hearted*] person. (➤ 前者は「楽しい」, 後者は「気立てのいい」の意) ‖ 電車の中で若者が年配者に席を譲っているのを見るのは気持ちのいいものだ It is *good* to see a young person give his or her seat to an elderly person on the train. ‖ 対話「蛇は好き?」「まさか! 気持ち悪いわ」"Do you like snakes ?" "Oh, no. They *give me the creeps*. ／They are *disgusting*." (➤ give ... the creeps は「…をぞっとさせる」) ‖ ゴキブリは気持ち悪い Cockroaches *are gross* [*yucky*]. ‖ 弟は気持ちよくお使いに行ってくれた My brother *willingly* went on the errand.
3【自分の好意を謙遜して, また, 相手の心づかいを指して】
▶気持ちはうれしいが, 大丈夫です I appreciate *the thought*, but no thanks. ‖ 対話「気を遣わないでください」「いいえ, ほんの気持ちです」"You shouldn't have (gone to the trouble)." "Oh, no. *It's just a small token of my appreciation*."
✉ **お礼のしるしにちくわをお送りしました. ほんの気持ちばかりですが, お受け取りください** Please accept the fish cake I sent you *as a token of my gratitude*.
4【ほんの少し】a little ▶(写真撮影で) 右肩を気持ち上げてみてください Please raise your right shoulder *a little* [*a tad*].

きもったま 肝っ玉 ▶肝っ玉かあさん a *gutsy* mom ‖ うちの息子は肝っ玉が小さくてがっかりだ I'm disappointed that my son is such *a coward* [*wimp*]. ‖ 三浦は肝っ玉の太い男だ Miura *has guts* [*grit*].

☛ 肝（→見出語）

きもの 着物 **1**【衣服】clothes /kloʊz, kloʊðz/ ▶着物を着なさい [脱ぎなさい] Put on [Take off] your *clothes*. ／Get dressed [undressed].
2【和服】a kimono /kɪmóʊnə/ (➤ 英語化している) ▶彼女は浩平の誕生日会に着物姿で出た She attended Kohei's birthday party *wearing a* (*Japanese*) *kimono*. 《参考》kimono は《米》では「(女性用の)ゆったりした化粧着」の意で用いられることがある.
✉ **お正月には着物を着ました** I *wore a kimono* during the New Year holiday(s).
✉ **今ではひとりで着物を着られる若い女性はほとんどいません** Nowadays there are hardly any young women who can *put on a kimono* without assistance.

きもん 鬼門 an inauspicious /ìnɔːspíʃəs/ [unlucky] direction ▶うちは玄関が鬼門にあるそうだ People say that our front door faces *an inauspicious* [*unlucky*] *direction*.

ぎもん 疑問 (a) question ; (a) doubt (疑い) ▶研究上の疑問 a research *question* (➤ 何を知りたいのか, 何を明らかにしたいのかといった疑問のこと) ‖ 親は子供たちの疑問に答えるよう努めるべきだ Parents should try to answer their children's *questions*. ‖ 授業中疑問に思うことがあったら, すぐ先生に質問しなさい If something comes up in class that you *don't understand*, ask the teacher right away.
▶彼が本当に UFO を見たかどうか疑問だ *I doubt that* he really saw a UFO. ‖ この発表には疑問がある *I have some doubts about* this briefing. ‖ その運転手の死因には疑問が残る The cause of the driver's death *is suspicious*. ‖ 彼女が有能であることには疑問の余地がない *There is no doubt* [*no question*] about her ability. ／Her ability leaves *no room for doubt*. ‖ 死刑廃止には疑問を感じます(＝賛成できない) *I can't agree* with the abolition of capital punishment. ‖**疑問詞** an interrogative /ìnṭərɑ́ːgəṭɪv/ ‖ **疑問符** a question mark ‖ **疑問文** an interrogative sentence, a question.

ギヤ a gear →ギア.

きゃあ 《驚きの声》Eeek /iːk/! →きゃっと.

きゃあきゃあ ▶子供はお気に入りのおもちゃをもらうとキャーキャー言って喜んだ When the child got his favorite toy, he *shouted with joy*. ‖ 若い女の子たちが人気歌手のあとをキャーキャー言いながら追いかけていった The young girls ran *squealing* after the popular singer. ‖女の子たちはその写真を見てキャーキャー笑いだした When they saw the picture, the girls began to *cackle* [*laugh and scream*].

ぎゃあぎゃあ ▶赤ん坊のギャーギャー泣く声で目が覚めた The baby's *crying* woke me up. ‖あんまり遅く帰るとおふくろがギャーギャー言うから，きょうはこの辺でさよならしよう My mom will *nag* at me [*get on my case*] if I go home too late, so I'll say good-bye to you now. (➤ nag は「うるさく小言を言う」, get on A's case は「人(A)にうるさく干渉する」).

きやく 規約 a **rule**.

きゃく 客 a **guest**; a **visitor**; a **customer**

◀解説▶「客」の言い方
(1) 日本語の「客」に対応する語はいろいろあり，使い分ける必要がある．家庭への訪問客やホテルなどの客は **guest** である．「訪問する人」の意味では **visitor** も広く用いられる．また「来客」の意味では **company** も用いるが，この語は常に Ⓤ 扱い．
(2) 商店などの「得意客」は **customer**，弁護士や会計士など専門職の人の客は **client** /kláɪənt/ という．

▶客を招待する invite *a guest* ‖きょうは客が２人来る We're expecting two *guests* today. ‖《電話で》ごめんなさい，今お客さんが来ていてお話できないの．あとで電話するわ I'm sorry, but I *have a guest* now, so I can't talk. I'll call you (later). ‖昨晩，うちに(不意の)客があった We had a (*surprise*) *visitor* yesterday evening. ‖週末に客がある予定だ We *are inviting some people* for the weekend.
▶そのスーパーは買い物客でいっぱいだ The supermarket is crowded with *customers* [*shoppers*]. ‖《店員などが》お客さん，お釣りですよ *Sir* [*Madam*], your change!

ぎゃく 逆 **the opposite**(左右対称のような対立); **the reverse**(裏と表のような反対側); **the contrary** (論旨が反対の); **the converse**(論理学などの命題における) 一形 逆の **opposite**; **reverse**; **contrary** → 反対

▶アラビア語の文章は英語とは逆の方向に読みます Arabic is read in the *opposite* direction from [of] English. ‖アルファベットを逆に言いなさい Say the alphabet *backward*. ‖その鍵は逆に回しなさい Turn the key *the other way*. ‖靴下を裏表逆に履いていることがわかり，うろたえてしまった I was embarrassed to find that my socks were *inside out*. ‖彼は新入りの頃，ぼくの使い走りをしていたが，今では立場が逆になった He used to be my gopher when he was newly hired, but now *the shoe is on the other foot*. (➤ the shoe is on the other foot は「形勢が逆転している」の意のインフォーマルな表現).
▶逆三角形の体 an *inverted* triangle body shape [triangle physique] ‖名簿のこの２人の名前は順序が逆だ The two names on the list here are *in the wrong order*. ‖きみの言ったことは事実とは逆だ What you have said *is contrary to* the truth. ‖阪神の優勝は我々の予想とは逆だった *Unexpectedly* [*Contrary to our expectations*], the Tigers won the pennant. (➤ unexpectedly は「思いがけなく，意外なことに」) ‖ ことわざ 逆もまた真なり The reverse is also true. ／The opposite is also [can also be] said.

ギャグ a **gag**; a **joke**(冗談) ▶私たちの英語の先生はいつも同じギャグを飛ばす Our English teacher always tells the same old *joke*.

きゃくあし 客足 ▶午後は雨で客足が鈍った *Customer traffic slowed* in the afternoon due to (the) rain.

きゃくあつかい 客扱い ▶彼女は客扱いがうまい She's good at *dealing with* [*handling*] *customers*.

きゃくいん 客員 ‖客員教授 a visiting [guest] professor ‖客員研究員 a visiting research worker (現地でほかの研究者たちと実際の研究に携わる); a visiting scholar (現地で主に自分だけで研究する).

きゃくえん 客演 ▶五島みどりはヨーロッパの主要オーケストラに客演している Goto Midori has *made guest performances* with major orchestras in Europe. ‖客演指揮者 a guest conductor.

ぎゃくこうか 逆効果 **the opposite effect** ▶がみがみ叱っては逆効果になるばかりだ Nagging usually has *the opposite* (*effect*) of the intended effect. ‖興奮している人に大声でどなるのは逆効果だ It only *makes matters worse* when you shout at an excited person. (➤「事態をさらに悪化させる」の意) ‖悪い点を取ったときに子供を叱るのは往々にして逆効果になりかねない It could be *counterproductive* to scold your child when he [she] has gotten a bad grade.

ぎゃくさつ 虐殺 **slaughter** /slɔ́ːtəʳ/; a **massacre** /mǽsəkəʳ/ (大虐殺) 一動 虐殺する **slaughter** +目, **massacre** +目 ▶ナチスによって数百万のユダヤ人が虐殺された Millions of Jews *were massacred* by the Nazis. 《参考》「ユダヤ人大虐殺」は the Holocaust /hóʊləkɔːst/ とか pogrom /póʊgrəm/ と呼ばれる.

ぎゃくさん 逆算する **count** [**calculate**] **backward**.

きゃくしつ 客室 a **guest room**(ホテル・旅館・個人の家などの); a **passenger cabin**(旅客機・客船などの) ‖客室係 a room clerk; a cabin boy(客船の) ‖客室乗務員 a flight attendant, a cabin attendant (➤ 乗務員をまとめて cabin crew と呼ぶ).

きゃくしゃ 客車 a **passenger car**,《英また》a **carriage**; a **coach** /koʊtʃ/ (➤《米》では「普通客室，２等車」,《英》では carriage の正式名).

ぎゃくしゅう 逆襲 a **counterattack** 一動 逆襲する **counterattack** (戦略的に); **fight back** (抵抗する) ▶彼はいじめっ子に逆襲した He *fought back against* the bully.

ぎゃくじょう 逆上 ▶彼に「うそつき！」と言われて私は逆上してしまった I *got* really *mad* [I really *saw red*] when he called me a liar. (➤ see red は「激怒する」の意のインフォーマルな表現).

きゃくしょうばい 客商売 a [**the**] **service industry**, **the hospitality industry**.

きゃくしょく 脚色 **dramatization** 一動 脚色する **dramatize** +目 ▶彼は川端の小説を脚色した He *dramatized* a novel by Kawabata.
▶《比喩的》彼女の話は脚色が多すぎる Her story has too many *embellishments*.

きゃくせき 客席 a **seat** ▶その劇場には客席が1500ある That theater has 1,500 *seats*. ‖役者のとちりに客席(＝聴衆)からやじが飛んだ When the actor blundered, (a storm of) catcalls arose from the *audience*.

ぎゃくせつ 逆説 a **paradox** /pǽrədɑ̀ːks/ ▶逆説的に聞こえるだろうが，気がせくと失敗をして結果的には余計に時間がかかるということなのだ It may *sound paradoxical* [*sound like a paradox*], but the more haste, the less speed.

きゃくせん 客船 a **passenger boat** [**ship**].

きゃくせんび 脚線美 **beautiful** [**shapely**] **legs** ▶リサ

は脚線美の持ち主だ Lisa *has beautiful legs*.
きゃくそう 客層 a **clientele** /klàɪəntél ‖ klìːɔn-/ (➤ 集合的に) ▶その店は多様な[若い]客層を引き付けている That store attracts a diverse [young] *clientele*.
ぎゃくそう 逆走する **run** [**drive** / **go**] **in the wrong direction.**
ぎゃくぞく 逆賊 a **rebel**(反逆者); a **traitor**(裏切り者).
ぎゃくたい 虐待 **ill-treatment** (ひどい処遇); **abuse** /əbjúːs/ (ことば・行為による虐待); **cruelty** (残酷な仕打ち) **一動 虐待する** **ill-treat** +㊐, **abuse** /əbjúːz/ +㊐ ▶動物が虐待されるのを見るのは耐えられない I can't stand seeing animals *treated cruelly*. ‖ 日本では幼児虐待が大きな社会問題となっている *Child abuse* is a growing social problem in Japan. ‖ 夫婦が2歳の息子を虐待していることが発覚した The fact that the couple had *been abusing* their two-year-old son came to light.
ぎゃくたまのこし 逆玉の輿 ▶逆玉(のこし)に乗る *marry a wealthy woman* / *marry money*.
ぎゃくたんち 逆探知 ▶警察は誘拐犯人の電話を逆探知しようと努めた The police tried to *trace* the call from the kidnapper.
きゃくちゅう 脚注 a **footnote.**
ぎゃくて 逆手 →さかて.
ぎゃくてん 逆転 ▶きみと彼の立場は逆転しているのに気がつかないのか Don't you realize that your position and his *are* now *reversed*?
▶《野球》広島は8回に4点をあげて試合を逆転, 中日に7対6で勝った The Carp rallied for four runs in the eighth to *turn the tables* on the Dragons and win the game 7-6. (➤ turn the tables は「形勢を一変する」) ‖ 西武はソフトバンクに6対4の逆転勝ちを収めた The Lions scored a 6-4 *come-from-behind win* over the Hawks.
きゃくひき 客引き a **tout** /taʊt/.
ぎゃくひれい 逆比例 an **inverse proportion** [**relation** / **ratio**]. →反比例.
ぎゃくふう 逆風 an **unfavorable** [**adverse**] **wind**; a **head wind**(向かい風) ▶逆風を突いてボートをこぐ row *against the wind* ‖ 風は逆風だ We have *an unfavorable wind*. / *The wind is blowing toward me* [*us*]. ‖ 今回の選挙は与党にとっては逆風だ *The wind is blowing against* the ruling party in the coming election.
きゃくほん 脚本 a **script**(劇・映画・放送などの); a **screenplay**, a **scenario** /sənǽriòʊ/ (映画の) ▶映画の脚本を書く write *a film scenario*.
‖脚本家 a scriptwriter, a scenario writer.
きゃくま 客間 a **drawing room** (応接間); a **guest room** (客を泊めるための部屋).
ぎゃくもどり 逆戻りする **turn back**; **revert** 《to》(立ち返る); **backslide** 《into》(悪い習慣に) ▶この道を逆戻りしていけば右手に白い建物が見えるはずです *Turn back* along this road, and you will see a white building on your right. ‖ きょうはまるで季節が冬に逆戻りしたみたいだ Today it seems as though winter *has returned*. ‖ そのブタは野生の状態に逆戻りした The pigs *reverted to* a feral state. ‖ 麻薬常用者は薬物使用に逆戻りすることが多い Addicts often *backslide into* drug use.
ぎゃくゆにゅう 逆輸入 **reimport** **一動 逆輸入する** **reimport** +㊐ ▶このモデルはアメリカからの逆輸入だ This model *is reimported* [is *a reverse import*] from the U.S.
きゃくよせ 客寄せ a **come-on**(目玉商品) ▶目玉商品は客寄せに使われる Loss leaders are used to *draw* (*in*) *customers*. ‖《慣用表現》彼はただの客寄せパンダだ He's just *a come-on man*.
ぎゃくりゅう 逆流 a **backward flow**; **reflux**(体液の), **regurgitation**(食べた物の; どちらも医学用語) **一動 逆流する** **flow backward(s)** ▶川の水が逆流した The river water *flowed back*.
きゃくりょく 脚力 **leg strength** ▶脚力を鍛える build one's *leg strength* ‖ 祖父は最近めっきり脚力が低下したと言っている My grandfather says that *his legs have become* much *weaker* recently. / My grandfather says *his ability to walk has decreased* a lot recently.
きゃしゃ 華奢な **delicate** /délɪkət/ (ひ弱な) ▶きゃしゃな体つきの女性 a woman of *slight* build ‖ 彼女はきゃしゃな手をしている She has *delicate* hands.
きやすい 気安い ▶古田君とは気安い間柄だから私から頼んでみよう Mr. Furuta and I *are on friendly terms*, so let me try asking him to do it. ‖ 俺のことを気安く「おい」なんて言うなよ You'd better stop saying 'Hey' to me, *as if we were close buddies*. (➤ buddy は「親友」の意のくだけた語) ‖ 静江はセミナーの教授の研究室をあまりにも気安く訪ねて行く Shizue visits her college seminar teacher's office too *freely*.
キャスター 1【家具などの脚部につけた車】 a **caster** (脚輪).
2【ニュースキャスター】 a **newscaster**, 《英また》 a **newsreader**(ニュースキャスター); an **anchor(person)**(ニュース番組の総合司会者).
キャスティングボート **the casting vote**(➤ 英語では「賛否同数の場合に議長が投じる決定票」を意味する) ▶《慣用表現》共産党議員がキャスティングボートを握っている The communists have *the deciding vote*.
キャスト a **cast**(配役全員); **casting** (役の割りふり) ▶その正月映画は豪華キャストだった The movie made for the New Year had a *star-studded cast*. ‖ その劇のキャストは決まりましたか Has the *casting* been decided for the play?

> **危ないカタカナ語✹ キャスト**
> **1**「配役」の意味の「キャスト」は英語の cast とは用法が異なる. cast は集合的に配役全体を指す. したがって, 配役の1人は a member of the cast という.
> **2** 個々の役は role とか part という.「メインキャスト」(主役)も役の1つなので a leading role [part] となる.

きやすめ 気休め ▶気休めを言わないで私の病気について本当のことを言ってちょうだい Don't give me *empty consolations*. Please tell me the truth about my illness.
きやせ 着痩せ ▶彼女は着痩せする(＝着物を着ると実際よりも細く見える) She *looks thinner* (*than she really is*) *when dressed*. / Clothes make her appear *thinner* (*than she really is*).
きゃたつ 脚立 a **stepladder.**
きゃっか 却下 (a) **rejection**, (a) **dismissal** (➤ 後者は法律用語) **一動 却下する** **reject** +㊐, **dismiss** +㊐; **disallow** +㊐ (要求・証拠などを) ▶その案は却下された The proposal *was rejected*. ‖ 証拠不十分で訴えは却下された The suit *was dismissed* due to lack of evidence. ‖ その納税者の異議は却下された The taxpayer's objection *was disallowed*.
きゃっかん 客観 ▶客観的な見方 an *objective* view

‖わが子を**客観的**に見るのは難しい It is hard to look at one's own child *objectively*. ‖ジャーナリズムで**客観性**を保つのは容易ではない It's not easy to maintain *objectivity* in journalism.

‖**客観テスト** an objective test.

きゃっきゃっ ▶子供たちは**キャッキャッ**と笑っていた The children were *shrieking* [*shouting*] *with laughter*. (➤ shriek は不快な「金切り声を出す」) ‖猿たちは**キャッキャッ**と鳴いていた The monkeys were *chattering*.

ぎゃっきょう 逆境 **adversity** ▶**逆境**と闘う struggle with *adversity* ‖ **逆境**に打ち勝つ overcome *adversity* ‖貧しい家に生まれた人は**逆境**に強いという It is said that people born into poor families are stronger in the face of *adversity*.

きゃっこう 脚光 **footlights**(舞台の足元の照明)；**limelight**(人々の注目を浴びること) ▶清水君は有望なピアニストとして**脚光を浴びている** Mr. Shimizu *has come into the limelight* as a promising pianist.

1**ぎゃっこう 逆行** ▶そんな校則は時代に**逆行している** School regulations of that kind *run counter to* [*go against*] the trend of the times.

2**ぎゃっこう 逆光** **backlight**(対象の背後から当たる照明) ▶この写真は**逆光**が効果的に用いられている This photo makes good use of the *backlight* from the sun. ‖それは**逆光**じゃない？ Aren't you *shooting into the sun*?

キャッシュ **cash** ▶**キャッシュ**でお支払いください Please pay (*in*) *cash*.

▶**キャッシュレス社会** a *cashless* society.

キャッシュカード a **cash card**, a **bank card**, an **ATM card** 《参考》ATM は automated teller machine (現金自動預け払い機)の頭文字. インフォーマルでは**キャッシュカード**のことを plastic money, anytime bank card, 24-hour bank card などともいう. ▶**キャッシュカード**で銀行から 3 万円引き出す draw 30,000 yen from the bank with one's *cash card*.

キャッチ ▶無線を**キャッチする** *receive* a radio message ‖ボールを**キャッチ**し損なって転んでしまった I failed to *catch* the ball and took a tumble. ‖**ナイスキャッチ**！*Nice catch*! ‖そのニュースを**キャッチした**のは朝の 5 時だった It was five o'clock in the morning when I *got wind of* the news. (➤ get wind of は「(情報などを)聞きつける, 嗅ぎつける」). ‖あっ, 今**キャッチ**が入ったからちょっと待ってて！Could you hold for a moment? I've got *a call waiting*. (→**キャッチホン**).

キャッチコピー a **catchy phrase**, a (**movie**) **blurb**.

キャッチセールス ▶きのう, 街で**キャッチセールス**に遭ってしつこく勧誘された Yesterday I *was accosted by a salesperson* on the street who persistently pressured me to sign a contract. (➤ **キャッチセールス**は和製語).

キャッチフレーズ a **catchphrase**, a **catchword** ▶「我ら皆きょうだい」というのがその慈善音楽会の**キャッチフレーズ**だった "We are all brothers and sisters" was the *catchphrase* for the charity concert.

キャッチボール **catch** (➤ catchball とはしない) ▶**キャッチボール**をしよう Let's *play catch*.

キャッチホン a **call-waiting telephone**.

キャッチャー a **catcher**；《インフォーマル》a **backstop** (➤「バックネット」の意だが, 俗に「捕手」の意にもなる) ‖**キャッチャーミット** a catcher's mitt.

きゃっと ▶母は台所でゴキブリを見つけ**キャッ**と叫んだ My mother saw a cockroach in the kitchen and *screamed* [*shrieked*]. (➤「キャッ」という叫び声は eek で表す).

キャップ a **cap**(帽子；蓋). →**蓋**.

ギャップ a **gap** ▶世代間の**ギャップ** *a gap* between generations／the generation *gap* ‖ 2 人の考え方の間には大きな**ギャップ**がある There is a big *gap* [*difference*] in the thinking of those two.

キャディー a **caddie** [**caddy**].

キャバレー a **cabaret** /kǽbərèɪ, kæ̀bəréɪ/ 《参考》《英》ではナイトクラブや大規模レストランなどにおける floor show, stage show などの正式な余興を指すことが多い.

キャビア **caviar(e)** /kǽviɑːʳ/.

キャビネット a **cabinet** ▶ファイル**キャビネット** a file [filing] *cabinet*.

キャビン a **cabin**(船室・小屋).

キャプテン a **captain** ▶彼はチームの**キャプテン**に選ばれた He was chosen [was elected] *captain* of the team. (➤ この場合, 役職・身分を表すので a や the はつけない).

ぎゃふん ▶今度あいつに会ったら**ギャフンと言わせてやる** The next time I see him, I'm going to *cut him down to size* [*put him in his place*]. (➤ともに「身の程をわからせる」の意のインフォーマルな表現).

キャベツ (a) **cabbage** ▶**キャベツ** 2 個 two head(s) of *cabbage*／two *cabbages*.

キャミソール a **camisole**.

ギャラ a **fee**(謝礼)；**payment**(支払い, 報酬) ▶この映画は**ギャラ**が安かった My *fee* [*payment*] for this film appearance was low. (➤「ノーギャラだった」というのなら low を nil にする).

キャラクター **1**【性格】(a) **character** ▶愛すべき**キャラクター**の人 a person with a lovable *character* 《参考》「あの先生はキャラが濃い(＝個性が強い)」は character でなく, That teacher has a strong personality. がよい. ‖彼はその役にうってつけの**キャラクター**だ He is the perfect *character* for the part.／He is perfect for the part.

2【劇中などの人物】a **character** ▶『トイ・ストーリー』には愛すべき**キャラクター**が多数登場する Lots of lovable *characters* appear in Toy Story.

‖**キャラクター商品** products featuring popular characters, character goods.

キャラバン a **caravan**.

キャラメル a **caramel** /kǽrəməl ‖-mel/.

ギャラリー a **gallery**(画廊；見物人).

キャリア a **career** /kəríəʳ/ ▶彼女は看護師としての**キャリア**が長い She'*s had a long career* as a nurse. ‖彼は**キャリアアップ**のために大学院に行っている He's attending (a) graduate school to help *further his career*. (➤ further は「さらに推進する」).

‖**キャリアウーマン** a career woman.

> **危ないカタカナ語** **キャリア**
>
> **1** career /kəríəʳ/ は「生涯」とか「一生の職業」の意. 日本語の「キャリア」の発音は「運ぶ人」「保菌者」などの意の carrier /kǽriəʳ/ と誤解されるおそれがあるので要注意.
>
> **2** 専門の職業を持つ女性の「キャリアウーマン」は career woman でよい. また「外交官を生涯の仕事とする人」も career diplomat でよいが, 公務員の「キャリア組」「ノンキャリア組」は career 本来の意味からずれているのでそれぞれ elite [fast-track] bureaucrat, ordinary [non elite] bureaucrat などとする必要がある.

キャリーバッグ a **wheeled carry-on** (**bag**).

ギャル a **girl**(➤ 日本語の「ギャル」は英語の girl のくだけ

た形である gal に由来するが, 今では古風) ▶ギャルに人気の店 a store popular with *girls* [*young women*].

きゃんきゃん ▶子犬たちが母犬を捜してキャンキャン鳴いている The puppies are *yelping* for their mother.

き

ギャング a **gangster**(1人) ; a **gang** (一団) ▶あの男が銀行強盗のギャングの一員だったとは驚いた I was surprised to find [know] that he was a member of *a gang* of bank robbers.

> **危ないカタカナ語 ギャング**
> **1** 日本語では「暴力団」の意にも「暴力団員」の意にも用いるが, 英語の gang は前者のみを指し, 後者は gangster とか mobster という.「銀行ギャング」は gang of bank robbers で,「ギャング映画」は gangster film [movie] である.
> **2** 英語のgangはwork gang(作業員仲間)や road gang repairing streets(道路の補修工事をしている作業員の一団)のように, 仕事仲間を指すこともある.

キャンセル (a) **cancellation** 一動 **キャンセルする cancel** +目 ▶ホテルの予約をキャンセルする *cancel* the hotel reservation ‖ 私は注文をキャンセルした I *canceled* my order. ‖ 対話「あすの予約をキャンセルしたいのですが」「かしこまりました」"*I'd like to cancel* my reservation for tomorrow." "Yes, sir [madam]." ▶キャンセル待ちの乗客たち *standby* passengers / passengers *on the standby* [*waiting*] *list* ‖ キャンセル待ちで飛行機に乗る fly [go travel] *standby* on a flight. ‖ **キャンセル料** a cancellation fee.

キャンデー 《米》 **candy**, 《英》 **sweets** ▶このキャンデーを10個ください Could I have ten pieces of this *candy*, please? (Give me ... とすると物乞いをしているようで不自然). ‖ **棒つきキャンデー** a lollipop.

キャンドル a **candle** ▶結婚披露宴で2人はキャンドルサービスをした During the wedding reception, the couple *circulated around the room lighting the candles*. (➤ candle service は「ろうそくの火を用いた礼拝」をいう).

キャンバス a **canvas** (画布) ; (a **piece of**) **canvas** (帆布, ズック).

キャンパス a **campus** ▶この大学はキャンパスが広い This university has a spacious *campus*. ‖ キャンパスでは友だちとは英語で話します My friends and I speak (in) English *on campus*. (➤「キャンパスの外では」なら off campus).

キャンピングカー a **camper**, 《英 また》 a **caravan** 《参考》特に大型キャンピングカーは recreational vehicle 《略 RV》という.

キャンプ a **camp** ; **camping** (キャンプすること) ▶彼らは十和田湖畔でキャンプした They *camped* on the shores of Lake Towada. ‖ ことしの夏は軽井沢にキャンプに行きたい I would like to *go camping* in Karuizawa [*go* to Karuizawa *to camp*] this summer. ‖ 我々はキャンプファイアを囲んで歌を歌った We sang songs around the *campfire*. ‖ キャンプファイアをしよう Let's *make* [*build*] *a campfire*. ‖ 米軍キャンプ a U.S. *military camp*.
‖ **キャンプ場** a campsite, a camping site, a camping ground ‖ **キャンプ村** a camping village ‖ **キャンプ用品** a camping outfit ; camping equipment (装備全体).

ギャンブル a **gamble** ; **gambling** (ギャンブルをすること) ▶父はギャンブルで全財産を失った My father lost all his money *gambling*. (➤ この gambling は「ギャンブルをして」の意の現在分詞) / My father gambled away all his money.

キャンペーン a **campaign** (運動) ▶教育改革のキャンペーン *a campaign* for educational reform ‖「町をきれいに」のキャンペーンを始めよう Let's start a "Keep our town clean" *campaign*. ‖ **キャンペーンガール** a campaign model (➤「キャンペーンガール」は和製語) ‖ **キャンペーンセール** a sales campaign / a sales drive.

キャンベラ Canberra (オーストラリアの首都).

きゆう 杞憂 groundless fears (根拠の無い不安) ▶私の不安は杞憂に終わった My fears *proved groundless* [*imaginary*]. ‖ きみの心配は杞憂にすぎない I believe your worries are *just imaginary* [*just* (*in*) *your imagination*].

[1]**きゅう 灸** →おきゅう.

[2]きゅう 急

> **訳語メニュー**
> 急速な →rapid, fast **1**
> 非常事態 →emergency **2**
> 緊急の →urgent **3**
> 突然の →sudden, abrupt **4**
> 急角度の →steep, sharp **5**

1【急速な】rapid, fast 一副 **急に rapidly** ▶急な流れ a *rapid* stream ‖ 急成長を遂げる achieve *rapid* growth ‖ 急発進する *shoot* forward ‖ 急停止する stop *abruptly* ‖ 桂川の流れは急だ The Katsura River runs [flows] *rapidly*. / The current of the Katsura River is *very fast*. ‖ この辺りはここ数年で急に開けた This area developed *rapidly* in the last few years. ‖ 新庁舎の建設は急ピッチで進んでいる Construction work on the new government office building is progressing *at a fast pace*.

2【非常事態】(an) **emergency** ▶非常食と水を用意して急な場合に備える stock food and water for *emergencies* ‖ 友人の急を聞いて病院に駆けつけた I rushed to the hospital when I heard a friend of mine was *in critical condition*. (➤ critical は「命が危ない」).

3【短時間内の】urgent (緊急の) ▶急な会議 an *urgent* meeting ‖ 急な用事であすサウジアラビアへたちます I'm flying to Saudi Arabia tomorrow on *urgent* business. ‖ 災害復旧は最も急を要する問題だ Restoration of the disaster area is the most *urgent* issue. ‖《標語》飛び出すな. 車は急に止まれない Don't run out into the road. Cars can't stop so *quickly*.

4【突然の】sudden (急に起こる) ; **abrupt** (突然で予期されていない) 一副 **急に suddenly, abruptly** ▶急な車線変更をする change lanes *suddenly* ‖ 首相の急な辞任には驚いた I was taken by surprise by the prime minister's *abrupt* resignation. (➤ abrupt は驚き・不快のニュアンスが強い) ‖ 急な(=予期しない)来客で母は慌てた An *unexpected* visitor put my mother in a flurry. ‖ ブレーキがあまりにも急だったので, 後ろの車に追突された I stepped on the brake so *abruptly* that I was hit from behind. ‖ きょうは急に温度が上がった The temperature *suddenly* rose today. ‖ 写真を見ていたら急に恵子に会いたくなった Looking at the picture, I *suddenly* felt like seeing Keiko.
▶人質たちは無事解放されると急に泣きだした The hostages *burst into tears* when they were released unharmed. (➤ burst into は「突然…しだす」).

5【急角度の】**steep**（勾配が）; **sharp**（カーブなどが）▶急な坂 a *steep* slope ‖ 中国の寺院の屋根は日本の寺院の屋根よりも傾斜が急だ The slant of the roofs of Chinese Buddhist temples *is steeper* than that of Japanese ones. ‖ 私の車は急なカーブを何とか通り抜けた I negotiated the *sharp* curve.

3**きゅう 級** a **class**(クラス); a **grade**（等級, 程度）▶第一級のホテル a *first-class* [*first-rate*] hotel ‖ 5万トン級の船 a ship in [of] the 50,000-ton *class* ‖ 書道で3級になった I got a third *kyu* [a *Level-* 3 *qualification*] in calligraphy. ‖ 柔道で1級を取った I got *a first kyu* [*a brown belt*] in judo. 《参考》書道・柔道などの「級」は「段」とともに日本語で表すのがよいが, 予備知識のない人に対してはカッコ内のような言い方をするほうがわかりやすい.

4**きゅう 九** **nine**; **the ninth** /naɪnθ/（9番目）▶投手は9番目の野手と言われる The pitcher is said to be *the ninth* man on the field.

5**きゅう 球** a **sphere** /sfɪəʳ/.

6**きゅう 旧** ▶旧東京教育大学 *the former* Tokyo University of Education ‖ きょうが旧正月だ Today is *New Year's Day according to the lunar calendar*. ‖《新聞などで》災害現場が旧に復するにはまだ時間がかかりそうだ It appears that it will still be quite a while before the disaster area can *be fully restored*. ‖ 旧仮名遣い old kana usage [orthography] ‖ 旧版 an old edition.

キュー a **cue** ▶監督は語り手にキューを出した The director *gave* the narrator *the cue* [*cued* the narrator].

キューアールコード QR コード a **QR code** ▶スマホをかざしてQRコードを読み取る scan *a QR code* with [on] a smartphone.

きゅうあい 求愛 **courtship**（女性に言い寄ること; 動物の求愛行動にも用いる）一動 **求愛する** **court** +㊐, **woo** +㊐ ▶ルリ子はついに一郎の熱心な求愛を受け入れた At last, Ruriko accepted Ichiro's ardent *declaration of love*. ‖ あれはゴリラの求愛のポーズです That is a gorilla's *courtship* pose.
‖ 求愛ダンス a mating dance.

きゅうい 球威 ▶彼のボールには球威がある He pitches *overpowering stuff*. (➤ overpowering stuff は「威力のある球」の意のインフォーマルな表現) ‖ 打球は球威（＝球速）に負けてセカンドフライになった Overpowered by *the speed of the pitch*, he popped up to second.

きゅういん 吸引 **suction** 一動 **吸引する** **suck** +㊐, **suck in** ▶酸素を吸引する *suck* (*in*) oxygen.
‖ 脂肪吸引術 liposuction /lɪ́pousʌ̀kʃən/.

1**きゅうえん 救援** **help**（援助）; **rescue**（遭難者などの）; **relief**（困窮者などの）▶（彼らに）救援を求める ask (them) for *help* ‖ 彼の救援に向かう go to his *rescue* ‖ 救援活動に当たる carry out *rescue* [*relief*] *operations* ‖ 我々は飢えと渇きに苦しむ人々に救援の手を差し伸べるべきだ We should *give a helping hand to* those who are suffering from hunger and thirst. ‖ 救援物資が各国から続々と到着した *Relief supplies* [*goods*] poured in from many countries. ‖ 救援隊 a rescue [relief] party ‖ 救援投手 a relief pitcher, a reliever.

2**きゅうえん 休演** ▶主役が病気になったので公演は休演になった *The performance was canceled* due to the leading actor's illness. (➤「中止になった」の意) ‖《掲示》本日休演(します) *No Performances Today*.

きゅうおん 吸音 **sound absorption**
‖ 吸音材 sound absorbing material.

1**きゅうか 休暇** a **vacation**,《英》a **holiday**, **holiday(s)**（数日以上の）; a **day off**（仕事を休む日）

> **語法** (1)「休暇」に相当するのは《米》vacation,《英》holiday(s)で,《英》でも大学の休みには前者を用いる. (2) leave も「休暇」に相当するが主に公務員・軍人などに関連して用いられる. (3) 会社・工場などでウイークデーに取る休日をインフォーマルではday off という.

▶彼女は10日間の休暇をふるさとで過ごした She spent her ten days' *vacation* [《英》*holiday* / *leave*] in her hometown. ‖ 私たちは北海道でスキーをして休暇を楽しんでいます We are having a nice ski *holiday* in Hokkaido. ‖ 私たちは1日休暇を取って海水浴に行った We took *a day off* [*a day's holiday*] and went (off) to the sea. ‖ 来週は彼は休暇で旅行に出る予定です He will be away *on vacation* [*on holiday*] next week. ‖ 1日休暇が欲しい I want to take *a day off*. ‖ 対話「(夏の)休暇はどこへ行きますか」「沖縄へ行くつもりです」"Where are you going for your (*summer*) *vacation* [*holidays*]?" "(I'm going) to Okinawa."
☞ 有給休暇 (→有給)

2**きゅうか 旧家** an **old family** ▶山本家はこの町の旧家である The Yamamotos are *an old family* in this town.

1**きゅうかい 休会** (a) **recess** /rɪsés/; (an)**adjournment** /ədʒə́ːʳnmənt/（一時的な）▶国会は今月の末まで休会です The Diet will be *in recess* until the end of this month.

2**きゅうかい 球界** **the baseball world** ▶(日本)球界のご意見番 an outspoken [opinionated] commentator on (Japanese) *baseball* (➤ outspoken は「歯に衣(きぬ)着せない」, opinionated は「自説を絶対に曲げない」).

きゅうかく 嗅覚 **the sense of smell** ▶モグラは嗅覚を頼りに食物を探す Moles rely on their *sense of smell* to find food.

きゅうがく 休学 ▶しばらく休学する *leave school* [*college*] for a while (● for a while がないと「退学する」の意にもなる) ‖ 彼は大学時代に病気で2年間休学した He *took* two years *off* [*was absent* two years] *from college* due to illness.

きゅうかざん 休火山 a **dormant volcano**/vɑːlkéɪnoʊ/.

1**きゅうかん 急患** an **emergency case** ▶この病院は日曜日でも急患を受け入れる態勢ができている This hospital is ready [prepared] to accept *emergency cases* even on Sundays.

2**きゅうかん 休刊** ▶この雑誌はいつから休刊になってるんだい? How long has this magazine been *out of print*? ‖ きょうは新聞の休刊日だ There's *no newspaper* today.

3**きゅうかん 休館** ▶図書館はきょうは休館です The library *is closed* today.

きゅうかんちょう 九官鳥《鳥》a **myna(h)** /máɪnə/ (**bird**).

きゅうかんび 休肝日 a day to give one's liver a rest (by not drinking alcohol) (➤ 説明的な訳).

きゅうぎ 球技 a **ball game** ▶私はバレーボール, バスケットボール, サッカー, ラグビーなどの球技が好きだ I like *ball games* such as volleyball, basketball, soccer and rugby. 《参考》《米》では ball game といえば「野球」を連想する人が多い.

「球技」のいろいろ アメフト (American) football／ゴルフ golf／サッカー soccer, football／水球 water polo／ソフトボール softball／卓球 table tennis, ping-pong／テニス tennis／バスケットボール basketball／バドミントン badminton／バレーボール volleyball／ハンドボール handball／フットボール football／野球 baseball／ラグビー rugby

きゅうきゅう 救急 ▶この町の救急システムはまだ完全ではない This town does not yet have a fully-functioning *first-aid system*.
‖救急患者 →急患 ‖救急救命士 a paramedic／an emergency medical technician ‖救急処置 first aid ‖救急箱 a first-aid kit ‖救急病院 an emergency hospital.

ぎゅうぎゅう ▶そんなにぎゅうぎゅう押さないでください Please don't push so *hard*. ‖ぎゅうぎゅう詰めの電車で通勤するのは楽ではない To commute in *jam-packed* trains is no picnic. (➤この picnic は「楽な仕事」の意のインフォーマルな語) ‖野球の練習でコーチにぎゅうぎゅう絞られた The coach *pushed* us *to our limits*. (🏺The coach gave us a hard [rough] time ... とすると, コーチが選手たちの練習ぶりを見て叱責したような響きになる).

きゅうきゅうしゃ 救急車 an **ambulance** /ǽmbjələns/ ▶救急車を呼ぶ call *an ambulance* ‖救急車で病院に運ばれる be taken to the hospital *by ambulance* [*in an ambulance*] ‖事故があったので救急車をお願いします There's been an accident and we need *an ambulance*.

きゅうきょ 急遽 **hurriedly** ▶ジョンは父親の訃報を聞いて急きょイギリスへ戻った John *rushed back* [*hurriedly returned*] to Britain upon hearing the news of his father's death.

きゅうきょう 旧教 →カトリック.

きゅうぎょう 休業する **close** /klouz/ ▶《掲示》明日当店は休業いたします Our store will *be closed* tomorrow. ‖《掲示》本日休業 Closed (Today). (🏺(×)Close (Today)と書かないこと.「(きょうは)閉めよ」の意にしかならない. また,「10時開店, 8時閉店」の場合, (×)"Open at 10, Close at 8" とはせず, "Open 10 a.m. to 8 p.m." または "Hours : 10 a.m. to 8 p.m." などとする). ‖休業要請 a (temporary) business closure request ‖休業補償 compensation for a (temporary) business closure.

きゅうきょく 究極 ▶究極のスポーツカー the *ultimate* sports car ‖究極のところ人間も動物には違いない *After all* [*In the final analysis*], humans, too, are animals. ‖宗教は究極的には何を目指すのか What is the *ultimate* goal of religion?

きゅうくつ 窮屈

📖 訳語メニュー
小さすぎて →tight **1**
居心地が悪くて →uncomfortable **2**

1【小さすぎる】**tight** ▶このセーターは脇の下が少し窮屈だ This sweater *feels* a bit *tight* under the arms. ‖この制服は私には窮屈すぎる This uniform is too *tight* for me. ‖このベンチに5人で座るのは窮屈だ This bench is *a tight fit for* five people (to sit on). ‖少年は体が大きくなってズボンが窮屈になった The boy *has grown out of* his pants.
2【気詰まり】**uncomfortable** /ʌnkʌ́mftəbəl/ ▶窮屈な職場 a workplace where you *don't* [*can't*] *feel comfortable* ‖規則だらけで学校は窮屈だった There were so many rules in school I *couldn't feel comfortable* there [I *felt suffocated* there].

ぎゆうぐん 義勇軍 a **voluntary army**.

[1]**きゅうけい 休憩** (a) **rest**(休むこと) ; a **recess** /rɪsés/(休憩時間) ; a **break**(お茶などのための小休止) 一動 休憩する **take [have] a rest, take [have] a break** ▶ちょっと休憩しよう Let's *have* [*take*] *a* short *rest*. (➤山道を歩いているときなど)／Let's *have* [*take*] *a break* for a while. (➤仕事を中断するときなど) ‖我々は木の下で10分間休憩した We *rested* for ten minutes [We *had* a ten-minute *rest*] under a tree. 《参考》「10[5]分間休憩」と口頭で言う場合, Take ten [five]. とだけ言うこともある. ‖会議は30分休憩した The meeting *recessed* for 30 minutes.
‖(劇などの)休憩時間《米》an intermission,《英》an interval ‖休憩室 a lounge /laʊndʒ/ ‖休憩所 a rest place ; a lobby (劇場などの).

[2]**きゅうけい 求刑する** **demand a penalty** /pénlti/ ▶検事は被告人に対し死刑を求刑した The prosecutor *demanded the death penalty* for the accused.

[3]**きゅうけい 球形の** **round, spherical** ▶球形の物体 a *round* object.

きゅうげき 急激な **sudden**(突然の) ; **rapid** (急速な) ▶急激に変化する世界情勢 a *rapidly* changing world situation ‖山の天気は急激に変化するので注意が必要だ Mountain weather can change *suddenly*, so you have to be very careful. ‖この辺は人口が急激に増加している The population around this area is *rapidly* increasing.

きゅうけつき 吸血鬼 a **vampire** /vǽmpaɪəʳ/ ▶吸血鬼ドラキュラ Dracula the *vampire*.

きゅうげん 急減 a **rapid [sudden] decrease**.

きゅうご 救護 ▶けが人を救護する *rescue and give first aid to* an injured person ‖自然災害に備えて救護班を設置しておくべきです We should have *a rescue squad* to prepare for natural disasters.
‖救護活動 relief activities.

[1]**きゅうこう 急行** **1**【乗り物】an **express (train)** ▶急行に乗る get on [catch] *an express train* ‖横浜に急行で行く go to Yokohama *by express*／take *an express train* to Yokohama ‖8時30分発の仙台行き急行 the 8 : 30 [eight-thirty] *express* for [to] Sendai ‖渋谷発元町・中華街行き急行列車 *an express* from Shibuya bound for Motomachi-Chukagai.
‖急行券 an express ticket ‖急行停車駅 an express station ‖急行料金 express charges.
2【急いで行くこと】一動 急行する **rush** 《to》 ▶彼はカメラマンを連れて犯行の現場に急行した He *rushed to* the scene of the crime with a photographer.

[2]**きゅうこう 休講** ▶教授が病気できょうは休講だった The lecture *was canceled* [*was called off*] today because the professor was sick. (➤call off はインフォーマルな表現) ‖このクラスは来週は休講にします *I will not hold class* next week.／*There will be no class* next week.／*Class will not meet* next week. (🏺「このクラス」を文字どおり this class とすると,「今やっている[きょうの]クラス」となって不自然) ‖《掲示》村田先生本日休講 *No Class* Today. Mr. Murata／*Class Canceled* Today. Mr. Murata.

[3]**きゅうこう 休校** ▶台風のためきのうは休校になった *We had no school* yesterday because of the typhoon. ‖首相は全国すべての学校に1か月の休校を要請した The Prime Minister *asked* all *schools* in the country *to close* for a month.

‖**臨時休校** a temporary school closure.

4**きゅうこう 旧交** ▶《慣用表現》きのう10年ぶりで早乙女君に会い**旧交**を温めた Yesterday, I met Mr. Saotome who(m) I hadn't seen for ten years, and we *renewed our friendship*.

きゅうこうか 急降下 a **nose dive**(飛行機の) **一動 急降下する nosedive** ; **shoot down**(勢いよく下がる) ▶ジェットコースターはいちばん上までゆっくり上がり，**急降下した** The roller coaster went up slowly to the top, and (then) *shot down*.

きゅうこうち 休耕地 fallow land.

きゅうこく 急告 an **urgent notice**(➤ 表示するときは Urgent).

1**きゅうこん 求婚** a **marriage proposal 一動 求婚する propose**《to》▶愛子に**求婚する** *propose to* Aiko ‖ 娘がきょう会社の同僚に**求婚された** My daughter *received a marriage proposal* today from one of the people she works with.

2**きゅうこん 球根** a **bulb**(ユリ・チューリップなどの) ▶チューリップ[ユリ]の**球根**を植える plant tulip [lily] *bulbs*.

きゅうさい 救済 relief(困窮者などを救うこと) ; (a) **salvation**(霊魂の救済) **一動 救済する relieve** +目, **save** +目 ▶難民を**救済する** *relieve* [*give relief to*] refugees ‖ 親鸞は人は阿弥陀(あみだ)の慈悲によって**救済される**と教えている Shinran teaches us that people can *be saved* by the mercy of Amitabha. ‖ キリスト教はキリストへの信仰による**救済**を説いている Christianity teaches *salvation* through faith in Christ. ‖ 政府は失業者に対して十分な**救済策**を講じていない The government has not taken adequate *relief measures* for the unemployed. ／The government has not provided adequate *relief* to the unemployed.

1**きゅうし 急死** (a) **sudden death** ▶あんな元気な人が**急死する**とは信じられない I can't believe that a healthy man like him could have *died* so *suddenly*.

2**きゅうし 休止** a **hiatus** /haɪéɪṱəs/ (活動の) ▶作家は５年間の執筆活動**休止**を宣言した The writer declared a five-year *hiatus* from his writing. ‖ 火山噴火のため飛行機の運行は２日間**休止**だそうだ They say flights *have been suspended* for two days because of the volcanic eruption. ‖**休止符**《音楽》a rest ‖ (システムやサービスの)**休止期間** downtime.

3**きゅうし 臼歯** a **molar (tooth)**.

きゅうじ 給仕 a **(food) server**(人) ▶彼女はファミレスで**給仕**のアルバイトをしている She's *waiting tables* at a family restaurant as a part-time worker.

きゅうしき 旧式の old-fashioned(流行遅れの) ; **out-of-date**(時代遅れの) ; **obsolete** /ɑ̀:bsəlí:t ‖ ɔ́bsəli:t/ ((機械・単語の使用が)廃れた) ▶**旧式の**ピアノ an *old-fashioned* piano ‖ このコンピュータは2000年に設置したもので今ではもう**旧式**だ This computer, which was installed in 2000, is now *obsolete*. ‖ 彼女は**旧式**な考え方に固執している She clings to her *out-of-date* ideas. ‖ チップス先生は**旧式**な教え方をした Mr. Chips taught in the *traditional* way.

きゅうじつ 休日 a **day off** (勤めの無い日) ; a **holiday** (祭日) ⇀休暇 ▶父は**休日**に家の掃除をするのが好きだ My father likes to clean the house *on his day off*. ‖ 彼女は時々**休日出勤する** She occasionally *goes to work on* her *days off*.

きゅうしにいっしょう 九死に一生 ▶**九死に一生**を得る have *a narrow escape from death* ‖ 彼は崖から転落したが**九死に一生を得た** He fell over a cliff, but *miraculously escaped death*. (➤「奇跡的に死を免れた」の意).

きゅうしゃ 厩舎 a **stable**.

1**きゅうしゅう 吸収 absorption 一動 吸収する absorb** +目, **soak up**(➤ 後者は「吸い取る」に近い) ▶スポンジは水をすぐに**吸収する** Sponges *absorb* water very quickly. ‖ サナダムシは体表から栄養を**吸収する** Tapeworms *absorb* [*assimilate*] nourishment through their skin.

▶日本は明治時代，急速に西洋文明を**吸収した** Japan rapidly *absorbed* [*assimilated*] Western civilization during the Meiji era. (➤ assimilate は「自分のものにする」) ‖ このくらいの年頃の子供は知識をどんどん**吸収する** Children of about this age *absorb* [*soak up*] new knowledge very fast.

2**きゅうしゅう 急襲する make an assault** /əsɔ́:lt/ ; **make a surprise** [**sudden**] **attack** ▶織田信長軍は1560年，桶狭間で今川義元軍を**急襲した** Oda Nobunaga's troops *made an assault* [*a surprise attack* ／*a sudden attack*] on the army of Imagawa Yoshimoto at Okehazama in 1560. ‖ ハリケーンがその町を**急襲した** A hurricane *attacked* the town (with violent force).

‖**特殊急襲部隊** a speed assault team(➤略称SAT).

きゅうじゅう 九十 ninety ; **the ninetieth** (90番目) ▶**90年代**を振り返る look back on *the nineties*.

きゅうしゅつ 救出 rescue 一動 救出する rescue +目 ▶溺れた生徒を**救出する**ため先生が川に飛び込んだ A teacher jumped into the river to *rescue* the drowning student. ‖ **救出活動**は３日間続いたが，助かったのは２人だけだった The *rescue operation* lasted three days, but only two people were saved.

きゅうしょ 急所 1【命に関わる部分】a **vital organ** (心臓・頭部・肺など) ; **the groin**(股間) ▶幸い銃弾は彼の**急所**を外れていた Fortunately the bullet missed his *vital organs*. ‖ **急所**を打つのはボクシングのルールに反する It's against boxing rules to hit in *the groin*.

2【要点】a **key point** ▶この問題の**急所**だけ教えてください Could you tell me just *the key point* of this question?

きゅうじょ 救助 rescue 一動 救助する rescue +目, **save** +目 (➤ 前者は救助活動に，後者は人命確保に重点があり，rescue a person(人を救助する)，save a life(人命を救助する)という結びつきが基本) ▶その犬は溺れた少女を**救助した** The dog *saved* the drowning girl. ‖ **人命救助**が常に最優先です *Saving lives* is always (the) top priority. ‖ ３人ががれきの中から**救助された** Three people *were rescued* from the debris. ‖ 生存者はヘリコプターで**救助された** The survivors *were rescued* by helicopter. ‖ 彼は手を振って**救助**を求めた He waved his hands [arms] to *ask for help*.

‖**救助犬** a rescue dog ‖ **救助信号** a distress signal, a mayday, an SOS ‖ **救助隊** a rescue team [party] ‖ **救助艇** a life boat (海難事故に遭っている船から逃れようとする人を救助する) ／a rescue boat(海難事故に遭っている人を救助し，船に救い上げる).

きゅうしょう 旧称 an **old name**, a **former name** ▶ムンバイ，**旧称**ボンベイ Mumbai, *formerly called* Bombay.

1**きゅうじょう 休場** ▶その力士はけがで今場所は**休場**している That sumo wrestler *is absent from the ring* during this tournament because of (an) injury.

2**きゅうじょう 球場** a **ball park** ▶屋根付き**球場** a

domed *stadium* ‖ 甲子園球場 Koshien *Stadium* (➤ a や the はつけない).

3**きゅうじょう 窮状** a **desperate situation**; **distress** /dɪstrés/ (心配・不安による精神的苦しみ); a (**sorry**) **plight** (哀れな状態) ▶その国の**窮状**は目に余るものがある The *desperate situation* of that nation is all too apparent. ‖ 戦争で荒廃した地域の子供たちの**窮状**を思いみよ Consider the *plight* of children in the war-torn area.

1**きゅうしょく 給食** a **school lunch** (学校の) ▶あなたの学校は**給食**はありますか Does your school provide *school lunches*?

2**きゅうしょく 求職 job-hunting** ▶**求職**で来る学生たちはたいてい紺の背広を着ている Most of the students who come *looking for jobs* wear dark-blue suits. ‖ 兄は毎日**求職**のために歩き回っている Every day, my brother goes [is going] around *job hunting*. / Every day, my brother is *looking for a job*. ‖ たった10人の求人に対して100名の**求職者**があった There were one hundred *applicants* for only ten jobs. ‖ **求職者** a job-hunter / a job seeker.

3**きゅうしょく 休職** ▶病気療養のために**休職する** *take a leave of absence* to recover from an illness / *take a medical leave of absence* in order to recuperate (from an illness) (➤ leave of absence は勤務先からとる「休職許可」) ‖ うつ病で**休職する**教員が増えている There is an increasing number of teachers who *take leave from work* because of depression.

ぎゅうじる 牛耳る run [**boss**] **the show** 《**in, on**》 (取りしきる); **control** (指揮する) ▶この課を**牛耳っている**のは宮田氏だ Mr. Miyata *runs the show in* this section.

1**きゅうしん 休診** ▶この医院は木曜日に**休診する** This clinic *accepts no patients* [*is closed*] on Thursdays. ‖ 《掲示》本日**休診** No Office Hours Today / Closed Today / Office Closed.

2**きゅうしん 急進** ▶教育に関する彼女の意見はかなり**急進的**だ She is quite *radical* in her views on education. ‖ **急進論者**がフランス革命を起こした *Radicals* started the French Revolution.

3**きゅうしん 球審 the** (**home-**)**plate umpire** /ʌ́mpaɪəʳ/.

4**きゅうしん 急伸** ▶ここ数日，その会社の株価が**急伸している** The stock price of that company has *been rising rapidly* [*sharply*] the past few days. (➤ rapidly は「急速に」, sharply は「急カーブで」).

きゅうじん 求人 ▶新聞に**求人広告**を出したが1人も来なかった We put [ran] *a want ad* in the paper, but no applicants came.

きゅうしんりょく 求心力 centripetal force.

きゅうす 急須 a **teapot** ▶**急須**から茶を注ぐ pour green tea from *a teapot*.

1**きゅうすい 給水 water supply** ▶この湖から5つの町に**給水している** This lake *supplies water* for five towns. ‖ あすから10%の**給水制限**が始まる Starting tomorrow, *the water supply will be cut* by 10 percent. ‖ **給水管** a water supply pipe ‖ **給水車** a water (supply) truck / 《英また》 a water cart ‖ **給水所** a water distribution station ‖ **給水塔** [**タンク**] a water tower [tank].

2**きゅうすい 吸水** ▶**吸水性**のある歩道用れんが an *absorbent* sidewalk brick.

きゅうすう 級数 《数学》 a **series**
‖ 等比[幾何]級数 a geometric series.

きゅうする 窮する be at a loss (途方に暮れる) ▶金に**窮する** *be pressed* for money ‖ 財務大臣は返答に**窮した** The Finance Minister was completely *at a loss* for an answer.

ことわざ **窮すれば通ず** It's when you reach a dead end that you have [make] a breakthrough. (➤「突破口が見つかるのは行き止まりに来たときである」の意).

1**きゅうせい 急性の acute** /əkjúːt/ (➤反対の「慢性の」は chronic) ▶**急性**肝不全 *acute* liver failure.

2**きゅうせい 旧姓** one's **maiden name**; one's **former family name** (➤後者は性差のない言い方)
▶佐々木夫人，**旧姓**野中さん Mrs. Sasaki, *née* Nonaka (➤ née の発音は /neɪ/) ‖ 彼女は**旧姓**を名倉といいます Her *maiden* [*former*] *name* is Nagura. 《参考》結婚後の姓は married name という.

3**きゅうせい 急逝** a **sudden death** ▶著者はベルリンのホテルで**急逝した** The author *died suddenly* at a hotel in Berlin.

4**きゅうせい 旧制 the old system** ▶**旧制**帝大 an imperial university *under the old system*.

きゅうせいぐん 救世軍 the Salvation Army.

きゅうせいしゅ 救世主 the Saviour (キリスト教の); **the salvation** (救済者) ▶きみこそまさにわが社の**救世主**だ You have really been our *salvation*.

きゅうせかい 旧世界 the Old World (➤「新世界」は the New World).

きゅうせき 旧跡 a **historic spot** [**site**] (史跡); **ruins** (廃墟); **remains** (過去から残された物).

きゅうせっきじだい 旧石器時代 the Old Stone Age, the Paleolithic /pèɪliəlíθɪk/ **age.**

きゅうせん 休戦 an **armistice** /ɑ́ːʳmɪstɪs/ (短期の); a **truce** (長期の); a **cease-fire** (停戦) ▶**休戦**の仲介をする broker *a truce* [*cease-fire*] ‖ 両国は**休戦協定**に調印した The two countries have signed *an armistice* [*a truce*] *agreement*.

きゅうせんぽう 急先鋒 an **active leader** ▶そのグループは環境運動の**急先鋒**だ The group is *in the vanguard* of the environmental movement. (➤ vanguard は「先駆，先頭」).

きゅうそ 窮鼠 ▶ ことわざ **窮鼠**猫をかむ A cornered rat will bite a cat. (➤日本語からの直訳).

きゅうそう 急送する send ... immediately ▶ご要望があり次第商品見本を**急送いたします** A product sample will *be sent* to you *immediately* on request.

1**きゅうぞう 急増** a **sudden increase** ▶生徒の**急増**に対処するために新校舎を造っているのです They are building a new schoolhouse to keep up with the *sudden increase* in enrollment. ‖ その会議ではアフリカの人口**急増**(問題)について話し合いが行われた The African *population explosion* was discussed at the meeting.

2**きゅうぞう 急造する build ... in a hurry.**

1**きゅうそく 急速な rapid, quick** 一副 **急速に rapidly, quickly** ▶遺伝子工学は近年**急速な**進歩を遂げた Genetic engineering has made *rapid* progress in recent years. ‖ 山では夜になると**急速に**気温が下がる Temperature drops *rapidly* in the mountains at night. ‖ 母の病気は**急速に**快方に向かった My mother recovered *rapidly* [*quickly*] from her illness. ‖ **急速冷凍** quick freezing.

2**きゅうそく 休息** (a) **rest** ▶十分な**休息**を取る get plenty of *rest* ‖ きみに必要なのは一晩ゆっくりと**休息する**ことだ What you need is a good night's *rest*. ‖ 日曜日は**休息日**と決めています I keep Sunday as *a day of rest*. (→休憩).

きゅうだい 及第 ▶試験に**及第する** *pass* the examination ‖ きみの成績ではこの授業の及第点はやれないよ With your scores, I can't give you *a passing grade* for the class.

きゅうたいいぜん 旧態依然 **the same as always has been** ▶人々は旧態依然たる慣習に縛られている People are still constrained by *age-old* customs [customs *that never change*].

[1]**きゅうだん 球団** **a ball club** ▶セ・パ両リーグとも6球団だ The Central and Pacific Leagues have six *clubs* each. (➤ この場合は ball は自明なので不要).

[2]**きゅうだん 糾弾** **denouncement** /dɪnáʊnsmənt/ (公の) ; **censure** /sénʃəʳ/ (厳しい非難) **一動 糾弾する denounce** +⾃ ; **censure** +⾃ ▶市民は汚職をした市長を糾弾した Citizens *denounced* the corrupt mayor.

[1]**きゅうち 窮地** **a (tight) corner** ; **a difficult situation** (苦境) ▶人を窮地に追い込む *drive* a person *into a (tight) corner* ‖ おじは事業に失敗して窮地に陥っている Since my uncle failed in business, he *is* now *in a difficult* [*tight*] *situation.* ‖ 彼は借金がかさんで窮地に陥っている He's run up big debts and *is* now *in financial trouble* [*difficulty*]. ／He's *over his head* [He's *drowning*] in debt.

[2]**きゅうち 旧知** ▶私は須田さんとは旧知の間柄だ I *have known* Mr. Suda *for a long time*. ／Mr. Suda is *an old acquaintance* of mine. (➤ acquaintance は通例 friend ほど親しくない).

きゅうちゃく 吸着 **adhesion.** ‖ (ゴムなどでできた)**吸着盤** a suction cup ‖ **吸着力** suction.

きゅうちゅう 宮中 **the Imperial Palace** (皇居) ▶宮中晩さん会 a banquet at *the Imperial Palace*.

ぎゅうづめ ぎゅう詰め ▶ラッシュアワーには電車はすべてぎゅう詰めである All trains *are jam-packed* during rush hours.

[1]**きゅうてい 宮廷** **the Court**
‖**宮廷文学** court literature.

[2]**きゅうてい 休廷** (an) **adjournment** ▶その日はそこで休廷となった *The court* (*was*) *adjourned* for the day.

きゅうていしゃ 急停車 ▶線路の前方に人が倒れていたので列車は急停車した Since a man was lying on the tracks ahead, the train *was brought to a sudden stop*.

きゅうてん 急転 ▶事態が急転して両国は戦争に突入した The situation *changed suddenly* and both nations plunged into war. ‖ 真犯人が現れて事件は急転直下解決した The real culprit emerged and the case *suddenly* cleared up.

きゅうでん 宮殿 **a palace** ▶バッキンガム宮殿 Buckingham *Palace*.

キュート キュートな **cute.**

[1]**きゅうとう 急騰** ▶地価の急騰で地所を入手するのが難しくなった The *sharp rise* [*jump*] in land values has made it difficult to buy a plot.

[2]**きゅうとう 給湯** (a) **hot water supply**
‖**給湯器** a water heater ‖ **給湯室** a place where you can get hot water ‖ **給湯設備** a hot water (supply) system.

きゅうどう 弓道 *kyudo* ; **Japanese archery.**

ぎゅうどん 牛丼 a **beef bowl**, a bowl of rice topped with beef and onions simmered in mildly sweet sauce (flavored with soy sauce, mirin (sweet rice wine) and dashi (fish and seaweed stock)) (➤ 説明的な訳).

きゅうなん 救難 (a) **rescue** ‖**救難訓練** a rescue drill.

きゅうに 急に ⇀急.

ぎゅうにく 牛肉 **beef** ; **veal** (子牛の) ▶牛肉を2キロ買う buy two kilograms of *beef*.

きゅうにゅう 吸入 **inhalation 一動 吸入する inhale** +⾃ ▶機上で酸素吸入器をつける wear *an oxygen inhaler* in the airplane cabin ‖ 患者に酸素吸入を行った We *gave* the patient *oxygen*. ／We *had* the patient *inhale oxygen*.

ぎゅうにゅう 牛乳 **milk** ▶牛乳1パック a carton of *milk* (➤「牛乳パック」は a milk carton) ‖ 私は毎日牛乳を3杯飲む I drink three glasses of *milk* every day. ‖**牛乳瓶** a milk bottle ‖ **牛乳屋** a milk shop (店) ; a milk deliverer (配達人).

きゅうは 急派する **dispatch** +⾃ ▶医療チームを急派する *dispatch* a medical team.

きゅうば 急場 an **emergency** ; a **crisis** (危機) ▶急場を救ってくださってありがとうございます Thank you very much for helping us out of the *emergency* [*crisis*]. ‖ そんな急場しのぎの方法は感心しないね Such *stopgap* [*makeshift*] ways don't impress me (favorably). (➤ stopgap は「間に合わせ」) ‖ この金で月末まで急場をしのいでくれ Use this money to *tide* you *over* till the end of the month. (➤ tide A over は「人(A)の窮地を切り抜けさせる」).

キューバ Cuba ‖**キューバ人** a Cuban.

きゅうはく 窮迫 **extreme poverty** [**financial pressure**].

きゅうばん 吸盤 a **sucker** ▶イカやタコは足に吸盤がある Cuttlefish and octopuses have *suckers* on their tentacles.

きゅうひ 給費 ‖**給費生** a scholarship student ‖ **給費制度** a scholarship program.

キューピー a **kewpie** /kjúːpi/ **doll.**

キュービスム **cubism.**

きゅうピッチ 急ピッチ ▶地下鉄新線の建設作業が急ピッチで進んでいる Construction work on the new subway line *is progressing rapidly*.

キューピッド **Cupid.**

きゅうびょう 急病 a **sudden illness** ▶インドへ行って急病になったらどうしよう What should I do if I *suddenly get sick* in India ? ‖ 陸上競技大会で急病人が出た *A medical emergency* arose at the track meet.

[1]**きゅうふ 給付** (a) **grant** (補助金・奨学金などの) ; (a) **benefit** (医療・社会保障などの) **一動 給付する grant** +⾃ ; **pay** +⾃ ▶失業給付 unemployment *benefits* (⇀手当て) ‖ **医療給付**を受ける receive *medical benefit*(*s*).

[2]**きゅうふ 休符** 《音楽》 a **rest**
‖**全[2分]休符** a whole [half] rest.

きゅうへん 急変する **change abruptly** [**suddenly**] ▶山の天候はよく急変する The weather often *changes abruptly* in the mountains. ‖ 金は無いと言うとその男の態度が急変した When I said I had no money, the man's attitude *changed suddenly*. ‖ おじの病状が急変した(＝悪化した) My uncle's condition *took a sudden turn for the worse*.

きゅうぼ 急募 ▶《掲示》アルバイト若干名急募 Several Part-timers *Urgently Wanted*.

きゅうほう 急報 an **urgent message** [**report**].

きゅうぼう 窮乏 **poverty** /pάːvəʳṭi/ (貧困) ; **acute** /əkjúːt/ **shortages** (深刻な不足) ▶世界には窮乏にあえぐ国が多い Many countries are groaning under *extreme poverty*. ‖ 被災地の人々は今でも窮乏生活を送っている People in the disaster area are still suffering from *acute shortages*.

キューポラ a **cupola.**

きゅうぼん 旧盆 **the Bon Festival according to the**

lunar Chinese calendar. →盆.

きゅうみん 休眠 dormancy 一形 **休眠状態の** dormant ▶休眠状態に入る go into *dormancy*.

きゅうむ 急務 urgent business ▶お客様からの信用を回復するのが我々の急務だと思う I believe the most *urgent business* before us is to regain customer trust.

1**きゅうめい 究明** (an) investigation 一動 **究明する** investigate +目 (捜査する) ; find out (見つける) ▶事故の原因を究明する *investigate* the cause of the accident ‖ 真相を究明する *find out* the truth ‖ なぜ10代の自殺者がこんなに多いのか究明する必要があります We should *find out* why there are so many teenage suicides.

2**きゅうめい 救命** ‖**救命具** a life preserver, life-saving equipment (➤総称) ‖ **救命胴衣** a life jacket ‖ **救命袋** an escape chute ‖ **救命ボート** a lifeboat ; a life raft (ゴム製の).

きゅうやくせいしょ 旧約聖書 the Old Testament.

きゅうゆ 給油 refueling 一動 **給油する** refuel (+目) ▶そのジャンボジェットは成田で給油した The jumbo jet *refueled* at Narita.‖**給油所** a gas [filling] station.

1**きゅうゆう 級友** a classmate ▶礼子さんと私は高校時代級友でした Reiko and I were *classmates* in (senior) high school.

2**きゅうゆう 旧友** an old friend ▶水野君は私の小学校からの旧友です Mizuno is *an old friend of mine* from elementary school. ‖ ゆうべは高校時代の旧友たちと酒を飲んだ Last night I had a drink with *some old high school friends*.

きゅうよ 給与 pay ; a salary (定期的で定額の) ; wages (賃金) ▶彼の給与を上げる *give* him *a (pay) raise* [(英) *rise*] (➤ (pay) raise [rise] は「昇給」) ‖ 給与を上げていただきたい I would like *a (pay) raise*. ‖ 経営難のため今月の給与は支給されなかった We *didn't get paid* this month because of financial difficulties. ‖ あの会社はとても給与水準が高い *Pay levels* at that company are very high.
‖**給与支払明細書** a detailed statement of one's salary ; a pay slip (1枚の簡略な) ‖ **給与所得** earned income, employment income ‖ **給与所得控除** (an) employment income deduction ‖ **給与所得者** a salaried employee, an employment income earner.

1**きゅうよう 急用** urgent business ▶急用でコンサートに行けなかった *Urgent business* kept [prevented] me from going to the concert. ‖ 社長は急用で不在ですが, ご伝言はございますか The president is out *on urgent business*. May I take a message? (May I ...? の代わりに Shall I ...? とすることもできるが, 丁寧度が下がる) ‖ 急用 (＝緊急) 以外は会社に電話をするな Don't call me at the office unless there's *an emergency*.

2**きゅうよう 休養** (a) rest 一動 **休養する** rest, take a rest ▶このプロジェクトが終わったらゆっくり休養したい When this project is finished, I want to *have a* good *rest*. ‖ きみは働き過ぎだ. たまには休養を取りなさい You always work too hard. You'd better *take some time off* (every once in a while).

きゅうらい 旧来の old (古い) ; conventional (従来ふうに行われた) ▶この変化の激しい時代に旧来の商売のやり方は通用しない *Old* ways of doing business won't get you anywhere in this rapidly changing age.

きゅうらく 急落する drop sharply, plummet /plʌ́mɪt/ ▶内閣支持率が急落した The approval rating of the Cabinet *dropped sharply* [*plummeted* / *plunged*].

きゅうり 胡瓜 a cucumber /kjúːkʌmbəʳ/ ▶キュウリの漬物を漬ける make *pickled cucumbers*.

きゅうりゅう 急流 rapids, a rapid stream ▶いかだで急流を下るのはスリルがあって愉快だ Shooting down *rapids* on a raft is a thrilling experience.

1**きゅうりょう 給料** pay ; a salary (サラリーマンなどの) ; wages (労働者などの現金給与) ▶高い [安い] 給料 a high [low / small] *salary* ‖ あしたは給料日だ Tomorrow is *payday*. / I get paid tomorrow. ‖ 今月は給料が上がった I *got a pay raise* [(英) *rise*] this month. ‖ あの会社は給料がよい [悪い] The *pay* is *good* [*bad*] at that company. / That company *pays* [*doesn't pay*] *well*. ‖ 彼はいい給料を取っている He gets *a big salary*.

2**きゅうりょう 丘陵** a hill
‖**丘陵地帯** hilly country / hilly terrain.

きゅうれき 旧暦 the lunar Chinese calendar (➤ the old calendar とはいわない) ▶旧暦の正月 New Year's Day *in the lunar Chinese calendar*.

きゅっと ▶鉢巻きを頭に巻いてきゅっと締めた I wound a *hachimaki* towel around my head and pulled it *tight*.

ぎゅっと ▶彼女はぼくの手をぎゅっと握り,「好きよ」と言った She squeezed my hand *tightly* and said, "I love you."

キュロット culottes /kjúːlɑːts ‖ kjulɔ́ts/ ▶キュロット姿の少女 a young girl *in culottes*.

きゅんとする キュンとする ▶彼の笑顔を見るとキュンとする I *get butterflies in* my *stomach* [My *heart pounds*] whenever I see him smile.

きよ 寄与 (a) contribution ▶医学の進歩に寄与する *make contributions to* medical development ‖ キュリー夫人の科学への寄与は絶大であった Madame Curie's *contributions* to science were great.

きょ 虚 ▶テロ集団は奇襲部隊に虚を突かれた The terrorist group *was caught off guard* by the commandos.

きょあく 巨悪 a great evil ▶巨悪と戦う battle [fight] against *a great evil*.

きよい 清い pure (純粋な) ; clean (清潔な) ▶清く澄んだ泉の水 *clean* and clear spring water ‖ 心の清い者は顔に現れる *The pure in heart* look pure. (➤「the ＋形容詞」で「…の人々」を表す) ‖ (我々の) 生徒には清い交際をしてほしい We want (our) students to have *chaste* relationships (with each other). (➤ chaste /tʃeɪst/ は「純潔な」の意の堅い語) ‖ 皆さんの清き一票をお願いしたい I want *honest votes* for me from all of you. ‖「清く, 正しく, 美しく」Live *cleanly*, righteously and beautifully. (➤宝塚歌劇団のモットー).

1**きよう 器用な** dexterous /dékstərəs/ (手が) ; skillful (熟練した) ▶きみは器用だがぼくは全く不器用だ You are quite *dexterous*, but I *am all thumbs*. (➤ be all thumbs は「ひどく不器用だ」の意のインフォーマルな表現.「不器用な」は clumsy) ‖ 彼女は手先が器用だ She *is skillful with her fingers*. / She *has nimble fingers*. ‖ 彼はテレビやラジオを器用に直す He is *skillful* at [*is skilled* in] repairing TV and radio sets. ‖ ジュディーさんは箸を器用に (＝上手に) 使う Judy uses chopsticks *well* [*skillfully*]. ‖ 山田さんは器用貧乏というやつで結局係長止まりだった Mr. Yamada is *a Jack of all trades* (*and master of none*). In the

end, he never got above a low-level supervisory position. (➤「何でもこなす人は名人にはなれない；多芸は無芸」という英語のことわざから).
☞ 不器用 (→見出語)

2**きよう 起用する** **appoint** ＋目 (任命する) ▶このプロジェクトに新人を**起用**したのが当たった *Appointing* [*Putting*] a new staffer to this project worked out well.

3**きよう 紀要** a **bulletin** (大学の；学会などの会報・定期報告書の意でも用いる)；**the proceedings** (学会などの記事録・論文集).

1**きょう 今日** **today, this day** ▶きょう田辺先生は薄化粧をしてきた *Today* Miss Tanabe came to school wearing a little make-up. ‖ きょうは忙しい I'm busy *today*. ‖ きょうはこれまで That's all *for today*. ／Let's call it a day. ‖ きょうから新学期が始まった The new school term began *today*. (● begin は始まる1時点を示すので from today としない) ‖ きょうから1週間禁酒します *Starting* (*from*) *today*, I won't drink (alcohol) for a week. ‖ きょう中に仕事を終えなさい Finish the work *by the end of the day*. ／Finish the work *today*. ／Finish the work *before the day is over* [*out*].
▶きょうは5月10日水曜日です *Today* is Wednesday, May 10. (➤ 通例日付より曜日を先に言う. May 10 は May (the) tenth と読む). ‖ 対話「きょうは何日ですか」「4月1日です」"What's the date *today*? ／What's *today's* date?" "Today's April 1." (➤ April (the) first と読む. 単に「18日です」と日付だけのときは the 18th と言う) ‖ 対話「きょうは何曜日ですか」「月曜日です」"What day is *today*? ／What day of the week is it *today*?" "Today's Monday. ／It's Monday today."
▶きょうの午後成田をたちます I'm leaving from Narita (Airport) *this afternoon*. ‖ きょうの夜は空いてますか Are you free *tonight* [*this evening*]? ‖ いいこと. あすでなく, きょうの夜8時よ Don't forget, it's *eight o'clock tonight*, not tomorrow. ‖ 来週[来年]のきょう *this same day* next week [next year] ‖ 先週のきょう a week ago *today* ／*this day* last week ‖ その事件が起きたのは5年前のきょうだ It was five *years ago today* that the incident occurred.

2**きょう 卿** **Lord** (➤ イギリスの侯爵以下の貴族の正式の肩書き) ▶テニソン卿 *Lord* Tennyson (● 正式には通例 Lord の次には姓だけを置くが, 名も入れるときは *Lord* Alfred Tennyson または Alfred, *Lord* Tennyson とする).

3**きょう 興** ▶先生は興に乗って, カラオケで続けて3曲歌った Our teacher *got into the spirit of things* and sang three songs in a row at the karaoke center. ‖ 主賓の長話に我々はすっかり興をそがれた The long speech by the guest of honor *threw a pall* over the gathering. (➤ pall は「(棺などに掛ける)布」が原義) ‖ 観客は相手チームが回の浅いうちに大量点を取ったので興をそがれてしまった The spectators *lost interest* in the game when the visiting team scored lots of [a bunch of] runs in the early innings. (➤ a bunch of は「(まとまって) 大量の」).

4**きょう 凶** **bad** [**ill**] **luck, bad** [**ill**] **fortune**；**misfortune** (災難) ▶その寺でおみくじを引いたら「凶」と出た When I picked a fortune slip at the temple, it said "*Bad Luck*."

5**きょう 経** a **sutra** ▶法華(ほけ)経 the Lotus *Sutra*.

-きょう -強 ▶ 30キロ強の荷物を3階まで運ぶのはきつかった It was tough work to carry my baggage weighing *30 kilograms or more* up to the third floor. ‖ パーツはすぐに届いて, 修理に1時間強かかった The part came quickly and the repair took *a little over an hour*.

ぎょう 行 a **line** ▶ 8ページ5行目 page 8, *line 5* ‖ 20ページの10行目から読んでください Start reading at *line* 10 on page 20. ‖ 10ページの下から3行目をご覧ください Look at *the third line* from the bottom on page 10.

きょうあく 凶悪な **atrocious** /ətróʊʃəs/, **brutal** ▶凶悪な犯罪 an *atrocious* [*a heinous*] crime ‖ 凶悪犯人の顔写真がテレビで放映された The face of the *brutal criminal* was broadcast on TV. 《参考》「(凶悪犯人の)顔写真」のことをインフォーマルでは mug とか mugshot という.

きょうあん 教案 a **teaching plan**.

1**きょうい 驚異** a **wonder**, a **marvel** (➤ 後者は「信じ難い」という気持ちをより強調する) ▶自然の驚異 *wonders* of nature ‖ ドバイのブルジュ・ハリファはまさに工業技術の驚異だ The Burj Khalifa in Dubai is *a marvel* of engineering. ‖ 月ロケットの打ち上げは20世紀科学の驚異だった Launching a rocket to the moon was one of the *most amazing* scientific *achievements* of the 20th century. ‖ ロボット工学は近年驚異的な進歩を遂げた There has been *amazing* [*marvelous*] progress in robotics in recent years. ‖ 親たちは幼い子供たちの英語習得の速さに驚異の目を見張った The parents *were amazed at* the rapidity with which their kids picked up English.

2**きょうい 脅威** a **threat**；a **menace** /ménəs/ (敵意を感じさせるほどの) ▶戦争の脅威が無くなる日が来ればと思う I long for the day when there is no *threat* of war! ‖ ダンプカーはほかのドライバーにとって脅威だ Dump trucks are *a menace* to other drivers.

3**きょうい 胸囲** one's **chest measurement** ▶彼は胸囲が95センチある His *chest measurement* is 95 centimeters. ／He measures 95 centimeters *around the chest*.

きょういく 教育 (an) **education** (主に学校教育)；(an) **upbringing** /ʌ́pbrìŋɪŋ/ (家庭での養育) 一動 **教育する** **educate** ＋目 ▶子供を教育する *educate* children ‖ 教育上の問題 an *educational* problem ‖ 誰にも教育を受ける機会はある Everyone has the chance to *get an education*. ‖ この雑誌は子供には教育上好ましくない This magazine is not good for children *from an educational point of view*. ‖ 教育のある人が良い市民であるとは限らない A *highly-educated* person does not necessarily make a good citizen.
▶日本の教育制度は戦後大きく改革された The Japanese *educational* [*education*] *system* was drastically reformed after the war. ‖ 彼女は教育ママだ She is *an education-minded* [*a grade-conscious*] *mother*. ‖ 家庭教育(＝家庭でのしつけ)は教育の重要な一部を成す *Discipline in the home* is an important part of education. ‖ 当社では新入社員に語学教育を実施しています We provide new employees with *foreign language education* in this company. ‖ 性教育には賛否両論がある There are pros and cons to *sex education*. ‖ 大学の入学試験はもっと教育的見地から議論されるべきだ College entrance exams should be discussed from more of *an educational point of view*.
‖教育委員会 the Board of Education ‖ 教育改

革 educational reform ‖ **教育学部** the School of Education ‖ **教育課程** a curriculum /kəríkjələm/ ‖ **教育漢字** basic kanji taught in elementary school ‖ **教育機関** an educational institution ‖ **教育基本法** the Fundamental Law of Education ‖ **教育産業** education-related industries ‖ **教育実習** practice teaching, teaching practice, teaching practicum, professional practice (➤どれを用いるかは学校によって異なる) ‖ **教育実習生** a student [practice / practicum / trainee] teacher, a teacher trainee ⇀**教生** ‖ **教育者** an educator ‖ **教育心理学** educational psychology ‖ **教育政策** education policy ‖ **教育大学** 《米》a teachers college, 《英》a college of education ‖ **教育長** 《米》a superintendent of schools, 《英》a chief education officer [director] ‖ **教育番組** an educational program ‖ **教育費** educational [school] expenses ‖ **職業教育** vocational education ‖ **初等教育** primary [elementary] education.

> **逆引き熟語 ○○教育**
> **ＩＴ教育** IT education／**英才教育** special education／**遠隔教育** distance education [learning]／**義務教育** compulsory education／**公教育** public education／**高等教育** higher education／**再教育** reeducation／**生涯教育** lifelong education／**スパルタ教育** harsh discipline／**性教育** sex education／**通信教育** a correspondence course／**幼児教育** early childhood education

きょういご 強意語 an **intensifier**, an **intensive word**.

きょういん 教員 a **teacher**

> **語法** (1)「教員」を指す最も一般的な語は teacher であるが, a member of the faculty [teaching staff] のようにもいう. (2)教員全員を指す場合は the teachers of a school [a college] / the faculty / the teaching staff などのようにいう.

▶父は高校の教員です My father is *a high school teacher*. ‖ **教員会議** a teachers' meeting ‖ **教員室** a teachers' room, a faculty room ‖ **教員免許更新制** the license renewal system for teachers, the teaching license renewal system (➤そのための講習なら system を course に換える) ‖ **教員免許状** a teacher's license [certificate], a teaching certificate.

きょうう 強雨 **intense rain(fall)**.

きょううん 強運 ▶強運の持ち主 a person with *incredible luck*.

1**きょうえい 競泳** a **swimming race** [**event**] ▶彼女は競泳の選手としてオリンピックに参加した She participated in the Olympic *swimming events*.

2**きょうえい 共栄** **co-prosperity**.

きょうえきひ 共益費 a **maintenance fee** (維持費).

1**きょうえん 共演する** **co-star** ▶渡辺謙と映画で共演する *appear* in a film *with* Watanabe Ken / *co-star* in a film *with* Watanabe Ken (➤後者は主役に対する助演であることを意味する). ‖ **共演者** a co-star.

2**きょうえん 供宴** a **banquet**.

きょうおう 供応する **entertain** +目 (接待する); **treat** +目 (おごる).

1**きょうか 強化する** **strengthen** /stréŋkθən/ +目 (強くする); **reinforce** /riːɪnfɔ́ːʳs/ +目 (補強する) ▶筋力[防衛]を強化する *strengthen* one's muscles [the defense] ‖ 彼らは 2 人のアメリカ人選手を入れてチームを**強化した** They *reinforced* [*beefed up*] their team with two American players. (➤ beef up はインフォーマルな表現) ‖ うちの野球チームは 3 か月ごとに**強化練習**を行う Our baseball team has *intensive training* every three months.

2**きょうか 教科** a **subject** ‖ **教科課程** the school curriculum ‖ **教科担当** a subject teacher, a specialist teacher (➤後者は音楽・美術・体育など, 特殊技能を要する教科担当の場合). ⇀**学科**.

1**きょうかい 境界** a **boundary** (地図などに示される国境線); a **border** (山や川などの地理的特徴に基づいた境界, 国境(地域)) ⇀**国境** ▶この 2 つの畑の**境界**をもっとはっきり決めましょう Let us define the *boundary* between these two farms more clearly. ‖ その町はテキサス州とアーカンソー州との**境界線上にある** The town is *on the border* between Texas and Arkansas. (➤「境界線」は boundary [border] line). ▶《比喩的》その候補は当落の**境界線上**にいる That candidate has a *borderline* chance of being elected. (➤「当選する見込みは五分五分だ」の意).

2**きょうかい 教会** a **church** ▶彼らは霊南坂**教会**で結婚式を挙げた They got married at Reinanzaka *Church*. ‖ 父は日曜ごとに**教会に行きます** My father *goes to church* every Sunday. (➤礼拝が目的で教会に行く場合の church は a や the はつかない).

3**きょうかい 協会** an **association**, a **society** ▶日本相撲**協会** the Japan Sumo *Association* ‖ 当**協会**は会員が 1 万名を超えています The *society* has more than 10,000 members.

ぎょうかい 業界 **the industry** /índəstri/ ▶宅配便**業界**は今や過当競争に入っている *The home delivery service industry* is now highly competitive. ‖ **業界紙** a trade paper ‖ **業界用語** industry jargon.

1**きょうがく 共学** **coeducation** ▶(男女)**共学**については今も賛否両論がある There are still pros and cons regarding *coeducation*. ‖ ぼくは男子校出なので, **共学校**に通っていた人が羨ましかった Being from an all-boys school, I was (always) jealous of people who went to *coeducational schools*. 《参考》男女別学校は single-sex school という ‖ **対話**「皆さんが通っているのは男子校, 女子校, それとも共学(校)?」「共学(校)です」"Is your school for boys only, girls only, or *co-ed*?" "*Co-ed*." (➤ /kóʊed/ と発音).

2**きょうがく 驚愕** **astonishment** 一動 **驚がくさせる** **astonish** +目 ▶少年の銃乱射事件は住民を**驚がくさせた** The boy's shooting rampage *astonished* the residents.

ぎょうかく 行革 **administrative reform**.

きょうかしょ 教科書 a **schoolbook**, a **textbook**, 《米また》a **text** ▶数学の**教科書** a math *textbook* ‖ **教科書**の28ページを開けなさい Open your *textbook(s)* to [《英》at] page 28. ‖ **教科書検定制度** the system of textbook authorization ‖ **教科書無償支給** the free supply of school textbooks.

きょうかつ 恐喝 **extortion**; **blackmail** (秘密をばらすと脅して); a **threat**, **intimidation** (脅し) 一動 **恐喝する** **blackmail** +目 ▶きみの言い方はまるで**恐喝**じゃないか You sound like you're trying to *threaten* [*intimidate* / *blackmail*] me. ‖ その男は**恐喝**して老夫婦から金を巻き上げた The man *extorted* money from the elderly couple. (➤ extort A from B は「B(人)から A(物)を脅し取る」).

[1]**きょうかん 共感** empathy；sympathy(同情) **—動 共感する** empathize《with》, sympathize《with》 ▶私はその映画の主人公に共感を覚えた I *empathized with* [*felt empathy for*] the main character in that movie. ‖ その本は全国の女性の共感を呼んだ That book *resonated with* women all over the country.

[2]**きょうかん 教官** a teacher, a member of the faculty [teaching staff]；the faculty, the teaching staff (➤ 集合的に) →教員 ▶国立大学の教官 *a teacher* at a national university ‖ 自動車教習所の教官 a driving *instructor*.

ぎょうかん 行間 ▶行間の意味を読み取ることができなければ文学は本当にはわからない You cannot truly appreciate literature unless you *read between the lines*. (➤ unless は「…しない限り」).

[1]**きょうき 凶器** a weapon /wépən/；a murder weapon (殺人に使われた).

[2]**きょうき 狂気** madness, insanity (➤ 後者はややフォーマルな語で，実際の精神病に関連して用いられることが多い) ▶有り金残らず浮浪者にやるとは狂気の沙汰だ You must be *crazy* to have given all your money to a bum.

[3]**きょうき 狂喜** ▶日本チームの決勝ゴールにスタンドのサポーターは狂喜した The supporters in the stands *went wild* when the Japanese team scored the winning goal.

[1]**きょうぎ 競技** a game, a match (試合；後者は主に《英》. ただし，テニス・ボクシング・ゴルフなどは《米》でも後者がふつう)；a contest, a competition (競技会；後者はやや堅い語)；an event (競技の種目) →試合
▶野外[屋内]競技 a field [an indoor] *game* ‖ 陸上競技 track and field *events* ‖ 体操の競技会 a gymnastics *competition* ‖ 国際スポーツ競技会 an international sports *competition* ‖ 彼女はテニス競技大会で1位になった She took first place in the tennis *tournament*. ‖**競技者** an athlete(陸上の), a player(球技などの) ‖ **競技場** a field；a (sports) stadium (観客席を含んだ).

[2]**きょうぎ 協議** (a) discussion(討論)；(a) deliberation (入念な討議)；(a) consultation (専門家などに相談すること)；a conference (意見の交換)；a negotiating session(折衝の会合) **—動 協議する** discuss ▶徹夜の協議 an all-night *negotiating session* ‖ 私たちは協議離婚することになりました We agreed to *divorce by mutual consent*. ‖**協議会** a conference ‖ **協議事項** the agenda (議題)；a topic [subject] for discussion (討論の主題).

[3]**きょうぎ 狭義** a narrow sense.

[4]**きょうぎ 教義** (a) doctrine；(a) dogma(絶対視される教条)；teachings(教え) ▶キリスト教の三位一体の教義 the Christian *doctrine* of the Trinity.

ぎょうぎ 行儀 manners(作法；複数形に注意.「行儀」や「マナー」の意で単数形 manner は用いない)；behavior (行い) ▶お行儀はどうしたの？ *Where are* [*Where's*] *your manners?* (➤ 子供を叱るときの決まった言い方で，文法には外れるが後者もよく用いられる) ‖ 行儀よくしなさい *Behave yourself!* ／*Be a good boy* [*girl*]. ‖ (誕生日会によばれて行くわが子に)お行儀よくするんだよ *Remember your manners*. ／*Mind your manners*. ‖ 近頃の若者は行儀作法を知らない(＝行儀が悪い)者が多い Many young people today *have no manners*. ／Many young people these days *do not know how to behave*. ‖ 道子はとても行儀がよい Michiko *has such good manners*. ／Michiko *is extremely well-behaved* [*well-mannered*].

きょうきゃく 橋脚 a (bridge) pier.

きょうきゅう 供給 (a) supply(必要品・不足品の) **—動 供給する** supply ＋目

> **【文型】**
> 人(A)に物(B)を供給する
> supply A with B
> supply B to [for] A

▶この発電所は首都圏に電力を供給している This power station *supplies* the metropolitan area *with* electricity [*supplies* electricity *to* the metropolitan area]. ‖**供給過剰** an oversupply, an excess supply, a supply glut.

きょうぎゅうびょう 狂牛病 mad cow disease(➤ 正式名は bovine spongiform encephalopathy(牛海綿状脳症)で，その頭文字を取って BSE と呼ぶ).

ぎょうぎょうしい 仰々しい exaggerated /ɪgzǽdʒəreɪṭɪd/ (誇張した)；ostentatious /ɑ̀:stentéɪʃəs/ (派手な) ▶店の前に仰々しい看板を出す put up an *ostentatious* [*a garish*] sign in front of the store (➤ garish /géərɪʃ/ は「けばけばしい」) ‖ 彼女の仰々しい物の言い方は嫌いだ I don't like her *exaggerated* way of speaking. ‖ こんな小さな間違いをそう仰々しく騒ぎ立てるな Don't *make such a big fuss* [*deal*] about such a small mistake.

きょうきん 胸襟 ▶胸襟を開いて話し合う *have a heart-to-heart talk*.

きょうく 教区 a parish (1つの教会の)；a diocese /dáɪəsɪs/ (主教・司教が管轄する大きな区域).

きょうぐう 境遇 surroundings；circumstances /sə́:ˈkəmstænsɪz/ (環境) ▶彼女は幸せ[不幸せ]な境遇に育った She was brought up in happy [unhappy] *surroundings*. ‖ どんなつらい境遇にあっても夢はもち続けなさい Continue to hold on to your dreams no matter how bleak the *circumstances* (are). ‖ **対話**「時間は有るけど，金が無いんだ」「ぼくだって同じ境遇だよ」"I have time, but no money." "I'm *in the same boat*."

きょうくん 教訓 a lesson ▶この交通事故で私は貴重な教訓を得た I *learned a* precious *lesson* from this traffic accident. ‖『イソップ物語』には多くの教訓が含まれている "Aesop's Fables" contains many *good lessons* [*moral lessons*].

きょうげき 京劇 the Peking [Beijing] opera；classical Chinese opera.

ぎょうけつ 凝血 clotted [coagulated] blood.

[1]**きょうけん 強肩** ▶その捕手は強肩だ The catcher can throw a very fast ball. ／The catcher *has a rifle arm*. (➤ともに「速い球を投げる(ことができる)」の意).

[2]**きょうけん 強健な** strong；sturdy(頑丈な) ▶彼は強健な肉体の持ち主だ He has a *strong* [*sturdy*] body.

[3]**きょうけん 狂犬** a rabid [mad] dog.

きょうげん 狂言 1【能狂言】 a Noh comedy.
2【偽り，見せかけ】 ▶狂言自殺をする *fake* a suicide ‖ あの強盗事件は被害者の狂言だった That robbery case proved to be *a put-up job* on the part of the supposed victim.

きょうけんびょう 狂犬病 rabies /réɪbi:z/；hydrophobia /hàɪdrəfóʊbiə/ (恐水病) ▶狂犬病(予防)ワクチン a *rabies* (prevention) vaccine.

きょうこ 強固な strong(強い)；firm(堅固な)；solid (固体としての結合力が) ▶強固な土台を築く build a *solid* foundation ‖ 強固な姿勢を貫く stick to a *strong* stance ‖ 強固な決意を持って行動する act with *firm* resolve ‖その計画に強固に反対し続ける continue to *strongly* oppose the plan ‖彼女は意志が強固でどんな誘惑にも動じない She *has a strong will* and isn't moved by [is immune to] any temptation.

ぎょうこ 凝固する coagulate (体液などが); solidify (液体·気体が) ▶血液は空気中では凝固する Blood *coagulates* in air. ‖たんぱく質は加熱すると凝固する Protein *coagulates* when heated.
‖凝固剤 coagulant.

1きょうこう 強硬な firm (断固とした); strong (強い); resolute (決心の固い); vigorous (力強い) ▶大学当局は学生の要求に対して強硬な態度をとった The university authorities adopted an *unyielding* attitude toward the students' demands. ‖彼はいつも強硬なことを言い強硬なふるまいをする He always talks *tough* and acts *tough*. ‖学生たちはその決定に強硬に反対した The students were *strongly* [*firmly* / *resolutely*] opposed to the decision. ‖彼らはその商社に対して強硬に抗議した They protested *vigorously* against the trading company. ‖彼は強硬派の1人だ He is one of the *hard-liners* [*hawks*]. (➤ hawk は「タカ」の意で, ここでは比喩的に「タカ派の人」).

2きょうこう 強行する force through ▶制度の改革を強行する *force* a revision of the system *through* ‖こうなったらあの群衆の中を強行突破するしかない It looks as though the only thing to do is (to) *force our way through* that crowd.

3きょうこう 恐慌 (a) panic ▶強い地震が人々を恐慌状態に陥れた The strong earthquake precipitated *a panic*. ‖銀行の倒産は金融恐慌を招く Bank failure will lead to *a financial panic* [*a panic in the financial sector*].

4きょうこう 凶行 a (violent / vicious) crime ▶なぜ彼がそんな凶行に及んだかわからない I have no idea why he committed such *a* (*violent* / *vicious*) *crime*.

5きょうこう 教皇 the Pope, the Pontiff.

1きょうごう 強豪 ▶強豪チーム a *very strong* team, 《インフォーマル》a powerhouse ‖我々は来週強豪のＰＬ学園と対戦する Next week we're scheduled to meet the PL Gakuen *powerhouse* [*Goliath*]. (➤ Goliath /gəláɪəθ/ は「巨人」).

2きょうごう 競合 competition /kɑ̀:mpətíʃən/ ▶Ｓ社とは同じ製薬会社だが, 競合する商品は少ない S Company and we are both in the pharmaceutical business, but we don't have a lot of products *competing against each other*.

ぎょうこう 行幸 the Emperor's visit ▶この石碑は明治天皇の当地への行幸を記念したものです This stone monument commemorates Emperor Meiji's *visit* here.

きょうこうぐん 強行軍 a forced march ▶強行軍でやらないとこの仕事は期日までに上がらない *If we don't push ourselves to the limit*, we won't be able to finish this job by the deadline.

1きょうこく 強国 a strong country, a powerful nation, a (great) power ‖軍事強国 a military power.

2きょうこく 峡谷 a gorge /gɔ:ʳdʒ/; a canyon (深く大きい谷) ▶グランドキャニオンは世界で最も有名な峡谷の１つだ The Grand Canyon is one of the most famous *gorges* in the world.

きょうさ 教唆 (an) instigation ▶犯罪を教唆する *abet* a crime / *incite* [*instigate*] a person to commit a crime.

ぎょうざ 餃子 →ギョーザ.

1きょうさい 共催 cosponsorship, joint sponsorship [auspices /ɔ́:spɪsɪz/] ▶その展示会は平成大学と出版社の共催で開かれた The exhibition was held *under the* (*joint*) *sponsorship* [*auspices*] of Heisei University and a publishing company. ‖(サッカーの) 2002年ワールドカップは日本と韓国の共催で行われた The 2002 World Cup (Soccer) was *co-hosted* by Japan and South Korea.

2きょうさい 共済 mutual aid [benefit]
‖共済組合 a mutual aid [benefit] association.

きょうざい 教材 teaching materials ‖視聴覚教材 audio-visual aids ‖音声 [ビデオ] 教材 audio recordings [video materials] used for teaching.

きょうさいか 恐妻家 a henpecked husband ▶彼は大変な恐妻家で, 奥さんの前ではいつもおどおどしている He is such *a henpecked husband* who always gets nervous in front of his wife.

1きょうさく 凶作 a bad [poor] crop ▶去年は米は凶作だった We had *a poor* rice *crop* last year. / The rice *crop* was *a failure* last year.

2きょうさく 狭窄 《医学》a stricture.

きょうざめ 興醒め ▶部長の長話に私たちは興ざめしてしまった The general manager's long-winded speech *spoiled our fun*. (➤ spoil は「台なしにする」) ‖素顔の美しいみゆきが厚化粧して現れたのでみんな興ざめした All of us *were turned off* when Miyuki, who looks so pretty without makeup, showed up plastered with heavy makeup. (➤ turn off は「(人を)うんざりさせる」).

きょうさん 協賛 support (支援); cooperation (協力) ▶花火大会は岡崎商工会議所の協賛を得て行われた The display of fireworks is held *with the support of* [*in cooperation with*] the Okazaki Chamber of Commerce and Industry. (➤ 前者は金銭的援助があったことを意味する).

きょうさんしゅぎ 共産主義 communism
‖共産主義国 a communist country [state] ‖共産主義者 a communist.

きょうさんとう 共産党 the Communist Party.

きょうし 教師 a teacher →教員 ▶中学 [高校] の教師 a junior [senior] high school *teacher* ‖英語の教師 an English *teacher* / *a teacher* of English (→英語) ‖私は地元の小学校で教師をしています I *teach in the* local *elementary school*. / *I teach elementary school* here.

1きょうじ 教示 instruction ▶A博士に臓器移植の注意点についてご教示をお願いした We asked Dr. A to *instruct* us about the matters that require attention in organ transplants.

2きょうじ 矜持 pride ▶きょうじを保つ maintain one's *pride*.

ぎょうし 凝視 a stare (大きく開けた目でじっと見つめること); a gaze (驚いたり感嘆したりして見つめること) ▶人を凝視してはいけません. 失礼です You mustn't *stare* at people. It is rude.

1ぎょうじ 行事 an event ▶ことしは行事が多くて忙しい I am busy with many *events* this year. ‖花火大会はこの町の年間行事の１つだ The fireworks display is this town's *annual events*.
‖学校行事 a school event.

「学校行事」のいろいろ 入学式 entrance ceremony / 始業式 opening ceremony / 健康診断 physical checkup / 開校記念日 anniversary of the school's founding / 中間試験 midterm exam(ination)／遠足 outing／期末試験 term [end of term] exam(ination)／大掃除 general cleaning／終業式 closing ceremony／夏休み summer vacation／合唱コンクール chorus competition／修学旅行 school excursion [trip]／体育祭 field day, sports day／水泳大会 swim meet／球技大会 ball game tournament／文化祭·学校祭 school festival／弁論大会 speech contest／消防訓練 fire drill／冬休み winter vacation／学年末試験 final examination／実力テスト proficiency test／卒業式 graduation ceremony／春休み spring vacation

2**ぎょうじ 行司** a **sumo referee** /rèfərí:/ ▶行司の軍配は白鵬に上がった *The referee's decision* went to Hakuho. ‖立(た)て行司 the head sumo referee.

きょうしきょく 狂詩曲《音楽》a **rhapsody.**

きょうしつ 教室 a **classroom**(部屋); a **class**(講習会) ▶教室で騒ぐな Don't be noisy in the *classroom*. ‖音楽の教室(＝音楽室)はどこですか Where is the *music room*? ‖彼女はヨガの教室を開いている She *teaches yoga*. ／She *gives yoga classes*. ‖ＬＬ教室 a language laboratory [lab] (➤ lab はインフォーマルな語).

きょうしゃ 強者 the strong(➤総称); a **strong** [an **overbearing**] **person** ▶強者をくじき弱者を助けるために我々は戦っている We are fighting for the weak against *the strong*. ／We are fighting *the strong* to help the weak.

ぎょうしゃ 業者 a **salesperson**(販売員); a **manufacturer**(製造業者); a **dealer**(販売業者)(➤日本語に相当する英語の言い方はない) ▶その関係の業者に当たってみましょう I'll check with *people in that line of work* [*companies in that line of business*].

ぎょうじゃ 行者 an **ascetic** /əsétɪk/.

きょうじゃく 強弱 strength and weakness(強さと弱さ); a **stress**(強勢); a **rhythm** /ríðəm/ (リズム) ▶詩の朗読では強弱のリズムが重要な役目を果たす *The rhythm of strong and weak beats* plays a very important part in poetry recitation.

1**きょうじゅ 教授 1**【大学の教員】a **professor** (➤肩書きとしては Professor Ishida のように姓の前につけるか, Prof. Ishida Taro のように表記する. 姓に直接つけるときは Prof. と略さない) ▶哲学科の教授 *a professor* in the Department of Philosophy ‖M大学の英語の教授 *a professor* of English at M University (● 「M大学の」の「の」を of としないこと) ‖きのう教授会があった We had *a faculty meeting* yesterday. (➤ faculty /fǽkəlti/ は「教授陣, 全教授」).
‖教授室 a faculty room ‖客員教授 a visiting professor ‖兼担教授 an adjunct professor ‖特任教授 a professor by contractual appointment, a specially appointed professor. (→准教授, 助教授).
2【教えること】▶彼女はサンチェス先生からスペイン語の個人教授を受けている She takes *private lessons* in Spanish from Mr. Sánchez. ‖彼女は自宅でダンスを教授している She *gives lessons in dancing* at home. ‖教授法 a teaching method.

2**きょうじゅ 享受する enjoy** +名 ▶我々は民主的な社会で自由を享受している We *enjoy* freedom in a democratic society.

ぎょうしゅ 業種 a **type of industry,** a **category of business.**

きょうしゅう 郷愁 nostalgia /nɑːstǽldʒə/ ▶母の写真を見て突然強い郷愁に駆られた When I saw a picture of my mother, I *was* suddenly *seized by* strong *nostalgia*. ‖この絵を見ると子供の頃への郷愁を感じる This picture *makes* me *nostalgic* for my childhood.

きょうしゅうじょ 教習所 ▶自動車教習所 a driving *school* ‖ダンス教習所 a dancing *school*.

きょうしゅく 恐縮 ▶ご迷惑をおかけして大変恐縮です *I'm* awfully *sorry* to have troubled you. ／*I must apologize to you* for having given you so much trouble. ‖遠路わざわざお見舞いにおいでいただき恐縮です *It's very kind of you* to come all the way to visit me in the hospital. ‖恐縮ですが車で名古屋駅まで送っていただけませんか *I hate to ask*, but could you possibly give me a ride to Nagoya Station?
✉ **結構な品を頂き主人も大変恐縮しております** My husband *is* also *much obliged to you* for your lovely gift. ➤ be obliged to は改まった言い方で「…に(深く)感謝している」の意.

ぎょうしゅく 凝縮 condensation 一動 **凝縮する condense** +名 ▶このデジカメには現代科学の粋が凝縮されている The latest technology *is condensed* into this digital camera.

きょうじゅつ 供述 a **statement**(申し立て); **testimony**(法廷での証言) 一動 **供述する state** +名, **testify** (+名) ▶彼女は警察にうその供述をした She *made a false statement* to the police. ‖彼は彼女がホテルから出て来るのを見たと供述した He *testified* that he had seen her come out of the hotel.

きょうしょ 教書 a **(Presidential) message**(米国大統領の); a **(papal) bull**(ローマ教皇の) ▶米国大統領の一般(年頭)教書 the U.S. President's State of the Union *Address* [*message*] (➤慣習上, 演説という形式で行われるので State of the Union Address という).

きょうじょう 教条 a **dogma.**

ぎょうしょう 行商 peddling ▶彼は薬の行商をして生計を立てている He earns his living by *peddling* medicines. ‖行商人 a peddler.

きょうしょく 教職 the teaching profession ▶きみは本当に教職に就きたいのですか Do you really want to *be a teacher* [*to go into teaching*]? ‖教職を天職と考えている先生方が多い Many teachers consider their *profession* a vocation. ‖この大学には教職課程がない This university does not have *a teacher-training course*.
‖教職員 the staff of a school, the staff [faculty] of a university, educational personnel ‖教職員組合 a faculty [teachers'] union.

きょうじる 興じる enjoy +名 ▶公園で老人たちがトランプに興じていた Seniors were *enjoying* playing cards in the park.

きょうしん 共振 resonance ▶大地震の共振現象で西湖に津波が発生した The *resonance* induced by the great earthquake triggered [generated] a tsunami in Lake Sai.

きょうじん 強靱な strong, tough (➤後者には「打たれ強い, へこたれない」というイメージがある) ▶あれだけ侮辱されても平気だとはきみの神経は強じんだね You must have *nerves of steel* [You must *be tough*] to keep cool in the face of such insult. (➤ nerves of steel は「鋼の(ような)神経」が原義) ‖マラソン選手は強じんな心臓を備えていなければならない Marathon runners have to have *strong hearts*.

き

きょうしんかい 共進会 a **competitive exhibition** ▶農業共進会 an agricultural [a country] *fair*.

きょうしんざい 強心剤 a **heart stimulant**.

きょうしんしょう 狭心症《医学》**angina pectoris** /ændʒàɪnə péktərɪs/《参考》日常的には単に angina ともいう.

きょうしんてき 狂信的な fanatic /fənǽtɪk/ ▶狂信的集団 a *fanatic* group ‖ 狂信的宗教集団 a *fanatic* cult.

ぎょうずい 行水 ▶行水を使う take *a bath in a portable tub*.

きょうする 供する serve +目(飲食物を); **offer** +目(提供する) ▶このワインは魚料理と一緒に供するのに最高だ This wine is best *served* with a fish dish. ‖ モルモットを実験に供する *utilize* guinea pigs in lab experiments.

1**きょうせい 強制 compulsion**(余儀ない); **enforcement**(嫌がったり抵抗したりしている人への) 一動 **強制する compel** +目, **force** +目 →無理 ▶彼らはその島で労働を強制された They *were compelled* [*forced*] to work on that island. ‖ 私たちに強制的に勉強させようとしても無駄よ It's no use trying to *force* us to study. ‖ 彼はロンドンから日本に強制送還された He *was forced to return to* Japan from London. ‖ そのジェット機は強制着陸させられた That jet plane *was forced down* [*was forced to make a landing*].
‖強制執行 compulsory execution ‖ 強制保険 compulsory insurance.

2**きょうせい 矯正** (a) **correction** 一動 **矯正する correct** +目 ▶遠視の矯正は難しい It is difficult to *correct* farsightedness. ‖ 彼女は現在歯を矯正している She *is having her teeth straightened*. ／She *wears braces*. (➤ braces は「歯列矯正器」).

3**きょうせい 教生** a **student** [**practice** ／ **practicum** ／ **trainee**] **teacher**, a **teacher trainee** /trèɪníː/ ▶母校に教生に行く *do practice teaching* at one's alma mater.

4**きょうせい 共生 symbiosis** /sìmbaɪóʊsɪs/.

5**きょうせい 強勢** (a) **stress**(音声学の) ▶第1音節に強勢を置きなさい Put [Place] *a stress* on the first syllable. ‖ important という語は第2音節に強勢がある The word 'important' *is stressed* on the second syllable.

ぎょうせい 行政 administration ▶この問題は行政の貧困から起きた This problem came about because of poor [bad] *administration*. ‖ この食糧問題を解決するには行政措置をとる必要がある *Administrative measures* should be taken to settle this food problem. ‖ 政府は行政改革を進めている The government is going ahead with *administrative reform*. ‖行政機関 an administrative organ ‖ 行政区 an administrative ward ‖ 行政権 administrative power ‖ 行政サービス administrative service ‖ 行政刷新会議 the Government Revitalization Unit ‖ 行政指導 administrative guidance ‖ 行政書士 an administrative scrivener (➤ 英米にはこれに対応する職業は無い. したがって gyoseishoshi lawyer と表記するのも一策) ‖ 行政処分 administrative disposition.

ぎょうせき 業績 achievements; **results** (結果); **contributions** (貢献) ▶彼女は栄養学の分野ですばらしい業績を上げた She has produced remarkable *achievements* in the field of dietetics. ‖ わが社のことしの業績ははかばかしくなかった Our business *results* this year have not been satisfactory. ‖ うちの会社は業績がいい[悪い] Our company *is doing well* [*poorly*]. ‖ 彼は世界平和のために多大な業績を残した He has made great *contributions* toward world peace. ‖ あの人にはしっかりした学問的業績は何もない He has no solid *academic achievements* [*record*].

きょうそ 教祖 the founder of a religion [**religious sect**] ▶その男はカラス真実教の教祖とあがめられている That man is revered as *founder of the* Crow Holy Truth *Sect*.

1**きょうそう 競争 competition**, a **race** 一動 **競争する compete** 《with》 ▶競争が無ければ値段は下がらない Prices won't come down without *competition*. ‖ その2軒の店は競争でスマートホンを売っている The two stores *are competing* to sell smartphones. ‖ 英語では小林君とはまるで競争にならない I'*m no match for* Kobayashi in English. ／There's *no way I can compete* with Kobayashi in English. (➤ ともに「小林君のほうが上だ」の意) ‖ 弟とどちらが速く泳げるか競争してみた My (younger) brother and I *had a race* to see which of us could swim faster. ‖ わが校はことし競争率が2倍だった *The rate of competition* for admissions to our school this year was 2 to 1. ‖ ファッションデザイン界はとても競争が激しい The world of fashion designing is very *competitive*. ‖ 競争力のある価格 a *competitive* price.
‖競争相手 a rival (同じ分野で競い合う, あるいは, 一方しか勝ち残れない競い合いの); a contestant (コンテストの); a competitor (スポーツ競技の); a contender (優勝を目指して争う) ‖ 軍備競争 the arms race.

2**きょうそう 競走** a **race** 一動 **競走する race** 《with》, **have a race** ▶競走に勝つ[負ける] win [lose] *a race* ‖ クラスメートたちと競走する *have* [*run*] *a race with* one's classmates ‖ 誰が100メートル競走で1位になりましたか Who took first prize in the *100-meter dash*? (➤ 短距離競走は dash という).

きょうぞう 胸像 a **bust**《参考》胴だけの彫像は torso /tɔ́ːrsoʊ/, 全身像は statue という.

ぎょうそう 形相 a **face**, a **look** ▶「もう別れよう」と言うとぼくの彼女は必死の形相ですがりついてきた When I said we should break up, my girlfriend clung to me with *a desperate look* (*on her face*).

きょうそうきょく 協奏曲 a **concerto** ▶ピアノ[バイオリン]協奏曲 a piano [violin] *concerto*.

きょうそくぼん 教則本 an **instruction book**; a **manual**(便覧, 解説書) ▶ギターの教則本 a guitar *manual* (➤「ギターの練習本」なら a guitar drill [practice] book).

きょうそん 共存 living in harmony(仲よく生活すること); **coexistence**(利害が衝突するものどうしが折り合っていくこと) 一動 **共存する live in harmony**; **coexist** ▶共存共栄の精神 the spirit of *coexistence* and coprosperity ‖ 日米の平和共存 the *peaceful coexistence* of Japan and the U.S. ‖ すべての人間は共存すべきだ All human beings should *live in harmony*.

きょうだ 強打 ▶人の頭を強打する *deal* a person *a heavy blow* on the head ‖ 壁に頭を強打する *hit* one's head *hard* against the wall.
‖(野球の)強打者 a hard hitter, a slugger.

1**きょうだい 兄弟・姉妹** a **brother**(男の); a **sister** (女の)

《解説》「きょうだい」と brother
(1) 日本語の「きょうだい」は, 兄弟・姉妹の両方を意味するが，英語ではふつう男女を区別する．区別しない sibling はやや改まった語．(2) 日本語では「兄」「弟」「姉」「妹」のように年上・年下の関係がはっきり表されるが，英語では長幼の順を特に問題とするとき以外はふつう older [younger] brother のような言い方はしない．

▶石原兄弟 the Ishihara *brothers* ‖ きょうだい間の競争意識 *sibling* rivalry ‖ 父は男４人兄弟です My father has three *brothers*. (➤ この場合は本人を除いて数える) ‖ 対話「きょうだいは何人ですか」「姉と，弟が２人です」"How many *brothers and sisters* [*siblings*] do you have ?" "One sister and two brothers." ‖ 彼女は４人姉妹の上から２番目だ She is the second (oldest ／eldest) of four *sisters*. ‖ きょうだいげんかしちゃだめ！ Don't *fight with your brother(s)* [*sister(s)*]！(➤ fight はつかみ合いのけんかでも口げんかでもよい)．

2 **きょうだい 強大な** great, mighty ▶その政治家は実業界に強大な勢力を持っている That politician has *great* influence in [on] the business world. ‖ ローマ帝国は強大(な帝国)だった The Roman Empire was a *mighty* one.

3 **きょうだい 鏡台** (米) a dresser, (英) a dressing table 《参考》(英) の dresser は食器戸棚の一種．

1 **きょうたく 教卓** a teacher's desk.

2 **きょうたく 供託** ‖ 供託金 a deposit.

きょうたん 驚嘆 amazement (びっくり仰天)；wonder (美しさ・すばらしさなどに圧倒されること) 一動 驚嘆する be amazed 《at, by》；wonder 《at》 ▶彼女の歌のうまさには驚嘆した I *was amazed at* how beautifully she could sing. ‖ 彼らは彼の腕前に驚嘆した They *wondered at* his skill. ‖ 彼が独力でアラビア語をマスターしたとは驚嘆に値する *It's* quite *amazing* that he has mastered Arabic by himself.

1 **きょうだん 教壇** a platform ▶教壇に立って30年になります It has been thirty years *since I became a teacher*. (➤「先生になってから」と考える)．

2 **きょうだん 凶弾** ▶彼は知事公邸を出たところで凶弾に倒れた He was shot down by *an assassin's bullet* as he left the governor's mansion. (➤「暗殺者の弾丸」の意)．

3 **きょうだん 教団** a religious organization [sect]；a (religious) cult (いかがわしい新興宗教)．

きょうち 境地 a state ▶無我の境地を経験したいものだ I'd like to experience *a state of perfect selflessness*. ‖ もう何もかも諦めの境地です I'm *at the point of giving up on* everything.

きょうちくとう 夾竹桃 《植物》 an oleander.

きょうちゅう 胸中 ▶アンネ・フランクの胸中を思うと胸が痛む It breaks my heart to imagine *how Anne Frank felt*.

きょうちょ 共著 ▶この本は三木氏と私の共著です This (is a) book I wrote *in collaboration with* Mr. Miki. 《参考》共著による書物を joint work という. ‖ 共著者 a coauthor, a joint author, a co-writer.

1 **きょうちょう 強調する** emphasize +目；stress +目 (重点を置く) ▶首相は忍耐と寛容を強調した The Prime Minister *emphasized* patience and generosity. ‖ 私たちの英語の先生は発音を強調し過ぎる Our English teacher *places* too much *stress* [*emphasis*] *on* pronunciation.

2 **きょうちょう 協調** cooperation (協力)；harmony (一致) ▶きみは協調性が足りないね You'*re not cooperative* enough. ‖ 協調性が無いと集団の仕事はできない If you lack *the will to cooperate* [*the spirit of cooperation*], you cannot work in a group. ▶このクラスの協調を乱さないでほしい Please don't disturb the *harmony* of this class.

きょうつう 共通の common (共有する)；universal (全体に通じる)；mutual (お互いの) ▶英文法とドイツ語文法には共通する部分が多い The grammars of English and German have much *in common*. ‖ その２つの会社は共通の利害で結ばれている The two companies are united by *common* interests. ‖ 音楽は人類に共通のことばである Music is a *universal* language among humans. ‖ 野田君はぼくたちの共通の友人です Noda is our *mutual* friend. ‖ 背が高いという点では２人は共通している (＝似ている) They *are alike* in that they are both tall. ‖ その２者には共通点はない [が多い] The two *have nothing* [*much*] *in common* with each other.

✉ **あなたと私は趣味が共通してますね** You and I have many interests *in common* [*common* interests], don't we ? ➤「共通の関心をもつ」の意. ✉ **私たちって共通点が多いですね** We *have a lot* (*of things*) *in common*, don't we ?

きょうつうご 共通語 a common language (共有する言語)；a lingua franca (異なる言語を話す者どうしが共通して用いる第３の言語) ▶英語はヨーロッパの共通語だ English is the *lingua franca* in Europe.

1 **きょうてい 協定** (an) agreement ▶両者の間に協定が成立した The two parties have arrived at *an agreement*. ／*An agreement* has been reached between the two parties. ‖ 彼らは協定価格でワインを売買している They buy and sell wine at the *agreed price*.

2 **きょうてい 競艇** a speedboat race (➤ motorboat は「エンジン [モーター] で動く船」を一般的にいう)．

きょうてき 強敵 a powerful rival [enemy].

きょうてん 経典 a sutra (仏教の)；a scripture (キリスト教以外の)；the Bible (キリスト教の聖書)．

ぎょうてん 仰天する be astounded ▶私は和男が淳子と心中したという知らせを聞いて仰天した I *was astounded* [*was flabbergasted*] at the news that Kazuo and Junko had committed suicide. (➤ 後者はインフォーマルな表現)．

きょうと 教徒 ▶彼は仏教徒 [キリスト教徒] だ He is *a Buddhist* [*a Christian*]. ‖ イスラム教徒は豚肉を食べない *Muslims* do not eat pork.

1 **きょうど 郷土** one's hometown；one's native region (生まれた地方) ▶彼は郷土の英雄だ He's the hero of *our hometown*. ／He's our *local* hero. ‖ 私は郷土史に興味をもっている I am interested in our *local history*. ‖ 郷土色豊かな祭り a festival full of *local color* ‖ あなたの国の郷土料理にはどんなものがありますか What kind of *traditional dishes* are there *in your country* ? ‖ 郷土芸能 a performing art peculiar to a locality.

2 **きょうど 強度** strength；intensity (熱・音・光などの) ▶このビルは鉄骨の強度に問題がある There is a problem with the *strength* of the steel frame of this building. (➤ 英語としては The problem is a lack of strength in this building's steel frame. のように表現するほうが自然) ‖ 彼は強度の近視だ He is *very* nearsighted.

きょうとう 教頭 (米) a vice-principal, (英) a deputy headteacher (●「教頭」を headteacher と訳さないこと．この語は (英) では「校長」(headmaster (男性) ／headmistress (女性)) の意であるから要注意)．

きょうどう 共同・協同 cooperation ▶彼はそのグループ

と協同で実験を行った He *cooperated* with the group in the experiment(s). ／He carried out the experiment (s) *in cooperation with* the group. ‖そのアパートの住人は風呂［トイレ］を共同で使う The residents of that apartment house *share* the bathroom. ‖両親は共同で子供のしつけの責任を取らなければならない Parents should *share* responsibility for teaching their children how to behave. ‖私たちは4人共同でヨットを買った *The four of us got together* to purchase a sailboat.

‖**共同企業体** a joint venture ‖**協同組合** a cooperative society,《インフォーマル》a co-op(➡**生協**) ‖**共同作業** group work ‖**共同作戦** concerted operations ‖**共同事業** a joint enterprise [undertaking] ‖**共同社会** a community ‖**共同住宅**《米》an apartment house,《英》a block of flats ; a tenement house(大都市の安アパート) ‖**共同生活** community life ‖**共同声明** a joint statement [communiqué] ‖**共同体** a community ‖**共同電話** a party-line telephone ‖**共同募金** the community chest ‖**共同募金運動** a community chest drive ‖**共同墓地** a (public) cemetery.

きょうねん 享年 **the number of years** one **lived** (生存した年数) ; **age at death** (死亡時の年齢) ▶小川氏は昨日がんで亡くなりました. **享年56歳** Mr. Ogawa died of cancer yesterday. *He was 56* (*years old*). (➤過去形に注意).

きょうばい 競売 (an) **auction** /ɔ́:kʃən/ ▶ピカソの絵を**競売に掛ける** *put* a Picasso *up for auction* ‖この家具は**競売に出される**予定です This piece of furniture is going to *be sold at auction*.

きょうはく 脅迫 a **threat** /θret/ 一動 **脅迫する threaten** ＋目 ▶きみは私を脅迫するつもりか Do you mean to *threaten* me? ‖彼らは夫に秘密をバラすぞと言って彼女を脅迫した They *threatened* her saying that they would reveal her secret to her husband. ‖**脅迫状**［**電話**］a threatening letter [telephone call].

きょうはくかんねん 強迫観念 (an) **obsession** ▶彼女はいつも誰かに見張られているという**強迫観念にとらわれている** She'*s obsessed with the idea* that she is always being watched by somebody.

きょうはん 共犯 **complicity** ▶彼はその犯罪の共犯の容疑で告訴された He was accused of *complicity* in the crime. ‖**共犯者** an accomplice /əkɑ́:mpləs/.

きょうふ 恐怖 (a) **fear** ; **terror, horror** (身の毛のよだつような怖さ) ▶彼は恐怖のあまり体中がぶるぶる震えていた He trembled *with fear* [*horror*] from head to toe. ‖子供たちにホラー映画を見せて**恐怖心を与えて**はいけない You shouldn't *frighten* young children by letting them see horror films. ‖彼女は**コンピュータ恐怖症だ** She *has a computer phobia*. ／She *is computer allergic*. ‖ぼくは**高所恐怖症**だ I *have a fear of heights*. ／I *have acrophobia* /ækrəfóʊbiə/. ‖**外国人恐怖症** xenophobia ‖**対人**［**人間**］**恐怖症** anthropophobia ‖**広場恐怖症** agoraphobia ‖**閉所**［**密室**］**恐怖症** claustrophobia ‖**水恐怖症**(**恐水症**) hydrophobia.

きょうぶ 胸部 **the chest** 一形 **胸部の chest, thoracic** /θərǽsɪk/ ▶**胸部レントゲンを受ける** have a *chest* X-ray.

きょうふう 強風 a **strong wind**, a **high wind** (➤後者がより強い) ; a **gale** (➤主に気象用語) ▶その強風で多くの木が倒れた Many trees toppled in the *strong wind*. ‖**強風注意報** a strong wind warning [advisory].

きょうへん 共編 **coeditorship** ‖**共編者** a coeditor, a joint editor.

きょうべん 教鞭 ▶**西教授はM大学で30年間教べんを執ってこられました** Professor Nishi has *been teaching* at M University for thirty years.

きょうほ 競歩 a **walk**, a **walking race** ; a **race walking** ▶彼は1万メートル競歩で優勝した He won the championship in the 10,000-meter *walk*.

[1]**きょうぼう 共謀** (a) **conspiracy** 一動 **共謀する conspire** ▶これはAとBの共謀による犯罪である This crime was committed by A *in conspiracy with* B. ‖彼が誰と共謀して大統領を暗殺しようとしたのか警察で取り調べ中だ The police are investigating who *conspired* with him in the plot to assassinate the President.

[2]**きょうぼう 凶暴な・狂暴な** **fierce** ; **savage** /sǽvɪdʒ/ (どう猛な) ; **violent** (乱暴な) ▶**凶暴な犬** a *fierce* [*savage*] dog ‖彼は酔うと**狂暴になる** He gets *violent* when he gets drunk.

きょうほん 教本 a **textbook**(教科書) ; a **manual**, an **instruction book**(教則本) ; a **drill** [**practice**] **book**(練習本).

ぎょうまつ 行末 **the end of a line**.

きょうみ 興味 (an) **interest** 一形 **興味深い interesting**

【文型】
物事(A)に興味がある
have an interest in A
be interested in A
【解説】have an interest in では interest の前に, **special**(特に) ; **great**, **strong**(大いなる)や **no**(全く…ない), **little**(ほとんど…ない)などの形容詞をつけることがある.

▶私はダリの絵に**大変興味がある** I *have a great* [*strong*] *interest in* the Dali's paintings. ／I *am extremely interested in* the works of Dali. ‖私は政治にはほとんど［**全然**］**興味がない** I *have little* [*no*] *interest in* politics. ‖弟はやっと勉強に**興味が湧いてきた**ようだ My brother seems to be finally *beginning to show some interest in* studying. ‖パソコンにはもう**興味を失った** I *have lost interest in* personal computers. ‖彼はぼくの新車に大いに**興味を示した** He seemed really *interested in* my new car. ／He *showed* a great *interest in* my new car.

▶彼女がいつ誰と結婚するかはみんなにとって**興味津々だった** When and who(m) she was going to marry were *questions of great interest* to us all. ‖彼女が誰と結婚しようとぼくは**興味**(＝関心)**がない** It is *no concern* of mine who she chooses to marry. ‖父はよくインドでの**興味深い**体験話をしてくれた My father often told us about his *interesting* experiences in India. ‖彼はその記事を**興味本位で**書いた He wrote that article *just for fun*. (➤「興味本位のテレビ番組」は a sensational TV program).

✉ **あなたはどんなことに興味がありますか** What are your *interests*? ／What are you *interested in*? ✉ **どういう訳で日本に興味をもつようになられたのですか** How did you *get interested in* Japan? ／What made you (*get*) *interested in* Japan?

きょうむ 教務 **school affairs** ‖**教務課** the educational affairs department ; the registrar's office (大学の) ‖**教務手帳** a teacher's record book, a class record book ‖ **教務部長** the head of the educational affairs department.

ぎょうむ 業務 **business** ; **duties**（自分の任務としての）▶**業務上の事故** an *on-the-job* accident ‖ **業務用の車** a car *for business use* ‖ **業務を拡張する** *expand* [extend] one's *business operations* ‖ 会社の**業務**を怠る neglect one's *duties* at the office ‖ B社と**業務提携**をする enter into *a business tie-up* with B Company. ‖**業務用出入口** a service exit.

きょうめい 共鳴 **1**【振動】**resonance** /rézənəns/.
2【共感】**sympathy** ▶彼の過激思想には**共鳴できない** I can't *sympathize* [*go along*] *with* his radical ideas. ‖ 彼の生き方を書いた本に**共鳴して**私は政治家になった The story of his life *inspired* me to become a politician.

[1]**きょうやく 協約** an **agreement** ▶**労働協約を結ぶ** [守る／実行する] reach [keep／carry out] *a labor agreement*.

[2]**きょうやく 共訳** a **joint translation**.

きょうゆ 教諭 a **teacher** ▶小学校 [中学校／高校] **教諭** an elementary school [a middle school／a high school] *teacher*（➤《英》では「小学校」は primary school がふつう）.

きょうゆう 共有 **joint ownership**（共同所有）**一動 共有する** **share** +目 ▶弟と部屋を**共有する** *share* a room *with* one's brother ‖ 我々3人でこの別荘を**共有している** The three of us *own* this vacation house *jointly*. ‖ この車はきみとぼくの**共有**ということにしよう Let's be *joint owners* of this car.／Let's buy this car *jointly*.（➤後者はこれから購入する場合）‖ 必要な情報をすべて**共有すること**が重要だ It's important that we *share* all the necessary information. ‖ 漢字は日本と中国の**共有**（＝共通）の文化である Kanji are (a) part of the *common* culture *shared by* Japan and China.（⇀**共同**）.

きょうよ 供与する **supply** +目, **provide** +目 ⇀**供給** ▶その国に医療機器を**供与する** *supply* [*provide*] that country *with* medical devices.

[1]**きょうよう 教養** **culture** ▶**教養を身につける** acquire *culture* ‖ **教養の高い女性** a *highly cultured* woman／a woman *of refined culture*／a *well-educated* woman ‖ 彼は大学教育は受けていないが，なかなか**教養がある** He doesn't have a college education, but he *is* quite *cultured* [*cultivated*]. ‖ 私は広く本を読んで**教養を深めたい** I want to *cultivate myself* by reading extensively.
‖**教養学部** the college [school] of liberal arts ‖ **教養科目** the liberal arts ‖ **教養番組** an educational program.

[2]**きょうよう 強要する** **coerce** /kouə́ːʳs/ +目（脅して…させる；堅い語）; **force** +目, **compel** +目（無理やり…させる；後者のほうが堅い語）▶私は寄付を**強要された** I *was compelled to* make [*was coerced* into making] a donation. ‖ 自白を**強要されて**罪をかぶる人もいる Some people *are forced into* confessing [*are forced to* confess] to a crime (they didn't commit).／Some people confess to crimes *under duress*.

[3]**きょうよう 共用する** **share** +目 ▶私たちの寮では台所と風呂は**共用です** We *share* the kitchen and the bathroom in our dormitory.

きょうらく 享楽 **enjoyment**
‖**享楽主義者** a hedonist /híːdnɪst/.

きょうらん 狂乱 ▶爆弾が破裂すると群衆は**狂乱状態**になった The bomb explosion threw the crowd into *a panic*. ‖**狂乱物価** steeply inflated prices.
☛ **半狂乱**（⇀見出語）

きょうり 郷里 one's **hometown** ▶**私の郷里は雪が多い** We have a lot of snow in *my hometown*. ‖ 私は1年に一度しか**郷里**の鹿児島に帰らない I only return to [visit] my *native* Kagoshima once a year.

きょうりきこ 強力粉 **high-gluten hard wheat flour**.

きょうりゅう 恐竜 a **dinosaur** /dáɪnəsɔ̀ːʳ/ ▶**恐竜**の中には空を飛ぶものもいた There were some *dinosaurs* that flew. ‖ **恐竜の骨**を掘り当てる dig up *dinosaur* bones.

きょうりょう 狭量な **narrow-minded, petty**（➤前者は他人の意見や指摘を受け付けないような狭量さを，後者は自分に気に入らないことがあるとすぐに感情を害するような狭量さを指すことが多い）▶**狭量な考えを持つな** Don't be *narrow-minded* [*petty*].

[1]**きょうりょく 協力** **cooperation** ; **collaboration**（学術・芸術分野での）
一動 協力する **cooperate** /kouɑ́ːpərèɪt/《with》, **collaborate**《with》; **work together**（一緒に働く）; **pull together**（力を合わせて働く）▶この計画はみんなの**協力が必要だ** This project requires everybody's *cooperation*. ‖ **ご協力ありがとう** Thank you for your *cooperation*.／Thank you for *helping* me. ‖ その子供を捜すためにみんなが警察と**協力した** Everyone *cooperated with* the police to find the child. ‖ 彼女は父親と**協力して**その本を書いた She *collaborated with* her father in writing the book. ‖ 昔，田植えは他の人の**協力**なしには不可能であった In the old days you couldn't plant rice without the *cooperation* of other people. ‖ みんなで**協力すれば**この仕事は今日中に終わる If all of us *pull together*, we'll be able to finish this job today.
▶共同募金に**ご協力をお願いします** Please donate money to the community chest. ‖ 全員が**協力すれば**この仕事は1週間で終わるだろう If everybody *works together*, this job will be completed in a week. ‖ 彼は私たちのクラブにとても**協力的だ** He is very *cooperative* toward our club. ‖**協力者** a cooperator, a collaborator, a supporter（➤「執筆[編集]協力者」は an editorial supporter).

[2]**きょうりょく 強力な** **powerful**, **strong** ▶**強力なモーター** [武器] a *powerful* motor [weapon]（➤カッコ内の語は比喩的にも用いる）‖ **強力な電波** a *strong* electric wave ‖ 仙台育英高校の打線は**強力だ** The Sendai-Ikuei's batting lineup *is powerful*. ‖ 彼は住民の**強力な**支持を受けて市長に選ばれた He was elected mayor of this city thanks to the *strong* support of the citizens. ‖ この薬は効き目が**強力だ** This medicine *is extremely effective*.

きょうれつ 強烈な **strong**（強い）; **severe**（激しい）▶**強烈な地震** a *severe* earthquake ‖ **強烈なパンチ** a *strong* punch ‖ 彼女と出会ったとき私は**強烈な印象**を受けた She left a *strong* impression on me when I met her.

ぎょうれつ 行列 **1**【並んだ列】a **line**,《英また》a **queue** /kjuː/（順番待ちの）; a **procession**, a **parade**（行進の列）▶女性たちはスーパーの前で**行列をつくっていた** Women stood in *a line* [formed *a queue*] in front of the supermarket. ‖ 当日はちょうちん**行列**が行われる *A lantern procession* will be held on the day.
2【数学の】a **matrix** ‖**行列式** a determinant.

きょうわこく 共和国 a **republic**（国王・天皇など君主がいない）▶アメリカは（連邦）**共和国**である The United

States is a (federal) *republic*. ‖ 共和制 a republican system.

きょうわとう 共和党 《米》 **the Republican Party, the Grand Old Party** 《略 GOP》
‖ 共和党員 a Republican.

きょえいしん 虚栄心 **vanity** ▶虚栄心の強い若者 a *vain* young person ‖ あの歌手は虚栄心の塊だ That singer has *a massive ego*.

ギョーザ 餃子 ***gyoza*** ; a Chinese-style meat-and-vegetable (fried) dumpling (➤ 説明的な訳) ; a **potsticker**(焼きギョーザ).

きょか 許可 **1**【許すこと】**permission, leave** (➤ 後者がより堅い語) 一動 許可する **permit** /pəʳmít/ +目 (積極的に) ; **allow** /əláʊ/ +目 (消極的または暗黙のうちに) ; **authorize** +目 (正式な手続きを経て) ▶プールで泳ぐときは先生の許可を得なさい Get your teacher's *permission* when you (want to) use the pool. ‖ 先生は早退の許可をくれなかった The teacher didn't *give* me *permission* to leave the class early. ／The teacher wouldn't *let* me leave the class early. (➤ let は「好きなようにさせる」) ‖ 寮母さんは私に午後11時まで外出してよいという許可をくれた My dorm mother gave me *permission* [*leave*] to stay out until eleven p.m. ‖ 「許可なく入室を禁ず」と書いた紙がドアに張ってあった There was a sign on the door, "No Entrance *Without Permission*."

【文型】
人(A)が…するのを許可する
permit A **to** do
allow A **to** do

▶両親は愛子がアルバイトするのを許可した Aiko's parents *permitted* her *to* work part time. ‖ 未成年者には酒やたばこの販売が許可されていない It *is not permitted to* sell minors alcoholic drinks or cigarettes. ／Minors *are not allowed to* buy alcoholic drinks or cigarettes. (➤ 後者は「買うのを許されていない」) ‖ 取材班は工場内部の撮影を許可されなかった The reporters *were not permitted* [*allowed*] *to* videotape the inside of the factory. ‖ 避難者たちの多くは帰宅を許可された Most evacuees *were allowed to* return to their homes.
▶警官は拳銃の携帯を許可されている Police officers *are authorized to* carry a gun.
2【免許】**license,** 《英》 **licence** ▶このスーパーでは酒類の販売が許可されている This supermarket *is licensed* to sell liquor. (➤「酒類販売許可証」は a liquor license). ‖ 許可証 a permit ; a license, 《英》 a licence(免許証).

逆引き熟語 ○○許可
(コンピュータへの)アクセス許可 access permission ／営業許可 a commercial [business] license ／外出許可 a leave ／結婚許可(証) a marriage license ／建築許可(証) a construction [building] permit ／銃器所持許可証 a gun permit ／駐車許可(証) a parking permit ／通行許可 a pass ／入学許可 admission ／入室許可 an entrance permit ／労働許可(証) a work permit

ぎょかいるい 魚介類 **fish and shellfish** (➤ 複数扱い) ; **seafood**(海産物).

きょがく 巨額 a **large sum** [**amount**] **of money**
▶彼はその慈善団体に巨額の寄付をした He donated *a large sum of money* to the charitable organization. ‖ 市は巨額の借金を抱えている The city is saddled with *enormous debt(s)*.

ぎょかく 漁獲 ▶ことしのサンマの漁獲は例年よりよかった The Pacific saury *catch* was better than usual this year. ‖ 漁獲高 a catch (of fish).

ぎょがんレンズ 魚眼レンズ a **fish-eye lens.**

きょぎ 虚偽の **false** ▶きみが虚偽の報告をしたことはわかっている I am aware that you made a *false* report.

きょぎょう 虚業 a **high-risk speculative business** [**company**].

ぎょぎょう 漁業 **fishing, the fishing industry** (➤ fishery, fisheries はそれぞれ「養魚場」「漁場」の意で用いることが多い) ▶この村は漁業で成り立っている This village is built on *fishing*. ／This village depends solely upon *fishing*. ‖ 漁業協定 a fisheries agreement ‖ 漁業組合 a fishermen's [fishers'] union ‖ 漁業権 fishery [fishing] rights.

きょきょじつじつ 虚々実々 ▶市長選挙では虚々実々の駆け引きが行われた In the mayoral election campaign, there was *a shrewd battle of wit and cunning*.

1**きょく 曲** (a **piece of**) **music** ; a **tune** (単純で短い旋律) ▶歌詞に曲を付ける *set* the words *to music* ‖ 大バッハは1100曲ほどの作品を残した The great Bach left behind about 1,100 *pieces of music* [*musical works*]. ‖ 今夜のコンサートは曲もよかったが演奏もよかった Both the *music* and the performance were wonderful at the concert this evening. ‖ 彼はリサイタルでまずサティの曲を弾いた He first played *a* Satie *piece* at the recital. ‖ 1曲歌ってください Sing me *a song*, please.

2**きょく 局** ▶ちょっと局(＝郵便局)にこの手紙を出しに行ってくる I'm (just) going to run to *the post office* to mail this letter. ‖ 原氏は本局に異動になった Mr. Hara was transferred to *the central* [*main*] *bureau*. (➤ bureau /bjʊ́əroʊ/ は官庁の局).

ぎょぐ 漁具 **fishing equipment** [**gear**].

きょくいん 局員 a **clerk** ; **staff**(全員) ▶郵便局員 a postal [mail] *clerk*.

きょくう 極右の **extreme** [**ultra**] **-right**
‖ 極右派 the extreme [ultra]-right.

きょくげい 曲芸 **acrobatics** ; an **acrobatic feat** (個々の芸当) ; a **stunt** (離れ業) ; a **trick**(早業, 芸当) ▶オットセイの曲芸 a seal's *tricks*. ‖ 曲芸師 an acrobat.

1**きょくげん 極言** ▶今度世界戦争が起きたら人類は破滅すると極言する人もいる Some people *go so far as to say* all humankind will be destroyed if another world war should break out.

2**きょくげん 極限** a **limit** ▶極限まで努力してみないと自分の能力の程はわからないものだ You have to push yourself to your *limits* to learn the true extent of your capabilities. ‖ 人間は極限状態になると何をしでかすかわからない Nobody can tell what a person will do when (he or she is) *pushed to the limit*.

きょくさ 極左の **extreme** [**ultra**] **-left**
‖ 極左派 the extreme [ultra]-left.

ぎょくさい 玉砕 ▶この島では日本軍が玉砕した The Japanese platoon on this island *died rather than surrender*. (surrender を surrendered とするのは一般的ではない).

きょくしょ 局所 →局部.

きょくしょう 極少の **minimal** ▶幸いわが社の損失は極少であった Luckily, our losses *were minimal*.

ぎょくせきこんこう 玉石混交 a **mixture of chaff and grain**(もみ殻と穀物との混合；価値あるものと無価値なものとの混合)；**uneven quality**(等質でないこと) ▶あの作家は多作だが，作品は玉石混交だ The novelist is prolific, but the quality of his works *is uneven*.

きょくせつ 曲折 twists and turns(紆余(うよ)曲折) ▶多少の曲折を経て，新経営陣が決まった A new management team was formed after a few *twists and turns*.

きょくせん 曲線 a **curve**, a **curved line** ▶ヘンリー・ムーアの彫刻は美しい曲線で知られる Henry Moore's sculptures are well-known for their graceful *curving lines*. ‖曲線美で知られる女優 an actress known for her *beautiful curves*.

きょくたん 極端 (an) **extreme** 一形 極端な **extreme** ▶それは極端な例だ That is an *extreme* case. ‖極端な話だけど，もしお父さんが死んだらあなたたちはどうやって生活するつもり？ *This may be an extreme case*, but supposing your father were to die, how would you get by? ‖何事も極端に走るのはよくない You should not *go to extremes* [*excess*] in anything. ‖彼女は犬を極端に嫌っている She has an *extreme* dislike for dogs. ／She abhors dogs. (➤ abhor は「ひどく嫌う」).

1**きょくち 極致** ▶その建物はロココ調の極致を見せてくれている That building shows *the perfection* of Rococo style.

2**きょくち 極地 the polar regions**
‖極地探検 a polar expedition ‖極地探検家 a polar explorer.

きょくちてき 局地的 ▶梅雨前線が局地的な大雨を降らせた The seasonal rain front caused *local* downpours [caused heavy rains *in some areas*]. ‖その大雪は局地的なものだった That heavy snowfall was *limited to a small area*.

きょくちょう 局長 the head of an office [**a bureau**]；**the chief** [**general director**] **of a bureau** (官庁の)；a **postmaster** (郵便局の).

きょくど 極度の extreme ▶極度の女嫌い an *extreme* woman-hater ‖おやじは極度に雷を恐れている My dad has an *extreme* fear of thunder. ‖私は極度の近視でほとんど物が見えない I am *extremely* nearsighted and can hardly see. ‖私はそのときは極度に緊張していた I was under *extreme* pressure at that moment.

きょくとう 極東 the Far East.

きょくどめ 局留め 《米》**general delivery**；《英》**poste restante** /pòust restɑ́:nt/ (➤いずれも封筒に書く文句).

きょくのり 曲乗り circus riding (馬の)；**trick riding** (自転車などの)；**stunt flying**(飛行機の).

きょくばん 局番 a **telephone exchange number**, 《米》 an **area code**, 《英》 an **STD code** (➤ STD は Subscriber Trunk Dialling(長距離ダイヤル直通システム)の略) ‖市外局番 《米》 an area code, 《英》 a dialling code.

きょくぶ 局部 a **part**(一部)；one's **private parts** (➤「性器」の婉曲(えんきょく)語) ▶局部的な痛み a *local* pain ‖局部麻酔 *local* anesthesia /æ̀nəsθí:ʒə ‖ -ziə/.

きょくめん 局面 the situation ▶この難しい局面を首相はどうやって切り抜けるのだろう How will the Prime Minister get through this *difficult situation*? ‖日米関係は新しい局面を迎えた The relationship of Japan and the U.S. entered *a new phase*.

きょくもく 曲目 a (**concert**) **program** (曲目表)；a **number**(個々の曲) ▶そのコンサートの全曲目を教えてください Could you let me know *the whole program* of the concert? ‖浅田さんの次の曲目はシューベルトの「菩提(ぼだい)樹」です Ms. Asada's next *piece* will be Schubert's "The Linden Tree."

きょくりょく 極力 ▶ご要望に添えるよう極力手を尽くしてみます I will *put my utmost efforts* into complying with your request. ／I will *do my utmost* to comply with your request.

ぎょくろ 玉露 *gyokuro*；the highest-quality green tea(➤説明的な訳).

きょくろん 極論 ▶極論すれば— *If I may put it in the strongest terms*, … . ‖それは極論だよ That's *going too far*.

ぎょぐん 魚群 a **school of fish**
‖魚群探知機 a fish finder.

きょげんへき 虚言癖 habitual lying.

1**きょこう 虚構** (a) **fiction** ▶それは全くの虚構だ It's pure *fiction*. ‖これは三島由紀夫が作り上げた虚構の世界だ This is *a fictitious world* Mishima Yukio invented.

2**きょこう 挙行** ▶2人の結婚式は4月に挙行される予定です Their wedding ceremony is going to *be held* [*take place*] in April.

ぎょこう 漁港 a **fishing port.**

きょしき 挙式 ▶挙式の日取りは決まりましたか Have you decided the date for your *wedding*? ‖2人は来月挙式する They're going to *hold their wedding* next month.

きょしてき 巨視的な holistic；**macroscopic** /mæ̀krəskɑ́:pɪk ‖ -skɔ́p-/.

ぎょしゃ 御者 a **driver**；a **coachman** (大型四輪馬車の)；a **cabman** (昔のつじ馬車・一頭立て2人乗り二輪馬車の).

きょじゃく 虚弱な weak, **delicate** ▶虚弱な子 a *weak* child ‖彼女は生まれつき虚弱体質だったが，頭はとても良かった Though she was born with *a delicate constitution*, she was very intelligent.

きょしゅ 挙手 raising of one's **hand** ▶質問のある［賛成の］人は挙手してください Please *raise your hand* if you have a question [if you agree]. ‖我々はデモに参加すべきかどうかを挙手で決めた We decided whether or not to take part in the demonstration *by a show of hands*. (➤ by a show of hands は「(賛否などを決めるとき)挙手で」に相当する決まり文句).

きょしゅう 去就 ▶去就を明らかにする decide on one's *course of action* ‖問題発言をした大臣の去就が注目される People are curious about *whether or not* the minister will *remain in office* after his controversial statement [remark].

きょじゅう 居住 ▶東京都の居住者 *a resident* of Tokyo ‖居住地 one's place of residence.

きょしゅつ 拠出 (a) **contribution**
‖拠出年金制度 a contributory pension system.

きょしょう 巨匠 a (**great**) **master**；a **maestro** /máɪstroʊ/ (特に大作曲家，大指揮者) ▶黒沢明は世界の映画界の巨匠の1人だった Kurosawa Akira was one of the *masters* of the international film world.

ぎょじょう 漁場 a **fishing ground** ▶日本近海は世界四大漁場の1つだ The waters around Japan constitute one of the world's four greatest *fishing grounds*.

きょしょく 虚飾 ostentation/ɑ̀:stentéɪʃən ‖ ɔ̀s-/ ▶虚飾に満ちた暮らしをする have an *ostentatious* lifestyle.

きょしょくしょう 拒食症 anorexia /æ̀nəréksiə/ (食

欲不振症）▶彼女は拒食症にかかっている She has *anorexia*.

きょじん 巨人 1【大男】a **giant**.
2【偉人】a **great figure** ▶アーネスト・ヘミングウェーはアメリカ文学の巨人の１人だ Ernest Hemingway is one of *the greatest figures* in American literature.

きょしんたんかい 虚心坦懐 ▶虚心坦懐にご意見をお聞きしたい I'd like to listen to what you have to say *with an open mind*.

1**きょせい 虚勢** **bluff**；a **bluff**（➤ 虚勢を張る人）▶あんまり虚勢を張るものじゃない Don't *bluff* so much.

2**きょせい 去勢** **castration** 一動 **去勢する castrate**＋目.

3**きょせい 巨星** a **giant star** ▶赤色巨星 a red *giant* (*star*) ‖（日本画壇の）巨星墜(ぉ)つ *A great man* [*woman*] (in the Japanese art world) has passed.

きょぜつ 拒絶 (a) **refusal**, (a) **rejection**（➤ 後者はぴしゃりとはねつけること）一動 **拒絶する refuse** ＋目, **reject** ＋目 ▶彼らは我々の要求を拒絶した They *refused* [*rejected*] our request. ‖その死刑囚は新聞記者との面会を拒絶した The condemned man *refused* to see the journalists. ‖彼女に結婚を申し込んだが，にべもなく拒絶された I proposed to her but she *gave* me *a flat refusal*. ‖心臓移植した患者に拒絶反応が出た The transplanted heart *was rejected* (by the patient). ‖その女優はヌードシーンに拒絶反応を示した That actress *was averse to* doing nude scenes.（➤ be averse to は「…を嫌がる」）.
‖《医学》**拒絶反応** (a) rejection.

ぎょせん 漁船 a **fishing boat**.

1**きょぞう 虚像** a **virtual image**（光学でいう，「実像」に対して）；an **unreal image**（本当でない姿）▶ぼくは彼女の虚像に恋をしたのだろうか Did I fall in love with *an unreal* [*imagined*] *image* of her？‖その女性歌手は虚像と実像の落差が大きい That woman singer's *public image* and private self are two very different things.

2**きょぞう 巨像** a **gigantic statue, a colossus**［複 **colossi**］.

ぎょそん 漁村 a **fishing village**.

きょたい 巨体 a **big body**, a **bulk** ▶鯨が海面に巨体を現した The *huge bulks* of whales came up to the surface of the sea.

きょだい 巨大な **huge**；**enormous**（並外れて大きい）；**gigantic** /dʒaɪɡǽntɪk/（とてつもない）▶巨大な旅客機 a *huge* airliner ／a *jumbo* jet ‖巨大企業 a *gigantic* [*mammoth*] enterprise ‖こんな巨大なカボチャは見たことがない I've never seen such an *enormous* [a *monster* ／a *giant*] pumpkin.

きょだく 許諾 **permission**（許可）；**consent**（同意）；**authorization**（公認）▶著作権で保護されている作品を使用するのに許諾を得る obtain *permission* to use a work protected by copyright ‖この本のいかなる部分も出版社の許諾なしに複製してはいけません You may not reproduce any part of this book without *permission* of the publisher.

ぎょたく 魚拓 a **rubbing of a fish** one **has caught**, an **India ink impression of a fish** one **has caught**.

きょだつ 虚脱 ▶彼女は恋人を失って虚脱状態だった She was in *a state of collapse* after losing her lover.

きょっかい 曲解 **distortion** 一動 **曲解する distort** ＋目；**twist** ＋目（➤「ねじる」の比喩的用法）▶彼の発言は曲解されて伝わった His remark *was misinterpreted* [*distorted*]. ‖彼はいつも私の言うことを曲解する He always *twists* what I say. ‖彼女は私の言ったことを曲解したようだ She seems to *have gotten a twisted idea* of what I said.

きょっけい 極刑 **the maximum**［**highest**］**penalty**（死刑制度を廃止している国では単に「最高刑」の意になるので，「死刑」の意では次のように明確に言うほうがよい）；**capital punishment, the death penalty**（死刑）▶彼は極刑（＝死刑）に処せられた He *was executed* [*was put to death*].

ぎょっと ▶窓の所で妙な音がしたのでぎょっとした I *was startled* by a strange noise (coming) from the window. ‖その男に突然ナイフを突きつけられてぎょっとした I *was taken by surprise* when he suddenly pointed a knife at me. ‖ぎょっとするようなこと言わないでよ Don't *startle* [*alarm* ／*scare*] me by saying things like that.

きょてん 拠点 a **base** ▶彼らはその高台を半島探検の拠点にした They used the plateau as *a base* for their explorations of the peninsula.

きょとう 巨頭 a **leader**（指導者）；a **tycoon** /taɪkúːn/（実力者）；a **big shot**（大物）▶財界の巨頭 *a prominent figure* in the business world.
‖**巨頭会談** a summit conference [meeting].

きょどう 挙動 **behavior** ▶挙動不審な人物 a *suspicious* character ／a person who *behaves suspiciously*.

きょときょと ▶男はきょときょとと落ち着かない風だった The man appeared ill at ease, and *his eyes kept darting here and there*.

きょとん ▶なぜみんなが笑っているのかわからず彼女だけきょとんとしていた She *looked blank* not knowing why everyone was laughing.

ぎょにく 魚肉 **fish (meat)** ▶魚肉ソーセージ a *fish* sausage.

きょねん 去年

last year ▶うちでは去年家を新築した We built a new house *last year*. ‖去年の８月にニューヨークへ行った I went to New York in *August* (*of*) *last year*. ‖去年の今頃は何をしていたのかなあ I wonder what I was doing *about this time last year*. ‖グアムへ旅行したのが去年のきょうだった It was *a year ago today* that I went on a trip to Guam. ‖去年の夏は一度も泳ぎに行かなかった I didn't go swimming at all *last summer*.

1**きょひ 拒否** (a) **refusal** 一動 **拒否する refuse** ▶登校を拒否する子がみんな内向的だとは限らない Not all school children who *refuse* to go to school are introverts. ‖日本は国連安全保障理事会での拒否権がない Japan has no *veto* (*power*) in the United Nations Security Council.

2**きょひ 巨費** an **enormous amount of money** ▶政府は新しい事業に巨費を投じた The government pumped *an enormous amount of money* into the new project.

ぎょふ 漁夫 a **fisherman**, a **fisher**（➤ 後者は性差のない語）▶《慣用表現》彼らはライバルの２社に競争させておいて漁夫の利を得ようとしている They are encouraging competition between companies (that are) rivals to their own, in the hopes of reaping *a windfall profit*.（➤ windfall は「思いがけないもうけもの，棚ぼた」.「漁夫の利」は a windfall from others' conflicts のようにいえる）.

ぎょふん 魚粉 **fish meal**.

きょへい 挙兵する **take up arms**（武器をとって立ち上がる）；**raise an army**（兵を組織する）▶ついに西郷は挙兵を決意した At last, Saigo made up his mind to *raise an army*.

きよほうへん 毀誉褒貶 ▶政治家に毀誉ほうへんは付き物だ For politicians *a mix of praise and censure* comes with the territory. (➤ come with the territory は「当然のこととして受け入れることになる」の意の熟語).

きょぼく 巨木 a **giant** [**huge**] **tree** ▶「縄文杉」と呼ばれる巨木 *a giant tree* called 'Jomon cedar.'

きょまん 巨万 ▶巨万の富を築く make [pile up] *a vast fortune* / become a multimillionaire.

きよみずのぶたい 清水の舞台 ▶《慣用表現》清水の舞台から飛び降りるつもりでその骨とう品を買った I *took the plunge* [*took a chance*] and bought the antique.

ぎょみん 漁民 a **fisherman**, a **fisher**(➤ 後者は性差のない語).

きょむ 虚無 一形 **虚無的な nihilistic** /nàɪɪlístɪk/ ‖ **虚無主義** nihilism /náɪɪlɪ̀zəm/ ‖ **虚無主義者** a nihilist.

きよめる 清める **purify** /pjʊ́ərɪfaɪ/ ▶力士が塩をまくのは(儀式として)土俵を清めるためです The reason sumo wrestlers scatter salt on the ring is to (ritually) *purify* the space.

ぎょもう 漁網 a **fishing net**.

きょよう 許容 ▶その程度のミスなら許容できる That sort of error is *tolerable* [*acceptable*]. ‖ 総理のその暴言は許容範囲を逸脱している The Prime Minister's outrageous remarks are (*completely*) *intolerable*.

ぎょらい 魚雷 a **torpedo** /tɔːrpíːdoʊ/.

きよらか 清らかな **pure**(純な); **clear**(澄んだ) ▶心の清らかな人 a person *of pure heart* [*noble mind*] / a *pure-hearted* [*noble-minded*] person ‖ 故郷の川の流れは清らかだった The river in my hometown ran *clear* (*and clean*). ‖ 桃子は清らかな目をしている Momoko has *limpid* eyes. (➤ limpid は「澄んだ」の意の文語).

きょり 距離 (a) **distance** ▶コロナウイルス対策として社会的距離を保つ maintain social [physical] *distance* as a coronavirus countermeasure ‖ ここから名古屋までの距離はどのくらいだい? What's the *distance* from here to Nagoya? / *How far is it* from here to Nagoya? ‖ 郵便局は歩いて行くには少し距離がある The post office *is a little too far* [*too distant*] to walk (to) from here. ‖ 会社までは歩いて15分の距離です It's *a fifteen-minute walk* to my office. / *It takes fifteen minutes to walk* to my office. ‖ 月と地球との距離を知っていますか Do you know *how far* the moon is from the earth? / Do you know *how far it is* from the earth to the moon?
▶《慣用表現》正雄の家とは目と鼻の間 [先] の距離だ Masao's home is *a stone's throw away* from ours. (➤「石を投げれば届く距離」が原義).
▶我々の意見と彼らの意見にはまだだいぶ距離がある Our opinions and theirs still *differ* greatly. ‖ 最近彼女とは距離を置くようにしている I've been *keeping* my *distance* [*staying away*] from her. ‖ 彼とは距離を置いたほうがいいよ It would be better for you to *keep* him *at arm's length*. (➤ keep ... at arm's length は「…を敬遠する」).

ぎょるい 魚類 **fish** (➤ 種類をいうとき, またはまれに fishes となる).

きょれい 虚礼 **empty formalities** ▶虚礼を廃する abolish *empty formalities*.

きょろきょろ ▶きょろきょろしないで黒板の文章を書き写しなさい Stop *looking around* and copy down these sentences from the blackboard.

ぎょろぎょろ ▶あの目のぎょろぎょろした怖そうな人は誰ですか Who is that scary person *with goggle eyes*?

ぎょろめ ぎょろ目 ▶彼はぎょろ目だ He is *goggle-eyed*. / He has *goggle eyes*.

ぎょろり ▶おじいさんは眼鏡の奥からぎょろりと私を見上げた The old man looked up at me *with a glare* from behind his glasses.

きよわ 気弱な **faint-hearted**.

1**きらい 機雷** an **underwater** [**a floating**] **mine**.

2**きらい 嫌い** **1【好きでない】do not like** +目; **dislike** +目 (嫌う); **hate** +目 (憎む) ▶ぼくはシャンソンは嫌いだ I *don't like* chansons. ‖ 飛行機で旅行するのは嫌いだ I *don't like* traveling by air [by flying]. / I *dislike* flying. ‖ 彼女は勉強が嫌いのようだ She seems to *hate* studying. ‖ ああいう男性は私の嫌いなタイプなの That guy is the type I *don't care for*. (● hate は感情的になるほど「大嫌い」という強い意味なので人に対して使うときは要注意) ‖ 私は映画がすっかり嫌いになった (＝興味を失った) I've completely *lost interest in* movies. ‖ お願いだから嫌いにならない (＝嫌だと思わない) で Please *don't get tired of* me. ‖ 山田君の女嫌いは有名だ Mr. Yamada is well known for his *dislike of women*. ‖ 残念ながらうちの子はそろいもそろって勉強嫌いだ Regrettably, *none* of our children *like to study*. ‖ 対話 《ホームステイなどで》「何か嫌いなものありますか?」「いえ, 何でも頂きます / ええ, 鶏肉がちょっと」"Is there anything you *don't like to eat*?" "No, I like everything. / I'd rather not have chicken."

> **あなたの英語はどう響く?**
> 日本語では愛し合っている男女が「きみなんか嫌いだよ」とか「あなたなんか大嫌い!」と軽い気持ちで言うことがあるが, これを "I hate you." と訳すと大変なことになる. 相手の気を引くための「嫌い」は I don't like you. などと表現する. hate は非常に意味の強いことばなので, 相手と本当にけんか別れでもするとき以外は使わない. → 憎い.

2【気味, 傾向】▶この出版社の出す児童書は小学生には難しすぎる嫌いがある Children's books by this publisher are *a bit* too difficult for elementary school children. ‖ 彼は独走する嫌いがある He's *apt to* have his own way.

☞ **大嫌い** (→見出語)

> **逆引き熟語 ○○嫌い**
> **男 [女] 嫌い** a man- [woman-] hater / **外国 (人) 嫌い** xenophobia / **食わず嫌い** a dislike of something without having tried it / **魚嫌い** fish phobia / **動物嫌い** zoophobia / **飛行機嫌い** (a) fear of flying, aerophobia / **負けず嫌い** a person who hates to lose / **マスコミ嫌い** media-shy

きらう 嫌う **dislike** +目 (好まない); **hate** +目 (憎悪する; 人に対しては軽々しく使わない); **detest** +目 (ひどく嫌う) ▶なぜだか彼女はぼくのことを嫌う She *dislikes* me for some reason. ‖ 2人の兄弟は互いをひどく嫌っている The two brothers strongly *dislike* each other. ‖ 偉ぶった態度からあの店員を多くの客が嫌っている That salesclerk's haughty attitude *puts* a lot of shoppers *off*. ‖ 嫌いなものは嫌い (理由などない) I *simply dislike it for no special reason*. ‖ サボテンは湿気を嫌う Cactuses *do* *not do well* in humidity. ‖ 電気製品は湿気を嫌う Electrical appliances may *malfunction* in humid areas. (➤ malfunction は「うまく機能しない」) ‖ 父は混んでいる急行を嫌って始発の各駅停車で座っていく My father *hates* overcrowded express trains, so he takes a local train starting at his station and (always) gets a seat. ‖ あの先生は生徒から嫌われている That teacher *is disliked* by (all) the students. ‖ 彼は近所でいちばんの嫌われ者だ He is the most *disliked boy* in our neighborhood.

▶友引の日の葬式は嫌われる People *avoid* holding funerals on *tomobiki* days (one of the inauspicious days according to the lunar calendar).

きらきら ▶きらきら光る星 *twinkling* stars ‖ きらきら光る才能 *glittering* talent ‖ 幼いモーツァルトの才能はきらきらと輝いていた The young Mozart's genius *was brilliant*.

ぎらぎら ▶ぎらぎらの太陽 a *glaring* sun (➤「焼けつくような」は scorching, broiling, searing などを用いる) ‖ 翌日は朝から太陽がぎらぎらと照りつけた The following day, the sun beat down *brightly* from morning on. ‖ 飢えたトラは獲物を前にして目をぎらぎら光らせた The hungry tiger *glared* at its prey.

きらく 気楽な **easy** (緊張・心配などがない) ; **comfortable** /kʌ́mfəʳt̬əbəl/ (楽な気持ちになっている) ▶気楽な暮らし a *comfortable* life ‖ 私は独身なので気楽だ I'm single and *carefree*. ‖ 彼女は田舎で気楽に暮らしている She is living *comfortably* [*in comfort*] in the countryside. ‖ どうぞ気楽になさってください Please *make yourself at home* [*at ease*]. (➤ 来客に言う決まり文句) ／Just *relax* (*and take it easy*). ‖ どうぞ気楽にいつでもおいでください You are always welcome. (Come by anytime.) ‖ あまり無理しないで気楽に行こうよ Let's not push ourselves too hard and *take things easy*.

きらす 切らす **run out** 《of》 ▶ちょっと塩を切らしてしまったので貸してくださいませんか I've just *run out of* salt. Could you spare me some? ‖ 《商店などで》 すみません. それは切らしております Sorry, we'*re out of* that. ▶そんなに息を切らしてどうしたの? What made you so *breathless*?

ぎらつく **glare** ▶ぎらつく光 *glaring* light ‖ 太陽がぎらついている The sun is *glaring*. ‖ 彼はどでかいもうけ口は無いかといつも目をぎらつかせている He is always *on the lookout for* a big profit. (➤ on the lookout for は「(獲物などを)得ようと見張って」の意).

きらびやか ▶きらびやかなドレスを着た女性たち women in *gorgeous* dresses.

きらめく **glitter** (きらきら輝く) ; **twinkle** (星などが光る) ▶きらめく宝石[星] a *glittering* gem [star] ‖ この作品には作曲者のきらめくばかりの才能があふれている This piece shows off the composer's *dazzling* talent.

きらり ▶暗闇の中にきらりと光るものがあった There was something that *glinted* in the darkness. ‖ 彼女の指にダイヤの婚約指輪がきらりと光った Her diamond engagement ring *sparkled* on her finger.

¹きり 霧 (a) **fog** (ふつう, 前が見通せないほど濃い霧 ;「濃い」は thick, heavy, dense など,「薄い」は light で, thin は用いない) ; (a) **mist** (薄い霧, かすみ) ▶霧の深い夜 a *foggy* night ‖ ゆうべは霧が深かった There was a dense *fog* last night. ‖ 霧が出てきた It's getting *foggy*. ／The *fog* is coming in. (➤ 後者は海や湖についていう) ‖ 朝霧が晴れて赤城山がくっきりと姿を現した The *morning mist* lifted to reveal the sharp outline of Mt. Akagi. ‖ 港は霧に包まれていた The port was shrouded in *fog*. ‖ スカートに霧吹きで霧を吹いてからアイロンをかけた I ironed the skirt after *spraying* it *with water*. ‖ 《比喩的》 政界の黒い霧 *shadows* on the political scene.

²きり 錐 a **(hand) drill** ; a **gimlet** /gímlət/ (T字型の柄の付いた木工きり) ; an **awl** /ɔːl/ (革に穴をあける靴屋などの) ▶きりで板に穴をあけた I bored a hole through the board with *a hand drill*.

³きり 桐 《植物》 **paulownia** /pɔːlóʊniə/ ▶総ギリのたんす a chest of drawers *made entirely of paulownia wood*.

⁴きり 切り **1** 【際限】 an **end** (終わり) ; a **bound** (限界) ▶欲を言えば切りがない *There's no end to* the things we'd like to have. ／Desire (for things) *knows no bounds*. (➤ 後者は堅い表現) ‖ その問題はいくら議論しても切りがない *There is no end to* the argument on that matter. ‖ 悩みだしたら切りがないよ Once you start worrying, *you can't stop it*. ‖ ピーナッツは食べ始めると切りがない If you eat one peanut, *you will eat another and another*.

2 【区切り】 ▶切りのいい数字 a *good* [*nice*], *round* number (➤ round は50, 100などの「端数のない」) ‖ 切りのいいところで少し休憩しよう Let's take a break *when we come to a good spot*. ‖ きょうはここで切りをつけて帰ろう Let's *call it a day*. (➤ call it a day は「(仕事などを)打ち切る」の意のインフォーマルな表現).

-きり ▶私は1人きりで映画を見ていた I was watching the movie *all alone*. ‖ みんな家に帰り, ぼくたち2人きりになった Everybody went home and *the two of us* were left *alone*. ‖ 兄は3年前イタリアへ行ったきり連絡もしてこない My older brother went to Italy three years ago, and I *haven't* heard anything from him *since*.

ぎり 義理 **1** 【社交上のルール】 (a) ***giri*** **(obligation)**

> **《解説》「義理」と obligation**
> (1) 日本語の「義理」は「人と付き合っていく際に守らなくてはならない世の中のルール」の意であり, 広義には「付き合い, 交際」の意でもあるが, これらの意を表す特定の語は英語にはない. 英語の obligation は「契約・約束・道徳的責任などに縛られて果たさなければならない義務」, duty は「良心・職責などから生じる義務(感)」の意で,いずれも日本語の「義理」にぴたりとは対応しない.
> (2) したがって, 日本語の「義理」には *giri* (obligation) か *giri*(-type) obligation を用いるのがよい.
> →人情.

▶多くの日本人は義理を時としてやっかいなものと思っている Many Japanese feel that *'giri' obligations* are occasionally bothersome. ‖ あすは上司の披露宴に義理で出席しなくてはならない Tomorrow I must attend my boss's wedding reception purely *out of social obligation*. ‖ あの人には義理があって嫌とは言えないのです I can't say no (to his request) because I'm under *obligation* to him. ‖ 日本人はよく義理と人情の板挟みになって苦しむ Japanese are often torn between *'giri' obligations and personal feelings*. ‖ 彼はとても義理堅い He *has a* very *strong sense of duty*. ／He never forgets to fulfill his *'giri' obligations*. (➤「義理堅い人」を a stickler for duty [obligation] ということもある) ‖ 私に義理立てしてきみまで会社を辞める必要はないよ You don't have to leave the company along with

me because you *feel* [you *are*] *obligated* to me. ‖この土地の人々は**義理人情にあつい** These local people are *loyal and warmhearted*.
▶バレンタインデーには同僚の男性たちに**義理チョコ**を贈った On St. Valentine's Day, I gave my male colleagues *chocolate as a matter of obligation* [*chocolate just to be nice*]. (➤後者は「単に親切心で」の意) ‖ (その絵は)**義理にも**うまく描けているとは言えないね *Even social obligation* won't make me say the picture is well done. (➤「社交上の義務でも言えない」の意) ‖彼は**お義理で**そのパーティーに出席した He went to the party *just* (*trying*) *to be nice*. ／He went to the party *as a social obligation*. (● 第1文の訳例のほうが日本語の「お義理で」の感じがよく出せる) ‖ 対話「オートバイ買ってくれないなら, 大学行かないからな」「養ってもらってるくせに, 親に向かってそんなことが言えた**義理か**」"I'm not going to college if you don't buy me a motorcycle." "*How dare you say that to me?* Who do you think is supporting you?"
2【続き柄の】-in-law ▶**義理の父** a father-*in-law* ‖ **義理の兄**［妹］a brother［sister］-*in-law* ‖ **義理の両親** *in-laws* (➤ parents-in-law とはあまりいわない).
☞ **不義理** (→見出語)

-ぎり -切り ▶豆腐を四つ**切りに**する *cut* the tofu *into four* (*pieces*).

きりあげる 切り上げる 1【区切りをつけてやめる】 **leave (off)**; **knock off**(仕事を中断する) ▶彼はいつもより早く仕事を**切り上げた** He *left* (*off*) work earlier than usual. ‖わあ, もう10時よ. きょうはこの辺で**切り上げましょう** Come on, it's ten already. Let's *knock off* for the day [*call it a day*].
2【上の位にする】▶26円を30円に**切り上げる** *round* 26 yen *up* to 30 yen.

きりうり 切り売りする divide and sell ▶ピザを**切り売りする** *sell* pizza *by the slice*.

きりえ 切り絵 cutting out paper; a **paper cutout**(切り抜いた作品).

きりおとす 切り落とす cut［**chop**／**saw**］**... off**(➤ chop は「おのなどでたたき切る」, saw は「のこぎりで切る」場合) ▶あの枯れ枝を**切り落として**ください Please *cut* [*chop*／*saw*] that dead branch *off*.

きりかえ 切り替え a **change**, a **change-over** ▶十進法への**切り替え** *a changeover* to the decimal system ‖運転免許の**切り替え**(＝更新) *renewal* of a driver's license ‖時勢に後れないためには頭の**切り替え**が必要だ You have to *switch* your way of thinking to keep abreast of the times.
‖**切り替えスイッチ** a changeover switch.

きりかえす 切り返す turn back ▶ハンドルを右に［左に］**切り返す** *turn* the steering wheel *back* to the right［left］(➤具体的にいうのが一般的) ／*swerve* (one's car) to the right［left］‖冴子の鋭い皮肉に私は**切り返す**ことばもなかった I was at a loss for *a reply* to Saeko's vicious sarcasm.

きりかえる 切り替える change ＋㊐ (改める); **switch** ＋㊐ (ぱっと, あるいは, 思い切りよく変える) ▶ギアを**切り替える** *switch* gears ‖あすから夏服に**切り替える**ことになっている We are going to *change* to summer uniforms tomorrow. ‖きみは旧式な物の見方をやめて頭を**切り替える**べきだ You should *change* your old-fashioned way of looking at things.

【文型】
A から B に切り替える
switch from A **to** B

▶機長は操縦を自動から手動に**切り替えた** The captain *switched from* automatic pilot *to* manual control. ‖私はブランド薬からジェネリック薬に**切り替えた** I *switched from* brand-name drugs *to* generic ones.

きりかぶ 切り株 a **stump**(木の); a **stubble**(稲・麦の).

きりかわる 切り替わる ▶あすから新制度に**切り替わる**予定だ This system is to *be replaced* by a new one tomorrow. ／We're *changing over to* a new system tomorrow.

きりきざむ 切り刻む cut［**chop**］**up**(➤後者は強く大まかに切ることをいう); **mince** ＋㊐ (ミンチにする) ▶野菜を**切り刻む** *cut*［*chop*］*up* vegetables.

きりきず 切り傷 a **cut** 《参考》深い切り傷は gash, かみそりなどによる深い傷は slash という.

ぎりぎり ▶生活費を**ぎりぎりまで**切り詰める cut living expenses *to the bare minimum* ‖宿題を**ぎりぎりまで**延ばしてはいけない Don't put off doing your homework *to the last minute*. ‖彼はその式に**ぎりぎりに**着いた He got there *just in time* for the ceremony. ‖3時の列車に**ぎりぎりで間に合った** I *just made it* onto the 3 o'clock train. (➤ make it は「(時間などに)間に合う」) ‖**ぎりぎりいくらまで**負けてくれますか *How far* [*How much*] can you knock the price down? ‖坂本はレフト線**ぎりぎりに**二塁打を放った Sakamoto smashed a sizzling double *just inside the left foul line*.

きりぎりす (虫) a **grasshopper**.

きりきりまい きりきり舞い ▶彼は仕事が忙しくて一日中**きりきり舞いした** He *was extremely busy with his work* all day. ／His work kept him on the go all day. (➤ on the go は「動き回って, 働きづめで」の意のインフォーマルな表現).

きりくずす 切り崩す level ＋㊐ (ならす) ▶数台のブルドーザーが一夜のうちにその小山を**切り崩して**しまった A few bulldozers *leveled* that hill overnight.

きりくち 切り口 a **cut end**(木の); a **section**(断面).

きりこ 切り子 a **facet** /fǽsɪt/
‖**切り子ガラス** cut glass.

きりこむ 切り込む ▶彼らは敵陣深く**切り込んだ** They *fought their way deep* into enemy territory. ‖学生の1人がその点について講演者に鋭く**切り込んだ** One of the students *sharply questioned* the lecturer on that point.

きりさく 切り裂く rip ＋㊐ ▶布をずたずたに**切り裂く** *rip* a piece of cloth into pieces ‖闇を**切り裂く**ような叫び声 a *piercing* shriek［scream］.

きりさげる 切り下げる reduce ＋㊐ (数量・価格などを); **devalue** ＋㊐ (平価を); **cut (away)**(削除する) ▶価格を**切り下げる** *reduce* a price ‖円を**切り下げる** *devalue* the yen.

きりさめ 霧雨 a **drizzle** ▶**霧雨が降っていた** It was *drizzling*.

キリシタン a **Christian** ▶隠れ**キリシタン** hidden *Christians* (of Japan).

ギリシャ Greece(➤正式な国名は the Hellenic Republic) ‖**ギリシャ語** Greek ‖**ギリシャ人** a Greek ‖**ギリシャ神話** Greek mythology.

きりすてる 切り捨てる ▶端数を**切り捨てる** *discard* [*omit*] fractions.
▶できないからといって子供を**切り捨てる**のは真の教育からは程遠い *Ignoring* children just because they are slow learners is far from true education.

キリスト (Jesus) Christ /kraɪst/ (➤呼びかけは Our Lord). ‖**キリスト降誕劇** a (Christmas) nativity play.

キリストきょう キリスト教 Christianity ▶キリスト教を信仰する believe in *Christianity*.
‖キリスト教徒 a Christian.

きりそろえる 切り揃える trim, cut evenly.

きりたおす 切り倒す cut down ; chop down(おの・なたなどで) ▶木を切り倒す *chop* [*cut*] *down* a tree.

きりだし 切り出し ▶スピーチは切り出しが肝心だ *How you start off* a speech is most important. ／The *beginning* of a speech is the most important part. ‖切り出しナイフ a pointed knife.

きりだす 切り出す ▶金を貸してくれと切り出すのはタイミングが難しい It is not easy to decide when to *broach* the subject of borrowing money. (➤ broach は「(話題などを)持ち出す」).

きりたつ 切り立つ ▶切り立った崖 a *vertical* [*perpendicular*] cliff ／a precipice /présəpɪs/.

ぎりだて 義理立て →義理.

1 **きりつ 起立** ▶起立！*Stand up!* ‖《法廷などで》全員起立！*All rise!* ‖先生が入って来ると，皆起立した Everyone *stood up* when the teacher came in.

2 **きりつ 規律 a regulation, a rule** (規則) ; **discipline** /dísəplɪn/ (風紀) ▶諸君には本校の規律をきちんと守ってもらいたいと思います You should observe the *regulations* [*rules*] of this school faithfully. ‖この学校は規律がやかましい This school is strict about *regulations* [*rules*]. ／*Discipline* is strictly enforced in this school.

きりつける 切り付ける slash 《at》▶暴漢が飛び出してきて演説中の首相に切りつけた A thug leaped out and *slashed at* the prime minister while he was delivering a speech.

きりっと ▶きりっと締まった顔 a face with *clearly defined* [*clear-cut* ／*finely-chiseled*] features.

きりつめる 切り詰める ▶利益を増やそうと思うなら支出を切り詰めなさい You should *cut back* [*down*] *on* your spending if you want to produce a large profit. ‖結婚式のために極力切り詰めています We're *pinching pennies* [*every penny*] for our wedding. ‖彼らは爪に火をともすような切り詰めた生活をしている They are *pinching and scraping*. ‖経費を切り詰めればいい辞書はできない We can't make an excellent dictionary if we *cut corners*(➤ cut corners は「手間や費用面で，手抜きをする」).

きりどおし 切り通し《米》**a cut,**《英》**a cutting.**

きりとりせん 切り取り線 a perforated line(➤ 通常の表示は cut here).

きりとる 切り取る cut out ▶手術で悪い所を切り取る *cut out* the bad part in an operation ／*remove* the affected part by surgical procedure (➤ remove は「除去する」) ‖息子がこの本から絵を切り取ってしまった My son *cut* the picture *out of* this book.

きりぬき 切り抜き a clipping,《英また》**a cutting**
▶新聞［雑誌］の切り抜き newspaper [magazine] *clippings* ‖切り抜き帳 a scrapbook.

きりぬく 切り抜く clip 《out of》(記事などを) ; **cut out**(ある形に) ▶新聞の音楽欄を切り抜く *clip* [《英また》*cut*] a music column *out of* the paper.

きりぬける 切り抜ける ▶難局を切り抜ける *get out of* [*tide over*] a difficult situation ‖大谷はワンアウト満塁のピンチを切り抜けた Ohtani *got out of* a bases-loaded jam with one out.

きりばな 切り花 a cut flower.

きりはなす 切り離す separate +㊊ ▶第一段ロケットが打ち上げ後 3 分で切り離された The first stage of the rocket *separated* three minutes after launching. (➤ separate は「(結合していたものが)分離する」の意だから, was separated とする必要はない) ‖その 2 つの問題は切り離して考えるべきだ The two issues should be discussed *separately*.

きりばり 切り張り・切り貼り ▶その論文はネットで集めた情報を切り貼りしたものだった The paper was made up of *copy and pasted* information gathered from the Net.

きりひらく 切り開く open up ; develop +㊊ (開発する) ▶山を切り開いて宅地にする *develop* a mountain into housing lots.
▶新しい学問分野を切り開く *open up* [*pioneer*] a new field of study ‖半導体の発明はエレクトロニクスの新分野を切り開いた The invention of the semiconductor *opened* new fields in electronics.

きりふき 霧吹き a **sprayer** ; an **atomizer**(噴霧器，香水吹き).

きりふだ 切り札 a **trump (card)**(トランプの) ▶最後の切り札を使う *play one's trump card* ‖我々には最後の切り札がある We have *a trump card*.

きりぼし 切り干し ▶切り干し大根 *shredded and dried* daikon.

きりまわす 切り回す manage +㊊ (処理する) ; **run** +㊊ (経営する) ▶チームのことは彼女が全部切り回している She *manages* everything that has to do with our team. ／She is the team manager [assistant]. (➤ 後者は「彼女はチームのマネージャーだ」の意 ; manager をこの意で使うのは主に《米》だが，文脈によっては「監督」の意になる) ‖この大きな店を切り回しているのがあの小さなおばあさんだって？Is that the little elderly woman who *runs* this big store?

キリマンジャロ (Mount) Kilimanjaro(アフリカの最高峰).

きりみ 切り身 a **slice**(薄い) ; a **fillet** /fílɪt, fɪléɪ/ (厚い) ▶サケの切り身 *a slice* [*fillet*] of salmon.

きりもみ 錐揉み ▶飛行機はきりもみ状態で墜落した The plane *went into a spin* and crashed.

きりもり 切り盛り ▶妻は家計の切り盛りが上手だ My wife is good at *housekeeping*. ／My wife is a good housekeeper. (➤単に housekeeper だと「家政婦」の意) ‖この家を切り盛りするのは15歳の少女には荷が重すぎる It is too much for a 15-year-old girl to *manage* this house.

きりゅう 気流 an air current ‖上昇［下降］気流 an ascending [a descending] air current.
☛ 乱気流 (→見出語)

きりょう 器量 1【美貌】(good) looks(美しい顔立ち) ; **appearance**(容貌) ▶彼女は器量がいい［悪い］She's *good-looking* [*plain-looking* ／*homely*].
‖器量よし a good-looker(➤ 男性にも用いる) ; a good-looking girl [woman].
2【人間としての大きさ】caliber →うつわ ▶あの政治家は指導者としての器量に欠けている That politician does*n't have what it takes to be a leader*.

ぎりょう 技量 skill ; an **ability** (能力) ▶技量を磨く hone one's *skill*(*s*) ‖彼は技量を認められて昇進した He was promoted when his *abilities* were recognized.

きりょく 気力 willpower(精神力) ; **drive** (やる気) ; **energy** (精力) ▶気力の乏しい人 a person who lacks *willpower* ‖その病人は気力だけで生きていた The patient held on through sheer *willpower*. ‖30代は気力がいちばん充実する People have the most *drive and energy* in their thirties. ‖この頃

年のせいか気力が続かない It may be because of my age, but these days I *can't bring myself to stick with anything for very long*.

きりわける 切り分ける cut +㊀ ; slice (up ／off)(薄く切る) ; carve +㊀ (肉などを) ▶ケーキを子供たちに切り分けてちょうだい Could you *slice up* the cake for the children ?

きりん 《動》a giraffe /dʒəræ̀f/ ▶お母さん, キリンの首はなぜ長いの? Mom, why are *giraffes*' necks so long ?

[1]きる 切る

> 📖 訳語メニュー
> 切断する, 傷つける →cut **1, 2**
> スイッチを切る →turn off **3**
> 電話を切る →hang up **3**
> 縁を切る →break off **6**
> 下回る →(be) under **7**

1【切り離す】 cut +㊀ ; slice +㊀ (薄く) ▶はさみでひもを切る *cut* a cord with scissors ‖ タマネギを薄く切る *slice* onion ‖ パンを 1 切れ薄く切る *slice off* a piece of bread ‖ 豚肉のブロックを包丁でたたき切る *chop* a large piece of pork with a cleaver ‖ 小枝をチョキンと切る *snip* a twig ‖ 針金をパチンと切る *snap* a wire ‖ 丸太をのこぎりで切る *saw* a log.

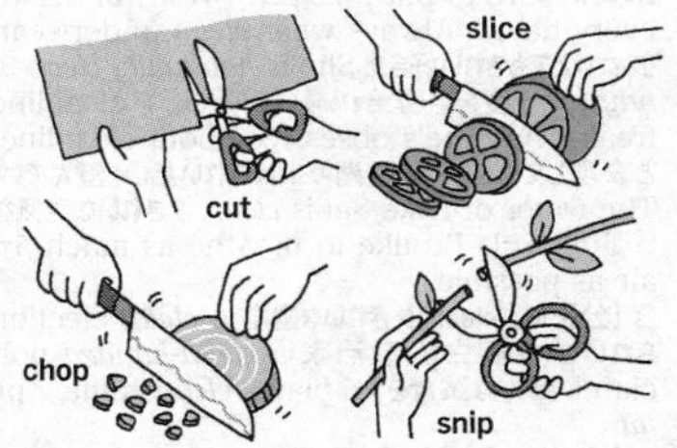

▶このスイカを 4 つに切りなさい *Cut* this watermelon into four pieces. ‖ 引退した力士は髪を短く切った(＝切ってもらった) The retired sumo wrestler *had* his hair *cut* short. ‖ 父は胃潰瘍で胃を半分切った(＝切り取った) My father *had* half of his stomach *removed* because of an ulcer.
▶私に来た手紙の封を切ったのだあれ? Who *opened* [*cut open*] the letter addressed to me ?
▶先頭を切って走っているのは上野選手です It's Ueno *taking* [*in*] *the lead !* ‖ 大学入試のトップを切って, きょう関西の私立大学の入試が行われた Private Kansai universities *kicked off* the entrance exam season today. ‖ マラソン選手たちは正午にスタートを切った The marathon runners *started* at noon.

2【刃物で傷つける】 cut +㊀ ; slash +㊀ (切り裂く) ▶ナイフで親指を切る *cut* one's thumb with a knife ‖ 弟は転んで顎を切った My little brother fell (down) and *cut* his chin. ‖ 少女は手首を切って何度か自殺しようとした The girl tried to commit suicide several times by *slashing* her wrist(s). ‖ 昔の武士は自分で腹を切って死んだ Old-time warriors killed themselves *by harakiri*.

3【流れを分断する】 turn off (スイッチなどを) ; hang up (電話を) ▶スイッチ [テレビ] を切りなさい *Turn off* the switch [TV]. ‖ 非常事態が起こると発電所は電気を切ることがある The power station may *cut off* electricity in an emergency. ‖ じゃあ, 電話を切るよ I've got to *hang up* now. ‖ 《電話を》切らずにそのままお待ちください *Hold on*, please. ／*Hold the line*, please. ‖ 亜希, きみがトランプを切る番だよ Aki, it's your turn to *shuffle the cards*.
▶連絡船が青い波を切って進んでいく The ferryboat is moving forward, *cutting through* the blue waves. ‖ レーシングカーが急カーブを切って疾走していく The racing cars are zooming ahead, *negotiating hairpin curves*. ‖ 彼は自転車のハンドルを切り損ねて電柱に激突した While riding on his bike, he *lost control of the handlebars* and crashed into a utility pole.

4【水や油をふるい落とす】 drain +㊀ ▶ホウレンソウを水切り籠に取り, よく水を切りなさい Put the spinach in a strainer and *drain* it well.

5【区切る, 限定する】 ▶彼には期限を切って100万円融資した I loaned him one million yen *with a definite payback date* [*date by which he had to pay me back*].

6【関係を断つ】 break off(関係を) ; break up《with》(人と別れる) ▶首を切る(＝解雇する) *fire* a person ／*give* a person *the ax* [《英また》*the sack*] ‖ おまえとは完全に縁を切る I'm *breaking off all relations* with you. ‖ 健作とは手を切ったわ I *broke up with* Kensaku. ‖ 《慣用表現》富士山と桜は日本と切っても切れない関係にある Mt. Fuji and cherry blossoms *are inextricably linked* to Japan. (➤ inextricably は「解きほぐせないほどに」) ‖ 吉田君とぼくとは切っても切れない仲です Yoshida and I are such good friends that *nothing can separate us*. ／Yoshida and I are *inseparable* friends.

7【下回る】 ▶原価を切って売る sell *below* cost ‖ 10秒を切る記録を出す set a record *under* 10 seconds.

8【伝票などを出す】 ▶小切手を切る *issue a check* ‖ 出張旅費の伝票を切る *fill out a form* asking for one's business trip expenses.

[2]きる 着る

1【身に着ける】 put on ; wear, have ... on

> **語法** **put on** は「着る」という動作を表し, **wear, have ... on** は「着ている」という状態を表す. また, wear は進行形でよく用いる.
>
> put on　　wear

▶上着を着る *put on* one's coat ‖ 姉はめったにスーツを着ないが, その日はダークスーツを着ていた My sister rarely wears a suit, but she *was wearing* a dark one that day. ‖ 彼女は美しい和服を着ていた She *was dressed* in a beautiful kimono. ‖ 同窓会に何を着ていこうかしら What should I *wear* to the class reunion ? (➤「着る」という動作が問題でなく, 「着終

わった状態［姿］」をイメージしているので wear を用いる）‖その子はパジャマを着るのに時間がかかる He [She] takes a while to *put on* his [her] pajamas. ‖コートを着るから（ちょっと）待っていて Please wait (a moment) while I *put on* my overcoat. ／Please wait (a moment). I'd like to *put on* my overcoat.

▶父はグレーの背広を着て出かけた Dad went out *in* his gray suit. ‖美奈子は服を着たまま寝てしまったわ Minako fell asleep *with* her clothes *on*. ‖コートは着たままでお入りください Please come in. Don't (bother to) take your coat off. (➤「脱がなくても結構です」の意) ‖ **対話**「この服を着てみてもいいですか」「どうぞ」"May I *try* this dress *on*?" "Sure. (Please) go ahead."

2【身に引き受ける】▶罪を着る *take* the blame ‖今晩泊めてくれれば恩に着ます I'*d be obliged* if you would put me up for the night.

-きる -切る ▶ヘアリキッドを1瓶使い切る *use up* a bottle of hair tonic ‖『源氏物語』を読み切るのは大変だ It's no easy matter to *read* "The Tale of Genji" *from beginning to end*.

▶相次ぐ不祥事に首脳陣は弱り切っている The top management *is greatly annoyed* by the series of scandals. ‖彼女は疲れ切っているように見えた She looked *absolutely exhausted*.

キルティング **quilting** /kwíltɪŋ/.

キルト a **quilt** /kwɪlt/.

きれ 切れ 1【切れ味】▶このナイフは切れが悪い This knife *doesn't cut well* [*is dull*]. ‖あいつは頭の切れがいい He is *quite smart*. ／He is *sharp as a tack* [《英》*a needle*]. ‖藤川のフォークは切れがいい Fujikawa's forkball is extremely *sharp*.

2【断片】▶木の切れ *a chip* [*piece*] *of* wood.

3【布】 **cloth**；**remnants**（はぎれ）.

-きれ -切れ ▶紙切れ *a piece of paper* ‖パン1切れ *a slice* of bread ‖マグロの刺身3切れ *three slices* of raw tuna ‖1切れの肉 *a piece* [*chop*] *of* meat ‖ローストビーフをもう1切れ頂けますか Could I have *another slice of* roast beef?

▶もう時間切れだ We are *running out of time*.

きれあじ 切れ味 ▶このナイフとあのナイフではどっちが切れ味がいいですか Which knife *cuts better*, this one or that one?

きれい 奇麗・綺麗

訳語メニュー
美しい →beautiful 1
かわいらしい →pretty 1
清潔な →clean 2
公正な →clean 3

1【美しい】 **beautiful**（完全無欠で美しい）；**pretty**（感じがいい，かわいらしい）；**lovely**（愛らしい，すばらしい，うっとりする；主に女性が用いる語）▶きみ，きょうはすごくきれいだよ You look really *pretty* today. ‖何てきれいなドレスでしょう What a *beautiful* [*pretty*] dress (this is)! ‖野は一面のひなげしの花盛りでとてもきれいだった The field was covered with poppies in full bloom and was really *beautiful*. ‖ **対話**「この絵本どう？」「きれい！」"What do you think of this picture book?" "*It's lovely*." ‖あの子きれいね She is *pretty* [*good-looking*], isn't she? ‖淳子はきれいな足をしている Junko has *nice* legs. ‖清彦は心がきれいだ Kiyohiko is a *good-hearted* person.

直訳の落とし穴「きれいになりたい」
「きれいになりたい」は文字どおりには I want to be [become] beautiful. であるが，この文は「私はきれいでない」ということが前提になっていなければならない．これは「金持ちになりたい」「背が高くなりたい」がいずれも現在「金持ちでない」「背が高くない」を意味していることからもわかる．したがって，コマーシャルなどで十分きれいな女優が「きれいになりたい」と言っているせりふを英語で表すには「もっときれいになりたい」と解釈して，I want to be more beautiful. としなければならない．なお，未来を示す語句があれば，現実は違う，という含みはもたず，I want to be happy after I get married.（結婚して幸せになりたい）は「今幸せでない」を意味しない．また同様に，「いつまでもきれいでいたい」は I want to be [stay] beautiful for as long as possible. が近い．→いつまでも.

▶彼女は字がきれいだ She *has good handwriting*. ‖健太郎，部屋をきれいに片づけなさい Kentaro, *straighten up* your room. ‖ゆかりの部屋はいつもきれいに片づいている Yukari's room is always *neat and clean*.

2【汚れがない】 **clean** ▶きれいなハンカチ a *clean* handkerchief ‖手をきれいに洗う wash one's hands (*clean*) (➤ wash だけできれいにする含みがあるので clean は省略してよい) ‖下着はいつもきれいにしておきなさい Be sure to put on *clean* [*fresh*] underwear every day. ／Always wear *clean* underwear. ‖彼女はとてもきれい好きだ She is *habitually clean and tidy*. (➤「度を越したきれい好き(の人)」を cleanliness freak という. She's obsessive about cleanliness. と表現してもよい) ‖西湖の水はきれいだ（＝澄んでいる）The water of Lake Sai is *clear*. ‖きれいな空気を思い切り吸いたい I'd like to breathe as much *fresh* air as possible.

3【公正な】 **clean** ▶きれいな選挙 a *clean* election ‖きれいな（＝潔白な）政治家 a *clean-handed* politician ‖きれいな試合をする play a *clean* game ／play *fair*.

4【すっかり】▶少年は山盛りのご飯をきれいに平らげた The boy *has wolfed down* the whole bowl of rice. ‖借金をきれいに返す *pay off* all the loan ‖入試が終わったら何もかもきれいに忘れてしまった Once the entrance exams were over, I forgot *everything* I had learned. ‖あの子のことはきれいさっぱり忘れたほうがいい You should put her *completely* out of your mind.

ぎれい 儀礼 **courtesy** /kə́ːṭəsi/ ▶彼らは儀礼をとても重んじる They place great value on *courtesy*. ‖答礼訪問は儀礼的なものだった The return visit was just *a formality*.

きれいごと きれい事 ▶経営の立て直しはきれい事では済まない Rebuilding management cannot be achieved by *fine words* (alone).

きれぎれ 切れ切れ ▶切れ切れの記憶をたどる［つなぎ合わせる］trace back [combine] one's *fragmentary* memories.

きれこみ 切れ込み a **notch**, a **slit**.

きれじ 切れ痔 **bleeding hemorrhoids** /hémərɔɪdz/ [**piles**].

きれつ 亀裂 a **crack**（割れ目，裂け目）；a **breach**（堤防・城壁などの）；a **rift**（関係をこわす）▶壁の亀裂は次第に大きくなっている The *crack* in the wall is getting wider. ‖道路に亀裂が生じて通行止めになった The road *was fissured* and had to be closed to traffic. ‖金銭的なトラブルで彼らの友情に亀裂が生じた

Trouble over money caused *a rift* [*a breach*] in their friendship.

-きれない -切れない ▶この少年のほうが悪いとばかりは言い切れない You *can't say for sure* that this boy is in the wrong. ‖こんなに食べ切れないよ This *is more than I can eat*. ‖少女はこらえ切れずに泣きだした The girl *could not stand it any longer* and burst into tears. ‖あと2週間で夏休み. もう待ち切れない Just two more weeks until (my) summer vacation, *I can hardly wait*.

きれなが 切れ長 ▶切れ長の目の人 an *almond-eyed* person (● 日本人や中国人などの目の形容にはこの almond-eyed(文字どおりには「アーモンド形の目をした」の意)を用いる. slit-eyed とすると, いかにも陰険・隠微な人物を連想させるので使用を避けたほうがよい).

きれはし 切れ端 ▶彼は紙の切れ端に電話番号を書いた He scribbled his telephone number on *a scrap of paper*. ‖小鳥たちはパンの切れ端をついばんだ The birds picked at *pieces of bread*.

きれま 切れ間 ▶雲の切れ間から鎌のような月が見えた The crescent moon was visible [was poking] through *an opening* in the clouds.

きれめ 切れ目 ▶雲の切れ目から満月が見えた I saw the full moon through *a break* [*a rift*] in the clouds. ‖何キロも切れ目なく続く車の列で道路はいっぱいだった The road was packed with cars lined up for miles and miles *without a break*. (➤ 英文は「何マイルも」).

きれもの 切れ者 ▶あの若社長はなかなかの切れ者だ That young company president is a really *sharp man*.

きれる 切れる

📖 訳語メニュー
よく切れる →cut **1**
切断される →break **2**
品切れになる →run out **5**
期限が切れる →expire **5**
関係が切れる →be through **6**

1【切る能力がある】cut ▶《刃物が鋭利である》この包丁はよく切れる This kitchen knife *cuts* well [is sharp]. ‖このかみそりはよく切れない This razor is *dull*. ‖《頭がよい》林さんの娘さんは切れる Hayashi's daughter is *smart* [*has a sharp mind*]. ‖彼はかみそりのように切れる男だ He is *sharp as a tack* [《英》*a needle*].

2【切った状態になる】break ▶糸はいちばん弱いところで切れる Thread *breaks* at its weakest point. ‖綱引きの最中に綱が切れて大勢がけがをした The rope *snapped* in the middle of a tug-of-war game and many people were injured. (➤ snap は「ぷつりと切れる」) ‖地滑りで電線が切れた The landslide *severed* the electric lines. (➤ sever /sévəʳ/ は「切断する」) ‖この電球, 切れてるよ This (light) bulb *is out* [*dead*]. ‖私が電話口に出たときには電話は切れていた The line *was dead* when I answered the phone. ‖洪水で堤防が切れた The riverbank *gave way* [The levee *broke*] due to the flood. (➤ give way は「崩れる」).
▶《比喩的》「俺, もうキレそうだ」と修二は言った "I'm about to *lose it*," Shuji said. (➤ lose it は「かっとなる」の意の俗語) ‖先生に何度も注意され, その生徒はとうとう逆ギレした When the teacher kept scolding him, the student finally *snapped* back.

3【傷つく, だめになる】 ▶かみそりの刃にちょっと触れただけで指が切れた Though I touched the razor's edge only slightly, I *cut* my finger. ‖このメーカーのストッキングはすぐ切れる(＝伝線する) The (panty) hose produced by this maker *run* easily.

4【流れが途切れる】 ▶家並みの切れた所に麦畑が広がっていた There were large wheat fields where the row of houses *ended*. ‖電話が途中で切れた We *were cut off* in the middle of a phone call. ‖この治療器は15分で自動的にスイッチが切れるようになっている This medical device automatically *turns itself off* after fifteen minutes. ‖100メートル走っただけで息が切れた I *got winded* after running only 100 meters.

5【尽きて無くなる】run out ; expire (➤ 満了する, 期限切れになる) ▶ガソリンが切れて通りで立ち往生してしまった Having *run out of* gas, I (was) stalled on the street. ‖**対話**「その問題集を100冊注文したいのですが」「すみません, 目下在庫が切れておりまして」"We'd like to order one hundred copies of this workbook." "I am sorry, but we're *out of stock*."
▶あと10日で契約の期限が切れる The contract *expires* [*runs out*] in ten days. ‖《駅員が男性客に》お客さん, 定期の期限が切れてますよ Sir, this pass *has expired*. ‖提出期限が切れてからレポートを出しても無駄です It is pointless to hand in your term paper *after the deadline*.

6【関係が無くなる】break up《with》(別れる) ; **be through**《with》(関係を断っている) ▶**対話**「おまえ, 浩二とまだ付き合っているのか」「あら, とっくの昔に切れているわよ」"Are you still going out with Koji?" "Oh no. We *broke up* long ago." (➤ Our relationship ended long ago. としてもよい) ‖正式に離婚して, 彼とは縁が切れた I got divorced and *cut (off) all ties* with him. ‖サイモンとは縁が切れている *I'm through with* Simon.

7【切ることが可能である】 ▶フランスパンはふつうの包丁ではなかなか切れない It's *hard to cut* a French baguette with an ordinary kitchen knife. ‖弟は全く不器用なのでトランプがうまく切れない My brother is all thumbs, so he *can't shuffle* cards. ‖《慣用表現》政治家と金とは切っても切れない関係らしい It seems that you *can't separate* politicians and money.

8【曲がる】 ▶松坂のカーブはよく切れる Matsuzaka's curveballs *break* sharply.

¹きろ 帰路 ▶帰路に就く *start* [*leave*] *for home* ‖ロサンゼルスからの帰路, 私はハワイに寄るつもりだった I was planning to stop over in Hawaii *on my way home* from Los Angeles.

²きろ 岐路 a **crossroads** ▶人生の岐路に立つまでは人生について考えることなどないものだ People never think much about life until they come to a *crossroads*.

キロ a **kilo** (➤ kilogram の短縮形 ; kilometer は短縮しないのがふつう) ▶ここから駅まで3キロ(＝キロメートル)ある It is three *kilometers* from here to the train station. ‖彼は時速140キロで高速道路を飛ばしていた He was driving his car (at a speed of) *140 kilometers per hour* on the superhighway.
▶私は体重が60キロ(＝キログラム)ある I weigh sixty *kilos* [*kilograms*].

きろく 記録

1【書いた物】a record /rékəʳd/ ; a **document** (文書) 一動 **記録する record** /rɪkɔ́:ʳd/ ＋目 ▶この本はオウム事件の記録です This book is *a record* of the Aum incidents. ‖う

き

ちの蔵には江戸時代の古い記録がたくさんある There are a lot of historical *documents* of the Edo era in our storehouse. ‖ 事件を記録した記録映画が公開された The documentary film that *recorded* [*chronicled*] the incident was released. (➤ chronicle は「時系列で記録する」; 🔵 that recorded は recording と, また that chronicled は chronicling としてもよい) ‖ 新聞記者たちは首相の発言をすべて記録に取った The news reporters *wrote down* everything the Prime Minister said. (➤ write down は「書き留める」).

‖記録映画 a documentary (film).

2【スポーツの成績】 a **record** (➤ しばしば「最高記録」を意味する) ▶自己の記録を更新する better one's *record* ‖ スピードスケートで世界新記録を出す set *a new world record* in speed skating ‖ 彼の100メートルの自己最高記録は10秒3だ His *best record* in the 100-meter dash is 10.3 seconds. (➤ ten point three seconds と読む) ‖ 彼女は女子100メートルバタフライの世界記録保持者だ She is the world *record holder* in the women's 100-meter butterfly. ‖ 1万メートルで彼は日本記録を破った He broke the *Japanese record* in a 10,000-meter race. ‖記録係 (＝計時係) a timekeeper.

3【慣用表現】 一形 記録的な **record**, **record-setting** ▶記録破りのベストセラー a *record-breaking* best seller ‖ 九州地方に記録的な大雨が降った The Kyushu district had a *record* rainfall. ‖ ことしは記録的な米の豊作だった We had a *record* rice crop this year. ／This year's bountiful rice crop was *a record breaker*.

ギロチン **the guillotine** /gíləti:n/.

ぎろん 議論 (a) **discussion** (話し合い); (an) **argument** (相手の説得や自己主張を目的としたもの) 一動 議論する **discuss** +目, **argue** 《about》 ▶それじゃあ議論の余地がない That leaves no room for *discussion*. ‖ 私たちはその映画について長々と議論した We *had a* long *discussion* about the movie. ／We *discussed* the movie for a long time. (➤ (×)discussed about とはしない) ‖ 脳死の問題について白熱した議論が行われた There was *a heated discussion* over the problem of brain death. ‖ ライオンとトラはどちらが強いかで, 弟とぼくは議論になった My (younger) brother and I *got into an argument* over which was stronger, a lion or a tiger.

-ぎわ -際 ▶窓際にいるあの男性は誰ですか Who is that man *by the window*?

▶別れ際に彼女は耳元で何かささやいた She whispered something in my ear *when we parted*.

ぎわく 疑惑 **suspicion** (「…であろう」という疑い); **doubt** (「…ではないだろう」という疑い); (a) **scandal** (スキャンダル); an **allegation** (証拠を示さない告発・申し立て) ▶汚職疑惑 *allegations* of corruption ／corruption *allegations* ‖ 不正疑惑 a cheating *allegation* ‖ 疑惑の人, X氏 Mr. X, *a man under suspicion* ‖ 世間の疑惑を招くような行動をとるな Don't do anything to *arouse* public *suspicion*. ‖ 生徒たちはその先生を疑惑の目で見ていた Students looked at the teacher *suspiciously*. ‖ 私はこの疑惑を晴らしたい I want to clear myself of this *suspicion*. ‖ またまた与党内で贈収賄疑惑が明るみに出た Yet another bribery *scandal* has surfaced in the ruling party.

きわだつ 際立つ ▶女優の中でも彼女は際立って美しい She *stands out* among actresses for her exceptional beauty. (➤ stand out は「目立つ」) ‖ 彼女の肌は際立って白い Her complexion is *strikingly* fair. ‖ 織田信長は日本史上の際立った人物の1人だ Oda Nobunaga is one of the *outstanding* figures in Japanese history.

きわどい 際どい **close** /klous/ (接戦の) ▶うちのチームは際どい勝ち方をした Our team won a *very close* [*narrow*] victory. ／Our team won by a *narrow margin*. ‖ 彼は際どい判定で柔道の決勝に勝った He won the judo final by a *close* decision. ‖ 彼はいつも際どい冗談ばかり言っている He tells *dirty* jokes all the time. ‖ 際どいところでその子は死なずに済んだ The child *narrowly* escaped death. ‖ 際どいところで帰りの最終バスに間に合った I was *just* in time for the last bus home. (➤ home は「家の方へ向かう」の意の副詞).

きわまる 極まる・窮まる ▶この話は不愉快極まる This story is *extremely unpleasant*. ‖ 進退窮まってきみの所に来たという次第だよ I'*m in a terrible fix* and have come to ask for your advice.

きわみ 極み **the extreme** (極端, 極度); **the height** (絶頂, 極致) ▶貧困の極み *the extreme* of poverty ‖ ご出席いただき恐縮の極みです I *am most grateful and honored* for your presence (at this gathering).

きわめつき 極め付き ▶極め付きの (＝評判の高い) ミュージカル a musical *widely acknowledged for its excellence* ／a musical to end all musicals (➤ 後者は「すべてのミュージカルをしのぐ(ミュージカル)」の意).

きわめて 極めて **very** (非常に); **extremely** (極度に); **awfully** (ものすごく) →とても, 非常に ▶これは極めて重要な問題だ This is a *very* [an *extremely*] important issue. ‖ 彼には人をだますのは極めて容易なことだった It was *quite* easy for him to deceive people. ‖ 電話帳の上手な利用法を知っている人は極めて少ない *Very* few people know how to make good use of telephone directories. ‖ きみがクラブを退会したのは極めて残念だ I am *awfully* sorry that you left the club.

きわめる 究める・極める・窮める ▶その山の頂上を極めることができたのはほんの2, 3人の登山家だけである Only a few climbers were able to *reach* [*conquer*] *the summit* of the mountain. ‖ 芸を窮めるには一生かかる It takes a lifetime to *perfect* an art. ‖ 1つの外国語を究めるのは容易なことではない It's no easy task to *master* a foreign language. ‖ 栄華を極めた平家もついに滅んだ *Despite all its glory*, the Heike clan perished in the end. ‖ 我々の仕事は困難を極めた We met *extreme* difficulties in our work. ‖ 先生たちは美恵子を口を極めて褒めた The teachers *praised* Mieko *to the skies*. (➤ praise ... to the skies は「褒めちぎる」の意の熟語).

きをつけ 気を付け 《号令》 **Attention!** (➤ この場合は /ətènʃʌ́n/ と発音) ▶「気をつけ」の姿勢を保ちなさい Keep standing *at attention*. (➤ この場合は /əténʃən/).

きをつける 気を付ける **be careful** (注意する); **watch (out)** 《for》 (通例動くものを注意して見る) ▶気をつけて運転する drive *carefully* ‖ 外国へ行ったらパスポートを無くさないように気をつけなさいよ *Be careful* not to lose your passport in a foreign country. ‖ 会社訪問のときはことばに気をつけなさい *Be careful* (about) what you say when you visit a company for a personal interview. ‖ 《人から注意を受けて》今度から気をつけます I'll *take more care* [*be more careful*] from now on. (➤ pay more attention または be more attentive とし

てもよい) ‖ 運転するときはスピードに気をつけなさい *Watch* your speed when driving. ‖ 車に気をつけるのよ *Watch out for* cars. ‖ じゃあ気をつけて, バイバイ *Take care*. Bye-bye.

1きん 金 gold 一形 金の gold, golden(➤「金でできた」は前者を用いるのに対し,「金色の」や比喩的な意味で用いる場合は後者がふつう) ▶金の延べ棒 a *gold* bar／*gold* bullion ‖ 金の卵 a *golden* egg ‖ この像は金でできている This statue is made of *gold*. ‖ 彼女は金の指輪をはめている She wears a *gold* ring.
ことわざ 沈黙は金, 雄弁は銀 Speech is silver, silence is golden.
☛ 金メダル (→見出語)

2きん 菌 a germ ; bacteria (バクテリア) ; a fungus(キノコ, カビの類 ; 複数形は fungi, funguses) ▶体の中にはさまざまな病原菌がすみついている There are many kinds of *germs* in our body.

きん- 筋- ‖筋萎縮症《医学》amyotrophy /èımaıá:trəfi ‖ æmı-/, muscular atrophy /ǽtrəfi/ ‖ 筋ジストロフィー《医学》muscular dystrophy ‖ 筋無力症《医学》myasthenia /màıəsθí:niə/.

ぎん 銀 silver ▶銀のスプーン a *silver* spoon.

きんいつ 均一 ▶市内のバス料金は均一200円だ A *uniform* [*flat*] 200-yen bus fare is charged on all city buses. ‖ Tデパートでは5000円均一セールをやっている T Department Store is having *a 5,000-yen-for-any-item sale*. ‖ 全品100円の均一料金です All items are *a flat rate* of 100 yen each.

きんいっぷう 金一封 ▶委員会は彼に賞状と金一封を授与した The committee presented him with a certificate of merit and *a monetary award*.

きんいろ 金色 golden color, gold 一形 金色の golden, gold ▶金色の太陽 a *golden* sun.

きんうん 金運 luck with money ▶その神社で金運アップを願った I prayed (to the kami) at the Shinto shrine for *better luck with money*.

きんえい 近影 ▶著者近影 *a recent photograph* of the author.

きんえん 禁煙 ▶《掲示》禁煙 No Smoking／Thank you for not smoking.／Smoking Forbidden(➤最後の例は権威主義的な表現) ‖《掲示》館内歩行禁煙 No smoking while walking in this building. ‖《掲示》車内禁煙にご協力ください Passengers are requested *not to smoke*.／Please *refrain from smoking* inside the train. (➤前者はバスの場合にも使える. 後者をバス用の掲示にするには inside the train を on the bus にする) ‖ 何度も禁煙しようとしたがくじけた I tried to *quit smoking* many times but failed.
‖禁煙コーナー a no-smoking [nonsmoking] area ‖ 禁煙車 a no-smoking car,《インフォーマル》a nonsmoker ‖ 禁煙席 a non-smokers' section.

きんか 金貨 a gold coin.

ぎんか 銀貨 a silver coin.

ぎんが 銀河 the Milky Way ▶銀河は無数の星から成る *The Milky Way* is made up of countless stars.
‖銀河系 the Galaxy.

1きんかい 近海 ▶日本近海には時々ロシアの船が出没する Russian ships occasionally appear in *the seas near Japan*.
‖近海漁業 inshore [coastal] fisheries.

2きんかい 金塊 a gold nugget ; a gold bar, gold bullion (延べ棒).

きんかぎょくじょう 金科玉条 the golden rule.

きんがく 金額 an amount of money ▶被害金額は予想をはるかに上回った The *amount* of damage far exceeded what we had estimated.

きんがしんねん 謹賀新年 (I wish you a) Happy New Year!／Happy New Year to you!《参考》キリスト教国ではクリスマスカードを送るときに新年を祝う上のようなことばを添えるのがふつう.

ぎんがみ 銀紙 silver foil ; tin foil(スズはく) ; aluminum foil(アルミホイル).

1きんかん 近刊 ▶近刊書目 a list of *forthcoming* [*up coming*] books(➤すでに出版された場合は recently published books).

2きんかん 金柑《植物》a kumquat /kʌ́mkwɑ:t ‖ -kwɔt/.

きんがん 近眼 →近視.

きんかんがっき 金管楽器 a brass instrument ; the brass(➤集合的に).

きんかんしょく 金環食 an annular eclipse /ǽnjələʳ ıklíps/ (➤annular は「環状の」).

1きんき 近畿 Kinki ▶近畿地方 the *Kinki* district.

2きんき 禁忌 a taboo ▶禁忌を破る break *a taboo*.

ぎんき 銀器 silverware.

きんきゅう 緊急 urgency /ə́:ʳdʒənsi/ (差し迫っていること) ; (an) emergency (非常時) 一形 緊急の urgent ▶父は緊急の用事で札幌へ行った My father went to Sapporo on *urgent* business. ‖ 緊急の際はこの戸を開けなさい Open this door *in an emergency* [*in case of emergency*]. ‖ 本日5時から緊急会議を開きます We will hold *an emergency meeting* at five today. ‖ 市当局は洪水に対して緊急対策をとった The city authorities took *emergency measures* [*steps*] to deal with the flood. ‖ 私たちの飛行機は羽田空港に緊急着陸した Our plane *made an emergency landing* at Haneda Airport. ‖ 緊急連絡先の電話番号 an *ICE* (phone) number(➤ICE は in case of emergency の頭文字).
‖緊急救助隊 an emergency task force ‖ 緊急地震速報 an early earthquake warning.

きんぎょ 金魚 a goldfish [複 goldfish] ▶夜店で金魚を買う buy some *goldfish* at a night stall ‖ 金魚をすくう scoop *a goldfish*《参考》「金魚すくい」は英米には無い遊びだが, goldfish-scooping と訳せばよい. ▶《慣用表現》少女たちは金魚のふんのように先生のあとについていった The girls *tagged along* behind [after] their teacher wherever he went. ／The girls *were stuck to* their teacher *like glue*.
‖金魚鉢 a goldfish bowl.

きんきょう 近況 ▶兄から近況を知らせる手紙が来た I got a letter from my brother telling (me) *how he was doing* [*was getting along*].
✉ 家族の近況をお知らせしましょう Let me tell you *the latest news* about my family. ➤「最新のニュース」の意.

きんきょり 近距離 a short distance ▶学校は近距離なので歩いて登校できる My school is (*at*) *a short way* from my house so I can walk. ‖近距離列車 a local train.

きんきらきん ▶きんきらきんのアクセサリー *bling-bling* accessories.《参考》きらきらして高価そうなものを bling(-bling)という.

きんきん ▶隣の奥さんのきんきん声を聞くと食欲が無くなるよ The *shrill voice* of the lady next door ruins my appetite.

きんく 禁句 a taboo(ed) word [phrase] ▶課長の居る所で身長の話は禁句だぜ Don't bring up the subject of height around the section chief. It's *taboo*.

キングサイズ (→かこみ記事)

危ないカタカナ語✹ キングサイズ
1 日本では男性服の特大判のことを「キングサイズ」と呼ぶが, 英語の king-size(d) はたばこの長さやベッドの大きさについていう語である. ベッドではおよそ1.98 m × 2.03 m のものを指す.
2「LL サイズ」も日本式の言い方で, 英語では extra large(略して XL)と呼ぶ.

きんけい 近景 the foreground(前景) ▶近景の人物 a figure in *the foreground*.

きんけつ 金欠 ▶ぼくは慢性の金欠病にかかっている(＝いつも金がない) I'm always (*flat*) *broke*. (➤ flat は「完全に」の意で, これがあるほうが意味が強い).

1**きんけん 近県** a nearby [neighboring] prefecture (➤ 後者は「隣接している」).

2**きんけん 金券** a cash voucher.

1**きんげん 謹厳な** serious(真面目な) ; sober(自制心があり冷静な) ▶謹厳な先生 a *serious* teacher ‖ 彼の取り柄は謹厳実直なところだ His strong [good] points are his *seriousness and honesty*. 《参考》英語では「極めて謹厳な」という場合, judge(裁判官)を例にとり be (as) sober as a judge のようにいう.

2**きんげん 金言** an adage(広く受け入れられている) ; an axiom /ǽksiəm/.

きんけんせいじ 金権政治 money politics ▶金権政治はもうごめんだ No more *money politics* !
‖ 金権政治家 a money-oriented politician.

1**きんこ 金庫** a safe [複 safes] ‖ (銀行の)金庫室 a bank vault ‖ 金庫破り a safecracker, 《英また》a safebreaker ‖ 貸し金庫 a safe(ty)-deposit box.

2**きんこ 禁錮** imprisonment ▶彼は3年の禁錮刑を受けた He was sentenced to three years of *imprisonment* [to *imprisonment* for three years].

1**きんこう 均衡** balance ▶力の均衡が崩れると中近東は再び戦乱のちまたになるだろう If *the balance of power* should be destroyed, the Middle East will be plunged into war again.
▶《野球》6回の裏, 1対1の均衡を破って阪神が2点追加した In the bottom of the sixth inning, the Tigers broke the 1-to-1 *deadlock* by scoring 2 runs. (➤ deadlock は「同点」).
☛ 不均衡 (→見出語)

2**きんこう 近郊** a suburb /sʌ́bəːʳb/ → 郊外 ▶村田さんはロス近郊に住んでいる Mr. Murata is living in *a* Los Angeles *suburb*. ‖ 大都市の近郊は人口が急増している The population in *the suburbs* of big cities is rapidly increasing. ‖ 私の家は大阪の近郊に在る My house is *on the outskirts of Osaka*.

3**きんこう 金鉱** a gold mine(金山); gold ore /ɔːʳ/(鉱石).

1**ぎんこう 銀行** a bank ▶銀行から金を下ろす withdraw money from *a bank* ‖ 銀行から金を借りる borrow [loan] money from *a bank* ‖ 私は明海銀行に10万円預けた I deposited [put] 100,000 yen in (my account with) *Meikai Bank*.
‖ 銀行員 a bank clerk [officer] (➤ officer は主に《米》で, やや気取った言い方) ; a cashier /kæʃíəʳ/, a teller(➤ ともに「出納係, 窓口係」の意で, 後者は主に《米》で好まれる) ‖ 銀行家 a banker ‖ 銀行券 a bank note ‖ 銀行口座 a bank account, an account with a bank(➤「銀行口座を開く」は open a bank account) ‖ 銀行強盗 a bank robber(人) ; a bank robbery(事件) ‖ 銀行預金 a bank deposit(➤「彼女には約200万の銀行預金がある」は She has about two million yen in bank deposits.) ‖ 銀行ローン a bank loan(➤「彼は家を買うために1500万の銀行ローンを借りた」は He took out a fifteen million yen (bank) loan to buy a home. なお, (bank) loan の代わりに mortgage(住宅ローン)を使ってもよい).

2**ぎんこう 吟行** ▶箱根に1泊2日の吟行をする *go on an* overnight *trip* to Hakone *to get inspiration for composing haiku* [*waka*].

きんこく 謹告 ▶《掲示》謹告, 3月末日をもって閉店いたします. 長らくのご愛顧に心より御礼申し上げます *Dear customers*, We will close the store on the last day of March. We'd like to express our heartfelt gratitude for your patronage for many years. (➤ 読者に告げるときは Dear readers, で始める).

きんこつ 筋骨 ▶筋骨たくましい男 a man *of sturdy build* / a *muscular* man.

きんこんしき 金婚式 a golden (wedding) anniversary ▶両親の金婚式を祝う celebrate one's parents' *golden* (*wedding*) *anniversary*.

ぎんこんしき 銀婚式 a silver (wedding) anniversary.
✉ 銀婚式おめでとう Happy *Silver Anniversary* ! / Happy *25th Wedding Anniversary* !

きんさ 僅差 a narrow margin ▶アントラーズは僅差でレッズに勝った The Antlers *beat* the Reds *by a narrow margin*. / The Antlers *edged out* the Reds.

きんさく 金策 ▶彼は毎日金策に駆け回っている He's been spending each day trying to *round up money*. (➤ round up は「かき集める」).

1**きんし 禁止** prohibition, a ban(➤ ともに法律や公の機関による禁止をいうが, 後者には「良くないことだから」という含みがあることが多い) 一動 禁止する prohibit +目, ban +目 ; forbid +目 (親・教師・医師などが) →禁じる.
▶この道路での駐車は終日禁止されている Parking *is prohibited* [*is banned*] on this street 24 hours a day. ‖ 未成年者の喫煙は法律で禁止されている The law *prohibits* smoking by minors. / Smoking by minors *is prohibited* under law.

【文型】
人(A)が…するのを禁止する
prohibit A from doing
ban A from doing
forbid A to do
forbid A from doing

▶16歳未満の者の結婚は法律で禁止されている The law *prohibits* anyone *from* marry*ing* before age 16. ‖ 公務員は副業を禁止されている Public workers *are prohibited* [*banned*] *from* tak*ing* a job on the side. ‖ 英語の授業中は日本語を話すのを禁止されています We *are forbidden to* speak Japanese during English class. (➤ forbidden は forbid の過去分詞形 ; 「先生が禁止している」ならば Our English teacher forbids us to speak [from speaking] Japanese during class.).
✉ 私たちの学校では髪を染めることは禁止されています Our school *forbids* students *from* dye*ing* their hair.
▶清川先生は教室に漫画本を持ち込むことを禁止している Mr. Kiyokawa *does not allow* students *to* bring comic books into the classroom. (➤「許していない」の意) ‖ 彼はそのオリンピックへの出場を禁止された He *was barred* from the Olympics. (➤ ban がものや

事を禁止するのに対して, bar は人を禁止の対象とする).

逆引き熟語 ○○禁止
飲食禁止 No Food or Drink ／**右折禁止** No Right Turn ／**追い越し禁止** No Passing ／**許可無き者の立ち入り禁止** Authorized Person Only ／**携帯電話(スマートフォン)の使用禁止** No Talking on Smartphones [Mobile Phones]; No (Mobile) Phone Zone ／**ごみ捨て禁止** No Litter [Littering] ／**撮影[写真]禁止** Photography Prohibited ／**私語禁止** No Talking [Whispering], Please Refrain from Talking ／**進入禁止** Do Not Enter, Wrong Way ／**立ち入り禁止** Off-Limits, Keep Off ／**駐車禁止** No Parking (Allowed) ／**停車禁止** No Standing ／**貼り紙禁止** No Posters ／**ペット同伴禁止** No Pets, Please. ／**メール禁止** No Texting ／**遊泳禁止** No Swimming (Allowed)

2**きんし 近視** 《米》 **nearsightedness**, 《英》 **shortsightedness**; **myopia** /maɪóʊpiə/ (➤ 医学用語)
▶私は10歳の頃から**近視**になった I have been *nearsighted* [*shortsighted*] since I was ten years old. ‖ きみの目は**仮性近視**だよ You are suffering from *false* [*temporary*] *nearsightedness*.
▶**近視眼的**な意見 a *nearsighted* [*myopic*] view.

きんじち 近似値 an **approximate quantity**, an **approximation**.

きんしつ 均質 **homogeneity** /hòʊmədʒəníːəṭi/ 一 形 **均質の** **homogeneous** /hòʊmədʒíːniəs/.

きんじつ 近日 ▶《掲示》『パイレーツ・オブ・カリビアン5』**近日公開** Pirates of the Caribbean 5 *Coming Soon*. ‖ その本は**近日中**にお返しします I'll return the book *in a few days*. (➤「数日たったら」の意) ‖ **近日中**にお目にかかりたいと思います I'd like to meet you *one of these days*. (➤「近いうちに, そのうちに」の意).

きんじとう 金字塔 a **monument** ▶彼女の理論は生物学において**金字塔**を打ち立てた Her theory became *a landmark* [*monumental*] *achievement* in biology.

1**きんしゅ 禁酒** ▶私は医者から**禁酒**するよう言われている The doctor told me to *stop* [*give up*] *drinking*.

2**きんしゅ 筋腫** 《医学》 a **myoma** /maɪóʊmə/.

3**きんしゅ 金種** a **denomination of money**.

きんしゅく 緊縮 ▶**緊縮**政策を実行する take *austerity measures* ／ put *austerity measures* into practice ‖ **緊縮予算** an *austerity* budget ／a *reduced* budget.

きんじょ 近所

neighborhood /néɪbəʳhʊd/ (自分の隣近所); **vicinity** (前者より広い地域) ▶**近所**の子供たち some *neighborhood* children ‖ **近所の人** *a neighbor* ‖ **近所の町** a *neighboring* town ‖ **近所付き合いの良い[悪い]人** *a good* [*bad*] *neighbor*. ‖ 《電話で》**近所**に来てるの? Are you in the *vicinity*? ‖ 学校の**近所**に釣り堀が在る There is a fishing pond *near* [*close to*] the school. ‖ 昨夜この**近所**で火事があった There was a fire *in my neighborhood* last night. ‖ カラオケは**近所迷惑**のこともある Karaoke can be *a nuisance to* everyone in *the neighborhood*. **対話**「この**近所**に郵便局は在りませんか」「この道の突き当たりに在ります」"Is there a post office *near here*?" "Yes, there's one at the end of this road."

きんしょう 僅少 ▶**残部僅少** *Only a small number of copies are left*.

ぎんじょう 吟醸 ‖**吟醸酒** a specialty brew of sake (rice wine).

きんじる 禁じる **prohibit** +目, **forbid** +目, **ban** +目

語法 prohibit は堅い語で, 法律や公の機関によって「禁止する」の意. ban も法律などによって公的に禁止することをいうが,「良くないことだから禁じる」という含みがある. forbid は日常的な語で,「(親・教師・医師などが)許さない」の意. ➡禁止.

▶学生は大学構内に車を乗り入れるのを**禁じられている** Students *are prohibited from* driving onto the college grounds. ‖ この薬は法律によって販売を**禁じられている** The sale of this medicine *is prohibited* by law. ‖ 父は医者から酒を**禁じられている** My father's doctor *has forbidden* him to drink. ／My father's doctor *does not allow* him *to* drink. ‖ 市当局はすべての公共建物での喫煙を**禁じた** The city *has banned* smoking in all public buildings.

1**きんしん 謹慎** ▶人に**謹慎**を命じる order a person to *be on his* [*her*] *best behavior* ‖ 私は体育館での喫煙を発見され, 3週間の**自宅謹慎**を命じられた I was caught smoking in the gym and *was confined to my house* [*was grounded*] for three weeks. (➤ ground は「(罰として, 子供)を外出禁止にする」).

2**きんしん 近親** ▶彼の**近親者**にすぐ連絡を取ってください Please contact his *close relatives* at once. ‖**近親結婚** intermarriage ‖**近親相姦**(かん) incest /ínsest/.

1**きんせい 均整** **symmetry** /símətri/ ▶西洋の美は**均整**にあり, 日本の美は**不均整**にある The Western idea of beauty lies in *symmetry* and the Japanese one in *asymmetry*. ‖ かおるは**均整のとれた**体をしている Kaoru is *well-proportioned*.

2**きんせい 金星** **Venus** /víːnəs/ (➤ 俗に the morning [evening] star とも呼ぶ).

3**きんせい 禁制** a **ban** 一 形 **禁制の** **prohibited**
▶女人**禁制**を解く lift *a ban on women's admittance* ‖ (江戸城の)大奥は将軍以外**男子禁制**だった The inner precincts of the castle *were barred to all men* except the shogun. (➤ bar は「…にかんぬきをする」が原義).
‖**禁制品** prohibited articles [goods]; contraband goods (密輸品).

4**きんせい 近世** **(early) modern times** [**ages**].

ぎんせかい 銀世界 ▶目を覚ましたら辺り一面**銀世界**だった I awoke to find the whole place *covered with snow*.

きんせつ 近接 ▶**近接**した村 a *nearby* village.

1**きんせん 金銭** **money**; **cash** (現金) ▶彼はすべてを**金銭**の尺度で見る傾向がある He tends to look on everything in terms of *money*. ‖ 彼女は**金銭感覚**がゼロだ She has no *concept of* (*how to use*) *money*. ‖ **金銭感覚**のまひした政治家もいる Some politicians *have a distorted sense of the value of money*.

2**きんせん 琴線** ▶彼女の歌は多くの聴く者の**琴線に触れる** Her songs *tug at the heartstrings* of many listeners.

きんせんか 金盞花 《植物》 a **common** [**pot**] **marigold**.

1**きんぞく 金属** (a) **metal** ▶プラチナは有用な**金属**だ Platinum is a useful *metal*.
‖**金属音** a metallic noise ‖ **金属元素** a metallic element ‖ **金属探知機** a metal detector ‖ **金属疲労** metal fatigue.

2**きんぞく 勤続** ▶私はこの会社に**勤続25年**になる I *have worked* for this company *for exactly 25 years*. ‖ 父はあす**勤続40年**で表彰される My father is to be given an award by the company tomorrow *in recognition of his 40 years of service*.

きんだい 近代 **modern ages, the present days** 一形 **近代の modern** ▶この町には近代的な工場が多い There are a lot of *modern* factories in this town. ‖ 大都市の近代化がこのような問題を引き起こしたのだ The *modernization* of big cities has brought about these problems. ‖近代英語 Modern English (1500年頃以降の英語) ‖ 近代音楽 modern music ‖ 近代国家 a modern state ‖ 近代思想 modern ideas ‖ 近代文学 modern literature.

きんたいしゅつ 禁帯出 **For reference only**(➤「参考にするため調べるのみ」の意).

きんたま 金玉 **balls** (➤ 日本語の「きんたま」に相当する俗語). →こう丸.

きんだん 禁断 ▶禁断の木の実は甘い *Forbidden fruit* is sweetest.
‖禁断症状(麻薬の) withdrawal symptoms.

きんちゃく 巾着 a **money pouch.**

きんちょう 緊張 **tension** 一動 **緊張する be tense ; be [get] nervous** (神経質である[になる]) ▶1杯のコーヒーは精神的な緊張をほぐすのに役立つ A cup of coffee helps relieve nervous *tension*. ‖ テストの前はいつも緊張する I *am* always *tense* [*nervous*] before a test. ‖ 就職面接を受ける前, ぼくは緊張した I *felt* [*was*] *tense* before (having) the job interview. ‖ 緊張しないで歌ってごらん Don't *get nervous*, just sing. ‖ 大勢の人の前でスピーチをするときは誰でも緊張するものだ Everyone *gets nervous* when making a speech in front of a large group of people [audience]. ‖ サッカー選手たちは緊張していた The soccer players *were keyed up*. (➤ tense はマイナスイメージだが, keyed up はよい意味の緊張にも用いる) ‖ 演奏するときは肩の力を抜いて, できるだけ緊張をほぐすようにしなさい When performing, try to let the tension out of your shoulders and *relax*. ‖ 緊張した関係 a *strained* relationship ‖ 国際間の緊張を緩和する ease *the international tensions* ‖ 両国間の緊張が高まっている The relationship between the two countries has *become tense*. ‖ 大使館には緊張感がみなぎっていた *A tense atmosphere* could be felt throughout the embassy. ‖ 小澤氏は緊張感をもって指揮した Mr. Ozawa conducted *with intensity*.
‖緊張緩和 détente /deɪtɑ́:nt ‖ déɪtɔnt/.

きんてい 謹呈する **present** +目 ▶学生らは教授に金時計を謹呈した The students *presented* their professor with a gold watch. ‖ 著者謹呈 *With the author's compliments* / *With compliments from the author* (➤ 贈呈本などに書くことば).

きんてんさい 禁転載 **No part of this book may be reproduced without permission.**

1**きんとう 近東** **the Near East**(➤ 現在では the Middle East(中東)に含める).

2**きんとう 均等** ▶みんなでこのお金を均等に分けましょう Let's divide this money *equally* among us all. ‖ 彼らはパーティーの費用を均等に負担した They shared the expenses of [from] the party (*equally*). (➤ share だけで「均等に分ける」の意味合いになるので equally はつけなくていい) ‖ この国では教育の機会均等が保証されている In this country, *equal opportunity* for education is guaranteed. ‖ 均等割りした(=文頭文末をそろえた)テクスト *justified* text.

きんトレ 筋トレ a **muscle-building workout** ▶兄はこのところ熱心に筋トレをやっている My brother has *been working out* hard *to build his muscles*.

> 「筋トレ」のいろいろ 腕立て伏せをする《主に米》do push-ups [《英》press-up] / スクワットをする do squats / 腹筋運動をする do crunches (浅い) ; do sit-ups (完全に起き上がる) / ベンチプレスをする do the bench press / 懸垂運動をする do pull-ups [《米》chin-ups]

ぎんなん 銀杏 a **ginkgo** [**gingko**] /gíŋkoʊ/ **nut.**

きんにく 筋肉 a **muscle** /mʌ́səl/ ▶ももの筋肉を鍛える develop the thigh *muscle(s)* ‖ 筋肉をほぐす relax one's *muscles* ‖ 筋肉硬直を起こした運動選手 a *muscle*-bound athlete ‖ きのうの重労働で体中の筋肉が痛い Every *muscle* in my body aches after yesterday's hard work. (➤「筋肉痛」は muscle pain) ‖ 彼は筋肉が発達している He has well-developed *muscles*. ‖ 彼女は筋肉質だ She*'s muscular*. ‖ 私は頭脳労働より筋肉労働のほうが向いている I'm more suited to *physical* [*manual*] *labor* than mental work. ‖ 兄は筋肉もりもりだ My brother *has muscles* (*popping out*) *all over* him. / My brother *is muscular*.
‖筋肉増強剤 a muscle-building drug.

> 「筋肉」のいろいろ 外腹斜筋 external oblique / 広背筋 broadest of back / 三角筋 deltoid /déltɔɪd/ / 上腕三頭筋 triceps /tráɪseps/ of arm / 上腕二頭筋 biceps /báɪseps/ of arm / 僧帽筋 trapezius /trəpí:ziəs/, traps / 大円筋 larger round / 大胸筋 greater pectoral /péktərəl/ / 大腿四頭筋 quadriceps /kwɑ́:drɪseps/, quads / 大臀筋 greatest gluteal /glú:ṭəl/ / ハムストリング hamstrings / ヒラメ筋 soleus /sóʊlɪəs/ / 腹直筋 abdominal rectus /réktəs/, abs

きんねん 近年 ▶ことしの米作は近年にない不作だ This year's rice crop is the worst we have had *in recent years*. ‖ 近年地球環境の悪化がますます進んでいる The deterioration of the earth's environment has been advancing *in recent years*.

きんば 金歯 a **gold tooth.**

1**きんぱく 緊迫する** **become tense** ▶緊迫した空気 *tense* mood ‖ 緊迫した米・イラク関係 *strained* relations between the U.S. and Iraq.

2**きんぱく 金箔** **gold foil**(やや厚めの) ; **gold leaf** (薄い).

きんぱつ 金髪 **blond hair** ▶金髪の女性 a *blond* woman / a blonde(➤ 後者の場合男性は blond とつづる) ‖ 彼女は金髪だ She is *a blonde*. / She is *blond*. / She's got *fair hair*. →ブロンド.

ぎんぱつ 銀髪 **silver hair** ▶銀髪の紳士 a *silver-haired* gentleman.

ぎんばん 銀盤 a **silver plate**(銀の皿) ; a **skating rink** (スケート場) ▶銀盤の女王 a queen of *the ice*.

きんぴか 金ぴか ▶金ぴかの指輪 a *gilded* ring.

きんぴらごぼう ***kinpira-gobo*** ; shredded burdock root and carrot stir-fried and sauteed in soy sauce(➤ 説明的な訳).

きんぶち 金縁の **gold-rimmed** (眼鏡の) ; **gilt- framed** (額縁の) ▶金縁の眼鏡 *gold-rimmed* glasses.

きんぷん 金粉 **gold dust.**

きんべん 勤勉 **hard work, diligence** /dílɪdʒəns/ (特定の仕事などに熱心) ; **industry** /índəstri/ (性格的に仕事好き) 一形 **勤勉な hardworking, diligent, industrious** /ɪndʌ́striəs/
▶勤勉な学生 a *hardworking* [*serious*] student ‖

靖彦はとても勤勉だ Yasuhiko *is a hard worker*. ／Yasuhiko *works* very *hard*. ‖ 勤勉だからといって必ず成功するとは限らない *Hard work* does not always bring success. ‖ 彼が昇進したのは勤勉のおかげだ His promotion is due to his *diligence* [*hard work*].

きんぺん 近辺 **neighborhood, vicinity** ▶箱根近辺の温泉旅館 hot spring resorts in *Hakone and thereabouts* ‖ 銀座近辺の地図 a map of *Ginza and its vicinity* ‖ この近辺は工場ばかりだ There is nothing besides factories *in this area*.

ぎんまく 銀幕 **the silver screen.**

ぎんみ 吟味する **examine** +㊐ (調査する) ; **select** +㊐ (精選する) ▶植物標本を吟味する *examine* a botanical specimen ‖ 料理の材料を吟味する *select* ingredients for cooking.

きんみつ 緊密な **close** /kloos/ ▶両国が緊密な連絡を取り合ってこそ平和を保つことができる The best way to keep peace is for both nations to keep in *close* contact with each other.

きんみゃく 金脈 a **gold vein**, a **vein of gold** (鉱脈) ; a **financial supporter** [**backer**] (金づる) ; a **gold mine** (もうかる仕事).

きんみらい 近未来 **the near future.**

きんむ 勤務 **work** (仕事) ; **service** (会社などのために働くこと) 一動 **勤務する** **work** ▶彼は私と同じ会社に勤務している He *works* in the same company as I do. ／He and I *work* for the same company. ‖ 彼は一日の勤務が終わると, 決まって行きつけのカラオケバーに行く He always goes to his favorite karaoke bar after finishing *a day's work*. ‖ 勤務先はどちらですか *What company* [*Who*] do you work for? (➤ 会社を尋ねて) ／Where do you work? (➤ 場所を尋ねて) ‖ 勤務時間は 9 時から 5 時までです *Working hours* are from 9 to 5. ‖ 勤務中は私用電話をしないに越したことはない It is preferable not to make private phone calls *during working hours* [*while at work*]. ‖ 私は夜間勤務でもかまいません I don't mind *working* (*on*) *the night shift*. (➤ shift は「(交替制の) 勤務時間」).

‖ **勤務状況** an attendance record ‖ **勤務条件** working conditions ‖ **勤務成績** service merit ‖ **勤務場所** a work place ‖ **勤務表** a work schedule ‖ **勤務評定** (an) efficiency rating ‖ **時間外勤務** overtime work.

> **あなたの英語はどう響く?**
> 「X 社に勤務しています」の代表的英訳を 2 例挙げれば, I work for X Company. と I'm with X Company. になる. 後者の言い方の場合, 話し手の会社での地位は高いことが多い. したがって, 新入社員などは前者を使うのが無難.

きんむく 金無垢 **solid gold.**

きんメダル 金メダル a **gold medal** ▶その体操選手はオリンピックで金メダルを 2 個獲得した That gymnast won two *gold medals* in the Olympics.

きんモール 金モール **gold braid.**

きんもくせい 金木犀 《植物》 a **fragrant orange-colored olive.**

きんもつ 禁物 ▶胃が悪いならたばこは禁物だ If you have a weak stomach, you *mustn't* smoke [smoking *is out*]. ‖ 大きな揺れは収まったがまだまだ油断は禁物だ The big quake has passed, but *we mustn't let our guard down* yet.

きんゆ 禁輸 (a) **trade embargo** ▶北朝鮮に対して全面禁輸を実施する impose *a total trade embargo* on North Korea.

きんゆう 金融 **finance** /fáɪnæns/ 一形 **金融の** **financial** ▶日本の金融情勢の見通しは明るくない The prospect is not bright for Japanese *finance*. ‖ 政府は金融引き締め政策をとった The government took *a tight-money policy*. (➤「金融の引き締めを行う」は tighten the money supply).

‖ **金融街** a financial district ‖ **金融緩和政策** an easy money policy ‖ **金融機関** a banking agency, a financial [lending] institution ‖ **金融危機** a financial crisis ‖ **金融業** the finance [moneylending] business ‖ **金融業界** the financial industry ‖ **金融業者** a financier /fìnənsíəʳ ‖ faɪnǽnsiə/, a moneylender ‖ **金融公庫** a finance corporation ‖ **金融再生委員会** the Financial Reconstruction Commission ‖ **金融支援** financial assistance ‖ **金融資産** a financial asset ‖ **金融市場** the money [financial] market ‖ **金融システム** a financial system ‖ **金融商品** a financial instrument ‖ **金融政策** a monetary policy (➤ 中央銀行主導の ; 政府主導の財政政策は a fiscal policy. また, a financial policy は金融監督政策) ‖ **金融庁** Financial Services Agency.

ぎんゆうしじん 吟遊詩人 a **minstrel** /mínstrəl/.

きんよう(び) 金曜(日) **Friday** 《略 Fri., Fr.》 ▶来週の金曜日は創立記念日で学校が休みだ Next *Friday* we will have no classes because it is the foundation day of our school. ‖ きょうは花の金曜日 (花金) だ *Thank God it's Friday*. (➤「ありがたい, きょうは金曜日だ」の意で TGIF と略記される). →曜日.

きんよく 禁欲 **abstinence** /ǽbstɪnəns/ (節制) ; **celibacy** /séləbəsi/ (性交をしないこと) ; **asceticism** /əsétɪsìzəm/ (禁欲主義) ▶禁欲的な生活を送る lead an *ascetic* life.

‖ **禁欲主義者** an ascetic, a stoic.

きんらい 近来 ▶それは近来まれに見る大事件だ That is an incident *unlike any we have had for* [*in*] *years*.

きんり 金利 an **interest rate** ▶金利を引き下げる cut an *interest rate* ‖ 普通預金の金利は現在いくらでしょうか What is the present *interest rate* on ordinary accounts? ‖ 昨年は金利が下がって借りるほうは得をした Last year borrowers lucked out when *interest rates* were lowered. ‖ **金利変動リスク** an interest rate risk ‖ **貸し出し金利** a lending rate ‖ **高** [**低**] **金利** high [low] interest.

1きんりょう 禁猟 ‖ **禁猟期** the closed [《英》 close] season ‖ **禁猟区** a game preserve.

2きんりょう 禁漁 a **fishing ban**

‖ **禁漁期** a closed [《英》 close] season ‖ **禁漁区** a no-fishing zone.

きんりょく 筋力 **muscular strength** ▶筋力トレーニングをする work out to strengthen [build up] one's *muscles*.

きんりん 近隣の **neighboring** /néɪbərɪŋ/ ▶近隣諸国 *neighboring* countries.

きんろう 勤労 ▶こんな安月給じゃ勤労意欲が湧かない Getting such a low salary *takes away my will to work*. ／I *hardly feel like working* for this low salary. ‖ きょう勤労者の集いがあります A meeting for *workers* will be held today.

‖ **勤労学生** a student worker ‖ **勤労感謝の日** Labor Thanksgiving Day ‖ **勤労所得** earned income.

く・ク

1く 区 a **ward** /wɔːʳd/ (都市の) ; a **zone**(区画) ; a **constituency** /kənstítʃuənsi/ (選挙区) ▶東京には23の区がある Tokyo has 23 *wards*. ‖ 私は目黒区に住んでいる I live in Meguro *Ward*. (➤ 手紙の宛名などでは Meguro-ku のようにローマ字で書くほうがよい).
▶彼は千葉第３区から立候補した He ran as a candidate in *the third constituency* of Chiba.
‖**区議会** a ward assembly ‖ **区議会議員** a member of a ward assembly ‖ **区長** the head [mayor] of a ward ‖ **区民** a resident [an inhabitant] of a ward ‖ **区役所**(→見出語).

2く 苦 **worry** /wə́ːri ‖ wʌ́ri/ (心配) ; **pains** (苦労) ; **suffering**(苦しみ) ; **anxiety**(不安) ▶つまらないことを苦にする *worry about* [*over*] a little thing ‖ 大したことではないのだから, そんなことは苦にするな It's not important ; don't *worry about* [*over*] it. ‖ 少年は病気を苦にして自殺した *Worry* [*Anxiety*] *over* his illness drove the boy to suicide. ‖ 仏教では現世は苦に満ちていると考える In Buddhism, it is thought that the present world is filled with *suffering* [*pain*].
▶私には長時間労働は苦にならない Working long hours *is no trouble* for me. ／I *don't mind* working long hours. ‖ 彼女はその数学の難問を苦もなく解いた She solved the difficult math problem *easily* [*with no trouble at all*].
ことわざ 苦あれば楽あり No pain, no gain.

3く 句 a **phrase**(語句) ; a **haiku**(俳句) ▶一句浮かんだぞ! Listen, *a haiku poem* has just come to me!

4く 九 **nine**. →きゅう.

1ぐ 愚 ▶そんな話を信じるなんて愚の骨頂だ It is *the height of folly* to believe such a story. ‖ 愚にもつかぬことを言うな Don't talk *nonsense*.

2ぐ 具 **ingredients**(料理の材料).

ぐあい 具合 **1**【体調】▶きょうはあまり具合がよくありません I do*n't feel* very *well* today. ／I'*m not feeling* very *well* today. ／I'*m feeling* a bit *under the weather* today. ‖ どこか具合でも悪いの? *Is there something wrong* [*the matter*] ? ‖ 対話「きょうはお体の具合はいかがですか」「まだ頭痛が残っています」"*How do you feel* today?" "I still have a headache." ‖ 対話「和代さんの具合はどうですか」「おかげさまで, だいぶよくなっています」"*How's* Kazuyo?" "She's a lot better, thanks." ‖ 医者が言うには彼女は腎臓の具合が悪いそうです The doctor says she *has kidney trouble*.
2【状態】▶ 対話「商売の具合はどうですか」「おかげさまで好調です」"*How is* business?" "We're doing well, thank you." ‖ 対話「新しい眼鏡の具合はいかがですか」「ぴったりです」"*How are* your new glasses?" "They're perfect." ‖ 対話「勉強の進み具合はどうですか」「何とかかんとかやっています」"*How are* (your) studies *coming along*?" "All right."
3【都合, 体裁】▶ここで彼女に会うのはちょっと具合が悪い It would be a bit *awkward* if I met her here. ‖ 結婚式にジーパンじゃあ, 具合が悪い *It's not proper* to wear blue jeans to a wedding. ‖ うまい具合に雨が上がった *Luckily*, the rain has stopped.
4【方法】▶ほら, ラケットはこういう具合に握るんだ Look! *This is how* you grip a racket.

グアテマラ **Guatemala** /gwɑːṭəmɑ́ːlə/ (中央アメリカの共和国).

グアムとう グアム島 **Guam** /gwɑːm/ (太平洋, マリアナ諸島の島 ; アメリカ領).

クアラルンプール **Kuala Lumpur**(マレーシアの首都).

1くい 杭 a **stake**(棒くい) ; a **pile**(建物の土台用などの) ; a **post**(主に支柱や目印用の) ▶地面にくいを打ち込む drive *stakes* [*piles*] into the ground ‖ 彼はテントを張るためにくいを立てた He put up *posts* for pitching the tent.
ことわざ 出るくいは打たれる The nail [stake] that sticks out gets hammered down [(back) in]. (➤ 日本語からの直訳) ／Stick your neck out, and it'll be chopped off. (➤「首を突き出すとはねられてしまうぞ」の意). 《参考》英語にはこれと反対の You can't keep a good man [woman] down. (才能あるものを抑えておくことはできない(いつか頭角を現す)) ということわざがある.

2くい 悔い (a) **regret** ▶精いっぱいやったのだから負けても悔いはない I did my best, so I *have no regrets* even though I lost. ‖ 彼は科学者として悔いのない一生を送った He lived a *full and satisfying* life as a scientist. ／He *had no regrets* about his life as a scientist. ‖ 彼女はオリンピックで実力を出し切れず悔いの残る試合をしてしまった She *regretted* that she had not been able to show her full ability in the Olympic competition.

くいあらためる 悔い改める **repent** (後悔し反省する) ; **mend** one's **ways**, **turn over a new leaf**(行いを改める) ▶キリストは人々に悔い改めよと教えた Christ taught people to *repent* and reform (themselves).

くいいじ 食い意地 ▶彼は食い意地が張っている He's *very greedy*. ／All he ever thinks about is food.

くいいる 食い入る ▶その男は私の顔を食い入るように見つめた He *stared into* my face. ／He *devoured* me *with his eyes*. (➤ devour /dɪváʊəʳ/ は「貪り食う」が本来の意味).

クイーン a **queen** ▶スペードのクイーン *a queen* of spades ／the spade *queen*.

くいき 区域 a **zone**(外観・特徴などによって隣接地域と区別された) ; an **area** /éəriə/ (用途・性格などによってほかと区別された) ; a **district**(行政・選挙などのために区分された) ▶町の住宅区域 *a residential district* [*area*] of a town ‖ あそこで泳いではいけないよ. 遊泳禁止区域だから Don't swim there. It is *a swimming prohibited zone*.

ぐいぐい ▶ぐずる子を母親がぐいぐい引っ張って連れていった The mother *dragged* her cranky child after her.
▶父は酒をぐいぐい飲んだ My father *gulped* (*down*) [*downed*] *one* cup of sake *after another*. (➤ one ... after another は「コップ１杯また１杯と」の意).

くいこむ 食い込む ▶肉に食い込んだ足のつめ an *ingrown* [《英》*ingrowing*] toenail ‖ ロープが彼の手首

に食い込んだ The rope *bit into* his wrists. (➤ bit は bite の過去形). ‖ 授業が延びて休み時間に食い込んだ The class *stretched on into* break time. ‖ 200メートル平泳ぎで日本の選手はどうにか 6 位に食い込んだ The entrant from Japan managed to *climb into* 6th place in the 200-meter breaststroke.

くいさがる 食い下がる ▶その小兵力士は横綱に食い下がった The small sumo wrestler *hung on to* the yokozuna. (➤ hang on to は「…にしがみつく」). ▶彼は先生に質問してしつこく食い下がった He *harassed* [*bugged*] the teacher with questions. (➤ bug は「質問などで悩ます」).

くいしばる 食い縛る ▶彼は歯を食いしばって痛みをこらえた He *clenched* [*gritted*] *his teeth* against the pain.

くいしんぼう 食いしん坊 a **big eater**, a **glutton** ▶こんな大きなお餅を10個も食べたの？ 食いしん坊ね！ You ate ten of these big rice cakes ? *What a pig !* (➤ pig は「豚」から転じて,「食いしん坊」の意のインフォーマルな語).

クイズ a **quiz** /kwɪz/ ▶クイズを解く answer *a quiz* ‖ クイズの答えを考える guess the answers of the *quiz* ‖ 今度はきみがクイズを出す番だ Now, it's your turn to *give* me *a quiz* [to *quiz* me].

‖**クイズ番組** a quiz show [program] 《参考》「クイズ番組の司会者」は quizmaster,「クイズ番組の解答者・出場者」は quiz panelist とか quiz competitor と言う。

くいたりない 食い足りない ▶あれだけ食べて, まだ食い足りないのかい You ate that much and still *don't think you've had enough*? ▶今の仕事は食い足りない I find my present job *too easy* (for me). ‖ この特派員報告は食い足りないことおびただしかった This correspondent's report was woefully *inadequate* [*incomplete*]. (➤ inadequate /ɪnǽdɪkwət/ は「不十分な」, incomplete は「不完全な」).

くいちがい 食い違い (a) **discrepancy**(本来, 同一であるべきものの不一致) ; (a) **difference**(違い) ; (a) **contradiction**(矛盾) ▶健太郎と雄太の間には多少意見の食い違いがある There is a slight *difference of opinion* between Kentaro and Yuta. ‖ 二人の話には多少食い違いがある There is some *discrepancy* between the two accounts. (➤ 具体的に数えられるいくつかの食い違いならば, There are some discrepancies ... となる).

くいちがう 食い違う ▶将来の職業について私と父は意見が食い違った(＝一致しなかった) My father and I *disagreed* about my future job. ‖ 運転手の話は目撃者のそれと食い違っている The driver's account *contradicts* that of an eyewitness. ‖ 政治家の発言と行動は食い違う(＝矛盾する)ことがよくある What politicians say *is* often *inconsistent with* what they do.

くいちぎる 食い千切る **bite off** ▶熊は綱を食いちぎって逃げた The bear *bit off* the rope and escaped.

くいちらす 食い散らす ▶テーブルの上は食い散らしたままになっていた The table *was littered with half-eaten food*.

くいつく 食い付く **bite** 《on, at》 ▶犬は骨に食いついた The dog *bit on* a bone. (➤ bit は bite の過去形) ‖ 魚が餌に食いついているようだ I feel the fish *nibbling at* the bait. (➤ nibble at は「(魚などが)…を少しずつかじって食う」). ▶もうけ話をちらつかせたら, あいつはすぐに食いついてきたよ When I hinted at a money-making idea, he *bit* right away.

くいつなぐ 食いつなぐ ▶彼女はアルバイトで食いつないでいる She *ekes out a living* working part-time. (➤ eke /iːk/ out は「(暮らしを)辛うじて立てる」).

くいつぶす 食い潰す ▶彼は父親が残した財産を食い潰してしまった He *ran through* all the fortune [money] his father had left him.

くいつめる 食い詰める ▶彼は東京で食い詰めて故郷に帰った *Having failed to make a living* in Tokyo, he went back to his hometown. (● go back to one's hometown を return [go] home とすると「家に帰る」の意になるのがふつう).

ぐいと ▶私はそのひもをぐいと引いた I pulled the cord *with a jerk*. ／I jerked on the cord. ‖ 彼女はその男を背後からぐいと押した She *gave* the man *a hard push* from behind. ／She *shoved* the man from behind. ▶彼は日本酒をぐいと飲み干した He emptied a cup of sake *in one gulp*. ／He *gulped down* a cup of sake.

くいどうらく 食い道楽 **epicurism**, **epicureanism** (美食主義) ; an **epicure**, a **gourmet** /góəˈmeɪ/ (美食家 ; この意では前者はやや古風) ; 《インフォーマル》 a **foodie** (料理好き, 食通) ▶彼女は食い道楽だ She is *an epicure* [*a gourmet*]. ／She is *a food buff* [*foodie*]. →グルメ.

くいとめる 食い止める **check** ＋目 (阻止する) ; **prevent** ＋目 (防止する) ▶延焼を食い止める *check* [*stop*] the spread of a fire ‖ 被害を最小限に食い止める *minimize* losses ／*keep* losses *to a minimum* ‖ インフルエンザのまん延を食い止めるために医者たちは懸命に働いた Doctors worked hard to *prevent* the influenza *from* spreading.

クイナ 《鳥》 a **water rail**.

くいにげ 食い逃げ ▶レストランで男が食い逃げするのを見た At the restaurant, I saw a man *leave* [*skip out*] *without paying his bill*.

くいはぐれる 食いはぐれる ▶夜遅く帰ったら, 夕飯を食いはぐれた Since I came home very late at night, I *missed* supper. ▶この資格さえ取っておけば一生食いはぐれることはない If you get this qualification, you *will be assured of a living* throughout your life. ／This license will *assure* you *of a job* to the end of your working life. (➤ assure A of B は「A(人)にB(物事)を保証する」).

くいぶち 食い扶持 ▶食いぶちを稼ぐ *earn one's keep*.

くいもの 食い物 **1【食物】** **food** ▶食い物の恨みは恐ろしい Grudges over *food* are ugly [messy]. **2【犠牲】** a **victim** ; (a) **prey**(餌食) ▶労働者を食い物にする(＝搾取する) *exploit* workers ‖ 彼女はそのチンピラたちの食い物にされた She *was victimized* by the punks. (➤ be victimized は「犠牲になる」) ‖ あの男は年寄りを食い物にしている That guy is *preying on* elderly people. ▶その会社は暴力団の食い物になった The company *fell prey to* the gangsters.

くいる 悔いる **repent** 《of》 (過去の罪や過ちを反省する) ; **regret** ＋目 (失敗や間違いを悔やむ) ▶その囚人は自分の犯した罪を悔いた The convict *repented of* his crimes. ‖ 彼は則子と結婚したがすぐにそれを悔いた He married Noriko and immediately *regretted* it.

クインテット 《音楽》 a **quintet**.

[1]**くう** 食う

訳語メニュー
食べる →eat **1**
生計を立てる →live **2**
虫が刺す →bite **3**

1【食べる】eat +目 ▶一緒に昼飯を食おうよ *Let's eat* [*have*] lunch together. (eat lunch の場合, 具体的な食べる行為を指すので, やや露骨な響きがあり,「食う」には近いが, 実際の場面では have lunch と表現することが多い. こちらは味わいながら, あるいは, 楽しみながら, のニュアンスがある). ‖ そのキノコは食えないよ That mushroom is *not good to eat* [*is inedible*]. ‖ たまにはうまいものが食いたいなあ I wish I could *eat* something really good once in a while. ‖ たらふく食った I'*m stuffed*.

2【生計を立てる】live《on》▶ぼくの月給じゃ2人はとても食えないよ My salary isn't enough for two people to *live on*. ‖ 音楽で食っていくのは難しい It is difficult to *earn a living* as a musician. ‖ 息子もアメリカでどうにか食っているようだ My son seems to *be getting by somehow* (*or other*) in the United States.

3【虫などが穴をあける】eat +目 (衣類などを) ; **bite** +目 (刺す) ▶虫の食ったリンゴ a *wormy* apple ‖ 蚊に足を食われた My leg *was bitten* by a mosquito. ‖ このスーツは虫に食われてしまった This suit *is moth-eaten*.

4【被害を受ける】▶家賃を3か月払わなかったら追い立てを食ってしまった Because I hadn't paid my rent for three months, I *got hit with* an eviction notice. ‖ ぼくは課長からお目玉を食った I *got chewed out* by the manager. (➤「こっぴどくどなられる」の意) ‖ 夜遅く帰ったら閉め出しを食ってしまった I *got locked out* when I went home late at night.

5【負かす】▶その力士は上位力士を食うので有名だ That sumo wrestler is famous for *toppling* higher ranking wrestlers. (➤ topple は「倒す」).

6【費やす】▶うちの車はえらくガソリンを食う Our car *burns a lot of gas*. / Our car is *a gas guzzler*. (➤ gas guzzler は「ガソリンを食う車」の意のインフォーマルな言い方) ‖ 日本車はガソリンを食わないからよく売れるのです Japanese cars sell well because they are *fuel-efficient*. ‖ マージャンは時間を食うゲームだ Mahjongg is a *time-consuming* game. ‖ あすの授業の予習に時間を食われてしまった I *spent too much time* preparing for tomorrow's class.

7【慣用表現】▶ショービジネスの世界は食うか食われるかの(=競争の激しい)世界だ Show business is *highly competitive*. ‖ あいつはいつも人を食ったようなことを言う He always *makes snide* [*disparaging*] *remarks* about people. (➤ snide は「嫌みな」, disparaging は「人を見下すような」) ‖ 長い間食うや食わずの生活だった It was *a hand-to-mouth* existence for many years. ‖ 彼には一杯食わされた He completely *took* me *in*. (➤ take in は「…を欺く」の意のインフォーマルな表現) ‖ もうその手は食わないぞ I'm *not going to fall for that trick* twice. (➤ fall for は「(わななどに)はまる」).

☞ 食わせる (→見出語)

[2]**くう 空 space ; the air**(空中) ▶彼はぼんやり空を見つめていた He was staring blankly into *space*.

クウェート Kuwait /kuwéɪt/
‖**クウェート人** a Kuwaiti /kuwéɪṭi/.

くうかん 空間 (a) **space** ▶この辺りは家が立て込んでいて十分な空間が無い This area is quite built up now and it does not have enough *open space*. ‖ 私の車の後部座席には私の両親が足を伸ばせる空間がない The backseat of my car doesn't have enough leg *room* for my parents. ‖ 地球は宇宙という果てしない空間に浮かぶ小さな星にすぎない The earth is but a small body [a speck] floating in the vastness of *space*. (この場合の「星」に star(恒星)を当てることはできない. speck は「小さな点, 染み」の意) ‖《広告》わが社は快適な生活空間を創造します Our company creates comfortable *living spaces*.

くうき 空気 1【大気】air ▶汚れた空気 dirty *air* ‖ この教室は空気が悪いね. 窓を開けて風を入れよう The *air* is bad in this classroom. Open (up) the windows and let in some fresh air. ‖ 表に行って少し新鮮な空気を吸おう Let's go outside and get some fresh *air*. ‖ 大都市の空気は窒素酸化物でひどく汚れている The *air* in big cities is heavily polluted with nitrogen oxide. ‖ このタイヤは空気が抜けている This tire is *a little deflated*.
‖(自転車の)**空気入れ**《米》an air pump,《英》a bicycle pump ‖ **空気感染** airborne infection ‖ **空気銃** an air gun, a BB gun ‖ **空気清浄器** an air cleaner ‖ **空気枕** an air cushion.

2【雰囲気】(an) **atmosphere** /ǽtməsfɪəʳ/ ▶殺人の現場は一夜明けたけさも陰鬱な空気に包まれている The scene of last night's murder is still wrapped [enveloped] in a somber *mood* this morning. ‖ 警察署には一種独特の空気がある A police station has *an atmosphere* all its own. ‖ 木村さんは空気の読めない人だ Mr. Kimura *never reads people's moods and feelings*. / Mr. Kimura *never takes hints*.

くうきょ 空虚 emptiness —形 **空虚な empty** ▶人生とは空虚なものだ Life is *empty*.

ぐうぐう ▶父はグーグーいびきをかいている My father *is snoring loudly*. (➤ 漫画などでは眠っている音の「グーグー」を ZZZ で表す) ‖ 朝食を抜いてきたからおなかがグーグー鳴っている My stomach *is growling* because I skipped breakfast.

グーグル Google(検索エンジンの商標名) ▶そのレストランについてグーグルで調べる look up the restaurant on *Google*. →ググる.

くうぐん 空軍 an **air force** ▶米国空軍と英国空軍 *the United States Air Force* [*USAF*] and *the Royal Air Force* [*RAF*]. ‖**空軍基地** an air base.

くうこう 空港 an **airport** ▶成田空港に着陸する[から出発する] land at [take off from] *Narita* (*Airport*) ‖**空港バス** an airport bus ‖ **空港ビル** an air terminal building ‖ **空港ホテル** an airport hotel.

ぐうじ 宮司 the chief priest of a Shinto shrine.

くうしつ 空室 a **vacancy.**

くうしゃ 空車 an **empty car** [**taxi**] ▶ホテルの前には客待ちの空車の長い列ができている There's a long line of *empty taxis* (waiting for passengers) in front of the hotel. 《参考》英米ではタクシーの上部の TAXI のランプが点灯していれば空車の場合が多い.

くうしゅう 空襲 an **air raid**, an **air attack** (➤ 前者は「奇襲攻撃」のニュアンスが強い) ▶東京は太平洋戦争中アメリカ軍の空襲を受けた Tokyo *was bombed* by the U.S. Air Force during the Pacific War. (➤ bomb /bɑːm/ は「…を爆撃する」の意).
‖**空襲警報** an air-raid warning [alarm].

くうしょ 空所 a **blank** ▶空所に適語を入れよ Fill in the *blanks* with the appropriate words.

ぐうすう 偶数 an **even number** (➤「奇数」は odd number) ▶偶数ページ an *even* page／an *even-numbered* page.

ぐうする 遇する **treat** +㊐ (待遇する) ; **employ** +㊐ (雇う) ▶前政府高官を理事として遇する *employ* an ex-government official as director.

くうせき 空席 a **vacant** [an **empty**] **seat** ▶国立競技場には空席がほとんど無かった［目立った］ There were very few [There were a conspicuous number of] *vacant seats* at the National Stadium. ‖ **対話**「835便には空席はありますか」「はい, 1つございます」 "Do you have *a seat available* on Flight 835 ?" "Yes, we do have one." ‖《比喩的》彼の辞任で副社長の椅子が空席となった The post of vice-president *was vacated* by his resignation.

くうぜん 空前の **unprecedented** /ʌnprésədenṭɪd/ (前例のない) ▶空前のベストセラー an *unprecedented* best seller ‖ 空前の大惨事 an *unprecedented* disaster ‖ その映画は空前のヒットを続けている The film is enjoying *unprecedented* success. ‖ 王選手の868本のホームランは空前の記録だ Oh's 868 home runs are an *all-time* record. (➤ all-time は「史上最高の」) ‖ 村上春樹の"１Ｑ８４"は空前のヒットだった Murakami Haruki's "1 Q 84" was a *record-breaking* hit. (➤record-breaking は「記録破りの」).

ぐうぜん 偶然 (a) **chance** ; (an) **accident** (思いがけない出来事) ; **coincidence** (同時発生) 一副 **偶然に by chance, accidentally, coincidentally**

▶偶然の出会い a *chance* meeting ‖ ぼくたちが沖縄で会ったのは偶然だった *It was by chance that* we met in Okinawa. ‖ 私は偶然その事故現場に居合わせた I *happened to* be at the scene of the accident. ／ I was at the scene of the accident *by chance* [*by accident*]. ‖ 通りを歩いていて偶然真知子に出会った Walking along the street, I *happened to* meet [*ran into*／*bumped into*] Machiko. (➤ run [bump] into は「(人に)ばったり出会う」の意のインフォーマルな表現) ‖ 偶然我々は同じ職に応募した *By* [*In*] *an odd twist of fate* we applied for the same job. (➤ この by an odd twist of fate は「思いがけない運命の巡り合わせで」の意) ‖ 偶然にも両研究者は同一の解決法を同日に発見した *By coincidence*, both researchers discovered the same solution on the same day. ‖ 偶然にも彼女とぼくは同じ県の同じ町の出身だ She *happens to* come from the same prefecture and town as I do. ‖ 全く偶然にも私たち3人は誕生日が同じだ Quite *coincidentally*, the three of us were born on the same day. ‖ 彼は偶然と見せかけてわざと彼女の足を踏んだ He stepped on her foot *accidentally on purpose*. ‖ きみも12月3日生まれだって? 偶然の一致だね You were also born on December 3 ? What *a coincidence* !

くうぜんぜつご 空前絶後 ▶空前絶後の事件 an *unprecedented and never to be repeated* incident ／a *once-only* incident ‖『風と共に去りぬ』の製作費は当時空前絶後と言われた It was said that the production costs of "Gone with the Wind" were *unprecedentedly high* (for those days).

くうそ 空疎 ▶彼のスピーチは内容が空疎だった His speech *had no substance*. (➤ substance は「中身, 内容」) ‖ 見かけは立派だが内容の空疎な書物が多い There are a lot of books that look impressive but *have no real substance*.

くうそう 空想 a **daydream** (楽しい) ; a **fancy** (とっぴな, 奇想天外な) ; **imagination** (芸術的・創造的な) 一動 **空想する daydream** +㊐, **fancy** +㊐, **imagine** +㊐ ▶彼女は先生に当てられたとき空想にふけっていた She was *daydreaming* when the teacher called on her. ‖ 彼女はよくかわいいお姫さまになった自分を空想した She often *daydreamed* about being a lovely princess. ‖ ライト兄弟よりずっと以前から人間は空を飛ぶことを空想していた Humans *imagined* themselves flying long before the Wright brothers. ‖ **空想家** a dreamer ‖ **空想科学小説** science fiction.

ぐうぞう 偶像 an **idol** /áɪdl/ ▶偶像を崇拝する worship *an idol*. →アイドル.

ぐうたら ▶うちの人はぐうたらでね My husband is *a lazy slob*. (➤ slob は「だらしない人［やつ］」).

くうちゅう 空中に **in the air** ▶風船は空中高く飛んでいった［漂った］ The balloon went [floated] up *in the air*. ‖ 飛行機は空中分解した The airplane *disintegrated in midair*. ‖ **空中戦** an air battle ‖ **空中ぶらんこ** a (flying) trapeze /træpíːz ‖ trəp-/.

くうちょう 空調 **air-conditioning** ▶空調設備のある部屋 an *air-conditioned* room ‖ **空調機** an air-conditioning unit ／an air-conditioner.

ぐーっと ▶彼はビールをぐーっと飲んだ He *took a long pull* on his beer. →ぐっと.

ぐうているい 偶蹄類 《動物》 an **artiodactyl** /àːʳtioʊdǽktl/.

クーデター a **coup d'état** /kùːdeɪtɑ́ː/, a **coup** /kuː/ ▶軍事クーデター a military *coup d'état* ‖ クーデターを行う stage *a coup* ‖ クーデターに成功して軍部が政権を掌握した The military succeeded in *a coup* and seized power.

‖ **無血クーデター** a bloodless coup d'état.

くうてん 空転 ▶議論は空転した The discussion *went* (*around*) *in circles*.

くうどう 空洞 a **hollow** ; a **cave** (斜面にあいた洞穴) ▶中が空洞になった木 a *hollow* tree ‖ この大仏の内部は空洞です This statue of Buddha is *hollow* inside. ‖ 多くの会社が生産基盤を海外移転して, 国内産業が空洞化している Because many companies have moved their production bases overseas, domestic industries are *being hollowed out*.

ぐうのね ぐうの音 ▶彼女の喫煙反対論にぐうの音も出なかった I *couldn't counter* her argument against smoking.

くうはく 空白 a **blank** ▶空白を埋める fill in *a blank* ‖ 答えのわからないところは空白のままにしておきなさい Leave it *blank* if you don't know the answer.

くうばく 空爆 **aerial bombing** ; an **air strike** (1回1回の) ▶その町はＮＡＴＯ軍の戦闘機の空爆を受けた The town *was bombed* (*from the air*) by NATO jet fighters.

ぐうはつ 偶発 ‖ **偶発事故** an accident ‖ **偶発戦争** accidental warfare.

くうひ 空費 (a) **waste** 一動 **空費する waste** +㊐ ▶その会議は全くの時間の空費だった That meeting was a complete *waste of time*. ‖ 時間を空費しないように気をつけなさい Be careful not to *waste* your time.

くうふく 空腹 **hunger** 一形 **空腹の hungry** ▶空腹を覚える feel *hungry* ‖ 少年は空腹を訴えた The boy complained *that he was hungry*.

クーペ a **coupé** /kuːpéɪ/.

くうぼ 空母 an (**aircraft**) **carrier** ▶米軍の原子力空母

が横須賀に入港した The U.S. *nuclear-powered* (*aircraft*) *carrier* docked at Yokosuka.

くうほう 空包 a **blank cartridge.**

クーポン a **coupon** ▶このクーポン使えますか Can I use this *coupon*?／Will you accept this *coupon*? ‖クーポン券 a coupon.

くうゆ 空輸 **air transportation**; **airlift**(応急策としての) 一動 空輸する **transport ... by air, airlift** ＋目 ▶このカニは北海道から空輸したものだ This crab *was shipped by air* from Hokkaido. (➤ ship は「輸送する」の意で, 乗り物に関係なく使われる) ‖ 彼らは雪に閉じ込められたその村へ食料を空輸した They *airlifted* food to the snowbound village.

クーラー an **air conditioner**(エアコン); a **cooler**(冷却器) ▶この部屋はクーラーがよく効いている This room *is well air-conditioned*. ‖ 冬にもかかわらずこのデパートではクーラーをつけている They *have the air conditioning on* in this department store, even though it is winter. ‖カークーラー a car air-conditioner.

> **危ないカタカナ語✹ クーラー**
> 1 英語の cooler は一般に「冷却器」を指す. ワインを冷やしておく wine cooler などがそれで, 釣りなどに持参する携帯用の冷蔵庫も cooler である.
> 2 日本語では冷房装置のことも「クーラー」というが, 英語では air conditioner がふつう.

くうらん 空欄 a **blank** ▶次の空欄に最もふさわしい語を書き込みなさい Fill each *blank* with the most suitable word.

クーリングオフ a **cooling-off period**(期間).

クール **cool** ▶彼はいつもクールだ He is always *cool-headed* [*cool*]. (➤ He's cool. は「彼ってかっこいい」の意にもなる) ‖ そのアイドル歌手は熱狂的なファンの歓迎をクールな目で見ていた The popular singer responded to her fans' welcome *nonchalantly*. (➤「興味なさそうに, 冷淡に」の意).

クールビズ **the "Cool Biz" summer dress code.**

くうろ 空路 ▶彼らは空路帰国の途に就いた They left for home *by air* [*by plane*]. ‖ 彼はきのう空路鹿児島から東京へ戻ってきた Yesterday, he *flew back* to Tokyo from Kagoshima.

くうろん 空論 ▶それは机上の空論だ That's *a paper argument*.／That's *an impracticable plan*. (➤ 後者は「非現実的なプランだ」の意).

ぐうわ 寓話 a **fable**(動物を擬人化した); a **parable**(たとえ話); an **allegory** /ǽləgɔ̀ːri/ (抽象概念などを擬人化した).

クエスチョン・マーク a **question mark.**

くえない 食えない ▶役者一本では食えない I *can't make a living* on acting alone.
▶《慣用表現》あいつは煮ても焼いても食えないやつだ There's no way on earth to get along with him. He's *too crafty*.／He's *a tough customer*. (➤ それぞれ「とても悪賢い人」,「扱いにくい人」の意で, うまくやっていきたくてもいきようがない)／He's *slippery as an eel*. (➤「のらりくらりで, とらえどころがない」の意).

クエンさん クエン酸 《化学》 **citric acid.**

クオータ a **quota (system)**(割り当て).

クオーター 《球技》 a **quarter (of a game).**

クオーツ **quartz** /kwɔːrts/ (石英) ▶クオーツの腕時計 a *quartz* watch.

クオーテーション (a) **quotation** (引用); **quotation marks**(マーク).

クオリティー **quality** ‖クオリティー・オブ・ライフ quality of life《略 QOL》(➤ 日本語では「生活の質」と訳す).

くかい 句会 a **haiku gathering.**

くかく 区画 a **lot**(土地の1区画分); a **block**(街区) ▶1区画分だけ売れ残っている There is only *one lot* left for sale [one unsold *lot*]. ‖区画整理 rezoning of the land／land readjustment.

くがく 苦学 ▶祖父は苦学して大学[学校]を出たそうだ My grandfather says he *worked his way through college* [*school*]. 《参考》アメリカなどではアルバイトをして大学を出る人は別に珍しくないので, work one's way through college [school] には日本語の「苦学して大学[学校]を出る」がもつ暗いイメージはない. ‖苦学生 a working student.

くがつ 九月 **September**《略 Sept. または Sep.》.

くかん 区間 a **section**; a **leg**(リレー競走の) ▶バス代は1区間210円です The bus fare is 210 yen per *zone*. ‖ その区間は大雨のため電車が不通です Train service on that *section* has been suspended due to heavy rain. ‖ 彼はその駅伝競走で第5区間の新記録を作った He set [established] a record in the fifth *leg* of the ekiden. ‖区間記録 a section record ‖区間タイム section time ‖(鉄道などの)不通区間 a closed section.

くき 茎 a **stem**(草花の); a **stalk**(葉柄・花柄の細いもの).

くぎ 釘 a **nail**; a **peg**(掛けくぎ) ▶ここにくぎを1本打ってください Drive *a nail* (in) here. ‖ レインコートをくぎに引っ掛けた My raincoat got caught on *a nail*.／*A nail* snagged my raincoat. ‖ 帽子とコートはこのくぎに掛けてください Please hang [put] your hat and coat on this *peg*.
▶《慣用表現》どんなことがあっても約束は守るようにと息子にくぎを刺しておいた I *made doubly sure that* my son would keep his promise no matter what. ‖くぎ抜き (a pair of) pincers(やっとこ式の)／a nail puller(てこ式の).

くぎづけ 釘付け ▶子供たちはテレビの画面にくぎづけになった The children('s eyes) *were glued to* the TV screen. (➤ glue は「接着剤でくっつける」が原義) ‖ ショックのあまり私はその場にくぎづけになった Shock *riveted* me to the spot. (➤ rivet /rívət/ は「びょうで留めるように固定する」).

くきょう 苦境・苦況 **difficulties, a difficult situation** ▶会社の倒産で彼は苦境に陥った He fell into *great difficulties* [He found himself in *a tight spot*] when the company went bankrupt. ‖ ジャイアンツの苦境を救うのは誰だろう Who is going to pull [get] the Giants out of this *fix*? (➤ fix は「苦しい立場」の意のインフォーマルな語).

くぎょう 苦行 **asceticism** /əsétɪsɪ̀zəm/, **ascetic self-discipline.**

くぎり 区切り・句切り ▶仕事に区切りをつけて少し休もう Let's *stop* what we're working on *when we get to a convenient place* and take a short-break. ‖ これでようやくひと区切りついた This should put *an end* to things for a while. ‖ 彼は仕事の区切りがつかないと5時になっても帰らない He never leaves his office at five unless he *has finished* his work *for the day*.

くぎる 区切る・句切る **divide** ＋目 ▶彼の部屋はカーテンで2つに区切ってある His room *is divided* (into two sections) by a curtain. ‖ 垣根がうちの庭と隣の庭を区切っている A fence *divides* our garden from our neighbor's. ‖ 1行ごとに区切って読みなさい

Read (the passage), *pausing briefly at the end of each line.*

くく 九九 the multiplication table(s), the times-table(s) ▶九九を暗記する learn *the multiplication tables* by heart ‖ 九九を7の段まで言う say *the multiplication tables* up to 7 (times) ‖ 九九の練習をする work on *the times-tables.*

くぐりぬける 潜り抜ける ▶その車は猛スピードでガードをくぐり抜けた The car *passed under* the railroad overpass at full speed.
▶法の網をくぐり抜ける *evade* the law.

くくる 括る tie《up》, bind ▶この雑誌をくくって束にしなさい *Tie* these magazines *up* in a bundle, please.
▶省略できる単語をかっこでくくりなさい *Put* [*Enclose*] the words which can be omitted *in parentheses.* (➤ enclose は「(語などを)囲う」の意). ‖ その男は首をくくって死んだ The man *hanged himself.*

くぐる 潜る ▶鳥居をくぐる *go* [*pass*] *under* a torii ‖ 列車はトンネルをくぐった The train *went* [*passed*] *through* a tunnel.
▶犯人は警察の厳重な警戒網をくぐって逃走した The suspect *slipped through* the police's tight net of surveillance.

ググる Google, google +目 ▶その店をググる *Google* the store.

くげ 公家 a court noble.

くけい 矩形 a rectangle /réktæŋgəl/.

くげん 苦言 ▶一言あえて苦言を呈したい I hope you don't mind my giving you some *frank* [*blunt*] *advice.* (● 英語では「率直な忠告」と考える).

ぐけん 愚見 ▶愚見では *in my humble opinion.*

ぐげん 具現 ▶この校章は建学の精神を具現化したものです This school emblem *embodies* the founding spirit of our school.

ぐこう 愚行 a foolish act(常識・分別を欠いた行為); stupid behavior(頭の働きが鈍いとしか思えない行動).

くさ 草 grass(芝や牧草; 1本の草は a blade of grass); a weed(雑草) ▶草の生えた庭 a *grass-* [*weed-*] *grown* garden ‖ うちの庭は草がぼうぼうだ Our garden is overgrown with *weeds.* ‖ 我々は緑の草に覆われた土手に寝そべった We stretched ourselves out on the *grass-covered* bank. /We lay down on the *grassy* bank. ‖ 牧場で牛が草を食べている Cattle *are grazing* in the pasture. ‖ 父は庭で草むしり[草刈り]をしている My father *is weeding* [*mowing the grass* in] the yard. (➤ この weed は「(庭などの)草取りをする」の意の動詞; mow は「(庭の芝生を)刈る」意で用いられる. 鎌(scythe)を使って畑などで行う草刈りには mow でなく cut を用いるのがふつう).
☞ 草の根, 草野球 (→見出語)

くさい 臭い

📖 訳語メニュー
悪臭がする →smell, stink **1**
怪しい →suspicious, fishy **2**

1【臭う】 smell; be smelly ▶《物が臭う》臭い水道水 *smelly* tap water ‖ この肉は何だか臭い This meat *is* somewhat *smelly.* ‖ 汗臭いよ. シャワーを浴びなさい Take a shower. You *smell sweaty.* ‖ 彼の息はいつもたばこ[酒]臭い His breath always *smells of cigarettes* [*liquor*]. ‖ ごみ入れが臭い The garbage can *stinks* [*smells terrible*]. (➤ stink は「悪臭を放つ」の意の動詞) ‖《人が臭いと感じる》ガス臭いぞ. 窓を開けろ Open the window. I *smell gas.*

2【怪しい】 suspicious /səspíʃəs/, fishy ▶どうもあの男が臭い That man looks *suspicious.* /There is something *fishy* about that man. (➤ fishy はインフォーマルな語) ‖ この詐欺事件ではあのセールスマンが臭いと思う I *suspect* (that) that salesman is involved in this scam.

3【…の感じがする】 ▶あいつの話は何だかいんちき臭いね His story *sounds fishy,* doesn't it? ‖ いつまでたってもあの女優の演技は素人臭い After all this time, that actress still acts *like an amateur* [her acting is still *amateurish*].

4【慣用表現】 ▶臭い芝居 *a hammy* [*cheesy*] *performance* (➤ hammy は「わざとらしい, 演技過剰の」, cheesy は「安っぽい」の意のインフォーマルな語) ‖ 校長は臭い物に蓋をしよう(=スキャンダルをもみ消そう)としたがだめだった The principal tried to *cover up the scandal* but failed. ‖ あの男はこれまで2度臭い飯を食った(=刑務所で服役した)ことがあるらしい Somebody told me he's *done time* [《英》 he's *done porridge*] twice.

くさいきれ 草いきれ ▶むっとする草いきれ overpowering *scent of grass in the sun.*

くさき 草木 a plant; vegetation (➤ 集合的).

くさす run ... down ▶彼は奥さんのことをくさしてばかりいる He's always *running* his wife *down.*

ぐさっと ▶今のきみのことばはぐさっときたよ What you just said really *hit home.*

くさとり 草取り weeding 一動 草取りをする weed +目 ▶庭の草取りが必要だ We need to *weed* our garden. /Our garden needs *weeding.*

くさのね 草の根 ▶刑事は草の根を分けても犯人を捜し出すと言った The detective said that he would *leave no stone unturned* to find the culprit. (➤ leave no stone unturned は「すべての石をひっくり返す」の意).
‖草の根民主主義 grass-roots democracy.

くさばな 草花 a flowering plant(花の咲く植物); a flower(花) ▶庭に草花を植える plant *flowers* in the garden ‖ その画家は草花を好んで描く That painter prefers to paint *flowers and plants.*

くさはら 草原 a grass field; a grassy plain, grasslands(大草原) ▶公園の草原で弁当を広げる open one's box lunch on *a grassy spot* in the park (● 英語では単に eat on the grass と表現することが多い).

くさび 楔 a wedge ▶丸太にくさびを打ち込む drive *a wedge* into a log.
‖くさび形文字(古代ペルシャ・アッシリアなどの) a cuneiform /kjúːnɪfɔːrm/ (character).

くさぶかい 草深い grassy; overgrown with grass(草の茂った); remote(へんぴな) ▶私は草深い田舎に住んでいます I live *out in the remote countryside* [*in the sticks*]. (➤ 後者は俗語表現).

くさみ 臭み a smell; an odor(嫌な臭い) ▶ニンニクには独特の臭みがある Garlic has distinctive *odor* [*a smell* of its own].
▶《比喩的》あの人の文章は臭み(=気取り)があるから嫌いだ I don't like his *affected* style.

くさむしり 草むしり weeding. →草取り.

くさむら 草叢 the grass(草地); a thicket(茂み) ▶ボールが草むらに入って見つからなくなった We lost the ball in *the grass.* ‖ キツネは草むらに隠れた The fox hid in the *thicket.*

くさやきゅう 草野球 sandlot baseball(➤ アメリカではもと草地でなく砂地でやったことから) ▶ここでは子供たちの

間で草野球が盛んだ *Sandlot baseball* is very popular among children here.

くさり 鎖 a **chain** ▶鎖のついた時計 a watch *on a chain* ‖ネックレスの鎖が切れている The *chain* of my necklace is broken. ‖その犬を鎖でつないでください *Chain up* the dog. (➤「犬を鎖でつないでおいてください」なら Keep the dog on a chain. とする →リード3) ‖そのシカは鎖でつながれていた The deer was *on a chain*. ／The deer was *chained up*.

ぐさりと ▶強盗は店員をぐさりと刺して逃げた The robber *stabbed* the clerk and ran away. ‖母親のひと言がぐさりと胸にこたえた What my mother said *struck straight* to my heart [*struck home*]. (➤ struck は strike(打撃を与える)の過去形).

くさる 腐る **1【腐敗する】rot**；**go bad, spoil**(➤特に食物が悪くなる) 一形 **腐った rotten** ▶腐った肉 *rotten* meat ‖梅雨時は食べ物が腐りやすい Food easily *goes bad* [Food *spoils* easily] during the rainy season. ‖牛乳が腐ってしまった The milk *has gone* [*turned*] *sour*. (➤ go [turn] sour は「酸っぱくなる」) ‖この門柱は腐りかかっていて危険だ This gatepost is dangerous since it's *half rotted away*.

▶《慣用表現》シャープペンシルなら腐るほど持ってるよ If you want mechanical pencils, I have *tons* [*a ton*] *of* them. (➤ tons [a ton] of は「たくさんの…」の意のインフォーマルな表現) ‖彼のおじさんは腐るほどお金を持っている His uncle *has money to burn*. (➤「燃やすほどのお金」の意).

2【堕落する】▶根性の腐った男 a *corrupt* man ‖あいつは根性が腐っている He *is rotten* to the core. (➤ to the core は「しんまで」).

3【気力や意欲を無くす】▶彼は入試に落ちてくさっている He *is dejected* because he failed the entrance exam. ‖そんなにくさるなよ. 大学だけが人生じゃない Don't *be down in the mouth* [*down in the dumps*]. College isn't the only thing in life.

くされえん 腐れ縁 ▶あの男とは腐れ縁で付き合ってるんだ He and I *are hopelessly linked together*. ‖政治献金は政治家と財界の腐れ縁を生みがちだ Political contributions often create *unsavory ties* between politicians and the business world. (➤ unsavory tie は「(道徳的に)芳しくない結び付き」).

くさわけ 草分け ▶彼は日本野球界の草分け(＝先駆者)の1人だ He is one of the *pioneers* of the Japanese baseball world. ‖放送大学はイギリスが草分けだ The idea of the Open University *originated in* Britain. ‖彼女はほかの女性ジャーナリストにとって草分け的な存在だ She is *a trailblazer* for other female journalists.

1**くし 串** a **skewer**(焼き鳥用などの小さな)；a **spit**(鳥の丸焼き用などの大きな) ▶串に刺した肉 a piece of meat on *a skewer*.

‖串カツ deep-fried pork on a skewer.

2**くし 櫛** a **comb** /koʊm/ ▶このくしで髪をときなさい Comb your hair with this *comb*. (◉ Do your hair ... とすることもできるが, こちらは言われている相手が女性であることを連想させる).

3**くし 駆使** ▶彼は数か国語を駆使する He *has a good command of* several languages. ‖彼女はコンピュータを駆使してその絵を描いた She *made full use of* the computer in drawing the picture.

くじ 籤 a **lot**(順番などを決めるための)；a **drawing**(抽選)；a **lottery**(宝くじなどの)；a **chance game**(福引きなどの) ▶くじ引きをする draw *lots* ▶私たちはくじで高井さんを司会者に選んだ We chose [selected] Mr. Takai as master of ceremonies *by lot*. ‖弟はくじで香港旅行を当てた My brother won a trip to Hong Kong *in a drawing*. ‖彼らは野球の試合の先攻を決めるためくじを引いた They *drew lots* to decide which team would go (up) to bat first. ‖くじ引きの結果, 第1試合は2組と3組の対決になった *Lots* were drawn to determine that the first match would be between Teams 2 and 3. ‖私はくじ運がいい[悪い] I *have good* [*bad*] *luck in lotteries*.

☛ 空くじ (→見出語)

くじく 挫く **1【手足を】sprain** +目；**wrench** +目 /rentʃ/ (強くねじる) ▶転んで左の足首をくじいた I fell down and *sprained* my left ankle. ‖重量挙げの練習をしていて彼は手首をくじいた He *sprained* [*wrenched*] his wrist while practicing weight lifting.

2【気分や勢いを】crush +目 (打ち砕く)；**discourage** /dɪskə́ːrɪdʒ/ +目 (やる気を失わせる) ▶彼のそのひと言で私の意気込みはくじかれた That single remark of his *crushed* my initial enthusiasm. ‖弱きを助け強きをくじく Assist the weak and defeat [crush] the strong.

くしくも 奇しくも **by (a strange) coincidence** (偶然の一致で)；**strangely [oddly] enough** (不思議なことに) ▶くしくもその日は私の父の命日であった *By* (*a strange*) *coincidence*, that day fell on the anniversary of my father's death. (➤ by chance (たまたま) でもよい) ‖くしくも私たち2人は同じバスに乗り合わせた *By a quirk of fate*, the two of us were on the same bus. (➤「運命の気まぐれで」の意).

くじける 挫ける **be discouraged** ▶一度や二度失敗したからといってくじけちゃだめだ Don't *be discouraged* over a couple of failures. ／Don't let a couple of failures *get* you *down*. ‖くじけないで頑張れ! (Keep your) chin up!

くじびき くじ引き →くじ.

くじゃく 孔雀《鳥》a **peacock**(雄)；a **peahen**(雌).

くしゃくしゃ ▶彼はポケットからくしゃくしゃになった千円札を取り出した He took out a *crumpled* 1,000-yen bill from his pocket. ‖少女の顔は涙でくしゃくしゃだった The little girl's face *crumpled* with tears. ／The little girl *crumpled* into tears. ‖おばあちゃんはうれしさで顔をくしゃくしゃにしてぼくらを迎えてくれた Grandma's face *wrinkled up* in a smile as she came to greet us.

ぐしゃぐしゃ ▶雨上がりで校庭はまだぐしゃぐしゃだ The schoolyard is still *soggy* from the rain. ‖慌てて作ったのでこのオムレツはぐしゃぐしゃだ I made the omelet in a hurry, so it is *runny*. ‖《事故などで》彼女の車はぐしゃぐしゃになった Her car *was totaled* [*was a total write-off*]. (➤ write-off は「修理不能の自動車(など)」).

くしゃみ a **sneeze** 一動 **くしゃみをする sneeze** ▶こしょうの匂いを嗅ぐといつもくしゃみが出る I (start to) *sneeze* whenever I smell pepper. ‖清二は授業中にでかいくしゃみをした Seiji *sneezed* loudly [*gave a loud sneeze*] during (the) class. 《参考》英米には人がくしゃみをすると, その人に向かって「お大事に」の意味で (God) bless you! と言う習慣がある. 言われた人は Thank you. と答える. 「ハクション」は ahchoo /ɑːtʃúː/ という.

1**くじゅう 苦渋** ▶社長は苦渋に満ちた表情を見せた The company president looked *deeply troubled*. ‖首相は苦渋の決断を迫られた The Prime Minister had to make *a bitterly difficult decision*.

2**くじゅう 苦汁** ▶我々は M 社の製品にシェアを奪われて，市場から撤退を余儀なくされるという**苦汁をなめた** We *had a bitter experience* when we were forced to withdraw from the market after our market share was captured by M Company's product.

ぐじゅぐじゅ ▶雨のあと，校庭は**ぐじゅぐじゅ**だった The schoolyard was *soggy* after the rain.

くじょ 駆除 extermination 一動 駆除する exterminate +目，**get rid of** (➤ 後者はややインフォーマルな言い方) ▶害虫を**駆除する** *exterminate* pests ‖ うちでは昔はよく猫いらずでネズミを**駆除した** We used to use rat poison to *get rid of* rats at our home.

くしょう 苦笑 ▶いちばん凡庸な絵を褒められて画家は**苦笑した** The artist *gave a wry smile* when the picture he thought (was) the most mediocre was complimented. (➤ wry /raɪ/ は「苦々しい」).

くじょう 苦情 a complaint ▶携帯電話についての**苦情**が増えているようだ It seems that *complaints* about cellphones are on the rise. ‖ テレビの音を小さくしなさい. でないと近所から**苦情が出る**わよ Turn down the TV or the neighbors will *be on our backs*. (➤ be on ~'s back は「～にがみがみ言う」) ‖ 犬の鳴き声がうるさいので隣の家に**苦情を言いに行った** I went to the next-door neighbor's (house) to *complain* about their dog's barking. ‖ 彼らは部屋が狭すぎると**苦情を言った** They *complained* that the room was too small (for them).

ぐしょう 具象 ‖**具象画** a representational painting.

ぐしょぬれ ぐしょ濡れ ▶夕立に遭って**ぐしょぬれ**になった I was caught in a rain shower and *got soaked to the skin* [*got drenched*]. ‖ 彼女のドレスは**ぐしょぬれ**だ Her dress *is dripping wet*.

くじら 鯨《動物》**a whale** ▶**鯨**は魚ではなく哺乳類だ *Whales* are not fish, but mammals. ‖ **鯨**は息を吐くとき潮を吹く *Whales* spout when they exhale.

> 「鯨・イルカ」のいろいろ **イッカク** narwhal, sea unicorn ／**イワシクジラ** sei whale ／**コクジラ** gray whale ／**ゴンドウクジラ** pilot whale ／**ザトウクジラ** humpback whale ／**シャチ** killer whale ／**シロイルカ** white whale, beluga ／**シロナガスクジラ** blue whale ／**スナメリ** black finless porpoise ／**セミクジラ** right whale, bowhead whale ／**ツチクジラ** Baird's beaked whale ／**ナガスクジラ** fin whale ／**ハナゴンドウ** Risso's dolphin ／**バンドウイルカ** blue-white dolphin ／**マイルカ** common dolphin ／**マッコウクジラ** sperm whale ／**ミンククジラ** minke whale

くしん 苦心 pains（骨折り）; **efforts**（努力）**一動 苦心する take pains** ▶きみの英作文にはだいぶ**苦心の跡**が見えるね It looks like you *put a lot of effort into* this English composition. ‖ 我々は展覧会を成功させようと**苦心さんたんした** We *took great pains* to make the art exhibition successful. ‖ この役作りのどこにいちばん**苦心されましたか** What was the most *difficult part* of creating [playing] this role? ‖ このブロンズ像は彼の**苦心の作**だ This bronze statue is *the fruit of great labor* on his part. (➤ fruit は「結実」).

1**くず 屑 waste, rubbish,**《米》**trash** ▶紙くず *wastepaper* ‖ 糸くず *waste* (*piece of*) *thread* / *lint* ‖ パンくず *crumbs* /krʌmz/ ‖ 野菜のくず vegetable *scraps*. →ごみ.

▶《比喩的》弱い者をいじめるなんてあいつは**人間のくずだ** He is (*a*) *real scum* [*a real scum bag*] to pick on somebody weak like that. (➤ scum は「(沸騰・発酵の際にできる)浮きかす，あく」が原義) ‖ 社会のくず the *dregs* of society (➤ dregs はワインのびんやコーヒーカップの底に残る「かす」が原義).

‖**くず入れ**（路上・駅・公園の）《米》a waste can [basket],《英》a dustbin ‖ **くず籠**《米》a wastebasket,《英》a wastepaper basket ‖ **くず屋** a junk dealer,《英 また》a rag-and-bone merchant.

2**くず 葛**《植物》**kudzu**《参考》1876年のフィラデルフィア博覧会の日本庭園に出品されたのがアメリカに持ち込まれた最初. 成長が早い雑草としてアメリカ南部では問題化している.

ぐず a dawdler ▶あいつ，ほんとに**ぐず**なんだから! That guy's such *a dawdler*! ‖ おまえが**ぐず**だから何をやっても遅くなるんだ It's all because you're such *a slowpoke* [*a slowcoach*] that everything goes so slow. (➤ slowpoke, slowcoach ともに「のろま」に相当し，《英》では後者が好まれる).

くすくす ▶若い女の子たちがぼくを見て**くすくす笑っている** The young girls are looking at me and *giggling*. →笑う.

ぐずぐず 1【手間取ること】▶**ぐずぐずし**てないで早く寝なさい Don't *dawdle*. Get to bed right now. ‖ 何を**ぐずぐずし**ていたんだよ What's *taking you so long*? ‖ **ぐずぐずするな** *Stop dragging your feet*. ‖ **ぐずぐずし**ていると学校に遅れるわよ *Hurry up*, *or* you will be late for school. (➤「急ぎなさい，さもないと」の意) ‖ 今度の金曜日が締め切りです. **ぐずぐずしてはいられません** The deadline is this Friday. *We have* [*There is*] *no time to lose*. (➤ 後半を We'd better get on the stick [get cracking]. としてもよい) ‖ 政府は消費税の増税を**ぐずぐず先延ばしする**余裕などないはずだ The government can't afford to *procrastinate* on a consumption tax hike. ‖ 彼は仕事の誘いに対する返事を**ぐずぐずと延ばした** He *procrastinated* on replying to the job offer. (➤ procrastinate on doing は「…するのを先延ばしする」)

2【不平を言う】▶済んでしまったことを**ぐずぐず言う**な Don't *grumble* [*complain*] about what's done.

3【鼻が詰まる】▶**鼻がぐずぐずしている** *My nose is stuffed up*.

くすぐったい ▶脇腹が**くすぐったい** My side *tickles*. ‖ そんな所触ったら**くすぐったい**よ Don't touch [Stop tickling] me there. *I'm ticklish* (there). ‖ 足の裏は**くすぐったく感じる** The soles of the feet are *ticklish*.

▶あんまりみんなに褒められるので**くすぐったい気分になった** I *felt embarrassed* with everyone praising me.

くすぐる tickle +目 ▶赤ちゃんを**くすぐる**のはやめなさい Don't *tickle* the baby. ‖ 足の裏や脇の下は**くすぐられる**とくすぐったい It feels ticklish when someone *touches* [*fiddles with*] the sole of your foot or under the arms.

▶そのテレビニュースのシーンは彼女の母性本能を**くすぐった** The scene on the TV news *aroused* her maternal instinct.

くずす 崩す 1【壊す】tear /teəʳ/ **down, pull down** ▶我々は石垣を**崩して**道幅を広げなければならなかった We had to *tear down* the stone walls to widen the road. ‖ マンション建設のために裏山が**崩された** They *leveled* the hill behind our house to build apartments.

く

2【整っているものを乱す】▶どうぞ膝を崩して(楽にして)ください Please *sit more comfortably*. ‖ 姿勢を崩すな *Stand* [*Sit up*] *straight*. (➤ 後者は座っている人に) ‖ おいきみ, 列を崩すな Hey you, *don't get out of line*. ‖ 履歴書には楷書できちんと崩さずに書きなさい Write your Japanese résumé in block style characters, *not cursive* ones. (➤「続け字ではなく」の意).
▶平均台の上でバランスを崩す *lose* one's *balance* on the balance beam ‖ 彼はレース当日体調を崩し, 結局惨敗した He *was in bad shape* on the day of the race, and was trounced.
3【両替する】 break ＋⽬, change ＋⽬ ▶この5000円札を1000円札に崩していただけますか Could you *break* [*change*] this 5,000-yen bill *into* (five) 1,000-yen bills? ‖ 50ドル札を崩すことはできますか Would you happen to *have change* for a fifty? (➤ この change は「小銭」).

くすだま 薬玉 a ***kusudama***; a decorative hanging ball (for a celebratory occasion that rains confetti when it is split) (➤ 説明的な訳).

ぐずつく ▶子供がぐずついてなかなか寝てくれない The baby *is fretful* and won't go to sleep easily. ‖ ここ2, 3日天気がぐずついている The weather has been *unsettled* for the past few days. ‖ 天気はまだ2, 3日はぐずつくだろう The weather will *be changeable* for a few more days.

くずてつ 屑鉄 scrap iron ▶その古くなった車はくず鉄として売れた The old car was sold for *scrap*.

くすねる filch ＋⽬ (価値の低いものを); **pilfer** ＋⽬ (自分の職場などから) ▶鉛筆を1本くすねる *filch* a pencil ‖ レジの金をくすねる *pilfer* money from the cash register.

くすのき 楠 《植物》 a **camphor** /kǽmfəʳ/ **tree**.

くすぶる 燻る smolder ▶焼却炉のごみはまだくすぶっている The trash in the incinerator *is* still *smoldering*. ‖ すすでくすぶった天井 a *sooted* [*sooty*] ceiling.
▶長くくすぶり続けている国境紛争 a *long-smoldering* border dispute ‖ 賃上げが不十分で, まだ社員の間に不満がくすぶっている Discontent *is* still *smoldering* among employees because the pay raise was inadequate. ‖ きのうは一日中家でくすぶっていた I *was stuck at home* all day yesterday. (➤ be stuck は「思いどおりに動けないでいる」).

くすり 薬

1【薬剤】 (a) **medicine**, (a) **medication**, a **drug**

> 《解説》 (1) drug は医師や製薬会社が好んで用いる語. 一般には「麻薬」「薬物」の意で用いることも多い. medication は医師の「処方薬」で日常的には med ともいう. medicine は Ⓤ では「医学」の意のことが多い. (2) 薬の形状によって tablet (錠剤), pill (丸薬), capsule /kǽpsəl/ (カプセル), powdered medicine (粉薬), liquid medicine(水薬)のように呼ぶ.

▶薬が効いてきた The *medicine* is beginning to work. ‖ 胃痛にはどんな薬がいいでしょうか What *medicine* works best for stomachaches? ‖ 朝は薬を飲むのを忘れてしまった I forgot to *take* my *medicine* [*medication*] this morning. ‖ この薬を毎食後服用してください Take this *medicine* after meals. ‖ この薬を服用後, 車を運転しないでください Do not drive after taking this *medication*. ‖ 母は高血圧で薬の世話になっている My mother *is on medication* for high blood pressure. (➤ be on medication は「薬物治療を行っている」) ‖ 看護師さんにやけどをした腕に薬を塗ってもらった The nurse smeared *salve* [*ointment*] on the burn on my arm. (➤ salve /sæv ‖ sælv, sɑːv/, ointment は「軟こう」) ‖ ことわざ ばかにつける薬は無い There is no cure for a fool. ／Fools never learn.
‖**薬屋** a pharmacy, 《米また》 a drugstore, 《英また》 a chemist's (shop).

> 「薬」のいろいろ **胃薬** (a) medicine for stomachache ／**うがい薬** gargle ／**かぜ薬** cold medicine ／**下剤** purgative ／**解毒剤** antidote ／**解熱剤** antipyretic ／**抗がん剤** (anti-) cancer drug ／**抗生物質** antibiotic ／**消化剤** digestive ／**処方薬** a prescription drug [medication, medicine] ／**睡眠薬** sleeping pill ／**精神安定剤** tranquilizer ／**鎮痛剤** painkiller ／**トローチ** troche ／**軟こう** ointment ／**目薬** eye drops, eyewash

2【教訓】 a **lesson** ▶彼は校則に違反して3週間の停学になったが, いい薬になったようだ He was suspended from school for three weeks because he violated a school regulation. It seems to have been *a good lesson* for him. ‖ 彼に親切心など薬にしたくもない He does*n't have a shred of* kindness. (➤「みじんも無い」の意). ‖**薬箱** a medicine chest; a medicine cabinet(洗面台横の薬入れ戸棚).

くすりゆび 薬指 the third finger
《参考》 (1) 英語では親指を特に thumb /θʌm/ として区別するので, 薬指は「(人さし指から数えて) 3番目の指」という. (2) 結婚 [婚約] 指輪をはめることが多いことから, 左手の薬指を特に ring finger とも呼ぶ. →指.

ぐずる be peevish(だだをこねる); **fret**(むずかる); **grumble**(不平を言う) ▶太郎はきょうは学校へ行きたくないとぐずっている Taro *is being peevish* and says he doesn't want to go to school today. ／Taro *is grumbling* he doesn't want to go to school today.

-くずれ -崩れ ▶画家崩れ *a failed painter*(➤「成功しなかった画家」の意), *a painter manqué* ‖ 役者崩れ *an actor manqué* (➤ (1) manqué /mɑːŋkéɪ/ は「なり損ないの」の意のフランス語で堅い語. (2) ふつうは He didn't make it as a painter [an actor]. のように表現する).

くずれおちる 崩れ落ちる cave in; fall down, collapse.

くずれる 崩れる

1【壊れる】 fall down, collapse, give way ▶大雨で堤防が崩れた The embankment *gave way* because of the heavy rain. ／The heavy rain *broke* the embankment. ‖ トンネルが崩れて鉄道が不通になった The railroad was cut off when the tunnel *collapsed* [*caved in*]. ／The *collapse* of the tunnel cut off the railroad.
2【整っているものが乱れる】▶ケーキの形が崩れないように気をつけてください Be careful with these cakes so they don't *lose their shape*. ‖ この靴は5年も履いているのにまだ形が崩れない Though I've worn these shoes for (all of) five years, they'*ve kept their shape*. ‖ 彼の計画はもろくも崩れた His plan *collapsed* easily.
3【天気が】▶天気が崩れそうだ The weather is likely to *change* (*for the worse*). ／The weather is likely to *get worse*.
4【小銭に換えられる】▶ 対話 「この1万円札崩れます

か」「5千円札が入ってもいいですか」"Can you *break* this ten-thousand yen (bill) for me?" "Is it OK if I include a five-thousand-yen bill?" (➤「すみませんが, 崩れません」なら I'm sorry, I can't break it.).

くすんだ dark(黒が混じったような); dull (色がはっきりしない); smoky (曇った); somber (黒っぽくて地味な) ▶くすんだ色 a *dark* [*dull*/*smoky*/*somber*] color ‖部屋にはくすんだ茶色のカーテンが下がっていた The room was hung with curtains of a *dull* brown color.

くせ 癖 **1【習癖】** a habit →習慣 ▶父は酔うと泣く癖がある My father *has a habit* of crying when he gets drunk. ‖彼は何事につけても極端に走る癖がある He *is in the habit of* going to extremes in whatever he does. ‖私は最近, 夜更かしする悪い癖がついてしまった Recently I *have gotten into the bad habit* of staying up late. 《参考》「癖を直す」は break a habit. ‖たばこは吸いません. 癖になりますから I don't smoke because it's *habit-forming*. ‖息子は夏のキャンプから帰って以来, 爪をかむ癖がなくなった After summer camp, my son *stopped* biting his nails. (●「爪をかまなくなった」と考える) ‖ 対話「どう, このチーズケーキ?」「最高! 癖になりそう」"How do you like this cheesecake?" "Great! I'*m afraid that I'll get addicted to it*!"

2【変わった特徴】 ▶彼はすぐ腹を立てる癖がある He has *a tendency* to lose his temper easily. ‖彼は癖のある [ない] 英語を話す He speaks English *with* [*without*] *an accent*. ‖彼女はちょっと癖のある(=変わった)話し方をする She has a slightly *peculiar* way of talking. ‖ X教授はちょっと癖のある人だ Professor X has certain *idiosyncrasies*. (➤ idiosyncrasy /ìdiəsíŋkrəsi/ は「個人的な性癖」) ‖癖のないさっぱりしたワイン a *mild*, light-bodied wine.

3【折り目, 縮れ】 ▶私の髪, ちょっと癖があるのよね My hair is a little bit *curly*. ‖高校の卒業証書を丸めておいたらそのまま癖がついてしまった When I kept my high school diploma rolled up for some time, it *got a permanent curl* in it.

☛ -くせに, そのくせ, 一癖 (→見出語)

-ぐせ -癖 ▶あいつは酒癖が悪い He *can't handle alcohol*. / He *gets nasty* [*belligerent*] when he drinks. (➤ get nasty は「怒りっぽくなる」).

くせげ 癖毛 ▶私の毛は癖毛だ I have *frizzy* [*curly*/*wavy*] *hair*. (➤ frizzy は「縮れた」, curly は「巻いた」, wavy は「緩やかにウェーブした」).

くせつ 苦節 ▶苦節10年, 彼はついに司法試験に合格した Though it took *ten grueling years*, he finally passed the bar examination.

-くせに ⚠ **ぴったりの英語がないので,「…であるのに」(even though, though, although),「…であるときに」(when) などと解釈して英訳する.**

▶彼女は大学を出ているくせに英語で簡単な挨拶もできない *Even though* she is a college graduate, she doesn't even know enough English to make a short speech. ‖この子は小学生のくせに妙に大人びた口を利く This boy speaks like an adult *although* he is (just) an elementary school student. ‖知りもしないくせに余計な口をたたくな Don't talk *as if you knew everything about it*. ‖知ってるくせに! *As if you didn't know!* ‖ 対話「今度, 旅行しないか」「どうせ金も無いくせに」"How about a trip sometime?" "*As if* you *had* the money!" (➤「お金を持ってるみたいなことを言うじゃない」という意味の仮定法).

くせもの 曲者 ▶城にくせ者が忍び込んだ *A suspicious character* [*person*] sneaked into the castle. ‖あの部長はなかなかくせ者だから気をつけろ You have to be careful with that department head because he can be *sneaky*. ‖彼の優しいそぶりがくせ者よ *Don't be taken in* by his kindness. (➤「だまされるな」の意).

くせん 苦戦する have a tough game ▶M大はきのう対D大戦で苦戦した The M University team *had a tough game* yesterday with the D University team. ‖期末試験は苦戦だった I *had a tough* [*hard*] *time* in the finals. (➤ have a tough [hard] time は「難儀する」).

くそ 糞 shit, crap 《参考》日本語の「くそ」同様, 多くのくだけた表現に用いられるが, タブー的表現と見なされることも多いので注意を要する.

▶くそがしたくなった I've got to *take a shit* [*a dump*]. (➤日本語同様, 品のない言い方).

▶《慣用表現》くそっ, 負けるもんか! *Shit!* I won't give up. ‖くそ食らえ! *Go to hell!* / *Up yours!* ‖英語なんか, くそ食らえだ English *sucks*. (➤ suck は「全く最低である」「お話にならない」の意のインフォーマルな語) ‖このくそったれめ! You *asshole!* / You *shithead!* (➤どちらも, きわめて品のない語). ‖このくそばばあ [じじい]! You *old hag* [*goat*]*!* ‖くそいまいましい! *Dang* (*it*)*!* / *Shit!* ‖きょうも外はくそ暑い It's *too darned* [*damned*] hot outside today, too. ‖石田先生はくそ真面目だ Mr. Ishida is *ridiculously straitlaced*. ‖豊はくそ度胸がある Yutaka is a man of *reckless courage*. / Yutaka's got *guts*, that's for sure. ‖勝負の世界では先輩もくそもない Being a senpai [Seniority] *doesn't mean anything* in the world of competition. ‖くそ力 brute force.

くそみそ 糞味噌 ▶昇のことをそんなにくそみそに言うなよ Don't *run* Noboru *down*. / Don't *trash* Noboru.

くだ 管 a tube(細めの); a pipe(太めの) ▶竹の管で水を引く lead water through a bamboo *pipe* ‖《慣用表現》彼は酔うといつも管を巻く Whenever he gets drunk, he *becomes garrulous*. (➤ garrulous /gǽrələs/ は「多弁な」の意で, 軽蔑的な響きがある).

ぐたい- 具体- 一形 **具体的な** concrete (形のある, 抽象的でない); specific (細かく, そのものずばりの); definite (正確ではっきりした); practical (実際的な) ▶具体案を示してください Let us know your *definite plans*. ‖計画は具体化しつつある The project is now *taking shape*. ‖具体的な数字を挙げる give a *specific* figure ‖もっと具体的に言ってくれますか Will you be more *specific* about that? ‖具体的に行動を起こす take *concrete* action ‖もっと具体的な例を挙げて説明してください Could you please explain, giving some more *concrete* examples? ‖小田先生の話はいつも内容が具体的でわかりやすい Mr. Oda's lectures are always very *practical* [*full of practical examples*] and easy to understand.

ぐたいせい 具体性 concreteness; specifics, details (踏み込んだ詳細) ▶その候補者の演説は具体性に乏しかった The candidate's speech lacked *specifics* [*details*].

くだく 砕く break +目 (力を加えて); shatter +目 (破片が周囲に飛び散るほど粉々に); smash +目 (大きな力で瞬間的に) ▶母は氷を砕いて氷枕に入れた My mother *broke* (*up*) the ice and put it into the ice bag. ‖彼は力いっぱいハンマーを振り下ろし岩を粉々に打ち砕いた He struck the rock with the hammer with all his might and *smashed* it.

▶彼の野望はあえなく**砕かれた** His ambition has been miserably *shattered to bits*. ‖私は問題解決のため**心を砕いた** I *beat* [*racked*] *my brains* for a resolution of the problem.
▶相対性理論をもう少し**砕いて**説明しましょう Let me explain the theory of relativity more *plainly*.

くたくた ▶夏の合宿では**くたくたになった** I *was dog-tired* [*was dead tired*] during the summer training camp. ‖そのランナーはマラソンを走り抜いて**くたくたの様子だった** The runner looked *exhausted* [*worn-out*] after running the marathon.

くだくだ ▶あの人は酔うと決まって**同じことをくだくだ言う** Whenever he gets drunk, he always *says the same old thing over and over*. ／He always *repeats the same thing over and over* when he gets drunk. ‖例によってSさんは**くだくだ言い訳ばかりしている** As usual, Mr. S *is making endless excuses*.

くだくだしい lengthy(長ったらしい) ▶これは万人に知られた傑作です．**くだくだしい**説明は不要でしょう This is a masterpiece everybody knows. It doesn't need a *lengthy* [*long-winded*] explanation.

くだけた 砕けた informal(形式ばらない) ▶**くだけた**言い方 an *informal* expression ‖その短編小説は**くだけた**文体[英語]で書かれている The short story is written in an *informal* style [in *informal* English]. (➤ familiar でもよい) ‖私たちの先生は**くだけた人柄**で人気がある Our teacher is liked for his [her] *friendly and approachable* personality.

くだける 砕ける break (into pieces) ▶ポケットの中でビスケットが**砕けていた** There was a *broken* cookie in my pocket. ‖シャンデリアが天井から落ちてめちゃめちゃに**砕けた** The chandelier *shattered* when it fell from the ceiling. (➤ shatter は「破片を飛び散らせて砕ける」) ‖何事も**当たって砕けろ**だ *Go for broke* [*Go all out*] in everything you do. ／Whatever you do, *give it your best shot*.

ください 下さい

1【…を与えてほしい】▶水を1杯**ください** Could you please *give* me a glass of water? ／*Can* [*May*] *I have* a glass of water (, please)? ‖電話ですぐ返事を**ください** Please call me back as soon as possible [right away ／immediately]. (➤ 副詞はこの順で丁寧度が下がる) ‖少し考える時間を**ください** Please *give* me time to think it over. ‖(店で)この傘を**ください** I'll *take* this umbrella. (➤ 買い物するときは(×)Give me ... とは言わない) ‖コーラを**ください** I'll *have* a cola, *please*.

> **あなたの英語はどう響く?**
> (1)「…が欲しい」「…をください」のつもりで，すぐ I want ... とか Give me ... と言う人がいるが，これらは直接的すぎて非常にぶしつけに響く．「コーヒーをください」なら May I have some coffee? とか I'd like some coffee. などと言うべきである．ただし，ファーストフード店などで注文するときは Two donuts and a (cup of) coffee, please. (ドーナツ2個とコーヒーをください)でよい．
> (2)「…してください」と依頼するときも，may, can, could, would などを用いたほうが丁寧に響く．Please ... は命令文を丁寧に言っただけなので，自分のことで頼むときには用いないほうがよい．

2【…してほしい】 →くれる ▶電話番号を教えて**ください** *May I have* your phone number? ‖あまり夜遅くに電話をしないで**ください** (*Please*) don't call me so late at night. ‖この小切手を現金にして**ください** *I'd like* to have this check cashed. ‖(できたら)手伝って**くださいませんか** *Could you* help me? ／*Could you* give [lend] me a hand? ‖ **対話** 「窓を開けて**ください**」「いいですよ」"*Please* open the window." "O.K. ／Sure."
(➤ このほかに以下のような言い方があるが，最後の例が最も丁寧な表現: Open the window, *please*. ／*Will you please* open the window? ／*Could* [*Can*] *you* open the window, *please*? ／*Would you mind* opening the window?).

くださる 下さる ▶この辞書は原先生が**下さった**ものです This is the dictionary (that) Mr. Hara *gave* me.

くだす 下す 1【言い渡す】▶裁判官は殺人犯に**死刑の判決を下した** The judge *sentenced* the murderer to death. ／The judge *passed* the death sentence on the murderer.
▶将軍は**攻撃命令を下した** The general *ordered* them to charge.
2【自分の意志を決する】▶部長は一度**下した決定**はめったに覆さない Once our general manager *makes a decision*, he rarely changes it.
3【相手を負かす】 beat +㊀ ,down +㊀ (➤ 後者はインフォーマル) ▶うちのチームは初戦で強豪を**下し**，波に乗った Our team went great guns after *beating* an awesome opponent in the first encounter.
4【下方に移す】▶私は朝から**腹を下している** I have *had diarrhea* [*had the runs*] since (this) morning. (➤ 後者はインフォーマルな表現).

くたばる ▶おまえなんか，**くたばっちまえ**! You *go to hell*! ‖あの頑固じじいもとうとう**くたばった**か That stubborn old man finally *kicked the bucket*, eh? (➤ kick the bucket は「死ぬ」の意のくだけた，しかも，おどけた言い方).

くたびれもうけ ▶頑張ったのに**くたびれもうけだった** I worked hard, but *it was all in vain*. ／I *gained nothing* for all my effort.
ことわざ **骨折り損のくたびれもうけ** Great pains, but all in vain. ／A lot of pain, but no gain.

くたびれる 1【疲れる】 get tired ; be exhausted /ɪgzɔ́ːstɪd/ (くたくたに疲れている)
▶私は近頃すぐに**くたびれる** These days I *get tired* easily. ‖長時間歩いて彼女は**ひどくくたびれている**ようだ She looks *dead tired* after that long walk. ‖オーストラリア旅行で**くたびれてしまった** The trip to Australia *exhausted* me. ／I *was exhausted* by my trip to Australia. ‖東京スカイツリーを見上げていたら**首がくたびれた** I'*ve got a stiff neck* from looking up at Tokyo Skytree.
2【使い古されている】▶その刑事のレインコートは**相当にくたびれていた** The detective's raincoat was pretty *worn out*.

くだもの 果物 fruit

語法 fruit は集合的に単数形で用いることが多く，種類を指すときも複数形は少ない．「果物と野菜」は fruit and vegetables となる．
▶**果物**はスーパーで買います We get *fruit* at a supermarket. ‖いろいろな**果物**を食べたほうがよい You should eat various kinds of *fruit*.
‖**果物ナイフ** a fruit [paring] knife ‖**果物屋** a fruit shop.

「果物」のいろいろ **アボカド** avocado ／**アンズ** apricot ／**イチゴ** strawberry ／**イチジク** fig ／**オレンジ**

orange ／**柿**(かき) *kaki*, persimmon ／**キウイ** kiwi (fruit) ／**グレープフルーツ** grapefruit ／**サクランボ** cherry ／**ザクロ** pomegranate ／**スイカ** watermelon ／**西洋ナシ** pear ／**ネーブル** navel orange ／**ネクタリン** nectarine ／**パイナップル** pineapple ／**バナナ** banana ／**パパイヤ** papaya ／**ビワ** loquat ／**ブドウ** grapes ／**プラム** plum ／**プルーン** prune ／**マルメロ** quince ／**マンゴー** mango ／**ミカン** *mikan*, satsuma, mandarin (orange) ／**メロン** melon ／**桃** peach ／**リンゴ** apple ／**レモン** lemon

くだらない 下らない **trashy** (くず同然の); **foolish, stupid** (ばかげた); **worthless** (価値のない) ▶**くだらない**本[小説] a *stupid* book [novel] ‖ そんな**くだらない**ことに金を使うな Don't waste your money on such *foolish* things. ‖ **くだらないことを言わないでよ** *Don't talk nonsense.* ／ *Don't bullshit.* (➤ bullshit は「牛のふん」. 転じて「くだらないこと(を言う)」の意で, 若者がよく使う) ‖ そんな**くだらない** (＝ささいな) ことで悩むな Don't worry about such a *trivial* [an *unimportant*] matter. ‖ あいつは**くだらない男**だ He is *a worthless loser*.

くだり 下り **1【下降】**▶**下りの**エスカレーター the *down* escalator ‖ そこから道は**下りになった** The road *went downhill* from there. ／The road *went* [*sloped*] *down* there. ‖ 対話「このエレベーターは下りですか」「いえ, 上りです」"Is this elevator *going down*?" "No, it's going up."

2【中央から地方へ行くこと】▶**下り**列車 the *down* [*outbound*] train (➤ the down train は《英》に多い言い方で, 《米》では the train for Okayama (岡山行き列車) のように行き先をいう) ‖ **下り線**ホーム the *down* platform 《参考》《米》では track No. 2 (2番線ホーム) のようにホームの番号をいう. ‖ 東名の**下りは**30キロの渋滞だ Traffic is backed up for 30 kilometers on the Tomei Expressway *out of Tokyo*.

くだりざか 下り坂 a **downhill road** [**street** ／ **path**] ▶もう少し行くと急な**下り坂**になる If you go a little further (ahead), you'll come to a steep *downward slope*.

▶《比喩的》最近彼女の人気は**下り坂だ** Her popularity *is declining* these days. ‖ 天気は**下り坂だ** The weather is *going downhill* [*changing for the worse*].

くだる 下る **1【下方へ移動する】** **go down** ▶子供たちは大声で歌を歌いながら山を**下った** The children *went down the hill*, singing loudly. ‖ 山小屋は頂上から少し**下った所**にあった The mountain hut was (located) a little way *down from* the summit.

▶うちの犬はおとといから**おなかが下っている** Our dog has *had diarrhea* since the day before yesterday.

2【流れの先へ進む】▶川岸を400メートルばかり**下ると**木の橋がある If you *go down along* (the bank of) the river for about 400 meters, you will come to a wooden bridge. ‖ 我々は**舟で**阿武隈川を**下った** We *boated down* the Abukuma River.

▶時代が**下る**につれて武士は経済力を失った As time *passed* [*went by*], the samurai lost (their) economic power.

3【決定する】▶そのテロリストに死刑の判決が**下った** The death sentence *was passed* on the terrorist.

4【下回る】▶洪水による死者は100人を**下らなかった** *No less than* one hundred people were killed in the flood. ‖ 工事にかかった費用は10億円を**下らない** Construction costs totaled *more than* a billion yen.

くち 口 **1【人・動物の】** one's **mouth** ▶**口を大きく開ける** open one's *mouth* wide ‖ **口をすぼめる** pucker one's *lips* ‖ ものを食べているときは**口を閉じなさい** Close your *mouth* when you are chewing. ‖ 少女は叱られると**口をとがらせた** The little girl *pouted* when she was scolded. (➤ pout は子供や女性が不満などのしぐさとして「口をとがらす」の意) ‖ 犬が**口にボールをくわえている** The dog has a ball in its *mouth*. ‖ 木村さんは**口にパイプをくわえて立っていた** Mr. Kimura was standing (*with a*) *pipe in his mouth*. ‖ 子供たちは**口をぽかんと開けて**背の高いインド人を見上げていた The children stared at the tall Indian (man) *with their mouths open*. ‖ 全くあいつの非常識には**開いた口が塞がらないね** I *am dumbfounded* at his lack of common sense.

▶**口の中が渇く** My *mouth* is dry. ‖ **口の中が腫れている** *The inside of my mouth* is swollen. (➤ My mouth is swollen. とすると「口元[口の辺り]が腫れ上がっている」の意になる).

2【味覚】▶このお酒, **お口に合いますかしら** Does this sake *suit your palate*? ‖ **お口に合えばよろしいのですが** *I hope you like this dish.* ‖ その子牛の肉は私の**口に合わなかった** I *didn't care for* the veal. (➤ care for は「気に入る, 好む」) ／The veal *didn't suit my taste buds*. ‖ 彼女は**口が肥えている** She *has a discerning* [*sophisticated*] *palate*. (➤ ともに「味覚が鋭敏だ」の意).

3【物の口】 a **mouth**; a **spout** /spaʊt/ (やかんやポットの) ▶袋の**口** the *mouth* of a bag ‖ **口の広い**瓶 a *wide-mouthed* jar [bottle] ‖ この瓶の**口**は小さすぎる *The mouth* of the bottle is too small. ‖ 洞窟が**ぱっくりと口を開けていた** We came unexpectedly upon a cavern's *gaping mouth*. (➤ gape は「口を大きく開ける」).

4【受け入れ場所】▶いい仕事の**口**を見つける find a good *job* ‖ 非常勤講師の**口**を探していたら, 地方の私大に適当な**口**があった When I was looking for *a job* [*position*] as a part-time lecturer, I found a suitable *one* [*one* that fit the bill] in a private university in the country.

5【話すこと, ことば】▶その情報は**口から口へと**伝えられた The information spread *by word of mouth* [*from mouth to mouth*]. (→口コミ) ‖ **口の利き方に気をつけなさい** Be careful what you say [how you speak]. ／Keep a civil tongue in your head. (➤ 後者は自分よりも年下の者の口の利き方が悪い場合の決まり文句) ‖ そのときの恐ろしさは到底**口では言えません** I *could never express in words* how frightened I was then. ‖ おまえは**口ばかり**だ You're *all talk*! (➤「(口ばかりで)何もしない」と言うのなら and no action をつける) ‖ **親の口から言うのも何ですけど**, うちの子は優しいんですよ *Though I say so myself*, my son is a very kind boy. (➤「(親としての)自分がそう言っているだけだが」の意) ‖ 洋介の言うことなんて, どうせ**口から出任せ**だろ? Yosuke said so? But he just *says whatever comes into his head*. ‖ **世間の口はうるさいものだ** People will talk. (➤「人はしゃべるものだ」の意).

ことわざ **口は禍**(わざわい)**の門**(かど) Out of the mouth comes evil. ／(Careless) words can cause problems [trouble].

6【慣用表現】

口がうまい ▶あいつは**口がうまい**から気をつけろ He's *a*

smooth [*fast*] *talker*, so be careful. (● 前半を He can talk people into anything. と訳すこともできるが, 訳例に含まれるマイナスイメージは薄れる).
口がおごる ▶彼女は口がおごっている She*'s used to fine cuisine*. (➤「美食に慣れている」) ／ She*'s a gourmet*. **口が重い** ▶日本人は概して口が重い The Japanese *are*, on the whole, *reticent*.
口が掛かる ▶その高校野球の選手にいくつかのプロ球団から口が掛かった Several professional baseball teams *asked* that high school player to *join* them. ‖ クリスマスパーティーに来ないかと3人から口が掛かっている I *have received invitations* to three Christmas parties. **口が堅い** ▶うちの秘書は口が堅い My secretary *is tight-lipped*. ／My secretary *can keep a secret*. **口が軽い** ▶彼は口が軽くて秘密が守れない He *is a blabbermouth* and can't keep a secret.
口が裂けても ▶昔の恋人のことなど夫には口が裂けても言えない I would never tell my husband about my old boyfriends *no matter what*. (➤ no matter what は「何があっても」「絶対に」). **口が過ぎる** ▶ごめんなさい. ちょっと口が過ぎたわ I'm sorry. *I went* (*a bit*) *too far* when I said that. (➤ go too far は「度が過ぎる」). **口から先に生まれる** ▶母は口から先に生まれたような人だ (It seems like) my mother *was born with the gift of gab*. (➤ the gift of gab は「おしゃべりの才」).
口が悪い ▶山田さんは口は悪いが気持ちはいい人だ Mr. Yamada *has a sharp tongue*, but he is kind at heart. (● 訳例は「口は悪い」を「辛辣なことを言う」と考えて has a sharp tongue (is sharp-tongued でもよい)を当てているが, それを「皮肉を言う」と考えれば is sarcastic と訳せるし,「ことばづかいが汚い」と考えれば is foul-mouthed (has a foul mouth でもよい)とも訳せる. 文の後半の意味はずれるが「口うるさいが悪い人ではない」の意の慣用句を使って Mr. Yamada's bark is worse than his bite. と訳すことも可能).
口にする ▶もう2日間何も口にして(＝食べて)いない I have *eaten* nothing for two days. ‖ 彼は思ったことは何でも口にする(＝しゃべる) He *speaks* his mind. ‖ 彼女の家庭のことを口にしたのはぼくの不注意だった It was thoughtless of me to *mention* her family.
口の減らない ▶何て口の減らないやつだ He *is never at a loss for words*. (➤「ことばに詰まることがない」の意) ‖ おまえは口の減らない男［女］だね You *have a comeback for everything*. (➤「何に対しても言い返すね」の意).
口を利く ▶どうしたの？ もう1時間も口を利かない(＝しゃべらない)じゃないの What's the matter? You haven't *said a word* for the past hour.
‖ 私たちはけんかをして何日も口を利かなかった We had an argument and didn't *talk* [*speak*] to each other for days. ‖ 私たちはショックで口を利くこともできなかった The shock *left* us *speechless*. ‖ 赤ん坊が口を利きだした The baby is learning to *talk*. ‖ あの子は大人のような口を利く That child *sounds* [*talks*] *like an adult*. ‖ 就職なら俺が口を利いて(＝口添えして)やるよ I will *put in a good word* for you when you apply for a job. ‖ 彼とはときどき口を利く程度で, そんなによくは知らないんだ He and I *chat sometimes*, but we don't know that much about each other. (➤ He and I know each other casually. ともいう).
口を切る ▶長い沈黙のあとまず口を切ったのは社長だった The president was *the first to speak up* after a long silence. **口を酸っぱくして** ▶この子ったら, 私がいくら口を酸っぱくして言っても勉強しないんです I've *told* him *a thousand times*, but he just won't study (hard enough). **口を滑らす** ▶彼女は口を滑らして全部しゃべってしまった She *blurted out* everything. **口をそろえる** ▶家族や親類は口をそろえて早く結婚しろと言う All my family and relatives are *unanimous* (*in saying*) that I should get married soon. (➤ unanimous /junǽnɪməs/ は「(意見が)全員一致の」).
口を出す ▶お母さん, 私のことに口を出さないで. お母さんには関係ないでしょ！Mom, *don't butt in* ! This is not of your business ! **口をつぐむ** ▶総理は記者の質問に痛いところをつかれて口をつぐんだ The Prime Minister *clammed up* when a reporter's question hit a sore point. (➤ clam up はそれまで話をしていた人が急に貝のように口を閉ざすことをいう). **口を慎む** ▶少しは口を慎みなさい Watch your language. ／*Be* a little more *careful of your language*. **口をとがらす** ▶何を口をとがらしているんだい Why *are* you *pouting* ?
口を濁す ▶計画を実行に移すかどうかについては大臣は口を濁した The Minister *did not express himself clearly* about whether or not he would implement the plan. **口を挟む** ▶私たちの問題に口を挟まないでくれ Don't *interfere with* our problem. ／Don't *poke your nose into* our problem. ‖ ちょっと口を挟んでいいですか Can I just *come in* here ? **口を割る** ▶男は誰に頼まれてやったか, 口を割らなかった The man didn't *come clean about* who (had) asked him to do it. (➤ come clean は「白状する」の意のインフォーマルな言い方).

ぐち 愚痴 a **grumble**(不平不満) ; (a) **complaint**(不公正などに対する抗議) **一動 愚痴を言う grumble, complain**
▶きみの**愚痴**は聞き飽きたよ I'm sick and tired of your *grumbling*. ‖ **愚痴っぽい人**は嫌われる Nobody likes *a complainer* [*grumbler*]. ‖ 妻は**愚痴ひとつこぼさず**大所帯を切り盛りしてくれている My wife manages our large family skillfully *without ever complaining* (about the hard work).

-ぐち -口 ▶働き口を探す look for *a job*.
▶横浜駅を降りたら**東口**から駅を出てください When you get off at Yokohama, leave the station through *the east exit*.

くちあたり 口当たり ▶このウイスキーは**口当たりがいい** This whisky *is very smooth*.

くちうつし 口移し ▶ツバメが**口移し**でひな鳥に餌をやっていた A mother swallow was feeding her young, *beak to beak*. (➤ beak は「くちばし」) ‖ 彼女はその子守歌を祖母から**口移し**で教えられた She learned the lullaby *by ear* from her grandmother.

くちうら 口裏 ▶**口裏を合わせて**おこう Let's *make sure our versions of the story agree* [*are consistent*]. (● 文末に to avoid trouble(面倒なことにならないように)をつけ加えてもよい).

くちうるさい 口うるさい ▶**口うるさい**老女 a *nagging* old lady ‖ 母親は娘に身だしなみをきちんとするよう**口うるさく注意した** The mother *persistently nagged at* her daughter to take (better) care of her (personal) appearance.

くちえ 口絵 a **frontispiece** ▶本の**口絵** *a frontispiece* to a book.

くちかず 口数 ▶うちの母は**口数が少ない** My mother *doesn't talk* [*say* ／ *speak*] *much*. ／Mother *says* *very little*. ‖ 口数が多いよ！ Don't talk so much !

くちがね 口金 a **clasp** (かばんなどの) ▶ハンドバッグの口金が壊れた The *clasp* on my handbag is broken.

くちきき 口利き ▶おじの口利きで就職できた I got the job through a *recommendation* from my uncle. ／I got the job because my uncle *put in a word for* me.

くちぎたない 口汚い ▶友だちのことを口汚く言うのは聞き苦しい It is awful to hear someone *say bad things about* their friends. ‖ 彼は安川君を口汚く罵った He *called* Yasukawa *bad names*. (➤ call ... bad names は「…に悪態をつく」).

くちく 駆逐する **drive away, drive out** ▶ ことわざ 悪貨は良貨を駆逐する Bad money drives out good. ‖**駆逐艦** a destroyer.

くちぐせ 口癖 ▶私たちの担任の先生は「頑張れ」が口癖だ Our homeroom teacher's *favorite phrase* is "Go for it !" (➤ favorite phrase は「好きなことば」) ‖ おふくろは口癖のように「勉強しなさい」と言う My mother *is always saying* to me, "Study hard."

くちぐちに 口々に ▶生徒たちは口々に先生の名を呼び, 手を振って別れを惜しんだ *All* the schoolchildren called their teacher's name and reluctantly waved him good-bye.

くちぐるま 口車 ▶あの男の口車に乗るなよ Don't *fall for* that guy's *sweet* [*smooth*] *talk*. (➤ fall for は「(話などに) 引っ掛けられる」の意のインフォーマルな言い方).

くちげんか 口喧嘩 a **quarrel**, a **fight**, (主に《英》) a **row** /raʊ/ (➤ fight には「殴り合いのけんか」の意もある) ; an **argument** (自説を主張し合う) ▶私はそのことで三郎さんと口げんかをした I *had an argument* [*words*] *with* Saburo over the matter. ‖ 人前で口げんかをするのはおよしなさい Don't *argue* [*quarrel*] in public. ‖ あの夫婦はしょっちゅうお金のことで口げんかをしている That couple *is* always *fighting* over money.

くちごたえ 口答え **back talk, backchat** (➤《米》では前者, 《英》では後者が好まれる) 一動 **口答えする** **talk back** ▶私に口答えするな Don't *talk back to* me. ‖ 口答えしないで, 宿題をしなさい！ None of your *back talk* [*backchat*], do your homework !

くちコミ 口コミ ▶口コミによる宣伝 *word-of-mouth* [*mouth-to-mouth*] advertising ‖ その情報は口コミで広がった The information spread *by word of mouth* [*from mouth to mouth*]. ‖ その商品は口コミ宣伝で売れた The product sold *through word-of-mouth advertising*. ‖ あの店のラーメンがおいしいという評判がいつのまにか口コミで広がった Before we knew it, news had gotten out *through the grapevine* about how good the ramen was at that shop. (➤ through the grapevine は「うわさで」).

> **危ないカタカナ語✹ 口コミ**
> マスコミをもじって「口コミ」というが, mouth communication では通じない. 「口伝え」の意味だから by word of mouth とか from mouth to mouth のような熟語を用いる.

くちごもる 口籠もる **mumble** (＋目) ▶両親が離婚した和子は先生に家族のことを尋ねられて口籠もってしまった Kazuko, whose parents were divorced, *mumbled* a vague reply to the teacher's question about her family. ‖ 彼は口籠もりながらわびを言った He *mumbled* his apologies.

くちさがない 口さがない **gossipy** ▶会社の同僚たちは口さがない The people I work with *are gossipy*. ‖ 世間は口さがない Tongues will *wag*. (➤ wag は「うわさ話 [おしゃべり] をするために盛んに動く」).

くちさき 口先 ▶彼女は口先だけだ She *never means what she says*. (➤「口で言っていることと本心は別だ」の意) ‖ その独裁者は口先では民主主義を唱えている The dictator *pays lip service to* democracy. (➤ lip service は「口先だけの支持または約束」) ‖ 口先まで出かかっているんだけどね It's *on the tip of my tongue*.

くちさびしい 口寂しい ▶口寂しいときには彼はよくあめ玉をしゃぶる *When he has* [*gets*] *a craving to put something in his mouth*, he sucks on (a piece of) candy.

くちずさむ 口ずさむ ▶彼女は『赤いスイートピー』を口ずさみながら料理をしていた She was cooking while *singing* "Red Sweet Peas" *to herself*.

くちぞえ 口添え ▶久保田教授の口添えで就職できた I was able to get a job because Professor Kubota *put in a* (*kind*) *word for me*. (●「口添え」はあくまでも「口頭で推薦すること」なので, 口頭・書面いずれの推薦も指す recommendation をここで用いるのは不適当) ‖ 上司の口添えで2人の縁談がまとまった Their engagement has been made through the *good offices* of their boss. (➤ good offices は「尽力, 好意」の堅い言い方).

くちだし 口出し ▶私のことに口出ししないでよ. もう17歳よ Please *don't bother me* [Please *leave me alone*] ; I'm already seventeen. (➤ bother は「邪魔する」) ‖ 人のことに口出しするのはやめてくれ Keep your nose out of my business. ‖ 俺たちのけんかに口出しするな Don't *stick your nose in* our fight. ‖ 大国はしばしば小国の内政に口出しをする Major powers often *meddle in* the internal affairs of small ones. (➤ meddle in は「おせっかいを焼く」).

くちづけ 口付け a **kiss** 一動 **口づけする** **kiss** ▶2人は熱い口づけをした They *kissed* passionately. →キス.

くちづたえ 口伝え ▶その民話は口伝えで広がった The folk tale spread *from mouth to mouth*. ‖ わが国には何世紀にもわたって口伝えに伝えられてきたおもしろい話がたくさんあります In our country, we have a lot of interesting stories which have *been handed down by word of mouth* over the centuries. →口コミ.

ぐちっぽい 愚痴っぽい **grumpy, grouchy** (➤後者がよりインフォーマルな語) ▶年を取ると愚痴っぽくなる We *tend to get grumpy* as we get old.

くちどめ 口止め ▶私はその件については口止めされている I *was told to keep quiet* about it. ／I *am forbidden to talk* about it. ‖ 彼はその女性に口止め料として10万円支払った He paid the woman 100,000 yen *in hush money* [*to buy her silence*].

くちなおし 口直し ▶これは口直しにちょうどいい It's good for *refreshing* [*freshening*] *the mouth*. ‖ 私は薬を飲んだあと, 口直しにコーヒーを飲んだ After taking the medicine, I drank coffee to *kill* [*get rid of*] *the bitter aftertaste*. ‖ 肉料理が済んだあと, 給仕はお口直しにライムシャーベットを運んできた After the meat course, the server brought us lime sherbet to *cleanse* [*clear* ／*refresh*] *the palate*. (➤ cleanse [clear ／refresh] the palate は「コース料理の途中でさっぱりしたものを食べて口を爽やかにし, 次の料理を新たな気持ちで味わえるようにする」を表す).

くちなし 《植物》 a **gardenia** /gɑːˈdíːnjə/.

くちパク 口パク **lip-sync(h)ing, lip synchronization** ▶

審査員たちは彼女が口パクをしていると思っていた The judges suspected that she *was lip-synching*.

くちばし 嘴・喙 a **bill**(アヒルのように平たいもの) ; a **beak**(特に猛きん類の) ▶オオハシはくちばしが大きい Toucans have big *bills* [*beaks*].

▶《慣用表現》あいつはまだくちばしの黄色い男だよ He's still too *wet behind the ears*. (➤ wet behind the ears は「未熟な」の意のインフォーマルな表現 ; 新生児の耳の後ろがなかなか乾かないところから出た表現) ‖ 人のことにくちばしを入れるのはやめてくれ Please don't *stick your nose into* my affairs. / *Mind your own business*. (→口出し).

くちばしる 口走る ▶彼女はその男性教授がセクハラをしたとうっかり口走ってしまった She accidentally *let out* that the male professor had sexually harassed a woman.

くちはっちょうてはっちょう 口八丁手八丁 ▶ 彼は口八丁手八丁だ He *is both eloquent and efficient*. / He *is both a good talker and a hard worker*.

くちはてる 朽ち果てる ▶朽ち果てた寺 a *dilapidated* [*run-down*] temple ‖ 朽ち果てた木の橋 a wooden bridge *that had rotted away* ‖ その家はすっかり朽ち果てている That house *has fallen into disrepair*.

▶こんな田舎で朽ち果てる(＝世に知られないままで死ぬ)のは嫌だ I don't want to *die in obscurity* in the country like this.

くちはばったい 口幅ったい ▶口はばったいことを言うようですが, 私ならもっと早くできますよ *It may sound presumptuous*, but I could do it much faster. (➤「生意気に聞こえるかもしれないが」の意).

くちび 口火 a **pilot light** [**burner**] ▶湯沸かし器の口火をつけた I turned on the *pilot burner* of the boiler. ‖《慣用表現》私が最初の発言をして会議の口火を切った I made the first remark that *started off* [*kicked off*] the meeting. / I made the first remark that *triggered discussion* [*got the ball rolling*] at the meeting. (➤ get the ball rolling は「一番手となって議論や活動を始める」).

くちひげ 口髭 a **mustache** /mʌ́stæʃ/, 《英》 a **moustache** /məstɑ́ːʃ/ ▶彼は口ひげをつけて変装した He disguised himself with *a mustache*. ‖ 彼は立派な口ひげを生やしている He has a splendid *mustache*.

くちびる 唇 a **lip**(➤ 上下あるので通例複数形で用いる) ▶上[下]唇 the *upper* [*lower*] *lip* ‖ 彼女は唇が薄い[厚い] She has thin [thick / full] *lips*. ‖ 唇が荒れている My *lips* are chapped.

▶《慣用表現》100メートル競走で2着になって彼女は悔しそうに唇をかんだ She *bit her lip* in dismay at coming in second in the 100-meter race. (➤ bit は bite の過去形) ‖ 坊やは不満そうに唇をとがらせた The little boy *pouted* discontentedly. (➤ pout は子供っぽい動作).

くちふうじ 口封じ ▶口封じに弟に少し金を渡した I gave my kid brother some money *to silence* him [*to keep* him *quiet*].

くちぶえ 口笛 a **whistle** /hwísəl/ ▶曲を口笛で吹く *whistle* a tune ‖ 口笛を吹いて犬を呼ぶ *whistle* for one's [a] dog(➤「口笛を吹いて犬を呼び戻す」なら whistle one's dog back) ‖ 彼は口笛を吹くのが好きだ He likes to *whistle*.

くちぶり 口振り ▶彼女はそのことについて何もかも知っているような口ぶりだ She *talks as if* she knew everything about it. (➤ as if 節中の動詞は過去形) ‖ 北野さんは私を手伝ってくれそうな口ぶりだった Miss Kitano *hinted that* she would help me. (➤ hint は「ほのめかす」) ‖ あの口ぶりでは彼は手紙を見たらしい *Judging from his words* [*his way of talking*], he seems to have read the letter.

くちべた 口下手 ▶口下手な人 *a poor speaker* ‖ 私は口下手だからよく人に誤解される I'*m bad at expressing myself*, so I'm often misunderstood. ‖ 口下手だから人前で話すのは苦手です I don't like speaking in public since I'm such *a poor speaker*.

くちべに 口紅 (a) **lipstick**(➤ Ⓤ 扱いがふつう) ▶口紅をつけている wear *lipstick* ‖ 口紅を拭き取る wipe off *lipstick* ‖ パールのかかった口紅 (a) frosted *lipstick* ‖ 彼女は薄く[濃く]口紅をつけた She put on a little [a lot of] *lipstick*. / She applied *lipstick* lightly [heavily]. ‖ 彼女はまだ口紅をつける年ではない She is not old enough to *use lipstick*.

くちべらし 口減らし ▶口減らしに末子を養子に出す put one's youngest child up for adoption *to reduce the number of mouths to feed*.

くちほど 口程 ▶彼のピアノは口程のことはない His piano playing is*n't as good as he says* [*claims*] *it is*. ‖ 彼は口程にもない小心者だ He *talks big*, *but* he's just a coward. (➤ talk big は「大口を叩く」).

くちまね 口真似 ▶彼は総理大臣の口まねがうまい He is good at *imitating* the prime minister's *way of speaking*. / He can *mimic* the Prime Minister well. (➤ mimic はしゃべり方だけでなく, 表情やジェスチャーのまねを含む).

くちもと 口元 ▶その少女は口元が愛らしかった The girl had a charming *mouth*. ‖ 彼女は口元に微笑を浮かべて私たちを迎えてくれた She welcomed us with a smile on her *lips*.

くちやかましい 口やかましい ▶口やかましい女房 a *nagging* wife ‖ 母は礼儀作法をきちんと守りなさいと口やかましく言う My mother *nags* me [*tells* me *repeatedly*] to mind my manners.

くちやくそく 口約束 an **oral** [**a verbal**] **promise** ▶口約束は当てにならない You can't rely on *an oral* [*a verbal*] *promise* alone.

くちゃくちゃ ▶クチャクチャガムをかまないでよ Don't chew your gum so *loud(ly)*.

ぐちゃぐちゃ ▶息子が整理カードで遊んで順番をぐちゃぐちゃにした My son played with my filing cards and *messed up* [*screwed up*] the order. ‖ 道は雨でぐちゃぐちゃだ The road *is all mud(dy)*.

1**くちょう 口調** a **tone** ▶彼は激しい[丁寧な / とがめるような]口調で話した He spoke in a sharp [a polite / an accusing] *tone*. ‖ このコマーシャルの文句は口調がいい[悪い] The words for this commercial are *rhythmical* [*not rhythmical*].

2**くちょう 区長** **the head** [**chief**] **of a ward** ; **the mayor of a ward**(東京都の区の).

ぐちょく 愚直 ▶おじは愚直とも言えるような人だ My uncle is *too honest for his own good*. (➤「正直すぎて損をしている」の意).

くちよごし 口汚し ▶ほんのお口汚しですが, どうぞお召し上がりください *It's not much*, but please do have some.

くちる 朽ちる **rot**, **decay** (➤ 後者がより堅い語) ▶朽ちた木 a *rotten* [*decayed*] tree ‖ あの橋は朽ちかかっている The bridge is *on the verge of collapse*.

▶朽ちることのない名声 *lasting* fame.

ぐちる 愚痴る **gripe**《about》 ▶彼は俺の顔を見ると仕事のことを愚痴り始める Whenever he sees me, he starts *griping about* his job.

くつ 靴 **shoes**(➤ 片方は a shoe で, 1 足は a pair of shoes) ; **sneakers**(スニーカー) ▶**靴**を履く put on one's *shoes* ‖ ここで**靴**をお脱ぎください Please take off your *shoes* here. ‖ あの女優は高価な**靴**を100足も持っている That actress has 100 pairs of expensive *shoes*. ‖ 新しい**靴**を履き慣らさないといけない I need to break in my new *shoes*. ‖ 犬の散歩には履き心地のよい**靴**を履く I wear comfortable *shoes* when I walk our dog. ‖ この**靴**はとても履き心地がよい *These shoes* are [*This pair of shoes* is] comfortable. (➤ this shoes とはしない. また, are, is はそれぞれ feel, feels としてもよい) ‖ この運動**靴**はかかとが減っている The heels of these *sneakers* are worn down.

✉ **日本人は家の中では靴を履きません** The Japanese don't *wear shoes* in their homes.

‖**靴墨** shoe polish ‖**靴ひも** a shoestring, a shoelace ‖**靴べら** a shoehorn ‖**靴磨き** a shoeshine man [woman], a shoeblack ‖**靴屋** a shoe store.

くつう 苦痛 (a) **pain** ; **agony** /ǽgəni/ (ひどい苦痛) ▶ そのがん患者は**苦痛**を訴えた The cancer patient complained of (his／her) *pain*. ‖ この務めは私には**苦痛**だ This duty *is painful* for me. ‖ 小沢先生と話すのは**苦痛**だ Talking to Mr. Ozawa *is a pain*. ‖ 最近では満員電車での通勤も**苦痛**に感じなくなりました These days I *no longer mind* commuting in crowded trains. ／ Commuting in crowded trains *no longer bothers* me.

くつがえす 覆す **overturn** +⊞ (定説などを) ; **overrule** +⊞, **reverse** +⊞ (判決・決定などを ; 前者には「権力者が」という含みがあることが多い) ▶彼らの新しい発見は定説を**覆した** Their new discovery *overturned* the established theory. ‖ 高等裁判所は下級審判決を**覆した** The high court *overruled* the lower court's [district court's] decision. ‖ 決定を**覆す** *overrule* [*reverse*] a decision ‖ 議会は大統領の拒否権(行使)を**覆した** Congress *overrode* the president's veto.

くつがえる 覆る ▶現政権が**覆る**のも時間の問題だ It's only a matter of time before the government *is overthrown*. ／The government will *be overthrown* before long. ‖ 判決が**覆る**ことは間違いない It is certain that the judgment will *be reversed*.

クッキー **1**【菓子】a **cookie**, a **cooky** ; 《英》a **biscuit** ▶オーブンで**クッキー**を焼く bake some *cookies* in the oven.

2【コンピュータ】a **cookie**.

くっきょうな 屈強な **sturdy** ; **burly** (太って強い) ; **strapping**(背が高くて強い) ▶**屈強な**若者 a *sturdy* young man.

くっきり ▶きょうは富士山が**くっきり**と見える Mt. Fuji can be *clearly* seen today. ‖ 今度の先生, 目鼻だちの**くっきり**したすてきな男性よ Our new teacher is a nice *clean-cut* guy.

クッキング **cooking** ‖**クッキングスクール** a cookery [cooking] school.

ぐつぐつ ▶塩とこしょうで味付けして 2 時間ほど**ぐつぐつ**煮込めば出来上がりです Season to taste with salt and pepper, *simmer* for two hours, and then it's done. (➤ season to taste は「好みに応じて味付けする」).

くっさく 掘削 **excavation** 一⊞ **掘削する** **excavate** +⊞ ▶トンネルを**掘削する** *excavate* a tunnel.

くっし 屈指 ⚠「屈指の」は「指で数えられるほど数少ない優れた」の意なので「one of the ＋形容詞の最上級」で表現されることが多い.

▶日産は世界**屈指**の自動車会社だ Nissan is *one of the largest* automakers *in the world*. ‖ 広中博士は世界でも**屈指**の数学者だ Dr. Hironaka is *one of the greatest* mathematicians *in the world*. ‖ 川口君は高校球界**屈指**の好投手だ Kawaguchi is *one of the best* pitchers *among high-school baseball players*.

くつした 靴下 **socks**(短い), **stockings**(長い) (➤ 両語とも特に片方を指すとき以外は複数形で用いる) ▶お父さんはよく**靴下**を裏返しに履く Dad often puts on his *socks* inside out.

くつじょく 屈辱 (a) **humiliation** ; (a) **disgrace**(不名誉) ▶吉村君にマラソンで負けたのは**屈辱**だった It was *a humiliation* to lose to Yoshimura in the marathon. ‖ こんな**屈辱**感を味わったのは初めてだ I have never *felt* so *humiliated* [*disgraced*] (in my life). ‖ こんな**屈辱**的な待遇には我慢できない I can't bear this *humiliating* treatment. ‖ 自分の体が思い通りに動かなくなるという**屈辱**は祖父にとっては耐えがたいことだった The *humiliation* of losing control of his body was hard for my granddad to bear.

ぐっしょり ▶傘を持っていかなかったので頭のてっぺんから足のつま先まで**ぐっしょり**ぬれてしまった I went out without an umbrella, and came home *dripping wet* from head to toe.

クッション a **cushion** ; a (**throw**) **pillow** ▶**クッション**のついた座席 a *cushioned* seat ‖ この椅子は**クッション**がいい This chair *is well-padded*. ／This chair *is comfortable to sit in* [*sit on*].

> **危ないカタカナ語✸ クッション**
> **1** ソファーなどの上に置く装飾用のクッションは cushion でもよいが, 枕の形をしたものは throw pillow とか, 単に pillow ともいう.
> **2** 日本語では運動靴などが弾力があることを「クッションがいい」というが, これは「詰め物」のことであるから cushion でなく pad を用いる. ＣＤなどを入れて送る「クッション封筒」は padded bag または Jiffy bag という.

くっしん 屈伸 ▶スキーをする前によく膝の**屈伸**運動をしなさい Practice *bending exercise* for your knees before skiing. ／You should do some knee bends [knee *bend exercises*] before you ski.

グッズ **goods**.

ぐっすり ▶赤ん坊は**ぐっすり**眠っている The baby is *sound* [*fast*] *asleep*. ‖ ゆうべは**ぐっすり**眠れましたか Did you *get* [*have*] *a good night's sleep*? ／Did you *sleep well* last night?

くっする 屈する **yield** 《to》(暴力などに屈服する) ; **give in** 《to》(負ける) ▶彼は暴力に**屈する**ような男ではない He is not a man who *yields to* violence. ‖ 彼はいじめに**屈しなかった** He *was not defeated* by bullying. ‖ 市長は市民代表の要求に**屈した** The mayor *gave in to* the demand (s) put forth by the citizens' representative(s).

くつずれ 靴擦れ a **blister**(水膨れ) ▶靴がきつくて**靴擦れ**ができた These shoes are too tight and have given me *blisters*. ‖ **靴擦れ**がして痛い I've got a sore place (on my foot) where the shoe rubs.

くっせつ 屈折 **refraction** ▶光線は水の中を通ると**屈折する** Light *is refracted* when it passes through water. ‖ 彼は複雑な家庭環境の中で育ったため, 屈折した性格になった The complications of his childhood home environment *warped* [*distorted*, *twisted*] his personality. (➤ warp は「ゆがめる」).

くったく 屈託 ▶娘は何の屈託もない(＝心配事のない)寝顔をしていた In her sleep, my daughter looked completely *free from worry* [*carefree*].

ぐったり ▶彼は疲れてぐったりしていた He was *dead tired* [*exhausted*]. ／He was *tired out*. ‖ 子供たちは皆猛暑の中でぐったりしていた All the children were feeling *weak and draggy* in the severe heat. (➤ draggy は「活気がない」).

くっつく stick 《to》(貼りつく) ; **cling** 《to》(まといつく) ▶ぬれたシャツが肌にくっついて気持ちが悪い I feel uncomfortable with my wet shirt *sticking to* my body. ‖ 値札シールがぴったりくっついていて剝がせない The price sticker *is stuck on* so firmly that I can't peel it off. ‖ のりが指にべっとりくっついた Glue *clung to* my fingers. (➤ clung は cling の過去形) ／My fingers were covered with glue.

▶東京の下町では家の軒と軒がくっつきそうに並んで立っている In the old downtown district of Tokyo, the houses stand side by side so close that their eaves *look* like they're *about to join together*. ‖ きみたち 2 人が仲よくくっついて公園を歩いているのを見たぜ I saw the two of you walking *side by side* [*arm in arm*] in the park. (➤ side by side は「並んで」, arm in arm は「腕を組んで」) ‖ 私が図書館へ行くときはいつも妹がくっついて来る Whenever I go to the library, my sister *tags along*. ‖ 彼女は先頭の走者にぴったりとくっついていった She *stayed close on the heels of* the front runner.

くっつける stick (together) ▶木片を接着剤でくっつける *stick* pieces of wood *together* with glue ‖ 椅子を 2 つくっつければ 3 人座れる If you *put* two chairs *together*, there will be room (enough) for three to sit. ‖ 冷蔵庫をもう少し壁にくっつけて(＝近づけて)よ *Put* [*Place*] the refrigerator *closer to* the wall.

くってかかる 食って掛かる turn [**round**] **on** ; **lash out** 《at》(激しく非難する) ▶ストライクの判定を不服とした選手は審判に食って掛かった Disgruntled by the call of "strike," the player *turned on* [*challenged*] the umpire. (➤ challenge は「異議を申し立てる」) ‖ その子は母親に食って掛かった The boy *lashed out at* his mother.

ぐっと 1【一気に】▶彼は冷えたビールをグラスに 1 杯ぐっと飲んだ He gulped down a glass of cold beer *in* [*at*] *one gulp*.

▶このひもをぐっと(＝力いっぱい)引いてください Please pull on the rope *as hard as you can*.

2【一段と】▶そちらの品よりこちらのほうがぐっといいですね This article is *much* [*far*] better than that one.

3【「ぐっとくる」の形で】▶娘に「お父さん長生きしてね」と言われて, 私はぐっときた When my daughter said to me "Daddy, please live a long time," it really *touched* [*moved*] me. (➤ touch, move はここでは「気持ちを揺さぶる, 感激させる」の意 ; 「泣きそうになった」なら I almost cried. としてもよい).

グッピー 《魚》a **guppy** /gʌ́pi/.

くっぷく 屈服する yield 《to》(脅し・権力などに一時的に屈する) ▶そんな脅しなんかに屈服するものか We are not about to *yield to* such a threat.

くつろぐ 寛ぐ relax, make oneself comfortable [**at home**] ; **feel at ease** (のんびりする) ; **unwind** /ʌ̀nwáɪnd/ (緊張から解放されて)

▶彼と一緒だとくつろげない I can't *relax* with him. ‖ 《客に向かって》どうぞおくつろぎください *Please make yourself comfortable* [*at home*]. 《参考》英語圏では客をくつろがせるために Our [My] house is your house. と言うこともある. ‖ アメリカ人の家にホームステイしたときはくつろぐことができなかった I couldn't *feel at ease* when I stayed with an American family.

くつわ a **bit**.

ぐでんぐでん ▶彼はぐでんぐでんに酔っ払ってホームのベンチで寝てしまった He was *dead drunk* and fell asleep on the platform bench.

くどい 1【話などが】▶この文章は表現がくどい This writing is too *wordy*. (➤「冗漫な」の意) ‖ おまえは少しくどいぞ! You're *getting on my nerves*. (➤「だんだん私の神経に障ってきている」の意) ‖ くどいようですが, 交通費は出してもらえるんですね *I don't mean to harp on the subject, but* you cover the transportation cost, right? (➤ harp on は「繰り返して言う」; いらだって言う場合は I hate to nag, but ... のような言い方をする).

2【色・味などが】▶このブラウスは色がくどすぎて好きじゃない I don't like this blouse because the color is *too intense*. ‖ この料理はくどい This food *is seasoned too strongly*. (➤ seasoned は「味付けされた」) ／This food is *too spicy*. (➤ spicy は「香辛料が効いた」).

くとう 苦闘 a **struggle** 一動 **苦闘する struggle** ▶生活のために苦闘する *struggle* for existence ‖ 苦闘の末, 彼は栄光を得た He won glory after (great) *struggle*. ‖ 入植者たちの生活は長い苦闘の連続だった The settlers' lives were a long series of *hard struggles*.

くどう 駆動 (a) **drive** ▶四輪駆動の車 a car with *four-wheel drive*.

ぐどうしゃ 求道者 a **truth seeker** (真理探究者) ; a **spiritual seeker** (精神的探求者).

くとうてん 句読点 punctuation marks.

> 「句読点・記号」のいろいろ **アステリスク** asterisk (＊) ／**アポストロフィ** apostrophe (') ／**引用符** quotation marks, quotes (" " / ' ') ／**かっこ** parentheses (( )) ／**感嘆符** exclamation point [mark] (!) ／**疑問符** question mark (?) ／**コロン** colon (:) ／**コンマ** comma (,) ／**斜線** slash (／) ／**セミコロン** semicolon (;) ／**ダッシュ** dash (−) ／**中かっこ** braces ({ }) ／**波形ダッシュ** swung dash (〜) ／**ハイフン** hyphen (-) ／**ピリオド** period, 《英》full stop (.) ／**ブラケット** brackets ([ ]) ／**指印** index (☞)

[1]**くどく 功徳** ▶功徳を積む accumulate *virtue* (through good deeds).

[2]**くどく 口説く 1【異性に言い寄る】make advances** 《to》; **seduce** ＋目 (誘惑する) ; **smooth-talk** ＋目 (うまいことを言う) ▶女性を口説く *smooth-talk* a woman ‖ ぼくは麻衣子が好きなんだけど, 口説くだけの勇気がない I really like Maiko, but I don't have enough courage to *talk* her *into going out with me*. (💡「付き合ってほしいと言う勇気がない」と考えて訳例のようにする. talk 以下を make advances to her あるいは, make a pass at her とすると「性的な関係を持とうとして近づく」というニュアンスになる) ‖ 彼女はいつもガードが固くてなかなか口説けない She is always defensive; I *can't get anywhere* with her. (➤ get anywhere は「多少とも成功する」の意で, 否定文・疑問文で用い

る).

2【しきりに頼む】**urge** /ə:ˈdʒ/ +目 ▶市民は公園を作るよう市長を口説いた The citizens *urged* the mayor to build a park. ‖ 父を口説いてカメラを買ってもらった I *talked* my father *into* buying me a camera. ／I *persuaded* my father *to* buy me a camera. (➤ persuade A to do は「A(人)を説得して…させる」).

くどくど ▶父はぼくの顔を見るたびに「しっかり勉強しろよ」「時間を無駄にするな」などとくどくど言う Every time my father sees me, he *repeats over and over* that I should study hard, not waste my time, and so on. ‖ 彼女はくどくどと孫たちの話をした She *ran on* about her grandchildren. ‖ きのう会社の中であったことを彼はくどくどと繰り返した He *harped on* about what happened at work yesterday. (➤ harp on は「繰り返して言う」で on は継続を表す副詞) ‖ 彼女は遅れた理由をくどくどと言い訳した She *gave* me *a big song and dance* about why she'd been late. (➤ a song and dance は「長い言い訳」の意のインフォーマルな表現).

くないちょう 宮内庁 the Imperial Household Agency ‖**宮内庁御用達** a purveyor to the Imperial Household.

くなん 苦難 (a) **hardship** ▶幾多の苦難を経験する［に耐える］experience［endure］many *hardships*. ‖ 苦難を乗り越える overcome［go through］(*a*) *hardship*.

くに 国 1【世界の国家】a **country**(国土に重点を置いて)；a **nation**(民族的・政治的結合体としての)；a **state**(法的・理論的意味での国家；アメリカ・オーストラリア・ドイツなどでは「州」を表すことも多い)；a **province**(「伊勢」「土佐」「河内」などの日本の昔の「国」) 一 形 **国の national, state**(➤ 後者はアメリカでは多く「州」の意) ▶貧しい［豊かな］国 a poor［rich］*country* ‖ 世界には190以上の国がある There are more than one hundred and ninety *countries* in the world. ‖ 私たちの大学ではいろいろな国の人が学んでいる Students from various *countries* study at our college. ‖ 第二次大戦後ドイツは２つの国に分断された Germany was divided into two *nations* after World War Ⅱ. ‖ アフリカの国々のほとんどは以前は植民地だった Most African *nations* were once colonies. ‖ その国は国有鉄道を民営化した The *state* privatized the national railroad system. ‖ 国の代表チーム a *national* team ‖ 国の安全を脅かす threaten［endanger］*national* security.

2【中央政府】**the** (**national**) **government** ▶住民は国を相手取って裁判を起こした The residents filed a suit against *the government*. ‖ 彼は国の援助で留学した He studied abroad with financial assistance from *the* (*Japanese*) *government*.

3【地域，国土】a **land** ▶毎年晩秋になると白鳥が北の国から渡ってくる Swans migrate here from *the north* in late fall every year.

✉ **自然を保護して日本を緑と水の豊かな国のままにしたいと思います** We want to protect the natural environment and keep Japan *a country* of abundant greenery and water.

4【故郷】one's **home**；one's **hometown**(生まれ育った所) ▶夏休みは国に帰ります I'm going *home* during the summer vacation. (➤ この home は副詞. 次の例も同じ) ‖ 国のおふくろから手紙と荷物が届いた I received a letter and a parcel from my mom (living) *back home*. ‖ **対話**「お国では何をなさっているのですか」「小学校の教師です」"What do you do *where you're from*?" "I teach at an elementary school." (➤「お国では」の部分はくだけた会話では, back in Canada のように具体的に言うことが多い. in your country は改まった響きになる) ‖ **対話**「お国はどちらですか」「長崎県です」"*Where is your hometown*?" "It's in Nagasaki Prefecture." (➤ 英語では hometown(生まれ故郷の町)はどこかと聞いているので, それは長崎県にあると答えている. →お国).

くにがら 国柄 national character ▶彼らの身振り手振りにもフランスのお国柄がうかがえる Their gestures, too, reveal the *national character* of France.

くにくのさく 苦肉の策 ▶それは彼の両親が最後にとった苦肉の策だった It was *his parents' last resort*. (➤ last resort は「最後の手段」).

くにゃくにゃ ▶こんにゃくはくにゃくにゃしている Konnyaku is *rubbery*. (➤ rubbery は「(かんだ感触が)ゴムのような」の意).

ぐにゃぐにゃ ▶針金はぐにゃぐにゃに曲がってしまった The wire was bent (*all*) *out of shape*. (➤「元の形がすっかりわからなくなって」の意).

▶何てぐにゃぐにゃした頼りない男なんだ What a *spineless* man he is! (➤ spineless は「背骨の無い；優柔不断な」の意).

ぐにゃっと ▶床にぐにゃっと座り込む sit down *limply* on the floor.

くねくね ▶くねくねした坂道を上り詰めると小さな家が見えてきた As we climbed the *winding* path, a little house came into view. (➤ winding /wáɪndɪŋ/ は「曲がりくねった」) ‖ ヘビがくねくねと山道をよぎった A snake *slithered* across the trail. (➤ slither は「(ヘビのように)滑るように進む」).

くねらす wriggle ▶蛇は体をくねらせて鳥籠に入った The snake *wriggled* into the bird cage.

くのう 苦悩 anguish；suffering(病気・不幸のときなどに感じる)；**distress**(心配・不安による) ▶太宰治は苦悩に満ちた人生を送った Dazai Osamu lived *a life of great suffering*［*distress*］.

くばる 配る 1【物を】**hand out, pass out**(手渡す)；**deliver** +目 (配達する)；**deal** +目 (トランプで) ▶通行人にビラを配る *hand out* fliers to passers-by ‖《教室で先生が》このプリントを全員に配ってください *Pass out* these handouts. ‖《試験監督が受験生に》これから問題用紙を配ります The examination papers will now *be passed out*.

▶郵便配達人は１日１回郵便物を配って歩く The letter carrier *delivers* the mail once a day. ‖《トランプで》今度はきみがカードを配る番だ Next it's your turn to *deal*.

2【気・目などを】▶健康には十分気を配っています I *take good care of* my health. ‖ クラスの生徒全員に目を配るのは大変です It's not an easy task to *pay* (*careful*) *attention to* all the students in class.

くび 首 1【頸部(けいぶ)，頭部】**the neck；the head** (頭)

> **解説** (1) neck は頭と胴の中間の部分を指すが,「窓から首を出す」とか「首をかしげる」というように日本語の「首」は頭も含むことが多い.
> (2) 首の前部(喉頸(のどくび))は throat, 後部(襟首)は nape という別の語を用いる. →頭.

▶キリンは首が長い Giraffes have long *necks*. ‖ 彼女

は首が細い She has a slender *neck*. ‖ハワイに着くと美しい少女が首にレイを掛けてくれた Upon my arrival in Hawaii, a beautiful Hawaiian girl put a lei *around my neck*. ‖女の子は父親の首にかじりついた The girl *clung to the neck* of her father.

▶ひな人形の首がころりと落ちた The *head* of one of the *hina* dolls dropped off and fell. ‖日本人は人の言うことが理解できないときに首をかしげる Japanese *tilt their heads* when they don't understand others. ‖ホームズはその不思議な事件に首をひねった Holmes *was baffled* by that mystery. ‖世界の多くの文化では首を縦に振ると「はい」を意味し, 首を横に振ると「いいえ」を意味する In many cultures in the world, *nodding* indicates "yes" while *shaking* one's *head* means "no." ‖横綱の優勝パレードを見ようと大勢の人がビルの窓から首を出した Many people *stuck their heads* [*craned their necks*] out of the windows of the buildings to see the yokozuna's victory parade. (➤ 後者は「首を伸ばした」の意) ‖寒風に帰宅を急ぐ男は首をすくめた The man *ducked his head* against the cold wind as he hurried home. ‖注意すると, その男の子は恥ずかしそうに首をすくめた When I scolded the child, he *shrugged* (*his shoulders*) *with embarrassment* [*gave an embarrassed shrug*].

▶ようやく, うちの赤ちゃんは首が据わってきた Our baby is finally *able to hold up his* [*her*] *head*. ‖その会社は破綻寸前であったが, 支援企業が現れて, 首の皮一枚でつながった The company was on the brink of bankruptcy, but a company offering financial assistance appeared, and it *managed to keep its head above water*. ‖トップの首をすげ替えるだけでは問題は解決しない We won't solve any problems by just *replacing top management*.

2【解雇】一動 首にする fire +㊐, **sack** +㊐ (➤ ともにインフォーマルな語 ; →解雇) ▶労働者の首を切る *fire* a worker ‖おまえは首だ! *You're fired*! ‖多くの従業員が首になりそうだ A lot of the employees are likely to *be fired* [*be sacked*]. ‖あんまり社長に盾つくと, 首が危ないよ You *might get fired* if you contradict the president too much.

3【慣用表現】

首が回らない ▶おじは借金で首が回らない My uncle *is up to his neck* [*ears*] in debt. **首をしめる** ▶部長に苦情を言うのはやめておいたほうがいい. 自分の首をしめるようなものだ You shouldn't complain to the general manager. You're just *asking for trouble*. (➤ ask for trouble は「自ら災いを招く」). **首を突っ込む** ▶他人の家の争いに首を突っ込むな You shouldn't *stick your nose into* [*Keep your nose out of*] other families' disputes. **首を長くする** ▶裕子はサウジアラビアへ出張した夫の帰りを首を長くして待った Yuko *looked forward to* [*could hardly wait for*] her husband's return from his business trip to Saudi Arabia.

くびかざり 首飾り a **neck ornament** ; a **necklace**(ネックレス) 《参考》首にぴったりつく短いネックレスをインフォーマルでは choker と呼ぶ. ▶真珠の首飾りをする put on [wear] *a* pearl *necklace*.

くびきり 首切り beheading (首をはねること) ; **firing from work**(解雇) ▶リストラで管理職数名に首切りがあるというわさだ I heard a rumor that some managers would *be fired* [*be getting the axe*] due to corporate restructuring.

ぐびぐび ▶彼はウオツカをぐびぐび飲んだ He *gulped down* vodka.

くびすじ 首筋 the nape [**scruff**] **of the neck** ▶猫の首筋をつかんで外に出した I took the cat by the *scruff* of its neck and put it out. ‖首筋が痛い I feel some pain at *the back* [*nape*] *of the neck*.

くびったけ 首ったけ ▶私, 五郎に首ったけなの I'*m crazy about* Goro. / I *have a crush* on Goro. ‖ひろしは昌代に首ったけだった Hiroshi was *head over heels in love with* Masayo.

くびっぴき 首っ引き ▶辞書と首っ引きで『シャーロック・ホームズの冒険』を読んだ I read "The Adventures of Sherlock Holmes" *with a dictionary in my hand* [*by my side*]. / I had to *use a dictionary many times* to get through "The Adventures of Sherlock Holmes."

くびつり 首吊り ▶彼は人生に絶望して首つり自殺した He despaired of his life and *hanged himself* [*committed suicide by hanging*]. (➤ hang の過去形は hung がふつうだが,「首をくくって死ぬ, 絞首刑になる [する]」のフォーマルな言い方のときは hanged が用いられる).

くびねっこ 首根っこ ▶彼は母親に首根っこを押さえられている (=言いなりになっている) He'*s under his mother's thumb*.

くびれる ▶瓶の中には真ん中がくびれているものもある Some bottles *are narrow* in the middle. ‖私の母はとても太っていてウエストがくびれていない My mother is very fat and *has no waist*. 《参考》「くびれたウエスト」のことを wasp waist (スズメバチのようなウエスト) という.

くびわ 首輪 a **collar** /kɑ́ːləʳ/.

くふう 工夫 an **idea** (アイデア) **一動 工夫する devise** /dɪváɪz/ +㊐ (考案する) ▶この家は左利きの人が住みやすいように工夫してある This house was built to be easy for left-handed people to live in. ‖何とかして読書の時間を作る工夫をしなければならない We have to try to *find some way* to make time for reading. ‖彼は最も効果的な水泳の訓練法を工夫した He *devised* the most effective training method for swimming. ‖(教材や教え方などで)いろいろ工夫に富む先生 a *resourceful* teacher ‖このレイアウトおもしろくないね. もう少し工夫できないかね This layout is dull. Couldn't you *do a little more to improve* it?

くぶくりん 九分九厘 ▶九分九厘私たちのチームの優勝だ *Ten to one*, our team will win the victory. / *In all likelihood*, our team will win the championship.

くぶどおり 九分通り ▶彼の健康は九分どおり回復した He has *almost* recovered. ‖私のスピーチの原稿は九分どおり出来上がっている The manuscript for my speech is *nearly* finished.

くぶん 区分する divide +㊐ ; **classify** +㊐ (分類する) ▶町を住宅地と商業地に区分する *divide* the town into (separate) residential and business districts.

くべつ 区別

(a) **distinction 一動 区別する distinguish** +㊐ ; (**can**) **tell** +㊐ (見分ける)

> **【文型】**
> A と B を区別する
> **distinguish** A **from** B
> **distinguish between** A **and** B
> A と B の区別がつく
> **can tell** A **from** B

▶長母音と短母音を区別する *distinguish* long vow-

els *from* short vowels ‖ 政治家は**公私の区別がつかなく**なるようだ It seems that politicians find it difficult to *distinguish between public and private matters.* ‖ 抽象画は難しい. いいものと悪いものの**区別がつかない** Abstract paintings are difficult. I *can't tell* good *from* bad ones. ‖ 私には本物と偽物のグッチの**区別がつかない** I *can't tell* a genuine Gucci *from* a fake one. ‖ **善悪の区別**をはっきりつけなさい Make a clear *distinction between good and evil.* ‖ あの学生は男か女か**区別がつかない** It is difficult to *tell* whether that student is a boy or a girl.
▶このマラソンには**男女の区別なく**参加できます Anyone, *regardless of sex,* can take part in this marathon.

くべる ▶彼はその古いラブレターを火にくべた He *tossed* his old love letters *in* [*into*] the fire. ／He *consigned* his old love letters *to* the fire. (➤ consign は「ゆだねる, 処分する」) ‖ 暖炉にまきをもう少しくべてください Will you please *put* some more wood *in* [*into*] the fireplace?

くぼち 窪地 a **hollow** ▶少女はくぼ地に隠れてそのまま眠ってしまった The girl hid in *a hollow* (*in the ground*) and fell asleep.

くぼみ 窪み a **hollow**, a **depression**(➤ 両者は区別なく使うこともあるが, 後者は広がりのある地面・土地についていうことが多い) ; a **dent**(へこみ) ▶道路のくぼみ *a hollow* in the road ‖ くぼみに水がたまっている Water has pooled in *the depression.*

くぼむ 窪む **sink**(地面などが沈下している) ▶彼は過労のために**目がくぼんだ** He *has hollows under his eyes* [*has sunken eyes*] from overwork. (➤ sunken eyes はかなり深くくぼんだ状態) ‖ 道があちこちくぼんでいるから運転に注意しなさい The road *has sunk in* in places, so be careful when you drive. (➤ 斜体字の in は「中に」の意の副詞. in places は「ところどころ」).

1**くま 熊** a **bear** ‖子グマ a (bear) cub ‖ ハイイログマ(グリズリー) a grizzly (bear).

2**くま 隈** ▶疲労からか, 彼女は目の下にくまができている She *has dark circles* under her eyes, maybe due to fatigue.

くまで 熊手 a **rake** ▶熊手で落ち葉をかき集める *rake* dead leaves *together* ‖ 花壇を熊手でかきならす *rake* a flowerbed.

くまなく 隈なく ▶ぼくたちは無くなった本をくまなく捜した We searched *everywhere* for the missing book. ‖ **部屋中くまなく捜したが鍵は見つからなかった** I searched *every corner* [*every nook and cranny in the room*], but could not find the key.

くまんばち 熊ん蜂 a **large carpenter bee.**

くみ 組・組み

訳語メニュー
学級 →homeroom, class **1**
グループ →group, team **2**
ひとそろい →set **3**

1【学級】 a **homeroom**, a **class** ▶娘は富士見台小学校の**2年5組**に在学しています My daughter is in *Homeroom 5, 2nd grade*, at Fujimidai Elementary School. ‖ きのう組替えがあってぼくは**B組**になった Yesterday my *homeroom was changed* and I am now in *class B.* ‖ **対話**「あなたの**組の担任**の先生, 誰?」「斉藤先生よ」"Who's your *homeroom* [《英》 *form-room*] *teacher*?" "Mr. Saito." ‖ **対話**「高1のときは何先生の組だったの?」「山下先生の組よ」"Whose *class* were you in when you were a tenth grader?" "I was in Mr. Yamashita's *class.*"

2【グループ】 a **group**(少人数の) ; a **team**(競技などの) ▶**2人組** *a duet* ‖ **3人組** *a trio* ‖ **4人組** *a quartet* ‖ 3人ずつ組みになりなさい Form *groups* of three. ‖ 彼は男子100メートル予選**第3組**に出場した He competed in *the third group* of the men's 100-meter preliminary. ‖ 生徒たちは**赤組と白組**に分かれて綱引きをした The students split up into *a red and a white team* [*squad*] to play tug-of-war. ‖ きのうA銀行に**4人組みの強盗**が押し入った *Four* burglars broke into A Bank yesterday.

3【ひとそろい】 a **set** ; a **pair**, a **couple**(2つで1つのもの) ▶茶器を**1組み**買った We bought *a* tea *set.* ‖ このスプーンは6本で**1組み**になっています The spoons come in *a set* of six. ／Each *set* has six spoons. ‖ トランプが**1組み**欲しい I want *a pack* [*a deck*] of cards. ‖ 新婚夫婦**10組み** ten newlywed *couples.*

4【暴力団の】 a **crime organization** ▶川口組の組長 the big boss of the Kawaguchi *Gumi.*

グミ a **gummy** /gʌ́mi/ (**candy**) [複 **gummies**].

くみあい 組合 an **association** ; a **union**(労働者の) ▶組合に加入する become a member of *an association* [*a union*] ‖ **労働組合**を組織する organize *a* (*labor*) *union* [《英》 *a trade union*] ‖ この**組合の組合員**はおよそ500人です This *association* has about five hundred *members.*
‖**組合運動** a union movement ‖ **組合費** union dues(➤ 天引きされる組合費を特に check-off と呼ぶ) ‖ **生活協同組合** a cooperative society 《略 co-op /kóʊɑːp/》.

くみあう 組み合う ▶我々は円陣を作り, **腕を組み合って**キャンプファイアの歌を歌った We formed a circle, *linked arms together*, and sang campfire songs.

くみあげる 汲み上げる **draw**, **pump up**(水などを ; 後者は特にポンプであることを明確にするとき) ; **elicit** /ɪlísɪt/(意見を引き出す) ▶水を井戸から**くみ上げる** *draw* [*pump up*] water from a well ‖ 彼は部下の意見をくみ上げるのが巧みだ He's skillful at *eliciting* opinions from his staff.

くみあわせ 組み合わせ a **combination** ; a **matchup**(試合の) ▶白と黒の**組み合わせ** *a combination* of black and white ‖ ワールドカップの試合の**組み合わせ**が決まった Teams in the World Cup have *been matched up.*

くみあわせる 組み合わせる **combine** +(目) ; **match** +(目) (対戦させる) ▶月に秋草を組み合わせたデザイン a design that *combines* the moon and autumn flowers ‖ 彼らは石や木片などを組み合わせてオブジェを作った They *put together* some pieces of stone, blocks of wood, etc., and created a work of art. ‖ 高校テニストーナメントでわが校はB校と**組み合わされた** In the inter-high school tennis tournament, our team *was matched against* B High School team.

くみいれる 組み入れる **include** +(目) (含める) ; **incorporate** /ɪnkɔ́ːrpəreɪt/ +(目) (吸収して合体してしまう) ▶その観光地を旅程に**組み入れる** *include* that tourist spot in the itinerary.

くみおき 汲み置き ▶くみ置きの水 water *ready for use.*

くみかえる 組み替[換]える ▶遺伝子を組み換える *recombine* genes ‖ 時間表を組み替えなければならない

We have to *revamp* the timetable.

くみかわす 酌み交わす ▶しばらくぶりに父と酒を酌み交わした For the first time in a long while, my father and I *poured sake for each other* [*drank sake together*]. (● 英語国では酒を酌み交わす習慣は一般的ではないので, 英訳に当たっては訳例のように「お互いに酒を酌み合いながら」と考える).

くみきょく 組曲 a **suite** /swiːt/ ▶バッハのチェロ組曲 Bach's cello *suites*.

くみこむ 組み込む **include** +㊐ (全体の一部として) ; **contain** +㊐ (何かを含んでいる) ; **incorporate** +㊐ (一部として取り入れる) ▶新規事業の支出を来年の予算に組み込む *include* the expenditure for the new project in the budget for next year ‖ 1枚のチップには大量の情報が組み込まれている A single chip *contains* a large amount of information. ‖ その先端技術を高級モデルに組み込む *incorporate* the advanced technology into high-end models.

くみたいそう 組体操 a **gymnastic formation.**

くみだす 汲み出す **dip out**(手やおけなどで) ; **pump out** (ポンプで) ▶池の水をくみ出す *pump out* water from the pond ‖ ボートから水をくみ出す *scoop out* water from a rowboat.

くみたて 組み立て **assembly** (機械などの) ; **construction** (文などの) ; **structure** (構造) ▶この文の組み立ては複雑だ The *construction* [*structure*] of this sentence is complicated. ‖ 組み立て式の本箱が欲しい I want a *knockdown* bookcase. (➤ knockdown は「分解可能の」).

くみたてる 組み立てる **assemble** +㊐ ▶ステレオを組み立てる *assemble* a stereo set ‖ 機械 [プラモデル] を組み立てる *put* a machine [a plastic model] *together* (➤ put ... together は「ばらばらの物を1つに組み立てる」) ‖ 論理をしっかり組み立ててわかりやすい文章を書きなさい *Construct* a well-structured theory and write clearly.

くみつく 組み付く **tackle** +㊐ ▶彼は勇敢にも泥棒に組みついた He bravely *tackled* the thief.

くみとる 汲み取る **1**【水などをすくう】**dip up** (さっと) ; **scoop up** (ひしゃくなどですくう) ▶浴槽の水をくみ取る *dip* [*scoop*] *up* water from a bathtub.

2【推察する】▶他人の気持ちをくみ取る(＝理解する) *read* [*perceive*] another person's feelings ‖ 裁判官は被告の事情をくみ取った(＝考慮した) The judge *took* the defendant's circumstances *into consideration*.

くみひも 組みひも a **braid.**

[1]くむ 組む **1**【絡ませる】**cross** +㊐ (交差させる) ; **fold** +㊐ (折り曲げる) ▶腕を組む *fold* one's arms ‖ 足を組む *cross* one's legs ‖ 電車の中で足を組んで座るのはほかの人の迷惑になる Sitting on the train *with your legs crossed* is a (real) nuisance to others. (→ あぐら) ‖ 弘と由紀が腕を組んで大学構内を歩いていた I saw Hiroshi and Yuki walking *arm in arm* on campus. ‖ 彼らは肩を組んで寮歌を歌った They sang their dormitory theme song *with their arms over each other's shoulders*.

2【協力する】**pair up** 《with》, **team up** 《with》 (➤ 前者は2人で, 後者は2人以上で) ▶私はテニスの試合で松田君とペアを組んだ I *paired* [*teamed*] *up with* Matsuda in the tennis match. ‖ 彼は仲間数人と組んで新しく会社を作った He *tied up with* (several of) his friends and started a new company.

3【組み立てる】▶足場を組む *put up* scaffolding [staging] ‖ 夏休みのスケジュールを組む *make* a schedule for the summer vacation.

[2]くむ 汲む・酌む **1**【水などを】▶コップに水をくむ *get* water in a glass ‖ 井戸から水をくむ *draw* water from a well ‖ 小川から水をくんで来い *Bring* water from the stream. ‖ 私は佐藤部長のお茶をくむ(＝入れる)ために会社に入ったんじゃありません I was not hired to *serve tea* to you, Mr. Sato.

2【気持ち・事情などを】**consider** +㊐ ▶彼女の事情をくむ *take* her situation *into consideration* ‖ どうか娘の気持ちをくんでやってほしい I'd like to ask you to *consider* [try to *understand*] my daughter's feelings toward you.

くめん 工面 ▶あすの10時までにその金を工面しなければならない I have to *manage to get* the money *ready* by 10 o'clock tomorrow.

[1]くも 雲 (a) **cloud**

> **語法** 物質としての雲, または範囲の不明瞭な雲の場合は Ⓤ 扱いで **cloud**, 形や範囲が明瞭な一片 [ひと塊] の雲は **a cloud**, 漠然と多数の雲を指す場合は **clouds**, 特定範囲 [場所] の多数の雲全体を指す場合は **the clouds** のように用いる.

▶空には雲ひとつ無かった There was not *a single cloud* in the sky. ／Not *a cloud* could be seen in the sky. ‖ 月が雲に隠れた The moon went behind *a cloud*. ‖ 雨が降る前は空に灰色の雲が出ているのがふつうだ There are usually gray *clouds* in the sky before it rains. ‖ 午後には雲が出てくるでしょう It will *cloud up* in the afternoon. ／It will *get cloudy* in the afternoon. ‖ 雲が晴れた *The clouds* have lifted. ‖ 湖に雲が低く垂れこめている *The clouds* are hanging low over the lake. ‖ 富士山頂は厚い [薄い] 雲に覆われていた The top of Mt. Fuji was covered with *heavy* [*thin*] *clouds*.

▶ (慣用表現) 雲をつかむような(＝曖昧な)話 a *vague* story.

> **逆引き熟語 ○○雲**
> **雨雲** a rain cloud ／**きのこ雲** a mushroom (-shaped) cloud ／**白雲** a white cloud ／**入道雲** a thunderhead ／**飛行機雲** a contrail, a vapor trail ／**夕立雲** a shower cloud ／**雷雲** a thundercloud ／**綿雲** a fleecy cloud

[2]くも 蜘蛛 (虫) a **spider** ▶クモは虫を捕らえて食べるために巣を張る *Spiders* spin webs to catch insects for food.

▶ (慣用表現) 子供たちはくもの子を散らすように逃げた The children ran away *in all directions*. (➤「四方八方へ」の意).

‖ **クモの糸** a spider's thread ‖ **クモの巣** a cobweb ／a (spider) web ‖ **セアカゴケグモ** a red-backed spider.

くもがくれ 雲隠れ ▶彼は都合が悪くなるとすぐに雲隠れしてしまう Whenever the situation is unfavorable to him, he *disappears*. ‖ 今までどこに雲隠れしてたんだい? Where have you *been hiding*? (● 「今まで」を till now と訳す必要はない. 現在完了進行形がその意味を示している).

くもま 雲間 ▶雲間から日がさし始めた The sun is beginning to shine through *a break in the clouds*. ‖ 月は雲間に隠れてしまった The moon has disappeared *behind the clouds*. ／The moon has been hidden by the clouds.

くもまく 蜘蛛膜《解剖学》**the arachnoid** /ərǽknɔɪd/ **membrane** ‖ **くも膜下出血**《医学》subarachnoid hemorrhage /hémərɪdʒ/.

くもゆき 雲行き ▶雲行きがまた怪しくなってきた *The sky* [*weather*] is threatening again. ／*Clouds* are threatening again. ／It looks threatening again.

▶《比喩的》中近東で雲行きが怪しくなった *The situation* in the Middle East *is getting worse*.

くもり 曇り 1【天候の】cloudy ▶あすはたぶん曇りだ It will probably *be cloudy* tomorrow. ‖ 朝は薄曇りだった It was *a bit cloudy* in the morning. ‖ ここ数日曇りの日が続いている We have had *cloudy weather* [*days*] for the past several days. ‖ 晴れ後曇り Fair [Clear], later *cloudy*.

‖ **曇り空** a cloudy sky (➤「予報ではきょうは一日曇り空だ」は各地の空をイメージして複数形で The forecast calls for cloudy skies all day today. とするのがふつう).

2【ガラス・レンズなどの】 ▶私は窓ガラスの曇りをきれいに拭いた I *wiped* the windowpanes clean.

‖ **曇りガラス** frosted glass.

くもる 曇る 1【空が】become [**get**] **cloudy** ▶急に空が曇って雨が降りだした The sky suddenly *became cloudy* [*clouded over*] and it began to rain. ‖ けさ起きたとき空はどんよりと曇っていた When I got up this morning, *it was overcast* [the sky *was heavily clouded*].

2【ガラス・レンズなどが】fog (up) ▶湯気で浴室の鏡が曇った The mirror in the bathroom *fogged up* with steam.

3【表情が】 ▶その件に触れると彼女の顔が一瞬曇った Her face *clouded over* momentarily when I referred to the matter.

くもん 苦悶 agony(もがくほどの苦しみ) ; **bitter suffering**(精神的・肉体的苦しみ) ; **anguish**(激しい精神的苦痛) ▶患者は苦もんの表情を浮かべた The patient showed an expression of *agony* [*bitter suffering*] on his [her] face.

ぐもん 愚問 a **silly** [**stupid**] **question** (➤ silly, stupid は「愚かな」の意で区別なく用いることもあるが, 前者には「軽く笑い飛ばせる」という含みがあることが多い)

▶愚問を発する ask *a silly question*.

くやくしょ 区役所 a **ward** /wɔːʳd/ **office** ▶父は港区役所に勤めています My father works at the Minato *Ward Office*.

くやしい 悔しい ⚠ **他人に負けたり, ばかにされたり, 自分の欲求が満たされなかったりするときに感じる「悔しい」という気持ちを表す1語の英語はない. したがって, be disappointed (がっかりする), be humiliated (屈辱を感じる), be upset (不快である), be frustrated (フラストレーションを感じている, しゃくだ), regret that (残念に思う) などのような言い方で代用する.**

▶ああ悔しい! くじがまた外れた *How disappointing* [*frustrating*]! I drew a blank again. ‖ 入試に失敗して本当に悔しかった I *was* really *upset* [*frustrated*] when I failed the exam. ‖ 悔しいけどぼくの負けだ *I hate to say it, but* I lost. ‖ まさる君にシカトされたの. 悔しい! Masaru gave me the cold shoulder. (So) I *feel awful*. (➤ give ... the cold shoulder は「無視する」の意のインフォーマルな表現) ‖ おまえたち, あんなチームに負けて悔しくないのか! *Don't you feel ashamed* [*mortified*] that you lost to a team like that? ‖ 負けて悔しかった I *was so disappointed* that I lost. ‖ 悔しかったらおまえも自分でやってみろ *If it bothers you so much*, why don't you do it yourself?

くやしがる 悔しがる ▶妹は人気ロックグループのコンサートチケットが買えなくて悔しがっていた My sister *seemed very disappointed* because she could not get a ticket for the popular rock group's concert.

くやしさ 悔しさ ▶廊下に立たされた悔しさで, ゆうべは眠れなかった I was so *frustrated* about their making me stand in the hall that I couldn't sleep last night. ‖ あの悔しさは一生忘れないだろう As long as I live, I'll never forget that (*bitter*) *disappointment* [*how angry and humiliated* I was then].

くやしなき 悔し泣き ▶チームが決勝戦で負けたときは悔し泣きした When our team lost in the finals, we *cried with* [*from*] *frustration*.

くやしなみだ 悔し涙 tears of frustration [**regret** ／ **disappointment**] ▶悔し涙をこらえる keep back one's *tears of frustration* [*regret*] ‖ 侮辱されて悔し涙を流す *shed tears in one's humiliation*.

くやしまぎれ 悔し紛れ ▶悔し紛れに彼女はぼくに悪態をついた She called me names *out of spite*. (➤ out of spite は「悪意から」) ‖ 試合に負けて, 彼は悔し紛れにぼくらに八つ当たりした He *took out his frustration* [(*bitter*) *disappointment*] over losing the game on us.

くやみ 悔やみ →お悔やみ.

くやむ 悔やむ be sorry 《for》(残念に思う) ; **regret** +目 (後悔する) ▶失敗したのはおまえの努力が足りなかったのだ. 今頃悔やんでもしかたがないよ You failed because you didn't try hard enough. It's no use *being sorry* now. ‖ 彼はスクイズの失敗を悔やんでいる He *regrets* that the squeeze play did not work out.

くよう 供養 a **memorial service** ▶私たちは先祖の供養をした We *had a memorial service* for our deceased family members [for the departed souls of our ancestors].

くよくよ ▶小さなことでくよくよするな Don't *be bothered* by small [unimportant] things. ／Don't *sweat* the small stuff. (➤ sweat は「気に病む」の意のインフォーマルな語) ‖ 過ぎたことをくよくよ思い悩むな Don't *worry so much* about what's past. ‖ 対話 「入試, だめだったよ」「くよくよするな. もう1年頑張ればいい」"I failed the entrance exam." "*Don't let it get you down*. You can try again another year." (➤ get ... down は「…をがっかりさせる」. it は漠然と状況を指す. Don't let it bother you. と言ってもよい) ‖ 就職面接のことなどくよくよ心配するな Don't *lose sleep over* the job interview. (➤ lose sleep over は「眠れなくなるほどくよくよ心配する」) ‖ 何くよくよしてるんだよ? What's eating you? (➤決まった言い方).

¹くら 鞍 a **saddle** ▶馬にくらを置く put *a saddle* on a horse ／saddle a horse.

²くら 蔵 a **storehouse**.

☞ **お蔵入り** (→見出語)

¹くらい 位 1【地位, 等級】 (a) **rank** (官職の) ; a **grade** (等級) ▶位の高い人 a person *of high rank* ‖ A氏はB氏よりも位が上 [下] だ Mr. A *ranks above* [*below*] Mr. B. ‖ 1等陸佐は2等陸佐より位が1つ上だ A colonel *is one grade higher* than a lieutenant colonel. ‖ 位人臣(くらいじんしん)を極める *achieve the highest possible rank as a retainer*.

2【数値の桁】 a **decimal place** [**position**] ▶100の位 the hundreds *position* [*place*] ‖ 位取りを間違える

make a *decimal* mistake.

[2]くらい 暗い

📖 訳語メニュー
場所・色が暗い →dark **1, 2**
陰気な →gloomy **3**
いかがわしい →shady **4**

1【光が少ない】dark；**dim**（薄暗い）▶彼は暗くなるまで教室に残っていた He stayed in the classroom *till dark* ‖ジャングルの中は日中でも暗い *It is dark* in the jungle even in the daytime.（➤ 明暗を表すときは通例 it を主語にする）‖フクロウは暗い所が好きだ Owls like *dark* places. ‖彼女は暗くなってからの帰宅は禁じられている She is not allowed to stay out *after dark*. ‖空が暗くなってきた The sky is *getting dark*. ‖ステージが突然暗くなった The stage suddenly *darkened*. ‖私たちはキャンドルをともすために部屋を暗くした We *dimmed the lights* to light the candles.（➤ この dim は「暗くする」の意の動詞）.

2【色がくすんだ】dark ▶暗い赤 *dark* red ‖暗い色 a *dark* color.

3【心が暗くなるような】gloomy ▶暗いニュース *gloomy* [*depressing*] news（➤ 後者は「気のめいるような」）‖彼女は少し性格が暗い She *is* a bit *gloomy* by nature. ‖戦争の悲惨な話を聞いているうちに暗い気持ちになってきた I *began to feel depressed* hearing tragic war stories. ‖来年の景気の見通しは暗い The economic outlook for next year is *dim* [*gloomy*]. ‖人類の未来は暗いように思えるときもある The future of humankind sometimes seems *bleak*.

4【いかがわしい】shady ▶政治の暗い面 the *shady side* of politics ‖暗い過去をもつ人 a person with *a shady past*.

5【疎い】▶私は経済学には暗い I *don't know much about* economics.

-くらい

1【概数を示して】about, around, approximately /əprɑ́:ksɪmətli/（➤ around はインフォーマルで好まれ, approximately はやや堅い；→約）▶ **対話**「日本の人口はどのくらいですか」「1億2750万人くらいです」"*How large* [*big*] is Japan's population ? ／*What* is Japan's population ?" "It is *about* one hundred twenty-seven and a half million."（➤ big は子供の, または子供っぽい言い方）‖ **対話**「アルバイトで毎月どのくらい稼ぐの？」「3万円くらいです」"*How much* do you earn a month from working part-time ?" "*Around* 30,000 yen. ／Thirty thousand yen *or so*."（➤ or so は「…かそこら」の意）‖ **対話**「国連加盟国はどのくらいありますか」「190か国くらいだと思います」"*How many* member countries does the United Nations have ?" "*Approximately* 190." →どのくらい.

2【程度を比較して】▶あなたと同じくらい（上手に）英語が話せたらなあ I wish I could speak English *as well as* you do. ‖新球場は甲子園と同じくらいの大きさだ The new stadium is *as large as* Koshien (Stadium). ‖悲しくて泣きたいくらいだった I felt so sad that I *almost* cried.

▶清水君くらい車に夢中な人はいない Nobody is more crazy about cars *than* Shimizu. ‖外国でお金を無くすくらい心細いことはない Nothing makes you feel more helpless *than* losing money in a foreign country. ‖トレーニングのあとのシャワーくらい気持ちのいいものはない *There is nothing like* a shower after a (good) workout.

▶あいつに謝るくらいなら死んだほうがましだ I *would rather* die *than* apologize to him.

3【程度の軽いものを引き合いに出して】at least（せめて）▶一流のビジネスパーソンになるには外国語の1つや2つくらい自在に話せなくてはならない You should speak *at least one or two* foreign languages fluently if you want to become a top-notch businessperson. ‖どんなに忙しくても歯くらい磨いて出勤しなさい No matter how busy you are, you should *at least* brush your teeth before leaving for work. ‖そのくらいのことで泣くんじゃない Don't cry over *such a small thing*. ‖きみはそれくらいのことがわからないのかい Can't you understand *such a simple thing* ?

クライアント a **client**.

グライダー a **glider** ▶グライダーを飛ばす fly *a glider*.

クライマックス the climax ▶その芝居は主人公の死でクライマックスに達した That play reached its [*the*] *climax* with the death of the protagonist.

クラウチングスタート a **crouching start**.

クラウド・コンピューティング cloud computing.

クラウン a **crown**（王冠）；a **dental** [**tooth**] **crown**（歯のクラウン. 文脈によっては crown だけでよい）.

グラウンド a **playground**, a **field**；an **athletic field** [《英》**athletic ground**]（陸上競技用の）▶私は駆け足でグラウンドを1周した I ran around the *field*.（➤「3周」の場合は I ran three laps around the field. とする）‖雨でグラウンドコンディションが悪く, 試合は中止になった The game was canceled because *the condition of the ground*(*s*) [*field*] was poor after the rain.

> **危ないカタカナ語✹ グラウンド**
> **1** 単に「グラウンド」というときは field を用いることが多く, ground は playground（小・中学校の運動場など）, cricket ground（クリケット競技場）のように複合語になることが多い.
> **2**「グラウンド」は「グランド」ともいうが, grand は「壮大な」という意味の形容詞である.

くらがえ 鞍替えする ▶もっと給料のよい仕事にくら替えするつもりだ I'm going to *get* [*switch to*] a better-paying job.

くらがり 暗がり the dark, darkness ▶猫は暗がりでも目が見える Cats can see in *the dark*.

くらく 苦楽 ▶2人は50年間も苦楽をともにしてきた夫婦だ They *have shared joys and sorrows* for fifty years as husband and wife.

クラクション a **horn**（➤「クラクション」はもと商標名の Klaxon から）▶クラクションを鳴らす sound [blow ／honk] the *horn*.

くらくら ▶高熱で頭がくらくらした The high fever *made me dizzy* [*made my head reel*]. ‖初めてたばこを吸ったときは頭がくらくらした The first time I smoked a cigarette, it *made me feel dizzy*. ‖空手の一撃を顔に受けたらくらくらっとした I *saw stars* when I received a karate blow to my face.（➤ see stars は「目がくらむ」の意のインフォーマルな表現）.

ぐらぐら ▶この椅子はぐらぐらしている This chair *is wobbly* [*unsteady*]. ‖歯が2本ぐらぐらしている（＝抜けそうだ）Two of my teeth *are* (*coming*) *loose*. ‖夕食の最中に地震で家がぐらぐら揺れた Our house *shook* with an earthquake in the middle of supper.

▶やかんの湯がぐらぐら煮立っている The water *is boil-*

ing in the teakettle.

くらげ《動物》a **jellyfish** ▶海で泳いでいてクラゲに刺された I was stung by *a jellyfish* while swimming in the ocean.

‖電気クラゲ a Portuguese man-of-war.

くらし 暮らし (a) **life**(生活)；a **living**, (a) **livelihood**(生計) ▶暮らしを立てる earn [make] *a living* ‖都会より田舎のほうが暮らしは楽だ *Life* is easier in the country than in the city. ‖彼らの暮らしは物質的には豊かだが, 精神的には貧しい Their *life* is rich materially, but poor spiritually. ‖昔に比べて日本人の暮らし[暮らし向き]は楽になった The Japanese *are better off* these days than they used to be. (➤ be well off で「暮らしにゆとりがある」) ‖うちの現在の暮らし向き our present (*life*) *circumstances*.

▶その原発事故は何十万人の住民の命と暮らしを脅かした The nuclear accident threatened the lives and *livelihoods* of tens of thousands of residents. ‖暮らしに困る人は生活保護を受けることができる Those people who *find it difficult to make a living* [who *can't make ends meet*] can receive welfare. (➤ make ends meet は「何とかやりくりする」の意のインフォーマルな表現) ‖彼らはぜいたくな[貧しい]暮らしをしている They *live high* [*in poverty*]. ‖東京に出ている娘はどんな暮らしをしているのかしら I wonder *how* my daughter *is getting along* in Tokyo. (➤ get along は「やっていく」) ‖ローンの返済に追われて暮らしが楽でない人が多い Many people *have trouble making ends meet* because they have to pay off loans.

グラジオラス《植物》a **gladiolus** /glædióʊləs/.

くらしきりょう 倉敷料 a **storage charge** [**fee**](請求額)；a **storage cost**(負担額).

クラシック 1【古典】a **classic** 一形 クラシックな **classic** ▶彼女はクラシックな家具を集めている She collects *classic* furniture.

2【音楽】**classical music** 一形 クラシックの **classical** ▶私はポピュラー音楽よりもクラシック音楽のほうが好きだ I prefer *classical music* to popular music.

‖クラシックファン a classical music fan [buff].

くらす 暮らす **live**(生活する)；**make a living**(生計を立てる)；**get along**(日々を過ごす)

▶安楽に暮らす *live* comfortably ‖遊んで暮らす *idle one's time away* ‖1日寝て暮らす *spend* a [the] day *in bed* ‖彼女は若い頃外国で暮らした She *lived* abroad when she was young. ‖夫の死後, 彼女は幸せに暮らした She *lived* a happy *life* after her husband's death. ‖兄は京都でひとりで暮らしている My brother *is living* by himself in Kyoto. ‖おばは英語を教えて暮らしている My aunt *makes a living* (by) teaching English. ‖うちでは月25万円で暮らしている We *live* on 250,000 yen a month. ‖**対話** 「いかがお暮らしですか」「相変わらず何とかやっております」 "*How are you getting along*? ／*How have you been* (*doing*)?" "I'm managing to get by, same as always."

クラス 1【学校の】a **class**；《米》a **home classroom**, a **homeroom**,《英》a **form-room**(学級) ▶3Cのクラス *class* 3C ‖クラス対抗のリレー an *interclass* relay ‖このクラスには田中さんが3人いる There are three Tanakas in this *class*. ‖クラスは意見が分かれてしまった The *class* was [The members of the *class* were] divided in their opinions. ‖高田君はクラス一ののっぽだ Takada is *the* tall*est* (student) *in my class*. ‖堀野先生が私たちのクラスの担任です Mr. Horino is our *homeroom* [*form-room*] *teacher*. ／Mr. Horino is in charge of our homeroom [form-room].

‖クラス委員 a class representative ‖クラス会 a class meeting；a class reunion(同窓会) ‖クラス分けテスト a placement test.

2【等級, 階級】a **class** ▶初心者クラス *a class* for beginners ‖中[上]級クラス an intermediate [advanced] *class* ‖エコノミークラスの航空券 an *economy-class* airline ticket ‖D社はトップクラスの自動車会社だ D Company is a *first-rate* automobile company.

> **危ないカタカナ語✹ クラス**
> 1 学校用語としての「クラス」は「学級, 組」の意であり, 英語でも class を(the) 6B class(6年B組), class 2D(2年D組)のように使う. class はまた, math class, class in math のように「科目別クラス[授業]」も指す.
> 2《米》ではまた, class を「同期卒業生(全員)」の意で, class of 2012(2012年度卒)のようにも用いる. したがって, I was in the same class with her. ／She and I were in the same class. は「私は彼女と同期の卒業です」の意になる. これらの文は「彼女と私は同じクラスだった」の意にもなりうるが,「同じクラスだった」ことを明確に言いたい場合は She and I were in the same home classroom. のようにする.

[1]グラス a **glass**(コップ；ガラス製品).

[2]グラス **grass**(草, 芝)

‖グラスコート a grass court.

クラスター a **cluster**(➤ 集団, 群れ, 房のこと) ▶コロナウイルスのクラスター a coronavirus *cluster*.

グラスファイバー **fiberglass**, **glass fiber**(➤ 製品は前者がふつう) ▶グラスファイバーのスキー板 *fiberglass* skis.

クラスメート a **classmate** 【解説】アメリカの高校では個人個人が異なった授業を取るので, 日本のような1年間同一のクラスという感覚がない. したがって classmate という語はあまり使わない.

▶私たちは中学校でクラスメートでした We were *classmates* in junior high school. ‖彼女は私のクラスメートです She is my *classmate*. ／She and I are in the same class. 《参考》「学校(の)友だち」に相当するのは schoolfriend, schoolmate で, 後者はやや古風.

グラタン **gratin**

‖マカロニグラタン macaroni au gratin (➤ au gratin /oʊ grǽtn/ は「グラタン風の」).

クラッカー 1【ビスケット】a **cracker**.

2【火薬の入った】a **cracker**, a **firecracker** ▶クラッカーが盛んに鳴らされた *Firecrackers* were set off one after another.

ぐらつく **shake** (前後・左右・上下に揺れる)；**wobble**(椅子などが左右に揺れる) ▶このビルは弱い地震でもぐらつく This building *shakes* even in a slight earthquake. ‖その椅子に座っちゃだめよ. 脚が1本ぐらついてるから Don't sit on that chair—one of the legs *wobbles*.

▶彼の決意はぐらついていた His determination was *shaky*. ‖彼女のひと言でぼくの自信はぐらついた Her single comment was enough to *shake* [*undermine*] my confidence. (➤ shake は一時的, undermine はより長期間の打撃を暗示する).

クラッチ a **clutch**；a **clutch pedal**(クラッチを操作するペダル) ▶クラッチを入れる[切る] let in [out] the clutch ‖クラッチが入っている［いない］The *clutch* is in ［out］. ‖私はクラッチペダルを床いっぱいに踏み込んだ I pressed the *clutch* (*pedal*) to the floor. ／I floored the *clutch* (*pedal*). (➤「クラッチペダルを踏む」は step on the clutch (pedal)).

‖**ノークラッチ車** an automatic (transmission) car (➤「ノークラッチ」は和製語).

グラニューとう グラニュー糖 **granulated sugar.**

グラビア (a) **photogravure** /fòuṭəgrəvjúəʳ/, (a) **gravure**《参考》印刷法を表す専門用語.「グラビアページ」は photo page,「グラビアアイドル」は a "gravure idol" や a bikini model がよい.

クラブ **1**【同好会】a **club**《参考》英語の club は Rotary Club のような学外のスポーツや社交のためのクラブを指すことが多い.

▶うちの学校には将棋クラブがあります We have a Shogi *club* in our school. ‖加山君はテニスクラブの主将をしている Kayama is (the) captain of our tennis *club*. ‖わが校ではクラブ活動が盛んだ At our school, *club activities* are very popular. →部 ‖ 対話「何かクラブに入ってる?」「うん, グリークラブに入ってるよ」"Are you in ［Do you belong to］ any *clubs*?" "Yes. I'm in the glee *club*."

‖**クラブ員** a member of a club ‖**クラブ室** a clubroom ‖**クラブ費** club dues /dju:z/.

2【ゴルフの道具】a (**golf**) **club** ▶新品のゴルフクラブのセット a new set of golf *clubs*.

3【トランプの記号】**clubs** ▶クラブのクイーン the queen of *clubs*.

グラフ a **graph**; a **chart**(表) ▶人口増加の様子をグラフにしてみた We drew *a graph* to show how the population has increased.

‖**グラフ用紙** graph paper ‖**円グラフ** a circle graph, a pie chart ‖**帯グラフ** a rectangle graph ‖**折れ線グラフ** a line graph ‖**棒グラフ** a bar graph, a bar chart.

グラブ a **glove** /glʌv/. →グローブ.

グラフィック a **graphic**(➤ 通例 graphics の形で用いる) 一形 **グラフィックな** **graphic** ▶グラフィックな雑誌 a *graphic* ［*pictorial*］ magazine.

‖**グラフィックデザイナー** a graphic designer.

クラフトし クラフト紙 **kraft paper.**

-くらべ -比べ ▶力比べをしよう Let's see who is stronger. ‖こうなったらきみとぼくとの根比べだ Let's see which of us can hold out longer ［the longest］!

☞ **腕比べ**, **背比べ** (→見出語)

くらべもの 比べ物 ▶東京の冬の寒さなんか北海道の寒さとは比べ物にならない No matter how cold Tokyo's winters may be, they *are nothing compared with* those in Hokkaido. ／The winter cold in Tokyo *cannot be compared with* that of Hokkaido. ‖オリジナルの絵と複製画とでは比べ物にならない *There is no comparison* between an original painting and a reproduction. ‖そっちのほうが比べ物にならないほど大きい That one is *incomparably* larger. ‖わが校の野球チームはC高校のチームとは比べ物にならない Our baseball team *can't even compare with* the C High School team. ／Our baseball team *is no match for* the C High School team. (➤「相手にならない」の意).

くらべる 比べる **compare** +目 ▶私は買う前に数店で値段を比べてみた I *compared prices* at several stores before making a purchase. ‖隣の家のひろしと背の高さを比べた My neighbor Hiroshi and I *compared* our heights.

【文型】
A と B を比べる
compare A **with** ［**to**］ B
A と比べると,
, compared with ［**to**］ A
in comparison with A

▶この子を彼のお姉さんみたいな秀才と比べてはかわいそうよ It's unfair to *compare* him *with* his brilliant sister. ‖我々の売り上げは昨年に比べると5%増えた Our sales increased 5 percent, *compared with* ［*to*］ last year. ／Our sales rose 5 percent *over* last year. ‖オーストラリアと比べて日本は人口が多い Japan is densely populated *in comparison with* Australia.

▶答えが合っているかどうか, 解答と比べて(＝照らし合わせて)みよう Let's *check* the answers *against* the ones in the answer book to see if they are right. ‖きみとぼくと, どっちが足が速いか比べてみないか Let's *see* who can run faster, you or me.

1**グラマー**《豊満》▶あの女優, すごいグラマーだね That actress's *got a great* ［*sexy*］ *body*. ／That actress *has a great figure* ［*is voluptuous* ／*is curvaceous*］. (➤ voluptuous は「肉感的な」, curvaceous は「曲線美の」).

危ないカタカナ語 ✹ グラマー

1 日本語では, 主に胸が豊かな女性を指して「グラマー」というが, 英語の glamour にはその意味はない. glamour は「魅力的なこと」の意で, 体格とは関係がない. また, その形容詞形 glamorous も人だけでなく, 仕事や雰囲気についても用いられる.

2 日本語の「グラマー」の意味を表すには voluptuous や curvaceous を用いるのがよい.「均整がとれていて魅力的な」という場合は shapely.

2**グラマー**《文法》**grammar.**

くらます ▶その男が行方をくらましてから5年になる It has been five years since the man *disappeared*. ‖その事件が明るみに出て以来, 彼は姿をくらましている Ever since the case was brought to light, he *has been in hiding*. (➤ be in hiding で「隠れている」).

クラミジア《生物学》**chlamydia** /kləmídiə/.

くらむ 眩む **be dazzled**(強い光でまぶしい); **feel dizzy**(高度や速度でめまいがする); **be blinded**(一時的に目が見えなくなる) ▶目もくらむばかりのダイヤモンド a *dazzling* diamond ‖目のくらむような断崖絶壁 a *dizzyingly* sheer cliff (➤ sheer は「切り立った」) ‖太陽に目がくらむ *be blinded* by the sun ‖ヘッドライトの光で一瞬目がくらんでしまった I *was dazzled* by the headlights for a second.

▶《慣用表現》彼は欲に目がくらみ公金を横領した *Blinded by greed*, he embezzled public funds.

グラム a **gram** ▶この小包は重さが600グラムある This parcel weighs 600 *grams*.

くらもと 蔵元 a **sake brewery**(醸造所); a **sake brewer**(醸造人).

くらやみ 暗闇 **the dark**; **darkness** (暗さ) ▶暗闇にだんだん目が慣れてきた My eyes gradually adjusted to *the dark*. ‖私は暗闇の中で目を凝らした I stared ［peered］ into the *darkness*.

ぐらり ▶夜中にぐらりときた I *felt a tremor* in the (middle of) the night.

クラリネット a **clarinet** /klæ̀rənét/ ▶クラリネットを吹く play the *clarinet*.
‖**クラリネット奏者** a clarinet(t)ist.

くらわす 食らわす **punch** ▶彼は男の顎にパンチを食らわせた He *punched* the man in the jaw.

クランク a **crank** ▶クランクアップする *finish shooting a movie* ‖クランクインする *start shooting a movie*.

グランド →グラウンド.

グランドキャニオン **the Grand Canyon** /kǽnjən/ (アメリカ, アリゾナ州の大峡谷).

グランドピアノ a **grand piano**(➤「コンサート用グランドピアノ」は a concert grand (piano)).

グランプリ a **grand prix** /grɑ̀ːn príː/ [複 **grand(s) prix**] ▶彼は2010年度のグランプリに輝いた He won the *Grand Prix* for 2010.

1**くり 栗** 《植物》a **chestnut** /tʃésnʌt/ (実), a **chestnut tree**(木) ▶クリのいが the bur of *a chestnut* ‖くり色の髪 *chestnut* hair ‖クリ拾いに行く go *chestnut gathering*
‖**甘ぐり** a sweet roasted chestnut.

2**くり 庫裏** the living quarters (in a temple) of a Buddhist priest and his family (➤ 説明的な訳).

クリア **1【はっきりした】** 一形 **クリアな** **clear** ▶クリアな映像 a *clear* picture.
2【どかす, 越える】 一動 **クリアする** **clear** +⊞ ▶ボールをクリアする *clear* the ball ‖１度目の試技でバーをクリアする *clear the bar* on one's first try ‖すべての条件をクリアする(＝満たす) *meet* all the conditions ‖ドラクエ10を全てクリアする *complete* (all the quests in) Dragon Quest X.

くりあがる 繰り上がる ▶発売日が明日に繰り上がった The release date *was moved up* to tomorrow.

くりあげる 繰り上げる ▶２時限目の授業を１時限目に繰り上げる *change* a class from (the) second period to (the) first period ‖予定を繰り上げる *move up* the schedule ‖開会を１時間繰り上げましょうか Should we *start* the meeting one hour *earlier than scheduled*? ‖試合開始は１時間繰り上げられて午前10時になった The start of the game *was moved forward* by one hour to 10 a.m. ‖当選者の１人が失格になったので次点の人が繰り上げ当選になった Since one of the winning candidates was disqualified, the runner-up *was awarded the election* [*was given the seat*].

クリアランスセール a **clearance sale**.

グリース **grease**.

クリーナー a **cleaner** ‖**粘着クリーナー** a lint cleaner [remover].

クリーニング **cleaning** ▶スーツをクリーニングしてもらう *have* one's suit *cleaned* ‖スーツをドライクリーニングに出す *send* a suit *to a dry cleaner* [《英また》 *a dry cleaner's*] ‖このワイシャツをクリーニングに出してください Could you please *take* these shirts *to the cleaners* [《英また》 *cleaner's*]? ‖コートはクリーニング屋さんに出してありますよ Your overcoat is at the *cleaners* [《英また》 *cleaner's*].

クリーム **cream** ▶コーヒーにはクリームを入れますか Would you like [Do you take] *cream* in your coffee? (● 前者は今コーヒーを勧めている場合, 後者はいつもの習慣を聞いている場合. 前者に対しては Yes, please. (はい, お願いします) とか, No, thank you. I drink it black. (いいえ, 結構です. ブラックで頂きます) のように答える) ‖顔から首にかけてこのクリーム[日焼け止めクリーム]をたっぷり塗っておきなさい Apply this *cream* [*sunscreen*] liberally to (your) face and neck.
‖**クリームソーダ** a melon soda float (メロンソーダの) (➤ 日本独特のもの. 英語の cream soda はバニラ味の炭酸飲料).

くりいれる 繰り入れる ▶この経費は来年度の予算に繰り入れます This expense will *be carried forward* [*be transferred*] to next year's budget.

クリーン **clean** ▶あの政治家にはクリーンなイメージがある That politician has a *clean* image.
‖**クリーンエネルギー** clean energy.

グリーン **1【緑】** **green** ▶グリーンのスカーフ a *green* scarf ‖グリーン車は６号車です The "*Green Car*" is car No. 6. (● 日本だけの呼称なので, 英語では deluxe-class [first-class] car などと説明するとよい).
2【ゴルフの】 a (**putting** /pʌ́tɪŋ/) **green** ▶セカンドショットで彼はグリーンを捉えた He *made the green* on his second shot.

クリーンクルー a **cleaning person**; (高層ビルの窓の) a **window cleaner**(➤「クリーンクルー」は clean と crew を重ねた和製業界用語；室内や高層ビルの窓の清掃を行う人のこと).

グリーンピース **green peas** /píːz/.

クリーンヒット a **sharp single** ▶センター前にクリーンヒットを打つ *line a single* to center(➤ line の代わりに rifle, drill, drive などの動詞が状況に応じて使われる).

> **危ないカタカナ語✸ クリーンヒット**
> **1** clean hit は間違いではないが, 英語では sharp single(鋭いシングルヒット)とするか, 訳例のように動詞を使って表すほうがふつう.
> **2** ほかに, clothesline (ぴんと張った洗濯ひも), bullet-like hit(弾丸のようなヒット)などの言い方もある.

クリオネ 《動物》a **clione** /klaɪóʊni/.

くりかえし 繰り返し (a) **repetition**; a **refrain**(歌などの繰り返し部分) ▶言語の習得には繰り返しが絶対必要である *Repetition* is absolutely necessary in language learning. ‖ぼくは彼女からの手紙を繰り返し繰り返し読んだ I read her letter *over and over again*. ‖人生は繰り返しがきかない You can't *repeat* your life.

くりかえす 繰り返す **repeat**(+⊞) ▶同じ間違いを繰り返す *repeat* the same mistake ‖よく聞いて先生のあとに続いて繰り返して言ってごらんなさい Listen carefully and *repeat* after me. (➤ 教室での先生の指示) ‖ハワイのキラウエアが噴火を繰り返した Kilauea in Hawaii erupted *repeatedly*. ‖同じ失敗を繰り返さないようにしなさい Be careful not to make the same mistake *again*.
▶すみません, 最後におっしゃったことがわかりませんでした. もう一度繰り返していただけますか I'm sorry. I didn't catch your last remark. Could you *repeat* it? ‖すみませんが, 繰り返してくださいませんか *I beg your pardon* (, but would you mind repeating that)? 《参考》相手のことばを聞き返すときの決まり文句. pardon を尻上がりに言う. 下げて言うと「ごめんなさい」「失礼しました」の意味になるので注意. 単に Pardon? とか 《英》 Sorry? とも言う.

くりくり ▶赤ちゃんのくりくりした目が愛らしかった The baby's *big, round, sparkling* eyes were so cute.
→つぶら.

ぐりぐり a **hard lump**(しこり); a **stiff neck**(肩凝り) ▶乳房にぐりぐりができると乳がんの疑いがある If there is *a hard lump* in your breast, it may mean (you have) cancer.

クリケット cricket ▶クリケットの試合 a *cricket* match ‖ クリケットはイギリスで盛んです *Cricket* is popular in Britain.

グリコーゲン 《生化学》 glycogen /gláɪkədʒən/.

くりこす 繰り越す ▶余ったクラス会費を来年度へ繰り越すことにした We decided to *carry* the surplus membership fees *forward* to the next year.

くりごと 繰り言 rambling(s)（取りとめのない話）; grumbling（不平） ▶老いの繰り言 the *ramblings* of an old person.

くりこむ 繰り込む ▶巨人ファンが東京ドームに繰り込んだ Giants fans *filed* [*streamed*] *into* Tokyo Dome.（➤ file into は「列を成して入る」, stream into は「流れるように［続々と］入る」の意).

くりさげる 繰り下げる ▶朝の会議の予定を午後に繰り下げた The meeting scheduled for the morning *was put off* until [*moved to*] the afternoon. ‖ 日程を少し繰り下げよう Let's *move* [*set*] *back* the schedule.

クリスタル (a) crystal
‖**クリスタルガラス** crystal (glass).

クリスチャン a Christian ▶熱心なクリスチャン a devout *Christian*.

クリスマス Christmas; Christmas Day（クリスマスの当日）

> **《解説》** (1) クリスマスの期間 (Christmastime) は Christmas Eve（12月24日）から1月1日（イギリスでは1月6日）までを指し, 12月25日のクリスマス祭日は Christmas Day または単に Christmas という.
> (2) Christmas は広告文などでは Xmas とも書くが, X'mas の表記はややまれ.

✉ **メリークリスマス!** *Merry Christmas!* ／《英また》 *Happy Christmas!* ➤ クリスマスカードにはよく新年の挨拶も含めて I wish you a Merry Christmas and a Happy New Year. の文句が用いられる.

‖**クリスマスカード［ツリー］** a Christmas card [tree] ‖ **クリスマスキャロル** a Christmas carol ‖ **クリスマス休暇** the Christmas holidays [vacation]（➤ 後者は学生がしばしば用いる） ‖ **クリスマスケーキ** a Christmas cake ‖ **クリスマスプレゼント** a Christmas present [gift] 《参考》ストッキングに詰める比較的安価な品を a stocking filler とか a stocking stuffer という.

クリスマスカードには次のようにも書きます.
(1) *Merry Christmas and (a) Happy New Year!* ➤ a は省略することもある.
(2) *Season's Greetings and Best Wishes for the New Year!* ➤キリスト教徒でない人にも可.
(3) *Have a Merry Christmas!*

グリセリン 《化学》 glycerin(e) /glísərɪn/.

くりだす 繰り出す ▶村人たちは花見に繰り出した The villagers *went* (out) [*turned out*] to see the cherry blossoms.

クリック a click 一動 **クリックする** click 《on》 ▶マウスをクリックしてファイルを選択する *click* the mouse and select a file ‖ アイコンをクリックする *click on* an icon.

クリップ a (paper) clip ▶この書類をクリップで留めてください Please fasten these papers with *a clip*. ／ Please clip these papers together.

グリップ (a) grip ▶バットのグリップ the *grip* of a bat.

クリニック a clinic ▶歯科クリニック a dental *clinic*.

くりぬく くり貫く hollow (out) ▶木の幹をくりぬいて作った舟 a boat *hollowed* from a tree trunk ‖ 子供たちはカボチャをくりぬいてちょうちんを作った The children *hollowed out* pumpkins to make lanterns.

くりのべる 繰り延べる postpone +⊞, put off（➤ 後者は「延ばす」に近い） ▶修学旅行は7月に繰り延べられた Our school excursion *was postponed* [*was put off*] until July.

くりひろげる 繰り広げる ▶両チームは熱戦を繰り広げた Both teams *played* an exciting game. ‖ 文化祭はにぎやかに繰り広げられた The school festival *was held* with a huge crowd of students and visitors (in attendance).

くりょ 苦慮する worry 《about, over》 ▶事態の対策に苦慮する *worry* what measures to take to deal with the situation ‖ 学校当局はそのいじめ事件の対応に苦慮している The school authorities are *finding* the bullying incident *a difficult problem to deal with*.

グリル a grill (room)（焼き肉料理を主に出す食堂）; a grill（焼き網） ▶マスをグリルで焼く broil a trout on *a grill*.

1 **くる 来る** **1【人が向こうからやって来る】** come ▶彼女は日曜日ごとにここに来る She *comes* here every Sunday. ‖ 10時に待ち合わせたのに, 彼女はとうとう来なかった（＝現れなかった） We had a date for 10 (o'clock), but she *didn't show* [*turn*] *up*. ‖ ここならずっと前に一度来たことがあるよ Oh, I *did come* here once a long time ago.（➤ did come は came の強調） ‖ さようなら. また来るからね Good-bye. I'll *come* [*be*] *by* again.（➤ be by は come by と同じで, 「人の家へやって来る」） ‖ みんなでピクニックに行くんだけど, きみも来ないか We're all going on a picnic. *Why not come along*?

ことわざ **来る者は拒まず, 去る者は追わず** We [I] neither reject those who come, nor chase after those who leave.

✉ **今バルセロナに来ています. きょうは市内見物をしました** Now I'*m in* Barcelona. I did sightseeing in the city today. ‖ 対話「いつ金沢に来るの?」「来週行くよ」 "When *are* you *coming* to Kanazawa?" "Next week."

2【ものが向こうからやって来る】 come ▶ほら, バスが来たよ Hey, the bus *is coming*. ‖ ことしは年賀状が40枚来た I *got* 40 New Year's cards this year. ‖ 彼女に先月手紙を書いたが, まだ返事が来ない I wrote to her last month, but she *hasn't answered* yet. ‖ 入試合格の通知が来た I *received* notification that I had passed the entrance examination. ‖ こんなチャンスは二度と来ないだろう This kind of chance will *never come again*. ‖ 新聞は6時半頃に来たと思います I think (that) the newspaper *was delivered* at about six thirty. ‖ この様子だと一雨来るな (Judging) from the look of the sky, it's bound *to rain* (soon).

▶交渉は最終段階に来て暗礁に乗り上げた The negotiations deadlocked *at* the final stage. ‖ 五十音順では彼の名前はいちばん後ろに来る His name *comes* last in the order of the Japanese (kana) syllabary.

3【時刻・時期・順番などが近づく】▶ゆく年来る年 the outgoing year and the *incoming* year／the old year and the *new* year ‖ あと10日でお正月が来る The new year *will be here* in just ten (more) days. ‖ 今度の誕生日が来ると20歳になります I'll be twenty *on* my next birthday. ‖ 出かける時間が来た The time *has come* for us to go.／It's time to go. ‖ 2時間待ってやっと私の番が来た After waiting for two hours, my turn *came* at last. ‖ 来年の3月が来れば父は退職予定だ *Coming* next March, my father will retire (from his job).

4【感覚・身体に感じる】▶きみの案はどうもぴんと来ないね Your idea just *doesn't work* for me.／Your idea just *doesn't click* with me.

▶かぜが胃腸にきて，下痢が1週間止まらなかった The flu *affected* my stomach and I had diarrhea nonstop for a week.

5【起因・由来する】 **come**《from》▶豆腐は中国から来た Tofu *came from* China. ‖ 便秘は運動不足からくるそうだ I hear constipation *comes from* (a) lack of exercise. ‖「トナカイ」という語はアイヌ語から来ている The word 'tonakai' *comes* [*derives*] *from* the Ainu language.

6【「…してくる」の形で】▶「前に出て来い」と先生が言った "*Come to* the front of the class !" said the teacher. ‖ 後藤さんの所へ行って謝って来い *Go apologize* to the Gotos. (➤「go＋原形」は《米・インフォーマル》に多く，「go and ＋原形」よりもくだけた言い方) ‖ おさむ，アイスクリームを買って来いよ *Go buy* some ice cream, Osamu. ‖ 4月には新入生がたくさん入学してきます In April, many new students *enter* our school.

▶雨が降ってきたので急いで帰宅した *It began to rain*, so we hurried back home. ‖ ブドウが実ってきた The grapes *are ripening*.

▶この家もだいぶ傷んできた This house *has become* quite a bit (*the*) *worse for wear*. ‖ ぼくは千春さんが好きになってきた I*'ve gotten* [*come*] *to like* Chiharu. ‖ 親友の重要性がわかるようになってきた I*'ve come to realize* the importance of (having and keeping) close friends. (➤ come to do は「…するようになる」で，believe, know, realize, understand, expect, think などが do の部分にくることが多い) ‖ 息子も英語がおもしろくなってきたらしい It looks like my son *has come to find* English *interesting* [*has come to enjoy* (studying) English]. ‖ パ・リーグの優勝争いがおもしろくなってきた The Pacific League's pennant race *has turned out to be very exciting*.

7【…しに来る】 **come to** [**and**] **do** ▶おじが帯広空港まで迎えに来てくれた My uncle *came to meet* me at Obihiro Airport. ‖ 友子ちゃんはお母さんが呼びに来て帰った Tomoko's mother *came to* get her and they went home. ‖ たまには遊びに来いよ *Come and see* us some time.

☛ 来る日も来る日も，－ときたら (→見出語)

²くる 繰る ▶アルバムのページを繰っていると懐かしい昔がよみがえってくる As I *turn* (*over*) the pages of the album, the good old days come back to my mind.

ぐる ▶多くの土建業者がその汚職国会議員とぐるだった Many contractors *were in cahoots with* that corrupt Diet member. (➤ in cahoots with は「…と共謀して」の意のインフォーマルな表現).

くるい 狂い ▶エンジンに狂いが生じた There is *something wrong* with the engine. ‖ ロボットの仕事に狂いはない A robot does a *perfect* job.

▶《慣用表現》私の目に狂いはなかった I *was right* in my judgment.／There was *nothing wrong* with my judgment.

くるいざき 狂い咲き ▶1月に桜が狂い咲きしたそうだ I hear a cherry tree *blossomed out of season* in January.

くるう 狂う **1【気が】** **go crazy** [**mad**] ▶犬は狂ったようにほえた The dog barked *like crazy* [*mad*].

2【機械などの調子が】▶この磁石は狂っている This compass *is not working* [*is off*]. ‖ 私の時計は狂っている My watch *does not keep good time*. ‖ このピアノは音が狂っている This piano *is out of tune*.

3【予定・見込みなどが変わる】▶雪崩のためバスの運行予定が狂った The snowslide has *thrown* the buses *off schedule*. ‖ 吉田のやつ，変なことばかり言うから調子狂っちゃうよ Yoshida always says the funniest things and *throws* me *off pace*.

4【夢中になる】 **be crazy** ▶兄はロックに狂っている My brother *is crazy about* rock music. ‖ ぼくたちは皆踊り狂った All of us *danced like crazy*. ‖ 王子は既婚の女優との恋に狂った The prince *was madly in love with* a married actress.

クルー a **crew**(乗組員・乗務員などの1チーム全体).

クルーザー a **cabin cruiser** /krúːzəʳ/ ▶エーゲ海をクルーザーで一周したい I want to sail the Aegean Sea in *a cabin cruiser*.

グループ a **group** ▶彼らはいくつかのグループに分かれて出かけた They went out in (several) *groups*. ‖ 6人ずつのグループに分かれてください Make [Form] *groups* of six. ‖ 日本では人々はよくグループで行動する In Japan, people often act *in groups*. ‖ ぼくは「昆虫研究グループ」に加わった I joined the Entomological Study *Group*. ‖ 先頭グループは10キロ地点を過ぎた *The leading group* passed the 10 kilometer point.

▶あんな不良グループと付き合ってはだめだよ You must not hang around with that *bunch of delinquents*. (➤ bunch は「一団」).

グルーミング **grooming**.

くるくる ▶毛糸をくるくると巻いて玉にする *wind* woolen yarn into a ball ‖ 彼女の家を探して同じ所をくるくる歩き回った I *went round and round* the same area looking for her house. ‖ 少女はくるくる動く目でほほえんだ The girl smiled *as she darted her gaze about*. ‖ 木枯らしに枯れ葉がくるくる舞った A dead leaf *spun away* on [in] the harsh autumn wind. ‖ 社長は方針をくるくる変える The president *always* [*constantly*] *changes* his policy. ‖ イギリスの天気はくるくる変わる The weather in England *is changeable* [*fickle*]. (➤ fickle は「(天気などが)変わりやすい」).

ぐるぐる ▶こまがぐるぐる回っている The top is spinning *round and round*. ‖ 私たちは京都の町をぐるぐる歩き回った We walked *around* Kyoto. ‖ デモ隊は警察署の周りをぐるぐる回った The demonstrators *circled* the police station. ‖ 大したけがでもないのに腕を包帯でぐるぐる巻きにされた My arm *was heavily bandaged* though it was a slight wound.

くるしい 苦しい

1【肉体的に苦痛だ】▶胸が苦しい My chest *hurts* (me).／I *have a pain* in my chest. ‖ 息が苦しい I *find it hard to breathe*. ‖ お餅を5個も食べたら，胃の辺りが苦しくてしょうがない My stomach *feels heavy* after eating five sticky rice cakes.／I ate five sticky rice cakes and my stomach *feels heavy*. ‖ その走者はゴールインしたあと, ひどく苦しがった The runner *was in extreme pain* after reaching the finish line.

2【精神的に苦痛だ】▶我々は苦しい立場に追い込まれている We have been put in *a tight spot* [*a difficult situation*]. ‖ 多くの性犯罪被害者たちは苦しい胸のうちを明かせないでいる Most sex crime victims can't confide their *inner torment* to anyone.

ことわざ 苦しい時の神頼み People turn to religion in times of distress. (➤「人間は苦難のときには宗教に頼る」の意).

3【経済的・時間的に困難だ】▶生活が苦しいと感じる feel *pinched* ‖ 苦しい生活に耐える endure *a life of hardship* ‖ わが家は家計が苦しい Our household finances *are in bad shape*. ／We *are bad(ly) off*. (➤《米》のインフォーマルでは bad off が多い) ‖ 1か月でこの仕事を仕上げるのはちょっと苦しい It is rather *difficult* to finish this job in a month.

4【不自然だ】▶苦しい言い訳をする make *a poor* [*clumsy*] *excuse* ‖ 今のだじゃれはちょっと苦しい That pun was pretty *bad*.

くるしまぎれ 苦し紛れ ▶苦し紛れにうそをつかざるをえなかった Since I had *been pushed* [*driven*] *into a corner*, I had to tell a lie. (➤「窮地に陥って」の意) ‖ あれは苦し紛れに言ったうそです I told that lie *to get out of the pinch I was in*. (➤「窮地を脱するために」の意).

くるしみ 苦しみ (a) **pain, suffering** (苦痛 ; 後者がより堅い語) ; **torment** (主に精神的な極度の苦痛) ; **hardship(s)** (苦難) ; **trouble(s)** (悩み) ▶精神的な苦しみ mental *pain* [*suffering*] ‖ こんな苦しみは二度と味わいたくない I don't want to have to go through this kind of *suffering* [*torment*] again. ‖ 祖父はよく戦争中の苦しみは忘れられないと言う My grandfather often says he can never forget the *hardships* he experienced during the war. ‖ カウンセラーはきっときみの苦しみを理解してくれるよ I'm sure (that) the counselor will be able to understand your *troubles*.

くるしむ 苦しむ

1【肉体的に】suffer 《from》 ▶彼は長年ぜんそくで苦しんでいる He *has been suffering from* asthma for a long time. (➤「ぜんそくで苦しむ人」は an asthma sufferer) ‖ 精神的に苦しむ *suffer* mentally ‖ 激しいせきで2日間苦しんだ Violent coughing *made* me *suffer* for two days. ‖ 祖父は老衰で苦しまずに死んだ My grandfather died *painlessly* from old age.

2【困る, 骨折る】suffer 《from》 ▶ことしは雨が少ないので農家は水不足に苦しむだろう We have had very little rain this year. The farmers will *suffer from* the water shortage. ‖ 子供の登校拒否で苦しんでいる(＝心を痛めている)親がたくさんいる There are many parents who *are distressed* because their children refuse to attend school. ‖ 彼はいつも借金の返済に苦しんで(＝苦闘して)いた He *was* always *struggling* to pay back money he'd borrowed. ▶どうして彼が試験に落ちたのか理解に苦しむよ I *simply can't understand* how he failed the exam. ‖ 首相の答弁は玉虫色で解釈に苦しむところが多い The Prime Minister's answers are so vague, most of the time we *can hardly tell what they really mean*.

くるしめる 苦しめる ▶患者は長い間心臓病に苦しめられた The patient *suffered from* [*was troubled with*] heart disease for a long time. ‖ あの人たちは娘さんの非行に苦しめられている They *are distressed* by their daughter's (serious) misbehavior [antisocial behavior]. (◆「非行」を delinquency を用いて訳すと, 窃盗, 麻薬使用など, 違法行為を連想させるので, 訳例のように表現するほうがよい) ‖ そのチームは時々ジャイアンツを苦しめる The team occasionally *gives* the Giants *a hard time*.

グルテン gluten.

クルトン croutons /krúːtɑːnz/.

くるひもくるひも 来る日も来る日も ▶来る日も来る日も雨だった It kept raining *day after day* [*day in and day out*].

くるぶし 踝 an **ankle**.

くるま 車

1【自動車】a **car** (➤通例「乗用車」を指し, トラックやバスは含まない) ; a **taxi** (タクシー) ▶車に乗り込む get in *a car* ‖ 車を降りる get out of *a car* ‖ お宅まで車でお送りしましょう I'll *drive* you home. ‖ 彼女を家から病院まで車に乗せていった I *gave* her *a ride in my car* [I *drove* her] from her house to the hospital. ‖ ここへは車で来たの？ Did you *drive* here？‖ 父は毎日車で会社に行く My father *drives* to work every day. ‖ すぐ車で迎えに行くから郵便局の前に居なさい Stay in front of the post office. I'll *pick* you *up* right away. ‖ 小学生の女の子が車にはねられた An elementary school girl *was hit by a car*. ‖ 対話「山中湖までどうやって行くの？」「車で行くよ」"How are you going to Lake Yamanaka？" "(We're going) *by car*." ‖ 対話「空港からホテルまではどのくらいですか」「車で30分ほどです」"How long does it take to go to the hotel from the airport？" "About thirty minutes *by car*. ／It's about *a* thirty-minute *car ride*."

▶車に気をつけなさいよ Look out for *cars*. ‖ 車の運転中はよそ見をしないように Keep your eyes on the road *while you are at the wheel*. (➤この wheel は「ハンドル」の意 ; at the wheel で「運転して」の意味になる) ‖ ここは車が多い *The traffic is heavy* here. ▶車(＝タクシー)を呼んでください Please call *a taxi* for me. ／Please call me *a taxi*. ‖ 金曜の夜はなかなか車が拾えない It is very difficult to catch *a taxi* on a Friday night.

> **あなたの英語はどう響く?**
> 「ここへは車で来たんですか」を Did you come here by car？としがちだが, この英語は少々ぎこちない. by car は by train, by bus など, 移動の手段を対比するような文脈で用いるのがふつうだからである. 英語では Did you drive here？のほうが自然.

‖ **車代** a taxi fare (タクシー代) ; an honorarium /ɑːnəréəriəm/ paid as car fare (謝礼) ‖ **車止め** a car stop ‖ **車寄せ** a porte cochère /pɔːʳtkoʊʃéəʳ/.

2【車輪】a **wheel** ; a **caster** (キャスター) ▶ベビーカーには4つの車がついている A stroller has four *wheels*. ‖ 車のついたスーツケースが欲しい I want a suitcase with *wheels* [*casters*] (on the bottom).

くるまいす 車椅子 a **wheelchair** 《参考》《英》では病人用のほろ付き車椅子のことをその発祥地の名を冠して Bath chair と呼ぶ. ▶車椅子で利用できる公共図書館 a *wheelchair-accessible* public library ‖ メアリーは車椅子に乗っている Mary *is in a wheelchair*. ‖ 彼は車椅子でヨーロッパを旅行した He traveled Europe *in a wheelchair*.

‖ **車椅子用スロープ** a wheelchair ramp.

くるまえび 車海老 a **prawn** /prɔːn/.
くるまる ▶私は寒くて布団にくるまった I was cold and *wrapped myself up* in a futon. ‖ その女の子は毛布にくるまって震えていた The little girl was shivering *under her blanket*.
くるみ 胡桃《植物》a **walnut** ‖ **クルミ割り器** a pair of nutcrackers, a nutcracker.
-ぐるみ ▶町ぐるみで暴力反対運動をやっています *The whole town* is taking part in a campaign against violence. ／There is a *town-wide* anti violence campaign underway. ‖ 私は家族ぐるみでロンドンに行った I went to London *with my family*. ‖ 渡辺さんたちとは家族ぐるみの付き合いです The Watanabes *are like family* (to us ／for us).
くるむ wrap +㊐ ; **tuck** +㊐ (特に布などで) ▶私はそのお菓子を紙にくるんだ I *wrapped* the candy in paper. ‖ 看護師は生まれたばかりの赤ん坊をタオルでくるんだ The nurse *tucked* [*wrapped*] a towel around the newborn baby.
グルメ a **gourmet** /góəˊmeɪ/, a **gourmand**

> **危ないカタカナ語✸ グルメ**
> 1 フランス語の *gourmet* から来ているが, この語はワインなどの味がわかる本当の「食通」をいう. 似た語に同じくフランス語で *gourmand* があるが, こちらはどちらかといえば「美食家」「大食漢」のイメージ.
> 2 gourmet, gourmand とも英語になっているが, 日本語でいう「グルメ」は「おいしい物を食べるのが大好きな人」くらいの意味だから, food buff /bʌf/ といってもよい.
> 3「ご当地グルメ」という場合は the regional specialty.

くるりと ▶彼女は「さよなら」と言うとくるりと背を向けた She said, "Good-bye" and *turned around* to leave. ‖ 彼は態度をくるりと変えた He had a *complete* change of attitude.
ぐるりと ▶ぐるりと辺りを見回す look *around* ‖ 何十人という報道関係者がその容疑者の周りをぐるりと取り囲んだ Dozens of reporters *surrounded* the suspect.
くるわす 狂わす ▶その男との偶然の出会いが彼の人生を狂わせた A chance meeting with that man *threw* his life *off course* [*upset* the course of his life]. ‖ 一瞬のためらいが彼の手元を狂わせた A moment's hesitation caused him to *miss his aim*.
くれ 暮れ the end of the year (年末) ▶年の暮れは何かと気ぜわしい Things are always busy around *the end of the year*. ‖ 暮れには楽しいパーティーがある We will have an exciting party *at the end of the year*. ‖ 暮れのボーナスが待ち遠しい I can hardly wait for the *year-end* bonus. ‖ 父は昨年の暮れから病気で寝ている My father has been sick in bed since *the end of last year*.
グレー gray,《英》**grey** ▶彼はグレーの服がよく似合う He looks nice in *gray*.
クレーコート a **clay (tennis) court**.
クレーしゃげき クレー射撃 shooting clay pigeon /pídʒən/.
クレーター a **crater**.
グレードアップ ▶パソコンをグレードアップする *upgrade* a PC (➤「グレードアップ」は和製語).
クレープ a **crepe** /kreɪp/ (食べ物) ; **crepe** (織物).
グレープフルーツ (a) **grapefruit**.
クレーマー a **(problem) complainer** (➤ 英語の claimer は「請求者, 主張者」).
クレーム a **complaint** ▶細かいことにいちいちクレームをつけるなよ Don't *complain* [*grumble*] about every little thing. ‖ 新企画は課長はすんなりＯＫしたが, 部長のところでクレームがついた The section chief okayed the new project right away, but the department head *found fault with it*. (➤「けちをつけた」の意).

> **危ないカタカナ語✸ クレーム**
> 英語の claim は「要求, 請求」, 特にお金に関する賠償などの意味で使われ,「苦情, 文句, 反対」の意味はない. したがって「クレームをつける」というときは complain, make a complaint, あるいは object, raise an objection (抗議する) などとする必要がある.「彼はホテルのサービスにクレームをつけた」は He complained [made complaints] about the hotel service. である.

クレーン a **crane** ; a **derrick** /dérɪk/ (船などに貨物を積むときに使う)
‖ **クレーン車** a crane truck.
くれぐれも ▶くれぐれもお体を大切に *Be sure to* take (good) care of yourself. ‖ 運転にはくれぐれも気をつけて Please be *very* careful (when) driving.
✉ **ご両親さまにくれぐれもよろしくお伝えください** *Please give my best regards* [*wishes*] *to* your parents. ➤ 日本語と同じく改まった表現.
クレジット credit (掛け売り) ; a **credit** [**charge**] **card** (クレジットカード) ▶当店ではクレジットは扱っておりません We don't sell *on credit*. ‖ 現金になさいますか, クレジットになさいますか Would you like to pay with cash or *by credit card*? ／Will that be cash or *credit*? ‖ クレジットカードを受け付けますか Do you take *credit cards*? ‖ クレジット(カード)で払います I'll pay *by credit* (*card*). (➤ 実際には by VISA, by JCB のようにカード名を言うほうがより一般的) ‖ **6か月のクレジット**でオートバイを買った I bought a motorcycle using *a 6 month credit card loan*. →カード.
クレソン watercress (➤「クレソン」はフランス語の cresson から).
ぐれつ 愚劣な silly (ばかばかしい) ; **stupid** (愚かな) ▶愚劣な質問をするな Don't ask *stupid* questions. ‖ 何て愚劣なやつらだ! What a bunch of *idiots* (they are)!
くれない 紅の crimson /krímzən/, **deep red**.
くれなずむ 暮れなずむ ▶そのカップルは暮れなずむトレドの町を散策した The couple walked around Toledo *in the lingering twilight*.
クレバス a **crevasse** /krəvǽs/.
クレマチス《植物》a **clematis** /klémətɪs/.
クレムリン the Kremlin (モスクワにあるロシア大統領府のある宮殿).
クレヨン (a) **crayon** ▶この絵はクレヨンで描いてある This picture was drawn *in crayon* [*with crayons*].
[1]**くれる** 1【与える】**give** ▶その時計, 俺にくれよ *Give* me that watch. ‖ おじいちゃんが誕生祝いにテニスのラケットをくれた My grandfather *gave* me a tennis racket for my birthday. ‖ クラスの生徒たちがこのネクタイをくれました The students in my homeroom *gave* me this tie. ‖ お茶1杯くれる? Could you *get me* [*Could I have*] a cup of tea? ‖ 園田君がリスボンから電話をくれた Sonoda *called* [*phoned*] me from Lisbon. ‖ ブエノスアイレスに着いたら手紙[Eメール]をくれよ *Drop me a line* when you arrive at

[in] Buenos Aires.
▶こんなぼろ自転車, 欲しいやつにくれてやる Anyone who wants this beat-up bicycle [clunker of a bicycle] *can have it*.
2【「…してくれる」の形で】⚠「…してくれる」に相当する言い方は英語にはない. for ...(…のために)をつけて表す場合もあるが, ふつうは「動詞＋人」だけでその意を表すことができる.
▶母が手袋を編んでくれた My mother *knitted* a pair of gloves *for me*. ‖ 母が朝5時に起こしてくれた My mother *woke me up* at five in the morning. ‖ 友だちが昼食をおごってくれた A friend of mine *treated me* to lunch [*bought me* lunch]. ‖ 父がギターを買ってくれた My father *bought me* a guitar. ‖ シンガポールではみんな親切にしてくれた Everybody *was kind to me* in Singapore. ‖ よく来てくれたね I am glad you could come.
▶誘ってくれてありがとう Thank you for *asking* me *to* join you. ‖ 話してくれればよかったのに You should *have told me*.
3【「…してくれる?」と人に頼んで】

【文型】
…してくれませんか, くれますか
Can [Could] you do?
Will you (please) do?
Would you mind doing?

《解説》(1) 人に「…してくれませんか」と頼み事をするときには, Can you ～?, Will you ～? などの疑問文の形で聞く. can, will の代わりに could, would を使うと, 控えめなより丁寧な言い方になる. 気軽に頼むときは can, will でよいが, 多少とも相手を煩わすときは could, would にする.
(2) will, would はしばしば命令や指示で No. という返事を予想しない. can, could はお願いで断られることもありうる.
(3) Will you ～? はほかに相手の意思を聞くのにも用いる.「友だちになってくれませんか」は Will you be my friend? と言う.
(4) Please do ～. は「…してください, …してよ」などに当たる語調を和らげた命令形で, 家庭内や親友どうしなど以外では, 頼み事には使わないほうがよい. ただし, 相手に対し,「どうぞ…してください」と勧めるときには用いられる.
(5) 日本語では「…してくれませんか」と否定形でも,「…してくれますか」と肯定形でも言うが, 英語では依頼は肯定形で言う. Won't you do? は「…しませんか」という誘いの言い方であり, Can't you help me? は「手伝ってくれないの」という非難を込めた言い方になる.

▶この辺でどこかおいしい店を紹介してくれますか *Can you* [*Could you*] recommend a good restaurant near here? ‖ **対話**「ちょっと手伝ってくれない?」「今はだめよ」"*Can you* give me a little help (with this)?" "Not (right) now." ‖ (ぼくと)結婚してくれますか *Will you* marry me? ‖ **対話**「そのドア, 閉めてくれよ」「あ, はい」"*Will you* shut the door?" "OK. / Sure." (➤ 命令に近い依頼だから, この場合 (×) Could you ～? は不適当.「そのドアを閉めてくれますか」なら Would you mind closing the door?) ‖ ここで靴を脱いでくれませんか *Would you mind* taking your shoes off here? (➤ mind に強勢を置くと「…したらどうなのよ」と皮肉を込めた響きになるので注意;「上映中はおしゃべりをやめたらどうなの」は Would you mínd not talking during the movie?).

²くれる 暮れる 1【日が沈む】get dark ▶3キロも歩かないうちに日が暮れた We had not walked three kilometers before *it got* [*became*] *dark*. ‖ いつの間にか日はとっぷり暮れていた *Night had fallen* before I noticed it. ‖ 日が暮れないうちに帰ろう Let's go home *before dark*. (➤「日が暮れてから」は after dark).
2【年・季節が】▶あと1週間でことしも暮れる Only one week is left before the year *ends* [*comes to an end*]. ‖ いつしか秋も暮れようとしていた Autumn *had drawn to an end* before I knew it.
3【思案・悲しみに】▶終電に乗り遅れて途方に暮れた I missed the last train and *was at a complete loss*. ‖ 彼女は夫に死なれて悲嘆に暮れた She *was overwhelmed with grief* when her husband died.

ぐれる go astray ▶ぐれた若者 a *delinquent* youth ‖ 私は中学生のときにぐれかけた I *almost went astray* [*got into serious trouble*] when I was a junior high student. (➤ went astray は went wrong としてもよい).

クレンザー (a) **cleanser** /klénzəʳ/; (a) **detergent** (洗剤).

クレンジング・クリーム (a) **cleansing cream**, a **cleanser**.

くろ 黒 black ▶黒のスーツ a *black* suit ‖ 黒のドレスを着る put on a *black* dress.
▶結局, 彼は黒(＝有罪)なのか白なのか Well, is he *guilty* or not?
‖黒ダイ a black sea bream ‖ 黒土 black soil [earth] ‖ 黒パン brown [rye] bread ‖ 黒ビール dark beer; stout /staʊt/.
☛ 真っ黒 (⇀見出語)

くろい 黒い 1【色が】black; dark (黒っぽい) ▶黒い服を着た女性 a woman *dressed in black* / a woman *in a black dress* ‖ さおりは色が黒い Saori *is dark-skinned*. / Saori *has dark skin*. ‖ 由美子は黒い目と黒い髪をしている Yumiko has *dark brown eyes and black hair*. 《参考》(1) dark は人間の皮膚・目・髪などの色が濃いことを表す. 反対は fair. (2) dark hair の中でも black hair はずばり「黒髪」だが, black eye は「(殴られたりして)周りが黒くなった目」の意味に解釈されることが多い.
2【汚れて】▶彼のワイシャツは袖口が黒く汚れていた His shirts *were stained with grime* around the cuffs. (➤ grime は「汚れ, あか」).
3【不正な, いかがわしい】▶あの政治家にはとかく黒いうわさがついて回る That politician is always surrounded by *black* [*dark*] *rumors*.

クロイツフェルト・ヤコブ病 Creutzfeldt-Jakob /krɔ̀ɪtsfelt-jáːkoʊb/ **disease** (➤ 略称は CJD).

くろう 苦労 hardship (辛苦); **difficulty** (困難); **trouble** (面倒) **━動 苦労する have a hard time, have difficulty [trouble]** ▶父の一生は苦労の連続だった My father has led a life of continual *hardship*. ‖ 彼は長年苦労をともにした奥さんに先立たれてしまった He lost his wife, who had shared long years of *hardship* with him. ‖ 若い頃はぐれて親に苦労をかけた When I was a kid, I went astray [I was a bad kid] and *gave* my parents *no end of trouble*. ‖ 《夫が妻に向かって》おまえにもずいぶん苦労をかけたね I know I've *put you through* a lot of *trouble* through the years, dear. ‖ 優勝したことで選手たちの苦労は報われた The *hard work* of the players paid off when they won the championship. ‖ 彼はまだ**苦労が足りない**よ He *lacks experience*.

> **【文型】**
> A **で苦労する**
> **have trouble with** A
> …**するのに苦労する**
> **have trouble** doing
> **have difficulty** doing
> **《解説》** 前者は手間や面倒くささを, 後者は困難さをいうが, 後者のほうがやや堅いだけで意味に大差はない. 面倒くささや困難さの程度を some, great, no などをつけて表すことも多い.

▶英語のリスニング**に苦労する**生徒が多い Many students *have trouble with* English listening comprehension. ‖ きみのうちを見つける**のに苦労した**よ I *had trouble* find*ing* your house. ‖ 息子は**何の苦労もなく**新しい環境になじんだようだ My son seems to have *had no trouble* adapt*ing* to his new surroundings. ‖ 悪天候の中, パイロットは**苦労して**ジェット機を操縦した The pilot *had great difficulty* fly*ing* the jet in the bad weather. ‖ 50を過ぎると職探しには**苦労する** It's *hard* to find a job once you're over 50.

▶私は英語を習得するのにずいぶん**苦労した** I *had an extremely hard time* learning English. ‖ 彼は妻と離婚して以来**苦労している** He has been *having a hard time* since he divorced his wife. (➤ a hard time は「つらい時期や経験」) ‖ 彼は**金に苦労している**ようだ He seems to *be in financial difficulty*. ／He seems to *be financially strapped*. ‖ 彼女は**大した苦労もせずに**人気歌手になった She achieved popularity as a singer *without even trying*. (➤「その努力さえもしないで」の意).

▶**苦労して稼いだ金**は, ばかな使い方はふつうしないものだ *Money gotten through hard work* [*Hard-earned money*] is usually not spent foolishly. ‖ **苦労話**をする tell *a hard luck story* ‖ 母は**苦労して**私たち3人の子供を育てた My mother *struggled* to bring up the three of us. (➤ struggle は「苦闘する, 奮闘する」) ‖ どうして帰りが遅くなったのか言い訳するの**に苦労した** I *was hard put* to come up with an excuse for why I had come home so late. (➤ be hard put to do は「…するのに困る」の意のインフォーマルな表現) ‖ 祖母は**苦労性**だ My grandmother is *a worrywart*. (➤ worrywart は「苦労性[心配性]の人」).

☛ **ご苦労, 一苦労** (→見出語)

ぐろう 愚弄する **ridicule** +Ⓔ ▶公衆の面前で人を**愚弄する**つもりか Are you trying to *ridicule* me in public?

くろうと 玄人 a **professional**(プロ) ; a **specialist**(専門家) ▶結局素人は**玄人**にかなわない It's not easy for an amateur to beat [surpass] *a professional*. ‖ 彼は農業問題については**玄人**だ He is *a specialist* in the field of agriculture. ‖ 彼の絵は**玄人はだし**だ His painting would *put a professional artist to shame*. (➤ put ... to shame は「…を恥じ入らせる」).

くろうにん 苦労人 a **sadder but** [**and**] **wiser person** ; a **self-made man** [**woman**] (たたき上げの人) ▶彼は若いがなかなかの**苦労人**だ Though young, he's *been through a lot of hardships* [he *has seen a lot of life* ／he *has gone through a lot*].

クローク a **cloakroom** /klóʊkruːm/ (➤ cloak だけでは「マント」の意味にしかならない) ▶**クローク**にかばんとコートを預けた I checked my bag and coat at the *cloakroom*.

クローズアップ a **close-up** /klóʊsʌp/
▶テレビの画面にヒロインの顔が**クローズアップ**された *A close-up* of the heroine's face appeared on the TV screen.
▶《比喩的》ＰＴＡの集まりでいじめの問題が**クローズアップ**された(＝大きく取り上げられた) The problem of bullying *was highlighted* at the PTA meeting.

クローゼット a **closet**.

クローバー a **clover** ▶四つ葉の**クローバー**は幸せをもたらすと言われている *A four-leaf clover* is said to bring good luck.

グローバル グローバルな **global** 一副 **グローバルに** **globally** ▶**グローバルな**競争に生き残る survive *global* competition ‖ ビジネスを**グローバル**に展開する expand a business *globally*.
‖ **グローバルスタンダード** a [the] global standard.

グローブ a **glove** /glʌv/ ▶ショートは鮮やかな**グローブ**さばきを見せた The shortstop showed [displayed ／exhibited] brilliant *glove work*.

グローブボックス a **glove box**, a **glove** [**dash**] **compartment**.

クロール **the crawl** ▶**クロール**で泳ぐ *swim* [*do*] *the crawl* ‖ 彼女は**クロール**でプールを4往復した She swam four laps *doing the crawl* (*stroke*).

クローン a **clone** /kloʊn/ (個体) ; **cloning**(手法) ▶**クローン人間** *a human clone* ‖ **クローン技術** *cloning* technology ‖ 政府は**クローン**を規制する法律を制定すべきだ The government should enact laws to regulate *cloning*.

くろかみ 黒髪 **black hair** ▶**黒髪**の少女 a girl *with black hair*.

くろぐろ 黒々 ▶彼は真っ白い紙に**墨黒々**と「新春」と書いた He wrote "Shinshun" *in deep black* on a sheet of spotless white paper. ‖ 父は**黒々とした髪**をしている My father has *jet-black* hair (*with no traces of gray*).

くろこ 黒子 a ***kuroko*** ; person in black who assists a performer in kabuki or an operator in a puppet theater(➤ 説明的な訳).

くろこげ 黒焦げの **charred** /tʃɑːʳd/ ▶**黒焦げの**トースト a *charred* slice of toast ‖ チキンはオーブンの中で**黒焦げ**になった The chicken *was charred* [*was burnt black*] in the oven.

くろこしょう 黒胡椒 **black pepper**.

くろざとう 黒砂糖 **brown sugar**.

くろじ 黒字 a **surplus** /sə́ːʳplʌs/ (貿易などの余剰金)
▶ここのところ彼の会社は**黒字**を増やしている These days his company is enjoying increasing *profitability* [*profits*]. ‖ 今月は2万円の**黒字**だ We have gone twenty thousand yen *into the black* this month. ‖ わが家は今月は**黒字**だ We are [Our accounts are] *in the black* this month.
‖ **貿易黒字** a trade surplus.

くろしお 黒潮 **the Kuroshio Current, the Japan Current**.

くろず 黒酢 **black vinegar**.

クロスカントリー ‖ **クロスカントリースキー** cross-country skiing.

クロスゲーム a **close game**(➤ この close /klous/ は「小差の」の意 ; →**接戦**) ▶決勝戦では5対4の**クロスゲーム**でＰＬ学園が勝った PL Gakuen won the final 5-4 *in a close game*. (➤ 5-4は five to four と読

む).

クロスバー a **crossbar** ▶**彼のシュートはクロスバーに当たった** His shot hit *the crossbar*.

クロスプレー a **close play** (➤ この close /klous/ は「際どい, 間一髪の」の意) ▶**クロスプレーだったが三塁は間一髪タッチアウトだった** The runner was tagged out in *a close play* at third (base).

危ないカタカナ語✹ クロス
クロスゲーム, クロスプレーの「クロス」は cross ではなく close /klous/ であることに注意.「接近した」「互角の」の意である. また, テーブルクロスの「クロス」は cloth (布)である.

くろずむ 黒ずむ blacken ▶**黒ずんだ色の土** *dark* earth ‖ **目の縁が黒ずんでいるところを見ると, 彼はひどく疲れているに違いない** Judging from [by] the *dark* rings around his eyes, he must be very tired. ‖ **台所の白い壁が煙のせいでだんだん黒ずんできた** The white walls of the kitchen *have become blackened* from smoke. ‖ **ワイシャツの襟が黒ずんできた** My shirt collar *has developed a grimy ring*. (➤ grimy /grámi/ は「汚れた」, ring は「(あかなどでできた)輪」).

クロスレファレンス a **cross reference.**

クロスワードパズル a **crossword (puzzle)** ▶**クロスワードパズルを解く** do [work out] *a crossword* (*puzzle*) 《**参考**》「8のヨコ[タテ]を解く」は work out 8 across [down] という.

クロッカス 《植物》a **crocus** /króukəs/.

グロッキー groggy /grá:gi/.

くろっぽい 黒っぽい blackish ; **dark**(暗色の) ▶**黒っぽい鳥** a *blackish* bird ‖ **彼女は黒っぽい服ばかり着る** She always wears *dark* clothes.

グロテスク grotesque ▶**グロテスクな彫像** a *grotesque* statue.

くろてん 黒貂 《動物》**sable.**

くろびかり 黒光り ▶**彼女は木の彫刻を黒光りするまで磨いた** She polished the wooden carving until it *took on a dark* [*black*] *luster*. (➤ luster は「光沢, 輝き」).

くろふね 黒船 a **black ship (that came to Japan at the end of the Edo period).**

くろぼし 黒星 a **black spot**(黒い点) ; a **defeat**, a **loss**(敗北) ; a **black mark**, a **blot**(汚点) ▶**黒星を重ねる** *suffer defeat after defeat* / *have a losing streak* (➤ streak は「(不運・幸運などの)一続き」) / *have a string of losses*.

くろまく 黒幕 a **wirepuller**, a **mastermind** ▶**政界の黒幕** *a behind-the-scenes kingpin* in politics (➤ kingpin は「中心人物, 親玉」) ‖ **では, 一体誰が事件の黒幕なんだ** Well, then, who's *pulling the strings* [《ときに》 *the wires*] (*from behind*) ? (➤「誰が後ろで糸を引いているのか」の意) / Well, then, who's *working behind the scenes* ? (➤「誰が裏工作をしているのか」の意).

くろめ 黒目 ▶**黒目がちの少女** a girl *with big dark eyes*. 《**参考**》 black eyes は, 殴られたり, ぶつけたりして, 目の周りが黒あざになっている目の意味になる.

くろやま 黒山 ▶**校門の前は黒山の人だかりだった** There was *a large crowd* in front of the school gate.

クロレラ 《植物》**chlorella** /klərélə/.

クロワッサン a **croissant** /krwɑ:sá:nt/, a **crescent** /krésənt/ **(roll).**

¹くわ 鍬 a **hoe** /hou/.

²くわ 桑 《植物》a **mulberry** /mʌ́lbèri/ **(tree)** (木) ; a **mulberry**(実).

くわい 《植物》**arrowhead** ; an **arrowhead root**(食用にする根).

¹くわえる 加える 1【付け足す】add +目 ▶**スープにもう少し塩を加えてください** *Add* a little more salt to the soup. ‖ **3に4を加えると7になる** Three *plus* four equals [makes] seven. (➤ make は子供の, または子供っぽい言い方) ‖ **私もこのグループに加えてください** Please *let* me *join* this group. ‖ **犬や猫まで加える(=含める)とうちは10人家族です** There are ten in my family, if you *include* [*count*] dogs and cats. ▶**花田君は頭がいいが, それに加えてハンサムときている** Hanada is smart. *In addition* (*to that*) [*What's more* / *On top of that*], he's handsome.

2【与える】▶**チャンピオンは挑戦者の顎に一撃を加えた** The champion *landed a blow* to the challenger's chin. ‖ **この亀は人に危害を加えることがあります** This turtle may *harm* visitors. ‖ **教師は生徒に体罰を加えてはならない** Teachers must not *inflict* corporal punishment on students. (➤ inflict は「(打撃・被害など)を加える, 及ぼす」).

²くわえる 銜える・銜える hold [**have**] **... in** one's **mouth** ▶**ポチはその骨を口にくわえた** Pochi *took* [*held*] the bone *in his mouth*. ‖ **弟は鉛筆を口にくわえていた** My brother *had* a pencil *in his mouth*. ‖ **その男はパイプをくわえてその場を立ち去った** The man left the place *with a pipe in his mouth* [*pipe in mouth*].

くわがた 鍬形 《虫》a **stag beetle.**

くわけ 区分け classification(分類) ; **division**(区分) **一動 区分けする classify** +目, **divide** +目 ▶**資料をテーマによって区分けした** We *classified* the materials by topic.

くわしい 詳しい

1【詳細な】detailed /dɪtéɪld ‖ dí:teɪld/ ▶**詳しいことはあとでお知らせします** I'll let you know *the details* later on. ‖ **この点についてもっと詳しい説明の出ている参考書が欲しい** I want a reference book that explains this *in greater detail*.
▶**原子力発電についてもっと詳しく知りたい** I would like to *know more* about nuclear power generation. ‖ **そのことについてもっと詳しく説明してください** Would you *elaborate* on that ? ‖ **この辞書は説明が詳しくて使いやすい** This dictionary is very useful and *gives* (lots of) *detailed explanations*. ‖ **詳しくは「マガジンX」をお読みください** *For further details*, read "Magazine X." ‖ 《広告文などで》**詳しくは直接お問い合わせください** Apply in person *for further information*. (➤ in person は「本人自ら直接に」の意).

✉ **このことについては, この次にもっと詳しくお便りします** I'll write (to) you *in more* [*greater*] *detail* next time regarding this (matter).

2【よく知っている】▶**田久保先生はアメリカ西海岸に詳しい** Mr. Takubo *knows a lot about* [*knows his way around*] the West Coast of the United States. (➤ know one's way around は「(場所の)地理に詳しい」) ‖ **黒田君は野球[ジャズ]にとても詳しい** Kuroda *knows all about* baseball [jazz]. ‖ **コンピューターに詳しい総務部長** a computer-*savvy* general affairs manager ‖ **この辺りは詳しくないんです** I'*m a stranger* in this neighborhood. ‖ **この銀行強盗事件は内部事情に詳しい者の犯行に違いない** This bank robbery must have been committed by someone *with detailed inside information*.

くわずぎらい 食わず嫌い ▶生ガキが食べられないんだって？**食わず嫌い**だろう You can't eat raw oysters？I bet you'*re just prejudiced because you never tried them*.（➤「偏見をもっている」の意）‖ＳＦが嫌いなの？**食わず嫌い**よ，きっと You don't like science fiction？You'*re just prejudiced because you've never read any*.

くわせる 食わせる ▶腹がぺこぺこで死にそうだ．**何か食わせて**よ I'm starving. *Give me something to eat*, will you？‖彼には**食わせていかなければならない**大勢の家族がいた He had a large family to *support*.‖光雄のやつ，あんまりしつこいから**肘鉄食わせてやった**わ That Mitsuo！I *gave* him *the brush-off* for being such a pest.

▶《慣用表現》やつに**一杯食わせてやった**．ざまあみろ！I *played a trick on* him；it serves him right！

くわだて 企て an **attempt**(試み)；a **plan**(計画)

▶無謀な**企て** a reckless［desperate］*attempt*‖彼の**企て**は失敗に終わった His *attempt* ended in failure.

くわだてる 企てる **plan** ＋㊐（計画する）；**plot** ＋㊐（たくらむ）；**try** ＋㊐，**attempt** ＋㊐（試みる）▶彼らは何か悪いことを**企てている**ようだ They seem to *be planning*［*plotting*］something evil.／They seem to *be up to* no good.‖あの会社は海外進出を**企てている** That company *is planning* to expand overseas.‖囚人たちは脱獄を**企てた**が失敗した The prisoners *attempted* to escape but failed.（➤attempt という語そのものに不成功のニュアンスがある）.

くわわる 加わる **join** ＋㊐ ▶私はみんなの話に**加わった** I *joined* in their conversation.‖ぼくらの仲間に**加わらない**か？Would you like to *join* our group？／How about *joining* us？

▶大勢の人が**加わって**網を引いた A large number of people *joined* together to pull in the net.‖私はそんな陰謀に**加わる**ことは断じてできない I could never *take part in* such a plot.

▶暑さが一段と**加わった** It *got*［*grew*］markedly *hotter*.‖雨の上に風が**加わる**でしょう *In addition to* the rain, there will be some wind.

-くん -君

> **《解説》「…君」の呼び方**
> (1)日本語の「…君」のように主に同輩や目下の人につける特別な敬称は英語にはない．呼びかけるときは親しい間柄であれば名(given name)で呼ぶ．
> (2)少し改まって，例えば第三者(特に目上の人)に同輩・友人のことを話す場合は姓(family name)で呼び，状況に応じて Mr., Miss, Ms. などをつける．
> (3)教室などで日本人どうしが英語を話す場合は -kun としてもよい．

▶古賀**君**，おはよう Good morning, Koga.（➤英語国民の習慣では，古賀太郎ならば Good morning, Taro. のように言う）‖水野**君**，元気かい？How are you, Mizuno(*-kun*)？‖森田**君**は来月結婚する予定です（*Mr.*）Morita is going to get married next month.

1**ぐん 郡** 《米》a **county** /káʊnṭi/, 《英》a **district**

> **《解説》**(1) 日本の郡は county と表現してよいが，この語はアメリカでは州(state) の中の最大行政区画を指し，イギリスでは「州」そのものを指す．
> (2) 外国向けの手紙では差出人の住所の「郡」は下のように -gun とローマ字で書くほうがよい．
> (例)〒410-3512
> 静岡県賀茂郡西伊豆町一色12345
> 12345, Ishiki, Nishi-Izu-cho
> Kamo-gun, Shizuoka, 410-3512
> JAPAN

2**ぐん 群** ▶彼はバッティングに関しては**群を抜いている** When it comes to batting, he *is unrivaled*［*is ahead of the pack*］.‖ゆう子はクラスの中で**群を抜いて**英語がよくできる Yuko is *head and shoulders above* the rest of her class in English.（➤head and shoulders above は文字どおりには「…より頭と肩だけ(高い)」の意）‖彼はジャイアンツの投手の中でも**群を抜いて**コントロールがいい He has *by far* the best control among the Giants' pitchers.

3**ぐん 軍** an **army**（➤もとは「陸軍」の意）；**the forces**（陸海空軍）；**troops**（軍隊）▶連合(国)**軍** the allied *forces*‖空**軍** the air *force*‖国連**軍** the U.N. *forces*［*troops*］.

☛ 軍隊，軍部（→見出語）

ぐんい 軍医 an **army doctor**(陸軍の)；a **navy doctor**(海軍の).

ぐんか 軍歌 a **war song**, a **martial**［**military**］**song**.

くんかい 訓戒 a (**formal**) **warning** ▶カンニングすれば**訓戒**では済まないぞ If you cheat on the exam, you won't get away with just *a warning*.（➤warning は「警告」. admonition を使うと「穏やかな［好意的な］注意」の意になる）.

ぐんかん 軍艦 a **warship**.

ぐんき 軍紀 **military regulations**.

くんくん ▶その犬は鼻を**くんくん**させて食べ物を探し回った The dog *sniffed around* for food.

ぐんぐん ▶気温は**ぐんぐん**(＝急速に)上昇した The temperature rose *rapidly*.‖彼女は背が**ぐんぐん**伸びた She grew *taller and taller*.‖加代子が手伝ってくれたので仕事が**ぐんぐん**はかどった Kayoko lent me a hand so the work went *quickly*.

ぐんこう 軍港 a **naval**［**military**］**port**.

くんこく 訓告 (an) **admonition** 一㊍ **訓告する** **admonish** ＋㊐.

ぐんこくしゅぎ 軍国主義 **militarism**

‖**軍国主義者** a militarist.

くんし 君子 a **virtuous person**(有徳の士)；a **wise person**(知者) ▶ことわざ **君子危うきに近寄らず** A wise person does not court danger.（➤日本語からの意訳．この場合の court は「(災いなどを)招く」の意の古風な語）.

くんじ 訓示 **instructions** ▶社長は全社員に**訓示した** The president *gave instructions* to all the employees.

ぐんし 軍師 a **military strategist**.

ぐんじ 軍事 **military affairs** 一㊎ **軍事の** **military**

▶**軍事**演習を行う hold *military exercises*［*maneuvers*／*drills*］‖イスラエルはいつでも**軍事行動を起こす**態勢を整えている Israel is always prepared to *start*［*enter into*］*military action*.

‖**軍事介入** military intervention‖**軍事基地** a military base‖**軍事攻撃** a military strike‖**軍事裁判** a military tribunal‖**軍事作戦** a military operation‖**軍事支配** military rule‖**軍事情報** military intelligence‖**軍事政権** a military regime［government］‖**軍事費** military expenditure‖**軍事力** military power［force／might］.

ぐんしきん 軍資金 a **war chest**, **war funds**；**campaign funds**(運動費).

くんしゅ 君主 a **monarch** /mɑ́:nəʳk/ (王・女王・皇帝など) ; a **sovereign** /sɑ́:vrən/ (最高の支配者)
‖**君主国** a monarchy (➤ 日本のような「立憲君主国」は a constitutional monarchy という) ‖**君主制** monarchism, a monarchial system ‖**君主政治**[**政体**] monarchy ‖**専制君主** an absolute monarch.

ぐんじゅ 軍需 ‖**軍需工場** a munition(s) plant [factory] ‖**軍需産業** the munition(s) industry ‖**軍需品** war supplies, munitions.

ぐんしゅう 群衆・群集 a **crowd** ; a **mob** (暴徒) ▶1万5000の**群衆** *a crowd* of fifteen thousand ‖その男の姿はやがて**群衆**の中に見えなくなった The man soon disappeared in [among] *the crowd*.
▶**群集心理**が働いて, デモ隊は興奮して機動隊に投石を始めた *Mob psychology* was at work, and the demonstrators became excited and started throwing rocks at the riot squad.

ぐんしゅく 軍縮 **disarmament, arms reduction, arms limitation, limitation of arms** 《参考》disarmament は本来「武装解除」の意であるが, 国際政治用語としては「軍備縮小」を意味する.
‖**軍縮会議** a disarmament conference ‖**核軍縮** nuclear disarmament.

くんしょう 勲章 an **order** (勲位を示す) ; a **medal** (コイン形の) ; a **decoration** (飾りひも・胸飾りなどを含めた).
▶彼は武勲により**勲章を授けられた** He *was decorated* for bravery.

ぐんじょういろ 群青色の **ultramarine** /ʌ̀ltrəmərí:n/.

くんしらん 君子蘭 《植物》a **clivia** /kláɪviə, kliv-/, a **Kaffir lily.**

ぐんじん 軍人 a **soldier** (陸軍兵士を指すが, 時に海・空軍兵士を指す) ; a **sailor** (海軍の) ; an **airman** [**-woman**] (空軍の) ; a **serviceman** [**-woman**] (兵士に対する客観的な呼称) ; **service personnel** /pə̀:ʳsənel/ (➤ 集合的) ; an **officer** (将校) ; a **marine** (海兵隊員)
‖**職業軍人** a career /kəríəʳ/ soldier ‖**退役軍人** 《米》a veteran, 《英》an ex-serviceman.

くんせい 燻製の・薫製の **smoked** ▶サケのくん製 *smoked* salmon.

ぐんせい 群生 ▶その池の周りにはアヤメが**群生している** (Japanese) irises *grow thickly* around that pond.

ぐんそう 軍曹 a **sergeant.**

ぐんぞう 群像 a **lively crowd** ; 《彫刻》a **group sculpture** ▶青春の**群像** a youthful *crowd*.

ぐんたい 軍隊 **(armed) forces, the military** 《参考》陸軍, 海軍, 空軍はそれぞれ the army, the navy, the air force という. ▶**軍隊に入る** join [enlist in] *the military*.
‖**軍隊生活** military life.

-くんだり ▶アラスカくんだりまで何しに行ったんだい? What made you go *as far as* [*all the way to*] Alaska?

ぐんだん 軍団 an **(army) corps.**

ぐんて 軍手 **(cotton) work gloves.**

ぐんと ▶ちょっと見ない間に背が**ぐんと伸びた**ね I haven't seen you for a while. You'*ve gotten so big* [You'*ve really grown*]. ‖部長になったら彼の給料は**ぐんと増えた** His salary *shot up* when he became department manager. (➤ shoot up は「急上昇する」) ‖パートに出るようになってから母は**ぐんと若返った** My mother *looks years younger* ever since she started working part-time.

くんとう 薫陶 ▶大学では Y 教授の**薫陶を受けた** I *studied under* Professor Y at college. (「徳によって人を感化し, 教育すること」の意の薫陶は儒教の影響を受けたもので, 英語にはぴったりの対応語はない. したがって, 「…の下で学ぶ」と考えて例文のように訳すしかない).

ぐんとう 群島 a **group of islands,** an **archipelago** /ɑ̀:ʳkəpéləgoʊ/.

クンニリングス **cunnilingus.**

ぐんばい 軍配 a **referee's** [**an umpire's**] **fan in sumo wrestling** ▶行司は白鵬に**軍配を上げた** The referee *judged* (*that*) Hakuho *was the winner*. ／The referee's *judgment was in favor of* Hakuho.
▶ことしは白組に**軍配が上がった** *Victory went to* the White Team this year.

ぐんぱつじしん 群発地震 ▶ここのところその地方に**群発地震**が起きている Recently, there has been *a series of earthquakes* in that district.

ぐんび 軍備 **armaments** ▶**軍備を縮小する** reduce *armaments*.
‖**軍備拡張** the expansion of armaments ‖**軍備縮小** (→軍縮).
☛ **再軍備** (→見出語)

ぐんぶ 軍部 **the military** (➤ 集合的に) ; **the military authorities** (軍当局).

ぐんぷく 軍服 a **military** [**naval**] **uniform** (➤ naval は海軍の場合).

ぐんぽうかいぎ 軍法会議 a **court-martial** ▶その兵士は脱走して**軍法会議に掛けられた** The soldier *was court-martialed* for desertion.

ぐんゆうかっきょ 群雄割拠 ▶室町時代後半は**群雄割拠の時代**であった The latter half of the Muromachi period was the period of *conflict between regionally powerful lords*.

ぐんよう 軍用の **military** ; **for military purpose** [**use**]
▶**軍用車両** a *military* vehicle.
‖**軍用機** a warplane ‖(軍用犬などの)**軍用動物** a service animal.

ぐんらく 群落 a **colony** (植物などの) ▶野生のユリの**群落** *a colony* of wild lilies.

くんりん 君臨する **reign** /reɪn/ +㊐ ; **dominate** +㊐ (支配する) ▶彼はこれまで政界に**君臨してきた** He *has dominated* the political world. ‖イギリスの君主は**君臨する**が統治しない The British monarch *reigns*, but does not rule.

くんれん 訓練 **training** ; **drill** (集団で繰り返して行う)
━動 訓練する **train, drill** ▶そのマラソン選手は来シーズンに備えて**厳しい訓練**に入った The marathon runner has started *hard training* for the coming season. ‖冬山に登るには**体を訓練しておく**必要がある If you are going mountain climbing in winter, you must first *undergo physical training*. ‖彼女はスパイとしての**訓練を受けた** She *was trained* as a spy. ‖英語の上達には**耳を訓練する**ことが大切である It is important to *train* your ears if you want to improve your English. ‖彼は息子を優れた水泳選手にしようと**猛訓練中**だ He *is training* his son *very hard* to be a top swimmer.
▶きのう学校で**火災訓練**[**避難訓練**]があった We had *a fire drill* [*an evacuation drill*] at school yesterday.
‖(盲導犬などの)**訓練士** a trainer.

け・ケ

[1]**け 毛** (a) **hair**(体毛, 特に頭髪) ; **fur** /fəːr/ (動物の柔らかい毛) ; **wool** /wʊl/ (羊毛) ; a **feather** (鳥の羽毛) ; a **bristle** /brísəl/ (ブラシの)

語法 hair は1本1本数えるときは Ⓒ 扱いで a hair, two hairs とできるが, 全体をいうときは Ⓤ 扱いで, hairs とはしない.

▶脇の下に毛が生えてきた *Hair* has begun to grow in my armpits. ‖ 父はだんだん**髪の毛が薄くなってきた** My father's *hair* has gradually gotten [become] thinner. ‖ だいぶ毛が伸びてるから, 床屋へ行ったほうがいいよ Your *hair* has grown out, so it's time you went to the barbershop. ‖ 車の座席に**毛が1本落ちていた** I found *a hair* on the car seat. ‖ 私のスパゲッティに**毛が1本入っていた** There was *a hair* in my spaghetti. ‖ 母の**髪の毛**は柔らかいのに, 私の**髪の毛**は硬い My mother has soft *hair*, but my *hair* is coarse [stiff]. ‖ このセーターは**毛100パーセント**です This sweater is 100 percent *wool(en)*.

▶《慣用表現》私の家は**掘っ立て小屋に毛の生えた程度**の家だ My house is *barely better than a shack*.

‖**毛抜き** (a pair of) tweezers.

[2]**け 気** ▶妹にはぜんそくの**気がある** My younger sister has *a touch* of asthma. ‖ あいつは**ホモっ気がある** He *acts a bit gay*. ‖ 彼は**アル中の気がある** He is *something of an alcoholic*. ‖ わが家は**女っ気がない** Our family *is all males*. / *There's not* a *female* in our house.

-け -家 ▶**多田家** *the* Tadas (➤ the ~s で「～家の人々, ～夫妻」の意) ‖ **高松宮家**の一員 a member of *the* Takamatsu *imperial family* [*household*] ‖ **栗田家**では毎年正月を温泉で過ごす *The Kurita family* spends every New Year at a hot-spring resort.

げ 下 ▶うちはせいぜい**中流の下**だ Our family belongs to *the lower middle class* at best. ‖ 彼女の学校の成績は**下の下**だった Her school record was *the worst* [*poorest*] *of all*. ‖《慣用表現》そんなことをするようなやつは**下の下**だよ A person who would do such a thing is *the lowest of the low*.

-げ -気 ▶美知子はきょうは**悲しげ** [**寂しげ**] に見えた Michiko *looked sad* [*lonely*] today. ‖ 彼女は**うれしげ**に手紙を読んでいた She was reading a letter *happily*. ‖ **何か言いたげ**だね You *look as though you want to say something*.

ケア care

‖**ケアマネージャー** a care manager ‖ **緩和ケア** palliative care ‖ **在宅ケア** home care.

けあな 毛穴 a **pore**.

ケアレスミス a **careless mistake**.

[1]**けい 計** a **sum**(簡単な計算の結果) ; a **total**(合計された結果の全体 ; 大きな数量についていうことが多い) ▶書店にテキストを**計600冊**注文した I ordered *a total of* 600 copies of the textbook from the bookstore.

ことわざ **一年の計は元旦にあり** New Year's Day is the day to make your plans for the year. (➤ 日本語からの意訳).

[2]**けい 刑** **punishment**(刑罰) ; a **sentence** (宣告された刑, 判決) ▶**刑に服する** serve *a sentence* ‖ **実刑を科す** impose *a prison sentence* ‖ 彼の**刑は重すぎる** His *sentence* was too heavy [harsh]. ‖ 彼は殺人罪で**重い刑に処せられた** He *received a severe sentence* on a charge of murder. / He *was severely punished* for (the) murder.

[3]**けい 罫** a **line**(線) ; a **rule** (印刷のけい線) ▶**けいの引いていないノート** an *unruled* notebook / a notebook *without lines*.

[4]**けい 京** **ten quadrillion**(10の16乗の数).

-けい -系 ▶ **日系** [**フランス系**] のアメリカ人 a *Japanese-*[*French-*] American ‖ **保守系** [**革新系**] の候補者 a *conservative* [*progressive*] candidate ‖ このスーパーは**イオン系**だ This supermarket belongs to the Aeon *chain*. ‖(大学組織の) **人文社会系** Faculty of Humanities and Social Science(s) ‖ (大学組織の) **体育系** Faculty of Health and Sports Sciences [Sport(s) Science].

げい 芸 **technique** /tekníːk/ (技巧) ; **talent** (才能) ; a **trick** (犬などに仕込む) ▶役者が**芸を磨く**のは当たり前だ An actor [actress] ought to *hone* his [her] *artistic skill*. ‖ うちの会社は**芸達者**が多く, **芸のない**のはぼくだけだ Everyone in my company *has some special talent*; I'm the only person with *no talent* at all. ‖ 私は毎日犬に**芸を仕込んでいる** I *teach* my dog *tricks* every day.

▶《慣用表現》毎年毎年同じ文面の年賀状では**芸がない** Writing the same thing on New Year's cards year after year shows *one has no originality*. ‖ 画家は葉っぱを1枚1枚丹念に描いているよ. 全く**芸が細かいね** The painter drew every leaf elaborately. He*'s really meticulous*.

ことわざ **芸は身を助ける** Someone who has a skill is always able to make a living.

ことわざ **多芸は無芸** Jack of all trades and master of none. / A jack of all trades is a master of none. (➤「何でもこなす職人は名人にはなれない」の意で, ともに英語のことわざ).

ゲイ a **gay**

‖**ゲイバー** a gay bar ‖ **ゲイボーイ** a gay ; a host in a gay bar (ゲイバーで働くボーイ). →**ホモセクシュアル**.

危ないカタカナ語 ゲイ

1 日本語の「ゲイ」は「男性同性愛者, ホモセクシャル」を指すが, 英語の gay には女性の同性愛者 (レズビアン) も含まれる. gay は同性愛者が好んで用いる語で, 軽蔑的な含みはない.

2 男性同性愛者を表す語に queer ; 《米》 fag, faggot があるが, いずれも軽蔑的. ただし queer は, 当事者たちが自身を肯定的に捉える語として用いることがある.

けいあい 敬愛 ▶**敬愛の念** a sense of *respect and love* ‖ 私は高山さんを大学の先輩として**敬愛しています** I *love and respect* Mr. Takayama as one of the older graduates from my university.

[1]**けいい 敬意** **respect**(真価を認めて抱く尊敬の念) ; **deference**(年長者・目上の人などに対して持つ敬いの気持ち, また, その意見や判断を受け入れること) ▶客員教授に**敬意を表して**歓迎会が開かれた A welcoming party

was held *in honor of* the visiting professor. ‖私は彼の長年の頑張りに**敬意を表する** I *respect* him for his hard work over many years. ‖年長者に**敬意を表する** show *deference* to older people.

[2]**けいい 経緯** a **complete account**(一部始終の話); a **chronology** (発生順の概略) ▶今回の事件の**経緯**を説明します Let me give you *a complete account* [the *chronology*] of the incident.

げいいん 鯨飲 ‖**鯨飲馬食** drink like a fish and eat like a horse.

けいえい 経営 management 一動 経営する manage /mǽnɪdʒ/ +目, **run** +目; **own** +目 (所有する); **carry on**(事業を営む)

> **語法** (1) **manage** と **run** は経営行為に重点を置く語で, 所有者として会社などを経営しているのか, 雇われてその経営に当たっているのかは問わない. 一方, **own** は所有者であることを明示したい場合に用いる. (2) run は商店や小規模の会社などについて用いる傾向がある.

▶おじは会社を**経営している** My uncle *manages* [*runs*/*owns*] a company. ‖現在, 彼の会社は**経営難だ** Now his company *is in financial difficulty* [*difficulties*]. (➤「財政困難だ」の意;「経営難に陥る」は fall [get] into financial difficulty) ‖彼は**経営の才**がある He has *managerial* [*executive*] *ability*. ‖会社は**経営の多角化**に努めている The company is trying to *diversify its business*. 《参考》「経営の多角化」は business diversification という. ‖会社は**経営がしっかりしていて**成長を続けている The company is growing steadily thanks to *good management*. ‖その会社では新しい**経営陣**が就任した *A new management team* was put in place at that company. ‖**経営学** business administration ‖**経営コンサルタント** a management consultant.

けいえいしゃ 経営者 a **manager**; **(the) management** (経営者側); a **proprietor** (店主) ▶大企業の**経営者** *the management* of a big corporation ‖彼はこの会社の**経営者**だ He *manages* [*runs*] this company. (→経営) ‖労働者たちは賃上げを要求して**経営者側**と話し合いを行っている The workers are holding negotiations with *the management* for higher wages. ‖**労働者と経営者**(=労使)の間にトラブルが起こった Trouble arose between *labor and management*.

けいえん 敬遠する 1【避ける】avoid +目, **keep away** 《from》 (➤後者はややインフォーマル) ▶彼はしつこいので皆から**敬遠されている**(=皆が彼を避ける) He is so persistent that everyone *avoids* [*keeps away from*] him. ‖私は糖尿の気があるので甘い物は**敬遠している** I have a touch of diabetes, so I *stay away from* sweets.

2【野球で】walk +目 (歩かせる) ▶**敬遠の四球** an *intentional* walk (➤ intentional は「故意の」) ‖ピッチャーは4番バッターを**敬遠した** The pitcher *walked* the cleanup hitter *intentionally*. / The pitcher *gave* the cleanup hitter *an intentional walk*. ‖彼は**敬遠された** He *was intentionally walked*.

けいおんがく 軽音楽 light music.

けいか 経過 1【時間の】passage, a **lapse 一動 経過する pass** ▶父が亡くなってから5年が**経過した** Five years *have passed* [*gone by*] since my father passed away. (➤「父が亡くなって5年になる」ならば It's been five years since my father passed away.) ‖《柔道の試合》50秒**経過**, 残りあと10秒です Fifty seconds *passed*, ten seconds left. ‖**時が経過したが**私の悲しみはますます強まってきた Despite *the passage* [*lapse*] *of time*, my grief has grown all the more intense. ‖何日も**経過して**ようやく彼は帰宅した Many days *passed* [*elapsed*] before he came home.

2【物事の】progress (進行); **course** (成り行き) ▶試合の**経過** the *progress* of a game ‖和平会談は予想どおりの**経過**をたどった The peace talks took the expected *course*. ‖**経過報告のための会議** a *checkpoint* (*review*) meeting ‖ **対話**「お母さまの手術後の**経過**はどうですか?」「おかげさまで**経過は順調です**」"*How is* your mother *recovering* from the operation?" "She *is making good progress*. Thank you for your concern."

[1]**けいかい 軽快な light** ▶**軽快な**フットワーク *light* footwork ‖**軽快な**サンバのリズム a *light* samba beat ‖彼女は**軽快な足取りで**デートに出かけていった She went out on a date *with sprightly steps* [*with a spring in her step*].

[2]**けいかい 警戒 guard**(警備); **watch**(見張り); a **precaution** (予防対策) **一動 警戒する guard, watch** ▶空き巣狙いを**警戒する** *be on the watch for* [*be on one's watch against*] prowlers / *watch* (*out*) *for* prowlers ‖口のうまい人間は**警戒した**ほうがいい You should *be on your guard against* slick talkers. ‖《バレーボール》相手はサーブのいいのが多いから**警戒しろ** *Be on guard* [*Keep up your guard* / *Don't let down your guard*]. Many players in the opposing team have good serves. ‖大雨のときは洪水を**警戒しなければならない** When there is a heavy rain, we must *take precautions against* flooding.

▶木曽川は**警戒水位**に達した The water of the Kiso River rose to *the danger level*. ‖猫は**警戒心の強い**動物だ Cats are *cautious* animals.

‖**警戒警報** a precautionary warning.

けいがいか 形骸化する reduce to a (mere) shell ▶**形骸化した**君主制 monarchy *in name only* / monarchy *that has been reduced to a shell*.

けいかく 計画 a **plan** (➤複数形で使うことが多い); a **project** /prɑ́:dʒekt/ (大がかりなもの); a **scheme** /ski:m/ (投機的で未知数の大きい計画; 陰険な計画の含みを持つこともある); a **program** (ある具体的な目的のために作成された計画) **一動 計画する plan, project** /prədʒékt/ ▶**計画**を実行する carry out *a plan* ‖**計画**を実行に移す implement [execute] *a plan* / put *a plan* into practice.

> **【文型】**
> **A の計画を立てる**
> **make plans for** A
> **…しようと計画している**
> **be planning to** do
> **plan on** doing
>
> **【解説】**「…する計画を立てている」は be making plans to do で具体的に日時を決めたり, 必要な手配を行ったりしている, という含みになる. plan to do はやや具体性に乏しく「(いつか)…するつもり[予定]でいる」に近い. **be planning to** do と **plan on doing** はその中間で「計画がある」で, 具体的な準備などは始めていない.

▶ **対話**「何か夏休みの計画を立てましたか」「ええ, 九州旅行を計画しています」"Have you *made* any *plans for* the summer vacation?" "Yes, I'*m planning* (*to* take) a trip to Kyushu." ‖ 我々は新しいハイブリッド車を買おうと計画している We'*re planning to* buy a new hybrid car. ‖ サムさんはハワイにいるおじさんを訪ねようと計画している Sam *is making plans to* visit [*planning to* visit / *planning on* visit*ing*] his uncle in Hawaii.
▶彼らはその建設計画に反対のようだ It seems that they are against the building *project*. ‖ 新しい道路を造る計画が市議会に掛けられた The *scheme* for building the new highway was presented to the municipal assembly. ‖ 父の急死で私の留学の計画は狂ってしまった My father's sudden death upset my *plans* to study abroad. ‖ 昨日, 計画停電が実施された A *scheduled* [*planned*] blackout took place yesterday.
▶万事計画どおりに進んでいます Everything is going *according to plan* [*schedule*]. (➤ according to plan [schedule] は決まり文句) ‖ 計画どおりにいけばこのプロジェクトはことし中に終わる予定だ We should finish this project (sometime) this year if everything goes *as planned* [*as scheduled*]. ‖ 3か年計画で町の美化を図ることになった We have decided on *a three-year plan* to clean up [beautify] our town. ‖ その誘拐事件は計画的な犯行だった The kidnapping was *premeditated*.
☛ 無計画 (→見出語)

[1]**けいかん 警官** a **police officer**

> 語法 (1)police officer は性別に関係なく用いることができる. 特に性別を明示する場合は policeman (男), policewoman (女)とする.
> (2)警官に声を掛けるときの言い方は "Excuse me, officer." がよい.

▶警官隊は暴徒を鎮めるために催涙ガスを用いた The *police* used tear gas to put down the rioters.

[2]**けいかん 景観** a **scenic view** ▶ロープウエーからの芦ノ湖の景観はすばらしい From the ropeway, *the scenic view* of Lake Ashi is wonderful. ‖ あのビルがこの町の景観を損ねている That building mars the *scenery* of the town.

[3]**けいかん 桂冠** ‖ 桂冠詩人 a poet laureate.

けいがん 炯眼・慧眼 ▶けい眼の持ち主 a person *with a keen eye* / a person *of great insight*.

[1]**けいき 景気** **1【経済活動の状態】economy** (経済) ; **business** (会社での商品の売れ行き) ▶景気が後退[回復]し始めた The *economy* is beginning to slow down [recover]. ‖ 景気は上向きだ *Business* is picking up. / The *economy* is improving. ‖ うちの会社は最近景気がいい[悪い] Our *business has been going well* [*has been slow*] recently. (➤ slow は slack (不振の)とも置き換えられる) ‖ 景気の後退で失業者が増えた The *recession* has increased unemployment. ‖ 対話「景気はどうだい?」「まあまあだね」"*How's business* (*coming along*)?" "Not bad. / Pretty good."
2【威勢, 勢い】▶ずいぶん景気の悪い顔してるね You really *look down in the dumps* [*mouth*]. (➤ down in the dumps [mouth] は「ふさぎ込んで」の意のインフォーマルな表現) ‖ 景気づけに一杯やろう Let's have a drink *to cheer* (*us*) *up*. ‖ 私たちは新宿の居酒屋で景気よくパーッとやった We *partied hardy* at a tavern in Shinjuku. (➤ party hardy は「どんちゃん騒ぎのパーティーをする」) ‖ あんまり景気よく金を使うとあとで困ることになるよ If you spend your money so *freely*, you'll soon be in trouble.
☛ 好景気, 不景気 (→見出語)

[2]**けいき 計器** a **gauge** /geɪdʒ/ (数量を測るもの) ; a **meter** (使用量を測るもの) ; an **instrument** (飛行機などの) ‖ 計器灯 a dashboard light, a dash light ‖ 計器盤 a dashboard, an instrument board ‖ 計器飛行 instrument flying.

[3]**けいき 契機** an **opportunity** ▶これを契機としてアメリカ文化についてもっと勉強したい I'd like to *use this as an opportunity* [to *take this opportunity*] to study more about U.S. culture.

[4]**けいき 刑期** a **term of imprisonment** (禁錮の期間) ; a **prison term** (刑務所に入っている期間) ▶男は刑期を務めた The man *served time in prison*. ‖ 彼は10年の刑期を終えた He served a ten-year *sentence* [*term of imprisonment*].

けいききゅう 軽気球 a **balloon**.

けいきんぞく 軽金属 a **light (weight) metal**.

けいく 警句 an **aphorism**, an **epigram** ; a **witty remark** (機知に富むことば).

けいぐ 敬具

> 解説 (1)一般的な手紙の結び文句は **Sincerely yours**, または **Sincerely** と書くが, 後者のほうがくだけた形. ペンパルなど親しい人には **Love** / **Your friend** / **Yours** などを用いてもよい. なお love は恋愛感情を含まない単なる親しさを表す結辞で, 使用頻度は女性のほうが高いが, 男性も使う.
> (2)ビジネスレターでは, **Yours faithfully** → **(Very) truly yours** / **Yours (very) truly** → **Sincerely yours** → **Sincerely** の順で改まり度の低い結辞となる. ビジネス関連のEメールでは Best wishes や Best regards が多い.
> (3)《米》では yours をあとに置く形(例: Sincerely yours) が多く, 《英》では Yours が先に来る形(例: Yours sincerely) が多い.
> (4)以上, いずれの場合もあとにコンマをつけ, 次行に署名する.

げいげき 迎撃する **intercept** +目 ‖ 迎撃機 an interceptor ‖ 迎撃ミサイル an interceptor missile.

[1]**けいけん 経験** (an) **experience** ━動 **経験する** **experience** +目 ; **go through** (苦しみなどを)
語法 ある程度以上の年月にわたって蓄積された総体としての経験をいう experience は Ⓤ 扱いで, much, some, little, a lot of, long, extensive などで修飾することが多い. これに対して, Ⓒ 扱いの an experience は1回1回の, experiences は複数回の経験をいう.
▶彼の培った経験 his acquired *experience* ‖ 経験は最良の教師である *Experience* is the best teacher. (➤ 英語のことわざ) ‖ 彼は年は若いが経験は豊富だ Though he is young, he has broad [wide, a lot of] *experience*. ‖ 彼女は経験は浅いが非常に優秀な通訳だ Though she has little *experience*, she is a very capable interpreter. ‖ 私はシンガポールで3年間日本語を教えた経験がある I have three years' *experience* (in) teaching Japanese in Singapore. ‖ 父は教師の経験を生かして定年後学習塾を始めた Making use of his *past experience as a teacher*, my father set up a *juku* after retiring. ‖ 彼女はあまり恋愛の経験がない She does*n't* have *much* ro-

mantic *experience*. ‖ 対話「アルバイトの経験はありますか」「はい，ホテルで皿洗いをしたことがあります」"Do you have any part-time job *experience*?" "Yes. I have been a dishwasher at a hotel."

け

▶魚市場でのアルバイトはいい経験だった Working part-time at the fish market was *a very good experience* for me. ‖ アメリカをヒッチハイク中に苦い［楽しい］経験をした I had *a bitter* ［*pleasant*］ *experience* while hitchhiking in the U.S. ‖ 夫が交通事故死してから彼女は多くの苦しい経験をした She *went through* a lot since her husband was killed in a car accident.

▶若いうちにいろいろな経験を積みたいと思っている I want to *do lots of different things* while I am young. ‖ もっと経験を積めば上手に翻訳できるようになるよ *With more experience*, you'll become able to translate skillfully. ‖ 数年間はここで働いて経験を積み，ゆくゆくは自分の店を開きたい I'd like to work here for several years to *gain* ［*get*］ *experience*, and eventually, open my own shop someday. ‖ こんな暑さは経験したことがない This is the hottest weather we *have* ever *had* ［*experienced*］. ‖ 彼女はこれまでにそういった苦労を経験したことがなかった She has never *encountered* ［*run up against*］ that kind of difficulty before. (➤ run up against で「…に出くわす」) ‖ 寝たきり老人の介護がいかに大変かは経験した人でなければわからないだろう *Only a person who has actually experienced it knows* how hard nursing a bed-ridden elderly person is. ‖ 経験から言えば物価は今後も上昇し続けるだろう I'm *making an educated guess* that prices will continue to rise. (➤ educated guess は「経験や知識に基づく(正確性の高い)推測」).

▶人生経験の豊富な人 a person who has a wealth of *life experience* ‖ 《募集広告》経験者優遇 Persons with experience especially welcome. ‖ 経験不問 No experience required. ／Beginners welcome.

‖経験主義《哲学》empiricism.

☞ 未経験 (→見出語)

[2]**けいけん 敬虔な** **devout** /dɪváʊt/, **pious** /páɪəs/ (➤ 前者が常に心からの信心深さをいうのに対して，後者は時としてうわべの信心ぶりを暗示する) ▶敬けんなクリスチャン a *devout* Christian.

けいげん 軽減する **reduce** +⊞ ▶仕事の量を軽減する *reduce* the amount of one's work ／*cut down on* one's work ‖ 政府はサラリーマンの税負担を軽減しようとしない The government is making no effort to *ease* the tax burden of office workers.

けいこ 稽古 **practice**（反復練習）; a **lesson**（先生についての）; **training**（運動・技術などの）; a **rehearsal**（劇などの下稽古；「本稽古」は dress rehearsal）▶剣道［ピアノ］の稽古をする *practice* kendo ［the piano］ ‖ お花の稽古をする *take lessons* in flower arrangement ‖ 稽古をつけてやるから掛かってこい Come on! I'll *give you a workout*. (➤ workout は「(運動選手の)練習」) ／I'll *teach you a thing or two*. (➤「しごいてやる」の意) ‖ その力士は稽古不足で負けたのだ The sumo wrestler lost the bout because he *hadn't trained enough*.

‖稽古事 a lesson ‖ 稽古場 a rehearsal hall ［room］(劇団などの)；a practice room.

[1]**けいご 敬語** an **honorific** /ɑ̀:nərífɪk/ ▶敬語を使う use *honorifics* ／use *polite expressions*(➤ 後者は「丁寧表現を使う」).

> **《解説》英語の中の敬語**
> (1)英語にも敬語的表現はあるが，日本語の場合ほど体系として定型化されたものではない．
> (2) Mr., Mrs., Miss, Ms. などの敬称は尊敬語の一種と考えてよい．
> (3)丁寧表現としては，I am very much honored to meet you.（お目に掛かれて光栄に存じます）や，I am very much obliged for your help.（ご援助誠にありがとうございます）などがある．また，相手に対して依頼や要請をする場合に用いる Would ［Could］ you ...? や please，相手の許可を求める場合に用いる May ［Can］ I ...? なども丁寧表現と言える．

[2]**けいご 警護する** **protect** +⊞ ▶警護にあたる *act as security guard(s)* ‖ 首相はSPによって警護されている The Prime Minister *is protected* by Security Police personnel.

[1]**けいこう 傾向** a **tendency**(思わしくない，または好ましくない)；a **trend**（社会の流れ）

> 【文型】
> …する傾向がある
> **have a tendency to** do
> **tend to** do

▶どうも彼は食べ過ぎる傾向がある He *has a tendency to* eat too much. ／He *tends to* eat too much ［*to* overeat］. ‖ 入試の傾向について何か情報をお持ちですか Do you have any information about *what (sorts of) questions tend to be asked on the entrance examination(s)* ［*about the kinds of questions that tend to appear on the entrance examination(s)*］?

▶ことしのファッションの傾向をご存じですか Do you know what this year's *trends in fashion* are ［will be like］? ‖ 交通事故死はますます増加［減少］傾向にある Traffic fatalities *are on the rise* ［*on the decrease*］.

[2]**けいこう 蛍光** **fluorescence** /flɔ:résəns/

‖蛍光灯 a fluorescent light ［lamp］ ‖ 蛍光塗料 fluorescent paint ‖ 蛍光板 a fluorescent screen ‖ 蛍光ペン a highlighter (➤ 個々の色には，例えば fluorescent pink marker のようにいう).

げいごう 迎合 ▶大衆迎合の政治家 a *populist* politician ‖ 権力に迎合する *follow the wishes* of the powers ‖ 若者に迎合するテレビ番組が多すぎる Too many TV programs *pander to* the tastes of young people. (➤ pander to は「…におもねる」).

けいこうぎょう 軽工業 **light industry**.

けいこうひにんやく 経口避妊薬 an **oral contraceptive, the pill**.

[1]**けいこく 警告** (a) **warning**(危険を予告して警戒させるもの)；(a) **caution**（注意，忠告）— 動 警告する **warn** +⊞, **caution** +⊞ ▶《警官が違反者に》今回は警告で済ませておきましょう I'll let you off with *a warning* for this time. ‖《掲示》駐車違反者に警告．違反した車はレッカー移動します Parking violators *be warned*. Your car will be towed (away).

> 【文型】
> 人(A)に…しないようにと警告する
> **warn** A **not to** do
> **warn** A **against** doing
> 人(A)に～と警告する
> **warn** A **that** S + V

▶医者は彼に塩分をとり過ぎないようにと警告した The doctor *warned* him *not to* eat [*against* eat*ing*] too much salt. ‖ 外務省は国民にその国に旅行しないようにと警告している The Foreign Ministry *has warned* Japanese *against* travel*ing* to that country. ‖ ガイドは旅行者にすりやひったくりに用心するようにと警告した The tour guide *warned* the tourists *that* they should watch out for pickpockets and (purse) snatchers.
▶《比喩的》その事故は無謀なドライバーたちへの警告だった The accident served as *a warning* to reckless drivers.

[2]**けいこく 渓谷** a **ravine** /rəvíːn/ (峡谷) ; a **gorge** /gɔːʳdʒ/ (両岸が絶壁になった) ; a **canyon** (深く大きな).

げいごと 芸事 a **traditional (Japanese) performing art**
▶彼女は何か芸事を始めたいと考えている She's thinking of beginning to take lessons in some kind of *traditional performing art* or other.

けいさい 掲載する **carry** +目 ▶私の読書感想文が学校新聞に掲載された My impressions of a book I'd read *appeared* in our school paper.
▶この雑誌には村上春樹の短編小説が掲載されている This magazine *carries* a short story by Murakami Haruki.

けいざい 経済 **1**【生産・商業活動】**economy** /ɪkáːnəmi/ 一形 **経済の economic** /ìːkənáːmɪk/ (➤「経済学上の」の意にもなる) ▶日本の経済は危機に瀕(ひん)している The Japanese *economy* is (now) in crisis. ‖ その発展途上国はわが国に経済援助を仰いできた That developing country has asked for our *economic* [*financial*] *support*. ‖ (わが家の経済状態では)私立大学に進学するのは無理だ My parents *can't afford to* send me to a private university (on our *family's budget*). (➤ budget /bʌ́dʒɪt/ は「家計」).
2【倹約, やりくり】**economy** 一形 **経済的な economical** /ìːkənáːmɪkəl/ ▶どんなに経済を考えてやりくりしても月15万円はかかります We can't live on less than 150,000 yen a month, *no matter how much we scrimp and save*. (➤ scrimp and save は「切り詰めて金をためる」) ‖ そんな豪勢な車を買うことはうちの経済が許さない Such an expensive car is *beyond our means*. (➤ means は「資力」) ‖ 安い品物を買うことが必ずしも経済的とは限らない Buying cheap products is not always *economical*. ‖ うちの女房は経済観念がまるで無い My wife *hasn't got a sense of economy*. (➤ sense of economy は「(きちんと)家計のやりくりをする感覚」, concept of economy は「経済の仕組みや動きなどを理解する力」) ／My wife *has no head for money*.
‖**経済界** financial circles ‖ **経済学** economics /ìːkənáːmɪks/ ‖ **経済学者** an economist /ɪkáːnəmɪst/ ‖ **経済学部** the school of economics ‖ **経済危機** an economic crisis ‖ **経済産業省** Ministry of Economy, Trade and Industry ‖ **経済制裁** economic sanctions(➤「経済制裁を科する[解除する]」は impose [lift] economic sanctions) ‖ **経済成長** economic growth ‖ **経済大国** a major economic power, an economic powerhouse ‖ **経済発展** economic development ‖ **経済摩擦** economic friction.
☛ 不経済 (→見出語)

けいさつ 警察 **the police** ; **the police force** (組織) ; **the police department**(行政の一部門としての)

> **語法** (1)一般に警察という組織を指すときの police は複数扱い. ふつうは the をつけるが, 新聞英語では the をつけない. (2)集合的に警察官を指すときは単に police で複数扱い.

▶警察はその男を追っている *The police* are after the man. ‖ その男を警察に突き出せ Take the man to *the police*. ‖ 出て行け! でないと警察を呼ぶぞ Get out of here, or I'll *call the police*. ‖ 泥棒に入られたのですぐに警察に届け出た When our house was burglarized, we *reported* it *to the police* right away. ‖ 犯人を捜索するために警察官が更に動員された More *police* were called on duty to search for the criminal.
‖**警察学校** a police school ‖ **警察官** a police officer(→警官) ‖ **警察犬** a police dog ‖ **警察署** a police station ‖ **警察署長** a police chief, the head [chief] of a police station (➤後者は堅い言い方) ‖ **警察庁** the National Police Agency ‖ **警察手帳** a police handbook(日本の警察官・刑事が携帯する) ; a police (officer's) ID(➤前者の中の身分証の部分またはカード式の).

けいさん 計算 **1**【数の】**calculation, computation**(➤後者は堅い語で, 規模の大きなものやコンピュータを用いて行うものを連想させる) ; **figures** (数字) 一動 **計算する calculate** +目, **compute** +目 ▶エクセルで計算する *do calculations* in [on] Excel ‖ 家の新築費用を計算する *compute* the cost of building a new house ‖ 数学の試験でいくつか計算間違いをした I made a few *mistakes in calculation* on the math test. ‖ 私たちは結婚式にいくらかかるかを計算した We *calculated* how much it would cost to hold our wedding. ‖ 彼は計算が速い[遅い] He is *quick* [*slow*] *at figures*. ‖ 何回やっても計算(=数)が合わないんだ No matter how many times I redo the calculation, the *figures* [*numbers*] don't come out right. ‖ あなたの計算は間違っている You have gotten your *figures* wrong. ／You've miscalculated. ‖ 旅費は計算に入れたけど食事代を忘れてたよ We *figured in* the travel expenses, but forgot the cost of meals. ‖ きみは計算問題をもう少し練習する必要がある You need more practice in *arithmetic*. (⚫英語には「計算問題」に相当する語がないので arithmetic (算数)という語で表す) ‖ 父は店の売り上げを計算している My father *is adding up* his store's sales. (➤ add up は「合計する」) ‖ 彼はとても計算高い男だ He's a very *calculating* person.
‖**計算器** a calculator (単純計算用の小型のもの) ‖ **計算尺** a slide rule.
2【予測】**calculation** 《on》(予測する) 一動 **計算する calculate** ▶彼が反対派に回ることは計算に入れていなかった I didn't *calculate* [*figure*] *on* him joining the opposition group. ‖ 失敗した場合のことも計算に入れておかねばならない We must *take into account* the possibility of failure. ‖ 交通渋滞を計算に入れて早めに家を出た We *figured on* there being heavy traffic and left home early. (➤ figure on は「…を見込む」) ‖ ぼくにはぼくなりの計算があるんだよ I have my own way of *figuring things out*.

けいさんしょう 経産省 **the Trade Ministry, the Ministry of Trade** 《略》**METI**. →経済.

[1]**けいし 軽視する** **underestimate** +目 (過小評価する) ; **make little of, take ... lightly**(軽く見る) ; **disregard** +目

(重んじない, 考慮しない) ▶速度制限を**軽視する** *flout* speed limits ‖ 伸夫は授業を**軽視した**から成績が良くなかったのだ Since Nobuo *underestimated* the importance of his classes, he got poor grades. ‖ この病気を**軽視して**はいけません You shouldn't *take* [*treat*] this illness *lightly*. ‖ 若者よ, 生命を**軽視する**な You young people must not *disregard* (the value of) human life.

2**けいし 警視** an **inspector** ‖**警視総監** the Superintendent-General of the Metropolitan Police.

☛ **警視庁** (→見出語)

1**けいじ 刑事** a (**police**) **detective** (刑事巡査) ▶私服**刑事** a plainclothes *detective* ‖ あの男は**刑事事件**を起こしたことがある He once committed *a crime*. (➤犯罪を分類していうときは criminal case という) ‖ きみは自分の行為に対してもう**刑事責任を問われる**年齢だ You are old enough to *be criminally liable* for what you do. (➤「刑事責任」は criminal liability) ‖**刑事裁判** a criminal trial ‖ **刑事犯** a criminal offense.

2**けいじ 掲示** a **notice** (貼り紙) ; a **sign** (表示板) ; a **bulletin** (公示, 広報) 一動 **掲示する put up** ▶**掲示**を出す put up *a notice* [*a sign*] ‖ バザーの案内が学校の廊下に**掲示してあった** Announcements [Notices] of a bazaar *were put up* in the school corridors. ‖**掲示板** 《米》 a bulletin board, 《英》 a notice board ‖ **電子掲示板** a BBS (= Bulletin Board System).

3**けいじ 啓示** (a) **revelation** ▶神の**啓示** divine *revelation* (天啓).

けいしき 形式 a **form** (決められた方法) ; (a) **formality** (形式にこだわること) ▶あまり**形式にこだわる**な Don't *stick* too much *to forms* [*formalities*]. ／Don't be so *stiff and formal*. ‖ 友だちの間で**形式ばる**のはよそう We're friends so we don't need to *be formal with each other*. ‖ 結婚披露宴のスピーチは**形式ばった**ものになりがちだ Speeches at wedding receptions tend to become *empty formalities*. ‖ 警察官はいくつか**形式的な**質問をした The policeman asked several *routine* questions. ‖ 来週の会合は討論会**形式**になると思います Next week's meeting will take the *form* of a debate.

‖**形式主義** formalism ‖ **形式主義者** a formalist.

けいしちょう 警視庁 the Metropolitan Police Department 《参考》 ロンドン警視庁は通称 Scotland Yard という.

けいじどうしゃ 軽自動車 a **light car**, a **subcompact car**.

けいしゃ 傾斜 a **slant** ; a **slope** (坂や丘などの) 一動 **傾斜する slope, slant** →傾く ▶雪の多い地方では屋根の**傾斜**が急だ In snowy areas, roofs have a steep *slant*. ‖ 丘は湖に向かって緩やかに**傾斜している** The hill *slopes* gently toward the lake. ‖ その出来事があってから, 和子の心は次第に哲夫のほうに**傾斜していった** After that incident, Kazuko's feelings gradually began to *lean* [*tilt*] toward Tetsuo.

げいしゃ 芸者 a **geisha** (➤英語化している) ▶**芸者**を揚げて騒ぐ have a *geisha* party.

げいじゅつ 芸術 art (➤総称) ; an **art** (➤特定部門の芸術) ▶父は**芸術**がわからない My father does not appreciate *art*. ／My father has no *artistic sense*. ‖ 詩はことばの**芸術**といわれる Poetry is referred to as the *art* of words. ‖ 彼のお兄さんは**芸術家肌**の人だ His (older) brother is the *artistic type*. ‖ 彼女のスケーティングは**芸術品**だ Her skating is *a work of art*.

‖**芸術家** an artist ‖ **芸術学部** the college of fine arts and music ‖ **芸術祭** an art festival ‖ **芸術大学** an art college, a university of arts.

1**けいしょう 敬称** a **title** (**of honor**), an **honorific** (**title**) ▶お名前をお呼びする際は**敬称**を略させていただきます (For brevity's sake,) I will omit *titles* [*honorifics*] and just call your names. (➤for brevity's sake は「簡略化のため」).

2**けいしょう 軽傷** a **slight injury** [**wound** /wuːnd/] ▶彼はその事故で**軽傷を負った** He *was slightly injured* in the accident. ‖ 私は自動車事故の巻き添えを食ったが, 幸いにも**軽傷を負った**だけで済んだ I was involved in a car accident, but fortunately I escaped *with* only *slight injuries*.

3**けいしょう 軽症** ▶姉は肺炎にかかったが, ごく**軽症**で済んだ My (older) sister got pneumonia, but (fortunately) it was only a very *mild* case.

4**けいしょう 継承 succession** 一動 **継承する succeed** (**to**) ▶王位を**継承する** *succeed to* the throne ‖ エリザベス二世は父ジョージ六世から王位を**継承した** Queen Elizabeth II *succeeded* her father, King George VI. ‖**継承者** a successor.

5**けいしょう 警鐘** an **alarm bell**, a **warning bell** ▶地球温暖化に**警鐘を鳴らす** *sound the alarm* over global warming.

1**けいじょう 形状** (a) **shape**, **form**

‖**形状記憶合金** a shape memory alloy ‖ **形状記憶樹脂** shape memory resin /rézɪn/.

2**けいじょう 計上する appropriate** /əpróʊprieɪt/ +目 (割り当てる) ▶保育所開設の資金を**計上する** *appropriate* money to open day nurseries.

けいしょうち 景勝地 a **scenic spot**

✉ **近くの松島は景勝地として知られています. 日本に来られたときにご案内したいと思います** Nearby Matsushima is well known *for its scenic beauty*. I'd like to take you there when you visit Japan.

けいしょく 軽食 a **light meal** ; a **snack** (間食として食べるもの) ▶ぼくたちは**軽食**を取るために道路の縁に車を止めた We pulled over to the side of the road for *a snack*.

けいしょくどう 軽食堂 a **snack bar** (カウンター式の) ; a **cafeteria** /kæ̀fətíəriə/ (会社・工場・学校などのセルフサービス式の) ; a **lunchroom** (学校・工場などの) ; 《米》 a **coffee shop** (ホテルなどの).

けいず 系図 a **family tree** ▶彼女の先祖はすべてこの**系図**に出ている Her ancestors are all shown in this *family tree*. ‖ わが家の**系図** (= 歴史) は江戸時代まで遡ることができる My family can trace its *history* back to the Edo period.

1**けいすう 係数** 《数学》 a **coefficient**.

2**けいすう 計数** 《数学》 (a) **calculation**

‖**ガイガー計数管** a Geiger counter.

1**けいせい 形成 formation** 一動 **形成する form** +目 (何かを形作る) ; **shape** +目 (ある形にする) ▶水は凍ると氷を**形成する** Water *forms* ice when it freezes. ‖ 進化の第一段階は約46億年前の地球の**形成**だった The first stage of evolution was the *formation* of the earth about 4.6 billion years ago. ‖ 性格は環境によって**形成される** One's character *is formed* [*is shaped*] by one's environment. ‖ 良書を読むことは**人格形成**に役立つ Reading good books helps *develop* [*build*] (*good*) *character*. ‖**形成**

外科 plastic surgery ‖ **形成外科医** a plastic surgeon ‖ **人間形成** character building.

[2]**けいせい 形勢** circumstances（周囲の状況）; the situation（立場, 情勢）; the tide（事件・行動などの流れ）; things（事態）▶形勢が不利なときは行動を起こすな Don't take action when *circumstances* are unfavorable. ‖ 味方の形勢はますます悪くなった *The situation* for our side grew steadily worse.
▶形勢は逆転した *The tables have been turned.*（➤慣用的な言い方）‖ 形勢が一気に逆転してぼくたちのチームが有利［不利］になった *The tide* suddenly turned in our team's favor [against our team]. ‖ しばらく形勢を見よう I'll watch how *things* develop for a while. ‖ 彼はいつも形勢の有利なほうにつく He always manages to *come down on the right side of the fence*.（➤「旗色のよいほうに味方する」の意の熟語）.

けいせき 形跡 evidence（証拠）; a sign（人・事物が存在したことを伝える）; marks（跡, 痕跡）; tracks（人・獣などの足跡;《英》では trace が好まれる）▶その穴には動物がすんだ形跡があった There was *evidence* that some animals had lived in the cave. ‖ その部屋には争った形跡はなかった *There were no signs* of a struggle in that room.（➤この場合のように signs は否定文で用いることが多い）‖ 死体には乱暴された形跡はなかった There were no *marks* of violence on the body. / The body didn't show any *sign* [*trace*] of molestation.（➤ molestation は rape の婉曲（えんきょく）語）‖ 雪の上には死体を引きずった形跡があった There were *marks* on the snow where the corpse had been dragged.

[1]**けいせん 経線** a meridian.

[2]**けいせん 罫線** lines ▶紙にけい線を引く *rule lines* on paper.

けいそ 珪素《化学》silicon.

けいそう 軽装 ▶彼は軽装で雲取山に登った He climbed Mt. Kumotori *in light clothes*. ‖ 私はいつも軽装で旅行する I usually travel *light*.（➤ light は「軽い身なりで」の意の副詞）.

けいそうちゅう 係争中 ▶係争中の問題 the point *at issue* (*in the court case*) ‖ 両者は特許侵害を巡って法廷で係争中である They *are involved in a* copyright infringement *dispute*.

けいそく 計測 measurement 一動 **計測する** measure ＋目 ▶A地点とB地点の間の距離を計測する *measure* the distance between Points A and B.

けいぞく 継続する continue（＋目）, go on《with》（➤前者が日本語により近い）▶この問題は今後も継続して話し合うことになった We decided to *continue* discussions on the matter at a later date. ‖ 仕事は休まずに継続してください Don't stop. *Go* [*Carry*] *on with* your work. ‖ あなたは定期券の継続（＝更新）手続きが必要です You need to *renew* your commuter pass. ‖ **継続は力なり** Persistence [Continued effort] brings success. / (Continuous) practice makes perfect.（●直訳的には Continuation is power. だが, 英語としては不自然. 英語では訳例に示したように「持続性［努力の連続］は成功をもたらす」「やり続けることが完璧（な腕前）にする」と発想するほうがふつう）.

けいそつ 軽率な careless（不注意な）; rash（後先を考えない）; thoughtless（思慮不足の）; imprudent（無分別な）; hasty（性急な）▶軽率な行動 *careless* behavior ‖ 軽率な判断をするな Don't make a *hasty* judgment. / Don't judge *hastily* [*rashly*]. ‖ 私は軽率なことを言ったようだ I seem to have spoken *out of turn* [*inappropriately*].（➤ out of turn は「不作法に」, inappropriately は「場を考えないで」）‖ 彼に何もかも話してしまうとはきみも軽率だったね It was *imprudent* of you to tell him everything.

[1]**けいたい 携帯 1【持ち運ぶこと】** 一動 **携帯する** carry ＋目 ▶この傘は携帯にとても便利だ This umbrella is very handy to *carry around* [to *take along*]. ‖ **携帯品** one's belongings, one's things（➤後者はインフォーマル）‖ **携帯用医療器具** a portable medical instrument（→ポータブル）.
2【携帯電話】《米》a cellphone（➤インフォーマルでは単に cell ともいう）,《英》a mobile phone（➤インフォーマルでは単に mobile ともいう）; a portable telephone ▶友人に携帯電話を掛ける *make a cellphone call* to a friend ‖ きみのケータイの番号を教えてよ Can I have your *cellphone number*? ‖ 多くの若者にとってケータイの無い生活は考えられない Many young people can't imagine a life without *cellphones*. ‖ 彼女から携帯にメールが来た I *got a text* (*message*) from my girlfriend.（➤電話番号を利用する「携帯のメール」は text (message) という;「携帯メールの送受信」は text messaging, あるいは単に texting という. →メール）‖ 携帯電話が電池切れだ My *cellphone* battery is dead. ‖ 会議中は携帯電話が鳴らないようにしてください Please *silence your cellphone* during the meeting.（➤今日では携帯電話と特定しないで, スマホやタブレットなどを含めた mobile devices（モバイル機器）と表現することが多い）.
‖ **携帯サイト**《米》a cellphone website,《英》a mobile (phone) website ‖ **お財布携帯** a mobile wallet ‖ **カメラ付携帯** a camera phone.
ディベートルーム「生徒の携帯電話の使用はよくない」

[2]**けいたい 形態** a form ▶日本と韓国は政治形態が異なる Japan and South Korea have different *forms of government*.
‖ **形態素** a morpheme ‖ **形態論** morphology.

けいだい 境内 the grounds of a shrine [a temple]（➤ grounds は precincts /príːsɪŋkts/ でもよいが, これは社寺の建物を連想させる）▶神社の境内で落ち葉をたく burn fallen leaves in *the grounds* [*precincts*] *of a shrine*.

けいちゅう 傾注 ▶計画実現に全精力を傾注する *channel* [*put*] *all one's energy into* carrying out the plan.

[1]**けいちょう 傾聴する** listen attentively《to》, listen with an attentive ear ▶彼のことばは傾聴に値する What he says is *worthy of attention* [*worth listening to*].

[2]**けいちょう 慶弔** happy and unhappy occasions.

[3]**けいちょう 軽佻** ▶世にはびこる軽ちょう浮薄の風 the *shallow and frivolous* way of thinking that prevails in our society.

けいつい 頸椎《解剖学》cervical vertebrae /vɔ́ːrṭɪbreɪ/, a cervical spine.

けいてき 警笛 a whistle /hwísəl/（列車などの）; a horn（自動車などの）▶《掲示》警笛鳴らせ Sound [Blow] Horn.

けいと 毛糸 woolen yarn [thread] ▶毛糸の帽子 a *woolen* cap ‖ 姉は私に毛糸の手袋を編んでくれた My sister *knitted a pair of* (*woolen*) *gloves* for me.

[1]**けいど 経度** longitude ▶東京の経度は東経139度45分である The *longitude* of Tokyo is 139 degrees 45 minutes east. / Tokyo is situated at 139 degrees 45 minutes east *longitude*.

[2]**けいど 軽度の** slight, minor ▶軽度の捻挫 a *slight*

sprain.

1けいとう 系統 1【組織】a system ▶系統立った勉強 *systematic* study ‖もう少し系統立てて説明してください Please explain it a bit more *systematically*.
‖消化器系統 the digestive system ‖神経系統 the nervous system.
2【血統】▶彼は源氏の系統を引いている He *traces* his *ancestry back* to the Genji clan.
3【系列, 傾向】▶彼女は茶系統の服を好んで着る She likes wearing *brown tones* [*shades of brown*]. ‖私は理数系統は弱い I am weak in *mathematics and science*.

2けいとう 傾倒する admire +副 ▶彼はスティーブ・ジョブズに傾倒している He *admires* Steven Jobs *greatly*.

3けいとう 鶏頭《植物》a cockscomb.

4けいとう 継投する relieve +目 (救援する) ▶継投策が裏目に出た *Replacing the pitcher* backfired.

げいとう 芸当 a trick(曲芸); a feat (離れ業, 妙技) ▶アシカはいろんな芸当ができる A sea lion can do a lot of *tricks*.

けいどうみゃく 頸動脈《解剖学》a carotid artery /kərɑ́ːtɪd ɑ́ːr̩təri/.

けいトラック 軽トラック a mini [light／small] truck.

げいにん 芸人 an entertainer ▶うちの父は宴会の席ではなかなかの芸人です My father is quite *an entertainer* at parties.

けいねん 経年 the passing of the years; the lapse of time(時の経過)
‖経年変化 a change over the years; ag(e)ing ‖経年劣化 deterioration [degradation] over time(➤ over time は with age でもよい).

げいのう 芸能 (public) entertainment(娯楽); art (芸術) ▶今夜のテレビは低俗な芸能番組で占められている Most of the TV shows on tonight are lowbrow *entertainment programs*. ‖彼は日本の伝統芸能を研究している He is studying *traditional* Japanese *performing art* (*forms*). ‖芸能界 (the world of) show business ‖芸能記者 an entertainment reporter; a gossip columnist(ゴシップ記事の) ‖芸能人 an entertainer (→タレント) ‖芸能プロダクション a theatrical agency.

けいば 競馬 horse racing, the races (➤ 前者には単に「馬を走らせる競走」の意もある) ▶競馬でもうける[損をする] make [lose] money on *horse racing*.
‖競馬馬 a racehorse ‖競馬場《米》a racetrack, 《英》a racecourse ‖草競馬 a local horse race.

けいはく 軽薄な shallow(薄っぺらな); frivolous(真剣さがない); flippant (重要な事柄に対して不真面目な); superficial(表面的な) ▶あんな軽薄な人と付き合ってはだめよ You shouldn't associate with such a *shallow* [*superficial*] person. ‖そのお笑いタレントは軽薄さが売り物だ That comic entertainer's appeal lies in his *flippant humor*.

けいはつ 啓発 enlightenment(啓もう) 一動 啓発する enlighten +目 ▶人を大いに啓発する講演 a most *enlightening* lecture ‖木村教授の話には聞くたびに大いに啓発される Professor Kimura's lectures always *enlighten* me. ／I always *learn* a lot from Professor Kimura's lectures. ‖自己啓発 self help, self development [improvement](➤「自己啓発書」は a self-help book).

けいばつ 刑罰 a penalty; (a) punishment (処罰) ▶人に刑罰を科す impose *a penalty* on a person ‖彼はその犯罪に対して軽い[重い]刑罰を受けた He received a mild [heavy] *punishment* for the crime.

けいはんざい 軽犯罪 a minor offense, a misdemeanor /mìsdimíːnəʳ/ (➤ 後者は法律用語) ▶不法侵入は軽犯罪である Trespassing is *a misdemeanor*.
‖軽犯罪法 the Minor Offenses Law.

けいひ 経費 expense (s) (費用); overhead expenses (一般諸経費; 単に overhead ともいう); expenditure (出費) ▶経費を切り詰める cut down (on) *expenses* ‖会社の経費でゴルフをする play golf at the company's *expense* ‖経費削減を心がける try to *reduce expenses* ‖会社の経費で飲み食いする eat and drink on one's company's *expense account* ‖会社員は必要経費が認められない Office workers are not legally authorized to claim a deduction for *business expenses*.
▶芸能人は舞台衣装代を経費で落とす Entertainers can *deduct* the cost of their stage costumes *as business expenses*.

1けいび 警備 guard(監視); defense(防衛) 一動 警備する guard +目 ▶警備を強化する tighten *security* ‖日米首脳会議が近づきアメリカ大使館周辺の警備はいつになく厳重だ *Security* is unusually tight around the American Embassy because the Japanese-American summit conference is approaching.
‖警備員 a (security) guard(➤ guardman とはしない; →ガードマン) ‖警備会社 a security company ‖警備隊 a garrison.

2けいび 軽微な minor(重要でない); slight(ちょっとした); minimal(最小限の) ▶軽微な違反 a *minor* offense ‖損害は軽微だった The damage was *slight* [*minimal*].

けいひん 景品 a gift; a giveaway(拡販用に配るもの); a prize(くじなどの賞品) ▶これは大売り出しの景品でもらったハンカチです This handkerchief was *a gift* [*a freebie*] at a sale. (➤ freebie は「ただでくれるもの」の意のインフォーマルな語) ‖2000円以上お買い上げいただきますと景品にボールペンがつきます If your purchases total more than two thousand yen, we'll throw in a ball-point pen *as a gift* [*for free*]. (➤ throw in は「おまけにつける」, for free は「ただで」) ‖対話「3等の景品は何ですか」「5000円分の商品券です」"What's (the) third *prize*?" "A gift certificate worth five thousand yen."

げいひんかん 迎賓館 a state guesthouse(国有の).

1けいふ 系譜 a genealogical /dʒìːniəlɑ́ːdʒɪkəl/ table ▶彼女の家の系譜をたどっていくと, 本居宣長に行きつくそうだ It is said that you can trace her family's *genealogy* back to Motoori Norinaga.

2けいふ 継父 a stepfather.

けいぶ 警部 a police inspector.

けいふく 敬服 admiration 一動 敬服する admire +目 ▶あなたの勇気には敬服します We *have great admiration for* your courage. ‖彼の真面目ぶりには全く敬服するよ I really *admire* his earnestness.

けいべつ 軽蔑 contempt; scorn (相手を見下しての) 一動 軽蔑する despise +目 (品性などが下劣だと考えて; 怒りが感じられる); look down on(対等視しない; 怒りは感じられない); scorn +目 (➤ 文語) ▶軽蔑に値しない *be beneath contempt* ‖軽蔑すべき男 a *contemptible* man ‖うそつきを軽蔑する *despise* [*scorn*] a liar ‖私は倫理観念のない人を軽蔑する I *despise* people who lack any ethical sense. ‖学歴がないからって, 人を軽蔑しちゃあいけないよ You shouldn't *look down on* a person for not being well-educated. ‖彼が私を軽蔑したような目つ

きで見たのはそれでか That's why he looked at me *with contempt*. ／That's why he gave me a *contemptuous* look.

けいぼ 継母 a **stepmother**.

1**けいほう 警報** a **warning** /wɔ́ːʳnɪŋ/ ; an **alarm**（非常ベルなど）▶**暴風警報**が出た They issued［gave］*a storm warning*.（➤ they は気象関係者を漠然と指している）‖ **津波警報**は解除された The *tsunami warning*［*alert*］has been canceled［lifted］.

2**けいほう 刑法** **criminal［penal］law, the criminal［penal］code** ▶**刑法**第３条 Article 3 of *the Criminal*［*Penal*］*Code*.

けいぼう 警棒 a **baton** /bətɑ́ːn ‖ bǽtɔn/,《米また》a **nightstick** ;《英また》a **truncheon** /trʌ́ntʃən/.

けいみょう 軽妙な **light (and easy)** ; **witty**（ウイットに富んだ）▶DJ の**軽妙な**おしゃべりがリスナーを魅了した The DJ's *light and easy* chat charmed the listeners.

けいむしょ 刑務所 a **prison** ▶**刑務所に行く**（＝入る）*go to prison*（➤ 差し入れなどで刑務所に行く場合は go to the prison）‖ **刑務所に入っている** *be in prison* ‖ そんなことをしてると**刑務所行き**だぞ You'll *be sent to*［You'll *end up in*］*prison* if you continue behaving that way. ‖**医療刑務所** a medical prison ‖ **少年刑務所** a juvenile prison.

げいめい 芸名 a **stage name**（舞台［ステージ］名）; a **screen name**（映画俳優の）▶星野夢子は彼女の本名ではなく**芸名**だ Hoshino Yumeko is not her real name, but her *stage name*.

けいもう 啓蒙 **enlightenment** 一動 **啓もうする** **enlighten** ＋目 ▶**啓もう的な**本 an *enlightening* book ‖ 彼女の講演で聴衆は大いに**啓もうされた** Her lecture greatly *enlightened* the audience.

‖**啓もう思想** philosophy of the Enlightenment ‖ **啓もう時代** the Enlightenment.

けいやく 契約 a **contract** /kɑ́ːntrækt/（文書になった正式の）; a **lease**（借家・借地などの）一動 **契約する** **make［sign］a contract** ▶労働［雇用］**契約** a labor［an employment］*contract* ‖ **契約を更新する** renew *a contract* ‖ **契約を履行する**［無効にする］execute［void］*a contract* ‖ **契約の条件を破る** break the terms of *a contract* ‖ **契約書を作成する** draw up *a* (*written*) *contract* ‖ **契約書を交わす** exchange (*written*) *contracts*.

▶当社はその私立高校と体育館建設の**契約を結んだ** Our company *signed*［*made*］*a contract* with that private high school to build a gymnasium. ‖ 我々は2015年暮れまでにその**契約を履行し**なければならない We must *complete*［*fulfill*］*the contract* by the end of 2015. ‖ その監督は西武ライオンズと**3年契約を結んでいる** The manager *is under a three-year contract to*［*with*］the Lions. ‖ 私たちは**1年契約**でアパートを借りている We are renting the apartment *on a one-year lease*. ‖ もうすぐアパートの**契約が切れる** Our apartment *lease* will expire soon. ‖ その選手は１億2000万円で**契約を更改した** The player renewed *his contract*, for 120 million yen.（➤ contract のあとにコンマをつけないと「１億2000万円だった旧契約を更改した」の意にもなる）.

‖**契約違反** a breach of contract ‖ **契約金** contract money ‖ **契約者** a contractor, a contracting party ; a policyholder（保険の）‖ **契約社員** a contract worker,《インフォーマル》a temp. ‖ **契約者専用** Authorized Users［Parking］Only（➤ 駐車［駐輪］場などの掲示）.

1**けいゆ 軽油** **diesel fuel** ; **light oil**（重油に対して）.

2**けいゆ 経由** ▶ロンドン**経由**でパリに飛ぶ fly to Paris *via*［*by way of*］London（➤ via の発音は /váɪə/）.

1**けいよう 形容** **description** 一動 **形容する** **describe** ＋目 ▶オーロラの美しさは何とも**形容し難い** No words can *describe* the beauty of the Northern［Southern］lights.

‖**形容詞** an adjective /ǽdʒɪktɪv/.

2**けいよう 掲揚** ▶国旗を**掲揚する** *hoist*［*raise*］the national flag.

けいり 経理 **accounting** ▶父はその会社の**経理**を担当している My father is an accountant for the company. ‖**経理係** an accountant ‖ **経理士** a public accountant ‖ **経理専門学校** an accounting school ‖ **経理部** the accounting department.

けいりゃく 計略 a **trick**（冗談・悪意のたくらみ）; a **trap**（わな）; a **plot**（陰謀）▶敵の**計略**にはまる fall into the enemy's *trap* ‖ これは敵の**計略**に違いない This, no doubt, is［No doubt, this is］some *trick* of the enemy. ／I'll bet this is some *plot* hatched by the enemy. ‖ 新任の先生を驚かそうと生徒たちはあれこれ**計略を巡らした** The students *devised* various *tricks* to surprise their new teacher.

1**けいりゅう 渓流** a **mountain stream**, a **brook**（➤ 後者は文語）▶**渓流釣りをする** *fish*［*angle*］*in a mountain stream*.

2**けいりゅう 係留** **mooring** /mɔ́ərɪŋ/ ▶船を**係留する** *moor* a boat.

1**けいりょう 軽量** **light weight** ▶舞の海は**軽量**の力士だった Mainoumi was *light* for a sumo wrestler. ‖《ボクシングなどで》彼は**軽量級の選手**だ He is *a lightweight*.

2**けいりょう 計量する** **measure** ＋目（寸法・量を）; **weigh** ＋目（重さを）▶騎手は毎レース後に**計量する** Jockeys *weigh themselves* after every race.

‖**計量カップ［スプーン］** a measuring cup［spoon］‖（自動車のオイルの）**計量棒** a dip-stick.

けいりん 競輪 a **bicycle［cycle］race, keirin**（➤ 競技名として英語化している）▶きょうは川崎で**競輪**がある *Bicycle*［*Keirin*］*races* are being held in Kawasaki today. ‖**競輪場** a bicycle［cycle］race track, a keirin circuit ‖ **競輪選手** a professional cyclist, a cycle［keirin］racer.

けいるい 係累 a **dependent**,《英》a **dependant**（扶養家族）.

けいれい 敬礼 a **salute** 一動 **敬礼する** **salute** ＋目 ▶上官［国旗］に**敬礼する** *salute* a superior officer［the national flag］‖《号令》気をつけ！**敬礼**！(At) attention ! *Salute !*（➤ この場合の attention の発音は /ətènʃʌ́n/）.

☞ **最敬礼**（→見出語）

けいれき 経歴 a **career** /kərɪ́əʳ/（職業上の）; a **personal history**, a **background**（職歴・学歴など広い意味での）; a **record** /rékəʳd/（記録としての）▶その人はどんな**経歴**の人ですか What is his *career history*［*career background*］? ‖ 彼は変わった**経歴**の持ち主だ He has had an unusual *career*.（● unusual の代わりに varied を用いると「いろいろな（仕事に就いてきた）」の意になる）‖ 彼はテレビディレクターとしての長い**経歴**をもっている He has a long *career* as a TV director.（→**キャリア**）.

けいれつ 系列 ▶彼は三井**系列**の会社に就職を希望している He wants to get a job with a company in *the Mitsui group*.

‖**系列会社** an affiliated company.

けいれん 痙攣 a **convulsion**（体全体［数か所］の; 通

例複数形で）; a **spasm**, (a) **cramp**（➤ ともに筋肉のけいれんをいうが，後者はこむら返りを指すことが多い）; a **twitch**（顔面のぴくぴく）▶筋肉のけいれん a muscle *spasm*／《米また》a *charley horse*（➤ 多くはこむら返りを指す）‖その男の子はけいれんを起こした That little boy had *convulsions*. ‖けさ彼女はひどい胃けいれんを起こした This morning she had painful *spasms in her stomach* [*stomach spasms*]. ‖ゆうべ眠っているとき足がけいれんした（＝ひきつった）I *had* [*got*] *(a) cramp* in my leg while sleeping last night.（➤ a を省略するのは《英》用法）‖彼女のまぶたがぴくっとけいれんした Her eyelid *twitched*.

1**けいろ 経路** a **course**（進路）; a **route**（決まった道）▶彼女は植村氏と同じ経路をたどって北極点に行こうとした She planned to follow the same *course* to the North Pole as Mr. Uemura. ‖その病気の感染経路はまだよくわかっていない *The route of infection* of the disease is not yet well known.

‖**飛行経路** a flight path.

2**けいろ 毛色** **hair color**（髪の色）; **fur color**（動物の）▶珍しい毛色の馬 a horse *of a rare color*. ‖《慣用表現》彼は役人としては少し毛色の変わった男だ He's a government official, but he *isn't typical*.／He is *not just your typical* government official.

けいろう 敬老 ▶敬老の気持ちを忘れてはいけない Never forget to *respect old people*.

‖**敬老の日** Respect for the Aged Day, Senior Citizens' Day（➤ 英米にはない）.

けう 希有な･稀有な **rare** ▶これは日本の歴史上でもけうな事件である This is *a rarity* [*a rare case*] in the history of Japan.（➤ a rarity /réərəṭi/ は「珍しい物［事］」）.

ケーキ (a) **cake**（➤ 大きさに関係なく，丸ごと１つは a cake，切り分けたものは Ⓤ 扱い；切り取ったケーキ１個は a piece of cake という）▶母は私の誕生日にチョコレートケーキを焼いてくれた Mother baked *a chocolate cake* for my birthday. ‖もう１つケーキをどうぞ Have another piece of *cake*. ‖新郎新婦はウエディングケーキにナイフを入れた The bride and groom cut the *wedding cake*.

‖**ケーキ職人** a pastry /péistri/ chef, patissier（➤ ともに「菓子職人」. 後者はフランス語）‖**ケーキ屋** a pastry shop, a patisserie /pətí:səri/.

> 「ケーキ」のいろいろ **エクレア** éclair／**カップケーキ** cupcake／**シュークリーム** cream puff／**ショートケーキ** shortcake／**スポンジケーキ** sponge cake／**タルト** tart／**チーズケーキ** cheesecake／**チョコレートケーキ** chocolate cake／**デコレーションケーキ** fancy cake／**トルテ** torte／**パウンドケーキ** pound cake／**フルーツケーキ** fruitcake／**ホットケーキ** pancake／**レアチーズケーキ** a no-bake [an unbaked] cheesecake, a gelatin cheesecake／**レヤーケーキ** layer cake

げーげー ▶飲み過ぎてゲーゲー吐いてしまった I *threw up a lot* because I had drunk too much.／I *threw up everything* in my stomach after drinking too much.

ケース **1**【入れ物】a **case** ▶眼鏡のケース a glasses *case* ‖人形をガラスのケースに入れる put a doll in *a glass case*.

2【場合】a **case** ▶珍しいケース an unusual *case* [*example*] ‖典型的ケース a typical [classic] *case* ‖彼女の場合は特別なケースです Her *case* is a special one [one of a kind].

ケースバイケース ▶クレーム対応はケースバイケースです Complaints should be dealt with *on a case-by-case basis*. ‖ケースバイケースの（＝その場にふさわしい）対応をお願いします Please take *suitable* [*appropriate*] measures.

> **危ないカタカナ語✹ ケースバイケース**
> **1** 英語の case by case は「一件一件」「その都度，場合に応じて」の意味であり，on a case-by-case basis の形で用いられることが多い．日本語の「場合により」の意では as the case may be などが近い．
> **2**「それはケースバイケースだよ」のような文では case by case は使えない．That [It] depends (upon each individual case).（個々の事情による）とする．

ケースワーカー a **caseworker**.

ケータリング **catering**.

ゲート a **gate**（空港の搭乗口）.

ゲートボール **gateball**, a **croquet-like game**（➤ 日本で考案された競技）.

ゲートル **puttees** /pʌtí:‖pʌ́ti/, **gaiters** /géiṭəʳz/.

ケーブル a **cable**

‖**海底ケーブル** an undersea cable.

ケーブルカー a **cable car**（➤「ロープウェー」を含む；→ロープウェー）.

ケーブルテレビ **cable television**,《略》**CATV**.

ゲーム **1**【遊び】a (...) **game**《参考》英語の game はスポーツまで含めるため，ふつう，明確に card game, board game, video game のように言う必要がある．▶きょうは雨だから室内で（カード）ゲームか何かして遊ぼう It's raining today, so let's play a (*card*) *game* or something indoors.

2【スポーツ用語】a **game** ▶西武はオリックスに３ゲーム差をつけて［つけられて］いる The Lions are three *games* ahead of [behind] the Buffaloes. ‖ゲームセットになった The game is over.／The game ended.／《テニスで》Game and set.《参考》「ゲームセット」はテニスからきたと思われる日本独特の言い方．

‖**ゲーム機** a game console; a game device（携帯性のある）‖**ゲーム障害［依存症］** (a) gaming disorder ‖**テレビゲーム** a video game.

> 「室内ゲーム」のいろいろ **椅子取りゲーム** music(-al) chairs／**クロスワードパズル** crossword puzzle／**碁** Go／**ジェスチャーゲーム** charades／**将棋** *shōgi*, Japanese chess／**スクラブル** Scrabble／**ダーツ** darts／**チェス** chess／**テレビゲーム** video game／**ドミノ** dominoes／**トランプ** cards／**バックギャモン** backgammon／**ビリヤード** billiards, pool, snooker／**ビンゴ** bingo／**ブリッジ** bridge／**ポーカー** poker／**マージャン** mah-jongg／**モノポリー** Monopoly

ゲームセンター an (**amusement**) **arcade**.

> **危ないカタカナ語✹ ゲームセンター**
> **1**「ゲームセンター」は和製語．英語ではふつう amusement arcade といい，《米》では penny arcade ともいう．インフォーマルでは単に arcade と呼ぶことが多い．
> **2** テレビゲーム (video game) が中心のものは video arcade といってもよい．

けおとす 蹴落とす ▶競争相手を蹴落とす *dislodge* a competitor（➤ dislodge は「追い払う」）‖あなたは人を蹴落としてでも出世したいのですか Do you want to get ahead even *at the expense of others*? (➤「他人を犠牲にして」の意).

けおりもの 毛織物 **woolen** /wʊ́lən/ **goods**.

けが 怪我 an **injury**, a **hurt** (ともに事故などによる; 後者は痛みを伴うちょっとしたけがを指すことが多く, しばしば年少者が[に]用いる); a **wound** /wuːnd/ (戦争・凶器・武器などによる攻撃で受けた, 傷口の大きい) ⇀傷.

一動 けがをする be injured /ínʤəʳd/, **get hurt, be wounded** ▶彼女のけがは手当てを受ける必要があった Her *injury* [*wound*] required medical treatment. ‖弟は頭にけがをした My brother *injured* [*hurt*] his head. (➤ hurt は過去形・過去分詞形とも hurt) ‖交通事故で大けがが[軽いけが]をした I *was seriously* [*slightly*] *injured* in a traffic accident. ‖ 対話 「けがしなかった?」「指をけがしたけど, 大したことないよ」"Did you *get hurt?*" "I *hurt* my finger, but it's nothing." ‖その地震で40人のけが人が出た Forty people *were injured* in the earthquake. / The earthquake *injured* 40 people. ‖けが人たちは直ちに病院に運ばれた *The injured* were rushed to the hospital. (➤ the injured は集合的に「けが人」を指す).
▶《慣用表現》部屋を間違えたのがけがの功名で, それが私の彼女と知り合うきっかけとなった Entering the wrong room proved to be *a blessing in disguise*. That was the first time I met my girlfriend. (➤ 外見上は不幸に見えるが実は幸福である事態を表す決まり文句).

げか 外科 surgery ▶外科手術を受ける have *a surgical operation* / have [undergo] *surgery* ‖彼は脳[心臓/形成/美容]外科の第一人者だ He is a leading expert in *brain* [*heart* / *plastic* / *cosmetic*] *surgery*. ‖**外科医** a surgeon ‖**外科医院** a surgical clinic [hospital].

げかい 下界 this world (この世); **the earth, the land (below)** (地上) ▶雲間から下界を眺める gaze through the clouds at *the land below*.

けがす 汚す disgrace +目 (他人からの非難・悪評などで面目を失う); **dishonor** +目 (自分自身の行動で名誉・家名などに傷をつける) ▶そんなことをすると体面を汚すことになりますよ Such conduct will *bring disgrace* [*dishonor*] on you. ‖彼は万引きで捕まって学校の名誉を汚した He *dishonored* [*disgraced*] his school by being caught shoplifting.

けがに 毛蟹 a **hairy crab**.

けがらわしい 汚らわしい dirty (汚い); **disgusting** (忌まわしい) ▶触らないで, 汚らわしい Don't touch me, *you dirty man*. ‖そんな話は聞くのも汚らわしい What you told me is really *disgusting*. / It *makes me sick* just to listen to it.

けがれる 汚れる ▶汚れた一生を送る lead a *dirty* [*corrupt(ed)*] life.

けがわ 毛皮 fur /fəːʳ/ ▶毛皮のコート a *fur* coat.

1**げき 劇** (a) **drama** (戯曲); a **play** (芝居) ▶井上ひさしの劇 *a drama* by Inoue Hisashi ‖劇を上演する perform [put on] *a play* (➤ play a drama とはいわない) ‖**劇作家** a playwright, a dramatist.
☞ 劇団, 劇的 (⇀見出語)

2**げき 檄** a **written appeal** (文書による訴え); a **harangue** /həræ̃ŋ/ (大勢の人に向かっての熱弁) ▶社長は社員一同にもっと売れとげきを飛ばした The president *harangued* everyone in the company to sell more.

げき- 激- ▶激太り a *dramatic* weight gain ‖激やせ a *dramatic* weight loss ‖激ウマ *delish* / *finger-licking good* (➤ finger-licking は手で食べるものに使う).

1**げきか 劇化する dramatize** +目 ▶自分自身の生涯を劇化する *dramatize* the story of one's own life.

2**げきか 激化** ▶巨人と阪神の首位争いが激化している The struggle for first place between the Giants and the Tigers *is growing* more and more *heated* [*is escalating*]. ‖選挙戦はますます激化している The election race *is heating up* [*is intensifying*]. ‖シリアでは内戦が激化した Civil war *intensified* in Syria.

げきが 劇画 a **comic strip (with a plot)**.

げきげん 激減 a **sudden** [**rapid**] **decrease** /díːkriːs/ ▶ここ数年野生のトラの数が激減している The number of wild tigers *has decreased sharply* [*dramatically*] over the past few years. (➤ 動詞の decrease の発音は /dìːkríːs/).

げきしょう 激賞 a **rave review 一動 激賞する praise highly** ▶批評家たちは彼の新しい小説をこぞって激賞した All the critics *praised* his new novel *highly* [*raved about* his new novel].

1**げきじょう 劇場** a **theater**, a **theatre** (➤《英》では後者がふつう).

2**げきじょう 激情** a **violent** [**strong**] **emotion**.

げきしょく 激職 a **demanding** [**strenuous** / **grueling**] **job** (➤demanding は「きつい」, strenuous は「非常な努力を必要とする」, grueling は「へとへとに疲れさせる」).

げきしん 激震 ▶東京が激震に見舞われた Tokyo was hit by *a severe earthquake*. ‖《比喩的》スキャンダルで政界に激震が走った The scandal produced *a major shockwave* in the political world.

げきじん 激甚 ‖**激甚災害** a disaster of extreme severity, a devastating disaster.

げきせん 激戦 a **fierce battle** (戦闘の); a **hot contest** (選挙などの) ▶千葉県は今度の参議院選挙では激戦地である Chiba Prefecture is *a closely contested district* in this general election for the House of Councilors.

げきぞう 激増 a **sudden** [**rapid**] **increase** /ínkriːs/ ▶日本では百歳以上の人の数が年々激増している The number of centenarians in Japan *is increasing rapidly* every year. (➤ 動詞の increase の発音は /ɪnkríːs/) ‖首都圏の人口は過去60年間に激増した The population of the Tokyo metropolitan area *has grown enormously* in the last sixty years.

げきたい 撃退する repulse +目 ▶敵を撃退する *repulse* the enemy ‖しつこい販売員を撃退するにはどうすればいいですか How do you *get rid of* [*drive away*] pushy salespeople? ‖彼女は合気道を使って痴漢を撃退した She used aikido techniques to *repulse* [*ward off*] the molester. (➤ ward off は「防ぐ, かわす」).

げきだん 劇団 a **theatrical** [**dramatic**] **company**; a **troupe** /truːp/ (旅回りの) ‖**劇団員** a member of a theatrical [dramatic] company, a trouper.

げきちん 撃沈 ▶船を撃沈する (*attack and*) *sink* a ship.

げきつい 撃墜する shoot /ʃuːt/ **down** ▶アメリカ軍の爆撃機がアフガニスタンで撃墜された A U.S. bomber *was shot down* over Afghanistan.

げきつう 激痛 an **acute** [**a sharp**] **pain** ▶私は背中に激痛が走ってうめき声を上げた I groaned when I felt *an acute pain* in my back.

げきてき 劇的な dramatic ▶山田選手の劇的な満塁ホームラン Yamada's *dramatic* grand slam (home run) ‖ 2 人はローマで劇的な(＝感動的な)再会をした

The two had a *moving* reunion in Rome.

げきど 激怒 (a) rage, (a) fury(➤ 後者のほうが程度が激しい) ▶父は私がたばこを吸っているのを見て激怒した My father *flew into a rage* [*raged* at me] when he saw me smoking. (➤ fly into a rage は「急に激怒する」).

げきどう 激動 ▶激動の時代 a period *of turbulence* ／a *turbulent* period [years] ‖ 激動する世界情勢をわかりやすく解説した本 a book that gives an easily understandable explanation of *turbulent* situations throughout the world.

げきどく 劇毒 (a) deadly poison.

げきとつ 激突 a crash ▶車は石塀に激突して大破した The car *crashed* [*banged*] *into* a stone wall and was heavily damaged. (⇀衝突) ‖ あす優勝候補どうしが激突する These two favorites *are running up against each other* tomorrow.

げきは 撃破する ▶敵を撃破する *smash* the enemy.

げきへん 激変 a violent change ▶この数年で状況は激変した Things have *changed dramatically* over the past few years.

げきむ 激務 strenuous [grueling ／hard] work ; a demanding [strenuous ／grueling] job(激職) ▶激務に耐える endure *a heavy workload* ‖ 父は毎日会社で激務に追われているようだ My father seems to *be extremely busy* [*be swamped with work*] at the office every day.

げきやく 劇薬 a powerful medicine [drug](強力な薬品) ; a poison (毒薬) ▶劇薬につき注意 Caution. This is *poison*.

げきやす 激安の super cheap ; dirt-cheap(捨て値の) ; bargain-priced(特売価格の).

けぎらい 毛嫌い ▶母は長髪の若者を毛嫌いしている My mother *hates* [*has an aversion to*] boys with long hair. ‖ 宗教を毛嫌いしている日本人が多い Many Japanese *are allergic to* [*have a distaste for*] religion.

げきりゅう 激流 a raging [violent] stream, a torrent.

げきりん 逆鱗 ▶彼が何気なく言ったことばが上司のげきりんに触れた His casual remark *infuriated* [*enraged*] his boss.

げきれい 激励 encouragement 一動 激励する encourage +目 ⇀励ます ▶教師のたゆまぬ激励でその無気力な生徒は再び学習意欲を取り戻した The teacher's constant *encouragement* inspired the apathetic student (to) work hard again. ‖ 難病と闘う少女に全国から激励の手紙が寄せられた *Letters of encouragement* to the young girl, who was suffering from an intractable disease, poured in from around the country. ‖ 校長先生は選手たちを激励した The principal *gave* the players *a pep talk*. (➤ pep talk は「激励のことば, 発破」).

‖激励会 a pep meeting [rally].

げきれつ 激烈 ▶激烈な地震 a *violent* earthquake ‖ その2つの塾は生徒獲得のための激烈な競争を繰り広げている Those two *jukus* are carrying on *a fierce competition* [are competing fiercely] for students.

げきろん 激論 a heated discussion ▶少年法を改正すべきかどうかについて法学者間で激論が戦わされている There is *a heated discussion* among jurists about whether or not the juvenile delinquency laws should be revised.

けげん 怪訝な dubious(疑わしい) ; quizzical(不思議に思った) ▶彼は私の説明を聞いてけげんな(＝当惑したような)顔をした He looked *perplexed* at my explanation. ‖ 彼女はけげんそうに(＝半信半疑で)ぼくのプレゼントを見た She looked at my present *dubiously*.

げこ 下戸 ▶私は全くの下戸です I *don't* [*can't*] *drink at all*.

げこう 下校する leave school(➤「退学する」の意にもなるので使い方に注意) ▶もう下校する時間ですよ It is time to *go home* [*leave school*]. ‖ 同級生が下校の途中で交通事故に遭った One of my classmates was involved in a traffic accident *on his* [*her*] *way home from school*.

げこくじょう 下克上·下剋上 ▶わが社では下克上が起きている In our company, *people of lower rank* have begun *grabbing* [*wrenching*] *power from people of higher rank*. (➤「下位の者が上役から権力をもぎ取っている」の意).

¹けさ 今朝 this morning ▶私たちはけさ(早く)イスタンブールに着いた We arrived in Istanbul (*early*) *this morning*.

²けさ 袈裟 a ***kesa*** ; an oblong cloth worn over a Buddhist priest's robe(➤ 説明的な訳).

げざい 下剤 a purgative, laxative (➤ 前者は主に医学用語) ▶下剤を飲む take *a purgative*.

けさき 毛先 a tip of a brush (筆先) ; the ends of one's hair(髪の毛の先) ▶毛先が痛んでいる *The ends of my hair* [*My hair ends*] are badly damaged.

げざん 下山 ▶一行は下山の途中で事故に遭った The party met with an accident *while going* [*climbing*] *down the mountain*.

けし 芥子·罌粟《植物》a poppy.

☛ けし粒 (⇀見出語)

げし 夏至 the summer solstice /sɑ́ːlstɪs/.

けしいん 消印 a postmark ▶手紙に消印を押す *postmark* a letter ‖ 願書は2月15日の消印まで有効です Applications *must be postmarked* no later than February 15.

けしかける 1【犬などを】 set《on》,《米·インフォーマル》sic《on》▶その老人は子供たちに「畑から出て行かないと犬をけしかけるぞ」と言って脅した That old man threatened to *set* [*sic*] his dog *on* the children if they did not get out of his field.

2【唆す】 egg《on》▶彼はその2人の少年をけしかけてけんかをさせた He *egged* the two boys *on to* fight. (➤ egg A on to do は「A(人)に…するようけしかける」の意のインフォーマルな表現).

けしからん unpardonable(許せない) ; inexcusable(弁解の余地の無い) ; scandalous(もってのほかの) ; rude(無礼な) ; shameful(恥ずべき) ; terrible(実に悪い) ▶きみの態度はけしからん Your attitude is *unpardonable*. ‖ 警察官が犯罪人をかくまうとはけしからん It is *scandalous* for a policeman to hide a criminal. ‖ ノックもしないで入って来るとはけしからん It's *rude* of you to come in without knocking. ‖ 高校生がポルノを読むなんてけしからん. こちらに渡しなさい It's *shameful* [*inexcusable*] for a high school student to be reading pornography. Hand it over.

けしき 景色

a scene (具体的な場面, 光景) ; a view (一定の場所で視野に入る眺め) ; scenery (ある地域全体の美しい風景) ▶美しい田園の景色 a lovely country *scene* ‖ 景色のよい場所 a *scenic* spot ／a place of *scenic beauty* ‖ 夕焼けのグランドキャニオンはすばらしい景色だった The Grand Canyon at sunset *was magnificent*. ‖ この宿は窓からの景色がとてもいい The *view* from the window of this inn is wonderful. ‖ スコットランドの景色は美しい

The *scenery* in Scotland is beautiful. ‖ 頂上からは360度見事な**景色**を望める From the summit, you can enjoy spectacular *scenery* [*views*] in all directions.

けしきばむ 気色ばむ ▶記者の無礼な質問に首相は珍しく**気色ばんだ** The Prime Minister uncharacteristically *let his anger show* when a reporter asked a rude question. ‖ インタビューの受け手は**気色ばんで**席を立った The interviewee left his [her] seat *in a huff*.

げじげじ 《虫》 a **house centipede** ▶校長先生は**げじげじ眉**なのでとても怖い顔に見えます The principal looks so stern because of his *bushy eyebrows*. (➤ bushy は「密生した」).

けしゴム 消しゴム an **eraser**, 《英 また》 a **rubber** 《参考》 後者は《米》ではコンドームと解釈されがちなので, 前者を用いるのが無難. ▶間違いは**消しゴム**で消して直しなさい Rub out your mistakes with *an eraser* and correct them.

けしつぶ 芥子粒・罌粟粒 ▶3, 40秒後にはジェット機はけし粒ほどになって, やがて視界から消えた The jet became *a mere speck* after thirty or forty seconds and finally disappeared.

けしとめる 消し止める **put out** ▶消防士が火事を**消し止めた** The firefighters *put* the fire *out*.

けじめ **1** 【区別】 a **distinction** ▶彼は公私の**けじめ**が全くついていない He makes no *distinction* between public and private matters. ‖ 夏休みの間, 勉強と遊びの**けじめ**をきちんとつけなさい You should *make a clear distinction* between study and play during your summer vacation.

2 【事態の収拾】 ▶一体きみはこの問題にどう**けじめをつける**つもりかね How on earth are you going to *settle* the matter? ‖ 総理は公約違反の**けじめをつける**(=責任を取る)べきだ The Prime Minister should *take responsibility for* breaking his campaign pledge.

げしゃ 下車する **get off** (電車・バスなどから); **get out** 《of》 (タクシーから) ▶鎌倉で**下車する** *get off* at Kamakura ‖ 岡山で**途中下車**して後楽園を見学した I *stopped over* [*broke my journey*] at Okayama and visited Korakuen.

‖ **下車前途無効** No stopovers on this ticket.

げしゅく 下宿 a **boardinghouse** (食事付きの下宿屋); 《米》 a **rooming house** (部屋だけを貸す) 一動 **下宿する** **board** 《at, with》, 《米》 **room** 《at, in, with》; **live away from home** (自宅を出て生活している) ▶**下宿**を探す look for *a room* (*in a boardinghouse*) ‖ 私はおじの所に**下宿している** I *am boarding* [*am rooming*] *at* my uncle's. ‖ 友人のエリックは大学の近くに**下宿している** My friend Eric *lives in a boardinghouse* near the campus. ‖ 彼女は**下宿代**に月6万円払っている She pays 60,000 yen a month *for room and board*. (➤ room and board は「食事付きの下宿」) ‖ **下宿のおばさん** [**おじさん**] はとても親切だ Our *landlady* [*landlord*] is very kind.

げじゅん 下旬 **the last ten days of the month** ▶2月の**下旬**に in *late February* (● 英語では月を三等分する言い方は一般的ではなく, 下旬は late (終わりに近い) で代用する) ‖ その資格試験は**5月下旬**から6月上旬にかけて行われる予定だ Those qualifying examinations will be held from *the end of May* to the beginning of June.

けしょう 化粧 **make-up** 一動 **化粧する** **put on make-up**, **make oneself up** ▶**化粧**を落とす take off one's *make-up* / remove *make-up* from one's face (➤ 後者は堅い言い方) ‖ **化粧を直す** touch up one's *make-up* ‖ 電車内で若い女性が一心に**化粧をしている**のを見るのは興ざめです Seeing young women intently *putting on make-up* on the train really turns me off. ‖ 私たちの先生はほとんど**化粧をしていない**けれど, それでもきれいです Our teacher *wears little make-up*, but she is still beautiful. ‖ 特に若いうちは**化粧**は少ないほどいいと思います I think as far as *make-up* is concerned, less is more, especially while you're young. ‖ あの**化粧の濃い**女性は誰? Who is that woman with *the heavy make-up*? / Who is that *heavily made-up* woman?

‖ **化粧室** a powder room (➤ 古風な言い方. 「トイレ」の意では restroom がふつう) ‖ **化粧せっけん** toilet soap ‖ **化粧台** 《米》 a dresser, 《英》 a dressing table ‖ **化粧道具** a cosmetic tool ‖ **化粧品** cosmetics (➤ 1つは a cosmetic) ‖ **化粧品入れ** a vanity case [bag] ‖ **化粧品学** cosmetology ‖ **化粧品店** a cosmetic(s) store.

> 「化粧品」のいろいろ **アイシャドー** eye shadow / **アイライナー** eyeliner / **アフターシェーブローション** aftershave lotion / **オーデコロン** eau de Cologne / **おしろい** (face) powder / **口紅** lipstick / **クリーム** cream / **化粧水** skin [face] lotion / **香水** perfume / **コロン** cologne / **コンシーラー** concealer / **つけまつげ** false eyelashes / **デオドラント** deodorant / **乳液** milky lotion / **パンケーキ** pancake / **日焼け止め** sunscreen / **ファンデーション** foundation / **ヘアカラー** coloring, hairdye / **ヘアスプレー** hair spray / **ヘアトニック** hair tonic / **頬紅** blusher, rouge / **マスカラ** mascara / **マニキュア剤** 《米》 nail polish, 《英》 nail varnish / **眉墨** eyebrow pencil / **ムース** mousse / **リップグロス** lipgloss / **ローション** lotion

☛ **厚化粧, 薄化粧** (→見出語)

けじらみ 毛ジラミ 《虫》 a **crab louse** [複 **lice**].

けしん 化身 ▶その殺人犯は**悪魔の化身**に違いない That murderer must be *the devil in disguise*. (➤「変装した悪魔」の意).

けす 消す

> 📖 **訳語メニュー**
> 火を消す →put out **1**
> 電灯などを消す →turn [switch] off **2**
> 字を消す →erase **3**
> 姿を消す →disappear **5**

1 【火を】 **put out** ▶**火事を消す** *put out* [*extinguish*] a fire (➤ 後者は「消火する」に相当するフォーマルな語) ‖ 少女はろうそくの火を**吹き消した** The girl *blew out* the candle.

2 【電灯・ガスなどを】 **turn** [**switch**] **off** (➤ switch はスイッチ式になっているものを切る場合) ▶テレビ [ラジオ] を**消す** *turn* [*switch*] *off* the TV [radio] ‖ ガスの火を**消してね** *Turn off* the gas, please. ‖ 彼女は明かりを**消した** She *turned* [*switched*] *off* the light(s).

3 【字などを】 **erase** +目 ▶黒板(の字)を**消す** *erase* (the words on) the blackboard ‖ 《黒板などの注意書きで》**消すな** *Save*. ‖ 壁の落書きを**消す** *clean off* [*rub out*] the graffiti on the wall ‖ 山田先生は田代君の間違えた部分を**線で消した** Mr.Yamada *crossed out* Tashiro's mistakes. (➤ cross out は「×や線を引いて削除の印とする」) ‖ うっかり大事な録音

を消してしまった I *erased* an important recording by mistake.

4【消滅させる】▶この薬品で下水管の臭いを消せるでしょうか Will this chemical *remove* the smells from our sewage pipe ? ‖キニーネにはマラリアの毒素を消す作用がある Quinine *counteracts* the effects of malaria.（➤ counteract は「中和する」）‖彼女の悲鳴は激しい風雨に消された Her scream *was drowned* (*out*) by the heavy rainstorm. ‖あの事故の記憶を消してしまえたらいいのだが I wish I could *erase the memory* of that accident.

5【姿を】disappear ▶突然彼女は群衆の中に姿を消した All of a sudden, she *disappeared* in the crowd. ‖それ以来少年は村から姿を消した After that, the boy *disappeared* from the village.

6【殺す】▶俺に刃向かうやつは消す Anyone who opposes me will *get rubbed* [*snuffed*] *out*.

げす 下種・下衆 ▶げすなやつ a *vulgar* person ‖気にするな. ただのげすの勘ぐりだよ Don't worry ! It's only *a petty-minded suspicion*.

げすい 下水 sewage /sú:ɪdʒ/, **waste water** ; **drainage**（下水設備）▶下水管がまた詰まった Our *sewage* [*drain*] *pipe* was clogged again. ‖今日ほとんどの大都市は下水道が完備している Most big cities today have fully-functional *sewage systems*.

‖下水工事 drainage [sewer] work.

ゲスト a **guest** ; a **guest member**（臨時の参加者）▶彼女はアメリカのテレビ番組にゲストとして出演した She *appeared* on an American TV program *as a guest* (*member*). ／She *made a guest appearance* on an American TV program.

けずりとる 削り取る shave +㊐, **scrape off**.

けずる 削る 1【刃物を使って】sharpen +㊐（鉛筆などを）; **plane** +㊐（板をかんなで）▶ナイフで鉛筆を削る *sharpen* a pencil with a knife ‖かんなで板を平らに削る *plane* a board／*shave* a board *with a plane*.

2【一部を減らす】cut +㊐ ; **slash** +㊐（大幅に）; **delete** +㊐（文章などを）▶業績不振により予算の一部が削られた Part of the budget *was cut* due to slow business. ‖その教科書は検閲で数行削られた Several sentences in that textbook *have been deleted* by the censor [have been censored (out)]. ‖リストから彼の名前が削られた His name *was crossed off* [*was stricken from*] the list.

げせない 解せない incomprehensible ▶彼の真意がげせない I find him [his true intentions] *incomprehensible*.

けた 桁 1【単位】a **place**（位）; a **figure**, a **digit**（0から9までのアラビア数字の1つ ; 後者のほうが1つ1つの数字という感じが強い）▶5桁の数字 a five-*digit* number ‖計算で桁を取り違えた I got the *places* mixed up while calculating. ‖大学の入学金はついに7桁になった University entrance fees have finally gone into [risen to] seven *figures*.

▶《慣用表現》きみの家とぼくの家とでは財産の桁が違うよ In terms of wealth, your family'*s in an entirely different bracket* than mine.（➤ bracket は「(所得で分けた)層」）.

2【建築】a **(cross) beam**（梁(はり)）; a **girder**（橋の）.

☛ 桁違い, 桁外れ（→見出語）

げた 下駄 *geta*, (a pair of) clogs

日本紹介 ✉ **げたは伝統的な木製の履き物です. 2枚の歯と逆V字型の鼻緒がついています. 多くは桐(きり)の木で作ります. 夏, 浴衣を着たときに, 履く人が多いです** *Geta* (clogs) are traditional wooden footwear. They consist of two supports and 'inverted-V'-shaped thongs. Most *geta* are made of paulownia. People often wear *geta* when they are dressed in *yukata* in the summer.

▶げたを履いて歩く walk in *geta*.

▶《慣用表現》ぼくにげたを預けられても困るよ Don't *push* [*shove*] *everything off on* (*to*) me. ‖試験の点数にげたを履かせる *raise* test scores *intentionally*.

‖げた箱 a footwear [shoe] cupboard.

けだかい 気高い noble ▶気高い精神 a *noble* spirit ‖千姫は気高い心をもった女性だった Princess Sen had a *noble* mind.

けたたましい ▶ワライカワセミのけたたましい(＝甲高い)鳴き声が動物園の朝の静寂を破った The *shrill* cry of a laughing kookaburra pierced the morning silence in the zoo. ‖救急車のけたたましいサイレンでたたき起こされた *The blare* of an ambulance siren woke me up.（➤ blare は「耳障りな騒音」）‖拓郎のジョークに由紀はけたたましい声で笑った Yuki laughed *loudly* at Takuro's joke.

けたちがい 桁違い ▶タイソンは桁違いの強さだった Tyson's power was *extraordinary*.

げだつ 解脱 freedom from worldly desires 一動 **解脱する be free from worldly desires.**

けたはずれ 桁外れの extraordinary /ɪkstrɔ́:ˈdneri/ ▶桁外れな天才少年 a boy of *extraordinary* genius ‖桁外れにコミカルな映画 an *outrageously* comical movie ‖その爆弾の威力は桁外れに大きい The bomb is *extraordinarily* powerful. ‖このカメラは桁外れに安い The price of this camera is *ridiculously* low.

けだま 毛玉 a **pill (of wool)** ▶私のセーターにはすぐに毛玉ができる My sweater *pills* very easily.

けだもの 獣 a **brute**（野獣）; a **beast**（四足獣）▶けだもののような男 a *brutal* man ／a *brute of* a man（➤後者はいい意味で「強そうな大男」の意にもなる）‖《女性が男性に》けだもの！ You *beast* !／You *brute* !

けだるい ▶けだるそうに歩く walk *listlessly* ‖きょうはちょっとけだるい感じがする I feel a bit *listless* [*lethargic*] today. ‖それはけだるい夏の昼下がりだった It was a *sleepy* summer afternoon.

けち 1【物惜しみする】stingy, tight-fisted（➤後者は「きつく握って放さない」の意）▶けちな人 a *stingy* person ／*a miser*（➤後者は前者より意味が強く「守銭奴」に相当）／a scrooge（➤ディケンズの小説『クリスマス・キャロル』に登場する守銭奴 Scrooge より）‖あいつはすごいけちなので女の子にもてない He is not popular with girls because he is so *stingy* [*tight-fisted*]. ‖この, けち！ You *tightwad* !

2【卑小な】▶けちな手を使う play [use] *a dirty trick* ‖けちないかさま師 a *small-time* crook.

3【難癖】▶誰かが提案すると山口君はいつもそれにけちをつける Whenever somebody proposes something, Yamaguchi *finds fault with* [*criticizes* ／ *throws cold water on*] it. ‖もらい物にけちをつけるとは何という嫌なやつだ What an ungrateful guy to *look a gift horse in the mouth* !（➤「もらい物のあらを探す」の意の熟語）‖パンを焦がしたのが, けちのつき始めだった I burned my toast and it *kicked off a string of bad luck*. ／I *got off a poor start* when I burned my toast.

けちくさい けち臭い ▶あいつのけちくさい根性が気に入らない I don't like his *small-mindedness*. ‖あんまりけちくさいことを言うな Don't think so *small*. ／Don't be so *small-minded*.

けちけち ▶そんなにけちけちしなさんな Don't be so *stingy* [*cheap*]. (➤後者は《米・インフォーマル》に多い) ‖ けちけちして金をためたってあの世までは持っていけないんだよ *Even if you save* (*every penny*) *so stingily* [*No matter how much money you save by scrimping*], you can't take it with you (when you die).

ケチャップ **ketchup** /kétʃəp/《参考》catsup, catchup ともつづる ▶彼は何にでもケチャップを掛ける He puts *ketchup* on everything.

けちょんけちょん ▶演奏会はけちょんけちょんにたたかれた The reviews of the concert *tore* it *utterly to pieces*. ／The concert *was picked to pieces*. (➤ tear [pick] ... to pieces は「…をぼろくそにけなす」の意).

けちる **scrimp**《on》(金を) ▶タクシー代をけちって歩いたら途中で雨に遭った I tried to *scrimp on* the taxi fare by walking and ended up being caught in the rain on the way. ‖ このケーキを作るときはバターをけちっちゃだめよ When you make this cake, don't *skimp on* the butter. (➤ skimp on は「渋って必要量を使わない」).

けちんぼう けちん坊 a **tightwad**; a **miser** /máɪzəʳ/ (ため込んで出さない人) ▶清一のけちん坊！ You're such *a tightwad* [*a penny pincher*], Seiichi!

1**けつ 穴** **1【お尻】**《米》**the ass**,《英》**the arse** (➤ともにきわめて品のない語.《米》butt,《英》bum のほうが無難) ▶見ろよ！あの女, 象みたいなでっかいけつしてるぜ Look! That woman has *an ass* like an elephant. →尻.

2【慣用表現】▶おまえはけつの穴の小さいやつだな！ You *cheapskate*! (➤実際の「けつの穴」は品のない俗語で asshole, または, butthole という) ‖ 泥棒は家の者に見つかってけつをまくった Caught in the act by a family member, the burglar *turned defiant*. ‖ おいらの成績はクラスでけつから２番目だ I'm *second to* [*from*] *bottom* in my class.

2**けつ 決** ▶それでは決を採ります(＝採決します) We'll *take a vote on it* now.

けつあつ 血圧 **blood pressure** ▶父は血圧が高い［低い］ My father has high [low] *blood pressure*. ‖ 私の血圧は正常だ My *blood pressure* is normal. ‖ 血圧は上が120で下が80だった My *blood pressure* was 120 over 80. ‖ 血圧を測ってもらった I had my *blood pressure* taken. ‖ 塩辛いものばかり食べていると血圧が上がるよ You're going to *get* [*end up with*] *high blood pressure* if you eat salty food all the time. ‖ **血圧計** a sphygmomanometer /sfɪgmoʊmənáːmɪṭəʳ/, a sphygmometer /sfɪgmáːməṭəʳ/, a blood pressure meter.

☛ **高血圧, 低血圧** (→見出語)

けつい 決意 (a) **determination** (やり抜こうとする意志); **resolution** (揺るぎない決心) **━動 決意する** **determine**, **make up** one's **mind** →決心 ▶決意を新たに with new *determination* ‖ 私は是が非でも英語をマスターしようと決意している I *am determined* [I *have decided* ／I *have made up my mind*] *to* master English, no matter what. ‖ 事故は二度と起こさないと堅く決意しています We'*re absolutely determined to* avoid another accident. ‖ その若いインターンは無医村で働く決意を固めた The young intern *made up his mind* to work in a village that had no doctor.

けついん 欠員 a **vacancy** ▶英文科の准教授に欠員がある The English Department has *a vacancy* for an associate professor. ‖ 早急に欠員を補う必要があります We need to *fill* (*up*) *the vacancy* without delay.

けつえき 血液 **blood** /blʌd/ ▶A型の血液 type-A *blood* ‖ 祖母は血液の循環をよくするために足をこすった My grandmother rubbed her legs to get the *circulation* going. ‖ **血液学** hematology ‖ **血液銀行** a blood bank ‖ **血液検査** a blood test.

けつえきがた 血液型 a **blood type** [《英》**group**] ▶血液型を調べる check *one's blood type* ‖ 私, 血液型はB型よ I've got type B *blood*. ‖ 私の血液型はあなたのとは合わない My *blood type* is not compatible with yours.《参考》血液型による性格や相性などの判断は, 英米ではふつう行われない. したがってこの用例は血液型が医学的に適合しないと理解される. ‖ **対話**「あなたの血液型, 何型？」「AB型です」"What's your *blood type*?" "(It's) AB."

けつえん 血縁 ▶彼女とは血縁関係にあります I *am related to* her *by blood*.

けっか 結果

a **result** (試験などの具体的な数字); an **outcome** (勝敗などの全体的な状況); **the upshot** (経過をたどって行き着いたところ) ▶期末試験の結果はあまりよくなかった The *results* of my final exams were not very good. ‖ 首相の失言が選挙の結果に直接影響した The prime minister's gaffe directly influenced [affected] *the outcome* of the election [the election *results*]. ‖ 検査の結果はどうでしたか How were your *test results*? ‖ 実験は失敗という結果に終わった The experiment *resulted in* failure. ／The experiment *turned out to be* a failure. ‖ 我々の努力の結果, この川の水はきれいになった *As a result of* our efforts, the water of this river has become cleaner. ‖ 結果はどうあれ, 試合に全力を出し切ることが大切だ It's important to give our all in the game, *whatever the outcome*. ‖ 結果オーライということにしよう Let's just say *everything turned out fine*. ‖ 原因と結果 cause and *effect* (➤決まった表現).

▶結果的にひどい口論になった The *upshot* was a bitter quarrel. ‖ 結果的には物理学を選んだのが彼にとって最善だった *As it turned out*, choosing physics was best for him. ‖ 結果論だが祖母はほかの病院に入院させたほうがよかった *It's easy to say now*, but it would have been better to put our grandmother in another hospital. (➤「今言うのは簡単だが」の意).

けっかい 決壊する **give way** ▶その大雨で長良川の堤防が数か所決壊した The banks of the Nagara River *gave way* [*were broken*] in several places due to the heavy rain.

けっかく 結核 **tuberculosis** /tjubəːʳkjəlóʊsɪs/ (略 TB) ‖ **結核患者** a tuberculosis patient.

げつがく 月額 ▶私の小遣いは月額２万円です My allowance is 20,000 yen *a* [*per*] *month*.

1**けっかん 欠陥** a **fault** (欠点); a **gap** (欠落しているもの); a **defect** (簡単には修理できないような); a **flaw** (ささいな) ▶欠陥を補う(＝隙間を埋める) fill [stop ／supply] *a gap* ‖ このオートバイは欠陥だらけだ This motorcycle is full of *defective parts*. ／This motorcycle is a lemon. (➤ lemon は「欠陥品」の意のインフォーマルな語) ‖ この家は欠陥住宅だ This house is full of *problems* [*defects*]. ‖ 約2000台の欠陥車が修理のために回収された About 2,000 *defective cars* were recalled for repair. ‖ 彼女は性格的に大きな欠陥がある She has a serious character *defect*. ‖ **欠陥住宅** a defective house [home] ‖

欠陥商品 a defective product.

2**けっかん 血管** **a blood vessel** 《参考》日常的には vein (静脈)を「血管」の意味で用いる ▶**血管**が細い have narrow *veins* ‖ **血管**が詰まる have blocked *veins*. ‖**血管造影(法)** angiogram /ǽndʒiəɡræm/ ‖ **毛細血管** a capillary vessel.

1**げっかん 月刊の** **monthly** (➤ 名詞の前で用いる) ▶この雑誌は**月刊**(＝月刊誌)ですか, 週刊ですか Is this magazine *a monthly* or a weekly? ‖ 私は数種の**月刊誌**を購読している I subscribe to [get] several *monthly magazines*.

2**げっかん 月間** **a month** ▶火災予防**月間** Fire Prevention *Month* ‖ **月間**最優秀選手 the most valuable player *of the month*.

1**けっき 決起する** **rise in protest** 《against》 ▶核実験反対の**決起集会** a *protest rally against* nuclear experiments ‖ 住民はごみ焼却場建設に**反対して決起した** The residents *rose in protest against* the construction of a waste incineration plant.

2**けっき 血気** ▶**血気盛ん**な学生たち *high-spirited* students ‖ **血気にはやった**行動 a *rash* [a *hot-blooded*] action.

けつぎ 決議 **a resolution** ▶国連**決議** a U.N. *resolution* ‖ スト突入を**決議する** *decide* to start a strike ‖ 生徒会はその**決議案**を採択した Our student council has adopted the *resolution*.

けっきゅう 血球 《生理学》 a **corpuscle** /kɔ́ːrpʌsəl/.

げっきゅう 月給 **a monthly salary, monthly pay** ▶日本ではたいていの人が週給でなくて**月給**をもらっている In Japan, most people receive not a weekly, but *a monthly salary*. ‖ 父の**月給**は50万円だ My father *gets* [*is paid*] 500,000 yen *a month*. ／ My father's *salary* [*pay*] is 500,000 yen *a month*. ‖ 彼は**安月給**だ He *gets a low* [*poor*] *salary*. (➤ 高い月給なら形容詞を high または good に置き換える) ／He *is not well-paid*.

‖**月給日** (a) payday ‖ **月給袋** a pay envelope.

けっきょく 結局 **in the end** (最後には) ; **eventually** (結果としては) ; **in the long run** (長い目で見れば) ; **after all** (予想・期待に反して) ▶あきらは多くの女性と交際していたが, **結局**直美と結婚した Akira dated many girls, but *in the end* he married Naomi. ‖ **結局**その計画は中止となった *Eventually* the project was abandoned. ‖ 品質の良いもののほうが**結局**は長もちする Quality goods last longer *in the long run*. ‖ 日本サッカーチームは**結局**金メダルをとれなかった The Japanese soccer team wasn't able to win the gold medal *after all*. ‖ 2人の結婚は**結局**失敗に終わった Their marriage *ended* (*up*) a failure. (➤ end (up)で「最後に…するようになる」) ‖ **結局**次のようになる What it *amounts to* is this. (➤ amount to A で「結局 A になる」) ‖ **結局**きみは何を言いたいのかね *So* what is it (that) you want to say?

けっきん 欠勤 **absence from work** ▶彼女はよく**欠勤する** She *is* often *absent from work*. ／She often *stays away from work*. ‖ 彼はきのう会社を**無断欠勤した** He *was absent from* his office yesterday *without notice*. ／He *missed work* yesterday *and didn't even call in*. (➤ call in は「電話を入れる」) ‖ 彼は**長期欠勤**をしたあと, 会社をやめた He resigned from the job after *a long absence*.

けづくろい 毛繕い **grooming** 一動 **毛繕いをする** **groom** (＋目).

げっけい 月経 **menstruation** ‖**月経周期** a menstrual cycle [period] ‖ **月経不順** irregular menstruation (➤ have an irregular period と表現するのがふつう) ‖ **無月経** amenorrhea /əmenərí:ə/.

げっけいじゅ 月桂樹 《植物》 a **laurel**.

1**けっこう 結構** **1【よい, 優れた】** **good** ; **nice** (すてきな) ▶**結構な**味 *good* taste ‖ 先日は**結構な物**をありがとうございました Thank you very much for giving me such a *nice* present the other day. ‖ 忙しい年の瀬にゴルフとは**結構な身分**だね I *envy your being able to* [You *have it made being able to*] play golf at the end of the year when everyone else is so busy!

2【大丈夫, 十分な】 ▶レポートを提出した人は帰って**結構です** Those who have turned in their papers *may* leave. ‖ 現金でも小切手でも**結構です** You *can* pay either in cash or by check. (➤ この can を may にすると話し手が許可を与えているようで不適切) ‖ **対話**「いくらお入り用ですか」「10万円で**結構です**」 "How much do you need?" "One hundred thousand yen *will do*." (➤ will do で「用が足りる」の意) ‖ **対話**「支払いは現金でしましょうか, それとも小切手で?」「どちらでも**結構です**」 "Shall I pay in cash or by check?" "*Either will be fine.*"

3【婉曲(えんきょく)な拒絶】 **No, thank you.** ▶ **対話**「お茶をもう一杯いかがですか」「いえ, もう**結構です**. 十分頂きました」 "How about another cup of tea?" "*No, thank you*. I've had enough."

4【かなり】 **quite, rather, pretty** (➤ この順に意味は弱くなる) ▶彼女は**結構**英語がうまい She speaks English *quite* well. ‖ あいつは**結構**締まり屋だね He's *rather* tight-fisted. (➤ rather は好ましくない場合に用いることが多い) ‖ ねえ, 礼子. 今週の週末, アルバイトする気ない? **結構**いいお金になるわよ Say, Reiko. Are you interested in some work this weekend? It pays *pretty* well [It's *pretty* good money]. ‖ **対話**「あの店のハンバーガー, どう?」「うん, **結構**いけるよ」 "How are the hamburgers at that restaurant?" "Oh, they're *really good*." ‖ 私って**結構**美人だなって思うことがあるわ Sometimes I think, "I'm *pretty* good-looking [I'm *quite* a beauty]." ‖ パソコンなんか無くたって**結構**何とかやっていけるよ We can get along *well enough* without a computer in our house. ‖ あのビルは**結構**前からあそこにあったよ That building has been there *for quite a while*.

2**けっこう 決行** ▶クーデターを**決行する** *mount* a coup ‖ ストを**決行する** *carry out* a strike *resolutely* ‖ 赤城山行きは小雨なら予定どおり**決行します** The trip to Mt. Akagi will *go* as scheduled if there's only light rain. (➤ この go は「(事が)進行する」の意) ‖《競技会で》**小雨決行** The meet will be held as scheduled in case of light rain. ‖《掲示》**スト決行中** On Strike.

3**けっこう 欠航** **cancellation** 一動 **欠航する** **cancel** (取りやめる) ▶日本航空22便は台風のため**欠航となります** JAL flight 22 *will be canceled* because of the typhoon. ‖ 本日の粟島行きフェリーボートは**欠航いたしております** The ferryboat for Awashima *has been canceled* today. ‖ フェリーは何週間も**欠航している** Ferry service has *been suspended* for weeks.

4**けっこう 血行** **the circulation of (the) blood, circulation** ▶運動は**血行**をよくする Exercise promotes *circulation* [*the circulation of blood*].

けつごう 結合 (a) **combination** (化合, 組み合わせ) ; (a) **union** (団結, 合体) 一動 **結合する** **combine, unite** ▶水素は酸素と**結合して**水になる Hydrogen *combines with* oxygen to form water.

げっこう 月光 **moonlight, moonshine.**

1**けっこん 結婚** (a) **marriage**(➤ 制度や概念は Ⓤ, 前に形容詞がついて具体的にどういう結婚かをいうときは Ⓒ 扱い) **一動 結婚する marry** (+目), **get married** (➤ 自動詞としては後者のほうがふつう) ▶お二人で**結婚**について話し合うことがありますか Do you ever discuss *marriage*? (➤ (×)your marriage としない. your marriage は現在すでにしている結婚を表すので, 既婚者に対する質問になる) ‖ 彼の最初の**結婚**は離婚という結果になった His first *marriage* ended in divorce. ‖ 私, **結婚願望**があまりないみたい I don't seem to have much *desire for marriage* [*desire to get married*]. (➤ 後者の動詞表現がふつう) ‖ 彼女に**結婚を申し込んだ**が断られた I *proposed to* her [*asked* her *to marry* me], but I was turned down. (➤ propose には to が必要なことに注意).

> **【文型】**
> **結婚する**
> **get married**
> **人(A)と結婚する**
> **marry** A
> **人(A)と結婚している**
> **be married to** A

▶奈美恵は 20 歳で**結婚した** Namie *got married* at the age of twenty. ‖ 私は27か 8 で**結婚したい** I want to *get married* when I am 27 or 28. ‖ 私たち**結婚するんです** We're *getting married*. ‖ 由美子は近々アメリカ人の牧師**と結婚するそうです** I hear Yumiko is going to *marry* an American clergyman shortly. ‖ **対話**「私と結婚してくれませんか」「すみません. まだ結婚する気にならないんです」"Will you *marry* me?" "I'm sorry, but I'm not thinking of marriage yet." (➤ marry with me としない) ‖ あの方は独身ですか, それとも**結婚していらっしゃいますか** *Is* he single or *married*? ‖ 小百合は**結婚して**子供が 2 人いる Sayuri *is married* with two children. ‖ **対話**「結婚して何年ですか」「今月の10日でちょうど 7 年です」"How long have you *been married*?" "Exactly seven years (on) the tenth of this month." ‖ 彼女はイギリス人のダンサー**と結婚している** She *is married to* a British dancer. (● 意味内容を考えて Her husband is a British dancer. (彼女の夫はイギリス人ダンサーだ) と訳すこともできる) ‖ 彼女の父は娘を金持ち**と結婚させ**(=に嫁がせ)たがった Her father wanted to *marry* his daughter to a rich man.

▶**結婚のお祝い**に何を贈ろうか What should I give you as *a wedding gift*? ‖ 2 人は軽井沢の教会で**結婚式**を挙げた They held their *wedding ceremony* at a church in Karuizawa. ‖ 2 人の**結婚生活**は性格の不一致から失敗に終わった Their *married life* ended in failure because of their incompatibility. ‖ うちの両親は**見合い結婚**です My parents had *an arranged marriage*. (→見合い).

▶**結婚おめでとう**! *Congratulations* (*on your wedding*)! 《参考》 (1)これはもともと新郎に対して用いる挨拶で, 新婦に対しては例えば I hope you'll be very happy. (お幸せに) ／I wish you every happiness. (お幸せを祈ります) ／I'm very happy for you. (私もうれしい) などと言うのがふつうであったが, 最近は新婦に対しても Congratulations! と言うことが少なくない. (2)新郎新婦にいちどきに言う場合は, Congratulations! My (very) best wishes to both of you. とか Congratulations! My (very) best wishes for your future happiness together. のような言い方がよい. ‖ **結婚しました** (SNS などで) I [We] *got married*. ／We *tied the knot*. ／We *got hitched*. (➤ 最後のいい方はスラング的).

✉ **ついにこの10月隆夫と結婚することになったんです**! Guess what. Takao and I are finally *getting married* this October. ➤ Guess what. は「ねえねえ, いいこと教えてあげる」などの意で, ビッグニュースを伝えるときのくだけた慣用表現.

‖ **結婚相手** a marriage partner ‖ **結婚記念日** a wedding anniversary(➤「結婚記念日おめでとう」は Happy (wedding) anniversary!) ‖ **結婚式** a wedding (ceremony) ‖ **結婚相談所** a marriage [matrimonial] agency ‖ **結婚披露宴** a wedding reception ‖ **結婚指輪** a wedding ring [band] (➤ marriage ring は和製英語).

> **逆引き熟語 ○○結婚**
> **学生結婚** marriage between college students ／**駆け落ち結婚** (an) elopement, a runaway marriage ／**偽装結婚** a fake [bogus] marriage ／**国際結婚** an international [intercultural] marriage ／**職場[社内]結婚** a marriage between coworkers ／**政略結婚** a political marriage ／**早[晩]婚** an early [a late] marriage ／**できちゃった結婚** a shotgun marriage [wedding] ／**同性愛(者どうしの)結婚** same-sex [gay] marriage ／**二重結婚** bigamy ／**見合い結婚** an arranged marriage ／**恋愛結婚** a love marriage

2**けっこん 血痕** a **bloodstain** ▶**血痕**を取り除く remove *bloodstains* ‖ **血痕のついた手袋** a *bloodstained* glove.

1**けっさい 決済** (a) **settlement 一動 決済する settle** ▶現金による**決済** a cash *settlement* ‖ キャッシュレス**決済** cashless *payment*.

2**けっさい 決裁** **approval**(承認) ; a **decision**(決定) ▶その計画は社長の**決裁**が必要だ The project is subject to the president's *approval*.

けっさく 傑作 **1【優れた作品】** a **masterpiece** ▶ジョイスの『ユリシーズ』は20世紀最大の**傑作**の 1 つと言われる Joyce's "Ulysses" is said to be one of the *masterpieces* of the 20th century. ‖『細雪』は谷崎の**最高傑作**に数えられる "Sasame-yuki" is counted among Tanizaki's *best works*.

2【滑稽な】 ▶今度は帽子をかぶったまま海に飛び込むなんて**傑作だね** This time he jumped into the ocean with his hat on? *That beats everything*. [*Now I've heard everything*.] (➤ 後者は驚きの表現で「これは今まで聞いた中で最高の(最高におもしろい, すごい)話だ」の意) ‖ 《先生が生徒に》**傑作な**答えがいくつもあったぞ Some of your answers were *really funny* [*were hilarious* ／*out of the ordinary*].

けっさん 決算 **settlement of accounts** ▶半年ごとに**決算をする** *settle accounts* every six months ‖ 当社は 8 月**決算です** We *settle accounts* in August.

‖ **決算期** a fiscal term, an accounting period ‖ **決算日** a settling day ‖ **決算報告書** a report on final accounts.

☛ **総決算** (→見出語)

げっさん 月産 **monthly output** [**production**] ▶その自動車会社は**月産** 5 万台を生産している The automaker has a *monthly output* [*production*] of 50,000 cars. ／The automaker produces 50,000 cars a month.

けっし 決死 ▶当時は宇宙飛行士は**決死の覚悟**でスペースシャトルに乗り込んだ In those days, astronauts boarded the space shuttle *at the risk of their lives*. ‖ その青年は溺れかけている子を救うため**決死の覚悟**で海に飛び込んだ That young man jumped into the sea to save a drowning child *at the risk of his life*.

げつじ 月次の **monthly** ▶**月次報告** a *monthly* report.

けつじつ 結実する **bear fruit** ▶この桃の木は毎年**結実する** This peach tree *bears fruit* every year. ▶彼の長年の努力がついに**結実した** His efforts over many years finally *bore fruit*. (➤ bore は bear の過去形) ‖ この辞書は我々の多年の努力の**結実**(＝成果)である This dictionary is the *fruit* [*result*] of our years of efforts.

けっして 決して **never**(絶対に…しない)；**not at all** (少しも…でない)；**by no means**(どんなことがあろうと…しない) ▶**決して**諦めるな *Never* give up！‖ 芳美は**決して**12時前には床に就かない Yoshimi *never* goes to bed before twelve. ‖ ご恩は**決して**忘れません I will *never* forget your great kindness. ‖ 彼は**決して**カンニングをするような男ではない He *never* cheats on exams. ‖ もっと運動をするのは**決して**困難なことではない It is *not* difficult *at all* [*by no means* difficult] to get more exercise. ‖ 彼は**決して**ばかではないが, 少し思慮に欠ける He is *no* fool, but he is a little thoughtless. (➤ 名詞を no で打ち消すのは, not で be 動詞を打ち消すより意味が強くなる).

けっしゃ 結社 a **society** ▶**政治結社** a political *society* ‖ **秘密結社** a secret *society*.

げっしゃ 月謝 a **monthly fee**.

けっしゅう 結集 ▶我々は総力を**結集して**学園祭の準備をした We *concentrated all our efforts* on getting ready for the school festival. ▶組合員は代々木公園に**結集しよう** Union members, let's *meet* in Yoyogi Park.

げっしゅう 月収 a **monthly income** ▶彼女の**月収**は50万円です She *gets* half a million yen *a month*. ／She has *a monthly income* of a half million yen.

けっしゅつ 傑出する **excel** /ɪksél/ ▶**傑出した**物理学者 a *prominent* [*an outstanding*] physicist ‖ 彼は作曲家としてのみならず, ピアニストとしても**傑出している** He *excels* not only as a composer, but (also) as a pianist.

けつじょ 欠如 a **want**(欠乏)；a **lack** (不足) ▶彼は常識がひどく**欠如している** He *is* seriously *lacking in* common sense. ‖ 彼女の言動は他人に対する同情と理解の**欠如**を示している Her behavior shows *a lack* of empathy and understanding toward others.

1**けっしょう 決勝** **the finals, the final match** [**game**] ▶**決勝の**二塁打 a (*game-*)*winning* double ‖ 興南高校は全国高校野球大会で**決勝戦**に進出した The Konan High School team made it into *the finals* of the National High School Baseball Tournament. ‖ **決勝戦**は大阪桐蔭高校と光星学院高校の間で行われ, 大阪桐蔭が勝った *The final game* was played between the Osaka Toin High School and Kosei Gakuin High School teams, and Osaka Toin won. ‖**決勝点** the goal／the finish line (ゴール地点)；a (game-)winning run (野球の) ‖ **同点決勝戦** a play-off.

2**けっしょう 結晶** a **crystal** (結晶体) ▶**雪の結晶** a snow *crystal* ‖ 水は**結晶する**と雪になる Water *crystallizes* to form snow. ‖《慣用表現》リエは２人の愛の**結晶**です Rie is *the fruit of their love*.

3**けっしょう 血漿**《解剖学》(**blood**) **plasma** /plǽzmə/.

げっしょう 月商 **monthly sales** ▶**月商**１億の会社 a company with *monthly sales* of a hundred million yen.

けつじょう 欠場 ▶馬原はオールスターゲームを**欠場した** Mahara *didn't play* [*show up*] in the all-star game. ‖ 中田は左膝の痛みで試合を**欠場した** Nakata *sat out* the game with a sore left knee. (➤ sit out は「腰掛けたまま最後まで参加しない」が原義).

けっしょうばん 血小板《解剖学》(**blood**) **platelets** /pléɪtlət/.

けっしょく 血色 one's **complexion** (顔色) ▶**血色の**よい(＝ばら色の)顔 a *florid* complexion ‖ 彼は**血色がよい** [**悪い**] He *has a healthy* [*sickly*] *complexion*. ／He *looks healthy* [*pale*]. ‖ 彼女は**血色がよく** [**悪く**] なった She *gained* [*lost*] *color*.

げっしょく 月食 a **lunar eclipse** ▶今夜**月食**があるそうだ I hear there will be *a lunar eclipse* tonight. ‖**皆既月食** a total eclipse of the moon.

げっしるい 齧歯類《動物》**rodents** /róʊdnts/.

1**けっしん 決心** (a) **decision** (結論, 決定)；(a) **determination** (熟慮の末の決心)；(a) **resolution** (強固な決意) ━動 **決心する** **decide, make up** one's **mind, resolve** ＋目 ▶彼の**決心**は固い His *decision* is firm. ‖ どんなことがあっても私の**決心**は変わらないだろう Whatever may happen, I will not change my *mind*. ／Nothing will change my *decision* [*determination* ／ *resolution*]. ‖ 就職か進学か, なかなか**決心がつかない** I just *can't make up my mind* whether to get a job or to go on to college.

> **【文型】**
> …しようと決心する
> **make up** one's **mind to** do
> **decide to** do
> …しようと決心している
> **be determined to** do

▶２学期はもっと一生懸命勉強しようと**決心した** I *made up my mind* [*decided* ／ *resolved*] *to* study harder in the second term. (➤ resolve は固い決意を表すが, 堅い語) ‖ 今度こそ, たばこはやめようと**決心した** I *decided that* I would [I *decided to*] quit smoking this time or never. 語法 decide, resolve のあとは, that に導かれる節でも to 不定詞でもよい. ‖ 知事は被災地域再生の先頭に立とうと**堅く決心していた** The governor *was very determined to* take the initiative to revive the disaster-stricken area.

✉ **私は将来絶対プロゴルファーになろうと決心しています** I *am* absolutely *determined to* become a pro golfer in the future.

2**けっしん 結審** **the conclusion of a trial** ▶その裁判はきょう**結審した** The trial *concluded* today.

けっする 決する ▶試合を**決する**ホームラン a home run that *decides* the game ‖ きょうは両横綱が**雌雄を決する**日だ Today is the day when the two yokozunas will *combat to determine which is the better* [*stronger*] *man*.

1**けっせい 血清**《解剖学》(a) **serum** /síərəm/ (➤ blood serum ともいう) ▶**血清**(注射)を打つ have *a blood serum* injection.

2**けっせい 結成する** **form** ＋目, **organize** ＋目 (➤ 後者がより堅い語) ▶少年野球チームを**結成する** *form* a boys' baseball team ‖ 新しい政党を結成する *organize* [*form*] a new political party.

‖結成式 an inaugural ceremony.

けつぜい 血税 a **tax paid by the sweat of** one's **brow** (➤「額に汗して払った税金」の意) ▶あいつらは血税の無駄遣いをしている They're wasting the *taxpayers' hard-earned money*.

けっせき 欠席 **absence** ━動 **欠席する be absent** 《from》

> 【文型】
> 学校など(A)を欠席する
> **be absent from** A
> **miss classes**
> ➤「授業に欠席する」

▶《教室で》安田君, きのうはどうして欠席したの? Why *were* you *absent* (*from school*) yesterday, Yasuda? ‖ 対話 《出欠をとって》「高田君」「欠席です」 "Takada?" "He *is absent*." ‖《教室で》きょうの欠席は誰かな Who's *absent* [*missing*] today? (➤ missing は授業より部活の場合) / Who *isn't here* today? ‖《電話で》かぜのためきょうは欠席します I will *be absent* [I will *be staying home* (*from school*) today] because of a cold. ‖ 良雄君はきのう無断で欠席した Yoshio *was absent from school* [*missed classes*] without notice yesterday.

▶母はそのＰＴＡの会合を欠席した My mother *did not attend* the PTA meeting. ‖ 私は高校時代**1**日も欠席しなかった I *didn't miss a single day* when I was in high school.

‖欠席裁判 a trial in absentia (➤「人を欠席裁判に掛ける」は try a person in absentia) ‖ 欠席者 an absentee /æbsəntíː/ ‖ 欠席届 a notice of absence, an absence note.

2**けっせき 結石** ▶尿路結石 a urinary *stone* ‖ 腎臓結石 a kidney *stone*.

1**けっせん 決戦** a **decisive** [**final**] **battle**; a **deciding match** [**game** / **race**] (競技で).

2**けっせん 血栓** 《医学》 a **thrombus** /θráːmbəs/

‖血栓症 (a) thrombosis /θrɑːmbóʊsɪs/.

けつぜん 決然 ▶決然と行動する act *decisively* [*resolutely*] / act *with decisiveness* (➤ decisively / with decisiveness はともに「決意も固く」の意) ‖ いじめっ子には決然たる姿勢で臨むべきだ You should deal with bullies *in a decisive manner*. ‖ 彼らは決然と敵に立ち向かった They stood *resolute* against the enemy. (➤ resolute は「(ある目的のために)意を決している」の意).

けっせんとうひょう 決選投票 a **final** [**decisive**] **vote** ▶決選投票を行う take *a final vote*.

けっそう 血相 ▶血相を変える *change color* / *turn pale* (➤「青くなる」) / *go red* (➤「赤くなる」) ‖ 姉は血相を変えて私の部屋に飛び込んできた My sister rushed into my room *with a pale face* [*her face white with anger*]. (➤ 前者は「青い顔をして」, 後者は「怒りで青くなって」).

けっそく 結束 **unity** (統一); **solidarity** (団結) ━動 **結束する unite** ▶父親は3人の息子たちに結束して生きるようにと言った The father told his three sons to live *in unity*. ‖ その政党は結束が固い The party *is closely united*. / The party *has great solidarity*.

けつぞく 血族 a **blood relative** [**relation**] (人).

げっそり ▶長い闘病生活で彼は頬がげっそり痩せこけた His cheeks *were hollow* [*sunken*] from his long illness.

けっそん 欠損 a **deficit** /défəsɪt/ (金銭の不足); a **loss** (損失) ▶300万円の欠損を埋める cover up [make up] *a deficit* of three million yen ‖ わが社は欠損続きだ We have suffered a series [succession] of *losses*.

けったく 結託 **conspiracy** /kənspírəsi/ ━動 **結託する conspire** 《with》 ▶その政治家はゼネコンと結託して大金を手に入れた *Conspiring with* contractors, the politician pocketed a huge sum of money.

けつだん 決断 (a) **decision** (決定) ━動 **決断する decide** ▶彼は決断が早い He *makes decisions* quickly. ‖ 彼には決断力が欠けている He *is indecisive*. / He *lacks decisiveness* [*decision*]. (➤「決断力」の意では Ⓤ 扱い).

けっちゃく 決着をつける **settle** +目; **be settled** (決着する) ▶紛争に決着をつける *settle* a dispute / *get* a dispute *settled up* ‖《けんかで》表へ出て決着をつけるか? Do you want to step outside and *settle* this? ‖ その裁判はまだ決着していない The case has not *been settled* yet.

けっちょう 結腸 a **colon** ▶結腸がん (a) *colon* cancer ‖ S字[状]結腸 the sigmoid *colon*.

ゲッツー (→かこみ記事)

> **危ないカタカナ語✸ ゲッツー**
> **1** 野球でダブルプレーのことを俗に「ゲッツー」というが, これは「2人をアウトにする」の意の動詞表現 get two からきたと思われる. 英語としては double play が一般的. また「ゲッツーにする」も turn [get / complete] a double play on ... のようにいうのがふつう.
> **2**「ゲッツーコースの球」は double-play ball という.

けってい 決定 (a) **decision**; a **conclusion** (最終的な考え) ━動 **決定する decide**; **set**, **fix** (日取りなどを; 後者はインフォーマルな語) →決める ▶決定を覆す reverse *a decision* ‖ 我々は生徒会の決定に従わなければならない We must comply with [abide by] *the decisions* made by our student council. ‖ 留学についてはきみは自分で決定すべきだ You should *decide* for [by] yourself whether you (should) study overseas. ‖ その小説のタイトルはまだ決定していない The title of the novel *isn't* [*hasn't been*] *decided* yet. ‖ 修学旅行の日取りは5月21, 22日と決定した(=決まった) The date for our school excursion *was set* [*was fixed*] for May 21 and 22. ‖ 就職先が決定した I*'ve found* a job. ‖ 鹿島アントラーズの優勝が決定した The Antlers *have won* [*clinched*] the championship. (➤ clinch は「決着をつける」の意のインフォーマルな語) ‖ 広島カープの勝利は決定的になった The Carp's victory *is almost a sure thing*. ‖ 不正があったという決定的証拠は何もない There's no *conclusive evidence* of wrongdoing. ‖《野球の》決定打 a winning hit ‖ 決定的瞬間 a decisive [critical] moment.

けっていばん 決定版 a **definitive** [**final**] **edition** ▶和英辞典の決定版 a *definitive* Japanese-English dictionary ‖ 彼は近松研究の決定版と言われる本を書いた He wrote what's said to be *the definitive* book on Chikamatsu.

けってん 欠点 a **fault** (欠けているもの); a **shortcoming** (性格上の短所や物事の不完全さ); a **drawback** (人や物事の不愉快な, または不都合な点); a **weak point** (性格的な弱点) ▶欠点を直す correct one's *shortcoming*(*s*) ‖ 欠点だらけの人 a person with many *faults* ‖ 欠点の無い人はいない

Nobody is free from *faults* [*shortcomings* ／ *weak points*]. ‖ 内気なのが彼の**欠点**だ Shyness is his *weak point*. ‖ 彼の人の良さは**欠点**を補って余りある His good nature more than compensates [makes up for] his *shortcomings*. ‖ 日本の教育制度の最大の**欠点**は入試の重圧がかかり過ぎることだ The greatest *drawback* of the educational system in Japan is the enormous pressure of entrance exams.

1**けっとう 決闘** a **duel** /djúːəl/ ▶佐々木小次郎は宮本武蔵との**決闘**で敗れた Sasaki Kojiro was defeated in a *duel* with Miyamoto Musashi.

2**けっとう 血統** **blood** ▶小川家は学者の**血統**だ The *blood* of scholars runs in the Ogawa family. ‖ この柴犬は**血統書付き**だ This Shiba is a *pedigree* [*pedigreed*] dog. ‖ **血統書** a pedigree /pédəgrìː/.

3**けっとう 血糖** **blood sugar** ▶高**血糖** high *blood sugar* ／hyperglycemia(➤ 後者は医学用語) ‖ 低**血糖** low *blood sugar* ／hypoglycemia(➤ 後者は医学用語) ‖ **血糖値** a blood sugar level.

げつない 月内 **within the month**; **by the end of the month**(月末までに).

けっぱく 潔白 **innocence** 一形 **潔白な innocent** ▶身の**潔白**を証明する prove one's *innocence* ‖ 私は全く**潔白**だ I'*m* absolutely *innocent*. ‖ その件に関して彼は**潔白**であると私は信じている I believe that *his hands are clean* in that matter.

けつばん 欠番 an **omitted number**, a **missing number** ▶ 13番は**欠番**にしてあります The number 13 *is omitted* from the list.

けっぴょう 結氷 ▶湖が全面**結氷**した The lake *was* entirely *iced over*.

1**げっぷ 月賦** an **installment**; **the installment plan**, 《英また》(a) **hire purchase (system)**（分割払い方式）; 《インフォーマル》an **easy payment plan** →ローン ▶私は**月賦**でパソコンを買った I bought a personal computer *in monthly installments* [*on the monthly installment plan*]. ‖ このスキーは10か月払いの**月賦**で買った I bought this pair of skis *in ten monthly installments*. 《参考》月賦の場合の割り増し金を carrying charge という.

2**げっぷ** a **belch**, 《インフォーマル》a **burp**, 《主に英》a **wind**(➤ belch は後の2つよりも音が大きく下品な感じがし, 後の2つは乳幼児を連想するという人も少なくない) ▶赤ちゃんに**げっぷをさせる** *burp* [*wind*] a baby ‖ 食べ過ぎて**げっぷが出た** I *belched* [*burped*] after eating too much. 《参考》英米人は一般に食事中や食後のげっぷを不作法と考え, それが思わず出た場合には必ず Excuse me. とか I'm (awfully) sorry. と言う.

けっぺき 潔癖 **1**【きれい好きな】**cleanly** /klénli/ (➤ 比喩的に **2** の意でも用いる) ▶**潔癖性の人** a person who *is fastidious about cleanliness* ／a *cleanliness fanatic* [*freak*].

2【不正などを嫌う】**scrupulous**（極めて良心的な）; **fastidious**(うるさく感じられるほどきちんとした); **upright**(真っ正直な) ▶**潔癖**な政治家 a *scrupulous* politician ‖ うちの部長は**潔癖**な人で部下からのお歳暮を受け取らない Our manager is a very *upright* man and does not accept year-end gifts from his subordinates.

けつべつ 決別 ▶だらしない生活と**決別する** *break with* one's past slovenly life (🍎「だらしない生活」を loose life とすると「性にだらしない生活」と解釈されがち) ‖ その２人の友は誤解が元で**決別する**ことになった The two friends *parted ways* due to a misunderstanding.

けつべん 血便 **bloody stools**, (a) **bloody stool** ▶**血便が出る** *have blood in* one's *stool*(*s*).

けつぼう 欠乏 (a) **lack**, (a) **want**（➤《米》では前者,《英》では後者が好まれる）; (a) **shortage**（不足）一動 **欠乏する** **lack** ▶ビタミンＣの**欠乏** *lack* of vitamin C ‖ 貧血は鉄分の**欠乏**が原因であることが多い Anemia is often caused by an iron *shortage* [*a shortage* of iron]. ‖ 被災地では物資の**欠乏**が深刻だ There is a serious *shortage* [*lack*] of daily necessities in the disaster-stricken area.

1**げっぽう 月俸** a **monthly salary**.

2**げっぽう 月報** a **monthly report**.

けつまくえん 結膜炎 **conjunctivitis** /kəndʒʌ̀ŋktɪváɪṭəs/; 《インフォーマル》**pinkeye**（流行性結膜炎）.

けつまずく 蹴躓く **stumble**(何かをしている最中に足をとられる); **trip**(何かに足をとられてよろめく) ▶切り株に**蹴つまずいて**転んでしまった I *stumbled* [*tripped*] *over* a stump and fell.

けつまつ 結末 an **end**(終わり); an **ending**（小説・映画などの）▶彼のボクシング人生は悲劇的な**結末**となった His boxing career came to a tragic *end*. ‖ 推理小説は**結末**がわかってしまっては興味が半減する If you know the *ending* to a mystery (novel), it's not half as interesting. ‖ この物語の**結末**はどうなるの？ How does this story *end*?

げつまつ 月末 **the end of the month** ▶ 5000円貸してよ. **月末に**[**までに**] 返すから Could you lend me five thousand yen? I'll pay you back *at* [*by*] *the end of the month*.

げつめん 月面 **the surface of the moon** ▶人類は1969年初めて**月面**に降り立った Human beings set foot upon *the moon* for the first time in 1969. (➤ この場合, わざわざ surface といわなくてもよい).

‖ **月面車** a lunar rover.

けつゆうびょう 血友病 《医学》**hemophilia** /hìːməfíliə/.

げつよう(び) 月曜(日) **Monday** (略 Mon., M.) ▶**月曜日**は仕事に行くのがおっくうだ I don't feel like going to work *on Monday*(*s*). (➤ on Mondays は「月曜日はいつも」という習慣性が強く出る). →曜日.

けつらく 欠落 a **gap**(欠陥); a **lack**(欠如).

けつりゅう 血流 **the bloodstream**.

げつれい 月例の **monthly**

‖ **月例会** a monthly meeting.

けつれつ 決裂 ▶交渉はついに**決裂した** The negotiations *have broken down* [*have come to a rupture*] at last.

けつろ 結露 **condensation** ▶**結露**はコンピュータを傷める *Condensation* will damage your computer. ‖ 朝方, 窓に**結露**が見られた There was *condensation* on the windows in the morning.

けつろん 結論 a **conclusion** ▶**結論を急ぐ** *jump* [*rush*] *to conclusions* ‖ あしたまでに**結論**を出さなければならない We have to *reach* [*draw*] *a conclusion* by tomorrow. ‖ 結局その企画はやめたほうがいいという**結論に達した** We *came to* [*reached* ／ *arrived at*] *the conclusion* that we should give up the project. ‖ **結論的に言って**, きみの言うことは正しい *The conclusion is that* you are right.

げてもの 下手物 a **weird** [**an odd**] **food**

‖ **げて物食い** a weird food eater.

-けど **but**(しかし); **though**(…だけど) →-けれども ▶カラオケ？お付き合いしたいけど, きょうはレポートを書かなきゃならないの Karaoke? I'd like to go with you, *but* I have a paper to finish today. ‖ この靴は履きやすいよ, ちょっと高かったけど These shoes are comfortable. They were a little expensive, *though*. ‖ 英語は80点だったけど, 国語は60点だった I got 80 points in English, *but* (only) 60 in Japanese. ‖ それ私の傘ですけど *Excuse me*, (*but*) that's my umbrella. ▶私はそろそろ帰るけど, あなたはどうする？I think I'll be going home. What about you？(➤ 逆接関係ではないので, but や though を用いない).

げどく 解毒 ▶この薬草には解毒作用がある This herb *works as an antidote*. (➤ antidote /ǽnṭidòʊt/ は「解毒剤」).

けとばす 蹴飛ばす **kick (away)** ▶腹立ち紛れにその自転車を蹴飛ばした I *kicked* the bicycle in a fit of anger. ‖ 少年は小石を蹴飛ばした The boy *kicked away* a small stone.

けなげ 健気 ⚠「けなげ」は幼い, または弱い立場の者が困難にくじけずに, 立派にふるまう様子を褒めていう語であるが, これにぴったりの英語はない. したがって, **brave** (勇敢な), **praiseworthy** (感心な) などを用いて近い意味を表すしかない.

▶その少年はけなげにもあらゆる困難に耐えた That young boy *bravely* endured every hardship. ‖ 誰もがその少女のけなげな行為に心を打たれた All of us were deeply moved by that little girl's *praiseworthy* action.

けなす 貶す **run down** ; **criticize** +㊐ (批評する) ; **disparage** +㊐ (それとなく)

▶彼は人をけなしてばかりいる He's always *running down* (other) people. ‖ あなたの業績をけなすつもりはありません I don't mean to *disparage* your achievement. ‖ 私の作品はその批評家にひどくけなされた My work *was panned* [*was badly criticized*] by the critic. (➤ pan は「(批評家が劇・本などを)こき下ろす」の意のインフォーマルな語).

けなみ 毛並み ▶この馬は毛並みが良い This horse has a fine *coat* (*of hair*).

▶《比喩的》彼女は毛並みが良い She *comes from a good family*. ‖ 毛並みの良さだけがF氏の取り柄だ Mr. F's only merit is his *good family background*.

ケニア **Kenya** (アフリカ東部の国).

けぬき 毛抜き **tweezers**.

げねつ 解熱 ‖**解熱剤** an antipyretic /æ̀nṭipaɪréṭɪk/, an antifebrile /æ̀ntɪfíːbrɪl/ (drug).

けねん 懸念 **fear** (恐れによる心配) ; **concern** (相手 [多くの人] が抱く心配) ; **anxiety** (将来に対する漠然とした不安) ; **worry** (心痛) ▶多くの人が食品の安全に対して懸念を抱いている Many people *have concerns* [*are concerned*] about food safety. ‖ 地球の温暖化のため, 海水面の上昇が懸念されている *It is feared that* sea levels may rise due to global warming.

✉ **その件に関してはご懸念に及びません** *There is no need to worry* about that.

ゲノム 《生化学》**the genome** ‖**ヒトゲノム** the human genome.

けば 毛羽 a **nap** (織物などの) ; a **pile** (じゅうたんなどの) ▶毛羽立った布 cloth *with a rough nap* ‖ 毛羽立った畳 a tatami mat *with frayed fibers*. 《参考》毛羽を出す機械を nap-raising machine (起毛機) と呼ぶ.

けはい 気配 a **feeling** (感じ) ; a **sign** (形跡) ▶秋の気配 *a sign* of autumn ‖ 春の気配が感じられる Spring *is in the air*. ‖ 人の近づく気配がした I *felt* someone approaching. ‖ 彼らは一向に出発する気配がない They're not showing any *signs* of leaving. ‖ その家には人の住んでいる気配がなかった There were no *signs* of life in that house.

✉ **11月も中旬となり, どことなく冬の気配が感じられます** In mid-November there is *a feeling* of winter in the air.

けばい **flashy** ▶ケバい服 *flashy* clothes ‖ あいつは何であんなケバい女と付き合っているんだ Why is he going out with such a *flashy* girl？

けばけばしい **tawdry** /tɔ́ːdri/ (派手で安っぽい) ; **loud** (色などがどぎつい) ; **showy** (派手だが悪趣味の) ▶けばけばしいネクタイ a *loud* tie ‖ 彼女はいつもけばけばしい服装をしている She always wears *showy* clothes. ／She is always dressed *loudly* [*gaudily*].

けばだつ 毛羽立つ・毳立つ **get (a little) fuzzy** ▶このブラウスはごしごし手洗いしたらけばだってしまった After I vigorously washed this blouse by hand, it *got a little rough to the touch* [*a little fuzzy*].

げばひょう 下馬評 a **rumor** ▶下馬評は当てにならない *Rumors* cannot be relied on. ‖ 下馬評では鈴木氏がそのポストに就くということだ There are *rumors* that Mr. Suzuki will be appointed to the position.

けばり 毛鉤・毛針 a **fly**.

けびょう 仮病 ▶彼女はよく仮病を使って学校を休む She often *plays sick* to get out of going to school. ／She often stays away from school *pretending to be sick*. ‖ 父は仮病を使って仕事を一日休んだ My father *feigned sickness* to take a day off work. (➤ feign /feɪn/ は「…を装う」の意の堅い語).

げびる 下卑る ▶下卑た笑い a *coarse* laugh ‖ 下卑た目つき an *indecent* look ‖ あいつはいいやつだが言うことが下卑てるよ He's a good guy, but he *has a foul mouth* [*a mouth like a sewer*]. (➤ sewer は「下水管」).

げひん 下品な **vulgar** (粗野な) ; **indecent** /ɪndíːsənt/ (淫らな) ; **crude** (不作法な, 無礼な) ; **low** (卑しい, 低俗な) ▶下品な会話 a *vulgar* conversation ‖ 下品な連中と付き合う keep *low* company ‖ 下品なことばを使わないよう気をつけなさい Be careful not to use *vulgar* [*indecent*] language. ‖ 彼女は美人だが笑い方が下品だ She is a beautiful woman, but her laugh is *unrefined*. ‖ 皿をなめるのは下品だ (＝行儀が悪い) It is *bad manners* to lick the plate.

けぶかい 毛深い **hairy** ▶私は毛深いのが悩みの種です Being so *hairy* has been a constant issue for me.

ケベック **Quebec** /kwɪbék/ (カナダ東部の州, およびその州都).

けまり 蹴鞠 ***kemari*** ; an ancient Japanese-style of football (➤ 説明的な訳).

けむ 煙 ▶《慣用表現》彼の話にすっかり煙に巻かれてしまった I *was* quite *mystified* by his account. → けむり.

けむい 煙い **smoky** ▶この部屋, 煙いなあ What a *smoky* room！

けむくじゃら 毛むくじゃら ▶毛むくじゃらの犬 a *shaggy* dog.

けむし 毛虫 a **(hairy) caterpillar** ▶あの人たちはどうして彼女を毛虫のように嫌っているんだろう Why do they hate her *like poison*, I wonder？(➤ hate like poison は「毛嫌いする」).

けむたい 煙たい **1【煙で】** **smoky** ▶煙たいなあ, たばこは外で吸ってよ It's awfully *smoky* in here. Go outside to smoke. ‖ たき火の煙が煙たい Smoke from the open-air fire really *makes my eyes smart* [sting]. (➤ この smart は「ひりひり [ちかちか] する」の意の自動詞).

2【窮屈な感じ】 ▶青木先生はどうも煙たい I *don't feel*

at ease with Mr. Aoki. ‖ 私はどうも会社の若い人たちに煙たがられているようだ I seem to *be shunned* [*avoided*] by the younger people at work. (➤ shun /ʃʌn/ は「避ける」) ／It seems that the young people at the office *keep their distance from* me.

けむり 煙 **smoke** ▶煙突から煙が上がっている *Smoke* is rising up from the chimney. (➤「一筋の煙」なら a plume of smoke) ‖ 老婦人が煙に巻かれて死んだ An elderly woman was suffocated to death by *smoke*. ‖ 部屋に入るとたばこの煙にむせた I choked on *cigarette smoke* when I went into the room. (➤パイプたばこの煙には fumes を用いる) ‖ S L は黒い煙を吐いて走った The locomotive went its way, belching black *smoke*.

けむる 煙る **1**【煙が立つ】**smoke** ▶山小屋のストーブはひどく煙っていた The stove in the mountain hut *was smoking* terribly. ‖ 灰皿のたばこが煙ってますよ There are cigarette butts *smoldering* in the ashtray.

2【かすむ】▶東山が春雨に煙っていた Higashiyama *appeared dim* in the spring rain.

けもの 獣 a **beast**, an **animal**

‖獣道 an animal trail [path].

けやき 欅 (植物) a **zelkova** (**tree**).

けやぶる 蹴破る ▶戸を蹴破る *kick open* the door ／*break open* the door.

ゲラ a **galley** /gǽli/ ‖**ゲラ刷り** galley proofs(➤単に galley または proof ともいう).

けらい 家来 a **retainer**(昔の) ▶殿様は家来を大勢従えていた The lord was attended by a large number of *retainers*.

げらく 下落 a **fall**, a **decline**(➤ともに物価などの下落をいうが, 前者は落ち込みが大きく, 後者は傾斜しているニュアンスがある) ▶物価の下落 *a fall* [*decline*] in prices ‖ 大豊作のためキャベツの値段が下落した Because of the abundant harvest, cabbage prices *have plummeted*. (➤ plummet /plʌ́mɪt/ は「急に下がる」) ／The abundant harvest caused cabbage prices to *drop* [*fall*].

げらげら ▶ぼくのだじゃれに彼女はげらげら笑った She *laughed hilariously* at my pun. (➤ hilariously /hɪléəriəsli/ は「腹を抱えるほどおかしくて」).

けり ▶行けなくて悪いね. 今夜中にけりをつけなきゃならない仕事があるんだ Sorry I can't go. I've got some important work to *finish* [*get out*] tonight. ‖ その件はすぐにけりをつけたいんだ I *want* the matter *to be settled* quickly. ‖ 彼女とはもうけりをつけたほうがいいぜ You'd better *have it out with* her. (➤ have it out with A は「Aととことん話し合って決める」) ／You should *end your relationship with* her.

げり 下痢 **diarrhea** /dàɪəríːə/, 《インフォーマル》**the runs**, **the trots** (➤あとの2者はトイレに何度も駆け込むことをユーモラスに表現したもの) ▶私は下痢をしている I *have diarrhea*. ／I *have the runs* [*the trots*]. ‖ きょうは下痢気味なんだ I *have a touch of diarrhea* today. ／I *have loose bowels*. (➤後者は「おなかが緩い」) ‖ サルモネラ菌は激しい下痢を引き起こすことがある Salmonella can cause severe *diarrhea*.

‖**下痢止め** antidiarrhea(l) medicine [drug].

ゲリラ a **guerrilla** /gərílə/ (1人のゲリラ兵) ▶彼らは敵のゲリラ戦術にてこずった They were perplexed by the *guerrilla tactics* of their enemy.

‖**ゲリラ豪雨** a torrential downpour ‖**ゲリラ戦** guerrilla warfare ‖**ゲリラ部隊** a guerrilla band.

ける 蹴る **1**【足で】**kick** ＋㊐ ▶私は思い切りボールを蹴った I *kicked* [*gave a kick to*] the ball as hard as I could.

2【拒絶する】**turn down** ▶俺の申し出を蹴りやがった They *turned* my request *down flat*. (➤ flat は「きっぱりと」).

ケルト a **Celt** /kelt, selt/ **━** 形 **ケルトの** **Celtic** /kéltɪk, sél-/.

ゲルマニウム **germanium** /dʒəːˈméɪniəm/.

ゲルマン **ゲルマンの** **Germanic** ▶英語はゲルマン系の言語だ English is *a Germanic* language.

‖**ゲルマン民族** the Germanic race.

ケルン a **cairn** /keəˈn/.

げれつ 下劣な **mean** (卑劣な) ; **low-down** (低級な) ; **dirty** (わいせつな) ▶あんな下劣な男と付き合うのは真っ平だ I don't want anything to do with such a *dirty*, *low-down* man!

-けれど(も) **though** /ðoʊ/, **although** /ɔːlðóʊ/

語法 前者は一般的な語で, 文頭にも後半にも用い, 副詞としては文尾で単独で用いることもある. これに対して後者はやや堅い語で, 文頭に置くことが多く, 文尾で単独で用いることはない. →けど

▶彼女の目はきれいだけれどもちょっと冷たい *Though* her eyes are beautiful, they are a bit cold. ‖ 彼女はピアノを持っているけれどもめったに弾かない *Although* she has a piano, she rarely plays it. ‖ **対話**「彼って背が高くてハンサムね」「そうね. ちょっと冷たい感じだけれども」"He's so tall and handsome." "Yes, a bit cold, *though*." ‖ そのミュージカルは高かったけれどもおもしろかった That musical was expensive, *but* it was very enjoyable. ‖ ステーキを食べたかったけれどもお金が足りなかった I (really) wanted to have steak, *yet* I didn't have enough money (on me). (➤ yet は「それにもかかわらず」) ‖ 彼女は病気だったけれども旅行を続けた She continued her trip *in spite of* her illness. (➤ in spite of のあとには名詞句が続く).

ゲレンデ a **ski slope**(➤複数形で用いられることが多い) ▶このゲレンデは傾斜が緩やかで初心者向きだ The *ski slopes* here are gentle and suitable for beginners.

> **危ないカタカナ語✹ ゲレンデ**
> スキーのゲレンデはドイツ語の *Gelände* (地面)からきている. 英語では ski slopes とか ski runs という.

げろ **barf**(吐くこと ; 吐いた物) ▶日本では酔っ払いが路上や車内でげろを吐くことがある In Japan, drunks sometimes *barf* on the streets or in trains. →おう吐.

ケロイド 《医学》**keloid**, **cheloid** /kíːlɔɪd/.

けろり ▶あいつは5分前に先生にひどく叱られたばかりなのに, もうけろりとした顔をしている The teacher scolded him only five minutes ago but he already *looks as if nothing happened*. ‖ 医者が何でもないと言っただけで胃の痛みがけろりと消えた As soon as the doctor told me there was nothing wrong, the pain in my stomach vanished *as if by magic*. (➤「まるで魔法を使ったように」が原義).

けわしい 険しい **1**【急な】**steep** ▶険しい山 a *steep* mountain.

2【厳しい】**grim**(表情が) ; **fierce-looking**(目つきが) ▶「きょうこそは門限までに帰るんだぞ」と父は険しい顔で言った "Today, be back by curfew," said my father with *a grim look* on his face. (➤ today を強めて言う) ‖ 険しい目つきをした男 a *fierce-looking* man.

▶あの会社の前途は**険しい** The future of that company is *bleak*.

¹**けん 県** **prefecture** /príːfektʃəʳ/

> 【解説】(1)「県」の訳語に prefecture を当てることが多いが, この語はもともとフランスの行政区画を指す語で, 英米では一般になじみが薄い. したがって, 日本の「…県」は -ken と表記してもよい.
> (2)手紙の宛名の場合は -ken は不要.
> (例) 〒279-0013
> 千葉県浦安市日の出16-4
> 16-4, Hinode
> Urayasu-shi, Chiba, 279-0013
> Japan

▶熊本**県**人会 *an association of people from* Kumamoto-*ken* [*Prefecture*] ‖ 私は埼玉**県**の出身です I'm from Saitama *Prefecture*. ‖ 富士山は山梨と静岡の**県境**にある Mt. Fuji rises *on the border of* Yamanashi and Shizuoka prefectures.

‖**県営グラウンド** a prefectural athletic field ‖ **県知事** a (prefectural) governor.

☞ **県下, 県庁, 県立** (→見出語)

²**けん 券** a **ticket** (チケット) ; a **coupon** (切り取り券) ▶(掲示) **券**をお持ちでない方は入場できません Admission by *ticket* only.

³**けん 剣** a **sword** /sɔːʳd/ ; a **dagger** (短剣) ▶ハムレットは**剣**を抜いた [収めた] Hamlet drew [sheathed] his *sword*.

⁴**けん 件** a **matter** (事柄) ; a **subject** (議題, 話題) ; a **case** (事件) ▶例の**件**はどうなりましたか What has become of *the matter* [*case*]? ‖ その**件**はもう打ち切りましょう Let's close the *subject* now. ‖ 就職の**件**についてご相談したいのですが I would like to talk to you *about* a job. ‖ きょうの管内の交通事故はわずか2**件**だった There were only two traffic accidents in [within] the jurisdiction of this police station today. (➤この場合の「件」は訳出不要).

⁵**けん 腱** 《解剖学》 a **tendon** ▶アキレス**腱**を切る tear *an Achilles(') /əkíliːz/ tendon*.

¹**-けん -兼** ▶寝室**兼**居間 a bed-*cum*-living room (➤発音は /kʌm, kʊm/) ‖ 山本氏はその雑誌の編集長**兼**発行人だ Mr. Yamamoto is *both* (the) editor *and* publisher of that magazine.

²**-けん -軒** ▶この島には人家が20**軒**しかない There are only twenty *houses* on this island. ‖ 彼の家は角から2**軒**目だ His house is *the second house* [*two doors*] *from* the corner. / He lives *two doors* [*in the second house*] *from* the corner. ‖ 彼女は4**軒**先に住んでいる She lives *four doors away* [*down*]. →一軒.

³**-けん -圏** a **sphere** /sfɪəʳ/ ; a **bloc** (特定の政策・目的などをもった諸国家の結合体) ▶ロシアの**勢力圏** the Russian *sphere of influence* ‖ **首都圏**は人口密度が高い *The Tokyo metropolitan area* is densely populated. ‖**共産圏** the Communist bloc ‖ **大都市圏** a greater metropolitan area / a megalopolis ‖ **ユーロ圏** the euro zone [area].

☞ **圏外, 圏内** (→見出語)

¹**げん 弦** a **string** (楽器や弓の) ; a **chord** /kɔːʳd/ (円の) ▶ブラームスは重厚な**弦の響き**を好んだ Brahms preferred a heavy *string sound*.

‖**弦楽器** a string instrument.

²**げん 験** ▶彼は**験を担ぐ** He *believes in omens*. (➤「前兆や兆候を信じる」の意) / He is *superstitious*. (➤「迷信を信じる」の意) ‖ 彼は優勝するまで**験を担いで**ひげをそらないと言っている He's saying that, *for good luck*, he won't shave till his team wins the pennant.

げん- 現- **present** (現在の) ; **incumbent** /ɪnkʌ́mbənt/ (現職の) ▶**現**執行部 the *present* executives ‖ **現**アメリカ大統領 the *incumbent* President of the United States.

-げん -減 ▶今月の売り上げは2割**減**だった This month's sales *have fallen off* by 20%.

けんあく 険悪 ▶**険悪な**目つき a *grim* look ‖ **険悪な**ムード a *tense* [*menacing*] atmosphere (➤ tense は「緊迫した」) ‖ **険悪な**空模様 a *threatening* sky ‖ 2人の仲は**険悪になってきた** Their friendship is now *in danger*. ‖ 2人は兄弟なのに**険悪な仲だ** Even though they are brothers, *they have a rocky* [*difficult*] *relationship*.

けんあん 懸案 a **pending problem** [**question**] ▶それは日中間の**懸案**だ It's *a question pending* between Japan and China. ‖ それでは**懸案となっている**問題を検討しましょう Let's discuss the *pending* issue(s).

げんあん 原案 **the original plan** (当初の計画) ; **the original bill** (もともとの議案).

けんい 権威 **authority** /əθɔ́ːrəṭi/ (影響力, 権力) ; an **authority** (権威者) ▶**権威のある**辞書 an *authoritative* dictionary ‖ 彼は**権威に**弱い He is submissive to *authority*. ‖ この頃は親の(子供に対する)**権威**は落ちている Recently, parents' *authority* over their children has declined. ‖ 彼はバイオテクノロジーの世界的**権威**(者)だ He is a world-famous *authority* on biotechnology.

けんいん 牽引 **traction** 一動 **けん引する** **tow** /toʊ/ +目 (船・自動車などを) ▶トレーラーを**けん引する** *tow* a trailer ‖ 車が故障したので**けん引して**もらった My car broke down and I *had* it *towed*. ‖ 香川はチームの**けん引車**だ Kagawa is *the motive force* [*motive power*] of the team. (➤ motive force, motive power はともに「原動力」).

げんいん 原因

a **cause** /kɔːz/ ; **the root** (根源) ▶彼女の不注意がその自動車事故の**原因**だった Her carelessness was the *cause* of the car accident. / Her carelessness caused the car accident. ‖ 警察が事故**原因**を調査中だ The police are investigating *the cause* of the accident. ‖ 対話「出火の**原因**は何ですか?」「たばこの不始末です」 "What was the *cause* of the fire?" "A lighted cigarette." ‖ 対話「その紛争の**原因**は何ですか?」「国連が**原因**を調査中です」 "*What started* the dispute?" "The United Nations is looking into the *cause*." ‖ 2国間の領土紛争が戦争の**原因となった** The territorial dispute between the two nations *led to* war. (➤ lead to で「…を引き起こす」) ‖ 親子のコミュニケーション不足が子供の非行の**原因**だ Lack of communication between parents and children is *the root* of delinquency. ‖ 大雪が**原因で**首都圏の電車のダイヤが大幅に乱れた The train schedules in the Tokyo metropolitan area were considerably disrupted *because of* [*due to*] heavy snow. ‖ 彼らは**原因不明の**熱病で病院に収容された They were hospitalized for a fever *of unknown origin*.

げんえい 幻影 an **illusion** (幻想) ; **mirage** /mərɑ́ːʒ ‖ mírɑːʒ/ (妄想) ; a **vision** (幻) ▶彼女の息子が**幻影**となって現れた Her (deceased) son appeared in a *vision*.

けんえき 検疫 **quarantine** /kwɔ́:rənti:n/ ▶海外から日本に持ち込まれる動物は規定された期間の**検疫を受ける** Animals entering Japan from abroad *are put in quarantine* for a specified period of time.
‖**検疫所** a quarantine station.

げんえき 現役 ▶**現役**の軍人 a serviceman *on active duty* ‖彼は**現役**最古参の投手だ He is one of the oldest *active* baseball pitchers. ‖その親方は**現役時代**に多くの輝かしい成績をあげた That stable master produced many brilliant results in *his sumo-wrestler days*. (➤野球やサッカー選手なら one's player days とする).
▶彼女は**現役**でM大学に入った She passed the entrance examinations for M University *right after graduation from high school*. (➤「初めて受験して」なら on her first try).

けんえつ 検閲 (an) **inspection** (検査); **censorship** /sénsəʳʃɪp/ (内容チェック) 一動 **検閲する** **inspect** +目, **censor** +目 ▶中国政府はインターネットの**検閲を行っている** The Chinese government *censors* the content of some Internet sites. ‖この荷物は**税関の検閲**を通った This baggage passed *customs inspection*.

げんえん 減塩の **low-salt, low-sodium** ▶**減塩**しょうゆ *low-sodium* soy sauce ‖医者は私に**減塩食**を盛んに勧める My doctor strongly recommends that I eat *a low-salt diet*.

けんえんけん 嫌煙権 **the right to smoke-free air**(煙を含まない空気を吸う権利); **non-smoker's rights**(非喫煙者の権利).

けんえんのなか 犬猿の仲 ▶私の父とおじは**犬猿の仲**です My father and my uncle are *on very bad* [*on cat-and-dog*] *terms*. (➤日本語の「犬猿」が cat-and-dog となる).

けんお 嫌悪 (a) **dislike**; (a) **hatred**(敵意を抱くほどの); (an) **abhorrence**(忌み嫌うこと) 一動 **嫌悪する** **dislike** +目, **hate** +目, **abhor** +目 ▶多くの人は蛇を**嫌悪する** Many people *have a dislike for* [*of*] snakes. / Many people *dislike* snakes. ‖暴力を**嫌悪する** *hate* [*abhor*] violence ‖彼は**自己嫌悪**に陥っている He is sunk in *self-hatred*.

げんおん 原音 (an) **original sound** ▶音響機器の究極の目標は**原音**に忠実な再生だ The ultimate aim of audio equipment is to faithfully reproduce the *original sound*.

1**けんか 喧嘩** an **argument**, a **quarrel** (口論)(➤後者は前者の結果生じることが多い); a **fight**(いさかい, 時に殴り合い; 夫婦の口げんかはこの語で表すことが多い) 一動 **けんかする** **argue** 《with》, **quarrel** 《with》, **fight** 《with》 ▶2人の間で**けんか**が始まった *An argument* [*A quarrel*] arose between the two. ‖きみたち何を**けんか**してるんだ What *are* you *arguing* [*quarreling*] about? / What's all this *fighting* about? ‖酔っ払いが道で**けんか**してたよ Two drunks *were fighting* in the street. ‖子供たちは誰が先にぶらんこに乗るかで**けんか** [**取っ組み合いのけんか**] をしていた The children *were quarreling* [*grappling*] *with each other* about who would get on the swing first. ‖この兄弟はおもちゃのことでよく**けんか**をする These brothers often *fight* [*quarrel*] over their toys. ‖ゆうべ子供の教育のことで妻と**ちょっとしたけんか**をした Last night I *had a* (*little*) *spat* with my wife about our children's education. (➤spat は「ちょっとしたけんか」の意のインフォーマルな語).
▶**けんかの売り言葉** *fighting* words ‖**仲間どうしのけんか** a *quarrel* among friends ‖ぼくがうそをついたと言ってあっちが**けんかを吹っかけてきた**んだ They *picked a fight with* me, saying I had lied. ‖**けんかを売る**気ならいつでも買ってやるぜ *If you want a fight*, you've come to the right place. ‖彼らは私の部屋に**けんか腰**で入ってきた They came into my room (*as if they were*) *ready for a fight* [*an argument*]. ‖マイクは**けんかが強い** Mike is *a great fighter*. ‖何て**けんか早い**男なんだろう What a *quarrelsome* guy he is! ‖あいつとの**昔のけんかは水に流した** We *buried the hatchet*. (➤bury /béri/ the hatchet は「戦いをやめる」の意のインフォーマルな言い方) ‖私, 彼とは**けんか別れ**して5年も会ってないの It's been five years since I *broke up with him after a fight*. (➤break up は恋愛関係の人どうしが「別れる」) ‖最初のうちは彼らは友だちだったが, あとで**けんか別れ**した At first they were friends, but they *had an argument and ended their friendship*. ‖きょうだい**げんか**しちゃだめよ Don't *fight with your brother* [*sister*].
ことわざ **けんか両成敗** Both sides are equally to blame for this quarrel. / It takes two to quarrel [make a quarrel]. (➤後者は「けんかをするには2人が必要」という意の英語のことわざ).

> **あなたの英語はどう響く?**
> 「けんか」をいつも fight とすると殴り合いのけんかなのか, 口げんかなのかがはっきりしない.「口げんか」であることをはっきりさせるには argument または quarrel を用いる.

‖**親子げんか** an argument [a quarrel] between parent and child ‖**夫婦げんか** an argument [a row /raʊ/] between husband and wife / a marital spat.

2**けんか 県下** ▶Mの名は三重**県下**にとどろいた M's name was well known *throughout* Mie *Prefecture*.

3**けんか 献花** **the offering of a flower** [**flowers**]; a **floral tribute**(花の贈り物); **wreath-laying**(花輪を置くこと) 一動 **献花する** **offer flowers** [**a floral tribute**] ▶女王は慰霊碑に**献花した** The Queen *laid* [*placed*] *a wreath* at the monument. (➤「花束をささげる」なら offer a bouquet とする). ‖**献花式** a flower-offering ceremony; a wreath-laying ceremony ‖**献花台** the table for offered flowers.

1**げんか 原価** **the cost** ▶製品を**原価**で売る sell a product *at cost* ‖**原価を割って**売る sell *below cost* ‖この商品の**原価**は売値の20パーセントだ *The cost* of this product is 20 percent of the retail price.

2**げんか 言下** ▶彼らの提案を**言下**に拒絶する reject their proposal *promptly*(➤promptly は「即座に」の意).

けんかい 見解 an **opinion**(意見); a **view** (ものの見方) ▶それは**見解の相違**だと思います I guess we *have a different understanding* of this (point). ‖防衛問題については私は彼と**見解を異にする** My *views* about defense problems *differ from* his. ‖その問題について我々は**見解の一致を見た** We reach *consensus* on that issue.

けんがい 圏外 ▶大気**圏外**に出る fly into *outer space*.
▶ジャイアンツは**優勝圏外**に去った The Giants *lost their chance of winning the pennant*. ‖田中候補は**当選圏外**に落ちた Candidate Tanaka *is out of the running*. (➤be out of the running は「勝つ見込みがない」) ‖《携帯電話で》**圏外** *out of* (*the service*) *range*(➤表示としては No service).

1**げんかい 限界** a **limit**; **limitation(s)**(能力・活動などの;

通例複数形)；the end(力・数量などの限り) ▶人間の力には**限界**がある There is *a limit* to human power. ‖きみは自分(自身)の**限界**を知るべきだ You should know your (own) *limitations*. ‖科学の進歩にはほとんど**限界**がない There is hardly any *limit* to the progress of science. ‖もう我慢も**限界**だ My patience *has reached its limit*. ‖その監督は**我慢の限界**だった The coach had *reached* [was *at*] *the end of his patience*. ‖その選手は**体力の限界**を理由に現役を引退した The player retired from active play on the grounds that he *no longer had the strength* [*stamina*] to be a strong player.

2**げんかい 厳戒** strict guard [watch]；special police alert(警官による) ▶サミットの期間中は**厳戒態勢**が敷かれる The police are *on special alert* during the summit.

げんがい 言外 ▶**言外**の意味を読み取る *read between the lines*(➤「行間を読む」の意の慣用句で,「読む」だけでなく「聞く」場合にも使う) ‖父は自分の店の倒産を**言外ににおわせた** My father *hinted* that his store might go bankrupt. ‖その雑誌記事は彼が犯人だと**言外ににおわせていた** The magazine article *implied* [*made the implication*] that he was the culprit.

けんかく 剣客 a (samurai) swordsman.

けんがく 見学 a study trip [visit]；a field trip((生徒たちの)実地見学) 一動 **見学する** visit (for study) ▶ぼくたちは養鶏場を(**実地**)**見学した** We *made a study trip* [*visit*] to a chicken ranch. ／We *visited* a chicken ranch *on a field trip*. ‖工場内を**見学**させていただいてよろしいでしょうか May we *walk around* the factory? ‖国会議事堂**見学**を楽しんでください Enjoy your *tour* of the Diet Building. ‖この工場の**見学者**は夏期に多い This factory gets many *visitors* in summer.
▶かぜ気味なので体育の授業は**見学**にさせてください I'm catching a cold, so please let me *sit out* P. E. class today. (➤ sit out は「…に参加しない」).

1**げんかく 厳格な** strict (好ましい意味で)；severe /sɪvíəʳ/ (冷酷なほど)；stern (怖いほど)；rigid(変更を許容しない)；rigorous(融通性の全くない) ▶**厳格な**先生 a *strict* teacher ‖**厳格な**決まり a *rigid* rule ‖**厳格な**検査 *rigorous* testing ‖彼は子供に対し**厳格だった** He was *strict* [*severe*] with his children. ‖規則を**厳格に**守る observe a rule *strictly*.

2**げんかく 幻覚** a hallucination ▶薬のせいで**幻覚を見る** *have hallucinations* due to the medication ‖**幻覚**で海の怪物を見る *hallucinate* a sea monster ‖晩年のモーツァルトは**幻覚**や妄想に苦しめられた In his later years Mozart suffered from *hallucinations* and delusions.‖**幻覚剤** a hallucinatory /həlúːsɪnətɔ̀ːri/ drug ‖**幻覚症状** hallucinosis /həlùːsɪnóʊsɪs/.

1**げんがく 弦楽** ‖**弦楽合奏団** a string ensemble /ɑːnsɑ́ːmbl/ (小規模な)；a string orchestra (大規模な) ‖**弦楽器** a string(ed) instrument；the strings (総称) ‖**弦楽四**[**五**／**六**]**重奏曲** a string quartet [quintet／sextet].

2**げんがく 減額** (a) reduction 一動 **減額する** reduce +目；cut +目 (減らす) ▶市長の給与は10パーセント**減額された** The mayor's salary *was reduced* (by) ten percent.

げんかしょうきゃく 減価償却《経済》depreciation 一動 **減価償却する** depreciate +目 ▶コピー機を5年で**減価償却する** *depreciate* a copy machine over five years.

けんがん 検眼 an eye [eyesight] test(視力検査) ▶あす**検眼**してもらうつもりだ I'm going to *have my eyes* [*eyesight*] *tested* tomorrow.

1**げんかん 玄関** the front door, the genkan, the entrance；the hall (屋内)；the porch (屋外)

> **解説 「玄関」と hall**
> (1)英米の一般家庭では玄関のドア(**front door**)を開けて入ったすぐの所を **entrance hall** とか単に **hall** と呼んでいる. ここは日本家屋の「たたき」に相当するが, 日本家屋の場合と異なり上がりかまちは無く, したがって一段低くなっているわけではない. ここからすぐに廊下のような構造になっていることが多く **hallway** と呼ぶ. (2)玄関ドアの外側で張り出し屋根のある部分は **porch** と呼び, 玄関ドアの内外部分を一緒にして **main entrance** と呼ぶ. (3)日本の「玄関」をさして, the genkan を用いることもある.

▶**玄関**からお入りなさい Come in through *the front door* [*main entrance*]. ‖誰か**玄関**に来てるよ There's someone [There's a knock] *at the genkan*. ‖《慣用表現》歌手になりたいと思って有名な作曲家の家を訪ねたが, **玄関払いを食わされた** I wanted to be a singer, so I visited a famous composer, but I *was turned away* (*at the door*).
▶かつて長崎は日本の**表玄関**だった Nagasaki was once *the gateway* to Japan.

2**げんかん 厳寒** severe [intense] cold (➤ severe は「厳しい」, intense は「強烈な」) ▶私たちは北海道の**厳寒**の中でトレッキングした We hiked in *the severe cold* of Hokkaido.

けんぎ 嫌疑 (a) suspicion ▶**嫌疑**を晴らす clear oneself of *a suspicion* ‖彼に収賄の**嫌疑**がかかった He *was suspected of* taking bribes.

げんき 元気 **1**【健康】(good) health →健康 一形 **元気な** healthy；fine, well ▶**元気な**人 a *healthy* person ／a person *in good health* ‖うちのおばあちゃんは80歳になりますが, 至って**元気です** Though my grandma is 80, she *is* still very healthy [still *enjoying good health*]. ‖長い間お会いしていませんね. **お元気でしたか** I haven't seen you for a long time. *How have you been?*
▶祖父はすっかり**元気になった**(＝健康を回復した) My grandfather *recovered from his illness* completely. ‖早く**元気になってね** I hope you'll *get better* soon. ‖《別れの挨拶》いつまでも**お元気でね** *Stay well!* ‖ 対話 「**お元気?**」「ええ, おかげさまで. あなたは?」 *"How are you?"* "Fine [Quite well], thank you. And you?" (➤ このような返事のしかたを義務[事務]的で冷たいと感じる人も多く, 若い人たちは単に (I'm) OK. ／All right. ／Great! ／Not bad. などのように答えることが多い) ‖ 対話 「皆さん**お元気ですか**」「おかげさまでみんなすこぶる**元気です**」 *"How's* your family *(getting along)*?" "They*'re* all *very well.*"

✉ **お元気のことと思います** I hope you are doing well [fine]. ／I hope all [everything] is going well with you. ／I hope this will find you well [in good health]. ➤ 第2文は第1文よりも改まった言い方. 最後の例は「この便りがあなたが元気でいるのを見いだす」の意.

✉ **体調を崩されているとのこと, 心配しています. ゆっくり休んで早く元気になってください** I'm a little concerned because you wrote me you're not feeling well. I hope you can take a good rest and get well soon.

け

✉ **どうぞお元気で** With best wishes. ➤ 手紙の末尾の署名の直前に書く文句.

2【活力】energy /énəʳdʒi/, **spirits, vigor** /vígəʳ/ 一形 **元気な energetic** /ènəʳdʒétɪk/ ; **cheerful**（明るい）▶まり子はいつも**元気がいい** Mariko *is* always so *cheerful* [*high-spirited* / *energetic*]. ‖いくら年を取ってもまだおまえとテニスをやるくらいの**元気はある** No matter how old I get, I'll still *have the energy* to play tennis with you. ‖きょうは高田さんは**元気がない** Miss Takada *is in low* [*poor*] *spirits* today. / Miss Takada *has the blues* today.（➤ have the blues は「ふさぎ込んで」の意のインフォーマルな表現）‖**元気がないみたい**だけどどうしたの？ What's the matter? You look *depressed* [*spiritless*]. ‖山頂に着いたときは**疲れきって口を利く元気もなかった** When I got to the mountain top, I was *so exhausted I couldn't utter a word*. ‖暑くて**元気が出ない**よ It's so hot I *feel listless*.（➤listless は「けだるい」. lethargic を用いてもよい）.
▶我々はコーヒー1杯で**元気を回復した** We all *refreshed ourselves* with a cup of coffee. ‖ブランデーを一杯やると**元気が出る**よ A drink of brandy will *cheer* you *up*. ‖**元気を出せ**. そんなに悪い知らせじゃないよ *Cheer up!* The news isn't all that bad. ‖子供たちは**元気いっぱい**芝生の上を駆け回った The children ran about on the grass *in high spirits*. ‖彼女のそのひと言に大変**元気づけられた** That single word of hers *encouraged* me greatly. / What she said was a great encouragement to me.

げんぎ 原義 the original meaning.

けんぎかい 県議会 a **prefectural assembly** ‖**県議会議員** a member of a prefectural assembly.

けんきゃく 健脚 ▶**健脚の人** *a good* [*strong*] *walker* ‖山男の兄は**健脚を誇っている** My brother, who is a mountain climber, *takes pride in being a strong walker*.

けんきゅう 研究

(a) **study, research**（➤ 後者は do research on のような句で Ⓤ 扱いで用いるのがふつう）一動 **研究する study, do research**《on》▶**研究に忙しい** be busy with *research work* ‖《書名》『日本神話の**研究**』"*A Study* of Japanese Mythology" ‖姉はダニの**研究をしている** My sister is *doing research on* mites. ‖私は京都大学で物理学の**研究をしたい** I want to *study* physics at Kyoto University. ‖私の英語の先生は, 毎年東京で行われる夏の**研究会**に出席する My English teacher attends a yearly summer *workshop* in Tokyo. ‖きのう彼は花粉症に関する**研究発表をした** He *read a* [*his*] *paper on* pollen allergy yesterday.
▶古代史**研究家** *a scholar* [*a student*] of ancient history ‖料理**研究家** a food *specialist* ‖温泉**研究家** a hot-spa *critic*.
‖**研究員** a researcher, a research scholar ‖**研究開発** research and development, R & D ‖**研究機関** a research institute ‖**研究グループ** a research group ‖**研究室** a study (room), an office（主に大学教員の）; a laboratory（実験室）‖**研究所** an institute, a research institute ‖**研究資料** research material ‖**研究センター** a research center ‖**研究発表会** a conference [meeting] for research presentations ‖**研究費** research expenses（大学教員などに割り当てられる）; research funds（研究資金）‖**研究論文** a (research) paper.

¹げんきゅう 言及 (a) **reference** 一動 **言及する refer** /rɪfə́ːʳ/《to》, **mention** +目 ▶首相は増税には**言及しなかった** The Prime Minister did not *refer to* [*talk about*] a tax hike.

²げんきゅう 減給 ➝減俸.

³げんきゅう 原級《文法》**the positive degree.**

¹けんきょ 検挙する arrest +目, **apprehend** +目 ▶警察は彼を窃盗容疑で**検挙した** The police *arrested* him for theft. ‖警察は暴力団を**一斉検挙した** The police *rounded up* a group of gangsters. ‖その候補者は選挙違反で**検挙された** That candidate *was arrested* for violating the election law.

²けんきょ 謙虚 humility, humbleness（➤ 前者は万物の創造主である神の前では自分を卑小な人間と捉えておごらないことで, キリスト教徒の基本的徳目の一つ ; 後者は偉ぶらないで他の人に敬意を示すこと）; **modesty**（やり遂げたことや美点を自慢したり, ひけらかしたりしないこと）一形 **謙虚な humble**（おごらない）; **modest**（自慢しない）▶今度の校長は態度が**謙虚**だ The new principal is *humble* in his behavior. ‖その大学者は**謙虚な人柄**で学生に慕われている That great scholar is deeply respected by the students for his *humility* [*unassuming attitude*]. ‖我々は誰かの死を目の当たりにすると**謙虚になる** Seeing someone die makes us (feel) *humble*. ‖政治家は**謙虚**に世論に耳を傾けるべきだ Politicians should *humbly* listen to public opinion. ‖彼の態度には**謙虚さ**が全く感じられない I cannot detect the least *modesty* in his attitude.

けんぎょう 兼業 ▶彼の家は喫茶店と書店を**兼業している** His family *runs both* a coffee shop *and* a bookstore. ‖うちは**兼業農家です** My family does a job on the side besides farming.（➤ 農業が主の場合）/ My family does farming as a side job [on the side].（➤ 農業が従の場合）.

¹げんきょう 元凶 ▶入試制度が現在の教育をゆがめている**元凶**だと言われる It is said that *the prime cause of the evils* [*distortions*] apparent in education today is the entrance examination (system).

²げんきょう 現況 the current situation [**state** / **condition**] ▶日本の大学の**現況** *the current state* of Japanese colleges and universities.

けんきん 献金 a **contribution**, a **donation**（➤ 後者には「見返りを求めない」という含みがある）一動 **献金する contribute** /kəntríbjuːt/《to, for》（➤ to は直接に, for は第三者を介して献金する場合に用いることが多い）➝寄付 ▶自民党に500万円を**献金する** *contribute* [*make a contribution of*] five million yen *to* the LDP. ‖**政治献金** a political contribution.

¹げんきん 現金 1【お金】cash ▶このオートバイは**現金**で買った I paid for this motorcycle *in cash*. ‖**現金**でお買い上げの方は1割引きになります We'll give you a 10 percent discount if you pay *in cash*. ‖今**現金の持ち合わせがないんだ** I'*m out of cash* now. ‖私は**現金**は持ち歩かない I don't [never] carry *cash*. ‖この小切手を**現金にしてください** Could you please *cash* this check? ‖彼は失業中で**現金収入**がない He's out of a job and has no *cash income*.
‖**現金書留** cash registered mail《参考》英米ではこの種の郵便はない. ふつうの封筒に小切手を入れたり, ふつうの書留に現金を入れたりして送る. ‖**現金自動預け払い機** an automated teller machine,《略》ATM ‖**現金自動支払い機** a cash machine, a cash dispenser ‖**現金正価** a cash price ‖**現金取引** a cash transaction ‖**現金輸送車** an armored car, a cash transport truck.

2【損得に敏感】▶子供は**現金**なもので, ディズニーランドに連れていってやると言ったら, 息子はすぐに泣きやんだ

Children are really *mercenary*. When I told my son I'd take him to Disneyland, he stopped crying. ‖ 10個まとめて買うと言ったとたんに彼は愛想がよくなった. **現金な男**だよ When I told him I would buy ten of them, his attitude suddenly improved. *What a change* !

2**げんきん 厳禁** ▶麻薬所持は法律によって**厳禁されている** Having or carrying narcotics with you *is strictly prohibited* by law. ‖《掲示》教室での私語**厳禁** *No* Whispering in the Classroom ‖《掲示》貼り紙**厳禁** *No* Posters (*Allowed*) ／《英また》Post *No* Bills.

1**げんけい 原形** **the original form** ▶この前の大地震でその建物は**原形**をとどめぬまでに破壊された That building was damaged *beyond recognition* in the last big earthquake. (➤ beyond recognition は「見る影も無く」) ‖**原形質**《生物学》protoplasm ‖**動詞の原形** the bare form of the verb.

2**げんけい 原型** a **prototype** /próʊt̬ətaɪp/ ▶飛行機の**原型**はライト兄弟によって作られた The *prototype* of the airplane was built by the Wright Brothers.

3**げんけい 減刑** a **reduction in** one's **sentence**, (a) **commutation** ▶**減刑**を求める ask for *a commutation* ‖彼の刑は10年から8年に**減刑された** His sentence *was reduced* from ten to eight years.

けんけつ 献血 **blood donation** ▶輸血用の血液が不足しております. どうか**献血**をお願いします We're short of blood for transfusion. Please consider *donating your blood*. ‖**献血者** a blood donor ‖**献血車** a blood donation vehicle [van] ; a bloodmobile.

けんげん 権限 **power** (法律で定められた ; しばしば複数形で用いる) ; **authority** (他人に命令し服従を強制する力) ▶総理大臣の持つ諸**権限** the *powers* of the Prime Minister ‖警官には犯人を逮捕する**権限がある** A police officer *has the authority* [*is authorized*] *to* arrest criminals.

けんけんごうごう 喧々囂々 ▶総会は**けんけんごうごうの議論**になった The general assembly disintegrated into *loud arguments*.

けんご 堅固な **strong** (強い) ; **firm** (しっかりした) ▶エディンバラ城は**堅固な**とりでだった Edinburgh Castle was a *strong* fortress. ‖彼は意志が**堅固だ** He is a man of *unshakable will*. (➤ unshakable は「揺るぎない, 不動の」の意) ／He's a *strong-willed* [*resolute*] man.

げんこ 拳固 →げんこつ.

1**げんご 言語** (a) **language** (ある特定の) ; **speech** (話す力, 話すこと) ▶現在世界中でおよそ3000種類の**言語**が話されている About 3,000 *languages* are spoken in the world today. ‖**言語**を持つのは人間だけである Human beings alone have *the gift of language* [*speech*]. ‖遠征隊は**言語に絶する**猛吹雪に遭遇した The expedition party encountered a violent snowstorm *that defied description*. (➤ defied は defy (拒む)の過去形) ‖この子には少し**言語障害**がある This child has a slight *speech defect*.

‖**言語学** linguistics /lɪŋgwístɪks/, philology ‖**言語学者** a linguist ‖**言語聴覚士** a speech therapist ‖**言語能力** language [linguistic] ability, (language ／linguistic) competence.

2**げんご 原語** **the original language** ▶この小説を**原語**で読めたらなあ I wish I could read this novel *in the original*.

けんこう 健康 **health** 一形 **健康な** **healthy** ▶私は**健康です** I *am in good health*. ／I *am well*. ‖母は**健康がすぐれない** My mother *isn't well*. ‖祖母はめっきり**健康が衰えた** My grandmother's *health* has declined noticeably. ‖適度の運動は**健康によい** Moderate exercise *is good for your* [*the*] *health*. ／Moderate exercise *keeps you healthy*. ‖たばこは**健康に悪い** Smoking *is bad for your* [*the*] *health*. ‖病気になって初めて**健康のありがたみがわかる** We cannot appreciate *the blessing of health* until we lose it. (➤「失うまではわからない」の意) ／We only realize *the importance of health* when we get sick.

▶彼女は**健康を回復した** She (*has*) *recovered her health* [*from her sickness*]. ／She *is all right again*. ‖**ご健康を祝して!** (*To*) *your health!* (➤ 乾杯のときのことば) ‖過度の飲酒は**健康を損なう** Excessive drinking *harms one's health*. ‖**健康を保つ**ために私は毎朝ジョギングをしている I jog every morning to *keep in shape* [*keep fit*]. (➤ 体力・筋力維持をいう場合.「病気にならない」をいうのなら keep in good health または stay healthy とする) ‖彼女の**健康的な**笑顔が好きだ I like her *healthy* smiling face. ‖私の**健康法**は早寝早起きです My *secret for staying healthy* is keeping early hours.

✉ **どうかくれぐれも健康にご注意ください** Please *take* good *care of yourself* [*of your health*].

‖**健康食品** health food ‖**健康保険(証)** (a) health insurance (card).

☛ 健康診断, 不健康 (→見出語)

けんごう 剣豪 a **master swordsman**, a **sword fighter** (➤ 後者が性差のない言い方).

1**げんこう 原稿** a **manuscript** (略 MS) ; **notes**, a **draft** (草稿) ▶ワープロで打った**原稿** *a manuscript* written on a word processor ／a typewritten *manuscript* ‖出版社に**原稿を送る** send one's *manuscript* to a publisher ‖**原稿を棒読みする** read *a manuscript* in a monotone ‖**原稿なしで話をする** speak *without notes* ‖イギリスのポップスについての**原稿を書く** *write* about British pop music. ‖**原稿用紙** manuscript paper ‖**原稿料** a writer's fee.

2**げんこう 現行** ▶**現行の**(=現在運用されている)法律 the *existing* law ‖**現行の**(=現在使われている)教科書は評判がよい The textbooks *now in use* have a good reputation.

3**げんこう 言行** **words and deeds, speech and behavior** ▶**言行一致の人** a person *of his* [*her*] *word* ‖**言行の一致しない人** a person who *says one thing and does another* (➤「言うこととすることが違う」の意).

げんごう 元号 an **imperial era name**.

けんこうこつ 肩甲骨 a **shoulder blade**, a **scapula** /skǽpjələ/ (➤ 後者は専門用語) ▶彼は**肩甲骨**を折った He broke his *shoulder* (*blade*).

けんこうしんだん 健康診断 a **physical examination** [**checkup**] (➤ 略して a physical とも a checkup ともいう) ▶年に1回は**健康診断を受けましょう** You should have *a physical checkup* at least once a year.

げんこうはん 現行犯 ▶その男は盗みの**現行犯**で捕まった The man was caught *in the act of stealing*.

けんこく 建国 **the founding of a nation**

‖**建国記念の日** National Foundation Day.

げんこく 原告 a **plaintiff** ▶裁判は**原告**の敗訴となった Judgment was given [The court decided] against the *plaintiff*.

げんこつ 拳骨 a **fist** ▶彼はぼくを**げんこつ**で殴った He

struck me with his *fist*. ／He punched me. ‖ 今度あの子をいじめたらげんこつだぞ I'll give you *one* right to your head if you bully him [her] again. (➤ one は「げんこつ一発」の意のインフォーマルな語. right は「もろに」).

ゲンゴロウ 源五郎 《虫》 **a Japanese diving beetle.**

けんさ 検査 **a test**(一定の標準に合うかどうかを判断するための)；(an) **examination** (入念な)；(an) **inspection** (主に公的機関によるチェック) ━動 **検査する test** +目, **examine** +目, **inspect** +目 ▶ＨＩＶの**検査をする** *test* for HIV ‖ **身体検査**を受ける have *a physical examination* ‖ 胃を**検査して**もらう *have* one's stomach *examined* ‖ 視力の**検査**をしてもらったほうがいいよ You should *get* your eyes [eyesight, vision] *tested*. ／You should *have* your vision *tested*. ‖ 《医者が患者に》いくつか**検査**をしようと思います I'd like to run some *tests*. ‖ 持ち物を**検査**します. テーブルの上に置いてください Let me *inspect* your things. Please put them on the table. ‖ これらの商品は市場に出る前に再度綿密な**検査を受ける** These products *are given* another thorough *examination* [*inspection*] before they are put on the market. ‖**検査官** an inspector.

> **逆引き熟語 ○○検査**
> **アルコール[酒気帯び]検査** a breath test, breath analysis ／**ＭＲＩ検査** an MRI examination ／**会計検査** an audit ／**学力検査** an (academic [a scholastic]) achievement test ／**血液検査** blood testing, a blood test ／ **(着衣上からの)所持品検査** a pat-down, a body search, a frisk ／**身体検査** a physical [medical] examination, a physical checkup ／**水質検査** a water quality test ／**精密検査** a close examination ／**立ち入り検査** an on-the-spot inspection ／**知能検査** an intelligence test ／**ＤＮＡ検査** a DNA test ／**適性検査** an aptitude test ／ **(手)荷物検査** a baggage inspection, a security check [screening] ／ **抜き打ち検査** a spot check ／**抜き取り検査** a random check [inspection], a sampling inspection ／**レントゲン検査** an X-ray examination

[1]**けんざい 健在** ▶両親とも**健在です** Both my parents *are in good health* [*doing well*] (*and enjoying their lives*).

[2]**けんざい 建材** **building materials** ▶**建材**の値段は高くなっている The prices of *building materials* are going up.

[3]**けんざい 顕在** ▶問題点を**顕在化させる** *expose* a problem ‖ 年金制度の問題点が**顕在化してきた** Problems in the pension system *have become apparent* [*clear*].

[1]**げんざい 現在** **the present**(過去や未来に対して)；**today** (今日) ━形 **現在の present**；**current** /kə́ːrənt ‖ kʌ́r-/ (現行の)
▶過去・**現在**・未来 the past, *the present* and the future ‖ 私は**現在**の仕事に満足している I am satisfied with my *present* [*current*] job. ‖ 私は**現在**この銀行に勤めている I work for this bank *at present* [(*right*) *now*]. ‖ 新タワーは**現在**建設中です A new tower is *currently* [*now*] under construction. ‖ **現在**の物価は50年前のそれとは全く違う Prices *today* are quite different from those of fifty years ago. ‖ 死刑制度は**現在**のままでよいのだろうか I wonder if the death penalty system is all right *as it is* (*now*). ‖ 対話「**現在**までに博覧会の入場者は何人ありましたか？」「６月17日**現在**で, 100万人を突破しました」 "How many people have come to the Expo *so far* [*up to now*]?" "*As of* June 17, the number of visitors exceeded one million." ‖ **現在**, ヤクルトが３点リードしている The Swallows are leading by three runs *at the moment*. ‖ 《案内板などの掲示》**現在地** You are here. (➤「今あなたはここに居ます」の意). ‖ 《文法》**現在完了** the present perfect ‖ 《文法》**現在分詞** a present participle.

[2]**げんざい 原罪** **original sin.**

けんさく 検索 **search**(探すこと)；**reference**(参照) ━動 **検索する search** ▶**検索**に便利なようにすべてのキーワードにはマークがついている All the key words are marked for easy *search* [*reference*]. ‖ その辞書はCD-ROM になっているから**検索**が容易だ The dictionary is on CD-ROM, so *looking up words* is easy. ‖ グーグルで**検索**したが, 結果はゼロだった I *searched* on Google and got no result(s). ‖ **検索語**を入力してください Type in *a search word*.

げんさく 原作 **the original (work)** ▶このドラマの**原作**は赤川次郎の小説です This drama *is based on* a novel by Akagawa Jiro. (➤ be based on で「…を基にしている」) ‖ この翻訳は英語の**原作**に忠実だ This translation is faithful to the English *original*.

[1]**けんさつ 検札** **ticket inspection** ▶列車がトンネルを出たとき車掌が**検札**に来た When the train passed through the tunnel, the conductor came to *check* [*inspect*] *tickets*.
‖**検札係** a ticket inspector.

[2]**けんさつ 検察** **the prosecution**(検察側) ▶**検察側**の証人 a witness for *the prosecution*.
‖**検察官** a (public) prosecutor ‖ **検察庁** the Public Prosecutors Office ‖ **高等検察庁** the High Court Public Prosecutors Office ‖ **最高検察庁** the Supreme Public Prosecutors Office ‖ **地方検察庁** the District Public Prosecutors Office.

[3]**けんさつ 賢察** **your guess** ▶まさにご**賢察**のとおりです *Your guess* is absolutely correct.

けんさん 研鑽 **intense [thorough-going] study**
▶彼はＹ教授の下で**研さんを積んだ** He *pursued his studies* under Professor Y. ‖ 彼女は長年の**研さん**の結果, 新たな理論を作り上げた She developed a new theory after many years of *intense study*.

[1]**けんざん 検算** ▶時間があれば**検算**してください Please *check* [*go over*] *the accounts* if you have time.

[2]**けんざん 剣山** a ***kenzan***；a spiked flower holder (➤ 説明的な訳).

[1]**げんさん 原産** ▶コアラはオーストラリア**原産**の動物です The koala (bear) is a *native* Australian animal. ‖ 中国は茶の木の**原産地**である China is *the home* of the tea plant. ‖ トウモロコシの**原産地**はどこですか Where did corn originate? (➤ originate は「起源がある」) ‖ ジャガイモは南アメリカが**原産地**だ The potato *is native to* South America.

[2]**げんさん 減産する** **reduce [cut] production** ▶米の10パーセント**減産** a ten percent *reduction in* rice *production* ‖ 原油を１割**減産する** *cut* crude oil *production* by ten percent.

[1]**けんし 犬歯** a **canine** /kéɪnaɪn/ **(tooth)**；a **dogtooth** (➤ いずれも複数形は teeth).

[2]**けんし 検死** an **autopsy** ▶**検死**の結果, 被害者は暴行されていたことがわかった The *autopsy* showed that the victim had been sexually assaulted.

[1]**けんじ 検事** a **(public) prosecutor** /prɑ́ːsɪkjuːt̬ər/

‖**検事正** a chief (public) prosecutor ‖ **検事総長** the Public Prosecutor General ‖ **検事長** a superintending prosecutor ‖ **次席検事** a deputy superintending prosecutor ‖ **次長検事** a deputy (public) prosecutor.

2**けんじ 堅持** ▶党綱領を**堅持する** *firmly uphold* one's party platform ‖ 白鵬は全勝を**堅持している** Hakuho *has a firm grip* on his winning streak.

3**けんじ 顕示** ▶彼は自己**顕示**欲が強い He *really loves to show off*. ／He's *an exhibitionist*.

1**げんし 原子** an **atom** ━形 **原子の** **atomic** ▶水素**原子** a hydrogen *atom*.

‖**原子爆弾** an atomic [atom] bomb /bɑ́ːm/, an A-bomb ‖ **原子物理学** nuclear physics ‖ **原子炉** a nuclear reactor.

☞ 原子力 (→見出語)

2**げんし 原始の** **primitive** ▶その島の先住民は今なお**原始的**なわらづくりの小屋に住んでいる The indigenous people of that island still live in *primitive* straw huts. ‖**原始時代** the primitive age ‖ **原始社会** primitive society ‖ **原始人** a primitive human ; primitive man (➤ 総称) ‖ **原始林** a primeval /praɪmíːvəl/ forest.

3**げんし 幻視** a **visual hallucination**.

4**げんし 原資** **resource(s) funds** ▶年金**原資** pension *resources*.

5**げんし 減資** a **reduction in capital** ━動 **減資する** **reduce capital**.

けんしき 見識 **judgment** (優れた判断力) ; **insight** /ínsaɪt/ (洞察力) ; a **view** (見解) ▶**見識のある**人 a person *of good judgment* [*insight*].

けんじつ 堅実な **sound** (健全な) ; **steady** (しっかりした) ; **solid** (信頼できる) ; **good** (等級が「良」の) ▶**堅実な**考え a *sound* idea ‖ 彼は**堅実な**会社で**堅実な**仕事をしている He has a *good* job with a *good* company. ‖ あのショートは守備が**堅実だ** That shortstop *has solid fielding* (*skills*).

げんじつ 現実

(a) **reality** (実在のもの, 事実として存在すること) ; a **fact** (事実) ━形 **現実の** **real** ; **actual** ; **現実的な** **realistic** ▶**現実は**厳しい *The reality* is stark. ‖ 若者はしばしば理想と**現実**との隔たりにがく然とする Young people are often dismayed by the gap between (their) ideals and *reality*. ‖ 彼女の留学の夢が**現実のものになった** Her dream of studying abroad *became a reality* [*came true*].

▶環境汚染は厳しい**現実**だ Environmental pollution is *a fact of life*. (➤ a fact of life は「(人生の)厳しい現実」の意の決まり文句) ‖ きみはいつも人生の厳しい**現実**から逃避している You are always running away [trying to escape] from the *harsh* [*grim*] *realities of life*. ‖ ハイジャックの話はよく聞くが, **現実に**それに巻き込まれるとは思いもしなかった I had often heard about hijackings, but I never thought I would *actually* be involved in one. ‖ ベルの音で**現実に引き戻された** The sound of the bell *brought* me *back to reality*. ‖ このドラマは**現実にあったこと**を基にしている This drama is based on *real life* [*a true story*].

▶近頃の若者は**現実的だ** (＝現実的な考え方をする) Today's young people *think realistically*. ‖ きみの提案は**現実的だ** [**現実離れしている**] Your proposal is *realistic* [*unrealistic*]. ‖ **現実問題として**, 1か月3万円だけで暮らしていけますか *The real question is*, can you make it on only 30,000 yen a month?

‖**現実主義** realism ‖ **現実主義者** a realist (➤ 英語はプラスイメージを持つことが多い) ‖ **拡張現実** augmented reality (AR) ‖ **仮想現実** virtual reality (VR).

げんじてん 現時点 ▶これが**現時点**において採れる最良の策だ These are the best measures we can take *at the moment*. ‖ 事故による負傷者は**現時点で**30人に上っている *As of now*, casualties resulting from the accident number some 30 injured.

1**げんしゅ 厳守する** **observe strictly** (法律などを) ▶この町では子供のほうが大人よりも交通規則を**厳守している** The children in this town *observe* traffic rules more *strictly* than the adults (do). ‖ レポートの提出日を**厳守してください** Please *observe* the deadline for turning in your papers. ‖ 佐々木さんはいつも時間を**厳守する** Mr. Sasaki *is* always *punctual*.

2**げんしゅ 元首** a **sovereign** /sɑ́ːvrən/ (君主) ; a **head of state** (国家元首) ▶スペインの**元首**は王様である Spain's *head* of *state* is the King.

3**げんしゅ 原種** an **original species** ▶バラの**原種**は150から200種ほどある There are about 150 to 200 *original species* of roses.

けんしゅう 研修 **study** (研究) ; **training** (訓練) ; an **induction (course)** (新入社員などの) ▶ロンドンへ英語の**研修**に行く go to London to *study* English ‖ 新入社員**研修**を受ける take an *induction* (*course*) ‖ 社外**研修**を受ける have *off-site training* (➤「社内研修」は in-house training) ‖ 新入社員に英会話の**研修**が行われた The new employees were given *training* in speaking English.

‖**研修会** a workshop ‖ **研修所** a training institute ‖ **研修生** a trainee /trèɪníː/ ‖ **研修旅行** a study tour.

けんじゅう 拳銃 a **pistol**, a **handgun** ▶犯人は警官に**拳銃**を発射した The criminal fired his *pistol* at a police officer.

げんしゅう 減収 a **decrease in production** (収穫の減少) ; a **decrease in income** (収入の減少) ▶ことしは農作物の大幅な**減収**が予想される A considerable [sharp] *decrease* in crops is expected this year.

げんじゅう 厳重な **strict** ; **severe** (妥協のない) ▶**厳重な**交通取り締まり *strict* traffic control ‖ 試験でカンニングをした人たちは**厳重に**処罰された Those who cheated on the examination were punished *severely*. ‖ 戸締まりを**厳重にしなさい** *Be very careful about* locking up. ‖ 政府に対して**厳重に**抗議する protest *strongly* against the government.

げんじゅうしょ 現住所 one's **current** [**present**] **address** ▶**現住所**を教えてください Could you give me your *current* [*present*] *address*, please?

げんじゅうみん 原住民 a **native** (➤ しばしば軽蔑的な響きをもつ). →先住民.

げんしゅく 厳粛な **solemn** /sɑ́ːləm/ ▶式は**厳粛に**執り行われた The ceremony was conducted *in* [*with*] *great solemnity*. (➤ in のほうが改まった言い方) ‖ 私は自分の父親の死という**厳粛な**事実に直面した I faced the *harsh reality* of my father's death.

けんしゅつ 検出 **detection** ━動 **検出する** **detect** ＋目 ▶住民数名の頭髪から少量の放射性物質が**検出された** A small amount of radioactive material *was detected* [*was found*] in the hair of some inhabitants. ‖**放射線検出装置** radiation detection equipment ／a radiation detector.

けんじゅつ 剣術 **swordplay, sword fighting** ▶**剣術**の稽古をする practice *sword fighting* ‖ **剣術**ごっこをする

play sword-fighting.

げんしょ 原書 the original (work) ▶シェークスピアを原書で読む read Shakespeare *in the original*.

1**けんしょう 懸賞** a prize ; a price (人の首・命に懸けられた賞金) ▶懸賞に当たる win *a prize* ‖ 懸賞付きの問題 questions *with prizes* ‖ 懸賞金の懸かったお尋ね者 a man [woman] with *a price* on his [her] head ‖ 懸賞論文コンテストに応募する enter *an essay contest*.

2**けんしょう 検証** investigation (調査) ; (a) review (調査, 再調査) ; verification (確認) 一動 **検証する** investigate +目, review +目, verify +目 ▶事件を検証する *review* an incident ‖ 理論を検証する *verify* a theory ‖ 警察が交通事故の現場検証を行っている The police *are investigating the scene* of a traffic accident (for evidence).

3**けんしょう 憲章** a charter
‖ 国際連合憲章 the Charter of the United Nations ‖ 児童憲章 the Children's Charter.

4**けんしょう 健勝** ▶✉ 拝啓, 時下, ますますご健勝のこととお喜び申し上げます Dear Sir(s), I hope you'*re enjoying good health*.

5**けんしょう 顕彰する** recognize +目 ▶長年の功労を顕彰する *recognize* his [her] long years of service / *honor* him [her] for his [her] long years of service.

1**けんじょう 謙譲** modesty (控えめ) ; humility (謙虚) ▶謙譲の美徳が失われつつある *The virtue of modesty* is being lost.

2**けんじょう 献上する** offer +目 ▶皇室にリンゴを献上する *offer* apples to the imperial family.

1**げんしょう 現象** a phenomenon /fənɑ́:mənɑ:n/ [複 phenomena] (自然現象など) ; a phase (様相) ▶オーロラは極地にだけ現れる自然現象である An aurora is *a natural phenomenon* appearing only in the polar regions. ‖ おならは生理現象なのでしかたがない Passing gas is a *physiological phenomenon* that cannot be helped [avoided]. ‖ バレンタイン・デーに女性が彼氏, (男性の)同僚や上司, 夫, 女ともだち, そして, 自分にチョコレートのプレゼントをするのが一種の社会現象となった The custom of women giving chocolates to their boyfriends, male co-workers and bosses, husbands, women friends and themselves on Valentine's Day has become *a social phenomenon*. ‖ 現象学 phenomenology.

2**げんしょう 減少** (a) decrease /dí:kri:s/ 一動 **減少する** decrease /dì:krí:s/ ▶W大学の学生数は年々減少してきている The number of students at W University *is decreasing* every year. ‖ 過去10年間この市の人口は絶えず減少してきた For the past ten years, *there has been a steady decrease* in the population of this city. ‖ ことしの米の生産高は昨年に比べて２割減少した This year's rice crop *shows* a 20 percent *decrease* as compared with last year.

1**げんじょう 現状** the present condition, the status quo /stèiṭəs kwóu/ (➤ 後者はラテン語起源で気取った言い方) ▶現状を維持する maintain *the present condition(s)* [*the status quo*] ‖ きみたちは現状に満足しているのか Are you satisfied with *the status quo* [with *things as they are*] ? ‖ 賃上げは現状ではちょっと無理だ You can hardly expect a pay raise *under the present conditions* [*in the present state of affairs*]. (➤ conditions の代わりに circumstances でもよい) ‖ その投手の年俸は現状維持がやっとだった It was all the pitcher could do to *keep* his salary from being reduced below the current level.

2**げんじょう 原状** ▶賃借人には部屋を出る際, 原状回復義務がある Renters have an obligation to *restore* the apartment *to its original state* when they move out.

けんしょうえん 腱鞘炎 inflammation of the tendon sheath /ʃi:θ/, tenosynovitis /tènousinəváɪtəs/.

けんじょうしゃ 健常者 an able-bodied person, a non-disabled person.

1**げんしょく 原色** a primary color (基本色) ; a vivid color (鮮やかな色) ▶熱帯の花は原色のものが多い Most tropical flowers are of *vivid colors*.
‖ 三原色 the three primary colors.

2**げんしょく 減食** ▶さゆりは体重を減らすために減食している Sayuri *is cutting back on her meals* to lose weight. / Sayuri *is on a diet* [*is dieting*] to lose weight.

3**げんしょく 現職の** incumbent /ɪnkʌ́mbənt/ ▶現職の総理大臣 the *incumbent* Prime Minister ‖ 酒気を帯びた現職の警察官が交通事故を起こした A police officer under the influence of liquor caused a traffic accident. (➤ この場合「現職の」は訳出不要).

げんしりょく 原子力 nuclear [atomic] energy (➤ energy /énəʳdʒi/ の代わりに power も可) 一形 **原子力の** nuclear ‖ 原子力空母 a nuclear(-powerd) aircraft carrier ‖ 原子力潜水艦 a nuclear(-powered) submarine ‖ 原子力発電 nuclear (electric) power generation ‖ 原子力発電所 a nuclear power plant.

1**けんしん 検診** a medical examination, a checkup ▶乳がんの定期検診を受ける have *a periodical checkup* for breast cancer.

2**けんしん 検針** meter reading [inspection] 一動 **検針する** read a meter.

げんじん 原人 a primitive human
‖ 北京(ペキン)原人 Peking man.

けんしんてき 献身的 ▶少年が危険な状態を脱するまで母親は献身的に看護した The mother *devotedly* nursed her little boy until he got out of critical condition. ‖ 彼女はアフリカ難民のために献身的に働いた She *devoted herself to* helping the African refugees. (➤「身をささげた」の意 ; (×)to help とはしない).

けんすい 懸垂 a pull-up (通例, 順手で, しばしば肩幅以上に手を広げて体を持ち上げる) ; a chin-up (通例, 逆手で行う) ▶きみ懸垂何回できる? How many *pull-ups* can you do?

げんすい 元帥 《米》 a general of the army, 《英》 a field marshal (陸軍) ; 《米》 a fleet admiral, 《英》 an admiral of the fleet (海軍) ; 《米》 a general of the air force, 《英》 a marshal of the Royal Air Force (空軍).

げんすいばく 原水爆 atom(ic) and hydrogen bombs /bɑ:mz/ ; nuclear bombs (核爆弾)
‖ 原水爆禁止世界大会 the World Conference Against Atomic and Hydrogen Bombs.

けんすう 件数 ▶冬は火事の件数が多くなる The *number* of fires increases in winter.

げんすんだい 原寸大の full-size, full-scale (実物大の) ; life-size (等身大の) ▶宇宙カプセルの原寸大の模型 a *full-size* model of the space capsule.

げんせ 現世 this life, one's present life ▶現世の出来事 *worldly* affairs ‖ 現世と来世を行き来できたらなあ I wish I could travel in time between *this life* and my next life.

1**けんせい 牽制** 《野球》▶投手はけん制でランナーを一塁アウトにした The pitcher *picked* the runner *off* first base. (➤ pick ... off は「けん制で…を刺殺する」).

2**けんせい 権勢** ▶平安末期, 平家一門は権勢をほしいままにした The Heike clan *wielded power as they pleased* at the end of the Heian period.

3**けんせい 憲政** constitutional government.

4**けんせい 顕性の** 《生物学》 dominant ‖**顕性遺伝子** a dominant gene.

げんせい 厳正 ▶厳正な裁判 a *fair and just* trial ‖厳正な抽選 a *fair* drawing ‖厳正な判断を下す make a *fair and impartial* judgment.

げんぜい 減税 (a) tax reduction [cut] ▶わが党は減税の実現に努力します Our party will do its best to bring about *a tax reduction* [to *reduce taxes*].

げんせいどうぶつ 原生動物 a protozoan /pròuṭəzóuən/ [複 -zoa, ~s].

げんせいりん 原生林 a primeval /praɪmíːvəl/ forest.

けんせき 譴責 a reprimand /réprɪmænd/ ▶その学生は暴力事件を起こしてけん責処分を受けた The student *received an official reprimand* for his violent behavior.

げんせき 原石 raw ore /ɔːʳ/ (鉱石).

けんせつ 建設 construction (建造); establishment (設立, 創立) 一動 **建設する** construct +㊐, build +㊐; establish +㊐ ▶この川の上流に大きなダムが建設されるらしい I hear a large dam is to *be constructed* in the upper reaches of this river. ／I hear they're going to *build* a big dam on the upper reaches of this river. ‖わが校の体育館は今建設中です Our school's gymnasium *is* now *under construction*. ／Our school's gymnasium *is* now *being built*.
▶我々は平和国家の建設に貢献しなければならない We must contribute to the *establishment* of a peaceful nation. ‖知事は住民と建設的な話し合いをした The governor had a *constructive* dialogue with the residents.
‖**建設会社** a construction company, a constructor.

けんぜん 健全な sound; healthy (健康な); wholesome (健康そうな) ▶健全な考え *sound* [*healthy* ／ *wholesome*] ideas ‖心身ともに健全な若者 a young person (who is) *sound* in mind and body.
▶わが市は健全財政だ Our city is blessed with *sound* [*stable*] *finances*.

1**げんせん 源泉** a source /sɔːʳs/ ▶川 [温泉] の源泉 the *source* of a river [a hot spring] ‖知識の源泉 *a font* [*fount*] of wisdom ‖当館の温泉は源泉かけ流しになっております Our hot spring water flows directly from the *hot spring source*. ‖**源泉課税** 《米》(a) withholding tax, 《英》 pay-as-you-earn (➤ 通例 PAYE と略す) ‖**源泉徴収** deducting tax from income at source ‖**源泉徴収票** a certificate of tax deducted (from income at source).

2**げんせん 厳選する** select carefully ▶宇宙飛行士は多数の候補者の中から厳選される Astronauts *are carefully selected* from a great number of candidates. ‖厳選の結果, 最優秀映画はインドの作品に決まった After *careful screening*, the prize for the best film was awarded to an Indian movie. (➤ screening は「選考, 資格審査」の意).

げんぜん 厳然と solemnly /sáːləmli/ (厳粛に); gravely (重々しく) ▶神父は厳然たる口調で会衆に話しかけた The priest spoke to the congregation *with great solemnity*. ‖我々の能力に差があることは厳然たる事実である It is *an undeniable fact* [*a hard fact*] that there is a difference in our abilities.

げんそ 元素 an element
‖**元素記号** the symbol of an element ‖**化学元素** a chemical element ‖**放射性元素** a radioactive element.

けんそう 喧騒 a noise; a din (ジャンジャン [ガンガン, ドンドン] というやかましい音) ▶我々は大都会のけん騒と雑踏の中に住んでいる We live in the *din* and bustle of a big city.

けんぞう 建造 building; construction (かなり大きなもの) 一動 **建造する** build +㊐, construct +㊐ ▶潜水艦を建造する *build* [*construct*] a submarine ‖最近建造されたタンカー a tanker *of recent construction*.
☛ 建造物 (→見出語)

げんそう 幻想 (a) fantasy (空想); a dream (夢想); an illusion (思い込み) ▶幻想を追いかける pursue *an impossible dream* ‖幻想を抱く hold [have] *an illusion* ‖幻想的な音楽 *dreamy* music ‖その遊園地には幻想的な雰囲気が漂っていた There was *an air of fantasy* about that amusement park.
‖**幻想曲** a fantasy, a fantasia.

げんぞう 現像 developing 一動 **現像する** develop +㊐ ▶カラーフィルムを現像する *develop* color film ‖フィルムを現像に出す take film in for *developing*.
‖**現像所** a processing laboratory.

けんぞうぶつ 建造物 a structure, a building (➤ 前者には日本語の場合と同じく「堂々とした」という含みがある. 後者は建物一般を指す語) ▶法隆寺は世界最古の木造建造物だ Horyuji Temple is the world's oldest wooden *structure*. ‖彼は建造物侵入の容疑で逮捕された He was arrested on suspicion of *breaking and entering someone else's domicile*. (➤ domicile は「住居」の意の堅い語).

1**げんそく 原則** a principle; a (general) rule (一般に通用する規則) ▶自由は民主主義の根本原則だ Freedom is a *fundamental principle* of democracy. ‖アメリカでは原則として公園での飲酒は認められない *As a general rule*, no drinking is permitted in public parks in the U.S. ‖私は原則として金の貸し借りはしない I don't lend or borrow money *on principle* [*as a matter of principle*]. ‖原則的にはきみの言うとおりだ *In principle* you are right.

2**げんそく 減速** a slowdown 一動 **減速する** slow down ▶バスは時速30キロに減速した The bus *slowed* (*down*) to thirty kilometers an hour.

けんそん 謙遜 modesty ▶彼は謙遜してそう言ったのだ He said that *out of modesty*. ‖山崎さんはいつも謙遜した言い方をする Mr. Yamazaki always talks in a *modest* manner. ‖またまたご謙遜を Oh, you're *being too modest*.

げんそん 現存 ▶これは現存する世界最古のミイラと言われている This is said to be the world's oldest *existing* mummy. ／This mummy is claimed to be the oldest *in existence*. ‖現存の人でその事件を記憶している人は少ない There are few people *living* who remember that event.

1**けんたい 検体** a specimen /spésəmən/.

2**けんたい 献体** body donation 一動 **献体する** donate one's body (to a medical school).

げんたい 減退する decline ▶60歳を過ぎると体力は急激に減退する Your (physical) strength *declines* sharply after you reach sixty. ‖私は最近少し食欲が減退している Recently I have *lost my appetite* a little. ‖この頃記憶力が減退している My *memory is slipping* these days. ／I am *getting forgetful* these days.

け

げんだい 現代 the present age［day］, modern times 一形 **現代の** modern, contemporary（➤ 前者は「近代の」を表すことも多い．また，後者は「同時代の」の意でも用いる）▶**現代の**日本 *modern* Japan ／*present-day* Japan ‖**現代は**映像の時代であると言われる It is often said that *this* is the age of visual images. ‖**現代人は**情報過多に陥っている *People nowadays*［*Modern people*］are inundated with information. ‖**現代っ子は**コンピュータに強い *Today's kids* are good with computers. ‖郊外には**現代的な**家が目につく In the suburbs one sees many houses of (increasingly) *modern* design. ‖**現代社会**では家族の絆(きずな)が弱まっている Family ties have weakened in *contemporary*［*modern*］*society*. ‖あの社長はまるで信長の**現代版**だ That company president is just like a *modern-day* Nobunaga.

‖**現代英語** present-day［contemporary］English（➤ modern English は「近代英語」）‖**現代音楽** contemporary music ‖**現代文学** contemporary literature.

けんたいかん 倦怠感 ▶私はこの頃しばしばけん怠感に襲われる I often *feel weary*［*tired*］these days.

ケンタッキー Kentucky（アメリカ中東部の州；略 KY, Ky., Ken.).

けんだま 剣玉・拳玉 a cup and ball ▶けん玉をする play *cup-and-ball*.

けんたん 兼担 ‖**兼担教授** an affiliated professor（➤ 文学部所属の教授が法学部の授業をするような場合につけられる名称；→**兼任**）.

げんたん 減反 acreage reduction 一動 **減反する** reduce acreage.

けんち 見地 a standpoint, a point of view ▶教育的見地からすれば学校における体罰は何ら好ましい効果を生まない From an educational *standpoint*［*point of view*］, corporal punishment in schools has no favorable results.

[1]**げんち 現地** ▶**現地の**人たち the *local* people ‖記者は**現地で**撮った写真を電送した The reporter wired a picture taken *on the spot*［*at the site* ／*on the scene*］. ‖地図は**現地そのものではない** The map is not *the territory it stands for*. ‖**現地時間**は午前９時です It is 9 a.m. *local time*. ‖工場見学は**現地集合，現地解散です** Participants in the factory tour will *meet and break up at* the factory.

[2]**げんち 言質** a (verbal) commitment /kəmítmənt/ ; a promise（約束）▶首相は在任中は増税は行わないと**言質を与えた** The Prime Minister *made a commitment* not to raise taxes during his term of office. ‖私たちは市長からこの計画を実行するとの**言質を取った** We got the mayor's *promise* to carry out the project.

けんちく 建築 architecture /ɑ́ːrkɪtektʃər/（ある時代や文化を反映したり，芸術的価値をもったりする建築様式；集合的に建築物も指す）; a building（建物）; construction（建設）▶宇治の平等院は平安時代の代表的な**建築**だ The Byodoin Temple in Uji is a typical example of Heian period *architecture*. ‖この教会の**建築様式は**ゴシック様式だ This church is built in the Gothic style. ‖うちでは今マイホームを**建築中だ** We *are having* our house *built*.

語法 工務店や建築家に依頼して建てていることをはっきりさせた言い方．日常会話では We are building a (new) house. でよい．

‖**建築家** an architect ‖**建築学** architecture.

けんちくし 建築士 an architect ‖一［二］**級建築士** a first［second］class architect and building engineer ‖**木造建築士** a registered architect for wooden buildings.

けんちょ 顕著な outstanding（目立った）; remarkable（注目すべき）; conspicuous（ほかと違っていて人目を引く）; marked（目立つ；文語に多い語）; notable（はっきり人目につく）▶**顕著な**学問的業績 *outstanding* academic achievements ‖**顕著な**特徴 a *remarkable*［*conspicuous* ／*striking*］feature ‖**顕著な**効果を示す show a *marked* effect ‖その国は近年**顕著な**経済的発展を遂げた In recent years, that country has made *remarkable* economic progress.

[1]**けんちょう 県庁** a prefectural office［government］（➤ 前者は建物，後者は行政機関）

‖**県庁所在地** the prefectural capital ／the seat of the prefectural government.

[2]**けんちょう 堅調な** strong（力強い）; healthy（好調な）; robust（しっかりした）▶**堅調な**経済成長 *strong*［*robust*］economic growth.

げんちょう 幻聴 an auditory hallucination.

げんつき 原付き ‖**原付き自転車** a moped ‖**原付き二輪車** a motorbike with a motor of less than 50 cc.

[1]**けんてい 検定** ▶この教科書は中学校用として文部科学省の**検定を受けている**（＝認可された）This textbook *has been approved* by the Ministry of Education(, Culture, Sports, Science and Technology) for use in junior high schools.

‖**検定教科書** an authorized textbook（➤「教科書検定」は textbook authorization［vetting］）‖**英語能力検定試験** an English proficiency test［examination］.

[2]**けんてい 献呈** →**謹呈**.

げんてい 限定する limit +目（上限を設ける）; restrict +目（制限する）▶来館者の数を１日500人に**限定する** *limit* the number of visitors to 500 a day ‖会員は100名に**限定されている** Membership *is limited to* 100 people. ‖彼の行動は狭い範囲に**限定されている** The sphere of his activities *is restricted* within narrow limits.

▶そのチョコレートは期間**限定**販売です The chocolate is on sale for a *limited* time.（➤ limited time offer（略して LTO）は「期間限定特別提供価格」の意）‖この時計は数量**限定**生産です The production of this watch is *limited*.

‖**限定版** a limited edition（➤「限定500部」は a limited run of 500 copies).

[1]**げんてん 減点** ▶スペリングを間違えて３点**減点された** Three points *were subtracted* from my score because I made a mistake in spelling. ‖氏名を書くのを忘れたら５点**減点だぞ** I'll *take off* five points if you forget to write your name (on the paper).（➤ take off は「…を引く，下げる」の意のインフォーマルな表現).

▶スピード違反でまた**減点を食った**よ I *got another point deducted* for speeding.

[2]**げんてん 原点** the (very) beginning（最初）; the starting［fundamental］point（出発点）; basic fundamentals（根本原理）▶日本人は「**原点に戻って考え直そう**」

とよく言う Japanese people often say, "Let us go back to *the starting point* and rethink this." ‖ 座標軸の原点 *the origin* of the coordinates.

3**げんてん 原典** the original.

げんど 限度 a limit ▶何事にも限度がある There is *a limit* to [in] everything. ／Everything has its *limit*. ‖ 我慢するにも限度がある There is *a limit* to my patience. ‖ その国では最低限度の生活が保障されている That country guarantees its people *the absolute minimum level of subsistence*.

1**けんとう 見当** a guess /ges/ ▶道路が混んでいて, いつ向こうに着けるか見当がつかない The roads are so crowded it's *anybody's guess* when we'll get there. (➤ anybody's guess は「予測がつかないこと」の意のインフォーマルな表現) ‖ 彼はいつも調べもしないで見当でものを言う He is always shooting off his mouth without properly checking things (out). ‖ 対話「誰が教室でたばこを吸ったか見当がつくかい?」「いや, 全然見当がつかないよ」"Do you *know* [Can you *guess*] who smoked in the classroom?" "No, I *haven't the slightest* [*faintest*] *idea*." ‖ 先生の推測は見当違いだった Our teacher *made a wrong guess* [*guessed wrong*]. (➤ 推測が正しい場合は make a right guess ／guess right) ‖ 私の推測は全くの見当外れだった My guess *was* completely *off the mark* [*target*]. ‖ きみの意見はまるで見当外れだ Your opinion *is beside the point*.

2**けんとう 検討** (an) examination (調査) ; consideration (考慮) ; (a) review (念入りな審査) 一動 **検討する** examine +目, consider +目 ; review +目 ▶企画 [提案] を検討する *examine* a project [a proposal] ‖ 《教師が職員会議などで》彼女を退学にするかどうかについてはもう少し検討してからのほうがよいと思います I think we should *give* the matter further *consideration* [*study* the matter further] before we decide whether or not to expel her (from school). ‖ 答えが間違っているからもう一度検討して(=考えて)みなさい Your answer is wrong, so *think* it *over* again. ‖ きみのプランはおもしろそうだ. 検討してみよう Your plan sounds attractive. We will *consider* [*review*] it *carefully*. ‖ 彼らの提案についてはもう少し詳しく検討する必要がある We need to *look into* their proposal (a little) more closely. ‖ カナダ留学についてはまだ検討中です I'*m* still *considering* [*thinking about*] studying in Canada.
‖ 検討(委員)会 an investigative commission.
☛ 再検討 (→見出語)

3**けんとう 健闘** ▶我々のサッカーチームは健闘し, 初勝利をあげた Our soccer team *fought hard* and gained the first victory. ‖ 彼は健闘したが1回戦で敗退した He was eliminated in the first match though he *put up a good fight* [*made a great effort*]. ‖ 決勝での健闘を祈る *Good luck* in the finals!

けんどう 剣道 kendo (➤ 英語化している) ; Japanese fencing
日本紹介 ✉ **剣道はフェンシングに似た日本の武術です. 竹刀と呼ぶ竹製の刀を使います** Kendo is a Japanese martial art that resembles fencing. A '*shinai*,' which is a sword made of bamboo, is used.
▶剣道の稽古をする practice *kendo*.

げんとう 厳冬 a harsh winter.

げんどう 言動 ▶彼は近頃言動がおかしい He *is acting* [*behaving*] *strangely* these days. ‖ 言動を慎みなさい Be careful about *what you say and do*.

げんどうき 原動機 a motor.

けんとうし 剣闘士 a gladiator (古代ローマの).

げんどうりょく 原動力 ▶彼の活躍がチームの優勝の原動力となった His outstanding play was *the driving force* behind the team's victory.

けんない 圏内 ▶関東地方は午後8時暴風圏内に入った The Kanto district entered the *storm zone* at 8 p.m. ‖ この点数ならきみは合格圏内だよ With this score you're *within reach of passing* the entrance examinations.

げんなま 現生 cold [hard] cash.

げんなり ▶机の上に積まれた書類を見ると, それだけでげんなりしてしまう Just glancing at the mountain of paperwork on my desk *gets* me *down* [*bums* me *out*]. (➤ ともに「うんざりさせる」の意のインフォーマルな表現) ‖ 先生に「校庭をあと3周しろ」と言われてみんなげんなりした Everyone *felt like dying* when the teacher said, "Three times more around the field."

げんに 現に really (本当に) ; actually (意外かもしれないが) ▶ぼくは現にこの耳でそれを聞いた I *really* heard it. ／I heard it *with my own ears*. ‖ あの人たちは現にそう言ったんです They *actually* said it.

けんにょう 検尿 a urine /jʊ́ərɪn/ test.

けんにん 兼任 ▶田中氏は首相と外相を兼任した Mr. Tanaka *concurrently held the posts* of Prime Minister and Foreign Minister. ‖ 国語の先生が書道の先生を兼任している The Japanese teacher *also teaches* calligraphy. ‖ **兼任教授** an adjunct professor (➤ 大学外に本職を持つ人 ; →兼担).

げんば 現場 a scene (事故・事件などの) ; a spot (犯行地点) ; a site (工事などの) ▶警官はすぐ現場に駆けつけた The police rushed to the *scene*. ‖ 彼はまるで現場に居合わせたかのようにその事件について説明した He explained how the incident occurred as if he had *been on the spot*. ‖ 刑事は私に犯人はもう一度犯行現場に戻って来るものだと言った The detective told me that a criminal always returns to *the scene of a crime*. ‖ 彼は盗みの現場を押さえられた He was caught [was arrested] *in the* (*very*) *act of stealing*. ‖ 文科省は現場の教師の声をもっと尊重すべきだ The Ministry of Education should pay more attention to what *active teachers* have to say.
‖ **現場監督** a supervisor, a field overseer ‖ **現場検証** an on-the-spot investigation [inspection] ‖ **現場中継** a live /laɪv/ broadcast from the scene [spot] ‖ **建築現場** a construction site.

けんぱい 献杯する drink a toast to commemorate someone who has passed away.

けんばいき 券売機 a ticket machine.

げんばく 原爆 an atom(ic) bomb /bɑːm/, an A-bomb ▶8月6日は広島に原爆が落とされた日です August 6th is the day *an atomic bomb* was dropped on Hiroshima.
‖ **原爆症** radiation sickness ‖ **原爆の日** the Anniversary of Atomic Bombing ; the Day the A-Bomb Fell.

げんばつ 厳罰 severe punishment ▶あんな男は厳罰に処してもよい A man like that deserves *severe punishment*. ‖ 違反者は厳罰に処するべきだ Offenders must *be punished severely*.

げんぱつ 原発 →原子力.

けんばん 鍵盤 a keyboard (➤ けん1本は a key) ▶彼は鍵盤楽器なら何でもこなす He is able to play all kinds of *keyboard instruments*.

げんばん 原盤 a **master**(レコードの).

げんはんけつ 原判決 the original decision [**ruling**] ▶原判決を破棄する overturn *the original decision*.

け

げんび 兼備 ▶確かに彼女は才色兼備だが, てんぐになり過ぎている She *has* indeed *both talent and beauty*, but she's too proud of the fact.

けんびきょう 顕微鏡 a **microscope** ▶顕微鏡で大腸菌を調べる examine colon bacilli through *a microscope*.

‖顕微鏡検査 (a) microscopic examination ‖顕微鏡写真 a (photo)micrograph ‖電子顕微鏡 an electron microscope.

けんぴん 検品 (a) **product inspection** ▶当社では完成品をすべて検品しております We *inspect* [*check*] every finished product.

げんぴん 現品 a **displayed item**(展示品); an **item in stock**(在庫品); an **actual item**(現物) ▶現品半額 *All goods in stock*: Half price.

げんふうけい 原風景 archetypal /ɑ́ːʳkitaɪp/ **landscape**; **landscape in the original state**(人手が加わっていない); **primeval landscape**(太古のままの風景); a **primal scene**(子供が垣間見た両親の性行為の場面; 心理学用語) ▶北海道の原風景 Hokkaido's *primeval landscape*.

けんぶつ 見物 sightseeing 一動 **見物する see, see** [**do**] **the sights** (➤ the sights は「名所」) ▶ローマは見物して回る所が多すぎる There is too much to *see* in Rome. ‖私たちはきのうロンドン塔を見物した Yesterday we *saw* the Tower of London. ／Yesterday we *went sightseeing* at the Tower of London. ‖鎌倉見物に出かけよう Let's go *sightseeing* in Kamakura. ／Let's go to Kamakura to *see the sights*. ‖私たちはロンドンにいたとき1年間であらゆる所を見物して回ろうとした When we were in London, we tried to *take in* all the sights in one year. (➤ take in は「(名所などを)訪れる」の意のインフォーマルな表現) ‖東大寺には大勢の見物客がいた There were lots of *visitors* at Todaiji Temple. (➤ 大道芸人などを囲むような見物人は onlooker という).

▶手品をやってるよ. ちょっと見物していこう They're doing magic tricks. Let's go *watch* for a moment. (➤ 後半を Let's go *take a look*. としてもよい).

☛ 高みの見物 (→見出語)

げんぶつ 現物 the actual [**real**] **item**(➤ item の代わりに article でもよい) ▶現物は見本よりも少々長めだった *The actual item* was a little longer than the sample. ‖現物を見ないで物を買うのは賢明ではない Buying something *sight unseen* is not wise. (➤ sight unseen は「あらかじめ調べずに［見ずに］」)

‖現物支給 payment in kind ‖現物支給制 a truck system.

ケンブリッジ Cambridge /kéɪmbrɪdʒ/ (イングランド南東部の都市; ケンブリッジ大学の所在地).

けんぶん 見聞

✉ **この夏休み中にイギリスをあちこち見て回り, 英語教師としての見聞を広めたいと思います** During this summer vacation, I'd like to tour around Britain, visiting places and seeing things, and *widen my knowledge* as a teacher of English.

げんぶん 原文 the original (text) ▶日本語訳を原文と照らし合わせる compare the Japanese translation with *the original* (*text*).

げんぶんいっち 言文一致 the unification of the (Japanese) spoken and written language.

けんぺいりつ 建蔽率 a **building to land ratio**, a **(building) coverage ratio.**

けんべん 検便 a **stool test.**

1**けんぽう 憲法** a **constitution** (➤ 自国の憲法は the Constitution と大文字にする) ▶憲法第9条 Article 9 of *the Constitution* ‖それは憲法に違反していない［している］That is *constitutional* [*unconstitutional*]. ‖言論の自由は憲法で保障された権利である Freedom of speech is a *constitutional* right. ‖日本国憲法は1946年11月3日に公布された *The Japanese Constitution* was proclaimed on November 3, 1946. ‖彼らは憲法改正の機会をうかがっている They are looking for an opportunity to *revise the Constitution*.

‖憲法記念日 Constitution Day.

2**けんぽう 剣法 the art of fencing.**

げんぽう 減俸 a **salary** [**pay**] **reduction**, a **salary** [**pay**] **cut** ▶私は10パーセント減俸された *My salary* [*pay*] *was reduced* by 10 percent. ／I *took a salary reduction* [*cut*] of 10 percent.

けんぼうじゅっすう 権謀術数 cunning and deceitful tactics.

けんぼうしょう 健忘症 forgetfulness; **amnesia** /æmníːʒə/ (記憶喪失症) ▶祖父は年を取って健忘症にかかってしまった My grandfather has *become very forgetful* with age.

げんぼく 原木 raw lumber.

げんぽん 原本 the original; **the original document**(文書); **the original text**(原文) ▶この写しは原本と相違ありません This is an exact copy of *the original* (*document*).

けんま 研磨する grind, polish; **sand**(やすりで)

‖研磨機 a grinder, a sanding machine ‖研磨材 (an) abrasive material.

げんまい 玄米 brown rice, unpolished rice.

けんまく 剣幕・見幕 ▶そんなすごいけんまくでどならなくたっていいでしょう You don't have to shout at me so *fiercely* [*ferociously* ／*threateningly*].

げんみつ 厳密な strict; **rigorous**(全く手を抜かない); **close** /kloʊs/ (綿密な) ▶厳密な調査をする make a *close* [*careful*] investigation ‖聖書の厳密な解釈 a *strict* interpretation of the Bible ‖厳密な分析 a *rigorous* analysis ‖厳密な意味ではアノラックとパーカは違う An anorak and a parka are different from each other *in the strict sense of the word*. ‖厳密に言うとこれは誤りだ *Strictly speaking*, this is a mistake.

けんみん 県民 an **inhabitant of a prefecture**(個人); **the people of a prefecture** (総称) ▶高知県民はその知らせに大喜びした *The people of Kochi Prefecture* were overjoyed at the news. ‖同じ九州でも福岡と鹿児島では県民性が異なる Although both prefectures are in Kyushu, *the people* of Fukuoka and Kagoshima *have different characters*.

‖県民税 a tax on the residents of a prefecture.

けんむ 兼務 ▶その先生は両校の体育講師を兼務している That teacher *teaches* physical education *in both schools*. ‖あの人は2つの会社の社長を兼務している He is *concurrently* the president of two companies. (➤ concurrently は「同時に」の意の堅い語).

1**けんめい 賢明な wise**(知恵を備えた); **sensible**(分別

がある)；smart(りこうな；《米》に多い用法) ▶賢明なやり方 a *wise* [*smart*] move ‖ 賢明な判断をする make a *wise* [*smart*] decision ‖ 賢明な人ならそんなことはしない A *wise* [*sensible*] person would not do such a thing. ‖ 彼のプロポーズを拒否したのは賢明でしたよ It was *wise* of you [You were *wise*] to refuse his proposal. ‖ きみがあの大学を受験しなかったのは賢明だったよ You *made the right choice* in not taking the entrance exam for that university.

2**けんめい 懸命な** eager(熱心な) 一副 懸命に hard ⇀一生懸命 ▶幹雄は葉子を喜ばせようと懸命だった Mikio *was eager* to please Yoko. ‖ 警察の懸命な努力にもかかわらず犯人は捕まらなかった Despite the police's *strenuous* efforts, the culprit was not arrested.

3**けんめい 件名** a subject(➤ Eメールでは Re：と書く).

1**げんめい 言明する** declare《that》(宣言する) ▶市長は向こう3年間での市職員の2割削減を言明した The mayor *declared that* the city staff would be cut by 20 percent within three years.

2**げんめい 厳命** a strict order 一動 厳命する give a strict order.

げんめつ 幻滅 disillusion；disappointment(失望) 一動 幻滅する be disillusioned《at, by》；be disappointed《with》 ▶パリへ行ってみて幻滅した I *was disillusioned* when I got to Paris [by what I saw in Paris]. ‖ 息子の成績には大いに幻滅を感じている I *am* greatly *disappointed with* my son's grades.

けんもほろろ ▶我々の要求はけんもほろろに拒否された Our demand was *flatly* rejected.

けんもん 検問 a check, an inspection (➤ 後者は目で見て検査するだけの場合が多い) ▶爆破予告があったので，空港での検問が強化された There was a bomb scare, so *checks* at the airport were tightened. ‖ 検問所 a checkpoint.

げんや 原野 a wilderness /wíldərnəs/ (自然のままの荒野)；the wilds (ある地方の未開地) ▶原野を切り開いて鉄道を敷く cut a path through the *wilderness* to lay a railroad ‖ ぼくたちは北海道の原野でさまざまな珍しい動物を観察した We observed various rare animals in *the wilds* of Hokkaido.

けんやく 倹約 thrift(つましくすること；悪いニュアンスはない)；saving (使わずに節約すること) 一動 倹約する save；economize《on》(使う量を減らす) ▶彼は倹約して大金をためた He *practiced thrift* and saved a lot of money. ‖ ファミリーサイズの瓶を買って20円倹約した I bought a family-size bottle and *saved* twenty yen. ‖ 地球を救うためにもっと倹約して暮らす方法を学ぼう For the sake of the earth, let us learn how to live *less wastefully*. ‖ 最近物価が上がっているのでできるだけ倹約しなければならない Prices keep rising these days, so we have to *economize* as much as possible. ‖ 彼は倹約家だ He is *a thrifty person*. ／He is *a saver*.

げんゆ 原油 crude oil [《英》petroleum] ▶原油をサウジアラビアから輸入する import *crude oil* from Saudi Arabia.

けんよう 兼用 ▶父のトレーナーはパジャマ兼用だ My father's sweatsuit *also serves as* his pajamas.

けんらん 絢爛たる gorgeous；dazzling(目がくらむほどの)；brilliant(華々しい)；flowery (文体などが) ▶三島由紀夫のけんらんたる文体 Mishima Yukio's *flowery* style of writing ‖ 女王はその晩もけんらんたる衣装をまとっていた The Queen was *gorgeously* [*dazzlingly*] dressed (on) that evening, too. ‖ その王室の結婚式はけんらん豪華なものであった The royal wedding was *rich in pageantry*. (➤ pageantry /pǽdʒəntri/ は「華麗な見せ物」).

けんり 権利 a right ▶国民の知る権利を守る preserve the *right* of the people to know ‖ 権利を主張 [乱用] する assert [abuse] one's *right* ‖ すべての子供には教育を受ける権利がある All children have *a* [*the*] *right* to receive an education. ‖ 何の権利があってきみはそんなことをするのか *What right do you have* to do that? ／*How dare* you do such a thing? ‖ お母さんには黙ってぼくの部屋に入る権利は無いんだよ Mother, you have no *right* to enter my room without permission. ‖ 誰も他人の権利を侵すことはできない Nobody should *infringe on* other people's *rights*.

‖ 権利金 key money (貸家などの) (⇀礼金) ‖ 権利書 a deed(➤「家の権利書」は deed to a house).

げんり 原理 a principle ▶スパナはてこの原理を応用したものだ The wrench is an application of the *principle* of the lever. ‖ 飛行機が空を飛ぶ原理を知っていますか Do you know the *principle* which enables an airplane to fly? ‖ 原理主義 fundamentalism ‖ 原理主義者 a fundamentalist.

けんりつ 県立の prefectural /prɪféktʃərəl/ ▶茨城県立水戸第一高校 Ibaraki *Prefectural* Mito Daiichi Senior High School ‖ 岐阜高校は県立ですか，市立ですか? Is Gifu Senior High School *run by the prefecture* or by the city?

げんりゅう 源流 the source(発生の元)；the origin (始まり，出発点) ▶相模川の源流は山中湖である Lake Yamanaka is *the source* of the Sagami River. ‖ ヨーロッパ文明の源流の1つはキリスト教である One of *the sources* [*origins*] of European civilization is Christianity.

1**げんりょう 原料** raw materials(原材料)；ingredients ((料理の)材料) ▶白滝の原料は何ですか What are the *ingredients* to make 'shirataki'? ／What is 'shirataki' made from?

2**げんりょう 減量する** lose weight ▶あと3キロ減量したい I want to *lose* three more kilograms. ‖ 節食とジョギングで5キロの減量に成功した I succeeded in *losing* five kilograms by dieting and jogging.

けんりょく 権力 power(法律で定められた権限；支配力)；authority /əθɔ́:rəṭi/ (他人に命令し服従を強制する力) ▶ 1789年，フランスの民衆は国王の権力を奪った In 1789 the people of France deprived their king of his *power*. ‖ 彼は大統領としての権力をほしいままにした He wielded his *power* [*authority*] as president arbitrarily. ‖ 彼はこの町の権力者だが人気がない He *has great power* [*authority*／*influence*] in this town, but he is disliked by the citizens.

‖ 公権力 governmental [public] authority.

げんろん 言論 speech (and writing) ▶言論の自由 freedom of *speech* ‖ 当時は言論の取り締まりが厳しかった There was strict control of *speech and writing* in those days.

こ・コ

[1]こ 子 **1【人間の】** a **child**［複 **children**］,《インフォーマル》a **kid** ▶子を産む give birth to *a child*／have *a baby* ‖ 子を育てる bring up *children* ‖ うちの子は気が小さい *Our son*［*daughter*］is timid. ‖ 市川さんのところで女の子が生まれた The Ichikawas had *a baby girl*. ‖ あの子はいつも遅れる *He*［*She*］is always late.（「あの子」を that child と訳すこともできるが, 文脈からそれが誰を指すのかはっきりしている場合は, この例のように he, she を用いることも多い）‖ 対話「お子さんは何人いらっしゃいますか？」「２人, 男の子と女の子です」"How many *children* do you have?" "Two. A boy and a girl［A son and a daughter］."（➤ boy, girl を用いるのは子供が小さいときのみ）《参考》「お父さん子」を a daddy's［father's］boy（男の子）, a daddy's［father's］girl（女の子）,「お母さん子」を a mama's［mother's］boy, a mama's［mother's］girl という. なお, イギリス英語では mama's の代わりに mummy's という.

2【動物の】 **young**（➤ 総称）《参考》英語には puppy（犬）, kitten（猫・ネズミ・ウサギなど）, foal（馬・シカ）, calf /kæf/（牛・象など）, cub（ライオン・トラ・オオカミ・キツネなど）, lamb /læm/（羊）など, 動物の子を表す特別な語がある ▶象の子 a *baby* elephant／an elephant *calf* ‖ 猫の子は子猫である A *baby* cat is (called) a kitten.

3【若い女性】 ▶案内所の子に聞いてください Please ask the *young lady* at the information desk.

☞ いい子（→見出語）

[2]こ 弧 an **arc** /ɑːʳk/ ▶弧を描いている海岸線 an *arched* coastline.

こ- 故- **the late ...** ▶故長谷川氏 *the late* Mr. Hasegawa ‖ 故竹下首相 *the late* Prime Minister Takeshita.

[1]-こ -個 ▶リンゴ３個 three apples ‖ イチゴのケーキを５個ください I'd like *five pieces* of strawberry cake.（➤ 数えられない名詞の場合）‖ このオレンジは１個いくらですか How much do these oranges cost *apiece*［*each*］?（➤ apiece は「１個につき」）.

[2]-こ -戸 ▶１戸ごとに注文を取る take an order *at each house* ‖ 50戸の村 a village of *fifty households*［*families*］.

[3]-こ -湖 ▶琵琶湖 *Lake* Biwa（➤ the Lake of Biwa は一般的ではない）‖ エリー湖とオンタリオ湖 *Lakes* Erie and Ontario.

[1]ご 五 **five**; **the fifth**（５番目）▶毎日５回 *five times* a day ‖（野球）５回の表［裏］the top［bottom］of *the fifth*（*inning*）‖ 弟は５年生です My brother is *a fifth grader*.

[2]ご 語 **1【単語】** a **word** ▶この語の意味を教えて Can you tell me the meaning of this *word*? ‖ 空欄に適する語を補え Fill in the blanks with a suitable *word*.

2【言語】 a **language** ▶彼女は数か国語に通じている She knows *several languages*. ‖ メキシコでは何語が話されていますか？ What *language* do you speak in Mexico?／*What language* do they speak in Mexico?（前者はメキシコ人やメキシコ在住の人に向かって質問するような場合. 後者は例えば, 日本の英語学習の時間などに日本人に向かって質問するような場合. What language is spoken in Mexico? はその両方の場合に用いられる）.

[3]ご 碁 **Go**（➤ 英語化している）
日本紹介 ✉ **碁は２人が向かい合って座り, 交互に盤上に白黒２種の丸い石を置いて陣地を取り合うボードゲームです. 囲碁ともいいます** Go is a board game in which two people sit face to face across a square wooden board. The two players alternately place rounded black or white stones to secure their position. It is also called '*igo*.' ‖ トムさん, 碁を打ちましょう Let's *play Go*, Tom. ‖ 碁石 a Go stone ‖ 碁盤 a Go board.

-ご -後 **after ...**（…のあと）; **in**（…たてば）; **... later**（…あとで）; **away**（離れて）; **since ...**（…以来ずっと）→あと
《解説》after は出来事の順序を表して「…したあとで」の意. in は時間や期間を表す語を伴って,「…の時間［期間］が経過すれば」の意で主に未来形とともに用いる. later は話題となった時点より「あとになって, そのあとで」の意. away は「時間的に離れて」. ▶ぼくは夕食後にテレビを見る I watch TV *after* dinner［supper］. ‖ この橋は２か月後には完成する This bridge will be finished *in two months*［*two months from now*］. ‖ ２, ３日後, 上野でばったり陽子に会った *A few days later* I ran into Yoko at Ueno. ‖ 健次にはその後会っていない I haven't seen Kenji *since*（*then*）.（→その後）‖ 今から100年後, 地球はどうなっているだろうか I wonder what the earth will be like *a hundred years from now*. ‖ 会議は３日後だ The meeting is three days *away*［*from now*］.

直訳の落とし穴「10分後に」

「10分後に」= after ten minutes とする学習者が多いが, これが使える場面は多くない.「10分後に救急車が到着した」はふつう, An ambulance arrived ten minutes later. で, An ambulance arrived after ten minutes. はまれ.（×）An ambulance arrived ten minutes after. は不可. A police car arrived at 8:30 and an ambulance arrived ten minutes after that.（８時半にパトカーが来て, その10分後に救急車が到着した）のような使い方は自然.

また,「10分後には家に帰ります」のように, 現在を起点にして未来のことを言う場合には after や later は使えない. in ten minutes または ten minutes from now を用いて, I'm going home in ten minutes. または, I'm going home ten minutes from now. とする. なお, in ten minutes を「10分以内」と誤解している学習者がいるが, それを表すのは within ten minutes である.

コアラ《動物》a **koala** /kouáːlə/ **(bear)**.

[1]こい 鯉《魚》a **carp**［複 **carp**］, a **koi**（➤ 英語化している）《参考》日本人はコイを池で飼って観賞し, 勢いのいい魚として好むが, 英語の carp にはあまりよいイメージはない. 一般の英米人はコイを薄汚くて, 貪欲な魚として嫌うことが多い. 観賞用のコイは koi と呼ぶことが多い. ▶にしきごい (a) *nishikigoi*; a *colored carp* ‖ コイに餌をやる feed

the *koi*.

☛ **こいのぼり** (→見出語)

2**こい 恋** **love** 一動 (…に)**恋する** **fall in love** ((with)), **love**(+目) 語法 fall in love は男女が「恋に落ちる」. love は「愛する, 慈しむ」で, 恋人だけでなく, 夫婦や友人に対しても用いる.

▶本物の恋 true *love* ‖ 恋をしている女 a woman *in love* ‖ 私, 生まれて初めて恋をしちゃった I'*m in love* for the first time. ‖ 哲也は明美に恋をしている Tetsuya *is in love with* Akemi. ‖ 2人は初めて会った日に恋に落ちた The two *fell in love* (*with* each other) on the day they first met. ‖ 恋の病に薬なし There is no medicine to cure *lovesickness*. ‖ 恋は盲目とはよく言われることだ It's a common saying that *love is blind*.

✉ **あなたに会った瞬間, 私はそれが恋だとわかりました** The minute I laid eyes on you, I knew it was *love*.

3**こい 故意の** **intentional**(初めから意図した) ; **deliberate**(慎重に考えたうえでの) 一副 **故意に** **intentionally, deliberately** ; **purposely, on purpose**(はっきりとした目的をもって) ▶彼は故意に遅れてきた He was *intentionally* [*deliberately*] late. ／He came late *on purpose*. ‖ 私は故意に彼女をつまずかせたのではない I did not trip her *on purpose*. ／I did not mean to trip her. (➤ 後者は「つまずかせるつもりはなかった」の意) ‖ **故意犯** a crime of intention, a crime of intent (犯罪) ; a person who commits a crime intentionally (人).

4こい 濃い

📖 **訳語メニュー**
色が濃い →dark, deep **1**
味が濃い →strong, thick **1**
密度が濃い →dense, thick **2**
可能性が濃い →strong **3**

1【濃度が】 **dark** (色や暗さが強くて) ; **deep** (色が鮮やかで) ; **strong**(味などが) ; **thick** (液体がどろっとしている) ▶濃い緑色の服 a *dark* [*deep*] green dress ‖ この赤は濃すぎると思わないかい? Don't you think this red is *too dark*? ‖ ((比喩的)) 彼の表情には苦悩の色が濃かった He showed *the depth of* his *anguish* on his face. ‖ 濃いスープ *thick* soup ‖ 濃いお茶 *strong* (green) tea ‖ 東日本の人のほうが一般的に濃い味付けを好む People in eastern Japan generally prefer *strongly seasoned food*(*s*) [*dishes*]. (➤ season は「(食物に)味を付ける」) ‖ このコーヒーは私には濃すぎる This coffee is *too strong* for me.

‖ **濃茶** thick matcha tea.

2【密度が】 **dense**(気体の) ; **thick**(密集した) ▶外は濃い霧が掛かっている There's a *dense* fog outside. ‖ 彼はひげが濃い He has a *thick* [*heavy*] beard. (➤ heavy はつけひげであってもよい) ‖ おまえ最近化粧が濃くなったみたいだぞ You seem to be wearing *heavier make-up* these days. ‖ 内容の濃い報告書 a *substantial* report ‖ あの教授の講演はいつも中身が濃い(＝内容がある) That professor's lectures *are* always *substantial* [*meaty*].

3【可能性が】 **strong** ▶第一発見者が殺人の真犯人ではないかという疑いが濃かった *There was a strong suspicion* that the first person to find the body might be the real murderer.

ごい 語彙 (a) **vocabulary** /voʊkǽbjəleri/ (語の総数) ▶語彙を増やす increase [expand ／ enlarge] one's *vocabulary* ‖ 父は語彙が豊富だ My father *has a rich* [*large*] *vocabulary*. (➤「貧弱だ」なら rich, large の代わりに poor を用いる) ‖ あなたは英語の語彙はどのくらいありますか How many English *words* do you know? ／How large is your English *vocabulary*?

こいがたき 恋敵 a **rival in love**.

こいくち 濃口の **dark** ▶濃口しょうゆ *dark* [*strong*] soy sauce ／*dark* [*strong*] shoyu.

こいし 小石 a **small stone** ; a **pebble**(水流で丸くなった).

こいしい 恋しい ▶ああ, 麗子! きみが恋しいよ Oh, Reiko. You're such *a sweetheart* [*a dear*]. ‖ 恋しい彼氏と一緒にパリに行きたい I want to go to Paris with the man I'*m in love with*. ‖ 神戸に居るマキ子が恋しい I *miss* Makiko who's in Kobe. (➤ miss は「居ないので寂しく思う」の意で, 恋人とは限らず家族や友人にも使う) ‖ 田舎が恋しくなったら電話するのよ Be sure to phone me when you *get homesick*. ‖ こたつが恋しい季節になった The cold season has set in when we *long for* the warmth of the *kotatsu*. (➤ long for は「…が恋しい」) ‖ 子スズメが母親を恋しがって鳴いている A little sparrow is crying *for* its mother. (➤ for は「…を求めて」).

こいつ ▶こいつが悪いんだ It's *his* [*her*] fault. ‖ こいつ, また怠けてる *Hey, you*'re goofing off again. ‖ ((漫画などを見ながら)) こいつはおもしろい (Hey,) *this* is funny!

こいなか 恋仲 ▶恋仲の2人 a (*loving*) couple ／a couple (*in love*) (➤ couple には「恋愛関係にある」という含みがある).

こいにょうぼう 恋女房 one's **beloved wife**.

こいぬ 子犬 a **puppy**, a **pup**.

こいのぼり 鯉のぼり a **carp streamer**

日本紹介 ✉ **こいのぼりはコイの形をした紙や布製の大きなのぼりです. コイは滝をも勢いよく上る元気のよい魚とされています. 男の子の成長を願って祝う端午の節句(現在はこどもの日)に立てます** *Koinobori* are big carp-shaped streamers made of paper or cloth. It is believed that carp are vigorous enough to swim up even waterfalls. People set up *koinobori* at '*tango-no-sekku*' (formerly the Boys' Festival, now Children's Day) with the wish that their boys will grow up strong and healthy.

▶端午の節句にこいのぼりを立てる hang out [set up] *carp streamers* for the Boys' Festival.

こいびと 恋人 a **sweetheart**(➤ 少々古風だが lover よりロマンチックな語) ; a **boyfriend** (男の) ; a **girlfriend** (女の) ; a **lover** (➤ 男女どちらにも用い, 肉体関係があることを暗示することが多い) ▶ひろしとめぐみは恋人どうしだ Hiroshi and Megumi *are in love* (*with each other*). ／Hiroshi and Megumi are *lovers*. (➤ lovers はしばしば「深い」関係を連想させる. ただし, young lovers にはそのニュアンスはない ; love each other とも言えるが, これは親子・きょうだい・友だち間もありうる ; 恋人どうしでは love each other very much などとすることもある) ‖ セーヌの川岸には寄り添う恋人たちがたくさん居た I saw a lot of (*romantic*) *couples* cuddling on the banks of the Seine. ‖ 対話「恋人はいますか」「いえ, ただいま募集中です」"Do you have *a boyfriend* [*girlfriend*]?" "No, I'm looking for one." (➤ あまり知らない人にはこういった立ち入った質問はしないのが礼儀 ; 「付き合っている人がいるか」と聞くには Are you seeing anyone? とする).

✉ **私は6月に孝夫と結婚します. 彼は高校時代**

からの恋人なんです I'm getting married to Takao in June. He was my high school *sweetheart*.

✉《バレンタインカードで》ぼくの恋人になってください Will you be my valentine? ➤valentine は本来「バレンタインの贈り物の受け取り手に選ばれた人」の意. この表現はふつうは学校の子供どうしで交換するカードや子供が母親に贈るカードに使われるもので, 恋愛と関係がないことが多い.

こいぶみ 恋文 a **love letter**.

こいめ 濃いめ **deeper**(色が); **stronger**(茶・コーヒーなどが) ▶私は濃いめのお茶が好き I prefer *stronger* [*rather strong*] green tea.

コイル a **coil**.

こいわずらい 恋煩い・恋患い **lovesickness** ▶誠は恋わずらいでげっそり痩せてしまった Makoto has lost a lot of weight from *lovesickness*.

コイン a **coin** ▶コインを投げて(勝負・順番などを)決める toss (up) *a coin*.

コインパーキング a **coin-operated parking space**(➤1台分の空きを指す).

コインランドリー a **laundromat** (《商標》 **Laundromat**), a **coin(-operated) laundry** ▶コインランドリーで洗濯をする do one's washing at *a laundromat*.

危ないカタカナ語✹コインランドリー

1 英語では coin(-operated) laundry というが, 日常的には《米》laundromat, 《英》laund(e)rette と呼ばれることが多い. ほかに, self-service laundry とか, インフォーマルで coin-op という言い方もある.

2 同様に「コインロッカー」も英語では coin-operated locker といい, 日常的には単に locker あるいは pay locker という.

コインロッカー a **coin-operated locker** ▶コインロッカーに荷物を預ける leave one's things in *a locker*.

1**こう 甲** **1**【手足の】▶足の甲 *an instep*／the *upper side* of a foot ‖ 右手の甲が痛い I have a pain in the *back* of my right hand.

2【甲乙の】▶甲(＝A)は乙(＝B)に対して法律上の義務を負っている *A* has a legal obligation to B. (➤「甲＝前者」「乙＝後者」で表せる場合はそれぞれ the former, the latter).

2**こう 功** **success** ▶功を焦ってはいけない Don't be too eager for *success*. ‖ 積極策が功を奏した The aggressive tactics *proved to be successful*.

▶《慣用表現》彼は功成り名遂げて実業界を引退した He retired from the business world *after achieving success and winning fame*. ‖ さすがは年の功ですね You've obviously learned a lot over the years. (➤「年月を重ねて多くのことを学んだ」の意).

ことわざ 亀の甲より年の功 Age and experience teach [bring] wisdom. (➤「年齢と経験が知恵を授ける」の意の英語のことわざ).

3**こう 効** ▶その新薬は効を奏さなかった The new medicine *didn't work* [*proved* ineffective].

4**こう 幸** ▶幸か不幸か彼は苦労することなく出世できた *Whether or not it was a good thing*, he succeeded in his career without having to work too hard.

5**こう 項** an **item** /áɪṭəm/ (表などの項目); a **clause** (法律の条項); a **member**(数式の) ▶議題の第2項 *item* 2 on the agenda ‖ 憲法第9条第2項 Article 9, *clause* 2 of the Constitution.

6**こう 香** **incense** /ínsens/ ▶香をたく burn *incense*.

7**こう 綱** 《生物学》a **class**.

8**こう 請う・乞う** **ask** 《for》; **request** +㊐ (要請する) ▶神に許しを請うた I *asked for* God's forgiveness. ‖ 今回の映画は必ず評判を呼ぶと思います. 乞うご期待 This movie is sure to be a hit. *Please be sure not to miss it*. (➤「お見逃しのないように」の意).

9**こう 1**【このように】**like this**; **this way**(こんなふうに) ▶道を聞かれたらこう答えなさい When asked for directions, answer *this way*. ‖ 腕をこう曲げてください Bend your arm *like this*. ‖ こう言っちゃあ何だが, きみはやきもちを焼いてるんだよ You are jealous, *if you ask me*. (➤if you ask me は「言わせてもらえば」の意で, 表現を和らげるために用いる) ‖ 《いらだちなどを表して》いつもこうなんだから There you go again.

2【こんなに】▶こう暑く[寒く]てはかなわないよ *This* hot [cold] weather is too much for me. (➤「こんなに暑い[寒い]天気には我慢できない」の意) ‖ こう雨ばかりだと閉口しますね *This much* rain is too much for anyone. ／We've had nothing but rain and it's just awful.

こう- 好- ▶好天 *good* [*fine*] *weather* ‖ 好青年 *a fine* [*nice*] *young man* ‖ 猛勉強が好結果につながった My intensive studying *bore fruit* [led to *good results*]. (➤bear fruit は「実を結ぶ」) ‖ 今夜の西武・バファローズ戦は好ゲームだった Tonight's Lions-Buffaloes ball game was *a good* [*close*] *game*. (➤close /kloʊs/ は「際どい, 接近した」).

-こう -港 ▶長崎港に入港する enter *the port of Nagasaki* [*Nagasaki Port*].

1**ごう 郷** ▶ ことわざ 郷に入っては郷に従え When in Rome, do as the Romans do.

2**ごう 業** **karma**(➤仏教用語) ▶己の業を担う carry [bear] one's own *burden of karma* [*sin*].

▶《慣用表現》業を煮やして彼女は退室してしまった She *became unable to stand it any more* and left the room. (➤「それ以上耐えられなくなって」の意).

3**ごう 号** a **pseudonym** /sjúːdənɪm/ (筆名, 雅号).

1**-ごう -号** **the number**(番号); an **issue**(雑誌の) ▶雑誌『科学』の5月号 *the May number* [*issue*] of "Science" magazine ‖ メイフラワー号でアメリカへ渡る sail over to America on *the Mayflower* ‖ 博士号を取る obtain *a doctor's degree* ‖ 鈴木は今シーズン第10号のホームランを打った Suzuki hit his *10th* season home run.

2**-ごう -合** ▶米を3合炊く cook 3 *cups* of rice.

▶富士山の6合目 the sixth *station* of Mt. Fuji.

こうあつ 高圧 **high pressure**(圧力); **high voltage**(電圧) ▶高圧電流 *high-voltage* current.

▶高圧的な社長 a *high-handed* president.

‖高圧線 a high-voltage [-tension] (power) line.

こうあつざい 降圧剤 an **anti-hypertensive drug**.

1**こうあん 考案する** **devise** +㊐, **think up**, **invent** ▶新しい型の炊飯器を考案する *devise* [*invent*] a new type of rice cooker ‖ このビデオゲームはある会社員が考案したものだ This video game *was thought up* [*was invented*] by an office worker.

2**こうあん 公安** **public safety** [**security**／**peace**]; **law and order**(法と秩序) ▶公安秩序を守る maintain *law and order* ‖公安委員 a public safety [security] commissioner ‖ 公安条例 public safety regulations ‖ 国家公安委員会 National Public Safety Commission.

1**こうい 行為** an **act**, an **action**, a **deed**

> **語法** (1)**act** は1回1回の行為, **action** は一連の行動を指すが, 同義に用いることもある.
> (2)act や action は事の善悪に関係なく用いられるが, **deed** は courageous deed(勇敢な行為)とか noble deed (立派な行為)のように優れた行為について用いることが多い. (3)このほか, **behavior**(人のふるまい, 一般的行動), **conduct**(道徳的観点から見た行動)も可能だが, いずれも不可算名詞で, 1回の行為には用いない.

▶**テロ行為**を未然に防ぐ prevent *acts of terrorism* [*terrorist acts*] ‖親切な**行為**は見ていて気持ちがいい It's good to see a kind *act* [someone *act* kindly]. ‖彼の破廉恥な**行為**にクラスのみんなが迷惑した His shameless *action* disturbed the whole class. ‖自分の**行為**に責任をもつべきだ You should take responsibility for your *actions* [*what you have done*]. ‖きみの**行為**は高校生にふさわしくない Your *behavior* [*conduct*] is not appropriate for a high school student. ‖家庭内**暴力行為**をやめる put an end to domestic *violence*.

> **逆引き熟語 ○○行為**
> **違反行為** violation(s) ／**医療行為** a medical [clinical] procedure, medical treatment ／**詐欺行為** fraud, deceit ／**残虐行為** an act of cruelty ／**慈善行為** a charitable act, an act of charity ／**性行為** a sexual [sex] act ; sexual activity ／**テロ行為** a terrorist act, terrorism ／**犯罪行為** a criminal act ／**反社会的行為** antisocial behavior ／**非紳士的行為** ungentlemanly conduct ／**不正行為** wrongdoing, illicit [unfair] behavior ／**不法行為** an illegal [unlawful] act ／**報復行為** an act of revenge [retaliation] ／**暴力行為** an act of violence

[2]**こうい 好意** **goodwill, good wishes ; kindness** (親切心) **一形 好意的な friendly** (友好的な) ; **favorable** (賛意を表す) ▶この贈り物は彼らの**好意**の表れだ This gift is to express their *goodwill* [*good wishes*]. ‖人の**好意**を無にしてはいけない Do not ignore [Always repay] the *kindness* of others. ‖他人の**好意**に甘えてはいけない You shouldn't take advantage of other people's *kindness* [*goodwill*]. (➤ kindness は実際に親切な行為が行われたことを暗示する).
▶みんなその新人に**好意を示した** Everybody *was friendly to* the newcomer. ‖彼女がぼくに**好意をもって**くれているなんて信じられないよ I can't believe she *has good* [*friendly*] *feelings* toward me. (➤ ... she's fond of me. とすることもできる) ‖あの秘書は上司にひそかに**好意を寄せて**(=好いて)**いる** That secretary secretly *cares for* her boss. ‖日本人の大半は米国を**好意的に見ている** Most Japanese *have a favorable view* of the U.S.

[3]**こうい 厚意** **kindness**
✉ **ロンドン滞在中はいろいろとお世話になりました. ご厚意に深く感謝いたします** Thank you very much for everything you did for me while I was in London. I very much appreciate your *kindness*.

[4]**こうい 校医** a **school doctor** [**physician**].

[5]**こうい 皇位** **the imperial throne** ▶**皇位継承**問題 the issue of *the succession to the imperial throne* ／the *imperial succession* issue.

ごうい 合意 an **agreement** ; **consent** (承諾) ; a **consensus** (総意) **一動 合意する agree** ▶労使はその問題について**合意に達した** Labor and management *reached an agreement* on the issue. ‖**双方合意のうえ**でその夫婦は離婚した The couple divorced *by mutual consent*. ‖首相は国民の**合意**がなければ新税は導入しないと言明した The Prime Minister stated that he would not introduce a new tax without the *consensus* of public opinion.

こういう ▶**こういう**魚は見たことがない I've never seen *this kind of* fish before. ／This is my first time to see a fish *like this*. ‖**こういう**場合英語では何と言ったらいいのでしょうか What should I say in English in *such* a situation ? ‖**こういうこと**はお母さんに相談しなさい This is *the sort of thing* you should talk about with your mother.

こういき 広域 a **wide area**.

こういしつ 更衣室 a **changing room** ; a **locker room** (スポーツ施設のもので, ふつうはシャワー付き).

こういしょう 後遺症 **aftereffects** ▶手術の**後遺症** the *aftereffects* of the operation ‖彼女はいまだに交通事故の**後遺症**に悩まされている She still suffers from the *aftereffects of an injury sustained in a traffic accident*.
▶《比喩的》離婚の**後遺症**で, 今でも男性に話しかけるのに抵抗を感じる I'm still hesitant to speak to men —it's *a lingering effect* of my divorce.

こういつ 後逸 ▶ショートはゴロを**後逸した** The shortstop *let* the grounder *pass*.

こういっつい 好一対 ▶**好一対の夫婦** *a well-matched couple*.

こういってん 紅一点 ▶彼女はこのオフィスでは**紅一点**だ She is *the only girl* [*woman*] in this office.

[1]**こういん 工員** a **factory worker** [**hand**] ▶彼は町工場の**工員**だ He works in a small-scale factory (in a town).

[2]**こういん 行員** a **bank clerk** ; a **teller**(銀行の金銭出納係) (➤ banker は「銀行の経営者」).

[3]**こういん 光陰** ▶ ことわざ **光陰矢のごとし** Time flies (like an arrow). (➤ 矢にたとえるのは日本的で, 英語のことわざでは通例カッコ内はいわない) ／Time passes [goes by] very quickly.

ごういん 強引な **pushy**(押しの強い) ; **high-handed**(高圧的な) ▶彼は**強引すぎる** He is *too pushy* [*aggressive*]. ‖彼の**強引**なやり方をみんな腹立たしく思っている Everybody is angered by his *high-handed* manner [way of doing things]. ‖彼女のやり方は少し**強引すぎる** She is a little *too pushy* [*high-handed*]. ‖子供たちを**強引**に勉強させようとしても無駄だ It is no use trying to *force* [*compel*] children *to* study. ‖私は**強引**にテニス部に入部させられた I *was coerced into* joining the tennis club. (➤ coerce /koʊə́ːrs/ A into B で「A (人)を強制して B をさせる」) ‖拓郎は和美を**強引にくどいた** Takuro *came on strong to* [*with*] Kazumi. (➤ come on strong は「しつこく接する」の意のインフォーマルな言い方) ‖あのセールスマンは売り込み方が**強引**だ That salesman takes a *hard-sell* approach. 《参考》「強引なセールスマン」は hard-selling salesman という.

こうう 降雨 (a) **rainfall**, (a) **rain**
‖**年間降雨量** the annual rainfall. →**降水**.

ごうう 豪雨 a **heavy rain** ; a **torrential downpour**(猛烈な雨) ▶きのうの**豪雨**でその町は大きな被害を受けた The *heavy rain* yesterday did great damage to that town. ‖その**集中豪雨**で村中が水につかった The whole village was flooded by *a local downpour* [*a flash rainstorm*].

こううん 幸運 **good luck, good fortune** **一形 幸運な** **lucky, fortunate** ▶幸運な男 a *lucky* man ‖ 幸運を祈ります I wish you *good luck*. ／*Good luck* to you. ‖ 昔から四つ葉のクローバーは幸運をもたらすと言われている The four-leaf clover has long been regarded as a bringer of *good fortune*.
▶幸運にも当たりくじを引いた I *was* (*very*) *lucky to* draw a winning ticket. ‖ 交通事故にあって幸運にもけがをしなかった *Luckily* [*Fortunately*], I wasn't injured in the traffic accident. ‖ 幸運の女神が我らにほほえんだ *Lady Luck* smiled on us.

こううんき 耕耘機・耕運機 a **cultivator**.

1 **こうえい 光栄** an **honor** /ɑ́ːnəʳ/ (名誉) ; a **privilege** /prívəlɪdʒ/ (格別な栄誉) ▶《交換留学生たちへの挨拶で》皆さんをわが校にお迎えできて光栄です *We are honored* [*are privileged*] to welcome you all to our school. ‖ おいでいただいて光栄です *We're very honored* by your visit. ‖ この会にお招きいただき大変光栄に存じます *It's a* great *honor* for me to be invited to this meeting.
✉ **貴財団の奨学金を頂き, 誠に光栄に存じます** *It is a great honor* [*I feel very honored*] to be awarded a scholarship by your foundation.

2 **こうえい 公営の** **public** ▶公営のスポーツ施設 *public* sports facilities ‖ 私は公営住宅[アパート]に住んでいます I live in *public housing*. ／I live in *a council house* [*flat*]. (➤ 後者は《英》; 公営住宅全体を public housing, その1軒を行政では a unit of public housing と呼ぶこともある).
‖公営ギャンブル publicly [municipally] managed gambling(➤ municipally は市町村の場合).

3 **こうえい 後衛** a **back**(競技の) ; a **fullback** (サッカー・ラグビーなどのフルバック).

こうえき 公益 **public interest**
‖公益事業 public utilities [services] ‖ 公益法人 a public interest corporation.

こうえつ 校閲 ▶原稿を校閲する *read and correct* a manuscript.

1 **こうえん 後援** **support**(支援) ; **sponsorship** (発起人・主催者などになること) **一動 後援する** **support** +㊀, **sponsor** +㊀ ▶横綱白鵬の後援会 *a supporters' association* for Yokozuna Hakuho ‖ 松尾氏の後援会が結成された *A society* was formed *to support* Mr. Matsuo. (➤ 芸能人などの後援会は fan club) ‖ その展覧会は朝日新聞社の後援で開催された The exhibition was held *under the sponsorship* [*auspices*] *of* the Asahi Shimbun. ‖後援者 a sponsor.

2 **こうえん 公園** a **park** ▶山下公園へ散歩に行く go for a walk in Yamashita *Park* (➤ 固有名詞のときはふつう the はつけない) ‖ 知床国立公園 Shiretoko *National Park*.

3 **こうえん 講演** a **lecture**, a **talk**(➤ 後者はインフォーマル) ; a **speech** (公式の演説) **一動 講演する** **lecture** 《on, about》, **give** [**deliver**] **a lecture, make a speech** ▶原子力発電についてご講演願えますか Could we ask you to give *a lecture* [*talk*] on nuclear power generation ? ‖ 首相は日本の将来について長々と講演した The prime minister *made a* long *speech* on the future of Japan. ‖ 集会で講演する *address* a meeting ‖講演会 a lecture meeting ‖ 講演者 a lecturer, a speaker ‖ 講演料 a speaking fee →謝礼.

4 **こうえん 公演** a (**public**) **performance** **一動 公演する** **give a performance** ▶英語劇の公演 the *performance* of an English play ‖ 歌舞伎の海外公演 a kabuki *performance* in foreign countries ‖ ウィーン・フィルは東京と大阪で3回公演の予定である The Vienna Philharmonic is scheduled to give three *performances* in Tokyo and Osaka.

こうおつ 甲乙 ▶両者は甲乙つけ難い *There is hardly any difference* between the two. ‖ 若乃花と栃錦は甲乙つけ難い名横綱だった *It is hard to say which* [*who*] *was the greater* yokozuna, Wakanohana or Tochinishiki.

1 **こうおん 高音** a **high-pitched sound** ; a **high tone** [**note**] (音調) ▶ぼくはどうしても高音が出ない I just can't sing *high notes*.
‖高音部記号《音楽》a treble clef.

2 **こうおん 高温** (a) **high temperature** ▶コーヒー豆を高温でいる roast coffee beans at *a high temperature* ‖ 日本の夏は高温多湿である (The) summer in Japan is *hot and humid* [*is muggy*].

ごうおん 轟音 a **roar**, a **roaring sound** ▶ごう音を立てる make *a roaring sound* ‖ ジェット機がごう音を立てて飛び去った A jet (plane) flew away *with a roar*.

こうおんどうぶつ 恒温動物 a **homeotherm** /hóʊmiəθəːʳm/.

1 **こうか 効果** (an) **effect** ; a **result**(結果) **一形 効果的な** **effective** ▶宣伝の直接的な効果は何もなかった There was no direct *effect* from the advertising. ‖ ジョギングの効果はすぐには現れない You can't expect immediate *results* from jogging. ‖ しょうが紅茶はダイエットに効果てきめんと言う人がいる Some people say ginger tea *has a great effect* on losing weight [*is very effective* in losing weight]. (➤「即座に効果がある」ならば have an immediate effect といえる) ‖ 叱りつけるだけでは子供の教育に大した効果はない. それどころか逆効果になることも多い Scolding children *rarely serves any purpose*. In fact, it often has *the opposite effect* [*is* often *counter productive*]. ‖ 娘の海外留学を思いとどまらせようという彼の説得は効果がなかった His attempt at persuading his daughter to give up studying overseas *had no effect*. ‖ 体重を減らす何か効果的な方法を教えてください Could you tell me an *effective* way to lose weight ? ‖ バックの音楽が舞台効果を盛り上げた The background music added to the *stage effect*. ‖効果音 sound effects ‖ 音響[視覚]効果 sound [visual] effects.

2 **こうか 校歌** a **school song** ; a **college song**(大学の).

3 **こうか 硬貨** a **coin** ▶100円硬貨2枚 two 100-yen *coins* 《参考》アメリカでは1, 5, 10, 25の硬貨をそれぞれ penny, nickel, dime, quarter と呼ぶ.

4 **こうか 高価な** **expensive** ; **costly** (そのものの価値が高いために) ▶高価な宝石 an *expensive* [*a costly*] jewel ‖ その時計はずいぶん高価だったろう That watch must *have cost a fortune*. ‖《比喩的》彼はその計画を成功させるために離婚という高価な代償を支払わねばならなかった Divorce was the (*high*) *price* he had to pay for the success of that project.

5 **こうか 高架** ‖高架鉄道《米》an elevated railroad, 《英》an overhead railway.

6 **こうか 硬化する** **harden** ; **stiffen**(こわばる) ▶《医者が患者に》あなたは血管がお年のせいで多少硬化していますね In your case, the blood vessels *have hardened* a bit with age. ‖ 修は彼女のぞんざいな物の言い方に態度を硬化させた Osamu *stiffened* his attitude at her rude remarks. ‖動脈硬化 sclerosis /skləróʊsɪs/ of the arteries, arteriosclerosis,

hardening of the arteries.

7**こうか 降下** (a) **descent** 一動 **降下する descend, come down**(飛行機などが；後者はインフォーマル)；**fall, drop**(温度が；後者は「急激に」).

8**こうか 工科 the department of engineering**

‖**工科大学** a college of engineering, an engineering college.

こうが 黄河 the Yellow River, Huang Ho /hwɑ̀ːŋ hóʊ/.

ごうか 豪華な magnificent /mæɡnífɪsənt/ (豪壮な)；**grand** (壮大な)；**gorgeous** (華やかな) ▶**豪華な**宮殿 a *magnificent* [*grand*] palace ‖ **豪華**客船 a *luxury* passenger ship ; a *luxury* liner (定期船) ‖ **豪華な**ホテル a *luxury* [*luxurious* ／《英》*posh* ／*plush*] hotel (➤ともにインフォーマルな言い方)／a *luxury* hotel ‖ **豪華な食事** a *luxurious* [*lavish* ／*fancy*] meal(➤ luxurious は「ぜいたくな」, lavish は「ふんだんにある」, fancy は「高級な」) ‖ 彼女は**豪華に**着飾っていたのでみんなの注目を引いた She was dressed *gorgeously* [dressed *to the nines*], so she caught everyone's eye. (➤ be dressed to the nines は「最高にめかしこんでいる」). ‖ 今晩のテレビ番組は**豪華な顔ぶれだ** Tonight's TV show has a *star-studded* cast. (➤ star-studded は「スター総出演の」) ‖ 今夜は**豪華に**フランス料理といこう *Let's* dine *in grand style* tonight at a French restaurant.

1**こうかい 後悔** (a) **regret, remorse,** (a) **repentance** (➤ regret は一般語. remorse は regret より堅い語で, 後悔の気持ちも強い. repentance は「悔い改め」に相当するキリスト教イメージの語) 一動 **後悔する regret** +目, **feel regret** 《for》, **be sorry** 《for》 (➤ 最後の言い方はややくだけた言い方)；**repent** ▶彼の態度には**後悔している様子**が見られない I can't see any *sign of remorse* in his attitude.

> **【文型】**
> **あること(A)を後悔する**
> **regret** A
> **be sorry for** A ➤ Aは名詞
> **…したことを後悔する**
> **regret doing** ／**regret having** done
> **～であったことを後悔する**
> **regret that** S ＋ V
> **be sorry that** S ＋ V

▶あとで**後悔するぞ** You'll *regret* it later. ‖ きみはいつか自分の言ったことを**後悔する**だろう Some day you will *regret* [*be sorry for*] what you (have) said. ‖ この道を選んだことを決して**後悔しない** I'll *never regret* having chosen this career. ‖ 彼は高校を終えなかったことを**後悔している** He *regrets not* finishing [*not having* finished] high school. ‖ 彼のプロポーズを受け入れなかった**ことを後悔している** I *regret that* I didn't accept his proposal. ／I *regret* not accepting his proposal. ‖ 家族をこんな目にあわせて心底**後悔しています** I'*m* deeply *sorry* [I deeply *regret*] *that* I have put my family through this. (➤ regret は改まった語) ‖ あとで**後悔すること**がないように, この機会を十分に生かすつもりだ I'm going to make full use of this opportunity so that I don't *feel regret* [*have any regrets*] later. ‖ 私は自分のしたことは**後悔していない** I *have no regrets* about [for] what I've done. ／I *have no regrets for* my actions. ▶たばこを吸ってると今に**後悔するぞ** If you smoke now, *you'll pay for it* later. (➤「あとで代償を払うことになるぞ」の意)／Smoking *will catch up with you*. (➤ catch up with は「…に悪い結果をもたらす」の意).

ことわざ **後悔先に立たず** It's too late to be sorry. ／It's no use crying over spilt milk. (➤ cry over spilt milk は文字どおりには「ミルクがこぼれたと言って泣く」；英語のことわざ).

✉ **あなたにひどいことを言ってしまって後悔しています. ごめんなさい** I *feel bad about* having said [I *regret* saying] such a terrible thing to you. I'm really sorry. (➤ 前者のほうがくだけた表現).

2**こうかい 航海** a **voyage**(船旅)；**navigation** (航行) ▶**航海に出る** *go on* [*set out on*] *a voyage* ‖ その豪華客船は大西洋横断の**処女航海**に出た The deluxe liner set out on her *maiden voyage* across the Atlantic. ‖ 私たちは今インド洋を**航海中**です We *are* now *sailing* across the Indian Ocean. ‖ 彼の父は長い間**航海に出た**ままだ His father has been *out at sea* for a long time. ‖ **航海の無事**を祈ります I wish you *a safe voyage*! ／I wish you *bon voyage*! (➤ 後者はやや気取った言い方で bon voyage は /bɑ̀ːn vwaɪɑ́ːʒ/ とフランス語流に発音する).

‖**航海士** a (ship's) mate ‖ **航海術** the art of navigation ‖ **航海日誌** a logbook.

3**こうかい 公開** a **public showing** 一動 **公開する open ... to the public**(私物などを)；**release** +目 (封切る, 公表する) ▶芸術作品の**公開** *a public showing* of works of art (➤ 1語で exhibition ともいう) ‖ 情報を**公開する** *disclose* [*release*] information (➤ disclose は「伏せてあったものを明らかにする」) ‖ 寺の宝物を**一般に公開する** *open* the temple's treasure(s) *to the public* ‖ そのユキヒョウは来週の日曜日に**一般に公開されます** The snow leopard will *be shown to the public* next Sunday. ‖ 京都御所は通常**一般公開されていない** The old Imperial Palace in Kyoto *is not* usually *open to the general public*. ‖ 大学跡地の利用に関する**公開討論会**が来週開かれる *An open forum* on how to use the former site of the college will be held next week. ‖ 私はその記録映画の**公開**を心待ちにしている I am looking forward to the *release* of that documentary (film).

‖**公開講座** an extension course (大学の)；an open class(受講資格に制限のない) ‖**公開捜査** an open criminal investigation ‖**公開ヒアリング** an open hearing ‖**公開放送** public broadcasting.

4**こうかい 更改** ▶契約を**更改する** *renew* a contract.

5**こうかい 公海 international waters, the high seas**(➤ 前者が日常的な言い方).

6**こうかい 紅海 the Red Sea**(アフリカとアラビア半島との間の海).

7**こうかい 黄海 the Yellow Sea, the Huang Hai** /hwɑ̀ːŋhάɪ/.

1**こうがい 郊外 the suburbs, the outskirts**

> **語法** (1) suburbs は in the suburbs of ... の形で用いられることが多いが, ときには Richmond is a suburb of London. (リッチモンドはロンドンの郊外である)のような形で使われることもある. (2) suburbs は都市の中心から近いベッドタウン的なイメージがあるが, outskirts は中心から遠く離れた所という感じを伴う. (3) 郊外 (the suburbs of a city) やそこに住む人々 (the people who live in the suburbs) を suburbia ということがある.

▶その美術館は大阪の**郊外**にある That art museum is in *the suburbs* of Osaka. ‖ おじ夫婦は東京の**郊外**に住んでいる My uncle and his wife live on *the* *outskirts* of Tokyo. ‖ 私はジローさんをパリ郊外に訪ねた I visited Mr. Gireau *in a suburb of Paris* [*in a Paris suburb*]. ‖ 私は以前郊外の住宅地に住んでいた I used to live in a residential area *in the suburbs*. ／I lived in a residential suburb.

2 **こうがい 公害** (environmental) pollution (環境汚染) ▶低[無]公害車を開発する develop *a low-pollution* [*pollution-free* ／ *zero emission*] *car* (➤ -free は「…のない」の意) ‖ 自転車は経済的であるだけでなく, 公害を引き起こすこともない A bicycle is not only economical, but also *pollution-free*. ‖ 政府は公害対策をもっと積極的に推進すべきだ The government should take more aggressive *measures against pollution*. ‖ 有機水銀中毒は公害病に認定されている Organic mercury poisoning has been recognized as *a pollution-caused disease*. ‖ 私たちは騒音公害に悩まされている We are suffering from *noise pollution*. ‖ **公害病認定患者** an officially acknowledged victim of a pollution disease ‖ **公害防止条例** an antipollution ordinance ‖ **公害問題** a pollution problem.

3 **こうがい 口外** ▶彼はうっかり秘密を口外した He inadvertently *let out* his secret. ‖ これは誰にも口外するなよ Don't *tell* anybody *about* it. ／Mum's the word.

4 **こうがい 口蓋** the palate 一形 口蓋の palatal /pǽlətl/.

5 **こうがい 校外** 一形 校外の extramural 一副 校外で outside of school ‖ **校外学習** a field trip ‖ **校外活動** extramural activities.

6 **こうがい 梗概** a synopsis [複 synopses].

7 **こうがい 光害** light pollution.

ごうかい 豪快 ▶石原君はセンターオーバーの豪快な(＝でっかい)ホームランをかっ飛ばした Ishihara blasted a *tremendous* [*towering*] home run into the center stands. ‖ 彼は豪快に笑って「すべて俺に任せとけ！」と言った He laughed *broadly* and said, "Leave it all to me!"

ごうがい 号外 an extra (edition of a newspaper); a single-sheet extra (１枚のもの) ▶号外を出す issue *an extra edition*.

こうかいどう 公会堂 a public hall ▶渋谷公会堂 Shibuya (*Public*) *Hall*.
‖ **音楽公会堂** a music auditorium.

こうかがくスモッグ 光化学スモッグ photochemical smog ▶光化学スモッグ注意報が出ている *A photochemical smog warning* has been issued.

こうかく 降格 (a) demotion 一動 降格する demote ＋目 ▶M氏は失敗が重なって降格された Mr. M *was demoted* because he made one serious mistake after another.

1 **こうがく 高額** a large sum (of money) ▶高額の寄付 a *large* contribution ‖ **高額紙幣** a large denomination bill [《英》 bank note] ‖ **高額所得者** a person with (a) high income.

2 **こうがく 工学** engineering
‖ **工学博士** a doctor of engineering ‖ **工学部** the school [department] of engineering ‖ **遺伝子工学** genetic engineering ‖ **環境工学** environmental engineering ‖ **コンピュータ工学** computer engineering ‖ **システム工学** systems engineering ‖ **生物工学** biotechnology ‖ **電気[機械]工学** electrical [mechanical] engineering ‖ **電子工学** electronics /ɪlèktrɑ́:nɪks/ ‖ **土木工学** civil engineering.

3 **こうがく 光学** optics ‖ **光学機器** an optical instrument ‖ **光学ズームレンズ** an optical zoom (lens) ‖ **光学マウス** an optical mouse.

ごうかく 合格 success in an examination (試験の) 一動 合格する pass ＋目; succeed 《in》 ▶大学入試合格おめでとう Congratulations on your *success in* [*on passing*] the college entrance examination! ‖ 私の合格の知らせに母は大喜びだった My mother was overjoyed when she learned (that) I *passed the examination*. ‖ このオーディションに合格すればあなたを採用します If you *pass* this audition, we will hire you. ‖ そのおもちゃは安全審査に合格しなかった The toy didn't *pass* the safety inspection. ‖ きのう合格者の発表があったが, ぼくの名前はなかった The names of the *successful applicants* were posted yesterday but I could not find my name among them. ‖ きみは合格圏内にいるよ You *have a fair chance of success* [*stand a good chance of succeeding*] in the exam. ‖ 英語は何とか合格点が取れた I somehow managed to get *a passing grade* in English.
✉ **スタンフォード大学合格おめでとう!** Congratulations on your admission [acceptance] to Stanford University! (➤アメリカでは大学入試はなく, いくつかの大学に願書, 内申書などを提出して受け入れられたら「合格」ということになる).
☛ 不合格 (→見出語)

こうがくしん 向学心 desire for learning [to learn] ▶彼らは向学心に燃えている They *are very eager to learn*. ／They *have a strong desire to learn*.

こうがくねん 高学年 the upper grades ▶高学年の生徒たちは遠足で鷹取山に行った *The upper-grade students* went on an outing to Mt. Takatori.

こうかくるい 甲殻類 a crustacean /krʌstéɪʃən/.

こうかくレンズ 広角レンズ a wide-angle lens.

こうかつ 狡猾な sly /slaɪ/, cunning (➤後者は巧妙さを強調するため, 文脈によってはプラスイメージの語になる) ▶こうかつな人 a *sly* person.

1 **こうかん 交換** (an) exchange 一動 (…と)交換する exchange ＋目《for》, swap ＋目《for》(➤後者はくだけた語), trade ＋目《for》(何かを与えて代わりに何かをもらう); replace ＋目 (新しい物と取り替える)
▶金と物との交換 the *exchange* of money for goods (➤「物々交換」は bartering または the exchange of goods for goods) ‖ 手紙[意見／情報]を交換する *exchange* letters [opinions／information] ‖ ときどき会って情報交換をしましょう We should get together and *compare notes* every now and then. ‖ 試合後, 選手たちはジャージを交換した The players *exchanged* their jerseys after the game. ‖ 少年たちは漫画本を交換した The boys *swapped* their comic books. ‖ 少女たちはお互いに不要な衣料品を交換した The girls *traded* [*swapped*] clothes they didn't need (any more).

【文型】
物(A)を物(B)と交換する
exchange [trade／swap] A for B

▶《読者欄で》どなたかスキーと私のオートバイを交換してください Would anybody like to *trade* [*exchange*] a pair of skis *for* my motorbike? (➤ exchange はやや堅い響き) ‖ 彼は記念切手と交換にこの本をくれた He gave me this book *in exchange for* a commemorative stamp. ‖ この腕時計の電池を交換してください Could you please *replace* [*change*] the

battery of this watch?
‖(電話の)**交換手** an operator ‖**交換条件** a bargaining point ‖**交換台** a switchboard ‖**交換レンズ** an interchangeable lens.

2**こうかん 好感** **a good impression** ▶彼女のシックな服装はみんなに**好感**を与えた Her chic clothes *made a good* [*favorable*] *impression on* them all. (➤「心にしっかり刻まれる印象」には make を用いる. give は「間違った印象, 思い込み」に用いることが多い) ‖アメリカに**好感**を抱いている日本人は多い Most Japanese *feel friendly toward* the U.S. ‖人に**好感をもたれる**ような人間になりなさい Try to become the sort of person who *is* (*well*) *liked* by others. ‖弓子さんは**好感のもてる人**だ Yumiko is a *likable* person.
‖**好感度** likability.

3**こうかん 高官** ▶政府の**高官** *a high-ranking* government *official*.

4**こうかん 公館** **a government establishment**
‖**在外公館** a diplomatic establishment abroad.

こうがん 睾丸 **testicles**(➤通例複数形で, 袋の「陰のう」は scrotum /skróʊţəm/ と発音).

ごうかん 強姦 **rape**. →暴行.

こうかんかい 交歓会 a **social gathering**(社交の集まり); 《インフォーマル》a **get-together**.

こうかんしんけい 交感神経 a **sympathetic nerve**
‖**副交感神経** a parasympathetic nerve.

こうがんざい 抗癌剤 an **anticancer** /æ̀nţikǽnsəʳ/ **drug** [**agent**], a **chemo** /kíːmoʊ, kéː-/ **drug** (➤後者は患者が用いる語. chemo だけで集合的にも用いる)
‖**抗がん剤治療** chemotherapy (➤インフォーマルでは chemo と略す).

こうがんむち 厚顔無恥 ▶あの女は**厚顔無恥**も甚だしい What a *shameless* [*brazen*(*-faced*)] woman she is!

1**こうき 好機** a **good opportunity**; a **good chance**(偶然のチャンス) ▶**好機**はめったにやって来ない *A good opportunity* seldom comes around. ‖きみはこの**好機**を逃してはいけない You shouldn't miss this *good opportunity*. / Don't let this *good opportunity* slip through your fingers. (➤slip through one's fingers は文字どおりには「指の間からこぼす」) ‖彼が三振して私たちはまたとない**好機**を逸してしまった We lost our *best chance* to score because he (got) struck out.
ことわざ **好機逸すべからず** Never miss a chance. / Never let an opportunity slip by.

2**こうき 後期** **the latter period**(時代の); **the second semester** /səméstəʳ/ (2学期制の学校の); **the second** [**latter**] **half**(後半) ▶江戸時代**後期** *the latter period* of the Edo era ‖この絵はルノワールの**後期**の傑作だ This is one of the best works of Renoir's *later life*. / This is one of the best of Renoir's *later* works. ‖来月の終わりに**後期の試験**があります We will have *the second semester examinations* at the end of next month.

3**こうき 校旗** a **school flag** ▶**校旗**掲揚 the raising of *the school flag*.

4**こうき 高貴な** **noble** ▶彼女にはどこか**高貴**なところがある There is something *noble* about her. ‖彼は**高貴の出**だ He is *of noble birth*. / He *comes from a noble family*.

5**こうき 綱紀** **discipline** ▶**綱紀**粛正 the enforcement of *official discipline*.

1**こうぎ 抗議** (a) **protest** /próʊtest/ ━動 **抗議する** **protest** /prətést/ +目, **protest** 《against》, **make a protest** 《against》 ▶授業料の値上げに対して学生の間から**抗議の声**が上がった (*Voices of*) *protest* arose among the students against the hike in tuition. ‖雇い主の不当な決定に**抗議する**勇気のある者は1人もいなかった Nobody dared to *protest* [*make a protest*] *against* the employer's unfair decision. ‖彼らは低賃金に**抗議して**ハンストを行った They carried out a hunger strike *to protest* [*in protest against*] their low wages. ‖キャッチャーはアンパイアの判定に**抗議した** The catcher *protested* to the umpire on [about] the call.
‖**抗議集会** a protest meeting [rally] ‖**抗議声明** a statement of protest ‖**抗議デモ** a protest demonstration ‖**抗議文** a letter of protest.

2**こうぎ 講義** a **lecture** ━動 **講義する** **lecture** 《on, about》, **give a lecture** ▶退屈な**講義** a boring *lecture* ‖歴史の**講義** a history *lecture* ‖英語の**集中講義** *an intensive course* in English ‖**講義**を聴く listen to *a lecture* ‖**講義をサボる** *cut class* ‖現代アメリカ美術について**講義する** *give a lecture* on modern American art.
‖**講義要項** the course requirements.

3**こうぎ 広義** ▶パイロット養成所も**広義**では学校だ A pilot training center is also a school *in the broad sense* (*of the term*).

4**こうぎ 厚誼** ▶父生前のご**厚誼**に感謝いたします We'd like to thank you for your *great friendship* with my father (during his lifetime). (➤カッコ内は省略するのがふつう).

ごうぎ 合議 ▶日本の会社ではたいがい重役たちの**合議**で意思決定をする In Japanese companies, decisions are usually made after *consultation with the board members*.
‖**合議制** a collegial [council] system.

こうきあつ 高気圧 a **high** (**atmospheric**) **pressure** ▶**高気圧**が西日本を覆っている *A high atmospheric pressure* [*An atmospheric high*] is covering western Japan.

こうきしん 好奇心 **curiosity** ▶猫は**好奇心**が旺盛だ Cats have a keen sense of *curiosity*. / Cats are very curious. 《参考》Curiosity killed the cat. (好奇心が猫を殺した; 好奇心もほどほどに)ということわざがある ‖いつも**好奇心**が旺盛であれば年を取らない *Curiosity* will keep you young. ‖私たちは**好奇心に駆られて**その洞窟に入ってみた We entered the cave *out of curiosity*. ‖祖父の冒険談は子供たちの**好奇心をそそった** Their grandfather's tale of adventure *aroused* [*piqued*] the children's *curiosity*.

1**こうきゅう 高級な** **high-class** [**-quality**]; **first-class**(一流の); **fashionable**(上流人向きの); **exclusive**(金持ち専用の); **high-end**(最高品質で, その分値も張る); **luxury**(等級が豪華版の) ▶**高級車** a *high-class* car / a *luxury* car ‖**高級**腕時計 a *luxury* [*high-end*] watch (➤時計愛好家向けに限定数作られるものに designer watch がある) ‖**高級なワイン** a *high-quality* [*an expensive*] wine (➤expensive は「高価な」だが,「高級な」というイメージを伴うことが多い) ‖**高級な**雑誌 a *quality* magazine ‖**高級なホテル** a *fashionable* [*a first-class* / *an exclusive*] hotel ‖**高級住宅街** an *exclusive* residential district ‖**高級ブティック** a *high-end* boutique(➤higher-end ということもある) ‖彼女はいつも**高級品**を身に着けている She always wears *expensive* [*upscale*] *clothes* (*and accessories*).
▶その学者の話は**高級すぎて**私にはわからなかった What

that scholar said *was over my head*. (➤ over ~'s head は「難しすぎて～には理解できない」の意).

2こうきゅう 高給 a high [large] salary ▶彼を高給で雇う employ him at *a high salary* ‖ 彼は高給取りだ He *receives* [*gets*] *a high salary*. ／He *is highly paid*.

3こうきゅう 硬球 a hard ball.

4こうきゅう 恒久の permanent ▶恒久平和を願う hope for *permanent* peace.

5こうきゅう 公休 a day off authorized by a company [an organization] ▶忌引はふつう公休扱いになる A day or days you take in mourning for your relative is [are] usually *treated as a day* [*days*] *off authorized by your company*.

6こうきゅう 後宮 a seraglio /sərǽljoʊ/.

ごうきゅう 号泣する cry bitterly, wail.

こうきゅうび 公休日 a legal [public] holiday, 《英また》a bank holiday (公式の休日) ; a regular holiday (商店などの定休日).

こうきょ 皇居 the Imperial Palace
‖皇居前広場 the Imperial Palace Plaza.

1こうきょう 公共の public ▶公共の利益 the *public* good ‖ 公共の福祉のために働く work for *public welfare* [*the welfare of the public*] ‖ 公共交通機関を利用する take [use] *public transportation*.
‖公共事業 public works ; a public enterprise (➤ 後者は「公共企業体」の意にもなる) ‖ 公共施設 public facilities, a public institution ‖ 公共放送 public broadcasting ‖ 公共料金 public utility charges [rates].

2こうきょう 交響 ▶マーラーの交響曲第9番 Mahler's *Symphony* No. 9 ‖交響楽団 a symphony orchestra ‖ 交響詩 a symphonic poem.

3こうきょう 好況 prosperity ▶好況の続く業種 a *prosperous* [*thriving*] *business* ‖ コンピュータ業界は好況を呈している The computer industry *is thriving* [*flourishing*].

1こうぎょう 工業 (an) industry /índəstri/ 一形 工業の industrial /ɪndʌ́striəl/ ▶日本の自動車工業 Japan's *automobile industry* ‖ 工業化した国 an *industrialized* nation [country] ‖ 東南アジア諸国の工業化は目覚ましい The *industrialization* of Southeast Asian countries has been remarkable.
‖工業高校 a technical [an engineering] high school ‖ 工業高等専門学校 a college of technology ‖ 工業国 an industrial nation [country] ‖ 工業生産 industrial production ‖ 工業製品 industrial products ‖ 工業大学 a technical university, an institute of technology 《参考》technical college には「工業[実業]専修学校」といった響きがある ‖ 工業団地 an industrial park [《英》estate] ‖ 工業地帯 an industrial area [district] ‖ 工業デザイン industrial design ‖ 工業都市 an industrial city ‖ 工業用水 water for industrial use ‖ 日本工業規格 Japanese Industrial Standards《略 JIS》.

2こうぎょう 鉱業 the mining industry
‖鉱業所 a mining station.

3こうぎょう 興行 (a) performance, a show ▶彼の劇団はニューヨークで初の興行を行った His theatrical troupe gave its first public *performance* in New York.

こうきょういく 公教育 public education.

1こうきん 公金 public money ▶公金を横領する embezzle *public money*.

2こうきん 抗菌の antibacterial ▶抗菌グッズ *antibacterial* products ‖ 抗菌剤 an antibacterial [antimicrobial] agent.

3こうきん 拘禁 restraint ; detention (留置) 一動 拘禁する restrain +目 ; detain +目 ▶酔っぱらいを拘禁する *restrain* a drunken person.

ごうきん 合金 an alloy /ǽlɔɪ/.

こうぐ 工具 a tool (職人用の) ; an implement /ímplɪmənt/ (主に農業用の) ‖工具店 a machine-parts supplier ‖ 機械工具 a machine tool.

こうくう 航空 aviation ▶航空機は通常定められた航空路を飛ぶことになっている *Airplanes* normally fly on designated *flight paths* [*air routes*]. ‖ アメリカでは航空網が非常に発達している *Air transport* [*transportation*] in the United States is well developed. ‖ 小包を航空便で送る send a package (*by*) *airmail*.
‖航空会社 an airline company ‖ 航空券 an airline ticket ‖ 航空自衛隊 the Air Self-Defense Force ‖ 航空写真 an aerial photograph ‖ 航空書簡 an aerogram(me) /éərəgræm/ ‖ 航空地図 an aeronautical chart ‖ 航空母艦 an aircraft carrier ‖ 航空料金 [運賃] an airfare.

こうぐう 厚遇 ▶その医師は村人たちから厚遇を受けた The doctor *was treated hospitably* by [*received hospitable treatment* from] the villagers.

1こうけい 光景 a sight ; a scene (景色) ▶美しい光景 a beautiful *scene* ‖ 日本人観光客が集団で街を歩く姿は世界の至る所で見かける光景である You will often see Japanese tourists walking in groups in all parts of the world. ／Japanese tourist groups are now a familiar *sight* in all parts of the world.

2こうけい 口径 a caliber /kǽləbəʳ/ ▶45口径のピストル a .45-*caliber* revolver (➤forty-five caliberと読む).

3こうけい 後景 the background.

こうげい 工芸 industrial arts ‖工芸家 a craft [handicraft] artist, an industrial artist ‖ 工芸品 a crafted product (個々の) ; craftwork (➤ 総称) ‖ 手工芸品 a handicraft ‖ 伝統工芸 traditional crafts ‖ 美術工芸 art(s) and craft(s).

ごうけい 合計 a sum (簡単な計算の結果) ; a total (数・量が大きく, さらに完全な総計) 一動 合計する add [sum] up ▶値段を合計する *add* [*sum*] *up* the prices ‖ 計算器を使って合計を出しなさい *Figure out the sum* with [on] your calculator. ／*Add* [*Sum*] *up the total* using your calculator. ‖ 合計350名の乗客がそのジェット機に乗っていた *A total of* three hundred and fifty passengers were on board the jet. ‖ 私は合計(＝みんなで)300種類の切手を集めた I have collected three hundred different stamps *in all*. ‖ 対話 (店で)「合計でおいくらですか」「58ドルです」"How much is it *altogether* [*in all*]?" "Fifty-eight dollars." (➤ 問いの文は How much does the bill come to? や What's the total bill? も可) ‖ 請求書の合計は1万5000円だった The bill *amounted to* 15,000 yen.

こうけいき 好景気 prosperity ; a boom (にわか景気) ▶この好景気が続いてくれればいいのだが I hope this *prosperity* will last. ‖ 中国は好景気に沸いている China's *economy is booming*.

こうけいしゃ 後継者 a successor ▶後継者を育てる groom *a successor* ‖ 彼は社長のただひとりの後継者だ He is the only *successor* to the president. (➤ of でなく, to が来ることに注意) ‖ 伝統工芸は後継者不足だ There are few (young) *people who carry on* the traditional crafts.

こうげき 攻撃 **1【攻めること】** (an) **attack**; (an) **offense** (防御に対する; 堅い語) **一動 攻撃する attack** +目, **make an attack** ▶彼らは夜陰に乗じて敵を**攻撃した** They *made an attack on* the enemy under cover of night. ‖ミツバチの巣はスズメバチの**攻撃を受けた** The beehive *was attacked* by a swarm of wasps. ‖**攻撃は最善の防御なり** *Attack* [*Offense*] is the best defense. (➤英語のことわざ) ‖相手側に**総攻撃**をかける launch [make] an *all-out attack* on the opposition (➤ all-out は「全力を出しての」の意).

2【非難すること】 **criticism**; (an) **attack** **一動 攻撃する criticize** +目 ▶日本の輸入規制は外国の**攻撃**の的になった Japan's import controls became a target of *criticism* [*attack*] by other nations. ‖**個人攻撃**はしないことにしよう Let's not have any *personal attacks*. 《参考》有名人に対する誹謗(ひぼう)中傷の個人攻撃を character accusation (いわれなき人格非難), または character assassination (人格の暗殺行為)と呼ぶ. ‖私は彼女の**攻撃的な**態度が我慢できない I can't stand her *aggressive* [*pushy*] attitude.

3【スポーツ】 (an) **offense**, an **offensive** ▶**攻撃**が私の弱点だ *Offense* is my weak point. ‖ 7回の表, ヤクルトの**攻撃**です The Swallows *are at bat* in the top of the seventh inning. ‖現在, オリックスが**攻撃中**だ The BlueWave *are* now *hitting*. ‖中日の5回の**攻撃**はトップバッターから始まった The Dragons started their fifth inning *offensive* with the first batter in their lineup.

こうけつ 高潔な noble ▶人格高潔な男性 a man *of noble character* [*of great moral stature*] (➤後者の moral stature は「道徳的に到達した高み」のこと) ‖**高潔な人** a person of *integrity* (➤ honesty がうそをつかず真実を語る「正直」に対して, integrity は高い道義心に基づいた「言行一致」を指す) ／ a person of *high principle* (➤ principle は「行いの規範」).

ごうけつ 豪傑 a **brave man** (勇者); an **outstanding man** (並外れた男性) ▶**豪傑笑いをする** *roar with laughter* ‖嵐の中この海峡を泳ぎ渡ったとは大した**豪傑**だ It *took guts* (for him) to swim across the strait in the storm. (➤ guts は「肝っ玉, 根性」).

こうけつあつ 高血圧 high blood pressure, hypertension (➤後者は医学用語) ▶彼は**高血圧**だ He has *high blood pressure*. ／He suffers from *high blood pressure*.

1**こうけん 貢献** (a) **contribution** **一動 貢献する contribute** /kəntríbju:t/ 《to》 ▶地域社会に(大いに)**貢献する** *contribute* (tremendously) *to* one's community ‖T 氏は科学の進歩に**大きな貢献をした** Mr. T *made a great contribution to* the progress of science. ‖彼はチームの優勝に**大きく貢献した** (＝重要な役割を果たした) He *played an important part* [*role*] in the team's winning the championship.

2**こうけん 後見 guardianship.** →後見人.

3**こうけん 効験** ▶この稲荷(いなり)さんは**効験あらたか**という People say that if you pray to this inari god, *your wishes are sure to be granted*.

1**こうげん 高原 highlands**; **heights** (高地) ▶那須**高原** the Nasu *Highlands* ‖軽井沢の涼しい**高原**で夏を過ごす spend the summer in the cool *heights* of Karuizawa.

2**こうげん 公言する declare** 《that》 ▶社長は会社を日本一にすると**公言した** Our president *declared that* he is going to make the company the biggest in Japan.

3**こうげん 抗原** 《医学》 an **antigen.**

ごうけん 合憲の constitutional ▶日本では自衛隊が**合憲か否か**が時々議論になる Whether or not it is *constitutional* for Japan to keep its Self-Defense Forces sometimes becomes a subject of controversy.

こうげんがく 考現学 the study of modern phenomena.

こうけんにん 後見人 a **guardian** ▶私の**後見人**はおじです My uncle is my *guardian*.

‖**後見人制度** a guardian system ‖**被後見人** a ward.

こうげんびょう 膠原病 a **connective tissue disease** (結合組織病; 俗に collagen disease ともいう).

1**こうご 口語** **(the) spoken language** (話しことば; 書きことば(written language)に対するもの); **colloquialism** /kəlóukwiəlìzəm/ (くだけた話しことば); a **colloquial expression** (日常的なくだけた個々の表現) ▶**口語英語** *spoken English* ‖スペイン語の日常的な**口語表現**を使えるようになりたい I want to learn how to use everyday *colloquial expressions* of Spanish.

2**こうご 交互に alternately** /ɔ́:ltəˈnətli/ ▶パネラーは通訳と**交互に**話した The panelists and interpreters spoke *alternately*. ‖土手には桜と松の木が**交互に** (＝互い違いに) 植えられていた Cherry trees and pine trees were planted *alternately* along the riverbank. ‖きょうは電話が頻繁に掛かってきて妻と私が**交互に**電話に出た We had a great number of calls today and my wife and I *took turns* (at) answering the phone. ‖**男女交互に**並びなさい Line up *boy-girl boy-girl*. (➤英米の小学校などで生徒を交互に整列させるときによく用いる表現).

ごうご 豪語 ▶自分のチームが日本一強いと彼は**豪語している** He *boasts* [*brags*] that his team is the strongest in Japan.

1**こうこう 高校** 《米》 a **(senior) high school**, 《英》 an **upper secondary school** ▶**高校**2 [3] 年生 a second-[third-] year student in *senior high school* ／《米また》 an eleventh-[a twelfth-] grader (→学年) ‖**高校生になる** *enter* (*senior*) *high school* (➤ become は用いない).

▶私は**高校生**です I am *a* (*senior*) *high school student*. ‖彼女は**高校時代**バスケットボールに熱中した She was deeply involved in basketball *when she was a high school student*. ‖もうすぐ**高校野球**が始まるね *The National Senior High School Baseball Tournament* will start soon.

✉ **私は桜高校の2年生です. 私たちの高校は海の見える高台にあります** I am a second-year student at Sakura *Senior High School*. Our school is situated on the top of a hill with a (full) view of the ocean.

2**こうこう 孝行** ⚠**「孝行(する)」にぴったり当てはまる英語表現はない.** →親孝行 ▶**孝行息子** *a faithful son* ／*a good son* (➤前者のほうが日本語に近い) ‖彼は親に**孝行する**どころか, 放蕩(ほうとう)息子だった Far from *being thoughtful of his parents*, he was a prodigal son. (➤ be thoughtful of は「…を思いやる」) ‖たまには**女房孝行**しろよ You should *be good to your wife* once in a while.

ことわざ **孝行をしたいときには親はなし** By the time you want to be good to [take care of] your parents, they're gone. ／Children always think of their parents when it's too late. (➤ 後者は「子供はいつも手遅れになってから親のことを思う」の意).

3**こうこう 後攻** ▶《野球》うちのチームが**後攻**だ Our team *fields first*. (➤ 英語では「先に守備をする」という).

4**こうこう 口腔** **the oral cavity** (➤「口腔(こう)外科」は oral surgery).

5**こうこう 航行** **sailing** (船の) ; **navigation** (船・飛行機の) **一動 航行する** **sail, navigate** ▶太平洋を**航行する** *navigate* [*sail across*] the Pacific ‖ 船が**航行**できる川 a *navigable* river.

6**こうこう 皓々・皎々** ▶私たちはこうこうたる月光の下で砂漠を横切った We crossed the desert under the *bright* moonlight.

7**こうこう 煌々** **brightly, brilliantly** ▶満月がこうこうと輝いていた A full moon was shining *brilliantly*.

こうごう 皇后 **the Empress**
‖**皇后陛下** Her Majesty the Empress.

ごうごう 轟々 ▶貨物列車がごうごうと鉄橋を通過した A freight train passed the iron bridge *with a roar*.

こうごうしい 神々しい ▶**神々しい**光景 an *awe-inspiring* scene.

こうごうせい 光合成《生 化 学》 **photosynthesis** /fòʊṭoʊsínθəsɪs/ ▶植物は**光合成**で二酸化炭素を吸収する Plants absorb carbon dioxide through *photosynthesis*.

こうこうや 好々爺 a **good-natured old man.**

こうこがく 考古学 **archaeology** /àːrkiάːlədʒi/ ▶**考古学上の**発見 an *archaeological* discovery ‖ **考古学的に**貴重な発見 an *archaeologically* important discovery ‖**考古学者** an archaeologist.

1**こうこく 広告** an **advertisement** /ædvərtáɪzmənt ‖ ədvə́ːtɪs-/, 《インフォーマル》an **ad** ; **advertising** (広告活動) **一動 広告する** **advertise** /ǽdvərtaɪz/ (+📖) ▶誇大**広告** an exaggerated *advertisement* ／*hype* ‖ 新聞**広告**を見て物を買う buy things from newspaper *advertisements* ‖ 新製品の**広告をする** *advertise* a new product ‖ ラジオとテレビを使った**広告**キャンペーンを開始する begin a radio and television *advertising* campaign ‖ わが社はきのう新聞に新刊本の**広告を出した** We *put* [*ran*] *an ad for* our new book(s) in yesterday's newspapers. ‖ 新聞に**広告**のちらしが毎日たくさん入ってくる We receive many *advertising flyers* with the newspaper every day. ‖ 私は今の仕事を新聞の**求人広告欄**で見つけた I found my present job in *the help-wanted column* of the newspaper.
‖**広告業界** the advertising industry [world], 《主に英》《インフォーマル》adland (➤ 無冠詞) ‖ **広告代理店** an advertising agency ‖ **広告板** a billboard.

2**こうこく 公国** a **principality.**

3**こうこく 抗告する** **appeal to a higher court.**

こうこつ 恍惚 ▶その美しい音楽を聞いてこうこつとして天にも昇る思いがした The beautiful music *entranced* me, making me feel as if I were in (seventh) heaven. (➤ seventh heaven は「神と天使のいる最高天」が原義) ‖ 10代の少女たちはそのロックバンドの歌と踊りに**こうこつ状態**だった The teenage girls *were enraptured by* the singing and dancing of the rock band.

ごうコン 合コン a **group date (to seek a girlfriend or a boyfriend)** (➤「コン」は company に由来する和製語) ▶新体操部の人たちと**合コン**しよう Let's arrange *a group date* with some members of the rhythmic gymnastics club.

1**こうさ 考査** an **examination,** a **test.** →試験.

2**こうさ 交差する** **cross ; intersect** (線・面などが相交わる) ▶胸のところで腕を**交差させ**なさい *Cross* your arms in front of your chest. ‖ その地点で鉄道と道路が**交差している** At that point, the street *intersects* the railroad.
☛ 交差点 (→見出語)

3**こうさ 黄砂** **yellow dust** [**sand**] ▶きょう中国から**黄砂**が飛来した *Yellow dust* [*sand*] was borne by the wind from China to Japan today.

1**こうざ 講座** a **course** (講義) ; a **program** (番組) ▶当カルチャーセンターでは数多くの**講座**を設けております We offer a lot of *courses* [*programs*] at our culture center. ‖ 私はラジオの**英会話講座**を聴いて英語を勉強した I learned English by listening to *English conversation programs* on the radio.

2**こうざ 口座** an **account** ▶ F 銀行に**口座**を設ける open *an account* with F Bank ‖ 私の**口座**に20万円振り込んでください Will you transfer 200,000 yen to my *account* ? ‖ この用紙にあなたの**口座番号**を記入してください Please fill in your *account number* on this form. ‖ **銀行口座**から 3 万円を引き出す withdraw thirty thousand yen from one's *bank account* ‖ 公共料金の支払いは銀行の**自動口座振替**が一般的だ Utility bills are generally *paid by automatic bank transfer*. (➤ 欧米では ... are paid by auto bill pay [by direct debit] (on a monthly basis) という言い方が一般的.《英》では are paid by standing order ともいう).
‖**当座預金口座**《米》a checking account,《英》a current account ‖ **普通預金口座**《米》a savings account,《英》a deposit account.

1**こうさい 交際** **association** **一動 交際する** **go (out) with** (➤ out があれば男女の初期[長期]の交際を連想させ, out がなければ男女が結婚を前提として交際することを連想させる) ; **see** (未婚者・既婚者を問わず,「異性と頻繁に会う」の意) ; **associate with** (好ましくない人と付き合う)
▶《男女交際》ぼくと**交際して**くれますか Will you *go out with* me ? ‖ さゆりとは去年から**交際しています** I'*ve been going* (*out*) *with* Sayuri since last year. ／Sayuri and I *have been going together* since last year. (➤ go together は主語が複数のとき) ／I've *been dating* Sayuri since last year. ‖ 当時は女子は男子と自由に**交際する**ことが許されなかった In those days girls were not allowed to *go out with* boys freely. ‖ 父に淳とはもう**交際しない**ようにと言われた My father told me not to *see* Jun anymore.
▶《一般の交際》私どもはああいう人たちとは**交際しておりません** We *don't associate with* people like that. ‖ サマーズさんのご一家と**交際**を始めてもう10年になる It's been ten years since we *became friends* [*became acquainted*] *with* the Summers. ‖ 父は**交際範囲**が広い My father has a wide *range of connections*. ‖ 母はなかなかの**交際家**だ My mother is *a* very *sociable person*. ／My mother is *a good mixer*. ‖**交際費** social expenses (一般の ; 通例複数形) ; an expense account (会社の).

2**こうさい 公債** a **public bond** (➤「国債」は national [government] bond,「地方債」は municipal bond,「市債」は city bond).

3**こうさい 虹彩**《解剖学》an **iris.**

1**こうざい 功罪** **merits and demerits** (長所と短所 ; この

ように対比して用いた場合，後者の語は /díːmerɪts/ とアクセントが移動する）▶私たちは死刑の**功罪**を議論した We discussed the *merits and demerits* [*advantages and disadvantages* / *pros and cons*] of capital punishment.

2**こうざい 鋼材** steel（鋼鉄）.

1**こうさく 工作** **1**【作ること】handicraft（手仕事）；《米》(wood) shop,《英》woodwork（授業の）▶きょう**工作**で本箱を作った I made a bookstand in *wood shop* [in *a shop class*] today.
‖**工作機械** a machine tool.
2【働きかけ】maneuvering /mənúːvərɪŋ/, manipulating ▶陰で**工作する** *maneuver* behind the scenes ‖ 彼は**裏工作**をして当選した He *manipulated things* [*events*] to win the election.
‖**工作員** a secret agent.

2**こうさく 耕作** cultivation；farm work（農作業）一動 **耕作する** cultivate ＋目, farm ＋目 ▶この土地は**耕作**に適していない This piece of land is not suited for *cultivation*. / This patch of land is not arable.（➤ arable /ǽrəbəl/ は「耕作に適した」）.

3**こうさく 交錯** a mixture（混じり合ったもの）一動 **交錯する** mix；intermingle《with》（➤後者は受け身形で用いることが多い）▶悲しみと怒りの**交錯** *a mixture* of grief and anger ‖ 彼女の話には真実と虚構とが**交錯していた** Fact and fiction *were intermingled* through her story.

1**こうさつ 絞殺** strangulation 一動 **絞殺する** strangle ＋目；choke ... to death（窒息させて殺す）▶**少女絞殺事件** the *strangulation* of a young girl ‖ その男は少女を素手で**絞殺した** He *strangled* a girl [*choked* a girl *to death*] with his bare hands.

2**こうさつ 考察** consideration；study（研究）一動 **考察する** consider ＋目, study ＋目 ▶いじめの問題は多角的に**考察する**必要がある It is necessary to *consider* the problem of bullying from various angles.

こうさてん 交差点 a crossing, an intersection（➤前者は「横断歩道」の意でも用いる；後者はやや堅い語）▶**交差点**を渡る cross *an intersection* ‖ 交通量の多い**交差点**を突っ切る drive through a busy *intersection* ‖ 次の**交差点**を右折してください Turn right at the next *intersection* [*junction*].
‖**スクランブル交差点** a pedestrian scramble (crosswalk), a diagonal [six-way] crossing.

1**こうさん 公算** (a) probability（高い確率）；a chance（可能性）▶わがチームが勝つ**公算が大きい** *There is a high probability* that our team will win.（➤前に high, low などの形容詞がつくときは a をつける）/ (The) *chances are* (that) we're going to win.（➤インフォーマルな言い方；the は省略することが多い）.

2**こうさん 降参** ▶きみの質問には答えられない．**降参だ**（＝諦める）I can't answer your question. *I give up.* ‖ いいかげんに**降参しろ**！ Say [Cry] uncle！ →降伏.

1**こうざん 高山** a high mountain ▶**高山病**にかかる get *altitude* [*mountain*] *sickness*.
‖**高山植物** an alpine /ǽlpaɪn/ plant.

2**こうざん 鉱山** a mine ▶その**鉱山**は去年閉山した That *mine* was closed last year.
‖**鉱山労働者** a miner, a mine worker.

こうさんぶつ 鉱産物 a mineral product.

1**こうし 講師** **1**【講演者】a lecturer, a speaker ▶司会者が**講師**を聴衆に紹介した The emcee introduced the *lecturer* [*speaker*] to the audience.
2【大学などの】a lecturer；《米》an instructor（助教の下位）；a teacher（先生）▶五十嵐さんは M 大学の**講師**だ Mr. Igarashi is *a lecturer* at M University. ‖ 彼は D 大学のフランス語の**非常勤講師**だ He is *a part-time lecturer* in French at D University. / He teaches French as *a part-time lecturer* at D University. ‖ 英会話の**講師** an English conversation *teacher*.
‖**専任講師** →専任.

2**こうし 公私** ▶あの方には**公私にわたって**お世話になっております I am indebted to him *both in public and private matters*. ‖ 公費で温泉へ行くなんて**公私混同**も甚だしい It is outrageous to *mix (up) public and private matters* to the extent of going to a hot spring resort at public expense. ‖ **公私混同しない**でよ Don't *mix public and private* [*personal*] *matters*. / Please leave your private life at home.

3**こうし 行使する** use ＋目；exercise ＋目（権利などを）▶武力を**行使する** *use* force / *resort to* arms（➤ resort to は「…に頼る」）‖ 職権を**行使する** *exercise* one's authority ‖ 労働組合は**実力行使に出た** The labor union *moved into action*.

4**こうし 格子** a lattice；a grating（鉄の）
‖**格子じま** a check(ed) pattern ‖ **格子戸** a lattice door ‖ **格子窓** a lattice window.

5**こうし 公使** a minister ‖**公使館** a legation.

6**こうし 子牛** a calf /kæf/；veal（子牛の肉）▶**子牛のカツ**を注文する order *a veal cutlet*.

7**こうし 孔子** Confucius /kənfjúːʃəs/（➤『論語』は the Analects of Confucius,「儒教」は Confucianism）.

8**こうし 皇嗣** an imperial heir；a crown prince.

1**こうじ 工事** construction 一動 **工事する** construct；build（建造する）▶その高層ビルは目下**工事中**だ The skyscraper *is* now *under construction*. ‖ そのトンネル**工事**は20年かかった It took twenty years to *build* the tunnel. ‖ **工事現場**に近づかないでください Don't go near *the construction site*. ‖ 500メートル先で**道路工事**が行われています *Road construction* [*repair*] *work* is in progress five hundred meters ahead.（➤ repair work は「補修工事」の場合）‖《掲示》**工事中** Workers Ahead / Construction Ahead.（●かつては Men Working / Men at Work などと表示されることが多かったが，最近は訳例のような性差のない言い方がふつう）.

逆引き熟語 ○○工事
外装工事 exterior work / **解体工事** demolition work / **ガス工事** gas fitting (work) / **下水工事** sewer construction / **建設[建築]工事** construction work, building operations / **公共工事** public works / **手抜き工事** slipshod work, shoddy construction / **電気工事** electrical work / **道路工事** road construction (work), road work, road repair(ing) (work) / **土木工事** civil [public] engineering (work) / **内装工事** interior finishing, carpentry work

2**こうじ 公示** a public announcement [notice], an official notice 一動 **公示する** announce publicly [officially] ▶きょう総選挙が**公示された** The general election *was officially announced* today.
‖**公示価格** the declared value.

3**こうじ 小路** an alley；a narrow street（狭い道）▶あの**小路**を入った所に行きつけの飲み屋がある There's a little bar that I often go to down that *alley*.
‖**袋小路** a blind alley.

[4]**こうじ 麹** *koji*, malted /mɔ́:ltɪd/ rice (米こうじ) (➤「麦こうじ」は malted barley,「豆こうじ」は malted soybean) ‖**麹菌** *koji* mold.

ごうしがいしゃ 合資会社 《米》a joint-stock company, 《英》a limited partnership.

[1]**こうしき 公式** 1【数学などの】a formula ▶数学の公式 a mathematical *formula* ‖ 円周を表す公式 the *formula* for the circumference of a circle.
2【正式】一形 公式の official (公の); formal (改まった) ▶公式記録 an *official* record ‖ オリンピックの公式スポンサー *official* sponsors of the Olympic Games ‖ 公式のパーティー a *formal* party ‖ ウガンダ大統領が日本を公式に訪問された The President of Uganda paid an *official* visit to Japan. ‖ プロ野球の公式戦は4月に始まる The *regular season* of professional baseball starts in April. / The *pennant race* starts in April.
☛ 非公式 (→見出語)

[2]**こうしき 硬式** 《解説》(1)野球やテニスで硬式と軟式を区別するのは日本独特. 英米では baseball, tennis といえば常に硬式である. (2)両者を区別する必要がある場合は軟式のほうを説明的にいう. →軟式.

こうしせい 高姿勢 ▶フランス代表団はその会議で終始高姿勢だった The French delegation *took a high-handed attitude* throughout the meeting.

こうしつ 皇室 the Imperial Family [Household] (➤ the Royal Family という人もいる).

こうじつ 口実 an excuse /ɪkskjú:s/ (言い訳); a pretext (偽りの理由) ▶もっともらしい口実 a plausible *excuse* ‖ 忘年会を欠席したいけどうまい口実が見つからない I don't want to attend the year-end party, but I can't think up a good *excuse*. ‖ おなかが痛いのを口実にして音楽の授業をサボった I *used* my stomachache *as an excuse* to cut music class. ‖ 彼女はあれこれと口実を考えては会議を欠席した She absented herself from the meeting *on some pretext or other*.

こうして ▶こまはこうして(＝こういうふうに)回すのです You spin a top *like this*. ‖ こうして2人はめでたく結ばれ, 幸せに暮らしました *Thus* the two married happily, and lived happily ever after.

[1]**こうしゃ 校舎** a school building; a schoolhouse (主に田舎の小規模な) ▶木造校舎 a wooden *schoolhouse*.

[2]**こうしゃ 後者** the latter /lǽt̬əʳ/ ▶ターナーとコンスタブルは19世紀イギリスの代表的画家で, 後者はイギリスの自然を多く描いている Turner and Constable are representative painters of nineteenth century Britain. *The latter* painted a large number of English landscapes.

[3]**こうしゃ 公社** a public [government] corporation ▶公社を民営化する privatize *a public* [*government*] *corporation*.
‖**公社債** a public and corporate bond.

-ごうしゃ -号車 ▶お客様のお席は5号車です Your seat is in *car number five*. ‖ この列車の1, 2, 10号車は喫煙車です *Cars number* one, two and ten of this train are for smokers.

[1]**こうしゃく 公爵** a duke (イギリスの); a prince (イギリス以外の) ‖**公爵夫人** a duchess /dʌ́tʃɪs/ (イギリスの); a princess (イギリス以外の).

[2]**こうしゃく 侯爵** a marquis /mɑ́:ʳkwɪs/ (➤イギリスの侯爵は marquess とつづる)
‖**侯爵夫人** a marchioness /mɑ́:ʳʃənəs/ (イギリスの); a marquise /mɑ:ʳkí:z/ (イギリス以外の).

[3]**こうしゃく 講釈** a lecture (お説教) 一動 講釈する lecture 《on, about》 ▶彼は講釈が好きだ He likes *lecturing*.

[1]**こうしゅ 好守** slick fielding.

[2]**こうしゅ 攻守** offense and defense.

[1]**こうしゅう 公衆** the public ▶公園はいつも公衆のためにきれいにしておかなければならない We should always keep parks clean for the benefit of *the public*. ‖ 立ち小便は公衆道徳に反する Urinating outdoors is an offense against *public morality* [*decency*].
‖**公衆衛生** public health [hygiene] ‖**公衆電話** a public telephone, a pay phone ‖**公衆便所** a public lavatory [toilet], 《英 また》a (public) convenience ‖**公衆浴場** a public bath.

[2]**こうしゅう 講習** a course (連続的に行う); a class (クラス) ▶パソコンの講習を受ける take *a special course* [attend *a class*] in using personal computers ‖ 彼はダイビングの講習に通っている He is taking *a course* in scuba diving. / He is taking diving *lessons*. ‖ 私は夏期講習を受けるつもりだ I am going to attend *summer school* [*a summer course*].

[3]**こうしゅう 口臭** bad breath, halitosis /hæ̀lɪtóʊsɪs/ (➤後者は医学用語) ▶きみ, 口臭があるね Your *breath smells*. ‖ この歯磨きは口臭を消すのによい This toothpaste helps eliminate *bad breath*.

こうしゅけい 絞首刑 (death by) hanging 《参考》「絞首台」は gallows, gibbet という. ▶その男は絞首刑に処せられた That man was put to *death by hanging*. / That man was hanged.

[1]**こうじゅつ 口述** dictation (ことばを書き取らせること) 一動 口述する dictate /díkteɪt/ ＋目 ▶会長は秘書に返書を口述筆記させた The chairman *dictated* a reply letter to his secretary.
‖**口述試験** an oral (examination).

[2]**こうじゅつ 後述する** state [say / mention / describe] below [later] ▶後述のとおり *as stated below* [*later*].

こうじょ 控除 a deduction 一動 控除する deduct 《from》 ▶医療費の控除を受ける *have* medical expenses *deducted*. ‖**医療費控除** a deduction for medical expenses ‖**基礎控除** a basic deduction ‖**社会保険料控除** a deduction for social insurance premium ‖**所得控除** tax deductions and allowances ‖**扶養[配偶者]控除** a deduction for dependents [one's spouse].

[1]**こうしょう 交渉** 1【話し合うこと】negotiation(s) 一動 交渉する negotiate /nɪgóʊʃieɪt/; bargain (値切る, 掛け合う) ▶英語で交渉する *negotiate* in English ‖ X社の代表と直接に交渉する *negotiate* face to face with a representative of X Company ‖ 組合は会社側と賃上げ交渉に入った The union entered into [started] *negotiations* with the company over the wage increase. ‖ 両国の外交交渉は不調に終わった *Diplomatic negotiations* between the two countries ended in failure. ‖ 家主と交渉して何とか家賃をまけてもらった I *negotiated* [*bargained*] with the landlord [landlady] and managed to get him [her] to lower the rent. ‖ その件は先方と交渉中なので, もうしばらくお待ちください The matter is still *under negotiation* with the other party, so please wait a bit longer. ‖**団体交渉** collective bargaining.
2【交際】▶お隣とは交渉がありません I'*ve nothing to do with* the people next door.
‖**性(的)交渉** sexual relations (関係); (sexual) intercourse (性交).

2**こうしょう 校章** a **school badge.**

3**こうしょう 高尚な** **refined**（洗練された）; **deep**（考え方や感じ方が深い）; **lofty**（高遠な）▶チェロを弾くのはとても高尚な趣味だ Playing the cello is a quite *refined* hobby. ‖ 彼の言うことは高尚すぎてついていけない What he says is too *deep* for me to follow.

4**こうしょう 口承** ▶親から子へと口承されてきた民話 folk tales that have *been passed down orally* from parent to child.
‖**口承文学** oral literature.

5**こうしょう 公称** ▶その会社は年商10億円と公称している The company has *officially* [*publicly*] *announced* that its annual sales came to a billion yen.

1**こうじょう 工場** a **factory**, a **plant**（製造・加工の; 後者は大規模な）; a **mill**（製紙・製鋼・紡績などの）▶製紙工場 a paper *mill* ‖ 自動車工場 a car *plant* [*factory*] ／an auto (mobile) *plant* [*factory*] ‖ 工場で生産された家屋 a *manufactured* home ‖ 彼は工場で働いている He works in *a factory*. ／He's a *factory* worker.
‖**工場長** a factory [plant] manager.

2**こうじょう 向上** **improvement** 一動 **向上する** **improve** ▶最近彼のフランス語は著しく向上した Recently his French *has shown* remarkable *improvement*. ／ He has recently *made* remarkable *progress* in French. ‖ その国の生活水準は近年どんどん向上している The standard of living of that country has been *going up* quickly in recent years. ‖ 彼女は向上心が強い She has a strong *desire to improve* [*better*] *herself*. (➤ この better は「より良くする」の意の動詞).

ごうじょう 強情な **stubborn** /stʌ́bəʳn/（生まれつき頑固な）; **obstinate** /ɑ́:bstɪnət/（自分の意志・目的にこだわる）▶あの子は強情すぎるので将来が心配だ He is such a *stubborn* child that I am afraid for his future. ‖ そんなに強情を張るんじゃないよ Don't *be* so *obstinate*. ‖ この強情っ張りめ！ You *bullhead*!

こうじょうせん 甲状腺《解剖学》**the thyroid** /θáɪrɔɪd/ **gland.**

こうしょうにん 公証人 a **notary public.**
‖**公証(人)役場** a notary office.

こうしょきょうふしょう 高所恐怖症 a **fear of heights**, **acrophobia** (➤ 後者は医学用語) ▶彼は異常な高所恐怖症だ He has an abnormal *fear of heights*.

1**こうしょく 好色** ▶好色な男 a *lustful* [*lecherous*] man ‖**好色文学** pornographic literature, pornography, erotica.

2**こうしょく 公職** **public office** ▶公職に就く enter [take] *public office* ‖ 公職を退く retire from *public office* ‖ 公職を追われる be driven from *public office* ‖ 公職に就いている人 an *official* ／ an *officer* (➤ 前者は高級官僚, スポーツ審判員, 駅員など, 後者は警官, 将校, 会社役員などを指す).
‖**公職選挙法** the Public Office Election Law.

1**こうじる 高じる** ▶彼女は心配が高じてノイローゼになってしまった She *worried so much* that she had a nervous breakdown. ‖ 彼は趣味が高じてプロの民謡歌手になった He *became so interested* in *min-yo* (Japanese folk songs) that he actually became a professional *min-yo* singer.

2**こうじる 講じる** ▶市は水不足に対して緊急対策を講じた The municipal government *took emergency measures* to deal with the water shortage. ‖ 音声学を講じる（＝講義する）*lecture* on phonetics.

1**こうしん 行進** a **march** 一動 **行進する** **march** ▶日本選手団は厳かに行進して入場した The Japanese athletic delegation *marched in solemnly*. ‖**行進曲** a march ‖ **結婚行進曲** a wedding march.

2**こうしん 後進** **the younger generation**（若い世代）; a **junior**（若い人）▶今後はコーチとして後進の指導に当たるつもりです I'm going to work as a coach for *the younger generation*. ‖ 彼は後進のために職を退いた He resigned his post to make way for *younger employees*. (➤ younger employee は「(自分より)若い社員［従業員］, 後輩」の意). ‖ 宇宙開発の分野では日本はもう後進国ではない Japan *is* no longer *backward* [*far behind*] in the field of space research and development.

3**こうしん 更新** **renewal** /rɪnjú:əl/ 一動 **更新する** **renew** +⑪ ▶運転免許証の更新 the *renewal* of one's driver's license ‖ 運転免許更新講習 a driver's license *renewal* course ‖ 契約を更新する *renew* a contract ‖ パソコンのデータを更新する *update* data on a personal computer (➤ update は「…の内容を最新のものにする」) ‖ ブログを更新する *update* a blog ‖ 100メートル競走の世界記録を更新する *renew* [*break*] the world record for the 100-meter dash ／set a new world record for the 100-meter dash.

4**こうしん 交信** **communication**（通信）; **contact**（連絡）一動 **交信する** **communicate**《with》, **contact** +⑪ ▶私たちは宇宙飛行士たちと交信した We *communicated with* the astronauts. ‖ ハム仲間と交信する *contact* a ham radio friend.

5**こうしん 口唇** **(the) lips** (➤ 上下あるので通例複数形で用いる) ‖**口唇ヘルペス** oral herpes; a cold sore (一般語).

6**こうしん 亢進・昂進** **(a) rise**; **(an) acceleration.**

こうじん 公人 a **public official**（地位の高い公務員, 官僚）; an **office holder**（公務員, 役人）.

こうしんじょ 興信所 a **(private) detective agency**（探偵調査をする）; a **credit bureau** [**agency**]（信用調査をする）.

こうじんぶつ 好人物 a **nice** [**good**] **person**, a **good-natured person** (➤ 後者は特に「気立てのよい人」) ▶彼は好人物なのでみんなに好かれている Everybody loves him for his *good nature*.

こうしんりょう 香辛料 **(a) spice** ▶香辛料の効いた料理 a *spicy* dish.

こうず 構図 **composition** ▶構図のよい写真 a *well-composed* picture ‖ この絵の構図は整っている This painting has a good *composition*.

1**こうすい 香水** **(a) perfume** /pə́:ʳfju:m/ ▶甘い花の香りのする香水 *a perfume* with a sweet floral scent ‖ 私は香水をつけたことがない I have never *used* [*worn*] *perfume*. ‖ 彼女がぼくの横を通ったとき, ぷんと香水が匂った A whiff [hint] of *perfume* came to me as she passed nearby.

2**こうすい 降水** **(a) precipitation** ▶東京の午前中の降水確率は40％です There is a 40% *chance of rain* in Tokyo in the morning.
‖**降水量** (a) precipitation.

3**こうすい 硬水** **hard water.**

こうずい 洪水 a **flood** /flʌd/; a **deluge** /délju:dʒ/（大洪水）; a **flash flood**（鉄砲水）▶連日の雨で多摩川に洪水が起きた The long spell of rainy weather caused *a flood* in the Tama River. ‖ 洪水は次第に引いた The *flood* gradually subsided.
▶《比喩的》メールの洪水が起きる receive [have] a

こ

flood of emails ／ be［get］*flooded* with emails ‖ 都内の道路はいつも車の洪水だ The streets in Tokyo *are always packed with cars*. ‖ 現代人は情報の洪水に押し流されそうになっている People of today are inundated with *information*.

1**こうせい 構成** **structure**（構造）; **composition**（組み立て）▶文の構成 the *structure* of a sentence ‖ 彼女のレポートは構成がよくできている Her report *has excellent composition*［*is well-composed*］. ‖ 委員会は７人で構成されている The committee *is composed of*［*is made up of* ／ *consists of*］seven members. ‖ 対話「お宅の家族構成は？」「妻と猫５匹です」"*How many are there in your family?*" "My wife and five cats."

2**こうせい 厚生** **welfare** ▶その会館は子供たちの厚生のために建てられた The hall was built for the *welfare* of children. ‖ **厚生施設** welfare facilities ‖ **厚生年金** an employees' pension (plan) ‖ **厚生労働省** the Ministry of Health, Labour and Welfare ‖ **厚生労働大臣** the Minister of Health, Labour and Welfare.

3**こうせい 公正な** **just**; **fair**（えこひいきのない）▶公正な判決 a *just* decision ‖ 公正な取り引き *fair*［*square*］dealings（➤後者は「公明正大な」に近い）‖ 公正な裁判を望みます I want (to get) *a fair trial*.
‖ **公正証書** a notarial［notary］deed ‖ **公正取引委員会** the Fair Trade Commission.

4**こうせい 更生する** **reform oneself**（立ち直る）▶その非行少年はすっかり更生して立派なボクサーになった The delinquent boy completely *reformed himself* and became a great boxer.
‖ **更生保護(事業)** offenders' rehabilitation.

5**こうせい 後世** ▶その政治家は後世に名を残すだろう That statesman will *go down in history*. ‖ 兼好は『徒然(つれづれ)草』の作者として後世に名を残した Kenko *made his name immortal*［*immortalized himself*］as the writer of "Essays in Idleness."（➤「彼の名前を不朽のものにした」の意）‖ これは後世に残る本だ This is a book that will *be remembered forever*. ‖ 後世の人はこの事実を何と思うであろうか What will *future generations* think about this?

6**こうせい 恒星** a (**fixed**) **star**.

7**こうせい 校正** **proofreading** 一動 **校正する** **proofread** +目 ▶学生新聞の校正をする *proofread* the student newspaper. ‖ **校正者** a proofreader ‖ **校正刷り** a (printer's) proof, a galley (proof).

8**こうせい 攻勢** an **offensive** ▶軍事［外交］攻勢 a military［diplomatic］*offensive*.

1**ごうせい 合成** **synthesis** /sínθəsɪs/ 一動 **合成する** **synthesize** +目 ▶シンセサイザーはいろいろな音を合成することができる Synthesizers can *synthesize* various sounds.
‖ **合成画像** a composite image ‖ **合成写真** a composite photograph ‖ **合成樹脂** synthetic resin; plastic(s) ‖ **合成繊維** synthetic fiber ‖ **合成洗剤** (a) (synthetic) detergent /dɪtə́ːrdʒənt/.

2**ごうせい 豪勢な** **gorgeous, grand**（邸宅などが）; **luxurious** /lʌɡʒʊ́əriəs/（暮らしなどが）▶その俳優は豪勢な暮らしをしている The actor is enjoying a *luxurious* life. ‖ 朝食からローストビーフとは豪勢だね You're *living high* (*on the hog*) to be having roast beef for breakfast.

こうせいしんやく 向精神薬 a **psychotropic** /sàɪkətroʊpɪk/ **medicine**.

こうせいせき 好成績 **good grades**（良い評点）; **good results**（良い成果）▶健は好成績で高校を卒業した Ken graduated from high school with *good grades*. ‖ 兄はマラソンで好成績をあげた My brother *did well* in the marathon.

こうせいねん 好青年 a **fine**［**nice**］**young man** ▶三郎はなかなかの好青年だ Saburo is quite *a nice young man*.

こうせいのう 高性能 ▶高性能エンジン［ロボット］a *high-performance* engine［robot］‖ 高性能ガソリン *high-powered* gasoline ‖ 高性能カメラ a *high-efficiency* camera.

こうせいぶっしつ 抗生物質 an **antibiotic** /æ̀ntibaɪɑ́ːtɪk/ ▶抗生物質を処方する prescribe *antibiotics* ‖ 抗生物質に対して抵抗力をもつスーパーウイルスが出現した Superbugs that resist *antibiotics* have appeared.

1**こうせき 功績** **service**（貢献）; an **achievement**（業績）; **credit**（栄誉）▶彼は物理学の発展に大きな功績を残した He rendered *distinguished service* toward progress in physics. ‖ 彼は陶芸に関する功績が認められて，文化勲章を授与された He was awarded an Order of Cultural Merit for his *achievements* in pottery. ‖ 彼はその機械の発明に対して功績を認められた He got *credit* for inventing the machine.

2**こうせき 鉱石** **ore** ▶ウラン鉱石 uranium *ore*.

1**こうせつ 降雪** (a) **snowfall** ▶昨夜大量の降雪があった There was *a* heavy *snowfall* last night. ‖ この地域の年間平均降雪量は80センチだ The average annual *snowfall* in this area is 80 centimeters.

2**こうせつ 公設の** **public**
‖ **公設市場** a public market.

ごうせつ 豪雪 (a) **heavy snowfall** ▶新潟県の高田は豪雪で知られる Takada in Niigata Prefecture is famous for its *heavy snowfall(s)*.
‖ **豪雪地帯** an area of heavy snowfall.

1**こうせん 光線** a **ray**［a **beam**］**of light**; **light**（光）
‖ **光線銃** a ray gun ‖ **可視光線** a visible ray ‖ **レーザー光線** a laser beam.

2**こうせん 交戦** ▶スペインは当時イングランドと交戦中だった At that time, Spain was *at war with* England.

3**こうせん 公選** (an) **election by popular vote** ▶党総裁は公選で決めるべきだ The party president should be elected *by popular vote*.

4**こうせん 鉱泉** a **mineral spring, a spa**.

5**こうせん 高専** a **college of technology, a technical college** ▶国立豊田高専 Toyota National *College of Technology*.

6**こうせん 抗戦する** **resist** +目 ▶村人たちは侵略者たちに抗戦した The villagers *resisted* the invaders.

こうぜん 公然の **open**（あからさまな）; **public**（公の）一副 **公然と** **openly**; **in public**（人前で）▶そのカップルは電車の中で公然と抱き合っていた The couple were embracing *openly* on the train. ‖ 彼は政府の政策を公然と非難した He denounced the government's policy *in public*. ‖ A君がBさんと同せいしているのは公然の秘密だ It's *an open secret* that Mr. A is living with Miss B.

こうせんてき 好戦的な **warlike** ▶好戦的な国民 a *warlike* nation ‖ 好戦的な態度 a *belligerent* /bəlídʒərənt/ attitude.

1**こうそ 控訴** an **appeal** 一動 **控訴する** **appeal**（+目）▶控訴を退ける［取り下げる］dismiss［withdraw］*an appeal* ‖ 地裁の判決を高裁に控訴する *appeal* a district court ruling to a high court.
‖ **控訴人** an appellant ‖ **被控訴人** an appellee.

2**こうそ 公訴** **prosecution** ▶公訴を提起する institute *prosecution*.

3**こうそ 酵素** an **enzyme** /énzaɪm/ ▶消化酵素 a digestive *enzyme*.

1**こうそう 構想** a **plan**(案); a **plot**(小説や劇の粗筋) ▶政権構想 an administrative *plan* [*scheme*](➤ scheme は主に《英》で「公の機関による大規模な実施計画や事業」) ‖ 校長先生はスポーツ施設拡大の構想を語った The principal told us about his *plan* for expanding the sport facilities. ‖ その作家は目下新しい長編小説の構想を練っている That novelist is now working out the *theme and detailed plot* of a new novel. (➤「テーマと詳細な筋」の意).

2**こうそう 抗争** a **dispute**; a **feud** /fjuːd/ (長期にわたる); **strife** ▶暴力団どうしの血で血を洗う抗争 *a blood feud* between the two gangs.
‖内部抗争 internal strife ‖ 派閥抗争 factional strife [infighting].

3**こうそう 高層の** **high-rise**
‖高層住宅[マンション] a high-rise apartment building [condominium] ‖ 高層ビル a high-rise building, a high-rise, a skyscraper.

こうぞう 構造 (a) **structure**(全体の構成); (a) **construction**(組み立ててできた物) ▶文章の構造 the *structure* of a sentence ‖ その車のコンパクトな構造 the car's compact *construction* ‖ 最近のホテルはほとんどが耐震構造になっている Most hotels today are *earthquake-proof*. ‖ 数学者はふつうの人間とは頭の構造が違うようだ Mathematicians seem to have a different *mental makeup* [*mindset*] from ordinary people.

ごうそう 豪壮な **magnificent** ▶ベルサイユ宮殿は豪壮だ Versailles Palace *is magnificent*.

1**こうそく 校則** **school regulations** [**rules**](➤ 後者はややくだけた言い方. the school code と呼ぶこともある) ▶校則に違反する violate [disobey] the *school regulations*(➤ 後者は「従わない」の意) ‖ ピアスをするのは校則違反だ Wearing pierced earrings is *against the school regulations*. ‖ 私たちの学校の校則は厳しすぎる The *regulations* of our school are too strict.

2**こうそく 拘束** (a) **restraint** ━動 **拘束する** **restrain** +目; **restrict** +目 (制限・条件をつける) ▶身体の拘束 physical *restraint(s)* ‖ 他人の自由を拘束する *restrict* the freedom of other people ‖ 彼女は警察に身柄を拘束された She *was kept in custody* [*detained*] by the police. (➤ custody は「身柄の拘束／保護」, detain は「勾留する」).

3**こうそく 高速** **high speed** ▶車は高速で走った The car traveled [moved] *at high speed*. ‖ 我々は今東名高速(道路)を時速100キロで走っている We are now driving on *the Tomei Expressway* at (the speed of) 100 km per hour.
‖高速鉄道 high-speed rail, a high-speed railway, 《米また》 superfast rail ‖ 高速道路 《米》 an expressway, a freeway, 《英》 a motorway 《参考》 highway は都市間を結ぶ主要道路(→ハイ-).
ディベートルーム「高速道路はもっと増やすべきだ」

1**こうぞく 皇族** **the Imperial** [**Royal**] **Family**; **a member of the Imperial Family**(個人).

2**こうぞく 後続の** **following**(次へ続く); **succeeding**(続いて起こる) ▶先頭のランナーと後続グループとの間隔が広がっている The distance between the front runner and the *following* runners is increasing. ‖ 1台の車が急に止まったために, 後続の2台がそれに追突した One car made a sudden stop and the two cars *behind it* piled up in a crash.

3**こうぞく 航続** ‖航続距離 a cruising radius; a flying range (特に, 航空機の) ‖ 航続時間 the duration of a flight [cruise] (➤ 前者は飛行機, 後者は船の).

ごうぞく 豪族 a **powerful family**; a **clan**(一門).

こうそつ 高卒 ▶父も母も高卒です Both my father and mother are *high school graduates*. ‖ 高卒の資格を得る receive *a high school diploma*.

こうだ 好打 a **good** [**sharp**] **hit**
‖好打者 a good hitter, a sharp hitter.

1**こうたい 交代・交替** a **shift**(交代勤務) ━動 **交代する** **replace** +目, **take one's place** (入れ代わる); **take turns**(代わる代わる行う) ▶社長が石井氏から佐野氏に交代した Mr. Sano *replaced* [*succeeded*] Mr. Ishii as president. (➤ succeed は「跡を継ぐ」) ‖ 《車の運転で》ちょっと交代してくれないか Will you *take over* for a while? ‖ 彼らは交代制で働いている They work (*in*) *shifts*. ‖ パートタイマーは交代制だ Part-time workers are on *the shift system*. ‖ この工場は8時間3交代制で操業している This factory operates in *three 8-hour shifts*.

【文型】
交代で…する
take turns doing

▶私たち2人は交代で皿を洗う The two of us *take turns doing* the dishes [do the dishes *by turns*]. ‖ 対話「交代で運転しないか?」「いいとも. ぼくが先に運転するから2時間たったら交代してくれ」"Why don't we *take turns driving* (the car)?" "Okay, I'll drive [go] first. But *take my place* [*take the wheel*] after a couple of hours." (➤ take the wheel は「運転を代わる」の意).
▶《野球》ピッチャーが交代した The pitcher *was replaced*. ‖ 山本は林と交代した(＝救援してもらった) Yamamoto *was relieved by* Hayashi.

2**こうたい 後退する** **retreat**(軍隊などが退却する); **step back, back up** (後ろへ下がる; 後者は車などについても用いる) ▶もう少し後退してください Please *step back* [*back up*] a bit further. ‖ フランス軍はドイツ国境から20マイル後退した(＝退却した) The French troops *retreated* 20 miles from the German border.
▶その国は景気の後退に悩んでいる That country is suffering from *a recession*. ‖ 父は額が後退している My father *has a receding hairline*. (➤ a receding hairline は「後退してゆく生え際」の意).

3**こうたい 抗体** 《生理学》 an **antibody** ‖抗体検査 an antibody test.

こうだい 広大な **vast**(目の届かないほど広がった); **extensive**(広範囲の) ▶広大な国 a *vast* country ‖ 広大無辺の宇宙 the *vast and boundless* [*infinite*] universe ‖ 広大な砂漠がその土地の大部分を占めていた An *extensive* desert covered much of the land.

こうたいごう 皇太后 **the empress dowager**(皇帝・天皇の未亡人); **the Queen Mother**(現国王の生母).

こうたいし 皇太子 **the Crown Prince** ▶皇太子殿下はその式典で英語で演説をされた *His Imperial Highness the Crown Prince* delivered a speech in English at the ceremony. ‖皇太子妃 the Crown Princess 《参考》イギリスの皇太子は the Prince of Wales, 皇太子妃は the Princess of Wales という.

こうたく 光沢 **luster**(反射による光の輝き); **gloss**(表面の, 特に髪の); (a) **sheen**(布・髪・鉱物などの); **polish**

（磨いて出した）▶美しい光沢のある真珠 a pearl with a beautiful *luster* ‖ 光沢のある紙 *glossy* paper ‖ サテンの光沢 the *sheen* of satin ‖ 絹には美しい光沢がある Silk has a lovely *gloss*. ‖ 光沢のある美しい髪は女性の憧れです Having beautiful, *lustrous* [*glossy*] hair is a woman's dream. ／Having hair with a lovely *sheen* [*luster*] is every woman's dream.

ごうだつ 強奪する rob《A of B》（AからBを強奪する）▶彼らは銀行から１億円を強奪した They *robbed* the bank *of* a hundred million yen. ‖ ABC銀行で（現金）強奪事件が発生した *A robbery* occurred at ABC Bank.（➤「銀行強盗事件」は a bank robbery）.

こうだん 公団 ‖**公団住宅** an apartment building [《英》a block of flats] constructed by the Housing Corporation.

こうだんし 好男子 a **handsome (young) man**（美男子）; a **fine young man**（性格のよい若者）.

1**こうち 拘置 detention 一動 拘置する detain** +㊐ ▶彼は窃盗の容疑で拘置された The police *detained* him on a charge of theft.

‖**拘置所** a detention center ; a jail /dʒeɪl/,《英また》a gaol（留置所）.

2**こうち 耕地 cultivated land ; arable land, a field**（農耕地）.

3**こうち 高地 highlands ; a height**（➤しばしば複数形）; a **plateau** /plætóʊ/

‖**高地トレーニング** high-altitude training.

こうちく 構築 building, construction（➤後者には組織的で大型という含みがある）; **creation**（新しいもの・独創的なものの）**一動 構築する build** +㊐, **construct** +㊐, **create** +㊐ ▶理論を構築する *construct* [*build*] a theory ‖ 現代口語日本語のコーパスを構築する *build* [*create*] a corpus of modern spoken Japanese.

こうちゃ 紅茶 (black) tea（➤緑茶（green tea）と区別する必要があるときにのみ black をつける）▶紅茶を入れる make *tea* ‖ イギリス人はふつう紅茶にミルクを入れて飲む British people usually drink *tea* with milk (in it).

こうちゃく 膠着 (a) **deadlock, stalemate**（こう着状態；前者は「行き詰まり」「デッドロック」，後者はチェスが起源で「手詰まり」）; a **standstill**（停止）▶試合は０対０のままこう着状態に入っています The game is *at a deadlock* [*is stalemated*] with a score of 0 to 0.

こうちゅう 甲虫《虫》a **beetle**.

1**こうちょう 校長**《米》a **principal**,《英》a **headteacher**《解説》(1)《英》では男女を区別してそれぞれを headmaster, headmistress ということもあるが，今ではやや古風な言い方．(2) 副校長または教頭は《米》で vice [assistant] principal,《英》で deputy headteacher という．(3) 街の英語学校や日本語学校の校長は director という．‖**校長室** the principal's [headteacher's] office ‖ **民間人校長** a principal from the private sector.

2**こうちょう 好調** ▶好調な選手 a player *in good form* [*condition*] ‖ ジャイアンツは今のところ好調だ The Giants are *doing well* for now. ‖ この店は本の売れ行きが好調だ Books *sell well* at this bookstore. ‖《野球》松田は好調だが，明石は不調だ Matsuda is *in good form* but Akashi is in a slump now. ‖ 対話「新しい事業はうまくいってますか」「まずまず好調です」"How is your new business?" "*Pretty good*." ‖ 対話「稀勢の里関，今場所の好調の理由は何でしょう？」「よく稽古して，よく眠っていることですかね」"What do you think is the reason you're *doing well* in this tournament, Mr. Kisenosato?" "Probably it's because I practice hard and sleep well."

3**こうちょう 紅潮** ▶少年の頬は寒さで紅潮していた The boy's cheeks *were flushed* with the cold. ‖ 花嫁は幸せで顔を紅潮させていた The bride *glowed* with happiness.（➤ glow は「顔が輝く」）.

こうちょうかい 公聴会 a public hearing ▶所得税減税についての公聴会が開かれた *A public hearing* concerning income tax cuts was held.

こうちょく 硬直する become stiff ▶硬直した経済 *rigid* economy（➤ rigid には「曲げると折れる，無理をすると壊れる」という含みがある）‖ 恐怖で体が硬直した My body *became stiff* with terror.

▶彼の考え方は硬直している His way of thinking *lacks flexibility*.（➤ flexibility は「柔軟性」）.

‖**死後硬直**《医学》rigor mortis /rìgəʳmɔ́ːʳṭəs/.

こうつう 交通

traffic（人・乗り物の行き来）; **transportation**（輸送）▶東京のこの辺は特に交通が激しい (The) *traffic* is heavy, especially in this part of Tokyo. ‖ 日曜日の交通量はさほど多くない (The) *traffic* on Sunday is fairly light. ／There is not much *traffic* on Sunday. ‖ 新しい橋の開通で交通の混雑はだいぶ緩和されるだろう The opening of the new bridge will do much to help relieve (the) *traffic congestion* [(the) *traffic jams*].（➤ jam はインフォーマルな語）‖ 交通の便がよくなればもっと多くの人が郊外に住むようになるだろう If *public transportation* is improved, more people will live in the suburbs. ‖ 今度の家は交通の便がよくない My new house *is inconveniently located*.（➤「不便な所に位置している」の意）. ‖ 交通違反で１万2000円の罰金を取られた I was fined 12,000 yen for *breaking traffic regulations*. ／I got a traffic ticket for 12,000 yen.（➤ traffic ticket は「（交通）反則切符」）‖ 日本は公共交通機関がよく発達している *Public transportation facilities* are well developed in Japan. ‖ けさ友人が交通事故に遭った This morning a friend of mine had [met with] *a traffic accident*.（➤インフォーマルでは auto accident, car accident のようにもいう）.

‖**交通安全週間** Traffic Safety Week ‖ **交通遺児** children orphaned in traffic accidents ‖ **交通指導員** a crossing supervisor ‖ **交通渋滞** traffic congestion, a traffic tie-up（全般的に混み合って進みにくい状態）: a traffic jam（つかえて進めない状況；限定された地域の小規模なもの）‖ **交通情報**（ラジオの）a traffic report ‖ **交通信号** a traffic light [signal] ‖ **交通整理** traffic control ‖ **交通費** commutation expenses（通勤・通学など定期的な）; a commutation allowance（勤務先が定期的に出す）; transportation expenses（電車・列車・タクシー・バスなどを使った場合の）; travel(ing) expenses（出張旅費）‖ **交通標識** a traffic sign ‖ **交通法規** traffic regulations ‖ **交通網** a transportation network, a network of roads.

ごうつくばり 強[業]突く張りの stubborn /stʌ́bəʳn/ **and selfish**（強情で我を張る）; **greedy**（欲ばりの）▶この強突く張りめ You're really *greedy* [*stubborn and selfish*]!

こうつごう 好都合な convenient /kənvíːniənt/《for》▶会議をあすに延ばしてくれると好都合なんだが It would *be convenient for* me if you could put off the meeting till tomorrow. ‖ 対話「出かける用事があるから心斎橋で会おう」「それは好都合だ（わ）」"I'm going out on an errand now. So how about meeting at Shinsaibashi ?" "*That's very convenient for me.*/*That'll be perfect.*"(➤後者は女性が多く用いる).

1**こうてい 校庭** **a schoolyard** ; **a (school) playground**(主に小学校の) ; **a campus**(大学の構内) ▶広い[狭い]校庭 a large [small] *schoolyard*.

2**こうてい 肯定** ▶彼はカンニングの事実を肯定した(＝認めた) He *admitted* that he had cheated on the exam. ‖ 万引きしたのかと聞かれたが彼は肯定も否定もしなかった When (he was) asked if he had shoplifted, he *answered neither yes nor no*. ‖ 物事は肯定的に考えたほうがよい It's better (for you) to *take a positive view* of things. ‖ この肯定文を否定文に書き換えなさい Rewrite this *affirmative sentence* in (to) the negative. ‖**自己肯定感** self-affirmation ; self-esteem(自尊心).

3**こうてい 皇帝** **an emperor**
‖**ローマ皇帝** a Roman emperor.

4**こうてい 工程** **a process** ▶作業 [製造] 工程 *a* production [manufacturing] *process* ‖ 彼はワイン作りの工程を説明してくれた He explained to us the *process* of producing wine.

5**こうてい 公定の** **official**
‖**公定価格** an official price ‖ **公定歩合** an official discount rate, an official bank rate.

6**こうてい 行程** **a journey** (旅 程) ; **an itinerary** /aɪtínəreri/ (日程) ; **(a) distance**(道のり) ▶我々は10日間の行程で北海道を車で周遊する予定です We plan to make a 10-day *journey* by car around Hokkaido. ‖**行程表** an itinerary.

こうでい 拘泥 ▶過去に拘泥するのは感心しない It's not good to *be obsessed* with the past.

ごうてい 豪邸 **a luxurious** /lʌɡʒʊ́əriəs/ **mansion** ; **a palatial** /pəléɪʃəl/ **residence** (宮殿のような住まい) ▶北川さんは時価10億円の豪邸に住んでいる Mr. Kitagawa lives in *a* (*luxurious*) *mansion* worth a billion yen at current (market) prices. (➤ mansion は「大邸宅」の意で, 日本語の「マンション」とは異なる). ⇀マンション.

こうていえき 口蹄疫 **a foot** [**hoof**] **and mouth disease**《略 FMD》.

1**こうてき 公的な** **public** ; **official** (公務の) ▶公的な事業 a *public* enterprise.
‖**公的支援** public assistance ‖ **公的資金** public money ‖ **公的年金** a public pension ‖ **公的年金制度** a public pension plan ‖ **公的年金保険** public pension insurance.

2**こうてき 好適な** **suitable** ▶この土地の気候は米作に好適だ The climate here *is suitable* for growing rice. ‖ このクッキーは贈り物に好適です These cookies will make a *fine* gift. (➤「いい贈り物になる」の意).

こうてきしゅ 好敵手 **a (good) match**, one's (**closest**／**nearest**) **rival** ▶彼は私の好敵手だった He was *a good match* for me.

1**こうてつ 鋼鉄** **steel.**

2**こうてつ 更迭** **replacement**(取り替え) ; **(a) dismissal** (解雇) **一動 更迭する** **replace** ＋㊐, **dismiss** ＋㊐ ▶本日法務大臣の更迭があった The Minister of Justice *was replaced* [*dismissed*] today.

1**こうてん 好天** **good** [**fine**] **weather** ▶ハイキングは好天に恵まれた We *had nice weather* for hiking.

2**こうてん 好転する** **improve**(事態・病状などが) ; **take a favorable turn**(事情などが) ; **turn better**(天候などが) ▶日本経済は好転の兆しが見えない The Japanese economy shows no sign of *improvement*. ‖ 1か月たったが彼の病状は好転していない A month has passed, but his condition *has not* yet *improved*. ‖ 日ロ関係は次第に好転している Relations between Japan and Russia *are* gradually *improving*. ‖ 心配された天候が好転した The weather *has turned better*, though we were afraid it might rain.

3**こうてん 公転** **revolution 一動 公転する** **revolve** ▶太陽系のすべての惑星は太陽の周りを公転している All the planets in the solar system *revolve* [*go*] *around the sun*.

4**こうてん 荒天** **rough** [**stormy**] **weather.**

5**こうてん 交点**《数学》an **intersection.**

こうでん 香典 ***koden***
日本紹介 ✉ **香典はお葬式に会葬者が持参し, 香の代わりに死者の霊に供えるお金です. 特別の袋に入れて供えます. 後日, 喪主がその半額ほどのお礼の品で返礼をするのがふつうです** *Koden* is the monetary offering people bring to a funeral in a special envelope and offer to the soul of the deceased instead of incense. To show his [her] gratitude, the chief mourner customarily gives in return a gift that costs about half the amount received.

こうてんてき 後天的な **acquired** ▶後天的な病気 an *acquired* disease ‖ 性格は後天的に作られると思う I think a person's character is formed *over time*. (➤「時がたつうちに」の意).

こうど 高度 **1【高さ】**(an) **altitude** (海面・地面からの) ; **(a) height** /haɪt/ (物の高さ) ▶高度を上げる [下げる] elevate [lower] the *altitude* ‖ 飛行機は現在高度1万メートルを飛行中です The airplane is now flying at *an altitude* [*a height*] of 10,000 meters.
2【高水準】一形 高度の **advanced** ▶高度な数学の問題 an *advanced* problem in mathematics ‖ 高度なテクニック an *advanced* [*a high-level*] technique ‖ 日本の高度経済成長期 the *economic boom years* [the *years of rapid economic growth*] in Japan ‖ インカ帝国は高度な文明をもっていた The Inca Empire had a *highly sophisticated* civilization.

1**こうとう 高等** ▶イルカは高等な知能をもっているようだ Dolphins seem to have *a high level* [*degree*] *of* intelligence.
▶人間は高等動物である Human beings are *higher animals*.
‖**高等学校** a (senior) high school(⇀高校) ‖ **高等学校卒業程度認定試験** the certificate for Students Achieving the Proficiency Level of Upper Secondary School Graduates ‖ **高等教育** higher education ‖ **高等裁判所** a high court of justice ‖ **高等数学** higher mathematics.

2**こうとう 口頭の** **oral** ▶日英文化比較について口頭で発表する make an *oral* presentation on contrasts between Japanese and English cultures ‖ 校長先生には口頭で報告した I made an *oral* report to the principal.
‖**口頭試問** an oral examination.

3**こうとう 高騰** ▶物価の高騰に対処する cope with *soaring prices* ‖ その国では物価が高騰し続けている Prices *are skyrocketing* in that country.

4**こうとう 好投** **good pitching** ▶前田は好投して10勝目をあげた Maeda *pitched brilliantly* to collect his tenth win.

5**こうとう 喉頭**《解剖学》**the larynx** /lǽrɪŋks/ [複 **larynges** /lærínd͡ʒiːz/].

こ

1**こうどう 行動** (an) **action**(一連の); **behavior**(ふるまい); **conduct**(道徳的観点から見た) **一動 行動する act, behave; do**(あることをする) ▶今こそ**行動**を起こすべき時だ Now is the time for *action*. ／Now is the time to *act*. ‖ 軽率な**行動**は慎みたまえ Be careful not to *act* thoughtlessly [rashly]. ‖ 何が原因で彼があんな**行動**をとったのかわからない I don't understand what caused him to *behave* like that. ‖ きみは人の**行動**を気にし過ぎるよ You pay too much attention to *what other people do*. ‖ ぼくの父は**行動半径が広い** My father is involved in *a wide range of activities*. ／My father *is active in many fields*. ‖ 新大臣はなかなか**行動力がある** The new minister *is a true man* [*woman*] *of action*. ‖ 午後の２時間の自由時間のほかは**団体行動**になる Except for two hours' free time in the afternoon, we will be *moving together* [*in a group*]. ‖ その国に対して**軍事行動**をとる take *military action* against that country.

2**こうどう 講堂** an **auditorium** /ɔ̀ːdɪtɔ́ːriəm/, 《英また》 an **assembly hall** ▶生徒全員が**講堂**に集まった All the students gathered in the *auditorium*.

3**こうどう 公道** a (**public**) **road**; a **highway**(幹線道路).

4**こうどう 黄道** 《天文学》 **the ecliptic** /ɪklíptɪk/.

5**こうどう 香道** ***Kodo***; the Japanese incense ceremony (➤ 説明的な訳).

ごうとう 強盗 a **robber**(強奪者); a **housebreaker**, a **burglar**(押し込み泥棒); a **mugger**(路上で襲う) 《参考》「強盗行為」は robbery, burglary または mugging ▶ゆうべ彼の家に**強盗**が入った Last night *a burglar* broke into his house. ‖ 借金がたまってその男はついに**強盗を働いた** Accumulated debts drove him to *commit robbery* [*burglary*]. ‖ 年末が近くなるにつれて**強盗に入られる**銀行やコンビニが多くなる The number of banks and convenience stores that *are robbed* increases toward the end of the year. (➤「銀行強盗」は bank robber,「銀行強盗を働く」は rob a bank という).

‖**強盗殺人事件** a robbery and murder case.

ごうどう 合同 **1**【合体すること】**一形 合同の joint** ▶私たちのグループは別のグループと**合同**で春のコンサートを開いた Our group *joined* with another to put on a spring concert. (➤「合同演奏会」は joint concert という) ‖ 先生の１人が休んだのできょうの授業は２クラス**合同**で行われた Since one of the teachers was absent, the two classes *were combined* for today's lesson. ‖ ３つの大学が『ハムレット』を**合同公演**した Three universities presented *a joint performance* of "Hamlet."

2【数学】**congruence** /kɑ́ːŋgruəns/ ▶この２つの三角形は**合同**だ These two triangles *are congruent*.

こうとうがっこう 高等学校 a (**senior**) **high school**. ⇀高校.

こうとうぶ 後頭部 the back of the head.

こうとうむけい 荒唐無稽な ridiculous, absurd /əbsə́ːʳd/ (ばかばかしい); **nonsensical** (無意味な) ▶彼の説は**荒唐無稽**だ His theory is *ridiculous* [*absurd*].

1**こうどく 購読 subscription**(予約購読) **一動 購読する subscribe**《to》▶うちでは３種類の新聞を**購読**しています We *subscribe to* three different newspapers. (➤「取っています」なら subscribe to より get のほうが適切) ‖ そのスポーツ雑誌の**購読契約を更新した** I *renewed my subscription* to the sports magazine. ‖ **購読料**は月いくらですか How much is the monthly *subscription fee*?

‖**購読者** a subscriber.

2**こうどく 講読する read** +目 ▶ゼミで『オセロ』を**講読**する *read* "Othello" in a seminar.

こうとくしん 公徳心 a **sense of public morality** ▶老若を問わず, 近頃**公徳心**の欠如した人が多いのは嘆かわしい It's deplorable that many people today, whether young or old, lack *a sense of public morality*.

1**こうない 校内** ▶**校内で**ガムをかんではいけない You must not chew gum *at school* [*on the school grounds*]. (➤ 生徒に向かって注意する言い方. 校則違反であることを言うには It's against the rules to chew gum ... . となる. at school は「(授業を受ける場としての) 学校にいるとき」; on the school grounds は「学校の構内で」). ‖ 部外者は**校内に入ることを禁じられている** Outsiders are not allowed to *enter* [*go onto*] *the* (*school*) *campus*. ‖ **校内弁論大会** an *interclass* speech contest ‖ **校内放送**で全生徒は校庭へ出るよう指示があった There was *an announcement over the school PA system* that all students should go out to the schoolyard. (➤ PA system は public-address system (拡声装置) の略.「校内放送をする」は make a PA announcement) ‖ どうしたら**校内暴力**を少なくすることができるだろうか? What can we do to reduce *school violence*?

2**こうない 構内** **the precincts** /príːsɪŋkts/ (寺院や公共物の敷地内); **the premises**(建物と土地); **the campus**(大学や大きな学校の) ▶駅の**構内**で遊んではいけません It's prohibited to play on *the station premises*. ‖ その大学の**構内**にはたくさんのポプラの木がある There are a lot of poplars on that *college campus*. ‖ 《掲示》**構内立ち入り禁止** Keep off the Premises.

こうないえん 口内炎 a **canker sore**, a **stomatitis**(➤ 後者は医学用語) ▶私はよく舌の先 [横] に**口内炎**ができる I often get *canker sores* on the tip [side] of my tongue. (➤「口の内側に」なら on the inside of my mouth).

こうにゅう 購入 purchase /pə́ːʳtʃəs/ **一動 購入する purchase** ⇀買う ▶夫婦はマイホーム**購入**を検討している The couple is considering *purchasing* a home. ‖ その辞書の**購入者**は主に高校生だ *Purchasers* of that dictionary are mostly high school students.

1**こうにん 公認** ▶自民党**公認で選挙に立つ** *run on* the LDP *ticket*(➤ ticket は「公認候補者名簿」) ‖ 自民党はその候補者を**公認した** The LDP *endorsed* the candidate and *put* him [her] *on the ticket*. ‖ 彼女の記録は世界新記録として**公認された** Her time *was officially recognized* as a new world record. ‖ 学生が放課後プールで泳ぐことは**公認されている** Students *are allowed to* swim in the pool after school. ／Student swimming in the pool after school *has been approved* (*by* the school *authorities*). ‖**公認会計士** a certified public accountant《略 CPA》／《英》a chartered accountant《略C.A.》‖**公認記録** an official record.

2**こうにん 後任** a **replacement**(代わりの人); a **successor**(後継者) ▶**後任**の校長先生 an *incoming* principal ‖ 私たちはウィリアムズ先生の**後任**を探しています We are trying to find *a replacement* for Mr. Williams. ‖ 高木氏が吉田氏の**後任**としてチームの監督になった Mr. Takagi became the manager of our team as the *successor* to Mr. Yoshida. ／Mr. Takagi *succeeded* Mr. Yoshida as our team manager.

3 **こうにん 高認** (➤ 高等学校卒業程度認定試験の略) →高等.

こうねつ 高熱 **a high fever** [**temperature**] ▶母は高熱を出して寝ている My mother is sick in bed with *a high fever*. ‖ 娘は昨夜高熱を出した My daughter *had* [*got* / *ran*] *a high fever* last night.

こうねつひ 光熱費 **electricity** [**lighting**] **and heating expenses** ; **utility bills**(公共料金, すなわち電気・ガス・水道料金) ▶冬は光熱費がかさむ We have large *electricity and heating expenses* in winter. / Our *electricity and heating bills* run high in winter.

1 **こうねん 後年** ▶その画家は後年多くの傑作を物した The artist painted a lot of masterpieces in his *later years*.

2 **こうねん 光年** a **light-year** ▶あの星は地球から1万光年離れている That star is ten thousand *light-years* (away) from the earth.

こうねんき 更年期 **the change of life** ; **menopause**(閉経期) ▶母は更年期を迎えています My mother is going through *menopause*. ‖**更年期障害** menopausal symptoms (➤「更年期障害を経験する」は suffer menopausal symptoms).

こうのう 効能 an **effect** ▶この薬はすぐに効能が現れる This medicine will *take effect* [*start working*] quickly.

‖**効能書き** a statement of efficacy /éfɪkəsi/.

こうのとり 《鳥》 a **stork**

《参考》 欧米では赤ん坊はコウノトリが運んで来るとよく子供に言う. また子供の誕生のことを a visit from the stork と表現することもある.

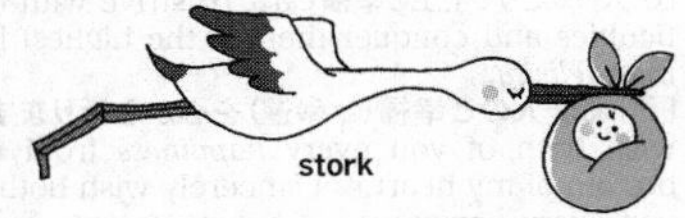

▶ 対話「ママ, 赤ちゃんはどこから来るの?」「コウノトリが運んで来るのよ」"Mommy, where do babies come from?" "The [A] *stork* brings them."

こうのもの 香の物 **(Japanese) pickles.**

1 **こうは 硬派** **1** 【政界などの】 **the hardliners** ; **the hawks**(タカ派).
2 【軟派に対して】 a **guy with a tough side** ; a **tough guy**(➤ ややマイナスイメージの語).

2 **こうは 光波** a **light wave.**

こうば 工場 →こうじょう.

1 **こうはい 後輩**

> **《解説》「後輩」について**
> (1)「後輩」は年功序列意識が強く, 家族主義的雰囲気が重要視される日本人社会の中で生まれた概念である. どの場合にも当てはまるような1語の英語はないので, 英訳する場合は自分と相手との年齢差や組織に属した時期のあと先などを言うことによって説明的に表現する. (2) 日本語の「後輩」を kohai としてそのまま用いることもある. →先輩.

▶彼女は学校の2年後輩でした She was *two years behind me* in school. ‖ 小野さんはぼくより年上だが, 演劇サークルでは後輩だ Mr. Ono is older than I, but he *joined* the drama club *later than I did*. (➤「私よりあとから入った」と考える) ‖ 彼は会社の(2年)後輩です He *joined* the company (two years) *after me*. / He *is junior to me* (by two years) at the office. (➤ junior は「年下の」あるいは「下位の」) ‖ 私たちは後輩たちの盛大な見送りを受けて3月に卒業した When we graduated from school in March, *the younger students* [*the kohai*] gave us a heart-warming send-off. ‖ あいつは後輩のくせに生意気だ He's got a lot of nerve for *a lowerclassman*. (➤ lowerclassman は「(高校・大学などの)下級生」).

2 **こうはい 荒廃** **devastation**(戦争・災害などによる) ; **ruin**(破壊・放置などによる) 一動 **荒廃する** **be devastated, fall into ruin** ▶内乱による国土の荒廃 the *devastation* of the country by civil war ‖ 荒廃した城 a *ruined* castle ‖ 戦争続きでその小国は完全に荒廃してしまった A succession of wars *has* completely *devastated* the small country.

▶戦争直後は人々の心も荒廃していた In the period immediately after the war, people were (lost) *in despair and desolation*. (➤ desolation は devastation と同義だが, 精神の荒廃にも用いる).

3 **こうはい 交配** **crossbreeding** 一動 **交配する** **cross** +目, **crossbreed** +目 ▶植物[鳥]を交配する *cross* plants [birds] ‖ オレンジとレモンを交配する *cross* an orange with [and] a lemon.

1 **こうばい 勾配** a **slope**(傾斜) ; 《米》 a **grade**, 《英》 a **gradient**(➤ ともに道路・鉄道などの傾斜度) ▶急な勾配 a steep *slope* ‖ この山道は勾配が緩やかだ This mountain path has a gentle *slope*. ‖ この坂は12度の勾配がある This slope has *a grade* [*a gradient*] of 12 degrees. ‖ この道は勾配が急だから, 雨が降ったときはドライバーは特に気をつけなければならない This road *is* (very) *steep*, so drivers must take extra care when it rains.

2 **こうばい 購買** **purchase** /pə́ːʳtʃəs/ ▶その広告は人々の購買欲をそそった The advertisement *enticed* people *into purchasing* the product. ‖ この本は購買部で売っています You can get this book at the *school store* [the *Co-op*]. (➤ Co-op は「生協」).
‖**購買力** purchasing power.

こうばいすう 公倍数 a **common multiple** ▶6と7の最小公倍数を求めよ What is *the least common multiple* of 6 and 7?

こうはく 紅白 ▶日本では祝い事をするときよく紅白のまん幕を張る In Japan, *red and white* decorative curtains are often hung on auspicious occasions. ‖ 昨年の NHK 紅白歌合戦は白組が勝った Last year in NHK's year-end *singing contest*, the all-male White team beat the all-female Red team.

こうばしい 香ばしい ▶その喫茶店の前を通るとコーヒーの香ばしい香りがする When you pass that coffee shop, you smell the *pleasant aroma* [*aromatic smell*] of coffee. (➤ aroma はコーヒーや香草のかぐわしい香りを表す語で, お煎餅が焼けるよい匂いを表す語はない).

こうはつ 後発 ▶後発部隊 a group *which departs later* ‖ その会社はパソコン業界では後発メーカーだ That company is *a latecomer* to the computer industry. ‖**後発医薬品** generic drugs.

1 **こうはん 後半** **the latter** [**second**] **half** ▶私たちは夏休みの後半を北海道で過ごした We spent *the latter half* of our summer vacation in Hokkaido. ‖ 後半(戦)5分にこちらのゴールが決まった We scored a goal five minutes into *the latter* [*second*] *half* (*of the game*).

2 **こうはん 公判** (a) **(public) trial** ▶その事件は公判に付

された The case *came* [*was brought*] *to trial*. ／The case *was tried*.
‖公判調書 a trial record.

[3]**こうはん 広範な** wide（幅の広い）; large（面積が大きい）; extensive（広大な）; wide-ranging（広範囲の）▶植物学に関する**広範な**知識 *extensive* [*wide*] knowledge of botany ‖ 地震の被害は**広範な**地域に及んだ The damage caused by the earthquake spread over a *large* area.

[4]**こうはん 鋼板** a steel plate.

[5]**こうはん 甲板** a deck ‖甲板員 a deckhand.

[1]**こうばん 交番** a police box [booth]（➤ 交番は日本独特のシステムで a Koban と表記されることも多い）▶この辺に**交番**はありますか Is there *a police box* near here? ‖ **交番**にすぐ届けたほうがいいですよ You should report it to the *police* (*box*) immediately.

[2]**こうばん 降板** ▶阿部投手は 7 回で**降板した** Pitcher Abe *was replaced* in the seventh inning.（➤「交代させられた」の意）‖ 松坂投手は 3 ホーマーを浴び**降板した** Pitcher Matsuzaka *was knocked out* when he was tagged for three homers.

ごうはん 合板 plywood /pláɪwʊd/（➤ 1 枚の合板は a plywood board）.

こうはんい 広範囲 a wide range ▶**広範囲**に及ぶ被災地 *extensive* disaster-stricken *areas* ‖ そのうわさは**広範囲**に広まった The rumor spread *far and wide*. ‖ その検定試験には**広範囲にわたる**知識が必要とされる *Wide-ranging* knowledge is needed for that certification examination. →広範.

[1]**こうひ 公費** public expense(s) ▶**公費**で旅行する travel *at public expense*.

[2]**こうひ 工費** a construction cost, construction costs.

こうび 交尾 mating（鳥・動物の）; copulation（動物の）
‖交尾期 the mating season（➤「交尾期の猫」は cat in [at／《英また》on] heat という）.

ごうひ 合否 ▶試験の**合否**は 1 週間後にお知らせします We'll let you know *the examination results* in a week.（➤ results は「結果」; 通例複数形にする）‖ 試験では 1 点が**合否を分ける**ことがある Sometimes one point *separates those who pass and those who fail* in an examination.

[1]**こうひょう 好評** a favorable reception（好意的な受け止め）; popularity（人気）▶このサイドリーダーは学生たちの間で**好評だ** This supplementary reader *is very popular* among students. ‖ 彼の提案はクラスで**好評だった** His proposal *was favorably accepted* by the class.

[2]**こうひょう 公表する** publish +目（発表する）; make ... public（公にする）▶生徒総会で役員の名前が**公表された** The names of the executives *were published* [*were made public*] at the general meeting of the student council.
▶その誘拐事件の真相はまもなく**公表される**だろう The facts of that kidnapping will *be made public* before long.

[3]**こうひょう 講評** (a) comment ▶きょう寺田先生が入試模擬テストの結果について若干の**講評をされた** Today Mr. Terada *made* several *comments* on the results of our trial entrance examinations.

[1]**こうふ 公布** proclamation（国家的重要事項の）; promulgation（法律などの）一動 **公布する** proclaim +目, promulgate /prɑ́:məlgeɪt/ +目 ▶日本国憲法は昭和21年11月 3 日に**公布された** The Constitution of Japan *was proclaimed* on November 3 in 1946 [the 21st year of Showa]. ‖ その法律は去年**公布さ**れたばかりである The law *was promulgated* only last year.

[2]**こうふ 交付する** issue +目 ▶旅券を**交付する** *issue* a passport ‖交付金 a grant.

[3]**こうふ 坑夫** a miner, a mine worker.

こうぶ 後部 the rear, the back ▶**後部**の座席 a *rear* [*back*] seat／a *back*seat.

こうふう 校風 (a) school tradition [spirit]《参考》school color はその学校を特徴づける制服やワッペンなどの色のこと →スクールカラー ▶その学校の**校風**は質実剛健だ The school traditionally encourages the students to be simple and sturdy.

[1]**こうふく 幸福** happiness; welfare（福祉）; felicity（非常な幸福; 改まった堅い語）一形 **幸福な** happy 一副 **幸福に** happily ▶他人の**幸福**を羨むな Don't envy the *happiness* of other people. ‖ 金で**幸福**は買えないと言うが…, They say money can't buy *happiness*, but ... ‖ 決して不幸ではないが「**幸福**ですか」と聞かれると返答に困る I'm not unhappy at all, but I find myself at a loss for an answer when (I'm) asked if I'm *happy*. ‖ 国民の**幸福**は政府の責任だ The *welfare* [*well-being*] of the people is the government's responsibility. ‖ 誰もが**幸福な**人生を送りたいと願っている Everybody hopes to lead [have] *a happy life*. ‖ 彼女は**幸福な**結婚生活をしている She is *happily married*. ‖ 彼はインドで**幸福に**暮らしている He is living *happily* in India. ‖ きみはいい奥さんに恵まれて**幸福な**（＝幸運な）人だね You are *fortunate* [*lucky*] to have such a good wife. ‖ 困難に立ち向かい, それを克服することは, 人間にとって至上の**幸福**である To strive with difficulties and conquer them is the highest human *felicity*.
✉ **お 2 人のご幸福（＝幸運）を心から祈ります** I wish both of you every *happiness* from the bottom of my heart. ／I sincerely wish both of you every *happiness*.

[2]**こうふく 降伏** surrender 一動（…に）**降伏する** surrender《to》▶敵はとうとう**降伏した** The enemy finally *surrendered*. ‖ 第二次大戦で日本は連合国に**無条件降伏した** At the end of World War Ⅱ, Japan *surrendered unconditionally to* the Allied Powers.

[1]**こうぶつ 好物** one's favorite (food／dish／delicacy)（➤ food は一般に「食べ物」, dish は主に皿に盛った「食べ物」, delicacy は「珍味」）▶すしは私の**好物**です Sushi is one of my *favorite foods*. ／I'm a (big) sushi fan. ‖ 妹は甘いものが大**好物**です My sister *is very fond of sweets*.／My sister *has a sweet tooth*.

[2]**こうぶつ 鉱物** a mineral ▶南アフリカは**鉱物**資源が豊富だ South Africa abounds in *mineral resources*.

こうふん 興奮 excitement 一動 **興奮する** get excited ▶接戦にみんな**興奮した** Everybody *got excited* at the close game. ‖ みんな**興奮して**叫んだ Everybody shouted *in excitement*. ‖ 自分たちのチームが優勝したときは**興奮して**我を忘れた We were beside ourselves *with excitement* when our team won the championship. ‖ そんなに**興奮するな**よ Don't *get* so *excited*. ‖ 彼女はすぐに**興奮する**たちだ She gets *excited* [*worked up*] easily. ‖ あのロックには全く**興奮する**よ That rock music really *turns* me *on*.（➤ turn on は「しびれさせる」の意のインフォーマルな表現）‖ 日本チームが勝ったとき, **興奮した**観衆がグラウンドになだれ込んだ When the Japanese team won, *excited* spectators surged onto the

field.
こうぶん 構文 the structure [construction] of a sentence, (a) sentence structure
‖**分詞構文** a participial construction.
こうぶんし 高分子 《化学》‖**高分子化合物** a high polymer.
こうぶんしょ 公文書 official papers; an official document(証拠となる書類) ‖**公文書偽造** the forgery of official papers [an official document].
こうへい 公平な fair; impartial /ɪmpɑ́ːrʃəl/ (えこひいきのない) ▶**公平な**裁き a *fair* judgment ‖両親はぼくたち子供に対して**公平だ** My parents *treat* all us children *fairly* [*equally*]. ／My parents *are impartial* toward us children. ‖教師は生徒を**公平に**扱わなければならない Teachers should deal *fairly* with their students.
▶その金はみんなで**公平に**(＝均等に)分けよう Let's divide the money *evenly* among us. ‖**公平に**(＝客観的に)言ってきみが間違っている *Objectively speaking*, you are in the wrong. ‖裁判官は**公平無私**であらねばならない Judges must be *fair and impartial* [*disinterested*].
☞ 不公平 (→見出語)
こうへん 後編 the latter [second] part; the latter [second] volume(後の巻); a sequel /síːkwəl/.
ごうべん 合弁の joint ▶この事業は日米の**合弁**(＝共同経営)です This business is under *Japanese-American joint management*. ‖わが社は日中**合弁事業**として発足した Our company started as a Japanese-Chinese *joint venture*. ‖**合弁会社** a joint corporation, 《英》 a joint company.
こうほ 候補 a candidate (立候補者); a nominee /nɑ̀ːmɪníː/ (指名推薦された人); an option(選択肢)
▶**候補者**を立てる field [put up] *a candidate* ‖金メダルの**最有力候補** a *favorite* to win the gold medal ‖**最終候補者リスト** a *short list*, a *shortlist* (➤「予選候補者リスト」は a long list) ‖**候補**の1つ one of the *options* ‖山村君を**委員長候補**に立てよう Let's nominate Mr. Yamamura as *a candidate for chairman* of the committee. ‖彼のデビュー映画はアカデミー賞の**候補になった** His first movie *was nominated* [*became a nominee*] for an Academy Award. ‖私たちの都市は次の次のオリンピックの**候補地**です Our city is one of *the sites bidding* for the second Olympic Games after next. ‖あの関取は横綱の**有力候補**の1人だ That sumo wrestler is one of the yokozuna *hopefuls* [*candidates*]. (➤ hopeful は「前途有望な人」) ‖阪神は来シーズンの**優勝候補の筆頭**だ The Tigers are *the top* [*foremost*] *contenders* for the next season. (➤ contender は「選手権や優勝」を目指して競う選手 [チーム]) ／The Tigers are *the favorite* [*are favored*] to win the pennant next season. (➤ favorite は「最有力候補, 本命」, favor は「… を本命と考える」).
[1]**こうぼ 酵母** yeast ▶パン**酵母** baker's *yeast* ‖醸造用**酵母** brewer's *yeast*.
‖**酵母菌** a yeast fungus /fʌ́ŋgəs/ (➤複数形は yeast fungi または yeast funguses).
[2]**こうぼ 公募** ▶標語を**公募する** *invite the public to submit* slogans [catchwords] ‖専任教授を**公募する** *advertise for* a full-time professor.
[1]**こうほう 後方** ▶1, 2歩**後方へ**退く take a step or two *backward* ／step *backward* a pace or two ‖**後方から**大きな声がした I heard a loud voice *from behind*. ‖彼女は列の**後方に**立っていた She was standing *near the back* of the line.
[2]**こうほう 広報** public information; public relations(広報活動)《略 PR》‖**広報課** the Public Information Section(市役所などの); an office of public relations(大学などの) ‖**広報誌** a PR magazine ‖**広報担当者** a publicist ‖**内閣広報官** the Cabinet public relations secretary ‖**内閣広報室** the Cabinet Public Relations Office.
[3]**こうほう 公報** an official report(公式の報告); a public bulletin /bʊ́lətn/ (官報)
‖**選挙公報** an election bulletin.
[4]**こうほう 工法** a construction method.
[5]**こうほう 高峰** a high [lofty] peak.
[1]**こうぼう 興亡** ▶ローマ帝国の**興亡** the *rise and fall* of the Roman Empire.
[2]**こうぼう 攻防** offense [attack] and defense
‖**攻防戦** a battle of offense [attack] and defense, an offensive and defensive battle.
[3]**こうぼう 工房** a studio, an atelier /æ̀t̬ljéɪ ‖ ətélieɪ/, a craft workshop.
ごうほう 合法の lawful; legal /líːgəl/ (法的な); legitimate(適法な, 正当な) ▶問題を**合法的な**手段で解決する solve a problem by *lawful* [*legal*] means ‖日本が自衛隊を持つことは**合法か非合法か**? Is it *legal or illegal* [*constitutional or unconstitutional*] for Japan to have the Self-Defense Forces?
ごうほうらいらく 豪放磊落な magnanimous /mægnǽnɪməs/ ▶彼のような**豪放らいらくな**人は少ない Few people are as *magnanimous* as he (is).
こうぼく 公僕 a public servant(公務員).
こうま 子馬 a young horse, a foal /foʊl/ (特に1歳以下の) 《参考》雄は colt, 雌は filly と呼ぶ. pony は種類としての小型馬.
こうまい 高邁な lofty(思想・目的などが); noble(気高い) ▶**高まいな**理想 a *lofty* ideal ‖彼は**高まいな**精神の持ち主だ He is a man of *noble spirit*.
こうまん 高慢な conceited(うぬぼれが強い); haughty /hɔ́ːt̬i/, 《インフォーマル》 high-and-mighty(人を見下した, 横柄な) ▶**高慢な**女 a *conceited* woman ‖あんな**高慢ちき**なやつは見たことがない I've never seen such a *haughty* man (as he). ‖彼女があんな**高慢ちきな**態度をとらなかったら, もっと友だちができるのに If she wouldn't act so *high-and-mighty*, she'd have more friends.
ごうまん 傲慢な haughty /hɔ́ːt̬i/ (人を見下した, 横柄な); arrogant(自分の力を過信して威張る); conceited (うぬぼれた) ▶**傲慢な**態度 a *haughty* attitude ‖あの男は**傲慢にも**自分が誰よりも優れていると思っている He is (really) *arrogant* and he thinks he is better than anyone else.
こうみゃく 鉱脈 a vein ▶石炭の**鉱脈** a coal *vein*.
[1]**こうみょう 巧妙な** clever(計画などが); cunning(機敏で巧みな;「こうかつな」という含みがある); crafty(ずる賢い); skillful(器用な) ▶**巧妙な**仕掛け a *clever* trick ‖**巧妙な**手口 a *crafty* [*cunning*] trick ‖彼は三塁線に**巧妙な**バントを決めた He laid down a *skillful* bunt on the third-base line.
[2]**こうみょう 功名** ▶彼は**功名**心が強い He's *very ambitious*.
[3]**こうみょう 光明** light ▶前途に**光明**を見いだす see the *light* at the end of the tunnel (➤「希望の光が見え始める」の意).
こうみん 公民 **1**【国民】 a citizen
‖**公民権** civil rights.
2【教科】 civics.

こ

こうみんかん 公民館 a **public hall.**
こうむ 公務 **official business** ▶公務でヨーロッパを旅行する travel in Europe *on official business.*
こうむいん 公務員 a **public official**; a **public employee** [**worker**].

> 《解説》中以上の地位の人を public official といい, それ以下の一般の公務員を public employee [worker] または civil servant という. しかし, 英語では政府・州・市など, 勤務先を具体的にいって, government official [employee], state [city] employee などとするほうがふつう.

こうむてん 工務店 a **building firm**, a **builder**; a **construction company**(会社組織の).
こうむる 被る ▶私は青木氏から多くの恩恵を被っている I *am* greatly *indebted to* Mr. Aoki. ‖農民たちはその台風で大きな損害を被った The farmers *suffered* great *losses* from the typhoon. (➤ suffer は「損害を被る」の意).
こうめい 高名な **famous, eminent** ▶高名な物理学者 an *eminent* physicist ‖あの人は世界的に高名な地球物理学者です He is a *world-famous* geophysicist. ▶ご高名(＝お名前)はかねがね承っております I have often heard of you. ／I have heard a lot about you.
こうめいせいだい 公明正大な **fair** ▶私たちは公明正大にプレーします We will *play fair* [*play cricket*]. (➤ play cricket はやや古風な《英》で,「(フェアなクリケットをする→)公明正大にふるまう」の意).
ごうもう 剛毛 a **bristle** /brísəl/.
こうもく 項目 an **item** /áɪṭəm/ (品物などの1点1点); a **head**, a **heading**(文章などの表題や見出し) ▶表の各項目に番号を振る number each *item* in a list ‖内容を項目別に分ける *itemize* [*classify*] the contents ‖**項目表** an itemized list.
こうもり 蝙蝠《動物》a **bat**
‖**こうもり傘** an umbrella.
[1]**こうもん 校門** a **school gate** ▶校門の所で彼女を待つ wait for her *at the school gate.*
[2]**こうもん 肛門** **the anus** /éɪnəs/ ▶肛門の病気 an *anal* /éɪnl/ disease.
ごうもん 拷問 **torture**; **the rack**(➤ 拷問台を rack ということから) ▶彼は拷問にかけられてすべてを白状した He confessed everything *under torture.* ‖面接試験はぼくには拷問のように感じられた The interview was sheer *torture* to me.
こうや 荒野 a **wilderness** /wíldəʳnəs/.
[1]**こうやく 公約** a **pledge**(誓約) 一動 **公約する** **pledge** ▶その政治家は選挙の公約を1つも果たさなかった That politician did not fulfill any of his *campaign pledges.* ‖首相は減税を公約した The Prime Minister *pledged* to reduce taxes.
[2]**こうやく 膏薬** a (**medical**) **plaster**, a **medicated patch.**
こうやくすう 公約数 a **common divisor** /dɪváɪzəʳ/ ▶12と9の最大公約数を求めよ What is *the greatest common divisor* of 12 and 9?
こうやさい 後夜祭 ▶学校祭のあとの後夜祭 *a closing party* after the school festival.
[1]**こうゆう 校友** a **schoolmate** (学友); an **alumnus** /əlʌ́mnəs/ (男子卒業生); an **alumna** /əlʌ́mnə/ (女子卒業生) (➤ alumnus の複数形の alumni /əlʌ́mnaɪ/ は男女共学校の卒業生にも用いる)
‖**校友会** an alumni association.
[2]**こうゆう 交友** ▶彼女は外向的で交友関係が広い She is outgoing and *has a large circle of friends.* ‖被害者の交友関係を当たってみなさい Check out the victim's (*circle of*) *acquaintances.*
[3]**こうゆう 公有** ▶この詩は公有財産になっている(＝著作権が切れている) This poem is in the *public domain.*
ごうゆう 豪遊 ▶その強盗は盗んだ金で豪遊している最中に警察に捕まった That burglar was arrested by the police while he was *having a* (*spending*) *spree* with the money he had stolen.
[1]**こうよう 紅葉** **autumn leaves** [**foliage** /fóulɪɪdʒ/], **autumn colors** [**hues**] ▶紅葉した木々 trees *in autumn* [*fall*] *colors* ／tree whose leaves *have turned red or yellow* ‖ことし京都の紅葉は美しかった The *autumn colors* in Kyoto were beautiful this year. ‖ことしはいつもより紅葉が早い This year *the leaves are turning* (*red*) earlier than usual. ‖この辺りは秋になると全山が真っ赤に紅葉する All the mountainsides around here *are ablaze with scarlet-tinged leaves* in (the) fall. (➤ ablaze は「燃え立って」).
✉ **京都の山々は美しく紅葉する頃が見頃です** The best season to see the hills of Kyoto is when they *are beautifully colored with autumn leaves.*
[2]**こうよう 公用** **official business** ▶父は公用で鹿児島に出張しています My father is in Kagoshima *on official business.* ‖インドでは英語は公用語の1つになっている In India, English is one of the major *official languages.*
‖**公用車** an official car.
[3]**こうよう 効用** (a) **use** /juːs/ (使い道); **good**(良さ, 長所); an **effect**(結果として生じた効果) ▶酒の効用の1つは憂さ晴らしになることである One of the *effects* of drinking is to make you forget your worries.
[4]**こうよう 高揚** ▶士気を高揚させる *boost* [*raise*] morale ‖大勝利に選手たちの気分は高揚した The players *felt high* [*felt exhilarated*] after a big victory.
こうようじゅ 広葉樹 a **broadleaf tree**
‖**広葉樹林** a forest of broadleaf trees.
ごうよく 強欲な **avaricious** /æ̀vəríʃəs/ ▶強欲な金貸し an *avaricious* moneylender.
こうら 甲羅 a **shell**(亀などの) ▶《慣用表現》海辺では若者たちが甲羅を干している On the beach, young people *are sunbathing* [*are basking in the sun*], *lying on their stomachs.*
こうらく 行楽 a **pleasure trip**; an **excursion**(通例団体の) ▶日本では5月の第1週がサラリーマンにとって最高の行楽シーズンだ In Japan, the first week of May is the best season for salaried workers to take *pleasure trips.* ‖房総の行楽地はどこも子供連れの行楽客でごった返していた Every *pleasure* [*holiday*] *spot* in Boso was crowded with *vacationers* [*pleasure seekers*] with children. (➤「行楽客」は《英》では holidaymaker ともいう) ‖きょうは絶好の行楽日和だ This is perfect *weather for making an excursion* [*taking a pleasure trip*].
[1]**こうり 小売り** **retail** /ríːteɪl/ ▶衣服の小売りをする *sell* clothes *at retail.* ‖**小売価格** a retail price ‖**小売業者** a retailer ‖**小売店** a retail store.
[2]**こうり 高利** **high interest** ▶高利で金を貸す lend money *at high interest.*
‖**高利貸し** usury /júːʒəri/ (➤ 行為); a usurer, 《インフォーマル》a loan shark(➤ ともに人).
[3]**こうり 公理** an **axiom** /ǽksiəm/.

ごうりか 合理化 streamlining（能率化），《英また》rationalisation；downsizing（規模縮小・人員削減）**一動 合理化する** streamline +目，《英また》rationalise, downsize +目 ▶その会社にはもっと思い切った経営の**合理化**が必要だ More radical *streamlining* [《英また》*rationalisation*] of management is an absolute must for that company.（➤《米》でのつづりは rationalization）‖ 雇い主は**合理化のため**50名を解雇した The employer dismissed fifty workers *as* (*part of*) *its streamlining* [*rationalization*] *program*.

こうりしゅぎ 功利主義《哲 学》utilitarianism /ju-tìlətéəriənìzəm/
‖**功利主義者** a utilitarian /jutìlətéəriən/.

1**こうりつ 公立の** public ▶**公立の**中学校 a *public* junior high school ‖ **公立**図書館 a *public* library.
‖**公立学校**《米》a public school（➤イギリスでは Eton, Harrow など一部の有名私立中等学校を指す），《英》a (publicly) maintained school.

2**こうりつ 効率** efficiency ▶**効率**をよくする improve *efficiency* ‖ 単に**効率優先**ではいい仕事はできない People who think *efficiency* is the only thing that matters can't do a good job. ‖ **効率のよい**仕事をする do *efficient* work ／work efficiently ‖ 広島はヒット３本で**効率よく**２点をあげた The Carp *efficiently* scored two runs on three hits.

こうりてき 功利的な practical（現実的な）；utilitarian（実利的な；軽蔑的に用いることも多い）▶**功利的な**考え方をする view things in a *practical* way ／take a *utilitarian* view of things.

ごうりてき 合理的な rational（理にかなった）；practical（現実的な）▶**合理的な**考え方をする have a *practical* way of thinking ／look at things in a *practical* way ‖ その考え方はとても**合理的**だが実行は難しい That idea sounds very *rational*, but it would be hard to put it into practice.

1**こうりゃく 攻略する** capture +目（捕らえる，奪う）▶（敵の）城を**攻略する** *capture* [*take*] a castle ‖ 由佳を**攻略する**には押しの一手しかなさそうだ (It) looks like you've got to be aggressive if you want to *capture* Yuka's *heart*.
‖（ゲームや試験を乗り切る）**攻略本** a strategy guide.

2**こうりゃく 後略** The rest is omitted.

1**こうりゅう 交流** **1【互いに行き来すること】**(an) exchange **一動 交流する** mingle《with》（打ち解け合う）；associate《with》（社交上・仕事上で付き合う）▶国どうしの**文化交流** *cultural exchange* among nations ‖ その歌手はファンとの**交流**を大事だと考えている The singer considers it important to *mingle with* his [her] fans. ‖ 当時は男子校と女子校の**交流**はなかった In those days boys' schools *did not associate with* girls' schools. ‖ あの人たちとは**交流**がない We *have nothing to do with* those people.
‖**交流試合** an interleague game（リーグ間の）.
2【電気の】 alternating current.

2**こうりゅう 拘留・勾留** custody, detention《参考》前者には「拘留」を当て，犯罪人を一定期間拘留場にとどめることをいい，後者には「勾留」を当て，被疑者・被告人を取り調べのために一定の場所にとどめることをいう
▶ 10人の学生が放火のかどで**拘留されている** Ten students are *in custody* on a charge of arson. ‖ その男は保釈金が用意できるまで**勾留された** That man *was kept in detention* [*was detained*] until he could raise bail.

3**こうりゅう 興隆** prosperity /prɑːspérəṭi/（繁 栄）**一動 興隆する** prosper；thrive（物事がうまくいく）▶平家一門の**興隆**と滅亡 the *rise* and fall of the Heike clan.

ごうりゅう 合流する join +目；merge《into》▶この川は３キロ先で富士川と**合流する** This river *joins* [*merges into*] the Fuji River three kilometers ahead. ‖ ここが２つの川の**合流点**です This is *where* the two rivers *meet*. ／This is the *juncture* of the two rivers. ‖ 彼らとは名古屋駅で**合流する**ことになっている We are supposed to *join* them at Nagoya Station. ‖ 正門前で３時に**合流しよう** *Let's all meet up* at the front gate at three.

こうりょ 考慮 consideration **一動 考慮する** consider +目（慎重に考える）；think over（時間をかけて考える）；take ... into account [consideration]（…を考えに入れる）▶決定する前にこれらの事情を**考慮**すべきだ Before we make a decision, we should *consider* [*think over*] these circumstances.

> **【文型】**
> **事情(A)を考慮に入れる**
> **take A into account [consideration]**

▶物事を決めるとき彼は妻の気持ちを**考慮に入れる** When making decisions, he always *takes* his wife's feelings *into account* [*consideration*].（➤ほとんど同じように用いられるが，account が「計算に入れる，要素に含める」に対して，consideration は「念入りに考える」というニュアンス）‖ 大学を選ぶときは地理的条件も**考慮に入れる**べきだ When choosing a college, its location should be *taken into consideration* too. ‖ 裁判官は被告が初犯であることを**考慮して**執行猶予付きの判決を出した The judge *took into account* that the defendant was a first offender and gave him a suspended sentence.
▶私が未経験だということを**考慮してください** Please *make allowance for* my inexperience.（➤ make allowance /əláʊəns/ for は「…を情状酌量する」）.

1**こうりょう 香料** (a) spice（香辛料）；(a) flavor（香味料）；(a) perfume（香水）.

2**こうりょう 荒涼たる** desolate（荒れ果てた）；dreary（うら寂しい）；bleak（寒々と何もない）▶**荒涼とした**原野 a *desolate* plain ／a wilderness ‖ **荒涼たる**月の景色 a *bleak* lunar landscape.

3**こうりょう 綱領** a platform（政党の方針）；fundamental principles（基本方針）▶党の**綱領** a party *platform*.

4**こうりょう 校了** completion of proofreading；OK（➤「校了」したことを表す）.

5**こうりょう 稿料** a manuscript fee（原稿料）.

1**こうりょく 効力** (an) effect ▶この薬は食前に飲まないと**効力がない** This medicine has no *effect* [doesn't work] unless you take it before meals. ‖ その契約はまだ**効力がある** The contract *is* still *valid*. ‖ この条例が**効力を発する**（＝実施される）のはことしの４月からです This regulation will *come into force* this coming April.

2**こうりょく 抗力**《航空》drag.

こうりん 後輪 a rear wheel.

1**こうれい 高齢** (an) advanced age ▶**高齢の**人 a person *of advanced age* [*years*] ／a person *advanced in years*（➤「高齢者」にも相当する）‖ **高齢者に優しい**町 an *age-friendly* city ‖ **高齢者に優しい**公共空間をつくる make *senior-friendly* public spaces ‖ **高齢**にもかかわらず彼は毎年富士山に登る Even though he is *very old* [*well advanced in years*], he climbs Mt. Fuji every year. ‖ 社員の**高齢化**がこの会社の問題点の１つだ *The rising aver-*

こ

age age of employees is one of the problems of this company. ‖日本の社会は急速に**高齢化**している Japanese society *is* rapidly *aging*. (➤この age は「加齢する」の意の動詞).
‖高齢(化)社会 an aging [《米》 graying ／《英》 greying] society ; a society with a high proportion of elderly people [seniors ／older people] (➤「超高齢社会」は super-aging society などと訳せる) ‖**高齢出産** late childbearing ‖**後期** [**前期** ／**中期**] **高齢者** a person in late old age [early old age ／middle old age].

2**こうれい 恒例** ▶試合の前に選手が宣誓をするのが**恒例**になっている It is *an established custom* that players take an oath before games. (🔔 1人が代表で宣誓をする場合でもほかにも選手がいるので players とする) ‖**毎年恒例**の新入生歓迎コンパを今度の土曜日に行います We're having our *annual* welcome party for freshmen next Saturday.

3**こうれい 好例** a **good example** ; a **case in point**(うってつけの例) ▶「つまらない物ですが」という表現は日本語の控えめな表現の**好例**である The phrase "Tsumaranai mono desuga" is *a good example* of a Japanese expression of modesty.

ごうれい 号令 a **command**(命令) ; an **order** (指図) ▶先生は生徒に始めの**号令を掛けた** The teacher *ordered* [*gave a command* to] his students to begin.

こうれつ 後列 a **rear row ; the last row** (最後列) ▶**後列**に座る sit in *a rear row* ‖**最後列**の人, テスト用紙を集めてください Those (sitting) in *the last row*, please collect the exam papers.

1**こうろ 航路** a **lane**(船·飛行機などの規定の) ; a **line** (船の定期の) ; a **course** (進路) ; a **route** /ruːt/ (道筋) ▶空の**航路** an air *route* ‖ヘリコプターは**航路を外れて飛んだ** The helicopter *flew off course*. ‖私たちの船は濃霧のため**航路を誤った** Our ship *got off course* because of the dense fog. ‖その航空会社はグアムへの**定期航路を開設した** That airline *has begun service* [*has opened a new route*／*has started regular flights*] to Guam. (➤ service は「便」).

2**こうろ 香炉** an **incense** /ínsens/ **burner**.

3**こうろ 高炉** a **blast furnace**.

こうろう 功労 **contribution**(貢献) ; **service** (尽力) ▶彼はスポーツの普及に**功労**があったので表彰された He was awarded a prize for his *contribution* to the popularization of sports. ‖彼らは国の発展に**功労があった** They *have done a great deal for* the development of the country. (➤「国の発展のために大いに尽くした」の意) ‖彼はこの地域のために**尽力した功労者**だ He is *a man who has rendered great service* to this community.

こうろうしょう 厚労省 **the Health Ministry, the Ministry of Health.** →**厚生**.

こうろん 口論 an **argument**(自説を論理的に主張し合う) ; a **quarrel**(口頭での言い合い) 《**参考**》 argument が quarrel に発展することは少なくない **一動 口論する argue, quarrel** ▶きみとは**口論**したくない I don't want to *pick an argument* [*a quarrel*] with you. ／I don't want to *argue* [*quarrel*] with you. ‖そんなつまらないことで**口論するな**よ Don't *argue* [*quarrel*] over such a small thing. ‖彼は父親と**口論して**家を飛び出した He *argued* [*quarreled*] *with* his father and ran out of the house. ‖彼は子供の教育問題について妻と**口論した** He *had an argument* [《主に英》 *a row*] with his wife about the education of their children. (➤ row /raʊ/ は「口げんか」の意のインフォーマルな語で主に《英》).

こうわ 講和 **peace** ▶**講和**を結ぶ sign *a peace agreement*. **‖講和条約** a peace treaty (➤「サンフランシスコ講和条約」は the San Francisco Peace Treaty).

ごうわん 剛腕·豪腕 **‖剛腕投手** a strong-armed pitcher ; a power pitcher (速球をびしびし投げる).

1**こえ 声** **1【人間の】** a **voice** ▶太い [大きな ／優しい ／美しい ／小さい] **声** a *deep* [*loud* ／*gentle* ／*sweet* ／*soft*] *voice* ‖**低い声で歌う** sing in a *low voice* ‖**声を限りに助けを呼ぶ** cry out for help *at the top of one's voice* ‖あの人は**声が大きい** He *has a loud voice*. ／He speaks *loudly*. ‖彼女はきのうからかぜをひいて**声が出ない** She caught (a) cold yesterday and *has lost her voice*. ‖緊張のあまり**声が震えた** I was so nervous that *my voice trembled*. ‖もう少し**静かな声**で話してください Could you speak more *quietly* [*tone* it *down*] ? ‖その英詩を**声に出して**読みなさい Read that English poem *aloud*. ‖その知らせを聞くと彼は**声を上げて泣き出した** When he heard the news, he *burst out crying*. ‖彼はたばこを吸っている娘を見て, 思わず**声を荒らげてどなった** When he saw his daughter smoking, he couldn't keep himself from *screaming at* her. ‖ **対話** 「駅前で1万円拾ったんだって?」「しっ, **声が高い**よ」"You found a 10,000-yen bill in front of the train station?" "Shh! Keep it under your hat!" (➤「秘密にしててよ, 黙っててよ」の意).
▶私たちは**声をそろえて**『ウィ·アー·ザ·ワールド』を歌った We sang "We are the World" *in chorus* [*in unison*]. (➤ chorus は「合唱」, unison は「斉唱」) ‖少女は**声を弾ませて**「私の絵が展覧会に入選したの」と言った The girl said *in a cheerful voice*, "My painting's been selected for the exhibition!" ‖彼女は会場の後ろまで**よく通る声**でスピーチした She gave a speech *in a clear voice* that carried to the back of the hall. (➤この carry は「声が(…まで)届く」) ‖どこかで若い女性の**泣く声**がする I can hear a young woman *crying* somewhere.
2【動物の鳴き声】 a **cry**(鳥や獣の大きな鳴き声) ; a **song**(小鳥のさえずり) ; a **chirp**(虫の) ▶宵闇が増すにつれて庭の**虫の声**がにぎやかになってきた As the darkness deepened, the *chirping of insects* grew louder in the garden.
3【意見】 ▶政府は物価高に憤る庶民の**声**に耳を傾けるべきだ The government should listen to the *complaints* of people who are angry about the high cost of living. ／The government should pay attention to (the) citizens' *anger* at the high cost of living.
4【慣用表現】 ▶新規プロジェクトは総理大臣の**お声がかり**でスタートした The new project was launched *thanks to the influence of* the Prime Minister. ‖政府は名もない国民の**声なき声**を無視してはいけない The government should not ignore *the voices* [*wishes*] of the silent majority.

逆引き熟語 ○○声
(動物などの)うなり声 a growl ／**うめき声** a groan ／**掛け声** a rallying cry ／**甲高い声** a high-pitched voice ／**キーキー声** a squeak, a screech ／**(女性の)黄色い声** a shrill voice ／**叫び声** a shout, a cry, a scream ／**しゃがれ声** a hoarse voice, a husky voice ／**わめき声** a yell, a shout, a howl ／**笑い声** laughter, a laugh

2**こえ 肥** **manure**(家畜のふん);**(night) soil**(人のふん)
‖**肥だめ** a manure pit.

ごえい 護衛 a **guard**; an **escort** /éskɔːrt/ (護衛団) ▶大統領を**護衛する** *guard* the President ‖ その特使には白バイの**護衛**がついていた That special envoy had *an escort* of motorcycle policemen. ‖ 彼らは**護衛**をつけてその大金を銀行へ運んだ They transported the large sum of money to the bank *under guard*. ‖ 首相は警官に**護衛されていた** The Prime Minister was *under police guard*.
‖**護衛兵** a guard.

こえがわり 声変わり a **change of voice** ▶息子は今**声変わりしている** My son's *voice is changing* now. ‖ 彼はまだ**声変わりしていない** His *voice hasn't changed* yet.

こえだ 小枝 a **twig**; a **sprig** (➤ twig より小さく葉や花のあるもの) ▶**小枝**に止まった鳥 a bird on *a twig*.

1**こえる 越える・超える** **1**【向こう側へ行く】**get** [**go**] **over**; **cross** +目 (横切る) ▶国境を**越える** *cross* the border ‖ この峠を**越えたら**温泉だぞ We'll be at the hot spring once we *get over* the pass. / The hot spring is right *over* the pass. ‖ この谷を**越えると**目的地はもうすぐだ We'll arrive at our destination shortly after *crossing* this valley. ‖ 飛行機は日付変更線を**越えた** The airplane (*has*) *crossed* (*over*) the (International) Date Line. ‖ 山下選手は 6 メートルのバーを軽々と**越えた** Yamashita *cleared* the 6-meter-high bar easily. ‖ 探検隊は死のタクラマカン砂漠を**越えて**旅をした The expedition made a dangerous trek *across* the Takla Makan Desert.
2【上回る】**be over**; **exceed** +目 (限度などを); **surpass** +目 (しのぐ) ▶聴衆は1000人を**超えた** The audience *exceeded* 1,000. / There *were over* one thousand people in the audience. ‖ あの人はまさか60歳を**超えて**はいないだろう That person can't *be over* sixty. ‖ この地では気温は夏でもめったに20度を**超えない** The temperature seldom *rises above* 20 degrees here even in summer.
▶制限速度を**超える** *exceed* the speed limit ‖ 師匠を**超える** *surpass* one's master ‖ 台風の被害は**予想を超えて**広い範囲に広がっていた The damage caused by the typhoon was *more* extensive *than we had expected*. ‖ 彼らは体力の限界を**超える**レースに果敢に挑戦した They boldly attempted the race which *pushed* them *beyond* their physical limits [which *challenged their physical limits*].

2**こえる 肥える** ▶この地方は土地が**肥えている** The soil is *rich* [*fertile*] in this area. ‖《慣用表現》彼は音楽にかけては**耳が肥えている** He *has an ear for* music. ‖ 彼女は**舌が肥えている** She *has a delicate palate*. / She appreciates fine cuisine. ‖ 私は絵を**見る目が肥えてきた** I've *acquired an eye for* art.

ごえん 誤嚥 **accidental swallowing**, 《医》 **aspiration** /æ̀spəréɪʃən/ ‖**誤嚥性肺炎** aspiration pneumonia.

ゴーカート a **go-cart**.

ゴーグル (**a pair of**) **goggles**.

ゴーサイン **the go-ahead**(進行命令) ▶政府は新しいプロジェクトに**ゴーサインを出した** The government *gave the green light* [*the go-ahead*] for the new project. (➤「ゴーサイン」は和製語).

コース **1**【道順, 進路】a **course** ▶ゴルフ**コース** a golf *course* ‖ ハイキング**コース** a hiking *trail* [*route*] (➤ trail は「山道」) ‖ 台風は**コースを外れた** The typhoon swerved from its *course*. ‖《野球》帆足は際どいコースへパームボールを投げてきた Hoashi pitched a palm ball across *the corner of* the plate.
2【競泳などの】a **lane** ▶彼女は第 3 **コース**を泳ぐ She is going to swim in *Lane* No. 3. (➤(×)Course No. 3 とはしない).
3【課程】a **course**, a **program** ▶初級**コース** an elementary *course* ‖ 大学進学**コース** *a course* for those who want to go on to college ‖ 彼女は**ドクターコース**の学生です She is a student in *the Ph. D. program*. ‖ 彼は人類学の**コースを取った**(= 人類学を専攻した) He *majored in* [《英》*read*] anthropology.
4【料理の】a **course** ▶フル**コース**の食事 a *full-course* meal.

> **危ないカタカナ語✹ コース**
> **1**「コース」に course を使えない場合がある. 例えば, 水泳や陸上競技の「コース」は lane で, プールの「コースロープ」は lane rope という. また, 野球の「インコースの球」「アウトコースの球」はそれぞれ inside pitch, outside pitch という.「パレードのコース」は parade route のほうがよい.
> **2** 料理用語としての「コース」は「決まった順序で出される料理」の意であるが, 英語の course は 1 品を指し, a five-course dinner, a dinner of five courses(5 品料理のディナー)のように用いる.

コースター a **coaster**(コップ敷き).

ゴースト ‖**ゴーストタウン** a ghost town ‖**ゴーストライター** a ghost(writer).

コーダ 《音楽》a **coda**.

コーチ a **coach** /koʊtʃ/ (➤ サッカーやアメフトでは coach は「監督」を指す) ▶テニスの**コーチ** a tennis *coach* ‖ ジャイアンツの**コーチを務める** *coach for* the Giants ‖ 彼は母校の野球チームを**コーチした** He *coached* the baseball team at his alma mater.
‖**ヘッドコーチ** the head coach.

コーディネーター a **coordinator** ‖**ファッションコーディネーター** a fashion coordinator ‖**移植コーディネーター** a transplant coordinator ‖**食品コーディネーター** a food coordinator.

コーティング **coating**.

コーデュロイ **corduroy** /kɔ́ːrdərɔɪ/ ▶**コーデュロイ**の上着 a *corduroy* jacket.

1**コート** 《上着》a **coat** /koʊt/; an **overcoat** (オーバー); a **raincoat** (レインコート) ▶**コートを着る** wear *an overcoat*.

2**コート** 《テニスなどの》a **court** /kɔːrt/ ▶アンツーカーの**コート** an all-weather *court*.

1**コード** 《ひも》an (**electric**) **cord** /kɔːrd/ (電気の) ▶テレビの**コード**をつなぐ *plug in* the TV set.
‖**延長コード** an extension cord.

2**コード** 《和音》a **chord** /kɔːrd/
‖**コード進行** a chord progression.

3**コード** 《決まり, 符号》a **code** /koʊd/ ▶バー**コード** a bar *code*(➤ これを読み取る器具を optical scanner という).

こおどり 小躍り ▶少女たちは思いがけないプレゼントに**小躍りして喜んだ** The girls *danced with joy* over the unexpected presents.

コードレス **cordless**
‖**コードレスホン** a cordless (tele)phone.

コーナー **1**【角, 隅】a **corner**; a **turn** (曲がり角); a **section** (区域) ▶《陸上競技》第 3 **コーナー**を回る round the third *turn* [*bend*] ‖《野球》(投手が)コ

ーナーぎりぎりを突く go for the *corners* ‖ 喫煙コーナーを設ける set up a smoking *section* ‖《テニス》錦織はコーナーぎりぎりにサーブを決めた Nishikori succeeded in putting his serve *right in the corner*.
‖《サッカー》**コーナーキック** a corner (kick).
2【売り場】▶彼女はそのデパートの**化粧品コーナー**で働いていた She works at *a cosmetics counter* in that department store. ／She worked in *the cosmetics department* [*section*] of that department store.
3【テレビ・ラジオの番組の】 a **segment.**
コーナリング **cornering.**
コーパス a **corpus**(言語資料) [複 **corpora, corpuses**]
‖**コーパス言語学** corpus linguistics.
コーヒー **coffee** ▶コーヒー1杯 a cup of *coffee* ‖《喫茶店で》コーヒー2つお願いします Two *coffees*, please. (➤店で注文するときは two cups of coffee よりもこのほうがふつう) ‖ コーヒーは濃い[薄い]のが好きだ I like my *coffee* strong [weak]. ‖ コーヒー入れようか？ Would you like some *coffee*? ‖ コーヒーでも飲みながら話さないか？ Shall we talk *over a cup of coffee*? ‖ コーヒー飲みに行こうよ Let's *go for coffee* [*go have some coffee*]. (➤ go have はインフォーマルな言い方).
‖**コーヒーカップ** a coffee cup ‖ **コーヒー牛乳** coffee-flavored milk ‖ **コーヒースタンド** a coffee stall [stand] ‖ **コーヒー豆** coffee beans ‖ **コーヒー沸かし** a coffee maker.
☛ ブラック (→見出語)
ゴーヤ《植物》a ***goya***; a **bitter melon.**
コーラ (a) **cola,**(a) **kola**; (a) **Coca-Cola,**(a) **Coke**(➤あとの2語は商標名であるが，日常的に多用される) ▶コーラを飲む drink *cola* ‖ コーラ1つちょうだい I'd like [I'll have] *a Coke* [*a Pepsi*], please. (➤ともに《商標》).
コーラス a **chorus** /kɔ́ːrəs/ ▶私たちはその歌をコーラスで歌った We *sang* the song *in chorus*.
コーラン **the Koran, the Quran** /kərɑ́ːn/ (イスラム教の教典；イスラム教徒は後者のつづりを好む).
こおり 氷 **ice** ▶氷は解けると水になる *Ice* melts into water. ‖ 池に氷が張り詰めている The pond *is frozen over*. ／The pond *is covered with ice*. ‖ 冷蔵庫から氷出して Could you get some *ice* from the refrigerator, please? ‖ 彼女の視線は氷のように冷たかった Her eyes were *as cold as ice*.
‖**氷砂糖**《米》rock candy,《英》sugar candy ‖ **氷枕** a pillow filled with ice, an ice bag.
こおりつく 凍りつく **freeze** ▶凍りついた道 a *frozen* street ‖ 道路は凍りついていて滑りやすい The road is *frozen over* and (is) very slippery. ‖ その夜の秋田市は凍りつくような寒さだった It was *freezing cold* in Akita City that night.
こおる 凍る **freeze** ▶ヨーグルトを凍らせる *freeze* yoghurt ‖ 凍らせたエンドウ豆 *frozen* peas ‖ 水は摂氏0度で凍る Water *freezes* at 0°C. (➤ zero degrees Celsius と読む) ‖ 諏訪湖は一面に凍っている Lake Suwa *is* (entirely) *covered with ice*. ／Lake Suwa *is frozen* [*is iced*] over. ‖ 寒さで水道管が凍ってしまった The water pipes *have frozen* from the cold.
ゴール a **goal**(主にサッカー・ホッケーなどの)；**the finish line**(レースの) ▶《サッカーで》ゴールに向かってボールを蹴る kick a ball at [toward] the *goal*(➤ 1語でいえば shoot) ‖《競走で》ゴールまであと20メートルだ You've got twenty meters (to go) to *the finish line*! 《参考》ゴールの幕などには FINISH と書くことが多い.
‖**ゴールキーパー** a goalkeeper(➤ keeper ともいうが，くだけた言い方は goalie) ‖ **ゴールポスト** a goalpost ‖ **ゴールライン** a goal line.
ゴールイン **1【スポーツ】**▶《ヨットレースで》ゴールインする *sail across the finish line*(➤「ゴールイン」は和製語) ‖《ランナーが》同時にゴールインする *cross* [*reach*] *the finish line* in a dead heat ／*finish* in a dead heat.
2【結婚する】▶2人は来春ゴールインする They are going to *get married* next spring.
コールスロー **coleslaw.**
コールタール **coal tar.**
ゴールデンアワー **prime time**(テレビ・ラジオの；「ゴールデンアワー」は和製語) ▶テレビ局はゴールデンアワーの視聴率獲得合戦をしている TV networks are in a battle for *prime-time* ratings.
ゴールデンウイーク ▶今度のゴールデンウイークにはどこかへいらっしゃいますか Are you planning to go somewhere this *Golden Week*?

> **危ないカタカナ語✹ ゴールデンウイーク**
> 「ゴールデンウイーク」は和製語であるが，日本関連の英語記事には Golden Week のままで用いられることもある. しかし文章中では the holiday-studded Golden Week(休日が散りばめられたゴールデンウイーク)または the Golden Week consecutive holiday のように書くほうがわかりやすい. the holiday week とも表現できる.

ゴールド **gold.**
コールドクリーム **cold cream.**
コールドゲーム《野球》a **called game** ▶試合は6回裏，雨のためコールドゲームとなった *The game was called* at the end of the sixth inning because of rain.
こおろぎ《虫》a **cricket** ▶コオロギの鳴く声が聞こえた I heard *crickets* chirping. 《参考》コオロギの鳴き声は英米では陽気で楽しげと聞かれるか，甲高い単なる雑音として聞き流される.
1**コーン**《トウモロコシ》《米》**corn,**《英》**maize** /meɪz/ 《参考》corns とすると「魚の目」‖**コーンサラダ** corn salad ‖ **コーンスープ** corn soup.
2**コーン** **1**《アイスクリームのカップ》a **cone** /koʊn/,《英また》a **cornet**(➤ cone は本来「円すい形」の意).
2《道路・工事現場などに置かれる円すいの標識》a **traffic** [**safety** ／**road** ／**construction**] **cone,** a (**traffic**) **pylon.** 《参考》「カラーコーン」は商標名.
ごーん ▶寺の鐘がゴーンと鳴った The temple bell *boomed*.
コーンスターチ **cornstarch.**
コーンフレーク **cornflakes.**
こがい 戸外 ▶戸外に出る go *outdoors* ‖ 冬でも子供たちは戸外で遊びたがる Even in winter, children want to play *outdoors* [*outside*].
1**ごかい** 誤解 (a) **misunderstanding**; (a) **misinterpretation**(誤った解釈) **一動 誤解する** **misunderstand** +㊐, **get ... wrong, misinterpret**(+㊐) ▶誤解を解く clear up *a misunderstanding* ‖ 2人の間に何か誤解があったらしい There seems to have been some *misunderstanding* between the two. ‖ 隠し事は誤解を招きかねない Secrecy can lead to *misunderstandings*. ‖ 彼は私の言ったことを誤解したに違いない He must *have misunderstood* [*misinterpreted*] what I said. ‖ 彼女はぼくを兄と誤解した She *took* [*mistook*] me *for* my older brother.

(➤ take [mistake] A for B で「AをBと間違える」) ‖ きみは個人主義というものを誤解している You *don't understand* what individualism means. ‖ 私の言うことを誤解しないでよ Don't *misunderstand* me. ／ Don't *get* me *wrong*. ‖ 彼の説明は誤解を招きやすい His explanation is *misleading*. ‖ ぼくがうそをついたなんて, それは全くの誤解だよ If you think I lied, you'*ve got* it all *wrong*.

2**ごかい** 《虫》 a **lugworm**.

こがいしゃ 子会社 a **subsidiary**, a **subsidiary company** ▶トヨタの子会社 a *subsidiary* of Toyota／a Toyota *subsidiary* ‖ 完全子会社 a wholly-owned *subsidiary*.

ごかいしょ 碁会所 a ***gokaisho*** ; a parlor where people meet to play Go (➤ 説明的な訳).

コカイン **cocaine** /koukéin/.

こがお 小顔 a **small face** ▶小顔に見せるメーク法 a makeup technique that *makes your face look smaller*. ⚠ **英米では small face はほめことばにならないので, 例えば, 次のように説明する必要がある. In Japan people (especially young women) prize and adore small faces and take pains to make their face look smaller. (日本では人々, 特に若い女性は, 小顔を尊び憧れて, 小顔になるためには努力を惜しみません)**

こがく 古楽 **early music.**

ごかく 互角 ▶両チームの実力は互角だ The two teams *are evenly matched*. ‖ 正男と和子の英語力は互角だ Masao and Kazuko *are about on a par* in their knowledge of English. (➤ on a par は「同等の」) ‖ 斎藤選手は山下選手と互角に戦った Saito *had a close match* with Yamashita. ‖ その試合は最後の瞬間まで互角だった The game [match] was *neck and neck* [《英》*nip and tuck*] until the last minute.

ごがく 語学 **language study** (➤ language は「ことば, 言語」) ▶語学の教師 a *language* teacher ‖ 語学の授業 a *language* lesson ‖ G大では語学と文学のどちらをやりたいのですか Which do you want to study at G University, *language* [*linguistics*] or literature? (➤ linguistics は「言語学」) ‖ ぼくは語学は弱い I am poor at (*foreign*) *languages*. ‖ 彼は語学の天才だ He is *a born linguist*. (➤ この linguist は「外国語のうまい人」) ／He has *a genius for languages*. ‖ 若いうちに語学をマスターしておきなさい Master *foreign languages* while young. (● 日本語ではよく「(外国語)をマスターする」というが, 英語の master は「(外国語)を完全に駆使する, 完璧に身につける」という含みが強い. したがって日本人のいう「マスターする」は learn (覚えて身につける)のほうが適切な場合が多い) ‖ これからはどんな仕事に就くにも語学力が必要だ From now on, *foreign language ability* will be required in many jobs. (➤「語学力」は linguistic skill のようにもいう).

‖**語学教育** language teaching [education] ‖ **語学実習室** a language lab(oratory) ‖ **語学者** a linguist.

ごかくけい 五角形 a **pentagon.**

こかげ 木陰 ▶涼しい木陰で昼寝する take a nap *in the cool shade of a tree* ‖ 私たちは大木の木陰で1時間ほど休んだ We took an hour's rest *under a big tree*.

こがす 焦がす **burn** +㊐ (焼く) ; **scorch** +㊐ (表面・一部を) ▶トーストを真っ黒に焦がしてしまった I *have burned* the toast. ‖ 私はうっかりたばこの火でズボンを焦がしてしまった I was so careless as to *scorch* my pants with a cigarette.

こがた 小型の **small** ; **pocket-size(d)** (ポケットに入るほどの) ▶小型の辞書 a *pocket-size* dictionary ‖ 小型のパソコン a *portable* personal computer (➤ portable は「持ち運び可能な」. 膝に載るサイズを lap-top, 手のひらサイズを palm(-top ／ -size)と呼ぶ) ‖ もう少し小型のデジタルカメラを見せてください Could you show me a *smaller* digital camera? ‖ パソコンはだんだん小型化してきている Personal computers are *getting* more and more *compact* [*miniaturized*].

‖**小型化** miniaturization ‖ **小型車** a subcompact car 《参考》アメリカでいう small car, compact car は日本のそれぞれ普通車, 中型車に相当する ‖ **小型トラック** a light [light-duty] truck.

こがたな 小刀 a **small knife** ; a **penknife**, a **pocketknife** (折り畳み式の).

こかつ 枯渇する **dry up** ▶川が枯渇した The river *dried up*. ‖ 化石燃料はいずれは枯渇する Fossil fuels will *be exhausted* someday. (➤ exhaust は「使い果たす」).

ごがつ 五月 **May** (➤ 略記しない) ▶5月にはツツジが満開になる Azaleas come into full bloom in *May*.

‖**五月人形** a samurai doll for the Boys' Festival ‖ **五月病** (mild) depression [apathy ／ anxiety ／ blues] that new employees and college freshmen experience in May (➤ 前後関係でわかる場合は "May syndrome" としてもよい).

こがね 小金 a **tidy sum of money** ▶小金をため込む save up *a tidy sum of money*.

こがねむし 黄金虫 a **gold beetle**, 《主に米》 a **goldbug** (➤ いずれも日本のものとは別種).

こがら 小柄な **short (in height)** ▶小柄な女性 a *petite* woman (➤ 褒めことばとして使う ; 発音は /pətí:t/).

こがらし 木枯らし a **cold winter wind, chilly blasts in late fall** ▶木枯らしに枯れ葉が舞っていた The fallen leaves were whirling in the *cold winter wind*.

-こがれる -焦がれる ▶私はアメリカの友だちと再会できるのを待ち焦がれている I *am looking forward to* seeing my friend in America again. ‖ 彼女はパーティーで会った美しい青年に恋い焦がれている She *is pining for* a handsome young man she met at the party. (➤ pine for は「…に恋い焦がれる」).

こかん 股間 one's **crotch.**

1**ごかん 語感** **1【ことばに対する感覚】** (one's) **sense of language**, (one's) **feel for language** ▶その詩人は並外れて鋭い語感をもっていた That poet had an unusually keen *sense of language*.

2【語のニュアンスや響き】 a **shade of meaning** ▶英語の decent という語は語感がつかみにくい The English word 'decent' has subtle *shades of meaning*. ‖「まろやか」は語感のいいことばです "Maroyaka" is a word that has a nice *ring* [*feel*] (to it).

2**ごかん 五感** **the five senses.**

3**ごかん 互換** ▶その2つのコンピュータには互換性がない Those two computers *are not compatible*.

こかんせつ 股関節 a **hip joint.**

こき 古希・古稀 **the age of seventy** (70歳) ▶古希を迎える reach *the age of seventy* ‖ 私たちは田島先生の古希を祝ってパーティーを開いた We gave a party to celebrate Mr. Tajima's *70th birthday*.

ごき 語気 a **tone of voice** ▶野党議員は語気鋭く首相を問い詰めた The opposition member grilled the Prime Minister *in a* (*sharp*) *tone of voice*. ‖ 彼は語気を強めて「自分は無罪だ」と言った He said *in a sharper tone*, "I'm not guilty."

ごぎ 語義 **the definition (of a word).**

こ

こきおろす こき下ろす put down; criticize ＋㊐ (非難する); 《インフォーマル》 trash ＋㊐ (…をくそみそに言う) ▶きみはどうして自分の父親をそんなにこっぴどくこき下ろすのかね Why do you *put down* [*criticize*] your own father so mercilessly? ‖ 彼の小説は1人の評論家にひどくこき下ろされた His novel *was* severely *criticized* [*panned*] by a critic. ‖ 批評家はその映画をこき下ろした The critic *trashed* the movie.

ごきげん 御機嫌 ▶何でそんなにご機嫌なんだい? How come you look so *happy*? ‖ 対話「浅田君, きょうはご機嫌いかがかね」「ええ, まあまあです」"*How are you feeling* today, Mr. Asada?" "Well, pretty good." ‖ おまえ, きのうの忘年会じゃずいぶんご機嫌だったぜ(＝上機嫌だった) You certainly *were enjoying yourself* at the year-end party last night. ‖ 奥さんのご機嫌ばかり取ってないで, たまには飲みに行かないか Instead of *trying to please* your wife *all the time*, why not come out drinking with us once in a while? ‖ 彼女はきょうはどうもご機嫌斜めみたいだね She does*n't* seem to be *in a very good mood* today, does she? ‖ ご機嫌よう *Good-by*(*e*)! ‖ 対話「かっこいい車ねえ」「うん, 性能もパワーもゴキゲンだよ」"What a cool car!" "Yeah, its performance and power are just *great* [*super*／*outstanding*]!"
✉ **ご機嫌いかがですか** *How have you been?*／How are you getting along?／How's everything?

こきざみ 小刻み ▶彼女の足は緊張で小刻みに(＝かすかに)震えていた She was so nervous that her legs were trembling *slightly*.
▶我々の野球チームは小刻みに(＝少しずつ)加点した Our baseball team added on runs *little by little*.

こぎたない 小汚い ▶おまえ, そんな小汚い格好であのレストランに入ろうってのかい? Are you going into that restaurant wearing such *seedy* clothes? ‖ そんな小汚い手はないよ! None of those *dirty tricks*!

こきつかう こき使う ▶看護師長は私たちを昼も夜もこき使った The head nurse *made* us *work* [*worked* us] *very hard* day and night. 《参考》部下をこき使う上司や社長をおどけて slave driver という.

こぎつける 漕ぎ着ける ▶つり橋はやっと完成にこぎ着けた They *managed to bring* the suspension bridge *to completion*. ‖ 労使はようやく合意にこぎ着けた Labor and management finally *reached* [*came to*] *an agreement*.

こぎって 小切手 《米》a check, 《英》a cheque ▶100万円の小切手を切る make out [write] *a check* for one million yen ‖ 私は銀行で小切手を現金に換えた I got my *check* cashed at the bank. ‖ 小切手で払ってもいいですか Can I pay *by check*?
‖米[カナダ]ドル建ての旅行者用小切手 a traveler's check in U.S. [Canadian] dollars ‖ 送金小切手 a remittance check [《主に英》cheque] ‖ 旅行者用小切手 a traveler's check.

ごきぶり 《虫》a cockroach ▶「きゃっ! ゴキブリ!」と妹が叫んだ "Eeek! *Cockroach*!" cried my (younger) sister. ‖ゴキブリ捕り a cockroach trap (トンネル仕掛け付きの); a cockroach-repellent spray (スプレー式の).

こきみ 小気味 ▶小柄のレスラーが大男を負かすのを見るのは実に小気味がよい I *get a kick* out of watching a giant beaten by a small wrestler. (➤ get a kick は「痛快でわくわくする」の意のインフォーマルな表現).

こきゃく 顧客 a customer, a client /kláɪənt/ (➤ 後者はより堅い語) ‖顧客サービス customer service ‖ 顧客満足 customer satisfaction ‖ 顧客リスト a list of customers [clients].

こきゅう 呼吸 1【息】breathing /bríːðɪŋ/ (息をすること); (a) breath /breθ/ (一呼吸); respiration (呼吸作用) 一動 呼吸する breathe /briːð/ ▶患者の呼吸が止まった The patient stopped *breathing*. ‖ 高地では呼吸が困難になる *It is difficult to breathe* [*People have difficulty* (*in*) *breathing*] at high altitudes.
‖呼吸器 the respiratory organs ‖ 呼吸器疾患 a respiratory disease ‖ 人工呼吸 artificial respiration ‖ 頻呼吸 tachypnea ‖ 無呼吸 apnea.
2【タイミング】▶ピッチャーとキャッチャーの呼吸が合わなかった The pitcher and catcher *were out of step* [*out of sync*] *with each other*. ‖『居酒屋』を歌ったとき2人の呼吸はぴったりだった The two sang "Izakaya" *in perfect harmony*. ‖ 釣りは合わせる瞬間の呼吸(＝こつ)を飲み込まないといけない In fishing, you must acquire the *knack* of raising the rod at the right moment.
☛ 深呼吸 (→見出語)

こきょう 故郷 one's home; one's hometown (故郷の町) ▶私が故郷を出てから5年になる It's been five years since I left *home*. ‖ きのう電話で故郷の両親と話した Yesterday I spoke over the phone with my parents *back home*. ‖ 故郷が恋しくなることはないかい? Do you ever *get homesick* [*miss your hometown*]? ‖ 博多は私の第二の故郷だ Hakata is my *second home*. ‖ いつかは故郷へ錦を飾りたい Someday I want to *return* [*go back*] *home as a successful man*.

こぎれい 小奇[綺]麗な tidy(きちんと整頓された); neat (よく手入れされた) ▶こぎれいな料理屋 a *tidy little* restaurant ‖ 妹はいつも部屋をこぎれいにしている My sister always keeps her room *neat and tidy*.

[1]こく body ▶こくのある酒 *rich* sake ‖ このワインは実にこくがある This wine has plenty of *body*. ‖ 彼のこの小説はなかなかおもしろいが, こく(＝深み)がない This novel of his is very entertaining but *has no depth*.

[2]こく 酷な cruel ▶あんなことを言うなんて酷だよ It was *cruel* of you to say that.／You were *cruel* to say that. ‖ 新人にホームラン20本を期待するのは酷だ It is *too much* to expect a rookie to hit 20 homers during the season.

こぐ 漕ぐ 1【船を】row ＋㊐ (オールで); paddle ＋㊐ (パドルで) ▶川でボートをこぐ *row* a boat on the river ‖ カヌーをこぐ *paddle* a canoe ‖ 《慣用表現》ほら, お父さんが本を読みながら舟をこいでる(＝居眠りしている)よ Look at Dad *nodding* over his book.
2【ペダルなどを】▶自転車をこぐ *pedal* a bicycle ‖ ぶらんこをこぐ *swing*.

[1]ごく 語句 words and phrases; an expression(表現).

[2]ごく 極 very, extremely(➤ 後者が強意); quite(全く) ▶中間試験はごく易しかった The mid-term examinations were *very* easy [were *a piece of cake*／were *a walk in the park*]. ‖ その事実はごく一部の人にしか知られていない The fact is known to only a *very* few. ‖ 日本人が英語の間違いをするのはごく当たり前のことだ It is *quite* natural that Japanese should make mistakes in English. ‖ この薬でごくまれに発疹(ほっしん)が出ることがあります This medicine causes a rash *in very rare cases*.

ごくあく 極悪の atrocious, villainous /vílənəs/ (➤ 後者は主に文語) ▶その悪人は極悪非道の限りを尽くした That villain committed *every atrocity imagina-*

ble. ‖極悪人 a (terrible) villain.

ごくい 極意 **mysteries**(奥義) ; a **secret** (秘けつ) ▶剣道の極意を窮めるには時間がかかる It takes a long time to master the *secrets* of kendo.

こくいっこく 刻一刻 ▶ロケット発射の瞬間が刻一刻と迫ってきた *Moment by moment*, the time for the launch(ing) of the rocket drew near.

こくえい 国営の **national** ; **state** (国有の, 国立の) ▶鉄道を国営にする *nationalize* railroads ‖この航空会社は国営です This airline company *is operated* [*is run*] *by the government*. ‖その国の国営放送局の伝えるところによると政府の指導者が交代したらしい According to what the *national radio station* of that country has reported, there seems to have been a change in government leadership.

‖国営企業 a state-run [-operated] enterprise ‖国営テレビ局 a state-run television station.

こくえき 国益 **national interest(s)** ▶国益を守る protect the *national interest* ‖私は米軍基地をそのままにすることは国益にかなうと思う [思わない] I [I don't] think keeping the U.S. bases *is in our national interest*.

こくおう 国王 a **king** ; a **monarch** /mɑ́:nəʳk/ (君主) ▶タイの国王 the *King* of Thailand / the Thai *King* (➤ 前者が正式な言い方).

こくがい 国外に **abroad** ; **overseas**(海外に) ▶国外に逃亡する take flight *abroad* ‖国外向けの放送 the *overseas* broadcasting service ‖彼の名前は国内よりも国外でよく知られている His name is better known *in foreign countries* than in his own country. / He is more famous *abroad* than at home. ‖その大統領は国外に追放された That president *was expelled from his* [*her*] *country*.

こくがく 国学 **the study of Japanese classical literature** [**Japanese thought and culture**].

こくぎ 国技 a **national game** [**sport**]

✉ **相撲は日本の国技で, 野球, サッカー, ゴルフとともに最も人気のあるスポーツの１つです** Sumo (wrestling) is the *national sport* of Japan and one of the most popular sports along with baseball, soccer, and golf. ➤ game は野球やフットボールなどのスポーツを指すので, この文では不適.

こくご 国語 **1**【日本語】**Japanese, the Japanese language** (➤ 後者は堅い言い方) ▶１時間目は国語だ We have *Japanese* class in the first period.

‖国語辞典 a Japanese dictionary.

2【自国語】one's **own language** ; one's **national language**(自分の国の言語, 国家語) ; one's **mother tongue**, one's **native language**(母語) ▶私たちは自分たちの国語に誇りをもつべきだ We should take pride in our *own language* [our *mother tongue*].

3【言語】a **language** ▶中野教授は数か国語を流ちょうに話す Professor Nakano speaks *several languages* fluently.

こくこく 刻々 →刻一刻, こっこく.

ごくごく ▶旅人は喉が渇いていたのでごくごくとコップの水を飲み干した The thirsty traveler *gulped down* a glass of water.

1**こくさい 国際** 一形 **国際的な** **international** ▶国際化の時代 the age of *internationalization* ‖国際的に活躍している歌手 a singer who is active *on the international* [*world*] *stage* ‖彼女は国際的に有名な女優だ She is an *internationally famous* [a *world-famous*] actress. ‖英語は世界中で使われている国際語である English is *an international language* (which is) spoken all over the world. ‖ゆうべのパーティーは実に国際色豊かだった The party held yesterday evening was *attended by people from all over the world* [*by people of all nationalities*]. (➤ それぞれ「世界中から来た人々」「あらゆる国籍の人々」の意) ‖自国のことをよく知らない国際人などありえないよ You cannot be *a citizen of the world* [*a global citizen*] unless you first know (something about) your own country. ‖中村さんは私が真の国際人と考えている人だ Ms. Nakamura is my idea of a true *cosmopolitan*. (➤ cosmopolitan /kɑ̀:zməpɑ́:lətn/ は「(国家的偏見にとらわれない)世界人」) ‖日本人はもっと国際性をもつ[国際感覚を身につける]必要があるとよく言われる It is often said that the Japanese people ought to *be* more *internationally minded* [*acquire a* more *international way of thinking*].

▶ソ連の崩壊で国際情勢は大きく変化した With the fall of the Soviet Union, *the international political situation* changed greatly. ‖そのパーティーは国際親善を図るために催されたものです That party was held to *strengthen the ties of international friendship*. ‖私はニューヨークの父に国際電話をした I made *an international* (*telephone*) *call* to my father in New York. ‖その計画は国際理解を深めるためのものである That program is intended to *deepen international understanding*. ‖今どき国際結婚など珍しくない Nowadays, it is no longer rare for (two) *people of different nationalities to marry* each other. (➤「国際結婚」は an intercultural [interracial / interethnic] marriageとするのがよい).

‖国際会議 an international conference ‖国際空港 an international airport ‖国際社会 the international community ‖国際収支 the balance of international payments ‖国際手配 an international [Interpol] hunt for a criminal ‖国際都市 a cosmopolitan city ‖国際便 an international flight ‖国際法 international law ‖国際連合 the United Nations《略 UN, U.N.》‖国際連盟 the League of Nations.

2**こくさい 国債** a **national** [**government**] **bond** ▶国債を発行する issue *national bonds* ‖赤字国債 a deficit-covering national [government] bond.

ごくさいしき 極彩色 ▶極彩色の熱帯の鳥 a tropical bird *with vivid colors*.

こくさく 国策 (a) **national policy**.

こくさん 国産の **domestic** ▶国産車 a *domestic* car / a *Japanese* car ‖国産品 *domestic* products [goods] / *domestically produced* goods ‖国産第１号のロケット the first rocket *made in Japan*.

こくし 酷使 ▶コンピュータ作業は目を酷使する Working on a computer *overworks* [*overtaxes*] the eyes. ‖そんなに体を酷使すると長生きできないよ If you *overwork yourself* like that, you won't live long.

1**こくじ 告示** a **notice** 一動 **告示する** **notify** +㊐ (知らせる) ; **announce** +㊐ (発表する) ▶告示板に告示を出す put up *a notice* on the *bulletin* [《英》*notice*] *board* ‖市長選挙がきょう告示された The mayoral election *was announced* today.

2**こくじ 酷似** ▶この一節は川端康成の『雪国』の冒頭に酷似している *There is a close resemblance* between this paragraph and the opening paragraph of Kawabata Yasunari's "Snow Country."

ごくし 獄死する die in prison.
ごくしょ 酷暑 severe heat ▶酷暑でビールの売り上げがぐんと伸びた Due to the *severe heat*, sales of beer rose dramatically.
こくじょう 国情 the condition of a country(国の状態); the situation [state of affairs] in a country(国内情勢) ▶彼女はタイの国情に詳しい She is quite familiar with *the situation* in Thailand.
ごくじょう 極上 ▶極上のワイン *choicest* wine / wine *of the best* [*highest*] *quality* ‖極上の牛肉 *choicest* [*prime*] beef(➤後者は特に牛肉を指すときに用いる).
こくじん 黒人 a black person; an African American (アメリカ人の) 一形 黒人の black; AfricanAmerican ▶黒人歌手 a *black* singer ‖キング牧師は自由と平等のために戦った偉大な黒人指導者だった Rev. Martin Luther King Jr. was a great *black* [*African-American*] *leader* who fought for freedom and equality. ‖新大統領は白人にも黒人にもヒスパニックにも等しく人気がある The new president is equally popular among whites, *blacks* and Hispanics.

直訳の落とし穴「黒人」とブラック
「ブラック」が黒人を指すことは多くの人が知っている. そこで,「ジムは黒人だ」のつもりで,(×) Jim is a black. と言いがち. black は通常, 単数形では用いない. 英語の black は「黒人の」の意味で形容詞として, a black student (黒人の学生)のように用いるか, 名詞としては白人(whites)やヒスパニック(Hispanics)などと対比して, 複数形 blacks の形で用いる. 単数の「黒人」は a black person (あるいは男性なら a black man, 女性なら a black woman)である. したがって, Jim is a black man. または, Jim is black. とする. また, 民族的なつながりを言って, アフリカ系アメリカ人であることを表して, an African American と言うこともある.「白人」を表す white も使い方は black と同様である.

こくすい 国粋 ‖国粋主義 ultranationalism ‖国粋主義者 an ultranationalist.
こくせい 国政 (national) administration(行政); government(政治) ▶選挙を通じて国政に参加する participate in *government* through elections.
こくぜい 国税 national taxes
‖国税審議会 the National Tax Council ‖国税審判所 the National Tax Tribunal ‖国税庁 the National Tax Agency《参考》アメリカで国税庁に当たるのは Internal Revenue Service で, イギリスのは Inland Revenue という.
こくせいちょうさ 国勢調査 a census ▶国勢調査を行う carry out *a census*.
こくせき 国籍 nationality; citizenship (公民としての身分, 公民権) ▶国籍を偽る disguise one's *nationality* ‖【対話】「彼女の国籍はどこですか」「カナダです」 "What is her *nationality*? / What *nationality* is she?" "She's Canadian." (➤「カナダ人です」と答える) ‖彼は日本で暮らしているが国籍はメキシコだ He lives in Japan, but is of Mexican *nationality*. ‖彼は5年前にアメリカの国籍を得た He acquired American *citizenship* five years ago.
☞ 多国籍 (→見出語)
こくせん 国選 ‖国選弁護人 a court-appointed lawyer(裁判所が任命した); a public defender(貧困などの理由で弁護人を選任できない刑事被告の公費弁護人).
こくそ 告訴 a charge(主に刑事事件の); (an) accusation(刑事・民事事件の); a complaint(特に民事の); a suit(訴訟) 一動 告訴する charge《with》, accuse《of》, sue《for》

【文型】
罪名(A)で人・会社(B)などを告訴する
charge B with A
file a charge of A against B
accuse B of A
sue B for A
【解説】charge は書類を調えての正式な, あるいは公式の告訴をいう. 特に, 検察による起訴を指す. accuse は違法あるいは犯罪行為などが行われたと訴えることで, 正式な告訴まで含む幅広い語. sue は賠償などを求めて裁判を起こすこと.

▶会社は元経理担当者を横領罪で告訴した The company *charged* a former accountant *with* embezzlement. / The company *accused* a former accountant *of* embezzlement. ‖彼女は暴行されたとしてそのセールスマンを告訴した She *filed a charge of* rape against the salesman. (➤ file は「(告訴状などを)提出する」の意) ‖彼らはその運転手を告訴して事故の損害賠償を求めた They *sued* the driver *for* (the) damages incurred in the accident. ‖彼は詐欺罪で告訴されている He *stands accused of* fraud.
▶うちの木を切らないでくれ. さもないと告訴するぞ Don't cut down our trees, or else we'll *file a complaint with* the police. (➤動詞 complain はふつう「苦情を言う, クレームをつける」). ‖告訴人 an accuser; a complainant (民事の原告).
[1]**こくそう 国葬** a state funeral.
[2]**こくそう 穀倉** a granary(穀物倉庫; 比喩的に「穀倉地帯」) ▶新潟は日本の穀倉地帯だ Niigata is *the granary* [*breadbasket*] of Japan. (➤ breadbasket は「パン籠」が原義).
こくたい 国体 the National Athletic Meet ▶千葉国体が開幕した The Chiba *National Athletic Meet* has started.
こくち 告知 (a) notice, (a) notification(➤後者はより堅い語) 一動 告知する notify +目, inform +目 ▶彼はがんの告知をされた He *was informed* that he had cancer.
こぐち 小口の small ▶小口の注文 a *small* order ‖彼は小口の預金をいろいろな銀行にしている He has *small* accounts with many banks.
こぐちぎり 小口切り ▶ネギを小口切りする *chop* a Japanese scallion *into thin pieces* starting from the root end.
[1]**こくちょう 国鳥** a national bird.
[2]**こくちょう 黒鳥** a black swan.
ごくっと ▶ビールをごくっと飲む *gulp down* beer ‖少年はテーブルの上のごちそうを見てごくっと生唾を飲み込んだ The boy's *mouth watered* when he saw the tasty-looking dishes on the table. (➤「口に唾がいっぱいたまった」の意).
ごくつぶし 穀潰し a good-for-nothing(役立たず).
こくてい 国定 ‖国定公園 a quasi-national park (➤ quasi- /kwéɪzaɪ-, kwɑ́ːzi-/ は「準…」の意).
こくてん 黒点 a black spot; a sunspot(太陽の).
こくど 国土 land(土地); a country (国) ▶国土を公害から守ろう Let us protect our *land* from pollution. (この例のように, 改まった日本語を訳す場合は Let's ... ではなく Let us ... とするのがふつう).

✉ **日本の国土の約67パーセントは山地で，多くは森林に覆われています** About 67% of Japan's *land area* is mountainous, and most of it is covered with forests.

‖**国土開発(計画)** national land development (planning) ‖**国土交通省** Ministry of Land, Infrastructure, Transport and Tourism.

こくどう 国道 a **national highway** ▶**国道**38号線 *National Highway* 38(➤ 地図や標識では Route 38 と書く).

こくない 国内の **domestic**；**home**(本国の) ▶**国内**および海外のニュース *domestic* and world news ‖**国内**でも海外でも *at home* and abroad ‖これは日本**国内**では見られない昆虫だ This is an insect which is not found *in Japan*.

‖**国内産業** domestic industries ‖**国内線** a domestic airline ‖**国内総生産** gross domestic product《略 GDP》‖**国内問題** a domestic issue.

こくなん 国難 a **national crisis**.

こくはく 告白 (a) **confession** 一動 **告白する** **confess**《to》(罪などを認める，白状する)；**declare** +目 (愛を)

> 【文型】
> 罪(A)を告白する
> confess to A
> ➤ Aは名詞・動名詞
> ～ということを告白する
> confess that S + V

▶自分の罪を**告白する** *confess* (*to*) one's crime (➤ 犯罪の場合)／*confess* one's sin(s) (➤ 宗教・道徳上の罪の場合；この場合，他動詞用法がふつう) ‖男は3人の女性を殺害したことを**告白した** The man *confessed to* killing three women. ‖夫は妻に，人妻と浮気したことを**告白した** The husband *confessed* to his wife *that* he had had an affair with a married woman. ‖もう彼女に愛の**告白**はしたのか？ Have you *declared your love* for her yet?

こくはつ 告発 a **charge**(主に刑事事件の)；an **accusation**(刑事・民事事件の) 一動 **告発する** **charge** +目，**accuse** +目 →告訴 ▶その会社は脱税で**告発された** That firm *was charged* with tax evasion.

‖**告発者** an accuser, a whistle-blower ‖**内部告発** an accusation from within an organization (➤ インフォーマルでは whistle-blowing という).

こくばん 黒板 a **blackboard**；《米》a **chalkboard**(色の薄い)；a **greenboard**(緑色の) ▶**黒板**を拭く erase the *blackboard*／clean [wipe] the *blackboard* (➤ erase は「(書いてあるものを)消す」) ‖あとで**黒板**を消しておいてくださいね Could you clean off the *chalkboard* later? ‖**黒板拭き**[**消し**] an eraser, 《英また》a (black)board rubber.

こくひ 国費 **government expense(s)** [**expenditures**] ▶私は10年前に**国費**留学をした I *was sent abroad to study at government expense* [*at the expense of the government*] ten years ago.

‖**国費留学生** a student studying abroad at government expense(国外に出ていっている)／a student from abroad studying here at government expense(外国から来ている).

こくび 小首 ▶**小首**をかしげたくなるような話 a *questionable* [*doubtful*] story ‖医者は彼女を丁寧に診察したあと，**小首をかしげた** The doctor *tilted his head questioningly* [*doubtfully*] after examining her carefully.

ごくひ 極秘 ▶その計画は**極秘**のうちに実行に移された The plan was carried out *in absolute secrecy*. ‖これ**極秘**だけど，彼女妊娠してるんだって *This is just between the two of us*, but I hear she's pregnant. (➤ インフォーマルな言い方).

‖**極秘情報** a top secret, top secret information ‖**極秘文書** a top secret document.

こくひょう 酷評 **severe criticism** 一動 **酷評する** **criticize ... severely** ▶彼の新刊本はある大学教授に**酷評された** His latest book *was criticized severely* [*was panned*] by a certain university professor. (➤ pan は「さんざんにたたく」の意のインフォーマルな語) ‖ 対話 「彼はすごく真面目だけど，頭が悪いよ」「それはまた**酷評だね**」"He's very honest but not bright." "Oh, you're *being too hard on* him."

こくひん 国賓 a **state guest** ▶米国大統領が**国賓**として来日した The U.S. President visited Japan *as a state guest*. ／The U.S. President came to Japan *on a state visit*.

ごくひん 極貧 ▶**極貧**生活をする live in *extreme* [*abject*] *poverty*.

こくふく 克服する **overcome** +目 (困難ののちに)；**conquer** +目 (打ち勝って支配する) ▶彼女は身体障害というハンデを**克服して**富士山登頂に成功した She *overcame* her physical disability and succeeded in reaching the summit of Mt. Fuji. ‖その病気が**克服される**日がやがて来るだろう The day will soon come when that disease *is conquered*. ‖彼はついに自分の内気な性格を**克服した** He finally *got over* [*beat*] his shyness. (➤ get over はインフォーマルな表現).

こくぶん 国文 ▶絵里子は C 大学の**国文科**の学生です Eriko is a student in *the Japanese literature department* of C University. ‖彼女は**国文学**を専攻しています She is majoring in *Japanese literature*.

‖**国文学史** the history of Japanese literature ‖**国文法** Japanese grammar.

こくべつしき 告別式 a **funeral ceremony** [**service**] ▶**告別式**を行う hold *a funeral* (*ceremony*).

こくほう 国宝 a **national treasure** ▶その建物は**国宝**に指定されている The building is designated as *a national treasure*.

‖**人間国宝** a living national treasure.

こくぼう 国防 **national defense**

‖**国防費** national defense expenditure ‖**国防予算** the national defense budget.

こくみん 国民

a **people**, a **nation** (全体)；a **citizen** (1人)

> 語法 社会的・文化的特徴などから見た場合は people を，政治的統一体としての国民をいう場合は nation をそれぞれ用いる.

▶**国民的**英雄 a *national* hero ‖アイルランド人の**国民性** the *national character* of the Irish people ‖日本人は勤勉な**国民**です The Japanese are *a* hard-working *people*. ‖公務員は**国民**のために働く Civil servants work for the *nation*. ‖私は日本**国民**です I am *a Japanese citizen*.

‖**国民栄誉賞** a People's Honor Award ‖**国民休暇村** a national vacation village ‖**国民健康保険** national health insurance ‖**国民宿舎** a *kokumin-shukusha*; a hotel that provides inexpensive accommodations in a resort area (➤ 説明的な訳) ‖**国民主権** popular sovereignty ‖**国**

民所得 national income ‖ **国民総生産** (the) gross national product《略 GNP》‖ **国民体育大会** →国体 ‖ **国民年金** a national pension ‖ **国民の祝日** a national holiday.

こくむ 国務 state affairs ‖ (アメリカの)**国務省** the Department of State ‖ **国務大臣** a minister of state ; a minister without portfolio(無任所大臣) ‖ (アメリカの)**国務長官** the Secretary of State.

1**こくめい 克明な** detailed ; minute /maɪnjú:t/ (微細な) ▶実験の結果を**克明**に記録する make a *detailed* [*minute*] record of the results of the experiment ‖ 戦時下の生活は彼女の日記に**克明**に記されていた Her diary gave a *minute and careful* description of life during the war.

2**こくめい 国名** a country name.

こくもつ 穀物 cereals /síəriəlz/ ;《米》grain,《英》corn(➤ともに集合的)

‖ **穀物畑** a grainfield, a field of grain.

こくゆう 国有の national ; state-owned, government-owned (➤ state-owned は《米》では「州有の」の意) ▶この庭園は**国有**(財産)です This garden is *government* [*national*] *property*. ‖ その**国有地**に新しい病院が建てられた A new hospital was built on the *government-owned site*. ‖ イギリス政府は1947年に鉄道を**国有化した** The British government *nationalized* the railways in 1947.

‖ **国有林** a national forest.

ごくらく 極楽 ▶このホテルは至れり尽くせりのサービスで, まるで**この世の極楽だ** This hotel is *an earthly paradise* with every kind of service at your fingertips. (➤ at one's fingertips は「手元にある」) ‖《温泉などにつかって》**極楽, 極楽** This is the life. (➤「これぞ人生」の意).

ことわざ **聞いて極楽, 見て地獄** When I heard about it, it sounded like (a) paradise, but when I saw it, it was really a hell. (➤ 日本語からの直訳) ／Things always look better from a distance. (➤「物事は常に遠くから見たほうがよく見える」の意).

▶ひいおじいさんは先週亡くなったが, まさに**極楽往生**だった My great grandfather passed away last week. I'm sure that he *has gone to Paradise*.

> **解説** **「極楽」と heaven, paradise**
> (1)「極楽」は本来,「あみだ仏のいる世界, 苦しみのない所」の意の仏教用語であるから, the (Buddhist) Pure Land とか the Land of Bliss [Happiness] のように訳すのがよい. (2) heaven は一般にはキリスト教でいう「天国」のことで, paradise はアダムとイブで連想される「楽園」.

‖ **極楽鳥**《鳥》a bird of paradise.

こくりつ 国立の national ▶あなたは**国立大学**へ行きますか, 私立大学へ行きますか Are you planning to go to *a national university* or a private one?

‖ **国立劇場** the National Theater ‖ **国立公園** a national park ‖ **国立病院** a national hospital.

こくりょく 国力 ▶**国力**の増強を図る try to develop *national power* [*strength*] ‖ 戦争は**国力**(＝国家資源)を疲弊させる War exhausts *the resources of a nation*.

こくるい 穀類 cereal(s) ; grain (➤集合的に) ;《英》corn(➤《米》では「トウモロコシ」の意).

こくれん 国連 the United Nations《略 UN, U.N.》(➤単数扱い) ▶日本は1956年に**国連**に加盟した Japan became a member of *the United Nations* in 1956. ‖ **国連安全保障理事会** the United Nations Security Council ‖ **国連決議** a United Nations resolution ‖ **国連憲章** the Charter of the United Nations ‖ **国連事務総長** the secretary-general of the United Nations ‖ **国連総会** the United Nations General Assembly ‖ **国連大学** the United Nations University ‖ **国連平和維持軍** a United Nations peacekeeping force (➤その兵士は peacekeepers) ‖ **国連本部** the United Nations Headquarters.

ごくろう 御苦労 ▶**ご苦労**だがこれを下に持っていってくれ *I'm sorry to trouble you*, but will you take this downstairs? ‖ 対話「館内を巡回してきました. 異状ありません」「**ご苦労**」"I've finished my round. Everything's OK." "*Good*." ‖ 対話「お申しつけの仕事, 終わりました」「**ご苦労さま**」"I've finished the job you asked me to do." "*Thanks* (*for your trouble*)."

こくろん 国論 public opinion (世論) ; (a) national consensus(国民的合意).

1**こけ 苔** moss ▶その寺の庭は一面に**コケ**が生えている The garden of that temple is covered with *moss*. ／*Moss* has grown all over the garden at the temple.

ことわざ **転石こけむさず** A rolling stone gathers no moss. (➤ 英語のことわざで,「職業や住居を転々と変えるのはよくない」の意であるが, アメリカ人の中にはこのことわざを「活動的な人は行き詰まることがない」の意に解する人が多い).

2**こけ 虚仮** ▶おまえ, 俺を**こけ**にするつもりか Are you trying to *make a fool of* me? (➤ make a fool of A で「Aを笑い物にする」).

ごけ 後家 a widow(未亡人).

こけい 固形の solid ▶**固形物**は食べないほうがいいですね It would be better for you not to eat *solid food*.

‖ **固形スープ** a stock [bouillon /bʊ́ljɑ:n ‖ bu:jən/] cube ‖ **固形せっけん** bar soap (粉せっけんなどに対して) ; a bar of soap (1個の棒状の ; 丸いものは a cake of soap) ‖ **固形燃料** solid fuel.

ごけい 互恵の mutually-beneficial ; reciprocal (相手から見返りを求めているという含みが強い) ▶**互恵関係** *mutually-beneficial* relationship ‖ **互恵通商協定** a *reciprocal* trade agreement.

こけおどし 虚仮威し (an) empty threat ; (a) bluff /blʌf/ (虚勢を張ること) ▶あいつの言ったことなど気にするな. ただの**こけおどし**だよ Don't worry about what he said. It's just (*a*) *bluff*.

こげくさい 焦げ臭い ▶**焦げ臭い**よ I *smell something burning*. ‖ 台所で**焦げ臭い**においがした The kitchen *smelled like something was burning*.

こけこっこー cock-a-doodle-doo /kɑ̀:kədù:dldú:/ ▶朝でもないのにニワトリが「**コケコッコー**」と鳴いた Although it wasn't morning, the rooster crowed "*cock-a-doodle-doo*."

こけし a *kokeshi* (doll)

日本紹介 ✉ **こけしは円筒形の胴体に丸い顔をつけた木製の素朴な人形です. 主に少女を表した姿で, 伝統的に日本の東北地方で作られます** *Kokeshi* are rustic wooden dolls with a cylindrical trunk and a round head. They mainly represent girls and are traditionally produced in the Tohoku district of Japan.

こげちゃ 焦げ茶 dark brown ▶**焦げ茶色**の紙袋 a *dark brown* paper bag.

こけつ 虎穴 ▶ ことわざ **虎穴に入らずんば虎子を得ず** If you don't enter a tiger's den, you can't catch a cub. (➤日本語からの直訳) ／Nothing ventured, nothing gained. (➤「思い切ってやらなければ何も手に入らない」の意).

こげつく 焦げ付く 1【焦げてくっつく】▶卵焼きがフライパンに焦げ付いてしまった The fried egg *has burned to the pan*.
2【回収不能になる】▶その会社に貸した1000万円が焦げ付いた Our 10 million yen loan to that company *turned sour*. (➤「焦げ付きの貸し金」のことを bad debt という).

コケティッシュ coquettish.

こげめ 焦げ目 ▶肉に焦げ目をつける *brown* the meat ‖畳にたばこの焦げ目がついていた There was *a cigarette burn* on the tatami mat.

こけらおとし 柿落とし ▶新劇場のこけら落としはシェークスピアの『ジュリアス・シーザー』だった *The first performance at the new theater, celebrating the completion of its construction*, was Shakespeare's "Julius Caesar." (「劇場の完成を祝う最初の公演」と考える).

こける 転ける fall ▶ジョギング中にこけて捻挫した I *fell* while jogging and sprained my ankle.
▶それは鳴り物入りの公演だったが見事にこけた(＝失敗した) The much-trumpeted theatrical performance turned out to be *a flop*. (➤much-trumpeted は「広く吹聴された」の意. flop は「失敗」の意のインフォーマルな語).

こげる 焦げる burn ; be burned (焼け焦げる) ; **be scorched** (きつね色に焦げる) ; **be charred** (黒焦げになる) ; **be singed** /sɪndʒd/ (表面が焦げる) ▶焦げたご飯 *scorched* rice ‖ステーキが焦げている The steak *is burning*. ‖電話をしてる間にカレーが焦げちゃったわ The curry *got burned* while I was talking on the phone. ‖トーストがすっかり焦げちゃったよ The toast *is* completely *burned*. ‖ぼくの歌集がキャンプファイアの中に落ちて焦げてしまった A songbook of mine *was charred* when it fell into the campfire.

こけん 沽券 ▶ここで音を上げては男のこけんに関わる To cry uncle at this point would *be beneath my dignity as a man*.

ごけん 護憲 the support [defense] of the Constitution
‖**護憲運動** the movement to support [defend] the Constitution.

ごげん 語源 the origin of a word, an etymology /èṭəmáːlədʒi/ ▶「カンガルー」という単語の語源を知っていますか Do you know the *origin* of the English word "kangaroo" ? ‖私は英単語の語源に興味をもっている I'm interested in the *etymology* of English words.
‖**語源学** etymology ‖**語源学者** an etymologist.

1**ここ 1【場所】here ; this place** (この場所) ▶ここへ来てください Come (up) *here*, please. ‖もう10分ここで待っててくれますか Can you wait *here* another ten minutes ? ‖《タクシーの運転手が客に》ここでいいですか Is *here* okay ? ‖ 対話 「わしの眼鏡はどこかな？」「ここにありますよ」"Where are my glasses ?" "(They're) *here*." (➤手渡すのなら "Here they [you] are." と言う) ‖ 対話 《建物を指して》「ここは何ですか」「外務省です」"What's *this* ?" "(It's) the Ministry of Foreign Affairs." ‖ 対話 「ここはどこですか」「銀座です」"*Where am I* ?" "(You're) in Ginza." (➤Where's here ? は一般的ではない) ‖ 対話 「ここから空港までどのくらいありますか」「約５キロです」"How far is it *from here* to the airport ?" "(It's) about five kilometers."
▶ここは日本だ. 俺は小田太郎だ. 太郎小田じゃない *This is Japan*. I'm Oda Taro, not Taro Oda.
2【部分・時点など】▶ここが肝心なところだ *This is* the crucial point. ‖ここが我慢のしどころだ *This is where* patience comes in. ‖《医者に》先生, ここが痛いんです Doctor, it hurts *here* [*this is where* it hurts]. ‖ここでひと休みしよう Let's take a break *now*. ‖きょうはここまで(にしよう) *That's all for today*. (➤授業・稽古などの終わりに先生が言う) ‖これはここだけの話にしましょう Let's *keep* this *between ourselves* [*between you and me*].
▶ここぞというとき打てなければ真の四番打者ではない You can't call a hitter a real cleanup if he can't get a hit *at the crucial moment* [*when the chips are down*]. ‖彼はここ一番というときには地力を発揮する When *it counts*, he shows his true ability.
3【最近】▶ここ３日間雨が降り続いている It has been raining *for the past* [*last*] *three days*. ‖ここ２，３日が山です *These few days* are crucial. ‖ここ２，３か月息子から電話がない I haven't had a (phone) call from my son *for the last few months*. ‖ここしばらくは暑い日が続くでしょう We'll have hot weather *for some time*. ‖ここのところ母は体調を崩しています My mother has been in poor health *these days* [*recently*].

2**ここ 個々** ▶それは大ざっぱな一般論であって, 個々の具体例には当てはまらない That is a rough generalization which does not apply to *each* specific example. ‖目的地まで個々に行きますか, グループで行きますか Shall we go there *individually* or in a group ?

こご 古語 an old word ; an archaic /ɑːˈkéɪɪk/ **word** (現代では使われない古風な語) ; an **obsolete** /ɑ̀ːbsəlíːt/ **word** (死語).

ごご 午後 afternoon ; p.m. (➤時刻のあとにつけて) ; **midafternoon** (午後の中ごろ, 午後３時から４時ごろ) ▶午後の一休み a *midafternoon* rest ‖彼は午後３時に到着した He arrived *at three in the afternoon*. ‖午後の早い時間に来てください Please come *early in the afternoon*. ‖日曜日の午後はたいてい暇です I am usually free *on* Sunday *afternoon* (*s*). ‖３月18日の午後にお伺いします I'll visit you *on the afternoon* of March 18. 語法 この２例のように特定の日の午後をいう場合, 前置詞は on になる.
▶きょうの午後はどちらへお出かけ？ Where are you going *this afternoon* ? 語法 this, tomorrow, yesterday, every などがつくと前置詞は不要.
▶あすの午後は時間があります I'll have some (free) time *tomorrow afternoon*. ‖きょうの午後はずっと家に居ます I'm going to stay home (*all*) *this afternoon*. ‖午後11時55分の列車が終列車です The 11 : 55 *p.m.* train is the last train. (➤p.m. は会話では通例用いない) ‖午後一で集まって打ち合わせをしよう Let's meet *first thing after lunch* and make arrangements.

ココア cocoa /kóʊkoʊ/ ▶ココアを１つください A cup of *hot chocolate* [*cocoa*], please.

> **危ないカタカナ語✹ ココア**
> 「ココア」はカカオの実(cacao)を煎り, 脂肪分を除いて粉末にしたもの. 飲み物としての「ココア」は cocoa でもよいが, 日常的には hot chocolate という.

ここう 孤高 ▶孤高の作家 a *solitary and high-minded* [*uncompromising*] writer (➤high-minded は「高潔な」, uncompromising は「妥協し

ない」).

ごこう 後光 a **halo** /héɪloʊ/.

こごえ 小声 a **low** [**small**] **voice** ▶彼女は「あなたが好きよ」とぼくの耳元で**小声で言った** She *whispered* in my ear that she loved me.

こごえる 凍える **freeze, be frozen** ▶手が**凍えた** My hands [fingers] are *numb with cold*. (➤ numb /nʌm/ は「感覚を失った」) ‖ かわいそうにマッチ売りの少女は**凍え死んだ** The poor little match-girl *froze to death*. (➤ froze は freeze の過去形) ‖ 外は**凍えそうな寒さ**だった It was *freezing cold* outside.

ここかしこ **here and there** ▶**ここかしこ**でジンチョウゲがほのかに香り始めた Daphnes have begun to give off a delicate fragrance *here and there*. ‖ **水仙や寒き都のここかしこ** (➤ 与謝蕪村(よさぶそん)の俳句) Narcissuses have begun to come out *here and there* in the still cold capital.

ここく 故国 one's **home (country)**.

ごこくほうじょう 五穀豊穣 a **rich harvest of (five kinds of) grain** ▶**五穀豊穣**を願う hope for *a rich harvest of grain*.

ここち 心地 ▶揺れが収まるまで [揺れが収まったあと] は**生きた心地がしなかった** I *was scared to death* until the quake stopped [*felt more dead than alive* after the quake stopped]. (➤ 前者は「死ぬほど怖かった」の意) ‖ 新居の**住み心地はいかがですか** *How does it feel to be* in your new home? ‖ この椅子は**座り心地がいい** This chair is *comfortable*. ‖ この車は**乗り心地がいい** This car *drives* [*rides*] *well*. (➤ drives は運転者の, rides は同乗者の意見の場合) ‖ 哲夫に愛を告白されたとき, 恭子は**天にも昇る心地**であった When Tetsuo declared his love for her, Kyoko *felt like she was walking on air*.

ここちよい 心地よい **pleasant** /plézənt/ (気持ちのいい) ; **comfortable** /kʌ́mfəʳtəbəl/ (楽な気持ちになっている) ▶**心地よい**そよ風が吹いてきた There is a *pleasant* cool breeze blowing. ‖ おばあさんは**心地よさそうに**眠っていた The old woman was sleeping *comfortably*.

こごと 小言 **1【叱ること】**▶ゆうべ帰宅が遅くなって父に**小言を言われた** Last night I *was scolded* by my father for coming home late. ‖ 社長はその社員がよく遅刻するので**小言を言った** The president *gave* the employee *a piece* [*a bit*] *of his mind* for being late for work often. (➤ give ... a piece [a bit] of one's mind で「…にひと言意見する」).

2【不平不満】▶彼はいつもあれこれ**小言ばっかり言っている** He *is* always *complaining* about this or that. 《参考》小言ばかり言っている人を grumbler とか griper /gráɪpəʳ/, あるいは whiner, 《英》whinger /wíndʒə/ という.

ココナッツ 《植物》a **coconut**.

ここら ▶**ここら**で一休みしようじゃないか Why don't we take a break *now*? ‖ **ここら辺** (=この辺) には高級マンションが多い There are a lot of luxury condominiums *around here* [*in this neighborhood*].

こころ 心

> **《解説》「心」と heart, mind**
> 喜怒哀楽など人間の感情の宿る場所をいうのが **heart**, 思考・意思決定などをする場所としての「心」が **mind**, 肉体に対する精神・気持ちを意味するのが **spirit**.

1【感情, 思いやり, 愛情】heart ▶そういう善行の記事を読むと**心**が温まる It warms my *heart* to read articles about good deeds like that. ‖ しばらく会わない間に彼の**心**は氷のように冷え切ってしまっていた His *heart* had cooled to the freezing point after the long separation. ‖ 彼女は**心の優しい**人だ She is a *gentle-hearted* person. / She is *kind-hearted*. ‖ 彼は見かけはいかついが, とても**優しい心の持ち主**だ He looks tough, but he *has a heart of gold*. ‖ 何年も付き合っていた彼女と切れて, **心にぽっかり穴があいた** I *feel an emptiness in my heart* after breaking up with my girlfriend who(m) I had been going with for several years.

2【意志, 考え, 本心】mind ▶彼女の**心**を読む read her *mind* ‖ 一生のうちには誰でも**心の病**にかかる可能性がある Anyone has the possibility of suffering *a mental illness* [*disorder*] at some point in their life. ‖ 自分は無実だと彼女は**心の中**で叫んだ *In her heart*, she screamed her innocence. ‖ 彼女はその秘密を**心の中にしまっておいた** She *kept* the secret *to herself*. ‖ 彼が**心の奥**で何を考えているのかわかりはしない He is inscrutable. / We can never know what he is thinking *at the back of his mind*. ‖ 彼は**心の奥底**では私を信用していないようだ He doesn't seem to trust me *in his heart of hearts*. / *Deep down*, he doesn't seem to trust me. ‖ **心から信頼できる**友人 a *staunch* friend.

［ことわざ］**親の心子知らず** Children do not understand parents' feelings.

3【意味, 精神】spirit (真意) ; **soul** (精髄, 本質) ▶彼の解釈は**この俳句の心**をとらえていない His interpretation doesn't capture the *spirit* of this haiku. ‖ 俳句や短歌は**日本の心**だ Haiku and tanka are expressions of *the Japanese soul*. ‖ 生け花を通して**日本人の心**を世界の人々に伝えたい I'd like to convey *the heart and soul of Japanese people* to the people around the world through Ikebana.

4【慣用表現】

心が痛む, 心を痛める ▶その悲しい知らせに心が痛んだ My *heart ached* [*broke*] at the sad news. ‖ 彼女の両親は彼女の不幸な結婚にひどく心を痛めている Her parents *are* very much *worried about* her unhappy marriage. **心が動く** ▶条件のいい商談を持ちかけられて, 彼は思わず心が動いた Having been presented with a good business proposal, he couldn't help *being interested*. **心が弾む** ▶楽しいピクニックに心も弾んだ I *was in a happy mood* at the picnic. **心が晴れる** ▶いくら友人に慰められても, 受験に失敗した雄二の心は晴れなかった No matter how much Yuji was consoled by his friends for failing the entrance exams, he couldn't *cheer* (*himself*) *up*. **心が広い** [**狭い**] ▶彼は心の広い [狭い] 人だ He is *broad-minded* [*narrow-minded*]. **心ここにあらず** ▶夫は妻の話を聞きながらも心ここにあらずというふうだった While his wife was talking to him, he looked as if *his mind were elsewhere*. **心に浮かぶ** ▶いいアイデアが心に浮かんだ A good idea *came to mind*. / I *came up with* a good idea. **心にかける** ▶いつもお心に掛けていただきまして, ありがとうございます Thank you so much for *being kind and helpful*, as always. / You are always so *very thoughtful*. I do appreciate it. **心に決める** ▶私はアイルランドに行くことを心に決めた I have *made up my mind* to go to Ireland. ‖ 私には心に決めた人がいます I already have *decided* (*in my heart*) *who to* *marry*. **心に留める** ▶今, 監督が言われたことをしっかり心に留めておこう Let's *keep* [*bear*] firmly *in mind* what the manager has told us. **心に残る** ▶祖母の顔は今でもはっきり心に残っている My grandmother's face is still *vivid* [*clear*] *in my mind*. ‖ これは私が今までに読んだ本の中でいちばん心に残る(=印象的な)ものです This is the most *impressive* book I've ever read. ／Of all the books I've ever read, this book has *made* the strongest *impression on* me. **心に触れる** ▶彼の俳句には心に触れるものが多い Many of his haiku *touch a chord within me*. (➤ touch a chord /kɔːʳd/ は「心の琴線に触れる」).

心を入れ替える ▶心を入れ替えてもっと勉強しなさい *Change your attitude* and study harder. **心を奪う** ▶聴衆は彼の弁舌に心を奪われるに違いない The audience will most probably *be carried away* by his eloquence. **心を配る** ▶もっと細かい点まで心を配って仕事をしなさい *Pay* more *attention to* small details in your work. **心を込める, 心の籠もった** ▶もう少し心を込めて仕事をしなさい *Put* a little more *spirit* in your work. ‖ これは私が心を込めて編んだセーターです I *put a lot of love* [*thought*] into knitting this sweater. ‖ 心の籠もった誕生日のプレゼントをどうもありがとう Thank you so much for the *thoughtful* birthday present. **心を閉ざす** ▶彼女は私たちに心を閉ざしてしまい, ろくに口も利かない She *has crawled into a shell* and hardly ever speaks to us. **心を引かれる** ▶ぼくは和服姿の楚々(そそ)とした女性に心を引かれる I *am attracted* to lovely young women dressed neatly in kimono. **心を許す** ▶俺にとって尾形は心を許した友だ To me, Ogata is a friend among friends. ‖ ぼくはまだあの男に心を許していない I'm not ready to *open myself up* to him.

☛ 心から (⇀見出語)

こころあたたまる 心温まる ▶心温まる話 a *heart-warming* story. **《参考》**日本人の中にはこの意味に heartful を使う人がいるが, この語は「心からの, 心のこもった」という意味はあるが「心温まる」という意味はない.

こころあたり 心当たり ▶犯人の心当たりはあるのかね? Do you have *any idea* who the criminal might be? (➤ この idea は「(…についての)見当」の意で, 主に疑問文・否定文で用いる) ‖ 誰か適任者の心当たりはありませんか *Can you think of* someone suited to the position? (➤ think of は「…を思いつく」) ‖ 黄色のセキセイインコを捕まえました. お心当たりの方は552-1234にお電話ください We have found a yellow budgie. The owner can claim it by calling 552-1234. (➤ claim は「自分の物だと言う」) ‖ どなたかこの時計にお心当たりの方はいらっしゃいませんか Do any of you *recognize* this watch? (➤ recognize は「見てだれのものかわかる」).

こころある 心ある **thoughtful** (思慮深い); **decent** (まともな) ▶心ある人はわが国の現状を憂えている *Thoughtful* people [*Thinking* people ／*Decent* people ／People *with* (*a*) *conscience*] are troubled by the present state of our country. ‖ 心ある人々によって村の社は守られている The village shrine is maintained by people *with a good heart* [by *decent* people]. ‖ 木下君が心ある人ならきっとその本をきみに返すはずだ If Kinoshita were a *decent* [*honest*] person, he would surely return the book to you.

こころいき 心意気 **(the) spirit** (気骨); **determination** /dɪtəːʳmɪnéɪʃən/ (決意) ▶その心意気だ *That's the spirit!* (➤「その調子だ」の意で人を励ますときの決まり文句) ‖ 最後までやり抜こうというきみの心意気が気に入った I'm impressed by your *determination* to carry it through to the end.

こころえ 心得 **1**【知識】**knowledge** ▶彼女はいくらか医学の心得がある She *has some knowledge of* medicine.

2【規則】a **rule** ▶ここでのキャンプ生活の心得をよく読んでください Read these *rules* about life here at camp carefully.

こころえちがい 心得違い ▶親を生きていることにして年金を受け取り続けるなど心得違いも甚だしい It's *totally outrageous* to continue to *accept* your parents' pensions, pretending that they're still alive.

こころえる 心得る ▶パソコンを持っていてもその使い方を十分に心得ていなければ何にもならない Even if you have a computer, it's useless if you don't *know* how to use it effectively. ‖ 穴あきジーンズで出社するとは, きみは会社を何と心得ているのかね You come to work wearing ripped jeans. *What do you think* the company is?

こころおきなく 心置きなく ▶《夫が妻に》ぼくが子供の面倒を見るから, きみは心おきなく(=心配せずに)同窓会を楽しんできなさい I'll be taking care of the kids. Go and enjoy yourself at the reunion *without worrying about* them. ‖ あの先生なら将来について心おきなく相談できる With that teacher I can talk about my future *freely* (*and without reserve*). ／I feel *comfortable* discussing my future with that teacher. (➤ 後者は「気楽に」).

こころがけ 心掛け (⚠ **ぴったりの対応語がないので, 状況に応じて「気持ちのもち方」「努力のしかた」などと意訳する**) ▶心がけ次第でどんなに忙しくても本は読めるものだ No matter how busy you may be, you can find time to read *if you really want to*. ‖ 国語の点数が20点だって? そりゃあふだんの心がけが悪いからだよ You got a score of 20 on the Japanese test? That's because you *didn't work hard enough*.

こころがける 心掛ける ▶いつも正しい姿勢を保つように心がけるべきだ You should always *try to* maintain good posture. ‖ 手紙をもらったらすぐに返事を出すように心がけなさい When you receive a letter, you must *strive* [*try*] *to* answer it promptly. (➤ strive は「懸命に頑張る」).

こころがまえ 心構え **(one's) (mental) attitude** (➤ ふつうは単に attitude) ▶心構えを変えない限りきみの成功はおぼつかない Unless you change your (*mental*) *attitude*, you have very little chance of success. ‖ 口頭試験を受ける心構えはできていますか Are you *mentally prepared to* [*ready to*] take the oral examination? (➤ be ready は「準備はできている」の意もある).

こころから 心から ▶彼は妻を心から愛している He loves his wife *with all his heart* [*from the bottom of his heart*]. ‖ ぼくは心から笑ったという記憶がない I don't remember the last time I *laughed wholeheartedly* [*from the bottom of my heart*]. (➤「思いきり笑う」の意味合いならlaugh heartilyでよい).

✉ **ご親切には心から感謝しております** I *sincerely* thank you for your kindness. ／I offer you my *heartfelt* thanks for your kindness.

こころがわり 心変わり **a change of heart, changing one's mind** ▶彼女は恋人の心変わりに気づいた She noticed that her boyfriend had *lost interest in* *her*. ／She noticed that her boyfriend's *love for her had shifted elsewhere*.

こころくばり 心配り consideration ▶お心配りありがとうございます Thank you for your *consideration*.

こころぐるしい 心苦しい ▶ご面倒をおかけして心苦しいのですが，私の英作文に目を通していただけますか I *hate to* trouble [*hate* troubl*ing*] you, but could you look over my English composition?

✉ **せっかくのお招きをお受けできず，心苦しく思っています** I deeply *regret* that I cannot accept your kind invitation.

こころざし 志 1【あることをしようと思う気持ち】 a wish(困難なことへの願望)；a desire(こうなりたいという欲望) ▶彼は父親の志を継いで陶芸家になった Following his father's *wishes*, he became a potter. ‖ 彼は志に反して家業を継がねばならなかった He had to take over his family business *in spite of his own desires*. ‖ いったん志を立てたら，簡単に諦めるな Once you *have made up your mind*, you should not give up [in] easily. ‖ 志を遂げるまでは故郷に帰らないつもりだ I am not going back home until I *achieve my goal* [*do what I set out to do*].

2【感謝，厚意】 ▶これはほんの志です．どうかお受け取りください Please accept this as *a token of my gratitude*. (➤「感謝のしるし」の意) ‖ お志はありがたいのですが，贈り物はご遠慮申し上げます I appreciate *your kindness*, but I have to decline the present.

こころざす 志す intend《to do》▶彼は若い頃はパイロットを志していた He *had intended* [*had wanted*] *to be* a pilot when he was young. (過去完了を用いることによってその志が実現しなかったという含みが出る) ‖ このオーディションは映画スターを志す人たちが受けます Those who *aspire to become* movie stars may take this audition. ／This audition is for those who *want to become* [*aim to be*] movie stars.

こころしずか 心静かに ▶その患者は心静かに最後の日々を過ごした The patient spent his [her] last days *peacefully*.

こころして 心して carefully ▶事故は起こしやすいということを忘れずに心して運転しなさい Drive *carefully*, keeping in mind how easy it is to have an accident.

こころづかい 心遣い consideration, thoughtfulness →思いやり ▶彼女にはお年寄りに対する心遣いというものが見られない She shows no *consideration* [*thoughtfulness* toward] for elderly people.

✉ **うちの子供たちにいろいろお心遣いをいただき，ありがとうございます** I appreciate your *thoughtfulness* [*kindness*] toward my children.

こころづくし 心尽くし ▶旧友を心尽くしの手料理でもてなす treat one's old friend(s) to *a lovingly prepared meal* ‖ 心尽くしのおもてなしを感謝します Thank you very much for your *warm* [*kind*] hospitality.

✉ **お心尽くしの品をお送りいただき，厚くお礼申し上げます** Thank you very much for sending me such a *nice present*.

こころづけ 心づけ a tip ▶彼は接客係に心付けを弾んだ He gave the concierge a big *tip*. →チップ.

こころづもり 心積もり ▶《旅行案内所などで》新婚旅行の費用はどれくらいのお心積もり(＝予定)ですか How much *are* you *thinking of* spending on your honeymoon?

こころづよい 心強い ▶きみが一緒に来てくれると心強いんだが I'd *feel reassured* if you'd come with me. ‖ きみからいいアドバイスがもらえて心強いよ Your good advice *encourages* me. ‖ (インターネットの掲示板などに) 心強いコメントをありがとう Thanks for your *encouraging* comments.

こころない 心無い cruel(むごい)；thoughtless(気遣いに欠けた) ▶心ない人々によって公園のコスモスは残らず摘まれてしまった Some (*thoughtless*) people picked all the cosmoses in the park. (こういうことは「心ない」人がやる行為だから，この例の場合はわざわざ thoughtless を用いなくても意味は通じる) ‖ その辛口の解説者は善戦した選手たちに対して心ない批判をした The harsh commentator *cruelly* criticized [berated] the players after they had put up a good fight.

こころなしか 心なしか ▶彼は心なしか寂しそうだった He looked lonely, but *I may have just imagined it*. (➤「私の気のせいかもしれないが」の意).

こころならずも 心ならずも against one's will(意志に反して) ▶私は心ならずも愛車を手放すはめになった I had to [was forced to] sell my car *against my will*. (➤「しかたなしに」という意味であれば，unwillingly, reluctantly などの1語の副詞を用いてもよい).

こころにくい 心憎い ▶新婚旅行のときと同じ部屋を取っておいてくれるなんて心憎いサービスね It was *absolutely marvelous* of them to give us the same room that we stayed in on our honeymoon. ‖ その8歳の少女のピアノは心憎いほど見事な演奏だった That eight-year-old girl gave an *admirable* performance on the piano.

こころにもない 心にも無い ▶心にもないお世辞を言うな Don't flatter me! ／Don't butter me up! (flatter, butter up が「本心からでない」の意を含んでいるので，「心にもない」は訳さなくてよい) 《参考》英語には Flattery will get you nowhere. (お世辞は何の役にも立たない)という慣用表現がある.

こころのこり 心残り (a) regret ▶決勝戦は最善を尽くして負けたのだ．心残りはない Because we gave our all in the final game, we *have no regrets about* losing.

こころばかり 心ばかり (⚠ **日本人はちょっとした贈り物をする場合にも，相当に高価な贈り物をする場合にもこの表現を用いるが，この日本的謙遜を表すのにぴったりの英語はない**). ✉ **心ばかりの品ですが，どうぞお納めください** Please accept this little present (*as a token of my gratitude*).

こころぼそい 心細い feel anxious (不安だ)；feel helpless(無力を感じる)；feel uneasy(気持ちが落ち着かない)；feel lonesome(寂しい気持ちになる) ▶外国旅行は初めてだったのでとても心細い思いをした Since it was my first trip abroad, I *felt* quite *helpless*. ‖ その夫婦は子供がいないので少々行く末を心細く思っている The couple have no children and *feel* a little *anxious* [*worry* a bit] about their future. ‖ 彼女は自分の将来を思うと心細くなった She *felt uneasy* about her future.

こころまち 心待ち →楽しみ ✉ **夏休みにお会いできるのを心待ちにしています** I'*m looking forward to* seeing you during the summer vacation. ➤ look forward to のあとには動名詞または名詞がくる.

こころみ 試み an attempt；(an) experiment (実験) ▶意欲的な試み an ambitious *attempt* ‖ これは今まで誰もやろうとしなかった新しい試みです This is a new *experiment* that nobody (has) ever attempted. ‖ それは男女の産み分けに挑んだ最初の試みであった It was the first *attempt* to choose the sex of children at conception. ‖生徒の提案を入れて, **試みに**4月から制服を廃止することになりました Accepting the students' proposal, we decided to *temporarily* abolish the school uniform rule *for a trial period*, beginning this coming April. (➤ temporarily は「一時的に」).

こころみる 試みる try, attempt (➤ 後者はしばしば失敗に終わることを暗示する) ▶彼はたとえ失敗してもたぶんもう一度**試みる**だろう Even if he fails, he will probably *try* again. ‖警察は人質犯たちに投降するようにと繰り返し説得を**試みた** The police repeatedly *tried* [*attempted*] to persuade the hostage-takers to surrender.

こころもち 心持ち **1【気持ち】**▶被災地の住民たちは不安な**心持ち**で一夜を過ごした The residents of the (disaster-) stricken area passed the night *in anxiety*.

2【ほんの少し】▶あの塀はこころもち左に傾いている That wall leans *somewhat* to the left.

こころもとない 心許無い ▶銀行に貯金がほとんど無いので**心もとない**(=不安だ) I *feel uneasy* because I have almost no savings in the bank. ‖新規事業を始めたいが資金繰りがどうも**心もとない** I'd like to set up a new business, but I'*m worried about* whether (or not) I can raise the necessary capital. ‖父は**心もとない手つき**でファックスを操作している My father operates the fax machine *clumsily* [*with clumsy hands*].

こころやすい 心安い ▶**心安い**レストラン one's *familiar* restaurant ‖滞米中に彼はある写真家と**心安くなった** He *got acquainted with* a photographer during his stay in the United States.

こころゆくまで 心行くまで ▶どうぞ**心行くまで**この別荘で夏休みをお過ごしください Please enjoy your vacation here in our summer cottage *as long as you like*. (➤「好きなだけ長く」の意) ‖私は**心行くまで**(その店の)インドネシア料理を味わった I enjoyed the Indonesian food *to my heart's content*.

こころよい 快い comfortable ; refreshing (爽やかな) ▶5月の**快い**風 the *refreshing* breeze of May ‖高原の澄んだ空気ほど**快い**ものはない Nothing is more *refreshing* than the pure air of the highlands. ‖私はソファーの上で**快い**気分でまどろんでいた I was *comfortably* dozing on the couch [was dozing on the couch in a *comfortable* mood].

こころよく 快く readily, willingly (➤ 前者は「進んで」の意に対し, 後者は「自分の意志で」または「自分の責務と考えて」の意で, 積極的な気持ちは前者が強い) ▶彼はぼくの頼みを**快く**承諾してくれた He *readily* [*willingly*] consented to my request. ‖妻はぼくがひとりでフィジーへ遊びにいったのを**快く思っていない**に違いない My wife must *be none too happy* about my having gone to Fiji without her. (➤none too は「あまり…でない」).

ここん 古今の ancient and modern (古代と現代の) ; of all ages (あらゆる時代の) ▶**古今東西**のあらゆる文献を渉猟する read every type of literature *ancient and modern, Western and Eastern* ‖大英博物館は**古今東西**の最高の芸術および考古学的貴重品を収蔵している The British Museum has a first-class collection of archeological artifacts and *ancient and modern art from around the world*.

ごこん 語根 the root of a word, a root.

ごさ 誤差 an error ▶このはかりは1000グラムにつき1グラムの**誤差**を生じる This scale has (*an*) *error* of 1 gram per 1,000. ‖この世論調査の**誤差許容範囲**はプラスマイナス3ポイントです The poll has *a margin of error* of plus or minus 3 percentage points.

ござ a (rush) mat ▶ござを敷く spread *a mat*.

コサージュ a corsage /kɔːrsɑ́ːʒ/.

ごさい 後妻 one's second wife (➤ 3人目なら third wife, 4人目なら fourth wife ... のようにする).

こざいく 小細工 tricks ▶つまらない**小細工**はやめろ Stop playing *petty tricks*!

コサイン 《数学》 a cosine /kóʊsaɪn/ (《略 cos》).

こざかしい 小賢しい shrewd /ʃruːd/ (抜け目がない) ; presumptuous /prɪzʌ́mptʃuəs/ (生意気な) ▶**こざかしい**策を巡らす work out a *shrewd* [*cunning*] scheme ‖**こざかしい**ことを言うんじゃないよ Don't say *presumptuous* things.

こさく 小作 tenant farming

‖**小作農** a tenant farmer.

こさじ 小匙 a teaspoon ▶小さじ3杯の塩 three *teaspoons* [*teaspoonfuls*] of salt.

こさつ 古刹 an old Buddhist temple.

こざっぱり ▶彼女はいつも**こざっぱりした**服装をしている She always dresses *neatly* (*and tidily*). ／She is always *neatly* dressed.

こさめ 小雨 (a) light rain ; a drizzle (霧雨) ▶外は**小雨**が降っていた *A light rain* was falling outside. ／It was drizzling [*raining lightly*] outside.

こさん 古参 ▶**古参**力士 a *veteran* sumo wrestler.

ごさん 誤算 (a) miscalculation ▶対立候補が出ないと踏んだのは町長の大きな**誤算**だった It was a big *miscalculation* by the mayor not to anticipate an opposing candidate.

ごさんけ 御三家 the top three (歌手などの) ; the three branch families in the Tokugawa Shogunate (徳川家の).

[1]**こし 腰** **1【腰部】** the waist /weɪst/, the middle (くびれた部分, ウエスト ; 後者はくだけた語) ; the (lower) back (背中の下部) ; the hip(s) (左右に張り出した部分)

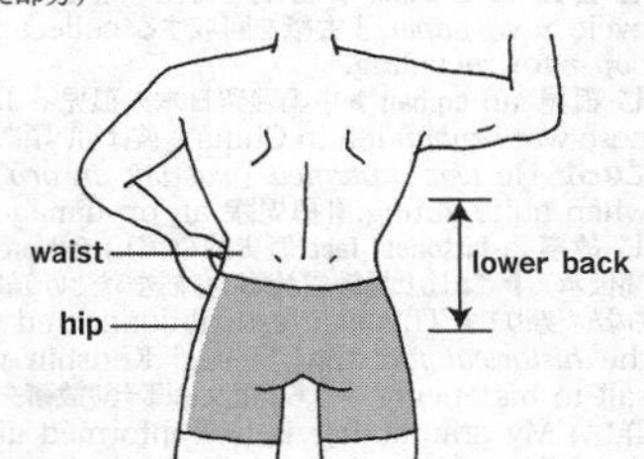

> **◀解説▶** 英語には日本語の「腰」に1語で対応する語はない. 日本語の「腰」は waist とその下の部分をも含んでいる. したがって, 英訳するときは和文の意味をよく考える必要がある. →ヒップ.

▶**腰が痛い** I *have a backache*. ／My *back hurts*. ‖めぐみは**腰が細い** Megumi has a slender *waist*. ‖祖父は年のせいで少し**腰が曲がっている** My grandfather *is* a little *bent* with age. ‖シートベルトはしっかりと**腰の低い位置**でお締めください Please fasten your seat belt tight and *low*. ‖フラの踊り子たちは音楽に合わせて**腰を振った** The hula dancers swayed their *hips* to the music. ‖雪道で滑って転び, **腰を打った** I slipped on the snowy road and *fell on my rear* [*hip*]. (➤ rear は「尻」) ‖**腰を伸ばして**深呼吸をしよう Let's stretch [straighten] *our backs* and take a deep breath. ‖ 彼のバッティングフォームは腰が安定していない His batting form is *wavering* [*shaky*].

2【強じんさ】▶髪が柔らかくてコシがないので, ブローしてもなかなか格好がつかない My hair *has no body*, and even if I blow-dry it, it doesn't hold a style. ‖ この餅はコシが強い This mochi is (*nice and*) *chewy*. (➤「コシの強いうどん」は firm [chewy] udon (noodles)).

3【慣用表現】

腰が重い[**軽い**] ▶彼は腰が重くてなかなか行動を開始しない He's awfully *slow* when it's time to get down to work. ‖ うちの夫は腰が軽くて用事を何でもやってくれる My husband *is always ready to pitch in* with any chore. (➤「いつでもすぐに取りかかる用意ができている」の意) **腰が低い** ▶会長は腰の低い人だ The president is very *modest*. **腰を上げる** ▶学校もようやく重い腰を上げていじめ問題に取り組み始めた Although it was initially hesitant [reluctant], the school finally *began* dealing with the bullying problem. **腰を落とす** ▶《綱引きで》みんな, 腰を落として! *Bend lower*, everyone! ‖ 腰を落として相手のサーブを待つ *crouch* waiting for a serve. **腰を折る** ▶人の話の腰を折るのは失礼です It's impolite to *interrupt* people while they are talking. (➤ interrupt は「人の話の邪魔をする」) **腰を下ろす** ▶ベンチに腰を下ろす *sit* (*down*) on a bench **腰を据える** ▶当分は田舎に腰を据えるつもりだ I'm going to *settle* in the countryside for a while. ‖ 私は腰を据えて医学の研究をしようと思う I'm going to *settle down* to study medicine *in earnest*. /I'm going to *apply myself to* studying medicine. **腰を抜かす** ▶母はその知らせを聞いて腰を抜かした My mother *was paralyzed with shock* at the news. (➤「驚きのあまり動けなくなった」の意).

[2]**こし 古紙** used paper ▶古紙を再生(利用)する recycle *used paper* ‖ 古紙を回収する collect *used paper* for recycling.

[1]**こじ 孤児** an orphan ▶中国残留日本人孤児 a Japanese war *orphan* left in China ‖ 彼は幼い頃に孤児になった He *was orphaned* [*was left an orphan*] when quite young. ‖ **孤児院** an orphanage.

[2]**こじ 故事** a historical fact(歴史的事実); folklore (民間伝承) ▶これは上杉謙信が敵に塩を送ったという故事にちなんだ祭りです This is a festival connected with the *historical fact* that Uesugi Kenshin gave salt to his enemy. ‖ うちの祖父は郷土の故事来歴に詳しい My grandfather is well-informed about the *folklore* [*legends* / *old tales*] *and history* of our hometown.

[3]**こじ 誇示する** show off ▶私, 胸毛を誇示する人は嫌いです I hate men who *show off* their hairy chests. ‖ あの男は何かと言うと権力を誇示したがる That man likes to *show off* his power whenever he gets the chance.

[4]**こじ 固辞する** refuse firmly ▶彼女は立候補の要請を固辞した She *firmly refused* to run in the election.

ごし 五指 ▶T先生は日本で五指に入る脳外科医です Doctor T is *among the top five* brain surgeons in Japan.

-ごし -越し **1【物・場所を隔てて】**▶その老婦人は眼鏡越しに私を見た The old woman looked at me *over her glasses*. ‖ 道行く人たちが垣根越しにうちの庭を見る Passers-by look into our garden *over the hedge*.

2【時間を隔てて】▶2人は10年越しの交際の末結ばれた The two finally got married after seeing each other *for ten years*.

ごじ 誤字 a wrong kanji(漢字の); a misspelled word (英単語などの); a misprint, a typo(誤植) ▶若者の書くメールには誤字が多い There are many *wrong kanji* in the e-mails young people write.

こじあける こじ開ける pry /praɪ/ ... open ▶箱の蓋をナイフでこじあける *pry* [《英また》*prise*] *out* the lid of a box with a knife ‖ 泥棒は鍵の掛かった扉をこじあけた The burglar *pried* [*prised*] the locked door *open*. ‖ 金庫はバールのようなものでこじあけられていた The safe *was pried open* with a crowbar-like tool.

こしお 小潮 a neap tide.

こしかけ 腰掛け a chair; a stool(背もたれの無いもの) ▶腰掛けに座る sit on *a chair* ‖ 腰掛けをガタガタさせるのはよしなさい Stop rocking the *chair*! ‖《比喩的》彼はただ腰掛け的に(=一時的に)その新聞社で働いていた He worked for the newspaper company just *as a temporary measure* [*as a stopgap*].

こしかける 腰掛ける sit (down), take a seat ▶腰掛けなさい *Take a seat*. (● その人の席として決まっている場合には Take your seat. とする) /*Have a seat*. ‖ 腰掛ける椅子が無かった There was no seat to *take*. / There were no seats left. (➤ 後者は「空席が無かった」の意).

こじき 乞食 a beggar, 《米また》a panhandler ▶こじきをする *beg* on the street /live as a beggar.

こしくだけ 腰砕け ▶国民の猛反発で増税論議は腰砕けになった Discussions about tax hikes *abruptly* [*suddenly*] *lost steam* because of a strong negative reaction from the people.

ごしごし ▶タオルで体をごしごし洗う *scrub* one's body with a towel.

こしたんたん 虎視眈々 ▶彼らは虎視たんたんと大統領暗殺の機会を狙った They watched *unwaveringly* for a chance to assassinate the president (*just like a tiger stalking its prey*).

[1]**こしつ 個室** a single room(ホテルの); a private room (私室) ▶病院の個室 *a private room* at a hospital.

[2]**こしつ 固執する** stick《to》▶父は古い考え方に固執するので困る The trouble is that my father *sticks to* the old-fashioned way of thinking. ‖ 彼女は自分の意見に固執し過ぎる She *is too attached to* her own opinions.

ごじつ 後日 later on(あとで); some other day (またいつの日か); in the future (将来) ▶この問題は後日話し合いましょう Let's discuss this problem *some other day*. ‖ その話には後日談があってね There's *more* [*a sequel*] to the story.

✉ **また後日お目にかかれるのを楽しみにしております** I'm looking forward to seeing you again *some time in the future*.

ゴシック Gothic(ゴシック様式の) ▶パリのノートルダム寺院はゴシック建築で有名だ Notre Dame in Paris is famous for its *Gothic architecture*. ‖ それはゴシック体(=太字)で書かれていた It was printed in *boldface*.

こじつけ ▶こじつけ話 *a far-fetched story* ‖ 彼女のあの文章の解釈は相当なこじつけだと思う I think her interpretation of that passage was rather *strained* [*distorted*].

こじつける distort(ゆがめる); strain(曲解する) ▶彼は話をこじつけるのがうまい He is skillful at *distortion*.

ごシップ (a) **gossip** ▶彼に関するゴシップはよく聞くね I hear a lot of *gossip* about him. ‖ゴシップは誰でも好きだ Everybody likes to *gossip*. (➤ この gossip は動詞).

ごじっぽひゃっぽ 五十歩百歩 ▶贈賄と収賄のどちらが悪いかなんて言えないよ. 五十歩百歩というところさ You can't say which is worse, giving or accepting a bribe. *It doesn't make any difference*.

こしぬけ 腰抜け a **coward** /káʊəʳd/, a **wimp**(➤ 後者は主に子供が用いる) ▶彼はどうしようもない腰抜け(＝臆病者)だ He is a hopeless *coward*.

こしばき 腰穿きする **wear** one's **pants low**; **sag** one's **pants** (➤ 後者はかなりずり下がった状態) ▶制服のズボンを腰ばきするのはだらしなく見える It looks sloppy to *wear your* school uniform *pants* so *low* [*below* (*your*) *waist*].

こしパン 腰パン **sagging** one's **pants** ▶彼はよく腰パンをする He often *wears his pants low* [*below his waist*]. ／He often *sags his pants*. (➤ 後者は極端に下げている印象がある).

こしゅう 固執 →こしつ.

1**ごじゅう 五十** **fifty**; **the fiftieth**(50番目) ▶50代の男 a man in *his fifties* ／a *fifty-something* man ‖50年代のファッション the fashions of *the 50s* / *50s* fashions.

2**ごじゅう 五重** ▶その寺の境内には五重の塔がそびえている *A five-storied pagoda* stands on the grounds of that temple. ‖五重奏[唱] a quintet(te).

ごじゅうおん 五十音 the 50 syllables in the Japanese phonetic writing system; the Japanese syllabary /sɪ́ləberi/ (五十音図).

ごじゅうかた 五十肩 a **frozen shoulder**.

ごしゅうしょうさま 御愁傷様 ▶この度は誠にご愁傷さまです I would like to express my sincere condolences to you. (● 日本ではこの言い方は決まり文句になっているが, 英語圏の人たちはこの言い方をあまり好まない. 口頭の場合は I miss your dad. (お父さんがいなくて寂しいな), I'm sorry that you lost your dad. (お父さんが亡くなって残念だ), また書きことばでは My heart goes out to you. (きみ[あなた]に同情します)のような, 紋切り型でないものが好まれる).

こじゅうと 小舅・小姑 a **brother-in-law** [複 **brothers-in-law**](兄弟); a **sister-in-law** [複 **sisters-in-law**](姉妹).

ごしゅきょうぎ 五種競技 **pentathlon**
‖近代五種競技 the modern pentathlon.

ごじゅん 語順 **word order** ▶この文の語順は正しくない The *word order* in this sentence is incorrect.

こしょ 古書 an **old book** (古い本); a **secondhand** [**used**] **book**(古本).

ごしょ 御所 **the imperial residence**; **the imperial palace**(宮殿).

ごじょ 互助 **mutual aid**
‖互助会 a mutual-aid society [association].

1**こしょう 故障** **trouble**; a **breakdown** (突然の) 一動 故障する **break down**; **go out of order** (主に公共性や共同使用性のある物が) ▶このファックスは故障している This fax machine *doesn't work*. ‖高速道路で車が故障した(＝えんこした) We *had a breakdown* on the expressway. ／Our car *broke down* on the expressway. ‖ぼくの車はエンジン故障を起こしたことがない My car has never had *engine trouble* [*an engine failure*]. ‖自動販売機が故障中で缶ジュースが買えなかった The vending machine was *out of order*, so I could not get a soft drink. ‖このミシンはどこか故障しているに違いない Something must *be wrong* with this sewing machine. ‖車両故障のため山手線は現在運転を見合わせています The Yamanote Line is now temporarily out of operation due to *technical problems* with one of the trains.
▶彼は足の故障でオリンピック出場が危ぶまれている We are afraid that he might not be able to take part in the Olympic Games because of his *leg trouble*. ‖故障者リストに載る[から復帰する] be put on [be taken off] *the injured reserve list* (➤「故障者リスト」は野球では the disabled list という).

2**こしょう 胡椒** **pepper** ▶白[黒]コショウ white [black] *pepper* ‖ラーメンにコショウを振りかける shake *pepper* on ramen ‖肉にお好みで塩・コショウします Season the meat with *salt and pepper* to taste.
‖コショウ入れ a pepper shaker ‖コショウひき a pepper grinder [mill].

3**こしょう 呼称** an **appellation**; a **name**(名前).

4**こしょう 小姓** a **page**.

こじょう 湖上 ▶湖上に数隻のヨットが見えた I saw several sailboats *on the lake*. ‖湖上には霧が立ちこめていた A mist hung *over the lake*.

ごしょう 後生 ▶後生だから行かないで! *For heaven's* [*goodness*(')] *sake*, please don't go! ‖彼女は古い日記帳を後生大事にしている She *treasures* her old diaries *more than anything else in the world*.

ごじょう 互譲 (a) **mutual concession** ▶互譲の精神でもめ事を解決する settle a dispute in the spirit of *mutual concession*.

こしょく 孤食 **eating alone**.

ごしょく 誤植 a **misprint**, a **typographical error**, 《インフォーマル》a **typo**(➤ あとの2語は「(キーボードでの)タイプミス」にも用いる) ▶その本は誤植が多い There are lots of *misprints* in that book.

こしょくそうぜん 古色蒼然 ▶古色蒼然とした寺 a temple *which appears hoary with age*(➤ hoary /hɔ́ːri/ は「古めかしい」).

こしらえる 拵える **make** +目(作る); **make up**(でっち上げる) ▶妹がこの人形をこしらえました My sister *made* this doll. ‖きょうはお父さんがごちそうをこしらえてあげるからね I'm going to *cook* [*fix*] you a delicious meal today. (● 日本語では父親本人が料理をする場合でも「お父さんが…」と言うが, 英語では訳例のように I'm ... と言うのがふつう) ‖ボーナスが出たら背広でもこしらえたら? When you get your bonus, how about *having* [*getting*] a suit *made*? ‖借金をこしらえる *incur* a debt ／*fall into* debt.
▶うまく話をこしらえて彼は両親から金をせしめた He *made up* [*framed up*] *a story* and cajoled money out of his parents.

こじらせる 拗らせる ▶かぜをこじらせて10日も寝込んでしまった My cold *got worse*, and I had to stay in bed for ten days. ‖子供のけんかに親が口を出して事態をこじらせてしまった The parents' interference in the children's quarrel *has complicated* the situation.

こじれる 拗れる **get worse**(悪化する); **go** [**turn**] **sour** (人間関係が) ▶両国の関係はこじれる一方だ Relations between the two countries *are getting worse* and worse. ‖彼らの関係はこじれてしまった Their relationship *soured* [*went sour*].

こじわ 小じわ **fine wrinkles** ▶目尻に小じわが目立つようになった *Fine wrinkles* [*Crow's feet*] have become conspicuous at the far corners of my eyes.

1**こじん 個人** an **individual** 一形 個人の **individual** (個

人個人の)；**personal**（個人に関する）；**private**（私的な）▶**個人**の権利 the rights of the *individual* ‖ 私**個人**としてはこの計画に賛成だ I am *personally* in favor of this plan. ‖ 1日にどのくらい睡眠が必要かは**個人差がある** The amount of sleep needed per day *differs for each individual* [*differs from person to person*]. ‖ **個人的な問題**には口を挟まないほうがよい It's better that you keep out of *personal problems* [*affairs*]. ‖ **個人情報**の扱いには細心の注意を払ってください You should be extremely careful when you deal with *personal information*. ‖ 英語の**個人**レッスンを受けたいんです I'd like to take *private lessons* in English. ‖ **個人経営**の店 a *privately run* store. ‖**個人企業** a private enterprise ‖ **個人競技** an individual event ‖ **個人主義** individualism ‖ **個人主義者** an individualist ‖ **個人タクシー** an owner-driven taxi, a taxi driven by its owner ‖ **個人面談** an individual conference ; a parent-teacher conference（親と教師の).

2**こじん 故人** **the deceased** /dɪsíːst/ (**man, woman**) ▶**故人**は誠実な方でした *The deceased man* was an honest person.

1**ごしん 誤診** a **wrong diagnosis** /dàɪəgnóʊsɪs/, a **misdiagnosis** ▶医者の**誤診**で手当てが遅れてしまった The patient's treatment was delayed because of his doctor's *wrong diagnosis*.

2**ごしん 護身** **self-defense**（自衛のため積極的に対抗すること）；**self-protection**（自衛に役立つものを用いて危害から身を守ること）▶**護身用**の催涙スプレー a tear gas sprayer *for self-defense* [*self-protection*].
‖**護身術** the art of self-defense.

3**ごしん 誤審** **misjudgment** ; a **miscarriage of justice** ▶アンパイヤは走者をセーフと**誤審した** The umpire *mistakenly called* the runner *safe*.

こじんまり →こぢんまり.

1**こす 越す・超す** **1**【越える, 渡る】**go over, cross** ▶私は5時間かかってその山を**越した** I *went over* the mountain in five hours. ‖ 多摩川を**越せば**川崎市です After *crossing* the Tama River, you are in Kawasaki (City). ‖ 私たちはハワイで冬を**越した** We *spent* the winter in Hawaii. ‖ 借金を始末せずに**年は越せない** I can't *greet the New Year* until I have cleared all my debts. ‖《慣用表現》仕事はようやく**峠を越した** We*'re through* [*done*] *with* the hardest part of the job.
2【引っ越す, 来る】**move** ▶彼は東京から大阪に**越した** He *moved* from Tokyo to Osaka. ‖ 隣に若いアメリカ人夫婦が**越してきた** A young American couple *has moved into* the house next door. ‖ ぜひまたお**越しください**よ Please do *come* again.
3【ある点を超える】▶彼は60を**超している** He *is over* [*past*] sixty. ‖ きのうの上野公園は1万人を**超す**人出があった *More than* ten thousand people thronged to Ueno Park yesterday. ‖ コウモリやイモリまで飼うとは, 彼女の動物好きは**度を超している** Keeping bats and newts, she's *gone way overboard* [*gone off the deep end*] in her love of animals.
4【勝る】▶給料は多いに**越したことはない** The bigger our salary, the better. ‖ そうと決まったら早くするに**越したことはない** Once you've made up your mind, (then) *the sooner you do it the better*.

2**こす 濾す・漉す** **filter** +目（ろ過する）；**strain** +目（こし器に通す）▶砂で雨水を**こす** *filter* rain water through sand ‖ 茶こしでお茶を**こす** *strain* tea with a strainer.

1**こすい 狡い** **cunning** /kʌ́nɪŋ/ ▶あの男には**こすい**ところがあるから気をつけろよ You must watch out for that man, because he has a streak of *cunning* [has a *sly* streak] in him. (➤ streak は「気味」) ‖ 彼は**こすい**ことをして金もうけをした He made money through *cunning* [*shifty*] means.

2**こすい 湖水** (**the water of**) **a lake** ‖**湖水地方** the Lake District（イングランド北西部の景勝地).

こずえ 梢 **a treetop, the top of a tree**（てっぺん）▶ニレの**こずえ**にモズが止まっていた I saw a shrike at *the top* of an elm.

コスタリカ **Costa Rica** /kòʊstə ríːkə/（中米の国).

コスチューム a **costume.**

こすっからい 狡っ辛い **crafty, sharp**（悪賢い）；**sneaky**（卑劣な）▶**こすっからい**政治家 a *crafty* politician.

コスト (a) **cost** ▶**コスト**を抑える keep *costs* down ‖ 生産**コスト**を減らす lower [reduce] production *costs* ‖ その会社は積極的に**コスト削減**をしている The company is aggressive about *cutting costs*.

コストパフォーマンス **cost performance.**

コスプレ **cosplay** ; playing dress-up often as an anime or cartoon character (➤ 説明的な訳).

ゴスペル **gospel** ‖**ゴスペル音楽** gospel music.

コスメチック **cosmetics** /kɑːzméṭɪk/（化粧品).

コスモス《植物》a **cosmos** /kɑ́ːzməs/.

コスモポリタン a **cosmopolitan** /kɑ̀ːzməpɑ́ːlətn/.

こする 擦る **rub** +目（手・布などで）；**scrub** +目（ごしごし磨く）；**scrape** +目（かする, 付着物をこすり落とす）▶そんなに目を強く**こすらない**の Don't *rub* your eyes so hard! ‖ 彼女は手を**こすって**温めた She warmed her hands by *rubbing* them. ‖ 塀に書かれた落書きをごしごし**こすった**が落ちなかった I *scrubbed* the graffiti on the wall, but it didn't come off. ‖ ハンドルを切り損ねて車のドアをビルの壁に**こすって**しまった I swerved out of control and *scraped* the door of the car against the wall of a building. ‖ 彼はタイヤの泥を**こすって落とした** He *scraped* the mud *off* the tire.

こせい 個性 **individuality**（人が生まれつき持っている特性）；**personality**（他人に印象づける個人的特徴, 人柄）▶生徒の**個性**を重んじる respect a student's *individuality* ‖ **個性**の乏しい男性 a man with little *individuality* ‖ **個性**のはっきりした人 a person of marked *individuality* ‖ 彼は**個性**が強すぎる His *personality* is too strong. ‖ 彼の絵には**個性**がはっきり出ている His paintings are marked by his distinct *individuality*. ‖ 彼女は**個性的な**顔だちをしている Her face shows *a strong personality*.

こせいだい 古生代 **the Paleozoic** /pèɪliəzóʊɪk ‖ pæl-/.

こせいぶつがく 古生物学 **paleontology** /peɪliɑːntɑ́ːlədʒi ‖ pæliɒntɔ́l-/.

こせき 戸籍 a **family register** ▶私は**戸籍上**ではおじの養子になっている *On the family register* I am listed as my uncle's adopted son.
‖**戸籍抄本** an extract from [a partial copy of] one's family register ‖ **戸籍謄本** a full copy of one's family register《参考》英米には日本の謄本に相当するものはないが, a birth certificate（出生証明書）がやや類似.

こせこせ ▶**こせこせした**人 a *fussy* person ／《インフォーマル》a *fussbudget* ‖ **こせこせした**町並み a *cramped* row of houses ‖ 私は**こせこせした**生活が嫌になった I'm really sick of my *cluttered* life.

こぜに 小銭 (**small**) **change**《参考》街頭募金箱に入れたり街頭音楽家に与えたりする小銭を特に spare change という ▶小銭をお持ちですか Do you have any *small change*? ‖小銭入れ a change purse, 《米また》a coin purse, 《英また》a purse (➤ ただし最後の語は主に女性用ハンドバッグ).

こぜりあい 小競り合い a **skirmish** ▶国境の周辺で小競り合いがあった There have been *skirmishes* along the border.

1**ごせん 五線** 《音楽》a **staff**, a **stave**
‖五線紙 music paper, a music sheet.

2**ごせん 互選** ▶役員を互選する *choose* officials *by internal vote* ‖議長を委員の中から互選する *elect* the chairperson *from among the members*.

ごぜん 午前 **morning** (➤ morning には「朝」の意もある；広義には夜中の 0 時から正午まで，あるいは，夜明けから正午または昼食時まで；しばしば in the morning の形で用いる)；**a.m.** (➤ 時刻のあとにつける) ▶午前5時頃はまだ真っ暗です It's still pitch-dark *at about five o'clock in the morning*. ‖結婚式は午前何時に始まるの？ *What time in the morning* does the wedding begin? ‖日曜の午前は教会に居ます I am at church *on Sunday morning*. (➤ 特定の日の午前の場合は前置詞は on になる) ‖娘はあすの午前にそちらに着きます My daughter will get there *tomorrow morning*. 語法 this, tomorrow, yesterday, every などがつく場合は前置詞は不要；→朝.

▶彼は午前11時の飛行機に乗るために8時に家を出た He left home at eight o'clock to get on the 11 *a.m.* plane. ‖私は午前中部屋の掃除をして過ごした I spent the *morning* cleaning my room. ‖そのレストランは午前中は閉まっている The restaurant is closed *during the morning*. / The restaurant does not open *before* [*until*] *noon*. ‖午前中いっぱいその問題を考えたが，いまだに答えがわからない I thought over the question *the whole morning*, but I still can't answer it.

▶《慣用表現》夫は時々はしご酒をして午前さまになる My husband barhops every now and then and *gets home in the wee* [*small*] *hours of the morning*. (➤ wee [small] hours は文字どおりには「(時計の)数字の小さな時間」).

こせんきょう 跨線橋 《米》an **overpass**, 《英》a **flyover**.

こせんじょう 古戦場 an **old battlefield**.

-こそ ▶きみこそうちの会社に欲しい人物だ You are *just* the person [the *very* person] we need in our company. ‖ 対話 「次回はもっとがんばらなくちゃね」「あなたこそ」"You'll have to try harder next time." "*The same goes for you*." (➤「同じことがあなたにも当てはまる」という場合に用いる) ‖ことしこそ合格するぞ I will pass the entrance examination *this year or never*. (➤「ことしがだめならもう二度とだめだ」の意) ‖それこそ私が言いたかったことだ That is *exactly* what I wanted to say. 《参考》自分の言いたいことを先に相手に言われたときなら，You took the words (right) out of my mouth. などと言う ‖きみのほうこそ謝れ！ *You're the one who* should apologize!

▶彼は年こそ若いがしっかりしている He *may be young, but* [*Young as* he *is*,] he's got a good head on his shoulders. (➤ 後者は極めて堅い言い方).

▶ママはあなたのためを思えばこそ勉強しなさいって言うのよ *The reason* that I push you to study so much *is because* I'm worried about your future. ‖今でこそ当たり前になったが，戦前は大学へ行く人はめったにいなかった *Although it is considered common* to go on to college *these days*, few people did so before the war.

☞ こちらこそ →こちら.

こぞう 小僧 a **brat** (悪ガキ) ▶あの酒屋の小僧 the *boy* from the liquor store (ご用聞きに来た小僧)；the liquor store *boy* (酒屋の男の子).

▶あいつはほんとうにいたずら小僧だ He's a real [*little*] *rascal*. / He's a really *mischievous boy*.

ごそう 護送 ▶犯人は刑務所に護送された The criminal *was sent* to prison *under guard*. ‖護送車 a police wagon, 《インフォーマル》a paddy wagon.

ごそうしん 誤送信 ▶誤送信のメール an email *sent to a wrong person* (*by mistake*) ‖eメールを誤送信してしまった I *sent* the email *by mistake*.

こそく 姑息な **stopgap** (一時しのぎの)；**makeshift** (間に合わせの) ▶彼はこそくな手段を使って自分の失敗の責任逃れをしようとした He tried to evade his responsibility for the mistake with *stopgap measures*.

ごそくろう 御足労 ▶署までご足労願いたいのですが *Would you mind coming* to the police station? ‖本日はご足労いただきありがとうございます Thank you very much *for taking the trouble to come here* today.

こそげる **scrape off** ▶鍋底のご飯のお焦げをこそげる *scrape off* the scorched rice at the bottom of a pot.

こそこそ ▶陰で彼にこそこそ会う meet him *surreptitiously* ‖警官の姿を見ると彼はこそこそとその場から逃げ出した When he saw the police officer, he *sneaked away* from the scene. ‖二度と陰でこそこそするな Never *go behind my back* again.

ごそごそ ▶暗がりの中で何かがごそごそ動いた Something *rustled* in the dark.

こそだて 子育て **child rearing** (子供を育て上げること)；**child care** (子供の世話)

✉ **私は今子育てに専念しています** These days, I spend all my time and energy *taking care of the baby*.

‖子育て支援 childcare support / parenting support.

こぞって ▶人々はこぞってパレードを見に集まった People turned out *in force* to watch the parade. (➤ in force は「大勢で」) ‖家族の者は私の留学計画にこぞって反対した *All of* my family were against my plan to study abroad.

ごそっと ▶林の中でゴソッと音がした I heard something large *rustling* in the woods.

▶たんすの中の物をごそっと盗まれた A thief had *made a clean sweep of* all the things in the chest of drawers [the dresser].

こそどろ こそ泥 a **sneak thief** (人)；(a) **petty theft** (行為) ▶銀行員がこそ泥をして警察に捕まった A bank teller was arrested by the police for committing *a petty theft*.

こそばゆい ▶授業中にみんなの前で先生に褒められてこそばゆかった I *felt embarrassed* [*awkward*] when the teacher praised me in front of the class. →くすぐったい.

ごぞんじ 御存じ ▶彼女をご存じですか Do you *know* her? ‖この近くでいい中華料理店をご存じじゃありませんか *Do you know of* a good Chinese restaurant around here? (● 日本文ではこのように否定形でも聞くが，英語では Do you know ...? とする. Don't you know ...? とすると「あら，知らないんですか」と非難の響きになる. know of は「(…のことを)聞いて知っている」).

✉ **ご存じかもしれませんが，日本では鶴と亀は長寿を象徴する生き物です** *As you may know*, in Japan the crane and the tortoise are symbols of longevity. ➤ as you know とすると，「知らないだろうから教えてあげよう」の含みをもつことがある．

1**こたい 固体** a **solid (body)** ▶水は液体だが，氷は**固体**である Although water is a liquid, ice is *a solid*.

2**こたい 個体** an **individual** ‖**個体差** an individual difference ‖ **個体数**（動植物の総数） a population（➤「野生のサイの個体数を維持する」は maintain rhino(ceros) populations in the wild）.

1**こだい 古代** **ancient times** ▶**古代**ギリシャの神々 the gods of *ancient Greece* ‖ ストーンヘンジは**古代**の神殿の跡だという説がある One theory holds that Stonehenge is the ruins of an *ancient* temple.
‖**古代史** ancient history.

2**こだい 誇大** ▶**誇大**広告を排除する exclude *exaggerated advertisements* ‖ 彼は**誇大**妄想の気味がある He is something of *a megalomaniac*.（➤ megalomaniac /mègələméiniæk/ は「誇大妄想癖の人」）.

こだいこ 小太鼓 a **snare drum** ▶**小太鼓**を打つ play the *snare drum*.

ごだいこ 五大湖 **the Great Lakes**（アメリカとカナダの国境にある大きな５つの湖；Erie, Huron, Michigan, Ontario, Superior の総称）.

ごたいそう 御大層な ▶一流ホテルで結婚披露宴とは**ご大層**なことだ I think holding a wedding reception at a top-notch hotel is (a little) *extravagant*.

ごたいりく 五大陸 **the five continents**.

こたえ 答え

1【解答】 an **answer**（質問に対する）; a **solution**（問題の解決法）▶正しい**答え**が言えたのは私だけだった I was the only one who could come up with the *right* [*correct*] *answer*. ‖（先生が生徒に）10分たったら**答えを合わせます**よ We are going to *check our answers* in ten minutes. ‖ この問題の**答え**がわかる人はいますか Does anyone [Do any of you] know the *answer* to this question? ‖ 一郎は私の答案の**答え**を見ようとした Ichiro tried to see my *answers*. ‖ その問題の**答え**は出ましたか Did you get the *answer* to the question [the *solution* to the problem]? ‖ **答え**をはぐらかすな Don't dodge [evade] my question.（➤日本語では「質問をはぐらかす」ともいうが，英語はそれに当たる言い方をする）.

2【返事】 an **answer**, (a) **reply**（➤ 後者は堅い語）▶お決まりの**答え** a stock *answer* ‖ 私の**答え**はノーよ My *answer* is "No." ‖ 何度もベルを鳴らしたが**答え**がなかった Though I rang the bell a number of times, nobody *answered* it [there was no *reply*].

こたえられない ▶ひと風呂浴びたあとのビールは**こたえられない** *There's nothing like* the taste of beer after a hot bath.（➤「…ほどいいものはない」の意）‖ インドネシアで食べたマンゴーは**こたえられない**ほどうまかった The mangoes I had in Indonesia *were out of this world*.（➤ out of this world は「天下一品」の意のインフォーマルな表現）.

こたえる 答える・応える・堪える

📖 **訳語メニュー**
返事をする →answer **1**
応じる →respond, meet **2**
影響する →tell on **3**

1【返事をする】 **answer**, **reply**《to》（➤ 後者は堅い語）▶私の問いに**答え**なさい *Answer* my question. ‖ 彼は「ぼくは何も知りません」と**答えた** He *answered* [*replied*] *that* he didn't know anything about it. ‖ 彼は私の質問にうまく**答えた** He *gave a neat answer* to my question.

2【応じる】 **respond** ▶聴衆の拍手に**応えて**オーケストラは更にアンコールを２曲演奏した *In response to* the audience's applause, the orchestra played two more encores. ‖ わがチームは郷土の期待に**応えて**優勝した Our team *responded* [*lived up*] *to the* expectations of local fans by winning.

✉ **残念ながらあなたのご要望にはお応えできません** I am sorry but I cannot *meet* [*comply with*] your request.

3【悪い影響を及ぼす】 **take a toll on**; **tell on** ▶重労働が**こたえて**きた Hard work is *taking a toll on* me [my health]. ‖ 前半飛ばしたのが**こたえて**，ランナーは途中でへばってしまった The runner's fast pace in the first half *took a heavy toll on* him, and he had to give up midway. ‖ 睡眠をよくとらないとそのうちに**こたえる**ぞ Your lack of sleep will *catch up with* you some day.（➤ catch up with は「…に悪い結果をもたらす」）.

こだかい 小高い ▶**小高い**丘 *a* (*small*) *hill*（➤ hill は「小山」だから small はつけなくてもよい）‖ 学校は川のそばの**小高い**所にあった The school was on *a slight rise* near the river.

こだから 子宝 ▶私のおじは**子宝**に恵まれている My uncle *is blessed with children*. ‖ 不運にも姉は**子宝**に恵まれなかった Unfortunately my (older) sister *had* [*bore*] *no children*.（➤ bore は bear(産む)の過去形）.

ごたく 御託 ▶あの人はすぐ偉そうに**御託を並べる** That man is always ready to *talk tediously* about anything.（➤ tediously は「うんざりするほど」）.

こだくさん 子沢山 ▶山田さんは**子だくさん**だ Mr. Yamada *has a large family*.

ごたごた (a) **trouble**（もめ事）▶彼の家は**ごたごた**が絶えない His family is never free from *troubles*. ‖ これ以上**ごたごた**を起こさないでくれ Please do not cause any more *trouble*.
▶**ごたごた**言うな *Don't grumble* [*complain*].

こだし 小出し ▶知恵を**小出し**にする give one's ideas *bit by bit* [*little by little*].

こだち 木立 (a **cluster of**) **trees**; a **grove**（小さな林）▶**木立**を通して明かりが見えた I saw a light through the *trees*.

こたつ 炬燵 a ***kotatsu***

日本紹介 ✉ **こたつは四角い木製のやぐらに布団を掛けた日本の伝統的な暖房具です．四角または長方形の上板はテーブル代わりにもなります．熱源は以前は炭でしたが，現在は電気がふつうです** A *kotatsu* is a Japanese traditional heating device that has a square wooden frame covered with a futon blanket. Usually a square or rectangular top is placed on it and it also serves as a table. The heat source used to be charcoal, but is usually electricity nowadays.

ごたつく ▶戦争直後でその国はまだ**ごたついていた** It was immediately after the war, and *there was* still *confusion* in the country.

こだて 戸建て a **house**.

ごたぶんにもれず 御多分に漏れず ▶**ご多分に漏れず**うちの娘も漫画が好きです My daughter, *just like everyone else*, loves comics.

こだま 木霊・谺 an **echo** /ékoʊ/ 一動 **こだまする** **echo** ▶子供らの歌声が谷間に**こだました** The children's song *echoed* through the gorge. ／The gorge *echoed* with the children's singing. ‖「オーイ!」と呼んだら「オーイ!」とこだまが返ってきた When we cried "Hello !", the mountain *echoed* it *back*.

こだわり ▶ぼくは自分よりも背の高い女性と付き合うことに**こだわりがある** I *have a hang-up* [*have a thing*] *about* going out with women who are taller than I am. (➤ hang-up は「コンプレックス, 悩み」の意のインフォーマルな語).
▶彼は豆腐に**こだわりがある** He's *particular about* tofu. ／He *has his favorite kind of* tofu. ‖ わが社は(製品の)**品質にこだわりがあります**. 一切の妥協はしません We are *committed to maintaining the* (*high*) *quality* (of our products). We do not compromise (on quality).

こだわる be particular [**choosy**] 《about》(➤ 後者はインフォーマル) ; **stick** 《to》 (…に執着する) ▶**美肌にこだわる** *be concerned about* [*obsess over*] beautiful skin ‖ **私は食べる物にはこだわらない** I *am not particular* [*choosy*] *about* what I eat. ‖ あの男はつまらぬことに**こだわる**からやりにくい I can't get along with that man because he *is too particular about* trivial things. ‖ 小さなことに**あまりこだわるな**よ Don't *attach too much importance to* trivial things.
▶自分が毎日着る物くらい**こだわりたい**(＝いいかげんにしたくない) I like to *be particular about* the way I dress every day. ‖ 当店では新鮮な食材に**とことんこだわっています** We *take painstaking care in* obtaining the freshest ingredients.

こたん 枯淡の ▶ブラームスの２つのクラリネットソナタは作曲者晩年の**枯淡の境地**を表している Brahms' two clarinet sonatas express the *refined simplicity* of the composer's later [twilight] years.

こちこち 1【硬い】▶この餅, こちこちで食べられないよ This rice cake is so *dry and hard* that it is impossible to eat. ‖ 池の水が**こちこちに凍っている** The pond has frozen *as hard as a rock*.
2【頑固】▶社長は**こちこちのがんこおやじだ** Our boss is a *hardheaded* [*stubborn*] old man.
3【緊張】▶彼女は英語のスピーチコンテストで**こちこちになってしまった** She *had stage fright* during the English speech contest.

ごちそう 御馳走 1【豪華な食事】 a **lavish meal** ; **wonderful food** [**dishes**] (すばらしい食べ物) ; **delicacies** (珍味) ; a **feast** (特別な祝宴などの) ▶テーブルにはいろんな**ごちそう**が並べてあった There were all kinds of *delicacies* spread on the table. ‖ 今夜は**ごちそうだよ** We're going to have *something special for dinner* tonight.
2【おごり】 a **treat 一動 ごちそうする buy** +㊐ (買う) ; **treat** +㊐ (おごる) ▶おばさんはぼくにアイスクリームを**ごちそうしてくれた** My aunt *bought* me (an) ice cream. ／My aunt *treated* me to (an) ice cream. ‖ 次回は私に**ごちそうさせてください** Let me *treat you* next time. ‖ きょうは**ごちそうする**から, 何でも好きなものを注文してよ Order anything you like. *You are my guest* today.
✉ **先日はごちそうになりどうもありがとうございました** Thank you so much for the delicious dinner you treated me to the other day.

ごちそうさま 御馳走様 ▶**ごちそうさまでした**. もう十分頂きました *Thank you very much*. I'm full. ‖ 《食事などをおごってもらって》**ごちそうさま** *Thanks* for the treat. ‖ 《のろけ話を聞かされて》**どうもごちそうさま** *Thanks* for all the juicy stories ! (➤「おもしろい話をありがとう」の意).

> **【解説】「ごちそうさま」について**
> 英語国民には食事のあとの「ごちそうさま」に当たる決まった挨拶はなく, 自分の家ではふだんは何も言わない. しかし, 招かれた客が料理を作ってくれた人などに向かって I enjoyed the meal very much. とか It [Everything] was delicious. (大変おいしい料理でした) ／That was a delicious meal. Thank you. (おいしいお食事でした. ありがとうございました) ／ Thank you for going to the trouble [making the effort]. (ご面倒をおかけしてありがとうございました) などと言うことはふつう. →**いただきます**.

ごちゃごちゃ ▶テーブルの上の写真を**ごちゃごちゃにしないでくれ** Don't *jumble* [*mix*] *up* the photos on the table. ‖ 一度に大勢の人に会ったので**頭の中がごちゃごちゃだ** I *got mixed up* [*got confused*] meeting so many people at one time. ‖ (私の部屋は)**ごちゃごちゃしてますけど**, どうぞお入りください Please come on in, though I'm afraid you'll find my room *quite a mess*. ‖ この公園は木が**ごちゃごちゃに植えてある** The trees in the park are planted *randomly*.
▶そこで何を**ごちゃごちゃ言ってるんだ** What are you *jabbering about* over there ? (➤ jabber は「(訳のわからないことを)ぺちゃくちゃしゃべる」).

ごちゃまぜ ごちゃ混ぜ ▶私の机の上の書類, **ごちゃ混ぜにしないでね** Please don't *jumble* (*together*) those papers on my desk. ‖ 彼はきのうのこととおとといのことを**ごちゃ混ぜにしている** He's *got* the events of yesterday and the day before that *all mixed up*.

こちょう 誇張 (an) **exaggeration 一動 誇張する exaggerate** /ɪgzǽdʒəreɪt/ +㊐ ▶彼女の言うことなんかあまり気にするな. いつも話をおもしろくしようとして**誇張するんだから** Don't pay too much attention to her. She always *exaggerates* to make what she says more interesting. ‖ **誇張ではなく**彼女は今まで会ったうちでいちばんの美人だ *Without exaggeration*, she is the most beautiful woman I have ever met. ‖ 私が今日あるのは野田先生のおかげだと言っても**誇張ではない** *It is not too much to say that* I owe what I am to Mr. Noda. ‖ 彼は**事実を誇張して話した** He *stretched the facts*. (➤stretchは「引き伸ばす」が原義).

1**ごちょう 語調** ▶彼は**語調を強めて**, それは自分の署名ではないと言った He *emphatically* denied that it was his signature. ‖ 彼は急に**語調を和らげて**,「話は変わりますが」と言った He suddenly *softened his tone*, saying, "Not to change the subject."

2**ごちょう 伍長** a **corporal**.

こちょこちょ ▶《赤ん坊や幼児の喉の辺りをくすぐって》こちょこちょ *Coochie, coochue, coo*.

こちら 1【話し手の側】 this ; **here** (この場所) ▶**こちら(の品)**はあちらより値が張ります *This* is more expensive than that. ‖ **こちら(の方)へどうぞ** *This way, please*. ‖ 学校は川の**こちら側**にある The school is on *this side* of the river. ‖ **こちらにいらっしゃってから**何年になりますか How long have you been *here* ? ‖ **こちら(の方)**は先ほどお話しした加古さんです *This* is Mr. Kako, who(m) I told you about a while ago.
2【話し手自身】 this ; **I** (私) ▶あとで**こちらからお電話します** *I*'ll call you back later. ‖ **こちらの言い分も聞いてくださいよ** I wish you would listen to what *I* have

to say, too. ‖ **こちらの身にもなってよ** Put yourself in *my position* [*in my shoes*]. ‖ 申し訳ございませんが, こちらでは輸入品は扱っておりません Sorry, but *we* don't carry imported goods. ‖《電話で》もしもし, こちらは辻井です Hello! *This* is Tsujii speaking. ‖ 対話「ご講演, ありがとうございました」「**こちらこそ**(ありがとうございました)」"Thank you for your speech." "*The pleasure was mine.* / *It was my pleasure.*" (➤ Thank you. とだけ答えてもよい. その場合, you を強く発音することで「こちらこそ」の意を表す) ‖ 対話《人とぶつかったときなど》「あ, すみません」「いや, **こちらこそ**」"Sorry." "That's all right — it was *my* fault (really)." / "Excuse me." "No, it was *my* fault." (➤ どちらの文もしばしば my を強く発音する).

▶そちらがそういう態度なら, **こちらにも考えがある** If that's your attitude [If you're going to be like that], *I know what I'm going to do.*

こぢんまり ▶こぢんまりとした家 a *cozy* [*snug*] *little* house(➤ ともに, 「小さいが温かい」という含みがある).

こつ a **knack** /næk/ ▶この戸を開けるにはこつがあるんだ There's *a knack* to opening this door. ‖ スカイダイビングは最初は難しいようだけど, 2, 3 週間もすればこつを覚えるよ Skydiving may seem difficult at first, but you'll get *the hang* of it after [in] a few weeks. (➤ get the hang of は「…の要領を覚える」の意のインフォーマルな言い方).

ごつい ▶レスラーの手はごつい Wrestlers' hands are (*big and*) *rough*.

1**こっか 国家** a **nation**(政治的統一体としての); a **country** (国土としての); a **state** (法律的・理論的意味での) 一形 **国家の national** ▶新しい国家 a new *nation* ‖ 国家のために身をささげる give one's life for one's *country* ‖ 国家どうしの争い conflicts between *nations* ‖ その年のいちばん大きな**国家的行事**は皇太子のご成婚であった The biggest *national event* of that year was the wedding of the Crown Prince.

‖**国家権力** national power, the power of the state ‖ **国家公務員** a national public [civil] servant, a national public [civil] official, a government official(➤ この順で地位が高くなる) ‖ **国家試験** a national [state] examination ‖ **国家主義** nationalism ‖ **国家戦略特区** a specific economic zone.

2**こっか 国歌** a **national anthem** ▶国歌斉唱 Let's sing the *national anthem* in unison.

3**こっか 国花** a **national flower.**

1**こっかい 国会 the Diet**(日本の; 日本の国会を Parliament という場合もある); **Congress** (アメリカの議会; the をつけない); **Parliament** (イギリス・カナダ・オーストラリアの議会; the をつけない); a **national assembly**(国民議会) ▶**臨時国会**を召集する convene *an extraordinary session of the Diet* ‖ **国会**は今開会中だ *The Diet* is now in session.

‖**国会議員** a member of the Diet (➤ 男性議員は a Dietman, 女性議員は a Dietwoman) 《参考》a member of the Diet をそのまま使って He [She] is a member of the Diet. とすると, 日本の制度に不案内な外国人は「食事療法」(diet)を実行している一員と解釈する可能性がある. 例えば, 「参議院 [衆議院] 議員です」と考えて, He [She] is a Congressman [Congresswoman]. のようにいえば誤解のおそれは減少する ‖ **国会議事堂** the Diet Building(日本の) ‖ **国会図書館** the National Diet Library.

2**こっかい 黒海 the Black Sea**(ヨーロッパ南東部にあり, 海峡で地中海と結ばれている).

こづかい 小遣い an **allowance** /əláʊəns/ (定期的に子供などに与える); **spending money, pocket money** (自分が使う) ▶私は月に1万円の**小遣い**をもらっている I get *an allowance* of 10,000 yen a month. ‖ 母はぼくの**小遣い**を月1万円に上げてくれた Mom increased my *allowance* to 10,000 yen a month. ‖ 私は**小遣い**で毎月 CD を2枚買う I buy two CDs every month *with my allowance*. ‖ 私は**小遣い銭稼ぎ**にアルバイトをやっている I'm working part-time *to earn pocket money* [*spending money*]. ‖ 私は**小遣い帳**をつけている I keep a record of my expenses. (➤「小遣い帳」を a petty cash book という).

こっかく 骨格 a **skeleton**(人や動物の; 建物の「骨組み」をいうこともある); a **framework** (建物の) ▶**骨格のたくましい**男性 a *sturdily-built* man / a *heavy-set* man.

▶来年度予算の**骨格**が固まった The *broad outlines* of the next fiscal year's budget were decided.

ごっかん 極寒の frigid ▶極寒の2月の朝 a *frigid* February morning ‖ **極寒**の地シベリアの冬は美しい The winter in *frigid* Siberia is beautiful.

1**こっき 国旗** a **national flag** ▶**国旗**を掲揚する hoist the *national flag* 《参考》アメリカの国旗は the Stars and Stripes または the Star-Spangled Banner と呼び, 俗に Old Glory という. また, イギリスの**国旗**は the Union Flag と呼び, 一般には the Union Jack という.

2**こっき 克己 self-control**(自制); **(self-) restraint**(自己抑制) ▶彼は**克己心**に富んでいる He has a lot of *self-control*.

1**こっきょう 国境** a **border**; a **frontier** /frʌntíəʳ/ (政治的・軍事的意味での); a **(national) boundary** (国境線) ▶**国境**を守る guard the *border* ‖ ドイツのフランスとの**国境地帯** the German *border* [*frontier*] with France ‖ ロシアと中国は**国境を接している** Russia and China *share a border*. ‖ 難民たちは歩いて**国境を越えた** The refugees *crossed the border* on foot. ‖ 「芸術に**国境**なし」とよく言われる It is often said that *art knows* [*has*] *no national boundaries.*

‖**国境紛争** a border [boundary] dispute.

2**こっきょう 国教** a **state religion**

‖**イングランド国教会** the Church of England, the Anglican Church.

こっきり ▶人生は**1回こっきり** You *only* live *once*.

1**コック**《料理人》a **cook** /kʊk/ ‖**コック長** a **chef** /ʃef/.

2**コック**《栓》a **tap**, 《米また》a **faucet** ▶**コック**をひねる turn on [off] the *faucet* 《参考》ガスや水道の栓の意味の「コック」は cock からだが, この語は俗語で男性器を意味するので不用意に使わないほうがよい.

こづく 小突く poke(+目); **nudge** +目 (注意を促すために肘で) ▶**小突く**なよ! Don't *poke* (*at*) me. ‖ 彼は妹を肘で**小突いた** He *nudged* his sister. / He *gave his sister a nudge*.

コックピット a **cockpit.**

こっくり ▶「おうちに誰か居ますか」と聞くと, その女の子は**こっくりとうなずいた** When I asked the little girl if someone was (at) home, she *nodded*. ‖ 父は新聞を広げたまま**こっくりこっくりし始めた** My father began to *nod* over the newspaper he was holding.

1**こづくり 小作り** ▶**小作り**の男性 a man of *slight build* / a man with *a small build* ‖ **小作りの顔**の女性 a woman with *small delicate features*.

2**こづくり 子作り** ▶**子作り**に励む be trying to *have a baby* / be trying for a baby.

こっけい 滑稽な funny(おもしろおかしい); **humorous** (ユーモアがある); **absurd**(話にならないほど非常識な); **ri-**

diculous（噴き出したくなるほどおかしい，ばかげた）；**comic, comical**（人を笑わせる；前者は「人を笑わせることを目的とした」，後者は「思わず知らず笑ってしまう」）▶**滑稽な**話 a *funny* story ‖ **滑稽な**歌 a *comic* song ‖ **滑稽な**顔 a *comical* face ‖ 彼はいつも**滑稽な**ことを言って人を笑わせる He always makes people laugh by telling (them) *funny* jokes. ‖ 英語を1年でマスターするなどという考えは**滑稽**だ It is *absurd* to think that one can master English in a year. ‖ おまえが歌手になるんだって！そりゃあ**滑稽な話**だ You want to be a singer? That's *ridiculous*.

こっけん 黒鍵《音楽》a **black key**.

こっこ 国庫《米》**the national treasury**,《英》**the exchequer** ‖**国庫補助** a government [state,《米また》federal] subsidy.

-ごっこ ▶お医者さん**ごっこをする** *play* doctor ‖ お店屋さん**ごっこをする** *play* shops ‖ さあ外で**鬼ごっこして遊ぼう**！Come on! Let's *play tag* outside! ‖ 子供たちはよく「**ごっこ遊び**」をする Children often play *games of make-believe*.

こっこう 国交 **diplomatic relations**（外交関係）▶**国交の正常化** the normalization of *diplomatic relations* ‖ その国と日本は**国交がない** There are no *diplomatic relations* between that country and Japan. ‖ アメリカは1980年にイランとの**国交を断絶した** The U.S. broke off (*diplomatic*) *relations* with Iran in 1980.

ごつごうしゅぎ ご都合主義 **opportunism** ‖**ご都合主義者** an opportunist.

こっこうしょう 国交省 **the Transport Ministry, the Ministry of Transport.** →国土.

こっこく 刻々と →刻一刻 ▶新しいニュースが現場から**刻々と送られてきた** The latest news was broadcast from the scene *in real time*. ‖ 世界情勢は**刻々と変化している** The international situation is changing *every moment* [*from moment to moment*]. ‖ 川の水は**刻々と増していった** The water of the river was rising *by the minute*.

1**こつこつ** ▶**こつこつ仕事をする** *plod* [*plug*] *away* at a task ‖ 何でも**こつこつ努力する**ことが大切だ It's important to work *slowly but steadily* in anything you do. ‖ **こつこつ**(＝少しずつ)ためた貯金が100万円になった I've been putting some money away *bit by bit*, and now it amounts to one million yen. ‖ きみは勉強を**こつこつ続けて**いればいい大学に入れるよ If you make *a steady effort* in your studies, you'll get into a good university.

2**こつこつ** ▶**コツコツという足音**が聞こえた I heard the *clicking* sound of heels. ‖ **コツコツと戸をたたく音**がした There was *a knock* on the door.

ごつごつ ▶**ごつごつした岩** *rough* rocks ‖ **ごつごつして険しい山道** a *rugged* mountain path ‖ **ごつごつした手** *rough and bony* hands.

こっし 骨子 **the gist** ▶計画の**骨子**は次のとおりだ *The gist* of the plan is as follows.

こつずい 骨髄 **the bone marrow** ▶《慣用表現》彼女に対してぼくは**恨み骨髄に徹している** I *hate* her *with all my soul*. ‖**骨髄移植** a bone marrow transplant ‖**骨髄炎** osteomyelitis /àːstioʊmàɪəláɪṭəs/ ‖**骨髄提供者** a marrow donor ‖**骨髄バンク** a bone marrow bank.

こっせつ 骨折 a **break**, a **fracture**（➤ 後者はやや専門的）**一動** **骨折する** **fracture**；**break (a bone)**（折る）▶軽い[ひどい]**骨折** a slight [nasty] *break* ‖ 左足を**骨折する** *break* [*fracture*] one's left leg ‖ 私は足を**骨折して**1か月間学校を休んだ I was absent from school for a month because I *had a fracture of my leg bone*. ‖ 彼は指を**骨折している** He's *got a broken finger*. ‖**複雑骨折** a compound fracture.

こつぜん 忽然 ▶金庫に入れてあった大金が**こつ然と消えた** A large sum of money in the safe *disappeared into thin air*.（➤「影も形もなく姿を消す」の意）.

こっそうがく 骨相学 **phrenology**/frənɑ́ːlədʒi ‖ -nɔ́l-/.

こつそしょうしょう 骨粗鬆症 **osteoporosis** /ɑ̀ːstioʊpəróʊsɪs/.

こっそり **secretly**（ひそかに）；**stealthily** /stélθɪli/（ずるいやり方で）；**on the sly**（ないしょで；インフォーマルな言い方）▶母は**こっそり**私に余分にお金をくれた My mother *secretly* gave me extra money. ‖ 彼女は授業中に**こっそりと**チョコレートを食べた During class, she ate a chocolate bar *on the sly*. ‖ 彼は**こっそりと**金庫室へ入るところを人に見られてしまった He was seen *sneaking* [*stealing*] *into* the bank vault. ‖ 彼女は教室から**こっそり抜け出した** She *sneaked* [*stole*] *out of* the classroom. ‖ 彼は英語の試験中に隣の人の答えを**こっそり盗み見た** He *sneaked* [*took*] *a peek at* the paper of the person next to him during the English exam.

ごっそり ▶泥棒に家のものを**ごっそり盗まれた** The burglar(s) *cleaned* us *out*.（➤ clean out は「(人のものを)ごっそり盗む」）‖ 泥棒に入られてお金を**ごっそり持っていかれた** Our house was broken into by a burglar and *all* of our money was stolen [was taken].

こった 凝った →凝る.

ごったがえす ごった返す ▶祭りで通りは**ごった返していた** *There was a lot of hustle and bustle* along the street because of the festival. ‖ 空港ロビーは海外からの帰国者で**ごった返していた** The airport lobby *was bustling* [*was very crowded*] *with* passengers returning from abroad.（➤ 前者は「活気づいて」，後者は「とても混んで」）‖ 江ノ島海岸は海水浴客で**ごった返していた** Enoshima Beach *was teeming with* bathers.（➤ teem with は「…であふれかえる」）.

ごったに ごった煮《米》a **hodgepodge**,《英》a **hotchpotch**.

こっち →こちら.

こづち 小槌 a **mallet** ▶打ち出の**小づち** a magic *mallet*.

ごっちゃ ▶これとこれ，**ごっちゃにしないでね** Please don't *mix* them *up*. ／Please don't *get* them *mixed up*. ‖ 記憶が**ごっちゃになっている** My memory is all *mixed up*. ‖ 公的なことと私的なことを**ごっちゃにするんじゃない**．わかったか Don't *confuse* public and private matters! Understand?!

こつつぼ 骨つぼ an **urn**（➤ funeral [cremation] urn ともいう）.

こづつみ 小包 a **(postal) parcel**, a **(postal) package**（➤ 箱に収めた荷物の場合は後者がふつう）；**parcel post**（小包便）▶**小包を出す** mail *a parcel* [*a package*] ‖ この本をアメリカへ**小包**で送りたいのですが I would like to send this book to the United States *by parcel post*.

こってり **1**【味・化粧などが濃い】▶**こってりした料理** *rich* food ‖ パンにバターを**こってりつける** spread butter *thickly* [*heavily*] on bread ／ spread bread *thickly* [*heavily*] with butter.
2【嫌というほど】▶カンニングしているところを先生に見つかって**こってり油を絞られた** The teacher *gave* me *a*

talking-to [*chewed* me *out*] when he caught me cheating.

こっとう 骨董 an **antique** /æntíːk/; a **curio** /kjóəriou/ (掘り出し物, 珍品) ▶骨とう品の時計 an *antique* clock ‖ 私のおじは骨とうに凝っている My uncle is crazy about *antiques*. ‖ この珍しいコインは骨とう屋で見つけました I found this rare coin at *an antique shop* [*a curio shop*]. 《参考》日本語では家具や置物などが古くなると「これは骨とう屋行きだ」と言うが, 英語では This is a museum piece.(博物館行きだ)と言う.

コットン **cotton.**

こつにく 骨肉 ▶父親の遺産を巡って醜い骨肉の争いが起きた *A family dispute* [*quarrel*] arose *among the children* over their father's legacy.

こっぱみじん 木っ端微塵 ▶彼は怒って花瓶を床に投げつけ, 木っ端みじんに砕いてしまった In anger, he threw the vase to the floor and broke it *into a thousand pieces* [*into smithereens*].

こつばん 骨盤 《解剖学》 a **pelvis.**

こっぴどく こっ酷く ▶万引きをしておやじからこっぴどく叱られた I *got a good dressing-down* from my dad for shoplifting. (➤ dressing-down は「叱りつけること」の意のインフォーマルな言い方).

こつぶ 小粒 ▶小粒のブドウ *small* grapes ‖ ことしの桃は小粒だが甘い This year's peaches are a little *smaller* (than last year's) but taste very sweet. ‖ うちの息子は小粒ですがやることは素早いですよ My son is *small*, but quick. ‖ 小粒な政治家ばかりが目につく You can see *small-time* politicians everywhere.

コップ a **glass** (ガラスの); a **mug** (取っ手のついた大型の) ▶水をコップに1杯持ってきてください Could you please bring me *a glass* of water?

‖**紙コップ** a paper cup.

危ないカタカナ語✹ コップ, カップ

1「コップ」は「杯」の意味のオランダ語 *kop* から日本語に入った. 一方,「カップ」は英語の cup からきている.「コップ」に当たるのは glass であるが, glass はもともと「ガラス」なので,「紙コップ」は paper cup とする必要がある.

2 cup は通例温かい飲み物用の茶わん(tea-cup など)や「優勝杯」を指す.

こっぷん 骨粉 **bone meal.**

コッペパン a **(bread) roll.**

コッヘル a **mess kit.**

こづれ 子連れ ▶木村さんは子連れでグアム旅行をした The Kimuras took a trip to Guam *with their child(ren)*. ‖ 彼女は子連れで再婚した She remarried and *brought children* [*a child*] *from her previous marriage*.

こつん ▶先生に頭をコツンとたたかれた The teacher *rapped* me on the head. / The teacher *gave* me *a rap* on the head.

ごつん ▶ジェーンはかもいに頭をゴツンとぶつけた Jane *bumped* her head on the lintel.

こて a **trowel** (壁を塗るときの); a **soldering** /sáːdərɪŋ ‖ sóldərɪŋ/ **iron** (はんだ付けの); a **curling iron** (カールをつける).

ごて 後手 ▶洪水被害者救済のための我々の対策は後手に回った Our efforts to rescue the flood victims *were too late*. (➤「遅すぎた」の意).

こてい 固定する **fix** +㊀ ▶この本棚がゆらゆらしないよう壁に固定してください I'd like you to *fix* these bookshelves to the wall so that they won't wobble. ‖ 固定観念にとらわれるな Don't be bound by *fixed ideas* [*stereotypes*]. ‖ このデパートは固定客が増えている The number of *regular customers* of this department store has increased.

‖**固定給** a fixed salary, regular pay ‖ **固定資産** fixed property [assets] ‖ **固定資産税** a fixed property tax ‖ **固定費** a fixed cost.

コテージ a **cottage.**

こてきたい 鼓笛隊 a **drum and fife** /faɪf/ **band.**

ごてごて ▶あのレストランは飾りつけがごてごてしていて落ち着かない That restaurant is so *overdecorated* [*gaudily decorated*] that I don't feel comfortable there. ‖ 彼女の部屋の飾りつけはごてごてし過ぎている The décor of her room is too *busy*.

こてさき 小手先 ▶そんな小手先のごまかしに引っかかるもんか I won't be deceived by such *a cheap trick*.

こてしらべ 小手調べ a **trial** (試し); a **tryout** /tráɪaʊt/ (試験的試み) ▶わがチームは小手調べにAチームと試合をした We played a game with A Team *to test our strength*.

[1]**こてん 古典** a **classic**; **(the) classics** (➤ 総称) 一形 **古典の classic** (古典的な, 伝統的に優れた); **classical** (文学・芸術が古典派の) ▶ギリシャ・ローマの古典 *the* Greek and Latin *classics* ‖ 古典的な小説 a *classic* novel ‖ 彼女は古典的な顔だちをしている She has a *classic* face.

‖**古典音楽** classical music ‖ **古典芸術** classical art ‖ **古典主義** classicism ‖ **古典文学** the classics (作品); classical literature(➤ 総称および学問).

[2]**こてん 個展** a **one-person exhibition** /èksɪbíʃən/ ▶9月に彼は銀座の画廊で個展を開く In September, he will *exhibit* his paintings at a gallery in Ginza.

ごてん 御殿 a **palace** ▶御殿のようなホテル a *palatial* /pəléɪʃəl/ hotel.

こてんこてん ▶あいつをこてんこてんにやっつけてやる I'll *make mincemeat of* him. ‖ 勝つ自信はあったのだが無名のチームにこてんこてんにやられてしまった Although we were confident we would win, we *were beaten to a pulp* [*were slaughtered* / *were massacred*] by an unknown team.

こてんぱん →こてんこてん.

[1]こと 事

《解説》「こと」と「もの」

(1) 日本語の「事」に相当する最も用法の広い語は **thing**. これよりもやや堅い語で, 特に「処理されるべき事柄」「関心を引かれる事柄」の意で用いられるのが **matter**,「自分に関係のある事柄」の意で用いられるのが **affair**,「ささいな, または異例な出来事」の意で用いられるのが **incident**.

(2) 日本語では「もの」と「こと」を使い分けるが, 英語の thing は両方の意味をもつ.

1【事柄】 a **thing**, a **matter**, an **affair**, an **incident** ▶大切なこと an important *thing* [*matter*] ‖ 取るに足りないこと a very small *thing* [*affair*] ‖ 事の真相を確かめる必要がある It is necessary to get to the truth of the *matter*. ‖ きょうはする事がたくさんある I have lots of *things to do* today. ‖ きょうは学校で何かおもしろいことあった? Did *anything* interesting happen at school today? ‖ いい事をすると気持ちがいいものだ It really feels good when you *do good*. ‖ おまえは自分のした事に責任が持てないのか Can't you ever assume responsibility for *what you've* *done*? ‖ あなたのご成功を**自分のこと**のように喜んでおります I feel as happy as if I *myself* had achieved your great success.

2【重大事, 事件】▶事の起こりはごくささいなことだった The *trouble* all began over a very trifling matter. ‖ 事が起こってからでは(＝今対応しないと)遅い *If we don't deal with this* (*problem*) *now*, it will be too late (to do anything about it) later. ‖ ゆかりとないしょで映画に行ったことが彼女の両親に知れたら**事だ** *There'll be hell* [*the devil*] *to pay* if Yukari's parents learn that she and I went to the movies on the sly.

3【事情】▶詳しいことは係の者にお尋ねください If you need *further information*, please ask the person in charge. ‖ 私は視力が弱い**こともあり**, 運転は好きではない I don't like driving, *partly because* my eyesight is poor. ‖ 私の**こと**ならご心配なく Please don't trouble yourself *about* me. ‖ 絵の**こと**はあまりよくわかりません I don't know much *about* art. ‖ **自分のこと**は自分でしなさい Look after *yourself*. ‖ **きみのことだから**3日ともたないね Well, *knowing you*, you won't last three days. ‖ **金銭のこと**はすべて妻に任せてある I leave all *financial* [*money*] *matters* to my wife. ‖ パソコン**のことになると**石井さんが頼りになる *When it comes to* personal computers, you can depend on Mr. Ishii. ‖ **事ここに至っては**辞職しかない *Now that it has* [*things have*] *come to this*, resigning is the only option.

4【ことばが意味する内容】▶きみたちにちょっと話したいことがある I have *something* to talk to you about. ‖ あなたのおっしゃる**こと**は正論[本当]だ *What* you say is right [true]. ／You are right. ‖ きみは上司の言う**こと**が聞けないのか Don't you even listen to *what* your boss *tells* you? ‖ これらの基本文を暗記する**こと**が大切だ It is important *to* learn these basic sentences by heart. ‖ きみのお父さんが最近亡くなった**こと**を曽根君から聞きました Mr. Sone told me *that* you lost your father recently.

5【文末に置いて】▶《女性が感動を表して》いい匂いのバラだ**こと**! *How* lovely this rose smells! ‖ いいお天気だ**こと**! *What* nice weather!

▶《「ことか」の形で強調して》あなたのお手紙を**何度**読み返した**ことか** *How often* I read your letter! ／I read your letter so many times. ‖ おまえのことを**どんなに**心配した**ことか** Do you have any idea *how* worried I was about you? ‖《決まりを示して》書類は青または黒のインクで**書くこと** *Fill out* the form in either black or blue ink. ‖ 当日は午前10時までに**集合すること** *You are to* be here [there] by 10 a.m. on the day. ‖ 最後に退出する者は**消灯のこと** The last person to leave *will turn off the lights*.

6【人の関連事項を示して】▶ゴジラこと松井秀喜 Matsui Hideki *who went by the name of* '*Godzilla*.'

7【別名】▶鴎外こと森林太郎 Mori Rintaro *a.k.a.* [*also known as*] Ogai.

8【「…したことがある」の形で】

> **【文型】**
> **(私は)…したことがある**
> I've done.
> **…したことがない**
> I've **never** done.
> **…したことがありますか**
> Have you **ever** done?

▶その映画は前に**見たことがある** *I've seen* the movie before. ‖ 私はハワイに**行ったことがありません** *I've never been to* [*I've never visited*] Hawaii. ‖ パッションフルーツは**食べたことがありません** *I've never eaten* (a) passion fruit. ‖ あんな背の高い男性には**会ったことがない** *I've never seen* such a tall man. ／He is the tallest man I have ever met. ‖ ワイエスの絵を**見たことがありますか** *Have you ever seen* a picture by Wyeth?

> **直訳の落とし穴「…したことがある」**
> 「ハワイに行ったことがありますか」を Have you ever been to Hawaii? と正しく言える学習者は多い. が, これに引っ張られて, 「ハワイに行ったことがあります」を(×)I've ever been to Hawaii. とするのは間違い. この ever は疑問文・否定文に用いるもので, 肯定文には用いない. I've been to Hawaii. でよい.

9【慣用表現】

…したことにする▶《虚構》彼はその日は病気だということにして家に居ようかと思った He thought of spending the day at home and *claiming* illness as an excuse. (➤ claim は「…と主張する」). **…したことになる**▶《結果》もう1度尾瀬へ行けば3度行ったことになる If I go once more, I *will have been to* Oze three times. **…したことに(は)**▶《感情を強調して》驚いたことには2人は親子でなく夫婦であった *To my surprise*, those two people were not father and daughter, but husband and wife. (➤ To one's ... は堅い文章語で, ふつうは I was surprised to learn [find out] that ... のように言う) ‖ 残念なことに彼女は入賞できなかった *To our disappointment*, she was not able to win a prize. (➤ We were disappointed because she didn't win a prize. がふつう). **…した(という)ことになっている**▶《建て前》先生というものは教えている学科のことは何でも知っていることになっている Teachers *are supposed to* know everything about the subject they teach. **…することがある**▶《可能性》朝ときどき頭痛とめまいで起き上がれないことがある *Sometimes* I can't get up in the morning because of a headache and dizziness. ‖ 乾電池を焼却炉の中に捨てると爆発することがあります Batteries *may* explode if they are thrown into the incinerator.

…することにしている▶《習慣》私は早寝早起きをすることにしています I go to bed and get up early. ／I keep early hours. (➤ 英語の現在形は1回限りの行為には用いず, いわば「習慣形」ともいうべきもので, 現在の習慣的行為を表す) ‖ 毎朝ラジオのフランス語講座を聴くことにしています I listen to a French radio course [program] every morning. ‖ 私は友人には金を貸さないことにしている I never lend money to friends.

…することにする▶《決心》高校生になったんだから, もう漫画は読まないことにしようと思う *I've made up my mind* [*I've decided*] to give up comics, now that I'm a high school student.

> **あなたの英語はどう響く?**
> 「…することにしている」にいつも make it a rule to do を用いる人が少なくない. 例えば, 「毎朝, 1時間散歩をすることにしている」を I *make it a rule to* take a walk for one hour every morning. とする類いである. しかし, これは「…するのを常とする」という日本語に当たる古くて大げさな言い方. 日常的には, I take a

walk for one hour every morning. のようにいう. ただし,「毎朝欠かさず」というのではなく,「例外的な朝もあるが」という気持ちでいうのなら, I *usually* [*generally* / *normally*] take ... のように「ふだんは」に当たる副詞を添える.

…することになっている ▶《予定》国王は明朝マドリードから成田に着くことになっている The king *is to* arrive at Narita from Madrid tomorrow morning. (➤ be to do で「予定」を表す) ‖《必要》運転するときは免許証を携帯することになっている People *are required to* carry their (driver's) licenses when driving. ‖ 夫か私のどちらかが会に出席することになっている Either my husband or I *am* [*are*] *expected to* be present at the meeting. (➤「当然のこととして求められている」の意; either A or B のあとの動詞は B に合わせて, ここでは am が文法に正しいが, 複数と受け止めて are にすることもある) ‖ 演奏会場内では飲食してはいけないことになっている You *are not allowed to* drink or eat in the performance hall. **…することはない** ▶《不必要》そんなに慌てて結婚することはないよ *There's no reason* to be in such a rush to get married. **…ということだ** ▶《伝聞》みどりは来年フランスへ留学するということだ *I hear* Midori will go to France to study next year. **…としたことが** ▶《似つかわしくない》私としたことが, 失礼いたしました *How thoughtless of me* ! / *How rude of me* !

☛ 事によると, 事もあろうに, 事もなげ (→見出語)

²**こと 琴** a **koto** (➤ 英語化している).

³**こと 古都** a **historic city** (歴史のある都市); an **old capital** (古い都).

¹**-ごと** ▶このトマトを皮ごと食べなさい Eat this tomato *with the skin on* [*skin and all*]. ‖ この小魚は骨ごと食べられます You can eat this small fish, *bones and all*.

▶アメリカ人はリンゴはふつう皮ごと(=むかないで)食べる Americans usually eat apples *without peeling them* [*with the peels on*]. ‖ 私は着替えをバッグごと盗まれた My extra clothes were stolen *along with the bag they were in*.

²**-ごと -毎** →-ごとに.

ことう 孤島 a **solitary** [an **isolated**] **island**; a **lonely island** (訪れる人が少ない); a **desert island** (無人島).

こどう 鼓動 **heartbeat, beating** ▶人間の心臓は1分間に約70回鼓動する The human heart *beats* with a frequency of about seventy times a minute. ‖ 昭彦と初めて口を利いたとき私の胸の鼓動は高まった The first time I talked to Akihiko, I *felt* my heart *beating* fast [I could *hear* my heart *pounding*].

こどうぐ 小道具 **props, (stage) properties** (演劇用の; 前者は後者の短縮語).

ごとうち ご当地 ▶よく知られたご当地ソング a well-known *local song* / a well-known *song with lyrics that mention local attractions*.

‖ご当地キャラ(クター) a local mascot character ‖ ご当地グルメ the regional specialty.

ことかく 事欠く **lack** ▶貧しくとも食べるものに事欠くことはない We are poor but don't *lack* enough to eat [but have enough to eat].

▶うちは農家だから新鮮な野菜に事欠くことはない As we are farmers, we *are never short of* fresh vegetables.

ことがら 事柄 a **matter** ▶この事柄については私は何も知りません I know nothing about this *matter*.

こときれる 事切れる **breathe** one's **last**; **pass away** (亡くなる) ▶彼は電話の受話器を手にしたまま事切れていた He *had passed away* holding the telephone receiver.

こどく 孤独 **solitude** (連れなどがいないこと); **loneliness** (ひとりぼっちで寂しいこと) 一形 孤独な **solitary, lonely** ▶孤独な生活をする lead a *solitary* [*lonely*] life ‖ ネコ科の動物は一般に孤独を愛する Animals in the cat family generally prefer *solitude*. ‖ 詩人は孤独を友とし愛した The poet loved *solitude*, regarding it as a friend. ‖ 大都会の片隅で孤独な一生を終える人もいる Some people end their *solitary* [*lonely*] *lives* in an out-of-the-way corner of a big city. ‖孤独死 passing away (at home) unnoticed by anyone.

ごとごと ▶かつて東京のあちこちを都電がゴトゴト走っていたものだ Streetcars used to *rattle* throughout the streets of Tokyo. ‖ 父が物置で何かゴトゴトやっている My father *is rattling about* in the storage room.

ことごとく ▶あいつは俺の提案にはことごとく逆らう He opposes *every single* proposal I make. ‖ 彼の予想はことごとく外れた *All* his projections turned out to be wrong.

ことこまかに 事細かに ▶彼はその日のことを事細かに私に語った He told me *in detail* (about) what had happened that day.

ことさら 殊更 ▶不動産屋は交通の便の良さばかりを殊更強調した The real estate agent emphasized *only* the good access to transportation (and didn't bring up anything else). ‖ こんなことを言って殊更きみの感情を傷つけようとしたわけじゃあないんだ I didn't *mean* to hurt your feelings (*intentionally*) by saying this. (➤ mean が「本気で…するつもりである」の意なので, intentionally をつけると冗漫になる).

ことし 今年 **this year** ▶ことしは人生で最も忘れ難い年になった *This year* has been one of the most unforgettable years of my life. ‖ ことしは寅(とら)年です *This is the year* of the Tiger. ‖ 父はことし50歳です My father turns 50 *this year*. ‖ ことしは雨が少ない We haven't had much rain *this year*. ‖ ことしこそは一生懸命勉強しようと心に決めた I have made up my mind that *this year* I'm going to study hard. (●「こそ」は訳出不要. 口頭では this を強く発音すればその感じが出せる) ‖ ことしから申し込み方法が変わります The application procedure will be changed *from this year on*. ‖ ことし中にこのビルは完成するでしょう This building will be completed *within the year* [(*sometime*) *this year*]. ‖ その歌手はことしの8月に引退した The singer retired from her professional singing career *this August*. ‖ ことしの夏はどこへいらっしゃるご予定ですか Where are you planning to go *this summer*?

語法 このように, this は過去にも未来にも使うが, はっきりさせたいときは過去は this past August, 未来は this coming summer のようにいう.

ことたりる 事足りる ▶わざわざ会いに行かなくても電話で話せば事足りる Don't bother to go (and) meet him [her]. Talking on the phone *should do* [*be enough*].

ことづかる 言付かる ▶父からこの荷物を言づかって来ました My father *asked* me *to bring* this package to you.

ことづけ 言付け a **message** ▶彼からぼくに何か言づけはありませんでしたか Did he leave you any *message* for me? ‖ 何かお言づけはございますか Would you like to leave *a message*? / Shall I take *a message*?

ことづける 言付ける leave a message《with》▶あす，彼に遊びに来るよう家の人に言づけてきた I *have left a message with* his family asking him to come to see us tomorrow.

ことなかれしゅぎ 事勿れ主義 ▶彼はいつも事なかれ主義だ His philosophy is to *not rock the boat*.（➤ rock the boat は「(わざわざ反対意見を出したりして)平穏を乱す」の意のインフォーマルな言い方）.

ことなる 異なる be different《from》, differ《from》; vary（同種のものが一様ではない）→違う
▶事態は以前のケースとは非常に異なっている The situation now *is very different from* what it was in the previous case. ‖ ギャンブルに関しては我々の意見は異なっている We *differ* [*disagree*] on gambling. ／We have *different* opinions on gambling. ／Our opinions on gambling *differ*. ‖ 山口県で使われている「直す」という語は，東京で使われているそれと意味が異なる The word 'naosu' has a *different* meaning in Yamaguchi Prefecture *than* it does [has] in Tokyo. ／The meaning of 'naosu' in Yamaguchi Prefecture is *different from* that [the one it has] in Tokyo.（➤ from のかわりに《英》では to も用いられる）‖ これには２つの異なるやり方がある We [You] have two *different* ways to do [of doing] it. ‖ なるべく異なった文化に触れて視野を広げなさい Try to expose yourself to *different* cultures in order to expand your horizons.
▶所得の高低により生活の水準も異なる Standards of living *vary* according to income. ‖ 国によって風俗習慣は異なる Each country has its own customs and manners.

ことに 殊に especially（ほかに比べて）; particularly（同種のものの中で）; exceptionally（例外的に）▶彼は野菜，殊にニンジンが嫌いだ He dislikes vegetables, *especially* carrots. ‖ 彼は殊にその点を強調した He *particularly* emphasized that point. ‖ ことしの冬は殊に雪が多かった It's been *exceptionally* snowy this winter.

-ごとに -毎に every →-置き ▶二日ごとに *every two days* ／ *every second day* ／ *every other day* ‖ 4年ごとに行われる祭り a *quadrennial* [《英》a *four-yearly*] festival ‖ 一雨ごとに暖かくなってきている It is getting warmer *every time it rains*. ‖ 彼は会う人ごとに娘の自慢をする He brags about his daughter *to every person he meets*. ‖ バスは20分ごとに出ている The buses leave *every twenty minutes*. ‖ 運転免許は３年または５年ごとに書き換えなければならない You have to renew your driver's license *every three or five years*. ‖ グループごとにリーダーを決めなさい Choose a leader for *each* group. ‖ 作業は日ごとに進んでいる The work is progressing *day by day*.

ことにする 異にする differ《from》▶この問題に関して彼は私とは意見を異にしている Regarding this issue, his opinion *differs* [*is different*] *from* mine.

ことによると 事によると ▶事によるとそのうわさは本当かもしれない The rumor *may* be true. ‖ 事によると父は胃がんかもしれない *Possibly* [*It is possible* that] my father has stomach cancer. →たぶん.

ことのほか 殊の外 exceptionally（例外的に）; extraordinarily /ɪkstrɔ́ːrdnérəli/（並外れて，異常に）▶ことしの米の作柄はことのほかよいようだ It looks like the rice crop is *extraordinarily* good this year.

ことば 言葉

訳語メニュー
言語 →language 1
単語 →word(s) 2
表現 →expression 2

1【言語】(a) language; speech（話すことば）; a dialect（方言）▶話しことば *spoken language* ‖ 書きことば *written language* ‖ 鹿児島ことば the Kagoshima *dialect* ‖ ことばの壁にぶつかる［を乗り越える］run up against [overcome] the *language barrier* ‖ ことばとは人間が自分たちの考えていることや感じていることをほかの人間に伝える手段である *Language* is a tool which people use to convey to others what they think and how they feel. ‖ 動物はことばを持たない Animals do not have *language*. ‖ 日本語には女ことばと男ことばがある Japanese has *female language* and *male language*. ‖ スワヒリ語はアフリカの多くの地方で話されていることばである Swahili is *a language* which is spoken in many parts of Africa.（➤ 日本語，英語など，１つの国やある地域で使われている言語(全体)の意では Ⓒ 扱い）‖ 初めてイギリスへ行ったときはことばが通じなくて困った When I first went to England, I had a hard time *making myself understood in English*.（➤「英語でわかってもらうのに苦労した」の意）.

2【語句・言い方など】 a word（単語）; an expression（表現）; one's remark（発言）; a [one's] vocabulary（語彙）▶きみは難しいことばをよく知ってるね You know a lot of difficult *words*. ‖ うまいことばが思いつかなかった I couldn't think of *a good word for it*. ／No *good expression* came to mind. ‖ あの人のことばにはとげがある His *words* are harsh. ／He has a harsh tongue. ／He speaks harshly. ‖ 上司の無神経なことばにはかちんとくる My boss's insensitive *remarks* get on my nerves. ‖ ことばに出して言わないほうがよい場合もある It is sometimes better to avoid *putting* things *into words* [better to *leave it unsaid*]. ‖ ぼくは由美子とはことばを交わしたことがない I have never *talked with* Yumiko. ‖ もう少しことばを慎みなさい You should *choose your words more carefully*. ‖ イングランドの田園はことばに表せないほど美しい The English countryside is beautiful *beyond words* [*beyond description*]. ‖ 彼女へのプロポーズのことばは何でしたか What did you *say* when you proposed to her?

3【慣用表現】▶おことばに甘えてそうさせていただきます Thank you very much. I'll be glad to accept *your kind offer*. ／I gratefully accept *your kind offer*.（●(1) 日本語特有の謙譲表現なので内容によって訳し方を工夫する必要がある．(2) 英語には Well, if you insist.（そうですねえ，ぜひにとおっしゃるなら）という古めかしい改まった言い方があり，これがユーモラスな感じで言うときの「それではおことばに甘えて」に相当することもある）‖ 彼女は人のことばじりを捉えて文句をつける癖がある She tends to *pick holes in what people say*.（➤「人のことばのあら探しをする」の意）／She tends to *pounce on other people's slips of the tongue*.（➤「人の言い間違いにすぐに飛びつく」の意）‖ おことばを返すようですが先生の説には少々矛盾があるように思われます *I am sorry to contradict you*, but your theory contains some inconsistencies. ‖ それは単にことばのあやだ That's just *a figure of speech*.

✉ **私の感謝の気持ちはことばでは言い表せません** Words are not adequate to express my gratitude. ➤「感謝を表すのにことばは十分でない」の

意.

ことばづかい 言葉遣い one's **language** ▶きみはもう少しことばづかいに気をつけたほうがいい You'd better *watch your language*. ‖ 彼女は上品［下品］なことばづかいをする She uses refined［vulgar］*language*. ‖ 祖母は最近の若者のことばづかいが理解できないと言う My grandmother says she can't understand the *language* of today's young people.

こども 子供 1【親に対して】a **child**［複 **children**], a **kid**（➤ 後者はくだけた語. 特に単数形 a kid は He's a good kid. のように褒めるときに用いることもあるが, 多くの場合, 丁寧さに欠ける品のない響きがあるので, a child を用いるのが無難；１人の場合「うちの子供」は my son, my daughter, my boy, my girl のように具体的に言う）; a **baby**（赤ん坊）▶子供を育てる raise one's *child(ren)* ‖ 彼女は結婚して３人の子供がいる She is married with three *children*. ‖ 対話「子供さんは何人ですか？」「娘が２人です」"How many *children* do you have?" "Two daughters." ‖ しばらく子供たちの面倒を見てくださる？ Will you please look after the *kids* for a while? ‖ 来月彼女に子供ができる（＝生まれる）She is going to *have a baby* next month.

2【大人に対して】a **child** ▶おまえはもう子供じゃないんだぞ You're no longer *a child*. ／You're not *a child* any more. ‖ 子供の頃よくこの川で泳いだものだ *When I was a child*, I often used to swim in this river. ‖ 私たちは子供の頃から互いによく知っている We have known each other well *since we were children*.

▶子供のときに覚えたことは一生忘れないものだ What is learned *in the cradle* is carried to the grave.（➤「揺りかごで覚えたことは墓場まで持ち込まれる」の意）‖ 彼は私を子供扱いする He *treats* me *as if I were a child*. ‖ 子供は風の子 Children like to play outside in every kind of weather.

▶子供心にも両親の間がしっくりいっていないことが理解できた *Though I was a child*, I understood that my parents were not getting along well with each other. ‖ そんな子供だましに乗るもんか I won't be taken in［fall for］by such *a childish*［*an obvious*］*trick*. 《参考》内容のない「子供だまし」のような本・映画・テレビ番組などのことをインフォーマルで pap という. ‖ そんな子供っぽいことではだめだ Don't be so *childish*.（➤一般に childish は悪い意味で, 次の例文の childlike は良い意味で用いる）‖ 最近の小学生には子供らしい天真らんまんさを無くしている者が少なくない Many elementary school children today lack *childlike* innocence. ‖ 私は子供時代を三重県で過ごした I spent my *childhood* in Mie Prefecture. ‖ その遊園地は子供連れでにぎわった The amusement park was crowded with *people with children*［*families*］.

‖**こどもの日** Children's Day ‖ **子供服** children's wear ‖ **子供部屋** a child's［children's］room, a nursery（➤ 後者は古めかしい言い方）.

こともあろうに 事もあろうに ▶事もあろうにこんな日に来るんだから He had to come today, *of all days*. ‖ 事もあろうに新婚ほやほやの先生を好きになるなんて！ *Of all people*, why did you have to get a crush on a teacher who's just married? 《参考》of all ... は「数ある…の中で」の意で, 当惑や驚きを表す.

こともなげ 事も無げ ▶「そんなの簡単だよ」と, 少年はこともなげに言った "That's quite simple," the boy said *as if it were nothing* (*to him*).

ことり 小鳥 a **little**［**small**］**bird**（➤ 単に bird で小鳥を意味することが多い）▶小鳥がさえずっている *Birds* are singing［chirping］.（➤ 後者は「チュンチュン［チーチー］」という短いさえずり；The birds are ... とすると「ふだんこの辺にいる小鳥」のニュアンス）.

ことわざ 諺 a **proverb**, a **saying**

> 《解説》proverb は一般的な真理を比較的わかりやすいことばで述べたことわざ, saying は一般人の生活の中でよく知られた言い習わしで賢明な常識や教訓を含むもの. proverb も saying の一部.

▶ことわざにもあるとおり「病は気から」ですよ Remember, *as the proverb has it*, "The mind rules the body." ‖「時は金なり」という古いことわざがある There is an old *saying* "Time is money." ／An old *saying* goes "Time is money."

ことわり 断り 1【拒絶】**refusal** ▶私は彼にすぐ断り状を出した I sent him *a letter of refusal* immediately. ‖（掲示）駐車お断り No Parking.

2【許可, 言い訳】**permission** ▶断りなしに入室しないでください Don't enter the room *without permission*. ‖ お留守の間, お断りもせずに（＝勝手に）自転車をお借りしました I *took the liberty of* using your bicycle while you were gone.

ことわる 断る 1【拒否・辞退する】**turn down**; **refuse** ＋目（拒否する）; **reject** ＋目（激しく拒絶する）; **decline** ＋目（丁重に辞退する）▶彼に車を貸してくれるように頼んだが断られた I asked him to let me use his car, but he *turned* me *down*. ‖ 彼はひどい格好をしていたので, レストランに入るのを断られた He *was refused* admission to the restaurant because he was so poorly dressed. ‖ 私は彼の招待［プロポーズ］を丁重に断った I politely *declined* his invitation［proposal］. ‖ 彼女にデートを申し込んだけど, あっさり断られちゃったよ When I asked her to go out with me, she *gave me a quick brush-off*.（➤ brush-off は「すげない拒絶」の意のインフォーマルな語）.

> 【文型】
> …することを断る
> **decline to** do
> **refuse to** do

▶俳優はマスコミが報道した離婚の可能性について話をするのを断った The actor *declined to* discuss the possibility of divorce that had been reported in the media. ‖ 殺人の容疑をかけられている男は取材を断った The alleged killer *refused to* be interviewed.

✉ **申し訳ありませんが, 寄付のご依頼はお断りさせていただきます** We are writing to *decline* your request for a donation. ／We are sorry to say we *cannot respond* to your request for a donation.（第２例の場合, cannot の代わりに will not とすることもできるが, cannot のほうが丁寧）.

2【前もって許可を得る, 通告する】▶ここにある本はどれでも貸してあげるが, 私にひと言断ってからにしてほしい You can borrow any book here, but please *let me know* first. ‖ 断っておくが金は貸さないよ *I'd like to make this clear*. I won't lend you any money.

こな 粉 **powder**（粉状のもの）; **flour** /fláuəʳ/（小麦粉）; **meal**（穀類の粗い粉）; **dust**（チョーク・金・炭などの）▶小麦を粉にひく grind wheat into *flour*.

‖**粉薬** powdered medicine, a medical powder ‖ **粉せっけん** soap powder ‖ **粉ミルク** powder (ed) milk；《米》(baby) formula(調合乳) ‖ **粉雪** fine snow(粒の細かい雪)；powder(y) snow(粒の細かいさらさらした雪).

こなごな 粉々に into［to］pieces ▶花瓶は落ちて粉々になった The vase fell and *broke into pieces* [(*was*) *smashed to smithereens*]. (➤ 後者はよりインフォーマルな言い方).

こなす do +目 (する)；finish +目 (終える) ▶**2人分の仕事をこなす** *do the work* of two people ‖ この仕事を1週間でこなすのは無理だ It is impossible to *finish* this work [*get* this job *done*] in a week.
▶彼女は英語を**自由に使いこなす** She *has an excellent command of* English. (● excellent の代わりに perfect や complete を用いると, 教養のあるネイティブスピーカーやバイリンガルの人を連想させる) ‖ ロデオで彼は見事に馬を**乗りこなした** He *managed* the horse admirably in the rodeo.

こなれる digest /daɪdʒést/ (食物が消化される) ▶**こなれやすい［こなれにくい］食べ物** *digestible* [*indigestible*] food.
▶《比喩的》最近彼も**人柄がこなれてきた** His character *has matured* [*mellowed*] lately. (➤ mature /mətʃʊə^r/ は「円熟する, 大人になる」) ‖ 彼女は**こなれた文章を書く** She writes in a *natural* style. ‖ ビルは**こなれた日本語を話す** Bill speaks *fluent* Japanese.

こにくらしい 小憎らしい irritating, annoying ▶横綱貴乃花はかつて**小憎らしいほど強かった** Yokozuna Takanohana was once so strong that some people *found* him *annoying* [some people *were annoyed* by him]. (➤ were annoyed の代わりに, were put off (うんざりさせた)を用いてもよい).

こにもつ 小荷物 a parcel, a package
‖**小荷物取扱所** a parcel(s) office.

ごにん 誤認 a mistake, an error(誤り)；misrecognition, (a) misperception(勘違い) ━動 **誤認する** mistake +目, misconceive +目 ▶それはきみの**事実誤認**だ That is your *misconception of the facts*. / You've made *a factual error*. ‖ 警察が**誤認逮捕**するということはありえる It is possible the police might *arrest the wrong person*.

こぬかあめ 小糠雨 a light drizzle ▶**こぬか雨が降っていた** It was *drizzling*. ‖ 岬馬がこぬか雨にぬれていた A *light drizzle* was falling on the Misaki horses.

コネ connections(縁故)；contacts(有力な知り合い)；influence,《インフォーマル》pull(影響力) ▶**コネで会社に入りたくはない** I don't want to join a company *through connections*. ‖ 彼女は音楽業界にたくさんの**コネを持っている** She has a lot of *contacts* in the music industry. ‖ 私はその銀行にちょっとした**コネがある** I have some *influence* [*pull*] with that bank.

こねこ 子猫 a kitten, a kitty(➤ 後者は主に幼児語).

コネチカット Connecticut /kənéṭɪkət/ (アメリカ北東部の州；略 CT, Conn.).

ごねどく ごね得 ▶市当局はその街区の住民に立ち退きを要求したが, 彼らは**ごね得を狙って**それを拒否した The municipal authorities asked the residents in that block to move out, but they rejected the request *thinking they would gain more money by taking a hard line*. (●「ごね得」に当たる英語はないので,「強硬路線を取ることによってより多くの金をもらおうと考えて」と考える).

こねる knead /ni:d/ +目 (練って混ぜる) ▶**粘土をこねてつぼの形を作る** *knead* (a lump of) clay into the shape of a pot ‖ 彼女は粉をこねてパン生地を作っている She is *kneading* flour into dough.

ごねる ▶彼は何かにつけてよく**ごねる** He can always find something to *complain* [*gripe* / *bitch*] *about*. (➤ bitch は「ぶつくさ言う」の意のインフォーマルな語).

この 1【物・事・人を指して】 this［複 these］▶**この辞書**はとても引きやすい *This* dictionary is very easy to use. ‖ きみの**この万年筆**はフランス製だね *This* fountain pen of yours was made in France, wasn't it? ‖ **このこと**をよく覚えておきなさい Keep *this* in mind. / Remember *this* well. ‖ **この子**はどこの子？ Who is *this* boy [*girl*]? (➤「この子」は this child とするよりも, 男女を分けて this boy, this girl とすることが多い) ‖ **この人たち**はこの部屋で何をしているのですか What are *these people* doing in *this* room? ‖ **この怠け者め！** What a lazy bum! / *You* lazybones!
2【最近の】 ▶**この3週間**とても忙しかった I have been very busy (*for*) *the past* [*the last*] three weeks. (● for these three weeks は古めかしく不自然な言い方になる).

このあいだ この間 the other day(先日)；a few days ago (2, 3日前)；recently, lately (最近)

> **解説「この間」と the other day**
> (1) 日本人は半月も1か月も前のことでも「この間」と言うが, 英語の the other day は通例2, 3日前か, 3, 4日前ぐらいの比較的近い過去を指す.
> (2)「この間はどうもありがとうございました」を Thank you (very much) for the other day. とするのは英語としては不自然. 下例のように感謝の具体的内容を言うこと. また, そもそもお礼はその場で言えば十分と考えており, 日本人のように日にちがたってから改めて言う習慣はない.

▶**この間**はお手伝いいただいてどうもありがとうございました Thank you very much for your help *the other day*. ‖ 彼は**ついこの間**アメリカから帰ったばかりだ He came back from the United States *quite recently* [*only a few days ago*]. ‖ 名古屋でその国際会議が開催されたのは**ついこの間**のことだった It was *only recently* that the international conference was held in Nagoya. ‖ **この間の**英語の授業, 私は出なかったんだ I didn't attend the *last* English class. ‖ 私, **この間から**ずっとかぜをひいているんです I've been suffering from a cold *for the past several days*. (➤ several days は5日から8日くらいまでを指すことが多い).

このうえ この上 ▶人からさんざん金を搾り取っておきながら, **この上**一体何が欲しいんだい After all the money you've sponged off of me, what *more* could you possibly want?

このうえない この上ない ▶皆さまに再びお目に掛かれたのは**この上ない喜び**です *Nothing* could please me *more than* seeing all of you again. ‖ 外国で親切な人に出会うのは**この上なくうれしいこと**だ *Nothing makes you happier* [*gives you more pleasure*] *than* meeting a kind person while abroad. ‖ 我々にとって品質は**この上なく重要**である Quality is of *the utmost* importance for us.

このかた この方 1【この人】 this ▶**この方**が鈴木さんです *This* is Miss Suzuki. (● 文頭でいきなり (×)She is ..., He is ... としない. また, 複数の人を紹介するときも This is で (×)These are としない).
2【…以来】 since ▶私は**生まれてこの方**入院したことがない I have never been in a hospital *in my entire life*.

このくらい この位 ▶《背丈を手などで示して》このくら

いの(背の)男の子ですが，見かけませんでしたか It was a boy *about this tall*. Have you seen him？‖このくらいの苦労でへこたれちゃいけない Don't let *such* a little problem get you down. (➤「こんな小さい問題でへこたれるな」の意)‖私にだってこのくらいできますよ Even I can do *this much*.‖申し訳ありませんが私がしてあげられることはこのくらいです I'm sorry, but *this is about as much* as I can do for you.

このご この期 ▶この期に及んで話し合いも何もないもんだ There can be no talks or anything like that *when things have gone this far*.

このごろ この頃 **recently, lately；these days, nowadays；today** →最近 ▶この頃謙治に会っていない I haven't seen Kenji *recently* [*lately*].‖この頃はわが社で弁当を持って来る人が増えてきている At our company, more people are bringing their lunch *these days*.‖この頃の若者は服装のセンスがいい Young people *today* have good taste in clothes.‖この頃のロックは私の理解を越えている *Recent* rock music is beyond my comprehension.

このさい この際 →際.

このさき この先 **ahead**(前方に)；**from now on**(今後), **in the future**(将来) ▶ 対話「M銀行はどこでしょうか？」「ずっとこの先です」"Where's M Bank？" "It's further (up) *ahead*." (➤「すぐこの先」なら It's only a little way ahead. とする)‖この先どうするつもりだい？What are you going to do *from now on*？

このたび この度 ▶西田氏はこの度文化勲章を受章されました Mr. Nishida has *recently* been awarded the Order of Cultural Merit.‖この度ドイツへ留学することになりました I am going to Germany to study *very soon*.‖この度は高校ご入学おめでとうございます Congratulations on your entrance into high school.‖この度はいろいろお手数をおかけしましてすみませんでした Thank you for all the trouble you've taken for me. (以上の2文では「この度」は訳出不要).

このつぎ この次 **next, next time** ▶この次は郡山に止まるんだったね The *next* stop is Koriyama, isn't it？‖この次の日曜日に海へ行きませんか Would you like to go to the beach *next* [*this coming*] Sunday？‖この次お会いするときにあの写真を差し上げます I'll give you that photo *next time* I see you. →今度.

このとおり この通り ▶このとおりやってごらん Just do it *like this* [*as I do*].‖わがチームはこのとおり(＝ご覧のように)まだ無得点です *As you* (*can*) *see*, our team hasn't earned any points yet.

このとき この時 **at this time** [**moment**] (➤過去の内容のときは at that time [moment] となる) ▶彼女はこのときとばかりに彼に話しかけた She *seized the opportunity* to speak to him.

このところ この所 **these days**(近頃)；**recently, lately**(最近) →最近，近頃 ▶このところ気分がすぐれない I don't feel well *these days*.‖このところ真紀子の姿を見ない I haven't seen Makiko *recently* [*lately*].

このは 木の葉 a (**tree**) **leaf**；**foliage**(木の葉全体) ▶風に舞う木の葉 *leaves* whirling in the wind.

このぶんでは この分では ▶この分では(＝このペースでは)もう1日ないとこれは終わらないよ *At this rate*, it will take one more day to finish this.‖この分では(＝現状のままでは)きみはとても試験に受からないよ *As things stand* (*now*), you won't be able to pass the examination.

このへん この辺 **1**【この付近に】**around** [**near**] **here；in this neighborhood**(この地域・地区) ▶私，この辺はよく知らないんです I am quite a stranger (*around*) *here* [*in this neighborhood*].‖この辺に稲垣さんという弁護士さんはいらっしゃいませんか Is there a lawyer named Mr. Inagaki who has an office *around here*？‖この辺には近寄らないほうがいいよ You'd better keep away from *this area*.

2【この程度，この時間】▶この辺で次の話題に進もう *Now* let's move on to the next topic.‖ではこの辺で失礼いたします I'm afraid I must say good-bye *for now*.‖きょうはこの辺で終わりにしましょう *That's all* for today.／*So much* for today.

このほか この他 ▶私はこのほかにもう1台［2台］携帯電話を持っている I have another cellphone [two more cellphones] *besides* [*in addition to*] *this* (*one*).

このまえ この前 **1**【前回】**last, last time** ▶この前お会いしたときとちっとも変わっていらっしゃいませんね You haven't changed a bit since I saw you *last*.‖この前彼女に電話したのは土曜日だった *The last time* I phoned her was Saturday.‖この前あの人に会ったときは元気そうだった He looked great (*the*) *last time* I saw him.
▶この前のレッスンは易しかったけど今度のは難しくなるよ The *last* lesson was easy, but the next one will be difficult.‖この前の首相は誰だっけ？ Who's *the former* Prime Minister？
✉ **この前のお手紙でなぜ日本人はカラオケが好きなのかお尋ねでしたね** In your *last* [*previous*] letter, you asked me why Japanese people like karaoke.

2【先日】▶この前はごちそうさまでした Thank you for your hospitality *the other day*. 《参考》英米人は後日になって感謝のことばを繰り返すことはしないのがふつう. →この間.

このましい 好ましい **favorable**(プラス評価の)；**desirable**(望ましい)；**suitable**(適している) ▶初めて彼女に会ったが，好ましい印象をもった This was my first time to meet her, but I had [got] a *favorable* impression.‖彼がこの会にとって好ましい人物だとはどうしても思えない I just can't consider him (as a) *desirable* person for this association.‖この町は大学の立地としては好ましくない This town is not *suitable* for (building) a new university.

このまま **as it is, as they are** ▶このテーブルはこのままにしておいてください Leave this table *as it is*.／Leave this table *untouched*.‖この金魚はこのままだとすぐ死んでしまうだろう This goldfish will die soon *if you leave it like this*.‖この枯れていく木々をこのままにしてはおけない *Something must be done* for these dying trees. (➤「何とかしなければならない」の意)‖このままでは締め切りに間に合わない I cannot meet the deadline *as things stand now*.

1**このみ 好み** one's **liking**；one's **taste**(趣味) ▶きみの好みにぴったりのドレスを見つけるのも楽じゃないよ It's not easy to find a dress exactly *to your liking*.‖このデザインは私の好みに合わない This design does not suit my *taste* [is not to my *taste*].‖それはあなたの好み？ Is that to your *liking*？‖好みのスパイスをお選びください Choose your *favorite* spice.‖吉田氏は好みがうるさい Mr.Yoshida is *hard to please*.／Mr. Yoshida is *choosy* [*picky*]. (➤ choosy, picky は「好みが難しい」の意のインフォーマルな語)‖あの子はぼくの好みじゃない That girl is not *my type*.／She's not the sort I *go for*. (➤ go for は「支持する」の意のインフォーマルな言い方)‖人の好みはさまざまだ Everyone to their own taste. ／To each his own. ／Tastes differ. (➤ 英語のことわざ) ‖ お好みで塩・コショウを加えてください Add salt and pepper *to taste*.

2**このみ 木の実** a nut.

このむ 好む like +㊐, be fond of, love +㊐ ⇀好き

【文型】
A より B を好む
like B better than A
prefer B to A
…するほうを好む
prefer to do ／prefer doing

▶彼は登山より水泳を好む He *likes* swimming *better than* mountain climbing. ／ He *prefers* swimming *to* mountaineering. ‖ 彼は家に居るほうを好む He *prefers* staying [*to* stay] home. (➤ 実際, 家に居ることが多い) ‖ 彼女は(どちらかと言えば)庭で過ごすことを好む She would *prefer to* spend her time in the garden.

▶父は私が夜外出するのを好まない My father *does not like* me to go out at night. ‖ 姉は恋愛小説を好んで読んでいる My (older) sister *is fond of* reading love stories. (⇀好んで) ‖ 若者は一般に冒険を好む Generally, young people *love* adventure. ‖ 私は都会の生活は好まない I *don't care for* city life. (➤ care for は通例否定文・疑問文に用いる).

▶《慣用表現》好むと好まざるとにかかわらずきみは健康診断を受けるべきだ You have to have a (physical) checkup *whether you like it or not*.

このよ この世 this world, this life ▶この世でいちばん大切なものは愛だ Love is the most precious thing *in this world*. ‖ その詩人は30歳でこの世を去った That poet *departed this world* [*this life*] at the age of thirty. ‖ 毎日をこの世での最後の日だと思って生きなさい Live every day as if it were your last day *on earth*.

このように like this ; (in) this way (この方法で) ▶瓶はこのように開けてください Please open the bottle (*in*) *this way*. (➤ インフォーマルでは in は省略することが多い) ‖ その実業家はこのようにして成功したのです *That is the way* he became a successful businessman. ‖ このようにして私はフランス語をマスターした *This is how* I learned French.

このんで 好んで ▶『イエスタデイ』は父が好んで口ずさむ歌だ "Yesterday" is a song my father *likes to* hum. ‖ 何を好んで世話役など引き受けたんだ *What will you get out of* volunteering to act as organizer? ／*What good will it do* (*for*) *you* to serve as organizer?

こはく 琥珀 amber ▶こはく色の液体 *amber* (*-colored*) fluid (➤ amber は《英》では信号の「黄」も表す).

ごばく 誤爆 accidental bombing.

ごはさん 御破算 ▶今まで言ったことはすべてご破算(＝取り消し)に願います Allow me to *withdraw* what I have said so far. ‖ 何もかもご破算に(＝だめに)なってしまった It all *came to nothing*. ‖ 両社の合併話はご破算になった Merger negotiations between the two companies *broke down* [*collapsed*]. ‖《そろばんで》ご破算で願いましては… *Starting* [*Beginning*] *afresh* ...

こばしり 小走り ▶私の姿を見て妹は小走りにやって来た When my sister saw me, she came *trotting* [*scurrying*] (up the street) toward me.

ごはっと 御法度 ▶うちの学校では漫画はご法度になっている(＝禁じられている) Comic books *are banned* [*are forbidden*] in my school.

こばな 小鼻 ⚠「小鼻」に相当する英語はないので, nostril (鼻の穴) を用いる. ▶父は怒ると小鼻をひくひくさせる My father *twitches his nostrils* when he gets angry.

こばなし 小話 a short (funny) story.

こばなれ 子離れ ▶最近は子離れできない親が多い Many parents can't *wean themselves from their children* [Many parents *cling to their children emotionally*] these days.

こはば 小幅 ▶小幅な値動きを見せる move *within narrow price limits* ‖ 円はきょうは小幅に上昇した The yen rose *slightly* today.

こばむ 拒む refuse +㊐, turn down (➤ 後者はインフォーマル) ; reject +㊐ (激しく拒絶する) ; deny +㊐ (認めない) ▶彼の要求を拒む *refuse* [*turn down*] his request ‖ 子供の給食費の支払いを拒む親がいる Some parents *refuse to* pay for their children's school-lunch expenses. ‖ 彼らはその建物への入場を拒まれた They *were denied* admittance to the premises.

こばら 小腹 ▶小腹がすく *be a little* [*a bit*] *hungry* ／《英また》be peckish.

コバルト cobalt /kóʊbɔːlt/
‖コバルトブルー cobalt (blue) (➤「コバルトブルーの海」は a cobalt (blue) sea).

こはるびより 小春日和 warm autumn [early winter] weather, an Indian summer.

こはん 湖畔 the lakeside, the lakeshore ▶湖畔のホテル a hotel *on the lakeside* ‖ 彼の別荘はその湖畔にあった His villa was situated *on the shore of* that *lake*. ‖ 私たちは山中湖畔でキャンプをした We camped *on the shores of Lake Yamanaka*.

こばん 小判 a ***koban*** ; an oval coin of gold used in the Edo era (➤ 説明的な訳).

ごはん 御飯 1【米飯】(boiled) rice ▶ご飯を炊く cook *rice* ‖ 私はパンよりご飯のほうが好きです I like *rice* better than toast. (● 日本人は「パン」の英語対応語を bread と考えがちだが, bread はトーストにする前の食パンを指す. したがって,「パン」と「ご飯」を対比して英訳する場合は,「パン」に toast, rolls などを当てるほうがよい) ‖ ほら, ほっぺたにご飯粒がついてるよ Look, there's *a piece of rice* stuck to your cheek.

2【食事】a meal ▶ごはんの支度をする prepare *a meal* ‖ もうごはんは済んだの? Are you through with your *meal*? (➤ 具体的に breakfast [lunch ／ supper] (朝[昼／晩]ごはん) とするのがふつう) ‖ ごはんですよ! *Dinner's ready*. ／Come and get it! (➤ 後者はくだけた言い方で,「食事だからいらっしゃい」の意).

ごばん 碁盤 a Go board ▶碁盤の目のような町並み streets laid out in *a grid*.

ごばんがい 五番街 Fifth Avenue (ニューヨーク市のマンハッタンを南北に貫く繁華街).

こび 媚 ▶部長にこびを売る *play up to* [*fawn upon*] a manager (➤「こびを売る人」を sycophant /síkəfənt/ という).

ごび 語尾 the ending of a word [an utterance] (➤ utterance は「発せられたことば」) ▶彼はことばの語尾がはっきりしない He *mumbles the end of everything he says*. (➤ mumble は「もぐもぐ言う」).
‖語尾変化《文法》inflection.

コピー 1【複写】copying (行為) ; a copy, a duplicate /djúːplɪkət/ ; a photocopy (コピー機での) ━動 **コピーする** copy +㊐, duplicate /djúːplɪkeɪt/ +㊐ (➤ 後者は「複写する」という日本語に近い) ▶この報告書を3部

コピーしてください Could you *make* three *copies of* this report, please?／Could you *run off* three *copies* of this report, please? (➤ run off は「複写機を動かしてコピーを取る」の意味合い) ‖ 原稿はお返ししませんのでコピーをお取りおきください Manuscripts will not be returned, so please *make a copy* for your files. (➤ for your files は「自分の整理用に」) ‖ 彼は私のノートを半分コピーした He *copied* half of my notebook. ‖ ソフトウェアは簡単にコピーできる Software *is* easily *duplicated*.
‖ **コピー機** a copy machine／a photocopier.
2【複製品】 a **copy**, a **reproduction** ▶海賊版のコピー a bootleg *copy* ‖ この絵のコピーが大量に出回っている There are a lot of *copies* [*reproductions*] of this painting going around.
‖ **コピー商品** a copied [pirated] product; a bootleg (レコード・CD・DVD・コンピュータソフトなど).
3【広告の文案】 **copy**
‖ **コピーライター** a copywriter.

> **危ないカタカナ語✸ コピー**
> **1**「複写」の意の「コピー」に当たる英語には copy, duplicate, photocopy があるが, 最初の2語は複写機を使わない手による「写し」も意味する. またこれら3語は「コピーする」という動詞にも使われる.
> **2** 絵画などの「複製品」の意味でも copy を使えるが, この意味では reproduction のほうが正確. 細部に至るまで本物と同じように作ったものは replica という.

こびじゅつ 古美術 **antique art**
‖ **古美術店** an antique store.
こひつじ 子羊 a **lamb** /læm/ ▶子羊のすね肉の蒸し煮 braised *lamb* shank.
こびと 小人 a **dwarf** /dwɔːrf/.
こびりつく **stick**《to》▶ガムが靴の底にこびりついている There is some chewing gum *stuck to* the sole of my shoe. (➤ stuck は stick の過去分詞) ‖ 彼の言ったことが頭にこびりついて離れない I *can't get* his words *out of my head*.
こびる 媚びる **flatter** +㊐, **butter up** (お世辞を言う); **fawn**《upon, on》(おもねる; 堅い語); **play up**《to》(機嫌をとる) ▶上司にこびる *flatter* [*butter up*／*fawn upon*／*play up to*] one's boss ‖ 彼は自分のためになりそうな人間にはいつもこびた言動に出る He always *plays* [*sucks*] *up to* people who may be able to help him.
[1]**こぶ 瘤** a **bump** (打撲による); a **lump** (腫れ物); a **hump** (ラクダの); a **gnarl** /nɑːrl/ (木の) ▶転んで頭に(ひどい)こぶができた I fell down and got *a* (bad) *bump* on the head.
▶《慣用表現》あいつは目の上のこぶだ He is *a pain in the neck* [*a thorn in my side*].
[2]**こぶ 鼓舞する** ▶自分はもっとよい記録が出せるはずと, その水泳選手は自らを鼓舞した The swimmer *encouraged himself* [*herself*], believing he [she] would be able to set a better record.
こふう 古風な **old-fashioned**; **antique** /æntíːk/ (古くて味わいのある); **archaic** /ɑːrkéɪɪk/ (語句・文体が古い) ▶古風な車 an *old-fashioned* car ‖ 古風な趣のある旅館 a *quaint* inn ‖ 古風で和服の似合う日本人女性 a Japanese woman who looks *conservative* and nice in a kimono ‖ 彼は考え方が古風だ His way of thinking is *old-fashioned*. ‖ 古風な掛け時計 an *antique* clock ‖ この叙事詩は古風な文体で書かれている This epic poem is written in an *archaic* style.

ごぶがり 五分刈り ▶五分刈りの男の子 a boy with *close-cropped hair*.
ごふくや 呉服屋 a **kimono fabric store**.
ごぶごぶ 五分五分の **fifty-fifty**; **even** (互角の) ▶彼の成功の見込みは五分五分だ He has a *fifty-fifty* chance of success. ‖ 試合中の両選手は五分五分だった The two players were *evenly matched* in the match.
ごぶさた 御無沙汰 ▶吉田先生にはもう3年もご無沙汰している I *haven't seen nor written to* Mr. Yoshida for three years. ‖ 対話 (久しぶりに会って)「ご無沙汰しています」「こちらこそ」"*Sorry I haven't been in touch*." "Me, too."
✉ **ご無沙汰してしまってごめんなさい** I'm sorry I haven't seen you for such a long time. ／It's been ages since I last wrote (to) you. Please forgive me. ➤ 前者は会っていない場合, 後者は便りをしていない場合の例.
[1]**こぶし 拳** a **fist** ▶拳を固める clench one's *fist* ‖ 拳大の石 a stone *about the size of a fist* ‖ いじめっ子が私に向かって拳を振り上げたとき先生が入って来た The teacher came in just as the bully *had* his [her] *fist raised to hit* me.
[2]**こぶし 小節** a ***kobushi***; a **distinctive vocal style** [**a voice-trembling technique**] **similar to ornamental vibrato** (➤ 説明的な訳) ▶小節を効かせて歌う sing *with delightful grace notes* (➤ grace notes は「装飾音」).
[3]**こぶし 辛夷**《植物》a ***kobushi*** **magnolia**.
こぶた 子豚 a **piglet**, a **little pig**.
こぶとり 小太り・小肥り ▶小太りの男の子 a *short and fat* boy／a *pudgy* boy. →太る.
こぶね 小舟 a **small** [**light**] **boat**.
コブラ《動物》a **cobra** /kóʊbrə/.
こぶり 小降り ▶午後には雨は小降りになるでしょう The rain will *let up* in the afternoon.
こふん 古墳 an **ancient tomb** /tuːm/, a **tumulus** /tjúːmjələs/ (➤ 小高い丘のような形の墓は tumulus mound または mound という) ▶明日香村の高松塚古墳 the Takamatsuzuka *Tumulus Mounds* at Asuka-mura.
[1]**こぶん 古文** **ancient** [**archaic**] **writings** (古代の諸作品); **(the) classics** (古典) ▶漢文は好きですが古文は苦手です I like Chinese classics but I'm weak in *Japanese classics*.
[2]**こぶん 子分** a **follower** (付き従う者); a **henchman** (暗黒街のボスの); a **flunky** (ぺこぺこする男); a **man** (部下) ▶親分子分の関係 the *boss-follower* relationship ‖ よし, きょうから俺の子分にしてやる OK, you're *my man* from now on.
ごへい 語弊 ▶彼はばかと言えば語弊があるが, 少なくとも利口ではない It *may not be entirely correct* to say he is stupid, but he's not (all that) bright either.
ごへいかつぎ 御幣担ぎ ▶彼は御幣担ぎだ He's *very superstitious*.
[1]**こべつ 戸別** ▶先生は生徒の家を戸別に訪問した The teacher visited *each* student's house. ‖ 販売員は家々を戸別に訪問した The salesperson went *from door to door* [*from house to house*].
‖ (選挙運動のためなどの) **戸別訪問** house-to-house canvassing.
[2]**こべつ 個別の** **individual** ▶私たちは先生と個別に面談した We had *individual* interviews with the teacher.／Each of us had a *one-on-one* talk with

the teacher. ‖**個別指導** individualized instruction (➤ man-to-man(マンツーマン) は「男どうしの腹を割った」の意).

コペルニクス **Copernicus** ▶**コペルニクス的**転回 the *Copernican* revolution.

コペンハーゲン **Copenhagen** /kóupənhèɪgən/ (デンマークの首都).

1**ごほう 語法** **usage** /júːsɪdʒ/ (用法) ▶現代日本語の**語法** modern Japanese *usage* ‖**語法**上の誤り incorrect *usage* in speech or writing.

2**ごほう 誤報** a **false report**(間違った報道) ▶津波警報は**誤報**であった The tsunami warning turned out *to be false*.

ごぼう 《植物》 a **burdock**(➤ 食用にする根の部分を特にいう場合は burdock root) 《参考》 英米では食用にしない. 食用にするのは「サルシフィ」(salsify)と呼ばれる, ゴボウに似た根菜. 別名 oyster plant, vegetable oyster. 日本のゴボウほど繊維質ではなく, 味の癖も少ない.

日本紹介 ✉ **ゴボウは根を食用にするために畑で栽培される根菜です. 棒状の木の根のような色と形をしています. 細く切ってニンジンと一緒に油でいため, しょうゆと砂糖で味付けし煮詰めたきんぴらが代表的な食べ方です** *Gobo*, or burdock root, is a root vegetable. It is in the shape and color of a tree root. A typical recipe using *gobo* is '*kinpira*.' To make it, *gobo* is cut into stick-like pieces along with carrot, fried in oil, seasoned with soy sauce and sugar and then simmered.

▶《慣用表現》機動隊は正門にピケを張っていたデモ隊を**ごぼう抜きにした** The police *cleared away* the demonstrators in the picket line at the front gate *one by one*. ‖彼は最後の200メートルで4人を**ごぼう抜きにした** He *overtook* four (other) runners in one spurt in the last 200 meters.

ごぼごぼ ▶詰まっていた流しの水が急に**ゴボゴボ**と流れ出した The water in the clogged sink suddenly started *gurgling* and drained out. ‖水を飲み過ぎておなかが**ごぼごぼする** I drank so much water (that) my stomach is *sloshing*. (➤ slosh は「(液体が)音を立てて跳ねる」).

こぼす **1**【漏らす, 落とす】 **spill** +㊀ (液体・粉末などを) ; **drop** +㊀ (食べ物などを) ; **shed** +㊀ (涙を) ▶あら嫌だ, コーヒー**こぼしちゃった**! Oh, no! I'*ve spilled* my coffee. ‖赤ん坊は食べ物をほとんど床に**こぼした** The baby *dropped* most of his food on the floor. ‖彼の身の上話を聞くうち, 私の母は思わず**涙をこぼしてしまった** As my mother listened to the story of his life, she *shed tears* in spite of herself.

2【不平を言う】 **complain** 《about, of》; **gripe** 《about》 (しつこく愚痴る) ; **grumble** 《about》 (ぶつぶつ言う) ▶忙しくて本を読む時間がないと**こぼす**人は結局読書が好きではないのだ Those who *complain* that they are too busy to read really don't like reading at all. ‖今月になって野菜が高くなったと**こぼす**主婦が多い Many homemakers *complain* [*gripe*] *that* vegetable prices have gone up this month.

こぼね 小骨 a **small** [**tiny**] **bone**.

こぼればなし こぼれ話 an **anecdote** /ǽnɪkdoʊt/.

1**こぼれる** **1**【あふれ出る, 落ちる】 **spill**(液体・粉末などが) ; **fall, drop**(涙などが) ▶あ, 花瓶の水が**こぼれる**! Watch out, the water in the vase is going to *spill* (*all*) *over*! ‖猫が瓶を倒したためにしょうゆが台所のテーブルに**こぼれた** The cat knocked over the bottle and *spilled* soy sauce on the kitchen table. (➤ この spill は「こぼす」の意の他動詞) ‖インクが机に**こぼれている** Some ink *is spilled* on the desk. ‖彼女の目から大粒の涙が**こぼれた** Large tears *dropped* [*fell*] from her eyes. ‖彼はビールをコップに**こぼれるくらいに**注いだ He filled the glass *to the brim* with beer. (➤ brim は「(コップの)縁」) ‖ボールはキャッチャーミットから**こぼれて**転々とファウルグラウンドへ転がった The ball *bounced off* the catcher's mitt and went rolling into the foul territory.

2【自然に外に出る】▶金メダルを手にして彼女の**白い歯がこぼれた** As she took the gold medal in her hand, her face *broke into a happy smile*. ‖樹間から暖かい春の日ざしが**こぼれている** Warm spring sunlight *is streaming through* the branches of the trees. ‖モス夫人は**こぼれんばかりの笑顔**で私を迎えてくれた Mrs. Moss met me *with a charming smile*.

2**こぼれる** ▶お母さん, この包丁**刃がこぼれて**て使い物にならないわよ! Mom, this knife is useless since it has *a nicked edge*.

ごほん ▶水野さんはかぜが治っていないらしく, まだ**ゴホン, ゴホン**とせきをしている Mr. Mizuno doesn't seem to have gotten over his cold, because he is still *coughing*.

《参考》漫画などでは「ゴホン, ゴホン」を cough, cough /kɔːf/ や coff, coff ／hack, hack などで表す.

こぼんのう 子煩悩 ▶**子ぼんのうな**父親 a *loving* [*fond* ／ *tender*] father (● doting father とすると「子供を溺愛する親ばかな父親」の意になる).

1**こま 駒** a **piece**, a **man** [**複 men**] (チェス・将棋の) ▶将棋の**駒**を動かす move *pieces* in shogi.

▶《慣用表現》水戸商業高校チームは決勝へ**駒を進めた** The Mito Commercial High School team *made it* into the finals.

2**こま 独楽** a **top** ▶**こま**を回す spin *a top* ‖**こま**が澄んでいる The *top* is sleeping.

3**こま** ▶四**こま**漫画 a *4-frame* comic strip.

‖**こま送り** single frame advance.

ごま 胡麻 **sesame** /sésəmi/ (**seeds**) ▶(すり鉢で)**ゴマ**をする grind *sesame seeds* (in a mortar) ‖**開け, ゴマ** *Open, Sesame!*

▶《慣用表現》ぼくに**ごまをすっても**だめだよ It's useless to *butter* me *up*. (→ごますり).

‖**ゴマ油** sesame oil.

コマーシャル a **commercial** ; an **advertisement** /ædvəˈtáɪzmənt ‖ ədvə́ːtɪs-/ (広告) ; a **spot** (番組の合間に入れる短いコマーシャル) 《参考》テレビ・ラジオなどでコマーシャルに出て商品を売り込む著名な人を pitchman [pitchwomen] という. ▶テレビ[ラジオ]の**コマーシャル** a TV [radio] *commercial* ‖最近は車の**コマーシャル**が多い These days we see a lot of *car commercials*.

‖**コマーシャルフィルム** a commercial film.

危ないカタカナ語✹ コマーシャル

1「コマーシャル」は commercial がそのまま使えるが, commercial message の略語とされる CM は日本でしか通用しない. 同様に CF も英語では用いない.

2「コマーシャルソング」は (commercial [advertisement]) jingle で, commercial song というと「商業的に売れる歌」の意味になる.

こまい 古米 **rice harvested in a previous year.**

こまいぬ 狛犬 a ***Koma-inu*** ; a Koma guardian

dog statue that is erected at the entrance of Shinto shrines to ward off evils (➤ 説明的な訳).

こまかい 細かい **1**【小さい】**fine** ; **small** (ほかに比べて) ▶細かい細工 *fine* [*detailed*] work ‖ 目の細かいレース *fine* lace ‖ 霧のように細かい雨 *fine* [*misty*] rain like fog ‖ 細かいことを気にするな Don't worry about *small things*. ‖ 細かい字を見ると目が疲れる Reading *fine print* is hard on the eyes. ‖ 彼女は肉と野菜を細かく切った She *chopped* the meat and vegetables (*into small pieces*).

2【詳細な】**detailed** /dɪtéɪld ‖ díːteɪld/ ▶支出の内訳を細かく書く write a *detailed* breakdown of the expenditures ‖ 細かいこと(=細部)はさておいて大筋を決めておこう Let's decide on an outline first and leave the *details* for another occasion. ‖ この調査は細かいところまで丹念に調べてある This study was conducted with painstaking attention to (*fine*) *detail*. ‖ 彼女は細かいところまでよく気がつく She'*s very perceptive*. / She'*s very attentive to other people's needs*. ‖ 彼女はとても神経が細かい She is very *sensitive*. ‖ 彼は金銭に細かい He is *strict about money matters*. / He is *tight with his money*. (➤ 後者は「けちけちしている」).

3【金銭が小額の】▶あいにく細かいお金の持ち合わせがありません Unfortunately, I have no *change* on me (right now).

ごまかし (a) **deceit,** (a) **deception** (➤ 前者のほうが否定的・軽蔑的ニュアンスが強い) ; **trickery** (詐欺, ぺてん).

ごまかす (⚠ **人の目を欺いたり, 不正を働いたりすることを「ごまかす」というが, この日本語に対応する1語の英語はない. 訳例で示したように文脈に応じて訳語を工夫する必要がある**) ▶会社の帳簿をごまかす *cook* (*up*) [*doctor*] the company books (➤ cook (up) は「でっちあげる」, doctor は「(不正に)手を加える」の意のインフォーマルな語) ‖ 税金をごまかしてはいけない Never *cheat on* [*dodge*] your taxes. (➤ cheat on は「…のことでいんちきをする」, dodge は「…からうまく逃げる」の意で, ともにインフォーマルな言い方) ‖ 彼女は年齢を5つもごまかしていた She *took* five years *off her age*. (➤ 少なめに言った場合) / She *added* five years *onto her age*. (➤ 多めに言った場合) (● 単に「年齢をごまかしていた」なら She misrepresented [lied about] her age. とする) ‖ 私はあの店でお釣りをごまかされた I *was shortchanged* at that store. (➤ shortchange は「釣り銭を少なく渡す」) ‖ これは笑ってごまかすようなことじゃないぞ This isn't something you can (just) *laugh off*. ‖ 彼は慌ててミスをごまかそうとした He hurried to *cover* [*conceal*] *his* (*own*) *mistake*.

こまぎれ 細切れ・小間切れ ▶豚肉のこま切れ (*finely*) *sliced* [*hashed*] *pork* ‖ 肉をこま切れにする *chop up* meat (*into small pieces*). ‖ 《比喩的》情報がこま切れ(=断片的)で被害の状況がよくわからなかった Little was known about the damage since the information was *fragmentary* [the information *came in bits and pieces*].

こまく 鼓膜 an **eardrum**, a **tympanum** /tímpənəm/ ▶鼓膜が破れそうなごう音 an *earsplitting* sound.

こまごま 細々 ▶家庭の中のこまごました雑用 household *chores* ‖ 父は留守中のことについてこまごまと注意を与えて旅行に出かけていった My father went off on a trip after leaving *detailed* instructions about what should be done in his absence. ‖ 彼は事件の経過についてこまごまと話した He *gave* me *a full account* of how the incident had developed.

ごましおあたま 胡麻塩頭 ▶(私を襲った)犯人はごま塩頭だったと思います I think the attacker had *salt-and-pepper hair*.

こましゃくれた **precocious** (子供がませている) ; **sassy** (生意気な) ▶何てこましゃくれた娘だろう What a *precocious* girl (she is)! ‖ こまっしゃくれた口を利くな! Don't give me that *sass*. / Don't sass me.

ごますり a **sycophant** /síkəfənt/ (おべっか使い) ; a **flatterer** (お世辞の上手い人) 《参考》俗語に an ass-kisser, a kiss-ass があるが, これは文字どおりには「(他人の)尻にキスする人」の意なので嫌う人も多い (➤ 行為としての「ごますり」は ass-kissing). apple-polisher という言い方もあるがやや古風. →ごま.

こまた 小股 ▶小股で歩く *shuffle* / walk *with short steps*.

こまどり 駒鳥 《鳥》a **Japanese robin**.

こまねく 拱く ▶湖の汚染が進むのをただ手をこまねいて見ているわけにはいかない We *just can't look on with our hands folded* [*just can't sit and do nothing*] while the lake is getting more polluted.

こまねずみ こま鼠 ▶母は一日中こまねずみのように動き回っている My mother *is* (*as*) *busy as a bee* [*a beaver*] all day. (➤ 英語では「ミツバチ[ビーバー]のように忙しい」という).

ごまめ ▶ごまめの歯ぎしり an underdog's chafing, protesting in vain.

こまめに ▶できるだけこまめに辞書を引きなさい Use your dictionary *whenever* it could possibly help you. ‖ こまめにデータを保存することをすすめます I advise you to save your data *frequently*. ‖ あの奥さんは一日中こまめに働くね That lady *works like a beaver* all day long, doesn't she? (➤ ビーバーは働き者とされる) ‖ 氷のうをこまめに取り替えてください Change the ice pack *often* (*enough*).

こまもの 小間物 **notions**
‖小間物屋 a notions store.

こまやか 細やか・濃やか ▶彼女は孤児たちにこまやかな愛情を示した She showed the orphans *tender affection*. ‖ 彼らの間にこまやかな友情が育った *A close friendship* grew between them.

こまらせる 困らせる ▶彼女は「あなたと別れるくらいなら, 私死にます」と言ってぼくを困らせた She *gave* me *a hard time* by saying, "I'll die if we split up." ‖ ドングリは泣いてドジョウを困らせた The acorn cried and *gave* the loach *much worry*.

こまりもの 困り者 a **nuisance** /njúːsəns/ ▶彼は一家の困り者だった He was *a nuisance* to his family. / He was *the black sheep* of the family. (➤ the black sheep of the family で「一家の持て余し者」).

こまる 困る **1**【悩む, 苦しむ】**have a problem, have difficulty** (悩んでいることがある) ; **be in trouble** (ひどく面倒なことになっている) (➤ problem は「困っている問題」, trouble は「困った状態」) ▶困ったことが起きた *A problem* has come up. ‖ 困ったことがありましてご相談したいのですが I'*ve got a problem* I'd like to talk over with you. ‖ 歯が悪くて[視力が弱くて]困っています *I'm troubled with* bad teeth [*by* poor eyesight]. ‖ 私, 今とっても困ってるんです I'*m in* big *trouble* now. ‖ 困ったことがあったら, いつでも相談に乗るよ *If you're ever in trouble*, I'll always be there for you. ‖ インドでいちばん困ったのは食事だった When I was in India, *the biggest problem I had* was (with) the food.
▶帰り道がわからなくてひどく困った I *had great diffi-*

culty finding the way back. (→苦労) ‖ 彼女は困ったときに頼りになる人です She is a person you can rely on *in* [*at*] *a pinch*. (➤ at は主に《英》) ‖ 妻の両親が１週間滞在すると聞いて, 彼はちょっと困った顔をした He *looked a little annoyed* [*unhappy*] when he heard that his wife's parents would stay for a week. ‖ 終電に乗り遅れ, そのうえ困ったことにはタクシーに乗る金が無かった I missed the last train, and *to make matters worse*, I did not have enough money to take a taxi. ‖ きみが居なくて本当に困ったよ I'*m* [We'*re*] really *lost* without you. ‖ 対話「浮かない顔をしてるけど, 何か困ったことでもあるのかい？」「レポートがまだ半分しかできてないんだ」"You look depressed. *Is anything wrong?*" "I've only finished half of my paper."

▶《同情して》それはお困りでしょう *I'm sorry for you*. (➤ I feel sorry for you. とすると相手を哀れんでいるような響きが強くなる) ／*That's too bad*. ／*What a shame!* ‖ 困っているときの友こそ本当の友 A friend *in need* is a friend indeed. (➤ 英語のことわざ; in need は「金・食べ物などに事欠く」の意).

2【迷惑・慨嘆している】▶困ったことにおじいちゃんは携帯を持っていない *The trouble* [*problem*] is my grandpa doesn't have a cellphone. ‖ 娘は30を過ぎたというのに結婚する気が全くない―困ったものだ My daughter is *a* (*real*) *headache* (to me); she's over thirty but has no intention of getting married. (➤「頭が痛い」の意) ‖ あれは困った(＝どうしようもない)やつだ He's [She's] *impossible*. ／He [She] is *a real problem*. ‖ 今更断られても困る *It's too late* for you to say no. ‖ 彼のように病気にあまり神経質なのも困る It is *not good* to be as worried [nervous] about health as he is. ‖ 私の言うことを聞いておかないと, あとで困ったことになりますよ *You'll be sorry* later if you don't follow my advice. ‖ 玄関の真ん前に車を止められては困ります *Do not* park your car in front of the entrance to our house. (➤「止めてくれるな」と断るとき; 「大変困ります」と丁重に言うには It causes us great inconvenience if you park your car ... とする).

3【当惑する】▶ぶしつけな質問をされ, 私は返事に困った I *didn't know* [*was at a loss*] *how* to reply to such a rude question. (➤ 前者のほうが自然) ‖ 彼女の難しい質問に私は困り果てた I *was extremely perplexed* by her difficult question. ／Her hard question *stumped* me. (➤ stump は「(人を)途方に暮れさせる」).

4【生活に困る・不便である】be hard up ▶彼は金に困っているらしい He seems to *be pressed* [*be in a fix*] *for money*. (➤ be in a fix はインフォーマルな表現) (●「…に困る」を be hard up for ... とすることもできるが, やや下品な言い方) ‖ 貯金どころか食うに困っている状態だ I *can hardly make a living*, much less save money. (➤ make a living は「生計を立てる」) ‖ 金に困って本を全部売り払った I sold all my books because I *needed money*. ‖ ぜいたくを言うな. 世の中にはもっと困っている人が大勢いるんだぞ You ask too much. There are a lot of *people* in the world *who are needier than you*. ‖ この地域は医者がいなくて困る This region *is in dire need of* doctors. (➤「ひどく不足している」の意).

こまわり 小回り ▶小回りの利く男 a *flexible* man ‖ こちらの車種は小回りが利きます This type of car *can turn in* tight *places*. ／This car *can turn on a dime*. (➤「10セント硬貨の上でも回転できる」が原義).

コマンド《コンピュータ》a **command**
‖**コマンドキー** a command key.

ごまんと ▶歌手志望の若者はごまんといる There are *countless* [*zillions of*] young people who want to be pop singers. ／Young would-be pop singers are *a dime a dozen*. (➤ a dime a dozen は「ごくありふれたもの」).

こみ 込み ▶全部込みでいくらですか How much is it *altogether*? ‖ 値段は配達料も込みになっています The price *includes* transportation. ‖ 初任給は税込み19万8000円だった My starting salary was 198,000 yen a month, *taxes included* [*before taxes*].
✉ **郵送料込みで3450円お送りください** Please send us 3,450 yen, *postage included*.

ごみ 塵・芥 **trash**(古新聞・紙・瓶・木片・段ボールなどの); 《米》**garbage**(特に台所から出る生ごみ); 《英》**rubbish**(家庭やオフィスなどから出るもの; 生ごみを含む); **refuse** /réfju:s/ (廃物; 堅い語); **litter** (紙くず; 散らかったもの); **waste**(廃棄物) ▶ごみを捨てる throw out the *trash* ‖ ごみを出す take out the *garbage* ‖《掲示》ごみを捨てるな No [Don't] Litter. ／No Dumping. (➤ 後者はごみ捨て場でない所に大量のごみが投棄してある場合などに多く用いられる) ‖ 燃えるごみ burnable *trash* ‖ 燃えないごみ nonburnable *trash* ‖ (コンピュータの)ゴミ箱フォルダ a trash folder ‖ ごみの日になるまでごみは出さないでください Don't put your trash [garbage] out before it's *trash* [*garbage*] *day*. (➤ この場合, garbage はゴミ一般であるが, 狭義では「生ごみ」. なお, アメリカでは多くの場合, 収集日は週１回で, リサイクルするものとそうでないものを分けて出す). ‖ あの空き地はごみの山になっている There is *a pile of trash* in that empty lot. ‖ 試合が終わったあとの球場はごみだらけだった After the ball game was over, we found the stadium full of *litter*. ‖ 目にごみが入ったみたいだ I think I have *something* in my eye.

‖**ごみ収集車**《米》a garbage truck [wagon], 《英》a dustcart ‖ **ごみ収集人**《米》a garbage collector, 《英》a refuse collector《参考》婉曲(えんきょく)に sanitation worker [officer] などともいう ‖ **ごみ焼却炉** an incinerator /ɪnsínərèɪṭəʳ/ ‖ **ごみ捨て場** a (garbage ／rubbish) dump, a dumping ground, 《英また》a (refuse) tip ‖ **ごみ箱**《米》a trashcan, a garbage can, 《英》a dustbin; a trash box (箱状の), a waste(-paper) basket (籠状の) ‖ **ごみ屋敷** a hoarding house, a hoarder [hoarder's] house, a trash house (➤ hoard は「密かに大量に溜め込む」; 最後の言い方が日本語に近いが, 他の語のほうが使用頻度が高い).

こみあう 混み合う **be crowded**《with》▶プラットホームは乗客で混み合っている The platform *is crowded* [*is jammed*] with passengers. ‖《車内のアナウンス》車内が混み合いましてご不便をおかけし, 申し訳ございません *The train is now packed to capacity*. We're very sorry for the inconvenience. (➤ 英米ではこのようなアナウンスはしない).

こみあげる 込み上げる ▶我知らず涙が込み上げてきた *Tears came to my eyes* in spite of myself. ‖ 我々が優勝したのだと知った瞬間喜びが込み上げてきた When I found out we won the championship, I *was filled with happiness*. ‖ その警官の暴言に怒りが込み上げてきた I *was filled with anger* when I heard the rude remarks of that police officer. ／The rude remarks of that police officer *filled me with anger*. ‖ お手紙を拝見して熱いものが込み上げてき

ました Your letter *brought* a lump to my throat. (➤ lump to one's throat は「喉が締めつけられるような感じ」).

こみいる 込み入る ▶この推理小説は筋が込み入っている The plot of this detective story *is* quite *intricate*. (➤ intricate /íntrɪkət/ は「複雑で難解な」の意) ‖ 彼らの離婚の裏には何か込み入った事情があるらしい There seems to be some *complicated* circumstances behind their divorce.

ごみごみ ▶新宿のようなごみごみした所は好きじゃない I don't like *crowded* places like Shinjuku.

こみだし 小見出し a subheading.

こみち 小道 a lane (細道) ; a path (野山の) ; a trail (森・山中の).

コミック a comic (漫画) ; a cartoon /kɑːˈtúːn/ (1コマの政治漫画)

‖コミック誌 a comic book [magazine].

コミッショナー a commissioner.

コミット コミットする commit《to》, make a commitment《to》.

こみみ 小耳 ▶ 対話「どうしてそれを知っているんですか？」「ちょっと小耳に挟んだもので」"How do you know that?" "*A little bird told me* (about it)." (➤ a little bird は「名は言えないがある情報源」といった感じで,「風の便り」に相当する).

コミュニケーション (a) communication ▶国際コミュニケーション international *communication* ‖ コミュニケーションの断絶 a breakdown in *communication* (切れること) ／a *communication* gap (隔たり) ‖ 外界とのコミュニケーション *communication* with the outer world ‖ 言語はコミュニケーションの手段である Language is a means of *communication*. ‖ 親子のコミュニケーションがない家庭は悲惨だ A family lacking *parent-and-child communication* is in sad shape. ‖ 耳の聞こえない人たちは手話によってコミュニケーションを行うことができる Deaf people can *communicate* with each other by means of sign language. ‖ 上層部と下の人たちとのコミュニケーションがうまくいっていないようだ It seems that *there is poor communication* between those at the top and those (working) in lower positions. ‖ マネージャーにはコミュニケーション能力が必要だ Managers need to have *communication skills*.

コミュニティ a community

‖コミュニティセンター a community center.

こむ 混む・込む 1【混雑する】 get [be] crowded《with》; be jammed [packed]《with》(詰め込まれている) ▶公園は花見客で混んでいた The park *was crowded with* cherry blossom viewers. ‖ (レストラン・デパートなどで) きょうは混んでるね It'*s crowded* today, isn't it? ‖ 電車が混んでいたので, 私はずっと立ちっぱなしだった Since the train *was crowded*, I had to stand the whole way. ‖ 道路がひどく混んでいたので, 私はここへ来るのにいつもより時間がかかった It took me longer than usual to get here because (*the*) *traffic was so heavy*.

2【細工が細かい】 ▶このペルシャじゅうたんはとても手が込んでいる This Persian rug is very *intricate* [*elaborate*].

ゴム gum /gʌm/ (材料としての) ; rubber (加工された) ▶この素材はゴムのような弾力がある This material has the resiliency of *rubber*.

‖ゴム印 a rubber stamp ‖ ゴム手袋 rubber gloves ‖ ゴム跳び elastic jumping [skipping] (➤ elastic は「伸縮性のある(もの)」の意) ‖ ゴムの木 a gum [rubber] tree ; a rubber plant (観葉植物) ‖ ゴムひも an elastic (string)《参考》ゴムひもなどを通すときに用いるピン状の道具を bodkin という. ‖ ゴムボート a rubber boat [raft] ‖ ゴムボール a rubber ball ‖ 天然 [合成] ゴム natural [synthetic] rubber ‖ 輪ゴム a rubber band,《英また》an elastic band.

こむぎ 小麦 wheat,《英また》corn ▶小麦を栽培する grow *wheat* ‖ 少女たちの肌は小麦色に美しく焼けている The girls *have beautiful golden suntans*.

‖小麦粉 flour.

こむらがえり こむら返り a leg cramp ▶泳いでいて足がこむら返りを起こした I *got* (*a*) *cramp* in my leg while swimming. (➤ a を略すのは主に《英》).

こめ 米 rice (➤「ご飯」は cooked [boiled] rice と訳せるが, 通常は文脈で区別し,「米」も「ご飯」も rice である) ▶ 1粒の米 a grain of *rice* ‖ 米をとぐ wash [rinse] *rice* ‖ 酒は米から造る Sake is made from *rice*. ／*Rice* is made into sake. ‖ この地域の農家では米と小麦を作っている The farmers in this area grow *rice* and wheat. ‖ うちでは月に20キロの米を食べる My family consumes twenty kilograms of *rice* each month.

✉ **日本人は米を主食としています** *Rice* is the staple food of the Japanese people.

‖米倉 a rice granary ‖ 米俵 a straw rice bag [sack] ‖ 米粒 a rice grain, a grain of rice ‖ 米どころ a prime rice growing region ‖ 米ぬか rice bran ‖ 米びつ a lidded container for rice, a rice bin [box] ‖ 米屋 a rice shop (店) ; a rice dealer (人).

こめかみ a temple ▶こめかみの辺りが痛い I have a pain in my *temple*(*s*).

コメディアン a comedian /kəmíːdiən/.

コメディー (a) comedy ▶このドラマはコメディータッチだ This drama has *a comic touch*.

こめる 込める 1【詰める】 load /loʊd/ +目, charge +目 ; include +目 (含める) →込み ▶猟銃に弾を込める *load* a shotgun.

2【集中する】 ▶心を込めて祈りなさい Pray *with all your heart*. ‖ 力を込めて押してごらん Push (it) *with all your strength*. ‖ もっと感情を込めて歌いなさい *Put* more *emotion into* your singing.

こめん 湖面 the surface of a lake ▶湖面に月影が映っていた The moon was reflected *on the surface of the lake*.

ごめん 御免 1【謝罪】 I'm sorry. ; Excuse me.

> **《解説》謝罪の表現**
> (1) 人の体に誤って触れたときなどに相手に軽く謝る場合は **Excuse me (, please)**. とか **Pardon me.** などと言う.《英》では単に **Sorry**. と言うことも多い.
> (2) 同様に軽く謝る **I beg your pardon**. は Excuse me. よりも上品な響きがあり, 必ず尻下がりに言う. これを尻上がりに言うと「もう一度言ってください」の意になるので注意.
> (3) **I'm sorry**. は自分の過失や落ち度を認めている場合に多く用いる. ほかに, I apologize. (謝ります) や Please forgive me. (許してください) も用いる.

▶きのうは本当にごめんね *I'm* really *sorry* about yesterday. ‖ びっくりさせてしまってごめんなさい *I'm sorry* for giving [to have given] you such a scare. ‖ この間お借りした傘を持って来るのを忘れてしまってごめんなさい *I'm sorry* I forgot to bring the umbrella I borrowed the other day. ‖「ごめんなさい」を言うときには相手の目を見なさい When you say *you are sorry* [*you apologize*], look the person in the eye. ‖ 対話「あ, ごめん. 足踏んじゃった?」「いや, 大丈夫」"Oh, *excuse me* [(*I'm*) *sorry*]! Did I step on your toe?" "No. I'm all right." ‖ 対話「アメリカに留学するんだって?」「うん, 黙っててごめんね」"What's this I hear about you going to the U.S. to study?" "Yeah. *I'm sorry* I didn't tell you." ‖ ごめんなさい. 私はあなたのお気持ちを傷つけるつもりはなかったんです *Please forgive me*. I didn't mean to hurt your feelings.

✉ **お便りが遅くなってごめんなさい** I'm sorry I didn't write you (any) sooner. ➤ 否定文で比較級に any をつけて「もう少し早く」の意.

2【断り】Excuse me. ▶お話し中, ごめんなさい *Excuse* [*Pardon* / *Forgive*] *me* for interrupting you. ‖ 対話《人の前を通るとき》「ちょっとごめんなさい」「どうぞ」"*Excuse me*." "Certainly." ‖《よその家を訪問して》ごめんください Excuse me. / Anybody home? / Hello! (➤ 後の 2 者はくだけた言い方).

3【拒否】▶人から指図されるのはごめんだ *I refuse* [*hate*] to be dictated to. ‖ 戦争はもうごめんだ *No more* war! ‖ 対話「健ちゃん, 正雄と仲いいんでしょ. デート断ってくれない?」「ごめんだね. 自分で言えよ」"Ken, you're pretty close to Masao. Could you tell him I don't want to go out with him?" "*No thanks*! Tell him yourself!"

コメンテーター a **commentator.**

コメント a **comment**; a **statement**(声明) 一動 **コメントする comment**《on》; **state** ▶私たちは市長にごみ処理場建設計画についてコメントを求めた We asked the mayor to *comment on* the construction of the waste treatment plant [facility]. ‖ ノー・コメント *No comment*. ‖ 首相はサミットは成功だったというコメントを発表した The Prime Minister released *a statement* saying that the summit was successful.

ごもく 五目 ▶五目並べをする play *gobang* (➤ gobang は日本語の「碁盤」から).

‖**五目ずし** vinegared rice mixed with various ingredients ‖ **五目飯** rice lightly seasoned and cooked with various ingredients ‖ **五目焼きそば** fried noodles with mixed ingredients.

こもごも 交々 →悲喜交々.

こもじ 小文字 a **small letter**; 《印刷》**lower case.**

こもち 子持ち ▶彼女も今では 3 人の子持ちだ She is now *the mother of three children*. / She has three children now.

▶子持ちカレイの煮付け *flounder with roe* simmered in soy sauce(➤ roe /roʊ/ は「魚卵」).

ごもっとも ▶あなたのおっしゃることはごもっともです You are *quite right*. / Your opinion is *quite correct*. ‖ お尋ねはごもっともです You *may well* ask that. ‖ お腹立ちはごもっともです You *have good reason* to be angry.

こもの 小物 1【小さい物】small articles; accessories(付属品) ‖ **小物入れ** an accessory case; a glove compartment (車の).

2【小人物】▶あんなの実に小物だよ He's just *small fry* [《米また》*small potatoes*].

こもり 子守 looking after a baby, baby-sitting(子守すること); a **babysitter**, 《英》a **childminder**(人) ▶バーバラは子守のアルバイトを見つけた Barbara found a job as *a baby-sitter*. ‖《妻が夫に》今度の土曜日は同窓会なの. 子守しててくれる? I have a class reunion this Saturday. Will you *look after* [*take care of*] *the kids*? ‖ **子守歌** a lullaby /lʌ́ləbaɪ/, a nursery song, a cradle song.

こもる 籠もる 1【閉じ籠もる】▶寺に籠もる *live in seclusion* in a temple ‖ どうして最近の子供たちはあんなに自分の部屋に籠もりたがるのだろう I wonder why young kids today like to *spend* so much *time alone in their own rooms*. ‖ ビルは妻の死後, 家に籠りきってしまった Bill *shut* himself *in* after his wife's death.

2【満ちる】▶窓を開けてくださる? 部屋に魚の臭いが籠もっているわ Would you please open the window? The room *reeks of* fish. [The room *is filled with the smell* of fish.] (➤ reek of は「…の悪臭がする」).

3【含まれる】▶心の籠もった贈り物 a *heartfelt* gift / a gift *from the heart* ‖ きみの演技は感情が籠もってないね Your performance *lacks feeling* [*is lifeless* / *is wooden*].

✉ **お心の籠もったご助言本当にありがとうございます** I very much appreciate your *considerate* [*thoughtful*] advice.

こもれび 木漏れ日 ▶地面に木漏れ日がさしていた *Sunlight streamed through the leaves* to the ground.

こもん 顧問 an **adviser**, an **advisor**; a **consultant**(コンサルタント) ▶彼の父は外務省の顧問をしている His father is *an adviser* to the Ministry of Foreign Affairs.

‖**顧問弁護士** a legal adviser(法律顧問); a corporation [《英》company] lawyer (会社で依頼している); a family lawyer (家庭で依頼している) ‖ **技術顧問** an expert adviser, a technical adviser.

こもんじょ 古文書 old documents.

こや 小屋 a **hut**(主に木造で粗末な); a **cabin** (丸太小屋); a **lodge** (山小屋); a **shed** (物置)

‖**犬小屋** a doghouse, a kennel ‖ **馬小屋** a stable ‖ **豚小屋** a pigpen.

こやく 子役 a **child actor**(俳優) ▶子役を演じる play *a child's part* [*role*].

ごやく 誤訳 a **mistranslation** 一動 **誤訳する mistranslate** +目 ▶彼はその翻訳の誤訳を 2, 3 か所指摘した He pointed out a few *mistakes* [*errors*] *in the translation*.

こやし 肥やし manure /mənjóəʳ/ (家畜のふんなど); **fertilizer** (化学肥料).

こやす 肥やす enrich +目; **fertilize** +目 (土を) ▶堆肥は土地を肥やすために用いられる Compost is used to *fertilize* the land [to *enrich* the soil]. ‖《慣用表現》たまには名画を見て目を肥やしたほうがいい It's a good idea to *cultivate your sense of beauty* by taking a look at famous paintings from time to time.

こやま 小山 a **hill**, a **hillock**(➤後者のほうがより小さい).

こやみ 小止み ▶雨は小やみなく降り続いた It went on raining *without a break*. →小降り.

こゆう 固有の one's **own**(それ自体の); **peculiar**《to》 ▶どの民族にも固有の文化がある Every people [ethnic group] has *its own* culture. ‖「万歳」は日本固有の風習だ Shouting "Banzai" is a custom *peculiar to* Japan. ‖ パンダは中国固有の動物だ The panda is *indigenous* [*native*] *to* China. (➤ indigenous /ɪndídʒənəs/ は「…に原産の」) ‖ 北方領土は日本固有の領土です The Northern Territories are an *integral part of Japan's territory*.

‖**固有名詞** a proper noun ‖ **固有種** an indigenous species.

こ

こゆき 小雪 a **light snow**; a **light snowfall** ▶けさ方小雪がちらついた We had *a light snow* (*fall*) this morning.

こゆび 小指 a **little finger**(手の); a **little toe** (足の). →指.

こよう 雇用 **employment**; a **job**(職) 一動 **雇用する** **employ** +目 →雇う ▶雇用を守る protect *jobs* ‖ 雇用を促進する promote *employment* ‖ 多くの日本の会社が終身雇用制を見直し始めている Many Japanese companies are reconsidering *the lifetime employment system*. ‖ そのアメリカ人選手の雇用期間は2年です *The period of employment* of that American player is two years.

‖雇用契約 an employment contract ‖ 雇用条件 the terms [conditions] of employment ‖ 雇用主 an employer ‖ 雇用保険 unemployment insurance ‖ 男女雇用機会均等法 the Equal Employment Opportunity Law ‖ 被雇用者 an employee /ɪmplɔ́ɪiː/.

1**ごよう 誤用** (a) **misuse** /mìsjúːs/ 一動 **誤用する** **misuse** /mìsjúːz/ +目. ▶若者に敬語の誤用が目立つ Young people often *misuse* honorific expressions.

2**ごよう 御用** ▶ほかにご用が無ければ失礼いたします I would like to excuse myself *if there is nothing more I can help you with*. ‖ 何か(ほかに)ご用はございませんか Is there anything (else) I can do for you? ‖ 何かご用でしょうか Can I help you (with anything)? ‖ 対話「ちょっと缶コーヒーを1個買ってきてくれないか?」「お安いご用だ」"Could you pick up a can of coffee (for me)?" "*Sure, no problem*."

ごようおさめ 御用納め ▶日本では12月28日が官庁の御用納めだ December 28 is *the last work* [*working*] *day of the year* at the government offices in Japan. (➤「御用始め」は the first work [working] day of the year).

ごようきき 御用聞き an **order taker**(御用聞きの人) ▶御用聞きに回る *go* [*do*] *the rounds of* one's *customers* ‖ 酒屋が毎金曜日の朝,御用聞きに来る The man from the liquor store *comes for orders* every Friday morning.

ごようたし 御用達 a **purveyor**

‖皇室御用達 a purveyor to the Imperial Family 《参考》イギリス王室が認めた商人に出す御用達の証を Royal Warrant of Appointment という.

ごようてい 御用邸 an **Imperial villa**.

コヨーテ 《動物》a **coyote** /kaɪóʊṭi ‖ kɔɪ-/.

こよなく **better than anything else** ▶こよなく晴れた青空 a *completely* clear blue sky ‖ 祖父はロンドンをこよなく愛した My grandfather loved London *better than any* other place on earth.

こよみ 暦 a **calendar** /kǽləndəʳ/ ▶暦の上ではもう春だ *Officially* [*According to the calendar*], it is already spring.

こより a **twisted paper string**.

こら ▶こら,待て! *Hey*! Stop! ‖ こら,何をしているんだ! *Hey*! What are you doing? ‖ こら,そんなことしちゃだめだぞ! *Look here*! None of that! ‖《子供に向かって》こらこら,けんかはよせ! *Hey there*, no fighting!

コラーゲン **collagen** /kɑ́ːlədʒən/ ▶豚足はコラーゲンが豊富だ Pork leg is rich in *collagen*.

コラージュ a **collage** /kəlɑ́ːʒ/.

こらい 古来 ▶その話は古来この地方に語り継がれている That tale has been handed down *from old* [*olden*] *times* in this district. ‖ 日本古来の食生活が見直され始めている The *traditional* Japanese diet is beginning to be re-evaluated.

ごらいこう 御来光 ▶私たちは山頂からの御来光を拝んだ We *reverently watched the sun rising* [*worshiped the sunrise*] on the summit of the mountain. (この日本語は「敬けんな気持ちで日の出を眺めた」と解釈すれば前者のように訳出することができるし,合掌するなど宗教的な行動を取ることを含めれば後者のように訳出することができる).

こらえしょう 堪え性・怺え性 **staying power** (耐久力); **endurance** /ɪndjʊ́ərəns/ (忍耐力); **perseverance**(粘り強さ) ▶彼はこらえ性がない He *has no staying power*. / He *isn't willing to endure hardship*.

こらえる 堪える・怺える **endure** +目 (継続的な苦痛などを); **hold back** (感情・涙などを); **stifle** +目 (笑い・あくびなどを) →我慢 ▶彼女は笑いたい[あくびをしたい]衝動をこらえた She *stifled* her urge to laugh [yawn]. / She *stifled* a yawn [laughter]. ▶私は痛みをじっとこらえた I *endured* [*bore*] the pain patiently. ‖ 父は怒り[涙]をこらえているようだった My father looked as though he were *holding back* his anger [tears]. ‖ 私は必死になって笑い[おしっこ]をこらえた I did all I could do to *keep from* bursting out laughing [urinating].

ごらく 娯楽 (a) **recreation**(休養・気晴らしになる趣味・スポーツなど); (an) **amusement** (ゲームなど); (an) **entertainment** (余興・遊びなど); (a) **pastime**(時間潰し的な) ▶月に1度釣りに行くのが父の唯一の娯楽だ My father's only *recreation* is going fishing once a month. ‖ きみは娯楽に金を使い過ぎる You spend too much money on *amusement(s)* [*entertainment*]. ‖ あの男は働くばかりで娯楽というものを知らない That man works all the time and doesn't know *how to enjoy himself*.

‖娯楽映画 an entertaining movie ‖ 娯楽産業 the amusement [entertainment] industry ‖ 娯楽施設 recreation facilities ‖ 娯楽室 a recreation room ‖ 娯楽センター an amusement center ‖ 娯楽番組 an entertainment program ‖ 娯楽費 amusement expenses ‖ 娯楽欄(新聞などの) the entertainment columns.

こらしめる 懲らしめる **punish** +目 (罰する); **teach ... a lesson**(思い知らせる) ▶子供のお尻をたたいて懲らしめる *punish* a child by spanking him [her] ‖ あいつ,今度会ったら(たっぷり)懲らしめてやるぞ That rat! I'll *teach* him *a* (good) *lesson* if I see him again! ‖ うそをついたから懲らしめてやった I *let* him *have it* because he had lied. (➤ have it は「罰せられる」の意のインフォーマルな言い方).

こらす 凝らす ▶目を凝らしてあれを見てごらん Look at that *closely*. / *Fix your eyes on* that. ‖ 生徒たちは学園祭のためにいろいろ趣向を凝らした The students *made elaborate plans* for the school festival.

コラボ a **collaboration**(共同制作); a **combination**(組み合わせ) ▶フランス料理と和食のコラボ *a combination* of French and Japanese cuisines ‖ そのショーは人気の華道家と有名作曲家のコラボであった The show was *a collaboration of* a popular artist in flower arrangement and a famous composer.

コラム a **column** /kɑ́ːləm/ ▶彼はその新聞に日本の詩についての短いコラムを書いている He writes a short *column* on Japanese poetry for that newspaper.

‖コラムニスト a columnist /kɑ́ːləmnɪst/.

ごらん 御覧 1【見る】▶絵をどうぞゆっくりご覧ください

Please take your time *looking at* [*enjoying*] the pictures. ‖ご覧に入れたい物があります I have something I *would like to show you.* ‖あの映画, もうご覧になりましたか *Have you seen* that movie yet?
▶ほらごらんなさい, ストーブのそばに近づいちゃいけないって言ったでしょ? *See?* I told you not to go near the heater.
2【…してみる】**try** ▶おいしいリンゴですよ. 召し上がってごらんなさい These apple slices are delicious. *Please try some.* ‖この新しいファックスを動かしてみてごらん *Try and see how* this new fax machine *works.* ‖(その曲を)もう一度初めから弾いてごらん *Try* (*playing*) that piece again from the top.

こり 凝り **stiffness** ▶肩の凝り *stiffness* in one's shoulder(s) ‖首筋に凝りがある I *have stiffness* in my neck. / I *have a stiff* neck.

コリアンダー 《植物》**coriander**《英》; **cilantro**《米》.

コリー 《動物》a **collie** (**dog**) (コリー犬).

ごりおし ごり押し ▶彼はいつも自分の意見をごり押しする He always *forces* his opinions *on others.*

こりかたまる 凝り固まる ▶あの連中は新興宗教に凝り固まっている(＝狂信者だ) They are a group of *fanatical* believers in a new religion.

こりこり ▶こりこりと歯応えのある食べ物 *hard, crunchy* food.

こりごり ▶いつも道に迷うし, 悪いやつにはだまされるし, もう東京はこりごりだ *I've had it* [*I'm fed up*] *with* Tokyo. I always get lost, or taken in by con artists.

こりしょう 凝り性 ▶彼は凝り性だから, いつもなかなか仕事が終わらない He is such *a perfectionist* it takes him forever to finish his work. (➤ perfectionist は「完全主義者」の意) ‖彼は何事にも凝り性だ He'*s very meticulous* about everything.

こりつ 孤立する **be isolated** /áɪsəleɪtɪd/ ▶谷間の村のいくつかが豪雪のため孤立した Several villages in the valleys *were isolated* by heavy snowfalls. ‖彼はクラスの中で孤立している He'*s isolated* [He *has no friends*] in his class.

ごりむちゅう 五里霧中 ▶その殺人事件は手がかりがなく捜査は五里霧中の状態だ There are no clues in the murder case and the investigators *are at a loss what to do next.*

ごりやく 御利益 ▶母が順調に回復しているのは御利益があったからだと思う My mother's being well on the way to recovery is (the result of) *a prayer answered*, I think. (➤「祈りがかなえられた」の意) ‖あの神社にお参りすれば御利益があるそうだ It is believed that visiting that shrine will *bring favors* [*blessings*] *from the gods.*

ごりょう 御陵 an **Imperial mausoleum** /mɔ̀ːsəlíːəm/ (➤ mausoleum は「壮大な墓」).

こりょうり 小料理 a **simple Japanese dish**
‖小料理屋 a small Japanese restaurant.

ゴリラ a **gorilla** /gərílə/ ▶ゴリラは見かけによらず内気な動物です *Gorillas* are more timid than they appear to be.

こりる 懲りる (⚠英語には1語で「こりる」を表す語がないので,「(失敗などから)教訓 (lesson) を得る」のように意訳する必要がある) ▶失敗して懲りる *learn a lesson* from one's failure ‖3回も事故を起こしたのに, まだ懲りない(＝学ぶところがない)のか You had three accidents, and you still *haven't learned anything* (from them)? ‖懲りないねえ, きみは You *never learn*, do you? ‖この苦い経験で彼も懲りるだろう This bitter experience will *teach* him *a lesson.* ‖これに懲りてサラ金からは金を借りないことだね *Let* this *be a lesson* to you never to borrow money from a loan shark.

ごりん 五輪 **the Olympics.** →オリンピック.

こる 凝る **1**【熱中する】**be into, be crazy**《about》▶私最近テニスに凝ってるの I'*m into* [I'*m crazy about*] tennis these days. ‖おばは新興宗教に凝っている My aunt *is involved in* [*is caught up in*] a new religion. ‖あの男は賭け事に凝って(＝はまって)すべてを失った That man *got hooked on* gambling and lost everything.
2【「凝った」の形で】**elaborate** /ɪlǽbərət/ ▶凝ったお料理ですね. どうやって作ったのですか This is such an *elaborate* dish. How did you make it? ‖藤井さんは凝った造りの家に住んでいる Mr. Fujii lives in a *well-designed* house. ‖彼の仕事はいつも凝り過ぎて失敗する He makes mistakes because he always *goes overboard.* (➤ go overboard は「度を越す」).
3【筋肉が痛む】**be stiff** ▶この頃どうも肩が凝る These days my neck and shoulders *are* always *stiff* (*and aching*). ‖《比喩的》ダークスーツを着て改まった席へ出ると肩が凝る I *feel ill at ease* [*feel uncomfortable* / *feel stiff*] whenever I have to attend a formal event in a suit.

コルク (a) **cork** ▶コルク栓を抜いてください Would you pull out the *cork*?

コルセット a **corset** /kɔ́ːˊsət/ ▶患者はコルセットを装着している The patient is wearing *a corset.*

ゴルフ **golf** ▶父は毎日曜日ゴルフをします My father *plays golf* every Sunday. ‖彼はゴルフが上手[下手]だ He *is a good* [*poor*] *golfer.* / He *is good* [*poor*] *at golf.* ‖今度の週末は伊豆にゴルフに行くつもりだ I plan to *go golfing* in Izu this weekend. ‖彼は社長杯を懸けたゴルフのコンペで2位になった He won the second prize in the *golf competition* for the President's trophy.
‖ゴルフ場 a golf course; golf links (海岸近くにある) ‖ゴルフ練習場 a (golf) driving range.

ゴルファー a **golfer**
‖プロゴルファー a pro [professional] golfer.

1 **これ** **this** [複 **these**] ▶これが金閣寺です *This* is (the) Kinkakuji Temple. ‖これがインドで撮った写真です *This* is a picture [*These* are the pictures] I took in India. (➤後者は写真が2枚以上ある場合) ‖《写真を見て》これ, 誰? Who's *this*? ‖これ2つください Could I have *two of these*? / *Two of these*, please. ‖これ, もらっていい? Can I keep [have] *this one*? (➤目の前のある具体的なものを指す場合は one をつけたほうが曖昧でなくてよい) ‖これこそ私の探していた本だ *This is just the* [*the very*] book I've been looking for. (➤ the very book は文学的な表現) ‖これ, 気持ちだけだけど, 私からのプレゼントなの *Here's* a little present for you. (➤決まり文句) ‖**対話**「私の物差し, 知らない?」「これかい?」"Do you know where my ruler is?" "*Is this it?*" (➤単に"This?"と言ってもよい).

2 **これ** **Hey!**, 《米》**Say!**, 《英》**I say!** ▶これ, 子供たち, 静かにしなさい *Hey* children, be quiet. 《参考》「これ, よく聞きなさい!」などという場合, 英語では"Listen carefully, Tom!"のように名前を呼んで注意を促すことも多い.

これから **from now on** (今後は, これ以降(ずっと)); **after this** (このあとで, このことがあってから; これを最後にして); **in the future** (将来は) ▶これからだんだん寒くなる *From* now on, the weather will get colder. ‖ これからはもう少しことばに気をつけなさい *From now on* [*In the future*], you should be more careful about what you say. ‖ ごめんね, 私これから約束があるの Sorry, but I've got an appointment *after this*. ‖ これからは英語以外の外国語も学ぶ必要がある It will be necessary to learn other foreign languages besides English *in the future*.

▶これから映画を見にいこう *Let's* go see a movie! (🍎 「これから」につられて from now をつけないこと. Let's ... には「これから, 今から」の意味が含まれている) ‖ これから言うことを書き取ってください Please write down what I'm about to say. ‖ これからそっちへ行ってもいい？ Would it be all right (for me) to drop in on you *now*? ‖ 父はまだまだこれからというときに死んでしまった My father died *just when he still had his whole life before him*. ‖ 最悪の事態はこれからだ The worst *is yet to come*. (➤ 決まった言い方).

これきり ▶持っている金はこれきり(＝これで全部)です *This is all* the money I have. ‖ あなたと会う［デートする］のはもうこれきり(＝これが最後)よ *This is the last time* I'll be seeing you.／This is our last date.

コレクション (a) **collection** ▶おじにはたくさんの絵のコレクションがある My uncle has a large *collection* of pictures. ‖ 私の趣味は鉄道切符のコレクションです My hobby is *collecting* railroad tickets.

コレクター a **collector** ▶美術品の熱心なコレクター an avid *collector* of art.

コレクトコール a **collect call** ▶ニューヨークにいる両親にコレクトコールをした I *placed* [*made*] *a collect call* to my parents in New York. ‖ コレクトコールで掛けていいよ You can *call* me *collect*. (➤ call ... collect で「…にコレクトコールをする」).

これくらい ▶これくらいの食料があれば十分だ *This much* food will be plenty. ‖ これくらいのことでへこたれはしないぞ I'm not giving up over *such a small thing*.

これこれ ▶これこれ, いたずらはやめなさい *Come, come* [*Come now*], stop fooling around.

▶彼はこれこれの日にこれこれの場所に行くように言われた He was told to go to *such and such* a place on *such and such* a day.

これしき ▶これしきのことで怒るんじゃないよ Don't get upset over *such a small* [*trivial*] *thing*. ‖ 何のこれしき！ *This is nothing*!

コレステロール **cholesterol** /kəléstəroʊl/ ▶悪玉［善玉］コレステロール bad [good] *cholesterol* ‖ 卵黄にはコレステロールが多い Egg yolks are high in *cholesterol*. ‖ アーモンドにはコレステロール値を下げる効果がある Almonds can help *lower cholesterol*.

これだけ **1**【これで全部】▶私の全財産はこれだけだ *This is all* the money I have.

2【最小限】▶これだけは言っておく I'll say *just this*. ‖ これだけは覚えておいてもらいたい I want you to remember *at least this*.

3【こんなにたくさん】▶これだけ言ってもまだわからないのか You still don't understand after *all* I've told you? ‖ これだけ雪が降ったのは久しぶりだ It's been a long time since we had *this much* snow.

これっぽっち ▶私はこれっぽっちもやましくない I *don't* feel guilty *in the least*. ‖ 対話「はい, お小遣い」「これっぽっちかよ」"Here's your spending money." "*This is it*?"

これで ▶あいつもこれで懲りたろう I think he learned his lesson from *this*. ‖ これで私の説明を終わります *This* concludes my explanation.／*This* is the end of my explanation. ‖ 《教室で》きょうはこれでおしまい *That*'s all for today.／*That* wraps it up for today.／*That*'s enough for today. (➤ 第3例は「きょうはもういいかな［いいでしょ］」という感じ. 日本語では「これで」であるが, (×) This is all for today. あるいは, (×) This wraps it up for today. のように this とはしない). ‖ きょうの仕事はこれで終わりにしよう Let's *call it a day*.

これでは ▶これではメンツが丸潰れだ *This* will mean a complete loss of face for me. ‖ これでは(＝この調子では)期日までに仕事を終えられないよ You'll never finish the job by the appointed day *at this rate*.

これでも ▶これでも中学時代は優秀なスプリンターだったんだぞ *Though you may find it hard to believe*, I was a top sprinter when I was a junior high school student. (➤「信じられないかもしれないが」の意).

これといった［いって］ ▶彼女は去年はこれといった収入が無かった She had no income *to speak of* last year. ‖ ちょっと寄ってみただけで, これといった用事(＝特別の理由)はありません I just dropped in. There's *no special* reason. ‖ この辺はこれといって見るところも無い There are no *particular* sights worth visiting around here.

これはこれは ▶これはこれはありがとう *Gee*, thanks a lot. ‖ これはこれはご親切に *Gee*. You're so kind.

これほど　これ程 ▶これほどおもしろいサッカーの試合は見たことがない I have never seen *such* an exciting soccer game *as this* (one). ‖ これほど大きな魚はめったにいないよ You rarely come across a fish *as big as this*. ‖ おまえがこれほどのワルだとは思わなかった I never thought you were *such* a bad guy. ‖ これほど説明してもわからないんなら勝手にしなさい If you still don't understand *after such a long explanation*, I give up.

これまで **1**【今まで】**up to now**; **all this while** (この間ずっと); **so far** (今までのところ) ▶これまで私はずっと幸運だった *So far* [*Up to now*] I've been lucky. ‖ これまで何をしていたの？ What have you been doing *all this while*? ‖ これはこれまで見た中でいちばんおもしろいテレビ番組だ This is the most interesting TV program I've *ever* seen. ‖ これまでの経過をご説明申し上げます Let me explain the process *through* [*up to*] *this point*.

2【おしまい】▶きょうの授業はこれまで *That's all* for today. (→これで) ‖ 彼の人生もこれまでだ *This is* [*will be*] *the end* of his life. (➤「彼の仕事人生は…」というニュアンスなら His career is over now.) ‖ 警官が追いかけてくるのを見て, 強盗犯人はもはやこれまでと観念した The robber resigned himself *to his fate* [The robber *gave up*] when he saw policemen running after him.

これみよがし　これ見よがし ▶彼女はいつも新しいコートをこれ見よがしに着ている She always wears her new coat *just to show off*. (➤ show off は「見せびらかす」).

コレラ **cholera** /kά:lərə/ ‖**コレラ患者** a cholera case [patient] (➤ 前者は「発症例」) ‖ **コレラ菌** a cholera germ.

ころ・ごろ 頃

▶私は若い頃は気が短かった I was quick-tempered *when* (I was) young. ‖ 私は小学生の頃は痩せていた I was skinny *when* I was in elementary school. ‖ 2時頃電話が鳴った The phone rang *around* [*about*] two. ‖ 11時頃オフィスにおいでください Please come to my office *at around eleven* [*at elevenish*]. ‖ この歌を聞くとケンタッキーに**居た頃**を思い出す This song reminds me of *my days* in Kentucky. ‖ 夕方**頃から**雨が降り出した *Toward* evening it started to rain. ‖ 来月の半ば**頃から**梅雨に入る The rainy season will set in *about* the middle of next month.

▶もう父が帰宅する**頃だ** *It's about time* for Dad to be getting home. ／My father should be home *any time* now. (➤「もう着いてもいいのに」のニュアンス) ‖ 彼女はもう結婚してもいい**頃だ** *It is about time* [*It's high time*] she got married. ／She is now old enough to marry. (● high time には非難の響きがあり, 日常的にはあまり使われない; あとの文は過去形にする).

ごろ 語呂 ▶ことわざはたいてい**語呂**がいい Proverbs usually have a nice *ring*. (➤ ring は「響き」) ‖ 彼は**語呂合わせ**が得意だ He is good at *making puns* [*making plays on words*]. (➤ pun は「語呂合わせの冗談」).

ゴロ 《野球》 a **grounder**, a **ground ball** ▶セカンド [ピッチャー] **ゴロを打つ** hit *a grounder to second* [*the pitcher*] ／ground to second [the pitcher] ‖ **ゴロを捕る** field *a ground ball*.

ころあい 頃合い 1【時間】▶**頃合いを見て**お父さんにそのことを話してあげるわ I'll *find a good time* to tell Dad about it.

2【手ごろ】▶**頃合い**の値段で**頃合い**の大きさのつぼを手に入れた I got a pot *of about the right size* at a *reasonable* price.

ころう 古老 an **elder**.

ころがす 転がす **roll** ＋㊐ ▶ボールを坂の上から**転がす** *roll* a ball down the slope ‖ スカラベはふんの玉を**転がす**習性がある A scarab has the habit of *rolling* a ball of dung.

▶《比喩的》土地を**転がして**(＝素早い転売で)大もうけする make a large profit by *rapid* [*quick*] *turnovers* in land [by *flipping* land].

ころがりこむ 転がり込む ▶テニスボールがよくうちの庭に**転がり込む** Tennis balls often *roll into* my garden. ‖ ばく大な遺産が彼のところに**転がり込んだ** A (big) fortune *fell into* his hands *unexpectedly*. ‖ 私は友人宅に**転がり込んだ** I *crashed at* a friend's house. (➤ crash at は「(人の家に)泊まりに押しかける」) ‖ 若い女性が助けを求めて交番に**転がり込んできた** A young woman *staggered into* the koban asking for help.

ころがる 転がる 1【回転して進む】**roll** ▶ボールは床を**転がった** The ball *rolled* across the floor.

2【存在する】▶岩が山道の至る所に**転がっていた** Rocks *lay scattered* all over the mountain path. ‖ あの程度の車ならどこにでも**転がってる**よ *There are lots of* cars like that. ／*You can find* that kind of car *anywhere*.

ころげおちる 転げ落ちる ▶階段から**転げ落ちる** *tumble down* the stairs ‖ ぼくはゆうべベッドから**転げ落ちた** I *fell out of* bed last night.

ころげまわる 転げ回る **tumble (about)**, **roll (about)** ▶犬が草むらで**転げ回っている** A dog *is rolling* (*about*) in the grass. ‖ 股間を蹴られて痛くて**転げ回った** I was kicked in the groin and *rolled* (*about*) in pain.

ころころ ▶ピンポン玉が椅子の下へ**ころころ転がった** The ping-pong ball *rolled* under the chair. ‖ **ころころとよく太った**赤ちゃんだこと! What a *chubby* baby! ‖ あいつの言うことは**ころころとよく変わる** He says something different every minute. ／He's *always changing his story*. ／He's *always flip-flopping*. (➤ flip-flop は日本語の「ころころ」に近い軽い感じの語).

ごろごろ 1【音を立てて】▶その岩は坂を**ごろごろ転がっていった** The boulder *rolled down* the slope. ‖ 遠くで雷が**ゴロゴロ鳴った** Thunder *rumbled* in the distance. ‖ 猫が**喉をゴロゴロ鳴らしている** The cat is *purring*. ‖ さっきからおなかが**ゴロゴロいっている** My stomach *has been growling* since a short while ago.

2【散在して】▶ゴルフボールがうちの畑に**ごろごろしている** There are golf balls *lying here and there* around my vegetable garden. ‖ 地面には兵士の死体が**ごろごろ転がっていた** The bodies of dead soldiers *were scattered across* the ground. ‖ あの程度のピアニストなら**世の中にごろごろいるね** Pianists like him [her] are a *dime a dozen*. (➤「1ダースで10セントの安物」が原義).

3【異物がある】▶コンタクトレンズにごみが入って目が**ごろごろする**(＝不快だ) A speck of dust has gotten in under one of my contact lenses and it's *causing me discomfort*.

4【怠けて】▶こんないい天気に家で**ごろごろしていて**もつまらない It's boring to *loaf around* at home on such a nice day.

ころし 殺し (a) **murder** (計画的な殺人); (a) **killing** (命を奪うこと).

‖**父親殺し** (a) patricide ‖**母親殺し** (a) matricide.

ころしもんく 殺し文句 a **clincher** (決定的なひと言); a **telling phrase** [**expression**] (効果的な文句) ▶どんな**殺し文句**でゆかりをくどいたの? What *line(s)* did you use to win Yukari's heart? (➤ line は「せりふ」).

ころしや 殺し屋 a **hired** [**professional**] **killer**; a **hit man** (男の), a **hit woman** (女の).

ころす 殺す 1【殺害する】**kill** ＋㊐; **murder** ＋㊐ (計画的に殺害する; 堅い語) ▶その男は5人の銀行員を銃で**殺した** He shot and *killed* five bank clerks. ‖ いたずらに昆虫を**殺してはいけない** Don't *kill* insects just for fun. ‖ 彼は妻に保険金目当てで**殺された** He *was killed* by his wife for his insurance money. ‖ 彼は自分の息子に**殴り** [**刺し**] **殺されてしまった** He *was beaten* [*stabbed*] *to death* by his own son. ‖ 彼女はネクタイで**絞め殺されていた** She had *been strangled* with a necktie.

2【抑える, だめにする】▶彼女はカーテンの陰で**声を殺して**泣いた She cried behind the curtain *trying to choke back her sobs*. ‖ 投手はけん制球で一塁**走者を殺した** The pitcher *picked the runner off* on his throw to first. ‖ そんなに酷評すると彼の貴重な**才能を殺す**ことになる Criticizing him so harshly like that will only *stifle* his special *talent*.

ごろつき a **ruffian**; a **gangster** (やくざ).

コロッケ a **croquette** /krookét ‖ krɔ-/ ▶カニコロッケ a crab *croquette*.

コロナウイルス **coronavirus** /kəróunəvàirəs/ ▶姉がコロナウイルスに感染した My sister got infected with *coronavirus*. ‖**コロナ禍** the COVID(-19) [the corona(virus)] pandemic ／ the COVID(-19) [the corona(virus)] crisis (➤ COVID-19 は coronavirus disease 2019 を表す) ‖**コロナ太り** quarantine weight gain (➤ quarantine は「感染症予防のための隔離」の意) ‖**新型コロナウイルス** new coronavirus.

ごろね ごろ寝 ▶兄は酔うとよく畳の上で**ごろ寝をする** When he gets drunk, my brother often *sleeps* on the tatami floor *without changing into his pajamas*. ‖ 父は日曜日は**ごろ寝をして過ごす** My father spends Sundays *lying around at home*.

ころぶ 転ぶ fall (down) ▶気をつけないと転ぶよ Watch your step, or you'll *stumble and fall*. ‖ そのおばあさんは石につまずいて転んだ The old woman stumbled over a rock and *fell*.

▶《慣用表現》彼は転んでもただでは起きない男だ He *learns* (*even*) *from his mistakes*. (➤「自分のしたミスからも何かを学ぶ」の意) ‖ どっちに転んでも損はない I have nothing to lose *either way*. ‖ ことわざ 転ばぬ先の杖(つえ) Prepare a cane to avoid falling down. (➤日本語の直訳)／Look before you leap.

ころも 衣 1【衣服，法衣】a **robe** ▶墨染めの衣をまとった僧侶が読経を始めた A (Buddhist) priest in black *robes* began to recite a sutra.

✉ **日本では生徒は6月1日に(夏服に)衣替えをします** In Japan, students *change to summer uniforms* on June 1.

2【皮】**batter, coating** (➤ともに天ぷらなどの衣をいうが，前者は「水で溶いたどろどろのもの」を，後者は「揚げたもの」をいう)；**breading** (パン粉の)；**icing, frosting** (菓子の).

コロラド Colorado (アメリカ西部の州；略 CO, Colo.).

ころりと ▶その力士は強そうに見えたが勝負が始まったらころりと負けてしまった The sumo wrestler looked strong but when the bout started he was *easily* beaten. ‖ マネージャーは女嫌いで通っていたのに彼女(の魅力)にはころりと参ってしまった Our manager had passed for a misogynist, but he *was a pushover* before her (charm). (➤ misogynist /mɪsɑ́ːdʒənɪst/ の代わりに woman-hater を用いることもできるが，この文脈ではこちらは強意すぎる. pushover は「簡単に負ける人」の意のインフォーマルな語).

コロン a **colon** (：の符号).

コロンビア Colombia /kəlʌ́mbiə/ (南米北西部の国).

コロンブスのたまご コロンブスの卵 Columbus's egg (➤英米ではこの表現も逸話もあまり知られていない) ▶これはまさにコロンブスの卵だ This is a perfect case of *Columbus's egg*.

こわい 怖い 1【ある物・人が恐ろしい】**frightening**；**scary** (恐怖心を呼び起こす)；**terrifying** (ぞっとするような)；**fierce** (表情などがものすごい，すさまじい)；**threatening** (脅すような) ▶怖い目に遭う have a *frightening* experience ‖ 怖い夢を見る have a *frightening* [*scary*] dream ‖ 怖い映画 a *scary* movie ‖ そんな怖い顔しないで！ Don't look so *fierce* [*threatening*]! ‖ 校長室に行くのって，怖いなあ Going to the principal's office *frightens me*. (➤ frighten は「ひどくおびえさせる」) ‖ 《慣用表現》彼はこわいもの知らずだ He *doesn't know what fear is*. ／He is *fearless*. ‖ 怖いもの見たさで少年はその洞穴をのぞき込んだ *Curiosity drove* the boy to look into the cave. (➤「好奇心が駆り立てた」の意).

2【態度が厳しい】**strict** (厳格な)；**stern** (融通の利かない厳格さをもった) ▶久野先生は怖い先生だった Mr. Kuno was a *strict* teacher.

3【人が怖がる】**be scared, be frightened** 《of》 (➤ともに一時的恐怖に用いる. 前者のほうがややくだけた言い方)；**be afraid** 《of》, **fear** +目 (➤恐れる；fear は改まった語；一時的恐怖には用いない) ▶わあ，怖い！ *I'm scared!* ‖ ぼくは突然怖くなって逃げ出した I suddenly *got frightened* [*got scared*] and ran away. ‖ 車が木に衝突するのではないかと怖かった I *was scared* that the car would crash into a tree.

【文型】
人・物(A)が怖い
be afraid of A／**fear** A
be scared of A

▶あの大きな犬が怖い I'*m afraid* [*scared*] *of* that big dog. ‖ たいていの人にとって死［死ぬの］は怖い Most people *are afraid of* death [dying]. ／Most people *fear* death. ‖ (我々は)仕返しが怖い We'*re afraid of* retaliation. ‖ 父は飛行機が怖くて乗らない My father *is afraid of* flying.

【文型】
怖くて…できない
be afraid to do
be too scared to do

▶この辺りは夜は怖くて外出できない People *are afraid to* go out at night in this area. ‖ 子供の頃は夜ひとりでトイレに行くのがとても怖かった When I was little, I *was too scared to* go to the bathroom alone at night.

こわいろ 声色 ▶《真似》彼は校長先生の声色を使うのが得意だ He is good at *imitating* [*mimicking*] our principal's *voice*.

こわがる 怖がる fear, be afraid 《of》 (➤後者が日常的) ▶子供はたいてい注射を怖がる Most children *are afraid of* injections. ‖ 英語を話すときは間違えるのを怖がってはいけない When speaking English, don't *be afraid of* making mistakes. (➤ be afraid of doing は「…しないかと心配である」の意) ‖ その子は怖がって溝を飛び越せなかった The child *was* too *afraid* to jump over the ditch. (➤ be afraid to do は「怖くて…できない」の意) ‖ 赤ん坊は雷の音を怖がった The baby *was frightened* by the roll of thunder. ‖ 彼女をいじめるのはよせ. 怖がってるじゃないか Stop picking on her. Can't you see she's *scared*? ‖ そのテロのあと，旅行者は飛行機を怖がって敬遠するようになった Travelers *were frightened away* from flying after the terror attacks. (➤ frighten A away で「A(人など)を脅かして追い払う」).

こわき 小脇 ▶彼は本を小脇に抱えていた He had a book *under his arm*.

こわけ 小分け ▶おじいちゃんは飲む薬を曜日ごとに小分けしている My grandpa *divides* his meds *in small portions* according to the days of the week.

こわごわ fearfully, with fear (びくびくして)；timidly (おずおずと) ▶こわごわ蛇に触る touch a snake *with fear* ‖ ビルのてっぺんからこわごわ下を見下ろした *Fearfully* [*Timidly*／*Gingerly*], I looked down from the top of the building.

ごわごわ ▶この浴衣はのりが効き過ぎてごわごわしている This yukata is *stiff* (*as a board*) with too much starch.

こわす 壊す 1【だめにする】**break** +目 (2つ以上に割る)；**destroy** +目 (破壊する)；**pull** [**tear**] **down, demolish** +目 (取り壊す)；**damage** +目 (損傷を与える)；**ruin** +目, **spoil** +目 (台なしにする) ▶おもちゃを壊す *break* a toy ‖ 箱を壊して開ける *break* a box open ‖ 彼は新しい家を建てるために古い家を壊した(＝解体してもらった) He *had* his old house *pulled* [*torn*] *down* in order to build a new house. (➤ torn は tear /teəʳ/ の過去分詞) ‖ 彼はブロック塀にぶつかって自転車を壊した He *damaged* his bicycle when he crushed into the concrete block wall. ‖ あのやかましい音楽がせっかくの雰囲気を壊した That loud music *ruined* [*spoiled*] the pleasant atmosphere. ／That loud music was a real wet blanket. (➤ wet blanket は「楽しい雰囲気を壊す物［人］」) ‖ 隣のビルのネオンサインがせっかくの庭園美を**壊して**しまった The neon sign on the tall building next door *destroyed* the unique beauty of the garden. ‖ 戦争が少年たちの未来の夢を**壊して**しまった The war *shattered* the boys' dreams for the future. (➤ shatter は「打ち砕く」).

2【健康を害する】ruin ＋㊐ ▶彼は働き過ぎて**体を壊し**た He *ruined* [*lost*] *his health* by working too hard. ‖ そんなに食べると**おなかを壊す**よ If you eat that much, you will *get a stomachache* [*an upset stomach*]. (➤「下痢をする」の意では get diarrhea).

こわだか 声高な vocal ▶その政治家は死刑制度に**声高**に反対している That politician is *vocally* [*vociferously*] opposed to capital punishment. (➤ vociferously /voʊsífərəsli/ はより堅い語).

こわばる ▶長旅のあとなので体が**こわばった**感じがする I *feel stiff* after the long journey. ‖ 彼女は恐怖のあまり顔が**こわばった** Her face *tightened* with fear. ‖ 彼の表情が**こわばった** His expression *became stiff* [*tense*]. (➤ 身構えたり，用心深くなったりする場合；tightened でもよい).

こわれもの 壊れ物 a **fragile article**；**breakables**（割れ物など）▶**壊れ物**—取り扱い注意 *Fragile*—Handle with Care (➤ 箱などの表示；fragile /frǽdʒəl ‖ -dʒaɪl/ は「壊れやすい」の意).

こわれる 壊れる

1【ばらばらになる】break, be broken；**be damaged**（部分的に損害を被る）；**be destroyed**（全壊する）▶安いおもちゃはすぐ**壊れる** Cheap toys *break* easily. ‖ 彼女の車の前の部分はその事故で**壊れた** The front of her car *was damaged* in the accident. ‖ 彼の家はその嵐で**壊れて**しまった His house *was destroyed* in the storm. ‖ この椅子は座ると**壊れる**よ This chair will *collapse* if you sit on it. (➤ collapse は「潰れる，崩れる」) ‖ このステンドグラスは**壊れやすい** This stained glass is *fragile*.

2【故障する】break down；**go out of order**（主に公共性や共同使用性のあるものが）▶車のエンジンが**こわれた** The engine of the car *has broken down*. ‖ そのテレビは**壊れていて**何も映らない That television *is broken* and there's no picture (on the screen). ‖ コンピュータが**壊れている** My computer is*n't working*. ‖ データが**壊れている**ようだ The data seems *corrupt*. ‖ この自動販売機は**壊れている** This vending machine *is out of order*.

3【だめになる】▶私たちの縁談は結局**壊れた** All the arrangements for our marriage *fell through*. ‖ 気分の**壊れる**ような話をしないでよ Don't say anything that might *disturb* [*ruin*] my good mood.

[1]**こん 根 1【根気】patience** ▶あまり**根を詰める**のは体によくないよ If you *push yourself* too *hard*, you'll make yourself ill. ‖ 刺しゅうは**根の要る**仕事だ Embroidery *requires patience*.

2【数学の】a **root** ‖ **平方根** a square root.

[2]**こん 紺 dark** [**deep**] **blue, navy blue** ▶**紺**のスーツ a *dark blue* suit.

こん- 今- ▶**今**シーズン *this* season ‖ **今**春 *this* spring.

こんい 懇意 ▶私は佐野氏と**懇意**にしている I *am good friends with* Mr. Sano. ‖ あの医者と父とは10年来**懇意**の間柄だ That doctor and my father *have been very close to each other* for ten years now.

こんいん 婚姻 matrimony /mǽtrɪmoʊni/ ▶ 2 人は 2 月 5 日に**婚姻届**を出した They *had their marriage registered* on February 5.

こんかい 今回 this time ▶前回のテストは合格者がなかったから**今回**は頑張りなさい No one passed the last exam, so (you all must) work harder *this time*. ‖ **今回**だけは大目に見てやろう I'll overlook it *just this once*. ‖ 引っ越しは**今回**で 3 回目だ *This* is the third time I've moved.

こんかつ 婚活 the activities necessary to find a partner and get married (➤ 説明的な訳)《**参考**》marriage partner [spouse] hunting ということもある. 日本社会をよく知る外国人の中には konkatsu を理解する人も少なくない. ‖ 彼女は最近婚活に励んでいる She's devoting herself to [concentrating on] *spouse hunting* these days. ‖ **婚活イベント** a marriage partner [spouse] hunting event.

こんがらかる ▶ひもが**こんがらかった** The string *got tangled up*.
▶その小説は筋が**こんがらかっている**から，頭の中まで**こんがらかってきた**よ The plot of that novel *is* so *intricate* [*complex*] that I'm *getting confused*.

こんがり ▶パンが**こんがり**焼き上がった The bread baked *to a nice brown*.

こんかん 根幹 a **basis**（基礎）；a **foundation**（土台）▶多数決は民主主義の**根幹**を成す Majority rule is the *foundation* of democracy.

こんがん 懇願する beg；**implore** ＋㊐（誠意を込めて必死に）；**entreat** ＋㊐（相手の決意を変えようと）；**appeal**（強く訴えて）▶彼は監督にもう一度チャンスが欲しいと**懇願した** He *begged* the coach for another chance. ‖ 私は援助してほしいと彼に**懇願した** I *implored* [*entreated*] him for help. ／I *appealed* to him to help me.

[1]**こんき 根気 patience** /péɪʃəns/（耐えること）；**perseverance** /pə̀ːˈsəvíərəns/（積極的な不屈の努力）▶よく**根気**が続くね I admire your *patience*. ‖ レース編みは**根気**が要る Lace knitting requires a lot of *patience*. ‖ この頃**根気が無く**なってきた I'm becoming *less and less patient* these days. ‖ 外国語は**根気よく**やれば身に付けることができる You can learn a foreign language *if you keep at it*.

[2]**こんき 婚期 marriageable age** ▶**婚期を逸する** *lose one's chance of marriage* [*to marry*] ‖ 彼はもうとっくに**婚期**を過ぎている He is long past *marriageable age*. →**適齢期**.

[3]**こんき 今期 this term** ▶**今期**の売り上げ目標額はほぼ達成された *This term* we managed to meet most of our sales targets.

[4]**こんき 今季 this season.**

こんきゅう 困窮 ▶都会には**住宅困窮者**がたくさん居る There are a lot of *people suffering from housing shortages* in large cities. ‖ 彼らは**生活困窮者**に救いの手を差し伸べた They extended a helping hand to *the poor and needy*.

こんきょ 根拠 grounds（客観的なよりどころ）；a **source**（実体のないものの出どころ）▶彼女の無実を証明する確実な**根拠**がある I have good [solid] *grounds* to vouch for her innocence. ‖ この情報には**根拠が無い** This piece of information is *groundless*. ／This news comes from an unreliable *source*. ‖ どんな**根拠**でこの説を信じるのですか *On what grounds* do you base your belief in this theory?
‖ **根拠地** a base.

ゴング a **bell**（ボクシングの）；a **gong**（どら）▶**ゴング**を鳴らす strike *a gong* ‖（ボクシングの）試合開始の**ゴング**が鳴った *The bell* sounded to mark the start of the match.

コンクール a **contest**, a **competition** ▶ショパン国際ピアノコンクール the Chopin International Piano *Competition* ‖ 私たちは全日本合唱コンクールで1位になった We won (the) first prize in the All-Japan *Chorus Contest*.

危ないカタカナ語 ✹ **コンクール**
1「コンクール」は「競争」とか「協力」の意味のフランス語 *concours* からきている. 英語では contest または competitionで表し, photo contest (写真コンクール), piano competition(ピアノコンクール)のようにいう.
2 主にゴルフで使う「コンペ」は competition を日本式に省略したもの.

こんくらべ 根比べ ▶こうなったらきみとぼくとの根比べだ Let's see which of us can *hold out longer!* (➤ hold out は「頑張る」).

コンクリート concrete ▶その寺は鉄筋コンクリート建てだ The temple is *a reinforced concrete building*.
‖コンクリートミキサー車 a concrete mixer.

ごんげ 権化 the embodiment, the incarnation, the epitome 《of》(➤それぞれ「性質・観念を具象化したもの」「性質・観念が人間の形をしたもの」「性質・観念の典型例」の意) ▶彼は物欲の権化だ He is *the embodiment* [*incarnation* / *epitome*] *of* greed.

こんけつ 混血 ▶彼は混血(児)だ He is (*of*) *mixed blood*. / He is *a child of mixed parentage*. (➤最近では He's of mixed ethnicity. / His ancestry is multiethnic. のような言い方が好まれる). →ハーフ.

こんげつ 今月 this month ▶今月は雨が多かった We've had plenty of rain *this month*. ‖ 今月の10日に私は富士山に登ります I will climb Mt. Fuji on the 10th of *this month*. ‖今月号 the current number [issue] of a (monthly) magazine.

こんげん 根源 a root ▶金は諸悪の根源だ Money is the *root* of all evil. (➤出典の聖書では The love of money is the root of all evil(s). となっている).

こんご 今後 from now on, after this(今から先は); **in the future**(将来は) →これから ▶今後絶対にそんなことをするな You must never do that *again*. ‖ 今後は一日置きに来ます I will come every other day *from now on* [*after this*]. ‖ 今後少なくとも5年間は海外生活だ We will be (living) abroad for at least five years. (🏺未来形を用いているので「今後」は訳出不要) ‖ 今後このソフトメーカーは発展すると思います I believe this software company will expand *in the future*. ‖ 今後の対策については何も決まっていない As for *future* measures, nothing has been decided yet.
▶《ビジネスで》今後ともよろしくお願いいたします I hope we will continue to enjoy good business relations. (🏺 (1)英米では商取引などの相手に対してこのように言うこともあるが, 単なる儀礼的な挨拶としては別れ際に It was nice meeting you. と言えば十分である. (2)日常会話で「今後ともよろしく」と言うのなら Let's keep in touch. (「連絡を取り合おう」の意)でよい).

コンゴ Congo(アフリカ中央部にある2つの国; コンゴ共和国とコンゴ民主共和国がある).

こんごう 混合 mixture 一動 **混合する mix** (+目); **blend** (+目) (同種類で多少の違いがあるものを) ▶油と水は混合できない You can't *mix* oil *with* water. / Oil does not *mix with* water. ‖ 銅と亜鉛を混合することでしんちゅうが得られる From the *mixture* of copper and zinc we get brass.
▶彼女たちはテニスの混合ダブルスに出場した They took part in the *mixed doubles* match.
‖混合(言)語 a mixed language.

コンコース a concourse /káːnkɔːʳs ‖ kɔ́ŋ-/ ▶東京駅のコンコース the *concourse* of Tokyo Station.

ごんごどうだん 言語道断 ▶彼の言語道断な(=けしからぬ)ふるまい his *outrageous* behavior ‖ 高校生が親に黙って外泊するなど言語道断だ(=許されるべきことではない) It's *unpardonable* [*inexcusable*] for a high school student to stay out overnight without telling his [her] parents.

[1]**こんこんと 懇々と earnestly**(熱心に) ▶彼女は息子の不心得を懇々と諭した She *gently and kindly* admonished her son for his misconduct.

[2]**こんこんと 滾々と・渾々と** ▶森でこんこんと湧き出る泉を見つけた In the forest, I found a spring *welling with fresh water*.

コンサート a concert ▶コンサートに行く go to the *concert* ‖ クラシック[ロック]のコンサートを催す hold a classical [rock] *concert* ‖ 嵐のコンサートのチケット a ticket for the Arashi *concert*.
‖コンサート会場 a concert venue ‖コンサートホール a concert hall ‖ガラコンサート a gala concert ‖野外コンサート an open-air concert.

こんざい 混在 ▶応募された俳句には優れたものと駄作が混在している The submitted haiku are *a mixture* of excellent and poor ones. / Among the submitted haiku, outstanding ones *are intermingled with* poor ones.

コンサイス concise(簡潔な).

こんさいるい 根菜類 root vegetables.

こんざつ 混雑 congestion 一動 **混雑する be crowded** 《with》 ▶週末のデパートはいつも買い物客で混雑する Department stores *are* always *crowded with* shoppers on weekends. ‖ 都会の大通りはいつも車で混雑している Main streets in big cities *are* always *busy with traffic* [always *congested*]. ‖ このバイパスは国道17号の混雑を緩和する目的で造られた This bypass was constructed to *ease the congestion* on Route 17.

コンサルタント a consultant(企業や組織が相手の); a **counselor**(個人的な問題の) ▶結婚コンサルタント a marriage *counselor* ‖ 彼はその出版社の経営コンサルタントです He is *a management consultant* for that publishing company.

こんじ 根治 a complete [**permanent**] **cure** ▶花粉症は根治が容易ではない Pollen allergy is not easy to *cure completely*.

コンシェルジュ a concierge /koʊnsjéəʳʒ/.

こんじき 金色の golden ▶金色に輝く仏像 a gleaming *golden* Buddhist statue.

こんじゃくのかん 今昔の感 ▶娘がハワイにダイビングに行くと言う. 自分が同じ年頃だった頃を思うと今昔の感がある My daughter says she's going to go diving in Hawaii. When I remember the days I was about her age, *I really feel how times have changed*.

こんしゅう 今週 this week ▶今週の金曜日に会合がある We have a meeting *this* Friday. (➤曜日の前に this や next がつくと on などの前置詞は不要) ‖ 今週は忙しくなりそうだ I expect (that) I'll be busy *this week*. ‖ 今週中にレポートを書き上げなければいけない I have to finish my paper *by the end of this week*.

こんじょう 根性 1【強じんな精神力】a lot of guts [**grit**]; (**strong**) **willpower**(意志); **fighting spirit**(気

概）; **tenacity**（粘り）▶あいつは**根性の無い**男だ That guy *has no guts*. ／That guy is *a wimp* [*spineless*]. ‖ けがを押して出場するとは見上げた**根性**だ He's got *a lot of grit* [*gumption*] to take part in the tournament with that injury of his. ‖ 彼は見かけによらず**根性がある** He is more *strong-willed* than he looks.

2【根本的な性格·考え方】 one's **nature**, one's **mind**; **mentality**（心理·考え方）▶島国**根性** an insular *mentality* ‖ **根性の曲がった**男 a man *with a twisted mind* ‖ **根性の汚い**男 a *malicious* man ‖ そんな狭い**根性**では世の中は渡れないよ You can't get anywhere in the world being so *narrow-minded*.

こんしん 渾身 ▶彼は燃え盛る家の中から**こん身の力を込めて**金庫を運び出した *Gathering every ounce of strength* (*in his body*), he carried the safe out of the burning house. ‖ 彼は**こん身の力で**ロープを引っ張った He pulled on the rope *with all his might*. ‖ ピカソは**こん身の力を込めて**ゲルニカを描いた Picasso *devoted himself entirely to* [*put all his energy into*] painting Guernica.

こんしんかい 懇親会 a **social** (**gathering**); a **get-together**（形式ばらない集まり）.

こんすい 昏睡 a **coma** /kóʊmə/ ▶やがて彼は**昏睡状態に陥った** Soon he *fell* [*went*] *into a coma*.

コンスタント constant ▶《野球》イチローは**コンスタントに**３割を打った Ichiro *constantly* hit over .300. (➤ three hundred と読む) ／Ichiro *constantly* maintains a batting average of over .300.

こんせい 混声 ‖**混声合唱** a mixed chorus.

こんせき 痕跡 traces; **marks**（しるし）▶彼らは部屋に殺人の**痕跡**を残さなかった They left no *traces* of murder in the room. ‖ その死体にはやけどの**痕跡**が無かった There were no burn *marks* on the dead body.

こんせつ 懇切 ▶そのパソコンは使用法についての**懇切な**（＝詳しい）説明書がついていた That personal computer came with a *detailed* manual. ‖ その女性は**懇切丁寧に**道を教えてくれた That woman *very kindly* showed me the way.

こんぜつ 根絶する eradicate ＋目（撲滅する）; **root out**（根こそぎにする）; **wipe out**（一掃する）▶性差別**根絶**のために努力を続けましょう Let's continue our efforts to *eradicate* [*root out*] sexism. ‖ 天然痘は1979年地球上から**根絶された** In 1979 smallpox *was wiped* [*stamped*] *out* (from the face of the earth).

コンセプト a **concept** ▶まず**コンセプト**を明確にする必要がある We need to clarify our *concept* first. ‖ この辞書の基本**コンセプト**は「見やすく，わかりやすく」です The *basic concept* of this dictionary is : easy to read and easy to understand.

¹**こんせん 混線する be crossed** ▶電話が**混線している** The lines *are crossed*.

▶《慣用表現》どうやら話が**混線して**（＝食い違って）いるようだね We seem to *be at cross-purposes*.

²**こんせん 混戦** ▶パ·リーグの６チームはペナントレースが４か月過ぎた今も**混戦状態**だ In the Pacific League, all six teams *are neck and neck* even after four months of the pennant race. (➤ neck and neck は「互角の」).

こんぜん 婚前 ▶彼らは**婚前旅行**でタヒチに行った They went to Tahiti on *a premarital trip*. ‖ あの夫婦には**婚前交渉**がなかったらしい I heard that couple didn't *have sex before their wedding* [*before getting married*].

こんぜんいったい 渾然一体·混然一体 ▶金沢は古さと新しさが**混然一体となって調和している** Kanazawa *is a happy* [*harmonious*] *blend* of tradition and modernity.

コンセンサス a **consensus**（➤ しばしば Ⓤ 扱い）▶臓器移植に関する**コンセンサスを形成する** build (*a*) *consensus* on organ transplants.

コンセント a (**wall**) **socket**; 《米》**an outlet** ▶テレビの**コンセントを抜く** *unplug* a TV set ‖ 壁の**コンセント**にプラグを差し込む put the plug in (to) *an outlet* on the wall（➤「壁のコンセントにテレビのプラグを差し込む」は plug the TV into a wall socket）.

> **危ないカタカナ語✹ コンセント**
> 電気プラグ用の差し込み口を「コンセント」というのは和製語. 英語では socket が一般的であるが，「電球用ソケット」と区別するために wall socket ということもある. 《米》では (wall) outlet, (plug) receptacle, 《英》では (power ／electrical) point ともいう.

コンソメ consommé /kɑ̀ːnsəméɪ/（➤ フランス語から）‖**コンソメスープ** consommé.

こんだく 混濁 muddiness; **cloudiness**（ワインなどの）‖**意識混濁** clouding of consciousness／mental fog.

コンダクター a **conductor**（指揮者，添乗員）.

コンタクト contact 一動 **コンタクトを取る contact** ＋目 ▶早速先方と**コンタクトを取って**みます I'll *contact* the other party at once.（➤ (×) contact to としない）.

コンタクトレンズ a **contact lens** ▶**コンタクトレンズ**をはめる [外す] put in [take out] *contact lenses* ‖ 姉は**コンタクトレンズ**を使っている My sister wears *contact lenses*.

こんだて 献立 a **menu** ▶**献立**を作る make out *a menu* ‖ 毎日毎日**献立を考える**のはとても面倒だ *Planning meals* day after day is a big bother.

‖**献立表** a menu.

こんたん 魂胆 an **ulterior** /ʌltíəriəʳ/ **motive**, a **secret purpose** ▶彼にＣＤをプレゼントしたからって別に**魂胆**があったわけじゃないわよ I had no *ulterior motives* in giving him the CDs. ／I had nothing particular in mind when I gave him those CDs. ‖ そんなおかしなことを言うなんて彼には何か**魂胆**があるに違いない He must have some *secret* [*hidden*] *purpose* to say such a strange thing.

こんだん 懇談 ▶先生と**懇談する** *have an informal talk* with one's teacher ‖ 父母と先生方との**懇談会**があす開かれる The parent-teacher *get-together* will be held tomorrow.（➤ get-together は「非公式な集まり」）／The *meeting* between parents and teachers will take place tomorrow.

コンチェルト a **concerto** /kəntʃéəʳtoʊ/（➤ イタリア語から）▶ピアノ**コンチェルト** a piano *concerto*.

こんちくしょう こん畜生 ▶「**こん畜生**！覚えていろよ！」と彼は叫んだ He exclaimed, "*Damn it !* You'll pay for this !" →畜生.

こんちゅう 昆虫 an **insect**, 《米·インフォーマル》a **bug** ▶兄は私に**昆虫採集**のしかたを教えてくれた My brother taught me how to *collect insects* [*make an insect collection*].

‖**昆虫学** entomology ‖ **昆虫学者** an entomologist ‖ **昆虫館** an insectarium.

「昆虫」のいろいろ **アブ** gadfly ／**アメンボ** water strider ／**アリ** ant ／**アリマキ** aphid /éɪfɪd/ ／**イナゴ**

locust／ウスバカゲロウ ant lion／蚊 mosquito／ガ moth／カゲロウ mayfly／カブトムシ beetle／カマキリ praying mantis／キリギリス grasshopper／クワガタムシ stag beetle／コオロギ cricket／ゴキブリ cockroach／シロアリ termite／スズメバチ hornet, wasp／セミ cicada／チョウ butterfly／テントウムシ ladybug／トンボ dragonfly／ノミ flea／ハエ fly／バッタ grasshopper／ブヨ gnat／ホタル firefly／マルハナバチ bumblebee／ミツバチ bee

こんてい 根底 **the root**（根源）; **the heart**（核心）; a **foundation**（根本, 基本）▶彼らの信頼は**根底**から揺らいだ Their faith was shaken *from the* (*very*) *foundation* [*core*]. ‖その暴動の**根底**には失業問題がある Unemployment was at *the root* [*heart*] of that riot.

▶日本人の心の**根底**には, 贈答の習慣は必要悪だとする考え方がある *Deep in the hearts* of Japanese people, there is a perception that the custom of exchanging gifts is a necessary evil. ‖彼の発見は従来の説を**根底から覆した** His discovery *completely* disproved the accepted theory [knocked the bottom out of the widely accepted theory].

コンディショナー **conditioner.**

コンディション **condition**; **shape**（体の; インフォーマルな語）▶体の**コンディション**を整える get oneself into good *physical condition*／get into *shape* ‖《試合前のスポーツ選手などが》きょうは体の**コンディション**がいい I'*m in top* [*good*] *form* today. 《参考》一般の人が「最近は体のコンディションがよい(＝健康だ)」なら I'm in good condition [shape] these days.

▶**コンディション**がよくないならマラソンには参加しないほうがいいよ It would be better for you not to take part in the marathon if you *don't feel well*. ‖私はベスト**コンディション**で試合に臨んだ I played the game *in top form*. ‖グラウンド**コンディション**不良のため試合は延期された The game was put off because *the field was not in good condition*.

コンテスト a **contest** ▶美人**コンテスト**に出る enter *a beauty contest* ‖フォト**コンテスト**で優勝する win a photo(graphy) *contest*.

‖**コンテスト出場者** a contestant.

コンテナ a **container** /kəntéɪnəʳ/ ‖**コンテナ車** a container truck [《英》lorry]; a container car（鉄道の）‖**コンテナ植物** a container plant（容器栽培された植物）‖**コンテナ船** a container ship.

コンデンサー a **condenser**, a **capacitor.**

コンデンスミルク **condensed milk.**

コンテンツ **content** /kάːntent/（➤「内容」の意では Ⓤ 扱い.「(容器の) 中身」「(本の) 目次」の意では contents がふつう）▶無料で**コンテンツ**を提供する offer *content* for free.

コント a (**comic**) **skit**, a (**comic**) **short play**（軽妙で風刺の利いた寸劇）▶**コント**を書く write *a* (*comic*) *short story* ‖**コント**を演じる stage *a* (*comic*) *skit*.

こんど 今度 **1**【今回, この度】**this time** ▶**今度**は上出来だ You've done (it) well *this time*. ‖**今度**だけは許してあげよう I will forgive you *just this once*.

▶**今度**の英語の試験は出来がよくなかった I didn't do well on [《英》in] the *last* English examination.（➤ last は「(現在にいちばん近い)この前の」）‖**今度**の先生はとても厳しい Our *new* teacher is very strict with us.

2【次回, 近い将来】**next time** ━形 **今度の next**（次の）

【文型】
今度…するとき
the next time S + V
➤ the を省くこともある
今度…したら(仮定)
if S + V **again** [**next time**]

▶**今度**モールにショッピングに行くときは誘ってね Please let me join you *the next time* you go shopping at the mall. ‖**今度**来るときは妹さんを連れていらっしゃい Bring your sister with you *next time* (you come). ‖ 対話「ママ, お菓子買って」「また, **今度**ね」"Mom, buy me some candy, please." "*Next time*."（➤ 大人の世界では "Maybe next time." は婉曲(えんきょく)な断りにもなる）‖**今度**一度飲みにいきましょう Let's go for a drink *the next time* (*we meet*). ‖**今度**うそをついたら許さないよ I won't let you get away with it *if* you lie (to me) *again*.／I'll make you regret it *if* you lie (to me) *again*.

▶**今度**の日曜日に遊びにいらっしゃい Come over *next* Sunday. ‖**今度**の大阪行きは何時に出ますか Please tell me when the *next* train for Osaka leaves. ‖**今度**はきみが鬼になる番だ *Now* it's your turn to be "it."

こんどう 混同する **mix up**, **confuse** ▶公私を**混同**してはいけない You must not *mix up* public and private matters. ‖きみは2つの全く違うものを**混同している** You *are confusing* [*mixing up*] two perfectly different things.

【文型】
A と B を混同する
confuse A **and** [**with**] B

▶フィクションと事実を**混同するな** Don't *confuse* fiction *with* fact.

コンドーム a **condom** /kάndəm ‖ kɔ́n-/; a **prophylactic** /pròʊfəlǽktɪk/（➤ 婉曲(えんきょく)な言い方. 俗語では rubber, skin ともいう）▶**コンドーム**を着ける wear [put on] *a condom*.

コンドミニアム a **condominium.**

ゴンドラ a **gondola** /gάːndələ/（ベニスの平底船; 気球などのつり籠）; a (**cable**) **car**（ロープウェーの）;《米》a **scaffold**,《英》a **cradle**（高いビルの窓掃除用の釣り作業台）▶停電で10人が**ゴンドラ**の中に閉じ込められた Ten people were trapped in *a cable car* due to the power failure.

コントラスト (a) **contrast** ▶赤い屋根が青い空と鮮やかな**コントラスト**を成している The red roofs make a vivid *contrast* with the blue sky.

コントラバス a **contrabass** /kάːntrəbeɪs/; a **double bass** /beɪs/（クラシック音楽の）; a (**string**) **bass**（ジャズなどの）.

コントラルト《音楽》**contralto.**

コンドル《鳥》a **condor** /kάːndəʳ/.

コントロール **control** /kəntróʊl/ ▶彼女は気が動転して自分の感情を**コントロール**できなかった She couldn't *control* her feelings because she was so upset.

▶《野球》あの投手は**コントロール**がいい［悪い］The pitcher *has good* [*poor*] *control*.

こんとん 混沌・渾沌 **chaos** /kéɪɑːs/ ▶当時の日本の政治情勢は**混とん**としていた The political situation in Japan at that time was *chaotic* [*in a state of chaos*]. ‖セ・リーグの首位争いは**混とん**としてきた The battle for first place in the Central League is *getting chaotic.*

こんな ▶こんな天気のいい日に家でごろごろしていたくない I hate to sit around the house on a beautiful day *like this* [on *such* a beautiful day]. ‖こんな漫画本は子供によくない Comic books of *this kind* [Comic books *like these*] are not good for children. ‖こんな数学の勉強が将来本当に役に立つのかなあ I wonder if studying *this kind of* math will actually be useful for me in the future. ‖ 対話 「お皿１枚貸してください」「こんなのでいいかしら」"May I borrow a dish [plate]?" "Will *this one* do?" ‖こんなに遅くまでどこへ行ってたの? It's late. Where have you been (*all this time*)? ‖悪いけどこんなにたくさんは食べられないよ I'm sorry, but I can't eat *this* much. (➤ この this は副詞) ‖こんなに長くお待たせしてすみませんでした I'm sorry to have kept you waiting *so* long [(for) *such* a long time]. ‖こんなふうに扱われるとは思わなかった I never expected to be treated *this way*. ‖どうしてこんなことになったんだ How did *this situation* come about? ‖《好ましくないことが起きたような場合に》こんなことってないよ *Things don't happen this way.* / *Things like this shouldn't happen.*

こんなん 困難 (a) **difficulty**; (a) **hardship** (苦難) 一形 **困難な difficult, hard**

▶困難な仕事 *difficult* work / a *hard* job ‖人生には多くの困難がある Life is full of *hardships*. ‖目的を遂げるためにはあらゆる困難に打ち勝つ必要がある You have to overcome every *difficulty* [*hardship*] to achieve your goal.

▶その問題を今月中に解決するのは困難だ It will *be difficult* [*hard*] to solve the problem within the month. ‖あなたの夢を実現するのは相当困難でしょう You'll *have* a lot of *difficulty* realizing your dream. ‖自動車事故に遭ったので彼はいくらか歩行が困難です Because of the car accident, he has some *walking difficulties* [some *trouble* (*with*) *walking*]. ‖困難に陥ったときにこそ, その人の真の実力がわかる People show their true ability *when the chips are down* [*when they are in a tight spot*]. (➤ when the chips are down は「いちばん大事なときに」の意のインフォーマルな表現).

こんにち 今日 today ▶今日の世界情勢 the world situation *of today* ‖今日の若者 young people (*of*) *today* / *today's* young people ‖今日の日本 *today's* Japan / *present-day* Japan ‖今日では多くの人がデジタルカメラを持っている *Today* [*Nowadays*], many people have a digital camera. ‖私の今日あるのは両親のおかげです I owe *what I am* (*today*) entirely to my parents. / My parents have made me *what I am* (*today*).

こんにちは 今日は Hello!, Hi!

> **◀解説▶「こんにちは」について**
> (1) Good day. や Good morning., Good afternoon. などが一応形の上では「こんにちは」に近い表現であるが, 最近ではこれらはあまり用いられず, Hello や Hi が軽い挨拶語として時間帯に関係なく広く使われている. (2) "Hello." と挨拶されたら同じく "Hello." と答えればよいが, 発音は尻上がりになる.

▶皆さん, こんにちは *Hello*, everyone! ‖ルーシーさん, こんにちは. ご機嫌いかがですか *Hello*, Lucy! How are you today?

こんにゃく *konnyaku*

日本紹介 ✉ **こんにゃくはコンニャクイモから作ったゼラチン状の食品です. 低カロリーで繊維質に富み, 腸内をきれいにすると言われています** *Konnyaku* is a gelatin-like food made from *konnyaku* yam. It is low in calories and high in fiber and is believed to clean the intestines.

こんにゅう 混入 ▶ワインに毒物を混入する *lace* wine *with* poison ‖ミネラルウォーターにかびが混入していた Some mold *was mixed in* with the mineral water.

コンパ a **party**; a **get-together** (形式ばらない集まり) 《参考》「コンパ」は「仲間, 交際」の意の company からきた語だが, 最近ではこの日本語自体が古風になりつつある →飲み会 ▶来週(クラスの)コンパをやろう Let's have *a* (*class*) *party* next week.

‖追い出しコンパ a farewell party ‖歓迎コンパ a welcome party ‖新入生歓迎 [新歓] コンパ a get-together to welcome freshmen.

コンバーター 《電気》 a **converter**.

コンパートメント a **compartment**.

コンバイン a **combine (harvester)**.

コンパクト 1【化粧用具の】a **compact**.

2【小型でまとまった】▶このデジタルビデオはコンパクトにまとまっていて使いやすそうだ This digital camcorder is *compact* and seems easy to operate. ‖このテントはコンパクトに折り畳める This tent folds *compactly*.

コンパクトディスク a **compact disc**, a **CD**

コンパス 1【製図用の】**compasses** (➤ 単数扱い), 《インフォーマル》 a **compass**.

2【脚】▶彼はコンパスが長い [短い] He *has long* [*short*] *legs*.

コンパニオン a **female guide** (催事場の); a **booth attendant** (展示コーナーの); a **(paid) female escort** [**entertainer**] (パーティー会場の; paid は報酬が出る場合) 《参考》日本ではイベントなどでの客の接待役を「話し相手」の意味で「コンパニオン」と呼んでいるが, companion にこの意味はない. 以上のように場合に応じた訳語を使うしかない.

こんばん 今晩 →今夜.

こんばんは 今晩は ▶石井さん, こんばんは *Good evening*, Mr. Ishii. 《参考》Good evening. は改まった挨拶で, 親しい間柄では時間に関係なく Hello. や Hi. が多く用いられる傾向にある. →こんにちは.

コンビ a **pair** ▶草野さんと星野さんはなかなかの名コンビだ Kusano and Hoshino are [make] *a good pair*. ‖A氏はB氏とコンビで会社を経営した Mr. A ran the company *in partnership with* Mr. B. ‖彼はかおりとコンビを組みたがった He wanted to *pair up with* Kaori.

コンビーフ corned beef, 《英また》 **salt beef** ▶コンビーフの缶詰 canned [《英また》 tinned] *corned beef*.

コンビナート an **industrial complex** (➤「コンビナート」はロシア語の *kombinat* から).

‖石油コンビナート a petrochemical complex.

コンビニ a **convenience store** (➤ c-store と表記することもある), 《英また》 a **cornershop** ▶このコンビニは24時間営業している This *convenience store* is open 24 hours a day. (➤「年中無休・24時間営業している」は be open 24/7 [twenty-four seven] という) ‖学校の帰りにコンビニに寄った I stopped in at *a convenience store* on my way from school.

コンビネーション (a) **combination** ▶絶妙なコンビネーション a perfect *combination*.

コンピュータ a **computer** ▶コンピュータにデータを入れる input [enter] data into *a computer* ‖コンピュータの

プログラムを組む write *a computer program* ‖ コンピュータでデータを処理する process data *by computer* (➤ a は不要) ‖ コンピュータ化された工場 a *computerized* factory [plant] ‖ 彼はコンピュータのような頭脳の持ち主だ He has a *computer-like* brain.／His mind is *like a computer*. (➤後者のmindは「理解[思考]力」).
‖ コンピュータウイルス a computer virus ‖ コンピュータグラフィックス computer graphics《略 CG》‖ コンピュータゲーム a computer game.

こんぶ 昆布 kombu, kelp, a (sea) tangle 《参考》英米人は日本人ほど昆布を食べない. また, 日本では昆布を祝儀に用いるが, 英米にはこの習慣はない.

コンプライアンス compliance
‖ 企業コンプライアンス corporate compliance.

コンプレックス an inferiority complex ▶その少年は背が低いことにコンプレックスを持っている The boy has *an inferiority complex* about his small stature. ‖ あの人たちは西洋人に対してコンプレックスを感じている They *feel inferior to* Westerners. ‖ 私, 鼻がぺちゃんこなのでコンプレックス感じてるの I've got *a complex* [*hang-up*] about my flat nose.

> **危ないカタカナ語✹ コンプレックス**
> **1** 単に complex だけには「劣等感」の意味はなく, 「強迫観念, 異常心理, 複合」の意味で使われる. したがって, 「劣等感」の意味のときは inferiority (劣等) をつける. 「優越感」は superiority complex [feeling] という.
> **2** ただし, インフォーマルな英語では complex が「過度の嫌悪 [恐怖] (感)」の意味で用いられる.

コンプレッサー a compressor.

コンペ a competition ▶ゴルフコンペ a golf *competition*.

こんぺき 紺碧 deep blue ▶紺ぺきの空にカモメが舞っていた I saw seagulls flying in the *deep blue* sky.

コンベヤー a conveyor ‖ ベルトコンベヤー a conveyor belt (➤ belt conveyor はまれ).

コンベンション a convention ‖ コンベンションセンター a convention center [《英》centre] ‖ コンベンションホール a convention hall.

コンポ stereo components
‖ カー・コンポ stereo components for a car.

こんぼう 棍棒 a club; a stick (細い); a nightstick (警棒).

こんぽう 梱包 packing 一動 梱包する pack +Ⓞ ▶こん包用資材 *packing* material.

こんぽん 根本 a foundation (物事の根底); a basis (基礎) ▶根本的な問題 a *fundamental* [*basic*] problem ‖ 健康は幸福の根本である Health is the *foundation* of happiness. ‖ 仏教とキリスト教では死生観が根本的に違う Views of life and death are *radically* [*fundamentally*] different in Buddhism and Christianity. ‖ きみは根本的に間違っている You are *fundamentally* wrong. ‖ 日本の教育制度は根本的な改革が必要だ *Drastic* reforms are needed in the Japanese educational system. (➤ drastic は「抜本的な, 思い切った」).

コンマ a comma (句読点の); a (decimal) point (小数点の) ▶この単語の前にコンマを打ちなさい Put [Use] *a comma* before this word. ‖ コンマ以下は切り捨てなさい Omit the fractions *below the decimal*. (➤「小数点以下の端数は省きなさい」の意).

こんまけ 根負け ▶彼の粘り強さには根負けするよ I *give up*, I can't beat his tenacity.

こんめい 混迷 confusion ▶首相の決断が政治の混迷に終止符を打った The Prime Minister's decision marked an end to the *political confusion*.

こんもり ▶こんもりと茂った松林 a *thick* pine grove ‖ 庭の隅の土がこんもりと盛り上がっていた In the corner of the garden, the earth rose *into a little mound*.

こんや 今夜 tonight, this evening (➤ evening は, 通例, 暗くなり出してから, 星が輝きを増す夕刻で, night の一部. 季節によっては 9 時, 10時でも用いられる) ▶今夜は外で食事しよう Let's eat out *tonight* [*this evening*]. ‖ 今夜は遅くまで勉強するぞ I'm going to study till late *tonight*. ‖ 今夜はここに泊まろうよ Let's stay here *for the night*. ‖「報道特集」は今夜 9 時からです "News Special" is on at nine *this evening* [*tonight*].

こんやく 婚約 an engagement《to》一動 婚約する be [get] engaged《to》▶ひろ子, 婚約おめでとう! Congratulations on your *engagement*, Hiroko! ‖ その相撲取りは歌手との婚約を発表した That sumo wrestler announced his *engagement to* a singer. ‖ 姉は弁護士と婚約した My sister *is engaged to* a lawyer. ‖ その映画俳優は婚約を破棄した The movie star *called off his* [*her*] *engagement*. (➤「婚約破棄」は a breach of promise) ‖ あの背の高い青年が由紀子さんの婚約者です That tall young man is Yukiko's *fiancé* /fìːɑːnséɪ/. (➤「女性の婚約者」は fiancée とつづる. 発音は同じ). ‖ 婚約指輪 an engagement ring [band] (➤「エンゲージリング」は和製語)《参考》アメリカなどでは婚約した女性は職場などで婚約指輪を同僚に見せ, 自分の婚約を知らせることが多い. 同僚は That's a beautiful ring. などと言う.

こんよく 混浴 mixed bathing /béɪðɪŋ/ ▶ここの露天風呂は混浴です In this open-air bath *people of both sexes bathe together*.

こんらん 混乱 (a) confusion (入り乱れた状態); disorder (位置・順序が乱れている状態) 一動 混乱する be confused ▶みんなが交通規則を守らないと大混乱が起きる If everyone fails to observe traffic rules, there will be *great confusion*. ‖ この混乱を早く収拾する必要がある We need to get this *chaotic situation* under control as soon as possible. ‖《相手の言っていることがわからないときなど》私, 頭が混乱しています I'*m getting confused*. ‖ 毎日忙しすぎて頭が混乱している I am so busy every day that *my head is spinning* [*my mind is in confusion*]. ‖ そんなにいっぺんにいろいろ言われると頭が混乱しちゃうよ I *get all mixed up* when you tell me so much all at once.

こんりゅう 建立 building, erection 一動 建立する build +Ⓞ, erect +Ⓞ ▶寺を建立する *build* a temple ‖ お墓を建立する *erect* a (family) grave.

こんりんざい 金輪際 ▶もう結婚なんて金輪際するものか *I'll be damned if* I ever marry again. (➤ 俗語的表現) ‖ 金輪際電話しないでくれ *Don't ever* call me up *again*.

こんれい 婚礼 a wedding, nuptials /nʌ́pʃəlz/ (➤ 後者は改まった語).

こんろ 焜炉 a (portable) cookstove,《英また》a (portable) cooking-stove ▶こんろで魚を焼く broil some fish on *a cookstove*.
‖ 電気 [ガス] こんろ an electric [a gas] stove.

こんわく 困惑する be at a loss (途方に暮れる), be embarrassed /ɪmbǽrəst/ (まごつく) ▶どう答えたらよいか困惑してしまった I *was at a loss* for an answer. ／I *was perplexed about* [*as to*] how to answer the question. (➤ 後者は堅い言い方) ‖ 私と顔を合わせたとたん彼女は困惑の表情を見せた When our eyes met, she *looked embarrassed*.

さ・サ

さ 差 (a) **difference**(違い)；a **gap** (隔たり)；a **margin** (得点・得票の開き) ▶年齢の差 (*a*) *difference* of [in] age ‖ 10分の差 *a difference* of 10 minutes ‖ 小 [大] 差で選挙に勝つ win an election *by a narrow* [*wide*] *margin* ‖ 1000円と980円の差は20円だが，その差が購買者に与える心理的影響力は大きい The *difference* between 1,000 yen and 980 yen is only 20 yen, but this *difference* has a great impact on customers. ‖ この２人の生徒には能力の差がほとんどない There is little *difference in ability* between these two students. ‖ この国では貧富の差が大きい There is a wide *gap between the rich and the poor* in this country.
▶中日は１点差で阪神に負けた The Dragons lost (the game) to the Tigers *by one run*. (➤ run は「(野球などの) 得点」) ‖ 50のターンを折り返して２位との差が大きくついた When he turned at 50 meters, he *had a big lead* on the second swimmer.
▶英語では森君にずいぶん差をつけられたよ Mori has *gotten* far *ahead of* me in English.

ざ 座 **1**【席】a **seat** ▶座に着く(＝着席する) take one's *seat* ／seat oneself ‖ 座を外す leave one's *seat*. ▶《慣用表現》みんなが黙っていると座がもたない When everybody keeps silent, *a party is like a funeral*. (➤「パーティーは葬式のようになる」の意).
2【地位，身分】▶政権の座につく take the *seat* of government.
3【星占い】an **astrological sign**, a **sign** ▶ 対話「きみ何座？」「水瓶(がめ)座よ」"*What sign* are you? [*What's* your (*birth*) *sign*?]" "(I am an) Aquarius."
《参考》十二宮 通例生まれた日の星座をいう場合，カッコ内の英語を使う.

牡羊座	the Ram	(白羊宮 Aries)
牡牛座	the Bull	(金牛宮 Taurus)
双子座	the Twins	(双子宮 Gemini)
蟹座	the Crab	(巨蟹(きょかい)宮 Cancer)
獅子座	the Lion	(獅子宮 Leo)
乙女座	the Virgin	(処女宮 Virgo)
天秤座	the Balance [Scales]	(天秤宮 Libra)
蠍座	the Scorpion	(天蠍(てんかつ)宮 Scorpio)
射手座	the Archer	(人馬宮 Sagittarius)
山羊座	the Goat	(磨羯(まかつ)宮 Capricorn)
水瓶座	the Water Bearer	(宝瓶(ほうへい)宮 Aquarius)
魚座	the Fishes	(双魚宮 Pisces)

さあ **1**【注意を促して】▶さあ，きみにこれをあげよう *Here* you are. ／This is for you. ‖ さあ，出かけよう *Now*, let's go. ‖ さあ，ホテルに着いたぞ *Here* we are at the hotel. ‖ さあ，バスが来た *Here* comes our [your] bus. ‖ さあ，子供たちは行った行った！ *Now* get along, kids!
2【言いよどんで】▶さあ，困ったことになったぞ *Well, well, well*. What a mess! ‖ 対話「美奈子さんはいつオーストラリアにたつのかしら？」「さあ，よくわかりません」"When is Minako leaving for Australia?" "*Well*, I'm not sure. ／*Well*, I don't really know."

サーカス a **circus** ▶サーカスの一座 a *circus* troupe ‖ サーカスを見にいく go to (see) *the circus*.

サーキット a **racing circuit** /sə́ːʳkɪt/ (自動車レース場)；a **circuit**(電気回路)
‖ サーキットトレーニング circuit training.

サークル a **circle**, a **club** ▶環境問題研究サークル an environmental problem study *circle* ‖ 聖書を読むサークル a Bible-reading *circle* (➤ これら２例のように circle は前に具体的な活動内容を表す語句を伴うのがふつう) ‖ 彼はぼくらのサークルの新入りだ He is a newcomer to our *club*.
✉ **私は学校でミステリー研究会に入っています．あなたはどんなサークルに入っていますか** I am a member of a mystery-story club at school. What kind of *school club activities* are you in?
➤ 部活動は extracurricular activity と表現してもよい.
‖ サークル活動 club [group] activities.

> **危ないカタカナ語✸ サークル**
> **1**「サークル」には circle, club の両語が当てはまる. circle は「小さな輪」の原義から「形式ばらない集まり，同好会」を指すのに対して，club は「こぶのようにまとまったもの」の意から「正式の組織を持つ集まり」を指す.
> **2** 学校の課外活動としての「…サークル」は music club, tennis club のように club を使うほうがふつう. なお，イギリスでは club を会員制の「社交クラブ」の意味で使うこともある.

ざあざあ ▶雨がザーザー降っている It'*s pouring* (down) rain. ／It'*s pouring*.

サーズ **SARS** /sɑːʳz/ (➤ severe acute respiratory syndrome (重症急性呼吸器症候群；通称，「新型肺炎」) の頭文字を取って付けた名).

サーチャージ a **surcharge** ▶燃油サーチャージ a fuel *surcharge*.

サーチライト a **searchlight**.

サード《野球》**third** (**base**) → 三塁 ▶サードを守る play *third* ‖ サードゴロ a grounder to *third*.

サーバー **1**【(球技で) サーブする人】a **server**.
2【給仕道具】a **server** (➤ server は「給仕人，ウエーター」も指す).
3【コンピュータ】a **server** ▶メールサーバー an email *server* ‖ インターネットサーバー an Internet [a Web] *server*.

サービス **1**【接客，接待】**service** ▶あのレストランはサービスが良い [悪い] The *service* at that restaurant *is good* [*poor*]. ／They *wait on you very well* [*poorly*] in that restaurant. (➤ wait on は「(人に) 給仕する」) ‖ 当方のサービスは最高でございます We provide the ultimate in *service*. ‖ お勘定はサービス料込みになっております The bill includes *service charges*.
▶日曜日は私の家庭サービスの日だ Sunday is the day (when) I *spend a lot of time with* my *family* [(when) *I do a lot of things for* my *family*].
‖ (高速道路などの) サービスエリア a service area ‖

サービス業 a service industry ‖ サービスステーション a service station ‖ サービス品 a freebie (ただの物), a giveaway (販売促進用の無料サンプル).

2【値引き, 無料】 a **discount** /dískaʊnt/ **一動** サービスする **give a discount, discount** (➤ 動詞の発音は /dískaʊnt, dɪskáʊnt/) ▶彼はスラックス1本がサービスで付いてくるスーツを買った He bought a suit with an extra pair of pants *thrown in*. (➤ throw in は「…をおまけに付ける」) ‖ 現金でしたらどの品も1割サービスさせていただきます We give a ten percent *discount* on all cash purchases. (➤ この意味で service は使えない) ‖ お客さん, きょうはサービスしとくよ! We'll give you a big *discount*, ma'am [sir]. /A special *discount* for you, ma'am [sir].

3【球技で】 a **service** ▶サービスエースを取る serve *an ace* (➤「サービスエース」は service ace または ace).

逆引き熟語 ○○サービス
アフターサービス after-sales service /インターネット接続サービス Internet-access service /オンラインサービス online service /介護サービス nursing (care) service /公共サービス public service /顧客サービス customer service /在宅介護サービス home care service /セルフサービス self-service /24時間サービス round-the-clock [24 hour] service /マイレージサービス a frequent flier [flyer] program /モーニングサービス a breakfast set [special] (→モーニング) /リップサービス an empty [insincere] compliment /ルームサービス room service

危ないカタカナ語✹ サービス
1 英語の service は「接客, 奉仕」の意味が基本で,「値引き」とか「無料」の意味はない. したがって「値引き」の意味では discount を,「無料」の意味では free などを用いる必要がある.
2 店の人などが言う「これはサービスです」は This is a complimentary gift. とか This is free. である. なお, レストランでの有料の「サービスランチ[ディナー]」は today's special と表現する.

サーブ a **serve**, a **service** ▶サーブは誰の番だ? Whose *serve* is it? ‖ あの選手はサーブがいい[悪い] That player has *a good* [*bad*] *serve*. /That player *serves well* [*badly*]. ‖ 彼女は速くていいサーブをする She has a good fast *serve*. ‖ ナイスサーブ! *Nice serve!* (➤ 会話では serve がより一般的; service はやや堅い語).

サーファー a **surfer**.

サーフィン **surfing** ▶湘南にサーフィンをしに行く *go surfing* at Shonan (Beach) (➤「サーフィンをする」は surf または ride a surfboard).

サーフボード a **surfboard** 《参考》 文脈から明瞭な場合は単に board と呼ぶことも多い.

サーベル a **saber**, 《英》 a **sabre**.

サーモスタット a **thermostat** /θə́ːrməstæt/.

サーモン **salmon** (鮭)
‖サーモントラウト a salmon trout.

サーロイン (a) **sirloin** /sə́ːrlɔɪn/ (牛の腰肉)
‖サーロインステーキ a sirloin (steak).

¹**さい 犀** 《動 物》 a **rhinoceros** /raɪnɑ́ːsərəs/, a **rhino** /ráɪnoʊ/ (➤ 後者はインフォーマルな語).

²**さい 差異** (a) **difference** ▶両者に大きな差異はない There's no big *difference* between the two.

³**さい 際** ▶お近くへおいでの際はぜひお立ち寄りください Be sure to visit us *when* you are in our area. ‖《掲示》緊急の際はガラスを割って中の赤いボタンを押してください *In case of* emergency, break glass and push red button. (➤ glass と red button には the をつけるのが文法的であるが, 掲示のときには略す) ‖ この際全部片づけよう Let's clear everything up *this time*. ‖ この際はっきり言っておきたいことがある I'd like to take *this occasion* to make something clear.

⁴**さい 才** (a) **talent**; a **gift** (天賦の) ▶彼には音楽の才がある He has *a talent* [*a gift*] *for music*.

⁵**さい 賽** a **die** [複 **dice**] ▶さいは投げられた *The die* is cast. →さいころ.

さい- 再- **re-** ▶再調査 *re*examination (➤ 動詞は reexamine) /a *re*survey ‖ 再入学する *re*enter (a) school ‖ 証明書を再発行する *reissue* a certificate ‖ パソコンを再起動する *reboot* [*restart*] a computer.

-さい -歳 ▶私は16歳です I'*m* 16 *years old*. (➤ インフォーマルでは years old を省略することも多い) ‖ 10歳の男の子 a boy of ten /a ten-*year-old* boy (➤ ten-years-old とはしない) ‖ お兄さんは何歳ですか *How old* is your (older) brother? ‖ 祖父は82歳で死んだ My grandfather died *at the age of* eighty-two [when he was eighty-two *years old*].

ざい 財 **wealth**; (a) **fortune** (ばく大な資産) ▶上田氏は一代で財を成した Mr. Ueda *amassed* [*accumulated*] *a big fortune* in his lifetime.

ざい- 在- ▶在日外国人 a foreign national [citizen] *living* [*residing*] *in Japan*.
✉ **在米中は大変お世話になり, ありがとうございました** I'd like to thank you very much for all you did for us *while we were in the U.S.*

さいあい 最愛の **beloved** /bɪlʌ́vd/ ▶彼は最愛の息子を交通事故で亡くした He lost his *beloved* [*much-loved*] son in a traffic accident.

さいあく 最悪の (**the**) **worst** ▶最悪の事態に備えておく be prepared for *the worst* ‖ 最悪の場合は家族がばらばらになるかもしれない *If* (*the*) *worst comes to* (*the*) *worst*, our family might be split up. (➤ the を省略するのは主に《米》) ‖ 史上最悪の海難事故が南シナ海で起こった *The worst* sea disaster in history occurred in the South China Sea.
▶中間試験は最悪の出来だった I *did absolutely terrible* on the midterm exams. ‖ この前の数学のテスト, 最悪だったよ My last math test was *a disaster*. (➤「全くの失敗」の意) ‖ **対話**「きのうの映画はどうだった?」「サイアク!」"How was the movie you saw yesterday?" "(It was) *the pits*!" (➤ the pits は「非常に不愉快なもの」の意の俗語; ● 人に言及して「サイアク!」と言う場合は "A disaster!" のような言い方をする).

ざいあく 罪悪 a **sin** (道徳・宗教上の); a **crime** (法律上の); a **vice** (悪徳) ▶(モーセの)『十戒』によれば, うそをつくことは罪悪である According to the Ten Commandments, lying is *a sin*. ‖ 人をだますことは罪悪だ (=間違っている) It's *wrong*(*ful*) to deceive people. ‖ 父はギャンブルを罪悪視している My father *sees* gambling *as a vice*. ‖ 彼は1人だけ救命ボートで脱出して罪悪感にさいなまれた He *had a guilty conscience* after being the only one to escape in a lifeboat.

ざいい 在位 **reign** /reɪn/ ▶後醍醐天皇の在位中に *in* [*under*] *the reign* of Emperor Godaigo ‖ その横綱は在位10場所を数える The yokozuna has *held his rank* for 10 consecutive tournaments.

さいうよく 最右翼 a **favorite** ▶金メダルの最右翼 a

gold-medal *favorite* ／*a favorite* for the gold ‖ 東氏が次期社長の**最右翼だ** Mr. Azuma *is favored* to be the next president.

[1]**さいえん 才媛** a talented [an intelligent] woman (➤ talented は「有能な」, intelligent は「知性が高い」) ▶新婦はT女子大をお出になったばかりのまれに見る**才媛**でいらっしゃいます The bride is *a lady of* rare *ability*, fresh from T Women's College.

[2]**さいえん 菜園** a vegetable [kitchen] garden《参考》いわゆる「家庭菜園」もこれでよい. ‖**市民菜園** a communal vegetable garden ‖**家庭菜園** a garden (vegetable) patch.

[3]**さいえん 再演** the second performance ▶その芝居の**再演**が決まった *The second performance* of the play has been decided. ‖その曲目は土曜の夜に**再演される** The program will *be performed again* [*be repeated*] on Saturday night.

[1]**さいかい 再会する** meet [see] again ▶**再会**を約束する promise to *meet again* ‖きみに**再会**できるとは夢にも思わなかったよ I never dreamed [Little did I dream] (that) I'd *meet* you *again*. ‖ほとんど1年ぶりで彼女と**再会した** I *met* her after an interval of almost a year. (➤「…のブランクがあったあとで」のような説明が続く場合は again は不要) ‖アリスとの**再会**を楽しみにしている I am looking forward to *seeing* Alice *again*.

✉ **あなたと再会できてとてもうれしく思いました** I was so happy [pleased] to *see* you *again*.

[2]**さいかい 再開する** start again, resume /rɪzjúːm/ (+目) (➤ 後者は堅い語) ▶雨で中断されていた試合が**再開された** The game which had been interrupted by (the) rain *started again*. ‖会議は休憩のあと**再開された** The meeting *was resumed* [(*was*) *re-opened*] after a break.

[3]**さいかい 最下位** ▶**最下位**の西武ライオンズ the *last-place* Lions ‖**最下位**を脱出する escape *the cellar* ‖あのチームはいつも**最下位だ** That team is always *in the cellar* [*at the bottom*].

さいがい 災害 a disaster ; a calamity /kəlǽməṭi/ (大災害) ▶大雨は地滑りや洪水などの**自然災害**を招く Heavy rains may cause *natural disasters* such as landslides and floods. ‖**災害**は忘れた頃にやって来る *Disaster* strikes when people begin to forget about it [when you least expect it]. (➤ 前者は日本語からの直訳. 英語では後者のように「全く思いもしないときに」とするのがふつう).

‖**災害保険** casualty insurance ‖**激甚災害** disaster of extreme severity ‖**二次災害** a secondary disaster ‖**労働者災害補償** industrial accident [injury] compensation.

ざいかい 財界 business [financial] circles, the business world

‖**財界人** a business [corporate] leader ; a financier (金融家) ; a businessperson (実業家).

ざいがい 在外 ‖**在外邦人** a Japanese expatriate, an expatriate Japanese (➤ expatriate は「海外居住者」で, インフォーマルでは expat という), a Japanese overseas.

さいかいはつ 再開発 redevelopment 一動 **再開発する** redevelop +目 ▶都市 [ウォーターフロント] の**再開発** urban [waterfront] *redevelopment*.

さいかく 才覚 resource (臨機応変の才) ; (a) talent (才能) ▶彼女は**才覚のある**人物だ She is a *resourceful* [*talented*] person. ‖彼は商売の**才覚がある** He has *a talent for business*. ／He has *business acumen*.

ざいがく 在学 ▶彼女はS大学に**在学している** She *is a student at* S University. ‖息子は中学に**在学中**だ My son *is* now *in* junior high school. ‖兄は大学**在学中**に通訳の資格を取った My (older) brother got an interpreter's license *while* (*he was*) *at college*. ‖**在学証明書** a certificate of student registration.

さいかくにん 再確認 reconfirmation 一動 **再確認する** reconfirm +目 ▶彼らは前回の打ち合わせ事項を**再確認した** They *reconfirmed* what had been discussed in their previous meeting. ‖忘れ物がないか**再確認しなさい** *Check again* [*Double-check*] that you don't leave anything behind. ‖近頃伝統的な日本食のよさを**再確認しています** Recently I've come to fully *recognize* the benefits of the traditional Japanese diet. ‖最近はたいていの航空会社では乗客による航空便予約の**再確認**を必要としない These days most airlines do not require passengers to *reconfirm* their reservations.

さいかどう 再稼働 reactivation (再活発化) ; restart(ing) (再始動) ▶原子炉を**再稼働する** *reactivate* [*restart*] a (nuclear) reactor (➤ 一般的には restart を用いる ; 厳密でない言い方では「原子力発電所を再稼働させる」というが, 再稼働させるのは運転することのできる機械や設備である原子炉である).

[1]**さいき 才気** ▶花嫁は**才気**煥発(かんぱつ)で, しかも美人です The bride is *brilliant* and, as you can see, beautiful.

[2]**さいき 再起** a comeback (復帰) ; (a) recovery (回復) ▶彼女は間違いなく舞台へ**再起**できるだろう She is sure to *make a comeback* on stage. ‖彼は**再起不能**だろうとうわさされている Rumor has it that he will probably *not be able to make a full recovery*.

さいぎしん 猜疑心 suspicion ▶うちの上司は**さいぎ心が強い** Our boss *doesn't trust people*. (●「人を信用しない」と考えればよい. 日本語に近く訳せば Our boss has a suspicious nature. とか Our boss is distrustful of others. となるが, 訳例のように言うのが自然).

さいきだいめいし 再帰代名詞 《文法》 a reflexive pronoun.

さいきどう 再起動 ▶コンピューターを**再起動する** *restart* [*reboot*] a computer.

さいきょう 最強の the strongest ▶世界**最強の**レスラー *the strongest* wrestler in the world.

さいきょういく 再教育 reeducation ; retraining (再訓練) ; in-service training (社内研修など) 一動 **再教育する** reeducate +目 ; retrain +目 ; give [provide] in-service training 《参考》教員の再教育(現職教育)は in-service (teacher) training という.

[1]**さいきん 細菌** a germ /dʒəːʳm/ (➤ 人体に有害な「ばい菌」の意の日常語), bacteria /bæktíəriə/ (➤ 単数形は bacterium).

[2]**さいきん 最近** 1 【近い過去】 recently, lately

語法 (1) recently は現在に比較的近い過去のある時に起こった事をいう場合に, 現在完了形または過去形とともに用いる. (2) lately は比較的近い過去のある時から現在まで続いているような事について, 通例現在完了形とともに用いる.

▶私の祖父は**最近**亡くなりました My grandfather passed away *recently*. (➤ この場合は継続的な事柄ではないので lately は不可) ‖**最近**玲子に会っていない I haven't seen Reiko *recently* [*lately*]. ‖**最近**とて

も忙しいんだ I've been quite busy *lately*. ‖ 私，つい最近ロンドンに行ってきたのよ I've been to London *quite recently*. ／I went to London *just recently*. ‖ 岡さんたちはつい最近越して行かれました The Okas moved out *quite recently*. (→近頃).

2【現代】today, these days(➤ どちらも通例現在形とともに用いる) ▶最近の若者は政治に関心がない *Today's* young people [Young people *today*] aren't interested in politics. (➤ recent young people とはしない) ‖ 最近の入試では小論文形式のテストを導入する傾向がある A *recent* trend in entrance exams is the introduction of essay-type tests. ‖ 最近は1人で海外旅行をする人がたくさんいる A large number of people travel abroad alone [by themselves] *these days*.

さいぎんみ 再吟味する reexamine +㊐.

さいく 細工 1【製作】a work (作られた物)；**workmanship** (技，細工の腕前) ▶このお盆はすばらしい細工だ This tray is a fine (piece of) *work*. ‖ このべっ甲細工は細工が良い[悪い] This tortoiseshell ornament is *of good* [*bad*] *workmanship*.

2【手直し】▶彼は自分の横領を隠すために帳簿を細工した He *changed* [*doctored*] the accounts to cover up his embezzlement. (➤ doctor は「不法に手を加える」の意のインフォーマルな語) ‖ 彼は自分のスキーがよく滑るように細工した He *made special modifications* to his skis so that they would go faster. (➤ modification は「部分的変更」).

さいくつ 採掘 mining ▶九州北部ではかつて多量の石炭が採掘されていた A great deal of coal used to *be mined* in Northern Kyushu.

サイクリング cycling ▶相模湖にサイクリングに行く *go cycling* at [around] Lake Sagami (➤ around のほうが周遊のイメージが強い．(×) to Lake Sagami としない) ／*go* to Lake Sagami *to cycle* [*for cycling*] (➤ 相模湖までは別の交通機関を利用し，目的地でサイクリングをする場合) ‖ 夏休みには友だちとサイクリングに行くつもりだ I am planning to *go cycling* [*go on a cycling tour*] with my friends during this summer vacation. ‖ **サイクリングロード** a bike way, a bike path.

サイクル a **cycle** ▶ファッションの流行には20年くらいのサイクルがある Fashions come and go in *cycles* of about 20 years. ‖ 彼はその試合でサイクルヒットを打った He *hit for the cycle* in the game. (➤「サイクルヒット」は和製語).

さいくん 細君 a person's **wife**.

さいぐんび 再軍備 rearmament 一動 再軍備する rearm(+㊐).

さいけいれい 最敬礼する give [**make**] **a deep bow** /baʊ/《to》; **bow deeply**《to》▶大使は天皇に最敬礼した The ambassador *made a deep bow to* the Emperor.

¹さいけつ 採決 voting；a **vote** (1回の) **一動 採決する vote**《on》, **take a vote** ▶国会で法案を強行採決する *force* [*steamroll* ／*railroad*] a bill through the Diet ‖ 国会でその法案の採決が行われた *A vote* was taken on the bill in the Diet.

²さいけつ 採血する collect [**gather**] **blood**(血液提供者から)；**draw blood**(検査のため血管から) ‖ **採血車** a bloodmobile.

³さいけつ 裁決 a **decision**(判断，決定)；a **judgment** (判決；judgement ともつづる).

さいげつ 歳月 ▶家を出てから10年の歳月が流れた *Ten years* have passed since I left home.

ことわざ 歳月人を待たず Time and tide wait for no man. (➤ 英語のことわざ；tide は「時期，季節」の意の古風な語).

¹さいけん 再建 rebuilding, reconstruction (➤ 後者は大きな建物のイメージが強い) **一動 再建する rebuild** +㊐, **reconstruct** +㊐；**reestablish** +㊐ (復興する) ▶会社を再建する *rebuild* [*reconstruct* ／ *reestablish*] a company ‖ 金閣寺は火災後再建された Kinkakuji Temple *was rebuilt* after a fire.

²さいけん 債券 a **bond**(公債)；a **debenture** (社債) ‖ **不良債券** a bad loan.

³さいけん 債権 a **credit** ‖ **債権国** a creditor nation ‖ **債権者** a creditor ‖ **債権放棄** debt forgiveness. (→債務).

¹さいげん 際限 a **limit**；an **end**(終わり) ▶人の欲望には際限がない Human desire *knows no limit*. ／ *There's no limit* to human desire. ‖ 議論は際限なく続いた The argument went on *endlessly*. ／ There was *no end* to the argument. ‖ その学者は際限なくしゃべり続けた The scholar talked *on and on*.

²さいげん 再現 (a) **reproduction 一動 再現する reproduce** +㊐ ▶忠実な色の再現 faithful color *reproduction* ‖ 過去の事件の再現 *the reenactment* of a past event ‖ 2人の対決はこの前のオリンピックにおける試合の再現だった The showdown between the two turned out to be *a replay* of their match in the last Olympics. (➤ replay は「再試合」).

ざいげん 財源 financial resources ▶この有名な温泉が地域の財源(＝収入源)だ This famous hot spring is *a source of income* for this district.

さいけんとう 再検討 (a) **review**(再吟味)；(a) **reexamination**(再検査) ▶校則を再検討する *review* the school regulations ‖ 彼らの提案は再検討する必要がある We need to *reexamine* their proposal.

さいこ 最古の (the) oldest ▶北海高校は北海道で最古の高校の1つです Hokkai High School is one of *the oldest* high schools in Hokkaido.

¹さいご 最後 1【いちばん終わり】the last；**the end** (終わり) **一形 最後の (the) last**；**final** (最終的な)

▶徳川最後の将軍 *the last* Tokugawa shogun ‖ 飛行機からの通信はそれが最後だった That was *the last* transmission (received) from the airplane. ‖ あなたにお会いできるのもこれが最後かもしれないわね This may be *the last time* I'll be able to see you. ‖ 対話「理恵さんは何番目に歌うの？」「最後から2番目だよ」"When (in the program) does Rie sing?" "She sings *second to last*."

▶彼と最後に会ったのは3年前だ It was three years ago that I saw him *last* [*for the last time*]. (➤ for the last time は「彼はその後死んだ」または「彼とはその後別れた」の含みになる) ‖ 歌手はコンサートの最後に聴衆とともに自分のヒット曲を歌った *At the end* of his concert, the singer sang his hit numbers along with the audience.

▶こつこつ勉強した者が最後には勝つんだ Those who study diligently will win *in the end* [*in the long run*]. (➤ 後者は「長い目で見れば」) ‖ 最後に皆さんのご多幸とご健康をお祈りして私の話を終わります I would like to *conclude* my speech by wishing all of you happiness and good health. (➤「締めくくる」の意の conclude が「最後に」の意を兼ねている) ‖ 最後の頑張りが勝利につながると思うよ Your *final* [*last-minute*] *efforts* will lead you to victory. (➤

last-minute は「土壇場の」).
▶その映画の最後はどうなるの？ *How* does the movie *end*？‖その映画はおもしろくなかったので最後までは見なかった The movie wasn't interesting, so I didn't see it *to the end*.‖私の言うことを最後まで聞きなさい *Hear* me *out*！‖私は最後の最後まで諦めないよ I will never give up *until the very* [*bitter*] *end*.
2【慣用表現】▶上司に嫌われたら最後だよ If you get on your boss's bad side, it will *be the end* of your career. (➤ get on ~'s bad side は「～に嫌われる」)‖ふさ子は話しだしたら最後，いつまでたっても止まらない *Once* Fusako starts talking, she never stops.

2**さいご 最期** one's **end** ▶彼は最期が近い He's near *his end*.‖スコットは南極探検で壮絶な最期を遂げた Scott met a brave *end* [died a heroic *death*] on his Antarctic expedition.‖私たちは昨夜祖父の最期をみとった We *were with* our grandfather *when he died* last night.

ざいこ 在庫 stock；a **stockpile**(山積みの) ▶ 対話「この本は在庫がありますか」「申し訳ありません．今，在庫切れになっておりまして」"Is this book still *in stock*?" "I'm sorry, sir [ma'am]. It is *no longer in stock*."
‖**在庫一掃セール** a clearance sale‖**在庫品** goods in stock, inventory.

1**さいこう 再考** ▶この問題は再考を要する This matter *needs to be reconsidered*.‖この企画全体を再考したほうがよいと思う I suggest we (should) *rethink* the whole plan.‖あなたの再考を促したい I urge you to *reconsider your decision*.

2**さいこう 最高** **1【いちばん高い［良い，多い］】(the) highest**；**(the) best**
▶キリマンジャロはアフリカで最高の山だ Kilimanjaro is *the highest* mountain in Africa.‖彼の最新作はこれまでで最高の出来栄えだ His latest novel is his *best* ever.‖万博はきょうが最高の人出だった *A record number of* people visited the Expo today.‖本日の最高気温は8度でした *Today's high* was 8 degrees. (➤天気概況のアナウンス)‖数学の最高点は誰が取ったの？ Who got *the highest score* [*mark*] in mathematics?‖彼女が100メートルの最高記録を持っている She holds *the* (*best*) *record* in the 100-meter dash.‖東名高速道路の最高制限速度は時速100キロだ *The maximum speed limit* on the Tomei Expressway is 100 kilometers per hour.
2【すばらしい】great, terrific, superb /supə́ːrb/
▶風呂上がりの冷たい麦茶．ああ最高！A glass of cold barley tea after a bath really *hits the spot* [*tastes great*]！／Ah, *there's nothing like* a glass of cold barley tea after a bath.‖そのバンドのニューアルバムは最高だ The latest album of that band is *awesome* [*superb*].‖あのレストランの料理，最高だぜ The food at that restaurant *is truly top-notch* [*out of this world*].‖彼女，サイコーだね She's *awesome*！‖最高に楽しい I'm having *the greatest* time.‖彼女，最高に幸せそうな顔をしていたぜ She looked as if she *was on cloud nine*. (➤be on cloud nine は「とても幸せな気分である」)‖ 対話「どう，調子は」「最高さ」"How's everything?" "*Couldn't be better.*／*Nothing could be better.*"

3**さいこう 再興 revival** 一動 **再興する revive** ＋目
▶浅野家の家臣たちはお家の再興を願った The Asano clan retainers hoped for the *revival* of the (Asano) clan.

4**さいこう 採光** ▶採光のいい部屋 a room that *gets plenty of* (*sun*)*light*‖私の部屋は窓が大きいので採光がよい My room *is light* with large windows.／My room *gets a lot of sunlight* thanks to the large windows.

ざいこう 在校 **1【学内にいること】**▶校長先生はご在校ですか *Is* the principal *at school*?
2【籍があること】▶この学校の在校生は何名ですか How many *students are enrolled in* this school?‖**在校生送辞** the farewell speech from the lower grades《参考》卒業式などで卒業生(a graduating student)と区別する場合の「在校生」は non-graduate student という．

さいこうさい(ばんしょ) 最高裁(判所) the Supreme Court‖**最高検察庁** the Supreme Public Prosecutors' Office‖**最高裁長官** the Chief Justice of the Supreme Court.

さいこうちょう 最高潮 a **climax, the peak** ▶4番打者が満塁ホームランを放って，試合は最高潮に達した The game *came to a climax* when the cleanup batter blasted a grand slam.‖日本チームが金メダルを取って観衆の興奮は最高潮に達した When the Japanese team won the gold medal, the excitement of the spectators *was at its peak*.

さいこうふ 再交付 a **reissue** 一動 **再交付する reissue** ＋目.

さいこうほう 最高峰 the highest mountain(いちばん高い山) ▶クック山はニュージーランドの最高峰だ Mount Cook is *the highest mountain* in New Zealand.
▶《比喩的》彼は現代画壇の最高峰だ He is *the greatest of all* painters today.‖『戦争と平和』は世界文学の最高峰の1つだ "War and Peace" is one of *the greatest masterpieces* of world literature.

さいごつうちょう 最後通牒 an **ultimatum** /ʌ̀ltɪméɪṭəm/ ▶反乱軍に最後通牒を出す issue *an ultimatum* to the rebel army.

さいころ a **die** [複 **dice**]《参考》さいころは通例2個一緒に用いるので複数形を多く使う．《英》では die は古語で単数形も dice を用いる ▶さいころを振るのは誰の番だ Whose turn is it to *throw* [*cast*] *the dice*?

さいこん 再婚 a **second marriage** 一動 **再婚する remarry, marry again** ▶彼女は子供たちのために再婚することにした She decided to *remarry* [*marry again*] for the sake of the children.

さいさき 幸先 ▶ヤクルトはジャイアンツを3対0で破り，幸先よいスタートを切った The Swallows *made a good start* by beating the Giants 3-0.

1**さいさん 再三** ▶子供たちは私が再三再四警告したにもかかわらずその池で泳いだ The children swam in that pond though I *repeatedly* cautioned them not to.

2**さいさん 採算 profit**(利益) ▶採算を度外視して売る sell without regard for *profit*‖この企画は採算が取れないかもしれない This project may not *pay off*.‖この事業を採算の取れるものに育てなければならない We must develop this business into a *profitable* venture.

ざいさん 財産 (a) **property**(主に不動産；Ⓒ扱いにすると具体的な「地所・土地(建物)」)；a **fortune** (ばく大な財産)；**wealth** (富)
▶国の財産 national [state-owned] *property*‖あの実業家には数十億円の財産がある That businessman has *property* worth billions of yen.‖彼は財産目当てに彼女と結婚した He married her *for her money* [*fortune*].‖ビル・ゲイツはコンピュータソフト

で一財産作った Bill Gates *made a fortune* on computer software. ‖ 彼は財産と名声の両方とも失ってしまった He has lost both his *wealth* and his fame. ‖ 私の全財産は850円だ *All I have* is 850 yen. ▶《比喩的》わが社の最大の財産は人だ Our company's greatest *asset* is its people.

‖財産家 a wealthy [rich] person, a person of means ‖財産管理人 a custodian (債務者全体の利益を代表する); a guardian (後見人).

さいし 妻子 one's **wife and child** [**children**] ▶家では妻子が待っている My *wife and child* [*children*] are waiting for me at home. ‖ 私は妻子(＝家族)を食べさせていかねばならない I have to support my *family*. ／I have *a family* to support. ‖ 彼女は妻子ある男と不倫している She's been having an affair with *a married man with a family*.

さいじき 歳時記 ***saijiki***; a collection of seasonal phrases(➤ 説明的な訳).

さいしけん 再試験 a **makeup exam** ▶私, あした再試験を１つ受けないといけないんだ I've got to take *a makeup exam* tomorrow.

さいじじょう 催事場 a **room for special events**(特別催し物会場); a **multi-purpose floor** [**room**／**space**] (多機能型催し会場).

さいじつ 祭日 a **holiday**; a **national holiday** (国の); a **festival day** (神社の).

ざいしつ 材質 ▶この床は材質の悪い[良い]木が使ってある The *quality of the wood* used in this floor is poor [good]. ‖ 職人は材質によって木を使い分ける Craftspeople choose the type of wood that is most suitable in terms of its *properties*. ‖ スピーカーは木の材質によって音が大幅に変わる Speaker sound (quality) varies greatly according to *the characteristics* [*properties*] *of the wood used*.

さいして 際して on, when (➤ 前者には通例動名詞, 後者には節が続く) ▶記念碑の除幕に際して市長の挨拶があった The mayor gave a speech *on* [*upon*] unveiling the monument. ‖ 誰かの逝去に際して何を言うかは判断が難しい It's difficult to decide what to say *when* someone passes away. ‖ 緊急事態に際しては諸君は敏速に行動しなければならない *In case of* emergency, you (all) must act promptly.

さいしゅ 採取する take ＋㊐ ▶血液を採取する *take* blood (→採血) ‖ コップから指紋を採取する *lift* some fingerprints from a glass／fingerprint a glass.

1**さいしゅう 採集 collection** 一㊍ **採集する collect** ＋㊐ (注意深く選んで集める); **gather** ＋㊐ (１か所にかき集める) ▶昆虫を採集する *collect* insects ‖ 貝殻を採集する *gather* sea shells ‖ この地域では高山植物の採集は禁じられている *Gathering* [*Picking*] alpine plants is prohibited in this area.

2**さいしゅう 最終の (the) last** (いちばんあとの); **(the) final** (最終的な)

▶今すぐ行けば最終のバスに間に合う You can catch *the last* bus if you leave right away. ‖ きょうが展覧会の最終日だ Today is *the last day* of the exhibition. ‖ 野球の試合は最終回に入った The ball game is now in its *final inning*. (➤ 連続ドラマや読み物などの最終回は the last installment という) ‖ 最終的には彼女もオーケーするだろう She'll give me the OK *in the end*. ‖ 最終的にメリーはトムのプロポーズを受け入れた Mary *eventually* accepted Tom's proposal (of marriage). ‖ 学校での最終責任は校長にある *The ultimate responsibility* at school lies with the principal.

‖(ごみの)最終処分場 a final disposal site.

ざいじゅう 在住する reside 《in》, **live** 《in》(➤ 後者は「住む」に相当) ▶ロンドン在住の日本人 a Japanese *resident in* London／a Japanese *living in* London.

さいしゅうしょく 再就職 ▶彼はその会社を辞めてから高校の英語教師として再就職した After quitting that company, he *got a job* as an English teacher at a senior high school. (🔘「～を辞めてから」と言っているので,「再」は訳出不要).

さいしゅつ 歳出 (annual) expenditure ▶歳出を削減する cut *expenditure(s)*.

さいしゅっぱつ 再出発する make a fresh [**new**] **start, start afresh** ▶きょうから新しい職場, 心機一転, 再出発です Now that I've begun to work at a new place starting today, I'd like to (turn over a new leaf and) *make a fresh start*. (➤ 後半を I'd like to make a fresh start with renewed determination. とすることもできる).

さいしょ 最初 **the beginning** 一㊋ **最初の (the) first**

▶私が飛行機で旅行をしたのはそれが最初だった It was *my first time* to fly [to travel by plane]. ‖ 最初に札幌に行き, それから根室に行った I went to Sapporo *first*, and then (on) to Nemuro. ‖ あのときがぼくにとって最初の北海道旅行だった That was my *first* trip to Hokkaido. ‖ 里谷選手は冬季オリンピックで金メダルを取った最初の日本人女性だ Satoya was *the first* Japanese woman to win a gold medal in the Winter Olympics. ‖ 最初は冗談かと思ったが彼は本気だった *At first* I thought he was joking, but it turned out that he was serious. (➤ at first はあとで状況などが変化したことを表す).

▶最初からもう一度歌いなさい Sing (the song) *from the beginning* (again). ‖ 最初から(＝やる前から)諦めてはだめよ Don't give up *before you try*. ‖ これはうまくいかないだろうって最初から言っただろう I told you *from day one* that this would never work. ‖ 最初からやり直しだ It's back to *square one*. ‖ その映画を見て私は最初から最後まで泣きっぱなしだった That movie made me cry *from beginning to end*. ‖ 私たちは最初はうまくいっていたのだが, すぐに口論をするようになった *Things started off well*, but we soon began to quarrel. ‖ ことわざ 最初が肝心 A good beginning is what matters.／A good beginning makes a good ending. (➤ ともに日本語からの意訳).

さいじょ 才女 a **talented** [**an intelligent**] **woman**; a **woman of ability**(有能な女性).

1**さいしょう 宰相** a **prime minister**.

2**さいしょう 最小の (the) smallest** ▶最小の数 *the smallest* number ‖ 世界最小の鳥 *the smallest* (species of) bird in the world. ‖最小公倍数 the least common multiple《略 L.C.M.》.

3**さいしょう 最少の (the) least** ▶最少の努力で最高のものを得るようにしなさい Try to get the most with *the least* effort. ‖ きょうのゴルフでは彼が最少得点者だ He had *the lowest* [*the best*] *score* in today's golf game.

1**さいじょう 斎場** a **funeral hall**.

2**さいじょう 最上の (the) best** (いちばん良い); **(the) top** (いちばん上の) ▶それが最上の方法だ That is *the best* way. ‖ これは最上の生地だ This is *the finest* cloth you can find. ‖ 事務所は最上階にあります My office is on *the top floor*. ‖ 彼は最上級のことばを使

ってておおげさに話した He talked in *superlatives*.
‖《文法》**最上級** the superlative (degree).

ざいじょう 罪状 ▶**罪状を認める**［**否認する**］*plead guilty* [*not guilty*] ／*enter a* [*not*] *guilty plea*.
‖**罪状認否** arraignment.

さいしょうげん 最小限 a［the］**minimum** ▶損害を**最小限に食い止める**ことが大事だ It is important to *keep* damage *to a minimum*. ／It is important to *minimize* damage. ‖**最小限**（＝せめて）これだけは言っておきたい I want to say this, *at least*.

さいしょく 菜食 a **vegetarian**［**vegetable**］**diet** ▶彼女は健康のために**菜食**を続けている She is on *a vegetarian diet* for her health. ‖彼女は（厳格な）**菜食主義者**だ She is *a* (strict) *vegetarian*. (➤ 肉・魚のほかに卵・チーズ・牛乳などもとらない徹底した菜食主義者を a vegan /víːgən/ という).
‖**菜食主義** vegetarianism.

ざいしょく 在職 ▶彼の市長**在職**は３期にわたった（＝３期務めた）He *served* three terms as mayor. ‖安倍氏は首相**在職中**にアメリカを数回訪問した Mr. Abe visited the U.S. several times *during his tenure* as prime minister. ‖**在職中**は大変お世話になりました Thank you very much for everything you did for me *while I was in office*. (➤ in office は官職の場合).

さいしょくけんび 才色兼備 ▶確かに彼女は**才色兼備**だが, 少々てんぐになり過ぎている She is *both intelligent and beautiful*, but she is too proud of it.

1**さいしん 最新の the latest**（最近の）; **the newest**（いちばん新しい）; **the most up-to-date**（いちばん新しいものに更新した）▶**最新の**流行 *the latest* [*newest*] fashion ‖**最新（の）**情報［技術］*the most up-to-date* information [technology] ‖ただ今, **最新の**ニュースが入りました *The latest* [*breaking*] news has just come (in). ‖彼女は**最新型の** BMW を運転していた She was driving *the latest* model BMW.

2**さいしん 再審** (a) **retrial** /rìːtráɪəl/ ▶その政治家は**再審**で有罪となった The politician was found guilty in *a retrial*. ‖最高裁は**再審**を命じた The Supreme Court ordered *a retrial*.
‖**再審請求** a petition for retrial.

3**さいしん 細心の careful**（注意深い）; **meticulous**（入念な）▶**細心の**注意 *careful* [*meticulous*] attention ‖車を運転するときは**細心の注意を払い**なさい You must *be very careful* when you drive (a car).

4**さいしん 再診** a **repeat visit** ▶**再診の**患者 a (*previously*) *registered* patient.

サイズ (a) **size** ▶標準**サイズ** an average [a standard] *size* ‖L**サイズの**シャツ a *large-size*(*d*) [an *L-size*(*d*)] shirt ‖フライドポテトの L**サイズ** *large* French fries ‖**サイズを測る** take the *size* ‖**私の体に合うサイズの**ジーンズはありますか Could you show me some [Do you have] jeans *in my size*? ‖この靴は**サイズ**が１つ大きい［ぴったりだ］These shoes are one *size* too large for me [are just my *size*]. ‖どの**サイズ**でコピーしますか What *size* do you want your copies in? ／What *size* copies do you want?
▶彼女の（**体のスリー**）**サイズ**はバスト84, ウエスト62, ヒップ88だ Her *measurements* [*vital statistics*] are 84-62-88. (➤ 後者は前者をおどけて言ったもの).

ざいす 座椅子 a ***zaisu***; a seat with a back but no legs (➤ 説明的な訳).

さいすん 採寸する take a person's **measurements** ▶**採寸して**もらえますか Could you *measure* me? ／Could you *take my measurements*?

さいせい 再生 1【新たにできる】▶トカゲのしっぽは切れても**再生する** A lizard's tail *grows back* [*regenerates*] if (it is) cut off.
2【再び使うこと】**recycling** 一動 **再生する recycle** ＋目 ▶ガラス瓶は**再生利用できる** Glass bottles *can be recycled*. ‖**再生医療** regenerative medicine ‖**再生可能エネルギー** renewable energy ‖**再生紙** recycled paper.
3【プレーバック】a **playback** 一動 **再生する play (back)** ▶そのユーチューブ動画は**再生回数**が100万回を超えている The YouTube video *has* over a million *views* [*hits*]. ‖前の晩に録画した映画を**再生して見た** I *played* (*back*) the movie (I had) recorded the previous night.
‖**再生装置** playback equipment（録音・録画の）.

ざいせい 財政 finance /fáɪnæns/ ▶その市の**財政**は健全だ The city's *finances* are sound. (➤「財政状態」の意のときは複数形にする) ‖県の**財政はひっ迫している** The prefecture is *under financial pressure*. ‖彼の会社はまもなく**財政危機**に陥った His company soon fell into *financial troubles* [found itself in *a financial crisis*]. ‖**財政学** (public) finance ‖**財政政策** a fiscal policy（政府主導の）‖**緊縮財政** fiscal austerity.

さいせいき 最盛期 the golden age（黄金時代）; **the season**（出盛り）▶大英帝国の**最盛期**はビクトリア女王の治世であった *The golden age* of the British Empire was during the reign of Queen Victoria. ‖ブドウは今が**最盛期**だ This is *the* grape *season*. ／Grapes are now *in season*.

さいせいさん 再生産 reproduction.

1**ざいせき 在籍** ▶うちの学校には2000人以上の生徒が**在籍しています** Over 2,000 students *are enrolled* in our school. ‖４月１日現在, 本校**在籍の生徒**は1200名です As of April 1, we have *an enrollment* of 1,200 (students). (➤ enrollment は「在学者総数」).
‖**在籍証明書** a certificate of (student) registration, a student registration certificate（学校の）; a membership certificate（団体などの）.

2**ざいせき 在席** ▶ **対話**《電話で》「吉田さんは**ご在席**ですか」「申し訳ありません. ただ今外出中です」"Is Mr. Yoshida *at his desk*?" "I'm sorry, but he's out right now [at the moment]."

さいせきじょう 採石場 a **quarry** /kwɔ́ːri/.

1**さいせん 再選 reelection** 一動 **再選する reelect** ＋目 ▶彼女の委員長**再選**（＝再選されること）は確実だ It is certain that she will *be reelected* chair (person).

2**さいせん 賽銭** ▶神社に**さい銭をあげる** *make an offering of money* at a Shinto shrine.
‖**さい銭箱** an offertory chest [box].

さいぜん 最善の (**the**) **best** ▶ステージであがらない**最善の**方法は観客をカボチャやナスと思うことだ *The best* way not to get stage fright is to regard the audience as pumpkins or eggplants. ‖常に**最善を尽くせ** Always *do your best*!

さいぜんせん 最前線 the forefront ▶その若い兵士たちは戦闘の**最前線**にいた Those young soldiers were on *the front line* of the battle [were on the battle*front*]. ‖彼はがん研究の**最前線**にいる He is at *the forefront* of cancer research.

さいせんたん 最先端 the leading［**cutting**］**edge** 一形 **最先端の** (**the**) **latest**（最新の）; **state-ofthe-art**（技術・装置などが最新式の）▶日本は電気自動車の分

さ

野で最先端を行っている Japan *is a leader* in the field of electric cars. ‖ あの子は流行の最先端を行っている She follows *the latest fashion.* ‖ このロボットは最先端の技術を駆使して作られている This is a *state-of-the-art* robot. ／This is a *cutting-edge* robot.

さいぜんれつ 最前列 ▶その大講義室では最前列に座る学生はほとんどいなかった Hardly any students sat in *the first* [*front*] *row* in that lecture hall.

1**さいそく 催促する** **urge** /ə:ʳdʒ/ +目《to do》, **press** +目《to do》(➤ 前者のほうが相手を説得しようとする感じが強い) ▶その店は彼にたまった請求書の支払いを催促した The store *pressed* [*urged*] him *to* pay his overdue bill. ‖ 彼女はぼくにキスを催促した She *urged* me to kiss her. ‖ 彼は手紙を書いて父親に金を催促した He wrote his father a letter *asking for* money. ‖ 大家は彼に部屋を出ていくよう催促(＝要求)した The landlord *demanded* that he (should) leave the apartment. ‖ 彼は催促されるまで家賃を払わなかった He did not pay his rent till he *was urged* to do so. ‖ **催促状** a reminder.

2**さいそく 最速** ▶世界最速のコンピュータ *the fastest* computer in the world.

3**さいそく 細則** **detailed regulation.**

さいた 最多の **(the) most** ▶彼はオールスターゲーム最多出場を果たした He has made *the most appearances* in all-star games.

サイダー (→かこみ記事)

危ないカタカナ語✹ サイダー

1 英語の cider /sáidəʳ/ からきているが, cider は《米》ではリンゴジュースを指す(soft cider とも言う). また《英》ではリンゴ酒(hard cider とも言う)の意味で使われ, 日本では「シードル」の名で売られている. いずれもいわゆる「サイダー」とは別物.

2 日本の「サイダー」に一致するものはないが, 味の点で近いものに Sprite や 7-UP がある(いずれも商品名). 一般的には soda (pop)(炭酸飲料)と言えばよい.

1**さいたい 妻帯** ▶妻帯者 a *married* man.

2**さいたい 臍帯** an **umbilical** /ʌmbílɪkəl/ **cord** (へその緒) ‖ **臍帯血** umbilical blood.

さいだい 最大(の) **(the) largest, (the) biggest** (最も大きな; 後者はインフォーマルな語で前者を誇張した言い方); **(the) greatest** (最も重大な[目立つ]); **(the) strongest** (最も威力のある); **(a, the) maximum** (最大限) ▶アジアで最大級のスポーツ施設 *the largest-scale* sports facility in Asia ‖ 今世紀最大の発見 *the greatest* discovery of this century ‖ オリンピックは世界最大のスポーツイベントだ The Olympics are *the world's biggest* [*largest*] sporting event. ‖ サッカーでブラジルの最大のライバルはアルゼンチンだ The Argentine soccer team is Brazil's *biggest* [*greatest*] *rival*. ‖ スペリオル湖は北米最大の湖だ Lake Superior is *the largest* lake in North America. ‖ ピカソは20世紀最大の画家の1人だ Picasso is [was] one of *the greatest* artists of the 20th century. ‖ これは私たちが経験したうちで最大の地震です This was *the strongest* earthquake (that) we've ever experienced.

‖ **最大公約数** the greatest common divisor《略 G.C.D.》‖ **最大(瞬間)風速** the maximum (instantaneous) wind speed.

さいだいげん 最大限 ▶こんなチャンスはめったにないから最大限に利用しなさい It is a chance in a million, so *make the most of* it. ‖ 何をするにも最大限の努力をすべきだ You should *make the greatest* [*maximum*] *effort* in whatever you do. ／You should *try your hardest* [*best*] no matter what you do. ‖ 彼らは初出場ながら, 持てる力を最大限に発揮してベスト4に残った Although it was their first appearance in the tournament, they *gave it all they had* and made it to the semifinals.

さいだいもらさず 細大漏らさず ▶彼女は日記にその日の出来事を細大漏らさず記入している She writes *in great* [*minute*] *detail* what has happened that day in her diary. (➤ 形容詞 minute /maɪnjú:t/ は「詳細な」).

さいたく 採択 **adoption** 一動 **採択する** **adopt** +目 ▶重役会はそのプランを採択した The board of directors *adopted* the plan.

ざいたく 在宅する **be at home** ▶あすはご在宅ですか Will you *be in* [*be at home*] tomorrow? ‖ コンピュータを利用して在宅勤務をする *work at home* with the aid of computers《参考》「コンピュータの端末を自宅に置いて会社の仕事をする人」を telecommuter や teleworker と言い, その場合の自宅を flexiplace という.

‖ **在宅医療** home medical care ‖ **在宅介護** home nursing care.

さいたる 最たる **prime** (第一の); **outstanding** (目立った) ▶子が親に先立つのは親不孝の最たるものだ A child's dying before his [her] parents is a *prime* example of not repaying the debt that is owed to (his [her]) parents.

さいたん 最短の **(the) shortest** ▶最短距離 *the shortest* distance ‖ 私たちは目的地までの最短コースを取った We took *the shortest route* to our destination. ‖ 線路の復旧には最短(＝少なくとも)1週間かかる It will take *at least* a week to restore rail service.

1**さいだん 裁断** **1**【布を裁つこと】**cutting** 一動 **裁断する** **cut** +目 ‖ **裁断機** a cutter.

2【判断】**(a) judgment** ▶この件は社長の裁断を仰ごうではないか Let's ask the president to *judge* [*decide on*] this matter, shall we?

2**さいだん 細断** ▶文書を細断する *cut* a document *into small pieces* ／ *shred* a document.

3**さいだん 祭壇** an **altar** /ɔ́:ltəʳ/ ▶祭壇を建てる erect [set up] an *altar* ‖ 祭壇に向かって礼をする bow toward an *altar* ‖ 祭壇に供え物をする make an offering at *the altar* ‖ 祭壇で祈る pray at *the altar*.

ざいだん 財団 a **foundation** ▶日本財団 the Japan *Foundation* ‖ **財団法人** a legally incorporated foundation.

さいちゅう 最中 ▶食事の最中にスマホをいじるのはやめなさい Stop using your smartphone *while* you're eating. ‖ その選手は試合の最中に倒れた The player fainted *in the middle of* the game [*while* (he was) playing the game]. ‖ オートバイは今修理の最中です My motorcycle *is being repaired* now.

ざいちゅう 在中 ▶《封筒の表示》写真[請求書]在中 *Photo(s)* [*Bill*] *enclosed* ／ *Enclosed : photo(s)* [*bill*] (➤ 単に Photos, Bill とするだけでもよい).

さいちょう 最長の **(the) longest** ▶日本最長の橋 *the longest* bridge in Japan ／ Japan's *longest* bridge.

1**さいてい 最低** 一形 **最低の** **(the) lowest** (最も低い); **(the) worst** (最悪の); **(the) minimum** (最小の)

▶その生徒は化学の試験ではクラスで最低点だった The student got *the lowest* score in class on the chemistry test. ‖息子を東京の大学にやるには**最低**(＝少なくとも)月15万はかかる Sending our son to college in Tokyo costs us *at least* 150,000 yen a month. ‖共同生活では**最低限**守るべき規則がある In communal living there are *minimum* rules that must be followed. ‖この試験の**最低合格点**は100点満点の50点です *The minimum passing score* in this examination is 50 out of 100. ‖この成績なら卒業に必要な**最低条件**を満たせるかもしれない With these grades, you may be able to meet *the minimum requirements* for graduation.

▶年寄りをだますなんてあいつは**最低**なやつだ He is *the lowest of the low* to have cheated senior citizens. ‖この1週間は本当に**最低**だった This past week was a total *disaster*. ‖あの先生, **サイテー**ね! That teacher's *the meanest of all*! ‖ 対話「調子はどうだい?」「**最低**だよ」"How are you doing?" "*Terrible.* / *Things couldn't be worse.*"

‖**最低価格**(＝底値) a rock-bottom price ‖**最低気温** the lowest temperature(➤ 放送などでは today's low のように言う) ‖**最低賃金** minimum wages ‖**最低料金** minimum charge [rate].

2**さいてい 裁定** a **decision**(一般に); a **ruling**(裁判の)

▶委員会の**裁定**には従わねばならない The committee's *decision* must be obeyed.

さいてき 最適の (the) **most suitable** (最もふさわしい); **perfect** (申し分ない); **optimum, optimal**(成長・繁殖にとって)

▶松田さんはきちょうめんなのでこの種の仕事には**最適**だ Since he is attentive to detail, Mr. Matsuda *is cut out for* [*is most suitable for*] this sort of work. (➤ be cut out for は「生来…にとても向いている」) ‖こちらはご贈答には**最適な**品々でございます These items would make *perfect* gifts. ‖彼女は校長には**最適の**人だ She is *just* the woman for principal. ‖バラのせんていに**最適な**時期 the *optimum* [*optimal*] time to prune a rose tree ‖ハードディスクを**最適化する** *optimize* [*defragment*] a hard disk (drive) (➤ 後者は「断片化を解消し, 再配置する」).

‖《言語学》**最適性理論** Optimality Theory.

ざいテク 財テク **money management** ▶**財テク**で上手に資産を殖やす increase one's assets by skillful *money management*.

1**さいてん 採点** 《主に米》**grading**, 《主に英》**marking** 一 動 **採点する grade** ＋目, **mark** ＋目 ▶先生方は答案の**採点**で忙しい Our teachers are busy *grading* [*marking*] the exam papers. ‖あの英語の先生は**採点が甘い** That English teacher *is an easy grader* [*marker*]. (➤「辛い」の場合は hard grader) ‖答案は20点満点で**採点した** I *graded* [*marked*] the (exam) papers on a 20-point basis.

‖**採点簿** a grade [mark] book.

2**さいてん 祭典** a **festival** ▶音楽の**祭典** a music *festival* ‖若人の**祭典** *a festival* for young people.

サイト 《インターネット》a **site**, a **website** [**web site**] ▶人気ロックグループの公式**サイト**にアクセスする go to the official *site* of a popular rock group ‖**サイトを立ち上げる**[**公開する**] set up [open] *a site* ‖おもしろい**サイト**を見つける find an interesting *site*.

さいど 再度 **again**(もう一度) ▶K大学に**再度**挑戦してみるつもりだ I am going to try to pass the entrance examination for K University *again*. (➤「2回目」の場合は, again を使わずに I am going to make a second attempt to pass ... としてもよい).

サイド ‖**サイドカー** a sidecar ‖**サイドスロー**《野球》sidearm throw [delivery] ‖**サイドテーブル** a side table ‖**サイドビジネス** a side business, (a) business on the side, a sideline ‖**サイドブレーキ** a hand brake, a parking brake, an emergency brake ‖**サイドボード** a sideboard ‖**サイドミラー** a sideview mirror, 《英また》a wing mirror 《参考》side mirror は sideview mirror ほどには使われない. door mirror ということもあるが, やはり一般的ではない.

さいどく 再読する **read again** ▶**再読**してみて初めてこの本のよさがわかった I didn't find this book of any value until I *read* it *again* [*reread* it].

さいなむ 苛む **torture** (**mentally or spiritually**)

▶私は罪の意識に**さいなまれている** I *am tortured* by remorse for my crime.

さいなん 災難 a **misfortune**(不幸); **bad luck** (不運); a **disaster** (大災害); an **accident**(事故)

▶とんだ**災難**に遭った I met (with) an unexpected *accident*. ‖私はちょうど家を留守にしていたので危うく**災難**を免れた I narrowly escaped the *disaster*, because I was away from home when it happened. ‖彼はあれ以来**災難続き**だ Ever since (that), he has had *a series of misfortunes* [*a run of bad luck*]. ‖ 対話「階段から落っこって眼鏡を壊しちゃったよ」「それは**災難**だったね(＝大変だったね)」"I fell down the stairs and broke my glasses." "*What a bummer* [*mishap*]!"

ざいにち 在日 ▶**在日**韓国人 a South Korean *living in Japan* / a South Korean citizen [national] *living* [*residing*] *in Japan* ‖**在日**アメリカ人 an American *living in Japan* / a U.S. citizen [national] *living* [*residing*] *in Japan* ‖**在日**米軍 the U.S. forces *in Japan*.

さいにゅう 歳入 (**annual**) **revenue**.

さいにゅうこく 再入国 **reentry** (to Japan)(日本への).

さいにん 再任 ▶井上氏が議長に**再任された** Mr. Inoue *was reappointed* chairperson.

ざいにん 罪人 a **criminal**(犯罪者); a **sinner**(道徳上・宗教上の).

さいにんしき 再認識 ▶海外を旅行してみれば日本がどんなにせわしない国か**再認識する**ことでしょう If you travel overseas, you will *come to realize* [*fully recognize*] how hectic life is in Japan.

さいねん 再燃する ▶彼の不用意な発言によって人種間の緊張が**再燃した** His careless remark *rekindled* racial tensions. (➤ rekindle は「…に再び火をつける」).

さいねんしょう 最年少の (**the**) **youngest** ▶彼はチームで**最年少**だがいちばん頼りになる Although he's *the youngest* on the team, he's the one we depend on (the) most.

さいねんちょう 最年長の (**the**) **oldest** ▶立候補者の中では森氏が**最年長**だ Mr. Mori is *the oldest* of the candidates.

さいのう 才能

(a) **talent** (持って生まれた能力); a **gift** (天分); **aptitude** (適性); **ability** (能力; 努力によって伸ばすことができる); (a) **facility**(もの覚えのよさ, 器用さ)

▶**才能**のある人 a person *of talent* / a *gifted* person / a person *of ability* [*abilities*] (➤ しばしば複数形で用いられる) ‖歌の**才能** *an ability* to sing ‖彼は音楽の**才能**がある He has *a talent* [*a gift* / *an aptitude*] for music. ‖彼女には本当に語学の**才能**がある She has great [real] *ability* in learning languages. / She has a great [real] *facility* for (learning) languages. ‖ 息子は絵の**才能がある**ようだ My son seems to *be talented* [*be gifted*] in painting. ‖ 彼女は娘のバレエの**才能を伸ばす**ためフランスへ留学させた She sent her daughter to France to (study and) *develop her talent* for ballet.

さいのかわら 賽の河原 ***Sai-no Kawara*** ; **the shores of the Sanzu River.**

さいのめ さいの目 ▶ジャガイモを**さいの目に切る** *dice* [*cube*] a potato.

サイバー **cyber** ‖ **サイバー攻撃** a cyberattack, a cyberassault ‖ **サイバースペース** cyberspace ‖ **サイバーセキュリティ** cybersecurity ‖ **サイバーテロ** cyberterrorism ‖ **サイバーテロ対策** measures against cyberterrorism.

さいはい 采配 ▶岸さんがこの仕事の**采配を振っている** Mr. Kishi *is running the show* [*is in control*] on this job. (➤ run the show は「切り盛りする」) ‖ きょうの試合は監督の**采配ミス**で負けた Today's game was lost due to *poor instructions* from the manager.

さいばい 栽培 **cultivation, culture** 一動 **栽培する** **grow** +目, **raise** /reɪz/ +目, **cultivate** +目 (➤ この順に堅い語になる) ▶母は庭でバラを**栽培している** My mother *grows* [*takes care of*] roses in the garden. ‖ 彼らはビニールハウスで野菜を**栽培している** They *grow* [*raise*] vegetables in a plastic greenhouse. ‖ この地域では茶が盛んに**栽培されている** Tea *is* widely *cultivated* in this district.

‖ **水栽培** water culture, hydroponics.

☛ **促成栽培** (→見出語)

さいはつ 再発する **recur** /rɪkə́ːʳ/ (病気・問題などが) ; **relapse** (病気が悪化する) ▶その種の原発事故は**再発する**おそれがある There is a possibility of that sort of nuclear accident *recurring* [*happening again*]. ‖ 持病の腰痛が**再発した** I *have had a return* [*a relapse* / *another attack*] of my old problem with lower back pain. ‖ がんの**再発** *a recurrence* of one's cancer.

ざいばつ 財閥 a **zaibatsu** (➤ 英語化している) ; a **financial conglomerate** (➤conglomerate /kənglɑ́ːmərət/ は「複合企業」の意) ▶住友**財閥** the Sumitomo *financial conglomerate*.

さいはっけん 再発見する **rediscover** +目 ▶最近ジャズの楽しさを**再発見している** I've recently been *rediscovering* the pleasure of jazz.

さいはて 最果て ▶北海道の**最果て**にはまだ原生林が残っている Virgin [Primeval] forests still remain in the *farthest reaches* of Hokkaido.

1 **さいはん 再犯** a **second** [**subsequent**] **offense**

‖ **再犯者** a repeat offender ‖ **再犯率** a recidivism rate.

2 **さいはん 再版** **the second edition** ; a **reissue** (再発行).

さいばん 裁判 (a) **judgment** (審判 ; 判決) ; a **trial** /tráɪəl/ (公判) ▶事件を**裁判にかける** *take* a matter *to court* (➤ court は「法廷」) ‖ **裁判に勝つ** [**負ける**] win [lose] *a suit* (➤ suit は「訴訟」) ‖ **裁判**は公平でなければならない *Judgment* [*A trial*] must be impartial. ‖ **裁判**(**の結果** [**判決**])はどうでしたか What was the *judgment* [the *verdict*]? (➤ verdict は「(陪審員による)評決」) ‖ その事件は目下**裁判中**です The case is *on trial* now. ‖ そのもめ事は**裁判沙汰に**なった The dispute *was put on trial* [*was taken to court*]. ‖ その件は**裁判**で争うことになった The case went to *trial*.

‖ **裁判員制度** a citizen [lay] judge system ‖ **裁判官** a judge, a justice (➤ 後者は《英》では高等法院判事, また《米》では最高裁判所判事を指す) ‖ **裁判長** the presiding /prɪzáɪdɪŋ/ judge, the chief justice.

> **逆引き熟語 ○○裁判**
> **簡易裁判** a brief trail, a summary proceeding / **軍事裁判** a military [war] trial / **刑事裁判** a criminal trial / **公開裁判** an open [a public] trial / **弾劾裁判** an impeachment trial / **つるし上げ裁判** a kangaroo court / **非公開裁判** a closed (-door) trial / **見せしめ裁判** a show trial / **民事裁判** a civil trial / **模擬裁判** a mock trial

さいばんしょ 裁判所 a **(law) court** (法廷) ; a **courthouse** (建物)

‖ **家庭裁判所** a family court, a domestic relations court ‖ **簡易裁判所** a summary court ‖ **高等裁判所** a high court ‖ **国際刑事裁判所** the International Criminal Court ‖ **最高裁判所** the Supreme Court (➤「最高裁判所長官」は the Chief Justice of the Supreme Court) ‖ **地方裁判所** a district court.

さいひ 採否 ▶あなたの**採否**は追ってご連絡します We will notify you later of *our decision on your application*. ‖ その案の**採否**は社長が決める Our (company) president will decide *whether or not to adopt the plan*.

さいひょうか 再評価 **reevaluation** ; **reassessment** (再査定) 一動 **再評価する** **reevaluate** +目, **reassess** +目 ▶彼の科学上の業績は**再評価されて**しかるべきだ His scientific achievements should *be reevaluated* [*reassessed*].

さいひょうせん 砕氷船 an **icebreaker.**

さいふ 財布 a **wallet,** 《米また》 a **billfold** (札入れ) ; a **coin** [**change**] **purse** (小銭入れ)

wallet

coin purse

▶満員電車の中で**財布**を盗まれた I had my *wallet* stolen [My *wallet* was stolen] on the jampacked train. ‖ **財布**が軽けりゃ気が重い A light *purse* makes a heavy heart. (➤ 英語のことわざ). ▶《慣用表現》うちではぼくが**財布のひもを握っている** I *hold the purse strings* in my family. ‖ きみは**財布のひもを締める**べきだ You should *tighten your purse strings* [*be more frugal*]. ‖ 当店では**お財布に優しい**ワインを各種取りそろえております We carry a wide range of wines that *are easy on the wallet*.

> **直訳の落とし穴「財布を忘れる」**
> 財布＝purse と覚えて,「家に財布を忘れた」のつもりで, I left my purse at home. などという男性の英語学習者がいる. purse は《米》では女性の持つ小さめのハンドバッグを指し,《英》では女性用の財布を指すので, He opened his purse ... などというと奇妙に響く. 札入れは wallet または,《米》billfold なので, I left my wallet [billfold] at home. とする. なお, coin purse (小銭入れ) は《米》でも通じる.

さいぶ 細部 **details**(➤ 通例複数形で用いる) ▶細部をおろそかにするな Pay attention to *details*. ‖この絵は細部まで丹念に描かれている Each *detail* of this picture is carefully painted. ‖美は細部に宿る Beauty lies in *the details*.

さいぶんか 細分化する **subdivide** +㊐ (分ける) ▶今の医学は非常に細分化している Medical science today *is* highly *specialized*. (➤「専門化している」の意).

さいへんせい 再編成 **reorganization**(組織換え) ; (a) **realignment** /rìːəláɪnmənt/ (組み直し) **━動 再編成する** **reorganize** +㊐ ▶政界再編成 a political *realignment* ‖監督は投手陣の再編成を迫られている The manager is being urged to *reorganize* his pitching staff.

さいほう 裁縫 **sewing** /sóʊɪŋ/ ; **needlework** (針仕事) ▶比呂は裁縫はとてもうまいが料理はだめだ Hiro is very good at *sewing* [*needlework*], but not (at) cooking. ‖**裁縫道具** a sewing set ‖**裁縫箱** a sewing box [basket].

さいぼう 細胞 a **cell** ▶人間の体は37兆の細胞からできているといわれている The human body is said to be made up of 37 trillion *cells*.
▶患者の胃のポリープからがん細胞が発見された *Cancerous cells* were found in a polyp in the patient's stomach.
‖**細胞分裂** cell division ‖**iPS細胞** an iPS cell (induced pluripotent stem cell の略) ‖**幹細胞** a stem cell ‖**単細胞** a single cell.

ざいほう 財宝 **treasure**(宝物) ▶埋蔵された財宝を探す look [search] for buried *treasure*.

さいほうそう 再放送 a **rebroadcast** ; a **repeat**, a **rerun** (➤あとの 2 語にはそれぞれ「(公演などの)再演」,「(映画の)再上映」の意もある).

サイボーグ a **cyborg** /sáɪbɔːʳg/.

サイホン a **siphon**.

さいまつ 歳末 **the year-end, the end of the year**
‖**歳末大売り出し** a year-end sale ‖**歳末助け合い運動** a year-end charity campaign [drive].

さいみつが 細密画 a **miniature**.

さいみんじゅつ 催眠術 **hypnotism** /hípnətìzəm/ ▶きみは催眠術にかかりやすいタイプだね You are the type that *is* easily *hypnotized*.
‖**催眠術師** a hypnotist.

さいむ 債務 a **debt** /det/ ; an **obligation**(法律上の)
‖**債務国** a debtor nation ‖**債務者** a debtor ‖**債務帳消し** debt forgiveness. (→債権).

ざいむ 財務 **financial matters**
‖**財務部** a financial division ‖**財務官** the Deputy Vice-Minister for Financial Affairs ‖**財務省** Ministry of Finance ; (米国)**財務省** the Department of the Treasury ‖**財務大臣** the Minister of Finance／the Finance Minister ‖(米国)**財務長官** the Secretary of Treasury.

さいもく 細目 **details**.

ざいもく 材木 **wood** ;《米》**lumber**,《英》**timber**(建築用に加工したもの)
‖**材木置き場**《米》a lumberyard,《英》a timberyard ‖**材木商** a lumber [《英》timber] dealer.

さいゆうしゅう 最優秀 ▶弟はT中学を最優秀の成績で卒業した My (younger) brother graduated from T Junior High School *with top honors*. ‖彼は4月の月間最優秀選手に選ばれた He was voted the monthly *MVP* for April. (➤ MVP は Most Valuable Player の略).
‖**最優秀新人賞** the Rookie of the Year Award /əwɔ́ːʳd/ ‖**最優秀選手賞** the Most Valuable Player Award.

さいゆうせん 最優先 ▶最優先課題 a *top-priority* issue ‖その問題を最優先させる give *the highest priority* to the issue.

さいよう 採用 **1【雇うこと】** **employment** **━動 採用する** **employ** +㊐,《米また》**hire** +㊐ ▶当社はことし大卒の学生を80名採用した Our company *hired* [*employed*] 80 college graduates this year. ‖彼女はX社の採用試験を受けたが, 採用されなかった She took *an employment test* for X Corporation, but *was not accepted* [*was turned down*].
‖**採用通知** (a) notification of employment.
2【取り上げること】 **adoption** **━動 採用する** **adopt** +㊐ ▶わが校では新しい教授法を採用することにした Our school decided to *adopt* a new teaching method.
▶この教科書は多くの学校で採用されている This textbook *is used* in many schools. (➤ adopt は一時的な行為を表し, 採用後は use を使う) ‖採用の詩には薄謝進呈 A small compensation will be awarded for any poem *used*.

さいらい 再来 ▶ウクレレブームの再来 *another* boom (of interest) in the ukulele ‖あの魅力的な映画スターはマリリン・モンローの再来と言われている That gorgeous movie star is said to be *a second* Marilyn Monroe. (➤「第二の…」と考える).

ざいらい 在来 ▶在来種のトマト *a native species of* tomato.
‖**在来線** a conventional [an old] railroad [railway] line ‖**在来工法** a traditional construction method.

ざいりゅう 在留する **live, stay** ‖(日本)**在留外国人** a foreign resident (in Japan).

さいりよう 再利用 **reuse** /rìjúːs/ ; **recycling** (再生利用) **━動 再利用する** **reuse** /rìjúːz/ +㊐, **recycle** +㊐ ▶空き缶を再利用する *reuse* [*recycle*] empty cans ‖たくさんの再利用できる製品がごみとして捨てられている A lot of products that *can be recycled* are thrown away as trash.

[1]**さいりょう 最良の** **(the) best** ▶英語を覚える最良の方法は何でしょうか？ What is *the best* way to learn English？
✉ **ことしがあなたにとって最良の年でありますように** I hope this will be *the best* year of your life.／I hope this year will be *your best* yet.

[2]**さいりょう 裁量** **discretion** /dɪskréʃən/ ▶その選択はきみの裁量に任せるよ I'll leave the selection up to your *discretion*.

ざいりょう 材料 **1【原料】** (a) **material** ; **ingredients** (料理用の) ▶材料費 *materials* cost ‖原材料 raw *materials* ‖建築材料 building *materials* ‖不安材料(＝原因) *a cause* for anxiety.
▶料理では良質の材料を使うことが大事だ In cooking, it is important that you use good-[high-]quality *ingredients*.
2【資料】 **data, material** ▶彼は新しい論文の材料集めのためにヨーロッパに滞在中です He is staying in Europe to collect *data and material* for his new thesis.

ざいりょく 財力 **financial power**,《米》**green power** ▶大手玩具メーカーが財力に物を言わせてわが社を乗っ取ろうとしている A large toy manufacturer is planning to take over our company *using its financial* *power* [*financial muscle*]. ‖ あの男性は財力に富んでいるといわれている That man is said to *have deep pockets*.

ザイル a (climbing) rope (➤「ザイル」はドイツ語の *Seil* から) ▶岩壁をザイルを使って登る[下りる] *rope up* [*down*] the wall ‖ 2人の登山家は体をザイルで結んでいた The two climbers *were on the* (*same*) *rope* [*were roped together*].

さいるいガス 催涙ガス tear /tɪəʳ/ gas ▶群衆に催涙ガスを発射する fire *tear gas* into the crowd.

さいるいだん 催涙弾 a tear gas grenade.

さいれい 祭礼 a festival.

サイレン a siren /sáɪrən/ ▶甲子園球場に決勝戦開始のサイレンが鳴り渡った The *siren* sounded the beginning of the final (game) at Koshien Stadium. ▶ゆうべはパトカーのサイレンで目が覚めた *A police siren* woke me last night.

サイレント ▶knife の k はサイレントだ The "k" in knife is *silent*. (➤ isn't pronounced でもよい).
‖**サイレント映画** a silent film [movie / picture] ‖**サイレントマジョリティー**(物言わぬ大衆) the silent majority.

サイロ a silo [複 silos] ▶穀物サイロ a grain *silo*.
‖**核ミサイルサイロ** a nuclear missile silo.

さいろく 採録する record +目(記録する); write down(書き留める) ▶沖縄の方言を採録する *record* Okinawa dialect.

さいわい 幸い **1**【幸せ】▶2, 3日中にお目にかかれれば幸いです *I would be happy* if we could meet in the next few days. ‖ 心の清い人たちは幸いである *Blessed* are those whose hearts are pure. / *Blessed* are the pure of [in] heart. (➤ 聖書のことば; blessed は「神の祝福を受けた」の意で, 発音は /blésɪd/).

✉ **本状に早めにお返事いただければ幸いです** *We would appreciate* [*be grateful for*] your prompt reply. / *We hope* to hear from you soon. ➤ 後者はインフォーマルな言い方.

2【幸運】一形 幸いな lucky, fortunate (➤ 前者はややインフォーマル) 一副 幸いに luckily, fortunately ▶再検査を告げられたが, 幸い何の異常もなかった I was told to have a reexamination, but *fortunately* nothing was wrong with me. ‖ 人生, 何が幸いするかわからない You can't tell what will *benefit* you in your life.
▶雨が降り出したが, 幸い折り畳みの傘を持って来ていた It started to rain, but *luckily* I had my folding umbrella with me.

1**サイン** **1**【署名】a signature /sígnətʃəʳ/ (書類・手紙などの); an autograph (有名人などからもらう) 一動 サインする sign, autograph
▶この書類にサインをしなければならない I must *sign* [*put my signature to*] these papers. ‖ 石川遼のサインをもらった I got Ryo Ishikawa's *autograph*. ‖ 《有名人に》サインしていただけますか May I have your *autograph*, please?
▶《会社で》これにサインをお願いします Could I have your *signature* on this, please? / Would you *sign* this, please?
‖(有名人の)サイン会 an autograph session ‖ **サインペン** a felt-tip pen.

2【合図】a sign, a signal ▶サインを受ける catch [get] *a sign* ‖ サインを見破る steal *a signal* ‖ 監督はランナーに「走れ」のサインを出した The manager *signaled* to [for] the runner to run.

> **危ないカタカナ語✸サイン**
> **1** 名詞の sign は「しるし, 兆候, (星座の)…座」の意味で,「署名」の意味はない. したがって,「サインしてください」のつもりで "Give me your sign." とすると,「あなたの星座を教えてください」の意にとられる可能性がある. なお, 動詞の「サインする」の意味では sign を使える.
> **2** 書類にする「サイン」は signature で, 有名人からもらう「サイン」は autograph という.「サイン帳」は autograph album [book],「サイン会」は autograph session,「サインボール」は autographed ball という.
> **3** 野球用語の「サイン」(合図)は sign または signal である. 数学用語の「サイン」(正弦)は sine とつづる別の語.

2**サイン** 《数学》a sine (略 sin).

サウジアラビア Saudi Arabia /sàʊdi əréɪbiə/
‖**サウジアラビア人** a Saudi.

サウスカロライナ South Carolina (アメリカの州; 略 SC, S.C.).

サウスダコタ South Dakota (アメリカの州; 略 SD, S. Dak., S.D.).

サウスポー a southpaw, a left-handed pitcher, a left-hander 《参考》southpaw は《英》ではふつう「左利きのボクサー」の意.

サウナ a sauna /sɔ́ːnə, sáʊnə/ ▶サウナ風呂に入る use [take] *a sauna*.

サウンド sound ‖**サウンドトラック** a sound track.

-さえ **1**【…ですら】even ▶先生でさえその問題は解けなかった *Even* the teacher could not solve the problem. ‖ 3か月たった今でさえその問題は未解決のままだ *Even* three months later, the problem remains unsolved. ‖ 自分の計画のことは(他人はもとより)妻にさえ言っていない I haven't told anyone about my plans, not *even* my wife.

2【さらに】besides ▶雨が降っているうえに風さえ出てきた It is raining, and *besides* [*on top of that*] it is getting windy. (➤ on top of that には「困ったことに」の意味が含まれるが, besides にはその含みはない).

3【ただ…ならば】▶医者がもっと早くがんを発見してさえいれば彼は死なずに済んだろうに *If only* the doctors had found his cancer earlier, he could have survived. ‖ 白でさえあればどんな花でも結構です Any flower will do, *as* [*so*] *long as* it is white. ‖ きみさえ OK ならぼくはいい It's O.K. by me *if* it's O.K. by you.

> **【文型】**
> (あなたは)…しさえすればよい
> **All you have to do is (to) do.**
> **You only have to do.**

▶あなたはただここにサインしさえすればよいのです *All you have to do is* (*to*) sign here. ‖ データを保存するにはこのボタンを押しさえすればよい *You only have to* [*All you have to do is* (*to*)] push this button to store (the) data.

さえき 差益 (a) gain(もうけ) ▶円高差益 exchange rate *gains* [*profits*] from the strong yen.

さえぎる 遮る **1**【見えなくする】block +目(妨げる); shut out(締め出す); screen(遮断する) ▶あの高い木々が視界を遮っている Those tall trees *block* [*obstruct*] the view. ‖ その高層アパートがうちに当たる日光を遮っている The tall apartment building *blocks* the sunlight from our house. ‖ 日差しは黒いカーテンで**遮られた** The sunlight *was shut out* by the black curtains. ‖ 有害な紫外線を**遮る** *screen* (*out*) harmful ultraviolet rays.

2【邪魔する】 **interrupt** +目 ▶話を**遮らず**, 最後まで聞いてください Don't *interrupt* me. Hear me out. ‖ きみの行く手を**遮る**ものは何もない Nothing will *stand in your way*. (➤ stand in ~'s way で「~の道に立ちはだかる」の意).

さえずり 囀り a **song**; a **warble** (ヒバリやウグイスの声); **chirping** (チュンチュン; 小鳥の声); **twittering** (チチ; スズメの声) ▶都心では鳥の**さえずり**もめったに聞かれない We seldom hear the *songs* [*twittering*] of birds in downtown Tokyo.

さえずる 囀る **sing**; **chirp, twitter, warble** ▶うちで飼っている小鳥は午前中よく**さえずる** My (little) birds *sing* [*twitter* / *warble*] a lot in the morning.

さえる 冴える 1【澄んだ】 ▶**さえた**月が冬空高く懸かっていた A *clear* moon was rising high in the winter sky. ‖ バイオリンの**さえた**音色が演奏会場に鳴り響いた The *clear* notes of the violin filled the music hall.

2【頭·調子などがよい】 ▶きょうは頭が**さえている** My mind is *sharp* [I am *alert*] today. ‖ きょうは**さえてる**じゃない You're really *clear-headed* today, aren't you? (➤ clear-headed は「鮮明な頭をした」の意) ‖ きょうはちょっと**気分がさえない**んだ I *don't feel* so *sharp* today. ‖ **顔色がさえない**ね. どうかしたの? You *look depressed* [*pale*]. What's the matter? ‖ うちのおじさん? **さえない**中年男よ My uncle? He's just a *dull* middle-aged man.

3【目が覚めた】 ▶夜が更けるにつれてますます目が**さえて**きた As the night wore on, I became *wider and wider awake*.

さお 竿 a **rod**; a **pole** (物を支えたり押したりする)

‖ **竹ざお** [**さお竹**] a bamboo pole ‖ **釣りざお** a fishing rod ‖ **旗ざお** a flagpole.

さか 坂 a **hill** (坂道); a **slope** (斜面) 【解説】 (1) slope は厳密には「斜面」の「面」または横から見た「線」に注目した言い方で, 山の斜面やスキー場のゲレンデを連想させる. (2) 日本語の「坂」に相当するのは hill で,「上り坂」「下り坂」を区別する場合は uphill road [path], downhill road [path] のように言う.

▶急な[緩やかな]**坂** a steep [gentle] *hill* ‖ **坂を上る**[**下る**] go up [down] *a slope* ‖ サンフランシスコの町は**坂が多い** San Francisco is *hilly*.

▶彼は60の**坂を越して**いるに違いない He must be *over* sixty. / He must be *on the other* [*wrong*] *side of* sixty. (➤ おどけた表現).

さが 性 **nature** ▶いくつになっても美しい女性を見て心ときめかすのは男の**さが**だ It's a man's *nature* to feel his heart beat faster at the sight of a beautiful woman, no matter how old he gets.

さかあがり 逆上がり **forward upward circling** (鉄棒の) ▶彼は級友たちの前で**逆上がり**を見事にやって見せた He gave a beautiful demonstration of *forward upward circling* before his classmates.

さかい 境 a **border** (境界); a **boundary** (境界線) ▶リオグランデ川はテキサス州とメキシコの**境**をなす The Rio Grande River forms the *border* [*boundary*] between Texas and Mexico. ‖ 富士山は山梨県と静岡県の**境**にそびえる Mt. Fuji stands on the *border* between Yamanashi and Shizuoka Prefectures.

▶その日を**境**にして私たちの仲は険悪になった That day *marked* the last of our friendship. (➤ mark は「…の印をつける, …をしるす」) ‖ 父は心臓発作で1週間**生死の境をさまよった** My father *hovered between life and death* for a week after his heart attack.

さかうらみ 逆恨み ▶彼に忠告してやったのに**逆恨み**された I warned him, but he *unjustly resented* me for it. (➤「不当に恨んだ」の意).

さかえる 栄える **prosper** (事業などがうまくゆく); **flourish** /flə́:rɪʃ/ (盛んになる); **thrive** (繁栄する)

▶イギリスはビクトリア女王の時代に**栄えた** Great Britain *prospered* during the reign of Queen Victoria. ‖ 堺は室町時代に海外貿易の中心地として**栄えた** Sakai *flourished* during the Muromachi period as a center of overseas trade.

さがく 差額 **the difference**; **the balance** (収支) ▶降りるとき改札口で**差額**を払ってください Please pay *the difference* at the ticket gate in the station.

‖ **差額ベッド** an extra-charge bed. ‖ **収支差額** a net surplus.

さかげ 逆毛 《主に米》 (a) **teased hair**; 《主に英》 (a) **backcombed hair** ▶彼女は髪に**逆毛を立てた** She *teased her hair*. ‖ 《美容院で》**逆毛を立てて**ください I'd like to have my *hair teased* [*backcombed*].

さかご 逆子 a **breech baby** (赤ちゃん); a **breech birth** [**delivery**] (逆産).

さかさ 逆さに **upside down** (上下逆に); **backward** (後ろから逆に) ▶1枚の抽象画が壁に**逆さに**掛かっていることに気づいた I noticed one of the abstract pictures was hung *upside down* on the wall. ‖ "madam" のように**逆さから**読んでも同じ語を回文という A word like "madam" that reads the same *backwards* as forwards is called a palindrome.

‖ **逆さまつげ** ingrowing [ingrown] eyelashes.

さかさま 逆様に **upside down** (上下逆さまに); **headfirst** (頭から真っ逆さまに) ▶こっちが上よ. **逆さまに**しないでね Please hold this side up. Don't turn it *upside down*. ‖ 青い湖面に富士山が**逆さまに**映っていた Mt. Fuji was reflected *upside down* in the blue waters of the lake. ‖ お年寄りの男性が階段を**頭から逆さまに**落ちた The elderly man fell *headfirst* down the stairs. ‖ アルファベットを後ろから**逆さまに**言ってごらん Say the alphabet *backward*.

☛ **真っ逆さま** (→見出語)

さがしあてる 捜し当てる·探し当てる **find (out)** ▶ようやく彼女の居所を**捜し当てた** At last, I *located* her [*found out* where she was / *discovered* her whereabouts]. (➤ locate は「所在を突き止める」) ‖ さらに4人の中国残留孤児が肉親を**捜し当てた** Four more Japanese war orphans, who had been left in China, *found* their Japanese relatives. ‖ 私は彼女を悩ませているものを**捜し当てた** I *found out* what was troubling her. (➤ find out はこの例のように抽象的なことを目的語とするのがふつう).

さがしだす 捜し出す·探し出す **find** +目, **search out** (➤ 後者のほうが綿密な捜索を連想させる) ▶警察は行方不明の子をやっと**捜し出した** The police finally *found* [*located* / *discovered*] the missing child.

さがしまわる 捜し回る·探し回る ▶家中**捜し回った**が手帳は出てこなかった I *searched all over* the house for my pocket diary but it did not turn up.

さがしもの 捜し物 ▶おじいちゃんはしょっちゅう**捜し物**をしている Grandpa *is* always *looking for something*. ‖ 【対話】「**捜し物**ですか」「ええ, コンタクトレンズが見つからないんですよ」"*Are you looking for something*?" "Yes. I can't find my contact lens(es)."

さがす 探す・捜す **look for**(なくしたもの，欲しいものなどを)；**search for**(時間をかけて，注意深く；捜索する)；**look up**(辞書・地図などで必要な情報を得る)；**hunt for**(場所をくまなく)；**seek** +㊐(探し求める；やや堅い語)

【文型】
人・物(A)をさがす
look for A
物(A)を求めて場所(B)をさがす
search B for A

▶職を探す *look for* work [a job] ‖ 何［誰］を探しているのですか What [Who] *are you looking for*? ‖ 警察は殺人に使われた凶器を求めて家中をくまなく**捜した** The police *searched* all over the house *for* the murder weapon. (➤ look for a house は捜し場所としての家の中ではなく，住むための，あるいは，訪ねて行く「家そのものを探す」).

▶安井さんの家を地図で**探した**が，**探し出す**ことができなかった I *looked up* Mr. Yasui's house on the map, but I couldn't *find* it. ‖ 気に入ったジャケットはないかと街中を**探して回った** I *looked around* town *for* a jacket I really liked. (➤ look around は「…を見て回る」) ‖ 対話「お母さん，ハンカチがないよ」「よく**捜して**ごらんなさい．その辺にあるでしょ」"Mom, I can't find my handkerchief." "*Look around*. It's probably there somewhere."

▶ぼくはポケットに手を入れて車のキーを**捜した** I *felt* in my pocket *for* my car key. (➤ feel for は「…を手で触れて捜す」) ‖ 暗い部屋の中でフロアスタンドのスイッチを手探りで**探した** In the dark room, I *groped for* the floor lamp switch. (➤ grope は「手探りで探す」).

さかずき 杯 a **sake cup** ▶男は**杯**をぐっと飲み干した The man drained [emptied] his *sake cup* in [at] one gulp.

さかだち 逆立ち a **handstand**；a **headstand**(頭をつけてする) ▶彼は**逆立ち**ができない He cannot *stand on his hands* [*head*]. ／He cannot do *a handstand* [*a headstand*].

▶《慣用表現》泳ぎでは**逆立ち**しても父にはかなわない I *can't hold a candle to* my father as far as swimming is concerned. (➤ cannot hold a candle to で「…の足元にも及ばない」).

さかだてる 逆立てる ▶物音に反応して犬は毛を**逆立てた** The dog's fur *bristled* in response to the noise.

さかて 逆手 ▶鉄棒を**逆手**で握る *grip* the horizontal bar *from below*.

▶彼女は私の論法を**逆手にとった** She *used* my own argument *to attack* me.

[1]**さかな** 魚 a **fish** [複 **fish**]

語法 (1) 2匹以上の魚の場合も fish の形を用いるが，多種類の魚を指すときはまれに fishes を用いることもある．(2)「魚肉」の意味では常に Ⓤ で fish の形．

▶たくさんの種類の**魚** many different kinds of *fish* ／many different *fishes*(➤ 前者のほうがふつう) ‖ **魚の大群**が同じ方向に泳いでいる *A school of fish* is swimming in the same direction. (➤ この school は「(魚などの)群れ」の意) ‖ すしがポピュラーになるにつれて**生の魚**を好む外国人が増えている Now that sushi is getting popular, more foreigners like *raw fish*.

▶きのう**魚釣り**に行って25匹釣った I went *fishing* yesterday and caught 25 fish. (➤ 数詞を伴うときは 25 fishes と複数形にすることもある).

‖**小魚** small fish(小さい魚)；fry(かえったばかりの稚魚).

✉ **日本は島国なので魚は日本人にとって大切なたんぱく源となっています** Since Japan is an island country, *fish* is an important source of protein for the Japanese people.

「魚」のいろいろ **アジ** horse mackerel ／**アユ** *ayu* ／**イワシ** sardine ／**ウナギ** eel ／**カツオ** bonito ／**カレイ** flounder ／**コイ** carp ／**サケ** salmon ／**サバ** mackerel ／**サメ** shark ／**サンマ** Pacific saury (pike) ／**スズキ** Japanese sea bass [sea perch] ／**タイ** sea bream ／**タラ** cod ／**トビウオ** flying fish ／**ナマズ** catfish ／**ニシン** herring ／**ヒラメ** flatfish, sole ／**フグ** globefish, blowfish ／**フナ** crucian (carp) ／**ブリ** yellowtail ／**マグロ** tuna ／**マス** trout ／**メカジキ** swordfish ／**ワカサギ** smelt

[2]**さかな** 肴 ▶ビールの**さかな**には枝豆がよく合う Edamame go well with beer [are a good *side dish* for beer]. (➤ side dish は「添え料理」).

▶《慣用表現》彼らは無能な課長を**さかなにして**飲み明かした They drank the night away, *making* the incompetent section chief *the butt of all their jokes*. (➤ butt は「(嘲笑・批評の)的」).

さかなで 逆撫で ▶彼女はいつも人の神経を**逆なでする**ようなことをする She always *rubs* people *the wrong way*. (➤ rub ... (up) the wrong way は猫の毛を逆方向になでると怒ることから転じて「…を怒らせる」の意のインフォーマルな表現).

さかなや 魚屋 《米》a **fish dealer**,《英》a **fishmonger** (人)；《米》a **fish store**,《英》a **fishmonger's** (店)
《参考》fish shop は《英》では fish and chips (フライドポテトを盛り合わせた魚のフライ)を売る店を指すことが多い．

さかのぼる 遡る **1【上流に行く】go up, go upstream** ▶サケは川を**遡って**，砂に産卵する Salmon *go up* the river and lay their eggs in the sand. ‖ この川を4キロほど**遡る**と美しい渓谷に出ます If you *go upstream* along this river about four kilometers, you will reach a beautiful gorge.

2【過去や起源に戻る】go back《to》, **date back**《to》 ▶七五三の慣習は江戸時代に**遡る** The custom of "Shichi-go-san" *goes* [*dates*] *back to* the Edo period. ‖ 十種競技の**起源は**古代ギリシャに**遡る** The decathlon *traces its origins to* ancient Greece. ‖ 新しい規定は7月1日に**遡って有効だ** The new regulations are *retroactive* to July 1.

さかば 酒場 a **bar**；《米》a **saloon** /səlúːn/ (西部劇の)；《英》a **pub**.

さかみち 坂道 a **hill**；an **uphill road** [**path**] (上り坂)；a **downhill road** [**path**] (下り坂) ⇀坂 ▶**坂道**を上る［下る］walk up [down] *a hill* ‖ カーブの多い**坂道** a winding *hilly road* [*path*] ‖ ボールはその**坂道**を転がり落ちた The ball rolled down the *hill*.

さかもり 酒盛り a **drinking party** [**session**] (飲み会)；a **(drinking) binge**, a **drinking bout** /baʊt/ (はめを外した).

さかや 酒屋 a **liquor store**,《英》an **off-licence**
《参考》日本酒だけの酒屋なら sake shop でよい．

さかゆめ 逆夢 ▶彼女とデートする夢を見たが**逆夢だった** I dreamed I went on a date with her, but *the dream didn't come true*. (➤「夢は実現しなかった」の意).

さからう 逆らう **1【逆行する】go against** ▶走者たちは風に逆らって走らねばならなかった The runners had to run *against* the wind. ‖ 時流に逆らって何になる What's the use of *going* [*swimming*] *against the current?*

2【反抗する】disobey ＋目（従わない）; **oppose** ＋目（反対する）▶親に逆らう *disobey* [*go against*] one's parent(s) ‖ 誰一人部長の提案に逆らわなかった No one *opposed* the general manager's proposal. ‖ 監督はきょうは低気圧だから逆らわないほうがいいよ The manager is out of sorts today, so you'd better not *rub* him *the wrong way*. (➤ rub ... the wrong way は「…を怒らせる, …の神経を逆なでする」の意のインフォーマルな表現) ‖ 私たちは両親の意に逆らって結婚しました We got married *against* our parents' wishes.

さかり 盛り **1【頂点の時期】the peak; the prime**（最盛期）▶ブドウは今が盛りだ Grapes are *in season* now. ‖ 明治神宮のハナショウブは今が盛りだ The Japanese irises in the Meiji Shrine are *at their best* [*in full bloom*] now. (➤ in full bloom は「満開で」).

▶健作は青春真っ盛りだ Kensaku is *in the prime of youth*. ‖ 上野の桜は盛りを過ぎた The cherry blossoms at Ueno *are past their peak*.

✉ **今頃ニューヨークは夏の暑い盛りでしょう** You must be reaching *the peak* of the summer heat about now in New York.

2【交尾期】heat ▶うちの猫は今盛りがついている Our cat is *in heat* now.

-ざかり -盛り ▶遊び盛りの子供たち children *at their most playful age* ‖ おいはいたずら盛りだ My nephew is *at the mischievous age*. ‖ おじは40代の働き盛りだ My uncle is in his forties and *in the prime of* (*his*) *life*. (➤「働く」は強いて訳さず,「人生の最盛期」と表現するのがふつう).

さかりば 盛り場 a **busy shopping and amusement district**; an **entertainment district**（歓楽街）; a **downtown**（町の中心街, 繁華街）▶学校の帰りに盛り場をうろつく hang around the *entertainment district* on one's way home from school.

さがる 下がる

📖 **訳語メニュー**
下へ動く →go down, fall **1**
垂れ下がる →hang **2**
バックする →step back, back up **3**
状態·程度が下がる →come [go] down **4**

1【下方へ移行する】go down; fall（落ちる）
▶すきっ腹に冷たいビールを飲んだら, 胃の中を下がるのがわかった When I drank cold beer on an empty stomach, I could feel it *go down* into my stomach. ‖ 温度計の水銀は熱に反応して上がったり下がったりする The mercury in a thermometer rises and *falls* in response to heat. ‖ 彼は右肩が下がっている His shoulders *slant* to the right. (➤ slant は「傾く」) ‖ ゴムが切れてパンツが下がってきた The elastic broke and my underpants *came* [*fell*] *down*.
▶《慣用表現》彼の努力には頭が下がる I *take my hat off* to [*I'm impressed by*] his strenuous efforts. (➤ 前者は「脱帽する」, 後者は「感心する」の意).

2【上方からぶら下がる】hang
▶軒下につららが下がっている The icicles *are hanging* under the eaves. ‖ 窓からロープが1本下がっていた A rope *was hanging* out of the window. ‖ そのスーパーには歳末大売り出しの垂れ幕が下がっていた A banner advertising the end-of-year sale *was hanging* out in front of the supermarket.

3【後退する】step back（人が）; **back up**（人や車が）
▶もう少し後ろへ下がってください Please *step back* a bit further. ‖ 3歩下がってください Please *back up* three steps. ‖ 1歩下がってください *Take* a step *backward*.

4【状態·程度が下降する】come [go] down; fall（高い所から低い所へ）; **drop**（急速に）
▶彼女の熱は下がった Her fever *came down*. ‖ 日没後急に気温が下がった After the sun set, the temperature suddenly *dropped* [*fell* sharply]. ‖ 豊作のおかげでキャベツの値段が下がった Thanks to a bumper crop, the price of cabbage *has dropped* [*come down*／*fallen*].
▶2学期は成績がだいぶ下がった My grades *dropped* considerably in the second term. ‖ 最高の作品は古くなっても値打ちは下がらない The value of an excellent work of art does *not go down* [*diminish*] with age.

[1]**さかん 盛ん** **1【広く行われる様子】**▶マレーシアではゴムの生産が盛んだ The rubber industry is *flourishing* in Malaysia. ‖ 私たちの学校はスポーツが盛んだ Sports *are* (*very*) *popular* at our school. ／Our school encourages sports among students. (➤ 後者は「学校が生徒にスポーツを奨励している」の意).

2【熱心, 頻繁】▶私たちは行く先々で盛んな歓迎を受けた We were given a *warm* [an *enthusiastic*] welcome wherever we went. ‖ 彼らは現地の学生たちと盛んに討論を行った They had *active* discussions with local students. ‖ 国際交流計画をもっと盛んにする必要がある We should further *promote* [*increase*] international exchange programs.

3【勢いがある様子】▶雪が盛んに降っていた It was snowing *hard* [*heavily*]. ‖ キャンプファイアは星空の下で盛んに燃えていた The campfire was *blazing* [*burning briskly*] under the starry sky. ‖ うちの祖父は老いてますます盛ん(＝精力的)だ My grandfather is getting more and more *energetic* [*vigorous*] as he grows older.

[2]**さかん 左官** a **plasterer**, a **plaster craftsperson**.

[1]**さがん 砂岩** **sandstone**.

[2]**さがん 左岸** →右岸.

[1]**さき 左記** ▶合格者は左記のとおりです. 佐々木, 尾崎, 中島 The successful candidates are *as follows*: Sasaki, Ozaki, Nakajima. (➤「次のとおり」の意; ● 日本語の縦書きでは「左」だが, 英文では横書きなので「以下」と表す).

[2]さき 先

📖 **訳語メニュー**
先端 →point, end, tip **1**
前方に →ahead **2**
…より向こうに →beyond **2**
将来 →the future **2**
順序 →first **2**

1【先端】 a **point**（とがった先）; an **end**（端）; a **tip**（指·舌などの先端）▶先の太い [細い] サインペンで書く write with a *bold*-[*fine*-]*point* felt-tip pen ‖ 針の先で指を突いた I pricked my finger with (the *point* of) a needle. ‖ この棒は先がとがっている This stick *is pointed* [*has a sharp end*]. ‖ 棒の先にトン

ボが留まった A dragonfly alighted on the *end* [*tip*] of a pole. ‖ 舌の**先**をやけどした I burned the *tip* of my tongue.

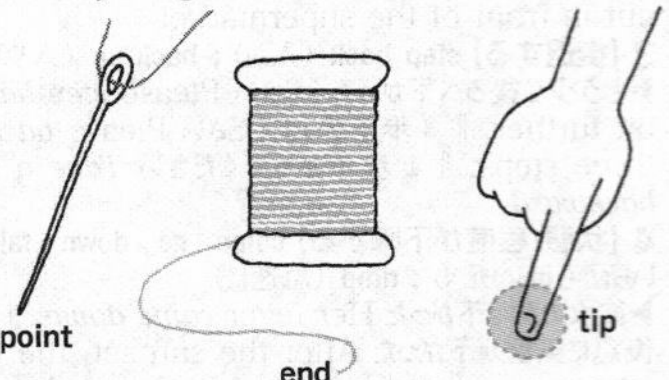

2【進行方向の前の方】▶《空間的》2キロ**先**に病院がある There is a hospital two kilometers *ahead*. ‖ 彼の家は**この先を**100メートルほど行った所にある His house is about 100 meters *down this street*. (➤ down this street は「この通りをまっすぐ行くと」) ‖《掲示》**この先工事中** Construction Ahead ‖ 浜辺は散歩道に沿って**ずっと先まで**広がっている A broad beach stretches *all the way* along the promenade. ‖ 霧が深くて**一寸先も**見えなかった The fog was so dense that we couldn't see *an inch ahead*. ‖ 私たちの学校はあのガソリンスタンドの**先**(＝向こう)です Our school is *beyond* that gas station. ‖ 新幹線は熱海から**先**が不通になっている (The) Shinkansen service is suspended *beyond* Atami.

▶《時間的》そんなぐうたらじゃあ**先**が思いやられるね Since you are so lazy, I'm a bit concerned [worried] about your *future*. ‖ **2年先には**大事な司法試験があるんだよ *In two years* [*Two years from now*], you will have to take the all-important bar exams. (➤ (×)two years after や (×)two years later は不可).

▶《順序》ぼくが**先**だよ I'm (*the*) *first*. ‖ 彼女がいちばん**先**に到着した She was *the first* to get here. ‖ **何より先に**宿題をやりなさい Do your homework *first of all*. ‖ 彼女は私より**先**にここに着いた She arrived here *before* me [*ahead of* me ／*earlier than* me]. ‖ もし私が遅れたら待たずに**先**に出発してください If I should be late, please go *ahead* without waiting for me. ‖ どうぞ**お先に** Please *go ahead*. ／After you. (➤ 後者は日本語とは逆の発想; ⇀**お先**). ‖ 鶏が**先**か卵が**先**か Which came *first*, the chicken or the egg? ‖ 荷物を**先に送った** I had my baggage [luggage] *sent on*. (➤ send on は「(物など)を前もって送る」) ‖ 暖かくなるのは**もう少し先**だ We have *only a little while to go* until it gets warmer.

▶《後続部分》**その先**(＝話の残り)はあす話すことにしよう I'll tell you *the rest* of the story tomorrow.

▶《遠くない過去》**先の**台風で土砂崩れがあり, 道は依然不通だ The road is still closed to traffic because of the landslide(s) caused by the *recent* typhoon.

3【慣用表現】 **先が知れる** ▶このまま会社にいても先は知れている If I continue working at this company, *I don't think I'll get very far*. ‖ 彼は父親にならって漁師になっても先が知れていると考えて, 勤めに出ることにした He decided to get a job as a salaried worker, considering that he *wouldn't have* (*much of*) *a future* if he followed in his father's footsteps as a fisherman. **先が見える** ▶仕事は山場を越えてようやく先が見えてきた Having completed the most difficult part of the job, I *can see the end* (*of the tunnel*) *approaching*. (➤ 後半を I can see the light at the end of the tunnel としてもよい) **先が短い** ▶彼は重病で先が短いらしい I hear that he is seriously ill and *doesn't have long to live*. ‖ その会社は先が短い The company's days *are numbered*. ／The company will *go out of business before long*. **先に立つ** ▶独り暮らしだと, 食事の支度も面倒くささが先に立つ Since I live alone, *not going to a lot of trouble comes first* [*not going to a lot of trouble is the most important thing*] when I prepare a meal. **先を争う** ▶人々は席を取ろうと先を争って講堂の中へ駆け込んで行った *Trying to push ahead of one another*, they rushed into the auditorium for seats. **先を越される** ▶彼女には先を越されたくないわ I don't want to *let* her *get ahead of* me [to *let* her *beat* me *to it*]. ‖ 新製品の開発競争ではライバル会社に先を越された Our rival company *beat* [*edged*] *us out* in developing a new product. **先を読む** ▶先を読むのは難しい *Predicting* (*the future*) is difficult.

[1]**さぎ 鷺**《鳥》a **heron** ‖ **アオサギ** a blue heron ‖ **シラサギ** an egret /íːgrət/.

[2]**さぎ 詐欺** a **swindle**(だまし取ること); (a) **fraud** /frɔːd/ (詐欺行為) ▶**詐欺を働く** *swindle* ／ *commit a fraud* ‖ 彼女は**結婚詐欺に遭って**300万円**だまし取られた** She *was swindled out of* three million yen *by a man who said he wanted to marry* her. ‖ 彼は**保険金詐欺**で訴えられた He was accused of carrying out *an insurance fraud* [*scam*].
‖**詐欺師** a swindler, 《インフォーマル》a con man [artist], 《英・インフォーマル》a wide boy; a fraud (地位・職業などを偽る人) ‖ **架空請求詐欺** a billing scam ‖ **還付金詐欺** a refund scam ‖ **なりすまし詐欺** an impostor scam.

-ざき -咲き ▶**遅咲き**のチューリップ *late-blooming* tulips ‖ この花は**早咲き**だ These are *early-blooming* flowers. ／These are *early-bloomers*. ‖ 桜の花はまだ**三分咲き**だ Only *a third* of the cherry blossoms *are in bloom*.

さきおくり 先送り ▶決定は**先送り**となった The decision *was put off* [*was postponed*].

さきおととい 一昨昨日 three days ago(3日前) ▶**さきおととい**は高い熱を出した I had a high fever *three days ago*. ‖ **さきおとといから**雨が降り続いている It has been raining *for three days*.

さきおととし 一昨昨年 three years ago(3年前).

さきがけ 先駆け ▶パリのファッションは婦人服流行の**先駆けとなる** Paris *leads* the world of women's fashion. ‖ マツユキソウは春の**先駆け**である The snowdrop is *a precursor* of spring. ‖ 木枯らしは冬の**先駆け**だ Chilly winds in late fall *herald* the coming of winter. (➤ herald は「先駆けをする」) ／ Chilly blasts are *a harbinger* of winter. (➤ harbinger は「先駆け」の意味だが, 好ましくないものの前触れというイメージがあることが多い).

さきがける 先駆ける ▶わが社は**時代に先駆けた**製品を作っている Our company creates products that are *ahead of their time*. ‖ そのメーカーは**世界に先駆けて**(＝世界で初めて)低公害車を売り出した The manufacturer was *the first in the world* to put low-pollution cars on the market.

さきこぼれる 咲きこぼれる ▶庭に萩(はぎ)が**咲きこぼれている** Bush clovers *are blooming all over* the garden.

さきごろ 先頃 recently, some days ago ▶道路の補修

は先頃終わった The repair work on the road was finished *recently*.

さきざき 先々 1【将来】▶先々のことを思い悩んでもしかたがない It is no use worrying about things *in the distant future*. ‖ 先々のために貯金しています I'm saving for *the future*.
2【先方】▶使節団は行く先々で(＝どこへ行っても)歓迎された The mission was welcomed *wherever it went*. ‖ 私は行く先々の都市で美術館を訪れた I visited art galleries in *every* city *I went to*.

サキソホーン a **saxophone**,《インフォーマル》a **sax** ▶サキソホーンを吹く play the *saxophone*.
‖サキソホーン奏者 a saxophonist.

さきそろう 咲きそろう ▶桜が咲きそろった The cherry blossoms *are all open* [*in full bloom*].

さきだつ 先立つ 1【前に来る】▶競技に先立って選手代表が宣誓を行った *Before* the games commenced, a player, representing the others, recited a pledge to play fair.
2【先に死ぬ】▶彼は妻に先立たれた His wife *has gone* (*on*) *before* him.
3【必要な】▶商売を始めたいが先立つものがない I'd like to start a business, but I lack *the wherewithal*. (➤ wherewithal は「(特定目的の)資金」) ‖ 何をするにも先立つものは金だ(＝金がなければ何もできない) We can't do anything without money.

さきどり 先取り ▶そのメーカーは若者の好みを先取りした新製品を売り出した That company has put out a new product which *anticipates* the preferences of young consumers. (➤ anticipate は「見越す」) ‖ 彼の考え方は時代を先取りしている His ideas are *ahead of the times*.

さきのばし 先延ばし (a) **postponement**(延期, 後回し); **procrastination**(やらなければならないことの; 当事者には「実行したくない」という気持ちがある軽蔑的な含みを持った堅い語) ▶計画の実行を先延ばしにする *postpone* the execution of the plan.

さきばしる 先走る ▶あんまり先走るな. ろくなことはないよ Don't *be* too *hasty* [Don't *jump the gun*]. No good will come of it. (➤ jump the gun は文字どおりには「ピストルの合図の前に飛び出す」の意).

さきばらい 先払い ▶家賃はふつう先払い(＝前払い)である Rent is generally *paid in advance*. (➤ pay in advance で「前払いする」).

さきほこる 咲き誇る ▶土手の桜が今を盛りと咲き誇っている The cherry trees on the bank *are in full bloom*.

さきぼそり 先細り ▶わが校への応募者はこれからまず間違いなく先細りになるだろう The number of applicants to our school will most probably *taper off* in the coming years.

さきほど 先程 a **little** [a **short**] **while ago**; **some time ago**(しばらく前に) ▶岡さん, 先ほど村瀬さんからお電話がありました Mr. Oka, there was a call from Ms. Murase *a short while ago*. ‖ 先ほどから江田さんという方がお待ちです A Mr. Eda has been waiting for you *for a while*. ‖ 彼女はつい先ほどここを出ました She left here *just a minute ago*.

さきまわり 先回り ▶友だちを驚かそうと先回りしてじっと待った I *arrived* there *before* my friends and waited to surprise them.

さきみだれる 咲き乱れる ▶バラの花が辺り一面に咲き乱れている Roses *are blooming* [*are in bloom*] all over the place.

さきもの 先物《金融》**futures** ‖先物取引 futures trading.

さきゅう 砂丘 a (**sand**) **dune** /djuːn/.

さきゆき 先行き ▶景気の先行きが不安だ Economic *prospects* are dark [gloomy].

さぎょう 作業 **work** ▶こんな単純作業はもう飽き飽きした I'm bored (to death) by this *simple work*. ／I'm tired of doing these *simple tasks*. ‖ 彼らは早朝から沈没した船の引き上げ作業に取りかかった They started *salvage operations* for the sunken ship early this morning. ‖ 父は作業中にひどいけがをした My father was badly injured *while at work*. ‖ 道路は修復作業中です The road is *under repair*. (➤ この場合の道路標識は Workers Ahead とか Work Ahead と出される).
‖作業員 a worker ‖ 作業時間 working hours ‖ 作業場 a workshop ‖ 作業台 a worktable ‖ 作業服[着] work(ing) clothes; overalls,《米》coveralls (つなぎ) ‖ 作業療法 occupational therapy ‖ 作業療法士 an occupational therapist.

さきん 砂金 **gold dust**.

さきんじる 先んじる **go** [**be**] **ahead**《of》▶彼の思想は同時代の人々に先んじていた His ideas *were ahead of* his contemporaries. ‖ [ことわざ] 先んずれば人を制す Take the lead and you will win. ／The early bird catches the worm. (➤ 後者は「先に行動を起こす者が成功を収める」の意の英語のことわざ).

[1]**さく 柵** a **fence**; a **railing**(横木の) ▶芝生に鉄の柵を巡らす put *an iron railing* around the lawn ／enclose the lawn with *an iron fence*.

[2]**さく 策** a **scheme** /skiːm/ (➤《米》では「悪だくみ」の含みがある); a **measure** (対策; しばしば複数形で用いる) ▶予防策をとる take a precautionary *measure* ‖ 政府を倒そうと策を練る *concoct* [*draw up*] *a scheme* to overthrow the government ‖ 彼らは地滑り防止の策を講じた They *took measures* to prevent landslides. ‖ こうなっては策の施しようがない As matters stand, *nothing can be done*.

[3]**さく 作** a **work**(作品) ▶これは彼の苦心の作だ This is *a work* he struggled to create. ‖ このつぼは唐九郎の作とされている This pot is believed to be *a work* by Tokuro.

[4]**さく 咲く** **bloom**, **come out** (花が); **blossom** (果樹の花が) ▶このチューリップは来週あたり咲くだろう These tulips will *bloom* around next week. ‖ ザクロの花は初夏に咲く Pomegranate blossoms *come out* in early summer. ‖ リンゴの花がちらほら咲き始めた Apple blossoms have begun to *appear here and there*.
✉ **ここ北海道では5月に一度にいろんな樹木の花が咲きます** Here in Hokkaido, many kinds of trees *bloom* all at once in May.

[5]**さく 裂く・割く** 1【破る】**tear** /teəʳ/ +目, **rip** +目 (乱暴に引き裂く) ▶彼女と別れてからぼくは彼女の手紙を全部ずたずたに裂いた After I broke up with her, I *tore up* all her letters [*tore* all her letters *to pieces*]. (➤ tore は tear の過去形) ‖ 彼女の両親はぼくたちの仲を裂こうとした Her parents tried to *break* us *up*.
2【分けて別のことに充てる】**spare** +目 ▶時間を割いて歯医者に行く *make time* to go to the dentist ‖ 10分ほどお時間を割いていただけませんか Could you *spare* me about ten minutes? ‖ 貴重なお時間を割いていただきありがとうございました Thank you very much for *giving me* some of your valuable *time*. ‖ 新聞は冬季オリンピックの記事に大きく紙面を割

いた The newspaper *gave a lot of space* to an article on the Winter Olympic Games.

さくい 作為 ▶この報告書は作為（＝作り事）の跡が歴然としている It is quite obvious that the report *was fabricated*. ‖あの男は言うことなすこといつも作為的だ What he says and does is always *deliberate* [*carefully contrived*].

さくいん 索引 an **index** /índeks/.

さくがら 作柄 a **crop**（作物）; a **harvest**（収穫）▶ことしの米の作柄は良好らしい I hear that we'll have a good rice *crop* this year. ／The rice *harvest* looks good this year.

さくげん 削減 **curtailment** ━動 **削減する** **curtail** /kəːʳtéɪl/ ＋目 ; **cut (down)**, **reduce** ＋目 ▶軍事費を削減する *curtail* military expenditures ‖売れ行きが低調で生産が20パーセント削減された Sales are sluggish, so factory production *has been cut* [*has been reduced*] by 20 percent. ‖多くの会社で経費削減は標語になっている *Cost-cutting* is a slogan at many companies.

さくさく ▶このクッキー，さくさくしてとてもおいしいわ These cookies are *crispy* and delicious. ‖父のパソコンはさくさく動く My father's PC runs *smoothly*.

さくさん 酢酸 **acetic acid**.

1**さくし 作詞する** **write words** [**lyrics**] ▶私たちの校歌は吉田先生の作詞によるものだ Mr. Yoshida *wrote the words* [*lyrics*] for our school song. ‖阿部太郎作詞，山田浩一作曲 *words* by Abe Taro and music by Yamada Koichi.

‖**作詞家** a songwriter, a lyricist /lírɪsɪst/.

2**さくし 策士** a **wheeler-dealer** ; a **schemer** /skíːməʳ/（陰謀者）; a **tactician**（戦術家）.

さくじつ 昨日 **yesterday**. →きのう.

さくしゃ 作者 an **author** /ɔ́ːθəʳ/, a **writer**（著者）; a **dramatist**（劇の）; a **novelist**（小説の）▶作者不詳の詩 a poem by an unknown *author* [*poet*] ／an *anonymous* poem.

さくしゅ 搾取する **exploit** /ɪksplɔ́ɪt/ ＋目 ▶労働者を[から]搾取する *exploit* the workers by making them work for less pay.

さくじょ 削除 **deletion** ━動 **削除する** **delete** /dɪlíːt/ ＋目 ; **remove** ＋目（取り除く）; **strike** ＋目（表・記録から）▶不要なファイルの削除 the *deletion* of unwanted files ‖リストから名前を削除する *delete* [*cross out*] a name from a list ‖この2語を削除すればもっと簡潔な文になります *Remove* [*Omit*] these two words to tighten up the sentence. ‖私は名前を名簿から削除してくれるように頼んだ I asked to *have* my name *removed* from the list.

さくず 作図する **draw a diagram** [**figure**].

さくせい 作成する **draw up** ; **prepare** ＋目（草稿を準備する）▶契約書は2通作成する必要があります The contract must *be drawn up* in duplicate. ‖《掲示》試験問題作成中につき生徒の入室を禁ずる No Students. Exam Papers *Being Prepared*.

さくせん 作戦 an **operation**（軍事行動）; (a) **strategy** /strǽṭədʒi/（全体の作戦計画・戦略）; a **tactic**（個々の戦術）▶作戦を立てる plan [work out] *a strategy* ‖作戦を変える change one's *strategy* ／change *tactics* ‖引き延ばし作戦 a stalling *tactic* ‖軍事作戦を立てる plan a military *operation* ‖販売作戦会議を開く hold *a sales strategy meeting* ‖作戦がまんまと成功した Our *plan* worked remarkably well. ‖試合は作戦どおりだった The game went *as planned*.

さくそう 錯綜 ▶（事故の）現場からの情報は錯そうしています The news from the accident site *is contradictory*.

さくづけ 作付け **planting**.

さくねん 昨年 **last year**. →去年.

さくばん 昨晩 **last night**. →昨夜.

さくひん 作品 a **work** ; an **opus** /óʊpəs/（特に音楽作品；通例 op. と略し，番号をつける）▶芸術作品 a *work* of art ‖文学[文芸]作品 a literary *work* ‖メンデルスゾーンのバイオリン協奏曲ホ短調作品64 Mendelssohn's Violin Concerto in E minor, *Op*.64 ‖太宰治の作品をどれか読んだことがありますか Have you ever read any of Dazai Osamu's *works*? ‖この絵はピカソの作品です This picture is *a* (*work of*) *Picasso*.

さくふう 作風 a **style** ▶独特の作風で知られる作家 a writer known for his [her] unique *style*.

さくぶん 作文 a **composition** ; an **essay**（エッセー，小論；感想文）▶私が書いた英語の作文を直してくださいますか Could you please correct my English *composition*? ‖『友情』という題で作文を書きなさい Write *an essay* entitled [with the title] "Friendship."

さくもつ 作物 a **crop**, **farm products**（➤後者は特に農場で収穫されたものをいう場合）▶作物を荒らす damage the *crops* ‖作物をトラックで市場へ運ぶ carry *farm products* [*produce*] to market in a truck ‖この土地は作物がよくできる This land yields good *crops*. ／This is good farming land.

‖**換金作物** a cash crop.

さくや 昨夜 **last night**, **yesterday evening**（➤ yesterday night とはしない．また，last evening もあまり好まれない）▶昨夜のテレビの特別番組は見ましたか Did you watch the special TV program *last night*? ‖昨夜から雨が降っている It has been raining *since last night*.

1**さくら 桜** **cherry blossoms** [**flowers**]（花）; a **cherry (tree)**（木）（➤ cherry だけでは「サクランボ」を指すことが多い）

日本紹介 ✉ **桜は日本人がいちばん好きな花です．春に薄いピンクの花をつけます．満開の時期はごく短く，散り際が愛(め)でられます．日本各地に桜の名所があります．この木の下で花を見ながら飲食するのが花見です** The Japanese love cherry blossoms best of all flowers. The cherry trees bloom light pink in the spring. Their period of full bloom is very short, and they are most admired when the petals begin to fall. There are many famous cherry blossom-viewing places around the country. Having a party [picnic] under cherry trees while viewing the blossoms is called '*hanami*.'

▶桜の咲く頃入学する enter school during *cherry blossom time* ‖井の頭公園の桜は今が満開だ The *cherry trees* in Inokashira Park are now in full bloom. ‖八幡市の背割堤の桜並木は毎年4月初めに，とてもきれいに花を咲かせます The *row of cherry trees* on the Sewari bank in Yawata bloom beautifully at the beginning of April every spring.

‖**桜前線** a cherry-blossom front ‖**八重桜** double cherry blossoms.

2**さくら** a **booster**（競売などで雇われて意図的に値段をつり上げる人）; a **plant**（観客に交じっていて選ばれて手品師などの手伝いをする人）; a **claque** /klæk/（劇場などに雇われて拍手喝采するグループ；1人を指す場合は a claqueur /klækə́ːʳ/）; a **shill**（大道商人などと組む人）.

さくらそう 桜草 《植物》a **primrose** 《参考》日本人は

サクラソウからはピンクの花色を連想するが，英語の primrose からは淡黄色を思い浮かべることが多い．

さくらん 錯乱 ▶彼女は一人息子の死のショックで**精神錯乱に陥った** Shocked by the death of her only son, she *went mad* [*became mentally deranged*]．(➤ カッコ内は医学用語)．

さくらんぼ 桜桃 a **cherry**.

さぐり 探り ▶彼に会ったら，うちに勤める気がないか**探りを入れてみてくれ** When you see him, *sound* him *out* about working for us. ‖ 彼らはライバル会社の経営状態に**探りを入れた** They *investigated* the financial conditions of their rival company.

さぐりあてる 探り当てる ▶私は暗闇の中で電灯のスイッチを**探り当てた** I *groped around and found* the light switch in the dark.

さぐりだす 探り出す search out ▶その企業の秘密を**探り出す** *ferret out* [*search out*] that company's secret (➤ ferret out は「(情報など)を探り出す」の意のインフォーマルな表現)．

さくりゃく 策略 a **trick**(たくらみ)；(a) **subterfuge**(ごまかしの手段) ▶彼らは社長を失脚させる**策略を巡らした** They *plotted* to bring down the president. (➤ plot は「たくらむ」)．

‖**策略家** a strategist ; a tactician (戦術家)．

さぐる 探る 1【見えないものを手足でさがす】feel, grope (手などで触れて；後者は「あちこちを手探りする」のニュアンスが濃い)；**search** (捜索する) ▶切符を取り出そうとポケットを**探った** I *felt* [*groped*] around my pocket *for* my ticket. ‖ スイッチを見つけようと壁を**探った** I *felt* [*fumbled*] along the wall to find the switch. (➤ fumble は「不器用にさがす」)．

2【事情などをひそかに調べる】▶人を**探る**ような目で見る look at a person *searchingly* ‖ 孝は友だちに友子の気持ちを何気なく**探ってほしい**と頼んだ Takashi asked a friend of his to casually *sound out* how Tomoko feels toward him. ‖ 彼らは佐々木氏の妻の行動を**探っていた** They were *spying on* Mr. Sasaki's wife.

さくれつ 炸裂 (an) **explosion 一動 さく裂する explode** ▶遠くで爆弾の**さく裂する**音が聞こえた We heard the bomb *explosion* [the bomb *going off*] in the distance.

ざくろ《植物》a **pomegranate** /pάːmɪgrænət/

‖**ザクロ石** (a) garnet.

[1]**さけ 酒** **alcohol** /ǽlkəhɔːl/ (ビール・ワイン・日本酒・蒸留酒など酒一般)；《主に米》**(hard) liquor,**《主に英》**spirits** (ウイスキー・ジンなどの蒸留酒)；**sake** /sάːki/ (日本酒；英語化している)；an **alcoholic drink** [**beverage**] (アルコール飲料) ▶**強い酒** *hard liquor* ‖ あのレストランは**酒を出さない** That restaurant doesn't serve *alcohol*. ‖ 未成年者は**酒を飲んではいけません** Minors may not *drink alcohol*. ‖ 私は**酒を飲みません** I *don't drink*. ‖ (体質的に)**酒は飲めません** I *can't drink*. ‖ 父は夕食前によく**酒を飲む** My father often *drinks* [*has a drink*] before dinner. ‖ 彼は**酒を飲んでも乱れない** He *can hold his liquor* (*well*). ‖ 父は**酒が強い** [**弱い**] My father *can drink quite a lot* [*cannot drink much*]. ‖ 父は**酒の勢いで**母とけんかした *Emboldened by drink*, my father had a fight with my mother. ‖ **酒の席で**仕事の話をするな Don't talk about work *while drinking*. ‖ 後藤さんはいつも**酒臭いね** Mr. Goto's breath always *smells* [*reeks*] *of alcohol*, doesn't it? ‖ 彼は**酒癖が悪い** He *gets bad-tempered* [*aggressive* / *argumentative*] *when he drinks*. ‖ [ことわざ] **酒は百薬の長** Sake is the best medicines. (➤ 日本語からの直訳) / Good wine makes good blood. (➤「良質のワインは良い血を作る」の意の英語のことわざ)．

> **直訳の落とし穴「酒を飲みすぎる」**
> 「酒」は sake として，英語にもなっているが，英語の sake は「日本酒」しか指さない．酒全般は alcohol または an alcoholic drink である．したがって，「彼は酒を飲みすぎる」は (×) He drinks too much sake. ではなく，He drinks too much (alcohol). とする．日本語で「酒を飲む」のことを単に「飲む」ということがあるように，英語でも coffee や water のような飲み物を指す目的語がない場合，現在形で習慣的な行為を表す He drinks a lot. (彼は大酒飲みだ) や He never drinks. (彼は飲まない)，あるいは I drink once or twice a week. (私は週に 1，2 回飲む) は酒のことである．また，名詞の単数形 a drink もしばしば「一杯の酒」「一種類の酒」を指し，have a drink (一杯やる)，go out for a drink (一杯飲みに出かける)，order a drink (酒を注文する) などのように用いる．複数形の drinks は紅茶や清涼飲料などを含む「飲み物」のことをいう．

> 「酒」のいろいろ **ウイスキー** whisky / **ウオツカ** vodka / **カクテル** cocktail / **シェリー** sherry / **シャンパン** champagne / **焼酎** *shochu* / **ジン** gin / **テキーラ** tequila / **日本酒** sake / **発泡酒** low-malt beer / **ビール** beer / **ブランデー** brandy / **ベルモット** vermouth / **マオタイ酒** mao-tai / **マッコリ** makgeolli, makkolli / **マティーニ** martini / **老酒**(らおちゅう) laojiu / **ラム酒** rum / **ワイン** wine

[2]**さけ 鮭**《魚》a **salmon** /sǽmən/ [複 **salmon**] ▶**サケのくん製** smoked *salmon* ‖**塩ザケ** salted salmon.

さげすむ 蔑む despise +目 (心の底から軽蔑する)；**look down on** (対等視しない) ▶彼は彼女を無知だと**蔑んだ** He *despised* her for being ignorant. ‖ 修は行儀作法のなっていない直美を**蔑んだ** Osamu *looked down on* Naomi for her poor manners. ‖ 彼女は**蔑むような目つきで**ぼくを見た She looked on me *with contempt*.

さけのみ 酒飲み a **(heavy) drinker** ; a **drunkard**(飲んだくれ) ▶**大酒飲み** a heavy *drinker*.

さけび 叫び a **cry** ; a **scream** (悲鳴)；an **outcry** (抗議の声) ▶無実の**叫び** *a cry* for innocence ‖ 核軍備反対の**叫び** *an outcry* [*a cry*] against nuclear armaments ‖ 助けを求める女性の**叫び声**が家の中から聞こえた A woman's *cry* [*scream*] for help came from inside the house.

さけぶ 叫ぶ 1【大声を出す】shout ; cry(主に恐怖や悲しみで) ▶「助けて！」と地震でけがをした女性が**叫んだ** "Help!" *shouted* a woman injured in the earthquake. ‖ 多くの人が助けを求めて**叫んだ** Many people *cried* [*shouted*] for help.

2【強く主張する】cry《for》, **clamor**《for》(➤ 後者は「何かを強く要求して叫ぶ」の意) ▶無実を**叫ぶ** *loudly claim* one's innocence ‖ 労働者たちが賃上げ要求を**叫んでいる** The workers *are clamoring for* higher wages. ‖ 生涯教育の必要性が**叫ばれている** The need for lifetime education *is being widely called for*. ‖ このところ日本では脱原発が声高に**叫ばれている** Recently, many people in Japan have *been vociferously demanding* [*been calling for*] the abolition of nuclear power plants.

さけめ 裂け目 a **crack**(割れ目，ひび)；a **tear** /teəʳ/, a

rip（布などの破れ）; a **crevasse** /krəvǽs/（クレバス）▶地震で堤防に**裂け目**が生じた The earthquake caused *a crack* in the bank.

さけよいうんてん 酒酔い運転 driving under the influence（略 DUI）; driving under intense influence（略 DUII）（➤ 後者は泥酔のとき）.

[1]**さける 避ける** avoid ＋目（危険などを意識的に）; stay [keep] away from（近づかない）; flinch from（…にひるむ，たじろぐ）▶危険を**避ける** *avoid* danger ‖ 利害の衝突を**避ける** *avoid* a conflict of interest ‖ 対決を**避ける** *avoid* a confrontation ‖ あんな卑劣な人は**避けた**ほうがいいわよ It's better to *stay* [*keep*] *away from* such a vulgar person. ‖ 父は胃の具合が悪いので刺激の強いものは**避けている** My father *stays* [*keeps*] *away from* spicy foods because he has stomach trouble. ‖ ルリ子とけんかをしてから顔を合わせるのも**避けている** Ever since I had an argument with Ruriko, I *have avoided* (seeing) her. ‖ ストライキは**避けられそうもない** It looks like a strike *is inevitable*. ‖ この問題は**避けて通れない** This is a problem we *cannot avoid* [we *have to face*].

【文型】
…するのを避ける
avoid doing

▶私たちはできるだけ化学添加物の使用を**避けるように**しています We're trying to *avoid* us*ing* chemical additives as much as possible. ‖ 彼は家族のことを話題に**するのを避けている**ように思える It seems to me that he *avoids* talk*ing* about his family.

[2]**さける 裂ける** tear /teəʳ/; rip（バリッと）; split（すぱっと両方に）▶この布地は簡単に**裂ける** This material *tears* easily. ‖ 強風で船の帆が**裂けた** The sail *ripped* under the force of the strong wind. ‖ 雷が落ちて木が 2 つに**裂けた** Lightning hit and *split* the tree in half.（➤ split は無変化動詞）.

▶《慣用表現》これ以上は口が**裂けても**言えない *Whatever happens*, you won't get another word out of me (on the subject).

さげる 下げる・提げる

訳語メニュー
低くする →lower **1**
つるす →hang **2**
（数量・価格・体重などを）減らす →reduce **4**
音量を絞る →turn down **4**

1【上方から下方へ移行させる】lower ＋目

▶額が曲がっているから，左側をもう少し**下げて**ください The frame is tilted. Can you *lower* [*bring down*] the left side a bit? ‖ 飛行機は空港に近づくと機首を**下げた** The airplane *lowered* its nose as it approached the airport.

2【上方からつるす】hang ＋目 ▶軒先に風鈴を**下げる** *hang* a wind bell under the eaves ‖ 肩からバッグを**提げる** carry a bag *slung over* one's shoulder ‖ 首にペンダントを**下げる**（＝身につける）*wear* a pendant around one's neck ‖ 隣人が菓子折りを**提げて**（＝持って）挨拶に来た Our (new) neighbor came to greet us *with* a box of sweets.

3【中心から離す】▶お皿を**下げて**ください Please *remove* the dishes. ／Please *clear* the table. ‖《ウエートレスが》（サラダのお皿を）**お下げして**よろしいですか Have [Are] you finished with your salad? ／Are you still working on your salad?（➤ 後者はインフォーマル）.

▶車を 2 メートルほど後ろに**下げて**ください Please *back up* your car about two meters.

4【状態・程度などを下降させる】▶もう少し値段を**下げて**くれませんか Could you *reduce* [*lower*] the price a little? ／Could you *knock* a bit *off* the price? ‖ 現金なら**値段を下げて**もらえますか Could you *give* me *a discount* for cash (payment)? ‖ 薬を飲んで**熱を下げた** I *brought my fever down* by taking some medicine.

▶生活水準を**下げる** *lower* the standard of living ‖ テレビの音を**下げて**くれませんか Will you *turn down* the TV? ‖ 彼は重要な取り引きで判断を誤ったため，地位を**下げられた** He *was demoted* because he made an error in judgment on an important deal. ‖ 浪人したくなかったら，もう少し受験校の**レベルを下げる**ことだね If you don't want to fail all the entrance exams, you should consider trying to get into an *easier* school [a *less competitive* school]. ‖ 英文のパラグラフは最初の行を数字分**下げる**のがふつうだ The first line of an English paragraph *is* usually *indented* by several spaces.

さげん 左舷 port（➤「右舷」は starboard）.

ざこ 雑魚 a small fish ▶《釣りで》きょうは**雑魚**ばかりだ I caught only *small fish* today.

▶《比喩的》**雑魚**は引っ込んでろ! *Butt out*, you *small fry*!（➤「小者」の意の small fry は集合的に用いる）.

ざこう 座高 ▶私は**座高**90センチだ My *height sitting down* [My *sitting height*] is 90 centimeters. ‖ 日本人は一般に**座高が高い** Japanese generally *have long torsos*.（➤ torso /tɔ́ːʳsoʊ/ は「胴」の意）.

さこく 鎖国 (national) isolation ▶**鎖国政策**をとる adopt *a closed-door policy* ‖ 徳川幕府は200年以上も**鎖国を行った** The Tokugawa Shogunate *isolated* Japan from (the rest of) the world for more than 200 years. ／The Tokugawa Shogunate *closed the door to* [*shut the doors against*] foreigners for more than 200 years.

‖**鎖国主義** isolationism.

さこつ 鎖骨 a collarbone, a clavicle /klǽvɪkəl/

‖**鎖骨骨折** a fracture of the collarbone.

ざこつ 座骨 an ischium /ískiəm/

‖**座骨神経痛** sciatica /saɪǽṭɪkə/.

ざこね 雑魚寝 ▶登山者たちは皆，山小屋で**雑魚寝した** The mountain climbers *were packed like sardines sleeping* on the floor of the hut.（➤ be packed like sardines /sɑːʳdíːnz/ は「（イワシの缶詰のように）びっしり詰まっている」の意）.

ささ 笹 bamboo grass; a bamboo leaf [blade]（葉）

‖**ささ舟** a bamboo-leaf boat ‖**ささやぶ** a bamboo thicket.

ささい 些細な trivial, trifling /tráɪflɪŋ/（➤ 前者がよりふつう）; small（小さな）▶彼らはいつも**ささいな**ことで口論する They always quarrel over *trivial* [*trifling*] matters. ‖ そんな**ささいな**ことでくよくよするな Don't worry about [over] such *small* things.

ささえ 支え a prop（つっかい棒）; (a) support（支えるもの）▶この植木には**支え**がいる This garden plant needs *a prop* [*a support*]. ／This garden plant needs to be propped up [be supported].

▶自動車事故で私たちは一家の**支え**を失った The car accident deprived our family of *support* [of the family *breadwinner*]. ‖ 金銭的な援助はできない

けど，**精神的な支えにはなってあげられると思う** I can't help you with money, but I can give you *moral* [*emotional*] *support*.

さざえ《貝》a **turban** [**top**] **shell**；a **sea snail**（巻き貝．サザエを指すことも多い）

▶**サザエのつぼ焼き** *a turban shell* broiled in its own shell.

ささえる 支える **support** +目（物理的に下から）；**carry** +目（重みなどを）▶**老人はつえで体を支えた** The elderly man *supported* himself with a stick. ‖ **あの 4 本の柱が屋根全体を支えている** Those four pillars *carry* the whole roof. ／The whole roof rests on those four pillars.

▶**彼女は 1 人で一家を支えている** She *supports her family* all by herself.

ささくれ a **hangnail** ▶**人さし指にささくれができちゃったわ** I've got *a hangnail* on my index finger.

ささくれる ▶**その椅子の修理で指がささくれてしまった** Repairing that chair *gave* me *hangnails*.

ささげもの 捧げ物 an **offering**.

ささげる 捧げる **offer** +目（神仏に供える）；**devote** +目（献身する）；**dedicate** +目（献呈する）▶**恋人に愛をささげる** *give* [*offer*] one's love to one's sweetheart ‖ **神前に玉串をささげる** *offer* a branch of a sacred tree to a Shinto god.

> **【文型】**
> **生涯(A)を活動(B)にささげる**
> **devote** A **to** B
> **dedicate** A **to** B
> ➤ B は名詞または動名詞
>
> **【解説】** **devote** が「(労力・時間などを)ささげて生涯を送る」ことに重点があるのに対し，**dedicate** は「ささげる決心や誓いを立てる」ことに重点がある．

▶**杉先生は教育に一生をささげてこられた** Mr. Sugi *has devoted* himself [his life] *to* education.（● Mr. Sugi devoted ... . と過去形にすると，当人は亡くなったという意味になる）‖ **本書を今は亡き前島先生にささげる** This book *is dedicated to* the late Professor Maejima.

▶**彼らは国のために命をささげた**（＝犠牲にした）They *sacrificed themselves* for their country.

ささつ 査察 (an) **inspection** 一動 **査察する** **inspect** +目．

さざなみ 小波 a **ripple** ▶**きょうの湖にはさざ波ひとつない** There isn't *a ripple* on the lake today. ‖ **そよ風で池の面にさざ波が立った** The breeze *rippled* the surface of the pond.

ささみ *sasami*；**sliced chicken breast.**

さざめく **chat and laugh merrily.**

ささやか ▶**私たちはささやかな暮らしをしています** We *live modestly* [*simply*]. ‖《**贈り物などを差し出して**》**ささやかな物ですが，お受け取りください** *This is just a small gift*, but please accept it.（➤ この small は「ささやかな，取るに足りない」の意）‖ **たとえささやかでも自分の家を持ちたいというのが庶民の願いだ** It is the dream of most people to have a house of their own, *however humble it may be*.

ささやき 囁き a **whisper**；a **murmur**（つぶやき）▶**風のささやきに耳を澄ましてごらん** Listen to the *whisper* of the wind. ‖ **試験中にささやき声が聞こえた** There was *a murmur of voices* during the test.

ささやく 囁く **whisper**（+目）▶**男は彼女の耳に何やらささやいた** The man *whispered* something in her ear. ▶**社長はもうすぐ辞職するとささやかれて**（＝うわさされて）**いる** It *is rumored* that the president is resigning soon.

ささる 刺さる **stick** ▶**魚の骨が喉に刺さった** A fish bone *is stuck* in my throat. ‖ **親指にバラのとげが刺さった** I *have got* a rose thorn in my thumb.

さざんか《植物》a **sasanqua** (**camellia**).

さし 差しで **face to face, tête-à-tête**（➤ 後者は堅い言い方）▶**部長と差しで話し合う** talk with the department head *face to face* [*one on one*].（➤ 後者は「一対一で」）.

さじ 匙 a **spoon**；a **tablespoon**（大さじ），a **teaspoon**（小さじ）▶**さじ 3 杯の砂糖** *three spoonfuls of* sugar. ▶《**慣用表現**》**医者もその患者にはさじを投げた** The doctor *gave up on* the patient. ‖ **彼女には両親もさじを投げている** She is *the despair* of her parents.（➤ この despair は「絶望させるもの」）／Her parents *have given up on* her.

さしあげる 差し上げる ▶**よろしければこれをあなたに差し上げます** If you like it, *you can have it*. ／*This is for you*, if you like it. ‖《**掲示**》**ご来店の方にはもれなく粗品を差し上げます** Gift *presented* to every customer. ‖《**店で**》**何を差し上げましょうか** *May I help you?*

✉ **またお手紙差し上げます** I will write (to) you again.

さしあたり 差し当たり **for the present** [**moment**], **for the time being**（当面）；**now, at present**（今は）▶**さしあたりこれで十分だ** This will do *for the present*. ‖ **さしあたり必要なものをそろえておきなさい** Get the things you need *for the time being*. ‖ **さしあたり予定はありません** I have no (particular) plans *for now* [*at present*].

さしいれ 差し入れ ▶**服役者への差し入れ** *things sent* [*brought*] to a person in prison.

さしいれる 差し入れる ▶**鈴木さんは仕事中の私たちにコーヒーとケーキを差し入れてくれた** Mr. Suzuki *brought* us coffee and cake *to have* while we worked.

さしえ 挿し絵 an **illustration**；a **cut**（カット）▶**挿し絵入りの本** an *illustrated* book.

‖**挿し絵画家** an illustrator.（→**イラスト**）.

さしおく 差し置く ▶**木村さんは課長を差し置いて社長と直談判した** Mr. Kimura *went over the head of* the section chief to negotiate directly with the president.（➤ go over the head of は「…を飛び越える」）‖ **何を差し置いてもこの仕事を片づけなければならない** *I cannot attend to anything else until* I have taken care of this.

さしおさえ 差し押さえ **seizure** /síːʒəʳ/, **attachment**（➤ 後者は主に法律用語）；**garnishment**（債権の）▶**裁判所は彼の全財産の差し押さえを命じた** The court ordered the *seizure* [*attachment*] of all his property. ‖ **荒木さんは財産の差し押さえにあった** Mr. Araki *had* his property *seized* [*attached*].

さしかえる 差し替える **replace** +目 ▶**この記事を最新のニュースと差し替えてはどうですか** Why don't you *replace* this article *with* some more recent news?

さしかかる 差し掛かる ▶**列車は鉄橋にさしかかったとき急停車した** The train stopped suddenly just as it *was approaching* the railway bridge. ‖ **選挙戦もいよいよ山場にさしかかった** The election campaign *has reached its climax* [*has come to the most important stage*].

さじかげん 匙加減 ▶**部長のさじ加減ひとつで彼の昇進**

が決まる It *is entirely up to* the general manager whether he will be promoted. ／His promotion *is entirely up to* the general manager. (➤ be up to ... は「…次第である」の意).

さしがね 差し金 ▶これは誰の差し金か Who *manipulated* [*led*] you to do that? ／Whose *idea* was it for you to do that?

さじき 桟敷 a **box** ▶私たちは桟敷席で相撲を楽しんだ We enjoyed watching sumo wrestling from *a box seat*. ‖**天井桟敷** a gallery (最も安い席) ‖**二階桟敷** a dress circle (特等席).

ざしき 座敷 a ***zashiki***

日本紹介 ✉ **座敷は畳を敷いた日本間のことで,特に客をもてなす部屋をいいます** A *zashiki* is a Japanese-style room floored with tatami mats. It is used especially to entertain guests.

さしきず 刺し傷 a **stab wound**.

さしこみ 差し込み 1【電気器具の】 a **plug**; an **outlet**, a **wall socket** (差し込み口) ▶そのコンセントに差し込みを入れてくれる? Could you insert *the plug* in that outlet? (→コンセント).

2【急な腹痛】 ▶腹に差し込みがきて,うずくまった I doubled over with *a sharp pain* in the stomach.

さしこむ 差し込む 1【はめ込む】 **insert** +目 ▶錠前に鍵を差し込む *insert* a key into a lock ‖扇風機のプラグを差し込んでちょうだい Can you *plug in* the (electric) fan, please? (➤ plug in で「プラグをコンセントに差し込む」).

2【光が入る】 ▶月の光が窓からさし込んでいる The moonlight *is streaming in* through the window. ‖日光が部屋いっぱいにさし込んでいる The sunlight *is pouring into* the room.

さしさわり 差し障り ▶差し障りのない話題 a *safe* topic (of conversation) ‖その件は差し障りがあるから言えない I won't mention the matter *for fear of giving offense*. (➤「気を悪くさせるのを恐れて」).

さししめす 指し示す **point** 《at, to》(指で); **indicate** (注意を向けさせる) ▶地図上の矢印は北を指し示している The arrow on the map *indicates* north.

さしず 指図 **directions** (指示); **orders** (命令) **一動 指図する** **direct** +目 ▶私の指図に従いなさい Follow my *directions*. ‖私たちは先生の指図を仰いだ We *asked for directions* from the teacher. ‖おまえの指図は受けないぞ I (will) refuse to take *orders* from you. ‖次に私が何をすればいいかなんて,あなたから指図されたくない I don't want you to *tell* [want you *telling*] me what I should do next. (➤ -ing 形にするのはややくだけた言い方).

さしずめ ▶彼がシャーロック・ホームズなら,きみはさしずめワトソン医師だな If he is Sherlock Holmes, you *must be* Dr. Watson. ‖さしずめ(＝さしあたり)これだけの金があれば生活には困らない This amount of money will get me by *for the time being*. ／I can live comfortably on this much money *for a while*.

さしせまる 差し迫る ▶入試が差し迫っている The entrance examinations *are approaching fast* [*are close at hand*]. ‖それは差し迫った問題ではない That is not an *urgent* [*a pressing*] matter.

さしだしにん 差し出し人 a **sender** ▶封筒には必ず差し出し人の住所を書きなさい You should always put the *sender's address* [*return address*] on the envelope.

さしだす 差し出す **hold** [**stretch**] **out**; **proffer** +目 (うやうやしく) ▶彼女は立ち上がって握手しようと手を差し出した She stood up and *held* [*stretched*] *out* her hand for a handshake. ‖セールスマンはその主婦に名刺を差し出した The salesman *held out* [*offered*] his business card to the housewife. (➤ 会社の受付などに名刺を差し出すような場合の動詞は present).

さしちがえる 刺し違える ▶2人の武士は刺し違えて死んだ The two samurai(s) *stabbed each other* and died.

さしつかえ 差し支え ▶勉強に差し支え(＝影響)があるならクラブ活動をやめるべきだ You should quit your club activities if they *affect* [*interfere with*] your studies. ‖お差し支えなければメールアドレスもご記入ください Please fill in your email address also *if you don't mind*. ‖お差し支えなければあすおいでください Please come tomorrow *if it is not inconvenient* (*for you*). ‖彼は天才だと言っても差し支えない *It may safely be said* [*You may safely say*] *that* he's a genius.

▶窓を開けても差し支えありませんか *Would you mind if* I opened the window? ／*Would you mind* my opening the window? (➤ if を使った言い方のほうが自然. 仮定法なので動詞は過去形になる).

さしつかえる 差し支える ▶いつまでもテレビを見てるとあしたの学校に差し支えるわよ If you watch TV so late, it'll *interfere with* your schoolwork tomorrow!

さして ▶それはさして重要な問題ではない That's *not* a *very* important problem.

さしでがましい 差し出がましい ▶差し出がましいようですが,お庭の手入れをなさったほうがよろしいのでは? *This may be none of my business*, but don't you think it would be better to take care of your garden? ‖差し出がましい口を利くな *You have no business saying such a thing* (*to me*). ／*Mind your own business!*

さしでぐち 差し出口 ▶我々のことで差し出口を利くな Stop *sticking* [*poking*] *your nose into* our business. (➤ stick [poke] one's nose into で「…に口出しする」).

さしとめる 差し止める **suspend** +目, **halt** +目 (一時中止する. 後者の方がより堅い語); **forbid** +目 (禁止する) ▶政府筋からの圧力でその雑誌の発行は差し止められた The publication of that magazine *was suspended* under pressure from the government. (➤「記事」の差し止めの場合には That article was forbidden [banned] ... となる).

さしのべる 差し伸べる ▶困っている友人に手を差し伸べるのは当然の義務だ It is our (natural) duty to *lend* [*give*] *a hand to* friends in trouble.

さしはさむ 差し挟む ▶人が話をしているときに口を差し挟むものではない You shouldn't *cut in on* other people's conversation. ‖彼女の証言には疑いを差し挟む余地がない Her testimony *leaves no room* for doubt.

さしひかえる 差し控える **refrain from**; **withhold**, **reserve** (保留する) ▶病み上がりだったので私は外出を差し控えた I *refrained from* going out because I was recovering from an illness. ‖外務大臣はその事件に関する発言を差し控えた The Foreign Minister *withheld* [*reserved*] comment on the incident.

さしひき 差し引き **the balance** (差し引き残高) ▶差し引き3000円の損[得]だ There is a *net* loss [gain] of 3,000 yen. (➤ net は「正味の, 純…」) ‖差し引きゼロになった The profits and losses *canceled* *each other out*.（➤ cancel out で「相殺する」）.

さしひく 差し引く **deduct** +㊔ ▶毎月約５万円を税金として給料から差し引かれている Some 50,000 yen *is deducted* [*is taken away*] from my monthly pay for taxes. ‖ 彼は税金を差し引いて10万円の臨時収入を得た He obtained a supplementary 100,000 yen income *after taxes*.

さしみ 刺身 **sashimi**（➤ 英語化している）

日本紹介 ✉ **刺身は鮮魚を薄切りにしたものです．お造りともいいます．タイ・マグロ・イカなどが好まれます．深い鉢に大根の千切りを敷き，その上に盛りつけます．わさびとしょうゆをつけて食べます** Sashimi is thinly sliced fresh raw fish. It is also called *'otsukuri.' Tai* (sea bream), tuna, and cuttlefish sashimi are very popular. The slices are arranged on finely shredded daikon (radish) in a deep dish. We dip sashimi in soy sauce flavored with *wasabi* before eating it.

▶タイを刺身にして食べる eat raw sea bream *after cutting it into thin slices* [*into sashimi*] ‖ 刺身の盛り合わせを注文する order a platter of *assorted sashimi*（➤ platter は「大皿」; assorted は「取り合わせた」の意）.

さしむかい 差し向かい ▶こうやって差し向かいで酒を飲むのは久しぶりだね It's been a long time since we last had a drink like this, *sitting across* (*the table*) *from each other* [*sitting face to face* (*across the table*)].

さしむける 差し向ける **dispatch** +㊔, **send** +㊔（➤ 前者が日本語に近い）▶新聞社は直ちに記者を現場へ差し向けた The newspaper *dispatched* [*sent*] reporters to the scene at once.

さしも ▶さしもの猛暑もようやく終わった The *unparalleled* summer heat has finally come to an end.

さしもどす 差し戻す ▶最高裁はその訴訟事件を下級裁判所に差し戻した The Supreme Court *referred* the case *back* [*returned* the case] to a lower court.

さしゅう 査収 ▶領収書を同封いたします．ご査収ください Enclosed is the receipt. *Please check* [*make sure*] *that it is correct*.

[1]**さしょう 査証** **a visa** /víːzə/ ‖**査証免除協定** visa-exempt arrangements.（⇀ビザ）.

[2]**さしょう 些少** **a small amount.**

[3]**さしょう 詐称** ▶年齢を詐称する（＝うそをつく）*lie* about one's age.

さじょう 砂上 ‖**砂上の楼閣** a home built on (the) sand, a house of cards（➤ 基礎のしっかりしていないもの）, a castle in the air（➤ 不可能なもの）.

ざしょう 座礁する **run** [**go**] **aground**, **ground**; **be stranded**; **go** [**run**] **on a rock**（暗礁に乗り上げる）▶船は三浦沖で座礁した The ship *ran aground* [*grounded*] off Miura. ‖ 船は座礁して大破した The ship *went* [*ran*] *on a rock* and broke in half.

さしわたし 差し渡し ▶橋［翼］の差し渡し *the span* of a bridge [a wing].

さじん 砂塵 **a cloud of dust.**

[1]**さす 差す・指す・挿す**

📖 **訳語メニュー**
花などを入れる ⇀put in **1**
方向を指さす ⇀point **3**
生徒などを当てる ⇀call on **4**
意味する ⇀mean **5**

1【物の中に入れる】 ▶チューリップを花瓶に挿す *put* a tulip *in* a vase ‖ 髪に花を挿す *wear* a flower in one's hair ‖ 鍋に水を差す（＝注ぎ足す）*put* some water *in* [*into*] the pot ‖ 昔の侍は腰に刀を差していた In the old days, samurai used to *wear* a sword at their side. ‖ 彼女からのラブレターが状差しに差してあった The love letter from her *was sitting* in the letter rack.

▶目薬を（目に）さしなさい *Apply* eye drops (to your eyes). ／ *Put in* eye drops. ‖ この自転車に油をさしなさい *Oil* this bicycle.

▶私たちの関係に水を差すつもり？ Are you trying to *come* [*put a barrier*] between us?

2【光などが入ってくる】 ▶この部屋は西日がさす The afternoon sun *comes into* this room. ／ This room *gets* the afternoon sun. ‖ 雲の切れ間から日がさしてきた The sun *began to shine* [*appeared*] from among the clouds. ‖ 心肺蘇生を施されて，その少年の顔に血の気がさしてきた After the boy received cardiopulmonary resuscitation, his face *regained color* [*color returned* to his face].

3【方向を示す】 **point**《to》▶磁石の針は常に北を指す The needle of a compass always *points* (*to* the) north. ‖ 駅はどっちですかと聞くと，その男性は何も言わずに右の方を指した When I asked the man which way the train station was, he *pointed to* the right without saying anything.

4【指名する】 **call on** ▶先生は私たちを順番に指した Our teacher *called on* us in turn. ‖ きょう数学の授業で指された I *got called on* in math class today.

5【意味する】 **mean**; **refer to**（指して言う）▶代数では *x* は未知数を指す In algebra, *x means* an unknown quantity. ‖ この「それ」とは何を指していますか What does this 'it' *refer to*? ‖ 准教授たちに対する批判は暗に教授を指してなされたものだ The criticism directed toward the associate professors was (in fact) covertly *meant* for the professors.（➤ covertly は「ひそかに」）.

6【将棋や碁を】 ▶彼とはよく将棋を指したものだ I often *played* shogi with him.

7【傘を】 ▶傘をさす *put up* [*open*] an umbrella（➤ put up は「掲げる」, open は「開く」）.

[2]**さす 刺す** **1【刃物などで】** **stab** +㊔（ぐさりと）; **prick** +㊔（ちくりと）▶強盗はその家政婦をナイフで刺した The robber *stabbed* the housekeeper with a knife. ‖ バラのとげで指を刺した I *pricked* my finger on a rose thorn. ‖ 鶏肉を串に刺し，たれをつけて焼いた I *skewered* some chicken meat, dipped it into the sauce, and broiled it.

2【虫が】 **bite** +㊔, **sting** +㊔ ▶蚊に刺された I *was bitten* [*was stung*] by a mosquitoe. ‖ 腕をハチに刺された I *got stung* on the arm by a bee.

3【刺激する】 ▶外は肌を刺すような寒さだった It was *piercingly* [*bitingly*] cold outside. ‖ 化学実験室に入ると強い臭いが鼻を刺した As I entered the chemical laboratory, a strong smell *hit* me [*assailed my nostrils*].

4【野球】 ▶ランナーを刺す *throw out* a runner ／ *put* a runner *out* ‖ 長野選手は三塁で刺された Chono *was thrown out* at third.

さすが 1【予想どおり】 ▶さすが有名なバイオリニストだけあってすばらしい演奏だった He played magnificently, *as* (*well*) *might be expected* of a famous violinist.（➤「有名なバイオリニストに当然期待されるとおり」の意）‖ さすがに彼は大冒険家だ He is *truly* [*indeed*] a great adventurer. ‖ 誰も知らなかったのに，父さんに聞いたらよく知っていた．**さすがは父さん！** Nobody else knew, but when I asked my father, he knew all about it. *That's my father* (*for you*)! ‖ **対話** 「弟のやつ，T大に受かったよ」「**さすがぁ！**」"My (younger) brother's been accepted by T University." "*Good for him*!"

2【…でさえも】▶**さすがの**コンピュータも独創性では人間の頭脳にはかなわないようだ It seems that *even* the best computer is no match for the human brain in originality. ‖ カレーライスは大好きだが，3日続けて出されると**さすがに**飽きる Even though I love curry and rice, *it's only natural* to get sick of it after being served it three days in a row. ‖ 由季はその時**さすがに**緊張していた Yuki was *understandably* nervous then. ／Yuki was, *as you can imagine*, nervous then.

さずかる 授かる **be awarded**（賞などを）
▶その画家は昨年文化勲章を**授かった** The artist *was awarded* the Order of Cultural Merit last year. ‖ 結婚後7年目にしてようやく**子宝を授かった** After seven years of marriage we *were* finally *blessed with a child*. ‖ **健康な体を授かった**ことを何よりも幸せに思います Nothing makes me happier than the fact that I *have been blessed* (*since birth*) *with good health*.

さずかりこん 授かり婚 a "**blessed-with-a-child**" **wedding**.

さずける 授ける **award** /əwɔ́ːʳd/ +㊁（賞などを）; **initiate**《into》（知識などを伝授する）▶彼に優等賞を**授ける** *award* him an honor prize ‖ 彼は父親から商売の秘けつを**授けられた** He *was initiated into* the secret of his trade by his father.

サスペンス **suspense** ▶スリルと**サスペンス**あふれる映画 a very thrilling film ／a thriller ‖ この小説は最後の1章まで**サスペンス**に満ちている This novel will keep you in *suspense* until the last chapter.

> **危ないカタカナ語✹ サスペンス**
> 英語の suspense は日本語の意味と異なり，ある事が決まらなかったり発表されなかったりすることからくる「気がかり，不安な状態」を指し，「謎に包まれたもの」の意味はない．いわゆる「サスペンスもの」に当たる表現は mystery または thriller である．suspenseful story は「先がどうなるかわからず，はらはらする物語」．

サスペンダー **suspenders**.

さすらう **wander** ▶ヨーロッパを**さすらう** *wander* around in Europe.

さする **rub gently**（前後・上下に優しく）▶私は祖父の腰を**さすった** I *gently rubbed* the lower part of my grandfather's back.

ざせき 座席 a **seat** ▶**座席に着く** *take a seat* ／*seat oneself* ‖ 私の**座席**を確保しておいてもらえますか Will you keep *a seat* for me? ‖《劇場などで》**座席はまだありますか** Are there any *seats* left [available]?
‖**座席指定券** a reserved-seat ticket.

させつ 左折 a **left turn** ━**動 左折する** **go** [**turn**] **left, make a left turn** ▶次の角を**左折して**ください Please *make a left turn* at the next corner.

ざせつ 挫折 (a) **failure**（失敗）; (a) **frustration**（くじくこと）▶公園建設計画は資金不足のため**挫折した** The plan to build a park *fell through* [*did not work out*] because of a lack of funds. (➤ fall through は「(計画が)失敗する」, work out は「うまくいく」) ／Because of a lack of funds, the plan to build a park *ended in failure*. (➤ end in は「結果的に…になる」) ‖ 彼はどの大学にも入学できず，深い**挫折感に襲われた** Since he could not get into any university, he was overcome with a deep *sense of failure*.

させる

> **【文型】**
> **人(A)に(無理やり)…させる**
> **make** A do
> **人(A)に(希望どおりに)…させる**
> **let** A do
> **人(A)に(説得して，頼んで)…させる**
> **get** A **to** do
> **have** A do
>
> **《解説》** **get** は「Aにいろいろ働きかけて…する状態に持っていく」, **have** は「ひと言頼めば，Aは…してくれる状態にある」という含みがある．**get** のあとには to do がくることに注意．意味の上からも persuade（説得して…させる）と同じ文型と覚えておくとよい．**get** と **have** は「…してもらう」に当たる場合も多い．

1【強制的に】**make**
語法 (1)目的語のあとに動詞の原形がくる．(2)受け身になると原形動詞の前に to をつける．
▶あの子たちを静かに**させて**くれ Please *make* those kids *keep* quiet. ‖ 私はグラウンドを3周**させられた**(=走らされた) I *was forced to* run three laps around the (athletic) field.

2【本人の希望どおりに】**let** ▶彼は娘の好きなように**させた** He *let* his daughter *do* as she pleased [liked]. ‖ 1つ質問**させて**くれ *Let* me ask you a question. ‖ 少し考え**させて**ください Please *give* me *time to think* about it. ／Please *let* me *think* (about it).

3【頼んで】**have, get**（➤ 後者を用いると高圧的に響くか，話し手が命令される人の上位者であることをほのめかすのがふつう；⇀**もらう**）▶あとで彼に**電話させ**ましょうか Shall I *have* him *call* you later? ‖ その件は息子に**調べさせ**ましょう I'll *have* my son *check* on it. ／I'll *get* my son *to check* on it. (➤ 前者では have に，後者では get に強勢を置く；to の有無に注意)．
▶私たちは彼女をくどいてクラブに**入部させた** We *talked* her *into joining* our club.

させん 左遷 **relegation**（隅へ追いやること）; (a) **demotion**（降格）▶支店長の**左遷**にほかの従業員は皆喜んだ The *relegation* [*demotion*] of the branch manager pleased the rest of the staff. ‖ 彼はある支店に**左遷された** He *was transferred to a lower position* in a certain branch office. (➤ transfer /trænsfə́ːʳ/ は「転任させる」)．

ざぜん 座禅 **Zen** [**zazen**] **meditation** (**in a cross-legged position**) ▶**座禅を組む** practice *Zen* [*zazen*] *meditation*.

さぞ ▶長旅で**さぞ**お疲れでしょう You *must be* very tired after the long journey. (🔘「きっと…に違いない」の意の must を用いる) ‖ 一年中春のような気候だったら自然は**さぞかし**単調なことだろう If we had spring-like weather all (the) year round, *how* monotonous nature *would be*! ‖ 亡くなった父も**さぞや**喜んでいることと思います I'm sure my late father *would* also *be* very pleased.

さそい 誘い (an) **invitation** ▶彼女は先約があったのでス

キーへの誘いを断った She declined *an invitation* to go skiing because of a previous engagement.

さそいあわせる 誘い合わせる ▶彼女らは友だちと誘い合わせて花見に出かけた They *asked* (all) their friends and went cherry blossom viewing.

さそいこむ 誘い込む ▶彼はまだ13歳のときに悪の道に誘い込まれた He *was tempted into* wrongdoing when he was only thirteen. ‖ セイレンは甘い歌で男たちを誘い込み，岩礁に乗り上げさせて死に至らしめた The Sirens *lured* men to their death on the rocks with sweet songs.

さそいだす 誘い出す ▶その晩は悪友に誘い出された Some bad friends *lured* me *out* [*talked* me *into going out*] for the evening.

さそう 誘う 1【勧める，招く】**ask** +目，**invite** +目（➤ 後者は「招待する」に近い）

【文型】
人(A)に…しようと誘う
ask [**invite**] A **to** do
人(A)を活動(B)に誘う
invite A **to** B

▶釣りに行こうと彼を誘った I *asked* him *to* go fishing with me. ‖ 彼は両親をレストランのディナーに一緒に行こうと誘った He *invited* his parents *to* dinner at a restaurant. ‖ 太郎はフィアンセを映画に誘った Taro *invited* his fiancée [*asked* his fiancée out] *to* a movie. ‖ 友だちを数人誕生パーティーに誘った I *invited* [*asked*] several friends *to* my birthday party.
▶ママ，日野君にデートに誘われちゃった Mom, Hino *asked* me *out* (*on a date*). ‖ あの人たちから夏休みに北海道旅行をしないかと誘われている I *have been asked* to take a trip to Hokkaido with them during the summer vacation. ‖ 私はある仕事をしないかと誘われている I *have been offered* a job. ‖ 誘ってくれてありがとう Thanks for *asking* [*inviting*] me.

2【働きかける】▶彼女の身の上話は聞く者の涙を誘った (Hearing) the story of her life *brought tears to* the listeners. ‖ 好天に誘われて何万人もの人が海へ泳ぎに出かけた The fine weather *brought* [*lured*] tens of thousands of people *out* for swimming in the sea.

ざぞう 座像 a **seated statue**（彫像）; a **seated image**（絵）.

さそり 蠍 a **scorpion**.

さそりざ 蠍座 (a) **Scorpio** ▶さそり座の女性 *a female Scorpio* ／*a Scorpio woman*.

さそん 差損 (a) **loss** ‖為替差損 a foreign currency (transaction) loss.

さた 沙汰 ▶雷が鳴っているのにゴルフをするなんて正気の沙汰じゃないね He *must be crazy* [He *is not all there*] to play golf when there is thunder (and lightning). (➤ be not all there は「常識に欠ける」の意のインフォーマルな表現) ‖ そんなことはするな．警察沙汰になるぞ Don't do that sort of thing, or you'll *get in trouble with the police*. ‖ 追って沙汰する *Judgment shall be passed* later.

さだか 定かな **clear** ▶そのあとのことはどうも記憶が定かでないんだ I just can't remember *clearly* what happened after that. ‖ 誰の差し金か定かでない It *isn't clear* who's pulling the strings.

さだまる 定まる **settle (down)** ▶天気はようやく定まったようだ The weather seems to *have settled* at last. ‖ ふらふらしていた息子の進路も2学期に入ってようやく定まった My son was not serious about his future direction, but he finally *became focused* when the second semester started. ‖ 方針がはっきり定まらないうちにスタートしないほうがいい You shouldn't begin something until the direction to take *has* clearly *been determined* [*set*]. ‖ 最近は天気が定まらない The weather is *changeable* these days.

さだめ 定め 1【決まり】▶私たちは法の定め（＝法律）に従わなければならない We must abide by [obey] *the law*.

2【運命】**fate** ▶こんなぐうたらな男と一緒になるのが私の定めかもしれないわね I guess I'*m fated* [I'*m destined*] to have such a lazy husband.

さだめる 定める **establish** +目 ▶住まいを定める *establish* a residence ‖ 法律を定める *establish* a law ‖ 狙いを定めて矢を射る *take aim* [*aim at the target*] and shoot an arrow ‖ 目標を定めて勉強したほうがよい It is better to study *with a fixed goal*.

ざだんかい 座談会 a **round-table discussion**; a **symposium** /sɪmpóʊziəm/（聴衆を前にした）.

さち 幸 **happiness** ▶わが国は海の幸，山の幸に恵まれている Japan is (abundantly) blessed with *products from land and sea*. ‖ お2人の船出に幸多かれと祈ります I wish both of you *happiness* at the start of your new life.

ざちょう 座長 a **chair(person)**（議長）; a **troupe leader**（劇団などの長）.

さつ 札 《米》a **bill**,《英》a **(bank) note** ▶1万円札を5000円札2枚に替える change [break] a 10,000-yen *bill* [*note*] into two 5,000-yen *bills* [*notes*]. ‖札入れ a wallet,《米また》a billfold.

-さつ -冊 a **copy**（部）▶ノート3冊 *three* notebooks ‖『ニューズウィーク』最新号を1冊買った I bought *a copy* of the latest "Newsweek" (magazine). ‖ この本を5冊ください Please give me *five copies* of this book. (● these five books は5冊の（違う）本を買う場合) ‖ 理髪店で順番待ちをしている間に漫画本を3冊読んでしまった I read *three* comic books while waiting for my turn at the barbershop. (➤ 3冊の別々の本なので three copies とはしない).

ざつ 雑な **careless**（神経の行き届かない），**sloppy**（いいかげんな）; **shoddy**（安っぽい，見かけ倒しの）▶雑な仕事 a *sloppy* [*careless*] job ‖ 彼は仕事が雑だ He *is careless and untidy* in his work. ／His work *is sloppy* [*slipshod*]. ‖ このキャビネットは作りがずいぶん雑だ This cabinet *is* rather *shoddy*. ‖ 雑に扱わないで Don't treat it *carelessly*. ／You should treat it more carefully. ‖ きみは雑だなあ You're so *sloppy*.

さつい 殺意 **murderous intent** [**intentions**] ▶男は彼女に対する殺意はなかったと言い張っている The man insists that he *didn't have murderous intent toward* her.

さつえい 撮影 **photography** /fətá:grəfi/（写真の）; **shooting**（映画の）一動 **撮影する** **take a photograph** [**picture**]《of》（写真を）; **shoot** +目（映画を）
▶私は友人の披露宴の写真を撮影した I *took photographs* [*pictures*] *of* my friend's wedding reception. ‖ 私たちは湖畔で記念撮影をした We *had a souvenir photograph* [*picture*] *taken* on the shore of a lake. ‖《掲示》撮影禁止 Photography prohibited. ／No photos. (➤ さらに具体的に言うには Photography and videotaping [filming] prohibited. ／No videorecorders or cameras (allowed).).
▶新作映画の撮影は来月開始予定です *Shooting* on [for] the new film is scheduled to start next

month.
‖撮影所 a movie studio.

ざつえき 雑役 an **odd job, chores** /tʃɔ́ːrz/ ‖**雑役婦** a cleaning woman ‖**雑役夫** a handyman.

ざつおん 雑音 **noise**; **static** (電波障害; 口うるさい批判)《参考》テレビ放映終了後の雑音を特に white noise と呼ぶ. ▶ラジオにひどく**雑音**が入るんだ There's a lot of *noise* [*static*] on the radio.
▶《比喩的》周りの**雑音**は気にするな Don't pay attention to all that *static*.

さ

さっか 作家 a **writer**; an **author** (著者); a **novelist** (小説家)
‖**絵本作家** a picture-book author ‖**陶芸作家** a ceramic artist ‖**流行作家** a popular writer.

ざっか 雑貨 **miscellaneous** /mìsəléɪniəs/ **goods, sundries** ‖**雑貨店** a variety [general] store, a dime store, a five-and-ten (➤ あとの2つは《米・インフォーマル》).

サッカー **soccer,**《英また》**(association)football**
▶**サッカー**は今小学生の男の子の間で人気が高い Playing *soccer* is now popular among elementary schoolboys. ‖**サッカー選手** a soccer player; eleven(チーム全員).

「サッカー用語」のいろいろ **アディショナルタイム** additional time /**イエローカード** yellow card /**ウイング** winger /**延長戦** overtime /**オウンゴール** own goal /**オフサイド** offside /**キックオフ** kickoff /**クロスバー** crossbar /**コーナーキック** corner kick /**ゴール** goal /**ゴールキーパー** goalkeeper,《米》goaltender /**ゴールキック** goal kick /**ゴールポスト** goalpost /**サイドバック** fullback /**サポーター** supporter /**シュート** shot /**スイーパー** sweeper /**ストライカー** striker /**スライディング** sliding tackle /**スローイン** throw-in /**センタリング** center /**タックル** tackle /**タッチライン** touchline /**ディフェンダー** defender /**得失点差** goal difference /**トラップ** trapping /**ドリブル** dribble /**ハーフタイム** halftime /**パス** pass /**ハットトリック** hat trick /**ハンド** handball /**PK戦** shootout /**ピッチ** pitch /**フェイント** feint /**フォワード** forward /**フリーキック** free kick /**ヘディング** header /**ペナルティー** penalty /**ペナルティーキック** penalty kick /**ボレー** volley /**ミッドフィールダー** midfielder /**レッドカード** red card

さつがい 殺害する **kill** +㊐; **murder** +㊐ (計画的な); **assassinate** +㊐ (特に要人を暗殺する) ▶その男は同僚を**殺害**して逮捕された That man was arrested for the *killing* [*murder*] of his co-worker. ‖2人のテロリストが大統領の**殺害を企てた** Two terrorists *attempted to assassinate* the president.

さっかく 錯覚 an **illusion**; **imagination** (気のせい) ▶目の**錯覚** an optical *illusion* ‖誰かがドアをノックしたと思ったが**錯覚**だった I thought someone had knocked on the door, but it was just my *imagination*. ‖あの新人歌手は人気を実力と**錯覚して**(=混同して)いる That new singer *is confusing* her popularity *with* real ability.

ざつがく 雑学 ▶映画の**雑学的知識** movie *trivia* ‖あの人は**雑学の大家**だ(=何でもよく知っている) He is *a storehouse of trivia* [*miscellaneous information*]. (➤ storehouse は「(知識の)宝庫」).

サッカリン **saccharin** /sǽkərɪn/.

ざっかん 雑感 **miscellaneous** /mìsəléɪniəs/ **impressions** [**thoughts**].

[1]**さっき 殺気** ▶**殺気立った**群衆は警官に石を投げ始めた The *wildly excited* mob began to throw stones at the police. ‖武蔵は**殺気**(=危険が起こりそうな気配)を感じて身構えた Apprehending *imminent danger*, Musashi assumed a posture of defense.

[2]**さっき** a **little** [**a short**] **while ago**; **some time ago** (しばらく前) ▶石原さんは**さっき**帰りましたよ Miss Ishihara left for home *a little while ago* [*some time ago*]. (➤「たった今」なら just now) ‖**さっきはごめんね** I'm sorry about what I said [did] to you *a little while ago*. ‖妹さんが**さっきから**そこで待っているよ Your (younger) sister has been waiting there *for a while* now. ‖**対話**「**さっきから**どこへ行っていたの?」「トイレ」 "Where have you been *all this time* [*while*]?" "In the rest room." (➤ rest room はレストランやデパートなどのトイレをいう).

ざっきちょう 雑記帳 a **notebook**.

さつきばれ 五月晴れ **nice weather in May** (5月の); **nice weather during the rainy season** (梅雨の晴れ間) ▶きょうは**五月晴れ**だ It's *nice May weather* today.

さっきゅう 早急に **immediately** (時を移さずに); **promptly** (速やかに) ▶**早急に**その計画を実行に移してくれ Implement that plan *immediately*. ‖状況を**早急に**調査する必要がある We need to investigate the situation *without delay*.

さっきょく 作曲 **composition** 一㊀ **作曲する** **compose** +㊐, **write music** ▶モーツァルトは8歳で最初の交響曲を**作曲した** Mozart *composed* his first symphony at the age of eight. ‖この歌はバーニー・トーピンが歌詞を書き, エルトン・ジョンが**作曲した** Bernie Taupin wrote the words of the song and Elton John *set* them *to music*. ‖その歌手は自分で**作詞作曲した** That singer *wrote both the words and the music* for his [her] song.
‖**作曲家** a composer.

ざっきょビル 雑居ビル an **omnibus building**, a **multipurpose building**(多目的ビル).

さっきん 殺菌する **sterilize** /stérəlaɪz/ +㊐; **pasteurize** /pǽstʃəraɪz/ +㊐ (低温で) ▶ふきんを熱湯で**殺菌する** *sterilize a* dish towel in boiling water ‖加工牛乳は**低温殺菌されている** Processed milk *is pasteurized*.

ざっきん 雑菌 **harmful germs** ▶**雑菌**の繁殖 (the) propagation of *bacteria*.

サックス a **sax**(➤ saxophone の短縮語)
‖**サックス奏者** a saxophonist /sǽksəfoʊnɪst/.

ざっくばらん ▶土井さんは**ざっくばらん**な人柄なので話しやすい Mr. Doi is a *frank* [an *outspoken* / a *straightforward*] person and easy to talk to. (➤ いずれも「率直な, 思ったとおりに言う」の意) ‖**ざっくばらんに**話し合おう Let's talk *frankly*. ‖**ざっくばらんに**言えば, 今の息子さんの成績では K 大学(入学)は無理です *Frankly*, with your son's current grades, it won't be possible for him to get into K University.

ざっくり ▶**ざっくり**編んだセーター a *loose-knit* sweater ‖**ざっくり**言えば *roughly* speaking ‖**ざっくり**したスケジュールを教えてください Please tell [give] me the *rough* schedule. ‖サメの仕業だ. 網を**ざっくり**食いちぎられている The net *has been chewed to pieces*. It must have been done by sharks.

ざっこく 雑穀 **minor cereals** ▶**雑穀**ご飯 rice cooked with *minor* (*cereal*) *grains*.

さっこん 昨今 ▶**昨今**の(=現在の)経済情勢では大幅な賃上げは期待できない We can't expect a substantial pay raise under *current* economic conditions.

さっさと **at once**(直ちに); **quickly** (速く) ▶何て散らかっているの！さっさと部屋を片づけなさいよ What a mess! Tidy up [Straighten up] your room *at once* [*quickly*]. ‖彼女はさっさと買い物を済ませた She did her shopping *quickly* [*on the run*]. (➤後者はインフォーマル) ‖さっさと寝なさいよ！Go to bed *right now*! (➤怒っているような場合) ‖さっさとやりなさい！Do it *right now*! ／*No resting*! ‖彼女は仕事が終わるといつもさっさと帰宅してしまう She always *hurries* home after work. ‖彼はさっさと金を払った He paid the money *right away*.

¹**さっし 察し** **guessing, anticipatory perception** ▶美津子は察しがいい Mitsuko *is quick at guessing*. ／Mitsuko *is a good mind reader*. (➤mind reader は「読心術者」) ‖察しがいいねえ *You're quite perceptive*. ‖おまえのたくらんでいることはだいたい察しがつく I *have a rough idea* of [I *can guess*] what you are up to. ‖お察しのとおりです *You've guessed right*. ‖日本文化は「察しの文化」と言われる Japanese culture is described as a *mind-reading* culture. (➤a culture of consideration [anticipatory perception] ともいう).

²**さっし 冊子** a **book** ‖小冊子 a booklet.

サッシ a **sash** ▶アルミサッシ *an aluminum* (*window*) *sash* ‖サッシの窓 a *metal-framed* glass sliding window.

> **危ないカタカナ語✹ サッシ**
> **1**「金属製の窓枠」の意味の「サッシ」は英語の sash からきているが, 開口部に取り付ける枠は英語では window frame という.「サッシの窓」は sash window とはいわず, 訳例のようにする.
> **2** sash window は英米に多い「上げ下げ窓」のことで casement window (開き窓)に対する表現. 日本に多い左右に動く「引き違い窓」は sliding window という.

ざっし 雑誌 a **magazine**; a **journal** (専門的な); a **periodical** (定期刊行物) ▶電車の中で漫画雑誌を読んでいる人が多い Many people read *comic magazines* on the train.
‖雑誌記者 a magazine reporter [writer] ‖医学[科学]雑誌 a medical [scientific] journal ‖学術雑誌 a scientific [an academic] journal ‖男性[女性]雑誌 a men's [women's] magazine.

ざつじ 雑事 ▶雑事を片づける do the *chores* (➤chores /tʃɔːʳz/ は「家庭内の日常の雑用」) ‖このところ身辺の雑事に追われていて忙しい I am busy with *personal business* [*affairs*] these days.

ざっしゅ 雑種 ▶この犬は雑種です This dog is *a mongrel* [*a crossbreed*]. (➤mongrel は特に犬についていう) ‖ラバは馬とロバの雑種(＝交配種)だ A mule is *a cross* between a horse and a donkey. ／A mule is *a hybrid* of [from] a horse and a donkey.

ざっしゅうにゅう 雑収入 a **miscellaneous** /mìsəléɪniəs/ **income**; a **miscellaneous revenue** /révənjùː/ (➤企業の雑収入).

さっしょう 殺傷 ▶このおもちゃの改造拳銃には殺傷力がある This converted toy gun *can wound or kill people*.

さっしん 刷新 (an) **innovation** (革新, 新機軸); (a) **complete reform** (全面改革) ▶校風を刷新する *reform* the school tradition(s) ‖政治の刷新を行う carry out *a complete reform* in politics ‖会社で人事の刷新が行われた There has been *a personnel reshuffle* [*shake-up*] in our company. (➤後者はインフォーマル) ‖今こそ政界の刷新を図るべき時だ Now is the time for *a cleanup* of politics.

さつじん 殺人 **murder** (計画的な); **manslaughter** /mænslɔ̀ːṭəʳ/ 《解説》(1) 法律用語では murder は殺意をもって犯された計画的殺人をいい, manslaughter は一時の激情で人を殴ったりした結果, 相手が死んでしまったというような場合をいう. (2) 両者を含めて homicide /hɑ́ːmɪsaɪd/ と総称する.
▶殺人を犯す commit *murder* ‖殺人容疑でその男を告訴する file a *murder* charge against the man ‖彼は殺人(未遂)の容疑で逮捕された He was arrested on suspicion of (*attempted*) *murder*. ‖森刑事がその殺人事件を担当した Detective Mori took charge of the *murder* (*case*). ‖殺人犯は警察によって刑務所に護送された The *murderer* was sent to jail under police escort.
▶殺人的な暑さ *murderous* heat ／a *murderous* [*killer*] heat wave ‖殺人的なスケジュール a *killing* [*killer*] schedule ‖電車は殺人的な混雑ぶりだった The train was *deadly* [*terribly*] *crowded*.

さっする 察する ▶口ぶりから察して, 彼は真相がわかっていないようだ *From his words* [*From the way he talks*] I gather he does not know the truth. (➤gather は「推測する」) ‖彼女がどんなに失望しているか察するに余りある I *can just imagine* how disappointed she must be.
✉ **心中お察しいたします** I *deeply sympathize with* you.
✉ **奥さまを亡くされ, どれほどお寂しいことかお察しいたします** I *can imagine* how much you miss your wife.

ざつぜん 雑然 ▶雑然とした町並み *haphazard, sprawling* streets (➤「無計画に広がる一方の」の意) ‖弟の部屋はいつも雑然としている My brother's room *is* always *a mess* [*in disorder*]. ‖棚に雑誌が雑然と置かれていた Magazines *were* all *mixed up* on the shelf.

さっそう ▶彼はいつもさっそうとした身なりをしている He is always *smartly* dressed. ‖今度の先生は大学を出たばかりでさっそうと(＝きりりと)している Our new teacher is just out of college and *looks very sharp*. ‖真知子は新しいドレスを着てさっそうとパーティーに出かけていった Machiko put on her new dress and went off *jauntily* [and *danced off*] to the party.

ざっそう 雑草 a **weed** ▶空き地は雑草に覆われていた The vacant lot was overgrown with [was full of] *weeds*.
▶庭の雑草を取るのに2時間かかった It took me two hours to *weed* the garden. (➤この weed は「雑草を除く」の動詞).
▶雑草のようにたくましく生きよ In life, you've got to be tough like *a weed*. (➤意訳).

さっそく 早速 **immediately**; **at once** (すぐに) ▶早速彼のメールに返事をした I responded to his email [text message] *immediately* [*at once*]. (➤text message は携帯電話のメールを指す) ‖そちらに着きましたら早速お電話いたします I'll call you *as soon as* I get there.
✉ **早速お返事いただきありがとう** Thank you for writing me back *so soon* [*quickly*].
✉ **早速ご返事を賜りありがとうございました** I

appreciate your *prompt* reply. ➤ 改まった表現で商用文などに使われる. prompt は「迅速な」の意.

ざった 雑多 ▶**種々雑多な**コインの収集 a collection of *miscellaneous* coins [*a miscellany* of coins] ‖ あの店では**種々雑多な**物を売っている That store carries *all kinds of* goods.

さつたば 札束 《米》 a **wad of bills**, 《英》 a **wad of (bank) notes** ▶銀行強盗は**札束**をかばんに突っ込んだ The bank robber thrust *wads of bills* into his bag.

さ

ざつだん 雑談 **small talk** (会話のきっかけ作りや場を和ませるための, 短い世間話) ; **chitchat** (軽い肩のこらない会話 ; chit-chat ともつづる) ; 《インフォーマル》 a **chat** (談笑) ▶到着した客と**雑談をする** *make small talk* with one's guest who has arrived ‖ 成績のいい販売員は往々にして**雑談**も得意だ Good salespeople are also good at making *chitchat* more often than not. ‖ 私たちはコーヒーを飲みながら**雑談した** We had *a chat* over coffee.

さっち 察知する **sense** +㊀ ▶彼らは警察の捜査があることを事前に**察知していた**ようだ It seems they had *sensed* the fact that there was a police investigation going on.

さっちゅうざい 殺虫剤 (an) **insecticide** /ɪnséktɪsaɪd/, 《インフォーマル》 a **bug killer** [**spray**] ▶そこのゴキブリに**殺虫剤をかけて**! *Spray* that cockroach !

さっと ▶**さっと**夕立が来た A shower came on *suddenly*. ‖ 涼しい風が**さっと**吹き込んできた A cool wind blew in. (➤ この場合「さっと」は訳出しなくてよい) ‖ ホウレンソウは**さっと** (= 軽く) **ゆでる**のがよい Spinach should *be boiled lightly* [*be parboiled*]. ‖ 彼は**さっと**身をかわして落石をよけた He *nimbly* dodged the falling rock.

ざっと **1 【おおよそ】** **about** (約…) ; **roughly** (概算で) ▶披露宴の費用は**ざっと**200万円かかる My wedding reception will cost *about* [*roughly*] two million yen.

2 【おおまかに】 **briefly** (簡単に) ; **roughly** (大ざっぱに) ▶彼に問題点を**ざっと**説明した I explained the problem *briefly* [*roughly*] to him. ‖ 私は毎朝, 新聞に**ざっと目を通す** I *skim over* [*glance over*] the newspaper every morning.

▶《難しい仕事などをやり終えて》 **ざっとこんなもんだ** *That should be it*. (➤ it を強めて言う. 「これで完成」) ／ *That should do it*. (➤ do を強めて言う. 「これで申し分なし」) ／ *It was a piece of cake*. (➤「朝飯前だった」).

さっとう 殺到する **rush** 《to》 (突進する) ▶生徒たちは行列を見ようと窓際へ**殺到した** Students *rushed to* the windows to see the procession. ‖ 番組終了後テレビ局に苦情が**殺到した** Complaints *poured into* [*flooded*] the TV station after the program. (➤ pour in [into], flood は「(手紙や申し込みが) どっと [あふれるほどたくさん] 来る」の意) ‖ ショーが終わると少女たちはその歌手の周りに**殺到した** When the show was over, young girls *swarmed* round the singer. (➤ swarm は「群がる」).

ざっとう 雑踏 a **crowd** (人混み) ▶私たちは**雑踏**をかき分けて進んだ We pushed our way through the *crowd*. ‖ 都会の**雑踏**を逃れて湯沢の温泉に出かけた We went to a hot spring in Yuzawa to get away [escape] from the *hustle and bustle* of the big city. (➤ hustle and bustle は「押し合いへし合い」).

ざつねん 雑念 ▶彼は**雑念**を払って仕事に専念した He put all *the other thoughts* out of his mind and concentrated on his work. ‖ 座禅を始めるとすぐに**雑念** (= 邪念) に捕らわれてしまった Just after I began to meditate, I was seized by *stray* [*worldly*] *thoughts*.

さつばつ 殺伐 ▶**殺伐とした**風景 *dreary* [*desolate*] scenery.

さっぱり

1 【快適な】 **refreshed** (気分が爽やかな) ; **relieved** (安心した) ▶シャワーを浴びたら? **さっぱりする**よ Why don't you take a shower ? You'll *feel refreshed*. ‖ 言いたいことを言ったら**さっぱりした**よ I said what I wanted to say and *felt relieved*. ／I *felt relieved* after I had said my piece. (➤ say one's piece で「言いたいことをはっきり言う」) ‖ 15分ほどうとうとしたら**さっぱりした** I dozed for about fifteen minutes and now I'*m refreshed*.

2 【味があっさりした】 **plain** (淡泊な) ; **light** (腹にもたれない) ▶**さっぱりした**味の料理 *lightly seasoned* food ／*plain* (*seasoned*) food ‖ 冷ややっこは**さっぱりして**いておいしい Hiyayakko is *light* and *refreshing* (to the palate).

3 【性格が淡泊な】 ▶彼女は性格が**さっぱりしている** She *has an easy-going* [*an optimistic* ／ *an open* (*-hearted*) ／ *a straight-forward*] *personality*. (➤ ぴったりの 1 語はない) ／She *has an open, positive personality*.

4 【全く】 **(not) ... at all** ▶私は数学が**さっぱりわからない** I do *not* understand math *at all*. ‖ 彼の言うことが**さっぱりわからなかった** I *could not make head or tail of* what he said. (➤「全然わからない」の意のインフォーマルな言い方 ; make heads or tails of ともいう) ‖ この物理の問題, **さっぱりわかんないわ** This physics problem *beats me*. (➤ beat は「困らせる」の意のインフォーマルな語) ‖ 一日中釣り糸を垂れていたが, 獲物は**さっぱりだった** I had my line(s) out all day, but *didn't get even a nibble*. (➤ a nibble は「一かじり」の意味) ‖ 彼女のことはきれい**さっぱり**忘れた I *completely* forgot *all* about her. ／I have *completely* forgotten about her. ‖ 対話「景気はどうだい?」「**さっぱりだね**」 "How's business ?" "*There isn't any*. ／*It's awful* [*terrible*]."

ざっぴ 雑費 **miscellaneous** /mìsəléɪniəs/ **expenses** ; **incidental expenses** (臨時経費) ▶今月は**雑費**がかさんだ *Incidental expenses* added up to a considerable sum this month.

さつびら 札びら ▶うちのバーに来るたびに彼は**札びらを切っていく** Whenever he comes to our bar, he *spends money ostentatiously*. (➤「これ見よがしに金を使う」の意).

さっぷうけい 殺風景な **dreary**, **drab** (わびしい) ; **dull** (変化のない) ; **bare** (飾り気のない) ▶**殺風景な**眺め a *dreary* [*dull*] sight ‖ この部屋は家具が1つもなく**殺風景だ** This room *is bare* [*drab* ／*cheerless*] without any furniture. (➤ cheerless は「陰気な」).

ざつぶん 雑文 **miscellaneous essays** [**writings**].

さつまあげ 薩摩揚げ ***satsuma-age*** ; a fried fish cake mixed with finely chopped carrot and burdock (➤ 説明的な訳).

さつまいも 薩摩芋 **a sweet potato** ▶**サツマイモ**をふかす steam *a sweet potato*.

ざつむ 雑務 **miscellaneous** /mìsəléɪniəs/ **duties** [**tasks**].

ざつよう 雑用 **odd jobs** ; **chores** /tʃɔːʳz/ (家庭内の) ▶ここ3日ばかりは**雑用**に追われててね I've been running around doing *odd jobs* for the last three days. ‖ 家のこまごました**雑用**で忙しい I'm busy with a thousand *little jobs* around the house. (➤ little job は「ちょっとした仕事」).

さつりく 殺戮 extermination(根絶, 皆殺し) ; carnage (特に戦争による大虐殺) ; a massacre(大虐殺) 一動 **殺りくする** exterminate +㊐ ‖ **殺りく兵器** weapons of extermination ‖ **大量殺りく** mass extermination ‖ **無差別大量殺りく** indiscriminate mass murder [slaughter].

さて well, now(➤ 訳出しないことが多い) ▶**さて**, 次の問題に移ろう *Well* [*Now*], let's move on to the next subject. ‖ **さて**, どうしたものか What shall I do *now*? ‖ 言うだけなら簡単だが, **さて**自分でやってみると言われるとたんに困ってしまう It is easy to say, but *when* I try doing it myself, I suddenly run into difficulty.

さてい 査定 (an) assessment 一動 **査定する** assess +㊐ ▶車のディーラーは私の車を 5 万円と**査定した** The car dealer *assessed* my car at 50,000 yen.

さておき ▶冗談は**さておき**, どうしてきみはそんなにしつこく自分の意見にこだわるんだい? *All joking apart* [*aside*], why do you have to be so stubborn about it? ‖ 何は**さておき**, できるだけ早くその問題を片づけてしまう必要がある *First of all*, we should settle that matter as soon as possible.

さてつ 砂鉄 iron sand.

さては ▶**さては**ぼくをだましたのはきみだったのか *So* [*Then*] it was you who deceived me! (➤ so, then は「では, それじゃあ」).

さと 里 **1【田舎】** countryside (田園地帯) ; a village (村) ; a rural area (農村地域).

2【実家】 one's home(town)(故郷) ; one's parents' home (実家) ▶妻は子供を連れて**里**へ帰った My wife went back to *her parents' home*, taking the children with her.

サド sadism(加虐性愛) ; a sadist(人).

さとい clever(賢い) ▶彼は利に**さとい** He *has a good* [*quick*] *eye* for profit.

さといも 里芋 a taro /tá:roʊ/.

[1]**さとう 砂糖** sugar ▶スプーン 2 杯の**砂糖** two spoonfuls of *sugar* ‖ **砂糖**の入っていないチョコレート *sugarless* chocolate ‖ **砂糖**をまぶしたドーナツ a *frosted* [*an iced*] doughnut ‖ コーヒーに**砂糖**入れる? Do you take [like] *sugar* in your coffee?

‖ **砂糖きび** (a) sugarcane ‖ **砂糖大根** (a) sugar beet ‖ **砂糖つぼ** a sugar pot.

[2]**さとう 左党** a drinker(酒飲み).

[1]**さどう 作動する** operate, run, 《インフォーマル》 work ▶この芝刈り機のモーターはスムーズに**作動しない** The motor of this lawn mower doesn't *run* smoothly. ‖ 何らかの理由で安全装置が**作動しなかった** The safety device did*n't work* [*function*] for some reason or other. / The safety device *malfunctioned* for some reason or other. ‖ たばこの煙で火災報知機が**作動する**場合があります Your cigarette smoke may *activate* [*trigger*] the fire alarm. ‖ ガス警報機は保証期間を過ぎると, **誤作動を起こす**可能性があります Gas alarms might *malfunction* after the warranty period expires.

[2]**さどう 茶道** (the) tea ceremony

日本紹介 ✉ **茶道は作法に従って抹茶をたてて味わう芸道です. 16世紀に千利休によって完成されました. 初めて抹茶を飲んだときに感じるのは思った以上に苦いということでしょう** *Sado* (the tea ceremony) is the ritualistic making and drinking of *matcha* [powdered green tea]. Sen'no Rikyu perfected the art of *Sado* in the sixteenth century. When you taste *matcha* tea for the first time, you may find it more bitter than you expected.

さとおや 里親 a foster parent ▶子供を**里親**に預ける leave a child with *foster parents*.

さとがえり 里帰り ▶今度 3 年ぶりに**里帰りする**つもりなの I'm *going home to see my parents* for the first time in three years.

さとご 里子 a foster child ▶子供を**里子として育てる** *foster* a child.

さとごころ 里心 ▶**里心がつく** *get homesick* / *miss* one's *home*.

さとす 諭す admonish +㊐ (➤ 堅い語) ▶父親は息子の不心得を懇々と**諭した** The father *admonished* his son gently for his misbehavior. / The father earnestly *lectured* his son on his misbehavior. (➤ 後者は前者よりくだけた言い方).

さとやま 里山 *satoyama* ; a hilly wooded area between farmland and mountain foothills (➤ 説明的な訳).

さとり 悟り (spiritual) enlightenment ; satori (➤ 英語化している) ▶**悟りを開いた**人 an *enlightened* person ‖ 長年座禅を組んだ末ようやく彼は**悟りを開いた** After years of Zen meditation practice, he *attained satori* [(*spiritual*) *enlightenment*].

さとる 悟る **1【悟りを開く】** ▶**真理を悟る** *attain spiritual enlightenment* ‖ きみはいかにも**悟った**ようなことを言うね You *talk like a philosopher*. / You *talk like you know it all*. (➤ philosopher /fɪlá:səfəʳ/ は「哲学者, 悟った人」; 後者は皮肉のこもった言い方) ‖ 「男なんてあんなものよ」と彼女は**悟った**ように言った "Men are like that," she said *philosophically*.

2【感づく】 notice +㊐ (〈見聞きしたり感じたりして〉気づく) ; realize +㊐ (〈考えて, 判断して〉実感する) ▶あとをつけているのを彼に**悟られない**ように気をつけた I was careful not to *let* him *notice* I was following him. ‖ 彼は金を払って数週間たってからだまされたと**悟った** He *realized* that he had been taken in a few weeks after paying the money.

サドル a saddle ▶**サドル**を高くする [低くする] raise [lower] *a saddle*.

さなか 最中 ▶冬の**さなか** in *the middle* of winter / in *mid*winter / in *the dead* [*the depths*] of winter (➤ いちばん寒い時期).

さながら ▶**さながら**映画のワンシーンのような光景 a scene *just like* a movie still(➤ still は「映画のスチール写真」の意).

さなぎ 蛹 a chrysalis /krísəlɪs/ (特にガやチョウの) ; a pupa /pjú:pə/ [複 pupae] (昆虫全般の) ▶**さなぎ**がかえって蝶になった *A chrysalis* morphed into a butterfly. / *A chrysalis* broke and a butterfly came out [emerged].

サナトリウム a sanatorium.

さのう 左脳 the left brain, the left hemisphere of the brain.

さは 左派 the left (wing) (集合的) ; a left-winger, a leftist (個人)

‖ **左派政党** a left-wing [leftist] party.

さば 鯖 a mackerel /mækrəl/ ▶《慣用表現》彼女は年を 3 歳**さばを読んだ** She *fudged* (*on*) *her age* by three years.

サバイバル survival ▶**サバイバル術** the art of *survival* (技術) / a *survival* tactic [strategy] (戦術).

‖サバイバルキット a survival kit.

さばき 裁き (a) **judgment** ▶裁きの庭 a *law* court／a court of *law* ‖ 裁きを受ける *be tried*.

-さばき -捌き ▶みごとな包丁さばき skillful knife *handling* ‖ 足さばき *footwork* ‖ 手綱さばき *handling* of the reins.

1**さばく 砂漠** (a) **desert** /dézəʳt/ ▶サハラ砂漠 the Sahara (➤ Sahara はアラビア語で「砂漠」の意だから, Sahara Desert とする必要はない) ‖ アフリカ中部では砂漠化が年々進んでいる In central Africa, each year, more and more *land is being lost to the desert*. (➤「砂漠化」を1語で desertification という).

2**さばく 捌く** **1【手でうまく分ける】**▶コピー用紙をさばく *loosen and even up* copy paper ‖ その騎手は巧みに手綱をさばく That jockey *handles* the reins skillfully.

2【処理する】do +㊐, **deal with** ▶難問をうまくさばく(＝解決する) *settle* a difficult matter successfully ‖ 彼は事務をてきぱきとさばく He *does* [*deals with*] his work efficiently.

3【売る】sell +㊐ ▶慈善コンサートの切符を100枚さばくのは大変だ *Selling* 100 tickets for a charity concert is no easy thing.

3**さばく 裁く** **judge** +㊐ ▶事件を裁く *give a judgment* in the case ‖ その事件は最高裁によって裁かれることになった The case has *come up before* the Supreme *Court*.

さばける 捌ける ▶宣伝が効いて在庫品は2日でさばけた(＝売り切れた) Thanks to effective advertising, all the goods in stock *were sold out* in two days. ▶彼はさばけた男だ He's a *sensible* [*down-to-earth*／*straightforward*] guy.

さばさば ▶ごたごたが片づいてさばさばした(＝ほっとした) I *felt relieved* when all the loose ends were taken care of. (➤ loose ends は「未解決の問題」).

サハラさばく サハラ砂漠 the Sahara.

サバンナ a **savanna(h)** /səvǽnə/.

1**さび 錆** **rust** —㊒ **さびた rusty** ▶さびをこすって落とす rub off the *rust* ‖ さびだらけの自転車 a *rusty* bicycle ‖ 門扉にさびが出てきた The doors of our gate are *getting rusty*.

[ことわざ] それは身から出たさびだ You asked for it. (➤ ask for it は「自分から面倒を引き起こす」)／You've made your bed and you must lie in it. (➤「自業自得」の意の英語のことわざ).

2**さび 寂** ▶さびのある声 a *deep, well-trained* voice.

さびしい 寂しい **1【孤独で心が痛む】lonely, lonesome** (➤ともに「寂しい」の意の一般語として用いるが, 後者は特に「人が恋しくて[話し相手がいなくて]寂しい」の意) ; **deserted** /dɪzə́ːʳtɪd/ (人の往来がなくて)

> **【文型】**
> 人・物(A)が(い)なくて寂しい
> **miss** A
> …できなくて寂しい
> **miss** doing

▶きみがいなくてとても寂しかったよ I *missed* you very much. (➤ miss は「人がいなくて[物がなくて]寂しく思う」の意) ‖ 優しい母さんがいなくて寂しい We *miss* (having) our loving mother. ‖ あなたが行ってしまうと寂しくなります *I'm going to miss* you (when you're gone). ‖ 一緒にお仕事ができなくて寂しいです I *miss* work*ing* with you. ▶寂しい山村 a *lonely* mountain village ‖ (人通りの絶えた)寂しい通り a *deserted* street ‖ 話し相手がいないと寂しい I *feel lonely* when I have no one to talk to [with]. ‖ あなたが休暇でいなかったとき, 私寂しかったわ I *was lonesome* [*felt sad*] when you were away on vacation.

✉ **お姉さんが大学に入学して家を離れられたとのこと, きっとお寂しいでしょうね** You say your (older) sister has left home for college. You must *miss* her [You must *be lonely* without her].

2【物足りない】▶正解者が3名とは寂しい限りだ I *feel* extremely *disappointed* that only three of you gave the correct answers.

▶《慣用表現》きょうは懐が寂しい I am *short of* [*on*] *money* today. ‖ 何となく口が寂しいのでガムをかんだ I somehow *felt a need to put something into my mouth*, so I chewed some gum.

さびしがりや 寂しがり屋 ▶私の父さんは寂しがり屋です My father is *a man who can't stand being alone*. ／My father *doesn't like being* (*left*) *alone*.

さびしがる 寂しがる **miss** +㊐

✉ **あなたがアメリカへ帰られたので, 家中が寂しがっています** The whole family [Everyone in our family] *misses* you now that you have gone back to the U.S.

さびしさ 寂しさ **loneliness** ▶少年はじっと寂しさをこらえていた The boy endured (his) *loneliness*. ‖ 彼女は寂しさを酒で紛らした She drowned her *loneliness* in drink.

さびつく 錆つく **rust, get rusty** ▶ドアがさびついてしまって動かない The door has stuck *with rust*.

▶《比喩的》私の中国語はもうさびついているよ My Chinese *has gotten rusty*.

さびどめ 錆止め a **rust preventive** (剤) ; **rustproofing** (作業).

ざひょう 座標 **coordinates** ▶座標を求める search for the *coordinates*.

‖座標軸 a coordinate axis.

さびる 錆びる **rust, get rusty** (➤後者はややインフォーマル) ▶この包丁はすぐさびる This kitchen knife *rusts* [*gets rusty*] easily. ‖ そこにあるくぎはみんなさびているよ Those nails *have* all *rusted* (*away*).

さびれる 寂れる ▶この温泉街は年々寂れてきている This hot-spring resort is *declining* [is *going downhill*] year by year. (➤ go downhill は「没落する」) ‖ あの温泉旅館はすっかり寂れてしまった That hot spring inn has really *gone to seed*. (➤ go to seed は「(最盛期が過ぎて)衰える」).

サファイア (a) **sapphire** /sǽfaɪəʳ/.

サファリ (a) **safari** /səfɑ́ːri/

‖サファリパーク《米》an animal [a wildlife] park, 《英》a safari park ‖ サファリスーツ[ジャケット] a safari suit [jacket].

ざぶざぶ ▶子供たちが池でざぶざぶ水の掛けっこをしていた Some children were *splashing water over each other* in the pond. ‖ クロクマがざぶざぶ小川を渡った A black bear *splashed across* the river.

サブタイトル a **subtitle** (➤ subtitles は「字幕」という意味でも用いる).

ざぶとん 座布団 a ***zabuton*** ; a Japanese (square sitting) cushion that is put on a tatami floor (➤説明的な訳).

▶座布団に座る sit on *a zabuton*.

サブプライムローン a **subprime loan.**

サプライズ a **surprise** ▶お母さんの誕生日にはすてきなサプライズをあげよう We'll give Mom a nice *surprise* on her birthday. ‖ あなたにサプライズがあるのよ I have *a surprise* for you.

サフラン (a) **saffron.**

サブリミナル **subliminal.**

サプリ(メント) a (**dietary**) **supplement.**

ざぶん ▶彼はプールに頭からザブンと飛び込んだ He dived into the pool *with a splash*. (➤ splash は水のはねる音を表す語) ／He plunged headfirst into the pool.

さべつ 差別 **discrimination** ; **segregation** (人種差別) 一動 **差別する** **discriminate** 《against》 ▶人種[肌の色]による**差別** racial [color] *discrimination* ‖ **差別的な発言** a *discriminatory* remark ‖ **男女差別**[**性差別**]は法律では禁止されているが, 実際にはまだ存在する *Gender* [*Sex*] *discrimination* is prohibited by law, but still exists in reality. ‖ 雇用者は年齢や性別を理由とする**差別**をしてはならない Employers cannot *discriminate* on (the) basis of age or sex. ‖ 女性を**差別**している国がある Some countries *discriminate against* women. (➤ discriminate against は「…を差別待遇する」) ‖ 両親はぼくを弟と**差別している** My parents *treat* my (younger) brother and me *differently*. ‖ 競合他社と**差別化を図らなければならない** It's important to *differentiate* ourselves from our competitors [from rival companies]. ‖ **差別語** a discriminatory word ‖ **逆差別** reverse discrimination ‖ **逆人種差別** reverse racism ‖ **女性差別主義** sexism ‖ **女性差別主義者** a sexist ‖ **年齢差別** age discrimination.

さほう 作法 **manners** (マナー ; 複数形で用いる) ; **etiquette** (礼儀作法 ; →エチケット) ▶食事の**作法** table *manners* ‖ 日本式の**作法** Japanese *etiquette* ‖ スープを飲むときに音を立てるのは**作法にかなっていない** It is *bad manners* to make (a) noise [to slurp] when you eat soup. ‖ 隣の家の子たちは**作法が身についている** The next-door neighbor's children *have* [*know*] *good manners*.

さぼう 砂防 ‖ **砂防ダム** a mudslide-control dam ‖ **砂防林** an erosion-control forest.

サポーター a **supporter** (サッカーチームなどを応援する人) ; an **athletic supporter**, a **jockstrap** (男性器用帯革 ; 後者はもともとスポーツ俗語).

サポート **support** ▶起業家を資金面で**サポートする** *support* an entrepreneur financially ‖ **テクニカル・サポート** technical support.

サボタージュ 《米》 a **slowdown**, 《英》 a **go-slow** ▶賃上げを要求して**サボタージュを行う** *go on slowdown* (*strike*) demanding higher wages [salaries ／ pay]. →サボる.

> **危ないカタカナ語✹ サボタージュ**
> 1 「サボタージュ」はフランス語の *sabotage* (操業妨害)に由来するが,「怠業」の意味はない. 日本語での意味を表すには slowdown や go-slow を使う.
> 2 「授業をサボる」はこの「サボタージュ」からきているが, 英語では cut school, cut [skip] class, play hook(e)y などとする.

サボテン 《植物》 a **cactus** /kǽktəs/ [複 **cactuses**, **cacti**].

さほど ▶きょうはさほど寒くない It isn't *all that* cold today. ／It's not *so* [*very*] cold today. ‖ 郷里はこの20年間さほど変わっていない My hometown has not changed *so much* in the last two decades. ‖ プロ野球にはさほど興味はない I am *not very much* [*not particularly*] interested in pro baseball.

サボる **1** 【**授業などを**】 **cut** +目, **skip** +目, 《主に米》 **play hook(e)y**, 《主に英》 **bunk off** ▶4時限目の授業を**サボる** *cut* [*skip*] one's fourth *class* ‖ 部活を**サボる** *skip* [*ditch*] one's club activities ‖ 彼はよく学校を**サボる** He often *cuts* [*skips*] *school*. ／He often *plays hook(e)y from school*. ‖ 彼はけさの英語のクラスを**サボった** He *cut* his English class this morning. ‖ 大学時代には時々**授業をサボった** When I was in college I *cut classes* now and then. (→サボタージュ).

2 【**勉強や仕事などを**】 **goof off** (怠ける) ; **play truant** (**from work**) (無断欠勤する) ▶**サボってないで仕事をしろ** *Stop goofing off* and get to work ! ‖ あいつ, **サボってばかりいる** He's *a goof-off*. (➤ goof-off は「怠け者」の意のインフォーマルな語) ‖ 雄二は掃除当番を**サボって**スケートに行った Yuji *skipped* his cleanup duty and went skating.

ザボン a **pomelo** /pɑ́:məloʊ/ ; a **shaddock.**

さま 様 ▶彼はどんなスポーツをやっても**様になっている** Whatever sport he plays, he does it *in style*. ‖ 彼女は何を着ても**様になる** She *looks really good* in whatever [everything] she wears. ‖ 彼女の和服姿は全く**様になっていなかった** She was *a sight* in her kimono. (➤ a sight は「(悪い意味で)見もの」の意) ‖ 美川, おまえ, なかなか**様になってるぞ** You're really *something*, Mikawa.

-さま -様 **Mr.** 〜 (➤ 男性に ; Mister の略) ; **Mrs.** 〜 (➤ 既婚女性に ; Mistress の略), **Miss** 〜 (➤ 未婚女性に), **Ms.** 〜 (➤ 未婚・既婚を問わず女性に)

> **解説 敬称のつけ方**
> (1) Mr., Mrs., Miss, Ms. のいずれも, 例えば Mr. Tanaka (Akio) のように姓または姓名の前につける. 名前だけのときはつけない.
> (2) Mr, Mrs, Ms のあとにドットを打つのは《米》に多く,《英》では打たないのがふつう.
> (3) ビジネスでは Ms. を, 社交では Mrs. を, というように2つを使い分けている女性も多い.

▶失礼ですが, 斎藤さまでいらっしゃいますか Excuse me. Are you *Mr*. [*Mrs*. ／*Miss* ／*Ms*.] Saito ? ‖ **お父さまはご在宅ですか** Is *your father* in ? (● この「さま」は訳出不要) ‖ おまえ, いったい**何さまだと思ってるんだい** *Who do you think* you are ?

ざま ▶ありゃあ, **何てざまだ** *What a mess* ! ／*What a sorry* [*sad*] *sight* ! ‖ 女房にまで逃げられて**全くざまはない** Your wife ran out on you ? *What a mess you've gotten* (*yourself*) *into* ! ‖ **何てみっともない死に様だろう** What *an* undignified *way to die* [*go*] ! ‖ **対話**「俺, 数学のテスト, 落としちゃったよ」「**ざまを見ろ**. 人の答案を写そうとするからだよ」 "I failed the math test." "*Serves you right* for trying to copy off my test paper." (➤「当然の報いだ」の意. 言う相手によって代名詞を him, her などに変える).
▶白洲次郎の生き様には学ぶべき点がある There's something to learn from *the way* (that) Shirasu Jiro lived (his life).

サマータイム 《米》 **daylight-saving** (**s**) **time**, 《英》 **summer time.**

さまがわり 様変わり ▶この町ももう2, 3年すればすっかり**様変わりする**だろう This town will *look* quite *different* in two or three years.

さまさま 様々 ▶うちの店は中尾君でもっているようなものだ. まさに中尾さまさまだ Our store would be nowhere without Nakao. The rest of us *have to take our hat off to* him. (➤ take one's hat off は文字どおりには「脱帽する」).

さまざま 様々な various ▶リンゴ, ナシ, そのほかさまざまな種類の果物 apples, pears, and *various* other kinds of fruit ‖ 大小さまざまのジャガイモ potatoes *of all* [*various*] *sizes*.

さ

直訳の落とし穴「さまざまな(種類の)ワイン」

various にはしばしば「さまざまな」「いろいろな」さらには「多様な」などの訳語を与えられるために,「さまざまな」=various と考えて,「あの酒屋さんはさまざまな(種類の)ワインを置いている」を That liquor store carries various (kinds of) wines. でよいと思っている人が多い. various は several different (いくつかの異なった)とオーバーラップしながら, それより少し多めという感覚で, 非常に多いという意味はない. また, 最近は酒屋さんにワインが何種類もあるのはごく当たり前なので, この英文は意味をなさない. 種類が豊富なことをいうには, many kinds of wines でもよいが, That liquor store carries a wide variety of [a wide range of / a wide selection of] wines. とする. 同様に,「小笠原諸島にはさまざまな珍しい動植物が生息している」も A wide variety [Many kinds] of rare animals and plants live in the Ogasawara Islands. となる.

▶世間のさまざまな人 *people from all walks of life* (➤「あらゆる職業・社会的地位 [階級]」など) ‖ この問題はさまざまな(=違った)角度から検討する必要がある This problem has to be examined from *different* angles. ‖ 人の心はさまざまだ So many people, so many minds. (➤「十人十色だ」の意の英語のことわざ).

さます 冷ます・覚ます・醒ます **1**【冷やす】cool ▶このスープは熱すぎる. 少し冷ましたほうがいい This soup is too hot. Better *let* it *cool* (*off*) a little. (➤ cool it とすると冷蔵庫などで「冷やす」ことになり, ここでは不適当).

2【目を覚ます】wake up ▶けさは5時に目を覚ました I *woke up* at five this morning. ‖ 赤ん坊は目を覚ましている The baby *is awake*.

▶《慣用表現》何度だまされたらわかるんだ. いいかげんに目を覚ませよ How many times do you have to be deceived? Isn't it *about time you woke up* (and smelled the coffee)? (「目を覚ませ」は日英語で似た発想をするが, 英語では訳例のように後ろに and smell the coffee (そしてコーヒーの香りをかぎなさい)がくることも多い).

3【平静に戻す】▶俺がきみの迷いをさましてやろう I will *bring* you *to your senses*. ‖ 酔いをさますために冷たい水を飲んだ I had a glass of cold water to *sober myself up*.

さまたげ 妨げ an obstacle ▶あまりに美人すぎるとかえって結婚の妨げになることもある Being too beautiful can actually be *an obstacle* in finding a husband. ‖ ぶっきらぼうな態度が彼の出世の妨げとなっている His bluntness *stands in the way* of his promotion.

さまたげる 妨げる disturb +⽬ (安眠などを); obstruct +⽬ (通行などを); prevent [keep] 《A from doing》 (A(人・物)が…するのを妨げる; keep はややインフォーマル) ▶近所の学校のスピーカーがしばしばうちの赤ん坊の眠りを妨げる The loudspeakers from the neighboring school often *disturb* my baby's sleep. ‖ 落石が通行を妨げた A fallen rock *obstructed* traffic.

【文型】
人・物(A)が…するのを妨げる
prevent A from doing
keep A from doing

《解説》 prevent は「完全に止めて行わせない」を意味するのに対して, keep は邪魔などをして「人に…させない」の意. →させる.

▶観客のブーイングが打者の集中を妨げた The spectators' booing *kept* the batter *from* concentrat*ing*. ‖ 炎に妨げられて消防士たちは建物に突入できなかった Flames *prevented* the fire fighters *from* enter*ing* the building. ‖ 大雪が彼らの前進を妨げた A heavy snowfall *hampered* [*impeded*] their progress. ‖ 悪天候に妨げられて山登りができなかった Bad weather *prevented* [*kept*] us *from* going mountain climbing. / Bad weather *prevented* our going mountain climbing.

さまよう さ迷う wander (当てもなく歩き回る); hover (2つの状態の間を) ▶その老人は道に迷って幾日も山の中をさまよった The old man lost his way and *wandered* in the mountains for days. ‖ 患者はこの3日間生死の境をさまよっている The patient has been *hovering between life and death* for the past three days.

さみしい 寂しい →さびしい.

さみしがりや 寂しがり屋 →さびしがりや.

さみだれ 五月雨 (an) early summer rain ▶《慣用表現》その広告への応募者が五月雨式に来ている Respondents to the advertisement *are trickling in* (*like early summer rain*). (➤ カッコ内は「五月雨式」をあえて訳したもので, 英語の発想ではない).

サミット the Summit [summit] (主要国首脳会議) ‖サミット参加者 a summiteer /sʌmɪtíəʳ/ ‖ G8サミット the Group of 8 summit (meeting).

さむい 寒い

cold; chilly (不快なほど); freezing (凍りつくように) ▶旭川はとても寒い所だが, 私は寒い気候が好きだ Asahikawa is a very *cold* place [*It's* very *cold* in Asahikawa], but I like the *cold* climate. ‖ ことしは寒い冬になりそうだ We'll likely have a *colder* winter this year. ‖ 朝晩めっきり寒くなりました Mornings and nights have gotten noticeably *colder*. ‖ このホールは凍りつくように寒い It's *freezing* in this hall. ‖ 寒くなるといけないからセーターを持って行きなさい Take your sweater with you in case it *gets cold*. ‖ 外出するときは寒くないようにして行きなさい *Keep* yourself *warm* when you go out. (➤「温かくする」と考える) ‖ 私たちは寒い所で1時間も待たされた We were kept waiting *in the cold* for an hour.

✉ **だんだん寒くなってまいりました. お体には十分お気をつけください** It's growing *colder*. Please take good care of yourself.

▶《慣用表現》お隣に強盗が入ったと聞いて背筋が寒くなった *I felt a chill going down my spine* [*My blood ran cold*] when I learned a burglar had broken into the house next door. ‖ その(テレビの)お笑い芸人は寒いギャグを連発した That TV comedian fired off a series of *lame* [*feeble* / *unfunny*] jokes.

☛ お寒い（→見出語）

さむえ 作務衣 a *samue*; a Zen monk's working clothes that are now also worn by ordinary people as casual or working wear（➤説明的な訳）.

さむがり 寒がり ▶彼女は沖縄育ちだから**寒がり**なんだ She grew up in Okinawa and *is very sensitive to the cold* [*can't tolerate the cold*].

さむけ 寒気 a **chill**（悪寒）▶**寒気**がする I feel *chilly*.（➤I have the chills. は医学的な表現）‖ 対話《病院で》「どうしました？」「少し**寒気**がして頭が痛いんです」"What seems to be the trouble?" "I *feel chilly* and have a headache."

さむさ 寒さ **cold**; **cold weather**（寒い天候）▶厳しい**寒さ** the severe *cold* ‖ 過酷な**寒さ** the brutal *cold* ‖ きょうは**寒さ**がとても厳しい *It is very* [*awfully*] *cold* today. ‖ **寒さ**が薄らいできた The *cold* (*weather*) has begun to let up. ‖ 子供たちは**寒さ**に震えていた The children were shivering with *cold*. ‖ 私はシカゴの**寒さ**に耐えられなかった I couldn't stand the *cold weather* in Chicago. ‖ 彼らは**寒さ**しのぎに腕立て伏せをして温まった They did push-ups to warm themselves *against the cold*.

✉ **日ごとに寒さが募るこの頃ですが，お変わりありませんか** *It's getting colder* every day. I hope you are well.

さむざむ 寒々 ▶**寒々**とした冬景色 the *dreary* winter landscape ‖ 女性のいない家はどことなく**寒々とした**感じがする There is something *cheerless* about a house without a woman.

さむぞら 寒空 ▶この**寒空**に，野良猫たちは食べ物にありついているだろうか I wonder if the stray cats are managing to get something to eat in *cold* [*frosty*] *weather* like today's.（➤ frosty は「霜の降りる」）.

さむらい 侍 a **samurai**（➤英語化している）; a **warrior**（武士，戦士）▶《比喩的》あの男，なかなかの**侍**だ（＝気骨と魂がある）He's really *a man of backbone and spirit*. ／He's *a* real *warrior*.

さめ 鮫 a **shark** ‖ **さめ皮** sharkskin ‖ **さめ肌** rough skin ‖ **シュモクザメ** a hammerhead shark ‖ **ジンベエザメ** a whale shark ‖ **ホオジロザメ** a great white shark.

1さめる 冷める・覚める・醒める

📖 **訳語メニュー**
冷たくなる →get cold **1**
目覚める →wake up **2**
酔いが消える →sober up **3**

1【冷たくなる】get cold, cool (down) ▶どうぞ召し上がってください．料理が**冷め**ますから Please eat your dinner before it *gets cold*. ‖ 誰も風呂に入らないものだから，お湯が**冷めて**しまった Since the hot bath was left sitting for a while, the water *cooled down* a bit.

2【意識がはっきりする】wake up（目が覚める）▶5時に目が**覚める** *wake up* at five (o'clock) ‖ 麻酔から**覚める** *wake up* [*come to*] from the anesthetic ‖ ゆうべは救急車のサイレンで**目が覚めた** The siren of an ambulance *woke me up* last night. ‖ 急な断崖から突き落とされて絶叫したところで，**夢から覚めた** I *woke up from my dream* when I was pushed off a steep cliff and screamed.

▶《慣用表現》これだけだまされてもまだ**目が覚めない**のか You still do*n't realize the truth* [*haven't woken up* (*and smelled the coffee*)] after having been deceived so much?（➤Can't you wake up after having ...? としてもよい；→覚める）.

▶知子は目の**覚める**ような黄色のドレスを着ていた Tomoko was wearing a *stunningly bright* yellow dress. ‖ 目の**覚める**ような美人に道を聞かれた I was asked for directions by a *dazzlingly* beautiful woman.

3【平静に戻る】sober up（酔いが）; **cool off** [**down**]（興味などが）▶彼，もう**酔いはさめた**かな Has he *sobered up* yet? ‖ あなたの忠告を聞いてやっと**迷いからさめました** Having listened to your warning, I finally *came to my senses*. ‖ 彼女のこと，本当に好きだったよ．でももう**冷めちゃった**んだ I really loved her, but I'*ve cooled off* now. ‖ 彼は熱しやすく**冷めやすい**タイプだ He easily gets excited but *cools off quickly*.

▶信雄にはどこか**冷めた**ところがある There is something *cool* and *unemotional* about Nobuo. ‖ みんなが興奮の渦の中にあっても，恵子だけはいつもひとり**冷めていた** Although everybody else was excited, Keiko *remained calm*.

2さめる 褪める **fade** ▶強い日ざしを受けてカーテンの色が**さめて**しまった The color of our curtains *faded* in the strong sunlight.

さも ▶彼は**さも**不愉快そうにそっぽを向いた He turned away *as if* he were [*like* he was] displeased.（➤この like は「まるで…かのように」の意のインフォーマルな接続詞）‖ 弟はその箱を**さも**大事そうに抱え込んでいた My little brother was hugging the box tightly *as if* it were something special to him.

さもしい ▶**さもしい**動機 a *base* [*mean*] motive ‖ そこまで**さもしい**ことをしなくてもいいでしょう You don't have to *stoop* that low.

さもないと **or (else)**, **otherwise**（➤ともに命令文のあとで用いる）▶もっと急いでくれ．**さもないと**あいつに先を越されちゃうよ！Hurry up, *or* he'll get ahead of us! ‖ すぐに出ていけ．**さもないと**警察を呼ぶぞ Get out of here at once, *otherwise* I will call the police. ‖ 私の言うとおりにしなさい．**さもないと**. Do what I tell you, *or else*.（●「さもないと」のあとに続く節（例えば「どうなるか知らないよ」）を省略した形）.

> **直訳の落とし穴「さもないと」**
> 「命令文＋さもないと」の「さもないと」には，or else と otherwise があるが，otherwise は前の命令文が否定形の場合には使えない．otherwise は「もしそうしないと」という意味で，初めから否定の意味が入っており，否定の文を受けない．or else は前の文の逆を想定するので，否定文でもよい．したがって，「食べ過ぎはやめなさい，さもないと太るよ」は（×）Don't overeat, otherwise you'll get fat. とはできず，Don't overeat, or else you'll get fat. とする．otherwise を使うときには，Stop overeating, otherwise you'll get fat. と前を肯定の命令文にする．

さもん 査問 (an) **inquiry**.

1さや 莢 a **shell**, a **pod**（➤前者は硬いさやに用いるのがふつう）▶そこにある豆の**さや**をむいてくれる？Could you *shell* those peas (for me)?（➤この shell は動詞）.

‖ **サヤインゲン**《米》a string bean,《英》a runner bean ‖ **サヤエンドウ** podded peas, snow peas.

2さや 鞘 a **sheath** /ʃiːθ/, a **case**（小刀の）▶侍は刀を**さや**に収めた［**さや**から抜いた］The samurai *sheathed* his sword [*drew* his sword].

▶《慣用表現》恋のさや当て *rivalry between two lovers* for a woman's affection ‖ 彼女は前の恋人と元のさやに収まったらしい I hear she *got back together* with her former boyfriend.

ざやく 座薬 a **suppository**.

さゆ 白湯 **plain hot water**.

さゆう 左右 **1【右と左】right and left**（➤ left and right とすることもある）▶道路を横断するときは左右をよく見なさいよ You must look *right and left* [*left and right* / *both ways*] carefully before you cross the street. ‖ 道の左右(＝両側)に桜の木が植わっている Cherries are planted on *either side* [on *both sides*] of the street.

2【影響, 支配】▶彼女は他人の意見に左右されやすい She *is easily influenced* by other people's opinions. ‖ 今回の選挙は日本の将来を左右(＝決定)する大事な選挙だ This is an extremely important election which will *decide* the future of Japan.

ざゆう 座右 ▶座右の書 a book *kept by* [*at*] one's *side* ‖「意志あるところに道は開ける」が彼の座右の銘だ *What he always tries to remember* is, "Where there is a will, there is a way."

さよう 作用 (an) **action**(働き)；an **effect**（影響）━ 動 **作用する act**《on》▶作用と反作用 *action* and reaction ‖ 酸がこの金属に化学作用を及ぼした An acid exerted *a chemical action* on this metal. ‖ 空気中の酸素が金属に作用してさびを作る Oxygen in the air *acts on* metals to rust them. ‖ たばこの煙は人体に有害な作用を及ぼす Tobacco smoke *has a harmful effect* [*an injurious effect*] *on* the human body. ‖ この薬には眠くなる作用がある This medicine will *make you sleepy*.

さようなら **Goodbye!**（➤ Good-bye, Goodby とつづることもある）；《インフォーマル》**See you (later)!** ▶彼はさようならも言わずに出ていった He left without even saying *goodbye* to us. ‖ 出発ロビーで彼女はホストファミリーにさようならと手を振った In the departure lobby, she *waved goodbye* to her host family. →さよなら.

> **《解説》「さようなら」について**
> (1) 別れの挨拶には goodbye のほかに (I'll) see you (later). / See you tomorrow. / So long.（➤ 目上の人には用いない）/ Take care (of yourself). / Take it easy.（➤「気楽にやれよ」の意）/ Have a nice day. / Good night.（➤ 夜別れるとき）などがある.
> (2) 親しい間柄では Bye. / Bye-bye.（➤ もとは幼児語）/ Bye (for) now. なども言う.
> (3) イギリスでは Good morning. / Good afternoon. / Good evening. を尻下がりに言って「さようなら」の意味に使うことがある. また Cheerio! はイギリス独特の親しい間柄の別れの挨拶である.

さよきょく 小夜曲 (a) **serenade**.

さよく 左翼 **the left wing**; **the left**（思想の）; a **leftist**, a **left-winger**（左派の人）; **left field**（野球の）▶左翼の学生 a *leftist* student.
▶左翼を守る play *left field*.
‖**左翼思想** leftism ‖ **左翼手** a left fielder ‖ **左翼団体**［**運動**］a leftist organization [movement]（→右翼）.

さよなら **1【別れ】goodbye, farewell**（➤ 後者は挨拶としては「さらば, ごきげんよろしゅう」に近い古風な言い方；今では用例のような複合語を作るときに用いることが多い）▶さよならパーティー *a farewell party* ‖ さよなら公演 *a farewell performance* [*concert*] ‖ あの連中とはもうさよならだ(＝会わない) *This is the last time I will ever see* them.

2【野球】▶阪神は糸原のさよならホームランで巨人を5対4で破った The Tigers defeated the Giants 5–4 on Itohara's *game-ending home run*.

さら 皿 a **dish**（深皿）; a **plate**（平皿, 銘々皿）; a **saucer**（受け皿）; a **platter**（大皿）

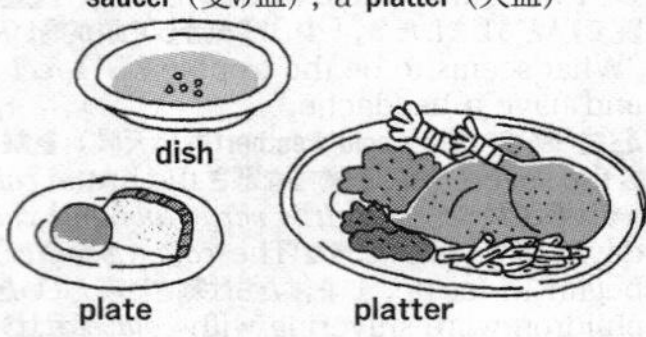

▶サラダを盛った皿 *a dish* filled with salad ‖ 食後は食卓の皿を片づけなさい You must *clear* (*the dishes from*) the table after meals.（➤ the dishes は「食器類」の意）‖ 母が皿を洗うのを手伝った I helped my mother *do the dishes*. ‖ 皿洗いのバイトをした I worked part time as *a dishwasher*. ‖ 牛肉と野菜の料理を1皿注文した I ordered a beef-and-vegetable *dish*.（➤ この dish は「料理」の意）.
▶《慣用表現》彼女は落としたコンタクトレンズを目を皿のようにして捜した She looked for her contact lens *with her eyes wide open*.
‖**皿洗い(機)** a dishwasher. ‖ **紙皿** a paper plate.

ざら ▶そんな事件はざらにある Such incidents *are quite common*. ‖ これほどの名馬はざらにはいない You *won't find* a fine horse like this *every day*. / A fine horse like this *is rarely to be found* [*is a rare find*].

さらいげつ 再来月 **the month after next** ▶兄は来月か再来月にはイギリスから帰ります My brother will be back from Britain next month or *the month after* (*next*).

さらいしゅう 再来週 **the week after next** ▶雨天のときは遠足は再来週まで延びてしまう If it rains, the excursion will have to be put off *until the week after next*.

さらいねん 再来年 **the year after next** ▶再来年までには家を改築しようと思っている I'm planning to rebuild my house *by the year after next*.

さらう **1【奪い去る】kidnap** +目（誘拐する）; **carry** +目《away, off》（運び去る）▶彼らは金持ちの子をさらって人質にし, 身代金を要求した They *kidnapped* a rich man's child and held him for ransom.（➤ -pp- とつづるのがふつう）‖ 大勢の人がその津波にさらわれた Many people *were carried off* [*were swept away*] by the tidal wave. / A lot of people *were snatched away* by the tsunami.
▶無名チームが優勝をさらった An unknown team *carried off* the first prize. ‖ パンダは依然として子供たちの人気をさらっている Pandas *are* still *overwhelmingly popular* among children. ‖ 彼女はほんの端役だったが, すっかり観衆の人気をさらった She played just a small part, but *stole the heart* of everyone in the audience.

2【きれいにする】clear +目 ▶どぶをさらう *clear* (*out*) a ditch.

3【復習する】go over, review +目 ▶今のところをもう一度さらってみなさい *Go over* what you've just learned. ‖ 先週の課をおさらいましょう Let's *review* last week's lesson.

サラきん サラ金 a **loan shark**(➤「高利貸し」の意のインフォーマルな語) ▶サラ金から金を借りる borrow money from *a loan shark*.

さらけだす さらけ出す **reveal** +㊀ ▶彼女は他人に自分をさらけ出すことは決してしない She never *reveals* [never *lays bare*] her true self to others.

さらさ 更紗 **calico**(➤「サラサ」はポルトガル語から).

[1]**さらさら** ▶智子はさらさらの髪をしている Tomoko has *silky smooth* hair. (➤ silky は「絹のような」) ‖ 小川がさらさら流れている A brook *is murmuring down through low hills*. ‖ 父は筆でさらさらと一句書いた My father wrote a haiku *with ease* with his flowing brush.

[2]**さらさら 更々** ▶大学院へ行こうなんていう気はさらさらないね I have *no* intention *whatsoever* of going to graduate school. ‖ 文句を言う気はさらさらないが, このレストランの店主は金もうけ主義だね *Far be it from me to* complain, but the owner of this restaurant only cares about making money.

ざらざら ▶畳の上が砂でざらざらしている The tatami is *gritty* with sand. ‖ 猫の舌はざらざらする Cat tongues *feel (rough) like sandpaper*.

さらしもの 晒し者 ▶昔は罪人はさらし者にされていた In the past, criminal offenders *were put in the pillory* [*on public display*]. (➤ pillory /píləri/ は「さらし台」).

さらす 晒す・曝す **1【風雨・危険などに】expose** +㊀ ▶駅前にたくさんの自転車が雨にさらされて放置されていた In front of the train station there were lots of bikes left *exposed to the rain*. ‖ 彼は多くの危険に身をさらしながら写真を撮り続けた He went on taking pictures, *exposing himself to* many dangers. ▶わが社は倒産の危機にさらされている Our company *is threatened with* [*is under the threat of*] bankruptcy.

2【あくを抜く, 白くする】▶タマネギの薄切りを水にさらす *soak* thin onion slices in water ‖ 古い浴衣を漂白剤でさらす *bleach out* an old yukata.

3【人目に】▶人前で恥をさらすようなことはしたくない I don't want to *disgrace myself* in public. ‖ ゆうべは飲み過ぎてとんだ醜態をさらしてしまった I drank too much last night and *made a fool of myself*.

サラダ (a) **salad**(➤ 種類や1人前をいうときは Ⓒ, たくさん作ったものを小分けしたときは Ⓤ) ▶野菜サラダを作る make [prepare] *a salad*(➤ サラダは野菜がふつうなので, わざわざ vegetable salad とはしない. 葉物のサラダは green salad という).

‖**サラダ油** vegetable [salad] oil ‖ **サラダ菜** butter lettuce ‖ **サラダボウル** a salad bowl ‖ **ポテトサラダ** (a) potato salad.

さらち 更地・新地 **vacant land**; a **vacant lot**(空き地; 1区画).

ざらつく ▶砂ぼこりで廊下がざらついている The hall is *sandy* with dust. ‖ このナシは舌にざらつく(=ざらざらする)感じだ This pear is *rough* to the tongue. / This pear has a *coarse* texture. (➤ coarse は「きめの粗い」).

さらに 更に **1【重ねて】further** ▶この問題は更に検討しなければならない This problem requires *further* consideration.

2【ますます】even, still (➤ いずれも比較級を強める) ▶夕方にかけて風は更に強まった The wind became *even* stronger toward evening. ‖ 私は彼より若いが, 彼女は更に若い I'm younger than him, but she is *even* younger [younger *still*]. ‖ その温泉はバス停から更に6キロ行った所にある That hot spring is six kilometers *beyond* the bus stop. ‖ 彼らは道に迷い, 更に悪いことに雨さえ降り出した They lost their way, and *what was worse* [*to make matters worse*], it began to rain.

さらば **Farewell!** /fèəˈwél/ (➤ 日本語同様, 古めかしい挨拶) ▶さらば友よ *Farewell*, my friend(s)! ‖ さらば故国! *Farewell* to my homeland! ‖ この会社ともいよいよおさらばだ The day *I leave* this company has arrived at last. ‖『武器よさらば』*A Farewell to Arms*(➤ ヘミングウェイの小説の題名).

サラブレッド a **thoroughbred** /θə́:roobred/ (純血種の動物, 特に馬) ▶尾上菊之助は歌舞伎界のサラブレッドと言われている Onoe Kikunosuke is said to be *a thoroughbred* [*a blue blood*] in the kabuki world.

サラミ **salami** /səlɑ́:mi/ ▶サラミ1切れ a slice of *salami* ‖**サラミソーセージ** (a) salami sausage.

さらり ▶さらりとした肌触りの絹のスカーフ a silk scarf which is [feels] *smooth* to the skin [touch] ‖ この梅酒はさらりとした飲み口だ This ume liqueur is *mild, smooth, and not syrupy*.

▶過ぎ去った嫌なことはさらりと忘れたほうがよい You should *completely* forget about unpleasant things in the past. ‖ 彼女は人の言いにくいことをさらりと言ってのける She says *with no difficulty* what other people hesitate to say.

サラリー a **monthly salary**(月給); an **annual salary**(年俸).

サラリーマン a **company employee**, an **office worker** (会社員); a **white-collar worker** (ホワイトカラー); a **salaryman** ▶父はサラリーマンです My father is *a company employee* [*an office worker*]. / My father works in an office.

> **危ないカタカナ語✹ サラリーマン**
>
> **1** 日本のサラリーマンを指して salaryman を使うことはあるが, 一般化した英語ではない. 「サラリー(月給)をもらって働く人」の意味で salaried man [worker, employee] は可能だが, これらも英米ではそれほど使われていない. 英語としては office worker, company employee, white-collar worker などが抵抗がない.
>
> **2** 日本人男性は職業を聞かれたとき, 「サラリーマンです」と答えることが少なくないが, 英語ではふつう I work for G Company. (G社に勤めています)のように具体的に社名を言うか, I'm an engineer. のように職種を言うことが多い.

サリー a **sari** /sɑ́:ri/ ▶緑のサリーを着た女性 a woman in a green *sari*.

ざりがに 《動物》a **crayfish**, 《米また》a **crawfish**, a **crawdad**.

さりげない ▶彼女はいつもさりげないおしゃれをしている She always dresses well in an *inconspicuous* way. (➤ inconspicuous は「目立たない」) ‖ 彼のさりげない優しさが大好きです He has a *natural* kindness that I just love. ‖ 彼女がぼくのことをどう思っているか, さりげなく聞いてみてくれ Will you sound her out *casually* about her feelings toward me? ‖ 林先生は板書の間違いをさりげなくごまかした Miss Hayashi tried to cover up her error on the chalkboard *with feigned unconcern*. (➤ with feigned unconcern は「平然と」).

1さる 猿 a **monkey**(尾のある); an **ape** /eɪp/ (尾のない猿, 類人猿) ▶猿がキャッキャッと鳴いている *Monkeys* are chattering. ‖人間は猿から進化した Human beings evolved from *apes*.

ことわざ 猿も木から落ちる Even a monkey sometimes falls from a tree. (➤日本語からの直訳) ／Even Homer sometimes nods. (➤「ホメロスのような大詩人でもうっかりすることがある」の意の英語のことわざ; このことわざの真意を理解して, No one is infallible. (過失を犯さぬ者はない)と訳すことも可能).

2さる 申 ▶申年 the year of the *Monkey*.

3さる 去る 1【離れて行く】**leave**(+㊐)(場所・地位・職などを) ▶彼は東京を去った He *left* Tokyo. (➤ left は leave の過去形.「A (場所・地位など)を去る」は leave A で (×)leave from A とはしない) ‖台風12号は去った Typhoon No.12 *has passed*. ‖夏が去り, 秋が来た Summer *is over*, and autumn has come. ‖彼は長患いのため職場を去らなければならなかった He had to *leave* his company because of a long illness. ▶おじは昨年この世を去った My uncle *passed away* last year.

ことわざ 去る者は追わず Don't run after a person who is leaving. ／Don't hold back someone who wants to leave. ‖去る者は日々に疎し Out of sight, out of mind.

2【消える】▶母の死後, 私の悲しみはいつまでも去らなかった My sorrow *has lingered* long after my mother's death. (➤ linger は「いつまでも残る」) ‖敵軍の兵士が撤退したので, ようやく危機は去った The enemy soldiers left (here), and the danger has finally *disappeared*.

3【過ぎ去った】▶姉は去る5月に結婚した My sister got married *last* May. ‖兄は去る10日に中国にたった My (older) brother left for China on the 10th *of this month*. (➤「今月の10日」の意).

4【「-去る」の形で】▶愛する人の思い出を消し去るのは不可能だ It is not possible to *wipe away* [*efface*] the memory of a loved one. (➤ efface は堅い語) ‖覆面をした2人組の男がその金を奪い去った Two masked men *took* the money and *ran away*.

ざる 笊 a *zaru*; a **bamboo** [**plastic**] **colander** (➤ colander は「水切りボウル」) ▶母はイチゴをざるに入れて洗った My mother washed strawberries in the *bamboo colander*.

‖ざるそば *zaru-soba*; buckwheat noodles served on a sieve-like bamboo tray with a chilled dipping sauce (➤説明的な訳) ‖ざる法 a law full of loopholes (➤ loophole は「抜け穴」).

さるぐつわ 猿ぐつわ a **gag** ▶その泥棒は守衛に猿ぐつわをかませて逃走した The burglar *gagged* the guard [*put a gag on* the guard], then made his escape.

さるしばい 猿芝居 ▶下手な猿芝居はやめろ Lay off [Knock off] *the cheap tricks*!

さるすべり 百日紅《植物》a **crape myrtle** /kréɪp mə̀ːʳtl/ (➤日本通の外国人の間では a monkeyslide tree として知られている).

サルタン a **sultan**.

さるぢえ 猿知恵 **low cunning**, a **harebrained idea**.

サルビア《植物》a **salvia**, **a scarlet sage**.

さるまね 猿真似 ▶あいつのすることはすべて社長の猿まねだ That fellow *apes* the boss in everything he does. (➤ ape は「(下手に)まねる」) ／He is *a copycat*—he does everything his boss does. (➤ copycat は「猿まねする人」).

サルモネラ ‖サルモネラ菌 salmonella ‖サルモネラ中毒 salmonella poisoning.

-ざるをえない →-せざるをえない.

されど ▶たかが10円されど10円. 10円玉がなくて用が足りないこともある It's only ten-yen, *but* ten-yen is ten-yen. (Someday,) you may find yourself in a jam just because you don't have a ten-yen coin.

される 1【受け身】

【文型】
…される
be ＋過去分詞
物(A)を…される
have A done

【解説】(1)「～は…される」という, いわゆる受け身形[受動態]は「**be 動詞＋過去分詞**」で表す.「Aによって」が必要な場合はあとに by A を付ける.
(2) go (行く), come (来る), run (走る), sit (座る) など,「…を」に当たる語(目的語)をとらない動詞(自動詞)は受け身形は作れない. しばしば, make A *do* (人(A)に…させる)など能動態を使って表現する. →させる.
(3) **have** A *done* は受け身形の代用になる言い方だが, 事故・災難など苦い体験を表すことが多い. また, この言い方は「人(A)に…してもらう」の意でも使う. →もらう.

▶彼は父親にひどく叱られた He *was* [*got*] *scolded* severely by his father. ‖彼は繰り返しスピード違反をして免許証を没収された He *had* his driver's license *taken away* for repeated speeding violations. ▶世の中にはまだ解明されない謎が数多くある There are so many *unsolved* mysteries in the world. (→-れる, -られる).

2【尊敬】▶奥村先生はこの春退職されました Mr. Okumura *retired* this spring. (英語には尊敬の助動詞「-れる」に相当する一般的表現がないので,「先生は退職した」と訳すしかない).

▶天皇陛下は伊勢神宮に参拝され, 私どもの旅館に宿泊されました (His Majesty) the Emperor paid a visit to the Grand Shrine of Ise, and *did us the honor of* staying at our inn. (➤ honor に尊敬の意がこもる).

サロン a **salon** /səlɑ́ːn ‖ sǽlɔn/.

さわ 沢 a **mountain stream**(谷川); a **marsh** (湿地, 沼地) ▶沢歩きをする *walk along* [*by*] *a mountain stream*.

さわがしい 騒がしい **noisy** ▶騒がしい音楽 *noisy* music ‖通りが騒がしくてきみの言うことが聞き取れない It is so *noisy* on the street (that) I can't hear what you are saying. ‖騒がしくするな Don't *be noisy*. ‖この頃世の中が騒がしくなってきた The world has become *chaotic* [*topsy-turvy*] these days. (➤ともに「混乱状態で」の意; 後者はインフォーマル).

さわがせる 騒がせる ▶あの事件は世間を大いに騒がせた That incident *caused* a great *sensation*. ‖どうもお騒がせしました I'm sorry about *all the fuss*. (➤騒ぎ立てたことをわびる場合) ／I'm sorry to *have bothered* [*have troubled*] you. (➤相手をうるさがらせたり相手に面倒をかけたりした場合).

さわぎ 騒ぎ 1【騒音】(a) **noise** ▶この騒ぎは何ですか

What is this *noise* [*racket*] about?
2【もめ事】(a) **fuss**(騒ぎ立てること); (an) **excitement**(興奮); (a) **panic**(慌てふためき); a **scare**(不安に陥れる事態)▶**爆弾騒ぎ** *a bomb scare* ‖ **離婚騒ぎ**でその歌手は人気が落ちた That singer's popularity has declined because of the *fuss over his* [*her*] *divorce*. ‖ B高校が優勝してわが町は大変な**騒ぎ**だった B High School's victory caused great *excitement* in our town. ‖ 去年の6月にコレラ**騒ぎ**があった There was *a cholera panic* [*outbreak*] in June of last year. (➤ outbreak は「大発生」).
▶《慣用表現》市民プールは大変な人出で, 泳ぐどころの**騒ぎではなかった** There was such a crowd out in the city swimming pool I *didn't even think of* swimming.
☛ **大騒ぎ**(→見出語)

さわぐ 騒ぐ **1【やかましくする】make noise**(騒ぎ立てる); **make a fuss**(つまらぬことで大騒ぎする)
▶2階の学生たちが**騒いでいる** The students living upstairs *are making noise*. ‖ 野球でR大が勝ったので, 彼らはそれを祝って**騒いでいる**のです They *are partying hearty* [*whooping it up*] to celebrate R University's victory in the baseball game. (➤ party hearty は「大騒ぎして楽しむ」, whoop it up は「(酒を飲んだりして)どんちゃん騒ぎする」の意のインフォーマルな言い方) ‖ このくらいのことで**騒ぐ**んじゃない! Don't *make a fuss* over such a small thing!
2【不満や要求を叫ぶ】clamor ▶授業料値上げに**反対して学生たちが騒いでいる** The students *are clamoring against* an increase in tuition fees. ‖ 彼らは首相の退陣を**要求して騒いでいる** They *are clamoring for* the resignation of the Prime Minister.
▶故郷で大きな地震があったというニュースを聞いて私は**胸が騒いだ** *My heart jumped* (*into my mouth*) at the news that a strong earthquake had struck my hometown.
3【もてはやす, 評判にする】▶俺も若い頃はずいぶん女の子に**騒がれた**もんさ When I was young, I *was* very *popular* with the girls.

ざわざわ ▶ざわざわしていた生徒たちは先生の姿を見て静かになった The *noisy* students quieted down when they saw the teacher.

ざわつく ▶授業が始まったのに教室はまだざわついている Although class has started, the classroom is still *noisy*. ‖ 開演前のホールはざわついていた *There was a buzz of conversation* in the hall before the curtain rose. (➤ buzz は「ざわめき」).

ざわめく ▶人のざわめく声(=ざわめき)が隣の部屋から聞こえてきた *A hum of voices* came from the next room. ‖ 本命が2位と決まった瞬間, 場内はざわめいた *There was a ripple* through the crowd when it was learned that the favorite had placed second. (➤ ripple は「さざめき」).

さわやか 爽やかな **refreshing**(天気・人などがすがすがしい); **crisp**(天気や風が); **fresh**(空気などが汚れていない); **refreshed**(気分がさっぱりした) ▶**初夏の爽やかな朝** a *refreshing* morning in early summer ‖ **爽やかな風** a *crisp* breeze ‖ **爽やかに晴れた秋の日** a *crisp and clear* autumn day ‖ **さわやかな笑顔** a *delightful* [*pleasant*] smile ‖ **さわやかな人** a *pleasant* [*refreshing*] person ‖ 私たちは高原の朝の**爽やかな**空気を胸いっぱい吸い込んだ We took deep breaths of the *fresh* [*bracing*] morning air in the highlands. (➤ bracing は「身が引き締まるような」) ‖ クレイダーマンのピアノ曲は人を**爽やかな気分にする** Clayderman's piano music *makes* you *feel refreshed*.

1さわら《植物》a **sawara**.

2さわら《魚》a **Japanese Spanish mackerel**.

1さわり 触り ▶その話のさわりだけを教えてあげよう I'll tell you only *the best* [*most impressive*] *part*(*s*) of that story.

2さわり 障り ▶勉学に**障りがある**といけないので, デートはほどほどにしておきなさい You should date less frequently, or it may *affect* your schoolwork.

さわる 触る・障る **1【触れる】touch** +㊐; **feel** +㊐(触って調べる) ▶子供たちは柔らかいウサギの毛に**触った** The children *touched* the rabbit's soft fur. ‖ しこりがないかどうか首に**触ってみた** I *felt* my neck to see if there was a lump. (➤ felt は feel の過去形) ‖《掲示》**触るな** Hands Off ‖ **触らないでよ**, エッチ! *Don't touch me* [*Keep your hands off me*], you dirty creep!
ことわざ **触らぬ神にたたりなし** The gods left alone do not curse. (➤日本語からの直訳) / Let sleeping dogs lie. (➤「眠っている犬はそのまま眠らせておけ」の意の英語のことわざ).
2【害する】be bad [**harmful**] ▶酒を飲み過ぎると**体に障る**よ Drinking too much *is bad for* [*is harmful to*] *your health*. ‖ 彼はぼくの**気に障る**ようなことばかり言う He always says things that *annoy* [*irritate*] me. ‖ **気に障った**のならごめんなさい I'm sorry if I'*ve offended* you. ‖ 弟の口笛がぼくの**神経に障った** My (younger) brother's whistling *got* [*grated*] *on my nerves*.

さわん 左腕 a **southpaw**. →サウスポー.

1さん 三 **three**; **the third**(3番目) ▶**3分の1** *a third* ‖ **3分の2** *two-thirds* ‖ **第三者** *a third party* ‖《文法》**三人称** the third person.

2さん 酸 (an) **acid**.

1-さん -産 ▶**外国産**の小麦 *foreign-grown* wheat (➤「国産の」は home-grown, または domestic) ‖ **オーストラリア産**の牛肉 beef *from* Australia (➤ from は「出どころ」を表す) ‖ このオレンジはカリフォルニア**産**だ These oranges *are from* [*are a product of*] California. ‖ このサツマイモはどこの**産**かわかりますか Do you know *where* these sweet potatoes *are grown*?

2-さん -山 **Mount** 〜《略 **Mt.** 〜》▶**鳥海山** *Mount* [*Mt.*] Chokai.

3-さん **Mr.** 〜(➤男性に); **Mrs.** 〜(➤既婚女性に), **Miss** 〜(➤未婚女性に), **Ms.** 〜(➤未婚・既婚を問わず女性に) →-様

> **解説 敬称のつけ方**
> (1)日本語の「-さん」と「-さま」は丁寧さにおいてかなりの違いがあるが, 英語の Mr., Mrs., Miss, Ms. はその両者に使える.
> (2)大人の人を姓で呼ぶ場合には Mr. などをつけるのが礼儀で, 電話や手紙・自己紹介などでは自分を指す場合にもつけることがある.
> (3)英語には(姓でなく)名前につける「-さん」に相当する語はない. 日本をよく知っている外国人との会話などでは姓または名に -san をつけてもよい. →-君.

▶天知**さん**, ご面会の方がいらしてますよ *Mr.* [*Mrs.* / *Miss* / *Ms.*] Amachi, there's a gentleman [lady] here who would like to see you. ‖ 美代子**さん**, ちょっと来て! Miyoko-*san*, come over here.
▶《母親が子供に》ほら, **お猿さん**よ Look at the mon-

key. ／Look, there's a monkey over there.
《参考》「犬さん」,「豚さん」,「小鳥さん」はそれぞれ doggy, piggy, birdie のように小児語で言う. また,「クマさん」は teddy,「ウサギさん」は bunny,「アヒルさん」は quack-quack などと言う.

さんい 三位 third place ▶競走で3位になる get *third place* in a race ‖ **3位**決定戦 a *third place* play-off.

さんいつ 散逸する ▶バッハのカンタータの楽譜は多くが**散逸した** The scores of many Bach cantatas *were scattered and lost*.

さんいん 産院 a maternity hospital［home］.

サンオイル suntan oil ▶体に**サンオイル**を塗る put［spread］*suntan oil* on oneself.

1**さんか 参加** participation 一動 **参加する** participate /pɑːˈtísɪpeɪt/《in》, take part《in》(➤後者はややインフォーマル); join《in》(加わる); enter ＋目 (競技などに) ▶討論集会に**参加する** *join* a teach-in ‖ コンテストに**参加する** *enter* a contest ‖ 私たちの討論に**参加して**ください Please *join* (*in*) our discussion. ‖ オリンピックは勝つことより**参加する**ことに意義がある In the Olympic Games, *participation* is more important than winning. ‖ その国はかつて黒人の**政治参加**に反対してきた That country has formerly opposed the *participation* of blacks *in politics*. ‖ 私は長年ボランティア活動に**参加して**きた I *have participated*［*have taken part*］*in* volunteer activities for many years. ‖ そのレースには20人が**参加した** Twenty people *entered*［*participated in* ／*took part in*］the race. ‖ ディベートの**参加者たち** *participants* in a debate.

2**さんか 酸化** oxidation 一動 **酸化する** oxidize ▶この金属は**酸化し**やすい This metal easily *oxidizes*.
‖**酸化物** (an) oxide /ɑ́ːksaɪd/ ‖ **酸化ナトリウム** sodium oxide ‖ **酸化マグネシウム** magnesium oxide.

3**さんか 産科** obstetrics /əbstétrɪks/
‖**産科医** an obstetrician /ɑ̀ːbstətríʃən/ ‖ **産科病棟** a maternity ward.

4**さんか 賛歌** a song of praise (たたえる歌); a hymn (賛美歌) ▶愛の**賛歌**を歌う sing *a hymn to love* ‖ 自由の**賛歌**を歌う sing *a paean to liberty*.

5**さんか 傘下** ▶多国籍企業の**傘下に入る** *get under the umbrella* of a multi-national corporation ‖ それらの国々は軍事的には NATO の**傘下にある** Those countries *are under the* military *umbrella* of NATO.

6**さんか 惨禍** a disaster(大災害); a calamity (悲惨な事態); horror(s) (恐ろしいこと) ▶戦争の**惨禍**を後世に伝える tell future generations of the *horrors* of war.

1**さんが 山河** mountains and rivers, natural surroundings ▶故郷の**山河** *the mountains and rivers*［*natural surroundings*］of one's native place.

2**さんが 参賀** ▶一般**参賀** well-wishers' *visits to the Imperial Palace*.

1**さんかい 山海** ▶彼らは**山海の珍味**でもてなしてくれた They entertained me with *delicacies from both* (*the*) *land and sea*.

2**さんかい 散会** ▶3時**散会** *Breaks up* at three.

さんがい 三階《米》the third floor,《英》the second floor ▶3**階**建てのビル a *three-storied* building ／a building of three stories ‖ 私の部屋は3**階**です My room is on *the third*［《英》*second*］*floor*. (→階).

ざんがい 残骸 the wreckage /rékɪdʒ/, a wreck; the remains (残留物) ▶墜落したヘリコプターの**残骸**が山中で見つかった *The wreckage* of the crashed helicopter was found on the mountain.

さんかいき 三回忌 the second anniversary of a person's death(追悼日); a Buddhist memorial service held on the second anniversary of a person's death (➤説明的な訳).

1**さんかく 三角** a triangle /tráɪæŋɡəl/ ▶**正三角形** *an equilateral triangle* ‖ **直角三角形** *a right* (*-angled*) *triangle* ‖ 丸・**三角**・四角 a circle, *a triangle* and a square ‖ **三角形**の面積は底辺掛ける高さ割る2である The area of *a triangle* is half the base times the altitude［height］.
▶《慣用表現》ないしょだけど, 俺, 会社の女性2人と**三角関係**になってるんだ This is just between us. I'*m in a love triangle* with two girls at the office.
‖**三角関数** trigonometric functions ‖ **三角巾** a triangle bandage ‖ **三角定規**《米》a triangle,《英》a set square ‖ **三角州** a delta ‖ **三角波** a chopping wave ‖ (ヨットの)**三角帆** a triangular sail ／a jib ／a lateen sail.

2**さんかく 参画する** participate《in》, take part《in》(➤前者が日本語に近い) ▶経営に**参画する** *participate*［*take part*］*in* management. (→参加).

さんがく 山岳 ▶**山岳地帯**の天候は急変する The weather in *mountain*［*mountainous*］*districts* is very changeable.
‖**山岳部** a mountaineering［an alpine］club.

ざんがく 残額 the balance(差し引き残高); the remainder (借金などの残金) ▶銀行預金の**残額**は20万円ある I have *a balance* of 200,000 yen in my bank account. ‖ あす**残額**を支払います I'll pay you *the remainder* of my debt tomorrow. ／Tomorrow I'll pay (you) *the rest* of what I owe you. (➤前者が「残額」という日本語により近く, 後者は「残りを払う」に近い).

さんがくきょうどう 産学協同 cooperation between industry and academia［businesses and universities］.

さんがつ 三月 March《略 Mar.》▶私はことしの**3月**に高校を卒業した I graduated from senior high school *this March*［*in March of this year*］. ‖ 私たちは**3月3日**にひな祭りのお祝いをした We celebrated the Doll Festival *on March 3*.

さんがにち 三が日 the first three days of the New Year (➤説明的な訳).

1**さんかん 山間** ▶**山間部**では雪が2メートルにも達した In *mountainous regions*［In *the mountains*］snow accumulated as deep as two meters.

2**さんかん 参観** ▶英語の授業を**参観する** *observe* an English class ‖ きょうは父母の**授業参観日**だ Today the parents are going to visit their children's classes. 《参考》英語圏では「授業参観日」のことを visiting［school visitation］day, school open house, open house (at school), open school parents' day, class visit, parents' observation day など, いろいろな名称で呼んでいる.

3**さんかん 三冠** a Triple Crown(➤ふつう大文字で書く) ▶野村は日本で初の**三冠王**になった Nomura became the first *Triple Crown winner* in Japan.

さんかんしおん 三寒四温 a late winter［early spring］cycle of three cold days followed by four warm days (➤説明的な訳).

ざんき 慚愧 ▶当社におけるこの度の不祥事は誠に**ざんきに堪えません** I［We］deeply *regret* (*and am*［*are*］*ashamed* of) the recent scandal at our company.

さんぎいん 参議院 the House of Councilors, the Upper House of the Diet ▶上田氏は参議院議員選挙に当選した Mr. Ueda has been returned to *the House of Councilors* in the election. (➤ return は「(国会議員として)選出する」).

‖**参議院議員** a member of the House of Councilors ‖**参議院議長** the President of the House of Councilors.

さんきゃく 三脚 a **tripod** /tráipɑ:d/ (カメラなどの) ▶三脚を据える set up *a tripod*.

ざんぎゃく 残虐な **cruel** (むごい) ; **brutal** (獣のように残忍な) ; **atrocious** (ショッキングな) ; **heinous** /héinəs/ (極悪な) ▶残虐な犯罪 a *brutal* [*heinous*] crime ‖侵攻してきた軍隊は罪のない女性や子供に多くの残虐行為を働いた The invading army committed many *brutalities* [*cruel acts*] against innocent women and children.

さんきゅう 産休 **maternity leave** ▶1年間の産休を取る take a one-year *maternity leave* ‖岸さんは産休中です Ms. Kishi is on *maternity leave*.

サンキュー **Thank you.** ▶ 対話「皿洗いしといたよ」「サンキュー」"I've washed the dishes for you." "*Thanks*." (➤ 文字どおりには Thank you. だが, この日本語のもつ軽い感じは Thanks. のほうが出る).

さんぎょう 産業 (an) **industry** /índəstri/ (➤ Ⓤ扱いで総称としても用いる ; 個々の産業は Ⓒ) 一形 **産業の** **industrial** /ɪndʌ́striəl/ ▶娯楽産業 the entertainment *industry* ‖自動車 [レジャー] 産業 the automobile [leisure] *industry* ‖新しい産業を興す build up a new *industry* [new *industries*] ‖地場産業を振興する promote *local industries* [*local industry*] (➤ 後者の industry は総称) ‖政府はもっと国内産業を守るべきだ The government should further protect *domestic industries* [*domestic industry*].

▶日本の産業の多くが国際競争力を失いつつある Many Japanese *industries* are losing international competitiveness. ‖産業スパイは産業界の秘密を探る機会を常に狙っている *Industrial* [*Corporate*] *spies* are always watching for a chance to ferret out *industrial* [*corporate*] secrets.

‖**産業革命** the Industrial Revolution ‖**産業再生機構** the Industrial Revitalization Corporation of Japan《略 IRCJ》‖**産業道路** an industrial road ‖**産業廃棄物** industrial waste ‖**産業廃棄物処分業者** an industrial waste disposal operator ‖**産業廃棄物処理施設** a treatment facility [plant] for industrial waste ‖**基幹産業** key [basic] industries.

ざんきょう 残響 **reverberation** ▶残響の豊かなホール a hall with ample *reverberation*.

ざんぎょう 残業 **overtime** [**extra**] **work** 一動 **残業する** **do** [**work** / **put in**] **overtime** ▶サービス残業する *work* [*do*] *overtime* for free / *work* [*do*] unpaid overtime ‖きょうは2時間残業した Today I *did* [*worked* / *put in*] two hours' *overtime*.

‖**残業手当** overtime pay, an overtime allowance /əláuəns/ ‖**サービス残業** unpaid overtime work. ‖**ノー残業デー** a no overtime day.

ざんきん 残金 ▶借金の残金 the *remainder* [*balance*] of one's debt.

さんきんこうたい 参勤交代 a system under which feudal lords [daimyo] had to spend every other year in Edo [Tokyo] (➤ 説明的な訳).

サンクチュアリー a **sanctuary** ▶野生動物のサンクチュアリー a wildlife *sanctuary*.

サングラス (a **pair of**) **sunglasses** ▶スキーのときはサングラスをかけたほうがいいよ When skiing, you should wear *sunglasses*.

さんけ 産気 ▶妻が産気づいた My wife has started to *get* [*feel*] *labor pains*.

ざんげ 懺悔 (a) **confession** (罪の告白) ; **repentance** (後悔) 一動 **ざんげする** **confess** /kənfés/, **repent** 《of》▶神に罪をざんげする *confess* one's sin(s) to God.

[1]**さんけい 参詣する** **go to pray at a shrine** [**a temple**] ; **visit a shrine** [**a temple**] (➤ 文脈がなければ単に「訪れる」の意になる) ▶毎年元旦には家族で神社に参詣する Every year on the morning of New Year's Day I *go to pray at a shrine* with my family. ‖原宿駅前は明治神宮への参詣人でごった返していた There were swarms of people in front of Harajuku Station on their way to visit the Meiji Shrine.

[2]**さんけい 三景** ▶日本三景 *the three most beautiful scenic spots* in Japan.

さんげき 惨劇 a **disaster**, a **tragedy**.

さんけつ 酸欠 (an) **oxygen shortage** [**deficiency**] ▶地下の作業員たちは酸欠にならないように新鮮な空気を取り入れ続けた The workers underground kept taking in fresh air in order to avoid *a lack of oxygen* [*(an) oxygen deficiency*].

さんけん 三権 ▶憲法の三権分立の原則 the Constitutional principle of the separation of *powers* (➤「三」は表現しないのがふつう).

さんげんしょく 三原色 **the three primary colors** ▶光の三原色 *the three primary colors* of light.

[1]**さんご 珊瑚** **coral** ▶サンゴ礁の海に潜る dive around *a coral reef* / dive in the sea around *a coral reef* ‖**サンゴ島** a coral island.

[2]**さんご 産後** **after delivery** [**giving birth**].

‖**産後うつ** postpartum depression ‖**産後ケア** postpartum care.

さんこう 参考 (a) **reference** ▶欄外の注を参考にしながらその詩を読んだ I read the poem *referring to* its marginal notes. ‖きみの意見はとても参考になった(=役に立った)よ Your comments *were* quite *helpful* [*were of* great *help*] to me. ‖ご参考までに申し上げますと, このベンツのお値段は800万円です *Just for your information* [*reference*], this Mercedes costs 8 million yen.

‖**参考書** a reference book (➤ 辞書・年鑑などの図書をいい, いわゆる「学習参考書」は study-aid (book), handbook for students, study guide などという ; →あんちょこ) ‖**参考資料** reference materials [data] ‖**参考人** a witness ‖**参考文献一覧** a bibliography /bìbliɑ́:grəfi/.

ざんこく 残酷 (a) **cruelty** 一形 **残酷な** **cruel** (むごい) ; **brutal** (獣のように残忍な) ; **merciless** (無慈悲な) ▶残酷な刑罰 a *cruel* punishment ‖残酷な行為 a *brutal* act / an act of brutality ‖残酷な運命 (a) *cruel* fate ‖戦争の残酷さ *the cruelty* of war ‖兵士たちは残酷にも多数の住民たちを殺した The soldiers *were cruel enough to* kill many residents. / The soldiers killed many residents *in cold blood*. (➤ in cold blood は「平然と」) ‖人が苦しんでいるのを見て喜ぶなんてあなたも残酷な人ね It's *cruel* of you to like watching people suffer.

さんこつ 散骨 **scattering of ashes** ▶私が死んだらオホー

ツクの海に散骨してほしい I want *my ashes to be scattered* over the Sea of Okhotsk.

さんさい 山菜 edible wild [mountain] plants.

1さんざい 散在 ▶山あいに農家が散在している The valley *is dotted with* farmhouses.

2さんざい 散財 ▶大変散財をおかけして申し訳ありません I'm afraid (that) I've *put* you *to terrible expense*. ‖ 彼女はデパートに出かけて散財した She went *on a spending spree* at a department store. ／She *splurged on a lot of* (*unnecessary*) *things* at a department store.

さんさく 散策 a walk, a stroll (➤ 後者が「ぶらぶら歩き」のニュアンスが濃い) ▶庭園を散策する *take a stroll* in the garden ‖ セーヌの川べりを散策する *stroll* along the banks of the Seine.

‖散策コース a walking path.

さんざし 《植物》a hawthorn.

ざんさつ 惨殺 ▶男は惨殺されていた The man *was brutally murdered*.

さんさろ 三差路 ▶この道路はこの先で三差路になる This road *divides* [*branches off*] *into two* further ahead. ／You will come to *a fork* in the road ahead.

さんさん 燦々 ▶日がさんさんとテラスに降り注いでいる The sun is shining *bright* [*brightly* ／*brilliantly*] on the terrace. (➤ bright はややインフォーマル；brilliantly は brightly をより強調した形).

さんざん ▶少年たちはその少女をいじめたことでさんざん叱られた The boys were *severely* scolded [got a *good* dressing-down] for bullying the girl. ‖ おじにはさんざん迷惑をかけてきた I've caused my uncle *a great deal of* trouble. ‖ 彼らはさんざんその大臣の悪口を言った They criticized the Minister *bitterly*. ▶試験の結果はさんざんだった The results of the exam *couldn't have been worse*. ‖ きのうは定期はなくすわ, 財布はすられるわで, さんざんな目に遭った What with losing my commuter pass and my pocket being picked, I really *had a hard time* [*a tough day*] yesterday.

ざんざん ▶外はざんざん降りだ It's *raining torrentially* [*raining buckets*] outside.

さんさんくど 三々九度 *san-san-kudo*; the exchange of sake cups by the couple at a Shinto wedding (➤ 説明的な訳).

さんさんごご 三々五々 by [in] twos and threes ▶町内会が終わって出席者は三々五々引き上げていった The neighborhood association meeting ended and the attendees left *in twos and threes*.

1さんじ 惨事 a disaster; a tragedy (悲劇的事件) ▶流血の惨事 *bloodshed* ‖ 通勤列車の正面衝突事故は史上最悪の惨事となった The head-on collision between two commuter trains turned out to be the most terrible railroad *disaster* ever.

2さんじ 賛辞 (a) tribute; praise (賞賛); admiration (感嘆) ▶人々は彼の勇気に惜しみない賛辞を送った People paid (a) high *tribute* to his courage. ／People gave high *praise* for his courage. ／People loudly *admired* (him for) his courage. (➤ loudly は「声に出して」).

3さんじ 三時 three o'clock ▶三時(のおやつ)にしよう Let's have some *afternoon snacks*.

4さんじ 参事 a counselor, 《英》 a counsellor

‖参事官 a counselor; the deputy director general (国土地理院の) ‖ 副参事官 a deputy counselor.

さんしきすみれ 三色菫 a pansy.

さんじげん 三次元 three dimensions; the third dimension (第三次元) ▶三次元の世界 the *three-dimensional* world(➤ 形容詞の場合, 3-D, three-D とつづることもある；→スリーディー) ‖ よくできた三次元(3D)映画は私たちに新しい映画体験を与えてくれる A well-made *3-D movie* can provide us with a new cinematic experience.

‖三次元映像 [空間] a three-dimensional image [space].

さんしすいめい 山紫水明 scenic beauty ▶山紫水明の地 a place of *scenic beauty*.

さんじせいげん 産児制限 birth control ▶産児制限を国策として奨励している国もある Some countries encourage people to *practice birth control* as (a) national policy.

さんじゅ 傘寿 ▶曽祖父の傘寿を祝う celebrate our great-grandfather's *80th birthday*.

1さんじゅう 三十 thirty; the thirtieth (30番目) ▶彼は30代後半[30前]だ He is in *his late thirties* [*is under thirty*].

2さんじゅう 三重の triple

‖三重唱[奏] a trio ‖ 三重衝突 a three-car pile-up ‖ 三重の塔 a three-storied pagoda.

さんしゅつ 産出する produce +㊐ ▶石油産出国 an oil-*producing* country ‖ この油田は多量の石油を産出する This oil field *produces* a lot of oil.

‖産出高 output, production.

さんじゅつ 算術 arithmetic /əríθmətɪk/.

さんじょ 賛助 ▶さだまさしの公演に加山雄三が賛助出演した Kayama Yuzo *made a guest appearance* [*appeared as a guest star*] in Sada Masashi's performance.

‖賛助会員 a supporting member.

ざんしょ 残暑 ▶ことしの残暑は例年になく厳しい The *lingering summer heat* [The *heat of late summer*] is unusually severe this year.

✉ **残暑厳しき折からお変わりありませんか** How are you getting along in *this severe lingering heat of summer*?

1さんしょう 参照する refer /rɪfə́ːʳ/ to ▶詳細は下記リストを参照のこと For further details, please *refer to* the following list. ‖ 22ページを参照(せよ) *See* p.22 ／*cf.* p.22 (➤ cf. はラテン語 *confer* の略で, 英語の compare に相当し, ふつう /kəmpéəʳ/と読む).

‖相互参照 a cross reference.

2さんしょう 山椒 Japanese pepper(香辛料); a Japanese pepper tree (木)

[ことわざ] **さんしょうは小粒でもぴりりと辛い** A Japanese pepper fruit may be tiny, but it is very hot. (➤ 日本語からの直訳) ／A little body often harbors a great soul. (➤「小さな体が偉大な精神を宿していることがしばしばある」の意).

3さんしょう 三唱 ▶万歳を三唱する *call* 'banzai' *three times* 《参考》英語には three cheers があるが, これは応援で Hip! Hip! Hooray! を3度叫ぶこと.

1さんじょう 惨状 ▶事故現場の惨状に思わず目を背けた I could not help turning my eyes away from the *horrific* [*terrible*] *scene* of the accident.

2さんじょう 三乗 cube ▶5の3乗は125 5 cubed is 125. ／The *cube* of 5 is 125.

さんしょううお 山椒魚 a salamander.

さんしん 三振 a strikeout 一動 **三振する** strike out (➤「三振させる」の意にもなる) ▶スライダーで三振する *strike out* on a slider ‖ 大谷投手は3イニングで7人

を三振に打ち取った Ohtani *fanned* [*struck out*] seven (batters) in three innings. (➤ fan は「三振に切って取る」) ‖ 畠山は二死満塁で三振に倒れた Hatakeyama *struck out* with the bases loaded after two outs.

ざんしん 斬新な novel ▶斬新なアイデア a *novel* [*a new and original*] idea ‖ 彼女はいつも斬新なデザインの服を着ている She always wears clothes that are *novel* in design.

1**さんすい 散水する** sprinkle water ▶地面に散水する *sprinkle water* on the ground / *sprinkle* the ground *with water*.
‖散水器 [車] a sprinkler.

2**さんすい 山水** a landscape (風景；風景画) ▶山水画 a *landscape* painting. →枯れ山水.

さんすう 算数 arithmetic /əríθmətɪk/ (学科)；counting, calculation, 《インフォーマル》sums (計算)；figures (数字) ▶私は算数 (＝計算) が苦手だ I am poor at *arithmetic*. /I have a poor head for *counting* [*calculation* / *figures*]. / I'm no good at *figures*.

サンスクリット Sanskrit.

さんずのかわ 三途の川 the *Sanzu-no Kawa*；the River of the Three Buddhist Hells (仏教の) ▶さんずの川を渡る cross *the Sanzu-no Kawa* (➤ 意味を伝えるだけなら die の 1 語でもよい).

さんする 産する produce ＋Ⓜ ▶小豆島は良質のオリーブを産する Good olives *grow* [*are produced*] on Shodo Island.

1**さんせい 賛成** agreement (同意)；approval /əprúːvəl/ (承認) ━動 賛成する agree 《with》；approve of (…を良いと認める)；second (提案・動議などを採用することに賛成する)

【文型】
人・意見(A)に賛成する
agree with A
人・案(B)に賛成である
be for [**in favor of**] B

《解説》 **agree with** は「同じ考えである」の意. **be for** や **be in favor of** は「その考え方を支持している, 味方である」の意. for の逆は against.

▶私はきみに全く賛成だ I completely *agree with* you. /*I'm* all *for* your idea. /I *couldn't agree* (*with* you) *more*. (➤ 最後の文は「これ以上賛成しようがない(くらい賛成だ)」の意) ‖ その意見に賛成ではありません I don't *agree with* that opinion. ‖ その点では彼に賛成です I *agree with* him on that. ‖ 山川君, きみはこの案に賛成? 反対? Yamakawa, *are* you *for* or against this proposal? ‖ 私はその動議に賛成です I *second* the motion. ‖ それは賛成できる考えだ It's a *supportable* idea.

▶先生は私たちの企画に賛成してくれた Our teacher *approved of* our project. ‖ 公共の場所での喫煙には賛成できない I *don't approve of* smoking in public places. ‖ 全員が賛成しているというわけではなかった Not all *were in agreement*.

▶賛成の人は手を挙げてください *Those who approve*, please raise your hands. ‖ 中井さんはあなたの考え方に賛成の演説をぶったよ Mr. Nakai made a speech *in support of* your opinion. ‖ 法案は賛成155, 反対21で可決した The bill was passed by a vote of 155 to 21. (➤「賛成」の意は was passed で表されている) ‖ **対話**「今夜は外に食事に行こう」「賛成!」"Let's eat out tonight." "*O.K.* / (*That's a*) *great idea!*"

☛ 不賛成 (→見出語)

2**さんせい 酸性** acidity ━形 酸性の acid /ǽsɪd/ ▶そのせっけんは酸性ですか, アルカリ性ですか Is that soap *acid* or alkaline? ‖ その液体からは酸性反応が出た The liquid showed *an acid reaction*.
‖酸性雨 acid rain ‖ 酸性食品 acid [acidic] food ‖ 酸性土壌 acid soil.

3**さんせい 三世** a sansei ▶日系三世(のアメリカ人) a *third-generation* Japanese-American. →二世.

さんせいけん 参政権 the right to vote (投票する権利)；suffrage /sʌ́frɪdʒ/ (➤ その権利を享受するというニュアンスもある)；the franchise /frǽntʃaɪz/ (➤ その権利の法的有効性を強調する語).
‖女性 [婦人] 参政権 female [woman('s)] suffrage.

さんせき 山積 ▶仕事が山積している I*'ve got tons of* [*a lot of*] work to do. /I *have a pile of* work to do. ‖ 難問が山積している Many difficult problems *have piled up*.

さんせん 参戦する participate in a war ▶多くの国が第二次大戦に参戦した Many countries *participated in World War II*.

さんぜん 燦然 ▶優勝カップは勝者の手の中でさん然と輝いていた The cup shone *brightly* [*brilliantly*] in the champion's hands.

さんそ 酸素 oxygen /ɑ́ːksɪdʒən/ ▶患者は手術中酸素吸入を受けた The patient *received oxygen* during the operation.
‖酸素マスク an oxygen mask.

さんそう 山荘 a mountain villa [cabin] (➤ villa のほうが大規模で高級).

ざんぞう 残像 an after(-)image.

さんぞく 山賊 a bandit ▶山賊の一味 a group of *bandits*.

さんそん 山村 a mountain village.

ざんだか 残高 the balance ▶銀行の残高は今15万円だ *The balance* on my account [My bank *balance*] is 150,000 yen. ‖ IC カードが残高不足で自動改札を通れなかった I couldn't pass through the automatic ticket gate because there was *not enough balance* [*money*] on my IC card.
‖(ATMの)残高照会 Show Balance.

サンタクロース Santa (Claus)；《英 また》Father Christmas ▶子供の頃はサンタクロースがいると信じていました When I was a child, I thought *Santa* (*Claus*) truly existed.

サンダル (a pair of) sandals ▶サンダルを履く put on *sandals*.

さんたん 惨憺たる wretched /rétʃɪd/ (悲惨な)；miserable (惨めな)；horrible (見るも無残な)；appalling (ぞっとするような) ▶惨たんたる生活を送る lead a *wretched* [*miserable*] life ‖ 惨たんたる光景 a *horrible* sight ‖ 爆発現場は惨たんたるありさまだった The scene of the explosion was *appalling* [*horrific*]. (➤ horrific は「(人に)恐怖と嫌悪を起こさせる」).

▶練習不足がたたって試合は惨たんたる結果に終わった Our team *was soundly defeated* in the game because we didn't practice enough. (➤ soundly は「したたか(に), ひどく」) ‖ 苦心惨たんしてやっと問題を全部解いた I *had a* (*really*) *hard time* solving all the problems.

さんだんじゅう 散弾銃 a shotgun.

さんだんとび 三段跳び the triple jump ; the hop, step and jump.

さんだんろんぽう 三段論法《論理学》**a syllogism** /sílədʒìzəm/.

1**さんち 産地** ▶山梨県はブドウの**産地**だ Yamanashi is a grape-*producing district*. ‖ これは**産地直送**の桃です These peaches *were shipped directly from the producers*.

▶秋田は美人の**産地**として知られる Akita is famous for (its) beautiful women. (➤「美人で有名」の意).

2**さんち 山地 a mountainous** /máʊntnəs/ **region** [**area**] ▶中国**山地** the Chugoku *mountainous region* [*area*].

さんちょう 山頂 the top [**summit**] **of a mountain**, **a mountaintop** ; **a peak**(とがった山の) ▶白根**山頂**は雪に覆われていた *The top* [*summit*] of Mt. Shirane was covered [capped] with snow. ‖ **山頂**まで3時間くらいかかった It took us about three hours to reach *the top of the mountain*.

さんちょく 産直の farm-fresh ▶**産直**の野菜 *farm-fresh* vegetables / vegetables *fresh from the farm*.

‖**産直市場** a farmer's market.

ざんてい 暫定 ▶**暫定**予算 a *stopgap* budget ‖ 校長が急病のため**暫定的に**教頭が校長の代理を務めることになった On account of the principal's sudden illness, the vice principal will take over for the principal *temporarily* [*for the time being*]. (➤「しばらくの間」の意) ‖ 現内閣は**暫定政権**だといわれている The present regime is said to be *a caretaker* [*stopgap*] *government*.

サンディエゴ San Diego /sæ̀n diéɪgoʊ/ (アメリカ, カリフォルニア州の都市).

サンデー 1【曜日】**Sunday.**

2【アイスクリーム】**a sundae**(➤ つづりに注意).

さんど 三度 three times ▶私はその映画は3**度**も見た I saw the movie *three times*. ‖《離れて生活している子供に》きちんと**三度三度食事をしている**か? Are you *eating right* [*regularly*] ?

▶《慣用表現》兄貴は野球を見るのが**三度の飯より好き**だ My (older) brother *would rather go hungry than* miss a baseball game. ‖「**三度目の正直**」で司法試験にパスした As they say "*Third time lucky*," I passed the bar examination on my third attempt.

サンドイッチ a sandwich ▶昼食にハムとレタスの**サンドイッチ**を食べた I ate *a ham and lettuce sandwich* for lunch. ‖**サンドイッチマン** a sandwich man ; sandwich board advertiser(➤ 性差のない言い方).

さんとう 三等 (the) third prize (3等賞) ; **(the) third place** (第3位) ; **third class** (3等級) ▶彼女はスピーチコンテストで**3等賞**を得た She got [won] (*the*) *third prize* in the speech contest.

1**さんどう 賛同 approval 一動 賛同する endorse**(➤ 公に支持を表明する ; 堅い語) ▶彼女の提案は多くの人たちの**賛同**を得た Her proposal had the *approval* of many people. ‖ 我々の趣旨にご**賛同**いただけますか Will you *support* [*endorse*] our aim ?

2**さんどう 参道 the approach**《to》▶清水寺への**参道** *a road* to Kiyomizu Temple ‖ 明治神宮の表[裏]**参道** *the front* [*rear*] *approach to* (the) Meiji Shrine.

ざんとう 残党 the remnants, the surviving members, the survivors.

さんにゅう 参入する enter +目 ▶別の1社がスマートフォン市場に**参入した** Another company *entered* the smartphone market.

ざんにん 残忍な brutal(冷酷無比の) ; **atrocious** (凶悪な) ▶**残忍な**殺人 a *brutal* murder ‖ **残忍な**独裁者 a *brutal* dictator ‖ 皇帝ネロは本当に**残忍な**性格だったのだろうか I wonder if (the) Emperor Nero really had a *brutal* personality.

さんにんしょう 三人称《文法》**the third person** ▶**三人称**単数現在形 *a third person* singular present-tense form.

ざんねん 残念

【文型】
～であることは残念だ
I'm sorry (that) S + V.
It's too bad (that) S + V.
It's a shame (that) S + V.

《解説》(1) **I'm sorry** は「(私は)気の毒に思う, 残念です」と同情・遺憾・後悔・謝罪などを表す.「我々は残念です」ならば We are sorry のように主語を変える.
(2) **It's too bad** はちょっとした困ったことに対して使い, 極めて深刻なことには使わない. 会話では単に Too bad とも言う. **It's a shame** もくだけた言い方.
(3)「…することは」の場合には (that) S + V が to do (不定詞)に変わる.

1【気の毒だと思う】**be sorry**《to do, for》

▶**残念ですが**お手伝いすることはできません *I'm sorry*, but I can't help you. / *Unfortunately*, I am unable to help you. (➤ unfortunately は「あいにく」) ‖ **残念ながら**きみは不合格だね *I'm sorry to* (*have to*) *tell you this*, but you didn't pass the exam. ‖ **残念!** 外れくじでした *Too bad !* You've drawn a blank. / You have *unfortunately* drawn a blank. (➤ 後者のほうがフォーマルな言い方) ‖ 対話「入試だめだったよ」「それは**残念だったね**」"I failed the entrance exam." "*I'm sorry to hear that*. / *That's too bad*. / *What a shame !*" (➤ a shame は「恥」ではなく「残念なこと」の意).

✉ **あなたのチームが優勝を逃したのは残念でしたね** *I'm sorry* [*It's regrettable*] *that* your team lost the championship. ➤ It's a pity that ... ともいうが,《米》では古風.

2【心残りがする】**一形 残念な regrettable**

▶両親はあなたと英語でお話しできないのを**残念がっています** My parents *are sorry that* they can't [My parents *regret* not being able to] talk to you in English. (➤ 後者はやや堅い言い方) ‖ 我々の間に誤解があるのは**残念だ** *It is a shame* there is [there has been] a misunderstanding between us. ‖ 力を出し切れなかった生徒がいたことを**残念に思います** *It is a shame* [*It is too bad* / *It is a pity*] *that* some of the students couldn't demonstrate their true potential.

▶**残念なことに**ドラゴンズはことしも優勝を逃した *Unfortunately*, [*Regrettably*, / *To my disappointment*, / *It's too bad that*] the Dragons failed to win the pennant this year too. ‖ 彼女, きみに会えなくて**残念がってた**よ She *is sad* she couldn't see you.

‖**残念賞** a consolation prize.

3【けしからんと思う】▶《校長の訓話》本日, 校内でとても**残念な事件**がありました I'm sorry to tell you that a very *regrettable* [*unfortunate*] incident occurred on campus today. ‖ 警察官がこのような事件を起こして誠に**残念に思います** *It's* really *regrettable that* a police officer caused an incident like this.

さんねんせい 三年生 a **third-year student** (中・高・大の) ; 《米》 a **third-grade student, a third grader** (小学校の) ; a **junior** (アメリカなどの 4 年制の大学・高校の) →学年 ▶息子は岡山高校 **3 年生**です My son is *a third-year student* [is *in his third year*] in Okayama Senior High School. ‖ 彼女は B 大学の **3 年生**です She is *a junior* at B University.

✉ **来年は 3 年生！高校の受験勉強をしなくてはなりません** I'll be *in* (*the*) *ninth grade* next year! I have to prepare for high school entrance exams. ➤ 英語圏の人と文通するときは「中学 3 年」は (the) ninth grade, 「高校 3 年」は (the) twelfth grade とするほうが理解されやすい.

サンバ a **samba** ▶**サンバ**を踊る dance the samba.

さんばい 三倍 **three times** ; **triple** (数量) ▶ 2 の **3 倍**は 6 Two times three is [equals] six. ‖ 私のもうけ [借金] が **3 倍**になった My profits [debts] *have tripled*.

さんぱい 参拝 ▶元日はいつもその神社は**参拝客**でにぎわう The shrine is always crowded with *worshipers* on New Year's Day. (→参詣).

ざんぱい 惨敗 ▶マラソンで優勝候補が**惨敗**を喫した The favorite for the marathon *was soundly beaten*.

サンバイザー a **sun visor**.

サンパウロ **São Paulo** /saʊm páʊloʊ/ (ブラジルの都市).

さんばがらす 三羽烏 ▶彼らは相撲界の**三羽がらす**と言われる They are referred to as *the three pillars* of the sumo world. (➤ pillar は文字どおりには「柱」).

さんばし 桟橋 a **pier** /pɪəʳ/ ; a **landing stage** (浮き桟橋) ▶大型汽船が竹芝**桟橋**に横付けになった A large passenger steamer came alongside the Takeshiba *Pier*.

さんぱつ 散髪 a **haircut** ▶私は 3 日前に**散髪した** I *had* [*got*] *a haircut* three days ago. ／I *had my hair cut* three days ago. (➤ 前者のほうが多用される) ‖ 私の弟は**散髪嫌い**だ My (younger) brother *does not like to go to the barbershop* [《英》 *barber's*].

ざんぱん 残飯 **food scraps, scraps of food** ▶動物たちにやる**残飯** *the scraps of food* [*the leftovers* ／ *the leavings*] for animals.

さんび 賛美 **praise** ; (an) **admiration** 一動 **賛美する praise** +目 ▶神を**賛美する** *praise* God ‖ 詩人たちは恋人を**賛美する**たくさんの詩を作ってきた Poets have composed numerous poems *in praise of* their beloveds.

さんぴ 賛否 ▶議長はこの件に対する**賛否**を問うた The chairperson *put* the matter *to the vote* [*took a vote* on the matter]. (➤「票決に付した」の意) ‖ 男女産み分けには**賛否両論**がある There are *arguments* (*both*) *for and against* [*the pros and cons* in] *choosing* the sex one's children will be.

さんびか 賛美歌 a **hymn** /hɪm/ ▶礼拝堂で**賛美歌**を合唱する sing *hymns* in chorus at a chapel.

‖ **賛美歌集** a hymnal, a hymnbook.

さんびょうし 三拍子 **triple time** [**meter**] ▶ワルツは**三拍子**だ Waltzes are in *triple time* [*meter*].

▶《慣用表現》巨人の元三塁手の長嶋は走・攻・守の**三拍子そろった**名選手だった The former Giants third baseman Nagashima was a great all-round player with perfect fielding, batting, and (base) running.

さんぶ 三部 **three parts** ‖ **三部合唱** a chorus in three parts ‖ **三部作** a trilogy.

さんぷ 散布する **scatter** +目 (まき散らす) ; **sprinkle** +目 (振りかける) ; **spray** +目 (吹きかける) ; **crop-dust** +目 (飛行機などで農薬を) ▶ナスに殺虫剤を**散布する** *spray* the eggplants with insecticide.

さんぷく 山腹 a **mountainside**, a **hillside** ▶彼の別荘は六甲山の**山腹にある** His cottage *stands halfway up* (the) Rokko Hill.

さんふじんか 産婦人科 **obstetrics and gynecology** /gàɪnəkɑ́:lədʒi/

‖ **産婦人科医** an obstetrician-gynecologist, 《インフォーマル》 an ob-gyn /òʊbigám/.

さんぶつ 産物 a **product** ▶落花生と米がこの地方の**主要産物**だ Peanuts and rice are *the main products* [*produce*] of this district. (➤ produce /próʊdjuːs/ は集合名詞で「農産物」を指す).

サンフランシスコ **San Francisco** /sæn frənsískoʊ/ (アメリカ, カリフォルニア州の都市).

サンプル a **sample** ; a **giveaway** (無料サンプル) ▶**サンプル**を見せてください Could you show me *a sample*, please? ‖ **サンプル**無料提供 Free *samples* (available).

‖ (レストランの店頭などの) **食品サンプル** a food replica (➤ 日本独自のもの).

さんぶん 散文 **prose**

‖ **散文作家** a prose writer ‖ **散文詩** a prose poem.

さんぽ 散歩 a **walk** ; a **stroll** (ぶらぶら歩き) 一動 **散歩する take a walk** ▶早朝の**散歩**は健康によい It is good for the health to *take a walk* early in the morning. ‖ **散歩に出かけよう**よ Let's *go* (*out*) *for a walk*. ／Let's *have* [*take*] *a walk*. ‖ 父は今**散歩** [**日課の散歩**] に出ております My father *has gone out for a walk* [*for his daily walk*]. ‖ 私は**散歩がてら**本屋に立ち寄った *While taking a walk*, I dropped in at a bookstore. ‖ 私は毎朝犬を**散歩させます** Every morning I *take* my dog *out for a walk* [*walk* my dog].

‖ **散歩道** a walk ; a promenade.

さんぼう 参謀 **1【軍の】** a **staff officer** ; **the staff** (➤ 総称) ‖ **参謀本部** the staff headquarters (➤ headquarters だけだと「司令部」の意になる) ‖ **参謀会議** a staff officers' meeting.

2【相談役, 助言者】 a **counselor**, an **adviser** ; a **strategist** /strǽtədʒɪst/ (軍師).

さんぽう 三方 ▶私の生まれた町は**三方**を小高い山に囲まれていた The town I was born in was surrounded by hills *on three sides*.

さんぼんじめ 三本締め ***sanbonjime***

日本紹介 ✉ **三本締めは, 会合や取引, その他のイベントの締めくくりとして, またはその会などが成功裡に終わったことを祝すために行われる慣習です. 幹事の合図で参加者全員がそろって「だだだ, だだだ, だだだ, だ」のリズムで手を叩きます. そしてこれをさらに 2 回繰り返します** *Sanbonjime* is a custom to conclude or celebrate a successful meeting or deal, or other event. It involves clapping hands in unison at the cue of the person in charge by all present with a beat of da-da-da, da-da-da, da-da-da, and ending with one da, then repeating the same process two more times.

さんま 秋刀魚《魚》a **Pacific saury** ▶サンマを塩焼きにする broil [《英》grill] *a saury* (*pike*) with salt.

-ざんまい -三昧 ▶おばあちゃんは近頃カラオケ三昧だ Grandma'*s completely wrapped up in karaoke* these days. ‖ 彼女はぜいたく三昧に育てられた She *was raised to think it natural to be surrounded by every luxury*.

さんまいめ 三枚目 a **comedian**(「喜劇役者［俳優］」の意ではあとの2語と同義); a **comic (actor [actress])** (喜劇俳優) ▶私はそこではとんだ三枚目(=ピエロ)を演じてしまった I was *a* real *clown* there.

さんまん 散漫 ▶あの男は注意力が散漫なのでしょっちゅうミスを犯す He often makes mistakes because he is *not careful enough*.

さんみ 酸味 **acidity; sourness** /sáʊəʳnɪs/ (酸っぱさ) ▶このリンゴは酸味が強すぎる These apples are too *sour* [*tart*]. (➤ tart はぴりっとするような鋭い酸っぱさをいう).

さんみいったい 三位一体《宗教》**Trinity**.

さんみゃく 山脈 a **mountain chain [range]** ▶我々は日高山脈の上空を飛んだ We flew over *the* Hidaka *Mountains*. (➤ the ... Mountains で「…山脈」を表す).

ざんむ 残務 **remaining business** ▶週末までに残務整理をしなくてはならない I have lots of *remaining business* [have *a backlog of work*] *to clear up* by the weekend. (➤ backlog は「(仕事の)滞り」).

さんめんきじ 三面記事 **general [local] news**, 《米また》**city news**.

さんめんきょう 三面鏡 a **three-sided mirror**.

さんもん 三文 ▶この絵は三文の値打ちもない This painting is *not worth a cent* [《英》*a straw*]. ‖ 三文判で結構です *A ready-made hanko* will do. (→判).

‖三文小説 a dime [cheap / pulp] novel.

さんや 山野 **mountains and fields**.

さんやく 三役 ▶党三役 *the three top officers* [*posts*] in a party.

さんゆこく 産油国 an **oil-producing country**, a **petroleum-producing country**.

さんよ 参与 a **counselor** ‖副参与 a deputy counselor ‖ 内閣官房参与 a special advisor to the Cabinet.

さんようすうじ 算用数字 **Arabic numerals**.

[1]さんらん 産卵する **lay eggs** (鳥などが); **spawn** (+自) (魚・カエルなどが) ▶サケは産卵のためにこの川を遡っていく Salmon go up this river to *spawn*.

‖産卵期 the egg-laying season, the spawning season.

[2]さんらん 散乱する **be scattered** ▶爆発現場はガラスの破片や壊れた家具などが散乱していた The scene of the explosion *was littered with* fragments of glass, broken furniture and the like. ‖ おもちゃが部屋中に散乱している Toys *are scattered* all over the room.

さんりゅう 三流の **third-class [-rate]** ▶三流の会社 a *third-rate* company / a company *of the third rank*.

▶彼女はティーンエージャーに人気があるが, 歌手としては三流だ She's popular with teenagers, but as a singer she's *third rate*.

ざんりゅう 残留 ▶残留農薬 *residual* agricultural chemicals (➤ residual /rɪzídʒuəl/ は「残余の」の意の堅い語) ‖ 中国残留日本人孤児 Japanese war orphans *left* in China ‖ 中国残留婦人 Japanese wives *left* in China (due to WW II) ‖ 瓶の底には残留物があった There was (*a*) *residue* on the bottom of the bottle. (➤ residue /rézɪdju:/ は主に化学用語).

さんりん 山林 a **(mountain) forest** ▶山林を切り開いて畑にする clear *a mountain forest* for planting.

さんりんしゃ 三輪車 a **tricycle**, 《インフォーマル》a **trike** ▶三輪車に乗る get on *a tricycle*.

さんるい 三塁 **third (base)** ▶三塁を守る play *third base* ‖ 彼は三塁線ぎりぎりのヒットを放った He singled down *the left foul line*.

‖三塁手 a third baseman ‖ 三塁打 a three base hit, a triple.

ざんるい 残塁 ▶4回の阪神の攻撃は3者残塁に終わった Three Tigers *were left* [*were stranded*] *on base*(*s*) in the fourth inning.

サンルーフ a **sunroof**.

サンルーム a **sunroom**.

さんれつ 参列する **attend** +自 (出席する) ▶卒業式に参列する *attend* the graduation ceremony [《米》the commencement] ‖ 川田氏の葬儀には多数の参列者があった There was a large *attendance* at the funeral for Mr. Kawada. / Many people *attended* Mr. Kawada's funeral. (➤ 後者のように表現するのがふつう).

さんろく 山麓 ▶八ヶ岳の山麓にはペンションがたくさんある There are many lodges at *the foot* of Mt. Yatsugatake.

し・シ

[1]**し 市** a **city** ―形 **市の city, municipal** /mjunísɪpəl/

> **《解説》**(1)英語では市名が New York City のように州名などと同じであるか，Salt Lake City のように City が市名の一部である場合以外は … City とはしない.
> (2)手紙の宛名では -shi でよい. ただし，横浜市や名古屋市など大きな市は単に Yokohama, Nagoya などとするだけでよい.

▶**市の条例** a *city* ordinance ‖ **市の職員** a *city* worker [employee] ‖ 私は**武蔵野市**に住んでいます I live in *Musashino* (*City*) [*the City of Musashino*].
‖**市当局** the city authorities. →**市議会**.

[2]**し 死 1【死亡】**(a) **death** ▶**死**は避けがたい *Death* is inevitable. ‖ そのとき彼は**死**を覚悟していたに違いない He must have been prepared for *death* [must have been ready to *die*] at that time. ‖ 彼女は1つあとの飛行機に乗ったので危うく**死を免れた** She narrowly *escaped death* by taking the next plane. ‖ 一瞬の不注意が彼らの**死**を招いた A moment's carelessness caused their *death*(*s*). (➤複数形は「死亡の事例」に注目した場合) ‖ 遭難者たちは山中で**死に直面していた** In the mountains, the victims *were staring death in the face*.
‖**死の灰** radioactive fallout, atomic dust.
2【野球で】 an **out** ▶巨人は1**死**満塁のピンチに立った The Giants found themselves in a fix with one *out* and fully loaded bases.

[3]**し 詩 poetry**(➤集合的)；a **poem**（1編の）▶谷川俊太郎の**詩** the *poetry* of Tanikawa Shuntaro ‖ **詩的な表現** *poetic* phrasing ‖ 彼は若い頃は**詩**を書いていた He wrote *poems* in his youth. ‖ この小曲はさながら一編の**詩**だ This piece of music is just like *a poem*. ‖**散文詩** a prose poem ‖ **叙事詩** an epic ‖ **叙情詩** a lyric.

[4]**し 師** one's **teacher**(先生)；one's **mentor**(良き指導者)；a **guru**(教祖)；a **leader**(指導者) ▶私は小田先生を**師**と仰いでいます I look up to Mr. Oda as my *mentor*.

[5]**し 四 four** ▶《九九で》2，2んが**4** Two times two equals *four*. ‖ **四の五の言わずに**言われたとおりにやれ Do as I tell you (to do) *without complaining*. →よん.

[6]**し 氏 Mr.**(男性)；**Mrs.**(既婚女性)；**Miss**(未婚女性)；**Ms.**(既婚・未婚を問わず女性)(➤《英》ではピリオドを省くことが多い) ▶野田**氏** *Mr.* Noda ‖ 野田・小野両**氏** *Mr.* Noda and *Mr.* Ono.

[1]**-し** ▶彼はハンサムだ**し**，頭もいい He is handsome *and* bright, too. ／He is bright *as well as* handsome. ‖ 雨はやまない**し**パンクはする**し**，さんざんなドライブだった *What with* continuous rain *and* (*what with*) having a flat, we didn't enjoy our drive at all. (➤ what with A and (what with) B はよくないことの理由を列挙するときの言い方) ‖ 子供じゃあるまい**し**，自分のことは自分でしなさい Look after yourself. You're not a child anymore. ‖ **対話**「きのうのドライブ楽しかったわ」「道もすいてた**し**ね」"Yesterday's drive was really enjoyable." "*And* the roads weren't crowded."

[2]**-し -視** ▶異端**視**する *treat* … as a heretic [heretical] ‖ 過大**視**する exaggerate ‖ 疑問**視**する *view* … with suspicion ‖ 重要**視**する emphasize；*regard* … as important ‖ 敵対**視**する *regard* … as an enemy.

[1]**じ 字 1【文字】** a **character**(表意文字；漢字など)；a **letter**（表音文字；かななど）▶お母さん，この**字**(＝漢字)どう読むの？ How do you read this *character* [*kanji*], Mom？ ‖ この本は老人用に大きな**字**(＝活字)で印刷されている This book is printed in large *type* for elderly people. ‖ **字の読み書きができない人** a person who *is unable to read and write* ／an *illiterate* person (→**識字**).
2【筆跡】 **handwriting**；a **hand**（書体）▶部長の**字**は読みにくい Our boss's *handwriting* is hard to read. ‖ きみは**字がうまい**［**下手だ**］ね You *have good* [*poor*] *handwriting*. ／ Your handwriting is good [poor]. ‖ もっと**字をきれいに書きなさい** *Write* more *neatly*.
3【慣用表現】▶彼は芸術の**ゲの字**もわからない He doesn't know *the first thing about art*.

[2]**じ 地 1【地面】**(the) **ground**.
2【下地，地肌】 a **ground** ▶ブルーの**地**に真紅のバラをデザインする design a crimson rose on a blue *background* ‖ 小池さんは**地が黒い**ので，日焼けしても目立たない Mr. Koike *has a dark complexion* [*is dark-skinned*], so it's hard to tell when he has a tan.
3【本性】 one's **true self** ▶彼女は思わず**地が出て**しまった Her *true self came out* (despite her efforts to conceal it). ‖ フーテン役なら彼は**地で行けば**よい To act the role of a vagabond he just has to *be himself*.
4【実地】▶彼の生涯はロビンソン・クルーソーを**地で行った**ようなものだった His life was *just like* Robinson Crusoe's.
5【その土地】▶**地の農産物** *local* produce ‖ **地もの**の野菜 a *local* vegetable.

[3]**じ 痔 piles, hemorrhoids** /hémərɔɪdz/ (➤後者は医学用語だが，日常的にはこちらを用いる) ▶**痔を患う** suffer from *hemorrhoids*.

[4]**じ 辞** a **speech** ▶開会［閉会］の**辞**を述べる make *an opening* [*a closing*] *speech*.

-じ -時 ～ **o'clock** ▶ **対話**「今，何**時**ですか」「私の時計では10**時**です」"*What time* is it (now)?" "It is *ten o'clock* by my watch." (➤「何時ですか」は What is the time？ あるいは Do you have the time？と言ってもよい).
▶母は午前9**時**発の『のぞみ』号で博多に向かった My mother left for Hakata on *the nine a.m. Nozomi*.
▶(この薬は)空腹**時**に服用のこと Be sure to take this medicine *on an empty stomach*.

しあい 試合 a **game**(球技の)；a **match**（通例2人または2組で行う)；a **fight**（ボクシングなどの)；a **tournament** /tóərnəmənt / (勝ち抜き戦) ▶**試合**に勝つ［負ける］

win [lose] *a game* ‖ 巨人対阪神の**試合が始まった** *The game* between the Giants and the Tigers *started* [*began*]. ／ The Giants and the Tigers *took the field*. (➤ take the field は「競技を開始する」) ‖ 兄はテニスの**試合**で勝った [負けた] My brother won [lost] the *tennis match*. ‖ 私たちは千代田高校チームと**バスケットの試合**をする We are going to play *a basketball game* with the Chiyoda High School team.

逆引き熟語 ○○試合
開幕試合 the opening game, the opener ／ (野球の) **完全試合** a perfect game ／ **国際試合** an international game [match] ／ **再試合** a rematch ／ **親善試合** a friendly game [match] ／ **放棄試合** a forfeited game ／ **無効試合** no game ／ **練習試合** a practice game [match]

1**じあい 慈愛** **affection**; **benevolence** (慈悲心) ▶菩薩(ぼさつ)像のまなざしは**慈愛に満ちている**ように感じられた It seemed to me that the image of the Bodhisattva had a *benevolent* look on her face.

2**じあい 自愛**
✉ **猛暑の折からどうぞご自愛くださいませ** Please *take care of your health*, especially in this sweltering [terrible ／ scorching] heat.

3**じあい 時合** 《釣り》 the time frame when the fish are biting well (➤ 説明的な訳).

しあがり 仕上がり ▶ドラゴンズの投手陣の**仕上がり**は**上々だ** The pitching staff of the Dragons *is* [*are*] *in superb form*.

しあがる 仕上がる ▶仕事はどうにかこうにか**仕上がった** The work *got* [*was*] *finished* somehow.

しあげ 仕上げ **finishing** (仕上げること); (a) **finish** (仕上がり具合); **the finishing touches** (仕上げの加筆) ▶彼は絵に最後の**仕上げ**を施している He is putting *the finishing touches* on [to] the painting. ‖ どんな仕事も**仕上げ**が肝心だ For any task, *the finishing touches* are important. ‖ 彼女の仕事はいつも**仕上げ**が丁寧だ Her work is always nicely *finished*.

じあげや 地上げ屋 a **land shark**, a (**land**) **flipper**.

しあげる 仕上げる **finish**, **get ... done** (➤ 後者はインフォーマル); **complete** (完成する) ▶この仕事を**仕上げる**のにあと10日かかる It will take ten more days to *finish* [*complete*] this work. ‖ スーツは今週末までに**仕上げて**いただきたい I'd like to *have* my suit *finished* by the end of this week.

しあさって 明明後日 **three days from now** (3日後) ▶しあさってバンコクへたちます I'm leaving for Bangkok *three days from now*. (● three days from now を three days later とすると, 現在が起点ではなく「その3日後」の意味になる).

しあつ 指圧 **shiatsu** /ʃiáːtsuː/ (➤ 英語化している); **acupressure** [**finger-pressure**] **therapy**
‖**指圧師** a shiatsu therapist, an acupressure therapist.

シアトル **Seattle** (アメリカ, ワシントン州の都市).

しあわせ 幸せ **1【幸福】** **happiness** 一形 **幸せな** **happy** ▶人々は神社や寺で健康と**幸せ**を願って祈る People pray at shrines and temples for health and *happiness*. ‖ 人間何が**幸せ**かわからない People don't know what will make them *happy* [bring them *happiness*]. ‖ 私, きょうはとっても**幸せな**気分なの I feel so *happy* today. ‖ 《反語的》何も知らないとは**幸せな**やつだ In his case, ignorance is *bliss*. (➤ Ignorance is bliss. は「知らないのが無上の幸せ; 知らぬが仏」の意の英語のことわざ).
✉ **お2人のお幸せとご繁栄を祈ります** I wish both of you *happiness* and prosperity.
✉ **いつまでもお幸せに**! I wish you a long and *happy* married life. ／ I wish you everlasting *happiness*! ➤ 結婚した人への祝辞.

2【幸運】 **good fortune**, **good luck** (➤ 前者はやや堅い言い方) ▶よい家族に恵まれて**幸せだ** I'*m lucky* to have a good family.

1**しあん 私案** one's **plan** ▶**私案**ですが検討してみていただけませんか Won't you please consider this *plan of mine*?

2**しあん 試案** a **tentative plan**.

3**しあん 思案** **thought** (考え); **consideration** (熟考) ▶**思案に暮れる** *be lost in thought* ‖ ここが**思案のしどころ**だ This is *the point we must think over carefully*.

じあん 事案 a **case** (事例); an **issue** (議論すべき問題) ▶いじめと思われる**事案** a *case* presumed to be bullying ／ a *case* of presumed bullying.

しい 椎 《植》 a **Japanese chinquapin** /tʃíŋkəpɪn/.

1**じい 辞意** one's **intention to resign** ▶**辞意を撤回する** withdraw [retreat] *one's resignation* ‖ 首相は**辞意を表明した** The Prime Minister expressed *his intention to resign*.

2**じい 自慰** →オナニー.

ジーエヌピー **GNP**, **G.N.P.** (➤ gross national product (国民総生産)の略).

シーエム (CM) a **commercial** (**message**) (➤ CM は和製語) ▶**CMを流す** put on [show ／ run] *a commercial*.

しいか 詩歌 →詩.

しいく 飼育 **breeding** 一動 **飼育する** **breed** +目; 《米または》 **raise** +目 ▶岩手県では馬の**飼育**が盛んである In Iwate Prefecture *horse-breeding* is a flourishing industry. ‖ 彼はライオンの**飼育係**だ He is a lion *keeper*.

じいさん an **old man**; one's **grandfather** (祖父) ▶変なじいさん a strange *old man* ／ an *old coot* (➤ 後者は主に《米・インフォーマル》).

シージー **CG** (➤ computer graphics の略).

じーじー ▶セミが朝から**ジージー鳴いている** The cicadas have been *singing shrilly* since morning.

じいしき 自意識 **self-consciousness** ▶女の子がみんな自分の方を見ていると思うなんて, きみは**自意識過剰**だ Thinking every girl is looking at you shows your *excessive self-consciousness*.

シーズン a **season** ▶行楽**シーズン** the tourist *season* ‖ 野球の**シーズン**になった *The baseball season* is here [has come]. ‖ イチゴは今が**シーズン**だ Strawberries *are in season* now. ‖ ホテルの料金は**シーズンオフ**は割安だ Hotel rates in the *off-season* are lower. (➤ season-off とはしない).

シーソー a **seesaw** ▶**シーソーで遊ぶ** play on *a seesaw* ▶巨人は**シーソーゲーム**の末8対5で阪神を下した The Giants downed the Tigers in an 8-5 *seesaw game*.

しいたけ 椎茸 a **shiitake** (**mushroom**) (➤ 英語化している) ▶**シイタケを栽培する** grow [raise] *shiitake*.

しいたげる 虐げる **oppress** +目, **treat cruelly** ▶彼らは**虐げられた**人々を守るために立ち上がった They rose in revolt to protect the *oppressed* people.

シーチキン **canned** [《英》 **tinned**] **tuna** (缶詰のマグロ; 「シーチキン」は商標名).

シーツ a **sheet** ▶ベッドの**シーツ**を取り替える change the

sheets ／change a bed ‖ ホテルのメイドはベッドに清潔なシーツを敷いてくれた The (hotel) housekeeper put clean *sheets* on my bed.

しーっ **Hush !** /hʌʃ/, **Shh !** /ʃ/ (➤いずれも人を静かにさせるとき) ▶私は弟に「しーっ, 音を立てないで」と言った I said to my brother, "*Hush* [*Shh* ／*Sh*] *!* Don't make any noise."

しいて 強いて ▶強いて言えばビールより日本酒のほうが好きです *If I must choose*, I'd say I prefer Japanese sake to beer. ‖ きみの作文はよく書けているけど, **強いて欠点を言えば**ちょっと漢字の間違いが多いね Your essay is well composed, but *if I were to mention any faults in it*, I would have to say it has a few too many wrong kanji characters.

シーディー a **CD** (➤ compact disc の略) ▶ビートルズのＣＤをかける play *a CD* of The Beatles ‖ ＣＤをリッピングしてスマホに入れる rip *CDs* to a smartphone ‖ そのグループは来週ＣＤを出す予定だ The group is scheduled to release a *CD* next week.
‖**ＣＤプレーヤー** a CD player ‖ **ＣＤ－ＲＯＭ** a CD-ROM (➤ ROM は read-only memory の略).

しいてき 恣意的な **arbitrary** /ɑ́ːʳbətreri/ ▶工場主の恣意的な決定に従業員たちは腹を立てた The *arbitrary* decisions of the factory owner caused anger among the workers.

1**シート** 《四角い紙, 覆い》 a **sheet** /ʃiːt/ ▶切手のシート１枚 *a sheet* of stamps ‖ 彼は積み荷に(防水)シートを掛けた He put *a waterproof canvas* [*a tarpaulin* ／*a trap*] on the load.

2**シート** 《座席》 a **seat** /siːt/ ▶シートを倒す recline one's *seat*.

シード a **seed** 一動 **シードする** **seed** +目 ▶第１シードの選手 a *top-seeded* player ／a No. 1 seed (➤後者の seed は「シードされた選手」) ‖ 昨年わがチームは第２シードだった Our team was *seeded No. 2* last year. ‖**シード校** a seeded team, a seeded school (➤英語では順位もあわせて言うのがふつう).

シートノック ▶選手にシートノックをする give a player *fielding practice*.

シートベルト a **seat belt** ▶シートベルトを着用する wear [use] *a seat belt* ‖ シートベルトをするのを忘れないで Don't forget to *buckle up*. (➤《米》に多い言い方) ‖ まもなく離陸いたします. シートベルトをお締めください We'll be taking off shortly. Please make sure that *your seat belts are fastened*.

ジーパン (a **pair of**) **jeans** ▶彼はたいがいジーパンだ He usually wears *jeans*.

ジーピーエス **GPS** (➤ the global positioning system (全地球測位システム)の略).

ジープ a **jeep** (➤ 商標名で Jeep ともつづる).

シーフード (a) **seafood**
‖**シーフードレストラン** a seafood restaurant.

シーベルト 《物理学》 a **sievert** (人体への放射線被ばく線量の単位) ▶４シーベルトの放射線 4 *sieverts* of radiation.

ジーメン **G-men** (➤Government men の略で, ＦＢＩの捜査官を指す) 《参考》日本では単数・複数に関係なく「ジーメン」というが, 英語では単数は G-man (女性は G-woman), 複数は G-men (女性は G-women だが G-men で代表させることもある) ▶麻薬ジーメン a narcotics *investigator* [*detective*].

シーラカンス a **coelacanth** /síːləkænθ/.

シーリング a **ceiling** (天井；上限) (➤ 日本語の「概算要求基準」の意味で使われる「シーリング」は guideline for budget requests).

しいる 強いる **force** +目 ; **press** +目 (押しつける) ▶彼らは労働者に過酷な労働を強いた They *forced* hard labor on the workers. ／They *forced* the workers into hard labor. ‖ 人に酒を**強いる**のはよくない It is not good to *force* a person to drink [to *press* a drink on a person].

シール a **seal**, a **sticker** ▶かばんにシールを貼る stick *a seal* on one's bag.

しいれ 仕入れ **purchase** /pə́ːʳtʃəs/, **buying-in**
‖**仕入れ係** a buyer, a purchase clerk ‖ **仕入れ原価** purchase [buying] cost ‖ **仕入れ先** a supplier ‖ **仕入れ値** a purchase [buying] price.

しいれる 仕入れる **stock** +目 (在庫として持つ) ; **lay in** (買い込む) ; **buy** +目 , **purchase** /pə́ːʳtʃəs/ +目 (➤後者は「購入する」に相当する堅い語) ▶店に夏物を仕入れる *stock* a store with summer wear ‖ スマートフォンを大量に**仕入れる** *stock* a large number of smartphones ／ *purchase* a large stock of smartphones ‖ クリスマス用品を大量に**仕入れた** We've *stocked* a large amount of Christmas items. ‖ 卸売業者は製造元から商品を**仕入れ**, 小売業者に売る Wholesalers *buy* [*get*] merchandise from manufacturers and sell it to retailers.
▶どこでその最新情報を**仕入れた**の？ Where did you *get* that latest information ?

じいろ 地色 a **ground color**.

1**しいん 死因** **the cause of death** ▶祖父の死因は脳卒中だった A stroke was *the cause of* my grandfather's *death*. ／ My grandfather *died of* a stroke.

2**しいん 子音** a **consonant** /kɑ́ːnsənənt/.

3**しいん 試飲** **sampling, tasting** 一動 **試飲する** **sample** +目 , **taste** +目 ▶**試飲室**で数種のワインを無料で**試飲**できます You can *sample* several wines for free in *the tasting room*.

しーん ▶その家の中はしーんと静まり返っていた The house was *completely* [*utterly*] *silent*.

シーン a **scene** ▶感動的なシーン a touching *scene* ‖ 『タイタニック』のラブシーンは今もまぶたに焼きついている The *love scene* in "Titanic" is still vivid in my memory.

じいん 寺院 a **temple** (仏教・ヒンズー教など, キリスト教以外の) ; a **mosque** (イスラム教の).

じーん ▶きのう先生は胸にじーんとくる話をしてくれた Our teacher told us a *touching* story yesterday. (➤ touching は「感動的な」).

ジーンズ (a **pair of**) **jeans** ▶ブランドもののジーンズ designer *jeans* ‖ ぴちぴちのジーンズをはいた若者 a young man in skinny *jeans* ‖ ジーンズを２本買う buy two pairs of *jeans* (➤ふつう(×)two jeans とはしない) ‖ ぼくは一年中ジーンズで通す I wear *jeans* year around. ／I spend all my time in *jeans*.
‖**スキニージーンズ** (a pair of) skinny jeans ‖ **ストレートジーンズ** (a pair of) straight jeans ‖ **スリムジーンズ** (a pair of) slim jeans ‖ **ブーツカットジーンズ** (a pair of) boot-cut jeans ‖ **ベルボトムジーンズ** (a pair of) bell-bottom jeans ‖ **ルーズ(フィット)ジーンズ** (a pair of) loose-fit jeans.

じう 慈雨 a **welcome rain** [**shower**].

しうち 仕打ち **treatment** ▶おじからひどい仕打ちを受けた I received *harsh treatment* from my uncle. ／I was *treated harshly* by my uncle.

しうんてん 試運転 a **trial run** (➤ a test-drive は買う前の「試乗」) ▶新しい機械 [車] の**試運転をする** *give* a new machine [car] *a trial* (*run*).

シェア a **share**(占有率) ▶わが社は日本のデジタルカメラ市場で20パーセントのシェアを占めている Our company has *a* 20 percent *share* of the digital camera market in Japan.

しえい 市営の **city**; **municipal** /mjunísɪpəl/ (自治体の) ▶市営バス a *city* bus ‖ 市営プール a *municipal* [*city*] pool.

じえい 自衛 **self-defense** ▶その警官は自衛上やむをえず犯人に発砲した The police officer had no choice but to shoot at the criminal *in self-defense*. ‖ 彼は暴走族の少年２人に襲われたとき傘で自衛した When attacked by the two hot-rodders, he *defended himself* with an umbrella.
‖自衛官 a uniformed Self-Defense Force member, a Self-Defense Force personnel ‖ 自衛権 the right of [to] self-defense ‖ 自衛隊(→見出語) ‖ 自衛本能 the instinct of self-preservation.

じえいぎょう 自営業 ▶父は自営業です My father *is self-employed.* ／My father *has his own business.*

じえいたい 自衛隊 **the Self-Defense Forces**
‖自衛隊員 a Self-Defense Force member ‖ 陸上[海上／航空]自衛隊 the Ground [Maritime／Air] Self-Defense Force.

シェイプアップ ▶シェイプアップする *get in shape* (英語の shape up はインフォーマルで「はっきりした形をとる, 好都合に進展する」,「やる気を出す, しっかりやる」の意. 日本語と同じ意味はない).

シェーバー a **shaver**.

シェービングクリーム **shaving cream** [**foam**].

しえきどうし 使役動詞 《文法》 a **causative verb**.

ジェスチャー a **gesture** ▶V サインはよく知られたジェスチャーだ The V sign is a well-known *gesture*. ‖ 彼はジェスチャーでぼくに逃げろと合図した He *motioned* [*signaled*] me to run away.
▶彼の親切はジェスチャー(＝見せかけ)にすぎない His kindness is nothing but *a show* [*an act*].
‖ジェスチャーゲーム (a game of) charades.

ジェット ‖ジェットエンジン a jet engine ‖ ジェット機 a jet (plane) ‖ ジェット気流 the jet stream.

ジェットコースター a **roller coaster**, 《英また》 a **switchback**, a **big dipper** (➤ (×)jet coaster とはしない) ▶ジェットコースターに乗る ride *a roller coaster*.

ジェネリック a **generic** ▶ジェネリック医薬品 a *generic* drug.

シェパード a **German shepherd** /ʃépəʳd/ (**dog**), 《英》 an **Alsatian** /ælséɪʃən/ (**wolfhound**).

> **危ないカタカナ語✹ シェパード**
> 単に shepherd というと「羊飼い」か, 犬ならば一般的な「牧羊犬」(sheep dog)を指す. 日本語でいう「シェパード」は, 《米》では German shepherd (dog) か German police dog, 《英》では Alsatian (wolfhound) といっている.

シェフ a **chef** [複 **chefs**] ▶レストランのオーナーシェフ the *chef-owner* of a restaurant.

ジェラシー **jealousy**.

シェリー **sherry**(酒).

シェルター a **shelter** ‖核シェルター a fallout shelter (➤ fallout は「放射性降下物」).

シェルパ a **Sherpa** /ʃəːʳpə/.

しえん 支援 **support** 一動 **支援する** **support** ＋目, **back up** (➤ 後者は日本語の「バックアップする」に相当するややインフォーマルな言い方) ▶ご支援を賜りありがとうございます Thank you very much for your *support*.
‖支援団体 [グループ] a support organization [group].

ジェンダー **gender**. →性.

[1]**しお 塩** **salt** /sɔːlt/ ▶トマトに塩をつけて食べる eat a tomato with *salt* ‖ 母はキュウリを塩で漬けた My mother pickled [preserved] some cucumbers with *salt*. ‖ 肉に軽く塩こしょうをします Sprinkle [Season] the meat lightly with *salt and pepper*. (➤ season は「(調味料などで)味をつける」) ‖ 私はスープの塩加減を見た I *tasted* the soup to see how it was seasoned. ‖ 対話《食卓で》「お塩を取ってください」「はい, どうぞ」 "Pass (me) the *salt*, please." "Sure. Here you are."

[2]**しお 潮** **the tide**; a **current**(潮流) ▶潮の流れに乗って泳ぐ swim with *the current* ‖ 今は潮が満ちている *The tide* is full. ‖ 潮が満ちて[引いて]きている *The tide* is coming in [going out]. ‖ 江の島に近づくと潮(＝海)の香りがした As I came near to Enoshima, I breathed in *the smell of the sea*.
▶テレビで鯨が潮を吹くのを見た On TV, I saw whales *spouting* [*blowing*].
‖潮風 a sea breeze.

しおから 塩辛 ***shiokara***; fish or squid innards preserved with salt and fermented (➤ 説明的な訳; fermented は「発酵させた」) ▶イカの塩辛 *soused* squid(➤ souse /saʊs/ は「塩漬けにする」).

しおからい 塩辛い **salty** /sɔ́ːlti/ ▶父は血圧が高いので塩辛いものは控えている My father doesn't eat too much *salty* food because he has high blood pressure.

しおくり 仕送り ▶私は親から月10万円仕送りしてもらって生活している I live on the 100,000 yen that *my parents send* (*me*) every month. ‖ 彼は給料の一部を田舎の両親に毎月仕送りしている Every month, he *sends* part of his salary to his parents back home.

しおけ 塩気 ▶このみそ汁, 塩気が足りないね This miso soup needs *a touch of salt*. (➤ a touch of は「少量の」の意) ‖ ビールには塩気のある食べ物がよく合う *Salty* food goes well with beer.

しおさい 潮騒 **the sound of the waves** [**surf**] (➤ surf は「寄せ打つ波」) ▶潮さいを聞く listen to *the sound of the waves*.

しおづけ 塩漬け ▶キュウリの塩漬け cucumbers *pickled* [*preserved*] *with salt*.

しおどき 潮時 ▶今が政界から身を引く潮時だ *It is high time* I retired from political life. (➤ high time に続く節中の動詞は通例過去形) ‖ 何事にも潮時というものがある There is *a time* for everything. (➤ 英語のことわざ).

しおひがり 潮干狩り **clam** [**shellfish**] **digging** ▶海岸に潮干狩りに行く *go clamming* on the beach ‖ 私たちは午前中潮干狩りをした We *dug for clams* [*hunted for shellfish*] in the morning.

しおみず 塩水 **salt water** ▶塩水でうがいする gargle with *salt water*.

しおやき 塩焼き **fish sprinkled with salt and broiled** [《英》**grilled**] ▶サンマを塩焼きにする *broil* a (Pacific) saury *with salt*.

しおらしい ▶生徒たちはしおらしい態度で先生の話を聞いていた The students were listening to their teacher *in an* unusually *quiet manner*.

ジオラマ a **diorama** /dàɪərǽmə/.

しおり 栞 a **bookmark** ▶本の間にしおりを挟む put *a bookmark* between the pages.

しおれる wilt；**fade**(色あせる)；**droop** (ぐったりする) ▶水をやっていなかったので庭の花がしおれてきた The flowers in the garden are *wilting* [*drooping*] because they haven't been watered.

1**しか 鹿** a **deer** [複 **deer**]；a **buck**, a **stag**(雄ジカ)；a **doe**(雌ジカ)；a **fawn**(子ジカ) ▶シカの角 *deer* antler(s) ‖ シカの肉 *venison* ‖ シカのふん *deer* droppings.

2**しか 歯科 dentistry**(歯学) 一形 **歯科の dental** ▶彼は**歯科大学**を卒業して**歯科医**になり, **歯科医院**に勤務している He graduated from *a dental college*, became *a dentist*, and is working at *a dental clinic*. (➤「歯科医」は dental surgeon あるいは, D.D.S. (=Doctor of Dental Surgery)と呼ぶこともある).

‖**歯科衛生士** a dental hygienist ‖ **歯科技工士** a dental technician.

3**しか 市価 the market price** ▶テレビを**市価**の半値で買う buy a TV set at half *the market price* ‖ あの店では何でも**市価**の1割引きだ They sell everything at a discount of ten percent off *the market price* at that store.

-しか only (➤ 修飾する語・句のすぐ前に置くのが一応の原則) ▶歌舞伎は一度しか見たことがない I've seen kabuki *only* once. ‖ 父は3000円しか小遣いをくれなかった My father gave me *only* 3,000 yen in spending money. ‖ 時間どおりに来たのはきみしかいない You are the *only* one that came on time. ‖ 彼は金もうけにしか興味がないようだ Money is the *only* thing he cares about. ／He seems to be *only* out for (the) money. (➤ be out for は「…を得ようとやっきになっている」の意) ‖ その種の魚は南洋にしかいない That kind of fish exists *only* in southern seas.

▶弟はサッカーにしか興味がない My (younger) brother is interested in *nothing but* soccer. (➤「…のほかはない」の意) ‖ 最終バスに乗り遅れたときはタクシーに乗るしかなかった When I missed the last bus, I had *no choice but* to take a taxi. (➤「タクシーに乗る以外の選択はなかった」の意).

▶コアラはユーカリの葉しか食べない Koalas feed *exclusively* on eucalyptus leaves. (➤ exclusively は「専ら」) ‖ ぼくにはこれしか言えない That's *all* I can say. ‖ 彼はしらばくれているとしか思えない He *must be* playing innocent [possum]. ‖ 西は大阪までしか行ったことがない Osaka is the farthest west I have ever been.

1**じか 時価 the current price** ▶**時価**2000万円の絵が盗まれた A picture worth 20 million yen *in today's money* was stolen. ‖ この古い陶器は**時価**500万円する This ancient piece of pottery is *currently* [*now*] worth 5 million yen.

2**じか 自家** ▶その温泉宿には**自家発電装置**がある That hot-spring hotel has *its own power generator*. ‖ 社長は**自家用ジェット機**でグアムへ飛んだ The president flew to Guam in *his private jet*.

‖**自家受精** self-fertilization ‖ **自家中毒** autointoxication, autotoxemia.

☛ **自家製** (⇀見出語)

3**じか 直** ⇀じかに.

じが 自我 the self, the ego (➤ 後者は主に専門用語) ▶自我に目覚める become conscious of *oneself* ‖ 自我を確立する establish *a sense of identity* ‖ 彼は**自我が強い** He *is egotistic*(*al*) [*egoistic* ／ *self-centered*]. ‖ 息子も**自我を主張する**年頃になった My son is old enough to *assert himself*.

1**しかい 司会する chair** +目, **preside** /prɪzáɪd/《at, over》(議長を務める；後者は堅い語)；**emcee** /èmsíː/ (+目) (ショー番組や祝宴の；emcee は master of ceremonies の頭文字を読みつづった語) ▶武井さんが会議の**司会をした** Mr. Takei *chaired* the meeting. ／ Mr. Takei *presided at* [*over*] the meeting. ／ Mr. Takei *acted as chairman* at the meeting. (➤ 女性の場合は chairwoman や chairperson と言う) ‖ 座談会は青木さんの**司会**で行われた The round-table talk was held *under the chairpersonship of* Ms. Aoki. (➤ 男性の場合は chairmanship とも言う) ‖《結婚披露宴などで》私が**司会を務め**させていただきます It is my pleasure to serve as your *master of ceremonies* [*M.C.*] today. (➤ 女性の場合は mistress of ceremonies と言う. M.C. は男性にも女性にも使える) ‖ 坂田氏はその人気番組の**司会**を5年間**やっている** Mr. Sakata *has hosted* [*has been the host* of] that popular show for five years. (➤ 女性の場合も, hosted と言う).

‖**司会者** a chairperson, a chairman, a chairwoman (会議の；最初の語は男性にも女性にも使える)；a master of ceremonies, an M.C. (公式のパーティーの)；a host(ショー番組の)；a quizmaster (クイズ番組などの)；a moderator(討論会の).

2**しかい 視界 (the field of) sight**；**view**(視野に入ってくる光景)；**visibility**(見通し) ▶まもなく大島が**視界に入って**きた Soon Oshima Island *came into sight* [*view*]. ‖ 振り返るとその自動車は**視界から消えていた** The car was *out of sight* when I looked back. (➤「視界から消える」は go out of sight) ‖ 濃霧で**視界**が悪く, 飛行機は(途中で)羽田へ引き返した *Visibility* was so poor because of the dense fog that the plane had to return to Haneda.

3**しかい 死海 the Dead Sea**(イスラエルとヨルダンの間の塩水湖).

1**しがい 市外 the outskirts of a city, the suburbs** ▶彼は浦和の**市外**に10年来住んでいる He has lived *in the suburbs* [*on the outskirts*] of Urawa for ten years. (➤ outskirts は「うらぶれた, まだ開発の進んでいない」という意味で使うことが多い；⇀**郊外**).

‖**市外局番**《米》an area code,《英》a dialling code ‖ **市外通話** a long-distance call,《米また》an out-of-town call.

2**しがい 市街 the streets**(街路)；a **city**, a **town** (町中) ▶ソウル**市街**は人や車で混雑していた The *streets* of Seoul were crowded with people and cars.

‖**市街戦** an urban battle ‖ **市街地** a city area ‖ **市街地図** a city map ‖ **市街電車**《米》a streetcar,《英》a tramcar.

3**しがい 死骸** a **corpse**, a **(dead) body**；a **carcass** /káːʳkəs/ (動物の) 《参考》動物の死骸を remains ということもある. ⇀**遺体**.

1**じかい 次回 next time** ▶**次回**の作品に期待しています I am looking forward to reading your *next* work. ‖ 落選して残念だったけど, **次回**は頑張ってね Sorry to hear that your work was not accepted for the exhibition. Better luck *next time*!

▶《テレビ番組などの最後に》**次回をお楽しみに** To be continued. (➤ 画面文字) ／ See you next week! (➤ 画面文字, または口頭) ‖ **次回完結** To be concluded.

2**じかい 自戒する admonish** oneself ▶**自戒**を込めて言うのだが, 常に腹八分目を心がけよ *As I also say to* *myself*, you should always try to eat moderately.

じがい 自害 ▶男が銃を乱射して７人を殺傷したあと自害した A man went on a shooting rampage and *killed himself* after killing or wounding seven people.

しがいせん 紫外線 **ultraviolet** [UV] **rays** /ʌ̀ltrəváɪələt reɪz/.

し

しかえし 仕返し **revenge** **一動** **仕返しする** **take revenge**《on》,《インフォーマル》**get even**《with》;《インフォーマル》**pay back** ▶義彦にはかなわないので代わりにあいつの弟に仕返しをした I was no match for Yoshihiko, so I *took revenge on* his younger brother. ‖一生かかったって, あいつには仕返ししてやるぞ I'll *get even with* [*get back at*] him (even) if it takes the rest of my life. ‖あいつ, ぼくのこと先生に言いつけやがって. 仕返しをしてやるからな！ I'll *pay* him *back* for telling on me to the teacher！

1**しかく 四角** a **square** (正方形); a **rectangle** /réktæŋgəl/ (長方形); a **quadrangle**, a **quadrilateral** (四辺形) ▶四角い建物 a *square* building ‖真四角な机 a *square* desk ‖渥美さんは四角い顔をしていた Mr. Atsumi had a *square* jaw.

▶四角張った挨拶はこのくらいにしましょう Let's dispense with *excessive formalities*. ‖そんなに四角張らないでください Please *make yourself at home*. (➤ make oneself at home は「気楽にやる」).

2**しかく 資格** **1【必要条件】** **qualification(s)**, a **right** (権利); a **license** (免許); a **certificate** /səʳtífɪkət/ (免状) ▶入会のための資格 the *qualifications* to join an association ‖司書の資格を取る obtain a librarian's *license* ‖彼は医療を行う資格を持たない He is*n't licensed to* practice medicine. ‖体育の教師になるにはどんな資格がいるんですか What *qualifications* do I need to be a P. E. teacher？‖株主なら誰でも株主総会に出席する資格がある All (the) stockholders have the *right* to attend the general meeting.

▶《面接で》どんな資格をお持ちですか What *qualifications* do you have？／What are your *qualifications*？‖姉は珠算２級の資格を持っている My sister has a second rank *certificate* in the abacus. ‖おじはパイロットの資格を持っている My uncle has a pilot's *license*. ‖彼女は保育所を経営する資格を取るつもりだ She is going to *apply for a license* to run a day-care center.

2【ふさわしいこと】 ▶山を汚す者に山を楽しむ資格はない People who leave trash in the mountains *don't have the right* to enjoy them. ‖何の資格があって私にそんなことを言うの？ *What right do you have* to say that to me？／*How dare you* say such a thing to me？‖彼には父親と呼ばれる資格はない(＝父親の名に値しない) He *doesn't deserve* to be called a father.

☛ 無資格 (→見出語)

3**しかく 視覚** **(the sense of) sight, vision** (視力)
一形 **視覚の** **visual** ▶ヘレン・ケラーは生後19か月のとき熱病のため視覚と聴覚を奪われた Helen Keller was deprived of *sight* and hearing when she was nineteen months old because of a fever. ‖レーザーショーは視覚効果を狙っている Laser light shows aim at *visual appeal*.

‖**視覚教育** visual education ‖**視覚教材** visual (teaching) aids ‖**視覚障害** (a) visual impairment, impaired vision.

4**しかく 死角** a **blind spot** (盲点); a **dead angle** (➤ 日本語に相当するが軍事用語で日常性はない) ▶大型トラックでは車の直前部が運転手にとって死角になることがよくある The area immediately in front of a large truck is often *a blind spot* to the driver.

5**しかく 刺客** an **assassin**.

1**しがく 歯学** **dentistry, dental surgery**
‖**歯学部** the school [department] of dentistry.

2**しがく 私学** a **private school** [**university** ／**college**] ‖**私学助成金** governmental subsidies to [for] private schools.

3**しがく 史学** **history**.

4**しがく 詩学** **poetics**.

じかく 自覚 **consciousness** /kɑ́:nʃəsnəs/ (意識); (an) **awareness** (気がついていること) **一動** **自覚する** **be conscious** [**aware**]《**of**》▶その医者は自分が胃がんにかかっていることを自覚していた The doctor *was aware* that he had stomach cancer. ‖きみはチームリーダーとしての責任を自覚すべきだ You should *be conscious* [*aware*] *of* your responsibility as the team leader. ‖きみは日本代表としての自覚が足りないよ You *need to realize* that you are a representative of Japan. (➤「自覚する必要がある」の意) ‖肺がんは自覚症状の現れにくい病気だ Lung cancer is a disease which does not often reveal itself through *subjective symptoms*.

しかけ 仕掛け a **device**, a **gadget** (装置) (➤ 後者には「巧妙に作られた」という含みがあり, 時に軽蔑的に用いられる); a **mechanism** (機械装置); a **trick** (からくり) ▶釣りの仕掛け a fishing *device* ‖マジシャンは種も仕掛けもありませんと言った The magician said there were no *gimmicks* in his magic.
‖**仕掛け花火** set fireworks.

しかける 仕掛ける ▶ウサギのわなを仕掛ける *set a trap* for rabbits ‖誰かが空港内に爆弾を仕掛けたらしい I heard that someone *has planted a bomb* in the airport. ‖ぼくが悪いんじゃないよ. あいつからけんかを仕掛けてきたんだよ It wasn't my fault. He *started* [*picked*] *this fight*.

シカゴ **Chicago** /ʃɪkɑ́:goʊ/ (アメリカ, イリノイ州の都市).

しかし **1【逆接を示して】** **but, however** (➤ 後者はやや堅い語で文頭・文中・文尾で使用可能) ▶旅行は楽しかった. しかし疲れたね I've enjoyed the trip, *but* I'm tired. ‖きみの仕事は立派だった. しかし時間がかかり過ぎたね You did a good job. *However*, you took too long to do it.

2【感動を示して】 ▶しかし, このラーメンうまいねえ *But* (*really*), isn't this ramen great？

じがじさん 自画自賛 ▶自画自賛になるかもしれませんが私の手打ちそばはなかなかのものですよ This may sound *self-praising* [sound like I'm *tooting my own horn*], but my buckwheat noodles are quite delicious.

じかせい 自家製 ▶自家製のクッキー our *homemade* cookies ‖このクッキー, 自家製なの I *made* these cookies *myself*. (➤「私が自分で作った」の意).

じがぞう 自画像 a **self-portrait** ▶自画像を描く paint one's *self-portrait*.

しかた 仕方 a **way** (**of** doing [**to** do]); **how to** do (…のしかた) →-方(かた)

【文型】
…するしかた, …のしかた
a way of doing [**to** do]
how to do

▶私は日本の選挙運動のしかたが気に入りません. 候補者の名前を大声で連呼するやり方です I don't like *the way* (that) Japanese election campaigns are conducted. They (just) repeatedly shout the candidates' names. ‖ ぼくは兄から車の**運転のしかた**を教わった I learned *how to drive* from my brother. ／My brother taught me *how to drive*. (➤ 後者のほうが英語的).

しかたがない 仕方がない **1【ほかに方法がない】can't help (it)**

◀解説▶「しかたがない」について
「しかたがない」は諦めの心境を表す, 極めて日本的な表現である. 一般に英米人は積極性を重んじ, このような消極的な表現はあまり好まない. 例えば, 日本人は「また入試に失敗してしまった. 実力がないのだからしかたがないや」などと言いがちだが, 英米人なら I flunked the entrance exams again. I just wasn't lucky. I'll try one more time. (入試にまた落ちたけど運がないだけさ. もう一度やってみよう)などと言うだろう.

▶彼はまだ日本語の勉強を始めたばかりだから間違えたって**しかたがない** *It can't be helped* [He *can't help it*] if he makes mistakes while speaking Japanese because he has just started studying it. (➤ この help は「避ける」) ‖ 監督に命令されればバントするよりしか**たがなかった** I *had to* make a sacrifice bunt because I could hardly ignore the manager's order. ‖ きみにそれが理解できなくても**しかたがない**よ I *don't blame* you for not understanding that. (➤「非難しない」の意).

【文型】
…してもしかたがない
It is [There is] no use (in) doing.
➤ in は省略するのがふつう. 「むだである」の意
There is no point in doing.
➤ in は省略することもある. 「意味, 理由, 狙いなどが見当たらない」の意

▶我々にはどうしようもないのだから心配して**もしかたがない** Since there's nothing we can do about it, *there is no use* worry*ing*. ‖ 泣いたって**しかたがない**よ. あいつはもう帰って来ないのだから *There's no point in* cry*ing*. He'll never come back to you. ‖ 両者が全く譲らないのだから, これ以上, 交渉を続けても**しかたがない** Since both parties won't concede a bit, *there is no point in* continu*ing* the negotiations. ‖ 水がないので泥水を飲む**よりしかたがなかった** We drank the muddy water because *there was no other choice*. ▶もう済んでしまったことは**しかたがない**けど, 今後はお金をなくさないようにしてね *It won't do any good to cry over spilt milk* [*What's done is done*], but (next time) try not to lose money again. (➤ cry over spilt milk は「こぼれたミルクを嘆く」が原義) ‖ **してしまったことはしかたがない**(＝元に戻せない) What is done cannot be undone. (➤ 英語のことわざ) ‖ ベストを尽くして負けたんだから, **しかたがない** I tried my best, but I lost the match. *That's how* [*the way*] *it goes*. (➤「世の中はそんなものだ」の意) ‖ **対話**「新幹線に間に合わないかもしれないよ」「だったら**しかたがない**. タクシーだ」"We may not make the Shinkansen train." "Then we'll *have to take* a taxi."

2【たまらない】▶暑くて**しかたがない** It's *unbearably* hot. ‖ ゆうべは12時までクラブで踊っていたからきょうは眠く**てしかたがない** I danced until midnight at a club last night, so I'm *incredibly* sleepy. (➤ incredibly は「ものすごく」) ‖ 彼は一人娘がかわいく**てしかたがない** He loves his only daughter *very much* [*to pieces*]. (➤ love ... to pieces は「大好きである」のインフォーマルな言い方) ‖ きみに会いたく**てしかたがない**よ I *am dying to* [I *can't wait to*] see you. (➤ どちらもくだけた表現) ‖ 孤児の話を聞くと泣け**てしかたがなかった** When I listened to the orphan's stories, I *couldn't help but* shed tears. →しようがない.

しかたなく 仕方なく **unwillingly** (嫌々ながらも) ; **reluctantly**(気が進まぬままに) ; **against** one's **will**(意志に反するが) ▶私は**しかたなく**諦めた I gave up *unwillingly* [*reluctantly*]. ‖ 私は**しかたなく**書類に署名なつ印せざるをえなかった I was forced to sign and seal the document *against my will*.

じかたび 地下足袋 ***jikatabi***; cloven-toed cloth work boots with rubber soles (➤ 説明的な訳).

じかだんぱん 直談判 ▶私がきみのお母さんに**直談判**して説得してみよう Let me *talk* to your mother *personally* to persuade her.

しかつ 死活 ▶これ以上この湖の汚染が進めば周辺漁民にとっては**死活問題**になる Any further pollution of this lake will be *a matter of life or death* [*a life-and-death problem*] to the fishermen around it.

しがつ 四月 **April** 《略 Apr.》 ▶日本の新学年は**4月**から始まる In Japan the new school year begins in *April*. ‖ **四月ばかの日** April Fool's [Fools'] Day.

じかつ 自活する **self-support** ▶彼は15歳で住み込みの新聞配達人になって**自活**を始めた He became a live-in newsboy at fifteen and began to *support himself* [*earn his living*]. ‖ 姉は**自活**している My (older) sister is *living on her own*.

しかつめらしい **solemn** ▶**しかつめらしい顔**で with *a solemn* [*a stiff and earnest*] *expression* (● 後者は「堅苦しく真面目な表情」と解した場合の訳).

シカト ▶声をかけたのに礼子に**シカト**されちゃった I said hello, but Reiko just *cut* me *dead* [*(completely) ignored me*]. ‖ あいつ, 絶対こっちに気がついてたぜ. **シカトしやがって** He noticed us for sure. *Acting as if he didn't see* ….

しがない **petty** ▶俺は**しがない**サラリーマンさ, と兄は冗談めかして言った My brother jestingly said that he was only a *run-of-the-mill* salaried worker.

じかに 直に ▶この鍋は熱いから**じかに**触ってはいけません This pot is very hot, so don't touch it *with bare hands*. ‖ 彼は**素肌にじかに**ワイシャツを着る He wears a shirt *on* (his) *bare skin* [*next to his skin*]. ‖ この書類は部長に**じかに**(＝直接)お渡し願います Please hand this document *directly* to the manager. ‖ この問題については彼と**じかに**(＝直接本人と)話し合うべきだ You should discuss this problem with him *in person* [*personally*].

じがね 地金 **substrate metal**(基板になる金属) ; **bullion** /bóljən/ (金・銀の延べ棒) ▶**金の地金**の値段が急騰した The price of *gold bullion* [*gold ingot*] has skyrocketed.
▶**地金**(＝本性)を出す show one's *true colors*.

じかび 直火 ▶肉を**じか火**で焼く broil [《英》grill] meat *over an open fire* (➤ broil, grill は「じか火または焼き網に載せて焼く」).

しがみつく **cling** 《to》(ぴったりくっつく ; 執着する) ; **hang on** 《to》(しっかり握って[捕まえて]離さない) ▶幼児は母親に**しがみついた** The little child *clung* (*tightly*) *to* his [her] mother. (➤ clung は cling の過去形).

▶《比喩的》T氏は党内の批判を意に介さず総裁の椅子にしがみついていた Mr. T disregarded the criticism of his party and *clung to* the presidency.

しかめっつら しかめっ面 a **grimace** /grɪméɪs/ ; a **frown** /fraʊn/ (眉をひそめること) ▶彼女は**しかめっ面**をして「痛いっ！」と言った She said "Ouch !" *with a grimace*. ‖ 母親は子供の不作法な態度に**しかめっ面をした** The mother *frowned at* her child's bad manners.

grimace　frown

しかめる **frown** /fraʊn/《at》▶先生は私の宿題を見て**顔をしかめた** The teacher *frowned* when he [she] saw my homework. ‖ 弟は歯痛に**顔をしかめて**(＝ゆがめて)いた My brother's *face was twisted* with pain from a toothache.

しかも (**and**) **moreover** (加えて；堅い言い方)；(**and**) **what's more** (おまけに；前者のややくだけた言い方)；**besides (that)** (その上)；**as well** (同様に)；《インフォーマル》**plus** (それに) ▶彼女は教育も知性も極めて高く，**しかも**プロフェッショナルである She is highly-educated, highly-intelligent, *and moreover*, she is professional. ‖ あそこのラーメンはうまくて**しかも**安い The ramen at that shop is good, *and what is more*, it's cheap. ／The ramen at that shop is good, *plus* it's cheap. ‖ このスマホはデザインが気に入らない. **しかも**厚すぎる I don't like the design of this smartphone. *Besides*, it's too thick. ‖ その生徒は能力がある. **しかも**よく勉強する That student has ability, *and* he works hard, *too*. ‖ あの作家は受賞後は作品数が少なく，**しかも**，それらは質的にも劣る The works that author has produced since winning a prize are few, *and besides that*, inferior.

じかようしゃ 自家用車

【解説】「自家用車」は a private [privately-owned] car (個人所有の車), a family car (家族共用の車), one's own car (自分だけが使う車)などのように訳せるが，英語ではあまりこれらの語は用いず，He drives to his office. (彼は自家用車で通勤する), My uncle has three cars. (おじさんは自家用車を3台持っている)のように言うのがふつう.

しがらみ **fetters** (足かせ)；**obstacles** (障害物) ▶**しがらみを断つ** break one's *fetters*.

しかりつける 叱りつける **tell off** →叱る ▶母親は息子が言うことを聞かないので**叱りつけた** The mother *told* her son *off* for not doing as he had been told.

しかる 叱る **scold** ＋目, **tell off**, **talk to**

【語法】(1)**scold** は親や教師が子供を叱る場合に用いるのがふつう. その場合，特に「がみがみ叱る」のなら **nag at** を用いる. (2)**tell off** と **talk to** は類似だが，叱り方や叱るときのことばの調子は前者のほうがきつい. (3)人をどなりつけて叱るような場合は **yell at** を用いる. (4)「叱責する」の意では **reprimand** /réprɪmænd/ ＋目 がふつう.

▶子供を**叱る** *scold* a child ‖ 怠けていて母に**叱られた** I *was scolded* by my mother for being lazy. ‖ 店長はレジ係がいいかげんな仕事をするので**厳しく叱った** The manager *told* the cashier *off* [*reprimanded* the cashier] for doing sloppy work. ‖ 先生はその少年がまた試合に遅れたので**叱った** The teacher *talked to* the boy [*gave* the boy *a talking-to*] about being late for the game again.

▶先生に見つかったら**叱られるぞ** You'll *catch it* [*get it*] if the teacher finds out what you've done. (➤ catch it は子供が［子供に］使うことが多い) ‖ 会議に遅れてこっぴどく**叱られちゃったよ** I *got bawled out* for arriving late for the meeting. (➤ bawl out は大人がインフォーマルな表現で用いることが多い) ‖ 上司に**叱られた** My boss *got upset with me*. ‖ 監督は選手を**大声で叱った** The manager *yelled at* the players.

しかるに 然るに **however** (しかしながら)；**on the other hand** (もう一方において).

しかるべき 然るべき **1**【相応の】**appropriate** (条件・目的にかなった)；**proper** (社会通念上正しい)；**suitable** (周囲の状況にふさわしい)；**respectable** (不体裁ではない) ▶向こうがそういう態度なら，こちらは**しかるべき**手段を取らざるをえないだろう If they take that attitude, I think we'll have to take *appropriate* measures.

2【…して当然だ】▶無事に帰国したのなら連絡があって**しかるべきだ** If he has returned home safely, he *ought to* let me know.

[1]**しかん 士官** a **commissioned officer**
‖**陸軍［海軍］士官** a military [naval] officer ‖ **陸軍［海軍］士官学校** a military [naval] academy ‖ **士官候補生** a cadet.

[2]**しかん 弛緩** **looseness**；**laxity** (緊張の欠如) 一動 **弛緩する** **relax** ‖**筋弛緩剤** a muscle relaxant.

しがん 志願する **volunteer**《for》；**apply**《for》(申し込む) ▶リチャードの父はイラク戦争が始まったとき陸軍に**志願した** When the Iraq War broke out, Richard's father *volunteered for* the army. ‖ 500人以上の生徒がその学校を**志願した** More than 500 students *applied* (*for* admission) to the school. ‖ M大学の入学**志願者**数は1万人を超えた The number of *applicants* for entrance to M University was more than ten thousand.

[1]じかん 時間

訳語メニュー
時，時刻 →time **1**, **2**
1時間 →hour **3**
時限 →period **4**

1【時】**time** ▶**時間**がたつのは全く早い *Time* really flies. ‖ きょうは**時間**がたつのも忘れるほど楽しかった I've had so much fun today that I lost track of the *time*. ‖ **時間**があったらお寄りください Come over if you have *time*. ‖ この病気を治すには**時間がかかる** It will *take time* to cure this disease. ‖ どんなに**時間がかかって**も仕事は仕上げてしまいます I'll finish the job no matter how long *it takes*. ‖ マージャンは**時間がかかる**［**時間を食う**］ゲームだ Mah-jongg is a *time-consuming* game. ‖ **時間がたっぷりある**から昼寝しよう We *have plenty of time*, so why not take a nap? ‖ もう**時間がない**. 急ごう We don't have much *time* left. Let's hurry (up). ‖ 今は**時間がない**(＝忙しい)からその話はあとにしてくれ *I'm tied up* now, so let's talk about it later. ‖ **時間が残り少なくなってきた** We *are running out of time*. ‖ きょうは時

間に追われている I've *been pressed for time* today. ▶その容疑者が白状するのは**時間の問題**だ It's just *a matter of time* before the suspect confesses. ‖ きみは家族のためにもっと**時間を作る**べきだ You should *make* more *time* for your family. ‖ もっと**時間をかけて**問題を考えなさい I think you should *spend* a little *more time* thinking about the problem.

> **【文型】**
> **…する時間がある**
> **have time to** do
> **…する時間を作る［見つける］**
> **make［find］time to** do
> **《解説》** (1)あとに名詞・動名詞がくると, **have time for** の形になる. この形は否定文・疑問文で使うことが多い.
> (2)時間を「作る」では **have** の代わりに **make** を, 「見つける」では **find** を用いる. 時間が「かかる」では It を主語に **take** を使う.
> (3)この **time** は「暇, ゆとり」の意.「…するのに必要な, それだけの時間」の意で, **have the time to** *do* とする場合もある.
> (4)Do you have the time ? は「いま何時ですか」の意.

▶きょうの午後は**買い物をする時間が十分にある** We *have* plenty of *time to* shop this afternoon. ‖ そんなくだらないことに付き合っている**時間はない** I *don't have time* for such nonsense. ‖ 彼は家族と1日**過ごす時間を作った** He *made time to* spend a whole day with his family. ‖ その問題をよく考えてみますので**時間をください** Please *give me some time* to think it over. ▶私のために**お時間を取って**くださりありがとうございます I want to thank you for *taking the time to* see me. (➤ 親しい間柄では単に Thanks for the time. と言うことも多い) ‖ 論文を書くのに**時間を取られた** Writing the paper *took* (me) *a lot of time*. ‖ 私たちは野球の試合が始まるまでゲームセンターで**時間を潰した** We *killed time* at the amusement arcade until the baseball game started.

▶将棋の試合は**時間切れ**で引き分けとなった Our shogi game ended up (in) a tie because *the clock ran out*. ‖ 試験の最後の問題を終えたところで, ちょうど**時間切れとなった** Just as I finished the last question on the test, *the time ran out* [*was up*]. ‖ 対話 「少しお**時間を頂けますか**. お話ししたいことがあります」「今は**時間がない**から, あすにしてくれないか」 "May I talk with you *for a few minutes* ?" "I'm sorry, but *I'm tied up at the moment*. Could you make it tomorrow ?"

2【時刻】time ▶野球の試合が始まる**時間**を教えてください Please tell me *what time* the baseball game starts. ‖ 彼女との約束の**時間を間違えて**1時間早く原宿に着いた I *mistook the time* [I *made a mistake on the time*] and arrived at Harajuku an hour early.

▶きょうはもう**時間が遅い**から, このくらいにしよう *It's late*, so why don't we call it a day ? ‖ **時間が来た**ので答案を提出しなさい (*The*) *time's up*. Hand in your test papers. ‖ **こんな時間に**人に電話をしてはいけません You shouldn't call other people *so late at night*. ‖ 彼は**時間にルーズ**だ He *isn't punctual*. ／He *is never on time*. (➤ 後者は「いつも時間どおりでない」の意) ‖ 彼女は**時間をきちんと守る** She *is punctual*.

▶《待ち合わせなど》あした4時ね. **時間を間違えないでね** We're meeting at four tomorrow. *Be on time*.

> **【文型】**
> **人(A)が…すべき時間だ**
> **It's time for** A **to** do.
> **It's (about) time** A did.
> **人(A)がとうに…すべき時間だ**
> **It's about time** A did.
> **《解説》** 上の2つは時間になる前から「そろそろ…すべき時間だ」と言うとき, 下は時間がとうに過ぎて, いらだちを表すときの言い方で, time を強く発音する.

▶もう**寝る時間ですよ** *It's time for* you *to* go to bed. ／*It's* (*about*) *time* you *went* to bed. (➤ 後者は「寝ていなければいけない時間」という気持ちを表して, 文の後半を過去形(＝仮定法過去)にする) ‖ とっくに来ていなければいけない**時間だぞ**. 何を手間取っていたんだ *It's about time* you *got* here. What took you so long ? ‖ そろそろ彼が現れても**いい時間だ** *It's about time* (that) he *showed* up. ‖ 子供たちはもう**寝る時間だよ** *It is high time* (that) the kids *went* to bed. (➤ 上の2例とも time に続く節中は仮定法過去).

▶飛行機が**時間どおりに**到着するといいのだが I hope the plane will arrive *on time*.

3【1時間】an hour ▶**1時間**は60分である *One hour* has 60 minutes. ‖ 東京からロサンゼルスまで飛行機で**10時間**ほどかかる It takes almost ten *hours* to fly from Tokyo to Los Angeles. ‖ 京都までバスで**何時間かかりますか** *How long* [*How many hours*] *does it take* to get to Kyoto by bus ? ‖ **1時間当たりの平均賃金**は学生の場合750円くらいです The average wage for students is about 750 yen *per hour*.

4【授業】a period（時限）; (a) **class**（授業）▶次の**時間**は化学です The next *period* is chemistry. ‖ 月曜日の**3時間目**は化学です We have chemistry (*in the*) *third period* (on) Monday. ‖ 彼は世界史の**時間**に携帯メールを送った He sent text messages during world history *class*.

‖**時間外** after hours ‖ **時間外入り口** the after hours entrance ‖ **時間外手当** overtime pay ‖ **時間外労働** overtime ／extra work after business hours ‖ **時間給** hourly [time] wages.

> **逆引き熟語 ○○時間**
> **移動時間** travel time ／**運行時間** operation hours ／**営業時間** business [operating] hours ／**お茶の時間** coffee time [break], tea time ／**開演時間** curtain time ／**開店時間** opening time ／(機械などの)**稼動時間** operating time ／(料理などの)**加熱時間** heating time ／(会社などの)**休憩時間** an intermission, a break ／**勤務[就業]時間** working [business ／ office] hours ／ **質疑応答時間** a question-and-answer period [session] ／**上映時間** running time ／**消灯時間** lights-out ／**睡眠時間** sleeping hours ／**スタート時間** starting time ／**閉店時間** closing time ／ (テレビなどの) **放送時間** air time, broadcasting hours ／**面会時間** visiting hours ／ (学校などの) **休み時間** recess (time)

²じかん 次官 an **undersecretary**
‖**政務次官** a parliamentary vice minister ‖ **外務事務次官** the administrative vice minister of foreign affairs. →**大臣**.

³じかん 字間 ▶**字間を空ける**［**詰める**］put more *space* [reduce *space*] *between the characters* [*words*].

じかんわり 時間割り 《米》 a (**class**) **schedule** /skédʒuːl ‖ ʃédjuːl/, 《英》 a (**class**) **timetable** ▶**時間割り**を変える change *a timetable* ‖ **時間割りを組む** set [arrange] *a schedule*.

1**しき 式** **1**【**儀式**】a **ceremony**；a **wedding**（結婚式）▶姉は5月に市内のホテルで**式を挙げた** My (older) sister *held her wedding* at a hotel in the city last May.

2【**方式**】a **style**(様式)；a **way**(流儀) ▶フランス**式の**やり方 the French *way* of doing things ‖ 仏**式で**葬儀を行う perform a funeral ceremony in a Buddhist *style* ‖ ヘボン**式**ローマ字 the Hepburn *system* of romanization ‖ これが**イタリア式の**もてなし方です This is *Italian* hospitality. ‖ **日本式の**経営では集団の和が尊重される Harmony is important in *Japanese(-style)* management. ‖ 今では日本の多くの家庭に**洋式の**便所がある Nowadays there's a *Western-style* toilet in most Japanese homes.

3【**数学などの**】an **expression**；an **equation**（等式）；a **formula**（公式）

▶**数式** a *numerical expression* ‖ 硫酸の**分子式**は H_2SO_4 である The *molecular formula* for sulfuric acid is H_2SO_4.

2**しき 四季** **the** (**four**) **seasons** ▶**四季の変化**がなければ私たちの生活はどれほど単調なことだろう Without *the change of the seasons* [*the seasonal changes*], we would find our life extremely monotonous. ‖ この寺は**四季を通じて**（＝1年中）多くの観光客が訪れる This temple gets many visitors *year round* [*all* (*the*) *year around*].

> **直訳の落とし穴「日本には四季がある」**
> 「日本には四季がある」は日本人が大好きな表現の1つで，日本を紹介するときの典型的な文である．文字どおりには Japan has four seasons. で，こう表現する学習者が多いが，これを聞いた英米人は初めきょとんとし，また何度も聞かされるとうんざりする．英米をはじめ世界の多くの国にも四季はあり，春夏秋冬に当たる単語がある．なにも四季は日本に特有のものではない．Japan has four distinct seasons.（日本にははっきりした四季がある）とすればずっとましであるが，これも判で押したようにたびたび話題にするのは避けたい．

3**しき 指揮** **1**【**楽団の**】━**動 指揮する** **conduct** /kəndʌ́kt/ (＋目) ▶オーケストラ［交響曲］を**指揮する** *conduct* an orchestra [a symphony] ‖ サイモン・ラトル**指揮の**マーラーの交響曲第5番 Mahler's Fifth Symphony *conducted by* [*under the baton of*] Simon Rattle ‖ 私たちの音楽の先生は地元で青年合唱団を**指揮している** Our music teacher *conducts* [*directs*] a chorus for the youth in his community. ‖**指揮者** a conductor ‖ **指揮台** a podium ‖ **指揮棒** a baton /bətáːn/.

2【**指示**】**command**(軍隊などの)；**direction**（指図）━**動 指揮する** **command** ＋目，**direct** ＋目 ▶作戦の**指揮を執る** *take command* of an operation ‖ 艦隊を**指揮する** *command* a fleet ‖ 米軍を**指揮する** *command* American forces ‖ うちの会社ではすべて社長の**指揮で**仕事をする In our company, each of the staff members follows the president's *directions* [*orders*] in everything. ‖ 社長自ら大掃除の**指揮を執った** The president of the company himself *led* (the employees) in the general cleaning of the office.（➤ led は lead の過去形）.

‖**指揮官** a commander.

4**しき 死期** one's **end** ▶彼は自分の**死期が近い**ことを知っているようだった He seemed to know that *he was near his end* [that *his death was approaching*].

5**しき 士気** **morale** /mərǽl/ ▶**士気を高める** boost [improve／raise] (one's) *morale* ‖ 連戦連勝で選手たちの**士気が上がってきた** *Morale* among the players has improved after a string of victories (in consecutive games).

シギ 鴫 《鳥》 a **snipe**.

1**じき 時期** **time**；**the season**（季節）▶**時期が来れば**きみにもそれがわかるよ *In time* you will understand. ‖ **時期が来たら**きみにすべてを話すよ I'll tell you everything *when the* (*right*) *time comes*. ‖ 毎年**この時期は**天気がよい We have a lot of lovely days at *this time* of year. ‖ キャンプに出かけるには今がいちばんよい**時期だ** This [Now] is the best *season* for going camping. ‖ カキはもう**時期外れだ** Oysters are *out of season* now. ‖ 本大学で大学院を設置するのは**時期尚早だ** It is still *premature* to establish a graduate school at this university.

2**じき 時機** an **opportunity**(チャンス) ▶**時機をうかがう** bide one's *time* ‖ 彼は転職の**時機を**狙っている He is waiting for *an opportunity* [*a good chance*] to change jobs.

3**じき 磁気** **magnetism** ▶録画したテープは**磁気を帯びた**物の近くに置かないでください Do not expose recorded tapes to *magnetic* sources.

‖**磁気嵐** a magnetic storm ‖ **磁気ディスク** a magnetic disk ‖ **磁気テープ** (a) magnetic tape.

4**じき 磁器** **porcelain** /pɔ́ːrsəlɪn/, **china**（➤後者は主に食器類を指す）‖**磁器製品** porcelains.

5**じき 次期** ▶B氏は**次期**総理の呼び声が高い Mr. B is widely expected to be *the next* prime minister. ‖**次期大統領** the President-elect(➤ -elect は「当選したがまだ就任していない」の意で，名詞のあとに置く).

6**じき 直** ▶正月ももう**じきだ** The New Year is *just around the corner* [*is close at hand*]. ‖ その角を曲がれば大学は**じきですよ** Turn that corner and you'll *soon come to* the college.

☞ **じきに**（→見出語）

じぎ 時宜 ▶**時宜を得た**，その画家の回顧展 a *timely* retrospective exhibition of the artist's work.

しきい 敷居 a **threshold** /θréʃhoʊld/, a **doorsill**(ともに玄関の)；a **wooden groove for a sliding door**(障子・ふすまの) ▶《慣用表現》こんなうちの**敷居**なんか二度とまたぐか！ I will never cross the *threshold* of this house again!／I will never enter this house again! ‖ どうも妻の実家は**敷居が高い** I *don't feel at home* at my parents-in-law's. ‖ 借金を返していないから，どうも彼の所の**敷居が高くてね** I'*m* rather *hesitant to visit his place* because I haven't returned the money I borrowed from him.

しきいし 敷石 a **paving stone**.

しぎかい 市議会 a **city** [**municipal**] **assembly**(➤ city council とすると「市参事会」の意になる場合があるので，このような言い方のほうがよりよい).

‖**市議会議員** a member of a city [municipal] assembly.

しきかくいじょう 色覚異常 **color blindness**.

しききん 敷金 a (**security**) **deposit** ▶2か月分の**敷金**を入れていただきます Please pay [make] *a deposit* of two months' rent.／The (*security*) *deposit* is two months' rent.

しきさい 色彩 **1**【**彩り**】**color** ▶鮮やかな**色彩の**ポスター a *brightly-colored* poster ‖ この画家は**色彩感覚が**こ

とのほか優れている The artist has an extraordinary *sense of color*. ‖ スリランカの寺院の絵画は色彩豊かだ The paintings in Sri Lankan temples are *very colorful*.

2【傾向】▶彼らの風習には宗教的な色彩がある Their customs *are colored* [*influenced*] by religion.

しきざき 四季咲きの perpetual ▶四季咲きのダリア a *perpetual* dahlia.

しきし 色紙 a ***shikishi*** ; A square piece of cardboard covered with rice paper. One side of it is used for writing a haiku, a tanka, an autograph, or farewell messages, etc. (➤ 説明的な訳).

1**しきじ 式辞** an address /ədrés/ ▶式辞を述べる give *an address*.

2**しきじ 識字** literacy(読み書きできる能力) ▶識字運動を推進する promote (activities for) *literacy* ‖ その国は(国民の)識字率が高い[低い] The *literacy rate* in that country is high [low].

‖ **非識字者** an illiterate (person).

じきじき 直々に personally (他人を介さずに) ; in person (面と向かって, 差し向かいで) ; directly (直接に) ▶社長がきみとじきじきに話したがっているよ The president wants to talk with you *personally* [*in person*].

しきしゃ 識者 an intellectual(知識人) ; an expert(専門家) ; knowledgeable people (有識者 ; 総称) ▶識者の意見を聞く ask for *an expert opinion*.

1**しきじょう 式場** ▶結婚式場を予約する reserve *a wedding hall for one's wedding* ‖ 体育館が入学式の式場に充てられている The gymnasium will *be used* for the entrance ceremony.

2**しきじょう 色情** (a) sexual desire ; lust(強い欲情).

しきそ 色素 (a) pigment ‖ **メラニン色素** melanin.

じきそ 直訴 a direct appeal ▶社長に賃上げを直訴するつもりだ We will *appeal directly* to the president for better pay.

しきそう 色相 a hue(色合い).

しきたり (a) tradition(伝統) ; (a) convention(慣行, 慣例) ; (a) custom(社会的習慣) ▶その村の人たちは古くからのしきたりを守っている The villagers observe all the old *traditions*.

じきでし 直弟子 a direct pupil [disciple].

しきち 敷地 a site(用地) ; a lot (土地の一区画) ▶ここは学校を建てるにはもってこいの敷地だ This is an ideal *site* [*place*] for building a school. ‖ 彼の家は600坪の敷地に立っている His house stands on *a lot* which is 600 *tsubo* (nearly 2,000 square meters).

しきちょう 色調 a tone, a (shade of) color ▶落ち着いた色調の壁 a wall painted in a quiet *color* [in quiet *colors*].

しきつめる 敷き詰める ▶床には深紅のじゅうたんが敷き詰めてあった The floor *was covered* (*wall to wall*) with scarlet carpeting. ／The floor *was covered* with scarlet *wall-to-wall* carpeting.

しきてん 式典 a ceremony.

じきに 直に soon, before long. ⇀すぐ.

じきひつ 直筆 one's own handwriting ▶記念館には詩人の直筆の原稿が保存してある In the memorial hall, they keep manuscripts *written in* the poet's *own hand*. (➤ handwriting を使うと, 前に written があるのでくどい).

しきふ 敷布 a sheet. ⇀シーツ.

しきふく 式服 formal wear.

しきぶとん 敷き布団 a futon (mattress), a ***shikibuton***.

しきべつ 識別 discrimination, distinction 一動 **識別する** discriminate [distinguish]《A from B》, tell A from B (➤ 後者はインフォーマルな言い方) ▶善と悪を識別する *discriminate between* good *and* evil ／*distinguish* good *from* evil ‖ 私はチョウとガの識別ができない I *can't tell* butterflies *from* moths.

しきもの 敷物 a carpet ; a rug (小型の) ▶彼は床に敷物を敷いた He covered the floor with *a carpet*. ／He carpeted the floor.

じぎゃく 自虐 self-torture(自分を苦しめること) ; masochism /mǽsəkìzəm/ (自分を苦しめて快感を感じること, マゾヒズム).

1**しきゅう 子宮** the womb /wuːm/, the uterus /júːtərəs/ (➤ 後者は解剖学用語)

‖ **子宮がん** uterine cancer ‖ **子宮筋腫** fibroid /fáibrɔid/ ‖ **子宮頸(けい)がん** cervical cancer.

2**しきゅう 支給する** supply +目 ; pay +目 (支払う) ▶制服は会社で支給します Uniforms *will be supplied* by the company. ‖ ボーナスは15日に支給します Your bonuses *will be paid* on the 15th.

3**しきゅう 至急** urgently /ə́ːrdʒəntli/ (緊急に) ; immediately(間を置かないで) 一形 **至急の** urgent, immediate ▶至急の用事 *urgent* business ‖ これを至急清書してください Please make a clean draft of this *as quickly as possible*. ‖《新聞広告》和美, 万事解決した. 至急連絡せよ Kazumi. Everything solved. Contact us *at once* [*immediately*]. (➤ 前者は「今すぐ」) ‖ これを大至急頼むよ Please do this *as fast as you can*. ‖《タクシーで》大至急頼むよ *Step on the gas!*

4**しきゅう 四球** ⇀フォアボール.

5**しきゅう 死球** ⇀デッドボール.

1**じきゅう 時給** hourly pay ▶時給いくらですか What is the *hourly pay*? ‖ アルバイト学生には時給800円が支払われる The working students are paid 800 yen *per hour*. ‖ 私は時給で払ってもらっている I'm paid *on an hourly basis*.

2**じきゅう 自給** ▶石油の自給率 *self-sufficiency rate* [*level of self-sufficiency*] in oil ‖ 日本は食糧の自給自足ができていない Japan is not *self-sufficient* in food. (➤「食糧自給率」は the food self-sufficiency rate).

3**じきゅう 持久** ▶試合は持久戦になった The game turned into *a test of endurance*. ‖ 私は最近持久力に欠けている These days I lack *stamina* [*staying power*].

しきゅうしき 始球式 ▶首相による始球式でことしの日本シリーズが開幕した This year's Japan Series started after the Prime Minister *threw out the ceremonial first pitch*.

しきょ 死去 one's death 一動 **死去する** die, pass away ▶けさ恩師の死去を電話で知らされた This morning I got a phone call informing me of my former teacher's *death*.

✉ **去る3月20日祖父は脳出血で死去いたしました** My grandfather *passed away* from a stroke [*died* of a stroke] on March 20.

じきょ 辞去する say farewell and leave.

しきょう 司教 a bishop ‖ **大司教** an archbishop.

しぎょう 始業 ▶始業のベルが鳴っている *The beginning bell* [*The bell for classes*] is ringing. ‖ うちの会社は9時始業の5時終業だ At our company, we *start work* at 9 a.m. and end at 5 p.m.

し

‖**始業式** the opening ceremony (of each term) (➤ 英米にはない).

じきょう 自供 confession **―動 自供する** confess /kənfés/ (+目) ▶容疑者は全面的に犯行を**自供し**始めた The suspect began to *confess* to all the charges against him. ‖ **自供**によれば彼はその殺人事件に加わっていた By [According to] his own *confession*, he took part in the murder. ／He *confessed* to having taken part in the murder.

じぎょう 事業 business (商売, 企業による生産・販売などの活動) ; an enterprise /énţəʳpraɪz/ (企て) ; an undertaking (仕事) ▶**事業**に成功 [失敗] する succeed [fail] in *business* ‖ **事業**(＝会社)を営む run *a business* (➤「店, 会社」の意味では a をつける) ‖ 私はA氏の援助を受けてこの**事業**を興した I started this *business* [*enterprise*] with the help of Mr. A. ‖ しっかりした辞書を作ることは一大**事業**だ It is a great *undertaking* to make a really dependable dictionary.

‖**事業家** a businessman (実業家) ; an entrepreneur /ὰ:ntrəprənə́:ʳ/ (事業を興す人) ‖ **事業資金** business funds ‖ **事業仕分け** government project screening [review] ‖ **事業部** a department, a division ‖ **公共事業** public works ‖ **出版事業部** a publishing division ‖ **慈善事業** charity work, charity ‖ **製品開発事業部** a product development division.

しきょうひん 試供品 a sample ▶このクリームの**試供品**はありますか Do you have a *sample* of this cream ?

しきよく 色欲 (a) sexual desire ; lust (強い欲情).

しきょく 支局 a branch (office) ▶彼は大阪**支局**に転勤になった He has been transferred to *the Osaka branch office*.

‖**支局長** the head of a branch office.

1**じきょく 時局** situation.

2**じきょく 磁極** a magnetic pole.

しきり 仕切り a compartment (箱・たんすなどの) ; a partition (部屋などの隔壁) ; a screen (ついたてなど) ▶**仕切り**のカーテン a *partitioning* curtain ‖ 私のかばんは**仕切り**が3つある My bag has three *compartments*. ▶《相撲で》両力士は土俵上で**仕切り**に入った The two sumo wrestlers have *squared off*. (➤ square off はボクシングなどで「身構える」の意).

しきりに 1【たびたび】 frequently (➤ やや堅い語で, 時間の間隔が比較的短いことを暗示する) ; often (よく, しばしば) ▶少女は私が話している間**しきりに**うなずいた While I was talking, the girl *frequently* [*repeatedly*] nodded to me. (➤ repeatedly は「繰り返し」) ‖ 母は**しきりに**外の様子を気にしているようだった It seemed that my mother *frequently* paid attention to what was going on outside. ‖ 兄は最近仕事が忙しすぎるとしきりにこぼす My brother *often* complains that he is too busy at work these days.

2【熱心に】 eagerly ; strongly (強く) ▶販売員は金の延べ棒を買えと**しきりに**勧めた The salesperson *eagerly* [*strongly*] urged me to buy gold bars. ‖ 子供たちは**しきりに**ディズニーランドに行きたがっている The children *are eager* [*are impatient*] *to* go to Disneyland. (➤ impatient は「待ち切れなくて」).

しきる 仕切る divide +目《into》(等しく分割する) ; partition +目《off》(仕切りで分ける) ; screen +目《off》(ついたてなどで分ける) ▶教室を2つに**仕切る** *divide* a classroom into two ‖ 部屋を**仕切って**納戸を作る *partition off* a closet from the room ‖ 部屋の一部は**仕切られている** Part of the room *was screened off*.

▶このプロジェクトは社長が直接**仕切っ**ている The boss is *handling* this project himself. ／The boss is *running the show* in this project.

しきん 資金 funds (財源) ; (a) capital (資本金) ▶商売を始めたいのだが**資金**が足りない I want to start a business but I don't have enough *funds* [*capital*]. ‖ 父は僅かな**資金**で商売を始めた My father started his business with very little *capital*. ‖ 彼女の店は父親が**資金を出し**ている Her shop *is financially supported* by her father. (➤「店を始めるときに父親が出資した」という意なら Her father *put out the money* for her shop.) ‖ どの会社も**資金繰り**が苦しいらしい It looks like all companies are having difficulties with *raising operating funds*.

‖**運転資金** a working [an operating] fund ‖ **結婚資金** a nest egg for getting married (➤ nest egg は「(将来のための)準備金」) ‖ **政治資金** a political fund (➤ 政治運動などの「買収資金」は slush fund という) ‖ **選挙資金** campaign funds.

しぎん 詩吟 *shigin*

日本紹介 ✉ **詩吟は中国人および日本人が作った古典的な漢詩を日本の古典風に朗唱する芸です. 近年では短歌や日本の近代詩の朗唱も行われます** *Shigin* is the art of chanting the classical Japanese version of classical Chinese poems composed by both Chinese and Japanese. In modern times, it includes chanting *tanka* and modern Japanese poetry.

しきんきょり 至近距離 point-blank range ▶犯人は**至近距離**から警官を撃った The criminal fired *point-blank* at the policeman. ‖ 彼は何者かに**至近距離**から撃たれた He was shot by someone *at* [*within*] *point-blank range*.

しきんせき 試金石 a touchstone (真価を計るもの) ; an acid test (試す機会, 試練) ▶この交渉をどうまとめるか, 彼にとってはこれが部長としての**試金石**だな How he handles these negotiations will be *the acid test* of what kind of an administrator he really is.

しく 敷く 1【平らに広げる】 spread +目 ; lay +目 (鉄道・敷物などを) ▶子供たちは庭にござを**敷いて**ままごと遊びをしている The children *spread* a (straw) mat in the yard and are now playing house on it. (➤ この spread は過去形) ‖ 彼は座布団を**敷く**とその上にあぐらをかいた He *put down* a zabuton and sat cross-legged on it. ‖ 自分の布団は自分で**敷き**なさい *Lay out* [*Put down*] your own bedding. (⇀布団) ‖ 神社の参道には玉砂利が**敷かれている** Gravel has *been spread* on the path leading to the shrine.

2【広く行き渡らせる】 ▶戒厳令が**敷かれて**夜の12時から朝6時までの外出が禁止になった Martial law *was imposed* [*declared*], with a curfew between twelve midnight and six in the morning.

じく 軸 1【心棒】 an axis /ǽksɪs/ (回転体の) ; an axle (車輪の) ; a shaft (機械の) ▶マッチの**軸** matchwood ／a matchstick (マッチ1本) ‖ 地球の**軸**が少し傾いていることが, 季節の変化する一因となっている The fact that the earth's *axis* tilts a bit is one cause of the changing of the seasons.

2【中軸, 中心】 ▶チームの**軸**となる選手が病気で欠場した The team's *core player* did not appear due to illness.

3【数学の】 an axis ▶縦[横]軸 *the vertical* [*horizontal*] *axis*.

じくあし 軸足 a pivot foot.

じくう 時空 **time and space.**

しぐさ 仕草 a **gesture**（身振り）; a **movement**（動作）▶わざとらしいしぐさ affected [artificial] *gestures* ‖ 彼は滑稽なしぐさで私を笑わせた His funny *gestures* made me laugh. ‖ その小さな女の子はしぐさがかわいかった *The way* that little girl *behaved* [*moved*] was very cute. ‖ パンダはしぐさがとてもかわいらしい The panda's *movements* are adorable.

ジグザグ a **zigzag** ▶ジグザグの道 a *zigzag* (path) ‖ 険しい山道が山頂までジグザグに延びていた A steep path *zigzagged* up to the top of the mountain. ‖ デモ隊は通りをジグザグ行進した The demonstrators *marched in a zigzag fashion* along the street [*marched* along the street *swaying from left to right*].

じくじ 忸怩 ▶わが処女作は若書きが目立ち, 内心じくじたるものがある My first work is filled with youthful shortcomings and *I feel very ashamed of it*.

しくしく ▶胃がしくしく痛む have an *incessant dull* pain in the stomach (➤「絶え間のない鈍痛がある」の意) ‖ 小さな女の子がしくしく泣いていた A little girl *was whimpering*.

じくじく ▶傷口がうんでじくじくしている The cut has become infected and *is oozing pus*.

しくじる **fail**（+目）;《米・インフォーマル》**flunk**（+目）（特に試験などに）; **blunder**（大失敗をする）▶きょうの英語の試験, しくじっちゃったよ I *failed* [*flunked*] the English exam today. ‖ その若手女優は舞台でしくじった The young actress *blundered* on (the) stage. ‖ しくじるなよ! *Don't blow it*.

ジグソーパズル a **jigsaw (puzzle)** ▶ジグソーパズルをする put [piece] together a *jigsaw puzzle*.

しくつ 試掘 ▶石油を探して試掘する *prospect* for oil.

シグナル a **signal** ▶彼にシグナルを送る *give* [*send*] *a signal* to him ‖ 子供たちが自殺を図る前に出すシグナルを見落とさないようにしなければならない We must not miss the *signals* children send before they attempt suicide.

しくはっく 四苦八苦 ▶レポートを書くのに四苦八苦した I *had a very hard time* writing the paper. ／I *struggled to* write the paper. ‖ うまい口実を見つけるのに四苦八苦した I *racked* [*wracked*] *my brains* trying to think up a good excuse. (➤ rack one's brains は「脳みそを絞る」) ‖ 彼は四苦八苦して(＝やっとのことで)その数学の問題を解いた He solved the math problem *with difficulty*.

しくみ 仕組み a **mechanism**（メカニズム）; **structure**（構造）▶機械の仕組み the *mechanism* of a machine ‖ 世の中の仕組み the *structure* of society ‖ 日本語と英語とではことばの仕組みが根本的に違っている Japanese and English are fundamentally different in their *linguistic structures*.

しくむ 仕組む ▶巧みに仕組まれたわな a cunningly *designed* trap ‖ 社長は部長一派の仕組んだわなにかかって辞任に追い込まれた The president of the company was forced to resign because he was caught in a trap *engineered* by the department manager's followers.

シクラメン《植物》a **cyclamen** /síkləmən/.

しぐれ 時雨 ⚠ **秋の終わりから冬の初めにかけて降ったりやんだりする雨をこう呼ぶが, これにぴったりの英語はないので, 次のように文脈でその意を表す.**
▶時雨の降る寒い初冬の午後だった It was a cold, early winter afternoon *with intermittent showers*. (➤ intermittent は「断続的な」の意) ／It was a cold *drizzly* afternoon in early winter. (➤ drizzly は「霧雨の降る」の意の形容詞).

しけ 時化 a **storm**（嵐）▶漁船は海上でしけに遭った The fishing boats were caught in *a storm* at sea. ‖ 海はしけ模様だ The sea *looks stormy*.

しけい 死刑 **the death penalty, capital punishment**（→極刑）▶死刑を廃止すべきと考える人もいる Some people maintain that *capital punishment* should be abolished. (➤「死刑廃止」は the abolition of capital punishment) ‖ 裁判官は彼に死刑の判決を言い渡した The judge passed the *death sentence* on him. ‖ 彼は強盗殺人の罪で死刑を宣告された He *was sentenced to death* for robbery and murder. ‖ その死刑囚はけさ死刑を執行された The *condemned criminal was executed* this morning.
ディベートルーム「死刑は絶対に必要である」

じけい 次兄 one's **second oldest** [《英》**eldest**] **brother**.

じけいだん 自警団 a **neighborhood watch group**; a **vigilante group**（自分たちで勝手に裁く）‖ **自警団員** a neighborhood watch group member.

じけいれつ 時系列 a **time series**, a **temporal sequence** ▶時系列で *in chronological order*.

しげき 刺激

1【体や感覚器官に対する作用】 **stimulation** 一動 **刺激する** **stimulate** /stímjəleɪt/ +目 ▶景気を刺激する *stimulate* the economy ‖ 景気刺激策 an *economic stimulus package* (➤ package は「一連の法案や政策」, 1つの策は「計画」は plan や program,「法案」は bill) ‖ その詩は彼女の想像力を刺激した That poem *stimulated* her imagination. ‖ 隣の家で魚を焼く匂いが食欲を刺激する The smell of broiling fish from next door *whets my appetite* [*makes my mouth water*]. (➤ whet は「(食欲などを)そそる」; make ~'s mouth water は「～によだれを出させる」) ‖ この溶液には刺激臭がある This solution has *an irritating* [*pungent*] *odor*. ‖ 胃の悪い人はコーヒーのような刺激物は避けたほうがよい People with stomach trouble should avoid *stimulants* such as coffee.

2【感情に働きかける力】 **stimulation**; **excitement** 一動 **刺激する** **stimulate** +目, **excite** +目; **provoke** +目（怒らせる）▶東京は田舎の子には刺激があり過ぎる Tokyo is too *stimulating* [*exciting*] for young people from the country. ‖ 若者たちは村の刺激のない生活には耐えられない Young people can't stand *a dull life* [*a life without excitement*] in a village. ‖ これ以上先方 [バス乗っ取り犯] を刺激しないほうがいい We shouldn't further *provoke* the other party [the bus hijacker]. ‖ お父さんは今低気圧だから刺激しちゃいけないよ Your father is in a bad mood, so don't *irritate* [*annoy*] him. (➤ irritate は「いらいらさせる」; annoy は「むっとさせる」) ‖ その映画は私には刺激が強すぎた That movie *was too much* [*too exciting*] for me.

3【意欲を起こさせること】 動 **刺激する** **inspire** +目（感化する）; **motivate** +目（やる気を起こさせる）; **encourage** +目（励ます）▶ケネディ大統領の演説は多くのアメリカ人にとって刺激となった President Kennedy's speech *inspired* [*motivated*] many Americans.

しげしげ **1【頻繁に】** ▶彼はしげしげとその女性のもとに通った He *often* [*frequently*] went to see the woman. (➤ 後者はやや堅い語で, 時間の間隔が比較的短いことを暗示する).
2【じっと】 ▶老人は私の顔をしげしげと見た The elder-

ly man studied my face *intently*.

しけつ 止血《医学》**hemostasis** /hìːmoʊstéɪsɪs/,《英》**haemostasis** ▶止血する *stop bleeding*.

じけつ 自決 ‖**民族自決権** the right to [of] self-determination. →自死.

しげみ 茂み bushes(低木の); a **thicket**(雑木林)▶茂みで用足しをする relieve oneself in the *bushes* ‖ 木の茂みに隠れる hide in *a thicket*.

1**しける 湿気る** ▶この煎餅しけてるよ These *senbei* (rice crackers) *have gotten soft* [*soggy*]. ‖この味付けのりは缶に入れておかなかったからしけてしまった These sheets of seasoned nori *have gotten soft* [*soggy*] since I forgot to put them in the can.

2**しける 時化る** ▶海がしけて(=荒れて)いる The sea is *rough* [*stormy*].

▶しけた顔するな! Don't look so *glum*! ‖ 徹夫おじさんのお年玉, 3000円しかなかったよ. しけてんの(=けちだ) Uncle Tetsuo gave me only 3,000 yen as a New Year's gift. He's quite *tight*.

しげる 茂る grow thick ▶雑草が庭一面に茂っている Weeds *grow thick* everywhere in the garden. /The garden *is overgrown with* weeds. ‖ 構内のクスの木が青々と茂っている The camphor trees on the campus *are thick with green foliage*. ‖ 向こうにこんもりと茂った丘が見える You can see a *thickly-wooded* hill over there.

1**しけん 試験** **1【学校などの】** an **examination**, an **exam**(通例大きい試験); a **test**(主に実力テスト);《米》a **quiz**(小テスト)

> **語法** (1)一般語は examination で, インフォーマルでは exam と短縮することが多い.
> (2)test は exam(ination)と同意で用いることも多いが, 入試のような選抜試験には用いられない. →**入試**.

▶試験に受かる[落ちる] pass [fail] *an exam* ‖ 英語の試験を受ける take [have] an English *examination* ‖ 試験がなければ高校生活はもっと楽しいのに High school would be a lot more fun if we had no *examinations*. ‖ 来週物理の小試験がある We're going to have [take] *a quiz* in physics next week. ‖ 試験の範囲は教科書の50ページから150ページまでです The *test* will cover pages 50 to 150 of the text. ‖ ここは必ず試験に出る This part will surely *be on the test*. ‖ 今は試験勉強で忙しいんだよ I'm busy *preparing* [*cramming*] *for the exam*. (➤ cram は「詰め込み勉強をする」) ‖ 彼は試験中にカンニングして見つかった He was caught cheating *during the test*. ‖ **対話**「世界史の試験はどうだった?」「まあまあだな」"How was the world history *exam*?" "Not that bad, I guess."

▶**【一般の】** 姉はきのう運転免許試験に合格した My (older) sister passed her *driving test* yesterday. ‖ 外交官試験は難関だ *Examinations to enter the diplomatic services* are extremely difficult. ‖ 妹は国家試験にパスしてスペイン語のガイドになった My sister passed *the national examination* and became a Spanish-speaking guide. ‖ 英語教師になるには筆記試験のほかに英語の面接試験にパスしなくてはなりません You have to pass *an interview* in English as well as *a written exam* to become an English teacher. (➤「口述試験」は oral exam).

2【性能検査】 a **test** ▶この車の試験運転をあす行います We are going to *test-drive* this car tomorrow. ‖ リニアモーターカーはまだ試験段階だ The linear motor car is still in the *experimental stage*.

‖**試験科目** an examination subject ‖ **試験官** an examiner(➤「試験を監督する人」は proctor という) ‖ **試験場** an examination room(試験を行う部屋); an experiment station(試験して研究する建物) ‖ **試験問題** an examination problem [question] ‖ **試験用紙** an examination paper ‖ **学年末試験** a final examination ‖ **期末試験** a term-end [an end-of-(the-) term] examination / a final examination ‖ **教員免許試験** a teacher certification exam ‖ **資格試験** a qualifying examination ‖ **司法試験** a bar exam ‖ **就職試験** an employment examination ‖ **昇進試験** a promotion exam ‖ **選抜試験** a selection [screening] examination ‖ **卒業試験** a graduation exam, an exit exam ‖ **追試験** a makeup [supplementary] examination.

☛ **再試験, 試験管, 無試験**(→見出語)

2**しけん 私見** one's (**own**) **opinion** [**view**] ▶地球温暖化に関して私見を述べる give one's *opinion* on global warming.

しげん 資源 resources ▶天然資源 *natural resources* ‖ 海底資源 *submarine resources* ‖ 人的資源 *human resources* ‖ 水[石油]資源 *water* [*oil*] *resources* ‖ 資源を開発する develop (the) *resources* ‖ 日本は鉱物資源は乏しいが, 水産資源は豊かだ Japan is poor in *mineral resources*, but rich in *marine resources*. ‖ 地下資源には限りがある There is a limit to *underground resources*. ‖ 私たちは地球上の木材資源を浪費している We are wasting the earth's *timber resources*.

じけん 事件 an **event**(特別な出来事); an **incident**(異常, または不愉快な事); a **happening**(偶発的な); a **case**(殺人など, 警察が捜査する)▶事件を調べる investigate *an incident* ‖ 2012年の最も重要な事件は何だったと思いますか What do you feel was the most important *event* of 2012? ‖ 猫がこの1週間帰って来ないのは, わが家にとって重大事件だ Our cat has been missing for the past week. It's *a major incident* [*happening*] for our family. ‖ 私はその事件とは何の関わりもありません I have nothing to do with that *incident*. ‖ 弟は15歳のときに事件を起こした My younger brother *got into trouble* [*caused an incident*] when he was fifteen. ‖ その殺人事件が発生したのは5年前の6月である That *murder* (*case*) occurred in June five years ago. ‖ 以前近所の銀行で強盗事件があった There once was *a robbery* [*a holdup*] at a nearby bank. (➤ この文では「事件」は訳語としては現れない).

> **逆引き熟語 ○○事件**
> **暗殺事件** an assassination / **医療過誤事件** a (medical) malpractice case / **汚職事件** a corruption scandal [case] / **刑事事件** a criminal case / **詐欺事件** a fraud case / **殺人事件** a murder (case), a homicide / **贈収賄事件** a bribery case / **テロ事件** a terrorist incident / **盗難事件** a burglary(忍び込み); a theft(窃盗) / **発砲事件** a shooting incident

1**じげん 時限** **1【時を限ること】** ▶空港で強力な時限爆弾が爆発して, 5人が死亡した A powerful *time bomb* went off at the airport, killing five people. ‖**時限スト** a limited-time strike, a time-limited strike ‖ **時限装置** a timing device; a

timer (device).
2【学校の】 a **period**, an **hour**; (a) **class**（授業）▶きょうの1時限目は休講です Today's *first class* is canceled. ／We have no class in *the first period* today.

2**じげん 次元** a **dimension**（数学の）; a **level**（レベル）▶四次元 *the fourth dimension* ‖三次元の空間 *three-dimensional* space ‖高［低］次元の *high-*［*low-*］*dimensional*.
▶《比喩的》彼らの会話は次元の低い［高い］ものだな It sounds like they're having a *lowbrow*［an *elevated*］conversation.

しけんかん 試験管 a **test tube** ▶試験管を使った実験 an *in vitro* experiment ／an experiment *in vitro*（➤ in vitro /ɪn víːtroʊ/ は「ガラス器の中の［で］」の意味のラテン語から）.
‖試験管ベビー a test-tube baby（⇀体外受精）.

しこ 四股 (sumo) **warm-up stamping** ▶しこを踏む *do warm-up stamping exercises*.

1**しご 私語** ▶演奏中は私語を慎むべきだ You should *not talk* during the performance. ‖授業中の私語は耳障りだ The *talking*［*whispering*］in class is distracting.

2**しご 死後** ▶シューベルトの『未完成交響曲』は彼の死後37年たってから世に出た The "Unfinished Symphony" by Schubert saw the light of day 37 years *after his death*. ‖この傑作は彼の死後に出版された This masterpiece of his was published *posthumously*.（➤ 発音は /pɑ́ːstʃəməsli/）‖死後硬直は死後2時間で始まる *Rigor mortis* sets in［starts］about two hours after death.（➤ /rìgəʳ mɔ́ːʳṭɪs/ と発音）.

3**しご 死語** a **dead language**（現在使われていない言語; 例えばラテン語）; an **obsolete** /ɑ̀ːbsəlíːt/ **word**（廃語）▶お父さん,「アベック」なんてもう死語よ Dad, nobody says 'abekku' anymore.

1**じこ 自己** **self** ▶自己を過信してはいけない Don't be too sure of *yourself*. ／Don't be overconfident. ‖彼女は自己顕示欲が強い She *wants to stand out*.（➤「目立ちたがる」の意）‖彼は自己主張が強い He *is very self-assertive*. ‖彼はいつも自己中心的で, 他人に対する思いやりがない He is *self-centered*［*egocentric*］and (is) inconsiderate of others. ‖自己紹介をします Let me *introduce myself*. ／May I *introduce myself*? ‖交通費は自己負担してください Please *pay your own* fare. ‖彼は自分の学業成績に自己満足していた He *was complacent* about［with］his performance at school.（➤ 現状に満足して怠けるのは complacent. 類語の self-satisfied は達成したことに満足してうぬぼれることで, さらに上を目指さないわけではない）‖ボランティア活動をするときは, 自己満足で終わらぬよう気を付けるべきだ When you take part in volunteer activities, you shouldn't be *self-satisfied*［you shouldn't *congratulate yourself*］just because you are taking part in them.（➤ congratulate oneself は「自分で自分をほめる, よくやったと胸を張る」）. ‖彼は試験に失敗して以来自己嫌悪に陥っている Since he failed the exam, he's been wallowing in *self-hatred*［*self-hate*］. ‖私のチェロは全くの自己流です I *taught myself* the cello and *play* it *in my own style*.
‖自己暗示 autosuggestion ‖自己啓発 self-development ‖自己実現 self-fulfillment［self-actualization ／self-realization］（➤ 後者二者は意志と努力で偉業を達成する意味が含まれる）‖自己批判 self-criticism ‖自己弁護 self-justification.

2**じこ 事故** an **accident**; a **mishap**（小事故）▶事故に遭う have *an accident* ‖事故を起こす cause［bring about］*an accident* ‖それは事件それとも事故? Is it an incident or *an accident*? ‖30分も遅れるなんて, 何か事故があったに違いない They're 30 minutes late. They must have had *an accident*. ‖私たちの修学旅行は何の事故もなく済んだ Our school excursion ended *without any mishaps*.
▶水難事故 an *accident* at sea［on a river ／on a lake］（➤ 海での［河川での ／湖での］事故）‖耕一はスピードを出し過ぎて交通事故を起こした Koichi speeded and caused *a traffic accident*. ‖友人は自動車事故で重傷を負った A friend of mine got seriously injured in *a car accident*. ‖その列車事故で3人が死亡し, 20人が負傷した Three people were killed and twenty injured in that *railroad accident*. ‖飛行機事故が怖いから飛行機には乗りたくない I don't like to travel by air because I'm afraid of being in *a plane crash*.（➤ crash は「墜落」）‖警察はこの町で事故防止運動を進めている The police are now promoting *a safety-first movement* in this town.
‖事故多発地帯《米》an accident-prone area ／high-accident zone;《英》a black spot.
☛ 無事故（⇀見出語）

じご 事後 ▶彼は父に結婚の事後承諾を求めた He asked his father for *approval after he got married*. ‖管財人は倒産の事後処理に追われている The receiver is busy *dealing with the aftermath* of the company's bankruptcy.
‖事後報告 an ex post facto report（➤ ex post facto は「事後の」の意のラテン語起源の慣用句）.

1**しこう 思考** **thought**, **thinking**（➤ 前者には「思考力」の意もある）**一動 思考する** **think** ▶思考と行動 *thought* and action ‖明せきな思考 clear *thinking* ‖プラス［マイナス］思考 positive［negative］*thinking* ‖動物には思考力はないのだろうか I wonder if animals have the *ability to think*. ‖疲れてくると思考力が鈍る The more tired you get, the *less well you can think*. ‖私は(突然)思考停止に陥った My brain froze［stopped working］. ／I (suddenly) became unable to *think*.

2**しこう 施行** **enforcement** **一動 施行する** **enforce** +目（法を）; **put ... in force**［**operation**］（効力を発揮させる）▶法律［規則］を施行する *enforce* a law［a rule］‖その法律は2009年から施行されている The law *has been in force* since 2009. ‖新しいダイヤは4月1日から施行される The new schedule *goes into effect* on April 1.
‖施行期間 an implementation period.

3**しこう 嗜好** a **taste**（好み）▶年を取るにつれて食べ物のしこうがすっかり変わった As I have grown older, my *tastes* in food have completely changed. ‖たばこ, コーヒーなどのしこう品 cigarettes, coffee and other *non-essential items*.

4**しこう 志向の** **-oriented**（➤ 名詞のあとにつけて「…志向の」の意で用いる）▶福祉志向の国 a welfare-*oriented* country ‖ステファニーはブランド志向の女性だ Stephany is a brand-［designer-］*conscious* woman. ‖現代の若者は仕事第一よりマイホーム志向型が多い Young people today are more *home oriented* than work oriented.

5**しこう 至高の** **supreme** ▶ミケランジェロは彫刻こそ至高の芸術と信じていた Michelangelo believed that sculpture was the *supreme* art.

6**しこう 歯垢** **plaque** /plæk, plɑːk/ ▶歯こうを取る remove *plaque*.

1**じこう 時効** **the period of limitations**（刑事訴訟において公訴できる期限）; **prescription**（民事訴訟における権利・義務などの時効）▶その事件は来年**時効になる**ので, 警察は解決に躍起になっている The police are redoubling their efforts to solve the case because *the statute of limitations runs out* next year.（➤ the statute of limitations は「公訴できる期限を定めた法律」）‖ 彼は**時効により**その借金から解放された He has been released from that debt *by prescription*.

▶《比喩的》もう**時効**だと思うから言っちゃうけど, 彼女, 学生時代すごく遊んでたのよ It's *ancient history* now, so I'm sure it's OK to tell you. She played around a lot when she was in college.（➤ ancient history は「遠い昔の話」の意のインフォーマルな言い方）.

2**じこう 事項** a **matter**（事柄）; an **item**（項目）; a **subject**（題目）▶**討議事項** an *agenda item* ／a *topic of discussion* ‖ 続いて**関連事項**を討議しましょう Let's go [move] on to discuss *related matters* [*subjects*]. ‖ まず**注意事項**をよく読みなさい First, read *the directions* carefully.

3**じこう 時候** ▶時候の挨拶表現 a *seasonal* greeting.

じごう 次号 **the next issue**（雑誌などの）▶**次号に続く** To be continued.

しこうさくご 試行錯誤 **trial and error** ▶新製品は**試行錯誤**の繰り返しの中から生まれることが多い New products often result from a process of *trial and error*.

じごうじとく 自業自得 ▶そりゃあ**自業自得だ** *You asked for it*. ‖ おまえが失敗したのは**自業自得**だよ Your failure *is your own fault*. ／Your failure is *of your own making*. ‖ だからあんな男と結婚するなと言ったのに！夏子の**自業自得**なんだからほっときなさい I told Natsuko not to marry such a man! She *made her bed, so let her lie in it*.（➤ 決まり文句）.

しごき **hard training**（きつい訓練）; **hazing**（新入生に対するいじめ）▶空手部のしごきにより学生の１人が死亡した A student died during *hazing* [while *being hazed*] by other karate club members.

1**しごく** **1**【**勢いよく引きこする**】▶あのおじいさんはよく顎ひげをしごいていたものだ That old man would often *stroke* his beard.

2【**厳しく鍛える**】▶上級生が新入部員をしごいた The older students *worked* the new members of their club *hard*. ／The older students *hazed* the new members of their club.（➤ 後者は「いじめ」の場合）.

2**しごく 至極** ▶彼が怒るのは**至極**当然だ It is *quite* natural that he should get angry. ‖ ２人の仲は**至極円満だ** The couple are getting along *extremely well* [getting along *famously*] (with each other).（➤ get along [on] famously は「馬が合う」や「意気投合する」に当たる決まった言い方）.

1**じこく 時刻** **time** ▶約束の［出発の］**時刻** the appointed [starting] *time* ‖ 今, **時刻**は11時半です The *time* is 11：30. ‖ 正確な**時刻**を教えていただけますか Could you tell me the exact *time*?

‖**時刻表**《米》a time schedule（➤ 列車・バスなどを明示する場合は time の代わりに train, bus などを用いる）,《英》a timetable.

2**じこく 自国** one's **own country**, one's **native land** ▶外国語を**自国語のように**話すのは不可能ではない It is not impossible to speak a foreign language *like a native* [*with native fluency*].（➤ native は「本国人(の)」）‖ **自国語** one's mother tongue, one's native language. → 母国語.

じごく 地獄 **hell**

> 【解説】「地獄」は仏教では, 現世で悪業を重ねた者が死後その報いを受けるとされる所, また, 前世における罪業の結果としての現状や境遇をいう. これに対して, hell はキリスト教で, 救われない魂が落ちて永遠にさまよう恐ろしい世界をいう.

▶この世の**地獄** (*a*) *hell* on earth ‖ そんな悪事を働くと**地獄に落ちるぞ** If you do such an evil thing, you'll *go to hell*.（➤ 多くのキリスト教徒は地獄を信じているので, こういうことは軽々しく言わない. 悪行を悔悟して地獄に落ちないように努める）.

［ことわざ］**地獄の沙汰も金次第** Even the judgment of hell depends on money.（➤ 日本語からの直訳）／Money makes the world go (a)round.（➤「金は世の中を動かす」の意の英語のことわざ）.

▶《比喩的》いじめられてばかりいる生徒にとって学校は**地獄だ** For those schoolchildren who are always being bullied, school is (*a*) *hell*. ‖ この会社を興すときに彼は**地獄の苦しみを味わった** He *went through hell* to build (up) this company. ‖ 日本のサラリーマンの大半は**通勤地獄**に耐えねばならない Most Japanese office workers have to endure the daily *hell of crowded commuter trains*. ‖ この子供たちもやがては**受験地獄**に立ち向かわねばならないのだ These children will have to take *a frightful series of exams* [will have to face *the hellish examination system*] soon.（➤「受験［試験］地獄」は直訳して examination hell ともいう）‖ そのうわさなら彼女はとうに知っていたよ. **地獄耳**だからね She already knew that rumor. *She hears everything*, you know.

しこしこ ▶アワビのしこしこした歯触り the *chewy quality* of abalone (flesh).

▶彼女, しこしこ宿題やってるよ She'*s plugging away at* her homework.（➤ plug away at は「…をこつこつやる」）.

しごせん 子午線 a **meridian** /mərídiən/.

しこたま ▶彼らはその取り引きでしこたまもうけた They *made a killing* [*a good haul*] on the deal.

しごと 仕事 **1**【**勤め, 職業**】a **job**, **work**

> 【語法】(1) job が「(収入を伴う)具体的な仕事」「勤め口」の意であるのに対し, work は「職」「働くこと」の意の抽象概念を表す. １つの仕事は a task.
> (2) work は「仕事」の意では常に Ⓤ.

▶軽い**仕事** an easy *job* ‖ 給料のいい**仕事** a high-paying *job* ‖ 新しい**仕事を探す** look for a new *job* ‖ **仕事を辞める** leave [quit] one's *job* ‖ **仕事を持つ** [**持っている**] hold [have] *a job* ‖ 私は今**仕事がない**（＝失業している）I'm *out of work* [*a job*] now. ／I am *unemployed* [*jobless*] now. ‖ **仕事を持つ女性が増えている** The number of *working women* [*women with jobs*] has increased. ‖ **仕事を次から次へと変える**のは望ましいことではない *Job-hopping* is not advisable. ‖ 教師はやりがいのある**仕事**（＝職業）です Being a teacher is a fulfilling [rewarding] *occupation*. ‖ 〔対話〕「お仕事は何をなさっていますか」「公

認会計士です」"What do you do (for a living)?" "I'm a certified public accountant."

あなたの英語はどう響く?
知り合ってすぐの外国人に「お仕事は何をなさってますか」と聞くとき, What is your occupation? とすると, 相手には税関などで係官に職業を尋ねられているように響くことがあるので要注意. 上の対話例のように聞くか, What kind of work do you do? のように聞く. 日本への観光客には, 例えば Are you here on business [vacation]? (仕事[休暇]でいらっしゃったのですか) のような無難な質問から始めて, 次第に話題を広げていくほうがよい.

2【働くこと】work (遊びに対する) ; **business** (商売すること) ; a **task** (必ずしなければならないこと) ; **duties** (任務) ; **household chores** (家での毎日の雑用) 一動 **仕事をする work** ▶彼は**仕事**第一だ *Work* is his No.1 priority. ‖ この**仕事**はきょう中に終えなければならない This *job* [*task*] has to be finished today. ‖ さあ**仕事を始めよう** Let's *get to work*. ‖ 彼は**仕事をせずに**家でごろごろしている He *doesn't work* and lies around at home. ‖ あの女の子は**仕事が遅い** That young woman *is a slow worker*. ‖ 彼女は**仕事がよくできる** She *is a capable worker*.
▶困難な**仕事**を成し遂げる accomplish a difficult *task* ‖ 兄は**仕事に追われて**恋人とデートする暇もない My brother is *so busy* he doesn't even have time to take his girlfriend out. ‖ **仕事で**あすマレーシアへ行きます I'm leaving for Malaysia *on business* tomorrow.
▶合宿では洗濯と掃除は1年生の**仕事**です At training camp, washing clothes and cleaning the room are freshmen *duties*. ‖ 子供には**家の仕事**をさせたほうがよい You should have your children do *household chores*. ‖ 彼は**仕事の鬼**だ He's *a workaholic*. (➤ 文脈によっては「仕事中毒の人」の意になる) ‖ 姉は**仕事の話ばかりしている** My sister always *talks shop*. (➤ talk shop は文字どおりには「自分の店の話をする」だが,「(時・所をかまわず)仕事の話をする」の意で用いられる) ‖ 父にとっては何事よりも**仕事**優先だ For my father, *work* takes priority over everything else. ‖ **仕事中**は面会できません I can't see you *while I'm on duty*. ‖ **仕事中**にたばこを吸ってはだめだよ Don't smoke *on the job* [*while you are working*]. ‖ 彼女は**仕事柄**いろいろな人と会う *Because of the nature of her business*, she meets various kinds of people.
‖**仕事着** work clothes ‖ **仕事場** a workshop, a place of work ‖ **仕事始め** (新年の) the first working day of the New Year ‖ **仕事部屋** a workroom ; a studio /stjúːdioʊ/ (アトリエ).

しこな 醜名・四股名 a sumo wrestler's ring name (➤ 説明的な訳).

しこむ 仕込む 1【覚えさせる】teach +目 ; **train** +目 (訓練する) ▶妹は犬に芸を**仕込む**のがうまい My sister is good at *teach*ing dogs tricks.
2【準備する】ready +目 ; **stock up** (買い込む)
▶前の晩に**仕込んだ**材料 ingredients *readied* the night before ‖ キャンプ用に食料をたっぷりと**仕込んだ** We *stocked up on* food for camping.
3【身につける】▶新知識を**仕込む** *acquire* [*pick up*] new knowledge.

しこり 1【腫れ物】a lump ▶彼女は乳房に**しこり**を発見したので医者に行った She went to the doctor after finding *a lump* in her breast.
2【気まずい感情】▶そのもめ事は2人の間に**しこり**を残した That conflict left some *hard* [*bad*] *feelings* between the two.

じこりゅう 自己流 →自己.

じこる 事故る ▶彼女は新車に乗り始めてすぐ**事故った** She *had* [*caused*] *an accident* soon after she began driving around in her new car.

しさ 示唆 (a) **suggestion** 一動 **示唆する suggest** +目 ▶彼の講演は**示唆に富んでいた** His lecture was *thought-provoking* [*stimulating*]. ‖ 首相は増税の可能性を**示唆した** The Prime Minister *suggested* [*hinted at*] the possibility of a tax increase.

じさ 時差 time difference ▶ 対話「東京・シドニー間の**時差**はどのくらいですか」「1時間ですが, サマータイム中は2時間です」"What's the *time difference* between Tokyo and Sydney?" "An hour, but two hours during daylight saving(s) time."
▶私はまだ**時差ぼけ**で困っている I am still suffering from *jet lag*. (➤「時差ぼけする」は have jet lag) ‖ わが社は冬の間は**時差出勤を採用している** Our company *staggers the commuting time* of its workers in wintertime. (➤ stagger は「ずらす」).

¹**しさい 司祭** a **priest** /priːst/.

²**しさい 子細 detail(s)** ▶交渉経過を**子細に記す** note down the progress of the negotiations *in careful detail*.

¹**しざい 私財** one's (**own**) **money** [**funds**] ; one's (**private**) **property** (全財産) ▶彼は**私財をなげうって**この学校を創立した He *donated* his *own funds* to found this school.

²**しざい 資材 materials**
‖**建築資材** building materials.

じざい 自在 ▶彼女はスウェーデン語を**自由自在に操る** She speaks Swedish *fluently*. / She *has* (*a*) *good command of* Swedish. (➤ 後者は「駆使する能力がある」の意に近い堅い言い方) ‖ このスポーツシャツの生地は**伸縮自在だ** This sport shirt *is made of stretch* [*stretchy*] *fabric* [*cloth*].

¹**しさく 思索 thought, thinking** ▶彼は今**思索にふけっている** He is *deep in thought* [*contemplation*]. (➤ contemplation は「熟考」の意) ‖ 彼はどちらかと言うと**思索の人**だ He is, if anything, *a man of thought* [*a thinking man*].

²**しさく 試作 trial manufacture** [**production**]
‖**試作品** a prototype (ひな型) ; a sample (見本).

³**しさく 施策** a **policy** (政策) ; **measures** (対策) ; a **program** (事業計画) ▶政府は景気浮揚のための有効な**施策を打てないでいる** The government hasn't yet adopted [carried out] effective *measures* to boost the economy.

じさく 自作 ▶年賀状に**自作**の俳句を書く write *one's own* haiku on a New Year's greeting card ‖ 彼は**自作自演**の歌で我々を楽しませてくれた He entertained us by singing songs *he had written himself* [*of his own composition*]. ‖ これは竹田氏の**自作自演**の映画だ Mr. Takeda *both directed and starred* in this movie. ‖**自作農** a land owner [an independent] farmer.

じざけ 地酒 local [**locally-made** / **locally-brewed**] **sake**.

¹**しさつ 視察** (an) **inspection** (査察) ; **observation** (観察) 一動 **視察する inspect** +目 ▶学校を**視察する** *make an inspection of* a school ‖ 産廃処理工場の**視察に出かける** *go for a tour* around an industrial

waste treatment plant ‖ 会長自ら新工場を**視察した** The chairman *inspected* the new plant personally. ‖ 大臣は被害状況をつかむため**現地を視察した** The Minister *made an on-site inspection* [*an inspection tour*] *of the disaster area* to find out the real situation. ‖ 社長は現在カナダを**視察旅行中**です The president is *on a survey* [*an inspection*] *tour* in Canada.

‖**視察団** an inspection team, a group of inspectors, an observation group.

2**しさつ** 動 **刺殺する** **stab ... to death**；《野球》**put ... out**（➤ 名詞形は put-out）.

じさつ 自殺 (a) **suicide** /sú:ɪsaɪd/ 一動 **自殺する** **commit suicide, kill** oneself ▶**自殺を図る** attempt *suicide* ‖ **首つり自殺をする** *hang oneself* (*to death*) ‖ **集団自殺する** *commit a mass* [*group*] *suicide* ‖ 新興宗教の信者たちの**集団自殺** *the mass suicide* of cult members ‖ **ピストル自殺をする** *shoot oneself to death* ‖ **服毒自殺をする** *kill oneself* [*commit suicide*] *by taking poison* ‖ **ガス自殺をする** *commit gas suicide* ／ *kill oneself by turning on the gas heater* 《参考》自動車の排気ガスによるガス自殺を a motor vehicle exhaust gas suicide という.

▶彼はノイローゼにかかり**自殺した** He suffered from a nervous breakdown and *committed suicide*. ‖ 軽装で冬の北アルプスに登るなんて**自殺行為だ** It is *suicidal* to climb the Northern Alps in winter in very light clothing.

✉ **日本では学校でのいじめが原因の自殺が増えてきています** In Japan, there has been an increasing number of *suicides* caused by bullying in schools.

✉ **《悩み事相談で》時々本気で自殺したくなることがあります** There are times when I really *want to kill myself*.

‖**自殺者** a suicide ‖ **自殺未遂** an attempted suicide.

1**しさん 資産** a **fortune**；**assets**（個人・会社の）；**property**（有形財産）▶当社の創業者は一代で**資産を築いた** Our founder *made a fortune* in his lifetime. ‖ 閣僚の**資産**が公開された The Cabinet ministers' *assets* were made public. ‖ 彼女は**資産家**と結婚した She married *a rich* [*wealthy*] *man*.

‖**固定資産** fixed [permanent] assets ‖ **流動資産** current assets.

2**しさん 試算** a **trial estimate**, a **calculation** 一動 **試算する** **make a trial estimate** ▶私の**試算**では旅費は10万円で十分でしょう According to my *trial estimate* [my *calculation*], 100,000 yen should be enough for our traveling expenses.

しざん 死産 a **stillbirth** ▶彼女の最初の子は**死産だった** Her first child *was stillborn*.

じさん 持参する **bring** +目（持って来る）；**take** +目（持って行く）▶当日は必ず印鑑をご**持参ください** Don't forget to *bring* your hanko stamp *with* you on the day. ‖ 全員弁当**持参**だった Each of us *brought* our own lunch.

‖**持参金** a dowry /dáʊri/.

しし 獅子 《動物》a **lion**；a **lioness**（雌）

‖**獅子鼻** a pug nose ‖ **獅子舞** *shishimai*, a dance performed with a lion's mask（➤ 説明的な訳）.

☛ **獅子座**（⇀見出語）

1**しじ 支持** **support**（応援, 励まし）；**favor**（是認, 引き立て）一動 **支持する** **support** +目, **favor** +目 ▶有権者の広範な**支持**を得る win broad *support* from the voters ‖ その運動を**支持して**スピーチをする make a speech *in support of* the movement ‖ 私は校長を**支持します** I *support* the principal. ‖ あなたはどの党を**支持していますか**？ Which party do you *support*？ ‖ 私はその計画を**支持する** I *favor* the plan. ‖ ぼくは木下君の案を**支持します** I'*m in favor of* Kinoshita's proposal. ‖ クラス全員の**支持**を受けて高橋君が生徒会長に立候補した Having the *support* [*backing*] of his whole class, Takahashi stood for President of the student council. ‖ その内閣の**支持率**は15パーセントまで急降下した The government's *approval rating* has plunged to 15%.

‖**支持者** a supporter；an advocate /ǽdvəkət/（主義・説などの）.

2**しじ 指示** **directions**（ことばによる指図）；**instructions**（やり方に関する具体的な指示）一動 **指示する** **direct** +目, **instruct** +目 ▶**人の指示に従う** follow a person's *directions* ‖ 私は部長の**指示**で書類を焼却した I burned the documents *as directed* [*instructed*] by the general manager. ‖ **指示**をよくお聞きください Listen carefully to the *instructions*. ‖ 医者は患者にすぐ精密検査を受けるよう**指示した** The doctor *instructed* the patient to have a thorough (physical) examination immediately. ‖ **指示語**《文法》a demonstrative ‖ **指示代名詞**《文法》a demonstrative pronoun.

3**しじ 師事** ▶私はロンドン大学のQ教授に**師事して**英語学を学んだ I studied English linguistics *under* Professor Q at the University of London.

4**しじ 私事** a **personal matter** [**affair**] ▶**私事**で恐縮ですが, 来月第１子が生まれます Excuse me for bringing up a *personal matter*, but our first baby will be born next month.

じし 自死 a **voluntary death** ▶**自死を選ぶ** choose a *voluntary death* ／choose to *voluntarily die*. ‖ 彼は**自死した** He *ended his* (*own*) *life*.（➤「自ら命を絶った」と「一生を終えた」の両方の意味がある）.

じじ 時事 ▶この雑誌では**時事的な**問題はあまり扱わない This magazine doesn't deal much with *current* events [*topical* issues].

‖**時事英語** English for current topics（➤ current English とすると modern English（現代の英語）の意に解される）／(standard) English used in the media, media English.

じじこっこく 時々刻々 ▶**時々刻々**変化する世界情勢を伝えるのがマスコミの役割だ It's the media's duty to report the *constantly* changing world situation.

ししざ 獅子座 (a) **Leo** /lí:oʊ/, **the Lion**.

ししつ 資質 a **talent**；a **gift**（天賦の）▶彼はリーダーとしての**資質**がある He has *a talent* for leadership.

しじつ 史実 (a) **historical fact** ▶これは**史実**に基づいた小説である This is a novel (which is) based on *historical fact*.

じじつ 事実 1【**実際に起こったこと**】(a) **fact**；**truth**（真実）▶**事実を調べる** check *a fact* ‖ それは**事実**に反する It is against [contrary to] the *facts*. ‖ **事実**は小説よりも奇なり *Fact* [*Truth*] is stranger than fiction.（➤ 英語のことわざ）‖ 私は確かな**事実**が知りたい I want hard *facts*.（➤ hard は「厳然たる」）‖ 今私が言ったことは**事実**です What I have told you so far is *factual*. ‖ それが**事実か事実でないか**調べてください Please investigate this and find out *if it is true or not* (*true*). ‖ 正直に**事実**を述べなさい Be honest and tell the *truth*. ‖ きみがよく

出席していたのは**事実**だが，宿題をやらなかったね *It is true* that you had good attendance in the class, *but* you did not do the assigned homework. (➤ It is true (that) ... のあとに, but ～ がくる形もよく使われる) ‖ **事実関係**を調べよう Let's investigate *what really happened*. ‖ 彼のぼくに対する非難は**事実無根**だ His criticism of me *has no basis in fact* [*is groundless*].

2【実際に, 本当に】▶**事実**私は何も知らないのです *Really* [*In fact* ／*Actually*], I don't know anything (about it).

3【実際の】▶英語は**事実上**世界語である English is the *de facto* global language. (➤ de facto は「事実上の」) ／English is *virtually* the global language. (➤ virtually は「ほとんど…同然」の意) ‖ 上田社長は名前のみで木村氏が**事実上の**社長です Mr. Ueda is the president in name only. Mr. Kimura is the *real* [*de facto*] president. ‖ 斉藤対近藤の試合が**事実上の**決勝戦だった The match between Saito and Kondo was *in reality* the final match.

しじみ《貝》a ***shijimi*** ; a **kind of small freshwater clam.**

1**ししゃ 死者** a **dead person** (1人) ; a **fatality** /feɪtǽləṭi/ (事故などによる死亡者数) 《参考》「死者」は総称的には the dead(複数扱い)という.「(最近)亡くなった人」というような敬意を込めた表現は the deceased. これは通例1人を指すが, 複数にも用いる.

▶**死者**にむち打つなかれ Speak well of *the dead*. ‖ 幸いその事故で乗客に**死者は出なかった** Fortunately, *none* of the passengers *were killed* in the accident. ／Fortunately *there were no fatalities* in the accident. ‖ その飛行機墜落事故は**多数の死者を出した** *Many lives were lost* in the plane crash. ／The plane crash *took many lives* [*a heavy toll of lives*]. (➤ life は「人命」; toll は「犠牲」).

2**ししゃ 支社** a **branch (office)** ▶大阪**支社** the Osaka *branch office* ‖ ぼくの父はトヨタのニューヨーク**支社**に駐在しています My father works at Toyota's New York *office*.

‖**支社長** a branch (office) manager.

3**ししゃ 試写** a **preview** /príːvjuː/ ▶あす, この映画の**試写会**を行います We will give *a preview* of this film tomorrow.

4**ししゃ 使者** a **messenger** ▶**使者**を送る send *a messenger* ‖ ウグイスは春を告げる**使者**です The bush warbler is a [the] *messenger* [*herald*] of spring. (➤ herald は「先駆け」の意の文語).

ししゃく 子爵 a **viscount** /váɪkaʊnt/

‖**子爵夫人** a viscountess /váɪkaʊnṭəs/.

じしゃく 磁石 a **magnet** (マグネット) ; a **compass** /kʌ́mpəs/ (コンパス) ▶**磁石**で北の方角を知る find north with *a compass* ‖ この飾りは**磁石になっている**ので冷蔵庫にくっつく This ornament *is magnetized* so you can stick it on the refrigerator.

ししゃごにゅう 四捨五入 rounding ▶4.7を**四捨五入する**と5になる 4.7 can *be rounded off* [*up*] to 5. (➤4.7は four point seven と読む).

ししゃも《魚》a ***shishamo*** **smelt.**

ししゅ 死守 ▶40%のマーケットシェアを**死守する** *keep* [*defend*] one's 40% market share *at any cost*.

1**じしゅ 自主** ▶**自主**独立の精神 an *independent* spirit ‖ 彼には**自主性**がない He doesn't have any *initiative*. ／He never *initiates* things. ‖ 生徒の**自主性**を尊重すべきだ We should respect our students' *autonomy*. ‖ **自主的な**(＝自発的な)行動 a *voluntary* act ‖ 自動車業界はアメリカ向け輸出を**自主規制した** The automobile industry *voluntarily restricted* (its) exports to the U.S. ‖ **自主的に考えて**行動しなさい Think and act *on your own judgment*.

2**じしゅ 自首** ▶警察に**自首する** *surrender* (*oneself*) to the police ／*give oneself up* to the police.

1**ししゅう 刺繍 embroidery** /ɪmbrɔ́ɪdəri/ **一動 刺しゅうする embroider** ▶金[花]の**刺しゅう** gold [floral] *embroidery* ‖ かわいい**刺しゅう**のついた買い物袋 a shopping bag covered with pretty *embroidery* ‖ 彼女はハンカチに自分のイニシャルを**刺しゅうした** She *embroidered* her initials on a handkerchief.

2**ししゅう 詩集** a **collection of poems** ▶『ロバート・バーンズ**詩集**』(書名) (*Collected*) *Poems* by Robert Burns.

1**しじゅう 四十 forty.** →よんじゅう.

2**しじゅう 始終 always, all the time.** →いつも.

1**じしゅう 自習** ▶きょうは午後の授業が**自習時間**になった The afternoon classes were changed into *self-study* [*free-study*] *hours* today. ‖ 12章は**自習して**おきなさい *Study* [*Do*] Chapter 12 *on your own*.

‖**自習室** a study hall 《参考》《米》では study hall は「自習室での学習, 自習時間」の意味で, have study hall のような用い方もする.

2**じしゅう 次週 next week** (来週) ; **the next week** (その次の週). →来週.

しじゅうから 四十雀《鳥》a **great tit** (ヨーロッパ・アジア産) 《参考》北米産の鳥ではよく似た chickadee /tʃíkədiː/ (アメリカコガラ) が同様に親しまれている. なお, tits は俗語で女性の「おっぱい」の意があるので注意.

しじゅうそう 四重奏 a **quartet** /kwɔːrtét/ (➤曲の意にも四重奏団の意にもなる) ‖**弦楽四重奏** a string quartet ‖ **ピアノ四重奏** a piano quartet.

ししゅうびょう 歯周病 a **periodontal disease.**

ししゅく 私淑 ▶私はその哲学者に**私淑している** I *admire* the philosopher *in my heart and respect* him *as my mentor*.

じしゅく 自粛 self-restraint ▶景品付きの販売競争は**自粛す**べきだ Companies that compete for sales by offering freebies should *exercise self-restraint*. ‖ その会社はホラーフィルムの輸入を**自粛した** The company (*voluntarily*) *refrained* from importing horror films.

ししゅつ 支出 expenses, 《米また》(an) **outgo,** 《英また》**outgoings** ▶先月は**支出**が多かった I had heavy *expenses* last month.

ししゅんき 思春期 puberty /pjúːbərṭi/ (肉体的に成熟して大人になり始める時期, 人によって年齢は異なるが, 一般的に, 11歳から16歳くらい) ; **adolescence** /ædəlésəns/ (子供期から脱した青年期の前半, 13歳から21歳くらいの期間) ▶**思春期**の女の子 a girl *at adolescence* ／an *adolescent* girl ／a *pubescent* girl ‖ **思春期**の思い出 memories of *one's adolescence* ‖ 息子も**思春期**にさしかかり, だんだん難しい年頃になってきた Our son is approaching (*the age of*) *puberty* and is becoming more and more difficult (to handle). (➤「思春期に達する」は reach [hit] puberty ともいう).

1**ししょ 司書** a **librarian** /laɪbréəriən/.

2**ししょ 支所** a **branch (office)** ▶パリに**支所**を設ける establish *a branch* (*office*) in Paris.

1**じしょ 辞書** a **dictionary** ; a **lexicon** (古典語の) ; a **glossary** (特定の用語辞典) ▶**辞書**を引く consult

[use／look up a word in] *a dictionary*(➤ consult は堅い語で, 主に書きことばで用いられる) ‖ 辞書に当たる refer to *a dictionary* ‖ この辞書には日常語がたくさん載っている This *dictionary* contains a lot of everyday vocabulary. ‖ 辞書と首っ引きで『あしながおじさん』を読み終えた I read through "Daddy-Long-Legs" with *a dictionary* (in my hand).
‖辞書学 lexicography(➤「辞書編集(法)」の意でも用いる) ‖ 辞書編集者 a lexicographer ‖ 電子辞書 an electronic dictionary.
ディベートルーム「電子辞書は紙の辞書に勝っている」

2**じしょ 地所** a **lot**(区画)；(a **piece of**) **land**(土地)；an **estate**(大所有地) ▶彼は事業に失敗して先祖伝来の地所を売ってしまった After failing in business, he sold the *land* that had been handed down from his ancestors.

3**じしょ 自署** one's **signature** ▶最後に自署願います Please *sign* [put *your* (*own*) *signature*] at the end.

じじょ 次女 one's **second daughter** ▶次女は大学生です *My second daughter* is a college student.

1**ししょう 支障** a **hitch**(深刻でないトラブル)；a **problem**(問題)；(a) **hindrance**(妨害, 障害)；(an) **inconvenience**(不都合, 不便) ▶総会は何の支障もなく進行した The general meeting went off *without a hitch*. ‖ このパソコンは少し古いが, メールのやり取りには支障がない Although this computer is a little old, there's *no problem* with sending or receiving emails. ‖ 彼の的外れな発言が会議の進行に支障をきたした His irrelevant remarks *hindered* the progress of the conference. (➤ hinder は(物事)を妨げる, 遅らせる) ‖ 彼の仕事に(大きな)支障となるもの *a* (serious) *hindrance* to his work ‖ 今度の日曜日は支障がある(＝都合が悪い) Next Sunday *is inconvenient* for me.

2**ししょう 師匠** a **teacher** 《参考》master も可能だが, この語は芸術の巨匠を指すことが多い. 日本の稽古事の師匠は teacher でよい ▶あの方は私の琵琶(びわ)のお師匠さんよ She is my *biwa teacher*.

1**しじょう 市場** a **market** ▶新しい市場を開拓する develop a new *market* ‖ わが社はこの春, ビデオカメラの新製品を市場に出す Our company will *market* a new model (of) video camera this spring. ‖ 米大統領は日本にアメリカ製品の市場開放を迫った The U.S. President pressed Japan to *open its market wider* to American products.
‖市場価値 market value ‖ 市場占有率 market share ‖ 市場調査 market research ‖ 売り手市場 a sellers' market ‖ 買い手市場 a buyers' market ‖ 株式市場 the stock market ‖ 金融市場 the financial market ‖ 国内[海外]市場 the home [overseas] market ‖ 住宅市場 the housing market ‖ 新興市場 an emerging market ‖ 強気[弱気]市場 a bull [bear] market.

2**しじょう 私情** **personal feelings** ▶私情にとらわれてはいけない Don't be overly influenced by your *personal feelings*. ‖ 私情を交えずお話ししましょう Let me talk to you *impartially*. (➤「公平な立場で」の意).

3**しじょう 史上** ▶テレシコワは史上初の女性宇宙飛行士だ Tereshkova was the first woman cosmonaut (*in history*). ‖ ガリレオは科学史上に永遠に名をとどめるだろう Galileo will be remembered forever *in the history of science*.

4**しじょう 紙上** ▶紙上の身上相談欄 a personal advice column *in the newspaper* ‖ 2人の婚約のニュースが紙上をにぎわせている The news of their engagement has been *in the headlines*.

5**しじょう 詩情** ▶詩情豊かな作品 a work of *poetical* [*lyrical*] *feeling* ‖ フォーレの音楽には豊かな詩情が感じ取れる *A rich poetic sensibility* is evident in Fauré's music.

6**しじょう 至上** ▶至上命令 *a supreme order*／*an order from the very top* ‖芸術至上主義 art for art's sake(➤「芸術のための芸術」の意) ‖ 白人至上主義者 a white supremacist.

7**しじょう 試乗** a **test-drive**(車などを買う前の) 一動 試乗する **test-drive** ＋目 ▶スポーツカーに試乗する *test-drive* a sports car ‖ 車を借りるときは試乗するほうがよい You should *drive* the car before you rent it. (➤ この場合, test-drive という必要はない).

じしょう 自称 ▶自称骨とう品収集家 a *self-proclaimed* antique collector ‖ その詐欺師は陶芸家と自称していた The fraud had *called himself* a ceramist.

1**じじょう 事情** **circumstances** /sə́ːˈkəmstænsɪz/(状況)；**conditions**(状態)；(a) **reason**(理由) ▶こういう事情では卒業式は延期せざるをえない *Under the circumstances* [*As things stand*], we will have to postpone the graduation ceremony. ‖ 私はやむをえない事情で大学をやめた I quit college because of *circumstances beyond my control*. ‖ どんな事情があってもおじいさんの葬儀には参列しなさい You must attend your grandfather's funeral *at any cost*. ‖ 対話「彼はなぜ来られないんですか?」「何か事情(＝理由)があるんでしょう」"Why can't he come?" "There must be some *reason*."
▶彼女は家庭の事情で高校を中退した She quit high school *for family reasons*. ‖ 担当者がいないので詳しい事情はわかりません The person in charge is not here, so (I'm afraid) I cannot give you any *details* just now. ‖ 彼は内部事情に通じている He *is in the know*. ‖ 新しい交通規則のおかげで交通事情がよくなった *Traffic conditions* are now better, thanks to the new traffic rules. ‖ その国は食糧事情がひどく悪い The *food situation* in the country is very bad. ‖ 彼はラテンアメリカの事情に詳しい He *knows a lot about* Latin America.／He *is well informed about what's going on* in Latin America.

2**じじょう 自乗** a **square** 一動 自乗する **square** ＋目 (➤ 通例受け身形) ▶3の自乗は9だ The *square* of 3 is 9.／Three squared is [makes] nine. →二乗.

3**じじょう 自浄** ▶与党には自浄能力がない The ruling party doesn't have *the ability to cleanse itself*.

ししょうしゃ 死傷者 **casualties**(➤ 複数形で用いる)；a **toll**(死傷者数) ▶乗客から数人の死傷者が出た We had several *casualties* among the passengers.／Several passengers were either killed or injured. ‖ 列車が脱線したが幸運にも死傷者はなかった The train (was) derailed, but fortunately there were no *casualties*. ‖ 地震による死傷者は数千人に上った The *toll* from the earthquake rose to thousands of people.

ししょうせつ 私小説 an **"I" novel**.

ししょく 試食する **try** ＋目(試す)；**taste** ＋目(味わう) ▶このピザを試食してみてください *Try* [*Have a taste of*] this pizza. ‖《掲示》どうぞご試食ください Taste it for free. (➤「無料で味見する」の意).
‖試食会 a tasting [sampling] party.

じしょく 辞職 **resignation** /rèzɪgnéɪʃən/ **一動 辞職する** **resign** /rɪzáɪn/ (+目) ▶辞職願を出す hand in one's *resignation* ‖ 大学の総長を辞職する *resign* as president of a university (➤ この as は「…としての」の意で, 資格や地位を表す) ‖ 彼は汚職事件の責任を取って辞職した He took the blame for the corruption scandal and *resigned his post*.
☛ 総辞職 (→見出語)

じじょでん 自叙伝 an **autobiography** /ɔ̀:t̬əbaɪɑ́:grəfi/ ▶松下幸之助の自叙伝 Matsushita Konosuke's *autobiography*.

ししょばこ 私書箱 a **post-office box** (➤ 略語は P.O.B. または P.O.Box) ▶元町郵便局私書箱28号 Motomachi *P.O.Box* 28.

1**ししん 私信** a **private** [**personal**] **letter** (➤ private は「私的な」, personal は「個人的な」).

2**ししん 指針** a **needle** (磁石盤・メーターなどの針) ; a **guide** (手引き) ; **guidelines** (公的な指標) ▶父の生き方は私の良き指針となっています My father's way of life is a good *guide* for me.
‖安全指針 safety guidelines.

1**しじん 詩人** a **poet** ▶彼は詩人肌の人間だ He is *something of a poet*. (➤ something of a は「ちょっとした(能力をもつ)」の意).
‖吟遊詩人 a minstrel /mínstrəl/.

2**しじん 私人** a **private citizen** (公職に就いていない一市民) ▶私人と公人の区別をしっかりつける distinguish clearly between *private* and public *persons* ‖ 私人としてその神社に参拝する *pay a private visit* to the shrine ‖ その委員は私人としては歯科医である The committee member is a dentist *in* (his [her]) *private life*.

1**じしん 地震** an **earthquake**, 《インフォーマル》 a **quake** (➤ ともに大きな, または比較的大きな地震を指す), 《米また》 a **temblor** ; an **earth tremor** (弱い地震) ; a **megaquake** (巨大地震) ▶火山国では地震が多い There are many *earthquakes* in countries with active volcanoes. ‖ ゆうべ11時頃弱い地震があった There was *a slight earthquake* [*an earth tremor*] at around eleven last night. ‖ 昨夜かなり強い地震が関東一円を襲った *A* fairly *strong* [*powerful*] *earthquake* shook the Kanto area last night. ‖ その地震の規模はマグニチュード5.8で, 揺れは30秒続き, 強い余震が2回あった The *earthquake* measuring 5.8 on the Richter scale [The *earthquake* with a magnitude of 5.8] lasted thirty seconds and was followed by two powerful aftershocks. →震度.
▶地震学者たちは大規模地震を予知するための研究を行っている *Seismologists* have been doing research to predict *large* (*-scale*) *earthquakes*. (➤ seismologist の発音は /saɪzmɑ́:lədʒɪst/).
▶地震, 雷, 火事, おやじ Four dreadful things : *earthquakes*, lightening, fire and the old man. ‖ 首都直下型地震 an *earthquake* directly under the capital.
‖震源 the focus of an earthquake ; the seismic center [focus] ‖ 免震構造 a seismically isolated structure ‖ 免震工法 seismic isolation ‖ 横揺れ (a) lateral vibration ‖ 余震 an aftershock.

✉ **日本は地震国です. あなたは地震というものを経験したことがありますか** Japan is *a land of earthquakes*. Have you ever experienced *an earthquake*?

✉ **このところ日本のいくつかの地域では頻繁に(弱い)地震があります** There have been frequent *tremors* in some parts of Japan recently.

> **あなたの英語はどう響く?**
> 「地震」をいつも earthquake とすると誤解を招くおそれがある. earthquake は阪神淡路大震災や東日本大震災クラスの大地震を指すのがふつう. 日常的な小さな「揺れ」は (earth) tremor という.

2**じしん 自信** **(self-)confidence** ▶私はドイツ語の会話には自信がある I *have confidence* [I'*m confident*] in my ability to speak German. ‖ 数学なら満点を取る自信がある *I know I can* get a perfect score on math exams. ‖ 猛練習するうちに自信がついてきた I *gained confidence* through hard training. ‖ 由美子は自信を喪失している Yumiko *has lost self-confidence* [*confidence in herself*]. ‖ その勝利で彼らは自信を取り戻した The victory restored their *confidence*. ‖ 木村さんは自信家だ Mrs. Kimura is *a* (*self-*) *confident woman*. ‖ 自信過剰は禁物だぞ Don't get *overconfident*. / Don't be *too sure of yourself*. ‖ 孝夫は自信満々だった Takao *was full of confidence* [*was very sure of himself*]. ‖ 対話「あしたはいよいよ入試だ」「受かる自信はあるの?」"Tomorrow I'll be taking the entrance exam at last." "*Are* you *confident* you'll pass ?"

3**じしん 自身** **self** ▶私 [私たち] 自身の物 my [our] *own* things / things *of* my [our] *own* ‖ 私自身, 最初はそう思ってたんだ I thought so *myself* at first. ‖ 彼自身, そのことは知らない *He himself* doesn't know about it. / He doesn't know about it *himself*.

ししんけい 視神経 **the optic nerve**.

じすい 自炊する **1**【食事を作る】**cook for oneself** ▶私は自炊には慣れている I am accustomed to *cooking for myself*. ‖ 兄は東京で自炊生活をしています My (older) brother lives in Tokyo and *does his own cooking* [*fixes his own meals*].
2【データ化する】《コンピュータ》 **scan and digitalize pages** [**books**] **(and turn them into PDF files) for personal use.**

しずい 歯髄 **(dental) pulp**.

しすう 指数 an **index**
‖知能指数 an intelligence quotient /kwóʊʃənt/ 《略 IQ》 ‖ 不快指数 a temperature-humidity index 《略 THI》 / a discomfort index 《略 D.I.》 ‖ 物価指数 a price index ‖ 感情指数 emotional (intelligence) quotient 《略 EQ》.

しずか 静か **1**【音がない】**quiet** (音がほとんどなく; ひっそりとしていて), **silent** (音が全くなくて) ; **still** (音も動きもなくて) **一副 静かに** **quietly, silently** ▶静かな部屋 a *quiet* room ‖ 今夜は何て静かなんだろう It's so *quiet* [*still*] tonight. ‖ 太極拳が静かなブームを呼んでいる Tai chi is enjoying *quiet*, *but steady popularity*. ‖ あの子は静かにさせるのが大変だ I have a hard time *keeping* him *quiet*. ‖ 主人公が息絶えると静かに幕が下りてきた As the hero breathed his last, the curtain began to fall *silently*. ‖ みんな, 静かに(してください) (Please) *be quiet*, everyone.
2【穏やかな】**soft** (穏やかな), **calm** /kɑ:m/ (冷静な) ; **gentle** (優しい) **一副 静かに** **softly, calmly, gently** ▶静かな音楽 *soft* music ‖ 海はこの1週間とても静かだ The sea has been very *calm* for the past week. ‖ 母はいつも静かな口調で話す My mother always speaks

softly [in a gentle voice]. ‖ ひどいかぜをひいたときは静かに寝ているのがいちばんだ When you catch a bad cold, the best thing is to stay *quietly* in bed.

しずく 滴 a **drop** ▶ぬれたタオルから滴がたれている *Water is dripping* from the wet towel. ‖ 少女の頬をひと滴の涙が伝った *A tear* slid down the girl's cheek.

しずけさ 静けさ **stillness, quiet(ness)** →静か ▶夜の静けさ the *stillness* [*still* / *silence*] of the night.

▶《慣用表現》これは嵐の前の静けさかもしれない Maybe this is *the calm before the storm*. (➤ calm /kɑːm/ は海や天候の「静かで穏やかな状態」).

しずしず ▶花嫁は父親に手を取られてしずしずとチャペルに入ってきた The bride, escorted by her father, walked *quietly and gracefully* into the wedding chapel.

システム a **system** ▶電話とコンピュータを使う新しい診断システムが開発された A new computer-telephone *diagnostic system* has been developed. ‖ この結婚相談所のシステムがどうなっているか教えてください Could you tell me *how* this matrimonial agency *is organized* [*works*]?

‖**システムエンジニア** a systems engineer ‖ **システムキッチン** a custom kitchen (➤「あつらえの台所」の意. (×)system kitchen は和製語) ‖ **システム工学** systems engineering.

ジステンパー **distemper**(犬の急性感染症).

ジストロフィー 《医学》**dystrophy** /dístrəfi/.

じすべり 地滑り a **landslide,** 《英また》a **landslip**

▶長野県北部で地滑りが起きて30人の死傷者が出た *A landslide* occurred in the northern part of Nagano Prefecture and 30 people were killed or injured.

▶《慣用表現》自由民主党が地滑り的勝利を収めた The LDP *won by a landslide*.

しずまりかえる 静まり返る ▶指揮者が指揮棒を構えるとホールはしーんと静まり返った *A hush fell* over the hall when the conductor raised his baton. (➤ hush は「静けさ」) ‖ 夏休みで子供たちのいなくなった小学校は静まり返っていた *A dead silence reigned* in the elementary school with all the children away for the summer vacation.

しずまる 静まる・鎮まる **calm down** ▶波[嵐]は朝までには静まるだろう The rough sea [The storm] will *calm down* before morning. ‖ 気が静まるまでそっとしておいてあげなさい Don't bother him until he *calms down*.

▶暴動は鎮まった(＝鎮圧された) The revolt *was quelled* [*was suppressed*]. ‖ 路上の騒ぎは鎮まった The commotion on the street *died down*.

しずみこむ 沈み込む ▶かわいそうに少女はあの事件以来沈み込んでいる The poor girl has been *gloomy and depressed* ever since that incident.

しずむ 沈む **1【水面や地平線の下に】sink, go down** (➤ 後者はややインフォーマル); **set** (太陽・月などが)

▶水より比重の大きい物はすべて水に沈む Anything with a specific gravity greater than water will *sink* (in it). ‖ こういうふうに手足を動かせば沈まないよ If you move your arms and legs this way, you *won't sink* [you *can keep yourself afloat*]. ‖ きょうの新聞は地中海で遊覧船が沈んだと報じている Today's newspaper reports that a pleasure boat *sank* [*went down*] in the Mediterranean Sea. ‖ 太陽が西に沈んだ The sun *set* in the west. ‖ 真っ赤な太陽が地平線に沈もうとしている The bright red sun *is* now *sinking* below the horizon.

2【気分が】feel gloomy [**blue**] (憂鬱になる); **feel sad** (悲しくなる) ▶父親の持病のぜんそくが出ると私は気分が沈んでしまう I *feel sad* whenever my father has one of his recurring asthma attacks. ‖ 母の死後, 父は悲しみに沈んでいる Since my mother's death, my father *has been submerged in grief*. ‖ そんなに沈んじゃって, どうしたの? You *look down*. What's bothering you? / You *look* so *down in the mouth*. What's the matter? (➤ down in the mouth は「意気消沈して」の意のインフォーマルな表現) ‖「1回戦で負けました」と彼は沈んだ声で言った "I lost the first match," he said *dejectedly*.

[1]**しずめる 沈める** ▶戦艦を沈める *sink* a battleship ‖ 彼は疲れきってソファーに深々と身を沈めた He *sank* deep into the sofa exhaustedly. ‖ チャンピオンは強烈なカウンターで挑戦者をマットに沈めた The champion *laid* the opponent *on the mat* with a hard counterblow.

[2]**しずめる 静める・鎮める** **calm** /kɑːm/ +㊐; **relieve** +㊐ (痛みを); **suppress** +㊐ (騒ぎを)

▶猟師は気の立っている犬を静めた The hunter *calmed* [*quieted*] the excited dogs. ‖ 私は話題を変えて彼の怒りを鎮めようとした I changed the subject trying to *calm* his anger [*calm* him *down*]. ‖ 彼女は目を閉じて気持ちを静めようとした She closed her eyes to *calm* [*compose*] *herself*. ‖ 彼女は神経を静めるためによくバッハを聴く She often listens to Bach to *settle her nerves*. (➤ Bach は /bɑːk/ と発音する) ‖ 気を静めて最初から話してごらん *Pull yourself together* and tell me the whole story from the beginning.

▶彼はひどい頭痛を鎮めるためにアスピリンを飲んだ He took aspirin to *relieve* [*ease*] his severe headache. ‖ 軍隊はその暴動を鎮めることができなかった The army wasn't able to *suppress* [*put down*] the riot.

じする 辞する ▶一身上の都合で[健康上の理由で]公職を辞する *resign from public office* for personal [health] reasons.

[1]**しせい 姿勢** **posture** ▶あなたは姿勢がいいわね You *have really good posture*. / You *carry yourself really well*. ‖ 姿勢が悪いよ! Watch your *posture*! ‖ 彼は直立不動の姿勢で1時間演説した *Standing perfectly straight*, he delivered an hour-long speech. ‖ 姿勢を正しなさい *Sit* [*Stand*] *up straight*. / *Straighten up*.

☛ 高姿勢, 低姿勢 (→見出語)

[2]**しせい 施政** ▶首相は施政方針演説をした The Prime Minister delivered his *speech on his administrative policies*.

[3]**しせい 市制** a **municipal** /mjunísɪpəl/ **system** ▶2つの町と3つの村が集まって市制を敷いた Two towns and three villages came together to *form* [*make up*] *a municipality*.

[4]**しせい 市政** **city government**(市の政治); **city administration**(市の行政) ▶横島市政には我々の意見が反映されていない Our opinions are not reflected in the Yokoshima *City* [*Municipal*] *Government*.

[5]**しせい 死生** **life and death** ▶死生観 one's view of *life and death*.

[6]**しせい 私製の** **private, privately made** ▶私製はがき a *postcard* (→官製).

[1]**じせい 時勢** **(the) times** ▶時勢に逆らう *swim against the current* (*of the times*) / *go against the times*

‖時勢に遅れないようにする keep up [move／keep pace] with *the times*.

²**じせい 時制** 《文法》 a **tense** ▶過去 [現在／未来] **時制** the past [present／future] *tense*.

³**じせい 自生の wild** 一動 **自生する grow wild** [**naturally**] ▶この湿原には珍しい植物が**自生している** Some rare plants *grow wild* in this marsh.

⁴**じせい 辞世** ▶**辞世の句** a haiku [tanka] *composed at the point of death*／a death [farewell] poem ‖**辞世のことば** one's *last* words.

⁵**じせい 自制 self-control** 一動 **自制する control** oneself ▶ここは**自制**が肝心だ It's important to *control yourself* [*your emotions*] now.

⁶**じせい 自省 self-examination, self-reflection, soul-searching** 一動 **自省する examine** oneself, **search** one's **soul**.

⁷**じせい 時世 times, days** ▶物騒なご**時世**だ These are dangerous *times*.

⁸**じせい 磁性 magnetism** ▶**磁性体** a *magnetic* body [substance].

しせいかつ 私生活 one's **private life** ▶私たちの**私生活**に立ち入るのはよしてください Stop poking your nose into our *private life*, will you?

しせいじ 私生児 an **illegitimate** /ìlədʒítəmət/ **child** (➤ a child of unmarried parents のような言い方のほうが好ましい).

じせいしん 自制心 self-control ▶やつらに何を言われても**自制心**を失うな Don't lose (your) *self-control* whatever they may say to you.

¹**しせき 史跡** a **historic place** [**spot**] ▶鎌倉には**史跡**が多い Kamakura has many *historic places* [*spots*].

✉ **日本にいらっしゃったときは，いくつかの史跡をご案内したいと思います** When you come to Japan, I'd like to take you to some *historic places*.

²**しせき 歯石 tartar** /tɑ́ːʳt̬əʳ/ ▶**歯石**をとる remove *tartar*.

¹**じせき 自責 self-reproach** ▶**自責**の念に駆られる suffer from (feelings of) *self-reproach* [*remorse*／*guilt*].

²**じせき 次席** →二位.

じせきてん 自責点 《野球》 an **earned run** 《略 ER》.

じせだい 次世代 ‖**次世代型テレビ** a next-generation [an advanced] TV.

¹**しせつ 施設 facilities** (設備) ; an **institution** (公共機関, 建築物) ; a **home** (母子家庭・老人などの)

▶教育 [厚生／スポーツ] **施設**を拡充する expand *educational* [*welfare*／*sports*] *facilities* ‖**軍事施設**を撤去する dismantle *military facilities*.

‖**公共施設** public facilities, a public institution.

²**しせつ 私設** ▶**私設**応援団 a *private* cheering squad [group] ‖**私設図書館** a *private* library.

³**しせつ 使節** a **mission** ; an **envoy** /énvɔɪ/ (外交上の) ▶劇団は友好 [親善] **使節**として来日した The theatrical troupe came to Japan on *a goodwill mission*.

¹**じせつ 自説** one's (**own**) **view** ▶ガリレオは最後まで**自説**を曲げなかった Galileo held to *his views* to the end (of his life).

²**じせつ 持説** one's **pet theory**.

じせつがら 時節柄

✉ **時節柄どうかお体を大切に** Please take care of yourself *in this cold* [*hot*] *weather*. ➤ 英語にはこのような決まり文句はない.

¹**しせん 視線** ▶**視線**(＝目)が合うと, 彼女はうれしそうににっこりした When *our eyes met*, she smiled happily. ‖彼女は私から**視線をそらした** She *averted her eyes* from me.／She *avoided eye contact* with me. ‖彼らの**冷たい視線**を浴びて, 私は居たたまれなくなった Under their *cold stares*, I felt extremely uneasy.

²**しせん 支線** a **branch line** ; a **spur** (鉄道や道路の) ▶幹線道路 [鉄道] の**支線** a highway [rail] *spur*.

³**しせん 死線** ▶彼はチフスにかかって2日間**死線をさまよった** Having caught typhus, he *was hovering between life and death* [*was on the verge of death*] for two days.

しぜん 自然 **1** 【山・川など】 **nature** 一形 **自然の natural** ▶**自然**豊かな山村 a mountain village with *a* rich *natural environment*／a mountain village (that is) rich in [with] *natural beauty* ‖南極の**自然**は厳しい *Nature* in Antarctica is harsh. ‖東京もこの辺はまだ僅かに**自然**が残っている There's still a bit of *nature* left in this part of Tokyo. ‖グランドキャニオンは**自然**が造った大彫刻だ The Grand Canyon is a great sculpture carved by *nature*. ‖田舎に住めば**自然に親しむ**ことができる You can *be in touch* [*close contact*] *with nature* if you live in the country(side). ‖洪水が起こるたびに**自然の恐ろしさ**を感じる I realize *the terrifying power of nature* every time there is a flood. ‖**自然破壊**から地球を守ろう Let's protect the earth from *the destruction of nature*.

▶この町には**自然がいっぱいある** This town *is in a very natural setting*. ‖村は**豊かな自然**に囲まれている The village is surrounded by a *rich* [*abundant*] *natural environment* [by *abundant natural beauty*]. (➤ 日本語では「豊かな自然」「美しい自然」というが, (×)rich [abundant] nature, (×)beautiful nature とはいわない ; natural abundance, natural beauty とはいう) ‖**自然界**には微妙なバランスがある There's a delicate balance in *the natural world*.

‖**自然界** the natural world, the world of nature ‖**自然科学** natural science ‖**自然現象** a natural phenomenon ‖**自然光** natural light ‖**自然災害** a natural disaster ‖**自然死** (a) death from natural causes ‖**自然主義** naturalism ‖**自然食品** natural foods, organic foods ‖**自然数** a natural number ‖**自然淘汰** [**選択**] natural selection.

2 【人工的でない, 無理のない】 一形 **自然な natural** 一副 **自然に naturally** ▶**自然な**動作はすべて優美である All *natural* movements are graceful. ‖デーブの日本語は**自然だ** Dave's Japanese is *natural*.／Dave *speaks* Japanese *very naturally* [*fluently*]. ‖状況から判断して彼女は自殺したと見るのが**自然だ** Judging from the circumstances, one would *naturally* assume that she committed suicide. ‖年を取って耳が遠くなるのは**自然なことだ** It is *natural* to lose some hearing as one grows older.

▶**自然の成り行きに任せた**ほうがいい You should *let nature take its course*.／You should let things take their course. ‖人前で抱き合うことはふつうの日本人には**自然にはできない** Hugging in front of other people doesn't come *naturally* to the average Japanese. ‖ 対話 「おまえ, 彼女とどうやって知り合ったんだい?」「**ごく自然にだよ**」 "How did you get to know her ?" "*Very naturally*." ‖その映画であの新人はごく**自然体**で演じている That new actor performs very *naturally* in the movie. ‖気負うことなく，いつも**自然体でいよ** Don't try to look better than you really are. Always *be your natural self*.

3【放っておいても成就する様子】▶ドアが**自然に**開いた The door opened *by itself*. ‖頭痛は**自然に**治った My headache went away *by itself*.

じせん 自薦する recommend oneself 《for》.

1**じぜん 慈善** charity ▶彼らは**慈善**のためにコンサートを開いた They held a *charity* concert. ／They held a concert *for charitable purposes* [*for charity*]. ‖その女優は多くの**慈善事業**をしてきた The actress has been involved in many *charitable activities*.
‖**慈善団体** a charitable organization.

2**じぜん 事前に** beforehand ▶事前に十分な打ち合わせをする make good arrangements *beforehand* [*in advance*].
‖(選挙の)**事前運動** pre-election campaigning ‖**事前協議** prior consultation.

3**じぜん 次善の** the next [second] best ▶至急**次善の**策を講じよう Let's adopt *the next best policy* as quickly as possible.

しそ 紫蘇《植物》a shiso leaf.

しそう 思想 an idea (観念)；thought (考え方) ▶過激な**思想** radical *ideas* ‖フロイトの**思想**は精神科医に大きな影響を与えた Freud's *ideas* were a great influence on psychiatrists. ‖**キリスト教思想**は西洋文明に多大な影響を及ぼしてきた *Christian thought* has greatly influenced Western civilization. ‖19世紀には偉大な**思想家**が輩出した The 19th century produced a number of great *thinkers*.

しぞう 死蔵 ▶わが家では数枚のテレカを**死蔵している** We have several *unused* phone cards.

じぞう 地蔵 a *jizo*

日本紹介 ✉ **地蔵は高さ1メートルくらいの地蔵菩薩(ぼさつ)の石像です. 菩薩は子供や旅人の守護者とされます. 全国のあちこちの道端に置かれています** A *jizo* is a stone Buddhist statue about one meter tall of *Jizo*, a Bodhisattva, who is said to be a protector of children and travelers. You can find many such statues along roadsides across the country.

-しそうだ → -そう

> **【文型】**
> (たぶん)…しそうだ《推測》
> be likely to do
> (今にも)…しそうだ《確信ある予測》
> be going to do
> be about to do
>
> **【解説】** **be likely to** が不確実な気持ちを幾分残した，十分な可能性や見込みまたは傾向を表すのに対し，**be going to** と **be about to** は行為・動作などが(潜在的にせよ)行われ始めようとしていることを表す. **be going to** は様子から判断し「…しそうだ」という見込みを強調する. これに対して **be about to** は「(まさに)…するところだ」の意で差し迫っていることを強調し，通例時を表す副詞(句)を伴わない.

▶東京ではいい仕事が見つかり**そうだ** I'*m likely to* [I'*ll probably*] find a good job in Tokyo. ‖その美術館は人気の観光名所になり**そうだ** The art museum *is likely to* become a popular tourist spot. ‖曇っていて今にも雨が降り**そうだ** It's cloudy and looks like it'*s going to* rain any moment. ‖少女は今にも泣き出し**そうだった** The little girl *was about to* cry. ／The little girl *was on the verge of* tears [crying].

しそうのうろう 歯槽膿漏 pyorrhea /paɪərí:ə/ → 歯周病.

シソーラス a thesaurus.

じそく 時速 speed per hour (1時間当たりの速度) ▶新幹線の最高速度は**時速**320キロだ The Shinkansen has a maximum speed of 320 kilometers *per hour*. (➤ 320 k.p.h. と略す) ‖その列車は**時速**何キロで走りますか How many kilometers *per hour* does the train go ? (➤ How fast …? で聞くほうがふつう).

じぞく 持続する last (続く)；keep up (維持する) ▶その歌手の人気は**持続**しなかった The popularity of the singer didn't *last* long. ‖決心するのは容易だが，その気持ちを**持続させる**のは難しい It is easy to make a decision to do something but it's hard to *keep up* [*maintain*] your determination. ‖愛情を**持続させる**ことは難しい It is hard to *keep* love *alive*. ／It is hard to keep the flame of love burning. ‖**持続可能な開発目標** the *Sustainable* Development Goals (➤ 略称は SDGs).

しそこなう 仕損なう ▶道で先生に会ったが，挨拶し**損なった** I met my teacher on the street, but I *failed to* greet her.

しそん 子孫 a descendant /dɪséndənt/ ▶彼は平家の**子孫**であることを誇りにしている He is proud of being *a descendant* of the Heike clan. ‖この技法は何としても**子孫**(＝次の世代)に伝えたい We want to pass these techniques on to *the next generations* no matter what it takes.

しそんじる 仕損じる fail；blunder (へまをする)
ことわざ 急(せ)いては事を**仕損じる** Haste makes waste.

じそんしん 自尊心 self-respect；pride (誇り) ▶**自尊心**の強い人 a *self-respecting* [*proud*] person ‖彼は**自尊心**が強すぎる He has too much *pride*. ／He *thinks too highly of himself*. ‖彼のことばに**自尊心**を傷つけられた What he said hurt my *pride*.

1 した 下

> **訳語メニュー**
> 位置が低い → under, below **1**
> 位置が下降する → down **1**
> 内側 → under **2**
> 地位が低い → under **3**
> 年齢が低い → younger **4**
> 能力が低い → low **5**

1【位置が】 under (…の真下に)；below (…の下の方に)；down (下へ) ▶大木の**下**に避難した人の上に雷が落ちた Lightning hit a man who had taken shelter *under* a big tree. ‖飛行機の窓からラスベガスの街が**下**に見えた From the plane window, I saw the streets of Las Vegas *below*.
▶富士山の五合目から**下**は霧に覆われていた From the fifth station on *down*, Mt. Fuji was covered with fog. ‖展望台から**下を見る**と怖い *Looking down* from the observation tower is scary [makes me feel scared]. ‖**下の方を見てごらん.** 摩周湖が見えるよ *Look down there !* You can see Lake Mashu.
▶いちばん**下の**引き出しが開かない The *bottom* drawer

is stuck. ‖その語は38ページの下から5行目に出ている You can find the word in *the fifth line from the bottom* of [on] page 38.

▶《階下》下の喫茶店は10時まで開いています The coffee shop *downstairs* is open till 10. ‖私たちのアパートの下の階には吉田さん一家が住んでいます The Yoshidas live in the apartment *below* us. ‖晩ごはんですよ. 下に降りて来なさい Dinner's ready. Come *downstairs* [Come *down* and eat]. ‖このエレベーターは下へ行きます This elevator is going *down*.

2【内側】under (…のすぐ内側に) ▶警官たちは制服の下に防弾チョッキを着けた Police officers wore bullet-proof vests *under* their uniforms. ‖スパイは秘密情報を書いた紙片を入れ歯の下に隠した The spy hid a slip of paper on which secret information was written *under* his false teeth.

3【地位が】under ▶課長の下には5人の部下がいる The section chief has five people working *under* him. (● ... working *for* him とすれば work under ほど上下関係を意識させない言い方になる) ‖あんな品の悪い人の下で働くのは嫌だ I don't want to work *under* such a vulgar person. ‖アメリカの会社では, 決定は上部で行われて下に伝えられる In American companies, decisions are made at the top and *passed down* the ranks. (➤このような経営方式を a top-down management system (トップダウンの経営方式) という).

4【年齢が】younger ▶下の子 one's *younger* child ‖弟は私より3つ年が下です My brother is three years *younger* than I am [than me]. (➤文末の am は省略することが多い) ‖春夫はぼくのいちばん下の弟です Haruo is *the youngest* brother.

5【能力が】low ▶高校時代, ぼくの成績は平均より下だった My grades in high school were *below average*. ‖ぼくの打率は野村君より下です (=低い) My batting average *is lower than* Nomura's.

²**した 舌** **the tongue** /tʌŋ/ ▶舌の先 the tip of one's *tongue* ‖スープは舌をやけどするほど熱かった The soup was hot enough to burn your *tongue*. ‖彼はばつが悪くなり, ぺろっと舌を出した Embarrassed, he *stuck his tongue out*. 《参考》(1)日本人は自分の失敗にてれたときなどに舌を出すことが多いが, 英語の stick [put] out one's tongue は専ら「軽蔑」を表す子供っぽいしぐさである. (2)英米人はばつが悪い場合など, 手のひらを上に向けて両手を広げ, 両肩をすくめる(これを shrug one's shoulders という).

▶《慣用表現》**舌が肥えている** ▶彼は舌が肥えている He'*s a gourmet*. (➤ gourmet /góəʳmeɪ/ は「美食家」). **舌の根** ▶あの人は辞任すると言ったのに, その舌の根も乾かぬうちに辞めないと言い出した He said he would resign, but *in the next breath* he said he would stay in his post. **舌をかむ** ▶ロシア人の名前は難しくて舌をかみそうだ I *get tongue-tied* when I try to pronounce Russian names. / Russian names are real *tongue twisters* for me. (➤ tongue twister は「発音しにくいことば」). **舌を巻く** ▶彼の頭の良さには舌を巻く (=驚嘆する) I *am amazed* [*am astonished*] to see how smart he is.

☛ 舌足らず (→見出語)

しだ 羊歯 《植物》(a) **fern**.

じた 自他 ▶父は自他ともに許す釣りの名人だ My father *calls himself* an excellent angler and *everybody acknowledges it to be true*.

したあご 下顎 **the lower jaw** (全体); a **chin** (下顎の先) (➤「上顎」は the upper jaw).

したあじ 下味 ▶豚肉は酒としょうゆで下味をつけます *Season* the pork with sake and soy sauce *beforehand*.

¹**したい 死体** a **body**; a **corpse** /kɔːʳps/

> **語法** (1)body は「死体」を表す一般的なことばで, 文脈上紛らわしい場合にのみ dead body という.
> (2)corpse は人間のみに用いるが, 死体を物として見るという含みがあることが多い. 動物の死骸は carcass /kɑ́ːʳkəs/. また解剖用の人間の死体は cadaver /kədǽvəʳ/ という.

▶身元不明の死体 an unidentified *body* [*corpse*] ‖死体の身元を確かめる identify the *body* ‖行方不明者が死体となって発見された The missing person was found *dead*. (➤「死んで見つかった」の意) ‖死体に外傷はなかった The *body* had no apparent injury.

‖**死体遺棄(罪)** (the crime of) abandoning a dead body ‖**死体解剖** (検死のための) an autopsy /ɔ́ːtɑːpsi/.

²**したい 肢体** ▶肢体不自由の *orthopedically* impaired / *physically* impaired.

³**したい** **want to** do, **would like to** do (➤後者は前者の丁寧な言い方)

> **【文型】**
> …したい
> **want to** do
> **would like to** do
> **《解説》** **want to** は「…したい」という欲求・希望をストレートに表す. **would like to** は「…したいのですが」という控えめな希望を表す.

▶初給料をもらったら最初に何をしたいですか? What do you *want to do* first [first thing] after you get paid for the first time? ‖またお会いしたいですね I'*d like to* see you again. / Let's get together again. ‖おまえは何でもしたいことができるのにまだ何もやっていないじゃないか You can do whatever you *want* (*to*), but you haven't done anything yet, have you? ‖成功したいのなら懸命に働くことだ If you *hope to* succeed, you must work hard. (➤ hope to は「…することを希望する」).

▶彼女は娘にしたい放題のことをさせている She *lets* her daughter *do whatever she pleases* [*have her own way*]. ‖自分のしたいようにしたらいい (You may) do *as you wish* [*like*]. (➤ wish のほうがより丁寧な言い方).

> **【文型】**
> …したい気がする
> **feel like** doing

▶昼寝でもしたい気がする I *feel like* taking a nap now. →-たい.

¹**しだい 私大** a **private university** [**college**].

²**しだい 次第**

> **【文型】**
> 人・物(A)次第だ
> **depend on** A

1【事情】 ▶事と次第によっては校長の責任問題に発展するかもしれない *Depending on circumstances*, this may develop into a problem for which the principal must take responsibility. ‖岸田さんに

事の次第を話してもらいましょう Let Ms. Kishida tell us *how it happened*. ‖ こういう次第で会に行けませんでした *For those reasons* [*Under those circumstances*], I could not attend the meeting.
2【…によって決まる】▶練習次第であなたのピアノはうまくなる Your piano playing will improve *depending on* how much you practice. ‖ 旅行するかどうかは天気次第だ Whether we will go on a trip or not *depends on the weather*. ‖ 何事もきみの努力次第だ Everything *depends on your efforts*.
▶ **対話**「彼からのこの贈り物は返したほうがいいかな」「それはあなた次第だよ. 気持ちはどうなの？」「いい人なんだけど付き合う気になれないの」"Should I send him back this present？" "*It's up to you*. How do you feel about him？" "He is a good person, but I don't want to go out with him."
3【…するとすぐに】▶受け取り次第電話してください Please call me *as soon as* you receive it.
☛ しだいに（⇀見出語）

[1]**じたい 事態** a **situation**（状況）; **things**（事情）▶事態を見守る keep an eye on the *situation* ‖ 事態を収拾する get the *situation* under control ‖ 事態はますます抜き差しならなくなってきた *Things* are [*The situation* is] getting more serious. ‖ 緊急事態が発生した An *emergency* has arisen.

[2]**じたい 辞退する** **decline** ＋㊐ ▶せっかくのご招待ですが辞退させていただきます I'm sorry, but *I have to decline* your invitation. ‖《告別式の広告》弔花はご辞退申し上げます No flowers *by request*.（⇀固辞）.

[3]**じたい 自体** **itself** ▶彼女はけがが自体よりも心理的ショックで深く傷ついているようだ She seems to be hurt more seriously by the psychological shock than the wound *itself*. ‖ 金銭自体は善でも悪でもない Money is not good or evil *per se* [*in itself*].（➤ per se /pəːr séɪ/ はラテン語語源の語で,「それ自体, 本来」の意の堅い語）.

[4]**じたい 字体** a **form of a character**, a **typeface**.

[1]じだい 時代

> 訳語メニュー
> 歴史上の ⇀period, age, era **1**
> 生涯の一時期 ⇀days **2**
> 時勢 ⇀times **3**

1【歴史上の時期】a **period** /píəriəd/（特定の期間）; an **age**（歴史的にはっきりした特徴を持つ期間）; an **era** /íərə/（age と同義に用いることも多いが, 大事件・発見・発明などのあった時代を指すこともある）▶室町時代 the Muromachi *period* ‖ 鉄器時代 the Iron *Age* ‖ 明治［大正］時代 the Meiji [Taisho] *era*（➤ 明治・大正・昭和・平成・令和などは era がふつう）.
▶ 21世紀はハイテクの時代だ The twenty-first century is *an age of high technology*. ‖ 1945年に日本の軍国時代は終わった Japan's *age of militarism* ended in 1945. ‖ エリザベス女王（1世）の時代にイギリスはスペインの無敵艦隊を破った The British defeated the Spanish Armada during the *reign* of Elizabeth I.（➤ reign は「治世」）‖ 一般人が気楽に宇宙旅行ができる時代（＝時）が来ると思います I think *the time* will come when ordinary people can enjoy space travel. ‖ そのドラマは時代考証がしっかりしている The drama is *historically* well researched.
‖**時代劇** a period [costume／samurai] drama ‖ **時代小説** a period [historical] novel ‖ **時代精神** the spirit of the age ‖ **同時代**（⇀見出語）.
2【生涯の一時期】**days** ▶この映画を見ると高校時代が思い出される This movie takes me back to *my high school days*. ‖ 高校時代は何のクラブに入ってたの？ What club activities did you take part in *in high school*？（➤ days を使うより, この例や次例のように表現するほうが英語として自然）‖ 学生時代はよくずる休みをした I often played hooky *when I was a student*. ‖ 私にも暴走族に入っていた時代があった There was *a time in my life* when I was a hot rodder.
▶現役時代の長嶋はスーパースターだった Nagashima was a superstar *when he was an active player*. ‖ 新婚時代は狭いアパートに住んでいた *For some time after we got married*, we lived in a small apartment. ‖ ぼくたちは大学時代に知り合いました We got to know each other *during our college days*.
3【時勢, 時流】**(the) times** ▶時代は変わる *Times* change. ‖ そのデザイナーはいつも時代の先端を行こうとしている That designer always tries *to be on the leading edge* (of fashion) [to *be a* (fashion) *trendsetter*]. ‖ 父の考えは時代遅れだ My father's way of thinking is *behind the times* [*old-fashioned*／*out of date*]. ‖ 時代の寵児(ちょうじ) a *legend in* one's *own time*.

> **逆引き熟語 〇〇時代**
> ◆暗黒時代 the Dark Ages／子供時代 one's childhood／青春時代 (in) one's youth [young days]／バブル時代 the bubble era／古き良き時代 the golden age, good old days／（米国・旧ソ連の）冷戦時代 the Cold War era
> ◆旧石器時代 the Old Stone age , the Paleolithic era／原始時代 the primitive age／氷河時代［期］the ice age

[2]**じだい 次代** **the next [coming] generation**（次の世代）; **the next era**（次の時代）▶次代を担う若者たち young people who will shoulder the burden of *the next era*.

[3]**じだい 地代** (a) **ground rent**.

じだいさくご 時代錯誤 an **anachronism** /ənǽkrənìzəm/ ▶時代錯誤的な考え方 an *anachronistic* way of thinking ‖ あの人には時代錯誤的なところがある He is something of *an anachronism*.

しだいに 次第に **gradually** ▶最初はミュージカルは好きではなかったが, 次第に好きになってきた At first I didn't like musicals, but I've *gradually* come to like them.

したう 慕う ▶明子は道夫をひそかに慕っていた Akiko *was* secretly *attracted to* [*in love with*] Michio. ‖ チップス先生は生徒たちから慕われた Mr. Chips *was respected very much* by his students.
▶ 2人の弟は姉を慕って上京した The two brothers *followed* their (older) sister to Tokyo.

したうけ 下請け a **subcontract** ▶父は自転車製造の下請けをしている My father *gets subcontracts* from a bicycle manufacturer. ‖ うちの会社は仕事を下請けに出している Our company is *contracting* [*farming*] *out* work.
‖**下請け業者** a subcontractor ‖ **下請け工場** a subcontract factory [plant].

したうち 舌打ち ▶「いまいましい雨だ！」と彼は舌打ちしながら言った "Damn the rain！" he *clicked* [*clucked*] *his tongue* (*in annoyance*). **《参考》** 舌

打ちの音は tut-tut /tt/, tsk tsk /tə̀sk tə́sk/ で表す.

したえ 下絵 a (rough) sketch.

したがう 従う 1【後ろからついて行く】follow +目 ▶ボスの猿が歩くと多くの猿が従う When the monkey leader walks, a lot of monkeys *follow* him.

2【指示・命令・規則などに】follow +目; obey +目 (権威者・命令などに); observe +目 (法律などを守る) ▶標識に従う [従って歩く] *follow* the signs ‖ 火事のときは係員の誘導に従ってください In case of fire, please *follow* the instructions of the person in charge. ‖ 《折り紙などで》指示に従って折りなさい Fold *according to* instructions. ‖ 彼は監督の指示に従ってバントをした He bunted *as* his manager *told him to*. ‖ 両親の言うことに従うべきだと思いませんか Don't you think you should *obey* your parents [*do* what your parents tell you (to do)] ? ‖ 寮生は寮の規則に従わなければならない Residents must *obey* the dormitory rules. ‖ 交通法規には従わねばならない Traffic regulations must *be observed* [*obeyed*]. ‖ イギリス人は法によく従う国民である The British are a *law-abiding* people. ‖ 彼は医者の忠告に従って酒をやめた He stopped drinking *on* his doctor's advice.

☛ したがって (→見出語)

したがえる 従える ▶社長は部下を数人従えて会議室に入ってきた The president came into the meeting room *accompanied* [*attended*] *by* a number of his assistants. (➤ attend のほうがより文語的).

したがき 下書き a (rough) draft ▶テーブルスピーチの下書きをする make *a draft* for an after-dinner speech ‖ (絵の)下描きがほぼできたからそろそろ色をつけてみようかな The *rough sketch* is finished now, so maybe I'll begin putting in the color.

したがって 従って 1【それだから】so ; that's why ... ▶山間部は降雪がひどく, 除雪もままならなかった. したがって列車が遅延するのも無理はない A lot of snow fell in the mountains and was not cleared away, *so* it was only natural that the trains were delayed. ‖ あの男はミスが多すぎる. したがって首になったのだ He makes too many mistakes. *That's why* he was fired.

2【…につれて】as ; with (…ともに) ▶年を取るにしたがって記憶は衰えるものだよ *As* you grow older, your memory begins to fail. ‖ 科学が発達するにしたがって自然破壊も進んできた *Along with* advances in science, there has also come more destruction of nature. / Advances in science have *been accompanied by* the destruction of nature. (➤ 後者のほうが英語として自然).

したがる ▶彼は海外旅行をしたがっている He *is eager* [*anxious*] *to* travel overseas. →-たがる.

したぎ 下着 underwear, underclothes ; 《インフォーマル》undies /ʌ́ndiz/ (特に女性・子供の); lingerie /lɑ̀:ndʒəréi/ (女性用肌着類) ▶下着は毎日取り替えるんですよ You must change your *underclothes* every day.

したく 支度 preparation(s) ━動 支度する prepare 《for》, get ready 《for, to do》

▶旅行の支度をする *prepare for* a trip / *make preparations for* a trip (➤ 後者は大がかりな支度を暗示する) ‖ 8時よ. 早く支度しなさい It's eight. Hurry up and *get ready*. ‖ 私は母の夕食の支度を手伝った I helped my mother *fix* [*cook*] dinner. (➤ fix はインフォーマルな語 ; この場合 prepare を使うと改まった感じになる) ‖ そろそろ夕ごはんの支度をしなくっちゃ I have to start *get*ting dinner *ready*. ‖ いつでも出られるように支度をしておきなさい *Get* [*Have*] everything *ready* so we can leave at any time. ‖ 誕生会の支度はすっかりできている *Everything is set* [*ready*] for the birthday party. ‖ 百合子は支度に時間がかかる Yuriko takes time *to get ready* (*to go out*). →準備.

じたく 自宅 one's home ▶きょうは自宅にいます I'll *be* (*at*) *home* today. (➤ at をつけないと副詞) ‖ 大学へは自宅からバスで通っています I go to college by bus *from home*. ‖ ご自宅はどちらですか *Where do you live* ? ‖ ひろみさんの自宅を訪ねた I visited Hiromi at *her home* [*house* / *apartment*].

したげいこ 下稽古 a rehearsal ; a run-through (of a play) (通し稽古).

したごころ 下心 an ulterior motive /ʌltíəriəʳ mòʊṭɪv/ ▶彼の親切には何か下心があるに違いない There must be some *ulterior motive* for his kindness. (●「下心」を secret intention としないこと. 日本語の「下心」がマイナスイメージであるのに対して, 英語の secret intention はあくまでも「秘密の意図」ということで中立的イメージだからである) ‖ きょうはいやに優しいのね. 何か下心があるんでしょう? You are so nice today. You must *have something up your sleeve*. (➤「たくらみなどを隠している」の意) (→腹 腹に一物).

したごしらえ 下ごしらえ preparation(s) ▶夕食の下ごしらえをしてから夕刊を読み始めた After I finished *preparations for* dinner, I began to read the evening newspaper.

-したことがある →こと.

したさきさんずん 舌先三寸 ▶舌先三寸で世の中を渡る get through life *with the gift of* (*the*) *gab* (➤ the gift of (the) gab は「口達者」).

したざわり 舌触り (a) texture ▶滑らかな舌触り (a) smooth *texture*.

したじ 下地 a base (基部) ; a foundation (しっかりした土台) ▶下地クリーム *foundation* cream ‖ (ペンキの)上塗りは下地が乾いてからだ The top layer can only be applied after *the base* has dried.

▶子供の頃アメリカにいたなら英語の下地はできてるはずだね You must have a good *foundation* in English if you lived in the U.S. as a child.

しだし 仕出し a catered bento [box lunch] (弁当).

したしい 親しい close /kloʊs/ (親密な); friendly (気さくな) ▶親しい友人 a *close* [*good*] friend ‖ 彼と私は中学時代から親しい仲だ He and I *have been close friends* since junior high school. ‖ いちばん親しい友だちが卒業記念にこの時計をくれた My *best friend* gave me this watch for my graduation. ‖ 私の父は彼の父親とここ10年来親しくしている My father *has been friends with* his father for ten years. ‖ 私はパリ滞在中にある名の知れた画家と親しくなった I *made friends* [*became friendly*] *with* a well-known painter during my stay in Paris. (➤ friends と複数形にすることに注意) ‖ 私は彼らが親しそうに挨拶していたので親友に違いないと思った They greeted each other *with* such *familiarity* that I thought they must be close friends. ‖ 対話「岡田君とは親しいの?」「いや一度話しただけさ」"*Are* you *friends with* Okada ?" "No, we (have) talked only once."

▶親しき仲にも礼儀あり There must be courtesy even between *close* friends.

あなたの英語はどう響く?
「ぼくは彼と親しい」という文を I'm *intimate* with him. と訳す人がいるが, この場合の intimate は性的な関係を暗示させるので避けるのが賢明である. We're [We've been] good friends. とか I've known him (for) many years. のような言い方が無難. ただし, close が「気持ちの上で親しい」に対して, intimate はさらに強意で「隠し事がなく何でも打ち明け合う」というようなニュアンスがあり, ネイティブは特に女性どうしが「親しい」の意味で, We're intimate with each other. と言うことも多い.

したじき 下敷き **1**【文房具】a **plastic sheet** (➤ 英米では使わない) ▶《比喩的》この小説はほかの作家の作品を下敷きにしたものだ This novel *was based on* [*was modeled on*] the work of another writer.
2【敷かれること】▶彼はその大地震のとき倒れた家の下敷きになった At the time of the great earthquake, he *was trapped under* a collapsed house. ‖その車はダンプカーの下敷きになって押し潰された The car was crushed *under* a dump truck.

したしみ 親しみ ▶どうも数学の先生には親しみがもてない I just *can't get to like* my math teacher. ‖あきら君から親しみの籠もった手紙をもらった I received a *friendly* letter from Akira. ‖彼が同窓生だとわかって急に親しみを覚えた When I learned that he was from the same school as me, I suddenly *warmed to* [*felt* more *friendly toward*] him.

したしむ 親しむ **1**【仲よくする】▶一般にアメリカ人は大変親しみやすい Generally, Americans are very *friendly* people. ‖彼は親しみにくい人だ He is *hard to make friends with*.
2【身近に感ずる】▶隅田川は昔から東京の人に親しまれてきた The Sumida (River) *has* long *been close to* the hearts of Tokyoites. ‖子供はもっと自然に親しむべきだ Children should *be in closer contact* [*more in touch*] *with* nature. ‖野田さんはこの辺りの子供には『紙芝居おじさん』として親しまれている Mr. Noda *is popular with* the children around here who call him "the picture (card) story man." ‖もっと書物に親しみなさい You should *spend more time* on reading.

したじゅんび 下準備 **preliminary arrangements**
▶我々は来週アメリカから来る客を迎える下準備で忙しい We are busy making *preliminary arrangements* for some guests coming from the U.S. next week.

したしらべ 下調べ ▶会議に先立って下調べをする *do* one's *homework* before a meeting (➤ homework は「(会議・討論などのための)下調べ」) ‖ゆうべはとても眠くてきょうの(授業の)下調べをすることができなかった I felt so sleepy last night (that) I could not *prepare* (*for*) today's lessons.

したたか **tough** /tʌf/ ▶彼は転んでもただでは起きないしたたかな男だ He is the sort of *tough* guy that can turn even misfortunes to his advantage.
▶マガジンラックの角に向こうずねをしたたか打ちつけた I *banged* my shin (*badly*) on the corner of the magazine rack.

したたらず 舌足らず **1**【舌が回らない】▶彼女はまだ子供っぽい舌足らずな発音をする She still speaks with a childish *lisp*.
2【不十分】▶舌足らずな説明 an *unsatisfactory* [*inadequate* / *insufficient*] explanation (➤ それぞれ「不満足な」,「妥当でない」,「不十分な」に相当).

したたる 滴る **drip** ▶蛇口から水が滴っている Water *is dripping* from the faucet. ‖彼の額から汗が滴り落ちた Sweat *dripped* off [from] his forehead.

したつづみ 舌鼓 ▶外国から来た旅行者たちは日本の珍味に舌鼓を打った The tourists from overseas *ate* Japanese delicacies *with relish* [*gusto*]. (➤「賞味した」の意).

したっぱ 下っ端 an **underling**
‖下っ端役人 a petty official.

したづみ 下積み ▶あの作家は下積みが長かったらしい I hear the writer had lived in *obscurity* for many years. (➤ live in obscurity で「世に埋もれて生きる」).
▶《貼り紙》下積み禁止 *Keep* (this box) *on top*.

[1]**したて 下手** ▶ここは下手に出たほうが得でしょう We would do better to *take a humble attitude* here. ‖下手に出りゃあつけ上がりやがって! Don't let my *humble attitude* go to your head! (➤「私が控えめな態度に出ていることでいい気になるな」の意).
‖(相撲の)下手投げ *shitate-nage*, an under-arm throw.

[2]**したて 仕立て** **tailoring** (紳士服の); **dressmaking** (婦人・子供服の) ▶仕立て下ろしの服 a *brand-new* suit ‖あの教授はいつも仕立ての良い服を着ている That professor always wears *well-tailored* suits.
‖仕立屋 a tailor (紳士服の); a dressmaker (婦人・子供服の).

したてる 仕立てる **1**【服をこしらえる】**have ... made** [**tailored**] (作ってもらう) ▶このスーツは中島屋で仕立てた I *had* this suit *made* at Nakajima-ya.
2【養成する】**groom** +目 ▶彼の夢は息子を一流のスキーヤーに仕立て上げることだった His dream was to *groom* his son *to be* a first-class skier.

したどり 下取り a **trade-in** ▶古いカメラを下取りしてもらって最新型を買った I *traded in* my old camera *for* the latest model. (➤ 動詞の trade in は「下取りに出す」) ‖お手持ちの車の下取りもいたします We'll *give* you *a trade-in* on your old car.
‖下取り価格 a trade-in price ‖下取り品 a trade-in.

したなめずり 舌なめずり ▶ライオンはごちそうを前にして舌なめずりをした The lion *licked his chops* at the good meal set before him. (➤ chops は「(主に動物の)顎, 口」. 人間の場合には lick one's lips というのがふつう).

したぬり 下塗り an **undercoat** (**of paint**) ▶下塗りを施す apply an *undercoat*.

したばき 下履き (**outdoor**) **shoes** ▶下履きのまま上がって来ないで! Don't come in with your *shoes* on!

じたばた ▶じたばたすると命がないぞ *One false move*, and you're dead. / *Move* and I'll kill you. ‖《警官が犯人に》じたばたするな *Don't move* (a muscle)! / *Freeze!*

したばたらき 下働き ▶彼は父親の下働きをしながら家業を継ぐ準備をした He prepared to take over the family business by *working under* his father *as an assistant*. ‖いつまでもこんな下働きはごめんだ I don't want to keep on *working for other people* like this.

したばら 下腹 **the** [one's] **lower abdomen** [**belly**].

したび 下火 ▶火事はやっと下火になったようだ The fire seems to *be* finally *dying down*.
▶《比喩的》その歌手の人気はもう下火だ The popularity of that singer *is* already *on the wane*. (➤

原義は「月が欠けかかっている」) ‖ 韓流ブームもひところと比べると**下火になった** The popularity of South Korean movies and stars *has cooled down* [*is on the wane*] compared to what it was like before.

したびらめ 舌平目《魚》a **sole** ▶シタビラメのムニエル *sole* meunière /mʌnjéəʳ/ ‖ シタビラメはお好きですか Do you like *sole*? (➤ 食品としてはふつう Ⓤ 扱いで, a sole, soles などとしない).

-したほうがいい →ほう.

したまち 下町 ▶この辺りにはまだ東京の下町情緒が残っている This district still has the atmosphere of the *old downtown* Tokyo.

> **◀解説▶「下町」と downtown**
> 「下町」が downtown と訳されることがあるが, downtown は「中心街」「繁華街」に近く, 日本語の「下町」とは一致しない. 東京の浅草・神田・日本橋などの「下町」をいう場合は, He was born in the old downtown district of Tokyo. (彼は東京の下町生まれだ) のように説明的に表現するほうがよい.

したまわる 下回る ▶ことしの野菜の値段は平年を下回っている This year's vegetable prices are *lower than those of an average year*. ‖ 入場者数は我々の予想を下回った The number of visitors *was less than we had expected*.

したみ 下見 a **preliminary inspection** ▶彼らは土地の下見に行った They made *a preliminary inspection* of the land. ‖ 私たちは受験会場の下見に行った We *went to take a* (*preliminary*) *look at* the place where the examination(s) would be held.

したむき 下向き 1【下を向くこと】 ▶ホースの先を上に向けないで下向きにしなさい Aim the end of the hose *downward*, not upward.
2【下降すること】 ▶景気が下向きになり始めた The economy is *on the decline*. ／Business is *taking a downward turn*.

じだらく 自堕落 ▶自堕落な生活を送る lead a *degenerate* [*dissipated* ／ *dissolute*] life.

しだれざくら 枝垂れ桜 a **weeping cherry tree**.

しだれやなぎ 枝垂れ柳 a **weeping willow**.

したん 紫檀《植物》**rosewood**.

しだん 師団《軍》a **division**.

じたん 時短 **reduction of working hours, time shortening** ▶時短料理 *time-saving* cooking.

じだん 示談 (an) **out-of-court settlement** ▶その自動車事故は示談になった That car accident *was settled out of court* [*was settled privately*]. ‖ **示談金**は50万円だった *The money paid as* [*for*] *settlement* was five hundred thousand yen.

じだんだ 地団太 ▶妹が当たりくじを引き自分は空くじを引いたので, 姉はじだんだを踏んで悔しがった Since her (younger) sister drew a prize while she drew a blank, she *stamped her feet* in frustration.

1**しち 七** **seven**; **the seventh** (7番目) ▶7時のニュース the *seven o'clock* news.

2**しち 質** **pawn** /pɔːn/ (質入れ) ▶金の指輪を質に入れる *pawn* a gold ring ‖ そのカメラは質に入っている The camera *is in pawn* [*in hock*].
‖**質草** a pawn ‖ **質流れ** foreclosure (➤ 1つ1つの事例は Ⓒ) ‖ **質屋** a pawnshop.

じち 自治 **self-government**; **autonomy** /ɔːtάːnəmi/ (自治権) ‖(町の)**自治会** a neighborhood association ‖ **自治区** an autonomous region ‖ **自治領** an autonomous territory ‖ **地方自治体** a local government.

しちかいき 七回忌 the sixth anniversary of a person's death (追悼日); a Buddhist memorial service held on the sixth anniversary of a person's death (➤ 説明的な訳). →-回忌

しちがつ 七月 **July**《略 Jul.》▶七夕は7月7日だ The Star Festival is on *July* 7. ‖ この地域では7月に花火大会が行われる There are firework(s) displays *in July* in this area.

しちごさん 七五三 ***Shichi-go-san***
日本紹介 ✉ **七五三は11月15日に7歳・5歳・3歳の子供を神社に参拝させる伝統的な風習です. 子供は晴れ着を着て親とともに神社に行き, 健康を感謝し, 幸福を祈願します** *Shichi-go-san* is the traditional Japanese custom of taking children of seven, five and three years of age to a Shinto shrine on November 15. Dressed in their best clothes, the children are taken to the shrine by their parents who thank the god(s) for their good health and pray for their happiness.

しちじゅう 七十 **seventy**; **the seventieth** (70番目).

しちてんばっとう 七転八倒 ▶急な腹痛で一晩じゅう七転八倒した I spent the night *rolling about* [*writhing*] with acute stomach pain. (➤ writhe /raɪð/ は「のたうち回る」).

しちふくじん 七福神 **the Seven Gods of Fortune**; **the Seven Lucky Gods**
日本紹介 ✉ **七福神は幸運の神様として信仰されている7人の神様です. ふつう, 7人が一緒に宝船と呼ばれるめでたい船に乗った姿で, 絵や彫刻の題材とされます** *Shichi-fukujin* are the seven gods who are worshipped because they are believed to bring good luck [fortune]. They are usually depicted in pictures or carvings as a group aboard an auspicious boat called the '*Takarabune* (Treasure Boat).'
▶七福神巡りをする make the rounds of *the temples dedicated to the Seven Gods of Fortune*.

しちめんちょう 七面鳥 a **turkey** ▶アメリカでは感謝祭の日には七面鳥料理を食べる In America, people eat *turkey* on Thanksgiving Day.

しちめんどうくさい 七面倒臭い ▶しちめんどうくさい仕事 a *troublesome job*.

しちや 質屋 →しち.

1**しちゃく 試着する** **try on** ▶このスーツを試着したいんですが I'd like to *try* this suit *on*.
‖**試着室** a fitting room.

2**しちゃく 死着** **DOA** (➤ dead on arrival の頭文字語; 輸送した生物が到着時に死んでいること).

しちゅう 支柱 a **prop** ▶背丈の伸びたヒマワリに支柱を立ててやった I *propped* up the overgrown sunflowers with *sticks*.
▶その家族は事故で一家の支柱を失った That family lost *the family breadwinner* in that accident. (➤ breadwinner は「一家の稼ぎ手」).

シチュー (a) **stew** /stjuː/ ▶ビーフシチュー beef *stew* ‖ シチューを作る make *stew*.

しちゅうかんせん 市中感染 **community-acquired infection**.

1**しちょう 市長** a **mayor** /méɪəʳ/ ▶大阪市長選に立候補する run for *Mayor of Osaka*.
‖**市長選挙** a mayoral election ‖ **一日市長** mayor for a day.

²しちょう 試聴 ▶この CD, 試聴してよろしいですか May I *listen to* this CD *before I buy it*? ‖ この音楽配信サービスは10日間試聴できます You *can have* this music streaming service for a ten-day *free trial period*.

¹じちょう 自重 ▶二度とこのような失敗をしないよう自重してもらいたい *Act more cautiously* [*with more restraint*] so that you don't repeat this sort of mistake. ‖ もう高校生なのだから自重しなさい Now that you are a high school student, you have to *be more thoughtful* [*careful*].

²じちょう 次長 an assistant general manager.

³じちょう 自嘲する mock oneself ▶自嘲気味の口調で in a *self-mocking* tone.

しちょうかく 視聴覚の audio-visual ▶この学校では視聴覚教育に力を入れてきた This school has been putting special emphasis on *audio-visual education*.
‖視聴覚教材 audio-visual materials.

¹しちょうしゃ 視聴者 a (TV) viewer ; an audience(集合的に) ▶全国の視聴者 a nationwide *audience* ‖ 視聴者参加のクイズ番組 an *audience participation* quiz show (➤電話で参加する番組は call-in [phone-in] (program) という. ラジオの場合は listener-phone-in show) ‖ 視聴者から抗議の電話が殺到した A great number of *viewers* called (in) to protest.

²しちょうしゃ 市庁舎 a city government office.

しちょうそん 市町村 cities, towns and villages ; municipalities(地方自治体).

しちょうりつ 視聴率 an audience [viewer] rating ▶ゆうべのオリンピックの開会式の視聴率は30.2パーセントだった The *viewer* [*audience*] *rating* of the Olympic opening ceremony last night was 30.2 percent. ‖ そのテレビ番組は視聴率が高い [低い] That TV program *has a large* [*small*] *audience*.

しちりん 七輪 a *shichirin* ; an earthen cooking stove that uses charcoal (➤説明的な訳).

じちんさい 地鎮祭 a Shinto rite of purifying a construction site / a Shinto groundbreaking ceremony (➤説明的な訳).

¹しつ 質 quality ▶質のよい米 rice *of* (*good*) *quality* ‖ 最近のハリウッド映画は質が落ちた Recent Hollywood films have declined in *quality*. ‖ 研究員はその製品の質を向上させる努力をしている The researchers are working hard to improve the *quality* of the product.
‖画質 image quality.

²しつ 室 a room ▶ 521号室 *Room* 521 ‖ 室料 a *room charge*.

しっ ▶彼女は猫を台所からしっしっと追い払った She *shooed* the cat out of the kitchen.

じつ 実 ▶名を捨てて実を取る go for *the real thing* [*real achievement*] and throw aside mere reputation ‖ 彼は実のある人物だから約束は守ってくれるだろう He's a *sincere* [*solid*] person, so you should be able to trust him to keep his word.
▶実を言えば彼女はぼくのいとこなんだ *To tell* (*you*) *the truth*, she is my cousin. ‖ 実を言うと私はもう彼女の言うことを信用していないんです *The truth is*, I don't believe her any more. ‖ 実を言うとぼくは補欠入学なんだよ *Actually*, I was admitted to this school to fill up a vacancy. ‖ 彼は学生だが, その実全然勉強しない He is a student, but *as a matter of fact*, he doesn't study at all.

☛ 実に, 実の, 実は (→見出語)

しつい 失意 disappointment (失望) ; despair (絶望) ▶私が失意のどん底にいたとき, 彼は親身になって励ましてくれた When I was in the depths of *despair*, he warmly encouraged me.

じついん 実印 a registered seal (➤欧米には実印登録の慣習はない).

しつう 歯痛 dental pain.

じつえき 実益 ▶何か趣味と実益を兼ねた仕事がしたい I want to get a job that *both suits my interests and pays well*. / I want to do work that is *interesting as well as practical*.

じつえん 実演 a practical demonstration (実際にやってみせること) ▶消防署の人は主婦たちに家庭用消火器の使い方を実演してみせた The firefighters *gave* housewives *a practical demonstration* on how to use home fire extinguishers.
‖実演販売 demonstration sales.

しつおん 室温 ▶温かくして, または室温で供します Serve warm or at *room temperature*.

しっか 失火 a fire (火事) ▶その火事は失火ですか, それとも放火ですか *Was the fire accidental* or was it arson? (➤あえて放火と対比するときは accidental を加える).

じっか 実家 one's parents' home ; one's parents' family (家族) ▶産後 2 週間ほど実家に帰ってました I spent two weeks at *my parents' home* after giving birth. ‖ 実家は酒屋をやってます *My parents' family* runs a sake shop.

じつがい 実害 substantial damage [harm] ▶今回の台風では作物に実害はなかった The recent typhoon did [caused] no *substantial damage* to the crops.

しつがいこつ 膝蓋骨 a patella /pətélə/, a kneecap.

しっかく 失格 disqualification 一動 失格する be disqualified ▶彼は 2 度フライングをして失格になった He *was disqualified* for jumping the gun twice.
▶家庭をかえりみないで俺は父親失格だ Having paid little attention to [Having neglected] my family, I'm *a failure* as a father. (➤ a failure は「失格者」).

じつがく 実学 practical learning.

しっかり 1【堅固, ぐらつかない】▶このドイツ製の机はしっかりしている (=頑丈だ) This German-made desk *is sturdy*. ‖ この家のつくりはしっかりしている This house is *sturdily* built.
▶彼女はかぜ気味だったがしっかりした声で歌った She sang *clearly* even though she had a slight cold. ‖ 堀さんはお年だがしっかりした足取りで歩く Mr. Hori walks *steadily* despite his advanced age. ‖ いいか, このことをしっかり覚えておくんだぞ Now, keep this *firmly* in mind.
▶新社長は若いがしっかりしている (=信頼できる) The new president is young, but *trustworthy* [*dependable*]. ‖ うちの息子もしっかりしてきた My son *has become a reliable person*. ‖ 彼の娘さんはとてもしっかりしたお嬢さんだ His daughter is a very *sensible* [*together*] girl. (➤ sensible は「思慮分別があってしっかりしている」の意. together は「落ち着いてしっかりした」の意のインフォーマルな語).
▶しっかりしなさい *Cheer up*! / *Hang in there*! (➤落ち込んでいる人などを励ますとき) ‖ しっかりしろ, すぐに救急車が来るからな *Hang in there*. The ambulance will be here any minute. ‖ 祖父は死に際まで意識がしっかりしていた My grandfather was *conscious* un-

til (the moment) he died.

2【真剣，一生懸命】▶アメリカへ行ったら**しっかり**勉強しなさい Study *hard* in the United States. ‖テニスのトーナメント，**しっかりね**！*Good luck* in the tennis tournament. ‖**しっかりしなきゃだめじゃないか**！ You need to *shape up*！

3【固くくっついた様子】▶母は子供を**しっかりと**抱いた The mother held her child *tight(ly)*. ‖ジェットコースターに乗るときは横棒に**しっかり**つかまりなさい Hold on *tight* to the bar when you ride the roller coaster. ‖犬は**しっかり**木につないでください Please tie your dog *securely* to the tree.（➤ securely は「確実に，安全に」）.

4【十分】▶**しっかり**眠る［食べる］ sleep［eat］*well*.

しつかん 質感 **texture** ▶フェルメールは牛乳の微妙な**質感**まで見事に表現した Vermeer represented even the subtle *texture* of milk skillfully.

しっかん 疾患 (a) **disease**, an **ailment**.

じっかん 実感 ▶その本を読んで教育の重要性を**実感した** Reading that book *made* me *fully realize* the importance of education. ‖ロシアを旅行してみて，その広さが**実感としてわかった** When I traveled in Russia I *got a real feeling* for how big the country is. ‖ 対話「金メダルを取られてご感想はいかがですか」「まだ**実感が湧きません**」 "How do you feel about winning the gold medal?" "*It hasn't sunk in yet.*／*I still can't believe it.*"

しっき 漆器 **lacquerware** /lǽkəʳwèəʳ/, **japan ware**.

しつぎ 質疑 ▶講演のあと**質疑応答**の時間があります The lecture will be followed by a *question-and-answer* session.

じつぎ 実技 **skill** ▶**実技**の試験 a *skill* test ‖学科試験には受かったんだけど**実技(試験)**がだめだった I passed the written test but failed the *practical test*.（➤自動車の運転免許試験の実技は driving test または road test という；→実地）.

‖**体育実技** gymnastic exercises.

しっきゃく 失脚 ▶その政治家はかなりの実力者だったが今度の政変で**失脚したらしい** That politician used to be a big power in the government, but I hear he *has lost his position*［*has been ousted from power*］amid the recent political changes.（➤ oust /aʊst/ は「追放する」）.

しつぎょう 失業 **unemployment** 一動 **失業する** **lose** one's **job** ▶父は人員整理で**失業した** My father *has lost his job* due to cutbacks. ‖**失業中**なので**失業手当**をもらっている Since I am now *out of work*, I am receiving *unemployment benefits*［*an unemployment allowance*］.（➤後半は《英》では I am on the dole. ともいう）《参考》失業中であることをおどけて I'm between jobs at the moment.（文字どおりには「現在，仕事と仕事の合間にいる」と表現することがある．

‖**失業者** an unemployed person；the unemployed（➤総称）‖**失業対策** an unemployment (relief) policy ‖**失業対策事業** an unemployment-relief project ‖**失業率** an unemployment rate.

じっきょう 実況 ▶現場からの**実況放送** an on-the-spot *broadcast* ‖彼はサッカーの**実況放送**に聴き入っている He is listening to the *play-by-play broadcast* of the football［soccer］game. ‖事故現場の様子が**実況中継された** The scene of the accident *was aired live* /laɪv/.

じつぎょう 実業 **business** ▶**実業界**に入る enter *the business world*.

‖**実業家** a businessman(男), a businesswoman (女)；a businessperson［複 businesspeople］(男女共用) ‖**実業学校** a vocational school ‖**実業教育** vocational education.

しっきん 失禁 **incontinence** ▶彼女はジェットコースターに乗っていて思わず**失禁した** She *lost control of her bladder*［*wet herself*／*wet her pants*］while riding a roller coaster.（➤ wet を使う表現はインフォーマル）‖老人は寝たきりで**失禁症状がある** The old man *is* bedridden and *incontinent*.

シック **chic** /ʃiːk/ ▶彼女は新しい夏服を**シック**に着こなしている She looks *chic* in her new summer suit.

しっくい 漆喰 **mortar** /mɔ́ːʳṭəʳ/（モルタル；れんが・ブロックなどの接合材として用いる）；**plaster**（壁・天井などに塗る）；**stucco**（壁などに施す化粧用）▶壁に**しっくいを塗る** *plaster* walls.

シックハウス ‖**シックハウス症候群** sick house syndrome.

しっくり ▶進とはどうも**しっくりいかない**んだ I *cannot get along well with* Susumu. ‖彼女，ご主人と**しっくりいってない**みたいね She seems to *be on bad terms with* her husband. ‖この壁に抽象画ではいまひとつ**しっくりしない** Somehow an abstract painting just *does not go very well with* this wall. ‖この表現はどうも**しっくりこない**ね That way of putting it just somehow *doesn't get it right*［*capture the meaning*］.

じっくり ▶彼の話を**じっくり**聴く listen to him *carefully* ‖先生と**じっくり**話し合う *have a heart-to-heart talk with* one's teacher ‖何も急いで結論を出すことはない．**じっくり考えよう**よ We don't need to jump to conclusions. Let's *think it over* (*carefully*). ‖ 対話「このレポートはあすまでですか」「いや，**じっくりやって**，いいものに仕上げてくれ」 "Do I have to finish this report by tomorrow?" "No, *take your time* and do a good job."

しつけ 躾 **discipline** /dísəplɪn/ ▶家庭の**しつけ** home *discipline* ‖この学校は**しつけ**が厳しいので有名だ This school is well known for its strict *discipline*. ‖母は**しつけ**にやかましい My mother is strict about *how we should behave ourselves*.（➤ behave oneself は「行儀よくする」）‖あの子は**しつけがなっていない**みたいだ He［She］seems *not* to *have been taught any manners*.（➤「行儀作法を教わっていない」の意）‖厳しい**しつけ**の反動で，娘は最近私のいうことを聞こうとしない It may be a reaction to my strict *parenting*, but my daughter won't listen to me［obey me］these days.

しっけ 湿気 **humidity**；**damp(ness)**（不快な）；**moisture**（適度な湿り気）▶**湿気の多い**気候 *humid* climate ‖**湿気を含んだ**風 a *moist* wind ‖のりは**湿気**を嫌う Nori is vulnerable to *humidity*. ‖畳は**湿気**で傷んでいた The tatami mats had been damaged by *dampness*. ‖日本の夏は**湿気が多い** Japanese summers *are humid*. ‖カメラは**湿気のない**場所に置きなさい Keep your camera in a *dry* place.

しっけい 失敬 ▶トムはお父さんの秘蔵のワインを１本**失敬しちゃった**よ Tom *made off with* one of his father's treasured bottles of wine.（➤ make off with は「…を持ち逃げする」の意のインフォーマルな言い方）.

じっけい 実刑 **a prison sentence**（実刑判決）▶あいつは最低10年の**実刑判決**を食らいそうだ He is likely to get at least a 10-year *prison sentence*.

しっけつ 失血 **blood loss** ▶**失血**死する die from

し

blood loss [*loss of blood*].

しつける ▶(排便などを)よくしつけられた犬 a *toilet-trained* [*housebroken*] dog ‖ スカートの裾をしつける *baste* [*tack*] the hem of a skirt.

▶家でちゃんとしつけているのかしら. お行儀の悪い子たちだわ I wonder if they *are taught good manners* at home. They don't know how to behave themselves.

し

1**しつげん 湿原** a **marsh**; (a) **marshland** (湿地帯) ▶釧路湿原 Kushiro *Marsh*.

2**しつげん 失言** a **slip of the tongue** /tʌŋ/ (うっかり口を滑らせること); a **gaffe**, an **improper remark** (不適切な発言) ▶彼の不用意な**失言**で会議が中断した His careless *slip* (*of the tongue*) caused the meeting to be adjourned. ‖ 総理大臣の**失言**はアジア各国に大きな波紋を投げかけた The Prime Minister's *gaffe* [*inappropriate remark*] caused a great sensation in Asian countries. ‖ それはきみの**失言**だ That is *something you should not have said*. / You *put your foot in your mouth*. (➤ 後者は「へまなことを言う」の意のインフォーマルな表現).

1**じっけん 実験** an **experiment** (科学の); a **test** (試みとしての) **一動 実験する experiment, test 一形 実験の experimental**

> 【文型】
> 被験者(A)で実験する
> experiment on A
> 手法・材料など(B)を使って実験する
> experiment with B
> ➤ 後者は「…を試してみる」に当たることが多い

▶動物[ヒト]で**実験する** *experiment on* animals [humans] ‖ 新素材で**実験する** *experiment with* new materials.

▶**実験室**で化学の**実験をする** *do* [*carry out*] *a* chemical *experiment* in *a laboratory* ‖ 理科で静電気の**実験をする** *do an experiment* on static electricity in science class ‖ 核**実験**を行う conduct *a nuclear test*.

▶私はカロリー摂取についての彼の研究の**実験台**になった I became *a subject for an experiment* in his research on calorie intake. ‖ その方法を**実験的に**(=試験的に)採用してみたらどうだろう? How about using that method *on a trial basis*? ‖ **動物実験**の結果, その薬には重大な副作用がないことがわかった *Experiments on animals* [*Animal experiments*] proved the medicine to be free from any serious side effects.

‖**実験段階** an experimental stage ‖ **実験道具**(化学の) chemistry apparatus /æpəræ̀təs/.

2**じっけん 実権** **real power** ▶うちで**実権を握っている**のは母だ In our family, it is our mother who *holds real power* [*wears the pants*]. (➤ wear the pants は「(妻が)夫を尻に敷く」に相当するインフォーマルな表現) ‖ その会社では会長が**実権を握っていて**, 社長は頭が上がらない In that company, the chairman *actually controls the business* and the president has no say (in running it).

じつげん 実現 **realization 一動 実現する realize** (現実化する); **come true** (本当になる) ▶夢を**実現させる** *make* one's dream *come true* / *realize* [*fulfil*] one's dream ‖ 念願を**実現する** *realize* [*achieve*] one's ambition ‖ 真に民主的な社会の**実現は困難**だ A really democratic society is *difficult to realize*. ‖ ぼくのギリシャ旅行の夢は**実現し**そうだ It seems that my dream of traveling in Greece will *come true*. ‖ その計画は資金難のため**実現しなかった** The plan *fell through* because of financial difficulties. (➤ fall through は「ご破算になる」) ‖ 私が知りたいのはこの計画が本当に**実現可能**かどうかということだ I would like to know if this plan is really *feasible*. (➤ feasible は possible の堅い言い方) / All I want to know is whether this plan will really *work* (or not).

しつこい 1【執ような】 persistent /pəˈsístənt/ ▶しつこい販売員 a *persistent* [*pushy*] salesperson ‖ 酔っ払いにしつこく付きまとわれて困った I had a lot of trouble when I was followed by a *persistent* drunk. ‖ 父は私にK大学に行くように**しつこく言った** My father *kept saying* that I should go to K University. ‖ あの子は何でも**しつこく聞きたがる** He is an *inquisitive* boy. (➤「詮索好きな」の意).

▶今度のかぜはしつこくてなかなか治らない I can't get over [get rid of] my *stubborn* cold. (➤ stubborn は「頑固な」の意; 「しつこいかぜ」を a deep-seated cold ともいう) ‖ **対話**「一度だけでいいからデートしてくれない?」「しつこい人ね. 嫌といったら嫌よ!」"Couldn't we go on just one date?" "*Don't be so pushy*. No means no." (➤ pushy は「厚かましい」の意).

2【色・味などが】 heavy, rich; greasy (油っこい) ▶このロールキャベツは私には少ししつこい This stuffed cabbage roll is a little *heavy* for me.

1**しっこう 執行** **execution** /èksɪkjúːʃən/ **一動 執行する execute** /éksɪkjuːt/ +㊐ (主に死刑の) ▶刑を**執行する** *execute* a sentence ‖ 逮捕令状を**執行する** *execute* an arrest warrant.

‖**執行委員会** an executive committee ‖ **執行部** the executives.

2**しっこう 失効する** **expire** (期限切れになる) ▶私の運転免許証は書き換えを忘れて**失効した** My driver's license *expired* because I forgot to renew it.

1**じっこう 実行** **practice 一動 実行する carry out** ▶それはすばらしい考えだ. 早速**実行に移して**みよう That's a wonderful idea. Let's *try it* (*out*) [*put it into practice*] right away. ‖ お父さんには自分が言ったことを**実行して**ほしいと思います I hope my father will *carry out* [*keep*] his promise (to us) [will *do* what he said]. ‖ あの人は**言うだけで実行しない** He's *all talk and no action*. ‖ 公約を**実行する**(=果たす)政治家はあまりいないようだ Only a few politicians seem to *fulfill* [*carry out*] their campaign promises.

▶全く**実行不可能な**(=実行に移せない)アイデア a completely *impracticable* idea ‖ その計画はどちらも**実行不可能だ** *Neither* of those plans *is workable* [*feasible*]. (➤「採用できないし成功もしない」という含みがある) ‖ 私は**実行力のある人**を尊敬する I respect a man who *is capable of getting things done*.

‖**実行委員** (a member of) an executive committee ‖ **実行委員会** an executive committee ‖ **実行ファイル** an executable file.

☛ **不言実行** (→見出語)

2**じっこう 実効** ▶**実効性のある**(=効果的な)措置をとる take *effective* measures.

しっこうゆうよ 執行猶予 a **stay of execution** ▶被告人は懲役1年, **執行猶予3年**の判決を受けた The accused was sentenced to one year in prison *with a three-year stay* (*of execution*).

しっこく 漆黒の **jet-black, ebony**.

しつごしょう 失語症 **aphasia** /əféɪʒə/ ▶失語症の人 *an aphasic*.

じっさい 実際 **1**【現実, 実地】**practice**（理論に対して実地）; **actuality**（可能性に対して現実性）; **reality**（空想・理想像に対して現実）一 副 **実際に（は）** **practically, actually, really** ▶理論と実際は必ずしも一致しない Theory and *practice* don't necessarily go together. ‖ 彼女は忙しそうにしているが, 実際はほとんどすることがないのだ She pretends to be busy, but *in reality* [*actuality*] she has little to do. ‖ あの人は実際は老人ではありません. そう見えるだけです He [She] isn't *really* old. He [She] only looks old. ‖ これは島根県で実際にあった話です This is something that *actually* happened in Shimane Prefecture. ‖ その問題は一見易しそうに見えたが, 実際にやってみるととても難しかった The problem looked easy, but I found it very hard when I *actually* tried to solve it. ‖ 英語をいくら勉強しても実際に使えなければ何にもならない There is no point in studying English hard if you can't *put* it *to practical use*. ‖ 実際のところ私はそのグループと何の関係もありません *In fact*, I have nothing to do with the group. ‖ あの女優はテレビで見ると実際より大きく見える The actress looks taller on TV *than she actually is* [*than she does in person*].

2【実に】**really**; **very**（とても）▶彼のタイ旅行の話は実際おもしろかった What he told us about his trip to Thailand was *really* [*very*] interesting. (➤ His talk about ... とすると通例「彼の演説」の意味に受け取られる).

じつざい 実在 **existence**（存在）▶私は幽霊の実在を信じない I don't believe in (the *existence* of) ghosts. ‖ 実在しない町 an *unreal* [*imaginary*] town ‖ この小説のヒロインは実在の人物をモデルにしている The heroine of this novel is modeled after a *real* person.

しっさく 失策 an **error**, a **mistake**; a **blunder**（大失敗）▶三塁手の失策が敗因だった The *error* by the third baseman was the cause of the defeat. ‖ 彼は仕事の上で大失策をして首になった He committed *a big blunder* on the job and got fired.

しつじ 執事 a **butler**.

1**じっし 実施する** **conduct** +目 ▶アンケート調査を実施する *conduct* [*do*] research by sending out questionnaires ‖ 国勢調査はあす実施されます The census will *be conducted* tomorrow.
▶春の交通安全運動実施中 Spring Traffic Safety Campaign *Now* in full swing [*in effect*] ‖ 新しい列車ダイヤは4月1日から実施される（＝有効になる）The new train schedule *takes effect* [*goes into effect* / *becomes effective*] on April 1.

2**じっし 実子** one's **own** [**biological**] **child**.

じっしつ 実質 **substance** ▶形式より実質が大事だ *Substance* is more important than form. ‖ きょうは顔合わせだけで, 実質的な話し合いはあすからだ We just want to meet and get to know you today. Let's start the *actual* discussions tomorrow. ‖ 秘書という名目で雇われたが, 実質的には小間使いのような仕事だった I was hired as a secretary, but *actually* I was (more) like a maid.
‖**実質賃金** real wages.

しつじつごうけん 質実剛健 ▶わが校は質実剛健を校風にしている The motto of my school is *simplicity and fortitude*.

じっしゃかい 実社会 **the real world** ▶ここで学んだことを実社会で生かしてほしい I hope you'll use what you've learned here in *the real world*. ‖ 学生たちは大学を卒業し, 実社会へと巣立っていった The students graduated from university and moved out into *the working world*. ‖ 父は教育らしい教育は受けておらず, ほとんどの知識は厳しい実社会から得たものだ My father has had little schooling; almost all his learning came from *the school of hard knocks*. (➤ the school of hard knocks は「厳しい実社会という学校［道場］で」の意).

じっしゅう 実習 ▶中学校で教育実習をする *do practice teaching* at a junior high school ‖ きょうは家庭科の授業で調理の実習をした Today we had *practical training* in cooking in home economics class.
‖**実習生** a trainee /treɪníː/; an intern（医学の, また実地に職業経験をする）‖ **教育実習生** a student [practice / practicum / trainee] teacher, a teacher trainee.

じっしゅきょうぎ 十種競技 **the decathlon**.

しつじゅん 湿潤な **humid** ▶湿潤な気候 a *humid* climate.

しっしょう 失笑 ▶彼はとんちんかんな質問をして皆の失笑を買った His nonsensical questions *made* everyone *burst into laughter despite themselves*.

じっしょう 実証する **prove** /pruːv/ +目 ▶その理論の正しさがいくつかの方法で実証された The truth of the theory *was proved* in several different ways.
▶実証的研究を行う conduct *empirical* research.

じつじょう 実情 **the actual state**; **the real condition**; **the actual** [**real**] **state of affairs**（物事の実際の状況）▶国土交通大臣が災害の実情を視察した The Land, Infrastructure and Transport Minister inspected *the actual condition* [*situation*] of the disaster. ‖ 彼女はエチオピアの実情を話してくれた She told us *the* (*real*) *state of affairs* [*how things stand*] in Ethiopia. ‖ この国では現在10人に3人が失業しているというのが実情だ *As a matter of fact*, three out of ten people in this country are jobless.

1**しっしん 失神する** **faint** ▶そのロック歌手のコンサートで多くの女の子が失神した A lot of girls *fainted* at that rock singer's concert.

2**しっしん 湿疹** **eczema** /éksɪmə/ ▶背中に湿疹ができる get *eczema* on the back.

じっしんほう 十進法 **the decimal system, the base-ten system, base 10.** ➝一進法.

じっすう 実数 an **actual number**（実際の数）;《数学》a **real number**.

じっせいかつ 実生活 ▶彼らは映画で夫婦を演じたが実生活でも夫婦だ They played a husband and wife in the movie, and are married *in real life* too.

しっせき 叱責 (a) **reprimand**（上司による）一 動 **叱責する** **reprimand** +目; **scold** +目 ➝叱る ▶ぼくは上司から無断欠勤を厳しく叱責された I *was reprimanded* severely for being absent from work without notice.

じっせき 実績 an **achievement**（業績）; (a) **performance**（出来栄え）▶父は仕事上の実績が認められて部長に昇進した My father was promoted to division head in recognition of his outstanding *job performance*. ‖ M 教授はこれまで際立った実績を上げていない So far, Professor M hasn't *achieved* anything notable.

1**じっせん 実践** **practice** 一 動 **実践する** **practice** +目, 《英》**practise** +目 ▶理論を実践に移す *put* a theory *into practice* ‖ 快楽主義を**実践する** *practice* hedonism.

2**じっせん 実戦** **an actual match** [**game**](試合); **actual combat** [**warfare**](戦争) ▶**実戦**に備える prepare for *an actual match* [*game*] ‖ **実戦**さながらの演習を行う conduct maneuvers *as if in actual combat* ‖ 宮本武蔵は**実戦**に強かった Miyamoto Musashi was strong in *actual combat*.

3**じっせん 実線** a **solid line.** →破線.

しっそ 質素な **simple**(簡素な); 《英また》 **homely**(ぜいたくではない); **plain**(地味な); **humble**(みすぼらしい) ▶パンと牛乳だけの**質素な**食事 a *simple* [*plain*] meal of bread and milk ‖ 彼は金持ちなのに**質素な生活**をしている Though he is rich, he *lives simply* [*plainly* / *a simple life*]. (➤ 副詞 1 語でいうほうがより一般的) ‖ 彼女は**質素な**服装をしている She *is plainly dressed.*

1**しっそう 失踪** **disappearance** 一動 **失踪する** **disappear** ▶彼女の夫が**失踪**してから 5 年たった It has been five years since her husband *disappeared.* ‖ その男は妻子を捨てて**失踪した** He *walked out on* his wife and children, *and nobody knows his whereabouts.* (➤ walk out on は「…を(見)捨てる」; whereabouts は「居所」).

2**しっそう 疾走する** **move** [**run**] **at** (a) **high speed** ▶子供たちは50メートルを全力**疾走した** The children *ran* [*dashed*] fifty meters *with all their might.*

じつぞう 実像 ▶邪馬台国の**実像**に迫ろうとする試み the efforts to find *what the Yamatai Kingdom really was* ‖ 伝記などで語られている姿は詩人の**実像**とは大きくかけ離れている The descriptions of the poet that have been passed down in biographies differ greatly from *what he really was* [*what he was really like*].

しっそく 失速 **stall** 一動 **失速する** **stall** ▶飛行機は突然**失速して**, 急降下し始めた All of a sudden, the plane *stalled* and began losing altitude rapidly.

じつぞんしゅぎ 実存主義 **existentialism.**

しったい 失態 a **blunder** ▶彼は酔って**失態を演じた** He got drunk and *made a spectacle* [*fool*] *of himself.*

1**じったい 実態** **the truth** (真実); **the actual** [**real**] **state of affairs**(物事の実際の状況) ▶いつかあの会社の**実態**を明らかにしてやる Someday, I'm going to show the world *the truth* about that company. ‖ 旅行案内を読んでもその国の庶民の**暮らしの実態**はわからない Travelers' guidebooks don't tell us about *the actual life* of the ordinary people of the country.

2**じったい 実体** ▶**実体**のない会社 a company that isn't doing actual business / a *dummy* company.

しったかぶり 知ったかぶり ▶彼は何でも**知ったかぶり**をする He *pretends to know everything.* / He *is a know-it-all.* (➤ know-it-all は「知ったかぶりをする人」の意のインフォーマルな語).

しったげきれい 叱咤激励する **give a pep talk.**

じつだん 実弾 a **bullet** ▶この銃には**実弾**が入っている There are (*real*) *bullets* in this gun. (➤ real は入れないのがふつう) / This gun is loaded.

‖**実弾射撃** firing practice with live ammunition.

しっち 湿地 **marshy** [**boggy**] **ground,** (a) **marsh** ▶ツンドラの**湿地帯** a tundra *bog* ‖ この辺は昔は**湿地**だった This area used to be *a marsh.*

じっち 実地 ▶その理論を**実地に応用する** *put* [*carry*] the theory *into practice* ‖ 彼女には教育の**実地経験**がない She has no *practical experience* in teaching. ‖ (運転免許の)ペーパーテストはパスしたが, **実地試験**ではねられた I passed the written test but failed the driving test. ‖ 運転は理屈じゃない. **実地で覚える**んだよ You can't learn to drive on theory. You need *hands-on* practice. (➤ hands-on は「実地の」).

‖**実地調査** an on-the-spot survey.

じっちゅうはっく 十中八九 ▶**十中八九**あすは雨が降るよ *Ten to one* it will rain tomorrow. ‖ **十中八九**彼はちえみをパーティーに連れてくると思う *Chances are* [*Most likely*] he will bring Chiemi to the party.

じっちょく 実直な **honest**(正直な).

しっつい 失墜 **loss** 一動 **失墜する** **lose** +㊐ ▶教授はそのテレビ討論会での失態で権威を**失墜してしまった** The professor *lost* his prestige [*lost* credibility] because of his gaffe in that TV debate.

じつづき 地続き ▶太古この島は大陸と**地続き**だったといわれている It is said that in ancient times this island was *contiguous to* the continent. (➤ contiguous /kəntíɡjuəs/ は「隣接する」).

しってん 失点 a **run allowed**(許した得点) ▶その契約をとれなかったことは彼の職歴上の大きな**失点**となった His failure to land the contract became a big *setback* in his career.

しっと 嫉妬 **jealousy** /dʒéləsi/ 一動 **嫉妬する** **be** [**feel**] **jealous** 《of》; **envy** +㊐ (羨む) ▶彼女は**嫉妬**で物事の判断ができない She is blinded by *jealousy.* ‖ その子は**嫉妬心**から妹をぶった The child slapped his sister *out of* [*from*] *jealousy.* ‖ あなたって, どうしてそんなに**嫉妬深い**の? Why are you so *jealous*? ‖ 一郎は成績のよい和夫に**嫉妬している** Ichiro *is jealous of* Kazuo who does well at school. ‖ 彼女たちは真理子が美人なので**嫉妬した** Mariko's beauty *made* them *jealous* [*aroused* their *jealousy*].

しつど 湿度 **humidity** /hju(ː)mídəṭi/ ▶きょうは**湿度**が高い The *humidity* is high today. / It's *humid* today. ‖ **湿度**は62%だ The *humidity* is 62 percent.

‖**湿度計** a hygrometer /haɪɡrɑ́ːməṭər/.

じっと **1【静かにしている様子】**▶**じっとしている** *keep* [*hold*] *still*(➤「動かないでいる」の意) / *stay quiet*(➤「静かにしている」の意) ‖ ママが戻って来るまでここで**じっとしていて**ちょうだい *Stay put* until Mommy comes back. ‖ その蛇は**じっとして**動かなかったので死んでいると思った Since the snake *was laying still* [*wasn't moving*], I thought it was dead. ‖ そのまま**じっとしていなさい** *Hold it.* ‖ 子供は 5 分だって**じっとしてはいられない** Children can't *sit still* even for five minutes. ‖ パレードが来ると聞いて**じっとしていられなくなった** I *felt restless* when I heard a parade was coming this way.

2【精神を集中して】▶子供たちはその背の高いカナダ人を**じっと見つめた** The children *stared at* the tall Canadian. ‖ 彼女はその絵を**じっと見つめていた** She was looking *intently* at the painting. / She was *gazing* at the painting. ‖ 聴衆は石原氏の演説に**じっと耳を傾けた** The audience *listened to* Mr. Ishihara *attentively.*

3【我慢して】▶人々は戦争が終わるのを**じっと待った** People *patiently* waited for the war to end. ‖ 私は涙を**じっとこらえた** I tried *hard* to hold back my tears.

しっとう 執刀 ▶上田医師の**執刀**で手術が行われた Dr. Ueda performed the surgery personally.

じつどう 実働(時間) **hours actually worked.**

しっとり ▶**しっとり**した肌 *moist and supple* skin (➤ moist だけでは実際に湿り気を帯びている印象になる) ‖ 焼きたてのパンは**しっとり**していておいしい Freshly-baked bread is *moist* and tasty. ‖ 彼のお姉さんは**しっとり**と落ち着いた人だ His (older) sister is a *quiet and graceful* person. ‖ さっきの雨で庭が**しっとり**している The garden was [has been] *freshened* by the rain we just had.

じっとり ▶彼の額には汗が**じっとり**にじんでいた His forehead was *damp* with sweat.

しつない 室内の **indoor** /índɔ̀ːʳ/; **interior** /ɪntíərɪəʳ/ (家の内部の) **一副 室内で**［**に**］ **indoors** /ìndɔ́ːʳz/ ▶雨だったので息子は**室内で**遊んだ My son played *indoors* [*in the room*] because it was raining. ‖ 彼は一日中**室内に**閉じこもっていた He stayed *indoors* all day. ‖ 彼女は花で**室内**(＝部屋)を飾った She decorated the *room* with flowers.

‖**室内楽** chamber music ‖ **室内装飾** interior decoration, décor /deɪkɔ́ːʳ/ ‖ **室内遊戯** an indoor game.

じつに 実に **very**(とても; 最も一般的で, ややくだけた語); **extremely**(極端に; very の強意語); **really**(本当に, 全く); **terribly**(すごく; ややくだけた語); **awfully**(恐ろしく, ものすごく; ややくだけた語); **just**(全く; ややくだけた語) ▶**実に**美しい朝 a *very* beautiful morning ‖ あのレストランは**実に**高い That restaurant is *very* [*really*] expensive. (➤ 前者には「客観的に見てとても高い」, 後者には「自分には行けないほど高い」という含みがある) ‖ スペイン旅行は**実に**楽しかった I *really* [*very much*] enjoyed my trip to Spain. (➤ very enjoyed は不可) ‖ きょうは**実に**忙しい I am *extremely* [*terribly* / *awfully*] busy today. ‖ おまえがやろうとしていることは**実に**くだらんことだよ What you are trying to do is *just* absurd.

しつねん 失念 ▶彼と約束があったのをつい**失念した** It just *slipped my mind* that I had an appointment with him.

じつの 実の **real** ▶**実の**母 one's *biological* [*birth*] mother ‖ あの2人は**実の**姉妹よりも仲が良い They are even closer than *real* sisters.

▶**実のところ**, タコ(を食べるの)は好きじゃありません *The fact is* (*that*) [*To tell* (*you*) *the truth*,] I don't like (eating) octopus.

じつは 実は **in fact**(前文を強調, または訂正して); **as a matter of fact**(相手にとって意外なことを言うときや, 相手のことばを否定するとき); **actually**(相手の驚きや困惑などを和らげるために用いる; 実質的な意味をもたないことが多い).

▶その独裁者は病死したのではなく, **実は**毒殺されたのだった The dictator didn't die of illness; *in fact* [*actually*], he was poisoned to death. ‖ **実は**彼は彼女から大金も受け取っていたのです *As a matter of fact*, he also received a lot of money from her. ‖ 対話「アイスクリーム食べない?」「**実は**ダイエット中なの」 "How about some ice cream?" "*Actually*, I'm on a diet."

ジッパー **a zipper, a (zip) fastener** /fǽsənəʳ/, 《英また》 **a zip** ▶**ジッパー**は脇にあります The *zipper* is on the side. ‖ 太ってしまって**ジッパーが上がらない** I've gained weight and now I can't *zip* this *up*. ‖ 背中の**ジッパーを下ろして**くださる? Could you *zip down* [*unzip*] the back of my dress, please?

しっぱい 失敗 (a) **failure**; a **mistake**(間違い) **一動 失敗する** **fail**(＋自), 《米・インフォーマル》 **flunk**(＋自) ▶彼の冒険は**失敗**に終わった His adventure was *a failure*. (➤ 個々の失敗には a がつく) ‖ ロケット打ち上げは**失敗した** The rocket launch *failed*. ‖ 実験は**失敗した** The experiment *failed*. (➤「成功した」は The experiment was a success [successful].) ‖ 私は公務員の採用試験に**失敗した** I *failed* [*flunked*] the civil service examination. (➤「(試験)に落ちる」「(学科)を落とす」の意では単に fail または flunk で (×)fail [flunk] in とはしない).

▶あの会社の株は今上がっている. こんなことならもっと買っておけばよかった. **失敗したなあ** The value of that company's stock is now rising. I wish I had bought more shares. *I really blew it*. (➤ blow は「しくじる」の意のインフォーマルな語. (I) blew it! (しまった)と間投詞的にも使う) ‖ このオムレツ, **失敗しちゃった** This omelet *is a flop*. (➤ flop は「失敗作」の意のインフォーマルな語).

ことわざ **失敗は成功のもと** You learn from your mistakes. (➤「人は自分の失敗から学ぶ」の意) / Mistakes are stepping stones to success. (➤「失敗は成功への踏み石だ」の意).

✉ **一度失敗したからといってくよくよしないで, この次頑張ってください** Don't be discouraged just because you *failed* once. Try harder [your best] next time.

じっぱひとからげ 十把一からげ ▶ぼくをあいつらみたいなちんぴらと**十把一からげ**にしないでよ Hey, don't *lump* me *together* with punks like them.

じっぴ 実費 **actual expenses** ▶**実費**だけ頂けますか Could you pay us just the *actual expenses*? ‖ 交通費は**実費**が支給されます Transportation expenses incurred will be reimbursed. (➤ reimburse /rìːɪmbɔ́ːʳs/ は「(経費などを)返済する」).

しっぴつ 執筆する **write** ＋目 ▶校長先生に学校新聞のコラムの**執筆**をお願いした We have asked our principal to *write* a column for the school newspaper. ‖ 彼女は新聞の連載小説を**執筆中**です She *is writing* [She *is at work on*] a serial novel for a newspaper.

‖**執筆者** a writer ‖ (辞書などの) **執筆協力者** an editorial supporter.

しっぷ 湿布 a **compress** ▶腕に温［冷］**湿布**をする put *a warm* [*cold*] *compress* on one's arm ‖ お母さんが喉に**湿布**をしてくれた Mother applied *a compress* to my throat.

じっぷ 実父 one's **biological** [**birth**] **father** (➤ real father という言い方もあるが,「育ての父」への配慮を欠く表現という捉え方もある).

しっぷう 疾風 a **strong wind**, a **gale.**

じつぶつ 実物 ▶あの女優はテレビで見るより**実物**のほうがきれいだ That actress is much more beautiful *in person* than on TV. (➤ in person は「じかに」) ‖ この子猫の絵は**実物そっくりだ** This painting of a kitten is *true to life*. ‖ **実物大**の模型 *life-size* models ‖ このコインの写真は**実物大**です These photographs of coins are *actual size*.

しっぺがえし しっぺ返し ▶あいつに**しっぺ返し**をしてやったよ I *gave* him *tit for tat*. / I *got* [*hit*] *back at* him.

しっぽ **1【尾】** a **tail** ▶うちの猫は太くて短い**しっぽ**をしている Our cat has a stumpy *tail*. ‖ 犬が**しっぽ**を振って飛んで来た The dog ran to me *wagging its tail*. ‖ その

犬は私を見るとしっぽを巻いて逃げていった Seeing me, the dog ran away *with its tail between its legs*.
2【慣用表現】▶あいつ要領がいいけどいつかきっとしっぽを出すよ He's cunning, but I'm sure he'll *show his true self*［*true colors*］some day. ‖ 上司にしっぽを振るなんて真っ平だ There is no way I would ever *suck up to* my boss.（➤ suck up to は「…にごまをする」）‖ 警察を呼ぶぞと脅かしたら，その押し売りはしっぽを巻いて逃げ出した When I told him that I would call the police, the persistent salesman finally *gave up* and left.

じつぼ 実母 one's **biological**［**birth**］**mother**（➤ real mother という言い方もあるが，「育ての母」への配慮を欠く表現という捉え方もある）.

しつぼう 失望 (a) **disappointment**（落胆，がっかり）；《インフォーマル》(a) **letdown**（約束を実行できずに期待に背くこと） **一動 失望する be disappointed**《by, with》；**be discouraged**《by, at》（落胆する）；**lose** (one's) **hope(s)**（希望をなくす）▶阿部は満塁のチャンスに三振してファンを失望させた Abe *disappointed* the fans［*let* the fans *down*］by striking out when the bases were loaded.（➤ let ... down は「約束を実行してくれると当てにしていたのに，期待を裏切って…をがっかりさせる」で，disappoint より意味が強い）.

> **【文型】**
> 原因(A)に失望する
> **be disappointed by**［**with**］A
> 人(B)に失望する
> **be disappointed in** B
> ～ということに失望する
> **be disappointed that** S＋V
> ➤ 理由を表すときは because S＋V

▶オリンピックのマラソンの結果には失望した I *was disappointed by*［*with*］the results of the Olympic marathon. ‖ きみには失望した I'*m disappointed in* you. ／You've *disappointed* me［*let* me *down*］. ‖ 彼女はチームメンバーに加われなくて失望した She *was disappointed that* she didn't make the team. ‖ 多くのファンがチームの振るわない出だしに失望している Many fans *are disappointed*［*are discouraged*］*by* their team's poor start of the season.（➤ be disappointed が「結果が期待はずれである」に対して，be discouraged は「やる気や自信を損なう」）‖ 日本の柔道選手が外国人選手に負けたからといって失望するな *Don't lose your hope*(*s*) just because Japan lost a judo match to a foreign opponent.
▶あの俳優はミスキャストだ．失望したね *What a disappointment*［*letdown*］! The actor was miscast in that film. ‖ 彼は前途に失望して自殺した *Despairing*［*Despondent*］*about* his future, he killed himself.

しっぽうやき 七宝焼 cloisonné /klɔ̀ɪzənéɪ ‖ klwɑːzóːneɪ/ **work.**

しつむ 執務▶我々は執務中の携帯電話の使用を控えることを申し合わせた We agreed to refrain from using cellphones while we are *at work*.
‖執務室 an office.

じつむ 実務 (practical) business▶本田氏は経理の実務に通じている Mr. Honda *has* (*a*) *practical knowledge* of accounting. ‖ 彼には実務の才がある He has *business ability*［*acumen*］. ／He has a head for business. ‖ 部長は方針を決めるだけで，実務は我々に任されている The manager only decides the course of action and leaves *the nuts and bolts* (of implementing it) to us.（➤ the nuts and bolts は「実際の運営」）.

しつめい 失明する lose one's **sight**▶彼は交通事故で両目とも失明した He *lost his sight* in both eyes in a car accident. ／He *became blind* in both eyes in a car accident.

じつめい 実名 an **actual name**▶容疑者の実名を公表する release the suspect's (*actual*) *name*.

しつもん 質問 a **question 一動 質問する ask** (**a question**)▶質問があります I have *a question* to ask you. ‖ 問 3 の設問について質問があります I have *a question* about problem number 3. ‖ 質問してもよろしいですか May I *ask* you *a question*?（➤May I ask a question to you? とはしない；また May I ask a question of you? は日常的ではない）‖ 何か質問はありますか Do you have any *questions* (for me)?／Are there any *questions*? ‖ その歌手はファンの質問攻めにあった That singer *was overwhelmed by*［*was bombarded with*］*questions* from her［his］fans.

しつよう 執拗な persistent（しつこい）▶執ような（＝頑固な）抵抗に遭う meet with *obstinate* resistance ‖ 彼らは社長に謝罪するよう執ように迫った They *were insistent on* receiving an apology from the president. ‖ 男は少女に執ように付きまとった The man followed the little girl *persistently*.

じつよう 実用 practical use 一形 実用的な practical▶この装飾的なペーパーナイフは実用にはならない（＝実用的ではない）This decorative paper knife is of no *practical use*. ‖ このテーブルセンターは実用と装飾を兼ねている This centerpiece is *practical* as well as decorative. ‖ 新しいタイプの太陽電池を実用化する *put* a new type of solar battery to *practical use* ‖ この辞書の長所は実用的なところだ The good thing about this dictionary is its *practicality*. ‖ 彼は独学で実用英語を身につけた He has taught himself *practical English*. ‖ 母はお歳暮には実用品を贈ることにしている When my mother buys year-end gifts, she always chooses *useful*［*practical*］*items*.

じつり 実利 (an) **actual profit**（現実の利益）▶実利を上げる *make a profit*.

しつりょう 質量《物理》**mass**▶月の質量は地球の約 80分の 1 です The *mass* of the moon is about an eightieth of that of the earth.

じつりょく 実力 1【力量，能力】(real) ability, capability（➤ 後者は主に実務能力を指す）▶自分の実力を試す try［test］one's *ability* ‖ かぜのため，ソフトボールの試合では実力を出せなかった Because of my cold, I couldn't show my *real ability* in the softball game. ‖ 最後は実力が物をいう *Real ability* will win［tell］in the long run. ‖ ビジネスで大切なのは学歴ではなく実力だ What counts in business is not your educational background but your *capability*. ‖ 秋山君は数学の実力はあるが，英語の実力はない Akiyama *is good at* math, but *poor at* English. ‖ 英語の実力をつけるにはどんな勉強法がいいでしょうか What learning method do you suggest to improve my English *ability*? ‖ 彼は日本で実力ナンバーワンのレーサーだ He is the *strongest* racer in Japan. ‖ 彼は政界の実力者だ He is *an influential*［*a key*／*a prominent*］*figure* in politics.
‖実力主義 the merit system ‖ 実力テスト a proficiency［an achievement］test.
2【武力など】▶警察は放水車などを使い，実力でデモ隊を解散させた The police dispersed the demonstrators *by force*, using water cannons.

しつれい 失礼 **1【無礼】一形 失礼な impolite**（礼儀に反する）; **rude**（無礼な）; **ill-mannered**（行儀・作法が悪い）

【文型】
人(A)が…するのは失礼だ
It is rude of A **to** do.

▶私に年齢を聞くなんて，あの人**失礼しちゃうわ** *It was rude of* him to ask (me) my age.
▶食事中にげっぷをするのはとても**失礼**です It is extremely *impolite* to burp at the table. ‖《レストランの主人などが使用人に》お客さまに対して**失礼のないように**しなさい *Be polite* to customers. ‖ きみ，人の足を踏んでおいて謝らないとは**失礼**じゃないか！ Hey, it's *rude* to step on my foot and not apologize. ‖ パンダにそっくりだなんて**失礼しちゃうわ** *I'm insulted* that you (should) say that I look like a panda. (➤ insult は「侮辱する」).

2【謝罪】▶《手洗いに立つときや携帯電話がかかってきたときなど》ちょっと**失礼** *Excuse me.* ‖《話に割り込むときなど》ちょっと**失礼します** *Excuse me* for disturbing you. ‖ 昨日は留守をしまして**失礼しました** *I'm sorry* I wasn't home yesterday. ‖ 夜遅く電話をかけまして大変**失礼をいたしました** *I am* very *sorry* for calling you so late (at night). ‖ **対話**「どうも**失礼しました**」「いえ，大丈夫です」"*I'm sorry.*" "That's all right."
✉ **年賀状が遅くなり失礼いたしました** Please forgive (me for) my belated New Year's greetings. ➤「年賀状が遅くなってごめんなさい」なら I'm sorry I am so late in sending my New Year's greetings. のようにいうほうが日本語に近い.

3【人に尋ねるとき】▶**失礼ですが**，この辺に薬局はないでしょうか *Excuse me.* Are there any drugstores near here? ‖《電話で》**失礼ですが**どちらさまでしょうか *Excuse me.* May I ask who is calling?

あなたの英語はどう響く?
会社などで入室するときに「失礼いたします」と言うが，それを直訳して Excuse me. とするのは英語的ではない. Excuse me. は人の前を通るとき，席を外すとき，失礼をわびるとき，相手に反論するとき，人に話しかけるときには用いるが，部屋に入るような場合には用いない. Good morning [afternoon], Mr. Jones. とか，上司でも親しい間柄なら Hi [Hello], John! のように言うのがふつう.

4【別れるとき】▶じゃあ**失礼** *Bye now.* ‖ ではそろそろ**失礼します** Well, *I'd better be leaving now.* ‖ 私は先に**失礼します** I'll have to *leave a little earlier.* / *Good night*, everybody. (➤ 後者は夕方以降) ‖ この辺で**失礼しなくてはなりません** I'm afraid I have to *be going* now. (→**おいとま**) ‖ **対話**「私はもう**失礼していい**でしょうか」「もちろん，かまいません」"*May I be excused?*" "Of course."

じつれい 実例 an **example** ▶地球が自転していることを**実例**で説明しなさい Give *examples* to illustrate the fact that the earth rotates (on its axis).

しつれん 失恋する be disappointed in love（相手に思いが通じない）▶そっとしておいてやれ. やつは目下**失恋中**なんだ Leave him alone [Don't bother him]. He *is broken-hearted.* ‖ 次郎は**失恋の傷**を癒やすためにふらりと旅に出た To ease *the pain of a broken heart*, Jiro set out on a journey. ‖「また**失恋しちゃった**」とかおりが言った "I *got dumped* again," Kaori said. →**振られる.**

じつわ 実話 a **true story** ▶この小説は**実話**に基づいている This novel is based on *a true story.*

[1]**してい 指定する appoint** +目（会合などの時間や場所を）; **designate** +目（主に場所を）▶**指定された時間**に遅れてばつが悪かった I felt embarrassed when I failed to arrive by the *appointed* time [by the time we had promised to meet]. ‖ 明朝 7 時に**指定の場所**に集合のこと Please gather at the *designated* place at seven tomorrow morning. ‖ その仏像は国宝に**指定されている** The Buddhist statue *has been designated* as a national treasure. ‖《掲示》**指定**の場所以外では禁煙 No smoking except in *designated* areas. ‖ この特急は**全席指定**（席）だ *All seats are reserved* on this special express train. (➤「指定席」は reserved seat).
‖（授業用の）**指定図書** a book on reserve.

[2]**してい 師弟 master and pupil**（師匠と弟子）; **teacher and student**（先生と生徒）(➤ 個々の人でなく，関係を表す表現なので a をつけない) ▶二人は**師弟**関係にある Those two are *master and pupil* [*teacher and student*].

[3]**してい 子弟 children** ▶良家の**子弟** *children* from good families.

[4]**してい 私邸** a **private residence.**

しでかす ▶あの男，何を**しでかす**かわかったもんじゃない There's no telling what he will *do.* ‖ きみは何てことを**しでかしたんだ** What an awful thing you'*ve gone and done*! (➤ go and do は「…のようなばかなことをする」の意のインフォーマルな表現).

[1]**してき 指摘する point out** ▶おかしなところがあったら**指摘してください** Please *point out* any mistakes I may have made. ‖ 私は先生の誤りを**指摘した** I *pointed out* the teacher's mistake. ‖ **ご指摘のとおり**，s は c の誤りです *As you pointed out*, "s" was erroneously written where there should have been a "c."

[2]**してき 私的な personal**（個人的な）; **private**（公的でない）▶**私的な**意見を差し控える reserve one's *personal* opinion ‖ **私的な**用事で会社の電話を使ってはいけない Don't use the office phone for *private* calls. ‖ このページの内容はあなたの**私的使用**に限ります The content of this page is for your *personal* use only.

[3]**してき 詩的な poetic** ▶**詩的な**表現 a *poetic* expression.

してつ 私鉄 a **private railroad** [《英》**railway**] ▶**私鉄**で通学する go to school *by* [*on*] *a private* (*railroad*) *line.*

-しては for（…の割には）▶彼女は日本人に**しては**背が高い She is tall *for* a Japanese person. ‖ きょうは11月に**しては**暖かい It's unusually warm today *for* November. ‖ 私と**しては**その案に賛成しかねるね *As for me*, I'm against the plan.

-しても ▶きみの答案は間違いはあるに**しても**ごく僅かだ Your test paper has few mistakes, *if any.* ‖ どこへ行くに**しても**きちんとした服装で行くんだよ You should be dressed properly *wherever you go.* ‖ 何を買うに**しても**お金は有効に使うべきだ *Whatever you buy*, you should make good use of your money. ‖ どんなに頑張ったと**しても**数学では彼にかなわない *However* [*No matter how*] hard I (may) try, I am no match for him in math.

-してもらう →**もらう.**

してやられる ▶あいつにはまんまとしてやられた I *was* completely *taken in* [*had*] by him. (➤ be had で「だまされる」の意).

1**してん 支店** **a branch office, a branch** ▶彼の父はＳ銀行の**弘前支店長**になった His father became manager of *the Hirosaki Branch* of the S Bank [the S Bank's *Hirosaki office*]. ‖ わが社は来年, 海外に**支店を出す**予定だ Our company plans to *set up* an overseas *office* next year.
‖**支店長** a branch (office) manager.

2**してん 視点** **a point of view, a viewpoint** ▶**視点を変え**てその問題を考えてごらん Try to think of the matter *from another* [*different*] *point of view*.

3**してん 支点** **a fulcrum** /fʌ́lkrəm/ (てこの) ▶てこの**支点** the *fulcrum* of a lever.

しでん 市電 《米》**a streetcar,** 《英》**a tram.**

1**じてん 自転** **rotation** 一動 **自転する** **rotate** ▶地球の**自転**につれて昼と夜が交互に来る Day alternates with night as the earth *rotates*.

2**じてん 辞典** **a dictionary** ⇀辞書
▶**国語辞典**を引く consult [use] *a Japanese dictionary* (➤ consult は書きことばで, use は話しことばで用いることが多い) ‖ **英和辞典**でその語の意味を調べてみなさい Look up the meaning of that word in *an English-Japanese dictionary*.

3**じてん 事典** an **encyclop(a)edia** /ɪnsàɪkləpíːdiə/ ▶**生物学事典** *an encyclopedia* of biology ‖ **百科事典**を編さんする compile *an encyclopedia*.

4**じてん 次点** ▶クラブの部長選挙で私は**次点**だった I was (*the*) *runner-up* in the election for club president. (➤ runner-up は「次点者」).

5**じてん 時点** ▶5月3日の**時点**で為替レートは1ドル80円だった *As of* May 3rd, the dollar exchange rate was 80 yen. ‖ **現時点では**何とも言えない I can't say for sure *now*.

じでん 自伝 an **autobiography** /ɔ̀ːṭəbaɪɑ́ːgrəfi/.

じてんしゃ 自転車 **a bicycle,** 《インフォーマル》 a **bike**
▶**自転車**に乗る ride *a bicycle* ‖ **自転車**で通学する go to school *by bike* ／ride a bicycle to school ‖ **自転車**で買い物 [勤め] に行く use *a bicycle* for shopping [commuting] ‖ **自転車**を押して歩く walk [push] *a bicycle*.
‖**自転車競技** [**競走**] a bicycle race ‖ **自転車専用道路** a bikeway, a bike path ‖ **自転車操業** a business that's barely keeping afloat [surviving from day to day] ‖ **自転車店** a bicycle shop ‖ **自転車旅行** a bicycle trip, a cycling tour.

1**しと 使途** ▶**使途**不明金 an *unaccounted* expenditure ‖ 交際費の具体的な**使途**を明確にする explain clearly *how* business entertainment funds *were used*.

2**しと 使徒** a **disciple** /dɪsáɪpəl/.

しとう 死闘 ▶マングースとコブラは**死闘**を繰り広げた The mongoose *struggled desperately* with the cobra. ／The mongoose and the cobra *were in a life-and-death struggle*.

1**しどう 指導** **guidance** (助言) ; **direction** (指示) ; **teaching** (学科などの) 一動 **指導する** **guide** +🄾 , **teach** +🄾 ; **coach** /koʊtʃ/ +🄾 (スポーツなどを) ▶おばはその女の子にイタリア語を**指導**している My aunt *teaches* Italian to that girl. ‖ 彼は娘さんにテニスを**指導**している He *gives* his daughter tennis *lessons*. ‖ コーチの熱心な**指導**で一郎は野球がどんどん上達した Under the earnest *guidance* of the coach, Ichiro improved rapidly in baseball. ‖ 彼は近くの学校で野球チームの**指導**をしている He *coaches* the baseball team at the nearby school. ‖ 私たちは音楽の先生の**指導**で合唱コンクールのための練習をしている We are practicing for the chorus contest *under the direction* [*guidance*] *of* our music teacher. ‖ 鎌倉さんは**指導力**がある Mr. Kamakura *is a natural leader*. (➤「生まれついての指導者だ」の意 ; have leadership は「率先して [先頭に立って] やる」の意) ‖ この問題で首相の**指導力**が試される This issue will test the *leadership qualities* [*abilities*] of the prime minister. ‖ **進路指導**は田中先生の担当です Mr. Tanaka is in charge of *career guidance*.
‖**指導員** an instructor ‖ (卒論などの) **指導教授** an academic adviser, 《英》 a tutor /tjúːṭəʳ/ ‖ **指導者** a leader (リーダー) ; a tutor, an instructor (勉強の) ; a coach, a trainer (スポーツの) ‖ **指導主事** a teachers' consultant (日本の) ; 《米》 a supervisor (of school education) ; 《英》 a school inspector.

2**しどう 私道** **a private road** ▶《掲示》私道につき通り抜け禁止 *Private*: No Trespassing.

3**しどう 始動する** **start** (+🄾) ▶エンジンを**始動させる** *start* an engine ‖ 新制度が**始動した** The new system *has started*.

1**じどう 自動の** **automatic** /ɔ̀ːṭəmǽṭɪk/, **automated** ▶このドアは**自動**です This is an *automatic* door. ‖ 最近の石油ストーブは倒れると**自動的に**火が消える In modern kerosene heaters, the flame goes out *automatically* if the heater tips over. ‖ 給料は**自動振り込み**です My salary *is deposited automatically into my bank account*.
‖**自動改札機** an automatic ticket gate [barrier] ‖ 《文法》**自動詞** an intransitive verb ‖ **自動制御** automatic control ‖ **自動体外式除細動器** (AED) automated external defibrillator ‖ **自動販売機** a vending [《英》 slot] machine 《**参考**》投入したお金や釣り銭が戻ってこないときにおどけて The machine ate my money. (機械が私のお金を食べてしまった) と言うことがある ‖ **自動引き落とし** an automatic deduction service ‖ **現金自動預け入れ支払い機** an automated teller machine.

2**じどう 児童** **a child** [複 **children**] ; a **schoolchild** (学童) ▶**児童向き**の本 books *for children* ／*juvenile* books (➤ juvenile /dʒúːvənaɪl/ は「児童の」の意の堅い語). ‖**児童期** childhood ‖ **児童虐待** child abuse ‖ **児童教育** juvenile education ‖ **児童憲章** the Children's Charter ‖ **児童自立支援施設** a juvenile correctional facility ‖ **児童心理学** child psychology /saɪkɑ́ːlədʒi/ ‖ **児童手当** a child benefit [allowance] ‖ **児童買春** child prostitution ‖ **児童福祉法** the Child Welfare Law ‖ **児童文学** juvenile literature ‖ **児童ポルノ** child pornography ‖ **児童遊園地** an amusement park for children.

じどうしゃ 自動車 **a car,** 《米また》 an **automobile** /ɔ́ːṭəmoʊbìːl/, 《英また》 a **motorcar**

> **《解説》** (1) car が日常語で, 日本語の「クルマ」に当たる. automobile, motorcar は正式な語.
> (2) car はふつうは「乗用車」を指し, トラック, バスなどは含まない. ⇀車.

▶**自動車**を運転する drive *a car* (➤「自動車を運転して…へ行く」は drive to ... で, a car を省略することが多い) ‖ **自動車で通勤する** *drive to work* ‖ 山本君は自動車でアメリカを旅行した Yamamoto *drove around* the U. S. ／Yamamoto *traveled* around the U.S. *in a car*. ‖ 日本の**自動車産業**は東南アジア進出がめざましい The Japanese *car* [*auto*(*mobile*)] *industry* is rapidly expanding its business to [into] Southeast Asia. ‖ **自動車事故**は年々増加する一方だ *Car accidents* increase yearly. ‖ インディ500は有名な**自動車レース**だ The Indy 500 is a famous *auto race*. ‖ 関越**自動車道**にはトンネルが多い The Kan-etsu *Expressway* has a lot of tunnels. (➤ expressway は《米》で「高速道路」の意味で《英》では motorway). ‖ **自動車教習所** a driving school ‖ **自動車修理工** a mechanic.

「自動車」のいろいろ **オープンカー** convertible ／**キャンピングカー** camper ／**救急車** ambulance ／**ごみ収集車** garbage truck ／**ジープ** jeep ／**消防自動車** fire engine ／**乗用車** (passenger) car, automobile ／**スポーツカー** sports car ／**セダン** 《米》sedan, 《英》saloon (car) ／**タクシー** taxi (cab), cab ／**ダンプカー** dump truck ／**トラック** truck, 《英》lorry ／**トレーラー** trailer ／**バス** bus ／**パトカー** police car, patrol car ／**バン** van ／**ブルドーザー** bulldozer ／**マイクロバス** microbus ／**ミニバン** minivan ／**リムジン** limousine ／**霊柩**(れいきゅう)**車** hearse ／**レーシングカー** race [racing] car ／**レッカー車** tow truck, wrecker

しどけない **slovenly** /slʌ́vənli/ ▶彼女は**しどけない**姿で戸口に現れた She appeared in the doorway, *looking slovenly*.

しどころ ▶ここが我慢 [思案] の**しどころ**だ Now is *the time when* we need to exercise patience [we need careful consideration].

しとしと ▶きょうも春雨が**しとしと**降っている A *gentle* spring rain *is falling* again today.

じとじと ▶梅雨期に入って**じとじと**した日が続いている It has been *humid* [*damp*] since the rainy season began.

シドニー **Sydney**(オーストラリアの都市).

しとめる 仕留める **shoot down** ▶彼は一発でキジを**しとめた** He *shot down* a green pheasant with one shot.

しとやか 淑やかな **graceful** (優美な); **demure** /dɪmjʊ́əʳ/ (つつましい, おとなしい) ▶グレース・ケリーは物腰が**しとやかだった** Grace Kelly was *graceful*. ‖ 女の子はもう少し**おしとやかにする**ものよ! A girl should *be* more *demure*.

1**じどり 地鶏** (a) **local chicken**(➤ 鶏肉は Ⓤ).

2**じどり 自撮り** a **selfie** ▶**自撮りする** take *a selfie*.

しどろもどろ ▶休んだ理由を聞かれたが, **しどろもどろ**の返事しかできなかった When I was asked why I had been absent, I could only give a *confused* answer. ‖ 彼女の説明は**しどろもどろだった** Her explanation *went backward and forward*.

1**しな 品** **1**【品物, 商品】an **item** (個々の); an **article** (同種の物の1品); **goods** (商品) ▶お歳暮用の贈答の**品々** *items* [*articles*] for year-end presents ‖ この店は安くていい**品がそろっている** This store carries a wide range of inexpensive but good *items*. (➤「全品目そろった店, 品ぞろえの豊富な店」を full-line store という) ‖ この**品**はよく売れる This *product* [*item*] sells well.

✉ **結構なお品**(＝プレゼント)**をありがとうございました** Thank you very much for the nice *present*.

2【品質】**quality** ▶この毛皮のコートは**品がいい** This fur coat *is of high quality*. ／This fur coat *is quality merchandise*. ‖ この靴はそこいらの物とは**品が違う** These shoes *are in an entirely superior class*, compared to most.

2**しな 科** ▶**科を作る** flirt ; be coquettish.

-しな ▶帰り**しな**におばの家に寄った *On my way home*, I dropped in at my aunt's house. ‖ 寝し**な**にお茶は飲まないほうがよい It would be better not to drink tea *just before you go to bed*.

1**しない 市内** ▶**市内**には大学はありません There is no university *in the city*. ‖ **市内**は無料配達です We deliver free of charge *within* (*the*) *city limits*. ‖ 午後はバスで**市内観光**の予定です We will be taking a bus *tour of the city* in the afternoon. ‖ お住まいは福岡**市内**ですか Do you live *in the City of Fukuoka*? ‖ **市内通話** a local call.

2**しない 竹刀** a **bamboo sword** /bæ̀mbu: sɔ́:ʳd/.

しなう 撓う **bend** ▶木の枝は雪の重みで**しなって**(＝たわんで)いた The branches of the tree were *bent* under the weight of the snow. ‖ アユ釣りにはよく**しなう**竹の釣りざおがいちばんだ *Supple* bamboo poles make the best fishing rods for ayu-fishing.

しなうす 品薄 ▶**品薄である** be *in short supply* ‖ 豆乳は**品薄になっています** Soy milk is *running short*.

しなかず 品数 ▶あのデパートは有名ブランド品の**品数がそろっている** That department store *carries a large variety of* famous brand-name *products*.

しなぎれ 品切れ **be sold out**(売り切れである); **be out of stock** (在庫切れである) ▶売り出したばかりの新製品が早くも**品切れ**とは驚いた It is surprising that a product that has just come on the market should already *be sold out* [*be out of stock*].

しなさだめ 品定め ▶靴を見て客の**品定めをする** *size up* a customer by looking at his [her] shoes ‖ 店先で長々と**品定めをする**のはよくない It is not good to take too much time in a store *looking over a prospective purchase*. (➤ look over は「見て回る」).

しなびる **wither** ; **shrivel** (しわしわになる) ▶**しなびた**キュウリ a *withered* [*shriveled*] cucumber ‖ 大輪の朝顔が**しなびてしまった** The large-blossomed morning glories *have withered*.

しなぶそく 品不足 →**品薄**.

しなもの 品物 an **item**(同種の物の1品); a **product** (製品) ▶アメリカの会社に注文してあった**品物**が届いた I received the *item* [*product*] I had ordered from a U.S. company.

シナモン **cinnamon**.

しなやか ▶**しなやかな**竹 a *flexible* bamboo ‖ **しなやか**な髪をした少女 a girl with *soft* hair ‖ バレエ・ダンサーは**しなやかな**体をしている Ballet dancers have *supple* [*limber*] bodies.

じならし 地ならし ▶私たちはローラーを使って運動場の**地ならしをした** We *leveled* the playground with a roller. ▶《比喩的》彼がその計画の**地ならしをした** He *laid the groundwork* for the project.

じなり 地鳴り **the rumble of the earth** 一動 **地鳴りがする** **rumble** ▶山で**地鳴り**とともに地滑りが起きた A landslide came down the mountain with *a rumbling sound*.

シナリオ a **scenario** /sənǽrioʊ/ ▶映画の**シナリオを書く** write *a film scenario* ‖ 最悪の**シナリオ** a worst-case *scenario* ‖ **シナリオ**どおりに進んでくれるといいのだが I hope things go *according to* (*the*) *scenario*. (➤ 比喩的にも用いる).

‖シナリオライター a scenario writer.

しなん 至難 ▶この庭石を1人で動かすなんて至難の業だ It's *a herculean task* to move this garden stone by myself. (➤ herculean /hə̀ːrkjəlíːən/ は「ヘラクレスのような怪力を必要とする；非常に困難な」の意) ‖中国語を1，2年でマスターするのは至難の業だ *It's next to impossible* to master Chinese in a year or two.

じなん 次男 one's **second son** ▶あそこの家では次男に家業を継がせるつもりだ They intend to have *their second son* take over the family business.

シニア a **senior citizen**, an **elderly person** (年配者) 《参考》senior は最近では senior citizen (「お年寄り」のことで特に定年退職後の年金生活者をいう)の意味で使われることもある ▶シニア世代 older generations／people in late middle age ‖シニア向け分譲マンション a condominium catering to *seniors* [*senior citizens*].

しにがみ 死に神 the Grim Reaper.

しにぎわ 死に際 ▶死に際のことば one's *last* [*dying*] words ‖彼は死に際に「すばらしい人生をともにしてくれてありがとう」と妻に言った "Thank you for sharing a wonderful life," he said to his wife *in his last moments* [*on his deathbed*].

しにく 歯肉 gum ‖歯肉炎 gingivitis.

しにせ 老舗 ▶老舗ののれんを守る keep up the reputation of the *old store* ‖彼の家は和菓子の老舗だ His family runs *a long-established* Japanese confectionery *store*.

しにたい 死に体 lame-duck, half-dead.

しにたえる 死に絶える become extinct.

しにめ 死に目 ▶彼は父親の死に目に会えなかった He *was not able to be at his father's bedside when he died*.

しにものぐるい 死に物狂い ▶死に物狂いで勉強する study *like mad*／study *one's head off* (➤ one's head off は「気が変になるほど」) ‖彼は司法試験に合格しようと死に物狂いで頑張った He *studied like mad* [*threw himself into a last desperate effort*] to pass the bar examination.

しにわかれる 死に別れる be bereaved of.

しにん 死人 a **dead person** ▶ ことわざ 死人に口なし Dead men tell no tales.

[1]**じにん 辞任 resignation** 一動 **辞任する resign** /rɪzáɪn/ ▶市長は事件の責任を取って辞任した Taking responsibility for the incident, the mayor *resigned*. ‖市長が辞任しても問題は解決しない The *resignation* of the mayor will not solve the problem.

[2]**じにん 自認** ▶私は自分が短気であると自認しています *I acknowledge* [*admit*／*recognize*] *the fact that* I have a short temper.

[3]**じにん 自任** ▶彼女はピアノの名手だと自任している She *fancies herself* (as) an excellent piano player. (➤ fancy oneself は「うぬぼれる」).

しぬ 死ぬ

1【死亡する】die /daɪ/ ; **be killed** (事故などで)

> 語法 (1)「死ぬ」の一般語は **die** だが，戦争や事故などで死ぬ場合はしばしば **be killed** が用いられる.
> (2) **die of** は病気・飢餓・老齢などが原因で死ぬ場合に，**die from** はけがなどが原因で死ぬ場合に用いることが多いが，die of が die from の代わりに用いられることも多い.

▶父は35歳で死んだ My father *died* at the age of 35. ‖その俳人は若くして死んだ The haiku poet *died* young. ‖ジェームズ・ディーンは自動車事故で死んだ James Dean *died* [*was killed*] in an auto crash. ‖フレディ・マーキュリーはエイズで死んだ Freddie Mercury *died of* AIDS. ‖ジョン・レノンは銃で撃たれて死んだ John Lennon *died from* a gunshot.

▶工事現場で5人の人が砂の中に生き埋めになって死んだ Five people *were killed* when they were buried under the sand at the construction site. ‖雷に打たれてゴルファーが死んだ Lightning hit and *killed* a golfer. ‖その子猫は凍えて死んだ The kitten *froze to death*. ‖少年はいじめっ子に殴られて死んだ The boy *was beaten to death* by a bully. ‖彼は12階から飛び降りて死んだ(＝自殺した) He *killed himself* by jumping off the twelfth floor. (→自殺).

> **あなたの英語はどう響く?**
> 「そのとき私は死ぬかと思った」を I felt like dying at that time. としてはいけない. これでは「そのとき私は死にたいと思った」という意味になる. At that time I thought (that) I was going to die. が正しい訳である.

▶ゆうべずっと前に死んだ両親の夢を見た Last night I had a dream of my *long-departed* parents [parents *who died long ago*]. ‖死んだ魚が川に浮いていた *Dead* fish were floating in the river. ‖去年彼女は夫に死なれた She *lost* her husband last year. ‖私は3年前に妻に死なれた It has been three years since my wife *died* [*passed away*].／My wife has *been gone* for three years. (➤ 日本語の「(親などに)死なれる」は影響を受ける人の立場から述べる言い方だが，英語では受け身形にはしない) ‖私は父に早く死なれたので働きながら大学を出なければならなかった Since my father *died* when I was very young, I had to work my way through college. ‖彼女は自分の不注意で赤ん坊を死なせた It was her carelessness that *caused* the baby's *death*.

2【比喩的】▶鉱山が閉鎖されてから町はまるで死んだようだ After the mine was closed, the town *became like a ghost town*. ‖彼の目は死んでいる His eyes are *like a dead man's*. ‖このまま自然破壊が進めば山は死んでしまう If the environment is destroyed any further, mountain ecosystems will *die* [*be destroyed*]. ‖赤い花瓶に生けたんじゃ，せっかくの赤いバラが死んでしまうよ If you put those red roses in the red vase, *their beauty will be ruined* [*destroyed*].

3【慣用表現】▶仕事にありつけるかどうかはぼくにとって生きるか死ぬかの問題だ Finding a job is *a matter of life and death* for me. ‖死ぬ気になれば何だってできるさ You can achieve anything *if you're willing to die for it*. ‖きみと一緒になれるなら死んでもいい I *would die* for the chance to marry you. ‖暑くて死にそうだ I *can't stand* this heat. (➤「我慢できない」の意) ‖きみのことが死ぬほど好きだ I *love* you *more than anything in the world*. ‖彼の講演は死ぬほど退屈だった His speech *bored* me *to death*. ‖恥ずかしくて死んでしまいたいくらいだった I *could have died of* embarrassment. ‖死んで花実が咲くものか Once (a tree is) dead, how can it bloom or bear fruit?／Once you're dead, how can you achieve anything? ‖ 対話 「調子はどう？」「忙しすぎて死にそうだよ」 "How's it going?" "I'm so busy it's *nearly killing* me."

じぬし 地主 a **landowner.**

じねつ 地熱 →ちねつ.

しのぎ 鎬 ▶しのぎを削る販売競争 a *fierce* sales competition ‖ オリンピックを目指して候補選手たちはしのぎを削った The candidates for the Olympic team *competed fiercely*.

-しのぎ -凌ぎ ▶一時しのぎの地震対策 a *stopgap* earthquake countermeasure ‖ 寒さしのぎにオーバーを買う buy an overcoat *to keep out* [*to protect oneself from*] *the cold* ‖ 祖母は退屈しのぎによく古いアルバムを見ていた My grandmother used to look at old photo albums *just to kill time*. (➤ kill time は「時間を潰す」) ‖ 明らかに彼はその場しのぎの言い訳を言っているだけだ Apparently he is making an excuse *just to get out of a tight spot*.

しのぎやすい 凌ぎやすい ▶しのぎやすくなりましたね It's gotten *nicer* out, hasn't it?

✉ **朝晩めっきり秋めいて，しのぎやすい時候となりました** Now we feel fall is here because it is cool and pleasant in the mornings and evenings. ➤ 英語では手紙の冒頭で気候について述べる習慣はない.

しのぐ 凌ぐ **1【耐える，防ぐ】**▶この家は立派とは言えないが雨風をしのぐには十分だ I can't say that this house is a fancy one, but it's enough to *keep out the rain and wind*. ‖ 彼は救助隊が到着するまでの１週間，あめと雪どけ水で飢えをしのいだ He *staved off* his hunger with candies and melted snow for a week until the rescue team arrived. (➤ stave off は「(危険などを)食い止める」).

2【勝る】 **surpass** +Ⓔ ▶あの学生は先生をしのぐ英語力がある The student's English proficiency *surpasses* the teacher's. ‖ 日本には高さと美しさで富士山をしのぐ山はない There are no mountains in Japan that *surpass* Mt. Fuji in height and beauty.

しのばせる 忍ばせる ▶足音を忍ばせて歩く walk *stealthily* ／walk *with stealthy steps* (➤ stealthily /stélθɪli/ は「ひそかに」) ‖ 父と母は長い間声を忍ばせて話し合っていた My father and mother were talking *in whispers* for a long time. ‖ その中学生はポケットにナイフを忍ばせていた That junior high school student *secretly carried* a knife in his [her] pocket.

しのびあい 忍び逢い an **assignation** ▶２人はたびたび忍び逢いをした The couple often *met secretly*.

しのびあし 忍び足 ▶母親は忍び足で赤ん坊の寝ている部屋から出ていった The mother *tiptoed* out of the room where her baby was sleeping. (➤ tiptoe は「つま先でそっと歩く」).

しのびこむ 忍び込む **break into** ▶泥棒はトイレの窓から家に忍び込んだらしい It seems that the burglar *sneaked* [*broke*] *into* the house through the bathroom window.

しのびない 忍びない ▶彼の上司についての悪口は聞くに忍びない *It is almost unbearable to hear* him run down his boss like that. ‖ 彼女の泣いている姿を見るに忍びない I *can't bear to see* her crying. ‖ ハンターはその子ジカを撃つに忍びなかった The hunter *couldn't find it in his heart* to shoot the fawn. (➤「…する気になれなかった」の意の熟語).

しのびなき 忍び泣き ▶彼女は自分の部屋で忍び泣きしていた She *was weeping* [*crying*] *in secret* in her own room.

しのびよる 忍び寄る **sneak up**《on》▶彼は後ろから忍び寄って浩美をわっと脅かした He *sneaked* [*snuck*] *up on* Hiromi from behind and gave her a big scare. (➤ snuck は《米》で用いられる sneak の過去形) ‖ いつの間にか秋が忍び寄ってきていた Autumn *had crept up on* us unnoticed. (➤ crept は creep(はう)の過去分詞形).

しのびわらい 忍び笑い 一動 **忍び笑いをする** **snicker**《at》.

1**しのぶ 忍ぶ** **1【我慢する】** **put up with** ▶しばらく不便を忍ばねばならない We have to *put up with* inconveniences for a while. ‖ 恥を忍んでご相談します I will *swallow my embarrassment* and ask for your advice.

2【人目を避ける】▶彼は妻帯者だが時折人目を忍んで若い女に会っているらしい He is married, but I heard that once in a while he *secretly* sees a young woman. ‖ 泥棒は庭の植え込みに忍んで(＝隠れて)家人が出かけるのを待っていた The thief *hid* among the shrubbery in the yard and waited for the people in the house to leave.

2**しのぶ 偲ぶ** ▶亡き師をしのんで演奏会を催した We held a concert *in memory of* our teacher. (➤ in memory of は故人に対して使う.「亡き師をしのぶ会」なら a get-together in memory of our teacher) ‖ 久しぶりに母校を訪ねて昔をしのんだ(＝思い出した) For the first time in a long while, I visited my old school and *recalled my past days* there.

1**しば 芝** **(the) grass**(芝草)；a **lawn** (庭や公園の刈り込んだ草地)；(a) **turf**(競技場などの芝面) ▶アメリカでは芝刈りは夫の役目である In America, *lawn mowing* is a husband's job.

‖**芝刈り機** a lawn mower ‖ **芝地** a grass plot ‖ **人工芝** artificial turf. →芝生.

2**しば 柴** **brushwood** ▶柴刈りに行く go gather *brushwood*.

じば 磁場 a **magnetic field**.

1**しはい 支配** **1【治めること】** **rule** 一動 **支配する** **rule** +Ⓔ, **govern** +Ⓔ (➤ 後者は「法的に治める」に当たる) ▶インドは長い間イギリスの支配を受けていた India was under British *rule* for a long time. ‖ 25年間にわたってその国を支配した独裁者はついに暗殺された The dictator, who had *ruled* [*governed*] the nation for a quarter of a century, was finally assassinated.

‖**支配者** a ruler ‖ **支配人** a manager；a maître d' /mèɪtrə díː/ (特にホテルの) ‖ **総支配人** a general manager.

2【影響を与えること】▶自然界の生き物はすべて適者生存という法則に支配されている All living creatures in the natural world *are subject to* the law of the survival of the fittest. ‖ 誰だって感情に支配される(＝負ける)ことがある Everyone *is* sometimes *overcome* by emotion.

2**しはい 賜杯** a **trophy**(トロフィー)；a **cup**(賞杯).

しばい 芝居 a **play**, (a) **drama** ▶芝居(を見)に行く go to *a play* ‖ 彼女は大の芝居好きだ She is a regular *theatergoer*.

▶《比喩的》下手な芝居はよせ！ Quit putting on an act!／Enough of that (play)acting!

じばいせき 自賠責 **compulsory automobile liability insurance**.

じはく 自白 (a) **confession** 一動 **自白する** **confess** (+Ⓔ)(白状する)；**admit** +Ⓔ (認める) ▶犯行を自白する *confess* (to) one's crime ／*make a confession of* one's crime ‖ 容疑者はとうとう殺人を自白した The suspect finally *confessed to* the murder.

し

／The suspect *made a confession of* murder at last.

じばく 自爆する blow oneself up ▶そのテロリストは爆薬を体に縛りつけて自爆した The terrorist *blew himself* [*herself*] *up* with explosives tied to his [her] body.

‖**自爆テロ** suicide bombing (行為；行う人は suicide bomber)；a suicide bomb (爆弾).

し

しばざくら 芝桜 《植》 moss phlox.

じばさんぎょう 地場産業 (a) (traditional) local industry ▶地場産業の振興を図る try to promote (a) *local industry*.

しばしば often, frequently (➤ 後者は前者よりも堅い語で，時間の間隔が比較的短いことを暗示する) ▶ぼくはうなされて夜中に目を覚ますことがしばしばある I *often* wake up in the middle of the night with nightmares. ‖我々は日本国憲法についてしばしば議論を戦わせた We *frequently* had discussions on the Constitution of Japan.

しはつ 始発 ▶始発電車は何時ですか？ When does *the first train* leave？‖特急『ゆふいんの森』は博多が始発駅です Hakata is *the starting station* for the "Yufuin-no-mori" limited express trains.

じはつてき 自発的な voluntary /vɑ́ːlənteri/ ▶自発的行為 a *voluntary* act ‖妹は毎日自発的にピアノの練習をする My sister practices the piano *on her own initiative* every day. ‖彼は客を空港まで出迎えに行くと自発的に申し出た He *volunteered* to go to the airport to meet the guest. (➤ volunteer は /vɑ̀ːləntíəʳ/ と発音).

しばふ 芝生 a lawn (栽培して刈り込んだ草地)；(the) grass (芝草)；a turf (四角に切った) ▶彼は「芝生に入るべからず」の立て札を無視して芝生の上に寝転がった He ignored the "*Keep off the grass*" sign and lay down on the *lawn*. ‖芝生を刈ってちょうだい Will you mow the *lawn*？

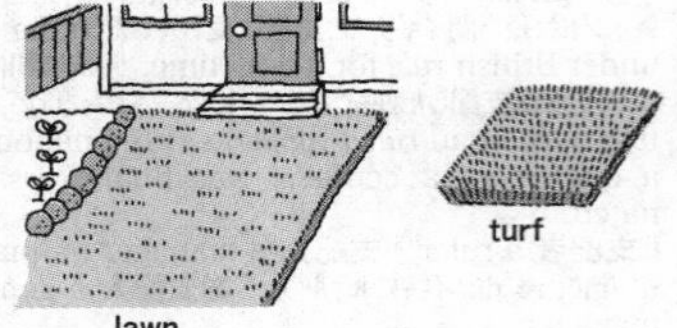

じばら 自腹 ▶先生はいつも自腹を切って私たちにごちそうしてくださった Our teacher always treated us *out of his own pocket*.

しはらい 支払い (a) payment ▶支払いを延ばす put off [postpone ／defer] *payment* (➤ 動詞はこの順に堅い語になる) ‖来週中に車の支払いをしなくてはいけない I have to make a car *payment* next week. ‖《レストランなどで》支払いは済ませたよ I'*ve paid the bill*. ‖「車の支払いが終わったら新しい冷蔵庫を買いましょうよ」と妻が言った "When we finish *paying off* the car, let's buy a new refrigerator," said my wife. (➤ pay off は「(借金などを)全部払う」).

‖**支払い期限** the due date ‖**支払い先** a payee ‖**支払い通知書** a notice of payment ‖**支払い人** a payer.

しはらう 支払う pay +目 ▶勘定を支払う *pay* the bill ‖残金は冷蔵庫を配達していただいたときに支払います I'll *pay* the balance when the refrigerator is delivered to my home.

しばらく 1【少しの間】for a (little) while；a [one] moment (ちょっと) ▶この雨はしばらく降り続くだろう It'll probably rain *for a while*. ‖しばらくお待ちください Please wait *a moment*. ‖しばらくすると雨は雪に変わった *After a while*, the rain changed to snow. ‖彼はしばらくすれば戻るだろう He'll be back *shortly* [*in a little while*].

2【長い間】for a long time ▶しばらくですね．お元気でしたか *I haven't seen you for a long time*. How have you been？‖やあ，しばらくぶりだね Hi！*It's been ages since I saw you last*. ／*Long time no see*. (➤ともにインフォーマルな表現) ‖私はしばらくぶりで帰省した I returned home *for the first time in a long time*.

しばる 縛る 1【結ぶ】tie /taɪ/ +目 (ひも・リボンなどで)；bind /baɪnd/ +目 (しっかり縛る) ▶傷を包帯で縛る *bind up* the wound with a bandage ‖髪をゴムで縛ってポニーテールにした I used an elastic string to *tie* [*make*] my hair into a ponytail. ‖まきは縄で縛ってあった The firewood *was bound* [*was bundled*] together with rope. (➤ bound は bind の過去分詞形) ‖家族全員が強盗に手足を縛られた Everyone in the family *was bound* hand and foot by the burglar.

2【束縛する】tie +目，bind +目；restrict +目 (制限する) ▶時間に縛られるのは嫌いだ I hate to *be tied down to the clock*. ／I hate *being a slave to the clock*. ‖生徒を不必要な規則で縛るのはよくない It's not good to *restrict* students with unnecessary rules.

[1]**しはん 市販する** sell [put／place] ... on the market；sell ... at a store [shop] (店で売る) ▶市販のかぜ薬 (a) cold medicine *on sale* [*over the counter*] (➤ over the counter は「処方箋なしで買える」の意) ‖この雑誌は会員の方にお配りするもので，市販はいたしておりません This magazine is for members only and *is not sold on the market* [*to the public*].

‖**市販品** a commercial item [product].

[2]**しはん 師範** an instructor.

じばん 地盤 the ground (地面)；the foundation (土台)；a stronghold (活動などの拠点)

▶ここは年間５センチくらいずつ地盤が沈下している *The ground* here *has been sinking* by some five centimeters every year. (➤「地盤沈下」は (land) subsidence).

▶あの代議士の地盤(＝本拠地)はこの辺の農村だ The farming villages around here are that Dietman's *stronghold*.

しはんき 四半期 a quarter ▶第１［２／３／４］四半期 the first [second ／third ／fourth] *quarter*.

じはんき 自販機 a vending machine ▶新聞を自販機で買う get a newspaper from *a vending machine*.

しはんせいき 四半世紀 a quarter century.

しひ 私費 ▶妹はイギリスに私費で留学した My sister went to England to study *at her own expense* [*paying her own expenses*].

‖**私費留学生** a foreign student who is studying at his [her] own expense (外国から来た)；a student studying overseas at his [her] own expense (外国へ行っている).

[1]**じひ 自費** ▶私は自費でロンドンへ行った I went to London *at my own expense*. ‖彼は詩集を自費出版した He *published* a collection of poems *at his own expense*. ／He paid to have a book of his

poems published.

2**じひ 慈悲** **mercy**; **pity**(哀れみ); **compassion**(仏の深い思いやり) ▶慈悲を請う beg for *mercy* ‖ 慈悲深い心 a *merciful* [*compassionate*] heart ‖ お慈悲ですから命ばかりはお助けを! *Have mercy on me and* spare my life, please!

シビア **severe**(厳しい) ▶アメリカの日本に対する見方はかなりシビアになってきている America's views on Japan have become quite *severe* lately.

じビール 地ビール (a) **local beer**, (a) **craft beer**.

じびか 耳鼻科 an **ear, nose and throat clinic**(耳鼻咽喉科医院), 《インフォーマル》an **E. N. T.**(➤ E.N.T. は ear, nose, throat の頭文字) ▶いい耳鼻(咽喉)科の先生をご存じないですか Do you know of a good *E.N.T. doctor*? (➤ 正式な名称は otolaryngologist /òʊţoʊlærɪŋgɑ́ːlədʒɪst/).

じびき 字引 a **dictionary**.

☛ 生き字引 (→見出語)

じびきあみ 地引き網 a **beach seine** ▶地引き網漁 *beach-seine* fishing.

じひつ 自筆 one's **own handwriting**; an **autograph**(有名人の自筆のサイン・原稿など) ▶徳川家康自筆の手紙 a letter *written by* Tokugawa Ieyasu *himself* ‖ テレビのスターに自筆のサインを頼む ask a TV star for his [her] *autograph* ‖ ここに自筆で氏名と住所を書いてください Please write your name and address (*in your own handwriting*). (➤ in your own handwriting は通常省く).

じひびき 地響き a **rumbling**(ゴロゴロという音); a **thud** /θʌd/ (ドスンという音) ▶大男は地響きを立てて倒れた The giant fell down *with a thud*. ／The ground shook when the giant fell down. ‖ 新燃岳が噴火したときは地響きがした When Mt. Shinmoe erupted, *the earth rumbled*.

しひょう 指標 an **index**, an **indicator** ▶経済指標 an economic *index* [*indicator*].

じひょう 辞表 a **resignation** ▶その監督は優勝できなかった責任をとって辞表を提出した Holding himself responsible for losing the pennant, the manager handed in his *resignation*.

じびょう 持病 an **old complaint**(長い間悩まされている病気); a **chronic disease** (慢性病)
▶糖尿病が彼の持病だ Diabetes is his *old complaint*. ／He suffers from chronic diabetes.
▶《比喩的》またあいつの持病の怠け癖が始まったらしい It looks like he's had *another attack* of his habitual laziness.

しびれ 痺れ **numbness** /nʌ́mnəs/ (無感覚)
▶長時間正座していたのでしびれが切れた My legs *are numb* [*asleep*] from sitting on them for a long time. ‖ 左手のしびれがまだ治らない My left hand is still *asleep*. ／I still have *no feeling* [*sensation*] in my left hand.
▶《慣用表現》1時間たっても彼が姿を現さなかったので，我々はしびれを切らして先に出発した After an hour, he still had not showed (up), so we *got tired of waiting* [*became impatient*] and went without him.

しびれる 痺れる **1**【感覚がなくなる】**go** [**become**] **numb** /nʌm/; **go to sleep**, **get** [**have**] **pins and needles**(正座のあとなどで; 後者は痛みを伴うもの)
▶畳に正座すると必ず足がしびれる Whenever I sit with my legs folded under me on the tatami floor, my legs *go numb* [*go to sleep*]. (➤ コンマ以下を I get pins and needles としてもよい) ‖ 寒さで手がしびれた My hands *are numb*(*ed*) with cold. ‖ その注射で足がしびれた The injection *has numbed* my legs.

2【興奮する, 陶酔する】▶あのロックにはシビレたね That rock music really *got* me *going* [*turned* me *on*].

しぶ 支部 a **branch** (**office**)(本部に対する); a **chapter**(クラブ・同窓会などの) ▶日本教職員組合九州支部 the Kyushu *branch* of the Japan Teachers' Union ‖ 申込書はカリフォルニア支部の阿部さん宛てに送ってください Please send your application to Mr. Abe of the California *Chapter*.
‖**支部長** the head of a branch office.

じふ 自負 ▶この絵は自分でもよく描けたと自負しています I *take pride in* having painted this picture nicely. (➤ take pride in は「誇りに思う」) ／I *am confident* that I painted this picture nicely. ‖ 腕のいい職人には自負心の強い人が多い Many skilled craftspeople are *very confident*.

しぶい 渋い

> **解説** 「渋い」の言い方
> (1)日本語の「渋い」にぴったりの英語はない. 食べ物や飲み物が「渋い」という場合は, 例えば「AがBの口をすぼませる」と考えて, A makes B's mouth pucker. のように表現する.
> (2)色合い・演技・質などを指していう「渋い」にもぴったりの語はない. 以下の例はすべて近似の英語である. 外国人の中には "*shibui*" をそのまま用いる人もいる.

1【味が】▶その柿, 渋くない? That persimmon *makes your mouth pucker*, doesn't it? ‖ このお茶は渋い This tea *tastes bitter*. (➤ bitter は「苦い, 舌を刺すような」).

2【地味で味わい深い】▶渋い色 a *quiet* color(➤ quiet は「(色合いが)地味な, 落ち着いた」) ‖ 母は渋い色のスーツを買った My mother bought an *elegantly plain* suit. ‖ 彼女は服装の好みが渋い She has *subdued* taste in clothes. (➤ subdued は「抑えた」) ‖ クラプトンは渋い声をしている Clapton has a *seasoned* voice. (➤ seasoned は「枯れた, 鍛えた」) ‖ その老優は渋い演技で観客をうならせた That old actor moved the audience deeply with his *low-key*(*ed*) performance. (➤ low-key(ed) は「抑えた」).

3【不機嫌な】▶父は思いどおりにいかないので渋い顔をしている My father *has a grim* [*sour*] *look on his face* apparently because things are not going as he planned. (➤ grim は「厳しい」) ‖ 母は私の通知表を見て渋い顔をした My mother *frowned* [*looked displeased*] when she read my report card.

4【けちな】▶彼は金に渋い He is *tight*(*-fisted*). (➤「渋ちん」に近い名詞が tightwad).

シフォンケーキ **chiffon cake**.

しぶがっしょう 四部合唱 a **chorus in four parts**.

しぶき 飛沫 **spray** ▶モーターボートはしぶきを上げて走った The speedboat plowed through the waves, sending up a cloud of *spray*. ‖ 波が岩に当たってしぶきを上げた The wave *splashed* on the rock. (➤ splash は「(水などが)飛び散る」).

1**しふく 私服** **plain** [**ordinary**] **clothes**(制服に対して); **civilian clothes** (軍服に対して); one's **own clothes**(自分の服) ▶その会には制服ではなく私服で参加してください Please attend the meeting wearing *your ordi-*

nary [*regular*] *clothes*, not your uniform.
‖私服刑事 a plainclothes (police) officer.

2しふく 私腹 ▶《慣用表現》彼は自分の地位を利用して私腹を肥やした He *lined his* (*own*) *pockets* [*feathered his nest*] by taking advantage of his position.

3しふく 至福 **bliss** ▶風呂上がりにビールを飲むのが父にとって至福の時だ For my father, drinking beer just after taking a bath is a moment of *bliss*.

ジプシー a **Gypsy** (➤今日では, 自称の Roma, the Romany が使われる) ▶ジプシー音楽 *Gypsy* music.

しぶしぶ **reluctantly** (気乗りはしないが) ; **unwillingly** (不満ながら) ▶弟は母に叱られてしぶしぶ自分の部屋へ入り勉強を始めた My (younger) brother was scolded by Mother and *reluctantly* went to his room to study. ‖おやじはぼくの外国留学にしぶしぶお金を出してくれた My father *coughed up* [*shelled out*] *the money* for my study overseas. (➤ cough up, shell out はともに「しぶしぶ(金などを)出す」の意のくだけた言い方).

しぶつ 私物 one's **personal belongings** [**effects**] (身の回りの品) ▶私物はみんな家に持ち帰ってください Please take home all *your personal belongings*. ‖その社長は社費で購入した絵画を私物化した That president *appropriated* (*for his personal use*) a painting which had been bought at the company's expense.

じぶつ 事物 **things** ▶日本固有の事物 *things* peculiar to Japan ‖百科事典にはいろいろな事物が詳しく説明してある An encyclopedia gives detailed information on various *things* [*subjects*].

ジフテリア **diphtheria** /dɪfθíəriə/.

シフト a **shift** ‖シフトキー a shift key.

しぶとい **stubborn** /stʌ́bəʳn/ (頑固な) ; **obstinate** /ɑ́:bstɪnət/ (自分の目的・意見などに固執する) ▶《容疑者に自白を強要して》何てしぶといやつだ You are one *stubborn* guy. (➤この one はあとの形容詞を強めて「非常な」という気持ちを表す形容詞) ‖レポーターはインタビューを拒否されたがしぶとく(=粘り強く)食い下がった The reporter was refused an interview, but he *persistently* kept on asking for one.

しぶる 渋る **hesitate** (ためらう) ; **grudge** (しかたなく認める) ▶彼はなぜか私と一緒に来るのを渋った For some reason, he *was unwilling* [*was reluctant*] to come with me. (➤ be unwilling (to do) は「気が進まない」; be reluctant (to do) は「気乗りはしないが, 義務感もあり迷っている」という含みがある) ‖彼女は彼のプロポーズに対して返事を渋った She *hesitated to give an answer* to his proposal. ‖彼は寄付金を出すのを渋った He *was reluctant* [*was hesitant*] to make a contribution. ／He *grudgingly* [*reluctantly*] made a contribution. (➤後者はいやいや出した場合).

じぶん 自分 oneself (自分自身) ; one's **self** (➤ふだんの, 本当の) ▶自分を(もっと)大切にしなさい You need to value [respect] *yourself* (more). ‖就職試験の面接では自分を売り込むことが必要だ At a job interview, you must try to sell *yourself*. ‖彼はいつもの自分ではないような気がした He didn't feel (like) his usual *self*.
▶自分でその問題を解きなさい Solve the problem *by yourself*. ‖私は自分で自分の車を修理した I repaired my car *by myself*. (➤ by oneself は「人の助けを借りずに単独で」の意) ‖私は炊事は自分でやっています I cook my *own* meals. ／I do all my *own* cooking.
▶自分の欠点は見えないものだ No one sees *his or her own* faults. ‖彼は自分の家がない He has no house *of his own*. ‖何でも自分の思うようにできるわけがない You can't have everything *your own way*. ／You can't expect everything to go *your way*. ‖自分のことは自分でしなさい *Look after yourself*. ‖パソコンを自分のものにする(=使いこなす)のに3週間かかった It took me three weeks to *master* the (personal) computer [to *become proficient at using* the computer]. ‖自分さえよければいいなんて考えじゃ世の中渡れないぞ You won't get far in the world if you *only think about yourself*. ‖病気をすると人は自分本位になりがちだ People tend to become *self-centered* when they get sick. ‖対話「部屋の掃除, 手伝ってよ」「自分でやれよ」"Help me clean my room, will you ?" "Do it *yourself*."
‖自分史 one's personal history.

じぶんかって 自分勝手な **selfish** ▶自分勝手な男 a *selfish* man ‖自分勝手は許さん! I refuse to let you *have your own way*. (➤ have one's own way は「自分の思いどおりにする」).

しへい 紙幣 **paper money** ; 《米》a **bill**, 《英》a (**bank**) **note** ▶5ドル紙幣 a five-dollar *bill*.

じへいしょう 自閉症 **autism** /ɔ́:tìzəm/
‖自閉症児 an autistic child.

じべた 地べた **the ground** ▶素足で地べたを歩くのは気持ちがいい It feels good to walk (right) on *the ground* with bare feet.

しべつ 死別 ▶彼は3歳のとき父親と死別した He *lost* his father when he was three (years old). ‖母との死別が彼女の人生で最も悲しい出来事だった The *loss* of her mother was the saddest event in her life.

シベリア **Siberia** /saɪbíəriə/.

しへん 詩編 《聖書》**the** (**Book of**) **Psalms** /sɑ:mz/.

しべん 至便 ▶交通至便 *very convenient* for public transportation.

じへん 事変 an **incident**, (a) **disturbance**.

じべん 自弁 ▶交通費は自弁のこと You'*re supposed to pay* your own transportation expenses.

しへんけい 四辺形 a **quadrilateral** /kwɑ̀:drəlǽṭərəl/
‖平行四辺形 a parallelogram.

しぼ 思慕する **long** 《for》(恋しく思う) ; **miss** (いなくて寂しいと思う) ▶少年は亡くなった母を今も思慕している The boy still *misses* his mother who passed away.

1しほう 司法 **jurisdiction**
‖司法解剖 an official autopsy ／ a legally-ordered autopsy ‖司法試験 the bar examination ‖司法書士 a judicial scrivener (➤一般にこの訳語を当てるが, 英米にはこれに対応する職業はない. したがって a *shiho-shoshi* lawyer と表記するのも一案) ‖司法取引 plea bargaining ‖国際司法裁判所 the International Court of Justice.

2しほう 四方 **all sides** [**directions**] ▶その広場からは四方に道が伸びている Streets run *in all directions* from that square. ‖彼の演説を聞くために四方八方から人が集まってきた People have gathered *from all quarters* to hear him talk. ‖四方八方捜したが, (猫の)タマは見つからなかった I *searched high and low* for Tama, but couldn't find her.
✉ **私の故郷は四方を山に囲まれているので夏はとても暑いです** It is very hot in summer in my hometown because it is surrounded by moun-

tains *on all sides*.

3**しほう 至宝** a **great treasure** [**asset**].

1**しぼう 脂肪** **fat**; **lard**(豚の) ▶植物性 [動物性] 脂肪 vegetable [animal] *fat* ‖ 脂肪のない肉 *lean* meat ‖ 低脂肪の食物 *low-fat* food ‖ この肉は脂肪が多すぎる This meat has too much *fat*. ／This meat is too fatty. ‖ この牛乳は乳脂肪分が3.5%だ This milk contains 3.5% *fat* [*butterfat* ／*milk fat*].

▶お父さんはおなかに脂肪がつき始めている My father is beginning to *put on weight* around the waist. ／My father is beginning to *get a paunch* [*a spare tire*]. (➤ 後者はインフォーマルな表現) ‖ うちの姉貴は脂肪太りだ My (older) sister is *fat and chunky*.

‖脂肪吸引 liposuction /lípoʊsʌkʃən/ ‖ 乳脂肪 butterfat ／milk fat ‖ 皮下脂肪 subcutaneous fat.

2**しぼう 死亡** **death** 一動 **死亡する** **die** ▶当時は結核で死亡する人が多かった Many people *died* of TB in those days. ‖ 彼は交通事故で死亡した He *was killed* in a traffic accident. (➤ 事故や戦争による死には be killed を用いる) ‖ 西日本を襲った台風で50人以上の人が死亡した A typhoon swept through western Japan, leaving over 50 people *dead* [claiming over 50 lives]. (➤ 前者は「50人以上の人を死なせて去った」の意) ‖ エイズは治療しないと死亡率の高い病気だ Untreated AIDS is a disease with a high *fatality* [*mortality*] *rate*.

‖死亡記事 [広告] an obituary /əbítʃueri/, 《インフォーマル》 an obit /óʊbɪt/ ‖ 死亡証明書 a death certificate, a certificate of death ‖ 死亡届 a report of a person's death.

3**しぼう 志望** (a) **wish** (➤ 実現の可能性の薄い場合や困難を伴う場合); a **desire** (強い望み) 一動 **志望する** **want, wish**; **desire** ▶息子は高校の英語教師を志望している Our son *wants to* be a high school English teacher. ‖ 私は建築家を志望している I *have a desire to* become an architect. (➤ 堅い言い方で, ふつうは I want to be an architect. という) ‖ 兄は志望どおり弁護士になった My brother became a lawyer *as he had wished*.

▶現役で志望校に合格したとは大したものだ It's wonderful that he was able to enter his *first choice college* on the first try. ‖ 第一志望の大学はどこですか Which university is your *first choice*? ‖ 私は第二志望の S 大学に合格しました I was accepted by the university *of my second choice*, S University. (➤「受け入れられた」の意).

じほう 時報 a **time signal** ▶時計をラジオの時報に合わせる set one's watch by the *time signal* on the radio. ‖ 正午の時報をお知らせします The time at the tone is twelve noon. (➤ tone はポーンやピーという発信音).

じぼうじき 自暴自棄 ▶高校生の頃は何もかも気に入らなくて自暴自棄になっていました When I was a high school student, every little thing annoyed me and I just *gave up on myself*.

しぼむ **close** (花が閉じる); **wilt** (植物がしおれる); **deflate** (風船が) ▶朝顔は日光に当たるとしぼんでしまう Morning glories *close* (when they're) in direct sunlight. ‖ 風船がいつの間にかしぼんでしまった The balloon *became deflated* before we knew it.

しぼり 絞り **1** 【カメラの】 an **iris diaphragm** /áɪrɪs dáɪəfræm/; **aperture** /ǽpərtʃər/ (レンズの口径, およびその開きの程度) ▶絞り2.8でシャッターを切ってください Please shoot at *F* 2.8. (➤ F は focal length number(焦点距離数)の略; 2.8は two point eight と読む) ／Please use *F* 2.8 for shooting. ‖ 絞りはいくつにしていますか What *aperture* are you using?

2 【染め方】 ▶絞りの着物 a *tie-dyed* kimono.

しぼりだす 搾り出す・絞り出す **squeeze** 《from, out of》 ▶チューブの歯磨きを搾り出す *squeeze* toothpaste *from* [*out of*] the tube ‖ 絞り出すような声で答える answer in a *forced* whisper ‖ その負傷者はことばを絞り出すようにして話した The injured person *forced out* his words.

しぼりとる 搾り取る **extort** +目 (金などを).

しぼる 絞る・搾る

📖 訳語メニュー
水気などを →wring, squeeze **1**
厳しく鍛える →work ... hard **3**
的を →focus **4**

1 【水分を取る】 **wring** /rɪŋ/ +目 (ねじって); **squeeze** +目 (押したり握ったりして) ▶タオルをよく絞りなさい *Wring* (*out*) the towel well. ‖ オレンジを絞ってジュースを作ってあげよう Let me *squeeze* some fresh orange juice for you.

2 【無理に出す】 ▶私たちはそのパズルを解くために知恵を絞った We *racked our brains* to work out the puzzle. ‖ コーチたちは知恵を絞って対阪神戦の作戦を練った The coaches *pooled their knowledge* to work out strategies to beat the Tigers. (➤ pool は「出し合う」) ‖ 暴力団員たちはその商店主から金を搾り取ろうとした The gangsters tried to *extort* money from the shopkeeper.

3 【鍛える, 責める】 **work ... hard** ▶《練習で》きょうはみっちり絞ってやる I'm going to really *work* you *hard* today. ‖ 今度の先生には絞られそうだなあ I can tell our new teacher is going to *work* us *hard*. ‖ 宿題を忘れて先生にたっぷり絞られた I *was chewed out* by the teacher for not having my homework done. (➤ chew out は「こっぴどく叱る」の意でインフォーマルなアメリカ英語).

4 【狭める】 **focus** +目 (焦点を合わせる) ▶警察は捜査の的を吉村氏に絞った The police *focused* the investigation on Mr.Yoshimura. ‖ 政界の焦点は誰が自民党の幹事長に選ばれるかに絞られてきた The interest of the political world *is* now *focused on* the question of who will be elected as the LDP's secretary-general. ‖ 我々は選択の幅を5人に絞った We *narrowed* the choice *down* to five people. (➤ 絞り込んでできたリストを short list という) ‖ ペナントレースは広島と巨人の争いに絞られてきた The pennant race *has boiled down to* a contest between the Carp and the Giants. (➤ boil down to は「…に煮詰まる」が原義).

▶もう少しテレビの音を絞ってくれないか Can you *lower* [*turn down*] the volume of the TV a little, please?

しほん 資本 (a) **capital** ▶資本を集める [投じる] raise [invest] *capital* ‖ 資本金10億円の会社 a company with (*a*) *capital* of one billion yen ‖ 私の父は僅かな資本で商売を始めた My father started (his) business *on a shoestring*. (➤ shoestring は「僅かな資金」の意のインフォーマルな語).

▶《比喩的》私は体だけが資本です(＝健康が私のただ一つの財産です) Health is my only *asset* [*capital*].

‖資本家 a capitalist ‖ 資本主義 capitalism.

1しま 島 an **island** /áɪlənd/

▶島の人々 *the islanders* ‖ 島に住む live on *an island* (➤ in は大きな島の場合) ‖ インドネシアは約1万3000の島から成っている Indonesia is composed of about 13,000 *islands*.

> **語法「…島」の言い方**
> (1)「…島」は -shima, -jima でもよいが, the Island [Isle /aɪl/] of ... とするほうが英語的(isle は詩的な響きを持つ語). 例えば, 佐渡島は Sadoshima (Island) とか the Island of Sado のようにいい, 三宅島は Miyake-jima (Island)とか the Island of Miyake のようにいう.
> (2)「…諸島」「…群島」は the ... Islands か the ... Isles を用いることが多く, 例えば沖縄諸島は the Okinawa Islands, イギリス諸島は the British Isles のようにいう. 尖閣諸島のような小島は the Senkaku Islets と表現するとよい. (➤ islet は /áɪlət/ と発音する).

2しま 縞 **stripes** ▶赤いしまのある白のブラウス a white blouse with red *stripes* ‖ しま柄のネクタイ a *striped* tie ‖ 極細のしまの入ったスーツ a suit with *pinstripes* / a pinstriped suit.

‖たてじま vertical stripes ; pinstripes (細いたてじま) ‖ よこじま horizontal stripes.

1しまい 仕舞い an **end** ▶しまいにはその村には老人だけが残された *In the end* [*Finally*], there remained only aged people in the village. ‖ しまいまで話を聞いてください Please *hear* me *out*. ‖ 自分勝手なことばかり言っていると, しまいには怒りますよ If you go on talking so selfishly, I'm going to get angry. ‖ きょうはこれでおしまいにしましょう Let's *call it a day*. / *That's all for today*.

☛ おしまい (→見出語)

2しまい 姉妹 **sisters** ▶石田姉妹 the Ishida *sisters* ‖ 私は3人姉妹の末っ子[真ん中]です I am the youngest [the middle] of *three sisters*. ‖ 神戸とシアトルは姉妹都市だ Kobe and Seattle are *sister cities* [《英》*twin towns*]. / Kobe is *a sister city to* [*of*] Seattle. ‖姉妹校 a sister school ‖ 姉妹編 a companion volume.

-じまい ▶ゆうべは忙しくて夕食を食べずじまいだった Last night I was so busy that I *had no time to eat* dinner. ‖『ボヘミアン・ラプソディ』はとうとう見ずじまいだった I *never got around to seeing* [I *missed*] "Bohemian Rhapsody." (➤ get around to は「…する時間[ゆとり]ができる」) ‖ その講演は最後までわからずじまいだった I sat through the whole lecture, but *still understood nothing* (*at the end*).

しまいこむ 仕舞い込む ▶直子はそのラブレターを引き出しのいちばん奥にしまい込んだ Naoko *tucked* [*stashed*] the love letter *away* in the innermost part of the drawer. (➤ ともにインフォーマルな語).

しまう 仕舞う 1【片づける】**put** (**away**) 《in》; **keep** +目 (しまっておく) ▶健次はおもちゃを戸棚にしまった Kenji *put* the toys (*back*) *in* the closet. ‖ 秋雄, 本を本箱にしまいなさい Akio, *put* the books *away in* the bookcase. ‖ この皿はどこにしまうの? Where do these plates *go*? ‖ 通帳をどこにしまったか思い出せない I can't think of where I *put* my bankbook. ‖ このこと, 胸の中にしまっておいてね *Keep* this to yourself. ‖ 対話「ここに置いてあるタオル, 何?」「あ, しまい忘れてたわ」"What's this towel doing here?" "Oh, I (just) *forgot to put it away*."

2【終わりにする】▶店をしまう *close* the store ‖ 台風が来ているから, きょうは早めに仕事をしまおうや A typhoon's coming, so let's *call it a day* early (today). (➤ call it a day は「(仕事などを)打ち切る, やめる」の意のインフォーマルな表現).

3【「…してしまう」の形で】▶夕方までにその仕事を片づけてしまいなさい *Get* the work *finished* [*done*] by evening. ‖『火花』は読んでしまいました I *have finished reading* "Hibana."

▶彼女から来た手紙を母に読まれてしまった My mother *went and read* the letter from my girlfriend. (➤ go and do は「勝手に…する」の意のインフォーマルな表現).

しまうま 縞馬 a **zebra** /zíːbrə/ ▶シマウマの群れ a herd of *zebras*.

じまえ 自前 ▶あのニュースキャスターの衣装は自前だそうだ I hear that newscaster *pays* for her dresses *herself*. ‖ 交通費は自前でお願いします Please *pay your own* travel expenses. ‖ 祖父の歯はすべて自前のものだ(=入れ歯ではない) My grandfather's teeth are all *his own*.

じまく 字幕 **subtitles**(せりふの訳 ; 複数形で用いる) ▶その映画には日本語の字幕がついている[ついていない] That movie has [does not have] Japanese *subtitles*. →スーパー.

しまぐに 島国 an **island country**

‖島国根性 insularity, insular mentality.

-しましょう

> 【文型】
> …しましょう
> **Let's** do.

▶休憩してお昼にしましょう *Let's* break for lunch. ‖ 先に進みましょう *Let's* move on. ‖ もう後ろは振り返らないようにしましょう *Let's not* look back anymore. (➤ 否定形は Let's not do. がふつう) / *Let's* stop looking back. (➤ Let's do. は相手の意向を確かめる「…しましょうか」に対して,「…しよう」という積極的な提案).

-しましょうか

> 【文型】
> …しましょうか (申し出て)
> **Shall I** do?
> **Can I** do?
> **Do you want me to** do? ➤ ふつうの言い方
> **Would you like me to** do?
>
> 解説 (1)**Shall I** do? は **Do you want me to** do? (…してほしいですか)の意で, 相手の意向を聞く言い方. Can I do? はもともと「…していいか」と許可を求める言い方.
> (2)申し出としては Shall I do? より **Can I** do? のほうが積極的で Yes. の返事を期待しているが, 相手の判断が必要な状況では **Shall I** do? を使うほうがよい. **Should I** do? を使う場合もある.

▶かばんをお持ちしましょうか *Shall I* take your bag? ‖ 何か飲み物を買ってきましょうか *Can I* get you something to drink? ‖ コンビニでお弁当買ってきましょうか *Do you want me to* get lunch for you at the convenience store? ‖ これ, 何部コピーしましょうか How many copies of this paper *do you want*? ‖ あすの朝, 起こしてあげましょうか *Would you like me to* wake you up tomorrow morning?

あなたの英語はどう響く?

「…しましょうか」の意味では, 英米ともに Shall I … ? の形を使うが, これはアメリカ英語ではかなり堅い言い方で, ふつうはむしろ Should I … ? とか Do you want me to … ? のような言い方が好まれる. 後者は「私に…してほしいですか」と言っているようで, 日本人には無礼に響くかもしれないが, 英語ではごく日常的な言い方. なお, イギリス英語では Shall I … ? はアメリカ英語の場合よりも日常的に使う.

-しませんか

【文型】
…しませんか
How about doing?
Why don't we do?
Would you like to do?

《解説》(1)上の2つは親しい人どうしで使う, ややくだけた言い方. **Would you …?** はより改まった丁寧な誘い方.
(2)いずれも Yes. の返事を予想している. 気軽には Sure. ／OK. (いいよ), Sounds great. (いいね), That's a good idea. (いい考えだ)などと言い, 少し改まっては I'd love to. (喜んで), That would be nice. (すてきでしょうね), I'd enjoy that very much. (楽しいでしょうね)などと言う. 断るときは, いきなり No. とは言わず, I'm afraid, but … (残念ですが…), I'd really like to, but … (したいのはやまやまですが…)などのあとに理由や都合を述べるのがよい.

▶この辺で一休みしませんか *How about* a break? ／*Why don't we* take a break? ‖ 一緒に旅行でもしませんか *Why don't we* take a trip together? ‖ 12時半に一緒にお昼を食べませんか *Would you like to* have lunch with me at twelve thirty? (➤ How about having … や Why don't you have … のほうがカジュアルで積極的な誘い) ‖ たまには会っておしゃべりでもしませんか *How about* getting together to have a chat once in a while?

しまつ 始末 **1【処理】**▶ごみを始末しなさい *Get rid of* [*Dispose of*] the garbage. ‖ 雪のあとの泥んこ道は**始末が悪い** Muddy roads after a snowfall are just *impossible*. ‖ あの子は**始末に負えない**子だ He is an *impossible* child. ／He *is hard to control* [*handle*]. ‖ 土産物をたくさんもらって**始末に困っている** *I don't know what to do with* all these gifts.
2【悪い結果】▶何だこの**始末**は? 足の踏み場もないじゃないか *What's all this mess?* I can't find anywhere to put my foot. ‖ 大失敗をして**始末書**を書かされた I had to turn in *a written apology* for my big blunder.

しまった ▶しまった! 電話番号を間違えた *Damn it* [*Oops*]! I dialed the wrong number. (➤ damn は /dæm/, oops は /ʊps/ と発音) ‖ しまった! 鍵を忘れた *Gosh* [*Shoot*]! I forgot the key. 《参考》My goodness! や Dear me! はかなり年配の女性が使うやや上品ぶった驚きの表現.

しまながし 島流し ▶**島流しにする** *exile* someone *to an island*.

しまらない 締まらない ▶**締まらない顔** a *stupid* face ‖ あんな男にだまされるなんて**締まらない話さ** What *a fool* I was to be taken in by such a man! (➤ be taken in で「だまされる」).

しまり 締まり ▶**締まりのない**ジーンズの若者たち youngsters in *loose* jeans ‖ 彼は**金に締まりのない**男で, 3万や5万の金は一晩で使ってしまう He *has no sense of the value of money* and wastes thirty to fifty thousand yen a night.

しまりや 締まり屋 ▶彼女はなかなかの**締まり屋**だ She's *very careful with* (*her*) *money*. ／She's *a tightwad*. (➤ 後者は「けちん坊」の意).

¹しまる 閉まる **close** /kloʊz/, **shut** (➤ shut は close に比べやや乱暴な響きがあり, 閉まる動作に重点がある) ▶**閉まるドア**に挟まれないようご注意ください Please be careful not to get caught in the *closing door*. ‖ ドアは風で**バタンと閉まった** The door *slammed* in the wind. ／The wind *slammed* the door *shut*. ‖ その窓はなかなか**閉まらない** The window won't *shut*. ‖ 引き出しが**閉まらない** The drawer *is jammed* [*stuck*]. (➤ それぞれ「つかえている」「動かせない」の意) ‖ 詰め込み過ぎてスーツケースが**閉まらない** I can't *lock* my suitcase because I packed too many things in it. ▶そのスーパーマーケットは午後11時に**閉まる** The supermarket *closes* at eleven p.m. ‖ あいにくデパートは休みで**閉まっていた** Unfortunately, it was their day off and the department stores *were closed*.

²しまる 締まる・絞まる **1【きつくなる】**▶そんなにネクタイを引っ張らないでよ. **首が絞まっちゃう**じゃないか Don't pull my tie so hard; you're *choking me*. ‖ この瓶は**栓が固く締まっている** This bottle *is* tightly *corked*.
2【たるんでいない】▶彼女は年の割に**締まった体**をしている She has a *firm* body for her age. ‖ 健は**締まった顔**をしている Ken has a *sharp* face. ‖ 彼は筋肉が**締まっている** He has *firm* muscles.
▶監督はナインに「**締まっていこう!**」と声をかけた The manager shouted to his team, "*Hang in there* [*Get tough*]!"

じまん 自慢 **pride** 一動 **自慢する** **be proud** 《of》; **boast** 《of, about》(鼻にかける); **brag** 《about, of》(威張る) (➤ that の文がくることも多い)

【文型】
人・物(A)を自慢する
boast of [**about**] A
brag about [**of**] A
be proud of A
➤ Aは名詞・動名詞

《解説》(1)**boast of** はしばしば「鼻にかけて話す」という悪い意味になるが, 人以外の場所や物を主語にして「自慢できるものがある」という良い意味でも使う.
(2)**boast** は控えめでないことだが, brag は聞くに耐えないほど「オーバーに言う」という悪い意味で, 未熟な分別のないふるまいを連想させる.
(3)**be proud of** は「誇りに思う」ことで必ずしもそれを口にすることではない.
(4)**boast that** S＋V ／**brag that** S＋V ／**be proud that** S＋V で「…ということを自慢する」の意味になる.

▶彼女ったら, **自慢ばかりしてる**のよ She's *always boasting* [*bragging*] *about* herself. ‖ わが校の**自慢**は美しいチャペルです Our school's *pride and joy* is its beautiful chapel. (➤ one's pride and joy は「自慢できるもの」) ／Our school *boasts of* having a beautiful chapel. ‖ 鈴木さんは自分の娘を**自慢に思っている** Mr. Suzuki *feels proud of* his daughter. ‖ その母親は娘が有名大学出である**ことを自慢げに話す** The mother *brags that* her daughter graduated from a prestigious university. ‖ 息子は小学校入学以来, 無遅刻・無欠席が**自慢です** My son *is proud that* he has never been late for school nor missed classes since he entered elementary school. ‖ 祖母は入れ歯が１本もないことを**自慢している** My grandmother *is proud that* she doesn't have a single false tooth.

▶彼は体力が**自慢だ** He *prides himself on* his (physical) strength. ‖ 彼はよく故郷の**自慢話をする** He often *talks proudly about* how great his hometown is. ‖ 彼は新しいスニーカーを**自慢げに見せた** He *showed off* his new sneakers. (➤ show off は「見せびらかす」).

▶**自慢じゃないけど**ぼくは水泳では学校で１番なんだ *I don't mean to brag*, but I'm the best swimmer at school. ‖ 彼は父親の**自慢の息子**だ He is his father's *pride (and joy)*. ‖ あいつの**自慢話**は聞き飽きた I'm fed up with his *bragging* [*boasting*]. ‖ おまえが博識なのは知ってるけど, あんまり**自慢する**なよな I know you are well-informed, but don't *toot your own horn* [*blow your own trumpet*]. (➤ horn は主に《米》, trumpet は主に《英》用法).

✉ **私の自慢は誰とでもすぐ仲よしになれることです** One thing I *am proud of* is that I can make friends with anyone right off.

[1]**しみ 染み** a **stain**(変色して汚れた) ; a **spot** (点々とした) ▶**染みのついた**テーブルクロス a *stained* tablecloth ‖ ドレスにワインの**染みがついてしまった** The wine left *a stain* [*spot*] on the dress. ‖ **染みはなかなか抜けない**ものだ It is difficult to take out [remove] *a stain*. / *Stains* don't come out easily. ‖ 年を取ると皮膚にたくさん**染みができる** As people grow older, they get a lot of *age spots*.

[2]**しみ 紙魚** 《虫》 a **silverfish**, a **bookworm**.

じみ 地味な **quiet** (おとなしい) ; **plain** (装飾のない) ; **conservative** /kənsə́ːrvət̬ɪv/ (控えめな) ; **subdued**(抑えた, くすんだ) ; **inconspicuous** (人目を引かない) ▶**地味な**色 a *subdued* [an *inconspicuous*] color ‖ **地味な**服装をする dress in *quiet* [*conservative*] colors ‖ **地味な**商売 a *stable and conservative* job ‖ このネクタイはあなたには**地味**すぎます This tie is too *plain* [*conservative*] for you.

▶私たちの歴史の先生は**地味な**人柄だが, 考え方は進歩的だ Our history teacher is a *quiet* [*reserved*] person, but his ideas are progressive. ‖ あの女優は高校時代は**地味で目立たない**生徒だったそうだ They say that when the actress was in high school, she *didn't stand out* at all.

しみこませる 染み込ませる **saturate** +目 (水などをたっぷり) ; **impregnate** +目 (薬品などを) ; **instill** /ɪnstɪ́l/ +目 (思想・感情を) ▶スポンジに水を**染み込ませる** *saturate* a sponge *with* water ‖ ハンカチに香水を**染み込ませる** *infuse* [*impregnate*] a handkerchief *with* perfume ‖ 学生に愛国心を**染み込ませる** *instill* patriotism in the students ‖ ブランデーをたっぷり**染み込ませた**ケーキ a cake strongly *impregnated* [*infused*] *with* brandy.

しみこむ 染み込む **soak** 《into, through》 ; **permeate** +目 (浸透する) ▶雨は乾いた土に急速に**染み込んでいった** The rain water *soaked into* [*permeated*] the parched ground very quickly. ‖ 大根を味がよく**染み込む**までとろ火で煮込んでください Boil the *daikon* gently until the flavor *soaks* [*works*] *through*.

▶彼には儒教思想が**染み込んでいた** He *was imbued with* the philosophy of Confucius. (➤ be imbued with は「…を吹き込まれる」).

しみじみ **fondly**(懐かしく) ; **strongly**(強く) ; **deeply**(深く) ▶静かな夜にはふるさとが**しみじみ**と思い出される On quiet nights, I *fondly* recall my hometown. ‖ 私はアメリカ旅行をしたとき, もっと英語をきちんと勉強しておけばよかったと**しみじみ**感じた When I took a trip to America, I felt *strongly* that I should have studied English harder.

しみず 清水 ▶岩の間から**清水**がこんこんと湧いていた *Water* was gushing out (ceaselessly) from between the rocks. (➤ 英語には「清水」に当たる単語はない).

じみち 地道 ▶**地道な**努力の積み重ねがしばしば偉大な発見を生む *Slow, steady* efforts [*Persistent* efforts] often lead to a great discovery. ‖ 彼が成功したのは**地道な努力**のおかげだ His *perseverance* [*steady effort*] has brought about his success. ‖ 無理をしないで**地道にやりなさい** *Keep a steady pace* [*Keep plugging away* (*at your job*)] and don't overwork yourself.

しみつく 染みつく **be saturated** 《with》 ▶彼のＴシャツは汗が**染みついている** His T-shirt *is saturated with* sweat. ‖ このジャケットにはたばこの臭いが**染みついている** This jacket *smells of* cigarette smoke.

しみったれ ▶あんな**しみったれ**, 見たことないよ I've never seen such *a stingy guy* [*a cheapskate* / *tightwad*]! →**けちん坊**.

しみでる 染み出る **seep** (**out**), **ooze** /uːz/ (**out**) (➤ 後者は血などのどろっとした液体が) ▶古いゴムホースの裂け目から水が**染み出ていた** Water *was seeping out* through a tear in the old rubber hose.

しみとおる 染み透る **soak** 《through》 ▶雨が服に**染みとおり**, 私は寒くて震えた I shivered with cold because my clothes *were soaked through* with rain.

シミュレーション (a) **simulation** ▶その鉄道事故のコンピュータによる**シミュレーション** a computer *simulation* of the railroad accident.

しみる 染みる **1【液体が少しずつ入り込む】** **soak** ; **seep** (染み出る) →**染み込む** ▶雨が天井に**染みてきた** Rain *is seeping* through the ceiling. ‖ 兄は大学時代の汗の**染みた**ジャージーを大切にしている My brother treasures a *sweaty* jersey from his college days.

2【刺激して影響を与える】 ▶冷たいものは**歯にしみる** My teeth *are sensitive to* cold foods and liquid. ‖ その薬を塗ったら傷口に**しみた** The cut *stung* when I applied the ointment. (➤ stung は sting(刺すように痛む)の過去形) ‖ たき火の煙が目に**しみた** *My eyes smarted* [*burned*] from the smoke of the fire. (➤ burn は「ひりひりする」) ‖ 風が**身にしみる** The wind *is piercing(ly) cold*. / The wind *chills* me *to the bone*. ‖ 年取ったおふくろの忠告, 本当に**身にしみた**よ My old mother's advice really *came home to me*.

✉ **あなたの励ましのことばが身にしみてうれしかったわ. ありがとう** Your words of encouragement *touched my heart*. Thank you. / I *really appreciate* your words of encouragement.

-じみる ▶彼は話し方が**年寄りじみている**(＝年寄りみたいな話し方をする) He talks *like an old man*. ‖ **子供じみた**ことはやめろ Stop behaving [acting] *like a child*!

しみわたる 染み渡る **penetrate** +目, **sink (deep) into** ▶彼のことばは彼らの心に**染み渡った** His words *pene-*

trated [*sank deep into*] their minds. ‖ 芭蕉の句には禅の精神が染み渡っている Basho's haiku *are penetrated* [*filled*] *with* the spirit of Zen.

しみん 市民 a **citizen**(公民権を持った人) ; **the citizens** (➤ 総称) ; a **resident**(住民) ▶ボストン市民 the *citizens* of Boston ‖ 私は都内に勤めをもつ川崎市民です I am *a resident of Kawasaki* and work in Tokyo. ‖ 停電は市民の生活に重大な影響を与える Power failures have a serious effect upon the lives of *the people* [*the public*]. ‖ 彼は1990年にアメリカの市民権を得た He obtained American *citizenship* in 1990.

▶《比喩的》日本では「メタボリックシンドローム」という語は市民権を得ている The term "metabolic syndrome" has *become popular* [*widely accepted*] in Japan. ‖ 初対面での握手は今やわが国でも市民権を得ている Shaking hands when introducing yourself to somebody else *has gained popularity* in Japan, too.

‖ **市民運動** a citizens' movement ‖ **市民会館** a civic center ‖ **市民社会** (a) civil society ‖ **市民税** city [municipal] tax(es) ‖ **市民病院** a municipal hospital.

じみんとう 自民党 **the Liberal-Democratic Party**《略 LDP》▶自民党総裁 President of *the LDP*.

じむ 事務 **office** [**desk** / **clerical**] **work** ; a **desk job** (事務の仕事) ▶事務的なミス a *clerical* error ‖ 事務レベルの協議 *working-level* consultations ‖ 彼女は昼間パートで事務作業をしている She *works* part-time *as a clerk* during the day. (➤ clerk は「事務員」) ‖ 彼女は事務に向いている She *is cut out for clerical work*. ‖ その客は受付嬢のあまりに事務的な態度に腹を立てた The guest got angry with the overly *businesslike* attitude of the receptionist. ‖ 優子は小さな会社の事務員です Yuko *has a desk job* at a small company.

> **あなたの英語はどう響く?**
> 日本語で「事務的な態度」というと「冷たい」といったニュアンスを伴うが, これを businesslike と訳してもこのニュアンスは出ない. 英語の businesslike は「事務能力が優れた, てきぱきした」というプラスイメージの語だからである. 日本語のニュアンスを出すには overly businesslike や too businesslike とでもするしかない.

‖ **事務局** an executive office, the secretariat /sèkrətéəriət/ ‖ **事務局長** a secretary-general ‖ **事務次官** an administrative vice-minister ‖ **事務室**[**所**] an office ‖ **事務用品** office supplies.

ジム a **gymnasium** /dʒɪmnéɪziəm/,《インフォーマル》a **gym**(体育館) ; a **boxing gym**(ボクシングジム).

しむける 仕向ける ▶彼女は息子が医学を学ぶようにしむけた She *made* her son study medicine. ‖ 彼は太郎にその授業をサボるようにしむけた He *led* [*induced*] Taro *to* cut the class. (➤ induce は堅い語).

しめあげる 締め上げる **screw up** (ねじで) ; **fasten tightly**(ひもなどで) ;《インフォーマル》**put** [**tighten**] **the screws**《on》(人を厳しく責める).

1**しめい 氏名** a **(full) name** ▶この欄にあなたの氏名を書いてください Please write down your *(full) name* in this space. ‖ 新任の先生の住所氏名をご存じですか Do you know *the name and address* of our new teacher ? (➤ 語順に注意).

2**しめい 使命** a **mission** ; **duty**(務め) ▶重大な使命を帯びてその国に行く go to that country on an important *mission* ‖ 使命を果たす carry out one's *mission* ‖ この事件の全容を伝えるのが新聞記者としての私の使命だと思う I consider it my *mission* as a newspaper reporter to report the whole story behind this incident. ‖ 若い選手を育てるのが私の使命です It is my *duty* to train young athletes.

‖ **使命感** a sense of mission.

3**しめい 指名** **nomination**(推薦) ; **designation** (任命) ; **appointment**(選任) **一動 指名する** **nominate** +Ⓞ, **designate** +Ⓞ, **appoint** +Ⓞ ▶彼は大統領候補に指名された He *was nominated* for the presidency. ‖ 佐々木君が議長に指名された Sasaki *was designated* [*was named*] as chair(person). ‖ 彼らはジョンを委員会の議長に指名した They *appointed* John chair (person) of the committee.

▶みんなが一斉に手を挙げたので, 先生は誰を指名し(=当て)たらよいか迷った They raised their hands all at once, so the teacher did not know who to *call on*. ‖ ご指名により, 一曲歌います Thank you for *asking* me. I'll sing one of my favorite songs. ‖ **指名打者** a designated hitter《略 DH》‖ **指名通話** a person-to-person call ‖ **指名入札** a tender by specified bidders.

☛ **指名手配** (→見出語)

じめい 自明の **self-evident** ▶利益を上げることより安全の確保が大事なのは自明のことだ *It is self-evident* that guaranteeing safety is more important than making a profit.

しめいてはい 指名手配 ▶警察はその殺人容疑者を全国に指名手配した The police *started a nationwide hunt* [*search*] for [*issued an all-points bulletin* for] the suspected murderer.

‖ **指名手配者** a wanted criminal.

しめきり 締め切り a **deadline** ▶この原稿は締め切りに間に合わせられると思う I think I'll manage to *make* [*meet*] *the deadline* for this manuscript. ‖ 予約の締め切りは10月10日です *The closing date* for reservations is October 10.

▶《ドアなどの掲示》閉め切り Closed / No Entrance.

しめきる 締め切る **1**【打ち切る】**close** /klouz/ +Ⓞ ▶申し込みは10月末で締め切ります We will *close* applications on October 31. ‖ 当校への入学願書の受け付けはすでに締め切りました *The deadline* for acceptance of application to our school *has* already *passed*.

2【閉ざす】**close** +Ⓞ ▶彼らは戸を閉め切って何やら話をしていた They were talking about something *behind closed doors*. ‖ 夏場1日閉め切った部屋はむっとする A room whose windows and doors have *been closed* all day long in the summer feels stuffy.

しめくくる 締め括る **conclude** +Ⓞ ▶この会議を締めくくる意味でおことばを頂きたく存じます We'd appreciate it if you could give a short speech to *conclude* this meeting.

しめころす 絞め殺す **choke ... to death**(窒息させる) ; **strangle ... to death**(首を絞めて殺す) ▶アナコンダが牛を絞め殺した The anaconda *choked* the cow *to death*.

しめさば 締め鯖 **salted and vinegared mackerel.**

しめし 示し an **example**(手本) ▶兄さんがそんな行動をしたのでは弟への示しがつかないよ If you act like that, you'll *set a bad example* for your younger brother. (➤「悪いお手本になる」の意).

しめしあわせる 示し合わせる ▶少女たちは示し合わせて家出した The girls ran away from home, *as they had planned* (*to*). ‖ おまえは弁護士と示し合わせて(＝ぐるになって)俺をだましたな! You've been *in cahoots with* that lawyer to cheat me! (➤ in cahoots /kəhúːts/ with で「(人)と共謀して」).

しめしめ ▶「しめしめ. 金庫に鍵がかかってないぞ」と泥棒はつぶやいた "*Aha* [*I've got it made*] *!* The safe isn't locked," the burglar muttered.

じめじめ ▶じめじめした天気 *damp* [*wet*] weather ‖ じめじめした性格の人 a *gloomy* person.

[1]**しめす 示す** **1【はっきり見せる】show** ＋目 ▶その赤ちゃんはどんなおもちゃにも反応を示さない That baby *shows* no reaction no matter what toy you show him. ‖ まず先生がお手本を示して見せた First, the teacher *showed* an example of how to do it. ‖ 彼は私たちに立派な模範を示した He *set a* good *example* for us. ‖ 組合は会社側の示した(＝提示した)回答を拒絶した The labor union rejected the solution *proposed* by (the) management.

2【方向などを指す】 ▶けさ温度計は零下7度を示した The thermometer *showed* [*registered*] seven degrees below zero this morning. (➤ register は「(目盛り盤に)表示する」) ‖ 磁石は北を示して(＝指して)止まった The needle stopped moving and *pointed* north. ‖ 時計が6時を示している The clock *shows* [*says*] six o'clock.

3【意味する】mean ＋目 ▶赤信号は止まれを示す A red traffic light *means* "stop." ‖ この記号は学校を示している This *is the symbol for* school.

[2]**しめす 湿す** ▶タオルを湿して顔を拭く *wet* [*moisten*] a towel and wipe one's face with it.

しめた ▶寝言で英語が出るようになったのならもうしめたものだよ If you have come to the point where you speak English even in your sleep, then *you've got nothing to worry about* [*you've got it made*]. (➤「心配はいらない」の意).

しめだす 締め出す shut out ; lock out(鍵をかけて) ▶門限に遅れて寮から締め出された I *was locked out* [*was shut out*] from the dormitory when I failed to return before the curfew. ‖ 住民は団結して暴力団員たちをその町から締め出した The town residents united to *squeeze* the gangsters *out* (of their area).

しめつ 死滅する die out ▶恐竜は大昔に死滅した Dinosaurs *died out* eons ago. (➤ eons /íːənz/ ago で「大昔に」) ‖ 大腸菌は煮沸すると死滅する Colon bacilli *are destroyed* [*are killed*] by boiling.

じめつ 自滅 ▶そのピッチャーは連続4つのフォアボールを与えて自滅した The pitcher *cut his own throat* by giving up four consecutive bases on balls.

しめつける 締めつける tighten ＋目 ▶ねじを締めつける *tighten* a screw.
▶政府は国民を重税で締めつけている The government *is squeezing* [*oppressing*] its citizens with heavy taxes. ‖ きのう一時胸を締めつけられるような感じがした Yesterday I *felt my chest tighten* for a moment. ‖ 別離のシーンには胸を締めつけられる思いだった The parting scene *wrung* [*wrenched*] *my heart*. / The parting scene was *heart* (-) *wrenching*. (➤ 後者がふつうの表現. wrung /rʌŋ/ は wring(絞る)の過去形).

しめっぽい 湿っぽい **1【ぬれた】wet ; damp**(不快など) ▶洗濯物がまだ湿っぽい The laundry is still *wet*. ‖ お母さん, シーツが湿っぽいよ Mom, the sheets are *damp*. ‖ 日本の夏は湿っぽい Japanese summers are *humid*. (➤ humid は気候や空気が「湿度が高い」).

2【気がめいる】gloomy ▶そんな湿っぽい話を聞かせないでくれ Don't tell me such *depressing* [*gloomy*] things. ‖ 日本の演歌の多くは湿っぽいから嫌いだ I don't like Japanese *enka* songs because most of them are too *sentimental*.

しめて 締めて ▶締めて10000円です It *amounts to* [*totals*] 10,000 yen.

しめなわ 注連縄 a ***shimenawa***
日本紹介 ✉ **しめ縄は神社の社殿や鳥居, 家庭の神棚などに張る魔よけのわら縄です. ジグザグに切った白い紙をつけた花づなのようなものです** A *shimenawa* is a twisted rice-straw decoration for warding off evil spirits that is hung at the main hall of a shrine, on a torii gate, or on a family Shinto altar. It is like a festoon with zigzag strips of white paper.

しめやか ▶葬儀はしめやかに行われた The funeral was performed *with quiet solemnity*.

しめらせる 湿らせる moisten /mɔ́ɪsən/ ▶彼女はティッシュを湿らせて靴を拭いた She *moistened* a tissue and wiped her shoes with it.

しめりけ 湿り気 moisture(水分) ; **damp**(不快な) ▶梅雨時は押し入れの中まで湿り気がある During the rainy season, even the insides of closets *are damp*. ‖ 土は常に湿り気を帯びた状態にしておいてください Please keep the soil *moist*.

[1]**しめる 閉める** **shut** ＋目, **close** /kloʊz/ ＋目
語法 shut は close に比べ乱暴な響きがあり, 閉める動作に重点がある. close は「閉めた状態にする」の意.
▶その戸[窓]を閉めろ *Shut* that door [window]! ‖ カーテンを閉めましょうか Shall I *close* [*draw*] the curtains? (➤ draw は「開ける」ときにも使う) ‖ 香水の瓶の蓋はきっちり閉めなさい *Screw* the cap on [onto] the bottle of perfume tightly. / *Cap* the perfume tightly. ‖ ガスの元栓を閉めるのを忘れないでね Don't forget to *turn off* the gas main.
▶その床屋は8時に店を閉める That barbershop *closes* at eight. ‖ 不況には勝てず, とうとう店を閉めることになりました Defeated by the economic recession, the store finally had to *close* [we finally had to *close* the store].

[2]**しめる 締める・絞める** **1【きつく結ぶ】fasten** /fǽsən/ ＋目 ; **tie** /taɪ/ ＋目 (ひもなどで) ; **tighten** ＋目 (きつく) ▶シートベルトを締める *fasten* a seat belt ‖ 右の靴ひもが解けているよ. 締めなさい Your right shoelace is untied. *Tie* it. ‖ 1人でネクタイ[帯]を締められますか Can you *put on* a tie [an obi] by yourself? ‖ ねじが緩んでいるから締めておこう The screw came loose so I'll *tighten* it.
▶その男は妻の首を絞めて殺した The man *strangled* his wife.
▶《慣用表現》そんなことをしたら自分の首を絞めることになるよ(＝自殺行為だ) Doing that would be *suicidal*.

2【たるんでいるものを固くする】 ▶相手が弱いからといって油断しないように気持ちを締めていこう Don't let down your guard just because your opponent seems easy to beat. *Stay* [*Keep*] *on your toes*. (➤ on one's toes は「油断しないで」).

3【料理で】 ▶アジを酢で締める *firm up* the flesh of horse mackerel by soaking it in vinegar.

3**しめる 占める** **1**【ある位置に存在する】occupy ＋㊐ ▶新庁舎は繁華街の中心に一角を占めている The new Government building *occupies a space* in the downtown area. ‖その国は石油の産出で世界の第1位を占めている That country *stands first* in the world in the production of oil.

2【ある割合でもつ】occupy ＋㊐；account for（ある割合を）▶海は地球の表面の約7/10を占めている The sea *occupies* [*covers*] about seven-tenths of the earth's surface. ‖聴衆の2/3は女性が占めていた Women *accounted for* [*made up*] two-thirds of the audience. ／Two-thirds of the audience *were* women. ‖私たちのクラスは男子が多数を占めている The *majority* of the students in our class are boys.

3【ほかのものを入り込ませない】▶日本は長い間自民党が政権の座を占めていた In Japan, the Liberal Democratic Party *ruled* for a long time.

4**しめる 湿る** get damp [wet]（➤ wet は damp よりも湿り気が多い）；get moist（ほどよく）▶木は湿るとよく燃えない When wood *gets damp* [*wet*], it will not burn very well. ‖この靴下，まだ湿ってるよ These socks *are* still *damp*. ‖湿った風が窓から入ってきた A *moist* wind came in from the window. ‖この粉薬は湿らないようにしておきなさい Keep this powder medicine *dry*.

しめん 紙面 space；a page（ページ）▶見やすい紙面 legible *pages* ‖紙面に限りがあるのでこの件は次号にて論ずる Since *space is limited*, this topic will be discussed in the next issue.

じめん 地面 the ground ▶地面に穴を掘る dig a hole in *the ground*（➤ dig の目的語は hole, grave, tunnel, trench などで，英語には「地面を掘る」という表現はなく，（×）dig the ground とはふつう言わない）‖地面は雪と氷に覆われていた *The ground* was covered with snow and ice. ‖大雨で地面はぐしょぐしょだった *The ground* was soggy from the heavy rain.

しめんそか 四面楚歌 ▶改革案が支持されず，厚生労働大臣は四面楚歌の状況だ With nobody supporting his reform plan, the Minister of Health, Labour and Welfare has found himself *under siege* [*embattled by the enemy*].

1**しも 霜** (a) frost ▶ひどい霜 heavy *frost* ‖ゆうべ霜が降りた *It frosted* last night. ／*There was a frost* last night. ‖明朝は霜が降りるでしょう *There will be a frost* tomorrow morning. ‖秋の朝は芝生に霜が降りる *Frost forms* on the grass on autumn mornings. ‖霜がとけて道路はぐちゃぐちゃだった The *frost* thawed, leaving the road slushy. ‖葉は霜で少し傷んでいる The leaves are touched with *frost*. ‖霜取り装置《米》a defroster /dìːfrɔ́ːstəʳ/,《英》a demister.

2**しも 下** **1**【川下】▶この川のずっと下の方にダムがある There is a dam far *down* this river.

2【終わりの部分】▶下3けたを四捨五入する round off to the nearest thousandth ‖短歌の下の句を考える think up *the second* [*latter*] *verse* of a tanka. ‖下半期 the second [latter] half of the (fiscal) year.

3【下半身】▶父は病気のおじいちゃんの下の世話までしている My father even has to *help* my sick grandfather with *his bodily functions*.

‖下ネタ an off-color [dirty] joke.

しもがかる 下がかる ▶下がかった冗談 an *indecent* [*off-color*] joke ／a *dirty* joke ‖話が下がかってきた Our conversation *became indecent*.

しもごえ 下肥 human manure.

しもざ 下座 ▶下座に着く take *a seat far from the place of honor* ／take *a seat to the foot of the table*（➤ 後者は会食の席であることを明確にするような場合）.

しもて 下手 the right [R] (of the stage)（➤ 英語では客席に向かって「右」という）▶きみは下手から，彼女は上手から登場する You appear *from the right* and she, from the left.

じもと 地元の local ▶地元の野球チーム a *local* baseball team ‖地元の人々はその新しい橋の建設を喜んでいる The *local* people are pleased with the construction of the new bridge. ‖川沿いの朝市は地元の人たちにも観光客にもとても人気がある The morning market along the river is very popular with both *locals* and tourists.

しもばしら 霜柱 frost columns [ice needles] (on the ground)（● 英語には「霜柱」という概念はないので，「(地上にできた)霜の柱」と考える）▶けさ霜柱が立っていた There were *ice needles* [*frost columns*] *on the ground* this morning.

しもぶくれ 下膨れ ▶平安時代にはしもぶくれの女性が美人とされていた In the Heian period, women with *full-cheeked* faces were considered beautiful.

しもふり 霜降り marbled meat（肉）▶牛の霜降り肉 *marbled* beef.

しもべ a servant ▶神のしもべ a *servant* of God.

しもやけ 霜焼け frostbite, chilblains（➤ 後者はやや軽いもの）▶耳が霜焼けになった My ears *are frostbitten*.

1**しもん 指紋** a fingerprint ▶指紋を取る take one's *fingerprints* ‖指紋を取られることを拒否する refuse to *be fingerprinted* ‖ナイフに残された指紋と彼の指紋とが一致した The *fingerprints* left on the knife matched his.

2**しもん 諮問の** advisory ‖諮問委員会 an advisory committee [panel] ‖諮問機関 an advisory body [organization ／board].

じもんじとう 自問自答 ▶彼は次にどうすればよいのか自問自答した He *asked himself* what he should do next.

しや 視野 **1**【見える範囲】one's visual field, one's field of vision [view]（ともに「目を動かさないで見える範囲」）；view（視界）▶トンネルを出たとたんぱっと視野が開けた As we came out of the tunnel, *our field of vision expanded* [*widened*]. ‖西の方には視野を遮るものが何もなかった There was nothing to *block my view* to the west. ‖大きな鳥が視野を横切った A big bird *crossed my line of vision*. ‖遠くに島影が視野に入ってきた An island *came into view* in the distance.

‖視野狭さく visual field constriction.

2【見方】▶国際的視野をもったビジネスマン a businessperson with an *international perspective* ‖小田島先生は視野が広い［狭い］Mr. Odajima *looks at things from a broad* [*narrow*] *perspective*. ／Mr. Odajima *takes a broad* [*narrow*] *view of things*. ‖旅をすると視野が広がるよ Traveling will broaden your *horizons*.

しゃ 斜 ▶斜に構える assume a defiant [challenging] attitude.

じゃ 蛇 a snake ▶蛇(じゃ)の道は蛇(へび) A snake knows a snake's path.（➤ 日本語からの直訳）／It takes a thief to catch a thief. (➤ 英語のことわざ).

ジャー (⇀かこみ記事)

> **危ないカタカナ語✸ ジャー**
>
> **1**「魔法瓶」や「(ご飯などの)保温器」を「ジャー」といっているが, 英語の jar は単に「広口の瓶」のことで,「保温容器」の意味はない.「魔法瓶」の意味なら vacuum bottle, flask, thermos などとしなければならない.
>
> **2**「炊飯ジャー」の意味ならば rice cooker and warmer とする.

じゃあ ▶じゃあ, またね *Well*, I'll be seeing you. ／ *Well, then.* Good-bye ! ‖ じゃあね ! *See you (later)!* ／ *Take it easy!* ／ *Cheers!* ／ *Cheerio* /tʃìərióʊ/! (➤ 後者 2 つは主にイギリス英語).
▶じゃあ(＝それなら), 私も行きません *In that case*, I won't go either. ‖ じゃあ, 勝手にしなさい *Then*, suit yourself !

ジャーキー **(beef) jerky.**

じゃあく 邪悪な **evil** ▶邪悪な心 an *evil* mind.

ジャージ(ー) 《米》a **warm-up (suit)**, 《英》a **tracksuit** (スポーツ用上下) ; (a) **jersey** ; **jersey**(服地).

しゃあしゃあ ▶彼はしゃあしゃあとうそをついた He lied *shamelessly*. ‖ 二郎のやつ, 万引きして捕まってもしゃあしゃあとしていたらしいよ I hear that when Jiro got caught shoplifting, he just *acted as if nothing had happened* [*brazened it out*]. (➤ brazen it out は「そしらぬ顔で通す」).

じゃあじゃあ ▶水道の水をジャージャー流しっぱなしにする leave the water running(➤「ジャージャー」は特に考えなくてよい) ‖ お風呂の水がジャージャーあふれてるよ The water *is spilling over* the edge of the tub. ／The bathtub *is overflowing*.

ジャーナリスト a **journalist.**

ジャーナリズム **journalism** ; **the mass media** (テレビ・ラジオを含めて) ▶彼はジャーナリズム関係の仕事をしたがっている He wants to get a job in *journalism*.

シャープ **1【鋭い】**▶シャープな映像[画面] a (very) *sharp* picture ‖ あいつはなかなかシャープだ(＝切れる) He is a *smart* guy. ／He's (as) *sharp* as a tack.
2【音楽】 a **sharp** ‖ **シャープ記号** a sharp symbol [sign].

シャープペンシル (⇀かこみ記事)

> **危ないカタカナ語✸ シャープペンシル**
>
> 「いつもとがっている」の意の eversharp を社名にしたアメリカの Eversharp 社がこの語の起源と思われるが, sharp pencil は和製語で, これは「とがった鉛筆」の意にしかならない. 英語では mechanical pencil, automatic pencil, 《英また》 propelling pencil のようにいう.

シャーベット 《米》 (a) **sherbet**, 《英》 (a) **sorbet** /sɔ́ːʳbət ‖ -beɪ/.

シャーマニズム **shamanism.**

シャーレ a **petri dish**(➤「シャーレ」はドイツ語の Schale から).

しゃい 謝意 **gratitude**(感謝の気持ち) ; an **apology**(過ちをわびる気持ち) ▶企画にご協力いただいた皆さまに謝意を表したいと思います I'd like to express my *gratitude* to all the people who cooperated with me on the project.

シャイ **shy**(恥ずかしがり屋の ; 英米では短所と考えられることが少なくない) ▶彼女は 3 人姉妹の中でいちばんシャイだ She's the *shyest* of the three sisters.

ジャイロスコープ a **gyroscope.**

しゃいん 社員 an **employee** /ɪmplɔ́ɪiː/ (従業員) ; a **member of the staff**, an **office staffer** (➤ 後者はインフォーマル) ▶新入社員 *a new employee* ‖ 彼は当社の社員だ He *works for* this company. ／He is *an employee* of this company. ‖ 私はことしの 4 月, この会社の(正)社員になりました I *joined the staff* of this company this April. ‖ 私は今はこの会社でアルバイトをしているが, 将来は正社員になりたい I'm now working part-time for this company and hope to become *a full-time* [*regular*] *employee* in the future.
‖**社員食堂** a canteen /kæntíːn/ ; a cafeteria /kæ̀fətíəriə/ (セルフサービス式の) ‖ **社員旅行** a company trip.

しゃうん 社運 **the fate of a company** ▶このプロジェクトにはわが社の社運がかかっている *The fate of our company* depends on this project.

しゃおく 社屋 a **company's office building** ▶わが社の新社屋が完成した Our company's *new office building* was completed.

1**しゃおん 謝恩** ▶開店10周年を記念して謝恩セールを行っております We are having *a thank-you sale* celebrating our 10th anniversary.
‖**謝恩会** a thank-you party for the teachers [professors] (➤ 英米には学生が行う謝恩会に当たるものはない).

2**しゃおん 遮音** **sound insulation.**

しゃか 釈迦 **S(h)akyamuni** /ʃɑ́ːkjəmùːni, sɑ́ː-/ ; **(the) Buddha** /búːdə/.

ジャガー 《動物》a **jaguar.**

しゃかい 社会 (a) **society** ; **the world** (世間) ━ 形 **社会の social** ▶民主主義の社会 a democratic *society* ‖ 日本(人)の社会では義理が重んじられる 'Giri' is very important in *Japanese society*. ‖ 挨拶もきちんとできないようでは社会に出てから困るよ If you can't manage proper social greetings, you'll have trouble when you *get out into the world*.
▶社会の変化についていく keep up with *the changes in society* ‖ もっと社会の出来事に注意を払いなさい Be more aware of *social* [*world*] *affairs*. ‖ 日本は肩書き社会だ Japan is *a title-oriented society*.
▶社会学は社会科学の一分野である *Sociology* is one of the *social sciences*. ‖ ジョンソン氏は日本の社会制度を研究している Mr. Johnson is studying the *social systems* of Japan. ‖ 社会的地位の高い人が人格者とは限らない It is not necessarily the case that a person of high *social rank* has a good character. ‖ 彼は T 新聞社の社会部に勤めている He works for *the city desk* of the T Shinbun. ‖ 殺人や交通事故のニュースは社会面に載る Murders and traffic accidents are reported on *the city news page*. ‖ 児童虐待はますます大きな社会問題になっている Child abuse is a growing *social problem*. ‖ 林さんは交通事故で頭に重傷を負ったが, 2 年後に社会復帰を果たした Mr. Hayashi suffered a serious head injury because of a car accident, but he *returned to work* two years later. ‖ その犯人は服役後社会復帰した That convict *re-entered society* after serving his (prison) sentence. ‖ 過激派は反社会的行動をとる Radicals are engaged in *antisocial activities*. ‖ アリやミツバチは社会性をもった昆虫だ Ants and honey bees are *social* insects.

‖ **社会科** social studies ‖ **社会事業** social work ‖ **社会主義** socialism（➤北欧型の福祉を重んじる社会民主主義も含む）‖ **社会主義国** a socialist nation ‖ **社会主義者** a socialist ‖ **社会心理学** social psychology ‖ **社会生活** social life ‖ **社会福祉** social welfare ‖ **社会福祉士** a social worker ‖ **社会保険** social insurance ‖ **社会保障制度** a social security system ‖ **社会民主主義** social democracy.

逆引き熟語 ○○社会
学歴社会 an education-conscious society ／**競争社会** a competitive society ／**車社会** a car-oriented society ／**現代社会** modern society ／**高齢化社会** an aging society ／**市民社会** (a) civil society ／**少子化社会** a society with fewer children [with a declining birthrate] ／**情報化社会** an information society ／**男性社会** a male-dominant society ／**地域社会** a local community ／**父系社会** a patrilineal society ／**文明社会** a civilized society ／**母系社会** a matrilineal society

しゃかいじん 社会人 ⚠「社会人」に相当する英語はないので，**a working adult**（働いている大人）で代用する．▶社会人になる *become a working adult* [*a (working) member of society*] ／go out into the (working) world ‖ 4月から社会人だ I *start* [*begin*] *working* in April. ‖《社長などの訓示》きょうからは社会人としての自覚をもって行動してください From today, you should conduct yourself *with the awareness that you are a working adult* (*with social obligations*).

じゃがいも じゃが芋 a **potato** /pətéɪt̬oʊ/, an **Irish potato** ▶ジャガイモの皮をむく pare *a potato* ‖ ジャガイモ掘り *potato*-digging.

しゃかっこう 斜滑降 **traversing** ▶斜滑降する *traverse* (*down*) *a slope*.

しゃがみこむ しゃがみ込む **squat** (**down**) ▶彼女は気分が悪くなりしゃがみ込んだ She felt ill and *squatted* (*down*).

しゃがむ **crouch** /kraʊtʃ/ (**down**), **squat** (**down**) 《参考》 crouch は人が靴ひもを結ぶためにしゃがむような姿勢や動物が獲物に忍び寄るような身構えた姿を指す．squat は crouch の意味でも用いるが，排便の姿勢を連想させることも多い ▶犬は少年の前にしゃがんだ The dog *crouched* in front of the boy.（➤おびえているか，飛びかかろうとしているかのいずれか）.

しゃかりき ▶しゃかりきになって働く work *like mad* [*like crazy*].

ジャカルタ **Jakarta**（インドネシアの首都）.

しゃがれごえ しゃがれ声 a **husky voice** ▶しゃがれ声で歌う sing *in a husky voice* ‖ 応援のし過ぎでしゃがれ声になってしまった I cheered so much that my *voice became hoarse*. 《参考》 husky はかすれた声，hoarse /hɔːˈs/ はかぜをひいたときのようながらがら声をいう．

しゃがれる ▶私はどなり過ぎて声がしゃがれた I shouted myself *hoarse*.

しゃかんきょり 車間距離 ▶車間距離は十分に取るようにしなさい Keep a good *distance from the car in front of you*. ‖ 前の車との車間距離を縮めようとアクセルをぐっと踏んだ I stepped on the accelerator to narrow the *gap* [*distance*] between me and the car ahead.（➤gap は「隙間，隔たり」の意）.

じゃき 邪気 **negativity**, **negative** [**harmful**] **influences**（悪い気）; an **evil spirit**（悪霊）▶邪気を払う purge *negative* [*harmful*] *influences* ／drive [chase] away *evil spirits*（➤「邪気がつかないようにする」は ward off negativity [negative influences ／evil spirits]）.

しゃきしゃき ▶私のおばあちゃんはもうすぐ80歳になるが，まだ動作はしゃきしゃきしている My grandmother will soon be eighty years old, but she still *moves briskly*.
▶セロリはしゃきしゃきしておいしい Celery is delicious because it's so *crisp* [*crunchy*].

しゃきっと ▶きょうはどうも体がしゃきっとしない Today I just *don't feel right*. ‖ だらだら歩かないで，もっとしゃきっとしなさい Don't dawdle along like that. *Walk more briskly*.（➤dawdle along は「のんびり［だらだら］歩く」の意）.

しゃきょう 写経 **copying a Buddhist sutra**.

じゃきょう 邪教 a **false religion**, an **evil religion**.

1**しゃく 癪**

【文型】
人(A)がしゃくに障る
be annoyed with A
物事(B)がしゃくに障る
be annoyed at [**about** ／**by**] B
●解説●「しゃく」に当たるぴったりの語はない．annoy（うるさくして機嫌を損ねる），irritate（いらいらさせる，怒らす），bother（ちょっと困らす）などを使って表現する．

▶将棋では妹に負けてばかりでしゃくに障る I'*m* really *annoyed with* my sister because I always lose to her in (the game of) shogi. ‖ お隣の犬は朝早くから吠えまくっていて，全くしゃくに障る I'*m* really *annoyed by* the constant barking of the dog next-door from early morning. ‖ 彼のいいかげんなやり方はしゃくに障る I'*m annoyed* [*irritated*] *by* his sloppy way of doing things.
▶人の邪魔ばかりして，あいつは全くしゃくに障る He *gets on my nerves* because he's always in the way. ‖ 彼女の無礼な態度は全くしゃくだ（＝我慢できない）I *can't stand* her rudeness. ‖ あんなチームに負けるなんて全くしゃくだ（＝残念だ）*It's a shame* that we lost to a team like that. ‖ 明子だけがもてもてなのはしゃくだけど，美人で頭がいい上に気立てがいいのだからしかたがない *It* (*really*) *gets me* [*aggravates me*] that Akiko is the one girl who is so popular with the guys. But I guess it can't be helped because she's so bright, beautiful, and on top of that, has a great personality.（➤get, aggravate /ǽɡrəveɪt/ はともに「いらいらさせる」の意のインフォーマルな語）.
▶彼のことばを聞いてしゃくに障った What he said *made* me *angry*. ／His words *offended* me. ‖ あいつのやることはいちいちしゃくに障るね Everything he does *gets on your nerves*, doesn't it?（➤get on one's nerves は「…の神経に障る」の意のインフォーマルな表現）‖ 彼女は私のしゃくの種だ She is a *vexation* to me.（➤vexation /vekséɪʃən/ は「腹立ちのもと」の意で，日本語と同じく古風な語）.

2**しゃく 酌** ▶お酌しましょうか *Shall I pour you some sake?*

-じゃく -弱 ▶2メートル弱のサケ a salmon *a little under* two meters long ‖ けさはクラスの1割弱の生徒がインフルエンザで休んでいる This morning, *slightly less than* ten percent of our classmates are absent because of the flu.

じゃくし 弱視 poor vision, poor eyesight ▶弱視の人 a person with *poor vision*.
ジャグジー 《商標》 a **Jacuzzi**.
しゃくしじょうぎ 杓子定規 ▶彼は何でもしゃくし定規にものを考えたがる He likes to *stick to the rules* in everything. ‖しゃくし定規はやめましょう Let's stop *going by the book* (*and be more flexible*).
じゃくしゃ 弱者 the weak (➤ 総称) ▶彼はいつも弱者の味方だ He is always on the side of *the weak*. ‖**交通弱者** people (who are) vulnerable to traffic accidents (事故に無防備な人々) ‖**災害弱者** people (who are) vulnerable to natural disasters ‖**社会的弱者** socially weak [vulnerable] people.
しやくしょ 市役所 a **city** [**municipal**] **office** ; 《米》 a **city hall** ▶市役所職員 a *city office* worker [employee] ‖横浜市役所 the Yokohama *City Hall* (➤ 機能としての「市役所」と建て物としての「市役所庁舎」の2つの意味がある. 後者をより明確に表すために building を最後につけることもある).
じゃくしょう 弱小の small and weak.
じゃくしん 弱震 a **weak earthquake**.
しゃくぜん 釈然 ▶そんな説明では釈然としないね I'*m not satisfied with* [*convinced by*] that explanation of yours. ‖あいつの話はどうも釈然としない(＝うさんくさい) *There is something fishy* about his account.
じゃくたい 弱体 ▶この選挙に与党が負けると政権はさらに弱体化してしまう If the ruling party loses this election, it will further *weaken* the government.
しゃくち 借地 leased land, rented land (➤ 前者の leased は正式書類を作成して借りることをいう形容詞) ‖**借地権** leasehold ‖**借地人** a leaseholder.
じゃぐち 蛇口 《米》 a **faucet** /fɔ́ːsɪt/, 《英》 a **tap** ▶蛇口をひねって水を出す[止める] turn on [off] *a faucet*.
じゃくてん 弱点 a **weak point**, a **weakness** ; a **shortcoming** (ささいな短所) ▶人の弱点を突くのはひきょうだ It's cowardly to take advantage of other people's *weak points*. ‖誰にも1つや2つ弱点はある Everybody has *a weakness* or two.
しゃくど 尺度 a **measure** /méʒəʳ/ (物差し) ; a **standard**, a **yardstick** (基準) ▶ヤードやマイルは長さの尺度である The yard and the mile are *measures* of length. ‖人間はとかく自分を尺度にして他人を測ろうとする People have a tendency to judge others *by their own standards* [*criteria*].
しゃくどういろ 赤銅色 **bronze** (ブロンズ色) ; **brown** (褐色) ▶彼は赤銅色に日焼けしていた He was tanned (*brown*). ／He [His skin] *was bronzed* from the sun.
しゃくとりむし 尺取虫 《虫》 an **inchworm**, a **measuring worm**.
しゃくなげ 石楠花 《植物》 a **rhododendron** /ròʊdədéndrən/.
じゃくにくきょうしょく 弱肉強食 ▶弱肉強食の世界 *a dog-eat-dog world*.
しゃくねつ 灼熱の **scorching** (焼き焦がすような) ; **burning** (燃えるような) ▶熱帯のしゃく熱の太陽 the *scorching* [*brilliantly hot*] sunlight of the tropics ‖しゃく熱の砂漠 a *scorching* [*torrid*] desert ‖2人はしゃく熱の恋に身を焦がした The two were consumed by *scorching* [*burning*] *passion*. ／The two were having a *torrid affair*.
じゃくねん 若年 youth ▶若年人口 the *youth* population.
じゃくはい 若輩 ▶若輩者ですが頑張りますので, よろしくご指導ください Although I'm *young and inexperienced*, I'll work hard [do my best], and so I'd appreciate any advice [guidance] you could give me.
しゃくはち 尺八 a **shakuhachi** (➤ 英語化している)
日本紹介 ✉ **尺八は竹製の縦笛で, 表に4つ, 裏に1つ穴があいています. 主に日本民謡の伴奏楽器として使われます** A shakuhachi is a vertical bamboo flute with four holes in the front and one at the back. It is mainly played as an accompaniment to traditional Japanese folk songs.
しゃくほう 釈放 (a) **release** 一動 **釈放する** **release** +目 ; **set ... free** (…を自由にする) ▶囚人を釈放する *release* a prisoner ／*set* a prisoner *free* ‖その容疑者は3週間後に釈放された The suspect *was released* three weeks later.
しゃくめい 釈明 (an) **explanation** (説明) ; (an) **excuse** /ɪkskjúːs/ (弁明) ▶野党議員は総理の発言について釈明を求めた The opposition party members demanded *an explanation* from the Prime Minister of his previous statement. ‖彼は家賃が滞っていることの釈明をした He made *an excuse* for being behind in his rent. ‖きみは自分の行為をどう釈明するつもりですか How do you *explain* [*account for*] your conduct ? ‖私に釈明の機会を与えてください Please give me *a chance to defend myself*.
しゃくや 借家 a **rented** [**rental**] **house** ▶もう借家住まいはこりごりだ I don't ever want to live in *a rented* [*rental*] *house* again. ／I'm fed up with living in a *rented* [*rental*] *house*.
‖**借家人** a tenant /ténənt/.
しゃくやく 芍薬 《植》 a **peony** /píːəni/.
しゃくよう 借用する **borrow** +目 (無料で) ; **rent** +目 (有料で) ▶10万円の借用証書を書く write *an IOU* for one hundred thousand yen (➤ IOU は I owe you. (私はあなたに借金がある)の音訳).
‖**借用語** a loanword, a borrowing.
ジャグラー a **juggler**.
しゃくりあげる しゃくり上げる **sob** (**violently**) ▶その女の子は部屋の隅でしゃくり上げていた The little girl *was sobbing violently* in a corner of the room.
しゃくりょう 酌量 **take ... into consideration** (考慮に入れる). →情状酌量.
ジャグリング **juggling** ▶5つのボールでジャグリングをする *juggle* five balls.
しゃくる **scoop** +目 (すくう) ▶清水を手でしゃくって飲む *scoop up* spring water with one's hands and drink it.
しゃげき 射撃 **shooting** ▶ワイアット・アープは射撃の名手だった Wyatt Earp was *an expert marksman* [*a good shot*]. (➤ 後者はインフォーマルな表現) ‖射撃競技はクレー射撃とライフル射撃から成る The *shooting competition* consists of *clay shooting* and *rifle shooting*.
ジャケット a **jacket** ▶紺のジャケットにはグレーのズボンが似合う A dark blue *jacket* goes well with gray slacks. ‖**レコードジャケット** a record jacket.
しゃけん 車検 a ***shaken*** ; a **car safety check** [**inspection**] ▶車検を受ける have *a* (*car*) *safety inspection* ‖この車は2022年の3月まで車検が有効です This car is not required to have another '*shaken*'

[*official safety check*] until March, 2022. 《解説》日本の制度としての「車検」を正確にいえば the Japanese (governmentally required) car inspection《略称 JCI》だが, inspection には「外見的な点検」というニュアンスがあるので check を使うほうがよい. ただし, 任意の「安全点検」も a car safety check といえるので, 法定の車検は an official car safety check [inspection] とするほうが誤解がない. なお, アメリカには日本ほど厳密な車検はないが, ブレーキランプ, ヘッドライトなどの簡単な検査は毎年行われる. また, イギリスでは Department of Transport (運輸省) が行う検査がある.

‖車検証 a car inspection certificate, a JCI certificate (日本の).

じゃけん 邪険な・邪慳な **harsh** (無情な) ; **spiteful** (意地悪の) ; **hard** (厳しい) ▶彼に対する彼女の邪険な態度 her *spiteful* attitude toward him ‖ 彼女にそう邪険にすることないだろう You don't have to *be* so *harsh with* [*hard on*] her. ‖ 彼は部下を邪険に扱い過ぎる He *is* too *hard on* his subordinates. ‖ 邪険な人 ! What a *hardhearted* man !

しゃこ 車庫 a **garage** /gərɑ́ːdʒ/, a **carport** (➤ 後者は屋根と柱だけの) ; a (**train**) **depot** /díːpoʊ/, a **roundhouse** (電車の ; 後者は中央に転車台のあるもの) ▶車を車庫から出す get a car out of the *garage* ‖ この電車は車庫に入ります This train *is out of service* (for the day). ／This train *is on its way back to the roundhouse*.

シャコ《貝》a **mantis shrimp**, a **squilla** /skwílə/.

しゃこう 社交 一形 **社交的な** **sociable** ▶父は社交嫌い [非社交的] だが, 母はなかなかの社交家だ My father is *unsociable*, but my mother is quite *a good mixer* [*mixes well with other people*]. (➤ mixer は「人と交わる人」) ‖ 彼は社交性に欠ける He lacks *sociability*. ／He is a bad mixer. ‖ 社交的でなければセールスマンは務まらない If you aren't *sociable*, you won't make it as a salesperson.

‖社交ダンス social dancing, ballroom dancing.

しゃこうかい 社交界 a (**high**) **society**, a **fashionable society** (➤ マスコミに追いかけられる社交界の人々のことを the glitterati /ɡlìt̬ərɑ́ːt̬i/ という) ▶社交界にデビューする make one's debut in *society* ‖ 社交界の花 a *society* beauty.

しゃこうじれい 社交辞令 a **polite fiction** ▶皆がボブに彼は日本人よりもうまく日本語を話すと言うが, それが社交辞令であることを彼はわかっている People tell Bob that he speaks better Japanese than the Japanese (do). But he knows this is just *a polite fiction*. ‖ あいつがそう言ったのは単なる社交辞令だよ. 真に受けるやつがあるか He said it just to be *polite* [*diplomatic*]. Don't take him seriously.

しゃこうしん 射幸心 **gambling mania, passion for gambling.**

しゃさい 社債 a **corporate bond** ; a **debenture** (無担保の) ‖転換社債 a convertible bond.

しゃざい 謝罪 (an) **apology** 一動 **謝罪する** **apologize** /əpɑ́ːlədʒaɪz/ ▶新聞に謝罪広告を出す publish *an apology* in a newspaper ‖ 彼は約束を破ったことを謝罪した He *apologized* to me for breaking [not keeping] his promise.

しゃさつ 射殺する **shoot ... dead** [**to death**] ▶クマはその場で射殺された The bear *was shot to death* [*was gunned down*] on the spot. (➤ 後者はインフォーマルな表現).

[1]**しゃし 斜視** a **squint** ; a **cross-eye** (寄り目) ▶斜視の男 a *squint-eyed* [*cross-eyed*] man.

[2]**しゃし 社史** **the history of a company** [**a corporation**], a **company history.**

しゃじ 謝辞 ▶謝辞を述べる give [make] *a speech* expressing one's *gratitude* (➤「感謝のことばを述べる」の意 ;「お詫びのことば (を述べる)」なら one's apology とする).

しゃじく 車軸 an **axle** /ǽksəl/.

しゃじつ 写実 ▶その小説は写実的だ The novel is *realistic*. ‖写実主義 realism.

ジャジャーン ▶ジャジャーン ! ついにロンドンに英語の勉強に行くことに決めたぞ *Guess what*. I have finally decided to go to London to study English. (➤ Guess what. は「当たりっこないけれど当ててごらん」と, びっくりするようなニュースを伝えたいときに用いる).

じゃじゃうま じゃじゃ馬 ▶じゃじゃ馬 (娘) *a wild* [*reckless*] *young woman*.

しゃしゃりでる しゃしゃり出る ▶私がしゃべってるときに横からしゃしゃり出ないでよ Don't *cut in* [*butt in*] *with your comments* when I'm talking. (➤ butt in のほうがより失礼な印象を与える).

[1]**しゃしゅ 社主** a **company owner.**

[2]**しゃしゅ 車種** **the model** [**type**] **of a car.**

しゃしょう 車掌 a **conductor** ; a **guard** (イギリスの鉄道の) ▶《呼びかけ》車掌さん ! *Conductor !*

しゃじょうあらし 車上荒らし **car break-in** (**and theft**).

しゃしん 写真

a **picture**, a **photograph** /fóʊt̬əgræf/,《インフォーマル》a **photo** /fóʊt̬oʊ/ ▶自分のウェブページ [ブログ] に写真を載せる post *photos* on one's Web page [blog] ‖ エミ, きみの写真が欲しい Emi, give me *a picture* [*a photo*] of yourself. ‖ この写真はよく撮れている This *picture* came out well. ‖ きみのこの写真, よく撮れてるよ You look really good in this *picture*. 《参考》実物よりよく撮れている写真のことを flattering picture という ‖ 真子さん, 一緒に写真に入ってくれませんか Mako, would you be in the *picture* [*photo*] with us ? ‖ 西郷さんの銅像の前で写真を撮りましょう Let's *take a picture* in front of the statue of Saigo. ‖ 多くの見物人たちが携帯で写真を撮っていた Many onlookers were taking *pictures* with their cellphones. ‖ 対話「すみません. (私たちの) 写真を撮っていただけますか」「いいですよ」"Excuse me. Will you *take a picture* of us ?" "Sure."

> **あなたの英語はどう響く?**
> 外国旅行をしていて「(私のこのカメラで) 写真を撮っていただきたいのですが」と言う場合, I'd like to have my picture taken. と言う人がいるが, これは写真館などで, プロに撮ってもらう場合に用いることの多い表現で, 通りがかりの人に頼むと命令的に響く. Would you take [mind taking] a picture of me ? とか Could I ask you to (please) take my [our] picture ? のように言うのがふつう.

▶彼女は写真が嫌いだ She *is camera(-)shy*. (➤ 反対は camera-happy という) ‖ ちえみは写真写りがいい Chiemi *photographs well*. (➤ この photograph は「写真に写る」という動詞) ／Chiemi *is photogenic*. ‖ ぼくは写真写りが悪いんだ I *don't come out very good in photos*. ‖ 彼女は写真よりずっときれいだ She's much prettier in person than *in photographs*. ‖ 写真判定の結果その走者は 2 位だった In the *photo finish* it was revealed that the runner placed second. ‖写真1つ1つに短い説明がついている Each *photo* has a brief caption.

✉ **私の家族の写真を送ります．いちばん右にいるのが私です** I am sending you *a picture* of my family. I am the one on the far right.

✉ **(封筒の上書きで)写真在中** Photos／Photos enclosed／Enclosed : photos.

‖**写真家** a photographer →カメラマン ‖**写真館** a photo studio /stjúːdioʊ/ ‖**写真機** a camera ‖**写真集** a photograph collection ‖**写真店** a photo shop ‖**写真展** a photograph exhibition.

逆引き熟語 ○○写真
顔写真 a head-and-shoulders shot, a mugshot (犯罪者の)／**カラー写真** a color photo／**記念写真** a souvenir picture [photo]／**グラビア写真** a gravure picture／**航空写真** an aerial photo／**合成写真** a composite photo／**白黒写真** a black-and-white photo／**スナップ写真** a snapshot, a snap, a candid photo [picture]／**スピード写真** an instant photo／**全身写真** a full-length photo／**卒業写真** a graduation [yearbook] photo／**デジタル写真** a digital photo

じゃしん 邪心 **malicious intent**, an **evil heart** ▶邪心を抱く harbor *malicious intent*.

ジャス **JAS** (Japanese Agricultural Standards 日本農林規格).

ジャズ **jazz, jazz music** ▶クラシックをジャズ風に演奏する *jazz up* classical music ‖『聖者の行進』はジャズの名曲だ "When the Saints Go Marchin' In" is *a jazz classic*.

‖**ジャズ歌手** a jazz singer ‖**ジャズ奏者** a jazz musician /mjuːzíʃən/ ‖**ジャズダンス** jazz (dancing) ‖**ジャズバンド** a jazz band ‖**ジャズマニア** a jazz fan [buff] ‖**ジャズマン** a jazzman ‖**スイングジャズ** swing ‖**ディキシーランドジャズ** Dixieland jazz ‖**モダンジャズ** modern jazz.

じゃすい 邪推 ▶邪推もいいかげんにしろよ No more of your *stupid* [*foolish*] *suspicions*. ‖幹雄さんとは一緒に帰っただけ．変な邪推はやめて You can just stop that sort of *silly imagining* right now. All I did was (to) walk home with Mikio.

ジャスト (→かこみ記事)

危ないカタカナ語✸ ジャスト
英語の just と日本語でいう「ジャスト」には次のようなずれがあることに注意．
1「2時ジャスト」は exactly 2 o'clock か，2 o'clock sharp がよい．just 2 o'clock でもよいが，これは「まだ2時」の意にもなる．
2「2万円ジャスト」は exactly 20,000 yen で，just は使わない．just 20,000 yen とすると，「2万円だけ，2万円しかない」の意味になる．
3 野球の「ジャストミートする」は just は使わず hit a ball squarely とか，hit a ball right on the nose という．
4「ジャストプライス」を just price とするのは和製語．a good [reasonable] price とする．
5「このジャケットはジャストサイズだ」は This jacket fits (me) perfectly. という．

ジャスミン 《植物》(a) **jasmine** /dʒǽzmɪn/
‖**ジャスミン茶** jasmine tea.

しゃぜ 社是 a **company motto**, a **corporate creed**.

[1]**しゃせい 写生** **sketching** (スケッチすること)；**drawing** (絵を描くこと) 一動 **写生する** **sketch** (+目) ▶弟は公園へ写生に行った My brother went to the park to *draw pictures*.／My brother went *sketching* in the park. ‖この桜の花を写生しましょう Let's *sketch* these cherry blossoms.

‖**写生画** a sketch ‖**写生帳** a sketchbook, a sketchpad.

[2]**しゃせい 射精** **ejaculation** 一動 **射精する** **ejaculate**.

しゃせつ 社説 an **editorial**, 《英また》a **leading article** ▶社説で政府を批判する criticize the government in the *editorial* [*leading article*].

[1]**しゃせん 斜線** an **oblique** /əblíːk/ **line** [**stroke**]；a **slash**, a **slash mark** (／という形の小斜線) ▶次の図の斜線の部分の面積を出しなさい What is the total area of the *shaded portion*?

[2]**しゃせん 車線** a **traffic lane**, 《英また》a **traffic strip** ▶4車線の道路 a *four-lane* road [highway] ‖車線を変更する change (*traffic*) *lanes* (➤ 標識の「車線変更禁止」は No Lane Change [Changing]) ‖中央車線に入る[から出る] move in to [move out of] *the center lane*.

しゃそう 車窓 a **train** [**car**] **window** (➤ car は乗用車の場合) ▶私は車窓からアルプスの美しい景色を楽しんだ I enjoyed looking out (of) the *train window* at the beautiful scenery of the Alps.

しゃたい 車体 **the body** (**of a car**) ▶塀にこすって車体の片側にかすり傷をつける scrape the side of one's *car* on the wall.

しゃだい 車台 a **chassis** /tʃǽsi, ʃǽ-/.

しゃたく 社宅 a **company house** (一戸建て)；a **company apartment** (共同社宅)；**company housing** (何棟かになった全体).

しゃだつ 洒脱 ▶洒脱な文章[人柄] a prose style [a person] *of nonchalant elegance*.

しゃだん 遮断 ▶水道管が破裂したために道路の通行が遮断された Traffic on the road *was stopped* [*was interrupted*] because a water pipe had burst. ‖いい録音をするには外部の音を遮断する必要がある In order to make a good recording, we need to *exclude* outside sounds.

‖(鉄道の)**遮断機** a crossing gate [barrier].

シャチ 《動物》a **killer whale**, an **orca**.

しゃちほこ 鯱 a ***shachihoko***；an ornamental tile on the roof of a castle in the shape of an imaginary sea monster (➤ 説明的な訳).

しゃちほこばる しゃちほこ張る →しゃっちょこ張る．

しゃちゅう 車中 ▶車中で有名なテレビタレントを見かけた I caught a glimpse of a famous TV personality *on* [*in*] *the train*.

しゃちょう 社長 **the president of a company**, a **company president**, 《英》a **chairperson**；《インフォーマル》a **boss** (➤「上司」の意味にもなる).

シャツ an **undershirt** (肌着)；a **shirt** (ワイシャツ)
‖**シャツブラウス** a shirtwaist ‖**スポーツシャツ** a sport(s) shirt.

[1]**じゃっかん 若干** ▶父のほうがぼくより若干背が高い My father is *a little* (*bit*) taller than I am. ‖申し込み用紙は若干残っています There are *a few* application forms left.／We still have *some* application forms. ‖(掲示)アルバイト若干名募集 Part-time Workers Wanted.

[2]**じゃっかん 弱冠** ▶その小説は作者が弱冠20歳のときに

芥川賞候補になった That novel was nominated for the Akutagawa Prize when the author was *only twenty years old*.

ジャッキ a **jack** ▶ジャッキで車を持ち上げる *jack up* a car.

しゃっきん 借金 (a) **debt** /det/ (➤借金そのものは a debt だが,「借金状態」の意では Ⓤ) ; a **loan** (貸付金) 一動 **借金する** **borrow money, get** [**run**] **into debt** ▶**借金**を返す get out of *debt* ‖ **借金**を全部返す *pay* off one's *debt* ‖ **借金**を踏み倒す dodge paying one's *debt* ‖ **借金**を申し込む ask for *a loan* (➤ debt はすでに借りている金のことだからこの場合は使えない).

▶彼は多額の**借金**をしている He *is* deeply *in debt*. ‖ 彼は**借金**で首が回らない He is up to his ears [neck] in *debt*. (➤ ears のほうがふつう) ‖ 私は**借金はない** I *have no debts*. / I am *free of debt*. (● I am out of debt. とすると「借金を返し終わった」の意になる) ‖ この家は会社から**借金**して建てました I *borrowed money* from my company to build this house. ‖ 私は彼に20万円の**借金がある** I *owe* him two hundred thousand yen. ‖ 《野球》ヤクルトは5つ**借金**がある The Swallows are five games *below* [*under*] .500. (➤ .500 は five hundred と読む).

> **あなたの英語はどう響く?**
> 「彼に1万円の借金がある」を I borrowed ten thousand yen from him. としがちだが, この英語は「借金した」という事実を言っているだけで, 現在もまだ借りているのかどうかはわからない.「借金がある」ことを表すには owe を使って I owe him ten thousand yen. とする必要がある.

‖ **借金取り** a debt collector.

ジャックナイフ a **jackknife**.

しゃっくり a **hiccup**, a **hiccough** (➤ともに発音は /híkʌp/) 一動 **しゃっくりする** **hiccup, have (the) hiccups** ▶困ったことに彼女はしゃっくりが止まらなかった The trouble was that her *hiccups* wouldn't stop.

しゃっけい 借景 ***shakkei*** ; utilizing a background view as a part of a garden (➤説明的な訳).

ジャッジ a **judge** (審判員, 審査員) ; (a) **judgment** (審判すること) ▶私たちの英語弁論大会のジャッジをしていただけませんか Could you be *a judge* in our English speech contest?

▶バッターは主審のストライクのジャッジ(=判定)に文句をつけた The batter complained when the umpire *judged* [*called*] the pitch a strike.

シャッター **1**【カメラの】a **shutter** ▶すみません, シャッターを押していただけますか Excuse me, but could you press the *shutter* (button) here? ‖ シャッターチャンスだ! Here's *a chance for a good shot*!

2【店などの】a **shutter** ▶うちの店では午後7時にシャッターを下ろします We pull down the *shutter(s)* at 7 : 00 p.m. ‖ この商店街にはシャッターを下ろしたままの店が多い There are many stores whose *shutters* remain closed [stores that have gone out of business] along this shopping street.

しゃっちょこばる しゃっちょこ張る ▶そんなにしゃっちょこ張らないでくれ Don't *be* so *stiff and formal*.

シャットアウト a **shutout** ▶騒音をシャットアウトする *shut out* the noise.

▶千葉ロッテは今季3度目のシャットアウト負けを喫した The Marines suffered their third *shutout defeat* of the season. →**完封**.

しゃてい 射程 a **(firing) range** ▶**射程距離**500キロのミサイル a missile with a *range* of 500 kilometers.

しゃどう 車道 a **road(way)** ; a **street** (通り) ▶ここら辺は車道と歩道の区別がない There is no dividing line between *street* and sidewalk around here.

じゃどう 邪道 ▶納豆にマヨネーズを入れ(てかき混ぜ)るなんて**邪道**だよ Stirring mayonnaise into natto is *unthinkable*.

シャトル a **shuttle** ▶スペースシャトル a *space shuttle* ‖ シャトルバス a *shuttle bus* ‖ 無料シャトルバスが両会場を結んでいます A free *shuttle bus* links both venues.

1**しゃない 車内** ▶**車内**では携帯電話のご使用はご遠慮ください Please refrain from using cellphones *inside the car*. ‖ **車内**には危険物は持ち込まないでください Do not bring dangerous objects [substances] *into the train*. (● 日本語の「ください」に引かれて Please ... とする必要はない. 内容的には命令の一種である) ‖ これからお弁当, お飲み物などの**車内販売**をさせていただきます We will be coming down the aisles soon with box lunches, beverages, and other refreshments. (➤ aisle /aɪl/ は「(座席間の)通路」).

2**しゃない 社内** ▶彼女は**社内**の女性の中で最古参だ She is the most senior staff member [employee] *in the office* [*company*]. ‖ 増田君は**社内結婚**をした Mr. Masuda *married* [*got married to*] *a woman working in the same company*.

‖ **社内研修** in-house training ‖ **社内電話** an interoffice phone ‖ **社内報** an in-house newsletter.

しゃなりしゃなり ▶隣の奥さんがおしゃれしてしゃなりしゃなり歩いていくのが窓から見える From the window, I can see the lady next-door all dressed up and *sashaying* [*strutting*] down the street. (➤ sashay /sæʃéɪ/ も strut も「気取って歩く」の意).

しゃにくさい 謝肉祭 **the carnival**.

しゃにむに ▶彼はしゃにむに敵の中へ突っ込んでいった He dashed *recklessly* into the very midst of the enemy. ‖ 彼女はひとかどの学者になろうとしゃにむに頑張った She *went all out* to make a name for herself as a scholar [an academic]. (➤ go all out to do は「必死に…する」の意のインフォーマルな表現).

じゃねん 邪念 **an evil thought** (よこしまな考え) ; **a distracting thought** (雑念) ▶**邪念**にとらわれる be lost in *distracting thoughts*.

じゃばら 蛇腹 a **cornice** (建築などの) ; a **bellows** (カメラの).

しゃひ 社費 **the company's expense** ; a **corporate expense** ▶取引先を**社費**で接待する entertain one's customer(s) at *the company's expense*.

ジャブ a **jab** ▶ジャブを打つ *jab* at one's opponent.

しゃふう 社風 **corporate culture** ; a **corporate image** (会社のイメージ).

しゃぶしゃぶ ***shabu-shabu***

日本紹介 ✉ **しゃぶしゃぶは薄切りにした牛肉を箸で挟んだまま, 鍋に沸かした熱湯にさっとつけ, 軽く左右に振って引き上げ, たれにつけて食べる料理です** *Shabu-shabu* is a dish consisting of thinly sliced beef. You pick up a slice of beef with your chopsticks and briefly swish it around in a pot of boiling water before dipping it in a sauce and eating it.

じゃぶじゃぶ ▶川をジャブジャブ歩いて渡る *splash across* a river ‖ 彼女はジーパンをジャブジャブ洗った She *splashed* her jeans in the water as she washed them.

しゃふつ 煮沸 **boiling** ▶煮沸消毒 sterilization by *boiling* ‖ 布巾を煮沸消毒する *sterilize* dish towels *by boiling* them.

シャフト a **shaft**.

しゃぶる **suck** +目 (吸う) ; **gnaw** /nɔ:/ +目 (かじりつく) ▶あめ玉をしゃぶる *suck* (*on*) a piece of candy ‖ うちの息子は寝るとき親指をしゃぶる My son *sucks* his thumb while he sleeps. ‖ うちの犬は骨をしゃぶるのが大好きだ Our dog loves to *gnaw on* [*chew on*] bones.

しゃべる **talk** (人と話す) ; **chat** (気楽に) ; **chatter** (つまらないことをぺちゃくちゃと) ; **speak** (ことばを発する) ▶妹はボーイフレンドと電話で1時間近くしゃべっている My sister *has been talking* with her boyfriend for nearly an hour on the phone. ‖ 生徒たちは教室でぺちゃくちゃしゃべっている The students *are chatting* [*chattering*] *away* in the classroom. ‖ 旧友とワインを飲みながら2時間しゃべった I *had a chat* with an old friend for a couple of hours over some wine. ‖ 彼女はよくしゃべるが, 人のうわさはしない She is *talkative*, but never gossips about others. ‖ 彼はふだんはあまりしゃべらないが, 少し酒が入ると口が軽くなる Although he's usually *a man of few words*, after a few drinks he gets quite chatty.

▶赤ん坊がしゃべるようになった The baby has started to *talk*. ‖ 英語は全然しゃべれません I *can't speak* English at all.

▶あなたに言ったことは誰にもしゃべら(＝告げ)ないでね Don't *repeat* [*blab about*] what I've told you.

シャベル a (**hand**) **shovel** /ʃʌ́vəl/ (長い柄と幅広の刃がついた) ; a **scoop** /sku:p/ (穀物・石炭などをすくう ; shovel より小型) ; a **spade** (穴掘り用の) ; a **trowel** (園芸用の小さな) ▶シャベルで泥をすくう *shovel* dirt.

‖パワーシャベル [ショベル] a power shovel, a mechanical shovel.

しゃへん 斜辺 an **oblique** /əblí:k/ **side** ; a **hypotenuse** /haɪpɑ́:tnju:s/ (直角三角形の斜辺).

しゃほん 写本 a **manuscript** ▶中世の写本 a medieval *manuscript*.

シャボンだま シャボン玉 a **soap bubble** ▶子供の頃よくシャボン玉を飛ばしたものだ I used to blow (*soap*) *bubbles* quite often when I was little. ‖ 彼女の夢はシャボン玉のようにはかなく消えた Her dream vanished *like a bubble*.

じゃま 邪魔 (a) **disturbance** (うるさく騒いだりしての妨害) ; (an) **interruption** (割り込んで中断させること) ; an **obstacle** (障害物) **一動 邪魔をする disturb** +目, **interrupt** +目 ; **interfere** 《with》 (干渉したりして) ; **be in the way** (通行の邪魔をする)

▶勉強中だから邪魔をしないでよ Don't *disturb* [*bother*] me. I'm studying. (➤ bother は「迷惑をかける」) ‖ お邪魔じゃないといいんですが I hope I'm not *disturbing* [*bothering*] you. ‖ ちょっとお邪魔していい? Mind if I *interrupt* [*bother*] you? ‖ 酔っ払いがグラウンドに飛び降りて野球の試合の邪魔をした A drunken man jumped onto the baseball field and *interrupted* the game. ‖ 仕事の邪魔をするな Don't *interfere with* my work.

▶邪魔だよ. どいてくれ *You're in the way*. Move. / Get out of my [the] way. ‖ 前の人の頭が邪魔になって映画がよく見えなかった The head of the person sitting in front of me *blocked my view* [*got in the way*] and I couldn't see the movie screen very well. ‖ 箱が邪魔になってドアが開きません The box *is blocking* the door. (➤ block は「ふさいで邪魔をする」) ‖ 図書館の閲覧室で話をするとほかの人の邪魔になる You'll *disturb* other people if you talk in the reading room of the library.

▶子供が邪魔ばかりするのでゆっくり新聞も読めなかった The children *kept getting in my hair*, and I could not relax and read the paper. (➤ get in ~'s hair は「~の邪魔をして困らせる」の意のインフォーマルな表現) ‖ 私を邪魔者扱いしないでよ Don't treat me like I'm *a nuisance*. (➤ 発音は /njú:səns/).

☛ お邪魔 (→見出語)

ジャマイカ **Jamaica** /dʒəméɪkə/ (西インド諸島にある国).

しゃみせん 三味線 a **samisen**, a **shamisen** (➤ 英語化している) ; a three-stringed Japanese instrument resembling a banjo (➤ 説明的な訳).

ジャム **jam**, **preserves** ; **marmalade** (かんきつ類の) ; **jelly** (ゼラチン入りで透明度の高い) ▶リンゴジャム apple *jam* ‖ パンにジャムをつける spread *jam* on bread ‖ パンにジャムをつけて食べる have *bread and jam*.

‖ジャムパン a jam-filled bun.

> **危ないカタカナ語✸ ジャム**
> **1** 日本語の「ジャム」は英語の jam より広い意味をもつ. 英語の jam は果物を煮崩したものをいい, 果実の原形が保たれているものは preserves または conserves という. 特にオレンジの(皮も入れた)ジャムは marmalade である.
> **2** ゼラチン入りの透明なものは jam とはいわず, jelly という.

シャムねこ シャム猫 a **Siamese** /sàɪəmí:z/ **cat**.

しゃメ(ール) 写メ(ール) 《商標》 **Sha-mail** (普通名詞としても用いる) ▶写メ(ール)を送る send a *text message with a photo* / send a *picture message* / *text* someone *a photo*.

¹しゃめん 斜面 a **slope** ▶その村は山の斜面にある The village is on the *slope* of the mountain. ‖ 彼はスキーをしていて急斜面で転倒した He tumbled on *a steep slope* while skiing. (➤「緩い斜面」は an easy slope).

²しゃめん 赦免 a **pardon** **一動 赦免する pardon** +目.

しゃも 軍鶏 a **gamecock**.

しゃもじ 杓文字 a **rice paddle** [**scoop**].

¹しゃよう 社用で **on business** ▶父は社用で今東南アジアを旅行中です My father is traveling in Southeast Asia *on business*.

²しゃよう 斜陽 ▶輸出が減ってこの産業も斜陽産業となってしまった Because of decreasing exports, this industry has now joined the ranks of *declining industries* [the *sunset industries*]. (➤ 後者はインフォーマルな表現).

じゃらじゃら ▶ポケットの中で何をじゃらじゃらさせてるの? What's that *jingling* in your pocket? ‖ 当時ウエストに金の鎖を何重にもじゃらじゃら巻くのが流行していた Wearing gold plated chains wrapped around your waist that *made a clinking sound* was the style then.

じゃり 砂利 **gravel** ▶小道に砂利を敷く *cover* a path *with gravel* / *gravel* a path ‖ 砂利道は歩きにくい *Gravel roads* are hard to walk on.

‖砂利トラック a gravel truck.

しゃりしゃり ▶このレンコン, しゃりしゃりしておいしいわね This lotus root is deliciously *crisp*.

じゃりじゃり ▶貝に砂が入っていたのか口の中がじゃりじ

ャりする The shellfish must have had some sand in it. There is something *gritty* in my mouth.

しゃりょう 車両 a **car**, a **vehicle** /víːəkəl/ (➤ 前者は主に乗用車を指し, トラック・バスは含まない. それを含むのは後者 ; car には列車の車両も含まれる) ; a **carriage** (➤ 主に《英》で「客車」の意で用いられる ;《米》ではその意味には car をあてる) ▶後ろの**車両**がすいている The cars in the rear are less crowded. ‖ **大型車両**はこのトンネルを通行できない *Large vehicles* cannot pass through this tunnel.

しゃりん 車輪 a **wheel** ▶自転車の**車輪**を取り付ける［外す］put *a wheel* on［take *a wheel* off］a bicycle ‖（車の）右後ろの**車輪**が溝に落ちてしまった The back *wheel* on the right side (of my car) got stuck in a ditch.

しゃれ 洒落 a **joke**（ジョーク）; **humor** /hjúːməʳ/（ユーモア）; a **pun**（語呂合わせ）▶うまい［下手な］**しゃれ** a clever［bad］*joke* ‖ **しゃれを飛ばす** *make a pun*／*crack a joke* ‖ それ, **しゃれ**のつもり? Is that supposed to be *a joke*?／Are you saying that as *a joke*? ‖ **しゃれ**になんないよ It's like a bad *joke*. ‖ つまらない**しゃれ**はよせ No more *stupid jokes*, please! ‖ 日本の政治家には**しゃれ**のうまい人が少ない Few Japanese politicians are good at *making jokes*. ‖ **しゃれ**のわからない人ね! You can't take *a joke*!

☛ **おしゃれ, 駄じゃれ**（→見出語）

しゃれい 謝礼 a **reward** /rɪwɔ́ːʳd/（報奨金）; a **fee**（弁護士・医師・ピアノ教師など専門職の人への礼金）; **honorarium** /ɑ̀ːnəréəriəm/（講演などの ; 本人からの要求がない場合に出すような）▶うちの猫を見つけてくださった方には1万円の**謝礼**を差し上げます *A reward* of 10,000 yen will be given to the person who finds my cat. ‖ 財布を届けてくれた人にいくら**謝礼**をしたらいいかしら? I wonder how much money I should give as *a reward* to the person who returned my wallet.

しゃれき 社歴 ▶彼の**社歴**は30年だ He's *been working for the company for* 30 years.

しゃれた 洒落た **fancy**（凝った）; **elegant**（洗練された）; **stylish**（当世風の）; **fashionable**（流行の）; **smart**（服装がピシッときまっている ;《英》に多い）; **tasteful**（趣味のよい）▶**しゃれた**車 a *fancy* car ‖ **しゃれた**フランス料理店 an *elegant*［*fancy*］French restaurant ‖ **しゃれた**服 a *stylish* dress ‖ **しゃれた**ヘアスタイル a *fashionable* hairstyle ‖ **しゃれた**内装の部屋 a room with *tasteful* decor ‖ 彼女は**しゃれた**服装をしている She is *smartly* dressed. ‖ **しゃれた**時計をしているね That's a *nice-looking*［*fashionable*］watch you're wearing.

▶青二才のくせに**しゃれた**口を利くじゃないか I don't want any *smart* talk［any *lip*］from a kid like you!

しゃれっけ 洒落っ気 ▶うちの姉は全然**しゃれっ気**がない My (older) sister is quite *indifferent to her appearance*. ‖ 少しは**しゃれっ気**を出せよ Try to *pay* more *attention to your appearance*.

じゃれる **play**《with》▶子猫がテニスボールに**じゃれて**いる A kitten is *playing with* a tennis ball. ‖ 犬が子供たちに**じゃれて**いた The dog was *frolicking*［*frisking*］to get the children's attention. (➤ frolic は「ふざけ回る」の意) ‖（猫の）タマが**じゃれて**ぼくの手をかんだ Tama bit me on the hand *playfully*. ‖ 若いカップルが**じゃれ合って**いた The young couple *were touching each other playfully*.

シャワー a **shower** ▶**シャワー**を浴びる take *a shower*

‖**シャワー室** a shower room.

ジャンクション a **junction**.

ジャンクフード **junk food**.

ジャングル **the jungle**

‖**ジャングルジム** a jungle gym, monkey bars.

じゃんけん *janken* ; the game of 'rock-paper-scissors'［'scissors-paper-stone'］(➤ 説明的な訳)

日本紹介 ✉ **じゃんけんはゲームの勝ち負けや順番を決めるときに行います. かけ声のあとで, 片手ではさみ・紙・石の形のどれかを出します. はさみは紙に, 紙は石に, 石ははさみに勝ちます** *Janken* is a game people play to decide the winner or who plays first. While shouting "Jan Ken Pon", you put your hand out in the shape of scissors, paper or a rock［stone］. Scissors beat paper, paper beats rock［stone］, and rock［stone］beats scissors.

▶**じゃんけん**で決めよう Let's decide by *'rock-paper-scissors'*! 《**参考**》英米では順番などを決めるとき,「じゃんけん」でなく, コインを投げて表 (heads) が出るか裏 (tails) が出るかで決める. これを tossup といい, 声をかける場合は Let's toss for it! という.

じゃんじゃん ▶朝から**じゃんじゃん**電話がかかってきた Phone calls have been *pouring in* since this morning. ‖ **じゃんじゃん**飲んでくれよ Drink *as much as you want*.

シャンゼリゼ **the Champs Élysées** /ʃɑ̀ːnzeɪlizéɪ/（パリを代表する大通りの名前）.

じゃんそう 雀荘 a **mah-jongg parlor**.

シャンソン a **chanson** /ʃɑ̀ːnsɔ́ːn/

‖**シャンソン歌手** a chanson singer.

シャンデリア a **chandelier** /ʃændəlíəʳ/ ▶居間に**シャンデリア**をつるす hang *a chandelier* in the living room.

しゃんと ▶祖母は80歳だがまだ**しゃんと**している At eighty, my grandmother is still *spry*. ‖ 背筋を**しゃんと**伸ばしなさい *Straighten* your back.／Stand up straight.

ジャンパー a **(stadium) jacket**, a **windbreaker**（上着）; a **jumper**（跳躍選手）

> **危ないカタカナ語✸ ジャンパー**
> **1** スキーや陸上競技の跳躍選手の意味の「ジャンパー」は jumper でよいが, 上着の「ジャンパー」は varsity jacket や windbreaker が相当する. 日本語の「ジャンパー」のもとになった jumper は水夫・漁師・荷揚げ人夫などの作業用上着を指す語で, タウンウェアのイメージはない.
> **2** jumper は《米》ではまた女性の「ジャンパースカート」をも指す.《英》でいう pinafore (dress) のこと.

シャンハイ 上海 **Shanghai** /ʃæŋhάɪ/（中国の都市）.

ジャンプ a **jump** 一動 **ジャンプする** **jump**（上へ飛び上がる）; **leap**（跳び上がる, 跳んで越える）▶**ジャンプ**すれば天井に届くかもしれない You might reach the ceiling if you *jump*. ‖ あの道端の水たまりを**ジャンプ**してごらん Try and *leap across* that puddle on the road.

▶《スキーで》伊東, 伸ばしました. 130メートルの大**ジャンプ**です Ito has come a long way. It was *a great*［*fantastic*］*jump* of 130 meters.

‖**ジャンプスーツ** a jumpsuit ‖ **3回転半ジャンプ**（フィギュアスケートの）a triple axel.

シャンプー **shampoo** /ʃæmpúː/ ▶妹はほとんど毎朝**シャンプー**する My (younger) sister *shampoos her hair* almost every morning.（➤ 美容院などで「シャンプーをしてもらう」は have a shampoo という）.

シャンペン (a) **champagne** /ʃæmpéɪn/.

ジャンボ ジャンボな jumbo

‖**ジャンボジェット機** a jumbo jet.

ジャンボリー a **jamboree** /dʒæmbəríː/.

ジャンル a **genre** /ʒɑ́ːnrə/（特に芸術作品の）; a **category** /kǽṭəgɔ̀ːri/（部門）▶**蔵書をジャンル別に分類する** classify the books in one's library *according to category* ‖ **シェークスピアの『マクベス』は悲劇のジャンルに入る戯曲だ** Shakespeare's "Macbeth" is an example of the tragic *genre* of drama. ‖ **彼はファッション界で新しいジャンル**（＝**領域**）**を開拓した** He opened up *a new field* [*sphere*] in the fashion industry.

1**しゅ 主** ▶**うちの客は若い女性が主だ** *Most* of our customers are young women. ‖ **このクラブは相互の親睦を図ることが主目的です** The *main purpose* of the club is promoting mutual friendship.

‖**主成分** the main [principal] ingredient(s)（食品などの）; the main [major ／principal] component(s)（食品以外の）.

☛ **主として**（→見出語）

2**しゅ 主 the Lord**（キリスト教の神）▶**主イエス・キリスト** *our Lord* Jesus Christ ／*Lord* Jesus (Christ).

3**しゅ 朱 vermilion** /vəʳmíljən/（色）▶**原稿に朱を入れる** *correct* [*red-pencil*] a manuscript ‖ **朱塗りの盆** a *vermilion-lacquered* tray.

ことわざ **朱に交われば赤くなる** Good company makes you good and bad company makes you bad.（➤「よい仲間はあなたをよくし，悪い仲間はあなたを悪くする」の意）.

4**しゅ 種**《生物学上の分類》**species**（➤ 単複同形）▶**絶滅した種** an extinct *species* ‖『**種の起源**』"*The Origin of Species*"（➤ ダーウィンの著書）‖ **絶滅危惧種** an endangered *species*.

しゅい 首位 first place, the top ▶**首位を行く阪神** the *front-running* Tigers ‖ **広島は巨人を破って首位を奪回した** The Carp regained [reclaimed] *first place* by defeating the Giants.

‖**首位打者** a leading hitter.

しゅいしょ 趣意書 a **prospectus**.

しゅいん 主因 a **main cause** [**factor**].

1**しゅう 私有の private** /práɪvət/ ▶**その国では私有財産権が認められていない** *Private property* is not allowed in that country.

‖**私有地** private land.

2**しゅう 雌雄 male and female**（➤ 日本語との語順の違いに注意）▶《慣用表現》**いよいよ雌雄を決する時が来た** The time has come (for us) to *fight a decisive battle*.

‖**雌雄同体** a hermaphrodite /həːʳmǽfrədaɪt/.

1**しゅう 週** a **week** ▶**私たちは週40時間労働だ** We work 40 hours *a week*. ‖ **私は週２回英語塾に通っている** I go to a juku to study English *twice a week*. ‖ **この島には週に１度しか船が来ない** The ferry (boat) comes to this island *once a week*.

✉ **日本の公立学校は週５日制です** Japanese public schools have [have adopted] *a five-day school week*. ➤ 職場の週５日制［週休２日制］は five-day work week.

2**しゅう 州** a **state**（アメリカ・オーストラリアなどの）; a **county** /káʊnṭi/（イギリスの）; a **province**（カナダの）▶**アメリカ合衆国には50の州がある** There are 50 *states* in the United States of America. ‖ **ポールはオレゴン州出身だ** Paul is from (*the State of*) *Oregon*.（➤ Oregon State とは言わない）‖ **ニューヨーク州の州都はオルバニーだ** The *capital* of *New York State* is Albany.

‖**州知事** a state governor（アメリカの）; a premier（カナダ・オーストラリアの）.

3**しゅう 秀**《学業成績》**excellent, outstanding exemplary**（➤ 優は very good, 良は good, above average, 可は satisfactory, fair, average, 不可は unacceptable, unsatisfactory）.

しゅー ▶**風船がシューといってしぼんでしまった** The balloon *hissed* as it shrank.

1**-しゅう -周** ▶**地球を１周する** *go around* [《英》*round*] the earth ‖ **グラウンドを走って３周する** *run around* the field *three times* ‖ **この湖を船で１周するのに１時間半近くかかります** It takes about an hour and a half to *sail around* this lake.

2**-しゅう -宗 sect** ▶**日蓮宗** the Nichiren *sect*.

じゆう 自由 **1【ほかから束縛を受けないこと】freedom**（束縛や拘束からの）; **liberty**（権利としての）（➤ 個々の権利は freedom. liberty はより抽象的で格調高い語）**一形 自由な free** ▶**自由を守る** defend one's *freedom* [*liberty*] ‖ **アフリカ諸国は長い戦いのあと自由を獲得した** The African nations won *liberty* after long struggle(s). ‖ **世界には言論の自由や集会の自由が制限されている国がたくさんある** There are many countries in the world where *freedom of speech and assembly* are restricted. ‖ **軍事政権の下では自由に意見を述べることができない** People can't express their views *freely* under a military regime. ‖ **彼は刑期を終えて自由の身となった** After serving out his sentence, he *became a free man*. ‖ **３時から５時までは自由行動です** You *have free time* [You *are on your own*] from 3 to 5.

2【思いのままにできる】一形 自由な free ▶**自由な時間がもっと欲しい** I want to have more *free* time. ‖ **彼の家庭には自由な雰囲気がある** His home has a *free* atmosphere. ‖ **魚のように自由に海を泳ぎたい** I wish I could swim *freely* like a fish in the ocean.

> **【文型】**
> **自由に（＝気兼ねなく）…する**
> **feel free to** do
> **自由に…できる**
> **be free to** do
> A **をご自由にどうぞ**
> **Please help yourself to** A.
> ➤ A は食べ物や簡単に手に取れる物

▶**トイレはご自由にお使いください** *Feel free to* use the bathroom. ‖ **このマラソン大会は誰でも自由に参加できる** Anyone *is free to* [can *freely*] take part in this marathon. ‖ **パンフレットはどうぞご自由にお持ちください** *Please help yourself to* a brochure. ／*Please feel free to take* a brochure. ‖ **お代わりはご自由にどうぞ** *Help yourself to* seconds [refills].（➤ seconds は食べ物の, refills は飲み物のお代わり）.

▶**夏休みの自由研究** a project during the summer vacation（➤ 英語では単に summer project というのがふつう）‖ **当店では英語を自由に話せる女性を探しています** We are looking for a woman *with a good command of* (spoken) English. ‖ **何でも自由になると思ったら大間違いだ** If you think you *can* always *have your way*, you are very much mistaken. ‖

大学へ行くも行かぬもきみの自由だ(＝きみ次第だ) It's *up to you* whether (or not) you go to college. ‖ 1号車から6号車までは**自由席車両**です Cars numbered one to six are *non-reserved*. ‖ **対話**「このアルバム, 見ていいですか」「どうぞご自由に」"Can I have a look at this photo album?" "Sure, *go ahead*."

‖**自由意志** free will ‖**自由業** a freelance(r) ⇀**フリー** ‖**自由競争** free [open] competition ‖**自由作文** a free composition, an essay ‖**自由詩** free verse ‖**自由時間** free time ‖**自由主義** liberalism ‖**自由主義国** a free nation ‖**自由席** a nonreserved seat ‖**自由の女神像** the Statue of Liberty ‖**自由貿易** free trade.

☛ **自由化** (⇀見出語)

1**じゅう 十** **ten**; **the tenth** (10番目) ▶**10**まで数える count up to *ten*.

☛ **十代, 十人十色, 十年** (⇀見出語)

2**じゅう 銃** a **gun**; **firearms** (➤総称) ▶**銃を構える** have one's *gun* at the ready ‖ **野鳥を銃で撃つ** shoot a wild bird (with *a gun*) ‖ 例外を除いて, 日本では**銃**の所持は禁じられている With a few exceptions, *gun* possession by citizens is prohibited in Japan. ‖ 銀行員は**銃で脅されて**強盗に1000万円を渡した The teller handed over 10 million yen to the robber *at gunpoint*.

‖**銃規制** gun control.

3**じゅう 柔** ▶**柔よく剛を制す** Softness can gain the upper hand over hardness. (➤日本語からの直訳) ／A gentle approach is (often) more effective than a forceful one.

じゅー ▶焼き肉が**ジューと**おいしそうな音を立てて焼けてきた The meat *sizzled* deliciously as it cooked. (➤ sizzle は「ジュージューいう」).

1**-じゅう -中** **1【時間】** ▶きのうは**一日中**ロックを聴いていた I listened to rock music *all day long* yesterday. ‖ 彼らは**一晩中**マージャンをした They played mah-jongg *all night* [(*all*) *through the night*]. ‖ この頃はスーパーへ行けばどんな野菜でも**一年中**手に入る Nowadays, you can buy any vegetable you like *all year round* [*throughout the year*] at the supermarket. ‖ 最後列の学生たちは講義の**間中**居眠りしていた The students in the last row slept *through* the lecture. ‖ この校舎はことし**中**に完成する予定だ This school building will be completed *before the end of this year* [*within the year*]. ‖ **夏中**ニュージーランドに行っていた I went to New Zealand *for the summer*.

2【場所】 ▶**世界中**を旅する travel *all over the world* ‖ **世界中から**環境運動家たちが東京に集まった Environmentalists *from around the world* gathered in Tokyo.

▶その高校生は**顔中**ににきびがある That high school student has pimples *all over his face*. ‖ **体中**が痛むんだ My *whole body* aches. ／I ache *all over*.

▶彼女が暴走族に入っていることは**近所中**に知れ渡っている Everyone *in the neighborhood* knows that she belongs to a motorcycle gang. ‖ 美奈は**学校中**でいちばん足が速い Mina is the fastest runner *in our school*.

2**-じゅう -重** **-fold** ▶**二重**[**三重**]の結び目 a *double* [*triple*] knot ‖ 紙を**何重**にも折る fold a piece of paper *many times over* ‖ 母はその木箱を**二重**[**三重**]に包んだ My mother put *two* [*three*] *layers* of wrapping on that wooden box. ‖ このケーキはホイップクリームが**三重**になっている This cake has *three layers* of whipped cream.

しゅうあく 醜悪 **一**㊊ **醜悪な** **ugly** (醜い); **hideous** /hídiəs/ (ぞっとするほど醜い); **sordid** (あさましい); **despicable** (卑劣な) ▶**醜悪な**顔をした怪物 an *ugly* monster ‖ **醜悪な**デザイン a *hideous* design ‖ **醜悪な**権力闘争 an *ugly* [a *sordid*] power struggle ‖ **醜悪な**行為 a *despicable* act.

しゅうあけ 週明け **the beginning of a new week** ▶**週明け**はどうも学校に行きたくない I somehow don't feel like going to school *on Mondays* [*at the beginning of the week*].

じゅうあつ 重圧 **(heavy) pressure** ▶**重圧**に耐える bear *heavy pressure* ‖ 太郎にとって恩師のそのことばは大きな**精神的重圧**だった For Taro, the remarks his teacher made proved to be a great *psychological burden*.

しゅうい 周囲 **1【周り】** **circumference** /sərkʌ́mfrəns/ (円の); a **perimeter** /pərímət̬əʳ/ (四角形の) ▶その古木は幹の**周囲**が4メートルある The ancient tree trunk measures 4 meters *in circumference*. ‖ その池の**周囲**はどのくらいありますか What is the *circumference* of that pond? ／How much does that pond measure *around*?

▶アメリカの住宅は**周囲**にほとんど塀を巡らしていない You will see few walls *around* houses in the United States. ‖ 本校の2階建ての赤れんがの校舎は**周囲**の緑と美しい対照を成している Our school's two-storied red brick buildings make a beautiful contrast with the *surrounding* greenery. ‖ 日本は**周囲を**海に囲まれている Japan *is surrounded by* (the) sea [*by* water].

2【人を取り巻く環境】 (an) **environment** (人に直接影響を与えるような); **surroundings** (地理的・場所的な) ▶**周囲**に溶け込む blend in with one's *surroundings* ‖ 人は**周囲の**影響を受けるものだ People tend to be influenced by their *environment*. ‖ 彼は**周囲の**人々に好かれている He is loved by those *around* [*close to*] him. ‖ **周囲の**目をあまり気にするな Don't worry about what others *around you* think (about you).

じゅうい 獣医 a **vet**

‖**獣医学** veterinary science [medicine].

じゅういし 獣医師 《米》a **veterinarian** /vèt̬ərənéəriən/, 《英》a **veterinary surgeon** (➤「獣医」の正式名称).

じゅういち 十一 **eleven**; **the eleventh** (11番目).

じゅういちがつ 十一月 **November** 《略 Nov.》

▶山本氏は**11月**3日に文化勲章を受章した Mr. Yamamoto received the Order of Culture on *November 3*.

しゅうえき 収益 **proceeds** /próʊsi:dz/ (売上高から経費などを引いた額); a **profit** (利益) ▶**収益の上がる**仕事 *profitable* business ‖ このコンサートの**収益**はアフリカの飢きん救済に使われます All *proceeds* of this concert go to assist famine relief in Africa.

1**しゅうえん 終演** ▶**終演**は午後9時です *The curtain falls* at 9 p.m.

2**しゅうえん 終焉** **death** ▶人生の**終えん** the *end* of life ‖ ソビエト連邦の**終えん** the *end* [*demise*] of the Soviet Union (➤ demise /dɪmáɪz/ は堅い語).

じゅうおう 縦横 ▶イギリスでは鉄道が国中を**縦横に走っている** In Britain, railways *crisscross* the country. ／Britain has *a nationwide network* of railways. ‖ 猿飛佐助は画面いっぱい**縦横無尽に暴れ回った** On the movie screen, Sarutobi Sasuke *ran around* *in all directions.*

じゅうおく 十億 a **billion** →億.

じゆうか 自由化 liberalization 一動 自由化する liberalize +目 ▶貿易の**自由化** *liberalization* of trade (➤「貿易を自由化する」は liberalize trade) ‖ 政府は木材市場を**自由化する**ことを検討した The government considered the possibility of *liberalizing* [*opening up*] the lumber market.

し

しゅうか 集荷 package [**parcel**] **collection**(荷物の) ; **collection of produce**(農産物の).

しゅうかい 集会 a **gathering** ; a **meeting**, an **assembly** (会合) →会議 ▶政治的**集会** a political *assembly* ‖ きょうの午後講堂で**臨時集会**が開かれた There was *a special gathering* [*meeting*] held in the hall this afternoon. ‖ その**抗議集会**には全国から人々が集まった People from all over the country gathered at the *protest rally*. (➤ rally は「政治的示威を目的とする大集会」).

‖**集会所** a meeting place, an assembly hall.

1 **しゅうかく 収穫 1【取り入れ】** a **crop**, (a) **harvest** (➤ 前者は作物そのものを指すことが多いのに対して, 後者は作物を取り入れる行為や時期に重点がある) **一動 収穫する harvest** +目 ▶ことしはリンゴの**収穫**が少なかった[多かった] The apple *crop* was small [large] this year. ‖ 当地ではことしかなりのダイズの**収穫**が見込まれている This year a good *crop* [a rich *harvest*] of soybeans is anticipated in this area. ‖ 日本では農作物の**収穫期**は秋だが, 北欧では夏だ The *harvest season* is autumn in Japan, but summer in Northern Europe.

‖**収穫高** a crop.

2【成果】▶カンボジア旅行では大きな**収穫**があった I *gained* [*got*] a lot from my trip to Cambodia. ‖ あなたがアメリカ留学で大きな**収穫を得られる**ことを祈ります I hope your study in the United States will be very *beneficial* to you. (➤ beneficial は「有益な」) / I hope you will greatly *benefit* from your study in the U.S.

2 **しゅうかく 臭覚** →嗅覚.

しゅうがく 就学する enter school ▶**就学(年齢)前**の子供 a child *below school age*, a preschooler.

‖**就学児童** a child of school age, a school-age child.

しゅうがくりょこう 修学旅行 a **school trip**, an **educational trip** 《参考》(1)school excursion という言い方は一般的ではない. (2)英米には日本のような学年全体でする「修学旅行」はないが, 教科ごとに特定の施設や場所を訪ねて学習する field trip(見学旅行) はある ▶**修学旅行**では沖縄へ行きました We went to Okinawa on *a school trip*.

1 **しゅうかつ 就活 job hunting, job seeking** ▶**就活**に出かける[をする] go [do] *job hunting*.

2 **しゅうかつ 終活 end of life planning** ▶近年, 多くの人が**終活**を始めている Many people have started to do *end of life planning* in recent years.

じゅうがつ 十月 October《略 Oct.》▶ **10月**の日光は紅葉が美しい In *October* Nikko is beautiful with autumn colors. ‖ **10月10日**は学校の運動会です Our school's field day [sports day] will be held on *October 10*.

1 **しゅうかん 習慣** a **custom** (社会のしきたり) ; a **habit** (個人の) ▶風俗や**習慣**は国によって異なる Each country has its own manners and *customs*. / Manners and *customs* differ from country to country. ‖ 悪い**習慣**はすぐつくが, よい**習慣**を身につけるには大変な努力がいる Good *habits* require great effort to develop, while bad *habits* are very easy to acquire. ‖ **習慣で** 6 時に目が覚める I wake up at 6 o'clock *from force of habit*. (➤「習慣の力で」の意) ‖ 外出から帰ると必ずうがいをするのが**習慣になっている** I *am in the habit of* gargling whenever I come home from somewhere. ‖ 知らないことばにぶつかったら必ず辞書で調べる**習慣をつけ**なさい If you come across a word you don't know, *make it a habit* to look it up in the dictionary.

✉ **日本には人に会って挨拶するときにおじぎをする習慣があります** In Japan, *it is customary* for people to bow to each other and exchange greetings when they meet.

2 **しゅうかん 週間** a **week** ▶軽井沢に**1週間**行ってきた We have been in Karuizawa *for a week*. (➤ for one week は厳密に「7日間」, for a week はややあいまいに「6日から8日, 9日」くらいを指すので,「1週間ほど」に相当する. 日常的には for a week ということが多い) ‖ きみの学校では**1週間**に何時間英語を勉強していますか How many periods do you study English (*in*) *a week* at your school? ‖ 注文した本は**3週間後**に手元に届いた *Three weeks later* I received the book I had ordered.

▶あすから**読書週間**が始まる *Book Week* starts tomorrow.

‖**交通安全週間** Traffic Safety Week.

3 **しゅうかん 週刊の weekly** ▶その雑誌は**週刊**ですか月刊ですか? Is that magazine published *weekly* or monthly? ‖**週刊誌** a weekly (magazine).

1 **しゅうき 臭気** a **bad** [**an offensive**] **smell** ; an **odor** /óʊdəʳ/ (特に薬品などの悪臭) ▶この薬には独特の**臭気**がある This medicine has a peculiar *smell* [*odor*]. ‖ 腐った魚がひどい**臭気**を放っている The rotten fish is giving off *a disgusting* [*foul*] *smell*. / The rotten fish stinks. (➤ stink は「ひどい悪臭を放つ」の意の動詞).

2 **しゅうき 周期** a **cycle** ; a **period** /píəriəd/ (周期の長さ, 区切り) ▶元素の**周期** the *period* of an element ‖ 地球は約1年の**周期**で太陽の周りを回る The earth goes around the sun in an approximately one-year *cycle*. ‖ 台風は**周期的に**日本を襲う Typhoons hit [strike] Japan *periodically*.

‖**周期律** the periodic law.

-しゅうき -周忌 ▶祖父の**三周忌**にはみんなで集まる予定です We plan to get together to observe *the second anniversary of* our grandfather's *death*. →-回忌.

しゅうぎ 祝儀 1【祝い事】 a **ceremony**, a **celebration**.

2【心付け】 a **tip**, a **gratuity** /grətjúːəṭi/ (➤ 後者は堅い語) ▶大工さんたちにちょっと**ご祝儀**をあげてください Would you give *a tip* to the carpenters? / Would you tip the carpenters?

‖**祝儀袋** a gift(-giving) envelope.

じゅうき 銃器 small arms(小火器).

しゅうぎいん 衆議院 the House of Representatives ‖**衆議院議員** a member of the House of Representatives ‖ **衆議院議長** the Speaker of the House of Representatives.

しゅうきゃく 集客する attract [**pull in**] **customers** ▶**集客力** *customer drawing* power.

1 **しゅうきゅう 週休** a **day off** (**in a week**) ▶あなたの会社は**週休**が何日ありますか How many *days off* do you have *a week* in your company? ‖ うちの会社

は週休2日制です We have *a five-day (work) week* in this company.

2 **しゅうきゅう 週給** **weekly pay**; a **weekly salary** [**wage(s)**] (工員・店員などの) ▶今度の仕事は**週給**5万円です The *weekly salary* [*wage (s)*] at my new job are 50,000 yen.

じゅうきょ 住居 a **residence** (敷地が広く堂々とした); a **dwelling** (居住用建物; 主に文語) ▶金沢に**住居**を定める take up one's *residence* in Kanazawa ‖ 息子は結婚して横浜に**住居を定めた** Our son got married and *settled down* [*made his home*] in Yokohama. ‖ 弥生時代の**住居跡**が発見された *Remains of dwellings* from the Yayoi period were discovered.

しゅうきょう 宗教 (a) **religion** (➤ 個々の宗教は a religion); a **faith** (信仰) 一形 **宗教の religious** ▶日本人は概して**宗教**に無関心だ Generally, the Japanese are indifferent to *religion*. ‖ もともと祭りはほとんどが**宗教的な**儀式だった Most festivals were originally *religious* ceremonies. ‖ プロテスタントは16世紀の**宗教改革**に端を発する Protestantism began with *the Reformation* in the sixteenth century. ‖ 彼は**宗教上の理由**から牛肉は食べない He doesn't eat beef for *religious reasons*. ‖ 彼はある**新興宗教**に凝っている He's into one of those *new religions*.

‖**宗教音楽** religious [sacred] music ‖ **宗教家** a person of religion ‖ **宗教指導者** a religious leader ‖ **宗教団体** a religious organization [group].

あなたの英語はどう響く?
日本人は宗教心の希薄さから, 軽い気持ちで I have no religion. (無宗教です) と言うが, キリスト教など一神教を深く信じる人々にとって I have no religion. は I am an atheist. (無神論者です) と言うことに等しく, 積極的に神を否定することを意味する. I'm not very religious. または I don't have any strong religious beliefs. のような言い方が無難. 多くの日本人は宗教的行事や儀式は重んじながら, 信仰心は希薄であるが, キリスト教徒などにとっては信仰が第一である.

「宗教」のいろいろ **イスラム教** Islam / **カトリック教** Catholicism / **キリスト教** Christianity / **新教** Protestantism / **神道** Shinto / **チベット仏教** Tibetan Buddhism / **道教** Taoism / **ヒンズー教** Hinduism / **仏教** Buddhism / **ユダヤ教** Judaism

☞ **無宗教** (→見出語)

1 **しゅうぎょう 就業** ▶**就業中**は無駄話をしてはいけないことになっています No unnecessary chit-chat is allowed *during working hours*. / We are not allowed to gossip *at work*.

‖**就業規則** a work rule, an office regulation.

2 **しゅうぎょう 修業** ▶本校の**修業年限**は3年である Our school requires three *years of study*.

3 **しゅうぎょう 終業する** **close** /klouz/ ▶**終業のベル** the *closing* bell ‖ **終業式**は3月23日だ *School will let out* [*break up*] on March 23. (➤ 前者は主に《米》用法, 後者は主に《英》用法).

‖**終業式** a closing ceremony (held on the last day of the school term) (➤ 英米では終業式は行わない).

じゅうぎょういん 従業員 an **employee** /ɪmplɔ́ɪiː/; a **worker** (労働者); an **attendant** (ガソリンスタンド・駐車場などの) ▶私はこの工場の**従業員**です I *work* in this factory.

‖**従業員組合** an employees' union.

1 **しゅうきょく 終局** a **close** /klouz/ (計画的な終わり); an **end** (自然な終わり) ▶戦争は**終局**を迎えようとしていた The war was nearing [coming to] *an end*.

2 **しゅうきょく 終曲** a **finale** /fɪnǽli/ ▶交響曲の**終曲** the *finale* of a symphony.

しゅうきん 集金する **collect bills** [**money**] ▶新聞配達の人は月1回**集金**に来る The newspaper carrier comes to *collect* once a month. (● この collect は「集金する」の意の自動詞; collect bills とする必要はない).

じゅうきんぞく 重金属 a **heavy metal.**

じゅうく 十九 **nineteen**; **the nineteenth** (19番目) ▶彼女は19で未婚の母になった She became an unwed mother *at the age of 19*.

ジュークボックス a **jukebox** ▶**ジュークボックスをかける** play *a jukebox*.

シュークリーム a **cream puff**

危ないカタカナ語 ✱ **シュークリーム**
フランス語の *chou à la crème* (クリーム入りのキャベツ) に由来するが, 英語では cream puff という. 「シュークリーム」を英語だと思ってそのまま発音すると shoe cream (靴墨) と受け取られるおそれがあるので注意.

じゅうぐん 従軍する **go to the front** (前線に行く)

‖**従軍慰安婦** a comfort woman ‖ **従軍記者** a war correspondent.

しゅうけい 集計する **add up** (合計する) ▶投票を**集計する** *add up* the (total of) votes ‖ この数字を**集計してくれますか** Will you *add up* these figures?

じゅうけい 重刑 (a) **severe punishment**, a **stiff penalty.**

じゅうけいしょう 重軽傷 ▶その衝突で約200名の乗客が**重軽傷を負った** About 200 passengers *were seriously or slightly injured* in the collision.

しゅうげき 襲撃 an **attack**, an **assault** (➤ 後者が日本語により近く, 特に激しさを強調する); a **raid** (急襲) 一動 **襲撃する attack** +目, **assault** +目 ▶敵は我々を背後から**襲撃した** The enemy *attacked* us from the rear.

じゅうげき 銃撃 **shooting** ▶3人組のギャングが血みどろの**銃撃戦**で死んだ The gang of three (men) were killed in a bloody *shoot-out*.

1 **しゅうけつ 終結** an **end** (自然な終わり); a **close** /klouz/ (計画的な終わり) ▶この戦争はまさに**終結しようとしている** This war is about to *end*. ‖ 労働争議が**終結した** The labor dispute *drew* [*came*] *to a close*.

2 **しゅうけつ 集結する** **concentrate** /kɑ́ːnsəntreɪt/ ▶ゲリラはこの辺りの山岳地帯に**集結している** The guerrillas *are concentrated* in the mountains around here.

じゅうけつ 充血 **congestion** /kəndʒéstʃən/ (主に脳・内臓の) ▶目が**充血しているよ** Your eyes *are bloodshot*. ‖**脳充血** congestion of the brain.

じゅうご 十五 **fifteen**; **the fifteenth** (15番目) ▶9時15分前に駅に来てください Will you come to the station *at a quarter to* [《米また》 *of*] nine?

1 **しゅうこう 就航** ▶その豪華船は来週**就航する** The luxury liner will *set forth on her maiden voyage* next week.

2 **しゅうこう 周航する** **sail around, circumnavigate** +目.

3しゅうこう 集光する gather [condense] (rays of) light.

しゅうごう 集合 1【集まること】(a) gathering ; (a) meeting(時間・場所を決めての) 一動 集合する gather, meet ▶キャプテンが「全員集合！」と叫んだ The captain cried, "*Gather around !*" ‖《校内放送で》クラス委員は生徒会室に集合してください Class representatives, please *meet* in the council room. ‖部員は全員集合しました All the members *are here* now.

▶集合時間：7時, 集合場所：正門前. 時間厳守のこと *Meeting time* : 7 : 00, *Meeting place* : In front of the main gate. Be on time.

2【数学の】a set

‖集合論 set theory, the theory of sets.

1じゅうこう 重厚 ▶重厚な家具 a *solid-looking* piece of furniture ‖重厚な人物 a person *of depth* ‖読み応えのある重厚な作品 a *serious* work (well) worth reading.

2じゅうこう 銃口 the muzzle of a gun ▶市民に銃口を向ける aim [point] a *gun* at civilians.

じゅうこうぎょう 重工業 heavy industries.

じゅうごや 十五夜 a full moon night ; the harvest moon(中秋の名月).

じゅうこん 重婚 bigamy /bígəmi/.

ジューサー a juicer, a juice extractor.

しゅうさい 秀才 a brilliant person, a bright student (➤後者は学生の場合) ▶前田君は学校一の秀才だ Maeda is *the brightest student* in our school.

じゅうざい 重罪 a serious offense, a felony (➤後者は法律用語) ▶重罪を犯す commit *a serious offense* ‖中国では麻薬の密輸は重罪である Drug smuggling is *a serious offense* in China.

‖重罪犯 a felon.

しゅうさく 習作 a study ; an etude /eɪtjúːd/ (芸術での).

じゅうさつ 銃殺 an execution by shooting(銃殺刑) ▶スパイは銃殺された The spy *was executed by firing squad*.

しゅうさん 集散 collect and distribute ▶集散地 a *distributing* [*trading*] *center* ‖木材の集散地 a lumber *trading center*.

じゅうさん 十三 thirteen ; the thirteenth(13番目) ▶キリスト教徒は13という数字をキリストとその12人の使徒がとった最後の晩さんに結び付ける Christians associate *the number 13* with the Last Supper which was attended by 13 people—Christ and his 12 apostles. (➤「13日の金曜日」は Friday the thirteenth という).

1しゅうし 収支 income and outgo, earnings and expenses ; revenue and expenditure(歳入と歳出) ▶今月の収支はとんとんだ We have just *managed to make ends meet* this month. (➤make ends meet は「やりくりする」の意のインフォーマルな言い方).

2しゅうし 終始 ▶彼女はその会議の間終始口を閉ざしていた She remained silent *from the beginning to the end* of the meeting [during the *entire* meeting]. ‖会議は非難の応酬に終始した They exchanged sharp words *throughout* [*all through*] the meeting. ‖きみの主張は終始一貫していない Your argument *lacks consistency*.

3しゅうし 修士 a master's degree 《参考》理科系の修士は Master of Science (略称 M.S.), 文科系の修士は Master of Arts (略称 M.A.) という ▶彼は東北大学で心理学の修士(号)を取った[取得した] He got [received] *a master's degree* in psychology at [from] Tohoku University.

‖修士課程 a master's program (➤「博士前期課程」の訳語としても使える) ‖修士論文 a master's thesis.

しゅうじ 習字 calligraphy /kəlígrəfi/ ; penmanship (主にペン習字, その書法) ▶習字を習う take *calligraphy* lessons ‖父は習字がうまい My father *is a good calligrapher*. ‖私は中学時代, 英習字の練習をした I practiced *English penmanship* when I was in junior high school.

1じゅうし 重視する attach importance 《to》(重きを置く) ; value +㊐ (大事に思う) ; lay stress 《on》(強調する) ▶彼は今度の仕事を非常に重視している He *attaches great importance to* his new job. ／He *takes* his new job *very seriously*. (➤前者は「大事な仕事と考えている」, 後者は「真剣に受け止めている, 本気で当たっている」で, 実際に本気で打ち込んでいることをいう) ‖あの学校では人格形成を重視している That school *lays* [*puts*] *much stress on* character building. ／That school *attaches great importance to* character building. ‖私たちはお客様のご意見を重視しています We *value* our customers' opinions.

2じゅうし 十四 fourteen ; the fourteenth(14番目).

じゅうじ 従事する be engaged 《in》; devote oneself 《to》(専念する) ▶広瀬博士はＨＩＶ/エイズの研究に従事している Doctor Hirose *is engaged in* research on HIV/AIDS. ‖将来私はボランティア活動に従事するつもりだ In the future I'm going to *devote myself to* volunteer activities.

じゅうじか 十字架 a cross ; a crucifix(十字架上のキリスト像) ▶愛子はいつも十字架のペンダントを下げている Aiko always wears *a cross pendant*.

じゅうじぐん 十字軍 a Crusade /kruːséɪd/.

じゆうじざい 自由自在 ▶彼はエクセルを自由自在に使いこなす He uses Excel *with ease* (*and confidence*).

じゅうしち 十七 seventeen ; the seventeenth (17番目).

しゅうじつ 終日 all day long(一日中) ; from morning till night (朝から晩まで) ▶この前の日曜は終日ネットサーフィンをして過ごした Last Sunday, I surfed the Internet *all day* (*long*). ／Last Sunday, I spent *the whole day* surfing the Internet. ‖父は終日畑で働いている My father works on the farm *from morning till night*.

じゅうじつ 充実 ▶充実した食事 a *substantial* meal (➤「量の多い」の意) ; a *good satisfying* meal ‖充実した人生を送る lead a *fulfilling* life ‖充実した時を過ごす spend [use] one's time *well*(➤「自分の時間を上手に使う」の意) ‖人生を充実させる *enrich* one's life ／ *make* one's life more *fulfilling* ／ *enhance* (*the quality of*) one's life.

▶父は気力が充実している My father is *full of vigor*. ‖この案内書は内容が充実している This guidebook *is rich in content* [*is very informative*]. ‖そのチームの投手陣は充実している The team *has a powerful lineup* of pitchers. ‖わが社は今春新卒を20名募集してスタッフの充実を図ることにした Our company has decided to hire 20 new college graduates this spring to *strengthen* the staff.

‖充実感 a sense of fulfillment.

しゅうしふ 終止符 《米》a period, 《英》a full stop ▶《慣用表現》彼は35歳で独身生活に終止符を打った He *put a period to* his single life at the age of 35.

じゅうしまつ 十姉妹《鳥》《米》 a **society finch,** 《英》 a **Bengalese (finch).**

じゅうしゃ 従者 a **follower**; a **squire**(騎士の).

1**しゅうしゅう 収集** (a) **collection**(➤「収集品」の意味では a をつける) **一動 収集する gather** +目 (何でもかんでもかき集める); **collect** +目 (注意深く選んで集める; 気に入ったものを集める)

▶情報を収集する *gather* information ‖ ぼくは鉄道切符の収集に興味をもっています I'm interested in *collecting* railway tickets. ‖ 祖父は浮世絵をたくさん収集していた My grandfather used to *have a large collection* of ukiyoe.

‖収集家 a collector ‖ 収集癖 a collecting mania /méɪniə/.

2**しゅうしゅう 収拾する settle** +目 ▶調停委員会が事態収拾に乗り出した The mediation committee began trying to *settle* things. ‖ 討論は収拾がつかなくなった The discussion *got out of hand*. ‖ 国会は紛糾して収拾がつかない状態になった The Diet is in total chaos and *has become uncontrollable*.

しゅーしゅー ▶シューシューという音 a *hissing* sound (➤ hiss は「(蒸気などが)シューという音を立てる」).

じゅうじゅう 重々 ▶ご迷惑をおかけしましたこと重々おわび申し上げます I'm *extremely* sorry to have troubled you. ‖ そのことは重々承知しております I'm *very much* aware of that.

じゅーじゅー ▶ステーキはテーブルへ運ばれてきたときもジュージューいっていた The steak *sizzled* as it was brought to the table. (➤「ジュージューいっているステーキ」は sizzling steak).

しゅうしゅく 収縮 (a) **contraction 一動 収縮する contract**; **shrink** (縮む) ▶筋肉の収縮 a muscular *contraction* ‖ 寒さで血管が急に収縮すると脳出血を起こすことがある A sudden *contraction* of blood vessels due to cold can trigger a cerebral hemorrhage. ‖ 細胞は浸透圧が高くなると収縮する Cells *shrink* when osmotic pressure increases.

しゅうじゅく 習熟する become proficient 《in》 ▶ 3か国語に習熟する *become proficient in* three languages ‖ 彼はまだ車の運転に習熟していない He *is not* yet *skilled at* driving a car. ／He is still a learner driver.

‖習熟度 a degree of (academic) achievement; a skill level (技術の) 《参考》「習熟度別クラス編成」は class division based on the degree of academic achievement.

じゅうじゅつ 柔術 jujutsu, ju-jitsu.

じゅうじゅん 従順 obedience 一形 従順な obedient, docile ▶今どき従順なだけでは世の中を渡っていけないよ. 場合によっては意見をきちんと言わなきゃ These days, it isn't enough for you to be simply *obedient*. In some cases, you have to speak up [give your opinion].

じゅうしょ 住所 an **address** /ǽdres/ ▶住所と名前を書いてください Please write your name and *address*. (➤ 語順は日本語と逆になる) ‖ 住所が変わったら知らせてください Please let me know if you change your *address* [if you move]. (➤ 後者は「引っ越したら」) ‖ ご住所をおっしゃってください May I have your *address* (, please)? ‖ 彼の住所は知りません I don't know *where he lives*. (➤「どこに住んでいるのか」と考えた場合の例) ‖ すりの犯人は住所不定の男だった The pickpocket was *a man with no fixed address*. ‖ 郵便局に住所変更届を出した I reported my *change of address* to the post office.

‖住所録 an address book.

しゅうしょう 愁傷 ▶この度はご愁傷さまでございます I *would like to extend my deepest sympathy* (to you) in your bereavement. 《参考》極めて堅い言い方で, ふつうは I'm very sorry (about the loss of your son). のように言う. なお, bereavement は「死別」の意の堅い語.

✉ **ご尊父さまご逝去の由, 誠にご愁傷さまに存じます** *Please accept my sincere condolences* on your father's passing.

1**じゅうしょう 重傷** a **serious injury**(事故などによる); a **serious wound** /wuːnd/ (武器による) ▶彼は交通事故で重傷を負った He *was seriously injured* in the traffic accident. ‖ そのハイジャック事件で3名の乗客が重傷を負った Three passengers *were seriously wounded* in the hijacking.

2**じゅうしょう 重症の serious** ▶重症の患者 a *seriously ill* patient ‖ 救助された登山者は重症の凍傷にかかっていた The mountain climber who was rescued had *a severe case* of frostbite. ‖ 50名の患者の中には3名の重症者がいた There were three *serious cases* among the fifty patients.

▶《比喩的》えっ, 奥さんとけんかして1週間も口を利いてないんだって? こりゃ重症だ You haven't spoken to your wife for a week since you fought with her, eh? It must *be serious*.

1**しゅうしょく 就職 一動 就職する get a job [a position]** ▶彼に就職を世話する find [get] him *a job* [*a position*] ‖ きみはもう就職は決まったの? ぼくはまだ探してる最中なんだ *Have* you *found* [*gotten*] *a job* yet? I'm still busy job-hunting. ‖ 彼女は新聞社に就職した She *got a job* with a newspaper company. ‖ 私は商社に就職が決まっている I *have taken up a post* in a trading company. ‖ 彼はある大銀行に就職した He *got employed* in a well-known bank. ‖ 妹は旅行会社に就職している My sister *is working for* a travel agency. ‖ 大卒者は相変わらず就職難だ As usual, *it's hard* for college graduates *to find employment*.

✉ **ご就職おめでとうございます. 私は就職活動を始めたところです** Congratulations on your new job! I have just started job hunting [looking for a job].

‖(大学の)就職(斡旋(あっせん))課 a career placement office ‖ 就職口 a job ‖ 就職試験 an employment test ‖ (会社が行う)就職説明会 a job fair [festival] ‖ (大学の)就職部長 a dean of career development.

☛ **再就職, 就活** (→見出語)

2**しゅうしょく 修飾 ornamentation**(飾ること); a **flourish**(不必要な飾りことば); **modification** (文法の) **一動 修飾する modify** +目 ▶この文章は余計な修飾が多すぎる This piece of writing has too many unnecessary *flourishes*. ‖修飾語 a modifier.

じゅうしょく 住職 the chief priest of a Buddhist temple.

じゅうじろ 十字路 a **crossroads** ▶田舎の道をしばらく歩くと十字路に出た After walking a short distance along the country road, I came to *a crossroads*.

1**しゅうしん 終身** ▶被告は終身刑を言い渡された The accused was sentenced to *life imprisonment* [*imprisonment for life*]. ‖ 父はそのクラブの終身会員

です My father is *a life member* of the club. ‖ 日本の終身雇用制は崩れ始めた The *lifetime employment system* in Japan has begun to collapse.

2**しゅうしん 執心** ▶きみはあの娘にずいぶんご執心のようだね You seem to *be* very much *taken with* [You seem to *be crazy about*] that girl.

3**しゅうしん 就寝する** **retire**(➤ 堅い語；ふつうは go to bed という) ▶彼はふだん11時には**就寝する** He generally *retires* [*goes to bed*] at 11：00.
‖**就寝時間** time to retire (for the night).

1**しゅうじん 囚人** a **prisoner** /prízənə^r/ (拘置・収監された者)；a **convict** /kənvíkt/ (既決囚)；an **inmate** (入所者) ▶囚人を釈放する release *a prisoner*
‖**囚人服** a prison uniform.

2**しゅうじん 衆人** ▶衆人環視の中で男が刺殺された A man was stabbed to death *in full* (*public*) *view* [*with a crowd watching*].

1**じゅうしん 重心** **the center of gravity**；(a) **balance**(釣り合い) ▶重心を失う lose one's *balance* ‖ 丸太の上で重心を取る *balance oneself* [*poise oneself*] on a log ‖ このこけしは重心が高いので倒れやすい This kokeshi doll topples over easily because of its high *center of gravity*.

2**じゅうしん 銃身** a **barrel (of a gun)**.

1**ジュース** 《飲み物》**juice**；**drinks** (➤ 総称) ▶朝食はトーストとオレンジジュースで済ませた I had toast and *orange juice* for breakfast.

> **危ないカタカナ語✸ ジュース**
> **1** 日本語の「ジュース」と違い，英語の juice /dʒuːs/ は果汁100パーセントのものをいう．したがって炭酸の入ったものや果汁分の少ないものは soft drink とか pop という必要がある．
> **2** テニスやバレーボールなどの球技の「ジュース」は deuce /djuːs/ とつづる別語．フランス語の *deux*(「２」の意)が語源．

2**ジュース** 《球技の》**deuce** /djuːs/ ▶最初のゲームから両選手はジュースになった The two players *went to deuce* from the very first game.

1**しゅうせい 修正する** **correct** +目 (誤りを正す)；**amend** +目 (法律の語句などを)；**revise** +目 (改訂する)；**alter** +目，**modify** +目 (一部を手直しする)
▶スペルの間違いを修正する *correct* a spelling mistake ‖ 計画を修正する *alter* [*modify*] a plan (➤ modify には「改良」の含みがある) ‖ 議案を修正する *amend* a bill ‖ 予算案は衆議院本会議で修正され，可決された The budget passed the House of Representatives after it had *been revised* at the plenary session. ‖ 数字を修正した場合は訂正印を押しておいてください In case you *make any changes* in the figures, please put your *hanko* (seal) there to show that a correction has been made. (➤ この in case は「もし…ならば」の意で主に《米》) ‖ ロケットはコンピュータによって自動的に軌道を修正される The rocket can automatically *correct* its course with its computer.
‖**修正案** an amendment ‖ **修正液** correction [correcting] fluid, 《インフォーマル》whiteout (➤「間違いを直すのに修正液を使う」なら use whiteout to correct errors) ‖ **修正予算** a revised budget.

2**しゅうせい 修整する** **retouch** +目 (写真の原板を) ▶写真を修整する *retouch* [*touch up*] a photograph.

3**しゅうせい 習性** a **habit** ▶ミツバチの習性を研究する study the *habits* of bees ‖ 日本人は海外旅行でも集団行動を好む習性がある The Japanese have *a habit* of acting as a group even when traveling abroad. ‖ 冬に南へ飛んでいくのは一部の鳥たちの習性だ It is *natural* for some birds to fly south in winter.

4**しゅうせい 終生** **all one's life** ▶終生の友 a *lifelong* friend ‖ このご恩は終生忘れません I will be grateful to you *all my life*. ／I will be [I am] *forever* grateful to you.

しゅうぜい 収税 **tax collection.**

じゅうせい 銃声 **the report of a gun.**

じゅうぜい 重税 a **heavy tax** ▶当時国民の多くは重税に苦しんでいた In those days many of the people *were groaning under* (*the burden of*) *heavy taxes*.

しゅうせき 集積 ▶天の川は非常に多数の微光星が集積したものである The Milky Way is *an accumulation* of millions of faint stars.
‖**集積回路** an IC, an integrated circuit, a chip ‖ **大規模集積回路** a large-scale integrated circuit (略 LSI).

じゅうせき 重責 a **heavy responsibility** ▶重責を担う bear [assume] *a heavy responsibility*.

1**しゅうせん 終戦** **the end of a war** ▶祖父は終戦を岡山で迎えた On the day World War Ⅱ *ended*, my grandfather was in Okayama. (➤「第二次世界大戦が終わったとき，祖父は岡山にいた」の意).

2**しゅうせん 周旋** →あっせん ‖**周旋屋** a real estate [house] broker (不動産・家の)；an employment agency (仕事の).

しゅうぜん 修繕する **repair** +目 (複雑なものを)；**mend** +目 (比較的簡単なものを) ▶この靴を修繕してもらいたいのですが I would like to *have* these shoes *repaired*. →**修理**.

1**じゅうそう 縦走** ▶１週間かけて南アルプスを縦走する予定です We plan to spend a week *walking along the ridges* of the Southern Japan Alps.

2**じゅうそう 重曹** **baking soda, sodium bicarbonate.**

しゅうそく 収束・終息 ▶早期に混乱を収束させる必要がある We need to *clear up* the confusion as soon as possible. ‖ インフルエンザの大流行がようやく終息した The flu epidemic *is* finally *over*.

しゅうぞく 習俗 **manners and customs.**

じゅうそく 充足 **satisfaction** ▶欲望を充足させる *satisfy* one's desire ‖ 多くの現代人は心の充足を求めている Many people today are seeking (*self-*)*fulfillment*.

じゅうぞく 従属する **be subordinate** /səbɔ́ː^{r}dənət/ 《to》 ▶その王国は事実上隣の大国に従属している The kingdom *is*, in fact, *subordinate to* its powerful neighboring state.
‖《文法》**従属節** a subordinate clause.

しゅうたい 醜態 ▶ゆうべは飲み過ぎて人前で醜態を演じてしまった Last night I drank too much and *disgraced myself* [*made a fool of myself*] in public.

1**じゅうたい 重体の** **critical** (危篤の)；**serious** (重い，深刻な) ▶５人の乗客が負傷して重体だ Five passengers were injured and are in *critical* [*serious*] *condition*.

2**じゅうたい 渋滞** **traffic congestion,** 《インフォーマル》a **traffic jam** ▶ぼくらの乗ったタクシーは交通渋滞に巻き込まれた Our taxi got caught in *a traffic jam* [*heavy traffic*]. ‖ 道路は３キロにわたって渋滞している The road *is backed up* (with traffic) for three kilometers.

[3]**じゅうたい 縦隊** a **file**(➤「横隊」は rank) ▶学童が1列縦隊で歩いている Schoolchildren are walking *in single file*.

[1]**じゅうだい 重大な** **important, significant**(重要な；後者は影響力が大きいことを強調する)；**serious**(深刻な)；**gross**(甚だしい) ▶**重大な**問題 an *important* [a *serious*] problem [issue] ‖ダイオキシン汚染は**重大な**問題だ Dioxin contamination is a *serious* problem. ‖その判決は同様の訴訟に**重大な**影響を与えた That ruling had a *significant* effect on similar lawsuits. ‖彼は**重大な**過失で首になった He was fired for *gross* negligence. ‖彼らは事の**重大さ**[**重大性**]に気づいてないようだ I don't think they are aware of the *seriousness* of the problem.

[2]**じゅうだい 十代** **the years of** one's **age from ten to nineteen** (10～19歳)；one's **teens** (13～19歳) 《参考》英語では13歳から19歳まで，すなわち年齢を表す数字に -teen がつく人たちを teenager と呼ぶ ▶彼女はまだ**十代**だ She is still *in her teens*. ‖会場は**十代の男女**でいっぱいだった The hall was crowded with *teenagers*. ⇀ティーンエージャー，ハイティーン，ローティーン．

しゅうたいせい 集大成 ▶この本は私の10年にわたる研究を**集大成した**ものです This book is *a compilation* of all of my research over the past ten years.

じゅうたく 住宅 a **house**, a **residence** (➤後者は堂々として優雅な家を連想させる)；**housing** /háozɪŋ/ (➤集合的) ▶木造の**住宅** a wooden *house*／a *house* built of wood ‖東京の**住宅事情**は極めて悪い The *housing situation* in Tokyo is very bad.／*Housing* in Tokyo is a terrible problem. ‖**住宅難**がますます深刻になってきた The *housing shortage* is becoming more and more serious. ‖私たちの学校は**住宅地**にある Our school stands in *a residential area* [*quarter*].

‖**住宅金融公庫** the Housing Loan Corporation ‖**住宅手当** a housing allowance ‖**住宅ローン** a house [housing] loan, a mortgage /mɔ́:ʳgɪdʒ/ ‖**住宅ローン借り換え** mortgage refinancing ‖**集合住宅** a housing complex.

しゅうだん 集団 a **group** ▶学生の**集団** *a group* [*a mass*] of students ‖**集団で**登校する go to school *in a group* ‖ツバメは秋になると**集団を作って**南へ渡る Swallows *form groups* and migrate southward in fall. ‖うちの息子はこの夏初めて**集団生活**を経験した Our son experienced *living together with others* [*communal living*] for the first time this summer.

‖**集団検診** a group medical examination ‖**集団食中毒** mass food poisoning ‖**集団心理** mass psychology.

じゅうたん 絨毯 a **carpet**(部屋全体に敷き詰める)；a **rug**(小型の) ▶ペルシャ**じゅうたん** a Persian *carpet* [*rug*] ‖居間に茶色の**じゅうたん**を敷いた We spread [put] a brown *carpet* on the floor of our living room.

[1]**じゅうだん 銃弾** a **bullet** /bólɪt/ ▶彼はゲリラの**銃弾**に倒れた He *was gunned down* by the guerrilla.

[2]**じゅうだん 縦断** ▶自転車で日本列島を**縦断する** *travel the length of* Japan on a bicycle ‖その台風は本州を**縦断した**(＝北上した) That typhoon *moved up along* the main island of Honshu.

[1]**しゅうち 周知** ▶彼がそのすい星を発見したことは**周知の事実**である It *is known to everybody* [It is *common knowledge*] that he (first) discovered the comet. ‖**周知のとおり**もはや日本は世界第2位の経済大国ではない *As is widely known* [*As is commonly known*], Japan is no longer the world's second largest economy.

[2]**しゅうち 衆知** ▶ごみ問題の対策が**衆知を集めて**検討された *Asking for practical ideas* [*suggestions*] *from many people*, they discussed what should be done to deal with the garbage problem.

しゅうちしん 羞恥心 a **sense of shame** ▶電車内で女子高校生に痴漢行為をするなんてあの男には**羞恥心**というものがないのか I wonder if he has any *sense of shame* at all to have groped a high school girl on the train. ‖その女優は**羞恥心**をかなぐり捨てて体当たりの演技をした The actress overcame her *shyness* and gave an all-stops-out performance.

しゅうちゃく 執着 an **obsession**；(an) **attachment** (愛着) 一動 **執着する** **have an attachment** 《to, for》 ▶生への**執着**を示す[失う] show [lose] *attachment* to life ‖私は社長の地位には全く**執着していない** I *have no* great *attachment to* my position as president. ‖彼女は金銭に**執着し過ぎる** She *is too obsessed with* money. (➤ be obsessed /əbsést/ with で「…に取りつかれる」)．

しゅうちゃくえき 終着駅 《米》a **terminal (station)**, 《英》a **terminus** ▶人生の**終着駅** *the end* of one's life. ⇀終点．

しゅうちゅう 集中 **concentration**

一動 **集中する** **concentrate** /kɑ́:nsəntreɪt/ 《on》 ▶精神を**集中して**勉強しなさい *Concentrate on* your studies. ‖インドネシアでは人口の約60パーセントがジャワ島に**集中している** In Indonesia, about 60 percent of the population *is concentrated* in Java. ‖私は何事にも**集中できない** I *can't focus on* anything. ‖ゆうべは外の騒音で英語の宿題に**集中できなかった** The noise from outside *kept* me *from concentrating on* my English homework. (➤ keep A from B は「A(人)にBさせないようにする」の意) ‖手品師の手の動きに**視線が集中した** *All eyes were drawn toward* the movement of the magician's hands.

▶昨夜**集中豪雨**があった We had *a local downpour* last night. ‖その大臣は失言をしてマスコミの**集中攻撃を浴びた** The minister *came under heavy fire* by the mass media for making an improper remark. ‖私は今**集中的に**太宰治の作品を読んでいる I've been *concentrating on* reading the works of Dazai Osamu. ‖彼は**集中力**がある He has good *concentration*. ‖彼は**集中力に欠ける** He *lacks concentration*.

‖**集中講座** an intensive course (➤「英語の」なら in English) ‖**集中治療室** an intensive care unit 《略 ICU》.

しゅうちょう 酋長 a **chief**.

じゅうちん 重鎮 a **heavyweight** ▶文壇の**重鎮** a *heavyweight* in literary circles.

しゅうてん 終点 《米》a **terminal (station)**, 《英》a **terminus** ▶お客さん，起きてください．**終点**ですよ Sir, wake up please. *We are at the terminal.* ‖高山本線の**終点**は富山だ The *end* of the Takayama Main Line is Toyama. ‖この電車の**終点**はどこですか How far does this train go? ‖《車内・駅構内の放送で》この電車は当駅が**終点**です This train service *terminates* at this station.

じゅうてん 重点 **stress**(強調) ▶私たちのクラブでは今体力づくりに**重点を置いている** Our club now *lays* [*puts*] *stress on* building up physical strength.（➤ 動詞 stress または emphasize を用いてもよい）‖ きみは今何を重点的に勉強していますか What are you studying most *intensively* now？／What (subject) are you *concentrating on* now？

じゅうでん 充電する **charge** +目, **recharge** +目
《参考》charge は厳密には製造工程で第 1 回目の充電をすることをいい, 利用者が購入後にする充電は recharge を使うべきであるが, 実際には両者の区別が曖昧な場合が多い ▶充電式のシェーバー a *rechargeable* shaver ‖ バッテリーを充電してくれますか Could you *charge* [*recharge*] this battery？
▶《比喩的》あの作家はこの半年間別荘に籠もって充電した That writer has spent the last half year shut up in his vacation home *recharging his batteries*.
‖充電式電池 a rechargeable battery.

しゅうでんしゃ 終電車 **the last train** ▶大阪行きの終電車はこの駅を10時に出ます *The last train* for Osaka leaves here at ten.

しゅうと 舅・姑 a **father-in-law**（しゅうと）; a **mother-in-law**（しゅうとめ）;《インフォーマル》**in-laws**（しゅうと, しゅうとめ）.

シュート 1【バスケット・サッカーなど】 a **shot** ━動 **シュートする** **shoot**;《バスケット》**make a basket**（ボールをバスケットに入れる）▶《サッカーで》森君がシュートを決めてわがチームが勝った Mori *scored a goal* and our team won.
2【野球】 a **screwball** /skrúːbɔːl/

> **危ないカタカナ語✹ シュート**
> **1** サッカーやバスケットボールの「シュート」は shot で, 「シュートする」という動詞が shoot.「ロングシュート」は long shot,「ジャンピングシュート」は jump shot という.
> **2** 野球の「シュートボール」は screwball で, shoot とはいわない.
> **3**「ウォーターシュート」,「ダストシュート」は water chute, dust chute で, この chute /ʃuːt/ は「下方へ落とす装置」の意.

じゅうど 重度の **severe, massive** ▶重度のやけど a *severe* burn ‖ 重度の障害者 a *severely* disabled person／the *severely* disabled（➤ 後者は集合的）‖ 重度の心臓発作 a *massive* heart attack.

しゅうとう 周到 ▶周到に練り上げた計画 a *carefully* worked-out plan.

じゅうとう 充当する **appropriate** +目（予算を）▶その金を道路建設に充当する *appropriate* the money for road construction.

じゅうどう 柔道 **judo**（➤ 英語化している）▶柔道をする practice [do] *judo* ‖ 5 段の柔道家 a 5th-grade *black belt in judo*（➤ black belt は「(柔道や空手の)有段者; 黒帯」）／a 5th-dan *judoka* [*judoist*].
‖柔道整復師 a judo therapist, a bonesetter（➤ 前者がふつう）.

しゅうどういん 修道院 a **monastery**（男の）; a **convent**, a **nunnery**（女の; 後者は文語的）.

じゅうとうほう 銃刀法 **the firearms and swords control law.**

[1]**しゅうとく 習得する** **learn** +目; **master** +目（熟達する）; **acquire** +目（覚えて身につける; 堅い語）▶外国語を習得する *learn* [*master*] a foreign language ‖ 運転技術を習得する *acquire* driving technique.

[2]**しゅうとく 修得する** ▶単位を修得する *earn* college credit(s).

[3]**しゅうとく 拾得** ▶拾得物を交番に届ける take *a find* to the police box.

しゅうとめ 姑 a **mother-in-law.** →しゅうと.

じゅうなん 柔軟な **flexible** /fléksəbəl/, **pliable** /pláɪəbəl/（曲げたりねじったりが容易な）; **supple**（しなやかな）▶柔軟な体 a *supple* body ‖ 柔軟な考え方 a *flexible* way of thinking ‖ 柔軟な態度 a *flexible* attitude ‖ このプラスチックは柔軟性に富む This plastic is very *pliable*. ‖ 柔軟体操をしましょう Let's do some *stretching* [*flexibility*] *exercises*.

じゅうに 十二 **twelve**; **the twelfth**（12番目）▶1 ダースは12個だ A dozen is a group of *twelve*.
‖十二宮 the signs of the zodiac ‖ 十二進法 the duodecimal system.

じゅうにがつ 十二月 **December**《略 Dec.》▶冬至は12月22日頃だ The winter solstice is around *December* 22.

じゅうにし 十二支 **the twelve signs** [**symbols**] **of the Chinese zodiac**《参考》十二支の「子, 丑, 寅, 卯, 辰, 巳, 午, 未, 申, 酉, 戌, 亥」はそれぞれ rat, ox, tiger, rabbit, dragon, snake [serpent], horse, sheep, monkey, rooster, dog, boar とする.「私は子年生まれだ」は I was born in the Year of the Rat. と言えばよい. なお, 中国では亥は boar の代わりに pig を用いる. →えと.

じゅうにしちょう 十二指腸 a **duodenum** /d*j*ùːədíːnəm/ ‖十二指腸潰瘍 a duodenal ulcer /ʌ́lsəʳ/.

じゅうにひとえ 十二単 a ***junihitoe***; a formal layered kimono for court ladies in the Heian period（➤ 説明的な訳）.

じゅうにぶん 十二分 ▶ 対話「(ごはんは)もうよろしいですか？」「ええ, 十二分に頂きました」"Have you had enough？" "Yes. I've had *more than enough*."

しゅうにゅう 収入 an **income**（所得）; **proceeds** /próʊsiːdz/（売上高, 収益）▶去年は収入が少なかった [多かった] I had a small [large] *income* last year. ‖ 彼女は年間500万円の収入がある She has an annual *income* of five million yen. ‖ 彼には月々決まった収入がない He doesn't have a regular monthly *income*. ‖ 収入の範囲内で生活しなさい You should live *within your income* [*means*]. ‖ バザーの収入は50万円でした The *proceeds* from the bazaar were half a million yen.
‖収入印紙 a revenue stamp ‖ 収入役 a treasurer ‖ 実収入 a net income ‖ 総収入 a gross income.

しゅうにん 就任する **assume** +目（職務を引き受ける）; **take office**《as》（役職・公職に）; **be inaugurated**《as》（高い地位の就任式を行って）▶小田氏がその大学の学長に就任した Mr. Oda *assumed the post* of president of the university. ‖ 彼は45歳でその会社の社長に就任した He *took office* as president of that company when he was forty-five. ‖ 吉村氏は大阪府知事に就任した Mr. Yoshimura *was inaugurated as* governor of Osaka Prefecture.
‖就任演説 an inaugural address ‖ 就任式 an inauguration.

じゅうにん 住人 a **resident** ▶このアパートの住人は学生が多い Most *residents* of this apartment house are students.

じゅうにんといろ 十人十色 ▶食べ物の好みは十人十色だ Food preferences *differ from person to person*.
ことわざ 十人十色 So many men, so many minds.

／To each his own.（➤一般的には Everyone has different interests and tastes. のような言い方がわかりやすい）.

じゅうにんなみ 十人並み ▶ぼくのガールフレンドは決して美人ではないが，まあ十人並みだ My girlfriend is no beauty, but she's *not bad looking*. ‖ 彼は高校では十人並みの学生だった He was an *average* student in his high school days.

しゅうねん 執念 tenacity（執ようさ）; persistence（粘り強さ）▶執念深い男 a very *tenacious* man ‖ 執念がなければ人生で大きなことは望めない You can't achieve much in life without *persistence* [*stick-to-itiveness*].（➤ stick to it は「最後まで頑張る」で，stick-to-itiveness /stɪktúːətɪvnəs/ は「粘り強さ」）‖ あの刑事は事件の犯人を執念深く追い回している That detective is pursuing the suspect *doggedly*. ‖ 彼は50年来民俗音楽の研究に執念を燃やしている He has been studying folk music *intently* for the past fifty years.

-しゅうねん -周年 anniversary ▶開店1周年記念大売り出し a big sale celebrating *the first anniversary* of the opening of a store ‖ きょうは本校［本校創立］の30周年記念日だ Today is *the 30th anniversary* of our school [of our school's foundation].

じゅうねん 十年 ten years, a decade /dékeɪd/（➤後者は10年を一区切りにした言い方）▶私はここに10年前に引っ越して来た I moved here *ten years* [*a decade*] *ago*. ‖ 木村氏は10年ぶりにアメリカから帰国した Mr. Kimura returned to Japan from the U.S. *for the first time in ten years*.

▶《慣用表現》部長が宴会で歌うのは十年一日のごとく『北国の春』ばかりだ Our manager sings only "Kitaguni-no-Haru" at parties *year in and year out*. ‖ 十年一昔だ Ten years can bring a lot of changes.（➤「10年は多くの変化をもたらしうる」の意）.

しゅうのう 収納する store ＋目 ▶家庭用品を収納庫に収納する［しておく］ *store* [*keep*] household goods in a closet ‖ 私たちの新しい家は収納スペースが多い［少ない］ We have a lot of [don't have enough] *storage space* in our new house.

[1]**しゅうは 宗派** a sect（分派）; a denomination（教派；sect より大きい）▶仏教はいくつもの宗派に分かれている In Buddhism there are many *sects*.

[2]**しゅうは 周波**《電気》a (wave) cycle, frequency ▶高［低］周波 high [low] *frequency*.

☛ 周波数（→見出語）

しゅうはい 集配 collection and delivery

▶この地区では郵便の集配は1日2回です In this area the mail *is collected and delivered* twice a day.

じゅうばこ 重箱 a *jubako*; a tier of lacquered boxes（➤説明的な訳）▶《慣用表現》重箱の隅をつつくようなまねはするな Don't *split hairs*. ／Stop *nit-picking*.（➤後者のほうがより軽蔑的）.

しゅうバス 終バス the last bus ▶終バスに間に合う［乗り遅れる］ catch [miss] *the last bus* ‖ 終バスはここを午後11時半に出る *The last bus* leaves here at 11:30 p.m.

しゅうはすう 周波数《物理学》a frequency.

じゅうはち 十八 eighteen; the eighteenth（18番目）▶18歳未満は入場お断り No one *under eighteen* is admitted.

‖**18金** 18-karat gold.

じゅうはちばん 十八番 one's specialty [party piece] ▶『風に吹かれて』は父の十八番だ "Blowin' in the Wind" is my father's *specialty*. →おはこ.

[1]**しゅうばん 週番** ▶今週の週番は誰ですか Who is *on duty this week*? ‖ 週番（の人）はいつもより30分早く登校のこと *Students-on-duty this week* are requested to be at school 30 minutes earlier than usual.

[2]**しゅうばん 終盤** the final [last] stage ▶大相撲春場所もいよいよ終盤にさしかかってきた The Spring Grand Sumo Tournament has already reached *the* [*its*] *final stage*.

じゅうびょう 重病 a serious illness ▶社長は重病らしい The president is rumored to *be seriously ill* [to *be very sick*].

‖**重病患者** a serious case.

しゅうふく 修復 restoration（復元）; renovation（建物を修理して一新する）; repair（道路などの）**一動 修復する** restore ＋目, renovate ＋目, repair ＋目 ▶壁画の修復をする *restore* a mural ‖ 両国間の関係の修復を図る try to *repair* [*mend* ／ *restore*] relations between the two countries ‖ その橋の修復には6か月かかった It took six months to *restore* the bridge. ‖ 鎌倉市と逗子市の間の道路が修復工事中だ The road between Kamakura and Zushi *is under repair*.

じゅうふく 重複 →ちょうふく.

[1]**しゅうぶん 秋分** the autumn (al) equinox /ékwɪnɑːks/ ‖**秋分の日** Autumn(al) Equinox Day.

[2]**しゅうぶん 醜聞** a scandal.

じゅうぶん 十分

1【必要量いっぱい】 enough; plenty（たっぷり）**一形 十分な** plenty of（たっぷりの）; enough, sufficient（必要なだけ十分な；後者は堅い語）; ample（必要以上に十分な）▶健康を保つには十分睡眠をとらなければならない To stay healthy, you must get *plenty of* [*enough*] sleep. ‖ これだけあれば十分だ This is *plenty*. ／This should be *enough*. ‖（それだけ言えば）もう十分だ. それ以上責めるのはやめなさい *That's enough*. Stop picking on him. ‖ そのアパートには十分な収納スペースがついている The apartment comes with *ample* storage space.

▶自分の力を十分発揮するように心がけなさい Try to *make the most of* what you have.（➤ make the most of は「…を最大限に活用する」）‖ 彼女の努力は十分に報われた Her efforts paid off *well* [*fully* ／ *completely*]. ‖ 私はできることは十分にやった I did *the best* I could [did *my utmost*]. ‖ 十分な議論もなされないまま決定が行われた A decision was made without *enough* discussion.

> **【文型】**
> …するのに十分な
> **enough to do**
> ➤ enough は前の形容詞にかかる副詞として，または名詞あるいは形容詞として用いる

▶きみはもう善悪の区別が十分できる年頃だ You are *old enough to* tell right from wrong. ‖ パリには多くの観光名所を回れるほど（十分に）長く滞在できなかった I wasn't able to stay in Paris *long enough to* see many sights. ‖ そのお年寄りはプールを何往復も泳げるほど（十分に）元気だ The elderly man is *fit enough to* swim many laps in the pool. ‖ 1人でやっていくには十分な給料をもらっています I'm earning quite *enough to* get along on my own. ‖ 政府は景気をよくするのに十分なことをやっているだろうか I wonder if the government is doing *enough to* improve the economy. ‖トイレに行く**時間は十分**ある There is *enough time to* go to the restroom. ‖ 2人でマンションを買うのに**十分なくらい稼ぎたい**と思っています We hope to *make enough money to* buy a condo. ‖ USBメモリーには動画をコピーするのに**十分なゆとりがなかった** There wasn't *enough room* in the USB memory *to* copy the video data.

2【余地がある】▶その証拠は彼を有罪とするのに**十分で**ある The evidence is *sufficient* to convict him. ‖ そこなら8時過ぎに家を出ても**十分**間に合う Even if I leave the house a little after eight, I can get there *in plenty of time*. ‖ 子供にはこんな高い自転車はもったいない. そっちの安いので**十分だ** It's a waste of money to buy such an expensive bicycle for a child. The cheaper one over there would *be good enough*.

あなたの英語はどう響く?
外国人から Would you care for some more roast beef? (ローストビーフをもう少しいかがですか)と聞かれた場合,「もう十分頂きました」のつもりで I've had enough. とだけ答えないこと. これでは「もううんざりです」の意味に解釈されてしまう. No, thank you. I've had (more than) enough. とか No, thank you, I'm full. のように答えるのが礼儀. 相手からの申し出を断るには, まず礼を述べ, 次に断りのことばや理由を言う.

☛ 不十分 (→見出語)

しゅうへん 周辺 ▶皇居周辺には朝早くからジョギングをする人たちが大勢いる We see a lot of joggers *around* the Imperial Palace early in the morning. ‖ **この周辺には**柿の木が多い There are lots of persimmon trees *in this neighborhood* [*around here*]. ‖ 犯人は世田谷・目黒区**周辺で**犯行を重ねた The criminal committed crimes *in the vicinity of* Setagaya and Meguro wards.
‖(コンピュータの)**周辺機器** peripherals.

シューマイ 焼売 a steamed Chinese pork dumpling 《参考》中国語音表記では shaomai となる.

1**しゅうまつ 週末** **a weekend** ▶**週末**[**先週末**]どちらで過ごされましたか Where did you spend *the weekend* [*last weekend*]? ‖ **週末は**電車が混みます The trains are jam-packed *on weekends*. ‖ 私たちは**週末に**スキーに行った We went skiing *over* [*for*] *the weekend*. (➤「週末の間ずっと」の意).

2**しゅうまつ 終末** ‖**終末期ケア** end-of-life care ‖ **終末論** eschatology /èskətάlədʒi/.

1**じゅうまん 十万** **a [one] hundred thousand** 《解説》英語には「万」に相当する単語はなく, 1万は「1000の10倍」と考え ten thousand という. したがって「10万」は a [one] hundred thousand となる →億 ▶この市の人口は約**20万**です The population of this city is about *two hundred thousand*. (➤ thousands としない).

2**じゅうまん 充満** ▶その部屋はたばこの煙が**充満していた** The room was *full of* cigarette smoke. / Cigarette smoke *permeated* the room. (➤ permeate /pə́ːˈmièɪt/ は「…に行き渡る, 浸透する」の意) ‖ 部屋には異臭が**充満していた** The room *was filled with* an offensive [a foul] smell.

じゅうみん 住民 **a resident** ▶このマンションの**住民**は皆東京へ通勤している All the *residents* of this apartment building commute to Tokyo. ‖ 焼却炉の建設は地元**住民**の反対にあっている *The local people* are against plans to build an incinerator in the neighborhood. ‖ この問題は**住民投票**で決められることになっている This issue will be decided by (a) *referendum*. ‖ 引っ越しをしたら**住民登録をしなければ**ならない When you move to another area, you have to *register your name and address* with the local authorities. (➤ 住民登録をしている住所, 居住し納税する所のことを domicile という)
‖**住民運動** a citizens' movement ‖ **住民税** a resident tax ‖ **住民票** a resident's certificate, a certificate of residence.

しゅうめい 襲名する **succeed to the (stage) name of ...** ▶猿之助の**襲名**披露興行が行われた A performance was given to announce his *succession to the name of* Ennosuke.

しゅうもく 衆目 ▶**衆目の一致するところ**斎藤は日本球界を代表する投手になるだろう *As most people agree*, Saito will be a star pitcher in Japanese baseball. ‖ 彼が有能であることは**衆目の一致するところだ** *There is wide* [*general*] *agreement* that he is competent.

じゅうもんじ 十文字 **a cross** ▶机を**十文字に**並べる arrange desks *in a cross*.

しゅうや 終夜 **all night (through)** ▶電車は大みそかには**終夜運転をする** Trains *run through the night* on New Year's Eve. (➤「終夜運転」は all-night service という) ‖ 土曜日は**終夜営業しております** We *stay open all night* on Saturdays.

しゅうやく 集約 ▶皆の意見を**集約する** *make a concise summary* of all people's opinions.

1**じゅうやく 重役** 《米》 a **corporate executive** [**director**], 《英》 a **company director** ▶土井氏はわが社の販売担当**重役**です Mr. Doi is our company's *chief sales director* [*executive*]. ‖ 佐藤さんは**重役に**昇進した Ms. Sato was promoted to *director*. / Ms. Sato obtained a seat on the board of directors. (➤ the board of directors は「重役会」)
‖**重役会議** a directors' meeting, a meeting of (the board of) directors, a board meeting ‖ **社外重役** an outside director.

2**じゅうやく 重訳** **a secondhand translation, a translation of a translation** ▶英語訳からの**重訳** a *translation of* an English translation.

じゅうゆ 重油 **heavy oil.**

しゅうゆう 周遊 ‖**周遊券** 《米》 an excursion ticket, 《英》 a round-trip ticket.

1**しゅうよう 収容する** **accommodate** +㊀, **hold** +㊀ ▶そのホテルは1500名近く**収容できる** That hotel can *accommodate* [*hold*] nearly one thousand (and) five hundred people. ‖ この病院は1000名の患者を**収容できる** This hospital *has* one thousand *beds*. (➤「1000人分のベッドを持つ」の意) ‖ この劇場は何人**収容できますか** What is the *seating capacity* of this theater? (➤ seating capacity は「収容力, 座席数」).
▶彼は交通事故で負傷して**病院に収容された** He was injured in a traffic accident and *was hospitalized* [*was taken to* (*the*) *hospital*]. ‖ 救助隊は飛行機の墜落事故で亡くなった人々の遺体を**収容した** The rescue team *recovered* the bodies of those who died in the plane crash. (➤ recover は「遺体などを回収する」).
‖**収容所** a refugee camp (難民の); an internment camp (捕虜などの); a concentration camp (強制収容所).

[2]**しゅうよう 修養** ▶座禅は精神修養に有効だ Zazen is good for *strengthening yourself mentally* [*spiritually*].

[3]**しゅうよう 収用する** expropriate /ɪkspróʊprieɪt/ +目 ▶道路拡張用地を収用する *expropriate* land for the expansion of a road.

じゅうよう 重要 一名 **重要性** importance 一形 **重要な** important, significant /sɪgnɪ́fɪkənt/ (➤後者は堅い語) ▶重要な問題 an *important* issue／a *significant* issue ‖ 重要な役割を演じる play an *important* role [part] ‖ 教育の重要性を強調する stress the *importance* of education ‖ きたる選挙は国の民主化に向けての重要な一歩だ This coming election is a *significant* step toward the country's democratization. ‖ 沖縄はアメリカにとって戦略的に重要だ Okinawa has strategic *importance* for the U.S. ‖ 江田君のお父さんは会社で重要な地位に就いている Eda's father has an *important* position in the company. ‖ 絶えず己の技能を磨くことが重要だ It's *important* that you constantly improve your skills. ‖ 重要なのは何歳まで生きるかではなく, いかに生きるかだ *What counts* [*What is important*] is not how long you live, but how (well) you live.

‖**重要人物** a VIP, a very important person ‖ **重要文化財** an important cultural asset [property] ‖ **重要無形文化財** an important intangible cultural asset.

しゅうらい 襲来 (an) invasion (侵入) ; (an) attack (攻撃) ; a hit (台風などの) ▶関東に寒波が襲来した A cold snap *hit* the Kanto district. ‖ 日本は鎌倉時代に蒙古(もうこ)の襲来を受けた Japan *was attacked by* the Mongols during the Kamakura period.

じゅうらい 従来 ▶従来からわが社の製品は品質において信頼に足るものとされてきました Our products have *always* been considered to be reliable in quality. ‖ 今や従来のやり方をもう一度考え直してみる時です Now is the time to reconsider the *traditional* [*conventional*] method. ‖ このスマートフォンは従来の(＝現在市販されている)ものとどう違いますか？ What's the difference between this smartphone and others *currently in use*? ‖ 式は従来どおり午後1時に始まります The ceremony will start at one in the afternoon, *as usual*. (➤ as usual は「今までのように」).

しゅうらく 集落 a village ; a hamlet (小さな村).

しゅうり 修理 repair(s) 一動 **修理する** repair +目 (複雑なものを) ;《英また》mend +目 (比較的簡単なものを) ;《インフォーマル》fix +目 《参考》mend は《米》では布製品, 特に衣服の直し・繕いの場合に用いる.

▶おもちゃを修理する *repair* [*fix*] a toy ‖ 壊れた椅子を修理する *mend* a broken chair ‖ 父は器用で, 家で何でも修理してしまう My father is good with tools and *can fix almost anything* at home. ‖ ノートパソコンが動かないわ. 修理に出さなくっちゃ The laptop (computer) doesn't work. I'll have to *send* it *out to be repaired*. ‖ 学生寮の屋根は夏休み中に修理された The dormitory roofs *were renovated* during the summer vacation. (➤ renovate は特に古い建物を修理する場合に用いる) ‖ うちの車は今修理工場に行っている Our car is in the (*repair*) *shop*.／Our car is in the *garage*. (➤この garage は「車庫」ではなく「修理工場」の意) ‖《掲示》修理中 Under Repair.

‖**修理工** a repair person, a repairman, a repairer ; a mechanic (車の) ‖ **修理費** repair costs.

[1]**しゅうりょう 修了する** finish +目, complete +目 ▶娘もやっと義務教育を修了しました My daughter *has finished* [*completed*] compulsory education at last. ‖ 母はやっと自動車学校のコースを修了しました My mother managed to *complete* the driving course.

‖**修了証書** a diploma /dɪplóʊmə/ ; a certificate /səˈtɪ́fɪkət/ of (the) completion of the course of studies.

[2]**しゅうりょう 終了する** end (予定されていたものが) ; close (継続していたものが) ▶会合は5時に終了した The meeting *ended* [*finished*／*was over*] at five. ‖ 火災訓練は無事終了した The fire drill *ended* uneventfully. ‖ 本日の営業時間は終了いたしました I'm afraid we're *closed*.／*Closed*. (➤後者は看板の場合).

じゅうりょう 重量 weight ▶あの鐘は重量が350キロある That bell is 350 kilograms in *weight*.／That bell weighs 350 kilograms. (➤ weigh は「重量がある」の意の動詞) ‖ あの荷物の総重量はどのくらいありますか What is the *gross weight* of that load? ‖ 小錦の押しは実に重量感があった Konishiki's push was really *massive*. ‖ 彼は柔道の重量級で優勝した He won the first prize in the judo *heavyweight division*.

‖**重量挙げ** weight lifting ‖ **重量挙げ選手** a weight lifter ‖ **重量制限** a weight limit ; a load limit (積み荷の).

じゅうりょく 重力 gravity ; gravitation (重力の作用) ▶物が落下するのは重力のためである *Gravity* causes things to drop. ‖ 無重力状態では人間は宙に浮くことができる In *weightlessness* [Under *zero-gravity conditions*] humans can float in the air.

☛ 無重力 (→見出語)

じゅうりん 蹂躙する violate +目, infringe +目 (侵害する) ; trample on (踏みにじる) ▶人権を蹂躙する *trample on* [*violate*／*infringe*] human rights.

シュール シュールな surrealistic (超現実主義の) ; surreal (現実離れした) ▶シュールな絵 a *surrealistic* painting ‖ シュールな体験 a *surreal* experience.

じゅうれつ 縦列 a file ▶縦列駐車 *parallel* parking.

しゅうれっしゃ 終列車 the last train ▶かろうじて仙台行きの終列車に間に合った I just made *the last train* to Sendai.

しゅうれん 修練 discipline (鍛錬) ; training (何かに備えて体・精神を鍛えること) ; practice (ある技術・技能を身につけるための繰り返しによる練習) ▶修練を積む *discipline oneself*.

しゅうろう 就労 ▶日本には多くの不法就労者がいる There are many *illegally-employed workers* [*illegal workers*] in Japan.

‖**就労時間[日数]** working hours [days] ‖ **外国人就労者** a non-Japanese employee (in Japan).

じゅうろうどう 重労働 hard work (きつい仕事) ; (a) hard labor (刑としての).

しゅうろく 収録する 1【録音・録画する】record /rɪkɔ́ːˈd/ +目 ▶野鳥の声をDATに収録する *record* the singing of wild birds on a DAT ‖ このDVDは学校生活のすべてを収録したものです This DVD is *a* complete *recording* of my school life.

2【新聞・書籍などに記載する】▶この辞書は何語**収録**していますか How many words does this dictionary *contain*?

じゅうろく 十六 sixteen ; the sixteenth(16番目).

しゅうわい 収賄 (a) bribery(贈収賄) ▶彼は**収賄**の罪で逮捕された He was arrested on a charge of *bribery* [*taking bribes*].

しゅえい 守衛 a guard ▶大学の**守衛** *a guard* at a college.

じゅえき 樹液 sap.

じゅえきしゃ 受益者 a beneficiary

‖**受益者負担** payment by the beneficiaries.

ジュエリー jewelry ▶高価な金の**ジュエリー** expensive gold *jewelry*.

1**しゅえん 主演する** star, play the leading role ▶高倉健**主演**のやくざ映画が一時大人気だった Yakuza films *starring* [*featuring*] Takakura Ken were once quite popular.

‖**主演男優**［**女優**］**賞** the award for best actor [actress].

2**しゅえん 酒宴** a drinking party.

じゅかい 樹海 a wide expanse of forest.

しゅかくてんとう 主客転倒 ▶(お客さんに)ごちそうしてもらったんだって? そりゃあ**主客転倒**だよ Were you treated to a meal? That's *putting the cart before the horse*. (➤ 文字どおりには「馬の前に荷車をつける」の意).

1**しゅかん 主観** subjectivity 一形 **主観的な** subjective ▶**主観**だけでものを言ってもらっては困る Don't take such a *subjective view* in everything. ‖できるだけ**主観**を交えずに(=客観的に)書いてください Please write as *objectively* as possible.

2**しゅかん 主幹** the chief editor, the editor in chief(本などの) ; the editorial writer in chief(論説の).

しゅがん 主眼 the main purpose (主要目的) ; the chief aim(主な狙い) ▶この本の**主眼**は事実を知らせることである *The main purpose* of this book is to disclose the facts.

1**しゅき 酒気** ▶**酒気帯び運転**は違反です It is illegal to *drive under the influence* (*of alcohol*) [to *drive while intoxicated*]. (➤ それぞれ DUI, DWI と頭文字で書いたり言ったりすることも多い) ／*DUI* [*DWI*] is illegal.

2**しゅき 手記** notes(覚書) ; memories (回想録).

しゅぎ 主義 1【イズム】-ism(…主義 ; 接尾辞として) ▶**菜食主義** vegetarian*ism* ; vegan*ism* (動物性のものを食べない完全な) ‖**資本主義** capital*ism* ‖**マルクス主義** Marx*ism* ‖**社会主義者** a social*ist*.

2【堅く守る考え方】 a principle ; a belief (信念) ▶借金しないのが私の**主義**だ It is my *principle* [*policy*] not to borrow money. ／I do not borrow money *on principle*. ‖人の陰口をきくのは私の**主義**に反する It *is against my principles* to say bad things about people behind their backs. ‖**主義主張**を貫くことは難しい It is difficult to *stick to your own ideas and principles*. ‖彼は自分の**主義**を曲げない男だ He is *a man of principle*. ／He doesn't sacrifice his principles. (➤「彼は自分の主義を犠牲にしない」の意)

▶あの学校はもうけ**主義**だそうだ They say that that school *is profit oriented*. (➤ oriented は「…優先の」) ／They say that that school *puts profit above everything else*.

1**じゅきゅう 受給する** receive +目 ▶厚生年金を**受給**する *receive* an employees' pension.

‖**受給者** a recipient (➤「生活保護受給者」は a welfare recipient,「年金受給者」は a pensioner).

2**じゅきゅう 需給** supply and demand.

1**しゅぎょう 修行** training(鍛錬) ; ascetic /əsétɪk/ discipline(禁欲的修養) ▶永平寺には外国から**修行**に来ている青年が何人かいる At Eiheiji Temple, there are some young people from overseas who came for *religious training* [to practice *ascetic discipline*]. ‖きみはまだ**修行**が足りないようだね It seems *there are a few things you have yet to learn*. (➤「まだ学ばなければならないことがある」の意).

2**しゅぎょう 修業** →しゅうぎょう.

じゅきょう 儒教 Confucianism /kənfjúːʃənìzm/.

じゅぎょう 授業

a lesson(個人授業にもいう) ; a class(教室での) ; teaching (教えること) ▶英語の**授業** an English *lesson* [*class*] ‖きょうは 4 時まで**授業**がある We have *classes* until four today. ‖ぼくたちは**授業**が終わるとすぐ野球の練習を始めます We begin practicing baseball right after *classes* are over. ‖あすは陸上競技大会のため**授業**はありません There will be no *classes* tomorrow because of the athletic meet. ‖**授業**では若いカナダ人の先生が英語の勉強の手助けをしてくれています A young Canadian teacher helps us learn English *in class*. ‖きのうは**授業**をサボった I *cut* [*skipped*] *class* yesterday. ／I *played hook*(*e*)*y* yesterday. (➤ cut [skip] class の表現で時間数をはっきり言うときは, 1 時間なら a class, 2 時間なら two classes のようになる) ‖ **対話**「どの先生の**授業**が好きですか」「古賀先生の生物の**授業**です」"Whose *class* do you enjoy most?" "Mrs. Koga's biology *class*."

▶三田先生は**授業**がうまい Mr. Mita *is a good teacher*. ‖佐々木先生の**授業**はつまらない Mr. Sasaki's *class* is boring. ‖物理の**授業**は難しくてついていけない The *physics class* is too difficult for me to keep up with. ‖きょうの体育の**授業**は先生の病欠で自習になった Today's *PE class* was canceled because the teacher was sick and we had a free study period. (➤ PE は Physical Education の略 ; gym class ともいう).

▶ 2 時間目の**授業**(=第 2 時限)は 9 時40分に始まる *The second period* starts at 9 : 40. ‖きょうはこれで**授業**を終わります That will be all for today. ／That's all for today. ‖**授業中**にガムをかむ生徒がいる Some students chew gum *during class*. ‖斉藤先生は**授業中**よくくしゃみをする Mr. Saito often sneezes *while teaching*. ‖私の高校の**授業時間**は50分です Our high school has 50-minute *periods*. ‖公立高校の**授業料**を無償化する make public high schools *tuition* free (➤「公立高校の授業料無償化」なら public high school tuition waiver) ‖うちの高校の**授業料**は年額40万円です The *tuition* at our high school is 400,000 yen a year. (➤ The tuition fees ... are ... も可).

‖**授業参観日** a parents' open [visiting] day ‖**課外授業** an extracurricular class ‖**短縮授業** shortened school hours.

しゅぎょく 珠玉 a gem ▶**珠玉の短編** *a literary gem*.

しゅく- 祝- ▶**祝卒業** *Congratulations* on your graduation ‖**祝優勝** *Congratulations* on winning the championship.

じゅく 塾 a juku ; a cram school

《解説》「塾」の訳し方
(1)英語には「塾」にぴったりの語がないので juku をそのまま用いるか, cram school (詰め込み学校) で代用するが, マイナスイメージがあるのであまり使われなくなった.
(2)特に「進学塾」を説明する場合には juku [cram school] which offers preparatory courses for entrance exams のように, また「補習塾」なら juku which offers supplementary lessons [individualized tutoring] after regular school hours とする.
(3)英米にある塾のような補充的学習を行う場は a learning center または a tutoring center と呼ばれる.

▶小学生対象の塾 *a juku* [*a cram school*] for elementary school students ‖自宅で塾をやる set up *a juku* [*a tutoring service*] in one's own home ‖私は放課後, 英語塾に行っている After school I go to *a juku to study English*. ‖おじはそろばん塾を開いています My uncle runs *a private abacus school*.
‖**塾長** the manager [operator] of a *juku*(運営している人) ; the headteacher of a *juku* (先生).

しゅくえん 祝宴 a **feast** ; a **banquet** /bǽŋkwɪt/ (格式ばった) ▶祝宴を催す give [hold] *a feast* [*banquet*].

しゅくが 祝賀 (a) **celebration** ▶祝賀会に参列する attend *a celebration* ‖きょうは会社設立10周年の祝賀会が開かれる Today we are going to *hold a party to celebrate* the tenth anniversary of our company's establishment. (➤「祝賀会」は a celebration だが, この文では「…を祝う」と考える).
‖**祝賀パレード** a celebration parade.

しゅくがん 宿願 ▶ヨーロッパの古城巡りをするのが私の宿願だった It was my *long-cherished wish* [*dream*] to visit old castles in Europe. ‖私は昨年その宿願を果たした I realized that *ambition* of mine last year.

じゅくご 熟語 an **idiom**, a **set phrase**.

しゅくさいじつ 祝祭日 a **public** [**national**] **holiday** ; a **red-letter day**(➤暦に赤字で示すことから). →祝日.

しゅくさつばん 縮刷版 a **reduced-size edition** ; a **pocket-sized edition**(ポケット版).

しゅくじ 祝辞 a **congratulatory speech** [**greeting**] ▶彼の成功に対し祝辞を述べたのは彼のライバルだった The person who gave the *speech congratulating* him on his success was his rival.

しゅくじつ 祝日 a **national holiday**, a **public holiday**, 《英また》a **bank holiday**.

「祝日」のいろいろ **元日** New Year's Day ／**成人の日** Coming-of-Age Day ／**建国記念の日** National Foundation Day ／**天皇誕生日** the Emperor's Birthday ／**春分の日** Spring Equinox Day ／**昭和の日** Showa Day ／**憲法記念日** Constitution (Memorial) Day ／**みどりの日** Greenery Day ／**こどもの日** Children's Day ／**海の日** Marine Day ／**山の日** Mountain Day ／**敬老の日** Respect-for-the-Aged Day, Senior Citizens' Day ／**秋分の日** Autumn(al) Equinox Day ／**スポーツの日** Sports Day ／**文化の日** Culture Day ／**勤労感謝の日** Labor Thanksgiving Day
㊟どれも特に決められた言い方はない.

[1]**しゅくしゃ 宿舎** a **place to stay**(泊まる場所) ; a **hotel** (ホテル) ; an **inn**(宿屋, 旅館)
‖**公務員宿舎** housing for public employees ‖**国民宿舎** a folk hostel, a nationally designated hostel.

[2]**しゅくしゃ 縮写** (a) **reduction** ▶案内図を縮写コピーする make a *reduced*(*-size*) copy of a guide map.

しゅくしゃく 縮尺 ▶テキサス州の縮尺25万分の1の地図が欲しい I'd like (to buy) a map of Texas on *a scale of 1 to 250,000*. (➤地図販売店の店員には I'm looking for a map ... のように言うことが多い).

しゅくしゅく 粛々と **solemnly** (厳かに) ; **without** (**making**) **a fuss**(騒ぎ立てることなく).

しゅくじょ 淑女 a **lady** 一形 淑女のような **ladylike**.

[1]**しゅくしょう 縮小** (a) **reduction** 一動 **縮小する** **reduce** +目 (減じる) ; **cut down** 《on》(費用などを) ▶図版を3分の2に縮小する *reduce* an illustration *to* two-thirds' *size* ‖防衛費を縮小する *cut down on* the national defense budget ‖事件発生後3年が経過して捜査陣が半分に縮小された Three years have passed since the incident happened and the investigation team *has been cut* in half.

[2]**しゅくしょう 祝勝** **the celebration of a victory** ▶祝勝会を催す hold a *victory celebration*.

しゅくず 縮図 ▶安土城の縮図 *a reduced copy* of Azuchi Castle.
▶《比喩的》学校は社会の縮図である A school is a miniature version [*a microcosm*] *of society*. (➤ microcosm は「小宇宙」).

じゅくす 熟す **ripen** /ráɪpən/, 《インフォーマル》**get ripe** 一形 **熟した** **ripe** ▶柿は秋に熟す Persimmons *ripen* in autumn. ‖このバナナはもう何日か置いたら熟すと思うよ These bananas will *ripen* [*get ripe*] if you leave them for a few more days. ‖このアボカドはよく熟していて食べ頃だ This avocado *is ripe* enough [is ready] to eat. ‖メロンはまだ熟していない The melons *are* still *green* [*unripe*].
▶我々の計画はまだ熟していない Our plan *is* still *unripe*. ‖新しい販売キャンペーン開始の機は熟した *The time is ripe* for a new sales campaign.

じゅくすい 熟睡 ▶ゆうべは熟睡していて地震にも気づかなかった I *slept* so *soundly* last night that I didn't feel the earthquake. ‖熟睡できましたか Did you *have a good night's sleep*? ‖彼女は熟睡しているようだ She seems to *be fast* [*sound*] *asleep*.

しゅくする 祝する **celebrate** +目 ▶太郎君の成功を祝して乾杯! Here's to Taro's success! →祝う.

しゅくせい 粛清 a **purge** 一動 **粛清する** **purge** +目.

じゅくせい 熟成 **aging**, **maturation** 一動 **熟成する** **age**, **mature** ▶ワインは熟成するにつれてまろやかになる Wines become mellow as they *age*.

しゅくだい 宿題

1 【学校の】homework, 《米また》a (**homework**) **assignment** (➤単に assignment ともいう)

語法 (1)homework は Ⓤ なので, (×)a homework とか (×)homeworks とはしない. 数えるときは a piece of homework, two pieces of homework のようにする.
(2)一方, assignment は Ⓒ なので one (homework) assignment, two (homework) assignments とできる. なお, assignment の基本的な意味は「課題」である.

▶きょうは数学の宿題がある I have *math homework*

today. ‖きょうは2つ宿題があるんだ I have *two* (*homework*) *assignments* today. ‖もう宿題はやったの？ Have you *done* your *homework* yet？‖松田先生はあまり宿題を出さない Mr. Matsuda doesn't *give* us *much homework* [*a lot of* (*homework*) *assignments*].

✉ **夏休みは宿題が山ほどあります** I have piles of [a mountain of] *homework* to do during summer vacation.

2【未解決の問題】▶この問題は次の会議まで宿題としましょう Let's *leave* this matter *for consideration* at the next meeting. ‖その件はまだ宿題になっている That matter *is pending* [*has been left open*].

じゅくたつ 熟達する master ＋目 (修得する) ▶短期間で外国語に熟達するのはほとんど不可能だ It's almost impossible to *master* [*become proficient in*] a foreign language in a short time. ‖彼は商業英語に熟達している He *is* (*well*) *versed in* business English. (➤ be versed in は「…の経験・練習を積んでいる」).

じゅくち 熟知 ▶山を熟知している人でも冬山は危険である Mountain climbing in winter is dangerous, even for those who *know* mountains *well*. ‖この辺の地理なら熟知しております I *know everything about* this area. ／I know my way around here.

しゅくちょく 宿直 night duty (夜勤) ▶今夜は宿直だ I *am on duty* tonight. ／I *am on the overnight shift* today. ‖**宿直室** a night-duty room.

しゅくてき 宿敵 an old enemy ; a sworn enemy (決して許さないと誓った敵).

しゅくてん 祝典 a celebration ; a festival (祭り) ▶祝典を催す observe *a celebration* ‖会社創立150周年の祝典を催した We *celebrated* the 150th anniversary of the foundation of our company.

しゅくでん 祝電 a congratulatory telegram, a telegram of congratulations ▶慶子に「ご結婚おめでとう」と祝電を打った I sent Keiko *a telegram congratulating her* on her wedding. ／I sent Keiko *a congratulatory telegram* that said "Congratulations on your wedding."

じゅくどく 熟読 ▶彼女はその記事を熟読した She *perused* the article. ‖憲法を熟読する *read* the Constitution *carefully*.

じゅくねん 熟年 late middle age to early old age (➤ 説明的な訳) ▶熟年夫婦 an *older* [*a more mature*] couple ／a couple *in their golden years* (➤ golden years には「楽しく過ごせる定年後」のニュアンスがある) ‖**熟年離婚** *late-(in-)life* divorce.

しゅくば 宿場 a stage ▶宿場町 a post(ing) station.

しゅくはい 祝杯 a toast ▶皆さん，この若い2人のために祝杯をあげましょう Everybody, let's *drink a toast to* this young couple !

しゅくはく 宿泊する stay《at, with》(➤ 英語では「友人の所(に)」などと言うとき「with ＋友人」と表現することができる.「場所に」は「at ＋場所」) ▶北海道を旅行したときはユースホステルに宿泊した We *stayed at* youth hostels when we traveled in Hokkaido. ‖彼は博多の友人の家に宿泊した He *stayed with* his friend in Hakata. (➤ 前置詞 with に注意) ‖ホテルの宿泊客は全員無事脱出した All the *guests that were staying* at the hotel escaped safely. ‖ 対話 「宿泊料はシングル1泊でいくらですか」「朝食付きで80ドルです」"How much is a single for one night ?" "A single room with breakfast is 80 dollars." (➤「宿泊料」は「定められた料金」は hotel rates,「かかった料金」は hotel charges.《英》ではホテルなどの料金(表)を tariff とも言う).

‖**宿泊施設**《米》accommodations,《英》accommodation ‖(ホテルなどの)**宿泊者名簿** a register.

しゅくふく 祝福 a blessing 一動 **祝福する** bless ＋目 ; congratulate ＋目 (祝う) ▶両親は2人の結婚を祝福した The couple's parents *congratulated* them on their marriage. ‖司祭は2人を祝福した The priest *blessed* the couple. ‖その赤ん坊は家族みんなの祝福を受けた The baby had the *blessing* [received the *good wishes*] of all the family members.

しゅくほう 祝砲 a salute /səlúːt/.

しゅくぼう 宿坊 a lodging in a temple.

しゅくめい 宿命 fate (しばしば死や不運を暗示する) ; destiny (良い意味でも用いる) ; karma (仏教でいう「業(ごう)」) ▶宿命のライバル *an old rival* ‖それがきみの宿命なのだ It's your *fate* [*destiny* ／*karma*]. ‖きみと出会い恋に落ちるのがぼくの宿命だったのだ It was my *destiny* to meet and fall in love with you.

‖**宿命論** fatalism.

しゅくやく 縮約する abridge ＋目

‖**縮約版** an abridged edition.

じゅくりょ 熟慮 careful consideration 一動 **熟慮する** think carefully《about》; think over ▶熟慮を要する問題 a problem which requires *careful consideration*.

じゅくれん 熟練 skill (磨いた技術) ▶漆塗りは大いに熟練を要する Lacquering requires much *skill*. ‖彼は熟練した歯科技工士だ He is an *expert* [*experienced*] dental technician.

‖**熟練工** a skilled worker.

¹しゅくん 殊勲 ▶その小さな力士は2横綱を破って殊勲賞を獲得した The small wrestler was awarded *the Outstanding Performance Prize* for defeating two yokozunas. ‖彼のそのヒットが殊勲打(＝決勝打)となった His hit proved to be *a game-winning one* [*the one that won the game*].

²しゅくん 主君 one's (liege) lord ▶主君に仕える serve one's *lord*.

じゅくんしゃ 受勲者 a recipient of an order [a decoration].

しゅげい 手芸 handicrafts ▶祖母は手芸が趣味だ My grandmother's hobby is *handicrafts*. 《参考》「編み物」は knitting,「刺しゅう」は embroidery という ‖**手芸品** handicrafts, a handcrafted article ; fancywork (刺しゅうなど).

しゅけいかん 主計官 a budget examiner.

しゅけいきょく 主計局 the Budget Bureau.

じゅけいしゃ 受刑者 a convict (服役者) ; an inmate (入所者), a prisoner.

しゅけん 主権 sovereignty /sɑ́ːvrənti/ ▶主権在民が日本の政治の根幹である Japan's government is based on the political philosophy that *sovereignty rests with the people*. ‖選挙は主権者である国民の真意を問う重要な手段である Elections are a very important means of assessing the real feelings (about issues) of the citizens, who *hold sovereign power*. ‖中国がその島の主権を主張している China claims *sovereignty* over the island.

じゅけん 受験

一動 **受験する** take [《英また》sit for] an examination ▶M大を受験する *take the entrance examination* for M University ‖ うちの息子は来年**大学を受験する** Our son is going to *take university entrance examinations* next year. ‖ 弘は去年**受験に失敗して**今は予備校に通っている Hiroshi *failed the entrance examination* last year and is going to a *yobikō* now.

▶その大学の**受験科目**は英語・国語・社会である The *examination subjects* of that college are English, Japanese and social studies. ‖ この高校は**受験校**なので, 学校側は生徒を全員 4 年制大学に入れようとしている Since this senior high school *is interested in educational advancement,* it is eager to see every student enrolled in a four-year college. (●「受験校」に相当する英語はないので説明的になる) ‖ 文科省は**受験地獄**を緩和する方法を真剣に考慮すべきだ The Ministry of Education should think seriously of a way to alleviate "*examination hell.*" (➤ alleviate は「緩和する」) ‖ **受験勉強**は本当の勉強とはいえない *Studying for entrance examinations* isn't real studying.

‖**受験者** an examinee /ɪgzæmɪníː/ ; an applicant (志願者) ‖ **受験生** a student preparing for entrance examinations ‖ **受験戦争** an examination war ‖ **受験番号** a placement number ‖ **受験票** an admission card to an examination ‖ **受験料** an examination fee.

しゅげんじゃ 修験者 a **mountain ascetic.**

[1]**しゅご 主語** 《文法》 a **subject** ▶文の**主語**・述語 the *subject* and predicate of a sentence.

[2]**しゅご 守護 protection** ‖**守護神** a guardian god.

しゅこう 趣向 a **plan** (計画) ; an **idea** (アイデア) ; a **device** /dɪváɪs/ (工夫) ▶オリンピックの開会式はいつも新しい**趣向が凝らされている** Every Olympic opening ceremony *is elaborately planned with a novel* [*an original*] *theme.*

しゅごう 酒豪 a **hard** [**heavy**] **drinker.**

じゅこう 受講 ▶ラジオのスペイン語講座を**受講する** *take* a radio course in Spanish ‖ 冬期講習を**受講する**者は何人ですか How many people are going to *attend* the winter session?

しゅこうぎょう 手工業 handicraft industry, manual industry.

しゅこうげい 手工芸 handicrafts ‖**手工芸品** handicrafts ‖ **手工芸店** a handicrafts shop.

ジュゴン 《動物》 a **dugong** /dúːgɑːŋ/.

しゅさ 主査 the chief examiner (論文などの) ; a **project leader** (事業・計画などの) ▶私の修士論文の**主査**は前島教授です Professor Maejima will be *the chief examiner* responsible for my master's thesis.

[1]**しゅさい 主催する organize** +㊐ (計画・準備する) ; **promote** +㊐ (発起人となる) ; **sponsor** +㊐ (後援する) ▶その花の品評会は農協の**主催**で行われた The flower show was held *under the sponsorship* [*auspices*] *of* the agricultural cooperative association. (➤ sponsorship, auspices はともに「後援」の意).

‖**主催国** the host country ‖ **主催者** an organizer, a promoter, a sponsor.

[2]**しゅさい 主宰** ▶劇団を**主宰する** *manage* [*run*] a theatrical company.

しゅざい 取材する cover +㊐ (記者が事件などを報道する) ; **gather material** [**data**] (材料を集める) ▶部長はその火災の**取材**に田島君を派遣した The general manager sent Tajima out to *cover* the fire. ‖ 彼女は新しい小説を書くために長い時間をかけて若者の生活を**取材した** In order to write a new novel, she spent quite a long time *gathering material* [*data*] for an article on young people's lifestyles. ‖ この物語は沖縄の歴史に**取材している** This story *draws from* the history of Okinawa.

‖**取材記者** a (news) reporter.

しゅざん 珠算 calculation on the abacus ▶**珠算をする** *calculate on the abacus.*

[1]**しゅし 趣旨 the purpose, the aim** (目的) ; **the point** (意図) ▶彼はその運動の**趣旨**を説明した He explained *the purpose* [*aim*] of the movement. ‖ 私の**趣旨**はおわかりいただけたでしょうか Did I make my *point* clear enough? ‖ 彼は愛は世界を変える**という趣旨の**演説を行った He gave a speech *to the effect that* love can change the world.

[2]**しゅし 主旨 the** (**main**) **point** (要点) ; **the gist** /dʒɪst/ (要旨) ▶講演の**主旨** *the point* [*gist*] of a lecture ‖ 彼女は私と結婚しない**という主旨の**手紙を送ってきた She sent me a letter *stating that* she would not marry me. (➤ state は「(正式に) 述べる」の意で, say より形式ばった書き物・発言について使われる).

[3]**しゅし 種子** a **seed** ▶かぼちゃの**種子** a pumpkin *seed.*

しゅじ 主事 ‖**指導主事** a teacher's consultant ‖ **社会教育主事** a social education officer ‖ **社会福祉主事** a social welfare officer ‖ **職業指導主事** a career counselor ‖ **進路指導主事** an academic counselor ‖ **生徒指導主事** a student (guidance) counselor.

じゅし 樹脂 resin /rézɪn/

‖**合成樹脂** synthetic resin.

しゅじい 主治医 a **physician in charge** ; a **family doctor** (かかりつけの医者).

しゅじく 主軸の key ▶**主軸の**選手 a *key* player.

しゅしゃ 取捨 choice (選択) ; **selection** (多くの中から吟味しての選択) ▶タイトルをいろいろ考えてみましたが, **取捨**はそちらにお任せします I've thought of many titles, but I'd like to leave the *choice* (up) to you. ‖ 情報は**取捨選択**してこそ価値がある Information is valuable only when it *is carefully selected.*

シュシュ a **scrunchie** [**scrunchy**].

しゅじゅ 種々の various (いろいろな) ; **manifold** (数多くの, かついろいろな種類の) ▶彼の**種々の**任務 his *manifold* duties ‖ この奇病の原因については**種々の**説がある There are *various* theories as to the cause of this rare disease. ‖ **種々の**理由で, その仕事はお引き受けできません There are *many* [*a number of*] reasons why I cannot accept the job. ‖ あの店では**種々雑多な**舶来品を扱っている That shop carries *a wide range of* [*all kinds of*] imported goods.

しゅじゅつ 手術 surgery (外科手術) ; an **operation** (1回1回の) 一動 **手術する perform an operation, operate** 《on》 (医師が患者に) ; **have surgery** [**an operation**], **undergo an operation** (患者が手術を受ける ; undergo は堅い語) ▶**緊急手術を受ける** have [undergo] emergency *surgery* ‖ **手術**は成功した The *operation* was successful. ‖ 私は盲腸炎の**手術を受けた** I *had an operation* [*I was operated on* / *I had surgery*] for appendicitis. / I had an appendectomy. (➤ appendectomy /æpəndéktəmi/ は「虫垂切除」の意の専門用語) ‖ 患者は**手術中に**死んだ The patient died *during the operation* [*on the operating table*].

‖**手術室** an operating room (➤ 略語は OR), 《英また》 an operating theatre.

じゅじゅつ 呪術 (a) (**magic**) **incantation** /ìnkæntéɪʃən/（魔術）.

1**しゅしょう 首相** a **prime minister**

> ❰解説❱「首相」の意では prime minister が一般的. premier /prɪmíəʳ/ は一部の国, 例えば中国の首相(Chinese Premier)を除き, 主として新聞の見出しでのみ用いる. chancellor はドイツ, オーストリアの首相を指す.

▶菅首相 *Prime Minister* Suga（➤ 自国の首相を指すときや, 固有名詞の前につけるときは大文字で書くのがふつう）‖現在のイギリスの首相は誰ですか Who is *the prime minister* of the UK now?

‖**前首相** the former prime minister, the ex-prime minister（➤「元首相」も former prime minister または ex-prime minister）‖**首相官邸** the official residence of the Prime Minister.

2**しゅしょう 主将** a **captain** ▶彼はわがチームの主将だ He is (the) *captain* of our team.（➤ 補語のときはしばしば the を省く）.

3**しゅしょう 殊勝な commendable**; **praiseworthy**（賞賛に値する）▶きみが献血したのは殊勝な心がけだ It *was commendable* [*praiseworthy*] of you to donate blood.

1**じゅしょう 受賞する・受章する win a prize**（賞を獲得する）; **be awarded** /əwɔ́ːʳdɪd/（賞を与えられる）▶スピーチコンテストで1等賞を受賞する *win* (*the*) *first prize* in a speech contest ‖こんな立派な勲章を受章できて光栄です I am highly honored to *be awarded* this fine medal.

‖**受賞者** a prizewinner（➤「受賞作品 (a prize-winning work)」の意にもなる）.

2**じゅしょう 授賞・授章** ▶かぜで授賞式には出席できなかった I couldn't attend the *award ceremony* because of a cold.

しゅしょく 主食 a **staple**, a **staple food**（基本［必需］食品）《参考》英米には日本のような「主食」「副食」という考え方はない ▶米は日本人の主食です Rice is *a staple* of the Japanese diet. ‖戦前までは多くの日本の家庭が和食中心で, 米を主食とし, 魚・野菜・みそ汁・漬物を副食としていた Before World War II, most people in Japan ate traditional Japanese meals of rice supplemented by fish, vegetables, miso soup, and pickles.

しゅしん 主審 a **chief umpire** /ʌ́mpaɪəʳ/; a **plate umpire**（特に野球の球審）.

しゅじん 主人 1【店・旅館などの】an owner, a **proprietor** /prəpráɪəṭəʳ/（➤ 後者は堅い語）▶旅館の主人 the *proprietor* of an inn ‖あの店の主人は私と小学校で同級だった That *storekeeper* was a classmate of mine when we were in elementary school.

2【夫】 one's **husband** ▶主人は公務員です *My husband* is a government employee. ‖ご主人によろしくね Please say hello to *your husband* for me.

1**じゅしん 受信 reception 一動 受信する receive** +目 ▶衛星放送を受信する *receive* satellite broadcasts ‖この辺は AFN の電波があまりよく受信できない AFN *reception* isn't very good in this area. ／We don't get AFN very clearly in this area.

‖**受信機** a receiver ‖**受信料** a receiving [subscription] fee.

2**じゅしん 受診する see a doctor**（➤ 歯科・眼科など特定の科を受診する場合は see a dentist, see an eye doctor などとなる）▶歯科を受診したいんです I'd like to *see a dentist*.

しゅじんこう 主人公 a **hero** /híːroʊ/（男性）; a **heroine** /héroʊɪn/（女性）; a **protagonist**（物語などの）▶この映画の主人公は犬です The *hero* [*heroine*] of this movie is a dog.

しゅす 繻子 satin.

じゅず 数珠 a (**Buddhist**) **rosary**, (a **string of**) **prayer beads** ▶《慣用表現》前方で事故があったために, 車が数珠つなぎになっていた Due to an accident on the road ahead, the traffic was *bumper-to-bumper*.

しゅすい 取水する draw [**take**] **water**《from》▶取水制限する control the amount of *water taken*.

しゅぜい 酒税 a **liquor tax.**

じゅせい 受精・授精 insemination; **fertilization**（繁殖）**一動 受精する be fertilized** ▶人工授精 artificial *insemination* ‖体外受精 external [in vitro] *fertilization* ‖**受精卵** a fertilized egg.

1**しゅせき 首席の top, chief, lead**; **principal**（楽団・劇団の）▶彼女は大学を首席で卒業した She graduated from university *with top honors* [*first in her class*].

‖**首席研究員** a chief [lead] researcher ‖**首席指揮者** a principal conductor ‖**首席奏者** the principal player ‖**首席バイオリン奏者** the principal violinist.

2**しゅせき 主席 the Chairman**（政府の長）

‖**国家主席** the president《参考》中国の習近平主席は President Xi Jinping と表すのがふつう.

しゅせんど 守銭奴 a **miser** /máɪzəʳ/ ▶あの守銭奴が寄付をするとは驚いたね I can't believe that that *miser* made a donation.

じゅぞう 受像する receive an image [**a picture**] ▶このテレビの受像状態はよい［悪い／弱い］We get good [poor／weak] TV *reception*.

しゅぞく 種族 a **tribe** ▶種族間の争い a *tribal* [an *intertribal*] war（➤ 後者は「異種族間の」に相当）‖種族保存の本能 the instinct for *tribal preservation*.

しゅたい 主体 ▶1年生主体の若いチーム a young team, *composed mainly of* freshmen ‖そのデモは一般市民が主体となった The *majority* of the demonstrators were ordinary citizens. ‖その問題に対して主体的な行動をとる *take independent action* [*act independently*] on that issue ‖18歳ならそろそろ主体性があってもいい頃だ Since you are now 18, it is high time you had *an independent spirit* [*an identity of your own*]. ‖彼女は主体性がない She *doesn't have a mind of her own*. ／She's *easily influenced by others*.（➤「たやすく人の影響を受ける」の意）.

しゅだい 主題 a **subject**（全体の）; a **theme** /θiːm/（話・文章などの底流を成す考え, テーマ）▶中心主題 a central *theme* ‖主題と変奏 a *theme* and (its) variations（➤「主題に基づく変奏」は variations on a theme）‖この映画は人間と大自然との闘いを主題にしている The *theme* of this film is the struggle of humans against nature.

‖**主題歌** a theme song.

じゅたい 受胎 conception

‖《キリスト教で》**受胎告知** the Annunciation.

じゅだく 受諾 acceptance 一動 受諾する accept +目 ▶H氏はそのチームの監督就任要請を受諾した Mr. H *accepted* the proposal that he become manager of the team. ／Mr. H *agreed* to become manager of the team.（➤ proposal に続く that

節内の動詞は原形).

しゅだん 手段 a **means**; a **measure**(対策); a **way**(やり方) ▶集中力を高める有効な**手段** an effective *means* of enhancing concentration ‖ 使える**手段**は何でも使え Use any *means* available to you. ‖ 言語は意思を伝達する**手段**である Language is *a means* of communication. ‖ ほかの方法が見つからないので**思い切った手段**をとらねばならないだろう I will probably have to take *drastic measures* [*action*] since I can find no other way. ‖ 笑顔は異性の愛情を手に入れるための有効な**手段**だ A smiling face is *a* good *way* to capture the heart of someone of the opposite sex.

▶医者は**最後の手段として**手術を行った The doctor performed an operation *as a last resort*. ‖ **どんな手段に訴えてでも**原子力空母を入港させないぞ We *will do anything* to keep the nuclear aircraft carrier out of the port. ‖ あの男は金もうけのためには**手段を選ばない** He will *stop at nothing* to make money. (➤ stop at nothing は「どんなことでも平気でやる」の意).

じゅちゅう 受注する **receive an order** ▶不景気で**受注**がめっきり減った The recession has drastically reduced [decreased] the number of *orders*. ‖ **受注生産の**靴 [コンピュータ] *made-to-order* shoes [computers] (➤「受注生産」は production by [on] order).

1 **しゅちょう 主張** (an) **assertion**(個人的確信に基づく); (an) **insistence**(自己の考えへの固執); (an) **argument**(説を述べること) **━動 主張する** **assert** +目, **insist** 《on》 (➤ that の文がくるときは insist that); **argue** +目 (理由を挙げたり, 筋道を立てたりして); **claim** +目 (権利があるとして); **maintain** +目 (異論にもひるまず)

▶権利を**主張する** *assert* one's right(s) ‖ 彼は20年間無実を**主張し**続けている He has continued to *assert* his innocence for 20 years. ‖ 彼は**自分の意見を主張する**ばかりで, 他人の意見を聞こうとしない All he does is (to) *assert his* (*own*) *views*; he won't listen to those of anyone else.

【文型】
～であると主張する
assert [**insist, argue, claim, maintain**] **that** S + V

▶被告は無罪を**主張した** The defendant *insisted that* he was innocent. / The defendant *insisted on* [*asserted* / *maintained*] his innocence. ‖ 暗記が重要であると**主張する**教育者もいる Some educators *argue that* memorization is important.

▶彼女はそのつぼはある人からもらったものだと**主張した** She *claimed that* the vase had been a present from someone. ‖ 母は自分の健康には菜食がいちばんいいと**主張している** My mother *maintains that* a vegetarian [vegan] diet is best for her health.

2 **しゅちょう 首長** a **head** ▶地方自治体の**首長** the *head* of a local government.

しゅっ ▶シュッと一吹き, いっぺんにゴキブリを退治した *One spray* and the cockroach was dead [gone].

じゅつ 術 ▶水 [火] 遁(とん)の**術**を使う practice *water* [*fire*] *magic* ‖ あいつは**世渡りの術**にたけている He is skilled at the *art of getting along in* the world.

じゅっ ▶熱い鉄板にエビを載せると**ジュッ**といって丸まった When I placed the shrimp on the hot griddle, it *sizzled* and instantly curled up.

しゅつえん 出演する **appear** ▶きみがテレビに**出演する**ってほんと? Is it true that you are going to *appear* [*be*] on TV? ‖ 彼はリア王の役で舞台に**出演した** He *appeared* on stage as King Lear.

‖**出演者** a performer (1人); the cast (全体) ‖ **出演料** pay, a performance fee (➤ 後者はやや堅い語).

1 **しゅっか 出火** ▶妙なことにその火事はトイレからの**出火**だった Strangely enough, the *fire started* in the bathroom. ‖ **出火の原因**は依然として不明である *The cause of the fire* remains unknown.

2 **しゅっか 出荷** **shipping** **━動 出荷する** **ship** +目 ▶石巻から東京へマグロが**出荷される** Tuna *are shipped* [*sent*] from Ishinomaki to Tokyo. (➤ ship は, 特に《米》では, 船に限らずどんな輸送手段のときにも使えるが, 一般的には send を用いるほうが無難).

じゅっかい 述懐する **reminisce** 《about》 ▶彼女はアメリカ留学時代を**述懐した** She *reminisced about* the days she spent studying in the U.S.

しゅっかん 出棺する **carry a casket out** (of the deceased's home [of the funeral home]) ▶**出棺**を見送る *see a casket off*.

しゅつがん 出願 (an) **application** **━動 出願する** **apply for** ▶特許を**出願する** *apply for* a patent ‖ (願書の) **出願手続き**は済ませましたか Have you sent in your *application* yet?

‖**出願期日** the deadline [the time limit] for application ‖ **出願者** an applicant.

1 **しゅっきん 出勤する** **go to work**(会社へ行く) ▶父は今月は日曜日も**出勤した** My father even *went to work* on Sundays this month. (➤ この work は「勤務先」の意の名詞; 次例も同様) ‖ けさは**自分の車で出勤した** I *drove my car to work* this morning. ‖ 私はたいてい9時**出勤**です I usually *come to the office* at nine. (➤「会社に着くのが9時だ」の意で, 本人が会社にいて言う場合. 会社以外の場所にいて, 出社時間を言っている場合は come でなく go になる) ‖ 今度の土曜日は**出勤日**だ This Saturday is *a working day* [*workday*] for me. ‖ 姉は看護師なので**深夜出勤**のときもある Since my older sister is a hospital nurse, she sometimes *works the graveyard shift*. (➤ the graveyard shift は「(3交替制における) 深夜勤務」の意のインフォーマルな語).

‖**出勤時間** clock-in time ‖ **出勤日数** the number of days worked.

2 **しゅっきん 出金** ▶旅費を**出金する** *allocate money to* [*for*] one's travel expenses.

しゅっけ 出家 ▶彼は退職後に**出家した** He *became a Buddhist priest* after (his) retirement.

しゅつげき 出撃 a **sortie**(主に航空機の), a **sally**

▶**出撃する** *sortie* / *make a sortie* ‖ **出撃**! Go and attack (the enemy)!

1 **しゅっけつ 出血** **bleeding** **━動 出血する** **bleed**

▶時々上の歯茎から**出血する** Sometimes my upper gums *bleed*. ‖ 彼はその事故で大けがをしておびただしく**出血した** He was seriously injured in the accident and *lost* a large quantity of *blood*. ‖ その男性は**出血多量で死んだ** That man died *from loss of blood* [*excessive bleeding*]. / The man *bled* to death. ‖ **出血サービス**を行う sell ... *at a loss* [*at a sacrifice*].

2 **しゅっけつ 出欠** ▶**出欠を取る** *call the roll* / *take* [*check*] *attendance*.

✉ **出欠を4月末日までにお知らせください** Please let us know by the end of April *whether* *or not you can attend.*

しゅつげん 出現 **appearance** **―動 出現する** **appear** ▶思わぬ強敵が**出現した** An unexpected powerful opponent *appeared* [*emerged*]. ‖またまたロシアから天才ピアニストが**出現した** Yet another brilliant Russian pianist *has come on the scene.* ‖コンピュータの**出現**は我々の日常生活に一大変化をもたらした The *advent* of the computer revolutionized people's daily lives. (➤ advent /ǽdvent/ は「(重要人物・事件などの)出現」の意).

しゅっこ 出庫する **1【品物を】take ... out of storage.** **2【車庫から】leave a depot.**

1**じゅつご 術語** **a technical term**; **terminology**(➤集合的に) ▶医学**術語** a medical *term* / medical *terminology*.

2**じゅつご 述語** 《文法》**a predicate.**

3**じゅつご 術後** ▶患者は**術後**の経過は順調です The patient is making good progress *after the operation.*

1**しゅっこう 出航する** **sail, set sail** ▶大東丸は4時に**出航**の予定です The Daito-maru is scheduled to *sail* at 4 : 00.
‖**出航時間** departure time.

2**しゅっこう 出港する** **leave port** ▶悪天候で船は**出港**できなかった Bad weather prevented our ship from *leaving port*.

3**しゅっこう 出向** ▶彼は子会社に**出向させられた** He *was sent on loan* [《英》*was seconded*] to a subsidiary company. ‖こちらには1年間の**出向で来ております** I'm here *on loan* for a year. / 《英》I'm here *on secondment* for a year.

じゅっこう 熟考 →**熟慮.**

しゅっこく 出国する **leave a country** ▶昔は共産主義諸国は**出国**も入国も難しかった Formerly it was hard both to *leave* and enter communist *countries*.
‖**出国手続き** departure formalities.

しゅつごく 出獄する **leave prison**(出所する); **be released from prison**(釈放される).

じゅっさく 術策 **a trick**; **a trap**(わな) ▶**術策**にはまる be entrapped / fall into a *trap*.

しゅっさつ 出札 ‖**出札係** a ticket clerk, 《英また》a booking clerk ‖**出札口** a ticket window, 《英また》a booking window.

しゅっさん 出産 **childbirth**; (a) **delivery**(分べん) **―動 出産する** **give birth** 《to》 ▶その女優は未婚の母として**出産した** That actress *gave birth* as unmarried. ‖彼女は**出産後**, 腰回りが少し太めになった She got a little bigger around the waist *after childbirth* [*after she gave birth*].

> **【文型】**
> **赤ちゃん(A)を出産する**
> **give birth to** A

▶純子は3400グラムの女の子を無事**出産した** Junko successfully *gave birth to* a baby girl weighing 3,400 grams.
▶妹さんはいつ頃**出産の予定**ですか When *is* your sister *expecting* her baby [*going to have* a baby] ? (➤ be expecting は「産む予定である」の意) ‖私は4月に2人目の子を**出産する予定**です I'*m expecting* my second child in April.
✉ **ご出産おめでとう** Congratulations on your *new baby*!
‖**出産祝い** a celebration of a birth (祝い事); a gift [a present] for a newborn baby (贈り物); a baby shower (近く出産する母親のために贈り物を持ち寄るパーティー) ‖**出産休暇** (a) maternity [paternity] leave (➤後者は夫の) ‖**出産予定日** a due date.

しゅっし 出資 (an) **investment** **―動 出資する** **invest** (+目)(投資する); **finance** +目 (資金面で支える) ▶ある事業に多額の**出資をする** *invest* a large amount of money [*invest* heavily] in a project / *make* a large *investment* in a project ‖共同事業に**出資する** *finance* a joint venture ‖政府**出資のプロジェクト** a government-*financed* [-*sponsored*] project ‖私の父はその事業に20パーセントの**出資をしている** My father *has* a twenty percent *interest* [*stake*] in that business. (➤ interest, stake は「権利, 株」).
‖**出資金** an investment ‖**出資者** an investor.

しゅっしゃ 出社 ▶来週の月曜日は7時までに**出社して**もらいたい I want you to *come to the office* by seven next Monday. ‖山田はまだ**出社して**おりません Yamada hasn't *come to the office* yet. →**出勤.**

じゅっしゅきょうぎ 十種競技 →**じっしゅきょうぎ.**

しゅっしょ 出所 **1【出どころ】the source** ▶**出所**の怪しい記事を新聞に載せるわけにはいかない We cannot print an article from an unreliable *source* in our paper. ‖この文の**出所**は夏目漱石です This passage *comes from* Natsume Soseki.
2【刑務所から出ること】▶彼はきのう**出所した**ばかりだ He *was released from prison* only yesterday.
‖**仮出所** release on parole.

しゅっしょう 出生 **birth** ▶**出生**の秘密 the secret of a person's *birth* ‖**出生届**を忘れずに出してください Please don't forget to *register the birth* of your baby. (➤「出生届」は the registration [report] of a birth(届け出ること), a birth registration form (届け出用紙)という) ‖この国の**出生率**は極めて低い The *birthrate* in this country is very low. ‖**出生地** one's birthplace.

しゅつじょう 出場する **participate** 《in》, **take part** 《in》(➤ともに「参加する」; 後者はインフォーマル); **enter** 《for》(参加を申し込む) ▶彼はオリンピックの体操競技に**出場した** He *participated* [*took part*] *in* an Olympic gymnastics competition. ‖M校はその試合に勝って甲子園大会**出場を決めた** M High won the game to *clinch a berth in* [to *make it to*] the Koshien tournament. (➤ berth は「出場権」, make it to ... は「…へ進む」) ‖私はそのオートバイレースに**出場を申し込んだ** I *entered* [I *was entered*] *for* the motorcycle race. (➤ be entered for と受け身形で使うことも多い) ‖その選手はピッチャーを殴って10日間の**出場停止になった** The player *was suspended* for 10 days for hitting the pitcher.
‖**出場者** a participant / an entrant.
☛ **初出場** (→見出語)

しゅっしょく 出色の **outstanding** (傑出した); **brilliant**(すばらしい) ▶彼女は最近では**出色のピアニスト**だ She is one of the most *outstanding* pianists that we've seen in recent years. ‖彼の演技は**出色の**出来栄えだった His performance was *brilliant*.

しゅっしょしんたい 出処進退 ▶**出処進退**を決めるのは首相自身である It's the prime minister himself who will decide to *resign or not*.

しゅっしん 出身

1【出身地】▶セリーヌ・ディオンはどこの国の**出身**か知っていますか Do you know *what country* Celine Dion *comes from*? ‖ **対話** 「どちらのご出身ですか」「北海道です」"*Where do you come from?*" "(I'm from)

Hokkaido."（➤ カッコ内は通例言わない）.

あなたの英語はどう響く?
出身地を聞くつもりで Where *did* you come from? としがちだが，これは「どこからやって来たの?」の意味になる．日本を旅行中の外国人なら "Kyoto." などと答えるかもしれない．どこで生まれ育ったのかを聞くには Where do you come from? または Where are you from? とする．さらに詳しく知りたいのであれば Where did you grow up?（どこで育ったのですか）とか，What country are you from?（どこの国からいらっしゃったのですか）と聞けばよい．また，出身国がわかっている場合は What part of the United States do you come from? ／ Where(abouts) in the United States are you from?（アメリカはどちらの出身ですか）という言い方もある．ただし，外国人の中にはこのような身元調査のような質問を嫌う人も多いので注意が必要．

2【出身校】▶大和中学校の**出身です** I *graduated from* Yamato Junior High School.（➤ graduate from は「…を卒業する」）‖元ジャイアンツのエースの桑田氏はＰＬ学園高等学校の**出身です** Mr. Kuwata, a former Giants ace pitcher, *is a graduate of* PL Gakuen High School.（➤ graduate は「卒業生」）‖私の**出身高校**は以前は女子校だった My *alma mater* used to be a high school for girls.（➤ alma mater /ælmə mɑ́ːṭəʳ/ は「母校」；大学にも使える）‖兄の銀行はＨ大学の**出身者**が多い At my brother's bank, there are a lot of *graduates* [*alumni*] from H University.（➤ alumni /əlʌ́mnaɪ/ は alumnus /əlʌ́mnəs/（男子の卒業生）の複数形．「女子の卒業生」は alumna /əlʌ́mnə/ で複数形は alumnae /əlʌ́mniː/）‖ **対話**「どちらの大学のご出身ですか」「立命館です」"*What university did you graduate from?*" "Ritsumeikan University."

3【その他】▶新内閣の大臣中５人は**官僚出身だ** Five ministers of the new cabinet *were former government officials*.‖彼は労働組合**出身**の議員だ He is a Dietman (originally) *from* a labor union.
‖**出身国** the country where one was born and raised; one's country of origin（➤ 後者は母国のほか，原産国，生産国の意味もある）; one's country of birth（出生国）.

しゅつじん 出陣する take the field ▶いざ**出陣**! It's time to *take the field*! ／It's time to *go into battle*!

じゅっしんほう 十進法 →十進法(じっしんほう).

しゅっせ 出世 success in life; promotion（昇進）**一動** **出世する** succeed in life, get ahead in life（➤ 後者はインフォーマル）; be promoted（昇進する）▶**会社で出世する** *climb up the corporate ladder* ‖**出世**(すること)ばかりが人生じゃない *Getting ahead* is not everything in life.‖彼は**出世**が早かった He *earned quick* [*rapid*] *promotion*.‖きみは友人を裏切ってまで**出世**したいのか Do you want to *get ahead in life* even at the expense of your friends?‖しっかり働かないと**出世**できないぞ! If you don't work hard, you can't *make it in the world*!（➤ make it は「成功する」の意のインフォーマルな言い方）‖彼は**出世コース**を歩んでいる He *is on the fast track*.（➤ the fast track は「出世街道」に相当する）‖きみは私たちのクラスの**出世頭**だね You are *the most successful* among our classmates.‖ヘミングウェーの**出世作** a *work that established* Hemingway *as an author* ‖ここの勘定は**出世**払いでいいよ You can *pay me back after you've been promoted* [*after you have made it to the top*].

しゅっせい 出生 →しゅっしょう.

しゅっせうお 出世魚 a fish whose name changes as it grows larger（➤ 説明的な訳）.

しゅっせき 出席 attendance, presence **一動** **出席する** attend +目; be present《at》（出席している）▶会議に**出席する** *attend* a meeting ‖授業に**出席する** *attend* [*go to*] class ‖私は池田教授の授業には必ず**出席する** I always *attend* Professor Ikeda's class. ／I never miss Professor Ikeda's class.‖その会議は20名が**出席して**行われた The meeting was held with twenty people *present*. ／Twenty people *attended* the meeting.‖**出席を取ります** I'll *call the roll* [*call your names* ／*take attendance* ／*check attendance*].‖友だちの誕生会に**出席していた人たち**の中には，何人か見たことのない顔もあった I saw some unfamiliar faces among *those who were present* at my friend's birthday party.‖その集会は**出席者**が多かった A large number of *people attended* the rally. ／The rally had a large *turnout*.（➤ turnout は「(集会などの)出席者，人出」）‖ **対話**《先生が教室で》「上田君，**出席していますか**」「はい」"*Is* Ueda *present* [*here*]?" "Yes. ／Present. ／Here."
✉ **披露宴へのご招待ありがとうございます．喜んで出席させていただきます** Thank you for inviting me to your wedding reception. I'll be delighted to *attend*.
‖**出席簿** a roll (book).

しゅっそう 出走 ▶100メートル走に**出走する** *run* a 100-meter dash ‖**出走馬** a starter.

しゅつだい 出題 ▶《先生がクラスで》南北戦争は今度の世界史のテストには**出題しない** There will be no *questions* on the Civil War on the coming examination.‖佐藤先生はいつも難問を**出題する** Mr. Sato always *gives* students hard *questions*.

じゅっちゅう 術中 ▶彼はまんまと敵の**術中**にはまった He *fell* right *into* the enemy's *trap*.

じゅっちゅうはっく 十中八九 →じっちゅうはっく.

しゅっちょう 出張 a business trip（商用の）; an official trip（公務による）**一動** **出張する** go ... on business, make a business [an official] trip ▶先月は２度札幌へ**出張した** I *went on* [*made*] *a business trip* to Sapporo twice last month. ／I *went to* Sapporo (*on business*) twice last month.（➤ 同僚や仕事仲間どうしの会話なら後者，それもカッコ内を言わないほうがふつう）‖父は**海外出張**が多い My father often *goes* [*travels*] *abroad on business*.‖**出張所** a branch office ‖**出張旅費** a traveling allowance, travel(ing) expenses.

しゅってい 出廷する appear in court.

1**しゅってん 出典** the source（出所）; a reference（参考にしたもの）▶この句の**出典**がわかりません I don't know *the source* of this phrase.‖**出典**を明らかにしてください Please give *references*.

2**しゅってん 出展** (a) display（陳列）; (an) exhibition /èksɪbíʃən/（公開）**一動** **出展する** display +目, exhibit +目 →出品 ▶油絵を**出展する** *exhibit* [*show*] one's oil painting (at an exhibition).

3**しゅってん 出店する** ▶ユニクロが銀座に**出店した** UNIQLO *opened a store* at Ginza.

しゅつど 出土する be excavated ▶このつぼは建築現場から**出土した**ものだ This pot *was excavated* [*was*

unearthed] at the construction site.
‖出土品 an excavated article [item ／artifact], a finding.

しゅっとう 出頭 ▶その容疑者は両親に付き添われて警察に出頭した The suspect *reported to* [*presented himself at*] *the police* accompanied by his parents.

しゅつどう 出動 ▶事件発生の知らせにすぐさま数台のパトカーが出動した Several police cars *were dispatched* as soon as the incident was reported. ‖政府は地震の被災者救出に自衛隊を出動させた(＝動員した) The government *mobilized* the Self-Defense Forces to rescue the victims of the earthquake.

しゅつにゅうこく 出入国 ▶乗客は全員出入国管理事務所を通らなければなりません All the passengers must go [pass] through *immigration*. ‖出入国記録カード an embarkation, a disembarkation card ‖出入国管理 immigration control.

しゅつば 出馬する run《for》▶鈴木氏が市長選に出馬するとは思わなかった I had no idea that Mr. Suzuki would *be running* in the mayoral election [*be running for* mayor].

しゅっぱつ 出発 departure 一動 出発する leave (+目) (場所を離れる；日常用いる語)；depart《from》(➤主に列車・飛行機などに用いる；日常語としては堅い語) ▶日曜日まで出発を延ばしたい I would like to put off my *departure* until Sunday.

> 【文型】
> A を(B に向かって)出発する
> leave A (for B)
> ➤ leave A for B も可能だが, leave A または leave for B で用いることが多い
> depart from A (for B)

▶翌朝, 私たちはオックスフォードを出発してロンドンに向かった The next morning, we *left* Oxford *for* London. ‖一行はきのうカトマンズを出発した The party *left* Kathmandu yesterday. ‖ニューヨークへはいつ出発？ When are you *leaving for* New York？(➤ leave New York(ニューヨークを発つ)との違いに注意) ‖その飛行機は正午にアトランタに向かって出発した The plane *took off* [*left* ／*departed*] *for* Atlanta at twelve noon. (➤ take off は「離陸する」) ‖このフェリーはあと30分したら出発します This ferryboat is *sailing* [*departing*] in half an hour. ‖あすの朝早く出発しよう Let's *set out* early tomorrow morning. ／Let's *get an* early *start* tomorrow morning. ‖《遠足などで》全員そろったかな？ では出発！ Is everyone present？ O.K. *Let's start* [*go*]！
‖出発点 a starting point；a place of departure (出発地) ‖出発ロビー a departure lounge.
☛ 再出発 (→見出語)

1 **しゅっぱん 出版** publication(出版すること)；publishing(職種) 一動 出版する publish +目 ▶詩集を自費で出版する *publish* a book of poems at one's own expense ‖出版の自由 freedom of *the press* ‖この辞書は2か月前に出版されたばかりの最新の辞書だ This is the most up-to-date dictionary *published* just two months ago. ‖その小説はもう出版されていません(＝絶版である) That novel *is out of print* now.
‖出版界 the publishing world ‖出版社 a publishing company, a publisher ‖出版物 a publication.

2 **しゅっぱん 出帆する** sail《for》, set sail《for》▶豪華客船は神戸からホノルルに向け出帆した The ocean liner *sailed* [*set sail*] from Kobe *for* Honolulu.

しゅっぴ 出費 expenses ▶出費を切り詰める cut down (on) *expenses* ‖今月は出費がかさんだ The *expenses* have piled up this month. ‖テレビが壊れて, 買い換えのために思わぬ出費をした Because our TV set was broken, we had to *spend money* unexpectedly to buy a new one.

しゅっぴん 出品 ▶絵を出品(＝展示)する *exhibit* a picture ‖展覧会に絵を出品する *send* [*submit*] a picture to an exhibition.
‖出品物 an exhibit /ɪgzíbɪt/.

しゅっぺい 出兵 ▶紛争地域に出兵する *send* [*dispatch*] *troops* to a war zone.

しゅつぼつ 出没 ▶最近この辺りにクマが出没する These days, bears *appear now and then* in this area.

しゅつりょう 出漁 ▶この嵐に出漁するなんて無茶だよ You must be out of your mind to *go out fishing* in this storm！

しゅつりょく 出力 ▶出力150馬力のエンジン a *150-horsepower* engine ／an engine *with a capacity of 150* horsepower.
▶《コンピュータで》多量のデータを出力する *output* a lot of data ‖データ[文書]をプリンターで出力する *print out* data [a document].

しゅつるい 出塁する get on base ▶山崎は4度出塁し, 4度とも生還した Yamasaki *got on base* four times and scored each time. ‖イチローは出塁率が高い Ichiro *has a very high on-base percentage*.

しゅと 首都 a capital ▶モスクワはロシアの首都である Moscow is the *capital* of Russia. ‖ペルーの首都はどこですか What is the *capital* of Peru？(➤ 名称を聞くので What ...？とする. Where ... ？とすると地理的な位置を聞くことになる) ‖首都圏の土地は高くてとても手が出ない Land in *the capital region* [in *the Tokyo metropolitan area*] is too expensive for us to buy. ‖首都大学東京 Tokyo Metropolitan University.

しゅとう 種痘 a smallpox vaccination /væ̀ksɪnéɪʃən/.

しゅどう 手動の manual ▶この機械は自動ですか, 手動ですか Is this machine automatic or *manual*？‖このボタンを押せば扉は手動でも開けられます By pressing this button, you can open this door *manually*.

しゅどうけん 主導権 the leadership(指導者の地位・任務)；the initiative /ɪníʃəṭɪv/ (先導) ▶主導権争いをする struggle for *the leadership* ‖彼はそのプランの提案に主導権を取った He *took the initiative* [*the lead*] in proposing the plan. ‖わが家では母が主導権を握っている My mother *wears the pants* in our house. (➤ wear the pants は「(妻が)亭主を尻に敷く」) ‖《テニス》ジョコビッチが錦織のサービスをブレークし, 主導権を握った Djokovic *took charge* by breaking Nishikori's serve.

じゅどうたい 受動態《文法》the passive voice.

じゅどうてき 受動的な passive ▶受動的な態度 a *passive* attitude.

しゅとく 取得する obtain +目 ▶ダイビングの免許を取得する *obtain* a diver's license.

しゅとして 主として mainly, chiefly(主に；後者がより堅い語)；mostly(大部分が) ▶この雑誌は主として女子学生に読まれている This magazine is *mainly* read by female students. ‖乗客は主としてアメリカ人だった The passengers were *mostly* [*for the most part*]

Americans. ／*Most* of the passengers were Americans. →主.

じゅなん 受難 **martyrdom** /má:ʳt̬əʳdəm/ (殉教, 苦難) ; **the Passion** (キリストの) ; **sufferings** (苦労) ▶それはとんだ**受難**だったね That was *hard luck*.

ジュニア **1【若い人】** a **young man** [**woman**] ; **young people** (複数の) ▶**ジュニア**向けの映画 a movie for *young people* ‖ 私の妹はテニスの**ジュニアクラス**で優勝した My sister has won the *junior* tennis tournament.

‖**ジュニア・オールスター** Junior all-star game.

2【二世】 ▶サミー・デービス・**ジュニア** Sammy Davis, *Jr.*

3【プロボクシングの】 ▶**ジュニア**ウェルター [ミドル／ライト] 級 the *junior* welterweight [middleweight／lightweight] class.

> **危ないカタカナ語✸ ジュニア**
> **1** 日本語の「ジュニア」は中学・高校生ぐらいの若い人を指すが, 英語の junior にはこの意味はない.
> **2**「若い人」の意味での「ジュニア」は young man [woman], youngster (主に少年), young people などで表すのがよい.「ジュニア向きのスタイル」などというときは teenage style のように teenage を用いる.
> **3** 英語の junior は「(年齢・地位が) ほかの人より下の (人)」,「(ハイスクールや大学で) 最終学年のすぐ下の学年にいる (生徒・学生)」などの意の形容詞または名詞として用いる.

しゅにく 朱肉 vermilion inkpad [stamp pad] for a hanko (➤ 説明的な訳).

じゅにゅう 授乳する **nurse** +㊐, **breast-feed** +㊐, **suckle** +㊐ (➤ 最後は動物にも使う) ▶**授乳**は３時間置きにしています I *nurse* my baby every three hours. ‖ 赤ん坊に**授乳している**母親 a mother *nursing* [*breast-feeding*] her baby.

しゅにん 主任 a **chief**, a **head** (➤ ともに「長」の意だが, 権威・権限という含みは前者が濃い) ; **the chairperson** (教科主任, 主任教授) ; a **manager** (会社・商店などの) ▶英語 (科) の**主任** the *chairperson* [*head*] of the English department ／ the *chief* English teacher ‖ ３学年の**学年主任**はどなたですか Who is *in charge of* the third *year* (students) ?

‖**主任弁護人** the chief counsel.

しゅぬり 朱塗りの **vermillion-lacquered** (赤漆の) ; **red** (赤い) ▶**朱塗りの**鳥居 a *red* torii [shrine gate] →朱.

ジュネーブ **Geneva** /dʒəní:və/ (スイスの都市 ; Genève はフランス語).

しゅのう 首脳 a **leader** (指導的地位にある人) ; a **head** (首位にある人) ; **the top** (最高位の人 ; ややくだけた語) ▶政府**首脳**が一堂に会してその問題を話し合った *The leaders of the Administration* [*The leading members of the government*] met to confer on the matter. ‖ ８か国**首脳会談**がジュネーブで開かれた The Group-of-Eight *summit conference* was held in Geneva. ‖ 中国は日本との**首脳会談** [**会議**] を拒否した China refused to hold *summit talks* [a *summit meeting*] with Japan.

‖ (会社の) **首脳会議** an executive [a top-level] meeting ‖ (会社の) **首脳陣** the chief [top-level] executives (of a company).

シュノーケル a **snorkel** /snɔ́:ʳkəl/ ▶**シュノーケル**をくわえて潜る dive using *a snorkel* ／go snorkeling.

じゅばく 呪縛 a **spell** ▶**呪縛**を解く break the *spell*.

しゅはん 主犯 **the principal offender**.

しゅひ 守秘 **secrecy** ▶公務員には**守秘義務**がある Public employees are bound by *confidentiality obligations*.

[1]**しゅび 守備** (a) **defense** ; **fielding** (野球の) ▶**守備**に就く *take to the field* ‖ そのチームは**守備**が固い [弱い] ことで知られる That team is known for tight [shaky] *fielding*. ‖ そのバレーボールチームは**守備**が上手だ The players on the volleyball team have good *defensive* skill. ‖ その選手は**守備範囲が広い** The player *covers* [*fields*] *a wide area*.

[2]**しゅび 首尾** ▶彼は**首尾よく**父親の勤める会社に潜り込んだ He *successfully* got a position in the company his father works for. ‖ 子供の言うことだ. **首尾一貫していなくてもしかたがないよ** A child is a child. You can't blame him [her] for not being *consistent*.

じゅひ 樹皮 **bark**.

ジュピター **Jupiter**. →木星.

じゅひょう 樹氷 an **iced-up tree**, a **tree covered with** (**snow and**) **ice** (木) ; (a **coat of snow and**) **ice on a tree** (氷) ▶山の木々は**樹氷**に覆われていた The mountain trees were coated with *ice* (*and snow*).

しゅひん 主賓 **the guest of honor, the chief guest** ▶**主賓**のスピーチ a speech given by *the guest of honor*.

[1]**しゅふ 主婦** a **housewife**, a **homemaker** (➤ 後者は婉曲 (えんきょく) 語で, 男性の「主夫」も指す) ▶**主婦**向けのテニス教室 a tennis class for *housewives* ‖ パートで働く**主婦**がますます増えてきている More and more *housewives* are taking up part-time jobs.

《参考》「働きに出ている主婦」を working wife ということがある.

‖**専業主婦** a (full-time) housewife [homemaker] ; a stay-at-home mother [mom].

[2]**しゅふ 主夫** a **house husband**, a **homemaker** (後者は婉曲 (えんきょく) 語で,「主婦」も指す).

[3]**しゅふ 首府** a **capital**. →首都.

シュプレヒコール a **chorus of shouts** (➤ 日本語はドイツ語 *Sprechchor* から) ▶プラカードを持って**シュプレヒコール**を叫ぶ carry signs and *chant* [*shout*] *slogans*.

じゅふん 受粉 **pollination** ▶ミツバチを使ってリンゴの木に**受粉させる** use honeybees to *pollinate* the apple trees.

[1]**しゅほう 手法** a **technique** /tekní:k/ (芸術上の) ; **technical skill** (技法) ; an **approach** (問題などの取り上げ方) ▶問題解決のために思い切った**手法**をとる take a bold *approach* to solving a problem.

[2]**しゅほう 主峰** **the highest** [**main**] **peak** ▶アルプスの**主峰**モンブラン Mont Blanc, *the highest peak* of the Alps.

しゅぼうしゃ 首謀者 a **ringleader** ▶麻薬密売の**首謀者** the *ringleader* of [behind] the drug dealing.

しゅみ 趣味

1【娯楽】 a **hobby** ; an **interest** (興味のあること) ; a **pastime** (気晴らし, 退屈しのぎ) ; (a) **recreation** (レクリエーション) ; **pleasure** (楽しみ) ▶私の**趣味**は古銭収集と船の模型を作ることです My *hobbies* [*interests*] are collecting old coins and building model ships. ／I collect old coins and build model ships as *hobbies*. ‖ 父の**趣味**はゴルフだ Playing golf is my father's *favorite pastime*. ／ My father plays golf as *a pastime*. ／My father plays golf for *recreation*. ‖ 将来は**趣味と実益を兼ねて**旅行会社に就職したいと思う In the future, I plan to *combine work and pleasure* by working for a travel agency.

あなたの英語はどう響く?

「あなたの趣味は何ですか」を What is your hobby? と訳す人が多いが, How do you spend your free time? や What do you do in your free time? (暇なときは何をしていますか)のような言い方が好ましい. hobby は切手などの収集や, スキューバ, ガーデニングなどのように自分で積極的に作業したり, かなり長期間にわたって打ち込んできたりしたことを指し, 読書・映画・音楽鑑賞などは通例含まない(それらを指すのは pastime). したがって, What is your hobby? と聞けば, I don't have one. (ありません)と答える人がいても不思議ではない. ただし, Do you have a hobby [any hobbies]? と趣味があるかどうかを聞くことはふつう.

2【好み】taste ▶あなたは服装の**趣味がいい**ですね You *have refined* [*fine*] *taste* in clothes. ／You *have* such *good taste* in clothes. (「趣味がいいね!」なら Good taste!) ‖ 彼はひどく**趣味の悪い**冗談をよく言う He often tells very *tasteless* jokes. ‖ 金縁眼鏡に金時計なんて**趣味が悪い**ね Gold-rimmed glasses and a gold watch—*what bad* [*awful* ／*terrible*] *taste!* ‖ この絵は私の**趣味じゃない**わ This painting *isn't to my taste*.

「趣味」のいろいろ **生け花** ikebana ／**エアロビクス** aerobics ／**映画鑑賞** watching movies ／**絵(を描くこと)** painting, drawing ／**園芸** gardening ／**音楽鑑賞** listening to music ／**カラオケ** karaoke ／**切手収集** stamp collecting, philately ／**キャンピング** camping ／**ゴルフ** golf ／**サーフィン** surfing ／**茶道** tea ceremony ／**写真** photography ／**手工芸** handicrafts ／**乗馬** horse riding ／**ジョギング** jogging ／**書道** calligraphy ／**スケートボード** skateboarding ／**ダイビング** diving ／**短歌** tanka ／**ダンス** dancing ／**釣り** fishing ／**手品** magic, trick ／**テニス** tennis ／**陶芸** ceramics, pottery ／**登山** mountain climbing ／**ドライブ** driving ／**バードウォッチング** bird-watching ／**ハイキング** hiking ／**俳句** haiku ／**盆栽** bonsai ／**ヨット** yachting ／**レース編み** crocheting

☛ **悪趣味, 多趣味, 無趣味** (→見出語)

じゅみょう 寿命 life(生命); a **life span**(命の長さ) ▶象は**寿命が長い** Elephants *live for many years*. ／Elephants *have long lives*. ／Elephants *are long-lived* [*live to a great age*]. ‖ おばはがんであと**半年の寿命**だ My aunt *has only half a year to live* because of cancer. ‖ 先日の大地震のときは**寿命**が10年縮まる思いがした That big earthquake we had the other day took ten years off my *life*. ‖ 医学の目覚ましい進歩によって日本では**平均寿命**が年ごとに伸びている Medical breakthroughs keep pushing *life expectancies* higher each year in Japan. (➤ life expectancy はある年齢の人が平均あと何年生きられるかを表す数字).

▶このバッテリーもそろそろ**寿命が来た**な This battery *is almost dead*. ‖ LED電球は白熱電球の40倍**寿命があります** LED light bulbs *last* forty times longer than incandescent ones. ‖ この機械の**寿命**は5年と言われている The *life* of this machine is said to be five years.

しゅもく 種目 an **event** ▶彼は運動会で5**種目**に出場した He competed in five *events* in the athletic meet.

じゅもく 樹木 trees ▶その島は**樹木**に覆われている That island is covered with *trees*.

じゅもん 呪文 (an) **incantation**(一連のまじないの文句; それを唱えること); a **spell** (魔法をかけるときのことば); a **charm** (悪いことを取り除くためのことば) ▶**呪文を唱える** utter *an incantation*.

しゅやく 主役 the leading part [**role**](中心となる役); **the leading actor** (男の), **the leading actress** (女の) ▶その映画の**主役**は13歳の少女が演じた A thirteen-year-old girl played *the leading part* in that film. ／A thirteen-year-old girl starred in that film. ‖ その交渉で**主役を務めた**のは通訳者だったと言っても過言ではないだろう It is not too much to say that interpreters *have played a very important role* in the negotiations.

じゅよ 授与 ▶卒業証書を**授与する** *present* a diploma ‖ 鈴木博士はノーベル化学賞を**授与された** Dr. Suzuki *was awarded* the Nobel Prize for chemistry. ‖ 私の修士号はS大学より**授与された**ものです My M.A. degree *was granted* by S University.

1しゅよう 主要な important(重要な); **principal**(最も重要な); **leading**(先頭に立つ); **major**(規模が大きい); **main**(全体の中で主な); **staple**(中心的な) ▶**主要**科目 an *important* subject ‖ その劇の**主要な**幕 the *principal* act of the play ‖ 静岡県の**主要**産業 the *leading* industry of Shizuoka Prefecture ‖ 私はB先生の講義の**主要な点**をメモした I took notes on the *main* [*key*] *points* of Mr. B's lecture. (➤ key は「重要で欠くことのできない」) ‖ わが社では**主要な**ポストはすべて女性が占めている Women occupy all the *leading* [*key*] positions in our company. ‖ 米は新潟県の**主要産物**の1つだ Rice is one of the *staple* [*main*] *products* of Niigata Prefecture. ‖ うちは全国の**主要都市**(＝大都市)に支店がある We have branch offices in *major* [*principal*] *cities* across the nation.

2しゅよう 腫瘍 a **tumor** /tjúːmər/ ▶良性[悪性]の**腫瘍** a benign [malignant] *tumor* ‖ 胃に**腫瘍**ができたので切ってもらった I got a stomach *tumor* and had to have it operated on.

1じゅよう 需要 demand ▶**需要と供給**のバランス *supply-and-demand* balance (➤日本語と語順が逆の場合が多い) ‖ **国内の需要**を満たすために日本は多くの農産物を輸入している Japan imports a great deal of farm products to meet *domestic demand*. ‖ ウイスキーの**需要**が増えている[減っている] The *demand* for whisky is rising [falling]. ‖ 手作りの家具はこのところ**大いに需要がある** Handmade furniture *is in great demand* these days. ‖ レコードプレーヤーは置いてないんですよ. 最近ではあまり**需要がない**もんですから We don't stock record players—*there isn't much demand for* them nowadays.

2じゅよう 受容する adopt(採用する); **accept**(受け入れる) ▶日本はさまざまな外来文化を**受容してきた** Japan *has adopted* [*accepted*] (elements of) various foreign cultures.

‖**受容性** [**力**] receptivity.

しゅよく 主翼 the wings of an airplane.

しゅらば 修羅場 a (**bloody**) **battlefield**(血生臭い戦場) ▶夫の浮気がばれて, 夫婦はその夜**修羅場を演じた** The night when the husband's affair was found out, the couple *had an ugly* [*a messy*] *fight*.

ジュラルミン duralumin /djurǽljəmən/ ▶3億円の入った**ジュラルミンの箱** *a duralumin box* containing three hundred million yen.

じゅり 受理する **accept** +目 (納得して受け取る) ; **receive** (単に受け取る) ▶入学願書を受理する *receive* an application for admission (to a university) ‖申請書は受理されなかった The application *was not accepted*.

じゅりつ 樹立する **establish** +目 ▶南スーダンとの国交を樹立する *establish* diplomatic relations with South Sudan ‖新政権を樹立する *form* [*establish*] a new government ‖彼は三段跳びで日本新記録を樹立した He *established* a new Japanese record in the triple jump.

しゅりゅう 主流 **the mainstream** (思想や運動の) ▶自民党の主流派 the *mainstream faction* of the LDP ‖主流のプロテスタント宗派 a *mainstream* Protestant denomination ‖10年後には電気自動車が主流になるかもしれない Electric cars may *become mainstream* ten years from now. ‖ 5年前はスカートはロングが主流だったが, 今はミニが復活した Five years ago long skirts *were the vogue*, but now miniskirts have come back into fashion. (➤ vogue は「流行」) ‖赤ちゃんには母乳がいちばん良いという考え方が現在では主流を占めている Today it is the *predominant* [*mainstream*] view that mother's milk is best for babies.

しゅりゅうだん 手榴弾 a **grenade** /grɪnéɪd/, a **hand grenade**.

1**しゅりょう 狩猟** **hunting**, **shooting** 《解説》hunting はアメリカでは銃猟(hunting with a gun)を, イギリスではキツネ狩り(fox hunting)をそれぞれ指す. イギリスでは銃猟は shooting という ▶狩猟に出かける *go hunting* [*shooting*].

2**しゅりょう 首領** a **leader** ; a **ringleader** (首謀者) ▶あの男は犯罪組織の首領だ He is the *leader* of a crime ring. / He is the *ringleader* of a criminal organization.

じゅりょう 受領 ▶金参万円確かに受領いたしました *Received* the sum of thirty thousand yen. ‖受領証 a receipt /rɪsíːt/.

しゅりょく 主力の **main** ▶ことしは小型車の販売に主力を注いでもらいたい This year I want you to *concentrate on* selling small cars. ‖彼は日本チームの主力選手だ He is a *key player* on the Japanese team.

‖主力商品 main items, main products.

じゅりん 樹林 a **forest** ▶針葉[落葉]樹林 a coniferous [deciduous] *forest*.

しゅるい 種類 a **kind**, a **sort** ; a **species** (生物学上の「種」) ▶世間には2種類の人がいる—犬の好きな人と猫の好きな人と There are *two kinds of* people in this world—those who like dogs and those who like cats. ‖私はああいう種類の映画は見ません I don't watch *that kind of* movies. / I don't watch movies *of that kind*. (➤ 後者は主に書きことばでの言い方) ‖ぼくはあいつらがあんな種類の人間だとは思わなかった I did not think they were *that sort of* people. (➤ sort は kind よりくだけた語で, ときに軽蔑的なニュアンスをもつ) ‖彼はあらゆる種類のツバキを育てている He grows *all kinds of* camellias [*every variety of* camellia]. (➤ variety は同類ではあるが細かな点で異なっている場合) ‖ 対話 「おたくの店にはどんな種類の花が置いてありますか」「季節の花ならいろいろありますよ」"What *kinds* of flowers do you carry in your shop?" "We sell a wide range of seasonal flowers."

▶この種類のトンボはこの地方にはいない This *species* of dragonfly is not found in this area. ‖イルカはクジラと同じ種類の動物だ The dolphin belongs to the same *species* as the whale. ‖犬は種類が多い There are many different *breeds* of dogs. (➤ breed は「(動植物の)品種」).

> **直訳の落とし穴「500種類の切手」**
> 「私は500種類以上の切手を集めた」を I have collected more than five hundred kinds of stamps. としがち. 英語使用者の感覚ではここで言う stamp はどれも postage stamp で1種類(あるいは, 記念切手・通常切手など数種類)なので, kinds を用いず, I have collected more than five hundred different stamps. とするのが自然. 同様に, 「私は2種類の英字新聞を読んでいる」も I read two kinds of English-language newspapers. ではなく, I read two (different) English-language newspapers. とする.

じゅれい 樹齢 **the age of a tree** ▶この桜の木は樹齢150年と言われている This cherry tree is said to be one hundred and fifty *years old*.

シュレッダー a **shredder** ▶文書をシュレッダーにかける *put* a document *into a shredder* / *shred* a document.

しゅろ 棕櫚 《植物》a **hemp palm** /pɑːm/.

しゅわ 手話 **sign language** ▶彼らは手話で話をしていた They were talking in *sign language*.

じゅわき 受話器 a **receiver** ▶受話器を取ったとたん電話が切れた The instant I picked up the *receiver*, the connection was broken. (➤「受話器を戻す」は put down the receiver) ‖受話器はそのままでお待ちください *Hold on*, please. (➤ 決まった言い方).

しゅわん 手腕 (an) **ability** ▶大臣として見事な政治的手腕を発揮する show one's outstanding *political ability* as a minister ‖いよいよきみが手腕を発揮するときが来たぞ Now is the time to *show your stuff*. (➤インフォーマルな言い方).

しゅん 旬 (the) **season** ▶旬の味 the delicacies of *the season* ‖サンマは今が旬だ Pacific saury *are in season* now. ‖野菜は旬のものがいちばんおいしい Vegetables are more delicious *in season*. ‖果物は旬を過ぎると風味が落ちる Fruits don't have as much flavor when they are *out of season*.

1**じゅん 順** **order** (順序) ; one's **turn** (順番) ▶背の順に並びなさい Stand *in order of height*. / Line up *in order of short-to-tall*. ‖カードをアルファベット順に並べなさい Put the cards *in alphabetical order*. ‖先着順にお座りください Please sit *in order of arrival*. ‖私はサラダ, 魚, フルーツの順に食べた I ate the salad *first*, *then* fish, *then* fruit. ‖どうぞ順にお入りください Come in *in turn*, please. (➤「順番に」の意) / Come in *one at a time*, please. (➤「1人ずつ」の意).

▶《試験後に》解答用紙を順に前に送って *Pass* your answer sheet *forward*, everyone! ‖順を追って話をしていただけませんか Could you give us your account *in order*, please? →順不同.

2**じゅん 純** ▶純日本風の家 a house in *pure* Japanese style / a *100 percent* Japanese-style house ‖純日本風の髪型 a *purely* Japanese hairstyle ‖彼女は純な娘だと思っていたらかなりすれていた Though I thought she was (just) an *innocent* girl, she turned out to be quite experienced.

じゅん‐ 準‐ semi- /sémi, sémaɪ/ (半…, やや…) ▶準公式試合 a *semi*regular-season game ‖ 準ミス東京 the Miss Tokyo *runner-up* ‖ クラブの準会員 *an associate member* of a club ‖ 準優勝する *take second place* (➤「準優勝者」は the second winner).

じゅんあい 純愛 pure and innocent love ▶2人の愛は純愛だった Their love was *pure and innocent*. ‖純愛物語 a pure love story.

じゅんい 順位 (a) ranking (序列, ランキング) ▶今週のヒットチャートの順位を教えてよ Tell me the *rankings* (of the songs) in this week's hit chart. ‖ 私は成績の順位は(＝成績では)クラスでトップです I'm at the top of my class *in grades*. ‖ 駅伝には20校が参加して順位を争った Twenty schools took part in the *ekiden* race and *contended for the lead*. ‖(同点者間の)順位決定戦 a play-off ‖(スポーツの)順位表 standings.

じゅんえき 純益 a net profit.

じゅんえん 順延する postpone +㊐, 《インフォーマル》 put off ⚠「順繰りに期日を延ばすこと」の意の「順延」にぴったりの英語はないので, 用例のように「いついつまで」のような説明語句を添える. ▶雨のため試合は来週まで順延となった Because of the rain, the game *was put off* till next week. ‖ 雨のため日本シリーズは(好天になるまで)順延された The Japan Series *was postponed* till the first clear day.

じゅんおくり 順送り ▶回覧板を順送りにする *pass on* a circular notice.

しゅんが 春画 a *shunga*, a sexually explicit picture (➤ 説明的な訳).

じゅんかい 巡回 round(s) ; patrol (警官の) ▶巡回中の警官 a police officer *on patrol* (*duty*) [*on his* [*her*] *beat*] ‖(自動車による)巡回図書館 a mobile library, 《米》 a bookmobile.

しゅんかしゅうとう 春夏秋冬 ▶アファンの森は春夏秋冬の趣がある Afan Woodland has a charm of its own, *through spring, summer, autumn and winter* [*all year round* / *through the year*].

じゅんかつゆ 潤滑油 lubricating oil, (a) lubricant /lúːbrɪkənt/ ▶《比喩的》赤ん坊があの(仲のよくない)夫婦の潤滑油らしいよ I'm told their baby is *what holds their marriage together*.

しゅんかん 瞬間 a moment, an instant (➤ 後者のほうがより短い) ▶決定的瞬間 a decisive *moment* ‖ 最大瞬間風速60メートルを記録した A *maximum instantaneous wind speed* of 60 meters per second was recorded.
▶息子の悲しそうな顔を見た瞬間私ははっとした *The moment* [*instant*] I saw my son's sorrowful face, I was startled. (➤ The moment [instant] ... は As soon as... と同意で,「…した瞬間」) ‖ ちょうど電話を切った瞬間, 彼が部屋に駆け込んで来た *Just as* [*The moment*] I hung up the receiver, he ran into the room. ‖ 今この瞬間にもどこかでたくさんの子供たちが餓死しようとしている Somewhere *this very moment* lots of children are dying of starvation.

じゅんかん 循環 circulation 一動 循環する circulate ▶入浴は血液の循環をよくする Taking a bath is good for the *circulation*. ‖ 血液は絶え間なく人体を循環している Blood *is* constantly *circulating* through the human body.
‖循環器 a circulatory organ ‖ 循環器科 a cardiovascular clinic ‖ 循環バス a loop-line bus.
☛ 悪循環 (→見出語)

じゅんかんごし 准看護師 《米》 a licensed practical nurse, 《英》 a state enrolled nurse.

しゅんき 春季 springtime ; spring (春) ▶春季合宿 a *spring* training camp ‖ 春季交通安全運動 a *spring* traffic safety campaign.

じゅんきゅう 準急 a semi-express train.

じゅんきょ 準拠 ▶この問題集は教科書に準拠して作成してある This workbook has been compiled *based on* [*in accordance with*] the textbook.

1**じゅんきょう 殉教する** become a martyr ▶殉教者 a *martyr* /máːʳṭəʳ/.

2**じゅんきょう 順境** a favorable [an ideal] environment ▶順境で育つ grow up *in an ideal environment*.

じゅんぎょう 巡業 a tour /tʊəʳ/ ▶私たちの劇団は地方巡業中です Our theatrical company is *on the road* [*on tour in the provinces*] right now.

じゅんきょうじゅ 准教授 an associate professor (➤ 大学によっては准教授を上級准教授 senior associate professor と准教授 associate professor とに分けている).

じゅんきん 純金 pure gold ▶純金のネックレス a necklace of *pure gold*.

じゅんぐり 順繰り ▶兄弟が多かったので服はいつも順繰りにお下がりになった As I had many brothers, our clothes were always handed down *in turn* [*by turns*].

1**じゅんけつ 純潔** virginity (処女[童貞]であること) ; purity (道徳的汚れのないこと) ▶純潔を守る[失う] keep [lose] one's *virginity*.

2**じゅんけつ 純血の** full-blooded
‖純血種 a thoroughbred, a purebred.

じゅんけっしょう 準決勝 a semifinal (1試合), the semifinals (全体) ▶準決勝に駒を進める make it into *the semifinals*. →準々決勝.

しゅんこう 竣工 completion of construction ▶しゅんこう1999年8月 *Completed* in August, 1999 ‖ 新しい橋のしゅんこう式が行われた *A ceremony was held to celebrate the completion* of the new bridge.

じゅんこう 巡航する cruise /kruːz/ ‖巡航速度 a cruising speed ‖ 巡航ミサイル a cruise missile.

じゅんさ 巡査 a police officer, a policeman (男), a policewoman (女), 《英 また》 a police constable /kʌ́nstəbəl/
‖巡査長 a senior policeman [policewoman] (日本の), 《米》 a master police officer, 《英》 a sergeant /sɑ́ːʳdʒənt/ ‖ 巡査部長 a police sergeant (日米の), 《英》 a senior sergeant.

しゅんじ 瞬時に instantly (ほんの一瞬で) ; with no time lag (時間のずれもなく) ▶インターネットを使えば瞬時にアメリカの友人にEメールを送ることができる You can send email *instantly* to your friends in America through the Internet.

じゅんし 殉死する kill oneself on the death of one's lord (主君に) ; die a martyr (殉教者として).

じゅんじ 順次 ▶急を要するものから順次話し合っていこう Let's discuss the problems *one by one* according to their urgency. ‖ 試合の進行状況は順次報告します I'll keep you informed on the game *as it progresses*.

じゅんしせん 巡視船 a patrol boat.

じゅんしゅ 遵守する abide by (忠実に守る) ; obey +㊐ (従う) ▶ルールを遵守する *abide by* the rule ‖ 日本人の多くは法律を遵守する Most Japanese are *law-abiding* people.

1 **じゅんじゅん 諄々と** ▶息子に喫煙の危険性をじゅんじゅんと説いた I explained the danger of smoking *over and over* to my son so that he would understand it well.（➤over and over は「何度も」）.

2 **じゅんじゅん 順々に** **in turn**（順番に）; **one by one**（一つ一つ）▶学生たちは順々に立ち上がって名前を言った The students stood up *in turn* and gave their names. ‖順々に仕事を済ませていきましょう Let's do the jobs *one by one*.

じゅんじゅんけっしょう 準々決勝 a **quarterfinal**（１試合）, **the quarterfinals**（全体）.

じゅんじょ 順序 **order** ▶家を建てるには順序というものがある There's a certain *order* in building a house. ‖数字の順序が狂っている The numbers are *out of order* [*in the wrong order*]. ‖もう一度初めから順序立てて話してください Can you start from the beginning again and tell me what happened *in order*?

じゅんじょう 純情 ▶純情な乙女心を傷つけるとは悪い男だ What a lout he is to hurt [have hurt] the feelings of such a *pure, sweet* girl! ‖あなたって意外に純情ね！ I'm surprised that you're so *naive*.（➤ naive は「純真な, うぶな」の意だが,「単純で無知な」という含みがあることも多い）.

1 **じゅんしょく 殉職** ▶警官２人がライフル銃を持った男の手にかかって殉職した Two policemen *were killed in the line of duty* by a man with a rifle.（➤ in the line of duty は「職務中に」）.

‖殉職者 a victim to one's duty.

2 **じゅんしょく 潤色** **embroidery** ▶話を潤色する *embroider* a story.

じゅんじる 準じる **1【同じ扱いをする】**▶当社ではパートの労働者も正社員に準じて（＝正社員同様に）支払われている In our company, part-time workers are *as well* paid *as* regular employees.

2【ある規則に応じる】▶我々は収入の額に準じて税金を納めなければならない We have to pay taxes *proportionate to* our income.（➤ proportionate は「釣り合った, 比例した」）.

じゅんしん 純真 ▶純真な青年 an *unsophisticated* young man ‖子供の純真な笑顔は心を和ませる The *innocent* smile of a child is heart-warming.

じゅんすい 純粋の **pure** /pjʊəʳ/（まじりけのない）; **genuine** /dʒénjuın/（本物の）▶純粋のアルコール *pure* [*100%*] alcohol ‖彼の純粋なところが好き I like him because he's *genuine and sincere*.（➤ sincere は「表裏のない, 正直な」. He's pure. は「彼は純潔だ」の意にもなる）‖彼女は純粋のペルシャ猫を飼っている She has a *pedigree* [*pure-blooded*] Persian cat.（➤ pedigree は「血統書付きの」の意 ; pedigreed ともいう）.

じゅんせい 純正の **pure**（純粋の）; **genuine**（本物の）

‖純正部品 genuine parts ‖純正食品 (a) pure food.

しゅんせつ 浚渫 ▶運河をしゅんせつする *dredge* a canal ‖しゅんせつ船 a dredger.

じゅんぜん 純然 ▶これは純然たる（＝明白な）詐欺行為だ This is *outright* fraud.

しゅんそく 俊足 a **fast runner**（足の速い人）▶江田君は俊足だ Eda is *a fast runner*. ‖走者は俊足を飛ばして一塁から一挙にホームインした The runner *raced* home all the way from first.（➤ race は「全速力で走る」）.

じゅんたく 潤沢な **ample**, **abundant** ▶潤沢な資金 *ample* funds.

じゅんちょう 順調 ▶順調にいけば, この仕事はことし中に終わるでしょう *If things go well*, I will finish this job sometime this year. ‖仕事は順調に進んでいますか Is your work moving along [proceeding] *smoothly*? ／Is your work coming along *well*? ‖すべて順調です Everything *is going all right* [*O.K.*]. ／Things *are going well*. ‖患者は順調に快方に向かっている The patient is *well* on the way to recovery.

じゅんて 順手 ▶順手に握る grip (a horizontal bar) *overhand*.

しゅんと ▶余裕しゃくしゃくだった山口君もテストの結果が悪くてしゅんとなってしまった After swaggering around as if the test would be so easy for him, Yamaguchi really *felt small* when he got a bad score on it.（➤ feel small は「しょげる」）.

じゅんど 純度 **purity** ▶純度95パーセントの金 95 percent *pure* gold ‖金を95パーセントの純度に精製する refine gold to 95 percent *purity*.

しゅんとう 春闘 a **spring (labor) offensive.**

じゅんとう 順当 ▶横綱・大関陣は順当に勝ち進んだ The yokozuna(s) and ozeki(s) went on winning *as might have been expected*.（➤「予想どおり」の意）.

じゅんのう 順応する **adapt** (oneself)《to》▶環境に順応する *adapt* [*adjust* ／ *accommodate*] *oneself to* one's environment（➤ adjust には自分を巧妙に適応させるというニュアンスがある）‖彼女は順応性に欠けている She lacks *adaptability*. ‖人間は最も順応性のある動物の１つだ Humans are one of the most *adaptable* animals.

じゅんぱく 純白の **pure white**; **snow-white**（雪のように白い）▶彼女は純白のウエディングドレスに身を包んでいた She wore a *pure white* wedding dress.

しゅんぱつりょく 瞬発力 **instantaneous muscular strength.**

じゅんばん 順番 one's **turn**（自分の番）; **order**（順序）▶きちんと順番を待ちなさい Wait your *turn* properly. ‖彼は献血の順番を待っていた He was waiting (for) his *turn* to donate (his) blood. ‖名簿の順番が狂ってるよ These names are *in the wrong order*. ‖生徒たちは順番にバスに乗った The students got on the bus *in order* [*one after another*].（➤ 前者は「順序よく」, 後者は「１人ずつ」; →順々に）‖生徒たちは順番に教室の前に出て自分の俳句を発表した The students came to the front of class *in turn* to recite their haiku(s). ‖私にもそれ使わせてよ. 順番でしょ！ Let me use it now! *It's my turn* [*We're supposed to take turns*]! ‖その保育園（の入園）は順番待ちの状態です The day care center has *a waiting list*.

じゅんび 準備

preparation (s) 一動 **準備する** **make preparations**《for》, **prepare**《for, to do》, **get ready**《for, to do》

> **語法「準備する」の言い方**
> (1) 大がかりな[正式な]準備を必要とする場合は make preparations, 大して大がかりな[正式な]準備を必要としない場合は prepare, またはそのややインフォーマルな言い方である get ready を一応の目安にするとよい. (2) 朝食や昼食のようなごく日常的な準備には, インフォーマルな動詞の fix を用い, かなりの準備を必要とする夕食なら prepare や get ready を用いるとよい.

▶大統領訪問の準備をする *make preparations for*

the president's visit ‖ 結婚披露宴は準備が大変だ A wedding reception involves a lot of *preparation*. ‖ 会議の準備はこれで整いましたね We have made all the necessary *preparations for* the meeting, haven't we? ‖ クラス全員が体育祭の準備に大わらわだ All the members in the class are in a hectic rush *preparing for* the athletic meet. ‖ 私たちは学園祭のためのあらゆる準備をした We *got* everything *ready for* our school festival. ‖ カナダ旅行の準備はできましたか *Are* you *ready for* your trip to Canada? ‖ いつでも出発できるように準備しておきなさいよ *Be prepared* to leave at any time. ‖ 夕食の準備ができました Dinner *is ready*. ‖ 準備完了 (*It's*) *all set*. ／*Everything's ready now*.

▶母は昼食の準備をしている My mother *is fixing* [*cooking*] lunch. ‖ 泳ぐ前には必ず準備運動をすべきだ You should always do some *warm-up exercise* before swimming. ‖ あのレストランはまだ準備中だ(＝開いていない) That restaurant *is not open yet*.

じゅんぷう 順風 a **fair** [**favorable**] **wind** ▶ヨットは順風に乗って帆走していた The yacht was sailing *with the wind*.

▶《比喩的》私たちの結婚生活は必ずしも順風満帆ではありませんでした Our marriage life was not all *smooth sailing*. (➤ smooth sailing は「順調な航海」の意で, 比喩的にも用いられる).

じゅんふどう 順不同 ▶ 対話 「この名前はあいうえお順になっていますか」「いえ順不同です」 "Are these names put in a-i-u-e-o sound order?" "No, they are *in random order*."

《参考》掲示の「順不同」は Not in order. とか, Names are given in random order. といえばよい.

しゅんぶん 春分 **the spring** [**vernal**] **equinox** /ékwɪnɑ̀:ks/ ‖ 春分の日 Spring Equinox Day.

じゅんぶんがく 純文学 **serious literature, belles-letters.**

じゅんぽう 遵法 ‖ 遵法闘争 《米》 a work-by-the-book tactic, 《英》 a work to rule.

じゅんぼく 純朴 ▶チベットの人たちは純朴だ (The) Tibetans are *plain and honest* people.

しゅんみん 春眠 ▶春眠暁を覚えず Spring slumber doesn't know daybreak.

しゅんめ 駿馬 a **fast** [**speed**] **horse**.

じゅんもう 純毛 **pure wool** /wʊl/ ▶純毛のセーター a sweater *made of pure wool*.

じゅんようかん 巡洋艦 a **cruiser** /krú:zəʳ/.

じゅんれい 巡礼 a **pilgrimage** /pílgrɪmɪdʒ/ (旅); a **pilgrim** (人) ▶四国巡礼の旅に出かける go on (*a*) *pilgrimage* in Shikoku.

じゅんろ 順路 a **route** /ru:t/ ▶順路に従って進む follow *the* (*regular*) *route* ‖ お客さま, そちらは出口になります. こちらが順路です Excuse me, sir. That's the exit. This is *the route to follow*.

しょ 書 **calligraphy, Japanese calligraphy** (書道); **penmanship** (ペン習字の場合).

しょあく 諸悪 ▶官僚(機構)が諸悪の根源だと言う人もいる Some people say bureaucracy is *the root of all evil*.

じょい 女医 a **woman doctor** [複 **women doctors**]

《参考》ふつうは Mrs. Norman is a doctor. のように単に doctor という.

しょいこむ 背負い込む ▶何もきみが責任を全部しょい込むことはないよ You don't have to *shoulder* all the responsibility by yourself. ‖ やっかいな仕事をしょい込んだものだね What a difficult job you'*re saddled* [*stuck*] *with*!

ジョイント a **joint** (継ぎ目, 継ぎ手)

‖ ジョイントコンサート a joint concert ‖ ジョイントベンチャー a joint venture.

[1]**しよう 使用** **use** /ju:s/ 一動 **使用する** **use** /ju:z/ ＋目 ▶使用済みの乾電池 a *used* battery ‖ 使用していない部屋 an *unused* room ‖ そのテストでは辞書の使用は許されなかった The *use* of [*Using*] a dictionary was not allowed during the test. ‖ この傘は自由にご使用ください Please *make free use of* [*help yourself to*] these umbrellas. ‖ このパソコンの使用法を教えてください Please show me *how to use* this PC. ‖ この電話番号は現在使用されておりません This telephone number *is no longer in service* [*in use*]. ‖ トイレは使用中だった The lavatory *was occupied*.

《参考》トイレ・浴室・暗室などに「使用中」の札を下げる場合は Occupied または Engaged とする ‖《掲示》使用禁止 Do Not Use ‖《エレベーターなどの》使用中止 Out of Use ‖《トイレなどの掲示》従業員も使用いたします Please pardon our appearance.

‖ 使用者 a user (利用者); a consumer (消費者); an employer (雇い主) ‖ 使用 [取り扱い] 説明書 instructions, an instruction manual ‖ 使用人 an employee /ɪmplɔ́ɪi:/; a servant (召し使い) ‖ 使用料 the rental fee (コピー機などの); the rental charge (スキー・スケートなどの); a royalty (著作権使用料).

[2]**しよう 私用** **private use** 一形 **私用の** **private** ▶会社の電話を私用に使わないように Don't use the office telephone *to make personal calls* [*for private purposes*]. ‖ 彼女が大阪へ行ったのは仕事ではなく私用だった It was not on company business, but on *private business* [*on a private errand*] that she went to Osaka.

[3]**しよう 試用** ▶あの運転手を1週間試用してみたらどうですか Why don't you *take* that driver *on trial* for a week? ‖ 試用期間 a trial period.

[4]**しよう 仕様** **1** 【方法】 a **way** ▶返事のしようがないので私は黙っていた There was no *way* I could answer, so I kept my mouth shut. →しようがない.

2 【仕立て】 ▶特別仕様の車 a car *with specific modifications* ／a car made to meet *specific needs*.

‖ 仕様書 specifications.

[5]**しよう 枝葉** **unimportant** [**minor**] **details** (さまつ); **branches and leaves** (枝と葉) ▶枝葉末節にこだわる be too concerned about *minor details*.

-しよう **1** 【勧誘】 **Let's ...** ▶これから15分間休憩しよう *Let's* take a fifteen-minute break. ‖ もうけんかはやめにしよう *Let's stop* fighting. ／*Let's not* [*Don't let's*] quarrel with each other any more. (➤ Don't let's は主に《英》) ‖ きょうの午後私の家で勉強しようよ *Why not* study at my house this afternoon?

2 【意志】 ▶きょうは雨が降っているから洗濯はあしたにしよう I'*ll* do the laundry tomorrow since it's raining today. ‖ これ以上あの生徒を問い詰めないことにしよう I *won't* question that student any more. → -よう.

[1]**しょう 性** ▶教師という職業は私の性に合っている I think that teaching *is right for* me. ‖ ぜいたくは私の性に合わない Luxury *doesn't suit* me.

[2]**しょう 賞** a **prize** (主に試合・レースなどの勝者への); an **award** (正式な審査員によって決定された) ▶賞を取る win *a prize* ‖ グラミー賞を取る take a *Grammy* ‖ 誰

が1等賞を取ったのかな I wonder who won (*the*) *first prize*. ‖あの作家は直木賞を受賞した That writer was awarded *the Naoki Prize*.

‖アカデミー賞 an Academy Award ‖2020年のアカデミー作品賞 the Best Picture Academy Award for 2020 ‖金［銀／銅］賞 a gold [silver／bronze] (award) ‖ノーベル物理学［平和］賞 a Nobel prize for physics [peace].

³しょう 章 a **chapter** ▶この物語は8つの章から成っている This story is made up of eight *chapters*. ‖第2章を要約しなさい Summarize *Chapter II* [*the second chapter*].

⁴しょう 商《数学》**the quotient** /kwóuʃənt/.

⁵しょう 省 a **ministry**(日本・イギリスの), a **department**(アメリカの) ▶外務［財務］省 *the Ministry* of Foreign Affairs [Finance] ‖(アメリカの)商務省 *the Department* of Commerce.

> 日本の「省」のいろいろ 総務省 Ministry of Internal Affairs and Communications／法務省 Ministry of Justice／外務省 Ministry of Foreign Affairs／財務省 Ministry of Finance／文部科学省 Ministry of Education(, Culture, Sports, Science and Technology)／環境省 Ministry of the Environment／厚生労働省 Ministry of Health, Labour and Welfare／農林水産省 Ministry of Agriculture(, Forestry and Fisheries)／経済産業省 Ministry of Economy, Trade and Industry／国土交通省 Ministry of Land, Infrastructure, Transport and Tourism／防衛省 Ministry of Defense

⁶しょう 小 ▶(生ビールは)大・中それとも小にしますか Large, medium, or *small*? ‖高山は「小京都」として一般に知られている Takayama is popularly known as '*Little Kyoto*.'

¹-しょう -性 ▶私の肌は脂性だ I have *greasy* [*oily*] *skin*. ‖母はひどく心配性だ My mother is *a worrywart* [*a* (terrible) *worrier*].

²-しょう -勝 a **win** ▶我々のチームは3勝1敗だった Our team had three *wins* and one loss. ／Our team *won* three games and lost one (game). ‖阪神は中日には8勝5敗だ The Tigers are *8-5* against the Dragons. ‖その投手は今季8勝目を上げた The pitcher chalked up his *8th win* this season.

じよう 滋養 **nourishment**(栄養分).

¹じょう 上 ▶わが家の暮らしは中の上といったところです We are in the *upper-middle* class. ‖弟の成績はクラスで上の部に入る My brother is *one of the top students* in his class. ‖《すし屋で》握りの上をお願いします I'd like '*jo*-nigiri' (*better-quality* nigiri), please.

²じょう 情 **emotion**(感情); **affection** (愛情) ▶情の籠った手紙 an *affectionate* letter ‖情のある人 a *warmhearted* person ‖彼女は情にもろく, すぐほろりとする She is *emotional* [*tenderhearted*／*soft* (-) *hearted*] and is easily moved to tears. ‖この詩は親子の情を表現したものだ This poem expresses the *affection between parent and child*. ‖この不況下, 彼を解雇するのは情に忍びない I *don't have the heart* to dismiss him in this recession. ‖長い年月一緒に暮らしていると他人といえどもお互いに情が移るものだ Although we're not related, we have *grown close* to each other after living together for so many years.

³じょう 錠 **1**【錠前】a **lock** ▶泥棒は特殊な道具でその金庫の錠を開けた The thief opened the *lock* of that safe with a special tool. (➤ふつうに「錠を開ける」は unlock) ‖その物置小屋は中から錠が下ろしてあった The shed *was locked* from the inside. ‖このドアはなかなか錠がかからない This door will not *lock*. →鍵.

2【錠剤】a **tablet** ▶アスピリンを2錠飲んでおきなさい Take two *tablets* of aspirin. ／Take two aspirins.

¹-じょう -上 ▶地球上で話されているあらゆる言語 all (the) languages spoken *on the earth* [*planet*] ‖金銭上の問題 a question [matter] *of money* ‖これは理論上は可能だが, 実際上は不可能だ *In theory* this is possible, *in practice* it is not. ‖それが彼女の性格上の大きな欠点だ That is a serious defect *in her character*. ‖車両には構造上の欠陥が生じている The cars have developed *structural* defects.

²-じょう -条 ▶日本国憲法第9条 *Article 9* of the Japanese Constitution.

³-じょう -乗 **the ...th power** ▶3の6乗 *the 6th power* of 3／3^6 (➤後者は three (raised) to the sixth power または three to the power of six と読む) ‖4を2乗する *raise* four *to the second power*.

⁴-じょう -畳 ▶8畳間 an *eight-tatami* [*eight-mat*] room ‖この部屋は何畳ですか *How many* (*tatami*) *mats* does this room have?

じょうあい 情愛 **affection** ▶夫婦の情愛 *affection* between husband and wife.

しょうあく 掌握する **seize** +㊐ ▶その政党がついに政権を掌握した That political party has finally *seized* [*assumed*] power. ‖あの監督は選手たちをしっかり掌握しているとは思えない That manager doesn't seem to *have* [*to be in*] *control* over the players.

じょうい 上位 ▶上位に食い込む climb into *higher ranks* ‖上位3名の選手 the *best three* players ‖この100名の中から上位10名を学校代表とします We'll select *the top ten students* out of these 100 to represent our school. ‖今は多方面にわたって女性上位の時代だ This is the age of *female dominance* in many different fields.

じょういかたつ 上意下達の **top-down** ▶上意下達の組織 a *top-down* organization.

しょういだん 焼夷弾 a **firebomb**, an **incendiary bomb**.

しょういん 勝因 **the cause of victory** ▶白鵬関, ずばり勝因は何ですか *What* exactly *made you win*, Hakuho-zeki? ‖楽天イーグルスの勝因としてはまず第一に田中の好投が挙げられる The primary *cause of* the Eagles' *victory* was Tanaka's good pitching.

¹じょういん 上院 **the Upper House**(各国共通); **the Senate** /sénət/(アメリカ・カナダ・オーストラリア・イタリア・フランスなどの); **the House of Lords**(イギリスの)

‖上院議員《米》a Senator,《英》a member of the House of Lords.

²じょういん 乗員 →乗務員.

しょううちゅう 小宇宙 a **microcosm** /máikrəkɑ̀:zəm/ ▶人間は各自一種の小宇宙である Each human being is a kind of *microcosm*.

じょうえい 上映する **show**(+㊐) (➤「(映画が)上映される」という自動詞の意もある) ▶スバル座で上映中の映画 a film *currently showing* at the Subaru-za ‖その映画は近日上映の予定です The film is scheduled to *be shown* in a few days. (➤「近日上映の

映画」は a forthcoming film) ‖ 当劇場では子供向けの映画しか上映しません Our theater *shows* only films for children. ‖ あの劇場では今何の映画が上映されていますか What movie *is* now *showing* at that theater?

しょうエネ 省エネ energy saving [conservation] ━ 形 **省エネの energy-efficient, energy-saving** ▶省エネ照明 *energy-efficient* lighting ‖ 省エネビル an *energy-efficient* building ‖ 省エネにご協力お願いします Please help to *save* [*conserve*] *energy*. (➤ conserve は「長くもつように大切に使う」) ‖ 省エネのため室温は摂氏28度に保っています In order to *save energy*, the room temperature is kept at 28℃.

じょうえん 上演する stage +㊐ ▶国立劇場で上演中の芝居 a play *currently running* at the National Theater ‖ この芝居はパリで上演され好評を博した This play *was staged* in Paris and was well received (there).

じょうおん 常温 room temperature(室温).

しょうおんき 消音器 a **silencer**, 《英》 a **muffler** (車の); a **silencer**(銃の).

1**しょうか 消化** 1【食物の】**digestion** ━ 動 **消化する digest** /daɪdʒést/ (+㊐) ▶この薬は消化を助ける This medicine helps the [your] *digestion*. ‖ うどんは体が温まるし消化もよい Udon noodles warm you up and *are easy to digest*. ‖ あの子はナッツを食べ過ぎて消化不良を起こしたから, 2, 3日は消化のよい食べ物をとらねばならないでしょう He has *indigestion* because he ate too many nuts. He will have to have only *light* meals for a few days.

‖消化器官 digestive organs; the digestive system (器官全体) ‖ 消化剤 a digestive.

2【十分に理解すること】▶その本はまだよく消化していないので, もう一度読むつもりです I haven't fully *understood* the book, so I plan to read it once more.

3【処理すること】▶こんな過密スケジュールはとても消化できない I can't *manage* a tight schedule like this.

2**しょうか 消火する extinguish** +㊐; **put out**(消す) ▶風が強くて消火に2時間かかった It took two hours to *put out the fire* because of the strong wind.

‖消火器 a fire extinguisher ‖ 消火訓練 a fire drill ‖ 消火栓 a (fire) hydrant /háɪdrənt/.

3**しょうか 昇華** ▶性欲をスポーツに昇華させる *sublimate* sexual desire through sports ‖ 2人は友情を愛に昇華させた Their friendship *blossomed sublimely into love* [*blossomed into sublime love*].

4**しょうか 唱歌 singing**; a **song**(歌) ▶唱歌集 a collection of songs; a songbook (歌本).

‖文部省唱歌 songs authorized by the Ministry of Education.

しょうが 生姜 ginger /dʒíndʒər/ ▶ショウガ入り煎餅 a *ginger-flavored* rice cracker.

じょうか 浄化する purify +㊐ ▶水を浄化する *purify* water.

▶政治の浄化はどの国でも共通の課題だ *Cleaning up* politics is a task shared by all countries.

‖浄化槽 a septic tank(下水の) ‖ 浄化装置[設備] purifying facilities.

1**しょうかい 紹介** 1【人の】**introduction** ━ 動 **紹介する introduce** +㊐, **present** +㊐ (➤後者は堅い語) ▶新任の平田先生を紹介します (Boys and girls,) let me *introduce* your new teacher, Mr. Hirata.

直訳の落とし穴「わが社を紹介します」

(1)introduce は人を引き合わせて名前を教えること, あるいは, 司会者がゲストの略歴などを披露すること. したがって,「わが社[故郷]の紹介をさせてください」は(×)Let me introduce my company [hometown]. ではなく,「…について話す」と考えて, Let me *tell* you *about* my company [hometown]. とする.

(2)紹介の際に気をつけたいことが1つある. Let me introduce my friend Jane to you. (友だちのジェーンを紹介します)に続く文で, 例えば, She comes from Australia. (彼女はオーストラリアからやって来ました)などとすぐ代名詞に置き換えるのは不自然. 最初の文はいわば話の枕で, 実際の紹介は2番目の文からなので, ここはもう一度, Jane comes from Australia. とするのが自然. そのあとは She にしてかまわない.

【文型】
人(A)を人(B)に紹介する
introduce A to B

▶ねえ, あの若い女性をぼくに紹介してよ Please *introduce* me *to* that young woman. (➤ introduce that young woman to me も間違いではないが, 英語では「ぼくをあの若い女性に紹介して」と発想するのがふつう) ‖ 親友が私を現在の妻に紹介してくれた My best friend *introduced* me *to* my present wife. ‖ 担任の先生はぼくを校長先生に紹介してくださった My homeroom teacher *presented* me to the principal. ‖ 弟の春夫を紹介します *This is* my brother Haruo. (➤いきなり He's ... としない) / I'd like to *introduce* [I'd like you to meet] my brother Haruo. (➤ I'd like ... の言い方は正式な紹介の場合; meet を使うのが日常的なくだけた言い方).

▶彼は先生の紹介で入社した He joined the company *through his teacher's introduction*. ‖ 友人の紹介で知り合った男性と結婚することになりました I am going to marry the man *my friend introduced to me*. / I am going to marry a man *I met through a friend*. ‖ 1人ずつ自己紹介してください I'd like each of you to *introduce yourself*.

▶ただ今ご紹介にあずかりましたララ社の吉野でございます I am (Mr.) Yoshino from RARA Company. I *am particularly honored to have been introduced* to you. 《参考》これは日本的表現で, 英米では司会者によって聴衆にすでに紹介されている場合, 改めて自己紹介することは一般的ではない. ただし, Thank you, Mr. Chairman. とか, First, may I thank you for your generous introduction. などと言って, 紹介してくれた人に謝意を述べることはある. また, 現代英語では敬称を付けず姓だけで話しかけることはふつうはしないので, 自分に対しても Mr. [Ms., Mrs., Miss] Yoshino として,「吉野」が姓であることを示すのが親切. ‖ 対話「皆さん, 紹介します. 新しく加わった田上君です」「(田上です.)どうぞよろしく」"*I'd like* you (all) *to meet* Mr. Tagami who has joined us recently." "Nice to meet you."

✉ **ウィルソン教授に紹介状を書いていただけないでしょうか** I wonder if you could write *a letter of introduction* to Professor Wilson for me?

✉ **私の教え子の田中小百合さんを紹介させていただきます** I'd like to [I am writing to] *introduce* my student, Tanaka Sayuri.

‖紹介状 a letter of introduction.

2【物事の】introduction 一動 紹介する introduce ＋目；**tell** ＋目（人に知らせる）▶彼は日本に初めてラテンアメリカの文学を紹介した１人だ He is one of the people who first *introduced* Latin American literature to Japan. ‖ 私のふるさとを紹介します Let me *tell* you about my hometown. ‖ ぜひ紹介したい便利グッズがあります There are some useful items I'*d like to tell* you *about*. ‖ この本はきょうの新聞に紹介されて（＝書評されて）いる This book *was reviewed* in today's newspaper.

[2]しょうかい 照会 (a) **reference**（人物・身元などの）；(an) **inquiry**（問い合わせ）**一動 照会する refer** /rɪfə́ːʳ/ 《to》；**inquire** ＋目 ▶その件につきましては本部までご照会ください Questions on that matter *should be referred to* the head office. ‖ 電話でご照会いただいてもお答えできません We cannot answer *inquiries* made by telephone.

[3]しょうかい 商会 a **company**；a **firm**（２人以上で構成される）▶スミス商会 Smith & *Co.* ‖ クラウン貿易商会 Crown Trading *Co.*

[1]しょうがい 生涯 a **life** ▶ダイアナ妃は波乱に富んだ生涯を送った Princess Diana led an eventful *life* [*a life* full of ups and downs]. ‖ 私は悔いのない生涯を送りたい I'd like to live my *life* without regrets. ‖ 祖父は昨年亡くなりました．82年の生涯でした My grandfather passed away last year. He was 82 (at the time). ‖ 彼は生涯をイルカの研究にささげた He devoted his *life* to the study of dolphins.
▶彼は生涯カナダのケベックで暮らした He lived *all his life* in Quebec, Canada. ‖ ご恩は生涯忘れません I will never forget your kindness *to the end of my life* [*as long as I live*]. ‖ 生涯現役で過ごしたいと思います I'd like to lead an active life [work actively] *as long as I live*. (➤ 後者は働き続ける場合) ／I'*d like to continue* to actively contribute to society. ‖ 大槻文彦は日本語の辞書作りを生涯の仕事とした Otsuki Fumihiko made compiling a Japanese dictionary *his life work* [*lifework*].
‖**生涯教育** lifelong education, continuing education. →一生.

[2]しょうがい 障害 1【妨げ】an **obstacle**, a **barrier** /bǽriəʳ/ ▶私たちの結婚にはいろいろな障害があった There were lots of *obstacles* [*barriers*] in the way of our marriage. ‖ 体が弱いのが障害となって彼は大成しなかった His poor health was *an obstacle* to his success. ‖ 英語ができないのが彼の昇進の障害となった（＝昇進を妨げた）His poor English ability *prevented* his promotion. ‖ 私の父は事業に成功するまでにさまざまな障害（＝困難）を乗り越えてきた My father overcame [got over] a lot of *difficulties* before he became a successful businessman. ‖ 我々の計画は障害にぶつかった Our plan *hit a snag*.
‖**障害物競走** an obstacle race（運動会の）；a steeplechase（競馬の）.

2【身体の，あるいは精神の】(a) **disability**（機能不全；個々の障害はⓒ）；an **impediment**（主に歩行・言語の）；(a) **disorder**（病的状態）；**impairment**（機能の障害）.
【解説】身体，あるいは精神の「障害」を表すいちばん普通の語は a disability で，人が「障害のある」を表すのは disabled,「障害をもつ」は with a disability である．複数の障害があれば with disabilities となる．
▶重い障害をもつ人 a person *with a severe disability* ／people *with severe disabilities* (➤ a severely disabled person を当てることもできる) ‖ 精神障害の人 a *mentally disabled* person ‖ 視覚障害の人 a *visually disabled* person ／a person *with impaired vision* [*visual impairment*] ‖ この子は言語障害を抱えている He has *a speech impediment* [*disorder*]. ‖ 祖父は脳出血で倒れて以来，右半身に障害が残った（＝まひしている）My grandfather *has been paralyzed* on his right side since he had a stroke. ‖ 彼女は下半身まひという障害を乗り越えてパラリンピックで金メダルを獲得した She won a gold medal at the Paralympics *despite her disability* of being paralyzed in the lower half of her body. (➤ 文字どおり「障害を乗り越える［克服する］」は overcome one's disability).
‖**障害者** a disabled person, a person with a disability ‖ **障害児教育** education of disabled children ‖ **外傷後ストレス障害** PTSD (Post Traumatic Stress Disorder) ‖ **学習［精神／発達］障害** a learning [mental／developmental] disability ‖ **軽度認知機能障害** mild cognitive impairment (MCI) ‖ **睡眠障害** a sleep disorder ‖ **性同一性障害** gender [sexual] identity disorder ‖ **摂食障害** an eating disorder ‖ **パニック障害** panic disorder.

[3]しょうがい 傷害 (an) **injury**（傷つけること）▶あの男は過去に５度も傷害事件を起こしている He has *inflicted bodily injury on people* as many as five times. ‖ あの男は傷害罪で逮捕された That man was arrested *on a charge of injuring somebody*.
‖**傷害致死** (a) bodily injury resulting in death ‖ **傷害保険** accident insurance.

[4]しょうがい 渉外 public relations
‖**渉外課** a public relations department [section] ‖ **渉外係** a public relations person.

じょうがい 場外 ▶阿部選手は場外ホームランを放った Abe belted *a homer that flew over the stands* of the stadium. ／Abe slammed *a ball out of the stadium*. ‖ 場外乱闘もプロレスのショーのうちだ *Rough-and-tumble outside the ring* is also part of the show in professional wrestling.
‖**場外馬券売り場** an off-track [off-course] betting office.

しょうかく 昇格 (a) **promotion** →昇進 ▶野川氏は４月１日付けで人事部長に昇格した Mr. Nogawa *got a promotion* to head of the personnel department as of April 1. ／Mr. Nogawa *was promoted* to chief of personnel as of April 1.
▶この町は人口が５万を超えたので市に昇格した Since the population had grown to over 50,000, this town *was upgraded* to a city.

[1]しょうがく 少額・小額 ▶少額の金 *a small sum* [*amount*] *of* money ‖ 小額紙幣 a *small* bill [《英》note].

[2]しょうがく 商学 commercial science
‖**商学博士** a Doctor of Commercial Science ‖ **商学部** the school of commercial science.

しょうがくきん 奨学金 a **scholarship** (➤ 成績優秀者に与えられるもので，日本のそれとは性格が異なる)；a **fellowship**（大学院生への）▶きみは奨学金を受けていますか Do you have *a scholarship*? ／Are you a *scholarship* student? ‖ 彼は奨学金を得てUCLAに留学した He was sent to UCLA *on a scholarship*. ／He *got a scholarship* to go to UCLA. ‖ わが校は優秀な学生に月額３万円の奨学金を出している Our school offers [awards] *scholarships* of thirty thousand yen a month to exceptional students.

1**しょうがくせい 奨学生** a **student on a scholarship** [**fellowship**] (➤ scholarship は主に学部生, fellowship は主に大学院生) ▶彼はブリティッシュ・カウンシルの**奨学生**だった He studied [was *a student*] *on* a British Council *scholarship* [*fellowship*].

2**しょうがくせい 小学生** 《米》 an **elementary school student** [**child**], 《英》 a **primary school child** [**pupil**] 《参考》 男女を明確にしたい場合は student [child / pupil] の代わりに boy か girl を用いる. ▶**小学生のとき**は1キロ泳げた I could swim a kilometer *when I was in elementary school*.

しょうがつ 正月 **the New Year** (新年) ▶**正月**三が日 the first three days of *the New Year* ‖ **正月休み** the *New Year holidays* (➤ 《米》ではクリスマス直前から正月までの休みを the holidays と呼んでおり, 正月は元日だけが休みのことも多い) ‖ **正月気分**がなかなか抜けない I can't seem to get rid of *the New-Year-holiday mood*.

✉ **正月(=元日)は家族全員で神社に参拝します** All of my family go together to a shrine on *New Year's Day*.

しょうがっこう 小学校 《米》 an **elementary school**, a **grade school**, 《英》 a **primary school**

▶うちの娘も来年は**小学校です** My daughter will *start* [*begin*] *school* next year. 《参考》 start [begin] school は義務教育を始めることをいい, 日本語の「学校に上がる」に相当する. enter school はあまり用いない ‖ 妹は**小学校6年生**です My sister is *in the sixth grade*. / My sister is *a sixth grader*.

しようがない・しょうがない **1**【やむをえない】

▶「**しようがないや**」と彼は言った He said, "*It can't be helped*." ‖ あいつが危険を覚悟で報道写真家になると言うのだからしようがないよ He says he wants to be a news photographer even though he's fully aware it's a dangerous job, so *there's nothing I can do* (about it).

▶反論すると彼女はますますご機嫌斜めになりそうだったので, 私は黙っているよりしょうがなかった I *just had to* [*had no choice but to*] keep my mouth shut because she would have gotten even angrier if I had talked back.

2【ひどい】▶こんな問題も解けないなんてしようがない学生だね *Some* student you are! You can't solve even that easy problem. (➤ この some は「ひどい」の意を表す皮肉な用法) ‖ 対話「お母さん, また傘なくしちゃった」「しょうがないわね」"Mom, I lost my umbrella again." "*You're impossible*." (➤「あなたはどうしようもない」の意).

3【たまらない】▶きょうは寒くてしようがない *It's simply too cold* today. ‖ 兄貴はぐうたらでしようがない(=どうしようもないぐうたらだ) My brother is an *impossible* slob. ‖ 最近は暇でしようがない I have *way too much* free time [have *far too much* time on my hands]. (➤ 前者の way はあとの形容詞や副詞を強めて「とても」の意味. 後者の on my hands は「私の自由になる」の意) ‖ 彼は明日の面接のことが気になってしようがなかった He was *really* worried about his interview tomorrow.

4【成果を生まない】▶こんな議論はしてもしょうがない This kind of argument will *get* us *nowhere*. (➤ get ... nowhere は「…にとって無益である」) ‖ マージャンしたいのに我々3人だけじゃしょうがないな I want to play mah-jongg but *have to give up* (*on doing so*) because there are only three of us. ⇀しかたがない.

じょうかまち 城下町 a **castle town**

✉ **金沢は城下町として有名です** Kanazawa is well known as *a castle town*.

1**しょうかん 召喚する** **summon** +㊐, 《法律》 **summons** +㊐ ▶彼の雇用主が証人として**召喚された** His employer *was summoned* [*subpoenaed*] to appear in court (as a witness).

‖ **召喚状** a summons, a subpoena /səpíːnə/.

2**しょうかん 召還する** **recall** +㊐ ▶アメリカは中国大使を**召還した** The United States *recalled* its ambassador from China.

3**しょうかん 償還** **redemption** (債券の); **repayment** (融資の) 一動 **償還する** **redeem** +㊐, **repay** +㊐.

4**しょうかん 小寒** *shokan*; the second coldest two-week period in a year (according to the traditional Chinese calendar) (➤ 説明的な訳). ⇀大寒.

1**じょうかん 情感** **emotion, feeling** ▶その歌手は**情感を込めて**歌った The singer sang *with deep emotion*.

2**じょうかん 上官** one's **superior** [**senior**] **officer**.

1**しょうき 正気** **consciousness** /kɑ́ːnʃəsnəs/ (意識) ▶**正気を失う** lose *consciousness* (➤「気を失う」の意) ‖ **正気を取り戻す** *come to one's senses*.

▶自殺したいなんて, きみ**正気かい**? (You say) you want to kill yourself? Are you *in your right mind*? ‖ あんなことをするなんて彼は**正気でない**に違いない He must be *out of his mind* [*be crazy*] to do such a thing. ‖ 私は酔うと**正気では**言えないことを言ってしまう傾向がある When I am drunk, I am inclined to say things I wouldn't say *when* (*I am*) *sober*. (➤ sober は「しらふの」) ‖ あんな怪しげな会社に持ち金を全部投資するなんて**正気の沙汰ではない** It is *utter madness* to invest all your money in such a shaky company.

2**しょうき 勝機** a **chance** (**to win**) ▶**勝機**をつかむ seize *a chance* (*to win*) ‖ **勝機**を逸する lose *a chance* (*to win*).

しょうぎ 将棋 *shogi*, **Japanese chess** ▶**将棋**を指す play *shogi*.

▶《慣用表現》電車が急停車したので乗客は**将棋倒し**になった Since the train came to a sudden stop, the passengers *fell over like dominoes*. (➤ domino は「(ドミノ遊びで使う)ドミノ牌(はい)」).

‖ **将棋盤** a *shogi* board

日本紹介 ✉ **将棋は五角形の木の駒を動かして戦う, チェスに似た盤上のゲームです. キングに当たるのが王将で, 相手の王将を詰めれば勝ちです. 取った相手の駒も自分のものとして使うことができます** *Shogi* is a board game like chess in which you move pentagonal wooden pieces (on the board). The counterpart of the king is called '*osho*' and if you checkmate your opponent's *osho*, you win. You can use the pieces you've seized from your opponent as your own.

1**じょうき 常軌** ▶**常軌を逸した**ふるまい *insane* [*screwy*] behavior ‖ あんな幼い子を叱り飛ばすなんてきみも**常軌を逸している**よ You must *be off your rocker* [*be crazy*] to yell at such a small child. (➤ off one's rocker は「気が変になって」の意でややおどけた感じのする言い方).

2**じょうき 蒸気** **steam** ‖ **蒸気機関車** a steam locomotive ‖ **蒸気船** a steamship.

3**じょうき 上気** ▶ミスコンで優勝した彼女の顔は**上気**していた Her face *was flushed with excitement* at winning the beauty contest.

4**じょうき 上記の** above(-mentioned) ▶詳細は上記の住所までお問い合わせください For additional information, please make inquiries to the *above* address.

✉《商業文で》**上記のとおり, この遅延はボルチモアの港湾ストが原因であります** As stated [mentioned] *above*, this delay is due to the dock strike in Baltimore.

✉ **上記のとおり相違ありません** I hereby declare [affirm] the *above* statement to be true and correct.

じょうぎ 定規 a ruler ‖三角定規《米》a triangle, 《英》a set square ‖ T定規 a T square.

じょうきげん 上機嫌 ▶お父さんはジャイアンツが勝っている限り上機嫌だ My father is *in a good mood* [*in (a) good humor*] as long as the Giants are winning. ‖彼は仕事がうまくいったので上機嫌で帰宅した Since his work had gone well, he came home *in high spirits*.

しょうきぼ 小規模な small-scale ▶小規模な会社 a *small(-scale)* company ‖石川さんは小規模に商売をしている Mr. Ishikawa is doing business *on a small scale* [*in a small way*].

しょうきゃく 焼却する burn (up), incinerate /ɪnsínəreɪt/ +㊀ ▶この書類は一刻も早く焼却してください Please *burn* these papers as soon as possible. ‖ごみ焼却場 a refuse incineration plant ‖ ごみ焼却炉 an incinerator.

じょうきゃく 乗客 a passenger ▶この車両には乗客が１人もいない There are no *passengers* on this car. ‖乗客の安全が第一だ The safety of *passengers* comes first.

1**しょうきゅう 昇給** a pay increase ;《米》a raise in salary, a pay raise ;《英》a rise in salary, a pay rise (➤インフォーマルでは《米》,《英》とも後者が好まれる) ▶ことしの昇給はたったの5000円だったよ This year's *pay raise* [*rise*] was only 5,000 yen.

2**しょうきゅう 昇級** (a) promotion. →昇進.

じょうきゅう 上級 ▶小野田さんはB大学で私より２年上級だった Miss Onoda *was* two years *ahead of me* at B University. ‖彼は乗馬の上級コースへ進むためにテストを受けた He took a test to get into *an advanced course* in horseback riding. ‖中学・高校では３年生が最上級だ In junior and senior high schools the third year is *the top class*.

✉ **この大学には私と同じ高校出身の上級生が何人もいます** There are lots of *upperclass students* from my high school at this university.

‖上級裁判所 a higher court ‖上級生 an upperclass student.

しょうきゅうし 小休止 a pause(中断) ; a break(中休み).

しょうきょ 消去する erase +㊀ (書いたものを消す) ; clear +㊀ (きれいにする) ; delete +㊀ (削除する) ; eliminate +㊀ (除去する) ▶ (パソコンなどの) 画面に映しているものを消去する *clear* the screen ‖迷惑メールを消去する *delete* spam ‖妻は録画したテレビ番組をうっかり消去してしまった My wife accidentally *erased* a TV program I had recorded.

しょうぎょう 商業 commerce(商取り引き) ; business (商売) 一形 商業の commercial ▶この町はかつては商業が盛んだった *Business* was once thriving in this town. ‖日本ではクリスマスやバレンタインデーは商業化されている In Japan, Christmas and Valentine's Day have *been commercialized*.

‖商業英語 business English ‖商業銀行 a commercial bank ‖商業高校 a commercial high school ‖商業主義 commercialism ‖商業地区 a business district ‖商業通信文 a business letter ‖商業都市 a commercial city ‖商業美術 commercial art.

1**じょうきょう 状況・情況** a situation (事態, 情勢) ; circumstances (周囲の事情, 付帯状況) ; conditions (主に一時的な状態) ; state (人や物の状態) ▶現在の状況から判断して, あの会社との取り引きは中止しないほうが賢明だろう Judging from *the present situation*, it would be better not to break off our business relations with that company. ‖現在の状況ではどちらのチームが勝つかわからない *Under the present circumstances* [*conditions*], we can't tell which team will win. ‖彼は現場の状況をありのまま説明した He gave a blow-by-blow account of *what had happened* [*what was happening*]. (➤ blow-by-blow は「詳細な」) ‖そちらの現在の状況をお知らせください Please let me know *the current situation* [*the present state of affairs* / *how things are going*]. ‖状況は悪くなる一方だ *Things* are going from bad to worse. (➤ things は漠然と「事態」を表す).

‖状況証拠 circumstantial evidence.

2**じょうきょう 上京する** come [go] to Tokyo ▶18のときに上京して20年になります It's been twenty years since I *came to Tokyo* at the age of eighteen.

しょうきょくてき 消極的な passive (受け身な) ; negative(否定的な) ▶営業の仕事をしたいなら消極的ではだめだよ If you want to get a sales job, you will have to stop being *passive*. ‖彼女はどちらかと言うと消極的な性格だ I would say she has an *unassertive* personality. (➤ unassertive /ʌnəsə́ːrtɪv/ は「自己主張をしない」) ‖彼女は雅彦さんとの結婚には消極的なのよ She shows a *negative* attitude toward marrying Masahiko.

しょうきょほう 消去法 ▶この方法は消去法で選ばれた This approach was chosen by (a) *process of elimination*.

しょうきん 賞金 prize money(コンテスト・競技などの) ; a reward /rɪwɔ́ːrd/ (報奨金) ▶歌謡コンテストで私は10万円の賞金をもらった I won one hundred thousand yen in *prize money* in the singing contest. ‖お尋ね者の首に５万ポンドの賞金がかかった There was *a reward* of 50,000 pounds on the head of the wanted man. ‖18頭の馬が1億円の１着賞金を争った Eighteen horses competed for the 100-million-yen *first place prize*.

じょうきん 常勤の full-time ▶私は短大で常勤で教えています I teach *full-time* at a junior college.

‖常勤講師 a full-time instructor [lecturer].

じょうくう 上空 ▶上空で何かがきらっと光った Something glittered *in the sky*. ‖ただ今, 大島の上空を飛行中です This plane is now flying *over* the island of Oshima.

しょうぐん 将軍 a general(軍隊の) ; a shogun (幕府の ; 英語化している) ▶ゴードン将軍 *General* Gordon ‖15代将軍慶喜 Yoshinobu, the fifteenth Tokugawa *shogun*. ‖将軍家 the Shogunate.

じょうげ 上下 1【上と下】▶彼は絵を上下逆さまに壁に掛けた He hung the picture *upside down* on the wall. ‖私たちの飛行機は激しく上下に揺れた Our plane *pitched* violently. (➤ pitch は「縦に揺れ

る」).

▶株価はこの１週間大幅に上下した Stock prices *went up and down* [*fluctuated*] dramatically this week. ‖内閣の支持率は30%の辺りを上下している The approval rating for the cabinet has been *hovering* at about 30%.

2【上りと下り】▶東海道線は上下線とも不通だ Both *north* [*up*] *and south* [*down*] *trains* are stopped on the Tokaido line.

3【1組みのもの】▶このスーツの上下は注文で作った This *coat and pants* are [This *suit* is] made to order. ‖その小説は上下２巻で発行される The novel will be published *in two volumes*.

しょうけい 小計 a **subtotal**.

じょうけい 情景 a **scene** /siːn/ (一場面) ; a **sight** (目に映った光景) ▶50年たった今もあの日の情景が忘れられない Fifty years have passed and I still can't forget the *scene* I saw that day [*how things looked* that day]. ‖この作家は情景描写に優れている This author is very good at *scenic description*.

しょうけいもじ 象形文字 a **hieroglyph** /háɪərəglɪf/.

じょうげかんけい 上下関係 ▶軍隊には厳しい上下関係がある The military has a strict *hierarchical structure*. (➤ hierarchical は /hàɪərάːˈkɪkəl/ と発音).

しょうげき 衝撃 1【物理的】 a **shock**, an **impact** ▶衝撃波 a *shock* wave ‖車の正面衝突による衝撃で彼女は即死した She died instantly from the *shock* [*impact*] of the head-on collision.

2【精神的】 a **shock** ; an **impact** (影響) ▶夫の死は彼女にとって大きな衝撃だった Her husband's death was a great *shock* to her. ／She was deeply shocked by her husband's death. ‖その知らせを聞いても我々はほとんど衝撃を受けなかった The news had little *impact* on us. ‖これはＹ嬢の衝撃的なヌード写真だ Here is a *shocking* nude picture of Miss Y.

しょうけん 証券 **securities** ; a **bond** (債券) ; a **certificate** (株式証券)

‖**証券アナリスト** a securities analyst ‖**証券会社** a securities firm [company] (➤ security firm は「警備会社」の意) ‖**証券取引所** a stock exchange [market] ‖**抵当証券** a mortgage-backed [an asset-backed] security ‖**有価証券** marketable securities.

しょうげん 証言 **testimony** (法廷で証人がする) ; **witness** (証拠を挙げての) **一動 証言する** **testify** 《to》, **witness** 《to》 ▶彼の無実を証言する *testify to* his innocence ‖いくら無実だと言い張っても, おまえさんがやったと証言する人がいるんだよ Though you insist on your innocence, we have a witness to *testify that* you did it. (➤ この witness は「証人」) ‖彼は被告に不利な[有利な]証言をした He *testified against* [*for*] the accused. ‖彼女は私がその部屋にいるのを見たと証言した She *testified to* having seen me in the room.

▶私は絶対に現場にはいなかった. 同僚たちが証言してくれるよ I wasn't there at all—my co-workers will *bear* me *out*. (➤ bear out は「支持する」).

じょうけん 条件 a **condition** ; **terms** (支払いなどの条件) ; a **requirement** (必要条件, 資格) ▶支払いの条件 *terms* of payment ‖「ただし, １つ条件がある」"But I have one *condition*." ‖健康と勤勉は成功するための２つの重要な条件だ Health and hard work are the two important *conditions* [*prerequisites*] of success. (➤ 後者は「前提条件」の意) ／The two key *requirements* for success are health and hard work. ‖匿名を条件に話をする speak *on condition of* anonymity ‖吉田君が手伝ってくれるという条件でぼくは議長の役を引き受けた I have accepted the post of chairman *on* (*the*) *condition that* Yoshida help me. (➤ on (the) condition that ... のあとは通例仮定法現在形) ‖１つ条件を付ける impose [attach] one *condition* ‖先方は１つ条件付きで我々の提案を受け入れた The other party accepted our proposal with one additional *condition*. ‖いくつかの条件付きで彼の申し出を受け入れた I accepted his proposal *on several conditions*. ‖わが社は英語の知識があることが昇進の必要条件の１つだ In our company a knowledge of English is among the *requirements* for promotion.

‖**条件反射** a conditioned reflex [response].

☛ **悪条件, 無条件** (→見出語)

じょうげん 上限 **the upper limit** ▶うちの会社では残業手当は月10万円が上限だ Our company has a 100, 000 yen *limit* on overtime pay.

1 **しょうこ 証拠** **evidence**, (a) **proof** (証明 ; 後者が確証性が高い) ; a **sign** (印) ▶検察側は十分な[明確な]証拠があるとしてその男を起訴した Public prosecutors indicted him when they felt that they had collected enough clear [positive] *evidence*. ‖泥棒はお金だけ盗んで何の証拠も残さずに逃げた The thief stole only money and made off without leaving the slightest *evidence* behind. ‖証拠不十分により本件は却下する *Insufficient evidence*. Case dismissed.

▶俺が間違っているという証拠でもあるのか Do you have any *proof* that I am wrong ? ／Can you prove me wrong ? ‖約束を忘れるなんてだらしがない証拠だよ That you forgot your promise *proves* you're unreliable. ‖あくびは退屈している証拠だ Yawns are a *sign* of boredom.

‖**証拠物件** material evidence ‖**状況証拠** circumstantial evidence ‖**物的証拠** physical evidence.

2 **しょうこ 礁湖** a **lagoon**.

しょうご 正午 **noon** ▶正午の時報 the *twelve o'clock* time signal ‖私は正午過ぎまで目が覚めなかった I didn't wake up until *after noon*. ‖正午に彼女と会うことになっている I'm scheduled to meet her *at twelve noon*. (➤ at noon を強めた言い方).

1 **じょうご 漏斗** a **funnel** /fʌ́nl/.

2 **じょうご 上戸** a **heavy drinker** ‖**怒り上戸** an angry drunk.

☛ **泣き上戸, 笑い上戸** (→見出語).

1 **しょうこう 将校** a **commissioned officer**, an **officer** ▶陸軍将校 a military *officer*.

2 **しょうこう 焼香** ▶お葬式で焼香する *burn incense* at a funeral.

1 **しょうごう 称号** a **title** ; a **degree** (学位) ▶サーの称号 the *title* of sir.

2 **しょうごう 照合する** **check** +目 ▶答えを照合する *check* one's answers *with* [*against*] the correct ones ‖この指紋の照合をお願いします Could you *check* this fingerprint ?

じょうこう 条項 a **clause** (条文) ; an **article** (箇条).

しょうこうかいぎしょ 商工会議所 a **chamber of commerce (and industry)** (➤ 外国ではカッコ内はふつう省略) ▶大阪商工会議所 the Osaka *Chamber of*

Commerce and Industry.

しょうこうきゃく 乗降客 ▶新宿駅の乗降客は1日何人ですか How many *passengers get on and off* (*trains*) every day at Shinjuku Station?

しょうこうぎょう 商工業 ▶名古屋は中部地方の商工業の中心地だ Nagoya is the center of *commerce and industry* in the Chubu district.

しょうこうぐち 昇降口 an **entrance**; a **hatch**(船の).

しょうこうぐん 症候群 a **syndrome** /síndroum/ ▶AIDS(エイズ)は「後天性免疫不全症候群」の略だ AIDS stands for Acquired Immune Deficiency [Immunodeficiency] *Syndrome*.

逆引き熟語 〇〇症候群
エコノミークラス症候群 economy class syndrome, deep vein thrombosis / 過敏(性)腸症候群 irritable bowel syndrome / 月経前症候群 premenstrual syndrome(PMS) / シックハウス症候群 sick-house syndrome / 重症急性呼吸器症候群 severe acute respiratory syndrome (SARS) / 睡眠時無呼吸症候群 (obstructive) sleep apnea syndrome / ストックホルム症候群 (the) Stockholm syndrome / ダウン症候群 Down's syndrome / 乳幼児突然死症候群 sudden infant death syndrome(SIDS) / ピーターパン症候群 (the) Peter Pan syndrome / VDT 症候群 visual display terminal syndrome, computer vision syndrome(CVS) / 慢性疲労症候群 chronic fatigue syndrome (CFS) / メタボリック症候群 metabolic syndrome(➤ 専門的な言い方で英米では一般的でない) / 燃え尽き症候群 burnout syndrome

しょうこうじょうたい 小康状態 ▶彼の病気はここのところ小康状態にある His illness is in *remission*. / He's in *stable condition*. (➤ 後者は予断を許さないが安定しているという場合もある).

しょうこうねつ 猩紅熱 **scarlet fever**.

じょうこく 上告 an **appeal to a higher court**; an **appeal** [**a final appeal**] (to the Supreme Court) (最高裁への) ▶最高裁判所に上告する *appeal* to the Supreme Court. →控訴.

しょうこりもなく 性懲りもなく ▶あいつは何度肘鉄を食らっても性懲りもなく若い女を追いかけ回している He's gotten the cold shoulder many times, but he still chases young women. He *hasn't learned his lesson yet*. (➤ learn one's lesson は「教訓を得る」).

しょうこん 商魂 ▶商魂たくましい男 a *highly business-minded* [an *enterprising*] man ‖ 商魂たくましい塾 a *commercially-minded* juku ‖ こんな田舎にまで来てセールスするとはあの男も商魂たくましいね He must be *a born salesman* to be able to sell goods in this country town. (➤「生まれながらのセールスマン」の意).

1**しょうさ 小差** a **narrow margin** ▶穴井は柔道で小差の判定勝ちをした In the judo match, Anai won (on) a decision *by a narrow margin*.

2**しょうさ 少佐** a **major**(陸軍, 空軍, 海兵隊の); a **lieutenant commander**(海軍の).

1**しょうさい 詳細** **details** /dɪtéɪlz ‖ díːteɪlz/ ▶詳細は会ってから話します I'll give you the *details* when I see you. ‖ 彼女はその事故について詳細な報告をした She made a *full* [*detailed*] report on the accident.

✉ **貴社の商品についての詳細を知りたいので, カタログをお送りください** I would like to *know more* [*have more detailed information*] about your products, so please send me a catalog.

✉ **なお詳細については追ってお知らせします** *Details* [*Particulars*] will be sent to you later.

2**しょうさい 商才** **business ability** [**talent**] ▶商才にたけた男 a man of great *business ability* ‖ 兄は商才がある My (older) brother *has a talent for business*.

じょうさい 城塞 a **citadel**.

じょうざい 錠剤 a **tablet**, a **pill**(➤ 厳密には後者は丸薬のことだが, 前者を含む語として広く用いられる) ▶ビタミンの錠剤を飲む take a vitamin *pill*.

しょうさっし 小冊子 a **booklet**; a **pamphlet**(政治・社会問題などを扱う); a **brochure** /broʊʃʊ́əʳ ‖ bróʊʃə/ (宣伝用パンフレット).

じょうざぶぶっきょう 上座部仏教 **Theravada** /θèrəvάːdə/ **Buddhism**. →大乗仏教.

1**しょうさん 賞賛** **praise**; **admiration** (感心, 敬服) 一動 **賞賛する** **praise** +Ⓞ, **admire** +Ⓞ ▶その大学生の勇敢な行為は賞賛に値する That college student's brave deed is worthy of *praise*. ‖ 批評家たちは彼の優れた演技を賞賛した Critics *praised* him for his excellent performance. ‖ 彼女の親孝行ぶりは人々の賞賛の的だ Her devotion to her parents is *the object of much admiration*. →たたえる.

2**しょうさん 勝算** ▶そんな大きなことを言って, 本当に勝算はあるのかい? You're talking awfully big; are you really *sure of winning*? ‖ 勝算は十分あるよ [全くないよ] We have a good [no] *chance of winning*.

3**しょうさん 硝酸** **nitric** /náɪtrɪk/ **acid** ‖ 硝酸塩 a nitrate /náɪtreɪt/.

しょうし 焼死する **burn** [**be burned**] **to death** ▶昨夜火事で子供2人が焼死した Two children *died* [*were killed*] *in a fire* last night. ‖ 1人の若い女性が焼死体となって発見された The *charred body* of a young woman was found.

1**しょうじ 障子** a ***shoji***

日本紹介 ✉ **障子は木の格子に白い和紙を張った引き戸です. 直射日光を遮ると同時に部屋に必要な明るさを入れてくれます** A *shoji* is a sliding door covered with white Japanese paper over a wooden lattice. It shuts out direct sunlight but lets enough light (through the paper) into the room.

2**しょうじ 小事** a **small** [**trivial** / **trifling**] **matter**, a **trifle** ▶小事にこだわるな Don't get hung up on *small* [*trivial* / *trifling*] *matters*. / Don't sweat *the small stuff*.

3**しょうじ 正時** **the hour** ▶毎正時に every hour *on the hour*.

1**じょうし 上司** one's **boss**, one's **supervisor** (➤ 後者は警察・軍隊など大きな組織の長を連想させる) ▶井出さんは私の上司です Mr. Ide is my *boss*. / I work under [report to] Mr. Ide. (➤ report to は「…に仕事の報告をする」) ‖ その件は上司と相談してみます I'll talk with my *boss* about it.

2**じょうし 城址** **the ruins of a castle** ▶小田原城址 *the ruins of* Odawara *Castle*.

1**じょうじ 情事** a **love affair**; an **affair**(浮気) ▶秘書と情事にふける *have a love affair* with one's secretary.

2**じょうじ 常時** ▶パスポートは常時携帯のこと You should carry your passport *at all times*.

しょうしか 少子化 a **declining birth rate**(減少する出生率) ; a **decrease in the number of children** (子供の数の減少) ▶日本では**少子化傾向**が大きな問題になってきた The *declining birth rate* has become a big problem in Japan.

しょうじがいしゃ 商事会社 →商社.

じょうじき 正直 **1【真実や事実を隠さない様子】** **honesty** /ɑ́:nəsti/ **一形 正直な honest** ; **straightforward** (率直な) ▶**正直な**少年 an *honest* boy ‖ **正直**に何もかも話してごらん Try telling me everything *honestly*. ‖ コンピュータは**正直**だから間違った入力をすれば間違った結果しか出てこないよ Computers *don't lie*, so you'll always get the wrong results if you input wrong data.

ことわざ **正直の頭(こうべ)に神宿る** A god watches over (the head of) an honest person. (➤ 日本語からの直訳) ／Honesty is the best policy. (➤「正直は最良の策」の意の英語のことわざ) ‖ **正直者がばかを見る** An honest person often gets the short end of the stick. ／Honesty doesn't (always) pay. (➤ 後者は「正直は報われないことが多い」の意) ‖ **三度目の正直** Third time('s) lucky. ／Third time does the trick.

2【本心を打ち明ける様子】 ▶**正直に言えば**私はカキは好きじゃない *Honestly*, [*I must admit*] I do not like oysters. ／*To tell* (*you*) *the truth* [*To be frank*], I don't care for oysters. ‖ **正直言って**困ってるんです *To be honest*, I'm in an awkward position.

じょうしき 常識 **1【誰でも知っていること】** (a) **basic knowledge** 《**of**》(基礎知識) ; **common knowledge** 《**in**》((分野・場所において) 広く知られている知識, 周知のこと) ; **general knowledge** (一般的知識) ; **conventional** [**received**／**popular**] **wisdom** (世間一般に信じられている通念) ▶物理学の**常識** the *ABC's* of physics ‖ **常識**を覆す disprove the *conventional* [*received* / *popular*] *wisdom* ‖ そんなこと今じゃ**常識**になってるよ It's *common* [*general*] *knowledge* now. ‖ 私立では入学金100万円は**常識**なんだって It's *quite common* to have to pay one million yen as an admission fee to a private school. ‖ 対話「塩分をとり過ぎると胃がんにもなるそうですよ」「そんなの**常識**だよ」"I'm told too much salt can cause stomach cancer, too." "*Everyone knows that*."

‖ **常識テスト** a test of general knowledge.

2【良識, 思慮, 分別】 **common sense** ▶あの人は若いけれど**常識**のある人だ Although he is young, he has *common sense*. ‖ 祖父は教育はないが**常識**の豊かな人だった My grandfather had no formal education, but he *had a lot of common sense*. ‖ 彼は時々**常識**を欠いたことをする Sometimes he shows *a* (*total*) *lack of common sense*. ‖ 深酒をしたあと海水浴に行くなんて**常識外れ**だ It is *crazy* to go swimming in the ocean after drinking heavily. ‖ ほかの人が食べ終わるまで席を立たないのが**常識**だ It's *common courtesy* not to leave the table before everyone else is finished. (➤ common courtesy は「皆が共有すべき礼儀」).

しょうしつ 焼失 ▶絵巻物の多くが戦火で**焼失した** A lot of picture scrolls *were lost* [*were destroyed*] in the flames of war.

じょうしつ 上質 ▶**上質**の生地 cloth *of fine quality*

‖ **上質紙** quality [fine] paper.

じょうじつ 情実 ▶裁判官は**情実**(＝個人的感情)に流されてはいけない A judge is not supposed to be influenced by (his) *personal feelings*.

しょうしみん 小市民 a **petit** [**petty**] **bourgeois** /bóəʳ-ʒwɑ:/ ; **the petite** [**petty**] **bourgeoisie** /bòəʳʒwɑ:zí:/ (集合的).

[1]**しょうしゃ 商社** a **business company** [**firm**] ; a **trading company** [**house**] (貿易会社)

‖ **商社マン** a trading company employee ‖ **総合商社** a general trading company [firm] (➤ 扱う品目・材料が広範囲で多く, 日本独特の形態とされる).

[2]**しょうしゃ 小社** ⚠ **自分の会社を卑下した言い方だが, この用法は英語にはないので,「私どもは…」と考える.** ▶**小社**は電気器具を扱っています *We* deal in electric appliances. (➤ Our company ... はあまり一般的ではない) ‖ 郵送料**小社負担** Postage *paid*.

[3]**しょうしゃ 勝者** a **winner** ▶核戦争に**勝者**はない There is no *winner* in a nuclear war.

[4]**しょうしゃ 瀟洒な** **simple**(,) **but elegant** (家などが) ; **trim** (庭園などが) ▶しょうしゃなペンション a *simple but elegant* resort inn ‖ しょうしゃな庭園 a *trim* garden.

じょうしゃ 乗車する **get on** (大型の乗り物に乗り込む) ; **get in** [**into**] (比較的小型の乗り物に) ; **ride** (乗って行く) →乗る ▶バスに**乗車する** *get on* a bus (乗り込む) ／*ride* a bus (乗って行く) ‖ 電車に**乗車する** *get on* a train (乗り込む) ／*ride* a train (乗って行く) ‖ まちがって反対方向の電車に**乗車した** I *took* [*got on*] a train going in the opposite direction by mistake. (➤ take は「(移動手段として, 交通機関) を利用する」で,「乗って行く」にも「乗り込む」にもなる) ‖ そのバスは前のドアから**乗車して**, 後ろのドアから下車するようになっている Passengers *get on* at the front and get off at the rear of the bus. ‖ タクシーに乗ろうとしたが**乗車拒否にあった** I tried to get in a taxi, but *the driver refused to take me*. ／I tried to catch a taxi, but *none would stop*. (➤ 後者は止まらなかった場合) ‖《乗務員のことば》皆さん, (まもなく発車しますから)**ご乗車ください** *All aboard*, please. ‖ その少年は**無賃乗車**しているところを見つかった That boy was caught *stealing a ride*.

‖ **乗車券** a ticket ‖ **乗車賃** a fare.

じょうじゅ 成就 **fulfillment** (実現) ▶北極のオーロラを見るという私の長年の夢がことしは**成就しそうだ** My long-cherished dream to see the aurora borealis will *be fulfilled* this year.

[1]**しょうしゅう 召集・招集** ▶国会を**召集する** *convene* a Diet session ‖ 会議を**招集する** *call* a meeting ‖ けさ臨時教授会が**招集された** A special faculty meeting *was called for* this morning. ‖ おい, 社長から**招集**の声がかかったぞ Listen, the president *wants us to gather*.

[2]**しょうしゅう 消臭** **odor eliminating**

‖ **消臭剤** (a) deodorant, a deodorizer.

しょうじゅう 小銃 a **rifle** (ライフル)

‖ **自動小銃** an automatic rifle.

じょうしゅう 常習 ▶彼は麻薬の**常習者**だ He is a drug *addict*. ‖ 彼女は遅刻の**常習犯**だ She is *habitually* late for school. (➤ 会社などの場合は school の代わりに office や work を用いる) ／She is a *habitual* latecomer.

‖ **常習犯** a habitual criminal.

しょうしゅうかん 商習慣 a **business practice** [**custom**].

しょうじゅつ 詳述する **explain in detail**, **elaborate** 《**on**》 ▶これに関しては第 8 章に**詳述して**あります *A detailed explanation* is given in Chapter 8.

じょうじゅつ 上述の above(-mentioned) ▶上述のように *as mentioned* [*stated*] *above*.

[1]**しょうじゅん 照準** ▶彼女はT大に照準を合わせて猛勉強した She studied hard, *setting her sights on* entering T University.

[2]**しょうじゅん 昇順(で)** (in) ascending order.

じょうじゅん 上旬 the first ten days of the month ▶1月上旬に *early* in January / in *early* January / in *the early part* of January ‖ この本が出るのは来月上旬頃だ This book will be out *early next month*.

しょうしょ 証書 a **certificate** /sə'tífɪkət/ (証明書) ; a **diploma** (修了証書) ; a **bond** (債務の) ; a **document** (文書) ▶高校の卒業証書を手にする get a high school *diploma*.

しょうじょ 少女 a **girl** 《参考》girl は5歳くらいから高校生くらいの女子を指す語. 大学生以上は young woman が適当. little girl は生後まもない女児から8歳くらいまでの少女を, young girl は8歳くらいから12歳くらいまでの女子を指すが, 18歳くらいから20代前半の男性を young guy と呼ぶのに対して, その年代の女性を young girl と呼ぶこともある.
▶彼女はいまだに少女趣味の小物が好きだ She likes *girlish* accessories even now.

[1]**しょうしょう 少々** ▶塩とこしょうを少々加えてください Add *some* salt and pepper. ‖ すぐに戻りますので少々お待ちください I'll be back soon, so please wait *a moment* [*a minute*]. ‖ (電話で) 少々お待ちください *Please hold on*. ‖ 懐が寂しいんだ. 少々金を貸してくれないか I'm short of money. Could you lend me *some* [*a little*]? ‖ 彼は少々神経質だ He's *a little* [*a bit*] sensitive. ‖ 彼は少々のことでは音を上げない He's not the sort to give up over *a trivial matter*. ‖ 対話「ご趣味は?」「はあ, 空手を少々」"Do you have any interests?" "Well, I do *some* karate."

[2]**しょうしょう 少将** a **major general** (米英陸軍・空軍の; 米海兵隊の; 旧日本陸軍の) ; a **rear admiral** (米英海軍の; 旧日本海軍の) ; an **air vice-marshal** (英空軍の).

[1]**しょうじょう 症状** a **symptom** /símptəm/ ; **the condition (of a patient)** (容体) ▶(医者が) どんな症状ですか What are your *symptoms*? / What seems to be *wrong* [the *matter*]? ‖ あなたにはおうだんの症状が出ています You have *symptoms* of jaundice. ‖ 医者に慢性胃炎と言われたが, 自覚症状は全くなかった The doctor told me that I have chronic gastritis, but I haven't noticed any *symptoms myself*. (➤「自覚症状」は subjective symptoms) ‖ 娘が風疹になったが幸い症状は軽かった My daughter contracted rubella, but luckily hers was*n't a serious case*.

[2]**しょうじょう 賞状** a **certificate** /sə'tífɪkət/ **of merit** ▶賞状を額に入れて壁に飾る frame *a certificate of merit* and hang it on the wall.

[1]**じょうしょう 上昇** a **rise** 一動 **上昇する rise, go up** ▶気温がぐんぐん上昇している The temperature *is rising* [*is going up*] steadily. ‖ そのテレビ番組は人気上昇中だ That TV program *is rising* in popularity. ‖ 石油の値段が再び急上昇した The price of oil *jumped sharply* again. ‖ トンビは上昇気流に乗って舞い上がる Kites soar by taking advantage of *ascending air currents*. ‖ 上昇志向の若き企業家 a young *upwardly mobile* entrepreneur.

[2]**じょうしょう 常勝の** invincible.

[1]**じょうじょう 上々** ▶1学期の成績は上々だったが, 2学期は目も当てられなかった I got *good* grades in the first term, but did miserably in the second (term). ‖ 滑り出しは上々だ I have gotten off to a *good* start.

[2]**じょうじょう 上場** ▶株式を上場する *list* one's shares [stock]; *have* one's shares [stock] *listed*; *go public* ‖ わが社は東証一部に上場しています Our company *is listed* on the first section of the Tokyo Stock Exchange.

じょうじょうしゃくりょう 情状酌量 ▶彼には情状酌量の余地がある *Extenuating* [*Mitigating*] *circumstances* in his case can be taken into account [consideration]. (➤ extenuating circumstances は「酌量すべき情状」).

しょうじょうぶっきょう 小乗仏教 →上座部仏教.

しょうしょく 小食 ▶鳥は概して小食だ Birds are *light eaters*. / Birds generally *eat very little*. ‖ 健康のためには小食がいいようだ It seems that *eating light* is good for the health. ‖ あれ, きょうは小食だね Gee, you *have a poor appetite* today. / You're *eating like a bird* today.

じょうしょく 常食 ▶米を常食とする *live on* rice ‖ パンダは笹(ささ)を常食としている The panda *feeds on* bamboo grass.

しょうじる 生じる **occur** /əkə́ːr/ ; **happen** (起こる) ▶彼が定年退職して欠員が生じた A vacancy *occurred* because of his retirement. ‖ どうしてそんなことが生じたのでしょうか How did that *happen* [*come about*]? ‖ 思わぬ不都合が生じて会合に出席できなかった Something unexpected *came up* and I was unable to attend the meeting. ‖ 誤解が生じるような言い方をしないでほしい Don't say anything that might *be misunderstood*.

じょうじる 乗じる ▶震災に乗じて (=つけ込んで) もうける悪質な業者もあった There were some profiteering businesses that *took advantage of* the earthquake to increase profits. ‖ 相手の隙に乗じて, 我々は反撃に出た When the enemy let down their guard, we *saw it as an opportunity to* go on the counter offensive. ‖ 侵入者は暗闇に乗じて庭に忍び込んだ The intruder stole into the garden *under cover of darkness*.

[1]**しょうしん 昇進** (a) **promotion** 一動 **昇進する be promoted** 《to》 ▶兄は最近昇進した My (older) brother *got a promotion* recently. ‖ 島さんは課長に昇進した Mr. Shima *was promoted to* section chief. (➤ 地位・役職を表す名詞は Ⓤ 扱い) ‖ 彼は係長から一気に部長に昇進した He *jumped* [*leaped*] from chief clerk to general manager.

[2]**しょうしん 小心な** **timid** ▶小心な男 a *timid* man ‖ 英雄の誉れ高い人が実は小心であることが多い Great heroes often turn out to *be timid at heart*.

[3]**しょうしん 傷心** **grief** (人の死などが原因の) ; **(deep) sorrow** (強い悲しみ) ; **broken heartedness** (失恋による) ▶妻を失った傷心を癒やすため彼は長旅に出た He started on a long trip to *forget his deep sorrow* at having lost his wife.

[4]**しょうしん 焼身** ▶学生が抗議の焼身自殺をした A student *burned himself* [*herself*] *to death* in protest.

[1]**しょうじん 精進** ▶芸の道に精進する *devote oneself to* the pursuit of one's art.
‖**精進料理** a vegetarian dish traditionally prepared for religious reasons (➤ 説明的な訳).

2しょうじん 小人 a person of weak character［small caliber］, a person of little consequence［importance］ ▶小人閑居して不善をなす A person of weak character does bad things when idle. ／An idle mind is the workshop of the devil.
じょうじん 常人 an ordinary person（ふつうの人）; an average person（平均的な人）.
しょうしんしょうめい 正真正銘の authentic /ɔːθéntɪk/（真正の）; real（本物の）▶正真正銘の英雄［ばか］a *real* hero［fool］‖これは正真正銘，近藤勇の手紙だ This is an *authentic* letter by Kondo Isami. ‖正真正銘の菜食主義者 a *card-carrying* vegetarian（➤「会員証を持った」が原義で，ときにおどけた響きをもつ；「絶対菜食主義者」は vegan）.

じょうず 上手 一形 上手な good 一副 上手に well ▶上手な歯医者 a *good* dentist ‖理恵はピアノが上手だ Rie is a *good* pianist.

【文型】
物事(A)が上手だ
be good at A
be skillful at A
➤ A は名詞・動名詞

▶彼女は編み物も上手だ She *is good at* knitting, too. ‖健は車の運転が上手だ Ken *is skillful at* driving (a car). ／Ken is a *good* driver.
▶彼は字も文章も上手だ Not only is his handwriting *beautiful*, but he writes *well*, too. ‖あなたは英語が上手ですね You speak *good* English. ／You speak English *beautifully*. ‖英語がずいぶん上手になりましたね Your English *has improved* a lot, hasn't it？‖英語が上手に話せたらいいなあ I wish I could speak English *fluently*. ‖スーザンは上手に箸を使う Susan handles chopsticks *well*［*skillfully*］. ‖話し上手よりも聞き上手になれ Be *a good listener* rather than *a good talker*.
しょうすい 憔悴する become haggard ▶しょうすいした顔 a *haggard* face.
1じょうすい 浄水 water purification
‖浄水場 a water treatment plant［facility］.
2じょうすい 上水 running water（水道水）; clean water（きれいな水）
‖上水道 a waterworks（給水設備）.
1しょうすう 小数 a decimal ▶小数第何位まで求めるのですか *How many decimal places* do I have to count down to？‖小数点以下は切り捨ててください Don't count numbers *below the decimal point*. ／Discard decimals.
2しょうすう 少数の (a) few, a small number of

【文型】
少数の A
a few A
a small number of A
➤ A は複数形の名詞

▶彼を支持したのはほんの少数だった Only *a few* (people)［*a small number of* people］supported him. ‖少数の例外はあるが，それは有効な規則だ That's an effective rule with *a few* exceptions.
▶少数の人の意見も採り上げるべきだ You should listen to the opinion of *the minority*. （➤ minority は「少数派」;「少数意見」は a minority opinion）‖わが社では男性社員は少数派だ At our company, male employees are in *the minority*.
▶うちの営業チームは少数精鋭だ Our sales team consists of *few*, but excellent members.
‖少数民族 an ethnic minority, a minority (race).
じょうすう 常数《数学》a constant.
しょうする 称する ▶黒井と称する男 a man who *calls himself*［*goes by the name of*］Kuroi ‖進はクラスで一番の俊足だと称している Susumu *claims* to be the best runner in his class. ‖秋田県の角館は小京都と称される Kakunodate in Akita Prefecture *is called* 'Little Kyoto.'
▶彼はかぜと称して仕事を休んだ He took the day off from work *claiming* he'd caught a cold. （➤ 日英とも「本当はかぜではない」の意味合い）.
しょうせい 小生 Ⅰ（➤ 英語では自分をへりくだって表す表現は用いないのがふつう）.
1じょうせい 情勢・状勢 a situation; things（事態）▶世界の情勢 the world *situation* ‖中東情勢が険悪になってきた *The situation* in the Middle East has become tense. ‖目下の情勢では紛争は解決しそうにない Judging from［by］*the present situation*, the dispute is unlikely to be settled. ‖しばらく情勢を注意深く見守る必要がある We have to carefully watch *how things develop* for a while.
2じょうせい 上製の superior, deluxe.
1じょうせき 定石 a *joseki*（囲碁の）; standard moves［tactics ／practices］▶それは囲碁の定石だ That's *a joseki*［*a set sequence of moves*］in *Go*. ‖川崎は定石どおりバントで走者を2塁へ進めた *Playing by the book*, Kawasaki sacrificed the runner to second.
2じょうせき 上席 1【上座】▶上席に座る sit at *the head of a table*.
2【上の位】一形 上席の senior ▶上席研究員 a *senior* researcher.
1しょうせつ 小説 a novel（長編の）; a story（短編の）; fiction（創作物）▶小説を書く write *a novel*.
‖小説家 a novelist ‖私小説 an "I" novel ‖推理小説 a mystery［detective］story ‖短編小説 a short story ‖恋愛小説 a love story.
2しょうせつ 小節《音楽》a bar ▶最初の3小節を歌う sing the first three *bars*.
じょうせつ 常設の standing（常置の）; permanent（永久の）▶クロード・モネ常設展 a *permanent* Claude Monet *exhibition* ‖その美術館の常設展示品には有名なルネサンスの絵画もあります *The permanent exhibits* at the art gallery include some famous Renaissance paintings.
‖常設委員会 a standing committee.
じょうぜつ 饒舌な loquacious /loʊkwéɪʃəs/; talkative（おしゃべりの）▶田口君のじょう舌はお酒が入ると拍車がかかる Taguchi gets even more *talkative* when he gets drunk.
しょうせっかい 消石灰 slaked lime.
1しょうせん 商船 a merchant ship
‖商船大学 a mercantile marine college.
2しょうせん 商戦 a trade war ▶年末商戦 year-end shopping season.
しょうぜん 悄然 ▶男はしょう然として出廷した The *dejected* man appeared in court. （➤ dejected は「落胆した」）‖敗れたテニスチャンピオンはしょう然たるありさまだった The defeated tennis champion was *crestfallen*. （➤ crestfallen は「意気消沈して」の意；名詞の前では用いない）.
じょうせん 乗船する board, go［get］on board a

ship, go aboard a ship, embark +目 (➤ 最後の語は堅い言い方) ▶皆さん, **乗船する**時間ですよ Everybody, it is time we *boarded* [*got on board*] *the ship.* ／All aboard!

しょうそ 勝訴 ▶裁判では被告側が**勝訴した** The accused *won the case* [*suit*] in court.

じょうそ 上訴 (an) **appeal** ▶**上訴する** appeal (a case) to a higher court.

1**しょうそう 焦燥** **impatience**(いらいら) ; **frustration** (挫折感) ▶私は就職がなかなか決まらず**焦燥(感)に駆られている** I *am frustrated* at having a hard time finding a job.

2**しょうそう 尚早** ▶結論を下すのはまだ**時期尚早だ** *It is too early* to draw a conclusion.

しょうぞう 肖像 a **portrait** /pɔ́ːʳtrət/ ; an **image** /ímɪdʒ/ (彫像) ▶自分の**肖像画**を描いてもらう sit for one's *portrait* ‖ ケネディ大統領の**肖像**のある硬貨 a coin with *an image* of (U. S.) President Kennedy

‖**肖像画家** a portrait painter ‖ **肖像権** the right to one's portrait(s).

じょうそう 情操 ▶音楽は子供の**情操**を育てるのに良いそうだ Music is said to be good for promoting *emotional development* in children.

‖**情操教育** cultivation of aesthetic sentiments (➤ aesthetic /esθétɪk/ は「美的な」の意).

じょうぞう 醸造する **brew** /bruː/ +目 (酒・しょうゆなどを) ▶ビールを**醸造する** *brew* beer ‖ 日本酒は米を材料にした**醸造酒**だ Sake is a *fermented alcoholic beverage* made from rice.

‖**醸造所** a brewery (ビール・日本酒の) ; a distillery (ウイスキーの) ; a winery (ワインの).

じょうそうぶ 上層部 ▶会社の**上層部** *the top management* of a company ‖ 政党の**上層部** *the top leadership* [*upper echelons*] of a political party.

しょうそく 消息 (●「消息」には news や information が相当するが, 実際には用例のように動詞を使って表現することが多い) ▶彼は数年前は中東に赴任していたが最近**消息がわからない** I know he was stationed in the Middle East several years ago, but I *don't know how he is getting along* now. ‖ アメリカにいる息子からこの半年間**消息がない** I *haven't heard from* my son in the U.S. for the last six months. (➤ hear from は「(本人から)手紙・電話などをもらう」; うわさなどで消息を聞く場合は hear of) ‖ 彼らがアマゾンの奥地で**消息を絶って**から１か月になる It's been one month since we *last heard from* them in the depths of the Amazon. ‖ 彼は１週間前から**消息を絶っている** He *has been missing* for a week. (➤ missing は「行方不明の」) ‖ ３人が依然**消息不明**だ Three people are still *unaccounted for*.

▶あの人は芸能界の消息に通じている [消息通だ] He *is well informed of things* happening in the entertainment world.

1**しょうたい 招待** (an) **invitation** 一動 **招待する** **invite** +目

> **語法** **invite** は比較的規模の大きな祝宴・パーティーなどに関連して用いることが多く, 日常的には **ask ... to come** や **have ... over** などを用いることが多い.

▶ご**招待**ありがとうございます. 喜んで伺います Thank you very much for your *invitation.* I would be glad to come. ／I accept your *invitation* with pleasure. (➤ 後者は形式ばった表現).

> **【文型】**
> 人(A)を会・場所(B)に招待する
> **invite** A **to** B

▶我々は友人を新居に**招待した** We *invited* our friends *to* our new house. ‖ あすは友恵さんの結婚式に**招待されている** I'*m invited to* Tomoe's wedding tomorrow.

▶私は清君を夕食に**招待した** I *asked* Kiyoshi (*to come*) to dinner. ／I *had* Kiyoshi *over* for dinner. (➤ 後者は夕食会が済んだあとでの文) ‖ 誕生パーティーには友だち５人を**招待し**ようと思う I am going to *ask* five friends *to come to my house* for my birthday party. ‖ 近藤先生はボストン交響楽団の**招待**で渡米した Mr. Kondo went to the U.S. *at the invitation* of the Boston Symphony Orchestra. ‖ その映画の試写会の**招待券**が手に入った I got *a complimentary ticket* for a preview of that movie.

‖**招待客** an invited guest ‖ **招待試合** an invitation match [game] ‖ **招待状** an invitation (card) ‖ **招待席** a reserved seat for a guest ‖ **招待選手** an invited player.

2**しょうたい 正体** **1【本当の姿】** one's **true nature** [**character**] ; one's **identity**(身元) ▶その不思議な発光体の**正体**はまだつかめていない The *true nature* of that light-emitting substance is not known yet. ‖ 男は自分の**正体**を隠した The man hid his *identity.* ‖ あの偽善者はやがて**正体を現す**だろう That hypocrite will *reveal his true character* [*show his true colors*] before long. ‖ 悪党め, とうとう**正体を現し**たな! You bastard! *I've found you out* at last! ‖ あいつは**正体不明**だ He is *an enigma.* (➤ enigma /ɪnígmə/ は「謎の人」) ‖ **正体不明の物体**が地球に近づいている An *unidentifiable* object is approaching the earth.

2【正気】 ▶彼は**正体なく**眠って [酔って] いた He was *dead* asleep [drunk].

3**しょうたい 小隊** 《陸軍》 a **platoon** ▶**小隊長** a *platoon* leader [commander].

1**じょうたい 状態・情態** **condition(s)** (一時的な状況) ; **circumstances** /sə́ːʳkəmstænsɪz/ (周囲の状況と特定の人や事柄との関係) ; a **situation**(人や物を取り巻く周囲の状況) ; a **state** (人や物の状態) ▶天候の**状態** weather *conditions* ‖ わが社は財政的に**危ない状態**にある Our company is in *critical condition* financially. ‖ **現在の状態では**このプロジェクトはあと３年かかるだろう *Under the circumstances* [*As things are* ／ *As things stand*], this project will take three more years to finish. ‖ 祖母はここ数年**寝たきりの状態**です My grandmother *has been bedridden* for several years. ‖ その国の**経済状態**は年々悪くなっている *The economic situation* in that country is getting worse year by year. ‖ 祖父の**健康状態**がはかばかしくない My grandfather is in a weakened *condition.* ‖ その小国は内乱のため**混乱状態**にある The small country is in *a state of confusion* because of internal disturbances.

2**じょうたい 上体** **the upper part of the body** ▶患者はベッドで**上体を起こした** The patient *sat up* in bed.

しょうだく 承諾 **consent** /kənsént/ (同意) ; **permission** (許可) ; **approval** (賛成) 一動 **承諾する** **consent** 《to》, **agree** 《to》, **approve** +目 ▶生徒が修学旅行に参加するには**親の承諾**が必要だ Students must have *parental consent* to take part in the school trip. ‖ 午後早退することは担任の先生から**承諾**をもらっています My homeroom teacher gave me *permission* to leave early this afternoon. ‖ 校長はうなずいて**承諾した** The principal *nodded* (his) *approval*. ‖ 両親は私たちの結婚を**承諾してくれた** My parents *approved* our marriage.

‖**承諾書** a letter of consent.

じょうたつ 上達 **improvement** 一動 **上達する** **improve** (だんだん良くなる) ; **make progress** (➤ 主に人を主語にして) ▶彼女のテニスには**上達**の跡が見られない She shows no signs of *improvement* in tennis. ‖ どうやったら英語が**上達する**でしょうか How can I [What can I do to] *improve* my English ? ‖ 彼女はロシア語の**上達が早い** [遅い] She *is making rapid* [*slow*] *progress* in Russian.

しょうだん 商談 a (**business**) **deal** (取り引き) ; **negotiations** /nɪgòʊʃiéɪʃənz/ (交渉) ; a **business talk** (商売の話) ▶**商談をまとめる** strike a *deal* ‖ やっと**商談がまとまり**, 契約の運びとなった At last, *the deal was struck* [*closed*] and the contract (was) signed. ‖ このホテルはよく**商談**の場に使われる This hotel is often used for *business talks*.

じょうだん 冗談 a **joke** ; **humor** (ユーモア) ▶**冗談を飛ばす** *make* [*crack*] *a joke* ‖ **冗談はよせよ** Stop *joking*. ‖ **冗談が過ぎるよ** You're carrying the *joke* too far. ‖ それはきつい**冗談**だね That's a cruel *joke* for sure. ‖ 彼は私が**冗談半分**に言ったことを真に受けて怒った Though I said it *half jokingly* [*half in jest*], he took it seriously and got angry. ‖ あいつは**冗談がわからない**から付き合っていて疲れるよ Since he *lacks a sense of humor* [*can't take a joke*], he's tiring to be with. ‖ 気を悪くしないでくれ. 今のは**冗談**だよ (=本気ではない) Don't be offended. *I was only joking* [*pulling your leg*]. (➤ pull one's leg は「(〜を)からかう」の意) ‖ **冗談はさておき**本題に入りましょう *Joking aside* [*All kidding aside*], let's get down to business now.

▶**ご冗談でしょう**. 私の立場でそんなことができないことはご存じのはず *You must be kidding* [*joking*]. You know my position prevents me from involving myself in anything like that. ‖ 日曜日に出勤しろだなんて, **冗談じゃないよ** *There is no way* I would go to work on Sunday. (➤ There is no way ... は「…だなんて嫌だね, やなこった」に相当する).

[1]**しょうち 承知** **1**【知っている】 **know** ; **be aware** (気づいている) ▶私が健二さんと付き合っていることは親も**承知しています** My parents *are aware* that I'm dating Kenji. ‖ 彼が金を出す気がないのは初めから**百も承知**だ I *knew well* [*was well aware*] from the very beginning that he had no intention of paying. ‖ おまえはそれを**承知のうえで**やったのだから責任を取らなければいけないよ You did it *with your eyes open*, so you'll have to accept responsibility for any consequences. (➤ with one's eyes open は「何が起こるか知りながら」) ‖ **ご承知のように**私は元プロレスラーでした *As you know*, I used to be a professional wrestler. ‖ 対話「あすの朝までに仕上げてください」「**承知いたしました**」"Please finish it by tomorrow morning." "*Right*. / *Yes, sir*."

✉ **当社の工場をご案内する件, 承知いたしました** I'll *be pleased to* show you around our plant as you have requested. ➤「あなたのご要望どおりに喜んでご案内します」の意. 改まった表現.

2【許す】 **permit** +目 (許可を与える) ; **allow** /əláʊ/ +目 (何かが起こる[行われる]ことを許す) ; **forgive** +目 (罪などを許す) ▶今晩遅く帰ることを母は**承知してくれた** My mother *permitted* me [*gave me permission*] to come home late this evening. ‖ 両親は私の留学を**承知してくれない** My parents won't *allow* me *to* study abroad. ‖ この子をいじめたら**承知しないぞ** *I'll teach you to* bully him. (➤ I will teach you to do は, 叱ったり脅したりするときの文句で,「…するとどういうことになるかわからせてやる」の意) ‖ そんなことをしたら**承知しない**よ I will *never forgive* you if you do such a thing. (➤ 強い警告) / If you do that, then don't *look at me*. (➤ 軽い警告).

[2]**しょうち 招致** (an) **invitation** 一動 **招致する** **invite** +目 ▶冬季オリンピックを**招致する** *make a bid to host* the Winter Olympics (➤ make a bid は「提案書を出す」, host は「主催する」の意).

しょうちくばい 松竹梅 ***shochikubai*** ; pine, bamboo and plum, used as a decoration on a celebratory occasion (➤ 説明的な訳) 《参考》 料理などの等級を表す松・竹・梅は「松[竹 / 梅]のすしの盛り合わせ」を a deluxe [special / regular] sushi platter と表すことができる.

しょうちゅう 焼酎 ***shochu***

日本紹介 ✉ **焼酎は米・麦・サツマイモなどを原料とした, 比較的安価な蒸留酒です. お湯や水で割って飲むのがふつうですが, 炭酸水で割って飲むチューハイも人気があります** *Shochu* is relatively inexpensive distilled liquor made from rice, wheat or sweet potatoes. It is usually diluted with hot or cold water. '*Chuhai*,' a blend of *shochu* and soda water, is a popular drink.

じょうちゅう 常駐 ▶パリ**常駐**の特派員 a *regular* correspondent *in Paris* ‖ 外国の軍隊がその国の南部に**常駐している** Foreign troops *are* (*permanently*) *stationed* in the south of the country.

‖**常駐ソフト** a resident (software) program.

じょうちょ 情緒 **1**【雰囲気】 **atmosphere** /ǽtməsfɪəʳ/ ▶その洋館には**異国情緒**があふれていた That Western-style building had *an exotic atmosphere* [had *exoticism*]. ‖ この町にはかつて**江戸情緒** [古い東京の**情緒**] が残っていた This town was once rich in the *Edo atmosphere* [the *atmosphere* of old Tokyo].

2【感情】 ▶彼女は夫の死後**情緒不安定になった** She *has been emotionally unstable* since her husband died. ‖ 彼女は**情緒たっぷりに**『蝶々(ちょうちょう)夫人』を歌った She sang "Madame Butterfly" *with* (*persuasive*) *emotion*.

‖**情緒障害児** an emotionally disturbed child.

[1]**しょうちょう 象徴** a **symbol** ; an **emblem** (ある物を表す記号や図形) 一動 **象徴する** **symbolize** +目 ▶スマートフォンは現代科学技術の**象徴**である The smartphone is *a symbol* of modern scientific technology. ‖ ハトは平和を**象徴する**鳥だ A dove *symbolizes* peace. / The dove is the bird *symbolic of* peace. ‖ 象は共和党の**象徴**だ An elephant is the *symbol* of the Republican Party. ‖ オリンピック聖火は平和と希望を**象徴的に表している** The Olympic Flame *symbolically represents* [*symbolizes* / *is a symbol of*] peace and hope.

‖**象徴主義** symbolism.

[2]**しょうちょう 小腸** **the small intestine.**

[3]**しょうちょう 省庁** **ministries and agencies.**

じょうちょう 冗長な **long-winded** (長たらしい) ; **wordy, verbose** /vəːʳbóʊs/ (ことば数が多い ; 後者には

「極端に多い」という含みがある)；**redundant** /rɪdʌ́ndənt/ (繰り返しが多い) ▶冗長なスピーチ a *long-winded* [*verbose*] speech ‖冗長な文体 a *redundant* (writing) style.

じょうでき 上出来 ▶おまえにしては上出来だ *Very well done* considering your work up to now. ‖このケーキ, きみが作ったにしては上出来だね This cake isn'*t bad*, considering you made it. ‖ 対話「やっとお父さんの似顔絵ができたよ」「上出来, 上出来」"I finally finished drawing your portrait, Dad." "*You did a good job!* ／*That's great!*"

1**しょうてん 焦点** 1【レンズの】a **focus** ▶カバの鼻にカメラの焦点を合わせる *focus* the camera on the hippo's nose ‖市販のほとんどのカメラは自動的に焦点が合う Most cameras on the market *focus* automatically. ‖この写真は焦点がぴったり合っている [ぼけている] This picture *is in* [*out of*] *focus*.

‖焦点距離 the focal length [distance] ‖自動焦点カメラ an auto-focus camera, an automatic focusing camera.

2【的】▶焦点となっている問題 a *focal* issue ‖焦点の人 the person *under focus* ‖彼の話は焦点がはっきりしないからわかりにくい He *rambles* [*doesn't stick to the point*], which makes it hard to follow him.

2**しょうてん 商店** 《米》a **store**, 《英》a **shop**

‖商店街 a shopping street; a shopping center (郊外などにある)；a shopping mall (遊歩道式の) ‖商店主《米》a storekeeper, 《英》a shopkeeper.

じょうと 譲渡 (a) **transfer** (権利・財産などの)；(a) **handover** (権力・財産などの移譲) 一動 譲渡する **transfer** ＋目, **hand over** ▶球団はその選手との交渉権をドジャーズに譲渡した The ball club *transferred* its negotiating rights over the player to the Dodgers. ‖このチケットは他人に譲渡することはできません This ticket may not *be given or sold* to anyone.

じょうど 浄土 the Pure Land ▶西方浄土 *the Pure Land* in the west.

しょうとう 消灯 ▶消灯時間は10時です *Lights-out* (is) at 10 p.m. ‖もう消灯の時間ですよ It is time you *put out* [*turned off*] *the light*. (➤It is time のあとの節中の動詞は仮定法過去形)／It's time to *turn off* [*turn out*] *the lights*.

しょうどう 衝動 (an) **impulse** /ímpʌls/ (抑えがたい)；an **urge** /əːrdʒ/ (駆り立てられるような感じ) ▶衝動的犯行 an *impulsive* crime ‖衝動買いをするとろくでもない物をつかまされることになるよ If you *buy* something *on impulse* [*on the spur of the moment*], you'll end up with something that is not worth the money. (➤「衝動買い」は impulse buying；「衝動買いの癖がある」は have an impulse buying habit) ‖その中学生は衝動的に先生を刺した That junior high school student stabbed the teacher *on impulse* [*impulsively*]. ‖私は腹が立って純を殴りたい衝動に駆られた I got angry and *felt an urge* to hit Jun.

じょうとう 上等 1【優れた】**excellent, fine, good** ▶上等のワイン (an) *excellent* wine／(a) *good* [*superior*] *quality* wine／a *fine* wine ‖このスーツはあれより上等だ This suit *is superior to* [*is better than*] that. ‖もっと上等のを見せてください Could you show me a *better* one [something *of better quality*]?

2【十分である】▶3回戦までいったんだろ？そこまでいきゃあ上等だよ You've made it into the third round, haven't you? You *should be quite satisfied with that*.

じょうとうく 常套句 a **conventional phrase**; a **cliché** /kliːʃéɪ/ (陳腐な).

じょうとうしゅだん 常套手段 ▶スパムメールを使って個人情報を盗むのは詐欺の常套手段だ Stealing personal information by sending spam mail is *a standard ploy* [*trick*] used in fraud. (➤ploy は「(だましなどの)手」) ‖返事に困ると話をそらすのが彼女の常套手段だ Changing the subject is her *usual trick* [*ploy*] when she has a hard time coming up with an answer.

じょうとうへい 上等兵 《米》a **private first class** (陸軍の)；a **superior private** (旧日本軍の).

しょうどく 消毒 disinfection (殺菌)；**sterilization** (煮沸などによる)；**pasteurization** /pæ̀stʃərəzéɪʃən/ (パスツール式低温殺菌法) (➤あとの2語は専門用語). 一動 消毒する **disinfect** ＋目, **sterilize** /stérəlaɪz/ ＋目, **pasteurize** /pǽstʃəraɪz/ ＋目 ▶傷口を消毒液で消毒する *disinfect* a cut with (*an*) *antiseptic* ‖水道の水は塩素で消毒してある Tap water *is disinfected* with chlorine. ‖外科用器具は使用する前に消毒する必要がある Surgical instruments must *be sterilized* before use. ‖メスを煮沸消毒した We *sterilized* the scalpels *in boiling water*. ‖消毒器 a sterilizer ‖消毒薬 a disinfectant, an antiseptic.

じょうとくい 上得意 one's **best customer**.

しょうとつ 衝突

1【物と物の】a **crash** (大きな音を立てての)；a **collision** (両方から動いてきての)；a **smash** (特に車の大衝突) 一動 衝突する **hit** (ぶつかる；最も一般的な語)；**crash**, **smash** 《into》, **collide** 《with》; **run** 《into》 (ぶち当たる) ▶大きないん石が地球に衝突したらどうなるだろう What would happen if a large meteorite were to *hit* the earth?

【文型】
乗り物・物(A)と衝突する
crash into A
collide with A

▶スポーツカーがバスに衝突した A sports car *crashed* [*smashed*] *into* a bus. ／A sports car *collided with* a bus. ‖列車どうしが正面衝突した The two trains *crashed* (*into each other*) *head-on*. ／The two trains *collided head-on*.

2【意見・利害の】a **clash**, a **conflict** (➤後者は長い間のぶつかり合いを連想させる)；a **collision** (深刻なぶつかり合い) 一動 衝突する **clash** ▶意見の衝突 *a clash* of views ‖利害の衝突 *a conflict* of interest ‖お父さんとはよく意見が衝突する I often *have disagreements with* my father. ／My opinions often *clash with* those of my father. ‖あの2人は話し始めるといつも衝突する Whenever those two start talking, they *lock horns*. (➤lock horns は文字どおりには「(牛などが)角を交えて戦う」) ‖私は会社で仲間と衝突しないようにやっている I try hard to *get along with* my co-workers.

逆引き熟語 ○○衝突
◆空中衝突 a midair collision／正面衝突 a head-on collision [crash]／多重衝突 a multiple pileup [smash-up]／玉突き衝突 a pile-up, a multicar collision／二重衝突 a double collision／列車衝突 a train collision [crash]
◆意見の衝突 a clash of views／武力衝突 an armed conflict／利害の衝突 a conflict [clash] of interest(s)

しょうとりひき 商取引 a **business** [**commercial**] **transaction, business dealings** ▶我々は主に台湾の会社と商取引をしている We mainly *have business dealings* [We mainly *do business*] with companies in Taiwan.

じょうない 場内 ▶そのアナウンスを聞いて場内は騒然となった When people in the hall heard the announcement, there was an uproar.

しょうにか 小児科 **pediatrics** /pìːdiǽtrɪks/ ▶小児科医にかかる consult *a pediatrician* [*a children's doctor*] (➤後者はインフォーマルな言い方). 《参考》小児歯科医は a pediatric dentist.

しょうにまひ 小児麻痺 **polio, poliomyelitis** /pòʊlioʊmàɪəláɪtɪs/ (➤後者は専門用語) ▶小児まひにかかる contract *polio*.

しょうにゅうせき 鐘乳石 a **stalactite** /stəlǽktaɪt/.

しょうにゅうどう 鐘乳洞 a **limestone cave.**

1**しょうにん 商人** a **merchant**; a **tradesman**; a **storekeeper**

> 《解説》(1)日本語の「商人」も英語の merchant も意味範囲は広いが，一般には merchant は「貿易商人」を指す．(2)「小売り商人」に相当するのは tradesman [-woman] で，「商店経営者，商店主」に相当するのは《米》storekeeper,《英》shopkeeper である．

2**しょうにん 承認** **approval** (賛成); **permission** (許可); **consent** (承諾) 一動 **承認する** **approve** +㊐, **recognize** +㊐ ▶予算案は理事会で承認された The budget proposal *was approved* by the board of directors. ‖アルバイトをするには学校の承認がいる You need your school's *permission* before you can work part-time. ‖日本は新政府を承認した Japan *recognized* the new government.

3**しょうにん 証人** a (**sworn**) **witness** (➤sworn は「宣誓をした」) ▶X氏の証人喚問を要求する *demand* Mr. X's *appearance as a sworn witness* (➤「参考人」なら an unsworn witness;「証人喚問」は a summons of a witness) ‖彼は被告側の証人として裁判に召喚された He was called as *a defense witness* at the trial. ‖原爆の被害者は戦争という悲劇の生き証人だ The atom bomb victims are *living witnesses* to the tragedy of war.

4**しょうにん 昇任** (a) **promotion** 一動 **昇任する** **be promoted** ▶彼は最近管理職に昇任した He *was promoted* to a managerial position recently.

5**しょうにん 聖人・上人** a **holy (Buddhist) priest** ▶親鸞聖人 *Saint* Shinran.

じょうにん 常任の **regular** ▶母はPTAの常任委員を3年やっている For three years my mother has served as *a member* on the PTA *standing committee*.
‖**常任委員会** a standing committee ‖**常任指揮者** the resident [regular] conductor (of an orchestra) ‖**常任理事** an executive director ‖(国連)**常任理事国** a permanent member (nation) of the UN Security Council.

しょうにんずう 少人数 **a small number of people** ▶こんな少人数ではあいつらにかないっこないよ There's no way this *small number of people* [so *few people*] can win against them. ‖このクラスは少人数なので生徒は授業中に数回ずつ当てられる Since this is a *small* class, each student can be called on several times during class. ‖あの英会話学校は少人数制をとっている That English language school *has a policy of limiting class size*. ／That English language school *keeps their classes small*.

しょうね 性根 ▶あの男は性根まで腐っている He's rotten *to the core*. ／He's bad *through and through*. ‖性根を入れ替えて勉強しろ *Make a fresh start* [*Turn over a new leaf*] and work hard.

じょうねつ 情熱 **enthusiasm** /ɪnθjúːziæzəm/, **passion** ▶最近兄はバラの品種改良に情熱を傾けている Nowadays, my older brother is *pouring his passion* into [*is passionate* about] producing a new variety of roses. ‖彼女は演劇に情熱を注いでいる She's *enthusiastic about* drama. ‖パメラは情熱的な少女だった Pamela was a *passionate* girl.

しょうねん 少年 a **boy** 《参考》5歳くらいから19歳くらいまでの男子を指す語．little boy は生後まもない男児から8歳くらいまでの少年を指す ▶10歳の少年 *a boy* of ten ／a ten-year-old *boy* ‖私は津和野で少年時代を過ごした I spent my *boyhood* in Tsuwano. ‖少年犯罪は年々増加している *Juvenile crime* is increasing year by year.
‖**少年院** a reformatory,《米また》a reform school,《英また》a community home ‖**少年雑誌** a boys' magazine, a magazine for boys.

じょうねん 情念 (an) **emotion.**

しょうねんば 正念場 **the crucial moment** [**point**] ▶ことしこそこのプロジェクトの正念場だ This year will *be crucial* for this project.

1**しょうのう 小脳** **the cerebellum.**

2**しょうのう 笑納**
✉ **これはおもてなしいただいたお礼です．どうぞご笑納ください** This is something to express my thanks for your hospitality. I hope you'll like it. (🍎「どうぞご笑納ください」は日本語独特の手紙用語で，直訳すると滑稽なことになる．英語では率直に「気に入っていただけるといいのですが」と意訳するしかない)．

3**しょうのう 樟脳** **camphor** /kǽmfəʳ/.

じょうば 乗馬 **horseback riding** (➤日本語につられて horse riding としない) ▶彼女は乗馬を習っている She is learning *how to ride a horse*. ／She is learning *horseback riding*. ‖**乗馬クラブ** a riding club ‖**乗馬服** riding clothes.

1**しょうはい 勝敗** **victory or defeat** ▶勝敗にこだわるな Don't fret over [worry about] *victory or defeat*. ‖勝敗はともかく全力を尽くすつもりだ *Win or lose*, we are going to fight as hard as we can. ‖ちょっとしたミスで勝敗が決まることがある The smallest mistake can *decide* (*the outcome of*) *a game*.

2**しょうはい 賞杯** a **cup**, a **trophy.**

しょうばい 商売

1【商い】(a) **business** /bíznəs/ ▶商売を始める start [go into] *business* ‖商売繁盛を祈願する pray for *success in business* ‖兄は岡山で商売をしています My (older) brother *owns* [*has*] *a business* in Okayama. ‖母は衣類雑貨関係の商売をしている My mother *is doing business* related to clothes and sundries. ‖これ以上ドル安が続くと商売上がったりだ We will go *out of business* if the value of the dollar drops any more. ‖彼は根っからの商売人だ He's *a merchant* [*businessman*] at heart. ‖タレントは所詮人気商売だ In the final analysis, TV personalities sink or swim depending on their popularity. ‖翻訳家の私にとって辞書は大事な商売道具だ As a translator, dictionaries are important *tools of my trade*. ‖**対話**「商売のほうはどうですか」

「不景気でさっぱりです」"*How's business?*" "Awful, because of this economic slump."

2【職業】business ▶ **対話**「どんなご商売をなさっていますか」「ガソリンスタンドをやっています」"*What kind of business* [*What line*] are you in?" "I run a gas station." →**職業**.

しょうばつ 賞罰 reward and punishment
▶賞罰なし no *commendations* [*rewards*] *and punishment* (➤ 英語圏にはない慣習).

じょうはつ 蒸発 evaporation 一動 蒸発する evaporate ▶水が蒸発して雲になる Water *evaporates* to make clouds.
▶《比喩的》私が蒸発したって誰も寂しがってくれないだろうな I'll bet if I were to *disappear*, nobody would miss me.

じょうはんしん 上半身 the upper part of one's **body** ▶彼は上半身がたくましい He has a muscular *upper body*. ‖上半身裸になってください Please strip *to the waist* (➤ Please remove your shirt. のほうが自然).

しょうひ 消費 consumption 一動 消費する consume /kənsúːm/ +目 ▶灯油の消費(量)は冬に増加する *Consumption* of kerosene increases in winter. ‖真夏には多量の電力が消費される A great deal of electricity *is consumed* in the height of summer. ‖個人消費が鈍化し始めている Personal *consumption* [Consumer *spending*] is beginning to slow.
‖**消費財** consumer goods ‖**消費者** a consumer ‖**消費者運動** the consumer movement ‖**消費者価格** a consumer price ‖**消費者団体** a consumer group ‖**消費者庁** the Consumer Affairs Agency ‖**消費者物価指数** the consumer price index《略 CPI》‖**消費税** a consumption tax(日本の); a sales tax(アメリカなどの); a VAT(=value-added tax)(イギリスなどの).

ジョウビタキ《鳥》a **Daurian redstart.**

じょうびやく 常備薬 household medicine《参考》海外旅行などで「常備薬」という場合は non-prescription medicine(処方箋なしで買える薬)とか over-the-counter medicine(店頭で買える薬)などと表現する.

しょうひょう 商標 a **trademark.**

1**しょうひん 商品 goods, merchandise** (➤ 総称); a **product**; an **item for sale** (売り物) ▶外国商品 foreign *goods* ‖輸入商品 imported *goods* ‖おたくの店ではどんな商品を扱っていますか What kinds of *products* do you sell in your store? ‖あの店は商品がそろっている That store carries a wide variety of *goods* [*products*]. ‖今日では情報も商品である These days even information is (*an item*) *for sale*.
‖**商品券** a gift certificate ‖**商品市場** a commodity market ‖**商品取引所** a commodity exchange ‖**商品名** a brand [trade] name.

2**しょうひん 賞品** a **prize** ▶賞品を獲得する win a *prize* ‖ゴルフのコンペで優勝し, 数々の賞品をもらった I won the golf tournament and got lots of *prizes*. ‖1等の賞品は何ですか What's (*the*) *first prize*?

3**しょうひん 小品** a **small artistic work** ▶音楽の小品 *a short musical composition* [*piece*] ‖絵画の小品 *a small painting* ‖文学の小品 *a short literary work*.

じょうひん 上品 elegance (身につけた優雅さ); **grace** (天性の姿や態度の優美さ); **refinement** (洗練) **一形 上品な elegant, graceful, refined; delicate** /délɪkət/ (味などが) ▶上品な中年女性 an *elegant* woman in her mid-40s or 50s (● middle-aged woman はしばしば中年太りのイメージを伴うので, elegant とは結び付かない) ‖上品な和菓子 *delicate* Japanese (-style) confectionery ‖シカは上品な顔をしている The deer is a *noble*-looking animal. ‖兄嫁はいつも上品な服装をしている My brother's wife always wears *elegant* clothes [always dresses *in good taste*]. ‖彼女は物腰やことば遣いが上品だ The way she moves and speaks *are* (both) *refined*. / She behaves and speaks *elegantly*. ‖彼女には生まれながらの上品さが備わっている She has (a) natural *grace*. ‖あの子はすぐお上品ぶるから嫌いよ I don't like her because she *puts on airs*.

しょうふ 娼婦 a **prostitute** /prάːstətjuːt/.

1**しょうぶ 菖蒲**《植物》a **sweet flag**; a **Japanese iris** (花ショウブ).

2**しょうぶ 勝負** a **game,** a **match** (試合); a **bout** /baʊt/ (相撲などの一試合) →**試合** ▶勝負に勝つ[負ける] win [lose] *a game* ‖横綱どうしの一戦はなかなか勝負がつかなかった The two yokozunas *had a close bout* [*match*]. ‖井口君と坂本君の碁はいまだに勝負がつかない The *Go match* between Iguchi and Sakamoto *has not ended* [*finished*] *yet*. ‖勝負は時の運だ *Victory or defeat* [*Whether you win or lose*] depends upon chance. ‖よし, どちらが強いか勝負しようよ All right, *let's fight it out* to see who's stronger.
▶入試まであとわずか2か月. この冬休みが勝負だ There's only two months before the entrance exams and (how I study during) this winter vacation *will decide whether I succeed or fail*.
‖**勝負事** a game; gambling(賭け事).

じょうふ 情婦 a **mistress.**

1じょうぶ 丈夫

訳語メニュー
人が健康な →healthy, strong **1**
物が堅固な →strong **2**

1【健康な】healthy(心身ともに健康な); **strong**(筋骨たくましい, 力の強い); **robust**(壮健な) ▶丈夫な赤ちゃん a *healthy* baby ‖弟は体が丈夫だ My (younger) brother has a *strong constitution*. (➤ constitution は「体質」) ‖虚弱体質だった息子は成長するにつれて丈夫になった Our son, who had been (physically) weak, *became healthier* [*stronger*] as he grew older. ‖祖父は老齢にもかかわらず丈夫で働いている My grandfather *enjoys good health* and is still working despite his advanced age. ‖歯が丈夫でないと, このお煎餅は食べられない You have to *have good teeth* to eat this *senbei* (rice cracker).

2【堅固な】strong; durable(長もちする) ▶丈夫な箱 a *strong* box ‖このバッグは丈夫な素材でできている This bag is made of *strong* [*durable*] material. ‖ジーンズは丈夫だ Jeans *wear well*. ‖この傘は丈夫だ. 5年も使っているがどこも何ともない This umbrella *was made to last*. I've been using it for five years, and it is still (as) good as new. (➤ last は「長もちする」).

2**じょうぶ 上部 the upper part** ▶灯台の上部 *the upper part* of a lighthouse.
‖**上部構造** a superstructure.

しょうふく 承服する accept +目 (受け入れる) ▶公

園を潰して高層マンションを造るなんて計画にはとても**承服できない** We absolutely cannot *accept* this plan to do away with the park and build a high-rise condominium.

しょうふだ 正札 a **price tag** [**label**].

じょうぶつ 成仏 ▶おまえがいつまでもそんなふうにぶらぶらしてたら，亡くなったおまえのお父さんは**成仏できないぞ** If you go on leading an idle life like this, your father will *not be able to rest in peace*. (➤ rest in peace は「永眠する」; 英語では,「亡くなったおまえのお父さん」の「亡くなった」を dead とはいわないのがふつう).

しょうぶん 性分 (one's) **nature** ▶単刀直入に物を言うのは私の**性分に合わない** It is *not in my nature* to say things directly. ‖ 田舎暮らしが私の**性分に合って**いるらしい Living in the country seems to *agree with* me. ‖ 彼はどんな場合にもうそなどつけない**性分だ** He's *the kind of person* who never tells a lie, no matter what. ‖ あなたっていつも部下をかばっては部長に怒られてるんだから**損な性分ね** You're a real *loser*—always making the boss mad by covering up for your subordinates!

じょうぶん 条文 a **provision of a law.**

しょうへき 障壁 a **barrier**; an **obstacle**(障害物) ▶ことばの**障壁** a language *barrier* ‖ 人種的偏見が世界平和の主な**障壁**となっている Racial and ethnic prejudice is the chief *obstacle* to world peace. ‖ (貿易の)**非関税障壁** a non-tariff barrier.

じょうへき 城壁 a **castle wall** ▶古代ローマは厚い**城壁**に囲まれていた Ancient Rome was surrounded by thick *walls*.

しょうべん 小便 **urine** /jʊ́ərɪn/ (尿); **urination** (排尿) **一動 小便をする urinate** /jʊ́ərəneɪt/ 《参考》以上の語はいずれも主に医者に話すときの用語で, 日常語ではない. →**おしっこ** ▶ゆうべは2度**小便**に起きた I woke up twice to *pee* last night. (➤ go to the bathroom が日常語) ‖ 彼は**小便が近い** He needs to go to the bathroom frequently.

じょうほ 譲歩 (a) **concession 一動 譲歩する concede** /kənsíːd/ ▶両国は互いの**譲歩**によってその政治問題を平和的に解決した The two countries were able to settle their political problems peacefully through mutual *concession*. ‖ 家主は賃貸契約に関しては少しも**譲歩しなかった** The landlord *gave us no concessions* [*conceded nothing*] on the rental agreement. ‖ 我々は互いに**譲歩することにした** We decided to *meet halfway*. (➤ meet halfway は「折り合う, 歩み寄る」).

1**しょうほう 商法** **commercial law**(法律); a **business method**(方法) ‖ **マルチ商法** multilevel merchandising; pyramid selling(ネズミ講式販売).

2**しょうほう 詳報** a **detailed report.**

しょうぼう 消防 **firefighting**(消火活動) ▶**消防**にはいつも危険が伴う There is always some danger in *firefighting*. (➤よく言われる表現に Firefighting and danger go hand-in-hand. (消防と危険は切っても切れない関係だ)がある) ‖ 彼女は火事を見てすぐ**消防署**に電話した She called *the fire station* [《英》*the fire brigade*] right after she saw the fire.
‖ **消防士** a firefighter ‖ **消防自動車** a fire engine, a fire truck ‖ **消防隊** a fire brigade ‖ **消防団** a volunteer fire department [company / brigade] ‖ **消防庁** the Fire and Disaster Management Agency (➤ 総務省消防庁;「東京消防庁」は Tokyo Fire Department).

1**じょうほう 情報** **information**; 《インフォーマル》a **tip** (耳寄りな情報); **intelligence** (重要・秘密事項に関する); **news** (ニュース) ▶いくつかの**情報** several pieces of *information* (➤ information は数えられない名詞なので (×)several informations とはできない) ‖ 信頼できる[できない]**情報** reliable [unreliable] *information* ‖ **情報**を集める gather [collect] *information* ‖ 最新ファッション**情報** *tips* on the latest fashion(s) ‖ 事故についての新しい**情報**を得る obtain more *information* on the accident ‖ **情報**を交換する exchange *information* ‖ **情報網**を張り巡らす set up *an information* [*intelligence*] *network*.
▶成田空港で爆発事故があったという**情報**が入ってきた *News* has just come in of an explosion at Narita Airport. ‖ 博多のしゃれたレストランについて少し**情報**を教えてあげよう I'll give you some *tips* on posh restaurants in Hakata. ‖ 私はそのことについて**何の情報も持ち合わせていない** I *know nothing* about it *whatsoever*. ‖ 現代は**高度情報化社会**だと言われる It is said that at present we are living in *a highly information-oriented society*. ‖ 市に対して一層の**情報開示**を求めて運動している市民たちがいる Some people are conducting a campaign demanding more extensive *disclosure of information* from the city (government).
‖ **情報開示** (information) disclosure ‖ **情報科学** information science ‖ **情報革命** the information revolution, the IT revolution ‖ **情報管理** information management [control] ‖ **情報機関** an intelligence [a secret] service ‖ **情報機器** an information device ‖ **情報技術** information technology (➤ IT と略す) ‖ **情報源** a source of information ‖ **情報検索** information retrieval 《略 IR》 ‖ **情報公開条例** the Free Access to Information Ordinance ‖ **情報産業** the information industry ‖ **情報誌** an information(al) magazine (➤ 無料の地元情報誌は a free local information magazine) ‖ **情報時代** the information age ‖ **情報処理** information [data] processing ‖ **情報提供者** an informant; an informer (警察などへの) ‖ **情報量** the amount of data [information] ‖ **タウン情報誌** a listings magazine.

> **逆引き熟語 ○○情報**
> **遺伝情報** genetic information / **インターネット情報** Internet information [data] / **花粉情報** pollen information / **気象情報** weather information, a weather report / **求人情報** job information / **交通情報** traffic information, a traffic report / **顧客情報** customer information / **極秘情報** top-secret [classified / confidential] information / **個人情報** personal information / **最新情報** the latest [up-to-date] information / **役立つ情報** a useful tip [piece of information]

2**じょうほう 上方に** **above** (ある物から上の方に); **upward** (上向きに) ▶予測を**上方修正する** *revise* one's estimate *upward* (➤ 名詞としての「上方修正」は upward revision).

しょうほん 抄本 an **abridged copy**, an **extract.**

じょうまえ 錠前 a **lock** ▶鍵で**錠前**を開ける open *a lock* with a key.

しようまっせつ 枝葉末節 ▶そんな**枝葉末節**は後回し

にして大筋から議論して決めていこう Let's deal with *minor details* like that later. We should discuss and decide the main points first. (→枝葉).

じょうまん 冗漫な **verbose** /vəːʳbóʊs/ (くどい；堅い語)；**lengthy** (長たらしい)；**wordy** (ことば数が多い)；**diffuse** (散漫な)；**long-winded** (だらだらと続く)；**redundant** (余分な) ▶冗漫な報告書 a *verbose* report ‖ 冗漫なドラマ a *long-winded* [*wordy*] drama ‖ 冗漫なことばをカットする omit *redundant* words ‖ 頭を整理してから書かないと文章が冗漫になる If you don't organize your ideas before you begin (to write), your writing will *be wordy*.

1**しょうみ 正味の** **net** (重さや値段などが) ▶その塩は正味2キロあった The salt had *a net weight* of two kilos. ／The salt weighed two kilos *net*.
▶正味 (＝たっぷり) 3か月は情報収集に費やした I spent three *full* months (in) collecting information.

2**しょうみ 賞味** ▶《表示》賞味期限12月6日まで *Best before* December 6. 《参考》「賞味期限」は a best-by [best before] date.「消費期限」は業者から見た場合には sell-by date となり, 消費者から見た場合には use-by date となる.

じょうみゃく 静脈 a **vein** ‖**静脈注射** an intravenous /ìntrəvíːnəs/ injection ‖ **大静脈** the main vein ; the vena cava /vìːnə kéɪvə/.

じょうむ 常務 an **executive managing director.** →専務取締役.

じょうむいん 乗務員 a **crewperson**, a **member of the crew** (ともに1人)；**the crew** (全体) ▶この船には何名乗務員が乗っていますか How many *crewpersons* are there on board this ship? ‖ この列車の乗務員 (＝車掌) は態度が悪いね The *conductors* on this train are not polite. ‖ タクシーの乗務員 (＝運転手) a taxi *driver*.
‖(飛行機の) **客室乗務員** a flight attendant.

しょうむしょう 商務省 **the Department of Commerce, the Commerce Department** (米国の).

1**しょうめい 証明** **proof** 一動 **証明する** **prove** /pruːv/ ＋目 ▶フランクリンは雷が電気現象であることを証明した Franklin *proved* that lightning is a form of electricity. ‖ 誰かきみのアリバイを証明してくれる者はいないのか Is there anybody who can *support* [*back up*] your alibi? (➤ ふつう「支持する, 裏付ける」に当たる語を用いる) ‖ 実験によってその理論の正しいことが証明された The experiments *proved* the truth of the theory. ／The theory *was proved* to be true by experiment(s). ‖ 身元を証明するものを見せてください Please show *identification*. [*I.D.*] ‖ 私の大学では, 学生は試験中に身分を証明するために学生証明書を机上に置くことになっている In my university, students are required to put their *identification cards* on their desks while they are taking examinations as *proof* of their identity.
▶先生はその数学の定理を証明した (＝実証した) The teacher *demonstrated* the mathematical proposition.
‖**証明書** a certificate /səʳtífɪkət/ ‖ **成績証明書** a transcript of (academic) records, an academic transcript ‖ **卒業証明書** a diploma.

2**しょうめい 照明** **lighting** ; **illumination** (装飾的な) ▶ナイターの照明 *lighting* for a night game ‖ 照明の悪い部屋 a *poorly lit* [*lighted*] room (➤「照明のよい部屋」は a well-lit [-lighted] room) ‖ 学園祭の夜の校舎には色とりどりの照明が施されていた The school buildings on the festival night *were decorated with* colorful *lights*.
‖**照明係** a lighting technician ‖ **照明効果** lighting effects ‖ **直接** [**間接**] **照明** direct [indirect] lighting [illumination].

しょうめつ 消滅する **disappear, die out** (習慣などが)；**vanish** (今まで存在していたものが)；**expire** (期限が切れる)；**lapse** (権利が) ▶流行語は自然に消滅する Fad words (will) *disappear* in the course of time. ‖ 多くの日本の伝統が消滅しつつある Many Japanese traditions *are dying out*. ‖ 9月の時点で巨人の優勝の可能性は消滅した By September, the possibility of the Giants winning the pennant had *vanished*. ‖ 日本では原則, 著作権は著作者の死後50年で消滅する As a general rule, a Japanese copyright *expires* [*lapses*] 50 years after the author's death.

しょうめん 正面 **the front** ; a **facade** /fəsɑ́ːd/ (建物の前面；フランス語から) ▶これは私の家を正面から撮った写真です This is a picture of my house taken from *the front*. ‖ 美術館の正面には大きな彫像が立っていた A big statue stood *in front of* the art gallery.
▶文部科学省は教育改革に正面から取り組むべきだ The Ministry of Education, Culture, Sports, Science and Technology should work *hard* on educational reform. ‖ あの人に正面切ってそんなことは言えないよ I can't tell him that *straight to his face*. ‖ けさ駅のそばでタクシーどうしが正面衝突した Two taxis *crashed into each other head-on* [*had a head-on collision*] near the train station this morning.
‖**正面玄関** the front door [entrance].

しょうもう 消耗 **consumption** 一動 **消耗する** **consume** /kənsúːm/ ▶マラソンは体力を消耗するスポーツだ Marathon running is an *energy-consuming* sport. ‖ 15時間ぶっ通しに働いてすっかり体力が消耗してしまった I *was exhausted* from working fifteen straight hours. (➤「疲労困ぱいした」の意) ‖ 乾電池は消耗品だ Dry batteries are *consumption goods* [*items*]. ／Dry batteries are *consumable goods* [*consumables*].

1**しょうもん 証文** a **written pledge** (誓約書)；a **bond of debt** (借金の証書).

2**しょうもん 掌紋** a **palm print.**

じょうもんじだい 縄文時代 **the Jomon period.**

しょうや 庄屋 a ***shoya*** ; a village head(man) in the Edo period (➤ 説明的な訳).

しょうやく 抄訳 an **abridged translation**, a **translation of selected passages.**

じょうやく 条約 a **treaty** ▶ヴェルサイユ条約 the *Treaty* of Versailles ‖ 条約を結ぶ [破棄する] conclude [abolish] *a treaty* ‖ (平和) 条約に調印する sign *a* (*peace*) *treaty* ‖ 条約を批准する ratify *a treaty* ‖ 条約の交渉をする negotiate *a treaty*.
‖**修好条約** a treaty of amity [friendship] ‖ **日米安保条約** the Japan-U.S. Security Treaty [Pact]；《正式名》the Treaty of Mutual Cooperation and Security between Japan and the United States (日本国とアメリカ合衆国との間の相互協力及び安全保障条約).

じょうやど 定宿 one's **usual** [**regular**] **hotel** ▶ここが私の定宿です This is *the hotel* I *usually stay at*.

じょうやとう 常夜灯 an **all-night (street) light** (➤ 街路灯であることをはっきりさせる必要がある場合は street を

つける).

しょうゆ 醤油 *shoyu* (sauce), soy sauce ▶彼はハンバーグにしょうゆをかける He *puts shoyu* [*soy*] *sauce on* hamburgers.

> ◀解説▶ 日本のしょうゆは *shoyu* または *shoyu* sauce を用いるのがよい. soy sauce の soy も「しょうゆ」が英語化したものだが, soy sauce は中国や東南アジアのものをも含む語で, 味・香りとも日本のものとは異なる.

しょうよ 賞与 a **bonus** ▶年 2 回の**賞与**がなければわが家は生活していけない Our family cannot get by without the biannual *bonuses*. (→ボーナス).

じょうよ 剰余 a **surplus** ▶予算剰余 a budget *surplus*.

しょうよう 商用で **on business** ▶彼は商用でマレーシアへ行った He went to Malaysia *on business*.

じょうよう 常用 ▶これは私が常用している辞書だ This is the dictionary (that) I *always use*. ‖ この薬は常用すると体に毒だよ If you *take* this medicine *habitually*, your health will suffer. ‖**常用漢字** (a) kanji designated for everyday use.

じょうようしゃ 乗用車 a (**passenger**) **car**, an **automobile** /ɔ́ːt̬əmoʊbìːl/.

しょうようじゅりん 照葉樹林 a **broad-leaved evergreen forest**.

じょうよく 情欲 (a) **passion** ; **lust**(過度の色欲).

しょうらい 将来

the future 一形 **将来の future** ▶私たちは将来[遠からぬ将来]結婚するつもりです We are going to marry *in the future* [*in the* not-too-distant *future*]. ‖ **近い将来**あの軍事政権は倒されるだろう That military regime will be toppled *before long* [*in the near future*]. ‖ 将来(=大きくなったら)何になりたいの? What do you want to be *when you grow up*?

> **あなたの英語はどう響く?**
> 中学生以上の若者になら,「将来何になりたいの?」の意味で What do you want to be *in the future*? と聞くのはよいが, 小学生以下の子供にこう聞くのは大げさで不自然. What do you want to be *when you grow up*? と聞くのが自然である.

▶この子は将来が楽しみだ This child *has a bright future*. / This child *is promising*. (➤「将来性」の意では Ⓒ で通例 a future ; promising は「将来性がある」) ‖ 彼女には大きな**将来性**がある She has a lot of *potential*. (➤ potential は「可能性, 潜在能力」) ‖ グラフィックデザインは**将来性がある** *There is a future* in graphic design. ‖ 小川さんは新進ピアニストとして**将来が期待されている** Miss Ogawa is a newly debuting pianist *with a promising future*. ‖ 山崎氏はわが社の**将来の**社長だ Mr. Yamazaki is our *future* president. ‖ このルーキーは**将来性がある** This rookie *has a great future ahead* (*of him*). ‖ **将来性のある**会社に入りたい I want to join a company *with a bright future*.

しょうり 勝利 (a) **victory** ; (a) **triumph**(大勝利) ▶圧倒的な**勝利** *a landslide victory* ‖ これは全員で勝ちとった**勝利**だ This *victory* belongs to all of us. ‖ **勝利の栄冠**を手にするのはどちらのチームでしょうか Which team will win *the crown of victory*? ‖ レーザー治療は医学の**勝利**である Laser treatment is *a triumph* of medical science. ‖ 民主党候補が**勝利宣言**をした The Democratic candidate *declared victory*.

‖**勝利者** a winner, a victor (➤ 後者は文学的で, やや大げさな語) ‖ **勝利投手** a winning pitcher, a winner.

じょうりく 上陸 (a) **landing** 一動 **上陸する land** ▶コロンブスは1492年にサン・サルバドルに**上陸した** Columbus *landed* at San Salvador in 1492. ‖ 船が港に入ると多くの観光客が**上陸した** Many tourists *went ashore* [*went on shore*] when the ship arrived in port. (➤ go ashore は「陸に上がる」の一般的な言い方) ‖ 台風 9 号は昨夜三浦半島に**上陸した** Typhoon No. 9 *hit* [*struck*] the Miura Peninsula last night. (➤ struck は strike (襲う)の過去形).

しょうりつ 勝率 a **winning percentage** ▶その投手の通算勝率は 6 割である The pitcher has a .600 career *winning percentage*.(➤.600はsix hundredと読む).

しょうりゃく 省略 (an) **omission**(省くこと) ; **abbreviation** (簡略化) 一動 **省略する omit** /oʊmít/ +㊐, **abbreviate** 《to》 ▶その本の日本版には各章にいくつかの**省略**がある Several *omissions* are found through the chapters of the Japanese edition of that book. ‖ ここは冠詞を**省略してもいい** You may *omit* an article here. ‖ 細かい話は**省略します** Let me *skip* the details. / I will *omit* unimportant details. ‖ 住所と名前を**省略せずに**書きなさい Write your name and address *in full*. ‖ **以下省略** *The rest is omitted*.

▶European Union (欧州連合)はふつうＥＵと**省略される** 'The European Union' *is* usually *abbreviated to* 'the EU.' ‖ 彼の名前の「ジェフリー」はふつう「ジェフ」と**省略される** His name 'Jeffrey' *is* usually *shortened to* 'Jeff.' (➤ shorten は「長さを短くする」).

1**じょうりゅう 上流** **1**【川の】**the upper reaches** 一副 **上流に**[へ] **upstream** ▶利根川の**上流**で大雨が降った There was a downpour in *the upper reaches* of the Tone River. ‖ この川の**上流に**発電所がある There is a power plant *upstream* on this river. ‖ その釣り場はこの橋より少し**上流に**ある The fishing spot is *a little bit upstream* of this bridge.

2【社会的地位の】**the upper class** ▶B 君は**上流家庭**の子弟だ B is the son of *an upper-class family*.

‖**上流社会** high society.

2**じょうりゅう 蒸留** **distillation** 一動 **蒸留する distill** +㊐ ▶ブランデーはぶどう酒を**蒸留して**作る Brandy is made by *distilling* wine. / Brandy *is distilled* from wine. ‖ ウイスキーは**蒸留酒**だ Whisky is *distilled liquor* [*spirit*].

‖**蒸留水** distilled water.

しょうりょう 少量の **a small amount of** ; **a little** ▶**少量の**水 *a small amount of* water ‖ ボトルの中に**少量**のブランデーが残っていた There was *a little* brandy left in the bottle. ‖ 沸騰したら**少量の**塩を加えなさい Add just *a bit* [*a pinch*] *of* salt when it boils.

しょうりょくか 省力化 **labor savings** ▶ＯＡ機器の導入で企業の**省力化**が進んだ The introduction of office automation has encouraged *labor savings* [*a reduction of labor*] in companies.

じょうりょくじゅ 常緑樹 an **evergreen** (**tree**).

じょうるり 浄瑠璃 ***joruri*** ; a story-chanting performance with samisen accompaniment (➤ 説明的な訳).

1**しょうれい 奨励** **encouragement** 一動 **奨励する encourage** ; **recommend** (推薦する) ▶政府は国民に倹約を**奨励している** The government *is encouraging* people to be thrifty. ‖ ホラー映画は幼い子供に奨励

できるものではない Horror movies cannot *be recommended* for [to] young children. (➤ for は親に対して, to は子供たちに向かって直接).

2 **しょうれい 症例** a **case.**

じょうれい 条例 an [a **local**] **ordinance, (municipal) regulations,** a **by(e)law**(➤ イギリスでは最後の語を用いることが多い) ▶騒音条例 a noise *ordinance*.

じょうれん 常連 a **regular customer,** a **regular** (なじみの客) ▶その飲み屋は常連でいつもいっぱいだ That bar [pub] is always full of *regulars*. ‖ 仙台育英学園高校は甲子園の全国高校野球大会の常連だ Sendai Ikuei Gakuen High School *regularly competes* in the National High School Baseball Tournament at Koshien Stadium. (➤ compete は「(大会などで)競り合う」の意).

じょうろ a **watering can** [**pot**] ▶じょうろで植木に水をやる water plants with *a watering can*.

しょうろう 鐘楼 a **bell tower**; a **belfry** /bélfri/ (教会の).

しょうろん 詳論する discuss ... at (great) length.

しょうわ 昭和 Showa ▶父は昭和43年生まれです My father was born in *the 43rd year of Showa* [in 1968]. 《参考》日本独特の年号なので, 日本の年号制度を知らない外国人には西暦を用いて言うほうがよい.

しょうわくせい 小惑星 an **asteroid** ▶小惑星イトカワ *the asteroid* Itokawa.

じょうわん 上腕 the [one's] **upper arm** ▶上腕二頭筋 a *biceps*.

しょえん 初演 a **premiere** /prɪmíəʳ ‖ prémieə/ (芝居・映画・音楽の); **the first performance** (芝居・音楽の) ▶作品の世界初演を行う give the world *premiere performance* of a work.

じょえん 助演 a **supporting role** ▶助演する play a *supporting role*.

ショー a **show** ▶プロレスなんて単なるショーだね Professional wrestling is nothing but *a show*. ‖ あす, この劇場で氷川きよしショーが行われる A Hikawa Kiyoshi *show* will be held at this theater tomorrow. ‖ 自動車ショー an auto show, a car show.

じょおう 女王 a **queen** ▶エリザベス女王2世 *Queen* Elizabeth II (➤ the second と読む) ‖テニスの女王 *the queen* of tennis / a tennis *queen* ‖ この歌手は「フォークの女王」と呼ばれた This singer was called *the queen of folk* (*music*).

‖ 女王バチ a queen bee.

ショーウインドー a **show window,** a **shopwindow** ▶ショーウインドーには春物の新作が陳列してあった There was a new line of spring clothes on display in the *shopwindows*.

ジョーカー the joker (in a pack of playing cards).

ジョーク a **joke** ▶うまい[下手な]ジョーク a good [poor] *joke* ‖ くだらない[卑わいな]ジョーク a silly [dirty] *joke* ‖ ジョークを言う[飛ばす] make [crack] a *joke* ‖ 今のはジョークだよ I was only *joking*. / I said it just *for fun* [*for a joke*].

ショーケース a **showcase.**

ジョージア Georgia (アメリカ南東部の州; 略 GA, Ga.).

ショーツ panties(女性用下着); **shorts**(短パン).

ショート 1【電気の】a **short circuit**(短絡) ▶電気がショートして停電になった *A short circuit* caused a blackout.

2【野球】(a) **shortstop,** (a) **short** (➤ 守備位置は Ⓤ, 選手を指すときは a をつける) ▶ショートを守る play *shortstop*.

3【髪の】▶きみはショートにしたほうが似合うよ You'd look better if you had your *hair cut short* [look better with *short hair*]. (●「ショートカット」は short hair という).

ショートケーキ (→かこみ記事)

> **危ないカタカナ語✹ ショートケーキ**
> 1 shortcake の short は「(バターなどがたくさん入っていて)さくさくする」の意. 日本の「ショートケーキ」に似ているが, 土台が scone(スコーン)を使ったものが多い. 《英》では shortbread(バタークッキーの一種)の意でも用いる.
> 2 日本でいう「ショートケーキ」は strawberry layer cake とか, sponge cake topped with cream and strawberries などとする.

ショートパンツ shorts(➤「男性用下着」の意になることもある); **hot pants** (特に短いもの) ▶彼女はショートパンツにスニーカーという姿だった She wore *shorts* and sneakers.

ショール a **shawl** ▶ショールを肩に掛けている wear *a shawl* around one's shoulders.

ショールーム a **showroom** ▶車[電気製品]のショールーム a car [an electric appliance] *showroom*.

1 **しょか 初夏 early summer**

✉ **この2, 3日初夏を思わせるような陽気です** It's been so warm for the past few days I feel like it's already *early summer*.

2 **しょか 書架** a **bookshelf**; **(the) library stacks**(図書館の).

3 **しょか 書家** a **calligrapher** /kəlígrəfəʳ/.

じょがい 除外する exclude +Ⓞ (意図的に省く); **except** +Ⓞ (意図的に例外とする) ▶プロを除外して考えれば彼女がテニスの世界一だ *If* professional players *are excluded* [*Excluding* professional players], she is the best tennis player in the world. ‖ 13歳以下はこの法律の適用から除外される Those who are 13 or under *are exempt* [*are excepted*] from the application of this law. (➤ exempt は「除外された」の意の形容詞) / This law does not apply to those 13 or under.

しょがくしゃ 初学者 a **beginner** ▶この辞書は初学者向けです This dictionary is intended for *beginners*.

じょがくせい 女学生 a **female student** →女子.

しょかつ 所轄 jurisdiction

‖ 所轄官庁[警察署 / 税務署] the competent authorities [police station / tax office] (➤ この competent は「法的権限を有する」の意).

1 **しょかん 書簡** a **letter**; **correspondence**(➤ 集合的).

2 **しょかん 所感** one's **opinion** 《of, about, on》(意見) ▶教授は彼女の論文に対する所感を述べた The professor gave his *opinion on* her thesis.

1 **しょき 初期 the early days** [**years**]; **the beginning** ━ 形 **初期の early** ▶江戸時代の初期に *in the early years* of the Edo period ‖ 私たちの学校は明治初期に開校した Our school was opened *early in* the Meiji era. ‖ 初期にはこの学校は生徒数40人かそこらの小さな塾だった *In the beginning*, this school was a small *juku* with forty students or so. ‖ がんは初期(の段階)に発見できれば助かる Cancer can be cured if it is caught *in the early stages*. ‖ これは芥川の初期の作品だ These are Akutagawa's *early* works.

‖ (コンピュータの)初期設定 (a) default.

2 **しょき 所期** ▶我々は所期の目的を達成した We have

attained [achieved] our *intended* objectives.

3 **しょき 書記** a secretary /sékrəteri/
‖**書記長** a secretary-general.

しょきあたり 暑気あたり ▶母は暑気あたりで体調を崩している My mother has been in poor condition because *she was affected by the summer heat*.

しょきか 初期化 initialization (of electric media) ; formatting(フォーマット) **一動 初期化する** initialize +目 ; format +目 (フォーマットする) ▶外付けハードディスクを初期化する *initialize* an external hard disk.

しょきゅう 初級の elementary ▶初級フランス語 *elementary* French ‖初級者クラス[コース] a *beginners'* class [course] ‖『初級英語』(書名) English *for Beginners*.

じょきょ 除去 removal(取り除くこと) ; elimination(排除) **一動 除去する** remove +目, eliminate +目 ▶社会悪の除去 the *elimination* of social evils ‖事故車を除去する *remove* the cars involved in an accident ‖有害物質を除去する *remove* harmful substances.

じょきょう 助教 an assistant professor, a research associate(➤ どちらを用いるかは大学による).

じょきょうじゅ 助教授 an assistant professor, (英) a senior lecturer 《参考》(1)「助教授」は今は「准教授」と呼ぶ. (2)上の2つの英語の名称はいずれも今の「助教」(国立大系に多い)または「専任講師」(私立大系に多い)に充ててかまわない.

しょぎょうむじょう 諸行無常 All things in this world are transient.

じょきょく 序曲 an overture /óʊvərtʃʊər/ ▶モーツァルトの『フィガロの結婚』序曲 the *overture* to Mozart's "Le Nozze di Figaro".

じょきん 除菌 bacteria elimination, sterile filtration ; disinfection.

ジョギング jogging **一動 ジョギングする** jog ▶ジョギングに出かける go *jogging* ‖彼は毎朝1時間ジョギングをする He *jogs* an hour every morning.

しょく 私欲 self-interest ▶我々は皆私欲に走りがちだ We all tend to pursue our *own interest(s)*.

1 **しょく 職** **1【仕事, 職業】** a job ; an occupation (➤ 職種 ; 履歴書などで用いる堅い語) ; a position(会社などでの地位) ▶職を得る get *a job* ‖人員整理で職を失った I lost my *job* because of staff reductions. ‖父は来年定年になるので次の職を探している My father is looking for another *job*, since he will reach mandatory retirement age next year. ‖彼は職を転々としている He'*s a job-hopper*. ‖木村氏は議長の職を辞した Mr. Kimura *resigned* (*from his position*) as chairman.

2【技能, 技術】 a trade ▶手に職をつけたい I'd like to *learn a trade*.

2 **しょく 食** ▶かぜをひいているので食が進まない(＝食欲がない) I *don't have much appetite* because I've got a cold. ‖父は体が大きい割に食が細い My father is a big man, but he *eats very little* [*eats like a bird*]. ‖昔, 日本人は1日2食しかとらなかった Japanese people used to eat only *two meals* a day. ‖近年, 日本人の食生活は豊かになった[西洋化した] Recently, the Japanese *diet* has improved [has become westernized].

しょくあたり 食あたり food poisoning ▶食あたりできのう1日下痢をした Because of *food poisoning*, I had [suffered from] diarrhea all day yesterday.

しょくあん 職安 an employment (security) office [bureau].

しょくいき 職域 an occupational field.

しょくいく 食育 dietary education.

しょくいん 職員 a staff member, a member of the staff, a staffer(いずれも1人の) ; the staff, the personnel /pɜ̀ːrsənél/ (ともに職員全体を指すが, 後者は特に公共団体や官庁などの全職員) ▶母は区役所の職員です My mother *is on the staff of* [*works at*] the ward office. ‖兄は市の職員です My older brother *is a city employee* [*works for the city*]. ‖この学校には50人の職員(＝教員と事務職員)がいる This school has *a staff* of fifty.
‖**職員会議** a staff meeting ; a teachers' meeting (教員の) ‖**職員室** a teachers' room, a faculty room.

しょぐう 処遇 (a) treatment ▶彼女を冷たく処遇する *treat* her *coldly* / *give* her *the cold shoulder* ‖彼は自分に対する彼らの処遇に不満をもっているようだ He seems to have some complaints about *the way they are treating* him.

しょくえん 食塩 salt /sɔːlt/ ▶スイカに食塩を振りかける sprinkle *salt* over a piece of watermelon.
‖**食塩水** saline /séɪlaɪn/ solution(➤ salt water は「塩水」).

しょくぎょう 職業

an occupation (履歴書などに書く職種) ; a profession ; a trade (技能の熟練を必要とする職人仕事) ; a job (勤め口) ; a career /kəríər/ (実績を積み上げていく仕事)

> **《解説》** (1)「職業」に当たるやや改まった語は **occupation** で,「仕事」に当たるのが **job**.
> (2) **profession** は通例医師・弁護士・教師のような専門知識を必要とする職業を指す. したがって, 初対面の人に向かって What's your profession ? とはふつう言わない.

▶将来どんな職業に就きたいですか What kind of *job* do you plan to have [do] in the future ? ‖彼女は職業を転々とした末に歌手になった After *changing jobs* many times, she finally became a singer. ‖こちらに氏名, 年齢, 職業をご記入ください Please fill in your name, age and *occupation* here. ‖男は職業はトラック運転手と登録した The man listed his *occupation* as a truck driver. ‖父のような知的な職業に憧れています My dream is to have *an intellectual profession* like my father's. ‖彼女は教えることを職業にしたいと思っている She wants to make teaching her *career*. ‖町会長さんの職業は植木屋さんです The president of our neighborhood association is a gardener (*by trade*). ‖**対話**「ご職業は何ですか」「農業をやっています」"*What* (*kind of work*) *do you do ?*" "I'm a farmer."

> **あなたの英語はどう響く?**
> 相手の職業を聞くときは What (kind [type] of work) do you do ? が無難. What do you do for a living ? も使われる. What's your occupation ? は役人が尋ねているように響く. また, What are you ? は失礼な聞き方. What's your job ? は例えば相手が建設会社に勤めていることがわかっているような場合に,「具体的にどんな仕事をしているのですか」の意で聞く.

✉ **アメリカではどんな職業が大学生に人気がありますか** What kinds of *careers* are popular with [among] college graduates in the United States?

‖(公共)職業安定所 the (Public) Employment Security Office ‖**職業教育** vocational education ‖**職業訓練指導員** a vocational training instructor ‖**職業能力検定** a vocational ability test ‖**職業病** an occupational disease ‖**職業別電話帳** the yellow pages.

しょくご 食後 ▶《医師が患者に》錠剤を差し上げますから食後に飲んでください I'll give you some tablets to take *after meals*. ‖毎食後必ず歯を磨きなさい Make sure you brush your teeth *after each meal*.

1**しょくざい 食材** ingredients (材料); foodstuffs (食品) ▶できるだけ新鮮な食材を手に入れる obtain the freshest possible *ingredients* ‖当店では主に地元の食材を使用しております We mainly use local *ingredients*.

2**しょくざい 贖罪** atonement《for》(償いの行為); remorse(償いの気持ち); redemption(罪からの救済) ▶私の過去の行いに対するしょく罪の気持ち a sense of *remorse* for what I did in the past ‖キリストは全人類のしょく罪のために死んだ Christ died for the *redemption* of the whole human race.

しょくし 食指 ▶レストラン業には食指が動くが, 残念ながら資金がない I'*m interested in* the restaurant business, but unfortunately I don't have any funds.

しょくじ 食事 a meal(毎日の); a diet (➤ 日頃の食事の内容を意識して用いる語)

⚠ **日本語で「食事」で済ますところを英語では時刻に合わせて具体的に breakfast, lunch, supper を用いる場合が少なくない.**

▶医者は1日に3度きちんと食事するようにと言う My doctor advises me to *have* three regular *meals* a day. ‖ゆうべは外で食事した I *ate* [*dined*] *out* last night. ‖栄養があっておいしい食事作りを心がけています I try to cook nutritious and tasty *meals*. ‖姉は食塩抜きの食事をとっています My older sister is on *a salt-free* [*no-salt*] *diet*. ‖日本人には野菜と魚を中心とした伝統的な食事がいい The traditional *diet* based on vegetables and fish is good for Japanese people. ‖太り過ぎないように食事を控えめにすることにした I made up my mind to *eat moderately* so as not to gain too much weight.

▶食事ですよ *Breakfast* is [*Lunch* is / *Dinner* is] *ready!* ‖《職場で》田口は今食事(＝昼食)に出ております Mr. Taguchi is out for *lunch*. ‖5時だからそろそろ食事(＝夕食)の支度をしなくては It's five o'clock and time to *fix supper*. ‖食事の後片づけをしていたら電話がかかってきた I got a phone call while I *was washing the dishes* [*clearing the table* /《英また》*washing up*]. ‖家族そろっての食事は日曜日くらいのものです Sundays are about the only time my whole family gathers for *a meal* [for *dinner*]. (● 後者は夕食のことを指して言う場合; my whole family 以下を my whole family eats (dinner) together としてもよい).

✉ 《ラブレターで》**あなたが恋しくて食事も喉を通りません** I'm so much in love with you that I can't eat a bite [I have no appetite]. (➤ 前者は「一口も食べられない」の意).

▶食事中に政治や宗教の話はしないようにしなさい You should avoid discussing politics and religion *while you are eating* [*while you are at* (*the*) *table*]. (➤ the を省略するのは《英》) ‖食事時に人を訪問するのは失礼だ It is rude to visit people *at mealtimes* [*while they're at* (the) *table*].

▶祖父は糖尿病なので食事制限をしている Since my grandfather is diabetic, he is *on a restricted diet*. ‖胃潰瘍を治すには食事療法がいちばんだ The best way to cure a stomach ulcer is to follow *a* (*careful* / *special*) *diet*.

1**しょくしゅ 触手** a feeler(昆虫の); a tentacle (下等動物の) ▶《慣用表現》その会社は化粧品の分野に触手を伸ばそうとしている That company is going to *extend its operations* [*branch out*] into the field of cosmetics.

2**しょくしゅ 職種** an occupation ▶どんな職種をお探しですか What *type of occupation* are you looking for? ‖求人用のパンフレットは職種別に並べてあります The recruiting brochures are arranged *by* [*according to*] *occupation*.

しょくじゅ 植樹 ▶卒業生たちが卒業記念に植樹をした The graduating class *planted some trees* in commemoration of their graduation. ‖**植樹祭** a tree planting ceremony;《米》Arbor Day(植樹祭の日).

しょくしょう 食傷する get fed up《with》 ▶どのチャンネルも同じようなバラエティー番組ばかりで視聴者は食傷気味だ Viewers are *getting fed up with* TV. There's nothing but the same old variety shows on every channel.

しょくしん 触診 palpation **一動 触診する** palpate ＋㊐.

しょくせいかつ 食生活 one's diet ▶食生活を改善する improve one's *diet* ‖体重を減らすには食生活(＝食習慣)の改善が必要です You need to change your *eating habits* to lose weight.

しょくせき 職責 one's duties ▶職責を全うする discharge [fulfill / carry out] one's *duties*.

しょくぜん 食前 ▶医者は食前に飲むようにと言って薬をくれた The doctor gave me some medicine to take *before meals*. ‖食前には手を洗うこと Wash your hands *before you come to the table*.

‖**食前酒** an apéritif /əpèrətí:f/.

しょくだい 燭台 a candlestick, a candleholder.

1**しょくたく 食卓** a (dining) table ▶食卓につく *sit down at* (*the*) *table*(➤ the を省略するのは《英》) ‖食卓の用意をする *set the table* ‖食卓を片づける *clear the table* ‖久しぶりに一家がそろって食卓を囲んだ It has been a long time since my whole family *sat around the dinner table* [*sat down for a meal* together]. (➤ It has been を It is とするのは主に《英》; 前者は夕食の場合).

2**しょくたく 嘱託** a part-time employee, a nonregular employee ▶父は去年その会社を定年退職し, 現在そこの嘱託として働いています My father retired from that company last year and now works there as *a nonregular employee*.

しょくちゅうしょくぶつ 食虫植物 an insectivorous plant.

しょくちゅうどく 食中毒 food poisoning ▶彼は悪くなった肉を食べて食中毒にかかった He got *food poisoning* from eating meat that had gone bad. ‖近所の小学校で集団食中毒が発生した There was *a mass outbreak of food poisoning* in a neighboring grade school.

しょくつう 食通 a gourmet /gʊ́əˈmeɪ/ ▶彼は味にはう

るさいよ. 食通だからね He's finicky about what he eats because he's such *a gourmet*.

[1]**しょくどう 食堂** a **restaurant**(レストラン); a **cafeteria**(セルフサービスの); a **dining room** (食事をする部屋)
‖**食堂車** a dining car / a diner /dáɪnəʳ/; a buffet /bəféɪ ‖ bófeɪ/ (ビュッフェ) ‖**学生食堂** a school cafeteria ‖**社員食堂** a company [an employee] cafeteria.

し

[2]**しょくどう 食道** the **gullet**; the **esophagus** /ɪsɑ́ːfəgəs/ ‖**食道がん** (a) cancer of the esophagus, an esophageal cancer.

しょくにん 職人 a **craftsperson**(➤特に性を区別するときは craftsman, craftswoman とする), an **artisan** ▶昨今は職人かたぎの大工さんが少なくなってきた These days, there are fewer carpenters *who take pride in their work*.
‖**職人かたぎ** the artisan spirit ‖**職人芸** craft artistry, the skill of a craftsperson [craft artist], craftsmanship.

しょくのう 職能の functional
‖**職能給** pay for skill.

しょくば 職場 one's **place of work**, one's **workplace**; the **workplace**(➤「家庭」と対比して一般論に用いる表現) ▶職場でのセクハラ sexual harassment in [at] *the workplace* ‖父の職場は新宿にある My father's *place of work* [My father's *office*] is in Shinjuku. / My father works in Shinjuku. ‖私たちは職場結婚です We were working in the same company [office] when we got married. / I met my wife [husband] at work. (➤名詞としての「職場結婚」は a marriage between co-workers などと訳す) ‖伊藤さんは出産後1年で職場復帰した Ms. Ito returned to *work* one year after she gave birth. ‖きょう職場で男性が1人大けがをした Today one man was seriously injured in an accident *on the job*. (➤on the job は「勤務中に」).
‖**職場放棄** a walkout, a strike.

しょくばい 触媒《化学》a **catalyst** /kǽṭəlɪst/.

しょくはつ 触発する touch off ▶彼の犯行はテレビの過激な暴力番組によって触発された His crimes *were touched off* [*were triggered*] by excessively violent TV programs. (➤trigger は「…の引き金となる」).

しょくパン 食パン bread ▶食パン1枚 a slice of *bread* ‖食パン1個 a loaf of *bread* ‖**山型食パン** (a loaf of) round top bread.

しょくひ 食費 food expenses; the charge for board (下宿の) ▶一郎は食費を切り詰めて欲しい物を買った Ichiro cut down his *food expenses* to buy something he wanted. ‖毎月の下宿代は食費込みで9万円です I pay ninety thousand yen a month *for room and board*.

しょくひん 食品 (a) **food**
‖**食品安全** food safety ‖**食品衛生** food hygiene ‖**食品会社** a food company ‖**食品加工** food processing ‖**食品添加物** a food additive ‖**食品メーカー** a food maker [manufacturer] ‖**インスタント食品** instant foods ‖**加工食品** a processed food ‖**自然食品** natural foods ‖**冷凍食品** frozen foods.

しょくぶつ 植物 a **plant** ▶植物を育てる grow *plants* ‖植物に水をやる water (the) *plants* ‖熱帯のジャングルでは植物の成長が速い *Plants* grow quickly in tropical jungles. ‖私は6人の生徒を植物採集に連れていった I took six students for *plant collecting*.
▶手術中の手違いからその患者は植物状態になった A mistake during the operation put the patient *into a vegetative state*. (➤「植物状態の患者」は vegetative patient や patient in a vegetative state という).
‖**植物園** a botanical garden ‖**植物学** botany ‖**植物学者** a botanist ‖**植物性たんぱく質** a vegetable protein ‖**植物油** vegetable oil ‖**園芸植物** a garden plant ‖**観葉植物** a foliage plant ‖**高山植物** an alpine plant ‖**多肉植物** a succulent (plant) ‖**熱帯植物** a tropical plant.

しょくべに 食紅 red food coloring.

しょくぼう 嘱望 ▶将来を嘱望されている青年 a young man *with an assured future*.

しょくみんち 植民地 a **colony** ▶英国人は1607年に北米に植民地を建設した In 1607, the English established *a colony* in North America.

しょくむ 職務 one's **duty** ▶職務を果たす[怠る] do [neglect] one's *duty* ‖申し訳ありませんが, 職務上いくつかの質問をしなければなりません I'm sorry, but I have to ask you a few questions *as a matter of duty*. ‖**職務規定** office [service] regulations ‖**職務権限** official powers ‖**職務質問** questioning, a police checkup.

しょくもつ 食物 food ▶消化のよい食物 easily digestible *food* ‖米は日本人の主要食物である Rice is *a staple food* for Japanese people. (🍎「米は日本人の主食である」というのなら, 英語は Rice is a staple of the Japanese diet. となる) ‖**食物繊維** dietary fiber ‖**食物連鎖** a food chain.

しょくよう 食用 ▶彼らはその木の根を食用にしている They *use* the root of that tree *for food*. ‖この実は食用になりますか Are these berries *good to eat*? / Are these berries *edible*?
‖**食用油** cooking [edible] oil ‖**食用ガエル**(=ウシガエル) a bullfrog.

しょくよく 食欲 (an) **appetite** /ǽpɪtaɪt/
▶食欲を促す飲み物 an *appetizing* drink ‖私はきょうはあまり食欲がない[とても食欲がある] I *have a poor* [*good*] *appetite* today. ‖少し運動すれば食欲が出るだろう A little exercise will *give* you *a good appetite*.
▶彼女は死んだゴキブリを見て食欲をなくした She *lost her appetite* when she saw a dead cockroach. ‖うちの犬は食欲旺盛だ Our dog *has an excellent* [*a healthy*] *appetite*. ‖いよいよ食欲の秋だ Fall, *the best season for eating*, has come. (➤英米人には秋は食の進む季節だという感覚はない).

[1]**しょくりょう 食料 food**; **groceries**(食料雑貨類) ▶3週間分の食料 three weeks' supply of *food* ‖難民たちに食料・水・雨露をしのぐ場所を与える provide *food*, water and shelter to the refugees ‖母は食料品の買い出しに出かけています My mother has gone to buy *food*. / My mother is out *grocery* shopping.
‖**食料品店**《米》a grocery store,《英》a grocer's (shop) ‖**生鮮食料品** fresh food(s), perishable foods, perishables.

[2]**しょくりょう 食糧 staple food**(主食); **food** (食料); **provisions** (備蓄した食糧) ▶食糧を蓄える stock *provisions* ‖将来食糧危機[不足]が来ると予測する人もいる Some people predict that we will face *a food crisis* [*shortage*] in the future.

‖**食糧事情**［**問題**］the food situation［problem］‖**食糧生産** food production ‖**食糧庁** the Food Agency（日本の食糧庁は2003年に廃止）.

しょくりん 植林 **afforestation** ▶あの山は３年前に**植林**したばかりだ We *planted* that mountain *with trees* only three years ago.

しょくれき 職歴 an **occupational career**, one's **employment**［**work**］**history**；a **professional career**（専門職としての）；an **employment record**（雇用記録）.

しょくん 諸君 ▶**諸君**全員に話したいことがある I have to tell all of *you* something. ‖**諸君**，おはよう！ Good morning, *everyone*［*boys and girls*］！‖**満場の諸君**！*Ladies and gentlemen*！

じょくん 叙勲 **conferment** ▶彼は文化面での業績により**叙勲された** He *was decorated* for his cultural achievement.（➤この decorate は「勲章を授ける」の意）‖**叙勲者** a recipient of an order［a decoration］.

しょけい 処刑（an）**execution** /èksɪkjúːʃən/（死刑執行）**―動 処刑する execute** ＋目 ▶公衆の面前で**処刑**を行う carry out a public *execution* ‖その殺人犯は**処刑された** The convicted murderer *was executed by hanging*［*by firing squad*］.（➤絞首刑と銃殺刑の場合）.

‖**処刑場** a place of execution.

しょげる **get depressed** ▶彼はギャンブルで有り金を全部すって**しょげている** He *is depressed* because he lost all the money he had with him in gambling. ‖則子ちゃんどうしたの？きょうは**しょげた顔してる**じゃない What happened, Noriko-chan? You *look down in the mouth* today.（➤down in the mouth は唇の端を下げて意気消沈している様子を表すインフォーマルな表現）.

1**しょけん 所見** **1**【**意見**】an **opinion**；a **view**（見解）. **2**【**見立て**】▶医者の**所見**によると，ただのかぜだった The doctor *diagnosed* my illness as a mere cold.（➤diagnose は「(通例病気を)…と診断する」）.

2**しょけん 初見** **sight reading** ▶ピアニストはその曲を見事に**初見で弾いた** The pianist *sight-read* that music perfectly.

じょけん 女権 **women's rights.**

じょげん 助言 **advice** /ədváɪs/；a **tip**（お役立ち情報）**―動 助言する advise** /ədváɪz/ ＋目 ▶友人に**助言**を求める ask one's friend for *advice* ‖生徒に**１つの**［**いくつかの**］**助言**を与える give a student *a piece*［*some pieces*］*of advice*（➤advice は数えられない名詞なので，数えるときは piece を用いる）‖来年の夏カナダに行ってみようと思っているんだけど，何か**助言してくれない**？ I'm planning to go to Canada next summer. Will you *give me some tips*？‖私は彼女にその仕事を引き受けないよう**助言した** I *advised* her *against* taking［*not to* take］on the job.

‖**助言者** an adviser.

しょこ 書庫 a **library.**

じょこう 徐行する go slow(ly), drive slow(ly)（➤後者は車の場合）▶《掲示》**徐行** Slow Down／Go Slow ‖霧のため（車を）**徐行しなければならなかった** I had to *drive slow*(*ly*)［*slow down* my car］because of the fog. ‖注意信号が出たので電車は**徐行運転をした** The train *went slow* as the signal had turned yellow.

じょこうえき 除光液 nail polish remover.

しょこく 諸国（**various**）**countries** ▶このホテルの従業員には**東南アジア諸国**の出身者が多い Many employees at this hotel are from *Southeast Asian countries*.

しょこん 初婚 one's **first marriage** ▶花婿は**初婚**，花嫁は再婚です This is the groom's *first marriage* and the bride's second (marriage).

しょさい 書斎 a **study** ▶**書斎**に籠もる shut oneself up in one's *study*.

しょざい 所在 **whereabouts**（行方，在りか）▶彼の**所在**はわからない His *whereabouts* are［is］unknown. ‖彼女は先週から**所在をくらましている** She has *been hiding*［*missing*］since last week. ‖警察は盗まれたダイヤの**所在を突き止めた** The police found out *where* the stolen diamonds *were*.

▶**責任の所在**を明らかにしなさい Find out *who is responsible*［*where the responsibility lies*］. ‖その会社の電話番号はわかるが，**所在地**がわからない I know the phone number of that company, but I don't know its *location*.

しょざいない 所在ない ▶彼は待合室で**所在なさそうだった** He *looked bored* sitting there in the waiting room.

じょさいない 如才ない ⚠**「如才ない」にぴったりの英語はないので，smart か tactful を用いる．ともに「気が利く，機転が利く」の意だが，前者にはときに批判的なニュアンスがある．clever を用いてもよいが，これも「抜け目のない」のニュアンスがある．**
▶**如才なく**ふるまう act *tactfully*［*cleverly*］‖あの男，**如才ない**やつだね That guy's *smart*. ‖彼女にすぐ礼状を出すとはきみも**如才ないね** It's *smart* of you to send her a thank-you letter so soon.

じょさんし 助産師 a **midwife**, a **birth attendant**, a **birthing assistant.**

しょし 初志 one's **original intention** ▶**初志を貫徹する**のは容易でない It is not easy to carry out［stick to］*one's original intention*(*s*).

しょじ 所持 **possession** /pəzéʃən/ **―動 所持する possess** /pəzés/ ＋目 ▶その歌手は大麻の**不法所持**で逮捕された That singer was arrested for *illegal possession* of marijuana.

‖**所持金** money on hand ‖**所持品** one's personal effects, one's belongings.

1**じょし 女子** a **girl**；a **woman**（女性）《**参考**》特に小学生ぐらいの女子を young girl，大学生以上を young woman ということが多い ▶私たちの学校は男子より**女子**のほうが多い Our school has more *girls* than boys.

‖**女子会** a (young) women's party（➤飲み会ならば drinking party）‖**女子学生** a female student,《主に米》a coed /kóʊed/（共学の大学の；この語を差別的と考える人もいるので前者が好ましい）‖**女子校** a girls'［an all-girl］school ‖**女子高生** a female high school student, a high school girl ‖**女子従業員** a female worker［employee］‖**女子100メートル走** the women's 100-meter dash ‖**女子寮** a girls'［women's］dormitory.

2**じょし 助詞**《文法》a（**postpositional**）**particle.**

しょしがく 書誌学 **bibliography.**

しょしき 書式 a **form** ▶この**書式**に従って書いてください Please write it following this *form*.

じょじし 叙事詩 an **epic** (**poem**).

じょしだい 女子大 a **women's college**［**university**］（➤women's の発音は /wímɪnz/）▶彼女は**女子大出**だ She is *a graduate of a women's college*［*university*］.

‖**女子大生** a student at a women's college（女子大の学生），a college girl；a female student,

《主に米》a coed /kóʊed/（共学の大学の女子学生；coed は差別的と考える人もいるので female student を使う方が好ましい）.

じょしつ 除湿する dehumidify +目 ‖**除湿器** a dehumidifier（➤「加湿器」は humidifier）.

じょしゅ 助手 an **assistant**；a **research associate**［**assistant**］（大学などの）▶映画撮影の助手をする *work as* a person's film *assistant* ‖助手席に乗る *get in beside the driver* ／*take the seat next to the driver* 《参考》「助手席」は文字どおりには assistant driver's seat だが，英米では乗用車の場合，運転席以外の席はすべて passenger('s) seat と呼ぶ．したがって，「助手席に乗っている人」は front-seat passenger という．

‖**運転助手** an assistant driver ‖**外国語指導助手** an assistant language teacher（略 ALT）.

しょしゅう 初秋 **early fall**［《英》**autumn**］.

じょじゅつ 叙述 ▶形容詞の叙述用法 the *predicative use* of an adjective.

‖《文法》**叙述形容詞** a predicative adjective.

しょしゅん 初春 **early spring**.

しょじゅん 初旬 ▶4月初旬に *early* in April ／*at the beginning* of April.

しょじょ 処女 a **virgin**（性経験のない女性；この語は童貞の男性にも使う）；**virginity**（処女［童貞］であること）▶あの子は処女ではない She is not *a virgin*. ／She has already lost her *virginity*.

▶タイタニック号は1912年，処女航海の途中に沈没した The Titanic sank on her *maiden voyage* in 1912.

‖**処女作** one's maiden［first］work ‖**処女地**［**林**］virgin soil［forests］‖**処女峰** an unclimbed peak ‖**処女膜** the hymen /háɪmən/.

じょしょう 序章 a **prologue**.

じょじょう 叙情 ▶叙情的な歌曲 a *lyrical* song.

‖**叙情詩** a lyric.

じょじょに 徐々に **gradually**；**little by little**（少しずつ）；**slowly**（ゆっくりと）▶徐々に温度が上がり始めた The temperature began to rise *gradually*［*by degrees*］. ‖彼は徐々に具合がよくなっている He is getting better *little by little*. ‖悦子は徐々にではあるが着実にスウェーデン語を身につけつつある Etsuko is learning Swedish *slowly* but surely.

1**しょしん 所信** one's **view**［**opinion**］；one's **belief**（信念）▶新しい外務大臣が記者会見で所信を述べた The new Foreign Minister expressed his *views*［*beliefs*］at the press conference. ‖首相は所信表明演説をした The Prime Minister gave *a general policy speech*.

2**しょしん 初診** ▶初診の方ですか Is this your *first visit*（*to this clinic*）?／Are you a new patient?

‖**初診料** an initial（examination）fee.

3**しょしん 初心** ▶初心に返る get back to one's *original enthusiasm* ／get back to *the basics*.

［ことわざ］初心忘るべからず Don't forget your initial earnestness［resolution］.（➤「最初の熱心さ［決心］を忘れるな」の意）.

しょしんしゃ 初心者 a **beginner**；a **novice** /ná:vəs/（新米）▶初心者向けの英語講座 an English course for *beginners* ‖私はスキーはまだ初心者です I'm just a *beginner* skier.

‖（車の）**初心者マーク** a newly-licensed driver's sticker.

1**じょすう 序数** an **ordinal**（**number**）（➤「基数」は cardinal number）.

2**じょすう 除数**《数学》a **divisor**.

しょする 処する **1**【対処する】▶難局に処する *deal*［*cope*］*with* a difficulty.

2【罰する】▶その殺人犯は死刑に処せられた The murderer *was executed*.

1**じょせい 女性** a **woman**［複 **women** /wímɪn/］（➤一般的な言い方）；a **lady**（➤丁寧な言い方）▶女性ドライバー a *woman* driver ‖女性の社長 a *female*［*woman*］president（➤ female は単に生物学的に「女性の」を意味する）‖今私が挨拶した女性は母の友だちです The *woman*［*lady*］I just said hello to is a friend of my mother's. ‖彼女は本当に女性らしい女性だ She's very *feminine*［*ladylike*］.（➤ feminine, ladylike, womanly は通例「女性らしい」という好ましい意味だが，昨今は男女の特徴を表す言葉は差別的にとられることがあるので注意）‖彼女はお年寄りたちに女性らしい心遣いを見せた She showed *womanly* consideration for the elderly people. ‖あの男性のことば遣いやしぐさは少し女性的だ That man's words and actions are somewhat *feminine*［*effeminate*］.（➤ effeminate は軽蔑的）‖男性の女性化 *feminization* of［in］men（➤「女性化した男性」は feminized man）.

‖**女性誌**［**女性週刊誌**］a women's magazine［weekly］‖**女性ホルモン** a female（sex）hormone.

2**じょせい 女声** a **female**［**woman's**］**voice**

‖**女声合唱** a female［women's］chorus.

じょせいきん 助成金 a **grant**, a **subsidy** /sʌ́bsədi/（➤後者は通例，必要経費の一部を助成する場合）▶研究助成金 a research *grant* ‖本校は国の助成金を受けている Our school *is subsidized* by the government.

しょせいじゅつ 処世術 ▶あの男は処世術にたけている He *knows how to get on*［*along*］*in life*.

じょせいと 女生徒 a **girl student**, a **schoolgirl** ▶新任の数学の先生は女生徒に人気がある Our new math teacher is popular with the *girl students*.

しょせき 書籍 a **book** ▶書籍売り場は何階ですか What floor is *the book department* on?

‖**書籍市** a book fair ‖**書籍目録** a book catalog.

じょせき 除籍 ▶学生を除籍する *remove* a student's name *from the school register* ‖学則に違反した生徒2名が最近除籍（＝放校）になった Two students who violated the school regulations *were expelled* recently.

しょせつ 諸説 **various opinions**［**views**］▶その事故の原因に関しては諸説紛々としている *There are various opinions* on the cause of that accident. ‖邪馬台国の所在地については諸説がある *Opinion is*［*Opinions are*］*divided* on the location of Yamataikoku.

1**じょせつ 除雪** ▶道路の除雪をする *clear*［*remove*］（*the*）*snow* from the road ／*clear* the road *of snow* ‖除雪作業は大変な重労働だ *Snow-removal work* is hard work. ‖**除雪車**《米》a snowplow,《英》a snowplough /snóʊplaʊ/.

2**じょせつ 序説** an **introduction**.

しょせん 所詮 **after all**（やはり）；**eventually**（結局は）▶彼女のことは所詮かなわぬ夢だった She was far beyond my reach *after all*. ‖所詮，人間は死ぬ運命にある We are all destined to die *eventually*. ‖いくら頑張っても，所詮勉強じゃああいつにかなわないよ No matter how hard I may try, I'll *never* do better than him in schoolwork. ‖いくら頑張ってみても所

詮あんな大きな家は買えないよ *There's no way* for me *to* buy a big house like that no matter how hard I work. (➤ There is no way は to 不定詞を伴って「とうてい…できない」の意). →どうせ.

じょせん 除染 decontamination **一動 除染する** decontaminate ＋目 ▶その地域全体を**除染する** *decontaminate* the entire area.

しょぞう 所蔵 ▶この絵は林氏**所蔵**のものです This picture *belongs to* Mr. Hayashi. ／This picture is *in* Mr. Hayashi's *collection*.

1**じょそう 女装** ▶**女装**した男が新幹線ですりの現行犯でつかまった A man (who was) *dressed* [*disguised*] *as a woman* was caught pick-pocketing on the Shinkansen. 《**参考**》異性の服を着るのを好む人を transvestite /trænsvéstaɪt/ または cross-dresser (服装倒錯者)と呼ぶ.

2**じょそう 助走** an approach run ▶走り幅跳びの**助走** *an approach run* for the broad jump.

‖**助走路** a runway (走り幅跳びなどの) ; an approach (スキージャンプの).

3**じょそう 除草** weeding **一動 除草する** weed, remove weeds

‖**除草剤** (a) weed-killer ; a herbicide.

4**じょそう 序奏** an introduction ▶『ソルベーグの歌』のオーケストラの**序奏** *the* orchestral *introduction* to Solveig's Song.

しょぞく 所属する belong to ; be on (…の一員である, …で働いている) ; work for (…で働いている)

【**文型**】
団体(A)に所属する
belong to A

▶私は音楽クラブに**所属している** I *belong to* [*am a member of*] the music club. (→属する)

▶父は M 新聞の外信部**所属です** My father *is in* the Foreign News Department of the M Shimbun. ‖私は Q 芸能プロに**所属している** I *work for* the Q Talent Agency.

▶彼女はその交響楽団**所属の**バイオリン奏者だ She is a violinist *with* that symphony orchestra. (➤ with は所属を表す前置詞) ‖日本のビジネスマンはふつう自分の**所属先**と肩書を名刺に刷り込んでいる Japanese businesspeople usually have their company *affiliation* and position printed on their business cards. (➤ affiliation は「(企業・学校などの)所属先」).

しょぞん 所存 ▶最善を尽くす**所存です** I *intend* [*am determined*] *to* do my best.

1**しょたい 所帯** a family (家族) ; a household (使用人・間借り人なども含めた) ▶うちは**大所帯です** I *have a large family* [*household*]. ‖彼女は**大所帯**を切り盛りしている She runs *a large household*. ‖子供が 3 人になり彼女は近頃**所帯じみてきた** Having three children *has domesticated* her. ‖そろそろ**所帯を持ったら**どうだい Isn't it time to *get married and have a family of your own*?

‖**所帯道具** household goods ‖**所帯主** the head of a household [a family], a householder ‖**所帯持ち** a married [family] man (男), a married woman (女).

2**しょたい 書体** a font.

しょだい 初代の the first ▶**初代**菊五郎 Kikugoro *the First* ‖日本の**初代**首相は誰ですか Who was *the first* prime minister of Japan?

1**じょたい 女体** a woman's body.

2**じょたい 除隊** a discharge from the army [military] ▶**除隊になる** be *discharged from the army* [*military*].

しょたいめん 初対面 ▶森さんとはきょうが**初対面**だった I *met* Miss Mori *for the first time* today. ‖彼らは**初対面の挨拶**を交わした They exchanged *introductory greetings*.

しょだな 書棚 a bookshelf [複 bookshelves].

しょだん 初段 a *shodan* ranking ▶柔道**初段**の人 a *shodan* judoist ‖彼は剣道**初段**だ He's *a shodan* in kendo. ／He is a kendo-player of *the lowest qualifying grade*. (● the first grade とすると the top grade (最上級) の意に解釈されるおそれがある).

しょち 処置 **1【措置】** a measure (➤ 通例複数形で用いる) ▶違反者に対しては厳しい**処置**をとります We will take strong *measures* against offenders. ‖どうか**寛大なご処置**をお願いします We hope you will *be lenient*. (➤ lenient は「罪などに寛大な」) ‖いくら注意しても聞かないんだから, あいつはもう**処置なしだ** Since he won't listen to me at all, *there's nothing more I can do* for him. ‖その問題の**処置に困っています** I *don't know what to do about* [*how to deal with*] the problem.

2【治療】 (a) treatment ▶私は虫歯を**処置してもらった** I *had* my cavity *treated* [*filled*]. ‖救急隊員は救急車の中で患者の**応急処置**をする Paramedics perform *emergency* [*first-aid*] *treatment* inside the ambulance.

しょちゅうみまい 暑中見舞い ▶**暑中見舞い**のはがきを書く write *a summer greeting card* 《**参考**》英米には暑中見舞いの習慣はないが, 例えば How are you spending these hot summer days? (この暑い夏をどのようにお過ごしですか)のように書いて, 暑中見舞いの意を表すことはできる.

1**しょちょう 所長** the head, the director ▶彼は長年国立国語研究所の**所長**を務めた He served for years as *the head* [*director*] of the National Institute for Japanese Language and Linguistics.

2**しょちょう 署長** the head, the chief

‖**警察署長** the head [chief] of a police station ‖**消防**[**税務**]**署長** the head of a fire station [a tax office].

3**しょちょう 初潮** one's first period [menstruation] ▶娘は12歳で**初潮**を迎えた My daughter had her *first period* at the age of twelve.

じょちょう 助長する encourage ＋目 ▶テレビゲームの画面に出てくる暴力シーンは実際の暴力を**助長する**ように思う I feel that violence in video games *encourages* real violence.

1**しょっかく 触覚** the sense of touch ▶盲人は**触覚**が敏感だ The blind have a keen *sense of touch*.

2**しょっかく 触角** a feeler (広く「触手」も含めて) ; an antenna /ænténə/ (昆虫などの).

1**しょっかん 触感** the touch, the feel ; (a) texture (手触り) ▶ビロードのような**触感** a velvety *texture*.

2**しょっかん 食感** (a) texture (舌触り) ; mouth feel, feeling in the mouth ▶コリコリした**食感** a chewy *texture* ／a chewy *mouth feel*.

しょっき 食器 the dishes (皿類) ; tableware (皿・ナイフ・フォーク・スプーンなど)

‖**食器戸棚** a cupboard /kʌ́bəʳd/ (流し台の上方に取り付けられたような) ; a sideboard (サイドボード) ; a cabinet (陶磁器を飾る).

ジョッキ a (beer) mug ▶ジョッキにビールをつぐ pour beer into *a beer mug*.

危ないカタカナ語✸ ジョッキ

1 日本語の「ジョッキ」は取っ手のついたビール用の容器を指すが, これは英語の jug から出た語とされる. 英語では一般に mug, stein(陶製の), tankard(蓋つきの)などが用いられる.

2 英語の jug は《英》ではジョッキ型の水差し(pitcher)や牛乳容器(milk container)などを指し,《米》では細口で取っ手のついた, 通例コルクで栓をする陶製またはガラス製のつぼを指す.

ジョッキー a **jockey**(騎手).

ショッキング ▶ショッキングなニュース *shocking* news.

ショック (a) **shock**(➤日本語の「ショック」より意味が強いことも多い) ▶人にショックを与えるような行為 *shocking* conduct(➤「けしからぬ行為」の意) ‖ 息子の万引きは彼にとって大きなショックだった His son's shoplifting was a great *shock* to him. ‖ 私は彼女のがさつな態度にショックを受けた I *was shocked* by her crude behavior. ‖ その知らせにショックを受けて彼女は一言も口が利けなかった (*Being*) *shocked* at the news, she could not speak a word. ‖ 農夫は額をスズメバチに刺されてショック死した The farm worker was stung on the forehead by a hornet and *died of shock*. ‖ 対話「うちの工場が夏には閉鎖かもだって」「ほんと？ショックだなあ」"I hear that the plant we work at may be closed down this summer." "Really? *What a shock!*"

‖ショック療法 shock treatment [therapy].

1**しょっけん** **職権** (**official**) **authority** (立場上与えられている権限) ▶職権を行使する exercise (one's) *authority* ‖ そのような行為は職権の乱用だ Such action is *an abuse of authority*.

2**しょっけん** **食券** a **meal ticket** [**coupon**].

しょっちゅう ▶母はしょっちゅう私にがみがみ文句を言う My mother is *always* [*forever*] nagging at me. (➤ always や forever を進行形とともに用いると, 繰り返し行われる行為を表し, 怒りやいらだちを示す) ‖ 私はしょっちゅうかぜをひく I get colds *very often*. ‖ こんな上等なウナギ, そうしょっちゅうはありつけないね *It isn't every day* that I get a chance to eat such excellent eel (as this).

しょってる ▶しょってるう！ *You really think you're something, don't you?* (➤ something は「たいした人物」).

ショット《球技》a **shot** ▶ナイスショット！ *Good* [*Nice*] *shot!* (➤ Good のほうがふつう).

しょっぱい **salty** /sɔ́:lti/ ▶海の水はしょっぱい Seawater *is salty*. ‖ このスープ, しょっぱくないかしら Can you *taste much salt* in the soup? ／Do you think the soup *is too salty*?

しょっぱな **初っ端** **the very beginning** ▶彼は試合のしょっぱなに 2 ランホーマーを放った He hit a two-run homer *at the very beginning* of the game. ‖ 会議はしょっぱなから混乱した The conference fell apart *as soon as it began*.

しょっぴく ▶ 2 人の警官が路上でわめいていた男を交番にしょっぴいて行った Two police officers *took* the man who was shouting on the street to the koban.

ショッピング **shopping** ▶元町にショッピングに行く *go shopping* in Motomachi ／ *go* to Motomachi *to shop* ／*go* to Motomachi *to do* some *shopping*.

‖ショッピングカート a shopping cart,《英》a shopping trolley ‖ ショッピングセンター a shopping center ‖ ショッピングバッグ a shopping bag,《英また》a carrier bag ‖ ショッピングモール a (shopping) mall.

ショップ a **shop**, a **store** ▶100円ショップ a hundred-yen *store*(➤アメリカには dollar store がある).

しょてい **所定** ▶所定(＝規定)の用紙を使って応募のこと Applications must be made in the *prescribed* form. ‖ 所定の期日までにこの仕事を終えなくてはならない I have to finish this task *by the fixed* [*appointed*] *date*. (➤ ふつうは by the deadline という).

じょてい **女帝** an **empress**.

しょてん **書店**《米》a **bookstore**,《英》a **bookshop**.

じょてんいん **女店員** →店員.

1**しょとう** **初等の** **elementary**

‖初等科 an elementary course ‖ 初等教育 elementary [primary] education.

2**しょとう** **初冬** **early winter** ▶ツバキの中には初冬に花を咲かせるものもある Some kinds of camellia (s) bloom *in early winter*.

3**しょとう** **初頭** ▶その事件は20世紀初頭に起こった That incident occurred *at the beginning* of the 20th century.

4**しょとう** **諸島** a (**group of**) **islands**, an **archipelago** /ɑ̀:rkəpéləgoʊ/ ▶伊豆[ハワイ]諸島 the Izu [Hawaiian] *Islands*.

しょどう **書道** ***shodo***, **Japanese calligraphy**

‖書道家 a calligrapher.

日本紹介 ✉ **書道は毛筆と墨を使って漢字やかな文字を書く日本の美術です. 伝統的な様式のものと前衛的な様式のものとがあります** *Shodo* is Japanese brush calligraphy. You draw *kanji* or *kana* letters with a calligraphy brush and *sumi* ink. Some schools of *shodo* value the traditional style while others aim to be avant-garde.

じょどうし **助動詞**《文法》an **auxiliary** /ɔ:gzíliəri/ 「**verb**.

しょどうそうさ **初動捜査** an **initial investigation** ▶警察は初動捜査でつまずいた The police botched *the initial investigation*.

しょとく **所得** (an) **income** ▶彼女は年間500万円の所得がある She has a yearly [an annual] *income* of five million yen. ‖ 彼は所得が多い[少ない] He *has a large* [*small*] *income*. (➤「低[中間／高]所得の」は low-[middle-/high-] income といい,「低所得者層(の人々)」は people in low-income brackets という). ‖所得水準 an income level ‖ 所得税 an income tax ‖ 勤労[不労]所得 earned [unearned] income ‖ 国民所得 the national income ‖ 雑所得 miscellaneous income.

しょなぬか **初七日** **the 6th day after a person's death** ▶初七日の法事(最近は告別式と一緒に行われることも多い) the Buddhist memorial service held on *the 6th day after a person's death*; it is now often held on the same day as their funeral.

しょにち **初日** **the first** [**opening**] **day** ▶大相撲秋場所の初日, 横綱は負けた On *the first day* of the Autumn Grand Sumo Tournament the yokozuna lost his bout.

しょにんきゅう **初任給** a **starting pay** [**salary**] ▶大学新卒者の初任給は現在約20万円だ The *starting pay* [*salary*] for a college graduate is around 200,000 yen now.

じょのくち **序の口** ▶《相撲》序の口の力士 a sumo wrestler in *the lowest rank*.

▶《比喩的》こんなの序の口で, (仕事は)これからもっときつくなるよ This is *just the beginning* and it's going to get even tougher.

しょばつ 処罰 (a) **punishment**(懲罰); a **penalty**(刑罰・罰金刑など具体的な) **一動 処罰する punish** +目 ▶その警官は飲酒運転をして厳しい**処罰を受けた** The policeman *received* severe *punishment* [*was* severely *punished*] for drunk driving. ‖アメリカでは州によってマリファナ不法所持の**処罰**が違う In the U. S., the *penalties* for illegal possession of marijuana vary from state to state.

1**しょはん 初版 the first edition** ▶『ユリシーズ』の**初版本** *a first edition* (*copy*) of "Ulysses" (➤『ユリシーズ』の初版本 2 冊なら two first edition copies of "Ulysses").

2**しょはん 初犯** one's **first offense**.

じょばんせん 序盤戦 an **early stage** ▶ペナントレースはまだ**序盤戦**だ The pennant race is still *in its early stages*.

しょひょう 書評 a **book review 一動 書評する review a book** ▶彼女の新しい小説は**書評**ではおおむね好評だった Her new novel was favorably received in most *book reviews* [by most reviewers].

‖**書評家** a book reviewer ‖**書評欄** a book-review column.

しょぶん 処分 **1【始末すること】disposal 一動 処分する dispose of**; **get rid of**(…を取り除く); **destroy** +目 (けが・病気の, あるいは危険な動物を) ▶彼女はその古いテレビを**処分する**ことにした She decided to *dispose of* [*get rid of*] the old TV set. ‖乳牛300頭を**処分する** *destroy* [*cull*] 300 cows(➤ともに大量の殺処分に用いる. 遠回しに put to sleep や put down などを使っていうことも多い).

2【罰すること】(a) **punishment 一動 処分する punish** +目 ▶経理部員は帳簿をごまかして厳しく**処分された** The accountant *was* severely *punished* for cooking the books. ‖彼はたばこを吸っているところを見つかって**退学処分になった** He was caught smoking and *got expelled* from school.

じょぶん 序文 a **preface** /préfəs/ (著者自身による); a **foreword**(しばしば著者にゆかりの人による).

ショベル a **shovel** →シャベル

‖**ショベルカー** a power shovel, an excavator.

しょほ 初歩 the ABC('s); **the basics**(基礎) **一形 初歩の elementary** ▶a と the の使い分けは英語の**初歩**だが, これが意外に難しい The distinction between "a" and "the" is one of *the ABC's* of English, but it's actually quite difficult. ‖きみは算数を**初歩から**やり直したほうがいいね You had better review arithmetic *from the basics*. ‖これは**初歩の**コンピュータグラフィックスの本だ This is a book on *elementary* [*rudimentary*] computer graphics. ‖こんな**初歩的な**ミスを犯してはだめだ You shouldn't have made such a *basic* mistake.

しょほう 処方する(薬を) **prescribe** +目 ▶医師は私に抗うつ剤を**処方した** The doctor *prescribed* an antidepressant for me.

しょほうせん 処方箋 a **prescription** ▶医者にかぜ薬の**処方箋を書いてもらう** *have* a doctor *prescribe* medicine for a cold.

しょぼくれる ▶**しょぼくれた**中年男 a middle-aged man *with a worn face*(➤「やつれた[疲れた]顔をした」の意) ‖何でそんな**しょぼくれた顔をしてる**んだい? What are you *look*ing so *down in the mouth* about? (➤ down in the mouth は「しょげ込んで」).

しょぼしょぼ ▶祖父は**しょぼしょぼした目で**ぼくを見た My grandfather looked at me with *bleary* eyes. ▶きょうは一日中雨が**しょぼしょぼ**降り続いた It continued drizzling *gloomily* all day long today.

しょぼん ▶そのサッカー選手は日本代表メンバーに選ばれずに**しょぼんとしていた** The soccer player looked *discouraged* because he didn't make the Japanese national team. ‖**しょぼんだよ!** *What a bummer!* (➤思うようにいかなかったときの言い方).

じょまくしき 除幕式 an **unveiling ceremony** ▶けさ, 学校創立者の銅像の**除幕式**が行われた The school founder's, bronze statue was unveiled this morning.

しょみん 庶民 the (common / ordinary) people; **the masses**(一般大衆) ▶国産のマツタケは高すぎて**一般庶民**の手には届かない Domestic matsutake is so expensive it is out of reach of *the common people*. ‖政治家はもっと真剣に**庶民の声**を聞くべきだ Politicians should listen to *the voice of the people* [*the opinions of ordinary people*] more seriously. ‖その王子には**庶民的なところがある** That prince has *the common touch*. ‖新首相には**庶民性**がある The new Prime Minister has *the common touch*. ‖浅草は**庶民的な**町だ The Asakusa district has a *down-home* flavor. (➤ down-home は「気さくな, 気取らない」).

しょむ 庶務 general affairs ▶彼は**庶務**を担当している(=庶務係だ) He is in charge of *general affairs*.

‖**庶務課** the section of general affairs, the general affairs section.

1**しょめい 署名** a **signature**(書類などへの); an **autograph**(有名人のサイン) **一動 署名する sign** /saɪn/ +目, **autograph** +目 →サイン ▶その書類に**署名する** *sign* the document ‖この書類には保護者の**署名**が必要です Your guardian's *signature* is needed on this document. ‖《街頭などで》**署名をお願いします** Could you *sign* this petition? / May I ask you for your *signature*? ‖私はその請願書に**署名した** I *put my signature* on [to] that petition. ‖この契約書には**署名がない** This contract *is not signed*. ‖今, 市長をリコールするために**署名運動**が展開されている *A signature-collecting campaign* is now under way in order to recall the mayor.

2**しょめい 書名 the title** [**name**] (**of a book**) ▶『老人と海』という**書名**の本 a book *entitled* "The Old Man and The Sea."

1**じょめい 除名する expel** +目 (組織から追放する) ▶彼はスキャンダルに関与したため会から**除名された** He *was expelled* from the club for his involvement in a scandal. / He [His name] *was taken off from the membership list* of the club because he was involved in a scandal.

2**じょめい 助命** ▶死刑囚の**助命**を嘆願する petition to *spare* the condemned criminal's *life*.

しょめん 書面 ▶我々の要望への回答は速やかに**書面で**お願いいたします Please reply promptly to our request *in writing*. (➤口頭でなく「文書で」の意).

✉ **採用試験の結果は書面で通知いたします** We will [shall] send you notification *in writing* of the results of your examination for employment in our company.

しょもう 所望 a **wish** ▶旅人は 1 杯の水を**所望した** The traveler *asked for* [*expressed a wish for*] a glass of water.

しょもつ 書物 a **book**.

しょや 初夜 the wedding night ‖**結婚初夜** one's

wedding night.

じょやく 助役 ▶駅の助役 an *assistant* stationmaster(➤「副駅長」の意) ‖ 市の助役 a *deputy* mayor(➤「市長代理」の意).

じょやのかね 除夜の鐘 the watch-night bell
日本紹介 ✉ **除夜の鐘は大みそかの夜12時に寺でつく鐘です. 108あるといわれる人間の煩悩を取り除くため108回つきます** A *joya-no-kane* (watch-night bell) is a bell at a Buddhist temple that is rung at midnight on New Year's Eve. It is rung 108 times to free people from their 108 earthly desires.

しょゆう 所有 possession 一動 所有する own +⊞, **possess** /pəzés/ +⊞ (➤ 後者はより堅い語で, 所有物を自分の自由にできるというニュアンスが強い) ▶**所有欲の強い人** a *very possessive* person ‖ その家は松田氏の**所有だ** The house *is owned by* Mr. Matsuda. / The house *belongs to* Mr. Matsuda. ‖ その名刀は太田さんの**所有となった** The famous sword *came into* Mr. Ota's *possession*. / The famous sword *fell into* Mr. Ota's *hands*. ‖ 彼女はゴッホの絵を**所有している** She *owns* [*possesses*] a Van Gogh (painting). ‖ 彼女はその家の**所有権を引き継いだ** She *took* [*gained*] *possession* of the house. (➤「所有権」は (the right of) ownership ともいう) ‖ この土地はうちの会社の**所有物**ではありません This estate is not our company's *property*. ‖《文法》**所有格** the possessive case ‖ **所有者** an owner ‖《文法》**所有代名詞** a possessive pronoun.

じょゆう 女優 an **actress**(➤ 男女を区別しないで actor を用いることも多くなってきている) ‖**映画女優** a movie actress ‖ **舞台女優** a stage actress.

1**しょよう 所要** ▶こちらまでの**所要時間**は車で10分くらいです *It takes about* 10 minutes to get here by car.

2**しょよう 所用 business** ▶父は**所用**で銀座に出かけています My father has gone to Ginza *on business*.

しょり 処理する deal with ; handle +⊞ (取り扱う) ; **manage** +⊞ (うまく処理する) ▶消費者からの苦情を**処理する** *deal with* a consumer complaint ‖ こんな大量の仕事は1人では**処理**できない It is impossible for one person to *deal with* [*handle*] such a large amount of work. ‖ コンピュータのおかげで大量の情報が短時間で**処理**できるようになってきた The computer has made it possible to *process* large amounts of information in a short time. (➤ process は「コンピュータで情報を処理する」) ‖ 彼らはその事件を大ごとにならないよう巧みに**処理した** They *dealt with* the incident skillfully so that it would not develop into a serious incident. ‖ 大量のごみを**処理する**(=処分する) *dispose of* large quantities of garbage ‖ 日本はとても深刻な**廃棄物処理問題**を抱えている Japan has a very serious *waste disposal problem*.

じょりゅう 女流

> **《解説》「女流…」について**
> (1)かつては女流作家, 女流詩人, 女流飛行家をそれぞれ authoress, poetess, aviatrix などと言ったが, 今では, それぞれ author, poet, pilot のように, 性差のない言い方をするのがふつう. 例えば, 「彼女は女流作家だ」は She is an author. でよい.
> (2)どうしても「女流…」と言いたい場合は woman … などと言えるが, 実際にはこの言い方もあまり好まれない. lady … はときに軽蔑的.

じょりょく 助力 help, aid (➤ 後者は公的援助を指すことも多い) ; **assistance**(補助) ▶彼女の**助力を仰ぐ** *ask* her *for help* ‖ 専門家の**助力を求める** call in professional *aid* ‖ 内田氏の**助力**によって, 私はこの本を書くことができた I wrote this book with the *help* [*aid*] of Mr. Uchida.

しょるい 書類 papers, documents (➤ 前者は書いたり印刷したりした文書一般を指し, 記録として残す正式文書の意の後者を含む) ▶**書類**に目を通す look through the *papers* [*documents*] ‖ 私は必要**書類**を提出した I submitted the necessary *papers*. ‖ 彼女は**書類審査**はパスしたが面接で落ちた She was selected from among the applicants after the *document screening*, but was eliminated in the interview. ‖ 警察は被疑者を**書類送検**した The police *sent* [*submitted*] the suspect's (*case*) *file* to the prosecutors' office. ‖ 警察は**関係書類**を押収した The police seized *the papers* [*documents*] *connected with the case*.
‖**書類かばん** a briefcase ‖ **秘密書類** secret [confidential] documents.

ショルダーバッグ a **shoulder bag**.

じょれつ 序列 ranking ▶日本人は**序列意識**が強い Japanese people have a strong *consciousness of their seniority ranking*. (➤ seniority は「先輩であること」).

しょろう 初老 a person in his [**her**] **early 60s**《参考》日本語の「初老」はもとは40歳のことを言ったが, 現在では60歳くらいの人を指す ▶**初老の**紳士 a *late-middle-aged* gentleman.

じょろん 序論 an **introduction** ▶研究論文の**序論** an *introduction* to a study.

しょんべん ▶しょんべんする *take* [*have* / *go for*] *a leak* ‖ ちょっとしょんべんに行ってくるよ I'm just *going for a* quick *leak*!

しょんぼり ▶彼女は雨の中にしょんぼり(=ひとり寂しそうに)立っていた She stood there in the rain *forlornly* [*looking forlorn*]. ‖ 彼はしょんぼりと(=がっかりした様子で)立ち去った He went away *dejectedly* [*with a dejected look*]. ‖ 対話「あの子, どうしてしょんぼりしてるの?」「先生に叱られたんだって」"Why is she *looking* so *down in the mouth*?" "I heard that the teacher scolded her." (➤ look down in the mouth は「口の両端が下がっている」が原義で, 元気がなくしょげている様子を表す).

しら 白 →しらを切る.

じらい 地雷 a **mine**, a **land mine** ▶**地雷**を除去する remove [clear] *a mine* ‖ **地雷**を埋める[敷設する] lay [plant] *a land mine* ‖ **地雷**を踏む step on *a land mine* ; meet with an unexpected disaster (➤ 比喩として) ‖**地雷原** a minefield.

しらが 白髪 (a) **gray hair**(白髪交じりの髪) ; (a) **white hair**(白髪) (➤ Ⓒ は髪の1本1本を意識するとき) ▶きみも**白髪**がずいぶん増えたねえ You have gotten more *gray hairs*, haven't you? ‖ 近頃母の**白髪**が急に目立つようになった My mother's *hair has turned* [*gone*] noticeably *gray* lately. (➤ turn [go] gray で「白髪になる」) ‖ 彼は**若白髪**だ His *hair is prematurely gray*. / He has *premature gray hair*.
‖**白髪染め** a hairdye, blue rinse(➤ 後者は青色の白髪染めで, 英米の年配の女性が使うことが多い).

しらかば 白樺 a **white birch** ▶シラカバ林 a grove of *white birches*.

しらき 白木 plain [**unpainted**] **wood**.

しらけ 白け apathy /ǽpəθi/ (無感動) ▶しらけの世代

an *apathetic* generation.

しらける 白ける ▶彼の無責任な発言で座がしらけてしまった His irresponsible remarks *put a chill on* [*threw a wet blanket over*] *the whole room*. (➤ wet blanket は文字どおりには「(消火用の)ぬれ毛布」の意で, 比喩的には「座をしらけさせる人」の意) ‖ 部長が顔を出したとたん楽しかったパーティーの雰囲気がしらけてしまった The pleasant atmosphere of the party *was chilled* [*was spoiled*] when the manager showed up. (➤ chill は「興を冷ます」) ‖ 今の大学生の多くはしらけていると言われる Many college students today are said to *be apathetic* [*unenthusiastic*].

しらこ 白子 milt, soft roe.

しらさぎ 白鷺《鳥》a white heron.

しらじらしい 白々しい ▶よくもそんなしらじらしい(＝見え透いた)うそが言えるもんだね How can you tell such a *transparent* [*barefaced*] lie?

じらす 焦らす ▶あんまりじらさないで話の結末を教えてくれよ Tell me the end of the story right away, and don't *keep* me *hanging* [*in suspense*]. (➤ keep ... hanging で「…に気をもませる」) ‖ 対話「キスは今度ね」「うーん, いつまでもじらさないでくれよ」"Your kiss can wait for the next time, OK?" "Mm—don't *tease* me." (➤ この場合, tease には「異性をその気にさせて困らせる」の意もある).

-しらず -知らず ▶暑さ知らず *free from* (summer) heat ‖ 寒さ知らず *free from* (winter) cold.

しらずしらず 知らず知らず ▶このCDを毎日聴いていれば知らず知らずのうちに英語が身につきます If you listen to these CDs every day, you'll learn English *without realizing it* [*unconsciously*].

しらせ 知らせ news (最近の出来事に関する情報); a report (報告); word (ことばによる) ▶悲しい知らせだ. 覚悟して聞いてくれ There is sad *news* for you. Please brace yourself. ‖ 私は国から父の急死の知らせを受け取った I received *word* from home that my father had suddenly died. ‖ 病院からは妻の病状について何の知らせもない I have had no *word* from the hospital about my sick wife.

▶区役所からのお知らせ an *announcement* from the ward office ‖《放送のコマーシャルで》それではここでお知らせを入れさせていただきます We'll be right back after this *announcement*. (➤ commercial と露骨に言うのを避ける場合の言い方) ‖ NKK からのお知らせです Here's a *message* from NKK.

しらせる 知らせる

let ... know, tell +目, inform +目 (➤ 最後は堅い語); notify +目 (通知する)

> 【文型】
> 人(A)に事(B)を知らせる
> let A know B
> tell A (about [of]) B
> inform A of B

▶何かあったら知らせてください If something comes up, please *let* me *know* [*tell* me]. ‖ 昨夜は楽しい集まりでした. 次回の日時が決まりましたらお知らせします Our get-together last night was enjoyable. I'll *tell* you [*let* you *know*] the date and time of the next one once they have been decided. ‖ 妹が電話で父が入院したと知らせてくれた My sister called to *tell* me *that* my father had been hospitalized. ‖ 彼は検査結果を知らされた He *was informed of* the test results.

▶洪水の危険を知らせるサイレンが鳴った Sirens sounded a flood warning. (➤「警報を出した」の意) ‖ 賃貸契約が切れる前に引っ越す場合は, その1か月前までに家主に知らせなければならない If you want to move out of the house before the lease expires, you must *notify* your landlord one month beforehand. ‖ きみが緑さんと婚約したこと, みんなに知らせようか Do you want me to *pass the word* that you've gotten engaged to Midori? ‖ そのニュースは私が彼女に知らせよう I'll *break* the news to her. (➤ break は通例「悪い知らせや秘密などを切り出す」の意).

✉ **きみのEメールのアドレスを知らせてください** Please *let* me *know* your email address.

✉ **私儀, この度名古屋支店に転勤いたしましたので, お知らせ申し上げます** I'd like to *inform* you that I have been transferred to the Nagoya Branch.

しらなみ 白波《米》white caps,《英》white horses ▶海は荒れ気味で白波が立っている The ocean is a little rough [choppy] with *white caps*.

しらぬがほとけ 知らぬが仏 →ほとけ.

しらばくれる ▶《警察で》しらばくれても証拠は挙がってるんだぞ Don't *pretend you don't know anything*. [Don't *play dumb*. / Don't *play* [*act*] *innocent*.] We have (enough) proof. (➤ play dumb /dʌm/ は「とぼける」) ‖ しらばっくれて! *As if you don't* [*didn't*] *know!*

シラバス a syllabus /síləbəs/.

しらはた 白旗 a white flag ▶白旗を揚げる hoist [show] *the white flag*.

しらはのや 白羽の矢 ▶次期社長として堀氏に白羽の矢が立った Mr. Hori *was singled out* to be the next company president. (➤ single out は「選び出す」).

しらふ ▶彼はしらふのときは借りてきた猫のようにおとなしい He is (as) meek as a lamb when *sober* [*not drunk*]. (➤ lamb は「(おとなしい)子羊」).

シラブル a syllable. →音節.

しらべ 調べ **1**【調査】▶《警察で》調べはついてるんだぞ. さっさと吐いたらどうだ *We've found out everything*, so now it's time for you to fess up.

2【旋律】a melody; a tune (節回し) ▶横笛の妙(たえ)なる調べ a sweet *melody* on a flute.

しらべもの 調べ物 ▶父は書斎で調べ物をしています My father is *doing some research* in his study.

しらべる 調べる

> 📖 訳語メニュー
> 調査する →examine, investigate **1**
> ことばなどを調べる →look up **2**
> 点検する →check **3**

1【調査する】examine +目 (人・物・場所などを); look into, investigate +目 (事件などを組織的に)

▶雌しべを顕微鏡で調べる *examine* a pistil under a microscope ‖ 警察はその交通事故の原因を調べている The police *are looking into* [*investigating*] what caused the traffic accident. ‖ 彼は今警察官に調べられて(＝尋問されて)いる He's *being questioned* by the police.

2【ことばなどを調べる】look up ▶その単語の意味を辞書で調べましたか Have you *looked up* the word in the dictionary? ‖ アイルランドのことを知りたいのならネットで調べなさい If you want to know about Ireland, *look* it *up* on the Net. ‖ 彼は地図を調べ始めた

He began to *study* the map.（➤この study は「注意深く見る」）.
3【点検する】check +目；**go over**（綿密に）▶タイヤに異常がないかどうか**調べる** *check* the tires for problems ‖ 必要事項が漏れていないか**調べて**ください Please *check* to see whether anything important is missing. ‖ 会計監査人たちは帳簿を注意深く**調べた** The auditors *went over* the accounts with care. ‖ 会員名簿を見て会費を納めていない人を**調べた** I ran down the association list to *see* who has not paid the membership fees［dues］.

しらみ 虱《虫》a **louse** /laʊs/［複 **lice**］▶《慣用表現》脱獄犯を捕まえるため警察はその一帯を**しらみつぶしに調べた** The police *combed* the area for the escaped prisoner.（➤comb /koʊm/ は「(くしですくように) 徹底的に捜す」の意）.

しらむ 白む ▶東の空が**白み始めた** The eastern sky *is turning bright*.／Day *is beginning to break*.（➤break は「(夜が) 明ける」）.

しらをきる 白を切る ▶**しらを切って**もだめだぞ！It's no use *playing dumb*［*innocent*］!

しらんかお 知らん顔 ▶彼女はぼくが話しかけても**知らん顔**だったけど，何か怒らせることでもしたんだろうか She *ignored me*［*gave me the cold shoulder*］when I spoke to her. I wonder what I've done to make her so upset. ‖ 彼は弟さんが困っているのに**知らん顔をしている** Even though his (younger) brother is in trouble, he *couldn't care less*.（➤「少しも気にかけない」の意）‖ 今度あの人に会っても**知らん顔して**いなさい You'd better *give* him *the cold shoulder* the next time you meet him.

しらんぷり 知らんぷり ▶健ったら，道で会っても**知らんぷり**なのよ Ken *pretends* he does*n't know* me if I see him on the street.

しり 尻 **1【でん部】**one's **buttocks** /bʌ́ţəks/,《インフォーマル》one's **rear (end)**, one's **behind**, one's **bottom**,《米また》one's **butt**,《英また》one's **bum**（椅子に座ったとき座席に触れる部分；one's butt は時に品のない響きを帯びる）；**the hips**（ウエストから下の横に張り出した膨らみの部分で，腰を含む）⇀けつ ▶大きな**尻** large *buttocks*／《インフォーマル》a large *bottom*［*behind*／*rear* (*end*)］（➤a large derrière /dèriéəʳ/ というおどけた言い方もある）‖ **尻の穴** one's *anus* /eɪnəs/ ‖ 彼女は**尻**が大きい She has large *buttocks*［broad *hips*］.（➤《インフォーマル》では a big bottom［rear (end)／behind］）‖ 猿は**尻**が赤い The monkey's *bottom* is red. ‖ **尻**におできができた I have a boil on my *bottom*［*rear end*］.（➤「右の尻に」と言うときは on my right buttock）‖ 彼女は**尻**を振って歩くからセクシーだ She is sexy because she wiggles［sways］her *hips* when she walks.（➤wiggle のほうが sway よりも大げさで下品な印象）‖ きみのジーパン，**お尻のところ**に穴があいてるよ There's a hole in *the seat* of your jeans. ‖ ちゃんと**お尻**拭いたの？Have you wiped your *bottom*?（➤日本語と同様に，your bottom と明示するのはごく幼い子や認知症のお年寄りなどに向かって言う場合．ふつうは wipe yourself で通じる）‖ 母はぼくが悪いことをするとよく**お尻をたたいた**ものだ My mother often *spanked* me when I misbehaved.
2【びり】the bottom ▶息子の成績はクラスで**尻**（＝びり）から３番目だ My son has very low grades and is third from *the bottom* of his class.
3【慣用表現】▶**尻の軽い**女 a woman *of loose morals*／an *easy* woman ‖ きみも**尻の落ち着かない**人だね You just *can't sit still*, can you? ‖ 俊雄はいつもぐずぐずしていて**尻が重い** Toshio always *drags his feet*［*heels*］.（➤drag one's feet［heels］は「(わざと) のろのろやる」の意のインフォーマルな言い方）‖ ディーンは**女房の尻に敷かれている** Dean *is completely under his wife's thumb*［*dominated by his wife*］.（➤be under A's thumb は「人(A)の言いなりになっている」の意）／Dean *is a henpecked husband*.（➤「めんどりにくちばしでつつかれる夫」の意）‖ あいつは50を過ぎたというのにまだ**女の子の尻を追い回している** Though he is over 50, he *is* still *chasing after young women*. ‖ 妻に**尻をたたかれて**彼は病院へ行った *Nagged* by his wife, he went to the hospital.（➤nag は「うるさく言う」）‖ 締め切りが迫って**尻に火がついてきた** The deadline is approaching and *I have to double my efforts*. ‖ あの客はいつも**尻が長い** That customer always *stays longer than he*［*she*］*should*.（➤この場合は customer は「店の客」.「家の客」なら visitor）.

しりあい 知り合い an **acquaintance**（知人）▶私はニューヨークには**知り合い**が多い I have many *acquaintances* in New York. ‖ フランス語は**父の知り合い**のフランス人から教わっています I'm learning French from a Frenchman［Frenchwoman］*my father knows*. ‖ 私はそのパーティーで彼女と**知り合いになりました** I *got acquainted with* her at that party.／I *met* her at that party.（➤日常会話では後者がふつう）‖ **お知り合いになれてうれしく思います** *I'm glad*［*happy*］*to meet you*.（➤答えるほうは I'm glad［happy］to meet you, too. と too を強めて言う）‖ **対話**「マリーさんとはお**知り合い**ですか」「ええ，もう10年以上の**知り合い**です」"*Do you know* Mrs. Murry?" "Yes, I *have known* her［we'*ve known* each other］for more than ten years."

しりあう 知り合う **meet** +目（初めて会う，出会う）；**get acquainted**《with》（知己を得る）；**get to know**（人となりがわかってくる）.
語法 meet が最も一般的．get acquainted は改まった言い方．get to know は「(徐々に) どういう人物かわかるようになる」の意
▶高田さんとは共通のお友だちを通じて**知り合いました** I *met* Ms. Takada through mutual friends. ‖ 彼女とは私のお友だちの結婚披露宴で**知り合いました** I *got acquainted with* her at the wedding reception of a friend of mine. ‖ (人が) お互いによく**知り合う**ようになるには多少時間がかかる It takes some time for people to *get to know* each other.

しりあがり 尻上がり **1【あとになるほど良くなること】**▶演奏は**尻上がりに**良くなった The performance *got better and better* toward the end.
2【語尾の上昇】▶この文は**尻上がりの調子**で読みなさい Read this sentence *with* (a) *rising intonation*.（➤反対は with (a) falling intonation）.

[1]**シリアル**《食品》**cereal (s)** ▶朝食用**シリアル** (a) breakfast *cereal* ‖ 朝食に**シリアル**を食べる eat *cereal* for breakfast.

[2]**シリアル**《連番》a **serial**
‖**シリアルナンバー** a serial number.

シリーズ a **series** /síəri:z/ ▶日本の城を題材にしたテレビの**シリーズ番組** a TV *series* on Japanese castles ‖ 6回**シリーズ**のテレビ番組 *a serial* TV *program* in six installments ‖ そのラジオ番組は**シリーズ物**なの？Is that radio program *a serial*? ‖ ことしの**日本シリーズ**は千葉ロッテが優勝した The Chiba Lotte Marines won *the Japan Series* this year.

危ないカタカナ語✹ シリーズ
「シリーズ」は series と一致するが，出版物や放送番組の「続き物」は a series, a serial の両語が使われ，a series はその中でも各回完結タイプのもの，a serial は全体として連続していくものを指す．

しりうま 尻馬 ▶あいつはすぐ人の尻馬に乗る男だ He tends to *follow other people's opinions blindly*.

1**じりき 自力** ▶行方不明になっていた登山者が自力で下山してきた The missing climber managed to descend the mountain *by himself* [*without help*]. ‖父はぼくに，これから先は自力でやっていけと言った My father told me to *manage all by myself* [*fend for myself*] from now on.

2**じりき 地力** one's **real ability** ▶彼はここ一番というときには地力を発揮する When it counts, he *shows his real ability*.

しりきれとんぼ 尻切れとんぼ ▶時間切れで彼のプレゼンは尻切れとんぼになった Time ran out and his presentation *was left unfinished* [*was cut off midway*].

しりごみ 尻込み ▶彼は選挙に出るのを尻込みした He *hesitated* to run in the election. ‖道端で蛇を見たらたいていの人は尻込みをする(＝ひるむ)だろう Most people would *shrink back* [*recoil*] at the sight of a snake in their path. ‖あいつはいざとなるといつも尻込みする He always *chickens out* at the last moment. (➤インフォーマルな言い方).

シリコン 1【元素】**silicon** /sílɪkən/
‖シリコンチップ a silicon chip ‖シリコンバレー Silicon Valley (サンフランシスコ南部の盆地の異名).
2【合成樹脂】**silicone** /sílɪkòʊn/.

しりしよく 私利私欲 ▶あの男は私利私欲に溺れて身を滅ぼした That man ruined himself by pursuing only *his own self-interest*.

じりじり ▶じりじりしながら彼を待つ wait for him *impatiently*.
▶彼は2位の選手をじりじりと引き離しにかかった He *slowly but surely* labored to widen his lead over the runner in second place.
▶真夏の太陽がじりじり照りつけていた The midsummer sun was burning down *fiercely*.

しりすぼみ 尻すぼみ ▶勉強会もメンバーが1人抜け2人抜けして，次第に尻すぼみになってしまった Our study group *petered out* as its members left one after another. (➤peter out は「徐々に消失[消滅]する」).

しりぞく 退く 1【下がる】▶武蔵は1歩退いた Musashi *took* [*made*] *a step backward*. ‖野党首脳は新政策に反対して一歩も退かなかった Opposition leaders *held their ground*, protesting against the new policy. (➤hold one's ground は「主張を貫く」).
2【引退する】**retire** ▶第一線を退く *retire* from the front line ‖その選手は体力の衰えから現役を退いた The player *retired from active play* due to declining strength.

しりぞける 退ける 1【拒否する】**turn down, refuse** ▶新井先生は私たちの提案を退けた Mrs. Arai *turned down* [*refused*] our proposal.
2【負かす】**defeat** +㊐, **beat** +㊐ (➤後者は前者よりややくだけた語) ▶チャンピオンは挑戦者をあっさり退けた The champ *defeated* [*beat*] the challenger with ease.
3【遠ざける】▶彼ら2人は周りの者を退けて密談した The two of them *kept* the others *away* to talk secretly.

1**しりつ 私立の private** ▶兄は東京の私立大学に通っている My brother goes to *a private university* in Tokyo. ‖私立学校 a private school ‖私立高校[中学] a private senior high school [junior high school] ‖私立探偵 a private detective, 《インフォーマル》a private eye.

2**しりつ 市立の city, municipal** (➤後者は「地方自治の」の意．したがって「町・村立の」の意でも用いられる) ▶市立の学校 a *city* [*municipal*] school ‖市立病院 a *city* [*municipal*] hospital／a hospital *run by the city* ‖市立船橋高等学校 Funabashi *Municipal* High School ‖横浜市立大学 Yokohama *City* University.

じりつ 自立 independence 一動 **自立する become independent; support oneself** (経済的に) ▶経済的に自立したいと考える女性が増えてきている The number of women who want to *support themselves* [want to *be economically independent*] is increasing. ‖彼は自立して不動産業を始めた He *has established himself* [*has set himself up*] as a real estate agent.
‖自立心 a sense of independence.

じりつしんけい 自律神経 an **autonomic** /ɔ̀ːṭənɑ́ːmɪk/ **nerve** ▶彼は自律神経失調症にかかっている He suffers from *autonomic imbalance*.

しりとり 尻取り *shiritori*; a word-chain game ▶しりとり遊びをする play *shiritori*.
日本紹介 ✉ **しりとりは単語の最後の音を言いつなげていくことば遊びの一種です．日本語には「ん」で始まる単語がないため，「ん」で終わる語を言ったり，適切な単語を答えられなかったりすると負けです** *Shiritori* is a word game played by making a chain of words in which the last syllable of one word is used as the first syllable of the next. Because there is no word in Japanese that begins with the 'n' sound without a vowel, if you say a word that ends with an 'n' or can't think of a word to continue the chain, you lose.

しりぬぐい 尻拭い ▶きみのばかげた行動の尻拭いをするのはごめんだね I don't want to *foot the bill* for your stupid behavior. (➤foot the bill は文字どおりには「勘定を払う」) ‖父親は息子の借金の尻拭いをした The father *paid* his son's *debt for* him.

じりひん じり貧 ▶その水族館への来館者はじり貧になっている The number of visitors to the aquarium *has tapered off*.

しりめ 尻目 ▶ジョギング中の青年はやじ馬たちを尻目に走り去った The young jogger *glanced at* the curious onlookers and ran away. ‖不景気にあえぐ企業を尻目にその会社は最高益を上げた *In sharp contrast to* other businesses struggling in the recession, the company earned a record profit.

しりめつれつ 支離滅裂 ▶ぼくのおじさんは時々支離滅裂なことを言う My uncle occasionally *rambles* (*when he talks*). ‖彼の論文は支離滅裂で訳がわからない His paper *lacks coherence* [*consistency*]. (➤coherence /koʊhíərəns/ は「つながりがきちんとしていること」, consistency は「矛盾がないこと」)／His paper *wanders all over* and makes no sense.

しりもち 尻餅 ▶私は凍りついた道で滑って尻餅をついた I slipped on the frozen street and *fell on my* *bottom* [*rear*].

しりゅう 支流 a **tributary**(本流に流れ込む) ; a **branch** (本流から枝分かれした) ▶この川は富士川の**支流**だ This river is *a tributary* [*branch*] of the Fuji River.

じりゅう 時流 **the current** [**trend**] **of the times** ▶時流に逆らう go against *the current of the times* ‖ **時流に乗り遅れた**会社 a business firm which *failed to keep up with the times* ‖ 彼女は**時流に乗っている** She's *in tune* [*sync*] *with the spirit of the age*. ‖ 小説家村上春樹は**時流に合っている** Novelist Murakami Haruki is *in tune with the* (*trends of the*) *times*.

しりょ 思慮 **thought**(考え) ; **prudence**(分別) ▶彼女は**思慮に欠ける**ところがある She is a little *thoughtless* [*imprudent*]. ／She is a bit *lacking in prudence*. ‖ 若い女性にそんな淫らな冗談を言うなんて彼も**思慮が足りない**ね It's *thoughtless* of him to tell a dirty joke in front of [in the presence of] a young woman. ‖ 彼は**思慮深い人**だ He is *a prudent man*.

1**しりょう 資料** **material**(材料, 題材) ; **data**(判断・結論の根拠としての) ▶卒論を書くための**資料を集めています** I'm collecting [gathering] *material* for my graduation thesis. ‖ この件に関しては**資料が不足している**のではっきりしたことは言えません We cannot say anything definite because we lack sufficient *data* on the matter.

‖**資料室** a reference room.

2**しりょう 飼料** (a) **feed**(鶏・牛などの ; 1回分の場合は a を伴う) ; **fodder**(干し草・わらなど家畜の) ; **forage** /fɔ́ːrɪdʒ/(牛馬用飼い葉).

1**しりょく 視力** **sight**, **eyesight**(物を見る力) ; **vision**(物を見て認識[判断]する力) ▶私は**視力がいい**[**弱い**] I *have good* [*poor*] *eyesight*. ‖ 近頃**視力が衰えてきた** My *eyesight* is getting worse [is failing] these days. ‖ **視力は両目とも1.0だ** My *vision* in both my eyes is 1.0. (➤ 日本式の言い方) ‖ **視力は正常です** I *have normal eyesight*. 《参考》視力が正常であることを英語では My eyesight is [My eyes are] twenty-twenty. とか I have twenty-twenty vision. とも言う.「20フィートの距離から視力表が読める」の意で, 20/20とも書く.

▶彼はその事故で**視力を失った** He *lost his* (*eye*)*sight* in the accident. ‖ 車の運転免許を取るために**視力検査を受けた** I had *an eye test* in order to get my driver's license.

‖**視力検査** an eye test ‖ **視力障害** vision impairment ‖ **視力表** an eye chart.

2**しりょく 資力** **wealth**(富) ; **means**(財産) ; **funds**(手持ち資金) ; **financial resources**(財源) ▶彼は**資力に物を言わせて**名画を買い込んでいる He is buying famous pictures *using the power of* (*his*) *money* [*the power of his wealth*]. ‖ わが社は**資力が乏しい**ので新製品を多く出せない Since our company has limited *financial resources*, we can't put many new products on the market.

3**しりょく 死力** ▶**死力を尽くす** make *desperate efforts* ‖ 彼らは**死力を尽くして戦った** They fought *tooth and nail*. (➤ tooth and nail は文字どおりには「(動物が)歯と爪で必死に戦って」).

じりょく 磁力 **magnetic force**(**s**).

シリンダー a **cylinder**.

1**しる 汁** **juice**(果汁) ; **sap**(樹液) ; **soup**(吸い物) ▶レモンの**汁を絞る** press [squeeze] the *juice* out of a lemon ‖ このグレープフルーツは**汁が多い** This grapefruit *is juicy*.

▶《慣用表現》あいつはいつも**うまい汁を吸っている** He always *skims off the top*. (➤ skim off は文字どおりには「上澄みをすくい取る」).

2しる 知る

訳語メニュー
- 知識として持つ →know **1, 2**
- 知り合いである →know **3**
- 気がつく →notice **4**
- 経験する →experience **5**

1【情報を得る】 **know** +㊐ ; **learn** +㊐ (読んだり聞いたりして) ; **hear** +㊐ (聞いて知る) ; **find** +㊐ (状況などから)

▶国民は税金の使われ方を**知る**権利がある People have the right to *know* how their taxes are (being) used. ‖ 両親はいつも私がどこにいるかを**知っていたい**のです My parents want to *know* where I am at all times. ‖ テレビのニュースで日本の旅客機がハイジャックされたことを**知った** I *learned* [*found out*] on TV that a Japanese passenger plane had been hijacked. ‖ 羽生が優勝したのを**知っている**? *Did you know* that Hanyu won the competition ? (➤ この Did you know ...? は質問というより,「…ということを知っていた」に当たる事実を伝える言い方).

▶チリに巨大地震があったことを**知って驚いた** I was surprised *to learn* that a megaquake had hit Chile. ‖ 私はスキー靴がそんなに高いものだと**知って驚いた** I was surprised to *find* that ski boots were so expensive. ‖ その画家についてもっと**知りたい** I want to *learn* more about the painter. ‖ あなたがスタンフォード大学へ入学したことを**知れば**彼女は喜ぶでしょう She will be very happy when she *hears* [*finds out*] that you were accepted by [made it into] Stanford University.

直訳の落とし穴「きのう知った」
know =「知る」と覚えている人が多いので,「幸子が結婚することをきのう知った」のつもりで, (×)Yesterday I knew that Sachiko is getting married. などと言ってしまう. know は「知っている」という状態を表す. したがって, この英文は強いて解釈すれば「きのう(すでに)知っていた」を表すことにはなるが, いつ「知った」かは明らかでない.「きのう知った」は Yesterday I found out that ... と言う.

2【知識がある】 **know**(+㊐)

▶野村氏は野球のことは何でも**知っている** Mr. Nomura *knows* everything about baseball. ‖ バーバラは歌舞伎について**よく知っている** Barbara *knows a lot* about kabuki. ‖ 中山さんはアメリカの歴史について**よく知っている** Mr. Nakayama *has a good knowledge* of [*is knowledgeable* about] American history. ／Mr. Nakayama *is well versed in* the history of the U.S. (➤ be well versed in は学問や技術などに詳しい場合に用いる) ‖ 彼は**物をよく知っている**(＝物知りだ) He *is* a *knowledgeable* person. ／He *is knowledgeable about many things*. ‖ この辺りの地理は**よく知りません** I'm quite *a stranger* around here.

▶父はフットボールのルールについて**何も知らない** My dad *knows nothing* about football rules. ‖ **知らない所**へ行ったらまず旅行案内所へ行くのがよい When you arrive at *a strange place*, the first place you should go (to) is the Tourist Information Center. ‖ **私の知る限り**, 彼は10年前はボストンにいた *As far as I know* [*To the best of my knowledge*], he was in Boston ten years ago. ‖ 彼は新宿の**裏の裏まで知り尽くしている** He *knows* Shinjuku *inside* (*and*) *out*. ‖ 私はその詩人のことを**知れば知るほど**, その詩が好きになった *The more I've learned* about the poet, the better I've come to like him [her] poetry. ‖ これは**知る人ぞ知る**秋田の銘酒です This is an excellent sake [rice wine] from Akita that *is known to only a select few* [*known only to connoisseurs*]. (➤ connoisseur /kɑ̀ːnəsə́ːʳ/ は「通(つう)」).

3【知り合いである】know +目 ▶私は神田さんを個人的に**知っています** I *know* Kanda personally. ‖ 彼女のことは(一応)**知ってはいますが, よくは知りません** I *know of* her, but I *don't know* her (*well*). (➤ know of は「(人について)一応[聞いて]知っている」の意) ‖ ぼくが弘美を**知った**(＝知り合った)のはクラブででした I *got to know* Hiromi at a club. ‖ **知らない人**から誘われてもついて行ってはいけません Don't go with *a stranger* even if he [she] invites you to go someplace. ‖ **知らない人**から食べ物や飲み物をもらっちゃだめよ Don't take food or drinks from somebody you *don't know*.

直訳の落とし穴「よく知っている」
「よく知っている」は know well であるが, これは主に人に用いて, We know each other well. (私たちはお互いによく知っている)のように使う. 物事の場合は知識をいうことになり, know about を使うことが多く, 「よく知っている」は know a lot about となる. したがって, 「キーン教授は日本文学をよく知っている」は, Professor Keene knows a lot about Japanese literature. である. (×)knows well about とは言わない. なお, 人の場合もその人となりや生い立ち, 家族などその人に関する「知識」をいうときには I know a lot about him. (彼についてはいろいろなことを知っている)という言い方をする. また, 「ジェーンがどのくらい日本に滞在するかはよく知らない」も know well を使わず, I don't know exactly how long Jane will be staying in Japan. と言う.

4【気がつく】notice +目; **realize** +目 (自覚する); **be aware** 《of》(気がついている) ▶彼女がそんなひどいけがをしているとは**知らなかった** I *didn't notice* [*know*] that she had been so seriously injured. ‖ 彼は**知らないうちに**ＨＩＶに感染していた He had gotten HIV *without realizing it*. ／He *was unaware* that he had contracted HIV. ‖ 私の辞書, **知らない**? *Have you seen* my dictionary?

5【経験する】experience +目 ▶日本に来て初めて地震というものを**知りました** I*'ve experienced* an earthquake for the first time since I came to Japan. ‖ 私たちは戦争を**知らない**世代です Our generation *has never experienced* war. ‖ きみは苦労を**知らない** You *haven't experienced* any (true) hardships.

6【知られる】▶山梨はおいしいワインで**知られている** Yamanashi *is famous for* (its) good wine. ‖ そのレスラーは凶暴なことで**知られている** The wrestler *is notorious for* his violent nature. (➤ notorious は「悪名が高い」) ‖ 池田氏は**名の知られた**言語学者である Mr. Ikeda is a *well-known* linguist. (→有名).

7【「知ったことではない」の形で】▶きみの**知ったことではない** *That's none of* your *business*. ‖ きみが誰と付き合おうと私の**知ったことではない** I *don't care* whoever you associate with. ‖ あなたがいくら損をしようと, **私の知ったことではない** However much money you may lose, *it's no concern of mine*.

シルエット a **silhouette** /sìluét/.

シルク silk ‖ **シルクハット** a silk hat ‖ **シルクロード** the Silk Road.

しるこ 汁粉 ***shiruko***
日本紹介 ✉ **汁粉は小豆で作る食べ物です. 甘くしたあんを溶かした熱い汁の中に焼いた餅を入れ, スナックとして食べます** *Shiruko* is a sweet made with red azuki beans. You dilute some sweetened red bean paste with water, heat it, and put some grilled *mochi* (rice cake) in it and eat it as a snack.

しるし 印 1【記号, 兆候】a **mark** (○×などの); a **sign** (ある意味・内容を表す); 《米》a **check**, 《英》a **tick** (照合のための✓印)
▶英語の教科書の意味のわからない単語に赤い**印をつけた** I *marked* in red the words I didn't understand in the English textbook. ‖ 警官は事故現場に**印をつけた** The police officer *marked off* (the place) where the accident had taken place. ‖ 机にこの**印をつけたの**誰? Who made this *mark* on the desk?
▶彼が意地悪するのはあなたに気があるしるしよ His acting mean to you is *a sign* (that) he's interested in you.

2【形に表すもの】a **token**(謝意などを込めるもの)
✉ **感謝のしるしに私が編んだテーブルセンターをお送りします** I'm sending you this table runner that I knitted as *a token of my appreciation*. (●「ほんのおしるしですがどうぞお受け取りください」としたいのなら Please accept this *as a small token of my gratitude*. とすればよい).

しるす 記す 1【書きつける】put [**write**] **down** ▶ぼくは彼女の住所と電話番号を手帳に**記した** I *wrote* [*jotted*] *down* her address and phone number in my notebook.

2【跡を残す】▶1969年, 人類は月への**第一歩をしるした** In 1969, humankind *left its first footprints* on the surface of the moon.

ジルバ jitterbug /dʒítəʳbʌg/.

シルバー silver(銀) ▶シルバー(＝高齢者)市場 the *senior* market(➤ silver market は「銀市場」) ‖ シルバー人材センター a *senior* citizen human resource center ‖ **シルバー料金** a *senior* price [fare] (➤ fare は「運賃」).

危ないカタカナ語 シルバー
1 日本では「シルバー」で老齢を表すことが多いが, 英語では silver でなく golden や gray を使う. したがって, 「シルバーエイジ」は the golden years となる. ちなみに, 「老人パワー」は gray power である. (この gray は「白髪の」という意味).
2「シルバーシート」は表示としては priority [courtesy] seating(優先席)という. 1つの「シルバーシート」は a seat for elderly and disabled passengers という.

[1]**しれい 指令** an **order**; **instructions**(指図) **一動 指令する order** +目 ▶彼らは本部の**指令**で行動した They acted on *an order* [*instructions*] from headquarters. ‖ 消防隊長は隊員たちに対して炎上中の建物から退去するよう**指令した** The fire chief *or-*

dered his men to leave the burning building.

2**しれい 司令** a **command** ‖ **司令官** a commander, a commanding officer ‖ **司令船**(宇宙船の) a command module ‖ **司令長官** a commander in chief ‖ **司令部** (the) headquarters.

1**じれい 辞令** ▶4月1日付けの**転任の辞令**をもらった I received *transfer orders* [*papers*] dated April 1.

し

2**じれい 事例** an **example**(典型的な例) ; an **instance**(個々の例) ; a **case**(実際の事例) ; a **precedent**(先例) ▶過去の**事例**を研究する study past *examples* ‖ 今までそういう**事例**はありません There have been no such *precedents*.

しれつ 熾烈な **fierce**(きわめて激しい) ; **keen**(強烈な) ▶しれつな競争 *fierce* [*keen*] competition ‖ 韓国社会は**しれつな競争社会**だ South Korean society is *fiercely* [*highly* / *ultra*-] *competitive*.

しれつきょうせい 歯列矯正 **orthodontics** /ɔ:ʳθədɑ́:nṭɪks/ 《参考》「歯列矯正をする」は一般には have one's teeth straightened と表現する.「歯列矯正器」は braces. →**矯正**.

じれったい ▶ねえ, 教えてよ. **じれったいわね!** Oh, please tell me—I'*m dying of curiosity*. (➤「知りたくてしかたがない」の意) ‖ 係員の手際の悪さに**じれったくなった**(=いらいらした) I *felt* [*was*] *irritated* by the clerk's inefficiency. ‖ 竹下君の優柔不断には**じれったくなる** Takeshita's indecisiveness *is* really *irritating*.

しれる 知れる ▶愛子がオーディションに合格したことはすでに近所に**知れている** It *is* already *known to everyone* in the neighborhood that Aiko passed the audition. / *Everyone* in the neighborhood *knows* that Aiko passed the audition. ‖ 彼が会社の金を使い込んでいたことが**知れてしまった** It *was revealed* that he had embezzled company money.

▶《慣用表現》あいつは**えたいの知れない男**だ He is *a man of mystery*. / He's *an enigma*. ‖ そんな大事なことを両親に相談しないなんてきみの**気が知れない**よ I *don't understand* why you didn't discuss such an important matter with your parents. ‖ きみのことばがどんなに心強かったか**知れない**よ *I can't be grateful enough* for your words of encouragement.

じれる ▶そんなに**じれる**なよ. すぐきみの番が来るから Don't *be* so *impatient*. It will soon be your turn. ‖ 彼は仕事がはかどらないので**ひどくじれた** He *was on edge* because his work was not progressing smoothly. (➤ on edge は「いらいらして」の意のインフォーマルな表現).

しれわたる 知れ渡る ▶タイガー・ウッズの名は全世界に**知れ渡っている** Tiger Woods' name *is known* all over the world. ‖ 連続ドラマの舞台となってからその町は全国に**知れ渡った** The town was used as the scene of a TV serial drama and *became known* throughout the country. / The town's being used as the scene of a TV serial drama *put* it *on the map*. (➤ put ... on the map は「(町・地方を)世間に注目させる」).

しれん 試練 a **trial** ; an **ordeal** (厳しい) ; a **test** (試験) ▶人生の厳しい**試練**に耐える endure the severe *trials* [the *ordeals*] of life ‖ 今は彼女にとって**試練の時**だ This is *a trying time* for her.

ジレンマ a **dilemma** /dɪlémə/ ▶彼女は仕事と家族のどちらを選ぶかという**ジレンマ**に直面している. She is faced with the *dilemma* of choosing between work and family commitments.

> **危ないカタカナ語✹ ジレンマ**
> カタカナ語のジレンマは, 上からの命令と下からの突き上げで悩む中間管理職のように, どちらでも構わないが板挟みで選べない場合にもいうが, dilemma はどちらを取っても不利益につながる難しい選択を指す.『ハムレット』の "To be or not to be." (生きるべきか死ぬべきか) が典型的な dilemma である.

1**しろ 城** a **castle** /kǽsəl/ ▶**城を築く** build *a castle* ‖ ここは萩城の**城跡**だ This is *the site of* Hagi *Castle*.

✉ **日本の城はほとんどが戦争や自然災害で焼失し近年再建されたもので, その多くが一般に公開されています** Most *castles* in Japan were destroyed due to wars or natural disasters, and rebuilt in recent years. Most of them are open to the public.

2**しろ 白** **1【色の】** **white** ▶**白の**ドレス a *white* dress. **2【無罪の】** **innocent** ▶その容疑者は**白**と判明した That suspect was proved (to be) *not guilty* [*innocent*].

しろあり 白蟻 a **termite** /tə́:ʳmaɪt/ ; a **white ant**(➤俗称) ▶**シロアリ**を駆除する exterminate *termites*.

しろい 白い **white** ; **fair**(皮膚が) ; **gray**(髪の毛が) ; **blank** (何も書いてない) ▶**白いユリ** a *white* lily ‖ 奈緒子は**色が白い** Naoko *has a fair* [*light*] *complexion*. (➤ white は使えない) ‖ **白い紙**と鉛筆を持っておいで Bring me a sheet of *blank paper* and a pencil. ‖ 私は柵を**白く塗った** I painted the fence *white*. ‖ 彼女は**白い歯**を見せてほほえんだ She smiled, flashing her *white* teeth. ‖ 母は**髪が白くなってきた** My mother's *hair is getting* [*turning*] *gray*. ‖ 最近父は急に頭に**白いもの**が目立つようになった Recently, *the white* in my father's hair has become noticeable. ‖ 強盗は**白っぽい車**で逃走した The robber escaped in a *whitish* car.

▶《慣用表現》彼らは私のことを**白い目**で見た They gave me *icy looks*. / They looked *askance* at me. (➤ askance は「不信の目で」).

じろう 痔瘻 an **anal fistula**.

しろうと 素人 a **layperson**(専門家でない人, ある特定の職業の一員でない人 ; 男女を区別するのなら a layman, a laywoman ; 複数形は laypeople) ; an **amateur** /ǽmətʃʊəʳ/ (楽しみのためにやる人, 経験や能力がないままにやる人) ▶この本は**素人向け**だ This book is for *laypeople*. ‖ それは**素人の考え**だ Only *a layperson* would think [say] that. / That's *a layperson's* idea. / That's what all *new people* [*greenhorns* / *first timers*] think. (➤ greenhorn, first timer はともに「初心者」) ‖ この絵は何となく**素人臭い** This painting looks somewhat *amateurish*. ‖ **素人療法**はしないで医者に行ったほうがいいよ You had better avoid *home remedies*. You should see a doctor instead.

☛ **ずぶの** (→見出語)

しろくじちゅう 四六時中 ▶あの子は外で遊ばないで**四六時中**(=一日中)テレビゲームをしている That boy never goes out to play, but spends *all day* playing video games. ‖ 彼女は**四六時中**(=しょっちゅう)仕事のことでこぼしている She's *always* grousing about her job. ‖ コンビニは**四六時中**開いている Convenience stores are open *24 hours a day*.

しろくま 白熊 a **white bear** ; a **polar bear** (ホッキョクグマ).

しろくろ 白黒 **1【白と黒】**▶白黒テレビ a *black-and-white* TV ‖白黒の映画 a *monochrome* film／a *black-and-white* movie.
2【慣用表現】▶どっちが正しいか一度白黒をはっきりつけようじゃないか Let's *settle* once and for all which of us is right. ‖彼女はそのドレスの値段を聞いて目を白黒させた(＝驚いた) She *was shocked* to hear the price of that dress. ／*Her eyes* (*almost*) *popped out* when she heard the price of that dress. (➤pop out は「飛び出る」).

じろじろ ▶そんなに私をじろじろ見ないでください Please don't *stare at* me like that! ‖彼女はぼくの顔をじろじろ見た She *looked intently at* [*studied*] my face. (➤この study は「何かを探るように見る」の意).

シロップ **syrup** /sírəp/ ▶ホットケーキにメープルシロップをかける pour *maple syrup* over [on] a pancake.

しろつめくさ 白詰草 《植物》a **white clover.**

シロナガスクジラ 《動物》a **blue whale.**

しろバイ 白バイ a **white police motorcycle** ▶スピード違反で白バイ(の警官)に車を止められちゃったよ I was stopped by *a motorcycle cop* for speeding.

> **危ないカタカナ語✹ 白バイ**
> **1**「白バイ」の車そのものは white police motorcycle と表現できるが, 英米ではスピード取り締まりの警官のバイクは白と決まっておらず各色が使われているので, 単に police motorcycle でよい.
> **2** 白バイに乗っている警察官は motorcycle policeman [policewoman／police officer], motor cop, speed cop などという.

しろぼし 白星 ▶白星をあげる *win* [*gain*] *a victory* ／*win* ‖その力士は今場所は白星が先行した That sumo wrestler has gotten more *wins* than losses in this tournament.

シロホン a **xylophone** /záɪləfoʊn/ ▶シロホンを演奏する play the *xylophone*.
‖シロホン奏者 a xylophonist.

しろみ 白身 **egg white, the white of an egg** (卵の); **white meat** [**flesh**] (魚などの) ▶白身の魚 *white-fleshed* [*white-meat*] fish.

しろめ 白目 **the white of** one's **eye.**

1**しろもの 代物** ▶とんだ代物(＝ひどい物)をつかまされちゃったよ They palmed off *some awful stuff* on me! ‖こんなの食えた代物じゃあないよ This *is hardly* [*scarcely*] *fit to eat.*

2**しろもの 白物** **1【洗濯物】**▶白物と色物を分けて洗濯する wash *whites* and colors separately.
2【電気製品】▶白物家電 *home appliances* (家庭用電気器具).

じろりと ▶受付の人は私が入っていくとじろりと見上げただけで何も言わなかった When I entered, the receptionist fixed me *with a piercing look* and said nothing.

しろん 試論 an **essay** 《on》.

じろん 持論 one's **opinion** (自分が信じる意見・考え); one's (**pet**) **theory** (事実に基づく, あるいは, 証拠立てられる説や理屈) ▶子供は甘やかして育てるべきではないというのが私の持論だ *My opinion* is that children should not be indulged too much. ‖彼女はあくまでも持論(＝自説)を曲げない She (always) sticks to *her opinions* [*views*]. ／She won't budge from *her pet theories.*

しわ 皺 a **wrinkle** /ríŋkəl/ 一動 **しわになる wrinkle** ▶あの人は60に手が届こうというのに顔にしわひとつない He is nearly sixty, but he doesn't have *a wrinkle* on his face. ‖祖父の顔はしわだらけだ My grandfather's face is *full of wrinkles.* ‖長い間座っていたのでズボンがしわになってしまった I've been sitting for so long that my pants *are* all *wrinkled.* ‖彼は1万円札のしわを伸ばした He *smoothed out* the crumpled ten thousand yen bill. ‖ナイロンはしわにならない Nylon *does not wrinkle* [*crumple*]. (➤crumple は文字どおりには「くしゃくしゃになる」) ‖父は考え事をしているとき額にしわを寄せる My father *wrinkles* [*creases*] his forehead when he is thinking.

しわがれる 嗄れる **get** [**become**] **hoarse** ▶あんまりせきをしたので声がしわがれてしまった I coughed so much I *got hoarse* [*lost my voice*]. (➤ふつうはカッコ内のように言う).

しわくちゃ 皺くちゃ ▶曽祖母の顔はしわくちゃだ My great-grandmother's face is *full of wrinkles.* ‖彼はポケットからしわくちゃのハンカチを取り出した He pulled a *wrinkled* [*creased*] handkerchief from his pocket.

しわけ 仕分けする **sort** (**out**), **classify** ＋㊐ ▶郵便局で年賀状を仕分けするアルバイトをした I had a part-time job *sorting* New Year's cards in the post office. ‖彼女は洗濯物を色物とそうでない物とに仕分けした She *sorted out* the laundry into white(s) and colored clothes. ‖政府の事業を仕分けする *screen* government projects (➤「事業仕分け」は budget screening (予算精査), cost cutting (経費削減)のように言える).

しわざ 仕業 **the work** ▶これは子供の仕業に違いない This must be *the work* of a child. ／A child must have done this. ‖これは一体誰の仕業だ *Who* on earth *did* this? ／Just *who is responsible for* this?

じわじわ ▶川の水かさがじわじわと(＝ゆっくりと)増してきた The river is rising *slowly.* ‖わが軍はじわじわと後退した We began to retreat *little by little.*

しわす 師走 ***shiwasu*, December.**

じわっと **gradually** ▶幸福感がじわっと湧いてきた *Gradually* a feeling of happiness welled up in my heart.

しわよせ 皺寄せ ▶勉強を怠けているとあとでしわ寄せが来るよ If you are lazy in your studies, you'll *have to pay for it* later. (➤pay for は「…の報いを受ける」) ‖中小企業は不景気のしわ寄せを受けやすい Small and medium enterprises are often the first to *be hit* by (a) recession. (➤「打撃を受ける」と考える).

じわれ 地割れ a **crack** [**fissure**] (**in the ground**).

1**しん 真** (a) **truth** (真理) 一形 **真の true** ▶真・善・美 *truth*, virtue and beauty ‖真の友人 one's *true* friend ‖真の学者 a scholar *worthy of the name* (➤「その名にふさわしい」の意) ／a scholar *in the true sense of the word* (➤「本当の意味での」の意) ‖真の愛は古くならない *True* love never grows old. ‖その洞窟の中は真の(＝完全な)闇だった The cave was in *utter* darkness. ‖彼女の演技は真に迫っていた She acted *most vividly.* ／Her performance was *vivid* [*true to life*／*realistic*]. ‖その絵は真に迫っていた The painting *was true to life.* ‖まさかの(ときの)友こそ真の友 *A friend in need is a friend indeed.* (➤英語のことわざ).

2**しん 心** **1【精神】** **mind** ▶横綱は常に心・技・体の充実を求められる Perfection of *mind, technique and body* is expected of a yokozuna at all times. ／

Mental, technical and physical perfection is expected of a yokozuna at all times.

2【本質的な部分】the heart ▶彼は奥さんをしんから愛している He loves his wife *deeply*. ‖ 研二は口は悪いがしんはいいやつだ Kenji has a sharp tongue but he is good *at heart*. ‖ この仕事はしんが疲れる This work is *mentally exhausting*.

逆引き熟語 ○○心
愛国心 patriotism, a patriotic spirit／**競争心** a competitive spirit／**恐怖心** fear／**虚栄心** vanity／**警戒心** wariness, cautiousness, watchfulness／**好奇心** curiosity／**猜疑(さいぎ)心** suspicion／**自尊心** pride, self-respect [-esteem]／**嫉妬心** jealousy／**羞恥心** (a sense of) shame／**自立心** (a sense of) independence／**親切心** kindness／**敵対心** hostile sentiments

3**しん 芯** **lead** /led/ (鉛筆の) ; a **core**(ナシ・リンゴなどの) ; a **heart**(キャベツ・レタスなどの) ; (a) **wick**(ろうそく・ランプなどの) ▶ナシの芯を取る remove the *core* of a pear／take the *core* out of a pear／core a pear ‖ ジャガイモが芯まで煮えたら火を止めます Turn off the heat when the potatoes *are done*. ‖ この鉛筆はすぐ芯が折れる The *lead* of this pencil breaks easily. ‖ このご飯は芯がある This rice is *still hard in the center*. ‖ バットが折れるのはボールがバットの芯に当たっていないからだ The reason bats break is that the batter has not hit the *sweet spot*. ‖ 体のしんまで冷えきっていた I was chilled *to the bone* [*to the marrow*]. ‖ 彼女はおとなしそうだがしんはなかなか強い She looks gentle but *has a strong will underneath*. (➤ underneath は「下に, 内側に」).

4**しん 信** a **mandate** /mǽndeɪt/ (選挙民の信任) ; **confidence**(能力に対する信頼) ▶総選挙で国民の信を問う hold a general election to get [win] *a mandate* from the people.

1**しん- 新-** ▶新車 a *new car* ‖ 新内閣が発足した *A new Cabinet* has been formed. ‖ 彼の新著が先月出た His *latest book* came out last month. (➤ latest は「最新の」).

2**しん- 親-** ▶親英家 an Anglo*phile* ‖ 親米家 a *pro*-American(➤ -phile は「…を愛する人」を表す. pro- は「…を支持する」を表す).
☛ **親日** (→見出語)

ジン gin ‖ **ジンフィズ** gin fizz ‖ **ジントニック** gin and tonic(➤ gin tonic とは言わない).

1**-じん -人** ▶現代人 a *person of today* [*the present age*] ‖ 彼女は東北人だ She is *a Tohoku woman* [*a woman from Tohoku*]. ‖ 彼女はアメリカ人だ She *is American*. (➤ She is an American. よりも, このように形容詞を用いて言うほうがふつう ; 複数形も They are American.)／She *is from the U.S.* [*America*.] (➤「アメリカ出身だ」の意) ‖ あの男の人は何人ですか? *What's* his *nationality*? (➤「国籍はどこですか」の意)／*Where* does he *come from*? (➤「どこの出身ですか」の意).

2**-じん -陣** ▶教授陣 a teaching *staff* ‖ 報道陣 *a group* of reporters／the press (*corps*) (➤ corps の発音は /kɔːʳ/) ‖ 選手団の第一陣が出発した *The first group* of athletes departed.

しんあい 親愛 ▶犬が尾を振るのは親愛の情を表している The reason dogs wag their tails is to show their *affection*.

しんあん 新案 ‖ **新案特許** a new design patent.

しんい 真意 one's **real intention** (本心) ; **the true meaning**(真の意味) ▶きみはぼくの真意を理解していない You don't understand *my real intention* [*what I really mean*].

じんいてき 人為的 ▶人為的な災害 a disaster *caused by* (*human*) *carelessness* ‖ チェルノブイリの惨事は人為的ミスが原因だ The cause of the Chernobyl disaster was *human error*.

しんいり 新入り a **newcomer**(新参者) ; a **new member**(新しいメンバー) ; a **rookie** (スポーツの) ▶私たちのグループに3人の新入りが加わった Three *new members* joined our group.

1**しんいん 心因** ▶心因性の症状 a *psychogenic* symptom (➤ psychogenic は /sàɪkoʊdʒénɪk/ と発音).

2**しんいん 真因** **the true cause.**

じんいん 人員 **the number of people**(人数) ; **the staff, the personnel** /pə̀ːʳsənél/ (職員全体) ▶事務所の人員を増やす increase *the staff* [*personnel*] of one's office ‖ 人員の削減 cutbacks in *personnel* ‖ あの工場では最近人員整理があった *They have reduced* [*downsized*] *the workforce* in that plant recently.

しんうち 真打ち a **rakugo master.**

しんえい 新鋭 a **rising star** ▶新鋭のラグビーチーム a *new and powerful* rugby team ‖ 彼はプロゴルフ界の新鋭だ He is *a new star player* in the pro golf world. ‖ **新鋭機** a state-of-the-art plane (➤「最先端技術を駆使した」の意).

じんえい 陣営 a **camp**(主義などを同じくするグループ) ▶自由主義陣営 a liberal *camp* ‖ バイデン陣営 the Biden *camp*.

しんえいたい 親衛隊 a **bodyguard**(護衛する人) ; (**ardent**) **fans**((熱心な)ファン) ; **groupies**(芸能人などの追っかけ).

1**しんえん 深遠な** **deep, profound** (➤後者は堅い語) ▶釈迦(しゃか)のことばの深遠な意味 the *deep* meaning of Buddha's words ‖ 深遠な思想の持ち主 a person of *profound* thought.

2**しんえん 深淵** an **abyss.**

じんえん 腎炎 **nephritis** /nɪfráɪṭɪs/.

しんおう 震央 an **epicenter.**

1**しんか 真価** **true value, true worth**(➤ value と worth は「金銭的な価値」を表すときは同義に用いられるが, 一般的には前者は本質的価値［卓越性］を, 後者は有用性・利用価値を強調する ; true は real にしてもよい) ▶この彫刻の真価がわかる人は少ない Few people understand the *true value* of this sculpture. ‖ いよいよきみの真価が問われる時が来た The time has come when your *true worth* [*value*／*ability*] will be tested. ‖ 書物の真価はその商業的値打ちでは測れない The *true value* [*worth*] of a book cannot be measured by its commercial value.

2**しんか 進化** **evolution** 一動 **進化する** **evolve** 《from》 ▶あなたは人間が猿から進化したという説を信じますか Do you accept [believe in] the theory that human beings *evolved from* (the) apes? ‖ 日本の携帯電話は独自の進化をとげた Japanese cellphones have *evolved* (technologically) in their own unique way.
‖ **進化論** the theory of evolution ; Darwinism ‖ **進化論者** an evolutionist ; a Darwinist.

じんか 人家 a (**dwelling**) **house** ▶この地域は人家が密集している［まばらだ］This district is crowded [is scattered] with *houses*. ‖ ダンプカーが人家に突っ込

んだ A dump truck plowed into *someone's house*.

シンカー《野球》a **sinker.**

シンガーソングライター a **singer and songwriter,** a **singer-songwriter,** a **songwriter-singer.**

しんかい 深海 the deep sea ▶彼らは潜水艇で**深海**を実地調査した They explored *the deep sea* [*the ocean depths*] in a submarine. (➤ the ocean depths は「深み」に重点がある).

‖**深海魚** a deep-sea fish.

1**しんがい 心外** ▶きみがそんなことを言うとは実に**心外**だ I *never expected* at all that you would say such a thing. ／What you said is truly *disappointing* [*shocking*].

2**しんがい 侵害 violation, infringement**(権利などの；後者は主に法律用語)；**intrusion**(無許可・無理やりの立ち入り)；**invasion**(侵入) **一動 侵害する violate** +目, **infringe**《on, upon》, **intrude**《on, upon》, **invade** +目 ▶版権**侵害** a copyright *infringement* ‖プライバシーを**侵害する** *invade* [*violate*] someone's privacy ‖憲法で保障された権利の**侵害** *an infringement* of constitutional rights ‖政府は出版の自由を**侵害した** The government *infringed on* the freedom of press.

じんかいせんじゅつ 人海戦術 ▶期限に間に合わせるには**人海戦術**をとるしか手がない The only way to meet the deadline is to *resort to sheer manpower*. (➤ manpower は「人的資源」).

しんがお 新顔 a **newcomer**；a **stranger**(見知らぬ人) ▶あいつ，ちょっと見覚えないけど，**新顔**かい？ I don't think I have met him before. Is he *a newcomer*?

1**しんがく 進学** ▶高校へ**進学する** *go on to* senior high school ‖本校の生徒の大半は**大学へ進学する** The majority of students at this school *go on to college* [《英》*university*]. (➤ この英文は「本校は進学校です」に対する訳文と考えてもよい) ‖S高校は**進学校として知られている** S High School *is known for sending a large number of students* (*on*) *to college*. ‖これは**進学**希望者のクラスです This class is composed of *students who want to go on to college*. ‖日本では**高校進学率**は96パーセントを超えている *The percentage of students who go on to high school* is over 96 percent in Japan.

‖**進学塾** a juku [cram school] that prepares students for entrance examinations.

2**しんがく 神学 theology**

‖**神学者** a theologian ‖**神学校** a theological school；a seminary(キリスト教の).

じんかく 人格 character(品性，徳性から見た人となり)；**personality**(人柄) ▶**人格**を疑う have doubts about someone's *character* ‖**人格**を否定する disparage [denigrate] *someone* [*someone's character*] ／deny someone's *value* [*worth*] *as a human being* ‖彼の**人格**は申し分ない He has very good *character*. ‖1歳の赤ん坊でも立派に**人格**を持っている Even a one-year-old baby has his or her own *personality*. ‖森さんは**人格者**だ Mr. Mori is *a man of character*. ‖学校は**人格形成**の場だ School is a place for *character-building*.

‖**二重人格者** a person with a split personality ‖**多重人格者** a person with multiple personalities.

しんかくか 神格化 deification /dèɪɪfɪkéɪʃən/ **一動 神格化する deify** /déɪəfaɪ/ ▶王様を**神格化する** *deify* a king.

しんがた 新型 a **new model** [**style**]；**the latest model**(最新型) ▶**新型**インフルエンザ a *new strain* of influenza ‖その自動車メーカーはことし2種類の**新型**を出した That automaker has shown two *new models* this year. ‖このエアコンは**新型**だ This air conditioner is *the latest model*. ／This is the latest model air conditioner.

しんがっき 新学期 a **new term** [**semester**](➤ 後者は年2学期制の) ▶**新学期**が間近だ The *new term* [*semester*] is just around the corner. (「間近だ」を near at hand とすることもできるが，文学的な言い方になる).

✉ **日本では新学期は4月に始まります** In Japan, *the new school year* begins in April. ➤ この場合の「新学期」は「新学年」のこと.

シンガポール Singapore /síŋgəpɔːʳ/

‖**シンガポール人** a Singaporean.

しんがり the rear ▶私は入場行進で**しんがり**を務めた I *brought up the rear* in the entrance march.

1**しんかん 新館** a **new building**；an **annex** /ǽneks/《to》(建て増しの別館) ▶ホテル東京の**新館**が完成した *A new building* of [*An annex to*] the Hotel Tokyo was completed.

2**しんかん 新刊** ▶**新刊**の図書 a *new* book ／a *new* publication ‖**新刊紹介** a book review ‖**新刊目録** a list of new publications ‖**新刊予告** a notice of forthcoming books.

3**しんかん 信管** a **fuse** ▶時限爆弾の**信管**を取り除く *defuse* a time bomb.

4**しんかん 神官** a **Shinto priest.**

しんかんせん 新幹線 the Shinkansen service(営業)；a **Shinkansen train**(車両) ▶**新幹線**を札幌まで延長する extend *the Shinkansen* (*service*) to Sapporo ‖当車は博多行き**新幹線**「のぞみ」号です This is a Nozomi *Super Express* bound for Hakata. ‖**東北新幹線**で青森まで行き，普通に乗り換えた I took *the Tohoku Shinkansen* to Aomori, where I transferred to a local train.

しんき 新規の new, fresh ▶**新規**に2人採用する必要がある We have to employ two *new* [*two more*] people. ‖**新規まき直し**をしよう Let's *start all over again*. ／Let's *make a fresh start*.

1**しんぎ 審議** (a) **deliberation**(正式討議)；(a) **discussion**(意見交換)；(a) **debate**(意見が対立する者どうしの) **一動 審議する deliberate** /dɪlíbəreɪt/《on》, **discuss** +目, **debate**(+目) ▶問題を**審議する** *discuss* a matter ‖予算案は現在**審議中**だ The budget bill is presently *under deliberation*. ‖我々はその問題を慎重に**審議した** We *deliberated on* [*discussed* ／ *debated*] the problem carefully.

‖**審議会** an advisory council.

2**しんぎ 真偽** ▶うわさの**真偽**を確かめるべきです You should find out whether the rumor is *true or false*.

3**しんぎ 信義 faith** ▶**信義**に厚い人 a *trustworthy* person ‖ビジネスでは顧客に対して**信義を守る**ことが大切だ In business, it is important to always *act in good faith* toward the customers.

じんぎ 仁義 social ethics(社会倫理)；a **moral code**(道徳規範).

しんきいってん 心機一転 ▶**心機一転**やり直そうと思う I am going to *turn over a new leaf* and make a fresh start. (➤ turn over a new leaf は「新しいページをめくる」の意から，「心を入れ替える」).

しんきくさい 辛気臭い ▶辛気臭い仕事 a *tedious* task ‖ 辛気臭い話はやめにしよう Let's quit talking about such an *unpleasant* topic. ‖ 彼の話を聞いてるとこっちまで辛気臭くなるよ Just listening to him is enough to make anyone *gloomy*.

しんきじく 新機軸 a **new line**, a **new departure** (➤ departure は「(従来のものからの)変更」) ▶今度の指導者は新機軸を打ち出すものと期待されている The new leader is expected to *strike up a new* (*policy*) *line*.

1**しんきゅう 進級** ▶息子はことし 4 年に進級した My son *moved up to* the fourth grade [《英》year] this year. ‖ 彼女は出席日数が足りなくて進級できなかった Because she had not attended class the minimum required number of days, she *was held back in the same grade* (*for a year*). (➤ 後半を she was forced to repeat the same grade. としてもよい).
‖**進級試験** an examination for promotion.

2**しんきゅう 新旧** ▶新旧の思想 *old and new* ideas (➤ 語順に注意) ‖ 新旧の役員が一堂に集まった The *incoming and outgoing* committee members met together in the room. (➤ incoming は「後任の」, outgoing は「辞任する」) ‖ 幹部が新旧交代する時期だ It's time to *replace* the *old* managers *with new* ones. ／It's time for *a rotation* in management. (➤ 前者は旧幹部に対しての不満がある場合, 後者は期限切れ, あるいは旧幹部への不満がある場合).

3**しんきゅう 鍼灸** **acupuncture** /ǽkjupʌ̀ŋktʃəʳ/ **and moxibustion** /mɑːksəbʌ́stʃən/
‖**鍼灸師** a practitioner of acupuncture and moxibustion.

しんきょ 新居 a **new house**, a **new home** (➤ 前者は「新家屋」, 後者は「新家庭」のニュアンスをもつこともある) ▶私たちは郊外の新居に引っ越した We moved to *a new house* in the suburbs. ‖ 彼らは結婚して新居を構えた They got married and *made a new home*.

1**しんきょう 心境** a **mood**, a **frame of mind** ▶私は今ゆったりと音楽を楽しむ心境ではない I'm in no *mood* to sit back and listen to music. ‖ パパは今お小遣いの値上げを聞いてくれそうな心境じゃないわよ Your dad's not in *a frame of mind* to listen to a request for a bigger allowance. ‖ 彼は心境の変化で外国留学するのをやめた He *changed his mind* and decided not to study abroad. ‖ **対話**「現在の心境をお聞かせいただけませんか」「とても複雑な心境です」"Could you tell us *how you feel now*?" "I have very mixed *feelings*."

2**しんきょう 進境** ▶野田君のテニスは進境著しい Noda *has made remarkable progress* in tennis.

3**しんきょう 信教** **religion** ▶信教の自由は何人に対してもこれを保障する *Freedom of religion* is guaranteed to all. (➤「これを」は訳さなくてよい).

しんきょうち 新境地 **new ground** ▶新境地を開拓する break *new* [*fresh*] *ground*.

しんきょく 新曲 a **new piece** [**tune**], a **new song** ▶カニエ・ウェストの新曲が来週発売される Kanye West *new release* will be out next week. (➤ release は新しい楽曲や封切り映画などをいう).

しんきろう 蜃気楼 a **mirage** /mərɑ́ːʒ ‖ míraːʒ/ ▶しんきろうが砂漠に現れた *A mirage* appeared in the desert.

しんきろく 新記録 a **new record**; an **all-time high** (史上最高記録) ▶彼は100メートル競走で日本［世界］新記録を樹立した He set *a new Japanese* [*world*] *record* in the 100-meter dash. ‖ ことしの車の生産台数は新記録だ This year's production of cars has reached *an all-time high*. ‖ きょうの最高気温は過去30年間での新記録だった Today's temperature was *the highest* in the past thirty years [was a *record high* for the past thirty years].

しんきんかん 親近感 a **kinship** ▶私はその台湾からの留学生に親近感を覚えた I *felt a kinship with* the student from Taiwan. ‖ 子供たちは大石先生に親近感をもっているようだ The children seem to *be friendly to* [*feel comfortable with*] Ms. Oishi. ‖ 私は話しているうちにその人に親近感を覚えた As we were talking, I began to *warm to* him. (➤ warm (up) to で「…に対して温かい［親しい］気持ちになる」).

しんきんこうそく 心筋梗塞 **myocardial** /màɪə-kɑ́ːʳdiəl/ [**cardiac** /kɑ́ːʳdiæk/] **infarction** (➤ 一般には「心臓発作」の heart attack を, この意味にも用いる).

1**しんく 辛苦** **hardship(s)** ▶若い頃は辛苦のなめ通しだった I went through many *hardships* [had quite a hard time] in my youth. (➤ have a hard time は「つらい経験をする」).

2**しんく 深紅・真紅** **deep red, crimson** /krímzən/ ▶深紅の優勝旗 a *deep red* pennant.

しんぐ 寝具 **bedding**; **bedclothes** (敷き布団以外のシーツなど).

しんくう 真空 a **vacuum** /vǽkjuəm/ ▶宇宙空間は真空状態だ (Outer) space is *a vacuum*.
‖**真空管** 《米》a (vacuum) tube, 《英》a valve ‖ **真空管アンプ** a vacuum-tube amplifier ‖ **真空パック食品** vacuum-packed food.

じんぐう 神宮 a **Shinto shrine** ▶明治神宮 *the* Meiji *Shrine*.

ジンクス a **jinx** /dʒɪŋks/ (➤ 悪い意味にしか用いない) ▶私たちのチームは日曜日の試合には勝てないというジンクスをついに破った Our team finally broke the *jinx* that kept us from winning games played on Sunday.

シンクタンク a **think tank** ▶経済政策シンクタンク an economic policy *think tank*.

シングル シングルの **single** ▶ **対話** (ホテルで)「シングルの部屋はありますか」「あいにく, ツインしか空いておりません」"Do you have *any single rooms*?" "I'm sorry, but all we have are twin rooms."
‖**シングルキャッチ** a one-handed catch ‖ (レコードの)**シングル盤** a single ‖ **シングルベッド** a single bed ‖ **シングルマザー** a single mother.

シングルス **singles** ▶女子シングルス決勝 the women's *singles* final (match) ‖ テニスのシングルスの試合をする play *singles* in tennis ‖ 彼はテニスの男子シングルスに優勝した He won in the (men's) tennis *singles*.

シングルヒット 《野球》a **single** ▶レフトへシングルヒットを打つ hit [line] *a single* to left ／single to left.

シンクロナイズドスイミング **synchronized swimming** (➤ 2018年からアーティスティックスイミング (artistic swimming) に名称が変更された).

しんけい 神経

1【体の器官】 a **nerve** ▶感覚神経は味や匂いのような感覚を脳に伝える *Sensory nerves* transmit impulses relating to a sensation, such as a taste or a smell, to the brain. ‖ おじは神経科の医師です My uncle is *a neurologist*.

2【心の働き】 **nerve(s)** ▶私たちの担任の先生は神経が

細かい Our homeroom teacher *is sensitive*. ‖ ゆうべは**神経が高ぶって**なかなか寝つけなかった I *was* so *on edge* [*nervous* / *excited*] last night I couldn't get to sleep. ‖ あき子は**神経がずぶとい** Akiko *is bold*. / Akiko *has nerve*. ‖ 新幹線の騒音は**神経に障る** The noise from the Shinkansen trains *gets on my nerves*. ‖ この仕事は**神経をすり減らす** This job *is a great strain on my nerves*. / This job *is nerve-racking* [*-wracking*]. ‖ 現代人は複雑な人間関係に**神経をすり減らしている** People today *are worn out* [*are stressed out*] by complicated human relationships. ‖ そんなささいなことに**神経を使う**な Don't *worry about* such a small thing. ‖ 家でごたごたが続いて私の**神経はぼろぼろです** I've had no end of trouble at home and I'*m a nervous wreck*. (➤ nervous wreck は「神経がすり減った人間」の意) ‖ 彼は**神経過敏**だから人を遠ざけてしまう He turns others off because he is so *hypersensitive* [*high-strung*].

‖**神経科** the department of neurology ‖ **神経ガス** nerve gas ‖ **神経外科** neurosurgery ‖ **神経細胞** a nerve cell ‖ **神経症** an anxiety disorder (不安障害) ; a mood disorder (気分 [感情] 障害) (➤ neurosis は現在は病名としては用いない) ‖ **神経症患者** a patient with an anxiety disorder and [or] a mood disorder (不安障害, および [あるいは] 気分 [感情] 障害の人 ; neurotic は現在では医学用語としては用いない). ‖ **神経中枢** the nerve center ‖ **交感神経** a sympathetic nerve (➤「交感神経系」は the sympathetic nervous system) ‖ **視神経** the optic nerve ‖ **副交感神経** a parasympathetic nerve (➤「副交感神経系」は the parasympathetic nervous system) ‖ **末しょう神経** a peripheral nerve.

しんけいしつ 神経質な **overly sensitive, high-strung** (人の性質が) ; **nervous** (一時的にいらついている) ▶**神経質な**子供 a *high-strung* child ‖ 彼は**神経質だ** He *is overly sensitive* [*high(ly) strung*]. ‖ そんなに**神経質になる**ことはないよ Don't *be* so *sensitive* about that.

直訳の落とし穴「彼は神経質だ」
神経質な＝nervous から,「彼は神経質だ」を He's nervous. という人がいる. 日本語の「神経質」はその人の性格をいうが, be nervous は一時的に緊張したり, 心配したりして落ち着かないことで, 誰にでもあることである. したがって, He's nervous. は「彼は心配で落ち着かない」や「上がって神経質になっている」を意味する. 性格の神経質をいうには He's overly sensitive. (あまりに神経過敏である) などとする.

しんけいつう 神経痛 **neuralgia** /njuræ̀ldʒə/ ▶おばは**神経痛**に悩まされている My aunt suffers from *neuralgia*.

しんげき 進撃 an **advance** ▶優勝に向けて**快進撃**を続ける make a *drive* for the pennant ‖ 軍隊は敵に向かって**進撃**を開始した The army began to make *an advance* [began to advance] against the enemy.

しんけつ 心血 ▶医師はその難病の原因究明に**心血を注いだ** The doctor *devoted himself* to research on the cause of the intractable disease. ‖ ミケランジェロはシスティナ礼拝堂に絵を描くことに**心血を注いだ** Michelangelo *poured all his energy* [*his heart and soul*] into painting the Sistine Chapel.

しんげつ 新月 a **new moon**.

[1]**しんけん 真剣な** **serious** (真面目な) ; **earnest** (本気の) ▶そんな**真剣な**顔をしないでよ Don't look so *serious*. ‖ 結婚についてもっと**真剣**に考えなさい Be more *serious* about getting married. ‖ 彼は何をするにも**真剣**だ He does everything *in* (*dead*) *earnest*. (➤ in (dead) earnest は「(全く) 本気で」) ‖ 今度の試合は**真剣勝負**で臨む We consider this game *a do-or-die battle*.

[2]**しんけん 親権** **parental rights** ; **custody** (離婚, 別居, 死別した場合) ▶**親権**者 a person with *parental rights* ; a *custodial* parent ‖ **親権**争い a *custody* fight [battle].

[1]**しんげん 進言** a **suggestion** /səgdʒéstʃən/ 一動 **進言する** **suggest** 《that》 ▶別のやり方を**進言する** *suggest* a different approach ‖ 彼らは社長にその計画を変更するよう**進言した** They *suggested* [*proposed*] to the president *that* the plan be changed. (➤ suggest のほうが控えめ ; suggest や propose に続く節内では動詞は仮定法).

[2]**しんげん 震源** **the focus of an earthquake** ; **the seismic** /sáɪzmɪk/ **center** ▶その地震の**震源**は房総半島沖90キロ, **震源**の深さは20キロと特定されている *The focus of the earthquake* was determined to be 90 kilometers off the coast of the Boso Peninsula and 20 kilometers deep.

▶《比喩的》そのうわさの**震源地**は早川君だ (＝早川君から出た) The rumor *started with* Hayakawa. / Hayakawa *started* the rumor.

じんけん 人権 **human rights** ▶ (基本的) **人権**を守る [侵害する] defend [infringe upon] (*fundamental*) *human rights* ‖ 正当な理由もなく解雇されるとしたら, それは**人権問題**だ It is *a question of human rights* [*a human rights issue*] if an employee is dismissed without sufficient reason. ‖ 対話 「ちょっとカバンの中を見せてみろ」「林先生, それは**人権**じゅうりんですよ」"Let me see what's in the bag." "Mr. Hayashi, that's *an infringement of my human rights*."

‖**人権宣言** the Declaration of Human Rights.

じんけんひ 人件費 **personnel** /pə̀ːrsənél/ **expenses** [**costs**] ▶**人件費**を削減する cut down on *personnel costs* ‖ どこの会社でも**人件費**がどんどん高騰している In any company, *personnel expenses* [*labor costs*] are rapidly increasing.

しんご 新語 a **new word** ▶**新語**は次々と現れるが, その多くはじきに消えていく *New words* are coined one after another, but most of them soon disappear. ‖ **新語辞典** a dictionary of new words and phrases.

じんご 人後 ▶佐藤君は鉄道好きでは**人後に落ちない** As a railroad buff, Sato *is second to none*. (➤ be second to none で「誰にも負けない」の意).

[1]**しんこう 進行** **1【乗り物の】** ▶**進行中**の電車の窓から顔を出してはいけない Don't put your head out of the window of a *moving* train. (➤ ここでの「顔」は頭部のこと) ‖ (バスの) **進行中**は運転手に話しかけないでください Please refrain from speaking to the driver *while* the coach is *in motion*. ‖ 《車内アナウンス》お出口は**進行方向** (＝先頭に向かって) 左側でございます As you *face front*, exits are on the left.

2【物事の】 **progress** /prá:grəs/ 一動 **進行する** **progress** /prəgrés/ ▶そのプロジェクトは**進行中**だ The project *is* now *under way* [*in progress*]. ‖ 小児がんは**進行が速い** Cancer in children *progresses* *quickly*. (🔴 progress quickly を spread quickly とすると「転移が速い」の意になる) ‖ 対話「翻訳の進行状況はいかがですか」「予定どおり進行しています」"*How are you progressing with* your translation work ?" "It's *going* as planned."

‖**進行係** a program director ; a master of ceremonies (司会者) ‖《文法》**進行形** the progressive form.

し

2**しんこう 信仰** **belief, faith** (➤ 後者には「盲目的な信仰」の含みがあることが少なくない) **一動 信仰する believe in** ▶**信仰**を捨てる[守る] renounce [keep] one's *faith* ‖ 彼女はギリシャ正教を**信仰している** She *believes in* the Greek Orthodox faith. ‖ 祖母はとても**信仰心**があつい My grandmother is a very *devout* woman.

3**しんこう 振興** **promotion 一動 振興する promote** +⑪ ▶B 氏は郷土の産業の**振興**に力を尽くした Mr. B made every possible effort to *promote* the development of industries in his hometown.

4**しんこう 新興** ▶**新興**工業国 *newly* industrializing countries ‖ 私たちは西武線沿線の**新興住宅地**に住んでいる We live in *a newly-developed residential area* on the Seibu Line.

‖**新興国** a new [developing] country ‖ **新興宗教** a new [newly-risen] religion ‖ **新興勢力** (the) growing power ‖ **新興都市** a boom town.

5**しんこう 親交** **friendship** ▶彼はその政治家と**親交がある** He *is on familiar terms with* that politician. ‖ そのハイキングで彼らは互いに**親交を深めた** They *deepened their friendship* [*friendly relations*] with each other through the hiking trip.

6**しんこう 侵攻** an **invasion 一動 侵攻する invade** +⑪.

しんごう 信号 a **signal** ; a **traffic signal** (交通信号一般) ; a **traffic light** (信号灯) ▶アナログ[デジタル]**信号** an analog [a digital] *signal* ‖ 無線**信号** a radio *signal* ‖ **信号**を守る obey *traffic signals* ‖ 今**信号**は青[赤]だ The (*traffic*) *signal* is green [red] now. (➤「青信号」は green light という) ‖ **信号**が赤になった *The traffic light* turned red. ‖ **信号**が青のうちに渡ってしまおう Let's cross the street while *the light* is green. ‖ **信号が青になるまで待ちなさい** *Wait until the light turns green.* / *Wait for the green light.* ‖ ただ今**信号**待ちです We're *waiting for a green light.* ‖ 事故は相手の**信号無視**が原因だった The accident was caused by the other party's *ignoring the traffic light.* ‖ **信号**を無視して横断してはいけません Don't cross *against the light.* (➤「信号を無視する」は ignore a traffic light [signal]) ‖ 最初の**信号**を左です Turn left at the first *traffic light.* ‖ ピーという**信号音**が鳴ったらご用件をおっしゃってください Please leave your message after (you hear) the *beep*.

‖**信号機** a signal ‖ **遭難信号** a distress signal, a mayday signal ‖ **手旗信号** flag signaling.

1**じんこう 人口** (a) **population** (➤ 具体的な地域の人口をいうときは a がつく) ▶東京の**人口**はスウェーデン全体の人口より多い The *population* of Tokyo is larger than the entire population of Sweden. (➤ population を修飾するときは large, small を使う) ‖ この町は**人口**が増加[減少]している The *population* of this town is on the increase [decrease]. ‖ 日本の**人口**は急速に高齢化が進んでいる The Japanese *population* is aging rapidly. ‖ この町は**人口** 1 万である This town has *a population* of 10,000. ‖ 東京は世界で最も**人口の多い**都市の 1 つです Tokyo is one of the most *populous* cities in the world.

▶第三世界では**人口爆発**が続いている *A population explosion* is taking place in the Third World. ‖ 日本の**人口密度**はイタリアよりも高い Japan's *population density* is greater than Italy's. ‖ **喫煙人口**は世界的に確実に減少している The world's *smoking population* is showing a definite decrease. ‖ 日本の**俳句人口**は数百万人に達する The number of *haiku writers* in Japan is up in the millions. (➤ *haiku* lovers は作家でなく, 愛読者という印象になる). ‖ 対話「日本の**人口**はどのくらいですか」「およそ 1 億2600万人です」"What's [How large is] the *population* of Japan ? / How many people live in Japan ?" "About 126 million." ‖ 対話「東京とニューヨークではどちらが**人口**が多いと思う ?」「東京だと思う」"Which do you think has a larger *population*, Tokyo or New York (City) ?" "Tokyo, I think."

‖**人口過剰** overpopulation.

2**じんこう 人工の** **artificial, man-made**

> 語法「人工の」に相当する形容詞としては **man-made** が一般的であったが, man-made の man が男性を連想させるため, 最近ではこの語を避けて **artificial** (人為的な), **handmade** (手作りの), **mechanical** (機械で動く), **machine-made** (機械製の), **manufactured** (大量に生産された)などの語を用いる傾向が見られる.

▶**人工の**湖 an *artificial* [*a man-made*] lake ‖ **人工授精**で子供を生む have a child through *artificial insemination* ‖ 新宿の高層ビル群は**人工の美**の一典型である The cluster of skyscrapers in Shinjuku is a classic example of *man-made beauty*. ‖ この川のニジマスは**人工的に**ふ化したものだ The rainbow trout in this stream were *artificially* hatched. ‖ **人工呼吸**のやり方を知っていますか Do you know how to perform *CPR* ? (➤「人工呼吸」は文字通りには artificial respiration だが, 実際には CPR (cardiopulmonary resuscitation) (心肺蘇生法)ということが多い. また, 口対口蘇生 [口移し] 法は mouth-to-mouth resuscitation という).

‖**人工甘味料** (an) artificial sweetener ‖ **人工芝** artificial turf (➤ 商標名の Astroturf もよく用いられる) ‖ **人工心臓** an artificial heart ‖ **人工臓器** an artificial internal organ ‖ **人工知能** artificial intelligence ‖ **人工雪** artificial snow.

じんこうえいせい 人工衛星 an **artificial** [**a man-made**] **satellite** (➤ 文脈からわかるときは単に satellite ともいう) ▶**人工衛星**を打ち上げる launch [send up] *a satellite* ‖ **人工衛星**を軌道に乗せる put *a satellite* in orbit.

しんこきゅう 深呼吸 a **deep breath** (息) ; **deep breathing** (息をすること) ▶**深呼吸をして**ください *Breathe deeply.* / *Take a deep breath.* (➤ breathe の発音は /briːð/) ‖ **深呼吸**をして気持ちを鎮める calm oneself with *deep breathing* [*by breathing deeply*].

1**しんこく 深刻な** **serious, grave** (➤ 後者のほうが深刻さの度合いが強い) ▶私にとって太りすぎは**深刻な**問題だ Being overweight is a *serious* problem for me. ‖ 父はひどく**深刻な**顔をしていた My father looked very *serious* [*grave*]. ‖ 最近わが国の景気後退はます

ます深刻になってきた The recession in Japan is becoming more and more *serious*. ‖ 産科医不足が深刻だ There's a *severe* [an *acute*] shortage of obstetricians. ‖ そんなに深刻に考え込むことはないよ You don't have to *take* it so *seriously*. ‖ その国の経済状態は年々深刻化(=悪化)してきている The economic situation in that country is *getting worse* year by year.

2 **しんこく 申告** **declaration** 一動 **申告する** **declare** +目 (課税品を) ; **file** +目 (書類を提出する) ▶《税関で》申告の必要のあるものはこの用紙に書き込んでください If you have anything to *declare*, please enter [write] it on this form. ‖ 対話《税関で》「申告するものはありませんか」「ありません」"Anything to *declare*?" "No, nothing (in particular)." ‖ 所得税の確定申告は毎年3月15日までに済ませなければならない (*Final*) *income tax return* must be filed by March 15 of each year.

‖ **青色申告** a blue income tax form.

しんこん 新婚の **newly-married** ▶新婚(ほやほや)の夫婦 a *newly-married* couple / newlyweds ‖ 2人は新婚ほやほやで幸せそうだ They *have just gotten married* and look so happy. ‖ 新婚生活はいかがですか How are you enjoying your *newly-married life*? ‖ 私たちは新婚旅行でバリ島に行った We went to Bali on *our honeymoon*. ‖ そのホテルは新婚旅行客でいっぱいだった The hotel was full of *honeymooners* [*honeymoon couples*].

しんさ 審査 (a) **judgment** (優劣の判定) ; (a) **review** (検討・評価) ; (an) **examination** (検査) ; (a) **screening** (選別) 一動 **審査する** **judge** +目, **review** +目, **examine** +目, **screen** +目 ▶スピーチコンテストの審査をする *judge* [*help judge*] a speech contest (つぼ (1) コンテストでは複数の審査員がいるのがふつうなので, そのことをはっきりさせたい場合は help judge(審査を助ける)のほうを使うとよい. (2)「スピーチコンテストの審査員」は a judge in a speech contest) ‖ カラオケ大会の審査員を務める act as (*a*) *judge* in [for / at] a karaoke contest (➤ 審査員が1人のときは通例 a をつけない) ‖ 求職者たちの資格審査をする *screen* the job candidates ‖《コンテストで》審査の結果を発表いたします *The judges are ready to announce their decision*. (➤ この judge は「審査員」) ‖ あなたのエッセーは現在審査中です Your essay is *under review* now.

‖ **審査委員会** a judging committee, a screening committee.

しんさい 震災 an **earthquake** (地震) ; an **earthquake disaster** (地震による災害)

‖ **震災地** an earthquake-stricken area ‖ **東日本[関東 / 阪神・淡路]大震災** the Great East Japan [Kanto / Hanshin-Awaji] Earthquake.

じんさい 人災 a **man-made** [**human**] **disaster**, a **disaster caused by human carelessness** (➤ man-made が男性を連想させるため, これを避けて後者の言い方を用いる人もいる) ▶その事故は天災ではなくて人災だ That accident was not a natural disaster but *a man-made one*. ‖ その山火事は不注意による人災だった The forest fire was *a disaster caused by human carelessness*.

じんざい 人材 a **capable person** ; **talent** (➤ 集合的) ; **human resources** (人的資源) ▶その商社は若い人材を求めている The trading firm is in need of *capable young people*. ‖ あの大学の教授陣は人材がそろっている That university has *a talented* teaching *staff* [*faculty*].

‖ **人材銀行** an employment agency for people with special talent or skills ‖ **人材派遣会社** a temporary employment agency, a temp agency.

しんさく 新作 a **new** (**art** / **literary**) **work** ▶新作を発表する present [perform / exhibit / publish] *a new work* (➤ perform は「上演する」, exhibit は「展示する」, publish は「発行する」).

しんさつ 診察 a **medical examination** 一動 **診察する** **examine** +目 ▶医者は丁寧に診察してから特に悪いところはないと言った The doctor *examined* me carefully and said that there was nothing in particular wrong with me. ‖ 胃の調子がおかしいので医者に診察してもらった I had stomach trouble, so I *went to see a doctor*. ‖ その眼科医の診察時間は9時から正午までと2時から6時までだ That eye specialist's *office hours* are nine to twelve (noon) in the morning and two to six in the afternoon.

‖ **診察券** an appointment card ‖ **診察室** a consulting room,《米また》an office,《英また》a surgery ‖ **診察料** a consultation fee, a doctor's bill.

しんさん 辛酸 **hardship**(**s**) (苦難) ; **bitterness** (つらさ) ▶人生の辛酸をなめる go through *hardships* in life.

しんざんもの 新参者 a **newcomer**.

1 **しんし 紳士** a **gentleman** ▶紳士的なふるまい *gentlemanly* behavior ‖ 紳士気取りはやめろよ Don't *be snobbish*. ‖ 紳士服売り場はどこですか Where is *the men's clothing department*?

‖ **紳士録** a Who's Who.

2 **しんし 真摯な** **sincere** /sɪnsíəʳ/ (誠実な) ; **straightforward** (率直な) ▶首相は国民の審判を真摯に受け止めると語った The prime minister said he would take the people's judgment *seriously*.

じんじ 人事 ▶4月に人事異動を行う *reshuffle the staff* in April ‖ この4月に大幅な人事異動があった There was a large-scale *staff reshuffle* last April. ‖ 兄は人事異動で福岡に転勤になった As part of *the changes in the staff* my (older) brother was transferred to Fukuoka. ‖ 人事を尽くして天命を待つ Do everything humanly possible and leave everything to Heaven's will [divine Providence].

‖ **人事部** the personnel [human resources] department ‖ **人事部長** a personnel [human resources] manager.

1 **しんしき 新式** a **new type**.

2 **しんしき 神式** **Shinto rites**

‖ **神式結婚式** a Shinto-style wedding.

シンジケート a **syndicate**.

しんじこむ 信じ込む ▶さゆりはぼくが本当のことを言っていると信じ込んだ Sayuri *firmly believed* [*just took* (*it*) *for granted*] that I was telling the truth.

1 **しんしつ 寝室** a **bedroom**.

2 **しんしつ 心室** 《解剖学》a **ventricle** /véntrɪkəl/ ▶右[左]心室 right [left] *ventricle*.

しんじつ 真実 **1【本当のこと】** **truth** 一形 **真実の** **true** ▶私は真実を知りたい I want to know *the truth*. ‖ 真実は1つだが解釈は人によってさまざまだ *The truth* is one, but interpretations vary from person to person. ‖ きみの話には真実味がないね Your story *doesn't ring true* [*is incredible*]. ‖ 彼女から真実味(=真心)の籠もったことばは聞かれずじまいに終わった We never once heard a *sincere* word from her.

2【本当に】 ▶児童虐待, いじめ, そして老人虐待一この国の現状は真実情けない Child abuse, bullying and elder abuse. – I *truly* [*sincerely*] feel that this nation is in a sad [pathetic] state.

じんじふせい 人事不省 unconsciousness ▶彼は頭を打って**人事不省に陥った** He hit his head and *became unconscious* [*lost consciousness* / *went into a coma*]. (➤ coma は「こん睡状態」の意の医学用語).

しんじゃ 信者 a **believer**, a **devotee** /dèvətíː/ (➤ 後者は堅い語) ; a **follower**(信奉者) ▶ロムニーさんはモルモン教の**信者**です Mr. Romney is a Mormon. / Mr. Romney is *a believer* in [believes in] Mormonism.

▶《比喩的》私はバッハの**信者**です I'm *a devotee* of Bach. (➤ この devotee は「熱狂的ファン」の意).

じんじゃ 神社 a (**Shinto**) **shrine**

日本紹介 ✉ **神社は日本古来の宗教である神道の神や皇室の祖先の霊を祭った社です. 名高い武人や文人など個人を神として祭った神社もあります** A *jinja* is a shrine where the gods of Shintoism, the indigenous religion of Japan, or the spirits of the ancestors of the imperial household are enshrined. Some *jinja* are dedicated to individuals such as famous warriors or great men of letters.

▶この**神社**はどんなご利益があるのですか What will the god do for you [What sort of benefit will the god bring to you] if you pray at this *shrine*? ‖ 秋葉**神社**に参拝した I visited *the* Akiba *Shrine*.

✉ **多くの日本人は正月に神社へ行って商売繁盛と家内安全を祈ります** Most Japanese go to *Shinto shrines* during the New Year's holiday to pray for success in business and the welfare of their family.

‖**神社仏閣** (Shinto) shrines and (Buddhist) temples.

ジンジャーエール ginger ale.

しんしゃく 斟酌する make allowances [(an) allowance] 《for》 ▶彼が年少である点を**しん酌する**必要がある We need to *make allowance*(*s*) *for* his youth.

1 **しんしゅ 新種** a **new species** [**variety**] (➤ species は生物学での分類上の「種」, variety は同類のものの中の「種」) ▶**新種**の昆虫を発見する discover *a new species of* insect.

2 **しんしゅ 進取** ▶彼は**進取**の気性に富んでいる He has a highly *enterprising* [*entrepreneurial*] *spirit*.

しんじゅ 真珠 a **pearl** ▶**真珠**を養殖する culture *pearls* (➤「養殖真珠」は cultured pearl) ‖ **真珠の首飾り**をする wear *a pearl necklace*.

‖**真珠貝** a pearl oyster ‖ **真珠取り** pearl fishery ; a pearl diver (人) ‖ **真珠養殖場** a pearl farm.

じんしゅ 人種 a **race**, an **ethnic group** 《参考》後者は「(一国内の) 民族 (集団)」の意であるが, 言語・文化・出身国・宗教などが同じであることを強調できるので, 最近ではこの言い方を好む人が多い (⇀民族) 一形 **人種の racial** ▶その国には5つの異なる**人種**が住んでいる There are five different *ethnic groups* living together in that country. ‖ アメリカはよく**人種**のるつぼと言われる America is often referred to as *an ethnic melting pot*. ‖ 現代のイギリスにはいろいろな**人種**がいる Modern Britain *has great ethnic and racial diversity*. (➤ diversity は「多様性」).

‖**人種差別** racial discrimination (➤「人種隔離政策」は racial segregation という) ‖ **人種的偏見** racial [ethnic] prejudice ‖ **人種問題** a racial [an ethnic] problem.

しんじゅう 心中 a **double suicide**

《解説》キリスト教では人の生死は神の手にあって自分の命を自分で断つことは許されない行為だと考える. まして人を道連れにすることは殺人としか解釈されない. なかでも無理心中 (a forced double suicide) は特に異常と考えられている.

▶彼は愛人と**心中した** He *committed suicide* with his lover. ‖ **一家心中**の悲しい記事を新聞で読んだ I read a sad story of *a family suicide* in the newspaper. ‖ 彼女は自分の子供2人を道連れに**無理心中した** She *killed* her two children *and then committed suicide*.

しんしゅく 伸縮 ▶**伸縮自在**のベルト an *elastic* belt ‖ **伸縮性のある**ズボン *stretch* pants ‖ このジーンズは**伸縮性**があってはきやすい These jeans are *stretchy* [*elastic*] and easy to wear.

しんしゅつ 進出 ▶残念なことにわがチームは1点差で**決勝に進出**できなかった To our regret, our team was one point short of *advancing to* [*making it into*] *the finals*. (➤ make it into は「うまく…にたどり着く」の意) ‖ そのスーパーマーケットは千葉に**進出する**予定だ The supermarket chain is *expanding* its *business* to Chiba. / The supermarket chain is going to *open* its *first outlet* in Chiba. ‖ エジプトに**進出している**日本の企業を(どこか)知っていますか Do you know any Japanese companies that *have been doing business* in Egypt?

あなたの英語はどう響く?

企業が「海外市場へ進出する」というとき advance toward a new market abroad などとしがちだが, 誤解を招く. advance は「軍隊が進撃する」の意味で用いられることが多い語で, これを使うとひどく攻撃的なイメージを与えてしまう. find new markets abroad, expand business overseas などとするのがよい.

しんしゅつきぼつ 神出鬼没 ▶鞍馬天狗は**神出鬼没**だ Kurama-tengu *appears and disappears like the wind*.

しんしゅん 新春 the **New Year**(正月).

しんじゅんせい 浸潤性の 《医学》**invasive** ▶**浸潤性**のがん *invasive* cancer.

しんしょ 親書 a **personal letter**(私信) ; a **signed letter**(署名入りの手紙) ; an **official letter**(公式の手紙).

1 **しんしょう 心証** an **impression** ▶きみの態度は部長の**心証**を害したかもしれないよ Your attitude might *have made an unfavorable* [*a bad*] *impression* on the manager.

2 **しんしょう 心象** a **mental image** ▶**心象風景** one's *mental* imagery.

3 **しんしょう 辛勝** ▶ヤンキースはメッツに3対2で**辛勝した** The Yankees *edged* the Mets, 3–2.

1 **しんじょう 心情** one's **feelings** ▶**心情的**には理解できるが彼の行為には賛成できない I can understand *his feelings*, but I cannot approve of his conduct. ‖ **心情としては**彼を解雇するに忍びない I (*just*) *can't bring myself* to dismiss [fire] him.

2 **しんじょう 身上** ▶彼らはその女性の**身上調査**を行った They *looked into* that woman's *history and her family background*.

▶忍耐強いのが彼の**身上**(＝取り柄)だ Perseverance

is his *good* [*strong*] *point*.
‖**身上書** a personal information form.

3**しんじょう 信条** a **principle**(主義) ; a **belief**(信念) ; a **creed**, a **dogma**(宗教上の ; 前者は信者の側から, 後者は教会の側から見た) ▶生活**信条** a *guiding principle* of one's life ‖ 私は約束の時間に遅れないことを**信条にしている** I *strongly believe in* the importance of being on time for appointments.

4**しんじょう 真情** one's **true** [**real**] **feelings** ▶彼は私に**真情**を吐露した He revealed his *true feelings* to me.

じんじょう 尋常の **normal**(正常の) ; **ordinary**(ふつうの) ▶ことしの夏の暑さは**尋常ではなかった** It was *abnormally* hot this summer. ‖ **尋常のやり方**ではこの目標は達成できない This objective cannot be achieved by *ordinary* means.

しんしょうしゃ 身障者 a **physically disabled** [**challenged**] **person** ⇀障害 ▶**身障者用の**車 a *disability* car ‖ **身障者用の**駐車スペース a *disabled* parking space [place / spot] (➤「身障者用駐車場利用証」は disabled parking permit という) ‖ この席はお年寄りや**身障者**のための優先席です These seats are reserved for senior citizens and *physically disabled people*.

しんしょうひつばつ 信賞必罰 ▶当社は**信賞必罰**主義です Our principle is that *success should be rewarded and failure punished*.

しんしょうぼうだい 針小棒大 ▶あの人はいつも**針小棒大に言い触らす** He always *makes a mountain out of a molehill*.

1**しんしょく 寝食** ▶彼とは 4 年間**寝食をともにした** I *lived under the same roof* with him for four years. ‖ 牧野さんは**寝食を忘れて**その研究に没頭した Mr. Makino was so absorbed in his research that he (*often*) *forgot to eat or sleep*. / Mr. Makino *single-mindedly* devoted himself to his research. (➤ single-mindedly は「ひたむきに」).

2**しんしょく 浸食** **erosion** 一動**浸食する** **erode** 《away》 ▶海は何世紀にもわたってこの断崖を**浸食している** The sea has been *eating away at* [*eroding away*] this cliff for centuries. ‖ 川は岸を**浸食して**峡谷を作ることがある A river can *eat away* its banks and form a canyon. ‖ この岩は風雨の**浸食作用**で異様な形をしている This rock is carved in curious shapes by the *erosion* of wind and rain.

3**しんしょく 神職** a **Shinto priest**.

しんじる 信じる

訳語メニュー
ことばなどを真実と思う ⇀believe **1**
信仰する ⇀believe in **2**
人などを信頼する ⇀trust, believe in **3**

1【ことばなどを真実と思う】believe +⊜ ▶私の言うことを**信じてよ** *Believe* me, please. (➤ believe someone は「その人のことばを信じる」で「その人を信頼する」ではない. 後者は **3** の trust someone という)

【文型】
〜だと信じる
believe (**that**) S + V

▶私は子供の頃サンタクロースは本当に北極から来るものだと**固く信じていた** When I was a child, I firmly *believed that* Santa Claus really came from the North Pole. ‖ 久雄が人気歌手になったなんて**信じられないよ** It is *unbelievable that* Hisao has become a popular singer.
▶そんな迷信は**信じられない** That superstition *is incredible* to me. (➤ incredible は「(途方もない話で)信じられない」) ‖ **その話はあまりにうますぎて信じられない** That's *too good to be true*.

直訳の落とし穴「息子を信じています」
「信じる」= believe と考えて, 「私は息子を信じています」のつもりで, I believe my son. としがちだが, 「believe + 人」は「その人が真実を語っていると信じる」という意味である. したがって, この英文は「息子の言っていること [言ったこと] を信じている」を表す. 日本語は, 息子を信頼している, あるいは, 息子は道に外れたことをしないと, さらには, 息子がやがて自己実現をしてくれることを信じている, という意味がふつうであるから, この場合は I trust my son. (➤ 信頼を寄せている場合—現在に重点がある) または, I believe in my son. (➤ 人格的に信用している, また, 可能性や将来性を信じている場合—未来志向型) としなければならない. ⇀**3**

2【信仰する】believe in ▶イスラム教徒はアラーの神を**信じる** Muslims *believe in* Allah. (➤ believe in は「(宗教を)信仰する, (神の)存在を信じる」の意) ‖ キリスト教徒はキリストの復活を**信じる** Christians *believe in* the Resurrection. ‖ **信じる者は救われる** Those who *believe* (in God) will be saved. ‖ インドではヒンドゥー教を**信じる**人が多い Most people in India *believe in* Hinduism [embrace Hinduism as their religion].

3【人などを信頼する】trust +⊜ ; **believe in**(人柄・価値・存在などを, また, 人の将来性を) ▶私たちは監督を**信じています** We *trust* our manager. ‖ 半年間も行方不明だった息子が生きて帰ってきたときには, **自分の目が信じられなかった** I *couldn't believe my eyes* when my son who had been missing for half a year suddenly returned alive.

【文型】
A を信じている
believe in A
【解説】 **believe in** A は「A の価値を認める, A を善いものであると信じる, A の存在を信じる」ことで, I *believe in* him. は「彼の人柄を信頼する」の意. これに対して I *believe* him. は「彼の言ったことを信じる」の意.

▶**自分を信じなさい** You *have to believe in* yourself. ‖ 私は民主主義をよいものと**信じる** I *believe in* democracy. ‖ きみ, ＵＦＯの存在を**信じる**? Do you *believe in* UFOs?

1**しんしん 心身** **mind and body** ▶その若者は**心身ともに**健全だ That young man is sound [healthy] *both in mind and body*. ‖ 彼女は**心身ともに**疲労困ぱいしている She is exhausted *both mentally and physically*. ‖**心身症** (a) psychosomatic illness [disorder] ‖ **心身障害** physical and mental [psychological] problems ‖ **心身障害児** a child with physical and mental disabilities.

2**しんしん 心神** ▶**心神喪失の** insane ; non compos mentis
‖**心神耗弱** diminished mental capacity ; feeble mindedness.

3**しんしん 新進** ▶**新進の**ギタリスト an *up-and-coming*

[a *rising*] (*young*) guitarist ‖ **新進気鋭**の経済学者 a *young and promising* economist.

4**しんしん** ▶夜の間に雪が**しんしんと**降り積もった The snow fell *thick and fast* during the night.
▶夜が更けるにつれて**しんしんと**冷えてきた As the night went on, the cold *crept through* to my very bones.

1**しんじん 新人** a **newcomer**, a **new member**; a **new face** [**star**] (芸能人などの); a **rookie** /róki/ (野球などの) ▶**新人**が主役に抜てきされた *A new face* [*actor*] was singled out to play the leading role.
‖**新人賞** the New-Star-of-the-Year Award, the Rookie-of-the-Year Award ‖ **新人戦** a rookie game [match].
☛ **新人王** (→見出語)

2**しんじん 信心** (**religious**) **devotion**; **faith** (信仰); **piety** /páɪəṭi/ (敬けんなこと) ▶**信心深い**家庭 a *devout* [*religious*] family.

じんしん 人身 ▶彼は飲酒運転で**人身事故**を起こした His drunk driving resulted in *a traffic accident involving an injury or death*. ‖ **人身攻撃**は慎むべきだ You should refrain from making *personal attacks on others*.

しんじんおう 新人王 the rookie of the year ▶**新人王**のタイトルを獲得する win *the Rookie-of-the-Year title*.

1**しんすい 浸水する be flooded** ▶400戸以上が床上[床下]**浸水した** Over four hundred houses *were flooded* above [up to] the floor. ‖ 道路が**浸水している** The road *is under water*.

2**しんすい 心酔する worship** +㊀ (崇拝する); **adore** +㊀ (強く愛する); **idolize** +㊀ (偶像のように崇拝する) ▶彼女は学生時代にある新興宗教に**心酔した** (＝夢中になった) She *was very enthusiastic about* [*over*] a certain new religion when she was in college. ‖ 私は漱石に**心酔している** I *worship* Soseki. ／I *am an ardent admirer of* Soseki. ‖ 女の子はよく有名な映画俳優や歌手に**心酔する** Girls often *idolize* famous movie stars or singers.

3**しんすい 進水する launch** /lɔ:ntʃ, lɑ:ntʃ/
‖**進水式** a launching ceremony.

しんずい 神髄・真髄 the essence (本質); **the soul** (精髄) ▶バリ島でガムラン音楽の**神髄**に触れた I came to appreciate *the essence* of gamelan music in Bali.

1**しんせい 申請** an **application** 一㊁ **申請する apply** 《for》 ▶パスポートの交付を**申請する** *apply* [*make an application*] *for* a passport.
‖**申請書** a written application, an application ‖ **申請人** an applicant.

2**しんせい 神聖な holy, sacred** /séɪkrɪd/ (➤ 前者が神など, 崇拝する対象そのものについていうのに対して, 後者はやや間接的に神に関連したものについていう) ▶**神聖な**場所 a *holy* [*sacred*] place ／a sanctuary ‖ 猫は古代エジプトでは**神聖な**生き物と考えられた Cats were considered *sacred* in ancient Egypt.

3**しんせい 真性の genuine** /dʒénjuɪn/ ▶**真性**コレラ *a genuine case* of cholera.

4**しんせい 新星** a **nova** (星); a **new star** (新人).

5**しんせい 神性 divinity**.

6**しんせい 真正の genuine**; **authentic** (正真正銘の).

じんせい 人生 life ▶幸福[不幸]な**人生**を送る lead a happy [an unhappy] *life* ／live happily [unhappily] ‖ さまざまな**人生** (＝生き方) がある There are many different *ways of life* [*living*]. ‖ 一生懸命に働くだけでは充実した**人生**は送れない Hard work alone does not make for a fulfilling *life*. (➤ make for は「寄与する, 役に立つ」) ‖ 祖父の**人生**は苦難に満ちていた My grandfather's *life* was full of suffering. ‖ **人生**には良い時と悪い時 (＝浮き沈み) がある *Life* has its ups and downs.
▶まあ, **人生**はそんなものだよ Well, *such is life*. ／Well, *that's life*. ／Well, *that's the way life is*. (➤ 失敗や不幸があった際によく使われる表現) ‖ ユーモア作家のくせに彼は悲観的な**人生観**の持ち主だ He has a rather pessimistic *view of life* [*outlook on life*] for a humorist. ‖ 彼は会社を辞めて, 翻訳家として**第二の人生**に踏み出した He quit his company and started *a new life* as a translator.
‖**人生相談欄** an advice column, an agony column.

しんせいじ 新生児 a **newborn baby** [**child**].

しんせいめん 新生面 a **new field**, a **new phase**.

しんせかい 新世界 a **new world**; **the New World** (アメリカ大陸).

しんせき 親戚 a **relative** /rélət̬ɪv/, a **relation** (➤ 前者のほうがふつう) ▶あの女の子はぼくの**遠い親戚**に当たります She is one of my *distant relatives*. ‖ 彼女とは父方[母方]の**親戚**に当たる She is *a relative* on my father's [mother's] side.
ことわざ **遠くの親戚より近くの他人** A good neighbor is better than a relative [brother] far off.

じんせきみとう 人跡未踏 ▶**人跡未踏**の森林 a *virgin* [*an untrodden*] forest ‖ この国にはまだ**人跡未踏**の地域が多い There are still many *trackless* [*unexplored*] regions in this country.

シンセサイザー a **synthesizer**.

1**しんせつ 親切** (a) **kindness** 一㊇ **親切な kind, nice** ▶**親切な**人 a *kind* person ‖ 皆さんの小さな**親切**がこの町を住みよい場所にします Your small act of *kindness* will make our community a better place to live (in).

> **【文型】**
> 人(A)が親切にも…する
> **It is kind** [**nice**] **of** A **to** do.
> A **is kind** (**enough**) **to** do.

▶ご**親切**ありがとうございます Thank you very much. *It was* very *kind* [*nice*] *of* you (*to* do so). ／Thank you for your *kindness*. ‖ 彼は**親切にも**傘を貸してくれた He *was kind enough to* lend me his umbrella. ‖ 彼女は**親切に**構内を案内してくれた She *was kind enough to* show [*kindly* showed] me around the campus.
▶バスで気分が悪くなったら**親切な**女性が席を譲ってくれた When I got sick on the bus, a *kind* woman gave me her seat. ‖ アメリカへ行ったときそこの人たちはみんな私に**親切にしてくれた** When I visited America, everyone (I met) *went out of their way to be kind* [*nice*]. (➤ go out of one's way to do は「わざわざ…してくれる」の意のインフォーマルな表現) ‖ 人が**親切心**から忠告してやったのに彼は怒ってしまった I gave him advice *out of the kindness of my heart*, but he got angry with me.

あなたの英語はどう響く?
英語国にホームステイしての帰り際, 「ご親切にしていただいてありがとうございました」の意味で Thank you (very much) for your kindness. と言う日本人学生が少なくないようであるが，この場合の for your kindness は漠然とし過ぎて，どこか他人行儀なよそよそしさが感じられる．もう少し具体的に言わないと感謝も型どおりで本心からではないと受け取られかねない．したがって Thank you for a wonderful homestay. や Thanks for everything. などの言い方が親近感や温かみが感じられてよい．

☛ **不親切**（→見出語）

2**しんせつ 新設** ▶この区域の人口増加に伴って小学校が**新設された**（＝新しい小学校が設立された）To keep pace with the increase in population in this district, a *new* elementary school *has been founded* [*been opened*].
‖**新設校** a newly-established [newly-founded] school ‖**新設コース** a new course.

3**しんせつ 新雪** **fresh snow.**

しんせっきじだい 新石器時代 **the Neolithic**/niːəlíθɪk/ **Age.**

しんせん 新鮮な **fresh** ▶**新鮮な**野菜［空気］*fresh* vegetables [air] ‖この魚は**新鮮で**おいしい This fish is *fresh* and tastes good. ‖彼女の作品には全く**新鮮味**が感じられなかった I found nothing *new* [*fresh*] in her work.

しんぜん 親善 **goodwill, friendship**（友好）; **friendly relations**（友好関係）▶わが国は近隣諸国との**親善**をさらに図るべきだ Japan should promote *friendly relations* [strengthen the ties of *friendship*] with neighboring countries. ‖バレーボールの日中**親善試合**が行われた A *goodwill* [*friendly*] volleyball *game* was held between Japan and China. ‖わが大学に外国人留学生を受け入れることは**国際親善**に大いに役立つことと思います I believe that by accepting foreign students, our university will make a great contribution to *international friendship*.
‖**親善使節** a goodwill envoy [mission].

じんせん 人選 ▶彼の後任を目下**人選中です** We are now (*in the process of*) *selecting* the right person to be his successor. ‖残念ながら首相は財務大臣の**人選を誤った**ようだ Regrettably, the Prime Minister seems to *have picked the wrong person* for the post of Minister of Finance.（➤ pick は「選ぶ」).

しんぜんけっこんしき 神前結婚式 a **Shinto wedding (ceremony).**

じんぜんけっこんしき 人前結婚式 a **non-religious wedding (ceremony).**

1**しんそう 真相** **the truth** ▶**真相**はじきに明らかになるだろう *The truth* will soon come out. ‖彼は**真相**を明かさなかった He did not reveal *the truth*. ‖**真相**は依然謎に包まれている *The truth* remains a mystery. ‖警察は事件の**真相究明**に乗り出した The police set about *finding out the truth* [*getting to the bottom*] of the affair. ‖**真相**はこうだ *The facts* are [*The real story* is] like this.（➤ 具体的説明があとに続く).

2**しんそう 新装** ▶そのスーパーはあす**新装開店する** The supermarket will *open* tomorrow *after having been remodeled* [*refurbished*].（➤ refurbish は「化粧直しする」) ‖《広告などで》4月15日**新装オープン** *Completely redecorated.* Reopening April 15.（➤ redecorate は「飾りつけを新しくする」;（×）Refresh Open や（×）New Open は和製英語).

3**しんそう 深層** ‖（海洋）**深層水** deep ocean water ‖**深層心理学** depth psychology.

しんぞう 心臓

1【臓器】**the heart** ▶**心臓発作**で死亡する die of *a heart attack* ‖私は**心臓**が悪い I have a weak [bad] *heart*. ／I have *heart* trouble. ‖彼女の前に出ると**心臓**がどきどきする My *heart* beats [pounds] wildly when I'm around her. ‖近所に雷が落ちたときは**心臓が止まるくらい驚いた** When lightning struck nearby, *I thought I would die of fright*. ‖兄は**心臓外科**の専門医です My brother specializes in *cardiac surgery*. ‖急に冷たい水に飛び込むと**心臓まひ**を起こすよ If you jump into (the) cold water all at once, you might get [have] *a heart attack* [*have heart failure*].（➤ 心臓の冠状動脈が詰まって血流が滞る，心臓発作，心臓まひ，心筋梗塞は heart attack で，心臓のポンプ機能が低下する，心不全が heart failure ; ● 今まさに冷たい水に飛び込もうとしている場合は the が必要だが，一般論として冷たい水に飛び込むことの危険性を言っている場合は the は不要).
‖**心臓移植** a heart transplant ‖**心臓病** heart disease ‖**心臓ペースメーカー** a (cardiac) pacemaker ‖**心臓マッサージ** a heart [cardiac] massage.

2【中枢部】**the heart** ; **the center**（中心）▶このコンピュータ室はこの大工場を動かす**心臓部**です This computer room is *the heart* [*the center*] which moves everything in this large factory.

3【厚かましさ】**nerve, cheek, rudeness** ▶あいつは**心臓**だな How *impertinent* [*impudent* ／*rude*] he is! ／What (a) *nerve*! ‖ぼくの前にまた顔を出すとは，きみも**心臓の強い**男だね You *have a lot of nerve* to show your face in front of me, don't you?

1**じんぞう 腎臓** a **kidney** ▶父は**腎臓が悪い** My father *has kidney trouble*.
‖**腎臓がん** kidney cancer ‖**腎臓結石** a kidney [renal] stone ‖**腎臓病** kidney trouble, a kidney disease ‖**人工腎臓** a kidney machine.

2**じんぞう 人造の** **artificial, man-made** →人工 ▶これは**人造**ダイヤです This is an *imitation* [*artificial*] diamond. ／This diamond is *an imitation*.
‖**人造湖** an artificial [a man-made] lake.

しんぞく 親族 **a relative,** a **relation**（➤ 前者のほうがふつう）▶父が**親族**を代表して謝辞を述べた My father expressed his gratitude on behalf of all his *relatives* [*relations*].

> 「親族·親戚」のいろいろ **いとこ** cousin ／**おい** nephew ／**おじ** uncle ／**夫** husband ／**おば** aunt ／**親** parent ／**義兄［義弟］** brother-in-law ／**義姉［義妹］** sister-in-law ／**兄弟** brother ／**姉妹** sister ／**最近親者** next of kin ／**しゅうと** father-in-law ／**姑** mother-in-law ／**曽祖父** great-grandfather ／ **曽祖母** great-grandmother ／**祖父** grandfather ／**祖母** grandmother ／**父** father ／**妻** wife ／**配偶者** spouse ／**母** mother ／**ひ孫** great-grandchild ／**孫** grandson（男）, granddaughter（女）／**息子** son ／**娘** daughter ／**めい** niece

‖**親族会議** a family council [meeting] ‖**親族関係** kinship.

じんそく 迅速な **prompt**（遅滞のない）; **quick**（素早い）▶ご注文の品は**迅速に**配達いたします Your order will be delivered *promptly*.

しんそこ 心底 ▶こんなに**心底**から笑ったのは久しぶりだ I haven't *had a hearty laugh* like this in a long time. ‖**心底**，あの人のことが好きなの I love him *from* *the bottom of my heart*. ／I *really* love him.

しんそつ 新卒 a **new** [**recent**] **graduate**(新卒者) ▶新卒の社員 an employee *who has just* [*recently*] *graduated* ‖ 新卒の先生が私たちのクラスを担任することになった A new teacher, *fresh from college*, is going to take over our class.

1 **しんたい 身体** **the body** ▶兄は生まれつき**身体強健**だ My brother was born with *a strong body*. ‖ 機内に危険物を持ち込ませないために空港では乗客の**身体検査**をする At the airport, every passenger must undergo *a security check* so that nothing dangerous will be brought on board the plane. (➤ security check は体だけでなく荷物の検査も含む；⇀健康診断，ボディーチェック).

‖ **身体障害者** a physically disabled [challenged] person, a person with a physical disability. (⇀障害).

2 **しんたい 進退** **1**【進むことと退くこと】▶泥の中で軍隊は**進退窮まった** The troop *could move neither forward nor backward* [*could neither advance nor retreat*] because of the mud.

2【身の処し方】▶我々はきみたちと最後まで**進退をともに**しよう We will *be* [*We're*] *with you* all the way. ‖ 彼はその事件のあとすぐに部長に**進退伺い**を出した Right after the incident, he wrote *a letter* to his manager *asking whether he should resign*. (🔘英米には進退伺いを出す習慣がないので，訳例のように「辞職すべきかどうかを尋ねる手紙」のように意訳する).

しんだい 寝台 **a bed**；**a berth**, **a bunk** (列車・船の；両語とも「車内[船室内]ベッド」の意で用いるが，後者には壁に取り付けた段ベッドというイメージが強い)

‖ **寝台券** a berth ticket ‖ **寝台車** a sleeping car ／a sleeper ‖ **寝台料金** a berth charge.

1 **じんたい 人体** **the human body** ▶**人体実験**をする conduct *experiments on humans* ／conduct *human experiments* ‖ 農薬は**人体**に悪い影響を及ぼすこともある Agricultural pesticides sometimes harm *the human body*.

2 **じんたい 靱帯** 《解剖学》 **a ligament.**

じんだい 甚大な **serious** (深刻な)；**heavy** (多大の)；**extensive** (広範囲の)

▶台風はこの地域に**甚大な**被害を及ぼした The typhoon caused *extensive* [*heavy*] damage to this region.

しんたいそう 新体操 **rhythmic (sportive) gymnastics.**

1 **しんたく 信託** (a) **trust** ‖ **信託銀行** a trust bank ‖ **信託投資** an investment trust ‖ **信託統治** trusteeship ‖ **信託統治領** a trust territory.

2 **しんたく 神託** **an oracle.**

しんだん 診断 (a) **diagnosis** /dàɪəgnóʊsɪs/ 一動 **診断する** **diagnose** /dàɪəgnóʊs ‖ dáɪəgnoʊz/ +目 ▶正しい[間違った]**診断**をする make a correct [wrong] *diagnosis*.

> **【文型】**
> **人(A)が病名(B)にかかっていると診断される**
> A **is diagnosed with** B
> A **is diagnosed as having** [**suffering from**] B
> **病気(A)が病名(B)と診断される**
> A **is diagnosed as** B
> ➤ この文型で人を主語にする場合，B には形容詞がくる

▶彼は肺がんと**診断された** He *was diagnosed with* lung cancer [*as having* lung cancer]. ‖ 彼女の病気は結核と**診断された** Her illness *was diagnosed as* tuberculosis. (➤ as のときは A (illness) = B (tuberculosis) の関係にある；人を主語にして，She was diagnosed as having [suffering from] tuberculosis. も可能) ‖ 医者は父を肺炎と**診断した** The doctor *diagnosed* my father's illness *as* pneumonia. (➤ 英文は mistakenly や wrongly (誤って)などがないかぎり，病名がきちんとわかったことをいう) ‖ 祖母は関節炎にかかっていると**診断された** My grandmother *was diagnosed as having* arthritis [being arthritic]. ‖ 彼は躁うつ症と**診断された** He *was diagnosed as* maniac-depressive.

▶私は**診断書**を書いてもらった I had a *medical certificate* drawn up. ‖ どの学校でも１年に１回は**健康診断**を行う In every school the students have *a physical checkup* once a year [have *an* annual *physical checkup*].

じんち 陣地 a **position.**

しんちく 新築 ▶小西さんは郊外に家を**新築した** Mr. Konishi *has built a new house* in the suburbs. ‖ 私たちはチーフに**新築祝い**を贈った We sent [gave] our chief *a housewarming present*. (➤ housewarming は引っ越ししたときの「新居披露パーティー」).

✉ **ご新築おめでとう．新築祝いとして日本の版画をお送りします** Congratulations on *your new home*. I am sending a Japanese wood-block print as *a house-warming gift*.

じんちくむがい 人畜無害 ▶あいつは**人畜無害**なやつだよ He's a *harmless* guy. ‖ この消毒液は**人畜無害**だ This antiseptic *is harmless to humans and animals*.

しんちゃ 新茶 **the first tea of the season** ▶**新茶**を出す[摘む] serve [pick] *the first tea of the season*.

しんちゃく 新着の **newly arrived**

‖ **新着品**[本] a new arrival.

1 **しんちゅう 真鍮** **brass.**

2 **しんちゅう 心中** ▶彼女はいちばんの親友に**心中**を打ち明けた She unburdened herself [her *heart*] to her best friend. ‖ ご**心中**をお察しいたします I understand [share] your *feelings*. ／I know *how you feel*.

しんちゅうぐん 進駐軍 an **occupation army, occupation forces.**

1 **しんちょう 身長** **height** /haɪt/ ▶**身長**を測る measure one's *height* ‖ 娘はこの１年でずいぶん**身長が伸び**た My daughter *has gotten* [*has become*] much *taller* this year. ／My daughter *grew like a weed* this year. (➤ grow like a weed は子供の急成長を表すときによく用いる言い方) ‖ **対話**「**身長はどのくらいありますか**」「175センチです」"*How tall are you ?*" "(I'm) 175 centimeters (tall ／in height)." (➤ "What's your height ?" "(It's) 175 centimeters." でもよい).

2 **しんちょう 慎重な** **cautious** (用心深い)；**careful** (注意深い)；**prudent** (配慮が行き届いた) ▶母は何事にも**慎重**なたちだ My mother is *careful* about everything. ‖ **慎重にやれよ！** *Be careful !* ‖ 金の貸し借りは**慎重**でなければならない You must be *cautious* about borrowing or lending money. ‖ 政治家はコメントに**慎重**であるべきだ Politicians should be *cautious* in their comments. ‖ ガラス器は**慎重**に扱わなければならない Glassware must be handled *carefully* [*with care*]. ‖ 彼の行動は時折**慎重さを欠く** His conduct sometimes lacks *prudence*. ／He sometimes acts imprudently [*rashly*]. ‖ 財務大臣は減税には**慎重な**(＝保守的な)立場をとっている The Fi-

nance Minister has been taking a *conservative* stand on tax cuts. ‖彼の運転は**慎重**だ He's a *cautious* [*safe*] driver.

3**しんちょう 新調** ▶彼はグレーの背広を**新調した** He *bought* a new gray suit. ／He *had* [*got*] a gray suit *made*. (➤ 後者はあつらえた場合).

じんちょうげ 沈丁花《植 物》 a (**sweet-smelling**) **daphne** /dǽfni/.

しんちょくじょうきょう 進捗状況 ▶工事の**進捗状況**を報告する report on *the progress* of construction (➤「進捗状況の報告」は progress report) ‖捜査の**進捗状況**はどうなってるかね *How far has* the investigation *gotten* [*proceeded*]?

しんちんたいしゃ 新陳代謝 metabolism /mətǽbəlìzəm/ ▶彼は**新陳代謝**が高い［低い］He has a *fast* [*slow*] *metabolism*. ／He has a *high* [*low*] *metabolism*.
▶《比喩的》芸能界は**新陳代謝**(＝新旧交代)が激しい There is constant *turnover* in (the world of) show business.

しんつう 心痛 worry ▶母は弟が警察に補導されて**心痛**のあまり寝込んでしまった When my brother was placed under police guidance, my mother *was so sick with worry* she could do nothing but lie down (in bed).

じんつう 陣痛 labor (**pains**); **contractions** (子宮筋の収縮) ▶**陣痛**が始まった Her *labor* started. ‖**陣痛**は5分置きにやって来た *Contractions* came at five-minute intervals.

じんつうりき 神通力 ▶孫悟空は**神通力**を持っている Songoku has *supernatural powers*.

しんてい 進呈する present《with》▶この辞書をあなたに**進呈します** Please accept this dictionary as a gift. ‖**進呈**須藤様, 水上より *Presented* to Mr. Sudo with best wishes from Minakami. ‖**見本無料進呈** We *offer free samples*. ／《広告で》Write for free samples.

じんてき 人的 ‖**人的外傷** trauma /tráʊmə, trɔ́ːmə/ ‖**人的資源** human resources ‖**人的被害** a casualty.

シンデレラ Cinderella /sìndərélə/ ▶彼女の成功はまさに現代の**シンデレラ物語**だ Her success is a present-day *Cinderella story*. ‖**シンデレラボーイ** a boy who went from obscurity to success.

1**しんてん 進展する advance** (目標に向かってレベルを高めながら); **progress** (ある方向に向かったり, ある線に沿ったりして); **develop** (変わったり成長したりしながら)
▶捜査は意外な方向に**進展した** The investigation *advanced* [*moved* ／ *went*] in an unexpected direction. ‖その交渉は一向に**進展していない** The negotiations *haven't progressed* at all. ／The negotiations *have made no progress* at all [*are at a standstill*]. ‖事態は急速に**進展した** The situation *developed* rapidly.

2**しんてん 親展** ▶この手紙には「**親展**」と書いてある This letter is marked *"Confidential* [*For your eyes only*]."

しんでん 神殿 a **shrine**; a **pantheon** /pǽnθiɑːn/ (万神殿) ▶アポロンの**神殿** the *Shrine* of Apollo.

しんでんず 心電図 an **electrocardiogram**, a **cardiogram** ▶**心電図**をとってもらった I had my *electrocardiogram* taken. ／I had *an ECG* (taken). (➤ ECG は electrocardiogram の略; EKG もよく使われる).

しんてんち 新天地 ▶多くの移民が**新天地**を求めてアメリカに渡った Many immigrants went over to the U.S. seeking a *new life*.

1**しんと 信徒** a **believer** ▶キリスト教［仏教／イスラム教］**信徒** *a believer* in Christianity [Buddhism ／ Islam] ／a Christian [a Buddhist ／ a Muslim].

2**しんと** ▶洞穴の中は**しんとしている** All *is quiet* in the cave. ／*Not a sound can be heard* in the cave. ‖突然ライトが消えると場内は**一瞬しんとなった** When the lights went out all of a sudden, *a momentary hush fell* over the hall. (➤ hush は「静けさ」).

1**しんど 震度 seismic** /sáɪzmɪk/ **intensity**

> **《解説》** (1)「震度」は気象庁で定めた日本独特のもので, 土地の揺れ具合を調査地点で一定の基準に合わせて機械で計測し, 0 から 7 までの数値を用いて表す.
> (2)マグニチュード(magnitude)は地震規模の大きさを表す数値で, これを計る方法として欧米ではリヒタースケール(Richter scale)を用いる.

▶昨夜**震度** 4 の地震が東京を襲った Last night an earthquake with an *intensity* of four *on the Japanese scale* jolted Tokyo.

2**しんど 進度 progress** ▶授業の**進度**が速すぎて私はついていけない The class is *going* [*moving* ／ *progressing*] *too fast* and I can't keep up.
‖**進度テスト** a progress test.

じんと ▶その歌は私の胸に**じんときた** The song *touched my heart* [*me*].

しんどい ▶**しんどい**わ *I'm tired*. ‖**しんどい**仕事だ What a *tough* [*hard*] job this is! ／ This is *hard* work!

1**しんとう 浸透 permeation** (染み渡ること); **penetration** (染み込むこと) **1【液体が】**一動 **浸透する permeate** /pə́ːrmieɪt/ ＋目, **penetrate** /pénətreɪt/ ＋目 ▶電気製品への液体の**浸透**を防止する prevent *the permeation* [*penetration*] of liquids into electrical appliances ‖水は土壌にはよく**浸透する**が, 石にはあまり**浸透しない** Water easily *penetrates* soil, but not stone.
‖**浸透性** permeability.
2【考え方が】▶最近では公共の場での禁煙が世間に**浸透してきた** Recently, restrictions on smoking in public places *have become prevalent* [*widely accepted*]. (➤ prevalent は「広く行き渡っている」の意の形容詞).

2**しんとう 神道 Shinto, Shintoism** (➤ 英語化している) ▶**神道**の清めの儀式 a *Shinto* purification rite. (→神社).

3**しんとう 心頭** ▶**心頭を滅却すれば火もまた涼し** If you can clear your mind of all thoughts and distractions, you will find that even fire feels cool. ‖増税だなんて全く**怒り心頭**だ *I'm enraged* by the tax hike.

4**しんとう 親等 the degree of kinship** ▶1 [2 ／ 3] **親等**の親族 a relative [relation] *in the first* [*second* ／ *third*] *degree* (*of kinship* ／ *of consanguinity*) (➤ /kɑ̀ːnsæŋgwínəṭi/ と発音).

1**しんどう 震動・振動 1【揺れ動く】vibrate** (左右に速く); **shake** (上下または左右に) ▶線路脇の家屋は電車が通過するたびに**震動する** The houses along the track *vibrate* [*tremble*] whenever the train passes. ‖火山の爆発で大地が**震動した** The volcanic eruption *shook* the earth.
2【左右に振れる】swing ▶振り子は左右に**振動する** A pendulum *swings* back and forth [backward

し

and forward]. (➤ この場合 right and left とはあまり言わない).

2 **しんどう 神童** a child prodigy, 《インフォーマル》 a whiz kid ▶ [ことわざ] 十で神童, 十五で才子, 二十歳過ぎたらただの人 A prodigy at ten, brilliant at fifteen, just another guy [girl] at twenty.

じんとう 陣頭 ▶市長が陣頭に立って暴力団追放に当たった The mayor *took the lead* in [*spearheaded*] the anti-gangster campaign.

じんどう 人道 一形 **人道的な** humanitarian (博愛的な) ; humane (慈悲深い) ▶日本は人道的な立場からその国に食糧援助を行った Japan provided food aid to that country on *humanitarian* grounds. ‖ そのような行為は人道的に見て許されない (＝人道主義に反する) Such conduct is *against humanitarianism*. ／Such conduct is *inhuman*. ‖ 捕虜の人道的扱い (the) *humane* treatment of prisoners.

‖**人道支援** humanitarian assistance ‖ **人道主義** humanitarianism (→ヒューマニズム) ‖ **人道問題** a question of humanity.

じんとく 人徳 ▶人徳のある人 a person *of virtue* [*integrity*] ‖ 石井さんが PTA 会長に選ばれたのはあの方の人徳だと思う I believe Mr. Ishii has been chosen as Chairman of the PTA because of his *integrity* [*personal charm*]. (➤ personal charm は「個人的魅力」).

じんどる 陣取る ▶彼らはパレードを見るために最前列に陣取った They *secured a position* in the very front row so they could see the parade.

シンドローム syndrome ▶メタボリックシンドローム metabolic *syndrome*. →症候群.

シンナー (paint) thinner /θínəʳ/ ▶シンナーでそのペンキを薄めてくれる? Could you thin the paint with some *thinner*, please?

▶シンナーを吸う inhale *paint thinner* ‖ シンナー遊びは危険だ *Glue-sniffing* is dangerous. ／It is dangerous to *sniff glue*. (➤ glue は「接着剤」).

しんなり ▶キャベツがしんなりしたらスープを入れてください Add the soup when the cabbage has *become tender*.

しんに 真に truly →真 ▶博士のノーベル賞受賞は真に喜ばしいことです The doctor's winning the Nobel Prize is *truly* a cause for celebration.

しんにち 親日 ▶親日派 *a pro-Japanese group* [*person*] (➤前者は集団, 後者は1人) ‖ ジョン・レノンは大の親日家だった John Lennon was a real *Japanophile*. (➤ 発音は /dʒəpǽnoʊfàɪl/). →親-, 知日家.

1 **しんにゅう 侵入** (an) invasion 一動 **侵入する** invade +目 (領土などに) ; break into (家などに) ; trespass 《on》 (土地などに) ▶1979年, ソビエト軍はアフガニスタンに侵入した Soviet troops *invaded* Afghanistan in 1979. ‖ 泥棒はこの窓から侵入した The burglar *broke into* the house through this window. ‖ スパイはこっそりその国に侵入した The spy *sneaked into* the country. (➤ sneak into は「こっそり忍び込む」) ‖ すぐに出ていけ. きみは立入禁止区域に不法侵入している Get out of here immediately! You*'re trespassing*.

2 **しんにゅう 進入** ▶電車が1, 2番線ホームに同時に進入してきた At the same time the trains *came in* on Track One and Track Two. ‖ 《標識》進入禁止 Do Not Enter ／No Entry.

しんにゅう- 新入- ▶彼女は S 大学の新入生です She is *a new student* [*a freshman*] at S University. ‖ ことしの新入社員はいい人物ぞろいだ This year's *new employees* are all good people. (● 英語では「新入社員」はふつう freshman とは言わず, この場合のように new employee と言ったり, someone new to the company [firm], someone who joined the company [firm] と言ったりすることが多い).

1 **しんにん 信任** confidence ▶彼は課長の信任を得ている His section chief has *confidence* in him. ／He is trusted by his section chief. ‖ 政府の信任投票が行われることになるだろう *A vote of confidence* in the Government will be taken.

‖**信任状** credentials.

☞ **不信任** (→見出語)

2 **しんにん 新任** ▶新任の挨拶を述べる make *an inaugural address* (➤ inaugural は「就任の」) ‖ 私たちの新任の先生は若い女性だ Our *new* teacher is a young woman.

1 **しんねん 新年** a new year (新しい年) ; the New Year (特定の年の) ▶新年を北アルプスで迎える welcome *the New Year* in the North Alps ‖ 新年おめでとう (*A*) *Happy New Year*.

[語法] (1) 口で言う場合には A を省略するのがふつう. (2) この言い方はクリスマス終了後の年末から元日まで用いることができるが, クリスマスカードを送るときに添えるのなら, I wish you a Merry Christmas and a Happy New Year. の形にするのがふつう. (3) 言われたほうは, Same [The same] to you. のように答える.

▶彼は新年早々交通事故に遭った He got involved in a traffic accident *right after the start of the New Year*. ‖ 毎年のように彼は同じ新年の抱負を決め, 松の内が明ける前にそれを破る Every year he makes the same *New Year's resolutions* and breaks them before the New Year week ends. ‖ 家族全員そろって新年を迎えた Our whole family *greeted the New Year* together.

‖**新年会** a New Year's party.

2 **しんねん 信念** (a) belief ; (a) faith (全幅の信頼 ; 宗教的信念を指すことが多い) ; (a) conviction (確信) ▶彼は努力はやがて報われるという固い信念をもっている He has a firm *belief* that (his) efforts will be rewarded. ‖ 神は存在するという彼の信念が最近ぐらついてきた His *faith* in the existence of God has been shaken recently. ‖ おじは死ぬまで信念を貫いた [曲げなかった] My uncle stuck to his *convictions* until (the day) he died.

しんのう 親王 an Imperial prince

‖**内親王** an Imperial princess.

シンパ a (communist) sympathizer.

しんぱい 心配 1 【不安, 悩み】 worry (無用な心配, 心痛) ; concern (人や事柄に対する (しばしば, 多くの人が寄せる) 関心 ; 通例, worry ほど直接的あるいは深刻でない) ; anxiety (悪い結果を予想してもつ (頭から離れない) 不安感) 一動 **心配する** worry 《about》 ; be worried 《about》 ; be concerned 《about》 ; be anxious 《about》 ▶心配のあまり病気になる get sick from *worry* [*anxiety*] ‖ 私たちのいちばんの心配は息子の病気です Our *biggest worry* [*concern* ／*anxiety*] is our son's disease. ‖ 心配するな *Don't worry*.

> 【文型】
> **人・物(A)のことを心配する**
> worry about A
> be worried about A
> be concerned about A
> be anxious about A

《解説》 (1)**worry about** はふつう無用な心配をすることで,「心配するな」と否定の形で用いることが多い.
(2)**be worried about** は困ったことが起こりうると予測して気をもむこと. 何とか手を打たなければと思うことが多い.
(3)**be concerned about** は困ったことが起こりうるかもしれないと, その問題に対して「関心を持つ」あるいは「懸念を抱く」ことで, 原因や根拠が **be worried about** ほど明確でない分, 何とか対処しなければ, という心配の度合いは **be worried about** ほど強くはない.
(4)**be anxious about** は不安を持つこと, 気がかりでならないこと.

▶そんなささいなことを**心配するな** *Don't worry* [*fret*] *about* such small things. (➤ fret はささいなことで「思い悩む」) ‖ 人の心配よりも**自分の心配をしろ** You should *worry about yourself* rather than (*worry about*) others. ‖ あすの天気が**心配だ** I'*m worried about* tomorrow's weather. ‖ 私のこと**心配してくれてありがとう** Thanks for *worrying* [*being concerned*] *about* me. ‖ 娘の将来が**心配です** We *are concerned about* our *daughter's future*. (➤例えば現在の社会状況などから将来を思っていう場合. しかし, 娘が今非行や麻薬に関わっているなど, 重大な問題を抱えている親ならば, We are worried about ... という可能性がある) ‖ 子供たちの将来は**心配していません** I do*n't worry about* our children's future. (➤プラス思考の親の場合) / *I'm not worried about* our children's future. (➤子供の能力などに自信をもつ親の場合) ‖ 祖母の容態が**心配で心配で一睡もできなかった** I *was so worried about* my grandmother's condition that I couldn't get a wink of sleep. ‖ 多くの人が失業するのではないかと**心配している** A lot of people *are anxious about* losing their jobs.
▶「医者を呼びましょうか」と彼女は**心配そうに言った** She said *anxiously*, "Shall I call a doctor ?" ‖ そっちで地震が起きたというニュースを聞いて, **心配になって電話したんだよ** I *was worried* when I heard that an earthquake hit your city. That's why I called you.

【文型】
～ではないかと心配する
be worried [**concerned**] (**that**) S + V

▶日本では多くの人が近い将来また大地震が来るのではと**心配しています** Many people in Japan *are concerned that* another severe earthquake will hit in the near future. (➤根拠がより明確で心配がさらに強い場合は be worried) ‖ 高校時代はずる休みをして親に大変**心配をかけた** I *caused a lot of worry* for my parents in my high school days by playing hooky.
✉ **私はやっと健康を取り戻しました. どうか心配しないでください** I am back on my feet at last [I am finally recovered], so *there is no need for you to worry*. ➤ on one's feet は「(病後に)起き上がれるほど元気になった」の意.
▶ぐれた息子が**心配の種**だ My unruly son is *a constant worry* [*a headache*]. ‖ 何か**心配事**がおありですか Is there *something on your mind* ? / Do you have *anything on your mind* ? (➤ともに「心にかかっていること」の意) ‖ きみは**心配性**だね You are *a worrywart*, aren't you ?
2【**気遣い, 世話**】▶**どうぞご心配なく** Please *don't bother*. ‖ **いろいろとご心配をいただき, ありがとうございました** Thank you *for everything*. (➤「心配」は訳出不要).

じんぱい 塵肺《医学》**pneumoconiosis** /nù:moʊkòʊnióʊsəs/.

しんぱく 心拍(数) a **heartbeat** ▶熱いお湯につかると**心拍数が上がる** When you soak in a hot bath, your *heart beats* faster [your *heart rate* goes up].

しんばつ 神罰 ▶悪事ばかり続けていると, やつには今に**神罰が下るよ** If that guy continues doing evil deeds, *divine punishment* will surely fall on him [he will surely incur *divine punishment*].

しんぱつじしん 深発地震 a **deep-focus earthquake.**

シンバル **cymbals**(➤通例複数形で用いる) ▶**シンバルを鳴らす** strike *cymbals* / clash *cymbals* (together).

1**しんぱん 審判** **1**【**競技の**】▶松永氏が選手権試合の**審判を務めた** Mr. Matsunaga *umpired* [*acted as umpire* in] the championship game. ‖ 誰がこの試合の**審判をするのですか** Who is going to *referee* this game ?
‖**審判員** an umpire /ʌ́mpaɪəʳ/ (野球・テニス・バドミントンなどの) ; a referee /rèfərí:/ (ボクシング・サッカー・ラグビーなどの) ; a judge(競技・討論会などの).
2【**裁き**】**judgment** ▶(キリスト教の)**最後の審判** *the Last Judgment*.

2**しんぱん 侵犯** (an) **invasion**(侵入) ; (an) **violation**(侵害) **—動 侵犯する** **invade** +㊐, **violate** +㊐ ▶国籍不明の偵察機がわが国の領空を**侵犯した** A reconnaissance plane of unknown nationality *invaded* [*violated*] Japan's airspace.

3**しんぱん 信販** a **credit sale** ▶**信販会社** a *credit* company.

しんび 審美的な **aesthetic** /esθétɪk ‖ i:s-/ ▶彼女は**審美眼がある** She has an *eye for beauty*. / She has *discriminating taste*.

しんぴ 神秘 (a) **mystery** ▶深海の**神秘を探る** investigate the *mysteries* of the deep sea ‖ スティーヴン・ホーキングは**宇宙の神秘**を解き明かそうとしている Stephen Hawking has been trying to unravel *the mysteries of the universe*. ‖ モナリザの笑みは**神秘的だ** Mona Lisa's smile is *mysterious*.

しんぴょうせい 信憑性 **credibility** ▶この話は**信ぴょう性がある** This is a *reliable* account. ‖ その証拠はすべて**信ぴょう性を欠いている** All the evidence lacks *credibility*.

しんぴん 新品 a **new article** ▶この自転車, **ぴかぴかの新品だぞ** This is a *brand-new* bike. ‖ このカメラは**新品同様だ** This camera is *as good as new*. / This camera is *in near mint condition*. (➤ in mint condition は「(メダルなどが)作りたての」が原義).

1**しんぷ 神父** a **priest, Father**(➤ (1)カトリック・ギリシャ正教・ロシア正教での呼び名. (2)後者は敬称や呼びかけに用いる) →牧師 ▶彼は**神父になった** He was ordained *a priest*. ‖ **ブラウン神父** *Father* Brown ‖ はい, **神父さま** Yes, *Father*.

2**しんぷ 新婦** a **bride** ▶**新婦**がお色直しのため退場した The *bride* left the banquet hall to change into a different dress.

3**しんぷ 新譜** a **new release.**

ジンフィズ a **gin fizz.**

しんぷう 新風 ▶その新人はジャイアンツに**新風を吹き込んだ** The rookie *has invigorated* the Giants' play. (➤ invigorate は「…に活力を与える」の意).

シンフォニー a **symphony**(交響曲) ▶ベートーベンの第

5番のシンフォニーを演奏する play Beethoven's Fifth *Symphony*.

[1]**しんぷく 心服** ▶多くの学生がY教授に心服している Many students *hold* Professor Y *in high esteem*.

[2]**しんぷく 振幅**《電気学》**amplitude** ▶振幅の大きな揺れ a quake with big *amplitude*.

しんふぜん 心不全 heart [cardiac] failure ▶心不全で死ぬ die of *heart failure*.

じんふぜん 腎不全 kidney failure.

しんぶつ 神仏 Shintoism and Buddhism(神道と仏教) ▶伝統を重んずる日本の家庭では神仏が同居しており, 仏壇の前で先祖に祈り, 神棚の前で家族の無病息災を祈る Most Japanese families that value tradition have both *Shinto and Buddhist altars*. They pray for their ancestors before the Buddhist altar and pray for their family's health and safety before the Shinto altar.

じんぶつ 人物 1【人】a person ▶謎の人物 a mysterious *person* ‖ 歴史上の人物 a historical *figure* [*character*] ‖ あの子は将来ひとかどの人物になるでしょう He will grow up to be *an important person* [to be *somebody*]. ‖**人物画** a portrait ‖**重要人物** an important person.

2【人格, 人柄】(a) **personality**(人柄, 個性) ; **character**(道徳的に見た性格) ▶わが社では採用にあたっては学歴よりも人物を重視します When hiring, we put more emphasis on *personality* [*character*] than on educational background. ‖ 彼は人物が立派だから同僚に好かれる He is such a fine *person* that all his colleagues like him. ‖ 彼は人物はいいけれど, どうも優柔不断だね He is a good *individual*, but is very indecisive. ‖ 彼の人物は保証するよ I can vouch for his *character*. (➤ vouch /vaʊtʃ/ for で「…を保証する」).

☛ **好人物** (→見出語)

シンプル simple ▶シンプルなデザインの時計 a *simply* designed watch / a watch of *simple* design ‖ 彼女はそのドレスのシンプルなところが気に入った She liked the *simplicity* of the dress.

しんぶん 新聞 a newspaper, a paper ▶きょうの新聞のトップ記事は何ですか What's the lead (ing) story in *today's newspaper*? / What's the front page news in *today's newspaper*? (➤ 前者は第1面のトップ記事1つを指し, 後者は1つあるいは複数を指す) ‖ ベルリンフィルが日本へ来るって新聞に出てたよ I read *in the paper* that the Berlin Philharmonic Orchestra is coming to Japan. ‖ 姉はピアノのコンクールで優勝して新聞に載った My sister won the piano competition and *got in the newspaper*. ‖ そのニュースは新聞にでかでかと出た The news *made the headlines*. ‖ 彼はいつも新聞を見ながら朝食をとる He usually has breakfast *over the morning paper*. ‖ **対話**「新聞は何を取っていますか」「デイリー・ジャパンです」"What *newspaper* do you take [read] ?" "The Daily Japan." (➤ 新聞名には the がつくものが多いがつかないものもある).

▶新聞記事にも時に誤りがある Sometimes there are mistakes in *newspaper articles*. ‖ 児童虐待事件がしばしば新聞種になる Child abuse cases *are* often *reported in the newspapers*. ‖ スキャンダルは格好の新聞種になった The scandal became *fodder for the newspaper*. ‖ 高校時代に学校新聞の編集長をしました I was the editor-in-chief of *the school newspaper* when I was a high school student. ‖**新聞売り場** a newsstand ‖**新聞記者** a (newspaper) reporter, a journalist ‖**新聞紙** newspaper ‖**新聞社** a newspaper company ‖**新聞配達** newspaper delivery ‖**新聞配達人** a newspaper delivery person(➤ person の代わりに boy, woman など, 具体的な年代・性別を表す語を用いることも多い) ‖**新聞販売店** a newspaper shop, a newspaper sales agency ‖**英字新聞** an English (language) newspaper ‖**スポーツ新聞** a sports paper.

じんぶんかがく 人文科学 the humanities

‖**人文科学部[科]** the school [department] of the humanities.

じんぶんしゅぎ 人文主義 humanism.

しんべい 親米の pro-American

‖**親米家** a pro-American ‖**親米感情** pro-American sentiments ‖**親米政策** a pro-American policy.

しんぺん 身辺 ▶結婚する前にきみはまず身辺を整理すべきだ The first thing you must do before you get married is to *put your affairs in order*. (➤ affairs は「身辺の諸事」) ‖ 警察はその要人の身辺を警護した The police *placed* the VIP *under protective guard*.

しんぽ 進歩 progress /prá:grəs/ ; an **advance**(向上) ; **improvement**(上達) ―**動** **進歩する progress** /prəgrés/, **advance** ; **make progress**(➤ 主に人を主語にして) ▶科学技術の進歩 technological *progress* ‖ 科学が進歩するにつれて生活が便利になる The more science *progresses*, the more convenient our life becomes. ‖ 世の中が進歩するほど, 心のゆとりは失われていくようだ The more society *advances*, the less mental elbowroom [latitude] we have. (➤ elbowroom は「活動できる自由」の意) ‖ 私の英語は少しも進歩していない My English *has shown no improvement*. ‖ 彼女はこの1年でピアノが飛躍的に進歩した She *has made tremendous progress* in playing the piano. ‖ 彼は何年間も勉強したにもかかわらずドイツ語ではあまり進歩がない Despite his many years of study, he *hasn't made much progress* in German. ‖ 校長先生は高校教育について進歩的な考えをもっている The principal has *progressive* [*advanced*] ideas about high school education.

-しんぽう -進法 ▶**10進法** the decimal system / *the base*-ten *system* / *base* 10 ‖**2進法** the binary system / *the base*-two *system* / *base* 2 《参考》基本となる数 x を使って the base-x system または base x とする方法が簡便.

[1]**しんぼう 辛抱 patience**(長期間耐えること) ; **perseverance**(弱音を吐かずにやり抜くこと) ―**動** **辛抱する be patient, persevere** ▶もう少しの辛抱だ Just a little more *patience*. / We should *hold on* a little longer. (➤ hold on は「持ちこたえる, 頑張る」) ‖ 何事にせよ, やり遂げるには辛抱がいる To accomplish anything at all, you must have *perseverance*. ‖ 会社の待遇の悪さにはもうこれ以上辛抱できない I can no longer *stand* [*put up with*] the poor treatment I'm getting from management.

☛ **辛抱強い** (→見出語)

[2]**しんぼう 信望 popularity**(人望) ; **confidence**(信用) ▶信望の厚い人 a person of wide *popularity* ‖ 彼は部下の信望が厚い He *enjoys the confidence* of his staff.

[3]**しんぼう 心棒** an **axle**(車軸).

[4]**しんぼう 心房**《解剖学》an **atrium** /éɪtriəm/ [複 a-

triums, atria] ▶右[左]心房 the right [left] *atrium*.

しんぽう 信奉する embrace +目; believe《in》(…の価値を信じる) ▶鈴木先生はカントの信奉者だ Mr. Suzuki is *a follower* of [*a believer* in] Kant. / Mr. Suzuki embraces Kantism. ‖ 兄は菜食主義の信奉者だ My brother *believes in* vegetarianism. / My brother is a (dedicated) vegetarian.

じんぼう 人望 popularity ▶人望を得る[失う] win [lose] one's *popularity* ‖ 俊夫君はクラスでとても人望がある Toshio *enjoys* much *popularity among* [*is* very *popular with*] the students in the class. ‖ 彼女は人望がない *No one likes* her.

しんぼうづよい 辛抱強い patient; persevering (目標達成のための粘り強い) ▶辛抱強い父親 a *patient* father ‖ 辛抱強いところが彼女の取り柄だ Her best quality is her *patience*. ‖ 父はしょっちゅう辛抱強く頑張って勉強せよと言う My father often tells me to keep at my studies *with perseverance* [*patience*]. ‖ 一行は救援隊の到着を辛抱強く待った They *patiently* waited for the arrival of the rescue party.

しんぼく 親睦 friendship ▶私たちのクラブでは会員の親睦を深めるためにハイキングを計画している We are planning a hike to promote (*mutual*) *friendship* among the members of our club. 《参考》社員・職員が相互の親睦を図ったり, 祝い金・弔意金・見舞い金などを出したりする基金を welfare fund と呼ぶ.

‖ **親睦パーティー** a party, 《インフォーマル》 a get-together.

シンポジウム a symposium /sɪmpóʊziəm/ ▶地球温暖化に関する国際シンポジウムが先月東京で開かれた The *international symposium* on global warming was held in Tokyo last month.

シンボル a symbol

> **危ないカタカナ語✹ シンボル**
> 日本語の「シンボル」は英語の symbol と一致するが, 選挙などの「シンボルバッジ」は campaign button, 「シンボルカラー」は学校のものであれば school color, 候補者のものは candidate's color のように具体的に表現する. 「シンボルマーク」は symbol mark でなく, 単に symbol とするか, mark, emblem, logo, trademark などの語を使う.

▶オリーブの枝は平和のシンボルである The olive branch is the *symbol* [*emblem*] of peace. / The olive branch is symbolic of [symbolizes] peace.

しんまい 新米 a novice /nɑ́ːvəs/, a new [young] hand, a beginner (人) ▶新米教師 a *novice* teacher ‖ 私はこの仕事は全くの新米です I am quite *a new* [*young*] *hand* at this job. / I am very *new* to this job.

‖ **新米記者** a cub (reporter).

じんましん hives, (a) nettle rash, urticaria /ə̀ːṭəkéəriə/ (➤ 最後の語は医学用語) ▶サバを食べたら体中にじんましんが出ちゃったよ I got *hives* [(*a*) *nettle rash*] over my whole body from eating mackerel.

[1]**しんみ 親身** ▶上司は私が困っているとき親身に相談に乗ってくれた My supervisor listened *warmly* [*kindly*] to my problems and gave me some advice when I was in trouble.

[2]**しんみ 新味** originality (斬新さ); novelty (目新しさ); freshness (新鮮み) ▶あのクイズ番組は新味に欠ける That quiz show is lacking in *originality* [*novelty* / *freshness*].

しんみつ 親密な close /kloʊs/, intimate /ɪ́nṭəmət/ (➤ 後者は特に性的な関係があることを暗示する) ⇀親しい ▶日米間の親密な関係 the *close* relationship between Japan and the U.S. ‖ 2人は次第に親密な仲になった The two gradually became *closer* [more *intimate*] with each other. ‖ 彼らの交際は日に日に親密の度を加えていった Their friendship *grew in intimacy* day by day. / They *grew closer* each day.

じんみゃく 人脈 a human network; personal connections [relationship] (人間関係) ▶出身校の人脈を頼りに求職活動をする engage in a search for employment making use of *connections* from one's alma mater ‖ その実業家は政界との人脈があるらしい That businessman is said to have *personal connections* in the political world [have political *connections*]. (➤ 後者がふつうの言い方).

しんみょう 神妙 ▶神妙な顔つきをする assume a *grave* [*serious*] expression ‖ 生徒たちは担任の先生の話を神妙に聞いた The students listened to their homeroom [class] teacher *in a quiet and obedient manner*.

しんみり ▶黒沢先生のお別れの挨拶を聞いてみんなしんみりしてしまった Mr. Kurosawa's words of farewell *made* every student *sad* [*saddened* all the students].

しんみん 臣民 a subject ▶イギリス[英国]臣民 a British *subject*.

じんみん 人民 the people ▶「人民の, 人民による, 人民のための政治」とはリンカーンの有名なことばだ "*Government of the people*, *by the people*, *and for the people*" are Lincoln's famous words.

‖ **人民戦線** the people's [the popular] front.

しんめ 新芽 a new bud ▶バラの新芽が出てきた The roses *are budding* (*out*).

しんめい 身命 ▶若き兵士たちは国を守るために身命を賭して戦った Young soldiers fought *at the risk of their lives* to protect their country.

[1]**じんめい 人命** (a) life, (a) human life (➤ 抽象的な「生命」の意では Ⓤ 扱い, 個々の「人命」の意では Ⓒ 扱い) ▶その飛行機事故で500人以上の人命が失われた That plane crash *claimed* more than 500 *lives*. (➤ claim は「(事故などが人命を)奪う」) ‖ その犬は人命救助で表彰された The dog was honored for *saving a* (*human*) *life*. ‖ 消火活動においては人命第一が基本です Saving *human life* [*lives*] is the first [most important] thing in firefighting.

[2]**じんめい 人名** the name of a person, a person's name

‖ **人名辞典** a biographical dictionary ‖ **人名簿** a list of names, a directory /dəréktəri/.

しんもつ 進物 a gift ▶これを進物用に包んでいただけませんか Could you please wrap this *as a gift*? / Could you please *gift-wrap* this? (➤ gift-wrap は「進物用に包装する」の意の動詞).

じんもん 尋問 (an) interrogation; questioning (質問すること) 一動 **尋問する** interrogate +目, question +目 ▶彼は警察に厳しく尋問された He *was interrogated* [*was grilled*] by the police. ‖ 巡回中のその警官は1人の若者を不審尋問した That police officer on patrol *questioned* a young man. ‖ 証人たちは次々に反対尋問を受けた The witnesses *were cross-examined* one after another.

‖ **誘導尋問** a leading question.

しんや 深夜 (the) **dead of night**（➤ midnight は「夜中の12時」）▶彼は深夜に私を訪ねてきた He came to see me *late at night* [*in the dead of night*]. ‖この店は深夜まで開いている This store is open *till late at night*. ‖救出作業は深夜まで続けられた Rescue attempts went on *far into the night*.

‖**深夜番組** a late-night show ‖**深夜放送** midnight broadcasting ; a late-night radio [TV] program ‖**深夜料金** a late-night rate [charge].

しんゆう 親友 a **good** [**close**] **friend** ;《インフォーマル》a **pal**, a **buddy**, a **chum**（男の）（➤ an intimate friend は異性間では性的関係を暗示するので使わないほうが無難）▶田村君はぼくの親友だ Tamura is one of my *best friends*. ‖私たちはすぐ親友になった We soon *became great friends*. ‖彼は私の無二の親友だ He is my (*very*) *best* [*closest*] *friend*.

しんよう 信用

📖 訳語メニュー
信用 →trust, confidence **1**
良い評判 →credit **2**

1【信頼，信任】**trust, confidence**（➤ 前者には信用して頼るという含みがある）**一動 信用する**（人を）**trust** +目
▶その先生は学生の信用を得ている The teacher has won [earned] his students' *trust* [*confidence*]. ‖私は政治家を信用しない I *don't trust* politicians. ‖彼女は信用できる人だ She is *trustworthy*. ‖うちの子供たちはぼくの運転を信用していない My children don't *trust* the way I drive. ‖約束を破ってばかりいると信用されなくなるよ If you break your word so often, you won't *be trusted*.

2【良い評判】**reputation, credit**（➤ 後者は主にビジネス関係の信用状態をいう）▶そんなごまかしをすれば店の信用に関わる If we try a trick like that, it will *jeopardize our reputation*.（➤「評判を危険にさらすことになる」の意）‖そのスキャンダルで彼は世間の信用を失った The scandal *discredited* him with the public.

3【信じること】**一動 信用する**（ことばを）**believe** (+目) ▶彼女は人の言うことをすぐ信用する She *believes* others (*too*) *easily*. ／She *is gullible*. ‖わかったよ. 信用するよ OK. I *believe* you.

‖**信用格付け** a credit rating ‖**信用金庫** a credit bank（➤ 日本では Shinkin Bank を用いている）‖**信用組合** a credit union [association].

じんよう 陣容 a **lineup**（顔ぶれ）▶そのチームは陣容を一新した That team changed its *lineup* completely. ‖わが社では重役の陣容立て直しが行われた The executive staff *was reorganized* in our company.

しんようじゅ 針葉樹 a **needleleaf** [**coniferous**] **tree**（➤ coniferous /kounífərəs/ は「球果[松かさ]をつける」), a **conifer** ▶見渡す限りの針葉樹林だ There are *coniferous trees* [*Conifer trees* spread out] as far as the eye can see.

しんらい 信頼 **trust 一動 信頼する trust** +目 ; **rely** 《**on**》（頼りにする）▶信頼できる情報 *reliable* information ‖ぼくはみんなの信頼に応えることができなかった I failed to live up to the *trust* everyone had placed in me. ‖両親の信頼を裏切るようなことはできない I can't betray my parents' *trust*. ‖彼女は約束は必ず守るので友人たちから信頼されている Since she always keeps her promise(s), she *is trusted* by her friends. ‖上司は私を信頼して仕事を任せてくれた My boss *put* (his [her]) *trust in* me and [*Trusting* me, my boss] left the task entirely in my hands. ‖仕事ぶりから見て彼女は信頼できる人に違いない Judging from how she does her work, she must be a *reliable* [*dependable*] person. ‖論文の盗用で大学教授としての彼の信頼性は傷ついた His plagiarism of another person's thesis has damaged his *credibility* as a university professor.

しんらつ 辛辣な **severe** /sɪvíəʳ/（厳しい）; **sharp**（鋭い）; **bitter**（痛烈な）▶辛辣な批評 *severe* [*sharp*] criticism ‖その批評家は辛辣なことを言うので有名だ That critic is known for his *sharp* [*severe* ／ *biting*] remarks. ‖この芝居は現代の世相を辛辣に風刺したものである This play is a *bitter* [*keen*] satire on present society.

しんらばんしょう 森羅万象 **all natural phenomena** /fənɑ́:mənə/.

[1] **しんり 心理** one's **state of mind**（心の状態）; **psychology** /saɪkɑ́:lədʒi/（精神状態, 気分）; one's **mentality**（ものの見方, 精神構造）▶どうして彼はこんな手紙をよこしたんだろう. 彼の心理が全くわからない Why did he send me such a letter ? I can't understand his *state of mind* at all. ‖この小説は思春期の若者の心理を見事に描写している This novel superbly describes the *psychology* [*mentality*] of adolescents. ‖彼は人の心理（＝心）を読むのがうまい He's good at reading other people's *thoughts* [*minds*]. ／He's a good *mind* reader. ‖兄は女の子のデリケートな心理を全然理解していない My (older) brother has no understanding of a girl's delicate *feelings*. ‖母が寝室が真っ暗でないと眠れないというのは心理的なもののようだ My mother's idea that she cannot sleep unless her bedroom is completely dark seems to be *psychological* [*all in her head*]. ‖図書館の壁を真っ赤にするとどんな心理的影響があるだろうか I wonder what the *psychological effect* of painting the library walls bright red would be.

‖**心理学** psychology ‖**心理学者** a psychologist ‖**心理小説** a psychological novel ‖**心理療法**[セラピー] psychotherapy ‖**心理療法士**[セラピスト] psychotherapist ‖**群集心理** mob [mass] psychology.

[2] **しんり 真理** (a) **truth** ▶真理を探究する search for *truth* ‖きみの言うことにも一面の真理はある There is some [There is an element of] *truth* in what you say.

[3] **しんり 審理** (a) **trial**（裁判）; (an) **examination**（取り調べ）**一動 審理する try** +目, **examine** +目 ▶その事件は現在審理中です The case is now *on trial* [*under examination*]. ／The case *is being tried* [*heard*] now.

じんりきしゃ 人力車 a **rickshaw** /ríkʃɔ:/（➤ 日本語から）▶人力車に乗る ride a *rickshaw*.

しんりゃく 侵略 (an) **invasion**（侵入）; (an) **aggression**（争いなどを仕掛けること）**一動 侵略する invade** +目

‖**侵略者** an invader, an aggressor ‖**侵略戦争** a war of aggression ; an aggressive war.

しんりょう 診療 (a) **medical treatment** ; **medical care**
‖**診療時間** office hours ‖**診療所** a clinic.

しんりょく 新緑 **fresh green leaves, fresh greenery**, 《文》**fresh verdure** /vɔ́:ʳdʒəʳ/ ▶6月の信州は新緑が美しい Shinshu in June is beautiful with *fresh greenery*. ‖奈良は新緑の頃が特にいい Nara is especially beautiful in *the season of fresh green leaves*.

✉ **新緑が目にしみる５月になりました** May has arrived *with its piercingly green leaves*.

[1]**じんりょく 人力** **human power** ▶天災は人力ではいかんともしがたい Natural disasters *are beyond human control*.

‖**人力飛行** (a) human-powered flight.

[2]**じんりょく 尽力** **assistance**, **help**(人のために何かをすること；前者は堅い語)；(an) **effort**(困難なことを実現するための努力) ▶ご尽力に感謝いたします Thank you very much for your *assistance* [*help*]. ‖彼らはその紛争の円満解決のためにできるだけ**尽力する**と約束した They promised to *make* every possible *effort* for a peaceful settlement of the dispute.

しんりん 森林 a **forest**, **woods**(➤後者は通例前者より小さく,《米》では単数扱い) ⇀森 ▶深い森林 a deep [thick] *forest* ／ deep *woods* ‖**森林浴**に出かける go for *a walk in the woods* ／go and *bask in the woods* ‖日本は**森林**が国土の約67パーセントを占めている In Japan, *forests* [*woodlands*] cover about 67 percent of the (whole) country.

‖**森林資源** forest resources ‖**森林地帯** a forest area, a wooded country ‖**森林破壊** the destruction of forests, deforestation.

[1]**しんるい 親類** a **relative**, a **relation** (➤前者のほうがふつう) ▶彼女は私の遠い**親類**です She's a distant *relative* of mine. ‖ぼくは彼女とは**親類です** I'*m related to* her. ／She and I *are related*. ‖その夜, 彼の**親類縁者**が皆集まった That night all of his *friends and relatives* got together. ‖私のおじさんは**親類付き合いがよい**[**悪い**] My uncle *keeps* [*doesn't keep*] *in good contact with his relatives*. (➤ in good contact の代わりに in touch も使える) ‖自慢じゃないが, 私は知事と**親類付き合い**(＝親類同様の付き合い)をしているんだ I don't mean to boast, but I'*m almost like family to* [*almost on family terms with*] the governor.

[2]**しんるい 進塁** ▶大谷はヒットで出塁, バントとエラーで三塁に**進塁した** Ohtani singled and *advanced* [*moved*] *to* third on a bunt and an error.

じんるい 人類 **humanity**, **humankind**, **the human race**, **mankind**(➤最後の mankind は man- が男性を連想させるので, 最近では使用を避ける傾向がある) ⇀人間 ▶**人類**の自由, 繁栄, 福祉は誰もが切望していることだ Everyone earnestly hopes for the freedom, prosperity, and welfare of *humanity* [*humankind*]. ‖核戦争が現実に起これば**人類**は滅亡してしまうかもしれない If a nuclear war really breaks out, the entire *human race* may perish. ‖**人類**(＝ヒト)の起源はいつごろまで遡れますか When did *Homo sapiens* originate?

‖**人類学** anthropology /æ̀nθrəpɑ́ːlədʒi/ ‖**人類学者** an anthropologist ‖**文化人類学** cultural anthropology.

しんれい 心霊 ‖**心霊現象** a psychic /sáɪkɪk/ phenomenon [複 phenomena] ‖**心霊写真** a psychic picture.

[1]**しんろ 進路** a **course**(自然な流れに沿った)；a **way**(抽象的な意味での)；a **path**(細い道) ▶鹿児島地方は台風10号の**進路**に当たっている The Kagoshima area is right in the *course* of Typhoon No. 10.

▶人生の**進路**を決める decide one's *course* [*future direction*] in life ‖人生の**進路**を誤る take the wrong *course* in life ‖よく考えて**進路の選択**を誤らないようにしなさい Think hard and try to make *the* right *choice about what to do in the future*. ‖もう９月だというのに私はまだ**卒業後の進路**が決まらない Though it is already September, I haven't decided yet *what to do after graduation*. (➤「卒業後何をするか」と考える) ‖私の学校では３人の先生が生徒の**進路指導**に当たっている In our school, three teachers assist students in *planning for their futures* [provide *guidance counseling* to students].

[2]**しんろ 針路** a **course** ▶船は**針路**を北々西に取っている The ship is sailing [heading] NNW. ‖飛行機は正しい**針路**についている[から外れている] The plane is on [off] its right *course*.

[1]**しんろう 心労** (a) **worry** ▶息子のことで**心労**が絶えない My son is a constant source of *worry* to me. ‖母は**心労**が重なって病気になった My mother *worried so much* that she became ill.

[2]**しんろう 新郎** a **bridegroom** ▶仲人が**新郎**新婦の経歴を紹介した The matchmaker outlined the *bride and bridegroom*'s background.

しんわ 神話 a **myth** /mɪθ/ (個々の)；**mythology** (総称) ▶世界に天地創造にまつわる**神話**はたくさんある There are many creation *myths* in the world.

▶《比喩的》女性より男性のほうが運転がうまいというのは**神話**だ The idea that men are better drivers than women is *a myth*. ‖その事故で原発の安全**神話**は崩壊した The accident destroyed the *myth* that nuclear power plants are safe.

‖**ギリシャ**[**ローマ**]**神話** the Greek [Roman] myths；Greek [Roman] mythology ‖**不敗神話** the myth of one's invincibility.

じんわり **slowly**(ゆっくりと)；**lightly**(軽く)；**gradually**(徐々に) ▶運動をしたら**じんわり**汗が出てきた The exercise caused me to perspire *lightly*. ‖その薬は**じんわり**と胃に作用する The medicine affects the stomach *gradually*.

す・ス

[1]す 巣 a **nest**(鳥の)；a **(cob)web**（クモの）；a **(honey) comb** /koʊm/ (ハチの) ▶ツバメがせっせと巣を作っている Swallows are busy building their *nests*. ‖ 朱鷺(とき)が先週から巣ごもりを始めた A Japanese crested ibis started *nesting* last week.
▶《比喩的》ここが私たち二人の愛の巣だ This is our *loving home*. (love nest と直訳すると「(愛人・不倫関係にある者の)愛の巣」の意になるのがふつう) ‖ 都会の繁華街は犯罪の巣になる危険がある The entertainment district of a big city is at risk of becoming *a hotbed of crime*.

[2]す 酢 **vinegar** /vínɪgəʳ/ ▶キャベツの酢漬け cabbage *pickled in vinegar* ‖ このちらしずしは酢が効いていない This *chirashi-zushi is not* well *vinegared*. ‖ サバを酢で締める *firm up* a mackerel fillet *by marinating* it *in vinegar*.
‖酢だこ vinegared octopus ‖ 米酢 rice vinegar.

[3]す 鬆 a **pore** /pɔːʳ/ (気孔) ▶この大根, すが入っている This daikon is *porous*. (➤ porous は「小さな穴の多い」の意).

[4]す 素 ▶かっこつけることなく素の自分を出していきたい I always want to show my *true* self [the *real* me] without trying to impress people [trying to look good].

ず 図 a **drawing**(絵図)；a **diagram**(図形)；a **figure** /fígjəʳ/ (図形, 絵図)；a **chart** (図表)；an **illustration** (挿し絵) ▶惑星の位置を図に描きなさい *Make a drawing of* the planets and their positions. ‖ 彼はその理論を図を描いて説明した He *drew diagrams* to explain the theory. ／He *illustrated* the theory *with diagrams*. ‖ 第 6 図と比較 [を参照] せよ Cf. *fig*.6. (➤ fig. は figure の略).
▶《慣用表現》彼の計画は図に当たった His plan *worked well* [*hit the mark*]. ‖ あいつはおだてるとすぐ図に乗る He *gets swell-headed* [*It goes to his head*] when he is flattered. ‖ 図に乗ってやり過ぎると失敗するよ If you *push your luck too far*, you'll end up failing. ‖案内図 a guide, a sightseeing map (➤ 後者は特に観光用の) ‖ 設計図 a plan ‖ 天気図 a weather map.

すあし 素足 **bare feet** ▶祖父は真冬でも素足で通している My grandfather *goes barefoot*, even in the middle of winter. (➤ この barefoot は「素足で」の意の副詞) ‖ 彼女は素足にスニーカーを履いていた She was wearing sneakers *without socks*.

すあな 巣穴 a **burrow**, a **hole** ▶ウサギの巣穴 a rabbit *burrow* [*hole*].

ずあん 図案 a **design** ▶花柄の図案 a floral *design*.

[1]すい 粋 **the essence**(最も重要なもの)；**the best (part)** (最良の部分) ▶その美術展は韓国の文化の粋を集めたものである The art exhibition displays [showcases] *the essence* of Korean culture. ‖ H-2Aロケットは科学技術の粋を集めて作られている The H-ⅡA rocket is an embodiment of *the best* that science and technology have to offer. (➤ embodiment は「具体化されたもの」).

[2]すい 酸い **sour** /sáʊəʳ/ →酸っぱい ▶彼は人生の酸いも甘いもかみ分けた人だ He has tasted *both the bitterness and sweetness* of life.

ずい 髄 **marrow**(骨髄)；**pith**(植物の芯).

すいあげる 吸い上げる **1【吸って上げる】suck up** ▶植物は地中から水と栄養分を吸い上げる Plants *suck up* water and nutrients from the soil.
2【利益を取る】▶本部は私たちチェーン店の利益の約 3 割を吸い上げている The head office *absorbs* [*skims off*] about 30% of our store's profits.

すいあつ 水圧 **water pressure**
‖水圧計 a water-pressure gauge /geɪdʒ/.

[1]すいい 水位 **water level** ▶日照り続きで貯水池の水位がかなり下がった Because of the long dry spell, the *water level* in the reservoir has fallen considerably.

[2]すいい 推移 a **change** 一動 推移する **change** ▶しばらく事態の推移を注意深く見守る必要がある We need to carefully watch how the situation *develops* [*changes*]. ‖ このところ円相場は一進一退で推移している The yen is going up and down these days. (➤「推移している」は訳語に出ない).

ずいい 随意 ▶どうぞご随意に *Do as you please* [*wish*]. ／*Suit yourself!* (➤ 後者は「勝手にしろ」に近い) ‖ 果物をご随意にお取りください *Please help yourself to* the fruit.

すいいき 水域 **waters**(海域)；a **zone**(区域) ‖排他的経済水域 an exclusive economic zone.

ずいいち 随一 ▶当代随一の作家 *the foremost* [*greatest*] writer of the day (➤ 前者は「(地位・重要さが)第一の」, 後者は「最も偉大な」) ‖ 松島は東北地方随一の景勝地と言われている Matsushima is said to be *the most* picturesque place in the Tohoku district.

スイートピー《植物》a **sweet pea**.

スイートルーム a **suite** /swiːt/ (➤ ホテルの居間・寝室などが一続きになった豪華な部屋；「スイートルーム」は和製語；発音にも注意).

ずいいん 随員 a **retinue**, an **entourage** /àːntʊráːʒ/ (➤ ともに「随員団」の意).

すいえい 水泳 **swimming** ▶彼は水泳がとてもうまい He is very good at *swimming*. ／He is a very good swimmer. ‖ ここで水泳をするのは危険だ It is dangerous to *swim* here. ‖ 彼女は今水泳を習っている She *is learning how to swim* now. ‖ 私の娘は水泳教室に通っている My daughter *is taking swimming lessons*. (➤「水泳教室」は swimming class).
‖水泳選手 a swimmer ‖ 水泳大会 a swim meet, a swimming competition.

すいおん 水温 **water temperature** ▶プールの水温を計る measure the *temperature of* (*the water* in) the swimming pool ‖水温計 a (water) thermometer /θəʳmáːməṭəʳ/.

すいか 西瓜 a **watermelon** ▶スイカの種を取る remove seeds from a slice of *watermelon* ‖ 日本人は夏の浜辺でよくスイカ割りをする People in Japan like to play "*split the watermelon*" on beaches in the summertime. (日本独特の遊びなので, 書く場合には“　”をつけるとよい).
‖種なしスイカ a seedless watermelon.

すいがい 水害 a **flood** /flʌd/（洪水）; a **flood disaster**（災害）▶この地方は3年連続して水害を受けた This district has suffered from *floods* for three years in a row.（➤ in a row は「数詞＋複数形の名詞」のあとで「連続して」の意）‖台風による東海地方の水害はひどかった The *flood* [*flooding*] *damage* in the Tokai district caused by the typhoon was severe. ‖多くの家が水害に遭った Many houses *were flooded*.

すいかずら《植物》**Japanese honeysuckle.**

すいがら 吸い殻 a **cigarette butt** /bʌt/ [**end**] ▶《掲示》吸い殻をホームに捨てないでください Do not discard (*cigarette*) *butts* on the platform.
‖**吸い殻入れ** an ashtray.

すいきゅう 水球 **water polo** /póʊloʊ/.

すいぎゅう 水牛《動物》a (**water**) **buffalo** ▶水牛の角 a *buffalo* horn.

すいきょ 推挙する **nominate** ＋㊐ ▶岡本氏は全会一致で議長に推挙された Mr. Okamoto *was* unanimously *nominated* for chairman.

すいきょう 酔狂 ▶こんな嵐の日にジョギングするなんてきみもずいぶん酔狂だね You must be *crazy* to go jogging on a stormy day like today. ‖だてや酔狂でこんなことはできない This isn't something you can do *just for fun* [*just on a whim* / *just for the heck of it*].

すいぎん 水銀 **mercury**
‖**水銀柱**（温度計・気圧計の）the mercury ‖**水銀中毒** mercury poisoning ‖**水銀電池** a mercury battery ‖**水銀灯** a mercury lamp.

すいけい 推計する **estimate** ＋㊐ ▶日本の推計人口 Japan's *estimated* population.

すいげん 水源 **the source of a river** ▶その川の水源はどこですか Where is *the source* of the river? ‖その川は水源をロッキー山脈に発する The river has its *source* [The river originates] in the Rockies.

1**すいこう 遂行する** **perform** ＋㊐ ▶任務を遂行する *perform* [*carry out*] one's duties (➤ carry out は「成し遂げる」に近い).

2**すいこう 推敲** ▶原稿を入念に推こうする carefully *polish* one's manuscript.

ずいこう 随行する **accompany** /əkʌ́mpəni/ ＋㊐ ▶彼は外務大臣に随行して渡米した He *accompanied* the Foreign Minister to the U.S.
‖**随行員** an attendant, a member of a retinue; an attaché（大使・公使の）‖**随行団** a retinue.

すいこむ 吸い込む **suck up**; **breathe** /bri:ð/ **in**（息を）; **inhale** ＋㊐（空気や煙を）▶この古い掃除機はちっとも吸い込まない This old vacuum cleaner *has no suction* at all. ‖火事のときは煙を吸い込むな Never *inhale* [*breathe in*] smoke during a fire. ‖私は水に潜る前に大きく息を吸い込んだ I *took a deep breath* before diving.
▶吸い込まれるようにきれいな星空だった The night sky was so deep and starry that I felt *as if I were being swallowed up by it*.

すいさい 水彩 ▶彼は水彩（＝水彩絵の具）で絵を描いた He painted with *watercolors*. ‖**水彩絵の具** watercolors（➤通例複数形）‖**水彩画** a watercolor ‖**水彩画家** a watercolor painter.

すいさつ 推察 a **guess** /ges/ 一動 **推察する** **guess**（＋㊐）; **imagine**（＋㊐）（想像する）▶ご推察のとおりです You *guessed* right. / Your *guess* is right.
✉ **お母さまが重病と伺いました. ご心配のこととご推察申し上げます** I have heard your mother is very ill and I *can imagine* how worried you must be.

すいさん 水産 ‖**水産加工業** the fish [marine product] processing industry ‖**水産業** the fishing industry ‖**水産資源** fishery resources ‖**水産試験場** a fisheries experiment station ‖**水産大学** a fisheries college ‖**水産庁** the Fisheries Agency.

すいし 水死する **drown** /draʊn/ →溺れる ▶きのう利根川で小学生が水死した A schoolchild (*was*) *drowned* in the Tone River yesterday. (➤ be drowned は他殺・事故死の両方に解釈できる) ‖ことしの夏の水死者は50人以上に上っている Statistics show that more than fifty people *drowned* this summer.

すいじ 炊事 **cooking** 一動 **炊事する** **cook** /kʊk/ ▶自分で炊事できますか Can you *cook* for yourself? ‖兄は炊事洗濯すべてを1人でやっている My (older) brother does *his cooking and laundry* all on his own. ‖**炊事道具** kitchenware.

ずいじ 随時 ▶随時更新 *Constantly* updated. (➤ constantly は「絶えず」) ‖随時相談受け付け中 *Consultation* available on request. ‖志願者には随時（＝いつでも）面接を実施する We interview applicants *at any time*. ‖救急車は随時出動できる態勢をとっている Ambulances are ready to respond *to emergency calls at any time*.

すいしつ 水質 ▶川の水質を検査する examine [analyze] the *water* (*quality*) of a river(➤ quality をつけないほうが自然) ‖この湖は水質汚染が進んでいる The *water* in this lake *is very polluted* [*contaminated*].
‖**水質汚染** water pollution [contamination].

すいしゃ 水車 a **water wheel**
‖**水車小屋** a water mill.

すいじゃく 衰弱する **become** [**get**] **weak** ▶彼女はひどく衰弱していて口も利けなかった She was too *weak* to speak. ‖患者は日ごとに衰弱してきた The patient is *getting weaker* day by day.

すいしゅ 水腫《医学》**edema** /idí:mə/, **dropsy.**

すいじゅん 水準 a **level**（程度）; a **standard**（標準）▶日本の科学技術の水準 Japan's *level* of scientific technology ‖マヤの天文学は当時の世界の最高水準に達していた The Mayas' astronomy had reached *the highest level* in the world at that time. ‖あの大学院生の論文は水準以上［以下］だ The thesis by that graduate student *is above* [*below*] *standard*. ‖近年その国の生活水準は高くなってきている Recently the *standard of living* in that country has risen. ‖**水準器** a leveling instrument, a surveyor's level.

ずいしょ 随所 ▶この会場は体の不自由な方のための配慮が随所になされています We have considered the needs of the physically disabled *everywhere* in this venue. ‖このマラソンコースには随所に飲料水の補給所が設けられている Drinking water is provided *at various spots* along the course of this marathon.

1**すいしょう 水晶** **crystal** /krístəl/ ▶水晶の置物 a *crystal* ornament ‖（眼球の）**水晶体** a lens ‖**水晶時計** a quartz /kwɔ:ʳts/ watch [clock].

2**すいしょう 推奨** **recommendation** 一動 **推奨する** **recommend** ＋㊐ ▶私は彼を誠実で信頼に足る人物として推奨した I *recommended* him as a sincere and trustworthy person. ‖安上がりな健康法としてウォーキングを推奨します I *recommend* walking as an inexpensive way to stay fit [healthy].

すいじょう 水上 ▶アメンボウは水上を滑るように進む A water strider slides *over* [*on*] *the water*.
‖**水上競技** water sports ‖**水上警察** the water police ‖**水上交通** water [waterway] traffic ‖**水上スキー** water-skiing ‖**水上輸送** water transportation [transport] ‖**水上レストラン** a floating restaurant.

す

すいじょうき 水蒸気 vapor /véɪpəʳ/ (自然に蒸発する水分) ; steam (水を熱することにより発生する蒸気).

1 **すいしん 推進** (a) propulsion (前へ押し出すこと) ; (a) promotion (促進) ━動 **推進する** propel /prəpél/ +目, promote +目 ▶ロケットのジェット推進 jet *propulsion* of a rocket ‖このボートはディーゼルエンジンで推進される This boat *is propelled* by a diesel engine. ‖和平の推進 the *promotion* of peace ‖自然保護運動を推進する *promote* a conservation movement ‖省エネを推進する *promote* energy conservation ‖政府と民間企業の両方がそのニュータウン計画を推進した Both the government and private enterprises *pushed forward with* [*promoted*] the new town project. ‖トップバッターはチームの推進力だ The top batter is the *driving force* of his team.
‖**政治改革推進本部** the Political Reform Promotion Headquarters.

2 **すいしん 水深** the depth of water ▶湖の水深を測る sound the *depth* of a lake ‖彼らは水深4, 5メートルの所でサメに襲われた They were attacked by sharks at *a depth* of four or five meters. ‖水深10メートルの所ではいろいろな魚が泳いでいる *Ten meters down*, there are all kinds of fish swimming around.

スイス Switzerland (➤国名を Swiss としない) ━形 **スイスの** Swiss ‖**スイス人** a Swiss [複 Swiss] ; the Swiss (総称).

すいすい ▶すいすいと試験問題を解く *breeze through* the exam (➤「すいすいと試験に合格する」の意にもなる) ‖メダカが小川ですいすい泳いでいた I saw *medaka* swimming *swiftly* in the stream. ‖この企画はそうすいすいとは運ばないよ This project isn't going to go that *smoothly*. (➤ smoothly の発音は /smúːðli/).

1 **すいせい 水星** Mercury ▶水星は太陽に最も近い惑星だ *Mercury* is the planet nearest to the sun.

2 **すいせい 彗星** a comet ▶《慣用表現》そのピアニストは昨年, すい星のごとくデビューした That pianist made a *dazzling* debut last year. (➤ dazzling は「きらびやかな」) ‖**ハレーすい星** Halley's Comet.

3 **すいせい 水性** ‖**水性ペイント** water paint ‖**水性マーカー** a water-based [washable] marker, a Magic Marker《商標》.

4 **すいせい 水生** ▶水生植物 an *aquatic* [*a water*] plant.

1 **すいせん 推薦** recommendation ━動 **推薦する** recommend /rèkəménd/ +目
▶文科省推薦の映画 a film *recommended by* the Ministry of Education.

> 【文型】
> 人(A)に物・人(B)を推薦する
> recommend B to A
> 人(A)を役職者(B)として推薦する
> recommend A as B
> 人(A)を地位など(B)に推薦する
> recommend A for B

> 《解説》(1) **recommend** A B の文型は主に《英》で,《米》ではあまり用いられない.
> (2)《米》では **recommend** a person は「人に」ではなく,「人を推薦する」の意味で使うことのほうが多い.

▶山田先生がこの辞書を推薦してくれました Mr. Yamada *recommended* this dictionary *to* me. ‖彼は彼女をよい秘書だと推薦した He *recommended* her *as* a good secretary. ‖私は来年の会社の旅行には湯布院を推薦します I *recommend* Yufuin *for* next year's company trip. ▶彼は先生の推薦でその会社に入った He got a job with that company *on the recommendation of* his teacher. ‖イタリア料理を食べたいんだけど, どこかいい店を推薦してくれないか？ I'd like to eat Italian food. Can you *recommend* a good restaurant? ‖あの人はちょっと推薦できないな I'm afraid I *can't recommend* him.
‖**推薦者** a recommender ‖**推薦状** a letter of recommendation ‖**推薦入学** admission by [on] recommendation.

2 **すいせん 水洗** ▶その国では水洗便所はまだ普及していない In that country, *flush toilets* are still not common.

3 **すいせん 水仙** 《植物》a narcissus /nɑːʳsísəs/ ; a daffodil (ラッパズイセン) ; a jonquil (黄ズイセン).

4 **すいせん 垂線** 《数学》a perpendicular (line).

すいぜん 垂涎 ▶このレア物のＬＰはマニア垂ぜんの的だ This rare LP *is coveted* by LP record buffs.

すいそ 水素 hydrogen /háɪdrədʒən/ ▶水は水素と酸素の化合物である Water is a compound of *hydrogen* and oxygen. ‖**水素爆弾** a hydrogen bomb, an H-bomb /éɪtʃbɑːm/.

1 **すいそう 水槽** a water tank ; an aquarium /əkwéəriəm/ (養魚用の) ▶私は水槽で熱帯魚を飼っています I have tropical fish in *an aquarium*.

2 **すいそう 吹奏** ▶トランペットの吹奏で式典が始まった The ceremony was opened with *a flourish of trumpets*. (➤ flourish は「(トランペットの)ファンファーレ」) ‖勝者をたたえて国歌が吹奏された The national anthem *was played* to honor the victor.
‖**吹奏楽** wind (instrument) music ‖**吹奏楽団** a brass band.

すいぞう 膵臓 the [one's] pancreas /pǽŋkriəs/ ▶膵臓がん *pancreatic* cancer.

ずいそう 随想 random thoughts ▶随想録 *essays*.

すいそく 推測 a guess (想像に基づく) ; (a) conjecture (不確実な情報などに基づく) ━動 **推測する** guess (+目), conjecture +目 ▶当てずっぽうな推測 a wild *guess* ‖私の推測は当たった [外れた] My *guess was right* [*wrong*]. / I *guessed right* [*wrong*]. ‖おおよそのことは推測がつく I can *make a* (pretty) good *guess*. ‖私の推測ではＳ氏がその事件に絡んでいると思う My *guess* is that Mr. S is involved in the affair. ‖単なる推測を信じてはいけない You should not believe something that is mere *conjecture*. ‖この化石は恐竜のものと推測されている This fossil *is thought* to be that of a dinosaur.

すいぞくかん 水族館 an aquarium.

すいたい 衰退 (a) decline ━動 **衰退する** decline ▶その産業は衰退の一途をたどっている That industry *is on the decline*.

すいちゅう 水中 ▶水中で目を開けていられますか Can you keep your eyes open *under water*? ‖彼は溺れる子を助けようと水中に飛び込んだ He jumped

into the water to rescue the drowning child.
‖水中カメラ an underwater camera ‖水中撮影 underwater photography ‖水中眼鏡 swimming goggles ‖水中翼船 a hydrofoil (boat).

すいちょく 垂直の vertical(水平面に対して); perpendicular (他方と直角を成している) ▶垂直の絶壁 a *perpendicular* [*vertical*] cliff(➤ vertical は必ずしも正確に垂直でない場合にも用いる) ‖柱を地面に垂直に立てる put up a pole *at right angles* to the ground ‖ヘリコプターは垂直に上昇することができる Helicopters can rise *vertically* [*perpendicularly*] from the ground. ‖垂直線 a vertical [perpendicular] line ‖垂直跳び a vertical jump ‖垂直尾翼 a tail fin ‖垂直離着陸機 a VTOL /víːtɔːl/ (➤ vertical takeoff and landing の略).

すいつく 吸い付く be attracted(吸い寄せられる) ▶針は磁石に吸い付く A needle *is attracted* by a magnet. ‖その虫はまるでヒルのように足に吸い付いて離れない The worm is *sticking to* my leg like a leech. (➤ stick は「くっつく」).

スイッチ a switch ▶電灯のスイッチ a light *switch* ‖車のエンジンのスイッチを切る turn off the *ignition* (*switch*) ‖炊飯器のスイッチを入れてちょうだい *Switch* [*Turn*] *on* the rice cooker, please.
‖スイッチバック a switchback ‖スイッチヒッター a switch hitter.

> **危ないカタカナ語✸ スイッチ**
> **1**「スイッチ」は switch でよいが, 自動車の始動スイッチの場合は ignition switch または ignition が一般的で, switch とは通例いわない. ignition は「点火」の意.
> **2**「スイッチを入れる[切る]」は turn on [off], または switch on [off] だが, turn を使うほうがよりふつう.
> **3** リモコンの場合は zap on [off] ともいう.

すいてい 推定 an estimate /éstɪmət/ (概算); estimation (推定すること) 一動 推定する estimate /éstɪmeɪt/ +目 ▶目的地までの推定飛行時間 *estimated* flight time to the destination ‖昨夜の火事による損害は1000万円に上るものと推定される The loss from the fire last night *is estimated* at ten million yen. ‖地球は46億年ほど前にできたと推定されている It *is estimated* [*Estimates are*] that the earth was formed some 4.6 billion years ago. ‖雪崩の遭難者は死亡したものと推定される The avalanche victims *are presumed* to be dead. ‖このミイラの死亡時の推定年齢は20歳だ This mummy *is supposed* [*is estimated*] to have been 20 *years old* when he died.

すいてき 水滴 a drop of water, a water droplet ▶蒸気は冷えると水滴になる Steam changes into *droplets of water* when it cools. / Steam changes into *water droplets* when it is cooled.

すいでん 水田 a paddy field, a (rice) paddy.

¹すいとう 水筒 a water bottle; a canteen /kæntíːn/ (キャンプ用・兵士用などの); a thermos(魔法瓶).

²すいとう 出納 accounts, revenue and expenditure
‖出納係 a cashier /kæʃíəʳ/ (会社・団体・銀行の); a teller(銀行の).

³すいとう 水痘 《医学》chicken pox.

⁴すいとう 水稲 paddy rice.

すいどう 水道 water service [supply] (給水施設); city [tap] water(水道の水); a channel (海峡) ▶この辺はまだ水道が引かれていない We still *have no water supply* [*service*] in this area. ‖水道の本管が壊れたので水が全く出なかった *A water main* broke, so people were without (any) water. ‖栓をひねるだけで水道水が得られるのはありがたいことだ It's a great thing to be able to get *tap water* by just turning on the faucet. ‖水道を止めて[出して]ください Please *turn off* [*on*] *the water*.
▶浦賀水道 the Uraga *Channel*.
‖水道管 a water main(本管); a water pipe(引き込み管) ‖水道局 the Waterworks Bureau, the Board of Water Supply ‖水道工事 plumbing (work) (建物内の給排水); waterworks (地区などの) ‖水道料金 water charges (➤「水道料金の請求書」なら the water bill) ‖上下水道 city water and sewage /súːɪdʒ/.

すいとる 吸い取る soak up, absorb +目 (➤ 後者は「吸収する」に近い) ▶コットンはよく汗を吸い取る Cotton *absorbs* [*soaks up*] sweat well. ‖この掃除機は吸い取る力が強い This vacuum cleaner has (a) strong *suction* (*power*). ‖人のもうけを吸い取る *make* money *off* (*of*) a person.

すいばく 水爆 a hydrogen /háɪdrədʒən/ bomb, an H-bomb ‖水爆実験 an H-bomb test.

すいはんき 炊飯器 a rice cooker ▶電気[ガス]炊飯器 an electric [a gas] *rice cooker*. →ジャー.

ずいひつ 随筆 an essay ‖随筆家 an essayist.

すいふ 水夫 a sailor, a seaman(➤ 後者は特に男性であることを示す必要のあるときに用いる).

すいぶん 水分 water; (a) liquid (何かに含まれる) ▶このバスタオルは水分をよく吸収しない This bath towel doesn't absorb *water* well [is not very absorbent]. ‖グレープフルーツは水分が多い Grapefruits are *juicy*. ‖脱水症にならないように水分を十分にとりなさい Drink plenty of *liquids* so that you don't become dehydrated.

ずいぶん **1**【非常に】very, extremely(➤ 後者は前者の強意語); awfully (ものすごく); certainly (間違いなく) ▶彼はずいぶん具合が悪そうだ He looks *very* ill. ‖きのうの朝はずいぶん寒かった It was *very* [*extremely* / *awfully*] cold yesterday morning. ‖ちょっと見ないうちにずいぶん大きくなったわね Well, you've *certainly* grown since I last saw you. ‖ずいぶんひどい降りだね It's *really* raining hard, isn't it? ‖ずいぶん長いこと歩いたけどまだ宿に着かない We've walked *quite* a long way, but we still haven't reached the inn. ‖この仕事を見つけるのに彼はずいぶんと骨を折ってくれた He went to *quite a lot of* trouble to find this job for me. ‖転職すべきかどうかでずいぶん悩んだ I worried *quite a lot* over whether or not I should change jobs.
2【ひどい】▶先にひとりで帰っちゃうなんてずいぶんな人ね *Some friend you are*, to go home early and leave me alone. (➤ この some は「大した」の意で皮肉で言うような場合に用いる).

¹すいへい 水平の level, horizontal ▶この床は水平ではない This floor is not *level*. ‖お盆は水平に持って運びなさい Carry the tray *level*. ‖あの絵, 右下がりだよ. 水平に(=まっすぐに)しなくちゃ That picture is tilted to the right. Make sure it hangs *straight*. ‖水平線から朝日が昇った[に夕日が沈んだ] The sun has risen above [has sunk below] *the horizon*.
‖水平思考 lateral thinking ‖水平尾翼 a horizontal tail, a tail wing.

²すいへい 水兵 a sailor, a seaman 《参考》両者とも同義だが, 英米の海軍では水兵の階級名としては後者が用い

られる.

すいほう 水泡 ▶彼の不注意で我々の3年間の努力は水泡に帰した Due to his carelessness, our three years of work *went down the drain* [*came to nothing*／*evaporated into thin air*].

すいぼくが 水墨画 (a) **(monochrome) ink painting** ▶風景を水墨画で描く *paint* [*do*] a landscape *in ink*.

すいぼつ 水没 ▶ダムの建設によりその村は湖底に水没した The village *was submerged* in a lake after construction of the dam.

すいま 睡魔 sleepiness, drowsiness(➤ともに「眠気」をいうが, 後者は食事をしたり, 薬や酒を飲んだり, 暖かな場所にいたりしたときに襲ってくるような眠気をいうことが多い) ▶英語の授業中どうしようもない睡魔に襲われた I *got* unbearably *sleepy* during English class. ／I *was overcome by* irresistible *drowsiness* during English class.

すいみん 睡眠 (a) **sleep**(眠り) ▶私は5時間の睡眠で十分だ Five hours' *sleep* is enough for me. ‖きみは毎日何時間睡眠をとりますか How many hours' *sleep* do you *get* [How many hours do you *sleep*] every night? ‖ゆうべは十分に睡眠をとった I *got* [*had*] *a good night's sleep* last night. ‖私は睡眠時間を減らさなければならなかった I had to cut down on *sleep*. ‖睡眠不足がこたえてきた *Lack of sleep* is beginning to take its toll on me. ‖きょうは睡眠不足だ I *didn't get enough sleep* last night. (英語では「昨夜は十分に睡眠をとっていない」と考えて訳例のように表現する. I didn't sleep well last night. (昨夜はよく眠れなかった)としてもよい) ‖睡眠不足を補うためによく電車の中で仮眠をとる I often take a nap in the train to *make up* (*for*) *lost sleep*. **‖睡眠薬** (a) sleeping medicine; a sleeping pill(錠剤) ‖**ノンレム睡眠** NREM /énrém, nɑ́:nrém/ sleep, non-REM sleep (➤non-rapid eye movement sleep ともいう) ‖**レム睡眠** REM sleep /rém sli:p/ (➤rapid eye movement sleep, paradoxical sleep ともいう).

すいめん 水面 the surface /sə́:ʳfɪs/ **of the water** ▶赤潮のために魚が死んで水面に浮いていた Because of the red tide, fish were floating dead *on the surface of the water*.

すいもの 吸い物 ***suimono*; clear soup.**

すいもん 水門 a **water gate**; a **sluice gate**(ダムの); a **lock**(運河の); a **floodgate**(防潮堤).

すいようえき 水溶液 (a) **water solution** ▶アルカリ性[酸性]の水溶液 (an) alkaline [acidic] *water solution*.

すいよう(び) 水曜(日) Wednesday /wénzdeɪ/ 《略 Wed.》 ▶水曜日は5時間授業だ We have five classes *on Wednesday*(*s*). ‖先週の水曜日に健康診断を受けた I had a physical checkup *last Wednesday*. →曜日.

すいり 推理 reasoning(論理的に考え出された); **inference** /ínfərəns/ (情報などに基づいた); a **guess**(当て推量) 一動 **推理する reason, infer** /ɪnfə́:ʳ/, **guess** ▶ホームズは見事な推理で次々と事件を解決していった Sherlock Holmes solved one case after another with his brilliant *reasoning*. ‖きみの推理は正しい Your *reasoning* [*guess*] is right. ／You guessed right. ‖その時刻にそこにいることができたのは彼以外にはいないと私は推理した I *reasoned* [*inferred*／*guessed*] *that* only he could have been there at that hour. **‖推理小説** a detective story [novel], a whodunit /hù:dʌ́nɪt/ (➤Who done it? (=Who did it?)の非標準的な言い方; インフォーマル) ‖**推理力** reasoning powers [faculties].

すいりく 水陸 ▶この戦車は水陸両用です This tank is *amphibious* /æmfíbiəs/.

1**すいりょう 水量 the volume of water** ▶集中豪雨で川の水量が増した *The river rose* after the torrential downpour.

2**すいりょう 推量** a **guess** ▶残念ながらきみの推量は間違っている I'm sorry to say, but your *guess* is wrong. ‖当て推量でものを言わないでくれ Don't *guess wildly*. ／Cut out the *random guesswork*.

すいりょく 水力 waterpower **‖水力発電所** a hydroelectric power station.

すいれん 睡蓮《植物》**a water lily.**

すいろ 水路 a **waterway**; a **canal** /kənǽl/ (運河).

すいろん 推論 reasoning(論理的に考え出された推理). →推理.

スイング a **swing**(振ること); 《音楽》**swing music** ▶バッターは思い切りスイングしたが空振りだった The batter *took a* wild *swing* at the ball and missed it. ‖彼女はゴルフのスイングを改善した She improved her (*golf*) *swing*.

1**すう 数** a **number** ▶クラスの生徒数 the *number* of students in a class.

2**すう 吸う 1【気体を】breathe** /bri:ð/ **(in), inhale; smoke** (たばこを) →吸い込む ▶深く息を吸う *breathe* deeply ‖私は窓を開けて新鮮な空気を吸った I opened the window and *took a breath* of fresh air. ‖たばこを吸ってもいいですか May I *smoke*? ／Do you mind if I *smoke*?

2【液体を】suck(+目); **absorb** +目 (吸収する) ▶ミツバチは花の蜜を吸う Bees *suck* nectar from flowers. ‖ドラキュラは人の生き血を吸う吸血鬼だ Dracula is a vampire who *sucks* people's blood. ‖壁紙が湿気を吸って変色した The wallpaper changed color because it *absorbed* moisture.

3【比喩的】▶一度都会の空気を吸う(=経験する)と二度と田舎へ帰らない人が多い Once people *experience* life in a big city, many of them will never go back to their hometowns.

すう- 数- several ..., some ..., a few ...(➤それぞれの意味の違いについては「数年」の項の 語法 を参照) ▶数百人 hundreds of people ‖数千人 thousands of people ‖数万人 tens of thousands of people ‖数百万人 millions of people ‖数千万人 tens of millions of people. →数人.

▶奈良には数回行きました I have been to Nara *several times*. ‖私は彼女を数時間待った I waited for her *for several hours*. ‖今回の展覧会にマチスのデッサンが数十点出品されている *Scores* [*Dozens*] *of* sketches by Matisse are on display at the current exhibition.

語法 「数十」に tens of ～ は用いない. score は「20」, dozen /dʌ́zn/ は「12」であるが, scores of は40～80, dozens of は36～50くらいを漠然と表すのに用いられる.

▶過去数十年間日本は平和と繁栄の上にあぐらをかいてきた Japan has rested on the laurels of its peace and prosperity *for the past* [*last*] *several decades*. (➤rest on the laurels of は「…の栄誉に満足する」; decade /dékeɪd/ は「10年間」) ‖数年後, 街で彼にばったり会った I ran into him on the street *a few years later*.

☞ 数日, 数年 (→見出語)

スウェーデン Sweden /swí:dn/ (➤発音に注意) 一

形スウェーデンの **Swedish** /swíːdɪʃ/ ‖スウェーデン語 Swedish ‖ スウェーデン人 a Swede /swiːd/; the Swedish (総称).

スウェット ‖スウェットシャツ a sweatshirt (➤ 丸首のゆったりした上着のことを指す.「トレーナー」は和製語で, 英語ではそれを sweatshirt という) ‖ スウェットスーツ a sweat suit ‖ スウェットパンツ sweatpants.

すうがく 数学 **mathematics, math** (➤ 後者はインフォーマルな語;《英》では maths と s をつけるのがふつう) ▶数学の先生 a *math* teacher ‖ 数学の問題 a *mathematical* problem ‖ 数学の公式 a *mathematical* formula.
‖数学者 a mathematician /mæθəmətíʃən/.

すうき 数奇な **varied** /véərid/ (変化に富んだ) ; **checkered** (浮き沈みの多い) ▶北斎は数奇な一生を送った Hokusai led a *varied* [*checkered*] life. ／Hokusai lived a life *full of variety* [*full of ups and downs*].

すうききょう 枢機卿 a **cardinal.**

すうこう 崇高な **sublime** /səbláɪm/ ; **noble** (気高い) ▶崇高な音楽 *sublime* music ‖ 崇高な精神 *noble* mind.

すうし 数詞 《文法》a **numeral** /njúːmərəl/.

すうじ 数字 a **figure** (表記された) ; a **digit** (0から9までの数字の1つ) ; a **number** (数) ; a **numeral** (数字の体系) ▶1桁の数字 a single *figure* ‖ 数字の3 the *number* 3 ‖ 数8543589には7個の数字が含まれている The number 8543589 contains seven *digits*. ‖ 彼は数字に強い He is good at *figures*. ／He has a good head for *figures*. ‖ 小切手に金額をアラビア[漢]数字で書く write the sum of money in *Arabic* [*Chinese*] *numerals* on a check.

すうしき 数式 a **numerical** [**mathematical**] **expression** ▶次の数式を解きなさい Work out the following *numerical expression*.

すうじく 枢軸 an **axis** [複 **axes**] ▶枢軸国 the *Axis* (nations) ‖ 悪の枢軸 the *axis* of evil.

すうじつ 数日 **a few days, several days** ▶数日前さち子に会った I met Sachiko *a few* [*several*] *days ago*. ‖ ここ数日彼女は学校を休んでいる She has been absent from school *for the last few days*. ‖ 全線が復旧するには数日かかる模様だ It will be *several days* before normal service can be restored on the entire line.

すーすー ▶赤ちゃんがスースー寝息を立てて眠っている The baby is asleep, breathing *quietly*. ‖ この部屋, 何だかすーすーするね This room *feels* pretty *drafty*. ／Doesn't this room *feel drafty*? (➤ drafty は「隙間風が入る」).

ずうずうしい 図々しい **impudent** ; **pushy** (押しの強い) ; **shameless** (恥知らずな) ; **presumptuous** (差し出がましい) ▶あんなずうずうしいやつは大嫌いだ I can't stand that kind of *pushy* person. ‖ 隣のうちの猫はずうずうしいやつで, うちの犬の餌を食べて帰る The cat from next door *thinks nothing of* eating our dog's food before it leaves. ‖ 私にはとてもそんなずうずうしいことはできません I could never do such a *shameless* thing. ‖ よくもずうずうしくそんなことが言えるね *How dare you* say such a thing? (➤「よく思い切って言えるものだ」の意) ‖ 彼はずうずうしくもまた私に金を貸してくれと言ってきた He *had the nerve* [*impudence* ／*presumption*] *to* ask me to lend him money again. (➤ nerve は「厚かましさ」) ‖ 何てずうずうしいやつだ!《米》*He's got some nerve*! ／《英》*Bloody cheek*!

すうせい 趨勢 a **trend**, a **tendency** (傾向) ▶時代のすう勢は虚礼廃止の方向に向かっている The *trend* of the times is for people to dispense with meaningless formalities. ‖ 時代のすう勢で陰影のあることばがどんどん消えてゆく *As time goes by*, a lot of words with subtle nuances disappear.

ずうたい 図体 a **body** (体) ; a **frame** (体格, 骨格) ▶彼はずうたいはでかいが, 気は小さい Although he's *a hulk of a man* [*a stocky man* ／*a burly man*], he's rather timid.

すうだん 数段 ▶経営者としては彼は私より数段上だ As a manager he is *far* more capable than I. ／As a manager he is *several notches* above me. (➤ notch は「刻み目」が原義).

すうち 数値 《数学》**numerical value** ; a **reading** (計測器などの表示値).

スーツ a **suit** ▶三つぞろいのスーツ a three-piece *suit* ‖ よそ行きのスーツ a Sunday *suit* ／one's Sunday clothes [best] 《参考》いずれも教会に着ていくスーツから出た表現だが, 後者の2つは必ずしもスーツとは限らない.

スーツケース a **suitcase** ▶スーツケースに荷札を付ける tag one's *suitcase*.

すーっと ▶彼は闇の中にすーっと消えた He *vanished into* the dark. ‖ 誰かが後ろからすーっと入って来る気配がした I felt as though someone had *slipped in* behind me. ‖ ミントティーを飲んだら口の中がすーっとした The mint tea made my mouth *feel refreshingly cool*.

すうにん 数人 **several** [**some** ／**a few**] **people** ▶数人の男が突然会場に乱入してきた *Several* [*Some*] men burst into the meeting place.

すうねん 数年 **several** [**some** ／**a few**] **years**
語法 いずれも「数年」に当たるが, ふつう a few は3～5を, several は3, 4から7～10辺りまでの範囲を指す. some は数年であることをぼかして言っている.
▶この数年(間)暖冬が続いている We have had mild winters *for the last several* [*few*] *years*. ‖ 木村さん一家は数年前に大阪に越した The Kimuras moved to Osaka *several years ago*. ‖ おじは数年したらシンガポールから帰って来ます My uncle will return from Singapore *in a few years* [*in two or three years*].

スーパー ▶母は食料品を買いにスーパーに行っている My mother has gone to the *supermarket* to do some grocery shopping. (➤ ふつう super とはいわない).

> **危ないカタカナ語✹ スーパー**
> 1「超…」「特大…」の意味での「スーパー」は多くの場合 super でよいが, ultra /ʌ́ltrə/ などのほうが適切な場合もある(ultramodern など).
> 2 外国映画の「字幕スーパー」は superimposition からきているが, これは画面の上に別の画面や文字を重ねて焼き付けることを指す. せりふの訳そのものは通例 subtitles という.

スーパーマーケット a **supermarket.**

スーパーマン a **superman** (超人) ; **Superman** (漫画や映画の).

すうはい 崇拝 **admiration** ; **adoration** (深く愛すること) ; **worship** (神のようにあがめること) 一動 崇拝する **admire** +目, **adore** +目, **worship** +目 ▶太陽神を崇拝する *worship* the Sun God(dess) ‖ 成り金の多くは金を崇拝する Most nouveaux riches *worship* money. ‖ 彼はビートルズを崇拝している He *admires* [*wor-*

ships] the Beatles. ／He *is an admirer of* the Beatles.

スープ (a) **soup** ▶スープを飲む *eat soup*（➤ カップ入りのスープをカップに口をつけて飲むのなら drink soup でよい）‖スープを飲むときに音を立ててはいけない You must not slurp your *soup*.（➤ slurp は「ペチャペチャ音を立てて飲む［食べる］」）.
‖**スープ皿** a soup bowl [plate]（➤ 前者は椀(わん)のように深いもの）‖**キノコのスープ** mushroom soup ‖**コンソメスープ** consommé《フランス語》‖**チキンスープ** chicken soup ‖**豆のスープ** bean soup.

す

ズーム ▶ぼくはカメラで彼女を追い，顔をズームインした I followed her with my camera and *zoomed in on* her face. ‖**ズームレンズ** a zoom lens.

すうりょう 数量 (a) **quantity** /kwáːnṭəṭi/（分量）；(an) **amount**（総量）▶輸入品の数量を増やす［減らす］increase [decrease] the *quantity* of imported goods.

すうれつ 数列《数学》a **progression**, a **sequence**.

すえ 末 **1【終わり】the end** ▶兄は 6 月の末にロンドンから帰国する My (older) brother will come back (to Japan) from London *at the end of June*. ‖ 3 月の末頃郷里では桜の花が満開です *Toward* [*About*] *the end* of March, cherry blossoms are in full bloom in my hometown. ‖末の娘はことしで16になります My *youngest* daughter will be sixteen this year.（→末っ子）.
▶《慣用表現》こんなに汚職事件が続出するなんて世も末だね *What is the world coming to* with corruption scandals like this occurring one after another?（➤「世の中はどうなるのだろう」の意）.
2【将来】a **future** ▶あの子は末が楽しみだ The boy *has a bright future*. ／He is a *promising* boy. ‖今からこんなに勉強嫌いでは末が思いやられるね If you dislike studying so much now, *I hate to think how you'll do in your future*.
3【…の結果】▶慎重に考えた末，私は大学受験をしないことにした *After* careful consideration [*After* much deliberation], I decided not to take any university entrance examinations. ‖長年の苦心の末，彼はとうとう実験に成功した *After* years of hard work, he succeeded with the experiment at last.

スエード **suede** /sweɪd/ ▶スエードの靴 *suede* shoes.

すえおき 据え置き ▶（支払いなどの）据え置き期間 the period of *deferment* ‖公共料金は当分の間据え置きになるだろう Public utility rates will *be frozen* for the time being.（➤「凍結される」の意）.

すえおく 据え置く **freeze** +⊜（給料の額などを凍結する）；**leave ... unredeemed**（負債などをそのままにしておく）▶私たちの給料は長い間据え置かれたままです Our wages have *been frozen* for a long time.

すえおそろしい 末恐ろしい ▶あの新人は末恐ろしい存在だ That rookie *will make a name for himself someday*.（➤「いつか名を上げるだろう」の意）‖あの悪がきは末恐ろしいよ That brat *is likely to get worse as time goes on*.

スエズうんが スエズ運河 **the Suez Canal.**

すえたのもしい 末頼もしい **promising** ▶あの子は頭もいいし，よく勉強もするし，末頼もしいね He is a *promising* boy; he is so bright and hardworking.

すえつける 据え付ける **install** +⊜（器具などを）；**fix** +⊜（固定して）▶居間に加湿器を据え付けた I *installed* a humidifier in the living room. ‖食器棚を壁に据え付けてもらった I *had* a cupboard *fixed* to the wall.

すえっこ 末っ子 **the youngest son [daughter]**（➤ カッコ内は女の場合）▶彼は 4 人兄弟の末っ子だ He is *the youngest* of the four brothers.

すえながい 末永い
✉ **ご結婚のお知らせをいただき大変うれしく思いました. お二人の末永いお幸せを心よりお祈りいたします［末永くお幸せにお暮らしください］**
How wonderful it was to hear of your marriage! Best wishes to you both for *many years of* happiness [I hope you will live happily *for many, many years to come*].

すえひろがり 末広がり ▶八は末広がりで縁起のよい数とされています Because the number eight in kanji *becomes wider toward the foot*, it is considered to represent a bright future and is thus auspicious.

¹すえる 据える **1【しっかり置く】place** +⊜（決まった場所に）；**set** +⊜（きちんと正しく）；**install** +⊜（設備などを取り付ける）▶ここにその冷蔵庫を据えてください *Place* the fridge (over) here. ‖大広間に大きな座卓が据えてあった A large low table *was set up* in the banquet hall. ‖オフィスに新しいコピー機が据えられた A new copying machine *was installed* in the office.
2【地位に就ける】appoint +⊜ ▶きみの後釜には佐藤君を据えるつもりだ I'm going to *appoint* [*put*] Sato in your place.
3【慣用表現】▶もっと腰を据えて勉強しなさい *Settle down* and study.（➤ settle down は「本気になる」）‖度胸を据えろ You must *summon up your courage*. ／Don't be afraid.

²すえる **sour**（酸っぱくなる）；**go bad**（悪くなる）**━形 すえた stale, rancid** ▶すえたビール［チーズ］の臭い the smell of *stale* beer [*rancid* cheese].

ずが 図画 **drawing**（主に線画）；**painting**（絵の具で絵を描くこと）▶彼は図画が得意だ He is good at *drawing*. ‖図画の時間は楽しかった I used to have fun in *art class*.

スカート a **skirt** ▶スカートの丈を詰める shorten a *skirt* ／take up the hem of a *skirt* ‖理恵はピンクのミニスカートをはいていた Rie was wearing a pink *miniskirt*. ‖スコットランドでは正式な場ではキルトというスカートのようなものをはく男性もいる In Scotland, some men wear a kilt that resembles a *skirt* on formal occasions. ‖スカートめくりは性暴力行為です *Flipping up* the girls' *skirts* is equal to an act of sexual violence.
‖**ギャザースカート** a gathered skirt ‖**タイトスカート** a tight skirt ‖**膝丈のスカート** a knee-length skirt ‖**ひだ［プリーツ］スカート** a pleated skirt ‖**フレアスカート** a flared skirt ‖**巻きスカート** a wraparound (skirt).

スカーフ a **scarf** ▶スカーフを首に巻く wear *a scarf* around one's neck. →マフラー.

ずかい 図解 an **illustration**; a **diagram**（図表）**━動 図解する illustrate** /fləstreɪt/ +⊜ ▶ここに製造過程をわかりやすく図解してある Here is an easy-to-understand *illustration* of the production process. →イラスト.

ずがいこつ 頭蓋骨 a **skull** /skʌl/ ▶羊の頭蓋骨 the *skull* of a sheep.

スカイダイビング **skydiving** **━動 スカイダイビングをする skydive.**

スカイライン（→かこみ記事）

危ないカタカナ語✹ スカイライン
1 日本では高原などの見晴らしのよい所につくった観光道路のことを「スカイライン」と呼ぶことがあるが，この用法は英語の skyline にはない．これは日本人が「空のような高い所を走る線」と考えて造語したものであろう．英語の skyline は「空を背景にした山やビルなどの輪郭」または「地平線」の意味である．
2 日本語の「スカイライン」を訳すと mountain drive [route] とか scenic mountain highway などとなるが，「スカイライン」のもつ詩的なイメージはない．

スカウト a **scout** /skaʊt/（人）**━動 スカウトする scout**《for》▶有望な新人をスカウトする *scout* (around) *for* a promising new star ‖ その選手は無名の高校野球チームからスカウトされた The player *was scouted* from an unknown high school baseball team.

すがお 素顔 ▶菊池さんは素顔が美しい Miss Kikuchi is beautiful *with no make-up*.（➤「化粧をしないで」の意）‖ 彼女は写真より素顔のほうが美しい She's more beautiful *in person* than in (her) pictures.（➤ in person は写真などに対して「実物で」）‖《比喩的》この番組は日本の素顔を伝えようとしている This program tries to show *Japan as it is* [to give *a true picture of Japan*].（➤ 前者は「ありのままの日本」の意）.

すかさず the moment（…した瞬間）→すぐ ▶席が１つ空いたと思ったら，中年のおばさんがすかさず横から割り込んできて座った *The moment* a seat was vacated, a middle-aged woman barged in and sat down.

すかし 透かし a **watermark** ▶1000円札には野口英世の透かしが入っている The one-thousand-yen bill has *a watermark* of Noguchi Hideyo on [in] it.

すかしへ すかし屁 ▶おまえ，すかし屁をしたな！ You *let one go*, didn't you?

[1]**すかす 透かす・空かす** **1【間を空ける】**▶彼らは間を透かさずに椅子を並べた They placed the chairs *right next to each other* [*without space in between*].
2【通して見る】▶木の間を透かして湖が見えた We could see a lake *through* the trees. ‖ 誰がいるのかと暗闇を透かして見た I *peeped* [*peered*] *into* the darkness to see who it was. ‖ 彼女は中身が見えないものかと封筒を明かりに透かしてみた She held the envelope *to* [*against*] *the light*, trying to see what was inside.
3【おなかを減らす】get hungry ▶家では子供たちがおなかをすかして待っていた The children were waiting *hungry* at home.

[2]**すかす** ▶泣き叫ぶわが子をなだめたりすかしたりして，やっとのことでインフルエンザの予防注射を受けさせた I finally *coaxed* my crying son [daughter] into getting a flu shot.

すかすか ▶すかすかの大根 a *porous* daikon ‖ きみの本棚はすかすかだね Your bookshelf looks *empty*. ／You have scarcely anything on your bookshelf.

ずかずか ▶男の子たちがずかずか土足で部屋へ上がって来た The boys *barged* into the room with their shoes on.（➤ barge into は「(乱暴に)…に入り込む」）.

すがすがしい 清々しい bracing（空気などが）; **refreshing**（気分が）▶すがすがしい空気 *bracing* [*fresh*] air ‖ 一眠りしたのですがすがしい気分だ I *feel refreshed* after my nap. ‖ 嵐の歌を聞いているとすがすがしい気持ちになる I *feel refreshed* when I hear Arashi's songs.

すがた 姿 **1【格好，身なり】**a **figure**（体つき）; an **appearance**（風采）▶知世はほっそりした姿をしている Tomoyo has a slender [slim] *figure*. ‖ 姿や形で人を判断してはいけない You shouldn't judge people by their *appearance*. ‖ 鏡で自分の姿を見てごらん Look at *yourself* in the mirror. ‖ こんな姿で本当に人前に出られると思う？ Do you really think I can go out *looking like this*? ‖ 母は珍しく着物姿で出かけた Mother left *wearing a kimono*, which is unusual for her. ‖ 夕焼け空に富士山の美しい姿がシルエットになって浮かんでいた The beautiful *shape* of Mt. Fuji was silhouetted in the evening glow.
2【人や物の存在】▶本田君の姿が見えない（＝本田君を見かけない）が，どうしたんだろう？ I *don't see* Honda. I wonder what has happened to him. ‖ 声はすれども姿は見えず I hear voices but *don't see anyone*. ‖ 水平線の向こうから船が姿を現した A ship *appeared* over the horizon. ‖ 少年は素早く塀の陰に姿を隠した The boy quickly *hid* (*himself*) behind the wall. ‖ 彼は人混みの中に姿を消した He *disappeared* in the crowd. ‖ 裕子はあれ以来さっぱり姿を見せない I *have seen nothing of* Yuko since then. ‖ 彼女は約束の時間に姿を見せなかった She *didn't appear* [*turn up*／*show up*] at the appointed time.
3【ありさま】▶破壊された自然は容易には元の姿に戻らない Once the natural environment is severely damaged [degraded], it cannot easily be restored to its *former state*. ‖ その山はもう元の姿をとどめていない The mountain is no longer *what it used to be*. ‖ 日本のありのままの姿を見てください Just observe Japan *as it* (*really*) *is*. ‖ 私の祖国のありのままの姿をお話ししましょう I'll tell you honestly about *how things are* in my native country.

すがたみ 姿見 a **full-length mirror** ▶彼女は姿見で全身をチェックした She checked her appearance [how she looked] in the *full-length mirror*.

スカッシュ **1【スポーツ】squash (rackets)**.
2【飲み物】(a) **squash**. →レモネード.

すかっと ▶言いたいことを全部言ったら胸がすかっとした I *felt a lot better* [*felt great*] after I had said all I wanted to say. ‖ この清涼飲料水はすかっとする This soft drink *is refreshing*.

ずがら 図柄 a **pattern** /pǽṭəʳn/ ▶部屋の壁紙の図柄が気に入らない I don't like the *pattern* of the wallpaper in my room.

すがりつく cling《to》, **hang**《on to》▶女の子は蛇を見て父親にすがりついた When the little girl saw a snake, she *clung to* [*hung on to*] her father.（➤ clung は cling の，hung は hang の過去形）.

すがる **1【つかまる】hold on**《to》; **cling**《to》（しがみつく）▶足をくじいたので友人の肩にすがって歩いた I sprained my ankle, so I had to walk *holding on to* my friend's shoulder.
2【頼る】depend on ; turn to（…に助けを求める）▶人の情けにすがるような生き方はしたくない I don't want to live (*depending*) *on* the charity of others. ‖ 私には身寄りがないので，年を取っても誰にもすがれない I have no relatives, so I have no one to *turn to* in my old age.

すかれる 好かれる be liked ; be loved（愛される）▶誰からも好かれるような人になりなさい Try to become the type of person who *is liked* [*is loved*] by everybody. ‖ 彼は気立てが優しいので誰からも好かれて

いる Everybody *likes* him because he's so kind-hearted. ‖ 彼は近所の人たちに**好かれている**(＝人気がある) He *is popular* with his neighbors.

ずかん 図鑑 an **illustrated book**, a **pictorial book** ▶私は昆虫の名前を図鑑で調べた I looked up the names of the insects in *an illustrated book*. ‖**植物[動物]図鑑** an illustrated book of plants [animals].

スカンク 《動物》 a **skunk** ▶スカンクが悪臭を放った The *skunk* gave off a terrible odor.

スカンジナビア Scandinavia ‖**スカンジナビア半島** the Scandinavian Peninsula.

ずかんそくねつ 頭寒足熱 ▶昔から寝るときは**頭寒足熱**がいいと言われている Since long ago, people have said that when you sleep, you should have '*a cool head and warm feet*.'

1**すき 隙 1【空間・時間の空き】**an **opening**; a **gap**(隙間) ▶雨戸の**隙**(＝隙間)から朝日がさし込んできた The morning sunlight came streaming in through the *opening* [*gap*] in the shutters. ‖ ドアの**隙**から隙間風が入ってくる A draft comes in through the *gap* in the door. (➤ draft は《英》では draught とつづる) ‖ 図書館の前には**隙もない**くらい自転車が止めてあった The space in front of the library was *jam-packed* with bikes. ‖ 父はよく仕事の**隙を見て**ぼくのキャッチボールの相手をしてくれた Dad used to play catch with me *whenever he could get away* from work.

2【油断】▶バッグをひったくられたのはこちらに**隙があった**のだろう I think I might have *been off guard* [I *wasn't being careful enough*], and that is why I had my purse [bag] snatched. ‖ 敵に**隙を見せるな** Always *be on your guard against* your enemy. (➤「警戒せよ」の意) ‖ 迎賓館の**警戒は一分の隙もなかった** The state guesthouse *was closely guarded*.

3【機会】a **chance** ▶犯人は逃げ出す**隙をうかがっていた** The criminal was watching [waiting] for *a chance* to escape. ‖ 泥棒は**隙をうかがって**家に忍び込んだ The burglar *took the chance* to steal into the house. ‖ あの二人はいつも一緒なので私が**割り込む隙はない** Those two are always together, so *there's never a chance* for me *to get between them*.

2**すき 鋤・犂** a **spade**(シャベル状の); 《米》 a **plow**, 《英》 a **plough** /plaʊ/ (牛・馬・トラクターが引く) ▶**すきで**畑を**耕す** *plow* [*plough*] a field.

3**すき 好き 1【好む, 愛する】like** +Ⓜ, **be fond of**, **love** +Ⓜ; **prefer** /prɪfə́ːr/ 《to》 ((…より)…のほうを好む)

> **語法** **like** と **be fond of** は同義だが, 後者のほうが意味が強く, 《米》では女性の間で聞かれることが多い. **love** は「大好きだ」の意で, 人にも物にも用いる.

▶私はスポーツ[犬]が**好きだ** I *like* sports [dogs]. (➤ 目的語が Ⓒ のときは複数形にする) ‖ 由美はチョコレートが**大好きだ** Yumi *is very fond of* chocolate. ‖ ぼくはきみが**好きだ** I *love* you. ‖ 私, アイスクリームがとっても**好き**なの I *love* ice cream. ／I *have a passion for* ice cream. ／I *adore* ice cream. (➤ adore は女性の言い方) ‖ どの銘柄のビールが**好き**? What is your *favorite* brand of beer?

> **【文型】**
> …するのが好きだ
> **like** doing ／**like to** do

> **《解説》** 両方ともふつう同じ意味で用いられるが, doing は一般的・習慣的なことに, to do は特定の, または未来の行為に言及することが多い.

▶うちの子供たちはサッカーをするのが**好きだ** Our kids *like* play*ing* soccer. ‖ 私はモーツァルトの室内楽を聴くのが**好きです** I *like* [*love*] *to* listen to chamber music by Mozart.

> **【文型】**
> A より B のほうが好きだ
> **like** B **better than** A
> **prefer** B **to** A

▶夏より春のほうが**好きです** I *like* spring *better than* summer. ‖ 私はどの科目よりも地理が**好きです** I *like* geography *better than* any other subject(s). ‖ **対話**「きみは犬と猫のどちらが**好き**?」「猫さ」 "Which do you *like* better, dogs or cats?" "I like cats better." ‖ ハンバーガーよりサンドイッチのほうが**好きだ** I *prefer* sandwiches *to* hamburgers. ‖ サッカーは見るよりもするほうが**好きです** I *prefer* playing soccer *to* watching it. ‖ 納豆は**好きではありません** I *don't care for* natto. (➤ この意味の care for は通例否定文・疑問文で使われ, 肯定文では使わない) ‖ 私はあの人が住むこの町が**好きになった** I*'ve come to like* the town because he [she] lives here. ‖ 王女はその新聞記者を**好きになってしまった**(＝恋するようになった) The princess *fell in love with* the reporter. ‖ 私, 太郎君のことが**ずっと好きだった**の I*'ve been* Taro's *secret admirer*. (➤ secret admirer は「ひそかに慕う人」) ‖ 佑樹君が**好きで好きでたまらない** I *like* Yuki so much. *It's driving me mad*. ‖ 彼女にはもう**好きな人**(＝恋人)がいる She already has *a boyfriend*.

✉ **思い切って言います. 実はずっと前からあなたのことが好きでした** I have made up my mind to tell you something. The fact is that I*'ve been in love with* you for a long time.

▶ **対話**「あなたのいちばん**好きな**野球チームは?」「ホークスです」 "What is your *favorite* baseball team?" "The Hawks." (➤ favorite は「いちばん好きな」の意; most favorite, very favorite は特別に強調するとき以外は使わない) ‖ **対話**「きょうもカラオケに行ってきたよ」「おまえも**好きだねえ**」 "I've been to a karaoke room today too." "You*'re* really *fond of* it."

> **あなたの英語はどう響く?**
> 外国人観光客に会うとすぐ Do you like Japan? と聞く人がいるが, 相手は Yes. としか答えようがない. せめて How do you like Japan? (日本の印象はいかがですか)とか Are you enjoying your stay in Japan? (日本での滞在を楽しんでおられますか)と聞くべきである.

ことわざ **好きこそものの上手なれ** When you love doing something [When you love an art], you quickly become good at it.

2【思うまま】▶どうぞ**好きなだけ**召し上がってください Please eat *as much as you like*. ‖ 彼は独身だから**好きなように**(＝のんきに)暮らしている Being single, he leads a *carefree* [*an easygoing*] life. ‖ **好きなようにしなさい** Do *as you please*. ‖ **好きにしろ!** *Suit yourself!* ‖ おまえも20歳になったのだから**好きにやっていい**よ Now that you are twenty, you can do *as you like*.

☞ 大好き (→見出語)

すぎ 杉 a **Japanese cedar** /síːdəʳ/
‖**杉花粉症** cedar pollen allergy (→花粉) ‖ **杉並木** rows of Japanese cedars.

-すぎ -過ぎ 1【時間】**past**, **after** (➤主に時刻につけて); **over** (➤主に年齢につけて) ▶**50過ぎの男** a man *over* fifty ／a man in his fifties (➤後者は「50代の男」の意) ‖ **ぼくのおじはもう60過ぎだ** My uncle *is over* [*past*] sixty now. ／My uncle *is on the wrong side of* sixty. (➤ be on the wrong side of は「…過ぎである」の意のユーモラスな言い方；「…前である」なら wrong の代わりに right を用いる) ‖ **もう昼過ぎだ** It's already *past noon*. ‖ **今10時10分過ぎです** It's ten (minutes) *past* [《米また》*after*] ten. (➤「15分過ぎ」は fifteen past ten ではなく, 通例 a quarter past ten という) ‖ **5時過ぎにもう一度電話します** I'll call again *after* five (o'clock). ‖ **彼女は12時過ぎまで起きていることがよくあった** She would often sit up *till past* midnight. ‖ **来月の3日過ぎなら暇ができます** I will be free *after* the third of next month.
2【度を越すこと】▶**太りすぎは健康によくない** Being *overweight* is bad for the health. ‖ **ねえ, 大きな声出し過ぎよ** Hey, you'*re speaking too loud*. ‖ **ふざけ過ぎよ！静かにしなさい** *Stop fooling around!* Quiet down!

-ずき -好き ▶**彼は映画[野球]好きだ** He is *a movie* [*baseball*] *fan*. (➤「映画好き」は《主に米》moviegoer, 《主に英》filmgoer, cinemagoer ともいう) ‖ **豚はきれい好きだ** Pigs *love being clean*. ‖ **あの落語家は酒好きのうえに女好きときている** That rakugo-teller is not only *a heavy drinker* but (also) *a womanizer*. ‖ **日出夫は釣り好きで週末にはよく出かける** Hideo is *an avid angler* and usually goes fishing on the weekends. (➤ avid は「熱心な」).

スキー **skiing** (滑ること); (**a pair of**) **skis** (道具) 一動 **スキーをする** **ski** ▶**スキーを履く[脱ぐ]** put on [take off] one's *skis* ‖ **彼女はスキーがとてもうまい** She *is very good at skiing*. ／She *is a very good skier*. ‖ **毎年冬は志賀高原にスキーに行く** I *go skiing* at Shiga Heights every winter. (➤ (×)go skiing to Shiga Heights とはいわない) ／I *go* to Shiga Heights *to ski* every winter.
‖**スキーウエア** skiwear, a ski suit ‖ **スキー靴** ski boots ‖ **スキー場** a skiing ground ; a ski resort (リゾート地) ‖ **スキーヤー** a skier.

> 「スキー競技」のいろいろ **アルペン複合** Alpine combined ／**エアリアル** aerials ／**回転** slalom ／**滑降** downhill ／**クロスカントリー** cross-country skiing ／**ジャンプ** ski jumping ／**スーパー大回転** super giant slalom ／**スノーボード** snowboarding ／**大回転** giant slalom ／**ノルディック複合** Nordic combined ／**バイアスロン** biathlon ／**モーグル** moguls

すきかって 好き勝手 ▶**彼女はいつも好き勝手なふるまいをする** She always *gets* [*has*] *her way*. ‖ **ぼくの好き勝手にさせてよ** Please *let* me *do my own thing*. (➤「やりたいことや向いていることをやらせる」の意).

すききらい 好き嫌い **likes and dislikes** ▶**弟は食べ物の好き嫌いが激しい** My (younger) brother *has strong likes and dislikes* [*preferences*] in food.

すきこのんで 好き好んで ▶**私は何もすき好んでこんな会社で働いているわけではない** I'm not working in this sort of company *by choice*. ‖ **何もすき好んで(＝よりによって)あんな怠け者と一緒になることはないのに** *Of all the men* (*in the world*), why did you have to choose that lazy bum?

すぎさる 過ぎ去る **pass** 一形 **過ぎ去った** **past** ▶**過ぎ去った日の思い出が今も脳裏に焼きついている** *Memories of days past* are burned into my memory. ‖ **過ぎ去ったことはしかたがない** *Let bygones be bygones*. ／What's done cannot be undone. ／What's done is done. (➤英語のことわざ).

すきずき 好き好き (a) **taste** (好み) ▶**人にはそれぞれ好き好きがある** Everybody has *his or her own taste*. ‖ **どちらの色を選ぶかは好き好き(＝好みの問題)だ** Which color to choose is *a matter of taste*. ‖ **食べ物には好き好きがある** Everyone has (his or her) *likes and dislikes* about food.
ことわざ **たで食う虫も好き好き** There is no accounting for tastes. (➤「人の好みは説明がつかないもの」の意) ／Tastes differ. (➤「好みは異なるもの」の意).

ずきずき ▶**傷がまだずきずき痛む** The wound *is* still *throbbing with pain*. ／The wound still *smarts*.

すきっぱら 空きっ腹 an **empty stomach** /stʌ́mək/ ▶**すきっ腹にビールがこたえた** The beer hit my *empty stomach* hard.

スキップ a **skip** 一動 **スキップする** **skip** (＋自) ▶**通りを歌いながらスキップして行く** *skip* down the street singing ‖ **問3をスキップする** *skip* Question 3.

すきとおる 透き通る 一形 **透き通った** **clear** (澄んだ); **transparent** /trænspǽrənt, -péər-/ (透明な) ▶**サラ・ブライトマンの透き通った歌声** Sarah Brightman's *clear* [*transparent*] singing voice ‖ **水晶は透き通っている** Crystal is *transparent*. ‖ **昔この湖の水は透き通っていた** The water of this lake used to be *clear*. ‖ **エミリーは透き通るような青い目をしている** Emily has *clear* blue eyes. ‖ **彼女は透き通るような肌をしている** She has a *clear* complexion.

-すぎない -過ぎない ▶**私がもらったのは5000円にすぎない** I received *only* [*no more than*] 5,000 yen. ／I *only* received 5,000 yen. (➤話しことばでは後者がよりふつう) ‖ **10年前は彼はただの学生にすぎなかった** Ten years ago he was *only* [*nothing but*] a student. ‖ **彼女の病気は口実にすぎなかった** Her illness was *only* an excuse.

すきほうだい 好き放題 →好き勝手 ▶**うちの道楽息子は好き放題のことをしている** That dissipated son of mine is doing *as he pleases*.

すきま 透き間・隙間 an **opening** ; a **gap** (望ましくない隙間); a **crack** (割れ目) ▶**誰か塀の隙間からのぞいてるよ** There's someone peeping through *an opening* [*a slit*] in the fence. (➤ slit は「細長い穴」) ‖ **壁の隙間を石こうで埋めた** I filled the *crack* in the wall with plaster. ‖ **妹は歯と歯の間にだいぶ隙間がある** My (younger) sister has large *gaps* between her teeth. ‖ **動物たちがフェンスの隙間から逃げた** The animals escaped through *a* [*the*] *gap* in the fence. (● a は隙間が複数箇所あった場合の1つ, the は隙間が1つだけの場合) ‖ **どこからか隙間風が入って来るようだ** I feel *a draft* coming from somewhere. (➤ draft は《英》では draught /drɑːft/ とつづる) ‖**隙間市場** a niche /nɪtʃ ‖ niːʃ/ market ‖**隙間商品** a niche product.

スキマー a **skimmer** (クレジットカード不正読み取り機器) ▶**パート店員が客の ATM カードにスキマーと呼ばれる不正読み取り機器を使っていた** A part-time clerk used a device called *a skimmer* on the customers' ATM cards.

すきやき すき焼き **sukiyaki** (➤英語化している)
日本紹介 ✉ **すき焼きは薄切りの牛肉をネギ, シ**

イタケ，春菊などの野菜や焼き豆腐などと一緒に鍋で煮て，しょうゆと砂糖で味付けした料理です．テーブルの上で調理して，皆で一つ鍋をつつきます Sukiyaki is a dish made of sliced beef which is cooked in an iron pan with vegetables such as green onion(s), shiitake mushrooms, edible chrysanthemum leaves and grilled tofu. It is seasoned with soy sauce and sugar. Sukiyaki is cooked at the table and everybody serves themselves from the same pan.

スキャット《音楽》a **scat**.

スキャナー a **scanner**.

スキャンダル a **scandal**, **dirt**(➤ 後者はインフォーマル) ▶スキャンダルをもみ消す hush up *a scandal* ‖ 彼の対立候補のスキャンダルを探し出す dig up *dirt* on his political opponent ‖ あの政治家にはスキャンダルが絶えない That politician was involved in one *scandal* after another. ‖ その歌手はスキャンダルのために人気を失った The singer lost her popularity because of *a scandal*.

スキューバ a **scuba** ▶彼らはサンゴ礁の海でスキューバダイビングを楽しんだ They enjoyed *scuba diving* in the sea among the coral reefs. (➤「スキューバダイビングをする」は scuba dive).
‖スキューバダイバー a scuba diver.

スキル a **skill** ▶当社では社員のスキルアップを図るため研修を行っています Our company provides training for its employees to *improve* their *job skills*.

すぎる 過ぎる 1【通過する】**pass**, **go by**(➤ 後者はややインフォーマル) ▶眠っている間に列車は姫路を過ぎた Our train *passed* Himeji Station while I was asleep. ‖ ハイドパークはもう過ぎましたか Have we *passed* [*gone by*] Hyde Park yet? ‖ 先頭のランナーは中間点を過ぎた The front-runner *passed* the halfway point. ‖ 嵐が過ぎるまでこの町で待とう Let's wait in this town until the storm *blows over*. (➤ blow over は「吹きやむ」).

2【時刻・年月などが】**pass**, **go by**(➤ 後者はややインフォーマル) 一形 過ぎた **past** ▶時が過ぎて，街の様子は変わった Time has *passed* [has *gone by*], and the city looks different. ‖ 彼がこの町を去ってから 5 年が過ぎた It *has been* five years since he left this town. (➤《米》に多い言い方で，《英》では It is five years ... のような言い方がふつう) ／Five years *have passed* [*have gone by*] since he left this town. (➤ 堅い文語的表現) ‖ 春が過ぎて夏が来た Spring *is over* [*is gone*] and summer has come. (➤「済んで」「過ぎ去って」の意) ‖ 私たちの音楽の先生は 40 を過ぎている Our music teacher *is over* [*is past*] forty. ‖ 卒論の提出期限はとっくに過ぎている It *is well past* the deadline for submitting graduation papers. ‖ この本の貸し出し期限は 3 週間過ぎている This (library) book *is* three weeks *overdue*. ‖ 過ぎてしまったことはしかたがない Let *bygones* be bygones. ／*What's done* cannot be undone. ／*What's done* is done. (➤ 英語のことわざ).

3【度を越す】▶少し口が過ぎますよ I think you'*re saying* a little *too much*. ‖ きみはぼくには過ぎた女房だ You are *too good* a wife for me. (➤「too ＋形容詞＋ a ＋名詞」の語順に注意) ／You are a *better* wife *than I deserve*.
▶食べ過ぎないようにしなさいよ Be careful not to *eat too much*. ／Don't *overeat*. ‖ 彼は働き過ぎてノイローゼになった He *overworked* (*himself*) [*worked too much*] and had a nervous breakdown.

ことわざ 過ぎたるはなお及ばざるがごとし Too much is no better than too little.

> 【文型】
> A 過ぎて…できない
> **too** A **to** do
> ➤ A は形容詞・副詞
>
> 《解説》「…するには A 過ぎる」の意にもなる. to do の主語 (B) を示すにはその前に for B をつける. so A that 〜(非常に A なので〜)を使っても同様の意味を表せる. →-ので.

▶このお茶は熱すぎて飲めない This tea is *too hot* for me *to* drink. ‖ 彼は恋をするには若すぎる He is *too young to* be in love.

> 【文型】
> いくら A であっても A であり過ぎない
> **cannot be too** A
> いくら…しても…し過ぎない
> **cannot** do **enough**

▶火の元はいくら注意してもし過ぎることはない You *cannot be too* careful with fire. ‖ 彼についてはいくら褒めても褒め過ぎることはない We *cannot* praise him *enough*.
☞ -すぎない (→見出語)

スキン **skin**(肌)；a **rubber**(コンドーム) ▶スキンケア商品 a *skin-care* product.

ずきん 頭巾 a **hood** /hod/ ▶赤頭巾 Little Red Riding *Hood* (➤ 童話の題名).

スキンシップ (→かこみ記事) ▶彼女は息子とスキンシップがとれている She is *physically affectionate* with her son.

> 危ないカタカナ語✹ スキンシップ
> 1 肌の触れ合いによる交流という意味の「スキンシップ」は skin(皮膚)と -ship(状態，関係)から作った和製語とされている.
> 2 英語では physical contact, body [bodily] contact, さらに広い意味では personal contact, close contact などというが，いずれの表現にも「スキンシップ」のもつ「ぬくもり」のニュアンスはない.

ずきんずきん ▶かぜで頭がずきんずきんする My head *is throbbing* from a cold.

スキンダイビング **skin diving** ▶毎週日曜日に近くの海でスキンダイビングをします I enjoy *skin diving* in the nearby sea every Sunday.

¹すく 好く **like** ＋㊐, **love** ＋㊐.
☞ 好かれる，好き (→見出語)

²すく 空く・透く 1【混んでいない】▶ラッシュアワーを過ぎていたので電車はすいていた The rush hour was over, so the train *was not crowded*. ‖ グリーン車はすいていますか *Is there* still *room* in the 'green car'? ／*Are there empty seats* in the first-class car? ‖ 対話「東名(高速)，どうだった？」「思ったよりすいてたよ」"How was the Tomei Expressway?" "It *was less crowded* than I (had) expected."

2【暇になる】▶手がすいたら手伝ってよ *When you're free*, can you give me a hand?

3【腹が減る】**be hungry** ▶あー，おなかがすいた Oh, gosh! I'*m hungry* [*starved*].

4【隙間ができる】▶ぼくは歯と歯の間が透いている I *have gaps* between my teeth. ‖ 戸が透いていると隙間風が入って寒い When the door is *ajar*, the room gets chilly with drafts coming in. (➤ ajar は「(戸が)半開きで」; draft は《英》では draught とつづる).

3 **すく 梳く** **comb** /koum/ +目 ▶髪をすく *comb* one's hair ‖彼は両手で髪をすいた He *ran* his hands *through* his hair.

4 **すく 漉く** ▶和紙をすく *make* a sheet of Japanese paper.

すぐ 直ぐ **1【時間の隔たりがなく，直ちに】at once, right [straight] away, immediately** (➤最後はやや堅い語); **instantly**(即座に); **soon**(まもなく) (➤soon は文脈によって「そのうちに」の意にもなる) ▶(今)すぐ降りてらっしゃい Come downstairs *at once* [*right now / this minute*]. (➤これに答えて「すぐ行くよ」という場合は I'm coming. でよい) ‖検査の結果はすぐわかります We'll know the test results *in no time at all*. ‖ヤクルトはすぐ反撃して同点とした The Swallows *immediately* fought back and tied the score. ‖すぐ戻ります I'll be back *soon*. / I'll be *right* back. (➤後者のほうが戻るまでの時間が短い) ‖ちょっと失礼します. すぐに戻りますから Excuse me, I'll be back *in a minute*. ‖《久しぶりの友人に》やあ, 上田君！ すぐわかったよ Hi, Ueda! I recognized you *at once* [*right away / instantly*]. ‖彼を今すぐ病院へ連れていかなければならない We have to take him to the hospital *right away*. (➤right および right away はややくだけた言い方) ‖もうすぐクリスマスだ Christmas *is coming up* (*soon*). / Christmas *is just around the corner*. ‖もうすぐ新潟よ We'll *soon* [*shortly*] arrive in Niigata. (➤shortly は「じきに, まもなく」).

> **【文型】**
> **～するとすぐに**
> **as soon as** S + V
>
> **《解説》**「～するとすぐに」の言い方は **as soon as** を使うのが最もふつう. 文章で使うやや堅い表現には「**had no sooner** +過去分詞+ **than**」や「**had hardly** [**scarcely**] +過去分詞+ **when**」がある. (→-いなや) また, **when** だけでも「～するとすぐに」を表すことができる場合がある.

▶結果がわかったらすぐに知らせてちょうだい *As soon as* you know the results, please let me know. ‖玄関を入るとすぐに何か変だと気づいた I noticed that something was wrong *as soon as* I walked in the front door. ‖彼は起き上がるとすぐにまたひっくり返った He *had no sooner* gotten to his feet *than* he fell again. / He *had hardly* [*scarcely*] gotten to his feet *when* he fell again. ‖時計が12時を打つとすぐ, 彼は弁当箱を広げ始めた He began to open his bento *when* the clock struck twelve. ‖この薬は飲むとすぐに効いてくる This medicine starts working *right* [*immediately*] *after* you take it.

2【簡単に】easily ▶その寺はすぐわかった I found the temple *easily*. ‖奈々子はすぐにかぜをひく Nanako *easily* catches cold. ‖彼女はからかわれるとすぐ怒る She's *quick* to get angry when she is teased. ‖彼女はすぐに人を信じる She believes people *too easily*.

3【距離の隔たりがなく，すぐ近く】▶私の家はバス停からすぐ近くです My home is *very near* the bus stop. ‖本棚は机のすぐ脇にあります My bookcase is *just beside* my desk. ‖駅のすぐ向かい側にマクドナルドがある McDonald's is *right across from* the train station. ‖パパ, スピードを落として. 白バイがすぐ後ろに来ているよ Dad, slow down. A motorcycle cop is *right behind* us. ‖息子はすぐ近くに住んでいる My son lives *within a stone's throw of* my home. (➤「家から石を投げれば届く距離に」の意) ‖スーパーは家から歩いてすぐの所にある The supermarket is *a few minutes' walk* [*only a short step away*] from my home.

-ずく ▶男は老婦人から力ずくでハンドバッグを奪い取った The man took the handbag away from the old woman *by force*. ‖腕ずくでも金は取り返してやる I'll get our money back *even if I have to resort to violence*. ‖彼は何事も欲得ずくだ He *does* everything *out of selfish motives* [*for money*].

すくい 救い **help**(助け) ▶彼は私に救いを求めた He asked me for *help*. ‖恵まれない人々に救いの手を差し伸べよう Let's extend *a helping hand* to those (who are) less fortunate. ‖手伝ってくれてありがとう. きみはまさに救いの神だよ Thank you for helping me out. You're a real *life-saver*!
▶《慣用表現》今回の水害で死者が出なかったのがせめてもの救いだ The only *saving grace* is that there were no fatalities from the flood. (➤saving grace は「(欠点を補う)取り柄」).

すくいがたい 救い難い ▶あいつは救い難いばかだ He is a *hopeless* idiot.

スクイズ 《野球》a **squeeze play**, a **squeeze** ▶見事なスクイズをする stage *a squeeze play*.
‖**スクイズバント** a squeeze bunt.

1 **すくう 救う** **save** +目; **rescue** +目 (救助隊などが); **help**(手助けする) ▶彼は川に飛び込んで溺れる子を救った He plunged into the river and *saved* [*rescued*] a child from drowning. ‖この方が私の命を救ってくださったのです This woman *saved* my life. ‖人々を苦しみから救う(＝解放する)ため彼は僧になった He became a Buddhist priest to *relieve* people of their suffering(s). ‖おじはぼくの窮地を救ってくれた My uncle *helped* me *out of* my difficulties.
▶こんなに真面目に働いているのにボーナスなしじゃ全く救われないよ To get no bonus after all my hard work *is a* real *letdown* [*disappointment*]. (➤ともに「がっかりすること」の意).

2 **すくう 掬う** **scoop** /skuːp/《up》; **dip**《up, out》(手のひらやひしゃくで); **ladle** /léɪdl/ +目 (ひしゃくで) ▶私は両手で雪をすくった I *scooped up* some snow in my hands. ‖その子供は金魚を3匹すくった The child *scooped up* three goldfish. ‖谷川の水を手ですくって飲んだ I *cupped* my hands to drink the stream water. (➤この cup は「カップのような形にする」の意の動詞) ‖アイスクリームはそのスプーンですくって食べなさい Eat your ice cream *with the spoon*.

3 **すくう 巣くう** ▶盛り場に巣くう暴力団 mobsters who *hang out* in the entertainment district.

スクーター a **(motor) scooter**.

スクープ a **scoop**(特ダネ) 一動 (他社を)スクープで出し抜く **scoop** +目 ▶その記者はライバル紙をスクープで出し抜いた That reporter *scooped* the rival paper. ‖彼女はその贈収賄事件をスクープした She *got a scoop* on the bribery case.

スクーリング **classroom instruction**
▶当コースでは月に1回のスクーリングが必要です This course requires a day of *classroom instruction* per month. (➤schooling は「学校で教育を受けること」という意味で通信教育の「面接指導」の意はない).

スクールカラー a **school color**(校色) ▶H大学のスク

ールカラーはオレンジだ The *school color* of H University is orange. ‖ 私はあの学校のスクールカラー(=校風)は好きではない I don't like *the atmosphere* of that school.

> 危ないカタカナ語✹ スクールカラー
> 学校の旗やユニフォームなどの色(校色)の意味では school color でよいが,「校風」の意味では school spirit, school tradition, traditional atmosphere of a school などとする必要がある.

スクールバス a **school bus.**

すぐさま **promptly** →すぐ ▶真理にメールを送ったら,すぐさま返事が来た When I sent Mari an e-mail, she replied *promptly*. / Mari replied *shortly* after I sent her an e-mail. ‖ 火災報知器が鳴ると警備員がすぐさま駆けつけてきた The fire alarm had *barely* gone off *when* a security guard arrived. (➤ barely A when B で,「A するかしないうちに B する」を表す. A はふつう過去完了形, B は過去形).

すくすく ▶庭ではエンドウ豆がすくすく育っている Peas are growing *rapidly* in the garden. (➤「速く, どんどん」の意) ‖ 子猫たちは母猫のお乳を飲んですくすくと育っている The kittens are drinking their mother's milk and growing *steadily*. (➤「着実に」の意).

すくない 少ない **few**(数が); **little**(量が); **small**(数量や部分・%などが)

> 語法 (1)few も little も「ほとんどない」で, 否定的な意味が強い. a few, a little とすると「少しはある」という肯定的な意味になる.
> (2)数・量のほか, 金額や人数, 程度などについていうときには small も用いる.

▶彼女の英作文には間違いが少ない Her English composition has *few* mistakes. ‖ 東京は地価が高いので庭付きの家は少ない Land prices in Tokyo are high, so *few* houses have yards or gardens. ‖ 少ないチャンスを生かさなければ試合には勝てない If you don't make good use of the *few chances* there are to score in a game, you can't win. ‖ 今日でも100歳まで生きる人は少ない Even today *few* (people) live to be a hundred. (➤ 話す場合は few と a few の区別が聞き取りにくいので, not many people … というのがふつう) ‖ 今月は雨が少なかった We've had very *little* rain this month. ‖ 日本はインドネシアより住んでいる人が少ない Japan has *fewer* inhabitants *than* Indonesia does. ‖ 日本の人口はインドネシアより少ない The population of Japan *is smaller than* that of Indonesia. (➤ population には fewer ではなく smaller を用いる) ‖ カラオケが嫌いな人は少なくない *Quite a few* [*Not a few*] people dislike karaoke. (➤ quite a few は「かなり多数の」, not a few は「少なからぬ」に相当する文語的な言い方) ‖ 大都会の真ん中は緑の草地と樹木が少ない Green grass and trees are *scarce* in the middle of a big city. ‖ ことしはジャガイモの収穫が少なかった The potato crop was *poor* this year.

▶少ない給料 *small* salary ‖ 父は口数が少ない My father *talks very little*. / My father *is a man of few words*. ‖ 母は家にいることが少ない(=まれだ) My mother is *seldom* at home. ‖ 雨で行楽地はどこも人出が少なかった *There was a small turnout* at most resort areas due to the rain. ‖ 最近野鳥の数が目に見えて少なくなった Recently wild birds *have noticeably decreased in number*. ‖ 人手が少なくて困っている We are in a bind because we *are understaffed*.

すくなからず 少なからず ▶工場の海外移転を危ぶむ声は社内にも少なからずあった *Not a few* staff members voiced concern over relocating the manufacturing plants overseas.

すくなくとも 少なくとも **at least**(➤ at the (very) least の形でも用いる); **not less than, no fewer than**(➤「少なくとも…だけのもの」の意) ▶このオートバイの修理, 少なくとも 2 万円はかかると思うよ I would guess the repairs to this motorcycle will cost *at least* twenty thousand yen. ‖ 彼は少なくとも30は過ぎている He is over thirty *at the* (*very*) *least*. ‖ 彼女には少なくとも 3 人のボーイフレンドがいる She has *not less* [*no fewer*] *than* three close male friends. ‖ 少なくともそれくらいはきみにできることだ That's *the least* you can do. (➤ the least は「最小・最少」).

すくなめ 少なめ ▶食事は少なめにしたほうが体にいいよ It is good for your health to eat *lightly* [*moderately*]. (➤ それぞれ「軽く」「控えめに」の意) ‖ 《ホットドッグを注文して》からしは少なめにしてください *Easy on* the mustard, please. (➤ easy on は「(調味料などを)ほどほどに」の意) ‖ 私たちは校内英語弁論大会の参加者数を例年よりも少なめに見積もった We *estimated* the number of participants in the intramural English speech contest *to be smaller* than usual. (➤ intramural は「学内[校内]の」) ‖ 対話「ご飯のお代わりいかが?」「はい, 少なめにしてください」"How about another helping of rice?" "Yes, thank you. *A small one*, please."

すくむ 竦む ▶私はその光景を見て恐怖で身がすくんだ I *was petrified* [*was paralyzed*] with terror at the sight. (➤ petrify は「身動きできなくする」) ‖ 高い崖から見下ろしたら足がすくんだ When I looked down from the high cliff, I *felt my legs giving way* [*felt my legs turn to rubber*]. ‖ お化け屋敷で弘はすくみ上がって一歩も歩けなくなった Hiroshi *was so scared of* the haunted house *that* he *was frozen* in place. (➤ in place は「その場で」).

-ずくめ ▶きょうはいいことずくめだよ I've had *a run of good luck* today. ‖ 彼は黒ずくめの格好で戸口に立っていた *Dressed* (*all*) *in black*, he stood at the door. ‖ 規則ずくめの寮生活なんてとても耐えられません I can't stand dorm life *with all the rules*.

すくめる 竦める **duck** +目 (首を); **shrug** +目 (肩を) ▶ぼくはボールが飛んでくるのを見て首をすくめた I *ducked my head* when I saw the ball flying toward me. ‖ そのアメリカ人男性は肩をすくめただけで何も答えなかった That American gentleman just *shrugged his shoulders* and gave no answer. (➤ 英米人がよくやる困惑・不賛成・冷笑などのジェスチャー).

スクラップ **1**【くず鉄】**scrap iron** ▶私は車をスクラップとして売った I sold my car for *scrap*. ‖ その古い船はスクラップにされた The old ship *was scrapped*.
2【切り抜き】a **clipping,** 《英また》a **cutting** ▶その連載記事はスクラップしてあります That serial *was clipped and filed*. (➤ was scrapped といわない. clip は「(記事を)切り抜く」).
‖スクラップブック a scrapbook.

スクラム a **scrum,** a **scrummage** (ラグビーの); a **scrimmage** (アメリカンフットボールの).

スクランブル a **scramble**(軍用機の緊急発進)
‖スクランブルエッグ scrambled eggs(➤ 通例複

数の卵で作られるので，複数形で使われる）‖**スクランブル交差点** a pedestrian scramble, a six-way crossing (for pedestrians).

スクリーン a **screen** ▶ヒロインの顔がスクリーンに大写しになった A close-up of the heroine's face was flashed on the *screen*.

スクリプト a **script**.

スクリュー a **screw propeller** /prəpélər/ (➤単に screw または propeller ともいう) ‖**スクリューボール** a screwball(➤日本でいう「シュート」のこと).

すぐれもの 優れ物 a **smart gadget** ▶この栓抜きはなかなかの優れ物だ This cork extractor is quite *a* (*useful*) *gadget*.

すぐれる 優れる **1【優秀である】一形 優れた good ; excellent** (➤通例比較級・最上級では用いない) ▶優れた仕事 *excellent* work ‖フィレンツェでは多くの優れた芸術作品に接することができた I got to see many *excellent* [*outstanding*] works of art in Florence.

【文型】
A は B より優れている
A **is better than** B.
A **is superior to** B.

▶洋子は英語ではクラスメートの誰よりも優れている Yoko *is better than* any of her classmates in English. ‖正男はスキーの腕前では兄より優れている Masao *is* a *better* skier *than* his (older) brother. ‖これらの輸入品は国産品よりも優れている These imported products *are superior to* domestic ones. ‖ある文明がほかより優れているという考え方はしたくない I don't like to think that one civilization *is superior to* others. ‖このお茶のほうがそちらより品質が優れている This tea is *of higher quality* than that one.
▶シェークスピアは世界で最も優れた劇作家の1人である Shakespeare is one of *the best* [*greatest*] playwrights in the world. ‖鈴木博士は日本が生んだ最も優れた科学者の1人で，数々の優れた業績がある Dr. Suzuki is one of the most *eminent* [*distinguished*] scientists (that) Japan has ever produced and has numerous *achievements* to his credit. (➤eminent は「(存命中または亡くなったばかりで)極めて有名な」, distinguished は eminent の意のほかに「名誉ある地位を占めている」の意が加わることが多い; to one's credit は「自分の業績として」) ‖優れた詩は政治家を動かす力をもつ *Fine* poetry has the power to move politicians.
2【「すぐれない」の形で】 ▶きょうは気分がすぐれない I *don't feel well* today. ／I *feel under the weather* today. ‖祖母は気分がすぐれないと言って早めに床に就いた My grandmother went to bed early saying she *was out of sorts*. ‖父は最近健康がすぐれない My father *is in poor health* [*is under the weather*] these days. ‖顔色がすぐれないね You *look pale* [*unwell*].

スクロール ▶《コンピュータ》ウインドーをスクロールする *scroll* (*down* ／*up*) a window.

ずけい 図形 a **figure** /fígjər/ ▶ボールの図形を描く draw *a figure* of a ball ‖私は計算の問題より図形の問題のほうが好きだ I like (to solve) problems *in geometry* better than ones in arithmetic. (➤geometry /dʒiá:mətri/ は「幾何学」).

スケート **skating**(スケートをすること) ; (a **pair of**) **skates** (スケート靴) 一動 **スケートをする skate, ice-skate** ▶湖でスケートをする *skate* on the lake ‖スケートできる? Can you *skate* [*ice-skate*] ? ‖スケートに行こう Let's *go skating*. ‖父がスケート靴を買ってくれた My father bought me (*a pair of*) *skates*. ‖彼女は500メートルスピードスケートで3位に入賞した She won third place in the 500-meter *speed-skating race*.
‖**スケートリンク** a skating rink ‖**インラインスケート** in-line skates(➤底に車輪を縦1列に並べたスケート靴を使うローラースケート) ‖**フィギュアスケート** figure skating.

スケートボード a **skateboard**(板) ; **skateboarding**(遊び) ▶公園の舗装された道でぼくたちはスケートボードをした We *skateboarded* on the paved walk in the park.

スケープゴート a **scapegoat** ▶彼は今回の汚職事件のスケープゴートにされた He was made *a scapegoat* in the current corruption scandal.

スケール **1【規模】** a **scale** ; (a) **caliber** /kǽləbər/ (人の度量) ▶スケールの大きなプロジェクト a *large-scale* project ‖彼はスケールの大きい[小さい]男だ He is *a man of high* [*low*] *caliber*. (➤「スケールの大きい人」は broad-minded [big-hearted] person ともいう).
2【はかり】 a **scale**(重さを量る; しばしば複数形で用いる) ; a **ruler**(物差し).

スケジュール a **schedule** /skédʒu:l ‖ ʃédju:l/ (日程) ; a **plan** (計画) ▶ハードスケジュール *a tight* [*heavy*] *schedule* (➤hard schedule は一般的な言い方ではない) ‖夏休みのスケジュールを組む make *plans* for summer vacation ‖今月はスケジュールが詰まっている My *schedule* is full this month. ／I have a tight *schedule* this month. ‖この仕事はスケジュールどおりには終わらないだろう This job won't be finished *on schedule*. ‖今週は忙しくて仕事のスケジュールのやりくりがつかない I'm too busy this week to juggle my work *schedule*. ‖《社長が秘書などに》きょうの私のスケジュールはどうなってるかね What does my *schedule* look like today ?

すけすけ 透け透けの **sheer** ▶ 対話 「あの人，下着がすけすけじゃない」「あれがはやってんのよ」"That girl's underwear *is showing right through her clothes*." "That's the fashion (now)."

ずけずけ ▶彼，ずいぶんずけずけと物を言う人だね He *speaks bluntly*. ／He's very *outspoken*. (● outspoken は文脈によっては「率直にずばりと物を言う」の意で褒めことばになる. 例えば Mr. Benson has a reputation for being an outspoken politician. (ベンソン氏は率直な政治家だという評判だ)のような場合がそうである).

スケッチ a **sketch** 一動 **スケッチする sketch** (+⑪) ▶彼は浜名湖へスケッチに出かけた He went *sketching* at Lake Hamana. ‖私は湖畔の風景をスケッチした I *sketched* [*made a sketch of*] the view of the lakeside. ‖**スケッチブック** a sketchbook.

すけっと 助っ人 a **helper** ▶日本のプロ野球は外国人助っ人なしには成り立たない Japanese professional baseball can't do without the *help* of foreign players.

スケトウダラ 《魚》an **Alaska pollock** [複 ～s].

すげない ▶すげない(＝そっけない)返事 a *curt* answer ‖彼女はぼくにすげない(＝冷たい)そぶりをした She treated me in a *cold* [an *icy*] manner. ／She gave [showed] me the cold shoulder. (➤give [show] ... the cold shoulder で「…を冷たくあしらう」) ‖彼女は私の招きをすげなく(＝すっぱりと)断った She rejected my invitation *flatly*.

すけばん 助番 **(the leader of) delinquent girls.**

すけべえ 助兵衛 a **lech** /letʃ/, a **lecher** 一形 **助兵衛**

す

な **lecherous** ▶助兵衛おやじ *an old lech* ‖ 助兵衛な男 a *lecherous* man ‖ 助兵衛ね！その手，放しなさいよ！ *You lech* [*You dirty old man*] *!* Let go of me！‖ その男は私の胸を助兵衛ったらしい目で見た The man stared at my chest *like a real lech*.

スケボー →スケートボード.

すける 透ける ▶更衣室の中の様子がカーテンから透けて見えた You *could see* into the dressing room *through* the curtain. ‖ その泉の水は底が透けて見えるほど澄んでいた The water in the spring was clear *enough to see the bottom*. ‖ 彼女は肌が透けて見えるネグリジェを着ていた She was wearing a *see-through* nightgown.

スケルツォ 《音楽》 a **scherzo** /skéəˈtsoʊ/ [複 ～s].

スケルトン a **skeleton**. →骸骨.

スコア a **score** ▶ランナーがスコアリングポジションにいて with runners in *scoring position* (➤ ランナーが複数名の場合) ‖ その試合は5対2のスコアでわが校が勝った Our school won the game by *a score* of 5 to 2. ‖ ついに5対5のタイスコアとなった Finally *the score was tied* at 5 to 5.

‖スコアボード a scoreboard.

すごい **1【程度が甚だしい，すばらしい】great, terrific** (➤ 後者のほうが大げさ)；**wonderful, marvelous** (➤ 後者は《米》では女性に好まれる) ▶ TOEICで700点取ったの？すごい！ You scored 700 on the TOEIC? *Great* [*Terrific* ／ *Wonderful*] *!* ‖ すごい！斎藤がまた勝った *Wow!* Saito won again. ‖ すごい新人が現れた A *marvelous* rookie has come on the scene. ‖ こんなすごいミュージカル見たことないわ I've never seen such a *marvelous* musical. ‖ ゆうべの風，すごかったね The wind last night *was really something*, wasn't it? ／That was *quite* a wind last night, wasn't it? ‖ 彼，すごい車に乗ってるよ！ *You wouldn't believe* the car he drives！(➤「きみは信じないであろう」の意) ‖ あそこにすごい美人がいるぞ There is *an extremely beautiful woman* [*a stunning woman*] over there. ／The woman over there is *a real beauty* [*a knockout*]. ‖ 対話「彼，車椅子で富士山に登ったんだってよ」「すごい！」"He climbed Mt. Fuji in a wheelchair." "That's *great* [*wonderful*]!" (➤ 年配者には後者が好まれる) ‖ 彼の(いちばん)すごいところは，毎日野球の練習で忙しいはずなのに定期試験の成績がいいところです *What I* (*most*) *admire about him* is that he gets good grades on [《英》 in] regular exams, even though he must be busy with baseball practice every day.

2【恐ろしい】terrible (強い恐怖感を与える)；**dreadful** (ひどく嫌な) ▶ 2日前ここですごい交通事故があった A *terrible* [*dreadful*] car accident happened here two days ago.

☛ すごく (→見出語)

ずこう 図工 (an) **art**；**arts and crafts, drawing and manual arts** (図画と工作) ▶図工の教師 an *art* teacher.

すごうで 凄腕 ▶ここのママさんはあれでなかなかすご腕なんだ. 何しろ5年でこの店持ったんだから The mama-san is quite *a go-getter*. After all, she opened her own bar in only five years.

スコール a (**rain**) **squall** /skwɔːl/.

スコーン a **scone**.

すごく **awfully, terribly** (➤ 前者は女性が使うことが多い)；**extremely** (極端に；very の強意語) ▶きょうはすごく暑い It's *awfully* hot today. ‖ あの子は泳ぎがすごくうまい That boy [girl] is a *terrific* [a *real* good] swimmer. ／That boy [girl] is an *awfully* [a *very*] good swimmer. ‖ 彼女は今すごく落ち込んでいる She is *terribly* depressed now. ‖ あの映画はすごくおもしろかった I found that movie *extremely* [*really*] amusing. (➤ really は「実に」) ‖ 横っ腹がすごく痛いんだ I have a *bad* pain in my side. ‖ 先生の授業，すごく楽しかったです We *sure* enjoyed your class！

すこし 少し

訳語メニュー
数が少し →a few, some **1**
量が少し →a little, some **2**
時間が少し →a while **3**
程度が少し →a little **4**

1【数】a few (➤「少しはある」という肯定の気持ちを表す)；**some** (➤ 漠然と「いくつか」の意を表す) ▶私たちのクラスに左利きの人が少しいる There are *a few* left-handed people in my class. ‖ 私には友だちが少ししかいない I have *only a few* friends. (➤ I have few friends. でもよいが，会話では only a few と言うことが多い) ‖ タマネギを少し買ってきてちょうだい Go (and) buy *some* onions.

2【量】a little (➤「少しはある」という肯定の気持ちを表す)；**some** (➤ 漠然と「いくらか」の意を表す) ▶ガソリンは少ししか残っていない We have only *a little* gas left. ‖ 先週は雨が少ししか降らなかった We only had *a little* rain last week. ‖ 私はビールを少し飲んだだけで気分が悪くなる I get sick when I drink even *a little bit of* beer. ‖ 銀行で金を少し下ろしたい I'd like to withdraw *some* money from my (bank) account. ‖ 彼女は少しの投資で大もうけをした She made a lot of money from a *small* investment. ‖ きみに少し言っておきたいことがある There is *something* I have to tell you.

3【時間，距離】a while (時間)；**some distance** (距離) ▶少し(＝しばらく)休憩しましょう Let's take a rest *for a while*. ／Let's take a *short* break. ‖ 少しお待ちください *Just a moment* [*a second*], please. ‖ 《電話で》少しお待ちください Hold on, please. (➤「切らないでください」の意) ‖ ロスには少ししかいませんでした We were in LA *for only a short time*. ‖ 校長は少し前に帰りました The principal went home *a few minutes ago*. ‖ 彼が車から降りた少しあとで時限爆弾が爆発した *A little while after* he got out of the car, a time bomb went off. ‖ 飛行機が出るまでにまだ少し時間がある *We still have a little time* before the plane leaves. ‖ 駅までは少しあります(＝遠いです)よ It's *quite a way* [*quite a ways* ／ *some distance*] to the train station. ‖ 福岡の少し先まで行く予定です I'm going *a little farther than* Fukuoka. ‖ バークレーの駅から少し歩けばカリフォルニア大学に着く The University of California is *a few* minutes' walk from Berkeley Station.

4【程度】a little, a bit (➤ 後者はインフォーマルな言い方) ▶この帽子は私には少し大きい This hat is *a little* big for me. ‖ 英語は少し話せます I speak *a little* English. ‖ 私は少し(＝軽い)かぜ気味です I have a *slight* cold. ‖ 《妻が夫に》あなた，少し飲み過ぎですよ Honey, you are drinking *a little* too much. ‖ 少しは私のことも考えてください Try to consider my feelings *a bit more*. ‖ ドアを少しだけ開けておきなさい Leave the door open *a crack*. (➤ a crack は副

詞用法で「少し(だけ)」) ‖ もう少し背が高ければいいのだが I wish I were *a little* taller. ‖ あの人, 少しいい気になっているんじゃないの That man is *a little* too sure of himself [too cocky], isn't he? ‖ 少し静かにしてくれませんか Can you be *a little* quieter?／Can you tone it down *a little* (*bit*)?

☞ もう少し (→見出語)

すこしずつ 少しずつ little by little, bit by bit(➤後者はインフォーマルな言い方) ; gradually (徐々に) ▶少しずつ寒くなってきている It's getting colder *little by little*. ‖ リスは少しずつビスケットをかじった The squirrel nibbled up a piece of biscuit *bit by bit*. ‖ 彼は少しずつ回復している He is recovering *little by little* [*slowly*／*gradually*]. ‖ 彼女の健康は少しずつ衰えていった Her health *gradually* declined. ‖ 毎日少しずつ勉強しなさい Study *a little* every day.

すこしも 少しも not (...) at all, not (...) in the least(➤後者のほうが強意的でやや堅い言い方) ; not (...) a bit(➤インフォーマルな言い方) ▶きみは少しも悪くない You're *not* in the wrong *at all*. ‖ ぼくは彼を少しも恐れてはいない I am *not in the least* afraid of him. ‖ きみの作文には少しも誤りがない There are *no* [*not any*] mistakes *at all* in your composition. ‖ 少年たちには少しも反省の色がない The boys do*n't* appear to be sorry *in the least* [*at all*]. ‖ その日, 湖面には少しも風がなかった That day *there was not the least bit* [*puff*] *of* wind on the lake. ‖ 私は世間の言うことなんか少しも気にしない I *don't* care *a bit* what (other) people say. ‖ 運転手は英語が少しもわからない The driver does*n't know a word of English*.

すごす 過ごす 1【時を】spend +目 (はっきりした目的をもって) ; pass +目 (退屈しないように, 何となく)

【文型】
…して時間(A)を過ごす
spend A doing

▶午後はテレビを見て過ごした I *spent* the afternoon watch*ing* TV. (● (×)I spent watching TV in the afternoon. とはしない) ‖ ベーカーさんの一家は夏休みをフロリダで過ごした The Bakers *spent* [*passed*] their summer vacation in Florida. ‖ 春休みを有意義に過ごしたい I'd like to *spend* my spring break meaningfully. ‖ あれが, 私たちが3年間過ごした中学校です That's the junior high school where we *studied* for three years. ‖ だらだらと日を過ごしてはいけない You shouldn't just *idle your days away*.

✉ **いかがお過ごしでしょうか. お元気のことと存じます** *How are you getting along?* I hope you are doing well.

2【度を越す】▶ゆうべは酒を過ごしてしまった I drank *too much* last night.

☞ 見過ごす, やり過ごす (→見出語)

すごすご ▶次郎は父親に叱られてすごすごと部屋を出ていった Scolded by his father, Jiro went out of the room *dejectedly* [*with his tail between his legs*].

スコッチ(ウイスキー) Scotch (whisky).

スコットランド Scotland ━形 スコットランドの Scottish, Scots, Scotch

‖スコットランド人 a Scot ; a Scotsman(男), a Scotswoman(女) ; the Scots (全体) 《参考》スコットランド人は Scotch, Scotchman, Scotchwoman, the Scotch という言い方を好まない.

スコップ a (hand) shovel (シャベル) ; a scoop(小さめの) ; a trowel /tráʊəl/ (園芸用の移植ごて) ▶スコップで穴を掘る dig a hole with *a* (*hand*) *shovel*.

すこぶる very, extremely(➤後者のほうがより強意) ▶祖父はすこぶる元気です My grandfather is *extremely* hale and hearty [is in *robust* good health]. (➤ hale and hearty は老人について用いる) ‖ このマニュアルはすこぶる不親切だ This manual is *most* user-unfriendly. ‖ 次郎の姉さんはすこぶる付きの美人だ Jiro's sister is *quite a stunning* beauty. ／Jiro's sister is a beauty *with a capital B*. (➤ with a capital B の B は前の名詞(beauty)の頭文字を大文字で表す).

すごみ 凄み ▶すごみのある声 a *threatening* [*menacing*] voice(➤ともに「威嚇するような」の意) ‖ 岩田先生の怒った顔にはすごみがある Mr. Iwata *looks frightening* when he gets angry with us. ‖ ジャイアンツの打線はそれほどすごみがない The Giants batting lineup *isn't* that *threatening*.

すごむ 凄む threaten ▶その男は仕返しをしてやるぞと言ってすごんだ That man *threatened* to get back at me.

すこやか 健やかな sound, healthy(➤前者は「すべての面で」というニュアンスが濃く, 後者より強意的) ▶彼は心身ともに健やかな青年だ He is a young man of *sound* body and mind. ‖ 親は子供が健やかに育つことを心から願っている Parents' deepest wish is that their children will grow up *in good health*. ‖ どうぞ末永くお健やかに I hope you *stay healthy* for many years to come.

すごろく 双六 *sugoroku* ; a race-type board game played with two dice and one counter for each player(➤説明的な訳).

すさまじい tremendous(驚くほど強力な) ; terrible(耐え難い恐怖感を抱かせる) ; fierce(風雨などが激しい) ; terrific(ものすごい威力を持っていて恐ろしい) ; amazing(驚きとともに当惑・ろうばいを覚えさせる) ▶火はすさまじい勢いで広がった The fire spread with *tremendous* [*terrible*] speed. ‖ 橋はすさまじい音響とともに崩れ落ちた The bridge fell with a *tremendous* [*terrific*] crash. ‖ すさまじい風だった A *fierce* wind was blowing. ‖ その歌手の人気はすさまじいばかりだ That singer's popularity is simply *amazing* [*astounding*].

すさむ 荒む degenerate /dɪdʒénərèɪt/ ▶彼女の行動は最近とてもすさんでいる Her behavior *has degenerated* a lot recently. ‖ 彼は最近すさんだ生活をしている He is living a *wild* [*degenerate*／*dissolute*／*dissipated*] life these days. (➤それぞれ「奔放な」, 「堕落した」, 「自堕落な」, 「道楽にふける」の意).

ずさん 杜撰な sloppy, slipshod ▶ずさんな工事 *sloppy* [*scamped*] construction ‖ 彼はやることがずさんだ He is *careless* in everything he does. ‖ この家はずさんなつくりだ This house was built in a *slipshod* manner.

すし 寿司 sushi(➤英語化している) ▶すしを握る make *sushi* ‖ すしを巻く make rolled *sushi*.

日本紹介 ✉ **すしは酢と砂糖で味付けしたご飯の上に, 主に薄く切った生の魚介類を載せた食べ物です. 飯を一口大に軽く押し固め, 生の魚介などのネタを載せた「握りずし」や, ネタをご飯の上に載せ, のりで巻いた円筒形や円すい形の「巻きずし」などがあります** Sushi is a food made of boiled rice seasoned with vinegar and sugar, combined with various ingredients (mainly slices of raw fish or shellfish). One kind is called '*nigiri-zushi*,' in which the rice is lightly pressed into bite-sized morsels and topped with a slice of raw fish or shellfish or other ingre-

す

dients. Another kind is called *'maki-zushi,'* which is tube-shaped or cone-shaped sushi in which the ingredients are placed on rice and wrapped in a sheet of *nori*.

「すし」のいろいろ (すしの種類) かっぱ巻き *kappa-maki* (cucumber roll) /かんぴょう巻き *kanpyo-maki* (pickled gourd roll) /ちらしずし *chirashi-zushi*(assorted raw fish and vegetables over rice) /鉄火巻き *tekka-maki* (tuna roll) /手巻き *temaki*(hand-rolled cone of sushi rice and seafood wrapped in a sheet of *nori*) /握り *nigiri*(pieces of raw fish on oblong mounds of vinegared rice)
(すしのネタ) アオヤギ round clam, red clam /アジ horse mackerel /アナゴ conger eel /アマエビ raw shrimp /アワビ abalone /イカ squid /イクラ salmon roe /ウニ sea urchin /エビ prawn /カツオ bonito /カニ crab /サバ mackerel /シャコ mantis shrimp /スズキ sea bass /タイ sea bream /タコ octopus /トロ *toro*; fatty tuna meat /ハマグリ clam /ハマチ young yellowtail /ヒラメ flounder /ホタテガイ scallop /マグロ tuna

‖すし職人 a sushi chef ‖すし屋 a sushi restaurant [bar] ‖回転ずし a conveyor-belt [a *kaiten*] sushi restaurant /a sushi-go-round.
☛ すし詰め (→見出語)

すじ 筋 1【線】a **line**; a **stripe** (しま) ▶筋を引く draw *a line* ‖帽子の黒い筋 a black *stripe* around the cap ‖彼の顔に残る長い一筋の傷痕 *a long scar* on his face ‖一筋の光 *a beam of light*.
2【繊維質】a **string**; **fiber** (植物の) ▶サヤインゲンの筋を取る peel off the *strings* of the string beans ‖この肉は硬くて筋が多い This meat is tough and *stringy*. ‖筋の多い野菜をもっととりましょう Have more *fibrous* /fáibrəs/ vegetables.
3【筋肉や腱(けん)】▶柔道をしていて足首の筋を違えた While practicing judo, I *sprained* my ankle. ‖寝違えて首の筋を痛めた I *got a crick in my neck* while I was sleeping.
4【論理, 道理】**logic**(論理); **reason**(道理) ▶きみの言うことは確かに筋が通っている(＝論理的である)が, 賛成はできない What you say *makes sense* [*is logical*], but I can't agree with you. ‖労働者の要求は筋が通っていた The workers' demands were *reasonable*. ‖きみの言い分は筋が通らない Your theory *doesn't make sense* [*doesn't hold water*]. (➤ hold water は文字どおりには「(容器などが)水を漏らさない」の意で, 否定文・疑問文で用いることが多い) ‖きみはその点については筋を通すべきだ You should *be reasonable* on that point. →筋違い, 筋道.
5【物語の】a **plot**; a **story** (筋立て) ▶筋の込み入ったスリラー a thriller with a complicated *plot* ‖この映画の筋はよくわからない The *plot* [*story*] of this movie is not clear.
6【素質】▶彼のピアノは筋がいい He is a *born* pianist. (➤「生まれながらのピアニストだ」の意) ‖《テニスで》きみ, なかなか筋がいいよ You'*ve got a natural gift* [*a natural talent*] for tennis.
7【関係者】a **source**(情報源) ▶その情報は極めて信頼のできる筋から得たものだ I got the information from a very *reliable source*. ‖信頼すべき筋によれば首相は内閣を改造するつもりらしい According to *reliable sources*, the Prime Minister is going to reshuffle the Cabinet.
8【沿っている所】▶街道筋に松が植わっている There are pine trees planted *along the street*.

ずし 図示する illustrate +ⓐ (実例・図解を使って); **diagram** +ⓐ (図形・図表などを使って) ▶血液の流れを図示する *illustrate* the flow of blood *with a drawing* ‖自宅までの道順を図示する *draw a map* to one's house ‖彼は研究結果を図示した He *diagramed* the results of his research.

すじあい 筋合い ▶きみにそんなことを言われる筋合いはない *You have no business* saying such a thing to me.

すじがき 筋書き a **plot**, a **story** (ドラマなどの; 後者のほうが具体的); a **script** (台本) ▶このドラマの筋書きは平凡だ The *plot* of this drama is commonplace. ‖何事も筋書きどおりに運ぶとは限らない Not all things go exactly *according to script*.

すじがねいり 筋金入り ▶彼は筋金入りの反戦主義者だ He is a *staunch* [*a committed* / an *unyielding*] pacifist. /He is a peace lover *to the core*. (➤後者の文はややインフォーマル; to the core は「しんまで」の意).

ずしき 図式 a **diagram** ▶先生はその問題を図式で説明した Our teacher explained the problem with *diagrams*.

すじこ 筋子 salted salmon roe.

すじちがい 筋違い ▶きみが文句を言うのは筋違いだ Your complaint is quite *unreasonable*.

すしづめ 鮨詰め ▶通勤電車はすし詰めだった We *were packed like sardines* in the commuter train. (➤ packed like sardines は「(缶詰の)イワシのようにぎゅう詰めで」が原義) / The commuter train *was jammed* [*was jam-packed*] (*with passengers*).

すじみち 筋道 logic(論理); **reason** (道理) ▶筋道の通った意見 a *logical* opinion ‖彼の主張は筋道が通らない What he claims *doesn't hold water* [*isn't consistent* / *isn't reasonable*]. ‖筋道の通らないことを言うもんじゃない Don't say such *illogical* things. ‖彼はいつも筋道を立てて話す He always speaks *logically*.

すじむかい 筋向かい ▶その店はうちの筋向かいにあります That shop *is diagonally opposite* [*is kitty-corner from*] my house. (➤ kitty-corner は「対角線上の」の意. catty-corner ともいう).

すじめ 筋目 a **crease**(ズボンの) ▶きちんと筋目のついたパンツ sharply *creased* pants.

すじょう 素性 ▶素性の知れない男 an *unidentified* man (➤「身元のはっきりしない男」の意) / a man *with a dubious past*(➤「経歴の怪しい男」の意).

ずじょう 頭上 ▶ジェット機が頭上をごう音を立てて飛んでいった Jet planes flew *over us* [*overhead*] with a roar. ‖《掲示》頭上注意 Watch your head. / Danger Overhead.

ずしり ▶何が入っているのか知らないが箱を持ち上げるとずしりと重かった I don't know what is in the box, but when I lifted it, it *was heavier than I had expected*.

ずしん ▶大きな岩がずしんと地響きを立てて落ちてきた A huge rock came down *with a thud* and shook the ground. ‖彼女のそのひと言はずしんと胸にこたえた That remark [comment] of hers *was like a blow* to my stomach.

すす 煤 soot /sʊt/ (ばい煙); **dust** (ほこり, ちり) ▶煙突がすすで詰まったようだ The chimney seems to be clogged with *soot*. ‖私たちは天井のすすを払った We swept the *cobwebs* from the ceiling. (➤ cobweb は「クモの巣」) ‖この部屋はすすだらけだ This room is *full of soot* [*dust*].

1 **すず 鈴** a **bell** ▶鈴の音 the tinkle [jingle] of *a bell* ‖鈴を鳴らす ring *a bell.* ‖《慣用表現》誰が猫の首に鈴をつけるかWho is going to *bell the cat*?(➤bell the cat は「皆が尻込みすることを進んで引き受ける」の意).

2 **すず 錫** **tin.**

スズカケ 《植物》a **plane tree.**

すすき 薄 《植物》**Japanese pampas grass**

《解説》(1)英米にはススキはないが, pampas grass と呼ばれる背の高いアシの一種があり, これがススキに類似している. (2)英米人は pampas grass を見ても日本人のように秋の風情は感じない.

スズキ 《魚》a **Japanese sea bass** [**seaperch**].

すすぐ 濯ぐ・漱ぐ **rinse** /rɪns/ +㊐ ▶洗濯物をすすぐ *rinse* the laundry ‖水で口をすすぐ *rinse* (*out*) one's mouth with water.

▶汚名をすすぐ *clear* one's name of shame.

すすける 煤ける ▶すすけた天井 a *sooty* /sóṭi/ [*smoke-stained*] ceiling.

すずしい 涼しい **cool** ▶涼しい風 a *cool* breeze ‖きょう[ここ]はとても涼しい *It is* very *cool* today [here]. ‖朝の涼しいうちに出発しよう Let's leave *in the cool* of the morning.

✉ **朝夕めっきり涼しくなりました** The mornings and evenings are *getting* much *cooler* these days. / *It is* now much *cooler* in the mornings and evenings.

▶《慣用表現》涼しい目元をした少年 a boy with *clear* [*bright*] *eyes* ‖彼はあんな卑劣なことをしておきながら涼しい顔をしている He *looks unconcerned* [*nonchalant*] even after having played such a dirty trick.

すずなり 鈴生り ▶柿が鈴なりになっている The tree *is heavy with* kakis [persimmons].

すすむ 進む 1【前進する】**go** (**forward**), **advance**, **make** one's **way**

> 《語法》(1)「進む」を表す最も一般的な語が **go** で, forward, to など方向を表す副詞(句)を伴うのがふつう. go の代わりに **move** (動く)を用いることもある. (2)「ある目標に向かって進む」が **advance**.「徐々に進む」ことを表すやや堅い言い方が **make** one's **way** で, make の代わりに push (押し分ける)や elbow (肘で押し分ける)などを用いて進むときの様態を表す. (3)「音や光が進む(伝わる)」の意では **travel** を用いる.

▶ゆっくり進む *go* [*move*] slowly *forward* ‖立ち止まらずにどんどん進んでください Don't stop. *Keep on moving* [*Move on*]. (➤ on は行動の継続を表す副詞) ‖ナポレオンの軍隊はモスクワより先には進めなかった Napoleon's army couldn't *go* farther than Moscow. ‖亀井のバントで阿部が二塁へ進んだ Abe *moved to* second on Kamei's bunt. ‖2歩前へ進め! Two steps *forward*! ‖白線の所まで進んでください Please *advance* to the white line. ‖2人の子供は手をつないで森の奥へと進んでいった The two children *made their way* into the forest hand in hand. ‖稲妻は雷鳴より速く進む Lightning *travels* faster than thunder. ‖123便にご搭乗のお客様は45番ゲートにお進みください Passengers for flight 123, please *proceed* to Gate 45.

2【進歩する】**advance**; **develop** (発達する) ━形 **advanced** (技術が進んだ); **progressive** (考え方が進歩的な) ▶アメリカの宇宙科学は進んでいる American space science *is advanced* [*is highly developed*]. ‖もっと進んだ生徒のためのコースについて詳しい説明を聞きたい I'd like to have a full explanation of the course for *more advanced* students. ‖中国では近代化が進んでいる(=進行中だ) China *is undergoing* modernization. ‖その国の法律制度はわが国のものよりもずっと進んでいる The legal system of that country *is way ahead of* ours. ‖おじいちゃんからのこの携帯メール, 顔文字が使ってあるよ. 進んでるなぁ This text message from Grandpa is dotted with emojis. He*'s really hip* [*with it*]. (➤ be hip, be with it は《インフォーマル》で「時流に合わせている」の意).

3【はかどる】**go**; **progress** (進歩する) ▶勉強の進み具合はどうですか How *are* your studies *going*? / How *are* you *getting along* in your work? ‖論文の執筆がなかなか進まない I *haven't made much progress* on my paper. ‖天気がよいので橋の工事は順調に進んでいる Since the weather has been good, construction work on the bridge *is progressing* smoothly. ‖新空港の建設が進んでいる Construction of the new airport *is in progress* [*is ongoing*]. ‖ 対話 「先週はどこまで進みましたか?」「30ページまでです」"How far did we *get* last week?" "As far as page 30."

4【より高度なところへ移る】▶私は文学部へ進みたい I want to *enter* the school of literature. ‖日本では高卒者の約54パーセントが大学へ進む Some 54 percent of all high school graduates *go* (*on*) *to college* in Japan. ‖この子には音楽の方面へ進ませようと考えています We are thinking about *encouraging* our child *to pursue* a career in music.

5【積極的に行う】▶りえは今度の見合にはあまり気が進まないようだ Rie *doesn't* look so *enthusiastic about* her upcoming 'miai' meeting.

6【病気・被害などが深刻になる】**advance** ━形 **advanced** (病状が進んだ) ▶(症状の)進んだがんは治すのが難しい Cancer *in the advanced stages* [*Advanced* cancer] is difficult to cure. ‖彼の肝硬変は相当進んでいる His cirrhosis *is* quite *advanced*. ‖知床では自然破壊が進んでいる(=深刻になっている) The destruction [degradation] of the natural environment around Shiretoko *has become serious*.

7【時計が早くなる】**gain** ▶この時計は1日に1分進む This watch *gains* one minute a day. ‖あの柱時計は5分進んでいる The wall clock *is* five minutes *fast*.

☛ 進んで (→見出語)

すずむ 涼む **enjoy the cool air** ▶木陰で涼む *cool oneself* under a tree.

すずむし 鈴虫 a **bell-ringing cricket** 《参考》cricket はコオロギ科の昆虫の総称. 鈴虫は欧米にはいない.

すすめ 勧め **advice** /ədváɪs/ (忠告); **recommendation** (推奨) ▶医者の勧めで彼は伊豆へ静養に出かけた He went to Izu for recuperation on his doctor's *advice*. ‖先生の勧めで彼はイギリスへ留学した He went to Britain to study on the *recommendation* of his teacher.

‖お勧め品 a recommended item [product].

すずめ 雀 a **sparrow** ▶スズメがチュンチュン鳴いている *Sparrows* are tweeting. ‖《慣用表現》補償金はすずめの涙ほどでした The compensation was *mere peanuts* [was *a paltry sum of money*].

すずめばち 雀蜂 a **hornet** (大型の); a **wasp** (小型の).

1 **すすめる 進める** 1【前へ出す】**move ... forward** ▶車

を前へ進める *move* [*drive*] a car *forward* ‖ 馬を進める *urge* a horse *forward* (➤ urge は「(動物などを)せきたてる」) ‖《慣用表現》わが校は準決勝へ駒を進めた Our school *made it to* the semifinals. (➤ make it は「たどり着く」の意のインフォーマルな表現).

2【進展させる】▶会議を進める *go on with* a meeting / *continue* a meeting ‖ その方向で研究を進めてください *Proceed* [*Go ahead*] in that direction with your research. ‖ その仕事は3人の実行委員の手によって進められた The work *was carried forward* by the three members of the executive committee.

3【時計を早くする】▶時計を5分進めた I *set* the clock *ahead* [*forward*] by five minutes.

2**すすめる 薦める·勧める 1【誘い促す】recommend** +目 (推薦する) ; **advise** /ədváɪz/ +目 (忠告する) ; **urge** /əːʳdʒ/ +目 (しきりに勧める, または影響力などを行使して駆り立てる) ; **suggest** +目 (参考のためにまたは控えめに助言する) ; **encourage** +目 (勇気づけ励ますなどして困難なことに挑戦させる) ▶きみにこの辞書を薦めます I *recommend* this dictionary to you. / I *recommend* you this dictionary. (➤ 後者は主に《英》. →推薦).

> 【文型】
> 人(A)に…するように勧める
> **recommend that** A (**should**) do
> **advise** A **to** do
> **suggest that** A (**should**) do
> 《解説》《米》ではふつう should を省略し, あとの動詞は原形のまま使う. したがって, A が3人称単数でも -s をつけない. また, 過去形にしない.

▶海外に出かけるときは旅行傷害保険に入ることを勧めるよ I *recommend* (*that*) you (*should*) take out travel accident insurance when you go abroad. ‖ 医者は彼に毎日軽い運動をするように勧めた The doctor *advised* him *to* get some light exercise every day. (→アドバイス, 忠告) ‖ 先生は彼女にM大を受けるよう勧めた Her teacher *suggested* (to her) *that* she (*should*) take the entrance exams for M University. ‖ 彼は私にもう1泊していけとしきりに勧めた He *urged* me *to* stay another night. ‖ 医者に勧められて彼は玉川温泉で湯治することにした *On the advice of* a doctor, he decided to go to Tamagawa Onsen for a hot-spring cure. ‖ 母は私に詩を書くように勧めてくれた My mother *encouraged* me to write poems. (→励ます).

2【飲食物などをとるよう促す】offer /ɔ́ːfəʳ/ +目 ▶客に座布団を勧める *offer* a *zabuton* [a cushion] to a guest ‖ 彼女は私にお茶[ワイン]を勧めた She *offered* me a cup of tea [a glass of wine].

すずらん 鈴蘭《植物》a **lily of the valley**.

すずり 硯 an **inkstone** ‖ **すずり箱** an inkstone case.

すすりなく すすり泣く weep [**cry**] **softly**, **snivel** ; **sniffle** (➤ 単に「はなをすする」のこともある) ▶朋美は教室の隅ですすり泣いていた Tomomi was *crying softly* in a corner of the classroom.

すする 啜る 1【飲み物を】sip +目 ; **slurp** +目 (音を立てて飲む) ▶彼は熱いコーヒーをゆっくりとすすった He *sipped* the hot coffee slowly. (➤「すする」は通例音を伴うが, sip は「ちびちび飲む」の意で, 音は伴わない) ‖ スープをすすって飲むのは不作法だ It is bad manners to *slurp* soup. 《参考》日本人は「麺をすする」が英米人にとっては slurp noodles も無作法.

2【鼻水を】sniffle ▶その男の子ははなをすすった The little boy *sniffled*.

すすんで 進んで ▶彼は母親のためなら何でも進んでやる He *is ready* [*willing*] to do anything for his mother. (➤ be ready to do は心構えができていて「気持ちよく…する」だが, be willing to do は「務めだから, そのようにする」で積極性は希薄) ‖ 彼は合宿では進んで部屋の掃除をした During the training camp, he *volunteered* to clean the room.

すそ 裾 a **hem** (縁) ▶カーテンの裾 the *hem* of a curtain ‖ 浴衣の丈が長かったので少し裾を上げてもらった I *had* the yukata *taken up* because it was too long. ‖ 私はズボンの裾をまくってぬかるみを歩いた I walked through the mud *with my trousers rolled up*.

すその 裾野 the foot (麓) ▶そのペンションは富士山の裾野にあります The resort inn stands at *the foot* of Mt. Fuji.

スター a **star** ; a **hero** (ヒーロー) ▶フットボールのスター a football *hero* ‖ 今やキャスターはマスコミのスターだ Nowadays newscasters are (treated like) media *stars*. ‖ 田中は楽天のスタープレーヤーだ Tanaka is the *star player* of the Eagles. ‖ 彼女は映画スターに憧れている She has a dream of becoming *a movie star*. ‖ **アクションスター** an action star.

スターティングメンバー the starting lineup, the starters.

スタート (a) **start** ▶彼らはスタートラインに並んでいる They are *on the starting line*. / They are *lined up for the start*. ‖ 福島選手はいいスタートを切った Fukushima *made a* good *start*. ‖ 正午の時報とともに100人の選手が一斉にスタートを切った The 100 racers *started* all at once at the noon time signal. ‖ 新規事業はスタートからつまずいた The new project *got off to a shaky start*. (➤ shaky は「危なっかしい」) ‖ 鹿島アントラーズは開幕3連勝と, 好調なスタートダッシュを切った The Kashima Antlers *got off to a* good *start*, winning the three initial games of the season. (➤ 陸上競技での「スタートダッシュ」は initial spurt という).

✉ **転職をして新しいスタートを切る決心をしました** I have decided to change jobs and *make a fresh start*.

‖ **クラウチングスタート** crouch(ing) start ‖ **スタンディングスタート** standing start.

スタイリスト a **fashion stylist** (モデルや俳優につく) ; a **sharp dresser** (おしゃれな人).

スタイル 1【型】a **style** ▶これが若い女性向けの最新流行のスタイルだ This is the latest *style* in clothes for young ladies.

2【格好】a **figure** ▶彼女は美人のうえにスタイルもいい Besides being good-looking, she has a great *figure* [she is well-proportioned]. (🔔 (1) She has a good style. とすると「文体が優れている」の意になる. (2) 男性がスタイルがよい場合は great figure の代わりに good physique /fɪzíːk/ を用いる).

▶あなた, すごくスタイルがいいわね You'*re in great shape*. ‖ 私, スタイルが悪いから水着姿になるのは嫌なの I don't like to wear a bathing suit because I *don't look good* in one. (🔔「スタイルが悪い」は英語では have a bad figure よりも be short and fat とか be too fat のように具体的に言うのがふつう).

危ないカタカナ語✸ スタイル
英語の style は「(建築·文芸などの)様式」「(服装な

どの)型」「文体」などを指すことば. したがって「(人が)スタイルがいい」というときにこの語は使えない. figure などを使って例文のように表す.

スタウト **stout** (➤ビールの一種).

スタジアム a **stadium** /stéɪdiəm/ ▶ヤンキースタジアム Yankee *Stadium*.

スタジオ a **studio** /stjú:dioʊ/ 《参考》日本語のスタジオには,「撮影所」「放送室」「仕事場・アトリエ」の意味があるが, すべて studio でよい ▶映画スタジオ a movie *studio* ‖ダンススタジオ a dance *studio* ‖録音スタジオ a recording *studio*.

スタジャン a **varsity jacket**, an **award jacket**.

すたすた ▶彼はすたすた坂道を下りてきた He came *briskly* [*hurriedly*] down the hill. (➤ それぞれ「足早に」,「慌ただしく」の意).

ずたずた ▶ラブレターをずたずたに裂く tear love letters *to shreds* [*pieces*] ‖木に引っかかったたこはずたずたになっていた The kite that had gotten caught in the tree was *torn* practically *to shreds*.

すだつ 巣立つ **leave the nest**(鳥が) ▶ひな鳥はやがて巣立っていくものだ A young bird must *leave the nest* sooner or later. ‖《比喩的》毎年約2000人の学生がこの大学から社会に巣立っていく Every year about two thousand students *graduate from* [*leave*] this college *and go out into the world*.

スタッカート 《音楽》**staccato**.

スタッドレスタイヤ a (**studless**) **snow tire** [《英》**tyre**] (➤ snow は winter でもよい).

スタッフ **the staff**(➤ 集合的な言い方 ; 個々のメンバーは a staff member, a member of the staff または a staffer という) ; an **employee** (社員, 店員, 職員) ▶彼はその雑誌の編集スタッフの一員である He is on *the editorial staff* of the magazine. ‖あなたのところには何人のスタッフがいますか How many people do you have on *the staff*? (● (×)How many staffs do you have? とはしない) ‖彼女はこのプロジェクトのスタッフ(の1人)です She is *on* this project team. / She's *working on* this project. ‖ジョージはこの店のスタッフ(の1人)です George is *an employee* [George *works*] at this store.

スタミナ **stamina** /stǽmɪnə/ ▶スタミナをつける *build up stamina* ‖彼はスタミナがある[ない] He has a lot of [no] *stamina*.

スタメン **the starting lineup** →スターティングメンバー ▶松井はスタメンから外された Matsui was left out of *the starting lineup*.

すたる 廃る ▶5敗もしては横綱の名が廃る(=不名誉だ) Five losses would be *a disgrace to* the yokozuna's *name*. ‖このましっぽを巻いて退散では男が廃る(=男らしくない) To slink away with your tail between your legs is *not like a man*.

☞ 廃れる (→見出語)

すだれ 簾 a **bamboo blind** [**shade**] (竹の) ; a **reed blind** (葦(あし)の) ▶部屋に西日が入るので軒下にすだれを掛けた Since my room is exposed to the afternoon sun, I hung *bamboo blinds* from the eaves.

すたれる 廃れる **go out of use**(物・ことばが) ; **become obsolete** /ɑ̀:bsəlí:t/ (ことばが) ; **go out of fashion** [**vogue**] (習慣・流行が) ▶「ハイカラ」ということばはもう廃れた The word 'haikara' *has* already *gone out of use* [*has become obsolete*]. (➤「廃れつつある」なら is obsolescent /ɑ̀:bsəlésənt/) ‖その風習は廃れてしまった(=はやらなくなった) Those customs *are outdated*. (➤「廃れつつある」なら are becoming outdated) ‖この辺りではだるまストーブはもう廃れてしまった Potbellied stoves *have fallen into disuse* around here. ‖その寺は今では廃れて訪ねる人もまれだ The temple, (which is) *dilapidated* [*rundown*], rarely has visitors. (➤ dilapidated /dɪlǽpɪdeɪtɪd/ は「荒れ果てた」).

スタンガン a **stun gun**.

スタンス a **stance**.

スタンダード (a) **standard** ▶スタンダードナンバー a *standard*(➤ (×)standard number としない) ‖ジャズのスタンダードナンバー a jazz *standard*.

スタンディングオベーション a **standing ovation**.

スタンド **1**【観客席】**the stands**(➤ 通例複数形で) ; **the bleachers** (屋根のない安い席) ▶三塁側のスタンドは満員だった *The stands* near third base were full. ‖ボールは外野スタンドへ飛び込んだ The ball went into *the outfield stands*.

2【電気スタンド】a **desk** [**table**] **lamp** (卓上の) ; a **floor lamp** [**light**] (床に置く).

3【売り場】a **stand** (➤ しばしば合成語で用いる) ; a **counter** (カウンター) ▶駅のスタンドで新聞を買った I bought a newspaper at the *newsstand* [*kiosk*] at the train station.

‖ガソリンスタンド a gas [《英また》filling] station ‖コーヒースタンド a coffee stand [counter].

4【自転車などの】▶(自転車の)スタンドを立てる[下ろす] put up [down] *a stand*(➤ 従来のタイプのスタンドは regular stand, 1本の棒状のものは kickstand という).

スタンドイン a **stand-in**.

スタンドプレー a **grandstand play** 《参考》grandstand は競技場の正面の特別観覧席のこと. そこにいる客の受けを狙った派手なプレーを grandstand play という.

スタントマン a **stunt man** [**woman**] ; a **stunt person** [**performer**].

スタンバイ ▶ヘリポートにはけがをした登山者を病院に運ぶために救急車がスタンバイしている An ambulance *is on standby* at the heliport to take the injured climber to the hospital.

スタンプ a **stamp** ; a **postmark**(消印) ▶スタンプ帳に記念スタンプを押す put *a commemorative stamp* in one's *seal book* ‖ここにスタンプを押してください Please *stamp* here. ‖日本中を回ってすべての駅のスタンプを集めるのが彼の夢だ His dream is to go around the country and collect the *stamp seals* of all the railway stations in Japan.

スチーム **steam** (蒸気) ; a **steam heater**, a **radiator** (暖房器具).

¹スチール 《鋼鉄》**steel** ▶スチール製の本棚 *steel* bookshelves ‖スチール缶 a steel can.

²スチール 《盗塁》a **steal** ▶ダブルスチールを敢行する pull *a double steal* ‖ホームスチールをする *steal home*. →盗塁.

³スチール 《写真》a **still**.

スチュワーデス a **stewardess** /stú:ərdəs/.

> **危ないカタカナ語✸ スチュワーデス**
> 英語の stewardess からきているが, 現在では stewardess, airline hostess のような性別を明示する語を避けて flight attendant や cabin attendant を用いる航空会社がふつう. なお, スチュワーデス, パーサー(purser)などの乗務員をまとめて cabin crew と呼ぶ.

-ずつ **one by one**(一人一人, 一つ一つ) ; **each** (1人

［１つ］につき）; **each of ...**（…の一人一人，…の一つ一つ）; **little by little**（少しずつ）; **every ...**（…ごとに）▶１人ずつバスに乗りなさい Get on the bus *one by one*. ‖ おやじはぼくたちに3000円ずつくれた Dad gave us three thousand yen *each*. ／Dad gave *each of* us three thousand yen. ‖（本は）３人に１冊ずつしかありません We only have one copy for *every* three persons. ‖ 当時日本の人口は年に100万人ずつ増えていた In those days Japan's population was increasing *by* one million a year. ‖ 面接試験は一度に３人ずつ行われる The interview will be given to three applicants at a time. ‖ 彼らは２，３人ずつやって来た They came *by twos and threes*. ‖ 景気は少しずつ回復している Business is getting better *little by little* [*by* (*slow*) *degrees*].

ずつう 頭痛 a **headache** /hédeɪk/ ▶けさは頭痛がする I *have a headache* this morning. ‖ 母はひどい頭痛で床に就いている My mother is in bed with *a bad headache*. (➤「頭が割れそうな頭痛」は splitting headache) ‖《比喩的》どら息子が頭痛の種だ My wayward son is *a headache* [*a source of constant anxiety* ／*a pain in the neck*].

スツール a **stool**.

すっからかん ▶あいつ，カジノですっからかんになったそうだ I hear that he *lost his shirt* gambling at a casino. (➤ lose one's shirt は「すべてを失って丸裸になる，すってんてんになる」).

すっかり **completely**（完全に）; **quite**（全く）; **utterly**（全く；否定的・軽蔑的な意味の語を修飾することが多い）▶この町もすっかり変わってしまった The town has changed *completely*. ‖ しまった！デートのことすっかり忘れてた Shoot! I *completely* forgot (about) my date. ‖ 宿に着いたときにはすっかり暗くなっていた By the time I got to the inn, it had gotten *quite* dark. ‖ すっかりそのことを忘れていた I *clean* [*quite*] forgot about it. ／I forgot *all* about it. ‖ 彼女は何か月にもわたる病気の夫の看病ですっかり疲れていた She was *utterly* exhausted after taking care of her sick husband for many months. ‖ 彼女はぼくにすっかり（＝何もかも）打ち明けた She told me *everything*.

✉ **すっかりご無沙汰しておりますが，お元気でしょうか** I haven't seen you *for a long time* [*for ages*]. Have you been well?

ずつき 頭突き a **head butt** ▶彼は友だちの胸に頭突きをかました He *butted* his friend's chest *with his head*.

ズッキーニ a **zucchini**.

すっきり ▶彼の説明はどうもすっきり（＝はっきり）しない His explanation is not *clear* to me. ‖ ちょっと眠ったらすっきりした Having a catnap *refreshed* me [*cleared* my *head*]. ‖ いらない家具を処分したら部屋がすっきりした Getting rid of the unnecessary furniture made the room look *neat and tidy* [*uncluttered*]. (➤ いずれも「きちんと片づいて」の意) ‖《天気予報》きょうもすっきりしない天気が続きそうです The *overcast weather* is likely to continue today. (➤ overcast は「どんよりした」) ／It will continue to be *cloudy* today.

ズック **canvas**（布地）‖**ズック靴** canvas shoes.

すっくと ▶空に向かってすっくと立つポプラ a poplar that *stands tall* toward the sky ‖ 彼女はすっくと席から立ち上がって質問した She *resolutely* rose from her seat and asked a question. (➤ resolutely は「決然と」).

ずっこける ▶回答者のとんちんかんな答えにクイズの司会者はずっこけた The quizmaster *was thrown off* (*beat*) by a panelist's wacky answer.

ずっしり ▶父はずっしり重いかばんを提げて出張から帰って来た My father came home from his business trip carrying a *heavily packed* bag. ‖ カレーは胃にずっしりきた The curry lay *heavily* on my stomach.

すったもんだ ▶すったもんだ（＝大騒ぎ）のあげくにその記念碑建立は取りやめになった After *a great fuss* [*a big argument*], the plan to erect the monument was called off.

すってんころり ▶玄関の雪の上ですってんころりと転んでしまった I *slipped and fell* on the snow-covered porch.

すってんてん →すっからかん.

すっと ▶彼はすっと（＝不意に）席を立つとあっという間にいなくなった He *abruptly* stood up and was gone in an instant. ‖ 言いたいことを言ったら気分がすっとした I *felt satisfied* after having spoken my mind. ‖ ジャイアンツが負けるとすっとするという人もいる There are some people who *get a real kick* out of seeing the Giants lose.

ずっと **1【はるかに】** **much, far**（➤ともに次にくる比較級を修飾する）▶彼女は私よりずっと頭がいい She's *much* smarter than I am. ‖ スケートよりスキーのほうがずっとおもしろいと思う I think skiing is *much* [*far* ／*a lot*] more fun than skating. ‖ 弟はぼくよりずっと大食いだ My younger brother is a bigger eater than me *by a long shot*. (➤ by a long shot は「断然」の意のインフォーマルな表現).
▶父はずっと前から禁煙しています My father quit smoking *a long time ago*. ‖ 彼女が人妻であることを知ったのはずっとあとになってからだった It was only *much later* that I learned she was married. ‖ 夏休みはまだずっと先だ Summer vacation is still *a long way off*. ‖ 列の先頭はずっと先です The front of the line is *far ahead*.

2【長い間】▶彼女は和服を着たいとずっと（＝いつも）思っていた She *has always* wanted to wear a kimono. ‖ あすはずっと（＝一日中）家に居る予定だから，いつ訪ねて来てくれてもいいよ I'll be home *all day* tomorrow, so come (and) see me any time you like. ‖ 三郎は午後ずっとテレビゲームをして過ごした Saburo spent *the whole afternoon* playing video games. ‖ 東京から京都までずっと立ち通しだった I had to stand *all the way* from Tokyo to Kyoto. ‖ 少女はその間中ずっと黙ったままだった The girl remained silent *all the while* [*the whole time*]. ‖ 今までずっとどこに居たの？ Where have you been *all this while*? ‖ いとこは１週間前からずっと病気で寝ています My cousin has been ill in bed *for a week*. ‖ 彼女はずっと（＝永久に）フランスに住もうと考えている She is thinking of living in France *permanently*.

✉ **あれからずっとあなたのことばかり考えています** I*'ve been* think*ing* only of you since then.

すっとぶ すっ飛ぶ ▶電話をかけたら彼はすっ飛んで来た He *rushed* [*hurried*] *to* me soon after my call. ‖ ひどい列車事故の知らせを聞いて眠気がすっ飛んだ When I heard the news of a bad train accident, my drowsiness *disappeared instantly*.

すっとんきょう 素頓狂 ▶清は時々素頓狂な声を上げてクラスの者を笑わせる Kiyoshi often makes his classmates laugh with *sudden, funny shrieks* [*screeches*]. (➤ shriek, screech はともに甲高い叫び声だが，前者は恐怖・苦痛による悲鳴に近いもの，後者は物が擦れるような耳障りなもの).

すっぱい 酸っぱい **sour** /sáʊəʳ/ ▶この梅干しは**酸っぱい** This pickled *ume* is *sour*. ‖ 彼女は**酸っぱい**ものが好きだ She likes *sour* things. ‖ この牛乳は**酸っぱい味がする** This milk *tastes sour*. (➤ この sour は「腐敗しかけて酸っぱい」の意) ‖《慣用表現》父は弟にそんな仲間に加わるなと**口を酸っぱくして**言い聞かせた My father told my brother *a thousand times* [*over and over again*] not to join such a group.

すっぱだか 素っ裸の **stark-naked** ▶子供の頃この川でよく**素っ裸で**泳いだものだ When I was a kid, I used to *skinny-dip* [*swim stark naked*] in this river. (➤ stark は「すっかり, 全く」の意味).

すっぱぬく すっぱ抜く **blow the lid off** ; **expose** +目 (暴露する) ▶スキャンダルを**すっぱ抜く** *blow the lid off* a scandal ‖ 新聞が大臣の汚職事件を**すっぱ抜いた** The newspaper *exposed* the Minister's bribery. ‖ その女優は密会現場を写真週刊誌に**すっぱ抜かれた** The picture of the actress's secret meeting *was disclosed* [*was revealed*] in a weekly photo magazine.

すっぱり ▶たばこはもう**すっぱり**やめた I quit smoking *once and for all*. ‖ あの子のことは**すっぱり**忘れました I was able to get over her *completely*. (➤ この get over は「(元の恋人のことなどを)忘れる」の意味).

すっぴん 素っぴん ▶ちょっとお化粧するから待ってて. **すっぴん**じゃ出られないわ Wait a minute while I put my face on. I can't go out *without my make-up on*.

すっぽかす **stand ... up** ▶みち子と3時にデートの約束をしてたんだけど, **すっぽかされ**ちゃったよ I had a date with Michiko for three o'clock but she *stood* me *up*. ‖ きょうは絶対**すっぽかさない**でね Please *don't forget to meet* me today! ‖ 彼は仕事を**すっぽかして**映画を見にいった He *left* his work *unfinished* and went to the movies.

すっぽぬける すっぽ抜ける **fall off** ▶**すっぽ抜けた**カーブ a *hanging* curveball ‖ 田中のスライダーが**すっぽ抜けた** Tanaka *hung* a slider. ‖ 急いで走ったら靴が片方**すっぽ抜けた** As I ran in a hurry, one of my shoes *fell off*.

すっぽり ▶大阪の空はスモッグに**すっぽり**覆われていた The skies of Osaka were *completely* covered with smog. ‖ この箱が**すっぽり入る**ような袋を探している I'm looking for a bag *big enough to hold* this box. ‖ ゆうべはかぜ気味だったので布団を**すっぽり**かぶって寝た Since I was coming down with a cold last night, I covered myself *up* with a quilt.

すっぽん 《動物》a **soft-shelled turtle** ▶《慣用表現》うちの妹とリエさんじゃ**月とすっぽん**だ My sister and Rie are *as different as night and day*. (➤「夜と昼間ほど違う」の意. 「リエさんがすごい」と言っている).

すっぽんぽん ▶ 対話「今, お風呂から出たばかりだからあとでかけ直すね」「じゃ, 今**すっぽんぽん**なの?」"I've just gotten out of the bath, so I'll call you back later." "So now you're *in your birthday suit?*"

すで 素手 **bare hands** ▶池のコイを**素手**でつかんだ I grabbed the carp in the pond *barehanded* [*with my bare hands*]. ‖ その男は**素手**で(=武器なしで)そのクマと戦った The man fought with that bear *unarmed* [*empty-handed*].

ステーキ (a) **steak** /steɪk/ ; (a) **beefsteak** (ビーフステーキ) ▶私は**ステーキ**を注文した I ordered (*a*) *steak*. (➤「みんなの分の」は I ordered steak [steaks] for everyone. で Ⓤ も Ⓒ もある) ‖ あの**ステーキ**ハウスは最高の**ステーキ**を出す They serve great *steak* at that steak house. (➤ 集合的な使い方).

‖**ステーキハウス** a steak house ‖ **サーロインステーキ** a sirloin steak ‖ **ハンバーグステーキ** a hamburger steak, a Salisbury /sɔ́:lzbəri/ steak / a chopped steak.

ステージ a **stage** ▶生まれて初めて**ステージ**(=舞台)に立って歌を歌った I sang on *a stage* for the first time in my life. ‖ 今度の嵐の**ステージ**(=公演)は期待できる We're looking forward to Arashi's next *performance*.

ステータス **status** ▶ベンツを持つことがかつて**ステータスシンボル**としてもてはやされた Owning a Mercedes was once very popular [was popular at one time] because it was *a status symbol*.

すてがたい 捨て難い ▶どちらも**捨てがたい** It's *hard to choose* (because I like them both). ‖ フランス料理も**捨てがたい**が, あまりお金がないから今回はイタリア料理にしよう It's *hard to say "no"* to French food, but let's have Italian because I don't have very much money.

すてき 素敵 一形 **すてきな** **nice, lovely** (➤ 後者は《米》では主に女性が用いる) ; **wonderful** (非常にすばらしい) ▶**すてきな**セーター a *wonderful* sweater ‖ **すてきな**プレゼントをどうもありがとう Thank you very much for the *nice* [*wonderful*] present. ‖ ダンスパーティー, すごく**すてきだったわ** We *had a lovely* [*wonderful*] *time* at the dance. ‖ 家族そろってダイビングなんて**すてきね** *It's wonderful* that your whole family goes (scuba) diving. ‖ **すてきな人**が現れたらすぐに結婚します If *Mr. Right* [*Prince Charming*] comes along, I'll get married right away. (➤ Mr. Right は「夫としてふさわしい人」の意で女性なら Miss Right ; Prince Charming にはおどけた響きがある) ‖ 対話「今度の日曜日に箱根へドライブしない?」「まあ, **すてき**!」"How about driving to Hakone this coming Sunday?" "*That would be* [*That sounds*] *great*." ‖ 対話「玲子の彼って, どんな人?」「背の高い**すてきな**人よ」"What's Reiko's boyfriend like?" "He's a tall, *wonderful* guy."

✉ **この間はすてきな夜をありがとう** Thank you for the *wonderful* evening the other day.

> **あなたの英語はどう響く?**
> 外国人から, How do you like my new suit? (私の新しいスーツどうですか?) と聞かれた場合, 「すてきですよ」の意味で That's fine. と答えないこと. これだと「それで(も)いいですよ」の意味になる. It looks really great [fine]. のような答え方がよい.

すてご 捨て子 a **deserted child**, an **abandoned child** 《参考》拾われた「捨て子」を a foundling という.

すてじあい 捨て試合 a **giveaway game**.

すてぜりふ 捨て台詞 a **parting shot** ▶「今に見てろよ」と彼は**捨てぜりふ**を残して部屋を出ていった He went out of the room with the *parting shot*: "You're going to be sorry."

ステッカー a **sticker** ; a **sign** (掲示) ▶かばんに**ステッカー**を貼る put *a sticker* on a bag ‖ ショーウインドーに「セール」の**ステッカー**が貼ってあった There was *a sign* that said "Sale" in the show window.

ステッキ a (**walking**) **stick** ; a **cane** (籐(とう)の) ▶祖父は**ステッキ**を手にして出かけていった My grandfather went out *with a* (*walking*) *stick in his hand*.

ステップ **1** 【踏み段】a **step** ▶彼は列車の**ステップ**に立って手を振っていた He was standing on the *step* of the train and waving his hand.

すす

2【足の踏み方】a **step** ▶ワルツのステップ a waltz *step.*
3【段階】a **step** ▶最初のステップでつまずく make a mistake *in step one* [*in the first step*].

すててこ **(a pair of) *suteteko* underpants.**

すでに 既に **already** ▶駅に着くと列車はすでに出てしまっていた When I got to the station, the train had *already* left. ‖ それはすでに述べたとおりです I've *already* told you about that. ‖ あの手紙は今頃はすでにロンドンに着いているに違いない The letter must have reached London *by now.* ‖ 医者が到着したが時すでに遅かった The doctor arrived *too late.*

すてね 捨て値 ▶捨て値でノートパソコンを手放した I sold a laptop computer *dirt-cheap* [*for next to nothing*]. (➤ 後者は「ただ同然で」).

すてばち 捨て鉢 ▶その失敗で彼は捨てばちになった He became *desperate* after his failure. ／The failure drove him to *despair.*

すてみ 捨て身 ▶あんな大きなやつが相手じゃ捨て身でぶつかるしかないぞ You have to *go for broke* when fighting against so large an opponent. (➤ go for broke は「一か八(ばち)かやってみる」).

すてる 捨てる 1【不要なものを投棄する】**throw away**; **dump** +目 (ごみなどをどさっと); **get rid of** (取り除く) ▶この欠けたコーヒーカップは捨てましょう Let's *throw away* [*get rid of*／*discard*] these chipped coffee cups. ‖ 空き缶はくず籠に捨てなさい *Throw* empty cans into the trash can. ‖ 川にごみを捨ててはいけません Don't *dump* rubbish in the river. ‖ そのくず籠のごみを捨てておいてね Please *empty* the wastebasket. (➤ この empty は「空にする」) ‖ 止まれ，警察だ！銃を捨てろ！Freeze! Police! *Drop* your gun(s)! ‖《掲示》ごみを捨てないでください No Littering ／ No Dumping Allowed ／ No Garbage. ‖ 先入観を捨てる *get rid of* preconceived notions ‖ そんな甘い考えは捨てなさい *Get rid of* [*Give up*／*Abandon*] such wishful thinking.
2【放っておく】**forsake** +目 (親しい人・故郷などを；文語)；**abandon** +目 (➤「見捨てる」の意の一般語で堅い語) ▶彼が困っているのに捨てておけないよ I can't *forsake* him when he's in trouble.
3【顧みない】**abandon** +目；**leave** +目 (置いて行ってしまう)；**desert** +目 (法律上・道義上見捨ててはいけないものを)；**give up** (諦める)
▶家庭を捨てる *abandon* [*leave*／*desert*] one's family ‖ あなた，進に捨てられたのよ．諦めなさい Hey, Susumu *deserted* you! Forget about him. ‖ どんなにつらくても希望を捨てては(＝諦めては)いけない Never *give up* [*abandon*] hope no matter how hard things get. ‖ 最後まで試合を捨ててはいけない You should not *give up on* (winning) the game until the very end. ‖ 彼は今までの地位を捨てて，ボランティア活動のためにタイに渡った He *gave up* his (social) position and went to Thailand to work as a volunteer. ‖《慣用表現》西野君のドイツ語も捨てたものではない Nishino's German is *not too bad.* ‖ このクッキー，私が１人で作ったのよ．まんざら捨てたもんじゃないでしょう I've baked these cookies on my own. You see—*I'm not totally useless*!
ことわざ 捨てる神あれば拾う神あり Some gods may let you down, but others will pick you up. (➤ 日本語からの直訳) ／When one door shuts, another opens. (➤ 英語の慣用句).

ステレオ a **stereo** /stériou/ ‖ステレオ装置 a stereo set ‖ ステレオ放送 stereophonic broadcasting.

ステレオタイプ a **stereotype** /stériətaɪp/ ▶ステレオタイプの考え方 a *stereotypical* way of thinking.

ステンドグラス **stained** /steɪnd/ **glass** ▶ステンドグラス製のランプ a *stained glass* lamp.

ステンレス **stainless** /stéɪnləs/ **steel** ▶ステンレス製の流し a kitchen sink made of *stainless steel.*

スト a **strike**, a **walkout** (➤ 後者は労使交渉の決裂後，労働者たちが職場を放棄したり，スト突入の準備をしたりするなどのストの初期段階を指すことが多い) ▶ストを決行する go on *strike*／walk out ‖《掲示》スト決行中 On Strike ‖ 鉱山労働者たちは賃上げと労働条件の改善を目指してストを行っている The miners *are on strike* for more pay and better working conditions. ‖ 学生たちは学費値上げに反対してストに入った The students *went on strike* against the tuition hike. ‖スト破り strikebreaking (行為)；a strikebreaker (人).

ストイック **stoic.**

ストーカー a **stalker** ▶ストーカーに悩まされる be harassed by *a stalker* ‖ 彼女はこの数か月ストーカー行為に遭っている She*'s been stalked* for the past few months. (➤「ストーカー行為」は stalking).

ストーブ a **heater**, a **stove** ▶ストーブをつける[消す] turn on [off] *a heater* ‖ガスストーブ a gas heater ‖ 石油ストーブ a kerosene [《英》paraffin] heater ‖ 電気ストーブ an electric heater.

> 危ないカタカナ語✸ ストーブ
> 1 日本語の「ストーブ」は暖房器具を指し，英語の stove にもその意味はあるが，その場合は potbelly [potbellied] stove (だるまストーブ)のような旧式のものを指すことが多い．
> 2 日常的には stove は cooking stove, cookstove (ともに料理用レンジ)の意味で用いられる．
> 3 暖房器具を指す最も一般的な語は heater である．

ストーブリーグ a **hot stove league.**

すどおり 素通り ▶彼は私の家の前を挨拶もせずに素通りしていった He *passed* my house without even coming in to say hello. ▶《比喩的》この問題は素通り(＝無視)できない We cannot *ignore* this issue.

ストール a **stole** /stoul/.

ストッキング **stockings** (➤ 通例複数形で)；**pantyhose** /pǽnṭihouz/ (パンティーストッキング；複数扱い．hose とも) ▶ストッキングをはく[脱ぐ] put on [take off] *stockings.*

ストック 1【在庫品】(a) **stock** ▶このパソコンはもうストックがありません We don't have this (personal) computer in *stock* any more. ／We no longer *carry* this computer.
2【スキーの】a (**ski**) **pole** [**stick**] (➤ ふつうは複数形で使う)《参考》「ストック」はドイツ語 *Stock* から．
3【花】a **stock.**

ストックホルム **Stockholm** /stá:khoulm/ (➤ スウェーデンの首都).

ストッパー a **stopper** (栓；抑え投手；サッカーの守備選手).

ストップ **stop** ▶ストップ！この先は行き止まりですよ *Stop!* This is a dead-end street. ‖ 大雪のため列車がストップ(＝立ち往生)した The train *was held up* [*was stuck*] because of a heavy snowfall. ‖ 資金が足りなくなって，あの工事はストップしたままだ The construction work *has been stopped* due to a lack of funds.

ストップウォッチ a **stopwatch**, 《インフォーマル》a

clock ▶ストップウォッチを押す[止める] start [stop] *a clock* ‖ストップウォッチで100メートル走のタイムを計る time a 100-meter dash with *a stopwatch*.

すどまり 素泊まり ▶素泊まりの料金はいくらですか? How much is the room charge *without meals*?

ストライキ a **strike**. →スト.

ストライク a **strike** ▶《野球》ど真ん中のストライク *a strike* right down the middle ‖彼はワンボールツーストライクから次の球をホームランした He hit a home run on *a 1-2 count*. ‖《ボウリング》第5フレームでやっとストライクが出た I finally got *a strike* in the fifth frame.

ストライド a **stride**.

ストライプ a **stripe** ▶ストライプのワイシャツ a *striped* shirt ‖青地に白のストライプのスーツ a blue suit with white *stripes*.

ストラップ a **strap** ▶携帯ストラップ a cellphone *strap*.

ストリップ a **striptease** ▶ストリップを見にいく go (and) see *a strip* [*striptease*] *show*. ‖ストリップ小屋 a strip joint ‖ストリッパー a stripteaser, a stripper.

ストレート 1【まっすぐ】▶坂本は能見の3球目のストレート(=直球)をレフトスタンドにたたき込んだ Sakamoto slammed Nomi's third pitch, *a fastball*, into the left field stands. (➤ straight ball とはしない) ‖挑戦者の右ストレートがチャンピオンの顔面にさく裂した The challenger's right *straight punch* smashed into the champion's face.

▶綾子はK大にストレートで(=現役で)合格した Ayako went *directly* into K University. /Ayako got into K University *right after graduating from high school*. ‖そう怒るなよ. 彼は自分の気持ちをストレートに(=素直に)言えないだけなんだ Don't get so upset. He just can't be *frank* about his feelings.

2【続けざま】▶田中は中田をストレートの三振に打ち取った Tanaka fanned Nakata in three *straight* pitches. ‖青木はストレートの四球で歩いた Aoki walked on four *straight* pitches. ‖《テニスの試合で》ナダルはフェデラーにストレート勝ちした Nadal *beat* Federer *in three straight sets*.

3【薄めないこと】▶彼はウイスキーをストレートで飲んだ He drank whiskey *straight* [《英また》 *neat*].

ストレス (a) **stress** ▶現代人の生活にはストレスが多い People today are under great *stress*. /People today are living stressful lives. ‖胃潰瘍の多くはストレスが原因とされる Many gastric ulcers are caused by *stress*. ‖ストレスを感じることがありますか Do you sometimes *feel stressed*? ‖あまり仕事に集中しているとストレスがたまってくる *Stress* will build up if you keep working so hard. ‖学年末試験があった[ある]のでストレスがたまっている I'*m pretty stressed out* because of the final exams. ‖運動はストレスの解消に有効だ Physical exercise is effective in reducing *stress*. ‖ストレス障害 stress disorder.

ストレッチ a **stretch**; **stretching**(ストレッチすること) ▶泳ぐ前に少しストレッチをする *do* some *stretching* before swimming ‖ストレッチ体操をする do *stretching exercises*.

ストレッチャー a **gurney** /gə́ːrni/ (車輪つきの) (➤ stretcher は通例「担架」).

ストロー a **straw** ▶ストローでソーダ水を飲む sip soda water through *a straw*.

ストローク 《スポーツ》 a **stroke** ▶彼女は速くて着実なストロークで泳いだ She swam with swift, sure *strokes*.

ストロボ a **flash**, an **electronic flash**, (a) **strobe (light)** ▶ストロボ内蔵のAFカメラ an autofocus camera with a built-in *flash*.

すとん ▶犬がじゃれて飛びついた拍子に私はすとんと尻餅をついた When the dog lunged playfully at me, I fell *flat* on my behind.

ずどん ▶森の中でズドンという銃を撃つ音がした The *boom* of a gunshot was heard from the forest.

すな 砂 **sand** ▶この部屋の中は砂でざらざらだ This room is gritty with *sand*. ‖子供たちは公園で砂遊びをしていた The children were *playing in the sandbox* in the park. ‖砂嵐 a sandstorm ‖砂時計 a sandglass, an hourglass.

☛ 砂煙, 砂場, 砂浜 (→見出語)

すなお 素直 1【ねじけていない】

> **《解説》「素直」について**
> (1)この語にぴったりの英語はない. obedient が相当語とされることがあるが, この語には「従順な」の意味以外に「人の言いなりになる」という否定的なニュアンスもあり, 特に大人に対して用いる場合にその傾向が強い. 類語の meek (おとなしい)にも同様の否定的ニュアンスがある.
> (2)したがって, gentle (性質がおとなしい), docile /dάːsəl ‖ dóʊsaɪl/ (扱いやすい), mild (柔和な)などの形容詞を適宜用いるしかないが, いずれも日本語の「素直(な)」とはずれがある.

▶素直な子 an *obedient* child /a *gentle* [*docile*] child ‖素直な人 a *mild* person ‖素直に人の言うことを聞く *be willing to* listen to other people's advice ‖真紀子は素直な性格だ Makiko has a *gentle* nature. ‖どうしてあなたって, 素直じゃないの? Why *can't* you *take things just as they are*? (➤「なぜ物事をありのままに受け取ろうとしないのか」の意) ‖「もううそはつかないね」と言うと妹は素直にうなずいた When I said, "You won't lie any more, will you?" my (younger) sister shook her head *meekly*. ‖彼はその条件を素直に(=反抗せずに)受け入れた He accepted the conditions *without protesting* [*objecting*].

2【癖のない】▶ナオミの髪は素直で扱いやすい Naomi's hair is *soft* and easy to manage. ‖彼女は素直な字を書く She has *clear*, *natural* handwriting. /Her handwriting is *fluid and without any peculiarities*.

すなけむり 砂煙 a **dust cloud**, a **cloud of dust** ▶オートバイが砂煙を上げて通り過ぎた A motorcycle passed by me raising *a cloud of dust*.

スナック 1【店】 a **local bar**, a **bar (that serves light meals)** ▶スナックで一杯やっていこう Let's have a drink at the *bar*.

2【食べ物】 a **snack**, a **snack food** (軽食, スナック食品; スナック食品はカロリーばかり高くて栄養価が低いことから junk food とも呼ばれる).

> **危ないカタカナ語✸ スナック**
> **1** 英語の snack はサンドイッチなどの「軽食」または, ポテトチップなどの「スナック食品」の意で, 前者のような軽食とソフトドリンクを供する店を《英》では snack bar という. これは, 日本の立ち食いそば屋のような店で, 酒類は置いていないのがふつう. なお, スナック菓子はしばしば snack food という.
> **2** 日本では酒類を出す店を「スナック」と呼ぶが, これは (local) bar または pub というべきである.

スナップ **1【写真の】** a **snapshot**, a **snap** ; a **candid shot** [**photo**] (➤ candid は「隠し撮りの」の意味もある) ▶私は赤ん坊のスナップを何枚か撮った I took some *snapshots* [*snap photos*] of my baby.
2【手首のひねり】 ▶もっとスナップを効かせて投げてごらん *Snap* your wrist more when you throw the ball.
3【留め金具】 a **snap**.

す

すなば 砂場 《米》 a **sandbox**, 《英》 a **sandpit** ▶砂場で遊ぶ play in *a sandbox*.
すなはま 砂浜 a **beach** ▶砂浜を歩く walk along *a beach* ‖ 砂浜で遊ぶ have fun at *a beach*.
すなぶろ 砂風呂 a **sand bath**.
すなぼこり 砂ぼこり a **cloud of (fine) sand**.
すなやま 砂山 a **sand hill** ; a **(sand) dune** (砂丘).
すなわち 即ち **1【言い換えると】** **that is (to say)**, **namely** (➤ namely のほうがより詳細な説明を続ける場合に用いられる) ; **or** (➤ 前出の語をわかりやすく, またはより正確に言い換える場合に用いる) ▶百獣の王, **すなわち**ライオン the king of beasts, *that is* (*to say*), the lion ‖ 2つの都, **すなわち**パリとロンドンの物語 a story of two cities, *namely* Paris and London ‖ 切腹, **すなわち**腹部を切って自殺すること 'seppuku' *or* killing oneself by slashing the abdomen.
2【つまり】 ▶きみの幸せは**すなわち**ぼくの幸せでもある Your happiness *is* my happiness. / As long as you're happy, I am, *too*.
スニーカー 《主に米》 **sneakers**, 《主に英》 **plimsolls** /plímsəlz/, **training shoes** (➤ いずれも2つで1足なので通例複数形で).
ずぬけた **outstanding** →ずばぬける ▶彼女のピアノのテクニックは出場者の中でも**ずぬけていた** Her piano technique was really *outstanding* [*exceptional*] among the contestants.
すね 脛 **the leg** (脚部) ; **the shin** (向こうずね) ; a **shank** (すね肉) ▶すね毛 hair of *the legs*.
▶《慣用表現》彼は30歳にもなってまだ**親のすねをかじっている** Even after reaching the age of thirty, he still *lives off* [*sponges off*] *his parents*. (➤ sponge off は「小遣いをせびる」で批判的意味合いがある) ‖ 彼は**すねにきず持つ身**だ He *has a guilty* [*bad*] *conscience*. (➤「やましさを感じている」の意).
‖**すね当て** a shin guard [pad].
すねる 拗ねる **get sulky**, **sulk** ▶彼女は自分の思いどおりにならないとすぐ**すねる** She *sulks* [*gets sulky*] whenever she can't have her own way. ‖ 何を**すねてる**の? What *are* you *sulking about*?
ずのう 頭脳 **1【脳】** **the brain**, one's **brains** (➤ 後者はインフォーマルな言い方) ▶CPU (=中央処理装置) はコンピュータの**頭脳**だ The CPU works as *the brain* of a computer. ‖**人工頭脳** a mechanical brain.
2【知性, 知能】 a **mind** (➤ 優れた知力, 優れた知力の持ち主 ; best, brilliant, bright(est), creative, great(est) などの形容詞がつくことが多い ; 知力全般だが, 特に思考力, 創造力を連想する) ; a **brain** (➤「脳みそ」を思い浮かべ, 計算力や記憶力を連想する) ; a **head** (➤ 比喩的な意味での「頭(の働き)」) ▶この研究所には日本の**最高の頭脳**が集まっている Some of the *top* (*scientific*) *minds* in Japan are working together in this laboratory. ‖ その会議には**世界最高の頭脳**が集まった Some of *the world's brightest minds* gathered at the conference. ‖ スティーブン・ホーキングはすばらしい**頭脳**の持ち主だ Stephen Hawking has a brilliant *mind*. ‖ あの投手は**頭脳的な投球をする** That pitcher throws the ball *tactically*. ‖ 彼女は**頭脳明せき**だ She has *a clear head*. / She is *clear-headed* [*brilliant* / *very sharp*]. ‖ ぼくは**頭脳労働**には向いていないようだ I'm afraid I'm not cut out for *brainwork* [*mental work* / *intellectual work*].
‖**頭脳集団** a think tank ‖ (手相の) **頭脳線** the line of head, a head line ‖ **頭脳流出** a [the] brain drain ‖ **頭脳労働者** a brainworker.
スノーボード a **snowboard** (板) ; **snowboarding** (競技) ‖**スノーボーダー** a snowboarder.
すのこ a ***sunoko*** ; a board with spaced wooded slats (➤ 説明的な訳).
スノッブ a **snob**.
スパート a **spurt** /spəːrt/ 一動 **スパートする** **spurt** ▶先頭の走者は最後の1周で**スパートした** The front-runner *spurted* in the last lap.
☞ ラスト (→見出語)
スパーリング 《ボクシング》 **sparring**.
スパイ a **spy**, a **secret agent** (人) ; **espionage** /éspiənɑːʒ/ (スパイ行為) ▶ボスは私に**スパイ活動をする**ように命じた The boss commanded me to *work as a spy*. ‖**スパイ映画** a spy movie ‖ **スパイ衛星** a spy satellite ‖ **スパイ小説** a spy story ‖ **産業スパイ** an industrial spy.
スパイク **1【運動靴などの】** a **spike** (くぎ), a **cleat** (滑り止め) ; **spikes**, **spiked shoes**, 《米》 **cleats**, **cleat shoes** (スパイクシューズ ; 2つで1足なので通例複数形で). ‖**スパイクタイヤ** a studded (snow) tire.
2【バレーボールの】 a **spike** ▶木村の**スパイク**が見事に決まった Kimura's *spike* clinched it.
スパイス (a) **spice** ▶スープに**スパイス**を入れる add *spice* to the soup / spice the soup ‖ **スパイスの効いた**カレー *spicy* curry.
スパゲッティ **spaghetti** /spəgéṭi/ ‖**スパゲッティナポリタン** spaghetti with tomato sauce ‖ **スパゲッティミートソース** spaghetti with meat sauce.
すばこ 巣箱 a **birdhouse** (鳥の) ; a **beehive** (ミツバチの) ▶**巣箱を掛ける** put up *a birdhouse*.
すばしこい **quick** ; **agile**, **nimble** (身軽ですばしこい ; 前者がより強意的) ▶俊二は動作が**すばしこい** Shunji is *quick* [*agile* / *nimble*]. ‖ コイは**すばしこくて**, その子は手でつかまえることができなかった The carp were so *quick* that the child could not catch them with his [her] hands.
すぱすぱ ▶たばこを**すぱすぱ吸う** *puff away* at a cigarette ▶包丁を研いでもらったら**すぱすぱ切れる**ようになった Now that I've had this kitchen knife sharpened, it *cuts like a razor*.
ずばずば ▶彼は何でも**ずばずば**と言う人だ He's a person who *comes right out* and says what he thinks. / He does*n't mince his words*. ‖ あの人は誰にでも**ずばずば**ものを言う He [She] speaks *frankly* to anyone and everyone.
すはだ 素肌 **skin** ▶**素肌**に浴衣を着る wear a yukata *next to the skin* ‖ **素肌の美しい人** a person *with beautiful skin* [*a beautiful complexion*] (➤ complexion は特に「顔の色 [つやなどの状態]」).
スパッツ **leggings** (➤ spats は「ゲートル」または「口げんか」).
すぱっと ▶この包丁は**すぱっと**何でもよく切れる This kitchen knife can cut *right* through anything.
スパナ 《米》 a **wrench**, 《英》 a **spanner** ▶**スパナ**でボルトを締める fasten a bolt with *a wrench*.
ずばぬける ずば抜ける ▶彼は**ずばぬけた**才能の持ち主だ He has an *outstanding* [*a remarkable*] talent. ‖ 荻野は**ずばぬけて**足が速い Ogino is an *exceptional-*

ly fast runner. ‖ 彼は本校ではずばぬけてよくできる He is *by far* the best student in our school. ‖ 彼女はクラスの女子生徒の中ではずばぬけて背が高い She is *head and shoulders* taller than the other girls in class. (➤「頭と肩が(ほかの人より)上にあるほど」の意で, 成績などについても用いる) ‖ 彼はその試験でずばぬけていい成績を取った He *distinguished himself* in the examination. (➤「抜群の成績をあげた」の意).

スパムメール **spam (mail)**.

すばやい 素早い **quick, swift** (➤後者はやや文語的) ▶マジシャンは手さばきが素早い A magician is *quick* with his or her hands. ‖ リスは動きが素早い Squirrels are *quick-moving*. ‖ 犬は素早く逃げた The dog ran away *quickly* [*swiftly*].

すばらしい 素晴らしい **wonderful, great** (見事な; 後者のほうがよりくだけた語); **splendid** (際立った); **excellent** (非常に優れた); **gorgeous** (色彩・外観などが豪華・華麗な); **fantastic** (夢のような); **marvelous** (信じられないほどの; 女性が用いることが多く, この傾向は《米》に強い) ▶すばらしい景色 a *fine* [*grand*] view ‖ すばらしい業績 an *excellent* [*a marvelous*] achievement ‖ 彼の英語力はすばらしい He has a *wonderful* command of English. (➤ command は「自由に使いこなす力」) ‖ 彼はすばらしい家を東京の郊外に建てた He had a *splendid* [*beautiful*] house built in the suburbs of Tokyo. ‖ 北海道旅行中すばらしい体験をした[すばらしい人々に会った] I had a *wonderful* experience [met *wonderful* people] during my trip to Hokkaido. ‖ この映画は実にすばらしい This movie is *just great*. ‖ 彼女の結婚式はとてもすばらしかった Her wedding *was* (*just*) *fantastic*. ‖ きのうはすばらしい天気だった It was *a beautiful day* yesterday. ‖ 山頂からの眺めはすばらしかった The view from the top of the mountain *was marvelous*. ‖ すばらしい夕焼けよ, 見て! Look at the *gorgeous* sunset!

ずばり ▶ずばり(=率直に)言ってくれよ Please speak *frankly*. / Get to the point. ‖ ずばり言ってあなたの考えは間違っています *Frankly* [*To be frank with you*], you've got it (all) wrong. ‖ ずばり正解です *That's exactly right* [*correct*]. ‖ 彼の表現はそのものずばりで含蓄がない His writing (style) is *straightforward* and lacks suggestiveness. ‖ 彼は本当に頭がいい. ずばり天才だ He's really smart. A genius, *no less*. (➤ no less は名詞の後ろに置いて,「ずばり(そのもの)」の意の強調表現).

すばる 昴 《天文学》 **the Pleiades** /plíːədiːz ‖ pláɪə-/ (➤「プレアデス星団」とも; 複数扱い).

スパルタしき スパルタ式 ▶あの学校はスパルタ式教育で名高い That school is well known for its *disciplinary rigor* [*harsh discipline*]. (➤ discipline は「しつけ」).

> **危ないカタカナ語✹ スパルタ式**
> 「スパルタ(式)」は英語の Spartan からきているが, この語は Spartan simplicity [frugality] (スパルタ式簡素さ[つましさ]), Spartan life (簡素に徹した生活) などのように, 主に生活態度や食事内容を指すのに用い, 日本語の「スパルタ式(教育)」にあるような,「時には体罰さえ辞さないような厳しさ」といった含みはない. 日本語の「スパルタ式」は用例のように表現するのがよい.

ずはん 図版 a **plate** (本の全ページ大の図版); an **illustration** (挿し絵, 説明図); a **figure** (図形, 図解).

スパンコール a **spangle** ▶スパンコールを散りばめたレオタード a *spangled* leotard.

スピーカー a **(loud)speaker**; a **PA (system)** (駅や学校などの放送設備; PA は public-address の略) ▶その候補者はスピーカーを使って街頭演説をした The candidate made a speech on the street *through a loudspeaker*.

スピーチ a **speech** (演説); **a few words** (短い話, 挨拶) ▶晩さん会でスピーチをする *give* [*make* / *deliver*] *a speech* at a dinner party (➤ deliver は「行う」に近い堅い語) ‖ 市長が歓迎会(祝賀会)で歓迎の[お祝いの]スピーチをした The mayor *said a few words of welcome* [*congratulations*] at the reception. (➤ a few words は「二言三言」ではなく, 場合によって, 3分～5分程度の短い話で, 歓迎の「ことば」や「挨拶」に当たる) ‖ スピーチコンテスト a speech contest.

> **直訳の落とし穴「スピーチをする」**
> 「スピーチをする」は give [make] a speech であるが, 結婚披露宴で「さて, 次に新婦のご友人にスピーチをお願いいたします」のつもりで, Now a friend of the bride will make a (short) speech. などと紹介するのは, あまりにそのものずばりで座が白けるほど不自然に響く. ふつうは遠回しな表現として(3分から5分のものであっても), Now a friend of the bride will say a few words. という.「～さん, スピーチをお願いできますか」は Could you say a few words, Mr. [Ms.] ～? というのがふつう. 英語でも間接的な表現が好まれる場合があるのである. スピーチが終わったあと, It was a nice speech. (すてきなスピーチでした)というのは全く問題ない.

スピーディー **speedy** 一副 **スピーディーに** **speedily** ▶クレームにスピーディーに対応する handle complaints *quickly* [*without delay*].

スピード (a) **speed** ▶自動車は時速80キロのスピードで走っていた The car was going [traveling] at *a speed* of 80 kilometers an hour. (➤ was running としない) ‖ 私はフルスピードで車を飛ばした I drove *at full* [*top*] *speed*. ‖ ジェットコースターは次第にスピードを上げた The roller coaster gradually *speeded up* [*gathered speed*]. ‖ 車は突然スピードを落とした[スピードダウンした] The car suddenly *slowed down*. (● reduce speed ともいえるが (×)speed down とはいわない) ‖ この車はどのくらいスピードが出ますか *How fast* does this car go? ‖ 道路が凍結しているからあまりスピードを出すと危険だよ The roads are frozen over, so it's dangerous to *speed*. ‖ 彼はスピード違反[オーバー]で捕まった He was arrested for *speeding*. ‖ コンピュータの導入で事務がスピードアップした With the installation of the computer, our office work has *speeded up*. ‖ 《掲示》スピード落とせ Reduce Speed Now. ‖ スピードウェー a speedway ‖ スピードガン a speed gun (➤商標名) ‖ スピード狂 a speeder, a speed demon ‖ スピード写真 an instant photograph ‖ スピードメーター a speedometer /spɪdɑ́ːmət̬ər/.

ずひょう 図表 a **chart**; a **diagram** (図形) ▶結果を図表で表す show results using *a chart*.

スピリチュアル a **spiritual** (歌) 一形 **スピリチュアルな** **spiritual** ▶スピリチュアルな体験をする have a *spiritual* experience.

スピン (a) **spin** (回転) ▶ボールにスピンをかける *put* (a) *spin* on a ball / *spin* a ball.

スフィンクス **the Sphinx**.

スプーン a **spoon** ▶チャーハンをスプーンで食べる eat

fried rice *with a spoon* ‖ スプーン３杯の砂糖 *three spoonfuls of* sugar ‖ その男の子はアイスクリームをスプーンですくって口にもっていった The boy *spooned* some ice cream into his mouth.
‖スプーンレース an egg-and-spoon race.

ずぶずぶ ▶靴がぬかるみにずぶずぶとめり込んだ My shoes *got stuck* into the mud.

すぶた 酢豚 **sweet and sour pork.**

す

ずぶとい 図太い **bold**(大胆な) ; **impudent**(無礼な, 厚かましい) ▶彼は神経がずぶとい He is a *bold* man. ／He's *got some nerve*. (➤ nerve は「(ずぶとい)神経」) ‖ 彼女のずぶとい神経にはほとほとあきれた I was totally shocked by her *boldness* [*brazenness* ／*toughness*].

ずぶぬれ ずぶ濡れ ▶父はずぶぬれになって帰って来た My father came home *dripping wet*. ‖ 夕立に遭ってずぶぬれになった I was caught in a shower and *got drenched* [*got wet*] *to the skin*. ‖ 私, ずぶぬれになっちゃった I'*m soaked to the skin*.

ずぶの ▶ずぶの素人 a *total* layperson (➤ 専門知識のない人) ／an *absolute* [*a rank*] beginner (➤ 初心者).

すぶり 素振り ▶素振りの練習をする make *practice swings* (➤ 野球・テニス・ゴルフなどで) ／*brandish* a bamboo sword *in practice*(➤ 剣道で竹刀を振る).

スプリング **1**【ばね】a **spring.**
2【春】**spring.**
3【スプリングコート】a **light overcoat**, a **topcoat.**

スプリンクラー a **sprinkler** ; a **sprinkler system**(一体で動く設備) ▶天井にスプリンクラーを設置する install *a sprinkler system* on the ceiling.

スフレ a **soufflé** /sufléɪ/.

スプレー a **spray**(噴霧器) ▶スプレーを吹きかけてゴキブリを殺す kill a cockroach with (*a*) *spray*.
‖ヘアスプレー (a) hairspray.

すべ 術 ▶あまりの火の勢いになすすべがなかった The fire was blazing so fiercely that we *could do nothing but* watch it [*we were at a loss what to do* (*next*)].

スペア a **spare** ▶ 対話「あっ, 電池が切れそう」「大丈夫よ. 私スペア持って来たから」"Oh, no. The battery is just about dead." "No problem. I brought *a spare*." ▶《ボウリングで》スペアをとったよ I made *a spare* ! ‖スペアインク a refill for a pen ‖ スペアキー a spare key ‖ スペアタイヤ a spare tire [《英》tyre].

スペアリブ **spareribs.**

スペイン **Spain** 一形 スペインの **Spanish**
‖スペイン語 Spanish, the Spanish language ‖ スペイン人 a Spaniard ; the Spanish(全体) (➤「ホセさんはスペイン人 [スペイン人の建築家] だ」はそれぞれ, Jose is Spanish., Jose is a Spanish architect. という).

スペース (a) **space** ; **room**(空間) ▶この机はスペースを取り過ぎている This desk takes up too much *space*. ‖ ここにヒーターを据え付けるだけのスペースはない There is not enough *room* [*space*] to install a heater in here.
‖スペースシャトル a space shuttle.

スペード a **spade** ▶スペードのキング the king of *spades* ‖ スペードの７ the seven of *spades*.

スペクタクル a **spectacle.**

スペクトル a **spectrum** [複 **spectra** または ～ **s**].

スペシャリスト a **specialist.**

すべすべ ▶赤ん坊の肌は絹のようにすべすべしている A baby's skin is as *smooth* as silk.

すべて 全て **all, everything** 一形 すべての **all, every**(➤ 後者は常に単数名詞を伴い, 動詞も単数形) ▶問題はすべて英語で出された *All* the questions were [*Every* question was] asked in English. ‖ この事件の責任はすべてきみにある *All* responsibility for the incident rests with you. ／You are *entirely* to blame for the incident. ‖ 彼が言ったことはすべて間違っている What he said is *all* wrong. ‖ おじは火事ですべての財産を失った My uncle lost *all* his fortune in the fire. ‖ すべての人を喜ばせることは難しい It is hard to please *everyone*.
▶すべてがうまく行かなかった *Everything* went wrong. ／Nothing went well. ‖ 大地震で市のすべてが破壊された The *entire* [*whole*] city was destroyed by the great earthquake. (➤ entire は whole より堅い語) ‖《本などのタイトル》『ゴルフのすべて』"*All* about Golf" ‖ あなたのすべてを知りたいの I want to know *everything* about you. ‖ すべてお任せします I'll leave *everything* up to you. ‖ おまえのやっていることは神様はすべてお見通しだ God does*n't miss* what you're doing. ‖ 金がすべてだという考え方は嫌いだ I hate the idea that money is *everything*. (➤ この everything は「何よりも大切なもの」の意).

すべらせる 滑らせる **slip** ▶ハイカーが尾根で足を滑らせ谷に転落した A hiker *slipped* and fell from the ridge into the gorge.
▶《慣用表現》それは２人の秘密のはずだったのに, 彼はうっかり口を滑らせてしまった It was supposed to be a secret between us, but he *let it slip out*.

すべりこみ 滑り込み **1**【野球】**sliding** ▶選手たちは滑り込みの練習をしていた The players were practicing *sliding* (*into base*).
2【やっと間に合うこと】▶彼は滑り込みで列車に間に合った He caught the train *just in time*. ／He *just* made the train. ‖ けさは寝坊して遅くなったが学校へは滑り込みセーフだった I overslept this morning, but *managed to make it* to school *just in time* [*under the bell*]. ‖ 入試は滑り込み合格だったらしい I think I *narrowly passed* the entrance exams. (➤ narrowly は「やっと, かろうじて」).

すべりこむ 滑り込む **1**【野球】**slide**《into》▶周東は三塁に頭から滑り込んだ Shuto *slid into* third base headfirst.
2【やっと間に合う】▶終電車に滑り込む *catch* the last train *just in time* ／*make* the last train ‖ 私たちは時間ぎりぎりに空港に滑り込んだ We *arrived* at the airport *just in time* [*in the nick of time*].

すべりだい 滑り台 a **slide** ▶子供たちは遊び場の滑り台で遊んでいる The children are playing on *a slide* in the playground.

すべりだし 滑り出し a **start**, a **beginning** ▶滑り出しは順調でした We've *gotten off to a good start*.

すべりどめ 滑り止め a **skid**(車輪の坂道用の) ; a **nonskid** [**nonslip**] **strip** (階段・浴室用の) ; **cleats** (スポーツ靴用の) ▶《比喩的》私は滑り止めにその大学を受験した I took the entrance examination for that university *as insurance*. (➤ insurance は文字どおりには「保険」で「困らないようにする備え」の意) ‖ 滑り止めにほかの大学も受験しとけばよかった I should have *hedged my bets* by applying to other universities as well. (➤ hedge one's bets は「大きな損失を受けないように掛け金を分散する」が原義).

スペリング **spelling** ▶その単語のスペリングを教えてください Could you give me the *spelling* of that word? ／Could you tell me *how to spell* that word? ‖ ひろしは和文英訳で3つのスペリングミスを犯した Hiroshi *misspelled* three words [*spelled* three words *wrong*] in his Japanese-English translation. →スペル ‖スペリングテスト a spelling test.

すべる 滑る 1【滑らかに動く】**slide**; **ski**（スキーで）; **skate**（スケートで）▶少年は坂を滑って降りた The boy *slid down* the slope.（➤ slid は slide の過去形）‖《スキーで》きょうは何回滑ったの? How many times did you *ski down* the slope(s) [mountain] today?
2【つるりと滑る】**slip**; **skid**（車などのタイヤが）▶彼はバナナの皮を踏んで滑った He *slipped* [*had a slip*] on a banana peel. ‖ 滑りやすいから気をつけなさい Watch out. It's *slippery*. ‖ 手が滑って皿を割ってしまった The dish *slipped out of my hands* and shattered. ‖ 私のバイクが氷で滑った My motorcycle *skidded* on the ice.
3【口が】▶つい口が滑ったのです It was *a slip of the tongue*. ／The word *slipped out of my mouth* before I knew what I was saying.
4【試験に落ちる】**fail** ▶私はH大を受けたが滑った I *failed* [*flunked*] the entrance examination for H University.（➤ flunk は「試験に失敗する」の意のインフォーマルな語）.

スペル **spelling**（➤ spell は「つづる」の意の動詞または「呪文」,「(ある特定の天候の)期間」,「(発作などの)ひとしきり」の意の名詞）▶ワードで作成した文書のスペルチェックをする *check the spelling* in a Word document ／*spell-check* a Word document（➤ソフトは a spell-check(ing) program または a spell-checker）‖ お名前のスペルを教えてください May I ask how you *spell* your name? ／Could you [How do you] *spell* your name?（● (×)Tell me the spell of your name. としないこと）. →スペリング.
‖スペルミス a spelling mistake [error].

スポーク a **spoke**.

スポイト a **dropper**（少量の液体用）; a **syringe** 《参考》「スポイト」はオランダ語から.

スポークスマン a **spokesman**（➤男性を連想させるこの語を避けて spokesperson を用いることも多い）.

スポーツ **sports**,《英》**sport**（➤総称）; a **sport**（➤個々の）▶スポーツをする *practice* [*enjoy* ／*play* ／*do* ／*take part in* ／*participate in*] *sports*.
語法 (1)play は《米》では baseball, football など具体的なスポーツ名とともに用いることが多い. (2)do はインフォーマルな語でこの用法を好まない人も多いが, 日常的にはよく用いられる. (3)take part in, participate in は「参加する, 加わる」に近い堅い言い方だがよく用いられる. (4)enjoy には「見て楽しむ」の意もある.
▶あの学校はスポーツが盛んだ Students in that school are very active in *sports*. ‖ スポーツはするのも見るのも大好きです I love both doing and watching *sports*. ‖ 好きなスポーツは何ですか What is your favorite *sport*? ／What *sport* do you like best? ‖ スポーツは何をやっていますか What *sports* do you do [play]? ／What *sports* are you into?（➤この be into は「熱中している」の意）‖スポーツ医学 sports medicine ‖ スポーツウエア sportswear ‖ スポーツカー a sports car ‖ スポーツ界 the sports world ‖ スポーツ解説者 a sports commentator ‖ スポーツクラブ a sports club ‖ スポーツシャツ a sport(s) shirt ‖ スポーツ新聞 a sports paper ‖ スポーツセンター a sports center ‖ スポーツ大会 a sports competition [event] ‖ スポーツチーム a sports team ‖ スポーツ店 a sporting-goods store ‖ スポーツドリンク a sports drink ‖ スポーツニュース sports news, a sportscast ‖ スポーツバー a sports bar ‖ スポーツファン a sports fan ‖ スポーツ欄 the sports section.

危ないカタカナ語✹ スポーツ(マン)
1 日本語では「(主に勝敗を争う)運動」のことを「スポーツ」というが, 英語の sport は狩猟, 魚釣り, 競馬などを含むもっと幅の広いことばである. したがって sportsman はハンターや釣り師も含む.
2「彼はスポーツマンだ」にぴったりの言い方はないので, He is good at sports. とするか, athlete(運動選手)を用いて He is a good athlete. などと表現する.
3「スポーツマンシップにのっとり, 正々堂々と戦うことを誓います」は I pledge to practice [show] good sportsmanship and play fair. と言えばよい. sportsmanship の man が「男性」を連想させるのでこの語の使用を避けようとする人もいるが, 実際には男女共用であることが多い. →正々堂々

スポーティー **sporty** ▶スポーティーなクーペ a *sporty* coupe ‖ スポーティーなブルーのジャケット a *sporty* blue jacket ‖ 達也はスポーティーな格好で外出した Tatsuya went out in *casual clothes* [*in sportswear*].

ずぼし 図星 ▶ぼくは彼女に図星を指されどぎまぎした What she said *hit the bull's-eye* and embarrassed me greatly.（➤ hit the bull's-eye は「標的の中心円を射る」）‖ おまえはきのう学校を休んでサーフィンをしていた. どうだ, 図星だろう I bet you played hooky yesterday and went surfing. So did I *hit the mark* [*hit the nail on the head*] or not?（➤後者は文字どおりには「くぎの頭をたたいた」の意. play hooky は《米》で「学校をサボる」の意）.

すぽっと ▶ドアが開かないので強く引っ張ったら取っ手がすぽっと抜けた The door wouldn't open, so I pulled hard (at it), and the doorknob *popped off*. ‖ ゴルフボールをぐっと押したら小さな穴にすぽっとはまった I pressed the golf ball and it *popped into* the small hole.

スポット ▶《アナウンサーが》本日はファッション界にスポットを当てます We're going to *spotlight* [*highlight*] the world of fashion today. ‖スポット広告 a spot (announcement) ‖ スポットニュース spot news.

スポットライト a **spotlight** ▶そのバレリーナはスポットライトを浴びて舞台の中央で踊った The ballerina danced at the center of the stage *with a spotlight on her*.

すぼまる ▶その洞穴は出口がすぼまっている The cave *gets narrower* [*narrows*] at the exit. ‖ このジーンズは先がすぼまっている These jeans *taper off* [*slim off*] *toward the ankle(s)*.

すぼめる ▶雨がやんだので彼女は傘をすぼめた It stopped raining so she *closed* [*folded*] her *umbrella*. ‖ 母親は口をすぼめて子供の頬にキスした The mother *puckered her lips* and kissed her child on the cheek.

ずぼらな **slovenly** /slʌ́vənli/ ▶ルームメートはずぼらだ My roommate is *slovenly*. ‖ 仕事を放りっぱなしにしているとはなんてずぼらな男だ What *a slovenly person* he is to leave his work unfinished!

ズボン **trousers**,《インフォーマル》**pants**; **slacks**（上着と対でないカジュアルなもの. 男女ともに用いる）▶だぶだぶのズボン baggy *trousers* [*pants*] ‖ このズボンは大きすぎる These *trousers* are too large. ／This pair of

trousers is too large. (➤ 動詞の単複の違いに注意) ‖ 黒いズボンを1本買いたいのですが I'd like to buy *a pair of* black *trousers*. ‖ ズボンの前が開いてるよ Your *fly* [*zipper*] is open. →窓(社会の窓).
‖ズボン下 long johns ‖ ズボンつり (米) suspenders, 《英》 braces.

スポンサー a **sponsor** ▶そのテレビ番組のスポンサーはせっけん会社だ The *sponsor* of the TV program is a soap company. ／A soap company sponsors the TV program.

スポンジ a **sponge** /spʌndʒ/ ▶スポンジはよく水を吸う *A sponge* absorbs water easily. ‖ スポンジで体をきれいに洗いなさい *Sponge* yourself clean.
‖スポンジケーキ (a) sponge cake.

スマート **slender, slim** (ほっそりした) ▶スマートな女の子 a *slender* [*slim*] girl ‖ スマートな服装 *stylish* [*chic*] dress ‖ きみ, だいぶスマートになったね You've gotten quite *slim*. ‖ (IC チップを内蔵した)スマートカード a smart card ‖ スマートテレビ a smart television [TV] ‖ スマートフォン a smartphone.

> **あなたの英語はどう響く?**
> 日本語では細身の人を指して「彼はスマートだ」と言うが, それを直訳して He is smart. とすることはできない. この英語は「彼は頭がいい」の意味に解釈されるのがふつう. 「彼はスマートだ」に相当するのは He is slim [slender]. である.

すまい 住まい a **house**(家) ; a **home**(家庭生活の営まれる所 ; 《米》では home も house 同様, 「家」の意で用いられることが多い) ; (a) **residence**(➤「堂々として優雅な」という含みがある) ; a **place**(➤ 大邸宅にもアパートにも用いるが, 「うち」の意ではインフォーマルな語) ▶立派なお住まいですね What a fine [nice] *house* you live in! ‖ お住まいはどちらですか *Where do you live*? ‖ 新婚の二人は東京の郊外に住まいを持った The newly married couple *made their home* in a Tokyo suburb. ‖ 祖父は軽井沢にもちょっとした住まいを持っています My grandfather has a little *place* in Karuizawa too. ‖ 田舎住まいにも飽きました I am tired of *rural life* [*living in the country*]. ‖ 当分ホテル住まいになるでしょう I'll have to *stay at a hotel* for some time.

すましじる 澄まし汁 **clear soup, consommé** /kɑ̀ːnsəméɪ ‖ kɒnsɒ́meɪ/.

¹**すます 済ます** →済ませる.

²**すます 澄ます** **1【耳などを集中させる】**▶耳を澄ましてごらん *Listen carefully*.
2【気取る, 平気な顔をする】▶あの社長秘書はいつも澄まして(＝上品ぶって)いる That president's secretary *is* always *prim and proper*. ‖ 彼は「自分は関係ありません」と澄ました顔で言った He said *coolly*, "I have nothing to do with it."

すませる 済ませる **1【終わらせる】** **finish** +㊐, **get through** 《with》 (➤ 後者はインフォーマルな言い方) ▶仕事を済ませてからシャワーを浴びた After I *finished* my work, I took a shower. ‖ 夕食は済ませましたか *Have* you *had* [*finished*] your supper? ‖ 5時までに仕事を済ませなければならない I must *get through* (*with*) my work by five o'clock. ‖ 宿題は済ませたの? *Are* you *through with* your homework? ‖ これは早く済ませちゃおうよ Let's *get* this *over with* quickly. (➤ get ... over with は「嫌でもやらなければならないことを片づける」).
▶今のは冗談だったでは済まされないよ You *can't get away with it* by saying it's just a joke. (➤ get away with (it) は「持ち逃げする」の意から「(悪いことをして)罰を受けない」).
2【間に合わせる】▶その島では電気なしで済ますことになると思うよ I guess you'll have to *do without* electricity on that island. ‖ 昼はラーメンで済ませた I *had just* a light lunch of ramen. ／For lunch I *made do with* ramen. (➤ make do with は「不十分なもので間に合わせる, 我慢する」).

スマッシュ a **smash**(テニスなどの) ▶彼女は見事なスマッシュで加点した She scored more points with her marvelous *smashes*. ‖ 彼は相手のコートにスマッシュを打ち込んだ He *smashed the ball* into his opponent's court.

すまない 済まない ▶きみには本当にすまないことをした *I'm sorry for what I did* to you. ‖ すまないが, ちょっと席を外してくれる? *I'm sorry to ask you* [*Excuse me*], *but* could you please leave your seat(s) for a moment? ‖ すまないが少々金を貸してくれないか *Would you mind* lending me some money? ‖ 対話「ぼくの辞書使えよ」「そりゃすまないな」"Use my dictionary." "Great, *thanks*." (➤ 英語ではこのように感謝の表現になるのがふつう).

¹**すみ 隅** a **corner** ▶ (罰として)隅に立っていなさい Stand in the *corner*! ‖ 先生は隅の席に座っていた The teacher was sitting in a *corner* seat. ‖ 彼女は部屋の四隅に椅子を置いた She put chairs in the *four corners* of the room. ‖ 警察は彼の家を隅から隅まで捜索した The police searched his house *from top to bottom* [*every nook and cranny* of his house]. ‖ この辺りは隅から隅まで知っています I *know every inch* of this neighborhood. ／I *know* this neighborhood *like the back of my hand*.
▶ (慣用表現) 彼は無口だがなかなか隅に置けない男だ Although he's quiet, he's *a smart guy*. ‖ 対話「健次がこの頃リナちゃんと付き合ってるの知ってた?」「ほんとかよ. あいつも隅に置けないね」"Did you know Kenji's been going out with Rina recently?" "No kidding! We *shouldn't underestimate* him." (➤「軽く見てはいけない」の意).

²**すみ 炭** **charcoal** ▶炭を焼く process [make] *charcoal* ‖ 当店のウナギは炭火で焼いております We broil eels over *charcoal*. ‖炭焼き窯 a charcoal kiln.

³**すみ 墨** **1【墨汁】** ***sumi*-ink, Chinese** [**China**] **ink, India** [**Indian**] **ink** (液状) ; a ***sumi*-ink stick** (固形) ▶墨をする rub *a sumi-ink stick* back and forth ／ make *ink* ‖墨絵 (a) *sumie*, a *sumi*-ink drawing.
2【タコ・イカの】 **ink** ▶イカ墨 squid *ink* ‖ タコが墨を吐いた The octopus squirted *ink*.

すみか 住みか a **dwelling**, an **abode**(➤ 後者はより堅い語) ; a **den**(盗賊などの) ▶盗賊たちの住みかは森の中にあった The *den* of the thieves was found in the woods.

すみきる 澄み切る ▶澄み切った青空 a (*crystal*) *clear* blue sky.

すみごこち 住み心地 ▶このマンションは住み心地がいい This apartment is *comfortable to live in*. ‖ ご新居の住み心地はいかがですか *How do you like living* [*life*] in your new house?

すみこみ 住み込みの **live-in** ▶住み込みのヘルパー a *live-in* caregiver ‖ そのお手伝いさんは住み込みだ The maid *lives in*. ‖ このレストランには住み込みのコックさんが5人います There are five *live-in* cooks in this restaurant.

すみずみ 隅々 ▶本を隅々まで読む read a book *from*

cover to cover ‖ 隅々まで捜したが財布は見つからなかった I looked for my wallet in *every nook and cranny* [*all the corners*], but I couldn't find it. ‖ 新宿なら隅々まで知っている I know Shinjuku *like the back of my hand*. (➤ know ... like the back of one's hand は「自分の手の甲のように知っている」が原義) ‖ 柔道は今や世界の隅々まで知れ渡っている Today judo is known *all over the world* [*throughout the world*].

すみつく 住み着く settle ▶裏の林にタヌキがすみ着いている A tanuki raccoon *has settled* in the woods at the back of my house. ‖ この村に住み着いて20年になります It is [has been] twenty years since I *settled* [*came to live*] in this village.

すみなれる 住み慣れる ▶彼は住み慣れた家を出ていった He left his (*beloved*) house *where he had lived so long*. ‖ 住み慣れたわが家に戻るとほっとする It feels good to come back to your home where everything is *familiar* (*and comfortable*). ／It feels great to get back to your home sweet home.

すみません 1【謝罪】I'm sorry.

> 【文型】
> …してすみません
> I'm sorry to do.
> I'm sorry (that) S + V.

▶遅くなってすみません *I'm sorry* I'm late. (➤ I'm sorry to be late. ／I'm sorry for being late. も使われるが, I'm sorry I'm late. が一般的. また, Sorry I'm late. Thank you for waiting. のように, sorry を使った表現のあとに Thank you for waiting. をつけ加えることもある) ‖ お待たせしてすみませんでした. 道が混んでいてバスが20分も遅れたものですから *I'm sorry to* have kept you waiting [*I'm sorry* I have kept you waiting ／*I'm sorry* for having kept you waiting]. The bus was more than twenty minutes late because of heavy traffic. ‖ 夜分遅く電話してすみません *I'm sorry to* call you so late at night. ‖ 対話「お宅の犬がほえてうるさいんだけど」「すみません, 静かにさせます」"Your dog's loud barking is disturbing us." "*I'm sorry*. I'll try to keep him quiet." ▶ 対話(足を踏まれて)「痛い!」「すみません, 大丈夫ですか?」"Ouch !" "*I'm sorry*. Are you all right ?"

> **あなたの英語はどう響く?**
> 日本人は日常会話でよく「すみません」と言うが, 英語の I'm sorry. は自分の過失について非を認めたときの謝罪の表現である. 例えば車どうしの衝突で I'm sorry. と言えば自分が悪かったことを認めたことになり, 相手から損害賠償を求められるだろう. 相手の体にぶつかったときなどの「すみません」は Excuse me ! がふつう.

2【呼びかけ】excuse me ▶すみません, 学生食堂はどっちでしょうか *Excuse me*, but do you know where the student cafeteria is ? ‖ すみません, 高島屋に行く道を教えてください *Excuse me*, could you tell me how to get to the Takashimaya Department Store ? ‖ すみませんが窓を閉めてください *Would you please* close the window ?

3【感謝】thank you ▶ 対話(電車の中などで)「どうぞお掛けください」「まあ, どうもすみません」"Please have a seat." "Oh. *Thank you very much*." ‖ 対話「つまらないものですが」「いつもどうもすみません」"This is a little something for you." "*You're always so kind*."

すみやか 速やかな prompt ▶速やかな回答 a *prompt* reply ‖ 速やかに対策を講じる必要がある It's necessary to take some *prompt* measures (to deal with the situation). ‖ 速やかに(＝すぐ)退出しなさい Leave the room *immediately*.

すみやき 炭焼き charcoal-making (炭作り) ; a charcoal maker [burner] (人).

すみれ 菫《植物》a violet ‖ すみれ色 violet.

すみわたる 澄み渡る ▶澄み渡った空 a *vast expanse of clear* sky.

1 **すむ 済む** 1【終わる】end ; finish (完了・完結する) ▶この会議, 3時までに済むといいが I hope this meeting *ends* by three o'clock. ‖ すぐに済むよ It *takes little time*. ／It *takes almost no time*. ‖ 宿題はもう済んだの? *Have* you *finished* your homework yet ? ‖ 用件が済んだので私は帰宅した When I *finished with* my business, I went home. (➤ with を伴った言い方は finish だけの言い方と異なり「もう用がなくなった」の意を強く含む) ‖ 私の辞書, 済んだら返してね When you'*re done with* my dictionary, please return it to me. (➤ be done with は「…を終えている, 済ませている」の意のインフォーマルな表現) ‖ 期末試験が済んでほっとした I feel relieved now that the final examination *is over*. (➤ be over は「済んでいる」状況に力点がある) ‖ 新聞はもうお済みですか *Are* you *through with* the paper ? ‖ 済んだことはしかたがない *What is done can't be undone*. ／*It is no use crying over spilt milk*. (➤ ともに英語のことわざ) ‖ 済んだことは水に流そう *Let bygones be bygones*. (➤ 英語のことわざ).

2【逃れる, 間に合う】▶電話で話せばわざわざ彼に手紙を書かないで済む If you call him up, you *won't have to* write to him. ‖ 何とか借金をせずに済んだ I *got by* without borrowing money. (➤ get by は「(困難を)どうにか切り抜ける」) ‖ そうしてくれればまた出かけなくても済む That will *save* me (*the trouble* of) going out again. (➤ save A B で「A(人)のB(労力)するのを省く」の意) ‖ 車の修理代は1万円で済んだ Repairs on the car cost *only* 10,000 yen. ‖ ことしの夏は涼しかったのでクーラーなしで済んだ We *managed without* an air conditioner this past summer since it was not so hot. ‖ 息子が風疹にかかったが, 幸い軽くて済んだ Our son caught the German measles [rubella], but it *wasn't* very serious.

3【解決する】▶金で済む問題ではない It's not a problem that can *be solved* with money. ‖ 俺を殴って気が済むんだったら遠慮なくやってくれ If it *makes* you *feel better*, go ahead, hit me. ‖「すみません」じゃ済まない You *can't get away* with just saying you're sorry. ‖ すみませんで済むと思うのか You think just saying you're sorry is going to *make things right* ?

2 **すむ 住む** live《in, on》; inhabit +㊐ (集団で生息する) ▶彼の一家は木更津に住んでいる His family *live(s) in* Kisarazu. (➤ 進行形にしない ; 家族の一人一人を考えるときは live, 家族を全体として考えるときは lives) ‖ 関西に住んで10年になります It has been ten years since I came to *live in* the Kansai district. ‖ オットセイは北半球の寒い海にすむ Fur seals *live in* the cold waters of the Northern Hemisphere. ‖ あの人は住む家がない He has no house to *live in*. ／He has no place to *live*. ‖ この辺りに住んでるの? Do you *live* around here ? ‖ この辺りの森には今でもリスが住んでいる Squirrels still *inhabit* [are found in] this forest. (➤ inhabit は他

動詞なので，あとに場所を表す目的語がくる）．
▶この小さな島には人が住んでいない *There are no people living* on this small island. ‖ 湖のほとりに人の住んでいない家が１軒あった We found [There was] an *unoccupied* house by the lake. ‖ あなたは永久に日本に住む(＝定住する)つもりなの？Do you plan to *live* in Japan permanently？(⚠ live forever とすると「(死ぬことなく)永久に生きる」というナンセンスな文になる).

す

[3]**すむ 澄む** 一形 **澄んだ clear** ▶谷川の流れは川底が見えるほど澄んでいる The mountain stream is so *clear* that you can see the bottom. ‖ その日，空は青く澄んでいた That day, the sky was blue and *clear*. ‖ 彼女はよく澄んだ声で『峠の我が家』を歌った She sang "Home on the Range" in a *clear* voice.

スムージー a **smoothie** ▶果物とフルーツジュースだけで作ったスムージーは食間の飲み物として最適である *Smoothies* made solely with fruit and fruit juice are ideal between-meal drinks.

スムーズ smooth /smu:ð/ ▶仕事はスムーズに運んでいる The work is proceeding *smoothly*. ‖ 入国手続きはスムーズに済んだ I got through immigration *without any hitches*.

ずめん 図面 a **plan**(設計図)；a **blueprint**(青写真) ▶彼は新しいビルの図面を引いた He *drew* (*up*) the *plans* for a new building.

すもう 相撲 sumo(➤ 英語化している)
日本紹介 ✉ **相撲はレスリングに似た日本の伝統的な格闘技です．国技とされています．力士はちょんまげを結ってまわしをつけ，土俵に上がる動作も様式化されています．年に６回，プロの力士による大相撲があります** Sumo is a traditional Japanese combative sport like wrestling and considered the national sport. *Rikishi* (wrestlers) have a topknot (hairstyle) and wear a belt and make ritualistic movements in the ring. Professional sumo wrestlers compete in six grand tournaments held during the course of a year. ⇀大関，横綱．
▶相撲をとる have a *sumo* bout.
‖**相撲とり** a *sumotori* ／a sumo wrestler.

「相撲の決まり手」のいろいろ **足取り** leg pick ／**浴びせ倒し** backward force down ／**内掛け** inside leg trip ／**内無双** inner thigh propping twist down ／**うっちゃり** backward pivot throw ／**上手出し投げ** pulling overarm throw ／**上手投げ** overarm throw ／**送り出し** rear push out ／**押し倒し** frontal push down ／**押し出し** frontal push out ／**肩透かし** under-shoulder swing down ／**きめ出し** arm barring force out ／**切り返し** twisting backward knee trip ／**首投げ** headlock throw ／**けたぐり** pulling inside ankle sweep ／**小手投げ** armlock throw ／**小股すくい** over thigh scooping body drop ／**さば折り** forward force down ／**下手出し投げ** pulling underarm throw ／**下手投げ** underarm throw ／**下手ひねり** twisting underarm throw ／**すくい投げ** beltless arm throw ／**外掛け** outside leg trip ／**突き落とし** thrust down ／**突き倒し** frontal thrust down ／**突き出し** frontal thrust out ／**つり出し** lift out ／**とったり** arm bar throw ／**二枚げり** ankle kicking twist down ／**はたき込み** slap down ／**引き落とし** hand pull down ／**寄り切り** frontal force out ／**寄り倒し** frontal crush out
(日本相撲協会のホームページより抜粋)

☛ **大相撲** (⇀見出語)

すもぐり 素潜り diving without breathing apparatus；skin diving(➤ シュノーケルやフィンを用いるもの)．

スモック a **smock**.

スモッグ (a) **smog** ▶けさの北京はひどいスモッグが垂れこめている This morning in Beijing there is a heavy *smog* hanging low over the city. ‖ **光化学スモッグ**で目をやられた I've got sore eyes from *photochemical smog*.

すもも 李 《植物》a **plum**.

すやき 素焼き ▶素焼きの植木鉢 an *unglazed* flowerpot.

すやすや ▶赤ちゃんがベビーベッドの中ですやすや眠っている The baby is sleeping *soundly* in the crib.

-すら even ▶恐怖のあまり悲鳴を上げることすらできなかった I was so scared I could not *even* let out a scream. ⇀-さえ．

スラー 《音楽》a **slur**.

スライス a **slice**.

スライダー 《野球》a **slider**.

スライディング sliding ▶ヘッドスライディング headfirst *sliding*.

スライド **1【フィルムの】** a **slide** ▶祖父は子供時代のスライドを見せてくれた My grandfather showed me some *slides* of his childhood.
‖**スライド映写機** a slide projector.
2【コンピュータソフトの】 a **slide**(プレゼンテーションソフトの１ページ) ▶お好みのデジタル写真からスライドショーを作るのは難しくはないです It's not difficult to make [create] a *slide show* from your favorite digital photos. (➤ スライドショーはソフトウェアによって画像を順次表示すること)．
3【同じ比率で動かすこと】 ▶賃金を物価にスライドして上げる raise wages *in proportion to* prices.

ずらかる ▶ここからずらかろうぜ Let's *blow* this place！／Let's *get out of* here！‖ サツ(＝警察)だ！ずらかれ(＝逃げろ)！Cops！*Beat it！*

ずらす **1【動かす】** ▶ちょっと椅子をずらしてくれない？Could you *move* the chair a bit？
2【時間を変える】 ▶出発の日取りを１週間ずらそう Let's *postpone* [*move up*] our departure one week. (➤ postpone は「延期する」，move up は「繰り上げる」)．

すらすら fluently(流ちょうに)；**easily**(容易に)；**smoothly**(スムーズに) ▶すらすら言えるようになるまでこのパラグラフを暗記しなさい Memorize this paragraph until you can say it *fluently*. ‖ あの子はまだ１年生なのに，難しい本をすらすら読む Although the girl is only a first grader, she can read difficult books *easily*. ‖ 礼状くらいすらすら書けなくてはだめだよ You have to at least be able to write a thank-you note *smoothly*. ‖ 数学は易しい問題ばかりだったのですらすら解けた The math problems were all so easy that I solved them *with no difficulty*. (➤「困難もなく」の意)．

ずらずら ▶その生徒は宿題をしてこなかった言い訳をずらずら並べ立てた The student gave *one* excuse *after another* for not doing his homework.

スラッガー 《野球》a **slugger**.

スラックス slacks ▶セーターにスラックスの女性 a woman in a sweater and *slacks*.

スラッシュ a **slash**, a **slash mark**, an **oblique stroke** [**line**]，《英また》an **oblique**.

スラム a **slum** ▶大都市のスラム街では犯罪が多発する Many crimes are committed in the *slums* of big cities.

すらりと ▶木村君のお母さんはすらりとした美人だ Kimura's mother is a *slender* beauty. ‖直美はすらりとした足をしている Naomi *has long slender legs*. ／Naomi *is leggy* [a *leggy* girl].

ずらりと ▶部屋に入るとずらりと知っている顔が並んでいた When I entered the room, I saw *many* familiar faces.

すられる 掏られる ▶人混みの中で財布をすられた I *had* my wallet *picked* [*lifted*] in the crowd.

スラローム 《スキー》(a) **slalom.**

スラング **slang**(俗語；集合的に)；a **slang word**(1つの俗語) ▶英語のスラングを使うときには注意が必要だ You should be careful when you use English *slang*.

スランプ a **slump** ▶畠山はスランプに陥っている Hatakeyama has *hit a slump*. ／Hatakeyama is *in a slump*. ‖田中はついにスランプを脱した Tanaka finally *came out of* his *slump*.

すり 掏摸 a **pickpocket**(人) ▶《掲示》すりにご用心 *Beware of Pickpockets* ‖すりの一味 a band of *pickpockets* ‖混雑した電車の中ですりにやられた I *had my pocket picked* [*My pocket was picked*] in the jam-packed train.

ずりあがる ずり上がる **slide up** ▶あの男の子のセーターはおなかのところまでずり上がっている That boy's sweater *has slid up* to his stomach. (➤ slid は slide の過去分詞形).

スリーサイズ one's **measurements** (➤ (×) three size は和製英語).

スリーディー **3-D** ‖スリーディー映画 a 3-D movie ‖スリーディーテレビ a 3-D television. →三次元.

スリーバント 《野球》a **two-strike bunt**(➤「ツーストライクを取られたあとにやるバント」の意；three bunt とはしない) ▶スリーバントに成功する succeed in *a two-strike bunt*.

スリーラン 《野球》a **three-run homer** [**home run**](➤ three-run は「3点の」の意).

ずりおちる ずり落ちる **slip off**(するりと落ちる)；**slide down**(ずるずると落ちる) ▶毛布がベッドからずり落ちた The blanket *slipped off* the bed. ‖バッグが網棚からずり落ちた The bag *slipped off* the rack.

すりかえる 摩り替える **switch, change** ▶ファイルの中身が何者かによってすり替えられた Someone *switched* the documents in the file. ‖今の答弁は問題をすり替えているように思えます It seems that you are trying to *change* the subject when you answer like that.

すりガラス 磨りガラス **frosted** [**ground**] **glass.**

すりきず 擦り傷 a **scratch** ▶彼は転んで肘に擦り傷を負った He fell down and *scratched* his elbow(s).

すりきり すり切り ▶すり切り小さじ1杯の砂糖 a *level* teaspoonful of sugar.

すりきれる 擦り切れる **wear out** ▶ズボンの裾が少し擦り切れてきた My pants *are* a little *worn out* at the hem. ‖その刑事は擦り切れたコートを着ていた The detective was in a *threadbare* [*frayed*] coat.

すりこぎ すりこ木 a **wooden pestle.**

すりこみ 刷り込み 《動物学》**imprinting.**

すりこむ 擦り込む ▶足に軟こうを擦り込む *rub* ointment *onto* one's leg ／*rub* one's leg *with* ointment.

ずりさがる ずり下がる ▶ズボンがずり下がってきた My pants *are sliding down*.

スリッパ **slippers**(➤ しばしば, 寝室などで履く, かかとのある, あるいは, かかと覆いのある軽い上靴もさす；a slipper は片方を指す), 《主に米》**scuffs**；**mules**(➤ しばしば, 装飾的な凝ったもの). ▶スリッパの片方が見つからない One of this pair of *slippers* [*mules*] is missing. ‖スリッパのまま外へ出てはいけません Don't go outside in *slippers* [*scuffs*].

スリップ **1**【滑ること】a **skid**(車などの横滑り；英語では slip よりも skid を用いることが多い) ▶車は凍結した道路でスリップし, ガードレールにぶつかった The car *skidded* on the icy road and ran into a guardrail. ‖《掲示》スリップ注意 Slippery When Wet ‖雨の日はスリップ事故が多い On rainy days, there are many *accidents caused by cars skidding* [*skidding cars*].

2【女性の下着】a **slip.**

すりつぶす すり潰す **grind** /graɪnd/ +目 (すり鉢などでする) ▶ごまをすり潰す *grind* sesame seeds.

すりぬける 擦り抜ける **pass through** ▶狭い道をダンプカーがすり抜けていった The dump truck *passed through* the narrow street.

すりばち すり鉢 an **earthenware mortar** /mɔ́ːʳṭəʳ/ ▶すり鉢でニンニクを潰す crush garlic in *a mortar*. →うす.

すりへらす 磨り減らす **wear (thin), wear down** ▶靴をすり減らして歩き回ったが, いい仕事は見つからなかった I wandered about looking for a good job *until my shoes were worn thin* [I *almost wore my shoes out* looking for a good job], but I couldn't find one.

▶《比喩的》プログラミングは神経をすり減らす仕事だ Programming *wears out your nerves*. ／Programming *is nerve-wracking*.

すりへる 磨り減る **be worn (thin), be worn down** ▶靴底がすり減って薄くなった The soles of my shoes *were worn thin*. ‖まな板がすり減ってきた The cutting board *is worn down*.

すりみ すり身 ***surimi***；minced processed fish.

スリム **slim** ▶スリムな人 a *slim* person ‖スリムなズボン *slim-cut* pants [trousers] ‖経営をスリム化する *streamline* management ‖もっとスリムになりたい I want to *slim down*.

すりむく 擦りむく **skin** +目 (かすって)；**scrape** +目, **graze** +目 (こすって；後者は多少の出血があるのがふつう)；**scratch** +目 (引っかいたように) ▶私は転んで膝を擦りむいた I fell and *skinned* [*grazed* ／*scratched*] my knees.

▶きのうローラースケート中に転んで肘と膝を擦りむいちゃった Yesterday I *scraped* both my elbows and knees (while) roller-skating.

すりもの 刷り物 a **handout**(資料として配るもの)；**printed matter**(印刷物).

すりよる 擦り寄る **snuggle up** ▶少女はソファーに座っている母親に擦り寄った The girl *snuggled up* to her mother on the couch.

スリラー a **thriller** /θrɪləʳ/ ‖スリラー映画 a thriller movie.

スリランカ **Sri Lanka**(インド南方の島国) ‖スリランカ人 a Sri Lankan.

スリル a **thrill** ▶スカイダイビングはスリルに富んだスポーツだ Skydiving is a *thrilling* sport. ‖ジェットコースターはスリル満点だ Roller coasters are *very thrilling* [is *full of thrills*]. ‖大陸横断の一人旅なんてちょっとスリルがあるわね Traveling across the continent alone would be a *thrilling* adventure, wouldn't it?

[1]する

📖 **訳語メニュー**
行為をする →do **1**
球技をする →play **1**
人・物を…にする →make **2, 3**
職業とする →be **4**
金がかかる →cost **5**
形・性質などをもつ →have **8**

す

1【ある行為を】do +目 ▶きょうはすることが山ほどある I have millions of things to *do* today. ‖ 若い人の中には何もすることがないと不平を言う人がいる Some young people complain that they have nothing to *do*. ‖ 父は私に好きなようにしろと言った My father told me to *go ahead and do as I liked*. ‖ きょうはすることなすことうまくいかない Today *everything* is going wrong. ／Nothing is going right for me today. (➤ 後者がよりインフォーマルな言い方) ‖ 授業中はおしゃべりするな *Don't* talk during class. ‖ **対話**「ほら, ドライバーが出血しているよ. どうしようか?」「救急車を呼んだほうがいいよ」"Look! The driver's bleeding. *What are we going to do* [*What should we do*]?" "We'd better call an ambulance."
▶野球 [テニス] をする *play* baseball [tennis] ‖ 私は1日に1時間運動をする I *exercise* one hour [I *get* an hour of *exercise*] every day. ‖ 部活が忙しくて勉強をする時間がない I'm so busy with club activities I have no time to *study*.

2【人を…にする】make +目 (➤ 目的語のあとに形容詞か名詞がくる)

【文型】
人・物(A)を B にする
make A B
➤ Bは名詞・形容詞

▶ぼくはきみを幸せにする自信がある I'm confident that I can *make* you *happy*. ‖ 川村君をチームの主将にしよう *Let's make* Kawamura captain of the team.

3【物を…にする】make +目 ▶この機械は小麦粉を麺にする This machine *makes* noodles from flour. ‖ 父は骨とう品を売って金にした My father sold an antique to *get* money. ／My father sold an antique for money. ‖ 昼休みの時間に公園のベンチをベッドにして寝ているサラリーマンがいる Some office workers *use* park benches *as* beds during lunch time.

4【職業とする】be ▶兄は高校の英語の教師をしている My brother *is* a high school English teacher. ‖ 父は弁護士をしている My father *is* a lawyer.

5【金がかかる】cost +目 ▶このテレビ, 30万円もしたのよ This television *cost* me 300,000 yen. ‖ **対話**「この車はいくらしたの?」「200万だよ」"*How much was* this car?" "Two million yen."

6【時間がたつ】▶あと2週間すれば私は20歳になる I'll be twenty years old *in* two weeks. ‖ 1か月もすれば暖かくなりますよ It's going to get warm *in* a month. ‖ 父は5分もすれば戻ります My father will be back *in* five minutes or so.

7【感じる】▶がれきの下から人の声がする I *hear a voice* from under the rubble. ‖ けさから寒気がする I've *had a chill* since this morning. ‖ 喫茶店に入るとコーヒーのいい匂いがした I *smelled* the aroma of coffee when I went into the coffee shop.

8【形・色・性質など】have +目 ▶ヨーロッパ人は高い鼻をしている Europeans *have* long [large] noses. ‖ 毒のあるカエルには鮮やかな色をしているものがいる Some poisonous frogs *have* bright colors. ‖ 雅子は優しい性格をしている Masako *is* kind *by nature*. ／Masako *has* a sweet *nature*.

9【決める, 仮定する】▶(喫茶店で) 私はアイスティーにします *I'd like* some iced tea, please. ‖ じゃあ, こうしよう Then *let's do it* this way. ‖ 仮にその少女をBさんとしよう *Let's call* the girl Miss B.

[2]**する 擦る・擂る・磨る 1【こする】rub** +目 ; **grind** /graɪnd/ +目 (ひいて粉にする) ▶2本の棒を擦り合わせて火をおこす make fire by *rubbing* two sticks *together* ‖ ごまをする *grind* sesame seeds ‖ マッチを擦る *strike* a match.
2【損をする】lose +目, **blow** +目 (➤ 後者は俗語) ▶彼は競馬で有り金を全部すってしまった He *lost* [*blew*] all his money on horse racing.

[3]**する 掏る pick** +目 (…の中の物を抜き取る) ▶俺の財布をすったのはおまえだろ You're the one who *picked my pocket*, aren't you?

[4]**する 刷る print** +目, **run off** (➤ 後者はややインフォーマルな言い方) ▶ことしの年賀状には辰(たつ)の版画を刷った(=刷ってもらった) I *had* the Dragon *printed* on my New Year's cards for this year. ‖ 彼女はそのプリントを1000部刷った She *ran off* a thousand copies of the handout.

ずる ▶彼は試験でずるをやった He *cheated on* [《英》*in*] the exam. ‖ 彼はその試合でずるをやった He *cheated* in the game.

ずるい 1【計略を使う】crafty, sly (悪賢い) ; **dishonest** (不正直な) ▶ずるいやつは嫌いだ I don't like *crafty* [*sly* ／*dishonest*] people.
2【不正な】unfair ; **cheating** (人をだます) ; **dirty, underhanded** (汚い) ▶そんなのずるいよ That's *not fair*! ‖ 先に走り出すなんてずるいぞ That's *cheating* to start running before everyone else. ‖ ずるいことはやめよう *Let's play fair*. ／*Don't play dirty* [*foul*]. ‖ あの政治家はずるいやり方で当選した That politician won through *dirty* [*underhanded*] tricks.

スルー スルーする ignore +目 (無視する) ; **pay no attention** 《to》 (注意を払わない) ; 《インフォーマル》 **give** A **the go-by** (➤ A(人)を無視する)
▶スルーするにはもったいない申し出 an offer too good to *ignore* ‖ 人をスルーする *give* a person *the go-by* ‖ 母親の小言をスルーする *pay no attention to* the complaints of one's mother ‖ こんなチャンスをスルーしちゃあだめだよ. 二度とないかもしれないよ Don't *let* this chance *go by*. You may not have another one. (➤ この go by は「(機会などが) 見逃される」).

ずるがしこい ずる賢い crafty, sly (悪賢い) ; **tricky** (策略を用いる) ; **cunning** (悪知恵にたけた ; crafty, sly と違って, 良い意味で「戦略にたけた」にも用いる) ▶ずる賢い政治家 a *crafty* [*tricky*] politician ‖ あいつはずる賢いやつだ He is as *cunning* [*sly*] as a fox. (➤ 欧米でもキツネの性質は陰性でずる賢いとされる) ／He's a *slick* character.

ずるける ▶学校をずるけてゲームセンターへ行く *skip* school and go to an amusement arcade.

するする ▶ヤシの木のてっぺんから猿がするする降りて来た A monkey *slid down* from the top of the palm tree. ‖ その蛇は木をするすると登っていった That snake *slid* [*slithered*] *up* the tree. ‖ 旗はするするとポールを上った The flag *ran up* the pole. ‖ ひもを引っ張ったら結び目がするするほどけた I pulled the string and the knot came *loose*.

ずるずる ▶斜面をずるずると滑り下りる *slide down* a slope ‖ 重い箱をずるずる引きずる *drag* a heavy box ‖

少年はずるずると(＝次第に)悪の道にのめり込んでいった The boy was *gradually* drawn into the world of crime. ‖ 彼は何のかんのと言って返済をずるずると延ばしている He is *stalling on* repaying the loan by making up a bunch of excuses.
▶うどんをズルズルとすする *slurp* one's *udon* noodles (➤ slurp は「音を立てて食べる(飲む)」の意. 音を立てて飲食することは欧米では下品とされる).

ずるずるべったり ▶あんな男とずるずるべったりに付き合っていてはだめだよ You shouldn't *just go on* seeing such a man (*out of habit*).

すると ▶彼は犬の名前を呼んだ. すると犬は裏庭からすっ飛んで来た He called his dog's name. *Then* the dog came rushing to him from the backyard. ‖ すると(＝では), きみはぼくがそれを取ったと言うんだね *So*, you mean I stole it.

するどい 鋭い 1【鋭利な】**sharp** ▶このナイフは刃が鋭い This knife has (got) a *sharp* edge. ‖ トラは鋭いきばを持っている Tigers have *sharp* fangs.
2【強く突き刺さるような】**sharp** ▶その男は私を鋭い目つきでにらんだ The man stared at me with a *sharp* [*piercing*] look in his eyes. (➤ piercing は「突き刺すような」) ‖ ワシは鋭い目をしている Eagles have *keen* eyes. ‖ 胃に鋭い痛みが走った I felt a *sharp* [an *acute*] pain in my stomach. ‖ きみの観察力はなかなか鋭いね Your power of observation is very *sharp*. ／You have a *sharp* eye. ‖ なかなか鋭いご指摘ですね That's a *perceptive* [*incisive*] comment. (➤ それぞれ「洞察力のある」「的を射た」の意).
3【敏感な】▶母は勘が鋭い My mother's got *sharp* intuition. ‖ 犬は嗅覚が鋭い Dogs have a *keen* sense of smell. ‖ あの子は音に対して鋭い感覚をもっている That child is very *sensitive* to sound.

するめ a **dried squid** ▶するめをあぶって食べる grill *a dried squid* and eat it.

ずるやすみ ずる休み ▶彼はよく学校をずる休みする He often *plays hooky* [《英》*plays truant* (*from school*)]. ‖ 彼女は仕事をずる休みして彼とデートした She *skipped work* and went out on a date with her boyfriend. (➤ skip は「サボる」) 《参考》学校や職場を「ずる休みする」ことを《英・インフォーマル》では throw a sickie という.

するりと ▶その子はぼくの脇の下をするりと抜けて逃げていった That child *slipped out* right under my arm and ran away.

ずれ (a) **difference**(差, 違い); a **gap** (隔たり); (a) **lag** (時間の) ▶時間のずれ(＝時差) a time *lag* ‖ 日本人とアメリカ人では感覚にずれがあるのは当然だ It's natural that there should be *differences* in perception between Japanese and Americans. ‖ 世代間の(考え方の)ずれは親子の問題を引き起こしている *The generation gap* causes problems between parents and children.

スレート a **slate** ▶スレートぶきの屋根 a *slate-covered* roof／a roof *covered with slate*(*s*).

ずれこむ ずれ込む ▶予定よりちょっとずれ込んでいる We're *running* a little *late*. ‖ 編集作業が遅れているのでその辞書の発行は来年にずれ込むだろう The publication of the dictionary will have to *be put off* until next year because of a delay in editing. (➤「延期される」の意).

すれすれ 1【触れそうになって】▶ダンプカーがぼくの体すれすれに走り過ぎた A dump truck *almost grazed* me as it passed. (➤ almost は「もう少しのところで…しそうに」, graze は「かすめて通る」) ‖ カモメが水面すれすれに飛んだ The gulls *skimmed* (*over*) *the water*. (➤ skim は「…をかすめて飛ぶ」) ‖ ツバメが地上すれすれに飛んだ A swallow flew very low, *almost touching the ground*. ‖ 川の水位が堤防すれすれまで上がった The water level of the river rose *almost as high as its banks*.
2【ぎりぎり】▶彼はすれすれで合格した He *barely* passed the examination. (➤ barely は「かろうじて…する」) ‖ すれすれで列車に間に合った I was *just* in time for the train. ／I *barely* made the train. ‖ 数学はいつも合格点すれすれだ I always *get barely passing grades* [*marks*] in math. ‖ あの男はいつも犯罪すれすれのことをやっている That guy is always doing things that *almost touch on the law*.

すれちがう 擦れ違う 1【そばを通り過ぎる】▶列車は橋の上で擦れ違った The trains *passed each other* on the bridge. ‖ 彼女は私と擦れ違ったとき何も言わなかった She did not say a word when we *passed each other* [when she *passed by* me].
2【行き違う】▶私たちはこれまで話が擦れ違っていた We *have been talking past each other*. ‖ 議論が擦れ違って結論が出なかった We could reach no satisfactory conclusion because our arguments *were at cross-purposes*. ‖ 夫は夜勤が多いので, 昼間勤めている私とは擦れ違うことが少なくありません Since my husband is often on the night shift and I work in the daytime, we sometimes *miss each other* [*don't see each other*].

すれっからし ▶あんなすれっからしの女と付き合ってはだめだ You shouldn't go around with such *a shameless girl*.

すれる 擦れる 1【こすれる】**be worn** (**out**) ▶裾口が擦れてきた My sleeves are getting *worn*.
2【純真さを失う】**lose** one's **innocence, become sophisticated** ▶彼は都会の生活で擦れてしまった He *lost his innocence* [*became worldly-wise*] after living in the city. ‖ 彼女はバレーボール一筋に打ち込んできた, 擦れていない女の子だ She is a *simple and unsophisticated* girl who has devoted herself entirely to volleyball.

ずれる 1【位置・時間が動く】▶台風の進路は予報よりだいぶ東にずれた The typhoon *veered* [*went*] much *further* east [more eastward] than was forecast. ‖ メンバーの到着が遅れて会議の始まりが30分ずれた(＝遅れた) Our meeting *started* 30 minutes *late* because some members arrived late.
2【外れている】▶きみの考えは常識からずれているよ Your opinion *deviates* from common sense. ‖ 彼は感覚が少しずれている His sense *is* a bit *off*.

スローガン a **slogan**, a **watchword** ; a **catchword**(効果を狙って繰り返し用いることば) ▶「安全第一」が我々のスローガンだ "Safety first" is our *slogan* [*watchword*].

スロープ a **slope** ; a **ramp**(車椅子用などの) ▶ぼくは40度のスロープを一気に滑り降りた I skied down the forty-degree *slope* in no time. ‖ 車椅子のためのスロープ *a ramp* for wheelchairs.

直訳の落とし穴「玄関のスロープ」
slope は自然の坂やスキーのゲレンデ (ski slope) を指す. 日本語でいう「玄関のスロープ」のような, 地面と建物の入り口などをつないだり, 高速道路に乗ったりするための人工的な坂道は slope ではない. 後者は日本語でも「ランプ」と呼ぶが, 英語は ramp である.「玄関のスロープ」あるいは高速道路の入り口のランプは an en-

trance ramp で, 高速道路に乗るためのものは an on-ramp ともいう. 出口のランプは an exit ramp または, an off-ramp である. 車椅子用に作られたスロープは an wheelchair ramp という.

スローフード slow food.

スローモーション slow motion ▶ただ今の取組をもう一度スローモーションで見てみましょう Let's watch the bout again in *slow motion*.

スロットマシーン 《米》a slot machine, 《英》a fruit machine.

ズワイガニ a snow [queen] crab.

すわり 座り ▶こちらのテーブルのほうが座りがいい This table is more *stable* [is *stabler*]. ‖ この椅子は座りが悪い This chair *is unstable* [*rickety*].

すわりごこち 座り心地 ▶このソファーは座り心地がいい This sofa *is comfortable* (*to sit on*).
▶《比喩的》どうだい, 社長の椅子の座り心地は? *How do you feel sitting* in the president's seat?

すわりこみ 座り込み a sit-in ▶組合労働者たちが座り込みを行った The union workers staged a *sit-in* [*sit-down*] (*strike*).

すわりこむ 座り込む sit down ; crouch /kraʊtʃ/ (うずくまる) ; sit in (抗議して) ▶彼は市長に面会を求めて玄関口に座り込んだ He *sat down* in front of the mayor's residence to get an interview with him. ‖ 彼女は船酔いして甲板に座り込んでしまった She got seasick and *crouched* on the deck.

すわる 座る・据わる 1【腰を下ろす】sit down ; sit (座っている ; 状態動詞) ; take a seat, be seated (席に着く) ▶ベンチに座る *sit down* on a bench (➤ 動作は sit down で, sit on a bench はしばしば「ベンチに座っている」状態を表す) ‖ 椅子に座る *sit on* [*in*] a *chair* (➤ on は接触を表すので上に載る状態のとき, in は「中に」をイメージするので, 肘掛けのある椅子に座るときや, 体がのめり込むように深々と座るとき) ‖ 前列の人たちは座ってください People in the front row, *please sit down*. (➤ Sit! はふつう犬に向かってしか言わない) ‖ 彼は机に向かって座り, コンピュータの電源を入れた He *sat* (*down*) at his desk and switched on his computer. (➤ down は動作を表すとき) ‖ こちらに [そちらに] お座りください *Please sit* here [over there]. (➤ 動作よりも着席した状態(「座っていてください」)にポイントがあるので sit を用いる. 以下 2 例も同様) ‖ あの相撲取りがエコノミークラスの席に座るのは容易ではない It is not easy for that sumo wrestler to *sit* in an economy class seat. ‖ みんなで火の周りに車座になって座って歌を歌った We all *sat in a circle* around the fire and sang some songs. ‖ 母はロッキングチェアーに座って編み物をしていた My mother *sat* knitting in the rocking chair.
▶どうぞ席にお座りください Please *be seated*. / *Take your seat*(s), please. ‖ 立っていないで, どの席でもいいから座りなさい Don't stand around. Please *take any seat you like* (*and sit down*). ‖ 映画館は満員で座れなかった The movie theater was full and I *couldn't find a seat*. ‖ その列車は満員で名古屋から新大阪までずっと座れなかった The train was so crowded (that) I *had to stand* all the way from Nagoya to Shin-Osaka. ‖ この教室は30人しか座れない This lecture room *seats* [*accommodates*] only thirty. (➤ seat は「…だけの座席をもつ」).
▶きちんと座って! *Sit* (*up*) *straight*. ‖ 《犬に向かって》お座り! *Sit!*
2【地位に就く】▶誰が次に社長の椅子に座るのだろう Who will be (the) next to *occupy* the president's chair?
3【一か所にいて動かない】▶部長は腹の据わった人だ Our general manager is *courageous* [is a person *with guts*]. ‖ 彼女は度胸が据わっている She's *gutsy*.

すんか 寸暇 ▶彼は寸暇を惜しんで受験勉強に励んだ He *devoted every spare moment* to studying for the entrance examination(s). / *All his time was spent* on studying for the entrance examination(s).

ずんぐり ▶母はずんぐりした体つきだ My mother is *dumpy* [*short and pudgy*].

すんげき 寸劇 a skit ▶私たちは英語の授業で寸劇を演じた We did *a skit* in our English class.

すんし 寸志 a small token of thanks [gratitude] 《参考》「寸志」は自分の贈り物(金銭であることも少なくない)を謙遜していうことばで, ふつうは贈り物を包むのし紙に書くが, この習慣は英米にはない.

ずんずん ▶皆ずんずん先に行っちゃって, ぼくだけ置いてきぼりにされたんだ All of them *forged on ahead* and I got left behind.

すんぜん 寸前 ▶スタントマンは車が火に飛び込む寸前に脱出した The stunt man got out of the car *just* [*right*] *before* it ran into the fire. ‖ あのデパートは販売不振で倒産寸前だ That department store *is on the verge* [*on the brink*] *of* bankruptcy because of poor sales. (➤ verge, brink ともに「(崖などの)縁」が原義) ‖ 勝はキレる寸前だった Masaru *was just about to* lose it.

すんたらず 寸足らず ▶この浴衣はだいぶ寸足らずだ This yukata is much *too short*.

すんだん 寸断 ▶中央線は大雨のため線路があちこちで寸断された The railroad tracks *were disconnected* at several places on the Chuo Line because of the heavy rain.

すんづまり 寸詰まり ▶(洗って)寸詰まりになったセーター a sweater which *has shrunk* ‖ 彼のズボンは少し寸詰まりだ His trousers are a little *too short*.

すんでのところで ▶とっさに急ハンドルを切って, すんでのところで追突を免れた I turned the steering wheel quickly, and *just* missed hitting the car ahead. ‖ すんでのところで車にひかれるところだった I was *almost* run over by a car.

ずんどう ずん胴 ▶父はとても太っていてずん胴だ My father is so fat that he *has no waist* [he *is waistless*].

すんなり ▶こんなにすんなりいくとは思わなかった I didn't expect this would *go* so *well*. / I didn't think it would *go* so *smoothly*. ‖ 留学したいと言ったら父はすんなり承知してくれた My father agreed *readily* when I said I wanted to study abroad.

すんぶん 寸分 ▶次の皆既日食が起こる日時を寸分の狂いもなく予測できるのはすごい It's great to be able to predict the date and time of the next total solar eclipse *without the smallest miscalculation*.

すんぽう 寸法 measurements (測定値) ; (a) size (サイズ) ▶洋服屋はぼくの背広の寸法を取った The tailor *took my measurements* [*measured* me] for a suit. ‖ ワイシャツの寸法を教えてください Please give me your shirt *measurements*. ‖ 靴の寸法はいくつですか What *size* shoe do you wear? ‖ 《洋服店などで》寸法直ししてますか Do you do *alterations*? (➤ alterations は /ɔ̀ːltəréɪʃənz/ と発音する).

せ・セ

せ 背 **1【背中】the back** ⇀背中 ▶私は病気の娘を背におぶい，病院まで運んだ I carried my sick daughter on my *back* to the hospital. ‖ 男は背を丸めてとぼとぼと歩いていた The man plodded along *with his back hunched* (*over*). ‖ 彼女は私の方に背を向けて立っていた She stood *with her back to* me. ‖ 私は電柱に背をもたせかけた I *leaned against* the utility pole.

2【物の背】the back ; the spine(本の) ▶この椅子は背が壊れている *The back* of this chair is broken.

3【背後】▶私たちは校門を背にして写真を撮った We took a picture *with* the school gate in the background. ‖ 私たちの高校は富士山を背にして建てられている Our school is built *with its back to* Mt. Fuji.

4【身長】(a) **height** /haɪt/ ▶背の順に並びなさい Line up in order of *height*. ‖ しばらく会わないうちに，きみはずいぶん背が伸びたね You'*ve grown* quite *tall* since I last saw you. ‖ 母は背が低い My mother is *short*. ‖ この川は背が立たない You *can't reach* [*touch*] *bottom* in this river. ‖ 私のほうが父より背が高い I'm *taller* than my father (is). ‖ 対話「きみ，背(の高さ)はどのくらいあるの？」「180センチです」"*How tall* are you?" "(I am) 180 centimeters (tall)."

5【慣用表現】▶彼女は世間に背を向けている She *has turned her back on* the world. ‖ 彼は金持ちになると旧友たちに背を向けた(＝見捨てた) When he became rich, he *turned his back on* his old friends.

ことわざ 背に腹はかえられぬ A desperate situation calls for desperate measures. (➤「切羽詰まれば一か八かの手段にすがる」の意).

¹せい 性 **1【セックス】sex 一形 性の sexual** ▶今日ではテレビや雑誌に性が氾濫し過ぎている These days there is too much *sex* on television and in magazines. ‖ 性体験のある高校生が増えてきた The number of high school students who have had *sexual experiences* is increasing. ‖ 息子は性に目覚める年頃だ My son is about the age when boys becomes *sexually* aware. ‖ この映画は露骨な性描写が多すぎる This film has too much graphic *sex* in it.

2【男女の別】sex ; a gender(社会学上また文法上の) (➤ 生物的な「性」は sex，文化や社会的な「性」は gender) ▶年齢，男女の性を問わず誰でも応募できます Anybody can apply for it regardless of age or *gender* [*sex*]. ‖ 性差別が依然として残っているのが実情だ The reality is that *sex* [*gender*] *discrimination* still exists. (➤ 特に女性に対する差別を sexism という).

▶以前は日本では男女の性による役割分担はより明確に定まっていた In Japan, *gender roles* used to be (more) clearly defined. ‖ 薬の効き目には性差がある The effectiveness of the medication varies according to *sex*.

‖**性教育** (⇀見出語) ‖ **性差別主義者** a sexist ‖ **性生活** one's sex life ‖ **性染色体** a sex chromosome ‖ **性転換** a change of sex, a sex change ‖ **性同一性障害** gender identity disorder(GID) ‖ **性道徳** sexual morality ‖ **性犯罪** a sex crime ‖ **性犯罪者** a sex offender ‖ **性ホルモン** a sex hormone.

☛ **性的** (⇀見出語)

²せい 精 **1【元気】**▶朝早くからずいぶん精が出ますね *You've been* (*hard*) *at it* from early morning, haven't you? (➤ be (hard) at it は「熱心に働いている」の意；《米》では通例 hard を省く) ‖ もっと勉強に精を出しなさい Study *harder*. ／*Make a greater effort* in your studies. (➤ 後者は堅い表現) ‖ もっと精を出して働いてくれなきゃ困るよ I need you to work *harder*. ／*Put yourself into* your work. (➤ put oneself into は「…に身を入れる」).

▶《慣用表現》あの子を説得するのにもう精も根も尽き果てた I *am completely exhausted* [*worn out*] from trying to persuade him. (⇀精根).

2【妖精】a sprite, a fairy ▶水の精 a water *sprite* (➤ a nymph /nɪmf/ ともいう) ‖ 花の精 a flower *fairy*.

³せい 姓 one's **family name**, one's **last name**, one's **surname**

> 《解説》last name は first name(名)に対する言い方で，アメリカ人が好む．一方，surname はイギリス人に好まれる．日本人の場合は family name を用いるのがよい．

▶日本人の名前は姓が先にきます The *family name* comes first in Japanese names. ‖ 姓は車，名は寅次郎．人呼んでフーテンの寅と発します *My family name* is Kuruma and my given name is Torajiro. But people usually just call me Tora the Wanderer.

✉ **私の名前は鈴木清美．鈴木のほうが姓です．日本で最も多い姓の１つです** My name is Suzuki Kiyomi. Suzuki is my *family name*. It's one of the most common *family names* in Japan.

⁴せい 生 life ▶誰でも生への執着があるのは当然だ It is natural that everyone should cling to *life*. ‖ 生あるものは必ず死ぬ All *living things* are destined [bound] to die. ／ All human beings are mortal. (➤ 後者は人間の場合).

⁵せい **1【原因を示して】due to, because of, owing to** ▶あなたの頭痛は過労のせいだ Your headache *is due to* [*is caused by*] overwork. (● due to はこのように be 動詞のあとに用いるのが本来の用法だが，今では because of, owing to などと同様に用いることが多い) ／ Your headache *comes from* overwork. ‖ 事故のせいでその列車は50分遅れた The train was fifty minutes late *due to* [*owing to*] an accident. ‖ 祖母は最近年のせいか物忘れがひどくなった It may be *because of* her age [*because* she's getting old], but my grandmother has grown forgetful lately.

2【責任を示して】one's **fault** (落ち度) ; a **blame** (失敗などの責任の所在；非難することではない) ▶これはあなたのせいよ It's *your fault*. ‖ 自分のミスをひとのせいに

するな Don't *blame* others for your mistake(s). ／Don't *lay* [*put*] *the blame on* others for your mistake(s).

【文型】
失敗(A)を人・物(B)のせいにする
blame B **for** A
blame A **on** B

▶**妻は何もかも私のせいにした** My wife *blamed* me *for* everything. ‖ **それをぼくのせいにするのか** Are you *blaming* me *for* that？‖ **両国は緊張を高めたことを互いに相手方のせいにした** The two nations *blamed* each other *for* raising tensions (between them).

▶**私たちは成績がふるわなかったのは準備不足のせいとしたくありません** We don't want to *blame* our poor performance *on* our lack of preparation.(➤ blame するものが，人や人のグループでなく，失敗や問題などの場合は blame ... on の文型を用いる) ‖ **彼女は自分の失敗を病弱のせいにした** She *blamed* her failure *on* her poor health. ／She *attributed* her failure *to* her poor health. (➤ attribute A to B は「Aの原因はBにあると言う[考える]」の意で，やや堅い言い方) ‖ **本当にごめんなさい．すべて私のせいです** I'm very sorry. I'll take all the *blame*.

6**せい 正** **1【正式なもの】**▶**正のほうを提出し，副はそちらで保管しておいてください** Please hand in *the original* and keep the duplicate for yourself. ‖ **増田さんはその協会の正会員になった** Mr. Masuda became *a regular* [*full*] *member* of that association.
2【数字でプラスの】一形 正の positive ▶**正の整数** a *positive* whole number [integer].

せい- 聖- Saint ▶**聖ペテロ** *Saint* Peter.

1**-せい -製** ▶**紙製の人形** a *paper* doll ／a doll *made of paper* ‖ **外国製のたばこ** *foreign-made* [*imported*] cigarettes ‖ **ドイツ製の車** a *German* (*-made*) car ‖ **彼の背広はみんな英国製だ** His suits are all *made in Britain* [are all *of British make*]. (➤ 後者は堅い言い方) ‖ **その時計，どこ製なの？** *Where was* that watch *made*？

2**-せい -制** ▶**6－3(教育)制** the 6-3 *school education system* ‖ **4年制の大学** a *four-year* college ‖ **週休2日制** *a five-day week*.

3**-せい -世** ▶**リチャード三世** Richard *III* [*the third*] ‖ **ジャック・ダニエル二世** Jack Daniel, *Jr.* [*Junior*] ‖ **(アメリカの)日系三世** a *third-generation* Japanese American ／*a Sansei*.

ぜい 税 (a) **tax**；(a) **duty** (物品税) ▶**税の負担が公平でないと考えている人が多い** There are many people who feel *the burden of taxes* [*taxation*] is not fair. (➤ taxation は「課税」) ‖ **この額は税込みです** This amount *includes tax*. ‖ **きみの給料は税込みでいくらですか** How much is your pay *before taxes*？‖ **税引きの手取りはどのくらいになるか教えてください** Tell me how much my pay will be *after taxes*. ／Tell me how much my take-home pay will be. (➤ 後者は「税引き給与」の意).
☛ **税金** (→見出語)

せいあい 性愛 sexual love.

せいあくせつ 性悪説 belief in people's innate [fundamental] badness (➤ 説明的な訳).

せいあつ 制圧する bring ... under control ▶**機動隊は暴徒を完全に制圧した** The riot squad *brought* the mob *under* complete *control*. ‖ **彼女のがんは制圧できなかった** Her cancer could not *be controlled*.

せいい 誠意 sincerity /sɪnsérəṭi/ **一形 誠意のある sincere** /sɪnsíəʳ/

> **《解説》** 日本語の「誠意」には「自分の気持ちを抑えたり，偽ったりしても相手に実のあるところを示す」というニュアンスがあるが，英語の sincerity は「ごまかさないこと，裏表のないこと」の意で，両者には意味のずれがある．→**誠実**.

▶**あの人は誠意がない** He lacks [has no] *sincerity*. ／He is lacking in *sincerity*. ／He is insincere. (➤ 英語はいずれも「あの人は率直に物を言わない(したがって不正直だ)」と解釈される傾向が強い) ‖ **首相の答弁には誠意が感じられなかった** I don't feel that the Prime Minister's answer was *sincere*. ‖ **きみにけがをさせておきながら見舞いにも来ないなんて，彼の誠意を疑うね** After injuring you, he didn't even come to see you at the hospital. I have to doubt his *sincerity*. (➤ 日本では加害者が速やかに見舞いに行くことを誠意の表れと解釈する傾向が強いが，アメリカなどでは早々に自分の非を認めたと解釈されがちである) ‖ **誠意をもって話せば彼だってわかってくれるよ** He will understand if you speak *with sincerity* [speak *sincerely*]. ‖ **彼の誠意のない口約束なんかもう聞きたくない** I don't want to hear any more of his *empty* promises.

1**せいいき 聖域** a **holy** [**sacred**] **precinct** /príːsɪŋkt/ (神社などの)；a **sanctuary** (教会の).

2**せいいき 声域** a **vocal range** ▶**その歌手は声域が広い** The singer has a wide *vocal range*.

せいいく 生育・成育 growth 一動 生育する grow ▶**熱帯地方の植物は生育が速い** Plants in the tropics *grow fast*.

せいいっぱい 精一杯 ▶**2学期は精いっぱい頑張り(＝ベストを尽くし)ます** I'm going to *do my best* during the second term. ‖ **精いっぱい働きます** I'll work *as hard as I can* [*as possible*]. ‖ **女の子は拳を振り上げて精いっぱいの抗議をした** The girl protested *with all her might* by raising her fist. ‖ **毎日を精いっぱい(＝最大限に)生きたい** I want to live each day *to the full*. ‖ **自分一人食っていくだけで精いっぱいだ** Supporting myself *is* (*about*) *all I can manage*. ‖ **(眠くて)目を開けているのが精いっぱいだった** *It was all I could do* to keep my eyes open. ／I *struggled to* keep my eyes open.

せいう 晴雨 ▶**サッカーの試合は晴雨にかかわらず行われる** The soccer game will be held *rain or shine* [*whether it rains or not* ／*regardless of the weather*].
‖**晴雨計** a barometer /bərɑ́ːmɪṭəʳ/.

せいうち 《動物》 a **walrus.**

せいうん 星雲 《天文学》 a **nebula** /nébjələ/ ▶**ガス状[渦状]星雲** a gaseous [spiral] *nebula*.

1**せいえい 精鋭** ▶**そのマラソン大会には毎年世界の精鋭が参加する** Every year *the very top competitors* from all over the world participate in that marathon. ‖ **わがチームは精鋭がそろっている** All our players are *the cream* [*pick*] *of the crop*. (➤「えり抜き」の意).
‖**精鋭部隊** a crack unit.

2**せいえい 清栄・盛栄 prosperity**
✉ **貴社におかれましてはますますご清栄のこととお喜び申し上げます** Please accept our congratulations on the ever-growing *prosperity* of your corporation.

せいえき 精液 semen /síːmən/.

せいえん 声援 a **cheer** 一動 **声援する** **cheer**（+目），《インフォーマル》**root for** ▶我々はスタンドから彼に盛んに**声援を送った** We *cheered* him on enthusiastically from the stands. ‖ 沿道は走って来る選手に**声援を送る**人々でいっぱいだった The sides of the street were packed with people *cheering* the passing runners. ‖ 観衆の大半は地元チームを**声援していた** Most of the spectators *were rooting for* the home team. ‖ そのランナーは**大声援の中を**1位でゴールインした The first-in runner breasted the tape *amid great cheers*.

せいおう 西欧 **West(ern) Europe**（ヨーロッパの西部）; **Europe, the West**（西洋）
‖**西欧諸国** (the) West European countries [nations], the Western countries ‖ **西欧文明** Western European civilization.

せいおん 清音 a **voiceless sound**.

1**せいか 成果** (a) **result**（結果）; (a) **fruit**（所産，実り）▶彼の発明は長年にわたる研究の**成果**だ His invention is the *result* [*fruit*] of years of research. ‖ その首脳会談は何の**成果**も上げずに終わった The summit meeting ended in failure. ‖ **成果の多い**会議でした It was a *fruitful* conference. ‖ あなた方の協力のおかげでこのショーはすばらしい**成果を上げる**ことができました Thanks to your cooperation, this show was *a great success*.

2**せいか 正課** ▶当校では剣道は**正課**に取り入れられている Kendo is included in *the regular curriculum* at our school.

3**せいか 生家** ▶ここが伊藤博文の**生家**です This is *the house where* [*in which*] Ito Hirobumi *was born*. ‖ **生家を出た**のは15歳のときだ I *left home* at the age of fifteen.

4**せいか 聖火** **the Olympic Flame**（オリンピック会場の）; **the Olympic Torch**（聖火ランナーの持つ）
‖**聖火台** the Olympic Flameholder ‖ **聖火ランナー** a runner in the Olympic Torch Relay ‖ **聖火リレー** the Olympic Torch Relay.

5**せいか 盛夏** **the height of summer** 《参考》「盛夏」は「夏の暑い盛り」の意味で，「盛夏の候，…」のように改まった手紙の書き出し文句として使ったりするが，英語では the height of summer をこのように使うのはふつうではない.

6**せいか 青果** **(fresh) produce, fruits and vegetables**（➤ fruits が先の語順がふつう）
‖**青果市場** a produce market, a fruit and vegetable market.

7**せいか 聖歌** a **sacred song**; a **carol**（クリスマスの賛美歌）; a **hymn** /hɪm/（賛美歌）
‖**聖歌隊** a choir /kwáɪəʳ/ ‖ **グレゴリオ聖歌** Gregorian chant(s).

8**せいか 生花** **1【生け花】flower arrangement.**
2【人工のものでない自然の花】 a **natural flower**.

9**せいか 正価** a **net price** ▶当店は**正価**販売をしております We sell only at *net prices*.

10 **せいか 製菓** **confectionery manufacturing** ▶**製菓会社** a *confectionery company*.

11 **せいか 精華** **the quintessence** ▶ミロのヴィーナスは古代ギリシャ彫刻の**精華**である Venus of Milos is *the quintessence* of ancient Greek sculpture.

12 **せいか 声価** one's **reputation**（評判）▶**声価を高める** enhance one's *reputation*.

1**せいかい 正解** a **correct** [**right**] **answer** 一動 **正解する** **answer correctly** ▶このクロスワードパズルの**正解**がわからない I don't know the (*correct*) *answers* to this crossword puzzle. ‖ そのクイズは全問**正解者**が1人もいなかった Nobody could *answer* all the questions in the quiz *correctly*. ／There was nobody who *gave* all *the correct* [*right*] *answers* to the quiz.
▶《比喩的》電車を使わずバスを利用したのは**正解**だった Taking the bus and not the train was *the right choice*.（➤「正しい選択」の意）.

2**せいかい 政界** **the political world, political circles** ▶彼は30歳で**政界に入った** He *entered politics* [*political life*] at the age of thirty.（➤ entered は went into でもよい）.

3**せいかい 盛会** ▶きのうのクラス会はなかなか**盛会だった** Yesterday's class reunion *was well-attended* [*was a great success*].（➤ 前者は「出席者が多かった」の意）.

せいかいけん 制海権 **naval supremacy, command of the sea.**

せいかがく 生化学 **biochemistry** /bàɪoʊkémɪstri/
‖**生化学者** a biochemist.

1**せいかく 性格** **1【人の】** (a) **character**（道徳的観点から見た人格，品格）; (a) **personality**（個性としての性格，人格）; (a) **disposition**（気質）▶人の**性格**は子供の頃に形成される A person's *character* is formed in childhood. ‖ 人格者は尊敬され，**性格**のいい人は好かれる A person who has (a) good character is respected ; a person who has a good *personality* is popular. ‖ 生徒はそれぞれに**性格**が異なる Every student has a different *personality*. ‖ この絵には彼の**性格**が表れている His *personality* shows in this painting. ‖ 山田君は**性格**が明るい[暗い] Yamada has a sunny [gloomy] *disposition*. ／ Yamada is cheerful [gloomy].
▶私は息子とは**性格が合わない** My son and I *don't get along well*.（➤「仲良くやっていけない」の意）‖ 私たちは**性格的に合わない** We *are incompatible*. ‖ **性格の不一致**を理由に二人は離婚した They divorced on the grounds of *incompatibility*.
‖**性格俳優** a character actor [actress].
2【物事の】 **character** ; **nature**（性質）▶日本の仏教とタイの仏教は**性格**が異なっている Buddhism in Japan has a different *character* from Buddhism in Thailand. ‖ 2つの出来事は表面的には違うが同じ**性格**のものだ The two events seem quite different, but they are similar in *nature*.

2**せいかく 正確** 一形 **正確な** **accurate** /ǽkjərət/（注意が行き届いている）; **exact**（ぴったりの，厳密な）; **precise**（細かな点まで精密な）; **correct**（正しい）一副 **正確に** **accurately, correctly, exactly, precisely** ; **for certain** [**sure**]（確実に ; for sure のほうがややくだけた言い方）▶市の人口を**正確に**数える get an *accurate* count of the city's population ‖ あの人の仕事は速くて**正確だ** His work is fast and *accurate*. ／He works fast and *accurately*. ‖ 新聞の報道がいつも**正確**とは限らない Newspaper reports are not always *accurate*. ‖ 校正の仕事では**正確さ**が最も重視される In proofreading, *accuracy* is considered most important. ‖ **正確な時刻**を教えてください Could you tell me [Do you have] the *exact* time ? ‖ **正確な数字**は102ミリです The *precise* figure is 102 millimeters.
▶日本の鉄道は時間が**正確なこと**で定評がある Japanese railways are known for their *punctuality*. ‖ 未来を**正確に**予測できる人などいない No one can predict the future *accurately*. ‖ 何が起きたのか正

確に知る必要がある We need to know *precisely* what happened. ‖ McDonald's という語を正確に発音できますか Can you pronounce 'McDonald's' *correctly*?
▶彼女はボストンかそこら辺りで生まれたと思いますが，正確には知りません I think she was born in Boston or thereabouts, but I don't know *for certain* [*for sure*]. ‖ 正確に言うと今10時 4 分です It is, *to be exact*, four minutes past ten.
☞ 不正確（→見出語）

せいがく 声楽 vocal music ▶先生について声楽を習う *take vocal lessons* from a teacher.
‖声楽家 a singer ‖ 声楽科 the vocal music course.

せいかつ 生活 (a) life; a living, (a) livelihood（生計，暮らし）一動 生活する live, make a living ▶都会の［日常／家庭］生活 city [everyday／home] *life* ‖ 学生生活を楽しむ enjoy one's school *life* ‖ 鯨は海で生活する Whales *live* in the ocean. ‖ 将来，月での生活が可能になるかもしれない One day, we may be able to *live* on the moon.
▶日本の多くの大学生はのんきな生活を送っている Many Japanese college students lead a carefree *life*. ‖ 彼はだいぶ乱れた生活をしている He lives a pretty loose *life*. ‖ 彼はぜいたくな生活をしている He *lives* in luxury. ‖ 彼らは豊かな［苦しい］生活をしている They *are well-off* [*badly-off*]. ‖ うちは今かつかつの生活をしている We *are living on a shoestring* now.（➤ live on a shoestring は「僅かの金で生活する」の意）‖ 生活を楽しむ方法を知らない人もいる Some people don't know how to *enjoy life*. ‖ 私たちは常に患者さんの生活の質の向上を心がけています We always try to improve our patients' *quality of life*. ‖ 長い日照りで多くの農民たちの生活が脅かされている The long spell of dry weather is threatening the *livelihoods* of many farmers.
▶東京で 1 か月15万円で生活するのは難しい It is difficult to *live* in Tokyo on 150,000 yen a month. ‖ アメリカで 2，3 年生活すれば日常会話程度の英語はものになるよ If you *spend two or three years* in the U.S., everyday English (conversation) will become a part of you. ‖ 彼は塾の先生をして生活している（＝生計を立てている）He teaches at a *juku* for *a living*. ／He *makes a living* by teaching at a *juku*. ‖ 老後どう生活するか考えていますか Are you thinking about how you will *support yourself* in your old age?
▶あの老夫婦は生活に困っている That elderly couple is *having trouble making ends meet*.（➤ make ends meet は「何とかやりくりする」）‖ その老人は生活保護を受けている The elderly man [woman] is *on welfare* [《英》*on benefit*]. ‖ 生活困窮者は生活保護を受けることができる *The poor and needy* can receive *welfare*. ‖ 国が違えば生活習慣も異なる Different countries have different *customs*. ／*Customs* differ from country to country. ‖ その国の生活水準はいまだに低い The *standard of living* in that country is still low. ‖ あなたの生活費は誰が払っているの？ Who pays (for) your *living expenses*? ‖ 中国人の生活様式は急速に変わりつつある The *lifestyle* of the Chinese people [The Chinese *way of life*] is rapidly changing. ‖ きみにはまだ生活力がない You can't *live* [*make it*] *on your own* yet. ／You are not able to *earn* [*make*] *your own living* yet. ‖ 彼女は生活力がある She *has a lot of earning power*.
‖生活環境 one's living environment ‖ 生活給 a living wage ‖ 生活協同組合 →生協 ‖ 生活習慣病 lifestyle-related diseases ‖ 生活必需品 daily necessities ‖ 生活保護法 the Daily Life Security Act.

> **逆引き熟語 ○○生活**
> 海外生活 living abroad／学生生活 (one's) school life／家庭生活 (one's) family life／結婚生活 married life／質素な生活 a simple life／独身生活 single life

1**せいかん 生還する** return ▶宇宙飛行士たちは宇宙から無事に生還した The astronauts *came back* [*returned*] *safely* from space.
▶《野球》原君の三塁打で 2 者が生還した Two runners *scored* on Hara's triple.（➤ score は「(走者が)得点する」）／Hara hit a triple to *bring in* two runs.

2**せいかん 精悍** ▶その刑事は精かんな顔つきをしていた The detective looked *fearless* [*tough*].（「精かんな顔つき」は a look of fearless determination と言える．また「精かんな顔」は a sharp, masculine face）.

3**せいかん 静観** ▶事態を静観する *observe* a situation *calmly* ‖ その国で政変があったが，わが国は静観の態度をとった There was a coup d'etat in that country, but our country *took a wait-and-see attitude* [*observed the situation calmly*].

4**せいかん 性感** sexual feeling [excitement] ▶性感帯 *an erogenous zone*.

1**せいがん 請願** a petition 一動 請願する petition
‖請願書 a petition.

2**せいがん 誓願** a vow.

ぜいかん 税関 (the) customs（➤ 一般に《米》では単数扱い，《英》では複数扱い）▶税関を通る go [get] through *customs*／clear *customs* ‖ 税関で引っ掛かる get stuck [get held up] at *customs* ‖ 税関での手荷物検査に時間がかかった It took a lot of time to get my baggage through *customs*. ‖ 税関では外国で購入したもので申告が必要なものがある You are required to declare some items purchased abroad at *customs*.
‖税関検査 a customs inspection ‖ 税関申告書 a customs declaration (form), a customs form.

せいがんざい 制癌剤 an anticancer drug.

せいがんしゃ 晴眼者 a sighted person.

せいかんせんしょう 性感染症 a sexually transmitted disease（➤ 略語は STD）.

1**せいき 世紀** a century ▶21［20］世紀 *the 21st* [*20th*] *century* ‖ 19世紀の中頃ペリーが浦賀に来航した Perry visited Uraga *in the mid-nineteenth century*. ‖ ノルウェー王国が誕生したのは20世紀初めのことだ It was at *the beginning of the 20th century* that the Kingdom of Norway came into being [existence]. ／The Kingdom of Norway was born *early in the 20*th century. ‖ ヒエログリフ（象形文字）の意味は何世紀もの間謎であった Hieroglyphics were a mystery *for centuries*.
▶月ロケットは20世紀の大冒険だった Getting to the moon by rocket was *a great adventure of the twentieth century*.
‖世紀末 the end of a [the] century.

2**せいき 性器** the sex organs, the genitals /dʒénətlz/,

the genitalia(➤ 後者２つは専門用語)《参考》男性器は penis, 女性器は vagina.

3**せいき 生気** **life**;《インフォーマル》**pep**(元気) ▶春になると山の木々は**生気**に満ちる In spring trees in the mountains are full of *life*. ‖ 彼女は近頃**生気**のない顔をしている She lacks *pep* these days.

4**せいき 正規の** **regular**(本式の, 本職の); **formal**(正式の, 公式の) ▶**正規の**教育 *formal* [*regular*] school education ‖ **正規の**服装 *formal* wear ‖ 外国に入るには**正規の手続き**を踏まなければなりません There are *regular procedures* [*required formalities*] to go through before you enter a foreign country.

せいぎ 正義 **justice**(公正); **right**(正しさ, 善) ▶**正義**のために悪と戦う fight for *justice* [*right*] against wrong ‖ 最後には**正義**が勝つ *Justice* will prevail (in the end). ‖ スーパーマンは**正義の味方**だ Superman is *a champion* [*friend*] *of justice*. ‖ 彼は**正義感**が強い He has a strong *sense of justice*.

せいきぐん 正規軍 **a regular army**.

1**せいきゅう 請求** **charge**(料金の); (a) **request**(要望); a **claim**(権利としての) 一動 **請求する** **charge** ＋目, **claim** ＋目 ▶彼はその代金500円を私に**請求した** He *charged* me 500 yen for it. ‖ 私はオートバイの修理代に５万円**請求された** I *was charged* 50,000 yen to have my motorcycle repaired. ‖ **ご請求があり次第**カタログをお送りいたします We will send you our catalog(ue) *on request*. ／《広告文》Catalogs sent *on request*.

▶お買い上げから30日以内に**請求**がなければ払い戻しはいたしません Refunds made only if *requested* within 30 days of purchase. ‖ あの人たちはきっとあなたに損害賠償を**請求して**くると思います I am sure that they will *claim* damages from you. ‖ **請求書**をください Could I have the *bill* [《米また》*check*], please? (➤「売り渡し商品[明細記入]の送り状」の意の「請求書」は invoice /ínvɔɪs/ という).

2**せいきゅう 性急な** **hasty**(急いだ); **rash**(向こう見ずの); **impetuous** /ɪmpétʃuəs/ (せいた) ▶**性急な**決定 a *hasty* decision ‖ **性急な**人 an *impetuous* person ‖ そんな**性急な**結婚はどうせろくなことはない No good will come of such a *rash* [an *impetuous*] marriage.

せいきょ 逝去 **passing, death**

✉ **お父さまのご逝去を悼み謹んでお悔やみ申し上げます** Please accept my sincere condolences on your father's *passing*. ／ Please accept my deepest sympathy on the *loss* of your father.

せいぎょ 制御 **control** /kəntróʊl/ 一動 **制御する** **control** ＋目 ▶自分の感情を**制御する** *control* one's feelings ‖ パイロットは操縦かんの**制御ができなくなり**, 飛行機は山にぶつかった The pilot *lost control* of his plane and it crashed into the mountain.

▶宇宙船は小惑星にぶつかって**制御不能になった** The spaceship struck an asteroid and *went out of control*.

‖ **自動制御装置** an automatic control (device).

1**せいきょう 盛況** ▶バザーは**盛況**のうちに終わった The bazaar ended [was] *a great success*. ‖ そのミュージカルは毎晩**満員の盛況だ** The musical *is drawing a full house* every night. (➤ a full house は「大入り満員」).

2**せいきょう 生協** a **cooperative society**(組合); a **co-op** /kóʊɑːp/, a **cooperative**(売店) ▶大学の**生協**でパンツを買った I bought (a pair of) underpants at the university *co-op* (*store*).

せいきょういく 性教育 **sex education** ▶生徒に**性教育**をする *educate* [*teach*] students *about sex*.

せいきょうと 清教徒 a **Puritan**

‖ **清教徒革命** the Puritan Revolution.

せいきょうぶんり 政教分離 **the separation of religion and politics**(宗教と政治の分離); **the separation of government and religion**(政治[政体]と宗教の分離); **the separation of church and state**(教会と政治の分離; キリスト教が主要宗教になっている国々の).

せいきょく 政局 **the political situation** ▶内閣改造があっても**政局**に影響はないだろう The reshuffle of the Cabinet will not affect *the political situation*.

せいきん 精勤 **diligence** ‖ **精勤賞** a prize for good attendance (➤ 英米にはない).

ぜいきん 税金 (a) **tax**; (a) **duty**(関税) ▶**税金**を払う pay *a tax* [*taxes*] ‖ 年収が一定額未満だと**税金**が免除される You are exempt from paying *taxes* if your yearly income is under a certain amount. ‖ 日本は**税金**がかなり高い (*The*) *taxes* in Japan are quite high. (➤「税金の安い国」は tax haven (税金回避国)という) ‖ この商品には**税金がかからない** This product is *duty-free* [*tax-free*]. ‖ 政府は自動車に**高い税金**をかけている The government imposes [lays] *a heavy tax* on automobiles. ‖ 稼ぎの半分は**税金にもっていかれる** Half of my earnings *go to taxes*. →税.

「税金」のいろいろ **固定資産税** fixed assets tax (➤ 英米では property tax) ／**事業税** enterprise tax ／**自動車税** car [automobile] tax ／**住民税** resident [residential] tax ／**酒税** liquor tax ／**消費税** consumption tax (➤ 英米では sales tax) ／**所得税** income tax ／**相続税** inheritance tax ／**贈与税** gift tax ／**地価税** land value tax ／**土地保有税** land ownership tax (➤ 英米では real estate tax) ／**入湯税** bathing tax ／**法人税** corporate tax

せいく 成句 an **idiom**(熟語, 慣用句); an **idiomatic expression**(慣用表現); an **idiomatic** [**a set**] **phrase**(慣用句).

せいくうけん 制空権 **air supremacy, command of the air**.

せいくらべ 背比べ ▶私は毎年５月５日に弟と**背比べをする** I *compare my height* with my (younger) brother on the 5th of May every year. ‖ **背比べしよう** *Let's see who is taller*.

ことわざ **どんぐりの背比べ** There isn't much difference between the two. ／It's six of one and (a) half a dozen of the other. (➤「一方は６個で, もう一方は半ダース」, つまり差がないことのたとえ).

1**せいけい 生計** **a living** ▶ロベールはフランス語を教えて**生計を立てている** Robert *makes* [*earns*] *his living* by teaching French. ‖ 私は新聞配達をして**生計を助けた** I *helped support my family* by delivering newspapers.

2**せいけい 整形** **orthopedics** /ɔːrθəpíːdɪks/, **orthopedic surgery**(整形外科); **plastic** [**cosmetic**] **surgery**(美容整形) ▶彼女の鼻はあんなに高くなかった―きっと**整形した**んだわ I'm sure her nose was flatter before. She must have *had a nose job*. (➤ nose job は「鼻の美容整形」の意のインフォーマルな言い方).

‖ **整形外科医** an orthopedist, an orthopedic surgeon.

3**せいけい 西経** **the west longitude** ▶**西経**20度 twenty degrees *west longitude* (➤ 通例 long. 20° west

と書き longitude twenty degrees west と読む) ‖ ワシントンＤＣは西経77度にある Washington, D.C. is located at 77 degrees *west longitude*.

4 **せいけい 政経** politics and economics
‖**政経学部** the school [college] of political science and economics, the politics and economics department.

5 **せいけい 成型** molding.

せいけつ 清潔な clean ▶**清潔な**下着 *clean* underwear ‖ **清潔な**政治 *clean* politics ‖ 母は口癖のように「いつも手を**清潔に**しておきなさい」と言う My mother always tells me to *keep* my hands *clean*. ‖ ぼくは身なりの**清潔な**女の子が好きだ I like *neatly-dressed* girls.

せ

1 **せいけん 政権** a system of government(政体) ; (political) power (政治権力) ; a government, an administration (政府 ;《米》では大統領を中心とする政府を指す) ▶**政権**の交代 a change of *government* [*administration*] ‖ 軍事**政権** a military *regime* (➤ regime はしばしば軽蔑的に民主的でない政権を指す) ‖ フランスでは今どの政党が**政権を握って**いますか Which political party is *in power* in France now？‖ **現政権**の支持率は高い[低い] The approval rating of *the present administration* [*government*] is high [low].

2 **せいけん 政見** a political view [opinion] ▶野党指導者はテレビで**政見**を発表した The opposition leader expressed his *political views* on TV.
‖**政見放送** a broadcast of a candidate's election pledges.

せいげん 制限 a limit, (a) limitation (➤ 後者は無冠詞で「制限を設けること」の意にもなる) ; (a) restriction (何かにつけられた制限・条件) 一動 **制限する** limit +目, restrict +目 ▶出費を**制限する** *set a limit* [*limits*] to the expenses ／*limit* the expenses ‖ テレビを見る時間を**制限する** *place restrictions* in TV viewing ‖ 人数に**制限**があるため, 申し込み者多数の場合は抽選となります Because there is *a limit* to the number of people who can be accepted, we will decide by lot if there is a large number of applicants. ‖ 米国は日本の自動車輸出に何らかの**制限**を求めてきた The U.S. has asked Japan to put [place] some kind of *restrictions* [*limitations*] on its export of cars. ‖ 日本の高速道路ではスピードは時速100キロに**制限されている** In Japan, speed on the expressways *is limited* to one hundred kilometers an hour. ‖ 都心部での車の使用はもっと大幅に**制限する**必要がある The use of motor vehicles in the downtown area should *be* much more *restricted*.
▶この試験の**制限時間**は50分です *The time allowed* for this test is fifty minutes. (➤「許された時間」の意) ‖《相撲で》**制限時間いっぱい** (*The*) *time's up*. ‖ この道路の**制限速度**は時速40キロです The *speed limit* on this road is 40 kilometers per hour. ‖ (応募に)年齢**制限**はありません There's no *age limit* [*restriction*].
‖**産児制限** birth control.
☛ **無制限** (→見出語)

ぜいげん 税源 a tax (revenue) source.

せいご 生後 ▶**生後**８か月の赤ん坊 an *eight-month-old* baby ‖ その戦争孤児は**生後**３か月で母親と別れ別れになった The war orphan got separated from his mother at three months *after birth*. (➤ 後半は when he was only three months old としてもよい).

1 **せいこう 成功** (a) success 一動 **成功する** succeed《in》, be successful《in》; work out (うまく行く) ▶**成功した**実業家 a *successful* business-person ‖ 彼女は政治家として**成功した** She *succeeded* as a politician.

> **【文型】**
> 仕事(A)に成功する
> succeed in A
> ➤ Aは名詞・動名詞
> 事業(B)を成功させる
> make B a success

▶わが社は日本で初めて産業ロボットの開発に**成功した** We were the first company in Japan to *succeed in* developing an industrial robot. ‖ 学園祭を**成功させよう**！Let's *make* the school festival *a* (*big*) *success*！(➤ 囲みを参照)
▶そのスペースシャトルの打ち上げは**成功しなかった** The launch of the space shuttle *was not successful* [*was a failure* ／*failed*]. ‖ もしこの計画が**成功すれば**私たちの夢の一部が実現したことになる If this project *is successful* [*goes well*], our dream will be partially realized. ‖ 胃がんの手術は**大成功だった** The operation for stomach cancer *was a great success*.

> **直訳の落とし穴「キャンペーンを成功させる」**
> 「我々はこの販売促進キャンペーンを成功させねばならない」などと言うとき, 日本人はとかく「成功する」= succeed と考えて, (×)succeed in this sales campaign などと言いがちであるが, 英語らしい言い方は make ... a success を使って, We have to make this sales campaign a success. である.「学園祭を成功させる」も (×)succeed the school festival などとは言えず, make the school festival a success と言う.

✉ **成功を祈る** I wish you *success* [*good luck*].

2 **せいこう 性交** (sexual) intercourse,《インフォーマル》sex 一動 **性交する** have sexual intercourse《with》▶初デートでは相手と**性交(セックス)**をしないほうがいいよ It's better not to *have sex* on your first date.
《参考》性交を表す婉曲(えんきょく)表現には go all the way, make love, sleep with などがある. →セックス.

3 **せいこう 精巧な** elaborate /ɪlǽbərət/ (手の込んだ) ; exquisite /ɪkskwízɪt, ékskwɪzɪt/ (手が込んだうえに美しい) ▶飛行機の**精巧な**模型 an *elaborate* model of an airplane ‖ その金のブローチは細工が**精巧を極めている** The gold brooch is *of exquisite workmanship*.

4 **せいこう 性向** tendency (ある特定の傾向) ; inclination (行動・考えなどの傾向).

せいこううどく 晴耕雨読 ▶「**晴耕雨読**」が私の理想です "*Plowing when it shines, reading when it rains*" is my ideal (lifestyle).

せいごうせい 整合性 consistency ▶この調査結果は彼の説と**整合性がとれている**(＝一致している) These findings *are consistent with* his theory.

せいこうほう 正攻法 an orthodox method [approach].

せいごひょう 正誤表 (a list of) errata.

ぜいこみ 税込み →税.

せいこん 精魂・精根 ▶この絵は私が**精魂**を込めた作品で

す I put my *heart and soul* into this painting. ‖ このつぼにはその陶芸家の**精魂**が籠もっている The ceramist's *spirit* is embodied in this vase. ‖ スティーブ・ジョブズはマッキントッシュの開発に**精魂を傾けた** Steve Jobs *applied* [*devoted*] *all his energies to* developing the Macintosh.
▶マラソン走者は全員**精根尽き果てた**ようだった All the marathon runners seemed to *be at the end of their strength*.

せいさ 性差 gender [sex] difference(s) ▶**性差のない**語 a *genderless* word ‖ ヒトの脳には**性差**があるだろうか I wonder if there are *sex differences* in the human brain.

[1]**せいざ 正座** *seiza* ; sitting erect with one's legs folded under one (➤ 説明的な訳) ▶妹は私より長く**正座していられる** My (younger) sister always outlasts me in *sitting in seiza*. ‖ 我々は**正座して**説教を聞いた We *sat erect* [*straight*] *with our legs folded under us* and listened to the sermon. (● 「正座する」は文脈によっては sit on the floor Japanese style のように表現してもよい).

[2]**せいざ 星座** a constellation ; the signs of the zodiac (十二宮; →座, 星占い)
▶オリオン**星座** (the *constellation* of) Orion (➤ Orion の発音は /əráiən/).
‖**星座早見図** a star chart.

「星座」のいろいろ アンドロメダ座 Andromeda ／牛飼い座 Boötes (Herdsman) ／海蛇座 Hydra (Water Monster [Snake]) ／大犬座 Canis Major (Great Dog) ／大熊座 Ursa Major (Great Bear) ／オリオン座 Orion (Hunter) ／カシオペア座 Cassiopeia ／ケフェウス座 Cepheus ／ケンタウルス座 Centaurus (Centaur) ／小犬座 Canis Minor (Lesser Dog) ／小熊座 Ursa Minor (Little Bear) ／琴座 Lyra (Lyre) ／白鳥座 Cygnus (Swan) ／ペガサス座 Pegasus (Winged Horse) ／蛇座 Serpens (Serpent) ／わし座 Aquila (Eagle)
注 前の語はラテン名, ( )内は英語名.

[1]**せいさい 精彩** life ▶今夜の彼のピアノ演奏には**精彩がなかった** His piano playing *was lifeless* this evening. ‖ 彼のきょうのプレーは**精彩に欠ける** His play *is lackluster* today.

[2]**せいさい 制裁** (a) punishment ; sanctions (国に対する) ▶彼は規則を破ったため**制裁を受けた** He *received punishment* [*was punished*] for breaking the rules.
‖**経済制裁** economic sanctions.

せいざい 製材 《主に米》lumbering, sawing
‖**製材所** a sawmill, 《米》a lumbermill.

[1]**せいさく 製作・制作** **1**【製作】manufacture (工場などでの) ; production (工場での生産 ; 映画などの製作) ━動 **製作する** manufacture +目, produce +目, make +目 ▶当工場ではオフィス用の家具を**製作しております** We *manufacture* office furniture at this plant. ‖ 私たちは計測器具の**製作**が専門です We specialize in the *production* of measuring instruments. ‖ 映画の**製作**にはお金がかかる It costs a lot of money to *make a film*. ／*Film production* is costly.
‖**製作者** a maker, a producer.
2【制作】▶あの人は秋の展覧会に出す作品の**制作**に没頭している He is immersed in *painting* a work which is going to be exhibited in a fall exhibition. ‖『考える人』はロダンの**制作**による "The Thinker" is Rodin's *work* [was made by Rodin]. ‖ 彼女はアトリエで**制作中**です She is *at work* in her studio.

[2]**せいさく 政策** a policy ▶経済**政策** an economic *policy* ‖ 日本の対ロシア**政策** Japanese *policy* toward Russia ‖ 現内閣の**政策**をどう思いますか What do you think of the *policies* of the present cabinet ? ‖ 日本の**外交政策**には何の変化もない There is no change in Japan's *foreign policy*.
‖**政策立案者** a policy maker.

[1]**せいさん 生産** production ━動 **生産する** produce /prədjúːs/ +目 ; manufacture +目 (大工場で大量に) ▶**生産を増やす** [減らす] increase [cut] *production* ‖ うちの工場では毎月4000台のテレビを**生産している** Our factory *produces* [*manufactures*] four thousand TV sets a month. ‖ ブラジルは世界一のコーヒー**生産国**だ Brazil is the world's leading coffee *producer*.
▶**国内総生産**は国のものとサービスの**総生産高**である The *gross domestic product* is a nation's *total output* of goods and services. ‖ 昨年の米の**生産高はどのくらい**ですか *What was the yield* of rice last year ? ／*How much* rice *was produced* last year ? ‖ わが社は最新の機械を導入して**生産性**を高めている We are raising [increasing] *productivity* by using the latest machines.
‖**生産過剰** overproduction ‖ **生産管理** production control ‖ **生産工場** a production plant ‖ **生産者** a producer ‖ **生産能力** production capacity ‖ **生産物** a product ‖ **生産ライン** a production line ‖ **国民総生産** gross national product《略 GNP》‖ **大量生産** mass production.

[2]**せいさん 精算** adjustment ━動 **精算する** adjust the fare (運賃を) ▶もしもし, 料金不足ですよ. **精算所**で**精算してください** Excuse me. That fare is not enough. Please *pay the difference* on your ticket at the *fare adjustment window* [*office*]. ‖ ここはぼくが立て替えておくから, あとで**精算しよう** Let me pay (for it) now and you can *pay* me *back later*. ‖**精算書** a statement of accounts.

[3]**せいさん 清算する** clear a debt /det/ (借金を) ; liquidate (倒産会社を) ▶滞った借金を**清算する** *pay off* [*clear*] a long-standing debt (➤ pay off で「(借金を)完済する」) ‖ 会社を**清算する** *liquidate* a company.
▶和美は健太郎との過去を**清算しようとした** Kazumi tried to *put her past* (*relationship*) with Kentaro *behind her*.

[4]**せいさん 成算** (a) hope [chance] of success, (a) prospect ▶**成算** (＝成功の見通し) もなしに商売を始めるなんてむちゃだ It's absurd to start a business with no (future) *prospects*.

[5]**せいさん 凄惨な** gruesome /grúːsəm/ ▶せい惨な殺しのシーン a *gruesome* murder scene.

[6]**せいさん 正餐** a (formal) dinner.

せいざん 青山 ▶ ことわざ 人間到(いた)る所青山あり Leave your hometown and prove your worth [to try your fortune]. What difference does it make where in this (wide) world you [your bones] are buried ?

せいさんかくけい 正三角形 《幾何学》an equilateral /iːkwɪlǽtərəl/ triangle.

せいさんカリ 青酸カリ 《化学》potassium cyanide /pətǽsiəm sáiənaid/.

[1]**せいし 生死** life and death ▶**生死に関わる問題** a mat-

ter of *life and death* ‖ 兄はアフリカへ出かけたまま**生死不明**だ My (older) brother left for Africa and we *don't know whether he is alive or dead.* ‖ 被害者は意識不明のまま１週間**生死の境をさまよった** After losing consciousness, the victim *hovered between life and death* for a week.

2**せいし 制止する** restrain《from》(抑止する); stop +目, hold [keep] ... back (止める) ▶彼は真実を告げようとする彼女を**制止した** He *restrained* [*stopped*] her *from* telling the truth. ‖ 警備員はそのロックスターを見ようとして前へ出てくるファンたちを**制止しようとした** The security guards tried to *hold* [*keep*] *back* the fans who were pushing and jostling to see the rock star.

3**せいし 静止した** still, stationary (➤ 後者はやや堅い語, stationery (文房具)とのつづりの違いに注意) ▶朝もやの中で二人の恋人がキスしたとき時間が**静止した**かのようだった Time seemed to *stand still* when the two lovers kissed in the morning mist.
‖**静止衛星** a (geo-) stationary satellite ‖ (ビデオの)**静止画像** a still frame.

4**せいし 正視** ▶問題を**正視する** *look at* a problem *squarely* ‖ 事故現場の惨状は**正視に堪えなかった** The scene of the accident was so horrific that we *couldn't bear to look at* it [was too horrific to look at].

5**せいし 製紙** paper manufacture
‖**製紙会社** a paper-manufacturing company ‖ **製紙業** the paper industry ‖ **製紙工場** a paper mill.

6**せいし 製糸** spinning(紡績); silk manufacture (生糸の) ‖**製糸業** the silk-reeling industry ‖ **製糸工場** a silk mill.

7**せいし 精子** a sperm.

1**せいじ 政治** politics /pɑ́:lətɪks/; government (行政, 統治) 一形 **政治の** political /pəlíṭɪkəl/ ▶**政治**は民衆の生活と深く関わっている *Politics* is closely connected with people's lives. ‖ 最近は**政治**に進出する女性の割合が増えてきている The proportion of women who enter [go into] *politics* has increased recently. ‖ 一般に最近の若い人は**政治**に無関心だ Young people in general are indifferent to *politics* these days. ‖ **政治の世界**で働きたい I'd like to work in *politics* [*the political world*].
▶国民は真の**民主政治**を望んでいる The people hope for true *democratic government*. ‖ 石橋氏は長い間**政治運動**に関わってきた Mr. Ishibashi has been involved in *political movements* for a long time. ‖ S 代議士は汚職事件の**政治責任**を取り辞職した Dietman S took *political responsibility* for the bribery case and resigned.
▶その事件は両国間の**政治的な問題**に発展した The incident developed into *a political issue* between the two countries. ‖ 彼の**政治的手腕**は日本では並ぶ者がいない His *political skill* is unrivaled in Japan.
‖**政治改革** (a) political reform ‖ **政治学** political science ‖ **政治学部** the department of political science ‖ **政治献金** a political donation [contribution] ‖ **政治権力** political power ‖ **政治資金** a political fund ‖ **政治資金規制法** (the) political funds control law ‖ **政治犯** a political prisoner ‖ **政治評論家** a political analyst [commentator] ‖ **政治倫理** political ethics [morality].

2**せいじ 青磁** celadon porcelain ▶**青磁**の花瓶 a *celadon* vase.

せいじか 政治家 a politician /pɑ̀:lətíʃən/; a statesman, a stateswoman (尊敬を集める)

> **(解説)「政治家」の言い方**
> **politician** が最もふつうの言い方だが, 国家レベルの「優れた政治家」の意では **statesman** [**-woman**], **statesperson** (性差のない語)という.

▶彼は**政治家**を志している He seeks to pursue a *political career* [become *a politician*].

せいしき 正式の formal (形式に従った); official (公式の); regular (正規の); proper (作法どおりの, きちんとした) ▶**正式のパーティー** a *formal* party ‖ **正式な会員** (＝正会員) a *regular* member ‖ **正式な食事の作法** *proper* table manners ‖ その団体の**正式の名称**は何ですか What is the *official* name of the organization? ‖ 私はその園遊会に**正式に招待された** I was *formally* invited [I received a *formal* invitation] to the garden party.
▶私は**正式に**絵を習ったことはない I have never taken *formal* painting lessons. ／I have never *formally* studied painting. ‖ **正式な箸の持ち方**を知らない若者が多い Many young people don't know the *proper* way to hold chopsticks. ‖ きょう**正式**に昇格の通知があった I was *officially* notified of my promotion today.

せいしつ 性質 (a) nature (生まれつきの); (a) character (性格, 人格); a property (同種のものに共通な特性); quality (品質) ⇀性格
▶電磁波の基本的な**性質** the fundamental *properties* of electromagnetic waves ‖ 彼は穏やかな[頑固な／気まぐれな]**性質**だ He has a mild [stubborn／changeable] *nature*. ‖ 液晶は結晶の**性質**をもった液体である Liquid crystal is a liquid with the *properties* of (a) crystal.

せいじつ 誠実 sincerity /sɪnsérəṭi/, integrity /ɪntégrəṭi/ 一形 **誠実な** sincere

> **(解説)「誠実」について**
> (1) **sincerity** は「ごまかしや偽りのないこと」を, **integrity** は「(圧力に屈したり社会の風潮に流されたりしない)堅固な道義心」を意味し, 日本語の「誠実」にぴったりではない. (2) 日本語で「誠実な人」というと人格者のイメージがあるが, 英語の sincere person はむしろ「自分に忠実な人」「考えることを偽らずにことばに出せる人」という意で用いる. ⇀**誠意**.

▶この手紙には**誠実さ**が感じられない This letter shows no *sincerity* [doesn't sound *sincere*]. ‖ 校長先生は**誠実**な人柄で皆から尊敬されている The principal is a person of *integrity* and is respected by everyone. (➤ a person of integrity は「高潔な人」の意で, しばしば人物紹介に使う) ‖ 私は**誠実**な男性と結婚したい I would like to marry a *sincere* [an *honest*] man. (➤ honest は「正直な」) ‖ いつまでもきみに対して**誠実でいる**ことを誓うよ I promise I will remain *true* [*faithful*] *to* you forever. (➤ ともに「信頼を裏切らない」の意).
☞ **不誠実** (⇀見出語)

せいじゃ 聖者 a saint.

せいしゃいん 正社員 a regular [permanent] employee; a full-time employee (パートでない) ▶初めは派遣社員だったけど, 今は**正社員**なんだ I started out as a temp. Now I'm *full time*. →社員.

せいじゃく 静寂 quietness(静かなこと); silence(音がしないこと); stillness(動きがないこと) ▶夜の静寂を破る break the *stillness* of the night ‖ その神社の境内は静寂そのものだった Everything was *quiet* [*still*] in the precincts of the shrine. ‖ 辺りは完全な静寂に包まれていた There was complete *silence* all around.

ぜいじゃく 脆弱な weak(弱い); fragile /frǽdʒəl/(もろい) ▶ぜい弱な産業 a *fragile* industry.

せいしゅ 清酒 refined sake.

ぜいしゅう 税収 tax revenue ▶税収の落ち込み a decline in *tax revenue*.

せいしゅく 静粛 ▶静粛に願います *Please be quiet*. 《参考》会議で議長が注意するときは Order! Order!(議事規則を守って!)と繰り返す. ‖ (教室で教師が)みんな静粛に Class, *come to order*.

せいじゅく 成熟する mature /mətjúəʳ/(大人になる); ripen(主に果物が) ▶たいていの動物は人間より早く成熟する Most animals *mature* faster than humans do. ‖ 温室ではメロンは早く成熟する Melons *ripen* fast in greenhouses. ‖ 水着姿のかおりは成熟した女を感じさせた In her bathing suit, Kaori looked like a *full-grown* woman. (➤ mature woman は若くはない「成熟した女性, 熟女」).

せいしゅん 青春 (one's) youth; adolescence /æ̀dəlésəns/(思春期; 12, 3歳から17, 8歳くらいまで) ▶悩み多き青春を送る have a trying *adolescence* ‖ ぼくらは今青春の真っただ中だ We are in the prime [at the peak] of our *youth*. (● be in the heyday や be in the full bloom も使えるが, どちらも文語的) ‖ 若者は青春を思い切り楽しむべきだ Young people should fully enjoy *their youth*. ‖ 彼らは学生運動に青春のエネルギーをぶつけた They worked off their *youthful* energy in the student movement. ‖ 青春時代にもう一度戻れたらなあ If only I could return to the *days of my youth*. ‖ 青春は二度と来ない *You'll never be young twice*. / *We're* [*You're*] *only young once*. (➤ 後者は決まった言い方).

せいじゅん 清純な pure; innocent(邪気のない) ▶清純な乙女 a *pure and innocent* girl ‖ 彼女にはまだ少女の清純さが残っている She still has the *innocence* of a young girl.

[1]**せいしょ 聖書** the (Holy) Bible ▶聖書に誓う swear on *the Bible* ‖ 聖書の知識がなければ英米文学は十分に理解できない You cannot fully appreciate British and American literature without (a) knowledge of *the Bible*.
‖旧[新]約聖書 the Old [New] Testament.

[2]**せいしょ 清書** a clean [fair] copy ▶私はレポートを清書してから提出した I *made a clean copy of* the report and handed it in.

せいしょう 斉唱 unison /júːnɪsən, -zn/ ▶国歌を斉唱する *sing* the national anthem *in unison* ‖ 卒業式は校歌斉唱で始まった The graduation ceremony started with *the school song sung in unison*.

[1]**せいじょう 正常な** normal ▶被告は当時正常な心理状態ではなかった The accused was not in a *normal* state of mind at that time. ‖ どの機械も正常に動いている All the machines are running *smoothly* [working *normally*]. ‖ ダイヤが正常に戻るにはもう少し時間がかかります It will take a little more time for the train schedules to *return to normal*. ‖ 私の血圧は正常値より少し低い[高い] My blood pressure is a little below [above] *normal*. ‖ その国との国交を速やかに正常化するべきだ We have to *normalize* diplomatic relations with the country immediately.

[2]**せいじょう 清浄な** pure(不純物がない); clean(きれいな) ▶高原の清浄な空気 the *pure* air of the high plateau.
‖空気清浄器 an air purifier.

[3]**せいじょう 政情** a political situation(一時期の); political conditions(継続的な) ▶その発展途上国の政情は大変不安定だ The *political situation* in that developing nation is extremely unstable.

せいじょうき 星条旗 the Stars and Stripes; the Star-Spangled Banner (➤「米国国歌」の意味もある); Old Glory.

せいしょうねん 青少年 young people(若者たち); the younger generation(若い世代) —形 青少年の juvenile /dʒúːvənaɪl/ ▶青少年の犯罪は家庭内の不和と関係がある *Juvenile delinquency* [*crime*] is related to family discord.

[1]**せいしょく 生殖** reproduction
‖生殖器 the sex [reproductive] organs, the genitals ‖ 生殖細胞 a reproductive cell.

[2]**せいしょく 聖職** the clergy ▶聖職に就く *take holy orders* / *enter the Church* / *join the clergy*.
‖聖職者 a clergyman, a churchman (➤ a member of the clergy が性差のない語. clergy は集合的に「聖職者たち」).

[1]せいしん 精神

> 📖 訳語メニュー
> 知性・理性の働き →mind **1**
> 根本精神 →the spirit **2**

1【知性・理性の働き】 mind —形 精神の mental ▶精神は肉体をある程度コントロールすることができる The *mind* can control the body to some extent. ‖ その兵士は精神に異常を来していた The soldier was *mentally* [*emotionally*] *disturbed*. ‖ 感情の抑圧は精神衛生上よくない Repressing your feelings isn't good *for your mental health*. ‖ 哲夫は精神修養のため座禅をした Tetsuo practiced zazen to *train* [*discipline*] *his mind*.
▶彼はほとんど精神力(=意志の力)でその試合に勝った He won the game mostly through *mental strength* [*willpower*]. ‖ きみはきっと精神的に疲れてるんだ You must be *mentally* exhausted. ‖ 彼女は精神的にタフだ She's *mentally* tough. ‖ 彼女は精神的に(=情緒面で)成長した She has grown up [has matured] *emotionally*.
▶おまえたちは精神がたるんでるぞ You guys *are slacking off*. ‖ ボールを打つときはボールに精神を集中しなさい In batting, you have to *focus your attention on* the ball. ‖ 離婚後は姉が彼女の精神的な支えとなった After her divorce, her (older) sister was her *emotional* [*moral*] *support*. (➤ moral support は子供に対しては用いない).

2【根本精神, 意図】 the spirit ▶アメリカ人は独立の精神を決して忘れないだろう Americans will never forget *the spirit* of independence.
‖精神安定剤 a tranquilizer (➤ Prozac が有名) ‖ 精神科医 a psychiatrist /saɪkáɪətrɪst/ ‖ 精神鑑定 a mental competency test, a psychiatric evaluation ‖ 精神障害 a mental [emotional] disorder ‖ 精神遅滞 mental retardation ‖ 精神年齢

せ

one's mental age ‖ **精神病** (a) mental [psychiatric] illness [disease] (➤その患者は a mental [psychiatric /sàɪkiǽtrɪk/] patient) ‖ **精神病院** a psychiatric hospital [institution], a mental hospital ‖ **精神分析** psychoanalysis /sàɪkouənǽləsɪs/ ‖ **精神分裂症**（＝統合失調症）schizophrenia ‖ **精神保健福祉士** a psychiatric social worker.

逆引き熟語 ○○精神
アマチュア精神 an amateur spirit, a spirit of amateurism ／**開拓者精神** the pioneer [frontier] spirit ／**起業家精神** an entrepreneurial spirit ／**騎士道精神** a gallant spirit, (the spirit of) chivalry ／**サービス精神** a spirit of service, a service mindset ／**スポーツ精神** a spirit of honest fair play ／**不屈の精神** an indomitable spirit ／**武士道精神** the samurai spirit ／**法の精神** the spirit of the law ／**ユーモア精神** a spirit of (good) humor

2**せいしん 清新な** **new**（新しい）; **fresh**（生き生きした）▶その新人作家は**清新な**文体で注目された The new writer was noticed for his *fresh* style.

1**せいじん 成人** an **adult** /ədʌ́lt ‖ ǽdʌlt/（法律上の成人）; a **grown-up**（大人）**一動 成人する** **grow up**; **come of age**（成年に達する）▶彼女には**成人した**娘がいる She has a *grown(-up)* daughter. ‖ 息子さんもご立派に**成人なさいました**ね Your son *has grown up* to be a fine man.
▶娘も去年**成人に達しました** My daughter *came of age* [*reached adulthood*] last year. ‖ この映画は**成人向き**だ This film is *for adults only*. ／This is an *adult* movie.
‖ **成人教育** adult education ‖ **成人式** a coming-of-age ceremony（➤英米にはない）‖ **成人の日** Coming-of-Age Day（➤英米にはない）‖ **成人病** an adult disease.

2**せいじん 聖人** a **saint** ▶私は**聖人**君子ではないよ I'm no *saint*! ／I'm only human.

せいしんせいい 誠心誠意 ▶私は**誠心誠意**彼に忠告したが無駄だった I advised him *in all sincerity*, but it was in vain. ‖ 彼女は**誠心誠意**家族に尽くした She devoted herself *wholeheartedly* [*heart and soul*] to her family. ‖ **誠心誠意**やらせていただきます We'll *do our* (*very*) *best* to deal with the matter. ／We'll deal with the matter to *the best of our ability*.

せいず 製図 **drafting**（設計図などの下書き）; **drawing**（図面を引くこと）
‖ **製図家** a draftsman, a drawer ‖ **製図器械** a drawing instrument ‖ **製図板** a drawing board.

せいすい 盛衰 **rise and fall**; **ups and downs**（浮き沈み）; **good times and bad times**（よい時と悪い時）▶徳川幕府の**盛衰** the *rise and fall* of the Tokugawa Shogunate ‖ 長い歴史を誇るわが社にも**盛衰**があった Though our company can be proud of its long history, it has had its *ups and downs* [*good times and bad times*].

せいすう 整数《数学》an **integer** /íntɪdʒəʳ/, a **whole number**.

せいする 制する **control** ＋目（抑える）; **stop** ＋目（止める）; **dominate**（支配的立場に立つ）▶**制し難い**怒りを感じる feel *uncontrollable* anger ‖ ウィンドウズが OS 市場を**制している** Windows *dominates* the OS market. ‖ 早稲田が箱根駅伝を**制した**（＝に勝った）Waseda *won* in the Hakone ekiden.

1**せいせい 精製** **refinement** **一動 精製する** **refine** ＋目 ▶ガソリンは石油から**精製した**ものだ Gasoline *is refined* from petroleum.
‖ **精製所** a refinery.

2**せいせい 清々** ▶予定どおり全部終わって**せいせいした**（＝ほっとした）I've finished everything on time and *feel relieved*.（➤英語では現在形を使う）‖ 嫌な部長が退職して**せいせいした**（＝うれしい）I'*m glad* the disagreeable general manager has retired.

せいぜい 1【多く見積もっても】 **at (the) most**（➤以下の用例のように最上級を使って訳す）▶きみに金を貸してあげるとしても**せいぜい** 3 万円だな I can lend you thirty thousand yen *at* (*the*) *most*. ‖ 彼の船は**せいぜい** 6 メートルくらいの長さだ His boat is six meters *at the longest*.（➤ at the longest は「最長でも」）‖ 私には**せいぜい**このくらいのことしかできない *This is the best* [*the most*] I can do. ‖ わが校の選手は予選通過が**せいぜい**（＝精いっぱい）だろう *The most* [*best*] we can expect of our school's athletes is that some of them win the trial heats. ‖ 彼女は**せいぜい**20歳だ She is *not over* twenty. ‖ この程度のガイドブックなら**せいぜい**1500円ぐらいでしょう A guidebook of this kind costs *no* [*not*] *more than* 1,500 yen.
2【できるだけ】 ▶久しぶりの旅行，2 人で**せいぜい**楽しんでらっしゃい This is your first trip (together) in a long time, so enjoy yourselves *as much as possible* [to the full].（🍎 so 以下を so make the most of it と表現してもよい）.

ぜいせい 税制 a **tax** [**taxation**] **system**
‖ **税制改革** a tax reform, a tax system revision ‖ **税制調査会** the Taxation System Research Council.

せいせいどうどう 正々堂々と **fair(ly)** ▶わが校のチームは**正々堂々と**戦って敗れた Our school team played *fair and square*, but (unfortunately) lost the game. ‖《けんかで》**正々堂々と**勝負しようぜ Come on and fight *fair*!

せいせき 成績

a **score**（総得点）; a **mark**（点数）; a **grade**（総合評価；ＡＢＣによる評価にも用いる）; a **result**（テストなどの結果；しばしば複数形で）▶英語の試験で**いい成績を取る** get a high *score* [score high *marks*] on an English exam（➤《英》では in an English exam となる）‖ **成績のいい［悪い］**生徒 a *high* [*low*] *achieving* student（➤ high achiever, low achiever ともいう）‖ **成績のかさ上げ** *grade* inflation ‖ 3 学期は**成績**がぐんと上がった［下がった］My *grades* improved greatly [fell badly] in the third term. ‖ 純子は英語でいい［悪い］**成績**を取った Junko got *a good* [*bad*] *grade* in English. ／Junko got *good* [*bad*] *marks* in English. ‖ 文夫は学校の**成績**が良い［悪い］Fumio *does well* [*badly*] in school. ‖ 試験の**成績**はどうだった？*What grade* [*What score*] *did you get* on the test? ／*How did you do* on the test?（➤前者は I got an F.（F だった），後者は Awful.（さんざんだった）などと答える；《英》では in the test となる）‖ 彼女の英語の**成績**は B だった She got *a B* in English. ‖ 彼の**成績**はクラスで上位だ He *ranks high* in his class. ‖ 期末試験の**成績**はあす発表される The *results* of the final examinations will be announced tomorrow.
▶不況で**営業成績**が大幅に落ち込んだ Our *business performance* [*results*] declined drastically due to the economic recession. ‖ アジア大会では日本は

不本意な成績に終わった Japan *did poorly* in the Asian Games.
‖成績証明書 a transcript ‖成績表《米》a report card,《英》a school report.
☛ 好成績, 不成績（→見出語）
せいせっかい 生石灰《化学》**quicklime, calcium oxide.**
1**せいせん 精選** ▶お歳暮用に当店が精選したワインはいかがでしょうか For your year-end gifts, how about some of our *specially selected* [*special selection of*] wines?
2**せいせん 生鮮** ‖生鮮食料品 fresh food（新鮮な）; perishable food, perishables（「生もの」に近い）.
3**せいせん 聖戦** a **holy war, jihad**（➤後者はイスラム教徒が異教徒に対して行う）.
1**せいぜん 整然** ▶整然と片づいた部屋 a *tidy* [*an orderly*] room（➤後者はやや堅い言い方）‖日本選手団は整然と行進した The Japanese athletes marched *in an orderly manner*. ‖兄の家はすべてが整然としている Everything in my brother's home *is in perfect order* [*is kept tidy*]. ‖ワシントンの町並みは整然としている Washington is a *well laid-out* city.
2**せいぜん 生前** ▶これは祖父が生前愛用していたパイプです This is the pipe my grandfather always used *while he was alive* [*during his lifetime*]. /This was my grandfather's favorite pipe.（●「祖父」が故人であることが話者間で了解されている場合は，後者のように「生前」は訳さなくてよい）.
せいぜんせつ 性善説 belief in people's innate [fundamental] goodness（➤説明的な訳）.
せいそ 清楚 ▶清そなイメージの女優 an actress with a *well-mannered* [*refined*] image ‖あの子はいつも清そな装いをしている That girl is always *neatly and modestly dressed*. ‖ワスレナグサは清そな花だ Forget-me-nots are *trim little* flowers.
1**せいそう 清掃 cleaning** 一動 **清掃する clean (up)** ▶ボーイスカウトたちが毎月第3日曜日に公園を清掃する Boy Scouts *clean (up)* the park on the third Sunday of every month.
‖清掃作業員 a sanitation worker ‖清掃車《米》a garbage truck,《英》a dust cart.
2**せいそう 正装 full [formal] dress** ▶警察署長は正装で式典に現れた The chief of police appeared *in full dress* [*in full-dress uniform*] at the ceremony. ‖あしたのパーティー，正装して行く必要があるかしらね Do we have to *dress formally* for tomorrow's party?
3**せいそう 盛装する be dressed up (in gala attire** /ətáiəʳ/) ▶盛装の女性たち *exquisitely dressed* ladies.
4**せいそう 政争** a **political struggle.**
せいぞう 製造 production; manufacture（機械による大量の）一動 **製造する produce** +目, **manufacture** +目; **make** +目（作る）▶食品を買う前に製造年月日を確かめるといいですよ Before you buy food, you should check *when it was made*.（➤「製造年月日」は the date of production [manufacture] ともいう）‖この工場は半導体を製造している Semiconductors are manufactured [produced] in this factory.
▶父は自宅でウエットスーツの製造販売をしています My father runs a business at home *making and selling* wetsuits. ‖その製品について製造元へ電話で問い合わせた I inquired of the *manufacturer* about the product over the phone. ‖製造業 the manufacturing industry.
せいそうけん 成層圏《気象学》**the stratosphere** /strǽt̬əsfɪəʳ/.
せいそく 生息する live (in); inhabit +目（➤あとに場所を表す目的語がくる）▶日本に動物は何種類生息しているだろうか I wonder how many kinds of animals *live in* [*inhabit*] Japan. ‖この森は野生の猿の生息地です This forest is a *habitat* [*home*] for wild monkeys.
せいぞろい 勢揃い ▶親類が勢ぞろいして私の結婚を祝ってくれた All my relatives *gathered* [*came together*] to celebrate my wedding.
せいぞん 生存 existence（生きていること）; **survival**（生き残ること）一動 **生存する exist, survive** +目; **live**（生きる）▶水だけで何日くらい生存できると思いますか How many days do you think we can *exist* [*live*] on water alone?（➤exist には「生き続ける」の意味合いがある）‖山で遭難した人たちの生存が確認された The *survival* [*safety*] of the people who had been lost in the mountains was confirmed. ‖あの飛行機墜落事故では3人だけが生存していた Only three *survived* that plane crash.（➤survive は「(危機・災害などを)切り抜けて生き残る」の意の他動詞なので，次に前置詞は不要）/There were only three survivors of [in] that plane crash.（➤survivor は「生存者」）‖乗組員が生存している見込みはほとんどない There is little hope that any crew members *are alive*. ‖動物の世界は生存競争が激しい *The struggle* [*fight*] *for existence* is fierce in the animal world.
☛ 適者生存（→見出語）
1**せいたい 生態 ecology** /ɪkɑ́ːlədʒi/（生物と環境の関係）; a **mode of life**（生活の様子）▶象の生態を探る investigate the *ecology* [*the life and habits*] of elephants ‖現代の若者の生態を調べる study the *lifestyles* of today's young people.
‖生態学 ecology.
☛ 生態系（→見出語）
2**せいたい 声帯 the vocal cords [chords]** ▶有名歌手の声帯模写をする *mimic* a famous singer's *voice*.
3**せいたい 生体** a **living body**, a **live** /laɪv/ **animal**
‖生体解剖 vivisection /vìvəsékʃən/ ‖生体検査 a biopsy ‖生体実験 a (scientific) experiment on a living body ‖生体認証 biometric identification.
4**せいたい 政体** a **form [system] of government**
‖立憲政体 a constitutional government.
せいだい 盛大な grand ▶彼女の結婚披露宴は実に盛大だった Her wedding reception was very *grand*. ‖彼はアメリカに出発する前に盛大な見送りを受けた He received a *big* [*rousing*] send-off before leaving for America. ‖その政治家の祝賀会は盛大に行われた The politician's celebration was held *on a grand scale*. ‖その会は盛大だった The meeting was *well-attended*.（➤「出席者が多かった」の意）/The meeting was *a great success*.（➤「大成功だった」の意）.
せいたいけい 生態系 an **ecosystem** ▶石油流出は海洋の生態系を大きく損ないかねない An oil spill can severely damage an ocean *ecosystem*. ‖生態系は我々が思っているよりもぜい弱なものだ *Ecosystems* are more fragile [delicate] than we image.
ぜいたく 贅沢 luxury /lʌ́kʃəri, lʌ́gʒəri/; **extravagance** /ɪkstrǽvəgəns/（度を越えた）一形 **ぜいたくな luxuri-**

ous /lʌɡʒóəriəs/, **extravagant** ; **expensive**（高価な）▶ぜいたくな家に住む live in a *luxurious* house ‖ 彼女はニューヨークでぜいたくな暮らしにすっかり慣れてしまった In New York, she got used to *a life of luxury*. ‖ 私の祖母は生涯ぜいたくに暮らした人だった My grandmother *lived in luxury* all her life. ‖ ぜいたくをするから借金をするはめになるのだ Your *extravagance* [*expensive lifestyle*] has led you into debt. ‖ 彼は着る物にはぜいたくだ He *spends lavishly* on clothes.（➤ lavishly は「惜しげもなく」）‖ ベンツなんてぼくたちには手の出ないぜいたく品だ A Mercedes is *a luxury* we cannot afford.（➤「ぜいたく品」は luxury item ともいう）.

▶ぜいたくな悩み an *enviable* problem ‖ きょうはちょっとぜいたくしてステーキでも食べよう Let's *splurge* [*go on a splurge*] today and have steak. ‖ この料理はバターをぜいたくに使いました We used *plenty of* butter in this dish.（➤ plenty of は「たっぷりの」）‖ ぜいたくを言うな *Don't ask* [*expect*] (*for*) *too much*. ‖ ぜいたくを言えばきりがない One [We] *can never be perfectly satisfied*.

せいたん 生誕 **birth** ▶ワーグナー生誕200年（祭）the bicentennial anniversary of Richard Wagner's *birth* / the 200th anniversary of Richard Wagner's *birth*《参考》「100年祭」は centennial /senténiəl/ [《主に英》centenary /senténəri/],「300年祭」は tercentennial /tə̀ːrsenténiəl/ [《主に英》tercentenary /tə̀ːrsenténəri/] という.

せいだん 星団 a **star cluster**.

1**せいち 生地** one's **birthplace**.

2**せいち 聖地** a **sacred** /séɪkrɪd/ **place**, a **holy place**.

3**せいち 整地する** **level** +目 ▶学校は校庭を整地してテニスコートを造成した Our school *leveled* the playground to make tennis courts.

4**せいち 精緻な** **exquisite, delicate** ▶精緻な金細工 *delicate* gold work.

せいちゅう 成虫 an **imago** /ɪméɪɡoʊ/, an **adult insect**（➤ 前者は専門用語）▶そのさなぎは冬には成虫のガになる The pupae of that species will emerge as *adult moths* in winter.（➤ pupae は pupa の複数形）.

1**せいちょう 成長** **growth** ━動 **成長する** **grow** (**up**) ▶子供の成長は驚くほど早い Children *grow up* so quickly. ‖ 少年は立派な若者に成長した The boy *grew up* to be [*grew* into] a fine young man. ‖ 彼女は離婚を経験してから（精神的に）ずいぶん成長した She *matured* a great deal emotionally after she experienced a divorce.（➤ mature は「成熟する」）‖ その会社は近年急成長した That company *has grown rapidly* in the past few years.

▶彼は成長株の力士だ He is an *up-and-coming* sumo wrestler.（➤ 文字どおりの「成長株」は growth stock という）‖ この国の経済成長は目覚ましいものがある The *economic growth* in [of] this country is amazing.

▶アサガオの成長を観察する observe the *growth* of a morning glory ‖ この化学肥料はバラの成長を促す This fertilizer helps (to) promote the *growth* of roses.

‖**成長産業** a growth industry ‖ **成長ホルモン** a growth hormone ‖ **経済成長率** a rate of economic growth ‖ **ゼロ成長** zero growth.

2**せいちょう 清聴** ▶ご清聴ありがとうございました Thank you for your *attention*.

3**せいちょう 静聴** ▶ご静聴願います *May I have your attention, please?*

せいちょうざい 整腸剤 a **medicine for intestinal disorders**.

せいつう …に精通する **be versed in** ▶彼はクラシック音楽に精通している He *is well versed in* classical music. ‖ 彼女は数か国語に精通している（＝堪能だ）She *is proficient in* several languages. ‖ 彼はジャズの歴史に精通している He *is an authority on* the history of jazz.（➤「権威者だ」の意）.

せいてい 制定する **establish** +目 ▶憲法を制定する *establish* a constitution.

1**せいてき 政敵** a **political opponent** [**enemy**].

2**せいてき 性的な** **sexual** ▶性的嫌がらせ *sexual* harassment（→セクハラ）‖ 性的虐待 *sexual* abuse ‖ 性的興奮 *sexual* excitement ‖ 性的区別のない語 a *gender-neutral* word ‖ 彼女は知的なうえに性的魅力もある She is intellectual, and has *sexual appeal* as well. ‖ 女性［男性］と性的な関係を持つ have a *sexual* relationship [*sexual* relations] with a woman [a man].

3**せいてき 静的な** **static**.

せいてつ 製鉄 **iron** /áɪərn/ **manufacture**

‖**製鉄会社** an iron-manufacturing company ‖ **製鉄業** the iron industry ‖ **製鉄所** an iron foundry, an ironworks.

1**せいてん 晴天** **fine weather** ▶半月ばかり晴天が続いた We have had *fine weather* [*clear skies*] for the past half a month. / The weather has been fine for the past half a month.

2**せいてん 青天** a **blue sky** ▶《慣用表現》その映画監督の自殺は青天のへきれきだった The suicide of that film director was (like) *a bolt from the blue* [*a thunderbolt from a clear sky*].（➤ 非常に思いがけない出来事を晴れた空から落ちてきた雷にたとえた表現；日英共通の比喩）‖ 彼はようやく青天白日の身となった（＝無罪放免になった）He *was* eventually *acquitted* (of all charges).

3**せいてん 聖典** a **sacred book** ; **scriptures**（➤ 通例複数形）; **the** (**Holy**) **Bible, (the) Scripture**（キリスト教の）; **the Koran**（イスラム教の）; **the Buddhist scriptures**（仏教の）.

せいでんき 静電気 **static electricity** ▶髪をとかすと静電気が起こることがある When you comb your hair, *static electricity* is sometimes generated.

せいと 生徒 a **student** ; a **pupil**

> **語法 student と pupil**
> (1)《米》では小・中・高とも **student** でよいが，小学校の生徒は **pupil**, schoolboy（男），schoolgirl（女）ということもある. (2)《英》では小学校・中等学校（日本の中学・高校に相当）の生徒は pupil, schoolboy, schoolgirl が伝統的であったが，最近では，《米》の影響で student ということも多い.

▶彼ら［彼女たち］はS高校の生徒だ They're *students* at S High (School). / They're S High *students*. ‖ この小学校では生徒数が次第に減少している There has been a gradual decrease in *the number of students* [*pupils*] in this elementary school.（➤ イギリスでは「小学校」は primary school）‖ **生徒指導の先生** a teacher in charge of *counseling and guidance*.

▶生徒会の運営は生徒の自主性に任されている The administration of the *student council* is left up to the *students*. ‖ **生徒総会**は毎年５月に開かれる The *general students' meeting* is held annually in May. ‖ **対話**「あなたの学校には**生徒**は何人いますか」「750人です」"How many *students* are there in your school？" "There are seven hundred and fifty."

‖**生徒会長** the president of a student council, the school captain ‖ **生徒手帳** a student handbook, a student ID.

1**せいど 制度** a **system** ▶教育**制度** an educational *system* ‖ 健康医療**制度** a health care *system* ‖ 司法**制度** a justice *system* ‖ 選挙**制度** a voting *system* ‖ 封建**制度** the feudal *system*.

▶わが社には新入社員に対する**英会話の研修制度**がある Our company has an in-house *training course in conversational English* for new employees. (➤ in-house は「社内の」) ／Our company has *a system of training in conversational English* for new employees.

2**せいど 精度** **precision** ▶**高精度**の観測機器 a *high-precision* observation instrument.

1**せいとう 正当な** **fair**(不正のない)；**due**(当然の)；**valid**(妥当な, ちゃんとした根拠のある)；**sound**(法的に有効な)；**just**(十分な根拠のある)；**justifiable**(もっともと認められる) ▶彼が**正当な**手段でその土地を手に入れたとは思えない I don't think he got the property by *fair* means. ‖ その作家は死後50年にしてやっと**正当な**評価を得た That author has finally received *due* recognition 50 years after his death. ‖ 会社は**正当な理由**もなく彼を解雇した The company dismissed him *without a valid* [*sound* ／*just*] *reason*. ‖ この場合彼の行為は**正当だ** In this case, his act is *justifiable*.

▶どんな理由があろうとも暴力行使は**正当化されない** Whatever reason there may be, the use of violence *is* not *justified*. (●「暴力行使を正当化する」は justify the use of violence) ‖ 目的は手段を**正当化しない** The end doesn't *justify* the means. ‖ 彼女がその男を撃ったのは**正当防衛だ** It was in *self-defense* that she shot the man.

2**せいとう 政党** a **political party** ▶あなたはどの**政党**を支持しますか Which *political party* do you support？

‖**政党政治** party politics ‖ **保守**[**革新**]**政党** a conservative [progressive] party.

3**せいとう 正統の** **orthodox** /ɔ́ːrθədɑːks/；**legitimate** /lɪdʒɪ́t̬əmət/ (正統な血筋の) ▶狩野永徳は狩野派の**正統な**画家である Kano Eitoku is the *legitimate* head of the Kano school of painting.

‖**正統派** an orthodox school.

4**せいとう 正答** a **correct answer.**

5**せいとう 精糖** **sugar refining**(工程)；**refined sugar**(できた砂糖).

6**せいとう 製糖** **sugar production, sugar processing.**

1**せいどう 青銅** **bronze.**

2**せいどう 聖堂** a **church** ‖**大聖堂** a cathedral.

3**せいどう 正道** ▶奇をてらわず, 日本画の**正道**を歩む shun eccentricity and pursue *the right path* of Japanese painting.

せいとく 生得の **inborn, natural**(生まれたときから持っている；前者はやや堅い語)；**innate** /ìnéɪt/ (自然に当人の性質の一部になっている).

せいどく 精読 **intensive reading** ▶**精読**は多読と同様に大事だ *Intensive* [*Careful* ／*Close*] *reading* is as important as extensive reading. ‖ この詩を**精読し**なさい *Read* this poem *carefully* [*closely*].

▶父はその書類を**精読した** My father *perused* that document.

せいとん 整頓する **tidy** [**straighten**] **up** ▶部屋を**整頓する** *tidy* [*straighten*] *up* one's room ‖ 父の書斎はいつもきちんと**整頓してある** My father's study *is* always *neat and tidy* [*orderly*]. ‖ 身の回りの物をちゃんと**整頓して**おきなさい *Keep* your things *in good order*. (➤ やや堅い言い方).

せいなる 聖なる **sacred** /séɪkrɪd/ (神聖で冒してはならない)；**holy**(宗教的に神聖とされる) ▶(フランスの)ルルドには奇跡を起こすといわれる**聖なる**泉がある In Lourdes, France, there is a *holy* fountain which is believed to work miracles.

せいなん 西南 **the southwest** ▶私たちの学校は東京の**西南部**にある Our school is in *the southwest* of Tokyo. ‖ 淡路島は大阪の**西南の方角**にある The island of Awaji is (*to the*) *southwest of* Osaka.

ぜいにく 贅肉 **fat** (**flesh**), 《インフォーマル》 **flab** ▶最近おなかに**ぜい肉**がついてきた Lately, I've *gotten flabby* [*gotten a spare tire*] around my waist.

せいにくてん 精肉店 a **butcher.**

1**せいねん 青年** a **young man**(20代から30代にかけての男子)；a **youth** (主に10代半ばから後半の男子)；**the youth** (女子を含めた若い人たち) ▶**青年男女** *young men and women* ‖ 佐藤君はなかなか有能な**青年**だ Sato is a quite talented *young man*. ‖ 彼は**文学青年**だ He is *a young lover of literature*.

☛ 好青年 (⇀見出語)

2**せいねん 成年** ▶彼女はもう**成年に達している** [まだ**成年に達していない**] She *is an adult* now [*is* still *under age* ／*is* still *a minor*]. ⇀**成人**.

‖**成年後見制度** the adult guardianship system ‖ **成年** [**未成年**] **後見人** a guardian of an adult [a minor].

せいねんがっぴ 生年月日 one's **birthdate,** one's **date of birth** ▶ **対話**「**生年月日**をお願いします」「平成10年９月16日です」"What's *your date of birth*？" "It is September 16, 1998." (➤ "When were you born？" "I was born on September 16, 1998." としてもよい. 読み方は September the sixteenth [September sixteen], nineteen ninety-eight).

せいのう 性能 **performance** (機械の働き具合)；**efficiency** (効率) ▶**性能**のいいカメラ a *high quality* camera ‖ このシェーバーは前に使っていたのより**性能がいい** This shaver *has better* [*higher*] *performance* than the old one. ‖ この掃除機は新型なのに**性能が悪い** This vacuum cleaner *is inefficient* [*has low suction*] even though it is a new model. ‖ **エンジンの性能**のよい車を選びなさい I recommend you choose a car *with a high performance engine*.

直訳の落とし穴「性能を調べる」

「彼はポンプの性能を調べた」のつもりで (×)He inspected the performance of the pump. とする人がいる. inspect は物を主に目で見て, 欠陥や不都合がないかを「念入りに調べる, 点検する」の意. ここでは実際に運転したり試験したりするのであるから inspect は合わない. He tested [measured] the performance of the pump. とする. なお, ポンプに異常がないかを目視して調べた, の意では He inspected the pump. とすることはできる.

☛ 高性能 (⇀見出語)

せいは 制覇 ▶わが校は高校野球で5回目の全国**制覇**を成し遂げた Our school *won* the fifth *championship* in the national senior high school baseball tournament. ‖ 民主党は米上院を**制覇**した The Democrats *have won control of* the U.S. Senate.

せいはつ 整髪 hairdressing
‖**整髪料** hairdressing (一般的に) ; hair liquid (男性の液体整髪料).

せいはんたい 正反対の (completely) opposite /ɑ́:pəzɪt/ ▶彼はみんなと**正反対**の意見を出した He raised an opinion *directly opposite to* everyone else's. ‖ 妹と私は服装の好みが**正反対**だ My (younger) sister and I have the *completely opposite* tastes in clothing. ／My sister's taste(s) in clothes is *exactly* [*just*] *the opposite* of [to] mine. ‖ 私は姉とは**正反対**の性格です My personality is *the very opposite* of my (older) sister's. ‖ しばらくして我々は**正反対**の方向に歩いていることがわかった We discovered after a while that we were going in *the completely opposite* direction.

せいひ 成否 success or failure (成功か失敗か) ▶交渉の**成否**は次の会議にかかっている The *success or failure* of the negotiations depends on the outcome of the next meeting.

せいび 整備 maintenance (機械・建物・道路などの手入れ・保全) ; **service** (修理点検) **一動 整備する maintain** +⊞, **service** +⊞ ▶オートバイを**整備しておく** *maintain* one's motorcycle ‖ 会社の車を**整備する** *do maintenance* on a company car ‖ 飛行機の**整備**にはどんなに念を入れても入れ過ぎるということはない Airplane *maintenance* can never be too careful. ‖ 車は定期的に**整備してもらう**ことが大切だ It's important to *have* your car *maintained* [*serviced*] regularly. ‖ テニスの決勝戦に備えてコートを**整備した** They *put* the court *in good condition* for the coming tennis finals.
‖**整備士**[工] a mechanic ‖ **自動車整備工場** a garage.

せいひょう 製氷 ice making
‖**製氷機** an ice machine ‖ **製氷皿** an ice cube tray ‖ **製氷所** an ice plant.

せいびょう 性病 a **venereal** /vənɪ́riəl/ **disease** (➤ VD と略す. 現在では sexually transmitted disease, 《略》STD (性感染症)というのがふつう) **《参考》** 性病はかつては social disease (社会病)と呼ばれたが, 現在では social disease は social problem (社会問題)と同義に用いることが多い.

せいひれい 正比例 direct proportion ▶XはYに**正比例する** X *is directly proportional* [*is in direct proportion*] *to* Y.

1**せいひん 製品** a **product, manufactured goods** ▶外国**製品** a foreign *product* ／foreign-made [imported] *articles* ‖ この会社は原料を東南アジアから輸入し, **製品**は主にアメリカへ輸出している This company imports raw materials from Southeast Asia and exports the *products* [*manufactured goods*] chiefly to America. ‖ このテレビはタイの**製品**だ This TV set *was made* [*was produced*] *in Thailand*. ／This TV set *is a product of Thailand*.
‖**製品開発** product development ‖ **電気製品** electrical appliances ‖ **乳製品** dairy products.

2**せいひん 清貧 honest poverty** ; a **simple life** (簡素な生活) ▶**清貧**に甘んじる live contentedly in *honest poverty* ‖ 修道士[修道女]は**清貧**の誓いをした The monk [nun] took a vow of *poverty*.

せいふ 政府 a **government** (➤自国の政府のことをいうときは the Government) ▶**日本政府** *the Japanese Government* ‖ **政府**高官 a high-ranking *government* official ‖ **政府**当局 the *government* authorities ‖ **政府**は来年度に減税を行うと発表した *The Government* announced that a tax reduction would be carried out next year. ‖ **政府**は声明を発表する時機ではないと考えております The *Government* feels it is not time to make a statement.

1**せいぶ 西部 the west, the western part** ▶東海地方の**西部**は雨でしょう It will rain in *western* Tokai. ／It will rain in *the western part of* [《英》 in *the west of*] the Tokai area. ‖ **西部劇**はアメリカ**西部**開拓者たちを描いたものだ *Westerns* [*Cowboy movies*] depict *the pioneers of the American Old West*.

2**せいぶ 声部** 《音楽》 a **part** ▶三**声部**のミサ曲 a Mass in three *parts*.

1**せいふく 征服** (a) **conquest** /kɑ́:nkwest/ **一動 征服する conquer** /kɑ́:ŋkə^r^/ +⊞ ▶彼らは冬のエベレスト**征服**に成功した They succeeded in *conquering* Mt. Everest in winter. ‖ 人類が滅びたあと地球を**征服する**(＝支配する)のはゴキブリかもしれない It may be cockroaches that *rule* the world after the human race dies out. ‖ この夏は不得意科目を**征服する**(＝マスターする)よう努力するつもりだ I am going to do my best to *master* my weak subject(s) during this summer.
‖**征服者** a conqueror.

2**せいふく 制服** a **uniform** ▶**制服**を着た自衛官 a Self-Defense Force member *in uniform* ‖ **制服**姿の女子学生たち girl students *in school uniform* ‖ 神戸の松蔭女子高校は**制服**がおしゃれだ The *uniform* of Shoin Girls' Senior High School in Kobe is fashionable.
ディベートルーム **「生徒には制服が必要である」**

3**せいふく 正副** ▶書類を**正副**2通用意する prepare a document in duplicate.
‖**正副議長**[**会長**] the chairperson and vice chairperson, the president and vice president.

1**せいぶつ 生物** a **living thing** [**creature** ／**organism**] ; **life** (➤動植物の総称) ▶アルコールの中で生きられる**生物**はいない No *living thing* [*organism*] can live in alcohol. ‖ 月には**生物**はいない There is no *life* on the moon. ‖ 海には多くの**生物**がすんでいる The sea abounds with *life*. (➤ abound with は「…が多い」の意の堅い言い方, 「海の生物」は marine life [organisms]).
‖**生物学** biology /baɪɑ́:lədʒi/ ‖ **生物学者** a biologist ‖ **生物多様性** biodiversity, biological diversity ‖ **単細胞生物** a single-cell(ed) organism.

2**せいぶつ 静物 still life** (画材としての) ; a **still life** (静物画) ▶私は**静物画**を描くのが好きだ I like painting *still lifes*. (➤ (×) still lives としない) ‖ セザンヌは風景画と**静物画**のどちらにも優れていた Cézanne excelled both in landscape and in *still life paintings*.

せいふん 製粉する mill +⊞ ▶小麦を**製粉する** *mill* wheat *into flour*.
‖**製粉機** a (flour) mill ‖ **製粉業** the milling industry.

せいぶん 成分 an **element** (元素) ; a **component,** an **ingredient** (構成要素) ; a **constituent** (不可欠の構成要素) ‖**成分表示** an ingredient label.

せいへき 性癖 a **propensity** ▶あの子にはうそをつく**性癖**

がある The child has *a propensity* for lying [*a habit* of lying]. (➤日常的には tendency (傾向)や habit (習性, 癖)を用いる).

せいべつ 性別 (the distinction of) sex, (a) sex [gender] distinction →セックス ▶柔道部は**性別**に関係なくどなたでも入部できます Anybody can join the judo club regardless of *gender* [*sex*]. ‖ 人間の**性別**は精子の染色体によって決定される *Sex distinction* in humans is determined by the chromosomes in the sperm.

▶向かいに座っている若者の**性別**がわからなかった I couldn't tell the *gender* of the young person sitting across from me.

せいへん 政変 a political change ; a coup d'état /kù:deɪtɑ́:/ (クーデター) ; a change of government (内閣の更迭) ▶その国で**政変**があったようだ It seems there has been *a change of government* in that country.

1**せいぼ 歳暮** a *seibo*

日本紹介 ✉ **歳暮はお歳暮ともいい, 日頃世話になっている人に贈る年末の贈り物です. 7月初めにも同じように贈り物をしますが, こちらは中元といいます** A *seibo* or an *oseibo* is a year-end gift Japanese send to people to whom they feel indebted. Japanese also send gifts called '*chugen*' in early July.

2**せいぼ 生母** a birth [biological] mother (➤「養母」は foster mother).

3**せいぼ 聖母** the Virgin Mary (聖母マリア) ; Our Lady, the Blessed Mother (of God) (➤この2つは主にカトリック教徒が用いる).

1**せいほう 製法** a manufacturing process ; a recipe /résəpi/ (料理の作り方) ▶チーズの**製法**を教えてください Would you teach me *how to make* cheese?

2**せいほう 西方** the west 一形 **西方の** western ▶オランダはドイツの**西方**にある The Netherlands is (to the) *west* of Germany.

1**せいぼう 制帽** a school cap (学校の) ; a regulation cap (公式の).

2**せいぼう 声望** reputation (評判) ▶**声望**の高い外科医 a surgeon of high *reputation* ‖ **声望**を高める enhance one's *reputation*.

ぜいほう 税法 (a) tax law.

せいほうけい 正方形 a square ▶**正方形**の紙 a *square* sheet of paper.

せいほく 西北 the northwest

‖**西北西** the west-northwest.

せいほん 製本 bookbinding 一動 **製本する** bind +目 ▶この辞書は**製本**がしっかりしている This dictionary is *well-bound*.

‖**製本機** a bookbinding machine ‖ **製本所** a bookbindery.

せいまい 精米 rice polishing ‖**精米機** a rice polishing machine ‖ **精米所** a rice mill.

せいみつ 精密な detailed (詳細な) ; close /kloʊs/ (綿密な) ; precision /prɪsíʒən/ (計器などが) ▶**精密な**地図 a *detailed* map ‖ **精密な**調査を行う conduct a *close* investigation ‖ **精密検査**をしてもらう get *a complete physical* / have *a thorough checkup*.

‖**精密機械** a precision instrument ‖ **精密工業** the precision machinery industry.

せいむ 政務 the affairs of state

‖ (大臣)**政務官** a parliamentary secretary, a vice-minister.

ぜいむしょ 税務署 a tax [taxation] office

‖**税務署員** a tax clerk [officer] ‖ **税務署長** the superintendent of a tax office.

1**せいめい 生命** (a) life (➤「個々の人命」の意味では a がつく) ▶**生命**の起源 the origin of *life* ‖ あのジェット機墜落事故で多くの貴い**生命**が失われた Many precious *lives* were lost in that jet crash. ‖ 彼は**生命の危険を冒して**その子供を救った He saved the child *at the risk of his own life*. ‖ ほかの惑星にも**生命体**が存在するのだろうか Is there *life* on other planets? ‖ ゴキブリは**生命力**が強い Cockroaches have strong *survival ability*.

▶《比喩的》正確さは時計の**生命**だ Precision is the *life* (*and soul*) of a watch. ‖ 流行語の**生命**はせいぜい半年だ Trendy words will *last* for half a year at most. (➤この last は「持ちこたえる」の意) ‖ その歌手は声帯を痛めて**歌手生命**を絶たれた Her *career as a singer* [*singing career*] came to an end when she damaged her vocal chords. ‖ そのスキャンダルで彼女の**政治生命**は大きく損なわれた The scandal ruined her *political career*.

‖**生命維持装置** life support / a life support machine [system] (➤「患者は生命維持装置をつけている」は The patient is on life support [on a life support machine]. といい, 「生命維持装置を外す[切る]」は take ... off [remove ... from] life support あるいは switch off [turn off] a life support machine などで, インフォーマルでは pull the plug という) ‖ **生命線** a lifeline (➤「生死を分ける重要事項」のほか「(手相の)生命線」も表す) ‖ **生命保険** life insurance.

2**せいめい 声明** a statement (所信の表明) ; an announcement (公表, 公示) ▶首相は日本がその国の新政府を支持するとの**声明を出した** The Prime Minister *made a statement* [*announced* / *declared*] that Japan would support the new government of that nation. ‖ まだ**公式声明**は出ていない No *official statement* has been issued yet.

‖**共同声明** a joint communiqué [statement].

3**せいめい 姓名** one's (full) name →氏名 ▶ここに**姓名**を記入し, 判を押してください Please write *your name* here and then imprint your *hanko* [personal seal] here.

1**せいもん 正門** the main entrance ; the front gate (表玄関, 表門) ▶学校の**正門**前にバス停がある There's a bus stop in front of *the main entrance* to our school. ‖ どうぞ**正門**からお入りください Please enter through [by] *the front gate*.

2**せいもん 声紋** a voiceprint.

せいや 聖夜 a holy [sacred] night ; Christmas Eve (クリスマス・イブ).

1**せいやく 制約** (a) restriction (制限) ; a condition (条件) 一動 **制約する** restrict +目 ▶この会の会員になるにはいろいろな**制約**がある This society imposes several *conditions* for membership. ‖ 彼の行動は厳しい**制約を受けていた** His activities *were* severely *restricted*. ‖ 短歌や俳句には作法上の**制約**がある There are several *restrictions* [*constraints*] in composing tanka and haiku.

2**せいやく 誓約** a pledge ; a vow /vaʊ/ (神への誓い) ; an oath /oʊθ/ (聖書・神にかけての) ▶二度と無断欠勤はしないと**誓約書**を書かされた I was made to give *a written promise* not to be absent (from work) without notice ever again.

3**せいやく 製薬** medicine manufacturing, the production of medicine (and drug)

‖**製薬会社** a pharmaceutical /fɑ̀:ˈməsjú:ṭɪkəl/ [drug] company (➤「製薬会社のセールスマン」は pharmaceutical representative [rep] という) ‖**製薬業界** the pharmaceutical industry.

4**せいやく 成約** **the conclusion of a contract** ▶**成約する** *conclude* [*make*] *a contract*.

せいゆ 精油 1【石油】**oil refining** (石油を精製すること); **refined oil** (精製された石油)

‖**精油所** an oil refinery.

2【植物の油】**essential oil.**

せいゆう 声優 a **voice actor** [**artist**] (➤女性は a voice actress とも); a **radio actor** (➤ラジオの; 女性は a radio actress とも); a **dubber** /dʌ́bəʳ/ (映画の吹き替えをする人).

1**せいよう 西洋** **the West, the Occident** (➤後者は主に文語); **the Western countries** (西洋諸国) 一形 **西洋の Western** ▶日本の近代化はイコール**西洋化**であった Modernization in Japan has been equated with *Westernization*. ‖私たちの日常生活は大いに**西洋化されている** Our everyday life *has been* very much *Westernized*.

‖**西洋史** Western history ‖**西洋人** a Westerner; a European (ヨーロッパ人) ‖**西洋文明** Western civilization ‖**西洋料理** a Western dish, Western food.

2**せいよう 静養** (a) **rest** ▶田舎で**静養する** *take a good rest* in the country ‖父は**静養のため**那須へ行っている My father has gone to Nasu *for his health* [*for recuperation*／*to get back his health*]. (➤ recuperation は「(病後の)回復」).

せいよく 性欲 (a) **sexual desire**; a **sex drive** (性衝動) ▶強い[弱い]**性欲** a strong [weak] *sex drive* ‖**性欲を満足させる**[刺激する] satisfy [stimulate] one's *sexual desire*.

せいらい 生来 **by nature** ▶彼は**生来**の慌てん坊だ He is hasty *by nature*. ‖「坊っちゃん」は**生来**無鉄砲だ 'Botchan' was *born* reckless.

1**せいり 整理** 一動 **整理する tidy (up)** (きちんと整頓する); **put ... in order** (秩序立てて片づける) ▶帰る前にこの書類を**整理して**おいてください Can you *tidy* these papers (*up*) before you leave, please? ‖この部屋はいつも**整理が行き届いている** This room *is* always *kept tidy* [*in good order*]. (➤後者のほうが改まった言い方) ‖さっきもらった名刺が見つからないなんて, きみもかなり**整理が悪いね** You can't find that person's (name) card he just gave you? What a *disorganized* guy you are! ‖あまり突然のことなので, まだ**気持ちの整理がつかない** It was so sudden I *haven't put my feelings in order* yet. ‖彼女は恐ろしく**整理整頓のよい**女性だ She's a woman with exceptional *organizational skills*.

▶事故現場ではお巡りさんが出て**交通整理をしていた** A policeman *was directing traffic* at the site of the accident. ‖当社は人員の**整理**(＝削減)はしません We won't *reduce* the work force.

‖**整理券** a numbered ticket (given to people in order of their arrival) ‖**整理だんす** a chest of drawers.

2**せいり 生理** 1【自然の働き】▶私, 体臭の強い男は**生理的にだめ**なの I'm *physically* repulsed by men with strong body odor.

‖**生理学** physiology /fìziɑ́:lədʒi/ ‖**生理現象** a physiological phenomenon ‖**生理的食塩水** a physiological saline solution ‖**生理的欲求** a physical desire.

2【月経】one's **period** /píəriəd/ ▶今月はまだ**生理**がないの I haven't had my *period* yet this month. ‖**生理**が1週間遅れている My *period* is a week late. ‖私, **生理になっちゃった** My *period* has started.／I got my *period*. ‖彼女はいつも**生理がひどい** She always *has heavy periods*. ‖今**生理中**なの I'm *having my period*. 《参考》生理になったことを遠回しに, It's that time of the month. という.

‖**生理休暇** a period [menstrual] leave ‖**生理痛** menstrual cramps [pain] ‖**生理不順** menstruation disturbance ‖**生理用ナプキン** a sanitary napkin [pad], 《英》a sanitary towel ‖**生理用品** sanitary goods.

ぜいりし 税理士 a **licensed** [**certified**] **tax accountant.**

せいりつ 成立 (日本語では1つの形にまとまることを何かにつけ「成立」というが, これに対応する英語はない. 何が「成立」するかによって適切な動詞を選ぶ必要がある) ▶江戸幕府は1603年に**成立した**(＝樹立された) The Edo Bakufu *was established* in 1603. ‖先月イタリアで新しい内閣が**成立した** A new Italian cabinet *was formed* last month. ‖野村家の令息と安田家の令嬢との間に婚約が**成立した**(＝取り決められた) An engagement *has been arranged* between the Nomuras' son and the Yasudas' daughter. ‖その二国間に平和条約が**成立した**(＝締結された) A peace treaty *was concluded* [*was signed*] between the two countries. ‖来年度予算が昨夜**成立した**(＝承認された) The budget for the coming fiscal year *was approved* in (the) Diet last night. ‖4時間にわたる交渉の結果, その商談は**成立した**(＝協定が結ばれた) They *came to a* business *agreement* after four hours of negotiations. ‖委員の過半数が出席したのでその会議は**成立した**(＝有効となった) Because a majority was [were] present, the meeting *was considered valid*.

☛ **不成立** (→見出語)

せいりゃく 政略 a **political maneuver** (1つの); **political tactics** [**maneuvers**] (様々な) ▶総理は**政略にたけた人だ** The Prime Minister is *a skilled political tactician*.

‖**政略結婚** a marriage of convenience [political reasons].

1**せいりゅう 清流** a **crystal stream.**

2**せいりゅう 整流** 《電気学》**rectification**

‖**整流器** a rectifier.

せいりょう 声量 **the volume of** one's **voice** ▶彼女は豊かな**声量**に恵まれている She has a rich, powerful *voice*.

せいりょういんりょう 清涼飲料 a **soft drink**; a **carbonated drink**, a **soda pop** (炭酸の入った).

1**せいりょく 勢力** **power** (支配力, 能力); **strength** (強さ); **influence** /ínfluəns/ (影響力) ▶彼は閣内でなかなか**勢力がある** He has great *power* in the Cabinet.／He carries much *weight* in the Cabinet. (➤「顔が利く」の意). ‖台風は房総半島に上陸すると急速に**勢力が衰えた** The typhoon suddenly lost its *strength* after landing on the Boso Peninsula. ‖私の支持政党は前回の総選挙で目覚ましく**勢力を伸ばした** The party I support achieved remarkable *gains* in the last general election.

▶彼は医学界で大きな**勢力を振るっている** He wields

great *influence* [*power*] in the medical world. ‖ 彼らはもう10年も**勢力争いをしている** They *have been struggling for power* (for) ten years now. ‖ ケニアではキクユ族とマサイ族が二大**勢力**(＝種族)だ The Kikuyu and the Masai are the two *influential tribes* in Kenya.

²**せいりょく 精力** **strength** (体 力) ; (an) **energy** /énəʳdʒi/ (元気, エネルギー) ; **vitality** (生命力) ; **vigor** /vígəʳ/ (活動力) ; **drive** (やる気, 積極性) ▶見るからに**精力的な**中年男 a middle-aged man *of* obvious *strength and vigor* ‖ **精力**の有り余った若者 a young man with more than enough *drive* (➤ drive は「やる気, 積極性」;「性的エネルギー」の意味なら sexual [vital] energy) ‖ 彼は**精力**にあふれている He is full of *energy* [*vitality*]. ‖ 私はこの仕事に**全精力**を傾注した I concentrated *all my energies* on this task. ‖ 佐藤氏は**精力的**に選挙運動をした Mr. Sato campaigned *energetically*.

¹**せいれい 聖霊** **the Holy Spirit** (キリスト教の三位一体の第三位).

²**せいれい 政令** a **cabinet order** ‖ **政令指定都市** a government-designated large city (of over half a million population) (➤ 日本独自のもの).

せいれき 西暦 **the Christian Era, the Common Era** 《略 CE》(➤ 後者は宗教色を避けた言い方) ▶ジェフリー・チョーサーは**西暦**1400年に死んだ Geoffrey Chaucer died in *AD* 1400 [in the year 1400 *of the Christian Era*].

《参考》AD はラテン語 Anno Domini の省略で,「主キリスト生誕の年に」の意. 数字の前に置くのが正式であるが, あとに置くこともある. なお, 1400の読み方は fourteen hundred.

せいれつ 整列する **line up** ▶校門の前に**整列しなさい** *Line up* in front of the school gate. ‖ 少年たちは横[縦] 2 列に**整列した** The boys *stood* in two rows [lines].

せいれん 精錬する **refine** +目 (精製する) ; **smelt** +目 (溶解する)

‖ **精錬所** a refinery (精製所) ; a smelter (溶鉱炉).

せいれんけっぱく 清廉潔白 **complete innocence** ▶収賄で起訴された政治家はあくまで**清廉潔白**を主張した The politician, who was charged with bribery, maintained his *complete innocence* [claimed to be *completely innocent*].

せいれんのし 清廉の士 a **person of great integrity**.

せいろ(う) a ***seiro*** ; a circular or square cooking utensil made of wood or bamboo for steaming food (➤ 説明的な訳).

せいろん 正論 a **sound argument** ▶彼の言うことは**正論**だ What he said *was reasonable*. / His argument *was sound* [*reasonable*].

セイロン **Ceylon** /sılá:n/ (スリランカ共和国を成す島 ; スリランカ共和国の前の国名).

ゼウス 《ギリシャ神話》**Zeus.**

セージ 《植物》**sage.**

ゼーゼー ▶彼はぜんそくで**ゼーゼー言っている** He's *wheezing* from asthma. ‖ 日頃運動していないから, ちょっと走っただけで**ゼーゼー言って**(＝息が切れて)しまう I don't usually exercise, so I *get out of breath* if I run (even) a little.

セーター a **sweater** /swétəʳ/ ; a **pullover** (頭からかぶるタイプの) ▶カシミアの**セーター** a cashmere *sweater* ‖ **セーターを編む** knit a *sweater* ‖ **セーターを着る**[**脱ぐ**] put on [take off] *a sweater*.

セーヌがわ セーヌ川 **the Seine** /sem/ (パリを貫流する川).

セーフ **safe** ▶《野球》彼の二塁盗塁は**滑り込みセーフとなった** He took off for second and *was called safe* as he slid in feet first.

▶《比喩的》懸命に学校まで走ったので**滑り込みセーフだった** I ran for all I was worth and *just* [*barely*] *made it* to school *on time*.

セーブ 《野球》a **save** ▶岩瀬は37**セーブをあげた** Iwase was credited with 37 *saves*. ‖ キーパーは**ファインセーブを連発した** The goalkeeper made several [a series of] *spectacular saves*.

‖ **セーブポイント** a save point.

セーフティーバント →**ドラッグバント.**

セーラーふく セーラー服 a **sailor suit** (上下の子供服) ; a **middy (blouse)** (セーラー服型のブラウス) ; a **sailor's uniform** (水兵の).

セール a **(bargain) sale** (➤ bargain はつけないほうがふつう) ▶**在庫一掃セール** *a clearance* (*sale*) ‖ このネクタイは**セールで買った** I bought this tie *on sale* [*at a sale*]. ‖ どのデパートでも**クリスマスセールをやっている** Every department store is having *a Christmas sale*. ‖ 表通りの文房具屋さんでは**新学期セールをやっている** The stationer's on the main street is having *a new school term sale*.

セールストーク a **sales pitch, sales talk** (➤ 前者がふつう) ▶それはいい**セールストーク**になる That will make a good *sales pitch*.

セールスポイント a **selling point** ▶このビデオカメラは軽量なことが第 1 の**セールスポイント**だ The light weight of this camcorder is its prime *selling point*.

▶《比喩的》私の**セールスポイント**は明るい性格です My most *winning characteristic* is that I am bright and cheerful. (➤ winning は「人を引きつける」).

セールスマン a **salesperson** ; a **salesman** /séılzmən/ (男性), a **saleswoman** (女性) ▶車の**セールスマン** a car *salesman*.

> **危ないカタカナ語✸ セールスマン**
> **1** 英語の salesman は「外交販売員」だけでなく,「店員」も指すことば. 日常的には前者を sales representative, 後者を《米》 salesclerk,《英》 shop assistant と呼んで区別している.
> **2** 女性の「店員」は saleswoman, saleslady, salesgirl などというが, 最近では性別の明示を避けて salesperson (複数形は salespeople) や salesclerk という言い方が好まれる.

せおいこむ 背負い込む **shoulder** +目 ▶彼女はよく嫌な仕事を**背負い込む** She often *shoulders* [*takes on*] troublesome tasks.

せおいなげ 背負い投げ a **shoulder throw, *seoi-nage*** ▶彼は相手を**背負い投げ**で破った He *threw* his opponent *over his shoulder* (onto the mat).

せおう 背負う **1**【**背にのせる**】**have** [**carry**] ... **on** one's **back** ▶重いリュックを**背負う** *carry* a heavy backpack (*on one's back*) ‖ ぼくは妹を**背負って**川を渡った I crossed the stream *with* my sister *on my back*.

2【**引き受ける**】▶彼は事業に失敗して, 3000万円の借金を**背負った** He failed in business and had to *shoulder* [*take on*] a debt of thirty million yen. ‖ 彼はひとりで一家を**背負っている** He *supports* his entire family by himself. ‖ 彼女は仕事を**背負い過ぎて**体を壊した She *took* on too much work [too many tasks] and damaged her health.

せおよぎ 背泳ぎ **the backstroke, the back crawl** ▶**背泳ぎで泳ぐ** swim *the backstroke* ‖ 私はやっと**背泳ぎ**ができるようになった I finally learned how to *swim on my back*.

セオリー a **theory**.

せかい 世界 **1【地球上の国々】the world** ▶**世界**には200以上の国がある There are over 200 countries *in the world*. ‖ カナダは**世界**で２番目に大きな国である Canada is the *world's second largest* country. ‖ 松本選手は柔道で**世界一**になった Matsumoto became *the world* judo *champion*. ‖ 日本の先端技術は**世界中から**注目されている Japan's advanced technology draws attention *from around the world* [*from all over the world*]. (● (×)from the world としないこと) ‖ 彼はアメリカのデザイナーで, その作品は**世界中で**高く評価されている He is an American designer whose works are highly valued *worldwide* [*throughout the world*].

> **直訳の落とし穴「世界中から」**
> (1)「世界中から集めた製品」というとき商店ではしばしば (×)products from the world と書いてあるが, これは英語ではおかしい. なぜなら日本は世界の一部であるから. 例えば, 日本にある店で products from Japan と表示するとおかしいのと同じである. products from all over [from around] the world が正しい言い方. したがって,「京都には毎年世界中から百万人近い観光客が来る」は About one million tourists visit Kyoto from all over the world every year. となる.
> (2)同様に, 日本人が日本語で「アジアへ行く」と言うことがあるが, これをそのまま go to Asia と日本人が言うと, 日本はアジアの一部なので英語ではおかしい.「(ほかの)アジアの国々へ行って見聞を広めたい」は I want to go to other Asian countries and broaden my horizons. のように, other が絶対に必要である.

▶大気汚染は**世界的な**(＝地球的な)問題である Air pollution is a *global* problem. ‖ その国立公園は**世界的に有名な**観光地だ The national park is a *world-famous* scenic spot [a scenic spot *of worldwide fame*]. ‖ アメリカの水泳選手たちは多くの**世界記録**を作った American swimmers have set many *world records*. ‖ 英語は**世界語**である English is *an international* [*a global*] *language*.

2【住むところ, 社会】a world ▶私と彼女では住む**世界**が違う She and I live in different *worlds*. ‖ 金星は実際には**死の世界**だ Venus is actually *a dead world*. ‖ スポーツ選手は**勝負の世界**に生きている Athletes live in *a highly competitive world*.

▶**スポーツの世界** the *world* of sports ‖ **動物の世界**では生存競争が激しい In *the animal world*, the struggle for existence is fierce. ‖ 暴力が**子供の世界**にまで(＝子供たちの間で)広がっている Violence is spreading *among children*.

‖**世界遺産** World Heritage (➤ 総称) ; a World Heritage property (個々の) ‖ **世界一周旅行** a trip around the world, a round-the-world trip ‖ **世界観** a world outlook [view], an outlook [a view] of the world ‖ **世界史** world history ‖ **第一[二]次世界大戦** World War I [II], the First [Second] World War.

☛ **新世界, 全世界** (→見出語)

せかす 急かす **hurry (up), rush** +目 (➤ 後者が強意的) ▶息子を**せかす** *hurry* (*up*) one's son ‖ そんなに**せかすな**よ Don't *rush* me. ‖ **せかされる**のは嫌だ I don't like to *be rushed*.

せかせか ▶ニューヨークではみんな**せかせか**歩いている In New York everyone walk *hurriedly*. ‖ 彼女はいつも**せかせかして**落ち着かない She *is* always *rushing about busily* and never slows down.

せかっこう 背格好 **height and build** (➤ height は「身長」, build は「体のつくり」) ▶息子は父親に**背格好**がそっくりなんですよ My son resembles his father in *height and build*. ／My son and his father are very much alike in *build*.

ぜがひでも 是が非でも ▶この試合には**是が非でも**勝ちたい I want to win this game *no matter what it takes* [*by hook or by crook*]. (➤ by hook or by crook は「何としてでも, どうしても」の意のインフォーマルな言い方) ‖ この仕事は**是が非でも**期日に間に合わせてくれ Finish this work by the deadline *at any cost* [*no matter what*].

せがむ **pester** +目 ; **press** +目 (しつこく迫る) ▶子供たちは母親にお小遣いを**せがんだ** The children *pestered* [*pressed*] their mother for money. ‖ 彼女にディズニーランドへ連れていってくれと**せがまれている** She *has been pestering* me to take her to Disneyland.

せがれ 倅 a **son** /sʌn/ ▶**せがれ**が家業を継いでくれるといいんだが I would like to have *my son* take over the family business.

セカンド 《野球》→二塁.

セカンドオピニオン a **second opinion** (➤ 特に別の医師の見解, 診断) ▶**セカンドオピニオン**を求める [受ける] seek [get] *a second opinion*.

セカンドバッグ a **clutch bag**.

1**せき 席** **1【座席】a seat** ▶いい**席**が取れるように早く出かけよう Let's leave early so (that) we can get good *seats*. ‖ こちらの**席**, よろしいですか Is it all right if I take this *seat*? ‖ **席に着いて**ください *Sit down*, please. ／Please *take your seat* (*s*). ／Please *be seated*. (➤ 最後の例はやや改まった言い方) ‖ (生徒に) きみは**席**に戻りなさい Go back to your *seat*. ‖ **席を代わり**ましょうか Shall I *change seats* with you? ‖ あっちの**席**に移ってもいいですか Can I move to that *seat* over there? ‖ クラスの**席替え**をする *rearrange the desks* in the classroom (→席替え).

▶《電話で》小川は今**席を外しております** Ogawa *isn't in* [*isn't at his desk*] now. ／Ogawa *is away from his desk* just now. ‖ **席を詰めて**いただけませんか Would you mind *sliding* [*moving*] *over*? ‖ この**席を取って**おいていただけますか Will you *save* [*keep* / *hold*] this *seat* for me, please? (➤ 動詞に take を用いるのは不可) ‖ 少女はその老人に**席を譲った** The girl *gave* (*up*) [*offered*] *her seat* to the old man. ‖ ちょっと**席を外させて**いただきます Please *excuse* me for a minute [for a few minutes].

▶《レストランなどで》**席**はありますか *Do you have any tables*? ‖ お**席**にご案内するまでお待ちください Please wait *to be seated*. (➤ レストランなどでの掲示) ‖ **禁煙席**にしますか, それとも**喫煙席**にしますか Would you prefer *a non-smoking* (*seat*) or (*a*) *smoking seat*? ‖ 対話「この**席**ふさがってますか」「いいえ, 空いています」"*Is this seat taken*?" "No, it isn't."

2【場所, 場合】 ▶改まった**席**に出る attend *a formal event* [*occasion*] ‖ その作家が**公の席**に姿を現したのは3年ぶりである The writer appeared in *public* for the first time in three years. ‖ こういう**席**で仕事の話はやめよう Don't talk shop on this sort of *occa-*

sion.

逆引き熟語 ○○席
運転席 a driver's seat／**折り畳み席［補助席］** a fold-down seat, a jump seat／**外野席** the outfield bleachers／**観客席** a seat, seats／**記者席** a press box／**喫煙席** a smoking seat／**貴賓席** the royal box／**禁煙席** a non-smoking seat／**後部座席** a back [rear] seat／**最前席** the first- [front-] row seat／**指定席** a reserved seat／**助手席** a front passenger seat／**操縦席** a cockpit／**内野席** the infield bleachers／**優先席** a priority seat／**予約席** a reserved seat

2**せき 咳** a **cough** /kɔːf/ **一動 せきをする cough** ▶せきが少し出る I have a slight *cough.* ‖ けさからせきがひどいんです I've had a bad *cough* all [since] this morning. (➤ all を用いると午前中の発言になり, since を用いるとその日の遅い段階での発言になる) ‖ 彼は時々ひどいせきをする He sometimes *coughs* quite harshly. ‖ (やっと)せきが止まった I've gotten over my *cough.*
‖**せき止め** (a) cough medicine ; a cough drop (ドロップ) ; cough syrup (シロップ).

3**せき 堰** a **dam** ▶《慣用表現》観衆がせきを切ったようにグラウンドになだれ込んだ The crowd of spectators rushed onto the field *like a dam breaking* (*loose*). ‖ 部屋に入るなり彼女はせきを切ったように話しだした As soon as she came into the room, she *burst* (*out*) *into a torrent of words.*

4**せき 籍** a (**family**) **register** (戸籍) ▶戸籍に入れる enter one's name in a *family register* ‖ 私はT大に籍を置いている I *am enrolled at* T University. ‖ 彼は野球部に籍がある He *is a member of* the baseball club.
▶彼女はまだ彼と籍を入れていない She *hasn't registered* her marriage yet. (●「結婚したことを届け出ていない」と考える) ／She *isn't* (*legally*) *married* to him yet. (➤ legally は「法律上」).

5**せき 積**《数学》**the product** ▶3と7の積を求めよ What is *the product* of 3 and 7 ?

せきうん 積雲《気象学》a **cumulus cloud.**

せきえい 石英 quartz.

せきがいせん 赤外線 infrared /ìnfrəréd/ **rays**
‖**赤外線カメラ** an infrared camera ‖ **赤外線写真** an infrared photograph.

せきがえ 席替え (a) **change in seating** (**arrangements**) ▶学校では学期ごとに席替えがある We have a change in *seating* (*arrangements*) each term.

せきこむ 咳き込む have a fit of coughing ▶初めてたばこを吸うとたいていの人はせきこむ Most people *have a fit of coughing* when they smoke for the first time.

せきさい 積載 loading 一動 積載する load (＋目)
‖**最大積載量** a loading capacity.

せきじ 席次 (a) **seating order** (席順) ; (an) **order of precedence** (優先順).

せきしょ 関所 a **barrier,** a **checking station.**

せきじゅうじ 赤十字 a **red cross**
‖**赤十字社** the Red Cross (➤ 正式名は the International Red Cross Society) ‖ **赤十字病院** a Red Cross hospital ‖ **日本赤十字社** the Japanese Red Cross.

せきじゅん 席順 seating order ▶席順を決める decide *the seating order* ‖ 生徒の席順は生徒証の番号順です The students are seated according to I.D. number [in the order of their I.D. numbers]. (➤ I.D. は identification (身分, 身元) の省略形).

せきじょう 席上 ▶彼は重役会の席上で辞意を表明した He announced his resignation *at* the directors' meeting.

せきずい 脊髄 the [one's] **spinal cord**
‖**脊髄炎** myelitis /màɪəláɪţɪs/ ‖ **脊髄神経** spinal nerves.

セキセイインコ《鳥》a **budgerigar.**

せきせつ 積雪 snow ▶蔵王は今積雪3メートルです In Zao, *the snow is* three meters *deep* now. ／In Zao, *snow has accumulated to a depth of* three meters. ‖ 深い積雪のため交通が途絶えた Because of the *deep snow,* traffic was held up.

せきたてる 急き立てる rush ＋目, **urge** /əːʳdʒ/《to do》(➤ 後者にはしつこく勧めるという含みがある) ▶せきたてないでよ Don't *rush* me ! ‖ 子供たちは早く行こうと父親をせきたてた The kids *urged* their father *to* leave quickly.
▶母親は子供たちをせきたてて早く学校に行かせた The mother *packed* the children *off* to school. (➤ pack off は「急いで送り出す」).

せきたん 石炭 (a) **coal** ▶燃えている石炭 live *coals* (➤ live の発音は /laɪv/) ‖ ストーブに石炭をくべる put some *coals* in the stove.

せきつい 脊椎 the backbone ; the spine (脊柱) ; **the vertebrae** /vɔ́ːʳţɪbreɪ/ (脊椎骨)
‖**脊椎[無脊椎]動物** a vertebrate [an invertebrate] (animal).

せきてい 石庭 a **rock** [**stone**] **garden** ▶龍安寺の石庭には異なる大きさの15の石が白砂の中に注意深く配置されている In the *rock garden* at Ryoanji, fifteen stones of different sizes are placed carefully in white gravel.

せきどう 赤道 the equator /ɪkwéɪţəʳ/ ▶エクアドルは赤道直下にあるのでその名がある Ecuador is so called because it *is located right on the equator* [because it *straddles the equator*]. (➤ straddle は「またがる」).

せきとめる 塞き止める dam up ▶村人たちは川をせき止めて貯水池を造った The villagers *dammed up* the river to make a reservoir.

せきとり 関取 a ***sekitori*** ; a sumo wrestler in the top two divisions, *juryo* and *makuuchi* (➤ 説明的な訳).

せきにん 責任

1【任務, 義務】(a) **responsibility** ; (a) **liability** (法律上, 特に損害賠償の支払いをすること) ; **accountability** (自分の言動について釈明し正当化すること) ▶子供のしつけは親の責任だ It is the *responsibility* of parents to discipline their children. ‖ マネージャーは歌手のスケジュールに対して責任を負っている Managers *are responsible for* singers' schedules. ‖ 夫は妻の負債を支払う責任がありますか *Is* a husband *liable for* [*to* pay] his wife's debts ? ‖ 当社では能力ある女性は責任ある地位に就いています In our company, capable women employees hold *responsible* positions. ‖ 当社は責任感あふれる社員を求めています We need new employees with a strong *sense of responsibility.* ‖ この売り場の責任者はどなたですか Who is *in charge of* this department ? ／Who is the *manager* of this department ?
‖**責任者** the person in charge ‖ **企業責任** corporate responsibility ‖ **社会的責任** social re-

sponsibility ‖ **説明責任** accountability ‖ **道義的責任** moral responsibility.
2【負うべき責め】one's **fault**（過失の）; (a) **responsibility**（結果として負うべき）▶責任を逃れる avoid *responsibility* ‖ それは私の責任ではありません That's not my *fault*. ／I'm not *responsible for* that. ‖ 私たちが遅刻した**責任**はきみにある It is your *fault* that we are late. ‖ 娘の自殺は体育の先生に**責任がある**, とその父親は言った The father *put the blame for* his daughter's suicide on the P.E. teacher.

【文型】
行動·結果など(A)に責任をもつ［取る］
take responsibility for A
➤ A は名詞·動名詞. 動詞は assume, accept, take on などを用いる
行動·結果など(A)の責任は人(B)にあるとする
hold B **responsible for** A

▶誰が結果に**責任をもつ**のですか Who will *take* [*accept*] *responsibility for* the consequences? ‖ 自分でやったことなのだから自分で**責任を取る**よ I'*ll take responsibility for* what I have done. ／I've made my bed and *I'll lie in* [*on*] *it*. (➤ As you make your bed, so you (must) lie in [on] it.（自分の用意したベッドなのだから自分が寝よ）ということわざから) ‖ 大人は常に自分の行動に**責任をもつ**べきだ An adult should always *take responsibility* [*be accountable*] *for* his or her behavior. ‖ 彼は事故の**責任を取らされた** He *was held responsible* [*accountable*] *for* the accident.
▶他人に**責任を転嫁して**はいけない Don't *pass* [*shift*] *the blame to* [*onto*] *other people* for what you have done. ‖ 彼はいつも**責任を転嫁しよう**とする He always tries to *pass the buck*. (➤ pass the buck はインフォーマルな言い方で「他人に罪をなすりつける」の意) ‖ 社長は列車衝突事故の**責任を取って**辞任した The president *took the responsibility for* the train crash and resigned. ‖ 市長, もしあなたにこの汚職事件の**責任がない**と主張なさるのなら, 誰に**責任がある**のか明らかにしていただきたい Mr. Mayor, if you insist that you'*re not responsible for* this bribery case, could you make clear to us *where the responsibility lies*?

せきのやま 関の山 ▶そんな虫のいいことを頼みに行っても断られるのが**関の山だ** If you go (to him) with such a selfish request, you're bound to be refused *at best*. (➤ be bound to do は「きっと…する」; at best は「よくても, せいぜい」) ‖ あの力士は8勝が**関の山だろう** That sumo wrestler will win eight bouts *at* (*the*) *most*. (➤ at (the) most は数詞を含む語句とともに用いて,「多くて, せいぜい」の意) ‖ つかみ合いになればとてもかなわないから, 口で言い返すのが**関の山だった** I could never win if I grappled with him, so *the most I could do* was argue.

せきはい 惜敗 ▶サッカーで日本はアルゼンチンに**惜敗した** Japan *was defeated* by the Argentine soccer team *by a narrow margin*.

せきばらい 咳払い ▶部長は**せき払い**をしてから受話器を取った The manager *cleared his throat* and picked up the receiver.

せきはん 赤飯 ***sekihan***
日本紹介 ✉ **赤飯は餅米にゆでた小豆を入れて蒸したものです. ふつう, 誕生日, 結婚式, 祭りなどの祝い事があるときに作ります** *Sekihan* (red rice) is made from glutinous rice steamed together with boiled red azuki beans. It is usually prepared on celebratory occasions such as birthdays, weddings, and festivals.

せきばん 石盤 a **slate**.

せきはんが 石版画 **lithograph**.

せきひ 石碑 a **stone monument**（記念碑）; a **gravestone**（墓碑）.

せきひん 赤貧 **grinding poverty**.

せきぶつ 石仏 a **stone** (**statue of**) **Buddha**（釈迦（しゃか）の）; a **stone Buddhist statue**（仏教の）.

せきぶん 積分《数学》**integral calculus, integration**.

せきべつ 惜別 ▶**惜別の情** a feeling of sorrow at *parting* (with someone).

せきむ 責務 **duty**（義務）; (a) **responsibility**（責任）▶二度とこのような事件を起こさないようにすることが私たちの**責務**だと思います I think it is our *duty* to make sure that this sort of incident does not occur again.

せきめん 赤面する **blush, flush**（➤ 後者からは女性を連想し, 男性の場合は女性っぽさを感じるという人が少なくない）▶きまり悪くて**赤面する** *flush* [*blush*] with embarrassment ‖ あんなうそをついてしまって, あとで恥ずかしくなり**赤面した** Later, I *blushed* with shame for having told such a lie. ‖ **赤面の至りです** I am ashamed of myself [of what I did].

せきゆ 石油 **oil, petroleum** /pətróʊliəm/ ▶**石油**は最も重要なエネルギー資源の1つである *Oil* is one of the most important energy resources. ‖ **石油資源**は有限だ *Oil resources* are limited.
‖ **石油会社** an oil company ‖ **石油化学製品** petrochemical products ‖ **石油危機** the oil crisis ‖ **石油工業** the oil [petroleum] industry ‖ **石油コンビナート** a petrochemical complex ‖ **石油ストーブ** an oil [a kerosene] heater ‖ **石油タンク** an oil tank ‖ **石油ランプ** an oil [a kerosene] lamp.

セキュリティ **security** ▶**セキュリティ**を強化する increase [enhance ／ strengthen ／ tighten ／ beef up] *security*.

せきらら 赤裸々 ▶**赤裸々な**真実 the *naked* truth ‖ 彼女の**赤裸々な**告白は我々を驚かせた Her *frank* confession surprised us.

せきらんうん 積乱雲《気象学》a **cumulonimbus** /kjù:mjəloʊnímbəs/; a **thundercloud**（入道雲）.

せきり 赤痢《医学》**dysentery** /dísənteri/
‖ **赤痢患者** a dysentery patient ‖ **赤痢菌** dysentery bacilli /bəsílaɪ/（➤ 通例複数形で）.

せきりょう 席料 a **cover charge**（➤（×）table charge と言わない. これは和製英語）.

セキレイ《鳥》a **wagtail**.

せきわけ 関脇 a ***sekiwake***; a sumo wrestler in the third-highest rank（➤ 説明的な訳）.

せく 急く **rush, hurry**（➤ 前者が強意的）▶**せく**ことはないよ You don't have to *rush*. ／Don't *rush*.
ことわざ **せいては事を仕損じる** Haste makes waste. ／More haste, less speed.

セクシー **sexy** ▶**セクシー**な女の子 a *sexy* girl ‖ **セクシー**に体をくねらせる wriggle *in a sexy way* ‖ 彼女は唇が**セクシー**だ She's got *sexy* lips.

セクシャルハラスメント **sexual harassment** → セクハラ.

セクション a **section**.

セクター a **sector** ‖ **第三セクター** a joint public and private venture（官民の合弁会社）; the third sector（民間の非営利団体）.

セクハラ **sexual harassment** ▶**セクハラ**で男性を訴える

charge a man with *sexual harassment* ‖ 職場でセクハラを受ける *be sexually harassed* at work.

せけん 世間 1【世の中】**the world** ▶世間にはさまざまな人がいるものだ There are all kinds of people in *the world*. ／It takes all kinds [sorts] of people to make *a world*. (➤後者は「世の中には変わり者もいる」の意のことわざ) ‖ **世間は狭い** *It's a small world*. (⇀狭い) ‖ 彼女は**世間知らずだ** She *knows little of the* (*real*) *world*. ／She's *naive*. ‖ 彼は**世間をよく知っている** He *has seen much of the world*. ／He *is a man of the world*. ‖ この女の子はまだ12歳なのに**世間ずれしていて**かわいげがない Though this girl is only 12, she *is too sophisticated* for her age and doesn't have the endearing charm of a child. ‖ 佐久間さんは**世間離れしている**(＝世間のことに無関心だ) Mr. Sakuma is *indifferent to worldly affairs* [*uninterested in worldly matters*].

‖**渡る世間に鬼はない** ⇀鬼.

2【世の中の人々】**people** ▶**世間の口**はうるさいものだ(＝人はうわさ話が好きだ) *People* like gossiping. ／*People* will talk. ‖ **世間をあっと驚かすために**(＝注目されようと)隣家に放火したと少年は言った The boy said that he had set fire to his next-door neighbor's house in order to *attract attention*. ‖ **世間を騒がせた**通り魔が捕まった The phantom slasher who *had been stirring public fears* was finally arrested. ‖ 自分の意志を貫くためには, 時に**世間を敵に回して戦わねばならない** You sometimes have to fight *the general public* in order to realize your own ideas. ‖ 私の親は**世間体**を気にし過ぎる My parents pay too much attention to *what other people think*. ／My parents worry too much about *appearances*.

▶娘が結婚するときは**世間並みのこと**はしてやりたい When my daughter gets married, I'd like to do *as much* for her *as other parents do for their daughters*. ‖ 私は**世間並みの**(＝悪くない)給料はもらっている I get a *decent* salary. ‖ テーブルを囲んだ一同は**世間話に花を咲かせた** The people at the table were animatedly swapping *gossip* and making *small talk*. ‖ 対話「世間ではもうあの殺人事件の話をしてませんね」「世の中なんてそんなものだよ」"*People* aren't talking about the murder case any more." "That's the way it is [goes]."

せこ 世故 ▶世故に長(た)けた人 a *sophisticated* [*worldly-wise*] person.

せこい **tight-fisted**; **stingy** ▶せこい人, せこいやつ a *tightwad*; a *cheapskate*; a *penny pincher* ‖ バイト料が入ったんだろ? **せこいこと言わずに**パーッとやろう You got paid by your part-time job, right? *Don't be such a tightwad* [*a cheapskate* ／*a penny pincher*]. Let's live it up a little [Let's party]!

セコイア《植物》a **sequoia** /sɪkwɔ́ɪə/.

せこう 施工 **construction** ▶この野球場はわが社が施工したものです This ball park *was constructed* by our company.

セコンド a **handler**, a **second**, a **corner man**.

-せざるをえない -せざるを得ない 1【余儀なく…させられる】**be obliged** [**compelled** ／**forced**] **to** do (➤forced がいちばん意味が強い) ▶彼らは借金を返すために車を売らざるをえなかった They *were forced* [*obliged*] *to* sell their car in order to pay their debts. ‖ 悪天候で登頂は断念せざるをえなかった We *had to* abandon [give up] our attempt to reach the summit due to bad weather.

2【…せずにはいられない】**cannot help** doing, **cannot help but** do (➤後者はインフォーマル) ▶これだけ証拠があるのだから彼はうそをついていると考えざるをえない With all this evidence, we *cannot help* think*ing* that he is lying.

せし セ氏 ⇀せっし.

1**せじ 世事** ▶彼は世事に疎い He knows little of *the* (*real*) *world*.

2**せじ 世辞** ⇀お世辞.

せしめる **wheedle** ＋目 (うまいことを言って); **trick** ＋目 (計略を使って) ▶ 対話「おい, そのカメラどうしたんだい」「おやじからせしめたんだよ」"Hey, how did you get that camera?" "I *wheedled* my Dad *into* getting it for me."

せしゅ 施主 **the organizer of a Buddhist memorial service**(法事を仕切る人); one's **client**(建築の依頼主).

せしゅう 世襲の **hereditary** /hərédəteri/ ▶昔は財産や地位などは世襲だった In the past, it used to be that property and position *were passed down from father to son*.

▶天皇の位は世襲される The title [position] of emperor *is hereditary*.

‖**世襲制度** a hereditary system.

せじょう 施錠 **locking** 一動 **施錠する** **lock** ＋目.

せすじ 背筋 ▶背筋をしゃんと伸ばしなさい *Straighten your back*. ／*Straighten up*. (➤立っている人, 座っている人の両方に使える) ／*Sit up straight*. (➤座っている人の場合).

▶《慣用表現》自然破壊の進む地球のことを考えると**背筋が寒くなる** I *get chills down my back* when I think of the increasing destruction of nature on the earth. ‖ その話を聞いて**背筋が寒くなった** The story *sent shivers* [*the chill*] *down my spine*.

セスナ a **Cessna**.

ぜせい 是正する **correct** ＋目 ▶日米間の貿易不均衡を是正する *correct* the trade imbalance between the U.S. and Japan.

せせこましい 1【場所が】▶せせこましい路地 a *narrow and crowded* alley.

2【考え方が】▶せせこましい考え方 *narrow-minded* views.

ぜぜひひ 是々非々 ▶事に是々非々で対応する deal with matters *impartially* [*fairly and justly*].

せせらぎ ▶耳を澄ましてごらん. 小川の**せせらぎ(の音)**が聞こえるよ Listen carefully and you can hear the *murmur* of the stream.

せせらわらう せせら笑う **scoff** 《at》, **sneer** 《at》 ▶ぼくがひとりで丸太小屋を作ろうとするのを見て彼はせせら笑った He *scoffed* [*sneered*] *at* my attempt to build a log cabin on my own.

せそう 世相 **social conditions**(社会の状況); an **aspect of society**(社会の一面) ▶その小説には当時の**世相**が生き生きと描かれている The novel vividly describes the *social conditions* at that time. ‖ 流行歌は**世相**を反映する Popular songs reflect (various) *aspects of society*.

せぞく 世俗の **worldly** ▶世俗的な事柄 *worldly* matters ‖ 芭蕉は**世俗**(＝世間)の煩わしさから脱出しようとした Basho tried to get away from the problems of *the world*.

せたい 世帯 a **family**(家族); a **household** (一つ家でともに住む人々) ▶このマンションには80**世帯**が住んでいる Eighty *families* live in this apartment complex.

‖**世帯主** the head of a family [household]. ⇀

所帯.

せだい 世代 a **generation** ▶この家には3世代が住んでいる Three *generations* are living in this house. ‖私はあの歌手とは同世代だ That singer and I are *of the same generation*. ‖この歌はきっと若い世代に受けるよ This song will surely appeal to *the young* [*rising*] *generation*. ‖この小説は幾世代にもわたって読み継がれてきた This novel has continued to be read *by* (*several*) *generations*. (➤「何世代もの人々によって」の意) ‖わが家はここで何世代にもわたって農業を営んでいる We've been farming here *for generations*. ‖わが社で経営陣の世代交代があった Our company has had a *generational shift* in management. ‖きみは次の世代を背負って立つ人間の1人だ You are one of the people who are destined to lead *the next generation*. ‖この頃息子に世代のずれを感じている Recently, I have been feeling *a generation gap* between my son and me.

▶第3世代の製品 a *third-generation* product → 次世代.

せたけ 背丈 **height** /haɪt/ ▶うちの娘は年の割に背丈がある Our girl *is tall* for her age. ‖この1年で15センチも背丈が伸びた I *have grown* fifteen centimeters this year.

セダン a **sedan**, 《英》a **saloon**.

せちがらい 世知辛い ▶金が物を言うせちがらい世の中だ What a *hard* [*cold*] world we are living in! Money is everything.

¹せつ 説 a **theory** (学説); a **view** (見方); an **opinion** (意見) ▶日本語の起源についてはいろいろな説(＝諸説)がある There are a variety of *theories* concerning the origin of the Japanese language. ‖恐竜は哺乳動物だったという説がある One *theory* says that dinosaurs were mammals. ‖私は彼の説には賛成できない I can't agree with his *opinion*.

²せつ 節 **1【時】**▶こちらへお出かけの節はぜひお立ち寄りください Please come to see us *if* you are ever in this area. (➤「こっちに来たらぜひ寄ってね」なら If you happen to come this way, be sure to drop in.) ‖お引っ越しの節は当店にお任せください *When* you have to move [*When* moving], leave everything to us. ‖その節はどうも Thank you so much *for the other day*. (→この間).

2【文のくぎり】 a **paragraph** (段落); a **passage** (一節); a **section** (章の下位区分) ▶最初の節を読んでください Will you read the first *paragraph*? ‖この点については第5章第1節を見よ Refer to Chapter V, *section* 1.

3【信念】 one's **principles** ▶いくら圧力をかけられても私は節を曲げたくない I don't want to compromise *my principles* no matter how much I am pressured.

せつえい 設営 **construction** 一動 **設営する** **construct** +目 ▶地震の被災者たちのための臨時の収容所が設営された Temporary shelters *were constructed* for the earthquake victims.

ぜつえん 絶縁 **1【縁を切ること】**▶娘があのろくでなしと絶縁してくれてうれしい I'm glad that my daughter *has broken* (*off*) *relations with* [*is through with*] that good-for-nothing.

‖**絶縁状** a letter terminating a relationship; a Dear John letter (特に女性から男性への; インフォーマルな言い方).

2【電気を通さないこと】 **insulation**

‖**絶縁体** an insulator; a nonconductor (不導体) ‖**絶縁テープ** friction tape, insulating tape.

¹せっかい 切開 (an) **incision** /ɪnsíʒən/ 一動 **切開する** **incise** +目, **cut open** ▶腹部を切開する *incise* the abdomen / *cut* the abdomen *open* ‖医師は私のできものを切開した The surgeon *cut open* my abscess.

‖**切開手術** a surgical operation.

²せっかい 石灰 **lime** ‖**石灰岩** limestone ‖**消石灰** slaked lime ‖**生石灰** quicklime.

せっかく 折角 ▶きみがせっかく貸してくれた本を電車の中に置き忘れてしまった I left the book you (*so*) *kindly* lent me on the train. (➤「親切にも」と考える) ‖せっかく来てくれたのに留守をしていてごめんね I'm sorry that I wasn't home when you (so *kindly*) dropped by. 《参考》日本人は約束のなかった人が自分の留守中に訪ねて来ても,「せっかく来てくれたのに」と言う. これは約束をして訪問するのがしきたりの欧米にはない発想である.

▶せっかくためたお金をみんな盗まれてしまった All the money I *went to so much trouble to* save was stolen. ‖せっかくですが, お断りします *I'm sorry* I have to decline [cannot accept] your (kind) offer. ‖せっかくの(＝楽しみにしていた)遠足も雨で潰れた *Though I had been looking forward to* the outing, it was canceled due to the rain. ‖せっかくのチャンスを逃してしまった I missed a *rare* chance. ‖ 対話「ステーキはいかがですか」「せっかくですが, 肉は食べませんので」"Would you like a steak?" "*No, thank you*. I don't eat meat."

✉ **せっかくのお招きですが, お伺いできそうにありません** I appreciate your *kind* offer, but I don't think I can go. / Thank you very much for your *kind* invitation, but I'm sorry I cannot go.

せっかち ▶小沢君はひどくせっかちだ Ozawa *is* quite *impatient*. ‖あなたは何事にもせっかちね. 少し落ち着きなさいよ You *are* always *in a rush* about everything. Take it easy.

せっかん 折檻 **chastisement** /tʃæstáɪzmənt/ (➤「体罰」の含みがある) 一動 **せっかんする** **chastise** +目 ▶彼はよく子供をせっかんする He often *punishes* his child *severely*. / He often *chastises* his child.

せつがん 接岸する **come alongside a pier**; **berth** (船を停泊させる).

せっき 石器 a **stone implement**

‖**石器時代** the Stone Age ‖**新[旧]石器時代** the Neolithic [Paleolithic] Age.

せっきゃく 接客 ▶森は接客中です Mr. Mori *is meeting* his *customer* [*client*].

‖**接客業** the hospitality industry [business].

せっきょう 説教 **1【小言を言うこと】** a **lecture**; **preaching** (くだくだしい) 一動 **説教する** **lecture** (+目), **preach** (+目) ▶ぼくたちはいたずらをして先生に長々と説教された We *got a* long *lecture* from our teacher for having played a prank. ‖父は私の態度がよくないと説教した My father *lectured* me on my bad attitude.

▶あの人嫌い. 説教ばかりするんだから I don't like him. He always *preaches*.

2【教えを説くこと】 a **sermon**, a **preach** 一動 **説教する** **preach** ▶キング牧師は罪悪について説教した Reverend King *delivered* [*gave* / *preached*] *a sermon* on sin.

‖**説教者** a preacher.

ぜっきょう 絶叫 a scream ; a shriek(悲鳴) ▶そんなに絶叫しなくても聞こえるよ You don't have to *scream*. I can hear you.

せっきょくせい 積極性 →積極的.

せっきょくてき 積極的な assertive (自己主張ができる) ; positive (前向きの, 建設的な) ; active (活動的な) ▶弟は**積極的な**性格だが, 妹は消極的です My brother *is assertive*, but my sister is passive. ‖ 何事にももっと**積極的な**態度をとるようにしなさい Try to take [adopt] a more *positive* attitude toward everything. ‖ 彼女は授業中とても**積極的だ** She *is* very *active* in class.

直訳の落とし穴「もっと積極的になる」

(1)「積極的な態度」は positive attitude というが, positive は行動や性格でなく,「考え方が前向きな」「プラス思考の」を表す. 行動や性格の積極性には assertive (はっきり自己主張する)や outgoing (外交的な)を用いる. したがって,「サリーは引っ込み思案だ. もっと積極的になる必要がある」は Sally is shy and withdrawn. She needs to be more assertive [outgoing]. となる.

(2)「ボランティア活動に積極的に参加する」は参加の度合いをいうのであれば actively take part in volunteer activities で,「進んで」という意味では willingly take part in volunteer activities という. スポーツや販売では積極性は当然期待されることで, 攻撃性に近くなり, play aggressively (積極的にプレーする), an aggressive salesman (積極的な販売員)と aggressive が合う.

▶おじの会社は**積極的に**事業を拡大している My uncle's company is expanding its business *aggressively*. (➤ aggressively は「攻撃的に」だが, ビジネス・スポーツなどではよい意味で使うことが多い) ‖ 黙っていないで**積極的に発言して**ください Don't keep silent. *Speak out* [*Speak your mind*]. (➤ ともに「自分の意見をはっきり言う」の意) ‖ この生徒にもう少し**積極性**があるといいのですが I'd like this student to show a little more *assertiveness* [*assertion*].

せっきん 接近 **1【近づくこと】** approach 一動 **接近する** approach +㊐, come [go] near ▶**接近してくる**車 an *approaching* car ‖ 台風5号が日本に**接近している** Typhoon No.5 *is approaching* Japan. (➤ (×) to Japan としない) ‖ 暴風雨圏が関東地方に次第に**接近してくる** The storm *is coming nearer* [*closer*] *to* the Kanto district. ‖ 一緒にコンサートへ行ってから2人の仲は**急接近した** They *grew much closer to* each other after going to the concert together.
2【差が少ないこと】 ▶H高校とP学園は実力が**接近している** H High School is *almost as strong as* P Gakuen.

せっく 節句 a seasonal festival.

ぜっく 絶句 ▶息子が突然ゲイだとカミングアウトしたとき彼女は**絶句した** When her son suddenly came out that he was gay, she *was struck dumb*. ‖ きみのルーズさには**絶句する**よ Your sloppiness *leaves* me *speechless*.

セックス sex 一動 (…と) **セックスする** make love (to, with), have sex (with) ▶10代の**セックス**について考えよう Let's take up the subject of teenage *sex*. ‖ 彼らは**セックスに興味をもつ**年頃だ They are old enough to *be sexually aware*. ‖ 彼は女と**セックスし**たことがない He has never *had sex with* [*made love to*] a woman.
▶彼女, **セックスアピール**がすごいね She has strong *sex appeal*. / She is sexy.
‖**セックスシンボル** a sex symbol.

危ないカタカナ語 セックス

1 英語の sex の第一義は「性別」で, 書類の sex 欄には, 男性は M(Male), 女性は F(Female)と書く. 最近では, 社会的・文化的な意味での性差を gender という.

2「性行為」は sexual intercourse, sex act, 《インフォーマル》sex で, 日常的な動詞表現では have sex with, make love to [with] などを用いる. 遠回しな表現としては sleep with, sleep together も用いられる.

1**せっけい 設計** **1【建造物の】** (a) design (デザイン) ; a plan (設計図) 一動 **設計する** design +㊐, make a plan for ▶家を**設計する** *make a plan for* a house ‖ 彼女のご主人は乗用車の**設計**をやっている Her husband *designs* passenger cars. ‖ このビルはT氏の**設計**です This building was constructed (based) on the *design* of Mr. T. ‖ この庭園の**設計をした**のはあの人だ He is the one who *laid out* this garden. (➤ lay out は「配置を考えて設計する」).
‖**設計技士** a design engineer ‖ **設計者** a designer ‖ **設計図** a plan, a blueprint.
2【生活の】 ▶卒業後の**生活設計**はどうなっていますか What sort of *plans* do you have *for your life* after graduation?

2**せっけい 雪渓** a snow-covered ravine /rəví:n/.

ぜっけい 絶景 ▶**絶景**だなあ! What *a wonderful* [*magnificent* / *superb*] *view* this is! ‖ 伊豆から見た富士山はまさに**絶景だった** Mt. Fuji as seen from Izu *was beautiful beyond description*. (➤ beyond description は「ことばで表現できないほど」).

せっけっきゅう 赤血球 a red blood cell.

せっけん 石鹸 soap /soup/ (➤「せっけん1個」は a bar [cake] of soap のようにいう) ▶この**せっけん**は泡立ち[落ち]がよい This *soap* lathers [washes] well. ‖ **せっけん**でよく手を洗ったの? Did you wash your hands well *with soap and water*?
‖**せっけん水** soapy water ‖ **化粧せっけん** toilet soap ‖ **粉せっけん** soap powder ‖ **洗濯せっけん** washing [laundry] soap ‖ **薬用せっけん** medicated soap.

1**せつげん 節減** ▶経費を**節減する** *reduce* [*cut*] expenses ‖ 電力**節減**にご協力ください Please cooperate in *cutting down on* electricity.

2**せつげん 雪原** a snow(-covered) field.

ゼッケン a number cloth →背番号.

1**せっこう 石膏** plaster
‖**石こう模型** a plaster cast.

2**せっこう 斥候** a scout.

せつごう 接合 joining(じかの) ; connecting(媒体を使った) 一動 **接合する** join +㊐, connect +㊐ ; set +㊐(骨を) ▶2本のパイプを**接合する** *join* [*connect*] two pipes together ‖ 骨を**接合する** *set* a bone.

1**ぜっこう 絶交する** break off one's friendship (with)(友だち付き合いをやめる) ; break up (with)(友人・男女の関係をやめる) ▶奈美はいちばんの仲よしと**絶交した** Nami *broke up* [*broke off her friendship*] *with* her best friend. ‖ 真紀とは**絶交したよ** *I'm done* [*I'm finished* / *I'm through*] *with* Maki.
▶もうきみとは**絶交だ**(=関係をもたない) I *won't have*

anything more *to do with* you. ‖ 数日して彼から絶交状が来た A few days later, *a letter* came from him *in which he said he was breaking off our friendship*. ‖ 2人は長いこと絶交状態にある There has been a long *rupture in their friendship*. (➤ rupture は「決裂」).

2**ぜっこう 絶好の** perfect (完璧な) ; ideal (理想的な) ▶ハイキングには絶好の天気だ It is *perfect* [*ideal*] weather for going on a hike. ‖ ダイビングに絶好の場所を見つけたよ I've found the *perfect* spot for diving. ‖ ライオンズはダブルプレーで絶好のチャンスを逃した The Lions missed a *great* scoring chance by hitting into a double play.

‖絶好球 a fat pitch, a gopher ball.

ぜっこうちょう 絶好調 ▶巨人の長野は今絶好調だ Chono of the Giants *is* now *in top form* [now *really hot*].

せっこつ 接骨 bone-setting ‖接骨医 a bone setter ‖ 接骨院 an orthopedic clinic.

せっさたくま 切磋琢磨 ▶お互い切磋琢磨して頑張っていきましょう Let's *hone our abilities by competing* with each other.

ぜっさん 絶賛する praise highly ▶多くの批評家が彼のニューアルバムを絶賛した Many critics *praised* his new album *highly*. ／His new album *received rave reviews* from many critics. ‖ 絶賛上映中 Now showing amid enormous popular acclaim. (➤ 広告の決まり文句).

せっし 摂氏の Celsius /sélsiəs/, centigrade 《略 C》 (➤ 現在では前者が正式) ▶今の温度は摂氏5度だ The thermometer reads five (degrees) *Celsius* [*centigrade*] now. ／The temperature is now 5℃.

‖摂氏温度計 a Celsius [centigrade] thermometer /θəʳmɑ́:mətəʳ/.

せつじつ 切実な serious (重大な) ; urgent (緊急な) ; acute (深刻な) ▶太っているのが切実な悩みです Being overweight is a *serious* problem for me. ‖ 我々はここにガードレールをつけてほしいという切実な要求を出しました We have made an *urgent* request for a guardrail to be installed here. ‖ 水不足が切実な問題になってきた The water shortage has become an *acute* problem.

▶心の内を話せる友だちが欲しいと切実に思う I'm *badly* in need of a friend I can confide in. (➤ badly は「ひどく」) ‖ きみはまだ受験を切実に思っていないみたいだね It looks like you are not *taking* the entrance exams *seriously* yet. ／You don't appear to *be taking* [*studying* for] the entrance exams *in earnest* yet.

せっしゃ 接写の close-up /klóʊsʌ̀p/ ▶(カメラで)ボタンの花を接写する *take a close-up* of a peony

‖接写写真 a close-up.

1**せっしゅ 摂取** (an) intake, consumption (養分などの) ; ingestion (食物などの) ; assimilation (知識・文化などの) 一動 摂取する ingest +目, take in ▶砂糖の摂取を減らす reduce one's *intake* [*consumption*] of sugar ‖ 食物を摂取する *ingest* food (➤「食物の摂取」は ingestion of food) ‖ 植物は地中から水と養分を摂取する Plants *take in* water and nourishment from the soil. ‖ 明治以降日本は西洋文化の摂取に努めてきた Since the Meiji era, Japan has tried hard to *take in* [*assimilate*] Western *culture*.

‖(食物の)摂取量 the intake.

2**せっしゅ 接種** (an) inoculation 一動 接種する inoculate +目 ▶その赤ん坊はジフテリアの予防接種を受けた The baby *was inoculated* against diphtheria /dɪfθíəriə/.

3**せっしゅ 節酒** temperance ▶父は病気をしてから節酒・節煙を心がけるようになった Since his illness, my father has become more *temperate in drinking* and smoking [has *cut down on his drinking* and smoking].

せっしゅう 接収する requisition +目 ▶そのホテルは兵舎として一度接収されたことがある The hotel *was* once *requisitioned* as an army barracks.

せつじょ 切除 excision /ɪksíʒən/ 一動 切除する excise /ɪksáɪz/ +目 ; remove +目 (取り去る) ▶腫瘍の切除 the *excision* of a tumor ‖ 医者は私の胃から腫瘍を切除した The surgeon *removed* a tumor from my stomach.

1**せっしょう 折衝** negotiations /nɪgòʊʃiéɪʃənz/ (➤ しばしば複数形) 一動 (…と)折衝する negotiate 《with》 ▶私たちは新しい校則のことで校長と折衝中だ We *are negotiating* [*in negotiations*] *with* the principal about the new school rules. →交渉.

2**せっしょう 殺生** killing ▶動物を無益に殺生してはいけません Don't *kill* animals needlessly.

▶ぼくだけ留守番だなんて殺生だよ I have to stay here all by myself? You're really *mean* [*heartless*]. (➤ 前者は「意地悪な」, 後者は「薄情な」).

3**せっしょう 摂政** a regency (役職・期間) ; a regent (人).

ぜっしょう 絶唱 ▶平井堅の『瞳をとじて』は文字どおりの絶唱だった Hirai Ken's "Hitomi wo Tojite" was *sung superbly*.

せつじょうしゃ 雪上車 a snowmobile.

1**せっしょく 接触** 1 【触れること】 (a) touch ; connection (電流の) 一動 接触する touch +目 ▶電灯がついたり消えたりしているよ. どこか接触が悪いんじゃないのかい The light is going on and off. It looks like there's a bad *connection* somewhere. ‖ 電線が屋根に接触している A power line *is touching* the roof. ‖ 彼の車がトラックと接触事故を起こした His car was in *a small collision* with a truck.

2 【交渉をもつこと】 contact 一動 (…と)接触する contact +目, make contact with ▶自然との接触は子供にとって大切だ *Contact with nature* is important for children. ‖ あの先生とはふだんあまり個人的な接触はありません I don't usually have much *personal contact* with that teacher. ‖ その報道記者はついにロンドンでマフィアのボスと接触することができた The reporter finally *made contact* [*got in touch*] *with* a Mafia boss in London.

2**せっしょく 節食** a diet (食事の量や質を制限すること) ▶あなたは節食したほうがいいですよ You'd better *go on a diet*. ‖ 腹が出てきたので, 母は父に節食させた Mom *put* Dad *on a diet* to trim his spare tire. (➤ spare tire は「(腹の)ぜい肉」の意のインフォーマルな表現).

せつじょく 雪辱 ▶S高に春の試合では負けたが, 夏の大会では雪辱を果たした Although we lost the spring game, we *got even with* S High School in the summer tournament.

‖雪辱戦 a return game [match].

ぜっしょく 絶食 a fast, fasting 一動 絶食する fast, abstain from food (➤ 両者とも, 宗教上断食するというニュアンスがある) ▶イスラム教徒はラマダンの間絶食する Muslims *fast* during Ramadan. ‖ 痩せたい一心でその少女は絶食した The girl wanted to become thin so badly that she *refused to eat anything*.

せっしょくしょうがい 摂食障害 an **eating disorder**.

セッション a **session**.

せっすい 節水 water saving ▶水不足のため**節水**にご協力ください Please cooperate in *saving* [*conserving*] *water* as there is a water shortage.

せっする 接する 1【隣り合う】**border**《on》(境などを) ; **adjoin** +⊞ (土地・家などが) ; **touch** +⊞ (触れる) ▶フランスとスペインは国境を**接している** France and Spain *border each other*. ‖ 父の土地は墓地に**接している** My father's land *adjoins* [*borders*] a cemetery. ‖ 隣の家の軒がうちのベランダに**接している** The eaves of the house next door *touch* the balcony of my house.
▶《数学で》直線 *l* は円 O に**接する** Straight line *l touches* [*comes in contact with*] circle O.
2【人と出会う, 応対する】**meet** +⊞ (会ってことばを交わす, 日時を決めて会う) ; **see** +⊞ (姿を見かける) ; **come into contact**《with》(接触する) ▶彼女はテレビのレポーターとして毎日多くの人と**接する** As a TV reporter, she *meets* many people every day. ‖ 今日, 日本人は外国人と**接する**機会がますます多くなっている Today, Japanese have more opportunities to *see* [*come into contact with*] foreigners. ‖《上司が部下に》お客さんにあんな**接し方**はないだろ? That's not how you should *treat* a customer. ‖ 教師は公平な態度で生徒たちに**接する**べきである Teachers should *treat* their students fairly [*deal* impartially *with* their students]. (➤ deal with は「(人を)扱う」).
3【物事に出会う】▶テレビのおかげで我々は毎日世界の出来事に**接する**ことができる Television *keeps* us *in contact with* the daily events of the world. ‖ 級友が死んだという知らせに**接し**, がく然とした I was terribly shocked *to hear of* my classmate's death.

ぜっする 絶する ▶今回の地震の被害は**想像を絶する**ものであった The damage from the last earthquake was *worse than you can imagine*. ‖ 北極のオーロラは**言語に絶する**美しさだった The aurora borealis was beautiful *beyond words* [*description*].

1**せっせい 節制** ▶パパ, 少しお酒を**節制**してよね Dad, *watch* [*cut down on*] *your drinking*, please. ‖ 日常生活で**節制**を心がけるようにしなさい Try to *be moderate* [*temperate*] in your daily life. / Try to use *self-control* in your daily life.

2**せっせい 摂生** ▶長生きしたいなら**摂生**を心がけるべきだ If you want to live long, you should *be careful about your health* [*take* (*good*) *care of yourself*].
☛ 不摂生 (→見出語)

せつぜい 節税 tax saving ▶私どもの銀行では**節税**のご相談にも応じております Our bank offers *tax consultation*.
‖**節税対策** (a) strategy to minimize taxes.

ぜっせい 絶世 ▶**絶世**の美女 a woman of *matchless* [*peerless* / *unsurpassed*] beauty (➤「並ぶ者のない」の意).

せつせつ 切々 ▶**切々**たる訴え an *earnest* [a *passionate*] appeal ‖ たけしは友恵に**切々と**苦境を訴えた Takeshi *earnestly* appealed to Tomoe to understand his difficulties.

せっせと ▶**せっせと**働く work *hard* ‖ 海外旅行に行くために目下**せっせと**金をためています I'm *working hard to save money* to travel abroad.

1**せっせん 接戦** a **close game** [**match**] (➤ close の発音は /kloʊs/), 《インフォーマル》a **squeaker** ; a **seesaw game** (抜きつ抜かれつの) ▶試合は大変な**接戦**だった It was *a* very *close game*. / The game was very *close*. / It was *a* (real) *cliff-hanger*. (➤「はらはらするようなスリルに富んだ試合」の意) ‖ **接戦**の末, 引き分けた After *a seesaw game*, it ended in a draw.

2**せっせん 接線**《数学》a **tangent** (**line**).

せっそう 節操 principle ; **morals** (品行) ; **integrity** /ɪntégrəṭi/ (性格が高潔なこと) ▶2人の女を同時に追い回すとは! 彼も**節操**がないね Chasing two women at the same time! He certainly lacks *morals*.
☛ 無節操 (→見出語)

せつぞう 雪像 a **snow statue**.

せつぞく 接続 (a) **connection** 一動 (…に)**接続する connect**《with, to》▶列車の**接続**が悪く, 小郡で2時間も待った We had a bad *connection* and waited for two hours at Ogori. ‖ 秋田まで新幹線で行きますが, 男鹿までうまく**接続する列車**はありますか We are going to Akita by Shinkansen. Is there *a good connection* from there to Oga? ‖ この列車は岡山で「しおかぜ3号」松山行きと**接続しております** At Okayama this train *connects with* the "Shiokaze No. 3" bound for Matsuyama. ‖ プラグが電源に**接続されていません** The plug *is* not *in the socket*. / *The power is* not *connected*. (➤「プラグが外れてるよ」なら It isn't plugged in.)
‖**接続駅** a junction ‖ **接続業者** an Internet service provider ‖《文法》**接続詞** a conjunction ‖ **接続便** (飛行機の) a connecting flight ‖ **接続料金** a (dial-up) connection fee, an access charge ‖ **常時接続** an always-on connection.

せっそくどうぶつ 節足動物《動物学》an **arthropod**.

せったい 接待 entertainment (もてなし) ; a **reception** (応対) 一動 **接待する receive** +⊞, **have** +⊞ (客を迎える) ; **entertain** +⊞ (もてなす) ▶わが家ではあす20人の客を**接待する**ことになっている We are going to *have* [*receive*] twenty guests at home tomorrow. ‖ きのうアメリカ人夫妻を日本料理店で**接待した** I *entertained* an American couple at a Japanese restaurant yesterday. ‖ 新年会では社長が**接待役** (=主人役)を務めます Our president will *do the honors* at the New Year's party.
‖**接待係** a receptionist ‖ **接待費** entertainment expenses.

ぜったい 絶対 1【無条件, 完全】一形 **絶対の absolute** ; **complete** (完全な) ▶私は**絶対に**自分の娘を信じている I trust my daughter *absolutely*. / I have *absolute* trust in my daughter. ‖ ヒトラーは**絶対的な**権力を持っていた Hitler had *absolute* power. ‖ 医者は患者に**絶対安静**を命じた The doctor told the patient that he should have *complete bed rest*.
▶アラーはイスラム教の**唯一絶対**の神である Allah is *the one and only* god of Islam. ‖ うちでは父のことばは**絶対だ** My father's word *is law* in our house. ‖ この世の中に**絶対**はない There are no *absolutes* in this world.
‖**絶対音感** perfect [absolute] pitch ‖ **絶対温度** absolute temperature ‖ **絶対君主制** absolute monarchy ‖ **絶対多数** an absolute majority ‖ **絶対零度** absolute zero.
2【どうしても】**definitely** ; **by all means** (是が非でも) ▶**絶対に**バリ島には行ってみるべきだ You should *defi-*

nitely visit Bali. ／You ought to visit Bali *by all means*. ‖あすは絶対に来てよ Tomorrow you *must* be here. ‖この曲を聴いてごらんよ. 絶対に気に入るから You must listen to this piece. You'll love it *for sure*.
▶私はギンナンは絶対に食べない I *never* ever eat gingko nuts. ‖彼は絶対にうそはつかない He *is the last person to* tell a lie. ／He *would never* lie. ‖パスポートだけは絶対なくさないでね *Be sure not* to lose your passport. ‖私はその計画には絶対反対です I'm *definitely* against the plan. ／There is *no way* I can accept this plan. ‖その仕事は絶対きょう中に終わらせてくれ I'd like you to get that job done today, *no matter what*.
▶ 対話「約束は守るよ」「絶対だな？」「うん, 絶対」"I'll keep my promise." "Are you *positive?*" "*Positive*." ‖ 対話「お父さん, オートバイ買ってよ」「絶対にだめだ」"Dad, please buy me a motorcycle." "*No way!*"

ぜつだい 絶大な enormous, tremendous (➤後者のほうがくだけていて大げさな語) ▶絶大な権力 *enormous* power ‖スミス教授は女子学生に絶大な人気がある Professor Smith is *tremendously* popular among the girl students. ‖絶大なご支援ありがとうございました Thank you very much for your *most generous* support. (➤「惜しみない支援」の意).

ぜったいぜつめい 絶体絶命 ▶ばく大な借金を抱えて彼は絶体絶命のピンチだった His big debt(s) drove him *up against the wall*. (➤「借金が彼を壁際に追い詰めた」の意) ‖さあ, ピッチャーは絶体絶命のピンチです Now the pitcher is *in a terrible* [*real*] *jam*.

せつだん 切断する cut (off), sever +⊞; amputate +⊞ (手術で) ▶電線をペンチで切断する *cut* (*off*) a wire with pliers ‖悪天候のため島と本土をつなぐすべての通信網が2週間にわたって切断された All communication links between the island and the mainland *were severed* for two weeks due to bad weather. ‖外科医は少年の左足を膝の上から切断した The surgeon *amputated* the boy's left leg above the knee.

1**せっち 設置する** install +⊞ (設備を); set up (機関などを); provide《with》(備える) ▶コピー機を設置する *install* a photocopier ‖公園にごみ箱を設置する *place* trash cans in a park ‖このマンションでは各部屋に煙感知器が設置してある Smoke sensors *are installed* in every room of this apartment house. ‖教育委員会は学校でのいじめ問題に対処するため特別委員会を設置した The board of education *set up* a special committee to deal with the problem of bullying in the schools.

2**せっち 接地** 《米》grounding, 《英》earthing (避雷器などの) 一動 **接地する** 《米》ground +⊞, 《英》earth +⊞; touch the ground (地面に接する) ▶このアンテナは接地する必要があります This antenna needs to *be grounded* [*to be earthed*]. ‖このライトバンは接地性がよい[悪い] This minivan *holds* [*doesn't hold*] *the road well*. (➤悪路でのバウンドについていう).

せっちゃくざい 接着剤 (a) glue /gluː/, (an) adhesive /ədhíːsɪv/ ▶こけしの首を接着剤で胴につける *glue* the head of a *kokeshi* doll to the trunk.
‖瞬間接着剤 quick-drying glue [bond].

せっちゅう 折衷 a compromise /kάːmprəmaɪz/ (妥協) ▶最終プランは先生と生徒の意見を折衷してできた The final plan was *a compromise* between the teachers' ideas and those of the students. ‖現代の日本では和洋折衷の生活をする人がほとんどだ In present-day Japan almost all Japanese have *lifestyles that combine both Japanese and Western elements*.
‖折衷案 a compromise.

ぜっちょう 絶頂 the peak, the zenith /zíːnɪθ ‖ zén-/ ▶彼女は先月結婚して今幸福の絶頂にある Having gotten married last month, she is now enjoying *the happiest time of her life*. ‖その歌手は今人気絶頂だ The singer is now *at the height* [*the peak* ／*the zenith*] *of* his popularity.

せっつく →せがむ.

せってい 設定 a setting 一動 **設定する** set +⊞ ▶新たな[野心的な]目標を設定する *set* a new [an ambitious] goal ‖エアコンの温度を26度に設定する *set* the temperature of the air conditioner at 26 (degrees) centigrade ‖はがきに印刷するにはプリンターの設定を変える必要がある If you want to print a postcard, you need to alter *the settings* on the printer.
▶学校で火災が起こったという設定で避難訓練が行われた We had a fire drill at school, *simulating the situation* of our school being on fire.
‖初期設定 an initial setting; the default (setting) (ユーザーが変更する前の値).

セッティング a setting ▶会議をセッティングする *arrange* [*set up*] a meeting.

せってん 接点 a point of contact ▶イスタンブールは東西文明の接点とも言える Istanbul can be said to be *a point of contact* between Eastern and Western civilizations.

せつでん 節電 saving electricity, power saving ▶首相は国民に節電を呼びかけた The Prime Minister appealed to the whole nation to *save* (*on*) electricity.

セット **1【一そろい】** a set ▶ベストとスカートでセットになっています The vest and skirt *come in* [*as*] *a set*. ‖彼女の結婚祝いに6客のコーヒー(カップ)セットを送った I sent her a 12-piece *coffee cup and saucer set* as a wedding gift. (➤カップと受け皿が6個ずつなので合計 a 12-piece set となる) ‖彼女が腹筋運動をするときは, 10回を3セットする When she does sit-ups, she does 3 *sets* of 10 reps.

> **危ないカタカナ語 ✸ セット**
> **1**「そろいの物」の意味では set は日本語の「セット」よりも意味が狭く, a coffee set (コーヒーセット), a set of golf clubs (ゴルフクラブ1セット) など一組み[一式]を成すものに使用が限られる. 家具の一そろいの場合は suite /swiːt/ を用いて a bedroom suite (寝室家具セット), a three-piece living-room suite (応接3点セット) のように言うことが多い.
> **2** 日本的な広い意味で, 例えば喫茶店などでの「ケーキセット」は cake with coffee [tea] のように言う必要がある. また,「セット旅行」は package tour である.

2【テニスなどの】 a set ▶第1セットを6対4で勝つ win the first *set* 6-4 ‖さあ, 3回目のセットポイントだ This is the third *set point*.

3【作動するようにする】 一動 **セットする** set +⊞ ▶オーブンのタイマーを30分にセットしてちょうだい *Set* the oven timer for 30 minutes. ‖5時に鳴るように目覚ましをセットした I *set* the alarm clock to ring [go off] at 5 o'clock.

4【髪を整える】 ▶《美容院で》髪をセットしてください

I'd like to *have* my hair *set*. (➤ have ... set で「…をセットしてもらう」) ‖ 彼女の髪はセットしやすい Her hair *sets easily*.

‖ セットポジション《野球》a set position ‖ セットローション setting lotion.

せつど 節度 moderation (度を過ごさないこと) ; restraint (慎み) **一形 節度ある** moderate /mɑ́:dərət/ ▶節度のある行動をとる act with *moderation* [*restraint*] ‖ 学生は節度のある服装をしなければならない Students should dress *moderately*.

せっとう 窃盗 (a) theft ▶彼は窃盗のかどで起訴された He was *charged* with *theft* [with committing *theft*].

‖ 窃盗犯 a thief.

せっとうじ 接頭辞《文法》a prefix.

せっとく 説得 persuasion ; dissuasion (説得して思いとどまらせること) **一動 説得する** persuade /pərswéɪd/ +目, dissuade +目

【文型】
人(A)を説得して…させる
persuade A to do
talk A into doing
人(A)を説得して…するのをやめさせる
talk A out of doing
人(A)を説得して B をやめさせる
dissuade A from B
➤ B は名詞・動名詞

《解説》(1) 日本語の「説得する」は，説得によって相手がどんな行動をとったかまでは問題にしないが，英語の persuade to do は「説得して…させる」という結果まで表す．
(2) 軽い意味で「…するよう［しないよう］言い聞かせる」という場合は talk into [out of] を用いる．

▶私は彼を説得して警察に自首させた I *persuaded* him *to* give himself up [turn himself in] to the police. (➤「自首するよう説得してみた」なら I tried to persuade ... となる) ‖ ぼくは彼女を説得してわがテニス部に入部させた I *talked* her *into* join*ing* our tennis club. ‖ 私は彼氏と別れるのを思いとどまるよう彼女を説得した I *talked* her *out of* break*ing* up with her boyfriend. ‖ メキシコ留学を思いとどまるよう何度も説得したが彼の決心は変わらなかった I tried repeatedly to *dissuade* him *from* studying in Mexico, but I could not change his decision. ‖ 私は彼を説得して辞職を思いとどまらせた I *dissuaded* him *from* resign*ing*.

▶私が説得すれば，パパはママにあの指輪買ってくれるかもしれないわよ If I *work on* Dad, he may buy you that ring, Mom. (➤ work on は「…に働きかける」の意) ‖ あなたの文章は説得力に欠ける Your writing *is not persuasive* [*convincing*].

せつない 切ない ▶幼い息子との切ない別れ a *painful* parting with one's little son ‖ あなたに半年も会えないなんて切ないよ. I won't be able to see you for half a year. I'*ll really miss you*! ‖ 彼は芳江に切ない思いを打ち明けた He told Yoshie of his *longing* for her. ‖ 別れとはこんなにも甘く切ないものなのね Parting is such *sweet sorrow*. (➤『ロミオとジュリエット』の中のせりふ).

せつなる 切なる ardent (燃えるような) ; earnest (真剣な，本気の) ; eager, keen (非常に熱心な；後者はややインフォーマル) ▶彼女は歌手になりたいという切なる願い[切なる希望]を持っている She has an *ardent desire* [*fervent hope*] to become a singer.

せつに 切に eagerly (熱心に) ; earnestly (ひたむきに) ; sincerely (心から) ▶私たちは世界平和を切に願っています We *earnestly* hope for world peace.

せっぱく 切迫した pressing (直ちに着手する必要のある) ; urgent (すべてに優先させるべき緊急性を持った) ▶事態は一刻の猶予もならないほど切迫していた The situation was so *urgent* [Matters were so *pressing*] we had no time to lose. ‖ これは早期解決を要する切迫した問題だ This is an *urgent* problem that we must solve quickly.

せっぱつまる 切羽詰まる be in a pinch, be in a desperate situation ▶彼は金を使い果たし，せっぱ詰まって母親に電話した *In a pinch* after spending all his money, he called up his mother. ‖ 私はせっぱ詰まって(＝困り果てて)いた I was *in deep trouble*. ／I was *in a fix*.

せっぱん 折半 ▶2人で費用を折半する *split* the cost *between the two* ‖ 私は彼ともうけを折半した He and I *halved* [*split*] the profits. (➤ halve の発音は /hæv ‖ hɑ:v/) ／I *went fifty-fifty on* the profits with him.

ぜっぱん 絶版 ▶この本は今絶版になっております This book is now *out of print*.

せつび 設備 equipment (装置・備品など；不可算名詞なので，数えるときは a piece of ..., two pieces of ... とする) ; facilities (施設) ; conveniences (便利な設備) ▶設備のよいホテル a *well-equipped* hotel ‖ 産業廃棄物処理のための設備 treatment *facilities* for industrial waste ‖ この病院には新しい設備がいろいろ備わっている This hospital has a lot of new *equipment*. ‖ 我々の寮には冷暖房の設備がない Our dormitory has no *air conditioning*. (➤「設備」は考えなくてよい) ‖ このマンションはあらゆる最新設備が整っている This condominium is equipped [provided] with all *latest conveniences* [*amenities*].

‖ 設備投資 investment in (plant and) equipment (➤ 通常は business investment に含める).

せつびじ 接尾辞《文法》a suffix.

ぜっぴつ 絶筆 ▶8月30日発売の週刊誌のエッセーが彼の絶筆となった The essay in a weekly magazine published on August 30 was *the last writing he did* [*the last thing he wrote*] *before his death*.

ぜっぴん 絶品 ▶あの店のアユは絶品だよ *Ayu* served at that restaurant is *exquisite* [*incomparable*]. (➤ exquisite /ɪkskwízɪt/ は「実にすばらしい」，incomparable /ɪnkɑ́:mpərəbəl/ は「比類のない」の意).

せっぷく 切腹 seppuku, hara-kiri (➤ どちらも英語化している).

せつぶん 節分 *Setsubun*

日本紹介 ✉ **節分は(旧暦で)春の始まる日である立春の前日で2月3日頃です．日本の家庭ではこの日の夕方，悪鬼を払うため「豆まき」をします．これは煎った大豆を「鬼は外，福は内」と叫びながら，投げるものです** *Setsubun* is the day before *risshun*, the start of spring (according to the lunar calendar), which usually falls on February third or thereabouts. In the evening of this day, Japanese do '*mame-maki* (bean throwing)' at their homes to drive away evil spirits. People throw roasted beans, shouting, "Out with the devil! In with luck!"

ぜっぺき 絶壁 a cliff (主に海岸の) ; a precipice /présəpɪs/ (岩山の) ▶絶壁から見下ろす look down from *a cliff* ／look over the edge of *a cliff* ‖ 荒船

山は片側が絶壁になっている Mt. Arafune has *a precipice* on one side.

せっぺん 雪片 a **snowflake.**

せつぼう 切望する long《for, to do》▶彼女は幸福な結婚を切望した She *longed for* a happy marriage. ‖ 彼はコロンビア大学に入ることを切望していた He *longed* [*was eager*] *to* go to Columbia University.

せ

ぜつぼう 絶望 despair 一動（…に）**絶望する despair**《of》▶彼らはその国の政治には全く絶望している They'*re* completely *in despair* over (the state of) politics in their country. ‖ 彼は絶望の末［あまり］自殺した *In despair* he committed suicide. ‖ 王子は幽閉の身から解放されることを絶望視していた The prince *had despaired of* being freed from confinement.

▶人生に絶望して死を選ぶ若者がいることは痛ましい It is tragic that there are young people who *give up* on life and choose death.

▶ああ, もう絶望だ *All hope is gone*！‖ ぼくらのチームの優勝は絶望的だ We have *no hope* of victory. ‖ 10対 1 では逆転勝ちなど絶望的だ When the score is 10 to 1, we *don't stand a chance* of pulling off a come-from-behind victory.

ぜつみょう 絶妙な marvelous（見事な）; **perfect**（完璧な）▶彼は鉄棒で絶妙な演技を見せた He gave a *marvelous* performance on the horizontal bars. ‖ イチローは一塁線に絶妙のバントをした Ichiro pushed a *perfect* bunt down the first base line.

ぜつむ 絶無 ▶勝てる可能性は絶無だと思った We thought there was *no* chance *whatsoever* of winning.

せつめい 説明 (an) **explanation** ; a **version**（特定の個人［側］からの説明で, それに対立する説明があることを含みとするもの）**一動 説明する explain** +目 ; **illustrate** /íləstreɪt/ +目（図や表を使って）▶きみの説明は簡潔でわかりやすかったよ Your *explanation* was brief and easy to understand. (➤「説明不足だった」なら was insufficient) ‖ 警察はその事件について詳しく説明した The police *gave a detailed explanation* of the case.

> **【文型】**
> **人(A)に B を説明する**
> **explain B to A**
> ➤ B に that や wh- の文がくるときは A のあとにする

▶この句の意味を説明してください Could you please *explain* this phrase？／Please *explain to* me what this phrase means. ‖ 2 語の違いを説明していただけますか Could you *explain* the difference between the two words？‖ 何があったのか説明する必要があります You need to *explain* (*to* me) what happened.

▶彼はオオムラサキの成長を絵とグラフで説明した He *illustrated* the growth of a Sasaki's purple emperor butterfly with pictures and graphs. ‖ その事故についての 2 つの矛盾する説明がある There are two contradictory *versions* of the accident. ‖ きょうは就職説明会に行ってきた Today I went to *a job fair* [*festival*].

▶このデジカメの説明書はないの？ Do you have *an instruction manual* [*an operating manual*] for this digital camera？(➤ プラモデルなどの作り方の説明書は directions という).

ぜつめつ 絶滅 extinction 一動 絶滅する become extinct ▶スマトラトラは絶滅寸前だ Sumatran tigers are on the verge [brink] of *extinction*. (➤「絶滅危惧種」を endangered species という) ‖ ニホンオオカミは1905年に絶滅した The Japanese wolf *became extinct* [*died out*] in 1905. ‖ ネズミを絶滅させることは不可能だ It's impossible to *completely get rid of* [*eradicate*] rats. (➤ get rid of, eradicate はそれぞれ「駆除する」「根絶する」の意).

せつもん 設問 a **question** ▶以下の設問に答えなさい Answer the following *questions*.

せつやく 節約 economy 一動（…を）**節約する economize**《on》（経済的に使う）; **save** +目（無駄を省く）; **cut down**《on》（切り詰める）▶燃料を節約する *economize on* fuel ‖ 商売が振るわないので経費を節約するよう努めている Business is bad, so we are trying to *cut expenses* [*cut down on expenses*]. ‖ バスで行けば時間と労力の節約になる Taking a bus will *save* time and labor. ‖ 外で飲むコーヒーを減らすと月に2000円近い節約になる If I go out for coffee less often, it will *save* me nearly two thousand yen a month.

▶光熱費がかさんでいるので, 電気と水道を節約してください Our utility bills are getting too high, so please *go easy on* the electricity and water. (➤ go easy on は「…を加減して使う」の意のインフォーマルな言い方).

せつり 摂理 Providence ▶生あるものは滅びるは自然の摂理だ It is the natural *course of things* that all living things must perish.

せつりつ 設立する establish +目, **found** +目（➤後者は関係者が資金を出したというニュアンスが強い）▶本校は70年前に設立されました Our school *was established* [*was founded*] seventy years ago.

せつれつ 拙劣 ▶拙劣な文章 *clumsy* [bad] writing.

せつわ 説話 a **narrative**（語り聞かせの）; a **tale**（架空の物語）.

せとぎわ 瀬戸際 ▶彼は重大なミスをして首になるかどうかの瀬戸際に立たされている He made a terrible mistake and is *on the verge of* being fired.

‖瀬戸際外交 brinkmanship diplomacy ‖ **瀬戸際政策** brinkmanship.

せとないかい 瀬戸内海 the (Seto) Inland Sea.

せともの 瀬戸物 china（➤集合的に）; **porcelain** /pɔ́:ˈsəlɪn/（磁器）; **pottery**（陶器）

‖瀬戸物屋 a china shop.

せなか 背中 the back →背 ▶背中が痛い I have a *back*ache. ／My *back* hurts. ‖ 背中をしゃんと伸ばしなさい Straighten your *back*. ‖ 誰かが背中をぽんとたたいた Someone tapped me on *the back*.

▶彼の家は映画館と背中合わせになっている His house *backs onto* a movie theater. ‖ 子供は親の背中を見て育つという People say children grow up watching *their parents' backs* [watching *what their parents are doing from behind*].

ぜに 銭 money ▶私のおじは銭もうけしか頭にない My uncle never thinks of anything except *making money*.

ぜにん 是認 (formal) approval ▶わが党は到底その改革案を是認するわけにはいかない Our party can hardly *give its approval to* the reform measure.

ゼネコン a **general contractor**（➤日本の「大手ゼネコン」は a major [big] construction company とするほうが明確）.

ゼネスト a **general strike** ▶ 48時間のゼネストを実施する go on a 48-hour *general strike*.

せのび 背伸び 1【背を伸ばすこと】▶子供たちはパレードを見ようと**背伸びした** The children *stood on tiptoe(s)* [*craned their necks*] in order to see the parade. (➤ stand on tiptoe(s) は「つま先で立つ」, crane one's neck は「首を伸ばす」) ‖ 猫は気持ちよさそうに**背伸びした** The cat *stretched* comfortably.
2【実力以上のことをすること】▶おまえはいつも**背伸び**し過ぎるんだ You are always *trying to do more than you are able to do*. ‖ 俺は**背伸び**はしないことにしてるんだ I try not to *set my sights too high*. (➤「狙いを高すぎるところに置く」の意).

せばまる 狭まる **narrow, become** [**get**] **narrow** ▶川は町に入る所で**狭まっている** The river *narrows* [*gets narrow*] just at the outskirts of town. ‖ 不況のため就職の機会が**狭まっている** Due to the recession, job opportunities are *becoming limited*.

せばんごう 背番号 a **uniform number**; a (**player's**) **number** (ゼッケン) ▶松坂投手の**背番号**は18だ Matsuzaka wears *uniform number* 18. ‖ あの**背番号** 8 の走者は誰ですか? Who is that *number* 8 runner? / Who is that runner wearing *number* 8?

ぜひ 是非 1【どうしても】▶お誕生会には**ぜひ**来てね I'd *really* like you to come to my birthday party. / *I'd love* to have you at my birthday party.
▶来シーズンは**ぜひ**日本ハムに優勝してもらいたい I'd *very much* like the Fighters to capture the pennant next season. ‖ 彼に**ぜひ**会いたい *I'm dying to* see him. ‖ ハワイへ行ったら**ぜひ**真珠湾を見にいってね *Don't forget to* (go to) see Pearl Harbor if you go to Hawaii.
▶原稿は**ぜひとも** 5 月末には頂きたいのですが Please send us your manuscript by the end of May *no matter what* [*at any cost*]. (➤ at any cost を使うと強い要求になる).
✉ **日本に来られたらぜひわが家にお泊まりください** When you come to Japan, you *must* stay at my house. ➤ この must は「ぜひ…してほしい」の意で, 人を招待するときなどによく用いる. must を強く発音する.
✉ **文通だけでなくぜひ一度お会いしたいですね** I *do* hope we will not only write to each other, but also that we can meet sometime. ➤ do は強調を表す.
2【善悪】▶彼らは物事の**是非**がわかっていない They can't tell *right* from *wrong*. ‖ 我々は憲法改正の**是非**について討論した We discussed *whether* (*or not*) the Constitution should be revised.

セピア **sepia** /síːpiə/.

ぜひとも 是非とも →**是非**.

せひょう 世評 (a) **reputation** (評判); (a) **rumor** (うわさ) ▶**世評**の高い映画 a *highly acclaimed* movie (➤ acclaim は「高く評価する」).

せびょうし 背表紙 **the spine** (**of a book**).

せびる **bum**《off》; **pester**《for》(うるさく) ▶彼は友人に電車賃を**せびった** He *bummed* the train fare off his friend. ‖ 彼はいつも友人にお金を**せびっている** He is always *pestering* his friends *for* money.

せびれ 背鰭《解剖学》a **dorsal fin** ▶サメの**背びれ** the *dorsal fin* of a shark.

せびろ 背広 a (**business**) **suit**,《英また》a **lounge suit** (上下一そろい); a **jacket**, a **suit coat** (上着)《参考》business suit が「背広」に最も近い語だが, 日本語の「背広」は単に jacket, suit coat だけを指すことも多い. なお, suit は「上下そろいの服」の意で, 女性のスーツも指す.

せぼね 背骨 **the backbone, the spine**.

せまい 狭い **narrow** (幅が); **small** (面積が) ▶**狭い**部屋 a *small* room (➤ narrow room とすると「細長い部屋」の意味になる) ‖ 何て**狭い**階段なんだろう What *narrow* stairs! ‖ この通りは**狭い**からトラックは通れない This road is too *narrow* for trucks to pass.
▶わが家には**狭い**ながらに庭がある We have a yard though it's very *small*. ‖ この部屋は10人が入るには**狭すぎる** This room is *too small* for ten people. ‖ 東京は土地が**狭い**割に人口が多い Tokyo has a large population in its *limited* area.
▶《慣用表現》こんな所で会うなんて, **世の中狭いねえ**! Imagine meeting you here. *What a small world!*
▶心の**狭い**人間になるな Don't be *narrow-minded*. ‖ 彼は視野が**狭く**, したがって話題の範囲も**狭い** He has *a narrow outlook*, so he can only talk about a *limited* range of topics.

せまきもん 狭き門 a **narrow gate**; **the strait gate** (➤聖書マタイ伝から; 比喩的にも用いる) ▶外交官試験は数十人に 1 人の**狭き門**だ Only one out of dozens of applicants can pass *the narrow gate* of the Diplomatic Service Examination.
▶**狭き門より入れ** Enter by the narrow gate. (➤ 聖書のことば).

せまくるしい 狭苦しい **cramped**,《インフォーマル》**pok(e)y** ▶**狭苦しい**アパート a *pok(e)y* apartment ‖ こんな**狭苦しい**部屋からは一刻も早く脱出したいよ I want to move out of this *cramped* apartment as soon as possible.

せまる 迫る 1【近接している】▶私の家の裏には崖が**迫っている** *There is* a cliff *right behind* my house. ‖ この部屋からは富士山がすぐ近くに**迫って見える** From this room Mt. Fuji appears *very near*. ‖ 問題の核心に**迫る**質問が次々に出された Questions that got *to the core* [*heart*] of the issue were raised one after another.
2【時間的・空間的に近づく】▶修学旅行が**間近に迫っている** Our school excursion *is approaching* [*is around the corner* / *is near at hand*]. ‖ 入試が 1 週間後に**迫っている** The entrance examination *is only a week away* [*off*]. ‖ その犬は死期が**迫っている**ことを知っているようだった The dog seemed to know that death was *imminent*. (➤ imminent は「差し迫って」の意の堅い語)
▶その村に着いたときにはすでに夕闇が**迫っていた** When we got to the village, the evening dusk *was coming on* [*falling*]. ‖ 噴火で流れ出た溶岩が町に**迫って来た** Lava from the eruption *bore down on* the town. (➤ bear down on は「(危険なものなどが)…に急接近する」).
3【追い詰める】▶必要に**迫られて**彼はアルバイトで子供を教えている Necessity *drove* him *to* get a part-time job teaching children.
4【強く求める】**press**《to do》; **pressure**《to do》(圧力をかける); **make advances**《on, to》(言い寄る) ▶若い女性に**迫る** *make advances on* [*come on to*] a young woman ‖ 達彦は私に結婚を**迫った** Tatsuhiko *pressed* me *to* marry him. ‖ 彼らは私に即答を**迫った** They *pressured* me *for* a prompt answer.

せみ 蝉 a **cicada** /sɪkéɪdə ‖ sɪkáːdə/,《米また》a **locust**《参考》セミはイギリスでは南部で極めてまれに見られる程度であるが, アメリカではしばしば大発生する. しかし, 日

せ

本におけるような夏の盛りと重なるイメージはない. ▶セミが鳴いている The *cicadas* are chirping.

セミコロン a **semicolon**(➤ 記号は ;).

セミナー a **seminar**. →ゼミ(ナール).

ゼミ(ナール) a **seminar** /sémɪnɑːʳ/ ▶大学のゼミで『ユリシーズ』を読む read "Ulysses" in a university *seminar* ‖ 午後4時から経営学のゼミがある *A seminar* is to be given on business administration at 4 p.m.

危ないカタカナ語✸ ゼミ(ナール)

1「ゼミ(ナール)」はドイツ語の *Seminar* からきている. 英語では seminar といい, 大学での講習だけでなく, 広い意味での研修や研究会などをも指す.

2 予備校を意味する「〜ゼミ(ナール)」は日本的な用法. 〜 Preparatory School と訳せなくはないが, preparatory school は日本の予備校とは実態が異なる. cram school, 《英また》 crammer を使えば実態を伝えることができる.

セミプロ a **semiprofessional**, 《インフォーマル》 a **semipro**.

1**せめ 責め** **blame**(失敗などの責任) ; **responsibility**(責任) ▶責めは私が負います The *blame* [*responsibility*] is mine. / I accept (total) *responsibility* [*blame*] for this.

2**せめ 攻め** **offense, the offensive** ▶攻めに転じる go on [switch to] *the offensive*.

せめあぐむ 攻めあぐむ ▶清水東は格下のチームを相手に攻めあぐんだ Shimizu-higashi *couldn't carry out an effective offensive* against a team lower in the standings.

せめこむ 攻め込む ▶わが軍は敵陣に攻め込んだ Our troops *carried the attack* all the way to the enemy camp.
▶《ラグビーで》同志社はパントを上げて明治陣内深く攻め込んだ Doshisha punted and *bore down* deep *into* Meiji's territory.

セメスター a **semester**(2学期制の1学期) ▶セメスター制を採用する adopt a *semester system*.

せめたてる 責め立てる ▶警察は被疑者を責め立てて自白を引き出そうとした Trying to extract a confession, the police *tortured* the suspect.
▶きのうは借金取りにさんざん責め立てられた(=圧力をかけられた) My creditors *put the squeeze on* me yesterday.

せめて **at least**(少なくとも) ▶締め切りまでせめてもう1日欲しいところだ If only I had *at least* one more day before the deadline!
▶せめてわびくらい言えよ You might *at least* apologize. ‖ もうお帰りですか? せめてお茶くらい飲んでいってください Oh, so soon? *At least* have a cup of tea before you leave. ‖ このところ忙しくしているので, せめて日曜日くらいは朝寝坊がしたい Since I have been extremely busy these days, I *at least* want to sleep in on Sundays.
▶家は全焼したが, 命が助かったのがせめてもの救いだ The house was burned to the ground. *The only saving grace* was that we didn't die. (➤ saving grace は「(欠点を補う)取り柄」).

1**せめる 責める** **blame** +㊐ (…のせいにする, …に責任があるとする) ; **accuse** /əkjúːz/ +㊐ (一方的に非難する) ; **reproach** +㊐ (とがめる ; 堅い語) ; **scold** +㊐ (叱る) ; **nag** +㊐ (がみがみ小言を言う) ; **press** +㊐ (迫る) ; **pester** +㊐ (しつこく迫る)

【文型】
A のことで人(B)を責める
blame B **for** A
accuse B **of** A

《解説》 **accuse** は重大な過ちや倫理的に許されないことなどをしたと一方的に主張すること. それが事実かどうかは証明されるまではわからない.

▶彼は事故は私のせいだと言って責めた He *blamed* me *for* the accident. / He *blamed* the accident *on* me. ‖ 彼は私が彼を裏切ったと言って責めた He *accused* me *of* having betrayed him.
▶私を責めないでよ Don't *blame* [*nag* (*at*)] me. ‖ 選手たちを責めないでくれ, 負けたのは私の采配ミスだ *Don't blame* [*criticize*] the players. It's due to my misjudgments that we lost the game. (➤ blame は単に責任の所在をいう場合, criticize は敗戦の要因をいくつも挙げて選手たちを非難する場合) ‖ 自分ばかり責めることはない. みんなの責任なんだから *Don't just blame yourself*. Everyone is [All of us are] to blame.
▶父親はパソコンを壊したと言って息子を責めた The father *scolded* his son *for* breaking his personal computer. ‖ 彼女は息子が怠けていることをよく責める She often *nags* [*criticizes*] her son about his laziness. ‖ 彼は借金を返せと責められた He *was pressed* to repay the loan.

2**せめる 攻める** **attack**(+㊐), **make an attack** (攻撃する) ▶相手は側面から攻めてきた The opponent(s) *made a* flank *attack*. ‖ 彼らは城を攻め落とした They *attacked* [*made an attack on*] the castle *and overcame* the enemy.

セメント **cement** /səmént/ ▶このセメントはまだ固まっていない This *cement* hasn't set yet.

ゼラチン **gelatin(e)**.

ゼラニウム 《植物》 a **geranium**.

セラピー **therapy**
‖アニマルセラピー animal-assisted therapy.

セラピスト a **therapist**.

セラミックス **ceramics**.

1**せり 芹** 《植物》 **Japanese parsley** /pɑ́ːˈsli/.

2**せり 競り** (an) **auction, bidding** (競売) ; **competition** (競争) ▶彼は競りでピカソの絵を買った He got a painting by Picasso *at* (*an*) *auction*. ‖ 築地では毎朝魚の競りが行われる A fish *auction* is held every morning at Tsukiji.

せりあう 競り合う **compete** 《with》 ▶試験のたびに木村君は山田さんと1番を競り合っていた Every time they had an exam, Kimura *competed with* Yamada for the top [best] score.

ゼリー 《米》 (a) **jello**, (a) **Jell-O** /dʒélou/ (➤ 後者は商標名) ; 《英》 (a) **jelly**.

せりおとす 競り落とす ▶その美術商はミレーの絵を2千万円で競り落とした The art dealer *bought* a Millet (painting) *at* (*an*) *auction* for twenty million yen. ‖ つぼは100万円でその古美術店に競り落とされた The vase *was knocked down* to the antique shop owner for one million yen. ‖ そのマグロは500万円で競り落とされた The tuna was *auctioned off* for five million yen.

せりだす せり出す ▶せり出している軒先 *overhanging* eaves ‖ 運動をやめてからおなかがせり出してきた I *have gotten quite a paunch* [*a potbelly* / *a spare tire*] since I quit exercising.

せりふ 台詞･科白 **lines** ; a **speech**(長い) ▶第 3 幕で主演女優がせりふを忘れた[とちった] In the third act, the leading actress forgot her *lines* [faltered on a few *words*].

せる 競る **compete**(競う) ; **bid**《on, for》(入札する) ▶その 2 人のアンカーがゴール前で激しく競った The two anchors *competed* fiercely in front of the finish line.

セルフィー →自撮り.

セルフサービス **self-service**(➤形容詞として名詞の前で用いる場合 self-serve ともいう) ▶セルフサービスの店 a *self-service* [*self-serve*] store ‖ ここではすべてセルフサービス方式でやろう Let's do everything *on a self-service* [*self-serve*] *basis* here.

▶ 対話 「コーヒーを入れてくれない ?」「セルフサービスでどうぞ」"Can I have a cup of coffee ?" "*Please help yourself.*"

セルフタイマー a **self-timer.**

セルロイド **celluloid** /séljələ̀ɪd/ ▶セルロイド製のおもちゃ a *celluloid* toy.

セレナーデ 《音楽》 a **serenade** /sèrənéɪd/.

セレブ a **celebrity.**

セレモニー a **ceremony**(➤通例, 祝い事や記念の式典で, ことさら葬儀は指さない)

‖セレモニーホール a funeral hall.

ゼロ **1【数字の 0】**(a) **zero** /zíəroʊ/ ; (a) **naught,** 《英》(a) **nought** /nɔːt/ ▶ゼロ歳の赤ん坊 a baby still in his [her] *first year* ‖ この数字にはゼロが 8 個つく This figure is followed by eight *zeros*. ‖ 5 引く 5 はゼロだ Five minus five is *zero*. ／Five from five leaves *naught*. ‖ 私の電話番号は123-1007です My phone number is one-two-three, one-o-o-seven [《英また》 one-double o-seven]. (➤ o は /oʊ/ と読む).

▶私たちは 4 対 0 で負けた We were defeated *4 to 0* [*four to nothing*]. (➤ nothing の代わりに nil を使うこともある).

2【何もないこと】 **nothing** ▶彼は事務能力がゼロだ He has *no* clerical ability. ‖ またゼロから出発だ I have to start again *from scratch*. (➤ from scratch は「スタートラインから, 何もないところから」) ‖ ロシア語の知識はゼロに等しい I know *next to nothing* about Russian. (➤ next to nothing は「ないも同然」).

セロハン **cellophane** /séləfeɪn/.

セロハンテープ (an) **adhesive** /ədhíːsɪv/ **tape** (➤「ばんそうこう」の意もある) ; 《主に米》 (a) **Scotch tape,** 《主に英》 (a) **Sellotape** 《参考》 あとの 2 語はともに商標名. 小文字で普通名詞としても用いる.

セロリ 《植物》 **celery** /séləri/ ▶セロリ 1 本 a stick of *celery*.

せろん 世論 **public opinion** ▶政治家は世論に耳を傾けるべきだ Politicians should listen to *public opinion*. ‖ 首相は世論を無視してその政策を断行した The Prime Minister carried out his policy in defiance of *public opinion*.

‖世論調査 a public opinion poll [survey].

せわ 世話

> **訳語メニュー**
> めんどうを見ること →care **1**
> 手数 →trouble **2**

1【面倒を見ること】 **care** ━動 世話する **take care of** (心配りをする) ; **look after** (困らないように[安全なように]しっかり見守る)

> 【文型】
> **人･動物(A)の世話をする**
> **take care of** A
> **look after** A

▶子供たちがその犬の世話をしている The children *take care of* [*look after*] that dog. ‖ 老後は子供の世話になるのがかつて日本の習慣であった In Japan, elderly people used to *be taken care of* [elderly people *were* customarily *looked after*] by their children.

▶竹田さんは世話好きだ Mr. Takeda *likes helping* [*to do things for*] *other people*. ‖ 大学を出てからは親に世話してもらおうなどと考えるな(＝頼るな) Don't *depend upon* your parents after graduating from college. ‖ バンクーバーではウィルソンさんのところにお世話になった I *stayed with* the Wilsons in Vancouver. (● 英語では単に「泊まった」と考える).

▶年老いた母親の食事や風呂の世話をする *help* my elderly mother with [*assist* my elderly mother in] eating and bathing ‖ 下の世話をする *help* someone go to the toilet ／*assist* someone with bowel and bladder functions.

> **あなたの英語はどう響く?**
> 英語国で, 先生に向かって「息子がいつもお世話になっております」と言うつもりで, Thank you very much for taking care of [for your many kindnesses to] my son. のように言うと, 「あなたのお子さんの世話をする (take care of) のが私の仕事ですから」と言われる可能性がある. 単なる挨拶としての「お世話になっております」に当たる言い方はないので, 英語では例えば, My son really likes your class. (息子は先生のクラスがとても気に入っています)のように言う.

✉ **ホームステイ中はいろいろとお世話になりました** *Thank you for all you did for me* during my homestay with you [while I stayed with you]. ➤仕事の取引先などに「いろいろお世話になっております」ならば Thank you very much for working with us. という.

▶《慣用表現》大きなお世話だ *It's none of your business.* ／*Keep your big nose out of my business.* ／*Thanks for nothing.* ‖ 人が何時に起きようと大きなお世話だ *What a big nuisance !* What does it matter when I get up ? ／When I get up *is none of your business*.

▶肝心の通訳がひどい間違いをしたのだから世話はない The interpreter who we all depend on made terrible mistakes. He [She] was *helpless* ! ‖ CDを聴くだけで英会話ができるようになるなら世話はない If you could learn to speak English by just listening to some CDs, learning English would be *a simple matter* [*a piece of cake*].

▶この旅行の世話役(＝まとめ役)は木村さんです Mr. Kimura is the *organizer* of this trip. ‖ この夏休みに子供キャンプの世話役(＝監督者)をした I was *a supervisor* at the children's summer camp this year. ‖ 山田さんは近所で知られた世話好きだ Mrs. Yamada is known in the neighborhood as someone who *loves to do things for other people*.

2【手数, 迷惑】 **trouble** ▶息子は体が弱かったので本当に世話が焼けた Our son was sickly so we *had a lot of trouble taking care of* him. ‖ 美和は世話の焼けない赤ん坊で, 生後 3 か月めからは夜中に目を覚ますことはありませんでした Miwa was an *easy* baby. She slept through the night from her third month. ‖ **世話を焼かせて**悪いね［悪かったね］I'm sorry to *trouble you* [*to have troubled you*].

3【紹介, あっせん】▶私は有田さんの**世話で**妻の恵子と知り合いました Mrs. Arita *introduced* me to my wife Keiko. ‖ コックを１人**世話してください** Could you please *find* us a cook? ‖ 私は教授に**お世話いただいて**B銀行に入行しました I got a job at B Bank *through* my professor's *introduction*. ／My professor *helped* me *find a job* at B Bank. ‖ 日本では息子や娘の結婚の**世話**を友人や親類に頼む親がいます Some Japanese parents ask their friends or relatives to *look for* potential mates for their sons and daughters.

せわしい 忙しい busy; hectic（てんてこまいの）; restless（落ち着かない）▶年の瀬はいつも**せわしい** I always *feel busy* [*restless*] at the end of the year.
▶**せわしない**人ね. もう少しのんびりしたら？ What a *busy* person you are! Why not take it a little easier?

[1]**せん 線** **1【細く長い筋】** a line ▶この紙にまっすぐな［太い／細い］**線**を２本引きなさい Draw two straight [bold／thin] *lines* on this paper. (➤「細い線」は fine line ともいう;「曲がった線, 曲線」は curved [crooked] line,「波線」は wavy [wiggly] line という).
▶点と点を**線**で結びなさい Connect the dots with *a line*. ‖ 私の水着は紺地に白い**線**が１本入っている My swimsuit has a white *line* on a navy blue background. ⇀下線, 斜線, 点線, 傍線.

2【輪郭】 one's [a] figure（体形）▶**体の線が目立つ**［**目立たない**］ジーンズ *figure-enhancing* [*figure-forgiving*] jeans ‖ 彼女はまだ**体の線**が崩れていない She hasn't yet lost *her figure*.

3【鉄道・道路・電話などの】 a line; a lane（道路の走行車線）; a track（鉄道の番線）▶**中央線** the Chuo (Train) *Line* ‖ 昨夜高速道路の**下り**［**上り**］**線**は衝突事故で大渋滞した The *outbound* [*inbound*] *lanes* of the expressway were backed up (with cars) last night because of a collision. ‖ 金沢行きの急行は**３番線**から出る The express (bound) for Kanazawa leaves from *track* [*platform*] (*No.*) *3*. ‖ エジンバラに行くのは**何線**ですか *Which* (*train*) *line* goes to Edinburgh?

4【方針, 水準】 a line ▶新製品の宣伝方法は**その線**でいこう Let's use [try] that *line* of advertising for the new product. ‖《相手の提案に答えて》よし, **その線**でいこう OK. Let's *go with that*.

5【慣用表現】▶そのネクタイ, なかなか**いい線いってる**ね That tie *looks very good* [*nice*] *on* you. ／That tie *is very stylish*. ‖ 彼の作品は**いい線までいった**んだが, 結局最終選考には漏れた His (piece of) work *was near the top of the list* but in the end did not make it to the final selection. (⇀いい線) ‖ 芸術かわいせつかどこで**線を引くか**が難しい It is difficult to decide *where to draw the line* between art and obscenity.

[2]**せん 栓** a cap（瓶の）; a plug（穴をふさぐもの）; a stopper（おけ・瓶の）; a cork（コルク栓）▶ビールの**栓を抜いて**くれ Take the *cap* off (of) a beer bottle. (➤ of をつけるのはインフォーマル) ‖ ワインの**栓を抜いた** I pulled the *cork* out of the wine bottle. ／I opened the wine bottle.
▶風呂の**栓を抜こうか** Shall I pull the *plug* in the bathtub? ‖ ガスの**栓を閉めて**［**開けて**］ください Will you *turn off* [*turn on*] the gas? ‖ 少女は指で耳に**栓をした** The girl *stopped* [*plugged*] her ears with her fingers.

[3]**せん 千** a thousand ▶このホールは約**3000人**収容できる This hall holds [seats] about *three thousand people*. (➤ 数詞を伴うときは thousands としない) ‖ **何千という人**がその化石を見に来た *Thousands of* people came to see the fossil. (➤ thousands of で「何千もの…」) ‖ 当館には毎日**数千人もの**入場者があります *Several thousand* visitors come to this museum every day. ‖ あなたが**千番目**の入場者です You are *the thousandth* visitor. ‖ ことしは**2012年**です This is the year *two thousand* (*and*) *twelve*.
▶きみが手伝ってくれれば**千人力**だ With you as a member of our team, it's *like having a thousand supporters*.

[4]**せん 戦**

> **逆引き熟語 ○○戦**
> **オープン戦** open competition ／**決勝戦** the final(s), the final game ／**公式戦** an official competition [game] ／**市街戦** urban warfare, street fighting ／**新人戦** a rookie game [match] ／**早慶戦** Waseda Keio game ／**団体戦** team competition ／**リーグ戦** league competition

[5]**せん 腺**《解剖学》a gland.

[1]**ぜん 善** good（良いこと）; right（正しいこと）▶我々は皆心の中に**善**と悪の両面を持っている We all have both *good* and bad sides (to us). ‖ 常に**善をなす**よう心がけなさい Always try to *do good*. ‖ そうと決まれば「**善は急げ**」だ. すぐ彼と連絡を取ってくれ Well, if that's decided, then contact him immediately—*the sooner the better*, they say. (文字どおりには Do a good deed quickly. だが, 英語では訳例のように言うほうがよい).

[2]**ぜん 禅** Zen(➤ 英語化している)
日本紹介 **禅はれんげ座に座って心を静め, めい想して, (呼吸を整え)精神を統一して真理を悟るための仏教の修行をいいます** Zen refers to a type of Buddhist training to attain spiritual enlightenment. You sit in the lotus position to calm yourself, and meditate to achieve a high degree of mental concentration (usually by focusing on your breathing).
‖**禅宗** Zen Buddhism ‖ **禅僧** a Zen priest ‖ **禅寺** a Zen temple.

[1]**ぜん- 前-** ex-, former（役職・地位などが前の; 前者には「再選されなかった」とか「外へ出された」というマイナスイメージがあることがある）; pre-（以前の）▶**前首相** the *ex*-prime minister ／the *former* prime minister (➤ 後者は「元首相」の意にもなる) ‖ **前妻** one's *ex*-wife ‖ **前職** one's *previous job* (*or occupation*) ‖ 彼は**前近代的な**考え方をする His way of thinking is so old-fashioned, it's *premodern*.

[2]**ぜん- 全-** all, whole ▶**全日本**弁論大会 the *All-Japan* Speech Contest ‖ **全額**を返済する pay back a loan *in full* ‖ **全優**（＝オールA）を取る get *straight* A's.
☛ 全世界, 全日本, 全米（⇀見出語）

ぜんあく 善悪 right and wrong, good and evil ▶この男の子はまだ**善悪**をわきまえていない This boy still *cannot tell right from wrong*. (➤ tell A from B で「AとBを区別する」).

[1]**せんい 繊維** (a) fiber /fáɪbəʳ/ ▶便秘なら繊維の多いものを食べなさい If you suffer from constipation, eat a lot of *fiber*. ‖この布は繊維が粗い[細かい] This cloth has a coarse [fine] *texture*. (➤ texture は「織り方」) ‖ナイロンは人間が生み出した最初の合成繊維だ Nylon is the first artificial *synthetic fiber*.
‖**繊維工業** the textile industry (➤ textile は「織物(の)」) ‖**繊維工場** a textile factory ‖**繊維製品** textiles ‖**食物繊維** dietary fiber ‖**神経繊維** a nerve fiber.

[2]**せんい 戦意** fighting spirit, will to fight ▶戦意を喪失する lose one's *fighting spirit* ‖クリチコの相手は最初から戦意がまるで感じられなかった From the beginning, Klitschko's opponent apparently had no *will to fight*.

ぜんい 善意 good intentions [will] ▶善意の人々 *well-intentioned* [*well-meaning*] people ‖彼は善意で忠告してくれたのだ He advised me *out of good will* [*with good intentions*]. ／He *meant well* when he advised me.
▶彼の善意を無にしてはいけない Don't *let* his *good will go to waste*.

ぜんいき 全域 the entire [whole] area ▶その地震は東海地方全域を襲った The earthquake hit *the entire Tokai area*.

せんいん 船員 a seaman, a sailor (➤ ともに高級船員以外の者を指す) ; the crew (全乗組員)
‖**高級船員** an officer.

ぜんいん 全員 all (the members) ▶生徒全員がスキーに参加した *All* the students went skiing. ‖家族全員で温泉へ行ってきた Our *whole* family went to a hot-spring resort. ‖全員一致で竜也と友江は学校のベストカップルに選ばれた Tatsuya and Tomoe were chosen *unanimously* as the best couple in the school. ‖この行事は全員参加です This event *is mandatory*. (➤ mandatory /mǽndətɔːri/ は「強制的な」) ‖全員集合! *Let's all assemble here*. ／(*Everybody*) *fall in!* (➤ fall in は「整列する」の意の軍隊用語).

せんえい 先鋭 ▶先鋭化した若きイスラム教徒 a *radicalized* young Muslim.

ぜんえい 前衛 a forward (球技の) ; the avant-garde /àːvɑːngáːʳd/ (芸術の前衛派)
‖**前衛美術** avant-garde art.

せんえつ 僭越 ▶こんなことを申し上げるのはせん越ですが, お示しの計画には実現性がないと思います *If I may be so bold* as to say so, I think your plan is impracticable.
▶せん越ながら私が議長を務めさせていただきます I'll do my best to *prove myself worthy of the honor of* serving as chairman. (➤ 英語では「せん越ながら」に当たるへりくだった言い方(=self deprecating expression)はないが, 訳例は謙遜した言い方) ‖せん越ながらひとつ提案させていただきます *Please allow me to* make a suggestion.

ぜんおん 全音 《音楽》 a whole step, a whole tone.

ぜんおんかい 全音階 《音楽》 the diatonic scale.

ぜんおんぷ 全音符 《音楽・米》 a whole note, 《英》 a semibreve.

せんか 戦火 (a) war (戦争) ; (a) battle (戦闘) ▶その国と激しく戦火を交える *fight a* fierce *battle* with that country ‖それらの文化財は幸いにも戦火を免れた Fortunately, those cultural treasures *were spared from destruction in* [*by*] *war*.

せんが 線画 line drawing (描くこと) ; a line drawing (描いた絵).

ぜんか 前科 a criminal record ▶彼には窃盗の前科がある He *was once convicted* of theft. (➤ be convicted of は「…で有罪になる」) ‖あの男は前科3犯だ That man is *an ex-con with three previous convictions*. (➤ ex-con は ex-convict の省略形).
‖**前科者** an ex-convict.

せんかい 旋回 a turn 一動 **旋回する** turn ; circle (輪を描く) ▶飛行機は左に旋回した The plane *turned* [*made a turn*] to the left. ‖トンビが村の上を旋回していた A kite *was circling* over the village.

せんがい 選外 ▶私の建築デザインはコンテストで選外だった My architectural design *failed to win a prize* [*was not among the winners*] in the competition. ‖彼女はエッセーコンテストで選外佳作に入った She received *an honorable mention* in the essay contest.

[1]**ぜんかい 全快** (a) complete recovery 一動 **全快する** recover completely (from an illness) ▶かぜが全快したら出社します I'll go to work when I *get over* my cold *completely* [*recover completely* from my cold].

[2]**ぜんかい 前回** the last time 一形 **前回の** the last ▶きみは前回も同じ言い訳をしたね You made the same excuse *the last time* too, didn't you? ‖彼は前回の選挙では落選した He was defeated in *the last* election.

[3]**ぜんかい 全壊** ▶この前の台風で町の数軒の家が全壊した Several houses in the town *were completely destroyed* by the recent typhoon.

[4]**ぜんかい 全開** ▶エンジン全開で飛ばせ *Open up* the engine (*all the way*)!

ぜんかいいっち 全会一致 ▶その議案は全会一致で可決された The bill was passed *unanimously*.

せんがく 浅学 shallow learning.

ぜんかく 全角 ▶全角の文字 a *two-byte* character ／a *full-width* character.

ぜんがく 全額 ▶授業料の全額免除を受ける receive *full* exemption from tuition fees ‖私は銀行から預金を全額引き出した I withdrew my *entire* [*whole*] savings from the bank. ‖この施設の建設は全額(=全部)寄付金で賄われた This facility was built *entirely* on contributions.
‖**全額出資子会社** a wholly-owned subsidiary.

せんかくしゃ 先覚者 a pioneer ▶福沢諭吉は日本の教育の先覚者だった Fukuzawa Yukichi was *a pioneer* in Japanese education. ‖坂本龍馬は時代の先覚者だった Sakamoto Ryoma *was ahead of his time*. (➤「時代に先んじていた」の意).

せんかん 戦艦 a battleship.

せんがん 洗顔する wash one's face ▶にきびを防ぐには丁寧な洗顔が何より大切です Nothing is more effective in preventing pimples than *washing your face* thoroughly.
‖**洗顔クリーム** facial cleansing cream.

ぜんかん 全巻 a complete set ▶100冊の日本文学全集を全巻読破する read through a *complete* 100-volume *set* of Japanese literature.

せんき 戦記 a war chronicle.

[1]**ぜんき 前期** the earlier period (初期) ; the first semester (2学期制の学校の) ; the first half (前半) ▶この絵は室町時代前期のものです This painting belongs to *the earlier* Muromachi *period*.
‖**前期試験** first-semester exams.

[2]**ぜんき 前記の** above-mentioned, aforementioned,

aforesaid(➤ あとの2語は主に法律文書などで用いることが多い) ▶前記の例 the *above*(*-mentioned*) example／the example (*mentioned*) *above*.

1せんきゃく 先客 ▶事務所には先客があったので出直すことにした I decided to visit the office another time because there was (already) *another visitor* before me.

2せんきゃく 船客 a (ship's) passenger ▶フェリーの船客 a ferryboat *passenger* ‖さくら号の船客たち *passengers* on (board) the Sakura.

せんきゃくばんらい 千客万来 ▶大みそかのそば屋は千客万来の忙しさだ Soba noodle shops are busy *serving crowds of customers* on the last day of the year.

せんきゅうがん 選球眼 a batting eye ▶《野球》イチローは選球眼がよく，めったにボールに手を出さない Ichiro has a good *batting eye* and seldom swings at bad pitches.

1**せんきょ** 選挙 (an) election ▶選挙に出る run in *an election*／《英》stand for *election* ‖甲府市長の選挙に出る *run for* Mayor of Kofu ‖彼女は選挙でクラス委員に選ばれた She was chosen class representative *by election*. ‖衆議院選挙は7月10日に行われる *The election of representatives to the Lower House* will be held on July 10. ‖彼は150票差で選挙に勝った[負けた] He *won* [*lost*] *the election* by 150 votes. ‖生徒会長を選ぶために全校で選挙をした We *had* [*held*] *a general election* to choose the president of the student council.

▶私は17歳なのでまだ選挙権がない I don't have *the right to vote* since I'm only 17.

‖選挙違反 an election law violation, election irregularities(➤「選挙違反で逮捕される」は be arrested for a violation of the election law) ‖選挙運動 an election campaign, 《英また》election canvassing ‖選挙演説 a campaign speech, 《インフォーマル》a stump speech ‖選挙管理委員会 an election administration committee ‖選挙区 an electoral [a voting] district, a constituency (➤「小選挙区」は a single-seat [single-representative] constituency,「中選挙区」は a multi-seat constituency) ‖選挙公約 a campaign promise [pledge] ‖選挙資金 an election campaign fund ‖選挙戦 an election [electoral] campaign(➤「大統領選挙戦」は a presidential race) ‖選挙速報 hour-by-hour reports of the election returns ‖選挙妨害 election [campaign] obstruction.

☛ 総選挙, 被選挙権 (→見出語)

2せんきょ 占拠 occupation 一動 占拠する occupy +目, 《インフォーマル》take over ▶労働者たちは工場を占拠した Workers *occupied* [*took over*] the factory. ‖彼の一家はその土地を不法占拠していると見なされた His family was considered to *be in possession* of the land *illegally* [*be illegally occupying* the land].

せんぎょ 鮮魚 fresh fish.

せんぎょう 専業 ‖専業主婦[主夫] a full-time housewife [househusband], 《インフォーマル》a stay-at-home mom [dad] (➤ 男女を区別せず a full-time homemaker とすることもできる) ‖専業農家 a full-time farmer.

せんきょうし 宣教師 a missionary ▶ザビエルは宣教師として日本に派遣された Xavier was sent to Japan as *a missionary*.

1せんきょく 戦局 the war situation ▶小早川軍の寝返りで戦局は一変した *The war situation* changed completely after the Kobayakawa troops went over to the enemy.

2せんきょく 選曲 music selection, selection of music [songs／pieces of music] 一動 選曲する select (songs [pieces of music]).

せんぎり 千切り ▶ニンジンを千切りにする *cut* a carrot *into fine* [*thin*], *long strips*／*cut* a carrot *into julienne strips* (➤ julienne(千切りの)は /dʒùːlién/ と発音) ‖キャベツを千切りにする *shred* cabbage *finely* [*thinly*] (➤ shred はキャベツやレタスなどの葉野菜で主に用いられる).

せんく 先駆 the vanguard (各種運動の) ▶先駆的な研究[仕事]をする do *pioneering* research [work] ‖あの医師は遺伝子工学の先駆者の1人だ That doctor is one of the *forerunners* [*pioneers*] of genetic engineering.

1ぜんけい 全景 the whole view; a panorama /pænərǽmə ‖ -rάːmə/ (広々とした) ▶眼下に山中湖の全景が広がっていた *A panoramic view* of Lake Yamanaka spread out below us.

2ぜんけい 前景 the foreground.

ぜんけいしせい 前傾姿勢 ▶(スキーの)滑降では緩斜面でいかにうまく前傾姿勢をとるかがポイントだ The point is to be able to *keep a forward-leaning posture* [*keep leaning forward*] when you ski on a slight slope.

1せんけつ 先決 ▶何よりも人命救助が先決だ *The first thing to do is* save lives.／Saving lives *must come first*. ‖この問題のほうが先決だ This problem *must be settled first*.／*First of all*, we have to settle this problem.

2せんけつ 潜血 《医学》occult blood.

せんげつ 先月 last month ▶先月は忙しかった I was busy *last month*. ‖先月4日に彼は事故に遭った He had an accident on the fourth of *last month*.

‖先々月 (→見出語).

せんけんたい 先遣隊 an advance team; advance troops(兵).

せんげん 宣言 (a) declaration; proclamation (国家の重大事の) 一動 宣言する declare +目, proclaim +目; announce +目 (発表する) ▶(アメリカ合衆国の)独立宣言 *the Declaration of Independence* ‖その地域は独立を宣言した The region *declared* [*proclaimed*] *its* independence. ‖K氏は父親の代わりに次期選挙に立候補すると宣言した Mr. K *announced* that he would take his father's place as (a) candidate in the coming election.

▶彼は議長として開会を宣言した As the chair [chairperson], he *declared the meeting open*.／As the chair [chairperson], he *called the meeting to order*.

ぜんけん 全権 complete power ▶その将軍はクーデターで全権を掌握した The general *seized complete power* after successfully staging a coup.

‖特命全権大使 an ambassador extraordinary and plenipotentiary.

ぜんげん 前言 ▶前言を取り消すよ I *take back what* I *said*. ‖大臣は抗議を受けて前言を取り消すはめになった Drawing protest, the Minister had to *eat* [*take back*] *his* (*own*) *words*.

せんけんのめい 先見の明 foresight ▶前社長には先見の明があった The former president *was a man of foresight* [*was far-sighted*]. ‖もっと先見の明があったら, あの株は手放さなかったのに I wouldn't have sold that stock if I had had more *foresight*.

せんご 戦後の postwar 一副 戦後に after the war ▶彼らは戦後の食糧難時代を生き延びた They lived through a difficult period *after the war* when food was scarce. ‖戦後の日本の発展は世界を驚かせた *Postwar* Japan's development [Japan's development *after the war*] quite surprised the world.

ぜんご 前後 1【前と後ろに】back and forth（動きが前後に）; **before and behind**（位置が前後に）▶ボート選手たちの体はこぐとき規則的に前後に揺れる Boat rowers move rhythmically *back and forth* while rowing. ‖首相の前後には数人のボディーガードがついて歩いていた Several bodyguards were walking *before and behind* the Prime Minister. ‖車の前後にはバンパーがついている A car has two bumpers : one *in front*, and the other *at the rear*.

▶車の前後を横断するときは気をつけなさい Be careful when you cross *in front of or in back of* vehicles. ‖前後左右をよく見てから花火に火をつけなさい Look *around you* carefully before you light the fireworks.

2【時間のあと先】before and after ▶父は食事の前後に薬を飲む My father takes medicine *before and after* each meal. ‖純子が帰るのと前後して(＝間を置かずに)みどりがやって来た Midori came to see me immediately after [as soon as] Junko left.

3【順序が逆になること】▶話が前後しますが… Excuse me, but *I'd like to go back to our first subject*. ‖話を前後させないでくれますか Would you please *stay on* [*stick to*] *the subject under discussion*?

4【およそ】about, around ▶40前後の男 a man *somewhere around* forty ‖対話「アルバイト学生の平均賃金はどのくらいですか」「時給1000円前後です」"What's the average wage for student part-timers?" "*About* 1000 yen per hour." ‖対話「11月5日の夕方あなたは何時に会社を出ましたか」「6時前後です」"What time did you leave the office on the evening of November 5?" "(*At*) *around* 6 o'clock."

5【慣用表現】▶少年Aは前後の見境もなく少年Bを殴った *Too enraged to be rational*, boy A hit boy B. (➤「激情のあまり理性を失って」の意) ‖前後不覚になるほど酒を飲むな Don't drink so much that you *lose consciousness* [*pass out*]. (➤ pass out は「酔い潰れる」) ‖起こそうとしたが彼は前後不覚に眠り込んでいた We tried to wake him up, but he was sleeping *like a log*. (➤ like a log は「(丸太のように)ぐっすりと」の意).

‖前後関係 the context.

1**せんこう 専攻する**《米》**major in**,《英》**read** ＋目, **specialise in** ▶大学では何を専攻しましたか What did you *major in* [《英》*read* / *specialise in*] at college? / What was your *major* at college? ‖姉は大学でロボット工学を専攻している My (older) sister *is majoring* [《英》*specialising*] *in* robotics at college.

▶彼は歴史学専攻の2年生だ He is a sophomore (student) *majoring in* history. / He is a sophomore history *major*. /《英》He is a second-year student *reading* history.

> **語法** (1)《英》の specialise in は特定のテーマ, 例えば「産業革命」のような狭い範囲で勉強する場合や, 理数系の特定分野に関して用いられる.《米》でも specialize in は理数系に用いる傾向がある.
> (2) 大学院を出た人に対して,「何を専攻しましたか」と聞くときは What did you study? とか What kind of research did you do? のように言うことが多い.

‖専攻科目 one's major, one's specialty.

2**せんこう 選考 selection**（選択）; **screening**（資格審査）**一動 選考する select** ＋目, **screen** ＋目 ▶彼は選考に漏れたらしい He seems to have *been passed over*. ‖父はその賞の選考委員の1人です My father is one of the *screening members* of the prize (-awarding) committee. ‖たくさんの応募者の中から新しい専任教師を選考中である They are now *in the process of selecting* a new full-time instructor from among many candidates.

‖選考委員会 a selection [screening] committee.

3**せんこう 閃光 a flash** ▶夜空にせん光が走った *A flash* ran across the night sky. / A bright light flashed across the night sky. (➤後者の flash は「せん光を発する」の意).

4**せんこう 先行** ▶巨人が2回に2点を入れて先行した The Giants scored two runs in the second inning to *lead the game*.

▶あの女優は実力よりも人気が先行している As for that actress, her popularity *exceeds* her talent.

5**せんこう 先攻** ▶今夜はライオンズが先攻だ The Lions *are batting first* tonight.

6**せんこう 線香 an incense** /ínsens/ **stick** ▶線香を上げる[たく] offer [burn] *incense sticks*.

‖線香花火 a sparkler.

1**ぜんこう 全校 the whole school**（学校全体）▶全校で創立10周年を祝った *The whole school* celebrated the 10th anniversary of its foundation. ‖全校生徒を代表して上杉さんがトロフィーを受け取った Representing *all the students*, Uesugi accepted the trophy.

‖全校集会 an all-school assembly.

2**ぜんこう 善行 a good deed**（1回の行為）; **good conduct**（➤数えられない名詞; 行為そのものより行動することに力点がある）▶善行を積む do many *good deeds*.

‖善行賞 a prize for good conduct.

ぜんごう 前号 the last issue [number]（先月号）; **the preceding [previous] issue [number]**（ある号の前の号）▶前号より続く Continued from *the last issue*.

1**せんこく 宣告 a sentence**（判決の）**一動 宣告する sentence** ＋目; **pronounce** ＋目（宣言する）▶被告人は死刑の宣告を受けた The accused *was sentenced* to death. ‖彼は有罪の宣告を受けた He *was convicted*. ‖医者は患者の死亡を宣告した The doctor *pronounced* the patient dead. ‖医者にがんを宣告されたときは目の前が真っ暗になった When the doctor *told* [*informed*] me I had cancer, I was plunged into despair.

2**せんこく 先刻** ▶そんなことは先刻承知の上だ I was *already* aware of that.

ぜんこく 全国 ▶この大学の学生は日本全国から集まっている The students at this university come *from all parts of Japan* [*from all over Japan*]. ‖そのサッカーの試合の様子は全国にテレビ中継された The soccer game was telecast *nationwide* [over a *nationwide* network]. ‖けさは全国的に冷え込んでいます This morning it was bitter cold *all across the country.* ／A cold wave hit *the entire nation* this morning.

✉ **高山祭は全国的に有名です** The Takayama Festival is known *throughout Japan*.

‖**全国区** the national constituency ‖**全国紙** a national (news) paper ‖**全国大会** a national convention [conference] (集会); a national meet (競技会).

せんごくじだい 戦国時代 **the Sengoku period**; **the Warring States period**(中国の).

せんごくだいみょう 戦国大名 a **warlord of the Sengoku period.**

ぜんごさく 善後策 **corrective** [**remedial**] **measures** ▶早急に善後策を講じなければならない We must *take corrective measures* immediately.

ぜんざ 前座 ▶前座を務める work an *opening act* ／ be a *curtain raiser*.

センサー a **sensor** ▶このトースターはむらなく焼けるように電子センサーがついている This toaster has *an electronic sensor* to make sure the toast browns evenly. ‖**赤外線センサー** an infrared sensor ‖**光センサー** a light sensor.

1**せんさい 戦災** **war damage** ▶第二次世界大戦ではその国の大部分の都市が戦災を被った Almost every city in that country *suffered damage* [*was damaged*] during World War II. ‖京都が戦災を免れた理由を知っていますか Do you know the reason Kyoto *escaped damage* during the war?

‖**戦災孤児** a war orphan.

2**せんさい 繊細な** **delicate** /délɪkət/ (壊れやすい); **fine** (細かい); **sensitive** (敏感な, 感じやすい) ▶繊細な指 *delicate* fingers ‖外見に似合わず彼は繊細だ He's much more *sensitive* than you would think from his appearance [from his looks].

3**せんさい 先妻** one's **ex-wife.**

1**せんざい 洗剤** **detergent** /dɪtə́ːʳdʒənt/ (➤「洗濯洗剤」は laundry detergent,「皿洗い洗剤」は dish (washing) detergent ともいう; 通常は Ⓤ 扱い, 種類をいうときは Ⓒ 扱い)

‖**合成洗剤** a synthetic detergent ‖**中性洗剤** a neutral detergent.

2**せんざい 潜在** ▶生徒一人一人の潜在能力を引き出す bring out the *potential* of each student ‖インドの潜在能力は無視できない We must not ignore India's *potential power*.

‖**潜在意識** subconsciousness.

ぜんさい 前菜 an **hors d'oeuvre** /ɔːʳdə́ːʳv/ (➤ 通例複数形 hors d'oeuvres で用いる).

せんざいいちぐう 千載一遇 ▶わが社にとって千載一遇のチャンスが巡ってきた This is an *unprecedented* [*a one-in-a-million*] chance for our company. (➤ unprecedented は「前例のない, 空前の」の意).

せんさく 詮索する **stick** [**poke**] one's **nose** 《into》(首を突っ込む); **pry** 《into》(秘密などを; 軽蔑的ニュアンスの濃い語) ▶余計な詮索はやめてくれ Don't *stick* [*poke*] *your nose into* things that don't concern you. ／Keep your nose out of things that don't concern you. ‖他人の私事を詮索するのは失礼だ It is rude to *pry into* another person's private affairs.

▶あの人は本当に詮索好きな人だ He is really *an inquisitive* [*a nosy*] *man.* ／He's *a* real *snoop* [*snooper*].

せんさばんべつ 千差万別 ▶人の考え方は千差万別だ Each person has his or her *own way* of thinking. ‖指紋は人によって千差万別だ Everyone has a *unique* fingerprint [a fingerprint that is *unique* to them].

1**せんし 戦死** **death in battle** ▶彼の祖父は第二次世界大戦で戦死した His grandfather *was killed in action* during World War II. (➤ in action は「戦闘中に」).

‖**戦死者** a person killed in war [action]; the war dead (➤ 総称).

2**せんし 戦士** a **fighter,** a **warrior** /wɔ́ːriəʳ/ (➤ 後者は主に文語); a **soldier** (兵士)

‖**企業戦士** a corporate warrior ‖**自由の戦士** a freedom fighter, a soldier for freedom ‖**無名戦士の墓** 《米》 The Tomb of the Unknown Soldier, 《英》 The Grave of the Unknown Warrior.

せんしじだい 先史時代 **prehistoric times** ▶先史時代の洞窟絵画 a *prehistoric* cave printing.

せんしつ 船室 a **cabin**

‖1 [2] **等船室** a first-[second-]class cabin.

せんじつ 先日 **the other day**(➤「2, 3日前」を表すのでそれ以前を言うのならば several days ago がよい)

▶私は先日ジェリー君に会った I met Jerry *the other day* [*several days ago*]. ‖先日の台風では被害はなかったですか Did the typhoon *the other day* do any damage (to your house)? ‖母は先日来かぜで寝込んでいる My mother has been sick in bed with a cold *for several days*. ‖先日の(＝前回の)会で決まったことを話してください Will you tell me what was decided at the *previous* meeting?

あなたの英語はどう響く?

「先日は結構な物を頂いて, 本当にありがとうございました」は Thank you very much for (giving me) a nice present *the other day*. と訳せるが, 英語では, 贈り物を受け取ったその場で心からの礼を一度言えばそれで十分であり, 再度お礼を言わなくても失礼にはならない. したがって, 上のようなお礼の言い方はその場でお礼が言えなかった場合に限定したほうがよい. あまり何度も言うと,「また何かを欲しがっているのでは」と誤解されるおそれさえある.

ぜんじつ 前日 **the day before, the previous day** ▶朝になると前日からの雨はやんでいた When morning came, the rain that began falling *the day before* [*on the previous day*] had stopped. ‖彼女は結婚式の前日になって竜夫と一緒になるのは嫌だと言いだした *The day before* the wedding, she said she didn't want to marry Tatsuo. (➤「前々日に」というときは Two days before ... となる).

せんじつめる 煎じ詰める ▶きみが言っているのは煎じ詰めると金を貸してほしいということだな What you are saying *boils down to* the fact that you want me to lend you money. ／*In short*, you are saying you would like to borrow money from me. (➤ in short は「要するに」).

1**せんしゃ 戦車** a **tank.**

2**せんしゃ 洗車する** **wash a car**

‖**洗車機** a car wash ‖**洗車場** a car wash ‖**洗車用品** car-washing materials.

せんじゃ 選者 a **judge**(判定者); a **critic** (批評家).

ぜんしゃ 前者 **the former** (➤「後者」は the latter) ▶人間にはのんびり型とせっかち型の2タイプがある. 前者は

ゆっくりし過ぎて失敗し，後者は急ぎ過ぎて失敗する There are two types of people : those who take it easy and those who are always in a rush. *The former* make mistakes because they go too slow, and the latter make mistakes because they go too fast.

1**せんしゅ 選手** a **player**（球技などの競技者）; an **athlete** /ǽθliːt/（運動選手）▶野球［サッカー］の選手 a baseball［soccer］*player* ‖ 彼は中学校で野球の選手だった He *played baseball*［*was on the baseball team*］in junior high school. ‖ 山下はオリンピック選手だった Yamashita was *an Olympic athlete*［Olympian］.

▶《放送で》高橋選手がホームランを打ちました Takahashi hit a home run.（➤ 英語では Player Takahashi とはしない）.

☛ 選手権（⇀見出語）

2**せんしゅ 船首** **the bow** /baʊ/ **(of a ship)**; **the prow** /praʊ/（➤ 文語的な語）.

1**せんしゅう 先週** **last week** ▶先週私は忙しかった I was busy *last week*. ‖ 私は先週の火曜日彼を訪ねた I visited him *last* Tuesday［(on) Tuesday *last week*］.（➤ 金曜日や土曜日に言うときは前者は「今週の火曜日」の意になるので後者の言い方がよい）‖ 先週のきょうは雨だった It was rainy *a week ago today*. ／《英》It rained *this day last week*.

2**せんしゅう 選集** a **selection**; an **anthology**（異なった人の作品から選んで編んだ）▶現代日本戯曲選集 *selections* from modern Japanese drama ‖ 啄木選集 *selected* works of Takuboku.

ぜんしゅう 全集 ▶宮沢賢治全集 the *complete works* of Miyazawa Kenji ／a *complete edition* of Miyazawa Kenji's works.

せんしゅうがっこう 専修学校 a **special vocational school**.

せんじゅうみん 先住民 an **indigenous** /ɪndídʒənəs/ **people**（民族）.

せんしゅうらく 千秋楽 ▶大相撲秋場所千秋楽 *the last day* of the Autumn Grand Sumo Tournament ‖ 歌舞伎の3月興行の千秋楽 *the closing day* of the March kabuki performances.

せんしゅけん 選手権 a **championship**, a **title**（➤ 後者は本来は「選手権者の称号」の意）▶選手権を取る［失う］win［lose］*a championship* ‖ 2人は高校テニス選手権を争った The two competed for the inter-high school tennis *championship*.

‖選手権試合 a title match ‖ 選手権大会 a championship tournament ‖ 選手権保持者 a champion, a titleholder.

せんしゅつ 選出 **election** 一動 **選出する** **elect** +目 ▶彼は生徒会長に選出された He *was elected*［We elected him］president of the student council.（➤ 役職には a をつけない）‖ 彼女は岐阜県選出の代議士だ She is a Diet member *for*［*from*］Gifu Prefecture. ／She represents Gifu in the Diet.

せんじゅつ 戦術 **tactics**（実戦での個々の戦術）; **strategy** /strǽṭədʒi/（総合的な戦略）▶巧妙な戦術 a clever *tactic* ‖ 相手に勝つ戦術を練ろう Let's work out our *tactics* to defeat our opponent. ‖ ゲリラは多く奇襲戦術をとる Most guerillas adopt *a hit-and-run strategy*.

☛ 人海戦術（⇀見出語）

ぜんじゅつ 前述 ⇀前記.

せんしゅてん 先取点 ▶先取点をあげたのは熊谷高校チームだった It was the Kumagaya High School team that scored *the first point of the game*.（➤ 野球の場合なら通例 the first run を，サッカーなら the first goal を用いる）.

ぜんしょ 善処 ⚠「善処」とは適切な処置をとることだが，実際には何もしない場合にも「善処いたします」と言うことが多い．したがって直訳的に take the appropriate［proper］measures としても日本語のもつ一時逃れのニュアンスは伝わらないことに留意する．

▶この件は善処いたします I will *take the appropriate*［*proper*］*measures* to deal with this matter. ／I will *deal appropriately* with this matter. ／I'll *see what can be done*［*what I can do*］*to deal* with this matter.

1**せんじょう 戦場** a **battlefield**, a **battleground** ▶兵士を戦場に送る send soldiers to the *battlefield* ‖ 戦場で死ぬなんて俺は嫌だ I don't want to be killed *on the battlefield*.

2**せんじょう 洗浄する** **cleanse** /klenz/ +目, **irrigate** +目（➤ 後者は主に医学用語）▶胃を洗浄する *irrigate* the stomach ‖ 洗浄力の強い洗剤 a *powerful*［*strong*］detergent.

‖（コンタクトレンズの）洗浄液 a cleaning liquid, a liquid cleanser ‖ 洗浄器 a syringe /sɪríndʒ/（歯科医などが使う）; a bidet /bɪdéɪ/（ビデ）‖ 資金洗浄 money laundering.

3**せんじょう 船上で** **on board, on a ship** ▶船上検査 an *on-board* inspection.

1**ぜんしょう 全勝する** **win all the games**［**matches**］▶ぼくたちの野球部は今季全勝優勝した Our baseball team *gained a complete victory*［*made a clean sweep of the field*］this season. ‖ 新横綱が初場所で全勝優勝した The new yokozuna *won all 15 of his bouts*［*won with a perfect record*］at the New Year Grand Sumo Tournament.

2**ぜんしょう 全焼** ▶昨晩の火事で2軒の家が全焼した Two houses (*were*) *burned to the ground*［*burned down*］in last night's fire.

せんしょうこく 戦勝国 a **victorious nation**［**country**］.

ぜんしょうせん 前哨戦 a **preliminary skirmish**.

せんじょうち 扇状地《地質学》an **alluvial fan**.

せんじょうてき 扇情的 ▶扇情的な小説 a *sensational* novel ‖ 扇情的な(＝性的なことを連想させる)写真 a *suggestive* picture.

せんしょく 染色 **dyeing** /dáɪɪŋ/

‖染色工場 a dyeworks.

せんしょくたい 染色体《生物学》a **chromosome** /króʊməsoʊm/ ▶X染色体とY染色体 an X and a Y *chromosome*.

せんじる 煎じる **brew** /bruː/ +目 ▶この漢方薬は数時間煎じてから服用してください Please *brew*［*boil*］this herbal medicine for several hours before taking it.

1**せんしん 専心する** **devote oneself**《to》▶彼は英語の勉強に専心している He *devotes himself to*［*is devoted to*］studying English. ‖ きみは勉強に専心しなくてはいけない You must *concentrate on*［*put your mind to*］your studies.

2**せんしん 先進の，先進的な** **advanced**

‖先進医療 advanced medical care ‖ 先進技術 (an) advanced technology ‖ 先進工業国 a highly industrialized country ⇀先進国.

3**せんしん 線審** a **line judge**, a **linesman**.

1**せんじん 先陣** **the van(guard)** ▶彼らは公害企業に対す

る法廷闘争の先陣を務めている They *are in the vanguard* of the plaintiffs against pollution-causing companies.

2**せんじん 先人** a **predecessor**; **people who came before us**(先人たち).

1**ぜんしん 全身** the **whole body**; **every part of the body** (体のすべての部分) ▶スキーや水泳は全身の運動になる Skiing and swimming exercise *every part of the body*. ／Skiing and swimming provide good exercise for *the whole body*. ‖その火事で彼は全身にやけどを負った He suffered burns *over his whole body* in the fire.

▶寒さで全身ががたがた震えた The cold made me shiver *from head to toe*. ‖うちの猫は全身泥まみれになって帰って来た Our cat came home with mud *all over* her. ‖私はこの企画に全身全霊を打ち込んだ I devoted myself *heart and soul* to this project. ／I gave *my whole self* to the project.

▶彼女は手術のために全身麻酔を受けた She was given *general anesthesia* in preparation for the operation. ‖彼は自動車事故で全身まひになった He *was totally paralyzed* in a traffic accident.

2**ぜんしん 前進** (an) **advance**; **progress** /prá:grəs/ (進歩) 一動 **前進する advance, progress** /prəgrés/ ▶《上官が兵士に向かって》前進！*Forward*！‖兵士たちは敵陣に向かって前進した The soldiers *advanced* [*made their way*] toward the enemy lines. ‖車を少し前進させてください Will you *move* your car *forward* a little? ‖いかなる障害があろうとも我々は前進あるのみだ We must *move forward*, no matter what obstacles we may encounter.

▶きのうの会議は労使の和解に向けて一歩前進した Labor and management *moved a step forward* toward reconciliation in yesterday's meeting. ‖彼の研究には前進の跡が見られない His research shows no *sign of progress*.

3**ぜんしん 前身** ▶私たちの学校の前身は女学校です Our school *used to be* [*was originally*] a girls' school. ‖国際連盟は国際連合の前身であった The League of Nations was *the forerunner* to the United Nations.

4**ぜんしん 前震** a **foreshock** /fɔ́ːʳʃɑ̀:k ‖ -ʃɔ̀k/.

ぜんじん 全人 ‖**全人教育** an all-round education, education for the whole person.

せんしんこく 先進国 a **developed country** ▶先進国は発展途上国をもっと援助すべきだ The *developed countries* should give more aid to developing countries.

‖**先進国首脳会議** the G8／the eight-nation summit.

ぜんじんみとう 前人未到・前人未踏 ▶彼は62日間も木の上に座り続けるという前人未到の(＝前例のない)記録を達成した He set an *unprecedented* record of sitting in a tree for 62 days.

せんす 扇子 a **folding fan**.

センス (a) **sense**(感覚); (a) **taste** (好み) ▶彼は音楽のセンスがない He has no *musical sense*. ／He has no *ear for music*. ‖彼女は服装のセンスがいい[悪い] She *has good* [*bad*] *taste* in clothes. ／She *has good* [*bad*] fashion *sense*. ／She is always dressed *in good* [*poor*] *taste*.

▶彼，なかなかユーモアのセンスがあるね He has *a good sense of humor*, doesn't he? ‖彼女には美的センスがまるでない She has no *sense of beauty* [*aesthetic sense*]. ／She has no *eye for beauty*. (➤「…のセンスがとてもある」というときは has a good [great] sense of … ／has a good [great] eye for … を使う)

せんすい 潜水 diving 一動 **潜水する dive, go underwater** ▶鯨は1時間近く潜水していられる Whales are able to *stay underwater* without breathing for up to an hour. ‖私は海面下10メートルまで潜水した I *dived* [*dove*] 10 meters under the sea. ／I *dived* [*dove*] to a depth of 10 meters.

‖**潜水艦** a submarine ‖**潜水病** caisson /kéisɑ:n/ disease ‖**潜水夫** a diver ‖**潜水服** a diving suit.

せんする 宣する declare ＋目 (宣言する); **announce** ＋目 (発表する); **pronounce** ＋目 (宣告する); **call** ＋目 (判定する) ▶教頭は卒業式の開式を宣した The vice-principal *announced* the commencement of the graduation ceremony. ‖雨のため試合の中止が宣された *The game was called* (*off*) because of rain.

ぜんせ 前世 a **former** [**previous**] **life** ▶彼は前世犬であったと信じている He believes that he was a dog in *a former life*.

1**せんせい 先生** a **teacher** (教師); a **professor** /prəfésəʳ/ (大学の); an **instructor** (実技の指導者) ▶習字の先生 a calligraphy *teacher* ‖父はこの学校の先生です My father is *a teacher* at this school. (➤ (×)of this school とはしない) ‖兄は高校の先生です My (older) brother is *a high school teacher*. ／My (older) brother teaches at a high school. ‖平野先生は英語[数学]の先生です *Mr.* Hirano is an English [a mathematics] *teacher*. (➤ English teacher は English を強く発音する. 両方強く言うと「イギリス人の先生」の意味になる. a teacher of English なら紛らわしくない)

▶先生になって5年です I've been *a teacher* for five years. ‖林先生は老人医学の専門医です *Dr.* Hayashi is a specialist in geriatrics.

▶小田先生，窓を開けてもいいですか May I open the window, *Mr.*[*Mrs.*／*Miss*／*Ms.*] Oda? ‖《医者に》先生，どこか悪いのでしょうか Is anything wrong with me, *doctor*? 《参考》(1)英語では「…先生」という呼びかけには Mr., Mrs., Miss, Ms. を用いる. 通例 Teacher は用いない. Sir, Ma'am [《英》Madam] を「先生」という呼びかけに使うのは古風. ただし，日本で教えている外国人の中には，「先生」をそのまま sensei とつづり，例えば「小田先生」の場合なら Oda Sensei とする人も多い. 複数の場合は例えば Oda, Yamada and Ogawa Senseis と表記する. (2)医師に対しては Dr. [《英》では歯科医・外科医には Mr., Mrs., Miss, Ms.] を使う.

逆引き熟語 ○○先生

運転教習所の先生 a driving instructor ／**華道の先生** a teacher of *ikebana* [flower arrangement] ／**教頭先生** a vice [an assistant] principal, 《英》a deputy headteacher ／**高校の先生** a high school teacher ／**校長先生** a principal, 《英》a headteacher ／**大学の先生** a college [university] teacher ／**担任の先生** a class [homeroom] teacher, 《英また》a form teacher ／**病院の先生** a hospital doctor ／**幼稚園の先生** a kindergarten teacher

2**せんせい 宣誓** an **oath** /oʊθ/ (神などにかけての); a **pledge**(人との固い約束) 一動 **宣誓する take an oath, make a pledge** ▶新大統領は就任の宣誓をした The new president *took the oath of office.* ／The new president *was sworn in.* ‖**選手宣誓**！我々選手一同はスポーツマンシップにのっとり，正々堂々と競技することを誓います *The athletes' oath!* We promise to play fairly and squarely and observe sportsmanship at all times.

³**せんせい 先制** ▶ランナーを二塁に置いて畠山はライト前に**先制**のヒットを打った With a runner on second, Hatakeyama *singled* to right *to drive in the first run.* ‖米ロとも**先制核攻撃**を恐れている Both the U.S. and Russia are afraid of *a preemptive nuclear strike* from the other side.

⁴**せんせい 専制** **autocracy** /ɔːtɑ́ːkrəsi/；**tyranny**（暴政）
‖**専制君主** an autocrat, a tyrant, a despot ‖**専制国家** an autocracy.

⁵**せんせい 潜性の**《生物学》**recessive**
‖**潜性**［**劣性**］**遺伝** recessive inheritance［transmission］‖**潜性**［**劣性**］**遺伝子** a recessive gene.

¹**ぜんせい 全盛** ▶藤原氏が**全盛**を極めたのは平安時代だ The Fujiwara clan *reached*［*was at*］*the height of its prosperity* in the Heian period. ‖1960年代はロックミュージックの**全盛期**だった The 1960's were the *heyday* of rock music. ‖あの俳優は**全盛期**を過ぎたようだ That actor seems to have had *his day.*

²**ぜんせい 善政** **good**［**ethical**］**government** ▶**善政**を敷く *govern ethically.*

ぜんせいき 前世紀 **the last century**（現在の前の世紀）；**the previous**［**preceding**］**century**（ある世紀よりも前の世紀）；**prehistory**（先史時代）.

せんせいじゅつ 占星術 **astrology** /əstrɑ́ːlədʒi/
‖**占星術師** an astrologer. →**星占い**.

センセーショナル **sensational** ▶センセーショナルな記事 a *sensational* article ‖そのピアニストは12歳でセンセーショナルなデビューをした The pianist made her *sensational* debut at the age of 12.

センセーション a **sensation** ▶スピルバーグ監督の最新作映画はセンセーションを巻き起こした Director Spielberg's latest film created［caused］*a sensation.*

ぜんせかい 全世界 ▶オリンピック競技を見るために**全世界**からたくさんの人々がやって来る Many people come *from all parts of the world*［*from around the world*］to watch the Olympic Games. ‖グリム童話は**全世界**に知られている Grimm's Fairy Tales are known *all over the world*［*throughout the world*］.／Grimm's Fairy Tales are read *worldwide.*
▶**全世界**の人々がその事件の成り行きに注目した *The whole world*［*All the world*］paid attention to how that incident developed.

せんせき 船籍 a **ship's registry** ▶日本**船籍**の船 a Japanese *registered* ship／a ship *flying* the Japanese flag.

¹**せんせん 宣戦** a **declaration of war** ━動（…に）**宣戦する** **declare war**《on, against》▶日本はアメリカに対する**宣戦**の布告なしに真珠湾を攻撃した Japan attacked Pearl Harbor without *declaring war against* the United States.

²**せんせん 戦線** a **front** ▶共同**戦線**を張らなければ我々は選挙で与党に勝てない We cannot win the election unless we form *a united front* against the ruling party.

せんぜん 戦前の **prewar** ▶**戦前**の教育 *prewar* education ‖**戦前**は女性には選挙権がなかった Women did not have the right to vote *in prewar days*［*before the war*］.
‖**戦前派** the prewar generation.

¹**ぜんせん 前線** **the front (line)**；a **front**（気象の）▶若い兵士たちが**前線**に送られた Young soldiers were sent to *the front.*
‖**寒冷**［**温暖**］**前線** a cold［warm］front ‖**梅雨前線** a seasonal rain front.
☞ **最前線**（→見出語）

²**ぜんせん 善戦する** **fight well, put up a good fight** ▶彼は柔道大会で**善戦**したが決勝戦で敗れた He *put up a good fight* in the judo tournament, but was defeated in the final match.

³**ぜんせん 全線** ▶まもなく**全線**で運転を再開する見込みです *The whole line* is expected to be reopened soon. ‖工事のため8号線は**全線**通行止めです Route 8 is *entirely* closed due to construction (work).
▶総武線は**全線**不通です Train service has been stopped *along the whole length* of the Sobu Line.／The *entire* Sobu train line is out of service.

ぜんぜん 全然

1【**否定表現を伴って**】**not ... at all**（少しも…ない）；**never**（どんな場合も…しない）

> **解説** 日本語では「全然知らない」のように否定語を伴って動詞を否定するが，英語では **nothing** や **no** などを用いて名詞の部分を否定することが多い.

▶私はジャズには**全然**興味がない I have *no* interest in jazz.／Jazz does*n't* interest me *at all*［*in the least*］. ‖今週は**全然**雨が降っていない We have*n't* had *any* rain this week.／We've had *no* rain this week. ‖そんな奇妙な名前は**全然**聞いたことがない I have *never* heard of such a strange name. ‖誰がやったか**全然**見当がつかないよ I do*n't* have *the slightest*［*faintest*］idea who did it. ‖彼の言うことは**全然**信用できない I can'*t* believe him *at all.* ‖あの人の言っていることは**全然**わからない I can'*t* understand him［what he says］*at all.*
▶ **対話**「お邪魔じゃないかしら」「**全然**」"I'm afraid I might be disturbing you." "*Not in the least.*" ‖ **対話**「砂糖はあとどのくらいある？」「**全然**ないわ.（入れ物は）空よ」"How much sugar is there left?" "*None.* The jar is empty."（➤ 分量が「全然ない」は none で表し，nothing とはいわない）.

2【**否定表現を伴わずに**】**real, really**（非常に；前者は real の副詞用法で，くだけた語）▶わあ，おまえの妹［姉さん］，**全然**かわいいじゃん Gee, your sister's *real pretty.* ‖そのジーンズ，**全然**かっこいいよ You *look really cool* in those jeans.／Those jeans look *really* nice on you.

ぜんぜんかい 前々回 **the time before last, the second-last time, the second to last time** ━副 **前々回の…で** **two ... ago** ━形 **the ... before last.**

せんせんきょうきょう 戦々恐々 ▶彼は級友からのいじめに**戦々恐々**としていた He was *in constant fear* of being bullied by his classmates. ‖彼女がぼくのラブレターを友だちに見せはしないかとぼくは**戦々恐々**としていた I *was terribly afraid* that she might show my love letter to her friends. ‖犯人はいつ捕まるかと**戦々恐々**としているに違いない The offender must be *constantly afraid* wondering when he［she］will be arrested.

せんせんげつ 先々月 **the month before last** ▶彼女は**先々月**，大阪へ転校していった She was transferred to a school in Osaka *two months ago* [*the month before last*].

せんせんしゅう 先々週 **the week before last** ▶先々週は学校を休んだ I was absent from school *the week before last*. ‖先々週の日曜日は何日だったっけ？ What was the date *the Sunday before last*?

せんぞ 先祖 an **ancestor** /ǽnsestəʳ/ ▶先祖代々の墓 a *family* grave ‖彼の先祖は武士だった His *ancestors* were samurai. ／He is a descendant of a samurai family. (➤ descendant は「子孫」) ‖家屋敷を切り売りしてはご先祖さまに申し訳ない I would feel badly for *our ancestors* if we sold bits and pieces of the family land. ‖彼らは先祖代々この島に住んでいる They have lived on this island *for generations*. (➤「何代にもわたって」の意) ‖これは先祖伝来のつぼです This urn *has been handed down from my ancestors*. ／This urn *has been in the family for generations*.

1**せんそう 戦争** (a) **war** /wɔːʳ/ (国家間の大規模な戦い) ; (a) **battle** (局地的な戦い, 戦闘) ⇀戦闘 ▶戦争に勝つ[負ける] win [lose] *a war* ‖激しい戦争をする fight a fierce *battle* ‖誰もが平和を願っているのに, 世界のどこかできょうも戦争が行われている Even though everyone desires peace, even today there are *wars* going on in some part of the world.

▶人類はなぜ戦争をするのか Why do humans *go to war*? ‖戦争は何としても避けなければならない We must avoid *war* by all possible means. (➤平和に対して「戦争(状態)」をいうときは a や the を付けない) ‖かつて, 日本はアメリカと戦争をして負けた Japan once *fought* (*a war*) *against* the U.S. and lost.

▶《比喩的》受験戦争(＝競争の激しい入試)に打ち勝つ pass (*the*) *highly competitive entrance examinations*.

‖戦争映画 a war film ‖戦争孤児 a war orphan ‖戦争犯罪人 a war criminal ‖核戦争 (a) nuclear war ‖侵略戦争 an aggressive war ／a war of aggression ‖全面戦争 a total war.

2**せんそう 船倉** 《海事》 a **hold**.

3**せんそう 船窓** 《海事》 a **porthole**.

1**ぜんそう 前奏** a **prelude** ▶ピアノの前奏に続いて合唱が始まった The chorus began following *a prelude* of piano music [a piano *prelude*].

‖前奏曲 a prelude.

2**ぜんそう 禅僧** a **Zen priest**.

せんぞく 専属 ▶あのモデルには専属の美容師がいる That model has a hairdresser *who works for her exclusively*. (➤ exclusively は「独占的に, 専ら」) ‖彼はあのプロダクションの専属歌手だ He is a singer *under* (*exclusive*) *contract to* [*with*] that talent agency. (➤「(独占的に)契約している」の意).

ぜんそく 喘息 **asthma** /ǽzmə/ ▶ゆうべぜんそくの発作が起こった I had *an asthma attack* last night. ‖弟はぜんそくもちだ My brother is (an) *asthmatic*. (➤ an をつければ名詞, 取れば形容詞の用法) ‖ぼくは子供の頃小児ぜんそくだった I *had asthma* when I was a child. (➤「小児ぜんそく」に当たる英語はない).

ぜんそくりょく 全速力 **full** [**top**] **speed** ▶赤いスポーツカーが全速力で横を通り過ぎた A red sports car passed by me *at full speed*. ‖私は電車に間に合うように全速力で走った I ran *as fast as I could* [*for all I was worth*] to catch the train. (➤ for all one is worth は「全力を尽くして」).

センター 1【野球】**center, center field** (ポジション) ; a **center fielder** (選手) ▶センター前にヒットを打つ single to *center* ‖坂本はセンターオーバーのホームランを打った Sakamoto belted a homer *to the center field stands*.

2【総合施設】a **center**

‖センター試験 the center examination, the University Center National Standardized Entrance Examination (s) ‖センターライン the center line.

> **危ないカタカナ語✸ センター**
> 1 日本でよく使う「中心施設, 総合的な施設［建物］」の意味の「…センター」は英語でも … center [《英》centre] でよく, medical center (医療センター), recreation center (レクリエーションセンター, レジャーセンター), sports center (スポーツセンター), a community center (地域センター)などのようにいう. ただし, health center は「保健所」である.
> 2 trade center (貿易センター ; 貿易の中心地), commercial center (商業センター ; 商業の中心地)などでは center が「総合的な施設［建物］」と「…の中心地」の両方の意味をもつので, 後者の意味では a center of trade, a center of commerce のようにいって, 前者と区別することもある.

せんたい 船体 ▶船体(＝船)は右に[左に]大きく傾き, まもなく沈んだ *The boat* listed heavily to starboard [port] and sank soon after.

せんだい 先代 ▶先代の幸四郎 the *last* [*former*] Koshiro.

ぜんたい 全体 1【全部】**the whole** ━形 全体の **whole, entire** (➤後者は前者より堅い語) ▶地震が襲ったとき建物全体が激しく揺れた The *whole* [*entire*] building shook violently when the earthquake hit. ‖山全体が雪で覆われていた The mountain was *entirely* covered with snow. ‖部分的な仕組みだけでなく, この機械の全体の構造が知りたい I want to know about the *entire* structure of the machine, not just a part of it. ‖全体としてこの絵はよく描けている *On the whole* [*As a whole* ／ *Generally* ／ *Overall*], this picture is painted very well. ‖全体から見れば, それは小さな問題だ *All things considered*, it's only a small problem.

2【強調して】▶一体全体あいつは何者だ Who *on earth* [*in the world*] is he? ‖一体全体きみたちは何を考えてるんだ What *on earth* are you thinking about? ‖一体全体何が起こったんだ *Whatever* has happened?

‖全体主義 totalitarianism.

ぜんだいみもん 前代未聞の **unheard-of** ▶中学生が教師を殺すなんて前代未聞(の不祥事)だ It is *unheard of* for a junior high school student to kill his [her] teacher. ‖30か国語を話せる人なんて前代未聞だ I *have never heard of* a person who could speak 30 languages.

1**せんたく 洗濯** **washing** ━動 洗濯する **wash** (＋目), **do the laundry** /lɔ́ːndri/ [**washing**] ▶母は毎日たくさん洗濯します My mother *does* many loads of *laundry* every day. ‖卓は自分で洗濯します Taku *does the laundry* by himself. ‖アクリルの毛布は洗濯が利く Acrylic blankets are *washable*. ‖このセーターは洗濯しても縮みません This sweater will not shrink *if washed* [*in the laundry*]. ‖野球部の上級生は下級生にユニホームを洗濯させる The older members of the baseball club *have* the younger ones *wash* their uniforms.

▶洗濯代は1か月いくらぐらいかかりますか What's your monthly *laundry bill*? ‖洗濯物があったら洗濯機に入れなさい If you have *laundry*, put it in the *washing machine* [the *washer*]. ‖雨が降ってきたら洗濯物を取り込んでおいてちょうだい If it rains, bring *the wash* in. ‖洗濯した物を乾燥機で乾かしなさい Dry *the clean clothes* in the dryer. (➤ the washed clothes とはあまりいわない).

▶《慣用表現》山のすがすがしい空気を思い切り吸って久しぶりに命の洗濯をした I took a deep breath of the fresh mountain air, and for the first time in a long time *felt rejuvenated to the core*.

‖洗濯籠 a (clothes) hamper ‖洗濯業者 a laundry, the cleaners(店) ; a launderer(人) ‖洗濯せっけん laundry soap ‖洗濯ばさみ《米》a clothespin, 《英》a clothes-peg.

2**せんたく 選択** choice, selection ━動 **選択する** choose +目, select +目 (➤後者は特に「最適のものとして選ぶ」の意) ▶医者になろうと音楽家になろうとおまえの選択に任せる I leave it to your *choice* [leave it (up) to you] whether to become a doctor or a musician. ‖おいしそうなケーキばかりで選択に迷った The cakes all looked so good I had a hard time *choosing* one.

▶あの店は(いろいろな靴を取りそろえていて)選択の範囲が広い The store *has a large selection* of shoes. ‖ほかに選択の余地はない I *have no other choice*. ‖友人の選択は慎重でなければならない We must be careful in *choosing* [*picking*] friends. ‖新婚旅行で私たちはホテルの選択を誤った On our honeymoon, we *made a bad* [*wrong*] *choice* of hotels. ／On our honeymoon we chose [selected] the wrong hotel.

‖選択科目 an elective, 《英》an optional ‖選択式問題 a multiple-choice question.

せんたくき 洗濯機 a washing machine, a washer.

せんたくし 選択肢 a choice, an option ▶我々の選択肢は多くない We don't have many *choices* [*options*].

ぜんだま 善玉 a goody, a good guy ▶ちゃんばら映画では必ず善玉が悪玉をやっつけることになっている In samurai films, the *good guys* never fail to wipe out all the bad guys.

せんたん 先端 1【先の部分】a tip ; a point(とがった) ▶塔の先端 the *tip* [*point*] of the tower ‖その町は半島の先端にある The town is located at the *tip* of the peninsula.

2【時代などの】the forefront ▶あの方は時代の先端を行く哲学者です He is a philosopher at *the forefront* of our times. ‖彼女は流行の先端を行っている She *follows the latest fashion*.

‖先端技術 (a) high technology.

☞ 最先端 (→見出語)

センダン《植物》a chinaberry ; a sandalwood(ビャクダン) ▶せんだんは双葉より芳し Sandalwood trees are fragrant when they sprout. (➤日本語からの直訳) ／Geniuses shine from early childhood.

せんち 戦地 the (battle) front (前線) ; a battlefield (戦場) ▶戦地へ行く[送られる] go [be sent] to *the front*.

センチ a centimeter, 《英》a centimetre (➤記号は cm) ▶身長は173センチあります I am 173 *centimeters* [*cm*] tall.

ぜんち 全治する heal (up) completely (➤けがが主語の場合) ; recover from a wound /wuːnd/ (➤人が主語の場合) ▶彼は全治2か月の重傷を負った He suffered a serious injury that took two months to *heal*. (➤まだ2か月経過せず治療中の場合は took の代わりに will [would] take を使う) ‖あなたの足の傷は2週間で全治するでしょう You will *completely recover from* the wound in your leg in two weeks. ／Your leg will *be as good as new* in two weeks.

ぜんちし 前置詞《文法》a preposition.

ぜんちぜんのう 全知全能 ▶全知全能の神 *Almighty God*.

センチメートル a centimeter, 《英》a centimetre (➤記号は cm). →センチ.

センチメンタル sentimental ; mawkish (安っぽく感傷的な) ▶センチメンタルな映画 a *sentimental* [*tear-jerking*] movie (➤ tear-jerking は「お涙頂戴の」; 1語で a tear-jerker ともいう) ‖昔のことを思い出してちょっぴりセンチメンタルになった I *got* a bit *sentimental* remembering the old days.

せんちゃ 煎茶 *sencha* ; green tea of moderate quality (➤説明的な訳).

せんちゃく 先着 ▶先着100名様に映画の無料招待券を差し上げます Free movie tickets will be given to the *first* 100 persons. ‖席は先着順に割り当てます Seats will be assigned *on a first-come, first-served basis*. (➤「早い者勝ちで」の意) ‖先着順に並んでください Please wait in line *in* (*the*) *order of arrival*.

せんちゅう 戦中 during the war.

せんちょう 船長 a captain ; a skipper (小型商船や漁船などの).

1**ぜんちょう 全長** the total [full] length ▶このトンネルは全長約2キロです This tunnel is about two kilometers *long*. ／The *total length* of this tunnel is about two kilometers. ‖彼は全長6メートルのヨットで太平洋を横断した He crossed the Pacific in a *six-meter-long* sailboat.

2**ぜんちょう 前兆** an omen /óʊmən/ (兆し) ; a precursor (先触れ ; 堅い語) ▶良い[悪い]前兆 a good [bad] *omen* ‖連続して起こる小地震は大地震の前兆であることがある A series of small tremors is often *a precursor* of a big earthquake.

せんて 先手 1【囲碁などで】the first move ▶私は先手のときしか碁で勝てない I can only win *Go* games when I make *the first move*.

2【先に優位に立つ】▶先手必勝 Taking the offensive first is the sure way to win (a game). ／Victory goes to the swiftest. ‖特許を申請するつもりだったが, B社に先手を打たれてしまった We were going to apply for a patent, but B Company *beat us to it* [*to the punch*]. (➤ beat ... to it [to the punch] は「先制パンチを与える」の意のボクシング用語から).

1**せんてい 選定** selection ━動 **選定する** select +目, choose +目 ▶私たちの学校は英語教育のモデル校に選定された Our school *was selected* [*was chosen*] as a model school for English teaching.

‖選定基準 the criteria for selection ‖選定図書 good books selected for reading.

2**せんてい 剪定する** prune /pruːn/ +目 (刈り取る) ; trim +目 (刈りそろえる) ▶父はバラの木[生け垣]を毎年せんていする My father *prunes* the rosebushes [*trims* the hedge] every year.

‖せんていばさみ pruning shears.

ぜんてい 前提 a **premise** /prémɪs/; a **prerequisite** /priːrékwəzɪt/ (必要条件) ▶きみの主張は**前提**が間違っている You are arguing from false [wrong] *premises.* ‖ その仮定が正しいということを**前提**にして議論を進めよう Let's continue the discussion *on the premise that* this assumption is correct. ‖ 彼とは結婚を**前提**に(＝念頭に)付き合っています I'm dating him *with* marriage *in mind.* ‖ 数年の経験を有することがこの仕事の**前提条件**です Several years' experience is the *prerequisite* for this job.

せんでん 宣伝 **advertising** (宣伝行為) ; (an) **advertisement** /ædvəˈtáɪzmənt ‖ ədvə́ːtɪs-/ (個々の) ; **publicity** (広く知らせること, PR) **一動 宣伝する advertise** /ǽdvəˈtaɪz/ ＋㊐ ▶S自動車会社はテレビで盛んに新車の**宣伝**をしている S Automobile Company is doing a lot of *advertising* on TV for its new model. ‖ 町は**宣伝**のために駅に露天風呂を作った *For advertising purposes,* the town built an open-air [outdoor] hot spring bath at the train station. ‖ おたくの雑誌にうちの店のことを書いてもらえば大いに**宣伝**になる If you write about our shop in your magazine, we'll get a lot of *publicity.*
▶その会社は新しいコンピュータの**宣伝キャンペーン**を開始した The company started *an advertising campaign* for its new computer. ‖ あのポスターは**宣伝効果**が抜群だ That poster *is quite effective* [*is an effective advertising tool*]. ‖ **宣伝文句**に釣られてとうとうデジタルカメラを買っちゃった I was tempted [cajoled／coaxed] into buying a digital camera by the *advertising pitch.* ‖ 社長は事あるごとに息子のことを**宣伝**して(＝自慢して)回っている The president *brags about* his son on every possible occasion.
‖**宣伝カー** a sound car ‖ **宣伝ビラ** a handbill (ちらし) ; a leaflet (折り込み) ; a propaganda bill (政治的ビラ).

1**ぜんてん 全店** **all the stores** [**shops**].

2**ぜんてん 全点** **all the items** ▶あの店では**全点**３割引きをやっている They offer a 30 percent discount at that store.

3**ぜんてん 前転** a **forward roll.**

ぜんてんこうがた 全天候型の **all-weather** ▶**全天候型**テニスコート an *all-weather* tennis court.

せんてんてき 先天的な **innate** /ɪneɪt/ (才能が) ; **congenital** (病気が) ▶きみには**先天的**に音楽の才能がある You have an *innate* talent for music. ‖ 血友病は**先天的な**病気だ Hemophilia is a *congenital* disease.

せんと 遷都 **the transfer of the capital** **一動 遷都する** **transfer** [**move**] **the capital** 《to》.

セント a **cent**

> 《解説》アメリカやカナダなどの最小の貨幣単位で１ドルの100分の１, また欧州連合のユーロの100分の１. 記号はアメリカ・カナダでは ¢ で, 20¢ のように数字のあとにつける. ２ドル30セントは two dollars and thirty cents ($2.30) だが, 単に two thirty ということが多い. ユーロの100分の１はしばしば euro cents といい, 記号は c.

せんど 鮮度 **freshness** ▶生鮮食料品の**鮮度**を保つ *keep* perishable foods *fresh* ‖ この魚は目が死んでいる. **鮮度**が落ちているようだ The eyes of this fish look dull. It looks like it's *not quite fresh.*

ぜんと 前途 a **future** (将来) ; **prospects** (見通し) ▶きみたちの**前途**は明るい You have a bright *future* ahead of you. ／A bright *future* lies before you. ‖ 我々の**前途**は暗い Our *prospects* are bleak. (➤ bleak は「寒々とした」) ‖ 二人の**前途**を祝して乾杯しよう I'd like to propose a toast to the bride and groom. May they have a bright and happy *future.*
▶彼は**前途有望**な作家だ He is a *promising* novelist. ／He is a novelist *with a bright future* (*ahead of him*). ‖ 目標まで**前途遼遠**(りょうえん)だ The end is still *far off* [*far to see*]. ／We are still *far* from our goal. ‖ 会社を興したものの**前途多難**だ Although we've started a company, there are many problems *ahead of us.*

ぜんど 全土 **the whole of ...** ▶高気圧が日本**全土**を覆っている A high atmospheric pressure extended over *the whole of* Japan. (➤ (×) the whole Japan としない) ‖ 台風の被害は**九州全土**に及んだ Damage from the typhoon spread *over all of Kyushu* [*all over Kyushu*].

1**せんとう 先頭** **the head** (先端) ; **the lead** (首位, 先導, 率先) ▶《行列のトップの人を尋ねて》どちらが**先頭**ですか？ Where is *the head* of this line？ ‖ 《マラソンで》尾崎は30キロ地点で**先頭に立った** Ozaki *took the lead* in the marathon after thirty kilometers. ‖ 仮装行列では平井先生が**先頭**だった Mr. Hirai *led* the fancy-dress parade. (➤ led は lead (先頭に立つ) の過去形).
▶国旗を**先頭**に選手団が入場して来た The group of athletes entered *with* their national flag *at the head of the line.*

2**せんとう 戦闘** (a) **combat** (小規模な戦い) ; (a) **battle** (大規模な戦い) ▶西の国境で激しい**戦闘**が繰り広げられた A fierce *battle* was fought along the western border.
‖**戦闘員** a combatant ‖ **戦闘機** a fighter ‖ **非戦闘員** a noncombatant.

3**せんとう 銭湯** a *sento*, a **public bath**
日本紹介 ✉ **銭湯は大勢の人と一緒に入る有料の公衆浴場です. 男性用と女性用に分かれています. 近年は各家庭に風呂が普及しているので, 銭湯は少なくなっています** A *sento* is a public bath where many people bathe together. An admission fee is charged. *Sento* are divided into two sections : one for men, the other for women. Since many homes have private baths these days, the number of public baths is decreasing.
《参考》英米には日本と同様の銭湯はないが, イギリスには１つの建物の中に個室の浴室を多数並べた公衆浴場がある.

4**せんとう 尖塔** a **steeple**, a **spire** (➤ 後者は前者のとがり屋根の部分) ; a **pinnacle** (小尖塔).

1**せんどう 船頭** a **boatman** ; a **ferryman** (渡し船の) ▶ ことわざ **船頭多くして船山へ登る** When there are too many boatmen, the boat goes up a mountain. (➤ 日本語からの直訳) ／Too many cooks spoil the broth. (➤「コックが多すぎるとスープができ損なう」の意の英語のことわざ).

2**せんどう 扇動** **instigation** (唆すこと) ; **incitement** (刺激すること) ; (an) **agitation** (世論の喚起) **一動 扇動する** **instigate** ＋㊐, **incite** ＋㊐, **agitate** /ǽdʒɪteɪt/ ＋㊐ ▶群衆を**扇動する** *agitate* the masses ‖ その暴動は反政府軍の**扇動**によって起きた The riot *was instigated* by

the rebel forces.
‖扇動者 an instigator, an agitator.

3せんどう 先導する lead ＋目 ▶ガイドが皆さまを博物館まで先導します The guide will *lead* you to the museum. ‖白バイが祝賀パレードを先導した Motorcycle police officers *led* the celebratory parade.
‖先導車 the lead [leading] car.

ぜんとうよう 前頭葉 《解剖学》a **frontal lobe.**

ぜんどううんどう 蠕動運動 《生理学》**peristaltic motion.**

セントバーナード(犬) a **Saint Bernard.**

セントポーリア 《植物》an **African violet**, a **saintpaulia**(➤ 英名は前者がふつう).

セントラルパーク **Central Park**(ニューヨーク市マンハッタンの中心部にある広大な公園).

セントラルヒーティング **central heating** ▶彼は新しい家をセントラルヒーティングにした He installed *a central heating system* in his new house.
▶セントラルヒーティングの家が増えてきた The number of *centrally-heated* houses is increasing.

セントルイス **St. Louis** (アメリカ, ミズーリ州東部の都市).

せんない 船内 ▶私は船内で有名な歌手を見た I saw a famous singer *on board* (*a ship*) [*on a ship*].

ぜんなんぜんにょ 善男善女 **pious** [**devout**] **people** (信仰深い人々); **temple visitors**(参拝者).

ぜんにちせい 全日制 a **daytime-only schooling system** ‖全日制高校 a daytime-only (senior) high school.

ぜんにほん 全日本 **All Japan** ━形 全日本の **all-Japan** ▶全日本剣道連盟 the *All Japan* Kendo Federation ‖全日本選手権を獲得する win the *all-Japan* title ‖全日本チーム the *Japanese national* team.

せんにゅう 潜入 **infiltration** ━動 潜入する **infiltrate** ＋目 ▶そのスパイは敵陣に潜入した The spy *infiltrated* [*smuggled himself into*] the enemy camp.

ぜんにゅう 全入 ▶大学全入時代 the era *when all applicants to universities can be admitted.*

せんにゅうかん 先入観 a **preconception**; a **bias** /báɪəs/ (偏ったものの見方); a **prejudice** /prédʒədɪs/ (偏見) ▶行く前まではその国に対してばかげた先入観をもっていた I had silly *preconceptions* about the country before visiting it. ‖先入観をもって人を見てはいけない You must not judge people with *prejudice* [*bias*].
▶大人はあまりにも先入観にとらわれ過ぎているため, 私たち高校生がそれなりに環境問題に関心があることに気づかない Adults *have too many preconceptions* about us high school students to notice that we do have a pretty good level of awareness of environmental issues.

1せんにん 専任の **full-time** ▶私たちの学校にはアメリカ人の英語の専任教師がいる Our school has a *full-time* American teacher of English.
‖専任講師(大学などの) an assistant professor, 《英》a senior lecturer; a full-time instructor (高校などの).

2せんにん 仙人 a ***sennin***; a mountain hermit who has acquired the art of never-ending life (➤「不老不死の法を修めた山の隠者」という説明的な訳).

3せんにん 選任 (an) **election**(選挙などでの); (an) **appointment** (任命) ━動 選任する **elect** ＋目, **appoint** ＋目 ▶彼女は委員の1人に選任された She *was elected* [*appointed*] (as) a member of the committee.

4せんにん 先任 **seniority** (より長い勤務経験); a [one's] **predecessor**(前任者)
‖先任者 a senior member.

1ぜんにん 善人 a **good person**; a **good-natured person** (温厚な人) ▶彼は根っからの善人だ He is born *good*.

2ぜんにん 前任の **former, preceding** /prɪsíːdɪŋ/ ▶前任の校長 the *former* [*preceding*] principal / the *ex*-principal.
▶私は前任者の仕事を1か月前に引き継いだ I took over my *predecessor's* job a month ago. (➤ predecessor の発音は /prédəsesəʳ/).

せんにんりき 千人力 ▶彼さえうちのチームに入ってくれれば, それこそ千人力だ If he would only join our team, he would be *worth more than any number of others combined.*

せんぬき 栓抜き a **bottle** [**cap**] **opener** (瓶の); a **corkscrew** (コルク抜き).

せんねん 専念する **concentrate** 《on》(集中する); **devote** oneself 《to》(没頭する) ▶思い切って療養に専念したら? Why don't you put everything else aside and just *concentrate on* recovering your health?

> **【文型】**
> 仕事など(A)に専念する
> **devote oneself to** A
> **devote oneself to doing**

▶ジョン・レノンは5年間子育てに専念した John Lennon *devoted himself to* raising his son for five years. ‖女性は結婚したら家に居て家事に専念すべきだと思いますか Do you think that after marriage women should stay at home and *devote themselves to* housekeep*ing*?

ぜんねん 前年 **the previous year**(前の年); **last year** (昨年) ▶前年度の活動報告をします I will now make a report on (our) *last year's* activities. ‖私たちは私が小学校へ上がる前年にこちらへ越してきた We moved here *the year before* my entering elementary school.

せんのう 洗脳 **brainwashing** ━動 洗脳する **brainwash** ＋目 ▶彼は洗脳されて新興宗教団体に加入した He was *brainwashed* into joining a cult.

1ぜんのう 前納する **pay ... in advance, prepay** ＋目 ▶会費は前納でお願いします You are requested to *pay* the membership fee *in advance* [to *prepay* the membership fee]. / Membership fees to *be paid in advance.*

2ぜんのう 全能の **almighty,omnipotent** /ɑːmnípətənt/ (➤ 後者はより堅い語) ▶全能の神 *Almighty* [*Omnipotent*] God.

せんばい 専売 a **monopoly** ▶日本ではかつてたばこと塩は政府の専売であった In Japan, tobacco and salt used to *be monopolized* by the Government.
▶《比喩的》この落語は彼の専売特許(＝得意芸)だ This rakugo is his *specialty* [*forte*]. →特許.

せんぱい 先輩

> **【解説】「先輩」について**
> (1)日本語の「先輩」は同じ学校・勤務先などに先に入った人や, 自分と同じ学校を先に卒業した人などを指すが, この語は, 年功序列意識が強く, 家族主義的雰囲気が重視される日本人社会で生まれた独特の概念で

ある．したがって，平等原理に基づく西洋諸国には対応する一語の名詞はないので，文脈によって適宜その内容を英訳する必要がある．
(2) 日本語の「先輩」(*sempai*)をそのまま用いたほうが適切な場合もある．

▶江島さんは大学では私より２年**先輩**でした Mr. Ejima *was* two years *ahead of me* in college.／Mr. Ejima *was* two years *senior to* me in college.（➤ senior to は「…より年上である」の意になることもある）‖亀田さんは会社の３年**先輩です** Miss Kameda *has been* in the company three years *longer than I have*. ‖井上さんはぼくの**高校の先輩**です Mr. Inoue is one of the *older graduates from my senior high school*.（➤「先輩」は英語に訳せない日本語なので *sempai* をそのまま使うことが多い）．
▶佐藤君は私より年は若いが，仕事の面では**大先輩**だ Sato is younger than me, but *much more experienced* on the job. ‖私は**先輩たち**と一緒で窮屈だった I felt somewhat awkward in the company of *people* all *senior to myself*. ‖彼は**先輩**の１人と飲みに行った He went drinking with one of his *senior coworkers*. ‖それじゃあ**先輩**，これで失礼します Well then, *Sempai*, I must be going now. ‖彼と私とは**先輩・後輩の間柄**です He and I are *on a sempai-kōhai basis*. ‖あの人はいつも**先輩風を吹かせている** He's always *making much of his seniority*.（➤ make much of は「…を重大［重要］視する」）．

[1]**ぜんぱい 全敗する** lose all the games［matches］▶わがチームは**全敗**を喫した Our team *lost all its games*［*matches*］．

[2]**ぜんぱい 全廃** (total) abolition 一動 **全廃する** abolish (completely) ＋目，《インフォーマル》do away with ▶そんな校則は**全廃**すべきだ We should *do away with* such school rules.

[1]**せんぱく 船舶** a ship, a vessel（➤ 後者は大型の船を指し，前者より堅い語）; shipping（➤ 集合的に）
‖**船舶会社** a shipping company.

[2]**せんぱく 浅薄な** superficial（表面的な）; shallow（薄っぺらな）▶**浅薄な**知識 (a) *superficial* knowledge ‖**浅薄な**若者 a *shallow*［*superficial*］young person ‖**浅薄な**知識しかないくせに偉そうなことを言うな Don't talk so big when you know so *little*.

せんばつ 選抜 selection 一動 **選抜する** select ＋目 ▶彼女は2000人の応募者の中から**選抜された** She *was selected* from among 2,000 applicants. ‖わがサッカーチームは当県の高等学校の中から**選抜されて**全国大会に出ることになった Our soccer team *was selected*［*picked*］*out* of all the high schools in this prefecture to play in the national soccer tournament.
‖**選抜高校野球** the national invitational high school baseball tournament ‖**選抜試験** a selection［screening］test ‖**選抜チーム** an all-star team, a pickup team.

[1]**せんぱつ 洗髪** a shampoo /ʃæmpúː/ ▶私は美容院で**洗髪**してもらった I *had my hair shampooed*［*washed*］at a beauty parlor.

[2]**せんぱつ 先発** ‖**先発投手** a starting pitcher, a starter ‖**先発メンバー** starting players, the starting lineup.

せんばづる 千羽鶴 *senbazuru*
日本紹介 ✉ **千羽鶴は折り紙で作った千羽の鶴です．これに糸を通して，一つなぎにします．平和への祈願を込めて折ったり，病人の病室に全快への願いを込めて飾ったりします** *Senbazuru* refers to one thousand paper cranes made according to an origami technique. You thread the paper cranes to make a string of cranes. Some people fold cranes wishing for peace, and others hang them in the rooms of sick people they know to express hope for a complete recovery.

せんばん 旋盤 a lathe /leɪð/
‖**旋盤工** a latheman, a turner.

[1]**せんぱん 戦犯** a war criminal（人）．

[2]**せんぱん 先般の** recent ▶**先般の**増税 the *recent* tax increase.

ぜんはん 前半 the first half ▶試合の**前半**は勝っていた We took the lead in *the first half* of the game. ‖彼女はまだ20代の**前半**だ She is still in *her early twenties*.（➤「10代前半」は one's early teens）．

ぜんぱん 全般の general 一副 **全般に** generally, in general（➤ 後者はふつう文頭に置く）▶このクラスは**全般**に成績がよい *In general*, the students of this class do well. ‖**全般的に言って**女性は男性より長生きだ *Generally* (*speaking*), women live longer than men. ‖それは**社会全般**にわたる共通の問題だ It is a common problem of *society at large*. ‖いいところに就職したいのは大学生**全般**について言える We can say of *almost all* university students that they want to find a good job.（➤「ほとんどすべての大学生」の意）．

せんび 船尾 the stern.

せんびき 線引きをする draw a line ▶倹約することとけちであることの**線引き**は難しい It's difficult to *draw a line* between being thrifty and being cheap［stingy］．

[1]**ぜんぶ 全部** all, everything; the whole（全体）一形 **全部の** all, (the) whole; every（どの…も）→すべて ▶私は持っていた金を**全部**彼に与えた I gave him *all* the money I had. ‖**全部の**学生が勉強が好きなわけではない Not *all* the students like［Not *every* student likes］studying.（➤ not all［every］... で部分否定）‖彼はその物語を**全部**翻訳した He translated *the whole* story.（➤「１つの物語の全体」の意．「そこにあるいくつかの物語全部」ならば all the stories）‖漫画『テルマエ・ロマエ』のシリーズは**全部**持っています I have *a complete set* of the comic series "Thermae Romae." ‖**全部**きみたちに任せるよ I will leave *everything* to you. ‖彼女のことは**全部**（＝すっかり）忘れてしまった I have *entirely* forgotten about her. ‖ 対話「**全部**でいくらになりますか」「5000円です」"How much will it be *altogether*［*in all*］?" "It will be 5,000 yen."

直訳の落とし穴「全部の金」
「全部の」＝whole,「金」＝money と考えて，「全部の金」「金を全部」を（×）the whole money と言う人がいるが，こうはいわない．「強盗は全部の金を盗んだ」は The robber stole all the money. または The robber stole the entire sum［amount］of money. が正しい言い方である．

[2]**ぜんぶ 前部** the front (part) ▶事故で車の**前部**が大破した *The front* (*part*) of the car was crushed in the accident. ‖バスの**前部**座席 a seat *in the front* of a bus.

せんぷう 旋風 a whirlwind /hwə́ːrlwɪnd/（つむじ風）; a sensation（大反響）▶彼女の最新アルバムは若者たち

の間に旋風を巻き起こした Her latest album has created [caused] *a sensation* among young people.

せんぷうき 扇風機 an (electric) fan ; a ceiling fan (天井に取り付けられた) ▶扇風機をつける[止める] turn on [off] the *electric fan*. ‖首振り扇風機 an oscillating /ɑ́sɪleɪtɪŋ/ fan.

せんぷく 潜伏 1【隠れること】hiding ▶犯人は1か月間も市内に潜伏していた The criminal *had been hiding* in the city (*for*) as long as one month.
2【病気が現れないこと】incubation ▶ＨＩＶ／エイズは潜伏期間が長い HIV/AIDS has a long *incubation* [*latent*] *period*.

ぜんぷく 全幅 ▶選手は全員監督に全幅の信頼を置いている All the players have *total* [*complete* / *absolute*] *trust* in their manager.

1**ぜんぶん 全文** the full [entire] text.

2**ぜんぶん 前文** a preamble (憲法・条約の) ▶日本国憲法前文 the *Preamble* to the Constitution of Japan.

せんべい 煎餅 a *senbei*, a rice cracker
日本紹介 ✉ 煎餅は通例しょうゆで味付けして焼いた薄くて堅い米菓子です. よく茶うけとして食べます. かむとポリポリという音がします A *senbei* is a thin, hard rice cracker, (that is) usually flavored with soy sauce and baked. People often have them with green tea. They are so crisp they make a dry, crunchy sound when you bite them.

ぜんべい 全米 ▶彼は全米代表選手だ He is an *all-American* athlete. / He is a member of the *U.S. national* team. ‖全米から抗議の手紙がホワイトハウスに殺到した The White House was flooded with protest letters *from all over the U.S.* ‖全米オープン(テニス) the U.S. Open (Tennis Tournament).

1**せんべつ 餞別** a farewell [send-off] gift ▶せん別としてジャネットさんに日本人形を贈った I gave Janet a Japanese doll as *a farewell gift*. 《参考》せん別にお金を贈る習慣は英米にはない.

2**せんべつ 選別** selection (選択) ; sorting (分類) 一動 選別する select +目, sort +目 ▶産地では, 色・つや・大きさなどによるサクランボの選別作業が進んでいます In the cherry-growing area, people *are sorting* cherries according to (their) color, luster, size, etc.

ぜんぺん 前編 the former [first] part ; the former [first] volume (前の巻) ; a prequel /príːkwəl/.

せんぺんばんか 千変万化 ▶富士の姿は時刻や気象などで千変万化する The appearance of Mt. Fuji *changes in a myriad of ways* according to the time, the weather and so on.

せんぼう 羨望 envy 一動 羨望する envy +目 ▶羨望の的 the object of *envy* ‖彼女の美しさは級友たちの羨望の的だった Her beauty was the *envy* of her classmates. / Her classmates envied [were envious of] her beauty. ‖彼女は羨望のまなざしでその高価なネックレスを見た She gazed *enviously* at the expensive necklace.

1**せんぽう 先方** ▶先方に今晩電話してみます I'll call *them* [*him* / *her*] this evening. (➤ 相手の人数・性別によって訳語は変わる) ‖先方は我々の案に賛成しないだろう I don't think *they* [*the other party*] will agree to our proposal. ‖悪いのは先方であっても, けんかはするなと言われています I've been warned not to quarrel with others, even if the fault lies with *the other person*.

2**せんぽう 戦法** tactics, strategy. →戦術.

3**せんぽう 先鋒** a vanguard.

ぜんぼう 全貌 the whole story [picture] (全体の様子) ; (all the) details (詳細) ▶その殺人事件の全貌はまだわかっていない We do not know *the whole story* [*all the details*] of the murder case yet.

ぜんぽう 前方に ahead (自分の前の方に) ▶《掲示》前方道路工事中 Road Work *Ahead* ‖前方に美しい山並みが見えた We saw beautiful mountains *ahead* [*in front*] *of us*. ‖《バスガイド》前方に見えてまいりました山は磐梯山でございます The mountain that has come into view *in front of* us is Mt. Bandai. ‖彼は前方不注意で事故を起こした He caused an accident *because he wasn't watching where he was going*.

せんぼうきょう 潜望鏡 a periscope.

ぜんぽうこうえんふん 前方後円墳 a ***zenpokoen-fun*** ; an ancient imperial burial mound in the form of a square at the top and a circle at the rear (➤ 説明的な訳).

せんぼつしゃ 戦没者 a war victim (1人) ; the war dead (全体 ; 複数扱い).

ぜんまい 1【植物】(a) royal fern.
2【ばね】a spring ; clockwork (ぜんまい仕掛け) ▶ぜんまいを巻く wind *a spring* (➤ wind の発音は /waɪnd/) ‖ぜんまい仕掛けのおもちゃ a *clockwork* toy (➤ この英語には「他人の意のままに動く人」の意味もある) ‖この人形はぜんまいが切れているので動かない This doll does not move since the *spring* [*clockwork*] is broken.

せんまいどおし 千枚通し an eyeleteer /àɪlətíə^r/ ; an awl /ɔːl/ (革に穴をあける).

せんまん 千万 ten million (1千万) ; a countless number (無数) ▶1億2千万ドル one hundred and *twenty million* dollars ‖何千万の人々 *tens of millions of* people.

せんむとりしまりやく 専務取締役

> **解説 「専務取締役」の言い方**
> (1) 日本の会社組織からいえば **senior (executive) managing director** と表現するのがよいが, managing director は《英》では「社長」の意で用いられるので, イギリス系の会社を相手にする場合は chief executive (officer) とするのがよい. なお, chief executive officer, 《略》CEO は《米》では会社の「最高責任者」の意で, 実権をもつ会長または社長を指す. executive の発音は /ɪgzékjəṭɪv/.
> (2) アメリカの会社には vice president が複数いて, 日本の平取締役(時に部長級)であることが多いが, そのうちの **senior vice president** が「専務取締役」にやや近い.

せんめい 鮮明な clear (はっきりした) ; vivid (生き生きした) ▶鮮明な画像 a *clear* picture ‖鮮明な記憶 a *vivid* memory ‖この本は印刷が鮮明だ The printing in this book is *sharp and clear*. ‖スーパーハイビジョンの画像は驚くほど鮮明です The picture of the ultra high-definition TV is astonishingly *clear*. ‖このテレビは鮮明に映る This TV has a *clear* [*sharp*] picture. ‖祖父の顔はまだ鮮明に覚えている I still remember my grandfather's face *clearly* [*vividly*].
☛ 不鮮明 (→見出語)

ぜんめつ 全滅 **annihilation** /ənàɪəléɪʃən/ **一**動 **全滅する be annihilated** /ənáɪəleɪtɪd/ ▶ゴキブリを全滅させることは不可能に近い It is almost impossible to *wipe out* all cockroaches. ‖その戦闘で敵は全滅した The enemy *was annihilated* [*completely destroyed*] in the battle. ‖芽の出たばかりのトウモロコシはクマに踏み潰されて全滅だ The sprouting corn *has been totally stamped flat* by bears.

せ

せんめん 洗面 ‖**洗面器** a washbowl, a washbasin ‖**洗面台** a sink, a washstand ‖**洗面道具** toilet articles.

ぜんめん 前面 ▶建物の前面 *the front* [*façade*] of a building ‖新しい問題が前面に出てきた A new issue has *come to the fore*. ‖私は交渉の前面には出たくない I don't want to *head* the negotiations.

せんめんじょ 洗面所 a **bathroom**（家庭の）; a **rest room**（公共の場所の）. →トイレ.

ぜんめんてき 全面的な **complete**（完全な）; **total**（全くの）▶時刻表は全面的に改訂された The timetable has been *completely* [*entirely*] revised. ／There has been a *complete* revision of the timetable. ‖あなたのご意見に全面的に同意します I am in *complete* [*total*] agreement with you. ／I share your opinion *completely*. ‖被疑者は犯行を全面的に（＝すべて）認めた The suspect pleaded guilty to *all* charges. ‖あなたの全面的な協力をお願いいたします I would like your *full* cooperation.

ぜんもう 全盲 **total** [**complete**] **blindness** **一**形 **全盲の** **totally** [**completely**] **blind** ▶全盲の歌手 a *blind* singer.

せんもん 専門

《米》**specialty** /spéʃəlti/, 《英》**speciality** /spèʃiǽləṭi/ ; a **major**（専攻科目）→専攻 ▶私の専門は遺伝子工学です My *specialty* is genetic engineering. ‖加藤教授の専門は民法である Professor Kato *specializes in* civil law. ‖私はフロリダ大学でアメリカ史を専門に勉強した I *majored in* [*made a special study of*] American history at the University of Florida. (➤ major in は「専攻する」の意) ‖ 対話 「きみの専門（＝専攻）は何ですか」「コミュニケーション論です」"What's your *major*?" "Communication theory."

▶彼は東南アジアの歴史について専門的な知識をもっている（＝専門家だ）He *is an expert on* the history of Southeast Asia. (➤ 特定のテーマには on を, 学問分野には in を用いることが多い) ‖吉田博士は心臓の専門医である Dr. Yoshida is a heart *specialist*. ‖地質学は私の専門外です Geology is *not my field of study*. ／Geology is *not my specialty*. ‖きみたちは専門科目を60単位取得しなくてはならない You are required to earn sixty credits in your *major field*.

‖**専門家** a specialist, an expert ‖**専門学校** a vocational school ‖**専門店**《米》a specialty store, 《英》a speciality shop (➤ それぞれ a store specializing in ... , a shop specialising in ... のようにもいえる).

ぜんや 前夜 **the previous night, the night before** ; **the eve**（重要な出来事の）▶前夜の豪雪で学校は休校だった School was closed due to *the previous night's* heavy snowfall. ‖彼の結婚式の前夜, 友人たちは彼のために独身お別れパーティーを開いた His friends threw a bachelor party for him *on the eve of* [*the night before*] his wedding. ‖私たちは文化祭の前夜祭を祝った We celebrated *the eve* of our school festival.

せんやく 先約 a **previous engagement** [**appointment**] ▶ 対話 「あしたスキーに行こうよ」「ごめん, あしたは先約があるんだ」"Let's go skiing tomorrow." "Sorry, but I have *a previous* [*another*] *engagement* for tomorrow." (➤ (×) I have another schedule. とは言わない).

> **あなたの英語はどう響く?**
> 日本人は「先約があります」というとき, previous engagement や another engagement を使う傾向が強いが, そちらの (previous, another) 約束のほうが魅力的だと言っているように響いて不愉快だ, というネイティブスピーカーも少なくない. 日常的には I have something to do. のように言うか, I have a dental appointment. のように具体的に言うのが無難.

ぜんやく 全訳 (a) **complete translation** ▶その詩集の日本語の全訳が欲しい I want *a complete* Japanese *translation* of that book of poetry.

[1]**せんゆう 戦友** a **comrade in arms**.

[2]**せんゆう 専有** ▶この市ではわが社がN車の販売専有権を握っている Our company has *exclusive rights* for the sale of N cars [the *sole right* of selling N cars] in this city. ／Our company is the sole distributor [dealer] of N cars in this city. ‖私のマンションの専有面積は80平米です My condo is 80 square meters.

ぜんゆう 全優 **straight A's** ▶全優の学生 an *all-A* [a *straight-A*] student ‖彼女は大学を全優で卒業した She graduated from college *with straight A's*.

せんよう 専用 ▶夜間専用の自動預金機 an automatic deposit machine *for night use only* ‖この食堂は学生専用です This cafeteria is *for* students *only*. ‖この座席は非喫煙者専用です These seats are *exclusively for* nonsmokers. ／This is the non-smoking section. ‖ここは従業員専用の入り口です This entrance is *for employees only*. ／This is *the employees' entrance*.

‖**専用回路** a leased circuit ‖**専用機** a plane for one's personal use (➤「大統領専用機」は presidential plane) ‖**専用車** one's [a] private car.

ぜんよう 全容 **the whole picture** ▶事件の全容が明らかになった *The whole picture* [*story*] of what had happened became clear. ‖サリン事件の全容を解明する必要があった We needed to *uncover the whole truth* [*get the complete story*] of the sarin (poison gas) incident.

ぜんら 全裸の **naked** /néɪkɪd/ ▶その林の中で全裸の死体が発見された A *naked* body was found in the woods. ‖「火事だ！」と叫んで男は全裸のままホテルの部屋を飛び出した Shouting "Fire!", the man dashed out of the hotel room *with nothing on* [*stark-naked*].

せんらん 戦乱 a **war**（長期の）; a **battle**（個々の）.

せんりがん 千里眼 **clairvoyance** /kleəʳvɔ́ɪəns/ ; a **clairvoyant**（人）.

[1]**せんりつ 旋律** a **melody**, a **tune** (➤ 後者は前者よりも単純な旋律を指すことが多い) ▶覚えやすい旋律 a catchy *tune* ‖聴衆は美しい旋律に酔いしれた The audience was enraptured by the beautiful *melody*.

[2]**せんりつ 戦慄** ▶あの光景を目にしたときは戦慄が走った I *shuddered* [*trembled*] at that sight. ／*A shiver of fear ran through* me when I saw that sight.

ぜんりつせん 前立腺 《解剖学》a [one's] **prostate (gland)** ‖**前立腺炎** prostatitis /prɑ̀stətáɪtəs/ ‖前

立腺がん prostate cancer ‖ **前立腺肥大(症)** enlargement of the prostate, (benign) prostate hyperplasia.

せんりひん 戦利品 the spoils of war.

せんりゃく 戦略 (a) **strategy** /strǽṭədʒi/ (➤ 個々の「作戦」の意味では a をつける) ▶その会社は海外に進出するための**戦略**を練っている The company is working out *a strategy* [*a plan*] to expand its business overseas. ‖ **戦略上**その基地の存続は必要だ We have to keep the base *for strategic purposes*.

‖**戦略兵器** strategic /strətí:dʒɪk/ arms ‖ **販売戦略** a marketing [sales] strategy.

ぜんりゃく 前略

> 《解説》英語には「前略」に相当する表現はない.「拝啓」と同じように相手の名前を用いて, Dear Mr. [Mrs. ／Miss ／Ms.] ～ とするか, 親しい友人には Dear Tom のように書く. ビジネスの手紙でもできるだけ相手の名前を調べてそれを使うほうがよい. どうしてもわからないときは Dear Sir [Sirs ／Madam ／Sir or Madam] などで代用させる. ⇀**拝啓**.

せんりゅう 川柳 a *senryu*

日本紹介 ✉ **川柳はユーモアで味付けした俳句です. 世相や人間の弱点などをウイットや風刺を交えて詠んだものです** A *senryu* is a haiku spiced with humor. Favorite subjects include aspects of society and common human weaknesses described with wit or satire.

1**せんりょう 占領** **1** (占拠) **occupation** 一動 **占領する occupy** ＋目 ▶日本は戦後しばらくの間アメリカの**占領**下にあった Japan *was under* American *occupation* for a while after World War II.

2【独占】▶彼は3つの部屋を1人で**占領している** He *has* three rooms *all to himself*. ‖ 自分だけで座席を**占領するな** Don't *keep* the seat *all to yourself*. ／Don't *hog* the seat. ‖ 私の部屋は荷物に**占領されて**いて寝る所もない My room *is filled with* stuff and I can't find a place to sleep. ‖ わが家のテレビチャンネルは子供たちに**占領されている** The children *have taken over* the TV in our family. (➤ take over は「支配する」).

2**せんりょう 染料** (a) **dye** /daɪ/

‖**合成** [**天然**] **染料** (a) synthetic [natural] dye.

ぜんりょう 善良な good ▶**善良な**一市民 a *good* citizen ‖ 彼は**善良な**人柄で皆から慕われている He is loved by all for his *good* personality.

ぜんりょうせい 全寮制の boarding ▶うちの学校は**全寮制**(の学校)で, 生徒は全員学校の寮に入ることになっている Our school is *a boarding school*, and all students are required to live in the school dormitories.

せんりょく 戦力 military strength (兵力) ▶平和憲法にもかかわらず日本の**戦力**は増大しつつある Despite its peace [pacifist] Constitution, Japan's *military strength* is increasing.

▶チームの**戦力を強化する**ため, 彼らは有望な選手を数名入部させた They recruited several promising players to *beef* [*build*] *up* their team.

ぜんりょく 全力 ▶我々はけがをした少女を救助するために**全力を尽くした** We *did our best* [*did all we could*] to rescue the injured girl. ‖ 私たちは**全力を**尽くして練習してきました We have been practicing *as hard as we can*. ‖ 警察は凶器の発見に**全力を挙げた** The police *went all out to* find the weapon. (➤ go all out to do は「必死になって…する」の意のインフォーマルな表現) ‖ 彼はこの企画に**全力を傾ける**と言った He said that he would *devote all his energy* [*energies*] *to* this project.

▶彼らは**全力で**疾走した They dashed *with all their might*. ／They ran *for all they were worth*. (➤ for all one is worth は「精いっぱい」の意のインフォーマルな表現).

ぜんりん 前輪 a **front wheel**

‖**前輪駆動車** a front-wheel drive car.

1**せんれい 洗礼** **baptism** ▶私は高校のとき**洗礼を受けた** I *was baptized* [*I received baptism*] when I was in senior high school.

▶《比喩的》パリでシュールレアリスムの**洗礼を受けた**画家 an artist (who was) *influenced by* [*exposed to*] surrealism in Paris ‖ その投手は大リーグでの初登板で3連続ホームランの**洗礼を受けた** In his first major league game, the pitcher *allowed* three back-to-back [consecutive] home runs.

‖**洗礼名** a Christian [baptismal] name.

2**せんれい 先例** a **precedent** /présɪdənt/; a **previous example** [**instance**] (前の例) ▶**先例を作る** set [create ／establish] *a precedent* ‖ **先例にならう** *follow suit* [*a precedent*]. ⇀**前例**.

ぜんれい 前例 a **precedent** /présɪdənt/ (先例); a **previous example** [**instance**] (前の例) ▶**前例のない**事件 an *unprecedented* case ‖ **前例がない**からこそやってみる価値があるんだ The fact that *no one has done it before* is precisely why it's worth it for us to try (it) now.

ぜんれき 前歴 one's **past**, one's **past history** [**record**] ▶人の**前歴**を調べる check a person's *past history* ‖ 誰も彼の**前歴**を知らない Nobody knows his *past*. ‖ 彼は盗みで2回逮捕された**前歴**がある He has *a past* [*previous*] *record* of being arrested twice for theft.

1**せんれつ 戦列** ▶けがのためにその投手は残りシーズン**戦列を離れた** Because of an injury, the pitcher *was sidelined* for the rest of the season. ‖ その打者は**戦列に復帰した** The batter *made a comeback*.

2**せんれつ 鮮烈** ▶**鮮烈な**記憶 a *vivid* [*strong*] memory.

ぜんれつ 前列 **the front row** ▶写真を見てくれ. **前列の**右から3番目がぼくだ Look at the picture. I'm the third from the right in *the front row*.

☛ **最前列** (⇀見出語)

せんれん 洗練された polished (磨かれた); **sophisticated** (洗練されて高級な); **refined** (あか抜けした) ▶**洗練された**デザインのドレス a dress with a *sophisticated* [*an elegant*] design ‖ 彼女の物腰は**洗練されている** She has *refined* [*sophisticated*] manners. ‖ 彼は**洗練された**文章を書く He has a *refined* writing style.

せんろ 線路 a (**railroad** ／《英》**railway**) **line**, a (**railroad** ／《英》**railway**) **track**; a **single** [**double** ／**quadruple**] **track** (単 [複 ／複々] 線) ▶**線路を敷く** lay *a line* ／build *a railroad* ‖《掲示》**線路に入るな** Keep off the *tracks*. ‖ 私の家は**線路**沿いにある My house is along *a railroad line*.

‖**線路工夫** a trackman ‖ **線路標識** a track indicator.

そ・ソ

そ

そあく 粗悪な **poor,** 《インフォーマル》 **shoddy**; **poor-quality**（質の悪い） ▶粗悪品 *a shoddy product* ／*an inferior product* ‖ 粗悪な紙 *poor-quality* paper.

そあん 素案 a **(preliminary) draft.**

-ぞい -沿いに[の] **along** ▶川沿いの家 houses *along* the river ‖ 我々は海岸沿いに走った We ran *along the shore*. ‖ 国道が川沿いに（＝川と平行に）走っている A national highway runs *parallel with* [*to*] *the river*.

そいね 添い寝 ▶赤ちゃんに添い寝する *lie beside* one's baby (and sleep) (➤英米では赤ちゃんや幼児に添い寝する習慣はない).

1**そう 層** **1【地層などの重なり】** a **layer**; a **stratum** /stréɪṭəm/（地層；専門用語） ▶オゾン層 the ozone *layer* ‖ 関東ローム層 *the stratum of loam* in the Kanto District.

2【階層】 a **class**（階級）; a **bracket**（年齢・所得などの） ▶高額[中堅]所得者層 the high [middle] income *bracket* ‖ 多くの日本人は自分たちが社会の中間層に属していると思っている Most Japanese believe that they belong to *the middle class*. ‖ ヨーロッパのサッカークラブは選手層が厚い European soccer clubs have (good) *bench strength*. ‖ この雑誌は読者層が広い This magazine *has a wide* [*large*] *readership*.

2**そう 僧** →僧侶.

3**そう 相** a **phase**（変化するものの1つの）; an **aspect**（側面）; a **look**（外観） ▶景気循環の1つの相 a *phase* of business cycle ‖ 言語や文化の種々相 various *aspects* of language and culture ‖ 動詞の相 the *aspect* of a verb.

‖鬱(うつ)病相 a depressive phase ‖ 躁(そう)病相 a manic phase.

4**そう 沿う・添う** **1【川・道などをたどる】** ▶川に沿って細い道が続いていた A narrow path ran *along* [*parallel to*] the river.

2【方針・希望などに従う】 ▶両親の期待に添う *live up to* [*meet*] one's parents' expectations ‖ 私たちは家の方針に添って厳しく育てられた We were raised strictly *in line* [*in accordance*] *with* family policy. (➤in line [accordance] with は「(方針などに)合わせて」).

▶兄は両親の希望に添って裁判官になった My (older) brother became a judge *following* my parents' wishes. ‖ 誠に残念ながら，ご希望に添うことができなくなりました We are sorry to inform you that your application has *not been accepted*. (➤「申し込みは受け入れられない」の意) ／We are sorry to inform you that we *cannot comply with* [*meet*] your request.

5**そう 躁の** **manic** ▶その夜，彼は躁状態だった He was *manic* [in a *manic* state] that night.

6**そう** **1【そのように】** **so** ▶皆さん景気が悪いとおっしゃるが私はそうは思わない People say business is slow, but I *don't think so*. ‖ そうむきになるな Don't be upset *like that*.

▶ 対話「ミスがないかどうか作文をチェックしたほうがいいよ」「すみません．今後そうします」"You should check your composition for mistakes." "I'm sorry. I'*ll do so* from now on." ‖ 対話「遅いからタクシーにしたら？」「ええ，そうします」"It's late, so you should take a taxi." "(I think) I will." ‖ 対話「私たちは阪神の大ファンです」「私もそうです」"We are great Tigers fans." "*Me*(,) *too*. ／*So am I*." ‖ 対話「次のバッターはスクイズすると思うよ」「ぼくもそう思う」"I think the next batter will attempt a squeeze play." "I think *so*, too."

2【それほど】 **so** ▶M高校チームはそう強くない The M High team is not *so* [*that*] strong. (➤that のほうがよりくだけた言い方) ‖ オタワはモントリオールからそう遠くない Ottawa is not *very* far from Montreal.

3【肯定して】 **yes** ▶ 対話「あなた，チアリーダーなの？」「ええ，そうよ」"Are you a cheerleader?" "*Yes, I am*." ‖ 対話「きみ，最近痩せてきたね」「そうなんです．ダイエットしてるんですよ」"You've been losing weight recently, haven't you?" "*Yes, I have*. I'm on a diet."

▶ 対話「あなたゆうべ寝なかったでしょう」「そうなんだ」"You didn't sleep last night, did you?" "*No, I didn't*." (➤答えの内容が否定のときは，疑問文の形に関係なく No を用いる) ‖ 対話「東京はニューヨークより大きいよ」「そうだね」"Tokyo is bigger than New York." "(*That's* ／*You're*) *right*."

4【あいづちなどで】 **Really?** ▶ 対話「幹子さんから手紙をもらったんだ」「そう？ 何て書いてあった？」"I got a letter from Mikiko." "*Really*? What did she say?" (➤語尾を上げると驚きや関心を，語尾を下げると無関心を表す；次例も同じ) ‖ 対話「光一郎君は独身なんだよ」「あら，そうなの？」"Koichiro is single." "Oh, *is he* [*is that so*]?" (相手の言ったことを受けて疑問文にすると驚きを表す) ‖ そうなんだ *Is that right*?

▶ 対話「鹿児島へ行ってきました」「あ，そうですか」"I've been to Kagoshima." "Oh, *have you*?" (➤尻下がりに言うとそっけなくなる) ‖ 対話「きのうは出かけてたんだ」「ああ，そう．どこへ行ったの？」"I was out yesterday." "*Really*? [*Were you*?] Where did you go?"

> **あなたの英語はどう響く?**
> 日本人は「そうですか」の意味で I see. を多用する傾向があるが，これは数学の解説や解答などを聞いて「わかりました」と言う場合や，相手の言い訳が了解できたというような場合に使う客観的な言い方で，日常的に使うと冷たい感じがする．This button activates the safety device.（このボタンで安全装置が作動します）という説明を聞いて I see. のように答えるのが正しい用法．相手が I went to Hokkaido last week. と言った場合は Did you? とか Really?（尻上がりに）などのように答えるのが日本語の「そうですか」に相当する．

5【その他】 ▶そうか！ やっぱり犯人はあいつだったか *So* he was the culprit just as I thought. ‖ そうだ，ルミちゃんの誕生日にはベゴニアの鉢植えを贈ろう *I know!* [*I've got a good idea!*] I'll give Rumi a pot of begonias for her birthday. ‖ 《店員が》そうですねえ．これな

んかいかがでしょうか *Let's see.* How about this (one)? ‖ そうそう, あしたはきみの誕生日だったね. 忘れるところだったよ *Say* [*Wait a minute*], tomorrow is your birthday, isn't it? I almost forgot. (➤ Say は《英》では I say がふつう) ‖ 対話「昼飯はおごるよ」「そうこなくっちゃ」"I'll treat you to lunch." "*Sounds great.*"

そう- 総- ▶総ヒノキ造りの家屋 a house built *completely* of hinoki [Japanese cypress] ‖ 彼女の年間総所得は 2 千万円に達する Her *gross income* amounts to twenty million yen annually. ‖ 日本の総人口は約 1 億 2 千 7 百万人だ The *total population* of Japan is about 127 million.

‖ **総支配人** a general manager ‖ **総司令官** a supreme commander, a commander-in-chief (➤ 後者の複数形は commanders-in-chief) ‖ **総司令部** the general headquarters (➤ 略は GHQ) ‖ **総目録** a general catalog [list] ‖ **総量** the total amount.

☛ 総会 (→見出語)

-そう 1【…のようだ】**look, seem, appear** (➤ いずれも「外見上そう見える」の意だが, look と seem では後者が真実性・可能性が高く, appear は「思い違いや見間違いがあるかもしれない」という含みがある; →見える) ▶あなた気分が悪そうね You *look* sick. ‖ どうも熱がありそうだ I *seem* to have a fever. ‖ 彼は(実際は健康でないのかもしれないが, 一見)健康そうに見えた He *appeared* to be in good health. ‖ 雨が降りそうだ It *looks like* rain.

▶ぼくたちの野球チームは今度の試合には勝てそうだ *It looks like* [*It seems*] our baseball team could win the next game. (●「勝ちそうだ」と確率の高い予想をいうのなら could の代わりに is going to を用いる) ‖ 何だか吐き [かぜをひき] そう *I feel like* I'm about to throw up [to catch a cold].

▶この問題なら私にも解けそうだ *I think* even I can solve this problem. ‖ (話を聞いて) それ, おもしろそうね (It) *sounds* interesting. ‖ 彼女は今にも泣きだしそうだった She *was on the verge of* tears. (➤ on the verge of は「今にも…しそうで」).

2【「…そうな [に]」の形で】▶おもしろそうな映画だ That movie *seems* interesting. ‖ 彼女の言いそうなことだわ It's *just like* her to say that. ‖ 危うく口を滑らせそうになった I *almost* let it slip (out). ‖ 彼女は寒いのが苦手だからきょうは来そうにない Since she doesn't like the cold weather, she *is not likely to* come today.

3【…という話だ】**I hear that ...** (…だと聞いている); **They [People] say that ...** (世間では…と言っている) ▶バスの運賃が来月から上がるそうだ *I hear that* bus fares are going up next month. ‖ バス会社は赤字だそうだ *They say* [*People say* / *It is said*] *that* bus companies are in the red. (●It is said that ... は堅い言い方).

▶彼女は来週アメリカへ帰国するそうだ *I'm told that* she will be back in the United States next week. (➤「本人から聞いている」の意) ‖ 天気予報によればあすは雪だそうだ According to the weather report, it will snow tomorrow. / The weather report calls for snow tomorrow. (➤ call for は《米》で「予報する」の意).

☛ よさそう (→見出語)

1ぞう 象 **an elephant** ▶象は鼻が長い *Elephants* have long trunks.

2ぞう 像 **a statue** /stǽtʃuː/ (立像); **a figure** (人物像); **an image** /ímidʒ/ (画像, 彫像)

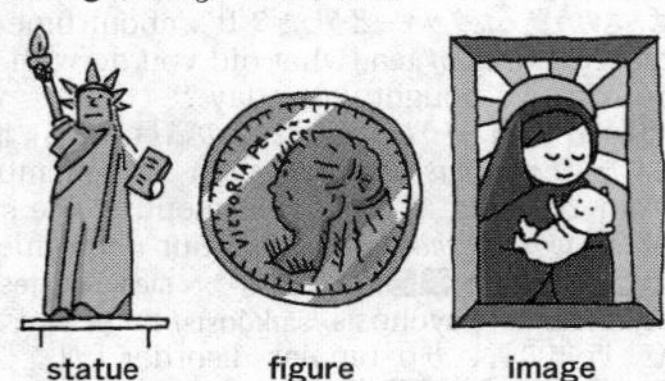

statue figure image

▶木 [石 / ブロンズ] 像 a wooden [stone / bronze] *statue* ‖ 聖母マリアの像 *a statue* [*an image*] of the Virgin Mary ‖ 上野公園には西郷隆盛の像が立っている There stands *a statue* of Saigo Takamori in Ueno Park. ‖ イギリスの貨幣には女王の像が彫られている British coins have *figures* of the Queen engraved on them.

-ぞう -増 ▶今月の売り上げは 2 割増だった This month's sales have *increased* by 20%.

そうあたりせん 総当たり戦 →リーグ(戦).

そうあん 草案 **a draft** ▶報告書の草案を作る make *a draft* of a report ‖ 憲法草案を討議する debate a *draft* constitution (➤ draft は「草案段階の」) ‖ クラブの会則はまだ大まかな草案ができたところだ The regulations of our club are still in *rough draft*.

1そうい 相違 **a difference** ▶大きな [かなりの] 相違 *a* big [significant] *difference* ‖ 2 人の間には意見の相違があった There was *a difference* of opinion between the two. ‖ 上記のとおり相違ありません I *affirm* [*certify*] the above *to be true* in every particular. (●certify は公証人などが言う場合) ‖ 彼が言ったことは事実と相違する What he said *goes against* [does *not agree with*] the facts.

2そうい 総意 **the general opinion** (大勢の人の意見); **the consensus** (一致した意見) ▶新しい法律は国民の総意に基づいて制定されたものだ The new law was enacted based on *a national consensus*.

3そうい 創意 **originality** ▶創意に富んだ作品を出品してください Please submit a really *original* work. ‖ 今回の出品作は全般に創意工夫に乏しい The works in the current exhibition are, on the whole, short on *originality and ingenuity*.

そういう **such, like that** ▶女性の前でそういう品の悪いことばを使わないでよ Please don't use *such* vulgar language in front of a lady. ‖ 井村? ここにはそういう人はいないね Imura? There is no *such* person here. ‖ そういうテレビ番組には興味はないね I'm not interested in *that kind* [*sort* / *type*] *of* TV program. ‖ きみにそういう才能があるとは想像もしなかったよ I never imagined that you had that kind of talent.

▶そういう訳で私は家を売ったんだ *That is why* I sold my house. ‖ そういう訳ならお母さんもわかってくれるさ *If so* [*If that is the case*], your mother will understand.

▶彼の親切をそういうふうに受け取っちゃいけないよ You shouldn't take his kindness *that way* [*like that*]. ‖ 人生とはそういうものだ (しかたがない) *That's life.* (➤ これに相当するフランス語の C'est la vie. もよく用いられる) / That's the way it is [goes].

そういえば そう言えば **come to think of it** (➤「考えてみると」の意のインフォーマルな言い方) ▶そういえば, あいつには 1 回会ったことがある *Come to think of it*, I met him once before. ‖ そろそろお茶の時間だな. そういえば, きのう買ったクッキーどうした？ It's about time for tea. *Speaking of* tea, what did you do with the cookies we bought yesterday?

ぞういん 増員 ▶うちの課では20名の職員が25名に**増員された** *There was an increase* in staff members from 20 to 25 at our department. ／The staff of 20 *was increased* to 25 at our department.

そ

そううつびょう 躁鬱病 《医 学》 **manic-depressive psychosis** (➤ psychosis /saɪkóusɪs/ は「精神病」の意. 近年の言い方は bipolar disorder「双極性障害」) ‖ **躁鬱(そう うつ)病患者** a manic-depressive.

そううん 層雲 《気象学》 a **stratus**, a **bank of clouds**.

ぞうえいざい 造影剤 《医学》 a **contrast medium**; an **imaging agent**.

ぞうえき 増益 (an) **increase in profit**, (an) **increased profit**, **earning growth** ▶今年度わが社は**増収増益**だった Our company reported an *increase in revenue and earnings* [*sales and profit*(*s*)] this past year.

ぞうえん 造園 **landscape gardening**
‖ **造園家** a landscape gardener ‖ **造園業** a landscape gardening business.

ぞうお 憎悪 (a) **hatred** /héɪtrɪd/, **animosity** (➤ 後者のほうが強意); **detestation** (強い憎悪) **一動 憎悪する hate** +目, **detest** +目 ▶彼はどういう訳か私に対して強い**憎悪の念を抱いている** He has an intense *hatred* of me [intense *animosity* toward me] for some reason or other. ‖ へつらうことは**憎悪すべき**悪徳だ Currying favor (with one's boss) is a *detestable* vice.

そうおう 相応 ▶働きに**相応した**収入が欲しい I'd like to be paid *according to* the work I do. ‖ **年相応**の格好をしなさい Dress in a way that *suits your age*. ‖ 化粧を落とすと彼女は**年相応に見えた** After removing her make-up, she *looked her age*. ‖ きみは**身分相応の暮らしをすべきだ** You should *live within your means*. ／You should *cut your coat according to your cloth*. (➤ どちらも「稼ぎの範囲内で生活する」の意).

そうおん 騒音 (a) **noise** (➤ いろいろな種類が入り交じった騒音は Ⓤ 扱い. はっきりした 1 種の騒音は Ⓒ 扱い) ▶通りの**騒音**がひどく, ゆうべはよく眠れなかった The street *noise* was very annoying and I couldn't sleep well last night. ‖ この辺の人々は新幹線の**騒音**に長い間悩まされ続けている The people in this neighborhood have been disturbed [troubled] by the *noise* of the Shinkansen for a long time.
‖ **騒音公害** noise pollution.

[1]**ぞうか 増加** (an) **increase** /íŋkriːs/ **一動 増加する increase** /ɪnkríːs/ ▶わが国では景気の後退で失業者の**増加**が深刻になってきた In our country, the *increase* in unemployment due to the recession has become a serious problem. ‖ がんによる死亡者数は年々**増加の一途をたどっている** The number of deaths from cancer *is increasing* [*is on the increase*] year by year. ‖ バードウォッチングの参加者は前回に比べ30パーセント**増加した** The number of participants in the bird watching (event) *has increased* by 30% over the last time.
‖ **増加率** a rate of increase.

[2]**ぞうか 造花** an **artificial flower**.

[1]**そうかい 総会** a **general meeting** [**assembly**]; a **plenary meeting** [**session**] (本会議) ▶生徒会の**総会**は土曜日の午後開かれる予定だ The *general meeting* of the student council is to be held on Saturday afternoon. ‖ **総会屋** a corporate racketeer [extortionist] ‖ **国連総会** the United Nations General Assembly.

[2]**そうかい 爽快な** **refreshing** ▶高原の朝の空気は**爽快だ** The morning air on the highlands is *refreshing* [*bracing*]. ‖ ゆうべはぐっすり眠ったのでけさは**気分爽快だ** I slept soundly last night and *am completely refreshed* this morning. ‖ ヨットの**爽快**さはたとえようがない Nothing can compare with the *exhilaration* of boat sailing. (➤ exhilaration /ɪɡzìləréɪʃən/ は「うきうきした気分」).

そうかいてい 掃海艇 a **minesweeper**.

そうがかり 総掛かり ▶課員**総がかり**で仕事をやってしまおう Let *all of us* in this section work together to finish this job. ‖ 私たちは**総がかり**でパーティーの準備をした We *all pitched in* to prepare for the party. (➤ pitch in は「協力して勢いよく取りかかる」).

そうがく 総額 **the total amount**; **the sum total** (合計額) ▶洪水による被害**総額**は 4 億円に上った *The total amount* of the loss from the flood was four hundred million yen. ‖ 年末セール中, **総額**2000万円の賞品が当たります During the year-end sale, we will give away prizes *totaling* twenty million yen.
▶私の年収は**総額**600万円だ My yearly income is 6 million yen *in total* [*in all*]. ／My annual income *totals* 6 million yen. ‖ その会社の資産**総額**は1000億円である That company's assets *amount to* (*a total of*) one hundred billion yen.

ぞうがく 増額 (an) **increase** ▶組合は賃金の**増額**を要求している The union is demanding *an increase* in wages. ／The union is demanding *a raise* [*a hike*] in their wages. ‖ 会社は接待予算を500万円に**増額した** The company *increased* its entertainment budget to five million yen.

そうかつ 総括 a **summary** (まとめ); **generalization** (一般論として言うこと) **一動 総括する summarize** +目, **generalize** +目 ▶問題点を**総括する** *summarize* the problems.
‖ **総括質問** a general interpellation (議会での).

[1]**そうかん 相関** a **correlation** ▶喫煙と肺がんとの間には密接な**相関関係**がある There is a close *correlation* between smoking and lung cancer. ‖『ハムレット』の登場人物の**相関図** a (*character*) *relationship chart* for "Hamlet" ‖ **相関図** a correlation diagram (➤ 物理・数学などの).

[2]**そうかん 創刊** ▶ 1930 年**創刊** *First published* in 1930 ‖ その雑誌は昭和39年に**創刊された** The magazine *made its first appearance* in the 39th year of Showa [in 1964]. (● The magazine was started ... としてもよい) ‖ ことしも新しい漫画雑誌が次々と**創刊された** New comic magazines *were published* one after another again this year.
‖ **創刊号** the first issue [number].

[3]**そうかん 壮観** a **spectacular view** [**sight**] ▶ナイアガラの滝はまさに**壮観**だ Niagara Falls presents *a spectacular view*. ‖ 何百頭もの象が草原を突き進む姿は**壮観**だった The hundreds of elephants rushing across the savannah were *a magnificent sight*.

[4]**そうかん 送還する** **deport** +目 (不法滞在者を); **repatriate** /riːpéɪtrieɪt/ +目 (捕虜などを) ▶政府は数百人の不法移住者を**送還する**決定をした The government decided to *deport* hundreds of illegal immigrants.

そうかん 増刊 ▶増刊号はきょう発売です *An extra edition* will be put out today.
‖**臨時増刊号** a special issue.

ぞうがん 象眼 (an) **inlay** /ínleɪ/ (➤動詞は /ìnléɪ/) ▶真珠の象眼を施したテーブル a table *inlaid* with mother-of-pearl.

そうがんきょう 双眼鏡 **binoculars** /bɪnɑ́ːkjələ^r^z, baɪ-/, 《インフォーマル》 **binocs** /bɪnɑ́ːks/ ; **field glasses** (小型の) ▶双眼鏡で野鳥を観察する watch wild birds through *binoculars* / bird-watch through *binoculars*.

そうかんとく 総監督 a **general manager**.

そうき 早期 an **early stage** ▶がんの治療では早期発見が大切だ *Early detection* is very important in the treatment of cancer. ‖英語の早期教育には賛否両論がある There are arguments for and against *teaching* English language *to* (*very*) *young children*.

1**そうぎ 葬儀** a **funeral (service)** ▶私たちは友人の父親の葬儀に参列した We attended the *funeral* of [for] our friend's father. ‖社長の葬儀には約300人の会葬者が集まった About 300 mourners gathered for our president's *funeral*.
‖**葬儀場** a funeral hall (➤英米では多くの人が集まるものは教会で行うのがふつう) ‖**葬儀屋** a funeral director, 《米》 a mortician, 《英》 an undertaker (以上, 人) ; 《米》 a funeral home, a mortuary (chapel).

2**そうぎ 争議** a **dispute** ▶争議を解決する settle *a dispute* ‖**労働争議** a labor dispute.

ぞうき 臓器 **internal organs** ▶臓器を提供する donate one's *internal organs* ‖臓器移植を行う carry out *an organ transplant* ‖この子は臓器移植する必要がある This boy [girl] needs *an organ transplant*.

ぞうきばやし 雑木林 a **thicket**(低木林) ; a **copse**, a **coppice**(小さな).

1**そうきゅう 送球** 《野球》 (a) **throw** ▶小田の本塁送球がそれて2者が生還した Oda's *throw* went wide of home plate to allow the two runners to score.

2**そうきゅう 早急な** **immediate** /ímíːdiət/ (即時の) ; **prompt**(迅速な) ; **urgent**(差し迫った) ▶早急にご返事を頂ければ幸いです I would appreciate a *prompt* reply. ‖早急に手術が必要です An operation is *urgently* needed.
▶この問題はできるだけ早急に解決しなければならない We must solve this problem *immediately* [*as soon as possible* / *without delay*].

1**そうぎょう 創業** **establishment, foundation** 一動 **創業する** **establish** ＋目, **found** ＋目 ▶その会社はことし創業100年を迎える The company will celebrate the 100th anniversary of its *foundation* this year. ‖明治20年創業 *Established* in the 20th year of Meiji / Since 1887.
‖**創業者** a founder.

2**そうぎょう 操業** an **operation** (➤しばしば複数形で) ▶操業時間を短縮する reduce *operating time* / shorten *operation hours* ‖あの鉄工所は操業を停止している That ironworks has stopped *operations*.

ぞうきょう 増強 a **buildup** 一動 **増強する** **build up** ▶軍備を増強する *build up* [*increase*] military strength (➤「軍備増強」は military buildup) ‖体力を増強する *increase* physical stamina [strength].

そうきょくせん 双曲線 《数学》 a **hyperbola** /haɪpə́ː^r^bələ/.

そうきん 送金 (a) **remittance** /rɪmítns/ 一動 **送金する** **send money, remit** ＋目, **make** [**send**] **a remittance** (➤remit 以下は堅い言い方) ▶小切手[為替]で送金する *send* [*make*] *a remittance* by check [by money order] ‖私は毎月息子に10万円送金している I *send* [*remit*] one hundred thousand yen to my son every month. ‖今月はまだ家からの送金がない I haven't received any money from home yet this month.
✉**ご送金いただきありがとうございました** Thank you very much for your *remittance* [for sending me the money]. ➤前者はビジネスレターの表現.
‖**送金受取人** a remittee /rɪmɪtíː/ ‖**送金人** a remitter /rɪmíṭə^r^/.

ぞうきん 雑巾 a **cleaning rag** ; a **floorcloth** (床用) ; a **duster** (から拭き用の) ▶その雑巾で床を拭いてちょうだい Wipe the floor with that *cleaning rag*.

そうぐう 遭遇 an **encounter** 一動 **遭遇する** **encounter** ＋目, **be confronted** 《with》 ▶しけに遭遇する *encounter* stormy weather ‖彼女は思わぬ事態に遭遇して途方に暮れた She was at a loss as to what she should do when *confronted with* an unexpected situation.

そうくずれ 総崩れ a **complete defeat, (a) rout** /raʊt/ (➤後者はやや堅い語) ▶投手陣が総崩れでわがチームはさんざんであった *One pitcher after another was batted out* and our team completely collapsed.

そうくつ 巣窟 a **den**(住みか) ▶悪の巣窟 *a den* of vice [iniquity].

そうけ 総毛 ▶家じゅうが荒らされているのを見て総毛立った When I found out my house had been ransacked, my *hair stood on end*.

ぞうげ 象牙 **ivory** /áɪvəri/ (➤「象のきば」そのものは tusk) ‖**象牙色** ivory, ivory white ‖**象牙細工** ivory work ‖**象牙の塔** an ivory tower.

1**そうけい 早計な** **premature**(時期尚早の) ; **hasty**(そそっかしい) ; **rash**(性急な) ▶人類に未来はないと考えるのは早計に過ぎる *It is premature* [(*overly*) *hasty*] to conclude that humanity has no future.

2**そうけい 総計** **the total** ▶この数字を全部足して総計を出してください Could you add up these figures and let me know *the total*? ‖その火災による被害額は総計2億円に達した Losses from the fire *amounted to* two hundred million yen.

そうげい 送迎 ▶空港のロビーは送迎の人々で混雑していた The airport lobby was crowded with *people who had come to meet or to see off passengers*.
‖**送迎デッキ**(空港の) an observation deck, a send-off deck ‖**送迎バス**(ホテルなどの) a pickup bus, a courtesy bus.

1**ぞうけい 造詣** ▶あの作家は日本の古典に造詣が深い That writer *has a profound knowledge of* Japanese classics. / That writer *is well versed in* Japanese classics.

2**ぞうけい 造形** **molding** ‖**造形美術** the plastic arts, the formative arts.

ぞうけつ 増結 ▶この電車には厚木駅で2両増結します Two cars will *be added* to this train at Atsugi Station.

そうけっさん 総決算 **the final settlement of accounts** (最終勘定) ▶《比喩的》この学園祭は私たちの高校生活の総決算です This school festival is the *culmination* of our high school life. (➤culmination /kʌ̀lmɪnéɪʃən/ は「(長年の)成果」).

[1]**そうけん 壮健な** **hale and hearty**（特に高齢者が）▶祖父は至って**壮健です** My grandfather *is hale and hearty*. ／My grandfather *is still going strong*. ‖ご**壮健**で何よりです I am very glad to hear that you are *in good* [*robust*] *health*.

[2]**そうけん 送検** ▶容疑者の身柄は１週間後に**送検された** The suspect *was sent to the* (*public*) *prosecutor's office* a week later. (➤ prosecutor /prɑ́:sɪkju:t̬əʳ/ は「検事」) ‖初犯だったので彼は**書類送検**だけで済んだ Since it was his first crime, he was released though *papers on his case were sent to the prosecutor's office*.

[3]**そうけん 双肩** **the shoulders** ▶この会社の将来は諸君の**双肩**にかかっている The future of this company rests on your *shoulders*.

そうげん 草原 **grassy plains, grasslands ; the prairies** /préəriz/（北米の）; **the pampas**（南米の）; a **steppe**（シベリアなどの）; a **savanna(h)** /səvǽnə/（熱帯・亜熱帯地方の）.

ぞうげん 増減 **increase and** [**or**] **decrease** ; (a) **fluctuation**（変動）▶会員数の**増減**が甚だしい There are sharp *fluctuations* in the number of members [in the membership]. ‖私の体重は多少の**増減**はあっても60キロ前後だ Although my weight *fluctuates* slightly, it stays at about 60 kilograms.

そうこ 倉庫 a **warehouse**（製品・商品用の）; a **storehouse**（貯蔵庫）▶その商品なら**倉庫**にストックがあります We stock that item in our *warehouse*.
‖**倉庫会社** a warehouse [warehousing] company ‖**倉庫業** the warehousing industry.

そうご 相互の **mutual** /mjú:tʃuəl/, **reciprocal**（➤後者は前者と異なり，相手からの見返りの意を強く含む）; **bilateral**（２国間の）▶会員**相互**の親睦を図るためダンスパーティーを開いた We gave a dance to promote *mutual* friendship among the club members. ‖国と国との**相互理解**を深める必要がある It's necessary to further *mutual understanding* between [among] nations. ‖きみたちは**相互に**（＝お互いに）助け合わなければならない You must help *each other*. ‖東急田園都市線と東京メトロ半蔵門線は渋谷で**相互乗り入れ**している The Tokyu Den-en-toshi Line and the Tokyo Metro Hanzomon Line *use the same tracks* beyond Shibuya.
‖**相互関係** a mutual [reciprocal] relationship ‖**相互作用** (an) interaction ‖**相互条約** a bilateral treaty ‖**相互扶助** reciprocal help.

ぞうご 造語 **coinage**（新語などを造ること）; a **coinage**, a **coined word**（造られた語）.

[1]**そうこう 草稿** a (**rough**) **draft** ▶演説の**草稿**を作る *draft* a speech.

[2]**そうこう 走行** ▶車の**走行距離**をチェックする check the *mileage* on the car (➤ mileage は /máɪlɪdʒ/ と発音する) ‖（自転車の前輪を上げて）**ウィーリー走行**する pull *a wheelie* ‖バスの**走行中**，窓から顔や手を出さないでください Do not stick your head or arm [arms] out of the window *when the bus is moving*. (➤掲示では Keep Arms In などとしている).
‖**走行距離計** an odometer /oudɑ́:mət̬əʳ/.

[3]**そうこう** ▶**そうこう**しているうちに in the meantime.

[1]**そうごう 総合** ▶事態を**総合的**に判断する take an *overall* view of the situation ‖目撃者の話を**総合**してみると犯人は眼鏡をかけた中年の背の高い男である When you *piece together* the witnesses' accounts, the suspect [culprit] is a tall middle-aged man wearing glasses. (➤ piece together は「(事実などを)つなぎ合わせる」).
‖**総合運動公園** a general [an integrated] recreation area with sports facilities, a public park with sports and recreation facilities ‖**総合学習（の時間）** (a period for) integrated study [learning] ‖**総合雑誌** an all-round [a general] magazine ‖**総合商社** a general trading company [firm] ‖**総合所得税** a consolidated [composite] income tax ‖**総合大学** a university ‖**総合病院** a general hospital.

[2]**そうごう 相好** ▶父は初孫を抱かせてもらい**相好を崩した** My father *was all smiles* [*broke into a smile*] when he held his first grandson in his arms.

そうこうかい 壮行会 a **farewell party** ▶フィリピンに赴任する吉田氏のために**壮行会**を開いた We had *a farewell* [*send-off*] *party* for Mr. Yoshida who is being transferred to a new post in the Philippines. (➤ send-off は「見送りの」に当たるインフォーマルな語).

そうこうしゃ 装甲車 an **armored car** [**vehicle**].

そうこん 早婚 an **early marriage** ▶一般にアメリカ人のほうが日本人より**早婚**だ Generally Americans *marry younger* [*earlier*] than Japanese (do).

そうごん 荘厳な **solemn** /sɑ́:ləm/ ▶パイプオルガンの**荘厳な**調べに圧倒された I was overwhelmed by the *solemn* music of the pipe organ. ‖戴冠式は**荘厳**に執り行われた The coronation was conducted *with solemnity*.

[1]**そうさ 捜査** a **search**（捜すこと）; (an) **investigation**（公的機関による究明）**━動 捜査する** **search**《for》, **investigate** ＋目 ▶警察は犯人に対する全国的な**捜査**を開始した The police began a nationwide *search* [*manhunt*] for the criminal. (➤ manhunt は「(大規模な)犯人捜査」) ‖**捜査**は難航している The *investigation* is facing difficulties. ‖その凶悪事件は12人の刑事が**捜査**に当たっている Twelve detectives have been assigned to *investigate* the vicious [heinous] crime.
▶警察は誘拐された少女の**公開捜査**に踏み切った The police launched *an open search* for the kidnapped girl. ‖銀行強盗が警察の**捜査網**に引っかかった The bank robbers were caught in the police *dragnet*.
‖**捜査課** the criminal investigation division ‖**捜査官** an investigator ‖**捜査本部** the investigation headquarters ‖**捜査令状** a search warrant.

[2]**そうさ 操作** **operation ; handling**（取り扱い）**━動 操作する** **operate** /ɑ́:pəreɪt/ ＋目, **handle** ＋目 ▶このＤＶＤレコーダーは**操作**が簡単だ This DVD recorder is easy to *operate* [*handle*]. ‖事故は機械の**操作ミス**によるものだ The accident was caused by *an error in operating* the machine. ‖彼は（車の）**ハンドル操作**を誤り，電柱に激突した He *lost control of the car* and crashed into a utility pole.
‖**遠隔操作** remote control.

ぞうさ 造作 ▶みそ汁を作るぐらいは**造作ない**（＝ごく簡単な）ことですよ Making miso soup *is extremely easy*.

[1]**そうさい 総裁** a **president** ; a **governor**（頭取）▶自民党**総裁** the *President* of the Liberal Democratic Party ‖日本銀行**総裁** the *Governor* of the Bank of Japan.

[2]**そうさい 相殺する** **offset** ＋目 ▶貸し借りを**相殺する** *offset* a loan against a debt ‖先月の売り上げ不振を今月の躍進で**相殺した** The slump in sales last

month *was offset* by this month's big jump. →帳消し.

そうざい 総菜 ***sozai***; **side dishes**; pre-prepared [pre-cooked] dishes usually eaten with rice (➤説明的な訳)

‖**総菜店** a sozai shop →おかず.

1**そうさく 捜索** a **search** 一動 **捜索する search** +目 (場所を); **search for**(人・物を) ▶彼らは警察犬を使って船の中を徹底的に**捜索した** They *searched* the ship thoroughly with (the help of) police dogs. ‖警察に家出した娘の**捜索願い**を出した I *asked* the police *to search for* my daughter who had run away from home. (● search my daughter とすると「所持品を調べるために娘の身体検査をする」の意になる) ‖彼は警察の**家宅捜索を受けた** *His house was searched* by the police.

‖**捜索隊** a search party.

2**そうさく 創作** **creation**(創作すること); an **original** [a **creative**] **work** (創作品) 一動 **創作する create** /kriéɪt/ +目 ▶このドラマは彼の**創作**ではなく別の作家の作品の翻案です This drama is not his *original work*, but an adaptation of a work by another novelist.

▶その話はすべて彼女の**創作**(=でっちあげ)だ The entire story is *a fabrication* by her.

ぞうさく 造作 **fittings**(建具類); **features**(顔立ち) ▶凝った**造作**の座敷 a tatami room with elaborate *fittings*.

そうさせん 走査線 a **scanning line**.

ぞうさつ 増刷 a **reprint** /ríːprɪnt/ 一動 **増刷する reprint** /rìːprínt/ +目.

そうざらい 総浚い ▶きょうは今までの課の**総ざらい**をしましょう Today, let's do *a general review* of the previous lessons.

そうざん 早産 **premature birth** ▶彼女は女の子を**早産した** She *gave birth prematurely to* a baby girl. ‖赤ん坊は(予定日より) 5 週間の**早産だった** The baby *was born* 5 weeks *premature*.

ぞうさん 増産する **increase production** ▶米の**増産**計画 a plan for *an increased yield* of rice(➤ yield は「収穫量, 生産高」) ‖その新製品は好評で, いくら**増産**しても注文に追いつかなかった The new product was so popular that no matter how much *production was increased*, they couldn't keep up with demand.

そうし 創始する **found** +目 ▶前島密は日本の郵便制度を**創始した** Maejima Hisoka *founded* the Japanese postal system. ‖あれは本校の**創始者**の像です That is a statue of the *founder* of this school.

1**そうじ 掃除** **cleaning** (きれいにすること); **sweeping** (掃くこと) 一動 **掃除する clean** +目 (きれいにする); **sweep** +目, **dust** +目 (ちり・ほこりを払って); **scrub** +目 (こすって); **mop** +目 (モップをかけて)

▶床に**掃除機**をかける *vacuum* [《英また》 *hoover*] the floor ‖たまには自分の部屋の**掃除**くらいしなさい You could at least *clean* your room once in a while.

▶佳代子は今, 自分の部屋の**掃除をしている** Kayoko *is* now *cleaning* (*up*) her room. (● up があるほうが「すっかり」というニュアンスが強くなる) ‖うちは毎年大みそかに**大掃除**をします We *do a thorough house cleaning* on the last day of every year.

‖**掃除機** a vacuum cleaner, 《英また》 a hoover ‖**掃除道具** cleaning implements [tools].

☞ **大掃除** (→見出語)

2**そうじ 相似** **resemblance**(似ていること); a **similarity** (類似点) ▶AはBの**相似形**である A is *similar* to B. ‖AとBとは**相似形**である A and B are *similar figures*.

3**そうじ 送辞** a **valedictory speech**.

ぞうし 増資 a **capital increase** 一動 **増資する increase capital**.

そうしき 葬式 a **funeral** (**service**) ▶**葬式**を出す hold a *funeral* ‖**葬式**に行く[出る] go to [attend] a *funeral*. →葬儀.

そうじしょく 総辞職 (a) **general** [**collective**] **resignation** ▶内閣の**総辞職**は10月になるだろう The *general resignation* of the Cabinet will take place in October. ‖内閣は**総辞職した** The Cabinet *resigned in a body* [*en bloc* / *en masse*]. (➤ en bloc /ɑ̀ːŋ bláːk/, en masse /ɑːn mǽs/ は「ひとまとめに」の意; ともにフランス語から).

そうしそうあい 相思相愛 ▶弘と恵美は**相思相愛の仲だ** Hiroshi and Emi *love each other*. / Hiroshi and Emi *are in love with each other*.

そうしたら ▶ここで降ろしてください. **そうしたら**駅まで歩きます Please let me off here. *Then* I'll walk to the station. ‖キスさせてくれよ. **そうしたら**家まで送ってあげるから Let me have a kiss—*if you do*, I'll drive you home.

そうしつ 喪失 **loss** 一動 **喪失する lose** /luːz/ +目 ▶処女[童貞]を**喪失する** *lose* one's virginity ‖彼は頭を打って記憶を**喪失した** He hit his head and *lost* his memory. ‖その役者は初舞台でやじられてすっかり自信を**喪失してしまった** The actor *lost* all (his) self-confidence after being jeered at his debut. ‖鈴木さんは奥さんをがんで亡くして深い**喪失感**を味わった[猛烈な**喪失感**に襲われた] Mr. Suzuki felt a profound *sense of loss* [was overwhelmed with a *sense of loss*] after he lost his wife to cancer.

‖**記憶喪失症** amnesia /æmníːʒə/.

そうして **1** 【それから】 (**and**) **then**; (**and**) **so** (それで) ▶私たちはまず映画を見にいきました. **そうして**食事をしました We went to the movies first, *and then* we had dinner. →そして.

2 【今の状態のまま】 **like that** (そのように); **as you are** (そのまま) ▶**そうして**ぐずぐずしている間に時間はどんどんたってしまいますよ You'll run out of time if you keep procrastinating *like that*. ‖**そうして**立っていなさい Keep standing *as you are*.

そうじて 総じて **on the whole**(総合的には, 全体として); **generally**(一般に) →概して ▶日本人は**総じて**シャイだ *On the whole* [*Generally*], the Japanese are shy.

1**そうしゃ 走者** a **runner** ▶第1**走者** the first *runner* ‖最終**走者** the last *runner* / the anchor (person) ‖中島は**走者**一掃の二塁打を放った Nakajima hit a double, driving in all three *runners*.

2**そうしゃ 奏者** a **player** ▶フルート**奏者** a flutist ‖打楽

器奏者 a percussionist ‖ オカリナ奏者 an ocarina *player*.

そうじゅう 操縦 **1【飛行機などの】一動 操縦する pilot** +⾃(飛行機を); **steer** +⾃(船などを) ▶飛行機を操縦する *pilot* a plane ‖ 船を操縦する *steer* a boat (pilot a boat というと「船の水先案内をする」の意になる) ‖ 彼はセスナ機の操縦ができる He can *fly* [*pilot*] a Cessna.

‖操縦かん a control stick [lever] ‖ 操縦士 a pilot ‖ 操縦席 the pilot's seat; a cockpit (操縦室) ‖ 副操縦士 a copilot.

2【人を操ること】▶渡辺氏は部下を思いのままに操縦している Mr. Watanabe *keeps* his staff *under his thumb*. (➤ under one's thumb は「(人を)顎で使って」の意) / Mr. Watanabe *holds a tight rein on* [*over*] his staff. (➤「しっかり掌握している」の意) ‖ 彼女は夫を意のままに操縦している She's *got* her husband *twisted around her little finger*. (➤ 女性が男性を思うままに操っている場合に使う).

ぞうしゅう 増収 an **increase in revenue**; an **increased income** (収入増) ▶今月は先月に比べ1割の増収だった This month our company reported [recorded] a ten percent *increase in revenue* over the previous month. →増益.

ぞうしゅうわい 贈収賄 bribery ▶贈収賄事件 a *bribery* case ‖ 建設業者と課長が贈収賄で逮捕[告発]された The contractor and the section chief were arrested for [were charged with] *bribery*.

そうじゅく 早熟な precocious /prɪkóʊʃəs/ ▶早絵は早熟な女の子だ Sae is a *precocious* girl. / Sae *has matured earlier* than other girls. ‖ 彼はまさに早熟の天才ピアニストだ He is really a *precocious* genius in playing the piano.

そうしゅこく 宗主国 a **colonial power** ▶旧宗主国 a former *colonial power*.

そうしゅつ 創出する create +⾃ ▶雇用を創出する *create* jobs ‖ アップル社はiPodやiPadで新市場を創出した Apple Inc. *created* new markets with the iPod and the iPad.

そうしゅん 早春 early spring ▶早春には木々は芽吹き, 人は桜の開花を待ちわびる In *early spring*, the trees bud and people grow impatient to see the cherry blossoms bloom.

そうしょ 草書 ***sosho***; (a) **cursive script**, (a) **grass script**; a **cursive** [**grass script**] **character** (1つの文字).

ぞうしょ 蔵書 one's **library**; a **collection of books** ▶約3000冊の蔵書 *a collection of* about 3,000 *books* ‖ H大学図書館の蔵書は500万冊だ The *library* of H University has five million books. ‖ 彼は蔵書家だ He *has a large library*.

そうしょう 総称 a **generic** [**general**] **term** ▶母乳で子を育てる動物を総称して哺乳類と呼ぶ 'Mammal' is *a generic term* for animals which feed their young with breast milk [animals that breastfeed their young].

ぞうしょう 蔵相 the finance minister.

そうじょうこうか 相乗効果 a **synergistic effect**, **synergism** /sínəʳdʒɪzəm/ (薬などの) ▶ペニシリンとストレプトマイシンの相乗効果が認められた *The synergistic effect* [*Synergism*] of penicillin and streptomycin was observed.

▶2社が電気自動車の発売に踏み切ったが, 相乗効果で市場が急速に拡大された The two companies started selling electric cars and *the synergistic effect* expanded the market rapidly.

[1]そうしょく 装飾 decoration 一動 装飾する decorate +⾃ ▶街路樹にはクリスマスの装飾が華やかに施されていた The street trees *were* festively *decorated* for Christmas.

‖室内装飾 interior decoration [design], décor /deɪkɔ́ːʳ/.

[2]そうしょく 草食の herbivorous /həːʳbívərəs/ ▶大型恐竜の多くは草食だった Most of the large dinosaurs were *herbivorous*. ‖ 息子は草食系だ My son is rather *passive toward women and dating*.

‖草食動物 a plant-eating [grass-eating] animal, a herbivore /hɔ́ːʳbɪvɔːʳ/.

ぞうしょく 増殖 multiplication 一動 増殖する multiply ▶顕微鏡をのぞくと菌がどんどん増殖しているのがわかる Through the microscope, you can see how rapidly the bacteria *multiply* [*reproduce*].

[1]そうしん 送信 transmission 一動 送信する transmit /trænsmít/ +⾃(信号を); **send** +⾃(送る) ▶メールを送信する *send* an email, email; *send* a text message (➤ 携帯電話からの) ‖ 船舶に最新の気象情報を送信する *transmit* the latest meteorological information to ships.

▶メールを送りましたが, 届いていないようなので再送信します I sent the email [the message], but it seems like it didn't arrive so I will *resend* it [I'm *sending* it *again*].

‖送信機 a transmitter ‖ 送信所 a transmitting station.

[2]そうしん 痩身 ‖痩身法 a weight-loss method, a way to lose weight →美容.

ぞうしん 増進する promote +⾃(促進する); **improve** (+⾃)(改善する); **increase** (+⾃)(増す) ▶適度の運動は健康の増進に役立つ Moderate exercise helps *promote* [*improve*] health. ‖ ぼくは夏になると食欲が増進する My appetite *increases* in the summer. / I have a better appetite in the summer. ‖ 2年になって急に数学の学力が増進した My math *has* suddenly *improved* since I entered the second year.

そうしんぐ 装身具 jewelry (宝飾類); **accessories** /əksésəriz/ (➤ 帽子やハンドバッグなどを含む; →アクセサリー).

[1]ぞうすい 増水する rise (水位が上がる); **swell** (水量が増える) ▶大雨で多摩川が増水した The Tama River *has risen* since [after] the heavy rain. ‖ 長良川が増水している The Nagara River *is swollen*.

[2]ぞうすい 雑炊 ***zosui***; rice soup simmered with chopped vegetables, fish, etc. (➤ 説明的な訳).

そうすう 総数 the total number ▶生徒の総数は何人ですか What is *the total number* of students? ‖ 応募総数は5000通に上った *The total number* of applicants reached 5,000.

そうすかん 総すかん ▶彼は紳士気取りでいるので女子社員から総すかんを食っている All the female employees in the company *have turned their backs on* him [*have given* him *the cold shoulder*] because he acts snobbish.

そうすると so (➤ 文頭で); **and** (➤ 命令文のあとで) ▶そうするときみはパーティーには来ないんだね *So* you're not coming to the party? ‖ そうすると彼女の言ったことは本当かもしれない *If so*, what she said may be true. ‖ まっすぐ行きなさい. そうすると左側に教会が見えます Go straight, *and* you'll see the church on the left. ‖ そうすると(=それでは)私も手伝いに行かなくちゃい

けないかしら *Then* maybe I should go and help him out, too.

そうすれば and(➤ 命令文のあとで)

【文型】
～しなさい, そうすれば…
命令文, and …

▶白状しなさい, **そうすれば**許してあげる Confess, *and* I'll forgive you. ／Come clean, *and* I'll let you off. ‖ 花瓶を割ったことを白状しなさい, **そうすれば**許してあげる Confess that you've broken the vase, *and* I'll forgive you. ‖ すぐに行きなさい. **そうすれば**終電に間に合うから You'd better leave right away, *and then* you'll make the last train.

そうせい 創世 creation ‖ **創世記**(聖書の) Genesis.

そうぜい 総勢 ▶私たちは**総勢**20名でした We were 20 *in all*. (➤ in all は「全部で」) ‖ **総勢** 5 万の軍隊が隣国に進攻した The 50,000-*strong* army advanced on the neighboring country. (➤「数詞 + strong」で「総勢…人の」の意；ハイフンは無しであけてもよい).

ぞうせい 造成する develop +㊐ (土地などを開発する) ▶海を埋め立てた場所は**造成されて**公園になっている The site reclaimed from the sea *has been developed* into a park. (➤ reclaim は「(海などを)埋め立てる」) ‖ 建設業者が山を削って宅地を**造成している** A building contractor is grading the hillside to *develop* land for residential lots.
‖ **造成地** land developed for building [housing] lots.

ぞうぜい 増税 a tax increase ▶近く**増税**があるようだ It seems we will have *a tax increase* pretty soon.

そうせいじ 双生児 twins (➤ 2 人の双生児のうちの 1 人は a twin) ▶あの双子は**二卵性双生児**だからあまり似ていない The twins do not look very much alike because they are *fraternal twins*. (➤「一卵性双生児」は identical twins という).

そうせつ 創設 establishment, foundation **一動 創設する** establish, found ▶津田梅子が津田塾大学を**創設した** Tsuda Umeko *established* [*founded*] Tsuda College. ‖ **創設者** a founder.

そうぜつ 壮絶 ▶**壮絶な**戦い a *violent* [*fierce*] battle ‖ **壮絶な**最期を遂げる die a *dramatic* [*heroic*] death(➤ 前者は「劇的な」, 後者は「勇ましい」).

ぞうせつ 増設 ▶電話を 3 本**増設する** *install* three *more* telephones ‖ ノートパソコンにメモリーを**増設する** *install* extra memory in a laptop computer ‖ 会社は支店を 5 か所**増設する**予定である The company plans to *set up* five *more* branch offices.

そうせん 操船する steer a boat [ship].

そうぜん 騒然 ▶会議場は**騒然としていた** The conference hall *was in a state of confusion*. ‖ 私が訪れたとき, その国は戦争直後でまだ**物情騒然としていた** When I visited the country, it was still *in a state of turmoil* after the war.

ぞうせん 造船 shipbuilding, a shipbuilder (➤ 前者は大きな会社をイメージさせるが, 後者は大小無関係)
‖ **造船会社** a shipbuilding company ‖ **造船技師** a shipbuilder, a marine engineer ‖ **造船業** the shipbuilding industry ‖ **造船所** a shipyard, a dockyard.

そうせんきょ 総選挙 a general election ▶**総選挙**で国民の信を問う take [submit ／put] a proposal to the people in *the general election* ‖ その党は**総選挙**で大勝した The party won big in *the general election*.

[1]**そうそう 早々** **1**【…してすぐ】as soon as ▶彼は帰国**早々**婚約を発表した *As soon as* he returned home from abroad [*On* his return from abroad], he announced his engagement. (➤ カッコ内は堅い言い方).
▶新年**早々**悪い知らせを受け取った I got (some) bad news *at the very beginning* of the year. ‖ 来月**早々**両親が上京する My parents are coming to Tokyo *early* next month.
2【急いで】hurriedly, hastily(➤ 後者には「分別を欠いて」という含みがあるのがふつう) ▶**早々**に立ち去る leave *hurriedly* [*hastily*] ‖ 2 人の雲行きが怪しくなったので我々は**早々**に引き揚げた We beat a *hasty* retreat because the two of them were getting quarrelsome.

[2]**そうそう 草々** ⚠ **英語には「前略」と同様,「草々」に相当する表現はなく,「敬具」に相当する表現で代用させる. →敬具.**

[3]**そうそう** ▶こんなにきれいな虹は**そうそう**見られるものではない You can't see a beautiful rainbow like this *so often* [*all that often*].

[4]**そうそう 葬送の** funeral ▶**葬送の**列 a *funeral* procession ‖ **葬送行進曲** a funeral march.

[1]**そうぞう 想像** (an) imagination **一動 想像する** imagine /ɪmǽdʒɪn/ (+㊐) (頭の中で考え・イメージなどを作る)；suppose《that》(仮定[想定]する) ▶太陽の無い世界を**想像できる**かい Can you *imagine* the world without the sun？‖ 奈良の大仏は**想像していた**よりも大きかった The Great Buddha of Nara was bigger *than I had imagined*. (●「想像していたとおりの大きさだった」だと, … was just as big as I had imagined) ‖ 猫ちゃん無しで生きていくことなんて**想像できない** *I can't imagine* [*It's hard for me to imagine*] living without my cat. (●(×)to live とはならない).

【文型】
～と想像する
imagine (that) S + V
➤ that 節の代わりに wh 節を用いることがある
人(A)が…することを想像する
imagine A doing
A が B であると想像する
imagine A as B

▶きみが宇宙にいると**想像してごらん** *Imagine* (*that*) you are in outer space. ／*Imagine* [*Picture*] yourself in outer space. (➤ picture A は「A を想像する, 思い浮かべる」の意. that 節が続くことは少ない) ‖ 彼が万引きするなんて**想像できない** I *can't imagine that* he would shoplift. (● この would は「まさかそんなことが」のニュアンスを出す；I can't imagine that he shoplifts [that he is a shoplifter]. だと「彼が(常習的に)万引きしているとは思えない」の意になる) ／I *can't imagine* him shoplift*ing*. (➤「彼が万引きしていることが想像できない」くらいの意味になる) ‖ 私の気持ちが**想像できる**？ *Can* you *imagine* how I feel？／*Can* you *imagine* my feelings？‖ 私はその本の著者が年配の男性だと**想像していた** I *had imagined that* the author of that book was an old man. ／I *had imagined* the author of that book *as* an old man.
▶彼は私が**想像**(＝予想)していたとおりの人でした I found him (to be) *exactly the kind of* person I *had expected*. ‖ 核戦争後の地球がどんなものか**想像も**

つかない I *don't have the slightest idea* what the earth would look like after a nuclear war. ‖ 対話「彼は何と言ってプロポーズしたんですか」「ご想像にお任せします」"What did he say when he proposed?" "I'll leave that (up) to your *imagination*."
▶一角獣は**想像上の**動物だ A unicorn is an *imaginary* animal. ‖ きみは**想像力が豊か**だね You are *quite imaginative*. ／You *have a rich imagination*. ‖ 彼女は**想像力**に欠ける She lacks *imagination*. ／She's unimaginative. ‖ **想像力**を働かせてごらん Use your *imagination*. ‖ あれは想像妊娠だったの That was *a false* [《英また》*phantom*] *pregnancy*. (➤「想像妊娠」を文字どおり imaginary pregnancy ということもある).

[2]**そうぞう 創造** creation /kriéɪʃən/ ; creativity (独創力) 一動 **創造する** create /kriéɪt/ +目 ▶天地創造 the *Creation* (of Heaven and Earth) ‖ 私は模型飛行機を作り上げて**創造**の喜びを知った I discovered the joy of *creating something* by making a model airplane. ‖ 模倣なしに**創造**などありえない *Creativity* comes after imitation. ‖ 芸術家は独創的なものを**創造する** An artist *creates* something original.

そうぞうしい 騒々しい noisy ; boisterous (特に子供が陽気で騒がしい) ▶**騒々しい**子供たちだこと！ What *noisy* [*boisterous*] children you are! ／You kids sure are *noisy*. ‖ そんなに**騒々しく**しないでよ Don't *be* so *noisy*. ／Don't *make* so much *noise*.
▶世の中が**騒々しく**なってきた The times have become *turbulent*.

そうそうたる 錚々たる ▶実業界の**そうそうたる**面々がそのパーティーに出席した *Prominent* figures from the business world attended the party.

そうぞく 相続 inheritance (遺産の) ; succession (地位の) 一動 **相続する** inherit +目, succeed to ▶彼女は父親からばく大な遺産を**相続した** She *inherited* [*succeeded to*] her father's large *fortune*. (🏺この意味での succeed to は堅い言い方) ／She *received* a large *inheritance* from her father. ‖ 専務が父親の跡目を**相続して**社長になった The senior managing director *succeeded* his father as president of the company. (🏺地位や物でなく, 人の跡を継ぐ場合は「succeed + 人」となる) ‖ 醜い**相続争い**はやめよう Let's not engage in any ugly *bickering over the inheritance*. (➤ bickering は「いさかい」).
‖**相続財産** an inheritance ‖ **相続税** an inheritance tax, 《米また》a death tax, 《英また》death duties ‖ **相続人** an heir /eəʳ/.

そうそふ 曽祖父 a great-grandfather.

そうそぼ 曽祖母 a great-grandmother.

-そうだ →-そう.

[1]**そうたい 総体** ▶**総体的に**女子は男子よりよく勉強する *On the whole* [*In general* ／*Generally* (*speaking*)], girls study harder than boys. (➤ on the whole は「概して」, カッコ内はともに「一般的に」の意) ‖ ことしの学園祭はいくつか問題はあったが**総体的には**(＝全体としては)成功であった Although we had some problems, this year's campus festival was a success *as a whole*.

[2]**そうたい 早退する** leave early ▶彼はきょう学校を**早退した** Today, he *left school before classes were over*. ‖ 彼女は会社を定時より１時間早く**早退した** She *left* the office one hour *earlier* than the (usual) quitting time.
‖**早退届** an early dismissal note.

[1]**そうだい 壮大な** grand ; magnificent (堂々としてすばらしい) ▶3000年前ここに**壮大な**宮殿があった There used to be a *grand* palace here 3,000 years ago.
▶モンブラン山頂からの眺めは実に**壮大**だった The view from the top of Mont Blanc was *magnificent*. ‖ 私たちは津軽海峡を泳いで渡るという**壮大な**計画をもっている We have a *grand* plan to swim across the Tsugaru Strait.

[2]**そうだい 総代** a representative, 《米》a valedictorian /vælədɪktɔ́ːriən/ (➤後者は成績最優秀者がなる) ▶野中さんは卒業生の**総代**に選ばれた Nonaka was chosen as *representative* [《米》*valedictorian*] of all the graduating students.

ぞうだい 増大 (an) increase 一動 **増大する** increase ▶最近赤ワインの需要が**増大している** Recently, the demand for red wine *has increased*. ‖ 近年の不況で雇用不安が**増大した** The recent recession *has increased* [*added to*] uneasiness about unemployment.

そうたいてき 相対的な relative 一副 **相対的に** relatively ▶ものを**相対的に**見る look at things *relatively* ‖ 早いとか遅いとか言ってもそれは**相対的な**ことだ The question whether it's (too) soon or (too) late is entirely *relative*.
▶**相対的に言って**この腕時計はほかのより安い This watch is *relatively* cheap compared with others. ‖ **相対的に言って**この県の人は保守的だ *Relatively speaking*, people in this prefecture are (socially) conservative.

そうだち 総立ち ▶レースが白熱し観客は**総立ち**となった As the race came down to a dead heat, *all* the spectators *rose from their seats at once*. ‖ 聴衆は**総立ちになって**指揮者に**拍手した** *All* the audience *gave* the conductor *a standing ovation*. (➤ standing ovation は「全員起立しての大喝采」).

そうだつ 争奪 a struggle (闘争) ; a competition (競争, 試合) ▶彼が辞めると, その空席を巡っての**争奪**が行われた When he resigned, there was *a struggle* for the newly vacant post. ‖ デビスカップの**争奪戦**が来月行われる The *competition* for the Davis Cup is scheduled for next month.

そうだん 相談

1【話し合うこと】 a talk, consultation 一動 (…と, に) **相談する** talk 《with, to》, consult /kənsʌ́lt/ +目

> 語法 (1)他動詞の **consult** は「権威者の助言を求める」の意で, 主に医師や弁護士に時に手短に相談する場合に用いる. (2)自動詞の **consult with** は「じっくり話し合う」のニュアンスになる. (3)「相談する」の意ではふつうは **talk with [to]** を用いる.

▶離婚のことで弁護士に**相談した** I *consulted* [*consulted with*] a lawyer about our divorce. ‖ 同僚に**相談しない**といけないだろうと思います I think I'll have to *consult with* my business partner(s).

> 【文型】
> **人(A)と B のことで相談する**
> talk with A about B
> talk over B with A

▶彼は今度の就職のことで両親と**相談した** He *talked with* his parents *about* his new job. ‖ みんなと相

談してからご返事します I'll give you my answer after I *talk it over with* the others. ‖ ねえねえ, 相談に乗ってくれる？ Look, I have a problem. *Can I talk it over with you*?
▶相談に乗って(＝助言して)くれる相手が欲しい I want someone to *give* me (*some*) *advice* [to *advise* me]. ‖ ちょっとご相談したいのですが If you have a moment, there's something I'd like to *ask your advice about* [I'd like to *talk to you about*]. ‖ 石田先生なら相談に乗ってくれるよ Mr. Ishida is a good person to go to *for advice*.
▶悩み事の相談は市役所で受け付けます You can bring your problems to City Hall. We would be glad to *talk with* you. ‖ 生徒相談室[市民相談室]は 3 階にあります The *student-counseling room* [The *counseling room for citizens*] is on the third floor.
‖ 相談役 a senior adviser.
2【慣用表現】▶費用はご相談に応じます The cost is *negotiable*. ‖ 今すぐ車を買ってくれといってもそれはできない相談だ I can't buy you a car right now, son. *That's asking a little too much*. ‖ ものは相談だけど, きみのビデオカメラとぼくのカメラを交換しないかい *It's just an idea*, but how about trading your camcorder for my camera?

そうち 装置 a **device**(特別の目的に考案された)；(an) **apparatus** /æpəræ̀ṭəs/ (組み立てられた器具装置)；**equipment**(機械設備；集合的に) ▶ガス漏れ警報装置 *a* leakage warning *device* ‖ 化学実験用の(機械)装置 *apparatus* for an experiment in chemistry ‖ 防火装置を取り付ける install *fire prevention equipment*.
‖ 安全装置 a safety device ‖ 制御装置 a control system ‖ 舞台装置 a stage setting ‖ 冷房装置 an air conditioner.

ぞうちく 増築する **build an addition** [**an extension**] (➤ extension は主に大きな建物の場合) ▶私は家の増築をK工務店に依頼した I asked K Builder's Office to *build an addition to* our house.
▶旧社屋に新しく一部が増築された A new *extension has been built* [*has been added*] onto the old company building. ‖ 校舎は目下増築中だ *An extension* to the school building *is* now *under construction*.

そうちゃく 装着する **wear** +㊐ ▶防弾チョッキを装着する *wear* a bulletproof vest ‖ 防護眼鏡を装着する *wear* protective goggles ‖ タイヤにチェーンを装着する *install* tire chains ／*put* chains on the tires.

1**そうちょう 総長** **the president (of a university), the chancellor (of a university)** 《参考》後者は《米》では限られた大学の学長を指すが,《英》では名誉職の総長を指す(実務を執る vice-chancellor が事実上の総長).

2**そうちょう 早朝** **early morning** ▶12月 5 日の早朝地震があった We had an earthquake *early on the morning* of December 5. ‖ あす早朝にオーストラリアへ出発します I'm leaving for Australia *early tomorrow morning*.

3**そうちょう 荘重な** **solemn** /sɑ́:ləm/ ▶荘重な儀式 a *solemn* ceremony ‖ 葬列は合唱隊の荘重な歌声に合わせて静々と進んだ The funeral procession advanced slowly to the *solemn* music of the choir.

4**そうちょう 曹長** a **sergeant major.**

ぞうちょう 増長する **get a swell(ed)** [《英》**swollen**] **head** ▶先生に褒められたからってあんまり増長するなよな Don't *get a swell*(*ed*) *head* just because the teacher praised you.

そうで 総出 ▶村じゅう総出で神社の境内を掃除した *All the people* in the village *went out* to clean the precincts of the shrine.

1**そうてい 想定** (an) **assumption**, (a) **supposition** 一動 (…と)想定する **assume** 《that》, **suppose** 《that》▶東海大地震を想定して避難訓練を行った We held an evacuation drill *on* [*under*／*with*] *the assumption that* the Great Tokai Earthquake had just occurred. ‖ 今回の災害を想定外の自然災害として説明するのは無責任なことだ It is irresponsible to explain this disaster as an *unforeseen* [*unexpected* ／ *unanticipated*] natural disaster. (● 「想定外として」だと as beyond our expectations) ‖ このような事態は想定の範囲内である(＝我われは想定していた) We *foresaw* [*anticipated*] *the possibility* of this kind of situation (happening).

2**そうてい 装丁** **binding**(製本)；(a) **design**(デザイン) ▶この本は装丁が非常にしっかりしている This book *is* very firmly *bound*. (➤ bound は bind(製本する)の過去分詞形) ‖ この詩集の装丁は有名な画家の手になるものです This anthology *was designed* by a famous artist.

ぞうてい 贈呈 **presentation** 一動 贈呈する **present** /prɪzént/ +㊐ ▶私たちは恩師にはと時計を贈呈した We *presented* a cuckoo clock *to* our teacher. ／We *presented* our teacher (*with*) a cuckoo clock.
‖ 贈呈式 a presentation ceremony ‖ 贈呈品 a present /prézənt/, a gift ‖ 贈呈本 a complimentary copy (of a book).

そうてん 争点 an **issue**；a **point of contention**(論点) ▶今度の蔵相会議では通貨介入問題が争点になりそうだ Currency interventions will be *an issue* [*a point of contention*] at the next meeting of finance ministers.

そうでんせん 送電線 a **power (transmission) line** [**cable**].

そうとう 相当

1【かなり】**pretty**；**very** (とても)；**considerable** (かなりの) ▶その歌手の家は相当大きいらしい I hear that singer's house is *pretty* big. ‖ 彼はその探検に相当自信がありそうだ He seems to be *very* confident in the expedition. ‖ おやじも若い頃は相当苦労したらしい My father seems to have had a *very* hard time when he was young. ‖ 彼はもう相当の年だ He's *well* advanced in age. ／He's *quite* [*rather*] old. (● rather は悪い意味の語を強めて使うことが多い) ‖ うちの娘は化粧品代に毎月相当な金を使っている My daughter spends *quite a lot of* [*a considerable amount of*] money on cosmetics every month. ‖ 北米には相当数の日本人がいる *Quite a few* Japanese live in North America. ‖ 内装にかかった費用は相当なものだった The amount of money spent on the decor was *considerable*.
2【当てはまること】一動 (…に)相当する **correspond** 《to》, **be equivalent** 《to》(…に当たる)；**be worth**(価値がある) ▶日本語の「義理」にぴったり相当する英語はない We can't find an English word which exactly *corresponds to* the Japanese expression 'giri.' ‖「頑張れ！」に相当する英語は何ですか What is the English word *for* [*equivalent to*] 'Ganbare'? (➤ この for は「…を表す」の意).
▶その強盗は800万円相当の宝石や時計を奪った The burglar stole jewelry and watches *worth* eight

million yen. ‖ 1ドルは100セントに相当する One dollar *is equivalent* [*equal*] *to* one hundred cents. ‖ きみの学力からすればR大学くらいが相当だろう I would say from your scholastic abilities that R University *is just right for* you.

そうどう 騒動 **trouble**(もめ事); (a) **turmoil**(大混乱, 騒ぎ); **confusion** (混乱); a **riot** /ráɪət/, a **disturbance** (暴動) (➤ 後者はしばしば前者の婉曲(えんきょく)語として用いる) ▶両家の間に騒動が持ち上がった *Trouble* erupted between the two families. ‖ わが家は騒動が絶えない There is no end of *turmoil* in our family. ‖ 先日, 両親がけんかして家じゅう大騒動になった The other day, our whole house *was thrown into confusion* because my parents had a fight. ‖ 学園騒動を鎮めるために警察が呼ばれた The police were called to quell the *disturbance at school*.

そうとう 贈答 an **exchange of gifts**; **gift-giving**(贈り物をすること) ▶日本では盆暮れに贈答が盛んだ In Japan, people *exchange* a lot of *gifts* at the *Bon* season and at the end of the year. ‖ このティーセットは贈答品として好適です This tea set is suitable for *gift-giving*. ‖ それ, 贈答用に包んでください Can you please *gift-wrap* it?
‖**贈答品売り場** a gift counter.

そうどういん 総動員する **mobilize** +Ⓞ ▶編集長は記者を総動員してその事件の取材に当たらせた The editor-in-chief *mobilized* all the reporters to cover the incident. ‖ 一家総動員で年末の大掃除をしました *The whole family* pitched in to do the year-end house cleaning.

そうとく 総督 a **governor general** (➤ カナダ, オーストラリアなどでは象徴元首であるイギリス(女)王の名代).

そうなめ 総なめ ▶その力士は上位陣を総なめにして優勝した That sumo wrestler *won the tournament by beating all* the higher-ranked wrestlers. / That sumo wrestler *won a sweeping victory over* the higher-ranked wrestlers.

そうなん 遭難 an **accident**(事故); (a) **shipwreck** (船の) **一動 遭難する** **meet with an accident**; **be wrecked** (船が) ▶うちの息子は谷川岳で遭難した Our son *met with* [*had*] *an accident* on Mt. Tanigawa. / Our son *lost his life* on Mt. Tanigawa. (💡 後者は死んだ場合) ‖ その船は三陸沖30キロの海上で遭難した The ship *was wrecked* 30 kilometers off (the coast of) Sanriku. ‖ ことしは飛行機の遭難事故が多かった There have been many *air accidents* this year.
‖**遭難救助隊** a rescue team [party] ‖ **遭難現場** the scene of an accident ‖ **遭難者** a victim.

ぞうに 雑煮 ***zoni***
日本紹介 ✉ **雑煮は正月を祝う料理の１つです. 野菜, 鶏肉, かまぼこなどを入れた汁に２～３個の餅を入れ, おわんに入れて出したものです** *Zoni* is one of the dishes cooked to celebrate the New Year. It is a bowl of soup containing vegetables, chicken, and kamaboko (steamed fish paste), along with two or three *mochi* (rice cakes).

そうにゅう 挿入 (an) **insertion** **一動 挿入する** **insert** /ɪnsə́ːʳt/ +Ⓞ (➤ 名詞の insert は「挿入物」の意) ▶鍵穴に鍵を挿入したが回らなかった I *inserted* the key into the keyhole, but it didn't work.

そうねん 壮年 ▶彼は50歳だからまだ壮年だよ He is fifty and still in *the prime of life*.

そうは 走破 ▶小田原・箱根間を２時間で走破する *run the entire distance* between Odawara and Hakone [*run all the way* from Odawara to Hakone] in two hours.

そうば 相場 **1【市価】** a **market (price)**; a **rate** (レート) ▶金の相場が上がって[下がって]いる The *market price* of gold is rising [falling]. ‖ ドルに対する円の相場が最近上がっている *The yen* has been rising [appreciating] against the dollar recently.
▶家庭教師の仕事は時給3000円が相場だ The *going rate* for tutors is 3,000 yen per hour. (➤ going rate は「現行の料金」).
‖**株式相場** a stock market ‖ **為替相場** the exchange rate.
2【投機】 **speculation** ▶相場でもうける make money through *speculation*.
3【通念】 ▶豆腐は白くて柔らかいものと相場が決まっている Tofu *is generally thought of* as being white and soft.

そうはく 蒼白な **pale** ▶彼女どうしたんだい? 顔面そう白だよ What's the matter with her? She *looks deathly pale* [*looks* (*as*) *white as a sheet*]. ‖ 彼はその悪い知らせを聞いて顔面そう白になった He *lost color* [*turned pale*] when he heard the bad news. → 顔面.

ぞうはつ 増発 ▶スキーシーズンにはバスが増発されます *There is a special* bus *service* during the ski season. / They run extra buses during the ski season. (💡 後者の場合, バス会社が言っているのなら主語は we).

そうばなてき 総花的 ▶総花的な政策 an *all around* policy ‖ 総花的な減税 an *across-the-board* tax cut *to please everybody* ‖ 新首相の施政方針演説は総花的で具体性に欠けていた The new prime minister's administrative policy speech was *intended to please everybody* [was *intended to make everybody happy*] and lacked concrete details.

ぞうはん 造反 ▶若手議員のグループが執行部に造反した A group of young Diet members *rebelled* against the party leadership.

そうび 装備 **equipment** /ɪkwípmənt/ **一動 装備する** **equip** +Ⓞ

> **【文型】**
> A に B を装備する
> **equip A with B**

▶車にカーナビを装備する *equip* a car *with* a satellite-based navigation system / *install* a satellite-based navigation system in a car ‖ 核兵器を装備した潜水艦 a submarine *equipped with* nuclear weapons ‖ 彼らは装備不十分のまま登山し, 遭難した They climbed the mountain and met with an accident *without getting proper equipment* [*getting properly equipped*]. ‖ このテレビは録画用ハードディスクを装備している(=内蔵している) This television set *has* a built-in hard disk for recording. (➤ built-in は「内蔵された」).

そうびょう 躁病 《医学》 **mania, manic disorder.**

[1]**そうふ 送付する** **send** +Ⓞ ▶書類は直ちに送付いたします We will *send* (*you*) the documents at once.

[2]**そうふ 総譜** 《音楽》 a **score**.

そうふう 送風 **ventilation** ▶送風機 *a blower*.

ぞうふく 増幅 **amplification**(電流の) **一動 増幅する** **amplify** +Ⓞ ▶音[信号]を増幅する *amplify* sound [signals]. ‖**増幅器** an amplifier(アンプ).

ぞうへい 増兵する increase the number of troops.

ぞうへいきょく 造幣局 a mint.

そうへき 双璧 ▶アメリカ史でワシントンとリンカーンは大統領の双璧だ In American history, Washington and Lincoln are ranked as *the two greatest* presidents. ‖キアヌ・リーヴス(の映画)といえば(私見では)「スピード」と「マトリックス」が双璧だ Speaking of (pictures starring) Keanu Reeves, "Speed" and "The Matrix" are *the two most outstanding ones* [*the two best ones*] (in my opinion).

そうべつ 送別の farewell ▶課長が一同を代表して送別のことばを述べた Our section chief made *a farewell speech* on behalf of all of us. ‖畑さんの送別会をやろう Let's have *a send-off* [*farewell*] *party* for Mr. Hata. (● farewell party はフォーマルな会を連想させる；打ち解けた送別会を good-by party, going-away party ということもある).

1**そうほう 双方** both sides [parties] ▶双方の合意に達する reach a *bilateral* agreement (➤ bilateral は「2国間の」) ‖双方の言い分を聞かないと真相はわからない You cannot learn the truth unless you hear what *both parties* have to say.
▶労使双方が歩み寄って交渉がまとまった There was a compromise made between *labor and management* and the negotiations were successfully completed.

2**そうほう 奏法** a way of playing a musical instrument.

そうほうこう 双方向の two-way, bidirectional ; interactive (相互に作用する) ▶双方向の交流プログラム a *two-way* exchange program ‖双方向のウェブページ an *interactive* webpage.
‖双方向通信 two-way [bidirectional ／interactive] communication.

ぞうほん 造本 bookmaking.

そうほんざん 総本山 the head temple [the headquarters] (of a Buddhist sect).

そうまとう 走馬灯 a revolving lantern ▶走馬灯のように *in rapid succession*.

そうむ 総務 general affairs
‖総務課 the general affairs section ‖総務省 the Ministry of Internal Affairs and Communications.

そうめい 聡明な intelligent (生まれつきものを理解するのが早い) ; brilliant, bright (賢い；前者のほうが意味が強い) ▶あの子はとても聡明な子だ He is a very *intelligent* [*bright*] boy.

そうめん 素麺 *somen*
日本紹介 ✉ **そうめんは極細の麺です．ゆでて冷水につけ，冷たくして出します．これを特製のつゆにつけて食べます．夏食欲の無いときに好まれます** *Somen* are very thin wheat noodles. After being briefly boiled, they are soaked in cool water and served cool. You dip them in a special sauce before eating. People like to eat *somen* in the summer when they have a smaller appetite.

ぞうもつ 臓物 entrails (動物の) ; giblets (鶏・七面鳥などの) ; the pluck (食用の).

ぞうよ 贈与する give +㊐, present +㊐, assign +㊐ (➤あとの語ほど堅い).
‖贈与税 a gift tax ; 《英》 a capital transfer tax.

そうらん 騒乱 (a) turmoil (混乱，騒ぎ) ; a riot (暴動) ▶政治的騒乱を引き起こす[鎮める] cause [put down] *political turmoil* ‖彼は騒乱罪で起訴された He was indicted *for causing a riot*.

ぞうり 草履 *zori*
日本紹介 ✉ **草履はわらやイグサで作る，鼻緒のついた日本の伝統的な履き物です．今では布・革・ゴム・プラスチックなどで作ります．海水浴のときはゴム製のものをよく履きます** *Zori* are traditional Japanese thong sandals made of woven rice straw or rushes. Today they are made from cloth, leather, rubber or plastics. People often wear rubber ones when they go to the beach for swimming.

そうりだいじん 総理大臣 the prime minister →首相 ▶菅総理大臣 *Prime Minister* Suga.

そうりつ 創立 foundation, establishment (➤後者がより堅い語) 一動 **創立する** found +㊐, establish +㊐ →創業 ▶この高校は明治6年に創立された This high school *was founded* in the sixth year of Meiji. ‖きょうは創立記念日で学校はお休みだ Today is *the anniversary of the founding of our school*, so we have no school. ‖学校の創立50周年を祝って市長が演説をした The mayor gave an address in celebration of the 50th anniversary of the *foundation* of the school.
▶この大学の創立者は誰ですか Who was the *founder* of this university? ／Who founded this university?

そうりょ 僧侶 a (Buddhist) priest /priːst/ ; a (Buddhist) monk (修道僧) ; a (Buddhist) friar (たく鉢僧).

そうりょう 送料 postage (郵送料) ; delivery charges (配達料) ▶この小包の送料はいくらですか What's the *postage* for this parcel? ‖これは5000円ですが送料は別です This costs 5,000 yen, but the *delivery charges* are extra. ‖送料[郵送料]込みで5000円です This will be 5,000 yen *including shipping* [*postage*] (*and handling*).

そうりょうじ 総領事 a consul general ▶英国総領事館 the British *Consulate General*.

そうりょく 総力 ▶双方総力を挙げての戦いは5年間続いた The *all-out* war continued for five years. ‖我々は総力を結集して調査に取り組んだ We *all combined our efforts* in conducting the investigation.
‖総力戦 a total [an all-out] war.

ソウル Seoul (大韓民国の首都).

そうるい 走塁 base running.

そうれい 壮麗な sublime /səbláɪm/ ▶朝日に輝く壮麗な富士 Mt. Fuji shining *gloriously* [*magnificently*] in the morning sunlight ‖アクロポリスの丘にはかつて壮麗な神殿が立ち並んでいた *Sublime* [*Magnificent*] temples once stood side by side on the hill of the Acropolis.

そうれつ 壮烈 ▶映画は織田信長の壮烈な最期で終わった The movie finished with Oda Nobunaga's *heroic* [*brave*] *death*.

そうろう 早漏 《生理学》 premature ejaculation.

そうろん 総論 general remarks ; an outline (概要) ▶その案には総論賛成，各論反対だ I *agree* with the plan *in general*, but not in the specifics.

そうわ 挿話 an episode ▶興味深い挿話 an intriguing *episode*.

ぞうわい 贈賄 bribery (賄賂を贈ること，また受け取ること) ; (a) payoff (賄賂の支払い) ▶建設会社の役員3名が贈賄罪で逮捕された Three construction company executives were arrested on a charge of *bribery* [*of offering bribes*].

そえがき 添え書き a caption (書画などの簡単な説

明）; a **postscript**（追伸）.

そえぎ 添え木 a **splint**（接骨用）.

そえもの 添え物 ▶あの 2 人の重役は単なる添え物だ Those two are directors *in name only*. ／Those two are *just decorative* directors.

そえる 添える **attach**《to》（添付する）▶花束にはカードが添えてあった A card *was attached to* the bouquet. ‖私は願書に写真を添えて提出した I sent in my application form *with* a photograph. ‖誕生パーティーに出席できなかったので，花束にメッセージを添えて彼女に送った Since I could not attend her birthday party, I sent her a bouquet *along with* a message. ‖母は豚カツにパセリと刻みキャベツを添えた My mother *garnished* the pork cutlet *with* parsley and shredded cabbage.（➤ garnish は「(料理に)つまを添える」）.

そえん 疎遠 ▶卒業後 2 人は次第に疎遠になってしまった The friendship between the two *has* gradually *cooled off* since graduation.

ソーシャルネットワーク a **social network**.

ソーシャルワーカー a **social worker**.

1**ソース**《料理にかけるもの》**sauce** /sɔ:s/ ▶コロッケにソースをかける put *Worcester sauce* on croquettes（➤ Worcester の発音は /wʊ̀stəʳ/）.
‖**ソース入れ** a sauce pot ‖**ホワイトソース** white sauce.

2**ソース**《出どころ》a **source** /sɔ:ʳs/ ▶その情報のソースは明らかにされていない The *source* of the information has not been revealed.

> **危ないカタカナ語✹ ソース**
> **1** 日本語の「ソース」は調味料の Worcester(-shire) sauce（ウスターソース）を指すのがふつうだが，英語の sauce は料理にかけ，味を引き立てる液状またはクリーム状のもの全般を指す．したがって，apple sauce, cranberry sauce, tomato sauce などのほか，アイスクリームにかける chocolate sauce なども sauce であり，サラダ用のドレッシングやマヨネーズも sauce の一種である．日本の「しょうゆ」は soy sauce というが，最近では shoyu という人もいる．
> **2**「ニュースソース」など「出どころ」を意味する「ソース」は source とつづる別の語．

ソーセージ (a) **sausage** /sɔ́:sɪdʒ/
‖**ウィンナソーセージ** (a) Vienna /viénə/ sausage, (a) wiener /wí:nəʳ/ ‖**フランクフルトソーセージ** a frankfurter, a hot dog.

ソーダ **soda**（➤ 炭酸ナトリウム，重曹，カセイソーダ，炭酸水を指す）‖**ソーダ水** soda (water); (soda) pop（甘み・香りをつけた飲料水）.

ソート ソートする **sort** +㊀ ▶《コンピュータ》顧客リストを年齢でソートする *sort* a customer list by age.

ソーラー **solar** ‖**ソーラーカー** a solar car ‖**ソーラーシステム** a solar heating system ‖**ソーラーパネル** a solar panel.

ゾーン a **zone**.

そかい 疎開 **evacuation** ▶祖父母は戦争中，田舎に疎開した経験がある My grandparents *were evacuated* to the countryside during the war.

1**そがい 疎外** **alienation** /èɪliənéɪʃən/ **━動 疎外する** **alienate** +㊀; **keep at a distance**（遠ざける）▶彼はクラスの仲間から疎外されている He *is avoided* [*is kept at a distance*] by his classmates. ‖彼女は強い疎外感に悩んでいる She is suffering from a strong *sense of alienation*.

2**そがい 阻害する** **hinder** +㊀ ▶領土問題が両国間の話し合いの進展を阻害している The territorial issue *has hindered* progress in talks between the two nations.

そかく 組閣 ▶首相は組閣に着手した The Prime Minister set about *forming* [*organizing*] *a new cabinet*.

そく 即 **1**【すなわち】▶色即是空 *Every form* (*in reality*) *is empty*.（➤「この世のすべては空(くう)である」の意）.
2【直ちに】**immediately** ▶私が働けなくなったら，即家族が路頭に迷う If I weren't able to work, my family would *immediately* become destitute. ‖彼は使い込みがばれて，即首になった When his embezzlement was found out, he was fired *on the spot*.（➤ on the spot は「その場で」）.

-そく -足 ▶《店で》靴下を 1 足ください May I have *a pair* of socks? ‖スニーカーは 5 足持っている I have *five pairs* of sneakers.

そぐ 削ぐ・殺ぐ **1**【斜めに薄く切る】▶ゴボウをそぐ *slice off* a burdock root ‖竹をそいでやりを作る *whittle* bamboo to make a spear ‖《理髪店で》後ろの髪をもう少しそいでください Could you *trim off* a bit more in the back? ‖耳をそがれた芳一は「耳なし芳一」と呼ばれた After his ears *were torn off*, Hoichi was dubbed 'Hoichi the Earless.'
2【失わせる】▶彼の話を聞いて我々はすっかり興味をそがれた We *lost* all *our interest* (in it) when we heard him talk about it.

1**ぞく 賊** a **thief**（こそ泥）; a **burglar**（押し込み泥棒）; a **robber**（強盗）▶ゆうべ家に賊が入った *A thief* broke into my house last night. ／My house was broken into by *a burglar* last night.

2**ぞく 俗な** **vulgar**（下品な）▶俗な考え a *vulgar* idea →俗っぽい.
▶《慣用表現》俗に言うように，タデ食う虫も好き好きだ *As is commonly said*, there is no accounting for tastes. ‖彼女は俗に言う「キャリアウーマン」だ She is *what is called* [*what you call*] a career woman.

3**ぞく 続** a **sequel** /sí:kwəl/《to》; **the second series**（続編）▶『続英作文十講』"Ten *More* Lectures on English Composition".

4**ぞく 属**《生物学》a **genus** [複 **genera**]《参考》「種」は species,「科」は family.

-ぞく -族 a **family**; a **tribe**（種族）▶ヨーロッパの王族 the *royal families* of Europe ‖その地方にはホピ族が住んでいる That area is inhabited by the Hopi (*people*).（● tribe は差別的用語とする人もいる）.

ぞくあく 俗悪な **vulgar** ▶俗悪なテレビ番組 a *vulgar* [*lowbrow*] TV program（➤ lowbrow は「低俗な」）‖何よ，そのネクタイ．俗悪ねえ！Wow, what a *vulgar* tie!

そくい 即位 (an) **enthronement** **━動 即位する** **ascend** [**accede to**] **the throne** ▶ビクトリア女王は1837年に即位した Queen Victoria *acceded to the throne* in 1837. ‖**即位式** an enthronement ceremony; a coronation ceremony（戴冠式）.

ぞくうけ 俗受け ▶俗受けを狙ったテレビ番組が多すぎる There are too many TV programs which try to *appeal to the vulgar tastes of the public*.

そくおう 即応 ▶時代の流れに即応した教育 education *adapted to* [*in pace with*] the current of the times.

そくおんき 足温器 a **foot warmer**.

ぞくご 俗語 **slang**（➤ 全体を指す; 数えられない名詞）;

a **slang word**(個々の俗語) ▶俗語っぽい表現 a *slangy* expression ‖ dough は**俗語**でお金のことだ 'Dough' is *slang* for money. ‖ ヘミングウェーの小説にはアメリカの**俗語**が多い Hemingway's novels are full of American *slang*.

そくざ 即座の **immediate** /ɪmíːdiət/ **一副 即座に** **immediately, at once, right away**(➤ この順にくだけた感じになる) ▶その質問に**即座に**答える answer the question *immediately* [*at once* / *right away*] ‖ 彼の申し出があまりにばかげていたので, 私は**即座に**(＝その場で)断った His offer was so ridiculous that I declined it (*right*) *then and there* [*on the spot*].

そくし 即死 **death on the spot** ▶彼はダンプカーにひかれて**即死した** He was run over by a dump truck and *was killed on the spot* [*instantaneously*]. (● この場合は (×)died としない).

そくじ 即時 ▶被疑者は**即時**釈放された The suspect was released *promptly* [*without delay*].

ぞくじ 俗事 **worldly matters** ▶父は学者肌で**俗事**に疎い My father is the scholarly type and doesn't know much about *worldly matters*. (➤ and 以下を is out of touch with everyday concerns. とすることもできる).

そくじつ 即日 ▶当店では**即日配達**いたします Our shop offers *same day delivery*. (➤ 広告・ちらしなどの文句. 口頭で用いてもよい) ‖ 市議会議員選挙は**即日**開票される In municipal elections, ballots are counted *on the day* of voting.

ぞくしゅつ 続出 ▶火山の噴火でホテルのキャンセルが**続出した** Due to the volcano's eruption, people canceled hotel reservations *one after another*. / The volcanic eruption resulted in *a flood of* hotel reservation cancellations. (➤ a flood of ... は「…の殺到」).
▶気温が高く, そのレースは途中棄権する走者が**続出した** *One* runner *after another* dropped out of the race due to the heat.

ぞくしょう 俗称 a **common name**, a **popular name**.

そくしん 促進 **promotion** **一動 促進する** **promote** +目 ▶世界平和を**促進する** *promote* world peace ‖ 植物の生長を**促進する**(＝速める) *accelerate* the growth of plants ‖ 強力な**発毛促進剤**が発売された A powerful *drug to promote hair growth* was put on the market. ‖ 我々は新商品の**販売促進**をするために地方回りをした We went on the road to *promote sales* of our new products. (➤「販売促進」は sales promotion).

ぞくしん 俗信 a **folk belief**; **superstition**(迷信) ▶この村にはたくさんの**俗信**が残っている There remain a lot of *folk beliefs* in this village. →**俗説**.

そくする 即する ▶きみの意見は現実に**即していない** Your opinion *isn't based on* reality. ‖ (もっと)時代に**即した**運動方針に切り替えねばならない We have to switch to policies that *meet* the needs of the times.

ぞくする …に属する **belong to**

> **【文型】**
> **団体(A)に属する**
> **belong to** A
> **《解説》** 人が組織や団体に属しているという場合は belong to よりも be a member of ... や be in ... が多く用いられる. 特に日常会話ではこの傾向が強い.

▶梅も桜もバラ科に**属する** Both the *ume* and the cherry tree *belong to* the rose family. ‖ 礼子はコーラス部に**属している** Reiko *belongs to* the chorus. / Reiko *is a member of* the chorus. / Reiko *is in* the chorus. (● chorus だけで「コーラス団」の意なので (×)chorus club とはしない).
▶私はまだどのサークルにも**属していない** I'm not *in* any group yet. ‖ ニュージーランドは英連邦に**属している** New Zealand *is a member of* the Commonwealth. ‖ アルジェリアはかつてフランスに**属していた** Algeria *was* once *under the rule of* France. (➤「支配下にあった」の意).

そくせい 速成 ▶3か月の英語**速成コース** a three-month *crash* [*intensive*] *course* in English (➤ intensive は「集中的な」).

ぞくせい 属性 an **attribute** /ǽtrɪbjuːt/.

そくせいさいばい 促成栽培 **forcing culture** ▶**促成栽培**の野菜は概して値段が高い *Forced vegetables* are generally high-priced.

1**そくせき 足跡** **1【足あと】** a **footprint**; a **mark**(影響, 感化) ▶円空は日本各地に**足跡**を残している Enku left his *marks* [*footprints*] in many places in Japan.
2【業績】 an **achievement** ▶先代社長が会社の歴史に残した**足跡**は消えることがないだろう The *achievements* of the former president will never be forgotten in the history of the company.

2**そくせき 即席の** **instant**(即座の); **ad-lib** /ædlíb/, **impromptu** /ɪmprάːmpt̮juː/ (即興の, 原稿や楽譜なしでの; ad-lib はややインフォーマルな語); **improvised**(即席で作った) ▶**即席の**飾り付け *improvised* decoration(s) ‖ **即席で**スピーチをする make an *ad-lib* [*impromptu*] speech / speak *off the cuff*(➤ off the cuff はインフォーマルな言い方).
‖**即席ラーメン** instant ramen.

ぞくせけん 俗世間 ▶**俗世間**は煩わしいことばかりだ *Life* is full of annoyances. ‖ 西行は**俗世間**を捨てて出家した Saigyo became a (Buddhist) priest after leaving *secular life*.

ぞくせつ 俗説 an **old wives' tale**; a **superstition**(迷信) ▶「ウナギと梅干しを一緒に食べるのはよくない」というのは**俗説**にすぎない The idea that eel and pickled plums should not be eaten together is just *an old wives' tale*.

そくせんりょく 即戦力 ▶企業は**即戦力**となる人材を求めている Companies want to recruit people who can *contribute to the company right away*.

1**ぞくぞく 続々** **one after another**(次から次へと) ▶生徒が**続々と**インフルエンザになっている *One* student *after another* has come down with the flu. ‖ コンサート後その歌手の楽屋にファンが**続々と**詰めかけた After the concert, there was *a steady stream* of fans rushing to the singer's dressing room. ‖ 赤十字社には日本中から見舞い金や見舞いの手紙が**続々と**寄せられている Money and letters of sympathy *have been flooding in* from all parts of Japan to the Red Cross (Society).

2**ぞくぞく** ▶かぜをひいたらしく背中が**ぞくぞくする** I must have caught (a) cold because I *feel shivers* [*a chill*] running down my back.
▶あすの決勝戦のことを考えると**ぞくぞくする** When I think about the final match tomorrow, I *get all shivery*. ‖ スピルバーグの映画は**ぞくぞくする**ほどおもしろい The movies made by Spielberg are *so thrilling* [*exciting*] *and fun*.

そくたつ 速達 **special delivery**, **express (delivery)** ▶

そ

《郵便局で》速達にしてください I'd like to send it (*by*) *special delivery*. ／Please send it *by express mail*.
‖速達郵便 special delivery mail, express delivery post 《参考》《英》では first-class mail もこの意でよく用いられる ‖ 速達料 a special [an express] delivery charge.

1**そくだん 速断** a snap decision [judgment] ▶この問題については速断は危険だ It is risky for you to *make a snap judgment* on this matter. ／It would be dangerous to *make a hasty decision* on this issue. ‖ 我々はその容疑者が犯人と速断すべきではない We should not *jump to the conclusion* that the suspect is the culprit.

2**そくだん 即断** a prompt decision 一動 即断する decide promptly, make a prompt decision.

ぞくっぽい 俗っぽい ▶俗っぽい小説 a *cheap* novel ‖ 俗っぽい人 a *worldly-minded* person ‖ あいつは俗っぽいやつだ He's *a snob*. ／He's *vulgar*. (➤「野卑な, 下品な」の意).

そくてい 測定 measurement 一動 測定する measure ＋目 ▶位置[高度]を測定する *measure* the position [altitude] ‖ 環状７号線の騒音を測定する *measure* the noise level on Belt Highway 7 ‖ 金曜日に体力測定をします We will have *a test of physical strength and fitness* on Friday.

そくてん 側転 a cartwheel ▶側転する *turn cartwheels*.

そくど 速度 (a) speed ; (a) pace (歩く[走る]速さ) ; 《物理学》velocity ▶私たちの乗った列車はトンネルを出ると速度を上げた Our train *picked up speed* as it came out of the tunnel. ／Our train *sped* [*speeded*] *up* as it came out of the tunnel. ‖ 列車は時速30キロに速度を落とした The train *reduced speed* [*slowed down*] to about 30 kilometers an [per] hour.
▶老人はかなりの[一定の]速度で歩いた The old man walked *at a good* [*fixed*] *pace*. ‖「のぞみ」号の最高速度は時速300キロである The Nozomi's *maximum speed* is 300 kilometers per hour. ‖ 制限速度を守ってください Please observe *the speed limit*. ‖ 運動量は質量かける速度と定義される Momentum is defined as mass times *velocity*. ‖ 対話「この飛行機の速度はどれくらいですか」「時速1000キロです」"*How fast* is this airplane flying ?" "A thousand kilometers per hour." (列車の場合は fly を move か go にする).
‖速度計 a speedometer /spɪdɑ́ːmət̬əʳ/ (自動車などの).

そくとう 即答 a ready [prompt] answer ▶即答を避ける[求める] avoid [demand] *a prompt answer* ‖ 申し訳ありませんが, 今即答はできません I'm sorry, but I can't give you *a ready* [*an immediate*] *answer*. ／Sorry, but I can't *answer that right off the top of my head*. (➤ right off the top of one's head は「とっさに, すぐに」の意のインフォーマルな言い方).

ぞくとう 続投 ▶《野球》ピッチャーはどうやら続投のようです It looks like the pitcher will *stay on the mound*.
▶《比喩的》外務大臣はM氏の続投になりそうだ The post of foreign minister will probably *be retained* by Mr. M *for another term*. (➤ retain は「維持する」).

そくどく 速読 speed reading 一動 速読する speedread ＋目 ▶易しい英語の小説を速読する *speedread* a story written in easy English ／*read* a story written in easy English *rapidly*.

そくばい 即売 an on-the-spot sale, a spot sale ▶きのう盆栽の展示即売会があった *An exhibition and* (*on-the-spot*) *sale* of bonsai was held yesterday. (➤この例では on-the-spot はないほうがふつう).

そくばく 束縛 (a) restraint (拘束) ; (a) restriction (制限) 一動 束縛する restrain ＋目, restrict ＋目 ▶私は一切の束縛から逃れたかった I wanted to free myself from all *restraints* [*restrictions*]. ‖ イタリアでは時間に束縛されて, 見たいものもろくに見られなかった Since I *had only a limited amount of time* in Italy, I was barely able to enjoy the things [places] I wanted to see.
▶束縛されるのが嫌だから, 子供はいらないわ I don't want children because they would *tie* me *down*. ‖ きみの自由を束縛するつもりは毛頭ないよ I don't have the slightest intention of *interfering with* [*restricting*] your liberty.

ぞくはつ 続発 ▶誘拐事件が続発している Kidnapping cases *are occurring one after another* [*in rapid succession*]. ／*There has been a series* [*a spate*] *of* kidnappings recently.

ぞくぶつ 俗物 a snob (上流社会人を気取り, 一般大衆を軽蔑する人間) ▶あの教授の俗物根性には我慢できない I cannot stand that professor's *snobbery*.

そくぶつてき 即物的な practical ; pragmatic (実用本位の) ; realistic (現実的な) ▶即物的な物の見方 a *practical* [*pragmatic* ／*realistic*] point of view.

ぞくへん 続編 a sequel /síːkwəl/ 《to》 ▶この小説の続編が読みたい I want to read the *sequel to* this novel.

そくほう 速報 a (news) flash ▶ベイルートからの最新速報によると人質の１人が撃たれたという *The latest* (*news*) *flash* from Beirut says one of the hostages has been shot. ‖ 《アナウンサーが》ニュース速報をお伝えします This is *a flash report*.

ぞくほう 続報 a follow-up report.

そくめん 側面 1【横の側】 a side ▶車体の側面に傷をつけた I put a scratch on the *side* of the car.
▶我々は遺児らを少なくとも側面から(＝間接的に)援助することはできる We can at least help the orphaned children *indirectly*.
‖側面図 a side view, a lateral plan.
2【別の面】 a side (一面) ; another side (もう１つの面) ▶祖父は生真面目な人でしたが, 時には競馬に出かけるという側面もありました My granddad was a very serious-minded person, but he had *another side* to his personality which took him to horse races now and again. ‖ 彼にあんなひょうきんな側面があるとは思いも寄らなかった I'd never imagined that he had such a humorous *side* to him.

そくりょう 測量 survey /sə́ːʳveɪ/ 一動 測量する survey /səʳvéɪ/ ＋目 ▶土地を測量する *make a survey of* the land ／*survey* the land.
‖測量技師 a surveyor ‖ 測量図 a survey.

そくりょく 速力 speed ▶列車は速力を増した The train *increased* [*gathered*] *speed*. ‖ 次第に船の速力が落ちてきた The ship has gradually *lost speed* [*slowed down*].
☞ 全速力 (→見出語)

そぐわない ▶この写真は記事の内容にそぐわない This photograph *does not fit well* [*is incongruous*] *with* the contents of the article. (➤ incongruous /ɪnkɑ́ːŋgruəs/ with は「…と不釣り合いな」の意の

堅い語）／This photograph and the article *don't match.* ‖ その彫刻はその場にそぐわない気がした I felt the sculpture was *out of place* there. ‖ 彼女のスピーチはその場［その場にいた学生たち］にはそぐわなかった Her speech *was not appropriate to* the occasion [*for* the students there]. ‖ あのたくさんの派手なちょうちんは桜の花の繊細な美しさにはそぐわない The many gaudy lanterns *mar* the delicate beauty of the cherry blossoms. (➤ mar は「損なう」の意で主に文語).

そげき 狙撃 **shooting, sniping** 一動 **狙撃する** **shoot** 《at》, **snipe** 《at》 ‖ **狙撃事件** a shooting incident ‖ **狙撃犯** a sniper(➤「狙撃兵」の意にもなる).

ソケット a **socket** 《参考》電球のソケットにも壁ソケット(コンセント)にもいうが, 後者と区別する必要がある場合には electric light socket とか lamp socket のようにいう →コンセント ▶ソケットに電球をはめてください Could you fit [screw] an electric light bulb into the *socket*? (➤ screw は「回してはめる」).

1**そこ 底** **1**【物の】**the bottom**；**the sole**(靴底) ▶その箱にそんなに詰めると底が抜けるよ If you stuff the box too full, *the bottom* will fall [come] out. ‖ 靴の底にガムがこびりついて取れないの I've got gum stuck to *the sole* of my shoe and can't get it off.

▶私は先生を心の底から尊敬している I respect my teacher *from the bottom of my heart.* ‖ 彼女は心の底ではぼくを憎んでいるようだ It seems that, *deep inside*, she hates me.

2【慣用表現】▶彼の中国史の知識は底が浅い He has only (a) *superficial* [*shallow*] knowledge of Chinese history. (➤ superficial, shallow はともに「浅薄な」) ‖ 彼には底の知れないところがある There is something *unfathomable* [*mysterious*] about him. (➤ unfathomable は「計り知れない」; →底知れない).

▶経済は底を打った The economy *hit rock bottom.* ‖ 売り上げが不振で会社の運転資金は底をついた We *are running out of* working funds because of sluggish sales.

2**そこ** **1**【その場所】**there**；**that place**(その場所) ▶そこはきみが行く場所ではない You're not supposed to go *there.* ‖ そこに何を隠したの？What did you hide *in there*? (● in は「中」であることをはっきりさせるとき) ‖ そのままそこに居なさいよ Stay *where you are.* ‖ そこは危険だ *That*'s a dangerous place. ‖ ポストならそこのコンビニの前にありますよ There's a mailbox in front of that convenience store *over there.* ‖ 香港まで飛行機で行き, そこから自動車で広州へ行きます I'll fly to Hong Kong and then drive to Guangzhou *from there.* ‖ そこから先へは行けません You can't go *any farther.* ‖ 対話「ぼくのボールペンが無いよ」「そこにあるじゃないか」"I can't find my ballpoint pen." "It's right *over there.*" ‖ 対話「NHKホールはどこでしょうか」「すぐそこですよ」"Where is the NHK Hall?" "It's *right over there.*" ‖ 対話「そこは何の部屋ですか」「父の書斎です」"What room is *that*?" "It's my father's study." ‖ 対話「どちらへお出かけですか？」「ちょっとそこまで」"Where are you going?" "Oh, *just down the road.*" (● 挨拶代わりのこのような会話は英米では一般的でない. 特にこの質問は尋問のように響く).

2【その点】**that** ▶そこが彼のいいところ［欠点］だ *That*'s his good point [weakness]. ‖ そこが彼らしいところだ *That*'s like him. ‖ 私たちがニュージーランドから学ぶべきところはそこなのです *That*'s what we should learn from New Zealand.

3【そのとき】▶先生の悪口を言っていたらそこへ先生が現れた The teacher showed up *just when* we were saying bad things about her.

4【慣用表現】▶春はもうそこまで来ている Spring *is just around the corner* [*is almost here*]. ‖ そこまで言うことはないでしょ！You went *too far* in what you said [in your comment]. ／What you said was *out of line.* ‖ そこまでは考えませんでした I didn't think *that far ahead.* ‖ そこへもってきて（＝もっと悪いことに）雨が降ってきた *What's worse*, it started to rain.

そご 齟齬 →齟齬を来す.

そこいじ 底意地 ▶彼女はおとなしそうだが底意地が悪い Although she looks meek, she is *mean* [*spiteful*] *at heart.*

そこう 素行 **conduct, behavior** ▶素行のよくない（＝非行）学生 a *delinquent* [*wayward*] student ‖ 彼は素行がよくない He *is a man of bad conduct* [*behavior*]. ‖ 素行を改めなさい You should *mend your ways* [*improve your behavior*].
‖ **素行調査** investigation of conduct.

そこかしこ ▶そこかしこにスミレが咲いている Violets are blooming *here and there.*

そこく 祖国 one's **homeland** ▶祖国へ帰る return to *one's homeland* (➤ motherland, fatherland, mother country, native country などともいう).

そこしれない 底知れない ▶ダ・ヴィンチは底知れない能力をもった人だった Da Vinci was a person of *immeasurable* [*fathomless*] ability.

そこそこ **1**【せいぜい】▶仙台まではあと10キロそこそこだ It's *only* 10 kilometers *or so* to Sendai. ‖ 彼は30歳そこそこで代議士になった He became a Dietman when he was *not much over* thirty. ‖ この指輪は１万円そこそこの（＝高くて１万円の）品だ This ring cost ten thousand yen *at most.*

2【一応】▶彼は初出場だったがそこそこの成績を収めた It was his first time to participate in a game, but he *did all right.* ‖ そこそこもうかっていますよ We're making a *modest* profit.

3【切り上げて】▶彼は話もそこそこに立ち去った He *cut his talk short* and hurriedly went away.

そこぢから 底力 **untapped** [**full**] **potential**；**real** [**underlying**] **strength**（本当の力）(➤ strength を power としてもよい) ▶わが校のバレーボールチームは土壇場で底力を出して試合を逆転した At the last moment, our school's volleyball team displayed [showed] all its *untapped potential* [*underlying strength*] and won a come-from-behind victory.

そこつ 粗忽な **careless**(不注意な)；**rash**(慎重に考えない)；**hasty**(性急な, そそっかしい) ▶彼は粗こつ者だから仕事にミスが多い He is *a careless person* who often makes mistakes in his work.

そこで **so**(だから) ▶翻訳にはずいぶん金がかかった. そこでわが社では機械翻訳システムを導入した Translation was very costly for our company, *so* we installed a machine translation system. ‖ そこできみの意見を聞きたいんだが… *Now*, I'd like to ask your opinion.

▶彼に言われて, そこで初めて気がついたんだ I *hadn't* noticed (it) *until* I heard of it from him. (➤「彼から教えられて初めて気がついた」の意).

そこなう 損なう **injure** /índʒəʳ/ ＋目 (傷つける)；**ruin** ＋目 (すっかりだめにする)；**damage** /dǽmɪdʒ/ ＋目 (損害を与える)；**mar** ＋目 (美観などを台なしにする)；**spoil**

+⊜（価値・品質などを下げてだめにする）▶過労のため**健康を損なう**サラリーマンが多い Many office workers *damage* [*ruin* / *lose*] *their health* through overwork.
▶このビルのために古都の美観が**損なわれている** This building *mars* [*spoils*] the beauty of the old capital. ‖ 彼女の**機嫌を損なわない**ようにいろいろ気を遣った I took every care not to *hurt her feelings* [not to *offend* her]. (➤ offend は「怒らせる」).

そ

-そこなう -損なう fail《to do》, miss +⊜

【文型】
…し損なう
fail to do
miss doing
➤ fail to do は「すべきことをしない, 怠る」, miss doing は「チャンスを逃す」

▶期限までに報告書を**出し損なった** I *failed to hand in* my report by the deadline. ‖ 先週の『まんが世界』を**買い損なった** I *missed buying* the "World of Comics" last week. ‖ きのう月食を**見損なった** I *missed seeing* the lunar eclipse last night. (「テレビ番組を見損なう」という場合は miss a TV program のように seeing を省略することが多い) ‖ 私はその電車に**乗り損なった** I *missed* [*didn't make*] the train. (➤ make は「間に合う」).
☞ **言い損なう, 聞き損なう, 見損なう** (→見出語)

そこなし 底無しの bottomless (➤ 比喩的にも用いる)
▶**底無しの**沼 a *bottomless* swamp.
▶彼は**底無しの**飲んべえだ He is an *insatiable* [a *bottomless*] drunk. / He drinks like a fish. (➤ 後者は「魚のように飲む」の意で, 決まった言い方).

そこぬけ 底抜け ▶あゆみは**底抜けに**明るい Ayumi is *full of* [is *bursting with*] cheer. ‖ 母は**底抜けの**お人よしだ My mother is an *extremely* good-natured person.

そこね 底値 a rock-bottom price.

そこねる 損ねる ▶彼女, 何で**機嫌を損ねた**んだろう? What *offended* her? / Why was she *in a bad mood* [*temper*]?

-そこねる -損ねる →-損なう.

そこのけ ▶料理にかけては彼は本職のシェフ**そこのけだ** As for cooking, he *is better than* a professional chef. ‖ 彼女のピアノはプロ**そこのけだ** Her (piano) playing would *put* (*even*) a professional pianist *to shame*. (➤ put ... to shame は「…を恥じ入らせる」の意).

そこはかとない ▶ビルに囲まれていても, 夕暮れの隅田川には**そこはかとない**風情が漂う The Sumida River, though surrounded by tall buildings, still has an *indefinable* charm at dusk. (➤ indefinable は「名状し難い」) ‖ 浴衣姿の裕美は**そこはかとない**色気を漂わせていた Wearing a yukata, Yumi exuded (a) *subtle* sex appeal.

そこびえ 底冷え ▶けさは**底冷えがする** I *feel chilled to the bone* this morning.

そこびきあみ 底引き網 a trawl (net).

そこら 1【その辺】▶その本ならどこか**そこらに**あるだろう The book should be *somewhere around there*.
2【約, 大体】... or so ▶費用は締めて３万円か**そこらだろう** It will cost 30,000 yen *or so* [*or thereabouts*] in all. (or so, or thereabouts は数詞のあとにつける).

そこらじゅう そこら中 ▶スパイは機密文書を捜して部屋の中を**そこら中**かき回して行った The agent rummaged *everywhere* in the room for the classified documents. ‖ 久しぶりに運動したので**体がそこら中痛かった** It was the first exercise I'd had in a long time so I ached *all over*. ‖ 彼は服を脱ぐと**そこら中に**放り出す When he undresses, he throws his clothes *every which way* [*all over the room*].

そごをきたす 齟齬を来す ▶外務大臣の発言は首相の答弁と**齟齬を来していた** The foreign minister's remark *was at variance* with the prime minister's answer. / *There was a contradiction* [*discrepancy*] between the foreign minister's remark and the prime minister's answer.

そざい 素材 (a) material ▶この靴の**素材**は合成ゴムです The *material* used in these shoes is synthetic rubber. ‖ このバッグの**素材**は何ですか What's the *material* used in this bag? ‖ この小説は民話を**素材に**している The *material* for this novel was taken from a folk tale.

そざつ 粗雑な sloppy; careless (不注意な) ▶**粗雑な**計画 a *sloppy* plan ‖ 彼女の調査は非常に**粗雑だ** Her research is very *careless* [*sloppy*]. ‖ そんな**粗雑な**考え方は困る I can't accept such *slipshod* thinking.

1そし 阻止する block +⊜; prevent《from》(…させない) ▶その法案の通過を**阻止する**ために野党が結束した The opposition parties united for the purpose of *blocking* the passage of the bill. ‖ 警官隊はデモ隊が国会議事堂になだれ込むのを実力で**阻止した** The police squad used force to *prevent* the demonstrators *from* surging into the Diet Building.

2そし 素子 an element, a device ‖**加熱素子** a heating element ‖ **半導体素子** a semiconductor device [element].

そじ 素地 the makings《of》(素質); a grounding《in》(基礎知識・基本技能) ▶彼には大指揮者の**素地がある** He has *the makings of* a great conductor. ‖ 彼女には生け花の**素地が**あったのでニューヨークで仕事を得るのに大いに役立った Her *grounding in* ikebana [Japanese flower arrangement] was a great help to her in getting her job in New York.

そしき 組織 1【秩序ある集団】an organization; a system (体系); structure (構造) 一動 **組織する** organize +⊜ ▶今日の政治**組織** today's political *system* ‖ 現代日本の**社会組織** the *social structure* of modern Japan ‖ 労働組合を**組織する** *organize* a labor union ‖ 英語の**組織的な**学習コース a *systematic* course in English.
▶生徒会は各クラスの代表が意見を交換する**組織**である A student council is *an organization* where representatives of each class exchange opinions. ‖ わが社の**組織**を説明しましょう Let me explain to you the *organization* of our company. (➤「(会社の)組織図」を organization chart という) ‖ その委員会は30人で**組織されている** The committee *is composed of* [*consists of*] thirty members. ‖ 私たちはいじめ対策委員会を**組織した** We *organized* a committee to combat bullying. (➤ combat は「…に取り組む」).
▶４月に**組織替え**があって, 私は営業へ配属された There was *a reshuffle* this April, and I was assigned to the sales division.
‖**組織犯罪** organized crime ‖ **犯罪組織** a criminal syndicate.
2【細胞の集まり】《生物学》tissue

‖**神経組織** nerve tissue ‖**結合組織** connective tissue.

そしつ 素質 **the makings**(あるものになる資質);(an) **aptitude**(適性);a **gift**(生来持っている才能)▶彼にはリーダーになる**素質**がある He has *the makings* of a leader. ／He has *what it takes* to be a leader. ‖彼女はよい歌手になる**素質**を持っている She has the *aptitude* to become a good singer. ‖私,語学の**素質**は無いみたい I seem to have no *gift* [*talent*] for languages.
▶ピカソは幼時から画家としての**素質**に恵まれていた Picasso was blessed with artistic *ability* [*talent*] from early childhood.

そして **and**; **and then**(それから)▶東京,大阪,**そして**京都 Tokyo, Osaka, *and* Kyoto ‖彼のスピーチは「**そして**」が多すぎる His speech included too many "*ands*."
☛ そうして(→見出語)

そしな 粗品 a **small gift**, a **little present** ⚠「粗品」にぴったりの1語の英語はないので,「ささやかな[小さな]贈り物」と考える. →つまらない ▶先着100名様に**粗品**を差し上げます The first 100 customers will be presented with *a small gift*. ／*Gifts* will be given to the first 100 customers.

そしゃく 咀嚼 ▶現代人は顎が小さくなり,**そしゃく力**が弱くなってきている Modern people *have a weaker bite* because their jawbones have become smaller.

そしょう 訴訟 a **suit**, a **lawsuit**(法廷に出された事件);(a) **litigation**(➤ 可算名詞としては前2者と同義. 不可算名詞としては訴訟過程)▶彼女はその損害賠償の**訴訟**に勝った[負けた] She won [lost] the damage *suit*. ‖その子の両親は病院を相手取って**訴訟を起こした** The parents of the child *filed a suit against* the hospital.
▶彼女は**離婚訴訟を起こした** She *filed for divorce*. (➤ file for は「…を申請する」) ‖アメリカは**訴訟好きな**社会だ American society is *litigation-happy* [*sue-happy*].
‖**訴訟事件** a legal case ‖**訴訟人** a suitor ‖**集団訴訟** a class suit, 《米また》a class action ‖**民事[刑事]訴訟** a civil [criminal] suit.

1**そじょう 訴状** a **complaint** ▶**訴状**によると被告はその会社から500万円をだまし取ったとされている *The complaint* says that the defendant cheated the company out of five million yen.

2**そじょう 俎上に載せる** **bring up ... for discussion.**

そしょく 粗食 a **plain** [**simple**] **diet** ▶修道士は**粗食**の割に長命だ Monks usually live long despite living on *a plain* [*simple*] *diet*. ‖**粗食**ばかりしていると体に悪い It is bad for the health to eat *unnourishing food* all the time. (➤ unnourishing は「栄養分の少ない[足りない]」).

そしらぬ 素知らぬ ▶久しぶりに会ったのにもかかわらず彼女は**そしらぬふりをした** I met her after a long time, but she *pretended not to recognize me* [but she *cut me dead*]. ‖彼は**そしらぬ顔をして**通り過ぎた He passed by, *completely ignoring me*.

そしり 謗り (a) **criticism**(批判)▶裏切り者の**そしりを受ける**(＝裏切り者として非難される) *be criticized* as a traitor.

そしる 謗る **criticize** ＋目(批判する);**speak ill of**(悪口を言う).

そすう 素数《数学》a **prime number.**

そせい 蘇生する **come back to life** ▶いったん心臓が停止しても,**蘇生する**ケースはよくあるらしい Apparently, there are quite a few cases of people *coming back to life* even after their hearts have stopped beating.
‖**人工蘇生(法)** artificial resuscitation ‖**心肺蘇生(法)** cardiopulmonary resuscitation(➤ 略語は CPR).

そぜい 租税 **taxes** ▶**租税**を徴収する collect *taxes* ‖**租税**を免除する exempt a person from *taxes*.

そせいらんぞう 粗製乱造 ▶あの会社では安っぽいおもちゃを**粗製乱造している** They *are mass-producing* [*are churning out*] toys *of inferior quality* in that company. (➤ churn out は「(良くないものを)どんどん作る」).

そせき 礎石 a **foundation stone** ▶**礎石を築く** lay the *foundation*.

そせん 祖先 an **ancestor**(1人);**ancestry**(➤ 集合的に)▶あの人の**祖先**は松平定信だ Matsudaira Sadanobu is one of his *ancestors*. ‖これは**祖先**から受け継いだ刀です This is a sword handed down from our *ancestors*. ‖現在の馬の**祖先に当たる**動物の化石が発見された A fossil of an animal *ancestral to* modern horses was discovered.
‖**祖先崇拝** ancestor worship.

そそう 粗相 **1【失礼, 失敗】**▶(店長が店員に)お客さまに**粗相のないように**注意してください Please be careful *not to offend* our customers *by any lapse of etiquette*. (●「作法を忘れて客を怒らせることのないように」と考える).
2【大・小便を漏らす】▶子供が玄関で**粗相をした** My child *had a little accident* in the hall.

1**そそぐ 注ぐ** **1【水が流れ込む】** **flow**《into》▶信濃川は新潟で日本海に**注ぐ** The Shinano River *flows* [*empties*] *into* the Sea of Japan at Niigata.
2【液体を流し入れる】 **pour** /pɔːʳ/ ＋目 ▶私は冷たいビールをコップに**注いだ** I *poured* cold beer into the glass.
3【努力などを集中させる】▶彼女は自然保護運動に**全力を注いだ** She *concentrated her energy on* [*poured her energy into* ／ *put her heart and soul into*] the ecology movement. ‖彼らは一人娘に有らん限りの**愛情を注いだ** They *showered* their only daughter *with* as much *love* as possible. ‖彼女はその子犬に**目を注いだ** She *turned* [*fixed*] *her eyes on* that puppy. (➤ fix はややインフォーマルな語).

2**そそぐ 雪ぐ** ▶汚名を**そそぐ** *clear one's name*.

そそくさ ▶彼は急用もないのに,ろくに話もせずに**そそくさと立ち去った** Even though he had nothing urgent to do, he *rushed away*, hardly saying a word (to me).

そそっかしい **careless**(不注意な);**hasty**, **rash**(軽率な);**scatterbrained**(注意散漫な)▶そんなうわさを真に受けるなんて,彼女ちょっと**そそっかしい**んだよ She was a bit *hasty* [*rash*] to have believed such a rumor.

そそのかす 唆す **incite**《to do》(扇動して…させる);《インフォーマル》**put** A **up to** B(A(人)を唆して B させる;B には名詞・動名詞が続く)▶その独裁者は軍部を**唆して**隣国と戦争をさせた The dictator *incited* the military *to* make war on a neighboring country. ‖悪友たちは彼を**唆して**万引きをさせた His bad friends *put* him *up to* [*talked* him *into*] shoplifting.

そそりたつ そそり立つ **rise** (**high**), **tower** ▶三陸海岸

では海面からそそり立つ崖が見ものだ The cliffs *rising* from the sea along the Sanriku coast are a spectacular sight. ‖ 原っぱの真ん中に大きな木がそそり立っている There is a big tree *towering* in the middle of the field.

そそる **excite** +目 (興味を) ; **whet** +目 (食欲を) ▶山腹にあいた洞穴は私の好奇心をそそった The cave in the mountainside *excited* [*aroused*] *my curiosity*.
▶この映画のタイトルには興味をそそられる The title of this movie *is really appealing to me* [*really appeals to me*]. ‖ 夏の暑いときでもカレーライスには食欲をそそられる Even in the hot summer, curry and rice *whets the appetite*.

そぞろ 漫ろ ▶あすのデートのことを思うと, かおりは気もそぞろだった(＝そわそわ落ち着かなかった) Thinking of the date planned for the next day, Kaori *felt uneasy* [*anxious*].

そだいごみ 粗大ごみ **outsized rubbish, bulky trash** [**refuse**] 《参考》英語には特に決まった言い方はない. なお refuse は「廃物」の意で, 発音は /réfju:s/.

そだち 育ち **breeding, upbringing** ▶彼は育ちが良い[悪い] He *is well-bred* [*ill-bred*]. ／He *is a man of good* [*ill*] *breeding*. ‖ 彼女はハワイ育ちか. 道理で英語がうまいと思った She *was raised* [*was brought up* ／*grew up*] in Hawaii ? No wonder that she speaks good English. ‖ 私は都会[田舎]育ちだ I'm *city-*[*country-*]*bred*. ／I'm *a city* [*country*] *boy*. ‖ 彼には育ち盛りの子供が 2 人いる He has two *growing* children.
▶ことしは冷夏で稲の育ちが極端に悪い Due to a cool summer, the rice *is growing* extremely *poorly* this year.

そだつ 育つ **grow ; grow up, be raised** (➤ 前者は「自然に大きくなる, 成長する」, 後者は「しつけや教育を受けて育つ」) ▶太陽光が無ければ植物は育たない Plants cannot *grow* without sunlight. ‖ 私は広島で生まれ大阪で育った I was born in Hiroshima and *grew up* in Osaka. (🔔「大阪で生まれ育った」は I *was born and raised* in Osaka. ということが多い) ‖ ぜいたくに育ったので彼女はわがままだ Since she *was brought up in luxury*, she is selfish. ‖ 母乳で育った子供は母乳から味覚を発達させる *Breast-fed* babies develop their taste buds from (flavors they are exposed to in) their mother's milk.
▶小さなサークルがやがて会員数10万人の組織に育った The small group *has grown into* an organization with 100,000 members. ‖ 少年の心に少しずつ正義感が育っていった A sense of justice *was* gradually *growing* in the boy's heart. ‖ (レスリングの)吉田選手は恩師の厳しい指導の下に育った The coach's strict training made a strong wrestler out of Ms. Yoshida.

そだてあげる 育て上げる **raise, bring up** (子供を) ; **train** +目 (訓練する) ▶彼女は 4 人の子供を立派に育て上げた She *has* successfully *raised* four children. ‖ その科学者は後継者を育て上げることに心血を注いだ The scientist devoted all his energy to *training* his successors.

そだてのおや 育ての親 a **foster parent** (里親) ; an **adoptive parent** (養子縁組をした養い親).

そだてる 育てる

raise /reɪz/ +目 (子供・動物・植物を ; 《米》で好まれる) ; **bring up** (子供を ; 《英》で好まれる) ; **grow** +目 (植物を) ▶子供はのびのびと育てたい We want to *raise* our children in a free atmosphere. ‖ 彼女はその子犬をドッグフードで育てた She *raised* the puppy on dog food. ‖ 父はおばの手ひとつで育てられた My father *was brought up* entirely by his aunt. ‖ 稲を育てるのは大変な仕事だ It is laborious work to *grow* [*cultivate*] rice plants. (➤ cultivate は「栽培する」).
▶優秀な選手を育てるにはよいコーチが必要だ To *make* [*produce*] a good athlete, you need a good coach.

そち 措置 **measures** (➤ 通例複数形で) ▶デフレに対して緊急措置を講じる take *emergency measures* against deflation ‖ 国民経済をよみがえらせるには思い切った措置(＝行動)をとる必要がある We need to take *drastic action* to revitalize the nation's economy. ‖ 政府は脱税には断固たる措置をとると約束した The government has promised to *crack down on* tax evasion. (➤ crack down on は「…を厳しく取り締まる」).

そちゃ 粗茶 ▶粗茶ですが, どうぞ *This tea is nothing special* [*just ordinary*], *but* I hope you like it. (🔔 日本語は謙遜表現として認知されているが, このような英語を使うと, 英米人は怪訝な顔をし, 逆に不快な印象を与えかねない. 勧める以上, I think this tea is very good. I hope you like it. などとすべきである).

そちら **1【相手の側】** **that ; over there** (その場所) ▶そちらの品はいくらですか How much is the one *over there* ? ‖ そちらの方は弟さんですか Is *that* your (younger) brother ?
2【相手の人】 **that, you** ▶ (電話で) もしもし, そちらは石井さんのお宅ですか Hello. Is *this* [(英) *that*] the Ishii residence ? (🔔 the Ishii residence は Mr. Ishii's residence としてもよい) ‖ 水曜日にそちらへ伺ってもよろしいですか May I visit [call on] *you* on Wednesday ?
✉ **そちらはいかがお過ごしですか. たまにはそちらの様子を知らせてください** How are *you* getting along ? Please let me know how things are going with *you* once in a while.

そつ ▶あの男は何をやらせてもそつがないね He is a man who does everything *faultlessly*. ‖ 彼女は事務的な仕事をそつなくこなす She performs office [clerical] work *carefully* [*flawlessly*].

そつい 訴追 (法律) **1【起訴】** **(the) prosecution** ━動 **訴追する** **prosecute** +目.
2【公務員を】 **impeachment** ━動 **訴追する** **impeach** +目 ‖ **刑事訴追** criminal prosecution.

そつう 疎通 ▶ビジネスを円滑に進めるためには意思の疎通が欠かせない (*Good*) *communication* is essential to doing business smoothly. ‖ 私はフランスで十分に意思の疎通を図ることができなかった In France, I had difficulty (in) *making myself understood*.

そつえん 卒園 **kindergarten** [**nursery school**] **graduation** (➤ 後者は保育園からの) ▶卒園する graduate from kindergarten [nursery school].
‖ **卒園式** a kindergarten [nursery school] graduation ceremony.

ぞっか 俗化する **be commercialized** (商業化する) ; **be popularized** (大衆化する) ; **be vulgarized** (俗悪化する) ▶その避暑地は最近だいぶ俗化してきた That summer resort area *has gotten* quite *commercialized* recently.

そっき 速記 **shorthand,** 《米また》 **stenography** /stənɑ́:ɡrəfi/ 《参考》shorthand はふつうの手書きを指す longhand に対していう
‖ **速記者** a stenographer.

そっきゅう 速球 a **fastball** ▶伸びのある速球 a rising *fastball* ‖(時速) 150 km の速球を投げる throw [hurl] a 150 k.p.h. *fastball* (➤ k.p.h. は kilometers per hour の略).

そっきょう 即興 improvisation ━形即興の **impromptu** /imprάːm*p*tjuː/ ▶私は即興でスピーチをするはめになった I had to make an *impromptu* speech. ／I had to speak *impromptu* [*ad lib*／*off the cuff*]. (➤ カッコ内はインフォーマルな言い方) ‖ジャズに即興演奏は欠かせない *Improvisation* is an integral part of (playing) jazz.

‖即興曲 an impromptu, an improvisation.

そつぎょう 卒業 graduation ━動卒業する **graduate** 《from》

> 語法 graduation および graduate は《米》では大学を含めて各種の教育機関を修了する意味に使うが,《英》では大学および大学レベルの高等教育機関についてだけ用い, その他の学校の場合は leave (school), finish [complete] (the course of ...)を使う.

▶姉はD大学(の経済学部)を卒業した My sister *graduated* (in economics) *from* D University. ‖弟は中学を卒業した My brother *graduated from* [*finished*] junior high school. ‖どこの高校を卒業したの? What [Which] high school did you *graduate from*?／Where did you go to high school? (● 大学なら What [Which] college did you *graduate from*?／Where did you *graduate* (*from*)? などという) ‖卒業したらまず何をやりたい? What do you want to do first (thing) *after you graduate* [*after graduation*]? ‖彼は単位不足で卒業できなかった He *couldn't graduate* because he didn't have enough credits. ‖彼女はN女子大の卒業生だ She is *a graduate* of N Women's University. (➤「大学卒業生」は university [college] graduate /grǽdʒuət/ という) ‖私は『カラオケと日本人』というタイトルで卒業論文を書いた I wrote my *graduation thesis* on "Karaoke and the Japanese." (→卒論).

▶《比喩的》もう漫画は卒業した I'*m through with* comics. ‖来週の金曜日に中野さんはこの番組を卒業します Ms. Nakano will *be leaving* this program next Friday.

✉日本では3月が卒業の月です In Japan, March is the month for *graduation*.

✉優等で卒業なさったなんてすごいですね It was great to hear that you *graduated* with honors. ➤ honors は「優等」の意.

‖卒業アルバム a yearbook ‖卒業式 a graduation [《米また》commencement] ceremony (➤「卒業式はいつですか」は When is the [your] graduation (ceremony)?;「卒業式の当日」は graduation day) ‖卒業試験 a graduation examination ‖卒業写真 a graduation photo [picture] ‖卒業証書 a diploma /dɪplóʊmə/ ‖卒業生 a graduate (➤「2012年度卒業生」は a graduate of the class of 2012 という) ‖卒業生総代 the representative of the graduating students, 《米》the valedictorian /vӕlədɪktɔ́ːriən/ (➤後者は成績最優秀者がなる) 《参考》送辞を述べる「在校生代表」を the representative of the non-graduates という.

[1]**そっきん 即金 cash**(現金) ▶即金でしたら1割引きにさせていただきます If you *pay in cash*, I can offer you a 10% discount. →現金.

[2]**そっきん 側近** an **aide** /eɪd/ (補佐する人); an **attendant** (従者) ▶首相の側近 an *aide* to the prime minister／a prime minister *aide*.

ソックス socks(➤ 通例複数形で) ▶ソックスを履く[脱ぐ] put on [take off] *socks*.

そっくり 1 【似ている】**look like**(見た目が); **be quite similar** 《to》 ▶あなたはお母さんにそっくりね You *look just like* your mother. ／You're *just like* your mother. ／You are *the spitting image* of your mother. ‖あなた, 横顔[声]がお母さんにそっくりね Your profile [voice] is *just like* your mother's. ‖彼かっこいいわね. マイケルそっくりよ He's cool. (He's) *just like* Michael.

▶きみのアイデアはぼくのとそっくりだ Your idea *is quite similar to* mine. ‖アンジェリーナ・ジョリーのそっくりさんがテレビに出てるよ There's *a look-alike* [*a double*] of Angelina Jolie on TV now. ‖ぼくの父は北島三郎のそっくりさんコンテストで優勝したことがある My father won the Kitajima Saburo *Look-Alike contest*. ‖あの像は実物そっくりだ That statue *is true to life* [*is lifelike*].

2 【そのまま全部】 ▶私は有り金をそっくり盗まれた I had *all* my money stolen. ‖盗まれた金がそっくり戻ってきたよ I got back the stolen money *intact*. (➤ intact は「損なわれずに」).

▶夫が外食してきたので, せっかく作った夕食がそっくり残ってしまった Because my husband had eaten dinner before coming home, the dinner that I had gone to the trouble of making for him *was left untouched*.

そっくりかえる 反っくり返る ▶彼は反っくり返るようにして歩く He walks *swaggeringly*. (➤「ふん反り返って」の意) ‖彼は社長の椅子に反っくり返っていた He sat in the president's chair *with his head held high*.

そっけつ 即決 a **prompt decision**(適切な時期の素早い決定); an **immediate decision**(遅滞のない決定); a **snap decision**(即座の決定; ややインフォーマルな言い方で,「よく考えないで」という含みがあることが多い) ▶重要な問題なので即決を避けた We avoided *making a snap decision* because of the importance of the problem.

そっけない 素っ気ない curt ▶そっけない返事 a *curt* answer ‖彼は近頃私にそっけない態度を見せる He *gives* me *the cold shoulder* these days. (➤ cold shoulder は「冷たいあしらい」).

[1]**そっこう 速攻** 1 【機敏な攻撃】a **swift** [**quick**] **attack**.

2 【すぐに】 ▶うちに帰ってからそっこう寝た I went to bed *immediately* [*right*] after I got home. ‖英語をそっこう覚える何かいい方法ある? Is there any good way of learning English *quickly and easily*? ‖何かあったらそっこう教えてよ If anything happens, let me know *right away*.

[2]**そっこう 即行** ▶計画の即行 the *immediate execution* [*carrying out*] of a plan(●「その計画を即行する」なら execute [carry out] the plan immediately).

ぞっこう 続行する continue ▶討議を続行してください Please *continue* [*go on with*] the discussion. (➤ 後者はインフォーマルな言い方) ‖雨は大したことがなかったので試合は続行された The match *was continued* as it was raining only lightly.

そっこうじょ 測候所 a **meteorological** /miːţiərəlάːdʒɪkəl/ **station**, a **weather station**.

そっこうやく 即効薬 a **quick-acting medicine**, an **instant**［**quick**］**remedy** ▶かぜの即効薬はない There is no *instant remedy* for a cold.

そっこく 即刻 immediately ▶彼は社長の顔をぴしゃりとやって，即刻首になった He was fired *immediately*［*on the spot*］for slapping the president.

ぞっこく 属国 a **tributary state.**

ぞっこん ▶私，久保田君にぞっこんなの I'*m crazy about*［I'*m head over heels in love with*］Kubota.／I *have a crush on* Kubota.（➤ 最後は思春期の若者特有の「のぼせ上がり，お熱」）‖彼はあの作曲家（の作品）にぞっこんほれ込んでいる He is *very keen on* that composer.

そつじゅ 卒寿 one's **90th birthday** ▶祖父の卒寿を祝う celebrate one's grandfather's *90th birthday*.

そっせん 率先 ▶彼は率先してその面倒な仕事に当たった He *took the lead*［*initiative*］in doing that troublesome task.

そっち 1【場所，物】over there（場所）；**that (one)**（物）▶よし，すぐそっちへ行くから待っていなさい I'm coming *over*（*to your place*）right away, so wait for me.／I'll be *over*（*there*）right away［I'll be *there* right away］, so wait for me.（🔴 聞き手が現在居る場所へ「行く」は通常 go ではなく come を使うが coming there と there を使うのは不自然に聞こえる）.

▶そっちのほうがこっちのよりずっといいよ *That one* is far better than this one. ‖そっちをください Give me *that one*. ⇀そちら.

2【相手の人】you ▶今度の日曜，そっちの都合はどう？ Can *you* make it next Sunday？／Is next Sunday all right with *you*？ ⇀そちら.

そっちのけ ▶彼女は仕事そっちのけでおしゃべりばかりしている She is always chatting and *neglecting* her work.

そっちゅう 卒中 a **stroke**,《医学》**apoplexy** /ǽpəpleksi/ ▶彼は卒中で倒れた He collapsed from a *stroke*. ⇀脳卒中.

そっちょく 率直 frankness 一形 **率直な frank**；**forthright**（ずばずば言う）；**straightforward**（正直な）；**outspoken**（ずけずけ言う）；**candid**（無遠慮なほど）▶率直な話し合いをする have a *heart-to-heart* talk ‖彼女は率直だから好きだ I like her because she is *frank*［*straightforward*］. ‖彼は回りくどい言い方はしない．いつも率直だ He doesn't talk in a roundabout way；he *is* always *straightforward*［*outspoken*］. ‖彼女の率直な発言は時として誤解を招く Her *candid*［*outspoken*］remarks sometimes invite misunderstandings. ‖率直に言ってきみはストレートに物を言い過ぎると思うよ *To be frank with you*［*Frankly*（*speaking*）］, you are too direct in your remarks. ‖きみが考えていることをもっと率直に言ってほしい I wish you would be more *forthright* and tell me what you think. ‖率直に話し合おう Let's talk *frankly*.

そっと 1【静かに，ひそかに】quietly（静かに）；**lightly**（軽く）；**softly**（柔らかく）；**gently**（優しく）；**secretly**（ひそかに）▶彼女は赤ちゃんを起こさないようにそっと歩いた She walked *quietly* so that she wouldn't wake the baby. ‖妹は赤ちゃんの頬にそっと触った My sister *softly*［*lightly*］touched the baby on the cheek. ‖中に何か入っているかどうか，箱をそっと振ってごらん Shake the box *gently* to see if there's anything inside. ‖私は父の顔色をそっとうかがった I *secretly* studied (the expression on) my father's face.

▶私はそっと部屋を出た I *sneaked*［*slipped*］*out of* the room.（➤ sneak は「こそこそ歩く」，slip は「そっと歩く」）‖英語の試験のとき，麻里はそっと直子の答案を見た During the English test, Mari *stole a glance at* Naoko's answers.（➤ steal a glance at は「…を盗み見る」）.

2【そのままにしておく】 ▶あいつはガールフレンドと別れたばかりなんだ．そっとしておいてやろうよ He just broke up with his girlfriend. Let's *leave* him *alone*.

ぞっと ▶あの男がそばに来るとぞっとするわ I *get the creeps* when that man comes near me. ‖蛇は見ただけでぞっとする The mere sight of a snake *gives me the creeps*［*gives me goose bumps*／*scares me to death*］.（➤ 2番目は「鳥肌を立たせる」，最後は「ひどく怖がらせる」の意）‖もう1便遅い飛行機に乗っていたら自分もあの事故に遭っていたと思うとぞっとした I *shuddered* when I thought that if I had been on the next flight, I would have been in the accident.

▶あまりぞっとしない（＝楽しめない）話だね Your story *leaves* me *cold*.

そっとう 卒倒する faint, pass out（➤ 後者はややインフォーマルな言い方）▶暑さのため数人の少女が卒倒した Several girls *fainted*［*passed out*］because of the heat. ‖何てざまだ．おふくろさんが見たら卒倒する（＝仰天する）ぞ What a sight！Your mother will *be shocked* when she sees you.

そっぱ 反っ歯 a **projecting tooth.**

そっぽ ▶「おっす」と声をかけたのに，上田のやつそっぽを向いて答えなかった I said "Hi!" to Ueda, but he *turned away* and gave no answer［*looked the other way* and did not reply］. ‖娘はこの縁談にそっぽを向いている My daughter *wouldn't listen to* this marriage proposal.

そつろん 卒論 a **graduation thesis**［**paper**］▶日本語の借用語について卒論を書く write *a graduation thesis*［*paper*］on loanwords in Japanese.

✉ **私は今卒論を書くために図書館にせっせと通っています** I am busy going to the library to work on my *graduation paper*.

そで 袖 a **sleeve**（衣服の）；**the wings**（舞台の）▶袖無しのブラウス a *sleeveless* blouse ‖長袖のシャツ a *long-sleeved* shirt ‖きみ，半袖で寒くないかい？ Hey, don't you feel chilly with just *a short-sleeved shirt* on？

▶子供はおびえて母親の袖にすがりついた The frightened child clung to his mother's *sleeve*. ‖このジャケットはまだ一度も袖を通したことがない I have never even *worn* this jacket. ‖彼は袖をまくり上げるとパン生地をこね始めた He *rolled up his sleeves* and began to knead the dough.

▶《慣用表現》袖にすがる depend on；turn to ‖袖にする give someone the cold shoulder／treat someone coldly. ‖ことわざ 袖振り合うも多生の縁 Even a chance meeting is predestined from a previous life.

▶ ことわざ 無い袖は振れぬ You can't wave your sleeves when you are in a sleeveless kimono.（➤ 日本語からの直訳）／You can't get blood out of a stone［turnip］.（➤「石［カブ］から血は出ない」の意の英語のことわざ）／I can't give you something I don't have.

‖袖口 a cuff.

ソテー ▶ポークソテー *sauté* pork／*sautéed* pork（➤

sauté の発音は /soʊtéɪ ‖ sɔːtéɪ/).

そてつ 蘇鉄《植物》a **cycad** /sáɪkæd/.

そと 外 **the outside**(外側) 一副 **外に**[**で**] **out, outside**; **outdoors**(戸外で) ▶**外**はひどく寒い It's freezing (cold) *outside*. ‖ **外**は暖かくていいお天気よ. どうして**外で遊ばない**の It's nice and warm *outside*. Why don't you play *outside* [*outdoors*]? ‖ かぜをひいているときは**外へ出**ないほうがいいよ When you have a cold, you shouldn't *go outside*. (●「屋外へ出る」の意; go out とするとある程度遠くへ行くことを意味する) ‖ **外から帰って来**たら手を洗うんですよ Wash your hands *when you come home*. ‖ 多くの主婦が**外に出て**パートとして働いている Many housewives work part-time *outside the home* [work *outside the home* at part-time jobs]. (●この場合, 建物を指す house は不可) ‖ たまには**外で食事**しようよ Let's *eat out* for a change. ‖ 男が**門の外に**立っている A man is standing *outside the gate*. ‖ 窓の**外を見て**ごらん *Look out* the window.
▶あの人はめったに**感情を外へ出さ**ない She seldom *shows her emotions*.

そとうみ 外海 **the open sea.**

そとがわ 外側 an **outer side, the outside**, an **exterior** (➤最後の語は堅い語) ▶このかばんは**外側**は革で, 内側は布だ This (hand)bag is leather on the *outside* and cloth on the inside. ‖ 刑務所の塀の**外側**は黒く塗ってあった The *exterior* walls of the prison were painted black.

そとづら 外面 ▶彼は**外面**はいいが, 内面が悪い He *puts on a pleasant face, in public*, but at home he's not pleasant [nice] at all.

そとば 卒塔婆 a ***sotoba***
日本紹介 ✉ **卒塔婆は長い板に仏教の神聖なことばが書かれたもので, しばしば戒名が漢字で書かれており, 時には梵字**(ぼんじ)**も併記されています. 故人の魂の安らぎを願って墓の脇に置かれます** A *sotoba* is a long wooden board on which sacred Buddhist words and often the kaimyo [posthumous Buddhist name] are written in kanji characters and sometimes also in Sanscrit letters. It is placed beside a grave for the repose of the deceased person's soul.

そとまわり 外回り ▶野田は午前中は**外回り**で午後から出社します Mr. Noda *is out making calls* in the morning and will come to the office in the afternoon. ‖ 父は営業マンなので**外回り**の仕事が多い Because my father is in the sales department, he works *outside* (*the office*) a lot.
▶上野で**外回り**の山手線に乗りなさい Take the *outer* Yamanote Line at Ueno.

そとみ 外見 ▶**外見**はよいが内側は安普請の建て売り住宅 a ready-built house *that appears nice from the outside*, but is cheaply built on the inside. ⇀外見(がいけん).

そなえ 備え **preparations**(準備) ▶周到な**備え**をして山に登る climb a mountain after making careful [thorough] *preparations* ‖ 私たちは常に地震に対して**備え**をしておくべきだ We should always *be prepared for* an earthquake.
ことわざ **備えあれば憂い無し** Preparation makes you free from worry. / Keep something [Save (up)] for a rainy day.

そなえつける 備え付ける **install** ＋目, **equip**《with》(➤前者は技術者など専門的技術・知識を持つ者の仕事を連想させる) ▶書斎にクーラーを**備え付けた** I *had* an air conditioner *installed* in my study. (➤ have ... installed で「…を備え付けてもらう」) ‖ パトカーには無線装置が**備え付けてある** Every patrol car *is provided* [*is equipped*] *with* a wireless radio. ‖ ヨーロッパの多くのアパートには(入居する前から)**家具が備え付けてある** Most European apartments *are furnished*. (➤ furnish は「(部屋に)家具を備え付ける」の意) ‖ **備え付けの**トイレットペーパーをお使いください Please only use the toilet paper *provided*.

そなえもの 供え物 an **offering** ▶仏前に**供え物をする** *place an offering* (of rice [water]) in front of the memorial tablet of a deceased family member. ⇀お供え.

1 **そなえる 備える**

📖 **訳語メニュー**
設備をもつ ⇀be equipped with **1**
準備をする ⇀prepare for **2**
才能がある ⇀be gifted with **3**

1【設備をもつ】be equipped《with》▶カーナビを**備えた**車 a car *equipped with* a navigation system ‖ わが校の語学ラボは最新の設備を**備えている** Our school's language laboratory *is fitted out with* the latest equipment. (➤ fit A out with B は「A(部屋など)にB(必要品)を取り付ける」). ⇀**備え付ける.**

2【準備する】prepare《for》; **provide**《for》(将来の災難などに) ▶期末試験に**備えて**猛勉強する study very hard to *prepare for* the end-of-term exam ‖ 彼女は毎日何時間も練習してテニスの試合に**備えた** She practiced for hours every day *in preparation for* the tennis match.
▶両親は老後に**備えて**貯金している My parents are saving money *to provide for* their old age. ‖ 雨に**備えて**傘を持って来たよ I've brought my umbrella *in case it rains*.

3【才能や能力がある】be gifted《with》▶コウモリは超音波で障害物をよける能力を**備えている** Bats *are gifted with* the ability to avoid obstacles by using ultrasonic waves.

2 **そなえる 供える** **offer** ＋目 ▶お彼岸に祖先の墓に花を**供える** *offer* flowers on the graves of one's ancestors during the equinoctial week. ⇀お供え.

ソナタ《音楽》a **sonata** ▶ソナタ形式 *sonata* form. ‖ **バイオリンソナタ** a violin sonata.

ソナチネ《音楽》a **sonatina.**

そなわる 備わる ▶このホールは最新式の設備が**備わっている** This hall *is provided* [*is furnished*] *with* the latest equipment. / The latest equipment *has been installed* in this hall.
▶彼女には音楽の才能が**備わっている** She *is gifted with* a talent for music. ‖ その女優には持って生まれた気品が**備わっている** The actress *has* natural grace.

ソネット a **sonnet.**

そねむ **get** [**feel**] **jealous** ▶彼の成功を**そねむ** *envy* his success.

その **the**; **that** [複 **those**]

解説 (1)本書ではしばしば「その」= the として,「その男」= the man のように使っているが, この「その男」は前に言及されたり, あるいは, 文脈上, どの男を指しているかがわかるということを前提としている. 英語の the は話し手だけでなく，聞き手にもどの個体（この場合「男」）を指しているかがわかる，というメッセージを伝える語で，指さすときに使うものではない．「その本」は相手の近くにある本も指すが，このように指示的に指すのは that book である．英語の指示語は話し手の近くにあるものを指す this と話し手から離れたものを指す that の２つで，前者は「この」，後者は「その」と「あの」に当たる．
(2) 食卓で「塩を取って」という場合，Pass me the salt, please. というのは，食卓に塩が１つしかなく，どれを指しているかがわかるからである．「その雑誌を取って」という場合，話し手が指さしていれば，Pass me that magazine, please. という．雑誌が何冊かある場合，Pass me the magazine, please. では，どれのことかわからず，Which magazine？と聞き返されてしまう．
(3)「テレビの音を小さくしてくれますか」は今見ていて音を小さくすべきテレビは状況でわかるので Could you turn down the TV？という．これをわざわざ，Could you turn down that TV？と明示すると，日本語で「そのテレビ」とはっきり言うときと同様に，わからないんですか，あなたが見ているそのテレビですよ，のような，いらだちを示す表現となる．

▶その絵は誰が描いたものですか Who painted *the* [*that*] picture？（💬 the picture はどの絵のことか聞き手にもわかるというメッセージを伝える．that picture は話し手から離れたものを指して使う）‖一体どうしたの，その傷？ How on earth did you get *that* cut？‖きみの前にあるそのズボンを取ってくれる？ Could you hand me *those* pants there in front of you？‖そのレディー・ガガって何者？ Who is *this* Lady Gaga？（➤ 今話題に上っているものを指すときは that は使わない）‖クラスの約３分の１が阪神ファンだが，私もその１人だ About one third of our classmates are Tigers fans, and I am *one of them*.

そのう ▶実はそのう，宿題を忘れました *Well*, to tell (you) the truth, I forgot my homework.

そのうえ その上 **besides, moreover**（➤ 前者は悪いことが重なる場合に用いることが多い．後者は前者より堅い語で，「加えて…」に近い）▶私たちの先生は厳しい．その上宿題が多すぎる Our teacher is very strict. *Besides*, he gives us too much homework. ‖カナダは広い．その上天然資源に富んでいる Canada is a large country; *moreover*, it has abundant natural resources.
▶校長先生はぼくたちを叱り，親を学校に呼びつけ，その上ぼくたちを１週間の停学処分にした Our principal scolded us, called our parents to school, and *what's more* [*furthermore*], suspended us for one week.（💬 furthermore はいくつかの状況が積み重なった場合に用いられる）．
▶大変ごちそうになりました．その上，お土産まで頂きまして Thank you for the wonderful meal *and also* for the nice present. ‖佐和子は美人で，その上頭もいい Sawako is beautiful and intelligent *as well*.（💬 as well は文尾に添える）‖夜もふけ，その上外は吹雪だった It was late at night, and *what was worse* [*to make matters worse*], there was a snowstorm outside.（➤「なお悪いことには」の意）．

そのうち 1【やがて】 **soon**（まもなく）; **before long**（そう日時がたたないうちに）; **someday**（いつか）▶そのうちたけしも帰って来るでしょうから，お茶でもどうですか How about a cup of tea or something？Takeshi will be back *soon*. ‖そのうちまたお目にかかりましょう I'll see you again *before long*. ‖そのうちディズニーランドに連れていってあげるよ I'll take you to Disneyland *someday* [*one of these days*]. ‖２人はそのうち（＝時間がたてば）仲直りするだろう They'll make up *in due time*. ‖そのうちにわかるよ *Time will tell*.（💬 相手に真実などをその場で伝えたくないようなときに用いる）‖「そのうち」は当てにならない *One of these days* is none of these days.
2【その中で】 ▶私たちは10人で富士登山をしたが，そのうち８人は富士山が初めてだった The ten of us climbed Mt. Fuji, eight *of whom* were climbing it for the first time.

そのかわり その代わり **instead** ▶この本は貸してあげられないけど，その代わりこのパンフをあげよう I cannot lend you this book, but I'll give you this brochure *instead*.
▶日本語教えてあげるから，その代わりに（＝お返しに）スペイン語教えてよ I'll teach you Japanese, so teach me Spanish *in return*. ‖きょうは残業してくれないか．その代わり（＝埋め合わせに）晩ごはんをおごるよ Could you work overtime today？I'll treat you to dinner *to make up for it*.

そのき その気 ▶その気でやればこんな仕事１時間で済みますよ *If you put your mind into it* [*If you try really hard*], you can finish the job in an hour. ‖ゴルフをしようと誘われているんだが，その気にならないんだ I have been invited to play golf, but I *am not interested* [*am not in the mood*]. ‖その気も無いのにずるずる付き合っちゃだめ You shouldn't go on seeing him [her] when you *have no interest* in marrying him [her].

そのくせ ▶彼女は痩せようとダイエットしているが，そのくせおやつのケーキは欠かさない She is on a diet to lose weight, *and yet* she never skips a cake at teatime. ‖その老人は口が悪い．そのくせ，自分のことを言われるとひどく怒る *Despite* his own harsh tongue, the old man gets furious whenever someone criticizes him.（➤ despite は「…にもかかわらず」）．

そのくらい その位 ▶《ご飯をよそってもらって》そのくらいで結構です *That* is enough [plenty] (for me). ‖**対話**「満員電車の中で靴を踏まれちゃったわ」「そのくらい我慢しなきゃ」"I got stepped on in a crowded train." "*You have to put up with* [*expect*] *things like that*."

そのご その後 **since (then)**（➤ since は通例現在完了の文で使う）▶その後彼女の消息を聞かない I have heard nothing of her *since* (*then*). ‖その後彼は責任を感じて辞職した *After that*, he resigned because he felt responsible. ‖その後数日して私は偶然マキに再会した I saw Maki again by chance *a few days later*.
✉ その後いかがお過ごしですか How have you been *since* (*then*)？

そのころ その頃 ▶その頃私，まだ起きてたよ *At that time*, [*Then*] I was still awake. ‖きょうはおじさんが６時にいらっしゃるからその頃までには必ず帰ってらっしゃい Your uncle is visiting us at six this evening. Be sure to come home *by then* [*by that time*]. ‖その頃のことは何も話したくありません I don't want to say anything about *those days*.

そのじつ その実 ▶彼は中国語が堪能と言うけれど，その実中国人とは話したことがないようだ He claims that his Chinese is excellent, but *the truth is* he has never talked to a Chinese person.

そのすじ その筋 **the authorities (concerned), those concerned** ▶その催し物の企画はその筋の命令により中止

された The plans for the event were canceled by order of *the authorities*.

そのせつ その節 ▶その節は大変お世話になりました Thank you very much for your help *the other day* [*at that time* / *on that occasion*]. (● 英語では last Tuesday(先週の火曜日は)とか, last Sunday (先週の日曜日は)のように具体的に言うほうがふつう. また, お礼はその場で言うのが原則で, 後日改めて言う習慣はない).

そのた その他 the others (ほかの人たち・物) ; the rest (残りの人たち・物) ▶大輝は華道部ただ 1 人の男子で, その他は皆女子だ Daiki is the only boy in the flower arranging club, and *the others* [*the rest*] are all girls. ‖ 正子は欠席したが, その他の生徒は出席した Masako was absent, but *the other* students were present. ‖ 係員は私に住所・氏名・年齢その他を尋ねた The person in charge asked me my name, age, address *and so on*. (➤ and so on は「…など」). →そのほか.

そのため 1【目的, 理由】▶ぼくはインドに留学したいんだ. お金をためているのはそのためだ I want to study in India. *That's why* I've been saving money. / I want to study in India and I've been saving money *for that purpose*.

2【結果】▶その朝はひどく雨が降っており, そのため試合は中止になった It was raining heavily that morning, *so* the game was canceled.

そのつぎ その次 ▶その次に会ったときはかおるは結婚していた *The next time* I saw Kaoru, she was married. ‖ 次は黒田さんで, その次が私の番です It's Mr. Kuroda's turn next and mine *after that*.

そのつど その都度 each time ▶このファックスを使うときはそのつど断ってください Please tell me *each time* you use this fax. ‖ 何かわからないことがあったらそのつど(＝いつでも)遠慮なく質問してください *Any time* you have questions, don't hesitate to ask me.

そのて その手 1【そのやり方】▶その手は食わないよ You can't play *that trick* on me. ‖ その手は古いよ *That's an old trick*. ‖ あいにくだが, その手には乗らないよ(＝おあいにくさま) Too bad for you! *I won't fall for that*.

2【その種類】▶学生はよくその手の間違いをする Students often make *that kind of* mistake [*those kinds of* mistakes].

そのとおり その通り ▶娘は私が最近太ってきたと言うが, 全くそのとおりだ My daughter says I'm getting fat these days, and *she's* absolutely *right*. ‖ 対話「彼は社長にはふさわしくない」「そのとおり」"He's not fit to be president of our company." "*You're right*." ‖ 対話「じゃあ, きみはこの企画にもっと金をかけろと言うのかい?」「そのとおり」"So you're saying we should spend more on this project?" "*Exactly*. / *That's right*." (➤ 相手が You're saying ...? と言って, こちらの考えを確認しているので, ここでは You're right. (あなたのいうことは正しい) と You で応じることはできない).

そのとき その時 then, at that time (➤ いずれも過去にも未来にも使える) ▶私はそのときまだ大学生だった I was still in college *then* [*at that time*]. ‖ そのとき若い男が家に飛び込んできた *At that moment*, a young man ran into my house. ‖ 先週の土曜日にパーティーに出てそのとき彼と知り合ったんだ I attended a party last Saturday and got to know him *then*. ‖ そのとき以来彼とは口を利いていない I haven't spoken to him (*ever*) *since*. ‖ あすすべてを話す. そのときまでこのことは秘密にしておいてくれ I'll tell you everything tomorrow. Please keep this (a) secret *until then*. ‖ 対話「入試に落ちたらどうするの?」「そのときはそのときさ」"What will you do if you fail the entrance exams?" "*I'll cross that bridge when I come to it*." (➤「その時が実際に来るまで気にしない」の意) ‖ 対話「もしお父さんに問い詰められたら?」「そのときはそのときよ(＝うまくやるわよ)」"If your father asks you about it, what will you do?" "*I'll play it by ear*." (➤ play it by ear は「臨機応変にやる」の意のインフォーマルな表現).

そのば その場 ▶火事が起きたとき数人の人がその場に居た Several people were *there* when the fire broke out. ‖ 彼が珍妙な格好で現れたのでその場に居合わせた人々は大笑いした *Those present* burst into laughter when he appeared in such a strange getup. ‖ 泥棒はその場で捕まった The robber was arrested *on the spot* [*then and there* / *red-handed*]. (➤ on the spot は「直ちに」, then and there は「その時その場で」, red-handed は「現行犯で」).

▶《慣用表現》その場しのぎの答弁 an *evasive* answer ‖ その場しのぎの措置 a *stopgap* measure ‖ その場逃れの言い訳 an excuse *just to get out of a tight spot* ‖ 問題が起きたら, その場その場で解決していこう Let's solve problems *as* [*when*] *they come up*. / When problems crop up, let's solve them *then and there*.

そのひぐらし その日暮らし ▶私はその日暮らしをしているが将来のことは全く気にならない I *live from hand to mouth* [*I just get through*] *each day*, and don't worry at all about the future.

そのへん その辺 1【その辺りに】around there ▶その辺にホチキスない? Is there a stapler somewhere *around there*? (➤ 日本語は「ない?」だが, 英語では単にあるかないかの質問には肯定形の Is を使って聞く. Isn't にすると,「あるはずなのにないの?」「ないのはおかしいでしょう, よく探してごらんなさい」などという含みになる). ‖ 兄ですか? 今出かけたばかりだからまだその辺に居るかもしれませんよ My brother? He just left, so he might be *just around the corner*.

▶その辺(のこと)はお任せしますよ I'll leave *it* to you.

2【その程度】▶その辺でやめたらどうだ. 食べ過ぎはよくないよ You should stop *there*. Eating too much is bad for your health. ‖ もうその辺で勘弁してやれよ. こいつもだいぶ反省しているようだから You should forgive him *now*. He seems to be really sorry for what he did [said].

そのほか その他 the others ▶そのことは 2 人だけが知っていたが, そのほかの人は知らなかった Two people knew about it, but *the others* didn't. ‖ そのほか何がありますか What *else* do you have? ‖ そのほかに何かご意見はありますか Do you have any *other* suggestions? →その他(た).

そのまま ▶彼女は人から聞いた話をそのまま話した She told the story *as* she had heard it. ‖ 私の部屋は(いじらないで)そのままにしておいてね Please *leave* my room *as it is*. ‖ そのままのきみが好きだ I like you *the way* [*as*] *you are*. ‖ どうぞそのまま(＝立たなくて結構です) Please *don't get up*. ‖ このジュースは薄めないでそのまま飲めます You can drink this juice without diluting it. (●「そのまま」は訳出不要) ‖ 兄はごろんと横になったかと思うと, そのまま寝込んでしまった The minute my (older) brother lay down, he fell asleep. (● この「そのまま」も訳出不要) ‖《電話で》

(切らないで)そのままお待ちください *Hold the line* [*Hang on*], *please*.

そのみち その道 ▶彼女はその道ではちょっとは知られた学者だ She is well known as a scholar *in that field*.

そのもの ▶彼は真面目そのものだ He is seriousness *itself*. ／He is *all* seriousness. (（×）He is seriousness. とはいわない) ‖ 彼女は健康そのものだ She is *the picture of* health. ‖ 花嫁は幸福そのものだった The bride *looked as happy as could be*. (「この上なく幸せで」の意. 現在形では as happy as can be).

そのような such, like that. →そんな.

そのように like that, in such a way. →そんなに.

そのわりに その割に ▶1週間ハワイに居たんだって? その割に焼けてないじゃない You're not very tanned, *considering* (that) you stayed in Hawaii for a week. (➤ considering は「その割には」の意の副詞).

1**そば 蕎麦** *soba* ; buckwheat noodles

日本紹介 ✉ **そばは, そば粉に水を加えてこね, 薄く延ばして細く切った麺です. ゆでて丼に入れたそばに熱いつゆをかけた「かけそば」と, ゆでてから冷たくしてざるに盛ったそばを濃いつゆにつけて食べる「盛りそば」が代表的です** *Soba* are noodles made of buckwheat flour and water, kneaded and finely cut. Typical ways of serving *soba* are '*kakesoba*' (briefly boiled soba in hot soup served in a bowl) and '*morisoba*' (briefly boiled then chilled soba that is served on a bamboo tray and dipped in a strongly-flavored shoyu-based sauce).

2**そば 側** **1**【傍ら】near, by (…のすぐ近くに) ; beside (…と並んで) ▶京都タワーは京都駅のすぐそばです The Kyoto Tower is *quite near* Kyoto Station. ‖ 母鹿のそばで子鹿が3頭じゃれていた Three fawns were playing *beside* their mother. ‖ 郵便ポストのそばに自動販売機がある There is a vending machine *beside* the mailbox. ‖ 展示品のそばにあまり近寄らないでください Please don't *get* too *close to* the display. ‖ こっちに来てそばに座ってよ Come and sit *by* me.

▶そばに寄らないでよ! *Keep away!* ‖ 1台の車が子供たちのそばを猛スピードで走り去った A car zoomed *by* the children at full speed. ‖ 母はすぐそばの美容院に行ってます My mother has gone to a *nearby* beauty salon. ‖ そばから口を出すな Don't *butt* [*horn*] *in*.

2【…するとすぐ】as soon as ▶息子は金が入るそばから使ってしまう My son spends his money *as soon as* he earns it.

そばかす freckles (➤ 通例複数形で) ▶麻美は鼻にそばかすがある Asami *has freckles* [*is freckled*] on her nose. ‖ 白人は日本人よりそばかすができやすい Caucasians *freckle* more easily than Japanese (do).

そばだてる ▶彼は自分の名前が挙がると耳をそばだてた When he heard his name mentioned, he *pricked up his ears*. (➤ prick up one's ears は「耳をそばだてる」の意のインフォーマルな言い方).

そびえる 聳える rise (up) ▶私たちの学校から空にそびえる新宿の高層ビル群が見える From our school, we can see the skyscrapers of Shinjuku *rising* [*towering*] *up* to the sky.

そびょう 素描 a (rough) sketch.

-そびれる ▶どうもそのことはみんなの前で言い出しそびれた I *missed* [*didn't get*] *a chance to tell* everyone about it. ‖ 彼女に聞きそびれてしまったので, その件についてはわかりません I don't know anything about the matter because I *failed to ask* her.

そふ 祖父 a [one's] grandfather →おじいさん.

ソファー a sofa /sóʊfə/, a couch /kaʊtʃ/ (➤ 厳密な区別はないが, 後者は《米》で好まれ, 片方だけ肘掛けがあるものを指すこともある) ▶ソファーで昼寝する take a nap on the *sofa*.

‖ソファーベッド a sofa-bed (背もたれの部分を倒してベッドにするもの) ; a daybed (背もたれを外してベッドにするもの).

ソフト ▶彼女はソフトな声で『夢やぶれて』を歌った She sang "I Dreamed a Dream" in a *sweet*, *low* voice. ‖ 会談は終始ソフトムードだった The talks proceeded in *a friendly atmosphere* from start to finish.

> **危ないカタカナ語✸ソフト**
> **1** 日本語では人の話し方や歌い方を「ソフト」と形容することがあり, 英語でも soft voice のようにいうが, 英語の場合は「静かな [優しい] 声」の意味であって, 日本語の「ソフト」とは少し意味がずれる.
> **2** 日本語では人の物腰も「ソフト」で形容することがあるが, 英語の soft はその場合, 否定的な意味になることが多い. 例えば, soft man は「女々しい男」であり, He is soft (in the head). は「頭が少し足りない」の意味である. したがって, 「ソフトムードの俳優」は gentle [quiet] actor とか mild-mannered actor のようにいう必要がある.
> **3** 「ソフトウェア」のことを略して「ソフト」というが, 英語では略さずに software という.

ソフト(ウェア) software (➤ 一つ一つのソフトウェアを指すときは a software program または a software という) ▶ゲームソフト game *software* ; a game *software* (program) ‖ 外国語学習のソフトウェア *software* for foreign language study ; a *software* (program) for foreign language study ‖ ソフトウェアの開発 *software* development ‖ ソフトウェア会社 a *software* company.

▶ワープロソフトを使う use word processing *software* ／use a word processing *software* (*program*) ‖ ウイルス対策ソフトを最新のものにする update an antivirus *soft-ware*.

ソフトクリーム soft-serve ice cream

《参考》円すい形のウエハースに入ったソフトクリームは厳密には soft ice cream in a cone [《英また》cornet] だが, ふつうは an ice cream cone といい, 味を表して vanilla cone (バニラ味の場合), chocolate cone (チョコレート味の場合) などといっている ▶ソフトクリームを食べる [なめる] eat [lick] an *ice cream cone*.

ソフトボール softball ▶ソフトボールをする play *softball*.

そふぼ 祖父母 one's grandparents, one's grandmother and grandfather.

ソプラノ 《音楽》(a) soprano /səprǽnoʊ/ (➤ 歌手は Ⓒ, 音域は Ⓤ 扱い) ▶明子はソプラノで, 久子はメゾソプラノだ Akiko is *a soprano* and Hisako is a mezzo-soprano. ‖ 彼女の声はソプラノだ She has a *soprano* voice.

‖ソプラノ歌手 a soprano.

そぶり 素振り a manner (様子) ; a sign (気配) ▶よそよそしいそぶり a distant *manner* ‖ 彼女のそぶりがおかしい There is something strange in her *manner*. ‖ ずいぶん勝手な頼みだったが彼は嫌なそぶりを見せなかった

My request was very selfish, but he showed no *sign* of being offended.

そぼ 祖母 a [one's] **grandmother** →おばあさん.

そぼう 粗暴な rowdy /ráʊdi/（乱暴な）; **rough** /rʌf/（荒っぽい）▶先生はジェームズの**粗暴な**ふるまいを戒めた The teacher rebuked James for his *rowdy* [*rough*] behavior.

そぼく 素朴な simple（簡単な；無邪気な）; **unsophisticated**（世間ずれしていない）▶私はタイで出会った**素朴な**村人たちが好きになった I came to like the *simple* [*unsophisticated*] villagers I met in Thailand. ‖ 村人は**素朴な**人たちばかりだった The villagers were (*just*) *plain folks*.

▶**素朴な**疑問だが, なぜ彼は彼女を助けてやらなかったのだろう This may be a *simple* question, but why didn't he help her?

そぼろ seasoned fish [**chicken**] **powder.**

そまつ 粗末 1【質が劣る】一形 粗末な poor（貧弱な）; **shabby**（みすぼらしい）; **humble**（質素な）; **plain**（あっさりした）▶**粗末な**食事 a *poor* meal ‖ 彼らは**粗末な**身なりをして**粗末な**小屋に住んでいた They wore *shabby* [*plain*] clothes and lived in a *humble* cottage. ／They dressed *shabbily* and lived in a *humble* cottage. ‖ **粗末な**ものですが, 召し上がってください *It's nothing fancy*, but please help yourself.（● 英語では「粗末なもの」と勧める習慣はない.「たくさんはないが」の意）.

2【大切にしない】▶自分の親を**粗末に**するんじゃない! Don't *treat* your parents *shabbily*! ‖ このつぼは家宝だから**粗末に**扱ってはいけない You shouldn't handle this vase *roughly* [*carelessly*] because it's a family treasure.

☛ お粗末（→見出語）

そまる 染まる dye /daɪ/（色が）▶酢を加えて加熱するとこの種の生地はよく**染まる** This kind of cloth *dyes* well if you add vinegar to the dye and heat it.

▶そのナイフは血に**染まっていた** The knife *was stained with blood*. ‖ 深山の紅葉が夕日に**染まって**輝いている The autumn leaves in the deep mountains *are glowing in the light of the sunset*.

▶この年齢の若者は悪に**染まりやすい** Young people this age *are* easily *misled into crime* [*delinquency*].

そむく 背く disobey +目（従わない）; **disregard** +目（無視する）▶両親の言いつけに**背く** *disobey* one's parents' instructions ‖ 自分の良心に**背く** *go against* one's conscience ‖ この命令に**背いた**者は厳罰に処する Those who *disregard* this order will be punished severely.

▶彼は親の期待に**背いて**家業を捨てた He *turned his back on* [*upon*] his parents and refused to take over the family business.

そむける 背ける ▶彼女は死んだネズミを見た瞬間, 目を**背けた** The moment she saw the dead rat, she *turned her eyes away* [*averted her eyes*]. ‖ 現実から目を**背けるな** Don't *turn your eyes away* from reality.

ソムリエ a sommelier /sʌ̀məljéɪ/（➤ フランス語から), a **wine steward.**

そめもの 染め物 dyeing（染めること）; **dyed goods**（染めた物）‖ **染め物**工場[屋] a dyehouse.

そめる 染める dye /daɪ/ +目 ▶髪を茶色に**染める** *dye* [*tint*] one's hair orange（● tint は髪の一部を染める場合）‖ 昔は草の汁で布を**染めた** In the past they used to *dye* cloth with the sap of plants.

▶彼女は恥ずかしさのあまり顔を赤く**染めた** She *blushed* [*turned red*] with embarrassment.

そもそも to begin with（まず第一に）; **on earth**（一体）▶**そもそも**きみがあんなことを言ったのが面倒の始まりだ It was your remark that caused all this trouble *to begin with* [*in the first place*]. ‖ **そもそも**誰がそんなことを言ったのかね Who *on earth* [Who *in the world* ／*Just* who] said that?

そや 粗野な coarse（品の悪い）; **rude**（不作法な）; **rough**（荒っぽい）▶**粗野な**ふるまい *rude* [*rough*] behavior ‖ 徹はよく**粗野な**ことばを使う Toru often uses *coarse* language. ‖ あの男は**粗野**でとっつきにくいが, 根はいい人間だ That man *has a rough manner* and seems inapproachable, but he's a good person at heart.

そよう 素養 knowledge（知識）; **accomplishments**（身につけたたしなみ, 芸）▶彼女には音楽の**素養がない** She *knows little* about music. ‖ 彼女には日本舞踊の**素養がある** She *has a* (*basic*) *grounding in* Japanese dance. ‖ 当社では中国語の**素養のある**人を1人求めている We are looking for a person *who knows some Chinese* [*who has some knowledge of Chinese*].

そよかぜ 微風 a gentle [**light**] **wind, a breeze** ▶**そよ風**が吹いている *A gentle* [*light*] *wind* is blowing. ／There is *a breeze* (blowing).

そよぐ rustle（さらさら鳴る）; **quiver, sway**（揺れる）▶木の葉が風に**そよいでいた** The leaves of the trees *were rustling* [*quivering*] in the wind. ‖ 稲穂が風に**そよいでいる** The rice plants *are swaying* in the wind.

そよそよ ▶春風が**そよそよと**（＝穏やかに）土手に吹いていた A spring breeze was blowing *gently* on the riverbank.

そよふく そよ吹く ▶**そよ吹く**風 a *gentle* breeze.

[1]**そら 空 1【天】the sky**; **the air**（空中）

語法 sky は通例そのとき頭上にある「空」と了解するので, the sky の形で用いるが, 形容詞を伴う場合は空のいろいろな様態の1つととらえて a cloudy sky（曇り空), a clear sky（晴れた空）などのように a をつけることがある.

▶雨がやんで**空**が明るくなった *The sky* lightened as it stopped raining. ‖ 青い**空**に白い雲が浮かんでいる White clouds are floating in *the blue sky*. ‖ **空**高くヒバリの鳴くのが聞こえた I heard a skylark singing *high up in the sky*. ‖ ツバメが**空**を飛んでいた Swallows were flying *through* [*in*] *the air*. ‖ 今回は快適な**空の旅**だった I had a pleasant *flight* this time.

‖ **空色** azure /ǽʒəʳ/, sky blue.

2【暗記】▶私は『平家物語』の冒頭を**そらで**言える I can recite *from memory* the beginning part of "The Tale of Heike." ‖ 彼女はその詩を**そらで**覚えた She *learned* the poem *by heart*. ／She *memorized* the poem.

☛ うわの空（→見出語）

[2]**そら**《注意を促して》**Look!, There!**; **Hey!**（呼びかけて）→ほら ▶**そら**! また電気, 消し忘れてる! *Hey!* You've forgotten to turn off the light again.

▶《キャッチボールなどで》**そら**, いくぞ! *Here* goes! ‖ **そら**見たことか（＝言わんことじゃない）I told you so.（→そら見ろ, それ見たことか).

そらおそろしい 空恐ろしい ▶地球温暖化がこのペースで進むと, 将来, 世界がどうなるか[地球の未来が]**空恐ろしい** I *feel very anxious* when I think about what will happen to the world [this planet] if global warming continues to progress at this rate.

[1]**そらす 逸らす** 1【脇へ向ける】▶彼女は彼に問い詰められて目をそらした When she was pressed for an answer, she *turned her eyes away* [*looked away*] *from* him. ‖ 注意をそらすな Don't *divert* your attention.
2【外す】▶キーパーはボールを後ろへそらした The goalkeeper *let* the ball *get past* him.
3【はぐらかす】▶話をそらさないで，きちんと答えなさい Give me a straight answer and don't *change the subject*.

[2]**そらす 反らす** bend backward ▶体を後ろに反らす *bend* oneself *backward* ‖ 彼は得意げに胸を反らせた He *stuck out his chest* [*squared his shoulders*] triumphantly.

そらぞらしい 空々しい thin, flimsy（➤ ともに「見え透いた」の意）▶空々しい言い訳をするな Don't make a *thin* [*flimsy*] excuse. ‖ 彼女はよく空々しいうそをつく She often tells *transparent* [*barefaced*] *lies*.

そらとぶえんばん 空飛ぶ円盤 a flying saucer ; an unidentified flying object（未確認飛行物体；《略》UFO）.

そらなみだ 空涙 crocodile tears（➤ crocodile は「ワニ」；ワニは獲物を食べながら涙を流すと信じられたことから）▶空涙を流す shed *crocodile tears*.

そらに 空似 a chance [coincidental] resemblance.

そらまめ 空豆 a broad bean, a fava bean.

そらみみ 空耳 ▶息子の声がしたと思ったが空耳だった I thought I heard my son's voice, but I *must have been hearing things* [it was *only my imagination*]. (● hear things は「幻聴が起こる」の意で通例進行形で用いる).

そらみろ そら見ろ ▶そら見ろ，言ったとおりじゃないか *You see ?* I told you so.

そらもよう 空模様 the look of the sky ; weather（天気）▶空模様が怪しくなってきた The *weather* looks threatening. ‖ この空模様ではあしたは雨だ Judging from *the look of the sky*, it will be rainy [we will have rain] tomorrow. (● 単に It looks like rain tomorrow. ということもできる) ‖ あすの空模様はどうだろう How will the *weather* be tomorrow ?

そらんじる learn ... by heart（暗記する）; recite ＋㊀（暗唱する）▶私は般若心経(はんにゃしんぎょう)をそらんじている I *know* the Heart Sutra *by heart*. ‖ 私は般若心経をそらんじることができる I can *recite* the Heart Sutra (*by heart*).

[1]**そり 橇** a sleigh /sleɪ/（馬が引く大型の）; a sled（小さいもの）; a sledge（➤《米》では通例荷物運搬用）▶そりで行く go on *a sled*.
‖犬ぞりレース a dogsled race.

[2]**そり 反り** a curve（曲線）; a warp /wɔːʳp/（ゆがみ）▶この椅子の背は少し反りがある The back of this chair *is* slightly *curved*. ‖ 暑い日ざしを受けて板に反りがきた The hot sun *has warped* the board.
▶《慣用表現》彼らは反りが合わない They *don't get along well*.

そりかえる 反り返る bend back（後ろへ体を曲げる）; warp /wɔːʳp/（板などが変形する）▶彼女はキスをされないように反り返った She *bent back* to escape being kissed. ‖ この板は乾燥して反り返ってしまった This board has dried and *warped*. ▶威張って椅子に反り返る *lean* [*sit*] *back pompously* in one's seat.

ソリスト a soloist /sóʊloʊɪst/（➤「ソリスト」はフランス語 *soliste* から）.

そりゃく 粗略な rough（乱暴な）; careless（不注意な）▶あの花瓶は大事なものだから粗略に扱ってはいけません That vase is precious, so don't handle it *carelessly* [*roughly*].

そりゅうし 素粒子（物理学）an elementary particle.

[1]**そる 剃る** shave ＋㊀ ▶ぼくは毎朝ひげをそる I *shave* (*myself*) every morning. ‖（理髪店で）顔をそってください I'*d like* (*to get* ／*to have*) *a shave*. ‖ 頭を坊主にそってください Please *shave off all my hair*. ‖ あの選手は縁起を担いで10日間も顔をそらずにいる That player goes *unshaven* [*without shaving*] for ten days as a good luck charm. ‖ この電気かみそりはよくそれる This electric shaver *shaves* very well. ／This electric shaver *gives* an excellent [a close] *shave*.

[2]**そる 反る** warp /wɔːʳp/（板などが）; curve（曲がる）; bend over backward（体などが）▶板が日に当たって反ってしまった The board *warped* in the sun. ‖ わあ！きみの体はよく反るんだね Wow ! You can *bend* your body *over backward*.

それ 1【相手に近い物を指して】that ; that one（そちらの物）▶それ，何ですか？ What's *that* ? ‖ これじゃなくてそれを見せていただけませんか No, not this one. Can you show me *that one ?*
2【話題に上った物・事を指して】it, that ▶ 対話「これ，誰の本？」「それ，私の」"Whose book is this ?" "*It's* [*That's*] mine." ‖ 対話「ピクニックに行こうよ」「それはいい考えね」"How about going on a picnic ?" "*That*'s a good [great] idea." ‖ 対話「あなたが捜しているもの，これ？」「あ，それそれ」"Is this what you're looking for ?" "Oh, yes. *That's it* [*That's the one*]." ▶《相手の唐突な発言などに》何，それ？ What do you mean ?
3【そのとき】▶それ以来奥田君には会っていない I haven't seen Okuda *since then*.
4【注意を促して】▶それごらん，言ったとおりでしょ *There now !* I told you so.
5【慣用表現】▶それもそうだが私としてはきみに賛成はできない *That may be true*, but I (still) can't agree with you. ‖ それがどうした？ *So what ?*

それから (and) then（次に）; after that（そのあと）; since（それ以来ずっと）▶私はまず宿題を済ませ，それから漫画を読んだ I did my homework first, *and then* read comic books. ‖ ぼくは去年の夏海辺で佳代と出会い，それからずっと付き合いを続けている I met Kayo at the beach last summer, and I have been going (out) with her *ever since* (*then*). ‖ 5月に金魚が1匹死に，それからまもなくもう1匹死んだ One goldfish died in May, and another died *soon afterward*. ‖ 初めて会ったとき宏美にはボーイフレンドがいたが，それから1か月後に彼とは別れたらしい Hiromi had a boyfriend when I first met her, but I heard she broke up with him *one month later*. ‖ 対話「学校を出たあと新宿へ行ったのさ」「それから？」"After school I went to Shinjuku." "*And after that ?* ／*And then ... ?*"

それきり 1【それだけ】▶話というのはそれきりかい（＝言いたいのはそれだけか）? Is that *all* you want to tell me ? ‖ 彼女からは以前1回電話があったがそれきりだ I got a telephone call from her once, but *that was all* [*it*].
2【それ以来】▶それきりその町には行っていない I haven't visited the town (*ever*) *since*.

それくらい ▶それくらい我慢しろ！ You can put up with *at least that* [*this*] *much* ! ‖ それくらいのことなら私にもできます Even I could do *something that* *easy*.（● この could は「（やってみれば）…できる」という仮定法で，I は強く発音する）‖ **それくらいのことがわからないのか** You can't *even* understand *that*? ‖ **それくらいのことで泣くな** Don't cry *over such a small thing*. ‖ **それくらいにしておきなさい** Leave it *at that*.（➤「もうよしなさい」の意）.

それこそ 1【まさにそれが】▶**それこそ地質学者たちが長い間探し求めてきた化石だ** *That is the very* fossil that geologists have long been searching for.
2【まるで】▶**彼女はそれこそ女王にでもなったかのようにふるまった** She behaved *as if* she were a queen. ‖ **お母さんに知れたらそれこそ大変だ** *I'll catch hell* [*There'll be hell to pay*] if my mom finds out (about it).（➤ hell to pay は「ひどく面倒なこと」の意のインフォーマルな言い方）.

それぞれ each, respectively（➤ 後者は通例文尾で用いる）▶**人はそれぞれ自分の人生観をもっている** *Each* person has their own view [philosophy] of life.（● 男女両方を含む場合，his or her が正確だが，この形をぎこちないと考えて，their を用いることが多い）‖ **彼らはそれぞれ自分の信念に従って生きている** *Each* of them lives their own life according to their beliefs. ／They *each* live their own life according to their beliefs.
▶**3人の姉たちはそれぞれ大学教授，ダンサー，看護師になった** My three sisters became a college professor, a dancer and a nurse *respectively*. ‖ **教え子たちはそれぞれの分野で頑張っている** My former pupils are doing their best in their *respective* fields.

それだから ▶**それだからあの先生が好きじゃないんだ** *That's why* I don't like that teacher.

それだけ 1【その程度】▶**それだけあれば2日分は十分だ** *That much* will be enough for two days. ‖ **それだけ言えばもういいだろう** I think you've said enough. ‖ **それだけなの，あなたが考えつくことって？** Is that *all* you can think of? ‖ **それだけの（＝そんなささいな）ことで彼がなぜあんなに興奮したのかわからない** I don't know why he got so excited *over such a trivial matter*. ‖ **私たちは別れたの．ただそれだけのこと** We broke up. *That's all there is to it*.
2【その物・事だけ】▶**ナマコ？ それだけはどうしても食べられません** Sea cucumber? I will eat *anything but that*.（➤「それ以外なら何でも食べる」の意）‖ 対話「このことはご両親に知らせるからな」「それだけは勘弁してください（＝そんなことをしないでください）」"I'll tell your parents about this." "Oh, please don't (do *that*)." ‖ 対話（店で）「ほかに何か？」「いや，それだけでいいです」"Will that be all, sir?" "Yes, *that will be all*."（● That's it. とか That's all. とだけ答えてもよい）.
3【その分】▶**良友と交わればそれだけ良い影響を受けるものだ** If you keep good company, you will have *that much more* good influence. ‖ **アイルランド留学には大金を使ったが，それだけのこと（＝値打ち）はあった** I spent a lot of money to study in Ireland but it *was* (*well*) *worth it*.

それっきり →それきり.

それっぽち ▶**それっぽちの金であたふたするな** Don't make a fuss over *a paltry sum of money like that*.

それで ▶**バスが来なかった．それで歩いてきた** The bus didn't come, *so* I walked all the way. ‖ **それで（＝そして）きみは何と答えたのかね？** What was your answer, *then*? ／*And* how did you answer, *then*? ‖（話を促して）**それで？** *Well*?

それでいて and yet ▶**あの野球選手は太っているが，それでいて足はとても速い** That baseball player is fat, *and yet* he can run very fast.

それでこそ ▶**よくやった．それでこそお父さんの子だ** Well done! *That's my boy* [*girl*]! ‖ **それでこそ友だちというものだ** *That's what* friends *are for*.

それでなくても ▶**きょうの出費は痛い．それでなくても今月は赤字なのに** Today's expenditure is quite a blow. *Even without it*, we are already in the red this month.

それでは ▶**それでは（＝そうすると）あなたは彼に会わなかったんですね** *So* you didn't see him, did you? ‖ **それでは次に，本日の講師をご紹介いたします** *Next* [*Now*], I'd like to introduce our lecturer for today. ‖ 対話「来年アメリカへ行きます」「それでは（＝それならば）もっと英語を勉強しなさい」"I'm going to the States next year." "*If so*, you should study English harder." ▶**それでは（＝じゃあ），さようなら** *Well*, I must say good-bye. ‖ **それでは，またあとで** See you later, *then*.

それでも but（しかし）; still（それでもなお）; even so（たとえそうでも）; all [just] the same（ともかく）; yet, and yet（それにもかかわらず；ともに堅い言い方だが，後者は前者より強意）; nevertheless（それにもかかわらず；堅い語で，前述したことに対する強い対照を表す）
▶**その企画は平凡だ．それでも出さないよりましだ** The plan is nothing new, *but* it's better than nothing. ‖ **それでも私はイタリアへ行きたい** *Still* [*Even so*] I would like to go to Italy. ‖「**それでも地球は動く**」とガリレオは言った "*Yet* the earth does move," said Galileo. ‖ **彼は3度失敗したが，それでもまだ諦めていない** He has failed three times, *yet* he hasn't given up.
▶**彼は疲れていて空腹だった．それでも歩き続けた** He was tired and hungry. *Nevertheless*, he kept on walking. ‖ **夏の北アルプスは人がいっぱいだ．それでもみんな行きたがる** In summer the Northern Japan Alps are crowded (with climbers and vacationers). *Even so* everybody wants to go there. ‖ **最新アルバムは大失敗作だった．それでも，私は彼らはすばらしいバンドだと思う** Their last album was a flop. *All the same*, I still think they're a great band.

それというのも ▶**きょう試験に遅刻してしまった．それというのもすべて目覚まし時計が鳴らなかったせいだ** I was late for the examination today. *It was* all *because* the alarm clock didn't go off.

それどころ ▶ 対話「そろそろ髪の毛，切ったら？」「忙しくてそれどころじゃないよ」"It's about time you got a haircut." "I*'ve got no time for that* now. ／I'm *too* busy *to think about it* right now."

それどころか on the contrary（反対に）; actually（事実は，実際は）; in fact（実を言うと，もっとはっきり言えば）▶**うちにはコンピュータはありません．それどころかテレビもないんです** We don't have a computer at home. *In fact*, we don't even have a TV set. ‖ 対話「あなたは会社に満足していますか」「いいえ，それどころかいつでも辞めたいくらいです」"Are you satisfied with your company?" "No, *actually* [*on the contrary*], I always want to quit."

それとなく ▶**それとなく彼女の意向を探ってほしい** I'd like you to sound out her real thoughts *in a roundabout way*.（➤「遠回しに」の意）‖ **彼にはそれとなく伝えておくよ** I'll *put a bug in his ear*.（➤「それとなく伝える」の意のインフォーマルな言い方）.

それとも or ▶**あなたはそれに賛成ですか，それとも反対ですか** Are you for *or* against it? ‖ **ロールパンにしますか．**

それともライスにしますか Would you like a roll *or* rice? (➤ 尻下がりに言う；一気に尻上がりに言うと「ロールパンかライスはいかがですか」と勧める言い方になる).

それなのに but ▶息子がしっかり勉強していると思って，私たちはお金を送り続けた．それなのに息子ときたら，毎日遊びほうけていたのだ We kept sending money to our son, believing that he was studying hard. *But* actually (it turned out that) he was goofing off every day. ‖ みんな最善を尽くした．それなのに(＝それでも) わがチームは負けてしまった Everybody did his best, *but even so* our team lost the game.

それなら ▶それなら問題はない *In that case* [*If so,*] there's no problem. ‖ それならそうと言ってくれればよかったのに *If that was the case*, you should have told me so. ／*If that's how it was*, why didn't you tell me so?

それなり ▶その映画はそれなりにおもしろい The film is interesting *in its own way*. ‖ 彼はそれなりによくやった He did *what he could*. ‖ わが課では各人がそれなりに評価されている In my department, each person is evaluated *according to his or her own true worth*. ‖ 彼の主張はそれなりに筋が通っている What he says is reasonable [makes sense] *up to a point*. (➤「ある程度までは」の意).

それに and；besides, moreover (その上；besides は好ましくない事柄を列挙する場合に用いるのがふつう) ▶ニンジンとトマト，それにリンゴをください Give me some carrots, tomatoes *and* apples, please. ‖ 風が強かったし，それに雨も降っていた It was windy, and *besides* (that) it was raining hard.
▶このセーターは色がとても気に入った．それに値段も手ごろだった I liked the color of this sweater. *What's more* [*Moreover*], the price was reasonable. ‖ 彼っていい人よ．それにお金持ちだし He's a really nice guy, *plus* he's rich. (➤ この plus はインフォーマルな用法).

それにしては ▶彼女は自分ではただのかぜだって言ってるけど，それにしては様子が変だ She says that she has a common cold and nothing else, but *even so*, she really looks sick.

それにしても even so；still (それでもなお)；at any rate (とにかく) ▶彼女，遅くなるとは言ってたけど，それにしても遅いなあ She said she would be late. *But even so*, this is too late. ‖ 彼女は運がよかっただけと言うが，それにしてもよくやったと思う She says she was just lucky, but I *still* think she did very well. ‖ それにしても所得税は高いねえ *At any rate*, income taxes are (too) high.

それにつけても ▶それにつけても残念なのは3回裏の暴投だ It is *still* regrettable that he threw a wild pitch in the bottom of the third inning.

それにひきかえ それに引き換え ▶杉本君はよく勉強して偉いわねえ．それにひきかえ，誰かさんはねえ… Sugimoto is a good hardworking student. *On the other hand*, what's-his-name [you know who]... (➤ what's-his-name は日本語の「誰かさん」「何とかさん」に相当する．女性の場合なら what's-her-name となる；you know who は「誰かさん」が聞き手を指す場合).

そればかりか ▶彼女は勉強家だ．そればかりかクラスの人気者だ She is a (real) hard worker, *and what's more* she is popular in her class. ‖ 早寝早起きは健康にいい．そればかりか，美容にもいい Going to bed and getting up early is good for your health, *and what's more*, it's good for your beauty.

それはさておき ▶それはさておき，2人の関係はどうなったの But, *leaving that aside*, what's going on between those two?

それはそうと ▶それはそうと(＝ところで)，けさのテレビニュースを見たかい？ *By the way*, did you watch the TV news this morning?

それはそれとして ▶それはそれとして，試験の結果はどうなんだ *Apart from that*, how did you do in the examination?

それはそれは ▶ 対話「息子が大学に合格しましてね」「それはそれはおめでとうございます」"My son has passed his university exam(s)." "*Congratulations.*" ‖ 対話「娘が家出をしましてね」「それはそれは…」"My daughter has run away from home." "*My goodness.* ／*Dear me.* ／*Well, well.*" (➤ いずれもやや古風).

それほど so, that much (➤ 後者はインフォーマル) ▶俺，それほど酔っちゃいないよ I'm not *as* drunk *as you think*. ‖ それほど彼女が好きなら，好きとはっきり言えばいい If you love her *that much*, you should say so clearly. (➤ この that は「そんなに」の意の副詞．次例も同じ) ‖ うちはそれほど金持ちじゃないのよ We are not *all that* well off. ‖ 対話「おなかすきましたか」「それほどでもありません」"Are you hungry?" "*Not very.*"

それまで 1【そのときまで】(up) until [till] then ▶それまで私は本を読んでいた *Up until* [*till*] *then* I had been reading a book. ‖ 講義は10時に始まりますから，それまでに教室へ来てください The lecture will start at ten. Please be in the classroom *by that time*. (➤ by は「…までに」という期限を表す) ‖ その魚はそれまで釣ったうちでいちばん大きかった The fish was the biggest I'd *ever* caught.
2【そこまで】▶それまでやることはないさ You don't have to do *that much*. ‖ それまでにしなさい(＝もう十分だ) *That's enough*.
3【それでおしまい】▶海外旅行もいいけれど，飛行機は落っこちたらそれまでだよ Going abroad is great, but if the plane crashes, *that's the end of it*. ‖ もう一度頼んでだめなら，それまでだ Let's ask once more, and if they refuse, then *let's give up* [*forget it*]. (➤「諦めよう[忘れよう]」の意).

それみたことか それ見たことか ▶それ見たことか．やっぱり失敗しただろう *I told you that would happen!* [*So there!* ／*Didn't I warn you?*] You screwed up (again). (➤ told は強く発音する) ‖ それ見たことか．準備しないで試験に受かろうったって無理だよ *I told you* it would be impossible to pass the exam without preparing.

それもそのはず ▶やつは俺の顔を見るなり逃げ出したが，それもそのはずだ．こないだ痛い目に遭わせてやったからな As soon as he saw me, he started to run away. *It was only natural* considering the (painful) lesson I taught him the other day.

それゆえ それ故 therefore, accordingly (➤ 後者は前者よりさらに堅い語)；thus (かくのごとく；堅い語).

それる 逸れる swerve(急に方向を変える)；miss(当たり損なう) ▶車は脇道へそれると急に速度を上げた The car *swerved* into a side road, and suddenly sped [speeded] up. ‖ 台風は東シナ海にそれた The typhoon *has swerved* [*veered*] to the East China Sea. ‖ (くぎを打っていて)手がそれて自分の指をたたいてしまった My hand *slipped* and I hit my finger instead of the nail. ‖ 不運にも矢は的からそれてしまった Unfortunately, the shot *missed the mark*.
▶話が脇道にそれてしまった We *have wandered from*

the main subject. ／We *have gotten off track*. ‖ **話はそれるけど**, 中学のときの先生今どうしているかなあ？ *By the way*, I wonder what our junior high teacher is doing now.

ソれん ソ連 **the Soviet Union.**

ソロ a **solo** /sóʊloʊ/ ▶ソロで歌う sing *a solo* ／sing solo (➤ 後者の solo は「ソロで」の意の副詞) ‖ ソロでピアノを弾く play a piano *solo*.

そろい 揃い a **set** ▶両親は娘が結婚する前に**家具一そろい**を買ってやった The parents bought their daughter *a set of furniture* before she got married.
☛ **お揃い** (→見出語)

-ぞろい -揃い ▶ブラームスの室内楽は傑作ぞろいだ *Most* of Brahms's chamber music works are masterpieces. ‖ いいなあ, きみは！美人ぞろいのクラスで How I envy you ! Your class is *full of* pretty girls. (●「イケメンぞろい」なら full of good-looking boys) ‖ この町の住民は金持ちぞろいだ *All* the residents of this town are wealthy.

そろう 揃う **1**【状態や行動が同じである】▶このリンゴは**粒はそろっていない**が味はよい These apples *are* (*all*) *different in size*, but they taste good. ‖ このひも, 長さがそろっていないよ These pieces of string *are not equal* in length. ‖ あの家の娘たちはそろって背が高い *All* the girls in that family are tall. ‖ 反対運動の**足並みがそろわない** We *can't get* the opposition movement *working smoothly* [*in unity*]. (➤ 運動参加者の発言) ／*There is a lack of unity* [*concerted effort*] in the opposition movement.
▶《慣用表現》うちの子は**そろいもそろって**足が遅い *Each* (*and every*) *one* of our children is a slow runner. ／*Without exception*, our kids are slow in running. ‖ おまえら, そろいもそろって腰抜けだな！ What *a bunch of* wimps !
2【全部集まる】▶全員そろったらすぐ練習を始めよう Let's start practice as soon as everyone *is here* [*has assembled*]. ‖ みんなそろったかな？ *Is* everybody *here* ? ‖ 夕食に家族全員がそろうのは日曜日くらいだ Sunday is the only day when all our family members *get together* [*gather together*] at the dinner table.
▶正月休みには**家族そろって**温泉に行った During the New Year's holidays, *my family and I* went to a hot spring *all together*. (● この場合の family は自分を除く家族の構成員) ‖ 私たちの学校にはいい先生がそろっている Our school *has a staff of* good teachers. ／Our college has a good faculty. (➤ 後者は主に大学の教員をいう場合).
▶もう１冊で『漱石全集』が全巻そろう One more volume and I will have a *complete* set of the works of Natsume Soseki. ‖ 客の数だけ皿がそろっていない We *don't have enough* dinner plates for all the guests. ‖ あの店にはマイルス・デービスの CD がかなりそろっている That store *has a large selection of* Miles Davis CDs.

そろえる 揃える **1**【きちんと並べる】**arrange** ▶カードを番号順にそろえる *arrange* the cards in numerical order ‖ 靴を脱いだらきちんとそろえておきなさい *Place* your shoes neatly *side by side* when you take them off.
2【１か所にまとめる】▶あすの遠足に持っていくもの, きちんとそろえたの？ Do you *have* everything (*ready*) for tomorrow's picnic ? ／Have you *gotten* everything you need for tomorrow's picnic ? ‖ 私は手塚治虫の『火の鳥』を全巻そろえたい I want to *get a complete set of* Tezuka Osamu's "Firebird."
▶あの店は質の良い品をそろえている That store *carries* quality goods [products]. (➤ carry は「(商品を)並べている」) ‖ このＴシャツは白, ピンク, ベージュ, それに薄いブルーをそろえています The T-shirts *come in* a range of colors : white, pink, beige and pale blue. (➤ come in は「…で手に入る」の意).
3【同じにする】▶ポスターを全部**同じ大きさに**そろえる *make* all the posters *the same size*(➤ 高さをそろえるときは size の代わりに height, 長さのときは length を使う) ‖ 前髪を切って**長さをそろえて**ください Could you trim [even out] my bangs so that they are *even* ? ‖ 子供たちは**声をそろえて**賛美歌を歌った The children sang hymns *in unison*. ‖ 彼らは**口をそろえて**悪いのはぼくだと言った They *unanimously* put the blame on me.

そろそろ **1**【ゆっくりと】**slowly** ▶水のいっぱい入ったバケツを手に持って彼女はそろそろと歩いた She walked *slowly*, carrying a bucket full of [filled with] water.
2【もうじき】**nearly, about** (➤ 後者は形容詞・名詞を修飾する場合はインフォーマル) ▶母はそろそろ50だ My mother is *nearly* 50. ‖ 横浜に来てそろそろ10年になる It has been *nearly* ten years since I came to Yokohama. (➤《英》では has been ではなく, It is ～ since ... と表現する) ‖ そろそろお昼だ It's *about* noon.
▶そろそろコートの(欲しい)季節です The overcoat season is *about here*. ‖ そろそろ桜の季節だ The cherry blossom season *is almost here* [*is just around the corner*]. ‖ そろそろおいとまします Well, *it's about time to* head on home. ‖ もうそろそろ彼が来てもいい頃だ *He should be here anytime* now. ‖ そろそろ行こうか *Shall we get going ?* ‖ 彼女もそろそろ(結婚してもいい)年頃だ She's (more than) *old enough to* get married.

> **あなたの英語はどう響く？**
> 「(そろそろ)帰ります」のつもりで, I'm going home. と言いがちだが, 進行形はすでに行動を起こしていることを表すので, 腹を立てて, 「私は帰る！」と言っているように響く. 「そろそろ帰ります」は行動に移る寸前であるから, 未来進行形を使って, (Well, I think) I'd better be going home. または, I think I'll be going home (now). とする. 同様に, 「(私たちの飛行機は)そろそろ成田に着く」は We'll be arriving at Narita before long. とする. また, 電話で長話をしたあとで, 「そろそろ切るね」のつもりで, 「切る」＝hang up を使って, I'm hanging up. とすると立腹して「切るよ！」と言っているように響く. 決まった表現はないが, I'd better be going. (終わりにするね) とか It was nice talking to you. (話ができてよかった) などとするとよい.

ぞろぞろ ▶私たちはみんなでぞろぞろと彼のあとについていった We all *filed along* behind him. ‖ 穴からアリがぞろぞろ出て来た (A procession of) ants came *pouring* out of the hole. (➤ pour は「多くのものがどっと出る」の意).

そろばん 算盤 an **abacus** /ǽbəkəs/ ▶そろばんを習う learn how to use *an abacus*.
▶《慣用表現》こんな値で売ったのではそろばんが合わない Selling at such a price *won't pay*.

ぞろめ ぞろ目 ▶ (さいころで) ぞろ目を出す throw a

double.

そわそわ ▶そわそわするんじゃありません Don't *fidget*! ／Don't *get fidgety*! ‖ 何をそんなにそわそわしてるの? Why *are* you so *fidgety* [*restless*]?

そん 損 1【利益を失うこと】(a) **loss** 一動 **損をする lose money** ▶株価が下がって50万円の損をした I *lost* [*suffered a loss of*] 500,000 yen when the stock prices fell. ‖ 安物を買うと結局は損をする If you buy cheap things, you end up *wasting money* [you *waste money* in the end]. ‖ 近頃は正直者が損をする(＝割が合わない) These days honesty *does not pay*.

▶これは損な仕事だ This job *doesn't pay*. ‖ あの男は決して自分の損になることはしない He never does *anything that isn't profitable* to him. ‖ せっかく猛勉強したのにテストをやらないなんて, 損しちゃったよ Though I had studied very hard, the teacher didn't give us a test. *All my efforts were wasted*. ‖ ことわざ 損して得取れ To catch a trout you have to lose a fly. ／Sow a loss, reap a gain.

2【不利】a **disadvantage** ▶国際社会では内気なのは損だ Being shy is *a disadvantage* in international society. ‖ 英語を習っておいて損はないよ You *have nothing to lose* (*and much to gain*) by learning English. ‖ 自分の意見をはっきり言わないと損をするよ If you don't express your opinion clearly, you'll *put yourself at a disadvantage*. ‖ 彼女は口が悪いのでだいぶ損をしている(＝人によく思われていない) Her sharp tongue *is a* real *disadvantage* to her.

☛ 大損 (→見出語)

そんえき 損益 a **profit and a loss** ▶損益勘定[計算書] a *profit and loss* account [statement].

そんがい 損害 **damage**(被害, 損害額); a **loss**(損失) ▶この災害による損害は10億円と推定される The *damage* caused by this disaster is estimated at one billion yen. ‖ 父の会社の損害は9千万円に上った The *loss* my father's company suffered amounted to ninety million yen. ‖ 火山の噴火はその村に大きな損害を与えた The volcanic eruption *did* [*caused*] *great damage* to the village. ／The village suffered great damage from the volcanic eruption. ‖ 被害者はK化学に総額5億円の損害賠償を請求した The victims *claimed damages* of five hundred million yen in total from K Chemicals. (●「損害賠償金」の意味では常に複数形).

そんぎかい 村議会 a **village council**.

そんけい 尊敬 **respect** /rɪspékt/ 一動 **尊敬する respect** +目, **look up to**(➤ 後者はインフォーマル) ▶尊敬すべき人 a person *worthy of respect* ／a person *we should respect* (● respectable は「(社会的に)まともな, きちんとした仕事をしている」の意なので使えない) ‖ 私たちは彼をリーダーとして尊敬している We *respect* him as our leader.

▶ホイットマンは偉大な詩人として尊敬されている Whitman *is looked up to* [*is highly thought of*] as a great poet. ‖ あの作曲家はベートーベンを非常に尊敬している That composer *has a high regard for* [*has a great respect for*] Beethoven. ‖ 尊敬する林先生があんな事件を起こしてショックです I'm shocked that Mr. Hayashi, whom I *highly* [*much*] *respect* as a teacher, could have caused such a scandal.

そんげん 尊厳 **dignity** ▶生命の尊厳を守る protect the *dignity* of life ‖ この不祥事はその裁判官の尊厳を著しく傷つけた This scandal markedly bruised the *dignity* of the judge.

‖**尊厳死** death with dignity (➤「尊厳死する」は die with [in] dignity).

そんざい 存在 1【いること, あること】**existence** 一動 **存在する exist** ▶宇宙人の存在を否定することはできない We cannot deny [rule out] the *existence* of extraterrestrials. ‖ 世界には飢えに苦しむ人々が多数存在していることを忘れてはならない We must not forget the fact that *there are* many people in the world who suffer from starvation.

▶幽霊なんて存在しないと思う I *don't believe in* ghosts. (➤ believe in は「…の実在を信じる」) ／I *don't think* ghosts *are real*. ‖ 一部のイギリス人は王室の存在意義を疑問に感じている Some British people question the *relevance* of the Royal Family. ‖ あの役者はちょい役でも存在感がある That actor sure has *presence*, even when he is playing only a small part.

▶この種の教養番組はすでに存在理由を失った Educational programs of this kind have already lost their *reason for being* [*raison d'être*]. (➤ 後者はフランス語をそのまま借用. 発音は /rèɪzoon détrə/).

2【人物】a **figure** ▶彼はこの会社では異色の存在だ He is *a unique figure* in this company. ‖ 彼女はクラスでは目立たない存在だった She *didn't stand out* in class at all.

ぞんざいな **rough**(荒っぽい); **coarse**(粗野な); **perfunctory**(おざなりの); **sloppy**(ずさんな); **careless**(不注意な) ▶ぞんざいな挨拶 a *perfunctory* greeting ‖ ぞんざいな仕事をする人 a *sloppy* [*careless*] worker ‖ あの人たちはことばづかいがぞんざいだ They speak *roughly*. ／They use *coarse* language. ‖ 彼は接客態度がぞんざいだ His manner toward customers is *rough*.

そんしつ 損失 a **loss** ▶彼の死はわが社にとって大きな損失である His death is *a* great *loss* to our company. ‖ 銀行の損失は10億円に上った The bank recorded *a loss* of one billion yen.

[1]**そんしょう 損傷** **damage**(物質的な); (an) **injury**(肉体的・精神的な傷) ▶自動車事故で脳に損傷を受ける suffer brain *damage* in a car accident.

[2]**そんしょう 尊称** an **honorific title**.

そんしょく 遜色 ▶彼女はパリの一流デザイナーに比べても少しも遜色がない She *can stand comparison* [*can hold her own*] with any top fashion designer in Paris.

そんじょそこら ▶この花瓶はそんじょそこらにあるような代物じゃない This is not *your average* vase. ‖ そんじょそこらの絵じゃないよ. 本物のマチスだよ It's not *just any painting*. It's a genuine Matisse.

ぞんじる 存じる ▶お2人はおたがいをご存じ? Do you two *know* each other? ‖ 小平先生ならよく存じ上げております I *know* Professor Kodaira *well*.

✉ **来月初めにお伺いいたしたいと存じます** I *am thinking of* visiting you early next month. ／I *would like to* visit you early next month. (➤ 前者は考えてはいるがまだ決心しておらず, 相手の都合を言外に尋ねている. 後者は話し手の意思を伝えている. なお「存じる」＝think と考えて, I think I would like to ... とするのは重複表現になる).

[1]**そんぞく** (a) **continuance** 一動 **存続する continue to exist**; **survive**(生き残る) ▶部員が減り, 野球部の存続が危うくなってきた The number of students in the baseball club has fallen, so it is uncertain whether we'll be able to *continue* the club [whether the club can *continue*].

[2]**そんぞく 尊属** an **ancestor** ‖ **直系**［**傍系**］**尊属** a lineal [collateral] ancestor.

そんだい 尊大な **arrogant**（自信過剰で高慢な）; **haughty**（優越意識が強い）▶**尊大な**態度 an *arrogant* manner ‖ **尊大な**男 an *arrogant* [a *haughty*] man.

そんたく 忖度する ▶彼は上司に**忖度している** He *is guessing* his boss's *feelings*.

[1]**そんちょう 村長** **the head of a village**, a **village mayor** ▶上野村の**村長**さん the *mayor* of Ueno Village.

[2]**そんちょう 尊重** **respect** /rɪspékt/ **一動 尊重する** **respect** ＋㊐ ▶民主主義の根本原則は個人の権利の**尊重**である The basic principle of democracy is to *respect* the rights of the individual. ‖ 両親は私の気持ちを**尊重してくれない** My parents *have* no *respect* [*regard*] *for* my feelings.（➤ have respect [regard] for は「…に敬意を払う」）‖ 高校ではもっと個性を**尊重した**教育をすべきだ High school education should *place more value on* individuality. ‖ 少数派の意見も**尊重されるべきである** The minority opinions should *be valued*, too.（➤ value は「重んじる」）.

そんとく 損得 **loss and gain**

> **《解説》** この語は loss and gain とか profit and loss のように訳せるが, 利益の内容によっては gain（有形・無形の利益）, profit（主に物質的または金銭上の利益）を, また利害関係を問題にしている場合は interest を用いて表すこともできる.

▶真の教育者はたいてい**自分の損得**には無関心だ True educators are usually indifferent to *personal gain*. ‖ **損得**は問題じゃない It doesn't matter *whether I gain or lose*. ‖ 彼のすることは全部**損得ずく**だ He does everything *for profit* [*money*]. ‖ 彼はすぐ**損得**を考える He is quick to think of his own *interests*.

そんな

such（既述した人・物などを指して）; **like that**, **that**（目の前の人・物などを指して）▶**そんな**人は知りません I don't know *such* a person. ‖ **そんな**（口先だけの）話は危ないよ *Such* talk is dangerous. ‖ ぼくは**そんな**うわさ話には興味がない I'm not interested in gossip *like that* [*like this*]. ／I'm not interested in *such* gossip. ‖ 男なんてみんな**そんなもの**よ Men are all *like that*. ‖ よく**そんなこと**が言えるわね How could you say *something like that*? ‖ **そんなことだろう**と思った I thought *as much*. ／I thought *so*.

▶**そんな**仕事, 私なら１日でできるよ One day would be enough for me to do *that* job. ‖ **そんな**ティムは嫌い I don't like Tim when he acts *like that*. ‖ **そんなわけで**ぼくはきみのことを怒っているんだ *That's why* I am angry with you.

> **直訳の落とし穴「そんな彼の性格」**
> 「そんな」＝such,「彼の性格」＝his character なので,「そんな彼の性格が好きだ」を（×）I like such his character. または,（×）I like his such character. などとするミスが多い. such のあとや前に所有格を置くことはできない. また,（×）I like such character of his. もおかしい. 日本語にぴったりの簡便な言い方はないが,「そのような彼の性格の一面」と考えて, I like that aspect of his character. とすることはできる. しかし, 英語ではむしろ具体的に「親切なところ」なら, I like his kindness.,「ユーモアのセンス」なら I like him for his sense of humor. などとするのが自然である.

▶ **対話**「そう, あなたって**そんな**人なの」「そうさ, ぼくは**そんな**男さ！」"So, *that's what kind of* person you are!" "Yes, *that's what* I am!" ‖ **対話**「新しい英語の先生, 27,8歳かなあ」「うん, まあ**そんなところだろうね**」"How old do you think our new English teacher is, 27 or so?" "Yeah, *that's probably about right*." ‖ **対話**「先生がこれから小テストをするって」「**そんなのないよ**」"He [She] says there's going to be a quiz." "*No way!* ／ *You're kidding!*"（➤ no way は no の強調形, you're kidding は「冗談だろ」の意）.

そんなに **so**,《インフォーマル》**that** ▶**そんなに**速く歩くなよ Don't walk *so* fast. ‖ **そんなに**怒らなくたっていいでしょう You don't have to get *so* angry! ‖ **そんなに**（＝きみが考えるほど）簡単じゃないんだよ It's not *as* [*so*] simple *as you think*. ／It's not *that* simple. ‖ 金もうけは**そんなに**楽じゃない Making money is not *all that* easy.（➤ この all は強調）‖ **対話**「駅まで２キロあるんだ」「**そんなに**遠いの？」"It's two kilometers from here to the station." "It's *that* far?"（➤ 上昇調で言う. この場合, Is it (really) that far? と疑問文にすると, 相手の言っていることに疑問を投げかけているように響く可能性がある）.

そんのう 尊皇・尊王 **the reverence for the Emperor**; **royalism**（主義）
‖ **尊皇攘夷**（じょうい）reverence for the Emperor and the expulsion of barbarians [foreigners] ‖ **尊皇派** the royalist party, the royalists.

そんぱい 存廃 **continuation** [**maintenance**] **or abolition**
‖ **死刑存廃論** a debate about whether to keep or abolish the death penalty.

ぞんぶん 存分に **to the full**; **to** one's **heart's content**（心ゆくまで）▶悲しかったら**存分に**泣きなさい If you are sad, have a *good* cry. ‖ 彼女は仕事を任されて**存分に腕を振るう**ことができた She was able to *give full scope to her ability* because the job was left entirely up to her.
▶私たちはハウステンボスで**思う存分**楽しんだ We enjoyed ourselves *to our hearts' content* [*to the full*] at Huis Ten Bosch. ‖ **思う存分**食べなさい Help yourself to *as much as you like*.

そんぼう 存亡 ▶これは社の**存亡**をかけた大プロジェクトだ This is a project so important that our company's *continued existence depends on* it [its success].

そんみん 村民 a **villager**, a **village's resident** [**inhabitant**].

ぞんめい 存命 ▶**存命**中に while someone *is alive* ‖ **存命中の**人物 a *living* [*real*] person.

そんらく 村落 a **village**; a **hamlet**（小さな）
‖ **村落共同体** a village community.

そんりつ 存立 **existence** ▶私立学校の**存立**を危うくする threaten the *continued existence* of private schools ‖ **存立**が見込める新しい公共企業体 a *viable* public corporation.

た・タ

1た 田 a **rice field**; a **(rice) paddy**, a **paddy field**(➤ ともに「水田」) ▶田に水を引く irrigate *a rice paddy* ‖農夫が田を耕している A farmer is plowing the *rice field*.

2た 他 **the rest**(残り); **the other**(2つのうちの「もう一方」; 一方が one, もう一方が the other); **the others**(2つ以上ある場合) **一形** **他の other**(➤ 複数名詞を修飾する); **another**(もう1つの; 単数名詞を修飾する) →その他, ほか ▶彼の発想のユニークさは他に例を見ない The uniqueness of his ideas *is unparalleled*.

たあいない 他愛無い →たわいない.

ダークホース a **dark horse**.

ターゲット a **target**(標的, 対象) ▶30代の女性をターゲットにした雑誌がよく売れている Magazines *targeting* women in their thirties are selling well. ‖ターゲットを絞ってそれに向かって頑張れ Zero in on the *target* and go for it. (➤ zero in on ... は「…に焦点を合わせる」).

ダージリン **Darjeeling** /dɑːʳdʒíːlɪŋ/ **(tea)**.

ダース a **dozen** /dʌ́zən/ ▶鉛筆をダースで売る sell pencils *by the dozen* ‖ 1ダース1000円 1,000 yen *a dozen* ‖鉛筆2ダース *two dozen* pencils (● dozen が形容詞的に用いられるときは複数形にしない) ‖ビール3ダース *three dozen* bottles of beer.

タータンチェック **tartan, plaid** /plæd/ ▶タータンチェックのミニスカート a *tartan* [*plaid*] miniskirt.

ダーツ **darts** ▶ダーツをする play *darts*.

タートルネック ▶タートルネックのセーター a *turtleneck* [《英また》 *polo-neck*] sweater.

ターバン a **turban** /tə́ːʳbən/.

ダービー **the Derby** ▶ダービーで大穴を当てる win big at *the Derby*.
‖**日本ダービー** the Japan Derby.

タービン a **turbine**.

ターミナル a **terminal**, a **terminus**
‖**エアターミナル** an air terminal.

> **危ないカタカナ語✹ ターミナル**
> **1** 日本語では「ターミナルビル」「ターミナルデパート」「ターミナルホテル」のように形容詞的に使うことが多いが, これらはいずれも和製語で, 英語の terminal の用法とは異なる. terminal は「始発[終着]駅(の建物)」を指し, bus terminal, air terminal のように用いる. ただし, terminal building を空港のターミナルビル (air terminal) の意で用いることはある.
> **2** 鉄道駅の「ターミナルビル」は building built above a railroad terminal,「ターミナルデパート」は department store at a railroad terminal,「ターミナルホテル」は hotel at a railroad terminal [railroad station] のように説明的にいう必要がある.

ターメリック **turmeric** /tə́ːʳmərɪk/.

タール **tar** ▶高[低]タールのたばこ a high [low] *tar* cigarette.

ターン a **turn** **一動** **ターンする turn, make a turn**.

1たい 鯛 a **sea bream** 《参考》(1) 日本語では「タイ」といえば「マダイ」を指すことが多いが, それを英語でいえば red sea bream となる. (2) sea bream 以外に porgy /pɔ́ːʳgi/, snapper などの名称で呼ぶ所もある.
日本紹介 ✉ **タイは形が美しく, 美味なことから魚の王様として珍重されています. また, タイという音が日本語で「めでたい」ということばに通じることから縁起物とされ, 結婚式などの祝い事に欠かせない魚となっています** *Tai* (sea bream) is prized as 'the king of fish' for its beautiful shape and tastiness. Because Japanese people associate '*tai*' with the Japanese word '*medetai* (auspicious),' *tai* is considered an auspicious fish. It is an indispensable fish for weddings and other celebratory occasions.
ことわざ **腐っても鯛** Even if it is off, sea bream is (still) sea bream. (➤ 日本語からの直訳. off は「傷んだ」の意) ／An old eagle is better than a young sparrow.

2たい 隊 a **team**, a **party**; a **corps** /kɔːʳ/ (軍団) ▶兵士たちは隊を組んで行進した The soldiers marched *in formation*. ‖**救助隊** a rescue team [party] ‖**捜索隊** a search team [party] ‖**登山隊** a climbing party.

3たい 対 ▶日本の対米政策 Japan's policy *toward(s)* the United States ‖**対空ミサイル** an *anti*aircraft missile ‖**法政対早稲田の試合** a game *between* Hosei *and* Waseda ／a Hosei *vs.* Waseda game(➤ vs. は versus /və́ːʳsəs/ の略).
▶3対1の比率 a ratio of three *to* one ‖我々は7対3で勝った We won 7 *to* 3. ‖《スポーツで》今, 何対何? *What's the score* now?
‖**対ゲリラ戦** counterinsurgency ‖**対敵情報活動** counterintelligence ‖**対テロ活動** counterterrorism.
☛ **対日** (→見出語)

4たい 他意 ▶ありのままを言っただけで, 別に他意はありません I meant just what I said and *nothing more*. ／I simply told the truth *with no ulterior motive*. (➤ ulterior motive は「隠れた動機, 下心」).

1タイ **1 【ネクタイ】** a **tie**, a **necktie** (➤ 前者のほうがふつう) →ネクタイ.
2 【同点】 a **tie** ▶3対3のタイで終わる end in a 3-3 *tie*(➤ 3-3 は three to three と読む) ‖棒高跳びで世界タイ記録を出す *tie the world record* in the pole vault ‖ 9回裏に得点は7対7のタイになった The score *was tied* at 7 to 7 in the bottom of the ninth inning.

2タイ **Thailand** /táɪlænd/ (➤ (×) Thai としない) **一形** **タイの Thai** ‖**タイ語** Thai ‖**タイ人** a Thai (person) (➤ 複数形は Thais または Thai people).

-たい **1 【自分が…したい】 want** 《**to** do》

> 【文型】
> **私は…したい**
> **I want to** do
> **I would [I'd] like to** do
> **I hope to** do
> ➤ (1) 積極的で強い願望を表す場合は I want to

do を, 少し控えめに「…したいものです」という場合には I would like to do を,「…できたらいいな」という希望を込めた願望を表す場合には I hope to do を用いる. (2) I would like to do は話しことばでは I'd like to do となることが多い.

▶私はカナダに留学したい(と思う) *I want to* study in Canada. ‖ きょうは学校へ行きたくないなあ *I don't want to* go to school today. ‖ みんなにお礼を言いたい *I'd like to* thank everybody [all of you]. ‖ 対話「将来何になりたいですか」「パイロットになりたいと思っています」"What *would you like to* be in the future?" "*I'd like to* be a pilot." ‖ 一刻も早く両親に会いたい *I hope to* see my parents as soon as possible. ‖ お茶をもう1杯頂きたいのですが *Could I have* another cup of tea? (●「…を頂けますか」に当たる Could I have … ? を用いる. →頂く 2) / *I'd like* (*to have*) another cup of tea. (● こちらは「欲しいな」と言っているだけなので, 例えば, 家で妻に言っても, Then serve yourself. (じゃ, ご自分でどうぞ)と言われるのが落ちである) ‖ 社長とお話がしたいのですが *I wish to* speak to the president. (➤ wish to do は want to do の改まった堅い言い方).

▶私のミスで試合に負けたときは泣きたい気持ちだった *I felt like* crying when we lost the game because of my error. (➤ feel like doing は「…したい気分である」の意) ‖ きょうは私がおごるから食べたいだけ食べていいよ I'm treating you today, so please eat (*whatever and*) *as much as you like*.

▶ 対話「今晩うちへ来ませんか」「行きたいけど少し頭痛がするんです」"Would you like to come over to my house tonight?" "*I wish I could*, but I've got a bit of a headache." (➤ I wish I could は「できるならそうしたい(ができない)」の意の仮定法).

2【人に…してもらいたい】**want … to do** →ほしい, もらう

【文型】
人(A)に…してもらいたい
I want A **to** do.
I would [I'd] like A **to** do.
➤ I want A to do. は命令形に近い

▶きみに謝ってもらいたい *I want you to* apologize. ‖ パソコンの調子が悪いので, (あなたに)チェックしてもらいたい Something is wrong with my computer. *I'd like you to* check it. (● 指示や, やや丁寧な口調の命令に響く. ふつうに頼むときは Could you check it (for me)? とする) ‖ 妻の和子をご紹介したいのですが *I'd like you to* meet my wife Kazuko.

▶彼にはこの失敗から学んでもらいたい *I hope* he learns from this mistake. (➤「…だといいな」の意; この場合, (×) I wish は使えない) ‖ 参考文献は巻末に示すので各自参照されたい *You should* refer to the references at [in] the back of the book. (➤「…するのがよい」の意).

[1]**だい 台 1**【物を置く台】a **stand**; a **pedestal** (台座)

▶譜面台 a music *stand* ‖ れんがを並べて植木鉢の台にした We arranged some bricks to make *a stand* for the potted plants. ‖ 証言台に立つ take the *witness stand*.

2【数・時間・金額などの範囲】▶私の貯金は100万円台に達した My savings reached the one million yen *mark*. ‖ 7時台は電車の本数が多い There are many trains *between* seven *and* eight. ‖ 平均点が40点台じゃ進級はおぼつかないね If your average score in the exams is 40-*something* [*somewhere between* 40 *and* 50], there is little hope of your moving up to the next grade. (➤ 40-something は「40何点」の意).

[2]**だい 題 1**【内容を表す名前】a **title** (タイトル); a **subject** (主題); a **theme** /θiːm/ (テーマ); a **topic** (話題)

▶「愛」という題の詩 a poem *entitled* "Love" ‖ 彼は「今日の若者」という題(＝テーマ)で講演した He spoke *on* (*the subject* [*theme*] *of*) "Youth Now." ‖ 何という題の本を読んでるの? What is the *title* of the book you are reading?

2【出題】▶数学のテストで2題(＝2問)解けなかった There were two *questions* on the math test (that) I couldn't answer.

[3]**だい 代 1**【世代】a **generation** ▶何代にもわたって *for generations* ‖ あのお菓子屋さんは代が替わって息子さんが跡を継いでいる That confectionery store *has changed hands*, and is now run by the son. ‖ 彼の家は父親の代には栄えていた His family prospered *in his father's time* [*days*]. ‖ 彼女の父親は一代で財産を築いた Her father built up a fortune *in his lifetime*. ‖ 彼女の母親は何代も続いた旧家の出だ Her mother comes from an old family *with a long history*. (➤「長い歴史をもつ」の意).

2【在職・継承の順序】▶綱吉は徳川幕府の5代目の将軍だ Tsunayoshi was *the fifth* shogun in the Tokugawa shogunate.

▶ 対話「リンカーンは何代目の大統領ですか」「16代目です」"*What number* president was Lincoln? / *Where* does Lincoln *come in the order of* American presidents?" "He was *the 16th* president. / He's *the 16th* (president)."

3【年代・年齢の10年単位】▶1980年代の初め[終わり]に in the early [late] 1980*s* [1980'*s*] (➤どちらも nineteen eighties と読む) ‖ 1970年代には2回の石油危機があった We had two oil crises in the 1970*s* [1970'*s*]. ‖ 彼女は10代[20代]で結婚した She got married in *her teens* [*her twenties*].

4【代金】a **fare** (運賃); a **charge** (かかった料金); a **rate** (一定の率に基づいた料金) ▶スマホ[ケータイ]代 the smartphone [cellphone] *bill* ‖ タクシー代 a taxi *fare* ‖ 電気代 the electric *rate* / the electricity *bill* ‖ 部屋代 rent ‖ ホテル代 hotel *rates* [*charges*] ‖ 私は本代に月に5000円使う I spend 5,000 yen a month *on books*. ‖ 月々の電話代がばかにならない Our phone *bill* comes to a considerable sum each month. (➤ bill は「請求書」) ‖ 対話「お代は?」「いりません」"*How much is it?* / *What's the price?*" "It's free (of charge)."

[4]**だい 大** ▶当店のピザには大中小の3サイズがあります We have three sizes of pizza—*large*, medium, and small.

▶その戦闘で両陣営とも大損害を被った Both sides suffered *heavy losses* in the battle. ‖ わが校は解決しなければならない大問題を抱えている Our school has *a serious* [*big*] *problem* to solve. ‖ すき焼きは私の大好物だ Sukiyaki is *one of* my *favorite foods*. (● 飲食物以外についていう場合は one of one's favorite things とする) / I *love* sukiyaki. ‖ (デジタルカメラの)このご時世にフィルムカメラを買ったのは大失敗だった It was *a real mistake* for me to buy a film camera in this era (of digital cameras).

▶その計画は失敗する可能性が大だ That plan *is very likely to* fail.

▶《慣用表現》誰にだって大なり小なり(＝いくらかは)欠

点があるものだ Everybody has some fault *or another*. ‖ 彼は草の上に大の字になった He *lay spread-eagled* on the grass. (➤「翼を広げたワシのように横たわった」の意) ‖ きのうこの地方で小石大のひょうが降った Yesterday we had hailstones *as big as rocks* [*of rock size*] in this area.

☛ 大の (→見出語)

だい- 第- ▶第 2 (の) *the second* [*2nd*] ‖ 5 月の第 2 日曜日 *the second* Sunday in [of] May ‖ 第 5 番 *No. 5*. (➤ 記号では #5 のように表す).

たいあたり 体当たり ▶私は体当たりしてひったくり男を倒した I knocked the purse snatcher down *by throwing* [*banging*] myself *against* him. / I knocked the purse snatcher down *with a tackle*.

▶《比喩的》体当たりでやる(=捨て身で当たる)しかないよ All you can do is *give it all you've got*. ‖ その新人女優は体当たりの演技で新人賞を獲得した The starlet *put everything she had into her part* and won the prize for best new talent. (➤「持てるすべてを役柄に注いだ」の意).

タイアップ a **tie-up** 《with》 ▶市はアニメ制作会社とタイアップして観光客を呼び込むために新しいキャラクターを作った The city *has tied up* [*partnered*] *with* an animation production company to create a new character in a bid to attract more tourists.

¹たいあん 大安 ***taian***

日本紹介 ✉ **古くから暦の 1 日 1 日には 6 種類の吉凶を表す呼称がつけられています. その中で大安は最も縁起の良い日とされ, 今でも結婚式はこの日を選んで行われます** From olden times, each day on the calendar has one of six kinds of names based on good and bad luck. *Taian* is considered the luckiest of them, and even now people try to pick a day designated as a *taian* day for their weddings.

²たいあん 対案 a **counterproposal** ▶対案を出す offer *a counterproposal*.

ダイアローグ (a) **dialogue**, 《米また》 **dialog**.

だいあん 代案 an **alternative** /ɔːltə́ːʳnətɪv/ **(plan)** ▶代案を考えておいてくれないか Can you prepare *an alternative plan*?

¹たいい 大意 **the general idea** (意図) ; an **outline** (概略) ; a **summary** (「内容の要約」の意の一般語) ; a **synopsis** /sɪnɑ́ːpsɪs/ (映画・演劇・本などの) ; a **résumé** /rézəmeɪ/ (論文・講演・公文書などの) ▶まずこの社説の大意をつかみなさい First of all, (try to) grasp *the general idea* [*the outline*] of this editorial. ‖ 意見書には大意を300語以内の英語でまとめたものを添付してください You are requested to attach an English *summary* of 300 words or less to your proposal.

²たいい 体位 a **physique** /fɪzíːk/ (体格) ; a **position**, (a) **posture** (姿勢 ; 後者は主に, 良い, 悪い, 正しいなど, 保ち方としての姿勢) ; a **(sexual) position** (性交の) ▶国民の体位の向上を図る plan to improve people's *physiques* ‖ 患者さんに楽な体位をとってもらいましょう Let a patient take a comfortable *position*. (➤床ずれを防ぐために「体位変換を行う」は change someone's position in bed).

³たいい 退位 **abdication** 一動 **退位する** **abdicate (from the throne)** ▶エドワード 8 世の退位 the *abdication* of Edward VIII. (➤ Edward the eighth と読む).

⁴たいい 大尉 a **captain** (陸軍) ; a **lieutenant** /luːténənt/ (海軍).

たいいく 体育 **physical training ; physical education** (科目としての ; P.E. または PE と略す) ▶体育は苦手の科目だ *PE* is one of my worst subjects.

‖**体育館** a gymnasium /dʒɪmnéɪziəm/, 《インフォーマル》 a gym ‖ **体育祭** [**大会**] 《主に米》 an athletic meet [festival], 《主に英》 an athletic meeting (競技会) ; 《主に米》 a field day, 《主に英》 a sports day (体育祭の日) ‖ **体育の日** Health-Sports Day (➤ 英米にはない. 2020 年から名称が「スポーツの日 (Sports Day)」に改められた).

だいいち 第一 **1** 【**最初の**】 **the first** ▶(交響曲の) 第一楽章 *the first* movement ‖ きょうは夏休みの第 1 日目だ Today is *the first day* of summer vacation. ‖ 東京の第一印象はいかがですか What is your *first impression* of Tokyo? ‖ オーストラリアに行って第一に感じることは土地が広大なことだ *The first thing* that strikes a visitor to Australia is the vastness of the country. ‖ まず第一に日本の政治制度について説明しておきましょう Let me *first* explain about Japan's political system. ‖ まず第一に彼女は若すぎる *To begin with*, she is too young. (●いくつかの理由を並べる場合の言い方).

2 【**重要な**】 ▶今のあなたには休養が第一です Rest is *the most important thing* for you now. / Rest is what you need *most* right now. (➤ 2 つ目の文の most は動詞 need を修飾する副詞) ‖ この本の第一の目的は良い英語の書き方を教えることだ The *primary* purpose of this book is to teach how to write good English. ‖ 高校時代は部活が第一で勉強は二の次だった When I was in high school, club [extracurricular] activities *came first*, and study second. ‖ 飛行機には安全が第一だ Safety must be *paramount* with any airplane. ‖ 《標語》 安全第一 *Safety First*.

3 【**そもそも**】 **in the first place, first (of all)** ▶ぼくは競馬なんてやらないよ. 第一金が無い I don't bet on horses. *In the first place* [*First of all*], I have no money.

だいいちにんしゃ 第一人者 ▶彼はこの道の第一人者だ He is *the leading authority* in this field.

だいいっせん 第一線 **the first** [**front**] **line** ▶彼は第一線の実業家だ He *is actively involved in the front line* of business. / He is a *leading* businessman. ‖ 彼は60歳だが, まだ芸能界の第一線で活躍している He is 60 and is still active at *the forefront* of show business. ‖ 彼は第一線(=現役)を退いて悠々自適の生活を送っている He has been living quite comfortably since he retired from *active life*.

だいいっぽ 第一歩 **the first step** ▶率直に話し合うことは相互理解を深める第一歩だ Talking with each other frankly is *the first step* to [toward] better mutual understanding. ‖ 彼は新しい人生の第一歩を踏み出した He *took the first step* toward a new life.

たいいほう 対位法 《音楽》 **counterpoint**.

¹たいいん 隊員 a **member of a party** ▶南極観測隊の隊員 *a member* of the Antarctic expedition party.

²たいいん 退院する **leave** [**get out of**] **(the) hospital** (➤ the を省略するのは《英》) ▶彼はきのう退院した He *left* (*the*) *hospital* yesterday. ‖ 彼女はまだ退院したばかりだ She is *just out of* (*the*) *hospital*. ‖ 彼女は入院して 2 週間後に退院した She *was released* [*was discharged*] *from* (*the*) *hospital* two weeks after she had been admitted. (● be released は「行

動が自由になる」, be discharged は「(退院の)許可が出る」のニュアンスを出したい場合に用いる).

ダイイングメッセージ a **dying message.**

たいいんれき 太陰暦 the **lunar calendar.**

[1]**たいえき 退役する** **retire** ▶ニックは昨年退役した Nick *retired* [*was discharged*] *from* military service last year.

‖**退役軍人** a retired soldier ; 《米》 a veteran ; 《主に英》 an ex-serviceman (➤ 《米》 では veteran よりも堅い語) ; a retired officer (退役将校).

[2]**たいえき 体液** **bodily fluid** /flúːɪd/ ; **semen** /síːmən/ (精液).

ダイエット a **diet** (食事制限) ▶ダイエットをする *go on a diet* (食事制限を行う) / try to lose weight (減量を図る) ‖ 今ダイエット中です I am *on a diet*. / I am *dieting*. ‖ 母はあと 3 キロ減らそうとダイエットしている My mother *is on a diet* to lose another three kilos. ‖ 急激なダイエットを行うのはとても危険だ Going on a crash *diet* is highly risky. ‖ サプリメントや水を飲むだけのダイエット法は信用しません I don't believe in such *weight loss methods* as only taking supplements or only drinking water.

‖**ダイエット食品** diet food.

> **危ないカタカナ語** ○○ダイエット
> 日本語のダイエットは「減量」や「痩せること」の意味で広く使われるが, diet は「日頃食べる食事」や「食事制限」のことなので, 食事に関係のないダイエットには diet は使えない. そこで「骨盤 [ヨガ] ダイエットをしています」は I'm trying to lose weight by doing pelvic stretches [by doing yoga]. などとする.

たいおう 対応 **1【釣り合うこと】** **correspondence** (一致) ; **equivalence** (相当すること) **一動 対応する** **correspond** 《to》 ▶ 1 対 1 の対応 one-to-one *correspondence* ‖ 対応する 2 つの辺 two *corresponding* sides ‖ 日本語の「小春日和」に対応する英語を書きなさい Write an English phrase *corresponding* [*equivalent*] *to* the Japanese "koharu-biyori."

2【反応・対処すること】 a **response** (応答) ; a **countermeasure** (対策) **一動 対応する** **respond** (応対する) ▶流行の変化に素早く対応していかないと, ファッション業界では生き残れない You cannot survive in the fashion world unless you *keep up with* changes in style(s). (➤ keep up with は「(遅れないで)ついていく」) ‖ 円高に対する政府の対応は後手後手に回っている The government's *response* to the yen's appreciation is always one step behind. ‖ この川は毎年氾濫しているのだから, 何らかの対応策を講じるべきだ This river floods every year, so some *preventive countermeasure*(*s*) should be taken.

だいおうじょう 大往生 ▶誰でも大往生したいと願う Everyone hopes for *a painless death after a long life*. ‖ 祖父は92歳で大往生した My grandfather *died peacefully* at the age of ninety-two.

ダイオード 《電気》 a **diode.**

ダイオキシン **dioxin** /daɪáːksɪn/ (➤ 複数形になることもある) ▶ダイオキシンは有毒で発がん性のある化学物質だ *Dioxin* is a toxic, carcinogenic chemical. → 体内.

たいおん 体温 (a) **body temperature** ▶鳥は人間より体温が高い Birds have a higher *body temperature* than humans (do). ‖ けさ体温計で体温を計ったら 38 度 3 分あった When I *took my temperature* with a thermometer this morning, I found it was 38.3℃. (➤ thirty-eight point three degrees Celsius /sélsiəs/ と読む. 華氏と誤解されるおそれがなければ C は省略してもよい).

‖**体温計** a (clinical) thermometer ‖ **低体温** (a) (very) low body temperature, 《医》 hypothermia.

[1]**たいか 大火** a **big** [**great**] **fire** ▶昨夜札幌で大火があった There was *a big fire* in Sapporo last night. / *A big fire* broke out in Sapporo last night.

[2]**たいか 大家** an **authority** /əθɔ́ːrəṭi/ (権威者) ; a (**great**) **master** (巨匠) ; a **great expert** (一流の専門家) ▶人類学の大家 *an authority* on anthropology ‖ 書道の大家 *a great master* of calligraphy / a master calligrapher.

[3]**たいか 退化** **degeneration, retrogression** (➤ ともに生物学用語) **一動 退化する** **degenerate, retrogress** ▶脳の退化 the *degeneration* [*atrophy*] of the brain ‖ 目が退化した魚 a fish with *degenerated* eyes ‖ 私は筋肉が退化してきた My muscles *have atrophied*.

[4]**たいか 耐火の** **fireproof**

‖**耐火建築** a fireproof [fire-resisting] building ‖ **耐火れんが** a firebrick.

[5]**たいか 大過** ▶大過なく with no *problems* [*mistakes*].

たいが 大河 a **big** [**great**] **river** ▶アマゾン川は世界有数の大河だ The Amazon is one of the *largest* [*greatest*] *rivers* in the world.

‖**大河ドラマ** an epic television drama.

だいか 代価 a [**the**] **price** (代償) ▶彼らは民主化のためにどれだけの代価を払えばよいのか What *price* will they have to *pay* for democratization ?

[1]**たいかい 大会** a **grand meeting** (大集会) ; a **general assembly** [**meeting**] (総会) ; a **tournament** (勝ち抜き式の競技大会) ▶労働組合の大会 the *general assembly* of the labor union ‖ わが校のバスケットボールチームは全国大会に出場した Our school basketball team took part in the *National* Basketball *Meet*. ‖ わが党は来月全国大会を開く Our party will hold its *national convention* next month. (➤ convention は「宗教や政治団体などの代表者たちが一堂に集まる大会」を指す).

> **逆引き熟語** ○○大会
> **カラオケ大会** a karaoke contest [competition] / **校内球技大会** intramural games / **世界大会** (スポーツなど) the world championship(s), (学術会議など) a world convention / **全国大会** (スポーツなど) a national meet, (学術会議など) a national convention [conference] / **たこ揚げ大会** a kite-flying contest / **(学会などの) 年次大会** an annual conference [convention / meeting] / **(素人) のど自慢大会** a [an amateur] singing contest / **花火大会** a firework(s) display / **弁論大会** a speech contest / **陸上競技大会** a track and field meet

[2]**たいかい 退会する** **withdraw** 《from》 ▶スポーツクラブを退会する *quit* a sports club / *withdraw from* a sports club membership (➤ 後者は堅い言い方) ‖ **退会届** a notice of withdrawal.

[1]**たいがい 大概** **generally** (一般に) ; **mostly** (大部分) → たいてい ▶ほらを吹くのも大概にしろ *Don't get carried away* with your big talk.

[2]**たいがい 対外** ▶わが校の野球部は部員の 1 人が万引きで捕まったため 1 年間対外試合を禁じられた The baseball team at our high school was prohibited

from playing *games with other schools* for a year because one of the team members was caught shoplifting.
‖**対外援助** a foreign aid ‖ **対外関係** foreign [international] relations ‖ **対外政策** a foreign policy.

たいがいじゅせい 体外受精 external [in vitro] fertilization (➤ in vitro /ɪn víːtroʊ/ はラテン語で「ガラス(＝試験管)内の」の意)
‖**体外受精児** a test-tube baby.

だいかいてん 大回転 《スキー》(a) giant slalom /slάːləm/.

たいかく 体格 (a) build ; (a) physique /fɪzíːk/ (体つき) ▶息子は年の割には**体格**がいい My son has a good *build* [*physique*] for his age. (➤「体格が悪い」なら poor) ‖日本の若者の**体格**は驚くほどよくなった The *physiques* of young Japanese have improved remarkably.

たいがく 退学する leave school, 《インフォーマル》 quit school (➤ 前者には「卒業する」の意もある) ▶高校を**退学する** *leave* [*quit* / *drop out of*] high school (➤ drop out of は「…から落後する」) ‖小林君は家庭の事情で大学を**中途退学した** Kobayashi *left* [*quit*] college *before graduation* for family reasons. ‖その生徒は飲酒運転で交通事故を起こして高校を**退学処分**になった The student *was expelled from school* after causing an accident due to drunk driving. (「退学処分」は expulsion from school) ‖三郎が万引きして**退学になった**こと知ってるかい? Did you know Saburo *was kicked out of school* for shoplifting? (前の訳例よりくだけた言い方) ‖**退学届** a notice of withdrawal from school ‖ **中途退学者** a dropout /drάːpaʊt/.

だいがく 大学 a university, a college

> 《解説》(1)総合・単科にかかわらず大学院が併設されていれば university, いなければ college を用いる.
> (2)インフォーマルでは大学院の有る無しにかかわらず college を用いる傾向がある.
> (3)理工科系の大学の中には institute を用いるところが少なくない.

▶**大学に行く** *go to* (*the*) *university* (the を省略するのは主に《英》) / *go to college* ‖いい**大学**へ行く go to *a* good *university* [*college*] ‖**大学**で教える teach at *a university* [*a college*] (at の代わりに in でもよい) ‖弟はK**大学**に入った[を出た] My brother got into [graduated from] K *University*. ‖**大学**ではどんなクラブに入っていますか What club are you in *at college*? ‖**大学生活**は楽しそうだね You seem to be enjoying *university* [*college* / *campus*] *life*. ‖ことしの**大学出**の初任給はいくらですか What is the average starting pay for *college graduates* this year? ‖今日では**大学教育**を受けた者が必ずしもいい職に就けるとは限らない Today people *with a college education* [*college-educated* people] don't always get a good job. ‖彼はバイトをしながらその金で**大学**を出た He put himself through *college* by working part-time. ‖母はスーパーで働きながら私を**大学**に行かせてくれた My mother put me through *college* while working for a supermarket. ‖ 対話「どこの大学に行っているの?」「ハワイ大学[東京工業大学]です」"What *college* do you go to? / Where do you go to *university* [*college*]?" "I go to the *University* of Hawaii [the Tokyo *Institute* of Technology]."
‖**大学教授** a (university / college) professor ‖ **大学生** a university [college] student 《参考》1年生は a first-year student または a freshman, 《インフォーマル》a fresher, 2年生は a sophomore, 3年生は a junior, 4年生は a senior という ‖ **大学入試** a university [college] entrance examination ‖ **大学入試センター** the National Center for University Entrance Examinations ‖ **大学ノート** a large-sized notebook ‖ **大学病院** a university hospital ‖ **国立大学** a national [《英また》state-run] university ‖ **女子大学** a women's university [college] ‖ **私立大学** a private university ‖ **短期大学** a junior college.

だいがくいん 大学院 a graduate school ▶**大学院**に行く go to *graduate school* ‖京大の**大学院**で政治学を修める study politics at the *graduate school* of Kyoto University. ‖彼女は**大学院**に在籍している She is in *graduate school*.
‖**大学院課程** a graduate course ‖ **大学院生** a graduate [《英また》postgraduate] student.

たいかくせん 対角線 a diagonal /daɪǽgənəl/ (line).

1**たいかん 体感** ▶新車に試乗して乗り心地を**体感する** test-drive a new car and *experience* its comfort ‖寒風が強く吹いているので**体感温度**は零度以下だ The cold wind is blowing hard, driving *the wind-chill temperature* [*factor*] down to below freezing.

2**たいかん 耐寒** ▶**耐寒**植物 a *cold-resistant* [*hardy*] plant.

3**たいかん 退官する** retire from government service ; retire from a national [public] university (国立[公立]大学などを).

4**たいかん 体幹** the core of the body, core muscles ▶**体幹**トレーニング *core* training.

1**たいがん 対岸** the opposite [other] side of a river ▶彼は川の**対岸**まで泳いだ He swam to *the opposite* [*the other*] *side* of the river. / He swam across the river to *the other bank*.
▶《慣用表現》我々はあの国での飢きんを**対岸の火事**と見なしてはいけない We shouldn't *remain indifferent to* the famine in that country. / We shouldn't think that the famine in that country doesn't concern us. (➤ 前者は「無関心でいる」, 後者は「ひと事と考える」).

2**たいがん 大願** ▶神社に参って**大願成就**を祈った I visited a Shinto shrine and prayed for *the fulfillment of my ambition*.

1**だいかん 大寒** *daikan* ; the coldest two-week period in a year (according to the traditional Japanese lunar calendar) (➤ 説明的な訳).

2**だいかん 代官** a *daikan* ; a local governor in the Edo period (➤ 説明的な訳).

たいかんしき 戴冠式 a coronation.

だいかんみんこく 大韓民国 →韓国.

1**たいき 大気** the atmosphere /ǽtməsfɪəʳ/ (地球を取り巻く空気の層) ; the air (空気) ▶**大気圏内**での核実験 an *atmospheric* nuclear test ‖ **大気の状態**が不安定ですのでシートベルトをお締めください Please fasten your seat belt as we may be passing through some *turbulence*. (➤ turbulence /təːʳbjələns/ は「乱気流」) ‖車の排気ガスが**大気汚染**の元凶だ Exhaust fumes from cars and trucks are the worst causes of *air pollution*.

2**たいき 大器** ▶彼はサッカー選手として**大器**(＝前途有

望)だと言われている He is said to be a soccer player *of great promise* [a *highly-promising* soccer player]. ‖ アントン・ブルックナーは**大器晩成型**の作曲家だった Anton Bruckner was *a late bloomer* as a composer.

3**たいき 待機する** **stand by** ▶彼らは自宅で**待機する**よう命じられた They were ordered to *stand by* at their homes. ‖ 混乱に備えて警官が**待機している** The police *are standing by* [*are on the alert*] in case of trouble. (➤ on the alert は「警戒態勢で」).
‖**待機電力** phantom load, standby [vampire] power.

たいぎ 大義 (a) **good cause** ▶イラク戦争を**大義**なき戦争と呼ぶ人もいた Some people said the Iraq war was one *without good cause*.

だいきぎょう 大企業 **big business**(➤ 総称) ; a **large** [《インフォーマル》**big**] **company**(個々の) ▶大卒予定者の多くが**大企業**への就職を希望している Many graduating college students want to find jobs in *large companies*.

だいぎし 代議士 a **Diet member**, a **member of the Diet**, a **Dietman** [**-woman**] (日本の), a **Congressman** [**-woman**] (アメリカの), a **member of Parliament** (イギリスの) ▶自民党所属の**代議士** *a Diet member* of the Liberal Democratic Party ‖ **代議士に立つ** *run for the Diet* ‖ 彼女は神奈川第2区選出の**代議士**だ She is *a representative* from the second electoral district of Kanagawa Prefecture.

だいきち 大吉 **excellent luck**. →おみくじ.

だいきぼ 大規模な **large-scale** ▶**大規模な**開発 *large-scale* development ‖ **大規模な**スーパーマーケット a *large-scale* supermarket ‖ **大規模な**核実験 a *large-scale* nuclear test ‖ **大規模な**世論調査が先月行われた A *large-scale* public opinion poll was conducted last month. ／Public opinion polls were conducted *on a large scale* last month.

たいぎめいぶん 大義名分 ▶彼らは人権擁護という**大義名分**(＝大目的)のために戦っている They are fighting for [in] the *great cause* of human rights.

たいきゃく 退却する **retreat** ; **withdraw**(撤退・撤兵する) ▶敵はついに**退却**を始めた Finally the enemy began to *retreat* from the battlefield.

たいきゅう 耐久 ▶**耐久性のある品物** *durable* goods ‖ ドイツ製の車はその**耐久性**で知られている German-made vehicles are known for their *durability*. ‖ その走者は**耐久力**に欠けていた The runner had no *stamina* [*staying power*]. ‖**耐久消費財** durable goods, consumer durables.

だいきゅう 代休 ▶木曜日にきょうの**代休**を取りたいのですが I'd like to *take a day off* on Thursday *to make up for today*.

1**たいきょ 退去する** **leave** +㊐ (立ち退く) ; **evacuate** +㊐ (危険区域などから) ▶不法占拠者は**退去**を命じられた The illegal occupiers were ordered to *leave* the building. ‖ 土砂崩れのおそれがあったため, 住民たちは**退去させられた** The residents *were evacuated* because of the danger of a landslide.

2**たいきょ 大挙** ▶サッカーのフーリガンが**大挙して**スタジアムに押し寄せた Soccer hooligans *crowded* [*thronged*] the stadium.／Soccer hooligans *came* to the stadium *in crowds* [*in large numbers*].

たいきょう 胎教 **prenatal training** ▶**胎教**にいい have a good influence on [be good for] *the* (*unborn*) *baby*.

たいきょく 対局 a **game of Go** [**shogi**／**chess**] ▶**対局する** *play Go* [*shogi*／*chess*].
‖**対局者** a player.

たいきょくけん 太極拳 **tai chi** /tàɪ tʃíː/ ; **tai qi** ▶毎日**太極拳を行う** *do* [*practice*] *tai chi* daily.

たいきょくてき 大局的 ▶**大局的**に物事を見る take a *broad* [*wide*] view of things／see things *in perspective*.

だいきらい 大嫌い ▶ニンニクは**大嫌い**だ I *hate* garlic. (➤「**大嫌い**な物」を one's pet hate ということもある) ‖ ピアノの稽古は**大嫌い**です I *hate* [*detest*] practicing the piano. (➤ hate は「憎悪する」, detest は「ひどく嫌う」) ‖ 母は嘘をつく政治家が**大嫌い**です My mother *loathes* lying politicians. (➤ loathe /loʊð/ は「ひどく嫌悪する」の意の堅い語).

直訳の落とし穴「あんな人, 大嫌い」

(1) 日本語では割合軽い気持ちで「あんな人, 大嫌い」「あの女優は大嫌い」などという言い方をする. これを「大嫌いである」＝hate と考えて, I hate him [that man／that actress]. としがち. しかし, hate は人に対しては「憎む」という極めて強い意味であり, 日常的に軽々しく「あの人が憎い」とは言わないように, 人に hate を使うのはかなり深刻な状況で, I hate you. はもう一生付き合うのはごめんだくらいの感情がこめられ, 人間関係を修復することは望めない可能性もある. そもそも, キリスト教では, 人を love せよが基本の教えであり, hate することは罪(sin)とされるために, 軽々しく, I hate だれだれ, という表現を口にしない. I dislike him [that actress] very much. が無難な表現である.

(2) 日本では, 約束を守らなかったりすると子供に「お父さんなんて大嫌い」と言われることがあるが, これは I don't like you one bit. (お父さんなんか, ちっとも好きじゃない)より, もっと具体的に Dad, you're mean. (お父さんの意地悪), You lied to me. (嘘をついた), Dad, you never keep your promises! (お父さんはちっとも約束を守らない)などと言われることが多いと思われる.

(3) 人以外の「ニンジンは大嫌い」は I hate carrots. でかまわない.

たいきん 大金 a **large sum** [**amount**] **of money**, 《インフォーマル》**a lot of money** ▶**大金**を持ち逃げする run away with *a large sum of money* ‖ 10万円は私には**大金**だった A hundred thousand yen was *a lot* to me.

だいきん 代金 **the price** ; **the charge**(サービスに対する料金) ▶**代金**はあとで結構です You can buy now and *pay* later. ‖ **代金はおいくらですか** *How much do I owe you?* ‖ (その品の)**代金は支払い済み**です It *has* (*already*) *been paid for*. ‖ 修理**代金を払う** *pay for* the repair.

だいく 大工 a **carpenter**
‖**大工技能専門学校** a carpentry (vocational) school ‖ **大工道具** carpenter's tools.

1**たいくう 対空の** **antiaircraft** ‖**対空兵器** antiaircraft weapons ‖ **対空ミサイル** an antiaircraft missile.

2**たいくう 滞空** ‖**滞空記録** a flight endurance record ‖ **滞空時間** flight duration ; time in flight [in the air] (スキー競技などの) ; hang time (フィギュアスケートなどの).

たいぐう 待遇 **1**【処遇】**treatment** ▶そんなひどい**待遇**には我慢できない I cannot put up with such *bad treatment* [*ill-treatment*]. ‖ 彼はタイでは国賓の**待遇**を受けた He *was treated* as a state guest in Thailand. ‖ 彼はそこで**特別待遇を受けた** He *was given*

VIP treatment there. (➤ VIP は very important person の頭文字).

2【職場の】▶あの会社は待遇(＝給料)が悪いので辞めた I quit my job (at that company) because I was *poorly paid* [because *the pay was low*]. ‖組合員は待遇改善を求めてストライキをした The union members went on strike for *better working conditions* [for *a raise in pay*]. (➤後者は「昇給」).

たいくつ 退屈な **tedious** /tíːdiəs/ (長たらしくてうんざりする); **dull** (おもしろくない); **boring** (うんざりさせるような); **uninteresting** (興味の持てない) **一動 退屈する get bored**

▶退屈な仕事 a *tedious* job ‖退屈な映画 a *dull* movie ‖通勤電車で退屈しないようにクロスワードパズルをする do some crosswords to *amuse oneself* on a commuter train (➤ amuse oneself は「…して楽しく過ごす」の意) ‖あんな退屈な男と付き合うなんて真っ平だわ I don't want to go out with such an *uninteresting* [*a boring*] guy. ‖近藤先生の講義はいつもと同じで退屈だった Mr. Kondo's lecture was *boring* [*dull*] as usual.

▶私は彼女の話に退屈した I got *bored* listening to her talk. ‖きょうは何もすることがなくて退屈な一日だった I've been *bored* all day long with nothing to do. ‖ああ, 退屈だ What *a bore*! (➤ bore は「(ひどく)退屈なこと［人］」) ／I'*m sooo bored*! (◉ (1) 退屈の程度を強調するため, 副詞の so を書くとき sooo のように 2 つ余分に o をつけて表すことがある. (2) I'm (so) boring. としないこと. これは「私は(とても)退屈な人間です」の意) ‖そのテレビドラマは退屈だった The TV drama *was a bore*. ‖小林さんは話し上手で聞き手を退屈させない Mr. Kobayashi is a good talker and never *bores* his listeners.

▶いいところへ来てくれたね. 退屈してたんだよ You came at just the right time. I *was bored* (*stiff*). (➤この stiff は「ひどく」の意) ‖退屈しのぎに(＝暇潰しに)漫画を読んだ I read comic books *to kill time*.

1**たいぐん 大群** a **large flock** (鳥・羊などの) ▶牛の大群 *a large herd* of cattle ‖ニシンの大群 *a large shoal* [*school*] of herring ‖イナゴの大群が作物を全滅させた *A large swarm* of locusts destroyed the crops. ‖渡り鳥の大群が南へ飛んでいった *A large flock* of migrating birds was flying southward. ／Migrating birds were flying southward in *large flocks*. →群れ.

2**たいぐん 大軍** a **large force** [**army**].

1**たいけい 体系** a **system** ▶賃金体系 a wage *system* ‖彼は近代医学を体系的に研究した He made a *systematic* study of modern medicine.

2**たいけい 体型** a **physique** (個人・人種の); a **figure** (容姿) ▶近頃はスリムな体型の若者が多い Many young people these days have slim [slender] *physiques*.

だいけい 台形 a **trapezoid** /trǽpɪzɔɪd/, 《英》 a **trapezium** /trəpíːziəm/.

たいけつ 対決 a **showdown** (紛争・スポーツなどの); a **battle** (戦い); a **fight** (格闘) **一動 対決する fight** 《against》 (…と戦う) ▶ワールドカップでのアルゼンチンとドイツの対決 the World Cup *showdown* between Argentina and Germany ‖クイズ番組で彼はチャンピオンの座を懸けて頭脳対決を繰り広げた On the quiz program, he was vying for the championship in *a battle* of brains. (➤ vie /vaɪ/ for で「…を得ようと争う」の意) ‖悪と対決する *fight against* evil ‖野党は政府に対して対決姿勢を強めた The opposition parties have strengthened their *stance against* the government.

たいけん 体験 (a) (**personal**) **experience** **一動 体験する experience** ＋目; **go through** (苦しみなどを経験する) ▶貴重な体験をする have a valuable *experience* ‖大津波を体験する *experience* [*go through*] a great tsunami ‖台所の火事［地震］を疑似体験する *experience a simulation* of a kitchen fire [an earthquake] ‖無料体験レッスンを受ける take a free *trial* lesson ‖私は医師としての体験からいろいろなことを学んだ I've learned a lot *from my experience*(*s*) as a doctor. ‖私はその村で奇妙な［ぞっとするような］体験をした I had a strange [terrifying] *experience* in the village. (◉ 1 回 1 回の体験は Ⓒ, 積み重ねた体験は Ⓤ 扱い) ‖(セックスの)初体験は何歳のとき? When did you *first have sex* [*have* your *first sexual experience*]?

‖体験学習 learning by experience.

たいげん 体現 **embodiment** **一動 体現する embody** ＋目; **personify** ＋目 (…の化身となる) ▶観音は慈悲を体現している Kannon *is the embodiment* of the spirit of compassion. ／Kannon *embodies* compassion. ‖彼の生涯はアメリカン・ドリームの体現だった His life *typified* the American dream. (➤ typify は「…を型によって示す」).

たいげんそうご 大言壮語 **bragging** (ほらの含まれた自慢話) **一動 大言壮語する brag**; **talk big** (大きなことを言う).

1**たいこ 太鼓** a **drum** 《参考》「大太鼓」は bass drum, 「小太鼓」は snare (drum)という ▶子供たちが太鼓をたたいている The children are *beating drums* [are *drumming*].

▶父は太鼓腹をしている My father has *a potbelly* [*beer belly*]. ‖太鼓橋 an arched bridge ‖太鼓持ち a jester (座をもたせる人); a sycophant /síkəfənt/, a toady (へつらう人).

2**たいこ 太古の** **primeval** /praɪmíːvəl/ ▶太古の昔から since *the dawn of time*.

1**たいこう 対抗する** **compete** 《with, against》 (競う); **match** ＋目 (互角である); **beat** ＋目 (負かす) ▶テニスで彼女に対抗できる者はいない No one *can compete with* [*match*／*beat*] her when it comes to tennis. ‖私は英語では陽子に対抗できない I *am no match for* Yoko in English. ‖こんな製品では他社のものに対抗できない A product like this cannot *compete against* rival products.

▶B 社は A 社に対抗して新しい 4 K テレビを発売した *In competition with* Company A, Company B put a new type of 4K television sets on the market. ‖彼女は私に強い対抗意識を抱いているようだ She seems to have *competitive feelings* toward me.

▶クラス対抗のソフトボール大会 an *inter-class* softball tournament ‖高校対抗テニストーナメント an *inter-high school* tennis tournament ‖大学対抗フットボール試合 an *intercollegiate* football game ‖日米対抗体操競技会 the *Japan-U.S.* gymnastic meet.

2**たいこう 対向** ▶対向する車の流れに突っ込む drive into *oncoming* traffic ‖《標示》対向車に注意 Beware of *oncoming cars*.

‖対向車線 the opposite lane ‖(見開きの)対向ページ the opposite [facing] page.

3**たいこう 退校** ▶その生徒は万引きをして退校処分となった The student *was expelled from school* for shoplifting.

4**たいこう 大公** a **grand duke**
‖**大公国** a grand duchy.
5**たいこう 大綱** an **outline, fundamental principles.**
1**だいこう 代行する act for** ▶彼は半年間会長の**代行**をした He was the *acting* president of the society for six months. (➤ acting は「一時的に代行する」の意の形容詞).
‖**代行運転** substitute driving ‖**代行機関** an agency ‖**代行サービス業** proxy service business (留守番をしたり, 犬猫・庭木などの世話をしたりする).
2**だいこう 代講** ▶前期は石川先生が井上先生の**代講**をした In the first semester Mr. Ishikawa *taught* us *in place of* Mr. Inoue [*substituted for* Mr. Inoue].
たいこうじあい 対校試合 a **game** [**competition**] **with another school** ▶B高とバレーボールの**対校試合**を行う play a volleyball *game with the B High team*.
たいこうば 対抗馬 a **rival horse** (競馬の) ▶《比喩的》伊藤氏は次の選挙で小野氏の**対抗馬**として出馬する Mr. Ito will run in the next election as *an opponent* of [as *a rival candidate* to] Mr. Ono.
たいこく 大国 a **big** [**great**] **power** (強国) ; a **large country** (広大な国) ▶経済的には日本は世界の**大国**の1つである Economically, Japan is among the *big* [*great*] *powers* of the world.
‖**経済** [**軍事**] **大国** an economic [a military] power ‖**地震大国** a highly seismic country ‖**生活大国** a great "quality-of-life" power.
だいこくばしら 大黒柱 the mainstay (支柱, 支える人) ▶青山君はピッチャーで4番. 文字どおりチームの**大黒柱**です Aoyama is our (main) pitcher and cleanup batter. He's literally *the mainstay* of the team. ‖伊藤さん一家は交通事故で**大黒柱** (=一家の稼ぎ手) を失った The Ito family lost their *breadwinner* in a traffic accident.
たいこばん 太鼓判 ▶彼女(の人柄)なら私が**太鼓判を押す** I can *vouch for* her. (➤「保証する」の意; vouch の発音は /vaʊtʃ/) ‖あの男は信用できるよ. ぼくが**太鼓判を押す** *Take my word for it*, he's a reliable man. (➤「ぼくのことばをそのまま信じなさい」の意).
だいごみ 醍醐味 ▶ハンググライディングの**だいご味** *the real pleasure* [*enjoyment*] of hang gliding ‖我々は大リーグの試合を観戦し, 野球の**だいご味**を味わった We experienced [felt] *the real thrill* of baseball when watching a U.S. major league game.
だいこん 大根 a ***daikon*** **(radish)**, a **mooli** /múːli/ (➤ radish は「ハツカダイコン」で, 日本の大根よりずっと小さく, 球形. また皮は主に赤色(中身は白)) ▶《慣用表現》彼女は**大根足**だ She has *stubby legs*. ‖彼は顔はいいが**大根役者**だ Though handsome, he is *a ham* [*horrible*] *actor*.
‖**大根下ろし** grated *daikon* (おろした大根) ; a *daikon* grater (おろし金).
1**たいさ 大差** a **great** [**big**] **difference** ▶両者に**大差**はない There's no big *difference* between the two. ‖きみの言ったことは彼の意見と**大差ない** What you said *is not much different from* his opinion. ‖きょうの気温はきのうと**大差ない** The temperature today *is about the same as* it was yesterday. ‖大学まではバスでも電車でも**大差はない** It *doesn't make much difference* [It *makes little difference*] whether you take the bus or train to the college.
▶わが校の野球部は**大差**で勝った Our baseball team won *by a wide margin*.
2**たいさ 大佐** a **colonel** /kɔ́ːˈnl/ (陸軍) ; a **captain** (海軍).
だいざ 台座 a **plinth** /plɪnθ/ (円柱の) ; a **pedestal** (像などを安置する).
1**たいざい 滞在** (a) **stay** 一動 (…に) **滞在する stay** 《in, at, with》 (➤ in, at は「場所」に, with は「人」に用いる) ▶その小説家は城崎に長期間**滞在していた** The novelist *stayed* a long time *at* Kinosaki. ‖私は今おじのところに**滞在している** I *am* now *staying with* my uncle [*at* my uncle's]. ‖私はアフリカ**滞在中**にマラリアにかかった I was stricken with malaria *during my stay* in Africa [while in Africa]. ‖ **対話**「どのくらいスペインに**滞在する**つもりですか」「2週間の予定です」"How long are you going to *stay in* Spain?" "(I plan to stay there) for two weeks."
✉ **そちらに滞在中はいろいろご親切にしていただき, ありがとうございました** Thank you for all your kindness *while I was there* [*during my stay there*].
‖**滞在客** a guest.
2**たいざい 大罪** a **serious crime** (法律上の) ; a **mortal** [**deadly**] **sin** (宗教上の).
だいざい 題材 subject matter (取り扱う内容, テーマ) ; **material** (材料) ▶作文の**題材** *material* for a composition ‖同性愛を**題材**にした小説 a novel *with* homosexual [same-sex] love *for its subject matter*.
1**たいさく 対策** a **measure** ; a **step** (段階的対策の1つ) ; a **countermeasure** /káʊnṭəˈmèʒəˈ/ (対抗策) (➤ いずれもしばしば複数形で用いる) ▶インフレ**対策** an anti-inflation *measure* ‖政府は石油価格の上昇に対して**対策を講じるべきだ** The government should *take measures* [*steps*] *against* the rise in oil prices. ‖来年は入試なのでそろそろ受験**対策**を考えなきゃあ Next year I'll be taking entrance examinations, so I'll have to start thinking about *a strategy* for passing. (➤ strategy は「戦略」) ‖警察は新たなハイジャック**対策**を練った The police have developed new *countermeasures against* hijackers.
▶村が鉄砲水に襲われ, 村役場に**災害対策本部**が設置された After the village was hit by a flash flood, *a disaster response headquarters* was set up in the village administrative office. (➤ 一時的な組織には headquarters は用いない).

> **逆引き熟語 ○○対策**
> **安全対策** safety measures ／**HIV** [**AIDS**] **対策** measures to combat HIV [AIDS] ／**公害対策** an antipollution measure ／**災害対策** disaster control [planning] ／**失業対策** an unemployment policy ／**ストーカー対策** an anti-stalking measure ／**テロ対策** an anti-terrorism measure, counterterrorism ／**防災対策** disaster measures ／**防犯対策** anticrime measures

2**たいさく 大作** a **great** [**grand**] **work** ▶ラウル・デュフィーの**大作**『電気の精』Raoul Dufy's *grand work* "La Fée Electricité."
だいさく 代作する write [**compose**] **for** ; **ghostwrite** (文芸作品などを)
‖**代作者** the actual writer [composer] of a work ; a ghostwriter (文芸作品などの).
たいさん 退散する disperse (群衆が) ; **leave** (立ち去

る); **run away**(逃げる) ▶暴徒は**退散した** The rioters *dispersed* [*left*]. ‖ 群衆を**退散させる**ために警察が呼ばれた The police were called in to *disperse* [*break up*] the crowd.

▶そろそろぼくたちも**退散**しようよ(=帰ろう) I think we too had better *be going* [*leaving*].

だいさんしゃ 第三者 a **third party** [**person**] (当事者以外の人); an **outsider** (部外者) ▶**第三者による調査** an *independent* investigation ‖ どちらの言い分が正しいか**第三者**に聞いてみたらどうだろう Why don't we ask *a third party* which opinion is right?

だいさんセクター 第三セクター a **joint public-private venture.**

たいさんぼく 大山木・泰山木《植 物》a **Southern magnolia.**

1**たいし 大使** an **ambassador** /æmbǽsədəʳ/ 《参考》 英連邦加盟国間では high commissioner が大使に相当する代表者 ▶駐米日本**大使** the Japanese *ambassador* to the United States ‖ A 氏は**駐英大使**に任ぜられた Mr. A was appointed *ambassador to Great Britain*. ‖ イギリス**大使館**にウォレン**大使**を訪ねた I went to visit *Ambassador* Warren at the British *Embassy*.

‖**大使館** an embassy ‖ **大使館員** a member of the embassy staff; the embassy staff (➤ 集合的).

2**たいし 大志** (an) **ambition** ▶**大志を抱く**人 an *ambitious* person ‖ 彼は**大志を抱いて**上京した He came to Tokyo *with great ambitions*.

1**たいじ 退治する** **get rid of**; **conquer** /kɑ́ːŋkəʳ/ +㊐(打ち破る) ▶ゴキブリを完全に**退治する**のは難しい It's difficult to *get rid of* cockroaches completely. ‖ 桃太郎は鬼**退治**に出かけた Momotaro set out to *conquer* the ogres.

2**たいじ 胎児** an **embryo** /émbrioʊ/ (妊娠3か月まで); a **fetus** /fíːṭəs/ (妊娠3か月以降).

3**たいじ 対峙する** **face** [**confront**] (**each other**).

だいし 台紙 a (**photograph**) **mount** (写真の).

だいじ 大事 **1**【大切】**一㊎ 大事な** **important**; **precious** (とても貴重な); **valuable** (価値のある) ▶**大事な会議** an *important* meeting / 《インフォーマル》a *big* meeting ‖ 私の**大事な**思い出 a *precious* memory of mine ‖ **大事な**データ *important* [*valuable*] data ‖ 本を読むときは必ず**大事な**ところにはアンダーラインを引くことにしている Whenever I read a book, I underline all the *important* points. ‖ このギターは私にはとても**大事な**ものです This guitar is very *precious* to me. ‖ 私たちにとって**大事な**ことは事実を知ることだ *What's important* [*The important thing*] is that we know the facts (of the matter). ‖ 出世は私にとってあまり**大事ではない** Achieving high social status *is not* very *important* to me. / Achieving high social status *holds little meaning* for me. / Achieving high social status *means little* to me. ‖ **人生には**金儲けより**大事なものがある** *There's more to life* than making money.

▶おじいちゃんとおばあちゃんを**大事にしてね** *Be kind* [*good*] *to* your grandparents. ‖ 友だちを**大事にしな**さいよ You should *cherish* your friends. ‖ ピーナツバター, **大事に**使ってよ. 月曜日までそれしかないんだから *Go easy on* [*with*] the peanut butter. It's all we have till Monday. (➤「加減して使え」の意のインフォーマルな言い方) ‖ 長い時間パソコンの画面を見ているなら**目を大事にした**ほうがいいよ If you spend a lot of time looking at a computer screen, you should *give your eyes a break*. (「目を大事にする」を「目を休ませる」と考える) ‖ **対話** (病人に)「どうぞお**大事に**」「ありがとうございます」"Please *take care of yourself*." "Thank you. I will."

2【重大事】▶火事は**大事に至らない**うちに消し止められた The fire was put out before it *got out of hand* [*got serious*]. (➤ get out of hand は「手に負えなくなる」) ‖ 航空機の不完全な修理が**大事**(=惨事)を引き起こした Incomplete repairs to the airplane were the cause of the *disaster*.

▶《慣用表現》けがは大したことはなかったが, **大事を取っ**て2日間入院した The injury was not serious, but I was hospitalized for two days *as a precaution* [*just to be on the safe side*].

ダイジェスト a **digest** /dáɪdʒest/ ▶長編小説の**ダイジェスト版** a novel's *digest*.

だいしきょう 大司教 an **archbishop.**

だいしぜん 大自然 (**Mother**) **Nature** ▶**大自然の懐に抱かれて生きる** live surrounded by *Mother Nature*.

たいした 大した **1**【すごい, すばらしい】▶7歳の子供にしては**大したものだ**(=よくやった) For a seven-year-old child, he *did really well*. ‖ 彼女の作品は**大したものだ** Her works *are really something*. (➤ something は「大したもの」の意のインフォーマルな語) ‖ 25歳で社長とは彼も**大したものだ** *It's quite an achievement* for him to be the president of a company at the age of 25. ‖《皮肉って》**大した友だちだよ, おまえは!** *Some* friend you are! ‖ **対話**「お父さん, ぼく英語で満点取ったよ」「そりゃ, **大したもんだ**」"Dad, I got a perfect score on the English exam." "Wow. *That's great!*"

2【「大した…ない」の形で】▶両者に**大した**(=大きな)**違いはない** There is *no big* [*not much*] difference between the two. ‖ 母の病気は**大したことはありません**(=重大ではない) My mother's illness *is not serious*. ‖ **遅れたって大したことはないよ** *It doesn't matter* if we are late. ‖ 彼は**大した学者ではない** He *is not much of a* scholar. (➤ not much of a ... はインフォーマルな言い方で「それほどの…ではない」) ‖ 被害は**大したことはなかった** There was *not much* damage. / We did*n't* have *much* damage. ‖《相手に贈り物をして》**大したものじゃないんですよ** *It's really nothing.* / *It's just a little something.* ‖ **大した車ではありませんが**, どうぞ私の車をお使いください You're welcome to use my car, *such as it is* [*though it is nothing fancy*]. (➤ such as it is は「大したものではないが, お粗末なものだが」の意の慣用句) ‖ 最近では1万円では**大した物は買えない** Ten thousand yen *doesn't go far* these days. (➤ go far は「使いでがある, 大いに役立つ」の意).

たいしつ 体質 a **constitution**; a **predisposition** (病気にかかりやすい素質) ▶私は丈夫な[弱い]**体質**だ I have a strong [weak] *constitution*. ‖ 私はかぜをひきやすい**体質**だ I have *a predisposition* to colds. / I catch colds easily. (インフォーマルな会話では後者がふつう) ‖ 彼は**アレルギー体質**だ He *has allergies*. / He's *allergic*. ‖ 香辛料の効いた食べ物は**体質的に合わない** Spicy foods *don't agree with* me. (この agree with は通例否定文で用いる) ‖ 私は**体質的に酒が飲めない** I have *very low tolerance for* [*resistance to*] alcohol.

▶《比喩的》金がすべてという党の**体質**(=考え方)を改善すべきだ We should change the party's *way of thinking* that money is everything. ‖ 証券業界の

古い体質(＝特徴) *the outdated characteristics* [*culture*] of the securities industry ‖ その政党の金権体質(＝金銭志向)は変わっていない The political party's inclination toward *money politics* has not changed.
‖企業体質 corporate culture.

¹たいして 大して **not very, not much** ▶外は大して寒くない It's *not very* cold outside. ‖ 雪は大して降らなかった It did*n't* snow *much*. ‖ 一日頑張っても仕事は大してはかどらなかった I worked hard all day but *didn't* make *much* progress [headway] in my work. ‖ 彼はその結果に大して満足していなかった He was *not so* satisfied with the results. ‖ 日本語の「よろしく」という表現には大して意味がないことがある Sometimes the Japanese expression "yoroshiku" does*n't* mean *much of anything*. (➤ not much of anything は not much を強めた, ややくだけた言い方で, 「ほとんど何もない」の含み) ‖ 誰が首相になろうと大して違いはない It does*n't make much difference* who the next prime minister is.

²たいして 対して **1**【向かって】**to, toward(s)** (● 行為などの方向性を明確にする場合は後者がふつう) ; **for** (好意・親切・お礼などを表す場合) ▶光夫は私に対してとても親切だ Mitsuo is very kind *to* me. ‖ 洋子は両親に対して反抗的な態度をとった Yoko took a defiant attitude *toward* her parents. ‖ 彼は私に対して好意を抱いているようだ He seems to have tender feelings *for* me. ‖ 彼は旧来の考え方に対して反対の立場をとった He took a stand *against* the conventional view. (● against は相手に対して敵意や反感を抱いているときに用いる).
2【対照】▶先月の火災件数28件に対して今月は19件だ There were 19 fires this month *compared with* [*as opposed to*] 28 last month.

たいしぼう 体脂肪 **body fat** ▶体脂肪を燃やす burn (one's) *body fat*.
‖体脂肪率 a body fat rate.

¹たいしゃ 退社する **1**【会社を辞める】**resign** /rɪzáɪn/《from》, **quit**(＋目) ▶中尾さんは先月一身上の都合で退社した Mr. Nakao *quit* [*left* / *resigned from*] the company for personal reasons last month.
2【仕事を終えて帰宅する】**get off work** (仕事を終える) ; **leave the office** [one's work] (会社を出る) ▶私たちの退社時間はタイムカードに記録される Our *check-out* [*punch-out*] *time* is recorded on time cards. ‖ 対話「何時に退社するの？」「たいてい 7 時頃だね」"What time do you *get off work*?" "Usually around 7 p.m."

²たいしゃ 代謝 **metabolism** /mətǽbəlìzəm/.

¹だいしゃ 台車 a **hand truck**, a **dolly**, a **cart**.

²だいしゃ 代車 a **substitute vehicle**, a **loaner**.

だいじゃ 大蛇 a **big snake**.

たいしゃくたいしょうひょう 貸借対照表《簿記》a **balance sheet**.

たいじゅ 大樹 a **big tree** ▶ ことわざ 寄らば大樹の陰 Seek shelter in the shade of a big tree.

¹たいしゅう 大衆 **the (general) public** (一般大衆) ; **the masses** (エリートに対して) ▶減税案は大衆の支持を得た The tax reduction policy won [gained] the support of *the* (*general*) *public*. ‖ スマートフォンがだんだん大衆化してきた Smartphones are *getting* more and more *popular*. ‖ 日本人の間で海外旅行が大衆化したのはそう遠い過去のことではない It's not so long ago that foreign travel *became popular* among Japanese people. ‖ S 紙は大衆的な新聞だ S Paper is geared *for the general public*.
‖大衆作家 a popular novelist [writer] ‖ 大衆雑誌 a mass magazine ‖ 大衆車 a popular car ; an economy car (経済的な車) ‖ 大衆社会 (a) mass society ‖ 大衆小説 a popular novel ‖ 大衆食堂 a cheap restaurant ‖ 大衆性 popularity ‖ 大衆文化 popular culture.

²たいしゅう 体臭 **body odor**《略 B.O.》▶彼は体臭が強い He has strong *B.O.* ‖ 彼は体臭に悩んでいる He has a *body odor* problem.

たいじゅう 体重 **weight** ▶体重どのくらい？ What's your *weight*? / How much do you weigh? (● 後者の聞き方がふつう. weigh は「体重がある」の意の動詞) ‖ 私は 3 か月で体重が10キロ増えた[減った] I have *gained* [*lost*] ten kilos in three months. (● kilo は kilogram の略. 米では体重にはキログラム(kilo)ではなくポンド(pound /paʊnd/), 英ではストーン(stone)を用いるのがふつう) ‖ 兄は身長は175センチあるのに体重は50キロしかない Though my brother is 175 centimeters tall, he *weighs* only 50 kilograms. ‖ きのう体重を量ったら62キロだった I *weighed* 62 kilos yesterday. ‖ 私は毎朝起きるとすぐ体重を量る I *weigh myself* as soon as I get up every morning.
‖体重計 the scale(s) (➤ 風呂場に置く体重計は a bathroom scale という).

¹たいしゅつ 退出 ‖退出時刻[時間] quitting time.

²たいしゅつ 帯出する **take out** ▶図書館から本を帯出する *take out* a book from a library. ‖《表示》禁帯出 not for loan / for reference only / in-library use only (図書館での場合).

たいしょ 対処する **cope**《with》▶難局にうまく対処する *cope with* a difficult situation ‖ 市長はその問題に前向きに対処すると約束した The mayor promised to *actively deal with* the problem.

¹たいしょう 対象 an **object** (的) ; a **subject** (主題) ▶研究の対象 *an object* of study ‖ 欲望の対象 *the object* of one's desire ‖ 絵を描くには対象をしっかり見なければいけない To draw a picture you must look over your *subject* carefully. ‖ その競技はアマだけでなくプロも対象としている The game is not only *for* amateurs, but *for* professionals as well. ‖ この辞書は高校生を対象としている This dictionary *is* (*intended*) *for* [*is aimed at* / *is targeted at*] high school students. ‖ その調査は5000人の大学生を対象に行われた The survey was conducted *on* 5,000 college students.

²たいしょう 対照 (a) **contrast** /kɑ́:ntræst/ 一動 (A と B を)対照する **contrast** /kəntrǽst/《A with B》; **compare**《A with B》(比較する)
▶彼女の白い肌は黒い髪と鮮やかな対照を見せていた Her fair complexion *contrasted* strikingly *with* her black hair. / Her fair complexion was *in* striking *contrast with* her black hair. / Her fair complexion and black hair *made a* striking *contrast*. ‖ 父の性格は母と対照的(＝正反対)だ My father is *just the opposite of* my mother in personality. ‖ 私は姉とは全く対照的でおてんばです I'm a tomboy, *the exact opposite of* my sister.
▶翻訳と原文を対照(＝比較)してみたらいくつかの間違いが見つかった When I *compared* the translation *with* the original, I found several mistakes. ‖ 日本語と英語の対照研究をする make *a contrastive study* of Japanese and English.

た

‖対照言語学 contrastive linguistics.

³たいしょう 対称 symmetry /símətri/ ▶チョウの羽には左右対称の模様がある Butterflies have *symmetrical* patterns on their wings.

⁴たいしょう 大将 a general(陸軍の); an admiral (海軍の) ▶《呼びかけ》よう大将, 元気かい? Hi (there)! How're you doing? 《参考》飲み屋, すし屋などの「大将」は「店主」に当たる owner や proprietor だが, 呼びかけには用いられず, 代わりに名前を言うのがふつう.

☛ お山の大将 (→見出語)

⁵たいしょう 大勝 a great victory ▶ヤクルトは巨人に大勝した The Swallows *won a great victory* [*had an easy victory*] *over* the Giants.

⁶たいしょう 大正 Taisho ▶祖父は大正14年生まれです My grandfather was born in the 14th year of *Taisho* [in 1925]. (● 日本の年号制度を知らない外国人には西暦を用いるほうがよい).

⁷たいしょう 大賞 a grand prize ▶コンテストで大賞を獲得する win *the grand prize* in a contest.

⁸たいしょう 隊商 a caravan.

たいじょう 退場する leave +⑪ (立ち去る) ▶舞台から退場する *leave* the stage ‖《ト書き》ロミオ退場 *Exit* Romeo (➤ 2人以上のときは Exeunt /éksiʌnt/ となる) ‖《野球で》審判はその選手に退場を命じた The umpire *ordered* the player *off the field* [*out of the game*].

¹だいしょう 大小 ▶港には大小さまざまな船が停泊している There are ships *of various sizes* at anchor in the harbor. ‖大小にかかわらず値段は同じです The price is the same *regardless of size*.

²だいしょう 代償 **1**【償い】compensation ▶彼女は私に損害の代償を要求した She demanded *compensation* from me for the damage.

2【犠牲, 代価】(a) price, (a) cost ▶それが手に入るならどんな代償を払ってもいい I want (to get) it *at any price* [*at any cost*]. / I *would give anything* to get it. ‖あんなむちゃな生活を続けていると彼はいずれは高い代償を払うはめになるだろう If he continues to lead such a wild life, sooner or later he'll *be made to pay a high price* for it. (➤ pay a [the] price は「代価[代償]を払う」という比喩的な意味に使うことが多い).

だいじょうぶ 大丈夫

all right ▶留守中は何が起こっても大丈夫なようにしてきた I made sure that *things would be all right* during my absence.

▶大丈夫だよ(=心配するな) *Don't worry*. ‖この木の実は食べても大丈夫なの? Are these nuts *safe to eat*? / Are these nuts *edible*? (➤ edible /édəbəl/ は「食べられる」) ‖ 対話「大丈夫ですか」「少しめまいがしましたが, 今はもう大丈夫です」"*Are you all right?*" "I felt a little dizzy, but I'*m all right* now. Thanks."

> **あなたの英語はどう響く?**
> 「何かお手伝いしましょうか」「いや大丈夫です」という対話を "Do you need any help?" "No, thank you." と英訳することのできる人でも, Are you sure? (本当に大丈夫ですか) と聞かれて「大丈夫ですとも」と言うつもりで Yes, I'm sure. のように返答してしまうことが少なくない. しかし, Yes, I'm sure. だけだと, 怒っているように響くか, ぶっきらぼうに響いてしまうおそれがある. Yes, but *thanks* anyway. と, ここでも感謝の気持ちを表すことばを添えるのが英語的.

だいじょうぶっきょう 大乗仏教 Mahayana /mɑ̀ːhəjɑ́ːnə/ Buddhism (➤ 上座部[小乗]仏教は Theravada /θèrəvɑ́ːdə/ Buddhism).

たいじょうほうしん 帯状疱疹 herpes /hə́ːʳpiːz/ zoster, shingles (➤ 単数扱い).

たいしょうりょうほう 対症療法 symptomatic treatment (治療).

¹たいしょく 退職 retirement (定年による); resignation (辞職) 一動 (…を)退職する retire《from》; resign《from》,《インフォーマル》quit work [one's job] ▶60歳で退職する *retire from one's job* [*business*] at the age of 60 ‖病気で退職する *quit* [*resign from*] *one's job* because of illness (➤ quit は自分の意志で, resign は何かやむをえない事情で退職するというニュアンスがある).

▶早期退職する *take early retirement* ‖退職する校長 an *outgoing* [*a leaving*] principal. ‖(大学を)退職した元教授 a *retired* professor ‖退職後の仕事を探す find a *post-retirement* job ‖退職年齢に達する reach *one's retirement age*.

✉ 私儀3月31日をもってXY銀行を退職いたしました I am writing to inform you that I *have retired from* XY Bank as of March 31. ➤ as of … は正式な日付に用いて,「…(日)現在, …(日)の時点で」の意.

‖退職金 retirement pay [benefits / money] (定年時の); termination pay (中途退職時の); a severance pay (解雇時の) ‖退職者 a retiree /rɪtàɪəríː/.

²たいしょく 大食 ▶彼は大食漢だ He is *a big eater* [*a glutton* / *a gourmand*]. (➤ glutton /glʌ́tn/ は軽蔑的) / He *eats like a horse*. (➤「馬のように食べる」の意).

³たいしょく 退[褪]色する fade ▶退色した壁紙 *faded* wallpaper.

たいしょこうしょ 大所高所 ▶問題を大所高所から判断する *judge* a problem *from a broad perspective* ‖年金制度を大所高所から見直す review the pension system *from a broad perspective* ‖政府はまず国防を大所高所から考えて, 沖縄の米軍基地問題に立ち向かうべきだと思う I think the government should first *take a broad view of* national defense, and then deal with the U.S. base issue in Okinawa.

たいしん 耐震の earthquake-resistant [-proof] ▶建物を耐震性のあるものにする make a building *earthquake-resistant* [*-proof*] ‖この高層ビルは耐震構造になっている This high-rise is *earthquake-resistant* [*-proof*].

‖耐震建築(物) an earthquake-resistant [-proof] building.

¹たいじん 対人 ▶彼女は対人関係がうまくいっていない Her *relationships with other people* aren't going well. / She has been having (some) problems in her *interpersonal relationships*. ‖彼女は対人恐怖症にかかっている She has *a phobia about meeting people*.

²たいじん 退陣 ▶彼らは首相の退陣(=辞職)を迫った They demanded the *resignation* of the prime minister.

だいじん 大臣 a minister, a secretary, a chancellor ▶外務大臣 the *Minister* of Foreign Affairs, the Foreign Minister (➤ 前者が正式名称) ‖経済産業大臣 the *Minister* of Economy, Trade and Industry 一省 ‖(日本の)副大臣 the Senior Vice *Minister*.

> 【解説】(1) 日本や欧州諸国の大臣は minister, アメリカの大臣に相当する職は secretary と呼ばれる. secretary は日本では「長官」と訳している. 一方 minister はアメリカでは「(プロテスタントの)牧師」の意がふつう.
> (2) イギリスでは minister, secretary, chancellor の 3 通りの大臣がある. ただし chancellor は the Chancellor of the Exchequer (大蔵大臣)のみ.

だいしんさい 大震災 a **great earthquake** ▶東日本[阪神・淡路]大震災 the *Great* East Japan [Hanshin(-Awaji)] *Earthquake*.

だいじんぶつ 大人物 a **great person** [**figure**] ▶青年の頃から彼にはすでに大人物の風格があった There was *something great* about him (even) when he was a young man.

だいず 大豆 a **soybean**
‖**大豆油** soybean oil ‖ **大豆畑** a soybean field.

たいすい 耐水の **water-resistant**; **watertight** (水を通さない) ▶この時計は耐水だが完全な防水ではない This watch is *water-resistant*, but not waterproof.

たいすう 対数 《数学》 a **logarithm.**

だいすう 代数 **algebra** /ǽldʒɪbrə/.

だいすき 大好きな **favorite** (いちばん気に入っている) ▶私の大好きな歌手[科目] my *favorite* singer [subject].

> 【文型】
> 人・物など(A)が大好きだ
> like A very much
> be very fond of A
> love A

▶私, あの人が大好き I *like* him *very much*. ／I *really like* him. ‖ 彼女は動物が大好きだ She's *very fond of* animals. ／She *loves* animals. (➤ love は主に女性が好む語) ‖ 智史は友達とサッカーをするのが大好きだ Satoshi *loves* playing soccer with his friends. ‖ 父は甘い物が大好きです My father *loves* sweets. ／My father has a sweet tooth. (➤ have a sweet tooth は「甘い物に目がない」の意のインフォーマルな言い方) ‖ 姉は野球が大好きだ My sister *is a great* [*huge*] baseball *fan*. ‖ 孝夫は車が大好きだ(＝車に夢中だ) Takao *is crazy* [《英》 *mad*] *about* cars.

たいする 対する **1**【応じた】**to, for** (➤ 前者は何かへの反応を, 後者は何かへの準備を表す) ▶きみの言ったことは私の質問に対する答えになっていない You are not answering my question. ／What you said is not an answer *to* my question. (● 前者の言い方がよりふつう).
▶地震に対する備えは万全ですか Are you prepared *for* an earthquake? ‖ この問題に対する(＝関する)あなたの考えを聞かせてください Could you tell us your views *concerning* this issue? →対して.
2【応対する】▶来賓の方に対するときは礼儀正しくしなさい Show good manners *to* guests.

[1]**たいせい 体制** a **system** (組織); **the establishment** (確立された権力機構; しばしば大文字で書かれる) ▶共産主義体制 a communistic *system* ‖ アメリカと中国とでは政治体制が異なる The U.S. and China have different *political systems*.
‖**反体制運動** anti-Establishment movement ‖ **反体制派** an anti-Establishment group; dissidents (➤ dissident は「反体制活動家」).

[2]**たいせい 体勢** a **position** (姿勢); a **footing** (足場) ▶あの体勢からシュートするのは難しい To shoot from such *a position* is difficult. ‖ 彼は体勢を立て直して一塁へ送球した He regained his *footing* and threw the ball to first.

[3]**たいせい 態勢** ▶飛行機は着陸の態勢に入った The airplane *prepared* to land. ‖ 選手団を受け入れる態勢は整った We *are prepared to* welcome the players.

[4]**たいせい 大勢** a **current** (一般的な流れ, 動向); a **trend** (主流的な傾向); **the general situation** (全体の形勢) ▶(世の)大勢に逆らう swim against *the current* (*of the times*) ‖ 試合の前半でほぼ大勢が決まった The *trend* was just about set in the first half of the game. ‖ 現在までのところ大勢に変化はない There has been no change in *the general situation* so far.

[5]**たいせい 大成する** **succeed** (成功する) ▶彼は後年, 画家として大成した He *achieved great success as an artist* [*became a great artist*] in his later years.

[6]**たいせい 耐性** **tolerance**; **resistance** (抵抗力) 一形 **耐性の** **resistant** ▶抗生物質に対する耐性 *resistance* to antibiotics ‖ サボテンは干ばつに対して耐性がある Cactuses *are tolerant* of drought. ／Cactuses *tolerate* droughts.
‖**耐性菌** drug-[antibiotic-] resistant bacteria (➤ 後者は「抗生物質への耐性の」の意).

[7]**たいせい 胎生** ▶胎生期に *during fetal life*.

たいせいよう 大西洋 **the Atlantic, the Atlantic Ocean** ▶大西洋を船で横断する cross *the Atlantic* by ship
‖**北大西洋条約機構** the North Atlantic Treaty Organization 《略 NATO》.

[1]**たいせき 体積** (**cubic**) **volume** ▶この球の体積はいくらか What is the *volume* of this sphere? ‖ この箱の体積は 1 立方メートルだ This box has a *volume* of one cubic meter.

[2]**たいせき 退席する** **leave** (one's **seat**) ▶すみませんが, 急用を思い出しましたので退席させていただきます Excuse me, but I've just remembered some urgent business and must *leave* (*my seat*).

[3]**たいせき 堆積** (an) **accumulation, sedimentation** (➤ 後者は地質学用語); a **pile** (物の積み重ね) 一動 **堆積する** **accumulate, pile up** ▶その都市では道路に石炭の粉塵(ふんじん)が堆積している The streets in the city *have huge piles* of coal dust on them. ‖ 三角州は河口に土砂が堆積してできる Deltas are formed when dirt and gravel *pile up* at the mouths of rivers.
‖**堆積岩** a sedimentary rock ‖ **堆積物** sediment, a deposit /dɪpάːzət/.

たいせつ 大切

一形 **大切な** **important** (重要な); **precious** (金銭では得られないほど); **valuable** (価値のある); **dear** (心から大切に思う) 一副 **大切に** **carefully** (注意深く)
▶大切な文書 an *important* document ‖ 彼女はぼくにとっていちばん大切な人です She's the most *important* [*dearest*] person to me. ‖ この文書には非常に大切なことが書かれている Matters *of great importance* are written in this document. (➤ of importance は堅い言い方) ‖ このビートルズのレコードは私の大切な宝物の 1 つです This Beatles record is one of my most *precious* possessions. ‖ 大切なものはロッカーに入れてください Please put *valuables* in the locker. (➤ valuables は複数形で「貴重品」) ‖ 問題文を丁寧に読んで筆者の主張をつかむことが大切だ

What's important [*What counts most*] is that you read the passage carefully and grasp the author's point.

▶教師が授業中に生徒を励ますことは**大切なことだ** *It is important that* teachers encourage (their) students during class. ／*It is important* for teachers *to* encourage (their) students during class.

▶《図書館で》本は**大切に**扱ってください Please handle books *carefully* [*with care*]. ‖ 両親を**大切に**しなさい You should *take good care of* your parents. (➤「よく世話をする」の意) ／*Be nice* [*good*] *to* your parents. (➤「優しくする, よくする」の意) ‖ これは私が**大切に**している写真です These are photos I *treasure*. (➤ treasure は「珍重する」) ‖ 水は**大切に**(＝無駄のないように)使いましょう Let's use water *sparingly*. ／Let's not waste water.

✉ **あなたからのプレゼント大切にします** I will *treasure* your present. ／I will *cherish* your gift. (➤ 後者は堅い言い方).

[1]**たいせん 大戦** a **great war**(大きな戦争)；a **world war** (世界大戦) ▶第二次**世界大戦** *World War* II (➤ II は two と読む. the はつかない) ／the Second *World War*.

[2]**たいせん 対戦する** **play**(＋目)；**have a game** [**match**] 《with》(試合をする)；**fight** 《with, against》(格闘技で) ▶ぼくたちは甲子園球場で松山商業と**対戦した** We *played* (*against*) Matsuyama Commercial High at Koshien Stadium. ‖ 彼らは来週中国チームと決勝で**対戦する** They will *have a game with* the Chinese team in the final next week. ‖ チャンピオンは金曜の夜に強敵と**対戦する** The champion will *fight* (*with*) a powerful rival this Friday night.

‖ **対戦相手** an opponent.

だいぜんてい 大前提 **the major premise** /prémɪs/ ▶わが国は天然資源に乏しいということがこの議論の**大前提**である The fact that our country has few natural resources is *the major premise* of this discussion.

[1]**たいそう 体操** **gymnastics** /dʒɪmnǽstɪks/, 《インフォーマル》**gym** (体操競技)；**exercises** (体を動かすこと)；**physical education** (教科としての「体育」；P.E. または PE と略すことが多い) ▶**ラジオ体操**をする do *exercises along with the radio* (➤ 英米には「ラジオ体操」はない) ‖ 彼は**器械体操**が得意だ He is good at *apparatus gymnastics*.

▶《慣用表現》このクイズは大いに**頭の体操**になる This quiz is effective in *exercising your brain*.

‖ **体操着** a gym suit ‖ **体操選手** a gymnast ‖ **体操用具** (a) gymnastic apparatus.

> 「体操競技」のいろいろ **あん馬** pommel [side] horse ／**段違い平行棒** uneven bars ／**跳馬** long horse ／**つり輪** rings ／**鉄棒** horizontal bar, the high bar ／**平均台** balance beam ／**平行棒** parallel bars ／**床運動** floor exercise

[2]**たいそう 大層** ▶娘さんは**大層**お出来になるそうですね I hear your daughter is doing *extremely* well. ‖ 彼は**大層**な金持ちだ He's a man of *considerable* [*enormous*] wealth. ‖ **大層なことを言う**(＝誇張する)な *Don't exaggerate*.

だいそう 代走 a **pinch runner**(代走者).

だいそつ 大卒 a **college** [**university**] **graduate** /grǽdʒuət/ (大卒者)；a **college** [**university**] **degree** (資格) ▶妹は**大卒です** My (younger) sister *is a college graduate*. / My (younger) sister *has a college* [*university*] *degree*. ‖ ことしは金融業界を志望する**大卒女子**が増えた The number of *female college graduates* hoping to get a job in the financial industry has increased this year.

だいそれた 大それた ▶彼らは世界の主峰をすべて征服しようという**大それた**望みを抱いている They have a *wild* ambition to conquer all the great mountains of the world. ‖ あの小心者にそんな**大それた**ことができるはずがない There is no way that coward could do such an *audacious* thing.

たいだ 怠惰な **lazy**(やる気がない)；**idle** /áɪdl/ (何もしていない, ぶらぶらしている) ▶**怠惰な**人 a *lazy* person ／a lazybones ‖ 彼女は依然**怠惰な**生活を送っている She is still leading an *idle* [*a lazy*] life.

だいだ 代打 a **pinch hitter**(代打者) ▶彼は投手の**代打**に出てホームランを打った *Pinch-hitting* for the pitcher, he belted a home run.

‖ **代打満塁ホームラン** a pinch-hit bases-loaded home run.

[1]**だいたい 大体** **1【おおよそ】** **about**；**almost** (もう少しで)；**generally** (たいてい)；**roughly** (大ざっぱに言って)；**more or less** (ほとんど；否定的意味合いで用いられることが多い) ▶私のクラスでは毎年**大体**20人が国立大学を志望する *About* 20 students in my class apply to national universities every year. ‖ 私は父と**大体**同じくらいの背丈だ I am *about* the same height as my father. ‖ 宿題は**大体**終わった I am *almost* finished with my homework. (➤ almost は「もう少しで(…する)」を表すので「もう少しで出来上がる」の意.「大体」はむしろ完了した大部分のほうに視点がある) ‖ 私は**大体**(いつも)したいことをさせてもらっている I am *almost always* allowed to do what I want. ‖ この学校の生徒は**大体**中流家庭の出だ Students in this school are *mostly* middle-class. ‖ その火事による損害は**大体** 4 千万円見当だ The loss from the fire is *roughly* estimated at forty million yen. ‖ 《話し終わって》**大体**こんなところです *That's about it*. ‖ 報告書は**大体**完成した I've *more or less* completed my report. ‖ **対話**「試験はどうだった?」「**大体**できたよ」"How was your test?" "I answered *most* of the questions."

2【そもそも】 ▶**大体**この計画は初めからずさんだった This plan was not well thought out *in the first place*. ‖ **大体**前提からして間違っていた We started with a false premise.

[2]**だいたい 代替の** **alternative**

‖ **代替医療** alternative medicine ‖ **代替エネルギー** alternative energy ‖ **代替燃料** an alternative fuel ‖ **代替品** a substitute.

[1]**だいだい 橙** 《植物》a **bitter orange** /ɔ́ːrɪndʒ/ 《参考》sour orange とすると「(腐って)酸っぱくなったオレンジ」ととられる可能性がある ▶**ダイダイ色の**スーツ an *orange-colored* suit.

[2]**だいだい 代々** **for generations**(何代にもわたって) ▶あの家は**代々**医者だ They have been doctors *for generations*. ／Being a doctor runs in the family.

だいたいこつ 大腿骨 a [one's] **thigh** /θaɪ/ **bone**, 《解剖学》**femur** /fíːməʳ/ [複 **femora**].

だいだいてき 大々的 ▶ＸＹ社は新製品を**大々的に**宣伝したXY Company advertised its new product *extensively* [*on a large scale* ／*in a big way*]. (➤ in a big way はインフォーマルな表現) ‖ 各紙がその大震災を**大々的に**取り上げた All newspapers *covered* the great earthquake *extensively*.

だいたいぶ 大腿部 the [one's] **thigh** /θaɪ/.

だいたすう 大多数 the majority ▶その案は大多数の賛成を得た *The* (*great*) *majority* of people were [was] for the plan. ‖ マラソン大会は参加者の大多数が完走した The *vast* [*great*] *majority* of the participants in the marathon completed the course.

[1]**たいだん 対談** a talk ; an interview (会見) ▶評論家は作家と2時間対談した The reviewer *had a* two-hour *talk with* the writer [*talked with* the writer for two hours]. ‖ 首相は記者団と対談した The Prime Minister *gave an interview* to the press corps.

‖**対談番組** a talk [chat] show.

[2]**たいだん 退団する** leave +目 ▶劇団「四季」を退団する *leave* the theatre troupe "Shiki."

だいたん 大胆な bold ; daring /déərɪŋ/ (向こう見ずな) ▶大胆な計画 a *bold* plan ‖ 独りで敵地に乗り込んで来るとは大胆不敵なやつだ He's a *daring* [*bold*] man to have entered the enemy territory alone.

▶大胆なデザインの服 a dress with a *bold* design.

[1]**だいち 大地** the ground ; the earth (天に対する地) ▶大地は一面雪に覆われていた *The ground* was completely covered with snow. ‖ 母なる大地 *Mother Earth.*

[2]**だいち 台地** a plateau /plætóʊ/, a tableland (➤ 前者はフランス語起源).

[1]**たいちょう 体調** (physical) condition, shape ▶体調が悪いのできょうは休ませていただきます *I'm not feeling well*, so I will be absent today. ‖ 私は今体調を崩している I'm *in bad condition* [*shape*] now. ‖ 運動選手はいつも体調を整えておく必要がある Athletes should always *keep themselves in good shape* [*in good condition*]. ‖ 体調はどう? *How's your health?* / *How are you feeling?*

[2]**たいちょう 隊長** a captain ; a leader (指揮者) ; a commander (司令官) ▶隊長! 全員そろいました *Captain*, we're all present. ‖ 彼は探検隊の隊長として活躍した He played an active part as (*a*) *leader* of an expeditionary party. (● 隊が複数あってその1人なら不定冠詞は省略しない).

[3]**たいちょう 体長** length /leŋkθ/ ▶そのミミズは体長が15センチあった The *length* of that earthworm was fifteen centimeters.

[1]**だいちょう 大腸** the large intestine /ɪntéstɪn/

‖**大腸炎** colitis /kəláɪṭɪs/ ‖ **大腸がん** colon cancer (結腸がん) ‖ **大腸菌** a colon [coliform] bacillus /bəsíləs/, E. coli bacteria (➤ colon は「結腸」.「大腸菌O157はE. coli O 157」) ‖ **大腸ポリープ** a colon polyp (結腸ポリープ).

[2]**だいちょう 台帳** a ledger(元帳) ; a register(名簿, 登録簿).

タイツ (a pair of) tights (➤ 複数扱い) ; a leotard /lí:ətɑ:ʳd/ (レオタード).

たいてい 大抵 usually, generally (一般に ; 後者は前者よりややくだけた語) ; mostly (大部分は) 一形 **たいていの** most ▶私はたいてい7時に朝食をとる I *usually* have (my) breakfast at seven. ‖ 最近の若者はたいてい親より背が高い Today's young people are *generally* [*mostly*] taller than their parents.

▶この学校ではたいていの(=ほとんどの)生徒が歩いて登校する *Almost all* [*Nearly all*] (*of*) the students at this school walk to school. (➤ almost は副詞なので (×)almost students とはしない.「過半数より多い」の意を漠然と示すのなら Most (of the) students ... とする) ‖ たいていの日本人は毎日風呂に入る *Most* Japanese take a bath every day. ‖ 彼が(オフィスなどに)いてよかったね. たいていは外出してるわ You're lucky to find him in. He's out *most of the time.*

たいてき 大敵 a great [powerful] enemy ; a great rival (競争者) ▶赤潮は漁業にとって大敵である Red tides are *a great enemy* of the fishing industry.

タイト tight ▶今週はスケジュールがタイトだ I have a *tight* schedule this week.

‖**タイトスカート** a tight skirt.

たいど 態度 1【動作・表情など】a manner ; an attitude /ǽṭətju:d/ (姿勢) ; behavior (ふるまい) ▶あの人の横柄な態度が気に入りません I don't like his arrogant *manner*. ‖ トニーは授業中の態度が悪いのでよく叱られる Tony is often scolded for his bad *attitude* [*behavior*] in class. ‖ 《相手の反抗的な様子をとがめて》何だ, その態度は! Who do you think you are! (➤「自分を何様だと思っているのか」の意).

▶市役所の窓口のおじさんは美人が来るところりと態度を変える The man at the counter in city hall changes his *attitude* completely when a pretty girl comes in. ‖ 彼は部長に対して反抗的な態度をとった He took *a defiant attitude* toward his manager. ‖ おまえは大して実力もないのに態度がでかいよ *You sure act big* for someone with so [such] little skill.

2【心構え】an attitude ; a stance(立場) ▶生活態度を改める change *one's attitude toward life* ‖ アメリカは貿易問題で中国に対して強硬な態度をとった The United States took *a firm stance* toward China on trade issues. (●「柔軟な態度」は flexible [accommodating] stance) ‖ あすまでにきみの態度を決めてほしい I want you to decide *how* [*where*] *you stand* by tomorrow. (➤ この stand は「(反対か賛成かの)態度をとる」)

[1]**たいとう 対等の** equal /í:kwəl/ ▶彼とぼくは腕力の点では対等だ He and I *are equal* in physical strength. ‖ 彼女は自分の子も他人の子も対等に扱う She treats her children and other children *equally*. ‖ 私はきみたちと対等の立場で話をしたい I want to talk to you *on an equal footing* [*on the same footing*].

[2]**たいとう 台頭** ▶世界における中国の台頭 the *rise* of China worldwide ‖ 大リーグではアジア出身の選手の台頭が目覚ましい Many players from Asia have begun to *make their presence felt* in the Major Leagues. (➤「存在感が増し始めている」の意).

だいどうげいにん 大道芸人 a street performer, 《英また》a (street) busker.

だいどうしょうい 大同小異 ▶候補者たちの政策は大同小異だ The candidates' policies *are essentially the same* [*are much alike*].

だいどうみゃく 大動脈 a main artery /ɑ́:ʳṭəri/, an aorta /eɪɔ́:ʳṭə/ ▶東名高速は日本の大動脈の1つだ The Tomei Expressway functions as one of Japan's *main arteries of transportation.*

だいとうりょう 大統領 a president (共和国の元首) ▶ジョー・バイデンはアメリカ合衆国第46代の大統領だ Joe Biden is the 46th *President* of the U.S.A. 語法 (1)特定の国の大統領を示す場合は大文字で始める. (2)呼びかけるときは Mr. [Madame] President! という.

‖**大統領官邸** the Presidential residence ; the White House (アメリカの) (➤ /hwáɪt haʊs/ と発音す

る. 第1アクセントが White にあることに注意) ‖ **大統領候補** a presidential candidate ‖ **大統領選挙** the presidential election ‖ **大統領夫人** the President's wife, 《米》 the First Lady ‖ **副大統領** a vice-president.

たいとく 体得 ▶彼は自動車修理の技術を3年で**体得**した He *mastered* auto repair skills through three years of work experience.

だいどく 代読する **read (a message) for [on behalf of] someone** ▶大使が天皇のおことばを**代読した** The ambassador *read out* a message from the Emperor [*on behalf of* the Emperor].

‖**代読サービス** reading service (for blind persons).

た

だいどころ 台所 a **kitchen** ▶**台所仕事**をする do *kitchen work* / work in the kitchen.

▶《慣用表現》わが家は今**台所が苦しい** Our *family finances are tight* now.

‖**台所用品** kitchen utensils /juténsəlz/, kitchenware.

「台所用品」のいろいろ **IH調理器** induction cooker / **圧力釜** pressure cooker / **泡立て器** whisk / **大さじ** tablespoon / **オーブン** oven / **オーブントースター** toaster oven / **おたま** ladle / **おろし金** grater / **缶切り** can opener / **キャセロール** casserole / **串** skewer / **計量カップ** measuring cup / **小さじ** teaspoon / **こし器** strainer / **コルク抜き** corkscrew / **こんろ** stove / **皿** dish, plate / **シチュー鍋** stew pot / **ジューサー** juicer / **タイマー** timer / **茶こし** strainer / **中華鍋** wok / **電子レンジ** microwave oven / **トースター** toaster / **鍋** pan, pot / **箸** chopsticks / **フードプロセッサー** food processor / **フライ返し** turner / **フライパン** frying pan, skillet / **ふるい** sieve / **ペーパータオル** paper towel / **包丁** kitchen knife / **まな板** cutting [chopping] board / **ミキサー** blender / **蒸し器** steamer / **麺棒** rolling pin / **やかん** kettle

タイトル **1**【題名】a **title** ▶その本の**タイトル**は何ですか What is the *title* of the book?

2【選手権】a **title**, a **championship** ▶**タイトル**を防衛する[失う] defend [lose] the *title* ‖ 彼はフライ級チャンピオンの**タイトル**を獲得した He gained [won] the *title* of flyweight champion.

‖**タイトルマッチ** a title match.

[1]**たいない 体内** ▶ダイオキシンは食物連鎖によって我々の**体内に入る** Dioxins *enter our* [*human*] *bodies* through the food chain. ‖ 3日過ぎても彼女の**体内時計**はまだロンドン時間だ Three days have passed, but her *biological clock* is still on London time.

[2]**たいない 胎内** **in the womb**

‖**胎内感染** prenatal infection.

だいなし 台無し ▶霜で作物が**台なしになった** The frost *ruined* the crops. / The crops *were ruined* by the frost. ‖ 雨で桜が**台なしになった** All the cherry blossoms have *been spoiled* by the rain. (➤ spoil は「損なう」) ‖ あの新しいビルは景観を**台なしにしている** That new building is *an eyesore* on the landscape [cityscape]. (➤ eyesore は「目ざわりなもの」) ‖ 不幸な結婚で彼女の一生は**台なしになってしまった** Her unfortunate marriage *has ruined* her life.

ダイナマイト **(a stick of) dynamite** /dáɪnəmaɪt/ ▶**ダイナマイト**で古いビルを爆破する use *dynamite* to blow up an old building.

ダイナミック **dynamic** /daɪnǽmɪk/ ▶**ダイナミックな演技** *dynamic* acting ‖ 北斎は押し寄せる波を**ダイナミックに**表現した Hokusai *dynamically* depicted the surging waves.

だいに 第二の **the [one's] second** ▶私の**第二の故郷** my *second* home (town) ‖ 父は会社の守衛として**第二の人生**に踏み出した My father started his *second* career as a company security guard.

たいにち 対日 ▶その国の**対日感情**は好転しつつある The nation's *feelings toward Japan* are [The nation's *sentiment toward Japan* is] changing for the better.

‖**対日関係** relations with Japan ‖ **対日貿易** trade with Japan.

[1]**たいにん 退任** **retirement** 一動 **退任する** **retire** (定年で) ; **resign** (辞職する) ▶**退任する**市長 an *outgoing* [*a leaving*] mayor ‖ 社長は**退任**を表明した The president announced his intention to *retire*.

[2]**たいにん 大任** a **heavy responsibility** ▶PTA 会長の**大任**をどうにか果たすことができた I managed to carry out my *heavy responsibilities* as (the) president of the PTA.

ダイニングキッチン → **かこみ記事**

> **危ないカタカナ語✸ ダイニングキッチン**
> dining room (食堂)と kitchen (台所)から作られた和製語. 日本語の「ダイニングキッチン」を表すには, 例えば kitchen with a dining area (食事をする場所のついた台所) とか, kitchen-cum-dining room (台所兼食堂)などとする. 英米では台所の一角で食事をする家庭も多い. → **エルディーケー**.

ダイニングルーム a **dining room.**

たいねつ 耐熱の **heatproof ; heat-resistant** (熱に強い)

‖**耐熱ガラス** heat-resistant glass.

だいの 大の **1**【非常な】**great** ▶ナポレオンは**大の**猫嫌いだった Napoleon was a *great* hater of cats. ‖ 私たちは**大の**仲よしだ We are *great friends*. ‖ 谷さんは**大の**ゴルフファンです Mr. Tani is an *avid* [*enthusiastic*] golf fan. (➤ avid /ǽvɪd/ は「熱心な」).

2【強調】▶その岩は**大の大人**が6人がかりで押してもびくともしなかった The rock wouldn't budge an inch even with six *fully grown adults* pushing it.

たいのう 滞納 ▶彼は2か月も家賃を**滞納している** His rent is two months *overdue*. / He is two months *behind* [*in arrears*] *with* the rent. (➤ in arrears は「滞って」) ‖ 彼は前期の授業料を**滞納している** He *is behind* on [in] his tuition payment(s) of the first semester.

‖**滞納金** arrears ‖ **税金滞納者** a tax delinquent [defaulter].

だいのう 大脳 **the cerebrum** /sərí:brəm/

‖**大脳皮質** the cerebral cortex.

だいのじ 大の字 ▶布団の上に**大の字になる** *lie* on the futon *with one's arms and legs stretched out* / *lie spread-eagled* on the futon.

たいは 大破 ▶衝突事故で彼の車は**大破した** His car *was greatly* [*badly*] *damaged* in the collision. / The collision *made a wreck* of his car.

ダイバー a **diver.**

[1]**たいはい 退廃・頽廃** **decadence** /dékədəns/ ▶**退廃的な映画** a *decadent* movie ‖ 今の社会は道徳的に**退廃している**ように思える Our (present) society seems (to *be*) morally *corrupt*.

[2]**たいはい 大敗** ▶うちのチームはB高校に**大敗を喫した**

Our team *was soundly defeated* by B High School.

たいばつ 体罰 corporal punishment ▶教師は生徒に体罰を加えてはいけないことになっている Teachers are not supposed to give *corporal* [*bodily*] *punishment* to their students.

たいはん 大半 most(半分より多い) ; almost all (ほとんどすべて) ; the greater part (半分以上) ▶この学校の生徒は卒業後大半が大学に行く *Most* students [*Most* of the students] in this school go to college after graduation. ‖参加者の大半は外国人だった The participants were *mostly* [*for the most part*] foreigners. ／*Almost all* (of) the participants were foreigners. ‖クラスの大半の者がインフルエンザにかかっている *Almost the entire* class has come down with the flu. ‖うちのおばあちゃんは１日の大半をテレビを見て過ごす My grandmother spends *most* [*the greater part*] of the day watching TV. ‖建築中のわが家は大半が完成した The construction of our new house is *nearly* completed.

たいばん 胎盤《解剖学》a placenta /pləséntə/ [複 placentas または placentae /plæsénti:/].

1**たいひ 対比** contrast /kɑ́:ntræst/ (対照, コントラスト) ; comparison (比較) 一動 (A と B を) 対比する compare《A with B》▶この画家は明と暗を巧みに対比させている This painter *contrasts* [*uses contrast* between] light and dark skillfully. ‖本年度の売り上げを昨年の実績と対比させてみましょう Let's *compare* the sales for this year *with* those from last year.

2**たいひ 堆肥** compost /kɑ́:mpoust/ ▶大きな堆肥の山 a large *compost* heap.

3**たいひ 退避** evacuation 一動 退避する evacuate, take shelter ▶津波警報が出て住民は高台に退避した People *evacuated* to higher ground after a tsunami warning was issued.

4**たいひ 待避** ▶貨物列車を待避させる *shunt* a freight train *into a siding* ／*leave* a freight train *in a siding*.

‖待避線 a siding, a sidetrack.

だいびき 代引き ▶代引きでお願いできますか Can I *pay cash on delivery*?

タイピスト a typist.

だいひつ 代筆 ▶ぼくは政雄にラブレターの代筆を頼まれた I was asked to *write* a love letter *for* Masao. ／Masao asked me to *write* a love letter *for* him.

たいびょう 大病 a serious illness ▶私は子供のとき大病をした When I was a child, I suffered from *a serious illness*.

だいひょう 代表 a representative /rèprɪzéntətɪv/ ; a delegate /déləgət/ (政治的な会議などの) 一動 代表する represent /rèprɪzént/ +目

▶光子は私たちのクラスの代表だ Mitsuko is the *representative* of our class. ‖彼女はオリンピック代表に選ばれた She was selected to go to the Olympics. ‖S 氏は日本の国連代表としてニューヨークへたった Mr. S left for New York as a Japanese *delegate* to the United Nations.

▶彼女はクラスを代表して生徒会に出席した She *represented* our class at the student council meeting. ‖父は一家を代表して謝辞を述べた My father offered a few words of thanks *on behalf of* my family. (➤ on behalf of は「…に代わって」) ‖彼は我々の課を代表するにふさわしい人物だ He is the best person to *head up* our section.

▶桜は日本の代表的な花です The cherry blossom is the *representative* flower of Japan. ‖この茶室は書院造りの代表的 (＝典型的) なものだ This tea-ceremony room is *typical of* Shoin-style architecture. ‖『金閣寺』は三島由紀夫の代表作だ "The Temple of the Golden Pavilion" is Mishima Yukio's *most famous work*.

‖代表権 representation power ‖代表団 a delegation, a representative body ‖代表電話 the main phone number ‖代表取締役 a representative director.

タイピン a tie pin ; a tie tack [tac] (留めびょう式の).

ダイビング diving ▶沖縄にダイビングしに行く go to Okinawa for *diving* [to *dive*].

▶《野球》青木はその飛球をダイビングキャッチした Aoki *snagged* the fly ball *with a diving catch*.

‖ダイビングスクール a diving school.

1**たいぶ 退部する** quit a club ▶彼はバスケット部を退部したいと思っている He intends to *quit* the basketball *club*.

2**たいぶ 大部** ▶大部な著作物 *a bulky book* ／*a tome* (➤ 後者は学術書や研究書を連想させる) ‖大部な (＝冊数の多い) 日記 *voluminous* diaries.

タイプ 1【型】 a type ▶芸術家タイプの人 an artistic *type* ‖このタイプのヘリコプター this *type* of helicopter ／a helicopter of this *type* (➤ 後者の言い方のほうが型が強調される) ‖桃子はぼくの好きなタイプじゃない Momoko is not *my type*. ‖ひろしはこつこつと地道に勉強するタイプではない Hiroshi is not the *type* to plug away at schoolwork. ‖あのタイプの男は女にもてるだろう That *type* of man is probably popular with women. ／He is the *type* girls like, I imagine. ‖久保田さんは重役タイプ (の人) だ Mr. Kubota is *the executive type*. ‖対話「今度, きみに吉田を紹介するよ」「悪いけどああいう人, タイプじゃないわ」"I'll introduce Yoshida to you next time." "No thanks. He is not (exactly) *my type*."

2【タイプライター】 a typewriter ▶私は１分間に50語タイプが打てる I *can type* 50 words a minute. ‖その手紙はタイプで打ってあった The letter *was typewritten*. ‖タイプミス a typo.

だいぶ 大分 very (とても) ; pretty (かなり) ▶映画が始まるまでまだだいぶ時間がある We still have *a lot of* time before the movie begins. ‖だいぶ疲れてるみたいだね You look *very* tired. ‖きょうはだいぶ気分がいい I feel *much* better today.

▶だいぶ待った? Have you waited *for a long time*? ‖ここから空港まではだいぶありますよ The airport is *pretty* far from here. ‖彼はだいぶ日本語がうまくなった His Japanese has improved *considerably*.

たいふう 台風 a typhoon /taɪfú:n/ ▶大型の台風が九州を襲った A big *typhoon* struck [hit] Kyushu. ‖強い台風が沖縄に接近している A powerful *typhoon* is approaching Okinawa. ‖台風10号が東シナ海で発生した *Typhoon No.10* originated in the East China Sea. ‖台風の目 [中心] the eye [center] of a typhoon.

《参考》(1) メキシコ湾・カリブ海方面の暴風雨は hurricane /hə́:rəkeɪn/, インド洋方面のものは cyclone /sáɪkloun/ という. (2) アメリカではハリケーンの発生順に男性名・女性名を交互につける.

だいふく 大福 *daifuku* ; a mochi [glutinous rice cake] stuffed with sweet bean paste (➤ 説明的

な訳).

だいぶつ 大仏 a **great** [**huge**] **statue of Buddha** /bú:də/ ▶奈良の大仏 the *Great Buddha* of Nara.

たいぶつレンズ 対物レンズ an **objective lens.**

だいぶぶん 大部分 **most**《of》(ほとんど); **the greater part**《of》(半分以上); **the majority**《of》(過半数)

【文型】
大部分の A
most A / **most of** A
the [**a**] **majority of** A
almost all (**of**) A

《解説》(1)あとに名詞が直接くるときは **most** A の形を使う. my や the などのついた名詞や us, them などの代名詞がくるときは most of A の形を使う.
(2)**most** (**of**) と **the majority of** は基本的には「50%より多い」の意で,「たいていの, 大半の」を表す.「100%に近い」の意を明確に表すには **almost all** や nearly all を使う. →ほとんど
(3)**almost** は「ほとんど」の意だが, むしろ「もう少しで」と解釈するとよい. 副詞なので直接, ふつうの名詞にはつけない.「当店の客は大部分が女性です」などというとき, (×) Our customers are *almost* women. とする誤りが多い. これでは「もう少しで一人前の女性たち」の意になってしまう. 数えられる名詞の前では *almost all* women のようにする.

▶**大部分の**日本人はアメリカ人に親しみを感じている *Most* Japanese feel friendly toward Americans. ‖ 現在は**大部分の**車が石油で動いている *Most* cars are powered by gasoline at present. ‖ アフリカ大陸の**大部分**は熱帯に属する *Most of* the African continent falls within the tropics. ‖ 私たちが食べるウナギは**大部分**が養殖ものだ *Most of* the eels we eat are farm-raised. ‖ 犯人は盗んだ金の**大部分**(=ほとんど全部)をすでに使ってしまっていた The criminal had already used up *almost all of* the stolen money. ‖ 本州の**大部分**は山だ *Most of* [*The greater part of*] Honshu is mountainous. (● the greater part of のあとにはふつう数えられない名詞がくる) ‖ 聴衆の**大部分**は女性だった *The majority of* the audience were women. (● the majority of は主に「人」に用いる).
▶私の考えは**大部分**彼の考えと一致する My views are *largely* [*mostly* / *for the most part*] in accord with his.

タイプミス a **typing error**; a **typo**(キーボードでのタイプミス).

タイプライター a **typewriter.**

たいへい 太平・泰平 ▶天下太平だ Peace reigns over the land. ‖ **太平**の世の中で, 人々の危機意識が薄れている *In these times of peace*, people have become insensitive to crises.

たいべい 対米 ▶その事件で日本人の**対米**感情が悪化した The incident caused *Japanese feelings* [*sentiment*] *toward the United States* to worsen. ‖ (日本の)**対米貿易** (Japanese) *trade with the United States* ‖ **対米輸出**を減らす reduce *exports to the United States*.

タイペイ 台北 **Taipei**(台湾の中心都市).

たいへいよう 太平洋 **the Pacific, the Pacific Ocean** ▶サンディエゴは**太平洋**沿岸にある San Diego is on *the coast of the Pacific*. ‖ きょうは(本州の)**太平洋側**はおおむね晴れるでしょう *The Pacific coast* will have mostly good weather today.
‖**太平洋戦争** the Pacific War ‖ **環太平洋** the Pacific Rim.

たいべつ 大別 ▶生物は動物と植物に**大別できる** Living things *can be classified* [*be divided*] *roughly* into animals and plants.

たいへん 大変 **1**【嘆かわしい】▶**大変な**(=恐ろしい)事件 a *terrible* accident ‖ きみは**大変な**(=ひどい)ことをしてくれたな You did an *awful* thing (to me).
▶**大変だ**! 津波が来る! *Oh my God* [*Oh, no*]! A tsunami is coming! ‖ 対話「お母さん, ガス止めた?」「あら, **大変**!」"Mom, did you turn off the gas?" "*Oh, no* [*Oh, dear*]!"

《解説》**「ああ, 大変だ」の言い方**
(1)緊急事態や驚くべき事件が発生した場合の「(それは)大変だ!」には **Oh my God, Oh God, Oh no, Oh my gosh, Oh my goodness** などを使う. ただし, Oh (my) God は神を汚すものとしてひどく嫌う人もいる. (2)軽い意味で「(それは)大変」という場合は **Oh no, Oh dear**(後者は女性的)などを用いるが, 話の内容によっては Oh, I'm sorry to hear that. や, That's too bad. なども「(それは)大変ですね」の意で用いられる. →しまった.

2【難しい】**hard, difficult** (➤ difficult のほうがやや堅い) ▶その大学に入るのは**大変だ** It is *hard* [*difficult*] to get into that university. ‖ そんなに夜遅くまで勉強とは**大変**ですね It must be *hard* [*tough*] to study until so late at night. ‖ この仕事は**大変だ** This job is *tough*. ‖ あれだけの家族を養っていくのは**大変なことだ** It is *no easy task* to support such a large family.

3【程度が甚だしい】▶縁日は**大変な**人出でにぎわった *A great many people turned out* [There was *a big turnout*] on the day of the festival. ‖ 北陸地方は**大変な**大雪に見舞われた There was *a terrible snowfall* in the Hokuriku district. ‖ 干ばつで米作は**大変な**(=深刻な)被害を受けた The drought *has severely damaged* the rice crop. ‖ 彼女は平均台の演技で**大変な**ミスをしてしまった She made *an awful mistake* during her performance on the balance beam. ‖ おふくろに見つかったら**大変だぞ** *There'll be hell to pay* if Mom finds out. (➤ hell to pay は「ひどくめんどうなこと」) ‖ 知事として務めるのは**大変な**責務である It's an *awesome* responsibility to serve as governor.

4【非常に】**very, very much** ▶楽しい一日を過ごさせていただき**大変**ありがとうございました Thank you *very much* for the wonderful day. ‖ その試合は**大変**いい試合だった It was an *extremely* exciting game. ‖ **大変**お世話になりました You've been *very* kind to me. / Thank you *very much* for everything. ‖ ご迷惑をおかけして**大変**申し訳ありません I'm *terribly* sorry for causing so much trouble.

だいへん 代返 ▶誰かが**代返**をしてくれないかなあ I wonder someone will *answer the roll in place of me* [*answer the roll call for me*].

1**だいべん 大便** **feces** /fí:si:z/, **excrement**; **stool(s)** (検便用の); a **bowel** /báuəl/ **movement**(便通; インフォーマルでは BM と略す) ▶**大便をする** *have a bowel movement* / *have a BM*. →うんち, くそ.

2**だいべん 代弁する** **speak for** ▶私の気持ちを日野君が**代弁してくれた** Mr. Hino *spoke for me*. / Mr. Hino *was my spokesman*.

1**たいほ 逮捕** (an) **arrest** 一動 **逮捕する** **arrest** +目 ▶その男は収賄の容疑で**逮捕された** The man *was ar-*

rested on a charge of accepting a bribe. ‖ 殺人犯はまだ**逮捕されていない** The murderer is still *at large*. (➤ at large は「逃げたままで」) ‖ 動くな，おまえを**逮捕する** Freeze ! *You are under arrest*.

‖**逮捕状** a warrant of arrest, an arrest warrant.

2**たいほ 退歩** **retrogression** ; **deterioration** (悪化) **一動** **退歩する** **retrogress, deteriorate.**

たいほう 大砲 a **gun** ; a **cannon** (旧式の) ▶**大砲**を撃つ fire [shoot] *a gun*.

1**たいぼう 待望の** **hoped-for** ; **long-awaited** (長らく待っていた) ▶**待望**の大型新人スター a *hoped-for* big new star ‖ **待望**の初舞台を踏む make one's *long-awaited* [*long-cherished*] debut on the stage ‖ 野田さんのところに**待望**の女の子が生まれた A *long-awaited* baby girl was born to the Noda family. ‖ 子供たちの**待望の** (＝楽しみにしていた) 夏休みが始まった The summer vacation the children *were eagerly looking forward to* [The children's *eagerly-awaited* summer vacation] has begun.

2**たいぼう 耐乏** **austerity** /ɔ:stérəṭi/ ▶**耐乏生活**を送る lead *an austere life*／lead *an austere way of life*.

たいぼく 大木 a **big** [an **enormous**] **tree** (➤ enormous は「びっくりするほど大きい」の意) ▶ケヤキの**大木** *a big* [*an enormous*] keyaki *tree*.

だいほん 台本 a **script** (脚本) ; a **scenario** /sənǽrioʊ/, a **screenplay** (映画の) ▶**台本**を書く write *a script*.

たいま 大麻 **hemp** (植物) ; **marijuana** /mæ̀rɪhwɑ́:nə/ (マリファナ ; 俗語では grass, pot などという) ▶**大麻**を吸う smoke *marijuana*.

タイマー a **timer,** a **time switch** ▶オーブンの**タイマー**を15分間にセットする set *the timer* on the oven for 15 minutes.

たいまい 大枚 ▶オペラのチケットを買うのに**大枚** 5 万円をはたいた I paid a *cool* fifty thousand yen [*to the tune of* fifty thousand yen] for an opera ticket. (➤ この cool は「たっぷりの」の意で金額を強調する).

たいまつ 松明 a **torch.**

たいまん 怠慢 **negligence** /néglɪdʒəns/ (不注意) ; **neglect** /nɪglékt/ (注意を怠って放置しておくこと) **一形** **怠慢な** **negligent** ▶当局の**怠慢**がこの事故を引き起こした *Negligence* on the authorities' part caused this accident. ‖ 彼は**職務怠慢**のかどで免職になった He was dismissed for *neglect of duty* [*professional negligence*].

だいみょう 大名 a *daimyo* ; a feudal lord (whose revenue was more than ten thousand *koku* of rice) (➤ 説明的な訳).

‖**大名行列** a *daimyo* procession ‖ **大名旅行** a junket (官費を利用しての観光旅行) ; a luxurious trip (ぜいたくな旅行).

タイミング **timing** ▶バス停に着くと**タイミング**よくバスが来た Just as I got to the bus stop, a bus came *with good* [*perfect*] *timing*. ‖ 肝心なのは**タイミング**だ The important thing is *timing*.

1**タイム 1**【**時間**】**time** ▶彼女は10秒78の**タイム**でゴールインした She crossed the finish line in [with] *a time* of 10.78 seconds. (➤ ten point seventy-eight と読む) ‖ 彼は初めてのマラソンで 2 時間10分の**好タイムを出した** He *posted a good time of* two hours and ten minutes in his first marathon. ‖ 日本チームは**タイムアップ**寸前に 1 点を追加した The Japanese team added one more point *right before the end of the game*.

▶このレストランは**ランチタイム**以外はすいている This restaurant is not crowded except for *lunch time*. ‖ 3 時から**30分間のタイムサービスを行います** We'll be offering *discount prices for 30 minutes*, starting at three o'clock.

2【**一時休止**】(a) **timeout** /tàɪmáʊt/ ▶**タイム** ! *Time out !* (試合中に作戦などのため)／*Just a moment*. (少し待ってください) ‖ 監督は審判に**タイム** (アウト) を要求した The manager called for *a timeout* to the umpire.

‖**タイムカプセル** a time capsule ‖ **タイムキーパー** a time keeper ‖ **タイムスイッチ** a time switch ‖ **タイムトライアル** a time trial ‖ **タイムマシン** a time machine.

2**タイム** 《植物》 (a) **thyme** /taɪm/ (➤ 香辛料のときは Ⓤ).

タイムカード a **time card,** a **time sheet** ▶**タイムカード**を押す punch *a time card*／clock in [out] (➤ out は退出するとき).

タイムリー ▶坂本は吉見の初球をたたいて同点**タイムリー**を放った Sakamoto jumped on Yoshimi's first pitch and tied the game with *a clutch RBI hit*. 《**参考**》 RBI は a run batted in (打点) の略. timely hit という言い方はあるが，あまりしない.

タイムレコーダー a **time clock,** a **time recorder** ▶**タイムレコーダー**で出勤時 [退社時] を**記録する** clock in [out]／punch in [out].

だいめい 題名 a **title** ; a **name** (名前) ▶『潮騒(しおさい)』という**題名**の本 a book with the *title*, "Sound of Waves"／a book *entitled* "Sound of Waves" ‖ 本に『希望の大地』という**題名を付ける** *title* the book "The Land of Hope."

だいめいし 代名詞 《文法》 a **pronoun** ▶関係 [疑問／指示／人称] **代名詞** a relative [an interrogative／a demonstrative／a personal] *pronoun*. ▶《比喩的》小野小町は美人の**代名詞**だ The name Ono-no Komachi is *synonymous* with "beautiful woman." (➤ be synonymous /sɪnɑ́:nəməs/ with は「…と同義の」の意)／Ono-no Komachi is *a symbol* of a beautiful woman.

1**たいめん 体面** **honor** /ɑ́:nə^r/ ▶先生は**体面**を保つために見え透いたうそを言った Our teacher told us a transparent lie to *save* (*his /her*) *face*. ‖ 両親は不仲だが**体面上**離婚しないでいる My parents are on bad terms, but *for appearances' sake* they have not divorced.

2**たいめん 対面する** **meet** +㊐ ▶**対面**交通の道路 a *two-way* road ‖ 20年ぶりで父と娘が**対面した** The father and his daughter *met* after twenty years' [a twenty-year] separation.

たいもう 体毛 **body hair** ▶**体毛が濃い** *be hairy* ‖ **体毛が薄い** have little *body hair*.

だいもく 題目 a **title** (絵・詩などの) ; a **topic** (議論・文章などの).

タイヤ 《米》 a **tire,** 《英》 a **tyre** ▶前 [後ろ] の**タイヤ** a front [rear] *tire* ‖ 空気の抜けた**タイヤ** a soft *tire* ‖ **タイヤ**がパンクした I had [got] a flat (*tire*). ‖ 自転車の**タイヤ**に空気を入れなくちゃ I have to pump up [put air in] the *tires* of my bicycle. (➤「…に空気を入れる」には inflate を用いてもよい).

‖**タイヤ痕** a skid mark ‖ **スタッドレスタイヤ** a studless tire ‖ **スパイク** [**スノー**] **タイヤ** a studded [snow] tire ‖ **スペアタイヤ** a spare tire.

ダイヤ 1【**鉄道の**】a (**train**) **schedule** /skédʒu:l ‖ ʃédju:l/ (列車の) ; a (**train**) **diagram** (運行図表) ▶首都圏の**ダイヤ**が乱れている *Train schedules* in the metropolitan area have been disrupted. ‖ 列車

た

はすべてダイヤどおりに運行している All (the) trains are running *on schedule*. ‖ 新幹線のダイヤは3月に改正された The *schedule* of the Shinkansen was revised in March. ‖ 大雪のため列車のダイヤ(＝運行)は混乱した A heavy snowfall disrupted *train schedules* [*service(s)*].

2【トランプの】a **diamond** /dáɪəmənd/ ▶ダイヤのエース the ace of *diamonds*.

☛ ダイヤモンド (→見出語)

たいやき 鯛焼き a ***taiyaki***; a fish-shaped pancake stuffed with sweet bean paste (➤ 説明的な訳).

[1]**たいやく 大役** an **important duty** ▶大役を仰せつかり恐縮しております I'm honored to have been charged with such *an important duty*.

[2]**たいやく 対訳** a **translation printed side by side with the original**.

だいやく 代役 a **substitute** /sʌ́bstɪtjuːt/ (代わりの人); a **stand-in** (映画などの); an **understudy** (補欠俳優) ▶彼女は主演女優が病気のため代役を務めた She acted as *a stand-in* for the leading actress who was ill. ‖ 彼女が私の代役として議長を務めた She *took my place* as chairperson.

ダイヤモンド 1【宝石の】a **diamond** ▶ダイヤモンドの指輪 a *diamond* ring ‖ 世界最大のダイヤモンドは3106カラットだ The world's largest *diamond* weighs 3,106 carats.

2【野球の】**the diamond** (➤ 時に球場全体も指す) ▶ダイヤモンドを1周する run around *the diamond*.

‖**ダイヤモンドダスト** diamond dust, ice crystals.

ダイヤル a **dial** ▶ダイヤルを回して104番に掛けたが話し中だった I *dialed* [*called*] 104, but the line was busy. ‖ あの国では大半のホテルはダイヤルイン方式です Most hotels in that country have *a direct dial system*. ‖ 《ラジオで》またあしたこの番組にダイヤルを合わせてくださいね Please *tune in to* our program again tomorrow.

☛ フリーダイヤル

たいよ 貸与する **lend** +⊞ ▶従業員には制服が会社から貸与されます Uniforms *are lent* to employees by the company. ‖ そのバイオリニストはJ財団から貸与されたアマーティを使用している The violinist uses an Amati *on loan* from the J Foundation.

[1]**たいよう 太陽** **the sun** 一形 **太陽の solar** ▶太陽は東から昇り西に沈む *The sun* rises in the east and sets in the west. ‖ 太陽が空に輝いている *The sun* is shining in the sky. ‖ 太陽がまぶしい The *sunlight* is really bright. ‖ あなたは私の太陽だ You are my *sunshine*. 《参考》太陽を描くとき日本の子供たちは通例赤色を用いるが, 英米の子供たちは通例黄色を用いる.

‖**太陽エネルギー** solar energy ‖ **太陽系** the solar system ‖ **太陽光発電所** a photovoltaic /fòʊṭoʊvɑ̀ːltéɪɪk/ power plant ‖ **太陽神** a sun god, a sun deity /díːəṭi/ ‖ **太陽電池** a solar cell [battery] ‖ **太陽熱発電所** a solar thermal power plant ‖ **太陽暦** the solar calendar.

[2]**たいよう 耐用** ▶この冷蔵庫の耐用年数は約10年です The *life* of this refrigerator is about ten years. / This refrigerator should last about ten years.

[3]**たいよう 大洋** **the ocean** ▶地球上には太平洋, 大西洋, インド洋, 南極海, 北極海の5つの大洋がある There are five *oceans* on (the) earth: the Pacific Ocean, the Atlantic Ocean, the Indian Ocean, the Southern Ocean, and the Arctic Ocean.

[4]**たいよう 大要** an **outline** (あらまし); a **summary** (まとめ); an **overview** (概観).

だいよう 代用する **substitute** /sʌ́bstɪtjuːt/ 《for》 (➤ substitute A for B で「AをBの代用にする, Bの代用にAを使う」) ▶マーガリンをバターの代用にする *substitute* margarine *for* butter ‖ 本箱が無かったので, こん包用の箱で代用した I didn't have a bookcase, so I *used* a couple of packing crates *as a substitute*. ‖ 父は厚い本を枕の代用にした My father *used* a thick book *as* a pillow.

‖**代用品** a substitute.

たいら 平らな **flat** (凸凹していない); **level** (水平な) ▶オランダは国土が平らだ The land is *flat* [*level*] in the Netherlands. ‖ ストーブは平らな所に置いてください Please place the heater on a *level* surface. ‖ 彼らは砂場を平らにならした They *leveled* the sandlot. ‖ 彼女はしわくちゃになった手紙を平らに伸ばした She *smoothed out* the crumpled letter.

▶人生は平らな(＝楽な)道ばかりではない Life is not always *smooth and easy*. / Life has its ups and downs.

たいらげる 平らげる **eat up**; **kill** +⊞ (酒を) ▶少年はポテトチップを1袋全部平らげた The boy *ate up* a bagful of potato chips.

だいり 代理 a **substitute**, an **agent**, a **deputy**

《解説》(1) substitute は「代役, 補欠」などの意味で用いる一般的な語. (2) agent はほかに代わって業務を遂行する人, deputy /dépjəṭi/ はほかの人に代わるよう任命された人.

▶係の者が休んでいますので, 代理の者を差し向けます The person in charge is not here so we will send *a deputy* [*someone in his place*]. ‖ 父の代理で葬儀に出席した I attended the funeral *in* my father's *place* [*on behalf of* my father]. ‖ 後藤氏は社長の代理で会議に出席した Mr. Goto *represented the president* at the conference. (➤ represent は「代理を務める」) / Mr. Goto attended the conference *for the president*. ‖ 担任の先生が病気なので鈴木先生がその代理をされた Mr. Suzuki *substituted for* our homeroom teacher who was sick. ‖ 副社長が社長の代理を務めた The vice-president served as *acting* president. (➤ acting は「代理の」).

‖**代理店** an agency; an agent (代理人) ‖ **代理母** a surrogate /sɚ́ːrəgət/ mother ‖ (自動車などの) **販売代理店** a dealer (shop) ‖ **旅行代理店** a travel agency [agent].

だいリーグ 大リーグ a **major** [**big**] **league**

‖**大リーガー** a major [big] leaguer.

たいりく 大陸 a **continent**; **the Continent** (ヨーロッパ大陸) ▶オーストラリア大陸 the Australian *continent* ‖ アジア大陸は世界で最も大きな大陸である Asia is the largest *continent* in the world. ‖ 大陸的な(＝小さなことにとらわれず, 度量の広い様子)考え方 an *expansive* way of thinking.

‖**大陸移動説** the theory of continental drift ‖ **大陸横断鉄道** a transcontinental railroad [《英》railway] ‖ **大陸性気候** a continental climate ‖ **大陸棚** a continental shelf ‖ **亜大陸** the subcontinent (➤ インド亜大陸は the Indian subcontinent).

だいりせき 大理石 marble ▶大理石のビーナス像 a *marble* statue of Venus ‖大理石を切り出す quarry *marble*.

たいりつ 対立 opposition ; a conflict /kɑ́:nflɪkt/ (衝突) 一動 **対立する** conflict /kənflɪ́kt/ 《with》 ▶産業廃棄物処分場の建設に関する賛成派と反対派の対立はますます深まっている *Conflict* is deepening between those supporting the construction of an industrial waste treatment plant and those opposing it. ‖ベルギーではフランス語系住民とオランダ語系住民が対立している In Belgium, the French-speaking and Dutch-speaking residents *are in conflict* [*are at loggerheads*]. ‖彼らの意見は全く対立している Their opinions *are* totally *against* [*opposed to*] *each other*. ‖彼らの政治的立場は我々とは対立するものだ Their political position *is opposite to* [*conflicts with*] ours. ‖彼女は前回の選挙で市長の対立候補だった She was the mayor's *opponent* in the last election.

1**たいりゅう 対流** convection (対流現象) ; convection currents (実際の流れ) ▶持ち運びのできるストーブをつけると対流によって部屋全体が暖まる When you turn on the portable heater, the entire room will warm up by *convection*.
‖対流圏 the troposphere /tróʊpəsfɪəʳ/.

2**たいりゅう 滞留** accumulation 一動 **滞留する** pile up ▶仕事が滞留しないようにしてください Keep your work from *piling up*.

1**たいりょう 大量の** large quantities of, a good [great] deal of (➤ あとの 2 例はややインフォーマルな言い方) ▶彼は自分で家を建てようと材木を大量に買い込んだ He bought lumber *in large quantities* to build a house by himself. ‖ジャンボジェット機は大量の貨物を輸送することができる Jumbo jets can transport *large quantities of* cargo. ‖サウジアラビアから大量の石油が輸入された *A great deal of* oil was imported from Saudi Arabia. ‖不況のためにその工場では従業員が大量解雇された *Many* employees were fired at the factory because of the recession.
‖大量殺りく (a) mass murder ‖大量生産 mass production ‖大量輸送システム a mass transit system.

2**たいりょう 大漁** a big [good] catch, a good haul ▶ことしはイワシが大漁だった *We had a big catch* [*a good haul*] of sardines this year.

たいりょく 体力 (physical) strength, stamina ▶体力をつける increase [build up] one's *strength* ‖毎朝のジョギングでだいぶ体力がついた I *have built up my strength* by jogging every morning. ‖私は近頃体力が衰えてきた My *physical strength* has recently declined. ／I have been getting weaker recently. ／ I don't have as much *stamina* as I used to. ‖彼は重労働に耐えるだけの体力がある He *is strong* enough to do hard labor. ‖彼女には手術に耐える体力がない She *doesn't have enough physical strength* to withstand the operation. ‖体力テスト a test of physical strength (and fitness).

タイル a tile ▶タイル張りの壁 a *tiled* wall.

ダイレクトメール direct mail (➤ 数えられない名詞なので a はつけない) ; an advertising letter (広告の手紙) ▶デパートからダイレクトメールが送られてきた I received *direct mail* from a department store. 《参考》しばしば開封しないでくず籠に捨てられることから, 受け取り手からは junk mail とも呼ばれる.

たいれつ 隊列 (a) formation ▶隊列を組んで行進する march *in formation*.

だいろっかん 第六感 a sixth sense ; a hunch /hʌntʃ/ (予感) ▶第六感が当たった My *sixth sense* worked well. ／My *hunch* proved right.

たいわ 対話 (a) dialog(ue) (劇中などの, または国どうしなどの) ; talks (国どうしの) 一動 **…と対話する** talk with ▶親子の対話 *dialog*(*ue*) [*communication*] between parents and children ‖市長はもっと市民との対話の場をもつべきだ The mayor should have more *dialog*(*ue*) with the public. (●「場」は訳出しなくてよい).

たいわん 台湾 Taiwan /tàɪwɑ́:n/ 一形 **台湾の** Taiwanese /tàɪwəní:z/ ‖台湾語 Taiwanese ‖台湾人 a Taiwanese [複 Taiwanese].

たうえ 田植え rice planting ▶今この辺りでは農家の人は田植えで忙しい The farmers around here are now busy *planting rice*.
‖田植え機 a rice-planting machine.

タウン a town ‖タウンウェア street clothes ‖タウン誌 a community magazine ‖タウン情報 information on things (going on) in town ‖タウンハウス a town house.

1**ダウン** **1【下がること】**▶2 学期は成績がダウンした My grades *fell* [*dropped*] during the second term.
2【倒れること】▶挑戦者は第 3 ラウンドでチャンピオンからカウント 8 のダウンを奪った The challenger *downed* [*floored*] the champ for an eight count in the third round. ‖母はかぜでダウンした Mom *came down with* a cold. ／Mom *took to her bed* with a cold. ‖私は疲労が重なってダウンした My fatigue accumulated and I *collapsed*.

> **危ないカタカナ語✹ ダウン**
> **1** 英語の down と一致する場合と, しない場合とがある. ボクシングの「ダウン」は一致する例で, 「彼は第 1 ラウンドでダウンした」は He was downed in the first round. と down を他動詞として使う. 同じ意味で be knocked down, be floored ともいう.
> **2**「成績がダウンする」というときの「ダウンする」には fall や drop を使う. また, 「かぜでダウンする」は come down with a cold という.
> **3**「イメージダウン」「コストダウン」などは和製語. それぞれ damage one's image, reduce [lower] the cost などとする必要がある. 「スピードダウン」「ペースダウン」はともに slow down となる.

2**ダウン** 《羽毛》 down
‖ダウンジャケット a down jacket.

ダウンしょう ダウン症 Down('s) syndrome
‖ダウン症児 a child with Down('s) syndrome.

ダウンロード download (+目) ▶このゲームソフトはインターネットでダウンロードした I *downloaded* this game software from the Internet. ‖このアプリは無料でダウンロードできる This app can *be downloaded* for free.

たえがたい 耐え難い intolerable, unbearable (➤ 前者は後者よりやや堅い語) ▶耐え難い苦痛 (an) *intolerable* [*unbearable*] pain ‖耐え難い寒さだった It was *unbearably* cold. ‖軍用機の騒音は多くの市民にとって耐え難いものだ The noise caused by military planes is *unbearable* to many people in the city.

だえき 唾液 saliva /səláɪvə/
‖唾液腺 salivary /sǽləveri/ glands.

たえしのぶ 耐え忍ぶ bear +目, endure +目 (➤ 後

者のほうが少しも屈せずに長い間耐え忍ぶというニュアンスが強い) ▶あらゆる苦難を耐え忍ぶ *endure* all hardships ‖ 彼女はその悲しみをじっと耐え忍んだ She *bore* the sorrow patiently. (➤ bore は bear の過去形).

たえず 絶えず always ; all the time (年がら年中) ▶彼女は絶えず人の悪口を言っている She is *always* saying bad things about others. ／She is badmouthing others *all the time*. (➤ 進行形とともに用いられた always, all the time, forever は「しょっちゅう」の意で, 通例不快な事柄に使う) ‖ 野村さんは絶えずぼやいている Mr. Nomura is *forever* griping. ／Mr. Nomura *never stops* complaining. ‖ 医学は絶えず(＝着実に)進歩している Medical science is progressing *steadily*. ‖ ファッションモデルの彼女は絶えずスタイルを保つ努力をしている As a model, she makes *constant* efforts to keep her figure.

たえだえ 絶え絶え ▶そのマラソン走者は息も絶え絶えに(＝あえぎながら)ゴールインした The marathon runner crossed the finish line *gasping for breath*.

たえなる 妙なる exquisite /ɪkskwízɪt, ékskwɪzɪt/ (絶妙な) ▶たえなる琴の音 the *exquisite* sound of a koto.

たえぬく 耐え抜く ▶海兵隊の訓練に耐え抜くには強い精神力が必要だ In order to *make it through* marine training, one must have strong willpower.

たえまなく 絶え間なく continuously ▶心臓は死ぬまで絶え間なく脈を打っている Our hearts beat *continuously* until we die. ‖ この1週間ばかり雨が絶え間なく降っている It has been raining *without (a) letup* for almost a week.

[1]**たえる 耐える・堪える** 1【我慢する】bear +㊐ (痛み・苦しみなどの重さに) ; stand +㊐ (自制心を働かせて) (➤ ともに通例否定文で用いる) ; endure +㊐ (長期の苦痛などに) ▶この暑さには耐えられない I *can't stand* [*bear*] this heat. ‖ 宇宙飛行士は孤独に耐えなければならない The astronaut must *endure* solitude. ‖ 彼女は上司のセクハラに耐えられず訴訟を起こした *Unable to bear* the sexual harassment from her boss, she filed a lawsuit against him.

▶《慣用表現》諸君の勝利の報に接し喜びに堪えません *I am truly delighted* to hear of your victory. ‖ あのサッカーの試合は退屈で見るに堪えなかった That soccer game was so boring I *couldn't bear to watch* it.

2【持ちこたえる】withstand +㊐, stand up to (➤ 後者はややインフォーマル) ; bear +㊐ (重い物を支える) ▶高温に耐えるビニール袋 plastic bags that *stand up to* high temperature ‖ この金庫は高熱に耐えられる This safe *is heat-resistant*. (➤「耐熱構造である」の意) ‖ 深海魚は大きな水圧に耐えられる Deep-sea fish *are able to withstand* great water pressure. ‖ この椅子, 私の重みに耐えられるだろうか? Will this chair *bear* my weight? ‖ その堤防は洪水に耐えられなかった The levee was unable to *hold back* the flood. (➤ hold back は「食い止める」).

3【価値がある, 可能である】▶この本は一読に堪える内容がある The book *is worth reading*. ‖ 日本ではまだ使用に堪える洗濯機やテレビなどが簡単に処分されている In Japan, washing machines, televisions and other things that are *still usable* are thrown away without a second thought. (➤ without a second thought は「よく考えないで」の意) ‖ 彼なら十分に委員長の任に堪えられるだろう He will *be fully able to perform* the chairman's duties.

[2]**たえる 絶える** 1【途絶える, やむ】▶山崩れで食糧の供給が絶えた The supply of food *was cut off* by the landslide. ‖ 彼女の消息が絶えてから久しい It's been a long time since we *lost* contact with her. ‖ 2人の間ではもめ事が絶えない There are *constant* troubles between the two. ／They have *no end* of troubles. ‖ わが家は笑い声が絶えない My home is *always* filled with laughter.

2【滅びる】die out ▶私の代でわが家の家名は絶える Our family name will *die out* in my generation.

だえん 楕円 an oval, an ellipse /ɪlíps/ (➤ 後者は専門語) ▶だ円形の長テーブル a long *oval* table ‖ ラグビーのボールがなぜだ円形なのか知っていますか Do you know why a rugby ball is *oval*?

たおす 倒す 1【立っている物を】cut down (切り倒す) ; blow down (吹き倒す) ▶木を切り倒す *cut down* a tree ‖ 強風で垣根が倒された The fences *were blown* [*were knocked*] *down* by the strong wind.

2【負かす, 滅ぼす, 殺す】throw down (投げ倒す) ; knock down (打ち倒す) ▶柔道を身につければ自分よりずっと大きな人を倒すことができる If you master judo, you can *throw down* a man who is far bigger than you. ‖ それまで無名だったボクサーが世界チャンピオンを倒した A boxer unknown up to then *knocked down* the world champion. ‖ 彼らはついにみごと独裁政権を倒した They finally succeeded in *overthrowing* the dictatorship.

タオル a towel /táʊəl/ (体を拭くための) ; a washcloth, a facecloth (体を洗うための) ▶タオルで体を拭きなさい Dry yourself with *a towel*.

‖タオル掛け《主に米》a towel rack,《主に英》a towel rail ; a towel ring (リング状の) ‖ バスタオル a bath towel. (→手拭い).

たおれこむ 倒れ込む collapse《into》▶ベッドに倒れ込む *collapse* [*flop*] *into* bed.

たおれる 倒れる 1【立っていた物が横になる】fall ; topple (バランスを失って) ; collapse (崩れる) ▶嵐で多くの木が倒れた Many trees *fell* in the storm. (➤ fell は fall の過去形) ‖ 強風で桜の木が何本か倒れた Some cherry trees *were knocked down* [*were blown down*] by the strong wind. (➤ 後者の blown は blow の過去分詞で,「吹き倒された」の意) ‖ 突風でクレーン車が倒れた A crane truck *toppled* in a sudden gust of wind. ‖ たんすが倒れないように壁に固定しておきなさい Fix the chest of drawers to the wall so that it doesn't *fall over*. ‖ この塀は倒れそうだから注意しなさい Be careful! This wall looks as though it might *collapse*. ‖ 難民たちは今にも倒れそうな小屋に住んでいる Refugees live in *ramshackle* shacks. ‖ 彼女は雪の上にあおむけに倒れた She *fell back* in(to) [on(to)] the snow. ／She *fell on her back* in(to) [on(to)] the snow. (雪に沈む場合 in または into を使う).

2【病気になる, 死ぬ】collapse (卒倒する) ; fall ill (病気になる) ; break down (ダウンする) ▶小谷先生は授業中に倒れた Mr. Kotani *collapsed* during class. ‖ 彼女は過労で倒れた(＝病気になった) She *fell ill* [*got sick*／*collapsed*] from overwork. ‖ メアリーはインフルエンザで倒れた Mary *came down* with the flu. ‖ 彼女は白血病に倒れた She *was stricken* by leukemia. ／She *fell victim* to leukemia. ‖ ジョン・F・ケネディは1963年凶弾に倒れた John F. Kennedy *was shot to death* in 1963. ‖ おなかがすいて倒れ(＝卒倒し)そうだわ

I'm so hungry (that) I think I'm going to *faint*.
3【組織が無くなる】▶S建設は多額の借金を抱えて**倒れた** S Construction Company *went under* after incurring its huge debts. (➤ go under は「倒産する」の意のインフォーマルな言い方) ‖ その国の政府は革命軍の攻撃によって**倒れた** The nation's government *was toppled* by the revolutionary army. (➤ topple は「(政府などを)倒す」).

[1]**たか 鷹**《鳥》a **hawk**; a **falcon**(狩猟用の) ▶**タカ狩りをする** hunt with *falcons*.
‖**たか匠** a falconer ‖ **鷹の爪**《植物》(a) cayenne /keɪén, kaɪ-/ pepper (トウガラシ).
☞ **タカ派** (→見出語)

[2]**たか 高** ▶彼は入試には受かるものと**たかをくくっている**(＝楽観している) He *is very optimistic about* passing the entrance exam. ‖ 易しい問題だと思って**たかをくくら**(＝軽視し)ないほうがいいよ Don't *make light of it* thinking it's an easy problem. ‖ 宇宙の広大さに比べたら人間が探査できる範囲など**たかが知れている** Compared with the vastness of the universe, the range humans can explore *is limited*.

たが 箍 a **hoop** ▶彼は**たがが緩んできた** He *has lost his tenacity*. ／ He *has become lax*. ‖ 近頃部員の**たがが緩んできている** *Discipline* among the team members *has become lax* recently. ‖ ここ数か月のその問題に対するテレビ報道の傾向は**たがははずれている**としか思えない The recent television reporting on that issue during the last few months can only be said to be *out of control*.

だが **but**; **though**, **although** (➤ 後者はやや堅い語) ▶彼は頭がいい. **だが**人間味に欠ける He is bright, *but* (too) impersonal. ／ *Though* [*Although*] he is bright, he seems to lack the human touch. ‖ 彼はウェスタンが大好きだ**が**奥さんは大嫌いだ He loves Westerns, *while* his wife hates them.

[1]たかい 高い

> **訳語メニュー**
> 高さが高い →high, tall **1**
> 程度が高い →high, advanced **2**
> 値段が高い →high, expensive **3**

1【人・物の高さが】tall(背が高い, 丈が高い); **high**(位置が高い)
解説 **tall** は人が「背が高い」, または, ものが「標準的なものに比べて(細長くて)丈が高い」で下から上までの全体がイメージされる. **high** は「位置的に高い」で, てっぺんが高いところにあることをいう. building(ビル), tree(木), tower(塔), utility pole(電柱), skyscraper(超高層ビル), glass(グラス)などには tall を, mountain(山)や peak(峰)には high を用いることが多い. altitude (高度)や ceiling (天井) は位置だけが問題となるので high を用いる.
▶**高い**ヤシの木 a *tall* palm tree (➤ (×)a high tree とはいわない. 逆は a small tree) ‖ **高い山** a *high* [*tall*] mountain (➤ mountain や peak は海抜をいうときは high がふつうだが, 険しい山のように, 山容から高いことをいうときには tall が自然に響く. 「低い山」は a low mountain) ‖ ミラーさんはとても**背が高い** Mr. Miller is very *tall*. (➤「背が低い」は short) ‖ 現在, 日本で**いちばん高いビル**は何というビルですか What is (the name of) *the tallest building* in Japan now? ‖ 棚は**高すぎて**少女が手を伸ばしても届かなかった The shelf was *too high* for the girl to reach. ‖ 彼はライトに**高いフライ**を打ち上げた He hit *a high fly ball* to right field. ‖ 私はマンションの**高い階**に住みたい I want to live on *an upper* [*a high*] *floor* of a condominium. ／I want to live in *an upper-floor* condominium (apartment).
▶西洋人は**鼻が高い** Westerners have *big noses*. (➤ high nose とはしない) ‖ きょうの江の島海岸は**波が高い** The waves at Enoshima Beach today are *high*.
2【程度・率などが】high, **advanced** ▶鳥インフルエンザの死亡率は**高い** The death rate for bird flu is *high*. ‖ 彼の体温は平均よりも**高い** His body temperature is *higher* than average. ‖ 日本の科学技術の**水準は高い** Japan has a *high level* of technology. ‖ 新工場は**高い**生産性を誇る The new plant boasts *high* productivity. ‖ この参考書はぼくには**程度が高すぎる** This reference book is of *too high* a level for me [is *over* my head]. (● too や so がつくと a の位置が変わることに注意).
▶彼は**理想が高い**(＝野心がある) He *is ambitious*. ／ He *has lofty ambitions*. ‖ 彼女は**学歴が高い** She is a *highly-educated* woman. ／She *has a high educational background*.
3【金額・値段が】high, **expensive** ▶日本の私立大学は**授業料が高い** Tuition at Japanese private universities is *high*. ‖ この指輪は**高すぎます**. もっと安いのを見せてください This ring is *too expensive*. Can you show me a cheaper one? ‖ アメリカに比べて日本は**食料品が高い** Prices of food are *higher* in Japan than in the United States. ‖ 大臣は**高い給料をもらっている** Cabinet ministers are *well* [*highly*] paid.

> **直訳の落とし穴「円が高くなる」**
> 「円が(ドルに対して)高くなってきた」を (×)The yen has gotten higher ... などという人がいる. 通貨の場合は high, low でなく, strong, weak を使うので, 正しい言い方は The yen has gotten stronger (against the dollar). または The yen has appreciated (against the dollar). である. 「円高」もいろいろな言い方があるが, 簡単には the strong yen や the yen's rise でよい.

4【声・音が】high ▶あの歌手の**声は高い** The singer has a *high* voice. ‖ 私にはそんなに**高い声**は出せない My voice doesn't go that *high*. ‖ ぼくにはこの曲は**キーが高すぎる** *The key* of this song *is too high* for me. ‖ しっ, **声が高い**よ Sh! *Lower* [*Drop*] your voice.
☞ **お高く止まる**, **高く** (→見出語)

[2]**たかい 他界する** **pass away** [**on**] (➤ dieの婉曲表現).

たがい 互い **each other**, **one another**
語法 (1) 3者以上ではどちらも区別なく用いるが, 2者では each other が一般的. (2) 日本語では「互いに」のように副詞として用いるが, 英語では代名詞扱いで, 目的語として, または所有格にして用いる.
▶私たちは**互いに**愛し合っている We love *each other*. (● 他動詞 love の目的語なので (×)with each other としない) ／ We're in love with *each other*. (● 後者は「ラブラブ」あるいは「ほれている」のように恋愛感情を強調する言い方) ‖ ロミオとジュリエットは初めて会ったとたん, **互いに**引かれ合った Romeo and Juliet were attracted to *each other* the instant they first met. ‖ 私たちは**お互いの**立場を尊重すべきだ We should respect *each other's* [*one another's*] positions. ‖ 両国の良好な関係は**互いの**(＝相互の)信頼の上に成り立

っている Good relations between both [*the two*] countries are based on *mutual* trust. ‖ 互いの健康を祝して乾杯！ *Here's to our health!*
☛ お互い, お互いさま (→見出語)

だかい 打開 ▶局面を打開するために全員力を合わせて頑張ろう Let's unite our efforts to *break the deadlock*. ‖ この局面の打開策を講じねばならない We have to *implement measures to cope with* this situation.

たがいちがい 互い違いに alternately /ɔ́:ltəʳnətli/ ▶彼女は赤と黄色のチューリップを互い違いに植えた She planted red and yellow tulips *alternately*. ／She *alternated* red and yellow tulips as she planted them. (➤ alternate /ɔ́:ltəʳnət/ は「交互にする」).

たかいびき 高鼾 a loud snore ▶日本では電車の中で高いびきの人もいる In Japan, there are people who *snore loudly* on trains.

たかが 高が ▶たかが数千円のことでがたがた言うな Don't make a fuss over *only* several thousand yen. ‖ たかがそんなつまらないことでキレるのはよくない It's not good to blow your top [lose your cool] over *such a trivial matter*. ‖ たかがこれくらいの仕事で弱音を吐くな Don't whine about *such a little* job. (➤ whine /hwaɪn/ は「泣き言を言う」の意) ‖ 東京人はたかがちょっとした雪くらいで大騒ぎしがちだ Tokyoites tend to make a big fuss over *a little* snow.

[1]**たかく 多角** ▶物事を多角的に考える consider a matter *from various angles* [*from various points of view*] ‖ 業務を多角化する *diversify* business operations.
‖多角形 a polygon /pɑ́:ligɑ:n/ ‖ 多角経営 diversified operation, diversification ‖ 多角貿易 multilateral trade.

[2]**たかく 高く** high ; highly (大いに) ▶鳥が空高く飛んでいる Birds are flying *high* (*up*) in the sky. (🔔 highly には場所的に「高く」の意味はないので, この文では使えない).
▶人を高く評価する think *highly* of a person ‖ 社長はきみのプランを高く買っているようだ The president seems to *think a lot of* your proposal. ‖ 彼はオートバイを高く(＝高値で)売りたがっている He wants to sell his motorcycle *at a high price*. ‖ 物価が年々高くなる Prices are *getting higher* every year.

たがく 多額の a large sum [amount] of ▶多額の出費[損失] *heavy* expenses [loss] ‖ 多額(＝大口)の寄付を行う make a *large* donation ‖ この計画には多額の資金が必要である *A large sum* [*amount*] *of* funds are necessary for this project.

たかさ 高さ

1【物の】(a) height /haɪt/ ; (an) altitude (地上からの高度) ▶東京スカイツリーの高さは634メートルだ (The) Tokyo Sky-tree *is* 634 meters *high* [*tall*]. ‖ 奈良の大仏の高さはどのくらいですか *How high* [*tall*] *is* the Great Buddha of Nara? ／*What is the height of* the Great Buddha of Nara? ‖ 飛行機は地上１万メートルの高さに達した The plane reached *an altitude* of 10,000 meters.

2【程度・率などの】▶湿度の高さでは山陰地方は東北よりも上だ The *level* [*degree*] *of humidity* in the San'in area is higher [greater] than that in the Tohoku area. ‖ 銃による死亡率の高さでは, アメリカは世界トップクラスだ The United States has one of the world's *highest gun fatality rates*. (🔔 top class は肯定的な意味合いで用いる) ‖ マカオの人口密度の高さはほかと比較にならないほどだ No other area in the world has a higher *population density* than Macau. ‖ この高校は京大合格率の高さを誇っている This high school is proud of the *high percentage* of its graduates who are accepted to [by] Kyoto University. ‖ 東京とロサンゼルスは緯度の高さ(＝緯度)ではほぼ同じだ Tokyo and Los Angeles lie at approximately the same *latitude*.

3【金額・値段の】▶東京の地価の高さは驚くほどだ(＝驚くほど高い) The price of land in Tokyo is astoundingly *high*.

4【音・声の】 pitch ▶声の高さ the *pitch* of a [one's] voice.

だがし 駄菓子 *dagashi* ; cheap sweets [candies].
‖駄菓子店 a penny candy store.

たかしお 高潮 a storm surge, a storm tide. →津波.

たかだい 高台 high ground (周囲よりも高地になっている所) ; a rise (周囲の地面より高い地点) ; a hill (丘, 小山) ▶高台に避難する[逃げる] evacuate to [run for] *high*(*er*) *ground* ‖ その城はちょっとした高台に在る The castle is [stands] on *a rise*. ‖ (鹿児島の)錦江湾高校は錦江湾を見下ろす高台にある Kinkowan High School is situated on *a rise* [*a hill*] that overlooks Kinko Bay.

たかだか 高々 at (the) most (多くて) ; only (たった) ▶たかだか 5, 6 千円でしょ. たまには外で食べましょうよ Let's eat out once in a while. It'll only cost five or six thousand yen *at most*. ‖ たかだか10万円くらいの金で大騒ぎするな Don't make such a great fuss over *only* a hundred thousand yen.

たかだかと 高々と high ▶勝者は誇らしげに両腕を高々と突き上げた The winner proudly thrust his arms *high*. (🔔 highly には比喩的用法しかないのでこの文では使えない).

だがっき 打楽器 a percussion instrument
‖打楽器奏者 a percussionist.

[1]**たかとび 高跳び** the high jump ▶走り高跳び the (running) high jump ‖ 棒高跳び the pole vault.

[2]**たかとび 高飛び** ▶犯人はすでに国外へ高飛びした(＝逃亡した)らしい The criminal seems to have already *escaped* [*fled*] overseas.

たかとびこみ 高飛び込みをする do the high dive.

たかなみ 高波 a huge wave ▶少年が高波にのまれた The boy was swallowed by *a huge wave*.

たかなる 高鳴る ▶恋人との再会を目前に静子の胸は高鳴った Shizuko's *heart pounded* at the thought of soon meeting her boyfriend again.

たかね 高値 a high price ▶私の車は予想以上の高値で売れた My car sold for *a higher price* than I had expected. ‖ より大きなアワビはより高値になる Bigger abalones *are priced higher*.

たかねのはな 高嶺[根]の花 ▶麗子はぼくには高根の花だ Reiko is *beyond my reach*. ／Reiko is *out of my league*. (➤ この league は「同じ部類」) ‖ フェラーリなんて庶民には高根の花だ A Ferrari is *out of the reach* of ordinary people.

たかのぞみ 高望み ▶あまり高望みをするな Don't *aim too high*. ／Don't be too ambitious. ‖ 高望みしなければどこかの大学に入れるよ If you don't *set your hopes too high*, you should be able to get into some university.

たかは 鷹派 a hawk (人) ▶その政治家は外交政策に関してはタカ派的だ The politician is *hawkish* on foreign policy. →ハト.

たかびしゃ 高飛車な high-handed ▶彼の高飛車な話

…方が嫌いだ I don't like the *high-handed* [*over-bearing*] way he speaks.

たかぶる 高ぶる ▶神経が高ぶってゆうべは眠れなかった I *was* so *excited* [*nervous* / *keyed up*] that I couldn't sleep last night.

たかまる 高まる rise ▶神尾のバイオリニストとしての評判が高まっている Kamio's reputation as a violinist *is rising* [*growing*]. ‖ コンサートの後半に入ると聴衆の興奮はより一層高まった The audience *got more excited* as the concert went on into the latter half. ‖ 消費税率アップに対する国民の反対の声が高まっている The people's opposition to the consumption tax hike has become *more and more* vocal. ‖ 両国間の緊張が再び高まっている Tensions *are building up* [*are increasing*] again between the two countries. ‖ その作品で彼の名声は大いに高まった The work *won* him great *fame*. ‖ 彼女の人気は高まりつつある Her popularity is *on the rise*.

たかみのけんぶつ 高みの見物 ▶彼は妻が自分の母親とけんかをしているのに高みの見物を決め込んだ He *just sat and watched* (*without getting involved*) while his wife was fighting with [quarrelling with] his mother.

たかめ 高め ▶あのアンパイアは高めの球をストライクにとる That umpire calls *rather high pitches* strikes.

たかめる 高める raise /reɪz/ +㊐; improve +㊐ (向上させる); increase +㊐ (増す) ▶生活水準を高める *raise* [*improve*] the standard of living ‖ 生産性を高めるために製造工程を全面的に機械化する mechanize the entire manufacturing process to *increase* productivity ‖ 学習効果を高めるには十分に睡眠を取ることが必要だ In order to study [learn] *more effectively*, you must get plenty of sleep. ‖ 読書は教養を高めるって本当でしょうか Is it true that reading *makes* you *more cultured*? / Is it true that reading *improves your* (*general*) *knowledge level*? ‖ 第 2 作はその小説家の名声を更に高めた The novelist's second work *further enhanced* his [her] reputation. (➤ enhance は「(価値)を高める」).

たがやす 耕す plow /plaʊ/ +㊐; cultivate +㊐ (開拓する) ▶耕うん機で畑を耕す *plow* fields with a cultivator ‖ 植民者たちは荒れ地を耕して畑を作った The colonists *cultivated* the wasteland and made it into a field.

たから 宝 (a) treasure ▶子供はどの親にとっても宝だ All children are *treasures* to their parents. ‖ 蔵にはわが家のお宝が詰まっている The storehouse is filled with our family *heirlooms*. (➤ heirloom は「先祖伝来の家宝」).
▶《慣用表現》コンピュータをゲームにしか使わないのじゃあ宝の持ち腐れだ It's *a waste of a good thing* to use a computer just to play games. (➤ a waste of a good thing が「宝の持ち腐れ」に相当する).
‖宝探し a treasure hunt ‖宝島 a treasure island.

だから **1**【それで】so; therefore (それゆえに; 堅い語) ▶彼は正直だ. だから私は彼の言うことを信じる He's honest, *so* I believe him. ‖ やっぱりテストに遅刻したの? だから早く行きなさいってあれほど言ったじゃないの I knew you were going to be late for the test! *That's why* I told you so many times to leave early.
2【…だから】because, since, as (since, as は because よりも意味が弱い. また as は多義で曖昧になるため, 《米》ではあまり好まれない)

> **【文型】**
> 〜 (A)だから…
> … because S + V
> … because of A ➤ A は名詞
> Since S + V, …
>
> **【解説】** since より **because** のほうが意味が強く, 直接の理由・原因を表す. 強調のため Because を文頭に出すこともあるが, 英語では「結論 [結果] + 理由 [原因]」の順に言うのがふつう. 文でなく名詞があとにくるときには because of になる. **since** はすでにわかっている理由を言うときに好まれ, Since 〜 の形で文の始めに置くことが多い.

▶彼は病気だから来られない He can't come *because* he is sick [*because of* sickness]. ‖ 私が怒ったのはきみが怠惰だったからではなく, 不正直だったからだ I was angry, *not because* you were lazy, *but because* you were dishonest. ‖ 彼がただ嫌いだからというだけで, 彼の意見まで軽視するのは間違っている You shouldn't discount his opinion *just because* you dislike him. ‖ きょうは日曜日だから郵便局は休みだ *Since* it's Sunday today, the post office is closed. / It's Sunday today, *so* the post office is closed. ‖ 彼女は末っ子だから甘やかされて育った *Since* she's [*Being*] the youngest daughter, she was pampered. ‖ 彼は太り過ぎだから走るのは得意でない He is not a good runner *since* [*as*] he is overweight.
3【慣用表現】▶彼がいつもみすぼらしい服装だからといって彼を見下してはならない You must not look down on him *just* [*simply*] *because* he is always shabbily [poorly] dressed. ‖ 相手のピッチャーはすごい, しかしだからといって必ずしも彼らが試合に勝てるというわけではない The opponents' pitcher is superb, but *it does not necessarily follow* that they'll be able to win the game. ‖ だから言わないこっちゃない *I told you so!* / *That's what I said!* ‖ 対話「俺は東大を出てるんだ」「だからどうだって言うの?」"I graduated from Tokyo University." "*So what?*"

たからか 高らか ▶M大学の学生たちは神宮球場で高らかに校歌を歌った M University students *belted out* their school song at Jingu Stadium.

たからくじ 宝籤 a (public) lottery; a lottery ticket (札) ▶彼は宝くじで500万円当てた He won five million yen in the *lottery*.

たからもの 宝物 a treasure ▶この貝殻は私にとって宝物です This shell is one of my *treasures*. ‖ 私はおばあさんの手紙を一生宝物にします I will *treasure* my grandmother's letters all my life. ‖ 誠実な友だちは宝物だ A true friend is *a valuable* [*precious*] *asset*.

たかる **1**【群がる】swarm /swɔːrm/ ▶道に落ちていたクッキーにアリがたかっていた Ants *were swarming* on the cookie lying in the street. ‖ 食物にハエがたかった Flies *collected* [*gathered*] on the food.
2【ねだる】bum [《英また》cadge /kædʒ/] (off) ▶彼はいつも周りの人にたかってたばこをせしめる He always *bums* [*cadges*] cigarettes *off* the people around him. / He always *sponges on* those around him for cigarettes.

-たがる want, would like 《to do》 (後者は前者よりていねいで控えめな表現) ▶彼女はきみと話したがっている She *wants to* talk to you. / She shows *interest* in talking with you. ‖ 彼女は来たがっているだろう I suppose she'*d like* to come. ‖ 彼女は子供の頃のことを話したがらない She *doesn't like to* talk about her childhood. (➤ like to do の否定形は「…する気がない」の意) ‖ 彼女はその件に関してはあまり話したがらない She'*s reluctant to talk* about the matter. ‖ 子供は何でも知りたがる Children *are eager to know* everything. ／ Children *are inquisitive*.

たかわらい 高笑い **loud** [**booming**] **laughter** 一動 **高笑いする** **laugh loudly, roar with laughter.**

たかん 多感な **sensitive** ▶彼女は今多感な年頃で難しいよ She is now at a *sensitive* age and very difficult to deal with. ‖ 詩人は金沢で多感な青年時代を送った The poet spent the *sensitive* period of his youth in Kanazawa.

1**たき 滝** a **waterfall, falls** (後者は固有名詞として用いるときは単数扱いが多い) ▶その滝は高さが150メートルある The *falls* are 150 meters high. ‖ ナイアガラの滝は新婚旅行地として人気がある *Niagara Falls* is a popular honeymoon spot.

▶彼女の顔を滝のような汗が流れた *Sweat poured down* her face.

‖滝つぼ the basin of a waterfall.

2**たき 多岐** ▶わが社が抱える問題は多岐にわたっている Our company *has a wide range of* problems.

だきあう 抱き合う **hug** [**embrace**] **each other** (➤ hug はあいさつ代わりの短いもの, embrace は「抱擁する」に当たる堅い言い方) ▶娘は大学入試合格の知らせに, うれしさのあまり母と抱き合った Hearing the news that she was accepted by the university, she and her mother *hugged each other* with [for] joy. ‖ 木陰で若いカップルが抱き合っていた A young couple *were embracing* under the shade of the tree. ‖ 彼らは抱き合って泣いた They wept *in each other's arms*.

だきあげる 抱き上げる ▶母親は泣いている赤ん坊を抱き上げた The mother *took* the crying baby *into her arms*. ‖ 赤ん坊は私が抱き上げると泣きやんだ When I *lifted* the baby *in my arms*, he [she] stopped crying.

だきあわせ 抱き合わせ ▶抱き合わせ販売 a *combination* sale ／ a *tie-in* sale ／ a *bundled* sale.

だきいぬ 抱き犬 a **lap dog.**

だきおこす 抱き起こす ▶看護師さんが私を抱き起こしてくれた The nurse *put her arms around* me *and helped* me *sit up*.

だきかかえる 抱き抱える ▶彼女は救急隊員に抱きかかえられて病院に運ばれた She was carried to the hospital *in* the rescuer's *arms*. ‖ 老婦人は大事そうに包みを抱きかかえていた The old woman *was holding* a package *in her arms* with great care.

たきぎ 薪 **firewood** ▶薪を燃やす burn *firewood* ‖ 薪を拾い集める gather *firewood*.

だきぐせ 抱き癖 ▶赤ちゃんが泣くたびに抱き上げると抱き癖がつくという人もいる Some people say if you cradle a baby in your arms whenever he or she cries, the baby will *want to be held all the time*. (後半は the baby will be unhappy unless he or she is being held. のように表現することもできる).

たぎご 多義語 a **word with multiple meanings.**

たきこみごはん 炊き込みご飯 rice cooked with fish [meat] and/or vegetables (➤ 説明的な訳).

だきこむ 抱き込む **win** [**bring**] **... over** ▶議長を抱き込むのがいちばん手っとり早い The quickest way is to *win* the chairperson *over to our side*.

タキシード a **tuxedo** /tʌksíːdoʊ/, a **di**
(英) では前者はまれ).

だきしめる 抱き締める **hug** +目, **embr**
後者は「抱擁する」に当たる堅い語) ▶母親は
抱き締めて泣いた The mother cried, *hugg*
bracing] her son *tightly*. ‖ (強く) 抱き締め
me tight. (➤ 恋人どうしの場合).

たきだし 炊き出しをする **prepare meals outdoors** ▶被災者にご飯の炊き出しをする *distribute* cooked rice to the disaster victims ‖ 炊き出し所を設ける set up *an emergency* [*a soup*] *kitchen* (➤ soup kitchen は英語圏に見られる「(貧者・被災者などのための) 給食施設」).

だきつく 抱き付く ▶1人の女の子がそのロック歌手に抱きついた A girl *threw her arms around* the rock singer. ‖ 子供は犬を怖がって父親に抱きついた (＝しがみついた) The child *clung to* his [her] father, scared of the dog. (➤ clung は cling の過去形).

たきつける 焚き付ける **1** 【火をつける】 **kindle** +目, **light** +目 ▶まきが湿っていてたきつけるのに時間がかかった Since the wood was wet, it took us a long time to *kindle* [*light*] it.

2 【唆す】 **egg on, incite** +目 (➤ 後者は堅い語) ▶友人たちは彼をたきつけてがき大将に挑戦させた His friends *egged* him *on* to challenge the bully. ‖ 報告書は容疑者Aが容疑者Bをたきつけて金を盗ませたと結論づけている The report concluded that Suspect A *incited* Suspect B to steal the money.

だきにんぎょう 抱き人形 a **hug-me-doll.**

たきのう 多機能 **multi-function** ▶スマートフォンは多機能だ Smartphones *are multi-functional*.

たきび 焚き火 a **fire** ; a **bonfire** (祭りのときなどの大きなもの) ▶たき火でイモを焼く roast sweet potatoes *in a fire* ‖ 私たちは落ち葉をかき集めてたき火をした We raked up fallen leaves and *built* [*made*] *a fire*.

だきゅう 打球 a **ball that has been hit,** a **batted ball** (➤ 文脈でわかるので単に the ball で表すのがふつう) ▶打球はレフトスタンドに飛び込んだ *The ball* went into the left-field stands.

だきょう 妥協 (a) **compromise** /kɑ́ːmprəmaɪz/ ; **give-and-take** (公平な条件下でのやり取り) 一動 (人と) **妥協する** **compromise** 《with》, **make** [**strike**] **a compromise** 《with》 ▶妥協的な [非妥協的な] 態度をとる take a *compromising* [*an unyielding*] attitude ‖ 両者の間に妥協の余地はない There is no room for *compromise* between the two. ‖ 我々は彼とその条件で妥協した We *compromised with* him on that condition. ‖ 私たちは品質に妥協することはありません We do not and will not *compromise on* quality. ‖ あの人とは妥協したほうが得ですよ It would be better [more advantageous ／ smarter] for you to *make a compromise with* him [to *meet* him *halfway*]. (➤ 後者のほうがインフォーマル) ‖ たいていのビジネス交渉では関係者双方の妥協が必要だ Most business negotiations involve *give-and-take* between the parties involved. ‖ 妥協案を探す find out *a meeting point* ／ work out *a compromise*.

‖妥協案 a compromise.

たきょくか 多極化 **multipolarization** 一動 **多極化する** **be** [**become**] **multipolarized.**

1**たく 宅** →お宅.

2**たく 焚く・炊く** **burn** +目 (燃やす); **build** [**make**] **a fire** (火をおこす) ; **cook** +目 (加熱して料理する) ▶落ち葉をたく *burn* fallen leaves ‖ 火をたいて体を温めた We *built* [*made*] *a fire* to warm ourselves. ‖ 今

どきまきで風呂をたく人はほとんどいない Nowadays, few people use wood to *heat* their *bath*.
▶多くの子供はご飯の炊き方を知らない Many children don't know *how to cook* [*boil*] *rice*. (● 炊飯器で炊く場合には cook rice といい, 直火で炊く場合には cook と boil の両方とも使える).

タグ a tag.

だく 抱く **hold** +目 (しっかり抱える) ; **hug** +目 (短時間ぎゅっと抱き締める) ; **embrace** +目 (情熱を込めて抱擁する) ▶赤ちゃん抱かせてくれる? Can I *hold* your baby? ‖ 赤ん坊は母親に抱かれてすやすやと眠っていた The baby was sleeping peacefully *in* its mother's *arms*. ‖ ねえ, しっかり抱いて! *Hold me tight!* ‖ 母親は赤ん坊を抱き寄せた The mother *snuggled* her baby.
▶鶏が卵を抱いている The hen *is sitting on* her eggs.

たくあん 沢庵 ***takuan***
日本紹介 ✉ **たくあんは干した大根を塩入りの米ぬかに漬けたもので, 日本では最も一般的な漬物の1つです. おいしいのですが, 匂いが強いのが難点です** *Takuan* are *daikon* that have been dried and pickled in salted rice bran. Takuan is one of the most popular pickles in Japan. Although it tastes good, its strong smell is a major drawback.

たぐい 類い ▶類いまれな才能をもった人 a person with *extraordinary* [*rare*] talent ‖ 類いまれな美女 a *matchless* [*rare*] beauty / a woman of *exceptional* beauty ‖ 彼はそういった類いの男ではない He is not *that sort* [*kind*] *of* (a) man.

たくえつ 卓越した **excellent** (非常に優秀な) ; **prominent**, **outstanding** (傑出した) ▶卓越した指揮者 an *excellent* [*outstanding*] conductor ‖ あの人は人物・技量ともに卓越している He *stands out* [*is distinguished*] in both character and ability.

だくおん 濁音 a **dull sound**, a **voiced sound** [**consonant**].

たくさん 沢山

> 語法 (1)「数がたくさん」は many, a lot of, lots of, plenty of で示す. このうち a lot of, lots of はインフォーマルな語法で好まれる.
> (2)「量がたくさん」は much, a lot of, lots of, plenty of で示し, a lot of, lots of はインフォーマルな語法で好まれる.
> (3) plenty of は「数・量」ともに用い,「有り余るほどの, たっぷりの」の意.
> (4)many, much は so, too, how などの語がつく場合や主語になる場合以外は, 否定文や疑問文に用いるのがふつう. →ごまんと.

1【数が多い】many, a lot of ▶たくさんの日本車がアメリカに輸出されている *Many* [*A lot of* / *A large number of*] Japanese cars are exported to the United States. ‖ その図書館には数え切れないほどたくさんの本がある The library has *countless* books. ‖ 英語の辞書はたくさんは持っていない I don't have *many* English dictionaries.

2【量が多い】much, a lot of ▶カレーはまだたくさんありますよ There's *a lot of* [*lots of*] curry left. ‖ お父さんは台湾のことをたくさん知っている Dad knows *a lot* about Taiwan. ‖ 酒はそんなにたくさんは飲みません I don't drink so *much* sake. ‖ 先月は雨がたくさん降った We had *a great deal of* [*plenty of*] rain last month. ‖ この辺りでは毎年この時期に雪がたくさん降る It snows *heavily* around here at this time of the year.

3【もう十分だ】▶試験はもうたくさんだ I'*m sick of* exams! / *No more* exams! (● 後者は文脈によっては「(ようやく)試験が終わった!」の意にもなる) ‖ けんかはもうたくさん. 少しは静かにしてよ *Enough of* your bickering! Can you please calm down a little? ‖ ハンバーガーはもうたくさんだわ I'm *fed up with* eating hamburger(s). (➤ be [get] fed up with は「…に飽き飽きしている[する]」の意のインフォーマルな言い方) ‖
対話「コーヒー, もう少しどう?」「いや, もうたくさん」"Some more coffee?" "*No, thank you.*" (● もう少し丁寧に断るときは I've had enough. / I'm full. Thank you. (十分頂きました. ありがとうございます)と言う. なお, enough を強く言うと「もううんざり」という意味になるので注意. また full は「おなかがいっぱいの」という意味).

たくじ 託児 ▶託児所に子供を預ける leave one's child in *a day-care center* [《英また》*a day nursery*] ‖託児施設 day-care facilities.

たくしあげる たくし上げる **tuck up** ; **roll up** ▶スカートをたくし上げる *tuck up* one's skirt ‖ 悪いけどぼくのシャツの袖をたくし上げてくれないか Sorry, but could you *roll up* my shirt sleeves?

タクシー a **taxi**, a **cab** (➤ 後者はややくだけた語) ▶タクシーで行こう Let's take *a taxi* [*cab*]. / Let's go by *taxi*. ‖ 雨が激しく降っていたので私たちはタクシーで帰宅した We *took a taxi home* [*went home by taxi*] because it was raining heavily. ‖ 駅の前でタクシーを拾った I *got* [*caught*] *a taxi* in front of the train station. ‖ 彼女は交差点の近くでタクシーを止めようとした She tried to *hail a taxi* near the intersection. (➤ hail は「声を掛けて止める」の意) ‖ タクシーを呼んでください Could you please call *a taxi* for me? / Could you please call me *a taxi*? ‖ この町には流しのタクシーは無い There are no *cruising taxis* in this town.
‖タクシー運転手 a taxi [cab] driver,《インフォーマル》a cabby ‖ **タクシー会社** a cab [taxi] company ‖ **タクシー乗り場** 《米》a taxi stand,《英》a taxi rank ‖ **タクシー料金** a taxi fare ‖ **個人タクシー** an owner-driven taxi.

たくじしょ 託児所 →託児.

たくじょう 卓上の **desk**
‖卓上カレンダー a desk calendar /kǽləndəʳ/ ‖ **卓上計算器** a tabletop [desktop] calculator ‖ **卓上スタンド** a desk lamp.

たくしょく 宅食 a **meal (kit) delivery service** (在宅配食. お弁当や下ごしらえずみの食材を配達してくれるサービス).

たくす(る) 託す(る) **entrust** +目 (責任を委ねる) ; **leave** +目, **commit** +目 (➤ 後者は堅い語) ▶あとのことを後任に託す *leave* [*commit* / *entrust*] things to the care of one's successor at work ‖ かなわなかった夢を若い世代に託す *commit* one's unfulfilled dream(s) to the younger generation ‖ 美香は子供を両親に託して夫と旅行に出かけた Mika went on a trip with her husband, *leaving* their child *with* her parents.

たくち 宅地 **housing land** ; a **housing site** (個々の用地) ; a **house** [**housing**] **lot** (通例1軒分の) ; **residential land** (すでに住宅が立っている) ▶宅地を造成する prepare *a housing site* / turn the [one's] land into *housing lots* (● 後者は1軒分ずつ区画することに

重点がある).
‖宅地造成［開発］業者 a (housing) developer ‖ 宅地分譲 sale of building lots.
だくてん 濁点 a **voiced sound mark.**
タクト a **baton** /bətɑ́:n ‖ bǽtɔn/ (➤「タクト」はドイツ語の *Taktstock* (指揮棒) から) ▶タクトを振る wave *a baton* (➤ 棒を振る) ／take *a baton* (➤ 指揮する).
たくはいびん 宅配便 **door-to-door delivery service, home delivery service** ▶これを宅配便で送ってください Please send this by *home delivery service*.
‖宅配便取扱所 a cargo collection agent.
たくはつ 托鉢する **go about begging for [seeking] alms** ‖托鉢僧 a begging monk [priest].
タグボート a **tugboat.**
たくほん 拓本 a **rubbing** ▶拓本をとる make *a rubbing*.
たくましい 逞しい 1【肉体が】**strong**; **robust** /roʊbʌ́st/ (体格のがっしりした); **sturdy** (屈強な); **powerful** (体力の優れた) ▶たくましい体格 a *strong* [*powerful*] build ‖ その少年はたくましい青年に成長した The boy grew up to be a *strong* [*robust* ／*sturdy*] young man. ‖ 徹はたくましい腕をしている Toru has *muscular* [*brawny*] arms. (➤ ともに「筋肉質の」の意. brawny は /brɔ́:ni/ と発音).
2【精神的に】**strong** ▶息子には逆境にめげないたくましい人間になってほしい I want my son to be a *strong* person—one who is not discouraged by difficulties.
3【甚だしい】▶やつらは商魂たくましい(＝いつも金もうけに躍起になっている) They *are always out to make money*. (➤ be out to do で「…しようと躍起になっている」の意).
4【思う存分する】▶想像をたくましくする *let* one's imagination *run wild*.
[1]**たくみ 巧みな** **skillful**; **clever** (巧妙な); **well-turned** (文章などが) 一副 **巧みに** **skillfully**; **cleverly** ▶巧みな手口［口実］a *clever* trick [excuse] ‖ 巧みな運転をする drive (a car) *skillfully* [*with skill*] ‖ 英語を巧みに話す人 a *good* English speaker ／a *good* speaker of English ‖ 父は書が巧みだ My father *is skilled* at calligraphy. ‖ セールスマンは巧みな売り込みで私に車を買わせようとした The salesman made a *skillful* sales pitch to try to get me to buy a car.
[2]**たくみ 匠・工** an **expert** [**accomplished**] **craftsman.**
たくらみ 企み a **plot** (陰謀; 比較的少人数による); a **trick** (計略; 悪意のないものを含む); a **scheme** /ski:m/ (主に利益を目的とした策略) ▶卑劣なたくらみ a mean *trick* ‖ 老人たちから金をだましとろうというたくらみを考えつく devise *a scheme* to cheat old people out of their money ‖ 首相暗殺のたくらみが発覚した An assassination *plot* against the prime minister came to light. ‖ 彼があいう笑い方をするときは何かたくらみがあるのよ He's always *got something up his sleeve* when he smiles like that. (➤ have (got) ... up one's sleeve は「(計画などを)隠し持っている」) ‖ きみのたくらみはわかっているよ I can see *what you are up to*. (➤ be up to ... は「(悪いことを)しようとしている」).
たくらむ 企む **plot** +目, **scheme** /ski:m/ +目 ▶殺人をたくらむ *plot* a murder ‖ 銀行強盗をたくらむ *scheme* to rob a bank ‖ 彼らは4人でハイジャックをたくらんでいた The four of them *plotted* a hijacking. ‖ あの子たちがおとなしいときはきっと何かたくらんでいるのよ Whenever those kids are quiet, they *are up to no good* [they *are up to something*]. (➤ be up to ... で「(悪いことを)しようとしている」).
だくりゅう 濁流 a **muddy stream** ▶多くの家が濁流に押し流された Many houses were swept away by the *muddy stream* [*waters*].
たぐりよせる 手繰り寄せる **draw in** ▶漁師たちが浜辺で網を手繰り寄せていた The fishermen on the shore *were drawing* the nets *in*.
たぐる 手繰る ▶ロープを手繰る *draw* [*haul*] *in* a rope ‖ ザイルを手繰って山頂へよじ登った I *hauled myself up* to the summit (hand-over-hand) *on* the climbing rope.
たくろう 宅浪 ▶彼は宅浪して大学に入った He got into a university *by studying at home* (*after he failed the entrance exams given the year he graduated from high school*). (● カッコ内は高校卒業の年の受験に失敗したことを説明的に言う場合).
たくわえ 蓄え **savings** (貯金); a **store** (貯蔵) ▶私にも多少の蓄えはある I have some *savings* [*some money saved*]. ‖ 食糧の蓄えが底をついた Our *stores* of food have run out. ／We've run out of food.
たくわえる 蓄える **store** (**up**) (貯蔵する); **save** +目 (取っておく, 貯金する) ▶アリは冬に備えて食べ物を蓄える Ants *store up* [*away*] food for the winter. ‖ 体力を蓄える *save* one's strength ‖ もしものときのためにお金は多少蓄えておいたほうがいいよ You'd be wise to *save* [*lay aside*] some money for a rainy day. (➤ for a rainy day は「不時の出費に備えて」の意のインフォーマルな表現).
[1]**たけ 竹** (a) **bamboo** /bæmbú:/ ▶竹を曲げて弓を作る bend *bamboo* to make a bow ‖ 竹が風にさやさや鳴っている The *bamboo trees* are rustling in the wind.
▶《慣用表現》彼は竹を割ったような性格の男だ He is an *open-hearted* man.
‖竹垣 a bamboo fence ‖ 竹細工 bamboo work ‖ 竹ざお a bamboo pole ‖ 竹筒 a bamboo tube ‖ 竹林 a bamboo forest ‖ 竹ぼうき a bamboo broom ‖ 竹やぶ a bamboo clump [grove].
☛ 竹馬, 竹の子 (→見出語)
[2]**たけ 丈** 1【長さ】**length** /leŋkθ/ ▶このコートは私には丈が長すぎる This coat is *too long* for me. ‖ 丈を直してくれますか Could you adjust the *length*? ‖ しばらく見ない間にずいぶん丈が伸びたね You'*ve grown* so *tall* since I saw you last. ‖ そのスカート, 少し丈を詰めたほうがすてきよ I think that skirt would look much nicer if you *took up the hem* a bit. (➤ hem は「へり」).
2【全部】▶彼はつかえていた思いの丈をぶちまけた He let out *everything* he had kept to [inside] himself.
-だけ -丈 1【…のみ】**only, just, alone**

> **語法** (1) only は修飾する語句の直前に置くのが原則. したがって位置によって文意が異なる.
> (2) インフォーマルでは動詞の前に置き, 強調したい語句を強めて発音することが多い.
> (3) just は only より緩やかな限定を表し, インフォーマルでよく用いられる.
> (4) alone は名詞・代名詞のあとに置く.

▶1度だけ *only* [*just*] once ‖ 私, あなただけが好きよ I love *only* you. ‖ ちょっとからかっただけだよ I was *just* kidding. ／I said it *just* for fun. ‖ 頼りにできるのはきみだけだ You're the *only* person I can count on. ‖ 本校では講義は英語だけで行われます Lectures are given *only* in English at our school. ‖ 別に用事じゃないんだ. ちょっと声が聞きたかっただけだよ I have no particular reason for calling. I *just* wanted to hear your voice. ‖ その犬を見たのはきみだけだ You were *the only one* who saw that dog. ／ *Only* you saw that dog. ／You *alone* saw that dog. ‖ それを信じているのはきみだけだ *Nobody* believes it *except you*. (➤「きみ以外誰も信じていない」の意).

【文型】
A **だけでなく** B **もまた**
not only A, **but also** B
B **as well as** A
➤ ともに B が強調される

▶英語圏の国だけでなく, スペイン語圏の国も旅してみたい I want to travel *not only* to English-speaking countries *but also* to Spanish-speaking countries. [*but* to Spanish-speaking countries *as well*] ／ I want to travel to English-speaking *as well as* Spanish-speaking countries.

▶お客さまはここにサインしていただくだけで結構です *All you have to do is* (to) sign right here. (● 英語では「しなければならないことは…だけ」と考える) ‖ 別れを考えただけで私は悲しい *The mere thought of* parting with you makes me sad.

▶難しそうというだけで諦めるべきではない You shouldn't give up on trying something *just because* it looks difficult. ‖ たまたま高い地位に就いているというだけで敬意を払われている人がいる Some people are respected *only* [*just*] *because* they happen to hold high positions.

2【程度, 限度】▶キャンディーはきみの好きなだけ取っていいよ You may take *as many* candies *as you want*. ‖ ちょっとだけでも来ていただけませんか Could you please come *just for a while*? ‖ 洋介は金が有ると有るだけ使ってしまう When Yosuke has money, he spends *all* of it [he always blows it]. (➤ blow は「(大金)を考えもなしにぱっぱっと使う」) ‖ やれるだけのことはやった I did *all I could* [*what I could*]. ‖ 私には家を買うだけの金は無い I don't have *enough* money to buy a house.

▶彼女は私より 2 センチだけ背が高い She's taller than I (am) *by* two centimeters. (➤ この by は数量の差の程度を表す) ／She's two centimeters taller than me.

3【…に比例して】▶チームが強くなればそれだけファンの数も増える *The* stronger our team becomes, *the* more fans we will have. (➤ この文の the はともに副詞で, 比較級の前にきて「それだけ」の意を表す ; 次例も同じ) ‖ ウイスキーは値段が高ければそれだけ味もいいと思われている People tend to think that *the* more expensive a whisky is, *the* better it tastes. ‖ ハードトレーニングをしただけのことはあった (＝効果があった) The hard workout *was effective* [*paid off*]. ‖ この投資はするだけのことはある (＝引き合う) だろう This investment will *pay off* [will *be worth doing*].

4【…にふさわしく】▶チャックは日本に長く居るだけあって日本語が上手だ Chuck speaks good Japanese (*as might be expected*), *since* he has been in Japan for a long time. ‖ 札幌の町は友人が自慢するだけあってとてもきれいだった I found Sapporo to be *as* beautiful *as* my friend had bragged it was. (● 英語では「自慢することばと同じくらい美しい」と考える).

たげい 多芸 **many talents** ▶多芸の人 a person of *many talents* ‖ 多芸な芸人 a *versatile* entertainer.

ことわざ 多芸は無芸 A jack of all trades is a master of none.

たけうま 竹馬 **(bamboo) stilts** (➤ 通例複数形で) ▶竹馬に乗る walk on *stilts*.

だげき 打撃 **1**【痛手】a **blow** ; a **shock** (衝撃) ; **damage** /dǽmɪdʒ/ (損害) ▶両親の離婚は私にとって大きな打撃だった Our parents' divorce was a great *blow* [*shock*] to me. ‖ 地震はその市に壊滅的な打撃を与えた The earthquake *devastated* the city. ‖ 銀行の貸し渋りで多くの中小企業はひどい打撃を受けた Many smaller businesses *were hit hard* by [*suffered serious damage* from] banks' reluctance to lend. ‖ 貿易規制が行われると日本企業が打撃を受ける Trade regulations will *hurt* Japanese business.

2【野球】**hitting, batting** ▶打撃練習をする take *batting* practice ‖ 彼は打撃はいいが守備はだめだ He *is a good hitter* but a poor fielder.

‖**打撃王** a leading hitter, a batting average leader ‖ **打撃戦** a slugfest.

たけだけしい 猛々しい ▶たけだけしい野武士の一団 a group of *ferocious* samurai living in the wild ‖ ぬすっとたけだけしいとはおまえのことだ You sure are *a brazen(-faced) thief*!

だけつ 妥結 (a) **settlement**(解決) ; an **agreement** (協定) 一動 **妥結する** **come to a settlement** [**an agreement**] ▶賃上げ交渉は1.2% でようやく妥結した The union and management finally *settled on* a 1.2 percent pay increase.

-だけど **but** ▶奇妙だけど本当の話 a strange *but* [*yet*] true story ‖ あの人は高名な学者だけど変人だ *Though* a celebrated scholar, he is an eccentric.

たけとんぼ 竹とんぼ a **toy bamboo dragonfly**.

たけなわ ▶スキーシーズンは今がたけなわだ The ski season *is* now *at its peak*. ‖ まさに宴たけなわだ The party is now *in full swing*. (➤ in full swing は「最高潮で」).

✉ **今, 日本は春たけなわです. 庭には花が咲き誇っています** Now spring is *in full swing* throughout Japan. The flowers in the garden are now in full bloom.

たけのこ 竹の子 a **bamboo shoot** [**sprout**].

☛ **雨後のたけのこ** (→見出語)

たける 長けている **proficient, skilled** ▶純はスポーツ全般にたけている Jun *is proficient in* almost any sport. ／ Jun *is skilled* [*good*] *at* almost all sports. ‖ 彼は商才にたけている He *is a shrewd merchant*. ／He *has a great talent for business*.

たげんごしゅぎ 多言語主義 **multilingualism**.

たげんごしようしゃ 多言語使用者 a **multilingual (person)**.

[1]**たこ 蛸** an **octopus** /ɑ́ːktəpəs/ (➤「足」は tentacle, 「吸盤」は sucker) ▶タコは 8 本の足で吸い付く *An octopus* clings to things with its eight tentacles.

▶《慣用表現》彼はコップ 1 杯のビールでゆでダコのように真っ赤になる He drinks one glass of beer and *gets as red as a boiled octopus*. (➤ 日本的な比喩なので, タコを食用としない英米人には伝わらない) ／He drinks one glass of beer and *gets as red as a beet* [*beet-red* ／*fiery-red*]. (➤「ビート[火]のように真っ赤になる」の意) ‖ 1 つのコンセントからたこ足配線をしてはいけない Don't put too many plugs in one outlet. ／Don't plug too many appliances into one outlet.

‖タコつぼ an octopus trap [pot].

[2]**たこ 凧** a kite ▶たこを揚げる [下ろす] fly [draw in] *a kite* ‖**たこ揚げ大会** a kite-flying contest.

[3]**たこ 胼胝** a **callus** /kǽləs/, a **callosity** /kəlɑ́:səṭi/ ; a **corn** (魚の目) ▶ラブレターを書き過ぎて中指にペンだこができた I have *a callus* [*A callus* has formed] on my middle finger from writing too many love letters.

▶《慣用表現》そのことは耳にたこができるほど聞いたよ I've heard *more than enough* of it. ／I'm sick (and tired) of hearing about it.

たこう 多幸

✉ **新年にあたりご多幸をお祈りいたします** I wish you all happiness in the New Year. ／ May the New Year bring you much [every] happiness. ➤ 第 2 文は「新しい年があなたにたくさんの幸せをもたらしますように」の意.

だこう 蛇行する **wind** /waɪnd/ ▶その川は平原を蛇行している The river *winds* [*meanders*] through the plain. ‖あの車, **蛇行運転してるぜ** That car is *swerving back and forth*. (➤ swerve /swəːʳv/ は「急に方向を変える」, またこの back and forth は「左右に」の意).

たこく 他国 a **foreign country**(外国) ; **other countries** (ほかの国々) ; **foreign land**(ほかの土地)

‖**他国者** a person from foreign land.

たこくせき 多国籍 ▶**多国籍**企業 a *multinational* company [corporation].

タコ(ス) a *taco*.

たこやき 蛸焼き ***takoyaki***

日本紹介 ✉ **たこ焼きは小麦粉に, タコ, ネギなどを刻んで入れ, 小さな球形に焼いた食べ物です. 特製のソースが掛けてあります** *Takoyaki* are a kind of little round pancake made of flour with chopped octopus and green onions. A special sauce is put on them.

たごん 他言 ▶**他言無用**に願います Please *don't tell anybody*. ／ Please *keep this a secret*.

[1]**たさい 多彩な** **various** /véəriəs/ (➤ 数の多さを更に強調するときは a wide range of ... などを用いる) →多種多様 ▶学校の創立50年を祝って**多彩な**行事が行われた In celebration of the 50th anniversary of the school's foundation, *various* events were held. ‖このパーティーには**多彩な顔ぶれ**が集まっている There are *people from all walks of life* at this party. (➤ walk of life は「職業, 階級」).

[2]**たさい 多才な** **versatile** /vəːʳsəṭl/ ; **multi-talented** (マルチタレントの) ▶**多才な人** a *versatile* [*multi-talented*] person ／a person *of many talents*.

ださい **hick**(やぼな) ; **crude** (粗野な) ▶あの格好見てよ. ださいよね Wow! Look at that. How *hick* [*crude*]! ‖ 対話「ださいな, その格好」「どうせ私はださいわよ」"That outfit is *dorky*." "You'd say I'm a *dork* anyway." (➤ dork, dorky は「ダサいやつ」「ダサい」).

ださく 駄作 a **failed artwork, rubbish** ▶はっきり言って, この映画は全くの**駄作**だ Honestly, this movie is *a total failure* [*absolute rubbish*]. (➤「完全な失敗作だ」の意).

たさつ 他殺 (a) **murder** ▶**他殺死体** a *murder* victim.

たさん 多産な **prolific, fecund** /fékənd, fíːk-/ ▶**多産な発明家** a *prolific* inventor.

ださん 打算的な **calculating** (計算高い) ; **mercenary** /mɑ́ːʳsəneri/ (金目当ての) ▶彼はとても頭の切れる**打算的な**男だ He's a very smart and *calculating* person. ／ He's a very intelligent person who always *looks out for number one*. (➤ look out for number one は「(他人のことよりも)自分のことを第一に考える」の意).

たざんのいし 他山の石 a **lesson to be learned from others' mistakes** ▶私たちはX社の倒産を**他山の石**とすべきだ We should *learn a lesson* from company X's bankruptcy.

たし 足し ▶私は日曜日にアルバイトをして小遣いの**足し**にした I *supplemented* my pocket money by doing a part-time job on Sundays. (➤ supplement /sʌ́plɪment/ は「補う」) ‖このお金は何かの**足し**にしてください I hope this money will *be of some help* to you. (➤「このお金が何かの役に立つといいのですが」の意) ‖これっぽっちのお金じゃ**何の足しにもならない**よ This little bit of money *is no help at all*.

[1]**だし 出し・出汁** **1【出し汁】(soup) stock ; broth** (肉・魚の) ▶昆布で**だしをとる** prepare *stock* from kelp.

2【手先, 口実】▶彼らは有名人を**だしにして**会員を集めた They *used* a famous personality *as a drawing card* [*a lure*] to attract people as members. (➤ drawing card は「客寄せ」, lure は「おとり」).

[2]**だし 山車** a **float** /floʊt/ ▶祭りには何台もの**山車**が出る Many *floats* appear in the festival parade.

だしあう 出し合う **pool** +目 (共同出資する) ; **chip in** (プレゼントなどをするためにみんなで ; インフォーマル) ; **share** +目 (分担する) ▶住人はマンションの将来の修理費用として1人月1万円**出し合っている** The condominium residents *are pooling* ten thousand yen per person a month (to pay) for future repairs. ‖私たちは各自1000円ずつ**出し合って**母の日のプレゼントを買った We *chipped in* 1,000 yen each for a Mother's Day present. ‖費用は各自**出し合いましょう** Let's *share* the expenses. ／Let's *pay* our own *share* of the expenses.

だしいれ 出し入れ ▶このつり戸棚は高すぎて, **物の出し入れ**に不便です This wall cabinet is placed too high, so that it's hard to *get things in and out*.

だしおしみ 出し惜しみする **grudge** +目 ▶彼はいつも慈善事業への寄付金を**出し惜しみする** He *is* always *unwilling* to donate money to charities. ／He always *stints on* money [contributions] to charities. (➤ stint は「けちけちする」の意) ‖ほかにどんなお宝を持ってるの? **出し惜しみしないで**全部見せてよ What other treasured items do you have? *Don't be so stingy about showing them*. Let me see them all.

たしか 確か

1【確信がある】一形 確かな certain, sure (➤ 前者のほうが客観的で意味も強い) **一副 確かに certainly, sure(ly)** ▶彼がカナダへ帰るのは**確か**だ *It is certain* that he will return to Canada. ／He *is sure* to return to Canada. ／ *I'm sure* he will return to Canada. ‖地球温暖化が起きているのは**確か**だ *It is certain that* global warming is happening. ‖スペイン語が世界の主要言語の1つであることは**確か**だ *It is true that* Spanish is one of the major languages in the world. ‖**確かなことは言えない** I can't say *for sure*. ‖ 対話「私はそんなことはしてません」「**確かだね**?」「絶対にしてませんよ」"I didn't do that." "*You're sure* [*positive*]?" "Absolutely sure [positive]." ‖ 対話「中国は世界中で存在感を増したね」「**確かに**」"China has made its presence felt worldwide." "*That's true*. ／ *It* *sure has.*"

▶原稿は11月21日に確かに受け取りました This is to *acknowledge* receipt of your manuscript on November 21. ‖ 書類は確かに秘書の方にお渡ししました I *definitely* handed the paper to your secretary. ‖ 弘は確かに頭はいいが他人に対する思いやりがない *I know* Hiroshi is bright, but he lacks consideration for other people. ‖ その本は確かに読んだが理解できなかった I *did* read the book, but I didn't understand it. (➤この did は強く発音する).

2【確実で信頼できる】一形 確かな reliable ; definite（はっきりした）▶**確かな人物** a *reliable* person ‖ **確かな筋からの情報** information from a *reliable* source ‖ きょうはきみから**確かな返事**を聞きたい I'd like (to have) a *definite* answer from you today. ‖ 軍事法廷は**確かな証拠**もないままに彼に死刑を宣告した The military tribunal sentenced him to death though they had no *strong* [*clear*] *proof* against him.

▶あの評論家の言うことなら**確かだ** *You can trust* what that critic says. ／What that critic says *is trustworthy.* ‖ この新聞記事は**確かだ**（＝正確だ）This newspaper article *is correct* [*accurate*]. ‖ あんなやつに金を貸しただなんて**気は確かかい**？ *Are you in your right mind*, lending money to a guy like that? ‖《酔っ払いに》**足元の確かなうちに**帰ったほうがいいよ You had better go home *while you can still stand*. ‖ うちの社長は**人を見る目は確かだ** Our boss *is a good judge of* people. ‖ あの歯医者さんなら**腕は確かだ**（＝信頼できる）*You can trust* that dentist's *skill*.

3【記憶が正しければ】▶彼女は**確か**真紀子という名前でした *If I remember correctly* [*rightly*], her name was Makiko. ‖ ペリーが浦賀へ来たのは**確か**1853年だった Commodore Perry came to Uraga in 1853, *if I'm not mistaken*.

☛ **不確か**（→見出語）

たしかめる 確かめる

check ＋目（チェックする）; **confirm** ＋目（陳述・証拠などを確認する）; **make sure**（念を入れる）▶答案を提出する前によく**確かめなさい** *Check* your paper carefully before you hand it in. ‖ 辞書で「マサチューセッツ」のつづりを**確かめた** I *checked* the spelling of [how to spell] "Massachusetts" in the dictionary.

> **【文型】**
> **～であることを確かめる**
> **make sure** (**that**) S ＋ V
> **check that** S ＋ V
> **～かどうかを確かめる**
> **check if** S ＋ V
> **物事(A)を確かめる**
> **check** (**on**) A
>
> **【解説】**(1)**make sure** は「間違いないと思うが, 念のため確かめる」の意. check に that の文を続けて同じ意味を表す. **check** (**if**) は「(わからないので)調べる, (異常がないかを)点検する」の意.
> (2)check のほかの意味と紛らわしくないように, check on や「十分, 念入りに」の意を込めて, check up on, check out の形も使う.

▶彼女, パーティーに出席すると言ってたけれど, 電話でもう一度**確かめた**ほうがいいよ She said she would attend the party, but you should call to *make sure* [*confirm* it]. ‖ 母はガスを止めたかどうか**確かめ**に家に戻って来た My mother came back to *make sure* [to *see if*] she had turned off the gas. ‖ 彼は手帳を見て, 次の日に何も予定が入っていないことを**確かめた** He looked at his planner to *check that* he had no appointments for the following day. ‖ ぼくに対する彼女の気持ちを**確かめたい** *I'd like to* know how she feels about me. ／*I want to be sure* about her feelings for me.

▶まずウイルス対策ソフトが最新のものになっているか**確かめて**ください First you should *check if* your antivirus software is updated. ‖ 彼は自分の防水スマホが本当に防水になっているか**確かめようと**水につけてみた He dipped his waterproof smartphone in the water *to check* [*to see*] *if* it was really waterproof. ‖ 彼の言い分を**確かめてみよう** Let's *check up on* his claim. (➤check up on は「…の真偽を確かめる」) ‖ そのことはまず息子に(聞いて)**確かめてみなければ** I've got to *check with* my son about it first. (➤check with で「…に聞いてみる」).

たしざん 足し算 addition ▶トムは**足し算**がちゃんとできない Tom is poor at *addition*. ／Tom can't *add* properly. (➤add は「足し算をする」).

だしじる 出し汁 stock ▶シイタケのだし汁 shiitake mushroom *stock*.

たじたじ ▶その学生の鋭い質問に教授は**たじたじ**となった The professor *was flustered* by the student's pointed question. (➤was flustered は「慌てた」の意).

だしっぱなし 出しっ放し ▶お湯を**出しっぱなし**にしないで Do not *leave* the hot water *running*.

たしなみ 嗜み accomplishments（芸道などの心得）▶彼女は茶道の**たしなみがある** She *is accomplished* in (the) tea ceremony.

たしなむ 嗜む ▶父は酒もたばこも**たしなみません** My father neither drinks nor smokes. ‖ 酒は**たしなむ**程度です I *drink a little* (now and then). (➤「時々少量を飲む」の意) ／ I *drink socially*. (➤「社交として飲む程度である」の意).

たしなめる reprove《for》; **politely tell**《to》（丁寧に言う）▶彼は息子の不注意を**たしなめた** He *reproved* his son *for* his carelessness. ‖ 車掌は車内でたばこを吸っていた乗客を**たしなめた** The conductor *politely told* the passenger who was smoking *to* stop.

だしぬく 出し抜く outwit /àʊtwít/ ＋目（計画の裏をかく）▶犯人は警察を**出し抜いて**逃亡した The suspect *outwitted* the police and escaped.

▶その会社は新製品を発売して他社を**出し抜いた**（＝他社の先を越した）The company *got the jump on* other companies by marketing a new product. ／ The company *got a head start* by selling a new product. (➤head start は「ほかより好調な出だし」).

だしぬけ 出し抜けに suddenly ▶彼が**出し抜けに**走り出したので, みんなあっけにとられた He *suddenly* started to run, leaving all of us open-mouthed [stunned]. ‖ あの先生は時々**出し抜けに試験**をする That teacher sometimes gives pop quizzes [tests]. (➤pop quiz [test] は「抜き打ち試験」) ‖ 彼は**出し抜けに**私に結婚してくださいと言った *Out of the blue* he asked me to marry him. (➤out of the blue は「青天のへきれきのように, 全く突然に」の意).

だしもの 出し物 a program ▶今月の帝劇の**出し物**は何ですか What's the *program* at the Imperial Theater this month? ／What's *on* at Teigeki this month? (➤on は「上演中で」) ‖ その祭りのいちばんの

出し物は大きな山車の行列です *The main feature* of the festival is the parade of big floats.

たしゃ 他者 **other people, others** ▶他者に共感する feel empathy for [empathize with] *other people*.

だしゃ 打者 a **batter**, a **hitter** ▶3割打者 a .300 (= three hundred) *hitter* ‖ ベイスターズは6回に打者9人を送り5点をあげた The BayStars sent nine *batters* to the plate in the sixth inning to score five runs.

だじゃれ 駄洒落 a **dumb** /dʌm/ [**dull**] **joke**; a **poor pun** (下手な語呂合わせ) ▶父はだじゃればかり飛ばしている My father never loses a chance to make *a pun*.

た

たじゅう 多重 ▶音声多重方式によるイギリス映画の日英2か国語放送 a bilingual—Japanese and English—(*multiplex*) broadcast of a British film. ‖ **多重衝突** a pileup ‖ **文字多重放送** teletext (➤ television text broadcasting の短縮形).

たしゅたよう 多種多様な **many kinds (of)** ▶あの店では手ごろで多種多様な服を扱っている That store sells *many different kinds of* clothing at reasonable prices. ‖ ドラッグストアでは薬以外にも多種多様な品物を売っている Drugstores sell *a wide range of* items besides medicine(s).

たしゅみ 多趣味 ▶井田さんは多趣味だ Mr. Ida *has a lot of interests* [*hobbies*]. / Mr. Ida *is interested in many things*.

だじゅん 打順 **the batting order** ▶次の回は1番からの好打順だ(=1番から始まる) The next inning will be opened by our lead-off batter.

たしょ 他所 **elsewhere.**

たしょう 多少 **1**【多いことと少ないこと】▶金額の多少にかかわらず寄付を歓迎します *Any amount* of contribution is welcome.

2【いくらか】**a few** (数えられるものについて); **a little** (数えられないものについて); **some** ▶ミュージカルに関する本なら多少持っている I have *some* [*a few*] books on musicals. ‖ 鍋の中にはスープが多少残っている There is *some* [*a little*] soup left in the pan. ‖ ディックは多少日本語ができる Dick can speak *some* Japanese. ‖ その件については私にも多少責任がある I have *some* responsibility [I am *somewhat* responsible] for the matter.

たじょう 多情な **sensitive passionate.**

たしょく 多色の **multi-colored.**

たじろぐ **flinch** 《from》 ▶女の子は大きな犬を見てたじろいだ(=尻込みした) The little girl *flinched* at the sight of a big dog. ‖ 彼は蛇を見てたじろいだ He *recoiled* at the sight of a snake. ‖ 彼はどんなことにもたじろがない He never *flinches* [*shrinks*] *from* anything. (➤ shrink from は「…にひるむ」の意で文語的).

だしん 打診する **sound out** ▶その問題について彼の意向を打診する必要がある We have to *sound out* his feelings [*sound* him *out*] on the matter.

たしんきょう 多神教 **polytheism** /pá:liθiìzəm/.

たす 足す **add** +目 ▶6に3を足す *add* three to six ‖ すき焼きに水を足す *add* water to sukiyaki ‖ 4足す2は6 Four *plus* two is six. / Four *and* two make(s) six.

▶お年玉に3000円足して携帯ゲーム機を買った I bought a handheld game console with the money I received for New Year's *plus* 3,000 yen. / I *added* 3,000 yen to the money I had received for New Year's to buy a handheld game console.

だす 出す

訳語メニュー
- 取り出す →take out **1**
- 提出する →hand in **2**
- 郵送する →send, mail **2**
- 金を支払う →pay **3**
- 宿題などを →give **4**
- 世の中に出す →issue **5**
- 表に出す →show **6**

1【内から外へ位置を移す】**take out** (取り出す); **put out** (外に出す); **stick out** (突き出す); **hold out** (手などを前に出す)

▶財布から小銭を出す *take* [*get*] some coins *out of* one's wallet (➤ get out は「しまい込んである所から出す」の意) ‖ 窓から顔を出す *stick* one's head *out of* the window (● head は首から上の部分をいう. face は顔面をいうのでここでは不可) ‖ ごみは収集日に出してください Please *put* the trash *out* on collection days. ‖ 子供は手を出して「お金を頂戴」と言った The child *held out his hand* saying, "Can I have some money?" ‖ 冷蔵庫からコーラを3本出して来なさい(=持って来なさい) *Bring* three Cokes from the refrigerator. ‖ 外に出してくれ! *Let me out*! ‖ 春になってユリの球根が芽を出した Spring has arrived and lilies *have begun to sprout*.

2【提出する, 渡す; 送る】**hand in**; **send** +目 ▶作文, 先生に出した? Have you *handed in* the composition to the teacher yet? ‖ 委員会に改革案が出された A reform plan *was submitted to* the committee. (➤ submit は「検討するために提出する」の意の堅い語) ‖ クリーニング屋にこのスーツを出しておいてくれる? Could you *take* this suit to the cleaners? ‖ 《路上で強盗が》金を出せ! *Hand over* [*Give me*] your money!

▶ファンレターを出す *send* [*write*] a fan letter ‖ 私は明治大学に願書を出した I *sent* [*submitted*] my application to Meiji University. / I *applied* (for admission) to Meiji University. (➤ 後者は「明治大学に出願した」の意) ‖ この小包を出してくださる? Would you *mail* [*post*] this parcel for me?

3【支払う】**pay** +目 ▶勘定はぼくが出すよ I'll *pay* [*foot*] the bill. ‖ 小林さんは老人ホームの建設にぽんと1000万円出した(=寄付した) Kobayashi gladly *donated* ten million yen for the construction of a home for the elderly.

4【与える】**give** +目 ▶数学の先生は宿題をたくさん出す Our math teacher *gives* [*assigns*] us a lot of homework. (➤ assign は「(課題)を与える」) ‖ 友だちの家に行ったら紅茶を出してくれた A friend of mine *served* meteaat her home. ‖ あの料理店はうまい刺身を出す That restaurant *serves* delicious sashimi.

5【人前・世の中に現す】**issue** +目 (印刷物を); **release** +目 (CDなどを); **publish** +目 (出版物を); **set up** +目 (看板などを); **come out** 《with》 (出版物・製品を)

▶記念切手を出す *issue* a commemorative stamp ‖ 看板を出す *set up* a sign ‖ 彼女は6月に新しいアルバムを出す She *is releasing* a new album in June. / Her new album *is coming out* [*will be released*] in June. ‖ その辞書の新しい版はいつ出すんですか When are you going to *come out* with a new

edition of the dictionary ? ‖ あの出版社は主に教育図書を出している That firm *publishes* mainly educational books. ‖ その英会話学校はよく新聞に広告を出す（＝載せる）That English conversation school often *puts* [*places*] advertisements in newspapers [advertises in newspapers].
▶監督は矢継早にサインを出した The manager *sent* one signal after another. ‖ きみでは話にならん. 責任者を出しなさい *Call* the manager. I'm wasting my time talking to you.
▶目撃者は名前を出さないように頼んだ The witness asked that his [her] name *be withheld*.
6【表面に現す】show ＋⊞ ▶ズボンをまくって膝を出してごらん Roll up your pant leg and *let me see* your knee. ‖ 見てごらん. あの女の人は背中を半分出しているよ Look ! Half of the woman's back *is showing*. ‖ 日本人は一般に感情を表に出さない Japanese people don't generally *show* their feelings.
▶元気を出せ！ *Cheer up !* ‖ 脇役があまり個性を出し過ぎると主役がかすんでしまう When a supporting actor is *too prominent*, he [she] overshadows the star. ‖ 彼女はスピードを出し過ぎて（＝スピード違反で）捕まった She was caught *speeding*.
7【熱・光・匂いなどを放つ】give off ▶懐中電灯は弱い光しか出さなかった The flashlight *emitted* [*gave off*] only a feeble light. ‖ 彼は熱を出して寝ている He is in bed *with a fever*. ‖ 応援団員は大声を出した The cheerleaders *yelled* [*shouted*].
8【生じさせる】produce ＋⊞ ▶S 大学は多数の著名人を出した S University *has produced* many distinguished people. ‖ 山口県は総理大臣を 9 人も出している Yamaguchi Prefecture *has produced* nine prime ministers. ‖ その鉄道事故は多数の死傷者を出した The railroad accident *left* many dead or injured. (➤ leave は「(ある状態に)する」) ／ A lot of people were killed or injured in the railroad accident. ‖ Y 商社は赤字を出した Y Trading Company *has gone into the red*. ‖ 私は梅田にすし屋を出した I *opened* a new sushi restaurant in Umeda. ‖ 火事を出さないよう気をつけなさい Be careful not to *start* a fire.
9【結果に行き着く】▶ついにこの問題の答えを出したぞ（＝問題を解いた）I finally *solved* this problem. ‖ あすまでには結論を出します We'll *arrive at a conclusion* [*make a final decision*] by tomorrow. ‖ 日本新記録を出す *set a* new Japanese *record*.

-だす -出す begin [**start**] **to** do（● to do の代わりに doing も用いる）▶とうとう雪が降り出した At last, it *began* [*started*] *to* snow. ‖ 悲しい知らせを聞いて, 彼女はわっと泣き出した She *burst into tears* when she heard the sad news.

たすう 多数の many, a lot of（➤ 後者はインフォーマル）▶バスの事故で多数のけが人が出たらしい I hear that there were *many* people injured in the bus accident. ／I hear *a lot* [*a large number*] *of* people were injured in the bus accident. ‖ 毎年多数の生徒がこの大学を受験します *Quite a few* students take the entrance examinations to this university every year.
▶このクラブでは女性会員が多数を占めている Women members are *the majority* in this club. ‖ 国民の大多数は増税案に反対している *The vast majority* of the nation is [are] against the tax increase bill. ／*Most people* in the country are against the tax increase bill. ／*Most* of the country is against the tax increase bill. ‖ その政党は衆議院の絶対多数を占めていた That political party occupied *an absolute majority* in the House of Representatives. ‖ **多数派** the majority.

だすう 打数 official times at bat（➤ 記録では a.b.（＝at bat）と略す）▶阿部は 5 打数 3 安打だった Abe had three hits in five *at bats*. ／Abe went 3 for 5.（➤ 後者は放送・新聞などでの表現）

たすうけつ 多数決 decision by majority ▶多数決で決める decide *by majority* [*by a majority vote*].

たすかる 助かる

訳語メニュー
救助される →be saved 1
生き残る →survive 1
助けになる →be a help 2

1【危険な状態から逃れる】be saved ▶バスが川に転落したが乗客は全員助かった（＝救助された）The bus fell into the river, but all the passengers *were saved* [*were rescued*]. ‖ 飛行機が山中に墜落し, 助かったの（＝生存者）は彼女 1 人だけだった The plane crashed in the mountains, and she was the only *survivor* [and she was the only one who *survived* (*it*)]. ‖ その患者は助からなかった The patient *didn't survive*. ‖ 父が助かる（＝回復する）見込みはあるのですか Is there any hope of [for] my father's *recovery* [any hope that my father will *recover*] ? ‖（愛犬の）マルが助かるといいんだが I hope Maru will *make it*.（➤ make it は「(困難などを)乗り切る」の意のくだけた言い方）.
2【助けになる】be a help ▶洋子がいてくれるととても助かる Yoko *is a* great [big] *help*. ‖ おかげで助かりました You'*ve been very helpful* [*a big help*]. ‖ 彼は英語がうまいので外国人の客が来たときは助かる He's very good at English, so he'*s a great help* when we have foreign customers. ‖ 息子の授業料が思ったより安いので助かる（＝ありがたい）I *am thankful* that my son's tuition is lower than I expected. ‖ これでだいぶ金が助かる（＝節約になる）This will *save* a lot of money. **対話**「このかばんを運ぶのを手伝いましょうか」「それはありがとうございます. そうしていただけると助かります」"Would you like me to carry this bag for you ?" "Thank you so much. *I really appreciate it.* ／ *That's so kind of you.*"
▶ひゃー, 助かった！岸先生, きょうは休みで試験は来週に延びたって *How lucky* [*What a relief*] *!* Mr. Kishi is absent today and the test has been postponed to next week.

たすき 襷 1【着物の袖をからげるためのひも】*tasuki* ; a cord [sash] for holding up tucked sleeves（➤ 説明的な訳）.
2【肩から腰へ斜めに掛ける布】a sash ▶《駅伝などで》アンカーにたすきを渡す hand one's *sash* over to the anchor ‖ たすき掛けの安全ベルト a *shoulder* belt.

たすけ 助け 1【救助】help ; rescue（救援隊による救出）▶私たちは助けを求めて叫んだが, 誰ひとり助けに来てくれなかった We cried for *help*, but nobody came to our *rescue*.
2【助力】(a) **help** ▶ぼくの助けが必要かい Do you need my *help* ? ‖ 彼女はとても私の助けになってくれる She is *a* great *help* to me.（➤ この help は「助けになる人」）‖ 私の助言など大して助けにならないと思うよ I'm afraid my advice wouldn't *help* much. ‖ この辞書は英語を書くときとても助けになるだろう This diction-

た

ary will *be* very *helpful* when writing in English. ‖ラファエロは弟子の助けを借りてその絵を完成させた Raphael completed the painting *in collaboration with* [*with the help of*] his pupils.

たすけあい 助け合い mutual help ; cooperation（協同）‖**歳末助け合い運動** a year-end charity drive [campaign].

たすけあう 助け合う help each other [one another]; cooperate /kouɑ́:pəreɪt/《with》(…に協力する) ▶2人は困ったときは助け合うことを誓った The two promised to *help each other* when in trouble.

たすけあげる 助け上げる ▶その若者は少年を穴から助け上げた The young man *helped* the boy *out of* the pit. (➤「穴から出るのを手助けした」の意) ‖彼らは漂流中を救助艇に助け上げられた They *were picked up* in the lifeboat while (they were) drifting.

たすけおこす 助け起こす ▶母親は転んだ子供を助け起こした The mother *helped* her fallen child *to his feet* [*helped* her fallen child *up*].

たすけだす 助け出す save +⽬; rescue +⽬ (救援隊などが) ▶消防士たちは2人の女の子を燃え盛る家の中から助け出した The firefighters *rescued* [*saved*] two girls from the burning house. →助ける.

たすけぶね 助け船 a lifeboat, a rescue boat ▶ありがたい. 助け船が来たぞ Thank goodness. Here comes *a lifeboat*.

▶《比喩的》先生は答えられない生徒に助け船を出した The teacher *offered a helping hand* to the student who couldn't answer the question.

たすける 助ける

1【危険から救う】 help +⽬ (手を貸して) ; rescue +⽬ (救援隊などが差し迫っている危険から救う) ; save +⽬ (危険・損失などから救う) ▶警官は川に飛び込んで溺れかけた女性を助けた The police officer jumped into the river and *saved* [*rescued*] the drowning woman. (➤ save は命が助かったことをいうが, rescue は救出されたあとに命を落とした場合にも使われる) ‖暗闇の中で誰かが「助けて!」と叫んだ Someone cried out in the dark, "*Help me!*" ‖井出博士が私の命を助けてくれました Dr. Ide *saved* my life. ‖私たちは地震の被災者を助けるため献金をした We donated money to *help* the earthquake victims [survivors].

2【手伝う】 help +⽬ ▶私は兄に助けてもらって宿題をやり終えた My brother *helped* me finish my assignment. / My brother *helped* me *with* my assignment. ‖本田氏は父親を助けて会社の経営を行っている Mr. Honda *helps* his father run the company. ‖家計を助けるため母はスーパーでパートをしている To *help financially* [*To help with the family finances*], my mother is working part-time at a supermarket. ‖豊富なイラストが本文の理解を大いに助けてくれる The abundant illustrations in the book *are* quite *helpful* in understanding the text. ‖リパーゼは脂肪の消化を助ける働きをする Lipase *helps* digest fat. →手伝う.

たずさえる 携える carry +⽬ ▶恩師の好きなチョコレートを携えて訪問した I visited my former teacher *with* a box of her favorite chocolates in my hand. ▶《慣用表現》アメリカと日本は手を携えて東アジアの安定に貢献しなければならない The U.S. and Japan must *join forces* to contribute to the security of East Asia.

たずさわる 携わる be engaged《in》▶彼女は英語の本を出版する仕事に携わっている She *is engaged* [*involved*] *in* publishing English books. ‖父は貿易関係の仕事に携わっています My father *is in* the trading business.

たずねびと 尋ね人 a missing person (1人) ; the missing (➤集合的に)
‖(新聞の)**尋ね人欄** a personal column.

¹たずねる 尋ねる・訊ねる

1【質問する】 ask +⽬

> **【文型】**
> **人(A)に物(B)を尋ねる**
> ask A B
> ➤ B にくる語句は question, something など, または wh- の文
> **人(A)に B について [B のことを] 尋ねる**
> ask A about B
> **人(A)に～かどうか尋ねる**
> ask A if [whether] S + V

▶ **対話**「ちょっとお尋ねしたいことがあるのですが」「いいですよ. どうぞ」"May I *ask* you *something* [*a* (*quick*) *question*]?" "Yes, go ahead." ‖私は京子に(彼女の身に)何があったのか尋ねた I *asked* Kyoko *what* had happened to her. ‖母は私にきょうの弁当はどうだったと尋ねた My mother *asked* me *how* the box lunch she had made for me today was. ‖たくさんの人がニックさんに日本に来て何年ですかと尋ねる Many people *ask* Nick *how long* he's been in Japan. ‖私は彼に彼の家族のことを尋ねた I *asked* him *about* his family. ‖姉はボーイフレンドのことを尋ねられて恥ずかしがっていた My (older) sister acted [seemed] embarrassed when she *was asked about* her boyfriend. ‖《掲示》詳細は店内でお尋ねください *Inquire* Within.

▶刑事はぼくにその男を知っているかと尋ねた The detective *asked* me *if* I knew the man. ‖叔父さんは少年に学校が好きかと尋ねた The boy's uncle *asked* him *if* [*whether*] he liked [likes] school. ‖医者は私にたばこは吸うかと尋ねた The doctor *asked* me *if* I smoked [smoke]. (●時制を一致させて, if の文の動詞を過去形にするのが原則).

2【さがし求める】 search《for》▶人々は行方不明の子供を尋ねて山を捜し回った People *searched* the mountain *for* the missing child. ‖一行は黄河の源流を尋ねる旅に出た The party left on a trip to *follow* the Yellow River to its source.

²たずねる 訪ねる

visit +⽬, pay a visit (➤後者はやや堅い言い方) ; call on (人を) ; call at (場所を)

> **語法** (1) visit は文語・《インフォーマル》のいずれでも用いられる. call on [upon], call at は《米》では堅い文章語で, 《英》ではビジネスなどの改まった会話で用いられる. (2)「人をひょっこり訪ねる」には drop in を, 「(古い記憶などを頼りに) 人を不意に訪ねる」には look ... up を用いる.

▶私はきのう戸田先生を自宅に訪ねた I *visited* [*called on*] Mr. Toda at his house yesterday. ‖淳子は求職のため職安を訪ねた Junko *visited* the employment office to look for a job [for work]. ‖来週鎌倉に居る彼女を訪ねることにした I've decided to *pay* her *a visit* in Kamakura next week. ‖横浜へいらっしゃることがあったらいつでも訪ねてください Any time you come to Yokohama, (please) *look* me *up*. ‖シャワーを浴びようとしたところへ友だちがひょっこり訪ねて来た A friend *dropped in on* me just as I was getting into the shower. (➤この on は迷惑を表す；→立ち寄る) ‖ 私が訪ねたとき彼女はテレビを見ていた She was watching TV when I *went to see her* [when I *visited*].

たぜい 多勢 ▶多勢に無勢，ここは逃げるにしかずだ *They far outnumber us.* We'd better flee now.

だせい 惰性 **1**【慣性】**inertia** /ɪnə́ːrʃə/ ▶摩擦や空気の抵抗が無ければ，こまは**惰性**で永久に回り続ける Without friction and the resistance of the air, a top would keep spinning forever *under its own inertia.*

2【習慣】▶私はろくに読みもしないのに**惰性**で毎週その雑誌を買っている I keep on buying the magazine each week *from* [*by*] *force of habit* though I barely read it.

だせき 打席 a **trip to the plate** ▶打席に立つ *come to bat* ／*step to the plate* ‖ 彼は5**打席**で4安打1四球だった In his five *trips to the plate* [In his five *at bats*], he had four hits and walked once.

だせん 打線 **the batting lineup** /láɪnʌp/ ▶7回，仙台育英高校の**打線**が爆発した In the seventh inning, the Sendai Ikuei *batting lineup* started hitting furiously. ‖ 中日ドラゴンズは**打線**が好調だ The Chunichi Dragons' *batting* is superb. ／The Chunichi Dragons *batters* are in top shape.

たぞうきふぜん 多臓器不全 **multi-organ failure.**

たそがれ 黄昏 **dusk** /dʌsk/；**(evening) twilight**（薄明かり）▶**たそがれ**の空に一番星が光っている The first star is shining in *the evening sky*.

だそく 蛇足 an **unnecessary addition** [**remark**] ▶彼の最後のことばは**蛇足**だった His last remark *was unnecessary.*

たた 多々 ▶医者に患者の病気の原因がわからないことは**多々ある** *There are quite a few* cases where a doctor doesn't know the cause of the patient's illness.

ことわざ **多々ますます弁ず** The more the better. (➤「多ければ多いほどよい」の意).

ただ 只・唯・徒 **1**【ふつうの】**ordinary**（平凡な）；**common**（ありふれた）▶父は**ただ**のサラリーマンです My father is an *ordinary* office worker. ‖ それは**ただ**のかぜだよ It's just a *common* cold. ‖ 渡辺氏は**ただ**の政治家ではない Mr. Watanabe is *no ordinary* [*isn't any ordinary*] politician. (●「ふつうの政治家ではない，特別に優れた政治家だ」の意．これを Mr. Watanabe is not an ordinary politician. とすると単に「ふつうではない」の意になるのがふつう) ‖ 私たち，**ただ**のお友達よ We're *just* friends. (➤ just に強勢を置く).

▶《慣用表現》弟をいじめるやつがいたら，**ただじゃおかない**ぞ If anyone has picked on my little brother, he's [she's] *in for it* (*from me*). (➤ be in for it で「仕返しを受ける」) ／If anyone picks on my little brother, he's *going to pay for it*.

2【無料の】**free** ▶そのコンサートの**ただ**の券 a *free* ticket for the concert ‖ このペンは**ただ**でもらった I got this pen *for nothing* [*for free*]. (➤後者はややくだけた言い方) ‖ その自動車は**ただ**同然の値で売られた The car (was) sold *for almost nothing* [*for a song*]. (➤ for a song は「捨て値で」).

ことわざ **ただより高いものはない** There is no free lunch. (➤「おごってもらえる昼食には裏がある」の含み).

3【単に】**just**；**only**（ただ…だけ）

▶ 30年ぶりに会った父子は**ただ**泣くばかりだった The father and his son *just* kept crying [could *only* cry] when they met after a thirty-year separation. ‖ 一度**ただ**話をさせてくれるだけでいい *All I ask* is that you let me talk to you once. ‖ この連休は**ただ**家でごろごろしていた During the (recent) consecutive holidays, I did *nothing but* lie around the house. (➤ nothing but は only と同じ) ‖ それは**ただ**の推測にすぎない It's *only* speculation. ‖ 彼女は**ただ**歌うばかりでなく作曲もする She *not only* sings, but (also) composes. (➤ not only A but (also) B で「ただAだけでなくBも」の意).

> **直訳の落とし穴「ただ…したいだけ」**
> 「ただ愉快にやりたいだけ」のような文をいうとき，日本人は just がすぐ口をついて出るようで，いきなり最初に持ってきて，(×)Just I want to have fun. などとする学習者が多い．英語では just は強める語の直前に置くのが原則で，通例主語のあと，(強勢のある)動詞の前である．be 動詞や完了形の have などではそのあとになる．したがって，I just want to have fun. とする．

4【数量が少ないことを誇張して】**only** ▶ゆかりは**ただ**一度の失恋に懲りて男嫌いになった Yukari came to dislike men after *only* a single experience of being heartbroken. ‖ ぼくは**ただ**の一度だってきみを裏切ったことはない I have *never* betrayed you. ‖ ボブさんはこの村に住む**ただ**1人の外国人だ Bob is *the only* foreigner living in this village.

5【補足説明して】▶ S ホールは音響効果がすごくいいよ．**ただ**駅から遠くてねえ S Hall has good acoustics. *The only bad thing about it* is that it is far from the train station.

だだ 駄々 ▶**だだ**をこねるんじゃありません Stop *whining.* (➤ whine /hwaɪn/ は「哀れっぽく泣く」) ‖ いくら**だだ**をこねてもきょうは何も買いませんよ I'm not going to buy anything for you today no matter how much you *whine.*

‖**だだっ子** a spoiled child [brat]（甘えっ子）.

ただい 多大な **great**；**serious**（深刻な）▶国連は世界平和のために**多大な**貢献をしてきた The United Nations has made a *great* contribution to world peace. ‖ その大地震は観光業界に**多大な**被害を与えた The big earthquake did *great* [*serious*] damage to the tourist industry. ‖ 先週は病気欠勤して皆さんに**多大な**ご迷惑 [ご心配] をおかけして申し訳ありません I'm sorry I caused *so much inconvenience* [*concern*] because of my absence from work due to illness last week.

だたい 堕胎 (an) **abortion** (➤個々の事例は C) →中絶 ━動 **堕胎する** **have an abortion, abort**（＋目）.

ただいま 只今・唯今 **1**【現在】**right now, now** ▶父は**ただいま**外出中です My father is out *right now* [*at the moment*]. ‖ 課長は**ただいま**戻りました Our (section) manager has *just* come back. ‖ 対話（レストランで）「ピザはまだですか」「**ただいま**お持ちします」"Is the pizza ready ?" "Coming *right* up !"

2【挨拶】▶お母さん，**ただいま**！ *I'm home*, Mom !

> **解説「ただいま」の言い方**
> (1)「ただいま」に当たる特に決まった言い方はないので訳例のように言ったり，Hi [Hello], Mom ! のように言ったりする．答えるほうも，例えば Hi, Yukio. How was your day ? のように答える．
> (2) I'm home ! の代わりに I'm back ! とも言えるが，後者は留守にしていた時間が前者の場合より短いことが多い．→お帰りなさい．

た

[1]**たたえる 称える** praise +目; admire +目 (感心・敬服する) ▶アラーをたたえる *praise* [*give praise to*] Allah ‖ 彼の勇気をたたえる *admire* [*praise*] his courage ‖ その詩人は自然の美しさをたたえる詩をたくさん書いた The poet wrote many poems *extolling* the beauty of nature. (➤ extol はpraiseの強意語).

[2]**たたえる 湛える** ▶満々と水をたたえた湖 a lake *full to the brim* ‖ 彼は満面に笑みをたたえていた He was *beaming* [*smiling*] *all over*. / He was *all smiles*.

たたかい 戦い・闘い **1【戦闘】**(a) **war** (戦争); a **battle** (局地戦); a **fight** (けんか) ▶桶狭間の戦い the *battle* of Okehazama ‖ 源氏は平家との戦いに勝った The Genji won their *battle* against the Heike. ‖ 不良グループはぼくたちに戦いを挑んできた The gang challenged us to *a fight*.

2【闘争】a **battle**, a **fight** 《against》 ▶時間との闘い a *race* against time ‖ シベリアの暮らしは厳しい自然との闘いである Life in Siberia is *a battle against* harsh nature. ‖ 医師たちはがんとの闘いを続けている Doctors are continuing their *fight* [*battle*] *against* cancer. ‖ 新婚時代は貧乏との闘いでした During the first days of our marriage, we were constantly *struggling with* [*fighting* (*against*)] poverty.

たたかう 戦う・闘う **1【戦争する, 勝負する】** **fight** 《against, with》

【文型】
敵(A)と戦う
fight against A
fight A

▶わが国は連合軍と戦った Our country *fought* (*a war*) *against* [*with*] the Allied Forces. (➤ fight with は「ともに戦う」の意味にもなる. fight は「戦争をする」の意味で, fight a war, fight a battle という言い方ができる) ‖ かつてわが国はロシアと戦った In the past, Japan *waged* (*a*) *war against* [*on*] Russia. ‖ 両チームは優勝を懸けて戦った Both teams *fought* [*battled*] *for* the championship. ‖ わがチームは正々堂々と戦った(=競技をした) Our team *competed fair and square*.

2【苦難に立ち向かう】fight, struggle ▶言論の自由のために闘う *fight* for freedom of speech ‖ おばは3年前から乳がんと闘っている My aunt has *been fighting* breast cancer for three years. ‖ 何人もの消防士が炎と闘っていた Several firefighters *fought the blaze*. ‖ その国は経済的かつ政治的困難と闘っている That country *is fighting* [*is struggling with*] economic and political difficulties.

たたき 叩き ▶アジのたたき *minced* horse mackerel ‖ カツオのたたき *lightly grilled* bonito.

たたきあげる 叩き上げる ▶たたき上げの人 *a self-made man* [*woman*] ‖ 彼は下積みからたたき上げて銀行のトップにまでなった He *worked his way up from the bottom* to the top of the bank organization.

たたきうり 叩き売り ▶道端で男がバナナのたたき売りをしていた A man was *selling* bananas *at a* (*big*) *discount* at the roadside.

たたきおこす 叩き起こす ▶彼は真夜中に隣の人をたたき起こした He *knocked at the door and woke up* his next-door neighbor at midnight. ‖ けさは4時におやじにたたき起こされた My father *rousted* me *out of bed* [*shook* me *awake*] at four in the morning. (➤ roust /raʊst/ は《米》で「たたき起こす」の意).

たたきおとす 叩き落とす ▶(ハエたたきなどで)ハエをたたき落とす *swat* a fly ‖ 柿の実をたたき落としたのは誰だ Who *knocked* all the persimmons *off the tree*?

たたきこむ 叩き込む **hammer** /hǽmər/ **into** (教え込む) ▶彼は子供の頃に礼儀作法をたたき込まれた Good manners *were hammered* [*were pounded*] *into* him in his childhood. ‖ この公式は頭にたたき込んでおけよ *Memorize* these formulas *so well that they are engraved in your memory* [*brain*]. (➤ engrave は「刻み込む」).

たたきころす 叩き殺す **beat ... to death** (殴って); **batter ... to death** (乱打して); **club ... to death** (こん棒で).

たたきだい 叩き台 ▶彼の案を討議のたたき台にしよう Let's use his plan as *a springboard* [*a basis*] for discussion. (➤ springboard は「足がかり, 出発点」).

たたきだす 叩き出す ▶そんなことをしたら家をたたき出されるよ If I ever did anything like that, I would *be kicked out of* the house. ‖ 福島は200メートルで日本新記録をたたき出した Fukushima *set a new Japanese record* in the 200-meter dash.

たたきつける 叩き付ける ▶彼はグラスを壁に[床に]たたきつけた He *dashed* the glass *against* the wall [*to* the floor]. (➤ dash は「激しくぶつける」) ‖ 投手はグラブを地面にたたきつけて悔しがった The pitcher *flung* his glove *to* the ground in (his) frustration. (➤ flung は fling (投げつける)の過去形) ‖ 小ぬか雨からたたきつけるような雨になった The rain started as a drizzle and turned into *a heavy downpour*. ▶(比喩的) 彼は上司に辞表をたたきつけた He *thrust* his resignation at his boss. (➤ thrust は「突きつける」).

たたきなおす 叩き直す ▶おまえのひねくれた根性をたたき直してやる I'm going to *fix* that perverse disposition of yours.

たたきのめす 叩きのめす ▶彼をたたきのめす *knock* him *down* / *floor* him *with a blow* / *give* him *a good* [*sound*] *thrashing*.

たたく 叩く **1【打つ】hit** +目 (狙いをつけて), **strike** +目 (➤ 後者のほうが堅い語, または法律用語); **clap** +目 (手を); **knock** +目 (拳などでトントンと); **tap** +目 (軽く); **slap** +目 (平手で); **beat** +目 (続けざまに)

【文型】
人(A)の B をたたく
hit A **on** [**in**] **the** B
➤ B は身体の部分. on は head, cheek, nose などに, in は head, face, stomach などに用いる. strike も同じ文型をとる

▶彼はいきなり私の頭をたたいた He suddenly *hit* me *in* [*on*] *the* head. (● hit my head のように, hit A's head ともいうが, これは何かが頭に当たる, または, (自分で)頭を何かにぶつける, の意味で使うのがふつう. 「背中をたたく」の場合も in [on] the back) ‖ 私は顔[胸]を強くたたかれた I *was hit* hard *in the* face [chest]. ‖ 彼は演説中, 何度もテーブルをたたいた He *struck* the table many times during his speech. (➤ struck は strike の過去形) ‖ 誰かがドアをたたいている Someone is *knocking on* [*at*] the door. ‖ ドラムをたたくのは楽しい *Beating* the drums is a lot of fun. ▶誰かが後ろから私の肩をぽんとたたいた Someone *tapped* me on the shoulder from behind. (→肩たたき) ‖ 水槽のガラスをたたかないでください Do not *tap* aquarium windows. ‖ 子供の頃はよく母親にお尻をた

たかれた My mother often *spanked* me when I was a child. (➤ spank は「罰としてお尻をたたく」) ‖ 彼女は彼の顔をぴしゃりとたたいた She *slapped* his face. ／ She *slapped* him on [across] the face. ‖ 激しい雨が窓ガラスをたたいている The heavy rain *is beating against* [*striking*] the windowpane.
▶サッカー選手たちがフィールドに入場すると観客は一斉に手をたたいた All the spectators *clapped their hands* [*applauded*] when the soccer players came onto the field [《主に英》 pitch]. (➤ applaud は「拍手喝采する」) ‖ 騎手はホームストレッチにかかると懸命に馬の尻をたたいた(＝むち打った) The jockey *whipped* the horse desperately at the stretch.
2【攻撃する】criticize +⑪ (批判する) ▶彼女の博士論文は教授からさんざんたたかれた Her Ph.D. dissertation *was* severely *criticized* [*was panned*] by the professor. (➤ pan は「こき下ろす」) ‖ 彼をたたくな. ベストを尽くしているんだから！ *Don't knock* him, he's doing his best！ ‖ 新聞はこぞってその談合入札をたたいた The newspapers were unanimous in *condemning* the rigged bidding. (➤ unanimous /junǽnɪməs/ は「全員が一致して」, condemn /kəndém/ は「厳しく非難する」の意).
3【値切る】▶この中古車, さんざんたたいて半値にまけさせたんだ I *haggled over the price* of this used car and got the price knocked down by half. (➤ haggle over は「しつこく値切る」).

ただごと 只事・唯事・徒事 ▶あの悲鳴はただごとではない Judging from the sound of that scream, it must be *something really bad*！ ‖ その状態はただごとではなかった The situation *was grave* [*serious*].

ただし but ▶この本, 貸してあげるよ. ただし汚さないでね I'll loan you the book, *but* don't get it dirty. ‖ 私は日本食が気に入っている. ただし納豆は別だ(＝納豆以外は好きだ) I like Japanese food, *but* natto is an exception. ／I like Japanese food *except for* natto. ‖ 本当のことをお話ししましょう. ただし録音・録画はしないこと I'll tell you the truth, *provided* you don't record or videotape the conversation. (➤ provided は「…という条件で」).
▶ただし書きに気をつけなさい Be careful of the *provisos* [the *fine print*]. (➤ proviso は /prəváɪzoʊ/ と発音. fine print は「(契約書などの)小さい文字で印刷された注意事項」の意で, small print ともいう).

ただしい 正しい correct, right, proper

> **解説** (1)一般に correct は「規準・標準的に見て正しい, 誤りがなくて正しい」, right は「真実・事実に一致していて正しい, 道徳的に見て正しい」の意であるが, 区別なく用いることもある.
> (2)proper は規則や作法にのっとっていて, 「適切な」「きちんとした」の意.

▶正しい答え the *correct* [*right*] answer ‖ 正しい手続きをとる follow the *proper* procedures ‖ あなたの英作文は文法的には正しい [正しくない] Your English composition is grammatically *correct* [*incorrect*]. ‖ 彼は正しいことと正しくないことの区別がつかない He can't tell the difference between *right* and *wrong*. ‖ あなたの言うことは正しい What you say is (absolutely) *correct* [*true*]. (➤ true は「事実である」) ／You are *right*. ‖ きみが正しいと思うとおりにやりなさい Do as you think *proper* [*fit*]. ‖ 紅茶の正しい入れ方を知っていますか Do you know the *proper* way to make tea？ ‖ 自分の名前を正しく書きなさい Write your name *correctly*. ‖ メキシコは正しくは(＝正確には)メキシコ合衆国という Mexico is the United Mexican States, *to be exact*.

¹ただす 正す correct +⑪ ▶不公平税制は正すべきである The unfairness of the tax system should be *corrected* [*rectified*]. (➤ rectify は correct よりも堅い語) ‖ 彼女は姿勢を正して挨拶した She *straightened up* and made her greetings.

²ただす 質す ▶彼女の真意をただす(＝確かめる)べきだ You should *make sure of* her true intention. ／ You should *find out* what she really means.

たたずまい 佇い appearance (外見); **atmosphere** /ǽtməsfɪəʳ/ (雰囲気) ▶この町にはまだ昔の城下町のたたずまいがある This town still has the *atmosphere* of an old castle town.

たたずむ 佇む stay [stand] still ▶彼女は湖畔にたたずんで, 向こう岸を見ていた She *stayed still* by the lake, looking across to the opposite shore.

ただただ ▶息子のサッカーへの入れ込みようにはただただ驚くばかりだ I'm *simply* amazed at my son's passion for soccer.

ただちに 直ちに 1【すぐに】immediately; at once, right away (➤ ともに「すぐに」に相当するが, 後者は前者よりもさらにくだけた言い方) ▶直ちに仕事に取りかかりなさい Get to work *right now* [*immediately* ／ *without delay*]. ‖ 直ちに武器を捨てて出て来なさい Put down your weapons *right away* and come out.
2【直接】▶家庭環境の悪さが直ちに子供の非行に結び付くとは限らない Juvenile delinquency is not always *directly* linked to a bad home environment.

だだっぴろい だだっ広い ▶だだっ広い家 a *huge* house ‖ 彼女はだだっ広い家にひとりで住んでいる She lives alone in a house which is *too big* for her. ／She lives in a house which is *far too big* [*spacious*] for a person living alone.

ただでさえ ▶暑い暑いって言わないでよ. ただでさえ暑いんだから Don't complain about it being hot. It's hot enough *without you saying so*. (➤「あなたが言わなくても」の意).

ただならぬ unusual (ふつうではない), **strange** (奇妙な) ▶ただならぬ音 an *unusual* [a *strange*] sound.

ただのり 只乗り a free ride ▶電車にただ乗りした I *sneaked* [*stole*] *a ride* on a train. (● 気づかれずに乗った場合) ／I *got a free ride* on a train. (● ただで乗せてもらえた場合).

ただばたらき 只働き ▶ただ働きをする *work for nothing* [*without pay*].

たたみ 畳 (a) tatami, a tatami mat
▶どうせ俺はたたみの上では死ねないだろう I probably won't be able to find a *decent place* to die.
日本紹介 ✉ **畳は稲わらで作った畳床をイグサで編んだ畳表で覆った, 和室専用の長方形のマットです. 和室の広さはこの畳が敷ける数で6畳間, 8畳間というように呼びます** Tatami are rectangular mats for Japanese-style rooms. They are made mainly of rice straw and covered with woven rush matting. The size of a Japanese-style room is calculated according to the number of tatami mats and are called, for example, six-mat rooms, eight-mat rooms, etc.

たたみかける 畳み掛ける ▶彼は畳みかけて質問した He *fired* questions (at me). ／He asked me *one* question *after another*. ‖ライオンズは畳みかけるような攻撃でこの回一挙に5点をあげた The Lions *got a string* of hits and scored as many as five runs in this inning.

たたむ 畳む **1**【紙や布などを】**fold** (**up**) ▶傘を畳む *fold* (*up*) an umbrella ‖洗濯物を畳む *fold* the laundry ‖布団は自分で畳みなさい *Fold up* [*Put away*] your futon by yourself. (➤ put away は「片づける」) ‖ぼくたちが朝食を用意する間にきみたちはテントを畳んでくれ Please *take down* the tents while we prepare breakfast.

2【閉める】**close** +㊐ ▶彼は店を畳んで田舎に引っ込んだ He *closed* his store and retired to the country.

た

ただもの 只者・唯者・徒者 ▶あの眼光鋭い侍はただ者ではない That samurai with sharp eyes *is no ordinary man*.

ただよう 漂う **1**【物が】**drift** ▶我々は水も食料も無く一昼夜海上を漂い続けた We *drifted about* [*were adrift*] for one whole day and night without water or food. ‖救命ボートは波間を漂っていた The lifeboat *was tossed about* by the waves. (➤ toss は「激しく揺する」) ‖白い雲が空に漂っている White clouds *are floating* in the sky.

2【香り・雰囲気が】▶香(こう)の香りが堂内に漂っていた The hall *was filled with* the scent of incense. ‖ケーキ屋さんの店内から甘い香りが漂ってきた A sweet aroma *drifted* out of the pastry shop. ‖この町には自由な空気が漂っている An atmosphere of freedom *pervades* in this town.

たたり 祟り a **curse**(呪い) ; **wrath** /ræθ/ (怒り) ▶お岩のたたりじゃ，あな恐ろしや How dreadful! Oiwa's *curse* is upon you. ‖あの山に入ると山の神様のたたりがあるぞ You'll suffer the *wrath* of the mountain god if you set foot on that mountain.

たたる 祟る ▶無理をするとあとでたたるよ If you continue overworking, it will *tell on* you later. (➤ tell on は「こたえる，影響を与える」) ‖日頃の不勉強がたたって期末テストの結果はさんざんだった My habitual laziness *resulted in* [*led to*] my doing very poorly in the final exams. ‖食べ過ぎがたたって胃を壊した I had stomach trouble *from* [*due to*] overeating. ‖彼は悪行がたたった He *got* what he deserved (for his misdeed(s)).

ただれる 爛れる **fester**(➤「(傷口が)うむ」の意でもある) ▶足の傷がただれてきた The wound on my leg began to *fester*.

▶彼女はただれた(＝だらしのない)生活を送っている She is leading a *dissipated* life.

1**たち 質** **nature**(性質) ; **temper** (気質) ▶父はすぐにかっとなるたちだ My father has *a hot* [*quick*] *temper*. ‖兄は頼まれると嫌と言えないたち(＝タイプ)だ My older brother is the *type* who can't say no to any request. ‖私はかぜをひきやすいたちだ I'*m prone to* colds. ／I catch colds *very easily*.

▶ことしのかぜはたちが悪い The colds going around this year are really *bad* [*nasty*].

2**たち 太刀** a ***tachi*** ; a long single-edged samurai sword (➤ 説明的な訳) ‖**太刀魚** a cutlass fish.

1**たちあい 立ち合い** ***tachiai*** ; an outset of a sumo bout (➤ 説明的な訳) ▶相撲は立ち合いで勝負が決まる The outcome of a sumo bout depends (on) how well the wrestlers do at the *tachiai* (*initial charge*).

2**たちあい 立ち会い** **presence**(同席，出席) ▶顧問弁護士の立ち会いのもとに遺言が読み上げられた The written will was read *in the presence of* the family lawyer [*with* the family lawyer *in attendance*]. ‖**立会演説会** a joint campaign-speech meeting ‖**立会人** an observer ; a witness (証人).

たちあう 立ち会う **be present**《at》▶交渉に立ち会う *attend* [*be present at*] the negotiations ‖誰が選挙の開票に立ち会うのですか Who will *be the witness* when the votes are counted? (➤ witness は「立会人，証人」).

たちあがる 立ち上がる **1**【起立する】**stand up** ; **rise** (腰を上げる) ▶私は急に立ち上がるとよくめまいがする I often feel dizzy when I *stand up* quickly. ‖先生に呼ばれて修一は席から立ち上がった When he was called on by the teacher, Shuichi *rose* from his seat [*got to his feet*]. ‖彼はほとんど反射的に立ち上がった He *sprang* [*jumped*] *to his feet* almost reflexively. (➤「ぱっと立ち上がった」の意).

2【行動を開始する】▶地元住民は干潟保護のために立ち上がった The local people *rose up* to preserve the tideland. ‖このコンピュータは立ち上がるのに時間がかかる It takes time before this computer *boots* (*up*) [*kicks in*].

3【回復する】▶彼女はいまだにその恐ろしいショックから立ち上がれないでいる She has not *recovered from* the horrible shock.

たちあげる 立ち上げる **boot** (**up**) +㊐, **start** (**up**) +㊐ (パソコンなどを；前者がよりくだけた言い方) ; **launch** +㊐ (事業などを) ▶パソコンを立ち上げる *boot* [*start*] (*up*) a personal computer ‖インターネットブラウザを立ち上げるのに数秒しかかからない It takes only a few seconds to *boot* my Internet browser. ‖新規事業を立ち上げる *start* [*launch*] a new business.

たちい 立ち居 **movements** ▶手術後，私は立ち居が不自由になった I had difficulty *getting around* after the operation.

たちいふるまい 立ち居振る舞い **bearing** (態度) ; **manner**(物腰) ; **carriage**(身のこなし) ; 《フォーマル》**deportment**(特に若い女性の) ▶立ち居振る舞いの堂々とした男性 a man of dignified *bearing* [*manner*] ‖あの娘は立ち居振る舞いがしとやかだ She has a graceful *bearing*. ／She is graceful in *movement*.

たちいり 立ち入り ▶《掲示》立ち入り禁止 Keep Out [Off] ／No Admittance (except on Business) ／No Trespassing ／Private ‖彼らはその会社の倉庫の立ち入り検査を行った They made *on-the-spot inspections* of the company's warehouses.

たちいる 立ち入る **1**【中へ入る】**enter** +㊐ ; **trespass**《on》(不法侵入する) ▶《掲示》立ち入るべからず Off Limits ／Keep Out ／No Admittance ‖危険地域には立ち入らないように *Stay clear* of high risk areas. ‖立ち入る者は処罰されます *Trespassers* will be prosecuted.

2【干渉する】▶他人のことに立ち入る *poke* [*stick*] *one's nose* in other people's business ‖立ち入ったことをお伺いするようですが，妊娠中ですか *Excuse me if I'm being too personal*, but are you expecting (a baby)?

たちうち 太刀打ち ▶私はチェスでは彼女に到底太刀打ちできない I *am no match for* her [*can hardly compete with* her] in chess.

たちおうじょう 立ち往生 ▶車が大雪で立ち往生した Cars and trucks *were stuck* [*were held up*] in the heavy snow. ‖ぼくたちはお金が無くなり，岩国で立ち往生した We ran out of money and *were* *stranded* in Iwakuni. (➤ be stranded は「途方に暮れる」).

たちおくれる 立ち遅れる·立ち後れる fall [lag] behind ▶その国の福祉政策は西欧諸国に比べて**立ち遅れている** That country's welfare policies *are behind* those of Western nations. ‖ 日本のサイバーテロ対策は米国に**立ち遅れている** Japan's anti-cyberterrorism measures *lag behind* those of the U.S.

たちおよぎ 立ち泳ぎ ▶**立ち泳ぎ**をする *tread water*.

たちかえる 立ち返る ▶我々は初心に**立ち返る**必要がある We need to *remember* our original enthusiasm.

たちがれる 立ち枯れる die; wilt(しおれる); **wither**(しなびる); **rot**(朽ちる)

‖**立ち枯れ病** a wilt disease.

たちぎえ 立ち消え ▶その計画は資金不足のため**立ち消え**になった The plan *came to nothing* [The plan *fell through*] for lack of funds. ‖ その選手のユベントス移籍のうわさは**立ち消えになった** The rumor of the player's transfer to Juventus *died out*.

たちぎき 立ち聞きする eavesdrop /íːvzdrɑːp/《on》(盗み聞きをする); **overhear** +目 (偶然に聞く) ▶彼らの話を**立ち聞きして**しまった I *overheard* them talking.

[1]**たちきる 断ち切る break**《off, with》▶悪い習慣を**断ち切る** *break* bad habits ‖ きみはあんな非行グループとの関係は**断ち切る**べきだ You should *break off* relations with [*break with*] such a group of delinquents. ‖ 彼はその女性に対する未練を**断ち切ろう**とした He tried to *give up* [*let go of*] his attachment to that woman.

[2]**たちきる 裁ち切る cut cloth [fabric]**.

たちぐい 立ち食い ▶駅のホームでそばを**立ち食いした** I *had* a bowl of soba noodles *standing* at a stall on the platform.

‖**立ち食いそば屋** a stand-up soba bar.

たちくらみ 立ち眩み ▶急に**立ちくらみがした** I suddenly *felt dizzy when I got to my feet*.

たちこめる 立ち籠める·立ち込める hang over ▶牧場に朝霧が**立ちこめていた** A morning mist *hung over* the meadow. ／The meadow *was veiled* [*was enveloped*] in a morning mist. ‖ 部屋にはたばこの煙が**立ちこめていた** The room *was heavy* [*thick* ／ *filled*] *with* cigarette smoke.

たちさる 立ち去る leave(+目); **go away** (行ってしまう) ▶彼女はひと言も言わずにその部屋を**立ち去った** She *left* [*walked out of*] the room without a word. ‖ (ここを)**立ち去れ**(=出ていけ)! *Get out* (*of here*)!

たちしょうべん 立ち小便 ▶**立ち小便をする**とはけしからん How inexcusable of him to *pee on the street* [*outdoors*]! (➤ pee は「おしっこする」の意. urinate /jʊ́ərəneɪt/ という堅い言い方もある).

たちすくむ 立ち竦む ▶私はそのむごたらしい光景に思わず**立ちすくんで**しまった I *was frozen* [*was petrified*] at the horrible sight. ‖ その男の子は猛犬にほえられてその場に**立ちすくんだ** When (he was) barked at by a fierce dog, the boy *stood rooted to the spot* with fear.

たちせき 立ち席 standing room. →立ち見.

たちつくす 立ち尽くす ▶彼女とけんか別れしたあと, 私は駅のホームで**立ち尽くした** After breaking up with her, I *stood absent-mindedly* on the platform of the station *for I don't know how long*.

たちっぱなし 立ちっ放し ▶私は博多までずっと**立ちっぱなしだった** I had to *stand all the way* to Hakata.

たちづめ 立ち詰め ▶電車は混んでいて1時間**立ち詰めだった** The train was so crowded that I *had to stand* for an hour.

たちどおし 立ち通し ▶売り場に立つ日は**立ち通し**で足が疲れる On days when I work at the sales counter, my feet get tired because I have to *keep standing the whole time*.

たちどころに 立ち所に then and there(その場で); **immediately**(直ちに) ▶ヒップホップのことなら彼は何を聞いても**たちどころに**答える He can answer anything about hip-hop *immediately*. ‖ その薬を飲むと痛みは**たちどころに**消えた The pain went away *like magic* as soon as I took the medicine. (➤ like magic は「魔法のごとく」の意).

たちどまる 立ち止まる stop; pause (一時的に) ▶彼女は**立ち止まって**ショーウインドーをのぞき込んだ She *stopped* [*paused*] to look at the shop window. ‖ **立ち止まらないで**進んでください *Move on* [*along*], *please*.

たちなおり 立ち直り resilience /rɪzíljəns/ (素早い原状回復); **recovery**(回復) ▶日本人は**立ち直りの早い**国民だ Japanese are a *resilient* people. ‖ だるま人形は**立ち直り**と我慢強さの象徴だ Daruma dolls are symbols of *resilience* and perseverance.

たちなおる 立ち直る get over, recover《from》▶事業の失敗から**立ち直る** *recover from* a business setback ‖ ちえみは(恋人との)別れのショックからやっと**立ち直った** Chiemi *has* finally *gotten over* the shock of her breakup. ‖ ピッチャーは3回から**立ち直った** The pitcher *regained his form* in the third inning.

たちならぶ 立ち並ぶ·建ち並ぶ ▶都心には高層ビルが**立ち並んでいる** Skyscrapers *stand in rows* [*side by side*] in the center of Tokyo.

たちのかせる 立ち退かせる evict +目 (法的手続きによって); **evacuate** +目 (危険地域などから) ▶暴力団をマンションから**立ち退かせる** *evict* a yakuza gang from an apartment building ‖ 住民を災害地域から**立ち退かせる** *evacuate* residents from a disaster area.

たちのき 立ち退き removal(移転); **eviction**(法的手続きに基づく); **evacuation**(危険地域などからの) ▶家主は彼が家賃を4か月滞納したため**立ち退き**を要求した The landlord demanded that he *move out* [*leave*] because he was four months behind in rent. (● demand that に続く文では《米》では should のない原形を用いる).

‖**立ち退き通告** an eviction notice.

たちのく 立ち退く move out《of》▶区画整理のために彼らはこの土地を**立ち退かなければならない** They have to *move out of* this place on account of a zoning adjustment.

たちのぼる 立ち上る go up, rise ▶煙突の煙が空にまっすぐ**立ち上った** The smoke from the chimney *went up* [*rose*] straight into the air.

たちのみ 立ち飲み a quick drink while standing up

‖**立ち飲み店** a standing bar, a bar with no seats.

たちば 立場 1【置かれている状況】a situation; a position (他人との関係で生じる) ▶友人に裏切られて私は苦しい**立場**に立たされた Betrayed by a friend, I was put in *a difficult situation* [*spot*]. ‖ 彼は微妙な**立場**に立っていた He found himself in *a very delicate situation*. ‖ 私はそのことについて目下何らコメントする**立場**にありません I'm not in the *position* now to make any comments about that. ／In my present *position*, I can't make any comments

about that.
▶少しは私の立場になってみてくれよ Please *put yourself in my place* [*in my shoes*]! (➤ put oneself in ~'s shoes は「人の身になって考える」の意のインフォーマルな言い方) ‖ 私がきみの立場だったら「ノー」と言うだろう *If I were in your place* [*If I were you*], I would say no.
2【ものの見方】 a **stand**, a **standpoint** (見地); a **point of view** (観点); a **stance** (態度) ▶彼は医師の立場から喫煙の害を説明した He explained the harm of smoking from the *standpoint* of a doctor [from a doctor's *point of view*]. ‖ 賛成なのか反対なのか立場を明らかにしてくれませんか Could you make your *standpoint* clear whether you are for or against it? ‖ この問題についてあなたの立場はどうですか Where do you *stand* on this question? ‖ 私はすでに自分の(政治的)立場を明らかにしている I have already made my (*political*) *stance* clear.

たちはだかる 立ちはだかる **block** +㊐ ▶出口に立ちはだかる *block* (the way to) the exit ‖ 彼は行く手に立ちはだかって, 私を通そうとしなかった He *stood in* [*blocked*] *my way* and wouldn't let me through.
▶多くの難問が我々の前に立ちはだかっている Many difficulties *lie ahead of* us. / There are many difficulties *in our way* [*on the road ahead*].

たちばなし 立ち話 ▶立ち話も何ですから, どうぞお入りください *It's not good to stand here talking*, so please come on in.

たちふさがる 立ち塞がる **stand in the way** ▶彼らの計画実現には多くの障害が立ちふさがっていた Many obstacles *stood in the way* of the realization of their plans. ‖ 彼は出入り口に立ちふさがっていた He *stood in* the doorway.

たちまち 忽ち **in a moment, in an instant** (一瞬にして); **at once** (すぐに) ▶風が強かったので火はたちまち広がった Since the wind was strong, the fire spread *in a moment* [*in an instant*]. ‖ その育毛剤はたちまち売り切れてしまった The hair restorers were sold out *at once*. ‖ うわさはたちまち学校中に広まった The rumor *spread* through the school *like wildfire*. (➤ spread like wildfire は「(野火のように)早く広がる」).

たちまわる 立ち回る ▶彼は如才なく立ち回って早く出世した He *acted in a smart and tactful way* and got speedy promotion. ‖ 帳簿のごまかしが見つからないように事務員はうまく立ち回った The clerk *played her cards well* so as not to be caught doctoring the accounts. (➤ play one's cards well は「事をうまく処理する」の意).

たちみ 立ち見 ▶《掲示》ただいま立ち見になります Standing Room Only (➤ SRO と省略; standing room は「立ち見席」) ‖ **立ち見客** a standee.

たちむかう 立ち向かう **face** +㊐, **confront** +㊐ ▶困難に立ち向かう *face* difficulties. ‖ がんに立ち向かう *confront* [*fight* / *stand up to*] cancer (➤ stand up to はインフォーマルな言い方).

だちょう 駝鳥 an **ostrich** /ɑ́:strɪtʃ/.

たちよみ 立ち読み ▶彼女はしょっちゅう書店で週刊誌を立ち読みする She often *stands reading* [*browses through*] weekly magazines in bookstores. (➤ browse /braʊz/ through は「拾い読みする」) ‖ 《掲示》立ち読みお断り No browsing.

たちよる 立ち寄る **drop in** 《at, on》 (➤ at の次には家などが, on の次には人がくる), **drop** [**stop** / **go**] **by** 《at》 (場所に); **stop over** [**off**] 《at》 (旅の途中などに短期間) ▶学校の帰りにパソコンショップに立ち寄った I *dropped in at* [*dropped into*] a computer shop on my way home from school. ‖ きょうの夕方, あなたのところに立ち寄っていいですか Can I *drop in on* you [*stop by* your place] this evening? ‖ 九州へ行く途中, 倉敷に立ち寄った I *stopped over* [*off*] in Kurashiki on my way to Kyushu. ‖ ブリストルに行く途中, 叔父のうちに立ち寄った On my way to Bristol, I *dropped in at* my uncle's home. ‖ 近くに来られましたらどうぞお立ち寄りください When you're in the neighborhood, please *stop by* [*drop in* / *drop by*] to see us. ‖ 容疑者は実家に立ち寄ったところを逮捕された The suspect was arrested when he *turned up at* his parents' home. (➤ turn up は「ひょっこり現れる」).

だちん 駄賃 a **reward** (報酬) ▶母親は使いをした息子に駄賃をやった The mother gave her son *a reward* for running an errand for her.

[1]たつ 立つ・建つ・発つ

📖 訳語メニュー
直立する →stand (up) **1**
建築される →be built **2**
出発する →leave **4**
立候補する →run for **4**
出てくる →rise **5**

1【人や物が直立する】 **stand up** (立ち上がる; 動作); **stand** (立っている; 状態) ▶みなさん, お立ちください Would you all *stand up*, please? ‖ 馬は生まれてすぐに立つことができる Horses can *stand* soon after they are born. (● 立ち上がるという動作よりも立っていられる能力をさすので stand が適当) ‖ 首相の後ろにはいつもボディーガードが 2, 3 人立っている A couple of bodyguards always *stand* behind the prime minister. ‖ バスで席が無かったので, ずっと立っていなければならなかった I couldn't find a seat on the bus, so I had to *stand* all the way. ‖ 大きくなったね. 立ってごらん You've grown tall. *Stand up* and let me have a look at you. ‖ 6 回の満塁のときにはファンは立って応援した The fans *stood up* and cheered when the bases were loaded in the sixth inning. ‖ **対話** (プールで) 「そっちは深いから危ないよ」「大丈夫だよ. 背が立つから」 "That side is deep. So it's dangerous." "Don't worry. I [My feet] *can touch the bottom*."
▶シェパードや秋田犬は耳が立っている The ears of German shepherds and Akitas *stick up*.
2【建築される】 **be built** ▶造成地にたくさんの家が建った Many houses *have been built* in the newly developed area. ‖ うちの前には10階建てのマンションが立っている *There is* a ten-story condominium in front of our house.
▶私たちの学校は丘の上に立っている Our school *stands* on a hill.
3【身を置く】 ▶《マラソンで》折り返し地点で私は先頭に立った I *took the lead* at the turn. ‖ ぼくは甲子園で初めてバッターボックスに立ったときは緊張した I got nervous when I *stood* in the batter's box at Koshien for the first time. ‖ 人の上に立つ人間になりたい I want to be *a leader*. ‖ 何事も相手の立場に立って考える習慣をつけなさい You should try to form the habit of putting yourself *in other people's shoes*. (➤ put oneself in ~'s shoes は「人の身に

なって考える」の意のインフォーマルな言い方).
4【行動を起こす】leave（+目）（立ち去る）; **run for**（立候補する）

【文型】
場所(A)をたって場所(B)に向かう
leave A for B

▶ロンドンに向けて東京をたつ *leave* Tokyo *for* London（➤ 実際の文では leave Tokyo または leave for London のどちらかで使うことが多い）‖いつ鹿児島へたちますか When are you *leaving for* Kagoshima?‖ゲストのスピーチが終わらないうちに**席を立つ**のは失礼です It is rude to *leave your seat* before the guest finishes his speech.
ことわざ **立つ鳥跡を濁さず** A bird that is going to fly away doesn't foul its own nest.
▶私は次の知事選に立つつもりです I'm going to *run for* governor in the next election.
5【発生する, 開催される】rise ▶何年も使われていない部屋を歩くとほこりが立った Dust *rose* when I walked through the room which hadn't been used for many years.（➤ rose は rise の過去形）‖波が立ってきた The waves *are rising*. / The sea *has become rough*.（➤ 後者は「海が荒れてきた」の意）‖最近彼にはよくないうわさが立っている Recently, *there is* a bad rumor about him *floating around* [*circulating*].‖あの男のことを考えるだけで**腹が立つ** The mere thought of him *makes me angry*.
▶週末はこの通り沿いに**朝市が立つ** *Morning markets are held* [*are opened*] along this street on weekends.
6【成り立つ】▶旅行の計画はまだ立たない Our travel plans *haven't been made* yet.
7【勃起する】get a hard-on.

2**たつ 経つ** **pass (by), go by**（経過する）▶祖母が亡くなってから７年たつ Seven years *have passed* since my grandmother died.（➤ 文語的な言い方）/ It has been [is] seven years since my grandmother died.（➤ is は主に《英》用法）‖時がたつにつれて悲しみも薄らいだ *As time went by*, my sorrow lessened.‖**時がたつのは速いなあ** *Time passes* [*goes*] *by* so quickly. / *How time flies!*‖何かに夢中になっていると時間はあっという間にたってしまうように思われる Time seems to *fly* when you are absorbed in doing something.
▶もう少したってからまた電話してくださいませんか Can you call me again *a little later*?‖ゆかりはもう10分かそこらたてば帰って来ますよ Yukari will come home *in* another ten minutes or so.（➤ この in は「(今から)…あとに」と時間の経過を表す）‖１週間もたたないうちに彼女はよくなるだろう She should be well again *in less than* a week.

3**たつ 断つ·絶つ** **1【切断する】cut off, sever** /sévəʳ/ +目（➤ 後者は堅い語）▶その台風のため通信網が断たれた Communications (network) *were cut off* because of the typhoon.‖日本はその国との国交を絶った Japan *cut off* [*severed*] diplomatic relations with the country.‖私は彼との交際を絶った I *broke up* [*broke it off*] with him.（➤ break up [break it off] with は「(人と)別れる」）‖そのジェット機は赤城山の付近で消息を絶った We *lost contact with* the jet near Mt. Akagi.‖歌手になりたがる若い女の子があとを絶たない *There's no end* of [*There's an unending stream* of] young girls who aspire to become singers.

2【やめる】give up ▶父は肝臓を悪くして酒を断った My father *gave up* [*quit*] drinking after having liver trouble.‖彼はこの10年間酒を断っている He has been *on the wagon* for the past ten years.‖彼は乏しい収入の中から貯金するためにすべての楽しみを断った He *denied himself* every pleasure to save from his meager earnings.（➤ deny oneself は「(楽しみなどを)自制する」）‖彼は十九の命を**自ら絶った** He *took his own life* [*killed himself* / *committed suicide*] at the age of nineteen.

4**たつ 裁つ** **cut** +目 ▶この布を寸法に合わせて裁ちなさい *Cut* this cloth to measure.

5**たつ 辰** **the Dragon**
‖**辰年** the year of the Dragon.

だつ- 脱- ▶彼は脱サラをしてすし屋を始めた He *quit* his *job as an office worker* and opened a sushi restaurant.
‖**脱原発** abandoning nuclear power generation（原子力発電の放棄）; changing nuclear power policy（原子力政策の転換）‖**脱ダム政策** anti-dam [non-dam] policy.

だつい 脱衣する **take off** one's **clothes**
‖**脱衣所** a changing room（更衣室）; a bathhouse（海水浴場などの）; a locker room（体育館などの）.

1**だっかい 脱会する** **quit** +目（辞める）; **leave** +目（去る）▶彼はその新興宗教団体を脱会することにした He decided to *leave* the new religious sect.

2**だっかい 奪回する** **recapture** /riːkǽptʃəʳ/ +目 ▶彼は次の試合でタイトルの奪回を目指している He aims to *recapture* the title in the next match.

たっかん 達観 ▶きみは人生を達観したようなことを言うね You sound like you *know all there is to know* about life. / You talk as if you've *become philosophical* about life.

だっかん 奪還する **recapture** +目; **regain** +目 ▶首位を奪還する *regain* [*recapture*] first place.

だっきゃく 脱却 ▶古い考え方から脱却する *shake oneself loose from* conventional ideas‖不況から脱却する *pull out* of a recession‖あの画家はまだ素人の域を脱却していない That artist *hasn't moved* beyond the level of an amateur yet.

たっきゅう 卓球 **table tennis, ping-pong**（➤ 前者が正式）▶卓球をする play *ping-pong*.
‖**卓球台** a ping-pong table.

だっきゅう 脱臼 **dislocation** 一動 **脱臼する** **dislocate** /díslәkeɪt/ +目 ▶彼は柔道をしていて左肩を脱臼した He *dislocated* his left shoulder practicing judo. / His left shoulder *went out* (*of joint*) while he was practicing judo.

タック a **tuck.**

ダッグアウト a **dugout.**

ダックスフント《動物》a **dachshund.**

タッグマッチ a **tag-team (wrestling) match.**

タックル a **tackle** 一動 **タックルする** **tackle** +目 ▶(そいつを)タックルしろ! *Tackle* him!‖ナイスタックル! *Nice tackle!*

たっけん 卓見·達見 an **excellent idea** ▶この論者がこの記事で述べていることはなかなかの卓見だ What the author is saying in this article is *excellent* indeed.

だっこ 抱っこ ▶女の子は「ママ, だっこして」と言った The girl said, "Mommy, *carry me* (*in your arms*)." / The girl said, "*Pick me up*, Mommy!"‖真希はいまだに縫いぐるみの犬をだっこして寝るんです Maki still goes to bed *with* a stuffed

toy dog *in her arms*. ‖ (あなたの赤ちゃん)だっこしていい? Can I *hold* her [him]?
‖だっこひも a baby strap [carrier].

だっこう 脱稿する finish writing a paper (論文を); finish [complete] a manuscript(原稿を).

だっこく 脱穀する thresh (+目)
‖脱穀機 a thresher, a threshing machine.

だつごく 脱獄する escape from [break out of] prison
‖脱獄囚 a prison [jail /dʒeɪl/] breaker, an escaped convict /kɑ́:nvɪkt/.

だっしにゅう 脱脂乳 skim milk
‖脱脂粉乳 powdered skim milk.

だっしめん 脱脂綿 absorbent cotton, 《英》 cotton wool ▶脱脂綿で傷口をきれいにする clean the cut with (*absorbent*) *cotton*.

たっしゃ 達者 1【上手なこと】▶彼は中国語が達者だ He *speaks* Chinese *fluently*. / He *is a good speaker* of Chinese. / He *is good at* Chinese. ‖この島の子供たちは皆泳ぎが達者だ All the children on this island are *good* swimmers. ‖政治家は口が達者でないといけない Politicians have to *be skillful* [*good*] *speakers*.
2【丈夫なこと】▶父は達者だ My father *is very healthy*. / My father *enjoys good* [*robust*] *health*. ‖お達者ですか Are you *in good health* [《英》 *in fine fettle*]? ‖祖父は足が達者で, 毎年富士登山をする My grandfather *has strong legs*, and he climbs Mt. Fuji every year. ‖どうぞお達者で I wish you *good health*.

だっしゅ 奪取 seizure /sí:ʒəʳ/ **━動 奪取する** seize /si:z/ +目 (力ずくで); grab +目 (いきなり) ▶政権を奪取する *seize* the government / *seize* power.

ダッシュ 1【記号】 a dash (—の記号); a prime (′の記号) ▶Bダッシュ B′ (➤ B prime /bì: práɪm/ と読む. ″であれば double prime).
2【突き進むこと】 a dash ▶栄冠へダッシュ! *A dash* toward victory! ‖走者はゴール前で猛烈にダッシュした The runner *made a* mad *dash* right before the goal.

だっしゅうざい 脱臭剤 (a) deodorizer /dióʊdəraɪzəʳ/, (an) air freshener (トイレなどの); a deodorant /dióʊdərənt/ (体臭用の).

だっしゅつ 脱出する escape 《from》 ▶奇術師は無事に箱から脱出できるだろうか Will the magician be able to *escape from* the box safely? ‖1日も早くこの安アパートから脱出したい I can't wait to *move out of* this cheap apartment (house).
▶都会のけん騒から脱出する *leave* the hustle and bustle of the city.

ダッシュボード a dashboard ▶車のダッシュボードにカーナビを付ける install a car navigation system into *the dashboard* of a car.

たつじん 達人 an expert /ékspəːʳt/ ▶彼はスケボーの達人だ He is *an expert* at skateboarding. / He's an expert skateboarder. ‖彼は語学の達人だ He is *a genius at languages*. / He is *a linguistic genius*.

だっすい 脱水 1【水分を取る】▶洗濯物を脱水機で脱水する *remove water from* wet clothes in a spin drier / *spin-dry* wet clothes.
‖脱水機 a spin drier, a spinner.
2【水分が不足する】▶その子は下痢が続いたために脱水症状になった The child *became* [*was*] *dehydrated* from continuous diarrhea. (➤ dehydrate /di:háɪdreɪt/ は「脱水する」,「脱水症」は dehydration).

たっする 達する 1【到達する】 reach +目, arrive at, get to
語法 (1) reach には arrive at と異なり「長い時間・苦労の末」という含みがある. (2) get to は arrive at のインフォーマルな言い方.
▶私たちはついに山頂に達した We finally *reached* [*made it to*] the top of the mountain. ‖骨に達するほどの深い傷だった The cut *went* nearly *to* the bone. ‖彼女の疲労はピークに達した Her fatigue *reached* a peak.
2【数・量が及ぶ】 reach +目; amount [run / come] to (総計…になる) ▶インドの人口は13億に達した The population of India *has reached* 1.3 billion. ‖地震による損害は50億円に達した The damage caused by the earthquake *amounted* [*ran* / *came*] *to* five billion yen.
3【達成する】 achieve +目 ▶私は病に倒れ, 目的を達することができなかった I fell ill and could not *achieve* [*accomplish*] *my goal*.

だっする 脱する ▶ピッチャーは打者をセカンドフライに打ち取ってピンチを脱した The pitcher held the batter with a pop fly to second and *got out of* the jam. ‖患者は危険な状態を脱した The patient *has gotten out of* critical condition.

たっせい 達成する achieve +目 (自分の能力・技能を用いて努力して); attain +目 (困難な目標を努力して); accomplish +目 (ある特定の仕事をうまく) ▶宇宙飛行士になるという目的を達成する *achieve* one's goal of becoming an astronaut ‖きみの目標を1年で達成するのはほとんど不可能だ It's next to impossible to *achieve* your goal in one year. ‖彼らはサハラ砂漠を車で横断するという偉業を達成した They *accomplished* the feat of crossing the Sahara in a car. ‖目標を達成するまで頑張ろう Let's keep at it until we *attain* [*reach*] our goal.
‖達成感 a sense of accomplishment.

だつぜい 脱税 tax evasion **━動 脱税する** evade (the payment of) tax ▶病院長が脱税で捕まった The director of a hospital was arrested for *tax evasion* [*evading taxes*].
‖脱税者 a tax evader [dodger].

たつせがない 立つ瀬がない ▶双方が譲ろうとしないのでは間に入った私の立つ瀬がない If both parties continue to refuse to make a concession, I'll *find myself in an awkward position* as an arbitrator.

だっせん 脱線 (a) derailment **━動 脱線する** be derailed ▶貨物列車が脱線した The freight train *ran off the rails* [*jumped the track* / (*was*) *derailed*].
▶(比喩的) 木村先生は授業中によく脱線する(=横道にそれる) Mr. Kimura often *goes off the subject* [*gets sidetracked*] in class. ‖少々脱線しておもしろいお話をいたしましょう I'd like to *digress* for a moment and tell you an interesting story. (➤ digress /daɪgrés/ は「脇道にそれる」の意の堅い語).

だっそう 脱走 escape; desertion (軍人の) **━動** (…から)脱走する escape 《from》, desert /dɪzə́ːʳt/ +目 ▶囚人が2人刑務所から脱走した Two convicts *escaped from* prison.
‖脱走者 a runaway ‖脱走兵 a deserter.

たった only, no more than (➤ 後者のほうが堅い言い方) ▶この町にはコンビニがたった1軒しか無い There's *only* one convenience store in this town. ‖彼はたった5冊しか本を持っていない He has *only* [*no more than*] five books. ‖皿を洗うのにたった5分しかかから

なかった It took *all of* [*just*] five minutes to do the dishes. (➤この all of は文脈によっては「たっぷり」の意になる) ‖ 彼女はたったひとりでアフリカ旅行に行った She went on a trip to Africa (*all*) *alone* [*by herself*].

▶たったそれだけしかお金持ってないの？ Is that *all* the money you have？‖ ひろみはたった今戻ったところです Hiromi has *just* come home. ／Hiromi came home *just now*. (➤just now は現在完了とともには用いないのがふつう).

-だった ▶母は昔看護師だった My mother *used to be* a nurse. ／ My mother *was* a nurse. (●「その母は今も健在である」という場合は前者,「その母はもう亡くなっている」という場合は後者を用いる).

だったい 脱退 **withdrawal** (退くこと) ; **secession** (党派・教会などからの) **━動 脱退する withdraw** [**secede**] 《from》; **leave** 《from》 ▶欧州連合からのイギリスの脱退 the *withdrawal* of the United Kingdom from the European Union ‖ 日本は1933年, 国際連盟を脱退した In 1933, Japan *withdrew from* the League of Nations. ‖ 彼はそのバンドからの脱退を表明した He announced that he *was leaving* the band.

タッチ 1【触れること】 a **touch ━動 タッチする touch** +㊀ ▶柔らかいタッチ a delicate *touch*.

▶《慣用表現》タッチの差でバスに乗り遅れた I missed the bus *by* (*a matter of*) *seconds*.

2【関係すること】 ▶私は父の事業にはタッチしていない I *am* not *involved in* my father's business.

3【野球で】 a **tag ━動 タッチする tag** +㊀ ▶彼はランナーにタッチしたが, 判定はセーフだった He *tagged* the runner but the umpire called it safe. ‖ 高橋は三塁盗塁を狙ったがタッチアウトになった Takahashi *was tagged out* in his attempt to steal third.

4【筆遣い】 a **touch** ▶軽妙なタッチの小説 a novel with a light and deft *touch* ‖ こまやかなタッチで描かれた絵 a painting with a delicate *touch*.

> **危ないカタカナ語✹ タッチ**
> **1**「私はその計画にタッチしていない」は I'm not involved in the project. とか I have nothing to do with that plan. などと表現し, touch は使わない.
> **2** 野球の「タッチ(する)」も touch ではなく tag という語を用いる(tag は「鬼ごっこ」が原義).「タッチアウト」も tag out が正しい.
> **3**「ワンタッチの」は automatic, push-button, instant などの形容詞を使う.
> **4**「タッチパネル」は touch screen [panel] といい, 形容詞としては touch-screen computer (タッチパネルのコンピュータ)などと用いる.

タッチアップ a **tag-up** (野球の) ; a **touch-up** (塗装・化粧品の手直し).

タッチダウン 《アメフト》 a **touchdown**.

タッチパネル a **touch screen**, a **touch panel** (➤文脈によって touch を省略することも多い) ▶タッチパネルをフリックする flick the *touch screen*.

タッチペン a **stylus (pen)** (スマートフォンやタブレット端末を操作するために使うペン).

だっちょう 脱腸 a **hernia** ; 《医学》 an **inguinal hernia, bubonocele** /bju:bánəsì:l/ (鼠蹊(そけい)ヘルニア).

タッチライン 《スポーツ》 a **touchline**.

たって ▶たってとおっしゃるならば言わせていただきます Well, *if you insist*, I will tell you what I think. ‖ 私は彼のたっての願いで生徒会長に立候補した I ran for president of the Student Council because he *begged* me to.

-たって ▶今すぐ出たって学校には間に合わないよ *Even if* you leave right now, you won't be in time for school. ‖ 逃げようったってそうはいかないよ You can't escape *no matter how* you try. ‖ 何てったってお客さまは神様だ *No matter what you say*, the customer is always right.

だって because ▶ **対話**「どうして食べないの」「だっておなかすいてないんだもの」"Why aren't you eating？" "*Because* I'm not hungry."

-だって 1【…でさえ】 even ▶そんなことは子供だって知っている *Even* a child knows that. ‖ 私は1日だって塾をサボったことはない I have never skipped *even* a single class at (my) juku.

2【…も】 ▶ **対話**「ああ喉が渇いた」「私だって」"Oh, I'm thirsty." "Me *too* [I am, *too*／*So* am I]." (● So am I. はやや堅い言い方) ‖ **対話**「私は英語が好きじゃない」「私だってそうだ」"I don't like English." "Me *neither* [*either*]. ／*Neither* do I." (●「…も…でない」と否定するとき).

3【伝聞】 ▶石井さんは12月で会社を辞めるんだって *I hear* Ms. Ishii is going to leave the company in December. ‖ あげたお金, もう使っちゃったんだって？ *Are you saying* that you spent all the money I gave you？

たづな 手綱 reins ▶手綱を締める [緩める] tighten [loosen] *the reins* ‖ 馬の手綱を取る *hold* [*lead*] the horse *by the reins*.

▶《慣用表現》手綱を引き締めてかからないと失敗するよ Unless you *keep a tight rein on yourself*, you will fail.

たつのおとしご 竜の落とし子 《動物》 a **sea horse**.

タッパ(ー) Tupperware 《商標》 (● 1つをいうときは a Tupperware container).

だっぴ 脱皮する shed its skin (蛇などが) ▶《比喩的》彼女はアイドルのイメージから脱皮し, 大人の歌手になろうとしている She is trying to *cast off* her image as a pop idol and become a mature singer.

たっぴつ 達筆 ▶達筆の手紙 a *beautifully written* letter.

✉ **お手紙ありがとう. きみが達筆なんで感心したよ** Thanks for the letter. I'm impressed with your *beautiful handwriting*.

タップダンス tap dancing ; a **tap dance** (1踊り).

たっぷり ▶きょうは昼食をたっぷりとった I ate a *big* lunch today. ‖ 私の家から駅までたっぷり2キロはある It is two *full* kilometers from my house to the train station. ‖ 良子が現れるまでぼくはたっぷり1 [2] 時間は待った Yoshiko kept me waiting for *a good* hour [*a good* two hours]. (➤a good は「たっぷり」) ‖ その報告書を仕上げるのにたっぷり5日かかった It took *all of* five days to write the report. (➤この all of は文脈によっては「たったの」の意になる) ‖ 慌てるな. 時間はたっぷりある Don't rush. There's *plenty of* time.

▶このセーターは袖がたっぷりしている This sweater has *very roomy* sleeves. ‖ スパゲッティはたっぷりのお湯でゆでるとよい Spaghetti should be boiled in *plenty of* water.

▶監督は勝てると自信たっぷりだった The coach was *fully* confident that his team would win. ‖ 彼の話しぶりは嫌みたっぷりだった His voice was *dripping with* sarcasm.

ダッフルコート a **duffle** [**duffel**] **coat.**
だつぼう 脱帽 ▶きみの根気のよさには脱帽するよ *I have to take my hat off to you* for your perseverance. ／*My hat goes off to you* [*Hats off to you*] for your perseverance. ／*I've got to hand it to you* for your perseverance.
たつまき 竜巻 a **whirlwind**,《米・インフォーマル》a **twister**; a **tornado** /tɔːˈneɪdoʊ/ (陸で起こる); a **waterspout** (海上で起こる) ▶きのうカンザス州で大きな竜巻があった A big *tornado* hit Kansas yesterday.
だつもう 脱毛 **hair loss**; **hair removal** ‖脱毛クリーム hair removal [depilatory] cream.
だつらく 脱落する **drop out** 《of》 ▶その走者は先頭グループから脱落し始めた The runner began to *drop out of* the lead group. ‖この電話帳は数ページ脱落している There are several pages *missing* from this telephone directory.
‖脱落者 a dropout.
だつりょく 脱力 **weakness** ▶脱力感がある feel *listless* [*exhausted*].
だつりん 脱輪 ▶脱輪して溝に落ちる *run off* the shoulder into a ditch ‖左前が脱輪した The left front wheel *came* [*flew*] *off*.

[1]たて 縦

> **《解説》「縦」と「横」**
> (1) 日本語では四辺形の上下の長さを指して「縦」, 左右の長さを指して「横」といい, その四辺形の向きを90度変えることによって「横」「縦」と呼ぶ辺も変わる.
> (2) これに対して英語では長方形の場合は長いほうを **length**, 短いほうを **width** といい, 正方形では上下を length, 左右を width という. また, 立体の場合は「縦」「横」のうち長いほうを length, 短いほうを width, 高さを height で表す. したがって, 日本語の「縦」「横」を英訳する場合は, length と width を適宜使い分ける必要がある.
> (3) 印刷用紙の向きを「縦」「横」というが, 英語ではそれぞれ portrait, landscape という.

一形 **縦の** **vertical** ▶このプールは縦が25メートル, 横が10メートルだ This swimming pool is 25 meters *long* [*in length*] and 10 meters wide [in width]. ／This swimming pool is 10 by 25 meters. ‖このドアは縦(＝高さ)が175センチ, 横が80センチある This door is 175 centimeters *high* and 80 centimeters across. ‖このカードをテーブルの上に縦に並べなさい Arrange these cards *lengthwise* [*lengthways*] on the table. ‖縦に1本線を引きなさい Draw a line *vertically*. ／Draw a *vertical* line. ‖縦2列に並んでください Line up *in two columns*, please.
▶縦向きの(パソコン)ディスプレー a *portrait* display ‖写真を縦向きに撮る take a *vertical* shot ‖文書を縦向きに表示する display a document *in portrait orientation*.
▶《慣用表現》日本人は縦の関係を重視する The Japanese consider *vertical relationships* important. ／Japanese people emphasize *hierarchical relationships*. ‖兄は横のものを縦にもしない My (older) brother *won't lift a finger* to do anything.
‖縦社会 a vertical society.
[2]**たて 盾** a **shield**; a **buckler**(丸盾) ▶盾で敵の矢を防ぐ defend oneself from arrows with *a shield*.
▶《慣用表現》先生方は校則を盾に取って私たちの要求を聞き入れてくれなかった The teachers rejected our demand, *giving* school regulations *as the reason*.
[1]**-たて -立て** ▶産みたての卵 a *newly-laid* [*fresh*] egg ‖炊きたてのご飯 *just-cooked* rice ‖ぼくはまだ大学を出たてです I am *just out of* college. ‖このパンは焼きたてだ This bread is *hot from the oven*. ‖これはとれたてのイチゴです These strawberries are *fresh from the farm*. ／These are *farm-fresh* strawberries.
[2]**-たて -立て** ▶ジャイアンツはタイガースに3たてを食った The Giants *lost* to the Tigers three *games in a row*.
たで 蓼 《植物》a **smartweed**
ことわざ たで食う虫も好き好き There is no accounting for taste(s). (➤「人の好みは説明できない」の意).
だて 伊達 ▶彼女はだて眼鏡をかけている She *wears glasses only for show* [*fashion*]. ‖彼女, だてに(＝無駄に)英語を勉強してはいないねえ. ちゃんと英語の手紙が書けるじゃないか She hasn't been studying English *for nothing*. It looks like she can write an English letter very well. ‖《慣用表現》だての薄着 a dandy loves to get dressed lightly (even in the cold).
‖だて男 a fop, a dandy(➤ 前者は軽蔑的).
[1]**-だて -建て** ▶米ドル建てのトラベラーズチェック traveler's checks *in* U.S. dollars ‖左へ曲がると5階建てのビルが見えます Turning to the left, you will see a *five-storied* [a *five-story*] building.
[2]**-だて -立て** ▶2頭[4頭]立ての馬車 a carriage and *pair* [*four*] ‖近頃2本立ての映画をやっている劇場は少ない Few theaters show *double feature* movies nowadays.
たてあな 縦穴・竪穴 a **pit**.
たていたにみず 立て板に水 ▶彼の話し方ときたら立て板に水だ He *talks very fluently* [*glibly*]. (➤ 後者は否定的なイメージの語) ／He *talks a mile a minute*. (➤「のべつ幕なしにしゃべる」の意のインフォーマルな表現) ／He *rattles on* (*and on*). (➤「おもしろくもないことをべらべらしゃべる」という含みがある).
たていと 縦糸・竪糸 **the warp**(➤ 集合的にいう語. 「横糸」は the weft または the woof).
たてうり 建て売り ▶建て売り住宅 a *ready-built* house ／a house *built for sale* 《参考》工場生産の規格品を現場で組み立てる方式のものは prefabricated house といい, 同じ場所に同じデザインで作られた建て売り住宅の1軒は tract house という.
[1]**たてかえる 立て替える** ▶悪いけど, 勘定立て替えておいてくれる? Sorry, but could you *get* the bill *for* me? I'll pay you back later. (➤「勘定を払う」は pay a bill だが, ここで pay では直截的すぎるので, 「勘定書を受け取る」の意味で get を用いるのがよい).
[2]**たてかえる 建て替える** **rebuild** +⊜, **reconstruct** +⊜ ▶わが家もそろそろ建て替えなくっちゃね It's time we *rebuilt* our house, isn't it? (➤ time 以下は仮定法過去形).
たてがき 縦書き **vertical writing** ▶縦書きの原稿 a manuscript *written vertically*.
✉ **日本では手紙は伝統的に縦書きですが, 最近は横書きにする人も多くなりました** In Japan, letters were traditionally *written vertically*, but recently the number of people writing them horizontally has increased.
たてかける 立て掛ける **lean** +⊜ ▶はしごを木に立てかける *lean* [*put* ／*set*] a ladder *against* a tree.
たてがみ 鬣 a **mane**(馬やライオンの).

たてかんばん 立て看板 a **standing signboard**.

たてぐ 建具 **fixtures**(作りつけの備品); **fittings** (家具); **joinery** (建具類) ‖**建具屋** a joiner.

たてごと 竪琴 a **harp**; a **lyre** /láɪəʳ/ (古代ギリシャの).

たてこむ 立て込む・建て込む ▶店は客で立て込んでいる The store *is crowded* [*is packed*] with shoppers. ‖今ちょっと立て込んでいますのであとにしてもらえませんか I'*m* a little *busy* [*occupied*] now. Could you make it later? ‖この辺は家が建て込んでいる This area *is* (*quite*) *built up*.

たてこもる 立て籠もる ▶乗っ取り犯は依然として飛行機の中に立て籠もっている The hijackers *are* still *holed up* in the plane. (➤ hole up は「(犯人などが)隠れる」の意のインフォーマルな表現).

たてじく 縦軸 a **vertical axis** [複 **axes**].

たてじま 縦縞 **vertical stripes** ▶縦じまのユニホーム a uniform with *vertical stripes* ／ a *vertical-striped* uniform.

たてつく 盾突く **contradict** /kɑ̀ːntrədíkt/ +目 (反論する); **defy** /dɪfáɪ/ +目 (反抗する) ▶彼はよく上司に盾つく He often *contradicts* his boss. ‖親に盾つくようなことはするな You should not *defy* your parents.

たてつけ 立て付け **fitting** ▶この窓は立てつけが悪い This window *is loose*. ／This window *doesn't fit well*.

たてつづけ 立て続けに **in a row**(連続して); **nonstop** (止まらずに); **in quick succession**(あまり間を置かずに) ▶《サッカー》そのチームは立て続けに4ゴールを決めた The team got four *straight* goals [got four goals *in a row*]. ‖彼女はさっきから立て続けにしゃべっている She's been talking *nonstop* [*without a pause*]. ‖彼は立て続けに水を3杯飲んだ He drank three glasses of water *in quick* [*rapid*] *succession*.

たてつぼ 建坪 ▶建坪100平米の家 a house *with a floor area* of 100 square meters.

たてなおし 立て直し・建て直し **reconstruction**, **rebuilding** ▶産業の立て直し industrial *reconstruction* ‖学校や病院の建て直し *rebuilding* of schools and hospitals.

[1]**たてなおす 立て直す** **1【再建する】**▶赤字財政を立て直す *reshape* a deficit budget ‖父は倒産寸前の会社を立て直した My father *put* the company, which had been on the brink of bankruptcy, *back on its feet*. ‖監督は3年で弱小チームを立て直した It took three years for the manager to *put* formerly weak team *back on its feet again*.

2【作り直す】▶我々はもう一度計画を立て直す必要がある We have to *rethink* our plan (from the beginning).

[2]**たてなおす 建て直す** →**建て替える**.

たてなが 縦長の **vertically long**; **oblong** /ɑ́ːblɔːŋ/ (長方形の) (➤ 英米では通例, 縦長, 横長を意識しない) ▶縦長の封筒 an *oblong* envelope (➤ 英米の封筒は横長がふつう).

たてなみ 縦波 a **longitudinal wave**.

たてぶえ 縦笛 a **recorder** ▶縦笛を吹く play the *recorder*.

たてふだ 立て札 a **sign**, 《英また》 (a) **notice** ▶「立ち入り禁止」の立て札を立てる put up *a* "KEEP OUT" *sign* ‖「通行止め」の立て札が立っていた There was *a sign* saying, "Closed to traffic."

たてまえ 建て前 **1【個人や団体の行動方針・原則】** **principles** ▶建て前を崩す [通す] give up [stick to] one's *principles* ‖役人の世界では建て前が何事にも優先する In bureaucracy *principles* have priority over everything else.

2【表向きの方針】 ***tatemae***, **public principles**

> **《解説》「建て前」について**
> 日本人は社会に対しての理想的な行動規範や原則を「建て前」と呼び, これを本心や実態, すなわち「本音」と対比することが多いが, 英語はこの場合の「建て前」,「本音」にぴったりの対応語をもたない. したがって,「建て前」には *tatemae* をそのまま当てるか, public principles (表向きの方針)や public appearances (表向きの見せかけ)などを用い,「本音」には *honne* をそのまま当てるか, true intention(s) (真の意向)や actual feelings (実際の気持ち)などを用いる. →**社交辞令**, **本音**.

▶建て前と本音は一致しないことが多い *What people say and what they really feel* is often different.

だてまき 伊達巻 a ***datemaki***; a rolled omelet with white fish (➤ 説明的な訳).

たてまし 建て増し (an) **extension**, (an) **addition** ▶わが家は今建て増しをしている We're *building an extension* onto our house. ／*An extension is being built* onto our house. ‖2階を建て増しした We *built on* a second story. ／The upstairs *was added on to* our house.

たてもの 建物 a **building**.

たてや 建屋 a **structure** [**building**] **for housing heavy machinery** ‖**原子炉建屋** a nuclear reactor building ‖**タービン建屋** a turbine building ‖**ディーゼル建屋** a diesel building.

たてやくしゃ 立て役者 a **leading actor** [**actress**] (中心役者); 《インフォーマル》 a **kingpin**(中心人物) ▶山本はチーム優勝の立て役者となった Yamamoto was the *key player* in the team's winning the championship. ／ Yamamoto became the team's *prize player*. (➤「賞に値する選手」の意).

たてゆれ 縦揺れ a **vertical jolt** [**shake**] (地震の); (**the**) **pitch** (船・飛行機の) ▶(地震で)突然, 激しい縦揺れが来た Suddenly the earth *shook up and down* violently. (● 飛行機なら Suddenly the airplane *pitched* violently. と表現する).

たてる 立てる・建てる・点てる

1【直立させる】 **set up**(しっかり固定する); **put** +目 (置く); **stand** +目 (垂直に立たせる) ▶柱を立てる *set up* a post ‖テレビのアンテナを立てる *set* [*put*] *up* a TV antenna ‖ケーキにろうそくを15本立てる *put* fifteen candles on a cake ‖学生たちは校門の前に大きな看板を立てた The students *put* a large signboard in front of the gate. ‖卵を立てるのは不可能に近い It's almost impossible to *stand* an egg. ‖茶碗のご飯に箸を立てるのは不快だ It is offensive to *stand* chopsticks in a bowl of rice. ‖コートの襟を立てて(＝折り返して)風を防ぐ protect oneself against the wind by *turning up* the collar of one's coat.

2【建築する】 **build** +目; **construct** +目 (大きな建築物を); **erect** +目 (主に直立したものを) ▶横浜に家を建てた We *had* our house *built* in Yokohama. ／ We *built* our house in Yokohama. (● 家は自分で建てるのではなく業者に依頼するのだから本来ならば「have＋目的語＋過去分詞」の形を用いるべきだが, We built our house. もふつうに使われるのでこれを用いてもよい).

▶我々は創立者の銅像を建てた We *erected* [*put up*] a bronze statue of the founder. ‖法隆寺は今から

1000年以上も前に建てられた (The) Horyuji Temple *was built* more than 1,000 years ago.
3【ある立場に就かせる】▶その党は今回の選挙で多くの女性候補を立てた(＝立候補させた) The party *ran* [*fielded*] many women candidates in this election. ‖あの人，会社の上司を仲人に立てて結婚を申し込んできたのよ He made a formal marriage proposal to me *using* his boss *as an intermediary*. (➤ intermediary は「仲介者」).
4【発生させる】▶音を立てる *make* a noise ‖ほこりを立てるな Don't *raise* dust. ‖父は私のいいかげんさに腹を立てたらしい My father seems to *have been upset* by my sloppiness.
5【目標などを定める】▶最初にしっかりした目標を立てることが重要だ It's important that you first *set a* clear *goal*. ‖目下，東北旅行の計画を立てているところです I'*m* now *working out* a plan for a trip around the Tohoku district.
6【面目を保たせる】▶彼を立てる *treat* him *with respect* ‖後輩が先輩を立てるのは日本人の習慣だ Younger Japanese customarily *keep a low profile* before older people. (➤ keep a low profile は「低姿勢を保つ」) ‖俺の顔を立ててくれ *Save* my *face*. (➤ save one's face で「体面を保つ」) ‖あの人はいつも他人への義理を立てることを第一に考えている He always *puts his obligations to other people* first.
[ことわざ] あちら立てればこちらが立たず You can't please everyone. (➤「全員を喜ばすことはできない」の意).
7【茶を入れる】▶茶をたてる *make* tea.

たてわり 縦割り ▶縦割り行政 a *vertically-divided* [*-segmented*] administrative structure.

だてん 打点 a **run batted in**《略 an RBI》▶山田は3試合で7打点をあげた Yamada batted in 7 *runs* [had 7 *RBIs*] in three games. ‖打点王 an RBI king ‖勝利打点 a game-winning RBI.

1**だとう 妥当な** **proper**(適切な)；**reasonable**(手ごろな) ▶妥当な意見[判断] a *sound* opinion [judgment] ‖私は彼のとった処置は妥当だと思う I find the measures he took *proper* [*appropriate*]. ‖50円の値上げなら妥当な線だ I think a 50 yen raise in price is *reasonable*.

2**だとう 打倒する** **defeat** ＋㊐ (敵を) ▶打倒ジャイアンツ! *Down with* the Giants!

たどうし 他動詞 a **transitive verb**(➤ 略語は vt. または v.t.).

たどうしょう 多動症 (an) **attention deficit disorder** (ADD).

1**たとえ 譬え・喩え** an **example**(例)；a **metaphor** (隠喩) ▶たとえは陳腐だけど，きみが宝くじに当たったとしてごらんよ I know this is a trite *example*, but suppose you won a lottery. ‖詩ではよくバラが愛のたとえになっている In poetry the rose is often *a metaphor* for love.
‖たとえ話 a parable(宗教的な)；an allegory /ǽləgɔ̀:ri/, a fable(教訓的な).

2**たとえ** **even if**(仮に…だとしても)；**even though** (…であることは知っているが；although の強調形)

> **【文型】**
> たとえ～だとしても
> **even if** S ＋ V
>
> **《解説》** if だけのときと同じように，ありうる条件のときは動詞は直説法，ありえないこと，現実ではないこと，実現が不可能に近いことなどには仮定法を用いる. ⇀もし.

▶たとえ雪が降ってもあすのラグビーの試合は行われます The rugby match will be held tomorrow *even if* it snows. ‖たとえ家族のみなが反対でも私は私の決めたことをやりぬくつもりだ *Even if* everybody in my family disagrees, I'm going to carry out what I've decided. ‖たとえ彼女がぼくを愛してくれていても，ぼくは彼女とは結婚しないだろう *Even if* [*Even though*] she does love me, I won't marry her. (🔵even if には「愛してくれているかどうかわからないが」, even though には「愛してくれているのは知っているが」の含みがある) ‖たとえ太陽が西から昇っても決心を変えるつもりはない *Even if* the sun *were to* rise in the west, I wouldn't change my mind.
▶たとえどんなことが起こっても私は希望を失わない *Whatever may happen* [*Whatever happens*], I will never lose hope.
▶《慣用表現》きみのためならたとえ火の中水の中，どんなことでも平気だ I'*d go through fire and water* for you.

たとえば 例えば **for example** (代表的な例を挙げると)；**for instance** (具体的には) ▶江戸時代には多くの優れた俳人が登場した一例えば芭蕉，蕪村，一茶など The Edo period produced many fine haiku poets, *for example* [*for instance*], Basho, Buson, and Issa. ‖例えば今ここに100万円あったらきみは何に使う? *For example*, if you had one million yen, how would you spend it? ‖例えばシャネルやプラダのようなブランド物の洋服は買いたくてもお金が無くて買えない Even if I wanted to buy brand-name clothes *such as* those made by Chanel and Prada, I couldn't afford them.
▶[対話]「空を飛べない鳥もいます」「例えば?」"Some birds can't fly (in the air)." "*For example?*" ‖[対話]「神の存在を信じるに足る十分な理由がたくさんあります」「例えば?」"There are many good reasons to believe in God." "*For example?* / *Such as?*" (🔵For example? がふつう. 素直に例示を求めているのに対し，Such as? は口調によって，皮肉的・懐疑的な響きになることもある. この場合は前の人の発言に疑念をもっての反応となる).

たとえる 喩える・譬える **compare**《A to B》

> **【文型】**
> A を B にたとえる
> **compare** A **to** B

▶ロマン派の詩人たちは恋人をしばしば花にたとえた Romantic poets often *compared* their sweethearts *to* flowers. ‖死はしばしば永遠の眠りにたとえられる Death *is* often *compared* [*likened*] *to* eternal sleep. (➤ liken は「なぞらえる」; sleep の代わりに rest でもよい) ‖この小説では独裁者を豚にたとえている This novel *uses* a pig *as a metaphor* for a dictator. (➤ metaphor は「隠喩」) ‖夕日はたとえようがないほど美しかった The sunset was beautiful *beyond description* [was *indescribably* beautiful]. / *Words can't express* how beautiful the sunset was.

たどく 多読 **extensive reading** ▶彼は精読よりも多読を心がけている His approach to reading is to *read extensively*, rather than to read intensively. / He always tries to *read many books*, rather than to read (just) a few carefully.

たどたどしい ▶たどたどしい説明 a *faltering* [*halting*] explanation ‖外国人がたどたどしい日本語で話しかけてきた A foreigner spoke to me in *broken*

Japanese. ‖ 酔っ払いがたどたどしい足取りで歩いていった A drunk *staggered* down the road [walked along the road *with unsteady steps*]. (➤ stagger は「よろよろ歩く」の意).

たどりつく 辿り着く reach +㊐ ▶6時間登ってついに山頂にたどりついた After six hours of climbing, we finally *reached* the top of the mountain. ‖ やっとのことで我々は山小屋にたどりついた We somehow *managed to arrive at* [finally *found our way to*] the lodge. ／We at last *made it to* the lodge.
▶この結論にたどりつくのに10年かかりました It took ten years to *come to* this conclusion.

たどる 辿る 1【道に沿って進む】follow +㊐ ▶山道をたどる *follow* [*go along*] a mountain path ‖ 警察犬は犯人の残した匂いをたどって隠れがを突き止めた The police dog successfully traced the hideout *following* the smell left by the criminal.
2【さがし求める】trace +㊐ ▶親鸞の足跡をたどる *trace* the footprints of Shinran ‖ この祭りは歴史をたどれば桃山時代に至る The history of this festival *reaches back to* the Momoyama period. ‖ 幼い頃のおぼつかない記憶をたどって生き別れになったおじを捜した *Relying on* vague childhood memories, I searched for my uncle who I had been separated from.
3【経る】▶その旧家は戦後没落の一途をたどった The old family *went down the road to ruin* after the war.

たな 棚 a shelf; a rack (網棚, 陳列棚) ▶それをいちばん下の棚に置く put it on the bottom *shelf* ‖ 彼は書斎の壁に棚をつった He fixed *a shelf* to the wall of his study. ‖ その男性は席に着くと荷物を棚に上げた After taking a seat, the man put his luggage on the *rack*.
▶《慣用表現》彼女はいつも自分のことは棚に上げて(＝目をつぶって)人のことを悪く言う She always *shuts her eyes to* her own shortcomings and speaks badly of others. ／She always speaks badly of others *while conveniently forgetting about* her own shortcomings.
☛ 棚ぼた (→見出語)

たなあげ 棚上げ ▶この問題は一時棚上げにしましょう Let's *shelve* [《米また》*table*] this matter for the moment. ／Let the matter ride for some time. (➤ 後者は「手をつけないでそのままにしておく, 様子を見る」の意) ／Let's *put* the matter *on hold* for a while. (➤ 時期が来たら再開したいという積極的なニュアンスがある).

たなおろし 棚卸し (an) inventory /ínvəntɔ:ri/, stocktaking ▶30日は棚卸しのため休業します This store will be closed on the 30th for *inventory*.

たなこ 店子 a tenant.

たなざらし 店晒し ▶この帽子はたなざらしになっていたに違いない一色があせている This hat must *have been sitting unsold for a long time*—its color has faded.

たなだ 棚田 a rice terrace; terraced rice fields [paddies].

たなばた 七夕 *Tanabata*, the Star Festival
日本紹介 ✉ **七夕は7月7日(地方によっては8月7日)に行われる星祭りで, 短冊という細長い紙に願い事を書いてササにつるします. 商店街で大々的にやるところもありますが, その中では仙台のものがいちばん有名です** *Tanabata*, the Star Festival, is celebrated on July 7 (in some districts, on August 7). People write their wishes on narrow pieces of paper called '*tanzaku*' and hang them on twigs of bamboo grass. Large-scale *Tanabata* festivals are held in some shopping districts. Of these, the one in Sendai is the most famous.

たなびく 棚引く ▶町の上にかすみがたなびいている Haze *is hanging over* the town.

たなぼた 棚ぼた a windfall ▶棚ぼた式の利益 a *windfall* profit ‖ 前任者の急死で大臣の椅子が棚ぼた式に彼のところに転がり込んで来た The sudden death of his predecessor brought him a cabinet post *in an unexpected piece of good luck*.

たなん 多難 ▶資金難で我々の前途は多難だ Our future will *be full of difficulties* because of lack of funds.

たに 谷 a (narrow) valley; a ravine /rəví:n/, a gorge /gɔ:ʳdʒ/; a trough /trɔ:f/ (気圧の) ▶谷には小川が流れていた A stream ran through the *narrow valley*.
‖谷川 a mountain stream ‖ 谷底 the bottom of a narrow valley.

> **《解説》「谷」について**
> (1)valley は山と山に挟まれた広い低地を指す語. したがって日本のような狭いくぼんだ土地をいうには narrow をつけたほうがよい. (2)ravine, gorge は両側が絶壁になった峡谷を指す.

だに 壁蝨 《虫》a tick, a mite.

たにし 田螺 《動物》a pond [mud] snail.

たにま 谷間 a valley (比較的なだらかな); a ravine /rəví:n/ (深く狭い) ▶谷間に花が咲いている Flowers are blooming in the *valley*.
▶《比喩的》(女性の両乳房の間にできる)胸の谷間 (a) cleavage /klí:vɪdʒ/ ‖ きょうは連休の谷間で通勤電車も閑散としている Since today *falls between two consecutive holidays*, commuter trains are nearly empty.

たにん 他人 others (ほかの人たち); a stranger (知らない人) ▶他人を当てにしてはいけない Don't depend on *others*. ‖ 美佐子はよく他人のおせっかいを焼く Misako often meddles in *other people's* affairs. ‖ 彼は面倒なことはすべて他人任せにする He *leaves* all troublesome tasks *to someone else*. ‖ 対話「きみたちよく似てるけど, 兄弟かい?」「いいえ, 赤の他人ですよ」"You two look alike. Are you brothers?" "No, we are *complete* [*total*] *strangers*."
▶《慣用表現》他人の空似というのはよくあることです It is not uncommon that two *strangers look quite alike*. ‖ マユミと思って挨拶したら他人の空似だった I thought she was Mayumi and said hello, but then I found that it was just *a chance* [*an accidental*] *resemblance*.
▶他人行儀はやめてケンと呼んでくれ Don't be so *formal*. Call me Ken.
ことわざ 遠くの親類より近くの他人 A near neighbor is better than a relative living far away. (➤ 日本語からの直訳).

たにんごと 他人事 →ひと事.

たにんずう 多人数 a large number of people, a lot of people.

たぬき 狸 a *tanuki*, a *tanuki* raccoon
日本紹介 ✉ **タヌキは日本の山地にすむアナグマに似た動物です. 民話では人間をだましたり, いたずらをしたりしますが, キツネのような冷たいず**

る賢さはなく, ユーモラスなイメージがあります A *tanuki* is a raccoon-like animal that lives in the mountains in Japan. In some folktales, a *tanuki* fools or plays tricks on people, but it has a humorous image in contrast to a fox, which is considered cold-hearted and sly.

▶《慣用表現》たぬき寝入りをする *pretend to be asleep* ／ *play possum* (➤ possum は「フクロネズミ」; 驚くと死んだふりをすると信じられたことから) ‖ あいつはとんだたぬきおやじだ He's *a crafty old man*. (➤ crafty は「ずるい」).

ことわざ 捕らぬたぬきの皮算用 Don't count your chickens before they hatch. (➤「卵がかえるまではヒヨコの数を数えるな」の意の英語のことわざ).

‖たぬきそば soba noodles with tempura crumbs in the broth.

たね 種 **1**【種子】a **seed**; a **stone**, a **pit**(梅・桃などの硬いもの); a **pip** (リンゴ・トマトなどの) ▶種無しスイカ a *seedless* watermelon ‖ 花壇にコスモスの種をまいた We planted some cosmos *seeds* in our flowerbed. ／We sowed cosmos in our flowerbed. (➤ sow /soʊ/ は「(種を)まく」) ‖ あす畑にトウモロコシの種をまこうよ Tomorrow let's *sow* the field *with* corn. (➤「sow＋場所＋with ...」の形は特に穀物の種をまくときに用いる) ‖ ヒマワリの種は食べられますが, アンズの種は食べられませんよ You can eat sunflower *seeds* but not apricot *stones* [*pits*].

ことわざ まかぬ種は生えぬ Nothing grows where no seed is sown. (➤日本語からの直訳) ／Nothing comes from [out of] nothing. (➤「無からは何も生じない」の意).

‖種牛 a stud bull ‖ 種馬 a stallion, a studhorse.

2【材料, 原因】a **topic** (話の); a **cause** (原因) ▶話の種が尽きて私たちはしばし沈黙した Having run out of *topics of conversation* [*things to talk about*], we remained silent for a while. ‖ 彼はいつもギャグの種をあさっている He's always searching for *material* for his jokes. ‖ 娘のことでは心配の種が尽きない My daughter causes me no end of *worry* [*anxiety*]. (● この場合,「種」の訳出は不要) ‖ 彼のひどい成績は両親の頭痛の種だ His poor school records are a constant *source of headache* to his parents. ‖ 歩美ばかりが男の子にもてるのがしゃくの種だ Ayumi's popularity with the boys is *a source of frustration* for me.／It's *frustrating* that Ayumi is always the one (that) the boys like.

3【手品などの仕掛け】a **trick**, 《インフォーマル》a **gimmick** /gímɪk/ ▶種も仕掛けもございません There's no *gimmick* behind this. ‖ 彼女はついに手品の種を明かした She finally showed us *how the trick was done*.

たねあかし 種明かし ▶それでは(手品の)種明かしをしよう I'll *show* you *my hand*. (➤ show one's hand で「手の内を見せる」) ‖ 種明かしをすると(＝本当のことを言うと), 彼が手紙を代筆してくれたのです *To give away the secret* [*To tell the truth*], he wrote the letter for me.

たねぎれ 種切れ ▶即席でスピーチをしたが, すぐ話題は種切れになった I began to speak off the cuff but I soon *ran out of* things to say. ‖ 対話《カラオケボックスで》「山岸さん, どうぞ歌ってください」「いや, 私はもう種切れです」"Mr. Yamagishi, please sing this time." "No. I *don't know any more songs*."

たねび 種火 a **pilot light** [**burner**].

たねまき 種蒔き **planting** ▶5, 6月はこの花の種まきの時期だ May and June are the *planting season* for [of] this flower.

たねんせいしょくぶつ 多年生植物 a **perennial (plant)**.

たのしい 楽しい **happy**(幸せな, うれしい); **pleasant** (喜びを与えてくれる); **enjoyable** (楽しめる); **exciting** (興奮が味わえる); **fun**(わくわくするようで) ▶楽しい思い出 *happy* memories ‖ あなたと一緒に居ると楽しいわ I *feel happy* when I'm with you. ／*It's fun to* be with you. (➤ fun は「おもしろいこと」の意の名詞) ‖ モーグルスキーはとても楽しい Mogul skiing *is a lot of fun* [*is very exciting*]. ‖ 友達とおしゃべりするのはとても楽しい *It's a lot of fun to* chat with friends. ‖『動物の謝肉祭』は聴いていてとても楽しい "The Carnival of Animals" is very *pleasant* to listen to. ‖ 楽しい時間はあっという間に過ぎる *Time* passes quickly *when you're enjoying yourself* [*having a good time* ／*having fun*]. ‖ ガーデニングはどの世代の人にとっても楽しいものだ Gardening is *enjoyable* for people of all ages. ‖ キャンプは夏のいちばん楽しい行事です Camping is the most *enjoyable* thing we do in summer. ‖ 彼女は(一緒に居て)楽しい人だ She is *a lot of fun* (*to be with*).

▶もうすぐ楽しい修学旅行だ I'*m looking forward to* the school excursion. (➤「旅行を楽しみに待っている」の意) ‖ では楽しい週末を! Have a *good* [*nice*] weekend! ‖ きょうはとても楽しかった I've *had a wonderful day* today. ‖ あなたと話ができて楽しかったわ It's *been fun* talking to you.

> **直訳の落とし穴「パーティーは楽しかった」**
> 「パーティーは(とても)楽しかった」はいろいろに表現できるが, 多くの学習者が (×) I enjoyed (very much) at the party. と間違った言い方をする. enjoy は他動詞用法がふつうなので, I enjoyed the party (very much). または I enjoyed myself (very much) at the party. とする.「楽しい時間を過ごした」の意味で I had a (very) good time at the party. または,「楽しい思いをした」の意味で I had (a lot of) fun at the party. とすることもできる.

▶父は引退後の生活を楽しく送って(＝楽しんで)います My father *is enjoying* retired life. ‖ 今夜は楽しくやろう *Let's have a great time* tonight. ‖ 子供たちは『ハッピー・バースデー』をいかにも楽しげに歌っている The children are singing "Happy Birthday to You" *cheerfully*. ‖ 対話「インド旅行はどうでした?」「とても楽しかったですよ」"How was the trip to India?" "It was *fantastic*." (➤ fantastic は「非常にすばらしい」の意のインフォーマルな語) ‖ 対話「見学旅行はどうだった?」「楽しくなかったよ」"How was the field trip?" "*I didn't enjoy* it."

たのしませる 楽しませる **entertain** ＋目 (芸・余興で); **please** ＋目 (喜ばせる); **amuse** ＋目 (おもしろがらせる) ▶その芝居は観客を大いに楽しませた The play *was* very *entertaining*. ／The play *entertained* the audience a lot. (➤ 前者が一般的な言い方) ‖ 水族館でのイルカのショーは(観客の)目を楽しませた The dolphin show at the aquarium was *a pleasure to watch* [*to behold*].

たのしみ 楽しみ **1**【楽しいこと】(a) **pleasure**; a **joy**(喜び); a **pastime**(気晴らし) ▶私の人生最大の楽しみは食べることだ My greatest *pleasure* in life is eating. ‖ 旅は私にとって何よりの楽しみだ Nothing gives me more *pleasure* than traveling. ‖ 若いうちに人生の楽しみも苦しみも経験した

ほうがいいね You should experience both the *joys* and agonies of life while you are young. ‖ 祖母のいちばんの楽しみは民謡を歌うことだ My grandmother's favorite *pastime* is singing Japanese folk songs.

2【心待ち, 期待】

> **【文型】**
> **物事(A)を楽しみにしている**
> **look forward to** A
> ➤ A は名詞
> **…するのを楽しみにしている**
> **look forward to** doing

▶母はこの夏のフランス旅行を楽しみにしている My mother *is looking forward to* her trip to France this summer. ‖ 子供の頃は夏休みを楽しみにしていたものだ When I was a child, I always *couldn't wait for* summer vacation to come. ‖ あなたからお返事をもらうのを楽しみにしています I *look forward to* hear*ing* from you.

▶母親は息子の将来をとても楽しみにしている The mother *places high* [*great*] *hopes on* her son's future. ‖ 私はそのパーティーが楽しみだった I *anticipated a good time* at the party. **対話**「ママ, お昼ごはん, 何?」「楽しみにしててね」"Mom, what's for lunch?" "*Wait and see.*"

✉ **飛行機は8日, 午後4時15分にロサンゼルス空港に着く予定です. あなたに会えるのを楽しみにしています** My plane will arrive at Los Angeles Airport at 4:15 p.m. on the 8th. I *am looking forward to* meeting [seeing] you. (➤ meeting は初対面のとき).

たのしむ 楽しむ **enjoy** +㊐, **have fun**

> **【文型】**
> **…して楽しむ**
> **enjoy** doing

▶1杯のコーヒーを時間をかけて楽しむ *enjoy* linger*ing* over a cup of coffee ‖ 姉は友達とよくテニスをして楽しむ My sister often *enjoys* play*ing* tennis with her friends. ‖ 祖母はイタリア語を楽しんで学んでいます My grandmother *enjoys* learn*ing* Italian.

▶週末はテニスと水泳をして楽しんだ We *enjoyed ourselves* [*had a lot of fun*] play*ing* tennis and swimming on the weekend. ‖ 先週末スノーボードをやって大いに楽しんだ Last weekend I went snowboarding. I really *enjoyed* it [I *had a great time* / I *enjoyed myself*]. ‖ 音楽はひとりで楽しむものだと私は思う I believe that music is something to *be enjoyed* on one's own. ‖ この映画は老人も若者も楽しめる This film *is enjoyable* for young and old alike. ‖ デパートを歩き回っていればただで一日中楽しめる I *can get* free *enjoyment* for a whole day just walking around a department store.

たのみ 頼み 1【依頼】a **request** ▶彼女は私の頼みを聞いてくれた[断った] She granted [declined] my *request*. / She said yes [no] to my *request*. (➤ 後者のほうがくだけた言い方) ‖ きみの頼みとあらば一肌脱がねばならないだろう If you're the one who *is asking*, I'm obliged to help you at any cost. ‖ **対話**「きみにひとつ頼みがあるんだ」「ああ, 何だい?」"*Will* [*Can*] *you do me a favor?* / *May I ask you a favor?*" "Sure. What is it? / Yes. Go ahead." (➤ 改まって「お願いしたいことがあるのですが」という場合は May I ask a favor of you? となる).

2【信頼】▶私にとってあなたは頼みの綱なんです You are my *last hope* [*last resort*]. (➤ last resort は「最後の手段, よりどころ」) ‖ 彼には支援グループが頼みの綱だった His support group was *a lifeline* for him.

たのみこむ 頼み込む ▶私は大学の先輩に就職を頼み込んだ I *begged* one of the older graduates from my university to help me find a job. ‖ お父さんに頼み込んでこれを買ってもらった I *begged and begged* until Father bought me this. (➤ 動詞を反復することで, その行為が繰り返し行われたことを表す).

たのむ 頼む 1【依頼する】ask +㊐

> **【文型】**
> **人(A)に物(B)がほしいと頼む**
> **ask** A **for** B
> ➤ 日本語では ask him for advice (彼に助言を求める)のように, 「人(A)に物(B)を求める」に当たることも多い

▶木田氏に援助を頼んだ I *asked* Mr. Kida *for* help [*to* help me]. ‖ 私は医者に大学病院への紹介状を書いてくれるように頼んだ I *asked* my doctor *for* a referral to a university hospital. ‖ 現状では社長にとても賃上げは頼めない As things stand, we can hardly *ask* our boss *for* a pay raise.

> **【文型】**
> **人(A)に…してくれと頼む**
> **ask** A **to** do
> **人(A)が…するように頼む**
> **ask that** A do
> ➤ A はものの場合もある. あとの動詞は原形

▶私たちはその少年にシャッターを押してほしいと頼んだ We *asked* the boy *to* take a picture. ‖ 父は人から何か頼まれると断れない性格です My father can't say no when someone *asks* him *to* do a favor. ‖ 通報者は名前を伏せておいてほしいと頼んだ The informer *asked to* remain anonymous [*for* anonymity]. / The informer *asked that* his [her] name be withheld. / The informer *asked that* he [she] not be identified. (➤「身元を明かさないでほしいと頼んだ」の意) ‖ 祖父は海に散骨してほしいと頼んであった My grandfather *asked that* his ashes be scattered over the ocean. ‖ 彼は頼まれないのに彼女を助けた He helped her *without being asked*. ‖ 彼女に頼まれて弁護士を紹介してやった *At her request*, I introduced her to a lawyer.

▶日出夫, ちょっと頼むよ(＝手を貸してくれ) Hideo, *give me a hand*. ‖ 小川君, 頼むからちょっと静かにしてくれないか *Could you please* quiet down, Ogawa? / Ogawa, *for heaven's sake*, be quiet! (➤ for heaven's sake はいらだちを表す).

▶コーヒーを1杯頼む(＝コーヒーをください) *Give* me a cup of coffee, please. ‖ 良夫, このノートのコピーを頼む(＝してくれる?) Yoshio, *can you* copy these notes for me? ‖ お母さん, 留守中子供を頼みます Mom, *could you look after* [*take care of*] the kids while I'm away? (➤「子供の世話をしてくれますか」の意) ‖ 飛行機の切符はもう頼んで(＝予約して)ある I have already *reserved* airplane tickets [*made* airplane *reservations*]. ‖ 出かけるからあとのことは頼んだよ Please *make sure that* there are no problems while I'm gone.

▶《レストランなどで》これは頼んで(＝注文して)ませんよ I

didn't *order* this. ／This is not what I *ordered*. ‖温泉旅館でマッサージを頼んだ I *called* a massage therapist (during my stay) at a hot spring hotel. ‖人手が足りないのでアルバイトを頼んだ Due to personnel shortage, we had to *hire* part-timers.

2【信頼する】▶吉田君は頼むに足る(＝信頼できる)人物だ You *can rely* [*count*] *on* Yoshida. (➤ count on は「当てにする」).

たのもしい 頼もしい **reliable** /rɪláɪəbəl/ (頼りになる) ; **promising** (有望な) ▶我々にとって彼は頼もしい味方だ He is a *reliable* [*dependable*] friend to us. ‖彼の娘さんは将来が頼もしいピアニストだ His daughter is a *promising* pianist. ‖頼もしい息子さんですこと! What a *wonderful* [*fine*] son (you have)! ／Your son is just *great*.

たば 束 a **bundle**(大きな束) ; a **bunch**(花・鍵などの小さな束) ; a **sheaf** (穀物などの) ▶手紙の束 *a bundle* of letters ‖鍵の束 *a bunch* of keys ‖彼はバラの花束を抱えてやって来た He came along with *a bunch of roses* in his arms. ‖この古本, 1束で100円だったわよ These secondhand books cost 100 yen *a bundle*. ‖彼らは干し草を束にして積み重ねた They piled hay *in sheaves*. (➤ sheaves は sheaf の複数形).

▶《慣用表現》我々が束になって掛かっても彼を倒せなかった Even all of us *put together* couldn't knock him down. ‖束になって掛かってこい Come on, I'll take you all on! (➤ take on は「(相手として)引き受ける」).

だは 打破する **break down** ▶因習を打破する *break down* old customs.

たばこ a **cigarette** /sígəret/ (紙巻きたばこ) ; a **cigar** /sɪgɑ́ːr/ (葉巻) ; **tobacco** /təbǽkoʊ/ (パイプ用の刻みたばこ) ; **smoking** (喫煙) ▶たばこに火をつける light *a cigarette* ‖たばこを1箱買って来てくれないか Get me *a pack of cigarettes*, will you? ‖私はたばこは吸わない I *don't smoke*. ／I'm a nonsmoker.

▶たばこ(＝喫煙)をやめたほうがいいことはわかっているが, なかなかやめられない I know I should give up *smoking*, but I just can't. ‖《そばの人に》おたばこを遠慮していただけますか Would you please *not smoke* [*refrain from smoking*]? ‖《放送で》車内でのおたばこはご遠慮ください Please [Kindly] refrain from *smoking* in the train. ／《掲示》No smoking. ‖《ホテル予約の際に》たばこが吸える部屋をお願いします I'd like a *smoking* room, please. (➤「禁煙になっている部屋」なら nonsmoking room) ‖灰皿はたばこの吸い殻と灰があふれていた The *cigarette butts* and ash were spilling over from the ashtray. ‖その火事は寝たばこが原因だった The cause of the fire was *smoking in bed*. ‖**対話**「たばこを吸ってもいいですか」「どうぞ」"May I *smoke*?" "Certainly." ／"Do you mind if I *smoke*?" "Not at all." (「困ります」ならば I'd rather you didn't (smoke). または I wish you wouldn't (smoke). のように言う).

‖**たばこ屋** a tobacco shop, a tobacconist's (店) ; a tobacconist /təbǽkənɪst/ (人).

たはた 田畑 **(the) fields** ▶田畑を耕す plow *the fields*.

たはつ 多発 ▶ここは交通事故が多発する場所だ This is a spot where traffic accidents *occur frequently*.

たばねる 束ねる **bundle** 《up》 ▶古新聞を1つに束ねる *bundle up* old newspapers ／*tie up* old newspapers *in a bundle* ／*bind* old newspapers *into a bundle* ‖直子は髪を後ろで束ねている Naoko *has* her hair *tied* [*fastened*] at the back.

▶由美はクラスの女の子たちを束ねる姉御的存在だ Yumi is like a big sister to her classmates ; she *brings everybody together*.

[1]たび 旅 a **trip**, **travel** ; a **tour**(観光・視察のための周遊旅行) ; a **journey**(比較的長い旅 ; 情緒的・文学的なニュアンスがある) →旅行 **一動** **旅をする** **travel, take a trip** ▶私は旅が好きだ I like *traveling* [*travel*]. ‖去年の夏, 北海道を1人旅した Last summer I *took a trip* to Hokkaido *alone* [I *traveled alone* to Hokkaido].

> **《解説》「すてきな旅」**
> 「すてきな旅」は a nice trip で,「すてきな旅を」の意味で Have a nice trip. などと用いる. travel は動詞用法が多く, 名詞ではふつう Ⓤ 扱いをして, overseas travel (海外旅行), business travel (商用旅行) など, 旅全般や旅の種類を指す語で, (×) a nice travel などと個々の旅には用いない. ただし, 複数形 travels は「遠方の各地への旅」の意で, しばしば用いるが, これはやや文学的な響きのある使い方.

‖空の旅より列車の旅のほうが好きです I like *traveling by train* better than *traveling by plane* [than *air travel*]. ‖空の旅［船の旅］はいかがでしたか How was your *flight* [*voyage*]? ‖彼は北欧一周の長い旅に出ていた He was on *a long journey* around Scandinavia.

ことわざ 旅は道連れ Good company makes the road shorter. (➤「楽しい同伴者が居れば長い道のりも短く感じる」の意).

ことわざ 旅の恥はかき捨て A person away from home need feel no shame. ／There's no need to worry about manners [how you act] when you travel.

‖**旅芸人** a traveling [touring] entertainer ‖**旅人** a traveler.

[2]たび 足袋 (a pair of) ***tabi*** ; Japanese-style socks worn with Japanese clothes (➤ 説明的な訳).

-たび -度

> **【文型】**
> **〜するたびに(いつも)**
> **every time** S + V
> **whenever** S + V

▶彼は来るたびに何か持って来てくれる *Every time* [*Whenever*] he comes, he brings us something. ／He *never* visits us *without* bringing us something. (➤ every time は「…するときはいつも」の意) ／He *never fails to* bring something when he comes. ‖この曲は聞くたびに新しい発見がある *Each time* I hear this piece, I discover something new. (➤ each time は「そのつど」の意).

だび 荼毘 **cremation** /krɪméɪʃən/ **一動** **だびに付す** **cremate** /kríːmeɪt/ ＋㊐.

タピオカ **tapioca** 《参考》熱帯植物キャッサバの根から作られるでんぷんのこと. 糊化したタピオカを丸めて作られる小さな球状のものは tapioca balls や tapioca pearls と言い, tapioca balls が入ったアイスティーやミルクティーのことは bubble tea と言う.

たびかさなる 度重なる ▶ミスがたび重なって彼は左遷された He was demoted *after making a series of* mistakes [*after making repeated* errors].

たびさき 旅先 ▶旅先から両親に手紙を書いた I wrote a letter to my parents *during the trip* [*while traveling*].

たびだつ 旅立つ **leave**《for》, **set off** [**out**]《for》(…に向けてある場所を離れる) ▶あす南米へ**旅立ちます** I'm *leaving* [*setting off*] *for* South America tomorrow. ‖彼はあの世に**旅立った** He *departed* this world [this life].

たびたび 度々 **often** ; **many times**(何度も) ▶彼は休暇中に**たびたび**遊びに来た He *often* [*frequently*] came to see me during the vacation. (➤ frequently は「足しげく」という感じの改まった語) ／He came to see me *many times* during the vacation. ‖**たびたび**お手数をかけてすみません I'm sorry to trouble you so *often*.

タヒチ **Tahiti** /təhíːṭi/ (南太平洋にあるフランス領の島) 一形 **タヒチの** **Tahitian**.

たびまわり 旅回り ▶**旅回り**の一座 a *touring* [*traveling*] troupe.

ダビング **dubbing** ; **copying** (複製すること) 一動 **ダビングする** **dub** +目, **copy** +目 ▶ビートルズの CD 貸してよ. **ダビングする**から Can you lend me a CD of the Beatles ? I'd like to *make a copy*.

タフ **tough** ▶ 3 日も徹夜できるとは**タフ**なやつだ He must be really *tough* [*hardy* / *strong-minded*] to be able to stay up all night three nights in a row.

タブ a **tab** ‖**タブキー** a tab key.

タブー a **taboo** /təbúː/ ▶**タブー**を犯す break *a taboo* ‖イスラム教社会では酒は**タブー**になっている Drinking is *taboo* in Muslim societies. (➤ a を省略する形容詞用法が多い) ‖曽根課長の居る所で髪の毛の話は**タブー**よ Talking about hair is *taboo* in front of manager Sone.

だぶだぶ ▶**だぶだぶ**のセーター a *loose* sweater ‖痩せたので上着もズボンも**だぶだぶ**だ My jacket and slacks have become *baggy* [*loose*] now that I've lost weight.

だぶつく ▶ことしは米が**だぶついている** There has been *a glut* [*an oversupply*] of rice (on the market) this year. (➤ glut /glʌt/ は「供給過剰」).
▶最近おなかの回りの肉が**だぶついてきた** I'm *getting flabby* around the middle these days.

ダフや ダフ屋 《米》a **scalper**, 《英》a **tout**.

たぶらかす 誑かす ▶あの男は老婆を**たぶらかして**金を巻き上げた He *swindled* [*cheated* / *conned*] an old woman out of her money.

ダブリン **Dublin**(アイルランドの首都).

ダブる ▶今月は日曜と祭日が**ダブった** The national holiday *fell on* a Sunday this month. (➤ fall on は「(ある日に)当たる」) ‖同じ座席番号の切符が 2 枚**ダブって発行された** *Two tickets were issued* for the same seat. ／ The seat was *double-booked*. ‖パソコンの画面を長いこと見ていたせいか, **物がダブって見える** *I'm seeing double*. Maybe it's because I've been looking at the computer screen for a long time. ‖《テニス・バレーボールで》**サーブをダブる** *make a double fault*.

ダブル **double** /dʌ́bəl/ ▶ (ホテルの) **ダブル**の部屋 a *double* room ‖**ダブル**の上着 a *double-breasted* coat ‖ウイスキーの**ダブル**(1 杯) a *double* whisky ‖ズボンの裾は**ダブル**にしてください Could you make the cuffs on the pants *double* ? ‖運賃の値上げと米の値上げで家計は**ダブルパンチ**を食らった The public transport fare increase and rice price hike have dealt *double blows* [*a double punch* / *a one-two punch*] to our family budget.
‖**ダブルスタンダード** a double standard ‖**ダブルデート** a double date ‖**ダブルベッド** a double bed ‖《ゴルフ》**ダブルボギー** a double bogey /bóʊgi/.

ダブルクリック 《コンピュータ》a **double click** ▶アイコンを**ダブルクリック**してソフトを起動する *double-click* (on) an icon to start a program.

ダブルス a **doubles** (**match** ／ **game**) ▶シングルスは負けたが**ダブルス**は勝った I lost in [at] singles but won the *doubles*. ‖**混合ダブルス**をしよう Let's play *mixed doubles*.

ダブルスチール a **double steal** ▶**ダブルスチール**で 1 点追加する add a run on *a double steal*.

ダブルプレー a **double play** ▶中日はその試合で 4 つの**ダブルプレー**を成功させた The Dragons executed four *double plays* in the game. ‖中田は三塁ゴロで**ダブルプレー**に打ち取られた Nakata grounded to third for *a double play*. (➤ ground は「ゴロを打つ」).

ダブルヘッダー a **doubleheader**.

タブレット 《コンピュータ》a **tablet**
‖**タブレット型パソコン** a tablet PC.

タブロイド ‖**タブロイド紙** a tabloid.

たぶん 多分 probably, likely, perhaps

> **語法** (1)「たぶん」に相当する英語には **probably, likely, perhaps** [**maybe**] があり, 可能性はそれぞれ約80%以上, 50～70%, 40～50%である.
> (2)probably は文中で, perhaps は文頭で用いられる傾向がある.
> (3)likely は文頭・文中のいずれでも用いられる(未来形では very, most などを伴う).

▶今晩徹夜すれば**たぶん**宿題は終わるだろう I will *probably* be able to finish my homework if I work on it all night. ‖彼は**たぶん**遅れて到着するだろう He *is likely to* arrive late. ／*It is likely* (*that*) he will arrive late. ‖**たぶん**彼女は今夜もカラオケに行くだろう *Perhaps* [*I think*] she will be at the karaoke place tonight, too. ‖あすは**たぶん**雨がやむだろう It will *probably* stop raining tomorrow. ‖**たぶん**彼は勝つだろう *The chances* [*Chances*] are (that) he will win. ‖ **対話** 「間に合うと思う？」「ええ, **たぶん** ／いいえ, **たぶん**だめね」 "Do you think we'll make it ?" "Yes, *I think so*. ／No, *I don't think so*."

たぶんかしゅぎ 多文化主義 **multiculturalism**.

たべあるき 食べ歩き ▶私たちは神戸で**食べ歩き**をした We enjoyed *visiting various restaurants* in Kobe. ／We made *an eating tour* of Kobe.

たべあわせ 食べ合わせ a **food combination** ▶ウナギと梅干しは**食べ合わせ**の悪いものの代表だ Eel and umeboshi (pickled plums) are considered *a bad combination* (in terms of digestion). ／ Eel and umeboshi are typical foods that are *hard to digest when you eat them at the same time*.

たべごろ 食べ頃 ▶このメロンはいつが**食べ頃**ですか When will this melon *be ripe* ? (➤ ripe は「熟して」の意) ‖イチゴは今が**食べ頃**です Strawberries are *at their best* now.

たべざかり 食べ盛り ▶うちには**食べ盛り**の子供が 3 人も居ます We have three *growing children with enormous appetites*.

たべずぎらい 食べず嫌い ▶刺身がだめだって言うけど, **食べず嫌い**じゃないの？ How can you say you don't like sashimi before you try it ? (➤「食べてもみないでどうして嫌いだとわかるの？」の意). → **食わず嫌い**.

たべすぎる 食べ過ぎる overeat ▶ああ, 食べ過ぎた. 苦しい I*'ve eaten too much* and my stomach feels heavy. ‖食べ過ぎておなかを壊した I had stomach trouble *from overeating*.

タペストリー a **tapestry**.

たべのこし 食べ残し leftovers ▶ 対話 「これ食べていいかい?」「いいわよ. 夕飯の食べ残しだけど」"Can I eat this?" "Sure, but it's *leftovers* from dinner."

たべほうだい 食べ放題 ▶この店は3000円で食べ放題飲み放題です At this restaurant, you can *eat and drink all you want* for 3,000 yen. (➤ 掲示で「3000円で食べ放題」なら All you can eat for ¥3,000. とする).

た

たべもの 食べ物 food ▶このホテルは食べ物がいい［悪い］This hotel serves good [poor] *food*. ‖食べ物を粗末にしてはいけません You shouldn't let (*good*) *food* go to waste. (この場合の good は「大切な(valuable)」の意で, 必ずしも「おいしい(delicious)」の意ではない) ‖何か食べ物が欲しい I want *something to eat*. ‖動物に食べ物を与えないでください Please don't *feed* the animals.

たべる 食べる 1【食物を取る】eat (+目), have (+目) (➤ have は eat の直接的な響きを避けた言い方で, 楽しんで食べるといった響きがある) ▶ほとんどの学生は学校の食堂で昼食を食べる Most students *eat* [*have*] lunch at the student cafeteria. ‖食べるのが速いね! You *eat* really fast! ‖うちの息子は全くよく食べる My son *eats a lot* [*eats like a horse*]. ‖今夜は外で食べよう Let's *eat* [*dine*] *out* this evening. (➤ dine は「食事をする」の形式ばった言い方) ‖すしを食べ過ぎた I *ate too much* sushi. ‖お昼を一緒に食べない? *Would you like to have* lunch with me? (have の代わりに eat を用いると, 単に「食べる」ことに焦点が当たってやや不自然) ‖(アレルギーなどで)食べられないものはありますか Is there *anything* you *can't eat*?

▶ちょっとこれ食べてみて *Try* this. (➤ try は「試しに食べる」) ‖ああ, よく食べた Boy, I really *stuffed myself*. ‖サンドイッチ, 好きなだけ食べてくださいね Please *help yourself to* the sandwiches. (➤ help oneself to は「…を自分で取って食べる」) ‖すぐ食べられる物を買わない? Why don't we grab *a bite* (*to eat*)? (➤ この bite は「軽い食事」の意).

▶食べられるキノコと食べられないキノコを見分けるのは難しい It is difficult to tell *edible* from *inedible* mushrooms. (edible /édəbəl/ は「毒でなく食用になる」の意. eatable (食べてもよい状態にある)と混同しないこと).

> 「食べ方」のいろいろ 急いで［がつがつ］食べる gobble (up) ／貪るように食べる devour ／むしゃむしゃ食べる munch ／ぽりぽり食べる crunch ／ツルツル［ズルズル］食べる slurp ／少しずつかじって食べる nibble ／かまずに食べる swallow

2【生活する】▶彼女は役者をして食べている She *makes her living* as an actress. (➤ make one's living は「生計を立てる」の意) ‖大学を出たらひとりで食べていく(＝独立する)ようにしなさい You have to *be independent* [*go it alone*] after graduating from college. ‖東京で親子4人が月15万円で食べていく(＝生活していく)のは難しい It is difficult for a family of four to *live on* 150,000 yen a month in Tokyo. ‖私の安月給では家族を食べさせていけない I can't *support* my family on my small salary.

だべる gab ▶喫茶店で3時間たっぷりだべった We *gabbed* for a full three hours at a coffee shop.

たべん 多弁な talkative, garrulous /gǽrələs/ (➤ 後者は通例軽蔑的に用いる).

だほ 拿捕 capture 一動 だ捕する capture +目 ▶数隻の漁船が日本海でロシア側にだ捕された Several fishing boats *were captured* by the Russians in the Sea of Japan.

たほう 他方 ▶田舎暮らしは平和だが, 他方ではちょっと退屈だ Living in the country is peaceful, but *on the other hand*, it's a bit boring.

たぼう 多忙な (very) busy ▶父は毎日多忙だ My father *is very busy* every day.

✉ ご多忙中大変申し訳ありませんが, 空港まで迎えに来ていただけないでしょうか I'm very sorry to trouble you, knowing *how busy you are*, but I wonder if you could come and pick me up at the airport.

たほうめん 多方面 ▶彼女の多方面にわたる活動 her *manifold* activities ‖池上さんは多方面で活躍している Mr. Ikegami is active *in many fields*. ‖彼女の趣味は多方面に及んでいる She has *a great variety of* [*a wide range of*] hobbies.

だぼくしょう 打撲傷 a **bruise** /bru:z/ ▶彼は顔面に打撲傷を受けた He *was bruised* on the face. ／He *got a bruise* on the face.

1**たま 玉** a **ball** (球状のもの) ; a **bead** (ガラスの小さい玉, ビーズ) ▶毛糸の玉 *a ball* of wool ‖そろばんの玉 an abacus *counter* ‖目の玉 *an eyeball* ‖百円玉 a 100-yen *coin*.

▶《慣用表現》彼は額に玉のような汗を浮かべていた He had *beads of sweat* on his forehead. ‖彼は体が弱いのが玉にきずだ His *only problem* is his poor health. ‖あいつはいいやつだが, 怠け癖があるのが玉にきずだ He's all right *except for* his laziness. ／He's a wonderful guy, but his laziness is *the fly in the ointment*.

ことわざ 玉磨かざれば光なし An uncut gem doesn't sparkle. ／If you don't hone your talent, it will be of little use to you.

2**たま 球** 1【ボール】a **ball** ; (a) **pitch** (投球) ▶球を打つ［捕る］hit [catch] *a ball* ‖あのピッチャーは球が速い That pitcher *throws a fast ball*. ‖彼の球は打ちやすそうだ His *pitch* looks easy to hit.

2【電球】a (**light**) **bulb** ▶球を換える change *bulbs* ‖球が切れた The *light bulb* has burned out.

3**たま 弾** a **shot** (散弾) ; a **bullet** /bólɪt/ (銃弾) ▶ピストルに弾を込める *load* a gun ‖弾が命中した The *shot* hit the mark. ‖彼は弾に当たって死んだ He was killed by *a bullet*.

たまぐし 玉串 ▶玉串を捧げる offer *a sprig of the sacred sakaki* [*Japanese cleyera*] *tree* to a god.

たまげる 魂消る ▶あの美人がきみの姉さんとはたまげたよ I'*m flabbergasted* to learn (that) that beautiful lady is your sister.

たまご 卵 1【鳥・虫などの】an **egg** ; **roe** /roʊ/ (魚卵) ▶(手で)卵を割る break *an egg* ‖パックの中の卵が1つ割れていた One of the *eggs* in the pack was broken [was cracked]. ‖ヒヨコが卵の殻を破って出て来た The chick cracked the *egg* and came out. ‖うちの鶏は毎日卵を産む Our hen *lays an egg* every day. ‖私はいつも熱いご飯に卵(＝生卵)をかけて食べる I like hot rice topped with a well-beaten *raw egg*. (➤ beat は「卵をとく」).

▶イクラはサケの卵を食塩水に漬けたものである Ikura is

salmon *roe* preserved in brine. ‖ カナリアが卵をかえした The canary *hatched her eggs*. ‖ **対話** (レストランで)「卵はどのようになさいますか」「いり卵［目玉焼き］にしてください」"How would you like your *egg*(*s*)?" "Scrambled [Sunny-side up], please."

‖**卵の殻** an eggshell ‖**卵焼き** eggs fried in layers ‖**(固)ゆで卵** a (hard-)boiled egg ‖**生卵** a raw egg ‖**半熟卵** a soft-boiled egg.

2【**まだ一人前でない人**】▶俳優［画家］の卵 a *budding* actor [artist] (➤ budding は「世間に認められ出した」) ‖ 教師の卵 a *new* teacher ‖ 政治家［医者］の卵 a politician [doctor] *in the making* (➤ in the making は「修業中の」のやや堅い言い方).

たまござけ 卵酒 ***tamago-zake***

日本紹介 ✉ **卵酒はエッグノッグのような飲み物です. 日本酒に卵を入れ, 砂糖を加えてかき混ぜ温めます. これを飲んで温かくして寝るとかぜが治るといわれます** *Tamago-zake* is a drink similar to eggnog. Eggs are put into sake and after some sugar is added, the mixture is stirred and heated. It is said that if you go to bed after drinking *tamago-zake* and keep yourself warm, you can shake off a cold.

たましい 魂 a **soul**(➤ 肉体と区別して); a **spirit**(➤ 精神の働き) ▶お盆は死者の魂(=霊魂)を慰める1年に一度の行事だ *Obon* is a festival held once a year to comfort the *spirits* of the dead. ‖ 刀は武士の魂とされた Swords were said to be the *souls* of samurai. ‖ 彼女の歌には魂がこもっている She sings *from the* [*her*] *heart*. (➤「心を込めて歌う」の意).

ことわざ **三つ子の魂百まで** The leopard cannot change its spots. (➤「ヒョウは自分のまだらを変えることはできない」の意の英語のことわざ) /The child is father of [to] the man.

ことわざ **一寸の虫にも五分の魂** A [Even a] worm will turn. (➤「虫でさえ(いざとなれば)反撃する」の意の英語のことわざ).

だます 騙す **trick** +目 (巧妙な策を使って); **deceive** +目 (うそをつくなど人を惑わして); **cheat** +目 (詐欺など不正なやり方で)

▶妻はセールスマンにだまされて高価な化粧品を買った My wife *was tricked* [*was deceived*] by the salesman into buying expensive cosmetics. ‖ 彼は人にだまされやすい He'*s easily cheated* by others. / He's an easy mark. (➤ easy mark は「お人よし, カモ」) ‖ 男はその老婦人をだまして金の延べ棒を取り上げてしまった The man *swindled* [*cheated*] the elderly woman *out of* her gold bars. /The man *tricked* the elderly woman *into* giving him her gold bars. ‖ きみが忠告してくれなかったらぼくはきっとだまされていたよ If you had not advised me, I'm sure I *would have been taken in* [*would have been had*]. (● ともにインフォーマルな表現で, 主に受け身形で使う) ‖ 彼は金をだまし取られた He *was cheated out of* his money.

▶この料理本当においしいのよ. だまされたと思って食べてみて This dish is really good. Just *take my word for it* and try some. (➤ take ~'s word for it は「人のことばを信じる」) ‖ 神経痛は持病だからだましだましやっていくしかないね Neuralgia is a chronic disease, so I have to *live with* it. (➤ live with は「(病気など)とうまく付き合う」).

たまたま 偶々 **by chance** ▶電車でたまたま昔教わった先生に出会った I met my former teacher *by chance* on the train.

> 【文型】
> たまたま…する
> **happen to** do

▶雑誌の広告でこういう製品のあることをたまたま知った I *happened to* learn of this product from an ad in a magazine.

たまつき 玉突き **billiards** ▶玉突きをする play *billiards* 《参考》(米)では pool, (英)では snooker /snóka^r/ が代表的な遊び方.

▶(比喩的) 高速道路で5台の車が玉突き衝突した There was *a pileup* of five cars on the superhighway. /Five cars were involved in *a rear-end pileup* on the superhighway. (➤ pileup は「多重衝突」). ‖**玉突き台** a billiard [pool] table ‖ **玉突き棒** a cue /kjuː/.

たまに 偶に **occasionally, once in a while** (➤ 後者はややくだけた言い方) ▶5月にはたまに大雨が降る We *occasionally* have heavy rain in May. ‖ たまには遊びに来いよ Come (and) see me *once in a while*. ‖ たまには外で食べようよ How about eating out *for a change*? (➤ for a change は「気分転換に」)

▶彼はごくたまにしか映画を見にいかない He *seldom* [*rarely*] goes to the movies. (➤ ともに「めったに…ない」の意) ‖ **対話**「鈴木さんにはよくお会いになりますか」「いいえ, たまに電話する程度です」"Do you often see Ms. Suzuki?" "No, we just call each other *once in a while*."

たまねぎ 玉葱 (an) **onion** /ʌ́njən/ ▶タマネギの皮をむく peel *an onion* ‖ タマネギやニンジンが苦手な子が多い Many children hate eating *onions* and carrots. ‖ タマネギを刻んでいたら涙が出てきた My eyes started to water as I was chopping *onions*.

たまの 偶の ▶たまの機会 a *rare* opportunity ‖ たまの訪問 an *infrequent* visit.

たまのこし 玉の輿 ▶彼女, 玉のこしに乗ったね She sure *married into a wealthy family* [(*into*) *money*], didn't she? (➤「金持ちの家に嫁いだ」の意).

たまひろい 玉拾いをする **collect balls for other players.**

たまむしいろ 玉虫色 an **iridescent color** 一形 **玉虫色の** **equivocal** (曖昧な) ▶玉虫色の返答 an *equivocal* answer.

たまもの 賜物 ▶当選は皆さまのご支援のたまものです My winning the election is the *result* [*fruit*] of your support and encouragement. ‖ 合格おめでとう. きみの努力のたまものだね Congratulations on your success in the entrance examination. Your *efforts have certainly paid off*.

だまらせる 黙らせる **silence** +目, **shut up** (➤ 後者はややぞんざいな響きがある) ▶彼は私を黙らせようとした He tried to *silence* me [to *shut* me *up*].

たまらない 堪らない **1**【**我慢できない**】▶私は歯が痛くてたまらない I *can't stand* [*bear*] this awful toothache. (➤ stand, bear は「我慢する」) ‖ 来月の旅行が待ち遠しくてたまらない(=待ち切れない) I *can hardly* wait for the trip next month. ‖ おばあちゃんは孫がかわいくてたまらないみたいだ Our grandmother is *just crazy about* her grandchildren. ‖ おかしくてたまらなかった I *could not help* laughing.

> 【文型】
> …したくてたまらない
> **be dying to** do
> ➤ be dying to do は「死ぬほど…したい」

た

▶彼はクイズの答えが知りたくてたまらなかった He *was dying* [*was desperate*] *to* know the answers to the quiz. ‖ ぼくは彼女に会いたくてたまらなかった I *was dying to* see her. / I *was desperate* [*anxious*] *to* see her.
▶夜帰って誰も居ない部屋の電気をつけるのはたまらなく寂しい I feel *really* lonely when I come home at night to a room with no one else there and turn the light on.
2【程度がひどくて嫌だ】▶こう騒がしくてはたまらない This noise is just *unbearable* [*intolerable*]. / It's *unbearably* noisy.
▶100万円もかかるんじゃたまらないなあ One million yen is *too much*. I *can't afford it*. (➤「そんなに出す余裕はない」の意).
3【こたえられないほどすばらしい】▶オードリー・ヘプバーンにはたまらない魅力があった Audrey Hepburn had *irresistible* charm. (➤ irresistible は「たまらないほど魅力的な」).

たまりかねる 堪り兼ねる ▶彼女は隣の奥さんの厚かましさにはたまりかねている She *cannot stand* [*bear*] the pushiness of the woman next door. / She *has no patience with* the pushy attitude of the woman next door. ‖ 父はその店員の横柄さにたまりかねて大声を上げてどなった *Unable to put up with* the salesclerk's arrogance, my father thundered at him.

だまりこくる 黙りこくる **remain silent.**

だまりこむ 黙り込む **fall silent** ▶父は朝からずっと黙り込んだままだ Dad *has been silent* since morning.

たまりじょうゆ 溜り醤油 **rich soy sauce.**

たまりば 溜り場 a **haunt** /hɔːnt/ (人がよく行く所); a **hangout** (たむろする所)
▶そのゲームセンターは不良のたまり場になっている That game center is a favorite *haunt* [*hangout*] of delinquents. ‖ B教授の研究室はよく大学院生のたまり場になる Professor B's office is often used as *a lounge* for graduate students. (➤ lounge /laʊndʒ/ は「休憩室」).

[1]**たまる 溜る 1【蓄えられる】**▶貯金箱にだいぶお金がたまった I've *saved up* quite a bit of money in my piggy bank.
2【滞る】 **accumulate** /əkjúːmjəleɪt/ (徐々に増える); **pile up** (積み重なる) ▶ドラム缶に雨水がたまっていた Water *had accumulated* in the drum. ‖ 窓枠にほこりがたまっている Dust *has collected* on the window frames. / *There is* a lot of dust on the window frames.
▶休んでいる間に仕事がどっさりたまった A lot of work *has piled up* during my absence. ‖ 疲れがたまって朝なかなか起きられない I have a hard time getting out of bed because I *can't sleep off* all my fatigue. (➤「疲れが取れなくて」の意) ‖ 家賃が3か月分もたまってしまった We*'re* three months *behind* with our rent. (➤ behind は「遅れて」) / Our rent is three months *overdue*. (➤ overdue は「期限が過ぎた」).

[2]**たまる 堪る** ▶死んでたまるか *I'll be* [*I'm*] *damned if* I will die! (➤ I won't die. の強意表現) ‖ 負けてたまるか *I'll be damned if* I lose!
▶そんなことがあってたまるか That's *impossible*! / That *can't be* (*true*)! ‖ 俺の気持ちがおまえなんかにわかってたまるか! *There's no way* you could understand how I feel.
▶安月給で朝から晩までこき使われるのはたまったもんじゃない I *can't stand* [It *really gets to* me] having to work morning to night [work day in and day out] for a (lousy) pittance. (➤ get to は「頭にくる」, pittance /pítns/ は「僅かな収入」の意).
☛ **堪らない** (→見出語)

だまる 黙る **1【ものを言わない】** **become silent**; **keep silent** [**quiet**] (静かにしている; quiet のほうがややインフォーマル) ▶容疑者は警察の取り調べに対して終始黙っていた The suspect *remained silent* while he was (being) interrogated by the police. / The suspect *never spoke* [*didn't say a word*] during his interrogation by the police. ‖ 子供は長い時間黙っていることはできない Children can't *keep quiet* for a long time. ‖ 先生は生徒たちに黙るように言った The teacher said to the class, "*Stop talking* [*No talking*], please." ‖ ちょっと黙ってなさい(=騒ぐのをやめなさい) (Please) just *be quiet* for a minute. ‖ 黙れ. おまえの愚痴にはうんざりだ *Shut up!* I'm fed up with your complaints. (➤ shut up はインフォーマルで, 日本語と同じくかなり乱暴な言い方).
▶「結婚してくれ」という浩二のことばに恵子は黙ってうなずいた Keiko just nodded (*silently*) when Koji said, "Will you marry me?" ‖ このことはほかの人には黙っていてね This is *just between you and me*, all right? (➤「ここだけの話」の意) ‖ 彼はそのことを黙っていた He *kept* it *to himself*. / He *kept* it *secret*.
2【許可を得ない】▶人のものを黙って使うな Don't use other people's things *without permission*. ‖ 俊男は親に黙ってバイクを買った Toshio bought a motorcycle *without telling his parents*.
3【反抗しない】▶あいつに侮辱されて黙っているつもりか Are you going to *take* his insults *lying down*? (➤ take ... lying down は「(ひどいことをされても)甘んじて受ける」の意. 否定文・疑問文で使う) ‖ おまえはいじめを黙って見ていたのか Did you just watch the bullying *without saying anything*?

たまわる 賜る **receive** +目 ▶厚情を賜る *receive* much kindness.

たみ 民 **(the) people.**

ダミー a **dummy**
‖ダミー会社 a dummy company [corporation].

だみごえ だみ声 a **thick voice** (濁った声); a **rasping voice** (耳障りな声).

だみん 惰眠 ▶惰眠を貪る *live* [*waste one's time*] *in idleness*.

ダム a **dam** (堤の部分) ▶ダムを建設する build *a dam*.
‖ダム湖 a reservoir, a lake ‖ ダムサイト a dam-site ‖ 貯水ダム a water-storage dam.

たむける 手向ける **offer** +目 (ささげる) ▶墓前に花を手向ける *offer* [*lay*] flowers at [in front of] the grave.

たむし 田虫 **ringworm** ▶足にたむしができた I have *ringworm* on my foot.

たむろ ▶こんな所にたむろして何しているんだ What are you doing *hanging out* [*loitering*] around here? (➤ loiter はしばしば取り締まりの対象になるようなものに用い, やや堅い語).

ため 為

訳語メニュー
利益 →for, for the benefit of **1**
目的 →to do, for **2**
原因, 理由 →because (of), due to **3**

1【利益を示して】for, for the benefit of（➤ 後者は形式ばった言い方）▶国のために戦う fight *for* one's country ‖ 貧しい人々のために働く work *for the benefit of* the poor（➤ for the benefit［sake］of とすると for だけよりも「利益」の意味が明確になる）‖ ためになる科学講演 a *worthwhile*［*an instructive*］science lecture

▶これはきみたちのためになる本だ This book *will benefit*［*be helpful for*］you.

▶先生は私たちのためを思って忠告するんだといつも言う Our teacher always says that he admonishes us *for our own sake*. ‖ そんなにウイスキーを飲まないほうが身のためだよ It will *do you no good* to drink that much whisky. ／You'*d better* go easy on the whisky.

2【目的を示して】(in order) to do, for

> 【文型】
> **人・物(A)が…するために**
> **(for A) to do**
> **in order (for A) to do**
> **so that A can［may］do**
> ➤ for A は文の主語と同じでないとき

▶山田はランナーを二塁に進めるためにバントした Yamada laid a bunt *to* advance the runner to second. ‖ 彼女はピアニストになるために音楽大学へ通っている She is attending a music college (*in order*) *to* become a pianist.（➤ in order to do は to do よりも形式ばった言い方）‖ 彼は試験に合格するために懸命に勉強した He studied hard *so that* he *could* pass［*in order to* pass］the examination. ‖ 彼女は音声学を学ぶためにロンドンへ行った She went to London *for the purpose of*［*with the intention of*］studying phonetics.（➤ purpose は「目的」, intention は「意図」; ともに形式ばった言い方でふつうは She went to London to study phonetics. のようにいう）‖ 私は時々何のために勉強するのかと思う I sometimes wonder *what* I am studying *for*. ‖ 対話「きみは何のためにアルバイトをしているのですか」「学費を稼ぐためです」"*Why* are you working part-time?" "*To* earn my tuition."

3【原因・理由を示して】because, due to ▶飲み過ぎたため, 数人の学生が病院に担ぎ込まれた Several students were rushed to the hospital *because* they had drunk too much (alcohol).

> 【文型】
> **理由・原因(A)のために**
> **because of A**
> **due to A**
> **on account of A**

▶長い内乱のためベイルートの街は荒廃した Beirut was devastated *because of* the prolonged civil war. ‖ 列車の遅れは雪のためです The train delay *was due to* the snow. ／ The train was late *because of* the snow. ‖ 輸血用の血液が不足しているため日本赤十字社は献血を呼びかけている *Due to* the shortage of blood for transfusions, the Japan Red Cross is appealing to people for donations. ‖ 遼はインフルエンザのためにそのトーナメントに出られなかった Ryo couldn't enter the tournament *on account of* the flu.

▶彼女は不注意のためにけがをした She hurt herself *through* her carelessness. ‖ 台風のため私たちの飛行機は離陸できなかった The typhoon *kept* our plane *from* taking off.（➤ keep A from B で「AにBさせないようにする」）.

だめ 駄目

1【役に立たないこと】no good 一形 **だめな no-good**（役立たずの）; **incompetent**（無能な）▶だめなやつ *a good-for-nothing* ‖ うちのマンションはだめだ. 雨漏りがする Our apartment *is no good*. The roof leaks. ‖ 私のパソコンはだめだ（＝壊れている）My (personal) computer *is broken*. ‖ 彼はだめなセールスマンだ He's an *incompetent* salesman. ‖ 子供が悪いことをしてもろくに注意もできないだめな親が多くなった There are a lot of *no-good*［*lousy*］parents nowadays who don't even scold their children when they are bad. ‖ 両親に甘やかされて彼はだめな人間になった He became a *good-for-nothing* after being spoiled by his parents.（➤ good-for-nothing は「役立たずでろくでなしの」）.

▶私って, 何をやってもだめなのかもね I guess I'm the sort of person who *can't do anything right*. ‖ だめね！彼, また三振しちゃったわ *Oh, my goodness!* He struck out again.

▶冷蔵庫に入れておかなかったから肉がだめになってしまった The meat *went bad*［*was spoiled*］since I forgot to put it in the refrigerator.（➤ go bad は「(食物が) 腐る」）‖ その霜で作物はだめになった The crops *were ruined* because of that frost. ‖ 物質的に恵まれ過ぎると人間はだめになる Too much material wealth *spoils* people.

2【無駄】no use 一形 **だめな useless**

> 【文型】
> **…してもだめだ**
> **It's no good doing.**
> **It's no use［useless］doing.**
> **There's no use (in) doing.**

▶言い逃れをしようとしてもだめだ *It's no good* try*ing* to talk your way out of it. ‖ 決まってからぐずぐず言ってもだめだ *It's no use* complain*ing* after something has been decided. ‖ 隠れてもだめだよ. お尻が見えてるよ *It's no use* hid*ing* anymore. I can see your bottom. ‖ 彼に説教してもだめだ. まるでこりない *There's no use* (*in*) lectur*ing* him. He never learns from his mistakes.（→しかたがない）.

▶涙を流したってだめだ You *can't fool me* with your crocodile tears.（➤ fool は「だます」, crocodile tears は「そら涙」の意）.

3【できない, 不可能】▶父は英語が全くだめです My father *cannot* speak English *at all*. ‖ 私, お料理はだめなの I'm a *bad*［*poor* ／ *terrible*］cook.（➤ terrible は「ひどく悪い」の意のインフォーマルな語）‖ 彼は料理は全然だめだ He is *hopeless* at cooking. ‖ これ以上はだめだというところまでがんばるよ I'll do my best until I *don't want to compete* any more. ‖ 救助隊は砂に埋まった少女を助けようとしたがだめだった The rescue team tried to save the girl from sinking into the sand but *failed*［*couldn't*］. ‖ だめでもともとだよ. 頑張って！ *You have nothing to lose*. Keep trying!（→駄目元）‖ 対話「お酒, いかがですか」「すみません, 私お酒はだめなんです」"How about a drink?" "I'm sorry. I *don't drink*."

4【絶望】▶もうだめだ！ *I'm finished!*（➤「私は終わりだ」の意）‖ ボートがひっくり返ったときにはもうだめかと（＝死ぬかと）思ったよ I thought I *was going to die* when the boat capsized. ‖ いろいろやってみたけど, だめだったよ I tried various approaches but *it was no good*. ‖ テニスの試合はまただめだった（＝負けた）I *lost*

た

the tennis match again. ‖ 彼女にプロポーズしたけどだめだった（＝断られた）I proposed to her but *was turned down*. ‖ **対話**「きょうの日本史の試験どうだった？」「だめだったよ」“How did you do on today's Japanese history test?” “I *didn't do* (*very*) *well*.”

5【禁止・必要を示して】▶そこで笑ってはだめだ *Don't* laugh at that. ‖ たばこなんかだめよ！Smoking? *You must be kidding*. (➤「冗談でしょ?，とんでもない」の意) ‖ あの男と付き合ってはだめだ You'*re not* going out with that man! (➤ この進行形は聞き手に対して話し手の決意・意志を通そうとする場合の用法) ‖ だめだと言ったらだめだ I said no and that's that. ‖ 晩ごはんまでに帰って来なくちゃだめだよ You *must* be home by dinner. ‖ そんなに急いで食べてはだめよ You *shouldn't* eat so quickly. ‖ 作文は今週中に提出しなければだめですか？*Do I have to* turn in my composition by the end of this week? ‖ **対話**「お父さん，車を借りてもいい？」「だめだ」“Dad, can I drive your car?” “*No, you can't*. ／*No way!*”

ためいき 溜め息 a **sigh** /saɪ/ ▶子供たちが無事と聞いて彼女はほっとため息をついた When she was told that her children were safe and sound, she *sighed with relief* [*gave a sigh of relief*]. ‖ その悲惨な事故の記事を読んで父は深いため息をついた Reading the article on the tragic accident, my father *heaved* [*breathed*] *a deep sigh*. ‖ ウエディングドレスを着た麻衣子さんはため息が出るほど美しかった Maiko was so beautiful in her wedding dress that she *drew sighs from everyone*.

ためいけ 溜め池 a **reservoir** /rézəʳvwɑːʳ/（貯水池）; an **irrigation pond**（かんがい用の）.

ダメージ damage /dǽmɪdʒ/ ▶輸出業者は円高で大きなダメージを受けた Exporters' profits *were greatly damaged* [*hit hard* ／*hard hit*] by the appreciation of the yen.

> **危ないカタカナ語 ダメージ**
> **1** 名詞の damage は「受けた損害，被害」の意味なので，「…にダメージを与える」は (×) give damage to ではなく，cause [do] damage to の形をとる。
> **2**「ダメージを受ける」は be damaged よりも be hurt（打撃を受ける）がふつう。特に「人」が主語のときは be damaged は使えない。

だめおし 駄目押し（野球）▶中日はだめ押しの2点を入れ，8対3で巨人を破った The Dragons added two *insurance* runs to beat the Giants 8-3. (➤ insurance は「勝利を確実にするもの」の意).

ためぐち ためロ ▶上司にためロで話す speak *too casually* to one's boss ／ speak *on equal terms* to one's boss.

ためこむ 溜め込む save +目；**stock up**（蓄えておく）▶彼女はうんと金をため込んでいるそうだ I hear she's *saved* (*up*) a lot of money. ‖ 彼らは万が一の場合に備えて生活必需品をため込んだ They *stocked up with* [*on*] necessities just in case.

¹ためし 例 ▶ぼくの彼女は時間どおりに来たためしがない My girlfriend *has never once* come on time. (➤「一度もない」の意) ‖ 今までわが社では女性がそのような要職に就いたためしがない There is no *precedent* for a woman holding such an important post at our company. (➤ precedent /présɪdənt/ は「先例」).

²ためし 試し・験し ▶お気に召すかどうか試しに2，3日使ってみてください Please use it for a few days *as a test* [*for a trial*] and see how you like it. (➤ trial は「試用」) ‖ 試しにやってみよう Let's *give* it *a try*. ／Let's *have a go at* it. ‖ サイズが合うかどうかその帽子を試しにかぶってみた I *tried* the hat on to see how it fit. (➤ try on で「試着する」) ‖ 試しに着てみていいですか May I *try* it *on*?

> **【文型】**
> **試しに…してみる**
> **try** doing

▶試しにこのはさみでそれを切ってみたら？Why not *try* cut*ting* it with these scissors? ‖ 試しに左手で書いてごらん *Try* writ*ing* with your left hand. ‖ 物は試し，やってごらんなさいよ You won't know if you don't try, right? (➤「試してみなければわからない」の意).

ためす 試す・験す test +目（テストする）; **try** +目（やってみる）▶ガス警報器がちゃんと作動するかどうか試してみた We *tested* the gas alarm to see whether it worked. ‖ 彼女ははさみの切れ味を試してみた She *tried out* [*tested*] the scissors to see how (well) they cut. (➤ try out は「試験的に使ってみる」).

だめだし 駄目出しをする order someone to redo a scene ▶女優は何度もだめ出しされた The actress *was asked to do the scene* over many times.

だめもと 駄目元 ▶失敗したってだめもとだ. やってみようよ *I have nothing* (*left*) *to lose*, so let's go ahead and give it a try.

ためらい 躊躇い (a) **hesitation**; (a) **reservation**（不安）▶彼は内部告発するのに何のためらいもなかった He had no *hesitation* in blowing the whistle. (➤ blow the whistle は「内部告発する，密告する」の意) ‖ 息子をアメリカの大学に送り出すことにはためらいがある I have some *reservation* about sending my son to a U.S. college.
‖ためらい傷 a hesitation wound.

ためらう 躊躇う hesitate /hézɪteɪt/, **be hesitant** ▶あの人のこと好きだけど，いざ結婚となるとためらうわ I love him but still *am hesitant* when it comes to marriage. ‖ 由紀子はためらいがちに彼にチョコレートの箱を渡した Yukiko handed him a box of chocolate *hesitatingly*. ‖ 彼女は本当のことを言うのをためらった She *hesitated* [*was hesitant*] to tell the truth. ‖ 彼は（少しも）ためらうことなくその金を赤十字に寄付した He donated the money to the Red Cross *without* (*the slightest*) *hesitation*.

ためる 溜める 1【蓄える】save +目（貯蓄する）; **collect** +目（集める）▶私はバイクを買うためにお金をためている I *am saving money* [*saving up*] to buy a motorcycle. ‖ ネットショッピングでポイントをためている I *earn* points by shopping online. ‖ 島の住民は雨水をためて生活用水に使っている The islanders *collect* rainwater for daily use. ‖ この貯水池は吉野川の水をためるために造られた This reservoir was built to *store* (*up*) the waters of the Yoshino River. ‖ ストレス[疲れ]をため過ぎないほうがいい You shouldn't *let too much* stress [fatigue] *build up*.

2【滞らせる】▶私は授業料を2か月分ためてしまった I'*m* two months *behind* in my tuition. ‖ 家賃を3か月ためて大家に文句を言われた I *had* three months of back rent *piled up* and got complaints from my landlord. ‖ 宿題［支払い／洗濯物］をためないようにしなさい Don't *let* your homework [bills ／washing] *pile up*.

ためんてき 多面的な many-sided ▶多面的な問題 a *many-sided* question ／a *multifaceted* problem

‖世界の出来事は多面的に見る必要がある You need to look at world events *from a variety of perspectives* [*angles*].

たもくてき 多目的の multipurpose ▶この棚はいろいろと多目的に使える This shelf can be used *for many purposes.* ／This is a *multipurpose* shelf.

‖多目的グラウンド an all-purpose ground ‖多目的ダム a multipurpose dam ‖多目的トイレ an accessible restroom [toilet].

たもつ 保つ maintain +㊐（何かをよい状態に）; keep +㊐（大事に守る）; hold +㊐（占める，保持する）▶世界の平和を保つ *maintain* world peace ‖健康を保つには十分睡眠をとることが必要だ Getting a good night's sleep is necessary to *maintain* [*keep*] one's health. ‖この部屋の温度は18度に保たれている The temperature of this room *is kept* at 18 degrees.

▶彼女は10年近く「テニスの女王」の座を保っていた She *held the title* of tennis queen for almost ten years. ‖母は若さを保つためにエアロビクスをしている My mother does aerobics in order to *keep herself young* [*stay young*].

たもと 袂 1【着物の】the bag of a sleeve（袋状の部分）; a sleeve（袖）. ▶《慣用表現》両社は提携を解消し，たもとを分かつことにした The two companies decided to end their partnership and *go their separate ways.*

2【そば】▶橋のたもとに大きな柳の木が立っている There stands a big willow tree *by* [*near*] the bridge.

たやす 絶やす ▶春子さんは笑顔を絶やさない人だ Haruko is *never without* a smile on her face. ‖彼らは寒い夜をしのぐために，火を絶やさなかった They *kept* the fire *alive* [*going*] to keep warm through the cold night. ‖娘の家では牛乳を絶やしたことがない At my daughter's house they *never run out of* milk [they *always keep* milk *in stock*].

たやすい easy ▶私にとってこれはたやすい仕事だ This is an *easy* task for me. ／I can do this *easily* [*with ease* ／ *without difficulty*]. ／This is *a piece of cake.*

たゆまぬ 弛まぬ ▶たゆまぬ努力 *untiring* efforts ‖太郎はたゆまぬ努力で優等で卒業した Taro *worked perseveringly* and graduated with honors.

たよう 多様な diverse /dəvə́ːˈs/（異なった種類から成る）▶多様な野鳥の種類 *a wide variety* [*range*] *of* wild birds ／ *many different kinds of* wild birds ‖スマートフォンは多様な機能を搭載している Smartphones are equipped with *a wide range of* [*many different*] functions. ‖世界には多様な民族が住んでいる There are *many different* ethnic groups in the world. ‖若いうちに多様な文化に触れることが大切だ It's important to experience *diverse* cultures while you are young. ‖島の生態系は多様な生物から成っている The island ecosystem is made up of *diverse* living organisms. ‖消費者の生活様式の多様化に合わせて多くの新しい製品が作り出された Numerous new products have been created to meet the *diversified* lifestyle needs of consumers.

‖多様性 diversity.

☛ 多種多様（→見出語）

¹たより 便り a letter（手紙）; news（消息）▶きのうインドに居る友人から便りがあった I got *a letter* from a friend in India yesterday. ‖その後姉から何の便りも無い I *have heard nothing from* my sister since.（➤ hear from で「（当人）から消息を聞く」）.

ことわざ 便りの無いのは良い便り No news is good news.

✉ 初めてお便りします This is my first *letter* to you. ／This is my first time to *write to* you.

✉ お便りありがとう Thanks for your *letter.* ／It was so nice to *hear from* you.

✉ お便りお待ちしています I am looking forward to your *letter.*

✉ たまにはお便りください Please *write* (to) me once in a while. ／Please *drop me a line* occasionally.

✉ またお便りします I'll *write* you again.

²たより 頼り reliance（信頼）; help（助け）▶頼りになる人 a *reliable* person ‖彼は本当に頼りになる人物だ He's a real *trouper.*（➤ real trouper は決まり文句）. ‖頼りがいのある友だちがいたらなあ I wish I had a *trustworthy* friend [a friend I could rely on].

▶辞書を頼りに英語で手紙を書いた I wrote a letter in English *with the help of* a dictionary. ‖父が一家の頼りです Dad is the *main support* of our family.（➤ support は「生活を支える人」）‖頼りにしてるよ I know I can *count on* you. ／ I'*m depending* [*relying*] *on* you.（●「頼りにしてたんだよ」なら I knew I could count on you. という）.

たよりない 頼り無い unreliable ▶母の運転は甚だ頼りない My mother's driving skills are completely *unreliable.* ‖あんな頼りない男と付き合うのはやめなさい Stop going out with such an *unreliable* guy.

たよる 頼る

1【依存する】depend《on》（寄りかかる）; rely《on》（信頼して頼りにする）

【文型】
人・物(A)に頼る
depend on A
rely on A

▶血液の供給は全面的に献血に頼っている We *depend* [*rely*] entirely *on* donations for the blood supply. ‖いつまでも人に頼るんじゃないよ You can't *depend* [*rely*] *on* others forever.

▶どんなに腹が立っても暴力に頼ってはいけないよ No matter how angry you are, you shouldn't *resort to violence.*（➤ resort to は「…の力に訴える」）.

【文型】
人(A)に必要なもの(B)を頼る
depend on A for B
人(A)に頼って…する
depend on A to do
rely on A to do

▶彼はいまだに生活費を両親に頼っている He still *depends on* his parents *for* his living expenses. ‖日本は石油を輸入に頼っている Japan *depends on* imports *for* oil. ‖彼は家計管理を奥さんに頼っている He *depends on* his wife *to* handle the household finances. ‖被災者たちは炊き出しをボランティアに頼っている The disaster victims *rely on* volunteers *to* distribute cooked rice.

2【援助を期待する】▶私にはあなたしか頼る人がいないの You're the only person I can *rely on* [*turn to*].（➤ turn to は「助けを求める」）‖私はおばを頼って上京した I came to Tokyo from the country *counting on* my aunt's help.（➤ count on は「…を当てにする」）‖私にはいざという時に頼れる親類がいない I have no relatives to *fall back on*. (➤ fall back on は「(いざという時に)よりどころとする」の意のインフォーマルな表現).

たら 鱈 (魚) a **cod**, a **codfish**
‖たらこ salted cod roe(食品).

-たら 1【仮定, 時点】**if**, **in case**(仮に…なら;後者は(主に米)で,(英)では非標準的);**when**(…のとき) ▶困ったことがあったら知らせてください *If* you (should) get into trouble, please let me know. (➤ should が入ると「万一…なら」の意になる) ‖雨が降ったら運動会は10月2日に延期になる *In case* it rains [*In case of* rain], the athletic meet will be postponed to October 2. (➤ in case of は堅い言い方) ‖これが両親にわかったらどうしよう *What if* my parents find out about it?
▶帰ったら電話するよ I'll phone you *when* I get home. (帰ることははっきりしているので if としない) ‖大学を卒業したら結婚しよう *After* we graduate from college, let's get married.
2【願望】**I wish**

【文型】
…たらなあ
I wish I were [did] …
If only I were [did] …
【解説】**I wish** が漠然とした「…であったらなあ」という一般的な願望に対して, **If only** はより強意で,「ただ…でありさえすれば」実現できたのに, あるいは, 別の結果になったのに, といった意味で用いる.

▶もっとお金があったらなあ *I wish I had* more money. ‖若かったらなあ *I wish I were* [*was*] young. (were が正式だが, くだけた文では was を用いることも多い) ‖若かったらエベレストに登れるのに *If only I were* young, I could climb Mt. Everest. (➤若くないことが唯一の障害という含み) ‖20代のときのパンツがはけたらなあ *I wish I could* fit into the pants I used to wear when I was in my twenties. ‖もっと英語がうまく話せたらなあ *I wish I were* a better speaker of English. / *If only I could* speak English better.
3【提案】▶美津夫, 髪が伸びたわね. 床屋さんに行ったら? Mitsuo, your hair is so long. *How about* going [*Why don't you* go] to the barber? (➤ Why don't you …? は穏やかな提案を表す).
4【驚き】▶横綱の強さったらない *Talking* [*Talk*] *about* strength! Look at the yokozuna! (➤ Talking about のほうが普通) ‖ことしの暑さったらなかったね *Talking* [*Talk*] *about* heat! This summer was horrible.

たらい 盥 a **washtub**(洗濯用のおけ) ▶(慣用表現)患者は病院をたらい回しにされた The patient *was sent from* one hospital *to* another. ‖その書類はあちこちの課をたらい回しにされた The documents *were shifted from* one section *to* another a number of times.

だらく 堕落 **corruption** 一形 堕落した **corrupt**, **rotten** (➤後者はややインフォーマル) ▶堕落した政治家 a *corrupt* politician ‖堕落した生活を送る lead a *decadent* [*rotten*] life ‖彼は酒とギャンブルで堕落してしまった He *was ruined* by drinking and gambling. ‖ローマは内部から堕落していった Rome *rotted* (*away*) from the inside.

-だらけ ▶この作文は間違いだらけだ This composition *is full of* mistakes. ‖公園は紙くずだらけだった The park *was littered with* wastepaper. ‖ぼくは欠点だらけの人間です I am *full of* faults. ‖家に入る前にその泥だらけの靴を脱いでちょうだい Take off your *muddy* shoes before you come in.

だらける ▶きょうは気持ちがだらけている I feel *sluggish* [*listless*] today. ‖生徒は試験が終わるとどうしても気分がだらける The students tend to *slack*(*en*) *off* after the tests. ‖試合はだらけてきた The game is becoming *dull*.

-たらしい ▶長ったらしいスピーチ a *lengthy* speech ‖うちの課長ったら, しょっちゅうすけべったらしい目で私を見るのよ My section chief gives me *lecherous* looks all the time. (➤ lecherous は /létʃərəs/ と発音) ‖嫌みったらしい言い方はよせよ Don't be so *sarcastic* [*nasty*].

だらしない 1【きちんとしていない】**slovenly**(手入れがされず汚い);**sloppy**(態度・服装・仕事などが);**untidy**(人・服装・習慣などが);**dissipated**(ふしだらな) ▶だらしない生活をする lead a *dissipated* [an *undisciplined*] life ‖だらしない服装は避けてください Please refrain from dressing *sloppily* [*untidily*]. ‖彼はお金にだらしない He is *careless* with his money. ‖私のルームメートはすごくだらしない My roommate is *a real slob* [*really slovenly*]. (➤ slob は「ぐうたら」).
2【ふがいない】▶そんなことぐらいで練習を休むなんてだらしないぞ *It's pretty pathetic* of you to skip practice for such a reason. ‖だらしない話だが, 碁では息子にかなわない *This is embarrassing*, but I'm no match for my son in Go. ‖ガールフレンドに自分の気持ちも言えないなんてだらしない(=意気地がない)ぞ What a *spineless* man you are not to even be able to tell your girlfriend your (true) feelings!

たらす 垂らす 1【ぶら下げる】**hang down** ▶窓からロープを垂らした I *hung* a rope *down* from the window. ‖私, 髪を肩に垂らそうと思うの I think I'll *let* my hair *hang* (*down*) *over* my shoulders.
2【液体を落とす】**drip** +目 ▶はけのペンキをたらしてしまった I *dripped* paint from the brush. ‖タコライスにタバスコを少したらすとおいしいよ Taco rice tastes better if you *add* a few drops of Tabasco. (➤ add は「加える」) ‖赤ちゃんはよだれをたらして寝ていた The baby was sleeping while *drooling*.

-たらず -足らず **less than**(未満の) ▶歩いて30分足らずの道のりだ It is a *less than* a 30-minute walk. ‖彼は2か月足らずで会社を首になった He was fired from the company *in less than* two months. ‖その赤ん坊は月足らずで生まれてきた The baby was born *prematurely*.

たらたら ▶彼は額から汗をたらたら流しながら働いている Sweat is *dripping* [*streaming down*] from his forehead as he works.
▶彼の口調はいやみたらたらだった His tone was *dripping* with sarcasm. ‖ふがいない夫をもって彼女は不平たらたらだ Her husband is such a spineless man that she's *forever griping* (about him). (➤ gripe /graɪp/ は「愚痴をこぼす」. また, この forever は「絶えず, しょっちゅう」の意).

だらだら ▶だらだら坂 a *long, gentle* slope ‖だらだら仕事をするな! Don't go about your work *so sluggishly*! ‖校長のだらだらした挨拶にはうんざりした I was bored to death by the principal's *long, rambling* speeches. ‖試合はだらだらと5時間も続いた The match *dragged on* for five hours.

タラップ a (**boarding**) **ramp** (飛行機の); an **accommodation ladder**(船の) (➤「タラップ」はオランダ語の *trap* から).

タラバガニ《動物》a **red king crab**; an **Alaskan king crab**.

たらふく ▶ドーナツをたらふく食いたいなあ I want to eat *as many* doughnuts *as I like*. ／ I want to eat *my fill of* doughnuts. ‖ たらふく食べて動けないよ I *stuffed myself* and can't move. ‖ たらふく食った! *I'm stuffed!*

だらりと **loosely** /lúːsli/ ▶突然横断幕の一方の側が外れて, だらりと垂れ下がった Suddenly the banner dropped at one end and hung *loosely*. ‖ 彼は酔っ払ってだらりと友だちの肩にもたれかかった He was drunk and *draped himself over* his friend's shoulder.

-たり ▶音楽を聴いたり本を読んだりして静かに一日を過ごした I spent the day quietly listening to music *and* reading books. ‖ 一日中雪が降ったりやんだりしていた *It snowed on and off* [*off and on*] all day. (➤ on and off, off and on は「断続して」) ‖ 彼女の家の玄関のベルを押す勇気がなくて家の前を行ったり来たりした I didn't have the courage to push the doorbell, and *went back and forth* in front of her house.

ダリア《植物》a **dahlia** /dǽljə ‖ déɪliə/.

たりきほんがん 他力本願 **reliance on other people** ▶他力本願では成功はできないよ You won't be successful if you always *rely on others*.

だりつ 打率《野球》a **batting average** ▶彼の打率は高い[低い] He has a high [low] *batting average*. ‖ 吉田は打率3割3分6厘で首位打者になった Yoshida won the hitting crown with a .336 *average*. (➤ .336 は "zero point three three six" と読む).

たりない 足りない **1**【不足している】**be short**《of》▶きみは卒業するには2単位足りない You *are* two credits *short* for graduation. ‖ お金が5000円足りない I *am* 5,000 yen *short*. ‖ 茶わんが3つ足りない We'*re short* three cups. ／We *need* three *more* cups. ‖ うちの店は人手が足りない Our store *is shorthanded* [*short of help*]. ‖ 食料が足りない We *don't have enough* food. ‖ インスタント食品はビタミンが足りない Instant foods *lack* [*are deficient in*] vitamins. (➤ ともに「欠けている」の意) ‖ あなたは熱意が足りないのよ You *lack* [*are lacking in*] enthusiasm. ‖ 私の試験の点数は合格点に25点足りなかった My test score *was* 25 points *below* the passing mark. ‖ きみはまだ勉強が足りないね You've still *got a lot to learn*. (➤「まだ学ぶことがたくさんある」の意) ‖ お客さん, 運賃が足りませんよ Sir [Ma'am ／Miss], you *haven't paid the full fare*. ‖ A氏の説など論ずるに足りない Mr. A's theory *is not* (*even*) *worth discussing*.
2【ばかな】▶彼, 少し(頭が)足りないんじゃない? Isn't he a bit *simple* [a little *stupid*]?
☛ 取るに足りない (⇀見出語)

たりょう 多量の **much**; **a large quantity** [**amount**] **of** ▶多量のワイン *much* wine ‖ わが国は多量の原材料を輸入している Our country imports *a large quantity* [*amount*] *of* raw materials. ‖ サウジアラビアは多量の(=豊富な)石油を産出する Saudi Arabia produces *abundant* oil. ‖ 玄米はビタミンBを多量に含んでいる Brown rice *is rich in* vitamin B.

だりょく 惰力 **inertia** /ɪnə́ːʳʃə/.

たりる 足りる **be enough** ▶4000円で足りるかしら Will 4,000 yen *be enough*? ‖ 私は睡眠は5時間あれば足りる Five hours' sleep *is enough* for me.
▶そんな用件ならわざわざ行かなくても電話で足りる If that's all you have to say, *you can say it on the phone* without going all the way out there.
☛ 足りない (⇀見出語)

たる 樽 a **barrel**(胴の膨れた); a **cask** (酒だる); a **keg** (小だる) ▶漬物のたる *a barrel* of pickles ‖ ビールのたる *a keg* [*barrel*] of beer ／a beer *keg* [*barrel*].

だるい ▶きょうは寝不足で体がだるい I *feel sluggish* [*feel exhausted*] today from lack of sleep. ‖ 一日中立っていたので足がだるい My legs *feel heavy* because I was standing all day.

たるき 垂木 a **rafter**.

タルタルステーキ **steak tartare**.

タルタルソース **tartar(e) sauce**.

タルト a **tart** ▶イチゴのタルトを焼く bake a strawberry *tart*.

だるま 達磨 a ***daruma***, a **Dharma doll**
日本紹介 ✉ **だるまは赤い張り子の人形で, 達磨大師の座禅姿をかたどったものです. 縁日に縁起物として売られます. 傾けてもまたまっすぐに起き上がります. そこから七転び八起きという表現と結び付き, 立ち直り(や逆境からの再起)を象徴しています. 人形の目の部分は白い2つの丸になっています. 最初に片方の目に墨を入れ, 願い事がかなったときにはもう一方の目も黒く塗ります** *Daruma* are red papier-mâché dolls. They are shaped like the Buddhist monk Dharma in Zen meditation. They are sold at Buddhist temple [Shinto shrine] festivals as good luck articles that are helpful in making people's wishes come true. They always return to an upright position when tilted over. Daruma dolls are associated with the phrase Nanakorobi-yaoki (Fall down seven times but get up eight times). They represent resilience (and recovering from adversity). The dolls have two white circles where the eyes should be. First, people paint in one eye with black *sumi* ink. If and when their wish is fulfilled, they paint in the other eye.

たるみ 弛み (a) **slack**(ロープ・ひもなどの); (a) **sag** (カーテンなどの) ▶ひもを引っ張ってたるみをなくしなさい Pull the string tight to take up the *slack*.

たるむ 弛む **slacken** ▶ロープがたるんでいる The rope *has slackened*. (➤「緩んでいる」の意にもなる) ‖ たるんだ太もも *flabby* thighs ‖ 小包のひもがたるんだ The cord around the parcel *became loose* [*slack*].
▶きみのこの書類は計算間違いが多すぎる. 近頃少したるんでるんじゃないか You've made a lot of calculation mistakes in these papers. I think you'*re getting* a bit *loose* [*slack*] these days.

たれ 垂れ **sauce**(掛け汁); **gravy** (肉汁) ▶肉をたれにつける dip meat in *sauce* ／*baste* meat (➤ baste は「(焼く[あぶる]前に)たれなどをつける」の意) ‖ 豚肉をゴマだれをつけて焼く *baste* pork *in a sesame sauce* and roast it ‖ (焼き鳥は)塩にしますか, たれにしますか? Would you like your yakitori salted or with *sauce*?

だれ 誰 **1**【疑問】**who**

> **語法** (1)疑問詞の who は主語・補語になる場合に用いられる. (2)他動詞や前置詞の目的語として用いられる場合には whom とするのが正式だが, これは堅い言い方. 形式ばらない日常英語ではいずれの場合も who が一般的.

▶あの人は誰？ *Who* is that man [woman]？‖この詩を書いたのは誰ですか *Who* wrote this poem？‖あなた, この頃誰と付き合ってるの？ *Who* are you going out *with* these days？／*Who* are you seeing these days？‖彼女誰と駆け落ちしたと思う？ *Who* do you think she ran away *with*？‖きみは困ったとき誰に相談しますか *Who* do you talk your problems over *with*？‖ぼくは誰に殴られたのかわかりません I don't know *who* hit me. ‖きみの尊敬している人は誰ですか *Who* do you respect？（➤「誰を」は whom であるが, 文頭では who を用いる）‖写真がボケていて誰が誰だかわからない The photo is so blurred [fuzzy] I can't tell *who's who*. ‖誰かと思ったよ *Is that really you?*

▶ 対話（ドアのノックに）「だあれ？」「あたし」"*Who is it?*" "It's me." ‖ 対話「誰からそんなうわさを聞いたの？」「知子からよ」"*Who* did you hear that *from*?" "From Tomoko." ‖ 対話「姉貴が結婚したんだ」「誰と？」"My sister got married." "*Who to?*／*To who?*"（To who？はくだけた言い方. To whom？にすると堅い言い方になる）‖ 対話「そのネクタイ誰にプレゼントするの？」「部長よ」"*Who* are you going to give that tie *to*?" "To the manager." ‖ 対話「この車は誰の（もの）ですか」「青木君のです」"*Whose* car is this?" "It's Aoki's." ‖ 対話「ゆうべは誰のアパートに泊まったの？」「小田君のアパート」"*Whose* apartment did you stay at last night?" "At Oda's." ‖ 対話「おまえたち, 誰をいじめてたんだ」「誰もいじめてません」"*Who* were you picking on?" "We weren't picking on anybody."

2【不特定の人】somebody, someone（肯定文で）; **anybody, anyone**（疑問文・否定文で）（➤ともに後者のほうが堅い語）▶お母さん, 玄関に誰か来たわよ Mom, there's *somebody* [*someone*] at the door. ‖誰か杉本さんの消息を知っていますか Does *anyone* know what has become of Sugimoto？‖会社にはまだ誰か居るかしら I wonder if there is *anybody* at the office. ‖誰か, ちょっと手を貸してくれないか Would *someone* lend me a hand？（➤疑問文で someone を使うのはその誰かが居ることを想定しているとき）‖誰かほかの人に聞いてください Ask *somebody else*.

【文型】
ほかの誰よりも…
... than anyone else

▶黒田さんはわが社でほかの誰よりも英語を話すのがうまい Ms. Kuroda can speak English better *than anyone else* in our office. ‖課長はほかの誰よりも早く出社する The section chief comes to work earlier *than anyone* [*anybody*] *else*.

▶野球のルールは誰だって知っている *Everyone* knows the rules of baseball. ‖がんばれば誰でも外国語を身につけることができる *Anybody* can learn a foreign language if they try hard.（➤ anybody は肯定文では「誰でも」の強意的な言い方になる）‖誰だって死ぬのは嫌だ No one wants to die. ‖誰でも出ていきたい人は出ていってよい *Whoever* wants to leave may leave. ‖誰でもいいから1人手伝いによこしてください Can you send me someone to help (me)? I *don't care who*. ‖誰にでも悩み事はある *Everybody* has one problem or another. ‖それは誰にでもできることではない Not *everyone* can do it. ‖私は今, 誰にも会いたくない I do*n't* want to see *anybody* now. ‖数学では誰にも負けたくない I *want to be the best* in mathematics. ‖体育館の中には誰も居なかった *Nobody* was in the gym. ‖学生たちは誰もその会に出席しなかった *None of* the students were present at the meeting.

▶彼女は誰彼構わず悪口を言う She speaks ill of *anyone and everyone*.

たれこむ 垂れ込む squeal /skwi:l/《to》（密告する）.

たれこめる 垂れ込［籠］める hang low ▶黒い雲が空に垂れこめている Black clouds *are hanging low* over the sky.

たれさがる 垂れ下がる hang (down) ▶旗がだらりと垂れ下がっている The flag *is hanging down* limply. ‖柿の木は実の重みで枝が垂れ下がっていた The branches of the persimmon tree *were drooping* [*sagging*] under the weight of the fruit.

たれながし 垂れ流し (a) **discharge**（排出(物)）▶生活排水の垂れ流し *a discharge* of untreated water containing household wastes.

たれながす 垂れ流す discharge ＋㊐ ▶その工場は未処理の廃水を川に垂れ流した The factory *discharged* untreated effluent into the river.

だれひとり 誰一人 nobody ▶誰ひとり私の気持ちを理解してくれなかった *Nobody* understood how I felt. ‖そのニュースを聞いて喜ばない者は誰ひとりいなかった *Everybody* was pleased to hear the news.

たれまく 垂れ幕 a **banner**; a **drop curtain**（劇場の）▶歓迎の垂れ幕が空港のロビーに掛かっていた There were welcoming *banners* in the airport lobby. ／Welcoming *banners* were hanging in the airport lobby.

たれる 垂れる 1【液体が滴る】drip ▶洗濯物から滴がたれている Water *is dripping* from the wet clothes. ‖彼女の額から汗がたれていた Her forehead *was dripping with sweat*. ‖帰宅したら床に点々と血がたれていた When I got home, I found *drops of blood* on the floor.

2【だらりと下がる】hang ▶耳の垂れた犬 a dog with *droopy* ears ‖垂れた肌［筋肉］*sagging* skin [muscles] ‖垂れた乳房 *sagging* breasts ‖彼女の髪は腰まで垂れている Her hair *hangs down* to her waist. ‖風が無いのでこいのぼりはだらりと垂れていた The carp streamers *were drooping* in the windless sky. ‖川に釣り糸を垂れて魚の掛かるのを待った I *dropped* [*lowered*] my line into the river and waited for a bite. ‖彼は申し訳なさそうに頭を垂れた He *hung his head* as if he knew there was no excuse for his behavior.

だれる ▶3時間が過ぎて会議はだれてきた After three hours, the meeting began to *drag*. ‖暑いと私はどうも気持ちがだれる The heat makes me *feel all dragged out* [*tired*].

タレント a **personality** ▶テレビタレント a TV *personality* [*star*] ‖タレント事務所に所属する belong to a *talent* agency.

危ないカタカナ語✸ タレント
1 talent は「才能」の意.「才能のある人」の意味もあるが主に集合的用法で, 一人一人を指すことは, まれ.
2 日本では映画やテレビに出る有名人のことを「タレント」といっているが, これに当たるのは personality, celebrity /səlébrəṭi/, performer, entertainer, star など.「テレビ［ラジオ］タレント」というときは TV [radio] を前につければよい.
3「タレント議員」は entertainer turned Diet member（タレントから転向した議員）のように説明する.

タロいも タロ芋 a taro.

-だろう 1【推量・想像を示して】I think(➤「…だと思う」の意の一般的な言い方) ▶ヤクルトはあすの試合には勝つだろう *I think* the Swallows *will* win tomorrow. ‖ 彼女はたぶんすぐに来るだろう She *will probably* be here in a minute. (➤ will は未来の確実なことを表す；probably が加わると「十中八九間違いない」の意になる) ‖ あの新人はきっと人気が出るだろう *I'm sure* the rookie *will* be very popular. (➤ I'm sure は話者が確信をもっている場合に用いる) ‖ 子供が生まれたら，きみはきっといい母親になるだろうね *I'm sure* you'*ll* be a good mother once you have a baby. ‖ 彼女，どこの学校だろう *I wonder* what school she attends. (➤ I wonder は「どこかな，なぜかな，誰かな」のような意味のとき用いる) ‖ 彼の言っていることは正しいだろうけど，賛成はできない He *may* be right [He is *probably* right], but I can't agree with him. (➤ may のほうが消極的) ‖ ビールを飲んでしまったのはおまえだろう You drank all the beer, *didn't you*?
▶クリスマスパーティーには来るんだろう？ You'll be at the Christmas party, *won't you*? ／I *suppose* I'll see you at the Christmas party. ‖ 対話「あの選手は来シーズン，ホームラン王になるだろうか」「まず，だめだろうな」"*Will* that player be the home run king next season?" "*Probably* not."
2【原因・理由の推量を示して】I wonder ▶どうしてみんな大学へ行きたがるんだろう I *wonder* why everybody wants to go to college.
3【仮定を示して】▶通信衛星が無かったら，テレビの同時中継でワールドカップを見ることはできないだろう Without communications satellites, we *would* be unable to watch the World Cup on TV in real time. ‖ あのとき現場に人が居たら大惨事になっていただろう If there had been people at the site, there *would have been* a catastrophe.
4【念押し・決めつけを示して】▶冗談だろ？ You *must* be joking. (➤ must は「…に違いない」) ‖ 泣くなよ．あしたがあるだろう Don't cry. Tomorrow *is* another day.

タワー a tower
‖タワーブリッジ (the) Tower Bridge (➤ ロンドンにある橋) ‖タワーマンション a high-rise condo [condominium] ‖ 東京タワー (the) Tokyo Tower.

たわいない 他愛ない ▶そのきょうだいはいつもたわいないことでけんかしている The siblings are always quarreling over *small* [*trivial*] matters. (➤ sibling は男女の別なく使える語) ‖ 少女たちはたわいないことで笑い合っていた The young girls laughed at any *little* thing. ‖ その男の子はたわいない(＝無邪気な)いたずらに興じた The boy amused himself by playing *innocent* tricks. ‖ 母は振り込め詐欺の手口にたわいなく(＝簡単に)引っかかった My mother was *easily* taken in by a bank transfer scam.

たわごと 戯言 nonsense ▶たわ言を言うんじゃない Don't talk *nonsense*. ／Don't be silly. ‖ そんなたわ言はもう聞きたくもない I am fed up with such *silly talk*.

たわし 束子 a scrub brush；steel wool(金属製の) ▶たわしで流しを磨く scour the sink with *a scrub brush*.

たわむ 撓む bend(全体が)；sag (down) (中央部分が) ▶木々の枝は雪の重みでたわんでいた The branches of the trees *were bent* under the weight of the snow. ‖ 本の重みで棚がたわんでいる The shelf *is sagging* under the weight of books.

たわむれ 戯れ play(遊び)；fun, (a) joke (冗談)；a jest(joke の古風な言い方) ▶たとえ戯れであってもそれは言わないでくれ Don't say that, even *in jest*.

たわむれる 戯れる play《with》▶子供たちが庭で犬と戯れている The kids *are playing with* the dog in the yard.

たわら 俵 a straw bag
‖米俵 a straw ricebag.

たわわ 撓わ ▶枝もたわわに柿がなっている The trees *are heavy with* ripe persimmons.

[1]たん 痰 phlegm /flem/ ▶たんを吐く cough out *phlegm* ‖ (病院で) たんが絡むんです My throat is full of *phlegm*. ／There's *phlegm* caught in my throat.

[2]たん 反 1【面積の単位】a *tan*；a Japanese unit of measurement for land area about 10 ares (➤ 説明的な訳).
2【反物の長さの単位】a *tan*；a Japanese unit of measurement for a roll of cloth nearly 12 yards (➤ 説明的な訳).

[3]たん 端 ▶けんかは誤解に端を発していた The quarrel *resulted from* a misunderstanding.

タン (a) tongue /tʌŋ/
‖タンシチュー stewed tongue, tongue stew ‖ 牛タン beef tongue.

[1]だん 段 1【階段の】a step；a rung(はしごの横棒) ▶本殿までは80段上らねばならない You have to go up 80 *steps* to get to the main shrine. ‖ 私は高い石段を1段ずつ上った I went up the high stone stairway *step by step*. ‖ 本箱のいちばん上の段(＝棚)の右端の本を持って来てちょうだい Can you please bring me the book on the far right *top shelf* of the bookcase?
2【武道などの】dan (➤ 英語化している) →初段 ▶柔道5段の人 a *5th-dan* judoist ‖ 彼女は剣道4段だ She is a kendo-player of *the fourth grade*.
3【段落】a paragraph ▶2段目から読んでください Please read aloud from *the second paragraph*.
4【九九の】▶3の段をやってみよう Let's run through *the threes*. ‖ 8の段がわかんないよ I don't know my *eight times table*.
5【…する場面】▶健は教室ではおとなしいが，野球をする段になるとがぜん張り切る Ken is unobtrusive in the classroom, but *when it comes to* (playing) baseball, he suddenly changes into a go-getter.

[2]だん 壇 a platform ▶(式典会場の)壇上の列席者たち(の1人) (a member of) a *platform* party ‖ 演説者が次々と壇に立った One speaker after another *took the platform*.

[3]だん 談 ▶X氏の談によれば Mr. X *says* ... ／*According to the account of* Mr. X ... ‖ 彼女は我々に経験談を聞かせてくれた She told us her *personal experiences*.

-だん -団 a group, a party ▶災害現場に調査団が派遣された *A survey group* has been sent to the scene of the disaster.
‖記者団 the press group [corps /kɔːʳ/]；a party of reporters ‖ 視察団 an inspection party [team] ‖ 青年団 a youth group ‖ 選手団 a delegation of athletes.

だんあつ 弾圧 suppression 一動 弾圧する suppress ＋目 (押さえつける)；persecute /pə́ːʳsɪkjuːt/ ＋目 (宗教・主義などを迫害する) ▶警察は反政府デモを弾圧した The police *suppressed* the antigovernment demonstration. ‖ 江戸時代, キリスト教徒は幕府によって弾圧された During the Edo period the Christians *were persecuted* by the shogunate.

たんい 単位 **1**【長さ・重さなどの】a **unit**（計量の）; a **measure**（度量の）▶ヤードは長さの単位である The yard is *a unit* [*a measure*] of length. ‖ 日本の貨幣の単位は円である The *denomination* of Japanese money is the yen.（➤ denomination は「通貨の単位」）‖ 単位を間違えて計算しないように気をつけなさい Be careful not to calculate *with the wrong unit*.

2【かたまり】▶校庭にはクラス単位で集合してください Meet in the schoolyard *in groups according to class*. ‖ 鉛筆はダース単位で箱に入っている Pencils are boxed *by the dozen*.

3【学科の】a **credit** ▶彼女は卒業に必要な単位をすでに取ってしまった She has already got enough *credits* for graduation. ‖ 4 単位足りないので卒業できないよ I'm four *credits* short, so I can't graduate. ／I'm four *credits* short for graduation. ‖ 英作文の単位(＝科目)を落とした I *flunked* [*failed*] my English composition (*course*). ‖ あの先生はすぐに単位をくれるよ He's [She's] *an easy grader*. ‖ この講座は何単位ですか *How many credits* do I get for this course?

たんいちでんち 単1電池 a **size D battery**.

たんいつ 単一の **single** ▶ダイヤモンドは単一の元素から成る Diamonds are made of a *single* element. ‖ 単一民族国家 an ethnically *homogeneous nation*.（➤ homogeneous /hòʊmədʒíːniəs/ は「同種の」の意.「異種の」は heterogeneous /hèṭərədʒíːniəs/）.

だんいん 団員 a **member** ▶彼女はすみれ座の団員だ She is *a member* of the Sumire-za.

たんおんかい 短音階 a **minor scale**.

1**たんか 担架** a **stretcher** ▶担架で運ばれる be carried on *a stretcher*.

2**たんか 単価** a **unit price** [**cost**] ▶そのメモ帳は単価100円です Those memo pads are 100 yen *each*. ／Those memo pads cost 100 yen *apiece*. ／The *unit price* for that memo pad is 100 yen.（➤最後の文は主にビジネスで用いられる）‖ 単価はいくらですか How much is it *for each*?

3**たんか 啖呵** ▶「俺に任せろ」と彼はたんかを切った "Leave it to me!" he *said confidently* [*defiantly*].（➤ confidently は「自信たっぷりに」, defiantly は「まあ見ていろと挑戦するように」）‖ 遠山の金さんは気持ちのいいたんかを切る Toyama-no Kin-san has a refreshingly *crisp way of speaking*.

4**たんか 短歌** a *tanka* (poem)

日本紹介 ✉ **短歌は1200年以上前からある短い日本の詩の一形式で5・7・5・7・7の31音からできています. 和歌とも呼ばれます. 自然の美しさ, 四季の移ろい, 恋愛などをよんだものが主流です** The *tanka* is a form of short Japanese poetry that originated more than 1,200 years ago. It consists of 31 syllables in five lines of either five or seven syllables arranged according to this scheme: 5-7-5-7-7. *Tanka* is also referred to as '*waka*.' The most common subjects for *tanka* are the beauty of nature, the changes of the seasons and love.

5**たんか 炭化** 一動 **炭化させる** **carbonize** ＋目 ▶炭は木を炭化させたものだ Charcoal *is carbonized* wood.

だんか 檀家 a ***danka***; one of the supporting families of a Buddhist temple（➤説明的な訳）.

タンカー a **tanker** ▶石油タンカー an oil *tanker*.

1**だんかい 段階** a **stage**（発達・進行などの一過程）; a **step**（目標などへの一歩）; a **phase** /feɪz/（局面）▶その計画はまだ全く研究の段階です The project is still in the purely research *stage*. ‖ 初期の段階で発見されれば容易に治るがんがある Some cancers can be cured easily if they are detected *in their early stages*. ‖ この英語コースは初級・中級・上級の3段階に分かれている The English courses (at our school) are divided into three *levels*: elementary, intermediate, and advanced. ‖ 宇宙開発は新しい段階に入った Space development has entered *a new phase*. ‖ その薬は臨床試験の最終段階に入っています The drug is in *the final stage* of clinical trials. ‖ 段階的な変化に気づく notice a *gradual* change.

2**だんかい 団塊** ▶団塊の世代 **the baby boomer generation** ／**the first post-war baby boomer generation**.

1**だんがい 断崖** a **cliff** ▶断崖絶壁 *a precipitous cliff*.

2**だんがい 弾劾** (an) **impeachment** /ɪmpíːtʃmənt/ 一動 **弾劾する** **impeach** ＋目 /ɪmpíːtʃ/ ▶クリントン大統領は弾劾された President Clinton *was impeached*.

たんかだいがく 単科大学 a **college**.

1**たんがん 嘆願** (a) **pleading**; (a) **petition**（署名による）一動 **嘆願する** **plead** ＋目（慈悲などを）; **implore** ＋目（誠意を込めて必死に）; **petition** ＋目（…してほしいと）▶両親は誘拐犯に息子を解放してくれるように嘆願した The parents *pleaded* with the kidnapper to release their son. ‖ 彼らは州知事にその男の死刑執行停止を嘆願した They *petitioned* the governor to stop the man's execution.

2**たんがん 単願する** **apply (for admission) to only one school** [**college** ／**university**].

だんがん 弾丸 a **bullet** /bʊ́lɪt/ ▶弾丸が彼の胸を貫いた *A bullet* went through his chest. ‖ 山田の弾丸シュートがゴールに突き刺さった Yamada's *bullet* pierced the target.

‖弾丸ライナー a line drive ‖ 弾丸列車 a bullet train.

1**たんき 短気な** **quick-**[**short-**]**tempered** ▶うちのおじいちゃんは短気だ My grandfather *is quick-tempered*. ／My grandfather *has a quick* [*hot* ／*short*] *temper*. ‖ どんなことがあっても短気を起こすな Don't *lose your temper* [Don't *become impatient*] whatever happens.

2**たんき 短期** a **short period** 一形 **短期の** **short, short-term** ▶ハワイへ短期留学する study in Hawaii *for a short period* ‖ きみは短期間でずいぶん英語がうまくなったね You've become very fluent in English *in no time*, haven't you?

‖短期借入金 a short-term loan, (a) short-term debt ‖ 短期講習 a short course ‖ 短期集中コース a crash course ‖ 短期大学 a junior college.

だんき 暖気 **moderate heat, warm weather**.

たんきゅう 探究［**探求**］**する** **search**《for》▶探究心の旺盛な子供 an *inquisitive* child ‖ 生きることの意味を探究する *search for* the meaning of life ‖ 大学は真理を探究する場所である A university is a place for the *pursuit* of truth.

たんきょり 短距離 a **short distance**

‖短距離競走 a short-distance race ‖ 短距離選手 a sprinter.

タンク a **tank**（容器; 戦車）‖タンクトップ a tank top ‖ タンクローリー a tanker,《米また》a tank

truck.
ダンクシュート a **slam-dunk**, a **dunk shot**.
タングステン **tungsten**.
だんけつ 団結 **union** ; **solidarity** (連帯) **一動 団結する** **unite** ; **get together** (まとまる) ▶みんなが団結して町から暴力団を追放した Everyone *came together* [*stood together*] to drive the gangsters out of town. ‖ 文化祭の成功のために一致団結しよう Let's all vow to *work together* for the success of the school festival. ／ Let's *all work together* to make the school festival a success. ‖ 団結は力なり In unity is strength. ／ Strength lies in unity.
1**たんけん 探検・探険** (an) **exploration** (未知の地の) ; (an) **expedition** (研究などを目的とする旅行) **一動 探検する** **explore** /ɪksplɔ́ːʳ/ +目 ▶宇宙探検によって数多くの事実が明らかになった *Space explorations* have revealed a lot of facts. ‖ ナンセンは北極を探検した Nansen *explored* the Arctic. ‖ 彼らは南極大陸へ探検に行った They *went on an expedition* to the Antarctic continent. ／They went on an Antarctic expedition.
‖探検家 an explorer ‖ 探検隊 an exploratory party, an expedition.
2**たんけん 短剣** a **dagger**.
たんげん 単元 a **unit**.
だんげん 断言する **assert** +目 (自信を持って主張する) ; **declare** +目 (公に, または真剣に言う) ; **affirm** +目 (証拠などに基づいて言う) ▶雅彦はユーフォーを見たと断言した Masahiko *asserted* [*affirmed*] *that* he had seen a UFO. ‖ その教授はこれまでに教えた学生の中でメアリーがいちばんよくできると断言した The professor *declared* Mary was the best student he had ever taught. ‖ 現時点で断言はできないが, 沈没前に船を脱出した人が数人はいると思う We *are not positive* [*sure*] at this point, but we believe several people escaped the ship before it sank. (前半を We can't say anything definite, のように言ってもよい).
たんご 単語 a **word** ▶「義理」に当たる英語の単語は何ですか What is the English *word* for "giri"? ‖ きみは英語の単語力をつける必要がある You need to *increase* [*build up*] your English *vocabulary*. (➤ vocabulary /voʊkǽbjəleri/ は「語彙」).
‖単語集 [帳] a wordbook.
タンゴ **the tango** ▶タンゴは踊れますか Can you do [dance] *the tango*?
‖アルゼンチンタンゴ Argentine /ɑ́ːʳdʒəntaɪn/ tango ‖ コンチネンタルタンゴ Continental tango.
だんこ 断固たる **decisive** /dɪsáɪsɪv/, **firm** ▶テロに対して断固たる処置をとる take *decisive measures* against terrorism ‖ 環境保護活動家はダム建設に断固反対した The environmental activists *were adamantly opposed to* [*were dead set against*] the building of a dam. ‖ 当局は脱税者を断固取り締まるべきだ The authorities concerned should *crack down on* tax evaders.
だんご 団子 a **dumpling** ▶ ことわざ 花より団子 Cake before flowers. ／ Substance over show. ／ Pudding rather than praise.
‖団子鼻 a snub nose (➤ 日本語がもつ愛きょうのニュアンスはない) ; a bulbous /bʌ́lbəs/ nose (➤「球根のような鼻」の意) ‖ 団子虫 a pill bug ‖ きび団子 a millet dumpling.
たんこう 炭鉱 a **coal mine**
‖炭鉱夫 a coal miner.
1**だんこう 団交** **collective bargaining** ▶組合側は会社側に団交を要求した The union demanded *collective bargaining* from the management.
2**だんこう 断行** ▶組合はストを断行した The union (*resolutely*) *carried out* the strike.
3**だんこう 断交** ▶わが国はA国と断交した Our nation *broke off diplomatic relations* with Country A.
だんごう 談合 **rigged bidding** (不正に操作された入札) ▶市庁舎の建設では談合が行われた The *bidding* for the construction of the city hall *was rigged*. ‖ 官製談合 government-initiated collusive bidding (➤ collusive /kəlúːsɪv/ は「なれ合いの」).
たんこうぼん 単行本 a **book** ▶私は自分のエッセー20編を単行本で出版した I published twenty essays of mine *in book form*.
たんごのせっく 端午の節句 **the boys' festival**.
たんこぶ a **wen** ; a **bump** (殴られてできる) ▶ (殴られて) 額に卵のようなたんこぶができた I've got an egg-like *bump* on my forehead.
▶《慣用表現》課長は目の上のたんこぶだ The section chief is *a pain in the neck*.
だんこん 弾痕 a **bullet mark** ▶車には弾痕があった The car bore *bullet marks* [*the marks of bullets*].
たんさ 探査 一動 探査する **explore** +目, **probe** +目 ▶深海を探査する *explore* the deep ocean.
だんさ 段差 ▶道路の段差 (部分) *an uneven part* on a road surface ‖《掲示》段差 (＝隆起) あり, スピード落とせ *Bump ahead* : go slow. ‖《掲示》段差がありますからご注意ください *Uneven pavement* [*floor*]. Watch your step. (口頭で言う場合は The pavement [floor] is not even, so please watch your step. などがふつう).
ダンサー a **dancer**.
たんさいぼう 単細胞 a **single cell**
‖単細胞生物 a monad ‖ 単細胞動物 [植物] a unicellular animal [plant].
たんさき 探査機 a **probe**
‖宇宙探査機 a space probe ‖ 金星探査機 a Venus probe ‖ 月探査機 a moon explorer.
たんさく 探索 an **investigation** ▶真犯人を探索する *carry out an investigation to find* the real culprit.
たんざく 短冊 a ***tanzaku*** ; a strip of thick paper on which a *tanka* [*haiku*] is written (➤ 説明的な訳) ▶ニンジンを短冊に切る *cut* carrots *into small sticks*.
タンザニア **Tanzania** /tæ̀nzəníːə/ (アフリカ東部の国).
たんさん 炭酸 **carbonic acid** ▶このミネラルウォーターは炭酸入りですか Is this mineral water *carbonated*? ‖ 炭酸飲料 carbonated beverages /bévərɪdʒɪz/, fizzy [bubbly] drinks, (soda) pop ‖ 炭酸ガス (→二酸化炭素) ‖ 炭酸カルシウム calcium carbonate ‖ 炭酸ナトリウム sodium carbonate.
たんさんでんち 単3電池 a **size AA battery**, a **double-A battery**.
たんし 端子 a **terminal** ▶入力 [出力] 端子 an input [output] *terminal*.
だんし 男子 a **boy** (少年) ; a **man** (成人の男) ; a **male** (男性) ▶男子・女子の順に交互に並びなさい Get into line—*boy, girl, boy, girl*.
‖男子学生 a male [boy] student ‖ 男子校 a boys' school, an all-boy(s) school.
タンジェント a **tangent** 《略》**tan**.
たんじかん 短時間 a **short time** ▶短時間で結論を出

す reach a conclusion *in a short time*.

だんじき 断食 a fast ▶ラマダンはイスラム教徒が日の出から日没まで断食する月だ Ramadan is the month during which Muslims *fast* [*practice fasting*] from sunrise to sunset.

だんじて 断じて **1**【肯定文で】▶私は断じて潔白だ I am *absolutely* innocent. ‖ それは断じて彼の誤りだ It is *certainly* his fault. ‖ 私は断じてわが道を行く I'll *firmly* [*resolutely*] go my own way.
2【否定文で】▶そんなことは断じていたしません I *would never* do that. ‖ きみを裏切ることは断じてない I'll *never ever* betray you. (➤ never ever は never の強調形).

た

たんしゃ 単車 a **motorcycle** ▶単車を飛ばす gun one's *motorcycle*. →オートバイ.

だんしゃく 男爵 a **baron** ‖男爵夫人 a baroness.

だんしゅ 断酒する **quit** [**give up**] **drinking**.

1**たんじゅう 胆汁**《生理学》**bile** /baɪl/.

2**たんじゅう 短銃** a **handgun**, a **pistol**, a **gun** (➤ あとの2語はインフォーマル).

たんしゅく 短縮 (a) **reduction** 一動 **短縮する reduce** +目; **shorten** +目 (短くする) ▶電子レンジを使って料理時間を短縮する *shorten* cooking time by using a microwave oven ‖ 従業員は労働時間の短縮を要求した The employees demanded *a reduction* in working hours. ‖ 労働時間は週38時間に短縮された The working hours *were reduced* [*were shortened*] to 38 hours a week.
‖**短縮形** a shortened form, a contracted form (➤ 後者は主に文法用語) ‖ **短縮授業** shortened school hours (「授業時間を短縮する」は shorten school hours. また, 短縮授業のある日は short school [early dismissal] day) ‖ **短縮ダイヤル** a speed dial, simplified dialing (➤ 短縮ダイヤル用の3桁の電話番号を 3-digit telephone number という).

たんじゅん 単純な **simple** ▶きみはこんな単純な問題も解けないの Can't you even solve a problem as *simple* [*uncomplicated*] as this (one)? ‖ サッカーは最も単純で, 最もおもしろいスポーツの1つだ Soccer is one of *the simplest* and yet most exciting sports. ‖ 私はそんなばかげたうわさを信じるほど単純じゃないわ I'm not so *simple* [*naive*] as to believe such a ridiculous rumor. (➤ この場合の simple, naive は「だまされやすい, 無知の」の意) ‖ 単純な機械 *a basic* machine ‖ イスラム教の単純すぎる説明 a *simplistic* [an *uncomplicated*] explanation of Islam.

1**たんしょ 短所** a **fault** (➤「欠点」の意の一般語); **shortcomings** (➤ ささいな欠点; 複数形で用いるのがふつう); a **defect** (fault より重大な欠点); a **weak point** (弱点) ▶誰にも何か短所があるものだ Everyone has their *shortcomings* [*faults*]. ‖ 飽きっぽいのが私の短所だ My *weak point* is that I lose interest in things quickly.

2**たんしょ 端緒** **the beginning** ▶端緒をつかむ find *a clue*.

だんじょ 男女 **man and woman** (男と女); **boy and girl** (少年少女); **both sexes** (男女両性) ▶この工場では500人の男女が働いている Five hundred *men and women* are working in this factory. ‖ 男女合わせて30人のボランティアがアフリカに派遣された A total of 30 volunteers, *male and female*, were dispatched to Africa. ‖ 男女(=性別)を問わず誰でも競技に参加できます Anybody can take part in the contest *regardless of gender* [*sex*]. ‖ このジャケットは男女兼用だ This jacket *can be used both by men and women*. (➤「男女兼用の服」は unisex clothes という) ‖ 男女雇用機会均等法は1986年に施行された *The Equal Employment Opportunity Law* came into effect in 1986.
‖**男女共学** coeducation (➤「男女共学の学校」は co-ed /kóʊed/ school) ‖ **男女共同参画** gender equality ‖ **男女同権** equal rights for men and women ‖ **男女平等** (the) equality of the sexes, gender equality.

たんじょう 誕生 **birth** 一動 **誕生する be born** ▶青木さん夫妻に男の子が誕生した A baby boy *was born* to the Aokis.
▶新しい政党の誕生 the *birth* of a new political party ‖ 地球の誕生は46億年前と言われる It is said that the earth *came into being* 4.6 billion years ago. ‖ 先月この町に公共図書館が誕生した A public library *was established* in this town last month. ‖ 誕生祝いにおじさんからカメラをもらった My uncle gave me a camera *for my birthday*.
✉ **お子さんのお誕生おめでとうございます** Congratulations on your new baby!
‖**誕生石** a birthstone ‖ **誕生パーティー**[**会**] a birthday party.

だんしょう 談笑する **have a pleasant chat**.

たんじょうび 誕生日 one's **birthday** ▶母の誕生日を祝う celebrate my mother's *birthday* ‖ 誕生日はいつですか When is your *birthday*? ‖ 私の誕生日は9月22日だ My *birthday* is (on) September 22nd. /(英) My *birthday* is September the 22nd [is (on) the 22nd of September]. ‖ きょうは父の45歳の誕生日だ Today is my father's forty-fifth *birthday*. ‖ 父親は娘の誕生日にセーターを買ってやった The father bought his daughter a sweater *on her birthday*. ‖ お誕生日おめでとう *Happy birthday* (*to you*)! (➤ カードなどでは Many happy returns (of the day)! も用いる.「きょうの良き日が何度も巡ってきますように」の意).
✉ **17歳のお誕生日おめでとう** My warmest wishes for [on] your 17th birthday!
✉ **ささやかですが, 誕生日のプレゼントをお送りしますのでお受け取りください** I'm sending a small *present for your birthday*. Please accept it (with my best wishes).

1**たんしょく 単色の** **monochrome**.

2**たんしょく 淡色** a **pale** [**light**] **color** 一形 **淡色の** **pale colored, light colored**.

1**だんしょく 暖色** a **warm color**.

2**だんしょく 男色** **male homosexuality**.

1**たんしん 単身** ▶彼女は単身ヨーロッパへ旅立った She set out on a journey to Europe *by herself* [*alone*]. ‖ 石田さんはニューヨークに単身赴任した Mr. Ishida was transferred to a new post in New York and had to *leave his family behind* (in Japan). ‖ 私はもう3年間単身赴任をしています I've *been working and living away from my family* [I've *been on a solo assignment*] for three years. ‖ 単身赴任の生活はつらい It's tough to *have to live apart from my family for work*. (「仕事の都合で家族と別れて暮らすこと」と考えて英訳する).

2**たんしん 短針** **the short** [**hour**] **hand** (➤「長針」は the long [minute] hand).

たんす 箪笥 a **wardrobe** /wɔ́ːʳdroʊb/ (洋服だんす); a **chest of drawers** (整理だんす); a **bureau** /bjʊ́əroʊ/, (米また) a **dresser** (鏡付き寝室用の).

ダンス a **dance**(踊り); **dancing** (踊ること) ▶洋子はダンスがうまい Yoko is good at *dancing.* ／Yoko is a good dancer. ‖ シンデレラは王子とダンスをした Cinderella *danced* with the prince. ‖ ダンスパーティーを開く give [throw] *a dance.*
‖**ダンス教師** a dancing instructor ‖ **ダンスホール** a dance hall ‖ **社交ダンス** social dancing, ballroom dancing.

> **危ないカタカナ語✹ ダンスパーティー**
> **1** 通例単に dance という. dance party は日本語の「ダンスパーティー」と異なり,「パーティーが中心でダンスもできるもの」の意.
> **2** 高校で行われる通常のダンスパーティーは high school dance というが, 学年末にあるクラス主催のダンスパーティーは prom. 正式の舞踏会は ball.

「ダンス」のいろいろ **カンカン** cancan ／**サルサ** salsa ／**サンバ** samba ／**ジャズダンス** jazz dance ／**ジルバ** jitterbug ／**スクエアダンス** square dance ／**タップダンス** tap dance ／**タンゴ** tango ／**チャールストン** Charleston ／**チャチャチャ** cha-cha ／**ハバネラ** habanera ／**ヒップホップ** hip-hop dance ／**フラダンス** hula ／**フラメンコ** flamenco ／**ブレークダンス** break dance ／**ベリーダンス** belly dance ／**ボサノバ** bossa nova ／**ボレロ** bolero ／**マンボ** mambo ／**リンボーダンス** limbo ／**ルンバ** rumba ／**ワルツ** waltz

たんすい 淡水 **fresh water**(➤「海水」は salt water)
‖**淡水魚** a freshwater fish.

だんすい 断水 ▶きのうから断水しています *The water has been cut off* since yesterday. ／The water supply *has been stopped* [*suspended*] since yesterday.

たんすいかぶつ 炭水化物 a **carbohydrate** /kɑ̀ːʳboʊháɪdreɪt/, 《インフォーマル》 **carb.**

たんすう 単数 **the singular** ▶ media の単数形は medium だ The *singular form* of 'media' is 'medium.'

1**たんせい 丹精・丹誠** ▶父が丹精こめて育てた菊が見事な花をつけた The chrysanthemums that my father *raised with great care* are blooming beautifully.

2**たんせい 端正な** **handsome**(きりっと整った) ▶あの歌舞伎役者は端正な顔立ちをしている That Kabuki actor has a *handsome*(, *clear-cut*) face.

1**だんせい 男性** a **man** [複 **men**] ▶彼, 信頼できる男性よ He is a trustworthy *man.* ‖ 早くすてきな男性が現れないかなあ I wonder if some *wonderful guy* will turn up soon. ‖ きのうハンサムな男性に会ったの I met a handsome *gentleman* yesterday. (➤ gentleman は敬意を込めた言い方).
▶女性の男性化 *androgenization* in women (● 「男性化した女性」は an androgenized woman) ‖ 彼の声は男性的だ He has a *masculine* voice. (➤ masculine は男性特有と考えられている性質を指す) ‖ アメリカンフットボールは男性的なスポーツだ American football is a *manly* sport. (➤ manly は「いかにも男性らしい」の意) ‖ 兄の男性用化粧品をちょっと使ってみた I tried using my brother's *men's cosmetics.*
‖**男性ホルモン** a male (sex) hormone (➤ male は生物的な性を強調する言い方).

2**だんせい 男声** a **male voice**
‖**男声合唱団** a male chorus [choir /kwáɪəʳ/].

3**だんせい 弾性** **elasticity** 一形 **弾性のある** **elastic.**

たんせき 胆石 a **gallstone** /gɔ́ːlstoʊn/.

だんぜつ 断絶する **break off** ▶隣国と国交を断絶する *break off* relations with a neighboring country ‖ 世代の断絶は大昔からあったようだ It seems that there have been *generation gaps* since the dawn of time.

たんせん 単線 a **single line** [**track**] ▶単線の鉄道 a *single-track*(*ed*) railroad.

たんぜん 丹前 a ***tanzen***; a cotton-padded winter kimono (➤ 説明的な訳).

だんせん 断線 ▶強風で電話が断線した The phone line *was cut off* by the strong wind.

だんぜん 断然 **1【はるかに】** **far**(形容詞・副詞(句)を修飾して); **by far**(比較級・最上級などを強めて) ▶耐久性ではこの車は他車より断然優れている This car is *far* [*much*] more durable than any other car. ‖ 3人のうちでは大輔が断然足が速い Daisuke runs *by far* the fastest of the three. (● 比較級を強めるときは much または far, 最上級を強めるときは by far がふつう). ‖ 彼女は断然トップの女優だ She is the best actress *by far* [*by a long shot*].
2【何としても】 ▶今度こそ断然禁煙するぞ I'm going to give up smoking *once and for all.* ／This time I'm *definitely* going to give up smoking.

1**たんそ 炭素** **carbon**
‖**炭素化合物** a carbon compound ‖ **一 [二] 酸化炭素** carbon monoxide [dioxide].

2**たんそ 炭疽** **anthrax.**

1**だんそう 断層** a **(geographic) fault** ▶二つの大きな断層がずれた Two major *faults* shifted.
‖**断層撮影** tomography ‖ **断層写真** a tomograph. →活断層.

2**だんそう 男装** ▶男装の女優 an actress *dressed in male attire.*

1**たんそく 短足** a **short leg** 一形 **短足の** **short-legged** ▶彼は短足だが足は速い He *has short legs* but runs fast. ／He is *short-legged* but fleet-footed. (➤ 前者の言い方のほうがふつう).

2**たんそく 嘆息** a **sigh.**

だんぞくてき 断続的な **intermittent** /ìntəʳmítnt/ ▶台風の影響で強い雨が断続的に降った Due to the typhoon, it rained hard *on and off.* ／The typhoon caused *intermittent* hard rains.

だんそんじょひ 男尊女卑 **dominance of men over women, male chauvinism** /ʃóʊvənìzəm/ ▶男尊女卑の社会 *a male-dominated society.*

たんだい 短大 a **junior college**
‖**短大生** a junior college student.

だんたい 団体 a **group**; a **party** (一行); an **organization** (組織体) ▶私は団体で行動するのは嫌いだ I don't like going around *in groups.* ‖ 35名以上の団体には団体割引がある *Group rates* [*discounts*] are available for *parties* of 35 or more. ‖ 私は中国への団体旅行に参加した I joined *a group tour* to China. ‖ 私は団体旅行中です I'*m traveling with a group.*
‖**団体競技** team sports ‖ **団体交渉** (→団交) ‖ **団体生活** group life ‖ **団体旅行客** a group [party] of tourists ‖ **宗教団体** a religious organization ‖ **婦人団体** a women's organization.

たんたん 淡々 ▶友人は自分の現在の心境を淡々と語った My friend *calmly* [*dispassionately*] expressed his present feelings. ‖ あの碁の名人は勝負に勝っても

負けても淡々としている That Go master *remains unaffected* [*unmoved*] whether he wins or loses.

だんだん 段々 **gradually ; more and more**（ますます）▶秋になって木の葉がだんだん色づいてきた With the arrival of autumn the leaves are *gradually* changing colors. ‖ 気温がだんだん上がってきた The temperature is rising *little by little*. (➤ little by little は「少しずつ」).

【文型】
だんだん…になる
get ＋ 比較級 ＋ and ＋ 比較級
become ＋ 比較級 ＋ and ＋ 比較級
get [come] to do

《解説》(1) **get** や **become** のあとに形容詞の「比較級＋ and ＋比較級」を続けて,「だんだん, ますます…になる」を表す. get のほうがくだけた語だが, 変化に重点があり, become のほうが変化後の状態に重点がある. →なる.
(2) 動詞を続けて「…するようになる」を表すには get または come のあとに to do を続ける.

▶だんだん暖かくなってきましたね It's getting warm*er and* warm*er*, isn't it? ‖ 話がだんだんおもしろくなってきた The story became *more and more* interesting. (➤「おもしろくなくなってきた」なら *less and less* interesting とする) ‖ 何度も聴くうちにこの歌がだんだん好きになってきた I'*ve come to* like this song after listening to it over and over. (➤ become to like としない).
‖段々畑 terraced fields.

たんたんめん 担々麺 **tan tan noodles** [**men**], **dandan noodles** [**mian**].

たんち 探知する **detect** ＋㊐ ‖逆探知機 a reversal detector ‖ 魚群探知機 a fish finder [detector] ‖ 電波探知機 a radar /réɪdɑːʳ/.

だんち 団地 an **apartment complex** /kɑ́ːmpleks/, a **housing complex** [**development**] ;《米また》a **project**（公営団地）▶私たちは団地住まいです We live in *a housing development*. ‖ 彼らは高層団地の 5 階に住んでいる They live in a unit on the fifth floor of *a high-rise apartment complex*.
‖団地族 inhabitants of a housing complex ‖ 工業団地 an industrial park.

だんちがい 段違い ▶テニスでは夏子は私より段違いにうまい I am *no match* for Natsuko in tennis. ／As far as tennis is concerned, I'm *not in the same class* [*league*] *as* Natsuko. (➤ be not in the same class [league] as ... は「…には遠く及ばない, かなわない」の意).
‖段違い平行棒 the uneven (parallel) bars.

[1]**たんちょう 単調な** **monotonous** /mənɑ́ːtnəs/ ; **dull**（退屈な）▶単調なリズム (a) *monotonous* rhythm ‖ 単調な仕事 a *monotonous* job ‖ この辺りの景色は単調だ The scenery around here *lacks variety*. ‖ 彼は単調な毎日の生活に飽き飽きしている He is tired of his *monotonous* [*dull*] everyday life. ／He is tired of the *monotony* of his everyday life.

[2]**たんちょう 短調** a **minor key** ▶短調の曲 a song *in a minor key* ‖ ト短調のフーガ a fugue in *G minor*.

[3]**たんちょう 丹頂**《鳥》a **Japanese crane**, a **red-crowned crane**.

[1]**だんちょう 団長** **the head** ; **the leader**（統率者）▶中国視察団団長 the *head* of the Chinese inspection party ‖ 野村氏を団長とする遠征チーム the visiting team *headed by* Mr. Nomura.

[2]**だんちょう 断腸** ▶中国市場から撤退を余儀なくされたのはまさに断腸の思いです *It is gut-wrenching* [*It really breaks our heart(s)*] that we have had to withdraw from the Chinese market.

たんてい 探偵 a **detective**,《インフォーマル》a **sleuth** /sluːθ/ 《参考》detective は「刑事」の意にもなるので, 明確にしたい場合は「探偵」を private detective,「刑事」を police detective とする.
‖探偵社 a detective agency ‖ 探偵小説 a detective story ‖ 私立探偵 a private detective [eye].

だんてい 断定 a **conclusion**（結論）**一動 断定する** **conclude** ＋㊐ ▶その証拠から裁判官たちは彼が有罪であると断定した From the evidence, the judges *concluded* that he was guilty. ‖ よく調べもしないで断定的な言い方をするのはけしからん He hasn't even looked into the matter so he shouldn't give his opinion in such a *decided* manner. ／He shouldn't make such a *categorical* statement when he hasn't done the proper research.

ダンディー ダンディーな (**middle-aged and**) **stylish** 《参考》英語の名詞としての dandy は「衣服や外貌に気を使う人」の意で古風な語.

たんてき 端的 ▶端的な表現 a *straightforward* expression ‖ 今回の事件は学校でのいじめの陰湿さを端的に（＝はっきりと）示している This incident *clearly* shows how sly and underhanded bullying at school is. ‖ 端的に言って, この作家の作品は読むに値しない *In brief* [*To be direct*], this author's works are not worth reading.

たんでん 炭田 a **coal field**.

[1]**たんとう 担当する** **take charge**《of》▶私は学園祭では放送係を担当する I *am in charge of* making announcements during the school festival. ‖ その殺人事件は原警部が担当している Inspector Hara *is in charge of* the murder case. ‖ この幼稚園で私は 3 歳児を担当している（＝世話をしている）I *take care of* three-year-old children in this kindergarten. ‖ 申し訳ありませんが, 担当の者はただいま外出中です I'm afraid *the person in charge* is out of the office right now. ‖ 英語の担当教員は清水先生だ Mr. Shimizu is a teacher (*in charge*) *of* English. ‖ その科目の担当は中野教授だ Professor Nakano *teaches* the subject. (●「中野教授が教える」と考えて訳す).

[2]**たんとう 短刀** a **dagger**.

[1]**だんとう 暖冬** a **mild winter** ▶暖冬で冬物が売れない Winter clothes are not selling well because of the *mild winter*. ‖ ことしは暖冬異変で, スキー場はどこも困っている It is *unusually warm* this winter, so all the ski resorts are having a hard time.

[2]**だんとう 弾頭** a **warhead**.

だんとうだい 断頭台 **the guillotine** /gɪ́lətiːn/.

だんどうだん 弾道弾 a **ballistic missile** /bəlɪ̀stɪk mɪ́səl/ (➤「弾道ミサイル」もこの訳でよい).
‖大陸間弾道弾 an intercontinental ballistic missile《略 ICBM》‖ 短距離弾道弾 a short-range ballistic missile《略 SRBM》‖ 中距離弾道弾 an intermediate /ìnṭəʳmíːdiət/ range ballistic missile《略 IRBM》.

たんとうちょくにゅう 単刀直入 ▶単刀直入な質問 a *direct* question ‖ 単刀直入に言ってくれ Please get *to the point*. ‖ 彼は単刀直入に用件を切り出した He *jumped right* into the main topic. ／He *cut straight to* the heart of the matter. ／He *cut to* *the chase.*

たんどく 単独の solo /sóʊloʊ/ **一副 単独で** alone (ひとりで) ; by oneself (独力で) ▶彼は単独で冬の富士山に挑んだ He attempted a *solo* ascent of Mt. Fuji in winter. ‖ そういうことは単独でやるべきではない You should not do that kind of thing (*all*) *by yourself.* (➤ この all は強調) ‖ 山での単独行動は危険だ It's dangerous to *go off* [*do things*] *by yourself* in the mountains. ‖ 修学旅行中は単独行動をしてはいけない During the school excursion, you must not *go off on your own.* (➤「ひとりで離れてしまう」の意) ‖ その誘拐事件は逮捕された男の単独犯行らしい It seems that the kidnapping *was carried out* [*committed*] by the arrested man *alone.*
‖ **単独会見** an exclusive interview ‖ **単独記者会見** a solo media [news] conference (➤ conference は記者団との会見) ‖ **単独飛行** a solo flight.

だんトツ 断トツ ▶彼女は1500メートル競走では断トツ(の1位)だった She was the winner *by far* in the 1,500 meters. ‖ 古川君はクラスの中で断トツに数学ができる Furukawa is *by far the best* at math in the class.

だんどり 段取り arrangements (手はず, 用意) ; a plan (計画) ▶彼は段取りが悪い He's bad at *making arrangements.* ‖ 葬式の段取りはすべて整った The funeral *arrangements* are all set. ‖ 祝賀会の段取りを決めよう Let's work out *a plan* for the celebration party.

だんな 旦那 a master (主人) ; a husband (夫) ▶旦那さま, お風呂が沸きました The bath is ready, *sir.* ‖ うちの旦那, きょうは帰りが遅いのよ My *husband* is coming home late today.

たんなる 単なる only, just (➤ 後者はよりくだけた語) ; mere (ほんの ; 形容詞として名詞の前で用いる) ; simple (単純な) ▶それは単なるうわさだ It's *only* a rumor. (➤「うわさであって, 事実ではない」の意) ／It's a *mere* rumor. (➤「どうということのないうわさである」の意 ; only との語順の違いにも注意) ‖ それは単なる言い訳にすぎない That's *just* an excuse. ‖ あれは単なる過失とは思えない It's hard to believe that was a *simple* mistake. ‖ 孝夫? (恋人じゃなく)単なる友だちよ Takao? Oh, he's *just* a friend.

たんに 単に only, merely (➤ 後者は前者よりも堅い語) ; simply (単純に) ▶単にそう言ってみただけです I *merely* [*only*] suggested it. ‖ 彼は単に金もうけのためにエロ小説を書いた He wrote an erotic novel *simply* for the money. ‖ あの男の子は単に頭がいいばかりでなく性格もいい That boy is *not only* smart *but* (*also*) good-natured.

たんにでんち 単2電池 a size C battery.

たんにん 担任 ▶クラスを担任する *take* [*have*] *charge of* a class ‖ 永田先生は私たちのクラスの担任です Mr. Nagata *is in charge of* our class. ／Mr. Nagata is our class teacher.
‖ **担任教師** a class [《米また》homeroom] teacher, 《英また》a form teacher.

タンニン 《化学》tannin.

だんねつ 断熱 ▶私の家は断熱してある My house *is insulated.* ／ My house *has insulation.* ‖ この発泡スチロールは断熱用です This styrofoam is used for *insulation.*
‖ **断熱材** insulation, insulating material.

たんねん 丹念な elaborate /ɪlǽbərət/ ; close /kloʊs/ (綿密な) ▶彼はそのデータを丹念に調べた He examined the data *closely.* ／He made an *elaborate* investigation into the data. ‖ 私は『雪国』を訳書のSnow Countryと丹念に(＝注意深く)突き合わせてみた I *carefully* compared "Yukiguni" with its translation "Snow Country."

だんねん 断念する abandon ＋㊐ ; give up (諦める) ▶資金不足のため我々はその企画を断念した We *abandoned* [*gave up*] the project for lack of money. ‖ その走者は足の故障で競技出場を断念した The runner *gave up* taking part in the race due to leg trouble. ‖ 私は彼女が登山部に入るのを断念させようとした I tried to *dissuade* her *from* joining [*convince* her *not to* join] the mountaineering club. (➤ dissuade A from B は「A(人)にB(事・行為)をしないように説得する」の意で, 堅い言い方).

1**たんのう 堪能** **1【上手なこと】**▶彼は英語と中国語に堪能だ He *is proficient in* English and Chinese. ／He *has a good command of* English and Chinese.
2【心行くまで楽しむ】一動 堪能する enjoy ＋㊐ ▶私たちは本場のフランス料理を堪能した We *enjoyed* [*feasted on*] genuine French food. ‖ ゆうべの『ローエングリン』は歌手, オーケストラ, 美術すべてがすばらしく, 十分に堪能した Yesterday evening we *enjoyed every moment* of "Lohengrin" including the singers, the orchestra, and the decor, which were all [all of which were] out of this world.

2**たんのう 胆嚢** a gall /gɔːl/ bladder
‖ **胆のう炎** cholecystitis /kàːlɪsɪstáɪtɪs/.

たんぱ 短波 a shortwave
‖ **短波受信機** a shortwave receiver [radio] ‖ **短波放送** shortwave broadcasting ‖ **極超短波** an ultrahigh frequency 《略 UHF》 ‖ **超短波** a very high frequency 《略 VHF》.

1**たんぱく 蛋白** protein /próʊtiːn/ (たんぱく質) ▶卵は理想的なたんぱく源だ Eggs are an ideal *source of protein.* ‖ ピーナツや卵はたんぱく質が豊富だ Peanuts and eggs are rich in *protein.* ‖ **動物** [**植物**] **性たんぱく質** animal [vegetable] protein.

2**たんぱく 淡泊な** plain (あっさりした) ▶私は淡泊な食べ物のほうが好きだ I prefer *plain* [*lightly seasoned*] food.

1**たんぱつ 単発** ▶単発の事件 an *isolated* incident ‖ そのドラマは単発で終わった It was a *one-off* drama.
‖ **単発機** a single-engine plane ‖ **単発企画** a one-off project.

2**たんぱつ 短髪** short hair **一形 短髪の** short-haired.

だんぱつしき 断髪式 the ceremony during which the top-knot of a retiring *rikishi* (sumo wrestler) is cut off (➤ 説明的な訳).

タンバリン a tambourine /tæ̀mbəríːn/ ▶タンバリンをたたく play [beat] the *tambourine.*

たんパン 短パン shorts.

だんぱん 談判 negotiations **一動** (…と) **談判する** negotiate 《with》 ▶昇給について社長と膝詰め談判した We *negotiated* [*had a talk*] *in person with* our president for a pay raise.

ダンピング dumping.

ダンプカー a dump(er) truck, a dumper, 《英また》a tip truck, a tipper lorry

> **危ないカタカナ語 ✹ ダンプカー**
> **1** car は乗用車を指すので「ダンプカー」は英語では dump car とはいわず, dump truck とか dumper (truck) という. 《英》ではまた tip truck とか tipper lorry ともいう.

2 dump car という英語も存在するが，これは「(石炭などを運搬する) 傾斜台付き貨車」のことである．

タンブラー a **tumbler**.

[1]**たんぶん 短文** a **short sentence**(短い一文)；a **short passage**(短い文章の一節).

[2]**たんぶん 単文**《文法》a **simple sentence**.

ダンベル a **dumbbell**.

たんぺん 短編 a **short story** ▶アーネスト・ヘミングウェーの短編集 the *collected short stories* of Ernest Hemingway ‖**短編映画** a short film ‖**短編作家** a short-story writer.

だんぺん 断片 a **fragment** ▶断片的な知識 *fragmentary* knowledge ‖断片的に小さい頃のことを思い出した I recalled my childhood *in fragments*. ‖話が断片的で事件の全貌がよくわからないんだ Stories came *in dribs and drabs*, and the full truth about the incident remained unclear. (➤ in dribs and drabs は「僅かずつ」の意のインフォーマルな言い方).

だんぺんか 断片化《コンピュータ》**fragmentation**.

たんぼ 田んぼ a (**rice**) **paddy**, a **paddy field** ‖**田んぼ道** a path between (rice) paddies.

たんぽ 担保 (a) **security**, (a) **collateral** /kəlǽt̬ərəl/；(a) **mortgage** /mɔ́ːʳɡɪdʒ/ (抵当としての不動産) ▶彼は家を担保にして借金した He *mortgaged* his house for money. ／ He *used* his house *as security* to borrow money. ‖この家は１千万円の担保に入っている This house *has a mortgage of* [*is mortgaged for*] ten million yen.

たんぼう 探訪 an **investigative visit** ▶京都へ歴史探訪に行く go to Kyoto to *find out about* [*explore*] *its history* ‖《テレビで》次にお送りするのはアメリカ人学生による渋谷探訪レポートです Coming up is an American student's *report* on his [her] visit to Shibuya.

だんぼう 暖房 **heating** ▶この部屋は暖房が効いていない [強すぎる] This room *is poorly heated* [*is overheated*]. ‖この部屋には暖房が無い This room *has no heat*(*ing*). ‖暖房中につき窓は閉めたままにしてください Please keep the windows closed as *the heating is on*. ‖この建物は集中暖房になっている This building has *central heating* [is centrally heated]. ‖**暖房装置** heating(設備)；a heater (器具).

だんボール 段ボール **cardboard** (ボール紙)；**corrugated** /kɔ́ːrəɡeɪt̬ɪd/ **paper** (波形の紙) ▶段ボール箱 a *cardboard* box.

たんぽぽ《植物》a **dandelion** /dǽndəlaɪən/ 《参考》欧米では芝生を荒らす雑草とされている.

たんまつ 端末 a **terminal**(コンピュータの) ‖**端末走査装置** a terminal scanner.

だんまつま 断末魔 ▶断末魔の叫び a scream *on the verge of death*.

たんまり ▶おばあちゃんから小遣いをたんまりもらった I got *tons of* pocket money from my grandmother.

だんまり 黙り **silence** ▶ここはだんまり戦術で行くのがいちばんよ *Keeping mum* [*quiet*] is the best strategy here. ‖彼女はその店での出来事についてはだんまりを決め込んだ She *clammed up* about the incident in the shop. (➤ clam up は「口を閉ざす」).

たんめい 短命の **short-lived** ▶カゲロウは短命だ Mayflies *are short-lived*. ／ Mayflies *have short lives*. ▶昔の人は大概短命だった Most people in the old days *had a short life* [*died young*]. ‖その内閣は短命に終わった The cabinet *did not last long* [did not *last for a long time*]. ／ The cabinet *was short-lived*.

たんめん 湯麺 ***tanmen***；Chinese noodles with stir-fried vegetables (➤ 説明的な訳).

だんめん 断面 a **cross section** ▶この映画はアメリカの現代社会の一断面を見せてくれる This movie shows *a cross section* of modern society in America. ‖それは歴史 [人生] の一断面だった It was *a slice of* history [life]. ‖**断面図** a cross section.

だんめんせき 断面積 a **cross-sectional area**.

たんもの 反物 a roll [bolt] of cloth for one kimono (➤ 説明的な訳).

だんやく 弾薬 **ammunition** /æmjəníʃən/ ‖**弾薬庫** a powder magazine, an ammunition dump.

だんゆう 男優 an **actor**, a **male actor**.

たんよんでんち 単４電池 a **size AAA battery**.

たんらく 短絡 a **short circuit**(電気のショート) ▶きみの考え方は短絡的すぎるよ You'*re jumping to conclusions*. ‖交渉決裂即戦争というのはあまりにも短絡的な議論だ The argument that the collapse of negotiations means immediately going to war is overly *simplistic*.

だんらく 段落 a **paragraph** ▶この文章は４つの段落から成る This composition is made up of four *paragraphs*.

だんらん 団欒 ▶地震が夕食後の団らんを襲った The earthquake struck just as families were *enjoying conversation* after dinner. ▶かわいそうにあの少女は一家団らんの楽しみを知らない That poor little girl has never experienced *a happy home*.

だんりゅう 暖流 a **warm current** ▶太平洋沖に暖流が流れている *A warm current* flows along the Pacific coast of Japan.

だんりょく 弾力 **elasticity** /ìːlæstísət̬i/ ▶ゴムには弾力がある Rubber has *elasticity*. ／Rubber is elastic. ‖これは弾力感のあるミートボールですね It is a *springy* meatball. ‖竹は弾力性に富み，たやすく曲がる Bamboo is *very flexible* and bends easily. ▶《比喩的》弾力に富んだ (＝柔軟な) 考え *flexible* thinking ‖何もそうしゃくし定規にやらないでもっと弾力的に考えたらどうですか Why don't you *be* more *flexible* and not try to do everything by the book？

だんれつ 断裂 a **rupture**, a **fracture**.

たんれん 鍛錬・鍛練 **discipline** (修養)；**training** (訓練) 一動 **鍛錬する** **discipline** ＋目, **train** ＋目 ▶身体の鍛錬 physical *training* ‖若いうちに心身を鍛錬しなさい *Train* your mind and body while young. ‖彼は精神を鍛錬するために座禅を組んだ He sat in Zen meditation to *discipline* his mind.

だんろ 暖炉 a **fireplace**.

だんわ 談話 (a) **talk** ▶この問題に関する外務大臣の談話が発表された *An informal talk* by the Foreign Minister on the matter was published. ‖**談話室** a lounge.

ち・チ

1 **ち 血** **1【血液】blood** /blʌd/ ▶彼のワイシャツには血がついていた There was some *blood* [There were some *blood stains*] on his shirt. (➤ blood stain は「血痕」) ／His shirt was stained with *blood*. (●「血のついたワイシャツ」は a blood-stained shirt) ‖傷口から血がほとばしり出た *Blood* gushed from the wound. ‖きみ, 手から血が出ているよ Look ! Your hand *is bleeding*. (●「手が出血している」と表現する) ‖ひげそり中に頰を切って血が出た My cheek *started bleeding* when I cut it while shaving. ‖傷口に包帯をしたが, 血(＝出血)は止まらなかった Though I bandaged the cut, the *bleeding* didn't stop. ‖被害者の顔は血だらけだった The victim's face was *covered with blood*.

2【血縁】blood ▶血は争えないものだ *Blood will tell*. (➤ 英語のことわざ) ‖彼らは血を分けた兄弟だ They are *blood brothers*. ‖松平さんは徳川家と血のつながりがある(＝親類だ) Mr. Matsudaira *is related to* the Tokugawa family. ‖彼女は小泉八雲の血を引いている(＝子孫だ) She *is descended from* Koizumi Yakumo.

［ことわざ］血は水よりも濃い Blood is thicker than water. →血筋.

3【慣用表現】▶血も涙もない独裁者 a *cold-blooded* [*merciless*／*ruthless*] dictator ‖血沸き肉躍るような冒険小説 a *stirring* [*thrilling*／*action-packed*] adventure story ‖彼は頭に血が上ると何をしでかすかわからない There is no telling what he'll do when he *loses his temper*. ‖あいつは血の巡りが悪い He is *slow-witted* [*dim-witted*]. ‖横田さんは司法試験に受かるために血のにじむような努力をした Mr. Yokota *struggled hard* [*sweated blood*] to pass the bar examination. ‖この試作品はスタッフ20人の３年に及ぶ血と汗の結晶だ This trial product is *the fruit of* the 20 staff members' *labor and efforts* over three years. ‖血の通った福祉政策 a *humane* welfare policy ‖もう少し血の通った行政をしてもらいたい I want the government to act more *humanely*. ‖彼は祭りが近づくと(自然と)血が騒ぐ His *blood begins to stir* when the festival approaches.

☛ 血の気 (→見出語)

2 **ち 地** **the ground**(地面) ▶私は去年初めてアフリカの地を踏んだ Last year, I *set foot* in Africa for the first time (in my life). ‖彼らはカナダを永住の地に決めた They made Canada their *permanent home*. ‖メキシコは私たち夫婦にとって思い出の地です Mexico *holds many memories* for us two. ／Mexico *has a special meaning* for my wife and I. (➤ 決まった言い方) ‖きみとなら地の果てまでも行くよ If you're with me, I'll go *to the ends* [*far corners*] *of the earth*.

▶《慣用表現》彼の考え方は地に足が着いていない His way of thinking *is impractical*. ／His ideas *are too fanciful*. ‖彼の人気も地に落ちた He *has entirely lost* his popularity. ／His popularity *has hit rock bottom*. (➤ rock bottom は「どん底」) ‖最近は子供に対する父親の権威も地に落ちた These days fathers *have no authority* over their children.

チアガール →チアリーダー.

チアリーダー **a cheerleader** 《参考》女子が多いが, 男子の場合もある. 日本では「チアガール」ともいうが, 和製語.

ちあん 治安 **law and order**(法と秩序) ; **security**(安全) ; **peace**(平和) ▶(警官・保安官など)治安の守り手 a *peace* officer [an officer of the *peace*] ‖社会の治安を乱す disturb the *peace* ‖警察は社会の治安を維持するのが仕事である The police are tasked with maintaining (*law and*) *order* in society. ‖東京はニューヨークに比べて治安がよい In comparison with New York, Tokyo *is safer to live* (*in*). ／*The crime rate* in Tokyo *is lower* than that in New York. (➤ 前者は「住んで安全だ」, 後者は「犯罪の発生率が低い」の意) ‖この辺りは特に夜間の治安が悪いから, 外出は控えたほうがいい This area *is* particularly *dangerous* at night, so you'd better refrain from going out (at night).

ちい 地位 **(a) position** ; **a post**(職) ; **a rank**(階級, 身分) ; **(a) status** /stéiṭəs/(社会的な) ▶地位を失う lose one's *position* ‖地位の高い人 a person of high *position* [*rank*] ‖最も高い地位にある高官 *the most senior* official ‖おじは会社で責任ある地位に就いている My uncle holds a responsible *position* [*place*] in his company. ‖次長は課長より地位が上だ An assistant general manager *ranks higher* [*has a higher rank*] than a section chief. ‖女性の社会的地位は少しずつ向上している The *social status* of women is improving little by little. ‖キャデラックは時に地位の象徴になる A Cadillac can be *a status symbol*.

ちいき 地域 an **area** /éəriə/ ; a **district**(行政上の区画) ; a **region**(気候などによって区別された) ▶人の住んでいない地域 an uninhabited *area* ‖地域のリーダー a *regional* leader ‖広い地域にわたって光化学スモッグが発生している A photochemical smog layer has formed over a wide *area*. ‖前市長は地域の発展に尽くした The former mayor devoted himself to the development of the *district*. ‖日本は面積が小さい割に気候の地域差が大きい Considering its small area, Japan has *large regional differences* in climate.

‖地域研究 area studies ‖地域社会 a local community ‖地域住民 a local resident.

ちいく 知育 **intellectual training.**

チーク 《植物》a **teak** /tiːk/(木) ; **teak**(木材) ▶チーク材の机 a *teak* desk.

チークダンス **cheek-to-cheek dancing** ▶チークダンスをする *dance cheek to cheek*.

ちいさい 小さい

訳語メニュー

大きさや程度が →small, little **1**, **4**
背が低い →short **1**
音が →low **2**
気が →timid, shy **3**
幼い →young **5**

1【大きさが】small, little（➤後者には「小さくてかわいい」のニュアンスがある）; **short**（背が低い）▶小さい箱 a *small* box ‖ 小さな犬 a *little* [*small*] dog ‖ 小さい男 a *small* [*short*] man（➤ small は比喩的に「狭量な」の意にもなる）‖ 彼はバスケットボールの選手としては小さい He is relatively *short* for a basketball player. ‖ 姉は小さくて細身です My (older) sister *is petite*.（➤ petite /pətíːt/ はフランス語から）‖ 去年買ったブラウスがもう小さくなってしまった I bought this blouse only last year and it's already *too small for* me. ／I have outgrown this blouse which I bought last year.（➤ outgrow は「…に合わないほど大きく成長する」）‖《手で高さを示しながら》こんなに小さかった頃のきみを覚えてるよ I can remember (you) when you were just *this high*.

▶《比喩的》ワンマン社長も家に帰ると妻と 4 人の娘の間で小さくなっている The autocratic president *cowers* [*shrinks*] when he is with his wife and four daughters at home.（➤ cower も shrink も「(恐怖などのために)縮み上がる」の意）.

2【音量が】low ▶彼女は小さな声で私に呼びかけた She called to me in *a low voice* [in *a whisper*].（➤ whisper は「ささやき」）‖ ラジオの音を小さくしてください *Turn down* the radio, please.

3【気・人物が】timid（臆病な）; **shy**（内気な）▶彼は気が小さくて人前で話せない He is too *timid* [*shy*] to speak in public. ‖ 私の同僚は人間が小さい(＝心が狭い) My colleague *is small-minded* [*petty*].

4【程度・規模が】small, trivial ▶父は小さい(＝ささいな)ことにこだわるたちだ My father tends to worry about *small* [*trivial*] matters. ‖ 台風の被害は小さかった The damage from the typhoon was *small* [*minimal*].（➤ minimal は「最小限の」）.

5【幼い】young ▶私は彼を小さい頃から知っている I have known him since he was *very young* [since he was *a child*]. ‖ 私は小さい子の世話をするのが好きだ I enjoy taking care of *small children*.

ちいさめ 小さめ ▶もう少し小さめのを見せてくれませんか Can you show me a slightly *smaller one*?

チーズ cheese ▶1 切れのチーズ a slice [piece] of *cheese* ／a wedge of *cheese*（➤三角形に切ったもの）.

▶《写真を撮るとき》はい, チーズ *Say cheese!*

‖**チーズケーキ** (a) cheesecake ‖ **チーズバーガー** a cheeseburger ‖ **チーズフォンデュ** cheese fondue（フランス語から）‖ **粉チーズ** powdered cheese, grated cheese(すりおろしたチーズ).

> 「チーズ」のいろいろ　エダムチーズ Edam cheese ／エメンタールチーズ Emmenthaler cheese ／カッテージチーズ cottage cheese ／カマンベールチーズ Camembert cheese ／クリームチーズ cream cheese ／ゴーダチーズ Gouda cheese ／ゴルゴンゾーラチーズ Gorgonzola cheese ／スティルトンチーズ Stilton cheese《商標》／スモークチーズ smoked cheese ／チェダーチーズ Cheddar cheese ／ナチュラルチーズ natural cheese ／パルメザンチーズ Parmesan cheese ／ファーマーチーズ farmer ('s) cheese ／ブルーチーズ blue cheese ／プロセスチーズ processed cheese ／モッツァレラチーズ mozzarella cheese ／ロックフォールチーズ Roquefort cheese《商標》

チータ《動物》a **cheetah** /tʃíːtə/.

チーフ the chief（長）▶うちの課のチーフ *the chief* of our section ‖ 彼女は全日空のチーフパーサーだ She is *a chief purser* with ANA.

チーム a **team** ▶チームを作る form *a team* ‖ 彼はそのサッカーチームのメンバーだ He is a member of the *soccer team*. ／He is on [《英》in] the *soccer team*. ‖ チームのメンバーは10時に競技場に集まることになっている *The team* [*The members of the team*] are to meet at the stadium at ten.（● The team is ... としてもよい）‖ 個人技よりもチームプレーを心がけるべきだ You should pay more attention to *playing for the* (*whole*) *team* than (showing off) your own skill. ‖ チームワークが勝利への鍵だ Good *teamwork* [*Working well together*] is the key to victory.

‖**チームティーチング** pair teaching, team teaching（➤日本人教師 1 名と母語話者 1 名による日本の外国語教授法には前者が適当）.

ちいるい 地衣類《植物学》**lichen** /láikən/.

ちえ 知恵 wisdom(賢明さ); an **idea**（思いつき）; **intelligence**(知性) ▶知恵のある人 a *wise* person ‖ 何かいい知恵はない? Do you have any *good ideas*? ‖ 私たちは最良の方法を見つけようと知恵を絞った We *racked our brains* to find the best way. ‖ あなたのお知恵をちょっと拝借したいのですが Would you give me some *advice*? ／Would you (kindly) share some of your *wisdom*? ‖ 我々は知恵を結集して地球温暖化に対処しなければならない We must draw on our combined *intelligence* to tackle global warming. ‖ うちのせがれに余計な知恵をつけないでくれよ Don't put *ideas* into my son's head.

ことわざ **三人寄れば文殊の知恵** Three people together (could) have the wisdom of *Monju*.（➤日本語からの直訳）／ Two heads are better than one.（➤英語のことわざ）.

‖**知恵者** a wise person ‖ **知恵熱** teething fever ‖ **知恵の輪** puzzle rings.

チェアマン a **chairman** ▶日本サッカー協会のチェアマン *the chairman* of the Japan Soccer Federation.

チェーン a **chain** ▶ドアのチェーン a door *chain* ‖ 登校の途中で自転車のチェーンが外れた My bicycle *chain* came [slipped] off on my way to school.（➤「外れたチェーンを掛ける」なら put the bicycle chain back on）.

▶彼はホテルのチェーンを持っている He owns *a chain of hotels* [*a hotel chain*].

‖**チェーンストア** a chain store,《英また》a multiple shop ‖ **チェーンソー** a chain saw ‖ **タイヤチェーン** a tire chain.

チェコ the Czech /tʃek/ **Republic** 一形 **チェコの Czech**

‖**チェコ語** Czech ‖ **チェコ人** a Czech.

チェス chess ▶チェスをする play *chess* ‖ **チェスの駒** a *chess piece* ／a *chessman* ‖ **チェス盤** a *chessboard*.

ちぇっ ▶チェッ, 定期券忘れちゃったよ *Darn it!* I forgot my commuter card. ‖ チェッ!(車が)ガス欠になりそうだ *Shoot!* I'm almost out of gas.

チェック 1【照合, 点検】a **check** ▶彼女は名簿の名前を順にチェックした She *checked* [《英また》*ticked*] *off* the names on the list.（● この訳例は「…の名前に順にチェックマークをつけた」という日本語にも対応する）‖ 答えを正解と比べてチェックしなさい *Check* your answers with the correct ones. ‖ 答案用紙は提出する前に必ずもう一度チェックしなさい Be sure to *check* your answer sheet again before you hand it in. ‖ 門の所で数人の教員が受験生かどうかをチェックしていた At the gate several teachers *were checking* to make sure the students were registered for the examination.

‖《コンピュータ》**チェックボックス** a checkbox.
2【**格子柄**】a **check** ▶**チェック**のスカート a *checked* [*checkered*] skirt／a skirt *with check patterns* ‖ 赤と白の**チェック**のスカート a skirt in red and white *checks* ‖ タータン**チェック**のマフラー a *plaid* /plæd/ [*tartan*] scarf.
3【**チェスで**】▶**チェック**(＝王手)！*Check*！

> **危ないカタカナ語 チェック**
> **1**「照合する, 点検する」の意味のチェックは check でよい. 照合の印であるチェックマーク(✓)も check (➤《英》は tick)という. この印は日本では時に「バツ, 不可」の意で用いるが, 英米ではほとんどの場合「OK」を表す.
> **2**「注意すべき点」の意味の「チェックポイント」は checkpoints または points to check とする. 前者には道路の「検問所」の意味もある.

チェックアウト (a) **checkout** 一動 **チェックアウトする check out**《of》▶《ホテルで》10時までに**チェックアウト**してください Please *check out* by 10 o'clock. ／《掲示》*Checkout* is 10 o'clock. ‖ **チェックアウト**は何時までですか When do I have to *be out of the room* by？／What time is *checkout*？／When is *checkout*？‖ 私は9時にホリデーインを**チェックアウトした** I *checked out of* the Holiday Inn at 9 o'clock. ‖ **チェックアウト**しますので, 会計をお願いします May I have my bill, please？ I'm *checking out*.
チェックイン (a) **check-in** 一動 **チェックインする check in**《at》, **check**《into》▶《ホテルで》**チェックイン**をお願いします I'd like to *check in*(, please). ‖ 前日は5時にヒルトンホテルに**チェックインした** We *checked in at* [*checked into*] the Hilton Hotel at five on the previous day. ‖ もう(＝早めに)**チェックイン**していいですか Is there any chance of *checking in* now？
チェックメート 《チェス》a **checkmate**.
チェルノブイリ Chernobyl /tʃəʳnóʊbəl/.
チェレスタ 《音楽》a **celesta** /səléstə/.
チェロ a **cello** /tʃéloʊ/ ▶**チェロ**を弾く play the *cello*.
‖**チェロ奏者** a cellist.
ちえん 遅延 delay 一動 **遅延する be delayed** ▶停電のため電車が1時間**遅延した** The train *was delayed* for an hour because of a power failure.
チェンジ a **change** ▶《テニスなどで》コートを**チェンジする** *change* courts ‖ 巨人は3者凡退で**チェンジ**, いよいよ9回の裏, 阪神の攻撃です Three Giants hitters *were retired* in order, and now the Tigers come to bat in the bottom of the ninth inning. 《**参考**》野球の「チェンジ」は日本独特の言い方. 英語では The side is retired. (片方の攻撃が終わった) のように言う.
‖(野球の)**チェンジアップ** a change up ‖ (自動車の)**チェンジレバー**《米》a gearshift (lever),《米また》a stickshift,《英》a gear lever (➤ change lever は古い英語).
チェンバロ a **harpsichord** /hɑ́ːʳpsɪkɔːʳd/ (➤ イタリア語起源の cembalo は一般的ではない)
‖**チェンバロ奏者** a harpsichordist.
¹**ちか 地下の underground** ▶**地下**駐車場 an *underground* parking lot ‖ 石油を求めて**地下**1000メートルまで掘る dig 1,000 meters *underground* for oil ‖ レストランは**地下2階**です The restaurant is on *the second basement level*. ‖ 本社ビルは地上20階, **地下**3階建てだ The head office building has 20 stories above ground and 3 *underground* [*beneath ground level*].
‖**地下街** an underground shopping mall ‖ **地下核実験** an underground nuclear test ‖ **地下資源** underground resources ‖ **地下室** a basement (地階); a cellar(食糧などを入れておくための地下貯蔵室) ‖ **地下水** ground [subterranean] water ‖ **地下組織** an underground organization(➤「地下に潜る」は go underground) ‖ **地下駐車場** an underground parking garage ‖ **地下道**《米》an underpass,《英》a subway(➤《米》では subway は「地下鉄」を意味する).
☛ **地下鉄** (→見出語)
²**ちか 地価 land prices, the price of land** ▶近頃の**地価**の下落はひどい The recent fall [decline] in *land prices* has been terrible.
¹**ちかい 地階** an **underground floor** ▶日本のデパートの多くは, **地階**で食料品を売っている Most Japanese department stores sell food on their *underground floor*(*s*).
²**ちかい 誓い** a **vow** /vaʊ/ (厳粛な約束); a **pledge**(誓約); an **oath**(宣誓); a **resolution** (決意) ▶**誓い**を守る[破る] keep [break] one's *vow* ‖ 禁煙の**誓い**を立てる *make a vow* not to smoke／*vow* not to smoke (➤ 後者の vow は動詞) ‖ **新年の誓い**を立てる make *a New Year's resolution* ‖ **忠誠の誓い** a *pledge of allegiance* ‖ 2人は緊張した面持ちで**誓い**のことばを述べた The couple appeared nervous as they *exchanged* (*their*) *vows*.
³**ちかい 近い** **1**【**距離が**】**near, close** /kloʊs/《to》(➤ 後者のほうがより接近している感じ)

> 【文型】
> **場所(A)に近い**
> **near** A
> **close to** A

▶その大学はお茶の水駅に [から] **近い** The college *is near* Ochanomizu Station. (● (×) near to とか (×) near from とはしない) ‖ ここから上野公園はもう**近い** Ueno Park *is near* here. ／We *are* quite *close to* Ueno Park.
▶火事は**近い**ぞ The fire *isn't far* from here. ‖ 虎の門病院へはこの道のほうが**近い**ですよ This is *a shorter way* to Toranomon Hospital. ‖ **近い**から歩いて行こう Let's walk. It's only *a short distance*. (● It's not far. としてもよいが, (×) It's near. とはしない).
▶《慣用表現》目が**近い**から新聞を読むと疲れる I get tired (from) reading newspapers since I'm *near-sighted*. ‖ 年を取るとトイレが**近く**なる As people grow older, they have to *go to the bathroom more often*.
2【**時間が**】**near, close**《to》▶卒業式も**近い** The commencement exercises *are drawing near* [*are around the corner*／*are near at hand*]. (➤ near at hand は堅い, また古風な言い方)／The commencement exercises will be held *soon*. ‖ 新しい体育館の完成は**近い** The new gym is *near* completion. ‖ 博覧会も終わりに**近い** The exhibition *is coming to an end*.
▶**近い**うちに一杯やろう Let's go out for a drink *one of these days* [*sometime soon*]. ‖ **近い将来**インドの人口は中国の人口を追い抜くだろう India's population will surpass that of China *in the near future*. ‖ きのう家に帰ったのは夜の11時**近かった** It was *nearly* [*almost*／*close to*] eleven when I got home last night. (● あとの2つのほうがより11時に近い).

3【数量・程度が】nearly, almost（ほぼ；後者はより近い感じ）▶日本では8200万人近い人が運転免許を持っている *Nearly* [*Almost*] eighty-two million people have driver's licenses in Japan. ‖ 姉はもう30に近い My sister *is* already *close to* thirty.／My sister *is almost* thirty.／My sister *is going on* [*is pushing*] thirty. ‖ きみの答えは正解に近い Your answer is *nearly* correct. ‖ この書類の山からその1枚を見つけるなんて不可能に近い It is *almost* [*next to*] impossible to find the sheet of paper in this pile.

4【関係が】close /kloʊs/ ▶オーストラリアとニュージーランドは政治的・文化的に近い関係にある Australia and New Zealand *are close* culturally as well as politically. ‖ チンパンジーは人間に最も近い動物だ Chimpanzees are the animals most *closely related to* human beings.

ちがい 違い

(a) **difference** 《between》 ▶両者の間には大した違いはない There is little *difference* [I don't see much *difference*] *between* the two. ‖ 年齢の違いなど気にするな Don't worry about *age differences*. ‖ この2種類の米の味の違いがわかりますか Can you *taste the difference* [Can you *distinguish*] *between* these two kinds of rice?（➤ この distinguish は「識別する」の意の自動詞）.

【文型】
A と B との違い
(a) difference between A and B

▶日本チームにとってこの試合に勝つと引き分けるとでは大きな違いとなる For the Japanese team, there is *a* big *difference between* winning this game *and* ending in a draw.

▶我々はお互いの違いを正しく認識しないといけない We have to appreciate each other's *differences*.（➤ 違いの多さ, 少なさをいうときは Ⓤ 扱いがふつうで, 違いの性格や種類をいうときは Ⓒ 扱い）.

▶ウイスキーは何を飲んでも違いがわからない I *don't know what's what*, when it comes to whisky.／I *can't tell* one whisky *from* another.（➤ tell A from B で「A と B を識別する, 見分ける」）‖ バスで行っても電車で行っても大した違い（＝大差）はない It *doesn't make a big difference* whether you go by bus or by train. ‖ Obama と Osama は1字違いだ Obama is *only one letter different from* Osama. ‖ 2分違いで電車に乗り遅れた I missed the train *by* two minutes.（ この by は実数などの「そば」の意から違いや差の程度を表す）‖ 姉と私は4つ違いです（＝離れている）My sister and I *are* four years *apart*.

☞ 大違い（→見出語）

ちがいだな 違い棚

a ***chigaidana***; staggered shelves in a tokonoma (alcove)（➤ 説明的な訳）.

ちがいない 違いない

must（➤ 未来についての推量には用いない）; **have (got) to**（➤ must よりややインフォーマルな言い方で, 相手を非難するニュアンスがあることが多い）

【文型】
…であるに違いない
must be
…であったに違いない
must have been

▶彼の言っていることは本当に違いない What he says *must* [*has* (*got*) *to*] *be* true. ‖ 彼女はここに住んでいたに違いない She *must have lived* here.／*I'm sure* she *lived* here. ‖ 僕はインフルエンザにかかったんだ─そうに違いない I've caught the flu. *I'm sure that is what it is*.

▶彼はあなたを知っているに違いない *I'm sure* he knows you. ‖ 彼らはきのう家に居なかったに違いない They *cannot have been* at home yesterday.（ 否定形の場合は must not でなく cannot を用いる）‖ あの子はきっと将来大物になるに違いない He *is sure to* become [*I bet* he'll become] a very important person in the future.（➤ 後者のほうがよりくだけた言い方）.

ちがいほうけん 治外法権

extraterritoriality /èkstrəterɪtɔːriǽləṭi/ ▶外国の外交官には治外法権が与えられている Foreign diplomats are granted *extraterritoriality* [extraterritorial rights].

ちかう 誓う

vow /vaʊ/ ＋㊐（厳粛に）; **swear** ＋㊐（神仏などに懸けて）; **promise** ＋㊐, **pledge** ＋㊐（固く約束して；後者は儀式ばった約束のニュアンスが強い）▶彼は二度と盗みをしないと誓った He *vowed* never to steal again. ‖ 彼は禁酒を誓った He *has sworn to* give up drinking.／He *has sworn off* drinking.（➤ sworn は swear の過去分詞形）‖ 彼らは結婚を誓い合った They *promised each other* to get married. ‖ 名誉に懸けて誓うが私は彼を裏切ってはいない I *pledge* [*give*] *my word of honor* that I am not the one who betrayed him. ‖ 私はそのことは秘密にしようと心に誓った I *am determined* to keep the matter secret.（➤ be determined は「決心している」）.

▶あの知事はよく「誓ってうそは申しません」と言う That governor often says, "*I swear* I'm not lying."

ちがう 違う

1【異なる】differ /dífəʳ/, **be different** 《from》; **vary** /véəri/（➤ differ は2者以上のものが本質的に異なることをいうのに対して, vary は同種類のものが一様でないことをいう）一形 違った **different**

▶アメリカでは州によって法律が違う Laws *differ* from state to state in the U.S. ‖ 立てた小指の意味は文化によって違う. インドでは「トイレに行くこと」を指す The meaning of an extended little finger *differs* from culture to culture. In India it signifies going to the bathroom. ‖ 雑煮の作り方は地方によって違う The way of making zoni *differs* according to region.

【文型】
A は B と違う
A is different from B.
A は B とは C が違う
A differs from B in C.

【解説】(1) **be different** は主に「全面的に異なる」ときに, **differ** は「ある部分, ある点で違う」または「どう違うか」をいうときに用いる.
(2) 第1の文型に in C をつけるか, A and B are different [differ] in C. の形で, 第2の文型と同じ文になる. in は on や over になることもある.

▶この家はモデルハウスとずいぶん違うじゃないですか This house is quite *different from* the model house. ‖ その小説は私が予想していたものとは大きく違っていた The novel *was very different from* what I expected [than I expected].（➤ 後者の言い方はややインフォーマル）‖ きょうの天気はきのうとあまり違わない The weather today *is not much different from* (what it was) yesterday.

▶ぼくたち夫婦は食べ物の好みがだいぶ違う My wife and

I *differ* greatly *in* (our) food preferences. ‖ このクラスの製品は最高級モデルとどこが違うのですか *How* [*In what ways*] do products in this class *differ from* high-end models ? ‖ 映画における女性の好みは男性とは少し違う Women's tastes in movies *differ* somewhat *from* those of men.
▶録音と生演奏ではやっぱり違うね After all, *there's a* (*big*) *difference* between a recording and a live performance.
▶ドルの値段は日によって違う(＝変化する) The value of the dollar *changes* [*varies*] every day. ‖ 習慣は土地土地で違う Customs *vary* from place to place. ‖ それじゃ約束と違うじゃないか That's *not* what you promised before. ‖ 彼は言うこととすることが違っている He says *one thing and* does *another*.
▶違った文脈 a *different* context ‖ テレビのニュースキャスターは毎日違う服を着ている TV newscasters wear *different* clothes every day. ‖ その件では私はきみと違った意見をもっている I have a *different* view from yours on the matter. ‖ なぜかこの電卓では計算するたびに合計が違う I don't know why, but I get a *different* sum each time I do the same calculation with this calculator. ‖ ぼくと違って, 弟はハンサムだ *Unlike* me, my younger brother is handsome.
▶彼女の生活スタイルは私と全く違わない Her lifestyle is *no different* from mine.
2【間違っている】be wrong 一形 **違った wrong ; incorrect**(不正確な) ▶住所録に載っている私の住所は違っています My address in the directory *is wrong*. ‖ 私はテストは結構できたと思ったのに, 返ってきた答案を見たらほとんど違っていたのがわかった I was confident about the test results, but when I got them back, I found that most of my answers *were incorrect*. ‖ 何か違うんじゃないかな Something's *not quite right*. ‖ 違っていたら謝ります I apologize if I'*m mistaken*.
3【否定の返事】no ▶ 対話「もしもし, 木村さんのお宅ですか」「いいえ, 違います. 番号違いではありませんか?」"Hello, is this the Kimura residence ?" "*No, it isn't*. I'm afraid you've got the wrong number."

[1]**ちかく 知覚 perception** 一形 **知覚の sensory** ▶人間には知覚できない電波 radio waves that are *imperceptible* to humans ‖ 知覚過敏の歯 a (*hyper*) *sensitive* tooth ‖ 知覚異常 sensory abnormality ; paresthesia /pærəsθíːʒə/ ‖ 知覚刺激 sensory stimulation ‖ 知覚神経 sensory nerves ‖ 知覚力 perceptivity.

[2]**ちかく 近く** **1【距離が】near, close** /kloʊs/ 《to》(➤ 後者のほうがより接近している感じ) ▶ (名古屋の)熱田高校は有名な熱田神宮の近くに在る Atsuta High School *is* (*situated*) *near* the famous Atsuta Shrine. ‖ その少年は家の近くで誘拐されたらしい I hear the boy was kidnapped *near* his house. ‖ 近くから見るとあの女優はちっともきれいじゃない Seen *close up* [*from a short distance*], the actress is not at all beautiful. (➤ この close up は副詞句で /klóʊs ʌp/ と発音) ‖ この近くに文房具屋さんは在りませんか Is there a stationery store *near here* [*nearby*] ? ‖ 正雄なら近くの喫茶店に行ってます Masao is at a *nearby* coffee shop.
✉(転居通知) **近く(＝近所)へおいでの節はぜひお立ち寄りください** When you are in the *neighborhood*, please stop by [drop by／drop in].
2【時間が】soon(まもなく) ▶私たちは近くハンガリーへ出発します We are leaving for Hungary *soon* [*shortly*]. ‖ この辺に近く高速道路ができることになっている An expressway is to be built around here *before long* [*in the near future*].
3【数量・程度が】about ; nearly, almost (➤ about は「その数字前後」, nearly と almost は「その数に少し足りない程度」を表すが, almost のほうが不足している点を強調する) ▶その選手は今月3割3分近くの打率をあげた The player's batting average is *about* .330 this month. (➤ .330 は three thirty と読む) ‖ 1時間近く待ってるのに彼女はまだ来ない I've been waiting for *nearly* an hour, and she hasn't come yet. ‖ スイス人のうち65パーセント近くの人がドイツ語を話す *Nearly* 65 percent of Swiss people speak German. ‖ 地震があったのは真夜中近くだった It was *almost midnight* when the earthquake struck. (→近い) ‖ 学生たちは夜中の2時近くまで飲み会で騒いでいた The students partied (noisily) until *nearly* [*almost*] 2 o'clock in the morning.

[3]**ちかく 地殻 the crust of the earth.**

ちがく 地学 earth science.

ちかごろ 近頃 recently, lately (→最近) **; these days, nowadays**(➤ ともに現在時制で用いる) ▶近頃淳子に会っていない I haven't seen Junko *recently* [*lately*]. ‖ 近頃彼, どうしてるかしら I wonder how he is doing *these days*. ‖ 近頃の若い者は敬語が使えない *Today's* young people [The young people of *today*] can't use honorific Japanese. ‖ 台風18号は近頃にない大型の台風だった Typhoon No. 18 was the biggest typhoon we have had *in* (*recent*) *years*.

ちかしい 近しい close /kloʊs/ ▶近しい友人が陸上自衛隊にいる *A close friend* of mine is in the Ground Self-Defense Forces.

ちかちか ▶睡眠不足で目がちかちかする My eyes *are irritated* due to lack of sleep.

ちかぢか 近々 before long, soon ▶ブラウンさん一家は近々オーストラリアへ帰るそうです I'm told Mr. Brown and his family are going back to Australia *before long* [*soon*].

ちかづき 近付き ▶お近づきのしるしに一杯やりましょう Let's have a drink *to celebrate our* (*new*) *friendship*. ‖ お近づきになれてうれしく思います I'm honored [It's a pleasure] to *meet* you. 《参考》初対面の人への別れ際の挨拶としては I'm very happy to have met you. とか Nice meeting you. のように言う.

ちかづく 近付く **1【接近する】come** [**go**] **near ; approach**(＋目) (接近する) ▶男が私に近づいて来た A man *approached* me. ‖ 私たちの乗った船は港に近づいていった Our ship *was approaching* [*getting closer to*] the harbor. (● 「…に近づく」は (×) approach to ... としない) ‖ 天気予報によると台風が近づいているそうだ According to the weather forecast, a typhoon *is approaching*. ‖ お年寄りが近づいて来て, 鎌倉駅への道を聞いた An old man *came up to* me and asked me the way to Kamakura Station. (● come up to は話しかけるなど何か目的があってまっすぐこちらの居る所まで来る場合) ‖ 津波警報が出ている間は海岸に近づくな *Keep* [*Stay*] *away* from the beach while a tsunami warning is in effect.

2【時期が近づく】get［draw］near（➤ draw near はやや堅い，または文語的な言い方）；**approach**（接近する）▶バレンタインデーが近づいて来た Valentine's Day *is getting*［*drawing*］*near*.／Valentine's Day *is just around the corner*. ‖ 我々がどう対処すべきか決定する時期が近づいて来た The time *is approaching* when we will have to decide what to do. ‖ その鉄道は完成に近づいている The railroad *is near*［*is nearing*］completion.（➤ 動詞用法の near は堅い語）．

✉ **夏休みも終わりに近づいて来ました** Summer vacation *is drawing to a close*. ➤「終わり」の意味の名詞 close は /klouz/ と発音．

3【親しくなる】▶あいつはうそつきだ．近づかないほうがいい He is a liar. You had better *keep*［*stay*］*away from* him. ‖ 監督は近づきやすい［にくい］Our manager *is easy*［*hard*］*to approach*.／Our manager *is easy*［*hard*］*to talk to*.

ちかづける 近付ける ▶明かりをもっと近づけてくれ *Bring* the light *closer*［*nearer*］*to* me. ‖ 子供を火のそばに近づけないでください Don't *let* the children *go near* the fire. ‖ 彼女は人を近づけない（＝人と付き合わない）She *associates with nobody*.／She *doesn't associate with anyone*.／She *keeps everyone at a distance*.

ちかてつ 地下鉄《主に米》a **subway**,《英》an **underground（railway）**；《インフォーマル》a **tube**（特にロンドンの）▶梅田まで地下鉄で行った I went to Umeda by *subway*.／I took the *subway* to Umeda.《参考》subway は《英》では「地下道」(underpass)の意であったが，最近では《米》と同じ「地下鉄」の意味でこの語を用いる人もいる．

ちかば 近場の ▶近場のスキー場 a *nearby* ski resort.

ちかみち 近道 a **shortcut**；**the shortest way**（いちばんの）▶遅刻しそうだから近道をして学校へ行こう It looks like we're going to be late for［to］school, so let's *take a shortcut*. ‖ 目白通りがここへ来るいちばんの近道ですよ Mejiro Street is *the shortest way* to get here.

▶《比喩的》入試合格への近道はあるだろうか Is there any *shortcut* to success in entrance exams?

ちかよる 近寄る **go［come］near** ▶私に近寄らないで！ *Stay away from* me.／*Don't come near* me. ‖ 夜道をひとりで歩いていたら酔っ払いが近寄って来た When I was walking alone at night, a drunken man *came up to* me. ‖《掲示》危険！近寄るな！ Danger! *Keep Off*!

▶制作中のその画家には近寄り難い雰囲気がある The artist seems *unapproachable* while at work.

ちから 力

訳語メニュー
- 物理的な力 →power, force **1**
- 肉体の力 →strength, power **2**
- 能力 →ability **3**
- 勢い，元気 →energy **4**
- 助力 →help **5**
- 権力，勢力 →power, influence **6**

1【物理的な力】power, force（➤ 後者はしばしば複数形で用いる）▶水の力 the *power*［*force*］of water ‖ 自然の破壊的な力 the destructive *forces* of nature ‖ このエンジンは3000回転で最大の力が出る This engine generates［produces］a maximum *power* of 3,000 revolutions. ‖ 自動車はガソリンの力で（＝ガソリンで）動く Cars run *on gas*. ‖ 水素爆弾はたった1個で全東京を破壊する力を持つ A single hydrogen bomb *can* destroy the whole city of Tokyo.

2【体力，腕力】strength, power（➤ 前者は人に蓄えられている力を強調する語）▶彼には戦う力が残っていなかった He had no *strength*［*power*］left to fight. ‖ あの兄弟は弟のほうが力が強い The younger brother *is stronger* than the elder. ‖ 私は病気をしてから力が無くなった（＝弱くなった）I *have become weak* since my illness. ‖ 近頃では若者は力仕事を嫌う Young people tend to dislike *manual labor* nowadays. ‖ 被害者は交番の前まではって来て力尽きた The victim came crawling up to the police box, and *breathed his last* just in front of it.（➤ breathe one's last は「死ぬ」の意の婉曲(えんきょく)な言い方）．

3【能力，才能】ability ▶考える力を養う（＝つける）nurture one's *ability* to think［one's thinking *ability*］‖ 彼には事業を取りしきるだけの力はとても無い He has no *ability* to manage a business. ‖ 小池君は数学の力がある［足りない］Koike *is good*［*poor*］*at* math. ‖ 彼にはその仕事を成し遂げる力は無い He *is incapable* of accomplishing the task. ‖ この頃だいぶ英作文の力がついたね You'*ve improved* a lot［*made* a lot of *progress*］in English composition recently. ‖ 自分の力でやってごらん Try and do it *yourself*. ‖ 力の限りこの地域のために働きます I'll work for the (local) community *to the best of my ability*［*as hard as I can*］.

▶《慣用表現》わが社は新素材の開発に力を入れている Our company *lays emphasis on* the development of new materials.

4【勢い，元気】energy /énəʳdʒi/ ▶力のこもった演説 an *energetic*［*a powerful*］speech ‖ チームが5連敗し，監督は力を落としている The manager *is discouraged* because his team lost five consecutive games.

✉《悔やみ状で》**お父さまが亡くなられてどんなにかお力落としのことと存じます** It must *be* very *hard* to have lost your father.

5【助力，支持】help；assistance（手伝い）▶何のお力にもなれず残念です I regret that I can'*t be of any help*［*assistance*］. ‖ 力を貸してくれてありがとう Thanks for your *help*. ‖ この店を出す際に彼女は本当に力になってくれた She *was a* great *help* to me in opening this shop. ‖ 彼は金の力で市長になったようなものだ He basically *bought his way into* the mayor's office.（➤ buy one's way into は「金の力で…を手に入れる」）‖ 薬の力に頼らずにかぜを治したい I want to get rid of my cold *without depending on*［*resorting to*］medicine. ‖ 人の力を借りようなんて思うな Don't *depend on* others. ‖ 困ったときは皆が力を合わせなければならない We have to *pull*［*work*］*together* in times of difficulties.

6【権力，勢力，武力】power, might（➤ 後者は文語）；**force**（実際に行使される力，武力）；**influence**（影響力）▶彼は力のある（＝勢力のある）政治家だ He is a *powerful*［*an influential*］politician. ‖ 民主勢力が力をもってきた The democratic forces are gaining *power*. ‖ 大統領は反対派を力で抑えつけた The president used *force* to suppress the opposition. ‖ 超大国は国際紛争の解決を力に頼るべきではない Superpowers should not *resort to force* in an attempt to solve international disputes. ‖ 力は正義なり *Might* makes［is］right.（➤「勝てば官軍」

に当たる英語のことわざ).

ちからいっぱい 力一杯 with all one's strength [might] (➤ might は文語) ▶少年はドアを力いっぱい押した The boy pushed the door *with all his strength* [*might*]. ‖ 私は学期末試験では力いっぱい頑張った I *did my best* on the term exam.

ちからかんけい 力関係 a power relationship, a balance of power.

ちからくらべ 力比べ a test of strength.

ちからこぶ 力瘤 the flexor muscle /flèksəʳ mʌ́səl/ (屈筋); the biceps /báɪseps/ (二頭筋) ▶ボディービルで鍛えたその女性は力こぶを作ってみせた The female body-builder *flexed her muscles* [*biceps*].

ちからずく 力ずくで by force ▶兄は力ずくで私のパソコンを取り上げた My brother took my (personal) computer from me *by force*. ‖ 警察は力ずくで暴徒を追い散らした The police *used force* to disperse the mob. ‖ その男は力ずくで部屋から連れ出された The man was *forcibly* removed from the room.

ちからぞえ 力添え support (支援); assistance (お金など物による援助) ▶私が成功したのはあなたのお力添えのおかげです I owe my success to your *support* [*assistance*].

ちからだめし 力試し ▶力試しにTOEICテストを受けてみたら, かなり良い成績だった I took the TOEIC Test *just to test my ability*, and I got a pretty good score.

ちからづける 力付ける encourage /ɪnkə́ːrɪdʒ/ +㊐ (勇気づける); cheer [pep] up (元気づける) ▶彼はM教授のことばに力づけられた He *was encouraged* by Professor M's remarks. ‖ 彼女が元気が無かったので力づけるために夕食に誘った She looked depressed, so I took her out for dinner to *cheer* her *up*.

ちからづよい 力強い strong (大変な力を持っている); powerful (力がみなぎっている); dependable (頼もしい) ▶浩は力強い腕で私をひしと抱いてくれた Hiroshi held me tight in his *strong* arms. ‖ この曲は力強いリズムが特徴だ This piece features a *strong* rhythm. ‖ 先生の力強い励ましのことばに私は元気づけられた My teacher's *strong* encouragement cheered me up. ‖ 「ご成功をお祈りします」と言うと, 彼は力強くうなずいた He bowed his head *with heartfelt* [*strong*] *emotion* when I said, "I wish you success." (● 「ご成功をお祈りします」の対象が勉強[仕事]なら, I wish you success に続けて in your studies [career] と言えばよい).

ちからなく 力無く weakly, feebly (➤ 後者は哀れみや軽蔑のニュアンスを含む) ▶刑事に「おまえがやったんだな」と問い詰められると, 容疑者は力無く「はい, やりました」と言った When the detective confronted him saying, "You did it, didn't you?", the suspect *weakly* assented, "Yes, I did."

ちからまかせ 力任せ ▶男は力任せにその太い金属の棒を曲げた The man bent the thick metal bar *with brute strength* [*force*]. ‖ ただ力任せにバットを振り回してもだめだ Just swinging the bat *with all your might* [*strength*] is useless.

ちからもち 力持ち ▶力持ちの男性 a man *with great* (*physical*) *strength* / a *strong* man ‖ うちの亭主, 気は優しくて力持ちよ My husband is kind and *strong*.

ちからわざ 力業 a feat of strength

1【強い力で】▶彼は力業で開かなくなっていた戸を開けた He managed to open the stuck door using *brute force*.

2【強引な手段で】▶公式を知っていればすぐに解けたはずの数学の問題を, 彼は力業で解いた He took *a rough and ready approach* to solving the math problem that he could have easily solved if he had known the formula.

[1]ちかん 痴漢 a groper, a pervert /pə́ːʳvəːʳt/, a molester /məléstəʳ/

> **◀解説▶「痴漢」について**
> (1) 日本語の「痴漢」は夜道で女性を襲う男や, 電車の中で淫らなことをする男を指すことばだが, これにぴったりの訳語はない.
> (2) 性的欲求を満たすために女性の体に触ることをインフォーマルな英語で grope といい, その行為をする人を groper というが, 電車の中の痴漢はこの語が近い. 夜道に出没する痴漢を含めるならば, pervert (変質者) を用いるのがよい.
> (3) 女性や子供に性的ないたずらや嫌がらせをする変質者は molester という.

▶けさ, 電車の中で痴漢にお尻を触られたのよ This morning in the train some *pervert* [*groper*] put his hand on my rear. ‖ 警察は電車内で女性たちに痴漢を働いていた男を捕まえた The police caught a man who *was molesting* women in the train.

[2]ちかん 置換 replacement 一動 **置換する** replace +㊐ (➤「AをBで置換する」は replace A with B の文型をとる) ▶「高校」という単語を「高等学校」に置換する *replace* the word "高校" with the word "高等学校".

ちき 知己 a good friend, a friend who truly understands you; an acquaintance (知人) ▶彼女とは20年来の知己だ She has been my *good friend* for twenty years.

ちきゅう 地球
the earth; the globe (➤ 丸さを強調する) ▶宇宙から見ると地球は美しい青い星だ (When it is) seen from outer space, *the earth* is a beautiful blue planet. (● 英語の star は自ら光を発する太陽のような恒星を指す語で, 地球は star ではない. したがって, この場合の「美しい青い星」を beautiful blue star とするわけにはいかない) ‖ 人間は皆同じ地球人なのだから, 殺し合いはやめるべきだ Humans are all *children of* (*the*) *planet Earth*, so we should stop killing each other. (● 科学的記事などでは the Earth または単に Earth とすることも多い. また Earth の代わりに the planet とも表す) ‖ ネズミは地球上の至る所に生息している Rats inhabit all corners of *the earth* [*the planet*]. ‖ 多くの科学者が地球外の生物が存在する可能性があると考えている Many scientists have speculated on the possibility of *extraterrestrial* life. ‖ 地球温暖化は深刻な問題だ *Global warming* is a serious problem. ‖ 地球に優しいエネルギー *earth-friendly* [*eco-friendly*] energy.

‖地球儀 a globe ‖地球物理学 geophysics /dʒìːəfízɪks/.

ディベートルーム 「地球温暖化は人類の発展上やむをえない」

ちぎょ 稚魚 fry (➤ 集合名詞) ▶アユの稚魚 ayu *fry* (➤ 文脈によっては「アユのフライ」の意にもなる).

ちきょう 地峡 ▶パナマ地峡 the *Isthmus* of Panama (➤ isthmus の発音は /ísməs/).

ちぎり 契り a promise (約束); a pledge, a vow (誓い) 一動 **契る** promise (+㊐), pledge +㊐, vow +㊐ ▶契りを交わす exchange *vows*.

ち

ちぎる 千切る tear /teəʳ/ +⾃ ▶ノートを1枚ちぎる *tear* a page out of a notebook ‖ もちを小さくちぎる *break* a rice cake into pieces ‖ 彼はパンを細かくちぎってハトにやった He *tore* the bread into (small) pieces and fed them to the pigeons. (➤ tore は tear の過去形) ‖ 彼は回数券を1枚ちぎり取った He *tore off* a coupon.

ちぎれぐも 千切れ雲 broken [scattered] clouds.

ちぎれる 千切れる tear /teəʳ/ off ▶引っ張ったら袖がちぎれてしまった The sleeve *tore off* when I pulled it. (➤ tore は tear の過去形) ‖ 雑誌を机から落としたら表紙がちぎれた The cover *came off* the magazine when it dropped from the desk. (● come off は自然に取れる場合に使う) ‖ 去年の冬の北海道は寒いなどというものではなく, 耳がちぎれるほどだった In Hokkaido last winter, it wasn't just cold. It was cold enough to *freeze your ears off*.

チキン chicken ‖ **チキンナゲット** a chicken nugget ‖ **チキンライス** chicken pilaf seasoned with ketchup ‖ **フライドチキン** fried chicken ‖ **ローストチキン** roast chicken.

ちく 地区 an **area** /éəriə/ (漠然と1つの地域を指して) ; a **district** (行政上の区画) ; a **zone** (特別な規定を持った, または他地域から区別される特徴などを持った) ▶彼は東海地区代表として全国英語弁論大会に出場した He represented *the Tokai district* in the All-Japan English Speech Contest. ‖ 我々の学校は閑静な住宅地区に在る Our school is in a quiet *residential area* [*district*].
‖**商業地区** a business district. ⇀**地域**.

ちく- 築- ▶このマンションは築20年だ This condominium [apartment] *was built* 20 *years ago*. / This condominium [apartment] *is* 20 *years old*. ‖ この家は築何年ですか *How old* is this house?

ちくいち 逐一 one by one (いちいち) ; in detail (詳細に) ▶大きな問題でなかったら逐一報告する必要はありません You don't need to inform me of *every* (*single*) problem unless it's a major one.

ちくごやく 逐語訳 (a) literal translation (文字どおりの訳出) ; (a) word-for-word translation (1語1語による訳出).

ちくざい 蓄財 an accumulation of money ; savings (貯金, 貯蓄) ▶その老人にはかなりの蓄財がある The old man *has accumulated quite a fortune* [*has saved quite a lot of money*].

ちくさん 畜産 stock raising [farming] (畜産業)
‖**畜産農家** a stock farmer.

ちくじ 逐次 one by one (1つずつ) ; one after another (次々に)
‖**逐次通訳** consecutive interpretation (➤「同時通訳」は simultaneous interpretation).

ちくしょう 畜生 **1**【けだもの】a brute (野獣) ; a beast (大きな四足獣) ▶あいつは畜生同然だ He is *a brute* (*of a man*).
2【罵り】▶チクショー! *Damn it!* (● 罵る対象によって it を you などに変える) ‖ チクショー. ことしは英語, 落としちゃうよ! *Oh, hell,* I'll probably flunk English this year! (➤ hell は「地獄」の意で, shit (「くそ」の意) 同様タブー語) ‖ チクショー. あの数学の試験, ほんとに頭にきたよ! *Shoot!* I'm really mad about that stupid math exam. (➤ shoot は shit を遠回しに言ったもの) ‖ チクショー, 誰がやりやがったんだ! Who *the hell* did this? (➤ これもタブー表現). ⇀**こんちくしょう**.

ちくせき 蓄積 accumulation (少しずつの) **一動 蓄積する** accumulate /əkjúːmjəleɪt/ +⾃ ; store (up) (将来使う目的で) ▶富を蓄積する *accumulate* wealth ‖ データを蓄積する *store* data ‖ 大量のデータを蓄積して, いつでも取り出せるようにしたものがデータベースだ A database is a system that allows you to *store* large amounts of data and retrieve it anytime.

チクタク a ticktock, a ticktack ▶時計のチクタクいう音 the *ticktock* [*ticktack*] of a clock ‖ 壁の時計がチクタク時を刻んでいた The clock on the wall *was ticking the minutes*.

ちくちく ▶ちくちくする痛み a *prickling* pain ‖ このセーター, 襟がちくちくして痛い The neck of this sweater is *scratchy*. ‖ 彼女, 新入社員をちくちくいじめて喜んでいるのよ She gets a kick out of *needling* the new employees.

ちくでんき 蓄電器 a capacitor, a condenser.

ちくでんち 蓄電池 a storage battery.

ちくのうしょう 蓄膿症《医学》empyema /èmpaɪíːmə/ (➤ 一般には paranasal sinusitis /sàɪnəsáɪţəs/ (副鼻腔炎) とか, chronic sinusitis (慢性副鼻腔炎) という).

ちくば 竹馬 ▶《慣用表現》竹馬の友 one's *childhood friend*.

ちぐはぐ ▶箱と蓋の大きさがちぐはぐで合わない The lid *doesn't fit* [*match*] the box. ‖ このネクタイ, スーツとちぐはぐじゃないかい? Isn't this tie *mismatched with* the suit? ‖ どうもあの2人の言うことはちぐはぐだ (=食い違う) Those two are *talking at cross-purposes*.

ちくび 乳首 a nipple (人の ;《米また》哺乳瓶の) ; a teat /tiːt/ (動物の ;《英また》哺乳瓶の).

ちくり ▶虫にちくりとやられた所が腫れてきた The place where I *was stung* by an insect swelled up.
▶嫁はしゅうとめに向かってちくりちくりと嫌みを言った The daughter-in-law *made some unpleasantly pointed remarks* to her mother-in-law.

ちくりん 竹林 a bamboo grove [thicket].

ちくる snitch《on》; tell《on》(告げ口する) ▶誰が俺のこと, 先生にちくったんだよ Who went to the teacher and *snitched on* me? ‖ おまえ, ちくりやがったな You *told on me*, didn't you?

ちくわ 竹輪 *chikuwa* ; steamed fish cake (➤ 説明的な訳).

ちけい 地形 geographical [natural] features, (a) topography ▶その地域の山岳地形 the region's mountainous *topography* ‖ 日本の地形は複雑だ Japan is *geographically* complex.
‖**地形学** topography ‖ **地形図** a topographical map.

チケット a ticket ▶この店で映画[コンサート]のチケットが安く買えるんだって I hear you can get movie [concert] *tickets* at a discount at this shop. ‖ あのミュージシャンのコンサートのチケットは売り切れです All the *tickets* for that musician's concert have sold out.
‖**チケット売り場** a ticket [box] office,《英》a booking office.

[1]**ちけん 治験** a clinical trial.

[2]**ちけん 知見** knowledge ▶知見を広める broaden one's *knowledge*.

ちけんしゃ 地権者 a landowner, a leaseholder.

ちこく 遅刻

一動 (…に) **遅刻する** be late《for, to》, be tardy《to, for》(➤ 後者は主に教師や学校関係者が用いる語で, 生徒・学生は前者を用いる) ▶けさは交通事故のため学校に15分遅刻した Because of a traffic accident, I *was* 15 minutes *late for* [*to*] school this morning. ‖ 彼女は約束の時間に遅刻した She *was late for* her appointment. ‖きょうの授業, **何分遅刻したんだい** *How late for* class *were you* today? ‖彼は毎日のように会社に**遅刻して行く** He *goes* to his office *late* almost every day. ‖けさは寝坊したが学校には**遅刻しなかった**(=間に合った) I overslept this morning, but I *was able to make it* to school *on time*. ‖雄太郎は**遅刻常習犯だ** Yutaro *is always* [*habitually*] *late*. (➤ late の代わりに tardy でもよい) ‖奈々は授業に**遅刻することがない** Nana *is* never *tardy to* class.

‖**遅刻者** a latecomer ‖**遅刻届** a tardy slip, a late note [slip].

ちこつ 恥骨 the pubic bone.

ちさんちしょう 地産地消 local production for local consumption, (the) local consumption of locally produced goods [food(s)].

ちし 致死の lethal /líːθəl/ ▶**致死率(性)の高い**化学兵器 a *lethal* chemical weapon ‖彼女は**致死量の**毒薬を飲んで自殺した She committed suicide by taking *a lethal dose of* poison.

‖**過失致死罪** accidental homicide, involuntary manslaughter.

ちじ 知事 a governor /gʌ́vəʳnəʳ/

▶祖父は3期連続福島県**知事**を務めた My grandfather served as the *governor* of Fukushima Prefecture for three consecutive terms. ‖ニューヨーク州**知事** the *governor* of New York.

‖**都道府県知事** a prefectural governor.

ちしき 知識 knowledge /nɑ́ːlɪdʒ/; information (情報); expertise /èkspəʳtíːz/ (専門的な) ▶私は星の**知識**が多少はある I have some *knowledge* of [I *know* something about] stars (and planets). ‖父はイスラム教に関する**知識**が全然ない My father has no *knowledge* of Islam. / My father knows nothing about Islam. ‖母は茶道について豊かな**知識**を持っている My mother has *extensive knowledge* of the tea ceremony. / My mother is *knowledgeable* about the tea ceremony. / My mother *knows a lot* about the tea ceremony. ‖この本はアメリカ映画に関する多くの**知識**を与えてくれる This book gives *a lot of information* about [on] American movies. ‖子供は**知識欲が旺盛だ** Children *are eager for knowledge*. / Children *have a thirst for knowledge*. ‖彼は**知識に飢えている** He *has a craving for knowledge*. (➤ craving は「渇望」の意) ‖この事件を解決するには医学的な**専門知識**が必要だ Medical *expertise* is needed to solve this case. ‖**知識は力なり** *Knowledge is power*. (➤ 英語のことわざ).

‖**知識階級** the intellectuals /ìnṭəléktʃuəlz/, the intellectual class ‖**知識人** an intellectual; an educated [a learned] person (教育のある人) ‖**予備知識** preliminary knowledge.

ちじき 地磁気 the earth's magnetism.

ちじく 地軸 the earth's axis.

ちしつ 地質 ‖**地質学** geology ‖**地質学者** a geologist ‖**地質調査** a geological survey ‖**地質年代** geologic(al) time 《参考》「古生代」は Paleozoic /pèɪliəzóʊɪk/, 「中生代」は Mesozoic /mèsəzóʊɪk/, 「新生代」は Cenozoic /sìːnəzóʊɪk/.

ちじょう 地上 ▶そのビルは**地上**60階, 地下3階建てです The building has sixty stories *above ground* and three underground. ‖ニューカレドニアは**地上の楽園**と呼ばれている New Caledonia is called *a paradise on earth* [*an earthly paradise*].

‖**地上戦** a ground war.

ちじょく 恥辱 humiliation ▶私は耐え難い**恥辱**を受けた I suffered unbearable *humiliation*.

ちじん 知人 an acquaintance /əkwéɪntəns/.

ちず 地図 a map (1枚の); an atlas (地図帳) ▶日本**地図** *a map* of Japan ‖世界**地図** a world *map* / *a map* of the world ‖白**地図** a blank *map* ‖道路**地図** a road *map* ‖**地図を描く** draw *a map* ‖その温泉は5万分の1の**地図**には出ていると思う I think the hot spring should be on a 1:50,000 scale *map*. (➤ one fifty-thousandth と読む) ‖アララト山がどこにあるか**地図で調べなさい** *Find* (*out*) *on the map* where Mount Ararat is.

ちすい 治水 flood control (洪水対策)

‖**治水事業** a flood-control project.

ちすじ 血筋 blood (血縁); a line (血統); stock, descent /dɪsént/ (家系) ▶彼は代々音楽家の**血筋**を引いている He comes from a long *line* of musicians. ‖彼女は**血筋が良い** She *comes from a good family*. ‖彼は夏目漱石の**血筋を引いている**(=子孫だ) He *is a descendant of* Natsume Soseki. ‖この子の目がぱっちりしているのは**母方の血筋だ** He has such big bright eyes. He *gets* it *from his mother's side of the family*. ‖**血筋は争えない** *Blood will tell*. (➤ 英語のことわざ).

1**ちせい 知性** intelligence /ɪntélɪdʒəns/ (知能); sense (良識, 分別); intellect /ínṭəlekt/ (知力, 理解力) ▶**知性的な人** an *intelligent* [*intellectual*] person ‖あの市長ときたら, **知性のかけらも無い**んだから That mayor does*n't have a shred of intelligence* [*sense*]. ‖アインシュタインはあらゆる時代を通じて最高の**知性人**の1人だ Einstein is among the greatest *minds* of all time. (➤ この mind は「知力の持ち主」の意).

2**ちせい 治世** a reign /reɪn/ ▶ビクトリア女王の**治世**は64年間に及んだ The *reign* of Queen Victoria lasted a full 64 years.

ちせいがく 地政学 geopolitics.

ちせつ 稚拙な poor (下手な); childish (子供っぽい) ▶**稚拙な**作文 a *poor* [*poorly-written*] composition.

ちそう 地層 a stratum /stréɪṭəm ‖ strɑ́ːt-/ ▶白亜紀の**地層** a Cretaceous /krɪtéɪʃəs/ *stratum*.

1**ちたい 地帯** a zone, a belt (目的・特徴で区分された地帯; 後者はある特定の作物ができる地帯であること, または区分された地帯が帯状であることを強調する); an area /éəriə/ (地域); a region (気候・地勢などによって区別された地帯) ▶綿花[小麦]のできる**地帯** a cotton [wheat] *belt*.

✉ **私たちの学校は周りに緑地帯がある美しい町にあります** Our school is in a beautiful town surrounded by *a greenbelt*.

‖**安全地帯** a safety zone ‖**工業地帯** an industrial area ‖**穀倉地帯** a breadbasket ‖**国境地帯** a border (area / region) ‖**山岳地帯** a mountainous region [area] ‖**森林地帯** a forest(ed) area ‖**田園地帯** a rural [farming] area ‖**農村地帯** an agricultural [a farming] area ‖**非武装地帯** a demilitarized zone.

2**ちたい 遅滞** (a) delay; arrears (支払いなどの).

ちだるま 血達磨 ▶彼は**血だるま**のまま病院に運ばれた He was taken to a hospital *covered* (*all over*) *with his own blood*.

チタン 《化学》 titanium.

1**ちち 父** a father →お父さん ▶私の**父**は医者です My *father* is a doctor. ‖**父**は毎朝6時に起きる *My father* wakes up at six o'clock every morning. ‖兄は25歳ですが, すでに3人の子の**父**です

My (older) brother is (only) twenty-five, but he is already the *father* of three children. ‖ 彼は父親のない［父親を失った］子供です He is a *fatherless* child.
▶力道山は日本プロレスの父と言われている Rikidozan is called *the father* of professional wrestling in Japan.
ことわざ この父にしてこの子あり Like father, like son.
‖ 父の日 Father's Day.

²ちち 乳 **1**【ミルク】milk ▶ヤギの乳 goat's *milk* ‖ この牛は乳の出がいい This cow *milks well* [*gives plenty of milk*]. ‖ 牛の乳を搾ったことある？ Have you ever *milked* a cow? ‖ 赤ちゃんがお乳を欲しがって泣いている The baby is crying for *milk* [*the breast*]. ‖ 母親が赤ん坊にお乳をやっている The mother is *breastfeeding* [*nursing*] the baby.
▶《慣用表現》あいつはまだ乳臭いガキだよ That guy *is* still *wet behind the ears*. (➤ be wet behind the ears は「未熟だ」の意のインフォーマルな言い方).
2【乳房】a breast ▶先生, 右のお乳のところにしこりがあるんです Doctor, I have a lump in my right *breast*.

ちちおや 父親 a father. →父.

ちちかた 父方の paternal ▶父方の祖父 a *paternal* grandfather／a grandfather on one's *father's side* ‖ 父方の祖父は今も健在です My grandfather *on my father's side* is still going strong.

ちぢかむ 縮かむ ▶寒さで手が縮かんだ My hands *became stiff* with cold.

ちぢこまる 縮こまる shrink (up) ▶寒くて体が縮こまってしまった I *shrank* [*curled*] *up* from the cold.／The cold made me *huddle up*.

ちちとして 遅々として discouragingly slow ▶政府の行政改革は遅々として進んでいない The government's administrative reforms are making *little* progress [are proceeding *at a snail's pace*].

ちちばなれ 乳離れ →ちばなれ.

ちぢまる 縮まる ▶冗漫なことばをカットしたら原稿が20ページも縮まった After I omitted redundant words, the length of my manuscript *was reduced* by as many as 20 pages. ‖ 彼女は力走したのでトップのランナーとの差がだいぶ縮まった She ran hard and *reduced* the first runner's lead remarkably. ‖ 走り幅跳びの世界記録と日本記録の差は一向に縮まらない The gap between the world record and the Japanese record for the broad jump *has not narrowed* at all.

ちぢみ 縮み shrinkage(縮小); crepe(織物).

ちぢみあがる 縮み上がる cower /káʊəʳ/; cringe (すくむ) ▶担任の先生にどなられてぼくらは皆縮み上がってしまった We all *cowered* [*cringed*] when our homeroom teacher yelled at us. (➤ cringe は /krɪndʒ/ と発音).

ちぢむ 縮む shrink ▶このセーターは洗っても縮まない This sweater doesn't *shrink* in the wash. ‖ ゴムは伸びたり縮んだりする Rubber *is elastic* [*stretches and returns to its original size and shape*]. ‖ あの突然の地震のときは命が縮む思いだった The sudden earthquake *scared the life out of me*.

ちぢめる 縮める shorten +目 (短くする); condense +目 (要約する); shrink +目 (縮小する) ▶コートの丈を3センチ縮めてもらった I *had* my coat *shortened* (by) three centimeters. ‖ きみの作文は長すぎるから原稿用紙5枚に縮めなさい Your composition is too long. *Condense* it into five pages on manuscript paper. ‖ 私はスーツのズボンを縮めてもらった I *had* my suit pants *taken in*.
▶シャクトリムシは体を伸ばしたり縮めたりして前進する The inchworm moves by *looping up* its body and then stretching it out. (➤ loop は「環状に丸める」の意).
▶彼女は記録を3秒縮めた She *bettered* the record by three seconds. (➤ better は「(記録などを)良くする」)／She *shaved* three seconds *off* the record. ‖ たばこは寿命を縮めるよ Smoking will *shorten* your life. ‖ インターネットは世界の距離を縮めた The Internet *has shrunk* the world.

ちちゅう 地中 ▶地中深く *deep under the ground*／*deep underground* ‖ 江戸時代に鋳造された金貨が地中に埋めてあるのが発見された Some gold coins minted in the Edo period were found buried *in the ground* [*the earth*].

ちちゅうかい 地中海 the Mediterranean /mèdɪtəréɪniən/ (Sea) ▶地中海沿岸諸国 the countries along *the Mediterranean* (*Sea*)／*Mediterranean* countries ‖ 地中海性気候 a *Mediterranean* climate.

ちぢらす 縮らす frizz(le), curl (➤ 前者のほうが縮れ方が細かい) ▶私たちの学校では髪の毛を縮らすことは禁止されています School regulations forbid us to *frizz(le)* [*curl*] our hair.

ちぢれげ 縮れ毛 frizzy [curly] hair (➤ frizzy のほうが縮れ方が細かい) ▶私は生まれつき縮れ毛です My hair is naturally *frizzy* [*curly*].

ちぢれる 縮れる frizz(le), curl (➤ 前者のほうが縮れ方が細かい) ▶アニーは髪の毛が縮れている Annie has *frizzy* [*curly*] hair.／Annie's hair is *frizzy* [*curly*].

ちつ 膣 the vagina /vədʒáɪnə/.

ちつじょ 秩序 order ▶社会の秩序を保つ［乱す］maintain [disturb] social *order* ‖ 指導者たちの抗争でその組織の秩序は乱れてしまった Conflicts among the leaders *disrupted* the organization [*caused disorder* in the organization]. ‖ 彼の考え方は秩序立っている His way of thinking is *systematic* [*methodical*].
☛ 無秩序 (→見出語)

ちっそ 窒素 nitrogen /náɪtrədʒən/
‖ 窒素酸化物 nitrogen oxide ‖ 窒素肥料 nitrogenous fertilizer ‖ 液体窒素 liquid nitrogen ‖ 二酸化窒素 nitrogen dioxide.

ちっそく 窒息 suffocation 一動 窒息する suffocate /sʌ́fəkeɪt/ (酸素が欠乏して); choke (首を締められたり, 鼻をふさがれたりして) ▶窒息しそうな毎日の生活 a *suffocating* everyday life ‖ 窓を開けてくれませんか. たばこの煙で窒息しそうです Could you open the window? I'*m suffocating* from all this cigarette smoke. ‖ その火災でたくさんの人々が煙に巻かれて窒息死した Many people *died of suffocation* in that fire.

ちっちゃな itty-bitty, itsy-bitsy; tiny (ごく小さな) ▶ちっちゃな家に住む live in an *itty-bitty* [*itsy-bitsy*] house ‖ ちっちゃな子猫 a *tiny* kitten. →小さい.

ちっとも ▶この本はちっともおもしろくない This book is *not* interesting *at all* [*in the least*]. ‖ ぼくはちっとも疲れてないよ I'm *not a bit* tired. ‖ 父さんは仕事の虫で私のことをちっとも構ってくれない My dad is so wrapped up in his work (that) he does*n't* pay *the least* attention to me.

¹チップ **1**【心付け】a tip /tɪp/ (➤ 発音に注意) ▶《ボ

ーイなどに》はい, チップです Here's *a tip* for you. ／Here's your *tip*. ‖ボーイさんにいくらチップをあげたらいいかしら How much should I *give* to the bellhop (*as a tip*)? ／How much should I *tip* the bellhop? (➤ 後者の tip は「チップをあげる」の意の動詞) ‖ウエーターにチップをあげるのを忘れないでね Don't forget (to *tip*) the waiter. ‖彼はウエートレスにチップを5ドルあげた He gave the waitress a five-dollar *tip*. ‖日本ではチップは不要です *Tipping* isn't necessary in Japan. ‖《掲示》チップは頂きません No Tips [No Gratuities] Accepted.

2【野球】**a tip** ▶バッターはボールをファウルチップした The batter *tipped* the ball *foul*.

²チップ **a chip** /tʃɪp/ (小片)
‖**ウッドチップ** wood chips ‖**コンピュータチップ** a computer *chip* ‖**メモリーチップ** a memory chip.

> **危ないカタカナ語✹ チップ**
> **1** 日本語の「チップ」には tip と chip が相当するので注意が必要.「心付け」の意味では tip である. 野球用語の「チップ」も tip で,「ファウルチップ」は foul tip という.
> **2** ポテトチップの「チップ」は chip で, 通例 chips と複数形にする (イギリスでは crisps といい, chips は細長い French fried potatoes のほうを指す). その他, chip はポーカーなどの「点数板」, コンピュータの「プリント小片」の意味でも使われる.

ちっぽけな **tiny** (ごく小さな) ; **itty-bitty, itsy-bitsy** (ちっちゃな) ▶ちっぽけな村 a *tiny* village ‖ちっぽけな町 a *one-horse* town (➤「おもしろみのない小さな町」の意の決まり文句).

ちてい 地底 **the bowels of the earth** ‖**地底湖** an underground lake, a subterranean lake.

ちてき 知的な **intellectual** (人が知性のある) ; **intelligent** (人・犬などが聡明(そうめい)な) ▶知的な仕事 an *intellectual* occupation ‖知的な生活に憧れる yearn for an *intellectual* life ‖きみんところの犬, なかなか知的な顔してるね Your dog looks very *intelligent*. ‖ジグソーパズルは知的能力の発達を促す Jigsaw puzzles stimulate the development of *mental* [*intellectual*] *abilities*.
‖**知的財産(権)** intellectual property (rights) ‖**知的所有権** intellectual property rights.

ちてん 地点 **a point** (点) ; **a spot** (場所) ; **a mark** (標識) ▶ベースキャンプから500メートル登った地点でそのパーティーは遭難した The party met with an accident at *a point* 500 meters from the base camp. ‖ここがまさに旅客機の墜落事故が起きた地点です This is the very *spot* [*place*] where the plane crash occurred. (➤ この very は後ろの名詞を強調する形容詞で「ちょうどその…」などの意) ‖鈴木は40キロ地点でスパートした Suzuki made a spurt at the 40 km *mark*. ‖ここがピューリタンたちの上陸地点です This is *where* the Puritans landed.
‖**着陸地点** a touchdown point [spot].

ちどうせつ 地動説 **the Copernican system [theory]** (➤「天動説」は the Ptolemaic /tɑ̀ːləméɪɪk/ system [theory]).

ちどり 千鳥《鳥》**a plover** /plʌ́vəʳ/.

ちどりあし 千鳥足 ▶彼は通りを千鳥足で歩いていった He *staggered* down [went *reeling* down] the street drunkenly. (➤ reel は「ふらふらと倒れそうに歩く」).

ちなまぐさい 血生臭い **bloody, gory** (➤ 後者は主に文語) ▶血生臭い戦闘 a *bloody* battle ‖新聞は毎日血生臭いニュースでいっぱいだ The newspaper is filled with *gory* news every day.

ちなみに 因みに ▶これはセザンヌの絵です. ちなみに値段は現在数億円と言われています This is a Cézanne. *Just for your information* [*Incidentally*], it would cost several hundred million yen if you bought it now. (➤ just for your information は「ご参考までに」, incidentally は「ついでながら」の意).

ちなむ 因む ▶私は息子を自分のふるさとの山にちなんで「いぶき」と名付けた I named my son Ibuki *after* [*for*] a mountain in my hometown. ‖理科の先生がハレーすい星にちなんだ話をしてくれた Our science teacher told us a story *connected* [*associated*] *with* Halley's comet.

ちにちか 知日家 **a Japan expert [specialist], an expert [a specialist] on Japan, a person well-informed about Japan.** →親日(家).

ちねつ 地熱 **the internal heat of the earth, geotherm** /dʒíːoʊθəːʳm/ (➤ 後者は専門用語)
‖**地熱エネルギー** geothermal energy ‖**地熱発電所** a geothermal power plant.

ちのう 知能 **intelligence ; mental faculties [abilities]** (知的能力) ▶彼の知能はふつうだ He has average *intelligence*. ‖イルカは知能が高い Dolphins *are very intelligent* [*bright*].
‖**知能指数** an intelligence quotient /kwóʊʃənt/ 《略 IQ, I.Q.》 ‖**知能テスト** an intelligence test, an IQ test ‖**知能犯** an intelligent [a smart] criminal (人) ; an intellectual crime (犯罪).

ちのけ 血の気 ▶あいつは血の気が多い He *is short-tempered* [*hot-tempered*]. ／He *easily loses his temper*. (➤ 後者は「すぐ腹を立てる」の意) ‖その手紙を読むと彼女の顔からさっと血の気が引いた Reading the letter, she *turned pale*. ／*The color* [*blood*] *drained* from her face as she read the letter.

ちのみご 乳飲み子 **a baby, a suckling** (➤ 後者は文語).

ちのり 地の利 **an advantageous location** ▶このコンビニは地の利を得ている This convenience store *has a great* [*an excellent*] *location*. ／This convenience store *is in a prime location*.

ちはい 遅配 ▶大雪のため郵便が遅配になった A heavy snow(fall) caused *a delay in mail delivery*. ／The mail was delayed by a heavy snow(fall).

ちばしる 血走る ▶血走った目 *bloodshot* eyes ‖兄の目は血走っていた My brother's eyes *were bloodshot*.

ちばなれ 乳離れ ▶私の子は乳離れしたばかりです My baby *has* just *been weaned*.
▶《比喩的》あの(男子)学生は20歳になるのにいまだに乳離れしていない (＝自立心がない) Although that student is twenty years old, he *is* still *not emotionally independent of his parents* [he *is* still *tied to his mother's apron strings*]. (➤ 後者は「母親べったりで」の意).

ちび **a shorty** (背の低い人) ; **a brat** (餓鬼) ; one's **little kid** (自分の子供) ▶このちび! 悔しかったら追いかけて来い Hey, *squirt*! Catch me if you can! (➤ squirt は「生意気な若者」の意のインフォーマルな語)

ちびちび ▶父はテレビを見ながらちびちびやるのが好きだ My father likes to *sip* sake while watching television.
▶墨汁が無くなりそうなのでちびちび使っている I'm *going*

easy on the sumi ink because I'm running short of [on] it. (➤ go easy on は「…を節約して使う」).

ちびっこ ちびっ子 a **little child** [**boy** / **girl**] (小さな子 [男の子 / 女の子]) ▶**ちびっ子のど自慢** a singing contest for *little kids* [*children*] (単数形の kid はかなりくだけていて, ぞんざいな響きがあるので安易に使わないほうがよい) ‖ 修は**ちびっ子**仲間の大将だ Osamu is the leader of a gang of *little kids*.

ちひょう 地表 **the surface of the earth.**

ちびりちびり ▶仕事のあとでウイスキーを**ちびりちびりやる**のは最高だ There's nothing greater than *sipping* a glass of whiskey after work. (➤ sip は「少しずつ飲むこと」の意) ‖ 父は1杯のブランデーを**大事そうにちびりちびり飲んだ** My father *nursed* a glass of brandy. (➤ nurse は「(酒などを大事そうに) ちびりちびり飲む」の意).

ちびる **1** 【**すり減る**】 ▶**ちびた**下駄(げた) *worn-out* geta ‖ **ちびた**鉛筆 a *stubby* pencil ‖ 鉛筆が**ちびてきた** The pencil is *getting stubby*.

2 【**けちけちする**】 **skimp** ▶ボーイへのチップを**ちびる**なよ Don't *skimp on* the bellhop's tip.

3 【**漏らす**】 ▶あいつジェット・コースターに乗ってて**小便ちびった**んだ He *wet his pants* while he was riding on the roller coaster!

ちぶ 恥部 **1** 【**陰部**】 **the private parts** ▶宗教画では, アダムとイブの**恥部**を隠すのにイチジクの葉が描かれている In religious images, fig leaves are used to hide Adam and Eve's *private parts*.

2 【**不名誉なもの**】 a **disgrace** ▶その辺りはかつてシカゴ最大の**恥部**と見なされていた That area was once considered Chicago's greatest *disgrace*.

ちぶさ 乳房 **breasts** (➤ 通例複数形で) ▶**豊かな** [**貧弱な**] **乳房の女性** an *ample-breasted* [*a small-breasted*] woman. ⇀**おっぱい**.

チフス **typhoid** /táɪfɔɪd/ (腸チフス) ; **typhus** /táɪfəs/ (発疹(はっしん)チフス) ; **paratyphoid** /pæ̀rətáɪfɔɪd/ (パラチフス) ▶**腸チフスにかかる** contract *typhoid*.

ちへいせん 地平線 **the horizon** /həráɪzən/ ▶太陽がゆっくりと**地平線**から昇ってきた The sun rose slowly above *the horizon*. ‖ 太陽が根釧原野の**地平線**に沈んだ The sun sank below *the horizon* on the Konsen Plateau.

ちほ 地歩 a **foothold** ▶かつて日本人移民はブラジル社会に**地歩**を占めようと奮闘した Japanese immigrants once struggled to gain *a foothold* in Brazilian society.

[1]**ちほう 地方** **1** 【**地域**】 an **area** /éəriə/ ; a **region** (気候・自然条件で分けられた) ; a **district** (行政区 ; 特徴のある区域) ▶この**地方**にはベイスターズのファンが多い There are a lot of BayStars fans in this *area* [in this *part of the country*]. ‖ 結婚式に関する習慣は**地方によって異なる** Wedding customs differ *from region to region*. ‖ **近畿地方** [**山岳地方**] はきのう豪雨に見舞われた It rained heavily in *the Kinki district* [*the mountainous district*] yesterday.

2 【**中央以外の**】 **the country** 一形 **地方の** **regional** ; **local** (地元の, その土地の) ; **rural** (農村地方の) ; **provincial** (田舎の) ▶**地方の新聞** a *regional* [*local*] newspaper (➤ local は「地元の」の意で「田舎の」というニュアンスはない) ‖ 発音の**地方差** *regional* variations of pronunciation ‖ **地方の人々** *country* people ‖ **地方出身**の学生たち students *from the country* [*from rural areas*] ‖ 私はその**地方の**支店に転勤になりました I was transferred to a branch office *in the country*. ‖ 彼はその**地方の**女子大の英文科で教えている He teaches in the English department of a local women's college. ‖ 青森のねぶたは実に**地方色**豊かな祭りである Aomori's "Nebuta" is a festival rich in *local character*. ‖ あの歌手も売れないうちは**地方回り**ばかりだった The singer spent a lot of time *on the road* before he became popular.

‖**地方行政** local administration ‖ **地方検察庁** a District Public Prosecutors Office ‖ **地方公共団体** a local public organization [body] ‖ **地方公務員** a local government employee ‖ **地方裁判所** a district court ‖ **地方自治体** a local government ‖ **地方都市** a rural [provincial] town (➤ provincial には「田舎臭い」という意が含まれることもある) ‖ **地方分権** decentralization of administrative power (from the central government to local governments).

[2]**ちほう 痴呆** ⇀**認知症** (➤ 近年,「痴呆」は「認知症」と言いかえられている).

ちまた 巷の ▶**ちまたの声** *public* opinion ‖ **ちまたのうわさでは**市長は重病だそうだ *Rumor has it* [*It is rumored*] that the mayor is seriously sick.

ちまちま ▶**ちまちま暮らして金をためる** *scrimp* and save (➤ scrimp は「金を出し惜しむ」).

ちまなこ 血眼 ▶彼は**血眼になって**無くしたパスポートを捜していた He was looking *desperately* [*frantically*] for his (missing) passport.

ちまみれ 血塗れの **bloody** ▶男が**血まみれになって**道路脇に倒れていた I found a man lying by the roadside *in a pool of blood*. ‖ 彼は**血まみれの**シャツのまま家に駆け込んで来た He ran into the house wearing a *blood-stained* shirt.

ちまめ 血豆 a **blood blister** ▶手元が狂って金づちで親指を打ち, **血豆**を作ってしまった I got *a blood blister* when I hit my thumb with a hammer by mistake.

ちまよう 血迷う ▶その息子は何を**血迷った**か, いきなり野球のバットを持って父親に襲いかかった The son, who had apparently *lost control of himself*, suddenly attacked his father with a baseball bat.

ちみち 血道 ▶息子はヒップホップに**血道を上げている** My son *is obsessed with* hip-hop.

ちみつ 緻密な **close** /kloʊs/ (観察などが綿密な) ; **precise** (精密な) ; **minute** /maɪnjúːt/ (詳細な) ▶**緻密な観察** a *close* observation ‖ 銀行強盗たちは**緻密な**計画を練った The bank robbers worked out an *elaborate* scheme. ‖ 彼女の案は発想はおもしろいけれども**緻密さに欠ける** As for her plan, the idea is interesting, but *the details have not been worked out sufficiently*. (➤「細部が十分に研究されていない」の意).

ちみどろ 血みどろの **bloody** ▶**血みどろの戦い** a *bloody* [*gory*] battle (➤ gory は主として文語).

ちみもうりょう 魑魅魍魎 **evil spirits of mountains and rivers.**

ちめい 地名 a **place name**

‖**地名辞典** a dictionary of place names.

ちめいしょう 致命傷 a **fatal injury** [**wound**] ▶彼は交通事故で頭に**致命傷**を負った (＝死んだ) He received [got] *a fatal injury* to the head in the traffic accident.

▶《比喩的》その汚職事件は彼の政治生命にとって**致命傷となった** The scandal *proved fatal* to his political career.

ちめいてき 致命的な fatal /féɪtl/ ▶致命的な過ちを犯す make a *fatal* mistake ‖ 力士にとって体重が軽いことは致命的だ Light weight is *fatal* to the career of a sumo wrestler.

ちめいど 知名度 ▶知名度の高い［低い］大学 a *well-known* [*little-known*] university ‖ 世界的に知名度の高いピアニスト a *world-famous* pianist ‖ ピアニストとしての実力の割には彼は知名度が無い Despite his ability as a pianist, he'*s not well known*.

ちもう 恥毛 pubic hair.

ちゃ 茶 tea(ふつうは紅茶)；green tea(緑茶) ▶薄い［濃い］茶 weak [strong] *tea* ‖ 父に茶を入れる *make tea* for my father ／*serve tea* to my father ‖ 彼は大きな湯飲みに茶をついだ He poured *green tea* into a large teacup.

ことわざ 茶腹も一時 Drinking green tea relieves hunger for a while.

‖茶会 a (Japanese) tea ceremony party；a tea party ‖ 茶菓子 cakes to have with tea ‖ 茶殻 used tea-leaves ‖ 茶器 (茶道具) tea things(➤一つ一つは teacup, tea kettle などと具体的にいうのがふつう) ‖ 茶こし a tea strainer ‖ 茶さじ a teaspoon ‖ 茶室 a tea house [hut／cottage](一軒家)；a tea ceremony room(建物の中の一室) ‖ 茶たく a Japanese teacup saucer ‖ 茶だんす a cupboard ‖ 茶筒 a tea caddy ‖ 茶摘み tea-picking ‖ 茶飲み a teacup ‖ 茶飲み友だち a friend one enjoys chatting with over tea.

☛ お茶, 新茶, 茶色 (→見出語)

チャーシュー char siu, (Chinese) roast pork, chashao.

チャーター charter ▶バスをチャーターする *charter* a bus ‖ チャーター機 a chartered plane.

チャーハン *chahan*；(Chinese) fried rice.

チャーミング (→かこみ記事)

> **危ないカタカナ語✸ チャーミング**
>
> **1** 日本語では主に若い女性について「チャーミング」というが, 英語の charming は表面的な美しさではなく, 物腰や態度が「感じがいい, 人を引きつける」の意で, 女性だけでなく, 男性や老人についても用いられる.
>
> **2** したがって,「チャーミングな女の子」の訳は charming girl よりも pretty [attractive] girl のほうが場合によっては適切.
>
> **3** 日本語でも最近は charming 本来の意味に近い使い方がされるようになった.「チャーミングなおばあちゃん」は a charming elderly woman でよく,「(こぢんまりとして)すてきな魅力のある」というような意味で「チャーミングなホテル［町］」は a charming hotel [town] でよい.

チャームポイント ▶えくぼが彼女のチャームポイントだ Her dimples are her *most attractive feature*. (🏺 (×) charm point は和製語)

チャイブ chive(食用ハーブの一種).

チャイム a chime ▶彼が教室に入って来ると同時に始業のチャイムが鳴った The moment he entered the classroom, the *chime* sounded. ‖ 玄関のチャイムがピンポーンと鳴った The *doorbell* went bing-bong. (➤ 玄関のチャイムも chime といえるが, doorbell のほうが誤解のおそれがない).

チャイルドシート a child seat.

ちゃいろ 茶色 brown；orange (明るい茶色) ▶焦げ茶色 *dark brown* ‖ 薄茶色 *light brown* ‖ 茶色の目 *brown* eyes.

ちゃがし 茶菓子 refreshment(s).

ちゃかす 茶化す make fun of(からかう)；spoof +目 (パロディーにして) ▶ちゃかすなよ, ぼくは本気なんだから Don't *make fun of* what I said. I meant it. ‖ その お笑いの寸劇は首相をちゃかしたものだった The comedy skit *spoofed* the Prime Minister. ‖ 彼は何でもちゃかして責任逃れをする He *turns* everything *into a joke* and tries to dodge his responsibility. (➤ dodge は「(義務や困難など)から逃げる」).

ちゃかっしょく 茶褐色 (dark) brown ▶茶褐色のスーツ a *dark brown* suit.

ちゃきちゃき ▶祖父はちゃきちゃきの江戸っ子だ My grandfather is a *real* [*genuine*] "Edokko" (which means that his parents and grandparents, including himself, were born and raised in the Shitamachi area of Tokyo).

-ちゃく -着 **1**【到着】▶この飛行機の成田着(＝成田に着くの)は午後 3 時だ This plane will *arrive at* Narita at 3 p.m. ‖ 飛行機は午後 2 時着の予定です The plane *is scheduled to arrive* [*is due*] at 2 p.m.

2【着順】▶彼はそのマラソンで 2 着になった He *finished second* [*placed second*] in the marathon (race). 《参考》競馬用語では馬が 2 着になることを place といい, 3 着(または 3 着以内)になることを show という. 1 着は win.

3【衣服の数】▶ジャケットを 1 着買った I bought *a* jacket. ‖ スーツは何着持っていますか *How many* (*business*) *suits* do you have?

ちゃくがん 着眼 ▶きみはいいところに着眼したね That's *the point*. (➤「そこが肝心な点だ」の意)／That's *a good observation*. ‖ 専門家はさすがに着眼点が違うね I can see that it takes an expert to know *where to look*.

ちゃくじつ 着実な steady 一副 着実に steadily；step by step (一歩一歩) ▶きみの英語の力は着実に伸びている Your English is improving *steadily*. ／You are making *steady* progress in your English. ‖ わがチームは後半に入ってからも着実に得点を重ねた Our team piled up points *steadily* in the second half of the game too.

ちゃくしゅ 着手する start (+目) (始める)；commence(+目) (開始する；堅い語) ▶仕事に着手する *get* [*set*] *to* work ‖ 新しい事業に着手する *start* [*launch into*] a new business.

‖着手金 a retaining fee, a retainer(弁護士などへの依頼などの)；a start-up fee(事業などの)；an initial fee(登録などの)；a deposit, earnest money (手付金).

ちゃくしゅつし 嫡出子 a legitimate child

‖非嫡出子 an illegitimate child.

ちゃくしょく 着色 (a) coloring(着色方法；着色剤) 一動 着色する color +目 ▶《表示》合成着色料使用 Contains Artificial Coloring.

ちゃくしん 着信 ▶携帯の着信音 a cellphone *ringtone*(➤「着信メロディー」も ringtone または musical ringtone) ‖ メールの着信を知らせる合図が鳴った A signal beeped informing me that I *had received* a text message [an email]. ／A beep announced *the arrival* of a text message [an email]. (➤ 前者は携帯電話のメール, 後者はパソコンの場合).

ちゃくすい 着水 (a) splash down(宇宙船などの) 一動 着水する splash down；make a water landing ▶(飛行機が)緊急着水する *make an* emergency *water landing*.

ちゃくせき 着席する sit down, be seated (➤ 後者がより丁寧な言い方) ▶ご着席ください Please *be seated*.

／Please *take your seats*.／*Sit down*, please. (➤ 最後の訳例はやや命令口調).

ちゃくそう 着想 an idea ▶着想の豊かな人 a person of *ideas*／an *idea* person.

ちゃくだん 着弾する hit +目, strike +目 ▶ミサイル数発が島に着弾した Several missiles *hit* [*struck*] the island.

ちゃくち 着地 landing. →着陸.

ちゃくちゃく 着々と steadily ▶工事は着々と進んでいる The construction work is progressing *steadily* [is making *steady* progress].／The construction work is *well* under way. ‖野村教授の糖尿病研究は着々と進んでいる Professor Nomura's diabetes research is progressing *steadily* [is making *steady* progress].

ちゃくにん 着任 ▶新店長は大阪からきょう着任した Our new store manager *arrived at his post* from Osaka today. ‖あの方が今度着任した新しい部長です He is the *newly appointed* head of our division.

ちゃくばらい 着払い collect [cash] on delivery《略 COD, C.O.D.》▶代金着払い *Payment* [*Payable*] *on delivery* ‖このサプリメントの代金は着払いで結構です You may *pay* for these dietary supplements *C.O.D.* [*upon delivery*.] ‖着払いで小包を送る send a parcel *C.O.D.*

ちゃくふく 着服する embezzle /ɪmbézəl/ +目, pocket +目 ▶彼女は店の金を着服して解雇された She was dismissed for *embezzling* [*pocketing*] store money.

ちゃくメロ 着メロ a (musical) ringtone.

ちゃくもく 着目 ▶刑事はタイヤについた泥に着目した The detective *focused his attention on* the mud on the tires. ‖いいところに着目したね! You've *noticed* a very important point.

ちゃくよう 着用する wear +目 ▶《掲示》生徒は登校の際制服を着用すること Students must *wear* school uniforms when coming to school.／Uniforms must *be worn* to school.

ちゃくりく 着陸 a landing, a touch-down (➤ 前者には「上陸」の意もある) 一動 (…に)着陸する land《at, in, on》▶月に着陸する *land on* the moon ‖飛行機はオルリー空港に定刻に着陸した The plane *made a landing* [*landed*／*touched down*] on time at Orly. ‖その飛行機はエンジンの故障で緊急着陸した The plane *had to make an emergency landing* due to engine trouble. ‖次の着陸予定地はホノルルだ The next *scheduled stop* is Honolulu.

☛ 軟着陸, 無着陸 (→見出語)

チャコール charcoal

‖チャコールグレー charcoal gray.

ちゃちな shoddy (見せかけだけの), cheap (安っぽい); flimsy (薄っぺらな, もろい) ▶ちゃちな家具 *shoddy* furniture ‖ちゃちな宝石箱 a *cheap* jewelry box ‖そんなちゃちな考えは捨てろよ Discard such a *flimsy* [*half-baked*] idea.

ちゃちゃ 茶々 ▶人が真面目な話をしているときに横から茶々を入れないで Don't *cut* [*butt*] *in with sarcastic remarks* when I'm talking seriously.

ちゃっかり ▶弟はちゃっかりしている My (younger) brother *is shrewd*. ‖彼はわが家にちゃっかり3日間も泊まった He *cleverly* managed to freeload on us for three days. (➤ freeload は「居候する」).

チャック a zipper, a fly (➤ 後者は「チャック[ボタン]隠し」の意だが, 前者と同義で用いることも多い) ▶(ズボンの)チャックが開いているよ Your *zipper* is open [down].／Your *fly* is open [down]. ‖チャックを上げなさい Pull up your *zipper* [*fly*].／Zip up your *fly*.

ちゃづけ 茶漬け *chazuke*

日本紹介 ✉ **茶漬けはお茶漬けともいい, 茶わんに盛ったご飯に熱い緑茶をたっぷりと掛けたものです. ご飯の上に載せる材料によって, サケを載せたものはサケ茶漬け, のりを載せたものはのり茶漬けなどと呼びます** *Chazuke*, or *ochazuke*, is a bowl of rice over which ample hot green tea has been poured. There are several varieties of *chazuke* depending on the additional ingredients used. These include '*sake-chazuke*' with salted salmon, and '*nori-chazuke*' with *nori* (dried pressed laver).

ちゃっこう 着工 ▶新校舎の工事は1月に着工し, 12月に完成した The construction of our new school building *was started* in January and completed in December.

チャット a chat 一動 チャットする chat ▶ネットのチャットに参加する participate in an online *chat* ‖ネットで友人とチャットする *chat* online with friends.

‖チャットルーム a chat room.

ちゃのま 茶の間 a living room; 《米》a family room (家族団らんの間) ▶そのコメディアンは茶の間の人気者です That comedian is *a popular TV star*.

ちゃのゆ 茶の湯 ▶茶の湯は茶道の別名である *Chanoyu* is another name for *sado*, the Japanese tea ceremony. →茶道.

ちゃば 茶葉 tea leaf ▶茶葉占いをする read the *tea leaves*.

ちゃばしら 茶柱 ▶ねえ見て! 茶柱が立ってる. きっといいことがあるわ Oh, look! There's a *stem* floating upright in my tea. Something wonderful is bound to happen. (➤ この場合は日本的な考え方だが, 英米には茶の葉が浮くと来客があるという俗信がある).

ちゃぱつ 茶髪 brown hair ▶茶髪の若者 a young man [woman] with *dyed brown hair*.

ちゃばん 茶番 a farce (茶番劇) ▶もし当選者が初めからわかっているとしたら選挙は茶番だ The election will be *a farce* if the outcome is a foregone conclusion. (➤ foregone conclusion は「初めからわかっていた結論」の意).

ちゃぶだい 卓袱台 a *chabudai*; a small round dining table that often has collapsible legs [has legs that can fold up] (➤ 説明的な訳).

チャペル a chapel (礼拝堂; 《英》ではプロテスタントの教会をいうことが多い).

チャボ 《鳥》a Japanese bantam.

ちやほや ▶彼女は一人娘でちやほやされて(＝甘やかされて)育った Her parents *pampered* her as she was an only child. ／She was a *pampered* only child. ‖日本に住んでいる多くの西洋人はちやほやされることを望んでいない Many Westerners living in Japan don't want to *be made much of*.

ちゃめ 茶目 ▶佳代はちゃめっ気たっぷりだった Kayo behaved in a *very mischievous* manner. ‖まあ, あなたっておちゃめね! Why, what a *mischievous* [*playful*] girl you are!

ちゃら ▶借金をちゃらにする *write off* a debt (➤「棒引きにする」の意).

ちゃらちゃら **1**【音】▶彼はポケットの中で硬貨をチャラチャラ鳴らした He *jingled* the coins in his pocket. **2**【態度・服装】▶ちゃらちゃらした服装の若者 a young man [woman] *wearing flashy* [*loud*] *clothes* ‖ ちゃらちゃらした格好で with a *flashy* appearance ‖ 彼はちゃらちゃらした嫌なやつだ He's a disgusting, *affected* guy.

ちゃらんぽらん ▶ちゃらんぽらんな仕事をする男 a man who does *sloppy* work ／a *sloppy* worker ‖ あきらは頭はいいが少しちゃらんぽらんなところがある Akira is smart, but half of what he says can't be taken seriously.

チャリティー **charity** ▶チャリティーコンサート a *charity* concert ‖ チャリティーショー a *charity* show.

ちゃりん ▶小銭がチャリンと床に落ちた A coin fell to the floor *with a clink*.

チャレンジ a **challenge**（挑戦） →挑戦 ▶K大にチャレンジする *try to get into* K University ‖ 来年はダイビングにチャレンジしようと思う I think I'll *try* (*my hand at*) [*take up*] scuba diving next year. ‖ 誰からのチャレンジだって受けてやる I'll take up the *challenge* from anyone. ‖ 彼はチャレンジ精神の塊だ *Challenge is* his *middle name*. (➤「チャレンジが彼のミドルネームだ」が原義で，彼を例えば，John Challenge Smith と呼んでもおかしくないほどの大きな特徴の意) ‖ 今度の仕事はチャレンジしがいのある仕事だ My new job is very *challenging*. ／My new job *challenges* me.

危ないカタカナ語✹ チャレンジ
1 日本語の「チャレンジ」は人が人に挑戦する場合にも，人が(難しい)事に挑戦する場合にも用いるが，視点はいずれも挑戦者にある．これに対して英語の challenge は難事が挑戦者に，あるいは強い相手が挑戦者にかける「かかってこい」という挑発をいう．したがって (×) I challenge my new job. とするのは誤り．
2 日本語の「チャレンジする」には try (one's hand at) を使ったほうが適切な場合が多い．例えば，「山登りにチャレンジする」は try to climb the mountain または try one's hand at mountain climbing でよい．「チャレンジ精神が旺盛だ」は be full of fight とか be enterprising という．

ちゃわん 茶碗 a **rice bowl**（ご飯用の）; a **teacup**（湯飲み） ▶ご飯はいつも茶わんに１膳です I always have *one bowl* of rice at each meal.
✉ **日本の家庭では各人自分の茶わんと箸を持っています** In a Japanese family, each person has his or her own *rice bowl* and chopsticks.

ちゃわんむし 茶碗蒸し a ***chawan-mushi***; a steamed egg custard containing various ingredients served in a teacup-like container (➤ 説明的な訳).

-ちゃん

《解説》愛称について
(1)「-ちゃん」は日本語独特の接尾辞なので -chan をそのまま使う．
(2) 英語の名前には慣用的な愛称があり，日本語の「-ちゃん」に相当する．例えば Thomas は Tom(my) に，James は Jim(my) に，Elizabeth は Betty, Bess(ie), Liz(zie) になる．
(3)「お父ちゃん」,「お母ちゃん」,「おじいちゃん」,「おばあちゃん」はそれぞれ Dad(dy), Mom(my), Grandpa [Granddad], Grandma [Grannie] という．
(4)「お兄ちゃん」,「お姉ちゃん」の場合は本人の名または愛称を使う．

▶一郎ちゃん，もう学校へ行く時間よ！Ichiro-*chan*, it's time to go to school!

ちゃんこなべ ちゃんこ鍋 a ***chankonabe***; a hot-pot dish containing vegetables, fish, meat, and other ingredients, mainly eaten by sumo wrestlers to gain weight (➤ 説明的な訳).

チャンス 1【機会】 a **chance**, an **opportunity** /ɑ̀ːpəʳtjúːnəṭi/

語法 (1) **chance** は偶然性を強調する場合，あるいは形式ばらない会話や書きことば(例えば親しい者への手紙)などでよく用いられる．
(2) **opportunity** は都合のよさを強調する場合，あるいは chance の堅い語として改まった会話や書きことばなどでよく用いられる．

▶チャンスをつかむ seize *a chance* [*opportunity*] ‖ 絶好のチャンス a golden *opportunity* ‖ 私たちはその後互いに会うチャンスが無かった After that, we had no *chance* [*opportunity*] to see each other. ‖ もしチャンスがあればもう一度バリ島へ行ってみたい If I have the *chance*, I would like to visit Bali again. ‖ 外国人と話をするチャンスはほとんど無い I have few *chances* to talk with foreigners. ‖ もう一度チャンスをください Please give me another [one more] *chance*. ‖ 今がチャンスだ Now is my [our] *chance*. ‖ このチャンスを逃すな Don't miss this *opportunity*. ‖ チャンスは一度だけだ You only get *one shot*. (➤ one shot は「１回のチャンス」の意).
2【スポーツで】 a **chance** ▶得点のチャンス *a chance to score* ‖ 中日は２度の絶好の得点チャンスをダブルプレーで逃した The Dragons let two perfect *scoring chances* slip by hitting into double plays each time. **《参考》** chance は「守備側のチャンス(刺殺・捕殺の機会)」の意でもあるので，攻撃側のチャンスは scoring chance (得点のチャンス)とする．

ちゃんちゃらおかしい ▶ちゃんちゃらおかしいよ That's *complete nonsense*! ／How *ridiculous*! ‖ あいつが生徒会長だって！ちゃんちゃらおかしいよ *He* is president of the student council? *You're kidding* (*me*) [*You're joking*]! (➤ He を強く発音する).

ちゃんちゃんこ a ***chanchanko***; a **padded winter vest**.

ちゃんと 1【きちんと】 **properly**（正しく）; **exactly**（正確に）; **regularly**（定期的に） ▶ちゃんとした食事 a *proper* meal ‖ あなた，ちゃんと顔を洗ったの？Did you wash your face *properly*? ‖ 良雄，ちゃんと勉強してる？Yoshio, are you studying *hard*? ‖ 言ったとおりにちゃんとしなさい Do *just* [*exactly*] as I told you. ‖ きみの言ったことはちゃんと覚えているよ I remember *exactly* what you said. ‖ 家賃はちゃんと払っています I pay my rent *regularly* [*on time*].
▶言いたいことがあったらちゃんと言いなさい If you have anything to say, *speak up* [*say it*]! ‖ ちゃんと座りなさい Sit up *straight*. ‖ 靴はちゃんとそろえて置きなさい *Neatly* arrange your shoes side by side. ‖ 約束，ちゃんと守ってよ *Be sure* to keep your promise. ‖ ちゃんとした服装をしていないと入れないレストランもある Some restaurants won't let you in if you are not dressed *properly*. (properly の代わりに decently を用いると「社会通念から見て非難されるところがない」という点を強調することになる) ‖ あの会社の経営状態はちゃんとしている That company *is in good shape*.
2【世間的に見てしっかりしている】 ▶ちゃんとした人たち *decent* people(➤「犯罪・売春などに無関係の」とい

う含みがある) ‖ 彼女はちゃんとした家庭に育った She grew up in a *respectable* family. (➤ respectable は「まともな, 卑しからぬ」) ‖ 兄はちゃんとした会社に就職した My brother got a job in a *reputable* company. (➤ reputable は「評判のいい」) ‖ 彼女のこと, ちゃんとしなさいよ *Do the decent thing* by her. (➤ 相手の女性が妊娠した場合などに社会的責任を取りなさいという意味で, やや古風な言い方).

チャンネル a **channel** /tʃǽnl/ ▶ (テレビの)**チャンネル**を1に替える change [turn] to *Channel* 1 (➤ channel one と読む) ‖ その番組は毎週金曜日午後9時から5**チャンネル**で放送している The program is televised *on Channel* 5 at 9 p.m. every Friday. ‖ そのドラマは何**チャンネル**でやっていますか *What channel* is the drama on? ‖ ぼくたちはいつも**チャンネル争い**をしている (=どの番組を見るかで争う) We always have an *argument over which program to watch*.

ちゃんばら a **sword** /sɔːʳd/ **fight** ▶**ちゃんばらごっこ**をする play at *sword fighting*.

‖**ちゃんばら映画** a samurai movie (with plenty of sword fights).

チャンピオン a **champion**, 《インフォーマル》 a **champ**; **championship** (選手権) ▶ボクシング [テニス] の**チャンピオン** a boxing [tennis] *champion* ‖ フライ級の**チャンピオン**になる become the flyweight *champion* / win the flyweight *championship*.

‖**チャンピオンベルト** a championship belt ‖ **世界チャンピオン** the world champion.

ちゃんぽん 1 【**交ぜること**】 ▶友だちの恵理はお父さんがイギリス人なので, 日本語と英語を**ちゃんぽん**に話す My friend Eri, whose father is British, speaks in *a mixture of* Japanese and English. ‖ 父はよく日本酒とウイスキーを**ちゃんぽん**に飲んでいます My father often drinks sake and whiskey *at the same time*.

2 【**麺料理**】 ***chanpon***; a Chinese noodle dish topped with stir-fried vegetables, pork and seafood (➤ 説明的な訳).

ちゆ 治癒する **cure** (病気が); **heal** (けがが) ▶**治癒**できない病気 an *incurable* disease / a disease *that cannot be cured* ‖ 傷が**治癒した** The wound *healed*. ‖ この病気は自然に**治癒する**のを待つしかない There is nothing for you to do but let the illness *cure* itself.

[1]**ちゅう 宙** **the air** ▶外へ出ると大きな飛行船が**宙**に浮いていた When I went outdoors, I saw a big airship floating *in the air*. ‖ 新郎新婦の周りでは紙吹雪が**宙**に舞っていた Confetti *was swirling through the air* over the bride and groom.

▶ 《慣用表現》 その問題は野党の審議拒否のために**宙に浮いたままだ** Because of the boycott by the opposition party, the question remains *up in the air*.

[2]**ちゅう 注** a **note** ▶本に**注**をつける add *notes* to a book ‖ この本はたくさん**注**がついている This book has copious *notes*.

‖**脚注** a footnote.

[3]**ちゅう 中** **the average** (平均) ▶私の成績はクラスでは**中**の上 [下] です I am above [below] *the average* in our class. ‖ 彼の学力は**中**ぐらいだ He is *average* in academic ability. ‖ わが家は**中の上**といったところだ My family is (in the) *upper-middle* class.

[4]**ちゅう 駐** ▶**駐**ロンドン特派員 a London (*-based*) correspondent.

[5]**ちゅう** a **kiss** ▶ママのほっぺに**ちゅう**して *Give* me *a kiss* on the cheek. ‖ パパはママのほっぺに**ちゅう**した Dad *pecked* Mom on the cheek. (➤ peck は「(人の)頬に軽くキスをする」の意のインフォーマルな語).

-ちゅう **-中** **1** 【**…の中**】 ▶木は空気**中**の酸素を増やしてくれる Trees help increase the amount of oxygen *in the air*. ‖ 100メートル走の参加者は8人**中**6人が黒人選手だ Six *out of* eight entries for the 100-meter dash are black athletes. ‖ 三浦君は**エリート中のエリート**だ Miura is *a member of the elite of the elite* [*the cream of the crop*].

2 【**…の間**】 **during, while**; **in** (…のうちに) ▶午前**中**に *in* the morning ‖ 戦時**中** *in* wartime / *during* the war ‖ **戦時中の配給** *wartime* rationing ‖ 夏休み**中**に大いにテニスをした I played tennis a lot *during* my summer vacation. ‖ 春休み**中**アルバイトをした I worked part-time *during* [*all through*] the spring vacation. (➤ all through は「…の間ずっと」の意) ‖ 妻の留守**中**は彼が子供の面倒を見た *While* his wife was away, he took care of the children. ‖ レポートは今週**中**に提出すること Turn in your papers *by the end of this week*. / Turn in your papers (*sometime*) *this week*. (⚠ within this week [month / year] などとは通例いわない).

3 【**…の最中**】 ▶ 《掲示》 **作業中** Road Construction Ahead (➤「前方道路工事中」) ‖ 《掲示》 **手術中** Operation in Progress ‖ 《掲示》 **放送中** On (the) Air ‖ 国会は**会期中**だ The Diet is *in session*. ‖ ストライキは**決行中**だ The strike *is* still *on*. ‖ 課長はただ今**会議中** [**電話中**] です The section chief is *in a meeting* [*on the phone*] now. ‖ 道路は**工事中**です The road is *under construction* [*under repair*]. (➤ 後者は「修復中」) ‖ 私たちの学校, 今**試験中**なんだ Our school *is having exams* now. ‖ **授業中**は静かにしなさい Be quiet *during* [*in*] class. ‖ 鈴木先生は今**授業中**です Mr. Suzuki *is teaching* [*in class*] now. ‖ 彼女たちは**食事中**だ They *are at* (*the*) *table*. (➤ the を省くのは主に 《英》) ‖ **対話** 「内線260をお願いします」「ただいまお話し中です」 "Extension 260, please." "(Sorry,) *the line is busy* [《英》 *is engaged*] now."

[1]**ちゅうい 注意**

訳語メニュー
精神を集中させること →attention **1**
用心 →care **2**
忠告 →advice **3**

1 【**精神を集中させること**】 **attention** ━動 **注意する** **pay attention** 《to》

【**文型**】
A に注意する, 注意を払う
pay attention to A
take notice of A

解説 (1)「関心を向け注意を払う」の意では **pay attention to** や **take notice of** が使われる. 後者は take no [little] notice of (全く [ほとんど] 注意を払わない) のように否定的に使うことが多い.
(2)「気を配って用心する」の意では take care of, be careful を使う. →**気をつける**.

▶英語を話すときはイントネーションに**注意しなさい** *Pay attention to* intonation when you speak English. ‖ 三塁のランナーには**十分注意しろよ** *Pay close atten-*

tion to [*Keep your eyes on*] the runner at third. ‖公報にあまり注意を払わない人が多い Many people *pay little attention to* [*take little notice of*] official bulletins. ‖小さな子供は注意力の続く時間が短い Young children have a short *attention* span. ▶手品師は観客の注意をそらすためにたばこに火をつけた The magician lit a cigarette to *divert* the audience's *attention.* ‖子供はみんなの注意を引こうとわざと騒いでみせることがある Children often make a fuss just to *get* [*attract*] *attention.* ‖AFN のニュースはよく注意していないと聞き取れない You can't understand the AFN news unless you listen to it *carefully* [*attentively*]. ‖《運転中に》ガソリンがあと少ししか無いよ. スタンドに注意してて We're low on gas. *Look out for* a gas station. (➤ look out for は「…を見落とさないようによく見ている」).

2【用心】care 一動 注意する take care《of》, **be careful**《of, to do》▶アスリートたちは特に健康には注意している Athletes *take* especially *good care of* their health [themselves]. (➤ take care of oneself で「体に気をつける」)／Athletes *are* especially *careful* about keeping in good health. ‖パスポートを無くさないように注意しなさい *Be careful* not to lose your passport. ‖このグラスの取り扱いにはもっと注意してくれないと困ります You have to *be more careful in* handling these glasses. ‖注意が足りないからけがをしたのだ You got hurt because you *weren't careful enough* [*paying enough attention*]. ‖《掲示》すり[雪崩]に注意 *Beware of* pickpockets [avalanches].

3【忠告】(a **piece of**) **advice** /ədváɪs/ ; a **rule** (規則) **一動 注意する warn** /wɔːʳn/ +目, **caution** +目 (警告する) ; **reprove** +目 (たしなめる)
▶先生の注意をよく聞きなさい Listen to your teacher's *advice.* ‖きみたちにひと言注意しておきます Let me *give* you *a piece of advice.* ‖《受験会場で》受験上の注意事項をよく読んでください (Please) read the exam *instructions* carefully. ‖試験官は受験生にカンニングをしないように注意した The supervisor *warned* [*cautioned*] the examinees not to cheat during the exam. ‖先生はその生徒の遅刻を注意した The teacher *reproved* the student for being late. ‖長電話をしないようにと注意された I *was told* not to talk long on the phone. ‖あんたはこれだけ注意されてもまだわからないの? I'*ve reminded* [*warned*] you hundreds of times and you still don't understand?

‖**注意書き** a note (注, 注釈) ; a cautionary statement, directions (商品についている文章 ; Caution または Warning で始まることが多い) ‖**注意欠陥[欠如]・多動性障害** attention deficit hyperactivity disorder (ADHD) ‖**注意報** a warning, an advisory ‖**安全注意事項** a safety precaution.

☛ 要注意 (→見出語)

²ちゅうい 中尉 a **lieutenant** /luːténənt/ (英陸軍) ; a **first lieutenant** (米陸[空]軍・海兵隊) ; a **sublieutenant** (英海軍) ; a **flying officer** (英空軍).

ちゅういぶかい 注意深い careful (用心深い) ; **attentive** (注意を払って見聞きする) ▶注意深いドライバー a *careful* driver ‖彼女は何をするにも実に注意深い She *is* very *careful* in everything she does. ‖誰もが彼女の話を注意深く聞いた Everybody listened *carefully* [*attentively*] to her. ‖この仕事をするには注意深くなくてはならない This work requires *careful attention.*

チューインガム (chewing) gum ▶彼は歯を磨く代わりにチューインガムをかんでいる He *chews gum* instead of brushing his teeth.

ちゅうおう 中央 the center [《英》 centre], the middle

一形 中央の central, middle

語法 (1)円や球体の場合, **center** は円周上のすべての点から等距離にある中心点を, **middle** は中心点とその周辺を含んだ「中心部, 中ほど」を指す. (2)部屋や地域についていう場合は center と middle はしばしば同義に用いられる.

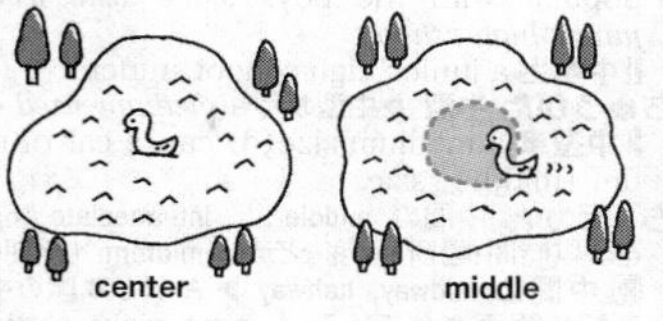

▶公園の中央に野外音楽堂がある There is an open-air concert stage in *the center* of the park. ‖体育館の中央に卓球台が置かれた A ping-pong table was placed in *the center* [*middle*] of the gymnasium. ‖大雪山は北海道のほぼ中央に位置する Mount Daisetsu is located almost in *the center* of Hokkaido. ‖私立大学数校が郊外から市の中央部に移転した Several private universities moved from the suburbs to *the heart* of the city. (➤ the heart は「中心, 真ん中」).

‖**中央アジア** Central Asia ‖**中央アメリカ** Central America ‖**中央委員会** a central committee ‖**中央気象台** the Central Meteorological /miːt̬iərəlάːdʒɪkəl/ Observatory ‖**中央銀行** a central bank ‖**中央集権** centralization (of power) ‖**中央政府** the central government ‖**中央広場** a central square [plaza] ‖**中央分離帯**《米》a median strip, 《英》a central reservation [reserve] ‖**中央郵便局** the Central Post Office.

ちゅうか 中華 ‖**中華街** (a) Chinatown ‖**中華人民共和国** the People's Republic of China (→中国) ‖**中華そば** Chinese noodles (with soup) ‖**中華鍋** a wok ‖**中華料理** Chinese food [dishes] ‖**中華料理店** a Chinese restaurant.

ちゅうかい 仲介する mediate /míːdieɪt/ ▶労使を仲介する *mediate* between labor and management ‖彼の仲介でその車を買った I bought the car *through* him.

ちゅうがえり 宙返り a **somersault** /sʌ́məʳsɔːlt/ (とんぼ返り) ; a **loop-the-loop** (宙返り飛行) ▶彼は子供たちの目の前で宙返りをして, 拍手喝采を浴びた He *did* [*turned*] *a somersault* in front of the children and received their enthusiastic applause. ‖飛行機は宙返りをした The plane *made a roll* [*a loop*] *in midair.* (➤ roll は側面宙返り, loop は前方宙返り).

‖**後(方)宙返り** a back(ward) flip [somersault] ‖**前(方)宙返り** a front flip [somersault].

ちゅうかく 中核 the nucleus /njúːkliəs/ ▶あと10年もすれば, きみたちがわが社の中核となるだろう In about ten years, your group will probably become *the*

ち

nucleus [*center*] of our company.

ちゅうがく 中学 a **junior high school**, a **lower secondary school** (➤後者は日本での正式英語名)；《米》a **middle school**,《英》a **secondary school** (➤後者は中学・高校共通) ▶息子は私立［公立］中学校に通っている My son goes to *a private* [*public*] *junior high school*. ‖ 謙は中学3年生だ Ken is in the third year of *junior high school*. ／Ken is in the ninth grade. (➤《米》では小学校から中学まで, 時には高校まで学年を通して数える) ‖ たけしは中学からの友だちだ Takeshi has been my friend *since junior high* (*school*). ‖ 彼女は中学時代男の子にとても人気があった She was very popular with the boys *while* (*she was*) *in junior high school*.

‖中学生 a junior high school student.

ちゅうがた 中型 ▶中型の犬 a *medium-sized* dog.

‖中型車 a medium-size(d) car, a car of medium [middle] size.

ちゅうかん 中間の **middle**；**intermediate** /ìnṭəʳmí:diət/ (時間・場所・程度などが)；**midterm** (学期の) ━副 **中間に** **midway**, **halfway** ▶A駅とB駅の中間に新駅が計画されている A new train station is planned *midway between* Stations A and B. ‖ 我々の車はそのつり橋の中間地点に差しかかった Our car was approaching *the midway* [*halfway*] *point* of the suspension bridge.

▶中間的な意見 a *moderate* opinion ‖ ぼくはきみと彼女の中間の立場をとる My stance is *midway* between yours and hers. ‖ 英語の中間試験はとても難しかった The English *midterm* [The *midterm* (*exam*) in English] was very hard. ‖ 中間色の内装を施された部屋 a room with a decor done in *neutral colors* ‖ 私は中間色が好きだ I like *neutral colors*. (➤neutral color は「くすんだやわらかい色」のことで,「2色の中間の色」なら intermediate color).

‖中間管理職 the middle management(➤集合的にその地位の人々をいうが, 1人を指す場合, He [She] is in middle management. といってもよい) ‖ 中間子《物理学》a meson /mí:zɑ:n/ ‖ 中間地点 the halfway point, a midpoint ‖ 中間報告［発表］an interim report [announcement].

[1]**ちゅうき 中期** **the middle** (**period**) ▶江戸中期に建てられた民家 a house built in *the middle* of the Edo period.

[2]**ちゅうき 注記** an **annotation** (短い説明)；a **note** (メモ書き).

ちゅうぎ 忠義 (**feudal**) **loyalty** ▶日曜出勤までして会社に忠義を尽くすことはないよ You don't have to *be* so *loyal* to your company that you work even on Sundays.

ちゅうきゅう 中級の **intermediate** /ìnṭəʳmí:diət/ ▶中級英語 *intermediate* English ‖ 中級コース the *intermediate* course ‖ クラスは初級・中級・上級と, 生徒の進度によって分けられる Students are assigned to elementary, *intermediate*, or advanced classes according to their proficiency level.

ちゅうきょり 中距離の **medium-range**

‖中距離ミサイル a medium-range missile.

ちゅうきんとう 中近東 **the Middle East**, **the Mideast**.

ちゅうくう 中空 a **hollow** (空洞)；**midair** (空中).

ちゅうけい 中継 (a) **relay** /rí:leɪ/ (中継放送)；(a) **hookup** (放送局間の, 放送網を結んでの) ▶ハワイからの中継 *a relay* from Hawaii ‖ 野球の中継放送 the *broadcast relay* of a baseball game ‖ そのサッカーの試合は全国ネットでテレビ中継された The soccer game *was televised* [*aired*] nationwide. ‖ オリンピックの開会式は全世界へ衛星生中継された The opening ceremony of the Olympic Games *was broadcast*(*ed*) *live* via satellite to all the countries of the world. ‖中継局 a relay station ‖ 中継車 an outside broadcast van ‖ 全国中継 a nationwide hook-up.

[1]**ちゅうけん 中堅** ▶彼は会社の中堅として将来を期待されている He's a *mid-level employee* with a promising future. ‖ わが社は印刷業界では中堅どころだ We are a *medium-size* [*midsize*] printing company.

‖中堅手 a center fielder(→センター).

[2]**ちゅうけん 忠犬** a **faithful dog**.

ちゅうげん 中元 a ***chugen***

日本紹介 ✉ **中元はお中元ともいい, 7月初めから中旬にかけて, 日頃お世話になっている人に贈る贈り物です** A *chugen* or an *ochugen* is a gift sent from early to mid July to someone to whom you have a social obligation or owe a favor. →歳暮.

‖中元大売り出し the special *chugen* sale, the midyear gift sale.

ちゅうこ 中古の **used**, **secondhand** (➤《米》では前者が好まれる) ▶中古の自転車 a *used* [*secondhand*] bicycle ‖ 私はポルシェを中古で買った I bought a Porche *secondhand*. (➤この secondhand は副詞用法；used にはこの用法はない) ‖ 中古住宅を買おうと思っている We are [I am] looking to buy an *older* [*existing*] home.

‖中古車 a used [secondhand, previously-owned] car(➤previously-owned は広告に多い) ‖ 中古品 a used article ‖ 中古品店 a secondhand store [shop].

ちゅうこう 中興 ‖中興の祖 a restorer.

ちゅうこういっかんきょういく 中高一貫教育 **unified lower and upper secondary school education**.

ちゅうこうせい 中高生 **junior and senior high school students**.

ちゅうこうねん 中高年 **people of middle and advanced age, the middle-aged and the elderly**. →中年.

ちゅうこく 忠告 (**a piece of**) **advice** /ədváɪs/ (➤こうしたらどう, という助言；数えられない名詞なので「1つの忠告」を an advice とはしない)；a **warning** (有害・危険なことに用心・警戒を促したり, 悪いことをやめさせるためのことば, 警告). ━動 **忠告する** **advise** /ədváɪz/ +目；**warn** +目 ▶きみにひと言忠告しておく Let me give you *a piece of advice*. ‖ 彼は友人の忠告に逆らって高校をやめてしまった He left high school against his friend's *advice*. (「忠告に従って」なら on his friend's advice とする) ‖ あいつは人の忠告を聞くようなやつじゃない He's not the type to *take advice from anybody*. ／He won't *listen to anybody's advice*. ‖ 彼の忠告に従っていれば事故は避けられたかもしれない If I had listened to his *warning*, I might have avoided the accident.

【文型】
人(A)に…するよう忠告する
advise A **to** do

▶今のうちに体を鍛えておけと兄に忠告された My (older) brother *advised* me *to* build up my body while I could [while I had the time]. ‖ 私は彼にたばこな

んかやるなと忠告した I *advised* him *not to* take up smoking. ／I *advised* him *against* taking up smoking. (➤ take up ... は「…を始める」の意).

ちゅうごく 中国 1【国名】**China** (➤正式名は the People's Republic of China)
‖**中国学** Sinology ‖**中国学者** a Sinologist (➤「中国問題研究家」の意でもある) ‖**中国語** Chinese, the Chinese language ; Mandarin /mǽndərɪn/ (標準中国語) ‖**中国人** a Chinese (man ／woman ／person) [複 Chinese (people)].
2【日本の中国地方】**the Chugoku district.**

ちゅうごし 中腰 ▶長い間中腰の姿勢でいると疲れる Keeping a *half-crouched* [*half-sitting*] position for a long time will make you tired.

ちゅうさ 中佐 a **lieutenant** /luːténənt/ **colonel** (陸軍・米空軍) ; a **wing commander** (英空軍) ; a **commander** (海軍・米沿岸警備隊).

ちゅうざ 中座 ▶お客さんが挨拶している最中に中座するのは失礼だ It is rude to *leave the room* before the guest speaker finishes his [her] speech.

ちゅうさい 仲裁 **arbitration** 一動 **仲裁する arbitrate** /ɑ́ːʳbɪtreɪt/ (+目) ▶紛争を仲裁する *arbitrate* a dispute ‖先生が(2人の)けんかの仲裁をした The teacher *arbitrated* (between the two in) their quarrel. →**調停**.

ちゅうざい 駐在 ▶彼は特派員としてロンドンに駐在している He *is stationed* in London as a correspondent. ‖《海外で自己紹介して》当地駐在員の岡本です I'm Okamoto and I *am working in our office here*.
‖**駐在所** a *chuzaisho* ; a (residential) police substation ‖**海外駐在員** an overseas worker.

ちゅうさんかいきゅう 中産階級 **the middle class** (➤時に複数形).

1**ちゅうし 中止** **stoppage** (停止) ; **cancellation** (予定行事などの) ; **suspension** (一時的な) 一動 **中止する stop** +目, **cancel** +目, **suspend** +目 ; **abort** +目 (任務・計画を) ▶作業の中止 a work *stoppage* ‖予定されていたテレビ放送の中止 the *cancellation* of a scheduled TV broadcast ‖試合は雨のため中止になった The game *was stopped* [*was called off*] because of rain. ／The game was rained out. ‖コンサートは歌手の病気のため中止になった The concert *was canceled* because the singer fell ill. ‖工事は豪雪のため一時中止された The construction work *was suspended* temporarily because of heavy snow. ‖点火15秒前に発射は中止された The launch *was aborted* 15 seconds before ignition.
▶彼女は病に倒れ, 5年間続けてきた研究を中止せざるをえなくなった She fell ill and had to *discontinue* the research she had been working on for the past five years. (➤ discontinue は「中断する」) ‖《掲示》使用中止 Out of Use ／Out of Order (壊れているとき).

2**ちゅうし 注視する** **stare** 《at》 ▶刑事は車内の不審な男を注視した The detective *closely watched* [*kept a close eye on*] a suspicious man on the train.

ちゅうじえん 中耳炎 (an) **inflammation of the middle ear, otitis** /oʊtáɪṭəs/ **media** (➤ inflammation は「炎症」. 後者は医学用語).

ちゅうじく 中軸の **key**
‖**中軸打者** a key batter [hitter].

ちゅうじつ 忠実な **faithful** (誓いをよく守る) ; **loyal** (忠誠心のある) ▶犬は飼い主に忠実だ Dogs *are faithful* [*loyal*] *to* their masters. ‖詩の訳は原文に忠実なだけではおもしろくない In the translation of poetry, being *faithful* to the original is not enough. ‖私は松本氏の忠告を忠実に守った I followed Mr. Matsumoto's advice *faithfully*. ‖その似顔絵はモデルに忠実に描かれている The portrait is (painted) *true to life*.

1**ちゅうしゃ 注射** an **injection,** 《インフォーマル》 a **shot** ▶診療所で注射をしてもらう get *an injection* [*a shot*] at the clinic ‖医者は私にペニシリンの注射をした The doctor *gave* me a penicillin *injection* [*shot*]. ‖きょう学校でインフルエンザの予防注射をした(=してもらった) We had *an inoculation* [*a vaccination*] against the flu at school today.
‖**注射器** a syringe /sɪríndʒ/ ‖**静脈注射** an intravenous /ìntrəvíːnəs/ injection.

2**ちゅうしゃ 駐車** **parking** 一動 **駐車する park** ▶ここは駐車できますか Can I *park* here? ‖この道路は両側とも駐車禁止だ *Parking is prohibited* along both sides of this road. ‖駐車違反車は(レッカー車で)移動される *Illegally-parked cars* will be towed. ‖あと30台駐車する余地がある There is enough *parking space* for 30 more cars. ‖車で行こうと思っていますが, 駐車する所はどうなっていますか I'm planning to drive. How's *the parking*? ‖《掲示》駐車禁止 No Parking (➤「駐車禁止区域」は no-parking area).
‖**駐車違反** a parking violation ‖**駐車許可証** a parking permit ‖**駐車券** a parking lot ticket ‖**駐車場** 《米》 a parking lot, 《英また》 a car park ‖**駐車料金** a parking charge ‖**縦列** [**平行**] **駐車** parallel parking ‖**二重駐車** double-parking (➤「二重駐車する」は double-park).

ちゅうしゃく 注釈 (an) **annotation** ; a **note** (注) ▶本に注釈をつける *annotate* a book ‖注釈つきのシェークスピアのテキスト an *annotated* edition of Shakespeare's works.

ちゅうしゅう 中秋・仲秋
‖**中秋の名月** the [a] harvest moon.

ちゅうしゅつ 抽出 **extraction** ; (an) **extract** (抽出物) ; **sampling** (見本の抽出) 一動 **抽出する extract** +目 ; **sample** +目 ▶ササの葉から抽出したエキスの入った健康ドリンク a health drink that contains essence *extracted* from bamboo leaves [contains bamboo leaf *extract*].
▶名簿から無作為に100人を抽出する *choose* the names of 100 people from the list *by random sampling*.

ちゅうじゅん 中旬 ▶その歌手は11月中旬に来日する The singer will visit Japan *in* [*around*] *the middle of* November [*in mid*-November]. (●「中頃」の意. 英語では1か月を10日ずつに分ける表現は一般的でない).

1**ちゅうしょう 中傷** (a) **slander,** (a) **libel** /láɪbəl/ 一動 **中傷する slander** +目 《参考》法律的には slander は口頭による中傷, libel は文書による中傷をいうが, 一般には区別なく用いられる ▶人を中傷するようなうわさ a *slanderous* rumor ‖人を中傷する(匿名の)手紙 a *poison-pen* letter ‖その報道はひどい中傷だ That report is a cruel *slander* [*libel*].
‖**中傷合戦** a mudslinging match.

2**ちゅうしょう 抽象** **abstraction** 一形 **抽象的な abstract** /æbstrǽkt/ ▶きみの論文は抽象的すぎて説得力に欠ける Your thesis is too *abstract* to be persuasive.
‖**抽象画** an abstract painting, an abstract ‖《文

ち

法》**抽象名詞** an abstract noun.

ちゅうじょう 中将 a **lieutenant** /luːténənt/ **general**(陸軍・米空軍・米海兵隊)；a **vice admiral**(海軍)；an **air marshal**(英空軍).

ちゅうしょうきぎょう 中小企業 small and medium-size(d) enterprises［**businesses**］▶**中小企業**の経営者 an employer of *a small or medium-size(d) business* ‖この不況下うちのような**中小企業**は苦しい *Small and medium-sized companies* like ours are having a hard time in this recession.(🏺日本語では「うちは中小企業です」といえるが, 英語では We're a small［medium-sized］business. と, 小か中かをはっきりいうしかない).

ち

ちゅうしょく 昼食 lunch ▶マクドナルドで**昼食**をとる have［eat］*lunch* at McDonald's ‖きょうは**昼食**にエビフライ定食とコーヒーを注文した I ordered the fried prawn set and coffee for *lunch* today. ‖きょうの**昼食**は抜きだった I skipped *lunch* today.

‖**昼食時間** lunchtime.

1**ちゅうしん 中心** **1**【**中 央**】**the center,**《英》**the centre**；**the heart**(中心部)；**the hub**(活動などの) ▶《数学》下の円の**中心**の座標を求めなさい Find the coordinates of *the center* of the circle below. ‖彼女の家は宇都宮市の**中心**に在る Her house is located in *the center*［*heart*］of Utsunomiya City. ‖私の会社は横浜の**中心**に在る My office is in *downtown* Yokohama.(➤ downtown は「商業の中心地, 市の中心地」の意) ‖私たちの住む町は城を**中心**に東西に広がっている Our town extends［spreads］to the east and west with the castle as its *center*. ‖世の中はおまえを**中心**に回ってるわけじゃないんだぞ！ You're not *the center* of the universe, you know!

▶**学生中心**の大学経営 *student-centered* college management ‖**男性中心の社会** a *male-dominated* society ‖**使用者中心**の和英辞典 a *user-friendly* Japanese-English dictionary ‖それは**輸出中心**の産業だ It is an *export-oriented* industry.(➤ -oriented は名詞に付けて,「…志向の」「…優先の」などの意) ‖この空港はアジアにおいて輸送の**中心**となるだろう This airport will be *a hub* of transportation in Asia.

‖**中心点**［**線**］the central point［line］.

2【**最も重要な部分・人**】**the center**；**the focus**(焦点) ▶**話題の中心** *the center*［*focus*］of a topic ／*the focus* of interest ‖グループの**中心人物** the *leader* of a group ‖この小説は島原の乱のことが**中心**になっている This novel *centers around*［*on*］the Shimabara Rebellion. ‖その町はかつて日本の**商業の中心地**だった The town was once *the commercial center* of Japan. ‖3年A組はクラス委員の雄二を**中心**によくまとまっている The 3-A class has come together very well *under* Yuji's *leadership* as a class representative.(🏺「リーダーシップのもとに」と考える) ‖彼女はそのプロジェクトで**中心的**な役割を果たした She played a *pivotal* role in the project.

2**ちゅうしん 衷心 the bottom of** one's **heart** ▶**衷心**より感謝いたします I'd like to express my *deepest*［*heartfelt*］gratitude.

3**ちゅうしん 忠臣** a **loyal retainer**［**subject**］.

ちゅうすいえん 虫垂炎 appendicitis /əpèndəsáɪtɪs/.

ちゅうすう 中枢 the center ▶その爆撃でコンピュータの**中枢**がやられた *The central operating system* of the computer was damaged in the bombing. ‖東京には政治や文化の**中枢機関**が集まっている *The central* political and cultural *institutions* are concentrated in Tokyo.

‖**中枢神経** the central nerves.

1**ちゅうせい 中世 the Middle Ages**(➤西洋史でほぼ西暦500〜1500年の期間) **一**形**中世の medieval** /mìːdiíːvəl/ ▶**中世の町**［**城**］a *medieval* town［castle］‖この寺院は**中世**に建てられた This cathedral was built in *the Middle Ages*.

2**ちゅうせい 中性の neutral** ▶男女の**中性化** *neutralization* of men and women.

‖**中性子** a neutron /njúːtrɑːn/ ‖**中性紙** acid-free paper ‖**中性子爆弾** a neutron bomb /bɑːm/ ‖**中性脂肪** a neutral lipid［fat］；《生化学・医学》a triglyceride. ‖**中性洗剤** a neutral detergent.

3**ちゅうせい 忠誠 loyalty**(個人的感情から発する)；**allegiance** /əlíːdʒəns/(義務感に基づく) ▶若き兵士たちは国家への**忠誠**を誓った The young soldiers pledged (their) *loyalty*［*allegiance*］to their country.

ちゅうせいだい 中生代 the Mesozoic /mèsəzóʊɪk/ (**era**).

ちゅうせきど 沖積土 alluvial soil.

ちゅうせつ 忠節 faithfulness.

ちゅうぜつ 中絶 **1**【**中止**】(an) **interruption**；**suspension**(一時中止) ▶計画を**中絶する** *suspend*［*abort*］a plan.

2【**妊娠の**】an **abortion** ▶**妊娠中絶をする** *have an abortion* ／*abort* a pregnancy(➤前者がふつう) ‖彼女は妊娠3か月で**中絶した** She *had an abortion* when she was three months pregnant.

ちゅうせん 抽選 (a) **drawing**(くじを引くこと)；a **draw**(1回1回のくじ引き)；a **lottery**(福引き) ▶宝くじ［福引き］の**抽選** a lottery［raffle］*draw* ‖**抽選**を行う hold *a drawing*［*lottery*］‖**抽選**でテレビを当てる win a TV set in *a lottery* ‖我々は**抽選**でキャプテンを決めた We *drew lots* to decide our captain. ／We decided our captain *by drawing lots*［*by lot*］.(➤ lot は「くじ」) ‖**抽選に当たった** I *drew a winning number*. ／I *won a raffle*［*lottery*］. ‖**抽選に外れた** I *drew a losing number*. ／I *drew a blank in the lottery*.

‖**抽選会** a raffle, a lottery(➤同義にも用いるが, どちらかといえば前者は慈善目的のものに, 後者は宝くじのような公共性のあるものに用いられる) ‖**抽選券** a raffle［lottery］ticket ‖**抽選番号** a raffle［lottery］number.

ちゅうぞう 鋳造 casting；**coinage**(貨幣の) **一**動**鋳造する cast** +目；**mint** +目(貨幣を) ▶青銅で**鋳造**した彫刻 a sculpture *cast* in bronze.

‖**鋳造所** a foundry.

ちゅうそつ 中卒 a **junior high school graduate** /grǽdʒuət/(中卒者) ▶うちの社長は**中卒**で身を起こした人だ Our boss built up the business *with only a junior high school education*.

ちゅうたい 中退する quit［**leave**］**school**(自分の意志でやめる)；**drop out**《**of**》(成績不良などが原因で) ▶父親が事業に失敗して学費を払えなかったため彼は大学を**中退した** His father's business failed and he could no longer pay tuition. So he *quit* college.(➤この quit は過去形).

‖**中退者** a dropout(➤「高校［大学］中退者」は high school［college］dropout).

ちゅうだん 中断する stop +目；**interrupt** +目(進行中のものを遮る)；**discontinue** +目(続いてきたものを中止する)；**suspend** +目(一時的に) ▶野球の試合は雨のため何度か**中断された** The baseball game *was* *interrupted* several times by rain. ‖勉強を中断して牛乳を1杯飲んだ I *stopped* studying (*for a while*) [*took a break* from studying] and had a glass of milk. ‖監督の急死で映画の撮影は中断せざるをえなかった They had to *discontinue* the shooting of the movie because the director died suddenly. ‖住民は建設工事を一時中断してもらうように決議した The residents decided to *have* the construction *stopped temporarily*. ‖交渉は休暇が終わるまで中断した The negotiations *were suspended* until after the holidays.

ちゅうちゅう ▶ネズミがチューチューいっている Mice *are squeaking*. ‖チューチュー音を立ててジュースを飲むな Don't *suck* the juice.

ちゅうちょ 躊躇 (a) **hesitation** 一動 ちゅうちょする **hesitate** /hézɪteɪt/ ▶私は一瞬ちゅうちょしてからその店に入った I *hesitated* for a moment, and then went into the store. ‖寒かったので彼女は水に入るのをちゅうちょした It was cold and she *hesitated* to go into the water. ‖彼はちゅうちょすることなくその車を買った He bought the car *without hesitation*.

ちゅうづり 宙吊り ▶宙づりの曲芸 *aerial* acrobatics ‖その登山者は足を滑らせて宙づりの状態になった The climber slipped and was left *hanging in midair*.

ちゅうてん 中点 《数学》 a **midpoint** ▶線分の中点 *the midpoint* of a line.

ちゅうと 中途で **halfway** ▶中途で引き返す turn back *halfway* ‖仕事を中途で投げ出してはいけない You should not *leave* your work *unfinished* [*half done*]. ‖次郎は高校を2年で中途退学した Jiro *quit* [*gave up*] high school when he was in the second year.

[1]**ちゅうとう 中東** **the Middle East, the Mideast**
‖中東諸国 (the) countries in the Middle East ／(the) Middle Eastern Countries ‖中東和平交渉 Middle East peace talks [negotiations].

[2]**ちゅうとう 中等の** **medium** (程度が); **middle-class** (階級が); **secondary** (教育が)
‖中等教育 secondary education.

[3]**ちゅうとう 柱頭** 《建築》 a **capital**.

ちゅうどう 中道の **middle-of-the-road**; **moderate** (穏健な) ▶アメリカの民主党は中道左派の政党だ The US Democratic Party is a *center-left* party. ‖青空党は中道政策をとっている The Blue-Sky Party is *middle-of-the-road* in politics.
‖中道政党 a middle-of-the-road party, a centrist party.

ちゅうどく 中毒 **1** 【毒物や食べ物の】 **poisoning**
▶ガス中毒で死ぬ die of *gas poisoning* ‖兄はフグで(食)中毒を起こしたことがある My brother once *got* (*food*) *poisoning* from eating globefish.
2 【依存症】 **addiction** ▶たばこ, いいかげんにやめたら? 中毒になるわよ Hadn't you better quit smoking before it's too late? You'll *get addicted*. ‖彼はアルコール中毒(＝依存症)だ He is *an alcoholic*. (➤ alcoholic は「アルコール依存症患者」;「アルコール依存症状」は alcoholism) ‖父はいわゆる仕事中毒だ My father is what you call *a workaholic*. (➤ workaholic は work と alcoholic から作られたことば) ‖兄は重症の活字中毒だ My big brother is a serious *book-addict*. (➤「書物中毒者」の意; addict の発音は /ǽdɪkt/).
‖たばこ中毒 nicotine [tobacco] addiction; a nicotine [tobacco] addict(人) ‖麻薬中毒 drug addiction; a drug addict(人) ‖薬品中毒 chemical poisoning.

ちゅうとはんぱ 中途半端 ▶何事も中途半端にしておいてはいけない You must not leave anything *half done* [*unfinished*]. ‖物事を中途半端にするな Don't do things *by halves*. (● halves /hævz/ は half の複数形. by halves はこの例のように否定文で使うことが多い) ‖中途半端な気持ちなら彼女と付き合うのはやめなさい Stop seeing her if you feel *halfhearted* about her [if you *are not serious* about her]. (➤ halfhearted は「気乗りのしない」).

ちゅうとろ 中とろ ***chutoro***; **medium-fatty tuna meat.**

ちゅうとん 駐屯する **be stationed**
‖駐屯地 a station; a garrison town (守備隊の配置された); a post (辺地の小部隊の); a base (長期駐留の基地) ‖駐屯部隊 a garrison; forces on station.

チューナー a **tuner** /tjúːnəʳ/
‖FMチューナー an FM tuner ‖テレビチューナー a TV tuner.

ちゅうなんべい 中南米 **Latin America, South and Central America** ‖中南米諸国 Latin [South and Central] American countries.

ちゅうにかい 中二階 a **mezzanine** /mézəniːn/
▶中二階のある家 a house with *a mezzanine*.

ちゅうにくちゅうぜい 中肉中背 ▶中肉中背の男 a man *of medium size* ‖母は中肉中背です My mother is of *medium height and build*.

[1]**ちゅうにち 駐日** ▶駐日アメリカ大使 the U.S. *ambassador to Japan*.

[2]**ちゅうにち 中日** ▶お彼岸の中日 an *equinox* /ékwɪnɑːks/ (●「春分」(the spring equinox) か「秋分」(the fall equinox) かを明示するのがふつう).

ちゅうにゅう 注入する **pour** ＋目 (注ぐ); **inject** ＋目 (注射する) ▶彼はライターにガスを注入した He *poured* lighter fluid *into* a cigarette lighter.

チューニング **tuning.**

ちゅうねん 中年 **middle age.**

> 【解説】日本語の「中年」が40歳前後から50代後半辺りまでを指すのに対して, 英語の middle age は40歳から65歳くらいの年齢を指し, 日本語の「中高年」に相当することも多い.

▶中年になる reach *middle age* ‖中年の男性[女性] a *middle-aged* man [woman] ‖祖父は70歳だが自分ではまだ中年だと思っている My grandfather is 70, but he still considers himself to be *middle-aged*. ‖彼は中年太りだ He has developed *a middle-age spread*.

ちゅうのう 中脳 **the midbrain.**

ちゅうは 中波 (a) **medium frequency, medium wave.**

チューバ a **tuba.**

ちゅうハイ 酎ハイ ***chuhai***; a *shochu* highball; a blend of *shochu* and soda water (➤ 説明的な訳).

ちゅうばん 中盤 **the middle stage** ▶ペナントレースも中盤にさしかかった The pennant race has entered *the middle stage*.

ちゅうび 中火 **medium heat** (熱); a **medium flame** (炎) ▶中火に掛けた鍋にバターを入れて溶かします Melt the butter in a saucepan over *medium heat*.

ちゅうぶ 中部 **the central part** ▶関東中部に大雨が降った There was a heavy downpour in *the central* Kanto area.

‖中部地方 the Chubu [Central] district ‖中部日本 Central Japan.

チューブ a **tube** ▶チューブ入りマスタード *a tube* of mustard ‖チューブから絵の具を搾り出す squeeze color from *a paint tube*.

ちゅうふう 中風 **paralysis** /pərǽləsɪs/ ; **palsy** /pɔ́:lzi/ (軽症のもの) ▶中風になる become *paralyzed*.

ちゅうふく 中腹 ▶そのホテルは山の中腹に在る The hotel stands *on a hillside* [stands *halfway up the hill*]. ‖我々は赤城山の中腹まで登ってそこで休憩した We went *halfway up* Mt. Akagi and took a rest there.

ち

ちゅうぶらりん 宙ぶらりん ▶たこが木の枝に引っ掛かって宙ぶらりんになっている A kite *is dangling* [*hanging*] from a branch. ‖その問題はまだ宙ぶらりんになっている The matter is still *pending* [*up in the air*].

[1]**ちゅうべい 中米** **Central America** ▶中米の数か国を訪問する visit several *Central American* countries.

[2]**ちゅうべい 駐米** ▶駐米日本大使 the Japanese *ambassador to the U.S.*

ちゅうへん 中編 ‖中編小説 a short novel.

ちゅうぼう 厨房 a **kitchen.**

ちゅうもく 注目 **attention, notice** (➤ 前者が意味が強い) 一動 注目する **pay attention** ((to)), **take notice** ((of)), **watch** +目 ▶注目すべき発言 a *noteworthy* remark / a remark *worthy of attention* [*notice*] ‖世間の注目を浴びて in *the public eye* ‖世間の注目を集める裁判 a *high profile* case ‖多くの科学者がこの新技術に注目している Many scientists *are paying attention to* this new technology. ‖世界は海洋汚染を論じるその円卓会議の成り行きに注目している The world *is watching* the progress of the roundtable talks on marine pollution. (➤「興味をもって見守っている」の意) ‖与党が公約を守るかどうか注目していこう Let's *keep an eye on* the ruling party *and see* [*to see*] if they carry out their campaign promises. ‖佐知子の美しい着物姿はその場に居合わせた外国人みんなの注目を引いた Sachiko in her beautiful kimono *drew* [*attracted*] *the attention* of all the foreigners there. ‖彼は僅か16歳で文壇にデビューして注目を浴びた He *became the center of attention* when he made his debut as a writer at (the age of) only sixteen. ‖当時この女優に注目した評論家はあまりいなかった At that time *few* critics *took notice of* this actress.

ちゅうもん 注文 **1【品物を作らせたり, 届けさせたりすること】** an **order** 一動 **注文する** **order** ▶注文に応じる fill *an order* ‖注文を取り消す cancel *an order* ‖((レストランなどで))ご注文はお決まりですか Are you ready to *order*? / May I take your *order*, please?

【文型】
人(A)のために物(B)を注文する
order A B
order B **for** A
品物(A)を店(B)に注文する
order A **from** B

▶私にはコーヒーを注文しておいてくれる? Can you *order* a coffee *for* me [*order* me a coffee]? ‖アマゾンに洋書を数冊注文した I *ordered* some foreign books *from* Amazon. ‖これは注文してないと思うんだけど I don't think I *ordered* this.
▶わが社はドイツの会社にその機械を注文した We *placed an order* for the machine with a German company. (➤ 堅い言い方) ‖注文したものが入ったら電話をくれますか Would you call me when my *order* comes [gets] in? ‖その辞書なら注文してある The dictionary *is on order*. ‖洋服はいつも注文して作らせます I usually *have* my clothes *made to order*. (→オーダーメード).

✉ ((通信販売などで))**貴社の春のカタログ13号より下記の3点の品を注文します** I would like to *order* [*place an order for*] the following 3 items from your spring catalog No. 13.

‖注文住宅 a custom-built house.

2【要求】 a **request** ▶家を新築するとき彼はあれこれ無理な注文をつけた When he was having his house built, he made all sorts of unreasonable *requests*. ‖ここまできて最初からやり直せというのは無理な注文だ If you want me to do it all over again at this stage, *you're asking too much*. ‖500万円貸せだって? そりゃあ無理な注文だ You want me to lend you five million yen. That's an *outrageous request*.

ちゅうや 昼夜 ▶捜索救助活動は昼夜兼行で行われた Search-and-relief efforts continued *day and night* [*around the clock*].
☛ 一昼夜 (→見出語)

ちゅうゆ 注油 **lubrication** /lù:brɪkéɪʃən/ (機械などに油をさすこと) ▶車に注油する *lubricate* [*grease*] a car.

ちゅうよう 中庸 **moderation** ▶彼の意見は中庸を得ている His opinion is *moderate*.

ちゅうりつ 中立 **neutrality** 一形 **中立の** **neutral** ▶中立を守る maintain *neutrality* ‖新聞は常に中立でなければならない Newspapers should always be *neutral*. ‖私が妻と口論したとき息子は中立の立場をとった When my wife and I got into an argument, our son *remained neutral* [*would not take sides*]. (➤ take sides は「どちらかに味方する」).
‖中立国 a neutral nation ‖永世中立 permanent neutrality ‖非武装中立 unarmed neutrality.

チューリップ a **tulip** ▶チューリップの球根 a *tulip* bulb ‖赤, 白, 黄色とチューリップが咲いている *Tulips* are blooming in red, white and yellow.

[1]**ちゅうりゅう 中流** **1【川の】** **the middle reaches** ▶中流に架かる橋 a bridge *halfway up* [*down*] *the river*.
2【社会の】 **the middle class** ▶彼は中流家庭に育った He was brought up in *a middle-class family*. ‖世論調査によると大抵の日本人は中流階級に属していると思っている(＝中流意識を持っている) According to opinion polls, most Japanese think that they belong to *the middle class*.

[2]**ちゅうりゅう 駐留する** **be stationed**
‖駐留軍 the occupation forces.

ちゅうりんじょう 駐輪場 a **bicycle parking lot.**

ちゅうわ 中和する **neutralize** /njú:trəlaɪz/ +目 ▶アルカリは酸を中和する Alkalis *neutralize* acids.

ちゅっと ▶人の頬にチュッとキスする *give* a person *a peck* on the cheek (➤ peck は「軽いキス」の意のインフォーマルな語 ; 「チュッ[プチュッ]とキスをする」は smack).

ちゅんちゅん チュンチュン鳴く **chirp** /tʃə:ʳp/ ▶スズメがチュンチュン鳴いている The sparrows *are chirping*.

-ちょ -著 ▶岡倉天心著『茶の本』"The Book of Tea" (*written*) *by* Okakura Tenshin.

ちょいちょい ▶彼は計算でちょいちょい間違いをする He

often makes mistakes in his calculations. ‖あの顔はテレビでちょいちょい(＝時々)見る顔だ That's a face that I see on TV *every now and then* [*from time to time*].

ちょいと →ちょっと.

ちょいやく ちょい役 a **bit part** [**player**]; a **walk-on part** [**role**] (せりふのない「通行人」の役).

ちょいわるおやじ ちょい悪おやじ a **slightly wild** [**dangerous**] **older man**; a stylish middle-aged man who enjoys being "a little bad" (➤ 説明的な訳).

1**ちょう 蝶** 《虫》a **butterfly** ▶アゲハチョウ a swallowtail (butterfly) (➤ 特に「キアゲハ」) ‖モンシロチョウ a cabbage butterfly.

▶《慣用表現》光代はちょうよ花よと(＝大事に)育てられた Mitsuyo was brought up *with the utmost care* (*and affection*).

‖ちょうネクタイ a bow tie ‖ちょう結び a bow.

2**ちょう 腸** **the intestines** /ɪntéstɪnz/ (大腸, 小腸); **the bowels** /báʊəlz/ (腸全体) ▶私は腸の具合が悪い There is something wrong with my *intestines*. ／I have *intestinal* trouble. ‖彼女は腸捻転[腸閉塞]を起こした She had *a twist* [*a blockage*] *in her intestines*.

‖小腸 the small intestine [bowel] ‖大腸 the large intestine [bowel].

3**ちょう 兆** a **trillion** ▶2兆円 two *trillion* yen ‖世界には何十億もの人間が居るが, 何兆ものネズミも居る The world now has billions of people, but also *trillions of* rats. →億.

4**ちょう 長** **1**【集団の頭】a **head**, a **chief** (➤ 後者は権威・権力などを連想させる); a **leader** (指導者) ▶グループの長 a group *leader*.

2【長所】a **merit**; an **advantage** (有利な点)

▶《慣用表現》対戦相手はディフェンス面で一日の長がある The enemy *has a slight advantage* [*edge*] in defense.

ちょう- 超- **1**【超-】**super-**, **ultra-** /ʌ́ltrə-/, **hyper** ▶超高速車 a *superfast* car (➤ Ferrari など) ‖超高感度テレビカメラ an *ultrasensitive* TV camera ‖超現実的なアートワーク a *hyper*-realistic artwork ‖彼女はジャズ歌手としては超一流だ As a jazz singer, she *is in a class of her own*. (➤「(実力的に)別格だ」の意) ‖彼のスキーの腕前は超高校級だ His skiing skill *far exceeds the usual level of high school students*. ／His (skill in) skiing *is outstanding for a high school student*. ‖超新星 a supernova ‖超大国 a superpower (nation).

2【チョー】▶チョーおいしいコーヒー *great* coffee ‖あいつ, チョーむかつくよ! He [She] *pisses me off*! ‖彼って, チョーかっこいい[お金持ち]! He's *super* cool [rich]!

1**-ちょう -庁** an **agency** ‖気象庁 the Japan Meteorological Agency ‖消費者庁 the Consumer Affairs Agency.

2**-ちょう -調** ▶モーツァルトのト長調[ト短調]交響曲 Mozart's Symphony in *G Major* [*G Minor*] ‖きみの論文は不自然な翻訳調が目立つね An awkward *translation-like style* is noticeable in your essay. ／Your essay reads like an awkward translation. ‖この戯曲のせりふは七五調で書かれている The lines of this play are written in *a seven-five syllable meter*.

3**-ちょう -朝** a **dynasty** ▶明朝 the Ming *Dynasty* ‖唐朝 the Tang *Dynasty*.

ちょうあい 寵愛 ▶楊貴妃(ようきひ)は玄宗皇帝の寵愛を一身に集めた Yang Guifei *received* all of Emperor Xuanzong's *affection*.

ちょうい 弔意 **condolences** /kəndóʊlənsɪz/ ▶遺族に弔意を表す express [offer] one's *condolences* to the victims' families.

ちょういん 調印する **sign** +㊐ ▶和平条約が両国の外務大臣によって調印された The peace pact *was signed* by the foreign ministers of the two countries.

‖調印式 a signing ceremony.

ちょうえい 町営の **municipal**, **town-managed** (➤ municipal は「地方自治体の」の意で,「市立の」にも当たる).

ちょうえき 懲役 **imprisonment with work** ▶裁判長は被告に3年の懲役刑を言い渡した The presiding judge sentenced the accused to three years' *imprisonment* (*with work*). ／The accused was sentenced to three years' *imprisonment* (*with work*). 《参考》imprisonment without work は「禁錮」.

‖無期懲役 life imprisonment.

ちょうえつ 超越 ▶時代を超越した知恵 *timeless* wisdom ‖日蓮上人は世俗を超越していた The Sage Nichiren *rose above* [*transcended*] worldly affairs. ‖彼女は利害を超越して社会に奉仕した She devoted her life to serving society, *disregarding* her own interests.

ちょうおんかい 長音階 《音楽》a **major scale**.

ちょうおんそく 超音速の **supersonic**

‖超音速旅客機 a supersonic transport, an SST.

ちょうおんぱ 超音波 **ultrasound**; **ultrasonic wave**

‖超音波検査 an ultrasound examination; ultrasonography.

1**ちょうか 超過** an **excess** /ɪksés/ 一動 **超過する** **exceed** +㊐ ▶今回のパーティーの費用は予算を超過した The expenses for this party *exceeded* our budget. ‖その遊覧船の乗客数は定員を50人も超過していた The number of passengers aboard the pleasure boat *exceeded* the legal capacity by 50 (people). ‖このスケート場では2時間を超えると1時間につき200円の超過料金を取られる At this skating rink, they charge 200 yen for each extra hour after two hours. (➤ extra は「追加の」) ‖輸入超過は今日アメリカ経済における深刻な問題である *An excess of imports* is a serious economic problem in America today.

‖超過勤務 overtime work (➤「超過勤務をする」は work overtime) ‖超過勤務手当 overtime pay, an overtime allowance ‖超過料金 an extra [additional] charge.

2**ちょうか 釣果** a **catch** (**of fish**) ▶大量の釣果 a large *catch* (*of fish*).

1**ちょうかい 懲戒** ▶彼は会社の金を使い込んで懲戒免職になった He embezzled company money and *was dismissed as punishment*. (➤「懲戒免職」は disciplinary dismissal という).

2**ちょうかい 町会** a **neighborhood association** ▶元町町会 the Motomachi *Neighborhood Association*.

3**ちょうかい 朝会** a **morning assembly** [**meeting**].

ちょうかく 聴覚 (**the sense of**) **hearing**, an **auditory sense** ▶聴覚障害の人 a *hearing-impaired* person ／a person *with hearing impairment*.

1**ちょうかん 朝刊** a **morning paper** (➤ 夕刊に対しては the morning edition).

[2]**ちょうかん 長官** ‖**宮内庁長官** the Grand Steward of the Imperial Household Agency ‖(アメリカの)**国務長官** the Secretary of State (➤日本の外務大臣に相当する) ‖**内閣官房長官** the Chief Cabinet Secretary.

ちょうかんず 鳥観図・鳥瞰図 a **bird's eye view.**

ちょうき 長期 a **long period** [**time**] **一形 長期の long (-term), long-range** ▶これまでのところ私はまだ長期の海外旅行をしたことがない I have never been on an *extended* trip abroad. ‖そのビルの工事は長期にわたりそうだ It will take quite *a long time* before the building is completed.

‖**長期休暇** a long [extended] vacation ‖**長期金利** a long-term interest rate ‖**長期計画** a long-range plan ‖**長期欠席** a long absence ‖**長期戦** a long-drawn-out [prolonged] war ‖**長期予報** a long-range forecast.

ちょうぎかい 町議会 a **town assembly** [**council**]

‖**町議会議員** a member of a town assembly [council].

ちょうきょう 調教 training ▶馬を調教する *train* a horse.

‖**調教師** a trainer.

ちょうきょり 長距離 a **long distance** ▶ニューヨークへ長距離電話を掛けた I made *a long-distance call* to New York. ‖父に長距離電話を掛けた I *called* [*phoned*] my father *long-distance*.

‖**長距離競走** a long-distance race ‖**長距離選手** a long-distance runner ‖**長距離トラックの運転手** a long-haul [long-distance] truck driver ‖**長距離バス** a long-distance bus ‖**長距離飛行** a long-distance [long-haul] flight ‖**長距離ランナー** a long-distance runner.

ちょうきん 彫金 chasing.

ちょうけい 長兄 one's **oldest** [**eldest**] **brother.**

ちょうけし 帳消し ▶借金を帳消しにする *cancel* a debt ▶彼のせっかくの名声も今回のスキャンダルで帳消しになった His good reputation *was wiped out* [*was destroyed*] by this scandal.

ちょうけつ 長欠 a **long absence** ▶彼は病気のため学校を長欠した He *was absent* from school *for a long time* because of his illness. ／He *took a long absence* from school due to illness.

‖**長欠児童** a child [a student] who has been absent from school for a long time.

ちょうげん 調弦《音楽》**tuning 一動 調弦する tune (up)** ▶オーケストラの調弦が始まった The orchestra has begun to *tune* (*up*). ‖オーケストラはオーボエのイ音に合わせて調弦する The orchestra *tunes* (*up*) to the oboe's A note.

[1]**ちょうこう 兆候・徴候** a **sign** (兆し); a **symptom** /símptəm/ (病気の症状) ▶景気は少しもよくなる兆候が無い The economy shows no *signs* of improving. ‖皮膚が黄色く変色するのはおうだんの兆候である A yellowish discoloration of the skin is *a symptom* of jaundice.

[2]**ちょうこう 聴講する sit in** 《**on**》(傍聴する); 《主に米》**audit** /ɔ́:dət/ +目 (➤試験や単位認定は受けない) ▶《大学で》Y 教授の講義を聴講する *sit in on* [*audit*] Professor Y's lecture ／*attend* Professor Y's lecture *as an auditor* [*an occasional student*] ‖あの人のシェークスピアについての講演を一度聴講したことがあります I once went to *listen to* [I once *heard*] her lecture about Shakespeare.

‖**聴講生** 《主に米》an auditor, 《主に英》an occasional [a special] student.

[3]**ちょうこう 長江 the Yangtze (River), the Chang Jiang.**

ちょうごう 調合する make up; **dispense** +目 (調剤する); **compound** +目 (成分を混ぜ合わせる) ▶処方薬を調合する《米》*fill* a prescription ／*make up* a prescription ‖薬草を調合して薬を作る *compound* a medicine from herbs ／*compound* herbs into a medicine ‖いかに有能な薬剤師でも頭のよくなる薬は調合できない Even the best pharmacist cannot *dispense* [*prepare*] a medicine to make people smarter.

ちょうこうそう 超高層

‖**超高層ビル** a skyscraper ‖**超高層マンション** a high-rise condominium [apartment building].

ちょうこく 彫刻 (a) **sculpture**, (a) **carving** (➤個々の作品の場合は a をつける) **一動 彫刻する sculpt** (+目), **sculpture** (+目) (主に, 大理石など硬いものに); **carve** (+目) (主に, 木に) ▶大理石の彫刻 a marble *sculpture* ‖彼は彫刻がうまい He is skilled in *sculpture*. ／He is a skilled sculptor. ‖この美術館にはロダンの有名な『考える人』の彫刻がある This museum has Rodin's famous *sculpture* "The Thinker."

‖**彫刻家** a sculptor ‖(木彫の)**彫刻師** a (wood) carver, a wood sculptor ‖**彫刻刀** a chisel /tʃízəl/.

ちょうさ 調査

a **survey** /sə́:ʳveɪ/ (実態調査); an **examination** (情報を得るための); (an) **investigation**, an **inquiry** (事故や犯罪などの) **一動 調査する survey** /səʳvéɪ/ +目, **investigate** /ɪnvéstɪgeɪt/ +目, **inquire** 《**into**》, **examine** +目 ▶その町の人口を調査する *make a survey of* the population of the town ／*survey* the population of the town ‖事故の原因を調査する *investigate* [*look into*] the cause of an accident ／*conduct* [*make*] *an investigation of* an accident ‖私どもの調査にご協力くださり感謝いたします We appreciate your cooperation in [with] our *survey*. ‖彼らは被害者の身元を調査している They *are inquiring* [*making inquiries*] *into* the victim's background. ‖その事件は現在調査中である The case is *being investigated* [*under investigation*]. ‖専門家が地滑りの現場を調査した The specialists *examined* the site of the landslide. (➤examine は「詳しく調べる」) ‖5年ごとに国勢調査が行われる The (*national*) *census* is conducted every five years.

‖**調査委員会** an investigating committee ‖**調査官** an advisor, an inspector ‖**調査結果** findings ‖**調査書** a transcript ‖**世論調査** a (public) opinion poll.

ちょうざい 調剤 《薬》**dispensing 一動 調剤する dispense** [**prepare**] **a drug** [**medicine**]; **fill a prescription** (処方箋を)

‖**調剤室** a dispensary.

チョウザメ 《魚》a **sturgeon.**

[1]ちょうし 調子

1【**具合, 状態**】**condition** (状態, コンディション); **form** (運動選手や馬などの); **shape** (体の; インフォーマルな語)

▶この車は調子がいい[悪い] This car *is in good* [*poor*] *condition*. ‖彼女は退院できるほどには調子はよくない She *is in no condition* to leave (the) hospital. ‖その走者はいつもの調子を取り戻したようだ The runner seems to have regained his usual *form*. ‖今シーズンのドラゴンズは調子がいい[よくない] The Dragons *are in good* [*poor*] *form* this

season. ‖ 私はどうも朝は**調子が悪い** I *can't function* in the morning.
▶このノートパソコンは**調子がいい**［**悪い**］This laptop *works* ［*doesn't work*］ *well*. ‖ エアコンの**調子がおかしい** *Something is wrong with* the air conditioner. ‖ きょうは体の**調子がいい** I *feel well* ［*feel fit*］ today. ／I'*m in good shape* today. ‖ 体の**調子が悪い** I *don't feel well* ［*good*］. ／I *feel bad* ［*out of sorts*］. ‖ きょうはどうもおなかの**調子が悪い** *Something is wrong with* my stomach today. ‖ 体の**調子を崩さない**ように毎日ジョギングをしています I jog every day *to stay* ［*keep*］ *in shape*. (➤ stay ［keep］ in shape は「体調を保つ」).
▶この頃**調子はどうですか**？ *How have you been* (*getting along*) lately？／*How are things* (*going*) *with you* these days？ ‖ 対話「**調子はどうだい**？」「まあまあだね」"*How are you getting along*？／*How's everything*？" "So-so. ／Not bad."
2【音調，拍子】tune（音の正しい調子）；a **tone**（音や声自体の調子）▶このギターは**調子が狂っている** This guitar is *out of tune*. ‖ この歌は**調子がよくて**覚えやすい This song is very *rhythmical* and catchy. ‖ 島倉さんは**悲しい調子で歌う** Shimakura sings *sadly* ［*in a sad tone*］. ‖ 彼は足で**調子をとりながら**ウクレレを弾いた He played the ukulele *beating time* with his foot. (➤ beat time は「拍子をとる」) ‖ あいつの歌はてんで**調子っぱずれ**で聞いていられない I can't stand his singing because he always sings *out of tune* ［*out of pitch*］.
3【口調，語調】a **tone** ▶山田監督は**強い調子で**審判の判定に抗議した Manager Yamada protested (against) the umpire's decision *in a sharp tone*. ‖ 野党は**激しい調子で**政府が約束を破ったことを非難した The opposition parties *condemned* ［*harshly criticized*］ the government for breaking its promise. (➤ condemn は「激しく非難する」).
4【慣用表現】▶**そうだ，その調子だ** *That's the way*. ／*That's the spirit*. (➤「その意気」の意) ／*Keep it up*！／*Keep up the good work*！(➤ あとの２例は「その調子で頑張れ」の意) ‖ あいつは全く**調子がいい** He is a (real) *smooth talker*. (➤ smooth talker は「口のうまい人」) ‖ 詐欺師は**調子のいいこと**ばかり言う Swindlers always talk *a good line* ［*story*］. ‖ 彼は飲むとすぐ**調子に乗る** When he drinks, he easily *gets carried away*. (➤ be ［get］ carried away は「興奮して我を忘れる」) ‖ 私は**調子に乗って**２時間カラオケで歌った I *got carried away* and sang karaoke for two hours. ‖ 彼は仕事が速いので**調子を合わせる**のが大変だ He works so fast that it is difficult to *keep pace with* him. (➤ keep pace with は「…に遅れないようについていく」).

2**ちょうし 銚子** a **ceramic sake bottle** (➤ ceramic は「磁器の」，「陶器の」は earthenware).

3**ちょうし 長姉** one's **oldest** ［**eldest**］ **sister**.

1**ちょうじ 弔辞** a **message of condolence** /kəndóʊləns/；a **eulogy** /júːlədʒi/（死者を褒めたたえることば）→追悼 ▶Ｔ氏に対する**弔辞を述べる** deliver *a eulogy* for Mr. T ‖ 彼は葬儀で友人一同を代表して**弔辞を読んだ** He read *a message of condolence* at the funeral on behalf of all his friends.

2**ちょうじ 寵児** ▶彼はＩＴの**寵児だ** He has *celebrity status* in the field of information technology. ‖ 当時スティーブ・ジョブズは時代の**寵児**だった Steve Jobs enjoyed *phenomenal popularity* ［*had supercelebrity status*］ at that time.

ちょうししゃ 聴視者 the (TV and radio) audience, the viewers and listeners《参考》テレビの視聴者，ラジオの聴取者を別々にいう場合はそれぞれ viewer, listener とする.

ちょうしぜん 超自然の supernatural ▶**超自然的な現象** a *supernatural* phenomenon.

ちょうしゃ 庁舎 ▶愛知県**庁舎** the Aichi Prefectural *Office Building* ‖ 目黒区**総合庁舎** the Meguro City *Office Complex*.

ちょうしゅ 聴取する hear ＋目；**question** ＋目（人に尋問する）▶警察はその事故について運転手から事情を**聴取した** The police *questioned* the driver about the accident ［*heard* what the driver had to say about the accident］.
‖（ラジオの）**聴取者** a radio listener.

ちょうじゅ 長寿 a **long life, longevity** /lɑːndʒévəṭi/ (➤ 後者は堅い語) ▶親族がみんな集まって祖父の**長寿を祝った** All my relatives met to celebrate my grandfather's *long life*. ‖ うちは**長寿**の家系です *Longevity* runs in my family.
‖**長寿番組** a long-lived program.

1**ちょうしゅう 聴衆** an **audience** (➤《米》では通例単数扱い.《英》では１つの集合体と見なす場合は単数扱いだが，一人一人の聴衆の集まりと考える場合は複数扱い) ▶**聴衆**はほとんどがティーンエージャーだった The *audience* was ［were］ mostly teenagers. ‖ **満員の聴衆**は出演者に盛大な拍手を送った *The capacity audience* gave the performers a big hand ［applause］. ‖ 自民党の候補者が**大勢の聴衆**の前で演説した An LDP candidate gave a speech before *a large audience*. ‖ その講演会には2000人もの**聴衆**が集まった About 2,000 *people* gathered to listen to the lecture.

2**ちょうしゅう 徴収する collect** ＋目（集める）；**levy** ＋目（税金・罰金などを；堅い語）▶ＰＴＡの会費［水道料金］を**徴収する** *collect* PTA dues ［the water bill］ ‖ 住民税を**徴収する** *levy* a residence tax.

ちょうじゅう 鳥獣 wildlife, birds and beasts
‖**鳥獣保護区** a wildlife sanctuary.

1**ちょうしょ 長所** a **strong** ［**good**］ **point**, a **strength**；(a) **merit**（利点，取り柄）；an **advantage**（有利な点）；(a) **virtue**（美点）▶**長所を伸ばす** develop one's *strong* ［*good*］ *points* ／enhance one's *strengths* ‖ 誰にも**長所**と短所がある Everyone has his or her *strong* and weak *points*. ／ Everyone has *strengths* and weaknesses. ‖ この製品には多くの**長所がある** There is a lot of *merit* ［There's (much) *merit*］ to this product. ‖ 大都会での生活には**長所**と短所がある Living in big cities has *advantages* and disadvantages.

2**ちょうしょ 調書** a **record**（記録）；a **report**（報告書）▶容疑者の**調書をとる** draw up *a report* by questioning the suspect.

ちょうじょ 長女 one's **oldest** ［**eldest**］ **daughter**（娘が３人以上の場合）；one's **older** ［**elder**］ **daughter**（娘が２人の場合）(➤《米》では oldest, older がふつう)；one's **first(-born) daughter**.

ちょうしょう 嘲笑 ridicule /rídɪkjuːl/, a **sneer** (➤ 前者は人をおどけてからかうことも含む) 一動 **嘲笑する ridicule** ＋目；**sneer**《at》▶彼は変な質問をしてみんなに**嘲笑された** He *was ridiculed* ［*was laughed at*］ by everybody when he asked a funny question. ‖ 彼は彼女を**嘲笑した** He *sneered at* her.

ちょうじょう 頂上 the top；**the summit**（これ以上ない

最高地点；堅い語)；**the peak**（とがった山頂）
▶あの丘の**頂上**まで競走しよう Let's race [have a race] to *the top* of that hill. ‖我々はマッターホルンの**頂上**を極めた We *gained the summit* of the Matterhorn. ／We *conquered* the Matterhorn. ‖キリマンジャロの**頂上**が雪をかぶっているのが見えた I saw Mt. Kilimanjaro *crowned* [*capped*] *with snow*.

ちょうじょうげんしょう 超常現象 a **paranormal phenomenon.**

ちょうしょく 朝食 **breakfast** ▶たっぷりした［軽い］**朝食**をとる have a hearty [light] *breakfast*(➤ U が原則だが, 種類をいうときはふつう C 扱い) ‖**朝食**の席に着く sit down to *breakfast* ‖わが家では毎朝７時頃に**朝食**をとる We *have* [*eat*] *breakfast* around seven every morning. ‖**朝食**にご飯とみそ汁, それに焼き魚を食べた I had rice, miso soup, and broiled fish *for breakfast*. ‖父は大抵**朝食**を食べながら新聞を読む My father usually reads the paper *over breakfast*. (➤ over は「(飲食などを)しながら」) ‖彼女は時々**朝食**を抜く She sometimes skips *breakfast*.

ちょうじり 帳尻 ▶何とかやりくりして**帳尻**を合わせた I managed to *get the accounts to balance*. ‖今月は何かと出費が多く, **帳尻**が合わなかった Since I spent too much money this month, I *couldn't make ends meet*. (➤ make ends meet は「収支を合わせる」).

1**ちょうしん 長身** ▶**長身**の男 a *tall* man ‖その投手は190センチの**長身**だ The pitcher is *tall*, with a height of 190 centimeters. ‖クーパー氏は**長身**を折り曲げて座敷に入った Mr. Cooper bent his *tall body* [*frame*] to enter the room.

2**ちょうしん 長針** **the long** [**minute**] **hand.**

ちょうじん 超人 a **superman**（男）, a **superwoman**（女）**━形** **超人的な** **superhuman** ▶彼は睡眠時間３時間で１日15時間働いている. まさに**超人**だ He works fifteen hours a day and sleeps only three (hours). He must be *superhuman*. ‖彼はこの仕事を完成するために**超人的な努力**をした He made *superhuman* [*Herculean*] *efforts* to finish this work. (➤ Herculean は「ヘラクレス(ギリシャ神話の怪力男)のような」の意).

ちょうしんき 聴診器 a **stethoscope** /stéθəskoʊp/ ▶**聴診器**を患者の胸に当てる apply *a stethoscope* to the patient's chest.

ちょうせい 調整 (an) **adjustment** **━動** **調整する** **adjust** /ədʒʌ́st/ +目 ▶写真の色と明るさを**調整する** *adjust* the color and brightness of a photo ‖部屋の温度を**調整する** *adjust* the room temperature ‖《掲示》**調整中** Scheduled Maintenance ‖ＤＶＤの音量を**調整する** *adjust* the DVD volume ‖メンバー全員が出席できるように日程を**調整します** We're going to *adjust* the schedule to make sure that all members can attend. ‖エンジンを**調整**してもらったほうがいい You should have the engine *tuned* (*up*). (➤ tune (up) は「(エンジンなどの機能を)正常に保つ」) ‖チャンピオンは防衛戦を控えて**調整**に余念がない The champion is intent on *getting in shape* with a defending match close at hand. (➤ get in shape は「体調を整える」).
‖**調整器** an adjusting device ‖**年末調整** the year-end tax adjustment.

ちょうせつ 調節する **adjust** /ədʒʌ́st/ +目（細かいところまで適合させる）；**regulate** +目（機械などを正確に作動するように）；**control** +目（制御する）▶サーモスタットを**調節する** *adjust* a thermostat ‖ヘビやトカゲは自分で体温を**調節する**ことができない Snakes and lizards cannot *adjust* their body temperature. ‖彼は椅子の高さを自分に合うよう**調節した** He *adjusted* the chair to his height. ‖このアイロンは旧式だから温度**調節**ができないのよ You can't *regulate* the temperature on this iron because it's an old model.

ちょうぜつ 超絶 ▶ピアニストは**超絶技巧**を披露した The pianist showed his [her] *transcendental technique*.

1**ちょうせん 挑戦** a **challenge** **━動** **挑戦する** **challenge** +目, **try** +目 ⇀**チャレンジ**（かこみ記事）▶テニスの試合でプロの選手に**挑戦する** *challenge* a pro to a game of tennis ‖難問に**挑戦する** *try* [*attempt*] to solve a difficult problem ‖重量挙げの世界新記録に**挑戦する** *try to establish* a new world record for weight lifting ‖スカイダイビングに**挑戦する** *try one's hand at* skydiving.
▶スウェーデン語に**挑戦**してみようと思うんだ I'm going to *try to* learn Swedish. ／I'm going to *challenge myself* to learn Swedish. (日本語に合わせて(×) challenge Swedish とするのは不可) ‖彼はチャンピオンに**挑戦状**をたたきつけた He flung down *a challenge* to the champion. ‖彼はいつも先生に対して**挑戦的な**(＝反抗的な)態度をとる He always takes a *defiant* attitude toward his teacher.
‖**挑戦者** a challenger.

2**ちょうせん 朝鮮** **Korea** /kərí:ə/
《参考》朝鮮民主主義人民共和国(＝北朝鮮)は正式には the Democratic People's Republic of Korea《略 DPRK》, 大韓民国(＝韓国)は the Republic of Korea《略 ROK》という. 両方を合わせて the two Koreas ということもある. ⇀**韓国, 北朝鮮** **━形** **朝鮮の** **Korean.**
‖**朝鮮語** Korean ‖**朝鮮人** a Korean ‖**朝鮮戦争** the Korean War ‖**朝鮮半島** the Korean Peninsula ‖**朝鮮労働党** the North Korea Workers Party.

ちょうぜん 超然とした **detached**（私情に溺れない）；**aloof**（非友好的な）▶みんなが騒いでいても, 次郎はいつもひとり**超然としている** Even when other people are making a fuss, Jiro always *remains aloof* [*detached*].

ちょうぞう 彫像 a **statue** ▶**彫像**を作る cast [carve] *a statue* (➤「鋳る」場合は cast, 「彫る」場合は carve).

ちょうそん 町村 **towns and villages**
‖**町村合併** the merger of towns and villages.

1**ちょうだ 長打** an **extra-base hit**, a **long ball** ▶阿部はセ・リーグ有数の**長打者**だ Abe is one of the outstanding *long*(*-ball*) *hitters* in the Central League.
‖**長打率** a slugging average.

2**ちょうだ 長蛇** ▶生徒たちは**長蛇**の列を作ってバスを待った The students waited for the bus *in a long line* [《英》*in a long queue*].

1**ちょうだい 頂戴** **1**【もらうこと】▶結構なものを**頂戴**いたしました *Thank you for* the nice present. ‖要らなければ, それ私に**頂戴** *Let me have it* [*Give it to me*] if you don't need it.
✉ **お手紙頂戴しました** I *received* your letter. ／Your letter *reached me*.
2【飲食する】▶十分**頂戴**しました *I'm full*. ／*I've had more than enough, thank you*. ‖コーヒーをもう

1杯**頂戴**したいのですが I'd like (to *have*) another cup of coffee, please.

3【…してください】▶ギターで何か1曲弾いて**ちょうだい** Can you play a tune on your guitar for me, *please*? ‖《食卓で》お塩を取って**ちょうだい** Pass me the salt, *please*. (➤ていねいな言い方は Could you pass me the salt(, please)?).

あなたの英語はどう響く?

日本語ではしばしば, 食卓で「塩を取って」と言ったり, 妻が夫に「ごみを出して」と言ったりするが, これを直訳して, (×) Pass me the salt., (×) Take out the garbage. としてはいけない. 身内の者を含めて, 人に何かを頼むときにこういう単純な命令形は用いない. これらは日本人が考える以上にぶっきらぼうできつく響く. もし子供が親や先生, あるいは目上の人に命令形で頼むと, 親はしつけの一環として, Pass me the salt, please. と please をつけて言うように注意する. please をつけるのは最低限のマナーである. また, Take out the garbage. では妻が立腹している響きになる. Could [Would] you take out the garbage?, Don't forget to take out the garbage. あるいは, Did you (remember to) take out the garbage? とすべきである. 親が子供に Clean up your room! (部屋を片づけなさい)と命令口調で言えば, 親が怒っていると子供は理解する. ふつうに言いつけているときは Please clean up your room., 少しきつめには, Will you please clean up your room? で, You need to [should] clean up your room. としてもよい.

[2]**ちょうだい 長大** ▶マーラーの長大な交響曲 a *grand* [*mighty*] Mahler symphony (➤ mighty は「長くて規模の大きい」の意).

ちょうたつ 調達する **raise** /reɪz/ +目(資金を); **procure** +目(物資などを); **provide** +目, **supply** +目(物資を) ▶武器を**調達する** *procure* weapons ‖ 新しい支店を開くための資金を**調達した** I *raised* funds to open a new branch store. ‖ 注文した品物をできるだけ早く**調達してください** Please *supply* the ordered item(s) [Please fill the order] as soon as possible.

‖**調達コスト** (a) procurement [sourcing] cost.

ちょうたんぱ 超短波 **ultrashort waves.**

[1]**ちょうちょう 町長** a **(town) mayor.**

[2]**ちょうちょう 長調** a **major (key)** ▶ハ長調のソナタ a sonata in *C major*.

ちょうちん 提灯 a **(paper) lantern**

日本紹介 ✉ **ちょうちんは一種の手提げランプです. 竹で作った球形の骨組みに和紙を貼り, 底の中央にろうそくを置いて明かりとします. しまうときにはアコーディオン式に小さく折り畳むことができます** A *chochin* is a kind of lantern. A globe-shaped bamboo framework is pasted and covered with Japanese paper and a candle is set in the center of the base as a source of light. A chochin collapses like an accordion and can be stored easily.

▶**ちょうちん行列**をする have *a lantern parade* [*procession*].

▶《慣用表現》彼はいつも上役の**ちょうちん持ち**をしている He is always *flattering his boss*.

ちょうつがい 蝶番 a **hinge** ▶戸の**ちょうつがい**が壊れているよ The door's *hinge* is broken.

[1]**ちょうてい 調停** **mediation** (第三者による仲裁の試み); **arbitration** (第三者を介しての紛争などの解決) **一動** (両者を)**調停する** **mediate** 《between》(+目), **arbitrate** 《between》(+目) ▶争いを**調停する** *mediate* a dispute ‖ 市当局は住民と会社側との**調停**に乗り出した The municipal authorities started *mediating* [*arbitrating*] between the local people and the companies concerned. (➤ arbitrate のほうが法的強制力をもつ) ‖ アメリカによる**調停**は不調に終わった U.S. *mediation* (*efforts*) failed.

‖**調停案** a mediation [an arbitration] plan ‖ **調停委員** a member of a mediation committee ‖ **調停委員会** a mediation committee ‖ **調停者** an arbitrator.

[2]**ちょうてい 朝廷** an **imperial court** ▶大和**朝廷** the Yamato *Imperial Court*.

ちょうてん 頂点 **the top**; **the peak** (特にとがった) ▶三角形の**頂点** the *apex* [*vertex*] of a triangle ‖ 彼女は今人気の**頂点にいる** She *is at the peak* of her popularity.

ちょうでん 弔電 a **telegram of condolence** /kəndóʊləns/ ▶遺族に**弔電を打つ** *send a telegram of condolence* [*telegraph one's condolences*] to the bereaved family.

ちょうでんどう 超電導・超伝導 **superconductivity** (超電導性)

‖**超電導体** a superconductor.

[1]**ちょうど 調度** **furnishings**; **furniture** (家具) ▶イギリスに半年以上住むのなら**家具調度付き**のアパートを借りたほうがいいよ If you're staying in Britain for more than half a year, you should rent a *furnished* flat.

[2]**ちょうど 丁度** **just** (まさに); **exactly** (正確に); **even** (端数のない) ▶今**ちょうど**8時30分です It's *exactly* eight thirty. (●この場合に just を用いると,「まだ」というニュアンスのいらだちや失望などが感じられる文になることがある) ‖ 私たちの乗る列車は**9時ちょうど**(=きっかり)に東京を出発する Our train will leave Tokyo at *nine o'clock sharp* [*on the dot*]. ‖ 急行は**毎時ちょうど**に出ます Expresses leave *every hour on the hour*. ‖ **ちょうど**20ポンドです *Exactly* £20. / £20 *even*. ‖ これは**ちょうど**私が知りたいと思っていたことです This is *just* [*exactly*] what I wanted to know. ‖ このワンピースは私に**ちょうどいい** This dress fits me *perfectly*.

【文型】
ちょうど…するところだ →所
be just doing
be just about [going] to do

▶映画が**ちょうど**始まるところだ The movie *is just* beginn*ing*. (➤ just は進行形を強めている) ‖ 帰宅したら**ちょうど**母が出かけようとしているところだった *Just* as I got home, my mother *was about to* go out. / I got home *just* as my mother *was about to* go out. ‖ まさに, グッドタイミング. **ちょうど**, 私も電話しようと思っていたところだ Great timing! I *was just about* [*going*] *to* call you.

▶**ちょうど**そのとき彼女の母親が姿を見せて私に挨拶した *Just then*, her mother showed up to greet me. ‖ **ちょうどいい**ときに来てくれたわね You came *at just the right moment*. ‖ **ちょうど**今来たところなんだよ I've *just* come. / I came *just now*. (●just now は現在完了形とともには用いない) ‖ さあ, 橋の**ちょうど真ん中**に来たわよ Now we are *right in the middle* of the bridge.

> **あなたの英語はどう響く?**
> 「今何時ですか」「ちょうど3時です」を英訳して "What time is it now ?" "It's just 3 o'clock." とする人が多い. まず, 質問文の中の now は不要である. また, 応答における just は文脈によっては「まだ」「やっと」といった含みを持つ. したがって,「ちょうど」を明確にする必要がある場合は, It's *exactly* 3 o'clock. ／ It's 3 o'clock *sharp*. のように言えばよい.

ちょうとうは 超党派の **nonpartisan**(どの政党にもくみしない); **bipartisan**(2大政党が協力する) ▶超党派のグループ a *nonpartisan* [*bipartisan*] group.

ちょうとっきゅう 超特急 a **superexpress (train)** ▶超特急のぞみ号 a Nozomi *superexpress* (*train*). ▶《比喩的》この仕事を超特急で仕上げてください Finish this job *with all possible speed*, please.

ちょうない 町内 ▶我々は同じ町内に住んでいる We live *on the same block*. ‖ご町内の皆さま, 本日は町長選挙の日です. 棄権しないで投票しましょう *Fellow citizens of this town*, today is the mayoral election day. Let's all go to the polls and exercise our (right to) vote!
‖町内会 a (local) neighborhood association.

ちょうなん 長男 one's **oldest** [**eldest**] **son**(息子が3人以上の場合); one's **older** [**elder**] **son** (息子が2人の場合)(➤《米》では oldest, older がふつう)《参考》(1)英米では日本の場合のように長幼の順をあまり問題にしないので, oldest [eldest], older [elder] のような形容詞は多用しない. (2) one's first(-born) son のようにもいえる ▶ぼくは長男です I am *the oldest son* (in my family).

ちょうにん 町人 **townspeople**(町民たち); a **merchant or a craftsman**(商人または職人).

ちょうのうりょく 超能力 (a) **psychic power**, (a) **supernatural power**; **telekinesis** /tèləkiníːsɪs/ (念動); **extrasensory perception** (超感覚的知覚; 略 ESP) ▶彼は超能力を使って自動車を動かした He moved a car with *telekinetic power*.
‖超能力者 a psychic; a person with psychic ability [supernatural power].

1**ちょうば 帳場** a **counter**; **the front desk** (旅館などの).

2**ちょうば 跳馬** 《競技》**the vault**; a **vaulting horse**, a **vault**(器具).

1**ちょうはつ 長髪** **long hair** 一形 長髪の **long-haired** ▶長髪の画家 a painter with *long hair*.

2**ちょうはつ 挑発** **provocation** 一動 挑発する **provoke** +目 一形 挑発的な **provocative** ▶挑発的な態度[ことば] a *provocative* attitude [remark] ‖挑発的な歌 a *provocative* [*suggestive*] song ‖牛は闘牛士の挑発に乗って暴れ出した The bull went wild at the *provocation* of the bullfighter.

3**ちょうはつ 調髪** a **haircut**(散髪); **hairdressing**(女性の髪の整え).

ちょうばつ 懲罰 **punishment**; **discipline** /dísəplɪn/ (懲戒; 折檻(せっかん)) ▶彼のとった行動は懲罰に値する His conduct deserves *punishment*.
‖(国会の)懲罰委員会 Committee on Discipline (➤一般の場合は disciplinary /dísəpləneri/ committee でよい).

ちょうふ 貼付する **affix** +目 ▶願書には写真を貼付すること *Affix* a photo to the application. (➤「てんぷ」は慣用読み).

ちょうふく 重複する **overlap** (+目) (重なる); **repeat** +目 (繰り返す) ▶あなたの説明は彼のと重複する箇所が多い Your explanation *overlaps* [*repeats*] his in many points. ‖作文を書く場合は同じ語句の重複は避けたほうがいいよ When writing a composition, it is better not to *repeat* the same words or phrases [it is better to avoid *redundancy*].

ちょうぶん 長文 a **long sentence**(長い一文); a **long passage** (長い文章の) ▶長文の手紙 a *long* letter ‖生徒の長文読解力をテストする give students a *long-passage reading comprehension* test.

ちょうへい 徴兵 《米》**draft**, 《英》**conscription** ▶祖父は21歳で徴兵されたそうだ I hear that my grandfather *was drafted* [*was conscripted*] when he was twenty-one.
‖徴兵制度 the draft system ‖徴兵猶予 (a) deferment (from military service).

ちょうへん 長編 a **long piece**
‖長編映画 a long film ‖長編作家 a novelist ‖長編小説 a long novel.

ちょうぼ 帳簿 an **account book**(➤文脈によっては単に a book となる) ▶帳簿に記入する enter accounts in *a book* ‖帳簿をつける *keep books* [*accounts*] ‖帳簿をごまかす doctor [cook] the *books* (➤インフォーマルな言い方)／falsify the *accounts* (➤堅い言い方).

1**ちょうほう 重宝な** **convenient**(手間が省けて便利な); **handy** (手元にあって便利な); **useful** (役に立つ) ▶スマートフォンは何かと重宝ですよ Smartphones are quite *convenient*. ‖あなたに頂いた修正液, 重宝しています That correction fluid you gave me *really comes in handy*. ‖彼は社内に顔が広いので何かと重宝がられている He *proves* himself *very useful* because he has lots of acquaintances throughout the company.

2**ちょうほう 諜報** **intelligence**
‖諜報活動 espionage /éspiənɑːʒ/ ‖諜報機関 an intelligence organization, a secret service ‖諜報部員 a secret agent, a spy.

ちょうぼう 眺望 a **view** ▶この丘からは町の眺望がすばらしい We can enjoy a wonderful *view* of the town from this hill. ／This hill commands a wonderful *view* of the town.

ちょうほうけい 長方形 a **rectangle**, an **oblong** (《米》では後者は「長円形」の意でも用いるので, 誤解を避けるには前者の言い方がよい).

ちょうほんにん 張本人 a **ringleader** (悪事の首謀者); an **author** /ɔ́ːθər/ (発案者) ▶警察は銀行強盗の張本人を捕まえた The police arrested the *ringleader* [*mastermind*] of the bank robbery. ‖アイヒマンはユダヤ人皆殺し計画の張本人として悪名が高い Eichmann is notorious as the *author* of plans to exterminate the Jews.

ちょうまんいん 超満員の **overcrowded** ▶超満員の通勤電車 an *overcrowded* [*a jam-packed*] commuter train ‖その日, 甲子園球場は超満員だった That day Koshien Stadium *was packed to overflowing* [*to over capacity*].

ちょうみりょう 調味料 a **seasoning**(塩, こしょう, しょうゆなど); (a) **spice** (香辛料) ‖化学調味料 a chemical [an artificial] seasoning.

ちょうみん 町民 **townspeople** (町の人々); a **resident of the town** (居住者).

-ちょうめ -丁目 ***-chome***.

ちょうめい 長命 a **long life**, **longevity**.

ちょうめん 帳面 a **notebook**.

ちょうもん 弔問 a **condolence** /kəndóʊləns/ **call**, a

call of condolence ▶遺族を弔問する *make a condolence call* on a bereaved family.

‖弔問外交 mourning [funeral] diplomacy ‖弔問客 a condolence caller.

ちょうもんかい 聴聞会 a hearing.

ちょうやく 跳躍 jumping, a jump **一動 跳躍する** jump ‖跳躍選手 a jumper ‖跳躍台 a springboard.

ちょうらく 凋落 ▶その歌手グループの人気のちょう落が甚だしい The *decline* [*fall*] of the singing group's popularity is dramatic.

ちょうり 調理 cooking **一動 調理する** cook (+目)(熱を加えて); prepare +目(下ごしらえする); clean +目(魚などの内臓を取り出す) ▶鶏肉を調理する *cook* chicken ‖魚を調理する *clean* a fish／*prepare* a fish for cooking ‖レトルト食品は調理の手間が省ける Retort pouches make *cooking* easy.

‖調理器具(一式) kitchenware, cookware, cooking utensils ‖調理師 a cook (➤調理師学校は culinary [cooking] school) ‖調理実習 cooking practice ‖調理場 a kitchen ‖調理法 a recipe /résəpi/.

1**ちょうりつ 町立の** municipal (➤「地方自治体の」の意で,「市立の」にも当たる) ▶町立桜が丘小学校 Sakuragaoka *Municipal* Elementary School ‖町立病院 a *municipal* hospital ‖町立美術館 a *town* [*municipal*] museum.

2**ちょうりつ 調律** tuning ▶ピアノを調律する *tune* a piano ‖調律師 a (piano) tuner.

ちょうりゅう 潮流 a (tidal) current (海流); a tide (潮の干満による流れ) ▶時代の潮流に乗る swim with *the current* [*the tide*] (●「…に逆らう」なら with の代わりに against) ‖暴力行為の潮流を食い止める stem *the tide* of violence ‖鳴門海峡は潮流が速い The *current* runs fast at the Naruto Strait.

ちょうりょく 聴力 hearing ▶聴力を失う lose one's *hearing* ‖父は年々聴力が衰えている My father's *hearing* is getting worse every year.／My father is getting harder of *hearing* every year.

‖聴力検査 a hearing test.

ちょうるい 鳥類 birds

‖鳥類学 ornithology ‖鳥類学者 an ornithologist ‖鳥類保護区 a bird sanctuary.

ちょうれい 朝礼 a morning assembly [meeting] ▶朝礼で校長先生は生徒たちにいろいろ注意をした The principal gave the students some advice at the *morning assembly*.

ちょうろう 長老 an elder ▶(国の)政界の長老 *an elder statesman* ‖村の長老 *a village elder*.

‖長老派教会 the Presbyterian /prèzbətíəriən/ church (➤その一員は a Presbyterian).

ちょうわ 調和 harmony **一動 調和する** harmonize《with》▶自然と調和して暮らす live *in harmony* with nature ‖あの看板は周囲の色彩と調和しない That billboard does not *harmonize* [*go well*] *with* the colors around it. ‖この絵は部屋のほかの絵との調和を考えて選びました I picked this picture to *harmonize with* the other ones in the room.

チョーク (a piece of) chalk ▶先生は黒板に書いた私の英文を赤いチョークで訂正した The teacher corrected my English passage on the blackboard *in red chalk* [*with a piece of red chalk*].

ちよがみ 千代紙 *chiyogami*; Japanese paper with colored figures or patterns (➤説明的な訳).

ちょきちょき ▶彼女ははさみで布をチョキチョキ切った She *snipped* the cloth with scissors. ‖植木屋さんが庭でチョキチョキやっている The gardener's shears are going *snip-snip* in the garden. (➤ snip-snip は「チョキチョキという音」).

1**ちょきん 貯金** savings (蓄え); a deposit /dɪpɑ́:zət/ (主に銀行への) **一動 貯金する** save (+目)(ためる); deposit +目(預け入れる) ▶私は少し貯金がある I have some *savings*. ‖ゆうちょ銀行に200万円の貯金がある I *have* two million yen [*have deposits* of two million yen] *in the* JP *Bank*. ‖私は毎月2000円ずつ貯金してきた I *have put away* 2,000 yen each month *for savings*. (➤ put away は「取っておく」)／I *have saved* 2,000 yen each month. ‖お年玉を全部ゆうちょ銀行に貯金した I *put* [*deposited*] all of my New Year's gift money *into my savings account* at the JP Bank. ‖海外旅行の[バイクを買う]ために貯金をしています I'*m saving up* for an overseas trip [to buy a motorcycle]. ‖トランペットを買うために貯金を5万円下ろした I *withdrew* [*drew*] 50,000 yen *from the bank* to buy a trumpet. ‖《比喩的》ヤクルトは5つ貯金がある The Swallows *have five games above* .500. (➤ .500 は five hundred と読む).

‖貯金通帳 a passbook (郵便局などの); a bankbook (銀行の) ‖貯金箱 a piggy bank, a moneybox ‖積立貯金 installment savings ‖郵便貯金 postal savings.

2**ちょきん** ▶指の爪をちょきんと切る *clip* a finger nail.

ちょくえい 直営 direct management ▶このホテルは全日空の直営だ This hotel *is under the direct management of* All Nippon Airways.／This hotel *is run* by All Nippon Airways.

ちょくげき 直撃 ▶台風10号が東海地方を直撃し,稲作に多大な被害を及ぼした Typhoon No. 10 *hit* [*struck*] the Tokai district *directly* and did a great deal of damage to the rice crop.

ちょくげん 直言する speak frankly, speak one's mind.

ちょくご 直後 right [immediately] after (➤ immediately はやや堅い語) ▶犯人は閉店直後に銀行に侵入したようだ The robber seems to have broken into the bank *right* [*immediately*] *after* it closed.

ちょくし 直視する face +目(向き合う); look straight at (まっすぐに見る) ▶事実を直視する(＝認める) *face* (the) fact(s) ‖きみは現実を直視しなければいけない You should *face* (*up to*) reality [*look squarely at* reality].／You should *accept* reality *as it is*.

ちょくしゃ 直射 ▶この植物は直射日光にとても強いです This plant is very tolerant of *direct sunlight*.

ちょくしん 直進する go straight ▶この通りを直進して突き当たりを右折してください *Go straight* along this street and turn right at the end. ‖直進車が優先です *Through traffic* has the right of way.

ちょくせつ 直接

一形 直接の direct, immediate /ɪmí:diət/ (➤後者のほうが媒介を挟まないという意味が強い) ▶直接の原因 a *direct* cause／an *immediate* cause ‖直接の上司 an *immediate* superior ‖その鍋はまだ熱いから直接触るとやけどするよ The pan is still very hot. You'll burn yourself if you touch it (*directly*). ‖文句があるなら彼と直接話し合ったほうがいいと思うよ If you have a bone to pick, you should talk with him *directly*. ‖私が東京の大学に通っていたときおじが直接・間接に援助してくれた My uncle helped me *directly*

and indirectly while I attended a university in Tokyo. ‖社長に直接お目に掛かりたいのですが I'd like to see the president *in person* [*personally*]. (➤ in person は「面と向かって」, personally は「他人を介さずに」の意) ‖ **対話** 「ロスに寄るのかい？」「いや, 直接シカゴに行く」"Are you going to stop over in Los Angeles?" "No, I'm going *straight* (*through*) to Chicago." (➤ straight は「まっすぐに」).
‖**直接税** a direct tax ‖ **直接選挙** (a) direct election ‖ **直接目的語** 《文法》 a direct object ‖ **直接話法** 《文法》 direct narration (➤《米》では direct discourse,《英》では direct speech ともいう).

ちょくせつほう 直説法 《文法》 **the indicative mood.**

ちょくせん 直線 a **straight line** ▶紙の上に直線を2本引きなさい Draw a pair of *straight lines* on the paper. ‖先頭のランナーは最後の直線コースでスパートを掛けた The front runner spurted in the *homestretch*. ‖家から学校まで直線距離で3キロだ It is three kilometers from my house to school *as the crow flies*. (➤ 文字どおりには「カラスが飛ぶように」) ‖**数直線** a number line.
☛ 一直線 (⇀見出語)

ちょくぜん 直前 **just** [**immediately**] **before** ▶彼の父は彼が大学を卒業する直前に亡くなった His father died *just before* he graduated from college.
▶車の直前を横断するのは危険だ It is dangerous to cross (*right*) *in front of* a car.

ちょくそう 直送 ▶リンゴは産地直送でお客さまにお届けできます We can *deliver* the apples *directly* to you *from our orchards*.

ちょくぞく 直属 ▶直属の上司 one's *immediate* superior ‖彼女は私の直属の部下だ She is under my *direct* [*immediate*] supervision. ／She is *on my staff*. ‖政府直属の機関 an organization *under the direct* [*immediate*] *supervision* of the government.

ちょくちょう 直腸 **the rectum** /réktəm/
‖**直腸がん** rectal cancer.

ちょくちょく ▶彼女はつまらない理由でちょくちょく会社を休む She's *often* absent from work for trivial reasons. ‖彼はここにちょくちょく顔を出す He comes here *from time to time*. ‖彼の作文にはちょくちょく誤字が見つかる You can find wrong characters *here and there* in his composition.

ちょくつう 直通の **direct** ▶空港まで直通バスが走っている There is (a) *direct* bus service to the airport. ‖今では世界中の主な大都市と直通ダイヤル通話ができる Nowadays, you can make *a direct telephone call* to most major cities in the world. ‖品川まではこの電車で直通で行けますよ This train goes *directly* to Shinagawa.
‖**直通電車** a through train (乗り換えなしの); a nonstop train (途中停車なしの).

ちょくばい 直売 ▶産地直売の野菜は安くて新鮮なものばかりだ The vegetables *sold directly by the growers* are all cheap and fresh.
‖**直売所** a farmer's market (➤ 生産者による直売市場).

ちょくはん 直販 **direct sales.**

ちょくほうたい 直方体 a **cuboid** /kjúːbɔɪd/, a **rectangular parallelepiped** /pærəleləpáɪped/.

ちょくめん 直面する **face** +㊐; **be faced with** (直面している) ▶トラは絶滅の危機に直面している Tigers *are faced* [*are confronted*] *with* extinction. ‖世界中のたくさんの人々が飢餓に直面している Many people throughout the world *face* [*are faced with*] starvation. ‖とりあえず今直面している問題を片づけなければならない First of all, we must settle the *problems before us*. ‖彼は自分の会社の倒産という事態に直面しても平然としていた He remained calm *in the face of* his company's bankruptcy. ‖私たちはたちまち資金難に直面した We soon *came up against* a shortage of funds.

ちょくやく 直訳 (a) **literal translation** ▶「行間を読む」は英語の read between the lines の直訳だ 'Gyokan o yomu' is *a literal* [*word-for-word*] *translation* of the English phrase "read between the lines."

ちょくゆ 直喩 a **simile** /síməli/. ⇀隠喩.

ちょくゆにゅう 直輸入 **direct import** /ímpɔːʳt/
▶当店の牛肉はオーストラリアから直輸入しております We *import* (our) beef *directly* from Australia. (➤ 動詞のときは /ɪmpɔ́ːʳt/).

ちょくりつ 直立する **stand straight** [**upright**] ▶高校の野球部員たちは直立不動の姿勢で監督の話を聞いた *Standing at attention*, the members of the high school baseball team listened to their manager.

ちょくりゅう 直流 **direct current** 《略 DC》 ▶乾電池の電流は直流である *Direct current* is used in batteries.

ちょくれつ 直列 **series** /síəriːz/ ▶電池は直列につないである The batteries are connected *in series*.
‖**直列回路** a series circuit.

ちょこちょこ ▶ちょこちょこ走る run *with short, quick steps* ‖彼女は夫と自分のためにちょこちょこっと夜食を作った She fixed a *quick* supper for her husband and herself. ⇀ちょいちょい.

チョコレート (a) **chocolate** /tʃɔ́ːklət/
‖**板チョコ** a chocolate bar.

ちょこん ▶彼は後ろから弟の頭をちょこんと(＝軽く)突っついた He poked his brother's head *lightly* from behind.
▶大きな椅子に小さな女の子がちょこんと腰掛けている A little girl is sitting *snugly* in an armchair. (➤ snugly は「こぢんまりと」).

ちょさく 著作 **writings** (作品); a **book** (本) ▶遠藤周作の著作 the *writings* of Endo Shusaku.
‖**著作権** copyright ‖**著作権侵害** an infringement of copyright, copyright violation ‖**著作権存続期間** the duration of a copyright.

ちょしゃ 著者 an **author** /ɔ́ːθəʳ/; a **writer** (執筆者) ▶著者不明の本 an *anonymous* book (➤ 発音は /ənɑ́ːnɪməs/) ‖その本の著者 *the author* of the book ‖ **対話** 「『幸福な王子』の著者は誰だか知っていますか」「オスカー・ワイルドです」"Do you know *who wrote* 'The Happy Prince'?" "Oscar Wilde did."

ちょじゅつ 著述 **writing** ▶彼は今歴史小説の著述に専念している He is now engaged in *writing* a historical novel.
‖**著述家** a writer.

ちょしょ 著書 **writings** (著作, 書いた作品); a **book** (本) ▶彼女には多くの著書がある She has written lots of *books*.

ちょすい 貯水 ‖**貯水槽** a water (storage) tank ‖**貯水池** a reservoir ‖**貯水量** the water storage volume (ためてある量); the water storage capacity (ためることのできる量).

ちょぞう 貯蔵する **store** (**up**) +㊐ (蓄える); **preserve** +㊐ (塩漬けなどにして保存する) ▶冬に備えて燃料を貯

蔵する *store* (*up*) fuel for the winter.
‖**貯蔵庫** a storehouse ; a cellar (地下の).

ちょちく 貯蓄 savings (➤常に複数形で) **—動 貯蓄する** save (up) ▶貯蓄に回す金なんか無いよ I don't have any money I can put into *savings*. ‖日本人は貯蓄好きとよく言われる It's often said that Japanese people like to *save* (*money*).

ちょっか 直下 ▶赤道直下の熱帯雨林 tropical rain forests *right on the equator* (● 英語では「赤道の真上の(地帯)」という).
‖**直下型地震** a direct-hit [near-field] earthquake, a major earthquake occurring directly under a city.

ちょっかい ▶他人のことにちょっかいを出す(＝干渉する)な Don't *meddle in* other people's affairs. ／Don't *poke your nose into* other people's affairs. ／Mind your own business. (➤ poke one's nose into は「…に首を突っ込む」. また, 最後の訳例はインフォーマルでかなり強い言い方) ‖彼女にちょっかいを出すなよ. 兄の彼女なんだから Don't *make passes at* her. She's my brother's girlfriend. (➤ make a pass at は「…に言い寄る」).

ちょっかく 直角 a right angle ▶この 2 本の線は直角に交わっている These two lines meet *at right angles* [intersect *at 90° angles*]. (➤読み方は ninety degree angles) ‖角ＡＢＣは直角である The angle ABC is *right*. ／ABC is *a right angle*.
‖**直角三角形** 《米》a right triangle, 《英》a right-angled triangle.

ちょっかつ 直轄の under direct control.

ちょっかっこう 直滑降 a straight downhill run, a schuss /ʃʊs/ ▶直滑降をする make *a schuss*.

ちょっかん 直感・直観 intuition /ìntʃuíʃən/ ; instinct (本能的な勘) ▶彼がうそをついているのが直感で[直感的に]わかった I knew *by intuition* [My *intuition* told me ／I *instinctively* knew] that he was telling a lie. ‖私はこの 2 人はうまくいかないのではないかと直感した I *felt in my bones* that the couple wouldn't get along well (with each other). ‖女の直感は鋭い A woman's *intuition* is keen.

チョッキ 《米》a vest, 《英》a waistcoat /wéskət, wéɪstkoʊt/ (➤「チョッキ」はポルトガル語から) ▶上着の下にチョッキを着る wear *a vest* under a jacket.
‖**防弾チョッキ** a bullet-proof vest.

ちょっきゅう 直球 a fastball (➤「ストレート」は和製語) ▶直球を投げる throw [hurl] *a fastball*.

1**ちょっけい 直径** a diameter /daɪǽmətəʳ/ ▶直径 5 センチの穴 a 5 cm-*diameter* aperture (➤ aperture は /ǽpəʳtʃəʳ/ と発音) ‖土俵の直径は4.55メートルです The *dohyo* has *a diameter* of 4.55 meters. ‖コンパクトディスクは直径12センチ, 厚さ1.2ミリだ Compact discs are 12 centimeters in *diameter* and 1.2 millimeters thick.

2**ちょっけい 直系の** direct ▶徳川吉宗は家康の直系の子孫ではなかった Tokugawa Yoshimune was not a *direct* descendant of Ieyasu. ‖このカーディーラーはトヨタ自動車の直系の子会社です This car dealer is *a wholly-owned affiliate* of Toyota Motor Corporation. ／This car dealer is under the direct control of Toyota Motor Corporation.

ちょっけつ 直結 ▶物価の上昇は生活に直結する重大な問題だ Price hikes are a serious problem *directly connected with* [*linked to*] our lives. ‖過密ダイヤは大事故に直結する A too tight train schedule *is bound to* cause a disastrous accident. (➤ be bound to は「きっと…する」の意) ／Excessively tight train schedules *directly lead to* big accidents.

ちょっこう 直行する go straight [directly] 《to》 ▶あすの朝は会社へは寄らず, 得意先に直行します Tomorrow morning, I'm going to *go straight* [*directly*] *to* one of our customers, without dropping in at the office. ‖彼女は直行便でニューヨークへ飛んだ She took *a direct* [*nonstop*] *flight* to New York. ／She flew nonstop to New York.

ちょっと **1【短時間】**(just) a moment [second] ▶ちょっと待ってね *Just a second* [*moment* ／*minute*], please. ‖ちょっとお時間頂けますか Can you spare me *a minute*? ／I wonder if I might have a few words with you. (➤後者は「ちょっとお話ができますか」の意) ‖ちょっと時間いい? Do you have *a moment*? ／Can I take your time *for a second*? ‖ちょっとよそ見してる間にバッグを取られた I looked away *for just a minute*, and my bag was stolen. ‖昔ちょっと銀行に勤めた I once worked for a bank *for a while* [*for a short time*]. ‖もうちょっとだけ待ってください Give me *a couple more minutes*.

2【少量】a little ▶彼女はちょっとしか食べない She eats only *a little*. ／She does*n't* eat *much* [is a *light* eater]. ‖私はちょっとウイスキーを飲むと心臓がどきどきする Drinking only *a small amount of* whisky causes my heart to thump. (➤ thump /θʌmp/ は「(心臓などが)鼓動する」) ‖最近は10万円ちょっとでヨーロッパ旅行ができる Nowadays you can enjoy a trip to Europe *for a little over 100,000 yen*.

3【僅かな程度】a little, a bit ; slightly (少しばかり) ▶この靴は私にはちょっと大きすぎる These shoes are *a little* too big for me. ‖もうちょっと奥へ詰めてください Move *a little* further to the rear, please. ‖ちょっと顔色が悪いね You look *a little* pale. ‖ちょっと到着が遅れますけど… I'm afraid I'll be arriving there *a little bit* late ... ‖ステーキはちょっと焼き過ぎだった The steak was *slightly* [*a little*] overdone. (➤「ちょっと焼き過ぎたステーキ」の場合は a slightly overdone steak といい, (×) a little overdone steak としない. 後に数えられる名詞が来ると a little は「小さな」の意味になる).
▶大丈夫, ちょっとけがしただけです I'm O.K. I've just gotten a *minor* injury. ／I'm fine. I just hurt myself *a little*. ‖彼はちょっとしたかぜが元で肺炎になった His *slight* cold developed into pneumonia. ‖旅人にはちょっとした親切がうれしい A *small* kindness makes a traveler happy. ‖もうちょっとで車にはねられるところだった I was *nearly* [*almost*] hit by a car. ‖動くな! ちょっとでも動いたら死ぬぞ! Freeze! *One move* and you're dead! ‖おばはちょっとのこと(＝ごくつまらないこと)で大騒ぎする My aunt makes a fuss about the *littlest things*. ‖母はちょっと顔をしかめたが, すぐにっこりした My mother *kind* [*sort*] *of* frowned but then smiled. (➤ kind of, sort of はインフォーマルな言い方で, 動詞・形容詞の前につける).

4【気軽に行動する様子】▶ちょっと聞いていいですか Could I ask you a *quick* question? ‖ちょっとお茶でも飲まない? How about a cup of tea *or something*? ‖この指輪, ちょっとはめてみてごらん Why don't you try on this ring? (➤ try on は「試しに着けて[着て]みる」) ‖ちょっとそこまで来たもんだから寄ってみたんだ I *happened* to be passing through *this neighborhood*, so I thought I'd just drop in.

5【可能性がない様子】not ... easily ▶この染みはちょっと落ちないよ This stain *won't* come out *easily*. (➤この won't は期待どおりにいかない状況を表す) ‖ これだけの小説はちょっとやそっとでは書けないよ You can't write a novel of this scope *as easily as you think*. ‖ この鉄扉はちょっとやそっとの衝撃ではびくともしない It *takes a bigger impact* [*shove*] *than that to make* this iron gate *budge*. ‖ 対話「すしはいかがですか」「私, 生の魚はちょっと」"How about sushi?" "I *don't much care for* raw fish." (● care for は「好む」で否定文で用いることが多い) ‖ 対話「今夜, 一杯どう?」「今夜はちょっと…」"How about a drink tonight?" "I'm afraid I *can't make it* tonight." (➤この make it は「都合がつく」).

6【程度がかなり高い様子】 ▶ちょっとした財産 a *small* fortune ‖ この1敗はちょっと(=かなり)痛い This loss is *quite* a blow to me. ‖ 松原さんの奥さんはちょっとした美人だ Mrs. Matsubara is *somewhat* of a beauty [*something of a* looker]. (● some beauty と表現すると「すごい美人」の意になる) ‖ 細田さんのマンションはちょっとしたものよ Hosoda's condominium is *quite something*. ‖ 彼女の洋服だんすの中にはちょっとした数のドレスがあった There were *quite a few* dresses in her wardrobe.

7【呼びかけ】 ▶ちょっと, みっちゃん! *Say* [《英 古風》I say], Mitchan! ‖ ちょっと, この借金どうしてくれるのよ *Hey*, how do you plan to pay back this money? (➤ Hey はくだけた呼びかけの表現) ‖ ちょっとすみませんが, 市役所はどちらでしょう *Excuse me, but* could you tell me where the city office is?

8【言いよどんで】 ▶ 対話「ゆうべ遅くまでどこに行ってたの?」「うん, ちょっとね」"Where were you till so late last night?" "Well, *I had things* [*something*] *to do*."

ちょっとみ ちょっと見 ▶ちょっと見にはこれが偽物とはわからない *A quick glance* won't tell you this is a fake.

ちょっぴり ▶彼女のことがちょっぴりかわいそうな気がした I felt *a little* (*bit*) sorry for her.

ちょとつもうしん 猪突猛進 ▶彼は猪突猛進型だ He is *a type of person who rushes headlong into things*.

ちょびひげ ちょび髭 a **small mustache** [《英》**moustache**].

ちょぼちょぼ ▶ひげがちょぼちょぼ生えてきた A *stubble* of beard is just beginning to show. (➤ stubble は「不精ひげ」).
▶彼はテニスではぼくとちょぼちょぼ(=同程度)だ He is *no better* at tennis than I am.

ちょめい 著名な famous(有名な); **well-known** (よく知られた); **distinguished** (特に科学・芸術などの分野で高名な) ▶あの老婦人は著名な作家だ That old lady is a *famous* [*well-known*] writer. ‖ 彼は著名な学者だ He is a *distinguished* scholar.
‖**著名人** a famous person [name]; a celebrity (芸能界・スポーツ界などの).

チョモランマ Chomolungma, Qomolangma (エベレストのチベット名).

ちょろい ▶ 対話「この数学の問題を解くの, 手伝ってくれる?」「よし, 任せろ. そんなのちょろいよ」"Can you help me with this math problem?" "Sure. Leave it to me. *It's a cinch* [*Nothing to it*]." (➤ cinch /sɪntʃ/ は「朝飯前」の意).

ちょろちょろ ▶川には水がちょろちょろ流れているだけだった There was a *mere trickle* of water in the river. (➤ trickle は「滴る」) ‖ 水道の水がちょろちょろ出っぱなしだ The faucet is left on and is *dripping*.

ちょろまかす pocket +Ⓣ (着服する); **filch** /fɪltʃ/ +Ⓣ (価値の低い物を); **pilfer** /pɪlfəʳ/ +Ⓣ (自分の職場などから) ▶その店員は高い値段を言って差額をちょろまかした The clerk charged extra and *pocketed* the difference. ‖ 彼女はその文房具屋で消しゴムをちょろまかした She *filched* [*pilfered*] an eraser from the stationery store.

ちょんぎる ちょん切る snip off [**at**] ▶その男の子はトカゲのしっぽをちょん切った The boy *snipped off* the tail of a lizard.

ちょんぼ ▶きょうのテストでちょんぼしちゃったよ(=へまをやらかした) I *made silly* [*stupid*] *mistakes* [*goofs*] on today's test.

ちょんまげ 丁髷 a **topknot** ▶力士はなぜちょんまげをしていると思いますか Why do you suppose sumo wrestlers *wear* their hair *up in a* (*top*)*knot*?

ちらかす 散らかす scatter +Ⓣ (まき散らす, ばらまく); **litter** +Ⓣ (ごみを); **make a mess** (乱雑な状態にする) ▶服を散らかす *scatter* clothes ‖ おもちゃを散らかすんじゃありません Don't *scatter* the toys *around*. ‖ 子供はテーブルを食べかすで散らかした The child *littered* the table *with* pieces of food. (➤ litter A with B で「A(場所)をB(物)で散らかす」) ‖ 部屋を掃除した先から子供たちが散らかしてしまう The kids will *make* the room *a mess* the moment I clean it.
▶散らかしっぱなしですけど, さあどうぞ I'm afraid the house [apartment / office] is a little *messy*, but please come on in. ‖ あまり散らかさないで Don't be a *litterbug*! (➤ litterbug は「ごみを散らかす人」) ‖《掲示》ごみを散らかさないでください Don't Litter / No Littering.

ちらかる 散らかる ▶部屋には紙くずがいっぱい散らかっていた The room *was littered* with bits of paper. ‖ あなたの部屋, 散らかってるわね. きれいに片づけなさい Your room *is a mess* [*is messy*]. You need to clean [tidy] it up. ‖ 散らかってますけど I hope you don't mind *the mess*.

ちらし 散らし a **flier**, a **flyer**, a **leaflet** (➤ leaflet は宣伝用以外の案内びらも指す); 《英》a **handbill** (街頭で手で配る); an **insert** /ɪnsəːʳt/ (新聞などの折り込み広告).

ちらしずし 散らし鮨・散らし寿司 ***chirashizushi***; a bowl of sushi rice topped with various kinds of sushi ingredients (➤説明的な訳).

ちらす 散らす 1【まき散らす】scatter +Ⓣ ▶木枯らしが吹いて芝生一面に落ち葉を散らした The winter gale *scattered* leaves over the grass. ‖ 肉に刻みパセリを散らします *Sprinkle* the meat with chopped parsley.

2【「…散らす」の形で】 ▶彼は友人たちに対してボスのように威張り散らしている He *lords it over* his friends. (➤ lord it over ... で「…に威張り散らす」) ‖ 酔っ払いたちが表でわめき散らしていた I could hear drunk(en) men *ranting and raving* outside. (➤ rant /rænt/ は「大声でわめき散らす」, rave /reɪv/ は「狂乱状態になってどなる」の意).

ちらちら ▶外では小雪がちらちら舞っている A light snow is falling outside. (●「ちらちら」は訳文には現れない).
▶この頃目がちらちらする My vision has *become blurred* [*blurry*] lately. (➤ blur /bləːʳ/ は「ぼやけさせる」).

ちらつかせる flash +Ⓣ (ちらりと見せる); **dangle** +Ⓣ

(見せびらかす) ▶強盗は私に刃物をちらつかせた The burglar *flashed* a knife at me. ‖ 彼は結婚をちらつかせて彼女を口説いた He tried to win her heart by *hinting at* (the possibility of) marriage. ‖ 彼らは札束をちらつかせて我々に立ち退きを迫った They urged us to move out, *dangling* a wad of money in front of us.

ちらつく ▶小雪がちらつき始めた A light snow began to *fall*.
▶遠くに家々の明かりがちらついている In the distance, I can see the *flickering* lights of (the) houses. ▶目を閉じると彼女の笑顔が目の前にちらつく Her smiling face *haunts* me whenever I close my eyes.

ちらっと →ちらり.

ちらばる 散らばる scatter ; be scattered (散らばっている) ▶ネックレスの糸が切れて真珠が散らばってしまった The necklace string snapped and the pearls *scattered* [*went every which way*]. ‖ ユダヤ人は世界中に散らばっている Jewish people *are scattered* all over the world. ‖ 書類が風で散らばらないようにおもしを載せた I put a weight on the papers so they would not *be scattered about* by the wind.

ちらほら ▶母の髪に白いものがちらほら見える My mother's hair *is flecked with* gray. (➤ be flecked は「点々とつく」) ‖ 梅の花がちらほら(＝あちこち)咲き始めました *Ume* blossoms are beginning to bloom *here and there*.

ちらり ▶彼はちらりと私のほうを見た He *glanced at* [*stole a glance at*] me. ‖ 人混みの中に彼女の姿がちらりと見えた I *caught a glimpse* of her in the crowd. (➤ glance が「ちらりと見ること(行為)」であるのに対し, glimpse /glɪmps/ は通例「glance の結果目に入るもの」の意) ‖ 彼が会社を変わったことをちらりと(＝偶然)耳にした I heard *by chance* (that) he had moved to another company.

¹**ちり 塵** dust (ほこり) ▶机の上にちりが積もっている The desk is covered with *dust*. ‖ テーブルのちりを払ってください *Dust* the table, please. (➤ この dust は動詞) ‖ 部屋は掃き清められてちり一つなかった The room was swept clean of (all) *dust*.
[ことわざ] ちりも積もれば山となる When the dust piles high enough, it makes a mountain. (➤ 日本語からの直訳) ／Many a little makes a mickle. (➤ 英語のことわざ ; mickle はスコットランド語で great の意).
☛ ちり取り (→見出語)

²**ちり 地理** geography /dʒiɑ́:grəfi/ (地理学 ; 地形) ▶地理の時間はおもしろい *Geography* class is interesting. ‖ 日本は島国だから地理的にはイギリスに似ている Japan is an island country, so *geographically* (*speaking*), it resembles Britain. ‖ 彼は大阪南部の地理に明るい He *knows his way around* the southern part of Osaka. ‖ この辺の地理は詳しくありません *I'm a stranger* here. (➤ stranger は「不案内な人」). ／*I'm not familiar with* [I *don't know*] this area.

チリ Chile (南米の太平洋側の国) 一形 チリの Chilean ‖ チリ人 a Chilean.

ちりがみ 塵紙 tissue (ティッシュペーパー) ; toilet paper [tissue] (トイレ用の).

チリソース chili sauce.

ちりちり ▶姉はちりちりにパーマをかけて美容院から帰って来た My sister came back from the beauty salon with a *frizzy* [*kinky*] permanent. →縮れる.

ちりぢり 散り散り ▶難民たちは上陸するとちりぢりになった The refugees *dispersed* [*went their separate ways*] upon landing. ‖ 大きな犬が近づいてきたので子供たちはちりぢりになって逃げた As a big dog approached, the children ran away *in all directions*.

ちりとり 塵取り a dustpan ▶ちり取りにごみを集める sweep the dirt into *a dustpan*.

ちりなべ ちり鍋 *chirinabe* ; a hotpot dish of fish (typically, cod or anglerfish), vegetables, tofu and broth (➤ 説明的な訳).

ちりばめる stud ＋目 ▶王様はお后(きさき)にダイヤモンドとルビーをちりばめた冠を与えた The king gave the queen a crown *set* [*studded*] *with* diamonds and rubies. (➤ set は「はめ込む」) ‖ その宝石箱は金銀がちりばめてある The jewelry box *is set with* gold and silver.

ちりめん 縮緬 《布》 crepe, crêpe.

ちりょう 治療 treatment ; a therapy (薬によらない治療法) ; a cure (完治法) 一動 治療する treat ＋目 ▶うつ病[乳がん]の治療をする *treat* depression [breast cancer] ‖ 放射線治療を受ける undergo *radiation therapy* ‖ あなたの潰瘍はすぐに治療する必要があります Your ulcer must *be treated* immediately. ／Your ulcer needs immediate (*medical*) *treatment* [attention]. ‖ 父は病院で糖尿病の治療を受けている My father *is being treated* for diabetes at the hospital.
▶《患者が医師に》治療は可能でしょうか Is it *treatable* [*curable*]? (➤ 後者は「治せるでしょうか」に相当) ‖ HIV／AIDSには完治させる方法は無いが, 有効な治療法は存在する There is no cure for HIV／AIDS, but effective *treatment* exists. ‖ 私は歯の治療をしなければならない I need to *have* (one of) my teeth *treated*. ／I need some dental work *done*.
‖ 治療費 a doctor's fee.

ちりょく 知力 intellectual power [capacity] (➤ しばしば複数形), mental ability ▶知力の優れた人 a person of great *intellectual power*(*s*) ‖ その老人は最近知力の衰えが顕著になった The elderly man's *mental ability* has been declining noticeably recently.

ちりんちりん ▶彼は自転車のベルをチリンチリン鳴らしながら細い道を通り抜けた He rode his bike down the narrow road *ringing* his bell [*making* his bell *go ting-a-ling*].

ちる 散る **1** 【花などが】 fall (落ちる) ; scatter (散らばる) ▶きのうの強風で桜が散ってしまった The cherry blossoms *fell* in yesterday's strong wind. ‖ 地面一面に花びらが散っていた The petals *lay scattered* all over the ground. ‖ 切れたコードから火花が散った Sparks *flew* from the severed cord.
▶《比喩的》その青年は戦地に散った(＝死んだ) The young man's *life was extinguished* on the battlefield.
2 【四方八方に去る】 disperse ▶試合が終わると観衆は散っていった The spectators *dispersed* after the game.
3 【気が散る】 ▶選挙カーの騒音で気が散って勉強ができない The noise from the election campaign trucks *distracts* me from studying. (➤ distract は「(注意を)そらす」).

チルド chilled ‖ チルド室 chill [chilled／chilling] compartment ‖ チルドワイン chilled wine.

¹**ちん** ▶ちんと洟(はな)をかむ blow one's nose *loudly*.

²**ちん 狆** 《動物》 a Japanese chin [spaniel].

ちん- 珍- ‖**珍客** a rare guest [visitor] ‖ **珍獣** a rare animal ‖ **珍品** a rarity ‖ **珍本** a rare book ‖ **珍問** an offbeat question (➤ offbeat は「とっぴな」).

ちんあげ 賃上げ 《米》 **a pay raise,** 《英》 **a pay rise** (➤ 文脈でわかる場合は pay を略すことが多い) ▶この不景気ではことしの**賃上げ**はほとんど望めないだろう Because of the recession, there is little hope of our getting *a* (*pay*) *raise* this year. ‖ 労働組合は5%の**賃上げ**を要求した The labor union demanded a 5 percent (*pay*) *raise* [*wage increase*]. (➤ wage increase は堅い言い方) ‖ 雇い主は彼らの**賃上げ要求**をのんだ The employer accepted their *demand for a* (*pay*) *raise* [demand for higher wages].

ちんあつ 鎮圧する suppress +目, **put down** (➤ 後者はインフォーマルな言い方) ▶軍隊がクーデターを**鎮圧した** The army *suppressed* [*put down*] the coup (d'état). ‖ 暴動はその日のうちに**鎮圧された** The riot *was suppressed* within the day.

ちんうつ 沈鬱 ▶試合に完敗し, 選手たちは**沈鬱な**表情でサッカー場を去った The players left the soccer field with *depressed* [*dejected*] looks on their faces after being decisively defeated. (➤ decisively は「決定的に」).

1**ちんか 沈下する sink, subside** (➤ 地面の場合, 後者は突然の陥没を意味するのがふつう) ▶地下鉄工事のために, この辺りの地盤が**沈下した** The ground in this area *has sunk* [*subsided*] because of the construction of the subway.

2**ちんか 鎮火する be extinguished** ▶火事は未明に至ってようやく**鎮火した** It was just before daylight that the fire *was* finally *extinguished* [*was put out*].

ちんがし 賃貸しする rent [**lease**] (**out**) 《**参考**》《英》では家を貸すことを特に let (out) という ▶彼は自分の家を友人に**賃貸ししている** He *is renting* (*out*) his house to a friend.

ちんぎん 賃金・賃銀 wages ; **pay** (給料) →**給料** ▶安い**賃金**で働く work at low *wages* [*pay*] ‖ 私は日給7000円の**賃金**で働いている I work for 7,000 yen a day. ／I am paid (*a wage* of) 7,000 yen a day. ／I *get* [*earn*] 7,000 yen a day. ‖ OL たちは男女間の**賃金格差**に抗議した The female office workers protested against the *wage gap* [*disparity*] between men and women.
‖**賃金カット** a wage cut ‖ **賃金凍結** a wage freeze ‖ **賃金抑制** wage restraint ‖ **最低賃金** a minimum wage.

ちんけ ちんけな good for nothing [**worthless**] ▶**ちんけな**男 a *good-for-nothing* man ‖ **ちんけな**商売 a *small-time* business.

チンゲンサイ 青梗菜 quiq geng cai.

ちんこん 鎮魂 praying for the repose of the soul(s) of the deceased ‖**鎮魂(ミサ)曲** a requiem.

ちんさげ 賃下げ a wage cut.

ちんしもっこう 沈思黙考 meditation.

ちんしゃ 陳謝 an **apology** 一動 **陳謝する apologize** ▶大臣は不適切な発言を**陳謝した** The minister *apologized* (*publicly*) for his improper statement.

ちんじゅ 鎮守 a **village protective deity**(神) ▶**鎮守**の森 a grove of a *village shrine*.

ちんじゅつ 陳述 a **statement** 一動 **陳述する state, give** [**make**] **a statement.**

ちんじょう 陳情 a **petition**(文書や署名などで要望を出すこと) ; an **appeal**(訴え) 一動 **陳情する petition** ; **make an appeal** 《to》 ▶私たちは市当局に下水道の整備を**陳情した** We *petitioned* [*made an appeal to*] the municipal authorities for the construction of sewer lines. (➤ sewer は /súːəʳ/ と発音) ‖ 政府は我々のダム建設反対の**陳情**をはねつけた The Government rejected our *petition* opposing the construction of the dam. ‖ 市民の代表が市長に**陳情書**を提出した The representatives of the citizens submitted *a petition* [lodged *a petition* with] to the mayor. ‖**陳情団** a group of petitioners ; a lobby (国会への).

チンする heat [**warm**] **in a microwave** (電子レンジで温める) ; 《米・インフォーマル》 **zap** ; **nuke.**

ちんせい 鎮静 calming (**down**) ; **remission**(痛み・症状などの) ▶彼のがんは**鎮静化している** His cancer is *in remission*. ‖**鎮静剤** a sedative ; a tranquilizer (精神安定剤).

1**ちんたい 沈滞 stagnation** ▶市場の**沈滞** *stagnation* in the market ‖ 景気が**沈滞している** The economy is *stagnant* [*in the doldrums*]. ‖ チームの**沈滞ムード**を破らなければならない We have to dispel the *depressed mood* among the team.

2**ちんたい 賃貸** ▶駐車場の**賃貸契約**をした I signed *a lease contract* for a parking space. ‖ 彼は**賃貸マンション**に住んでいる He lives in *a rental apartment*. (➤ 単に an apartment でもよい) ‖ その会議場の**賃貸料**(＝使用料)は1日2万円だ The *rent* for the conference room is 20,000 yen a day.
‖**賃貸業者** a rental agent.

ちんたら ▶**ちんたら**と仕事をするな Don't work (*so*) *inefficiently*. ‖ **ちんたら**歩くな Don't *dawdle*.

ちんちくりん ▶**ちんちくりん**の浴衣 a yukata that is (*a bit*) *short for a person* ‖ 英語の先生は**ちんちくりん**だ Our English teacher is *a shorty*.

ちんちゃく 沈着な calm /kɑːm/, **composed** ▶**沈着**冷静な人 a *calm*, self-possessed person ‖ 彼は**沈着**な態度を失わなかった He kept *calm* [《英また》 *unflappable*]. ／He kept his composure.

ちんちょう 珍重 ▶こんながらくたを夫がどうして**珍重する**のか理解に苦しむ I can't understand why my husband *treasures* junk like this *so much*. ‖ チョウザメの腹子はキャビアとして**珍重されている** Sturgeon roe *is prized* as true caviar.

ちんちん 1【音】▶どこからか**チンチン**と鉦(かね)の音が聞こえてくる I can hear the "*ding, ding*" of a bell ringing somewhere. ‖ この町にはまだ古風な**ちんちん電車**が走っている In this town, old-fashioned "*ting-a-ling trams*" still run.
▶やかんのお湯が**チンチン**沸いている The water in the kettle is boiling and *hissing*. (➤ hiss は「シューシュー音を立てる」).
2【犬の芸】▶ポチは**ちんちん**をしてソーセージをねだった Pochi *sat up* and begged for some sausage. ‖ ポチ, **ちんちん**! *Sit up*, Pochi!
☛ **おちんちん** (→見出語)

ちんつう 沈痛な sad, sorrowful ▶父は友人の死を聞いて**沈痛な**面持ちだった My father looked *sad* [*sorrowful*] at the news of his friend's death.

ちんつうざい 鎮痛剤 a **painkiller** ; (**an**) **aspirin** /ǽsprɪn/ (アスピリン) ▶**鎮痛剤**をのむ take *a painkiller* ／take *pain medication*. (➤ 後者は処方された薬を飲む場合).

ちんでん 沈殿・沈澱 sedimentation 一動 **沈殿する settle** ▶川底にへどろが**沈殿している** Sludge *has settled* on the riverbed. ‖ 瓶の底に白い**沈殿物**がある There is some white *sediment* at the bottom of the bottle.

ちんどんや ちんどん屋 a ***chindon-ya***; a small band of gaily-costumed musicians on the street hired to advertise the opening of a store, etc. (➤ 説明的な訳).

チンパンジー a **chimpanzee** /tʃìmpænzíː/, a **chimp** (➤ 後者はインフォーマル).

ちんぴら a **hoodlum**, a **petty criminal**, 《米また》 a **punk**, 《英また》 a **yobbo** /jáːboʊ/.

ちんぷ 陳腐な **trite** /traɪt/; **hackneyed** /hǽknid/ (使い古されたうえ, 退屈で品もない); **banal** /bənáːl/ (独創性のない) ▶**陳腐な言い回し** a *trite* [*hackneyed*] phrase ‖ 文章の上手な人は**陳腐な**表現は使わない Good writers try to avoid *trite* [*banal*] expressions. 《参考》陳腐な決まり文句のことを cliché /kliːʃéɪ/ という.

ちんぷんかんぷん ▶彼女の説明は私にはちんぷんかんぷんだ Her explanations are just *gibberish* to me. (➤ gibberish は「訳のわからないおしゃべり」) ‖ あの人の講演は私にはちんぷんかんぷんだった I *couldn't make heads or tails of* his lecture. ／His lecture *was all Greek* to me. (➤ cannot make heads or tails of は「…がさっぱりわからない」).

ちんぽ(こ) a **penis**, a **dick**, 《英》 a **willy**.

ちんぼつ 沈没する **sink**, **go down** ▶漁船が秋田沖で[太平洋で]転覆, **沈没した** A fishing boat capsized and *sank* off Akita [in the Pacific Ocean].

ちんまりした **cozy** (居心地のよい); **snug** (こぢんまりした) ▶**ちんまりとした**喫茶店 a *cozy* coffee shop.

ちんみ 珍味 a **delicacy** /délɪkəsi/; a **dainty** (特に風味が良い場合) ▶テーブルには山海の**珍味**が並べられた The table was spread with all kinds of *delicacies* from land and sea. ‖ うん, これはなかなか**珍味**だ Mmn. This is *a real delicacy*.

ちんみょう 珍妙な **strange** ▶その役者は**珍妙な**格好で番組に登場した The actor appeared on the program in a *strange* [*weird*] get-up.

ちんもく 沈黙 **silence** ▶深海の底は**沈黙の世界**だ The bottom of the deep ocean is *a world of silence*. ‖ 彼女は長い間の**沈黙を破って**真相を話し始めた She *broke her* long *silence* and began to tell the truth. ‖ 容疑者はその事件について**沈黙を守った** The suspect *kept silent* [*held his tongue*] about the incident. ‖ **沈黙は承諾のしるし** Silence gives consent. (➤ 英語のことわざ).

ことわざ (**雄弁は銀,**) **沈黙は金** (Speech is silver,) silence is golden.

ちんれつ 陳列 (a) **display** /dɪspléɪ/ 一動 **陳列する** **exhibit** /ɪɡzíbɪt/ ＋目, **display** ＋目 ▶ショーウインドーには高価なガラス器がたくさん**陳列してある** Many pieces of precious glasswork *are displayed* [*are on display*] in the show window. ‖ 博物館には先史時代の土器が**陳列してあった** Prehistoric earthen vessels *were exhibited* in the museum. ‖ 駅員は落とし物をいくつか棚に**陳列した** The station employee *set out* some of the lost items on a shelf.

‖**陳列ケース** a display case ‖ **陳列室** an exhibit hall, a display room; a showroom (ショールーム) ‖ **陳列台** a display stand ‖ **陳列棚** a display shelf ‖ **陳列品** an exhibit (➤ 集合的に指す語; 個々の陳列品は exhibit item または article [item] on display).

つ・ツ

ツアー a **tour** /tʊəʳ/; a **group tour** (団体旅行) ▶その史跡の**ガイド付きツアー**に出かける go on *a guided tour* of that historic site ‖ **スキーツアー**に参加する[申し込む] join [sign up for] *a ski tour* ‖ 来年は**ツアー**でヨーロッパ旅行をするつもりだ I'm thinking of traveling in Europe *on a group* [*package*] *tour* next year. ‖ その歌手は2年ぶりに**全国ツアー**に出た The singer went on his first *nation-wide* [*cross-country*] *tour* in two years.

‖**ツアーコンダクター** a tour conductor, 《英》 a courier /kʊ́riəʳ/.

> **危ないカタカナ語✹ ツアー**
> **1** 日本語では専ら「団体旅行」の意味で「ツアー」といっているが, tour は本来何か所かに立ち寄る「周遊旅行」の意味である. また観光旅行に限らず,「視察旅行」やスポーツチーム・劇団などの「巡業」の意味でも用いる.
> **2** 日本語でいう「ツアー」は group tour, package tour などのようにいう必要がある.

[1]**つい 対** a **pair** ▶**対**のペンダント pendants which make *a pair* ／*a pair of* pendants ‖ この湯飲みは夫婦用に**対になっている** These teacups *come in pairs* for use by married couples. ‖ 玄関に**一対**の置物がある There are *a pair of* ornaments in the hall.

[2]**つい 1【ほんの, 僅か】** **only**; **just** (ちょうど, まさに) ▶幸子は**つい今し方**出ていった Sachiko went out *just* [*only*] *a few minutes ago*. ／Sachiko *just* went out. ／Sachiko went out *just now*. ‖ その俳優の死を知ったのは**ついけさほど**のことだ It was *only this morning* that I learned of the actor's death. ‖ 彼が帰国することは**つい最近まで**知らなかった I didn't know *until quite recently* that he would be coming home. ‖ 彼は私の家の**つい**2, 3軒先に住んでいる He lives *only* a few doors down from my house.

2【うっかり】 ▶**ついうっかり**下りの電車に乗ってしまった I got on an outbound train *by mistake*. ‖ **ついうっかり**かばんを網棚に置き忘れてしまった I *carelessly* left my bag on the rack. ‖ 私は**つい**(＝思わず)笑ってしまった I laughed *in spite of myself*. ‖ 期末試験が迫ってきても新しい漫画本には**つい手が伸びてしまう** Even though the final exams are approaching, I still *can't stop* reach*ing* out for a new comic book. (→ついつい).

ツイート a **tweet** (➤ ツイッター(Twitter)上のメッセージ. 「つぶやき」ともいう).

ツイード **tweed** ▶**ツイードの服を着た**スコットランド人 a Scotsman in *tweeds* ‖ **ツイードのスーツ** a *tweed* suit.

ついおく 追憶 (a) **recollection** (記憶をたどって懸命に思い出すこと); (a) **reminiscence** /rèmɪnísəns/ (思い出に

ふけること)(ともに具体的に「いろいろ思い出す出来事」の意ではしばしば複数形)▶懐かしい昔の追憶にふける indulge in *recollections* of the good old days.

ついか 追加 an **addition** 一形 **追加の additional** 一動 **追加する add**《to》▶ビールをあと3本追加してくれ *Add* another 3 bottles of beer *to* our order, please. ‖ 広島は7回に追加点を2点あげ, ヤクルトを8対2で破った The Carp *added* two runs in the seventh to beat the Swallows 8-2. ‖ カラオケボックスでは追加料金を払えば時間を延長できる You can extend your rental of a karaoke room by paying *an extra fee*.

‖追加予算 the supplementary budget.

ついかんばんヘルニア 椎間板ヘルニア《医学》a **herniated disc** [**disk**] ▶椎間板ヘルニアになる[の手術を受ける] have [have surgery for] a *herniated disc*.

ついき 追記 a **postscript** 一形 **追記型の recordable** ▶追記型の CD a *recordable* CD.

1**ついきゅう 追及** an **investigation**(調査); (an) **interrogation**(長時間の尋問) 一動 **追及する investigate** +目, **interrogate** +目 ▶事故の責任を追及する *search for* the person (who is) responsible for the accident ‖ 飛行機墜落事故の責任が厳しく追及されている A strict *investigation* into who was responsible for the plane crash is being carried out. ‖ 警察はその容疑者を徹底的に追及した The police *thoroughly interrogated* the suspect.

2**ついきゅう 追究・追求 pursuit** /pərsjúːt/ 一動 **追究する・追求する pursue** /pərsjúː/ +目; **seek (after)**(時間・労力をかけて)▶真理を追究する *pursue* truth / *seek* (*after*) truth ‖ 利潤を追求する *seek* profit ‖ 誰もが幸福を追求する Everybody *pursues* [*seeks after*] happiness.

ついげき 追撃 ▶広島は3連勝して首位巨人を激しく追撃している Winning three games in a row, the Carp *are close behind* the Giants [the Carp *are edging* the Giants].

ついし 追試 a **supplementary examination,**《米・インフォーマル》a **makeup** ▶金曜日に英語の追試を受けないといけないんだ I have to take *a makeup* (*test*) in English this Friday. / I've got to *resit* an English *exam* this Friday. (➤ 後者は主に《英》).

ついじゅう 追従する follow.

ついしょう 追従 flattery ▶上司にお追従を言う *flatter* [*suck up to*] one's boss ‖ 多くの国がアメリカに追従して, その国連決議を支持した Many nations *followed* the U.S. lead and supported the U.N. resolution.

‖追従笑い an obsequious /əbsíːkwiəs/ smile.

ついしん 追伸 a **postscript,**《略》**PS, P.S.**

✉ **追伸―別便にてサクランボを1箱お送りします** *PS* I am sending you a box of cherries separately.

ついずい 追随 ▶わが高校は東大合格者の数では他の追随を許さない Our high school *can't be beat*(*en*) for the number of its students that make it into Tokyo University. / No other high school comes close to ours in the number of students it sends to Tokyo University.

ついせき 追跡 a **chase,** (a) **pursuit** /pərsjúːt/ (➤ 後者がより堅い語) 一動 **追跡する chase** +目, **pursue** /pərsjúː/ +目 ▶警官は泥棒を追跡した The police officer *chased* [*pursued* / *ran after*] the thief. ‖ 殺人犯は警察の追跡を逃れたらしい The murderer seems to have eluded the police. ‖ 犯人追跡中のパトカーがタクシーに追突した A police car *in pursuit of* the suspect hit a taxi from the rear.

‖追跡調査 a follow-up survey ‖ 追跡番号 a tracking number.

ついぞ ▶彼女は自分が間違っていてもついぞ謝ったことがない She *never* apologizes even when she is (in the) wrong.

ついそう 追想 reminiscence /rèmɪnísəns/.

ついたいけん 追体験 a **vicarious experience** (➤ vicarious /vaɪkéəriəs/ は「代理の」) ▶戦時中の生活を追体験する *experience for oneself* what life was like during wartime.

ついたち 一日 the first day of the month ▶8月1日 *the first* (*day*) of August / August 1 (➤ August (the) first と読む).

ついたて 衝立 a **screen**; a **partition**(仕切り) ▶部屋をついたてで仕切る partition the room (off) with *a screen*.

ついちょうきん 追徴金 money paid in addition, a **surcharge**; a **penalty**(罰金).

ついつい ▶このバッグ, あんまり安かったので, ついつい買っちゃった This (hand) bag was so inexpensive I *couldn't help* buy*ing* it.

ツイッター Twitter(➤ 商標名) →ツイート, つぶやき, つぶやく.

-ついて 1【…に関して】about, on (➤ 前者は話題とその周辺を指す. 後者は専門的なテーマに関して用いられることが多い) ▶学生たちは秋の学園祭について話し合った The students talked *about* the school festival in the fall. ‖ 瀬戸教授は現代ドイツ文学について講演した[本を書いた] Professor Seto gave a lecture [wrote a book] *on* modern German literature. ‖ 新しい首相についてどう思いますか What do you think *of* the new prime minister? ‖ 私たちは安楽死について討論した We discussed euthanasia. (discuss は他動詞なので, (×) discuss about などとしない. また, euthanasia は /jùːθənéɪʒə/ と発音).

2【…ごとに】per →-につき.

1**ついで 序で** ⚠「…のついでに」にぴったりの英語はないので,「…の途中で」「…のときに」などと考える.

▶駅へ行くついでに(=途中で)この荷物を出してくれない? Could you mail this package *on your way to* the train station? ‖ 横浜に来たついでにベイブリッジを見てみたい *Now* (*that*) I'm in Yokohama, I'd like to see the Bay Bridge. (➤ now (that) は「今…だから」).

✉ **ニューヨークへ行ったついでに留学中の娘に会いたいと思っています** *When* I visit New York, I'm (*also*) planning to see my daughter who is studying there.

▶おついでがありましたらどうぞお立ち寄りください Please drop in *when you have a chance to* [*when you happen to*] *come this way*. (➤「この方面に来る機会があれば」と考える) ‖ お代はおついでのときで結構です You may pay me *anytime at your convenience*. (➤ at one's convenience は「都合のいいときに」) ‖ ついでですが(=ところで)ちょっとご相談したいことがあります *Incidentally* [*By the way*], I'd like to ask for your advice about something. (by the way は重要な用件を切り出すときにも用いる).

2**ついで 次いで after**(…のあとに); **next to**(…の次に) ▶北岳は富士山に次いで日本で2番目に高い山だ *After* [*Next to*] Mt. Fuji, Mt. Kitadake is the highest mountain in Japan.

ついていく 付いて行く 1【後続する】**follow** +目; **tag along**（➤ 後者には「付きまとう」のニュアンスがある；→ついて来る）▶子供たちは先生のすぐあとをぞろぞろとついていった The children *followed* the teacher at his [her] heels.

2【同伴·同行する】**accompany** +目; **go (together) with**（一緒に行く）▶最近は大学入試を受ける子供についていく親がたくさんいる These days, there are many parents who *accompany* [*go together with*] their sons and daughters to university entrance examinations. ‖ 変なおじさんについていっちゃだめよ Don't *go* anywhere *with* a strange man.

3【遅れないようにする】**keep up** 《with》▶そんなに速く歩かないでよ. ついていけないよ Don't walk so fast. I *can't keep up*. ‖ あの教授の授業は難しくてついていくのが大変だ That professor's class is so difficult that I have a hard time *keeping up* (*with* it). ‖ 彼の考え方にはついていけない I *can't go along with* his way of thinking. (● 「賛成できない」の意) ／I *can't follow* his reasoning. (● 「理解できない」の意) ‖ もっと勉強しないとクラスの人についていけなくなるわよ If you don't work harder, you'll soon *fall behind* (*the others*) in your class. (● 「ほかの人に置いていかれる」の意).

1**ついている 付いている** ▶ほっぺたにご飯粒がついてるよ *There's* a piece of rice *stuck to* your cheek. (➤ stuck は stick (くっつける) の過去分詞形) ‖ 雪の上に車の通った跡がついていた *There were* tire tracks on the snow. ‖ この雑誌には付録が 3 つもついています *There are* three supplements to this magazine. ／This magazine *includes* three supplements. ‖ あなたのアパートには非常階段はついていますか Does your apartment *have* a fire escape? ‖ ランチセットにはコーヒーまたは紅茶がついています Coffee or tea *comes with* the lunch set.

2**ついて(い)る** **be lucky** ▶今夜はついてるぞ *I'm lucky* [*I am in luck* ／*Luck is with me*] tonight. ‖ ついてないわ! バス行っちゃったところよ *Today is not my day!* I have just missed the bus. ‖ 全くついてないなあ! きょうに限って休業だなんて *Just my luck!* Of all the days they could close, they've picked today. ‖ 対話 「きみ, 運がいいね」「うん, このところ怖いくらいついてるんだ」"You're very lucky." "Yeah, I've *been* so *lucky* recently that I'm a little scared."

> **あなたの英語はどう響く?**
> 相手に同情を示す場合の「残念だね」「ついてないね」に相当する英語は Bad [Hard ／Tough] luck! であるが, これに to you をつけて, Bad luck *to you*! とすると, 「おまえなんかくたばれ；こんちくしょう」といった意味になるのがふつう. ただし, *for* you ならばよい.

ついてくる 付いて来る **follow** +目; **tag along** 《with》（➤ 後者は「付きまとう」のニュアンス）▶この犬ったら, どこにでも私について来るのよ Wherever I go, this dog *follows* [*tags along with*] me. ‖ 俺について来い! *Follow* me! ／*Come* (*along*) *with* me! ‖ ついて来るの, やめて Stop [Quit] *following* me.

ついては **so, therefore**（だから；後者は堅い語）; **in this connection**（これに関して）▶当校は来年創立100年を迎えます. ついては卒業生の方々に寄付をお願いしたいと考えております Our school is going to celebrate the 100th anniversary (of its founding) next year, *so* we are thinking of seeking contributions from the alumni.

ついてまわる 付いて回る ▶我々にはどこまでも不運がついて回った We *were dogged* by misfortune(s) wherever we went. (➤ この dog は「付きまとう」の意の動詞) ‖ どこへ行っても彼にはあの大女優の息子(の1人)だということがついて回る Wherever he goes, he *cannot escape from* the fact that he is a son of the great actress. (● 一人息子の場合は the son となる).

ついとう 追悼 ▶故人への追悼の意を表す *pay tribute* to the memory of the deceased person ‖ おじが亡父への追悼の辞を述べた At my father's funeral, my uncle delivered *a eulogy* [*gave a memorial address*] for him. (➤ eulogy /júːlədʒi/ は「(死者に対する) 賞賛のことば」) ‖ 学校長の追悼式 [集会] *a memorial service* [*gathering*] for our school principal.

ついとつ 追突 a **rear-end collision** 一動 追突する **strike** [**hit** ／**collide with**] ... **from behind** ▶私の乗ったタクシーが観光バスに追突した The taxi I was in *struck* [*collided with*] a sightseeing bus *from behind*. ‖ 彼の車は追突されて大破した His car *was hit from behind* and was badly damaged.

ついに 遂に·終に·竟に **finally**（(思いのほか) 長いことかかって）; **at (long) last**（障害を乗り越えて, やっとのことで）; **after all**（期待や予想に反して, 結局）▶彼らはついに頂上に到達した They *finally* reached the summit. ‖ 初め反対していた父もついに折れた My father, who had been opposed (my plan) at first, *finally* agreed. ‖「ついにやったぞ」と彼らは叫んだ "We made it *at* (*long*) *last*," they shouted. ‖ 私たちは彼女を待ちに待ったが, ついに彼女は現れなかった We waited and waited, but she never did show up [she didn't show up *after all*]. (● after all には「期待していたのに」という含みがある；finally や at last は否定文では用いない). →とうとう.

▶だんだん暗くなりついには何も見えなくなってしまった It became darker and darker *until* we could see nothing. (● この until は結果を表す接続詞で「…してついに」の意. 前にコンマを打ってもよい) ‖ 彼は中米へ行ったままついに帰らなかった He went to Central America, *never to* return. (➤ この never to do は結果を表して「そして…することはなかった」の意).

ついばむ 啄む **peck** 《at》▶寺の境内では数羽のハトが豆をついばんでいた Inside the temple precincts, there were a few pigeons *pecking* [*picking*] (*at*) beans. (➤ precinct は /príːsɪŋkt/ と発音).

ついほう 追放する **expel** +目; **exile** /éksaɪl, égzaɪl/ +目 (政治的理由で国外へ); **banish** +目 (罰として国内外のどこかへ); **deport** +目 (外国人を国外へ); **purge** +目 (主に政党から); **remove** +目 (解任する) ▶アダムとイブはエデンの園を追放された Adam and Eve *were expelled* from the Garden of Eden. ‖ 国王はそのクーデターでイランから追放された The Shah *was exiled* from Iran because of the coup. ‖ 不法入国者は国外追放になった Illegal immigrants *were deported from the country*. ‖ 彼は党内から自分の敵になる者たちを追放した He *purged* the party *of* his enemies. ‖ 彼は聖職から永久追放になった He *was removed permanently* from ministry. ‖ 町民は暴力追放に立ち上がった The townspeople took action to *eliminate* [*get rid of*] *organized crime*. (➤ eliminate /ɪlímɪneɪt/ は「除去する」; ●「暴力」に violence を当てると, 家庭内暴力やいじめなどを連想させるので, 「暴力」を「組織犯罪」と考えて訳例のようにす

る）‖覚醒剤追放運動 *a campaign against* stimulant drugs.

ついやす 費やす **spend** ＋目（金や時間を）; **waste** ＋目（無駄に使う）▶こんなむだな議論に貴重な時間を費やすのはごめんだね I refuse to *spend* [*waste*] valuable time in such (a) useless argument. ‖画家はその壁画を完成するのに２年の歳月を費やした It *took* the artist two years to paint the mural.（➤「２年かかった」の意）‖そのビルは100億円を費やして完成した The building was completed *at a cost* [*at an expense*] of ten billion yen.

ついらく 墜落 a **fall**; a **crash**（墜落事故）**一動 墜落する** **fall**; **crash**（飛行機が）▶ジェット機は山中に墜落した The jet *crashed* in the mountains. ‖その飛行機墜落事故で乗客３名が奇跡的に助かった Three passengers miraculously survived the *plane crash*. ‖墜落現場 a crash site.

ツイン a **twin** ▶《ホテルで》シングルは空いておりませんが，ツインならございます All our single rooms are occupied now, but we can offer you *a twin*. ‖ツインの部屋に泊まりたいのですが We'd like to stay in *a room with twin beds*.

> **危ないカタカナ語✹ ツイン**
> **1** twin はもともと「双子」のことで，双子の兄弟［姉妹］は twin brothers [sisters] である（どちらか一方を指すときは単数形）.
> **2**「ツインベッドの１つ」は a twin bed である（通例 twin beds と複数形でいう）．また，「ツインの部屋」は twin room, twin-bedded room, room with twin beds などという．double (room) は「２人用の部屋」の意だが，《米》ではベッドが２台あるのが普通．

つう 通 an **authority** /əθɔ́ːrəṭi/ 《on》（…の権威者）; an **expert** /ékspəːʳt/ 《on, in》（…の専門家）; a **connoisseur** /kɑ̀ːnəsə́ːʳ/ 《of》（美術品や酒などの目利き）▶あの人は大変な財政通だ He is quite *an authority on* finance. ／He is very *well-informed* [*knowledgeable*] *about* finance. ‖キーン教授は日本通だ Professor Keene is *an expert on* Japan. ‖彼女はワイン通だ She is *a wine connoisseur*. ‖ビートルズのことなら安田君が通だ Yasuda *knows everything* about the Beatles.

つういん 通院する **go to (the) hospital** 《解説》go to (the) hospital は通例「入院する」の意なので，「通院する」の場合はあとに every day（毎日）や regularly（定期的に），または as an outpatient（外来患者として）などを補う必要がある．また see a doctor や go to a doctor's office を使って表すこともできる．▶足をくじいて２週間通院した After spraining my ankle, I had to *go to* (*the*) *hospital as an outpatient* for two weeks.

[1]**つうか 通過する** **1【通り過ぎる】pass** ▶次の列車は当駅を通過します The next train will *pass* (*through*) this station. ‖台風が通過してようやく風雨が収まった After the typhoon *passed*, the winds and rain finally died down. ‖《機内アナウンス》ただいま当機は岡山上空を通過しております We *are* (now) *flying over* the city of Okayama.
‖通過駅 a through station.
2【可決する，合格する】pass ▶その法案は小差で国会を通過した The bill *passed* the Diet by a narrow margin. ‖第一次審査を通過してあすは面接です I'*ve passed* the first screening and will be interviewed tomorrow.

[2]**つうか 通貨** (a) **currency** /kə́ːrənsi ‖ kʌ́r-/ ▶通貨を切り下げる［切り上げる］devalue [revalue] a *currency* ‖古代地中海地方では牛が通貨だった In the ancient Mediterranean region, the cow was used as *currency*. ‖イタリアの通貨はユーロだ The *currency* of Italy is the euro.
‖通貨危機 a monetary crisis ‖通貨制度 a monetary [currency] system.

> 「通貨」のいろいろ アメリカ dollar ／アルゼンチン peso ／ＥＵの一部の加盟国（イタリア，オーストリア，オランダ，スペイン，ドイツ，フランスなど）euro ／イギリス pound sterling ／インド rupee ／インドネシア rupiah ／エジプト Egyptian pound ／オーストラリア Australian dollar ／カナダ Canadian dollar ／韓国 won ／スイス Swiss franc ／スウェーデン krona ／タイ baht ／台湾 New Taiwan dollar ／中国 yuan ／デンマーク krone ／日本 yen ／ニュージーランド New Zealand dollar ／ノルウェー krone ／フィリピン peso ／ブラジル real ／ベトナム dong ／香港 Hong Kong dollar ／マレーシア ringgit ／メキシコ peso ／ロシア ruble

つうかあ ▶あいつと秋山はつうかあの仲らしい I hear he can *read* Akiyama's *mind*. ／I hear he and Akiyama *can communicate very well*. ／I hear he *knows exactly how* Akiyama *feels, and vice versa*.（➤ vice versa /vàisi və́ːʳsə/ は「その反対も同様」の意）.

つうかい 痛快 ▶痛快な映画 an *exciting* movie ‖あの鼻っ柱の強いチャンピオンがマットに沈んだときは実に痛快だった It *gave me great pleasure* [*satisfaction*] to see that overconfident champion sprawled on the mat.

つうがく 通学する **go to [attend] school**; **commute to school**（長距離を）▶通学の行き帰りにその神社の前を通ります I pass in front of the shrine *on my way to and from school*. ‖対話「通学はバスですか？」「いいえ，徒歩です」"Do you *go to school* by bus?" "No. I walk to school."（👄学校での対話なら Do you come to school by bus? となる）. ‖通学区域 a school district ‖通学路 a school route.

[1]**つうかん 痛感する** ▶最近歩くことの必要性を痛感している I *feel strongly* the necessity of walking. ‖外国人に道を聞かれて答えられなかったときは語学力の不足を痛感した My lack of language ability *came home to me* [I *realized fully* my lack of language ability] when a foreigner asked me the way, and I couldn't answer him [her].

[2]**つうかん 通関** **going through customs** ▶通関手続き *customs* procedures.

つうき 通気 **ventilation**（換気）▶このトレーナーは通気性に富んでいる This sweat suit *breathes well*.
‖通気孔 an air vent.

つうきん 通勤 **commuting**, 《米》**commutation** **一動 通勤する** **commute** /kəmjúːt/, **go to work** ▶電車で通勤する *commute* by train ‖車［徒歩］で通勤する *drive* [*walk*] *to work* ‖私は横須賀から有楽町に通勤している I *commute* from Yokosuka to Yurakucho. ‖通勤の便を考えて中野区に引っ越した I moved to Nakano Ward so (that) I could *get to my office easily*. ‖運悪く通勤ラッシュにぶつかった Unfortunately, I got caught in the *commuter rush* (*hour*). ‖遠距離通勤は全く疲れる *Commuting a long distance* [My *long commute*] tires me out.（➤後者の commute は「通勤

時間[距離]」)‖ **対話**「通勤にどのくらい時間がかかりますか」「1時間半かかります」"How long does it take you to *commute*?" "An hour and a half."
‖**通勤客** a commutation passenger ‖ **通勤圏** a commuter belt ‖ **通勤者** a commuter ‖ **通勤手当** a commutation [commuting] allowance /əláuəns/ ‖ **通勤定期**《米》a commutation [commuter] ticket,《英》a season ticket ‖ **通勤電車** a commuter train.

つうこう 通行 **traffic** ▶その通りは**通行止め**になっている The street *is closed to traffic*. ‖《掲示》**車両通行止め** Closed to All Vehicles／No Thoroughfare for Vehicles ‖ この道は**一方通行**になっている This is *a one-way street*. ‖《掲示》**一方通行** One Way ‖ 日本では車は**左側通行**です In Japan, cars and trucks *must drive on the left* (*side of the street* [*road*]). ‖《掲示》**左側通行** Keep to the Left／Keep Left.
‖**通行人** a passer-by [複 passers-by] ‖(高速道路などの)**通行料金** a toll(●「普通車の通行料金は700円です」なら The toll for cars is 700 yen.).

つうこく 通告 **notice, notification**(➤後者がより堅い語) **一動** **通告する** **notify** +㊐, **inform** +㊐ ▶市当局は不法占拠者に立ち退きを**通告した** The municipal authorities *notified* [*informed*] the squatters that they would have to evacuate the premises.

つうこん 痛恨 ▶それまで0点に抑えていただけに, あのカーブが斎藤には**痛恨の一球**になった That curve was *an extremely regrettable pitch* for Saito, who had been shutting out until then.

つうさん 通算 ▶**通算**2000万人以上の人が万博を訪れた *A total of* over twenty million people visited the international exposition. ‖ 祖父は**通算**38年間教師をした My grandfather spent *a total of* thirty-eight years as a teacher. ‖ 江夏投手の**現役通算成績**は206勝158敗193セーブだった Pitcher Enatsu had *a career* [*lifetime*] *record* of 206 wins, 158 losses and 193 saves.

つうじ 通じ a **bowel movement**(➤インフォーマルでは婉曲(えんきょく)に BM と略す) ▶冷たい牛乳は**通じをよくする** Cold milk will *promote regular bowel movements*. ‖ 私, きのうから**お通じがない**のよ I *haven't had a bowel movement* since yesterday. ‖ 野菜をたくさん食べて適度に運動することは**規則的なお通じを促す** Eating lots of vegetables and getting moderate exercise helps (to) *keep* you *regular*. (➤ keep A regular で「A(人)に規則的なお通じがある」).

つうじて 通じて **1【手段, 仲介】** **through** ▶私たちはインターネットを**通じて**多くの情報を得る We get a lot of information *through* the Internet. ‖ 友人を**通じて**彼女と知り合った I got acquainted with her *through* a friend of mine. ‖ 首相は**テレビを通じて**(＝テレビで)重大発表を行った The Prime Minister made an important announcement *on TV*.
2【通して】 **throughout** ▶奄美大島は**1年を通じて**暖かい It is warm *all* (*through*) the year in Amami Oshima. ‖ 山田選手は**シーズンを通じて**好調だった Yamada was in good shape *throughout* [*all through*] the baseball season.

[1]**つうしょう 通称** ▶この沼は**通称**「さぎ沼」という This marsh is *usually* [*commonly*] *called* "Heron Marsh."
✉ **私の名は江藤美樹, 通称ミッキーです** My name is Eto Miki. *Everybody calls me* "Mickey."

[2]**つうしょう 通商** **commerce**(大規模な商取引); **trade** (貿易) ‖**通商交渉** trade negotiations [talks] ‖ **通商条約** a commercial treaty.

つうじょう 通常 **usually**(ふだんは); **regularly**(定期的に) ▶**通常**仕事は7時に終えます *Usually* we finish work at 7 o'clock. ‖ 役員会は**通常**毎月第1木曜日に開かれる The board meeting is *regularly* held on the first Thursday of every month. ‖ 年内は**通常どおり**営業します Our store will be open *as usual* through the end of the year. ／Our store hours will be the same the rest of this year. ‖ あす雨ならば遠足は中止で**通常どおり**授業をします If it rains tomorrow, the outing will be canceled and we'll have classes *as usual*.

ツーショット ▶彼女は彼氏と**ツーショット写真**を撮った She took *a picture of* herself *and* her boy friend.

つうじる 通じる

1【交通・通信が届く】 **lead** 《to》(道が…に至る); **run**(交通手段が) ▶この道路は山形市に**通じている** This road *leads to* Yamagata City. ‖ 京都駅から国際会館までは地下鉄が**通じている** A subway *runs* between Kyoto Station and Kokusai-Kaikan. ‖ そのドアは裏庭に**通じています** That door *opens onto* the backyard.
▶電話回線が故障していて**電話が通じない** I *can't get through* because of a problem with the telephone lines. (➤ get through は「(電話などで)連絡がとれる」の意) ‖ 電柱の修理が終わってまた**電気が通じた** Now that the utility pole repairs are completed, we can *use* electricity again.
2【相手にわかる】 ▶シドニーではあなたの**英語は通じました**か Were you able to *make yourself understood* in English in Sydney?／Did people understand your English in Sydney? ‖ 父には冗談がまるで**通じない** My father *doesn't catch on to* jokes [*can't take* a joke]. (➤ catch on to は「…がすぐわかる」の意) ‖ 彼の皮肉は彼女には**通じなかった** His sarcasm *was wasted on* her. (➤「無駄だった」の意) ‖ この翻訳は**意味が通じない** This translation *doesn't make sense*. ‖ 弘はやっとの思いで愛情を告白したが, 彼女には彼の**気持ちが通じなかった** Hiroshi finally got up his courage to declare his love to her, but he *couldn't get his feelings across to* her clearly.
▶《テニスで》錦織はフェデラーには全然**通じなかった** Nishikori *was no match for* Federer. (➤ match は「競争相手」).
3【精通している】 ▶ドナルド・キーン氏は日本文学に**通じていた** Donald Keene *was well versed in* Japanese literature. ／Donald Keene *knew a lot about* Japanese literature. (➤後者はインフォーマルな言い方) ‖ 斎藤教授はアメリカの政治に**通じている** Professor Saito *is well informed about* [*on*] American politics.

つうしん 通信

(a) **communication**(交信); **correspondence**(手紙による) **一動** (人・乗り物と)**通信する** **communicate**《with》; **correspond**《with》▶宇宙船との**通信** *communication* with the spaceship ‖ パソコンによる**通信** *communication* using personal computers ‖ 台風のためすべての**通信**が途絶えた All means of *communication* [All *communications*] were cut off by the typhoon. ‖ 我々はその難破船と無線で**通信を続けた** We *kept in communication* [*kept in touch*] with the wrecked ship by wireless.
▶私は**通信教育**で翻訳を勉強しています I am taking *a*

correspondence course in translation. ‖彼女は通信教育で大学を卒業した She earned her college degree through *correspondence courses*. ‖私はこのかばんを通信販売で買った I bought this bag *by mail order* [*from a mail-order house*].

‖通信員 a correspondent ‖通信衛星 a communication(s) satellite /sǽṭəlaɪt/ (➤略して comsat ともいう) ‖通信社 a news agency ‖通信簿 →通知(表) ‖通信網 a communications network.

[1]**つうせつ 通説** **the accepted theory** ▶アメリカ先住民はアジア系民族だというのが通説だ It is *the accepted* [*a commonly accepted*] *theory* that Native Americans are (people) of Asian origin. ‖通説では日本列島は昔大陸と陸続きだった According to *the accepted theory*, the Japanese Islands were once adjacent to the Asian continent.

[2]**つうせつ 痛切** ▶海外旅行をしてみて語学の必要性を痛切に感じた While traveling overseas, I became *keenly* aware of the importance of studying foreign languages.

つうぞく 通俗的な **popular**; **lowbrow**(低俗な) ▶どのテレビチャンネルにも通俗的な番組があふれている All the channels are full of programs *geared to popular tastes* [*lowbrow* programs]. (「大衆の好みに合わせた番組」の意).

‖通俗小説 a popular novel ‖通俗心理学 popular psychology, pop psychology.

つうたつ 通達 (a) **notice**, (a) **notification** (➤後者は堅い語) ▶文部科学省は教師は生徒に体罰を加えてはならない旨の通達を出した The Ministry of Education (, Culture, Sports, Science and Technology) issued *a notice* [*a notification*] that teachers must not inflict corporal punishment on students.

つうち 通知 (a) **notice**, (a) **notification**(➤後者は堅い語) 一動 **通知する** **notify** 《of》, **inform** 《of》 ▶ABC社から正式な採用通知があった I received an official *notice* [*notification*] *of employment* from ABC Company. ‖文子さんから同窓会の通知を受け取ったよ. あなたのところにも何か通知があった? I got *a notice* of our class reunion from Fumiko. Have you *heard anything* about it? ‖1週間後には試験の結果を通知します We will *notify* you *of* [You will *be notified of*] the results of the exam in a week. ／We will *let* you *know* the results of the exam in a week. (➤ notify は堅い言い方で, 日常的には後者の let ... know を使うことが多い).

✉ **本大学に合格されましたのでご通知いたします** *It is our pleasure to inform you* that you have been accepted by our university.

✉ **大会の日程が変更されたことをご通知いたします** *This is to notify you* that the schedule of the convention has been changed.

‖通知表 《米》 a report card, 《英》 a school report.

つうちょう 通帳 a **passbook**(普通預金の); a **bankbook**(銀行の) ▶通帳を作る open a bank [a savings] account(➤「口座を開く」の意).

‖郵便貯金通帳 a postal savings account book.

ツードア ▶ツードアの車 a *two-door* (car).

つうどく 通読する **read through** ▶『大菩薩峠』を通読する *read* "Daibosatsu-Toge" *through* ‖この報告書を通読して感想をお願いします I would like to have your comment on this report after you *read* it *through*.

ツートンカラー 一形 **ツートンカラーの** **two-tone**(➤(×) two-tone color は和製語) ▶ツートンカラーの車 a *two-tone* car ‖白と青のツートンカラーの内装 a *white-and-blue* décor.

[1]**つうねん 通念** a **common idea**(広く知られた考え方); a **generally accepted idea** (一般に受け入れられている見解) ▶誤った通念 *a common* mistaken *notion* (notion は根拠のない漠然とした考えをいうことが多い) ‖女性が結婚後も仕事を続けることはすでに社会の通念になってきている It has *become generally accepted* for women to continue working [pursue their careers] after getting married.

[2]**つうねん 通年の** **all year, year-round**

‖通年国会 a year-round Diet session ‖通年採用 hiring throughout the year ／year-round hiring.

つうはん 通販 **mail order**. →通信.

ツーピース a **two-piece (suit)** ▶ツーピースの水着 a *two-piece* bathing suit ‖紺のツーピース a navy blue *two-piece* (*suit*).

[1]**つうふう 通風** **ventilation** ▶この部屋は通風がいい This room *is well-ventilated*. ‖通風管[孔] a ventilator /vénṭleɪṭəʳ/, an air vent.

[2]**つうふう 痛風** **gout** /gaʊt/ ▶痛風にかかっている suffer from *gout*.

つうぶん 通分 ▶$\frac{1}{2}$と$\frac{1}{3}$は通分すると$\frac{3}{6}$と$\frac{2}{6}$になる When you *reduce* $\frac{1}{2}$ and $\frac{1}{3}$ *to a common denominator*, you get $\frac{3}{6}$ and $\frac{2}{6}$. (➤ denominator /dɪnɑ́:mənerṭəʳ/ は「分母」. 「分子」は numerator /ɲjú:mərerṭəʳ/).

つうほう 通報 a **report**(警察などへ) 一動 (…に)**通報する** **report** 《to》 ▶《掲示》万引きは警察に通報します Shoplifters Will *be Reported* to Police ‖この男に似た者を見かけたらすぐ警察に通報してください If you happen to see anyone resembling this man, *report it to* the police [*inform* the police *of* it] right away.

‖通報ベル(銀行強盗防止用の) a silent bell.

つうやく 通訳 **interpretation, translation** (通訳すること); an **interpreter** /ɪntə́:ʳprəṭəʳ/, a **translator** (通訳者) 一動 **通訳する** **interpret** /ɪntə́:ʳprət/ +目, **translate** +目 《参考》 translate は厳密には「翻訳する」だが, 一般には「通訳する」を含めて translate という傾向がある.

▶通訳なしで講演する deliver a speech without *an interpreter* [without *interpretation*] ‖首相は加藤氏の通訳でフランス大使と会談した The Prime Minister talked with the French ambassador through the *interpreter* Mr. Kato. ‖彼があなたの通訳をしてくれます He will *interpret for* you. ／He will act as *interpreter* for you. (as のあとに役職名などが続くときは Ⓤ 扱い) ‖彼の言ったことを日本語に通訳してください Could you please *interpret* [*put*] his words *into* Japanese? (➤ put はややインフォーマル) ‖その会議では山内氏が同時通訳をした Mr. Yamauchi did *simultaneous interpretation* at the conference. (➤「同時通訳者」は simultaneous interpreter).

‖全国通訳案内士試験 the national examination for guide interpreters.

つうよう 通用 1 【通る】▶この理論は今日でも立派に通用する(=有効である) This theory *holds true* [*good*] even today. ‖そんな古い考えは今の若い人には通用しませんよ Such an old-fashioned idea *won't be accepted by* [*won't wash with*] today's

young people. (● wash は「受け入れられる」の意のインフォーマルな語で, 否定文で用いる) ‖ きみのわがままは社会に出たら**通用しない**(=許されない)よ Your selfish behavior will not *be accepted* once you start working. ‖ そんな子供だましはこの俺には**通用しない**ぜ Such a childish trick *won't work on* me. ‖ 私の片言英語はローマでは**通用しなかった** *Nobody* in Rome *understood* my broken English.
▶彼女は42歳だが, 20代でも十分**通用する** Although she is 42, she *can pass* for a woman in her twenties.
2【使われる】▶その国ではフランス語は**通用しない** French *is not used* in that country. ／They *don't speak* French in that country. ‖ 米ドルは世界中で**通用する**のですか Can U.S. dollars *be used* [*Are* U.S. dollars *accepted*] anywhere in the world? ‖ この500円玉はまだ**通用しますか** *Is* this 500-yen coin still *in circulation*?
▶この切符の**通用**(=有効)期間は5日間です This ticket *is valid* [*good*] for five days. ‖ 社員の方は**通用門**から出入りしてください Employees, please use *the service entrance* [*side gate*].

ツーラン《野球》a **two-run homer** [**home run**] (➤ two-run は「2点得点した」の意で, ホームランとは限らない).

ツーリスト a **tourist.**

ツーリング **touring.**

ツール a **tool** ▶情報**ツール** an information *tool* [*device*].

つうれい 通例 **usually, as a rule** ▶**通例**水曜日の午後は会議がある We *usually* hold a meeting on Wednesday afternoon. (● as a rule の場合は文頭か文尾に置く).

つうれつ 痛烈な **bitter**; **severe**(不寛容なまでに) 一副 **痛烈に** **bitterly**; **severely** ▶その打者はライトに**痛烈な**ライナーを飛ばした The batter drove a *hard-hitting* liner to the right. ‖ その批評家は彼女の新しい小説を**痛烈に批判した** The critic *bitterly* [*severely*] criticized her new novel.

つうろ 通路 a **passage**; a **way**(ある場所から別の場所へ行く道筋); an **aisle** /aɪl/ (劇場・教会・飛行機などの座席間の); a **catwalk**(舞台・工事現場などの頭上に架けた狭い足場); a **walkway**(公園・庭園などにある歩行者専用の) ▶**通路**に物を置くな Don't put things in the *passage* [*passageway*]. ‖ この箱は**通路**を邪魔している These boxes are blocking the *way*. ‖ すみませんが車椅子が通りますので**通路を空けて**(=通して)ください Excuse me, could you please let a wheelchair through? ／Excuse me, but could you *make way* for a wheelchair? ‖ **通路側の席** an *aisle* seat ‖ **通路**に立たないでください Don't stand in the *aisle*, please.

つうわ 通話 a (**telephone**) **call** ▶アメリカへの**通話料金**は3分ごとに160円です The *charge for a phone call* to the U.S. is 160 yen for every three minutes.
‖**通話記録** a telephone call record ‖ **通話料** telephone charges ‖ **市外通話** an out-of-town call ‖ **市内通話** a local call ‖ **指名通話** a person-to-person call ‖ **番号通話** a station-to-station call ‖ **ビデオ通話** a video call ‖ **無料通話** a no-charge call ‖ **料金先方払い通話** a collect call, 《英また》a reverse(d)-charge call.

つえ 杖 《主に米》a **cane**, 《主に英》a (**walking**) **stick** ▶**つえ**をついて歩く walk with *a stick* [*a cane*] ‖ 彼は**つえ**をつかずに歩けるようになった He began to walk without the help of his *cane*. ‖ 祖母は動き回るには**つえ**が要る My grandmother needs a *cane* to get around.
ことわざ **転ばぬ先のつえ** Look before you leap. (➤「跳ぶ前によく見よ」の意) ／(An ounce of) prevention is better than (a pound of) cure. (➤「予防は治療に勝る」の意. better than を worth(…に値する)に置きかえ可; ともに英語のことわざ).

[1]つか 柄 a **hilt** ▶刀の**つか** the *hilt* of a sword.

[2]つか 塚 a **mound**; a **burial mound**(墓).

つかい 使い **1【用事】**an **errand** /érənd/ ▶娘はいつも快く私の**使い**をしてくれる My daughter is always glad to *run* [*go on*] *errands* for me. ‖《子供に》郵便局までちょっと**お使いに行って**くれない? Will you run to the post office for me? (➤ 具体的な用事が念頭にあるときは run an errand ともいう; 州によって年齢は異なるが, 米国では幼い子供が1人で買い物に行ったり, 留守番をしたりすることは禁止されている).
2【使いの人】a **messenger** ▶神の**使い** a *messenger* of a god ‖ 彼は自分で来る代わりに**使い**をよこした Instead of coming himself, he sent *a messenger*. ‖ 私の荷物を受け取りにお宅まで**使いの者**をやります I'll send *someone* (over) to your house to pick up my baggage. (➤「誰かを派遣する」の意).
☞ **お使い** (→見出語)

つがい 番い a **pair**; a **brace** (猟鳥の) ▶**ひとつがい**のカナリア *a pair of* canaries ‖ **ひとつがい**のガン *a brace of* wild geese.

つかいかた 使い方 ▶この栓抜きの**使い方**が全然わからない I don't know at all *how to use* this corkscrew. ‖ 私はその単語の**使い方**を間違えた I *misused* the word. ‖ 彼は人の**使い方**がうまい[下手だ] He's good [poor] at *managing* people. ‖ 弟は自転車の**使い方**が乱暴なので貸したくない My brother *is rough with* bicycles that I don't like to lend him mine. (➤ be rough with は「(物を)乱暴に扱う」).

つかいがって 使い勝手 ▶**使い勝手のいい**パソコン an *easy-to-use* [*a user-friendly*] personal computer ‖ **使い勝手のいい**台所 a kitchen that *is easy to cook* [*work*] *in*.

つかいこなす 使い熟す **have a good command of**(言語などを); **handle** +目 (人・物を) ▶大人が英語を**使いこなせる**ようになるには大変な努力がいる It takes great effort for a grown-up to *acquire a good command of* English. ‖ 最近は小学生でもコンピュータを**使いこなせる** Even elementary school students *can handle* computers these days.

つかいこむ 使い込む **1【長く使う】**▶よく**使い込んだ**すりこ木 a *well-used* wooden pestle ‖ 万年筆は**使い込む**ほど書きやすくなる *The longer* you *use* a fountain pen, the easier it becomes to write with.
2【私用に使う】**embezzle** /ɪmbézəl/ +目 ▶男は会社の金を1000万円**使い込んだ** He *embezzled* ten million yen of the company's money. ／He *embezzled* ten million yen *from* the company.

つかいすて 使い捨ての **disposable**, **throwaway** (➤ 後者はインフォーマル) ▶**使い捨ての**紙コップ a *disposable* paper cup ‖ **使い捨て**ライター a *throwaway* lighter.

つかいたおす 使い倒す ▶この辞書を**使い倒す**ぞ I'll *get the most out of* this dictionary. (➤「最大限に活用する」の意).

つかいで 使い出 ▶この徳用瓶入りシャンプーは**使いで**がある This economy-sized bottle of shampoo *lasts long*. (➤「長くもつ」の意) ‖ 最近は1万円札の**使いで**

がない A ten-thousand-yen bill *doesn't go far* [*go a long way*] these days. ／You can't buy much with a ten-thousand-yen bill these days.

つかいにくい 使いにくい ▶使いにくい缶切り a can opener that *is hard to use*.

つかいはしり 使い走り a **messenger**,《インフォーマル》a **gofer**, a **gopher** /góufəʳ/ (人)(➤ gofer は go for のなまった発音に由来する語) ; an **errand** /érənd/ (用事) ▶彼女は上司の使い走りをさせられるのが嫌で会社を辞めた She quit the company because she hated being *a gofer* for her boss.

つ

つかいはたす 使い果たす ▶彼は給料日前に給料を使い果たしてしまった He *spent* [*used up*] *all* his salary before payday.

つかいふるし 使い古し ▶使い古しの歯ブラシ a *well-worn* toothbrush ‖ 使い古した表現 an *overused* [*a trite* ／*a corny*] expression.

つかいみち 使い道・使い途 (a) **use** /ju:s/ ▶この道具にはどんな使いみちがあるのですか What *use*(*s*) does this tool have ? ／What is this tool used for ? ‖ この箱は使いみちに困っている I am trying to find some *use* for this box. ‖ この圧力鍋は使いみちが広い This pressure cooker has many *uses*.

つかいもの 使い物 ▶刃がこんなにぼろぼろなんじゃあこの包丁は使い物にならないね With its blade all nicked like this, this carving knife *is useless*. ‖ 私のドイツ語はだんだん使い物にならなくなって(＝さび付いて)きている My German is *getting rusty*.

つかいやすい 使い易い ▶使いやすいコンピュータソフト an *easy-to-use* software program.

つかいわける 使い分ける ▶弟は「パパ」と「お父さん」を使い分けている My brother *uses* "Papa" or "Father" *depending on the occasion*. ‖ 日本語の敬語を使い分ける(＝正しく使う)のは難しい It is difficult to *use* (Japanese) honorific language *properly*. ‖ その外交官は 5 か国語を使い分ける The diplomat *has a good command of* five languages. (➤「使いこなせる」の意) ‖ 私は手帳は個人用と会社用を使い分けている I have two separate notebooks, one for personal use, and the other for business use.

つかう 使う・遣う

訳語メニュー
使用する →use **1, 3, 4, 8**
人を雇う →employ **2**
乗り物を利用する →take **5**
金・時間を消費する →spend **6**
無駄に使う →waste **6**

1【材料・道具として役立てる】use ＋目 ▶中華料理では野菜をたくさん使う A lot of vegetables *are used* in Chinese cooking. ‖ この靴には上質のバックスキンが使われています These shoes are made of good buckskin. (「良いバックスキンでできている」の意).
▶曽根さんは小説を書くのにコンピュータを使う Sone *uses* a computer to write novels. ／Sone writes novels on a computer. ‖ もっと頭を使えよ Try to *use* your brains [head] a little more. ‖ 道具は使うほどに手になじむ The more you *use* a tool, the more comfortable it feels (in your hands). ‖ この井戸は近所の人が共同で使っています The people in the neighborhood *share* this well. ‖ 対話「これは何に使うのですか」「ニンニクを潰すのに使います」"What's this thing (*used*) for ?" "It's for crushing garlic."
▶ポイントは食事, ホテルの宿泊, 航空券などに使えます Points *can be redeemed* for dining, hotel stays, airline tickets, etc. (➤ この redeem は「(商品券・引換券など)を商品 [現金] に換える」の意).

2【人を雇う】employ ＋目 ▶人件費が高いのでたくさんの人は使えない I can't *employ* many people because labor costs are high. ‖ あのファストフード店ではバイトを数人使っている That fast-food restaurant *employs* several part-time workers.

3【人などを働かせる】use ＋目 ; **handle** ＋目 (扱う) ▶各国とも大使館員を使って他国の情報を集めている Every country *uses* its embassy personnel to gather information about other countries. ／Every country *has* its embassy personnel *collect* information about other countries. (➤「have ＋人＋ do」で「人に…させる」) ‖ うちの監督は選手を使うのがうまい Our manager is good at *handling* the players.
ことわざ 立っている者は親でも使え If your father or mother happens to be standing nearby, use him or her to help you. (➤ 日本語からの直訳) ／Use anybody who is available.

4【ことばを話す】use ＋目 ; **speak** ＋目 (話す) ▶敬語を正しく使えない人が多くなってきている There's been an increase in the number of people who cannot *use* (Japanese) honorifics correctly. ‖ 彼は仕事では主に英語を使っている He mainly *uses* English in his job. ‖ パキスタンでは何語が使われていますか What language do they *speak* in Pakistan ? (パキスタン人に尋ねる場合は they を you に変える).

5【到達手段として利用する】take ＋目 ▶地下鉄を使う *take* a subway ‖ 国道16号線を使えば, そこへはもっと速く行けますよ You'll get there more quickly if you *take* [*follow*] Route 16.

6【お金・時間を消費する】spend《on》

【文型】
物(A)に金(B)を使う
spend B **on** A

解説 (1) on がふつうだが,「購入のために」の意では《米》では for を用いることもある. ただし, その場合も spend for より pay for を用いることが多い.
(2) 購入後の維持費としては **spend on** を用いる. **spend for** はその意味では用いない.

▶彼はステレオシステムに50万円使った He *spent* half a million yen *on* his stereo system. (spent ... for や paid ... for も可) ‖ わが家では食費に月 8 万円ほど使う We *spend* about eighty thousand yen *on* food a month. (spend ... for や pay ... for も可) ‖ この美術館の建設にいくらお金が使われたのですか How much money *was spent on* building this museum ? ‖ きみは月平均で携帯電話にいくら使っているの? How much (money) do you *spend on* your cellphone per month on average ? (➤ 接続料・通話料などをいうので spend on).
▶お金をむだに使うな Don't *waste* your money. ‖ 彼は空いた時間はほとんど小説を書くのに使っている He *spends* most of his free time writing novels. (→[1]かける, 過ごす) ‖ あげたお金, もう全部使っちゃったんだって? You mean you'*ve* already *gone through* (all) the money I gave you ? (➤ go through は「(金などを)使い果たす」の意のインフォーマルな言い方).

7【注意・心などを働かせる】 ▶同時通訳は神経を使う仕事だ Simultaneous interpreting is a *nerve-*

racking job. ‖ 日本人は外国人に対して**気を遣い過ぎる** Japanese people are *too anxious to please* foreigners. ‖ どうぞ**お気を遣わ**ないでください Please don't *bother*.

8【特別な技術・策などを用いる】use +⾃; **operate** +⾃（操作する）▶**魔法を使う** *use* magic ‖ あの腹話術師は巧みに人形を**使う** That ventriloquist *operates* [*manipulates*] his puppet skillfully. ‖ 彼はたびたび**仮病を使って**学校をサボる He often cuts classes (*by*) *pretending to be sick*. (➤ playing sick としてもよい).

¹**つかえる 使える** ▶わが社はみんなパソコンが**使える** Everybody in our office *can use* [*operate*] a computer.

▶そのパソコンはつないでないので**ネットが使えない** You *can't use the Internet* [*go online*] because the PC is not connected. ‖ 突然私のアカウントが**使えなくなった**（＝凍結された）My account *was disabled* [*suspended*] without notice. ‖ このボールペンはまだ**使える** This ballpoint pen still *works*. (➤ work は「(機械・道具が) 機能する」) ‖《店で》VISA カード, **使える**かしら Do you *take* [*accept*] VISA? ‖ 今ではほとんどどこでもカードが**使える** Credit cards *are* now *accepted* almost everywhere. ‖ 田中君はなかなか**使える**男だよ Tanaka is a very *capable* [*competent*] man.

²**つかえる 支える 1【通行の妨げになる】stick**《in》, **get stuck** ▶ピアノがドアに**つかえて**どうしても部屋に入らない We can't get the piano into the room because it's *stuck in* the door. (➤ stuck は stick の過去・過去分詞形) ‖ 餅が喉に**つかえた** A piece of rice cake *got stuck* [*got caught*] *in* my throat. ‖ 食べたものが**胸につかえている** What I ate *lies heavy on my stomach*. ‖ 洞窟の天井に頭が**つかえ**（＝触れ）ないように私たちは身をかがめて歩いた We walked bent over so that our heads would not *touch* [*hit*] the roof of the cave. ‖《電車のアナウンス》前に電車が**つかえて**おります We have another train *standing by on the track* ahead.

▶《慣用表現》彼に何もかも話したら**胸につかえていたもの**が取れた I felt relieved when I told him *what had been bothering me* [*weighing on my mind*].

2【ことばが滞る】▶**つかえたら**私が助け船を出すから，その英語の文章を一度読んでごらん Try reading through the English passage once. I'll help you if you *get stuck*. ‖ 彼はスピーチの途中で**つかえて**（＝口籠もって）しまった He *stumbled* in the middle of his speech.

³**つかえる 仕える serve** +⾃（奉公する）; **attend (on)**（主に貴人に；堅い語）▶犬の「クロ」は終生ひとりの主人に**仕えた** Kuro the dog *served* the same master throughout his life. ‖ 彼の妻は病気のしゅうとに10年も**仕えてきた** His wife *has taken care of* [*has attended* (*on*)] her sick father-in-law for ten years. (➤ has attended to だと「(人の) 世話をする」の意になる).

つかさどる 司る・掌る control +⾃（制御する）; **manage** +⾃（管理する）; **be in charge of**（担当する）

▶呼吸を**つかさどる**神経 nerves that *control* breathing.

つかずはなれず 付かず離れず ▶親とは**付かず離れず**というくらいのほうがうまくいくようだ It seems you get along better with your parents when you *are neither too close nor too distant from* them.

つかつかと boldly（大胆に）; **without hesitation**（ちゅうちょなく）▶彼女は有名芸能人を見つけると**つかつかと**歩み寄ってサインを求めた As soon as she spotted the celebrity, she *boldly* walked up and asked for an autograph.

つかぬこと 付かぬ事 ▶**つかぬこと**を伺いますが，以前どこかでお会いしなかったでしょうか *Excuse me* (*for asking*), but haven't I seen you somewhere before? (●「少し唐突に聞こえるかもしれませんが」の意).

つかのま 束の間の brief（短い）; **momentary** /móʊmənteri/（瞬時の）; **ephemeral** /ɪfémərəl/ ▶**つかの間**の出来事 a *brief* incident ‖ **つかの間の**幸せ *transient* [*fleeting*] happiness ‖ 人は皆**つかの間の**人生を精いっぱい生きているのだ We all live (out) our *brief* lives as best we can. ‖ 4か月ぶりに雨が降って農民がほっとしたのも**つかの間**，今度は大雨で洪水の心配が出てきた It *was just for a passing* [*brief*] *moment* that the farmers could feel relieved to have the first rain in four months. Now they are getting worried that the heavy rain might cause floods. ‖ 我々の人生は**つかの間の**ものだ Our life is *ephemeral*.

つかまえる 捕まえる

1【捕らえる】catch +⾃; **net** +⾃（網で）; **trap** +⾃（わなで）; **pick up, nab** +⾃（犯人などを；後者のほうがよりくだけた語）

▶ぼくを**捕まえて**ごらん! Try to *catch* me! ‖ 刑事たちはすりのグループを現行犯で**捕まえた** The detectives *caught* [*arrested*] a group of pickpockets red-handed. (➤ arrest は「逮捕する」に相当する堅い語) ‖ 警察はその泥棒を**捕まえた** The police *picked up* [*nabbed*] the thief.

▶タクシーを**つかまえる** *catch* a taxi / *hail* a taxi (➤ 後者は合図して止める).

2【すがりつく】cling to [**onto**], **hold to** [**onto**] ▶女の子は母親のスカートを**つかまえて**離さなかった The little girl *clung to* her mother's skirt and wouldn't let go. (➤ clung は cling の過去形) ‖ 孫娘の里沙はおじいちゃんを**つかまえて**離そうとしなかった My granddaughter Risa *held onto* her grandfather and wouldn't let go. (● 祖母が発したことば) ‖ 親を**つかまえて**（＝に向かって）「ばか」とは何事だ! How dare you call your father stupid!

つかませる 摑ませる ▶彼は私に粗悪な腕時計を**つかませた** He *fobbed off* an inferior watch on me. (➤ fob off A [fob A off] on B で「A (不良品など) を B (人) につかませる」) ‖ あの男は私に偽のダイヤを**つかませた** That man *palmed* a fake diamond *off* on me.

¹**つかまる 捕まる be caught; be arrested**（逮捕される）

▶泥棒が警察に**捕まった** A thief *was caught* by the police. ‖ 彼はスピード違反で**捕まった** He *was caught* [*was arrested* / *was stopped*] for speeding. (➤ be stopped は「(パトカーなどに) 停止を命じられる」) ‖ 殺人犯はまだ**捕まらない** The murderer *is* still *at large* [*on the loose*]. (➤ at large, on the loose はともに「(犯人などが) 逃走中で」の意).

▶彼は教室からこっそりと抜け出ようとしているところを**つかまった** He *was caught* sneaking out of the classroom. (➤ be caught doing は「(よからぬことを) しているところを見つかる」) ‖ 出かけようとしたところを話し好きのお隣さんに**つかまった** My talkative neighbor *got hold of* me just as I was leaving. ‖ けさから前田さんを捜しているけどまだ**つかまらない**んだ I've been looking for Maeda since this morning, but I *haven't gotten hold of* him yet. ‖ 夜12時を過ぎるとタクシーがなかなか**つかまらない** It's *hard to get* [*catch*] a taxi after midnight.

²**つかまる 摑まる** hold [hang] on 《to》 ▶電車が揺れますのでつり革におつかまりください The train may jerk, so please *hang* [*hold*] *on to* a strap.

つかみあい 摑み合い ▶子供の頃はよく兄貴とつかみ合いのけんかをしたものです I often *wrestled* [*grappled*] *with* my (older) brother when we were children. ‖ 2人の少年がつまらないことでつかみ合いを始めた The two boys started to *fight* over a trivial matter. ‖ 彼はレフェリーとつかみ合いのけんかをした He *had a dust-up* with the referee.

つかみかかる 摑み掛かる ▶怒った客はいきなり店員につかみかかった The angry customer suddenly *grabbed at* the store clerk.

つかみどころ 摑み所 ▶つかみどころのない人 a person *whose character is hard to define* ‖ つかみどころのない話 a *pointless* story.

つかむ 摑む **1【しっかり握る】** catch +目 (動いているものを) ; take +目 (手に取る) ; hold +目 (握って離さない) ; grab +目 (ひっつかむ) ; seize +目 (急に強く) ; grip +目 (強く握り続ける)

▶彼女はゴロを素手でつかんだ She *caught* the grounder with her bare hand(s). ‖ カーブで電車が揺れたのでとっさにつり革をつかんだ The train jerked when it went around a curve, so I *grabbed* [*caught hold of*] a strap. ‖ 息子はおびえて私の腕をぎゅっとつかんだ My son was afraid and *grabbed hold of* my arm. ‖ 彼は私の手をつかんで「結婚してください」と言った He *took* my hand and said "Will you marry me?" ‖ ケイトは私の手をつかんでリビングへ案内した Kate *took* me by the hand and led me into the living room. ‖ 警察官は銃をつかんだ The police officer *seized* the gun. ‖ 美雪はジェットコースターで彼の手をつかんだ Miyuki *gripped* her boyfriend's hand on the roller coaster. ‖ 溺れていた少年は私の投げたロープをつかんだ The drowning boy *took hold of* the rope I tossed to him.

2【手に入れる】 get +目 ▶宝くじに当たって大金をつかんだ I won the lottery and *got* a lot of money. ‖ 加藤投手はついに先発のチャンスをつかんだ Pitcher Kato finally *got* a chance to be the starter. ‖ 刑事は事件の重要な情報をつかんだ The detective *got hold of* some valuable information about the case. (➤ get hold of は「…を手に入れる」).

▶韓流スターはその映画で女性ファンのハートをぐっとつかんだ The South Korean star *captured* the hearts of women fans with the movie.

3【理解する】 grasp +目 ▶あの人の話は長くて要点をつかむのに苦労する He is so longwinded that I find it hard to *grasp* [*get*] his point. ‖ 彼は質問の要点をしっかりつかんでいないようだ He does not seem to have fully *understood* the point of the question.

つかる 浸かる・漬かる **1【水に沈む】** ▶《風呂で》肩までよくつかりなさい *Soak* up to your shoulders. ‖ 大雨で学校の地下室が水につかった The heavy rain *flooded* the school basement. (➤ flood は「水浸しにする」).

2【漬物になる】 ▶漬物は漬かり過ぎると酸っぱくなる Pickles become sour when they *are pickled* too long.

つかれ 疲れ fatigue /fətíːg/, tiredness ; exhaustion /ɪgzɔ́ːstʃən/ (極度の) ▶リラックスして疲れを取る relax and *refresh oneself* ‖ 最近は疲れがすぐには抜けない I can't shake off *fatigue* [*tiredness*] easily these days. ‖ 夏の疲れがまだ残っているようだ It seems like I still haven't gotten over my summer *fatigue*. ‖ 岸田教授は疲れを知らない人だ Professor Kishida *never gets tired*. ‖ 家に帰り着いたとたん, どっと疲れが出た The moment I got home, *tiredness* overcame me. ‖ 彼は長時間の会議のあとで疲れを感じた He *felt weary* after the long meeting. (➤ weary /wíəri/ は長時間の作業で「(精神的にも)疲れた」の意) ‖ 母は妹の看病疲れで寝込んでしまった My mother took to her bed from *exhaustion after taking care of* my (younger) sister when she was sick.

☞ お疲れさま (→見出語)

つかれはてる 疲れ果てる be exhausted /ɪgzɔ́ːstɪd/.

つかれめ 疲れ目 eyestrain /áɪstreɪn/ ▶疲れ目のときはぬれたタオルを目に当てるとよい It helps to put a wet towel over your eyes when you have *eyestrain*.

¹**つかれる 疲れる** get tired ; be tired (疲れている) ; be exhausted /ɪgzɔ́ːstɪd/ (くたくたに) ▶近頃はすぐ疲れる These days I *get tired* easily.

> **【文型】**
> **作業など(A)で疲れる**
> **be tired from [after] A** ➤ A は名詞または動名詞
> **(解説)**「疲れた状態になる」は **get tired**, 「疲れた状態になった」は **be tired. after** のあとには文が続くこともある.

▶長時間パソコンで仕事をすると目がとても疲れる My eyes *get* very *tired after* I work on a computer for a long time. ‖ きょうは次から次と人と会う約束があって疲れた I *was tired from* [*after*] having one appointment after another today. ‖ 午前中ずっとテニスをして(へとへとに)疲れた I'*m tired* (*out*) *from* [*after*] playing tennis all morning.

▶私はくたくたに疲れた I *am exhausted* [*am all worn-out* / *am dead tired*]. ‖ ブエノスアイレスからの空の長旅で父は(へとへとに)疲れた顔をしていた My father *looked tired* (*out*) *from* the long flight from Buenos Aires. ‖ その中年男は生活に疲れた顔をしていた That middle-aged man looked *weary of life*.

▶以前より疲れやすくなった I *get tired faster* than before. ‖ 私はちょっと運動しただけで疲れてしまう Just a little exercise *tires* [*wears*] me *out*.

²**つかれる 憑かれる** be possessed /pəzést/ 《by, with》 ▶兄はつかれたように受験勉強に取り組んでいる My (older) brother is studying for the entrance examination *like someone* [*a man*] *possessed*. / My (older) brother is studying *like mad* [*like crazy*] for the entrance examination. (➤ like mad, like crazy は「猛烈に」).

¹**つき 月** **1【天体の】** the moon

▶月の裏側 the other side of *the moon* ‖ 月のない夜 a *moonless* night ‖ 上[下]弦の月 *the moon* in the first [last] quarter (🔴 in の代わりに at でもよい) ‖ 今夜は月が明るい We have a bright *moon* tonight. (🔴 月の様相を表す形容詞がつくときはいろいろな月がありうるので, しばしば a ~ moon になる) / *The moon* is bright tonight. ‖ 月が欠けて[満ちて]きた *The moon* is beginning to wane [wax]. ‖ 三笠山に月[大きな丸い月]が出た *The moon* [*A big round moon*] appeared over Mt. Mikasa. ‖ 今夜は月が出ている[いない] *There is a* [*no*] *moon* tonight. ‖ 月は雲に隠れている *The moon* is hidden by clouds.

▶《慣用表現》お宅のお嬢さんとうちの娘では月とすっぽん

(＝大違い)ですわ *There's a world of difference* between your daughter and ours.

‖**月着陸船** a lunar module /lùːnər mάːdʒuːl/ (➤ LM と略すことが多い) ‖**月ロケット** a moon rocket.

2【1か月】 a **month** ▶**月1回**の健康診断 a *monthly* physical checkup ‖ 家賃は**月の初めに**払います I pay my rent *at the beginning of each* [*every*] *month*. ‖ **月に1度**はスキューバダイビングをします I go scuba diving *once a month*. ‖ 彼は**月に**5万円(も)貯金している He saves (as much as) 50,000 yen *every month*.

²つき 付き **luck, fortune**(運)(➤ 後者のほうが堅い語) ▶私にもようやく**つきが回ってきた**ようだ I think *luck is coming my way* now. ／I feel I'*m in luck* now. ／I think I'*ve got fortune* on my side now. ‖ このところ私には**つきがない** I'*m out of luck* these days.

³つき 尽き ▶あれが俺の**運の尽き**だった That was *the end of my luck*.

⁴つき 就き **1【…に関して】about** ▶あなたの経歴につき2，3お尋ねしたいことがあります I'd like to ask you a few things *about* [*concerning*] your personal history.

2【…ごとに】 ▶超過料金は**30分につき300円**です The extra charge is 300 yen *for every* half an hour [thirty minutes]. ⇀-につき.

-つき -付き 【…の付いた】with ▶**バス付きの**アパート an apartment *with* a bath(room) ‖ **ズーム付きの**カメラ a camera *equipped with* a zoom lens ‖ このストーブは1年間の**保証付き**です This heater *comes with* a one-year guarantee [warranty]. ‖ 弟は**おまけ付きのキャンデー**を買った My little brother bought a box of candies *that came with* a toy inside. ‖ この日本旅館の宿泊料は**1泊2食付きで**1万6000円だ This Japanese inn charges 16,000 yen for one night, *including* two meals.

¹つぎ 次 **1【順序があと】**一形 **次の (the) next, (the) following** 一副 **次に next**

▶**次の**ピッチャーは誰ですか Who's *the next* pitcher? ‖ **次の土曜日**に六本木へ行こう Let's go to Roppongi *next* Saturday. (🏺 (×) on next Saturday とはしない) ‖ 対話「神田は**次**ですか」「いいえ，**次**は東京です．神田は**次の次**です」"Is Kanda *the next* stop?" "No, *the next* stop is Tokyo. Kanda is *the one after that*." ‖ **次に何をすればいいの**ですか What should I do *next*?

▶我々はロンドンに1週間滞在し，**その次の週**パリへ向かった We stayed in London for one week and left for Paris *the next* [*the following*] week. ‖ **次の方**，どうぞ *Next* (*person*), please. ‖ それは**次に**(＝次回)会ったとき話すよ I'll talk to you about it (*the*) *next time* we meet. (🏺 文法的には the が必要だが，インフォーマルでは省略することがある) ‖ ピョンチャンオリンピックは私が高校に入った**次の年**に開かれた The Pyeongchang Winter Olympics were held (*in*) *the year after* I entered high school. ‖ **次から次へと**新型の車が出てくる New cars are coming out *one after another*. (➤「1つまた1つと」).

▶**次の**(＝以下の)文章を読んで問いに答えなさい Read *the following* passage and answer the question(s). ‖ 外務大臣の演説の要点は**次のとおり**です The gist of the Foreign Minister's speech is *as follows*: (🏺 このあとに改行して要点を述べた文章を続けるのがふつう).

2【順位などが次】next to, after ▶(学科は)現国の**次に**英語が好きです *Next to* modern Japanese, I like English best. ‖ カナダはロシアの**次に大きい国**です *Next to* [*After*] Russia, Canada is the largest country in the world. ‖ 富士山の**次に高い山**は何ですか *After* Mt. Fuji, what's the highest mountain?

☞ **その次** (⇀見出語)

²つぎ 継ぎ a **patch** ▶**継ぎだらけのシャツ** a shirt full of *patches*.

つきあい 付き合い **1【交際】**(an) **association** ⇀交際 ▶川田氏とは**付き合いが長い** I *have known* Mr. Kawada for many years. ／Mr. Kawada and I *have been friends* for many years. ‖ 私たちは学生時代からの**付き合い**(＝友だち)です We *have been friends* since we were college students. ‖ 金のことでけんかして彼との**付き合いをやめた**(＝絶交した) I *broke off* (*my relationship*) *with* him after having an argument about money matters.

> **あなたの英語はどう響く?**
> 「彼女とは長い付き合いです」と言うつもりで (×) I *have associated with* her for a long time. と言わないこと. associate with は社交上や仕事関係で交際する場合に用い，個人的な友人同士の付き合いという意味では，I *have known* her for a long time. ／She and I have known each other for a long time. ／She and I are old friends. などのように，また恋愛関係にあるなら，She and I *have been* (*going*) *together* [*seeing each other*] for a long time. のように言う.

2【行動を共にすること】 ▶**付き合いで**彼とカラオケに行った I went to a karaoke place with him (*just*) *to be sociable*. ‖ 彼女は**付き合いがいい** She *is a sociable person* [*a good mixer*]. (➤ good mixer は「交際上手な人」の意のインフォーマルな表現) ‖ 彼は宴会に全然出席しない. **付き合いの悪い男**だ He never goes to parties. He's *an unsociable guy*. ‖ 父は**付き合いで飲む**程度です My father is just a *social drinker*. ‖ 同僚との**付き合い**も大事だよ It's important to *socialize with* your co-workers. (🏺 社交としての仲間付き合いをいう) ‖ 友だち**との付き合い**もほどほどに You should *socialize with* your friends in moderation [without overdoing it]. ‖ 彼女は**仕事上の付き合いで**ゴルフをすることが多い She often plays golf *for business reasons*. ‖ 父は近所**付き合いがうまくない** My father *can't get along* (*well*) *with* his neighbors.

つきあう 付き合う **1【交際する】go (out) with; see** ＋目 (未婚者・既婚者を問わず，「異性と頻繁に会う」); **associate with**(通例好ましくない人と) ⇀**交際**

▶最近誰かと**付き合ってる**? Are you *seeing* anybody these days? ‖ 弟は直美ともう1年近く**付き合っている** My (younger) brother *has been going with* Naomi for nearly a year now. ‖ 彼女はうちの課長と**付き合っているらしい** They say she *is seeing* [*dating*] the chief of our section. ‖ **私と付き合ってもらえませんか** Will you *be my girlfriend* [*boyfriend* ／*steady*]? ／Will you go out with me? (🏺 前者は「本気で」，後者は「とりあえず」というニュアンス).

▶彼女は**付き合いにくい女性**だ She's a hard woman to *get along with*. (➤ get along は「仲よくやっていく」) ／She's unpleasant to *be with*. (➤ unpleasant は「不愉快な」) ‖ あの人たちとは二度と**付き合わない**でちょうだい I don't want you to *associate with*

them any more.
✉ **きみとはもうこれ以上付き合えなくなりました. さようなら** I'm afraid I won't be able to *see* [*meet*] you again. Good bye.
2【行動をともにする】▶みんなで飲みに行くんだ. おまえも**付き合え**よ We're going for a drink. Why don't you *join* us? ‖ 私は母の買い物に**付き合った**(＝一緒に行った) I *went* shopping *with* my mother. ‖ 兄がテレビの深夜映画を見ていたので, 私も**付き合って**夜更かしした Since my (older) brother was watching a late-night movie on TV, I stayed up *to keep him company*. ‖ ちょっとそこまで**付き合って**くれないか Would you mind *accompanying* me just down the street?
3【病気などとかかわり合う】▶祖母はこの10年間がんとうまく**付き合っている** My grandmother has been *living with* cancer for ten years.

つきあかり 月明かり moonlight ▶**月明かり**の夜 a *moonlit* night ‖ **月明かり**を頼りに山道を歩いた I walked along the mountain path with the help of (*the*) *moonlight*.

つきあげる 突き上げる ▶突然, 激しい腹痛が**突き上げ**てきた I *was* suddenly *attacked* by sharp abdominal pain. ‖ 突然**突き上げる**ような揺れがきた Suddenly the ground *heaved* (*upward*). / There was a sudden *vertical jolt*.
▶総会では執行部の弱腰が激しく**突き上げられた** The weak-kneed attitude of the executives *was* severely *criticized* at the general meeting.

つきあたり 突き当たり the end ▶お父さんの病室はこの廊下の**突き当たり**の右側です Your father's room is on the right at *the* (*far*) *end* of this corridor.

つきあたる 突き当たる ▶この道をまっすぐ行って線路に**突き当たったら**右へ行けば駅はすぐですよ Go straight along this street *till you come to* the railroad tracks *at the end* (of the street). Turn right and you'll see the train station.
▶その計画は資金面で**壁に突き当たった** We *hit a* financial *snag* in carrying out the project. (➤ snag は「(水中に没していて船の運航を妨げる倒木などの)障害物」が原義).

つきあわせる 突き合わせる **1【照合する】** check《with, against》▶翻訳を原文と**突き合わせてみた** I *checked* the translation *with* [*against*] the original. ‖ 新しい辞書を旧版と**突き合わせてみた** I *compared* the new dictionary *with* its old edition.
2【向かい合わせる】▶あいつらと**顔を突き合わせて**仕事をするのは嫌だ I don't like working *face to face with* them. ‖ 彼と**膝を突き合わせて**その件について相談した I *sat knee to knee with* him and talked over the matter. / We talked over the matter *face-to-face*.

つきおくれ 月遅れ ▶**月遅れ**の雑誌 *a back number* of a magazine ‖ うちの田舎では**月遅れ**のお盆を祝う The Bon Festival is celebrated (in August) *according to the lunar calendar* in my hometown. (➤「太陰暦[旧暦]に従って」と考える).

つきおとす 突き落とす ▶彼女は彼をプールに**突き落とした** She *pushed* him *into* the pool. ‖ モリアーティー教授はシャーロック・ホームズを崖から**突き落とした** Professor Moriarty *pushed* Sherlock Holmes *over* the cliff.

つきかえす 突き返す **1【こちらも突く】** poke back ▶突かれたので**突き返した** Someone poked [jabbed] me, and I *poked* [*jabbed*] him *back*.
2【受け取らない】 reject ＋目 (拒否する); send ... back (送り返す) ▶提出期限が過ぎていたので私のレポートは**突き返された** My paper *was rejected* [The teacher refused to accept my paper] because it was overdue. ‖ 歳暮を持って来たらみんな**突き返せ** If someone comes with a year-end gift, *thrust* it *back*.

つぎき 接ぎ木 grafting ▶サンザシの木にリンゴの枝を**接ぎ木する** *graft* a branch of an apple tree *onto* a hawthorn tree.

つきぎめ 月極めの monthly ▶**月ぎめ**の購読者 a *monthly* subscriber ‖ 彼は**月ぎめ**でその駐車場を借りた He rented the parking space *by the month*.

つききり →つきっきり.

つぎこむ 注ぎ込む put ... in [into], sink ... in [into] ▶彼は金を全部その会社に**つぎ込んだ** He *sank* all his money *into* the company. (● sink A into B は「A (資金など)をB (事業など)につぎ込む」の意で, しばしば回収が困難な場合に用いる) ‖ M社は大金を**つぎ込んで**新しいゲームソフトを開発した M Corporation *put* [*poured* / *funneled*] a lot of money *into* developing a new game software program.

つぎざお 継ぎ竿 a jointed fishing rod.

つきささる 突き刺さる stick《in》▶魚の骨が喉に**突き刺さった** A fishbone *stuck in* my throat. (➤ stuck は stick の過去形).
▶彼女のとげのあることばがぼくの心にぐさりと**突き刺さった** Her barbed remarks were like a knife *stabbing* me.

つきさす 突き刺す stick ＋目 (とがったもので物を); thrust ＋目 (強引に突く); stab ＋目 (刃物で人を)
▶ジャガイモにフォークを**突き刺す** *stick* a fork *into* a potato / *stick* a potato *with* a fork ‖ 強盗は学生をナイフで**突き刺した** The robber *stabbed* the student with his knife.
▶「裏切り者」という彼のひと言がぼくの胸を**突き刺した** His words "You traitor!" *pierced me* (*like a knife*).

つきすすむ 突き進む shove one's way ▶彼女は特売コーナー目がけて人混みの中を**突き進んだ** She *shoved her way* through the crowd to the bargain counter. ‖ 両国は武力衝突へと**突き進んだ** The two countries *were heading* (*straight*) *toward* an armed clash. ‖《ラグビー》ゴールに向かって**突き進め**! *Make a dash for* the goal!

つきせぬ 尽きせぬ ▶わが子に対する彼女の**尽きせぬ**愛情 her *undying* love for her child.

つきそい 付き添い an attendant (付き添い人; 通例貴人の従者); a helper (お手伝い); a chaperon(e) /ʃǽpəroʊn/ (未成年者に対するお目付け役);《主に米》a caretaker (介護人) ▶その患者には**付き添い**をつける必要がある The patient needs to have *a helper* to take care of him [her]. ‖《試験会場で》**付き添いの方**はこちらでお待ちください Would *those accompanying* [*escorting*] the students wait over here, please?

つきそう 付き添う attend (on); take care of (世話をする); accompany ＋目 (ついて行く); chaperon(e) ＋目 (未成年者のお目付け役として) ▶花嫁[花婿]に**付き添う** *attend* a bride [a bridegroom] (➤ 英米などの結婚式で花嫁に付き添う若い未婚の女性を bridesmaid, 花婿に付き添う若い男性を best man と呼ぶ) ‖ 入院中は娘が私に**付き添ってくれた** My daughter *took care of* me in the hospital. ‖ 少年は父親に**付き添われて**警察に自首した The boy turned himself in to the police *accompanied by* his father. ‖ そのスキー旅行では2名の教師がお目付け役として付き添った Two teachers *chaperoned* [*acted as chaperones* for] the ski trip.

つきたおす 突き倒す ▶兄は私を突き倒した My brother *knocked* [*pushed*] me *down*.

つきだす 突き出す 1【体の一部を】stick [thrust] out ▶胸を突き出す *stick* [*thrust*] *out* one's chest ‖ 車の窓から顔を突き出すな Don't *stick* your head *out of* the car window. ‖ 彼女は彼に向かって片腕［舌］を突き出した She *stuck out* her arm [tongue] at him.

2【突いて外へ出す】push out ▶横綱は相手を土俵の外へ突き出した The yokozuna *pushed* [*shoved* / *thrust*] his opponent *out of* the ring.

3【飛び出ている】jut out ▶細長い半島が太平洋に向かって突き出している A long and narrow peninsula *juts out into* the Pacific.

4【引き渡す】hand over ▶アパートの住人は自分たちで捕まえた泥棒を警察に突き出した The residents of the apartment house *handed* the burglar they had caught *over to* the police.

つぎたす 継ぎ足す・注ぎ足す ▶用紙が小さすぎたので継ぎ足した The paper wasn't big enough, so I *added more*. ‖ コードを継ぎ足さないとコンセントに届かない This cord won't reach the outlet unless we *connect another cord* [*an extension cord*] *to* it. ▶ビールはつぎ足すとまずくなる *Pouring* more beer *into a glass that hasn't been finished* ruins the taste (of the beer).

つきたてる 突き立てる ▶食べ物に箸を突き立てるのははしたない It is (very) bad manners to *spear* one's food *with* a chopstick.

つきづき 月々 ▶月々の小遣い a *monthly* allowance ‖ 父は月々10万円の住宅ローンの支払いに四苦八苦している My father has a hard time making our 100,000 yen *a month* mortgage payments.

つぎつぎ 次々に one after another ▶ランナーが次々にゴールインした The runners reached the goal *one after another*. ‖ 難題が次々に持ち上がった Difficulties came up *in succession*. / Problems cropped up *one after another*.

つきっきり 付きっ切り ▶父は入院中の母に付きっきりだった My father *took care of* my mother *around the clock* [was *in constant attendance upon* my mother] during her hospitalization. ‖ 私は付きっきりで子供たちの夏休みの宿題を手伝った I *sat by* the children *the entire time* and helped them with their summer vacation homework.

つきつける 突き付ける thrust 《against, at, on, into》 ▶ギャングは彼の背中にピストルを突きつけた The gangster *thrust* a gun *into* his back. ‖ 労働組合は10項目の要求を会社側に突きつけた The labor union *thrust* [*forced*] a ten-point demand *on* the management.

つきつめる 突き詰める ▶物事をあまり突き詰めて考える(＝真面目に考え過ぎる)な Don't *take* things too *seriously*.

つきでる 突き出る stick [jut] out ; project(…の上に) ▶庭の上に突き出たバルコニー the balcony *projecting* over the garden ‖ 穴から鉄棒が突き出ていた An iron bar was *sticking out of* the hole. ‖ 根室半島は太平洋にぐっと突き出ている The Nemuro Peninsula *juts* far (*out*) into the Pacific. ▶突き出たおなか［顎］a *protruding* belly [jaw].

[1]**つきとおす 吐き通す** ▶うそをつき通す *stick to* a lie.

[2]**つきとおす 突き通す** ▶畳に針を突き通す *pierce* a tatami mat *with* a needle / *stick* a needle *through* a tatami mat.

つきとばす 突き飛ばす ▶ひったくりは女性のバッグをひっつかむと彼女を突き飛ばして逃げた After snatching the woman's bag, the snatcher *shoved* her *out of his way* and fled.

つきとめる 突き止める find out ▶調査団は事件の真相を突き止めた The panel *discovered* [*found out*] the truth of the matter. / The panel *got to the bottom of* the matter. ‖ 警察は犯人の居所を突き止めた The police *located* the culprit [*discovered* the culprit's whereabouts].

つきなみ 月並みな hackneyed, trite /traɪt/ (陳腐な) ; **commonplace** (ありきたりな) ▶月並みな表現 a *hackneyed* [*trite*] expression ‖ その評論家は月並みなことしか話さなかった That critic made nothing but *trite* comments [*commonplace* remarks]. ‖ 月並みな言い方ですが, 健康第一ですよ *This may sound rather trite*, but nothing is more important than good health.

つきぬける 突き抜ける pierce, go through ▶くぎが靴の底を突き抜けて足に刺さった A nail *pierced* [*went through*] the sole of my shoe and stuck me in the foot. ‖ 数日もすればアスパラガスの芽が固い土を突き抜けてくる Asparagus shoots will *push through* the hard soil in a few days.

つきのわぐま 月の輪熊 《動物》an **Asian black bear.**

つぎはぎ 継ぎ接ぎ patching and darning ▶継ぎはぎだらけのズボン pants *with patches all over* / pants *patched all over* ‖ このクッション, 生地が足りなくて裏側は継ぎはぎなの I ran out of cloth so the backside of this cushion is *a patchwork*.

つきはじめ 月初め ▶月初めは懐が温かい We have a lot of money at *the beginning of the month*.

つきはなす 突き放す ▶時には子供を突き放すことも必要だ At times, it is necessary to *detach ourselves from* our children. ▶ジャイアンツは8回に2点を加え, カープを突き放した The Giants added two runs in the eighth inning to *break away from* the Carp. (➤ break away from は「引き離す, 差を広げる」).

つきばらい 月払い (a) **monthly payment** (➤「支払い金」の意では a がつく) ; a **monthly installment** (分割払い) ▶私はRVを月払いで買った I bought an RV on *a monthly installment plan*.

つきひ 月日 time ▶月日のたつのは早いものだ Time flies. (➤ 英語のことわざ) ‖ 父が死んで5年の月日が流れた *Five years* have passed since my father died.

つきびと 付き人 an **attendant** ▶白鵬の付き人 *an attendant* to Hakuho.

つぎほ 接ぎ穂・継ぎ穂 ▶Yes. や No. だけの返事では相手は話の接ぎ穂を失ってしまう If you answer with only a yes or no, the other person will find it difficult to *continue the conversation* [to *keep the ball rolling*].

つきましては →ついては.

つきまとう 付き纏う follow about, tag along 《with》 (➤ 後者はインフォーマル) ▶ストーカーに付きまとわれる *be followed* [*tailed*] by a stalker / be stalked ‖ あの歌手にはいつも親衛隊が付きまとっている Groupies always *follow* that singer *about*. / Groupies always *tag along with* that singer. (➤ tag along

には「喜ばれないのに」のニュアンスがある).
▶あの政治家には常に黒いうわさが付きまとう Black rumors constantly *surround* that politician. ‖ ぜんそくが母に長年つきまとっている Asthma has *been dogging* my mom for a long time.

つきみ 月見 ***tsukimi*** ; **moon-viewing.**

つきみそう 月見草《植物》an **evening primrose.**

つぎめ 継ぎ目・接ぎ目 a **joint** ; a **seam**(縫い目) ▶継ぎ目のないレール rails without *joints* ‖ パイプの継ぎ目からガスが漏れていた Gas was leaking from the pipe *joints*.

つきもの 付き物 ⚠「付き物」に当たる1語の英語はないので,「不可分だ」「…の一部だ」「…すれば必ず～する」などと考えて訳す.
▶学生に試験は付き物だ Tests and exams *are* (*an inevitable*) *part* of student life. (「学生生活の(避けられない)一部分」の意) ／Students *cannot do without* tests and exams. (「無しでは済ませられない」の意) ‖ 規則に例外は付き物だ *Every* rule *has* an exception.
▶おじはプロレスに八百長は付き物だと言う My uncle says that rigging *is inseparable from* pro-wrestling. (「切り離せない」の意) ‖ ラグビーにけがは付きものだ Injuries *are a part of* playing rugby. ／You *can't* play rugby *without* getting injured (once in a while).

つきやぶる 突き破る **break through** ▶暴走したダンプカーがブロック塀を突き破って家に飛び込んで来た A dump truck went out of control and *crashed through* the concrete block wall into the house. ‖ 私は100メートル12秒の壁がなかなか突き破れない I can't seem to *break through* the 12-second barrier in the 100-meter dash.

つきやま 築山 a ***tsukiyama*** ; artificial mound in a Japanese-style garden (➤ 説明的な訳).

つきゆび 突き指 a **sprained finger** ▶突き指をしたときは冷水につけるとよい When you *sprain a finger*, it helps to soak it in cold water.

つきよ 月夜 a **moonlit night** (➤ moonlit は文語的で詩的な語) ▶その夜は月夜だった It was *a moonlit* [*moonlight*] *night*. ‖ 今夜はいい月夜だ *The moon is very beautiful* tonight.

つきる 尽きる **run out** (資金・食糧・金などが無くなる) ▶資金が尽きてその候補者は脱落するはめになった The candidate had to drop out of the race when the funds *ran out*.
▶彼の運も尽きたようだ It looks like his luck has *run out*. ‖ 走者は力尽きて倒れた The runner collapsed *from exhaustion*.
▶この古地図を見ていると興味が尽きない I *never get tired of* looking at this old map. ‖ 久しぶりのクラス会で話は尽きなかった It was our first class reunion in a long time, so *there was no end of things to talk about*.

つきわり 月割り ▶うちのローンの返済額は月割りにすると10万円になる We make *monthly* payments of 100,000 yen on our loan.

[1]つく 着く・付く・就く・点く

> 📖 **訳語メニュー**
> 到着する →arrive, get to, reach **1**
> 手などが届く →reach, touch **2**
> くっつく →stick **3**
> 職などに就く →take, get **8**

> **【文型】**
> 場所(A)に着く
> **arrive at** [in] A
> **reach** A
> **get to** A
>
> **【解説】** 場所に「着く」の意では arrive と reach がともによく使われる. **arrive** は「到着する」で, 視点が到着点側にあるので to A とはいわずに, at A または in A という. 一方, **reach** の視点は行く側から到着点に向いている. reach は「…に到達する, …まで行く」を意味する他動詞なので, うしろに to, at, in などの前置詞をつけない. また reach は時に, 時間をかけて, 苦労して, などのニュアンスを伴うことがある. get to は3つのうちでいちばんくだけた言い方.

1【到着する】arrive《at, in》, **get to** ; **reach** +㊐ (長い時間・苦労の末に)
▶ホテルに着く *arrive at* a hotel (到達「地点」の意識の強い比較的狭い場所に着く場合の前置詞は at) ‖ アフリカに着く *arrive in* Africa (捕らえどころのない広い場所に着く場合には「中」を表す in) ‖ 目的地に着く *reach* one's destination ‖ ダブリンに着いたら電話をください Call me when you *get to* [*arrive in*] Dublin. ‖ 家に着いて初めてメキシコ地震のことを知った I first learned about the earthquake in Mexico when I *got home*. ‖ この列車, 何時に秋田に着くの? What time will this train *get to* Akita? ‖ ニューヨークに(ようやく)着いたよ. 今バスを待っているところ I *made it to* New York. I'm just waiting for the bus to arrive. (➤ make it to は砕けた言い方). ‖ **対話** (国際電話で)「もしもし, お母さん, 今ロサンゼルスに着いたとこ」「そう, そちらのお母さんによろしくね」"Hello, Mom. I've just *arrived in* Los Angeles." "Good. Please give my regards to your host family mother." ‖ そろそろ(目的地に)着く? *Are* we almost *there*? ‖ 小包がついたら知らせてください Let me know when the package *has arrived*. ‖ さあ, (駅に)着きましたよ *Here we are* (at the station). →到着.
✉ **ド・ゴール空港には7月28日の午後3時に着く予定です. できれば出迎えをお願いいたします** I'm scheduled to *arrive at* Charles de Gaulle Airport at 3 p.m. on July 28th. If possible, could you please meet me at the airport?

2【届く】reach +㊐, **touch** +㊐ ▶手が床に着くまで体を曲げてごらん Bend over until your hands *reach* the floor. ‖ あの外国人は背が高くてバスの天井に頭が着きそうだ That foreigner is so tall that his head almost *touches* the ceiling of the bus. ‖ 湖は足が(底に)着かないほど深いから落ちないように気をつけて Be careful not to fall into the lake because it's so deep (that) you *can't touch* (the) bottom.

3【物に物が付着する】stick ▶こののりはよくつく This glue *sticks* well. ‖ スーツにソースをこぼしたら染みがつい

てしまった I spilled sauce on my suit and *stained* it. (➤ stain は「染みをつける」) ‖ 手に血がついていた *There was* some blood on my hand. ‖ カーテンにたばこの臭いがついてとれない The curtains *have* a stale tobacco odor which won't come out.

4【付属する】▶スヌーピーの絵のついたセーター a sweater *with* Snoopy *on* it ‖ 毛皮の襟のついたコートを買った I bought a coat *with* a fur collar. ‖ 4月号には特大付録がつきます The April issue *is coming with* special supplements.

5【跡が残る】▶きちんと折り目のついたズボン *neatly-creased* [*well-pressed*] pants ‖ 雪道に点々とキツネの足跡がついている The snow-covered road *is dotted* with fox footprints. ‖ その地図で印のついている所が私の家です The place *marked* on the map is my house.

6【離れないようにする】▶この旅行にはガイドがつきます A tour guide will *accompany* you during the trip. ‖ 首相の周りにはいつもSPがついて離れない *There are* security police around the prime minister at all times. ／The prime minister is always *closely* guarded by security police.

7【場所を占める】▶どうぞ席に着いてください Please *take your seat*(s). ／Please *be seated*. (●後者は非常に丁寧な言い方) ‖ この頃は家族全員で夕食の食卓に着くことはめったにない These days all the members of the family seldom *gather at the table* for dinner. ‖ 位置に着いて, 用意, ドン! *On your mark (s)!* Get set! Go! ／《英また》*Ready!* Steady! Go! ‖ 全員, 配置に着け! Everybody, *take* your positions! ‖ 政治改革はようやくスタートラインに着いたばかりだ Political reform has barely *reached* the starting line.

8【職業・役職に携わる】 take +㊐, get +㊐ ▶大学を出てからどんな職業に就くつもりですか What kind of job are you going to *take* [*get*] when you graduate from university? ‖ 私たちの担任の先生は3年前教職に就いたと言っている Our homeroom teacher says he *entered the teaching profession* [*began his teaching career*] three years ago.

9【従う】▶この夏, 父について南米に行きました I went to South America *with* my father this past summer. ‖ 彼の行く先々悪いうわさがついて回る Wherever he goes, bad rumors follow [*dog*] him. (➤ この dog は「付きまとう」の意の動詞).
▶母は私と弟がけんかすると必ず弟につく(＝味方する) My mother always *takes* my brother's *side* [*sides with* my brother] whenever we fight. ‖ おまえには俺がついてるぞ I'm *behind* you [I'll *back* you *up*] all the way! ／I'll *stand by* [*behind*] you!
▶私は母についてピアノを習った I took piano lessons *from* my mother. ‖ 兄は江藤博士について心理学を研究している My (older) brother is studying psychology *under* [*with*] Dr. Eto.

10【新しいものが加わる】▶ことしもビワにたくさん実がついた The loquat tree *bore* a lot of *fruit* again this year. (➤ bore は bear(実を結ぶ)の過去形) ‖ あの銀行に預金すれば年に3パーセントの利子がつく If you deposit money in that bank, it will earn [*draw*] 3% interest a year. ‖ この問題集で大学受験の実力が確実に身につきます You can definitely *improve* [*develop*] your ability on entrance examinations with this drill book. ／This drill book will surely *help* you do well on entrance examinations. ‖ この頃寝そべって本を読む悪い癖がついた Recently, I *have formed* a bad habit of lying down to read.

11【目や耳に】▶彼は大きいから人混みでも目につく(＝目立つ) He's so tall that he *stands out* in the crowd. ‖ 高校生たちは先生の目につかない所で飲酒をした The high school students drank *where* they *could not be seen* by their teachers [*behind* their teacher's *backs*]. ‖ 車の騒音が耳について眠れない I can't get to sleep because the noise of traffic *bothers* me. ‖ どうもあいつの口癖は鼻につく His (peculiar) way of talking somehow *gets on* my nerves. ／I'*m put off by* his (peculiar) speech mannerism(s).

12【火・電気が活動状態になる】▶この懐中電灯, つかないよ This flashlight *doesn't work*. ‖ 門灯がついてないよ The gate light *isn't on*. ‖ しばらくすると明かりがついた After a while, the lights *came on*. ‖ 私は明かりがついていても眠ることができる I can sleep even with the lights *on*. ‖ 部屋に誰も居ないのにストーブがついたままになっている Even though there's no one in the room, the heater *has been left on*.
☛ ついている (→見出語)

2**つく** 突く・撞く・衝く **1【強く押したりたたいたりする】** push +㊐ (押す); thrust +㊐ (強く); prod +㊐, poke +㊐ (指などで軽く)
▶誰かがぼくの背中を突いた Someone *pushed* me from behind. ‖ 農園主は牛を棒で突いた The farmer *prodded* [*poked*] the cow with a stick. ‖ その力士は土俵際で相手の胸をどんと突いた The sumo wrestler *thrusted at* his opponent's chest at the ring's edge.
▶あの寺では朝6時と夕方6時に鐘をつく That temple *bell is rung* [*is struck*] at six in the morning and six in the evening. ‖ ボールを突く *bounce* a ball ‖ 判をつく *put* [*affix*] one's hanko to a document.

2【勢いよく刺す】 prick +㊐ (針などで); stab +㊐ (刃物で) ▶刺しゅうをしていてうっかり指を針で突いてしまった I carelessly *pricked* my finger with a needle while I was embroidering. ‖ アマゾンの現地人はもりで魚を突いて捕る The natives of the Amazon catch fish *with* spears.

3【棒状のもので支える】▶お年寄りがつえをついて歩いている An elderly man is walking *with a cane*. ‖ 彼は頬づえをついて窓越しに庭を眺めていた He was looking out (of) the window at the garden, *resting his cheek on one hand*. ‖ 母は食事のときいつも「テーブルに肘をつかないで」と言う When we sit down to eat, my mother always tells me not to *put my elbows* on the table.

4【弱点・重点などを攻める】▶進歩派の議員たちは大統領の政策の矛盾をついた Liberal Congressmen *attacked* the President for the contradic-tion(s) in his policy. ‖ 先生の批評は痛いところをついていた My teacher's remarks *got* me where it hurts [*hit* close to home]. ‖ 彼の意見は問題の核心をついている His opinion *touches* (*on*) the core of the issue. ‖ 先生は彼の意表をつく質問に口籠もってしまった The teacher was stumped by his *unexpected* question.

5【感覚や感情を刺激する】▶台所に入るときな臭い臭いが鼻をついた As I went into the kitchen, a burning smell *hit my nose* [*assailed my nostrils*].

6【障害を物ともしない】▶事件記者たちは激しい嵐をついて現場へ急行した The reporters rushed to the scene of the crime *in the face of* [*despite*] the terrible storm.

³つく 憑く possess +㊀(とりつく). ⇀つかれる.

つぐ 継ぐ・接ぐ・注ぐ・次ぐ **1【つなぎ合わせる】**▶息子が骨折したので,医者に骨を**接いで**もらった I had the doctor *set* my son's broken bone. ‖ よく見ると,この壁紙はここで**継いである** If you look carefully, you can see that this wallpaper *is joined* here.

2【主に液体を器に入れる】pour /pɔːr/ +㊀ ▶コップに牛乳を**つぐ** *pour* milk into a glass ‖ もう1杯コーヒーを**ついで**ください Please *pour* me another cup of coffee. ‖ 彼はコップにビールを**ついで**一気に飲んだ He *filled* the glass with beer and drank it in one gulp.

> **あなたの英語はどう響く?**
> 日本では酒やビールをお互いにつぎ合う習慣があるので,「ビールをおつぎしましょう」を直訳して, Let me pour you some beer. と言う人が少なくないが,英語圏ではそのような習慣はふつうではない. This is one of our customs.(私たちの習慣なんです)/This is Japanese style.(これが日本式です)/It's our custom to pour for each other.(つぎ合うのが日本の習慣です)などのことばを添えるほうがよい.

3【あとに続く】take over(譲り受ける); **succeed**《to》(継承する) ▶家業は弟が**継ぐ**ことになっている My brother will *take over* our family business. ‖ 兄は父の**跡を継いで**大工になった My brother *followed in* our father's *footsteps* and became a carpenter.

4【順序や地位が次である】▶彼は自民党内では総裁に**次ぐ**実力者だ In the Liberal Democratic Party, he's the most influential man *after* the president. ‖ 日本チームはカナダに**次いで**3位になった The Japanese team took third place *after* Canada. (⇀**次いで**).

つくえ 机 a **desk** ▶机の上を片づけなさい Tidy up your *desk*. ‖ 彼女とは小学校時代に**机を並べた**(=同級だった)ことがある She and I *were* once *in the same class* when we were elementary school students. ‖ たけしが**机に向かって**(勉強して)いるのを見たことがない I've never seen Takeshi studying *at his desk*.

つくし 土筆《植物》a **field horsetail**(スギナ).

-づくし -尽くし ▶カニ**尽くし**ツアー a *crab-eating* tour / a tour to *enjoy special crab dishes* ‖ マグロ**尽くし**ランチ a lunch with *assorted* tuna sushi ⇀心尽くし.

つくす 尽くす **1【十分に行う】**▶全力を**尽くす** *do* one's *best* ‖ 彼女はあらゆる手を**尽くして**いなくなった猫を捜した She *tried every possible means* [*left no stone unturned*] to find her missing cat.

▶このテーマはもう**論じ尽くされている** This subject *has* already *been fully discussed*. ‖ カイコは山のようなクワの葉を瞬く間に**食べ尽くした** The silkworms *ate up* a heap of mulberry leaves in a flash.

2【尽力・献身する】▶彼女は麻薬撲滅運動に**尽くして**きた She has *devoted herself to* the fight against drugs. ‖ 我々は生きている間は社会のために**尽くさなければならない** As long as we live, we should *contribute to* [*serve*] our society. ‖ 妻は私にかいがいしく**尽くしてくれる** My wife *waits on* me hand and foot.

つくだに 佃煮 ***tsukudani***; a preserved food made of seaweed, small fish, mushrooms or other ingredients boiled down in a sweetened soy-based sauce (➤説明的な訳).

つくづく ▶今の子供たちは変化の速い時代に生きていると**つくづく思う** I *really* think [*strongly* feel] that children today are living in rapidly-changing times. ‖ この会社が**つくづく嫌になった** I'*ve gotten sick and tired* of this company. ‖ 姉と一緒の部屋に居るのが**つくづく嫌になった** I'*m sick to death* of sharing a room with my big sister. (➤ to death は「死ぬほど,ひどく」).

▶客は床の間に飾られたつぼに**つくづくと**見入っていた The guests were gazing *intently* [*earnestly*] at the vase in the tokonoma.

つぐない 償い compensation(損害の賠償); **atonement**(贖罪(しょくざい)) ▶彼は大抵のことは金で**償いがつく**と考えている He thinks almost anything *can be compensated for* with money. (🔴 for が必要なことに注意; ⇀**償う**) ‖ きみは罪の**償いをしなければならない** You will have to *atone for* your crime [sin]. (➤ crime は法律上の罪, sin は道徳上・宗教上の罪) ‖ この**償い**(=埋め合わせ)**はするから** I'll *make* it *up* to you.

▶せめてもの**償い**にお食事を差し上げたいんですが I would like to treat you to dinner *as a token of my regret* (*for what I did*). (➤「遺憾の気持ちのしるしに」の意).

つぐなう 償う compensate /kɑ́ːmpənseɪt/ **for**(…の償いをする); **atone for**(贖罪(しょくざい)する); **make up for**(不足・損失などを補う); **pay for**(…の埋め合わせをする) ▶罪を**償う** *atone for* a crime [a sin] ‖ 彼らが被った損害はあなたが**償う**べきだ You should *compensate* them *for* the damage they suffered. ‖ 彼女は自分がかけた迷惑を**償おう**とした She tried to *make up for* all the trouble she had caused.

▶犯罪者は刑に服して罪を**償わねばならない** Offenders must *pay for* their crimes by serving (out) their sentences. ‖ その人は死をもって事故の**責任を償おう**とした He tried to *take responsibility for* the accident by taking his own life. **《参考》**このように死ぬことで責任を取ろうとする姿勢は,西洋ではむしろ責任回避と受け取られる.

つくね a **chicken meat ball**.

つくねんと absent-mindedly(ぼんやりと); **idly**(何もしないで); **(all) alone**(独りぼっちで) ▶おばあさんが**つくねんと**店番をしている An elderly woman tends the store *all alone*.

つぐみ 鶫《鳥》a **thrush**.

つぐむ 噤む ▶口を**つぐむ** *keep silent* / *keep* one's *mouth shut*.

つくり 作り・造り ▶れんが**造り**の家 a house *built of brick* / a *brick* house ‖ このテーブルは**作りが悪い** This table *is poorly made*.

つくりあげる 作り上げる ▶父は本棚を1日で**作りあげた** My father *made* a bookcase in one day. ‖ 誰がそんな話を**作りあげた**(=でっちあげた)のだろう I wonder who *made up* such a story.

つくりおき 作り置き ▶これは**作り置き**のできる料理です This dish can *be prepared in advance*.

つくりかえる 作り替える remodel +㊀ ▶父は300万円かけて居間を応接間に**作り替えて**もらった My father had the living room *remodeled into* a drawing room at a cost of three million yen. ‖ ウェブサイトを**作り替えた** I *revamped* our website. (➤ revamp は「刷新する」の意).

つくりかた 作り方 how to make ... ; a recipe /résəpi/（調理法）▶チーズケーキの作り方を教えてください Can you tell me *how to make* cheesecake?／Can you give me your *recipe* for cheesecake?

つくりごと 作り事 (an) invention ; a fabrication, an invented story（作り話）.

つくりざかや 造り酒屋 a sake brewery（工場）; a sake brewer（人）.

つくりだす 作り出す produce ＋目（商品・産物などを）; create ＋目（新しい物を）; simulate ＋目（人工的に自然な状況を）▶新製品を作り出す *create* a new product ‖ 黒澤監督は数々の名画を作り出した The director Kurosawa *produced* many excellent films. ‖ 映画の撮影では強風を作り出すのに巨大な扇風機が使われる When making movies, huge fans are used to *simulate* strong wind.

つくりつけ 作り付けの built-in ▶作りつけの食器棚 a *built-in* cupboard.

つくりばなし 作り話 a made-up [an invented] story ; (a) fiction（架空の話［物語］）▶作り話をする *make up a story* ‖ 彼の言ったことは作り話じゃなくて本当の話だ What he said is not *a made-up story* but a fact. ‖ 彼女の身の上話は全くの作り話だとわかった The story of her life turned out to be pure *fiction*.

つくりもの 作り物 ▶作り物の花 an *artificial* flower ‖ このドキュメンタリーは作り物くさい This documentary seems a bit *doctored*.（➤ この doctor は「手を加える」の意の動詞）.

つくりわらい 作り笑い a forced smile [laugh]（無理に作られた）; a plastic smile（取ってつけたような）▶彼女は彼に作り笑いをした She gave him *a forced smile* [*laugh*].（smile は表情, laugh は発声に注目した言い方）.

つくる 作る・造る **1【製造する】** make ＋目 ; manufacture ＋目（工場などで大規模に）; produce ＋目（商品や産物を生産する）▶模型飛行機を作る *make* a model airplane.

> 【文型】
> **人(A)に物(B)を作ってやる**
> make A B
> make B for A

▶私は弟に水鉄砲を作ってやった I *made* my little brother a water pistol.／I *made* a water pistol *for* my little brother.（後者は「誰に作ってあげるか」をはっきりさせるとき）.

> 【文型】
> **原料(A)から物(B)を作る**
> make B of A
> make B from A
> 【解説】of は原料・材料がそのまま生かされる場合, from は原料から製品へと質が変化する場合に用いられる.

▶この食器類の多くはプラスチックで作る（＝作られる）Most of this tableware *is made of* plastic. ‖ 豆腐は大豆から作る Tofu *is made from* soy beans. ▶その工場では自動車の部品を作っている The factory *makes* [*manufactures*] car parts. ‖ 父の会社はテレビを作っている My father's company *produces* TV sets. ‖ ミツバチは蜂蜜を作る Bees *produce* honey.

2【建造する】 build ＋目 ; construct ＋目（大きなものを）▶団地を造る *build* a new housing complex ‖ ビーバーは木の枝を集めてダムを造り, そこに巣を作る Beavers collect branches to *build* dams and *make* their homes in them. ‖ 郊外に新しい家がたくさん造られている Many new houses *are being built* in the suburbs. ‖ 市民はこの町に市民ホールが造られることを期待している The citizens are looking forward to the *construction* of a municipal hall in this city.

3【芸術作品・世論などを生み出す】 write ＋目（詩などを）; compose ＋目（曲を）; coin ＋目（新語を）▶詩を作る *write* a poem ‖ 山田耕筰は多くの曲を作った Yamada Kosaku *composed* [*wrote*] a lot of music. ‖ 流行語を作る *coin* a new buzzword ‖ 世論はマスコミによって作られる傾向がある Public opinion tends to *be formed* by the media.

4【育成する】 grow ＋目,《主に米》raise ＋目（栽培する）▶トウモロコシを作る *grow* [*raise*] corn ‖ 東北地方の農家はほとんどが米を作っている Most farmers in the Tohoku district *grow* rice.

5【料理する】 make ＋目 ; cook ＋目（火に掛けて）; prepare ＋目（用意する）▶サラダを作る make salad（cook は火を使って調理することを表すので生野菜のサラダには make を用いる）‖ 食事を作る *prepare* a meal ‖ おいしい夕飯を作ってあげるよ I'll *cook* you a good dinner.／I'll *cook* a good dinner *for* you. ‖ 姉がスープを作っている My (older) sister *is making* soup. ‖ さあ, 夕ごはんを作りましょう Let's *fix* supper.（➤ fix は「食事を作る」の意のインフォーマルな語）.

6【組織する】 organize ＋目 ▶会社を作る *establish* [*found*／*start*] a company ‖ クラブ［バンド］を作る *form* a club [a rock band] ‖ その組合は1950年に作られた The union *was organized* in 1950. ‖ 父は20年前に商事会社を作った（＝始めた）My father *started* a trading company twenty years ago.

7【赤ん坊を産む】 have ＋目 ▶私たちは経済的理由で子供をつくることができなかった We couldn't *have* children for economic reasons.

8【友情・家庭などを築く】 make ＋目 ▶大学では友だちをたくさん作りたい I want to *make* a lot of *friends* in college. ‖ 私たちはお互いに協力し合っていい家庭を作ります We will help each other and *make a happy home*.

9【ある形にする】 form ＋目 ▶人々は宝くじ売り場の前に長い行列を作った People *formed* a long line [《英また》queue] in front of the lottery booth. ‖ 子供たちは手をつないで輪を作った The children *formed* a circle by holding each other's hands.（➤ ふっ

うは簡単に The children joined hands in a circle. という).

10【制定する，樹立する】enact /mækt/ +目 (法律などを) ; **establish** +目 (記録などを) ▶新しい税法を作る *enact* [*make*] a new tax law ‖ 日本国憲法は1946年に作られた The Constitution of Japan *was enacted* in 1946.

▶記録を作る *establish* [*set*] a record.

11【用立てるために整える】make +目 ; **raise** +目 (金を調達する) ▶金をつくる *make* money (➤「もうける」の意にもなる) ‖ 月末までに30万円つくらなければならない I have to *get* 300,000 yen *together* [I have to *raise* 300,000 yen] by the end of the month. ‖ 今度暇を作って遊びに行くからね Some day I'll *make time* to come and see you.

12【わざとこしらえる】▶口実を作る *make* (*up*) an excuse ‖ 新任の先生は私たちの前で無理に笑顔を作った Our new teacher *forced herself* to smile in front of us. ‖ その強盗事件は店員が作った狂言だった The burglary was a story *made up by* the salesclerk.

つくろう 繕う 1【修理する】mend +目 ; **darn** +目 (靴下などを) ; **patch** +目 (継ぎ当てをして) ▶スカートのかぎ裂きを母に繕ってもらった I *had* my mother *mend* the tear in my skirt.

2【取り繕う】▶彼女はいつも世間体を繕うことばかり考えている She is always trying to *keep up appearances*. ‖ 出任せのうそをついてその場を繕った I *smoothed things over* by saying whatever came into my head.

つけ 付け 《主に米》 a **charge account**, 《主に英》 a **credit account** (➤ ともに an account とだけいうことが多い ; →クレジット) ▶付けを払う settle *an account* ‖ あの店にはだいぶ付けがたまっている I'*ve got* a lot *on my account* at that store. ‖ 酒やビールはその店で付けで買う I buy sake and beer *on credit* [*on the cuff* / *on tick*] at the store. (➤ on the cuff は《米》の, on tick は《英》の, ともにインフォーマルな用法) ‖ 付けにしてもらえます? Can you *charge* it (*to my account*)? / Can you *put* it *on my account*? (➤ Can you put it on my tab? は「付け」を表すこともあるが, on my bill と同様に,「(店を出るとき払うので) 請求書に付けておいてもらえますか」の意にもなる).

▶《慣用表現》1年生のとき怠けた付けが回ってきたようだ My laziness in the first year *has* finally *caught up with* me. ‖ そのうち付けが回ってくるぞ You'll *have to pay for it* someday. (➤ pay for は「…の報いを受ける」).

つげ 柘植 《植物》 a **box**.

1-づけ -付け ▶彼は6月1日付けで課長に昇進した He was promoted to section chief *on* June 1st.

✉ **3月18日付けのお手紙ありがとうございました** Thank you for your letter *of* [*dated*] March 18.

2-づけ -漬け ▶ナスの浅漬け *lightly pickled* eggplants / eggplants *pickled for a short time* ‖ 英語漬けの授業 an *English immersion* class ‖ 仕事漬けになっている be *knee-deep in work* / be *up to one's neck in work*.

つけあがる つけ上がる ▶成績がいいからってつけあがるんじゃないよ Don't *get* so *swell-headed* [*conceited*] just because your grades are good! (➤ conceited は「うぬぼれの強い」) ‖ 人が下手に出ればつけあがりやがって Just because I was nice and polite doesn't mean you should *take advantage of* me [go *lording it over* me]! (「私が優しく丁重にしたからといって, きみがつけ込んで [威張り散らして] いいということにはならないぞ」の意).

つけあわせ 付け合わせ a **garnish** ▶マッシュルームの付け合わせ *a garnish* of mushrooms.

つけあわせる 付け合わせる garnish 《with》 ▶コックは豚カツに刻みキャベツを付け合わせた The cook *garnished* the pork cutlet *with* shredded cabbage.

つけいる 付け入る take advantage of, 《ややインフォーマル》 **play on** [**upon**] ▶チャンピオンは相手につけいる隙を与えなかった The champion allowed his opponent no chance to *take advantage of* him. ‖ ヒトラーはドイツ民族の恐怖心につけいった Hitler *played on* [*upon*] the fears of the German people.

つけかえる 付け替える change +目 ; **replace** 《with》 (取り替える) ; **renew** +目 (新しくする) ▶お母さん, この(服の)ボタン付け替えてくれない? Mom, could you *replace* these buttons (*with other ones*)?

つげぐち 告げ口する tell 《on》 (➤ この on は「人にとって不利なことを」のニュアンス) ▶彼はいつもクラスメートのことを先生に告げ口する He always *tells* the teacher what his classmates have done. ‖ カンニングしたら先生に告げ口してやるからな If you cheat, I'll *tell* the teacher *on* you. ‖ ゆうべのことは女房には告げ口しないでくれよ Please don't *tell* my wife about (what I did) last night. ‖ 彼はすぐ告げ口をする He's *a tattletale*. (tattletale はふつうは「すぐ告げ口する子供」の意).

つけくわえる 付け加える add 《to》 ▶あなたの説明に付け加えることはありません I have nothing to *add* to your explanation. ‖ 最後にひと言付け加えますと, かおりさんは大のカラオケ好きです *One final addition*. Kaori is a great karaoke lover.

つけげ 付け毛 a **hair extension**, a **hairpiece**.

つけこむ 付け込む take advantage of (都合よく利用する), 《ややインフォーマル》 **play on** [**upon**] ▶他人の弱みにつけ込むのはよせ Don't *take advantage of* the weaknesses of other people. / Don't hit a man when he is down. (後者は「倒れているときに打つな」, 転じて「ひきょうな行為をするな」の意) ‖ 彼らは彼の人のよさにつけ込んだ They *took advantage of* [*played on*] his good nature.

つけたす 付け足す add +目 ▶手紙の末尾に書き忘れた用件を付け足した At the end of the letter, I *added* something I had forgotten to mention. →足す.

つけっぱなし 付けっ放し ▶父はよくテレビをつけっぱなしにしてうたた寝している My father often dozes off *with* the TV *on*.

つけとどけ 付け届け a **present**, a **gift** (贈り物)

✉ **付け届けは日頃恩義を受けている人に対して感謝またはその恩義の継続を願って行う贈り物のことです** A tsuketodoke is *a present* to someone (who) you feel indebted to in everyday life. It expresses your gratitude or wish for continued favor.

1つけね 付け根 ▶彼はその事故が原因で右腕を付け根から切断しなければならなくなった Because of the accident, he had to have his right arm amputated *at the shoulder*. ‖ 少女は際どい質問をされて耳の付け根まで真っ赤になった The off-color questions made the girl flush right *to the back of the neck*. (英語では「首の後ろまで」と表現する).

2つけね 付け値 →言い値.

つけねらう 付け狙う ▶彼はやくざに付け狙われている He *is being tailed* by a yakuza.

つけひげ 付け髭 a **false mustache**（口ひげ）; a **false beard**（顎ひげ）▶付けひげをつける［取る］put on［take off］*a false mustache* ‖ 私は付けひげをしてイメージを変えてみた I tried to change my image by wearing *a false mustache*［*beard*］.

つけまつげ 付け睫毛 **false eyelashes**（➤ 通例複数形で）▶付けまつげをつけている wear *false* (*eye*) *lashes*（● 「つける」なら put on を用いる）.

つけまわす 付け回す ▶佐藤選手はどこへ行ってもカメラマンに付け回されている Wherever he goes, Sato *is followed around*［《英》*about*］by photographers. ‖ 彼女はストーカーに付け回されている She *is being followed around*［*being tailed*］by a stalker.

つけめ 付け目 an **aim**（狙いどころ）; an **object**（目的）▶そこがやつのつけめなんだよ That's his *aim*［*goal*］. ／ That's what he's aiming at.

つけもの 漬物 **pickles**（➤ 通例複数形で）▶漬物を漬ける make *pickles* ‖ キュウリの漬物 *pickled* cucumbers.

つけやきば 付け焼き刃 ▶付け焼き刃の知識は実社会では通用しない The *knowledge you've crammed into your head* won't be very useful in the real world.（● 「急いで頭に詰め込んだ知識」の意）.

[1]つける 付ける・着ける

📖 訳語メニュー
- 付着させる →put ... on **1**
- 身に着ける →put on, wear **2**
- 取り付ける →install **3**
- 日記をつける →keep **5**
- 電気・ガスをつける →turn on **10**

1【付着させる】put ... on ▶彼女は通学かばんに目立つようにステッカーをつけた She *put* some stickers *on* her schoolbag so it would stand out. ‖ 傷口に軟こうをつけた I *put*［*applied*］ointment *on* my cut. ‖ ホットドッグにはマスタードをたっぷりつけてもらえますか Could you *put* extra mustard *on* my hot dog？‖ トーストにマーガリンをつけて（＝塗って）食べた I *spread* margarine on my toast and ate it. ‖ 満員電車の中でシャツに口紅をつけられた I *got* my shirt *stained with* lipstick on a jam-packed train.

2【身に着ける】put on ; wear ＋㊐（身に着けている）▶ネクタイを着ける *put* a tie *on* ／ *put on* a tie ‖ 警官たちは防弾チョッキを身に着けた［身に着けていた］The police officers *put on*［*wore*］bullet-proof vests.（● 身に着けるまでの動作をいうのなら put on, その結果として，装着した状態をいうのなら wore）‖ 本校の生徒は必ず胸に校章を着けなければならない The students in［at］our school have to *wear* the school badge on their jackets. ‖ エリザベスはダイヤのピアスを着けていた Elizabeth *wore*［*was wearing*］(a pair of) diamond pierced earrings.（➤ wore は wear の過去形）‖ あのリボンを着けた子がかわいいね That girl *wearing* a ribbon in her hair is pretty, isn't she？

3【取り付ける】put on ; install ＋㊐（設置する）

【文型】
物(A)に物(B)を付ける
put B **on**［**to**］A
attach B **to** A

▶玄関ドアに新しい錠をつける *put* a new lock *on* the front door ‖ このタイヤにスノー・チェーンをつけてくださる？Could you *put* snow chains *on* these tires？‖ 父親は娘の三輪車に風船をつけた The father *attached* a balloon *to* his daughter's tricycle. ▶アパートにエアコンをつけたい I want to *have* an air conditioner *installed* in my apartment. ‖ ママ，上着にこのボタンをつけてよ Mom, could you *sew* this button on my jacket？（➤ sew /soʊ/ は「縫い付ける」）.

4【跡を残す】▶ズボンにぴんと折り目をつける *put* a sharp crease in one's pants［slacks］‖ うっかりぶつかって高価な掛け軸に傷をつけてしまった I *damaged* an expensive scroll by carelessly bumping into it. ‖ カレンダーに試験日の印をつけた I *marked* the examination date on the calendar.

5【記入する】keep ＋㊐（記録して残す）▶お宅は家計簿をつけていますか Do you *keep* a record of your family expenses？／Do you *keep track* of your family budget？‖ 私は20年間日記をつけています I have *kept* a diary for twenty years.（● keep a diary は「（継続的に）日記をつけている」の意．「日記をつける」という1回1回の動作は write in a diary）‖ 勘定は付けておいてくれる？Can you *charge* it to my account？（➤「私の部屋につけておいてくれる？」なら to my account を to my room にする）‖ きみがわざと窓ガラスを割ったことはえんま帳に付けておくからな I'*m putting* you *on* my blacklist［in my little black book］for breaking the window on purpose.

6【そばに置く】▶きみにはボディーガードをつけてあげよう I'll *assign* a bodyguard to protect you. ‖ 母親たちはどうして子供に家庭教師をつけるんだろう I wonder why mothers *hire*［*employ*］tutors *for* their children.

7【跡をつける】follow ＋㊐ ; **shadow** ＋㊐（尾行する）▶私服の刑事はすりの跡をつけた The plain-clothes detective［police officer］*shadowed* the pickpocket.

8【新しいものを加える】▶庭のバラがつぼみをたくさんつけた The rose bushes in the garden *are covered with* buds. ‖ 体力をつけるためにジョギングをしています I jog to *build up my strength*.（➤ build up は「（健康を）増進させる」）‖ おまえは二軍へ行って力をつけてこい Go back to the farm team and *try to improve*.

9【与える，設ける】▶先生は彼の答案に90点をつけた The teacher *gave* him a score of 90 on the exam. ‖ その会社社長はブラマンクの絵に3億円の値をつけた The company president *offered* three hundred million yen for a picture by Vlaminck. ‖ 私たちは娘に麻里という名を付けた We *named* our daughter Mari. ‖ 彼は長い名を付けられた He *was given* a long name. ‖ 彼は何かと理由をつけて会議をサボる He always tries to skip the meetings *on some pretext* or other.（➤ pretext /príːtekst/ は「口実」）‖ 彼は契約に際してたくさんの条件をつけた He *set*［*attached*］many conditions in the contract.

10【火・電気を活動状態にする】turn on ▶ストーブをつける *turn on* the heater ‖ テレビ［電灯］をつけてちょうだい *Turn on* the TV［the light］, please.

11【解決させる】▶俺が行ってその話に決着をつけてくるよ I'll go and *settle* the matter. ‖ この試合，早く勝負をつけてほしいな I hope this game will *be decided* soon.

12【ある場所に到着させる】pull up《to, at》▶運転手はホテルの玄関に車を着けた The driver *pulled up* (his car) at the entrance of the hotel. ‖ できるだけ早くボートを岸に着けてくれ Please *bring* the boat to the shore as soon as you can.

²つける 浸ける・漬ける 1【浸す】soak +目; **dip** +目(ちょっと浸す); **immerse**(沈める) ▶そのシャツは洗う前にぬるま湯につけておいたほうがいいよ You'd better *soak* the shirt in lukewarm water before you wash it. ‖ 彼は顔を水につけた He *dipped* [*immersed*] his face in the water.

2【漬物にする】pickle +目; **preserve** +目(漬けて保存する) ▶母はキュウリを塩で漬けた My mother *pickled* cucumbers with salt.

つ

つげる 告げる inform +目, **tell** +目(➤ 前者は後者よりやや堅い語) ▶上司に会社を辞める考えを告げた I *informed* my boss *of* my intention to resign from the company. (➤ inform A of B で「AにBを告げる」) ‖ 監督はダッグアウトから出て審判に投手の交代を告げた The manager came out of the dugout to *inform* the umpire that he would replace the pitcher. ‖ 私は受付に自分の名前を告げた I *gave* my name to the receptionist. ‖ その男は名前も告げずに立ち去った The man went away *without giving* his name.

▶小鳥のさえずりが夜が明けたことを告げていた The chirping of birds *announced* the dawn. ‖ 時計が正午を告げた The clock *struck* (twelve) noon.

つごう 都合 1【事情, 便宜】convenience(好都合)

【文型】
日時(A)が人(B)に都合がいい
A **is convenient for** B.
A **is all right with** B.

《解説》(1)A には日時・場所や漠然と事情を表す it などがくる. **convenient** は「事物が人にとって都合がよい」の意であるから人を主語にして(×) If you're convenient ... とはいわない.
(2)**be all right** は「大丈夫, 結構」の意で, 親しい人どうしで使うくだけた言い方. be fine ともいう.

▶きょうは都合はいいですか *Is it convenient for* you today? ‖ **対話**「次の日曜はご都合よろしいでしょうか」「ええ, いいですよ」"Would next Sunday *be convenient for* you?" "Yes, it'*s all right with* me." ‖ みんなが都合のいい日を決めるのに苦労している I'm having a hard time setting *a date that is convenient for everybody*. ‖ **対話**「いつがいちばん都合がいいですか」「来週の木曜なら都合がいいのですが」"When would *be the best time* for you?" "Next Thursday would *be fine*." (● ふつうに「あなたはいつが[何時が/どこが]都合がよいですか」は When [What time/Where] is convenient for you? で, これを(×) When [What time/Where] are you convenient? とするのは学習者がよくするまちがい).

▶その日なら都合がいいよ That date *works for* [*suits*] me. / I'*m free* that day. ‖ あいにくあすは都合が悪いんだ I'm afraid I *can't make time* [*make it*] tomorrow. (➤ make time は「時間を作る」, make it は「都合をつける」の意のインフォーマルな言い方) ‖ 都合のいい日を月曜日以外で3日教えてください Please tell me three *available days* except Monday. ‖ ご都合のよろしいときに私どものオフィスまでおいでください Please come to our office *at your* (*earliest*) *convenience*.

▶あなたのご都合に合わせます At your convenience. / Any time is fine [OK]. (➤ あとの文はややインフォーマル) ‖ 都合がつき次第伺います I will visit you *as soon as I can* [*as soon as my schedule permits*]. ‖ きょうは都合がつきません(=予定がいっぱいです)ので, 会は欠席させてください I'm afraid I can't attend the meeting today because my *schedule is too tight*. ‖《店などの掲示》都合により本日は休ませていただきます Sorry. Closed Today.

▶彼女はよく自分の都合だけで物事を決めてしまう She often arranges matters just to suit *her own convenience*. ‖ 私は家庭の都合で会社を辞めました I quit the company *for family reasons*. ‖ 時間の都合でスピーチは各人2分に限らせていただきます *In the interest of time*, speeches will be limited to two minutes each. ‖ 説明の都合上, 詳細は省略いたします Let's skip the details *to make the explanation easier to understand*.

2【調達】▶1万円都合して(=貸して)くれないか Do you suppose you could *lend* me ten thousand yen? ‖ 何とか都合をつけて(=時間を見つけて)会えるようにするよ Somehow I'll *find time* to go (and) to see you.

☛ 好都合(→見出語)

つじ 辻 a **street corner**(街角); a **crossroads**(十字路).

つじぎり 辻斬り a ***tsujigiri***; a samurai who attacked and slashed passersby indiscriminately to try out his sword (➤ 説明的な訳).

つじつま 辻褄 ▶きみの話はつじつまが合わない Your story is *inconsistent*. / Your story *doesn't hold water* [*doesn't hang together*]. ‖ 彼女はつじつまの合わないことをよく言う She often talks *inconsistently*. / What she says often *fails to add up*. ‖ うそがばれそうになったので適当につじつまを合わせておいた My lie was about to be exposed, so I *managed to make my story more plausible*.

つた 蔦《植物》**ivy** ▶ツタのはう洋館 a Western-style house *covered with ivy* / an *ivied* Western-style house.

-づたい -伝いに along ▶私たちは駒ケ岳の尾根伝いに登った We climbed *along* the ridge of Mt. Koma. ‖ 猫は魚をくわえて屋根伝いに逃げた The cat made its escape *from roof to roof* [*along the rooftops*], fish in mouth.

つたう 伝う ▶ロープを伝って降りる climb down *along* a rope ‖ うれし涙が彼女の頰を伝って落ちた Tears of joy *ran* [*rolled*] *down* her cheeks. ‖ 泥棒は屋根を伝って逃走した The thief fled *along the rooftops*.

つたえきく 伝え聞く be told about something indirectly.

つたえる 伝える 1【知らせる】tell +目, **inform** +目(➤ 後者はやや堅い語) ▶彼女に先に行くからと伝えてください Please *tell* her that I'm going on ahead. / Please *inform* her that I'm going first. ‖ 私は彼に正午にここに来るように伝えた I *told* him to be here at noon. ‖ アメリカ大使は米国政府の意向を外務大臣に伝えた The U.S. ambassador *informed* the Minister of Foreign Affairs *of* the U.S. Government's intention. (➤ inform A of B で「AにBを伝える」) ‖ 私たちはその知らせを彼女に伝えないのが最善だと考えた We thought it best *not to tell* her [*not to let* her *know*] the news. ‖ みどりちゃんによろしく伝えてね *Say hello to* Midori for me.

✉ **皆さまによろしくお伝えください** *Give my*

best regards to everyone.

▶人間は意思を**伝え合う**のにことばを使う People use language to *communicate with* one another. ‖ 新聞の**伝える**ところによるとアエロフロート機がハイジャックされたそうだ *The newspaper says that* an Aeroflot aircraft was hijacked. ‖ **伝えられる**ところではハイジャック犯はテロリストグループの一味だそうだ The hijackers were *reportedly* [*allegedly*] members of a terrorist group. (●ともに新聞用語だが allegedly には非難のニュアンスがある) ‖ 首相はアメリカの大統領と会談したと**伝えられる** The Prime Minister *is reported* to have had [The Prime Minister *reportedly* had] a talk with the U.S. president.

2【電気や熱を】**conduct** ＋㊐ ▶ガラスは電気を**伝えます**か Does glass *conduct* electricity? ‖ 鉄は熱をよく**伝える** Iron *is an efficient conductor* of heat.

3【紹介する】**introduce** ＋㊐ ▶漢字がいつ頃日本に**伝えられた**かはっきりしたことはわからない It is not known exactly when Chinese characters *were introduced* into Japan.

4【後世に残す】**hand down** ▶民話は世代から世代へと**伝えられてきた** Folktales *have been handed down* from generation to generation.

つたない 拙い ▶社会人になっても**拙い**字を書く人が多い There are many adults whose handwriting is *messy* [*sloppy*]. ‖ **拙い**歌ですがお聞きください *I'll do my* (*poor*) *best to sing* you *a song*. (●I'm not very good at singing, but please listen to my song. とも訳せるが, このようなへりくだった表現は避けたほうがよい).

つたわる 伝わる 1【伝達される】**travel**(光や音が進む) ▶光は音よりも速く**伝わる** Light *travels* faster than sound.

▶ぼくの気持ちがあの子に**伝わった**だろうか I wonder whether my feelings for her *have gotten through* (*to* her). ‖ レース前の記者会見からも選手たちの意気込みが私たちに**伝わってきた** We *felt* the racers' enthusiasm even at the pre-race press conference.

2【広まる】**spread** /spred/ ▶総理大臣が内閣を改造するだろうといううわさが**伝わっている** *The rumor is spreading* that the Prime Minister is going to reshuffle the cabinet. / *There is a rumor going around* that the Prime Minister will reshuffle the cabinet.

3【受け継がれる】**come down** (後世に) ; **be handed down** (代々伝えられる) ; **be introduced**(よそからもたらされる) ▶東北地方に**伝わる**古い民話を集める collect folktales *handed down* from generation to generation in the Tohoku district ‖ この刀は曽祖父の代から**伝わった**ものです This sword *has come down* [*has been handed down*] to us from our great-grandfather.

▶唐草模様は遠くペルシャから**伝わってきた** Arabesque patterns *were introduced* [*came all the way*] from distant Persia.

つち 土 soil(土壌) ; **earth** (岩石に対して) ; **ground** (土地, 地面) ; **dirt** (汚れ) ; **clay** (粘土) ▶この辺は**土**が肥えている The *soil* around here is rich [*fertile*]. (➤「痩せている」は poor) ‖ 種は粒の細かな**土**にまきなさい Sow the seeds in fine *soil*. ‖ その木は湿気のある**土**に植えないといけない That tree must be planted in wet *ground*. ‖ 塀が**土**で汚れていた The wall was soiled with *dirt*. ‖ それは**土**に還る材質です That is a *biodegradable* material. / Those are *biodegradable* materials.

▶《慣用表現》きのうは横綱に**土がついた**(＝負けた) The yokozuna *was toppled* [*was beaten* / *was defeated*] yesterday. ‖ 江沢氏は30年ぶりに故国の**土を踏んだ** Mr. Ezawa *set foot in* [*on*] his homeland after an absence of 30 years.

つちかう 培う cultivate /kʌ́ltɪveɪt/ ＋㊐ ▶長年にわたって**培ってきた**伝統 traditions that *have been cultivated* over the years ‖ 部活動で**培った**体力 one's physical strength *gained through* school club activities.

つちくれ 土くれ a **clod**.

つちけむり 土煙 a **cloud of dust** ▶トラックは**土煙**を上げてあの道を走っていった The truck sped along the road, sending up *clouds of dust*.

つちふまず 土踏まず the arch of a foot.

つちぼこり 土埃 dust ▶ヘリコプターは**土ぼこり**を上げながら校庭に着陸した The helicopter raised *dust* as it landed in the school ground.

つつ 筒 a **long round vessel** ; a **cylinder** /sílɪndəʳ/ (円筒) ; a **pipe**(パイプ) ▶その容器は**筒状**になっている The container is *cylindrical* (in shape).

-つつ 1【進行中】▶地球は毎年少しずつ温かくなり**つつある** The earth *is getting* a little warmer every year. ‖ 新球場が建設され**つつある** The construction of the new ball park *is under way*.

2【…しながら】▶諸君の健闘を祈り**つつ**乾杯しよう Let's drink a toast *to your success* in the coming game. ‖ 彼女は悪いと知り**つつ**(＝思っていたけれども)姉の日記を読んでしまった She read her sister's diary *even though* she felt guilty about it.

つつうらうら 津々浦々 ▶かつて正月には寅さんの映画が**全国津々浦々**で上映されていた Tora-san films used to be shown *throughout* [*all over*] *the country* during the New Year holiday.

つっかいぼう 突っ支い棒 a **prop** ▶**つっかい棒**をしないと板塀が倒れそうだ The board fence will fall if you don't *prop* [*shore*] it *up*. (●shore は特に重い物のとき).

つっかえす 突っ返す ▶上司は彼が出そうとした辞表を**突っ返した** The boss *refused to accept* [*pushed back*] the letter of resignation he tendered.

つっかかる 突っ掛かる 1【向かって行く】▶牛はたけり狂って闘牛士に**突っかかって行った** The bull furiously *rushed at* [*launched himself at*] the bullfighter.

2【食ってかかる】**turn** [**round**] **on** ▶**突っかかる**ように言う speak *aggressively* ‖ 彼は上司によく**突っかかる** He often *turns* [*rounds*] *on* his boss. ‖ 思うように行かなかったからってそう俺に**突っかかる**なよ Stop *picking on* me just because things didn't go the way you wanted. (➤ pick on は「…に言いがかりをつける, 絡む」).

つっかけ 突っ掛け sandals(ひもつきの) ; **clogs** (木の台の) ▶**つっかけ**で出かける go out *in sandals*.

つっかけぐつ つっかけ靴 slip-on shoes.

つつがなく 恙無く ▶**つつがなく**お過ごしでしょうか(＝お元気でしたでしょうか) Have you been *doing well*?

つづき 続き a **continuation** (記事などの) ; a **sequel** /síːkwəl/ (続編) ; a **series** /síəriːz/ (続き物) ▶この記事の**続き**は12ページをご覧ください The *continuation* of this article is found on page 12. / Continued on page 12. ‖ これは 7 ページからの**続き**です This *is continued from* page 7. ‖ この小説の**続き**は次号に掲載されます The *sequel* to this novel will appear in

the next issue. (◎「前号[前回]の続き」という場合は continuation と表示) ‖ 続きをお楽しみに Don't miss the *sequel*. / You won't want to miss the *sequel*. ‖ 昨夜聞いた講演は5回続きの3回目だった The lecture I heard last night was the third in *a series of five*.
▶宝くじを続き番号で買う buy lottery tickets in *running* [*serial*] *numbers* ‖ この文章は続き具合がおかしい The sentences (in this paragraph) *don't tie together well*. ‖ 3週間の日照り続きのあとようやく雨が降った It rained after *a dry spell* that lasted three weeks. ‖ 困ったことにうちではこのところ不幸続きだ Unfortunately, we have had *a run of bad luck* recently.

つづきがら 続き柄 relationship ▶世帯主との続き柄 your *relationship* to the head of your household.

つっきる 突っ切る ▶彼女の家はこの公園を突っ切って行けばすぐです If you *cut across* this park, you will soon come to her house.

つつく 1【突く】peck at(くちばしで); nudge +Ⓞ(主に肘で); poke +Ⓞ(指などで) ▶鶏が餌をつついている Chickens *are pecking at* the food. ‖ ひなは殻をつついて穴をあける A chick *pecks a hole* in the shell. ‖ 彼は私の脇腹をつついて「しっ!」と言った He *nudged* [*poked*] me in the ribs and said, "Hush!"
2【殊更取り上げる】▶彼はすぐ人の欠点をつつく嫌なやつだ He is such a disagreeable man who is always *finding fault with* other people.

つづく 続く 1【時間的に継続する】continue, go on (動作・状態が; 前者のほうがやや堅い語); last (ある期間続く) ▶その団体交渉は5時間続いた The collective bargaining session *continued* [*went on*] for five hours. ‖ ベトナム戦争は21年間続いた The Vietnam War *lasted* [*continued*] for 21 years. (◎ last はふつう期間を表す副詞(句)を伴う) ‖ 微熱が1か月続いた A slight fever *continued* [*persisted*] for a month. (➤ persist は「しつこく残る」) ‖ (次号に)続く *To be continued*. ‖ 23ページに[から]続く *Continued* on [from] page 23. ‖ このよいお天気があと1週間続くといいですね I hope this fine weather will *last* [*hold* (*out*)] for another week. ‖ 先週は3日間続いて雪が降った It snowed for three days *in a row* last week. ‖ 雨が1週間降り続いている *It has been raining* for a week. / *It has kept on raining* (*nonstop*) for a week.
▶うちは曽祖父の代から続く和菓子の老舗だ My family runs an old Japanese confectionery shop *founded* by my great-grandfather. (◎「曽祖父によって創立された店」の意).
2【頻繁に起こる】▶このところ試験が続いたのでゆっくりテレビを見る暇もなかった I had no time for watching TV because we'*ve had so many* tests recently. ‖ このところ大きな余震が続いていて落ち着かない I can't feel at ease because we'*ve had so many* big aftershocks recently. ‖ ことし, 彼女の家ではおめでたいことが続いた *One* happy event *followed another* in her family this year.
3【空間的につながる】lead《to》▶この道はずっと金沢まで[県境まで]続いている This road *leads* [*continues*] all the way *to* Kanazawa [the prefectural border]. ‖ 見渡す限りススキの原が続いていた A field of Japanese pampas grass *stretched out* (before us) as far as the eye could see [in every direction]. ‖ 駅前には商店街が続いている The street in front of the train station is lined with stores. (➤ line は「一列に並べる」).
4【保つことができる, もつ】▶彼はあんなにぜいたくをしてよく金が続くね How can he *afford* such a luxurious lifestyle? / How can he *afford to* live so luxuriously? ‖ こう暑くては根気が続かない I *can't keep* my spirits *up* in this hot weather.
5【順位・順序がつながる】▶続いてお天気です *Next* we'll have a look at the weather. / Our weather report will *follow* the commercial. ‖ オーストラリアはアメリカに続く(=次ぐ)水泳王国だ Australia *comes after* the U.S. as a swimming superpower. ‖ 何とか釈明しようと思ったがことばがうまく続かなかった I tried to make [offer] an explanation, but *was at a loss for words*.

つづけざま 続け様に in a row (連続して); one (...) after another (次々に) ▶日本チームは続けざまにゴールを3つ決めた The Japanese team scored three goals *in a row*. ‖ 少年たちは続けざまに川に飛び込んだ *One* boy *after another* dove [dived] into the river. ‖ 続けざまに数発の銃声がした We heard several shots *in a row*.

つづける 続ける 1【時間的に継続させる】continue, go [keep] on (➤ continue のほうがやや堅い語)
▶私は結婚しても仕事を続けるつもりです I intend to *continue* work*ing* even after I get married. ‖ 仕事を続けなさい *Go* [*Carry*] *on with* your work. / *Keep on* work*ing*. ‖ 彼はコーヒーを一口飲んでから話を続けた He *continued* his talk after (he took) a sip of the coffee. ‖ きみは自分の得意とすることを続けるべきだ You should *stick with* what you're good at. (➤ stick with A は「A(仕事など)をこつこつやる」の意のインフォーマルな言い方).
▶投球の練習は続けてやらなければ意味がない You won't get anywhere if you don't *keep up with* your pitching practice. ‖ 近所で2件続けて火事があった Two fires broke out *in succession* in my neighborhood. ‖ 3日も続けて遅刻するとは, きみも相当なものだね You're really something to have come late three days *in a row*. ‖ 会議は昼休みのあと続けられた The meeting *was resumed* after the lunch recess. (➤ resume /rɪzjúːm/ は「再び始める」).
2【順序が次になる】▶満員のバスが通過したあと, すぐ続けてがらがらのバスが来た *Right after* a jam-packed bus passed (the stop), an almost empty one followed.

-つづける -続ける

【文型】
…し続ける
continue to do [doing]
keep (on) doing
go on doing

【解説】(1)**continue to** *do* と **continue** *do*ing は実際上, ほとんど区別なく使われる.
(2)**continue** は継続を客観的に表す, いわば無色透明な語.
(3)**keep** *do*ing は「その状態のまま…し続ける」を表す. 励ましや命令の文では continue よりよく使われる. on は「どんどん」の意で, これがあると「しつこさ」が加味されることがある.

▶村の人口は減り続けている The population of the

village *continues to* decline [*keeps* declin*ing*]. ‖彼女は古いマックのコンピュータを使い**続けている** She *continues to* use her old Mac computer. ‖そこで１時間以上**待ち続けた** I *kept* wait*ing* there for more than an hour. ‖彼は死ぬまで一家の大黒柱として**働き続けた** He *kept on* work*ing* to support his family until he died. (● keep on doing は keep doing よりも「しつこく[繰り返し]…し続ける」の意が強い) ‖話が終わったと思ったのに，彼はその後30分も話をし**続けた** I thought he had finished talking, but he *went on* (talk*ing*) for another 30 minutes.

▶私たちは４時間**歩き続けている** We *have been walking continuously* (for) four hours. ‖２人は**何時間も電話で話し続けた** The two talked on the phone *for hours on end*. (● on end は時を表す複数名詞のあとにつけて「立て続けに…間も」の意).

つっけんどん 突っ慳貪 **brusque** /brʌsk/ (ぶっきらぼうな) ; **abrupt, curt**(そっけない) ▶電話に出た人の言い方は**つっけんどんだった** The person who answered the phone was *abrupt* [*curt* ／ *brusque*]. ‖あの店員はいつも**つっけんどんな**口の利き方をする The clerk always speaks *curtly* [*brusquely*].

つっこみ 突っ込み **the straight man** [**woman**] (➤ 掛け合い漫才の中心の話し手. 相手の「ぼけ」は funny man [woman] または stooge あるいは goof).

つっこむ 突っ込む **1**【押し込む】**thrust, plunge** 《into》 (➤ 後者のほうが「突然強く押し込む」というニュアンスが強い) ; **stick** 《into》 (差し込む) ; **stuff** 《into》 (詰め込む)

▶ポケットに手を**突っ込む** *thrust* [*stick*] one's hand *into* one's pocket ‖熱いお湯にいきなり足を**突っ込んで**飛び上がった After *plunging* my leg *into* the hot water without thinking, I jumped out (of the bath). ‖彼女は洗濯した衣類をたんすに**突っ込んだ** She *stuffed* [*shoved*] the washed clothes *into* the chest of drawers. ‖保険の外交員は書類をかばんに**突っ込んで**(＝詰め込んで)出ていった The insurance salesman *stuffed* [*crammed*] his papers in his briefcase and left.

▶《慣用表現》他人の家庭の問題にあまり**首を突っ込まない**ほうがいいぞ You *shouldn't stick your nose into* [*meddle in*] other people's family problems.

2【突進する】**crash** 《into》 (すさまじい音を立てて) ; **plunge** 《into》 (急に) ; **run** 《into》 (衝突する) ▶その事故はバイクがトラックに**突っ込んで**起きた That accident was caused by a motorbike *crashing into* a truck. ‖彼は頭を水中に**突っ込んだ** He *plunged* his head *into* the water. ‖そのトラックは民家に**突っ込んだ** That truck *ran into* a house.

3【急所を攻める】▶首相は野党議員に**突っ込まれて**立ち往生した *Sharp questioning* by an opposition (party) member stumped the Prime Minister.

つつじ 躑躅 《植物》 ***tsutsuji*** ; a Japanese azalea /əzéɪliə/.

つつしみ 慎み **modesty**(控えめな態度) ; **prudence** (慎重) ; **discretion** /dɪskréʃən/ (思慮分別) ▶きみたちはもっと**慎み深く**なければいけません You should be more *modest* [*prudent* ／ *discreet*]. ‖ミニスカートであぐらをかくなんて**慎みのない**まねはやめなさい *Don't behave indecently* by sitting cross-legged in a mini skirt. (➤ indecent は「慎みのない」).

つつしむ 慎む **be careful** 《about, of》 (気をつける) ; **refrain** 《from》 (控える) ▶ことばを**慎みなさい** *Be careful of* your language. ／*Watch* [*Mind*] your language. ／*Watch* your tongue. ‖きみはもう少し口を**慎む**ことを学んだらどうだい Why don't you learn to *watch* [*be careful about*] *your language*? ‖その国では政治的な発言は**慎んだ**ほうがいいね You should *refrain from* talk*ing* about politics in that country. ‖胃を患ってからは暴飲暴食を**慎んでいます** I *have refrained from* eating and drink*ing* [I *have been careful not to* eat or drink] too much since I had stomach problems.

つつしんで 謹んで

✉ **謹んでおわび申し上げます** I *humbly* ask [beg] your forgiveness [I *humbly* apologize] for what happened.

✉ **謹んでお父上のご逝去をお悔やみ申し上げます** Please accept my deepest sympathy on your father's death.

✉ **謹んで新春のお喜びを申し上げます** I wish you a happy New Year.

つったつ 突っ立つ ▶ぼさっと**突っ立って**ないで掃除手伝えよ Don't just *stand* there, ―help me clean up.

つっつく 突っ突く →つつく.

つつぬけ 筒抜け ▶わが社の秘密情報は競争相手に**筒抜けだった** Some of our (company's) secret information *leaked out* to a rival company. ‖きみたちの話は隣の部屋に**筒抜けだったよ** Your conversation *could be heard in* [*could be heard all the way to*] the next room.

つっぱしる 突っ走る ▶東名高速をバイクで**突っ走る** *speed* [*race*] along the Tomei Expressway on one's motorcycle.

▶彼は何でもやり始めるとがむしゃらに**突っ走る**タイプだ He is the type who *rushes* headlong into whatever he does.

つっぱねる 突っ撥ねる **turn down** ▶きみはあんなべらぼうな要求はきっぱりと**突っぱねる**べきだった You should have *turned down* [*rejected*] such an outrageous demand outright.

つっぱり 突っ張り **1**【相撲】***tsuppari*** ; an open-armed thrust ‖**突っ張り合い** an exchange of (open-armed) thrusts.

2【若者の】**(juvenile) delinquency** ; a **(juvenile) delinquent**(人).

つっぱる 突っ張る **1**【強く張る】▶満員電車の中で私は窓に**腕を突っ張って**体を支えた I propped myself up in the jam-packed train by *steadying my arm* against a window. ‖きのう10キロ走ったので足の筋肉が**突っ張っている** My leg muscles *are* all *stiff* because I jogged ten kilometers yesterday.

2【反抗する】▶昌代はいつも**突っ張っている**が，根は優しい子だ Masayo *acts rebellious*, but at heart she is a softhearted girl.

つつましい 慎ましい **1**【控えめな】**modest**(謙虚な) ; **unassuming**(物静かで，でしゃばらない) ▶兄貴の彼女は**つつましい**感じの人だ My (older) brother's girlfriend seems a *modest* [an *unassuming*] person.

2【質素な】**simple** ▶彼女は大女優の割には**つつましく**暮らしている She lives a *simple* life for such a great actress. ‖その年の正月は**つつましく**祝った That year we celebrated the New Year holiday *modestly*.

[1]つつみ 包み 《主に米》 a **package,** 《主に英》 a **parcel** ▶父が大きな**包み**を抱えて帰って来た My father came home with a big *package* under his arm.

[2]つつみ 堤 a **bank**(川・湖などの) ; an **embankment**(川・海岸などの) ▶矢作川の**堤**をぶらつく walk along the Yahagi *embankment* [the *bank* of the Yahagi River].

つづみ 鼓 a ***tsuzumi***; a Japanese hourglass-shaped drum (➤ 説明的な訳).

つつみかくす 包み隠す ▶どんな小さなことでも**包み隠さず**に話しなさい Tell me everything *without keeping* [*hiding*] *anything from me*, no matter how insignificant (you think it is). ‖ 娘は妻には何もかも**包み隠さず**話すらしい My daughter seems to *talk* about everything with my wife *frankly* [*openly*].

つつみがみ 包み紙 **wrapping paper**; a **wrapper** (小さいもの) ▶キャンデーの**包み紙** a candy *wrapper* ‖ プレゼントをしゃれた**包み紙**で包む wrap (up) a present in fancy *wrapping paper*.

つ

つつむ 包む **wrap** /ræp/ (**up**)

【文型】
物(A)を紙など(B)に包む
wrap (**up**) A **in** B

▶彼女は赤ん坊を毛布に**包んだ** She *wrapped* her baby *in* a blanket. ‖ そのプレゼントはきれいな紙で**包んであった** The present *was wrapped up in* fancy paper. ‖ 贈り物を包装紙で**包んでもらった** I *had* a gift *wrapped in* wrapping paper. / I had a present gift-wrapped.

▶これを贈り物用に**包んでください** Please *wrap* this *up* as a gift. / Please *gift-wrap* this. (➤ gift-wrap /gíftræp/ は「贈り物用に包装する」の意の動詞) ‖ それ, **包まなくて結構です** You don't have to *wrap* it. ‖ 彼女は黒のドレスに**身を包んでいた** She *dressed herself* in black. / She *was dressed* in black.

▶友人の結婚式にはいくらくらい**包めばいいのだろう** How much money would be appropriate as a gift for my friend's wedding? (➤ 英米には結婚祝いとして現金を贈る習慣はない).

▶摩周湖は濃霧に**包まれていた** Lake Mashu *was wrapped* [*was veiled*] *in* thick fog. ‖ 事件は謎に**包まれていた** The affair *was wrapped* (*up*) [*was shrouded* / *was veiled*] *in* mystery. ‖ 家々は炎に**包まれた** The houses *were enveloped in* flames. ‖ コンサート会場は若者の熱気に**包まれていた** The concert hall *was filled with* the young people's excitement.

つづり 綴り **1【スペリング】** **spelling** →スペル
▶「サッカー」の**つづり**を知っていますか Do you know the *spelling* of [know *how to spell*] the word 'soccer'? ‖ 「ミシシッピー」の**つづり**はよく**間違えられる** 'Mississippi' *is* often *misspelled* [*misspelt*]. ‖ この単語の**つづりは間違っている** This word *is spelled incorrectly*. / This word *is misspelled*. ‖ きみの英作文は**つづりの間違い**が多いね There are a lot of *misspellings* in your English composition. ‖ ライトさん, お名前の**つづりを一字一字言って**ください Please *spell out* your name, Mrs. Wright.
2【とじたもの】 ▶この伝票は4枚**つづり**になっておりますので強くお書きください This carbon slip has four *sheets*, so press down hard when you write.

つづる 綴る **1【単語を書く】** **spell** ＋㊐ ▶あなたの名前はどう**つづり**ますか How do you *spell* your name?
2【文章を書く】 ▶私は幼い日の思い出をノートに**つづった** (＝書いた) I *wrote down* my childhood memories in a notebook.
3【とじる】 ▶ばらばらの書類を全部ファイルに**つづって**整理した I've arranged all of the loose documents *in a file*.

つて 伝 a **connection**(関係); **pull** (引き) ▶彼は**つて**で(＝コネで)会社に入った He got a job in the company *through connections* [*pull*]. ‖ 彼は高校を卒業すると親戚の**つてを頼って**上京してきた *Counting on* a relative [(his) relatives] for help, he came to Tokyo after he graduated from high school.

つど 都度 ▶私は京都へ年に2, 3回行くが, **そのつど**その和食の店に寄る I go to Kyoto a few times a year, and *whenever* I do, I drop in at that Japanese restaurant.

つどい 集い a **meeting** (会合); a **gathering**, a **get-together**(非公式で打ち解けた).

つどう 集う **gather** ▶公会堂にその歌手のファンたちが**集った** The singer's fans *gathered* at the public hall.

つとまる 務まる **be fit for**(…に適している); **be equal to**(…に対して十分能力がある) ▶彼には教師は**務まらない**よ He *is unfit to be* a teacher. ‖ 彼女くらい能力があればどんな仕事でも**務まる** A woman of her ability *is equal to* any task.

つとめ 勤め・務め **1【仕事】** a **job**, **work** →仕事

▶母は今パートの**勤め**を探しています My mother is now looking for a part-time *job*. ‖ インフルエンザで3日間**勤めを休んだ** I *took three days off from work* because of the flu. ‖ 姉は近くのスーパーに**勤めに出ています** My sister *is working* at a nearby supermarket.

▶**お勤めはどちらですか** Where do you work? / Who do you work for? (→勤める) ‖ 兄はやっといい**勤め口**を見つけた My brother has finally found *a* good *job* [*position*]. ‖ ここに**勤め先の電話番号**を書いてください Please write your *work* [*office*] *phone number* here. ‖ 父は**勤め人**です My father is *a white-collar worker*. (→サラリーマン).

2【義務】 (a) **duty**; **responsibility** (責任) ▶父はいつも「おまえの**務め**は勉強することだ」と言う My father always says that my *duty* is to study. ‖ 子供をできるだけしっかり育てるのは親の**務め**である It is *the responsibility* of parents to raise their children to the best of their ability. ‖ 彼はキャプテンとしての**務めを立派に果たした** He *fulfilled his duties* as captain *admirably*. / He *did a great job* as captain.

-づとめ -勤め ▶父は会社[銀行]**勤めをしている** My father *works for* a company [bank].

つとめて 努めて ▶お年寄りには**努めて**(＝できるだけ)親切にしてあげなさい Be *as* kind *as you can* [*as possible*] to elderly people. (● as possible より as you can のほうがくだけた言い方) ‖ 彼女は**努めて**冷静にしていた She *was making an effort* to compose herself.

つとめる 勤める・務める・努める

1【勤務する】 **work** ▶父は市役所に**勤めている** My father *works at* City Hall. ‖ あなたのお母さんは**勤めて**いらっしゃいますか, それとも家にいらっしゃいますか Does your mother *work outside* or stay at home? ‖ **対話**「どちらにお**勤め**ですか」「B社に**勤めています**」"Where do you *work*?" "I *work for* B Company." (● 答えの文は I work at B Company. としてもよい. work for は雇用主を意識した言い方で, work at は勤務先を意識した言い方(at のほうがふつう)).

2【役目を果たす】 **serve** ▶彼は国会議員を5期**務めた** He *served* five terms as a Dietman. ‖ 私がガイドを**務めましょう** Let me *act* [*serve*] as your guide. ‖ マ

イクがそのバラエティーショーの司会を務めた Mike *acted as* emcee [MC／M.C.] of the variety show. (● act as のあとの役目を表す語は通例 Ⓤ 扱い).

3【努力する】try《to do》

【文型】
…しようと努める
try to do
【解説】(1)「…しようと頑張る」は **try to** do で表せる. 注意したいのは **tried to** do という過去形の場合で, 日本語の「努めた」では結果についてはあまり関心がないが, **tried to** do では「努めたがうまくいかなかった」という結果まで暗示される. →努力
(2)「…しないようにする」は try not to do.
(3) try doing は「試しに…してみる」の意に用いるのがふつう.

▶私は毎日30分間, 適度な運動を行うように努めています I *try to* do moderate exercise for thirty minutes every day. ‖ わが校では節水・節電に努めています We*'re trying to save water and electricity* at our school. ‖ 何度も彼女に連絡をとろうと努めたが, だめだった I unsuccessfully *tried to* get in touch with her several times. ‖ 私は彼を説得しようと懸命に努めた I *tried my hardest* [*did my best*] *to* persuade him. (➤ 後者は「全力を尽くした」).

▶二度とこのようなことが起きないよう努めます I'll *do my utmost* to make sure such a thing never happens again. (➤ do one's utmost は「全力を尽くす」) ‖ 私たちはこれからもお客様のご要望にできる限り応えるよう努めて参ります (In the future,) we will *continue to strive to* do everything possible to meet our customers' needs. (● strive to は「懸命に努力する」の意の改まった言い方) ‖ 私たちは自分たちの社会をよくするように努めなければならない We should *endeavor* [*strive*] *to* improve our society. (● endeavor, strive は try より更に努力する必要があることを意味するやや堅い語).

つな 綱 a **rope**(太い) ; a **cord** (細い) ; a **leash**(主に犬をつなぐひもや鎖) ▶犬に綱をつけて散歩させる walk a dog on *a leash* ‖ 木に綱を張って洗濯物を干した We stretched *a rope* [*a cord*] between the trees to hang the washing. ‖ クライマーにとってザイルは命の綱だ Climbing ropes serve as *lifelines* for climbers.

☞ 綱渡り (→見出語)

ツナ tuna /túːnə ‖ tjúːnə/ (fish)

‖ツナサラダ (a) tuna salad.

つながり 繋がり a **connection**, a **relation**

▶犯罪と麻薬との間には密接なつながりがある There is a close *connection* [*relation*] between crime and drugs. ／Crime and drugs are closely connected [related]. ‖ 姓は同じですが, 彼女とは何のつながりもありません Though we have the same family name, I *am not related to* her in any way.

つながる 繋がる **1【結び付く】be connected**《with, to》▶徳島と淡路島は鳴門大橋でつながっている Tokushima and Awajishima (Island) *are connected* by the (Great) Naruto Bridge. ‖ このコンピュータはネットにつながっていますか Is this computer *connected* to the Internet? ‖ 私の家は祖父の家と渡り廊下でつながっている My house *is linked to* my grandfather's by a connecting passageway. ‖ なぜか彼女に電話がつながらない I *can't get through to* [*can't reach*] her *on the phone* for some reason. ‖ 07をダイヤルすればフロントにつながります Dial 07, and you'll *reach* [*be connected to*] the front desk.

2【間をあけずに続く】▶その機関車には貨車が25両もつながっていた As many as twenty-five freight cars *were connected* [*were attached*] *to* the locomotive. ‖ 車がつながっていて目的地に着くまで3時間かかった *The traffic was bumper-to-bumper*, so it took me three hours to reach my destination. ‖ 息子の通っている中学は高校・大学とつながっている My son's junior high school *is affiliated* [*is connected*] *to* a senior high school and a university.

3【関連する】be related《to》▶彼女は私と血はつながっていないが, 私にとって姉のような人だ Although she *is not related to* me by blood, she is like a sister to me. ‖ お金が幸福につながるとは限らない Money does not always *make for* happiness.

▶たばこの吸い過ぎは肺がんにつながることが多い Heavy smoking often *leads to* [*results in*] lung cancer. (➤ result in は「結果として…になる」) ‖ ウイルスの発見がその難病の克服につながった (=への道を開いた) The discovery of the virus *paved the way to* conquering the intractable disease.

つなぎ 繋ぎ a **stopgap** (間に合わせ) ; **overalls** (作業服) ; a **binder**(料理の) ▶材料のつなぎに小麦粉を使う use flour to *bind* the ingredients.

‖つなぎ資金 a stopgap [relief] fund.

つなぎとめる 繋ぎ止める ▶父は心臓バイパス手術を受けて命を繋ぎ止めた My father had a heart bypass operation that *saved* his *life*. ‖ 顧客の信用を繋ぎ止めることは難しい It's hard for us to *secure and keep trust* of our customers.

つなぎめ 繋ぎ目 a **knot**(結び目) ; a **joint**(継ぎ目) ▶パイプのつなぎ目が緩んでいる The *joint* in the pipe has loosened.

つなぐ 繋ぐ **1【連結する】connect** +㊐ (2つ以上のものを結合する) ; **join** +㊐ (じかに結びつける) ; **tie** +㊐ (結び目を作って縛る) ; **attach** +㊐ (くっ付ける)

▶ホースを蛇口につなぐ *connect* a hose to [onto] the faucet [《英》tap] ‖ おもちゃの線路をつなぐ *connect* the parts of a toy railroad ／*put together* a toy railroad (➤ put together は「組み立てる」) ‖ 手をつないで歩く walk *hand in hand* ‖ その2本のひもをつないでください Please *tie* the two pieces of string *together*. ‖ 子供たちは手をつないで輪を作った The children *joined hands* [*put their hands together*] to make a circle. ‖ 彼は自動車にトレーラーをつないだ He *attached* the trailer to his car.

2【くくりつける】tie +㊐ ▶牛をくいにつなぐ *tie* a cow to a stake ‖ ポチをしっかりつないでおいてよ, いいね? *Keep* Pochi securely *tied up*, OK? (●「鎖や革ひもなどに犬をつないでおく」は keep a dog on a leash) ‖ 数隻のボートが埠頭(ふとう)につないであった Several boats *were moored* to [at] the pier. (➤ moor は「(船をロープなどで)係留する」) ‖ 彼は無実の罪で10年間ろう獄につながれていた He *was in prison* for ten years on false charges.

3【通信機器を】connect +㊐, **put ... through** ▶コンピュータをネットにつなぐ *connect* a computer to the Internet ‖ 内線の1234につないでください Please *connect* me to extension 1234. ／Please *give* me extension 1234. ‖ この電話, 校長室につないでいただけますか Could you please *put* this call *through to* the principal's office? ‖ 電話を総務課につないでもらった I *had* my call *connected* [*put through*] to the General Affairs Department.

4【切れずに続くようにする】▶佐藤選手は敗者復活戦で勝ち, メダルに望みをつないだ Winning the consolation match, Sato *kept his hope(s) of* (*winning*) a medal *alive*. ‖ 母は点滴と輸血で辛うじて命をつないでいる My mother *is* barely *being kept alive* by IV drips and blood transfusions.

つなげる 繋げる **connect** ＋目 ▶コードをつなげて長くした I've extended the electric cord *by connecting* it to another.

つなひき 綱引き (a) **tug-of-war** ▶綱引きをする have [play at] *a tug-of-war*.

つなみ 津波 a **tsunami** /tsuná:mi/ (➤英語化している); a **tidal wave** 《解説》tsunami は日本語の「津波」から英語に入った語で, 地震などの影響による高波を指す(複数形は tsunamis か tsunami waves とする). tidal wave は本来は潮の干満によって生じる波のことであるが, 日常的には「津波」の意でも用いる.

▶壊滅的な津波が三陸沿岸を襲った Devastating *tsunamis* hit the Sanriku coast. ‖ 地震のため津波が発生した The earthquake caused *a tsunami*. ‖ その地震による津波の心配はありません There's no risk of a *tsunami* from that earthquake.

‖津波警報 a tsunami warning.

つなわたり 綱渡り **tightrope walking** [**dancing**] ▶綱渡りをする *walk* (*on*) *a tightrope* (➤比喩的に「危ない橋を渡る」の意にも使う).

つね 常 ▶私は夕食後犬を連れて散歩するのが常だ I *usually* take a walk with the dog after supper. ‖ 彼は夜遅くまで起きて勉強するのが常だった He *used to* stay up studying till late at night. ‖ 力を持つ者もいつかは滅びるのが世の常だ The powerful are overthrown sooner or later, and that is *the way of the world* [*the way it has always been*].

☛ 常に (→見出語)

つねづね 常々 **always** (いつも); **constantly** (絶えず) ▶常々心配していたことが現実に起きてしまった What we had *always* been worrying about came to pass. ‖ 常々父にはそう聞かされております That is what my father is *always* telling me.

つねに 常に **always** (いつも); **at all times** (どんなときでも) ▶太陽は常に東から昇り西に沈む The sun *always* rises in the east and sets in the west. ‖ 私は職業柄身だしなみには常に気を遣っています My profession being what it is, I *always* try to look neat. ‖ たいていの信号機は常に動いている Most traffic lights are on *all the time*.

つねひごろ 常日頃 **always** (いつも); **at all times** (どんなときでも) ▶常日頃から清潔を心がけなさい *Always* try to be clean. ／*Always* pay attention to cleanliness. ‖ 教養は一夜漬けで身につくものじゃない. 常日頃からの積み重ねだよ You cannot become a well-educated person by overnight cramming. It's the result of *constant* study.

つねる **pinch** ＋目 ▶夢ではないかとわが身をつねった I *pinched* myself to make sure I was not dreaming. ‖ 彼女は私の腕を思い切りつねった She *gave* me *a sharp pinch* on the arm.

ことわざ わが身をつねって人の痛さを知れ Pinch yourself to know the pain of others. (➤日本語からの直訳) ／Walk a mile in someone else's shoes. (➤「他人の靴で1マイル歩けばその人の気持ちがわかる」という意味).

つの 角 a **horn** (牛・羊などの); an **antler** (鹿の枝角) ▶水牛には長い角がある Water buffaloes have long *horns*. ‖ 雄鹿に角が生えてきた *Antlers* began to appear on the stag's head. ‖ カタツムリが角を出している A snail has put out its *horns*. ‖ このパイプは水牛の角製だ This pipe is *made of* water buffalo *horn*. (● 材料としての horn は無冠詞).

▶《慣用表現》妻と母が角を突き合わせているのを見るのはつらい I can't bear to see my wife and mother *locking horns with* each other. (➤lock horns は比喩的に「衝突する」の意) ‖ 早く帰らないと今ごろ奥さんが角を出してるぞ If you don't hurry home, your wife will *be furious*.

‖角細工 hornwork ‖ 角笛 a horn.

つのる 募る **1**【募集する】**recruit** /rɪkrú:t/ ＋目 (会員などを); **call for** (援助などを) ▶旅行のメンバーを募る *recruit* members for a trip ‖ 文化祭の出し物のアイデアを募ります We are *calling for* ideas for a presentation at the school festival. ‖ 動物園ではコアラの赤ちゃんの愛称を募っています The zoo *is inviting* everyone *to suggest* nicknames for the baby koala. ‖ 私たちは地震被災者のために寄付金を募った We *collected contributions* for the earthquake victims.

2【激しくなる】▶台風の接近に伴い, 風雨がますます募ってきた As the typhoon approached, the wind and rain *intensified* [the storm *gathered* (*force*)]. ‖ 夜が更けるにしたがって不安が募ってきた I *became more uneasy* as the night went on. ‖ フィアンセがロンドンに転勤になって半月, 彼女は恋しさが募ってきた Half a month has passed since her fiancé was transferred to London, and she *misses* him *more and more*.

¹つば 唾 **spit**; **saliva** /səláɪvə/ (唾液)

▶歩道に唾を吐いてはいけない You must not *spit* on the sidewalk. (➤この spit は「唾を吐く」の意の動詞) ‖ 男は手に唾をつけて, エイッとばかりに岩を押した The man *spat on his hands* and gave the rock a shove. (➤spat は spit の過去形だが, 《米》では spit の形も用いる) ‖ 私は梅干しを見ただけで唾が出てきた *My mouth watered* just looking at the sour *ume* pickles.

▶《慣用表現》その漫画はぼくが唾をつけてあるんだからね(＝先に読む番だ) (I've got) *dibs on* that comic book. (● dibs は「優先権」の意で, 子供が使う言い方).

☛ 生唾 (→見出語)

²つば 鍔 a (**sword**) **guard** (刀の); a (**hat**) **brim** (帽子の) ▶つばの広い帽子 a *broad-brimmed* hat.

つばき 椿 《植物》 a **camellia** /kəmí:liə/

‖つばき油 camellia oil.

つばさ 翼 a **wing** ▶ツルは翼を広げて一斉に飛び立った The cranes spread their *wings* and flew off (all) together. ‖ アホウドリは翼を広げると2メートル以上ある Albatrosses have *a wingspread* [*a wingspan*] of over two meters.

つばぜりあい 鍔迫り合い ▶両チームが激しいつばぜり合いを演じている Both teams *are fighting* [*competing*] fiercely. ‖ その決勝はつばぜり合いだった The final match was *closely fought*.

つばめ 燕 《鳥》 a **swallow**; a **martin** (イワツバメ) ▶ツバメの巣 a *swallow*'s nest.

つぶ 粒 a **grain** (穀物・砂・塩・砂金などの); a **drop** (水滴などの) ▶私たちは茶わんのご飯を1粒も残さずに食べるようしつけられた We were trained to eat (up) *every grain* of rice in our bowl. ‖ ことしのリンゴは粒が小さ

い The apples this year *are small* [*small-sized*].
▶《慣用表現》このチームは選手の**粒**がそろっている(=皆優れている) The players on this team *are all very good*. (→粒ぞろい).
☞ 大粒, 粒より (→見出語)

つぶさに ▶生存者たちはその事故の模様を**つぶさに**語った The survivors gave a *detailed* story of how the accident occurred.

つぶし 潰し ▶彼は何の技能もないので**潰しが効かない** He *can't switch* to any other job because he doesn't have any transferable skills. ‖ 経理は**潰しが効く**職種だ Accounting is a job with *transferable* skills.

つぶす 潰す **1【ぺしゃんこにする】crush** +目 (圧力をかけて押し潰す); **mash** +目 (ゆでたジャガイモなどを) ▶空き缶を**潰す** *crush* an empty can ‖ ジャガイモを**潰す** *mash* potatoes ‖ トマトを**潰して**ジュースを作った I *crushed* tomatoes to make juice.
2【だめにする】ruin +目; **spoil** +目 (甘やかして) ▶彼は放漫な経営のために4代続いた老舗を**潰した** His careless management *ruined* [*bankrupted*] the old store his family had kept for four generations. ‖ 子供の個性を**潰さない**ように伸び伸びと育てたい I would like to raise my children in a relaxed way so as not to *spoil* their individuality. ‖ 巨人はワンアウト満塁のチャンスをダブルプレーで**潰した** The Giants *ruined* a scoring chance with the bases loaded and one out by a double play. ‖ せっかくの休日が娘の学校の父母会で**潰された** A precious holiday *was spoiled* because of the PTA meeting at my daughter's school (on that day). ‖ その候補者は連日の選挙演説で**声を潰して**しまった The candidate *lost his voice* [The candidate's *voice was hoarse*] after making campaign speeches on several days in a row.
▶このお見合いを断るとお父さんの**顔を潰す**ことになりますよ You will *make* your father *lose face* if you decline to have this *omiai* with her [him].
3【時間をふさぐ】kill ▶テレビを見て**暇を潰す** *kill* [*waste*] *time* watching television ‖ この前の日曜日は一日中ぶらぶらして**時間を潰した** I *idled* [*loafed*] *away* the whole day last Sunday.
4【「…つぶす」の形で】▶その飼育係はゾウに**踏みつぶされた** The animal handler *was trampled to death* by an elephant. ‖ 彼は父親の遺産を5年で**食いつぶした** He *spent all* (of) the inheritance from his father in five years.

つぶぞろい 粒揃い ▶このブドウは**粒ぞろい**です These grapes *are of the same large size* (and high *quality*).
▶《比喩的》わがチームは**粒ぞろい**の選手ばかりだ All the members of our team are *first-rate*. / All our players are *the cream of the crop*. (➤ the cream of the crop は「選び抜かれた人」).

つぶつぶ 粒々 ▶このグレープフルーツジュースには**粒々**が入っている This grapefruit juice contains *pulp*. (➤ pulp は「果肉」).

つぶやき 呟き a **murmur**(低い声の); a **mumble**(ぼそぼそ言うこと); a **tweet**(ツイッター(Twitter)上でのメッセージ).

つぶやく 呟く **murmur**(低い声で言う); **mumble**(ぼそぼそ言う); **mutter**(不平を言う) ▶祖母はいつも何か独り言を**つぶやいている** My grandmother *is* always *murmuring* [*mumbling*] to herself. ‖ ツイッターで**つぶやく**(=ツイートする) *tweet* on Twitter.

つぶより 粒選り ▶**粒より**のイチゴ *choice* strawberries ‖ わがバレーボールチームは**粒より**の選手で構成されている Our volleyball team is composed of *excellent* [*our school's best*] players.

つぶら 円ら ▶**つぶらな瞳**の女の子 a girl with *cute round eyes*.

> **あなたの英語はどう響く?**
> 「つぶらな瞳」を beady eyes (ビーズのような目) と表現する人がいるが, これは間違い. 英語の beady eyes は「冷たく, 計算高い[怒っているような]目」を連想させることが多い. 日本語の「つぶらな瞳」はむしろ cute [lovely] round eyes のようにいうのがよい.

つぶる 瞑る **close** one's **eyes** ▶いいものあげるから, ちょっと**目をつぶってて** I've got something nice for you. So *close your eyes*. ‖《比喩的》深田先生はぼくのいたずらに**目をつぶってくれた**(=見ないふりをした) Ms. Fukada *overlooked* my prank.

つぶれる 潰れる **1【圧力で原形が壊れる】be crushed**; **collapse** (建物などが崩壊する) ▶その車は事故でぺちゃんこに**潰れた** The car *was crushed* flat [*totaled*] in the accident. ‖ 津波で20戸の家屋が**潰れた** Twenty houses *collapsed* in the tidal wave. ‖ 手のひらのまめが**潰れた** The blister on the palm of my hand *broke*.
2【だめになる】go bankrupt, go under (倒産する); **fold (up)**(事業などが失敗する) ▶この不況でうちの会社は**潰れそうだ** Our company is about to *go bankrupt* [*go under*] due to this recession. ‖ その会社は僅か1年で**潰れてしまった** That company *folded* after only a year in business. ‖ あの八百屋は**潰れた** That vegetable store *has gone out of business*. ‖ 海外旅行の計画は資金難で**潰れた** Our plan to travel overseas *fell through* because of a lack of money. (➤ fall through は「(計画が)だめになる」) ‖ 大声を出していたら**声が潰れた** I've *screamed* [*shouted*] myself *hoarse*. ‖ あまりにまぶしくて**目が潰れそうだ** The sun is so bright that I feel like I'*m about to go blind* [*lose my sight*]. ‖ 彼は**飲み潰れた** He *was dead drunk*.
▶きみが引き受けてくれなければ, ぼくの**顔が潰れて**しまうよ If you don't take the position [job], I'll *lose face*.
3【時間をとられる】▶洗濯で半日**潰れて**しまった I *lost* [*wasted*] half the day doing a lot of washing.

つべこべ ▶**つべこべ言わずに**言うとおりにしなさい *Don't talk back to me*—just do as I say. / *Don't give* me *any of your lip*. Just do as you're told. (● 後者のほうが怒りの程度が強い) ‖ **つべこべ言わずに**仕事に戻れ *Stop complaining* and get back to work.

ツベルクリン **tuberculin** /tjuːbə́ːrkjəlɪn/ ‖ **ツベルクリン検査** a tuberculin test ‖ **ツベルクリン反応** the tuberculin reaction.

¹つぼ 壺 **1【入れ物】** a **pot**; a **vase**(装飾用の花瓶など); a **jar**(広口の) ▶**つぼ**を焼く make [bake] *a pot* ‖ これは平安時代の**つぼ**です This *vase* is from the Heian period. (● pot では高価なイメージは伝えにくい).
2【急所】 an **acupressure point**, a **pressure point**(指圧の) ▶首筋の**つぼ**を押さえる press *acupressure points* at the nape of the neck ‖ 指圧には多くの**つぼ**がある There are many *pressure points* in shiatsu.
▶《比喩的》あのコメディアンは客を喜ばす**つぼ**(=こつ)を心得ている That comedian has *a knack* for entertaining an audience. ‖ あの人の話はいつも**つぼ**を外さ

ない He always keeps to *the point*.
☞ 思うつぼ（→見出語）

2つぼ 坪 a **tsubo**（➤面積の単位；約3.3㎡）▶坪当たり何百万円もする土地 a piece of land costing some million yen *per tsubo*（🏺日本事情に詳しくない外国人に説明する場合は，「1平方メートル当たり」と考えて per square meter とするとよい）‖うちの建坪は30坪だ The *floor space* of my house is thirty *tsubo*. ／The *floor space* of my house is about 99 *square meters*.（🏺日本語としての「坪」を知らない外国人には後者のような言い方がよい）.

つ

つぼみ 蕾 a **bud** ▶バラのつぼみ a rose *bud* ‖その花はまだつぼみだ The flowers *are* still *in bud*. ‖このバラはつぼみを5つつけている This rose has five *buds*. ‖公園の桜の木はつぼみをいっぱいつけている The cherry trees in the park *are covered with buds* [*are budding vigorously*]. ‖梅のつぼみはまだ堅い The *buds* of the *ume* trees are still in their early stages [are not open yet].（🏺英語ではこの場合の「堅い」を hard とはいわない）.

つぼむ 窄む **close** /klouz/ ▶朝顔は午後になると花がつぼむ Morning glories *close up* in the afternoon.

つぼめる 窄める →すぼめる.

1つま 妻 a **wife** ▶最愛の妻 one's beloved *wife* ‖別れた妻 one's *ex-wife* ‖私には妻も子もある I have *a wife* and children [and (a) child]. ／I'm married with one child [with children].（➤「妻のある男」は a married man）‖彼女はきっと彼の良き妻になるだろう I'm sure she will *make* him *a good wife*.（➤この make A B は「A(人)の B(人・物)になる」の意）‖ラフカディオ・ハーンは日本女性を妻にした Lafcadio Hearn *married* a Japanese woman.

2つま 妻 a **garnish** ▶刺身のつま *a garnish* served with sashimi.

つまさき 爪先 **the tip of** one's **toe**(s), one's **tiptoe**(s) ▶この靴はつま先がきつくて痛い These shoes pinch my *toes*.（🏺「足の指を締めつける」の意）‖私はゴッホの『ひまわり』を一目見ようとつま先で立った I *stood on tiptoe* to have a look at van Gogh's "Sunflowers." ‖家の者に気づかれないように私はつま先で廊下を歩いた I *walked on tiptoe* [I *tiptoed*] down the hallway so as not to be noticed by anybody in my family. ‖道はこの先つま先上がりになる The road *rises gently* [*slightly*] ahead.
▶《慣用表現》その紳士は頭のてっぺんから足のつま先まで非の打ちどころのない身なりをしている The gentleman is perfectly dressed *from head to toe*.

つまされる ▶自分にも小さい子供がいるだけに今度の事件では身につまされる思いがした I *felt a pang of sympathy* when I heard of the incident because I also have a small child.（➤pang は「心の痛み」）.

つましい 倹しい **frugal**, **thrifty**（➤前者のほうが「倹約」の意が強い）▶つましい生活を送る lead a *frugal* life.

つまずく 躓く 1【足をとられる】**trip**《over, on》; **stumble**《over, on》(よろめいて) ▶大きな石につまずく *trip over* a big stone ‖玄関マットにつまずく *trip on* the doormat ‖石につまずいて転んだ I *stumbled over* a rock and fell. ‖その男の子は足を突き出して彼女をつまずかせた That boy put his leg out to *trip* her.
2【失敗する】▶英語は何とかクリアーしたが，数学でつまずいた(＝落とした) I managed to pass English, but *flunked* math.

つまはじき 爪弾き ▶彼はひねくれているので，みんなからつまはじきにされている He is so hard to get along with, so *everybody gives him the cold shoulder*.（➤give the cold shoulder は「(人に)冷たくする，相手にしない」）.

つまびく 爪弾く ▶ギターをつま弾く *pick* [*strum*] a guitar（➤strum は「(下手に)かき鳴らす」）.

つまびらか 詳らか・審らか ▶事件の真相はいまだつまびらかではない We still don't have *a clear understanding* of [*clearly understand* the truth about] the incident.

つまみ 1【つまんだ量】a **pinch** ▶ホウレンソウをゆでるときにはお湯に塩をひとつまみ入れなさい When boiling spinach, it is best to put *a pinch* [*a bit*] of salt in the water.
2【つまんで持つ部分】a **knob** /nɑːb/ ; a **dial**（ダイヤル）; a **tab**（缶の蓋の）▶そのつまみを右に回してください Turn the *knob* [*dial*] to the right, please.
3【酒の】***tsumami*** 《参考》(1) 日本語の「酒のつまみ」にぴったりの英語はない. (2) hors d'oeuvre /ɔːʳdə́ːʳv/（オードブル）, appetizer（アペタイザー）はふつうは食前に出されるもので，食欲を刺激するものをいう. snack は「軽食」に相当する.

つまみぐい つまみ食い ▶私は焼きたてのクッキーを1個つまみ食いした I *pinched* one of the cookies hot from the oven. ‖男の子は母親の留守中にお菓子をつまみ食いした(＝こっそり食べた) The boy *sneaked* some candy [*ate* some candy *secretly*] while his mother was out.
▶《比喩的》その店員は店の金を長年にわたってつまみ食い(＝着服)していた The salesclerk had been *pocketing* [*filching*] money from the store for years.

つまみだす つまみ出す **pick out**（つまんで取り出す）; **throw out**（放り出す）▶スープに入った紙切れを箸でつまみ出す *pick* a small scrap of paper *out of* the soup with chopsticks ‖言うことを聞かないやつはつまみ出すぞ I will *throw* [*kick*] anyone *out* who doesn't listen to me.

つまむ 1【指先で持つ】**pick**《up》, **pinch** ＋㊐ ▶母は死んだゴキブリを恐る恐るはしでつまんだ My mother fearfully *picked* the dead cockroach *up* with chopsticks. ‖自分のしたおならがあまりに臭かったので思わず鼻をつまんだ My fart smelled so bad that I had to *hold my nose*.
2【食べる】▶どうぞお好きなものをつまんでください Please *help yourself to* whatever you like.

つまようじ 爪楊枝 a **toothpick** ▶人前でつまようじを使うのは不作法だと思う I think it's rude to *use a toothpick* [to *pick your teeth*] in front of others. 《参考》「糸ようじ」は dental floss と呼ぶ.

つまらない 詰まらない

1【おもしろくない】**uninteresting**（興味のもてない）; **boring**（飽き飽きするような）; **dull**（単調な）▶つまらない話題 an *uninteresting* subject ‖つまらない講義 an *uninteresting* lecture ／a *boring* [*dull*] lecture ‖その試合はつまらなかった The game *was boring* [*dull*]. ‖独りぼっちはつまらない Being alone is *boring*. ‖彼のいつものジョークはつまらない His old jokes *bore me*. ／I'*m bored* with [by] his old jokes.（🏺boring は「(物事が)つまらない」の意であるから，「自分がつまらないと思う」ときには I'm boring ではなく I'm bored を用いる）‖ああ，つまらないなあ What *a bore*! ／I *am sooo bored*!（🏺sooo は so を強調したもので，話しことばとしては伸ばして発音する）‖家に居て勉強ばかりするのはつまらない It's *boring* to stay at home and only study. ‖学生生活がつまらなくなった(＝嫌になった) I *got tired of* student life.
2【取るに足りない】**small**, **trivial**（ささいな）; **silly**（おろ

かな) ▶先生はどうしてそんなつまらないことを大げさに言うんだろう? Why does our teacher exaggerate such a *small* [*trivial*] matter? ‖ 彼女はつまらない男と結婚した She got married to a *worthless* [*good-for-nothing*] man. ‖ つまらないミスをする make a *silly* mistake ‖ 彼はつまらない物ばかり集めている All he collects is *junk*. (➤ junk は「がらくた」).

あなたの英語はどう響く?
日本人は他人に贈り物をする際,「つまらない物ですが」という言い方をするが, それを直訳して, This is a trifling [worthless] thing. とか This gift is nothing. などと言っても英語としては通用しない. Here's a little something for you. (心ばかりの物ですが) と言い, I hope you like it. (気に入っていただけるといいのですが) とか I thought you might like this. (お好きだろうと思いまして) などのようなことばを続けるのが英語的.

3【ばかばかしい】▶つまらないことを言うな Stop talking *nonsense*. ‖ けがをしてもつまらないからそんな危険なスポーツに手を出すのはやめておけ It would *be silly* to get hurt. So don't get involved in such a dangerous sport.

つまり in short(要するに); 《インフォーマル》 **in a nutshell** (簡単に言えば); **that is**(すなわち); **in other words**(言いかえれば) ▶何度デートに誘っても断ってくるということは, つまり彼女はぼくが好きじゃないんだ I've asked her out many times, but she has turned me down each time. *In other words* [*In short*] she doesn't like me. ‖ つまりそういうことだ That's it *in a nutshell*.
▶あの人は父の弟, つまり私のおじです That man is my father's brother, *that is*, my uncle.

つまる 詰まる 1【いっぱいになる】be stuffed 《with》; **be jam-packed** 《with》 (びっしり) ▶この貯金箱には1円玉がぎっしり詰まっている This piggy bank *is jam-packed with* 1-yen coins. ‖ 彼の頭には雑学の知識がいっぱい詰まっているらしい His head seems to *be stuffed* [*be filled* / *be jam-packed*] *with* a great deal of encyclopedic knowledge. ‖ 今週は予定が詰まっている I *am tied up* this week. / I *have a full schedule* this week. ‖ 仕事が詰まっているので残業しなければならない I must work overtime since *my work has piled up*.
2【ふさがる】▶かぜで鼻が詰まっています My nose *is stuffed up* due to my cold. ‖ 洗面所のトイレが1つ詰まっていて使えません One of the toilets in the restroom *is clogged* [*is plugged* / *is stopped*] *up* and can't be used. ‖ コピー機に紙が詰まっている The copy machine *is jammed*. ‖ 歯の間に何か詰まっていて気持ちが悪い There's something *stuck* in my teeth and it's bothering me. (➤ stuck は stick の過去分詞形) ‖ 祖父は餅が喉に詰まって窒息して死んだ My grandfather choked to death on mochi (*stuck* in his throat). ‖ 会議室はたばこの煙が充満していて息が詰まりそうだった The meeting room was full of cigarette smoke, and I *felt like I was suffocating*. ‖ 悲しい光景を見て胸が詰まった I *got all choked up* [*felt a lump in my throat*] when I saw the sad scene.
▶《慣用表現》いつも両親に見張られているようで息が詰まる I *feel stifled* because it seems as though I am being watched by my parents all the time.
3【行き詰まる】▶私は答えに詰まって床を見つめた I stared at the floor since I *didn't know what* [*how*] *to answer*. ‖ 突然マイクを向けられてことばに詰まった Facing a mike that had suddenly been held out to me, I *was at a loss for words* [*was stuck for words*].
4【縮まる】▶10キロを過ぎて, 先頭ランナーとの差がだいぶ詰まってきた The gap between the lead runner and the rest (of the runners) has *narrowed* [has *shrunk*] after ten kilometers. ‖ 彼の打球は詰まった当たりのセカンドゴロだった He hit a *slow* grounder to second.

つみ 罪 1【悪い行い】(a) **sin**(宗教・道徳上の); a **crime**(法律上の); an **offense**(規則違反) ▶うそをつくことは罪である Lying is *a sin*. (➤ キリスト教国ではうそをつくことは宗教上の罪とされる) ‖ 彼は罪を認めた He pleaded *guilty*. ‖ その男は家宅侵入の罪に問われた The man *was charged with* [*was accused of*] trespassing. ‖ 彼女は軽い罪を犯して罰金を取られた She was fined for (*committing*) *a minor offense*. ‖ 彼は殺人の罪を犯した He *committed* (*a crime* of) murder. ‖ 誘拐は非常に罪が重い Kidnapping carries *a severe punishment*. / Kidnapping is *a felony*. (➤ felony は「重罪」) ‖ 彼に罪があることは明らかだ It is clear that he *is guilty*. ‖ その件に関しては彼に罪(=責任)はない He *is not to blame for* that. / He *is not responsible for* that.
▶罪を憎んで人を憎まず Hate the offense, but not the offender. / Hate the sin, but love the sinner. (➤ 後者はキリスト教徒の使う表現).
▶罪のないいたずら a *harmless* trick / an *innocent* prank ‖ 罪のないうそ *a white lie* ‖ 罪のない笑顔 an *innocent* smile.
2【思いやりのない行い】▶大きくなって手に負えなくなったからといってペットのワニを川に捨てるとは罪なことをするものだ *It was really a crime* [*heartless*] to abandon a pet crocodile in the river just because it had grown too big to take care of.
☛ 罪滅ぼし (→見出語)

つみあげる 積み上げる pile up ▶れんがを積み上げる *lay* one brick *upon another* ‖ この漫画週刊誌の発行部数は全部積み上げれば富士山の3倍の高さになる This comic magazine has such a large weekly circulation that if you *piled up* all copies of one edition the stack would be three times as high as Mt. Fuji. →積み重ねる.

つみおろし 積み降ろし loading and unloading ▶アルバイトでトラックの荷物の積み降ろしをした I *loaded and unloaded* trucks as a part-time job.

つみかさなる 積み重なる pile up; **accumulate**(徐々に蓄積する) ▶テーブルの上には新聞や雑誌が積み重なっていた Newspapers and magazines *were piled up* on the table. ‖ 疲労が積み重なってダウンした *Accumulated* fatigue knocked me out.

つみかさね 積み重ね ▶語学が上達するには毎日の努力の積み重ねが大事だ It is important to *make continuous efforts* to make progress in learning a language. / If you want to make progress in language study, it is important to *keep* (*working*) at it *steadily*.

つみかさねる 積み重ねる pile [**heap**] **up**(➤ pile はきちんと縦に積み重ねる場合と, 雑然と山のように積み重ねる場合との両者に用いるが, heap は雑然と積み重ねる場合に用いることが多い; →山 2) ▶本を積み重ねる *pile* [*heap*] *up* books ‖ 悪事を積み重ねる transgress *repeatedly* ‖ 実験を積み重ねる *make a series of* experiments ‖ 経験を積み重ねて運転のこつをつかみなさい Get the knack of driving from *accumulated* experience.

つみき 積み木 (building) blocks ▶積み木をして遊ぶ play with (*building*) *blocks*.

つみこむ 積み込む load《with》▶彼らは私たちの荷物をトラックに積み込んだ They *loaded* the truck *with* our things. (文型に注意) ‖ トラックは救援物資を積み込んで被災地へ向かった The truck set off for the disaster-stricken area, *loaded with* relief supplies.

つみたて 積み立て savings(➤ 複数形で)
‖積立金 a reserve (fund) ‖ 積み立て貯金 installment savings, savings plan.

つみたてる 積み立てる save (up) (貯金する) ; put [lay] aside (使わずに取っておく) ▶私たちは修学旅行の費用として月々5000円を積み立てている We *save* [*put aside*] 5,000 yen a month for our school trip.

つみつくり 罪作り ▶お年寄りをだますなんて, 罪作りなやつだ What a *cruel* [*heartless*] man to swindle elderly people.

つみとる 摘み取る pick +⊜ (摘む) ; nip +⊜ (挟み取る) ▶イチゴを摘み取る *pick* strawberries.
▶《比喩的》悪の芽はつぼみのうちに摘み取るべきだ Evil [Wrongdoing] should *be nipped* in the bud.

つみに 積み荷 a load ; (a) cargo (主に船・飛行機などの) ; freight /freɪt/, 《英また》goods (主に列車・トラックなどの貨物) ▶トラックの積み荷を降ろす *unload* a truck.

つみのこし 積み残し ▶荷が多すぎて積み残しが出た There were too many things to be loaded and *some were left unloaded* [*behind*].

つみびと 罪人 a criminal (犯罪者) ; a sinner (宗教・道徳上の).

つみぶかい 罪深い sinful ▶そんな罪深いことを考えてはいけない You shouldn't think such *sinful* [*indecent*] thoughts. (後者は性的なニュアンスがある).

つみほろぼし 罪滅ぼし ▶過去の過ちの罪滅ぼしをする *atone for* one's past mistakes.
▶このあいだの罪滅ぼしに (＝埋め合わせに) あしたディズニーランドへ連れていくよ I'll take you to Disneyland tomorrow *to make up for* the other day.

つみれ (minced) fish ball ▶イワシのつみれ a sardine *ball*.

¹つむ 積む **1【物を重ねる】** pile [heap] up ▶あの子の部屋には漫画の本がどっさり積まれている Comic books *are piled* [*are heaped*] *up* in his room. ‖ 課長は山と積まれた書類を見て嫌な顔をした The section chief made a face when he saw the documents *piled up so high*. ／The section chief frowned at *the pile of* documents. (➤ frown /fraʊn/ は「眉をひそめる」). →積み重ねる.
▶《慣用表現》その職人はいくら金を積まれてもいやな仕事はしない The craftsperson wouldn't do a job he doesn't want to do *for all the tea in China* [*for all the gold in the world*]. (前者は「中国のお茶すべてと引き換えにしても」の意).
2【荷物として載せる】 load《A with B》(A に B を積み込む).

> **【文型】**
> **乗り物(A)に荷物(B)を積む**
> **load A with B**
> **load B onto [into] A**

▶引っ越し屋は彼の家財をトラックに積んだ The movers *loaded* their trucks *with* his household goods. ／The movers *loaded* his household goods *onto* their trucks. ‖ 原油を積んだタンカーが毎日その狭い海峡を行き来している Tankers (that *are*) *loaded with* crude oil pass through the narrow strait every day.
3【蓄積する】 ▶経験を積んだ教師 an *experienced* teacher ‖ 彼は長年修業を積んで一人前のコックになった He became an accomplished cook *after going through long years of training*. ‖ もっと練習を積まないとレギュラーになれないよ If you don't *practice more*, you'll never become a regular.

²つむ 摘む pick +⊜ (摘み取る) ; gather +⊜ (集める, 収穫する) ▶はしりのイチゴを摘んで東京へ出荷した We *picked* [*gathered*] the first harvest of strawberries and shipped them to Tokyo. ‖ 女の子たちはレンゲソウを摘んで花輪を作った Little girls *gathered* milk vetches to make garlands. ‖ イチゴ摘みに行こう Let's go (and) *pick* strawberries.
▶《比喩的》子供たちの創造力の芽を摘むのはよくない It's not a good thing to *nip* your children's creativity *in the bud*.

³つむ 詰む ▶目の詰んだ布 *finely-woven* cloth (➤ woven は weave (織る) の過去分詞形).
▶《チェス》あと 3 手で詰むだろう With three more moves, I'll *checkmate* my opponent.

つむぐ 紡ぐ spin +⊜ ▶糸車で糸を紡ぐ *spin* thread [yarn] on a spinning wheel.

つむじ 旋毛 a hair whorl (on the head) ▶《慣用表現》孝夫はすぐつむじを曲げるからみんなに嫌われている Takao is disliked by everybody because he easily *gets cross*. (➤ get cross は「不機嫌になる」) ‖ 彼みたいなつむじ曲がりには会ったことがない I've never met such a *cranky* [*difficult* ／*contrary* ／*perverse*] *man* as he. (➤ a cranky person は「気難し屋」の意のインフォーマルなアメリカ英語).
‖つむじ風 a whirlwind.

つむる 瞑る →つぶる.

¹つめ 爪 a nail (人の) ; a claw (動物の) ; a talon (猛鳥の) ; a hoof (ひづめ) ▶爪をかんじゃだめ Don't bite your *nails*. ‖ 爪が伸びたから切らないといけない My *nails* have grown long, so they need trimming [cutting ／clipping]. 《参考》手の爪は fingernail, 足の爪は toenail という.
▶ライオンやトラは鋭い爪を持っている Lions and tigers have sharp *claws*. ‖ 子猫はドアを爪でひっかいた The kitten scratched the door (with its *claws*). ‖ 猫がソファーに爪を立てた The cat dug its *claws* into the sofa.
▶《慣用表現》あの人には爪のあかほどの親切心もない She doesn't have *an ounce* [*the slightest bit*] *of* kindness in her.
▶お隣の秀才の爪のあかでも煎じて飲みなさい You should learn from [try to be like] that smart boy next door. (➤「見習いなさい」の意) ‖ M氏は爪に火をともすように暮らしている Mr. M *leads an extremely frugal life* [*is a penny pincher*].
☛ 爪痕, 爪切り, 深爪 (→見出語)

²つめ 詰め ▶(その計画は)詰めが甘かったようだ It seems that we were *not careful enough in the final stage* [*phase*] of the project. ／It seems that we did*n't do a good job on the finishing touches* of that project.

-づめ -詰め **1【詰めること】** ▶缶詰の果物 *canned* [《英また》*tinned*] fruit ‖ 瓶詰のビール *bottled* beer ‖

段ボール箱詰めのオレンジ oranges *packed in a cardboard box*.
2【…しどおし】▶満員で車内では立ちづめだった I *had to remain standing* in the packed train. ‖ きょうは朝から働きづめだった I *worked straight through* from this morning.
3【待機中の】▶父は警視庁詰めの新聞記者をしている My father is a newspaper reporter *assigned* (*to*) the Metropolitan Police Department.

つめあと 爪痕・爪跡 a **nail mark**; a **scratch**(ひっかいた痕) ▶彼の顔には猫にひっかかれた爪痕がある He has some *cat scratches* on his face.
▶《比喩的》地滑りの生々しい爪痕(＝傷痕)がまだ残っていた The vivid *scars* left by the landslide could still be seen.

つめあわせ 詰め合わせ an **assortment** ▶缶詰の詰め合わせ *an assortment* of canned food ‖ 彼女からチョコレートの詰め合わせが届いた I got a box of *assorted chocolates* from her.
▶《電車で》後ろのお客様もお乗りになれるようご順に中ほどまでお詰め合わせください Would everyone *move along* toward the center of the car to make room for those getting on (the train)?

つめえり 詰め襟 a **stand-up** [**cadet-style**] **collar** ▶詰め襟の学生服 a school uniform *with a stand-up* [*cadet-style*] *collar*.

つめかえる 詰め替える **refill** ＋目 (補充する); **repack** ＋目 (荷物を詰め直す) ▶シャンプーを詰め替えてくれる? Could you *refill* the bottle of shampoo? ‖ リンゴを新しい箱に詰め替える *repack* the apples in a new box.

つめかける 詰め掛ける **crowd** [**throng**] 《into》(➤ crowd は「1か所にあふれるように」, throng は「押し合いへし合いして」のニュアンス) ▶多数の買い物客がデパートのバーゲン会場に詰めかけた Many shoppers *crowded* [*thronged*] *into* the bargain floor of the department store.

つめきり 爪切り **nail clippers**; **nail scissors** /sízəʳz/ (はさみ状の) ▶爪切りで爪を切る cut one's nails with *nail clippers*.

つめこみ 詰め込み ▶私は試験のために徹夜で詰め込み勉強をした I *crammed* [*boned up* / 《英また》*swotted up*] for the exams all night. ‖ あの先生は詰め込み主義だ That teacher believes in *cramming knowledge* into students' heads.

つめこむ 詰め込む **pack** ＋目 (詰める); **cram** ＋目 (ぎっしり詰め込む)

> **【文型】**
> 物(A)を箱など(B)に詰め込む
> **pack** A **into** B
> **pack** B **with** A

▶彼は身の回りの品を段ボールに詰め込んだ He *packed* his belongings *into* a cardboard box. ‖ 洗濯物を袋に詰め込む *pack* a bag *with* dirty clothes.
▶あの先生は教育とはただ知識を詰め込むことだと思っているようだ That teacher seems to think that education is just *cramming* knowledge into his students. ‖ その子はうどんを腹いっぱい詰め込んで飛び出していった The boy went out as soon as he had *stuffed himself with* noodles. (➤ stuff oneself with は「…をたらふく食べる」の意のインフォーマルな表現).

つめしょ 詰め所 a **station**; a **guardroom**(衛兵の).

つめたい 冷たい **1【温度が低い】cold**; **chilly** (ひんやりする); **icy**(ひどく冷たい) ▶冷たい空気 *icy* air ‖ クーラーの風が冷たい The air blowing from the air conditioner *feels cold* [*chilly*]. ‖ 何か冷たい飲み物が欲しいな I'd like something *cold* (to drink). ‖ 井戸水は夏は冷たく感じる Well water feels *cool* in the summer. (● cool は心地よい冷たさをいう) ‖ 家族が発見したときそのお年寄りはすでに冷たくなっていた When the elderly man was discovered by his family, he was already *dead and cold*.
2【冷淡な】cold ▶冷たくあしらわれる *get the cold shoulder* ‖ 彼を冷たくあしらう *give* him *the cold shoulder* ‖ 都会の人は概して冷たい City people are *cold* [*unfriendly*] in general. ‖ 彼氏が最近冷たくなった My boyfriend *has become cold* toward me recently. ‖ あれほど心の冷たい人はめったにいない You rarely come across such a *cold-hearted* [*cold-blooded*] man as he. ‖ 姉はしゅうとめが冷たく当たるとこぼしている My (older) sister complains to me about how *coldly* her mother-in-law treats her.
▶冷たいことを言うな! *Have a heart*!

つめばら 詰め腹 ▶その不祥事で副社長が詰め腹を切らされた Taking the blame for the scandal, the vice president *was forced to resign* [*was made walk the plank*].

つめもの 詰め物 **padding**(クッション用の); **packing**(荷造り用の); **stuffing**(料理用・布団用の); a (**dental**) **filling**(歯科用の) ▶発泡スチロールの詰め物 Styrofoam /stáɪrəfoʊm/ *packing* ‖ チキンにセロリやニンジンの詰め物をする *stuff* a chicken with celery and carrots ‖ 詰め物をしたロールキャベツ a *stuffed* cabbage roll ‖ (歯の)金の詰め物がどこかに行っちゃった I've lost a gold *filling*.

つめよる 詰め寄る **press** ＋目 (しつこく迫る) ▶彼は計画を変更しろと私に詰め寄った He *pressed* me to change (my) plans.

つめる 詰める **1【いっぱいにする, ふさぐ】pack** ＋目 (かばん・容器などに); **fill** ＋目 (満たす); **stuff** ＋目 (無造作に) ▶ピーマンにひき肉を詰める *stuff* a green pepper *with* ground meat ‖ ごちそうを折りに詰める *put* (the) delicacies *into* a small wooden box ‖ 洋服と薬はもう旅行かばんに詰めました I'*ve* already *packed* my clothes and medicine into my traveling bag. ‖ 水筒に水を詰めてハイキングの用意をした I *filled* the canteen and got ready for the hike.
▶歯医者さんは私の歯に何か白い物を詰めた The dentist *filled* my cavity *with* something white. ‖ 段ボールの隙間に新聞紙を詰めて荷造りをした When I packed my household things, I *stuffed* the gaps in the cardboard boxes *with* newspaper.
2【押し込む】▶《バスの運転手などが》奥へ詰めてください *Move to the rear* [*Move down* / *Move along*], please. ‖《乗客が》もう少し(席を)詰めていただけますか Could you *sit* a little *closer*? / Would you mind *moving* [*sliding*] *over*?
3【話を進める】▶この話はもう少し先方と詰める必要がある This deal needs to *be discussed* a little *more in detail* with the other party. ‖ 詳細を詰めておきましょう Let's *firm up* the details.
4【切り詰める】▶スカートの丈を詰めてもらった I had my skirt *shortened* [made *short*]. ‖ ズボンはどのくらいお詰めしましょうか How much more should I *take in* your pants?
▶行間[字間]を詰める *reduce* space between the lines [characters] ‖ 文字を詰めて書く write with

minimal letter spacing.
5【待機する】▶あの交番には常時２人の警官が**詰めている**(＝配置されている) There are always two police officers *stationed* in that police box. ‖ 消防士は24時間, 消防署に**詰めている** Fire fighters *are on stand-by* at the fire station twenty-four hours a day. (➤ on stand-by は「待機して」).
6【慣用表現】▶奇術師が燃え盛る車から脱出するのを観客は**息を詰めて**見つめた The audience watched the magician escaping from the burning car *with bated breath*.

つもり **1【意図, 計画】一動**…**するつもりだ be going to** do ; **plan to** do, **be planning to** do ; **intend to** do, **intend** doing

> **【文型】**
> …**するつもりだ**
> **be going to** do
> **plan to** do ／**be planning to** do
> **intend to** do
>
> **《解説》**(1)**be going to** do は前もって決めた予定を表す. したがって, そのためにすでに準備が始まっていることを暗示する. しばしば混同される **will**（＝'ll）は発言するその場での意思決定(「…しよう」)や将来実行される約束(「…します, …してあげよう」)を表す. あらかじめの予定は表さないので,「…つもり」に当てはまることは, むしろ少ない.
> (2)**plan to** do は「…する計画［予定］だ」の意(→**予定**). plan on doing も使われる. **intend to** do は意図をいちばん明確に表す言い方だが, plan よりかたい文章語.

▶スーパーに寄る**つもりだった**が時間がなかった I *was going to* stop in at a supermarket but didn't have the time. ‖ **対話**「今度の休暇はどうする**つもりですか**」「インドを旅行する**つもりです**」"What *are* you *going to* do this coming vacation?" "I'*m planning to* travel to India." ‖ 私たちは夏休みはカナダで過ごす**つもりであります** We *intend to* spend our summer vacation in Canada. ／We'*re planning to* spend our summer vacation in Canada. ‖ ジョークの**つもりだった**が受けなかった My *attempt* at a joke fell flat.
▶どんな映画を見る**つもりなの**? What movie do you *have in mind*? (➤ have ... in mind は「…を心に決めている」の意) ‖ 黙って会社を休むとはどういう**つもりだ** *What are you trying to pull* [*What do you mean*] by taking a day off (from) work without notifying the company? (➤ pull は「人の目を欺くようなことをする, 良からぬことをする」で, この場合, 後者より非難の調子が強い) ‖ いつまで待たせる**つもり**? How long *are you going to* make me wait? ‖ あなたの気持ちを傷つける**つもりはありませんでした** I *didn't mean to* hurt your feelings. (🏺 mean to do は「本気で［本心から］…するつもりである」の意で, 否定文で「本心でない」を言うことが多い. intend to do よりくだけた言い方) ‖ この肖像画は妻を描いた**つもりです** This portrait *is meant to* be of my wife. ‖ たとえ招待されても彼女の誕生パーティーに出る**つもりはない** Even if I am invited, I *will not* go to her birthday party. (🏺 この will は前々からの予定ではなく, 発言したときの意志を表す).
2【仮想】▶彼は自分がチームのエースの**つもりでいる** He *thinks* he is [He *considers* himself] the ace pitcher of the team. ‖ 私たち, 互いにもっとわかり合えて**たつもりなのに** But *I thought* we understood each other better.
3【心構え】▶きみには来年キャプテンになってもらうから**そのつもりでいてくれ** We intend you to be captain next year, so *be prepared* [*keep that in mind*]. ‖ 今度エラーしたら二軍落ちだから**そのつもりでいろ** *Remember* that you'll be sent back to the farm team if you make another error.

つもる 積もる 1【重なって高くなる】pile《up》; **lie**(横たわる) ▶通りに雪が**積もった** Snow *piled up* on the street. ‖ そこでは雪が３メートル以上も**積もっていた** I found the snow *piled up* more than three meters deep on the ground there. ‖ 机の上にはほこりが厚く**積もっている** Our desks *are covered with* thick dust.
2【たくさんになる】▶彼女には父親に対して**積もる恨み**がある She has *pent-up resentment* toward [against] her father. ‖ あちこちから借りた借金が**積もり積もって**300万円になった The money I borrowed from here and there *has added up* to three million yen.

1つや 艶 gloss(表面の) ; **luster**(本来備わっている光沢) ▶母の髪は**つやがある** My mother's hair *is glossy*. ／My mother's hair *has a nice shine*. ‖ 病気のせいで祖父の顔は**つやがなかった** My grandfather's face *looked dull* [*sallow*] due to his illness. ‖ 彼女の自慢は**つやのある**声だ Her pride is her *mellow* voice. ‖ たんすを布で磨いて**つやを出した** I polished the cabinet with a cloth to *bring out the luster*.

2つや 通夜 a **wake** ▶親戚の**通夜**に行く attend *a* relative's *wake* **《参考》** 通夜はアイルランドなど一部の地域では行われるが, その他の英語圏ではあまり一般的ではない.

つやけし 艶消し ▶**つや消し**の黒 *matte* black.
▶せっかくのお祝いのパーティーに**つや消しなことを言う**(＝水をさす)な Don't *throw a wet blanket* over [*spoil the fun* of] the celebration.
‖**つや消しガラス** frosted [matted] glass ‖**つや消し電球** a frosted (electric) bulb ‖**つや消し塗料** flat paint(光沢のない塗料).

つやつや 艶々 ▶彼女の髪は手入れがいいので**つやつやしている** Her hair is *lustrous* [*shiny*] because she takes good care of it. ‖ 彼, まだまだ若いね. 肌が**つやつやだよ** He's still so young. His skin is *lustrous* [*glowing*].

1つゆ 露 dew /djuː/ ▶草は**露**でぬれている The grass is wet with *dew*. ‖ 庭には**朝露**が降りていた The *morning dew* covered the yard.

2つゆ 液・汁 soup(吸い物) ; **sauce**(そばなどのつけ汁) ; **broth**(だし汁) ▶牛丼の並みを**つゆ**だくでお願いします A medium beef bowl with *extra broth*, please.

3つゆ 梅雨 ***tsuyu*** ; **the rainy** [**wet**] **season**
日本紹介 ✉ **梅雨は日本における雨季の名で, 梅の実が熟する頃の雨というので, 梅の雨と書いて「ばいう」ともいいます. 6月から7月半ばにわたる時期で, 一年中で最もじめじめとして, カビの生えやすくなるときです** *Tsuyu* is the name of the rainy season in Japan. It is also called '*baiu*' (literally, *ume* (Japanese apricot) rain, because it is rain that falls when *ume* bear fruit). Tsuyu lasts from June to mid-July and it is the time of the year that is mostly damp and when things get moldy easily.
▶**梅雨**に入った［が明けた］ *The rainy season* has set in [has ended ／is over]. ‖ 関東地方では**梅雨**が明けたようだ The *rainy season* appears to be over in the Kanto region. ‖ ことしの**梅雨**入りは遅れそうだ It

looks like *the rainy season* is going to come late this year. ‖ きょうも関東地方には**梅雨空**が広がっています Today the *rainy season clouds* are again covering the Kanto area. ‖ きょう**梅雨明け**が発表された *The end of the rainy season* was announced today. ‖ ことしは**空梅雨**だった We have had *a dry rainy season* this year.

4**つゆ 露** ▶病気とは**つゆ**知らず(＝全然知らずに)彼を訪れた I visited him, *not knowing at all* that he was ill in bed.

つゆくさ 露草《植物》an **Asiatic dayflower.**

つよい 強い 1【力がある】**strong, powerful**(➤両者はほぼ同じ意味で, 交換可能) ▶**強い**腕 *strong* [*powerful*] arms ‖ **力の強い**男 a man *of strength* [*power*] ‖ 彼は**腕っぷしが強い** He is *strong.* / He is a *strong* [*powerful*] man. ‖ ジェットエンジンは**力が強い** Jet engines *are powerful.* ‖ 息子には逆境に負けない**強い**子に育ってほしい I hope my son will grow up to be someone *strong* enough to overcome adversity. ‖ **母は強し** *Mothers are strong.* ‖ ライオンズは相変わらず**強い** The Lions are *formidable* as usual. (➤formidable は「侮れない, 手ごわい」).

2【程度が激しい】strong ; intense(激しい, 強烈な) ; **severe**(耐え難いほどの) ▶**強い**光[熱] *intense* light [heat] ‖ **強い**意志 a *strong* will ‖ **強い**怒り[憎しみ] *intense* anger [hatred] ‖ **強い**布 *strong* [*tough*] cloth ‖ きょうは**風が強い** There's a *strong* wind today. / The wind is *strong* today. ‖ ゆうべ**強い**地震があった There was a *powerful* [*strong*] earthquake last night. ‖ 兄は**責任感が強い** My brother has a *strong* sense of responsibility. ‖ トイレは**強い**芳香剤のにおいがした There was a *strong* scent of air freshener in the bathroom. / The toilet smelled *strongly* of air freshener. ‖ その政治家は与党に**強い**影響力をもっている The politician has *great* influence [clout] with the ruling party. ‖ 私のお父さんはお母さんには**強い**ことが言えない My father is in no position to say anything *severe* to my mother. / My dad can't get *tough* with my mom. (➤後者は「強い態度に出る」) ‖ 父は**強い**酒が好きだ My dad likes *hard liquor*.

3【耐えられる】 ▶**干ばつに強い**品種のキュウリ a *drought-resistant* strain of cucumber (➤drought(干ばつ)は /draʊt/ と発音) ‖ この品種の稲は**冷害に強い** This type of rice *is highly resistant to* [*is strong against*] the cold. ‖ 私は夏が好きで, 暑さには**強い** I love (the) summer and *don't mind* [*can take*] *the heat.* (➤and 以下を the heat doesn't bother me. としてもよい) ‖ 私は**乗り物に強い**(＝酔わない) I *never get motion sickness.* ‖ 桐(きり)材は**湿気に強い** Paulownia wood *can withstand* humidity. (➤withstand は「持ちこたえる」) ‖ うちの家系は皆**酒が強い** All the members of my family are *heavy drinkers* [can *drink quite a lot* / *can hold their liquor*].

4【得意だ】 ▶彼女は数学に**強く**, ぼくは英語に**強い** She is *strong in* mathematics, while I am *good at* English.

つよがり 強がり ▶**強がり**はよせ Stop *bluffing.* ‖ 彼は**強がりを言っている**だけだ He's just *whistling in the dark.* (➤「暗闇で口笛を吹く」が原義 ; インフォーマルな表現).

つよがる 強がる ▶彼は**強がって**みせたが, 内心ではびくびくしていた He *put on a bold front*, but inside, he was quite frightened. (➤bold front は「大胆な態度」).

つよき 強気な aggressive(積極果敢な) ; **strong**(市況が) ▶販売員として成功したければ**強気**でなければだめだ You have to be *aggressive* if you want to succeed as a salesperson. ‖ 彼は誰に対しても**強気な**態度をとる He takes an *aggressive* attitude [a *firm* stand] toward everybody. ‖ 市況は**強気**だ(＝株価が上昇気味だ) The stock market is *bullish* [*strong*].

つよく 強く strongly ; hard(力いっぱい) ; **firmly**(断固として) ▶私は戸を**強く**押した I pushed the door *strongly.* ‖ そのひもを**強く**引っ張りなさい Pull the string *hard.* ‖ そのボクサーは頭を**強く**打たれて意識不明になった The boxer was hit *hard* on the head [received a *sharp* blow to the head] and became unconscious. ‖ 母親は子供を**強く抱き締めた** The mother *held* her child *tight(ly)* in her arms.
▶我々は原発に対して**強く**抗議する We *strongly* protest against nuclear power plants. ‖ すぐ医者に見てもらうようにと私は彼に**強く勧めた** I *strongly* advised him to see a doctor at once. ‖ 代表団は市長に回答を**強く迫った** The delegation *pressed* the mayor for an answer.
▶震災で両親をなくしたけれど, 私たちは**強く生きて**いくつもりです We lost our parents in the great earthquake, but we're going to *be strong and get on with our lives.*

つよさ 強さ strength, power(➤両者はほぼ交換可能) ; **intensity** (程度の激しさ) ▶ブラジルチームの**強さ**には驚いた I was amazed at *how strong* the Brazilian team was. ‖ 光の**強さ**はどんな器械で測るのですか What kind of instrument is used to measure the *intensity* of light? ‖ 「大和なでしこ」は日本人女性の可憐(かれん)さと**心の強さ**を表す美称だ Yamato-nadeshiko [Japanese (fringed) pink] is a beautified name for a Japanese woman representing her loveliness and *inner strength.*

つよび 強火 a strong fire, high heat (➤後者は電熱にもいえる) ▶中華料理は**強火**が決め手だ The most important thing in Chinese cooking is to use *high heat* [*a high flame*]. ‖ 魚を焼くときは**強火**の遠火にします When you broil fish, use *a high* [*strong*] *flame* at some distance. ‖ フライパンに油を入れて**強火**で熱します Put the oil in the skillet and heat it over *high heat* [over *a high flame*].

つよまる 強まる become strong(er) ▶風が**強まっている** The wind is [Winds are] *picking up.* ‖ 台風の接近で午後から風雨が**強まる**でしょう Due to the approach of the typhoon rain(s) and wind(s) will *become stronger* starting this afternoon. ‖ その条約により日米関係は**強まった** The treaty *strengthened* Japan-U.S. relations. ‖ あの政治家が賄賂を受け取ったという**疑惑が更に強まった** People *have become more suspicious* that the politician accepted a bribe.

つよみ 強み strength ; a strong point(長所) ; **an advantage**(有利な点) ▶ロシア語ができるのが彼の**強み**だ His *strength* lies in his Russian ability. ‖ 彼女の**強み**は顔が広いことだ Her *strong point* [*advantage*] is that she has a large circle of acquaintances.

つよめる 強める strengthen /stréŋkθən/ +⑩ ▶ガスレンジの火を**強める** *turn up* the flame on a gas range / *make* the flame on a gas range *stronger* ‖ その経験で彼女は自分の信念を**強めた** That experience *strengthened* her faith. ‖ 電車の爆破予告があったので警察は警戒を強めた The police *tightened* security after receiving threats to blow up the train.

つら 面 the mug ▶でかい面をする act *big* ‖ あの男の面見てみろよ Look at *the mug* on that guy. ‖ ちょっと面を貸せ Just *come along with me.* ‖ あいつ, どの面下げて俺のところに来られるんだ *How dare* he come to see me！(● How dare の後ろでは 3 人称・単数・現在にも -s はつけない).
☛ 面の皮 (→見出語)

つらい 辛い hard, tough (困難な；後者のほうがインフォーマルで, つらさを意識している程度が前者よりも大きい)；**painful** (精神的に苦しい)
▶つらい修業 *hard* training ‖ つらい人生を送る lead a *hard* life ‖ 早起きするのはつらい It's *hard* getting up early in the morning. ‖ 男はつらいよ It's *hard* [*tough*] being a man. ‖ 私, 彼と別れるのがつらいんです It's really *hard* [*painful*] for me to say goodbye to him. ‖ 私のつらい立場もわかってください I wish you would understand the *tough* [*difficult*] position I'm in. ‖ その仕事はつらかったが何とかやり遂げた That was a *hard* [*tough*] job, but I managed to complete it. ‖ 失業したときはつらかった It was a *painful* experience for me to lose my job. ‖ 疲れていて目を開けているのがつらかった I was so tired that I *had trouble* keeping my eyes open. (➤「苦労した」の意).
▶どうしてあの子につらく当たるの？ Why *are* you *hard on* her？／Why *are* you so *tough with* her？

-づらい →-にくい.

つらがまえ 面構え a **look** ▶男は一癖ありそうな面構えだった He was a sinister-*looking* guy.

つらさ 辛さ pain (苦痛)；**bitterness** (悔しさ) ▶失恋のつらさを味わう taste the *bitterness* [experience *the pain*] of a broken heart.

つらなる 連なる range (伸びる)；**stretch** (広がる) ▶日本アルプスは南北に連なっている The Japan Alps *range* [*stretch*] from north to south. ‖ 見渡す限り砂丘が連なっていた The sand dunes *stretched* as far as the eye could see.

つらぬく 貫く 1【貫通する】go [**run**] **through** ▶弾丸は彼の右肩を貫いた The bullet *went through* [*pierced*] his right shoulder. ‖ 淀川は大阪市の中心部を貫いて流れている The Yodo River *flows* [*runs*] *through* the heart of the City of Osaka.
2【やり遂げる】▶信念を貫く *stick to* one's convictions ‖ 彼は生涯自分流の生き方を貫いた He *stuck* [*kept*] *to* his own way of life till the end. (➤ stuck は stick の過去形) ‖ 彼は初志を貫いて医者になった He *carried out* his (original) intention [resolve] to become a doctor.

つらねる 連ねる ▶湖畔には土産物屋が軒を連ねていた Souvenir shops *were lined up* along the shore of the lake. ‖ 私たちは車を連ねて襟裳岬へドライブした A bunch of us *drove our cars together* to Cape Erimo. ‖ 私はそのリコール運動の賛同者として名を連ねた(＝載せた) I *entered my name* on the list of supporters of the recall campaign.

つらのかわ 面の皮 ▶面の皮の厚いやつ a *thick-skinned* [*shameless*] man ‖ あいつの面の皮をひんむいてやりたい I'd like to *take* him *down a peg or two.* (●「鼻っ柱をへし折る」の意).

つらよごし 面汚し a **disgrace** (不面目) ▶あいつはわが家の面汚しだ He [She] is *a disgrace* to our family. ‖ こういうスラム街があることは町の面汚しだ Such slums are *a disgrace* to [*a blot on the face* of] this town.

つらら 氷柱 an **icicle** /áɪsɪkəl/ ▶つららが軒先に下がっている *Icicles* are hanging from the eaves.

つられる 釣られる ▶販売員の甘いことばに釣られて多くの人たちがその品を買った Many people *were enticed* by the salesperson's sweet words [were sweet-talked] into buying the goods. ‖ 世間知らずは甘いことばに釣られ(＝だまされ)やすい Naive people easily *fall for* honeyed words. ‖ 人だかりができていたので, 私も釣られて見にいった I *was drawn* by the crowd and went to see what was happening. ‖ 男がおじぎをしたので, 私も釣られて頭を下げた The man bowed, *which led* me *to* bow also [, *which made* me bow *reflexively*, too].

つり 釣り 1【魚釣り】fishing ▶三浦へ釣りに行く *go fishing* at Miura (● to Miura とはしない)／*go* to Miura *to fish* (➤ この fish は「釣りをする」の意の動詞) ‖ 彼はグアムで釣りをしたり, ゴルフをしたりした He *fished* and played golf on Guam. ‖ 弟は渓流釣りに行ってイワナを釣ってきた My (younger) brother went *fishing in a mountain stream* and caught some char(r)s. ‖ アユ釣りが解禁になったからあの釣り場は釣り人でいっぱいだろう The *ayu fishing* season is now open, so *anglers* will crowd in on that *fishing spot*.
‖釣り糸 a fishing line ‖ 釣りざお a fishing rod ‖ 釣り道具 fishing tackle, a rod and reel ‖ 釣り仲間 a fishing companion [buddy] ‖ 釣り針 a fishhook (→見出語) ‖ 釣り船 a fishing boat (➤「相乗りの釣り船」は party boat という).
2【ネット上での挑発】《コンピュータ》**flamebait.**
☛ お釣り, 釣り(銭) (→見出語)

つりあい 釣り合い (a) **balance** (均衡)；**proportion** (比率) ▶綱渡りは長いさおを使って釣り合いをとる A tightrope walker uses a long pole to *keep his balance*. ‖ わが国は輸入と輸出の釣り合いがとれていない Our country's imports and exports are *not in balance* [are *unbalanced*]. ／Our country's exports are out of *proportion* to its imports. (● 後者は「輸出が断然多い」の意).
☛ 不釣り合い (→見出語)

つりあう 釣り合う balance；match (調和する) ▶去年のわが家の収入と支出は釣り合っていなかった Our income and expenditures didn't *balance* last year. ‖ こんなモダンな家具はこの家には釣り合わない Such modern furniture *doesn't match* [*suit*] the house. ‖ 2 人の結婚は家柄が釣り合わないと周囲から反対された Their marriage was opposed by everyone around them because their family backgrounds *did not match*.

[1]**つりあげる 吊り上げる 1【つるし上げる】lift** +目 ▶彼らは船荷をクレーンでつり上げていた They *were lifting* the cargo with a crane.
2【目・眉を】▶彼女はぼくの不注意なことばにきっと目をつり上げた She *glared at* me *disapprovingly* over my careless remark. (●「非難するようににらんだ」の意).
3【物価を】mark up, raise /reɪz/ +目 (➤ 前者には「価格を設定する」の意もある) ▶ブローカーは需要があると見るや商品の値をつり上げていった Seeing the growing demand, the broker began to *mark up* [*raise*] the price of the product.

[2]**つりあげる 釣り上げる land** +目 ▶大きなタイを釣り上げる *land* a big sea bream.

つりがね 釣り鐘 a **suspended temple bell** ▶釣り鐘を

つく strike *a temple bell*.

つりかわ 吊り革 a **strap** ▶この先電車が揺れますのでつり革におつかまりください The train will sway ahead. So please hold [hang] onto the *strap*.

つり(せん) 釣り(銭) **change** ▶釣りはいらないよ Keep the *change*. ‖ この釣り銭, 間違ってますよ I'm afraid this is the wrong *change*. (● 実際にはもっと具体的に Shouldn't it be 10 yen more?(あと10円足りなくない?)などと言うことが多い) ‖ この自動販売機は釣り銭が出ません This vending machine doesn't give *change*. (● 機械の構造上出ない場合) / This vending machine didn't give me my *change*. (● 機械が壊れて出なかった場合) ‖ あの店でまた釣りをごまかされた They *shortchanged* me again at that store. ‖《バスなどの掲示》お釣りのないように願います *Exact fare*, please. ‖ 対話「1万円でお釣りがもらえますか」「いいですよ」"Can you give me *change* for a ten-thousand-yen bill?" "Certainly."

つりばし 吊り橋 a **hanging bridge**; a **suspension bridge**(ケーブルなどによる規模の大きい橋).

つりばり 釣り針・釣り鉤 a **fishhook** ▶釣り針に餌をつける bait *a fishhook*.

つりぼり 釣り堀 a **fishing pond**, a **fishpond** ▶釣り堀で釣りをする fish in *a fishpond*.

つりわ 吊り輪 **the rings** ▶つり輪の演技 a performance on *the rings*.

1**つる 蔓** **1**【植物の】a **vine**(ツタなどのつる植物の); a **tendril**(キュウリなどの巻きひげ); a **runner**(イチゴなどの地をはう) ▶朝顔のつるはよく伸びる Morning glory *vines* grow fast. ‖ サツマイモをつるごと地面から引っこ抜いた I pulled out the sweet potatoes, *vines and all*.

2【眼鏡の】《米》a **temple**, 《英》an **arm**.

2**つる 鶴** 《鳥》a **crane**

日本紹介 ✉ **ツルは秋にシベリアから飛来し, 春に帰っていく渡り鳥です. 日本ではカメと同様に長寿とめでたさを象徴する動物とされ, 祝い事に関係する図案によく登場します** The (Japanese) crane is a migratory bird that flies from Siberia in the autumn and flies back in the spring. In Japan the crane, like the tortoise, is considered an auspicious animal that symbolizes longevity and happiness. It is often depicted in pictures (that are) related to celebratory occasions.

▶《慣用表現》お父さんの**鶴の一声**で家族全員でカナダへ移住することになった *One word* from Dad and the whole family decided to move to Canada.

☞ **折り鶴, 千羽鶴** (→見出語)

3**つる 吊る** **hang** +目 ▶棚をつる *put up* a shelf ‖ 私は2本の木の間にハンモックをつった I *hung* a hammock between two trees. (➤ hung は hang の過去形) ‖ その容疑者は首をつった The suspect *hanged himself*. (➤ hang は「首をつる」の意のときは規則変化) ‖ 彼は骨折した腕をつり包帯でつっていた He *had* his broken arm *in a sling*. ‖ 妹は目が少しつっている My sister has slightly *upward-slanting eyes*. / My sister's *eyes slant* slightly *upward*.

4**つる 釣る** **1**【魚を】**catch** +目(釣り上げる); **fish** +目(釣りをする) ▶スズキを釣る *fish for* sea bass (● fish は「魚を釣るために釣り糸を垂れる」の意で,「魚を釣り上げる」まではいわないので, fish sea bass は不可) ‖ スズキを5匹釣った I *caught* five sea bass.

2【甘言で誘う】▶セールスマンはうまいことばで学生を釣って英会話のDVDを買わせた The salesman *talked* [*smooth-talked*] the student *into* buying a set of English conversation DVDs. (➤ smooth-talk ... into doing は「うまいことを言ったり巧みな行動をとったりして…させる」の意のインフォーマルな表現).

☞ **釣られる** (→見出語)

5**つる 攣る** **have** [**get**] **a cramp**(けいれんを起こす) ▶私は睡眠中に足がつることがある I sometimes *get a cramp* [*get cramps*] in my leg while sleeping. (➤《英》では通例 a をつけない) ‖ 水泳中に足がつった I *got a cramp* in my leg while (I was) swimming.

つるし 吊るし ▶そのスーツ, あつらえ? それともつるし? Was that suit made to order, or was it *off the rack* [《英》*off the peg*]?

つるしあげる 吊るし上げる ▶みんなでスト破りをつるし上げた They *subjected* the strikebreakers *to a kangaroo court*. (➤ kangaroo court はカンガルーの跳躍から連想されてできた語で, 正規の裁判手続きを飛ばして人の責任などを追及すること).

つるす 吊るす **hang** +目 ▶洋服をハンガーにつるす *hang* one's clothes on a hanger ‖ 軒先に風鈴をつるす *hang* a wind-bell under the eaves.

つるつる **1**【滑るような音】▶そうめんをツルツル食べる *slurp down* (the) *somen* noodles.

2【滑る様子】▶つるつるした肌 *silky smooth* skin ‖ 道路が凍ってつるつるになっている The road is *slippery* with ice. ‖ おじいちゃんの頭はつるつるにはげている My grandpa is *as bald as an egg*.

つるはし 鶴嘴 a **pick**(両端のとがったもの); a **pickax** /pɪ́kæks/ (片方がとがったもの).

つるべ 釣瓶 a **bucket at the well** ▶ ことわざ 秋の日はつるべ落とし Dusk falls quickly in the fall.

つるむ ▶彼らはいつも3人でつるんでゲームセンターに遊びに行く The three of them always *hang out* at game centers.

つるり ▶彼は氷の上でつるりと滑った He *slid* on the ice. (➤ slid は slide の過去形) ‖ 日に焼けた肌がつるりとむけた The skin *peeled right off* where I'd gotten sunburned.

つれ 連れ ▶きょうは連れがあるんだ I have *someone with me* today. ‖ 人混みで連れ(=友だち)にはぐれてしまった I got separated from my *friend*(*s*) in the crowd. ‖ お連れさまが先ほどからお待ちです *Your party* has been waiting for you for some time. (➤ この party は「行動をともにしている相手」の意).

-づれ -連れ ▶彼女たちは3人連れで海外旅行に出かけた *The three* of them set out on an overseas trip. ‖ 夏休みに家族連れで北海道旅行をした I took a trip to Hokkaido *with my family* during the summer vacation.

☞ **子連れ** (→見出語)

つれあい 連れ合い one's (**help**)**mate**(➤ 日本語に近い文語的な語); one's **husband**(夫); one's **wife**(妻); one's **spouse** /spaʊs/ (配偶者; 法律関係や役所の書類などで使うことが多い) ▶去年連れ合いを亡くして寂しい思いをしているよ *My wife* passed away last year, so I feel lonely these days. (● 夫を指す場合は wife を husband に変える).

つれさる 連れ去る **take away**; **abduct** +目; **kidnap** +目 ▶私は男が女の子を連れ去るのを目撃したんです I saw a man *take* the girl *away*.

つれそう 連れ添う ▶私たち, 連れ添ってかれこれ20年になるわね We'*ve been married* for about twenty years, haven't we?

つれだす 連れ出す **take out** ▶私は彼女をお茶に連れ出した I *took* her *out* to have a cup of tea.

つれだつ 連れ立つ ▶家族と連れ立って動物園へ行った I went to the zoo *with* my family.

-つれて -連れて as(➤ あとに節がくる), with (➤ あとに句がくる) ▶人は年を取るにつれて忘れっぽくなる *As* we grow older, we become forgetful. ／The older we get, the more forgetful we become. ‖ 車の数が増えるにつれて交通事故も多くなる *As* cars increase in number, traffic accidents occur more frequently.

▶気圧は高度が増すにつれて下がる Atmospheric pressure decreases *with* altitude. ‖ 科学の進歩につれて生活様式も変化する Lifestyles change (*along*) *with* scientific progress.

つ

つれていく 連れて行く take +目 →連れる

【文型】
人(A)を場所(B)へ連れていく
take A to B

▶弟を東京ディズニーランドへ連れていった I *took* my brother *to* Tokyo Disneyland. ‖ そのお年寄りは私を最寄りの駅まで連れていってくれた The elderly man *showed* [*took*] me *to* the nearest train station. (➤ show は「案内する」).

つれてくる 連れて来る bring +目

【文型】
人(A)を場所(B)へ連れて来る
bring A to B

▶医者は助手を連れて来た The doctor *brought* an assistant with him. ‖ ママ, あしたお友だちを連れて来てもいい？Mom, can I *bring* a friend tomorrow?

▶彼は娘さんをパーティーへ連れて来た He *brought* his daughter *to* the party.

つれない cold ▶彼女は求婚者につれない返事をした She gave a *cold* reply to her suitor. ‖ このところ彼女はぼくにつれないんだ She's been *giving* me *the cold shoulder* lately. (➤ give ... the cold shoulder で「…を冷たくあしらう」) ‖ つれない人ね！What a *heartless* person you are!

つれもどす 連れ戻す bring back ▶警察は誘拐された幼い女の子を両親のもとへ連れ戻した The police rescued the kidnapped girl and *brought* her *back* to her parents. ‖ 家出をして連れ戻されたことがあります I have *been dragged back home* after running away. (➤ drag back home は「無理やり家に連れ戻す」).

つれられて 連れられて ▶少年は父親に連れられて警察に自首してきた The boy, *accompanied by* his father, turned himself in to the police.

[1]**つれる 連れる** take +目 (連れていく); bring +目 (連れて来る)

▶父さん, お願い, 野球を見に連れてってよ *Take* me to a ball game, Dad. Please! ‖ 私を連れてって *Will you let me go with you?* ‖ 東京スカイツリーに行くの？私も連れてって Are you going to Tokyo Sky Tree? *Can you take me* [*Can I join you*]?

▶娘が 2 人の孫を連れて遊びに来た Our daughter came to see us *with* two grandchildren *in tow*. (➤ in tow は「けん引された」が文字どおりの意味). ‖ 川沿いの散歩道は朝晩, 犬を連れて散歩する人が多い There are many walkers *with* their dogs on the promenade along the river in the mornings and evenings.

[2]**つれる 釣れる** catch +目 (釣る) ▶きのうハゼが20匹釣れた I *caught* twenty gobies yesterday. ‖ きょうは何匹釣れたの？How many fish did you *catch* today?

つわもの 兵・強者 a (mighty) samurai (武士); someone to be reckoned with (侮り難い人).

つわり 悪阻 morning sickness ▶女房は妊娠 3 か月目につわりがひどかった My wife had terrible *morning sickness* when she was in her second month of pregnancy. (→妊娠).

つんけん ▶そんなにつんけんしないでくれよ Don't *be* so *crabby*.

つんざく 劈く pierce +目 ▶耳をつんざくような喚声 an *earsplitting* roar ‖ オートバイの爆音が夜の静けさをつんざいた The sound of a motorcycle *pierced* the still air of the night.

つんつるてん ▶娘は背が急に伸びちゃって, どの服を着せてもつんつるてんなのよ My daughter has grown so quickly that anything she puts on is *too short*.

つんつん ▶あの娘はつんつんして(＝気取って)いて愛想も何もない That girl *is stuck-up* and is not the least bit friendly. ／That girl *is haughty* [*arrogant*] and not pleasant at all. (● 後者のほうが堅い言い方) ‖ 朝から何をつんつんしている(＝いらいらして人に当たる)んだ What have you *been on edge* about all morning?

つんと ▶つんと澄ました娘 a *conceited* [*stuck-up*] young girl ‖ 彼女はいつもつんとしている She is always so *prim and proper*.

▶ワサビが鼻の奥につんと来た！The wasabi *set* my sinuses *on fire* [*cleared* my sinuses]! (➤ sinus /sáɪnəs/ は「副鼻腔(こう)」の意).

▶病室に入ると消毒液の匂いがつんと鼻をついた When I entered the ward, the smell of disinfectant *assailed my nostrils*. (➤ assail /əséɪl/ は「(悪臭などが)襲う」の意).

つんどく 積ん読 ▶きみはいつもつんどくだね. たまには読んでみろよ You always *buy books and just pile them up*, don't you? Why don't you try reading them once in a while?

ツンドラ a tundra /tʌ́ndrə/.

つんのめる fall forward (前へ倒れる) ▶歩道のへり石に足をとられてつんのめった I tripped over the curb and *almost fell forward*.

て・テ

て 手

訳語メニュー
手, 人手 →hand 1, 3
手段 →means 4
計略 →trick 5

1【手, 腕】 a **hand** (手首から先) ; an **arm** (肩から先) ▶どうして日本の女性には笑うときに手で口を隠す人がいるのだろう I wonder why some Japanese women cover their mouths with their *hands* when they laugh. ‖ 男の子は両手に大きな犬を抱えていた The boy was holding a big dog *in his arms*. ‖ 手に取って見ていいですか Can I *pick* it *up*? ‖ どうぞ真珠を手に取ってご覧ください Please (feel free to) *take* the pearls *in your hands* and examine them.
▶この問題のわかる人がいたら手を挙げなさい Can anyone answer this question? If you can, *raise your hand*. ‖ 手を上げろ! *Hands up!* / *Stick 'em up!* (➤ "'em" は them の略でインフォーマル) ‖ 日本人は習慣的に手を合わせて祈る Japanese customarily *put their hands* [*press their palms*] *together* when they pray. (➤ palm /pɑːm/ は「手のひら」) ‖ 男の子はもっと欲しいと手を差し出した The boy *held out his hand* asking for more. ‖ お手を拝借! *Let's clap together!*
▶みんなは菅原さんの歌に合わせて手をたたいた Everyone *clapped their hands* in time with Sugawara's singing. ‖ ヒロミと手をつないで公園を歩いた Hiromi and I walked in the park *hand in hand*. ‖ ぼくはまだ女の子の手を握ったことがない I've never *held* a girl's *hand*.
▶ロープから手を離すな Don't *let go of* the rope. (➤ let go of で「…から手を離す」) ‖ 選手たちは観客の声援に手を振って応えた The players *waved* to the cheering crowds. (➤ wave だけで「手を振って合図する」の意になる) ‖ 《掲示》手を触れないでください Do Not Touch / Hands Off ‖ 《犬に》お手! *Shake!* / *Give me your paw!*
▶《比喩的》交通遺児に愛の手を! Extend *a loving hand* to children orphaned by traffic accidents.

2【行為】 ▶捜査の手はS土木会社に及んだ The *investigation* has been extended to S Engineering Company. (● この場合「手」は考えなくてよい) ‖ 中日は5点差がついても攻撃の手を緩めなかった The Dragons were winning by (as many as) five runs, but they did not *relax* their offensive [*break off* their offensive].

3【人手】 a **hand** ▶収穫期にはどうしても手(=労働者)が足りなくなる We are short of *workers* [We are short-handed] during the harvest season. ‖ お皿を洗うから手を貸してくれない? Will you *give me a hand* with the dishes? / Will you *help me* (to) do the dishes? ‖ **対話**「今, 手は空いてる?」「いや, どうしても手が離せないんだ」"*Are* you *free* now?" "Sorry, I'*m tied up* [*busy*] right now."
‖**働き手** a worker, an earner (稼ぎ手).

4【手段, 方法】 a **means** ▶あらゆる手は尽くした I have *tried every possible means*. / I have *left no stone unturned*. ‖ 救助隊はあらゆる手を尽くして山の遭難者を捜索した The rescue party *did everything in their power* to search for the missing mountaineer. ‖ 《将棋・チェスなどで》それはいい手だ That's *a good move*.

5【計略】 a **trick** ▶その手はもう古い That *trick* is already old hat. ‖ 汚い手を使って勝とうなんてひきょうだぞ It's mean of you to use *a dirty trick* to win. ‖ その手には乗らないよ I'm not going to be fooled by *that*. ‖ その手があったか! I should've come up with *that*! (思いつくべきだった) / Oh, of course! (ああ, なるほどね) / This is *it*! (まさにこれだ). ‖ それを利用しない手はない There's no *reason* not to take advantage of that.

6【着手】 ▶仕事が山のようにたまっていて, どこから手をつけていいかわからなかった I had such a pile of work to do that I didn't know *where to begin* [*start*]. ‖ 阪神が負けると仕事が手につかないという友人がいる There is a friend of mine who gets so discouraged when the Tigers lose a game that he *can't do any work*.

7【種類】 a **kind** ▶この手のバットは折れやすくて危険だ *This kind of* bat is dangerous because it breaks (too) easily. ‖ あの手の人は苦手だ I find it hard to deal with *that type of person* [*a man like him* / *a woman like her*].

8【その他の慣用表現】 **手がかかる** ▶手がかかる子供 a *troublesome* child ‖ 子供に手がかからなくなったので働きに出ることにした I have decided to get a job since my children are *old enough to take care of themselves*. **手がつけられない** ▶部屋は手がつけられないほど散らかっていた The room was so messy (that) I *didn't know where to start* (*putting it in order*). ‖ 彼はかっとなると手がつけられない He *gets out of hand* when he gets angry. (➤ out of hand は「手に負えない」).
手が出ない ▶そんな高い毛皮にはとても手が出ない I *can't afford* such an expensive fur. **手が早い** ▶あいつは手が早い(=けんかっ早い) He *is a quarrelsome guy*. ‖ あいつは女性に手が早い He *is fast with* women. **手が回らない** ▶けさは忙しくて, 部屋の掃除まで手が回らなかった I was very busy this morning, so I *couldn't get around to* cleaning my room. (➤ get around to doing は「…する時間ができる」). **手に汗握る** ▶日本シリーズの第7戦は手に汗握る試合だった The seventh game of the Japan Series was a really *exciting* one.
手に余る ▶おいっ子たちのお守りはぼくの手に余るよ Taking care of my nephews *is more than I can handle*. **手に入れる** ▶彼女は土地を売って大金を手に入れた She *got* a lot of money by selling a piece of land. ‖ そのサッカーの試合のチケット, ぼくが手に入れてあげるよ I'll *get* you a ticket for the soccer game. **手に負えない** ▶事態はすでに手に負えなくなっている The situation *has* already *gotten out of hand*. ‖ この仕事は私の手に負えません This is *more*

of a job *than I can handle*. ／This is *too tough* a job *for* me.
手にする ▶初めて給料を手にしたときは本当にうれしかった I was extremely happy when I *received* my salary for the first time. ‖ ぜひ全国高校野球大会の優勝旗を手にしたい(＝で勝ちたい) We really *want to win* the All-Japan Inter High School Baseball Tournament. 手に手を取って ▶2人は手に手を取って新婚旅行に出発した The couple departed on their honeymoon *hand in hand*.
手に取る ▶きみの考えてることは手に取るようにわかる I *can read* you *like a book*. 手に入る ▶念願のマイホームがやっと手に入った We finally *got* the house which we had wanted for so long. ‖ そのシャツはいろんなサイズのものが手に入る The shirts are *available* in many sizes. ‖ 日本では一般の人には銃器はほとんど手に入らない In Japan, civilians can almost never *get their hands on* guns. (➤ get one's hands on は get のインフォーマルな言い方).
手の込んだ ▶手の込んだモザイク a *complex* mosaic ‖ 手の込んだ刺しゅう *elaborate* embroidery. 手も足も出ない ▶500万円なんて値段じゃ私には手も足も出ないわ It costs five million yen ? *There's no way* I can come up with that ! ‖ きょうの英語の試験は難しくて, 私には手も足も出なかった Today's English exam was *too difficult* for me. ／Today's English exam was a (real) *killer*. (➤ killer は「ひどく難しいもの」の意の俗語).
手もなく ▶その力士は横綱に手もなく押し出された The sumo wrestler was *easily* pushed out of the ring by the yokozuna.
手を上げる ▶どんなに腹が立っても子供に手を上げるな No matter how angry you are, (you should) never *strike* a child. ‖ 彼は自ら手を上げてこの部署に異動してきた He (was) transferred to this department at his own *request*. ‖ 田中は文化祭実行委員に手を上げた Tanaka *volunteered* to become a member of the school festival organizing committee.
手を入れる ▶リンダは私の英作文に手を入れてくれた Linda *revised* [*corrected*] my English composition. (➤ revise は「大幅修正する」, correct は「(ミスを)訂正する」).
手を打つ ▶早急に手を打たないとこの川の汚染は取り返しがつかないことになる Unless prompt *countermeasures are taken*, the contamination of this river will reach a critical point. (➤ countermeasure は「対策」) ‖ その車を50万円で引き取ってもらうことで手を打った We *closed a deal* [*struck a bargain*] to trade in the car for 500,000 yen. (➤「話がまとまった」の意) ‖ 組合は1％の賃上げで手を打たざるをえなかった The union had to *settle for* a one percent hike. (➤ settle for は「希望どおりではないが受け入れる」).
手を替え品を替え ▶店員は手を替え品を替えて彼女にその商品を売りつけようとした That salesperson tried *every possible means* to talk her into buying the product. (➤ talk A into doing は「A(人)に話をして…させる」.「A(人)に話をして…するのをやめさせる」は talk A out of doing).
手を切る ▶息子には暴力団と手を切ってほしい I wish my son would *cut off all relations* [*connections*] *with* that gang. ‖ 芳恵と手を切ってくれないか Will you *break up with* Yoshie ? (➤ break up は「(男女が)別れる」). 手を下す ▶彼は自分で手を下さずに子分の1人にその犯罪をやらせた He got one of his underlings to commit the crime *without actually dirtying his own hands*. 手を組む ▶わが社はP社と手を組んで新規事業を開始した Our company started a new business *in cooperation with* P Company.
手を染める ▶彼は貧困から犯罪に手を染めた He *became involved* in crime due to poverty. 手を出す ▶彼は会社の金に手を出した He *embezzled* the company's money. ‖ 店長は新しく入ってきた女の子にすぐ手を出そうと(＝くどこうと)する The store manager always *makes advances to* [*on*] new female employees. 手を抜く ▶仕事の手を抜くな Don't *do a sloppy job*.
手を引く ▶当行はS商事の経営から手を引くことにしました Our bank has decided to *withdraw from* [*pull out of*] the management of S Trading Company. 手を広げる ▶上田さんは商売の手を広げようとしているらしい I hear Ueda plans to *expand* his business.
手を結ぶ ▶日本は第二次世界大戦でドイツ・イタリアと手を結んだ(＝同盟した) Japan *allied* [*formed an alliance*] *with* Germany and Italy during World War II. 手を焼く ▶きみには本当に手を焼くよ You are a big *headache* (to me). (➤「頭痛の種だ」の意) ‖ わが家のいたずらっ子たちにはほとほと手を焼いている I really *have a lot of trouble controlling* [*handling*] our mischievous children. ‖ 暴走族には警察も手を焼いている The police *are having difficulty* (*in*) *handling* the hot rodders. (➤ have difficulty (in) doing で「…するのに苦労する」; in は省略することが多い).
☛ その手, 手取り足取り, 手に手に, 手のひら (→見出語)

-て **1**【意味の発展を示して】and ▶まず私が発表して, 次に木村君が意見を述べた First, I made a presentation, *and* then Mr. Kimura made some comments.
2【原因・理由を示して】▶きみと知り合えて本当によかったよ I'm really glad (that) I met you. (➤ that は通例省略する) ‖ 私は授業をサボって父に叱られた I was scolded by my father *for* cutting classes.
3【前述したことの反対を示して】but ▶彼女は遊びに来ると言って来なかった She said she would come and see me, *but* she didn't.
4【前述したことへの付加を示して】and ▶この本はおもしろくてためになる This book is interesting *and* instructive. ／This book is *not only* interesting *but* (*also*) instructive.

¹で 出 **1**【出かけること, 出具合】▶縁日は人の出が多かった There was a large *turnout* at the festival. ‖ こんろを掃除したらガスの**出が良くなった** The gas burner *has been working better* since I cleaned it. ‖ この急須は**出が悪い** This teapot *doesn't pour well*. ‖ 夕方になると時々水の**出が悪くなる** Sometimes in the evening the water *doesn't flow well*.
2【出入り】▶ドミンゴは舞台の袖で静かに出を待っていた Domingo was waiting calmly in the wings for *his turn* to go on stage.
3【出身】▶所長は学者の家の出だそうだ The director is said to *come from* an academic family. ‖ うちの会社の社員は皆**大学出**だ In our company everyone is *a college graduate*.

²で ▶で, そのときぎみは何をしてたの? *And* [*So*], what were you doing then? ‖ 対話「それっきり彼ったらひ

と言も口を利こうとしないの」「で，あなたはどうしたの？」 "After that, he wouldn't say a word." "*So*, what did you do ?"

-で

📖 訳語メニュー
場所 →in, at, on 1
時間 →at, in, on 2
手段, 方法 →by, in, on, with 3
原因, 理由 →with, from, of 4
原材料 →of, from 5
金額 →for, at 6
年齢 →at 7
基準 →with, at, by 8

1【場所や所属を示して】in, at, on

語法 (1)基本的には「その中で」を意識する場所や地域，または立体的な物や空間の内部を指すときは **in**，広がりの意識のない地点または番地を指すときは **at**，「…の上で」というように物に接している状態を示したり街路名を指したりするときは **on** を用いる．
(2)広い地域でも，ちょっと立ち寄ったり，そこを通過地点としたりするようなときには **at** を用いる．

▶レストランで食事をする eat *in* a restaurant ‖ 広小路2丁目ですし屋を経営する run a sushi restaurant *in* Hirokoji Ni-chome ‖ 凍った池でスケートをする skate *on* a frozen pond.
▶彼は島原市で生まれ育った He was born and raised *in* the City of Shimabara. ‖ 彼女はそのとき蔵王でスキーをしていた She was then skiing *at* Zao. ‖ 飛行機は羽田で給油した The plane refueled *at* Haneda. ‖ 神宮球場で決勝戦が行われた The final game was played *at* the Jingu Stadium. ‖ きみの家でギターを弾こう Let's play our guitars *at* your home.
▶山中湖畔でキャンプをした We camped *on* [*by*] Lake Yamanaka. (➤ on は「湖に接した岸辺で」, by は「岸近くで」).
▶ 対話「どこでアルバイトしてるの」「東西デパートです」 "*Where* is your part-time job ?" "*At* Tozai Department Store." (● 単に「デパートです」なら "*At* a department store." と言う).
▶青梅街道で事故があった A traffic accident occurred *on* Ome Avenue. ‖ 現在東海道線で10分の遅れが出ています Currently, Tokaido Line trains are running ten minutes late. (●「東海道線の列車が遅れている」と考える) ‖ 私はＮＴＴで働いています I work *for* NTT. ‖ この製品はうちの会社で開発したものだ This product was developed *by* our company.

2【時間を示して】at, in, on(➤ 時刻には at, 朝・昼・晩や月・年・季節などには in, 曜日や日付などには on を用いる) ▶きょうはお昼で授業を終わります I'll finish my classes *at* noon. ‖ あと2時間で津に着く We'll be arriving in Tsu *in* two hours. (➤ この in は「ある日時が経過すれば」の意を表す) ‖ このレポートは1週間で仕上がります I can finish this term paper *in* a week.
▶私は来月で［8月で］17歳になる I'll be seventeen years old *next month* [*in August*]. ‖ この定期券は8月12日で切れる This commutation pass expires *on* August 12.

3【手段・方法を示して】by, in, on, with

語法 (1)「…によって，…を使って」の意で手段・方法などを表すのが **by, in, on**. これらは by car, by phone, in cash, on TV など慣用句化したものが多く，あとにくる名詞は Ⓤ 扱い.
(2)「…を使って」の意で，何かを表現するときの材料・手段などを表すのが **in, with**. 後続の名詞は，in の場合は in ink のように Ⓤ 扱い，with の場合は with a pencil のように Ⓒ 扱いがふつう.

▶小切手［現金］で払う pay *by* check [*in* cash] ‖ 電話で話す talk *on* the telephone ‖ アメリカ大陸をバスで横断してみたい I'd like to go across the United States *by* bus [*on* a bus]. ‖ 品川駅まで車でお送りします I'll take you to Shinagawa Station *in* my car [*by* car]. (● (×)by my car とは言わない) / I'll drive you to Shinagawa Station. (➤ 後者のほうがふつう) ‖ テレビのニュースでその俳優が自殺したのを知った *On* the TV news I learned that the actor had killed himself. ‖ 商品のご注文はお電話でお申し込みください Please place your order *by* telephone.
▶入学願書は黒インクで［ボールペンで］記入してください Please fill out the application for admission *in* black ink [*with* a ballpoint (pen)]. ‖ 男は持っていたナイフで突然警官に襲いかかった The man suddenly attacked the police officer *with* a knife. ‖ 私たちは『さくらさくら』を英語で歌った We sang "Sakura, Sakura" *in* English. ‖ 田中のバントでランナーは二塁に進んだ The runner advanced to second *on* Tanaka's bunt. ‖ 人を見かけで判断するな Never judge people *by* appearances. ‖ 彼女は鉛筆削りで指を切った She cut her finger *on* a pencil sharpener. (● on を with にすると故意に切ったことになる) ‖ 私は新聞広告でその仕事を見つけた I found the job *through* a newspaper ad. ‖ 対話「何でこの教室のことを知りましたか」「雑誌の広告で知りました」 "*How* did you find out about this course ?" "*From* an advertisement in a magazine."

4【原因・理由を示して】with, from, of ▶母が肺炎で［過労で］入院した My mother was hospitalized *with* pneumonia [*from* overwork]. ‖ 心臓病［がん］で死ぬ人がますます多くなってきている More and more people are dying *of* heart disease [cancer]. ‖ 輝彦は病気で欠席している Teruhiko is absent (from school) *because of* sickness. ‖ その暴力団員は武器の不法所持で起訴された The gangster was prosecuted *for* illegal possession of a weapon. ‖ (群馬県の)高崎は観音様で有名です Takasaki is famous *for* its statue of Kannon. ‖ 彼女は交通事故で［スキーで］左足を骨折した She broke her left leg *in* a traffic accident [*while* skiing]. (➤ 後者は「スキーをしていて」) ‖ 強風で倉庫が倒れた The storehouse was toppled (over) *by* the strong wind. ‖ 大きな笑い声で中野さんだとすぐわかった I recognized Mr. Nakano instantly *by* his big laugh.

5【原材料を示して】of, from ▶この財布は本物の革でできている This wallet is made *of* genuine leather. ‖ バーボンウイスキーは最低51％のトウモロコシで作られる Bourbon whiskey is made *from* at least 51 percent corn. (● 材料の質や成分が変化する場合は from, しない場合は of を用いる) ‖ このアパートは鉄筋コンクリートでできている This apartment house is built *of* reinforced concrete.

6【金額を示して】for, at

> 語法「…円で買う[売る]」というときの「で」には代金・交換を表す **for** を用いる. 品物の単価や変動する物の価格を表す場合は **at** を用いる.

▶このテレビは4万円で買いました I bought this television *for* 40,000 yen. ‖ あの店ではジーパンを半値で[2割引きで]売っている They sell jeans *at* half (the) price [*at* twenty percent off] at that store. ‖ 1万円でお釣りはありますか Do you have change *for* 10,000 yen [a 10,000-yen bill]?

7【年齢を示して】at ▶おじは60歳で運転免許を取った My uncle obtained a driver's license *at* (the age of) sixty. ‖ 彼は10代で有名になった He became famous *in his teens*.

8【基準を示して】with (…をもって); **at** (…の速度[度合い]で); **by** (…ぎめで) ▶13勝2敗で横綱が優勝した The yokozuna won the sumo tournament *with* 13 wins and 2 losses. ‖ この列車は時速300キロで走ります This train travels *at* 300 kilometers per [an] hour. ‖ パートの方には週給でお支払いします Part-timers are paid *by the week*.

9【動作・作用が行われる様態・条件を示して】▶お客さまには笑顔で接しなさい You should greet our customers *with* a smile. ‖ 強盗たちはその金を3人で山分けした The robbers divided the money *among* the three of them. ‖ 記者は興奮した口調で飛行機墜落のニュースを伝えた The reporter *excitedly* reported the news of the airplane crash.

10【語・文を接続して】and ▶北海道は広大で, その上変化に富んでいる Hokkaido is diverse *as well as* vast. ‖ 彼, ハンサムで, 背もとっても高いのよ My boyfriend is handsome *and* very tall.

11【話題・論題を示して】about, on (➤ 前者は一般的内容, 後者は専門的内容) ▶いろいろなテーマで話す talk *about* [*on*] various subjects ‖『恒久平和の条件』という題で論文を書く write an essay *on* [*entitled*] "Conditions of an enduring peace" ‖ その件であすもう一度話し合おう Let's talk *about* it again tomorrow.

であい 出会い an **encounter**, a **meeting** (➤ 前者のほうが偶然の感じが強い) ▶それは運命の出会いだった It was a fateful *encounter*. ‖ 聖書[山田先生]との出会いが私の生き方を変えた My *encounter* with the Bible [Mr. Yamada] changed my life. ‖ 人生にはさまざまな出会いがあり, 別れがある Life is full of *meetings* and partings.

であいがしら 出会い頭 ▶2人の生徒は出会い頭にぶつかった The two students bumped into each other *at the corner*.

であいけい 出会い系 ‖**出会い系喫茶** a dating cafe ‖ **出会い系サイト** an online dating site.

であう 出会う **meet** (+目) (初めて会う); **come across, run across, run into** (➤ いずれも偶然に) ▶彼女には3年前に福岡で初めて出会った I first *met* [*came across*] her in Fukuoka three years ago. ‖ きのう偶然昔の友人に出会った I *ran into* [*happened to meet*] an old friend yesterday. ‖ 意味のわからない単語に出会ったら必ず意味の見当をつけ, 辞書を引きなさい Whenever you *come across* a word you do not understand, guess the meaning and look it up in a dictionary.

てあか 手垢 ▶その日記帳は手あかで汚れていた The diary was stained with *finger marks*. ‖ 手あかのついた(=使い古された)表現 a *trite* [*hackneyed*] expression.

てあし 手足 **hands and feet**; **arms and legs** (腕と脚); **limbs** /lɪmz/ (四肢) ▶警備員は手足を縛られていた The guard was tied *hand and foot*. (➤ 熟語として単数形で用いる) ‖ 彼は手足が不自由だ He *has trouble using his hands and legs*.
▶《慣用表現》兄は病気の父の手足となって(=に代わって)働いている My (older) brother is working *in place of* my sick father. ‖ この秘書は長年代議士の手足となって働いてきた This secretary has been working for the Diet politician *as a close competent assistant* for a long time. (➤「身近にいる有能な援助者として」の意).

であし 出足 a **turnout** (人出); a **start** (滑り出し) ▶投票者の出足がよい[鈍い] There is quite a good [slow] *turnout* at the polls. ‖ 新しい支店の客の出足は好調だ We have a good number of customers *coming* to our new branch store. ‖ この車は出足がいい This car has *a very rapid pick-up* [*initial acceleration*].

てあたりしだい 手当たり次第に **at random** ▶私は手当たりしだいに推理小説を読んだ I read detective stories *at random*. ‖ 悔しさのあまり, 彼女は夫に本や雑誌を手当たりしだい投げつけた In her frustration, she threw *every* book and magazine *in sight* [*whatever* books and magazines *she could find*] at her husband.

てあつい 手厚い **warm** (温かい); **cordial** (心からの); **utmost** (この上ない) ▶負傷者は病院で手厚い看護を受けた The injured were nursed in the hospital with the *utmost* care. ‖ 我々はチベットで手厚いもてなしを受けた We were received *cordially* [*warmly*] in Tibet. ‖ 戦場に散ったその若き兵士は手厚く葬られた The young soldier who was killed on the battlefield was buried *with* (*the utmost*) *respect*.

てあて 手当(て) **1【治療】**(a) **medical treatment** [**care**] **一動 手当てする treat** +目 ▶けが人に応急手当てを施す give the injured *first aid* (*treatment*) ‖ 私は診療所でやけどの手当てをしてもらった I *had* my burn *treated* [*attended to*] at the clinic.

2【プラスの賃金】benefits, an **allowance** /əláʊəns/ ▶基本給のほかにどんな手当がつきますか What *allowances* do we receive besides base pay?
‖**家族手当** family benefits ‖ **危険手当** an allowance for hazardous work, 《米》danger pay, 《英》danger money ‖ **失業手当** unemployment benefits ‖ **児童手当** a child allowance ‖ **住宅手当** a housing allowance ‖ **退職手当** retirement benefits (定年による); severance pay (失業による) ‖ **超過勤務手当** overtime pay.

てあみ 手編みの **hand-knit(ted)** ▶手編みのセーター a *hand-knit*(*ted*) sweater ‖ 対話「そのセーター, 手編み?」「ううん, 機械編みよ」"Is your sweater *hand-knitted*?" "No, it's machine-knitted."

てあら 手荒な **rough** /rʌf/ ▶手荒なまねはよせ Don't *play rough with* him [her]. ‖ 彼女は誘拐犯に手荒な扱いを受けた She was treated *roughly* by the kidnapper.

てあらい 手洗い ▶セーターを手洗いした I *washed* my sweater *by hand*. ‖ 家族のみんなが頻繁に手洗いを励行するようにした I made regular *hand washing* a rule for everyone in my family. ‖ 正しい方法で手洗いをすることが, 最も効果的な風邪予防法だ *Washing your hands* properly is the most effective way to prevent colds. ☞ **お手洗い** (→見出語)

であるく 出歩く go out ; wander around (ぶらぶらする) ▶知美は一郎と日曜ごとに出歩く Tomomi *goes out* with Ichiro every Sunday. (➤ go out には「(男女が)定期的に交際をしている」というニュアンスがある ; ⇀交際) ‖この一帯は物騒なので1人で出歩かないように Since this area is not safe, please do not *wander around* [*about*] alone. ‖彼は友だちと遅くまで出歩いていた He *stayed out* late with his friends. (➤ stay out は「夜遅くまで外出している」).

てい 体 ▶体のいい言い訳 a *glib* excuse ‖彼がどう言おうとも, それは体のいい押し売りだよ(＝押し売りにほかならない) Whatever he may say, it's *nothing but* a hard sell.

てい- 低- ▶低価格 a *low* price ‖低所得 (a) *low* income ‖低賃金 *low* pay [wages] ‖低年齢層 people in the *lower* age group [bracket] ‖日本経済の低成長 the *slow growth* of the Japanese economy.

-てい -邸 one's residence ▶私は斎藤邸に案内された I was escorted [shown] to Mr. Saito's *residence*.

ティアラ a tiara.

ていあん 提案 a proposal ; a suggestion (控えめな) ━動 提案する propose ＋目, suggest ＋目 ▶彼の提案は一考の価値がある His *proposal* is worth considering. ‖母の提案で尾道で途中下車した We made a stopover at Onomichi at my mother's *suggestion*.

> 【文型】
> …しようと提案する
> propose [suggest] doing
> A が…するように提案する
> propose that A (should) do
> suggest that A (should) do
> 《解説》あとの2つの表現の場合,《米》ではふつう should のない原形を用いる.

▶彼女はほかの何人かの生徒に手伝ってもらうことを提案した She *proposed* get*ting* [*proposed* to get] some other students to help us. ‖私は地震被災者のために募金活動を行おうと提案した I *proposed* [*suggested*] *that* we (*should*) conduct a fund-raising campaign for the earthquake victims. ‖提案者 a proposer.

ティー 1【茶】(a) tea (➤ 種類や杯数をいうときは数えられる). ‖ティーカップ a teacup ‖ティーバッグ a tea bag ‖ティーポット a teapot ‖ティールーム a tearoom.
2【ゴルフの】a tee.

ディーエヌエー 《生化学》DNA (➤ deoxyribonucleic acid (デオキシリボ核酸)の略) ‖DNA 鑑定 DNA testing (手法) ; a DNA test (1回1回の鑑定) 《参考》「遺骨を DNA 鑑定する」は run DNA tests on the remains のようにいう ‖DNA サンプル a DNA sample ‖DNA 配列 a DNA sequence.

ディーエム direct mail (➤ DM は日本式略語で英語では用いない) ⇀ダイレクトメール ▶DMを送る send *direct mail*.

ディーケー ▶3DKのマンション a three-room apartment [《英》flat] with a kitchen-dining room. ⇀エルディーケー.

ディージェー a DJ ▶人気DJ a popular *DJ*. ⇀ディスクジョッキー.

ティーシャツ Tシャツ a T-shirt, a tee shirt ▶彼女はTシャツにジーパンという格好でやって来た She came wearing *a T-shirt* and jeans.

ティーじょうぎ T定規 a T square.

ティーじろ T字路 a T-junction [-intersection], a tee ▶そこのT字路を右に曲がってください Please turn right at the *T-junction*.

ディーゼル ‖ディーゼルエンジン a diesel engine ‖ディーゼルカー a diesel (car) ‖ディーゼル機関車 a diesel locomotive.

ていいち 定位置 a fixed position.

ティーバック Tバック ▶Tバックのビキニ a *thong* bikini.

ティーピーオー the occasion (場合, 場面) (➤ TPO は time (時間), place (場所), occasion (場合)の頭文字を取った日本式の略語) ▶TPOに応じた服装をすることが大切だ It's important to dress to suit *the occasion*.

ディーブイ DV (家庭内暴力) (➤ domestic violence の略だが, 英語では略さずに言うのがふつう).

ディーブイディー DVD (➤ digital versatile [video] disc の略) ▶DVDを掛ける play a *DVD* ‖データをDVDに蓄積する store data on a *DVD*.

ディーラー a dealer ▶車のディーラー a car [an auto (mobile)] *dealer*.

ていいん 定員 (a) capacity (収容能力) ; the total number 《of》 (総数) ▶この映画館は定員300名です This movie theater has *a* (*seating*) *capacity* of 300. ／This movie theater *seats* 300 (people). (➤この seat は「…人分の席がある」の意 ; 堅い表現では can accommodate ともいえる) ‖入場者はまだ定員に達していない The attendance has not reached *capacity* yet. ‖このバスの定員は何名ですか What is the (*seating*) *capacity* of this bus ? ／What's *the total number of passengers* on this bus ? ‖このエレベーターの定員は10人だ This elevator *can hold* ten people. (➤「収容できる」の意).
▶ヨーロッパツアーへの応募者はすでに定員を超過している The number of applicants for the package tour of Europe has already *exceeded the limit*. ‖そのコースは定員を超過した The course *was over-enrolled*. ‖警察の調べでその船は定員以上の客を乗せていたことが判明した The police investigation brought to light that the ship *had been overloaded* with passengers. ‖あの短期大学は定員割れになった That junior college *was underenrolled* [*failed to fill its enrollment quota*].
‖収容定員 an admission capacity.

ティーンエージャー a teenager, a teen ▶ティーンエージャーの息子 my *teenage* son ‖このテレビ番組はティーンエージャーに人気がある This TV program is popular among *teenagers* [*teens*].

> **危ないカタカナ語✹ ティーンエージャー**
> 1 日本では「ティーンエージャー」は漠然と十代の若者を指すものと思われているようだが, 英語の teenager は13歳から19歳の人のこと. すなわち, thirteen から nineteen までの -teen で終わる年齢層に限られる.
> 2 8歳から12歳の子供を tween ('tween ともつづる)ということがあり, 消費者層として認知され, マーケティングで使われ始めた語.
> 3 また, 10歳から12歳くらいまでを preteen(ager) や subteen といい, 13歳から15歳くらいを one's early teens, 16歳から19歳くらいをone's late teens という.
> 4 日本語のように「ローティーン」「ハイティーン」とはあまりいわない.

て

ていえん 庭園 a **garden** ▶日本庭園 a Japanese *garden*.

ていおう 帝王 an **emperor**（皇帝）; a **monarch** /mánəˈk/（君主）, a **king**（王）▶暗黒街の帝王 a gangland *kingpin*.（➤この kingpin は「中心人物, 親玉」の意）.
▶うちの2番目の子は**帝王切開**で産まれた Our second child was delivered by *Caesarean* (*section*).（➤発音は /sɪzéəriən/）‖彼女は**帝王切開**で子供を産んだ She had her baby *by Caesarean* (*section*). / She had *a Caesarean*.（➤後者は「帝王切開をした」の意）.

て

ていおうがく 帝王学 ▶皇太子に**帝王学**を授ける *groom* the Crown Prince *to be Emperor* ‖先代の社長は息子に**帝王学**を学ばせた The former president *groomed* his son *to be company president* [*to take over the company*]. / The former president *taught* his son (*lessons on*) *how to be a good company president*.

1**ていおん 低音** a **low voice** [**tone**], a **low-pitched sound**; **bass** /beɪs/（音楽の）▶彼は**低音**の魅力で有名だ He is famous for his charming *low* [*deep*] *voice*.

2**ていおん 低温** a **low temperature** ▶ことしの夏は異常な**低温**だった This summer (*the*) *temperatures have been* unusually *low*.

1**ていか 低下** a **drop**; a **decline**（衰え）**一動 低下する drop**（不意に）; **fall**（高い所から落ちる）; **decline**（衰える）▶気温は海抜が高くなるにつれて**低下する** The temperature *drops* [*falls* / *goes down*] as the elevation increases. ‖大学生の学力は年々**低下してきている**と言われる It is said that the academic level of university students *is declining* year by year. ‖高校に入ったら急に視力が**低下した** When I entered high school, my eyesight suddenly *worsened*.（➤「悪くなった」の意）‖厚着は病気に対する抵抗力を**低下させる** Dressing too warmly will *lower* your resistance to disease.

2**ていか 定価** a **fixed** [**set**] **price**; a **list price**（表示価格）▶**定価**の2割引きにしておきましょう We will give you a 20 percent off the *list price*. / We will give you a 20 percent discount.（🔘2文目では「定価の」は含意されている）.

1**ていがく 停学** (a) **suspension from school** ▶彼は1週間の**停学処分**を受けた He *was suspended from school* for a week. / He *was given* a week's *suspension from school*.

2**ていがく 定額** ‖**定額制** flat rate ‖**定額プラン** a flat-rate plan, a fixed rate plan.

3**ていがく 低額** a **small sum** (**of money**)
‖**低額所得者** a person with a small income.

ていがくねん 低学年 the lower grades ▶このお話は**低学年**向きに書き直してある This story is rewritten for *the lower grades*.

ていかん 諦観 resignation（諦め）▶人生を**諦観する** *resign oneself* to one's present way of life [lifestyle].

ていかんし 定冠詞《文法》a **definite article**.

1**ていき 定期の regular**（規則的な）; **periodic**(**al**)（周期的な, 決まった間隔を置く）▶歯の健康を保つためには**定期的**に歯科医の検診を受けるのがよい You should have a dental checkup *regularly* [*on a regular basis* / *periodically*] in order to keep your teeth in good condition. / To keep your teeth healthy, have a *regular* [*periodic*] dental checkup. ‖雑誌を**定期購読する** *take* [*subscribe to*] a magazine（🔘「定期」は特にいわなくてもよい）‖あすから**定期試験**が始まる Our *regular exams* begin tomorrow. ‖そこへの（飛行機の）**定期便**はありますか Is there *a scheduled* [*regular*] *flight* there?
‖**定期入れ** a pass holder ‖**定期演奏会** a regular concert ‖**定期刊行物** a periodical ‖**定期券**《米》a commuter pass [ticket], a season ticket [pass],《英・インフォーマル》a season; a train pass（電車の）; a bus pass（バスの）《参考》pass は駅員に提示するもので, いずれの場合も日常的には a monthly [weekly] pass のような言い方をすることも多い ‖**定期検診** a regular [periodic] medical checkup ‖**定期船** a liner ‖**定期預金** a time [fixed] deposit.

2**ていき 提起する bring up** ▶彼は重要な問題を**提起した** He *brought up* an important issue.

ていぎ 定義 a **definition 一動 定義する define** +目 ▶この辞書は「イエスマン」を「雇い主・指導者などの意見に常に同意する人」と**定義している** This dictionary *defines* the (word) 'yes-man' as 'a person who always agrees with his [her] employer, leader, etc.'

ていきあつ 低気圧 a **low** (**atmospheric**) **pressure** ▶《比喩的》父さんはきょうは**低気圧**だから話しかけないほうがいいよ Dad is *in a bad mood* [is *out of sorts*] today, so you'd better not speak to him.

ていきゅう 低級な low-class; **vulgar**（低俗な）; **cheap**（安っぽい）; **low-minded**（低俗なことに関心をもつ）▶**低級な**雑誌 a *vulgar* [*cheap*] magazine ‖きみたちの**低級な**おしゃべりにはへきえきするよ I am absolutely disgusted at your *low-minded* conversation.

ていきゅうび 定休日 a **regular holiday**, a **regular day off**（店の）▶Sデパートは水曜日が**定休日です** S Department Store *is closed* on Wednesdays.（➤on Wednesdays は「毎週水曜日に」のニュアンス）.

ていきょう 提供 an **offer 一動 提供する give** +目, **provide** +目, **offer** +目 ▶この雑誌はファッションの最新情報を**提供してくれる** This magazine *gives* the latest fashion information. ‖その機密情報を**提供して**くだされば100万円差し上げましょう We'll give you a million yen if you *provide* us *with* that secret information.（➤provide A with B で「AにBを提供する」）‖彼は親切にも自分の豪邸を次のダンスパーティーの会場に**提供しようと申し出てくれた** He has kindly *offered the use* of his luxurious mansion for the next dance party.
▶この番組はN生命保険会社の**提供**でお送りしました This program *has been brought to you* [*has been sponsored* / *has been presented*] *by* N Life Insurance Company.
‖（臓器の）**提供者** a donor（➤「（臓器の）被移植者」は donee /dòuníː/）.

テイクアウェイ →テイクアウト.

テイクアウト《米》a **takeout**,《英また》a **takeaway**（➤両者ともに「持ち帰り用の料理（店）」の意）▶テイクアウトのピザを注文する order a *takeout* pizza →持ち帰り.

ていくう 低空 a **low altitude** ▶住民は夜間の**低空飛行**に抗議した The residents protested against *low-altitude* night *flights*.

ディクテーション (a) **dictation** ▶英語のディクテーション (an) English *dictation*.

デイケア day care
‖**デイケアセンター** a day-care center.

1**ていけい 提携 cooperation**（協力）; a **tie-up**（業務上・

技術上の） **一動 提携する** cooperate /kouá:pərèɪt/《with》, tie up《with》▶当社はB社と**提携して**この薬品を開発した We developed this drug *in cooperation with* B Company. ‖ 当社はT社と**技術提携して**いる We *have a technical tie-up* [We *are in technical cooperation*] *with* T Company.

‖**提携先** a business partner.

2**ていけい 定形** a **standard** [**regular**] **size**（標準の大きさ）

‖**定形封筒** a standard size(d) envelope ‖ **定形郵便物** standard size(d) mail（➤ 1つ1つは a piece of standard size(d) mail や a standard size(d) letter).

ていけいし 定型詩 **fixed form poetry** [**verse**]（➤「自由詩」は free form poetry [verse]).

ていけつ 締結 (a) **conclusion** **一動 締結する** **conclude** +目 ▶平和条約を**締結する** *conclude* a peace treaty.

ていけつあつ 低血圧 **low blood pressure.**

ていけん 定見 ▶**定見**の無い人 a person without *definite* [*firm*] *views* / a person without *a guiding philosophy*.

ていげん 提言 a **proposal**（積極的な）; a **suggestion**（控えめな） →**提案** ▶組織の改革を**提言する** *put forward a proposal* that the organization (should) be reformed.

ていこう 抵抗 **1**【逆らうこと】**opposition**; (a) **resistance**（敵がい心をもった積極的な） **一動 抵抗する** **oppose**（+目）, **resist**（+目）▶工場労働者は産業ロボットの導入に強い**抵抗**を示した Factory workers showed strong *opposition* [*resistance*] to the introduction of industrial robots. ‖ 敵はあくまで**抵抗する**だろう The enemy will *resist* to the bitter end. ‖ マレーネ・ディートリヒはナチスに徹底的に**抵抗した** Marlene Dietrich consistently *resisted* [*opposed*] the Nazis. ‖ 無駄な**抵抗**はやめろ! It's no use *resisting*!（➤「無駄な抵抗をする」を fight a losing battle（文字どおりには「負け戦をする」）という） ‖ 健康な肉体は細菌や病気に対する**抵抗力**が強い A healthy body has great *resistance* to germs and disease(s).

2【違和感】▶ああいう物の言い方には**抵抗がある**ね That way of speaking *puts me off*.（➤ put ... off は「…を不快にする」） ‖ 若い女性の中には下着のような服で外出することに**抵抗がない**人もいるようだ Some young women seem to *have no qualms* about going out wearing underwear-like clothes.（➤ qualm /kwɑ:m/ は「ためらい」).

3【物理的な】**resistance** ▶電気**抵抗** electric *resistance* ‖ この車は空気の**抵抗**を減らすために流線型にしてある This car is streamlined to reduce *air resistance*.

☛ **無抵抗**（→見出語）

1**ていこく 定刻** **the appointed time**（指定の時刻）▶**定刻**までにお集まりください Please be here by *the appointed time*. ‖ 生徒総会は**定刻**に始まった The general students' meeting started *as scheduled* [*on time*]. ‖ そろそろ会議を始めましょうか. **定刻を過ぎて**いますし Shall we begin the meeting now? We are already running *behind schedule*. ‖ 彼女は**定刻**に5分遅れて[**定刻**5分前に]到着した She arrived five minutes *behind* [*ahead of*] *schedule*. ‖（飛行機の）305便は**定刻**どおりですか Is Flight 305 (flying) *on schedule*?

2**ていこく 帝国** an **empire** /émpaɪəʳ/ ▶395年頃ローマ**帝国**は2つに分裂した Around AD 395, *the Roman Empire* split (into two).

‖**帝国主義** imperialism /ɪmpíəriəlìzəm/ ‖ **帝国主義者** an imperialist ‖ **反帝国主義** anti-imperialism.

ていさい 体裁 (an) **appearance**（外見）; (a) **show**（見せかけ）▶**体裁**よりも実用性を重んじる consider practicality more important than *appearance* ‖ **体裁**を繕う keep up *appearances* ‖ 野田教授は**体裁**を気にしない Professor Noda doesn't care about his *appearance* [*what he looks like*]. ‖ そのスーツなら**体裁が悪くない**わ I think you *look quite presentable* [*decent*] in that suit. ‖ 彼の読書は**体裁だけ**のようだ He seems to read books *only for show*. ‖ ネクタイをしていないのは私だけだったので**体裁が悪かった** I *felt awkward* because I was the only person that had no tie on.（➤「気まずかった」の意).

ていさつ 偵察 **scouting** /skáʊṭɪŋ/, **reconnaissance** /rɪká:nəzəns/（➤ 後者は軍事用語） **一動 偵察する** **scout**（+目）, **reconnoiter** /rì:kənɔ́ɪṭəʳ/（+目）▶**偵察**に出かける go *scouting* ‖（国境を）**偵察してこい** Go *reconnoiter* (the border).

‖**偵察衛星** a reconnaissance satellite ‖ **偵察機** a reconnaissance [scout] plane ‖ **偵察飛行** a reconnaissance flight ‖ **無人偵察機** a reconnaissance drone.

ていし 停止 a **stop**; **suspension**（一時的な） **一動 停止する** **stop**, **suspend** ▶軍事活動の一時**停止** a temporary *suspension* of military activities ‖ バスは踏切で**一時停止した** The bus *came to a brief stop* at the railroad crossing. ‖ 飛行機が**完全に停止する**まで席を立たないでください Please remain seated until the plane *comes to a complete stop*. ‖ このビルは資金難で建築工事が**停止している** The construction of this building *is* now *stopped* [*is at a standstill*] because of a lack of funds.

▶彼は交通違反を犯して運転免許が90日**停止になった** Due to a traffic violation, his driver's license *was suspended* for 90 days. ‖ 工事のため体育館の**使用が停止になった** The gym *was* (temporarily) *closed* because of construction work. ‖ その選手は相手投手を殴って1週間の**出場停止になった** The player *was suspended from play* for a week after hitting the other team's pitcher.

‖**停止信号** a stoplight ‖（交差点などの）**停止線** an intersection line ‖（音楽プレーヤーなどの）**一時停止ボタン** a pause button ‖ **営業停止処分** a penalty shut-up, (a) suspension of business (as a penalty).

1**ていじ 定時** ▶私は毎日**定時**に（＝決まった時間に）退社する I leave the office *at a regular* [*fixed*] *time* every day. ‖ 列車は**定時**に（＝時間どおりに）到着した The train arrived *on time* [*on schedule*].

2**ていじ 提示する** **show** +目; **produce** +目（取り出して）; **present** +目（差し出す）▶構内に入るときは学生証を**提示してください** Please *show* [*present*] your student identification card when you enter the campus. ‖ 彼は身分証明書を**提示した** He *produced* his ID card.

デイジー《植物》a **daisy.**

ていしせい 低姿勢 ▶市長は陳情団に対して**低姿勢**で応対した The mayor adopted *a modest attitude* toward the group of lobbyists. ‖ 部長はきょうは低気圧だから, **低姿勢**でいったほうがよさそうだ The general manager has been in a bad mood today, so you'd better *keep a low profile*.（➤ low profile

て

/próʊfaɪl/ は「目立たない態度」).

ていじせい 定時制 ▶彼は定時制高校に通っている He attends *high school evening classes*.

ていしぼう 低脂肪の low-fat

‖低脂肪乳 low-fat milk.

ていしゃ 停車 a stop ; a halt(一時的な ; 堅い語) ━ 動 停車する stop, halt ▶車は停車した The car *came to a stop* [*a halt*]. ／The car *stopped* [*halted*]. ‖彼は車を停車させた He *brought* his car *to a stop* [*a halt*].

‖この列車は仙台で3分間停車します This train will *make a* three-minute *stop* at Sendai. ‖次の停車駅は福井です The next *stop* is Fukui. ‖3番線に停車中の電車は軽井沢行きです The train (*waiting* ／ *standing*) on Track No.3 is bound for Karuizawa. ‖《掲示》停車禁止 No Standing [Stopping].

☛ 各駅(停車), 急停車 (→見出語)

て

ていしゅ 亭主 one's husband, one's hubby /hʌ́bi/ (➤後者は「ハズ」に近いインフォーマルな語) ▶うちの亭主は働き者なのでありがたい I'm thankful for my *husband* because he works hard. ‖うちの主人は亭主関白です My husband is *the boss* in our family. ／My husband *rules the roost* [*wears the pants* ／ *wears the trousers*] in our house. (➤ rule the roost は「止まり木を支配する」, wear the pants [《主に英》 trousers] は「ズボンをはく」が原義).

ていしゅう 定収 a steady income ▶彼は会社を辞めてからは定収が無い He hasn't had *a steady income* since he quit the company.

ていじゅう 定住する settle down ▶定年後はスペインに定住することにしました I decided I would *settle down* [*live permanently*] in Spain after retirement.

ていしゅうは 低周波 《電気》 low frequency

‖低周波ノイズ low-frequency noise.

ていしゅく 貞淑な chaste ▶貞淑な妻 a *chaste* wife ／a wife who *is faithful to* her husband.

ていしゅつ 提出 submission ━ 動 提出する submit +目 ; turn [hand] in (レポートなどを) ▶辞表を提出する *submit* one's resignation ‖レポートは最後の授業のときに提出してください Please *turn in* [*hand in*] your papers to me at the last class. ‖願書の提出は今月末日までにお願いします *Applications should be submitted* [*filed* (*in*)] by the last day of this month. (➤ file (in) は「(願書・訴えなどを)公的な場所に出す」) ‖あすがレポートの提出期限だ The papers *are due* tomorrow. (➤ due は「期限になって」の意).

ていしょう 提唱する advocate /ǽdvəkeɪt/ +目 (公に主張する) ; propose +目 (提案する) ▶ラマーズ法を提唱する *advocate* the Lamaze method ‖PLOに新しい和平交渉を始めるよう提唱する *propose* that the PLO (should) begin a new round of peace talks.

‖提唱者 an advocate /ǽdvəkət/, a proposer.

1ていしょく 定職 a regular [steady ／ permanent] job ▶さくらは兄が定職に就くことを望んでいる Sakura wants her brother to have *a regular* [*steady* ／ *permanent*] *job*.

2ていしょく 定食 a set meal 《解説》高級レストランなどで出されるものは a table d'hôte /tɑ̀:bəl dóʊt/ (meal) とか a meal from the table d'hôte menu などというが, 一般食堂の定食は a set meal, a dinner [lunch] set, a meal from the set menu のようにいう ▶この定食にはコーヒーがつく This *set meal* comes with a cup of coffee. ‖私はA定食を注文した I ordered the *dinner set* A.

3ていしょく 抵触 ▶法に抵触する行為 an act that *is against* [*contrary to*] *the law* ／an *unlawful* act.

4ていしょく 停職 ▶そのニュースキャスターは不穏当な発言で1か月の停職になった The newscaster *was suspended from work* for one month for making an improper remark.

でいすい 泥酔する get dead drunk →べろんべろん ▶そのサラリーマンは泥酔して公園で一夜を明かした The office worker *got dead drunk* and spent the night in a park.

ていすう 定数 a fixed number(決まった数) ; a quota /kwóʊţə/ (定員) ; a quorum /kwɔ́:rəm/ (定足数) ; a constant(常数) ▶定数に達するまでにあと5人必要です We need five more people in order to meet [fill] the *quota* [*quorum*].

‖重力定数 the gravitational constant.

ディスカウント a discount /dískaʊnt/

‖ディスカウントストア[ショップ] a discount store [《英》 shop] ‖ディスカウントセール a discount sale.

ディスカッション a discussion ▶パネルディスカッションを行う hold a *panel discussion* ‖食の安全についてクラスでディスカッションをした We *had a discussion* on food safety in class. ‖彼女はクラスのディスカッションには積極的に参加する She participates actively in class *discussions*.

ディスク a disc, a disk 《参考》ともに円盤状の物を指し, ときに混用されるが, 通例 disc はコンパクト・ディスク (compact disc) や MD (MiniDisc ; 商標名), DVD (digital versatile [video] disc) など光ディスク (optical disk) に, disk はフロッピー・ディスク (floppy disk) やコンピュータのハードディスク (hard disk) などの磁気ディスクに用いられる.

ディスクジョッキー a disc [disk] jockey, a DJ, 《インフォーマル》 a deejay(➤いずれも人を指す) ▶レーガン氏は昔ディスクジョッキーをやっていた Mr. Reagan used to be *a DJ*.

ディスクロージャー disclosure(情報の公開).

ディスコ a disco, a discotheque /dískətek/.

ディスコグラフィー a discography.

ディズニーランド Disneyland(アメリカ, ロサンゼルス郊外にある遊園地).

ディスプレー a display ; a monitor(モニター)

‖液晶ディスプレー a liquid crystal display 《略 LCD》 ‖カラーディスプレー a color display.

ディスポーザー a disposer.

ていする 呈する present /prɪzént/ +目 ▶汚職事件は更に複雑な様相を呈してきた The corruption scandal *has presented* a further complication. ‖きみに1つ苦言を呈したい *Let me give* you a piece [bit] of candid advice.

1ていせい 訂正 (a) correction ━ 動 訂正する correct +目 ▶きみの報告書はだいぶ訂正の必要がある Your report needs a lot of *corrections*. ／Your report needs to *be corrected* in many places. ‖話の中でもし私の言うことが間違っていたら訂正してください Please *correct* me if I make any error in my speech. ‖《試験問題の設問文で》もし誤りがあれば訂正しなさい *Correct* errors, if any.

‖訂正記事 a correction.

2ていせい 帝政 imperial government ; czarism /zɑ́:rɪzəm/ (旧ロシアの)

‖帝政ロシア Czarist Russia.

ていせいぶんせき 定性分析《化学》**qualitative analysis.**

[1]**ていせつ 定説** an **established theory**(確立した学説など); a **widely accepted theory** (一般に受け入れられた説) ▶定説を覆す overturn *an established theory* ‖ たばこが健康に悪影響を及ぼすというのは定説になっている It'*s widely accepted* that smoking is bad for the health.

[2]**ていせつ 貞節** **fidelity**《to》 一形 (…に)貞節な **faithful**《to》.

ていせん 停戦 a **cease-fire** ▶停戦交渉 a *cease-fire* negotiation ‖ 停戦協定を結ぶ[守る] conclude [abide by] *a cease-fire agreement*.

ていそ 提訴する **take ... to court, bring ... before the court**(裁判に掛ける); **sue** +目, **file a suit**(告訴する) ▶彼らはその事件を金沢地裁に提訴した They *took* the case *to* [*brought* the case *before*] the Kanazawa District *Court*.

ていそう 貞操 **chastity** ▶貞操を奪われる lose one's *chastity* ‖ 貞操を守る remain *chaste* ‖ 彼女は貞操観念が強い She has high standards of *sexual morality*.

ていそく 低速 **low speed** ▶低速走行車は左の車線へ Cars traveling at *low speed* should use the left lane.

ていぞく 低俗な **vulgar**; **low**(卑しい, 下品な); **lowbrow**(ミーハー族向きの) ▶低俗な雑誌 a *vulgar* magazine ‖ 低俗な趣味 *low* tastes ‖ 低俗な番組 a *vulgar* [*lowbrow*] program ‖ 彼の好みは低俗だ He has *bad* taste.

[1]**ていたい 停滞** ▶景気が停滞している Business is *stagnant* [*sluggish*]. ‖ 梅雨前線は依然として日本の南岸に停滞している A rain front is still *hanging* [*hovering*] *over* the southern coast of Japan.

[2]**ていたい 手痛い** ▶支店長の急死は我々全員にとって手痛い打撃であった The branch manager's sudden death was *a serious blow* to us all. ‖ 5回にショートの手痛いエラーが出た The shortstop made a *costly* error in the fifth inning. (●「高くつく」と考える).

ていたく 邸宅 a **residence**(立派な家); a **mansion**(大邸宅) 《参考》英語の mansion は城のような「大邸宅」を指し, 日本語の「マンション」とは異なることに注意. →マンション.

ていたらく 体たらく ▶何という体たらくだ What *a sad state* (*of affairs*)! ／What *a sorry sight*!

でいたん 泥炭 **peat.**

ていち 低地 a **lowland** (**area**) ▶低地は水が出やすい *Lowlands* are prone to floods.

ていちあみ 定置網 a **fixed shore net.**

ていちゃく 定着する **take root**(根を下ろす) ▶散骨の習慣は日本には定着しないだろう The custom of scattering ashes probably wo*n't take root* [*won't become established*] in Japan. ‖ 携帯電話は我々の日常生活に定着した Cellphones have become a part of our daily lives. ‖ 文法的には誤りだがその言い方は定着した Though grammatically incorrect, that expression *is firmly established* [*is here to stay*].

[1]**ていちょう 丁重な** **polite, courteous** /kə́ːʳtiəs/ (➤ 後者のほうが丁寧度が高い); **hospitable**(手厚い) ▶丁重な話し方 a *polite* way of speaking ‖ 彼らはそのホテルで丁重なもてなしを受けた They were treated *courteously* [*hospitably*] at the hotel. ‖ 我々は彼女を丁重にもてなした We *gave* her *the red-carpet treatment*. ‖ 彼女は彼の結婚の申し込みを丁重に断った She *politely* declined his proposal of marriage. ‖ 事故の犠牲者は丁重に葬られた Those who had been killed in the accident were buried *with reverence*.

[2]**ていちょう 低調** ▶我々の商売は夏場は低調だ Our business *is* usually *slack* during the summer months. (➤ slack /slæk/ は「(景気などが)低迷した, 停滞した」の意) ‖ 最近の美術展の応募作品は全般に低調だ(＝質が落ちている) These days the *quality* of entries to art exhibitions *has fallen off* in general. ‖ 有権者の出足は最初は低調だった Voter turnout was initially *poor*.

ティッシュ(ペーパー) a **tissue** /tíʃuː/; a **Kleenex** /klíːneks/ (➤ 商標名) ▶ティッシュではなをかむ blow one's nose with *a tissue*.

> **危ないカタカナ語✹ ティッシュペーパー**
> **1** 日本語では「ティッシュペーパー」というが, 英語では単に tissue でよい. tissue paper というと, 本の図版に掛ける保護用の薄葉(うすよう)紙を指す.
> **2** Kleenex ともいうが, これは商標名が普通名詞になったもの.

ていっぱい 手一杯 ▶私は仕事で手いっぱいだ I'*m tied up* with work. ／I'*ve got my hands full* with work.

ていてつ 蹄鉄 a **horseshoe.**

ていでん 停電 a **power outage** [**failure**](電力供給停止); a **blackout**(➤「空襲時の灯火管制」の意味もある) ▶停電のために電車は2時間も立ち往生した The train was brought to a standstill for two hours because of *a power failure*. ‖ 突然停電になった Suddenly *the electricity was cut off* [*the lights went out*]. ‖ あ, 停電だ Oh, *the lights have gone*! ／Oh, *the power's out* [*off*]! ／Oh! It's *a blackout*! ‖ 約3時間の計画停電 a *planned power outage* [《英》*cut*] of about 3 hours(● 地域ごとに順次停電させる「輪番停電」に当たるのは rolling blackout).

ていど 程度 **1【水準】** a **level** (あるレベル); a **standard**(満足できるレベル) ▶これは中学程度の問題だ This is a junior high school *level* problem. ‖ その問題は中学1年生には程度が高すぎる The problem *is too difficult for* seventh graders. ‖ 彼女のゴルフの腕って, どの程度なの? *How* good a golfer is she? ／*How* good is she at golf?

2【度合い】 a **degree**(度合い); an **extent**(範囲, 限度) ▶地震でどの程度の被害が出たかはまだ伝えられていない The *extent* of the damage caused by the earthquake has yet to be reported. ‖ どの程度まで彼を信用していいのかわからない I don't know *to what extent* [*how far*] he can be trusted. ‖ 都会に住めばある程度の騒音は我慢するしかない When you live in a big city, you have no choice but to put up with noise *to some extent* [*degree*].

3【およそ】 ▶彼の送別会の予算は1人当たり5000円程度で済ませましょう Let's limit the budget for his farewell party to *about* five thousand yen a person.

ていとう 抵当 (a) **mortgage** /mɔ́ːʳɡɪdʒ/; (a) **security,** (a) **collateral** /kəlǽtərəl/ (物件) ▶彼の家は700万円の抵当に入っている His house *is mortgaged* for seven million yen. ‖ 私は家を抵当に入れて銀行から500万円借りた I borrowed five million yen from the

bank with my house *as security* [*as collateral*].
‖抵当流れ (a) foreclosure.

ていとく 提督 an **admiral**, a **commodore.**

ディナー (a) **dinner**
‖ディナーショー a dinner show ‖ディナーパーティー a dinner party.

ていねい 丁寧 **1【礼儀正しい】polite, courteous** /kə́ːrṭiəs/ (➤ 後者のほうが丁寧度が高く，真の親切心や他人に対する温かさが前者に加わる)；**civil** (➤ 無礼にならない程度に礼儀正しいという含みを持つことが多い) ▶丁寧な手紙 a *polite* letter ‖ もう少し丁寧なことばづかいをしなさい Use more *polite* language. ／Speak more politely [civilly]. ‖ 父は女性に対して丁寧だ My father is *polite* to women. ‖ 男の人に駅への道を聞いたら，その人は丁寧に教えてくれた When I asked a man how to get to the train station, he *politely* [*courteously*／*kindly*] told me the way.
✉ **先日はご丁寧に駅まで車でお送りいただき，ありがとうございました** *It was very thoughtful* [*considerate*／*kind*] *of you* to take me to the train station in your car the other day. ➤ thoughtful, considerate はともに「思いやりがある」の意.
‖丁寧語 polite language (ことばづかい)；a polite expression (表現).
2【注意深い】careful ▶彼は丁寧な仕事をする人だ He is a *careful* worker. ‖ 私はきょう学校で習ったことを丁寧に復習したよ I *carefully* reviewed what I studied in school today. ‖ 丁寧に扱ってください Handle *with care*. (➤ 壊れ物に対する注意書き) ‖ 芳美は丁寧な字を書く Yoshimi writes *neatly*.

ていねん 定年 the (**mandatory**) **retirement age** ▶うちの会社では重役には定年が無い There is no *retirement age* for directors in our company. ‖ 父は来年定年です My father will *reach retirement age* next year. ‖ 定年を60歳から65歳に引き上げる raise *the retirement age* from 60 to 65 ‖ わが社では従業員は65歳で定年になる Employees *are supposed to retire* at the age of sixty-five in our company. ‖ 定年後は好きなことをして暮らしたいと考えている人が多い Many people want to live doing what they like *after retirement*.
‖定年制 a retirement system ‖ 定年退職者 a retired person, a retiree /rɪtàɪəríː/.

ていはく 停泊する anchor /ǽŋkəʳ/ ▶その船は函館港に３日間停泊する The ship will *be* [*lie*] *at anchor* for three days in the port of Hakodate. ／The ship will *anchor* for three days in the port of Hakodate.
‖停泊地 an anchorage.

ていばん 定番 ▶定番のジーンズ *standard* jeans ‖ このショルダーバッグは定番商品です This shoulder bag is *a standard item* (*with an established reputation*). ‖ 日本でケーキといえば，イチゴのショートケーキが定番だ Speaking of cake in Japan, strawberry layer cakes are *the standard* [*most popular*] *type* of cake.

ていひょう 定評 an **established** [**excellent**] **reputation** ▶彼はバイオリニストとしてすでに定評がある He has *an established* [*excellent*] *reputation* as a violinist. ／He is a violinist with *an established reputation*. ‖ 彼は歌がうまいことでは定評がある *Everybody knows* [*says*] that he is a good singer. ‖ あの店のウナギはうまいことで定評がある The broiled eel served at that restaurant *has a reputation for* [*is known for*] its fine taste.

ディフェンス defense ▶そのサッカーチームはディフェンスが強い[弱い] The soccer team's *defense* is strong [weak].
‖ディフェンス陣[側] the defense (➤ 集合的に).

ディベート a **debate** ▶安楽死についてディベートを行う have *a debate* about euthanasia.

ていへん 底辺《数学》**the base** ▶三角形の面積は底辺×高さ÷２である The area of a triangle is *the base* multiplied by the height divided by two. ▶《比喩的》社会の底辺に住む人々 people at *the bottom* of the social scale [ladder].

ていぼう 堤防 a **levee**, an **embankment** (➤ 後者はハイウェー用の土手を指すことも多い)；a **dike** (人為的な)；a **bank** (自然に近い土手) ▶オランダは堤防で守られている The Netherlands is protected by *dikes*. ‖ 天竜川の堤防が数か所で決壊した The *banks* of the Tenryu River were broken in several places.

ていぼく 低木 a **shrub**, a **bush** (➤ 前者は公園・庭などの植え込みを形成していることが多い)；**shrubbery** (低木の一群).

[1]**ていほん 定本 the standard text**；**the definitive book** (決定版)；a **critical edition** (校訂版).

[2]**ていほん 底本 the original text.**

ていめい 低迷 ▶低迷する経済 a *slumping* [*stagnating*] economy ‖ 株価は依然低迷を続けている The stock prices are still *hovering at a low level* [are still *stagnant*].

ていめん 底面《数学》**the base.**

ていやく 定訳 a **standard translation** (基準となっている)；a **definitive translation** (最良で変えようのない).

ていよく 体よく tactfully (うまく)；**politely** (丁重に) ▶彼女は先約があるからと誘いを体よく断った She *tactfully* [*politely*] declined the invitation, saying that she had a previous engagement.

ていらく 低落 ▶内閣支持率は低落傾向にある The cabinet's approval rating *is dipping*.

[1]**ていり 定理** a **theorem** /θíːərəm/ ▶ピタゴラスの定理 the Pythagorean *theorem*.

[2]**ていり 低利 low interest** ▶どこか低利でお金を貸してくれるところ知ってる？ Do you know of a place where you can borrow money *at a low interest rate* [*at low interest*]?

でいり 出入り **1【出はいり】**▶このビルはテナントの出入りが激しい The tenant *turnover* (*rate*) in this building is high. (➤ turnover は「入れ替え」) ‖ その家は車の出入りが多い Cars are always *arriving at and leaving* that house. ／At that house cars are always *pulling in and out*. ‖ 私は彼女の家に出入りを許されているただひとりの人間だ I am the only person who is allowed free *access* to her house. (➤ access /ǽkses/ は「入る権利」) ‖ 彼はあるアメリカ人家庭にしばしば出入りしている He *is a frequent visitor* at the house of an American family.
▶うちには出入りの食料品屋があるのでめったに買い物に出ない Since a grocer *regularly comes to our home to take orders*, I rarely go shopping. (英米では御用聞きに回るという習慣は一般的ではないので「注文を取りにいつも家へ来る」と考える).
‖出入り口 a doorway (戸口)；an entrance (入り口).
2【支出と収入】▶年末は金の出入りが激しい *Money flows* fast at the end of the year.

ていりつげんぜい 定率減税 a **proportional tax reduction.**
でいりゅう 泥流 a **mudflow,** a **mudslide.**
ていりゅうじょ 停留所 a **stop** ▶**バスの停留所**はすぐそこを曲がった所にあります There is *a bus stop* just around the corner.
ていりょう 定量 a **fixed** [**given**] **quantity**
‖**定量分析** quantitative analysis.
ていれ 手入れ **1【良い状態にすること】care** ▶爪[顎ひげ]の手入れをする *trim* one's nails [beard] (➤ trim は「切りそろえる」の意) ‖ 姉は寝る前に必ず**肌の手入れをする** My (older) sister always does her *skin-care* routine before going to bed. ‖ 彼の自動車[家]は**いつも手入れが行き届いている** He always *keeps* his car [house] *in good repair*. ‖ 忙しくて**庭の手入れをする**暇がない I have been so busy I have no time to *take care of* the garden. ‖ この**庭は手入れが行き届いている** This garden *is well kept* [*tended*].
2【警察が踏み込むこと】a **raid** ▶麻薬密輸の容疑で彼のマンションに**警察の手入れがあった** The police *raided* his apartment on suspicion of drug smuggling.
ていれい 定例の **regular** ▶月曜に**定例の会議がある** We have a *regular* meeting on Mondays.
ディレクター a **director** ▶テレビの**ディレクター** a TV *director*.
ディレッタント a **dilettante**(趣味として文学や美術を愛好する人).
ティンパニー **timpani**(➤ 複数扱い, 時に単数扱い) ; a **kettledrum**(➤ 通例 2 つ以上用いたものを timpani と呼ぶ)
‖**ティンパニー奏者** a timpanist.
てうす 手薄 ▶空港の**警備が手薄だ** Security *is* rather *weak* [*slack*] at the airport. ‖ 生産不足のため新製品の在庫は**手薄になってきた** Stocks of the new product *have run short* because of underproduction.
てうち 手打ち ▶**手打ちそば**[うどん] *handmade* soba [udon] noodles.
デーゲーム a **day game.**
データ **data**
語法 (1) data は datum の複数形であるが, 特に《米》では単数扱いがふつう. (2) コンピュータのデータの意味では《英》《米》とも単数扱い. (3) 数える場合は a piece of data, two pieces of data のようにいう.
▶**最新のデータ** the latest [most recent] *data* ‖ **データを集める**[分析する] collect [analyze] *data* ‖ **コンピュータにデータを打ち込む** input [enter] *data* into a computer. ‖ 古い携帯の**データを新しいスマートフォンに移しました** I transferred the *data* from my old cell [mobile] phone to my new smartphone.
‖**データ処理** data processing ‖ **データ通信** data communications ‖ **データバンク** a data bank ‖ **データベース** a database.
デート a **date**(会う約束, デート ; デートの相手) ━ **動 デートする** **date** +目 (付き合う) ; **go (out) on a date**(デートに出かける ; 1回ごとのデートについていう) ; **see** +目 (付き合う, 頻繁に会う) ; **go (out) with**(方々に出かけて付き合う). 語法 out があれば初期または長期の交際を連想させ, out がなければ結婚を前提として交際することを連想させる.
▶悪いけどきょうは**彼女とデートの約束があるんだ** I'm sorry, but I *have to go out* [*I have a date*] *with* my girlfriend today. ‖ **彼女のデートの相手**, 誰だったと思う? Who do you think her *date* was? ‖ 私たちはずっと**週末にデートしている** We *are seeing* [*dating*] each other on weekends. ‖ ぼくはきのう神戸で由美子と**デートした** I *went out with* Yumiko in Kobe yesterday. (➤ I dated Yumiko … としない. 動詞 date は 1 回 1 回の個別のデートには用いない) ‖ **ぼくとデートしてくれませんか?** Will you *go (out) on a date with* me? ‖ 進君が**デートに誘ってくれない**かなあ I hope Susumu will *ask* me *out*.

> **危ないカタカナ語✹ デート**
> **1** date は「日付, 日時」が原義で, これから「(ある特定の日に)人と会う約束」の意が生じた. 会う相手はロマンチックな関係にある人でなくてもよい. ただし, インフォーマルでは「ロマンチックな相手とのデート」の意でも用いる.
> **2**《米・インフォーマル》では date は「デートの相手」の意味でも用いる.

テーピング **taping** ▶**左足をテーピングする** *tape* one's left leg.
テープ **1【粘着性のテープ】**(a) **tape** ▶粘着テープ (a roll of) adhesive *tape* 《参考》Scotch tape は《米》の, Sellotape は《英》の商標名で, 普通名詞や動詞としても多用される.
‖**絶縁用テープ** insulating tape ‖ **養生テープ** (a) curing tape ‖ **両面テープ** double-sided [double-faced] tape.
2【録音・録画用テープ】(a) **tape** ▶**テープを早送りする** fast-forward *a tape* ‖ **テープを巻き戻す** rewind *a tape* ‖ **テープ起こしをする** transcribe *a tape* ‖ 彼はこっそり 2 人の会話を**テープに録音した** He secretly *taped* [*tape-recorded*] the conversation between the two. / He secretly *recorded* the conversation of the two *on tape*.
▶彼女はその**音楽テープ**を何度も掛けた She played the *music tape* over and over.
‖**テープデッキ** a tape deck ‖ **カセットテープ** a cassette tape ‖ **磁気テープ** a magnetic tape.
3【紙テープ】(a) **tape** ; a **paper streamer**(航海の見送りのときなどの) ▶父さんが 1 着で**テープを切った** My father *breasted the tape* as the winner. ‖ 地元の名士たちがその高速道路の開通式で**テープカットをした** The local celebrities *cut the ribbon* at the opening ceremony of the expressway.
テーブル a **table** ▶**テーブルを拭いて**ちょうだい Could you wipe the *table*, please? ‖ ごはんですよ. **テーブルに着いて** Dinner is ready. *Sit at the table.* ‖ 私はいつも食後母が**テーブルの上を片づける**のを手伝う I always help my mother *clear the table* after meals.
‖**テーブルクロス** a tablecloth ‖ **テーブルタップ**(=電源タップ) a power strip(➤「テーブルタップ」は和製英語) ‖ **テーブルマナー**(→かこみ記事).

> **危ないカタカナ語✹ テーブル**
> **1**「テーブルマナー」は table manners, manners at table のように複数形にする. また,「テーブルチャージ」は cover charge,「テーブルセンター」は centerpiece という.
> **2**「テーブルスピーチ」も和製英語で, after-dinner speech や luncheon speech, あるいは speech at a dinner [luncheon] などという. 単に speech ということもある.

テープレコーダー a **tape recorder** ▶**テープレコーダーを掛ける** play *a tape recorder*.

テーマ a **theme** /θiːm/ ; a **subject**（主題）; a **topic**（話題）▶多くの作家が愛をテーマに小説を書いた Many writers have written novels with love as their *theme* [dealing with love]. ‖ 次回の討論会のテーマは「いじめ」です The *subject* [*topic*] of our next forum is "bullying." ‖ きみの卒業論文のテーマは何ですか What is the *theme* [*subject*] of your graduation thesis ?

‖**テーマ音楽** theme music ‖**テーマソング** a theme [title] song ‖**テーマパーク** a theme park.

て

テールライト a **taillight.**

ておい 手負い ▶手負いのクマ a *wounded* bear.

ておくれ 手遅れ・手後れ ▶彼のがんは手遅れだった His cancer was discovered *too late.* ‖ 手遅れにならないうちに医者に診てもらいなさい See your doctor *before it is too late.*

でおくれる 出遅れる get a late start ▶選挙運動に出遅れたのが彼には最後まで響いた His *delay in running for election* adversely affected his campaign until the end.

ておけ 手桶 a **bucket,**《米》a **pail.**

ておしぐるま 手押し車 a **pushcart**（籠付きで買い物用の）; a **handcart**（農場・工事現場などで物の運搬に使う二輪の）; a **wheelbarrow**（工事などに使う一輪の；通称「猫車」）.

ておち 手落ち a **mistake**（間違い）; **fault**（過失の責任）; (an) **oversight**（見過ごし）; a **slip,** a **slip-up**（ちょっとした間違い）▶申し訳ありません. これは私の手落ちです I'm very sorry. This is my *mistake* [*fault*]. ‖ 品質管理に手落ちがあった There was *an oversight* in the quality control. ‖ 警備の手落ちからその銀行は強盗に入られた The bank was robbed because of *faulty security.* ‖ 手落ちのないように頼んだよ See (to it) that *everything goes right* [that *nothing goes wrong*].

デオドラント a **deodorant.**

ており 手織りの handwoven /hǽndwóʊvən/（手で織った）; **homespun** /hóʊmspʌn/（家で紡いだ）▶手織りのネクタイ a *handwoven* tie.

‖**手織物** handwoven [homespun] fabrics.

でかい big, huge（➤ 後者は大きいことを誇張する語で「非常に大きな」の意）▶でかい音 a *big* sound ‖ 俺にはでかい夢がある I have a *big* dream. ‖ 彼はいつも態度がでかい He always acts *big.* ‖ そんなでかい声出すなよ Don't *yell.*

てかがみ 手鏡 a **hand mirror** ▶手鏡を見る look into *a hand mirror.*

てがかり 手掛かり・手懸かり a **clue** /kluː/（糸口）; a **key**（理解・解決の助け）; a **trace**（形跡）▶殺人犯は部屋に 1 つの手がかりを残した The murderer left *a clue* in the room. ‖ 彼の居場所についてはまるで手がかりがない We have no *clue* as to his whereabouts. ‖ いくら考えても問題を解く手がかりが見つからなかった No matter how hard I tried, I could not find *a key* to (solving) the problem.

▶行方不明の船について何の手がかりもない There is no *trace* of the missing ship. ‖ 肉親の手がかり（＝情報）を求めて孤児たちが中国からやって来た The orphans came from China looking for *information* about their relatives.

てがき 手書き handwriting 一形 **手書きの handwritten** ▶私は年賀状はいつも手書きです I always *write* my New Year's cards *by hand.* ‖ 手書きのレポートは受け付けません *Handwritten* papers are not acceptable.

でがけ 出掛け ▶出がけに電話が掛かってきてバスに乗り損ねた I got a phone call *just as I was about to leave* and missed the bus.

てがける 手掛ける handle +目, **deal with** ▶私は長年この種の仕事を手がけてきた I have been *dealing with* [*handling*] this kind of work for many years. ‖ 公害問題は手がけたことがない I *am unfamiliar* [*have no experience*] *with* pollution problems.

でかける 出掛ける go (out) ; **leave**（場所を離れる）; **step out**（ちょっと外出する）; **set off**（旅行などに）▶彼は毎朝早く仕事に出かける He *goes* to work [*leaves* (*home*) for work] early every morning. ‖ そろそろ出かける時間だ It's about time to *go.* ‖ 今から出かけるというときに玄関のベルが鳴った The doorbell rang just as I was *leaving.* ‖ オーストラリアにはいつ出かけるんですか When do you *leave* [*set off*] for Australia ?

▶兄は朝早くから釣りに出かけた My (older) brother *went fishing* early in the morning. ‖ 彼はエジプトへ出かけて留守だ He *is away* in Egypt. ‖ あいにく父は今出かけています I'm sorry, but my father *is out* now. ‖ 私の母は買い物に出かけています My mother *has gone* (*out*) *shopping.* ／My mother *is out shopping.*

▶お時間がおありでしたらお出かけ（＝おいで）ください *Come and see me* if you have time. ‖ **対話**「お出かけですか」「ええ, ちょっと出かけて来ます」"*Are* you *going out* ?" "Yes, I'*m* just *stepping out* for a minute."（➤ 英米人も社交辞令としてこのように言い合うことはあるが, 日本人ほど頻繁ではない）.

てかげん 手加減 ▶きみの相手は子供だ. 手加減してやれよ Your opponent is a child. *Go easy on* him. ‖ さあ, 掛かってこい. 手加減はいらないぞ Come on. *Don't pull your punches.*

でかした ▶でかしたぞ！ **Good job !**

でかせぎ 出稼ぎ ▶父は農閑期になると東京へ出稼ぎに行く During the (agricultural) off-season, my father *goes* (up) to Tokyo *to work.*

‖**出稼ぎ労働者** a seasonal worker（季節労働者）; a migrant worker（外国への）.

てがた 手形 1【証券としての】a **draft,** a **bill** ▶私は70万円の手形を振り出した I drew *a draft* [*a bill*] for 700,000 yen.

‖**手形受取人** the payee /peìː/ of a bill ‖**手形支払人** the payer of a bill ‖**空手形**（→見出語）‖**不渡り手形** a dishonored [bad] bill ‖**約束手形** a promissory note.

2【手の形】a **handprint** ▶これが双葉山の手形だよ This is Futabayama's *handprint.*

でかた 出方 a **move**（動き）▶相手の出方を見る wait for the other side to *make a move first* ‖ 相手の出方次第では訴えてやる Depending on what *move* the other side *takes,* I'll decide whether to sue them (or not).

てがたい 手堅い steady（堅実な）; **reliable**（信頼できる）; **trustworthy** /trʌ́stwə̀ːrði/（深く信頼できる）; **sure**（確実な）▶手堅い方法 a *sure* method ‖ 彼は手堅い男だ He is a *steady* [*reliable* ／ *trustworthy*] person. ‖ 彼は手堅い商売をしている He does *steady* business. ‖ 彼はランナーを手堅くバントで送った He *played* (*it*) *safe* and advanced the runner with a bunt.（➤ play (it) safe は「安全策をとる」）.

デカダンス decadence.

てかてか ▶ずいぶん長いことはいたのでズボンのお尻がてかて

かになった I've been wearing these pants so long (that) the seat is *shiny*. ‖ 橋本氏は頭にポマードをてかてかに塗りたくった Mr. Hashimoto smeared his hair with pomade *so that it shone*. (➤ shone は shine の過去形).

でかでか ▶選挙が間近なので候補者の名をでかでかと書いた車がよく通る Since the election will be held soon, cars with candidates' names displayed *in big characters* come by often. ‖ (新聞に)その事件のことがでかでかと出た The incident *made the headlines*. (➤ headline は「(新聞などの)見出し」). ‖ その写真は一面にでかでかと載った The picture *was splashed* across the front page.

てがみ 手紙 a **letter**; **mail**, 《英また》 **post**

> 語法 **mail, post** は手紙のほか, はがき, 小包などを含めて「郵便物」の意で用いる. ただし, これらは数えられない名詞扱いなので, ふつうは単数形.

▶順子, あなたに手紙よ Junko, here's *a letter* for you. (● Here's your letter. とすると, 順子が書いた手紙の意になる) ‖ きょうは珍しく手紙が 2 通来た I got two *letters* today, which is unusual for me. ‖ きょうは日曜日なので手紙が来ない There's no *mail* today because it is Sunday. ‖ 私に何か手紙来てる? Is there any *mail* [*post*] for me? ‖ 彼女の手紙には「最近結婚しました」と書いてあった *In her letter*, she said that she had gotten married recently. ‖ 彼とは 5 年ほど手紙のやり取りをしている I *have been corresponding with* him for nearly five years.

▶手書きの手紙 a handwritten *letter* ‖ ゆうべ友人に手紙を書いた Last night I *wrote to* a friend of mine. (➤ write to で「…に手紙を書く」) ‖ 近頃はメールばかりで, 手紙をめっきり書かなくなった These days, I send e-mails most of the time and I *hardly write* (*any*) *letters* at all. ‖ たまには手紙をくださいね Please *drop me a line* [*write to me*] once in a while.

▶この手紙を出して来てちょうだい Please *go and mail this letter* for me. / Please *post this letter*. ‖ 手紙はメールに大きく取って代わられた *Letters* have been replaced by email(s).

✉ **お手紙ありがとう. 毎日首を長くして待っていました** Thank you for *your letter*. I was looking forward to it every day.

✉ **お手紙うれしく拝見しました** I really enjoyed *your letter*. / I was delighted to hear from you.

✉ **この前の手紙に書きましたように, 日本では 4 月に学校が始まります** *As I said in my previous letter*, school starts in April in Japan.

> **直訳の落とし穴「手紙をくれる」**
> 「手紙」= a letter, 「くれる」= give であるが, 「息子はめったに手紙をくれない」を (×) My son rarely gives me a letter. とはできない. give a letter は「手紙を, 『はい, あげる』と言ってくれる」の意味である. 「手紙をくれた」は手紙を書いてよこすという意味であるから, My son rarely writes me (a letter). または, My son rarely writes to me. とする. なお, レストランで「メニューをください」もメニューをもらって帰りたいわけではないから (×) Please give me a menu. でなく, May I have a menu? と言う.

> **逆引き熟語 ○○手紙**
> 依頼の手紙 a letter of request / お祝いの手紙 a letter of congratulations / お悔やみの手紙 a letter of condolence [sympathy] / お見舞いの手紙 a get-well letter / お礼の手紙 a thank-you letter / お別れの手紙 a farewell letter / 苦情の手紙 a letter of complaint / 激励の手紙 a letter of encouragement / 謝罪の手紙 a letter of apology / 招待の手紙 a letter of invitation / 匿名の手紙 an anonymous letter

☞ 置き手紙 (→見出語)

てがら 手柄 **credit**(誉れ, 名誉) ▶そんなことをしても何の手柄にもならないよ You won't get the least *credit* for doing it. ‖ 手柄を独り占めにするな Don't take all the *credit* (for /to) yourself. ‖ 彼はその商談で手柄を立てた He *distinguished himself* in the business negotiations. ‖ お手柄だよ *Well done!*

てかる ▶私は顔がてかりやすいので, よく脂取り紙を使います My face tends to *be oily*, so I often use facial oil blotting paper.

てがる 手軽な **easy**(たやすい) 一副 **手軽に** **easily** ▶手軽な料理 an *easy-to-fix* meal / an *easily cooked* dish ‖ 手軽に作れる昼食 a lunch you can prepare *quickly* / an *easily* prepared lunch ‖ 昼食は宅配ピザで手軽に済ませた I ate a *quick* lunch of home-delivered pizza. ‖ この入浴剤のおかげで家庭で手軽に(=いつでも)温泉気分が味わえる Thanks to these bath salts, you can enjoy a hot spring atmosphere at home *anytime*. ‖ このデジカメは子供でも手軽に使えます This digital camera *is easy to use* even for children.

デカンター a **decanter**.

てき 敵 an **enemy**; a **rival** (競争相手); an **opponent** (スポーツなどの対戦相手) ▶ヤマアラシは敵に襲われると針を立てて身を守る When confronted with *an enemy*, porcupines protect themselves by erecting their spines. ‖ あの男を敵に回すと面倒だ If you *make an enemy* of that man, he'll cause you (a lot of) trouble. ‖ 山田選手は敵陣深く絶妙のパスを送った Yamada made a beautiful pass *deep into the opponent's side*. ‖ 私など彼の敵ではない(=とてもかなわない) I *am no match for* him.

▶《慣用表現》チャンピオンは向かうところ敵なしだ Nobody [Nothing] stands in the champion's way. (➤「立ちはだかるものがない」の意).

▶《比喩的》睡眠不足は美容の敵だ Lack of sleep is the *enemy* of beauty.

-てき -的 **1【…に関する】**▶金銭的には心配は要らない You need not worry *as far as money goes* [*is concerned*]. ‖ 認知症が科学的に解明され始めた Senile dementia has begun to be *scientifically* explained. ‖ 私的にはそれは名案だと思う *As for me* [*If you ask me*], I think it's a very good idea.
2【…のような】▶私の彼ってとても紳士的よ My boyfriend is very *gentlemanlike*. ‖ それはまさに天才的な作品だ It's truly the work *of a genius*.

でき 出来 ▶出来の良い[悪い]生徒 a *bright* [*dull*] student ‖ 出来の良い[悪い]作品 *well-made* [*poorly made*] work ‖ きみの作品, いい出来じゃないか Your work *is quite well done*. ‖ 対話「ひろしは学校の出来はどうだい?」「英語はいいけど, 数学がだめね」"*How is* Hiroshi *doing* in school?" "He's doing well in English, but badly in math." ‖ 対話「ことしの柿の出来はどうですか」「とてもいいですね」

"*How are* the kaki (persimmons) this year?" "It's a bumper year for them." (➤ bumper は「大豊作の」,「出来の悪い年」は lean year).

¹**できあい 出来合いの ready-made** ▶出来合いの総菜 *deli/prepared dishes* ‖ 出来合いのワイシャツは私の体には合わない *Ready-made* shirts do not fit me well.

²**できあい 溺愛する dote on** ▶彼女は猫のミミを溺愛している She *dotes on* her cat Mimi. ‖ 彼は祖母に溺愛されて育った He was raised by his *doting* grandmother.

できあがり 出来上がり (a) **finish** ▶出来上がりは上々だった It was a superb *finish*.

できあがる 出来上がる ▶私の服はいつ出来上がりますか When will my suit *be ready* [*be finished*]? ‖ 私の家は来月出来上がります My house will *be completed* next month. ‖ 《折り鶴を折っていて》はい, 出来上がり *OK, finished!* ‖ ピザが出来上がったよ The pizza *is done*. (➤ be done は「料理が出来上がる」).

▶やつ, すっかり出来上がってる(=酔っ払ってる)ぜ (It) looks like he's *plastered* [*loaded*].

てきい 敵意 hostility; (an) **animosity**(強い憎しみ) ▶敵意に満ちた顔つき a *hostile* look ‖ 彼は私に敵意を示した He showed his *hostility* toward [to] me. ‖ 彼はぼくに敵意を抱いているようだ He seems to have some *hostile feelings* toward [to] me. ‖ 親戚の者たちに対する彼女の敵意はすでに小さくなっていた Her *animosity* toward [against] her relatives was already diminishing.

テキーラ tequila /tɪkíːlə/.

てきおう 適応 adaptation(努力しての適合・順応); **adjustment**(微調整を行っての適合・順応) 一動 **適応する adapt**《to》, **adjust**《to》 ▶気候変動に適応する *adapt to* climate change ‖ 生物は環境に適応しながら進化してきた Living creatures have evolved by *adapting to* their environment. ‖ 彼はまもなく新しい生活様式に適応した He soon *adjusted to* his new way of life.

‖**適応障害** (an) adjustment disorder ‖ **適応性** adaptability.

てきおん 適温 (a) **suitable temperature**(適切な温度); (a) **moderate temperature**(程よい温度) ▶野菜を適温に保つ keep vegetables at *a suitable temperature*.

てきがいしん 敵愾心 hostile /hɑ́ːstl ‖ hɔ́staɪl/ **feeling, hostility**, (an) **enmity** ▶彼に敵がい心を抱く feel *hostility* toward [to] him.

¹**てきかく 的確な appropriate**(目的にかなった); **proper**(ふさわしい); **accurate** /ǽkjərət/ (正確な) 一副 **的確に accurately** ▶的確なアドバイス the *right* [*appropriate/proper*] advice ‖ 的確な判断 an *appropriate* [a *proper*] decision ‖ 自分の考えを的確に表現する explain one's opinion *correctly* [*clearly*] ‖ 彼はその件を的確に処理した He dealt with the case *properly*.

▶彼女はその評論の主旨を的確につかんでいない She hasn't grasped the point of the critical essay *accurately*. ‖ 上司は部下に的確な指示ができなければいけない Managers must be able to give their workers *clear* directions. ‖ 彼の批評は的確だ(=当たっている) His criticism *is to the point*.

²**てきかく 適格の qualified**(有資格の; ある基準に合っている); **competent**(あることを完璧に成し遂げることのできる); **eligible** /élɪdʒəbəl/ (…に選ばれるのにふさわしい) ▶ノーマンはリーダーとして適格だ Norman is well *qualified* to be a leader. ‖ 彼は教師として適格な人物であることを保証します I assure you that he is *competent* as a (school) teacher.

‖**適格者** a qualified person, an eligible (person).

てきぎ 適宜 ▶《黒板などの掲示》答案を提出した者は適宜帰ってよい Those who have turned in their answers may go home *whenever they like*. ‖ 適宜情報を書き入れてください Insert information *as appropriate*.

てきごう 適合 ▶ラクダは砂漠の生活に最も適合した動物だ The camel is the animal (that is) best *adapted to* life in the desert. ‖ これだけの条件に適合する人物を見つけるのは容易ではない It's not easy to find a person who *meets* all these requirements perfectly.

てきこく 敵国 an **enemy country, the enemy**

‖**敵国捕虜** an enemy prisoner of war.

できごころ 出来心 ▶彼は出来心で[ちょっとした出来心で]漫画を万引きした He shoplifted manga *on impulse* [*on the impulse of the moment*].

できごと 出来事 an **event**(特筆すべき); a **happening**(ちょっとした); an **incident**(ささいな, または異例の) ▶ことしの主な出来事 the chief *events* of this year ‖ 我々は世界の出来事をテレビで即時に知ることができる TV allows us to know *what is going on* [*what is happening*] in the world in real time. ‖ サマーキャンプであった愉快な出来事をお話ししましょう Let me tell you about some amusing *incidents* at summer camp. ‖ それは蒸し暑い夜の出来事だった It *happened* on a muggy evening.

てきざいてきしょ 適材適所 ▶彼は経験もあるし英語も堪能だからまさに適材適所だ Because he has experience and is proficient in English, he is *the right man for the job*.

テキサス Texas(アメリカ南西部の州; 略 TX, Tex.).

テキサスヒット《野球》a **Texas leaguer.** →ぽてんヒット.

てきし 敵視 ▶彼はぼくを敵視しているらしいが, ぼくは別に気にしていない He seems to *look upon* me *as an enemy*, but it doesn't bother me.

できし 溺死 drowning /dráʊnɪŋ/ 一動 **溺死する drown, be drowned**

▶彼は湖で泳いでいて溺死した He (*was*) *drowned* while swimming in the lake. (●事故の場合は was を省略するのがふつう) ‖ 彼女は溺死体となって発見された She was found *drowned*. (➤「溺死体」は a drowned body).

てきしゃせいぞん 適者生存 the survival of the fittest.

てきしゅつ 摘出 removal 一動 **摘出する remove** +目 ▶腫瘍の摘出 (*surgical*) *removal* of a tumor ‖ 弾丸を摘出する手術 surgery to *remove* a bullet.

てきじん 敵陣 enemy lines ▶敵陣深く攻撃[潜入]する strike [infiltrate] deep behind *enemy lines*.

できすぎ 出来過ぎ ▶その話は出来過ぎだ It *is too good to be true*. (➤「うますぎて, 本当とは思えない」の意) ‖ 彼女は佐々木君には出来過ぎた女房だよ She is *too good* to be Sasaki's wife./Sasaki doesn't deserve *such a good* wife. ‖ **対話**《野球の試合後のインタビューで》「きょうは100点満点のピッチングでしたね」「いやあ, 出来過ぎです」"Your pitching was perfect today, wasn't it?" "Well, *it was better than I thought it would be*."

テキスト a **textbook**,《米また》a **text**(教科書); a **text**(原文, 原本); **text**(コンピュータの文字のみのデータ) ▶英語のテキスト an English *textbook* ‖ テキストの5ページを開きなさい Open your *textbook(s)* to [《英また》at] page 5. ‖ 手書きの文書をテキストに変換する translate a written document into *text*.

‖**テキストファイル** a text file.

てきする 適する be suitable [**fit**]《for》▶次の□に適する1語を補え Fill in each square [box] with a *suitable* word. ‖ 問題はこの仕事があなたに適しているかどうかです The question is whether this job *suits* you or not. ‖ このゲレンデは初心者に適している This (ski) slope *is suitable for* beginners. ‖ この本は子供が読むのには適さない This book *is not suitable for* children to read.

▶彼は教師には適さない He *is not cut out to* be a teacher. ／He *is not fit to* be a teacher. (➤ 前者は「生まれつき向いていない」, 後者は「(性格的な欠点などがあって)不適だ」の意) ‖ うちではその仕事に適した人を1人探している We are looking for a person *suited for* the job. ‖ この水は飲用水として適していますか Is this water *all right* to drink? (● good to drink とすると「おいしい」という意にもなる) ／Is this water *drinkable* [*potable*]?

1**てきせい 適性** (an) **aptitude** ▶彼は語学に対する適性がある He has *an aptitude* for languages. ‖ 彼女に教師としての適性(能力)があることは疑いない There is no doubt that she has *competence* as a teacher.

‖**適性検査** an aptitude test ‖**職業適性** vocational aptitude.

2**てきせい 適正な appropriate** /əpróʊpriət/ (適切な); **proper** (正しい) ▶1ドル80円は適正なレートとは思われない An exchange rate of 80 yen to the dollar doesn't seem *appropriate*. ‖ テストだけで生徒の適正な評価はできない You can't evaluate your students *properly* with only tests.

‖**適正価格** a fair price.

てきせつ 適切な suitable(周囲の状況にふさわしい); **appropriate** /əpróʊpriət/ (条件・目的にかなった); **proper**(社会通念上正しい) ▶適切なことば a *suitable* word ‖ 適切な処置 *appropriate* measures ‖ 適切な判断 *proper* judgment ‖ 彼の言ったことは適切だ What he said *is to the point*. (➤ to the point は「的を射ている」) ‖ 彼は自分の考えを適切に表現する術(すべ)を心得ている He knows how to express his ideas *well*. ‖ 今の気持ちを表す適切なことばが見つからない I can't find an *appropriate* word for how I'm feeling now.

☛ 不適切 (→見出語)

てきぜん 敵前 ▶敵前で逃亡する desert *in the face of the enemy*.

‖**敵前逃亡者** a deserter in the face of the enemy, a deserter under (the enemy's) fire.

できそこない 出来損ない ▶出来損ないのシチュー *badly-cooked* stew ‖ このアップルパイは出来損ないだ This apple pie is *a failure* [*a flop*].

▶この出来損ないめ! You *idiot*!

てきたい 敵対する oppose +㊀ ▶党内には執行部に敵対するグループがある There exists a group in the party that *opposes* the executives.

できだか 出来高 ▶彼女の給料は出来高払いだ She is *paid on a piecework basis*.

できたて 出来立て ▶このパンは出来たてのほやほやです This bread is *fresh* [*straight*] *from the oven*. (➤「オーブンから出したばかり」の意) ／This bread is *freshly baked*.

▶《比喩的》この大学は出来たてのほやほやなので, 教授陣が手薄だ Since this college is *brand-new*, it has a rather weak teaching staff.

1**てきち 適地** a **good place**《for》, **land suitable**《for》.

2**てきち 敵地** (an) **enemy territory** [**land**].

できちゃったけっこん できちゃった結婚 a **shotgun marriage** (➤ 女性の父親が怒って銃で男性に女性との結婚を強要したところから), a **marriage due to an unintended pregnancy**.

てきちゅう 的中 ▶彼の弾丸は見事に的中した His bullet *hit the target* [*the bull's-eye*]. ‖ 彼女の予言は的中した Her prediction *has come true* [*proved right*]. ‖ 日頃の不安が的中した My longstanding concern *proved (to be) correct* [*well placed*].

てきど 適度の moderate /mɑ́:dərət/ ▶室内の空気は適度の湿り気を帯びているのがよい Room air should have *a certain amount of* humidity. ‖ 医者は私に毎日適度の運動をするように言った The doctor advised me to get [do] *moderate* exercise every day. ‖ 適度に飲めば酒も薬だ If you drink *moderately*, drinking can do you good [be beneficial].

てきとう 適当 **1**【**適切なこと**】**一形 適当な suitable**(周囲の状況にふさわしい); **proper** (社会通念上正しい); **reasonable** (金額が適正な) ▶「取り除く」の意味を表す最も適当な1語を選びなさい Choose the most *suitable* word that expresses the meaning of 'get rid of.' ‖ あそこは女子学生がひとりで行くには適当な場所ではない It is not a *proper* place for female students to go alone. ‖ 高校生にはお小遣いは月々いくらくらいが適当でしょうか How much do you think is *reasonable* as a monthly allowance for a high school student? ‖ 塩とこしょうを適当に加えなさい Add salt and pepper *to taste*. (➤ to taste は「好みに応じて」) ‖ このケーキ, みんなで適当に分けなさい Divide these cakes among yourselves. (● この「適当に」は訳す必要はない) ‖ **対話**「お昼(ごはん)どうする?」「何か適当に食べておくよ」"What are you going to do for lunch?" "I'll find *something or other* to eat."

2【**いいかげんなこと**】▶(知りもしないくせに)適当なことを言うんじゃない Don't *talk nonsense*. (➤ 決まり文句) ‖ 1問もわかんないよ. 適当に書いちゃえ I can't answer a single question, so I'll write *whatever pops into my head*. (➤「頭に浮かんできたことを」の意).

☛ 不適当 (→見出語)

てきにん 適任 ▶彼なら人望があるし, 監督に適任だ He is trustworthy and *suited* [*suitable* ／*qualified*] *for* the post of manager. ‖ 彼はこの仕事に適任だ[適任者だ] He *is the right man* for the job. ‖ 彼女はその仕事には不適任だ(=向いていない) She *is not cut out for* that job.

できばえ 出来栄え・出来映え ▶見事な出来栄えのつぼ a vase *of excellent craftsmanship* ‖ この菊人形は見事な出来栄えだ This chrysanthemum doll is *splendid* [*excellent*]. (➤ chrysanthemum は /krɪsǽnθɪməm/ と発音) ‖ きみのこの報告書はすばらしい出来栄えだ You'*ve done a wonderful job* on this report.

てきぱき ▶てきぱき仕事をする人 a *businesslike* person ／a person who *does his or her work efficiently and in a businesslike way* (● 日本語の「ビジネスライク」には「事務的な」という否定的含みがある

が, 英語の businesslike は「能率的な」などの肯定的な意味で通例用いる) ‖ もっとてきぱき(=速く)仕事をしなさい Do the job more *quickly* [*speedily*]. ‖ 店員のてきぱきした(=手際のよい)応対が気持ちよかった We found the salesclerk's *efficient* service quite refreshing. ‖ ガイドはツアー参加者の質問にてきぱきと(=きびきびと)答えた The guide *crisply* answered the questions of the tourists.

てきはつ 摘発する **expose** +⊜ ▶官僚による汚職事件が摘発された A scandal involving government officials *was exposed* [*was laid bare*]. (➤ lay bare は「明らかにする」の意).

てきびしい 手厳しい **severe** /sɪvíəʳ/ ▶手厳しい批判 *severe* [*relentless*] criticism ‖ 先生は私が時間にルーズだと手厳しくとがめた The teacher *severely* criticized my carelessness about time.

てきほう 適法の **legal** ▶マカオではギャンブルは適法だ Gambling is *legal* in Macau.

てきめん 覿面 ▶この薬を飲んでみろよ. 効果てきめんだから Take this medicine. It *works like a charm* [*works wonders* / *works miracles*]. ‖ 少し怠けたらてきめんに成績が落ちた I neglected my studies a little and *immediately* my grades went down.

できもの 出来物 a **boil**(おでき); a **sore** (腫れ物, ただれ) ▶首にできものができた I've got *a boil* on my neck.

1**てきやく 適役** ▶母親役には彼女が適役だ She *is suited for* the role of mother. ‖ 議長には杉田君が適役だ Sugita *is perfect for* the chairmanship. / Sugita is *the most suitable person* [*just the right person*] to be chairperson.

2**てきやく 適訳** an **appropriate translation**.

てきよう 適用 **application** —動 **適用する** **apply** /əplái/《to》▶この条項は外国人留学生には適用されない These articles *don't apply to* the foreign students. ‖ このことばは適用範囲が広い This word *is used widely*.

てきりょう 適量 ▶塩を適量加えます Add the *proper* [*suitable*] *amount* of salt. / Add salt *to taste*. (➤ to taste は「好みに応じて」の意) ‖ ぼくにはビールの小瓶1本が適量だ A small bottle of beer is the *right amount* for me.

できる 出来る

> 📖 訳語メニュー
> 生じる →have (got) **1**
> 作られる →grow, be made of [from] **2**
> 仕上がる →be completed **3**
> 能力がある →can, be able to do **4**
> 優れている →be good at **5**

1【生じる】 **have (got)** (ある); **appear** (現れる) ▶腕におできができた I'*ve got* a boil on my arm. (➤ have got は have の意で用いられるインフォーマルな表現) ‖ おでこににきびができた Pimples *have come out* on my forehead. ‖ 声帯にポリープができた A (small) tumor *has developed* in my throat. (➤ polyp は専門用語) ‖ 激しい雨のあと校庭には大きな水たまりができた After a heavy rain, a big puddle *appeared* on the school playground. ‖ ほら, 家の壁にハチの巣ができてるよ Look! A beehive *has been built* on the wall of our house.

▶急用ができたので, お先に失礼します Some urgent business *has come up*. Please excuse me. ‖ 泰彦は恥ずかしがり屋でなかなか彼女ができない Yasuhiko is so shy that he *can't find* a girlfriend. ‖ 大学ではきっといい友だちができるよ I'm sure you will *make good friends* at college. ‖ あなた, 私子供ができた(=妊娠している)の Honey, I'*m pregnant*. ‖ あの2人はどうもできてるらしい I hear those two are *a couple*. / I hear those two are (already) *lovers*. (➤ 肉体関係を指す場合) ‖ この頃きれいになったけど, 彼氏でもできたんじゃない? You're more beautiful than ever these days. Did you *find yourself* a boyfriend or something?

2【作られる】 **grow** (育つ); **be made** 《of, from》(作られる) ▶北海道の東部では厳しい気候条件のために米はほとんどできない Rice *doesn't* usually *grow* well in the eastern part of Hokkaido because of the harsh climate. ‖ ことしはミカンがよくできた We *had a bumper crop of* mikans this year.

▶八王子市に新しい団地ができた A new housing complex *was built* in Hachioji City. ‖ 駅前にマクドナルドができた(=オープンした) A new McDonald's *has opened* in front of the train station. ‖ 全国でクラフトビール店がどんどんできている Craft beer bars *are popping up* all over the country. (➤ pop up は「急に[ぱっと]現れる」) ‖ 日本の内閣制度は1885年にできた(=始まった) The Japanese cabinet system *started* in 1885. ‖ きみたちの学校はいつできたの When *was* your school *founded*? ‖ このミニカーはとてもよくできている This miniature car *is* well *made*. (➤ miniature car は「1人がやっと乗れる程度の小さな車」の意もある) ‖ 日本の製品はなかなか壊れないようにできている Japanese products *are made* so as not to break easily.

▶《材料を使って作られる》日本の伝統的な家屋は木と紙でできている Traditional Japanese houses *are made of* wood and paper. (🔔 be made of は通例原料の質や成分が変わらない場合) ‖ 洗剤は石油からできる Detergents *are made from* petroleum. (🔔 be made from は通例原料の質や成分が変わる場合).

▶俳句は5-7-5の17音節でできている A haiku *consists of* 17 syllables (5-7-5).

3【仕上がる】 **be completed** ▶新校舎がこの秋ようやくできた(=完成した) Our new school building *was* finally *completed* this fall. ‖ 皆さん, 夕食の用意ができましたよ Everyone, dinner *is ready*. ‖ 《クリーニング店で》このワイシャツ, いつできますか(=いつ取りに来たらいいですか) When can I *pick up* this shirt? ‖ 宿題, もうできたの! You'*ve done* your homework already? (🔔 この already は驚きを表す. 単に「もうできたかどうか」を尋ねるときは Have you done your homework yet? と言う) ‖ **対話** 「注文したステーキ, まだ?」「はい, すぐにできます」 "Isn't the steak I ordered ready yet?" "*It'll be ready in a moment*."

4【能力がある, 可能である】 **can, be able to** do

> 【文型】
> **…することができる**
> **can** do
> **be able to** do

▶私はウクレレはできるが, ギターはできない I *can play* the ukulele, but I *cannot* [*can't*] *play* the guitar. ‖ きみ, 腕立て伏せは何回できる? How many push-ups *can* you *do* at one time? ‖ 佐藤君はロシア語ができる Sato *can speak* Russian. (🔔 相手に「ロシア語はできますか」と聞くときは *Do* you *speak* Russian? とするのがふつうで, *Can* you ...? とすると失礼に響くことがある) ‖ やればできる. 思い切って挑戦してごらん You *can do* it if you try. Go for it！‖私にできることがあれば何なりと言ってください Please let me know if there is anything I *can do*.

語法 can と be able to
(1)「できる」という意味では，現在時制の can と be able to の両方が使えるが，主語が無生物の場合は前者が一般的．［例］She can [is able to] speak three languages.（彼女は3か国語を話すことができる）／This hall can hold 200 people.（このホールは200人を収容できる）．
(2)can は未来形と完了形がなく，ほかの助動詞に続くこともできないので，代用として be able to を使って will be able to, have [has] been able to とする．
(3)過去時制の could が過去を表す語句とともに用いられる場合，「過去に持っていた能力」を表す．［例］When he was a boy, he could play the piano, but now he can hardly play it at all.（彼は少年の頃ピアノが弾けたが，今はほとんど弾けない）．この場合 When he was a boy, he was able to play the piano .... としても同じ意味になる．
(4)ただし，He could run 100 meters in 12 seconds. のように過去を表す語句がない場合，「彼は走ろうと思えば100メートルを12秒で走れる」のような意味になり，「(現在)やろうと思えばできる」ことを表す．一方，He was able to run 100 meters in 12 seconds. だと，「彼は(実際に)100メートルを12秒で走ることができた」という意味になり，「(過去に)実際にできた［した］」ことを表す．
(5)また，can は「継続して何かができる」能力を意味するので，一度きりの経験には使えない．よって，「私は試験に合格できた」は(○)I was able to pass the exam. とするか，単に I passed the exam. となり，(×)I could pass the exam. は不可．
(6)「できなかった」の意である could not と was [were] not able to は同じように使える．［例］I couldn't [wasn't able to] get there by 3.（3時までにそこに着くことはできなかった）．

▶今きみにぼくの言うことが理解できなくても，もっと年を取れば理解できるようになるよ Even if you *can't* understand what I say now, you'*ll be able to* (understand it) when you're older. ‖9時の電車に乗ることができた I *was able to* catch the nine o'clock train.（● could にすると仮定法になって「乗ろうと思えば乗れる」という意味になるので注意）／I *made* the nine o'clock train.（➤「間に合った」の意）‖あの番組，ちゃんと録画できた？ *Did* you (*manage to*) record the TV program all right？
▶将来人間は宇宙に住むことができるだろう Humans *will* (*probably*) *be able to* live in space in the future. ‖その日はパンダの赤ちゃんを見ることはできなかった We *were not able to* [*couldn't*] see the baby panda that day. ‖警察はまだその泥棒を逮捕できないでいる The police *have not* yet *been able to* arrest the robber.
▶犬は遠くの物音を聞きつけることができる A dog *is capable* of hearing distant sounds. ‖あすの晩までに旅行から帰って来ることができますか *Is it possible* for you to return home from the trip by tomorrow evening？‖この博物館の中では写真撮影はできません(＝許可されていない) You *are not allowed* to take photographs [Taking photographs *is not permitted*] in this museum. ‖人々の民主化への熱望を無視することはできない *There is no ignoring* people's desire for democratization.（➤ There is no doing は「…することはできない」の意の文語）．
▶担保もなしにきみに100万も貸すなんてできない相談だ Lending you a million yen without security *is out of the question*.（➤ be out of the question は「問題外だ」の意）‖できればあすお返事を頂きたいのですが I would like to hear your answer tomorrow, *if possible*.
5【優れている】be good《at》▶(勉強の)できる生徒 a *bright* student／a *quick* learner ‖できない生徒 a *poor* student／a *slow* learner ‖木村君は理科が［どの科目も］よくできる Kimura *is good at* science [*does well* in all subjects]. ‖谷口さんはよくできる(＝有能な)人だ Ms. Taniguchi is a *competent* person. ‖長谷川氏は実によくできた人(＝人格者)だ Mr. Hasegawa is *a man of* (*good*) *character* indeed.

できるかぎり 出来る限り ▶子供の教育のためにはできる限りのことをしてやりたい I would like to do *whatever* [*as much as*] *I can* for my children's education.

できるだけ 出来るだけ as ... as one **can** [**possible**]

【文型】
人(A)ができるだけ…
as ... as A can
as ... as possible
➤ ... は副詞や形容詞など

▶学生時代にできるだけ多くの本を読みなさい Read *as many* books *as you can* while you are a student. ‖科学者は1つの真理に到達するのにできるだけたくさんの事実を集め検討しなければならない A scientist has to collect and examine *as many* facts *as possible* in order to reach a single truth. ‖できるだけ早く帰って来てね Come back *as soon as possible* [*as soon as* you can]. ‖きみのためにできるだけのことはするよ I'll do *all I can do* for you.／I'll do *everything* [*anything*] *I can* for you.

てきれい 適例 a **good** [a **suitable**／an **appropriate**] **example.**

てきれいき 適齢期 (a) **marriageable age**, a **proper age for marriage**

解説 英米人は「何歳(くらい)までに結婚するのがよい」とか「何歳が結婚適齢期だ」のようにはあまり考えない．よって，これらのことは話題にしないほうが賢明．

▶気がついたらうちの娘ももう適齢期になっていた Before I knew it, my daughter was *of marriageable age*.

できレース 出来レース a **fixed match** [**game**／**race**].

てぎれきん 手切れ金 consolation money(慰謝料)．

てぎわ 手際 ▶彼女は見ていていらいらするくらい手際が悪い(＝不器用だ) She *is* so *clumsy* that it's irritating to watch her. ‖彼はいつも手際よく仕事する He always does his work *skillfully* [*with skill*／*efficiently*].（➤ skillfully, with skill は「巧みに」，efficiently は「てきぱきと」）．

てぐすね 手ぐすね ▶息子が帰って来たら叱ってやろうと母親はてぐすね引いて待っていた The mother was waiting for her son to come home, all *set on* scolding him.（➤ set on は「…する固い決心で」）．

てくせ 手癖 ▶あいつは子供の頃から手癖が悪かった He *was light-fingered*, even when he was a little boy.

てぐち 手口 a **trick**(策略)；a **method** (方法) ▶これはよくある手口だ This is one of the classic *tricks.* ‖ その2つの犯行は手口が似ている The *methods* used for the two crimes are similar. (●「犯行手口」は専門用語では modus operandi といい, M.O. と省略する).

でぐち 出口 an **exit** /éksɪt, égzɪt/, 《英また》a **way out** ▶出口はあちらです The *exit* is over there. ‖ 出口で待っててちょうだい Will you wait for me at the *exit*? ‖ (選挙の)**出口調査** an exit poll.

てくてく ▶オートバイが故障したので, 私はきょうは会社までてくてく歩いた My motorcycle has broken down, so I *walked* to work today.

テクニカル ‖**テクニカルサポート** technical support ‖ **テクニカルターム** a technical term；jargon (➤ 後者はしばしば軽蔑的に用いられる) ‖ **テクニカルノックアウト** a technical knockout, a TKO ‖ **テクニカルライティング** technical writing.

テクニシャン a **technician.**

テクニック (a) **technique** /tekníːk/ ▶メッシのサッカーのテクニックはすばらしい Messi's soccer *techniques* are marvelous.

テクノ 《音楽》**techno.**

でくのぼう 木偶の坊 a **dummy** ▶このでくのぼうめが！ You *dummy.* ／You *good-for-nothing.*

テクノロジー technology ▶テクノロジーの発達は我々の生活をすっかり変えてしまった The development of *technology* has changed our daily life completely.

てくび 手首 a **wrist** /rɪst/ ▶彼の手首をつかむ seize him by the *wrist* ‖ 手首が強くないとテニスはできないよ You must have a strong *wrist* to play tennis.

でくわす 出くわす come across, run across, run into ▶林さんに道でばったり出くわした I *came across* [*ran into* ／*bumped into*] Hayashi on the street. (➤ bump into がいちばんくだけた言い方).

てこ 梃子・梃 a **lever** /lévəʳ, líːvə/ ▶てこの力 *leverage* ‖ 我々はてこを使って庭石を隅に移動した We moved the garden rock aside with *a lever.*
▶《慣用表現》彼はこうと決めたらてこでも動かない Once he makes a decision, he *won't budge an inch* [he *sticks to it*]. (➤ 前者は「びくともしない」, 後者は「固執する」の意).

てこいれ 梃入れ ▶景気のてこ入れが必要だ The economy must *be shored up* [*bolstered* (*up*)]. (➤ bolster (up) は「強化する」).

てごころ 手心 ▶彼はまだ若いんだから手心を加えてやりなさい You should *make allowances for* his youth. (➤ make allowances for は「…を考慮する」) ／ You should *be patient with* [*go easy on*] him because he's still young and inexperienced.

てこずる ▶康夫には全くてこずるわ Yasuo *has gotten* quite *out of hand.* ／Yasuo *is too much* for me. ／Yasuo *is* quite a *handful.* (➤ handful は「手に負えない子, 問題児」) ‖ 対話「数学のテスト, どうだった?」「証明問題にてこずったよ」"How did you do on the math test?" "I *had a lot of trouble* on the proofs."

てごたえ 手応え a **response**(反応) ▶釣り糸を垂れるとすぐ釣りざおに手応えがあった As soon as I cast the line, I got *a response* on my fishing rod. ‖ 彼は今回の交渉には確かな手応えを感じていた He felt sure he was getting *a positive response* in the current negotiations.

でこぼこ 凸凹 unevenness(平らでないこと) 一形 **凸凹の uneven, rough；bumpy**(特に道路がでこぼこの多い) ▶月の表面は凸凹だ The surface of the moon is *uneven.* ‖ 凸凹道で車が故障してしまった My car broke down on the *bumpy* [*rough*] *road.*

デコメール (a) **Deco-mail** (➤ 商標), (a) **decorated mail.**

デコる decorate +目 ▶彼女は携帯をデコっている She has a *decorated* cellphone.

デコレーション (a) **decoration**

> **危ないカタカナ語✸ デコレーション**
> **1** 日本語ではお祝い用のケーキのことを「デコレーションケーキ」というが, これは和製語. 英語では用途によって birthday cake (誕生日の), Christmas cake(クリスマスの), wedding cake(結婚式の)のようにいう. なお, クリスマスケーキを食べるのは日本的な習慣で, 《米》では Christmas cake は一般的ではない.
> **2**「飾りつけしたケーキ」の意なら decorated cake, 「華やかに飾りたてたケーキ」の意では fancy cake を用いる.

てごろ 手頃な reasonable, moderate (値段が；後者は「程よい」)；**handy** (扱いやすい)；**affordable**(値段的に手が届く) ▶手ごろな値段の中古車 a *reasonably* [*moderately*] *priced* used car ‖ この辞書なら持ち歩くのに手ごろだ This dictionary is *handy* to carry. ‖ ボウリングは手ごろなスポーツだ Bowling is a sport *that's easy and fun to play.* ／Bowling is an *easy-to-enjoy* sport. ‖ 手ごろな価格の住宅をもっとたくさん建てる build more *affordable* housing ‖ もう少し手ごろなものはないでしょうか Do you have anything more *affordable*? ‖ 私は一家3人が住むのに手ごろな家を探している I'm looking for a house (that is) *suitable for* my family of three to live in.

てごわい 手強い tough /tʌf/；**formidable** (侮り難い) ▶あいつは手ごわいぞ He is a *tough* [*hard*] customer. (➤ この customer は「(交渉などの)相手」) ‖ K商業は手ごわい相手だ K Commercial High School is a *formidable* opponent.

テコンドー taekwondo /taɪkwάːndoʊ/.

デザート dessert /dɪzə́ːʳt/, 《英・インフォーマル》**afters** ▶デザートは何がいいですか? What would you like for *dessert*? ‖ ダイエット中だからデザートはパスするわ Since I'm on a diet, I think I'll skip *dessert.*
‖**デザートメニュー** a dessert menu.

デザイナー a **designer,** a **stylist** ▶彼女はデザイナーブランドでまとめている She is dressed in *designer* (*brand*) *goods* from top to bottom. 《参考》「デザイナーブランドのジーンズ」は designer jeans という.
‖**インテリアデザイナー** an interior designer ‖ **ウエブデザイナー** a web designer ‖ **グラフィックデザイナー** a graphic designer ‖ **工業デザイナー** an industrial designer ‖ **商業デザイナー** a commercial designer ‖ **服飾デザイナー** a dress designer ‖ **ヘアデザイナー** a hair stylist.

デザイン a **design** 一動 **デザインする design** +目 ▶この服, 自分でデザインしたのよ I *designed* this dress (for) myself.
‖**デザイン(専門)学校** a school of design ‖ **工業デザイン** industrial design ‖ **商業デザイン** commercial design ‖ **ユニバーサルデザイン** universal design.

てさき 手先 1【手の先, 指】▶彼女は手先がとても器用だ She is very *clever with her hands.* ／She is very *dexterous*. (➤ dexterous は /dékstərəs/ と発音) ‖ 健二は手先が不器用だ Kenji is *clumsy with his hands* [*fingers*].

2【人に使われる者】a **pawn** /pɔːn/ (小者) ; a **tool** (道具) ; an **agent** (スパイ) ▶彼は自分がテロリスト組織の手先だと白状した He confessed he was *an agent* of a terrorist organization. ‖ 吉田なんかの手先になるのは嫌だ I don't want to be Yoshida's *pawn*. (➤ pawn はチェスの駒のひとつで, 将棋の歩に当たる).

でさき 出先 ▶出先から電話で連絡するよ I'll contact you by phone *on my way* [*from outside* (*of*) *the office*].

‖**出先機関** a local agency of the central government(官庁の) ; a branch (office)(支店).

てさぎょう 手作業 **handwork, manual work** ▶手作業で全部の票を数え直す recount all the votes *by hand*. ‖ この仕事は手作業で行われたもので, 機械ではありません This work was done *manually*, not by a machine.

てさぐり 手探りする **grope, feel** (➤ 手で触りながら探すというニュアンスは後者が強い) ; **fumble** (もぞもぞと, 不器用に) ▶彼女は暗闇でドアの取っ手を手探りでさがした In the dark, she *groped* [*felt* / *fumbled*] *for* the doorknob. ‖ 私たちは手探りで洞窟を探検した We explored the cave, *groping our way through*.

▶《比喩的》今度の事業はまだ手探りの状態です This (business) project is still in *its beginning stages*.

てさげ 手提げ・手下げ

‖**手提げかばん** an attaché case /æ̀t̬əʃéɪ keɪs/ (アタッシェケース) ; a briefcase (書類かばん) ; a tote bag(主に女性用の大型の) ; a suitcase (スーツケース) ‖ **手提げ金庫** a portable safe [cashbox] ‖ (デパートなどの)**手提げ袋** a shopping bag.

てさばき 手捌き ▶鮮やかな手さばきでマグロをさばく dress a tuna *with a deft hand* [*very deftly*].

テザリング **tethering** ▶このスマートフォンのテザリング機能を使えば, ノートパソコンやタブレット端末をインターネットに接続させることができる This smartphone can connect your laptop and tablet to the Internet using its *tethering* function.

てざわり 手触り a [the] **touch** ▶絹は手触りが柔らかい Silk *feels soft*. ‖ この布は手触りがすべすべしている This cloth is smooth to *the touch*.

でし 弟子 a **pupil**(教え子) ; a **disciple** /dɪsáɪpəl/ (特定の先生・学説の) ; an **apprentice** /əprént̬ɪs/ (徒弟) ▶モーツァルトは生活のために弟子をとった Mozart took *pupils* to support himself. ‖ 彼は10歳のとき小山名人に弟子入りした He *became an apprentice of* the master, Koyama, at the age of ten. ‖ 寺田寅彦は夏目漱石の弟子だった Terada Torahiko was *a disciple* of Natsume Soseki.

てしあげ 手仕上げ ▶手仕上げの表札 a *hand-finished* name plate.

てしお 手塩 ▶手塩にかけて育てた弟子 an apprentice who *has been trained with loving* [*great*] *care*.

デジカメ a **digital camera,** 《インフォーマル》a **digicam** ▶デジカメで写真を撮る take a photo with *a digital camera* [*digicam*] 《参考》デジタルカメラと区別する場合, フィルムカメラを conventional film camera と呼ぶ.

てしごと 手仕事 **manual work, handwork**(機械利用に対して) ; **handiwork** (手細工など) ▶あの子は手先が器用だから手仕事に向いている Since she is clever with her hands, she is suited for doing *work using her hands*.

てした 手下 one's **men** (➤ 複数形で集合的に) ; an **underling**(下っ端).

デジタル デジタルの **digital** ▶本をデジタル化する *digitize* [*digitalize*] a book ‖ デジタル時計には針がなく, 時間を数字で示す *A digital watch* [*clock*] doesn't have hands but shows the time in figures. ‖ (ロンドンの)ビッグベンはデジタル表示に変わると思いますか ? Do you think that Big Ben's numerals will ever *be changed to digital* ones ? ‖ 通信のデジタル化が急速に進んでいる Communications have *become* rapidly *digitalized*. ‖ 2011年にテレビ放送がアナログからデジタルに移行した TV broadcasting shifted from analog to *digital* in 2011.

‖**デジタルオーディオプレーヤー** a digital audio player 《略 DAP》 ‖ **デジタル写真** a digital photo ‖ **デジタル署名** a digital signature ‖ **デジタル信号** a digital signal ‖ **デジタルフォトフレーム** a digital photo frame ‖ **デジタル録音** digital recording.

てじな 手品 **magic**(総称) ; a (**magic**) **trick**(個々の) ▶トランプの手品 a card *trick* ‖ その手品の種を明かしてください Please explain the *trick*.

‖**手品師** a magician, a conjurer /kɑ́ːndʒərə^r/.

デシベル a **decibel**(音の強さの単位).

でしゃばる 出しゃばる ▶出しゃばるんじゃない Don't *be too forward*. / Don't *butt in*. (➤ butt in は「口を出す, 干渉する」) / Mind your own business. ‖ 私のような老人が出しゃばる幕ではありません This is no business for an oldie like me to *stick* [*poke*] *my nose in*. (➤ stick [poke] one's nose in で「首を突っ込む」).

てじゅん 手順 (a) **procedure** /prəsíːdʒə^r/ (手続き) ; a **process** (過程) ▶ある手順を踏む follow *a process* ‖ マニュアルの手順に従ってください Please follow the *procedure* indicated in the manual. ‖ まず最初に仕事の手順を決めよう First, let's decide *the order* in which the tasks should be done.

てじょう 手錠 (a **pair of**) **handcuffs** ▶容疑者はおとなしく手錠を掛けられた The suspect did not resist *being handcuffed*.

-でしょう →-だろう.

デシリットル a **deciliter**.

-です ⚠ **断定の「-だ」の丁寧な形で, be 動詞がこれに相当するが, 日本文が「-です」とあっても訳出不要の場合も多い. また, 日本文が「-です」でも英語では過去形になる場合もある.** ▶私は高校生です I *am* a high school student. ‖ 彼はとても親切です He *is* very kind. ‖ きょうは寒いですね *It's* cold today, isn't it ? ‖ その手紙を書いたのは健さんです It *was* Ken who wrote the letter. / Ken *was* the one who wrote the letter.

▶彼は日本語がわからないんです He cannot understand Japanese. ‖ そんな訳で照美は来なかったんです That's why Terumi didn't come. ‖ 彼には会えませんでした I couldn't see him.

てすう 手数 **trouble** ▶大変お手数をおかけすることになり[おかけしてしまって]申し訳ございません I am sorry to give [to have given] you so much *trouble*.

▶お手数ですが, この文を英語に訳していただけませんか *I am* (*very*) *sorry to trouble you*, but could you please translate this sentence into English ? ‖ お手数ですがよろしくお願いいたします *I hate to bother you*, but may I ask you to do it ?

てすうりょう 手数料 (a) **commission**(売買手数料) ;

a **fee**（報酬）; a **charge**（料金）▶車を1台売るといくら手数料がもらえるの？ How much *commission* do you get when you sell a car? ‖ 別に手数料が200円かかります We *charge* an additional 200 yen *for handling* this. ／There is an additional *handling charge* of 200 yen.

1**てすき 手透き・手隙** ▶手すきの人は手伝ってください Would anyone who is *free* please give me a hand? ‖ 今お手すきですか *Are you free* now?

2**てすき 手漉き** ▶手すきの和紙 *handmade* Japanese paper.

ですぎる 出過ぎる ▶出過ぎたまねをするな Don't be too pushy. ／Mind your own business.

デスク a **desk**(机); **the desk**, a **newspaper desk**(新聞社の編集部) ▶スポーツデスク the sports *desk*.
‖**デスクトップ(コンピュータ)** a desktop (computer) ‖ **デスクワーク** desk work.

でずっぱり 出突っ張り ▶第2幕では主人公は出ずっぱりだ The protagonist *stays on stage throughout* Act Two.

テスト a **test**, an **examination**,《インフォーマル》an **exam** ⇀試験

> **語法** (1) **test** は学校の試験だけでなく,「検査」「実験」などの広い意味で用いられる. (2)「学校の試験」の意味のテストは test でも **examination** でもよいが, 入試のような選抜試験には test は用いない. (3)「小試験」の意味では **quiz** も用いる.

▶テストに受かる［落ちる］ pass［fail］*a test* ‖ 英語のテストを受ける take an English *test*／take *a test* in English (➤後者は「英語で書かれたテスト」の意にもなる) ‖ スペリングのテスト a spelling *test*［*quiz*］‖ きょう数学のテストがあった We had a math *test*［*exam*］today. ‖ このロボット, ちゃんと動くかどうかテストしてみよう Let's *do*［*perform*／*carry out*］*a test* to see if this robot works properly. ‖ テストの点は思ったよりよかった My *test* scores were better than I expected.
‖**テストケース** a test case (➤裁判関係では「(その結果が判例となる)試験的な訴訟」の意で用いられる) ‖ **テストパイロット** a test pilot ‖ **テスト飛行** a test flight ‖ **期末テスト** a final test［exam］‖ **口頭テスト** an oral test［exam］‖ **体力テスト** a test for physical strength ‖ **多肢選択式テスト** a multiple-choice test ‖ **知能テスト** an IQ test ‖ **中間テスト** a midterm test［exam］‖ **抜き打ちテスト** a pop test［quiz］.

てすり 手摺り a **handrail**(階段や病院の廊下などの); a **railing**(柵); **banisters**(階段の手すりと支柱が一体になったもの) ▶《エスカレーターなどの掲示》手すりにおつかまりください Please Hold *Handrail* ‖ 手すりに寄りかからないでください Please do not lean on the *railing*.

てせい 手製の **handmade**(手で作った); **homemade**(自家製の) ⇀手作り ▶手製の時限爆弾 a *handmade* time bomb ‖ このクッキーは手製です These are *homemade* cookies. ‖ このスカートはあなたのお手製ですか Did you *make* this skirt *yourself*?

てぜま 手狭な **small**(狭い); **cramped**(狭苦しい) ▶手狭な台所 a *cramped* kitchen ‖ この部屋は私には少々手狭です This room is a bit (*too*) *small* for me. ‖ 家族が増えるにつれてわが家は次第に手狭になってきた My family has outgrown our house. (➤outgrow は「…に合わないほど大きくなる」).

てそう 手相 **lines on the palm** (➤palm /pɑːm/ は「手のひら」) ▶「あなたは長生きの手相をしています」と手相見は言った "You *have a long life line*," said the *palm reader*［*palmist*］. ‖ 手相を見てあげよう Let me *read your palm*. ‖ きみはいい［良くない］手相をしてるね You have *lucky*［*unlucky*］*lines on your palm*.
‖**手相占い** palmistry /pɑ́ːmɪstri/.

でぞめしき 出初め式 ***dezomeshiki***; the New Year's parade of fire brigades, the New Year Brigade Parade (➤説明的な訳).

でそろう 出揃う ▶予想された候補者が出そろった *All* the expected candidates *have entered* the election［*have announced* their candidacy］. ‖ 全員が会議に出そろった *All* the members *are present* at the meeting.

てだし 手出し ▶《けんかで》先に手出ししたほうが悪い The one who *started the fight* is to blame. ‖ 吉野君は私の彼よ. 余計な手出しはしないで! Yoshino is my boyfriend. *Don't make advances on him*［*Stay away from him*］.

でだし 出だし **the beginning, the start** ▶(その歌の)出だしをちょっと歌ってみてくれ Can you sing just *the beginning*［*the first part*］(of the song)? ‖ ヤクルトは出だし好調だ The Swallows *have gotten off to a good start*.

てだすけ 手助け (a) **help** ▶人の手助けをする *help* others ‖ この机を動かすにはもう1人手助けがいる We need one more *hand* to move the desk. (➤hand は「援助の手」) ‖ 避難者たちの手助けがしたい I'd like to *lend a hand* to the evacuees.

てだて 手だて a **way** ▶ほかに手だてはないものかな Isn't there any other *way*? ‖ 今のところ, HIV／エイズを完治させる手だてはない For the present, there is *no way* to cure HIV／AIDS.

でたて 出たて ▶大学を出たての若い子が仲間に加わった A young man［woman］, *fresh from college*, has joined our team.

でたとこしょうぶ 出たとこ勝負 ▶出たとこ勝負で行こう Let's *play it by ear*. (➤「臨機応変にやる」の意) ‖ 出たとこ勝負で試験を受けた I took the examination *cold*［*without making any preparations*］. (➤cold は「準備なしで」の意のインフォーマルな用法).

てだま 手玉 ▶心配するな, あんなやつ手玉にとってやるよ Don't worry. I'll *get* him *right under my thumb*. ‖ モニカは3人の男を手玉にとっている Monica has three guys *at her beck and call*. (➤at one's beck and call は「意のままに扱って」).

でたらめ ▶でたらめな生活を送る lead a *disorganized*［*haphazard*］life／live *irresponsibly* ‖ あいつの言うことはみんなでたらめだ Everything he says is *nonsense*. ‖ あいつの言ったことは全部でたらめだった Everything he said was (pure) *rubbish*［*bullshit*］. (➤bullshit は「うそ, でたらめ」の意の俗語) ‖ 彼女が教えてくれた電話番号はでたらめ(＝うそ)だった She gave me a *false* telephone number.
▶彼があんなでたらめな(＝無責任な)男とは思わなかった I didn't think he was so *irresponsible*. ‖ 恐怖に駆られて彼はでたらめに発砲した Being seized with fear, he fired *at random*. ‖ 事実を知りもしないくせにでたらめを言うな Don't *talk nonsense*! You don't know the facts.

てぢか 手近 ▶私はいつもその辞書を手近に置いている I always keep the dictionary *close at hand*. ‖ 手近な例を挙げればわかるでしょう You will understand it if I give you a *familiar* example.

てちがい 手違い a **mistake** ; a **slip-up**(ちょっとした間違い) ; a **mix-up**(混乱をもたらすような) ▶こちらの手違いでツアーをオーバーブッキングしてしまいました Due to our *mistake* [*oversight*], the tour was overbooked. ‖何か手違いがあったようだ It seems there was some kind of *slip-up* [*mix-up*].

てちょう 手帳 a (**pocket**) **notebook**,《英》a **pocketbook** ; a **pocket diary**, a **datebook**(日付入りの) ▶そのことはちゃんと手帳に控えてあります I made a note of that in my *notebook*.

‖**生徒手帳** a student handbook, a student's ID.

てつ 鉄 **iron** /áiəʳn/ ; **steel** (鋼鉄) ▶この橋は鉄でできている This bridge is made of *iron*. ／This is an *iron* bridge. ‖彼は鉄のような意志を持っている He has *an iron will*. ‖この野菜ジュースには鉄分が0.8ミリグラム含まれている This vegetable juice contains 0.8 milligrams of *iron*.

‖**鉄くず** scrap iron.

ことわざ **鉄は熱いうちに打て** Strike while the iron is hot. (➤ 英語は「好機, 逸すべからず」の意.「柔軟性のある若いうちにしっかり鍛えておけ」というのは日本特有の解釈).

てっかい 撤回する **withdraw** +㊐ (引っ込める) ; **retract** +㊐ (発言を) ▶要求を撤回する *withdraw* one's demand(s) ‖すまん, ぼくが間違っていた. 今のことばは撤回するよ I'm sorry, I was wrong. I *take* it all *back*. ‖市長はあとで発言を撤回した The mayor later *retracted* his [her] remark(s). ‖彼は間違いを証明されて自分が言ったことを撤回した He *ate his words* when he was proven wrong. (➤ eat one's words は「前言を取り消す」).

てつがく 哲学 **philosophy** /filá:səfi/ ▶「常に前進」—これが私の人生哲学だ Ever onward : this is my *philosophy of life*. ‖彼のものの考え方は哲学的だ His way of thinking is *philosophical*. ／He thinks *philosophically*.

‖**哲学者** a philosopher ‖**哲学書** a philosophy book.

てつかず 手付かず ▶自然を手付かずにしておく leave nature *untouched* ‖この市に地下鉄を造る計画はまだ手付かずだ Plans for building a subway in this city *haven't gotten off the ground* yet. ／Plans for building a subway in this city *remain on the drawing board*. (➤ on the drawing board は「計画の段階で」) ‖手付かずの仕事がたくさんある I have a mountain of work I *haven't gotten to yet*. (➤ get to は「(仕事に)取りかかる」).

てづかみ 手掴み ▶彼は漬物を手づかみで食べた He ate the pickles *with his fingers*. ‖彼が川で魚を手づかみで捕まえたのには驚いた To my surprise, he caught a fish in the river *with his hands*.

てっかん 鉄管 an **iron pipe** [**tube**].

てつき 手付き ▶ロングさんは危なっかしい手つきではしを使う Mr. Long uses chopsticks *awkwardly* [*clumsily*]. (●「慣れた手つきで」なら with a practiced hand) ‖彼は不器用な手つきでギターを弾いた He played the guitar *clumsily* [*awkwardly*]. (●「器用な手つきで」なら skillfully).

てっき 鉄器 **ironware**(集合的に) ; an **iron utensil**

‖**鉄器時代** the Iron Age.

デッキ **the deck**(船の) ; a **platform** (列車の) ; a (**tape**) **deck**(テープデッキ) ▶船のデッキで日光浴をする sunbathe *on deck* ‖《掲示》乗客の皆さまはこのデッキにお立ちにならないでください Passengers are not allowed to stand on this *platform*.

‖**デッキシューズ** deck shoes ‖**デッキチェア** 《米》a beachchair,《英》a deck chair.

てっきょ 撤去する **remove** +㊐ ▶警官隊はバリケードを撤去した The police force *removed* the barricade.

てっきょう 鉄橋 an **iron bridge**(鉄で造った橋) ; a **railroad bridge** (鉄道の橋).

てっきり ▶チャイムが鳴ったとき, てっきりパパが帰って来たのだと思った When the doorbell rang, I thought it was Dad coming home *for sure*. (➤ for sure は「間違いなく」) ‖その指輪はてっきり盗まれたとばかり思っていたが, きょうベッドの下から出てきた I thought that the ring *must* have been stolen, but today I found it under my bed. ‖なぜかてっきりあの人があなたの奥さんだと思い込んでいました For some reason or other, I *was under the impression that* she was your wife. (➤ 日本語同様, 英文も事実と違うという含みがある).

てっきん 鉄筋 ▶鉄筋コンクリート造りのビル a *reinforced concrete* [*a ferroconcrete*] building.

でつくす 出尽くす ▶意見が出尽くした Everyone *fully expressed* their ideas (on the topic). ／The topic *was exhaustively discussed*.

てづくり 手作りの **handmade** (手製の) ; **homemade** (主に食べ物が自家製の) ▶手作りの家具 *handmade* furniture ‖この人形は彼女の手作りだ She *made* this doll *with her own hands*. ‖手作りのクッキーですけど, いかがですか Here are some *homemade* cookies. Please help yourself.

> **直訳の落とし穴「手作りの」**
> 「手作りチーズケーキ」を (×) handmade cheesecake という間違いが多い. handmade は machine-made (機械製の) に対して用いる語で, a handmade sign (手作りの看板) や handmade wooden furniture (手作りの木の家具) とはいう. しかし, 手で作るのが当たり前の料理や菓子には合わない. 料理の手作りには「(買ったものでない) 自家製の」の意の homemade を用いて, homemade cheesecake とする. ただし, 店でも機械製でないという意味で handmade pasta (手打ちのパスタ) などと handmade を用いることはある.

てつけ(きん) 手付(金) a **deposit**, **earnest money** (➤ 後者は主に法律用語) ▶早めに手付けを打ったほうがいいだろう I think you'd better *make* [*pay* ／*leave* ／*put*(*down*)] *a deposit* on it soon. ‖そのソファーに1万円の手付金を払った I made [put down] a ten-thousand-yen *deposit* on that sofa. ／I put down ten thousand yen for that sofa. ‖この車はいくら手付けを払えばいいですか How much *deposit* should I put (down) on this car ?

てっこう 鉄鋼 **steel**

‖**鉄鋼業界** the steel industry.

てっこうじょ 鉄工所 an **ironworks**.

てっこつ 鉄骨 a **steel frame** (**work**) ▶鉄骨の橋 a bridge with *a steel framework*.

‖**鉄骨住宅** a house built on a steel frame.

デッサン a **sketch**(下絵) ; a **rough drawing**(鉛筆などで描いた概略的な絵) 《参考》「デッサン」はフランス語の *dessin* から ▶その屋敷をデッサンする make *a sketch* of the mansion ‖ピカソはデッサンの巨匠だ Picasso is a master of *sketching*.

てつじょうもう 鉄条網 a **barbed-wire fence**, **barbed-wire entanglements** (➤ barbed-wire は《米》では

barbwire ともいう）▶牧場の周りに鉄条網を張る put *a barbed-wire fence* around the ranch／fence the ranch with *barbed wire*.

てつじん 鉄人 an **iron man** ▶トライアスロンは鉄人レースと言われる The triathlon is called *the iron man race*.

てっする 徹する ▶彼は菜食主義に徹している He is a *strict* vegetarian. ‖ その商人は金もうけに徹している The merchant *puts his heart and soul into* making money.
▶地下鉄の復旧工事は夜を徹して行われた They worked *all night* to restore service on the subway.

てつせい 鉄製の **iron** ▶鉄製のフライパン an *iron* skillet［frying pan］.

てっそく 鉄則 a **hard-and-fast rule** ▶ゴロは正面で捕るのが鉄則だ The *hard-and-fast rule* is to take grounders right in front of you. ‖ あの場面ではバントが鉄則だ In a situation like that, the *ironclad rule* is to bunt.

てったい 撤退 (a) **withdrawal** /wɪðdrɔ́ːəl/（引き下がること）; a **pullout**（立ち退くこと）**一動 撤退する** **withdraw**《from》, **pull out**《of》▶即時撤退を求める call for *an* immediate *withdrawal* ‖ 軍隊はその国から撤退した The troops *withdrew* from［*pulled out* of］that country. ‖ わが社は南アフリカ市場から撤退することになった We decided to *withdraw* from the South African market.

てつだい 手伝い **help**（手伝うこと）; a **helper**（手伝う人）▶うちの娘は全く母親の手伝いをしたことがないので，ご飯の炊き方も知らない Since my daughter has never *helped* her mother, she doesn't even know how to cook rice. ‖ お手伝いしましょう Let me *give* you *a hand*.／Let me *help* you. ‖ 何かお手伝いすることはありますか Is there anything I can *do for* you?／Is there anything I can *help* you with?
▶あの人たちがこの災害を乗り切る手伝いをしたい *I'd like to help* them get through this disaster. ‖ 対話「お勤めですか？」「いいえ，家事手伝いをしています」"Do you work for a company?" "No. I *help my mother at home* (*with the housework*)."
☛ お手伝いさん（→見出語）

てつだう 手伝う **1【手助けする】help** ＋目

【文型】
人(A)が…するのを手伝う
help A do ➤ do は動詞の原形
人(A)の仕事(B)を手伝う
help A with B

▶私は父の夕食の支度を手伝った I *helped* my father prepare dinner. ‖ 私は姉の仕事を手伝った I *helped* my sister *with* her work.（日本語では「仕事を手伝う」と言うが，help のすぐあとにくるのは主に「人」で，helped my sister's work は不可）‖ この机を動かすのを手伝ってよ *Help* me move this desk.／*Give me a* (*helping*) *hand* in moving this desk. ‖ 妻が資料探しを手伝ってくれなかったらこの著作は完成しなかったでしょう Without my wife's *assistance* in searching for material, I wouldn't have been able to complete this book. ‖ パパ，ぼくが手伝ってあげるよ I'll be your *helper*, Dad.（➤ 子供っぽい言い方）.
2【加わる】▶心配事に過労も手伝って彼はついに病気になった *On top of* his worries, overwork caused him to get sick.／Overwork *aggravated* his worries, and he finally got sick.（➤ aggravate /ǽgrəvèɪt/ は「悪化させる」）.

でっちあげ でっち上げの **trumped-up**（罪などが）; **made-up**（話などが）▶でっちあげの新聞記事 a *trumped-up* newspaper article ‖ それはでっちあげだ．私は殺人犯じゃない It's *a setup*［*I was framed*］. I'm not a murderer. ‖ あいつの話は全くのでっちあげだった His story was a complete *fabrication*.（➤「でっちあげの話」は manufactured［made-up］story）.

でっちあげる でっち上げる **cook**［**make**］**up**; **fudge** /fʌdʒ/ ＋目（特に重要な数字・事実を改ざんする）▶彼は事実を隠すために話をでっちあげた He *cooked*［*made*］*up* a story to hide the fact. ‖ 彼は自分の理論に合うようにデータをでっちあげた He *fudged* the data to make it fit his theory.

てつづき 手続き (a) **procedure** /prəsíːdʒəʳ/; **formalities**（正式の）▶（飛行機の）搭乗手続き the boarding *procedure* ‖ アメリカの大学に留学するにはどんな手続きが必要ですか What *procedures* are necessary to be admitted to an American university? ‖ 私はまだ入学手続きを済ませていない I haven't finished the *admission procedures* yet. ‖ 今週中に手続きを完了します. I'm going to finalize the *procedure* within this week.

てってい 徹底 **1【妥協のないこと】一形 徹底的な** **thorough** /θə́ːroʊ, θʌ́roʊ/ **一副 徹底的に** **thoroughly** ▶あの男は徹底したけちだ He is an *absolute* cheapskate. ‖ 彼女は徹底した平和主義者だ She is a pacifist *to the bone*. ‖ 彼のやることはいつも徹底している He *is thorough*［He *goes all the way*］in whatever he does. ‖ 何をするにも徹底的にやれ Whatever you do, do it *thoroughly*［*completely*］. ‖ 私は教科書を徹底的に復習した I reviewed the textbook *thoroughly*.
▶原因を徹底的に調査してほしい We want you to investigate the cause *thoroughly*. ‖ 予算の徹底した見直しが必要です We need to review the budget *thoroughly*［conduct a *thorough* review of the budget］.
2【行き渡らせること】▶厚生労働省は各給食センターに食器の煮沸を徹底させた The Ministry of Health, Labour and Welfare *saw to it that* all dishes and implements used at all school lunch preparation centers were sterilized in boiling water.（➤ see to it that ... は「…となるよう注意を払う」）‖ 原発の危機管理が徹底されていなかった Crisis management at the nuclear power plant *was inadequate*.
☛ 不徹底（→見出語）

てっとう 鉄塔 a **steel tower**; a **pylon** /páɪlən/（高圧線用の）.

てつどう 鉄道《米》a **railroad**,《英》a **railway** ▶鉄道を敷く lay［construct］*a railroad* ‖ 日本は鉄道がよく発達している *Railroads* are very well developed in Japan. ‖ 鉄道運賃の値上げは家計に響く An increase in *train fares* affects our family budget. ‖ 彼らは中国旅行中に鉄道事故に遭った They had［met with］*a railroad accident* while traveling in China.
‖ **鉄道案内所** a railroad information office ‖ **鉄道公安官** a railroad security officer ‖ **軽便鉄道** a light railway.

てっとうてつび 徹頭徹尾 ▶私はその事件を徹頭徹尾調べ上げた I investigated the case *thoroughly*.／I made a *thorough* investigation of the case. ‖ 彼は徹頭徹尾(=初めから終わりまで)その計画に反対した He was against the plan *from beginning to end*.

デッドヒート ▶彼らはゴール直前までデッドヒートを演じた They *were in a dead heat* until just before the goal. (➤ dead heat は本来は「(勝者のない)同着のレース」だが, 最近は「大接戦」の意でも使われる).

デッドボール ▶鳥谷はデッドボールで一塁へ出た Toritani *was hit by a pitch* and got [was walked] to first base.

> **危ないカタカナ語✹ デッドボール**
> 1 英語の dead ball はファウルなど一時的にプレーが中断するボールのことで, 日本でいう「デッドボール, 死球」の意味ではない.
> 2 英語では The batter was hit by a pitch. (打者は投球に当たった) のように動詞で表現し, 通例, 名詞ではいわない(あえて訳せば a pitch which hits the batter となる). 「死球を受けた打者」は hit batsman [batter] で, 「死球による出塁」は記録上 hit by a pitch を略して HBP または HP という.

てっとりばやい 手っ取り早い ▶説明書を読むよりも彼に聞くほうが手っとり早い It's *easier and quicker* to ask him than to read the manual. ‖ カラオケが上達する手っとり早い方法を教えてください Could you teach me how I can *easily and quickly* become better at karaoke? ‖ 手っとり早く言えばお金を貸していただきたいのです *To put it simply* [*In a nutshell*], I'd like you to lend me some money. (➤ それぞれ「簡単に言えば」,「要するに」).

デッドロック a deadlock ▶話し合いはデッドロックに乗り上げた The negotiations *came to a deadlock* [*a stalemate*]. 《参考》「デッドロックに乗り上げる」という日本語は「ロック」を rock(岩)と誤解したことから生まれた表現.

でっぱ 出っ歯 a bucktooth.

てっぱい 撤廃 abolition(廃止) 一動 **撤廃する** abolish +目; lift +目 (禁止令などを解く) ▶不公平税制を撤廃する *abolish* an unfair tax system ‖ 政府は米の輸入禁止令を撤廃した The government *lifted* the ban on importing rice.

でっぱり 出っ張り a projection ▶壁のあの出っ張りは何ですか What's that thing *sticking out* on the wall?

でっぱる 出っ張る stick out, protrude (➤ 後者は堅い語) ▶出っ張った岩 a *protruding* rock ‖ だいぶおなかが出っ張ってきたなあ I'm *getting quite a potbelly* [*beer belly*].

てっぱん 鉄板 an iron plate, a hot plate
‖ 鉄板焼き *teppan-yaki*; steaks and other foods grilled Japanese-style (➤ 説明的な訳).

てつびん 鉄瓶 an iron kettle.

でっぷりした stout /staʊt/ ▶でっぷりした体格の紳士 a *stout* [*portly*] gentleman.

てつぶん 鉄分 iron ▶鶏のレバーは鉄分が豊富だ Chicken liver is high in *iron*.

てっぺい 撤兵 (a) troop withdrawal 一動 **撤兵する** withdraw (+目)(戦闘を避けるために); evacuate (+目)(安全な場所へ移動するために) ▶大統領はその国から2000人撤兵することを決断した The president decided to *withdraw* [*evacuate*] 2,000 troops from the country.

てっぺん 天辺 the top ▶私たちはその山のてっぺんまで登った We reached *the top* of the mountain. ‖ 校長先生は頭のてっぺんがはげている Our principal has a bald spot at *the top* of the head.
▶《慣用表現》彼は私を頭のてっぺんから足のつま先までじろじろ見た He looked at me *from head to foot*.

てつぼう 鉄棒 an exercise bar, a horizontal bar (体操用の); an iron bar (鉄製の棒) ▶鉄棒の練習をする practice on *an exercise* [*a horizontal*] *bar*.

てっぽう 鉄砲 a gun(ライフル・ピストルなど); a rifle(ライフル銃) ▶彼はウサギを狙って鉄砲を撃った He *fired* [*shot*] (*a gun*) at the rabbit.
‖ 鉄砲玉 a bullet ‖ 鉄砲水 a flash flood.

テッポウユリ 《植物》 an Easter lily.

てづまり 手詰まり a deadend; a stalemate ▶手詰まりになる[なっている] get [be] *stalemated*.

てつや 徹夜する stay [sit] up all night《doing》, pull an all-nighter (➤ 後者は《米・インフォーマル》で「徹夜で勉強[仕事]をする」の意) ▶徹夜で仕事をする work *all night* / work (*throughout*) *the whole night* ‖ 徹夜はこたえる *Staying up all night* is really hard on me. ‖ 若い頃はよく徹夜で勉強したものだ I used to *stay* [*sit*] *up all night studying* when I was young.
▶ 対話「疲れてるみたいだね」「徹夜できょうの試験の勉強をしてたからね」"You look exhausted." "I *was up all night* study*ing* [prepar*ing*] for today's exams."

てづる 手蔓 ▶就活のために手づるを求めて方々当たる turn to every acquaintance one has for *connections* to get a job.

でどころ 出所・出処 a source ▶そのニュースの出どころ the news *source* ‖ 税務署員は私に金の出どころについて尋ねた The tax office clerk asked me *where the money came from* [*how I got the money*]. ‖ 私はそのうわさの出どころを突き止めた I traced the *source* of the rumor [*where* the rumor *started*].

デトックス detoxification, detox ▶このお茶にはデトックス効果があると言われている This tea is supposed to *detoxify the body*.

テトラポッド a tetrapod, a wave impeding [dissipating] block(消波ブロック).

てどり 手取り ▶私の給料は手取りで20万円になります My salary is 200,000 yen *net* [*after taxes*]. / My *take-home* pay comes to 200,000 yen.

てとりあしとり 手取り足取り ▶きみが手取り足取り教えてやらなきゃ, 彼女にはその仕事はできないよ If you don't lead her *by the hand*, she'll never get the job done. ‖ 水泳の先生は私に手取り足取り(=一つ一つ親切に)教えてくれた The swimming instructor taught me *kindly, step by step*.

テナー 《音楽》 tenor /ténəʳ/; a tenor (歌手); a tenor (voice) (声); the tenor(声部)
‖ テナーサックス a tenor saxophone.

てなおし 手直しする revise +目 (大改訂または小改訂する); modify +目 (僅かな修正で改良する); improve +目 (欠陥などを矯正する); correct +目 (間違いを訂正する)
▶草稿を手直しする *revise* [*modify*] a draft ‖ その翻訳は手直しの必要がある That translation *must be revised* [*be modified* / *be improved*]. ‖ カレンは私の英文レポートを手直ししてくれた Karen *corrected* my English paper. ‖ その書類には手直しされた跡があった I found some places where the document *had been changed* [*modified* / *altered*].

でなおす 出直す ▶また出直して参ります(=また来ます) I'll *come to see* you *again*. ‖ 父は事業に失敗し, 一から出直す(＝やり直す)ことになった My father failed in his business and had to *make a fresh start* [had to *start again from scratch*].

てなげだん 手投げ弾 →しゅりゅうだん.

てなずける 手懐ける **tame** +⊞ (動物を) ; **win over** (人を味方にする) ▶野生のタヌキを手なずけるのは難しい It is difficult to *tame* a wild *tanuki* (raccoon). ‖ 課長は部下を手なずけようと必死だ The section chief is all out to *win* everyone in his section (*over*) *to his side*.

てなみ 手並み ▶テニスがお上手と伺っていますが, お手並みを拝見したいですね I hear you're a good tennis player—*let's see just how good* (*you are*) [*let's see your skill*].

てならい 手習い ▶60の手習いで最近水泳を始めたんですよ *Thinking it is never too late to learn*, I started (taking) swimming lessons recently. (➤「習うのに遅すぎるということはないと考えて」の意).

てなれた 手慣れた ▶彼のパソコン操作は手慣れたものだ He *is quite experienced* [*skilled*] in operating a personal computer.

テナント a **tenant** ▶《掲示》テナント募集中. 012-3456に電話してください *Space For Rent* [*To Let*]. Call 012-3456. (➤ for rent は主に《米》, to let は主に《英》).

てにいれる 手に入れる →手.

テニス **tennis** (➤ 通例硬式テニスを指す) ▶きのう洋一郎とテニスをした I *played tennis* with Yoichiro yesterday. ‖ テニスしない? How about *playing tennis*? ‖ あしたはテニスの試合がある We have *a tennis match* [*tournament*] tomorrow. (➤ 前者は「1試合」, 後者は「勝ち抜き戦」).

‖**テニスコート** a tennis court ‖ **軟式テニス** soft tennis (➤ 日本で考案されたもの).

「テニス用語」のいろいろ アドバンテージ advantage ／エース ace ／オーバーハンド overhand ／グラウンドストローク ground stroke ／グラスコート grass court ／クレーコート clay court ／サービス service ／サーブ serve ／サイドライン sideline ／シード seed ／ジュース deuce ／シングルス singles ／ストローク stroke ／スマッシュ smash ／スライス slice ／セットポイント set point ／タイブレーク tiebreaker ／ダブルス doubles ／ダブルフォールト double fault ／トップスピン topspin ／ハードコート hard court ／バックハンド backhand ／パッシングショット passing shot ／フォアハンド forehand ／フォールト fault ／ブレークポイント break point ／ベースライン baseline ／ボレー volley ／マッチポイント match point ／ラブ love ／ラリー rally ／リターン return ／ロブ lob

てにてに 手に手に ▶沿道の観客は手に手に小旗を持ってマラソン選手たちに声援を送った Spectators along the streets cheered the marathoners with small flags *in their hands*.

デニム **denim** ▶デニムのジャケット a *denim* jacket ‖ デニムのジーンズ denims.

てにもつ 手荷物 **baggage**, **luggage**

語法 (1) 前者は《主に米》, 後者は《主に英》だが, 航空機・船の場合は《英》でも前者を用いることが多い. なお《米》では luggage は荷物よりかばん類などの入れ物を指すことが多い. (2) ともに Ⓤ なので, 数えるときは a piece of baggage [luggage] のようにいう.

▶私の手荷物は博多駅に預けてある I have checked my *baggage* at Hakata Station. ‖ (一時預りで) 料金は手荷物1個につき500円です The charge is ¥500 for each *piece of baggage*.

▶手荷物はいくつ機内に持ち込めますか How many pieces of *baggage* can I take on the plane? (➤「持ち込み手荷物」は carry-on baggage または unchecked baggage という) ‖ 搭乗前には手荷物検査があります *All your baggage must be screened* before boarding.

‖**手荷物預かり証** a baggage claim tag ; 《主に英》 a luggage ticket ‖ (駅の) **手荷物一時預かり所** 《米》 a baggage room, 《英》 a left-luggage office ‖ (空港などの) **手荷物受取所** a baggage claim (area) ‖ (空港などの) **手荷物係** a baggage [luggage] handler.

てぬい 手縫いの **handsewn** /hæ̀ndsóʊn/ ▶手縫いのブラウス a *handsewn* [*handmade*] blouse.

てぬかり 手抜かり an **oversight** (手落ち) ▶大事なお客さまだから手抜かりのないように頼みます He's [She's] a very important guest, so make sure there are no *oversights* [*slip-ups*]. ‖ 手抜かりはないか Is everything all right [OK]? ‖ それは私の手抜かりでした It's my *fault*.

てぬき 手抜き **corner-cutting** ▶業者が手抜き工事をしたに違いない. 床が傾いている The builders must *have cut corners*. The floor isn't level. ‖ 父の手抜き料理はもううんざりだ I'm fed up with my father's *lazy cooking*.

▶仕事で手抜きをするな *Be conscientious* in your work. (➤ conscientious /kɑ̀ːnʃiénʃəs/ は「良心的な」の意).

てぬぐい 手拭い a ***tenugui*** ; a Japanese-style thin hand towel (made of cotton) (➤ 説明的な訳).

てぬるい 手緩い **easy** (言いなりになる) ; **lenient** (寛大な) ▶あの先生は遅刻の罰が手ぬるい That teacher *is too easy* [*lenient*] *on* (his) students who are late for class. ‖ そんな罰では違反者には手ぬるいよ. もっと厳しくしなくっちゃ That's *a mere slap on the wrist* for them. You should be tougher on offenders. (➤ a slap on the wrist は「なまぬるい罰」の意のインフォーマルな表現).

テネシー **Tennessee** /tènəsíː/ (アメリカ南東部の州 ; 略 TN, Tenn.).

てのうち 手の内 ▶交渉にあたっては手の内を見せては負けだ You lose out in negotiations if you *show your hand* [*put all your cards on the table*]. (➤ ともにトランプからきた表現).

テノール 《音楽》 **tenor** /ténəʳ/

‖**テノール歌手** a tenor. →テナー.

てのひら 手の平・掌 **the palm** /pɑːm/ (**of one's hand**) ▶女の子は手のひらにテントウムシを載せていた The girl had a ladybug on *the palm* [*flat*] *of her hand*.

▶《慣用表現》私が要求を断ると, 彼は手のひらを返すように急に態度を変えた When I refused his request, he suddenly *changed his tune*. (➤ change one's tune は「態度をがらりと変える」) ／When I turned down his request, *his attitude changed drastically* [*completely*].

デノミ(ネーション) **redenomination** ; **renaming of currency units** 《参考》 denomination は「貨幣単位」のこと. 「貨幣単位の呼称変更」の意味では redenomination とする.

-ては 1【条件を示して】▶そんなことを言われては黙っていられない I can't keep quiet *after* what they said to me. ‖ あの子と一緒でなくては映画に行きたくない I don't want to go to the movie *if* she doesn't go with me.
2【反復を示して】▶彼はうそをついては親に叱られている *Every time* he tells a lie, he gets scolded by his parents.
▶2人は何度となくけんかしては, またすぐ仲直りする They quarrel often, *but* soon make up (with each other).
▶《慣用表現》食っては寝, 食っては寝で, 夏の間に3キロも太った I *spent all the time eating and lying around the house*. That's how I gained three kilos over the summer.

-てば, -ってば ▶危ないってば It's dangerous, *I tell you*. ‖ ほんとうだってば It's *really* true.

では now, well (さて) ; then (それでは ; それで) ▶では本題に入りましょう *Now*, let's get to the main point. ‖ ではそろそろ失礼します *Well*, I must be going now. ‖ では始めよう *Well*, let's get started [let's start]. ‖ ではまた See you later. ／(I'll) be seeing you. ‖ ではお休みなさい Good night, *then*.
▶ではきみが行っても無駄だね *Then* it's no use your going. ‖ では, あなたは人種差別主義についてどう思われますか *Well then*, what do you think of racial discrimination?
✉ **またお便りします. ではまた** I'll write you again. Bye for now.
✉ **ではこの辺で** That's all for today. ／*Well*, I think that's all I have to say for now. ➤「今のところお話しすべきことはこれだけです」の意.

-では 1【場所を特定して】at, in (➤ 地点には at, 地域には in を用いるのがふつう) ▶甲子園球場では阪神・巨人戦が行われている A Tigers-Giants game is being held *at* Koshien Stadium. ‖ 神戸では晴れているが, 京都では曇りだ It's sunny *in* Kobe, but it's cloudy *in* Kyoto.
2【分野を特定して】▶スキーでは三浦君にかなう人はいない No one can beat Miura *when it comes to* skiing. (● when it comes to ... は「…ということになると」; to のあとは名詞または動名詞がくる) ‖ 彼は守備では優秀だが打撃がよくない He's very good *at* fielding, but not so good *at* batting.
▶首相は外交面では目覚ましく奮闘した The Prime Minister has been very active *on* the diplomatic front.
3【判断の基準を示して】▶300万円ではフェラーリは買えない You can't buy a Ferrari *with* only three million yen. ‖ こんな成績ではS大合格はおぼつかないな I'm not sure you will be accepted by S University *with* such grades.
▶私の考えではわが町の議員は多すぎる *In my opinion*, our city has too many (municipal) assembly members. ‖ きみたちのようなボールさばきでは(＝から判断すると)レギュラーにはなれないぞ *Judging from* the way you handle a ball, you can't make the regular team.
▶内閣官房長官の話では政府は減税を実施するそうだ The Chief Cabinet Secretary said that the government would reduce taxes. ‖ 来週では遅すぎる. 今週中に仕上げなさい Next week is too late. Finish it up this week.

デパート a department store, 《英また》a big store ▶私は母と梅田のデパートへ買い物に行った I went shopping at *a department store* in Umeda with my mother.

> **危ないカタカナ語✹ デパート**
> 「デパート」は英語の department からきているが, department は「部門, 売り場」の意味であって百貨店のことではない. 「百貨店」の意味では department store と必ず store をつける. イギリスでは big store, the stores ともいう.

てはい 手配 arrangements (手はず, 段取り ; 通例複数形で) ; preparation(s) (準備 ; 具体的な準備の意味のときは通例複数形) 一動 **手配する** arrange, prepare ▶新婚旅行の手配は全部旅行代理店に依頼した We asked a travel agency to make all the *arrangements* for our honeymoon. ‖ 彼らはいろいろと運動会のための手配をした They *made preparations* [*prepared*] for the athletic meet.
▶この荷物はきょう中に発送するよう手配しましょう We will *arrange* to send this parcel today. ／We will *see* (*to it*) *that* this parcel is sent today. (➤ see to it that ... は「…するよう取り計らう」の意) ‖ 警察はその男を指名手配した The police *put* the man *on the* (*most-*) *wanted list*. ／The police *put out an APB* on the man. (➤ APB は all-points bulletin (全部署緊急連絡, 全国指名手配)の略).
✉ **4月1, 2日パリに出張します. 宿泊の手配をお願いします** I will be making a business trip to Paris from April 1 to 2. I would appreciate it if you could *arrange* my accommodations.

てはじめに 手始めに ▶手始めにこれをやってごらん Try this *first* [*at the beginning*]. ‖ 手始めにクラブの持ち方から練習します Let's *start with* [*by*] practicing how to hold the club. ‖ 手始めに各自自己紹介をしましょう *First of all*, let's each introduce ourselves by turns.

てはず 手筈 arrangements (➤ 複数形で) ▶会議の手はずはすっかり整った Everything *is arranged* [*is set*] for the conference. ‖ 私たちは劇場の前で彼と会う手はずになっている We *are supposed to* meet him in front of the theater.

てばたしんごう 手旗信号 semaphore.

デパちか デパ地下 a department store's basement food floor.

でばな 出端・出鼻 ▶父親のそのひと言で彼女は出ばなをくじかれた That single word of her father's *killed her enthusiasm*. ‖ 1回の表に3点入れて中日は阪神の出ばなをくじいた With three runs in the top of the first inning, the Dragons *stopped* the Tigers *dead in their tracks*. (➤ stop A dead in A's tracks は「たちどころにAの動きを止める」の意のインフォーマルな表現).

てばなし 手放し ▶手放しで(＝手を放して)自転車に乗るのは危険だ It's dangerous to ride a bicycle *with no hands* [*without using* (*one's*) *hands*].
▶彼女の行動を手放しで褒めるわけにはいかない Her conduct *cannot* be regarded as *altogether* praiseworthy. (➤ not ... altogether で部分否定) ‖ 父の手術が成功したからといってまだ手放しでは喜べない Just because my father's operation went well *doesn't mean we can stop worrying and celebrate*.

てばなす 手放す・手離す part with (人手に渡す) ; sell ＋目 (売る) ▶母はしかたなくダイヤの指輪を手放した My mother had no (other) choice but to *part with* her diamond ring. ‖ この絵は100万円以下では**手放**せません(＝売れない) I can't *sell* this picture [can't *let* this picture *go*] for less than a million yen. ‖ 多くの人にとって携帯電話は片ときも**手放せない**(＝無しでは済ませられない) Many people *cannot do without* their cellphones [*are inseparable* from] even for a second.

てばなれ 手離れ ▶ようやく子供たちが大きくなって**手離れ**しました Now my kids have grown up and *no longer need our constant care and attention*.

でばぼうちょう 出刃包丁 a **kitchen knife with a pointed tip**.

てばやく 手早く **quickly**(機敏に); **speedily**(スピーディーに) ▶部屋の中を**手早く**片づける clean up the room *quickly* ／put the room in order *speedily* ‖ お酢を加えて**手早く**かき混ぜなさい Add vinegar and stir *quickly*. ‖ 父は帰宅が遅いときはハムサンドを**手早く**こしらえた When my father got home late, he *rustled up* a ham sandwich. (➤ rustle up は「(食事など)を手早くこしらえる」) ‖ 彼は**手早く**昼食をこしらえた He *threw together* a quick lunch. (➤ throw together は「(食事)を有り合わせのもので手早く作る」).

ではらう 出払う ▶あいにくうちのタクシーは全部**出払って**います I'm sorry but our taxis *are* all *out*.

でばん 出番 one's **turn** ▶《ステージで》さあ, あなたの**出番**よ Now it's your *turn* (to go on the stage). ‖ 先発投手が好調だったのでぼくの**出番**(＝登板の機会)はなかった I had no *opportunity to take the mound* because the starter was in good form.

てびかえる 手控える ▶宗教団体に対しては警察は捜査を**手控える**傾向にあった The police had a tendency to *refrain from* investigating religious organizations.

てびき 手引き **1【助けること・案内すること】**▶私はお年寄りを**手引きして**(＝手を引いて)病院内を歩いた I *led* the elderly man [woman] around the hospital *by the hand*. ‖ ジョンの**手引き**でシカゴの観光をした John *took* me sightseeing around Chicago. ‖ 美香の**手引き**で彼は銀行に就職できた He was able to get a job at a bank *through* Mika's *introduction*.

2【解説書】 a **manual**(使い方の); a **handbook**, a **guide(book)**(案内書) ▶(機械などの)使用の**手引き** an operating *manual* ／operating *instructions* ‖ 海外旅行の**手引き** *a guidebook* on traveling abroad ‖ 詳しくは**手引き**をご覧ください Please refer to the *manual* for further information.

デビットカード a **debit card**.

てひどい 手酷い ▶考えもなしに契約書に署名してあとで**手ひどい**目に遭った I *had a terrible time of it* because I signed the contract without really thinking (about it). ‖ その評論家は彼の新しい小説を**手ひどく**やっつけた The commentator *severely* criticized his new novel.

デビュー a **debut** /déɪbju:/ **一動 デビューする** **make** one's **debut** ▶**デビュー作品** one's *first work* ‖ **デビュー**したての女優 a *debuting* actress ‖ 彼女が映画界に**デビュー**したのは2年前のことだ It has been two years since she *made her debut* [she *first appeared*] in films. ‖『A・RA・SHI』は嵐の**デビュー曲**だ ARASHI *made their debut with the song* "A・RA・SHI."

てびょうし 手拍子 ▶私たちは**手拍子**をとりながら校歌を歌った We sang our school song *clapping with the beat*.

てびろく 手広く **on a large scale**(大規模に); **extensively**(広範囲に) ▶その会社は関東地区で**手広く**商売をしている That company is doing business *on a large scale* in the Kanto area. ‖ 彼らは**手広く**輸入業を営んでいる They are *extensively* involved in the import business.

でぶ a **fatty**(➤ 通例軽蔑的に); a **porky**(➤ 通例おどけて); a **butterball** (➤ 通例親しみを込めて); a **fatso** /fǽtsoʊ/ (➤ 通例軽蔑的, あるいはおどけて).

デフォルト《コンピュータ》(a) **default** ▶ワードの文書は**デフォルト**で doc や docx などの拡張子が付く The extension doc, docx and so forth are attached to a Word document *by default*.

デフォルメ (a) **deformation** (➤ 日本語はフランス語の déformer から) ▶ピカソの**デフォルメ**された女性の顔 a woman's *deformed* face by Picasso.

てふき 手拭き a **hand towel**.

てぶくろ 手袋 (a **pair of**) **gloves** /glʌvz/; (a **pair of**) **mittens**(親指だけ分かれたミトン) ▶**手袋**をはめる put on one's *gloves* ‖ **手袋**を脱ぐ take [pull] off one's *gloves* ‖ 彼女は**手袋**のまま私と握手した She shook hands with me *with her gloves on*.

でぶしょう 出不精・出無精 ▶妻は**出不精**です My wife *doesn't like going out*. ／My wife *is a homebody* [*a stay-at-home person*]. (➤ stay-at-home は「出不精の」) ‖ 彼女は結婚してから**出不精**になった After she got married, she became *a homebody* [*a stay-at-home person*].

てぶら 手ぶらの **empty-handed** ▶張り切ってバーゲンに行ったのに母は**手ぶら**で帰って来た My mother went out in high spirits hoping to buy a lot of things at a sale, but came back *empty-handed*. ‖ あす内輪のパーティーをやるんだ. **手ぶらで来いよ** We are having an informal party tomorrow. Please *just bring yourself*. (➤「手ぶらで来てください」の意の決まり文句). ▶日本では人の家を初めて訪問するとき**手ぶら**で(＝手土産を持たないで)行く人は少ない In Japan, there are few people who do*n't take* [*bring*] *a present* when they visit another person's house for the first time. (➤ take も bring も「持って行く」だが,take は持参者の出発点に視点があり,bring は受け取る人の到着点に視点がある).

デフラグ《コンピュータ》**defragmentation** ▶ハードディスクを**デフラグする** *defragment* a hard disk.

てぶり 手振り a **gesture**(しぐさ); a **hand movement**(手の動き).

てぶれ 手ぶれ **camera shake** ▶**手ぶれ**を防ぐ prevent *camera shake* ‖ **手ぶれ補正機能**付きカメラ a camera equipped with an *anti-shake* [*anti-blur* ／*image stabilizing*] *function*.

デフレ(ーション) **deflation** ▶**デフレ**への対策を講じる take measures against *deflation*.

デフロスター a **defroster**, a **demister**(➤ 冷蔵庫の霜取り装置の場合は英米ともに前者を, 車の場合は《米》では前者または defogger を,《英》では後者をそれぞれ用いることが多い).

でべそ 出臍 a **protruding belly button**.

テヘラン **Teh(e)ran** /terá:n/ (イランの首都).

てべんとう 手弁当 ▶ボランティアたちは**手弁当**で被災者支援に集まった Volunteers gathered to give the victims a helping hand, *each bringing their own box lunch*. ‖ **手弁当**で(＝報酬を当てにせずに)選挙の応援をする work on an election campaign *without pay* [*being paid*／*compensation*].

てほどき 手解き initiation, (an) introduction ▶父から碁の手ほどきをしてもらった I *was initiated into* the game of 'Go' by my father.

てぼり 手彫り ▶手彫りの人形 a *hand-carved* doll.

てほん 手本 an example(例)；a model(模範) ▶ほかの生徒のよい手本となるよう努めなさい Try to be a good *example* to the other students. ‖ 山野氏は私が医師として手本とする人です Mr. Yamano is my *role model* as a doctor. (➤ role model は「模範となるもの, 理想の姿」).
▶子供は両親を手本にして育つものだ Children grow up *following the example of* [*patterning themselves after*／*modeling themselves on*] their parents.

てま 手間 time(時間)；labor(労力)；trouble (手数) ▶プログラムの組み直しには手間がかかる Restructuring a program will take much *time and labor*. ‖ こんな手間のかかる仕事は嫌だ I hate this kind of *troublesome* job [*time-consuming* job]. ‖ ノートをコピーしてしまえば書き写す手間が省ける I'll make a photocopy of the notebook and that will *save* me the *trouble* of copying it (by hand).
‖**手間仕事** piecework (賃仕事) ‖**手間賃** pay, wages.
☛ 手間取る, 手間ひま (→見出語)

デマ a false [groundless] rumor ▶数日中に富士山が噴火するというデマが飛んだ There was *a false rumor* that Mt. Fuji was going to erupt in a few days. ‖ その女優が結婚したというううわさはデマだった(＝根拠がなかった) The rumor that the actress had gotten married turned out to *be groundless*. ‖ 誰がそんなデマを飛ばしたんだい Who *started a rumor* like that?
▶後継総裁選びについてデマが飛んでいるらしい *Rumors* seem to *be circulating* [*flying*] as to who will be chosen as the next president.

> **危ないカタカナ語✸デマ**
> **1**「デマ」はドイツ語の *Demagogie* から出た語. 英語にも demagogy /déməgɑːgi/ という語があるが, これは「政治的な民衆扇動」の意である.
> **2**「でたらめなうわさ, 中傷」「人を陥すためにわざと流すその知らせ」の意では false rumor や groundless rumor などを用いる.

てまえ 手前 **1**【こちら側】this side ▶橋の手前でタクシーを拾った I got a taxi on *this side* of the bridge. ‖ 彼女は浜松の1つ手前の駅で電車に乗る She gets on the train one station *before* Hamamatsu. ‖ 消防署の手前を左に曲がると駅に行けます You can get to the train station if you turn left *just before* the fire station.
▶わが社は今や倒産の一歩手前だ Our company is *on the verge* [*brink*] *of* bankruptcy.
2【他人に対する体裁】▶子供の手前, 夫婦げんかもできない I feel (that) I shouldn't quarrel with my husband *in the presence of* the children. ‖ 周囲の反対を押し切って始めた手前, この事業を今やめるわけにはいかない I can't quit this business now, *after* having started it against everyone's advice.

でまえ 出前 food delivery service；catering /kéɪt̬ərɪŋ/ service(パーティーなどへの仕出し) ▶あのそば屋は出前をする That *soba* shop *delivers* [*offers delivery service*]. ‖ すし屋に12時に出前をしてくれるよう頼んだ I asked the sushi shop to *deliver* sushi at noon. ‖ ピザの出前を取ろう Let's *call out for* pizza. (➤「電話して頼む」の意).
‖**出前持ち** a delivery person.

てまえがって 手前勝手な selfish(自分勝手な)；self-centered(自己中心的な). →自分勝手.

てまえみそ 手前味噌 ▶いささか手前みそになるが, 私の説は多くの人に受け入れられるだろう I may *be flattering myself*, but I expect my theory to be accepted by many people. ‖ 彼女はいつも手前みそばかり並べる She always *blows* [*toots*] *her own horn*. (➤ blow [toot] one's own horn は「自画自賛する」の意のインフォーマルな表現).

でまかせ 出任せ ▶あいつはいつも出まかせばかり言っている He's always *making irresponsible remarks*. ‖ 今までどこにいたのと聞かれて彼女は口から出まかせのうそをついた When asked where she had been, she came out with *a glib lie*. (➤ glib /glɪb/ は通例軽蔑して「うわべだけの」の意).

てまきずし 手巻きずし *temaki-zushi*；hand-rolled sushi (➤ 説明的な訳).

てまくら 手枕 ▶手枕で昼寝をする take a nap *using one's own arm as a pillow*.

でまど 出窓 a bay window；a bow window (弓形の).

てまどる 手間取る take time ▶鈴木先生の家を探すのにずいぶん手間取った It *took me a lot of time* to find Mr. Suzuki's house. ‖ 審査員たちはチャンピオンを決めるのに手間取った The judges *were slow* to decide who won the contest. ‖ 彼女は何を手間取っているんだろう What's *keeping* her? ‖ 入国審査で手間取った I *got held up* at customs. (➤ インフォーマルな言い方).

てまね 手真似 a gesture ▶彼はその外国人と手まねで話をした He communicated with the foreigner *with* [*through*] *gestures*. ‖ 彼は私に座れと手まねで言った He *made* me *a gesture to* sit down.／He *motioned* me *to* take a seat.

てまねき 手招き beckoning 一動 手招きする beckon /bekən/ ▶日本人は人を手招きするとき, 手のひらを下にして手を上下に動かします To *beckon* someone *over*, the Japanese move their hand up and down with the palm facing downward. ‖ 友だちがこっちへ来いと手招きをしている My friends *are beckoning* me to come over. ‖ 社長は手招きして私を部屋に呼び入れた The president *gestured* for me to enter his room.

てまひま 手間暇・手間隙 ▶手間ひまかけて育てたリンゴがこの台風8号で7割方落ちてしまった Because of Typhoon No.8, about 70 percent of the apples I had *spent so much time and labor* raising were windfalls.

てまり 手鞠・手毬 a *temari*；a small ball a girl enjoys bouncing (➤ 説明的な訳).

てまわし 手回し preparations(準備) ▶彼女は手回しがいいのでいつも感心している I am always impressed by the thoroughness of her *preparations*.

てまわりひん 手回り品 one's (personal) belongings, one's things ▶お手回り品にご注意ください Please keep an eye on *your belongings*.

でまわる 出回る ▶早くもブドウが出回っている Grapes are already *on the market* now. ‖ このバッグの類似品が出回っているらしい I hear there are a lot of bags *around* similar to this one. ‖ 偽札が出回っている Counterfeit bills *are circulating* [*are going around*].

て

デミグラスソース (a) **demi-glace sauce**.

てみじか 手短な brief ▶要点だけを手短に説明してください Please outline the main points *briefly*.／Please give a *brief* explanation of the matter. ‖ 手短に言うと2人は別れたんだよ *To make* [*cut*] *a long story short* [*In short*／*In brief*], they broke up.

でみせ 出店 a **branch**(支店); a **booth**, a **stand** (屋台); a **concession**(ショッピングセンター内などの).

てみやげ 手土産 a **present**, a **gift** (➤後者は前者より堅い語) ▶日本では人の家を初めて訪れるとき, よく手土産を持っていく In Japan, when people visit others for the first time, they usually bring *a present*.

て

てむかう 手向かう stand up to ▶誰もそのいじめっ子に手向かおうとしなかった Nobody attempted to *stand up to* the bully.

でむかえ 出迎え ▶空港までお出迎えに参ります I will (*come to*) *meet* you at the airport. ‖ 社長は空港で市長の出迎えを受けた The president *was greeted* by the mayor at the airport.

でむかえる 出迎える meet +⽬ (会う); **welcome** +⽬ (歓迎する); **receive** +⽬ (迎え入れる) ▶おじを大宮駅まで出迎えた I went to Omiya Station to *meet* my uncle. ‖ 町を挙げて優勝した野球部員たちを出迎えた The whole town *welcomed* the winning baseball team. ‖ 総理は賓客を玄関で出迎えた The Prime Minister *received* the guest at the entrance.

でむく 出向く go(行く); **come**(相手から見て) ▶私は彼女に会いにわざわざ彼女の郷里まで出向いた I *went* all the way to her hometown to see her. ‖ こちらから出向きますからそこでお待ちください I'll *come* to your place. Please wait there. (相手の場所へ「行く」は go でなく come).

テムズがわ テムズ川 the Thames /temz/ (ロンドンを貫流する川).

でめきん 出目金《魚》 **popeyed** [**telescope-eyed**] **goldfish** [複 **goldfish**].

デメリット a **disadvantage**, a **demerit**(➤前者が日常的に用いる語) ▶どの案にもメリットとデメリットがある Each plan has advantages and *disadvantages*.

-ても 1【…したとしても】**even if**(仮に…でも) ▶雨が降ってもぼくは行くからね I'll go [come] *even if* it rains. ‖ 年を取ってもゴルフは続けるつもりだ *Even after* I get old, I will keep on golfing. (この例のように必ず起こることをいう場合は even if としない).

> 【文型】
> (いくら)…しても
> **no matter** A
> ➤ A は what, how などの文
> 《解説》**no matter** who visits me (誰が訪ねて来ても), **no matter** where you go (どこへ行っても) など疑問詞の文を続ける. ただし, 「どんなことがあっても, 何が起きようと」は **no matter** what happens だが, しばしば **no matter** what で済ます.

▶何度聞かれても, 知らないものは知らないのです *No matter how many times* you ask, if I say I don't know, I don't know. ‖ いくら頭がよくても, 他人に対する思いやりがなければ人間として失格だ *No matter how* smart you are, if you don't have consideration for others, you are a failure as a person. ‖ 休日はどこへ行ってもすごい人だ On holidays, you run into crowds of people *no matter where* you go [*wherever* you go].

▶雨が降っても降らなくても, あすは外出します I'm going out tomorrow *whether* it rains *or* shines [*whether* rain or shine].

2【「…てもよい」の形で】▶この手紙を見てもよいが, 声に出して読まないでくれ You *can* read this letter, but don't read it aloud.

でも but ▶ 対話「プール行かない?」「うん, でもあした試験だしなあ」"How about going to the pool?" "Sounds good, *but* I have an exam tomorrow."

デモ 1【抗議の】a **demonstration**,《インフォーマル》a **demo** 一動 **デモをする demonstrate** ▶その河口堰(ぜき)建設反対のデモに参加する join [participate in] the *demonstration* against building a dam across the mouth of that river ‖ 数千のデモ隊がプラカードを持ち, シュプレヒコールをしながら雨の中を行進した Several thousand *demonstrators* marched in the rain, carrying signs and shouting [chanting] slogans. (➤「デモ参加者」は protesters を用いることも多い).

▶街頭デモを行う *hold a street demonstration*／*take to the streets* ‖ 抗議デモ(行進)を行う stage *a protest march* [*a protest demonstration*] ‖ 彼らは国会議事堂の前をデモ行進した They *marched in a demonstration* in front of the Diet Building.

‖デモ隊 demonstrators ‖ 反戦 [反政府] デモ an antiwar [antigovernment] demonstration.

2【販売促進用の】a **demo** [複 **demos**]

‖デモテープ a demo tape.

-でも 1【譲歩を示して】**even**, **even if** ▶そんなカーブはアマチュア選手でも打てる *Even* an amateur player could hit a curve ball like that one. ‖ あすは雨天でもラグビーの試合は行われます We are going to have a rugby match tomorrow, *even if* it rains.

▶旧式でもいいですからそのパソコンをください Please let me have the computer. I *don't care if* it's an old model. ‖ この仕事は残業してでも片づけたい I want to get this job done, *even if* I have to work overtime.

▶今でもきみを愛している I *still* love you.

2【どんな…でも】**any …** ▶必要なときはいつでもお手伝いします I can help you *any time* you need me. ‖ 冷蔵庫にあるものは何でも自由に飲んでください You can drink *anything* in the refrigerator. ‖ 社長は奥さんの言うことは何でも認めてしまう The president accepts *anything* his wife says.

3【最低限を示して】**at least** ▶あのとき手付金だけでも払っておくんだった I should have *at least* paid a deposit then.

4【…か何[誰]か】▶コーヒーでも飲もうか Let's have a cup of coffee *or something*. ‖ 映画でも見ようか Shall we go to the movies?／How about going to the movies? ‖ 吉田先生にでも相談してみたら? Why don't you try talking it over with, *say*, Mr. Yoshida?

デモクラシー democracy.

てもち 手持ち ▶手持ちのお金を全部お貸ししましょう I'll lend you all the money I *have with me* [*I have on hand*]. ‖ 手持ちの(=在庫の)品はみんなはけた The goods *in stock* have all been sold.

てもちぶさた 手持ち無沙汰 ▶手持ち無沙汰で(=ほかに何もすることが無くて)新聞を何度も読み返した I read the same newspaper over and over again because I *had nothing else to do*.

てもと 手元 ▶手元の現金 cash *in hand* ‖ 私はいつも

辞書を手元に置いている I always keep my dictionary (*near*) *at hand*. ‖ その資料は現在手元にございませんので, あすこちらからお電話します I'm sorry I don't have the data *with me* now. Let me call you tomorrow. ‖ 今ぼくの手元には2000円しかない I have only 2,000 yen *with* [*on*] *me* now. ‖ 詳しくはお手元にお配りしたパンフレットをご覧ください For further information, please refer to the brochure *that was given to you*.

▶手元が狂って弾丸は少しのところでイノシシに当たらなかった (*My aim was off* and) the bullet narrowly missed (hitting) the boar.

でもの 出物 a **bargain**(買い得品).

デモンストレーション **demonstration** ▶化粧品のデモンストレーション販売 cosmetic *demonstration and sales*. ‖デモンストレーション競技 a demonstration sport.

デュエット a **duet** /dju:ét/ ▶ボーイフレンドとデュエットで歌う sing *a duet* with one's boyfriend ‖ 妹とバイオリンとフルートのデュエットをした My (younger) sister and I *played a duet* for violin and flute.

てら 寺 a **temple** ▶秋に奈良の有名な寺巡りがしたい I want to visit the famous *Buddhist temples* in Nara this fall. ‖ 鎌倉の禅寺で座禅を組んだ I meditated [sat for meditation] at *a Zen temple* in Kamakura. 《参考》東大寺は (the) Todaiji Temple のようにいう.

テラ **tera-** ▶テラバイト *terabyte* (略 TB).

てらい 衒い a **affectation**.

てらう 衒う ▶博学をてらう *show off* one's profound knowledge ‖ あいつ, ちょっと奇をてらってるな He *pretends to be* a bit *strange*.

デラウェア **Delaware** /déləweəʳ/ (アメリカ東部, 大西洋岸の州 ; 略 DE, Del.).

テラコッタ **terracotta, terra-cotta**.

てらこや 寺子屋 a ***terakoya*** ; a private educational institution for commoners' children during the Edo period (➤ 説明的な訳).

てらしあわせる 照らし合わせる **check** +目 (照合する) ▶自分の答えと本の模範解答とを照らし合わせてみた I *checked* my answers against the model answers in the book. (➤ check A against B で「AとBとを照らし合わせる」).

てらす 照らす **1【光が】shine** 《on, over》(輝く) ; **light** +目 (明るくする) ▶満月が海を照らしていた The full moon *was shining on* the sea. ‖ 月が野原を照らしていた The moon *was shining over* the field. / The field *was moonlit*. ‖ 彼は懐中電灯でそのドアを照らした He *shined* a flashlight *on* that door. ‖ 懐中電灯で足元を照らしてごらん *Throw* (*some*) *light on* the trail ahead with the flashlight.

2【比較する】▶法律に照らしてみると彼のしたことは犯罪に相当する *According to* the law, what he did is a crime. / If we *judge* his conduct by the law, it must be considered a crime.

テラス a **terrace**, a **patio** /pǽṭioʊ/ ▶テラスで新聞を読む read a newspaper on the *terrace*.

‖テラスハウス《米》a row house, a town house, 《英》a terraced house, a terrace-house.

デラックス **deluxe** /dəlʌ́ks/ ; **gorgeous** (豪華な) ▶デラックスな車 a *deluxe* car ‖ デラックスなホテル a *deluxe* [*first-class* / *topnotch*] hotel ‖ デラックスなマンションに住む live in a *luxurious* [*deluxe*] condominium.

てり 照り 《料理》a **glaze**.

テリア 《動物》a **terrier** ‖フォックステリア a fox terrier ‖ヨークシャーテリア a Yorkshire terrier.

テリーヌ (a) **terrine** ▶フォアグラのテリーヌ (a) foie gras *terrine*.

てりかえし 照り返し **reflection** ▶舗道は照り返しが強烈だった The *reflected heat* on the sidewalk was fierce.

デリカシー **delicacy** ; **sensitivity** (思いやり) ▶デリカシーのない男性 a man without *delicacy* ‖ 彼はデリカシーに欠ける He *lacks sensitivity*. / He *is insensitive*.

デリカテッセン a **delicatessen**, 《インフォーマル》a **deli** (➤ delica とはいわない).

デリケート **delicate** /délɪkət/ ▶それはデリケートな問題で, 人前では話せない It is too *delicate* a matter to discuss in front of other people. ‖ 乙女心はデリケートだ A young girl's heart *is easily hurt*. (➤「傷つきやすい」の意).

> **危ないカタカナ語✹ デリケート**
> 「デリケートな (＝微妙な, 扱いにくい) 問題」は delicate matter でよいが,「(人の性格が)デリケートな」という場合の「デリケート」には sensitive を用いる. 人について delicate を用いると「きゃしゃな」「虚弱な」の意味にとられやすいので注意が必要.

てりつける 照り付ける **blaze down** ▶背中に太陽が照りつけていた The sun *was blazing on* [*down on* / *upon*] my back.

デリバリー **delivery**.

てりやき 照り焼き (a) **teriyaki** (➤英語化している) 《参考》teriyaki は英語になっているが, 日本料理の「魚の照り焼き」を説明的にいうと fish broiled after being marinated in *shoyu* [soy sauce] and *mirin* [sweet rice wine] となる.

てりゅうだん 手榴弾 →しゅりゅうだん.

てりょうり 手料理 ▶今夜は久しぶりにおふくろの手料理にありつける Tonight I'll get to eat Mom's *cooking* for the first time in ages.

てる 照る **shine** (輝く) ▶さっきまで降っていたのにもう日が照っているよ It was raining until just a few minutes ago, but *the sun is shining* now. ‖ 日が頭上にかんかんと照っている The sun *is burning down* on my head. / The sun *is baking* my head. ‖ 降っても照ってもあすは防火訓練が行われる *Rain or shine*, there will be a fire drill tomorrow. ▶《慣用表現》人生, 照る日もあれば曇る日もあるよ We all *have our ups and downs* in life. (➤ ups and downs は「浮き沈み」の意).

でる 出る

> **訳語メニュー**
> 外へ出る →go out of **1**
> 出発する →leave **2**
> 卒業する →graduate from **3**
> 到達する →come to **4**
> 出席する →be present at **5**
> 出演する →appear **6**

1【中から外へ移動する】go out 《of》, **get out** 《of》 ▶外へ出ろ! *Get out!* ‖ 出ていけ! *Get out of here!* ‖ 子供たちは一斉に雪の積もったグラウンドに出て遊んだ All the children *went out* to play on the snow-covered playground. ‖ できるだけ早くこの島を出たい I want to *get off* this island as soon as I can. ▶母は今出て(＝出かけて)います Mother is *out* now.

‖監督がダッグアウトから出て来た The manager *has come out of* the dugout. ‖赤いポルシェがその駐車場から出ていった A red Porsche *pulled out of* the parking lot. (➤ pull out は「(車や列車が)出ていく」)

▶横浜インターで東名高速を出た(＝降りた) I *got off* the Tomei Expressway at the Yokohama Interchange. ‖彼は18のとき東京へ出た He *went to* Tokyo at the age of eighteen. ‖彼らは燃えている店から出られなくなった They *were trapped* in the burning store. ／They *couldn't escape* from the burning store.

2【出発する, 去る】leave ＋目 ▶あなたは毎朝何時に家を出ますか What time do you *leave* your house every morning? (leave home だと「家出をする」の意にもなるので,「家を出発する」は訳例のような言い方がよい).

▶品川駅では京急久里浜行きの電車は１番線から出ます At Shinagawa Station, trains for Keikyu Kurihama *leave* from Platform No.1. ‖バスはたった今出たところです The bus *has* just *left*. ‖彼女はぼくを捨てて出ていった She *walked out on* me. (➤ walk out on は「見捨てる」の意のくだけた言い方).

3【卒業する】graduate《from》(➤《米》では高校・大学に,《英》では大学に用いる) →卒業 ▶ 対話「きみはいつ大学を出たの？」「３年前です」"When did you *graduate from* college?" "Three years ago." ‖ 対話「きみはどこの中学を出たの」「地元のＫ中学です」"What junior high (school) did you *go to* [*attend*]?" "K Junior High School, a local school."

4【到達する】come《to》; **lead**《to》(道が) ▶国道38号線を３時間走るとその湖に出る If you drive along Route 38 for three hours, you'll *come to* the lake. ‖この道を行くと駅に出ますか Will I *get to* the train station if I go down this street? ‖この道を行けば市の中心地に出る This road *leads* you *to* the center of the city. ‖42丁目に出るまでにまだ８ブロックあります You have eight blocks to go till you *get to* 42nd Street.

5【参加する, 出席する】be present《at》(居合わせる); **take part**《in》, **participate**《in》(参加する; 後者は堅い語); **attend** ＋目 (会合などに出席する; やや堅い語) ▶彼女は夫にパーティーに出てくれと頼んだ She asked her husband to *attend* the party. ‖彼はそのマラソンに出た He *took part* [*participated*] *in* the marathon. ‖うちのサッカー部は全国高校選手権大会に出た Our soccer team *participated in* the All-Japan Inter High School Soccer Championship(s). ‖私の代わりに部下が会議に出た One of my staff members *attended* the meeting instead of me. ‖明日の会議は(どうしても)出られないんだ I *can't make it* to the meeting tomorrow.

▶ 対話「きみ, きのうの経済学の授業に出た？」「うん, 出たよ」"Did you *attend* the economics class yesterday?" "Yes, I did." ‖ 対話「今度のパーティー, 出る？」「うん, 出るよ」"Are you *go*ing to the next party?" "Sure."

6【出演する】appear ▶彼女はきのうテレビに出た She *appeared* on television yesterday. ‖私はラジオのインタビュー番組に出たことがある I once *was on* a radio interview program. ／I was once interviewed on the radio. ‖この歌舞伎には団十郎が出ている Danjuro *is starring* in this kabuki play. (➤ star は「主演する」).

7【応答する】▶電話が鳴ってるわ. ちょっと出てくれない？ The phone is ringing. Will you please *answer* it?

8【雑誌などに掲載される】▶歌手のＹ. Ｋ. さんの婚約の記事が週刊誌に出ている Singer Y. K.'s engagement *is reported* [*is featured*] in a weekly magazine. (➤ 後者は特別記事として扱われた場合) ‖きみの名前がきょうの新聞に出てたよ I *found* your name in today's paper.

9【出版・発行される】▶この雑誌の最新号は金曜日に出る The latest issue of this magazine will *come out* on Friday. ‖宮部みゆきの新しい小説が出た Miyabe Miyuki's new novel *has been published* [*is out*].

10【与えられる, 供される】▶ことしの夏はボーナスがほとんど出ないらしい I hear we'll *be getting a very small* bonus this summer. ‖彼女の結婚披露宴には料理がたくさん出た A lot of dishes *were served* at her wedding reception. ‖化学の期末試験に難しい問題が出た *There were* some difficult problems on the final chemistry exam.

11【うわさなどが生じる】▶ 対話「その話はどこから出たんだい？」「信頼すべき筋から出たものです」"Where did you *get* the news?" "I *got* it from a reliable source."

12【よく売れる】sell ▶ことしはこの手のエアコンがよく出ます This type of air conditioner *is selling* well this year.

13【表面に見えるようになる】▶(子供に)シャツのボタンをちゃんと留めて. おへそが出てるわよ Button your shirt properly. Your belly button *is showing*. ‖この布団じゃ小さくて足が出てしまう This futon is too short, so my feet *stick out*. ‖月が出たがすぐに雲に隠れてしまった The moon *appeared*, but it was soon covered by clouds. ‖日こそ出ていたが風はとても冷たかった The wind was very cold though the sun was *out*.

▶水道管が凍って水が出ない The water pipes are frozen, so there is *no* water [we *can't get* water]. ‖建築現場から金貨や銀貨が出てきた Old gold and silver coins *were discovered* at [*were dug* from] the construction site. ‖チューリップの芽が出てきた The buds of the tulips *are coming out*. ／The tulips are budding.

▶彼は怒るとすぐ顔に出る When he is angry, it *shows* on his face. ‖いざ試合になるといつもの実力が出ない Whenever I compete in a match, I *can't do my best* [*can't show my ability*]. ‖前に知っていた名前が出てこない I can't *retrieve* a once-familiar name. ‖最近父は腹が出てきた These days my dad *is getting big* around the waist. ‖彼はここ数年で大いに貫禄が出てきた He *has gained* a lot presence [confidence] over the past few years. ‖その男の証言で真相が明るみに出た The real story (behind the case) *was revealed* by the man's testimony.

14【発見される】▶電車の中に忘れた傘が出てきた(＝戻ってきた) I *got back* my umbrella which I had left on the train. ‖きみが無くした時計, 出てきたの？ *Has* your missing watch *turned up*? (➤ turn up は「(紛失物などが)偶然見つかる」).

15【勢いなどが増す】▶この車はすぐにスピードが出る This car *picks up speed* [*accelerates*] quickly. (➤ pick up は「(速度を)増す」) ‖風が出てきた The wind *has started to blow*. ‖この調味料をスープに入

れるといい味が出る This seasoning *brings out* the flavor of the soup. ‖プレゼンが進むにつれて彼女は調子が出てきた As her presentation went on, she *got the hang of it* [*became more confident*]. (➤この hang は「要領, こつ」の意).

16【発生する】▶彼は熱が出たので学校を休んだ He *had a fever*, so he was absent from school. ‖この辺りにはしばしば痴漢が出る Perverts *hang out in* this neighborhood. ‖大掃除をしたら山のようなごみが出た We *had* heaps of rubbish after cleaning the whole house. ‖火事はレストランから出た The fire *started* in the restaurant. ‖地震で数百人の死者が出た Several hundred people *were killed* in the earthquake. ／The earthquake *claimed* hundreds of lives. (➤ claim は「(人命を)奪う」).

17【ある態度をとる】▶我々の提案に相手はどう出る(＝反応する)だろう I wonder how the other party will *react* to our proposal. ‖学校側はいじめっ子には強く出たほうがいい Schools should *take a firm attitude* toward bullies.

18【行き着く】▶ついに結論が出ました We'*ve* finally *come to* [*reached*] a conclusion.

19【体外へ排出される】▶タマネギを切っていたら目から涙が出た Tears *came* to my eyes when I was chopping onions. ‖転んで膝を擦りむいたら血がたくさん出た When I fell down, I skinned my knees and *bled* a lot. (➤ bled は bleed(出血する)の過去形) ‖早くして！おしっこが出そうなの Hurry up！I *can't hold my pee* anymore. (➤幼い子供のせりふ).

20【「-出る」の形で】▶躍り出る *take the lead* ‖警察に名乗り出る *give oneself up* to the police.

‖しゃしゃり出る(→見出語).

21【なくなる・いなくなる】▶そのお金はまるで羽が生えていたかのようにあったという間に出ていった The money *has gone* in a flash as if it had grown wings.

22【登場する】▶夢に出てくるような美しいお城 a beautiful castle that *appears* in a dream ‖シェイクスピアの『夏の夜の夢』に出てくるような妖精 the fairies that *appear* in Shakespeare's A Midsummer Night's Dream ‖昨夜, 死んだ父が私の夢に出てきた Last night my dead father *appeared* in my dream.

デルタ a **delta** ‖デルタ地帯 a delta region.

てるてるぼうず 照る照る坊主

日本紹介 ✉ **てるてる坊主は手製の小さな紙人形で, ふつう子供たちが運動会や遠足などの前日に好天を願って軒下につるします** A *teruteru-bozu* is a small handmade paper doll, which children usually hang under the eaves the day before a field day or an outing, hoping for good weather.

でるまく 出る幕 ▶大人の出る幕ではない This *has nothing to do with* grown-ups. ／Grown-ups *shouldn't butt in here*.

てれかくし 照れ隠し ▶照れ隠しに笑う習慣は欧米ではあまり一般的ではない Grinning *to cover one's embarrassment* is something that is not very common in Western countries. ‖彼は照れ隠しに関係のないことをしゃべり出した *To hide his confusion*, he began to talk about something totally unrelated.

てれくさい 照れ臭い ▶人前で歌を歌うのは照れくさいものだ Singing in front of others makes me (*feel*) *embarrassed* [*self-conscious*]. ‖空港できれいなハワイの女の子にキスされて, 彼は照れくさそうな顔をしていた He looked *embarrassed* [*awkward*] when a beautiful Hawaiian girl kissed him at the airport. ‖彼は褒められててれくさそうに笑った When he was praised, he smiled *shyly* [*bashfully*].

てれしょう 照れ性 ▶彼女はてれ性だから人前で話すのが苦手なんだ Because she *is bashful* [*shy*], she has a hard time talking in front of people.

でれでれ ▶女性と一緒だと, やつはいやにでれでれする When he is around women, he *goes soft in the head*.

テレパシー telepathy /təlépəθi/ ▶彼が何を考えているかテレパシーでわかった I knew *by telepathy* what he was thinking about.

テレビ (a) **television**, (a) **TV** /tìːvíː/

語法 (1)「テレビの受像機」の意味では a television だが,「テレビ放送」の意味では Ⓤ 扱い. (2) インフォーマルでは TV がふつうだが,《英》では telly ともいう. ▶テレビを見る watch *television* [*TV*] ‖テレビをつける turn on *the TV* ‖テレビを消す turn off *the TV* ‖テレビの音を大きく[小さく]する turn up [down] *the TV*.

▶大概の家では居間にテレビがある Most households have *a TV* (*set*) in their living room. ‖そろそろテレビを買い替えようよ It's about time to buy *a* new *TV*.

▶父は日曜日は一日中テレビを見ている My father spends Sunday watching *TV* all day long. ‖テレビはあまり見ません I don't watch much *television*. ‖その試合はテレビで見た I watched [saw] the game *on TV*. ‖対話「ワールドカップの試合, 見た？」「テレビで見たよ」"Did you see the World Cup game？" "Yes, I watched [saw] it *on TV*." ‖今夜はテレビでどんな番組がありますか What's *on TV* tonight？‖今夜テレビでいい映画がある There is a good movie *on TV* tonight. ‖あのタレントはよくテレビに出る That personality often appears *on TV*. ‖私はテレビの深夜映画をよく見る I often watch the late-night movies *on TV*.

▶テレビのチャンネルを1にして Change the (*TV*) *channel* to 1, please. ‖テレビ放送がアナログからデジタルに変わった *Television broadcasting* switched from analog to digital. ‖そのサッカーの試合はテレビで生放送された The soccer game *was televised live*. (➤ live /laɪv/ は「生で」) ‖息子はテレビゲームに夢中だ My son is crazy about *video games*. (●「テレビゲームをする」は play a video game).

あなたの英語はどう響く?

「今テレビで何やってる？」のつもりで (×)What's on *the* TV now？とするのは間違い. この文は「テレビの上に何が載っているか？」の意味になる. What's on TV now？が正しい.「テレビ放送」の意味では Ⓤ 扱いであることに注意.

‖**テレビアンテナ** a TV antenna ‖**テレビ映画** a telefilm, a made-for-TV movie ‖**テレビ会議** a TV conference, a video conference；a teleconference (➤電話会議にも使う) ‖**テレビカメラ** a TV camera ‖**テレビ局** a TV station ‖**テレビコマーシャル** a television commercial ‖**テレビショッピング** teleshopping(➤「テレホンショッピング」の意にもなる) ‖**テレビスタジオ** a TV studio /stjúːdioʊ/ ‖**テレビタレント** a TV personality ‖**テレビ電話** a videophone ‖**テレビ討論会** a TV discussion ‖**テレビドラマ** a TV [video] drama

‖テレビ番組 a TV program ‖テレビモニター a video monitor ‖テレビ欄 a channel guide ‖薄型テレビ a flat-screen TV ‖液晶テレビ an LCD [a liquid crystal display] TV ‖壁掛け(式)テレビ a flat-panel TV ‖高品位テレビ high-definition television (➤機器はⒸ) ‖3Dテレビ a 3-D TV ‖プラズマテレビ a plasma-panel TV ‖有料テレビ pay TV.

テレホン a **telephone** ▶テレホンショッピングでN社に品物を注文する place an order for an item with N Company *by phone* (➤「テレホンショッピング」を teleshopping ともいう. また, テレホンショッピングで品物を郵送してもらうことを telephone mail order という). ‖テレホンカード a telephone card, a phonecard.

てれや 照れ屋 a **shy person** ▶あいつてれ屋なんです He is *shy* [*bashful*]. ‖妹はひどいてれ屋で人に褒められると必ずどぎまぎする My (younger) sister is *a* very *shy person* and always feels embarrassed when praised by others.

てれる 照れる **be** [**feel**] **shy**(恥ずかしがる) ; **be** [**feel**] **embarrassed** (きまり悪がる) ; **be** [**feel**] **self-conscious** (注目されててれる) ▶花婿さん, そんなにてれないで Don't *be shy*, bridegroom ! ‖お母さんと一緒に出かけるとなると, ぼくはてれてしまう I'*m* really *embarrassed* when I have to go out with my mother.

▶そんなに褒められると, てれちゃう (=きまりが悪い) な When you praise me so much, I *feel embarrassed* [*ill at ease*].

テレワーク **telecommuting, working from home, telework(ing)**.

てれわらい 照れ笑い ▶デートの途中でばったり私に出会って息子はてれ笑いを浮かべた Running into me during his date, my son *smiled in embarrassment* [*smiled to cover his embarrassment*].

テロ **terrorism** /térərìzəm/, **terror** (➤後者は主にマスコミ用語) ▶テロとの戦い the war against [on] *terror(ism)* ‖ヨーロッパで爆弾テロが多発した *Terrorist acts using bombs* took place frequently in Europe. / There were frequent *terrorist bombings* in Europe.

‖テロ攻撃 a terrorist [terror] attack ‖テロリスト a terrorist ‖サイバーテロ cyber-terrorism, cyber terrorism ‖サイバーテロ対策 cyberterrorism countermeasures.

テロップ **superimposed text on the TV screen** (➤ Telop は商標名. captions (説明文), subtitles (字幕), scrolling tickers (ぐるぐる回って流れる速報ニュースや情報) などをそれぞれ用いる) ▶テロップを流す run *a ticker*.

てわけ 手分け ▶この仕事は我々3人で手分けしてやろう Let's *divide* the work among the three of us. ‖私たちは手分けして迷子を捜した We went *in several groups* [*parties*] to look for the missing child. / We *separated into groups* to search for the lost child.

てわたす 手渡す **hand** +㊐

> 【文型】
> 人(A)に物(B)を手渡す
> **hand** A B / **hand** B **to** A

▶先生は成績表を一人一人に手渡した The teacher *handed* each student his [her] report card. ‖この書類は郵送でなく直接木村さんに手渡してください Please *hand* these papers *to* Mr. Kimura directly instead of mailing them.

[1]**てん 天** **1**【空】**the sky, the heavens** (➤後者は主に文語) ▶天まで届くような高い山頂 a *sky-high* peak ‖星は天に輝く The stars shine in *the heavens*. ‖優勝と2位では天と地ほどの差がある There's *a world of difference* between winning the championship and coming in second.

▶最後のバッターが三振に倒れると監督は天を仰いでため息をついた When the last batter struck out, the manager *looked up at the sky* [*cast his eyes heavenward*] and sighed.

ことわざ 天高く馬肥ゆる秋 the pleasant season of autumn when the sky is clear and high and horses grow stout (on the rich grass) (➤日本語からの意訳).

2【神の国】**Heaven, heaven** ▶やっと子供ができた. 天からの授かりものだ At last we have a child. He [She] is *a gift from Heaven*. ‖祖母は天に召された My grandmother *died and went to heaven*. (➤「天国に行った」の意).

▶《慣用表現》ただ運を天に任せないで自分で頑張れるだけやってみなくてはだめだよ You shouldn't just *leave it up to chance*. You must try your best. ‖習字で金賞を取ったときは天にも昇る心地だった I *was on cloud nine* [*was walking on air* / *was in heaven*] when I won the gold(en) prize in the calligraphy contest. ‖天は自ら助くる者を助く *Heaven helps those who help themselves*. (➤ Heaven の代わりに God(神)ということも多い ; 英語のことわざ).

ことわざ 天は二物を与えず Heaven doesn't bestow two special talents. (➤日本語からの意訳).

[2]**てん 点**

> 訳語メニュー
> 小さい印 →dot **1**
> 点数 →point, score, mark **2**
> 得点 →score, point **3**
> 注目・言及すべき箇所 →point **4**
> 個数 →piece, item **5**

1【小さい印】a **dot** ; a **speck** (染みのような斑点) ; a **point**(地点) ; a **spot**(斑点) ▶飛行機からはグアム島が点のように見えた Guam looked like *a dot* when I looked down at it from the airplane. ‖空高く昇った風船が点のようだ The balloon high up in the sky looks like *a speck*. ‖文の残りを省略するときは点を4つつける Four *dots* are used to indicate that the rest of the sentence is omitted. ‖点Aから点Bまで直線で結びなさい Draw a line from *point A* to *point B*.

▶《慣用表現》携帯電話の請求書を見て彼は目が点になった *His eyes* almost *popped out of his head* when he saw the cellphone bill.

2【評価の点数】a **point** (1点) ; a **score** (得点) ; a **grade**, 《主に英》a **mark** (➤ABCによる評価にも用いる) ▶物理は点が悪かった My *score* in physics was bad. / My *grades* [*marks*] in physics were bad. (● 1科目の成績は単数形の grade だが, 複数回の試験の点数を念頭に置いているために1科目でも grades になっている) ‖世界史の試験でいい点[80点]を取った I got *a good grade* [*a score of* 80] on the world history test. ‖数学は平均点以下[平均点以上]だった I got *a below-average* [*an above-average*] *score* on the math test.

▶ピリオドをつけ忘れて1点引かれた I lost *one point*

for forgetting to put in … period. ／The teach-er took off [subtra…] a point because I forgot a period. ‖ … 小テストは何点だったの？」 … (score) did you get on … 「10点満点で4点だ」 got four (points) out of ten." [《英》in] the qui…

3【得点】a sc… point (バレーボ… 点；どのスポーツにも使える)；a … ラグビーなどの)；a **goal** (アイスホッケー・サッ… ; … run (野球・クリケットの) →得点 ▶2点を入… points ‖ 阪神に点が入るとファンは熱狂… gers … s went crazy when the Ti-…] a run. ‖ 私たちのチームはもう1点取… ve that our team will *score* … 国の体操選手は高い点をマークした … nast obtained a high *score*. ‖ … る？」「5対2で巨人が勝って［負け … the *score*?" "The Giants are … 5 to 2."

… (game-)winning run, the (game-) … the decisive run.

…べき箇所】a **point**；a **respect**(細かな … ートのどういう点がまずかったんでしょうか … of my report were not satisfac-… (＝観点)から見ると日本はヨーロッパ諸国 … れている From *that point of view*, Ja-… far behind European countries. ‖ その … なたと同意見です I agree with you *on that* …

どういう点で芭蕉の俳句が一茶のものより優れているのですか *In what respect* are Basho's haiku superior to those of Issa？‖ この車はあの赤い車よりデザインの点では優れている The styling of this car is better than that of the red one. (●「デザインが赤い車よりいい」と考える) ‖ 近年，学校の制服は色やスタイルの点で大いに変化している Recently, school uniforms have been changing remarkably *in* color and style.

▶資金の点ではご心配いりません *As far as* money *is concerned*, you don't have to worry. ／There is nothing (for you) to worry about *in terms of* financing. ‖ この店は1種類の料理しか出さないという点でユニークだ This restaurant is unique *in that* they serve only one dish. (➤ in that は理由を表す文を導く) ‖ 姉と私はすべての点で違う My (older) sister and I are different *in every way*. ‖ わからない点は(＝わからないことがあれば)遠慮なく聞いてください *If there is anything you don't understand*, don't hesitate to ask.

‖出発点 the starting point.

5【品物の個数】a **piece**, an **item** /áɪṭəm/ ▶衣類5点 five *pieces* of clothing ‖ 家具数点 *several pieces* of furniture ‖ ことしのバザーには100点以上の品物が集まった More than 100 *items* were collected for the bazaar this year.

テン《動物》a **marten**

‖黒テン a sable ‖ 白テン an ermine.

-てん -展 ▶サツキ展 an azalea *show* ／a *display* of azaleas ‖ あの美術館では今ダリ展をやっている That gallery is now holding *a Dalí exhibition*.

でんあつ 電圧 **voltage** /vóʊltɪdʒ/

‖電圧計 a voltmeter.

てんい 転移 **metastasis** /metǽstəsɪs/ ▶彼はがんが肺に転移したことを知らなかった He did not know that the cancer *had spread* [*had metastasized*] *to* his lungs. (➤「転移性のがん」は metastatic /mèṭəstǽṭɪk/ cancer).

てんいん 店員 a **salesperson**, a **salesclerk**, 《米また》a **store clerk**, 《英また》a **shop assistant** (➤ 以上は男女共用)；a **salesman** (男), a **saleswoman**, a **saleslady** (女) ▶兄はコンビニの店員として働いている My (older) brother works as *a salesclerk* [*an assistant*] in a convenience store. ‖ 彼女はギフトショップの店員だ She is a gift shop *attendant*.

でんえん 田園 **the country(side)** ▶この大都市も僅か30年前までは田園地帯だった This big city used to be *a rural* [*farming*] *area* only thirty years ago. ‖ 車で20分も行けば田園風景が広がっている A twenty-minute drive will take you into *the country* (*side*). ／If you drive for twenty minutes, a *pastoral landscape* will spread before you.

‖田園都市 a garden city.

¹てんか 天下 ▶江戸時代の日本は武士の天下だった During the Edo period, samurai *dominated* Japan. ‖ 秀吉は1590年，天下を統一した Hideyoshi *unified Japan under his rule* in 1590. ‖ 政宗は天下を取ることを夢見ていた Masamune dreamed of *seizing control of the nation* [*conquering the whole country*]. ‖ 天下国家を論じる discuss how to *create a better* [*a more just*] *future for one's country*.

²てんか 点火 **lighting**(火をつけること)；**ignition**(点火して一気に燃え上がらせること) 一動 **点火する light** ＋㊐, **ignite** /ɪgnáɪt/ ＋㊐ ▶聖火に点火する *light* [*ignite*] the Olympic flame ‖ このガスレンジは自動点火式だ This gas range is equipped with *automatic ignition*. ‖《ロケットの打ち上げで》3，2，1，0，点火！Three, two, one, zero, *ignition*!

³てんか 添加する **add** ＋㊐ ▶砂糖を添加した飲み物 a drink with *added* sugar ‖ このヨーグルトには添加物は入っていない This yogurt contains no *additives*.

‖食品添加物 a food additive.

⁴てんか 転嫁 ▶彼は自分の責任を私に転嫁した He *shifted* [*transferred*] his responsibility to me. ‖ うちの部長は罪を部下に転嫁して平然としている Our manager thinks nothing of *shifting* [*putting*] the blame *on* his subordinates. ‖ 責任転嫁はよしなさい Don't *pass the buck to others*. ／Don't *shift (the) responsibility to others*.

⁵てんか 転科 ▶中国語学科から日本語学科に転科する *change one's department* from Chinese to Japanese. →転部.

¹でんか 電化 **electrification** 一動 **電化する electrify** /ɪléktrɪfaɪ/ ＋㊐ ▶そのローカル線はようやく全面電化された At last the local line *has been electrified* along the whole line.

‖電化製品 electric(al) appliances ‖ オール電化住宅 an all-electric home.

²でんか 殿下 **His** [**Her**] **Highness**；**Your Highness** (➤ 呼びかけ) ▶皇太子殿下 (*His Imperial Highness*) the Crown Prince ‖ 英国皇太子殿下 (*His Royal Highness*) the Prince of Wales.

³でんか 伝家 ▶伝家の宝刀 *a trump card* (切り札) ‖ 伝家の宝刀を抜く play one's *trump card*.

¹てんかい 展開 (a) **development** 一動 **展開する develop** /dɪvéləp/ (進展する) ▶この技術の今後の展開は世間の注目の的となろう Future *developments* in this technology should attract a good deal of public attention. ‖ 事態は思わぬ方向に展開した The situation *took* an unexpected *turn*. ‖ それは最悪の展開だった That was the worst *scenario*.

‖《音楽》(ソナタ形式の)**展開部** a development.

2**てんかい 転回** a **turn**(方向転換); (a) **revolution**(大変革) ▶遺伝学は生物学に**一大転回**をもたらした Genetics brought about *a revolution* in (the study of) biology.

1**てんがい 天涯** ▶少年は震災で家族と親戚を亡くし, **天涯孤独の身**となった The boy lost his family and relatives in the devastating earthquake and was left *alone in the world*.

2**てんがい 天蓋** a **canopy** /kǽnəpi/
‖**天蓋ベッド** a canopy bed.

でんかいしつ 電解質《化学》an **electrolyte**.

てんかいっぴん 天下一品 **the best in the world** ▶おふくろの作る五目ずしは天下一品だ My mother makes *the best* gomoku-zushi (rice) *in the world*.

てんかふん 天花粉 **baby powder**.

1**てんかん 転換する** **change** (**over**) (**to**) ▶量から質への**転換** the *switch* from quantity to quality [from high volume to high value] ‖わが社は貸しビル・貸し部屋経営からホテル経営への**転換**を図っている Our company is planning to *change* (*over*) from renting buildings and offices *to* managing a hotel. ‖我々は考え方を180度**転換する**必要がある We need to *make a* complete *turnabout* [*an about-face*] in our way of thinking. (➤ turnabout は「方向転換」, about-face は「(思想などの) 180度の転回」) ‖その国は今**転換期**にある The country is at *a turning point* now. ‖**気分転換**に散歩したらどうだい Why don't you take a walk *for a change* (*of pace*)?

2**てんかん 癲癇** **epilepsy** /épɪlepsi/ 一形 **てんかんの** **epileptic** /èpɪléptɪk/ ▶**てんかんの発作**を起こす have *an epileptic fit* [*seizure*].

てんがんざい 点眼剤 **eye drops**.

1**てんき 天気** 1【空模様】**the weather** 語法 (1)通例 the weather の形で用いる. (2) good, bad などの形容詞がついても a は不要.

▶**天気**は良好です *The weather* is good. ‖今夜は**天気**が変わるかもしれない There may be a change in *the weather* tonight. ‖シアトルの**天気**はどうですか What is *the weather* like [How is *the weather*] in Seattle?

▶あしたの**天気**が気になるな I'm worried about tomorrow's *weather*. ‖週末は**天気**が崩れ[回復し]そうだ *The weather* is likely to go downhill [improve] on the weekend. (➤ go downhill は「下り坂になる」) ‖このところ**天気**がぐずついています *The weather* has been unsettled recently. (➤ unsettled は「(天候が)定まらない」).

▶あす**天気**がよかったら遊園地に行くんだ *If it is a nice day* tomorrow, we'll go to an amusement park. ‖**天気がよければ**日曜日にのみの市を行います We'll hold a flea market on Sunday, *weather permitting*. ‖**いい天気ですね** It's *a beautiful* [*wonderful* / *lovely*] *day*, isn't it? / What *lovely weather*! ‖**嫌な天気だねえ** It's *bad* [《英》*nasty*] *weather*, isn't it?

▶**天気**のよしあしにかかわらずラグビーの練習は行います We will have rugby practice *rain or shine*. ‖《テレビなどで》週末の**天気予報**をお知らせします Here is *the weather forecast* for the weekend. ‖**天気予報**によれば北陸は雪だそうだ *The weather forecast calls for* snow in the Hokuriku district. (➤ call for は《米》で「予報する」の意) ‖対話「きょうの天気はどう?」「晴れてるよ」"How is *the weather* today?" "Nice weather!" (➤ It's fin… ていない」の意味になることも… い).

2【晴天】▶あした**天気**になる… will *be nice* tomorrow. ‖… しらね I wonder if this … *bright*] *weather* will last … tomorrow. (➤ カッコ内の形容… れた」「雲一つなく澄んだ」「日光が…
‖**天気雨** a sun shower ‖**天気図** … [chart] ‖**天気相談所** the weath… bureau ‖**天気予報** a weath… weather report.

天気に関連する表現 アメダス AMeD… ice pellets / **異常気象** abnormal weather / **エルニーニョ** El Niño / **オゾン**… layer / **オゾンホール** ozone hole / **カ氏**… heit / **かすみ** haze / **雷** lightning / **寒**… wave / **干ばつ** drought / **気圧** atmos… pressure / **気圧計** barometer / **気圧**… trough / **霧** fog, mist / **霧雨** drizzle / … rainfall / **光化学スモッグ** photochemical sm… / **高気圧** high (atmospheric) pressure / **洪**… flood / **降水確率** probability of precipitation, probability of rain / **紫外線** ultraviolet (rays) / **湿度** humidity / **霜** frost / **集中豪雨** localized torrential rain / **スモッグ** smog / **セ氏** Celsius, centigrade / **前線** front / **台風** typhoon, hurricane, cyclone / **竜巻** tornado / **津波** tsunami, tidal wave / **低気圧** low (atmospheric) pressure, depression / **等圧線** isobar / **雪崩** avalanche, snowslide / **虹** rainbow / **熱波** heat wave / **ひょう** hail / **風速計** anemometer / **フェーン** foehn / **吹雪** snowstorm / **ヘクトパスカル** hectopascal / **みぞれ** sleet / **雷雨** thunderstorm / **雷雲** thundercloud / **ラニーニャ** La Niña / **乱気流** turbulence

☛ **お天気屋** (→見出語)

2**てんき 転機** a **turning point** ▶日本の金融政策は**転機**に立たされている Japan's monetary policy is at *a turning point*. ‖人生の**転機**はどこに転がっているかわからない You can't tell when *a turning point* will come in your life.

3**てんき 転記** ▶帳簿に**転記する** *make a transfer into* an account book.

1**でんき 伝記** a **biography** /baɪɑ́:grəfi/, a **life** ▶渋沢栄一の**伝記**を読んで感銘を受けた I was very much impressed when I read the *biography* [*life*] of Shibusawa Eiichi. ‖宮本武蔵や柳生十兵衛のような剣豪の**伝記**を読むのが好きだ I like to read the *biographies* of great swordsmen such as Miyamoto Musashi and Yagyu Jubee.

2**でんき 電気** 1【電 気】**electricity** /ɪlèktrísəṭi/; (**electric**) **power**(電力) 一形 **電気の** **electric**, **electrical** (➤ 両者は同義のこともあるが, 一般的に前者は直接電気で動くものに, 後者は電気に関する人・仕事などに用いることが多い) ▶**電気**を起こす generate *electricity* ‖この自動車は**電気**で動く This car runs on *electricity*. ‖エアコンは**電気**を食う The air conditioner consumes a great deal of *electricity*. ‖料金滞納で**電気**を止められてしまった Our *electricity* [The *electricity* in our house] was stopped because we hadn't paid the bill. ‖この鉄条網には**電気が通っている** This barbed wire is *live*. (➤ live

/laɪv/ は「電流が通じている」の意）‖先月は**電気代**がかさんだ We ran up a high *electric bill* last month.

2【**電灯**】a **light** ▶電気をつけて［消して］よ Turn on ［Turn off］ the *light*, please. ‖電気をつけたまま眠ってしまった I fell asleep with the *light* on.

‖**電気ウナギ**《魚》an electric eel ‖**電気釜** an electric rice cooker ‖**電気かみそり** an electric shaver ‖**電気機関車** an electric locomotive ‖**電気器具** an electric(al) appliance, electric(al) equipment（➤後者は集合的に「電気器具類」の意）; electrical goods ‖**電気技師** an electrician, an electrical engineer ‖**電気ギター** an electric guitar /gɪtάːʳ/ ‖**電気工学** electrical engineering ‖**電気自動車** an electric car ［vehicle］ ‖**電気ショック** an electroshock, an electric shock ‖**電気スタンド** a desk lamp, a table lamp（卓上の）; a floor lamp,《英》a standard lamp（フロアスタンド）‖**電気ストーブ** an electric heater ‖**電気抵抗** electrical resistance ‖**電気分解** electrolysis ‖**電気毛布** an electric blanket ‖**電気屋** an electric(al) appliance store ‖**電気用品** electric(al) supplies ‖**家庭用電気製品** home electric appliances, household appliances.

テンキー《コンピュータ》a **numeric keypad**.

でんきゅう 電球 a **(light) bulb** ▶60ワットの電球 a 60-watt *bulb* ‖裸電球 a bare *light bulb* ‖電球が切れたから取り替えてくれる？ The *bulb* has burned out. Could you change ［replace］ it？

‖**ＬＥＤ電球** an LED bulb.

てんきゅうぎ 天球儀 a **celestial globe**.

1**てんきょ 転居** a **move**, a **change of address** /ǽdres ‖ ədrés/ 一動 **転居する move**《to, into》→引っ越す ▶彼は仕事の都合で東京から大阪へ転居した He *moved* ［《英また》*removed*］ from Tokyo to Osaka for business reasons.

✉ **この度下記へ転居しました. お近くへお越しの節はぜひお立ち寄りください** I *have* recently *moved* to the address given below. Please drop in when you come this way.

‖**転居先** one's new address（➤郵便物の「転居先不明」の表示は Forwarding Address Unknown）‖**転居通知** a change-of-address notice,《英また》a removal notice.

2**てんきょ 典拠** a **source**（出典）; an **authority**（権威のある）▶この文にはきちんとした典拠があります The *source* of this passage is properly cited. ‖次の文の典拠をきちんと示してください Make sure to cite the *source* ［*authority*］ for the following (quoted) paragraph.

でんきょく 電極《電気》an **electrode** /ɪléktroʊd/, a **terminal**.

てんきん 転勤 a **transfer** /trǽnsfəːʳ/ 一動 **転勤する be transferred** /trænsfə́ːʳd/《to》▶転勤は3月と4月に多い *Transfers of personnel to other places* usually take place in March and April. ‖私, 今度福岡に転勤になるんです I'*m being transferred* ［*being moved*］ *to* Fukuoka.

てんぐ 天狗 a ***tengu***

日本紹介 ✉ **てんぐは人間に似た想像上の生き物です. 顔が赤く, 鼻が異常に長く突き出ていて, 2枚の翼を持ち, 深山に住んでいて, 神通力があり, 空を飛ぶことができると言われています** A *tengu* is a human-like imaginary creature with a red face, an extraordinarily long and protruding nose, and two wings. People say it lives deep in the mountains and that it has supernatural powers, including the ability to fly.

▶《慣用表現》彼は英語がうまいのでてんぐになっている He *is* rather *stuck-up* ［*conceited* ／ *puffed up*］ because he is good at English. ‖成功したので彼はてんぐになった The success *went to his head*.

テングサ agar /άːgəʳ ‖ éɪgə/（寒天の原料になる）.

でんぐりがえる でんぐり返る do a forward ［**backward**］ **roll**（でんぐり返しをする）; **turn head over heels**（ひっくり返る）.

1**てんけい 典型** a **type**（代表的なもの）; a **model**（理想としての見本）▶典型的な国際都市 a *typical* international city ‖彼女は典型的な日本美人だ She is indeed a *classic* Japanese beauty. ‖つくば研究学園都市は研究機関を集約した都市の典型だ Tsukuba Science City is the *model* of a research-intensive city.

2**てんけい 天啓** (a) **divine revelation**.

でんげき 電撃 an **electric shock** 一副 **電撃的に with lightning speed**

‖**電撃結婚** a sudden marriage ‖**電撃戦**（ナチスドイツの）a blitzkrieg ‖**電撃療法** electroshock ［electroconvulsive］ therapy.

てんけん 点検 a **check**; (an) **examination**（綿密な）; a **checkup**（機械などの）; (an) **inspection**（公式の検査）一動 **点検する check, examine** ▶（自動車の）安全点検 a car *safety check* ‖メーターを点検する *check* a meter ‖エンジンをよく点検する *examine* an engine closely ‖お荷物の中身を点検させていただきます Please *open* your baggage *for inspection*. ‖その車は定期点検を受けていますか Has the car had its *periodic* ［*regular*］ *checkup*？ ‖《掲示》点検中 Under Inspection.

でんげん 電源 a **power supply**（電力の供給）; a **plug**（差し込み）▶コンピュータを電源につなぐ *plug in* the computer ‖電源が入ってないんだから機械は動かないよ The machine won't work because *the power is off*. ‖電気器具を点検するときはまず電源を切ってください When you examine an electrical appliance, please *unplug it* ［*cut off the power supply*］ first. ‖電源を入れる turn on *a power switch* ‖この部屋に電源（＝コンセント）は無いの？ Don't you have any *outlets* in this room？

てんこ 点呼 a **roll call** ▶受講生の点呼をとる *take the attendance* of the participants in a course ‖看守は受刑者たちの点呼をとった The prison guard *took the roll call* of the inmates.

1**てんこう 天候 the weather** →天気 ▶我々は天候が回復するのを待った We waited for *the weather* to improve. ‖旅行中は天候（＝好天）に恵まれた We were blessed with *fine weather* during our trip. ‖悪天候のため試合は中止された The match ［game］ was canceled because of *bad weather*.（→悪天候）.

2**てんこう 転校する transfer** /trænsfə́ːʳ/《to》▶私は小学校時代に2度転校した I *changed schools* twice during elementary school. ‖彼は近く大阪の学校へ転校する He will soon *transfer* ［*change*］ *to a school* in Osaka.

‖**転校生** a transfer /trǽnsfəːʳ/ student.

3**てんこう 転向する** ▶あのゴルファーはプロに転向した That golf player *became* a professional ［*turned* professional］. ‖彼は俳優から転向した国会議員だ He is an actor-*turned*-Dietman. ‖彼は共産主義か

ら資本主義へ転向した He *has converted* from communism to capitalism. ⇀転じる.

でんこう 電光 (a flash [bolt] of) lightning (稲妻)
‖**電光掲示板** an electric bulletin [《英》notice] board ‖**電光ニュース** an electric board spelling out news items.

てんごく 天国 Heaven ; (a) paradise /pǽrədaɪs/ (楽園) ▶天国に行く go to *Heaven* [*paradise*] ‖ぼくのおじいちゃんは天国に居るんだよ My grandpa is now in *Heaven*.
▶この避暑地は地上の天国だ This summer resort is *like heaven* [*paradise*] *on earth*. ‖この牧場は子供たちにとっての天国だ This ranch is *paradise* for kids. ‖日本は温泉天国だ Japan is *a hot spring paradise*.
‖**歩行者天国** a vehicle-free pedestrian's mall.

てんこもり てんこ盛り ▶この海鮮丼は海の幸がてんこ盛りだ This seafood bowl *is piled high with* delicacies from the ocean.

でんごん 伝言 a message /mésɪdʒ/ ▶前田さまよりご伝言がございます I have [Here's] *a message* for you from Mr. Maeda. ‖(父に)何か伝言はありますか Can I take [Would you like to leave] *a message* (for my father)? ‖会田さんに伝言をお願いできますか Could you give *a message* to Mr. Aida? ‖彼は留守だったので奥さんに伝言を頼んできた As he was not at home, I left *a message* with his wife.
‖**伝言板** a message board.

1**てんさい 天才** (a) genius /dʒíːniəs/, a gift (生まれつき備わった才能) ; a genius, a whiz kid (天才の人 ; 後者は「若いやり手」の意だが「天才児」のインフォーマルな語としても用いる) ; a wizard (鬼才) ; a prodigy (並外れた神童) ▶彼は語学の天才だ He is *a linguistic genius*. ‖彼は音楽の天才だ He has *a gift* for music. ／He is *a* musical *genius*. ‖彼は犯罪にかけては天才だ He has *a genius* for crime. ‖アインシュタインは100年に1人の天才だった Einstein was the type of *genius* who comes along only once in a hundred years.
▶みどりは天才的バイオリニストであると誰もが認めている Everybody recognizes Midori as a *gifted* [an *exceptionally talented*] violinist. (➤ gifted は「生まれついての才能を持った」).
‖**天才教育** (the) education for gifted children ‖**天才児** a gifted child, a child [an infant] prodigy, a child genius.

2**てんさい 天災** a natural disaster [calamity] ▶その事故は天災か人災かでもめた There was a bitter dispute as to whether it was *a natural disaster*, or one caused by human neglect.
[ことわざ] **天災は忘れた頃にやって来る** Natural disasters occur when we least expect them. (「いちばん予期しないときに」の意. when we have forgotten all about them とすると, we が以前に天災を経験した人たちであるという含みが出る).

3**てんさい 転載** reproduction 一動 **転載する** reproduce +目 ▶《表示》無断転載を禁ず Reproduction of this publication without prior permission of the publisher is prohibited.

てんざい 点在する dot +目 (物が) ▶湾には小島が点在していた The bay *was dotted with* small islands.

てんさく 添削 (a) correction 一動 **添削する** correct +目 ▶私の作文を添削してください Could you please *correct* my composition? ‖彼女はスピーチの原稿を先生に添削してもらった She *had* her speech script *corrected* by the teacher. ‖彼は英作文の通信添削講座を受けている He is taking *a correspondence course* in English composition *that includes correction* (*of mistakes*).

でんさんき 電算機 a computer.

てんし 天使 an angel /éɪndʒəl/ ▶天使のような歌声[ほほ笑み] an *angelic* voice [smile] ‖看護師は「白衣の天使」と呼ばれる A nurse is called '*an angel in white*.'

1**てんじ 展示** (an) exhibition /èksɪbíʃən/, (a) display /dɪspléɪ/, (a) show 一動 **展示する** exhibit /ɪɡzíbɪt/ +目, display +目, show +目 ▶その美術館にはシャガールの絵がたくさん展示してある Many pictures by Chagall *are exhibited* [*are on show*] in the art gallery. (➤ be on show はインフォーマルな表現) ‖壁には生徒の作品が展示してある Students' works *are displayed* [*are on display*] on the wall. ‖私はTデパートへカトレアの展示会[着物の展示会]を見にいった I went to a cattleya *exhibition* [a kimono *show*] at T Department Store.
‖**展示場** an exhibition hall ‖**展示即売会** an exhibition and spot sale ‖**展示品** an exhibit (➤集合的に指す語. 一つ一つは an exhibited item).

2**てんじ 点字** Braille /breɪl/ ▶点字の本 a book (published) in *Braille* ‖私は点字を読むことができる I can read *Braille* (*type*) [*raised letters* / *raised characters*].
‖(プラットホームの)**点字ブロック** a raised stop line on the platform for the blind.

でんし 電子 an electron /ɪléktrɑːn/ 一形 **電子の** electronic /ɪlèktrɑ́ːnɪk/ ▶電子は素粒子の1つである The *electron* is one of the elementary particles. ‖DVDレコーダーがリモコンの指示をキャッチすると電子音がピッと鳴る You can hear *a beep* when the DVD recorder receives instructions from the remote control unit.
‖**電子オルガン** an electronic organ ‖**電子音楽** electronic music ‖**電子カルテ** an electronic medical record ‖**電子機器** an electronic device ‖**電子計算機** a computer ‖**電子掲示板** an electronic bulletin board ‖**電子顕微鏡** an electron microscope ‖**電子工学** electronics /ɪlèktrɑ́ːnɪks/ ‖**電子辞書** an electronic dictionary ‖**電子出版** desktop publishing《略 DTP》‖**電子商取引** electronic trading [commerce], e-commerce ‖**電子書籍** an electronic book, an e-book, a digital book ‖**電子書籍端末** an electronic reading device ‖**電子書籍リーダー** an e-(book) reader, an electronic reader ‖**電子手帳** an electronic datebook [diary], an electric (personal) organizer, a desktop organizer ‖**電子ブック** an electronic book ‖**電子マネー** electronic money, e-money ‖**電子メール** electronic mail, e-mail, email (➤携帯電話でやりとりするメールは text message または text といい, メールのやりとりは texting という ; ⇀イーメール) ‖**電子レンジ** a microwave oven /màɪkrəweɪv ʌ́vən/.

でんじしゃく 電磁石 an electromagnet.

でんじは 電磁波 electromagnetic waves.

てんしゃ 転写 transcription ▶ウイルス転写 virus *transcription*.

でんしゃ 電車 a train (車両が連結した) ; 《米》a streetcar, 《英》a tram(car) (1両だけの路面電車) ▶電車が来たよ Here comes *our* *train.* ／*Our train*'s coming [pulling] in. (➤ 後者の文のほうが近くに来ている感じが強い) ‖ 姉は**電車**で大学へ通っている My sister goes to college *by train.* ／My sister *takes the train* to college. ‖ 上野に行くにはどの**電車**に乗ればいいですか Which *train* should I take to go to Ueno? ‖ **電車**の中で携帯電話を使うのはやめましょう Let's refrain from using cellphones *on the train.* ‖ 満員**電車**での通勤はもううんざりだ I'm fed up with commuting on *jam-packed trains.*

▶終**電車**に乗り遅れないよう全力で走った We ran as fast as we could to catch *the last train.* ‖ **電車**賃は持ってる? Do you have enough money for *train fare*?

逆引き熟語 ○○電車
各駅停車の電車 a local train／**貨物電車** a freight [goods] train／**急行電車** an express (train)／**下り電車** an outbound [a down] train／**最終電車** the last train／**始発電車** the first train／**通勤電車** a commuter train／**特急電車** a limited express (train)／**上り電車** an inbound [up] train／**普通電車** a local train／**満員電車** a jam-packed train／**路面電車** a streetcar, a trolley (car)

てんしゃだい 転車台 a **turntable.**

てんしゅ 店主 《主に米》 a **storekeeper,** 《主に英》 a **shopkeeper** ; **the owner of a store** [**shop**] (➤ イギリスでは shop は小さな店, store はデパートなど大型店を指す).

てんじゅ 天寿 ▶祖父は**天寿**を全うした My grandfather *died a natural death* [*died of old age*]. (➤ die of old age は「老衰で死ぬ」).

でんじゅ 伝授する teach +㊐, **instruct** +㊐ (教える) ; **initiate** +㊐ (手ほどきをする) ▶秘策を**伝授する** *teach* a person a secret tactic.

てんしゅかく 天守閣 a **castle tower** [**keep**] 《参考》 西洋の中世の城の中央にある要塞の塔は donjon.

てんしゅつ 転出する move out ▶**転出**届を出す submit *a change of address notification.*

てんじょう 天井 a **ceiling** /síːlɪŋ/ ▶裸電球が**天井**からぶら下がっていた A bare light bulb was hanging from the *ceiling.* ‖ ヤモリが**天井**にはりついている There's a gecko *on the ceiling.* ‖ 最近はネズミが**天井**裏で走り回っている音を聞かない These days, we don't hear mice running about in the *attic.*

▶《慣用表現》ガソリンの価格の上昇は**天井**知らずだ Gasoline prices *are skyrocketing* [*soaring*].

‖**天井画** a painting on the ceiling.

でんしょう 伝承する pass down ▶民間に**伝承**された言い伝え a legend *passed down orally* among people

‖**伝承文学** oral literature.

てんじょういん 添乗員 a **tour conductor,** a **courier** /kóriəʳ/ ▶**添乗員**同行の旅 a trip with *a tour conductor* ‖ このツアーには**添乗員**はつきません There will be no *conductor* on this tour.

1**てんしょく 転職** a **change of job** [**career**] (➤ change of career は仕事のタイプを変える場合) ▶**転職**したいのなら30代に決意したほうがいい If you want to *change jobs* [*careers*], do so while you are (still) in your thirties. ‖ 日本では**転職者**は必ずしもいい待遇を受けていない In Japan, *job-hoppers* are not always treated well. (➤ job-hopper は「転々と職を替える人」).

2**てんしょく 天職** a **vocation** ▶父は仕立て屋の仕事を**天職**と考えている My father regards tailoring as his *vocation* [*calling*]. ⇀職業.

でんしょく 電飾 illumination ▶繁華街は**電飾**でこうこうと輝いていた The entertainment district *was* brilliantly *illuminated.*

でんしょばと 伝書鳩 a **carrier** [**homing**] **pigeon.**

テンション ▶アウトレットモールに買い物に出かけると真美は**テンション**が高くなる Mami *gets very excited* whenever she goes shopping at an outlet mall. ‖ なんか今日, **テンション**高いね You're kind of *hyper* today. (➤ hyper は若者がよく用いるインフォーマルな語) ‖ 彼女はなんか**テンション**が低いみたい She just seems really *down* [*depressed*]. ‖ けさは髪形が決まらなくて**テンション**が下がっちゃう This morning I just couldn't get my hair(style) right, so I'*m* (*kind of*) *feeling down* [*feeling blue*].

てんじる 転じる ▶話題を**転じる** *change* the subject ‖ あのテニス選手はアマからプロに**転じた** That tennis player *changed* [*went*] from amateur *to* professional.

てんしん 転身 ▶彼は野球選手からテレビタレントに**転身**した He *transformed himself* from a baseball player to a television personality.

でんしん 電信 telegraph, telegraphic communication

‖**電信技師** a telegraph operator ‖**電信送金** telegraphic transfer ‖**電信柱** a telegraph pole, a telephone pole, a utility pole.

てんしんらんまん 天真爛漫な innocent ▶子供たちの**天真らんまん**な笑顔を見ていると, この子たちの未来が明るいことを願わずにはいられない When I see children's *innocent* smiling faces, I can't help wishing them a bright future.

てんすう 点数 a **mark**(評点) ; a **grade**(テストの総合評価 ; ABC による評価にも用いる) ; a **score**(競技・テストの総合点) ; a **point**(競技の) ; a **run**(野球の) ⇀点 ▶彼は英語で高い**点数**を取った He got a high *score* [*grade*] in English. ‖ 塾の生徒はテストの**点数**を非常に気にする *Juku* students are particularly concerned about (their) *test scores.*

▶わがチームの**点数**は3点だ Our team scored three points. ‖ 対話「数学の試験の**点数**はどうだった?」「85点だった」 "What was your *score* on the math exam?" "85."

▶《慣用表現》近頃お父さんに優しくしていやに**点数稼い**でるじゃないか You're so nice to Dad these days. What are you trying to *score brownie points* for? (➤ brownie point は「上の人に取り入って得る信用」).

てんせい 天性の born(生まれついての) ; **natural** (生まれたときから持っている) ▶**天性**の名文家 a *born* stylist ‖ 彼女は**天性**の魅力を持っている She has a *natural* charm. ‖ 彼の絵に見られる気品は**天性**のものだ The elegance seen in his painting comes to him *naturally.* ‖ ことわざ 習慣は第二の**天性**である Habit is (a) second nature.

でんせつ 伝説 (a) **legend** ━形 **伝説の legendary** /lédʒənderi/ ▶**伝説**によるとこの山は一晩でできたそうだ According to *an old legend,* this mountain arose in one night. ‖ 雪女にまつわる**伝説**は多い There are many *legends* concerning the 'snow woman.' ‖ デービー・クロケットは**伝説**的な英雄だ Davy Crockett is a *legendary* hero.

てんせん 点線 a **dotted line** ; a **perforated** /pɑ́ːʳfəreɪtɪd/ **line** (ミシン目の入った切り取り線) ▶平均気温は**点線**で示してあります The *dotted line* shows the average temperature. ‖ 点線に沿って切り取ってください Please tear off along the *perforated line*.

[1]**でんせん 伝染** **contagion** /kəntéɪdʒən/ (接触による); **infection** (空気・水などによる感染) ▶かぜは伝染する Colds *are infectious* [*catching*]. / Colds *spread from person to person*. ‖ はしかは伝染病だ Measles is *a contagious* [*an infectious*] *disease*. / Measles is (highly) contagious. (➤ 日本語では「伝染病」よりも「感染症」という表現が一般的) ‖ 彼のあくびが伝染した I *caught* his yawning.

て

[2]**でんせん 電線** a **power line**(送電線); an **electric wire** (電灯の); a **telephone line** (電話の) ▶大雪のため各所で電線が切れた *Power lines* were severed in many places owing to the heavy snowfall. ‖ 電線にスズメが3羽止まっている There are three sparrows on the *telephone line*.

[3]**でんせん 伝線** a **run**, 《英また》 a **ladder** ▶あら, ストッキングが伝線してるわ Oh my! I *got a run* [*a ladder*] in my hose.

てんそう 転送する **forward** +㊐ (手紙・メールなどを); **transfer** +㊐ (データを) ▶田中さんからのメール, 携帯電話のほうにも転送しておいてくれる? Could you *transfer* [*send*] the e-mail from Mr. Tanaka to my cellphone? ‖ 休暇中に来た郵便物は転送しようか? Do you want your mail *sent on* while you're on vacation? (➤ send on は forward よりくだけた言い方).

▶ネットでの高速データ転送 high-speed Internet data *transfer* (➤ この transfer は名詞) ‖ このデータはコピーまたは別のハードディスクに転送することはできません This data may not be copied or *transferred* to another hard disk.

✉ **この手紙を下記の住所に転送してください** Please *forward* this letter to the following address. ➤ 簡単に Please forward to: のように表記して転送先の住所を添えてもよい.

‖**転送先** a forwarding address.

でんそう 電送 ▶写真を電送する *transmit* a picture / *send* a picture *by wire*.

‖**電送写真** a telephoto, a wire photo.

てんぞく 転属 ▶営業部へ転属になる *be moved* [*transferred*] *to* the sales department.

てんたい 天体 a **celestial body** [**object**], 《文》 a **heavenly body** ▶宇宙にはこの銀河系以外にも無数の天体がある There are countless *celestial bodies* in the universe besides those in our galaxy. ‖ 彼らはハレーすい星を撮影するために天体観測をした They made *astronomical observations* in preparation for taking pictures of Halley's comet.

‖**天体望遠鏡** an astronomical telescope.

> 「天体」のいろいろ **天の川** Milky Way / **衛星** moon, satellite / **銀河** galaxy / **恒星** (fixed) star / **準星** quasar /kwéɪzɑːʳ/ / **準惑星** dwarf /dwɔːʳf/ planet / **小惑星** asteroid / **新星** nova /nóʊvə/ / **すい星** comet / **星雲** nebula /nébjələ/ / **星座** constellation /kɑ̀ːnstəléɪʃən/ / **太陽系** the solar system / **超新星** supernova /sùːpəʳnóʊvə/ / **ブラックホール** black hole / **流星** meteor /míːt̬iəʳ/, falling [shooting] star / **わい星** dwarf / **惑星** planet

でんたく 電卓 a **desktop calculator**

‖**ポケット電卓** a pocket [hand-held] calculator.

でんたつ 伝達 **transmission** (送ること, 伝えること); **communication** (意思の疎通) 一動 **伝達する** **transmit**, **communicate** ▶今日では情報の伝達は容易である Nowadays, it is easy to transmit information. ‖ 言語は思想を伝達する We *communicate* [*convey*] our thoughts through language. ‖ 体育祭が延期になったことをクラス全員に伝達して(=知らせて)ください Please *inform* all the class members that the athletic meet has been postponed. ‖ 《学校で》本日は特に伝達事項はありません There's no special *message* for you today.

[1]**てんち 天地** **1** 【天と地】 **heaven and earth**; **the universe** (宇宙); **the world** (世界) ▶天地創造の神話 a myth about *the creation of the world*.

▶《慣用表現》容疑者の供述と目撃者の証言とでは天地の開きがある There is *all the difference* [*a world of difference*] between the statement of the suspect and that of the witness.

2 【場所, 世界】 ▶彼らは新天地を求めて海を渡った They sailed across the ocean in search of *a new land*.

3 【上下】 ▶壁の絵, 天地が逆(=逆さま)じゃないの? The picture on the wall seems to be hanging *upside down*. ‖ 《荷物などの表示》天地無用 This Side Up.

[2]**てんち 転地** **a change of air** ▶その医者は彼に温泉での転地療養を勧めた The doctor recommended that he (should) *go to* a hotspring *for a change of air* [*for his health*].

でんち 電池 a **battery**, a **cell** (➤ 後者の集合体が前者) ▶この電池は切れている This *battery* is dead. ‖ 携帯電話が電池切れを起こしている The *battery* on my cellphone has died [is dead]. ‖ そのおもちゃは電池で動く The toy is *battery-powered*.

‖**アルカリ電池** an alkaline battery ‖ **乾電池** (→見出語) ‖ **充電式電池** a rechargeable battery ‖ **水銀電池** a mercury (oxide) cell ‖ **太陽電池** a solar battery ‖ **単1電池** a D (size) battery 《参考》単2, 単3, 単4, 単5はそれぞれ C, AA, AAA, N と表示する.「この機器は単2電池2本で動く」は This device runs on two C batteries. という ‖ **蓄電池** a storage battery ‖ **リチウム電池** a lithium battery.

でんちゅう 電柱 a **utility pole**(電気・電話線用の); a **telephone pole**(電話線用の) ▶電柱に貼り紙をする stick a poster on *a utility pole*.

[1]**てんちょう 店長** a (**store**) **manager** ▶彼は横浜デパートの店長に任命された He was appointed *manager* of Yokohama Department Store.

[2]**てんちょう 転調** 《音楽》 **modulation** 一動 **転調する** **modulate** ▶シューベルトは転調の名手だった Shubert was a master at *modulation*. ‖ Cメジャーの曲を途中でAマイナーに転調する *modulate* [*change* (*keys*)] from C major to A minor in the middle of a piece of music.

てんで ▶彼女は私の言うことにてんで耳を借そうとしなかった She would *never* listen to what I said. ‖ 1000円の賃上げではてんで話にならない A 1,000 yen pay raise is *entirely* out of the question. ‖ 彼は横綱と戦ったがてんで相手にならなかった He *was no match for* the yokozuna. ‖ このホッチキスはてんで役に立たない This stapler is *completely* [*utterly*] useless.

[1]**てんてき 点滴** a **drip**, an **intravenous drip** (➤ intravenous /ìntrəvíːnəs/ は「静脈注射による」の意. 単に intravenous ともいい, その場合は名詞扱い. ともに IV

と略す) ▶病院で**点滴**を受ける get *a drip* [an IV drip / an IV] at the hospital ‖ 患者に**点滴**を行う put a patient on *a drip* / give a patient *an IV drip* [*an IV*].
ことわざ 点滴石をうがつ Constant drips of water will penetrate the rock. (➤ 日本語からの直訳).

2**てんてき 天敵** a **natural enemy** ▶マングースはコブラの**天敵**として有名だ The mongoose is known as the *natural enemy* of the cobra.

てんてこまい てんてこ舞い ▶開店を翌日に控えて店員はみんな**てんてこまい**だった Everybody in the shop was *extremely busy* [was *going crazy*] preparing for the shop's opening the next day. ‖ 今週は**てんてこ舞い**の1週間だった It has been a *hectic* week. (➤ hectic は「大忙しの」).
✉ **私はいつも仕事が忙しくててんてこまいしています** My work keeps me *terribly busy* all the time.

でんてつ 電鉄 an **electric railroad** [《英》 **railway**] **company** ▶小田急**電鉄** Odakyu *Electric Railway Co., Ltd.*

1**てんてん 点々** ▶廊下に血が**点々**と落ちていた There were *drops of* blood along the corridor. ‖ その手紙には彼女の涙の跡が**点々**とついていた The letter *was spotted with* her tears. ‖ その画家は**点々**で絵を描く The painter paints with *tiny dots*. ‖「び」はかなの「ひ」に**点々**を付けなさい Add the *two dots* to a kana "hi" to produce a kana "bi".

2**てんてん 転々** ▶各地を**転々**とさまよう wander *from place to place* ‖ 彼は職を**転々**とした He *drifted from job to job*. ‖ ボールは左中間に**転々**と転がった The ball *bounced* between the left and center fielders.

てんでんばらばら ▶修学旅行では**てんでんばらばら**に行動しないで,グループでまとまって行動するように When we go on our school trip, don't go *wandering all over the place*. (Try to) stay with the group as we move around. ‖ 兄の作るお握りは大きさが**てんでんばらばら**だ The *onigiri* my (older) brother makes are *of all sizes*.

でんでんむし でんでん虫 →**かたつむり**.

テント a **tent** ▶川原に**テント**を張る pitch [set up / put up] *a tent* on the shore of a river ‖ **テント**を畳むのを手伝ってくれ Help me pull [take] down the *tent*. ‖ **テント**は強風で潰れてしまった The *tent* collapsed in the strong wind. ‖ 彼らは森の中で1週間**テント生活をした** They *camped out* in the woods for a week.

でんと ▶おかみさんはいつもレジの前に**でんと**座っている The proprietress always sits in front of the register *imposingly* [*as if she were rooted there*].

1**てんとう 転倒する** **1**【倒れる】**fall down** ▶そのスケート選手は**転倒**して2位にとどまった The skater finished second, because he *fell down* [*took a fall*].
2【うろたえる】**be** [**get**] **upset** ▶その悪い知らせに彼女は気が**転倒**してどうしていいかわからなかった She *was* so *upset* when she heard the bad news that she didn't know what to do.

2**てんとう 店頭** ▶**店頭**ではリンゴの安売りをしていた *At the store front* there were apples on sale. ‖ まだ夏だというのに**店頭**には早くも毛皮のコートが飾られている Though it's still summer, fur coats are displayed *in the shopwindows* already.
‖**店頭小売価格** a retail price (小売価格); a shop price (店頭価格) ‖ **店頭販売** over-the-counter sales.

3**てんとう 点灯** ▶街路灯が一斉に**点灯**した All the street lights *came on* at once.

1**でんとう 伝統** (a) **tradition**; (a) **history** (歴史) ━形 **伝統の traditional** ▶古い**伝統**を重んじる respect old *traditions* ‖ **伝統**を守る maintain [preserve] a *tradition* ‖ **伝統**を打ち破る break with *tradition* ‖ 日本の**伝統芸術** Japanese *traditional art* ‖ わが社は創業以来70年の**伝統がある** Our company *has a history* of seventy years since its foundation. ‖ わが校のチームは**伝統的に**テニスが強い Our school team is *traditionally* strong in tennis.
✉ **ひな祭りは日本の伝統的な行事です** The Doll Festival is a *traditional* Japanese event.

2**でんとう 電灯** a **light**, an **electric light** ▶**電灯**をつける [消す] turn on [turn off] the *light*.

1**でんどう 伝導** **conduction** ▶銅は熱**伝導**率がよい Copper *is a good conductor* of heat.

2**でんどう 伝道** **missionary** [**mission**] **work** ▶彼はアフリカで**伝道**に携わっている He is engaged in *missionary work* in Africa. ‖ わが校の創始者はアメリカから日本に来てキリスト教の**伝道をした** Our school's founder came from America to Japan to *preach* [*spread*] Christianity.
‖**伝道師** a missionary.

3**でんどう 電動の** **electric** /ɪléktrɪk/ ▶この鉛筆削りは**電動**式ですか Is this an *electric* pencil sharpener?
‖**電動自転車** an e-bike, a battery-operated bike, a power bike ‖ **電動歯ブラシ** an electric toothbrush ‖ **電動モーター** an electric motor.

4**でんどう 殿堂** ▶学問の**殿堂** *a sanctuary* for learning ‖ 野球の**殿堂** the Baseball *Hall of Fame* (➤「殿堂入りした人」は a Hall of Famer).

てんどうせつ 天動説 《天文学》 **the Ptolemaic** /tɑ̀ːləméɪɪk/ **system, Ptolemy's** [**the**] **geocentric theory of the universe.** →**地動説**.

てんとうむし 天道虫 《虫》《米》 a **ladybug**, 《英》 a **ladybird**
‖**ナナホシテントウ(ムシ)** a seven-dotted [-spotted] ladybug.

てんとりむし 点取り虫 《米》 a **grind** /graɪnd/, 《英》 a **swot**.

てんどん 天丼 ***tendon***; a bowl of rice topped with tempura (➤ 説明的な訳).

てんにゅう 転入する **move in** ▶**転入**届を出す submit one's *moving-in notification*.
‖**転入生** a transfer /trǽnsfəːr/ student.

てんにん 転任 a **transfer** /trǽnsfəːr/ ▶高島先生は大阪の学校に**転任**になった Mr. Takashima *was transferred* to a school in Osaka. ‖ きょう宇井先生の**転任**の挨拶があった Today Mr. Ui made *a farewell speech* (*before his transfer*).

てんねん 天然の **wild** (野生の); **natural** (人工でない) ▶このアユは**天然**もので養殖ものではありません These are *wild* ayu, not farmed ones. ‖ **天然の**真珠 a *natural* pearl (➤「養殖の真珠」は a cultured pearl).
‖**天然ガス** natural gas ‖ **天然資源** natural resources (➤ 複数形で) ‖ **天然石** a natural stone ‖ **天然パーマ** naturally curly hair.

てんねんきねんぶつ 天然記念物 a **natural monument** (自然物); a **rare species** /spíːʃiːz/ **protected by law** (法律で保護されている動植物) ▶ニホンカモシカは特別**天然記念物**に指定されている Japanese serows *are protected by law* [*are designated as a rare spe-*

cies and protected by law].

てんねんとう 天然痘 《医学》 **smallpox.**

てんねんボケ 天然ボケ someone who unintentionally says stupid or funny things (➤ 説明的な訳).

てんのう 天皇 **the Emperor** 《解説》 (1) 日本の天皇には慣習的に the Emperor を用いるが, 厳密には emperor は「帝国(empire)を治める人」の意で, 西洋ではローマ帝国の皇帝またはナポレオンのように武力によって権力を握った人を指し, 歴史的には「独裁者」というイメージを持っている. (2) したがって, *Tenno* という表現を用いることも一案であるが, 現在ではまだ慣習に従ったほうが無難.
▶天皇は国民統合の象徴である *The Emperor* is the symbol of the unity of the people. ‖ あなたは天皇制についてどういう考えを持っていますか What do you think of the *Emperor system* of Japan? ‖ 天皇陛下が国体の開会を宣言された *His Majesty the Emperor* declared the National Athletic Meet open.
《参考》「天皇皇后両陛下」は Their Majesties the Emperor and Empress という.
‖天皇誕生日 the Emperor's Birthday.

てんのうざん 天王山 ▶ペナントレースもいよいよ天王山だ Now is *the crucial point* in the pennant race.

てんのうせい 天王星 **Uranus** /jóərənəs/ ▶天王星は1781年にハーシェルが発見した Herschel discovered *Uranus* in 1781.

[1]**でんぱ 電波** a **radio wave** ▶通信衛星のおかげで電波の届きにくい地域は少なくなった Thanks to communications satellites, fewer places *get poor reception.*
‖電波障害 static, interference ‖ 電波探知機 a radar /réɪdɑːʳ/ ‖ 電波時計 a radio-controlled watch ‖ 電波望遠鏡 a radio telescope ‖ 電波妨害 jamming.

[2]**でんぱ 伝播** **spread** ▶稲作文化の伝播 the *spread* of rice-growing culture ‖ ハエは病気を伝播する Flies *spread* disease.

てんばい 転売 (a) **resale** 一動 **転売する resell** ＋㊐ ▶彼女はブランド物を転売して利益を得ている She makes a profit by *reselling* brand-name products. ‖転売価格 a resale price.

てんばつ 天罰 **heaven's judgment** (天の裁き); a (**divine**) **punishment** [**retribution**] (当然の報い) ▶天罰てきめんさ See how swift *heaven's judgment* is. ‖ よりによって身寄りのないお年寄りをだますから, おかしな死に方をしたんだわ. 天罰よ If he died an unnatural death, *it's only just* [*he deserved it* / *he asked for it*], considering how he had deceived all those old and lonely people. (➤ just は「公正な」の意).

[1]**てんぴ 天日** **the sun, the sunshine** ▶ワカメを天日に干す dry *wakame* (seaweed) in *the sun* [*sunshine*].

[2]**てんぴ 天火** an **oven** /ʌ́vən/. →オーブン.

てんびき 天引き **deduction** ▶税金や各種保険金は給料から天引きされます Tax and various insurance payments will *be deducted* from your pay.

てんびょう 点描 ▶スーラは点描画 [点描画法] で有名だ Seurat is famous for his *pointillist paintings* [for his *pointillism*].

でんぴょう 伝票 a **slip** (取り引きの); a **bill**, a **check** (請求書) ▶この伝票の山, きょう中に処理しなくちゃ I have to deal with this pile of *slips* within the day. ‖ 伝票は別々にしてください Could we have separate *checks*, please?
‖売り上げ伝票 a sales slip.

てんびん 天秤 a **balance** ▶果物をてんびんで量る weigh fruit *on* [*in*] *a balance.*
▶《慣用表現》 仕事か結婚か, 彼女は2つをてんびんに掛けた Career or marriage? She *weighed the advantages and disadvantages* [*pros and cons*] *of each.* (➤「それぞれの長所と短所を検討した」の意) ‖ あいつ, また2人の女性を(両)てんびんに掛けているらしいよ I hear that he *is dividing his love between* two girls again. / I hear he's *stringing along* two women again. (➤ string along は「気を持たせる」).

てんびんざ 天秤座 (a) **Libra** /líːbrə/.

てんぶ 転部 ▶経済学部から法学部へ転部する *transfer* [*move*] from the School of Economics to the School of Law ‖ 夜間部から昼間部へ転部する *change* from the night division to the day division. →転科.

[1]**てんぷ 添付する** **attach** ＋㊐ ▶ワードで作成した書類を添付する *attach* a Word document ‖ 写真を添付したEメールを送る send an email with a photo *attached* (to it) ‖ 願書には推薦状を添付すること The application *must be accompanied by* [*must include*] a letter of recommendation. ‖ 添付した書類をご覧ください See *attached* documents. (➤ Eメールの「添付書類」は attachment).

[2]**てんぷ 貼付する** →ちょうふ.

[3]**てんぷ 天賦の** **gifted** ▶彼女は音楽に天賦の才がある She *is gifted with a talent for* music. / She *has a gift for* music. / She is a born musician.

てんぷく 転覆する **overturn** ▶東海道線の列車が静岡・浜松間で脱線し, 転覆した A Tokaido Line train derailed and *overturned* between Shizuoka and Hamamatsu.
▶船は横波を受けて転覆した The ship *was overturned* [*was capsized*] by side waves. / Side waves overturned [capsized] the ship. (➤ capsize /kǽpsaɪz/ は船が転覆し, 沈没する場合に多く用いられる) ‖ 車は氷の上をスリップして転覆した The car skidded on the ice and *turned upside down* [*turned turtle*].
▶軍の幹部が政府の転覆を謀った The leading members of the armed forces plotted to *overthrow* the government.

てんぶくろ 天袋 a ***tenbukuro***; storage space above an *oshi-ire* (➤ 説明的な訳).

てんぷら 天麩羅 **tempura** (➤ 英語化している)
日本紹介 ✉ **天ぷらは魚介類や野菜を使った揚げ物の1つで, 水で溶いた小麦粉の衣をつけてたっぷりの油でからっと揚げて作ります. ふつう, 大根おろしを入れたつゆに軽くつけます** Tempura is a deep-fried food consisting of seafood or vegetables, which are dipped into a flour-and-water batter and deep-fried until crisp, but not brown. Tempura is usually dipped into a light shoyu-based sauce containing grated *daikon* radish.

テンプレート a **template.**

てんぶん 天分 one's (**natural**) **gift**, **talent** ▶彼女は音楽の天分に恵まれている She has [is blessed with] a great *gift* for music.

でんぶん 伝聞 **hearsay.**

でんぷん 澱粉 **starch** ▶穀物にはでんぷんが多い Grains have a lot of *starch.*

テンペラ **tempera** (画法・絵の具); a **tempera** (1枚の画).

てんぺんちい 天変地異 (a) **natural disaster.**

てんぽ 店舗 《米》a **store**,《英》a **shop**
‖**貸し店舗** a store [shop] for rent (➤ 英米の貸し店舗にはしばしば "For Rent" の看板が掛けられている).

テンポ a **tempo** ▶テンポの速い[遅い]曲 a piece of music with *a* quick [slow] *tempo* ‖ 田舎と都会では生活のテンポが違う The *tempo* of life in the country is very different from that in big cities. ‖ うちの父は時代のテンポについていけないとこぼしている My father grumbles that he *can't keep up with the changing times*.

てんぼう 展望 1【見晴らし, 景色】a **view** ▶塩尻峠に着くと突然大展望が開けた When we arrived at Shiojiri Pass, *a panoramic view* suddenly *spread out before us*.
‖**展望車** an observation car ‖ **展望台** an observation tower [deck], an observatory /əbzə́ːʳvətɔːri/.
2【見通し】a **prospect** ▶彼はこの記事の中で日本経済の展望を詳しく述べている In this article, he gives a detailed explanation of the *prospects* for the Japanese economy.
▶今のままでは仕事の展望が開けない As it is, the *outlook* for my career looks bleak [I have no good career *prospects*]. (➤ bleak /bliːk/ は「(生活などが)暗い」の意).

でんぽう 電報 a **telegram**, 《米また》a **wire** ; a **cable** (海外電報) ▶挨拶のことばを電報で送る send a greeting *by wire* ‖ いとこが大学に入ったのでお祝いの電報を打った I sent *a congratulatory telegram* to my cousin, who had been accepted by a university.
‖**電報為替** a telegraphic transfer ‖ **お悔やみ電報** a telegram of condolence.

デンマーク **Denmark**(ヨーロッパ北部の王国) 一形 デンマークの **Danish**
‖**デンマーク語** Danish ‖ **デンマーク人** a Dane.

てんまく 天幕 a **tent** (テント) ; 《英》a **marquee** /mɑːʳkíː/ (園遊会などに用いる大型テント) ▶天幕を張る erect *a tent* [*marquee*].

てんまつ 顛末 ▶というのが事のてんまつだ This is *the full account of the event*. ‖ 事件のてんまつを知っている人は彼ひとりだ He alone knows *the whole story* [*all the details*] (*of the event*).

てんまど 天窓 a **skylight**.

てんめい 天命 (one's) **fate** ; (**Divine**) **Providence** ▶天命と諦める submit to one's *fate* ‖ ことわざ 人事を尽くして天命を待つ Do your best and leave the rest to *Providence*.

てんめつ 点滅する **blink** ▶あそこで点滅している赤い光は何ですか What is that *blinking* red light over there?

てんもん 天文 ▶ベルサイユ宮殿の建設費を今日の貨幣に換算すれば天文学的な数字になるだろう The construction costs of the Palace of Versailles would be *astronomical* [reach *astronomical figures*] in today's money.
‖**天文学** astronomy /əstrɑ́ːnəmi/ ‖ **天文学者** an astronomer ‖ **天文台** an astronomical observatory ‖ **天文ファン** a space enthusiast.

てんやく 点訳 ▶小説を点訳する *transcribe* [*put*] a novel *into Braille* /breɪl/.

てんやもの 店屋物 food delivered from a restaurant or a soba shop (➤ 説明的な訳).

てんやわんや ▶てんやわんやの(＝大忙しの)一日 a *hectic* day ‖ 時限爆弾の予告電話があって大使館の中はてんやわんやの大騒ぎとなった A warning call that a time bomb would go off threw the whole embassy into *utter confusion*. (➤「大混乱」の意).

てんよう 転用 **conversion** (用途・性質などの) ; **diversion** (方向・方針などの) 一動 転用する **convert** ＋目, **divert** ＋目 ▶農地を宅地に転用する *convert* farm land *to* residential use.

でんらい 伝来 ▶鉄砲はいつわが国に伝来したか知っていますか Do you know when guns *were introduced* into this country? ‖ これは先祖伝来の巻物だ These scrolls *have been handed down from my ancestors*.

てんらく 転落 a **fall** 一動 転落する **fall** ▶バスが川に転落し, 10人が死亡した The bus *fell* into the river, claiming the lives of 10 passengers. ‖ 彼は崖から転落して重傷を負った He *fell* over the cliff and was seriously injured.
▶賭け事が彼を転落させた Gambling was [led to] his *downfall*. ‖ ドラゴンズは3位から4位に転落した The Dragons *dropped* from 3rd to 4th place.

てんらんかい 展覧会 an **exhibition** /èksɪbíʃən/, a **show** ▶きのう展覧会を見に上野へ行った I went to Ueno to see an *exhibition* yesterday.
‖**展覧会場** an exhibition hall.

でんりそう 電離層 **the ionosphere** /aɪɑ́ːnəsfɪəʳ/.

でんりゅう 電流 an **electric current** ▶電流の通じている銅線 a *live* copper wire (➤ live の発音は /laɪv/) ‖ この電線には電流が通じている This wire is live. ／This wire is charged with *electricity*. (➤ 前者がふつうの言い方) ‖ ゴムは電流を通さない Rubber does not conduct *electricity*. ／*An electric current* will not flow through rubber.
‖**電流計** an ammeter /ǽmìːt̬əʳ/, a galvanometer /gæ̀lvənɑ́ːmət̬əʳ/.

でんりょく 電力 (**electric**) **power** ▶震災で電力事情がひっ迫した The *electric power situation* has worsened considerably due to the great earthquake. ‖ この車は電力だけで動く This vehicle runs on *electric power* alone. ‖ 電力不足により関東地方で輪番停電が行われた *The* (*electric*) *power shortage* resulted in rolling blackouts in the Kanto region.
‖**電力会社** an electric power company.

でんわ 電話 1【電話機, 回線】a **telephone**, a **phone** ▶この温泉宿にはまだ電話が引かれていない This hot spring inn doesn't have *a telephone* yet. ‖ 電話を引きたいのですが I'd like to have *a telephone* installed. ‖ 電話が鳴ってるよ The *phone*'s ringing. ‖(電話局の案内) この電話番号は現在使われておりません This *telephone number* is out of service. ‖ 対話「電話をお借りしたいのですが」「どうぞ」"May I use the *phone*?" "Sure."
2【通話】a (**phone**) **call** 一動 電話する **call**, **phone**, 《英また》**ring** ▶道子, 電話よ Michiko, *there's a call for you*! (● telephone は「電話機」のことなので, (×)there's a telephone は不可) ‖ 井出先生, 電話が入っていますので職員室までおいでください Mr. Ide, *you're wanted on the phone*. Please come to the teachers' room. ‖ 私から電話があったことを伝えてくださいますか Could you just tell him [her] that I *called*, please? ‖ 部長からちょっと遅れると電話があった The manager *called in* to say that he'd be a little late. (➤ call in は「電話で連絡する」の意) ‖ すみません. 電話がちょっと遠いのですが Sorry, *I can't hear you very well*.

て

▶**電話**で注文する place an order *by telephone* ‖ **電話**で(ホテルなどの)部屋を予約する reserve a room *by telephone* ‖ 至急の配達をご希望の方は**お電話**でお申し込みください For quick delivery, order *by phone*. ‖ **電話注文**を受ける receive *telephone orders* ‖ 私は彼にクラス会のことで**電話した** I *gave* him *a call* about the class meeting. ‖ 今度**電話していい**? Can I *give* you *a call*?

▶この商品をご希望の方は今すぐ**お電話でお申し込み**ください If you want this item, please *call* us with your order now. ‖ 結果は**電話**でお知らせします We'll *phone* you (with) the results. ‖ 課長はただいま**電話中です** The section chief *is on the phone* now. ‖ 矢野は今**別の電話に出ております** Yano *is* now *on another line*. ‖ 俊夫, **電話に出て**[を取って]ちょうだい Toshio, could you *answer* [*get* / *pick up*] *the phone*? ‖ きのう彼女に**電話を掛けた**が居なかった I *called* [*phoned*] her yesterday but she wasn't in. (● but 以下を but there was no answer とすることも可).

▶ 654-3210に**電話をください** Please *call* [*ring*] me at 654-3210. (➤ 番号は six-five-four, three-two-one-oh /oʊ/ と読む) ‖ 彼は怒って**電話を切った** He *hung up the phone* [*hung up on me*] angrily. (➤ hang up on は「一方的に切る」の意) ‖ **電話を切らないで**お待ちください Please *hold on*. / *Hold the line*, please. ‖ この電話, 広志と**代わってくれ** *Put* Hiroshi *on* (*the line*). (●「広志を呼んできます」「広志に代わります」は I'll get Hiroshi.).

▶**お電話ありがとうございました** Thank you for *calling*. ‖ あとでもう一度**お電話を頂けますか** Could you *call* me *back* later? ‖ ここへ**電話を頂ければ**連絡がとれます You can reach me *at this number*. ‖ あしたの朝いちばんに**電話をくれよ** *Give me a call* [*a ring*] first thing tomorrow morning. / *Call* [*Phone* / *Ring*] *me* (*up*) first thing tomorrow morning. (⇀**かこみ記事**) ‖ あとでこちらから**電話いたします** I'll *call you* (*back*) later. ‖ 緊急の際は110番に**電話して**ください *Call* [*Dial*] 110 in an emergency. ‖ 帰りが遅くなるようだったら(家に)**電話してちょうだい** Please *call home* if you're going to be late. ‖ **病気で休むって電話しといてね** Could you *call in sick* for me, please? ‖ **対話**「誰に**電話した**の?」「政夫さん. だけど**話し中**だったわ」"Who did you *call*?" "Masao. But the line was busy [I couldn't get through]."

▶《引っ越しセンターなどの宣伝文句》**お電話1本**くだされば**お手伝いに上がります** Help is just *a phone call* away. ‖ 麻子, あまり**長電話する**のはやめなさい Don't *be* too *long on the phone*, Asako. ‖ 台風で休校になったことを皆に**電話連絡して**ください Please *call* everyone *and tell* them that there is no school because of the typhoon. ‖ この子の両親とまだ**電話連絡がとれません** We can't *reach* his parents *by phone* yet. ‖ 彼女は最近**いたずら電話**に悩まされている She has recently been bothered by *prank* [*obscene*] *calls*. (➤ obscene は「いかがわしい」) ‖ マドリードに居るおじに**国際電話を掛けた** I *made an international* [*overseas*] *phone call* to my uncle in Madrid.

▶今のは**間違い電話**だった That was *a wrong number*. ‖ すみません. **電話番号を間違えました** Sorry. *I have the wrong number*. (● 相手が間違えている場合は I'm afraid you have the wrong number. などと言う) ‖ **電話番**なんて嫌だな I hate *being on phones*.

‖ **電話局** a telephone company ‖ **電話交換手** a telephone operator ‖ **電話セールス** telesales ‖ **電話帳** a telephone directory, 《インフォーマル》a phone book (➤ 日常的には後者がふつう) ‖ **電話番号** a telephone number ‖ **電話ボックス** a (tele) phone booth ‖ **電話魔** a telephone addict /ǽdɪkt/ ‖ **電話料金(請求書)** a telephone bill.

☛ **長電話** (⇀見出語)

あなたの英語はどう響く?

「あした電話を(掛けて)ください」の意味で (×) Give me a telephone tomorrow. と言うのは不可. telephone は「電話機」のことである. 「通話」の意の a call を使って Give me a call tomorrow. とするか, 単に Call [Phone] me tomorrow. と言う必要がある. また, Telephone me. のような言い方は一般的ではない.

逆引き熟語 ○○電話

◆**壁掛け式電話** a wall (tele)phone / **携帯電話** a cellphone, a mobile phone / **固定電話** a home phone (家庭の), an office phone (会社などの) / **テレビ電話** a videophone / **テレビ電話機能付き携帯電話** a video-equipped cellphone
◆**いたずら電話** a prank call / **インターネット電話** an Internet (tele)phone / **親子電話** a party line / **国際電話** an international [overseas] call / **市内電話** a local call / **私用電話** a personal [private] call / **長距離電話** a long-distance call / **長電話** a long [lengthy] phone call / **にせ(いたずら)電話** a fake call, a hoax call (爆弾予告など悪質な) / **間違い電話** a wrong number / **留守番電話** an answering machine

と・ト

[1]と 戸 a **door** ⇀ドア ▶戸を開ける［閉める］ open［close］ *the door*（● 日本の住居の和室に多い引き戸などの場合は slide *the door* open［shut］のようにもいえる）.
ことわざ 人の口に戸は立てられぬ People will talk.（➤「人はとかくうわさするもの」の意）.
‖引き戸 a sliding door.

[2]と 都 **the Metropolis** /mətrá:pəlis/（主要都市）━形 都の **Metropolitan** /mètrəpá:lətn/
《参考》「東京都」は Tokyo Metropolis または Metropolitan Tokyo ともいう. だが, 手紙などの住居表示は Metropolis なしで単に Tokyo だけでよい.
▶東京都教育委員会 the Tokyo *Metropolitan* Board of Education ‖都の人口は増加する一方だ The population of *Metropolitan Tokyo* is steadily increasing. ‖都（の当局）に工事の中止を陳情した We petitioned *the Metropolitan authorities* to stop the construction (project).
‖都議会（議員）(a member of) the (Tokyo) Metropolitan Assembly ‖都知事 the Governor of Tokyo ‖都庁 the (Tokyo) Metropolitan Government (Office) ‖都バス a Metropolitan bus.
☛ 都営, 都内, 都民, 都立（⇀見出語）

-と **1【列挙して】and** ▶犬と猫 a dog *and* a cat ‖ナイフとフォーク a knife *and* fork（● この場合のようにペアにしていうことが多いものは, あとの名詞に a をつけない）.
2【動作の相手を示して】with ▶浩は智子とデートした Hiroshi went out *with* Tomoko. ／Hiroshi dated Tomoko. ‖その件についてはコーチと相談します I'll talk it over *with* the coach. ‖学校には誰と一緒に行ってるの？ Who do you go to school *with*? ‖山川君は小野さんと結婚した Mr. Yamakawa married Miss Ono.（➤ marry with とはしない）‖横浜はあすは中日と試合する The BayStars are going to play (*against*) the Dragons tomorrow. ‖彼女はお金持ちと結婚している She is married *to* a rich man.
3【比較・選択を示して】and ; or（または）▶弟は私と身長が1センチしか違わない There is only one centimeter's difference in height *between* my (younger) brother *and* me. ‖私の自転車はきみのと同じだ My bicycle is *the same as* yours. ‖紅茶とコーヒー, どちらになさいますか Which would you like［prefer］, tea *or* coffee? ‖母の話と父の話は矛盾している What Mom said is contradictory *to*［inconsistent *with*］what Dad said.
4【考え・内容を示して】that ▶彼は先生に「カンニングはしていません」と言った He told his teacher *that* he hadn't cheated. ‖私はそろそろ受験勉強を始めなければと考えているところです I think (*that*) I should start preparing for the entrance exam.（➤ インフォーマルでは that は省略されることが多い）‖由希子は香奈を親友と思っている Yukiko thinks of［regards］Kana *as* a best friend.
5【結果を示して】▶彼女は抜てきされて局長となった She was chosen (*to be*) bureau chief.（●「(役職に)選ばれる」の意では通例役職名に a はつけない）.
6【…するとき】when ▶雨がやむと子供たちは運動場に飛び出した *When* it stopped raining, the children rushed out to play on the playground. ‖警官が近づくとその車は突然発進した *Just when* the police officer approached the car, it suddenly took off.
7【仮定・条件・譲歩を示して】if ▶のんちゃん, ママを手伝ってくれるとうれしいんだけど Non-chan, Mommy will be happy *if* you help me. ‖夜更かしすると（＝するのは）体に悪いよ It is bad for your health *to* stay up late at night. ‖急がないとバスに遅れるわよ You'd better hurry *or* you'll be late for the bus.
▶降ろうと降るまいと野球の練習は休まない We will have baseball practice, *whether* it rains *or* not. ／We will practice baseball, rain *or* shine. ‖人が何と言おうときみの思うとおりにしなさい Do what you think is right, *no matter what* other people may say (to you).
8【説明を求めて】▶「彼を雇いたくないな」「と言うと？」「彼はその仕事に向いてないよ」"I'd rather not hire him." "*Which is to say?*" "He's not suitable for the job."

ど 度 **1【回数】... times**（➤ 3 以上の数詞とともに用いる）▶本を1度［2度／3度］読む read a book *once*［*twice*／*three times*］‖彼女は日に2度しか食事をとらない She eats only *two* meals a day.
2【角度・温度など】a degree ▶30度の勾配の坂 a 30-*degree* slope／a slope of 30 *degrees* ‖この辺りでは冬でも平均気温は摂氏8度あります The average temperature in this area in winter is *8 (degrees) C.*（➤ 誤解が生じるおそれがなければ C（＝Celsius, Centigrade）は省略可）‖このウイスキー（のアルコール度数）は43度だ This whisky contains 43 *percent* alcohol. ／This whisky has an alcohol content of 43 *percent*. 《参考》英米では酒の濃度を proof で表す. これは日本の度数の倍の数値になるので, 上の例文は This whisky is 86 proof. と表現される ‖ 対話「体温はどのくらいですか」「6度5分くらいです」"What's your temperature?" "It's around *thirty-six point five* (degrees Celsius)."
3【眼鏡の強さ】▶度付きのサングラス *prescription* sunglasses（➤ prescription は「処方箋」）‖彼女は度の強い眼鏡を掛けている She wears *strong*［*thick*］glasses. ‖この頃近視の度が進んじゃってね My nearsightedness *has gotten worse*.
4【限度】▶彼の度の過ぎた気前のよさ his *over-the-top* generosity ‖ジョギングはよいが度を越す（＝やり過ぎる）と体を悪くする Jogging is good, but can be bad for you if you *overdo* it. ‖冗談にしても度が過ぎるよ You *carried* your joke *too far*.

ドア a **door** ▶玄関のドア a front *door* ‖ドアを閉めてください Shut［Close］the *door*, please. ‖誰かがドアをノックしている Someone is knocking on［at］the *door*. ‖（駅で）閉まるドアにご注意ください Mind the closing *doors*. ‖ドアをバタンと閉めるな Don't slam the *door*. ‖彼はドアを押さえて閉まらないようにしてくれた He held the *door* open for me.

‖ドアチェーン a door [night ／security] chain, a chainlock ‖ ドアホン an intercom(→インターホン) ‖ ドアマット a doormat ‖ ドアマン a doorman ‖ 回転ドア a revolving door ‖ 自動ドア an automatic door.

> 危ないカタカナ語✹ ドアボーイ
> 1 ホテルやレストランなどの出入り口にいて客の案内をする係の男性を「ドアボーイ」というが，これは和製語．英語では doorman である．
> 2 同様に「ドアガール」も和製語だが，これに対応する英語はない．「案内係」の意の attendant を使って door attendant とすれば通じるが，これは男女共通の語である．

と

どあい 度合い the extent (範囲)；the degree (程度) ▶強弱の度合いを計る measure the (*degree* of) strength ‖ 国際間の緊張の度合いは高まり［緩み］つつある International tensions are increasing [lessening]. (この文では「度合い」の訳出は考えなくてよい).

とあみ 投網 a cast net ▶投網を打つ cast *a net*.

とある →²ある.

¹とい 樋 a gutter (水平の)；a drainpipe (縦の).

²とい 問い a question ▶問いの２番がどうしてもわからなかった I just couldn't answer the second *question*. ‖ 以下の問いに答えなさい Answer the following *questions*. ‖ 問い５の答えは何ですか What's the answer to *question* five [the fifth *question*]?

といあわせ 問い合わせ (an) inquiry /ɪnkwáɪəri/, 《英》enquiry ▶問い合わせの手紙 a letter of *inquiry* ‖ 電話による問い合わせ *an inquiry* made by telephone ／a telephone *inquiry* ‖ 私はその製品について問い合わせをした I *made inquiries about* [*inquired about*] the product. ‖ お問い合わせは下記へどうぞ Please address *inquiries* to the following.
✉ **当社の新和英辞典についてお問い合わせを頂きありがとうございます** Thank you for your *inquiry* about our new Japanese-English dictionary.

といあわせる 問い合わせる ask, inquire /ɪnkwáɪəʳ/ 《about, of》(➤ 後者は前者より堅い語)；check 《at, with》(確認のために) ▶その事件についての情報が欲しいのなら国会図書館に問い合わせてみたら？ If you want information about that incident, how about *asking* [*checking*] at the National Diet Library? ‖ この件はどなたに問い合わせたらいいでしょうか Who should I *ask* [Who should I *inquire* to] *about* this matter? ‖ 彼女にその理由を問い合わせてみます I'll *ask* her the reason. ‖ 詳しいことはＢ大学のＣ教授に問い合わせて(＝連絡して)ください If you want more details, please *contact* Professor C of B University.

-という -と言う 1【そういう名前の】▶私は小笠原という男性を紹介された I was introduced to a man *named* Ogasawara. ‖ きょう鈴木さんという方が見えました *A* Mr. Suzuki came to see you today. (➤ この a は固有名詞とともに用いて話し手になじみでないことを表す) ‖ 『ライ麦畑でつかまえて』という小説は誰が書きましたか Who wrote the novel (*titled*) "The Catcher in the Rye"? ‖ これは何という花ですか *What is the name of* this flower? ／*What is* this flower *called*?
2【内容を示して】that ▶おじが死んだという知らせが届いた We received news [notification] *that* our uncle had died. ‖ 彼は金に困っているという手紙を私によこした He wrote me (a letter) *saying that* he was having money problems. ／He wrote me a letter *to the effect that* he was in financial difficulty. (➤ to the effect that ... は「…という趣旨の」の意で堅い言い方).
▶中国という大国 the great nation *of* China ‖ 年賀状を出すという習慣はクリスマスカードを送り合うという西洋の習慣に似ている The Japanese custom *of* sending New Year's cards is similar to the Western practice *of* exchanging Christmas cards.

ということは と言うことは ▶中央線が止まってるって？ということはバスと地下鉄の乗り継ぎだな The Chuo line isn't running? *That means* I have to take a bus and (then) a subway.

-というのに -と言うのに ▶まだ20代だというのに彼女には円熟した雰囲気がある *Though* she is still in her twenties, she acts quite mature.

-というより -と言うより ▶彼女はけちというより倹約家なのだ She is *not so much* stingy *as* thrifty. (➤ not so much A as B は「A よりむしろ B」の意).

-といえば -と言えば speaking [talking] of
語法 (1) この言い方は直前の話題に関連した話題を展開する場合に用いる．(2) そのような制約がない場合は下の第２，第３例の訳例のように表現するとよい．
▶野球と言えば，ことしの中日は実に強いね *Speaking of* baseball, the Dragons are very strong this year. ‖ ラフカディオ・ハーンと言えばすぐに松江を思い出す *If someone mentions* Lafcadio Hearn, I immediately think of Matsue. ‖ シカゴと言えばシアーズタワーを思い出します I associate Chicago *with* the Sears Tower.

といかえす 問い返す ask again (再び尋ねる)；ask back [against] (反問する).

といかける 問い掛ける inquire ＋目，ask ＋目．

といき 吐息 a sigh /saɪ/ (ため息) ▶映画が終わると客席から吐息が漏れた When the movie ended, *sighs* were heard from [came from] the audience.

といし 砥石 a whetstone；a grindstone (回転式の) ▶包丁をといしで研ぐ sharpen a kitchen knife on [with] *a whetstone*.

といただす 問い質す question ＋目 ▶数人の学生を呼んで問いただしてみましたが，やはり彼らも全く知らないということでした I called (in) several students and *questioned* them, but they said that they knew nothing (about it).

ドイツ Germany 一形 ドイツの German ▶ドイツの首相 the *German* chancellor ‖ 1989年ベルリンの壁が取り壊され，東西ドイツは再統一された In 1989, the Berlin Wall was demolished and East and West *Germany* were reunited.
‖ドイツ語 German ‖ ドイツ人 a German.

-といって -と言って ▶どこといって行きたい所はない There's no place *in particular* I want to go to.

-といっても -と言っても ▶白ワインといっても種類が実に多い There is a great variety of white wines. (この場合，とくに訳出する必要はない).

といつめる 問い詰める ▶刑事は男を問い詰めたが自白させることはできなかった The detective *grilled* the man, but could not get a confession. (➤ grill は「厳しく尋問する」の意のインフォーマルな語) ‖ 彼はカンニングをして先生に問い詰められた He cheated on an exam and *was questioned severely* by the teacher.

どいつもこいつも ▶どいつもこいつも無責任なやつばかりだな *Every one of them* is an irresponsible guy.

どいなか ど田舎 ⇀田舎.

トイレ a **bathroom**,《英また》a **toilet**; a **restroom**(公共の場所の); a **lavatory**,《米また》a **washroom**

> **《解説》トイレについて**
> (1)アメリカの家庭では bathroom が, イギリスの家庭では toilet がそれぞれ一般的. ただし最近ではイギリス人でも bathroom を用いる人も多い. なお, toilet は《米》では「便器」の意になる.
> (2)ホテルやレストランなどの公共の場所では restroom が最も一般的で,《米》では men's room(男用), ladies' room(女用),《英》では the gents(男用), the ladies(女用)なども用いられる. 学校では lavatory や washroom がふつうだが, カナダでは後者は bathroom と restroom の両方の意味で使われている.

▶トイレを流す(のを忘れる) (forget to) flush the *toilet* ‖ トイレ休憩をとる take a *bathroom* [*toilet*] break ‖ トイレの水が流れている *The toilet* is running. 《参考》「トイレの水」を toilet water とすると, 入浴後に体に振りかけるオーデコロンのような化粧水(cologne)だと誤解される恐れがある. したがって用例のようにいうのが普通. ‖ 祖母はトイレが近い My grandmother *constantly needs to go to the bathroom* [*toilet*]. ‖ ちょっと失礼. トイレに行ってくる. Excuse me. *Nature's calling*. (➤ 文字通りには「自然が呼んでいる」で, トイレに行きたいということを遠回しに, また少しおどけて言う表現) ‖《ドライブ中に》そろそろトイレに行きたい I *need a nature stop* pretty soon. (➤ nature stop は「トイレ休憩」) ‖《ホテル・レストランなどで》すみません, トイレはどちらでしょうか Excuse me, but could you tell me where *the restroom* is? ‖ ちょっとトイレ *I have to go to the bathroom* [*restroom*]. (➤「トイレ」という語を使わずに(Please wait) one minute. I'll be right back. (ちょっと失礼. すぐ戻ります)と言うことも多い.) ‖ 対話《個人宅で》「トイレをお借りできますか」「どうぞ. 階段を上がると右手にあります」"May I use your *bathroom* [*toilet*]?" "Sure. Go up the stairs—it's on your right."

トイレットペーパー (a roll of) **toilet paper** [**tissue**], a **toilet roll, bath(room) tissue** ▶二枚重ねの[ダブルの]トイレットペーパー 2-ply [double-ply] *toilet paper*.

1**とう 塔** a **tower**; a **steeple**(教会などのせん塔); a **pagoda** /pəgóʊdə/ (仏寺の塔) ⇀せん塔 ▶三重の塔 a three-storied *pagoda*.
‖ テレビ[広告]塔 a television [an advertising] tower.

2**とう 党** a (**political**) **party** ▶党を結成する form *a* (*political*) *party* ‖ きみは何党を支持しているの? What *party* do you support?
‖ 党員 a member of a (political) party, a party member ‖ 党首 the president of a (political) party, the party leader ‖ 党大会 the (national) convention of a party ‖ 党本部 the headquarters of a (political) party.

3**とう 籐** a **cane**, a **rattan** /rətǽn/ ▶籐の椅子 a *cane* chair / a *rattan* chair.

4**とう 当** ▶当(=この)大学の学生 the students at *this* college ‖ 当の本人はその問題に全く無関心だった *He himself* [*The man in question*] was quite indifferent to the matter. (➤ 女性なら She herself [The woman in question] ... となる) ‖《機内アナウンス》皆さま, 当機はあと15分ほどでロンドン・ヒースロー国際空港に着陸する予定でございます Attention, all passengers. *We*'ll be arriving at London Heathrow International Airport, in about 15 minutes.
‖ 当店 this store [shop / restaurant] (➤ this の代わりに our でもよい).

5**とう 糖** **sugar** ▶父は時々尿に糖が混じる My father sometimes has *sugar* in his urine ‖ 糖分を取り過ぎないように注意しなさい Watch your *sugar* intake.
‖ 糖類《化学》a saccharide /sǽkəraɪd/.

6**とう 唐** **Tang**; **the Tang Dynasty**(唐朝).

7**とう 薹** ▶とうの立った大根 a daikon that *has become tough and stringy*(➤ tough and stringy は「かたくて筋が多い」) ‖ あの女優はもうとうが立っている That actress *has passed her prime*. (➤ prime は「全盛期, 盛り」) ‖ オフィーリア役を演じるには彼女は少しとうが立ち過ぎている She's a bit *too old* to play Ophelia's part.

8**とう 問う** 1【尋ねる】**ask, inquire** /ɪnkwáɪəʳ/ ▶数学のテストで円とは何かを問う問題が出た In the math exam, we *were asked* what a circle is. ‖ わが子の安否を問う電話が次々と入った One phone call after another came from the parents *asking about* their children's *safety*.
2【問題にする】▶年齢は問いません. 能力のみを問います It *doesn't matter* how old you are. What *counts* is what you can do. (➤「重要なのは何ができるかだ」の意) ‖《広告で》経験は問いません *No* experience *necessary* [*required*].
3【法律上の罪がある】▶きみは偽証罪に問われているのだ You *are charged with* [*accused of*] perjury.

1**-とう -等** 1【等級】▶1等船室 a *first-class* cabin ‖ 特等席 a *special* seat / a box (seat)(➤ 劇場の) ‖ 対話「徒競走は何等だったの?」「2等だったよ」"*What place* did you come in [*Where* did you place] (in the race)?" "I came in *second*."
2【…など】**and so on** [**so forth**], **and others, etc.** /et séṭərə/ ⇀-など ▶柔道・空手・剣道等の日本の武道が今や世界中に広まっている Judo, karate, kendo, *and other* Japanese martial arts are practiced all over the world now.

2**-とう -頭** ▶2頭の馬 *two* horses ‖ 30頭の牛 thirty *head* of cattle(➤ この意味の head は単複同形).

1**どう 胴** **the body**(胴体部); **the trunk**(人間・動物などの); **torso** /tɔ́ːʳsoʊ/ (人の) ▶彼は胴が長い[短い] He has a long [short] *trunk*. ‖ 父は胴(=腰)が太い My father has a big *waist* [*torso*]. (➤「胴が細い」なら have a small waist [torso]).

2**どう 銅** **copper**
‖ 銅貨 a copper (coin) ‖ 銅山 a copper mine ‖ 銅産出国 a copper producer ‖ 銅線 copper wire ‖ 銅メダル a bronze medal(➤ bronze は「青銅」).

3**どう 道** 1【行政単位の】a **prefecture** ▶北海道立図書館 Hokkaido *Prefectural* Library ‖ 道議会 the Hokkaido *Prefectural* Assembly.
2【分野】a **way**, a **path**
‖ 華道 the way of flowers (➤ ふつうは flower arrangement という) ‖ 茶道 the way of tea(➤ ふつうは the tea ceremony という).

4**どう 堂** ⇀堂に入る.

5**どう** 1【状態・方法を尋ねて】**how, what**
▶《状態》学校, どう? *How are you doing* at school? / *How do you like* your school? (➤ 後者は「気に入っている?」というニュアンス) ‖ あれからどうしてる? 元気? *How have things been going* since

と

then？Are you doing well？‖この洋服どう？（＝似合うかしら）*How do I look* in this dress？‖《旅行中の観光客に》京都はどうですか？*Are you enjoying* Kyoto？／*How do you like* Kyoto？‖ 対話「英語の試験どうだった？」「バッチリだよ」"*How* did you do on the English exam？" "Perfect！"‖この絵，どう思う？*What do you think about* this picture？（➤（×）How do you think とはしない）‖私のこと，どう思ってる？*What do you think of* me？‖同性婚をどう思いますか？*What do you think of* same-sex marriage？／*Tell me your opinion about* same-sex marriage.

と

【文型】
A はどうか？
How is A？
What is A like？

▶ 対話「夏休みはどうだった？」「どうってことないね」"*How was* your summer vacation？" "*Nothing much.*"‖ 対話（電話・メールなどで）「そちらの天気はどうですか」「雨になりそうです」"*How's* the weather over there？／*What's* the weather *like* over there［where you are］？" "Looks like rain."

直訳の落とし穴「ハワイはどうでしたか」
様子や感想を聞いて「ハワイはどうでしたか」のつもりで，「どうですか」＝How about？と考え，How about Hawaii？などという人がいる．How about ...？は提案して「…はどうですか」というときに用いるので，いきなりこう聞くと何のことかわからず相手はぽかんとしてしまう（→**3**）．様子を聞くのは，How was Hawaii？である．また，旅行者などにその土地の印象を聞いて「金沢はいかがですか（＝お気に入りましたか）」も（×）How about Kanazawa？でなく，How do you like Kanazawa？という．

✉ **日本では今インフルエンザがはやっていますが，そちらではどうですか** There's flu going around in Japan now. *How is it over there？*
▶《方法》上野へはどう行くのですか *How* do［can］I get to Ueno？‖これをどう説明したらいいのかわからない I don't know *how to* explain it.（➤ how to do は「どう…したらよいのか，…のしかた」）‖どうしたらいいか自分でもわからない I don't have a clue *what I should do.*（➤ not have a clue は「さっぱりわからない」の意のインフォーマルな言い方）‖ 対話「この箱どうやって開けるの？」「そのつまみを引っ張るのよ」"*How* do you open this box？" "Pull the tab."
2【体調などを尋ねて】

【文型】
人・物（A）はどうしたの？
What's the matter with A？
What's wrong with A？
What happened to A？

《解説》（1）相手に「どうしたの？」と聞くときは単に **What's the matter？**という．with *you* をつけると，「どうかしているよ」と相手をとがめる気持ちが入ることが多い．
（2）**What's the matter？**はしばしば，単に相手を気遣って使う．**What's wrong？**は「どこが具合悪いの？」と故障などの原因や理由を聞くのに使う．**What happened to A？**は「A に何があった［起きた］の？」の意．

▶ 対話「どうしたの？ 顔色が悪いよ」「ちょっと寒気がするんだ」"*What's the matter？*［*What's wrong？*］You look pale." "I'm a little chilly."（➤「どうもしないよ」なら Nothing (is the matter).）‖ 対話「どうしたの（＝何かあったの）？」「彼女に振られちゃったんだよ」"*What happened？*" "She dumped me."
▶《医者・警官が》どうしました？*What seems to be the trouble*［problem］*？／What can I do for you？*‖手をどうしたんですか *What happened* to your hand？
3【勧めて】How［What］about ...？

【文型】
A はどう？
How about A？
What about A？

《解説》（1）様子を聞いたり，提案したり，意見・説明・判断を求めたり，さまざまに使われる．「…してはいかが」と勧める場合には，How about？を使う．
（2）What about？はより主張する意図が強く，しばしば，「そう言うあなたはどうなの？」という批判口調で用いる．

▶ 対話「もう済んだの？」「まだよ．あなたのほうはどう？」"Have you finished？" "Not yet. *How about* you？"‖ 対話「コーヒーでもどう？」「いいね」"*How about* some coffee？" "Sounds wonderful."‖私がばかですって？**あなたこそどうなのよ** You said I'm stupid？*What about you？／Look who's talking！*（➤後者は「そう非難めいたことを言うあなただって同じでしょ」の意）．
▶ 対話「テニスするのはどう？」「いいね」"*What do you say to* playing tennis？" "Sounds great."
4【問い詰めて】▶もっと行儀よくしたらどうなの？ You *should* behave more politely.／Where are your manners？‖《子供に》「ありがとう」はどうしたの？*What ever happened to* "Thank you"？‖ 対話「おまえ，服装がだらしないぞ」「そう言うおまえはどうなんだよ」"You are dressed like a slob." "*What about yourself？*"
5【疑念・疑問を示して】▶財布を忘れちゃった．どうしよう？I forgot my wallet. *What shall I do？*‖熱帯雨林がすべて破壊されたら地球はどうなるのだろう *What would become of* the earth if all the rain forests were destroyed？
▶また失敗したらどうなるんだろう *What if* I should fail again？（➤ What would happen if ...？のインフォーマルな言い方）‖チョコレートを食べ過ぎるとどうなるんだろう *What effects* does too much chocolate have on you？‖この話の最後はどうなるの？*How* does this story *turn out*？‖ 対話「彼，うまくいくかしら？」「さあどうかな」"Will he succeed？" "Well, *I don't know.*"
☛ **どういう，どうしようもない，どうでもいい，どう見ても**（→見出語）

どうあげ 胴上げ ▶優勝チームは全員で監督を胴上げした The members of the winning team *tossed* their manager *into the air* after the victory.
とうあつせん 等圧線《気象》an **isobar** /áɪsəbɑːʳ/.
とうあん 答案 an **examination paper**, a **paper** ▶答案を提出する hand in one's (*examination*) *paper*‖いつ答案を返してくれますか When will you return my *paper*？／When can I have my *paper* back？
‖**答案用紙** an answer sheet.
どうい 同意 **agreement**, **consent**（➤後者は前者より堅

い語で, 特に上位の人の承諾をいう) **一動**(…に)**同意する** agree《to》; consent《to》

【文型】
提案(A)に同意する
agree to A
accept A
consent to A
人(B)に同意する
agree with B

《解説》**agree to** と **accept** は「(提案や計画を)受け入れる, 認める」の意で, **agree with** は「(人や人の意見に)賛成する」の意. また agree to *do* は「…することを承諾する, …することで合意する」の意. **consent to** は立場の上の者が「進んで承認を与える」の意.

▶当会への入会申し込みには両親の**同意**が必要です Your parents must *agree* [*consent*] *to* your application for admission to this club. ‖ぼくはM大を受験するのに父の**同意**を得ることができなかった I failed to obtain my father's *consent to* take the entrance examinations for M University. ‖彼女は私の提案に**同意した** She *agreed to* [*accepted*] my proposal. ‖あなたの意見には**同意**(＝賛成)できません I can't *agree with* you [*with* what you say].

どういう what ▶**どういう**手順を踏んだらいいのでしょうか *What* procedure(s) should I follow?／*What* steps should I take? ‖それは**どういう**意味ですか *What* do you mean by that? (➤口論しているような場合には, この表現はいらだちを表す) ‖大学に行かないって, **どういう**こと? *What* do you mean, you won't go to college? ‖その人は**どういう**人ですか *What* is he [she] like?／*What* does he [she] look like? (➤前者は人の性格・外見を, 後者は外見を聞くのに用いる) ‖《妻が夫に》あの女の人, あなたとは**どういう**関係なの? *What* is your relationship with that woman? (● What is she to you? とすると, 「あの女の人, あなたにとってどれほどの(意味を持つ)人?」という含みを持った言い方になる).
▶**どういう**訳でこんなに遅れたの? *Why the heck* [*the hell*] did you come so late? ‖毎日毎日遅れて来て, **どういう**つもりだ *What's the big idea* [*What do you mean*] coming in late day after day! (➤ What's the big idea はこちらをいらつかせる行動の理由を聞くとき) ‖ 対話「**どういう**映画が好きですか」「ホラーもの以外なら何でも」"*What kind* [*sort*] *of* movies do you like?" "All kinds, except (for) horror movies."

どういご 同意語 a **synonym** /sínənɪm/ ▶ huge は enormous の**同意語**だ 'Huge' is *a synonym* for 'enormous.'

とういじょう 糖衣錠 a **sugar-coated pill** [**tablet**].

とういそくみょう 当意即妙 ▶**当意即妙**に答える *make a witty response*.

どういたしまして 1【感謝に対して】▶ 対話「手伝ってくれてありがとう」「**どういたしまして**」"Thanks for your help." "*You're* (*quite*) *welcome*.／*Don't mention it*.／*Not at all*.／*My pleasure*.／*Anytime*." (● You're (quite) welcome. は《米》で, Not at all. や Don't mention it. は《英》で好まれる傾向がある) ‖ 対話「留守中, 荷物を預かってくださってありがとうございました」「**どういたしまして**. はい, どうぞ」"Thank you so much for accepting my package while I was out." "*No problem!* Here it is." (➤ No problem. は「何でもないことです」「お安いご用です」の意).
2【謝罪に対して】▶ 対話「待たせてすまなかったね」「**どういたしまして**」"Sorry to keep [have kept] you waiting." "*That's* (*quite*) *all right*.／*That's OK*." (➤謝罪に対しては You're welcome. とは言わない).

とういつ 統一 **unity** (まとまり); **unification** (統合); **standardization** (規格化, 画一化) **一動 統一する** **unite** ＋㊐, **unify** /júːnɪfaɪ/ ＋㊐, **standardize** /stǽndəʳdaɪz/ ＋㊐ ▶服装を**統一する** *standardize* clothing ‖ファイルの保存形式を**統一する** *use a uniform* file saving format ‖秀吉は天下を**統一した** Hideyoshi *unified* the whole country.／Hideyoshi *brought* the country *under his rule*. ‖ヨーガは精神の**統一**を目指す Yoga aims at *mental* [*spiritual*] *centering*.
▶内装は白を基調にしていて**統一**感がある The décor was done using white as the basic color which gives *a sense of uniformity* ‖**統一**感 a sense of unity [*uniformity*] ‖**統一**地方選挙 a *combined* [*unified*] local election.
☛ 不統一 (→見出語)

どういつ 同一の **the same** ▶A教授の論文ではB教授と**同一の**事例を扱っている Professor A's paper deals with *the same* case *as* Professor B's. ‖その小川さんというのは, 私の知っている人と**同一**人物だろうか Is that Mr. Ogawa *the same* Mr. Ogawa that I know?／Is that the Mr. Ogawa *that* I know? ‖私はあなたと**同一**意見です My opinion is *the same* as yours.／You and I have *the same* opinion. ‖あんな男と**同一**視されてはたまらんよ I don't want to *be categorized* [*classified*] with him.／Don't *put* me *in the category* as him.

どういん 動員する **mobilize** /móʊbəlaɪz/ ＋㊐; **pull** (観客などを引き付ける) ▶東京サミットには何千人もの警官が**動員された** Thousands of police officers *were mobilized* for the Tokyo Summit ‖そのアメリカのバンドは大勢の観客を**動員した** That American band *pulled* (*in*) [*drew*] a large audience.
☛ 総動員 (→見出語)

とうえい 投影 (a) **projection** (映写); a **reflection** (反射) ▶池に**投影された**紅葉 autumn tints *reflected* in a pond.

とうおう 東欧 **Eastern Europe**
‖**東欧諸国** Eastern European countries《参考》かつて東欧に含まれていた, ポーランド, チェコ, ハンガリーなどは現在「中欧」(Central Europe)と呼ばれている.

どうおんいぎご 同音異義語 **a homonym**.

1**とうか 投下する** **drop** ＋㊐ ▶難民キャンプにヘリコプターから食糧が**投下された** The helicopter *dropped* food into the refugee camp. ‖1945年8月, アメリカは日本の広島と長崎に2つの原爆を**投下した**. In August 1945, the United States *dropped* two atomic bombs over the Japanese cities of Hiroshima and Nagasaki.

2**とうか 灯火** ▶**灯火**親しむべし Autumn is a good season for reading by a lamp.
‖**灯火管制** (a) restriction on lightning; a blackout (完全消灯); a brownout (減灯).

1**どうか 銅貨** a **copper** (**coin**).

2**どうか 1**【依頼・嘆願して】**please** →どうぞ ▶**どうか**そのことは忘れてください *Please* forget (about) that.／*I would appreciate it* if you would forget all about that. (➤後者は改まった言

い方；appreciate は「感謝する」).

✉ **どうか早くよくなってください** *I wish* you a quick recovery. ／*I hope* you will get well soon. ➤ 後者は前者よりもインフォーマル.

2【疑念を表して】 whether (or not), if ▶私はその仕事に就きたいのかどうかわからないんです I'm not sure *whether or not* [*if*] I want to take the job. ‖《警察・医師などが》どうかしましたか *What* seems to be the problem [trouble]?

3【正常でない】 ▶耳たぶ, どうかしたの？ 血が出てるわよ *What's wrong with* your earlobe? It's bleeding. ‖ゆうべは私どうかしてたわ I *wasn't myself* last night, you know. ／*Something was wrong* [*was the matter*] with me last night. ‖そんなに耳元で大声を出さないでくれ. 頭がどうかなりそうだ Don't speak in such a loud voice so close to my ears! *It drives me crazy.*

4【不賛成・疑問を示して】 ▶彼女のような世間知らずもどうかと思う *I wonder how* people (who are) as naive as she is will get along in the world. (➤ どうやって世渡りして行くのだろうか, の意).

☞ どうかすると, -かどうか (→見出語)

3**どうか 同化** assimilation **一動** (…に)**同化する** assimilate /əsíməleɪt/ 《into》 ▶帰国子女の中にはなかなか日本社会に同化できない人もいる Some returnee children cannot *assimilate into* Japanese society.

どうが 動画 ▶動画を再生する play *a video file* ‖携帯電話 [デジタルカメラ] で動画を撮る *videotape* with a cellphone [a digital camera] ‖YouTubeに動画をアップする *upload* [*post* ／*put up*] *a video* (*file*) on [to] YouTube.

‖**動画サイト** a video (web)site ‖**動画ファイル** a video file. →アニメ.

とうかい 倒壊 (a) collapse **一動 倒壊する** collapse, fall down, be destroyed ▶倒壊した家屋 a *collapsed* house ‖その地震では古いビルの倒壊が目立った The *collapse* of old buildings attracted attention in that earthquake.

1**とうがい 当該**

‖**当該商品** the product in question ‖**当該問題** the relevant issue(s).

2**とうがい 凍害** frost damage.

とうかく 頭角 ▶彼は20代で初当選してから党内で次第に頭角を現してきた After he was elected for the first time in his twenties, he gradually *distinguished himself* in the party.

どうかく 同格 ▶小川氏は私の先輩だが, 職位は私と同格だ Mr. Ogawa is my senior, but we *have the same rank* in the company. ‖文中のこの2語は同格です These two words in the sentence are *in apposition.*

‖**同格語**《文法》an appositive.

どうかすると ▶人はどうかすると(＝時々)ひどく悲観的になることがある People can be very pessimistic *on occasion*(*s*) [*at times*].

どうかせん 導火線 a fuse ▶導火線に点火する light *a fuse.*

とうかつ 統括・統轄 control **一動 統括する** control ＋目 (まとめる)；supervise /súːpərvaɪz/ ＋目 (監督する) ▶生産部門はすべて吉田さんが統括している Mr. Yoshida *supervises* the whole production line.

どうかつ 恫喝 intimidation **一動 恫喝する** intimidate ＋目.

とうがらし 唐辛子 (a) red (chilli) pepper, cayenne /keɪén/ (pepper) ▶七味トウガラシ seven-spice (*red*) *pepper.*

とうかん 投函する mail ＋目,《英また》post ＋目 ▶忘れずにこの手紙を投かんしてください Don't forget to *mail* [*post*] this letter, please.

とうがん 冬瓜 a winter melon.

どうかん 同感 ▶彼の言うことに同感(＝賛成)だ I quite *agree with* him. ／I'*m with* him all the way. ‖**対話**「入試制度は廃止したほうがいいと思う」「同感！」"I think the entrance examination system should be abolished." "*I agree.*" ‖**対話**「人生ではいつも前向きな姿勢が大切です」「同感です」"In life, I think it's important to always have a positive attitude." "*I feel the same way.*"

どうがん 童顔 a baby [childlike] face (子供っぽい顔) ▶彼は40歳だが, まだ童顔を残している He is forty, but he still has *a baby face.*

1**とうき 冬期・冬季** wintertime, the winter season (➤ 後者は「冬の季節」に相当) ▶この道路は冬期は通行止めになる This road is closed during *the winter* (*season*).

‖**冬季オリンピック** the Winter Olympics [Olympic Games] ‖**冬季休暇** the winter vacation [《英》holidays].

2**とうき 陶器** pottery **《解説》** (1) pottery は「陶器」の総称. 「陶磁器」は ceramics または ceramicware, 「磁器」は porcelain /pɔ́ːrsəlɪn/, 「土器」は earthenware という. また, 「瀬戸物」の意の俗称に china がある. (2) いずれも集合的な言い方なので, 数えるときは a piece of ..., two pieces of ... のようにいう.

3**とうき 投機** speculation ▶投機的事業 a *speculative* venture ‖投機性の強いゲーム a *gambling* game ‖名画が投機の対象になっているのは残念なことだ It is a pity that famous paintings have become the object of *speculation.*

4**とうき 騰貴** a rise (価格の)；(an) appreciation (土地・株などの) **一動 騰貴する** appreciate /əpríːʃieɪt/ ▶円の騰貴 the *appreciation* of the yen ‖その当時は土地が騰貴していた Land prices *were* [Land *was*] *rising* at that time. (➤「急騰していた」なら ... were skyrocketing.).

5**とうき 登記** registration **一動 登記する** register ▶購入した土地を登記する *register* a piece of land one has purchased.

‖**登記所** a registry [register] office (戸籍の)；a real property registration office (不動産の) ‖**登記簿** a register ‖**登記料** a registration fee.

6**とうき 投棄する** throw away, dump ＋目 (➤ 後者には「ぞんざいに投げ捨てる」というニュアンスが強い) ▶生ごみの不法投棄 unlawful *dumping* of garbage ‖その国は使用済み核廃棄物を海洋に投棄している That country *is dumping* nuclear waste in the ocean.

とうぎ 討議 (a) discussion, (a) debate (➤ 後者は最初から賛成・反対の立場を明らかにして意見を述べ合うこと) **一動 討議する** discuss ＋目, debate ＋目 ▶この件 [問題] については十分に討議してもらいたい I would like you to *discuss* this matter [issue] fully. (➤ discuss は他動詞なので (×) discuss about とはしない) ‖生徒たちは制服を廃止すべきかどうかを討議した The students *discussed* [*debated*] whether their school uniform should be abolished. ‖その問題は現在討議中だ The problem is *under discussion.*

1**どうき 動機** a motive ▶動機は何であれ, 万引きはいけない Whatever *the motive* is, shoplifting is wrong. ‖**対話**「きみが日本の歴史の勉強を始めた動機は何ですか」「わが国のことをもっと深く知りたかったからです」"What was your *motive* for [in] studying Japanese history?／What made you study Japanese history?" "Because I wanted to know (about) our country more deeply."

2**どうき 同期** 1【同じ年度】▶私たちは大学で同期だった We *were in the same class* in [at] college.／We *graduated* from college (*in*) *the same year*.
‖**同期会** a class reunion (➤「高校の同期会」なら a high-school reunion) ‖**同期生** a classmate →クラス.
2【同じ時期】▶ことし前半の交通事故による死亡者の数は昨年同期に比べて僅かに減少した The number of traffic deaths in the first half of this year has shown a slight decrease over (*the same period of*) *last year*. ‖輸入は前年同期比で8パーセント減少した Imports decreased 8% *from a year earlier*.
3【作動の時間的一致】▶iPadと2台のパソコンを同期する *sync* an iPad with [to] two computers (➤ sync は synchronize の短縮形).

3**どうき 動悸** (rapid) **heartbeat**, **palpitation** /pæ̀lpɪtéɪʃən/ (➤後者は医学用語) ▶階段を上ると動悸がする When I go up the stairs, my heart starts *pounding* [*palpitating*].

1**どうぎ 道義** **morality** ▶道義にもとる行為をする do something that *is against morality* [something *immoral*] ‖その件に関しては道義的責任を痛感しています I feel a great deal of *moral responsibility* for that matter.

2**どうぎ 動議** **a motion** ▶緊急動議を提出する make *an urgent motion*.

どうぎご 同義語 **a synonym**. →同意語.

1**とうきゅう 等級** **a grade**, **a class** ▶このリンゴは品質に応じて秀・優・良と等級がつけてある These apples *are graded* for quality as "excellent", "superior" and "good."

2**とうきゅう 投球** **pitching** (投げること); **a pitch**, **a delivery** (投げた球) ━動 **投球する pitch**.

とうぎゅう 闘牛 **bullfighting** (➤一つ一つの闘技は a bullfight という)
‖**闘牛士** a bullfighter; a matador /mǽtədɔːʳ/ (牛にとどめを刺す役) ‖**闘牛場** a bullring.

どうきゅう 同級 ▶高校で同級だった久米君にきのう何年かぶりで会った Yesterday I met Kume, *a classmate* from senior high school who(m) I hadn't seen in [for] years. (➤ classmate は「同級生」) ‖伸彦さんとは高校で同級でした I was *in the same class* as Nobuhiko in senior high school.
《参考》be in the same class は《米》と《英》で異なった意に用いられることが多い. →クラス.

どうきょ 同居する **live together** ▶わが家では犬もカナリアも人間と同居している At my house, dogs, canaries and people all *live together*. ‖きみはぼくの両親と同居するのは嫌かい? Would you be opposed to *living with* my parents?
‖**同居人** a housemate, a flatmate; a cohabitant (同棲者); a roommate (同室人).

1**どうきょう 同郷** ▶宮沢君と私は同郷です Miyazawa and I *are from the same town*. ‖同郷のよしみでこれからもよろしく *Since we come from the same part of the country*, I hope we will be good friends (from now on).

2**どうきょう 道教** **Taoism**.

どうぎょう 同業 ▶私は松原さんとは同業です Mr. Matsubara and I *are in the same business* [*trade*／*line of work*]. ‖彼は同業者(仲間)の間では有名だ He's well known in *the profession* [*trade*].
‖**同業者組合** a trade association.

とうきょく 当局 **the authorities** /əθɔ́ːrəṭiz/ ▶この件は関係当局[学校当局]に処理してもらうのが筋だ *The authorities concerned* [*The school authorities*] should take care of this problem. ‖市当局は子供たちのために公園を造ることを決定した *The city authorities* have decided to make a park for children. (➤ふつうは The city has decided ... という).

とうきょり 等距離 **be equally distant** [**equidistant**] **from** ▶名古屋は東京と大阪からほぼ等距離だ Nagoya *is* almost *equidistant from* Tokyo and Osaka.

どうぐ 道具 **a tool** (手で使う簡単な工具); **a utensil** /juténsəl/ (台所道具); **an instrument** (主に精密機械); **an implement** (農業・園芸用の) ▶大工道具 carpenter's *tools* ‖釣り道具一式 a set of *fishing tackle*／*fishing gear* (➤ gear /gɪəʳ/ は「道具一式」) ‖台所道具は立派なのに彼の料理はまずい He has all sorts of *kitchen utensils* [*cooking equipment*], but he is a terrible cook. ‖聴診器は医者にとっては大事な道具である A stethoscope is a valuable *instrument* for a doctor.
▶《比喩的》ことばは意思を伝達するための道具である Language is *a tool* for communication. ‖彼女はその男のたくらみの道具に使われたにすぎない She was used only as *a tool* in [for] that man's scheme.
‖**大道具** a (stage) setting ‖**家財道具** household goods ‖**小道具** (stage) properties, 《インフォーマル》props ‖**裁縫道具** a sewing kit (➤ kit は「一式」) ‖**テニス道具[用具]** tennis equipment.

とうくつ 盗掘 **tomb robbery** [**robbing**] ━動 **盗掘する rob a tomb**.

どうくつ 洞窟 **a cave**; **a cavern** /kǽvəʳn/ (大きくて深い) ▶今度あの洞窟を探検してみようよ Let's explore the *cave* someday.
‖**洞窟探検** caving, spelunking /spɪlʌ́ŋkɪŋ/.

とうげ 峠 1【山の】**a (mountain) pass** ▶碓氷峠を越えると浅間山が見えてきた As soon as we crossed (over) *the Usui Pass*, Mount Asama came into view.
2【ピーク】**the peak** (最高点); **the height** /haɪt/ (最も盛んな状態) ▶峠を越えたプロレスラー an *over-the-hill* pro wrestler ‖暑さもここ数日が峠だろう The heat will be at *its peak* [*height*] for the next few days.
▶暑さも峠を越したようだ It seems that the hottest season *is over* [*is gone*]. ‖このプロジェクトも峠を越えた The hardest part of this job *is over*.／We *are over the hump* with this project. (➤「難関を乗り切った」の意のインフォーマルな表現) ‖日本の経済は峠を越えたと思いたい We hope the Japanese economy *has turned the* [*a*] *corner*. (➤ turn the [a] corner は「危機を脱する」) ‖お父様の容体は峠を越えました Your father *has passed the crisis* [*is out of danger*].

どうけ 道化 **a clown** /klaʊn/ (サーカスなどの); **a buffoon** /bəfúːn/ (おどけ者) ▶あいつはパーティーではいつも道化者だ He always *plays the clown* [*buffoon*] at a party.
‖**道化師** a clown.

1**とうけい 統計** **statistics** /stətístɪks/ (➤複数扱い) ━形 **統計の statistical** /stətístɪkəl/ ▶統計をとる collect [take] *statistics* ‖最新の統計によると, 肺がんによ

る死者は増えている According to the most recent [the latest] *statistics*, deaths from lung cancer are on the increase. ‖統計によると中途退学する高校生が増えている *Statistics* [*Figures*] *show that* more students are dropping out of high school. (➤この訳例のように一般的な場合は the をつけない).

‖統計学 statistics (➤この意味では単数扱い) ‖統計資料 statistical material [data] ‖統計調査 statistical research ‖統計表 a statistical table.

2とうけい 東経 the east longitude ▶船は東経130度50分を航行中だ The ship is sailing at (*a longitude* of) 130 degrees 50 minutes *east* [*Long*. 130° 50′ *E*].

3とうけい 闘鶏 cockfighting (➤一つ一つの闘技は a cockfight という).

とうげい 陶芸 ceramic art ; (the craft of) making pottery

‖陶芸家 a ceramist, a potter.

どうけい 同系の affiliated (同系列の) ; similar (同じような) ▶わが社はトヨタ自動車と同系です Our company *is affiliated with* Toyota Motor Corporation. ‖同系の色 a *similar* color.

とうけつ 凍結する freeze (+目) ▶道路が凍結していたので車がスリップした Since the road *was frozen*, my car skidded. / My car skidded because the road was *icy*. (➤「凍結した道路」は a frozen [an icy] road).

▶《比喩的》ガソリンの価格を凍結する *freeze* gasoline prices / *place* [*put*] *a freeze on* gasoline prices ‖彼らはその企画を凍結した They *put* the plan *in cold storage*. (➤「冷凍貯蔵にした」が原義) / They *shelved* the plan. ‖その国は核開発計画の凍結に同意した The country agreed to *freeze* its nuclear program.

どうげつ 同月 the same month.

とうけん 闘犬 dogfighting (➤一つ一つの闘技は a dogfight という).

どうけん 同権 ▶男女が同権なのは言うまでもない It goes without saying that men and women have *equal rights*. (➤「男女同権」は equal rights for men and women).

‖男女同権主義 (equity) feminism.

1とうこう 登校する go to school ▶バスで登校する take the bus to school / *go to school* by bus (➤前者がふつう) ‖歩いて登校する *walk to school* ‖全校生徒は8時20分までに登校することになっている All students are supposed to *be at school* by 8:20. (「学校に来ている」と考える) ‖登校の途中で[登校中に]捨て猫を見つけた I found some abandoned kittens *on my way to school*. ‖いろいろな理由で不登校の生徒が増えている More and more students *don't attend* [*go to*] *school* for various reasons. ‖8月25日は登校日だ We *have to go to school* (on) August 25. (英米には日本のような休暇中の「登校日」はない).

✉ 私は自転車で約40分かけて登校します It takes me about 40 minutes to *get to school* on my bicycle.

☛ 不登校 (→見出語)

2とうこう 投稿 1【ネットへの】posting ; a post, a posting (投稿したもの) 一動 投稿する post (➤ post はサイト上に「掲示する」ことなので, 自分のサイトに自ら「書き込む」や「アップする」の意味にもなる) ▶YouTube に動画を投稿する *post* [*upload* / *put up*] a video on [to] YouTube ‖学校のウェブサイトにメッセージを投稿する *post* a message on the school's Website.

‖(ネットへの) 投稿者 a poster.

2【新聞・雑誌などへの】(a) contribution 一動 (…に) 投稿する contribute 《to》 ▶地元の新聞に川柳を投稿する *contribute* a senryu *to* the local paper.

‖(新聞などへの) 投稿者 a contributor ‖投稿欄 a readers' column.

3とうこう 投降する surrender oneself.

1とうごう 統合 integration 一動 統合する combine +目 (結び付ける) ; integrate /íntəgreɪt/ +目 (1つにまとめる) ▶昨年その2つの部署は1つに統合された Last year the two departments *were combined* [*consolidated* / *merged*] into one. ‖S小学校はT小学校に統合される予定だ S elementary is scheduled to *be integrated* into T elementary school. (➤ integrated school は人種差別のない「融和学校」).

‖統合ソフト《コンピュータ》integrated software (applications).

2とうごう 等号 《数学》an equal sign.

1どうこう 同行する accompany +目 ▶村田さんに同行して浜松まで行った I went to Hamamatsu *with* Mr. Murata. ‖《刑事が》署までご同行願います *Will you come* [*accompany us*] to the police station? ‖私も同行しましょうか Shall I *accompany* [*go along with*] you?

2どうこう 同好 ▶俳句が好きなのだが同好の士が見つからない I like (making) haiku, but I can't find *anyone who shares the same interest*. (➤「同好の士」は a like-minded people ということもできる) ‖柔道同好会 an amateur judo *club*.

3どうこう 動向 a trend ▶景気の動向 business *trends* ‖世論の動向 the *trend* of public opinion.

4どうこう 瞳孔 the pupil (of the eye).

とうこうき 投光器 a floodlight.

とうごうしっちょうしょう 統合失調症 《医学》schizophrenia /skìtsəfríːniə/

‖統合失調症患者 a schizophrenic /skìtsəfrénɪk/.

とうこうせん 等高線 a contour /káːntʊəʳ/ (line).

とうごく 投獄する put ... into jail, imprison +目 ▶彼は2年間投獄されていた He *was imprisoned* [*was incarcerated* / *was in prison*] for two years.

とうこん 闘魂 fighting spirit.

どうこん 同梱する bundle +目

‖同梱ソフト bundled software.

とうざ 当座 ▶当座しのぎの措置をとる take a *stopgap* measure ‖アメリカから帰って来た当座はホテル住まいをしていた I lived in a hotel *for a while* after returning from America. ‖これだけあれば当座の生活費には十分です This sum of money should be enough to cover my *immediate* living expenses.

‖当座預金 a checking [《英》current] account.

どうさ 動作 movement(s) ; action(s) (行動) ▶きびきびした動作 brisk *movements* ‖パンダは動作が緩慢だ Pandas move slowly. ‖彼は動作が機敏だ He is quick in *action*. / He is quick-moving.

‖動作環境 hardware requirements (ハードウェアの必要条件).

とうさい 搭載 ▶ミサイルを搭載した戦闘機 a fighter *loaded* [*mounted*] *with* missiles ‖このパソコンは最新・最速のペンティアム・プロセッサーを搭載している This personal computer *is equipped with* the latest and fastest Pentium processor.

とうざい 東西 east and west(東と西) ; the East and the West(東洋と西洋) ▶町は東西に延びている The town extends *from east to west* [*east and west*]. (➤ east and west はこの場合「東西(の方向)に」の意味の副詞句) ‖ イスタンブールは東西文化の接点にある Istanbul lies at the junction of *Eastern and Western* [*Oriental and Occidental*] *cultures*.
‖東西南北 north, south, east and west(➤ 語順に注意).

どうざい 同罪 ▶ 2 人は同罪である Both men *are equally to blame* [*equally responsible*].

1**とうさく 盗作** (a) plagiarism /pléɪdʒərìzəm/ 《参考》インターネット上にある他人の曲や詞を無断で使用することを plagiarhythm というが, これは plagiarize と rhythm の合成語. 一動 盗作する plagiarize ＋目, 《インフォーマル》crib ＋目 ▶その論文に盗作疑惑が持ち上がった *An allegation of plagiarism* in the paper has been made.

2**とうさく 倒錯** (a) perversion /pərvə́ːrʒən/ ; (a) deviation (➤ 前者のほうがより軽蔑的な響きがある) ▶フェティシズムは性的倒錯の一種だ Fetishism is one kind of *sexual perversion*.
‖性的倒錯者 a (sexual) pervert /pəːrvə́ːrt/.

とうさつ 盗撮 secret filming.

どうさつ 洞察 insight /ínsaɪt/ ▶ 50年後の今日を正確に予測するとは, 彼は何と洞察力のある人だったんだろう What *a man of insight* he was to predict precisely what would happen fifty years later!

1**とうさん 倒産** (a) bankruptcy /bǽŋkrʌptsi/ 一動 倒産する go bankrupt ▶また地方銀行が倒産した Another local bank *went bankrupt* [*went broke*].

2**とうさん 父さん** →お父さん.

どうさん 動産 movable property, movables ; 《英》one's personal estate.

1**とうし 闘志** fighting spirit ▶あのゴールキーパーは闘志の塊だ That goalkeeper has a lot of *fighting spirit*. ‖ 彼は闘志満々だった He was *full of fight* [*pep*]. (➤ pep は「元気」の意のインフォーマルな語) ‖ 生徒たちは甲子園出場へ闘志を燃やしている The students *are* all *fired up* about going to Koshien Stadium.

2**とうし 闘士** an activist(活動家) ; a champion(主義などのために戦う人).

3**とうし 投資** (an) investment 一動 (…に)投資する invest 《in》 ▶土地に投資する *invest* (*one's money*) *in* land ‖ 新技術の開発に多額の投資をする *invest* heavily *in* the development of new technology.
‖投資家 an investor ‖ 投資銀行 an investment bank ‖ 投資信託 an investment trust.

4**とうし 凍死する** freeze to death ▶ハイカーは八甲田山中で凍死体となって発見された The hiker *was found frozen to death* in the Hakkoda mountains.

5**とうし 透視する** see through(透かして見る) ▶ X 線で胸を透視する *look at* the chest *through the fluoroscope*(➤ fluoroscope は「蛍光透視鏡」).
‖透視能力 clairvoyance /kleərvɔ́ɪəns/ ; clairvoyant power.

1**とうじ 当時** then, at that time ; in those days(その時代) ▶当時(＝そのとき)の首相, 村山氏 Mr. Murayama, who was the prime minister *then* [the *then* prime minister] (➤ 後者の then は形容詞) ‖ 当時(＝その頃)の科学者は磁気が何であるか知らなかった The scientists *of those days* did not know what magnetism was all about. ‖ 1000円は当時としては大金だった One thousand yen was a lot of money *then* [*at that time* ／ *in those days*].

2**とうじ 冬至** the winter solstice /sɑ́ːlstɪs/
✉ **きょうは冬至です. 日本ではこの日にゆず湯に入り, かぼちゃを食べる習慣があります** Today is *the winter solstice*. It is a Japanese custom to take a hot bath scented with yuzu and to eat pumpkin on this day.

3**とうじ 湯治** ▶伊豆の温泉へ湯治に行く *go* to a hot-spring resort in Izu *to recuperate* [*to recover one's health*].
‖湯治客 a person at a spa to cure a disease ‖ 湯治場 a hot-spring resort.

4**とうじ 答辞** an address /ǽdres/ in reply, 《米》a valedictory /vælədíktəri/ (告別の辞) ▶彼女は選ばれて卒業式で校長の祝辞に対する答辞を読んだ She was selected to *make an address in reply* to the principal's address at graduation. 《参考》《米》では「答辞を読む」ことを deliver the valedictory at commencement といい, それを読む人を valedictorian /vælədɪktɔ́ːriən/ という.

5**とうじ 杜氏** a (chief) sake brewer.

1**どうし 動詞** 《文法》a verb ▶call は規則動詞だ 'Call' is *a regular verb*.
‖句動詞《文法》a phrasal verb ‖ 自動詞《文法》an intransitive verb ‖ 他動詞《文法》a transitive verb.

2**どうし 同志** a fellow member(政治運動などの) ; a comrade /kɑ́ːmræd/ (特に共産党の).

-どうし -同士 ▶お互いどうしで話し合って決めたら? You should talk it over and decide it *between yourselves*. ‖ 兄弟どうしでけんかになった The brothers began to quarrel *among themselves*. ‖ 彼らは敵どうしだ They are *mutual* enemies. (➤ mutual /mjúːtʃuəl/ は「相互の」) ‖ トラックどうしが衝突した Two trucks crashed into *each other*. ‖ 私たちはお隣どうしです We *live next door to each other*. ／ We are *next-door neighbors*. ‖ 私たちは友だちどうしです We are *friends*. ‖ 彼らはいとこどうしだ They are *cousins*. ‖ 男どうしでしか話せないこともある There are some things that you can only talk about *with other guys*. 《参考》男どうしの「(卑わいな)話」を guy talk, locker-room talk などという ‖ 彼らは似た者どうしだ They are *similar to each other*. ／They are *birds of a feather*.

どうじ 同時に **1**【同じときに】at the same time ; simultaneously(瞬間的に同時に) ; the moment (that) (…した瞬間 ; that は通例省略する) ▶ 2 か所で同時に放火があった There were two cases of arson *at the same time* in different places. ‖ 彼女の新しい CD は世界同時発売された Her new CD was released *simultaneously* worldwide. ‖ 地震の揺れを感じると同時に私は外へ飛び出した *The moment* I felt the earthquake, I rushed out of the house.
2【…であり, また…】▶この本はおもしろいと同時に教えられるところが多い This book is *both* interesting *and* instructive. ／This book is interesting *as well as* instructive. ‖ 車はとても便利なものだが同時に凶器にもなりうる Cars are useful, but they can become deadly weapons *at the same time*. ‖ 彼は社長であると同時に取締役会長でもある He is the president, and is *concurrently* serving as chairman of the board of directors. (➤ concurrently /kənkə́ːrəntli/ は「兼任して」).

とうしき 等式 an equation.

とうじき 陶磁器 ceramics, ceramicware ; pottery and

porcelain /pɔ́ːˈsəlɪn/ ; china（瀬戸物）（➤ いずれも種類を集合的に指し，1 個は a piece of pottery のようにいう）.

とうじしゃ 当事者 the party concerned ▶金の問題は当事者どうしで解決すべきだ The money issue [problem] should be settled by *the parties concerned*.

どうじだい 同時代の contemporary ▶同時代の人 *a contemporary* ‖シェークスピアと徳川家康は同時代の人だったということを知っていましたか Did you know that Shakespeare and Tokugawa Ieyasu were *contemporaries*?

と

とうじつ 当日 that day（その日）; the appointed day（定めた日）▶主賓は当日遅れて来た The guest of honor showed up late *that day*. ‖試合の当日は雨だった It rained (on) *the day* of the game.（➤ on はしばしば省略される）‖出発の当日になって慌てないように今から準備しておきなさい You'd better begin to prepare now, so that you won't get flurried on *the day* of departure.

▶当日雨天の場合は順延します If it rains on *the appointed day*, the event will be postponed till the next clear day. ‖この切符は発行当日限り有効です This ticket is good [valid] only for *the day of issue*.

‖当日券 a ticket sold on the day (of the performance [game／match]), a same-day ticket, a non-reserved ticket for the day.

1**どうしつ 同室** ▶彼女とは寮で同室でした I *shared a room* with her in the dormitory. ／She was my roommate in the dormitory. ‖私たちのグループはホテルで同室だった Our group all *stayed in the same room* at the hotel.

2**どうしつ 同質の** homogeneous.

どうじつ 同日 the same day.

どうじつうやく 同時通訳 simultaneous /sàɪməltéɪmiəs/ interpretation（仕事）; a simultaneous interpreter /ɪntɔ́ːˈprət̬əˈ/（通訳者）▶同時通訳する do *simultaneous interpretation* ‖小松氏が会議の模様を同時通訳した Mr. Komatsu *translated* the meeting *simultaneously*.

どうして

📖 訳語メニュー
なぜ →why **1**
どうやって →how **2**

1【理由】 why ▶どうして(＝なぜ)そう考えたのですか *Why* did you think so? ／*What made* you think so?（💡後者は「何がきみにそう考えさせたのか」の意で，英語的発想）‖どうして英語を勉強しなければならないのですか *Why* do we have to study English? ／*What* do we have to study English *for*?（➤ What ... for? は「何のために」）‖どうして大学へ行くためにこんなに一生懸命勉強しなければならないのでしょう *Why* do I have to study so hard to go to college?（➤ 口頭で言う場合は why に強勢を置く）.

▶どうしてオリンピックに野球がないのか知っていますか Do you know *why* baseball is not included in the Olympic Games? ‖きみはどうしてここに居るの? *How* do you *happen to* be here?（💡Why are you here? は詰問や非難のように響く）.

▶マレーさん，どうしてこの大学で教えるようになったのですか *How did you happen to* start teaching at this university, Mr. Murray? ‖どうしてそのことをご両親に話さなかったの? *How come* you never told your parents about that before?（➤ How come は「どうして」の意のインフォーマルな言い方で，あとは「主語＋動詞」の語順）.

▶ 対話「彼女，どうして言われたとおりにしなかったの?」「どうしてかわかんない」"*Why* didn't she do as she was told?" "I don't know *why*." ‖ 対話「あの男の子と付き合っちゃいけないよ」「どうして?」"You shouldn't go out with that boy." "*Why* (*not*)?"（💡「どうしていけないの?」の意味だから not が必要だが，略すこともある）.

2【方法】 how ▶どうして(＝どうやって)彼と知り合ったのですか *How* did you come to know him? ‖どうしていいかわからなかった I didn't know *what to do*. ‖失業してこれからどうして暮らしを立てていけばいいかわからない Now that I'm unemployed, *I don't know how* I will make a living (from now on).

3【反語的に】 ▶純子は一見か弱そうだが，どうしてなかなかしんの強い女の子だ Junko may look fragile, *but* she is *actually* a strong girl.

どうしてか ▶どうしてか私は彼女が嫌いだ *For some reason*, I don't like her.

どうしても

1【何が何でも】 ▶どうしてもこの試合には勝つぞ I'll win this match *no matter what*. ／I'll win this match *regardless of what happens*.（➤ ともに「何があっても，絶対に」の意のインフォーマルな言い方）‖この仕事はどうしてもきょう中に終えなければならない I must get this job done today *by all means*.（➤ by all means は堅い言い方）.

▶母はどうしてもそのネックレスが欲しいと言っている My mother says she *just has to have* that necklace.（➤ この just は強調の副詞で，「何が何でも手に入れなければならない」の意）‖息子はどうしてもあの人と結婚したいと言っている My son *would give anything* to marry her.（➤ would give anything to do は文字どおりには「…するためなら何でも手放す[与える]」の意）.

2【全く】 ▶どうしても答えがわからなかった I *simply* [*just*] couldn't work [figure] out the answer. ‖彼がなぜあんなことをしたのかどうしても理解できない I *don't have the faintest* [*foggiest*／*slightest*] *idea* why he did such a thing. ／I *can't understand for the life of me* why he did such a thing.（➤ for the life of me は「命を懸けても」が原義でやや大げさな言い方. 通例，否定であることを強調するときに用いる）.

3【とかく】 ▶人はどうしても過ちを犯しがちだ We *are* (all) *liable to* make mistakes. ‖最近睡眠不足が続いているので，食後はどうしても居眠りが出てしまう Since I haven't been getting enough sleep recently, I *can't help* dozing off after eating.

とうしゃ 当社 this [our] company ▶当社は家具全般を扱っております *We* deal [*Our company* deals] in all kinds of furniture. ‖当社はコンピュータソフトの開発を行っております *We* develop [*Our company* develops] computer software. ／*Ours* is a computer software development company.

1**とうしゅ 投手** a pitcher →ピッチャー ▶勝利投手 a winning *pitcher* ／a winner ‖先発投手 a starting *pitcher* ／a starter ‖敗戦投手 a losing *pitcher* ／a loser.

‖投手陣 a pitching staff ‖投手戦 a pitching [pitchers'] duel ‖救援投手 a relief pitcher, a reliever.

2**とうしゅ 党首** a party head [chair／president].

どうしゅ 同種の similar(似かよった) ▶今月に入って同

種の事件が3件起きた Three *similar* incidents have occurred this month.

とうしゅう 踏襲 ▶古いやり方を踏襲する *follow* the old ways.

1**とうしょ 投書** a **letter (from a reader) to the editor**(編集部への); an **anonymous letter** [**notice**](密告の) ▶読者からの**投書** *a letter* from a reader ‖ 新聞に**投書する** *write* (*a letter*) to a newspaper.

‖**投書欄** a letters-to-the-editor column, a readers' column.

2**とうしょ 当初** ▶あの男は**当初**から怪しいとされていた The man has been under suspicion *from the beginning*. ‖ 引っ越して来た**当初**はこの辺はまだ人家がまばらだった When I *first* moved here, there weren't as many houses as there are now.

1**とうしょう 凍傷** **frostbite**; a **chilblain** /tʃílbleɪn/ (軽度の) ▶耳が**凍傷**になった I got *chilblains* on my ears. ‖ 1月の立山登山でつま先が**凍傷**になった When I climbed Mt. Tate(yama) in January, my toes *got frostbitten*.

2**とうしょう 東証** **the Tokyo Stock Exchange** ▶わが社は**東証**一部に上場しています Our company is listed on the first section of *the Tokyo Stock Exchange*.

‖**東証株価指数** the Topix index.

1**とうじょう 登場する** **appear, make an** [**one's**] **appearance** ▶このドラマには3人のイタリア人が**登場する** Three Italians *appear* in this drama.

▶《脚本のト書きで》ハムレット**登場** *Enter* Hamlet. / Hamlet *enters*.

‖**登場人物** the characters(文芸作品の); the cast (演劇などの).

2**とうじょう 搭乗する** **board** +目 (飛行機に) ▶《搭乗口で》いらっしゃいませ. 本日はご**搭乗**ありがとうございます Good afternoon, sir [ma'am]. *Welcome aboard*. (➤ Good afternoon, sir. の部分は時間帯と乗客によって変わる) ‖ 乗客は全員**搭乗した** All passengers *are on board* now. ‖ **搭乗開始**は何時からですか What's the *boarding time*? ‖ **搭乗手続き**はここでできますか Can I *check in* here?

‖**搭乗アナウンス** boarding announcements ‖ **搭乗員** a crew member; the crew(乗務員全体) ‖ **搭乗ゲート**[ロ] a boarding gate ‖ **搭乗券** a boarding pass [card] ‖ **搭乗者** a passenger ‖ **搭乗者名簿** a passenger list ‖ **搭乗手続きカウンター** a check-in counter.

1**どうじょう 同情** **sympathy**; **compassion** (深い思いやり); **pity** (哀れみ) 一動 (…に)**同情する** **sympathize** 《with》; **pity** +目 (哀れむ) ▶**同情**の涙を流す weep from [for] *pity* ‖ 私は彼女に**同情しない** I have no *sympathy for* her. ‖ 今度の件に関してはきみに**同情している** I *sympathize with* you over this matter. ‖ **同情**なんかされたくないよ I don't want to *be pitied*. ‖ 被災者の皆さまに心よりご**同情**申し上げます We would like to express our deepest *sympathy* for the victims.

2**どうじょう 同乗** ▶社長のタクシーに**同乗**させてもらって駅まで行った The president *gave me a ride* [*a lift*] in a taxi to the train station. ‖ その自動車事故で**同乗**していた女性2人がけがをした Two girls who happened to *be in the car* were injured in the accident.

‖**同乗者** a fellow passenger.

3**どうじょう 道場** a **dojo** (➤ 英語化している); a **training hall** ▶柔道の**道場** a judo *school* [*hall*] ‖ 彼は日曜ごとに剣道の**道場**へ通っている He goes to a kendo *dojo* every Sunday.

‖**断食道場** a weight loss boot camp.

4**どうじょう 同上** **as above, the same as above** 《参考》リストなどでは ditto《略 do.》やその記号" (ditto mark)が使われる.

どうしょういむ 同床異夢 sleep together but have different dreams; appear to be allies but have divergent goals (➤ 説明的な訳).

どうしようもない ▶あいつはどうしようもない怠け者だ He's a *good-for-nothing* bum. ‖ また授業をサボったの? **どうしようもない**子ね You skipped class again? You're *impossible* [You're *a hopeless case*].

▶**どうしようもなくなって**(=困り果てて)相談に来ました I'*m totally at a loss* (*as to*) *what to do*, so I have come to ask for your advice. ‖ 今更**どうしようもない** *It's too late*. ‖ 家を出るよりほかどうしようもなかった(=やりようがなかった)んです I *had no other choice* but to run away from home. ‖ 私, あの人のこと**どうしようもなく**好きなんです I'm so (much) in love with him. I *can't help myself*. / I'm *head over heels* in love with him. (➤ be head over heels in love with... は「…に夢中だ」の意) ‖ 彼の詩の大半は**どうしようもなく**創造性に欠けている Most of his poems are *sorely* lacking in creativity.

どうしょくぶつ 動植物 **plants and animals, animals and plants** (➤ 前者の語順がふつう); **flora and fauna** (一地方・一時代の動植物の全種類).

とうじる 投じる **spend** +目, **invest** +目 (資金を); **throw** +目 (投げ込む) ▶その作家は私財を**投じて**郷里に図書館を贈った The writer *spent* [*used*] his own fortune to donate a library to his home. ‖ そのダム建設には巨費が**投じられた** A huge amount of money *was spent* on the construction of the dam [to build the dam].

どうじる 動じる ▶ものに**動じない**女性 an *unflappable* woman ‖ 私の姉は人前に出ても少しも**動じない** My sister *shows no sign of being nervous* in public. / Being in front of people does*n't faze* her. (➤ faze は「慌てさせる」).

1**とうしん 答申** a **report** 一動 **答申する** **submit** +目, **report** +目 ▶中央教育審議会は教育改革についての中間**答申**を首相に提出した The Central Education Council submitted *an interim report* on educational reforms to the Prime Minister.

‖**答申案** a draft of a report.

2**とうしん 投身** ▶中年男性がビルの屋上から**投身**自殺した A middle-aged man *threw himself to his death* from the top of the building.

どうしん 童心 ▶妻と私は**童心**に返ってシーソー遊びに興じた My wife and I *played* on a seesaw *as if we were children again*.

どうじん 同人

‖**同人誌** a literary coterie /kóʊt̬əri/ magazine.

どうしんえん 同心円 a **concentric circle** ▶**同心円**を描く draw *a concentric circle*.

とうしんだい 等身大の **life-size(d)** ▶**等身大**の肖像画を描く paint a *life-size* picture.

とうすい 陶酔 ▶聴衆はワーグナーの音楽に**陶酔した** The audience *was entranced* [*was spellbound* / *were mesmerized*] by the music of Wagner. (➤《英》では audience は聴衆1人1人を考える場合は複数扱いなので, were となる).

どうすう 同数 **the same number**.

どうせ ⚠ **この語は相手を侮蔑する気持ちや捨てば**

ちな気持ち, 悲観的な気持ちを込めて用いられることが多いが, これにぴったり対応する英語はない. したがって, 文脈により anyway (いずれにしても), at all (仮にも), after all (結局は) などを用いる. ▶どうせやらなきゃいけないんだから今すぐやっちゃおう Let's do it right now since we have to do it *anyway* [*anyhow*]. ‖ どうせ捨てようと思っていた雑誌だ. 要るんなら持ってってくれ I was going to throw away these magazines *anyway*. You can have them if you want.

▶どうせやるんならしっかりやれ If you do something *at all*, do your best.

▶いくら頑張ったってどうせ100点なんか取れっこないよ There's *no way* for me to get a perfect score, no matter how hard I try. ‖ カズはどうせ来やしないよ Kazu won't come *anyway*.

▶ 対話「こないだはすっぽかしてごめん, ついうっかり忘れてた」「どうせそんなことだろうと思ってたよ」"I'm sorry that I stood you up the other day. Our appointment slipped my mind." *"That's what I thought would happen.* / *I knew that would happen."* (➤ 後者は皮肉).

1**とうせい 統制** control (権力などによる) ; regulation (規制などによる) **一動 統制する** control +目, regulate +目 ▶米価を統制する *control* the price of rice ‖ 統制のとれた行進 *well-regulated* marching.

‖**思想統制** thought control.

2**とうせい 当世** ▶当世の若者 *today's* young people / young people (*of*) *today* ‖ 当世風のファッション the *latest* fashion(s).

1**どうせい 同性** ▶彼女は同性の間ではあまり評判がよくない She is not well liked by those of her *own sex* [*gender*].

‖**同性愛** homosexual love ; same-sex love (男女とも) ; lesbianism /lézbiənìzəm/ (女性の) ‖ **同性愛者** a homosexual (男女とも) ; a gay (主に男), a lesbian /lézbiən/ (女) ‖ **同性婚** (a) same-sex marriage. →ホモセクシュアル.

2**どうせい 同姓** ▶この地域には同姓の人が多い There are a lot of people with *the same family name* in this area. ‖ 私の学校には同姓同名の人が3人いる At my school, there are three students who have *the same family and given names*.

3**どうせい 同棲** cohabitation **一動** (…と) **同せいする** cohabit 《with》; 《インフォーマル》 live (together) 《with》 ▶同せいの相手 a *live-in* companion ‖ 何と彼の娘は20も年上の男と同せいしていた He was really astounded to find that his daughter *had been living* [*shacking up*] *with* a man 20 years older than her. (➤ shack up は「同せいする」の意の俗語で, 非難のニュアンスがある).

4**どうせい 動静** movements ▶警察はその男の動静に特別に注意を払っていた The police were paying special attention to his *movements*.

1**とうせき 投石する** throw a stone ▶3人の少年がホームレスの人たちに投石を繰り返して逮捕された Three boys were arrested for repeatedly *throwing stones* at homeless people.

2**とうせき 透析** dialysis /daɪǽləsɪs/ ▶透析を受ける undergo *dialysis* ‖ 透析を受けている be on *dialysis*.

どうせき 同席 ▶パーティーでぼくは彼女と同席した (=同じテーブルに着いた) I *sat at the same table* with her at the party.

とうせん 当選・当籤 **1【選挙の】** (an) election **一動 当選する** be elected ▶彼は市議会議員に(最高得票数で)当選した He *was elected to* the city council (at the head of the poll). ‖ 彼は衆議院議員選挙当選12回の古参議員である He is a senior statesman who *won* twelve *elections* for the House of Representatives. ‖ その立候補者は当選確実と見られている The candidate is considered *a shoo-in*. (➤ shoo-in /ʃúːɪn/ は《米・インフォーマル》で「楽勝が予想される候補者」「本命」の意).

2【懸賞に当たること】 ▶彼女は懸賞で1等に当選した She *won* (*the*) *first prize* in the contest. ‖ 私, オーストラリア旅行に当選したわ I'*ve won* a trip to Australia.

‖**当選者** a successful [an elected] candidate (選挙の) ; a winner (懸賞の) ‖ **当選番号** a winning number ‖ (アメリカなどの就任前の) **大統領当選者** a president-elect.

とうぜん 当然 **一形 当然の** natural

> 【文型】
> …が～するのは当然だ
> It is natural for … to do.
> It is natural that … (should) do.
>
> 〔解説〕 natural の前に強調の意味で **quite, only, very** などをつけることもある.

▶若者がお年寄りに席を譲るのは当然だ *It is natural for* young people *to* give their seats to elderly people. / *It is quite natural that* young people *should* offer their seats to elderly people. ‖ あのくらいの年の女の子が歌手や俳優に憧れるのは(ごく)当然だ *It is* (*quite*) *natural for* a girl of her age *to* aspire to become a singer or an actress. ‖ 彼女が大学まで車でお送りしましょうかって言ってくれたんだ. 当然, その申し出は受けたよ She offered me a ride to my university. *Naturally*, I accepted it.

▶そんなものを食べたらおなかを壊すのは当然だよ After eating something like that, *It's no wonder* you got sick. ‖ 彼はあんな失策をしたんだから会社を解雇されるのは当然だ He *deserves* to be dismissed from the company for making such a stupid mistake. ‖ 遅く出れば遅く着くのは当然だ *It stands to reason that* if you leave late you'll arrive late. (➤「理にかなっている」の意) ‖ それじゃあ彼女がきみを捨てるのも当然さ She left you *for a good reason*. ‖ きみたちの要求は当然だよ I think your demand *is reasonable*.

▶彼女に聞く必要なんかないよ. 当然やってくれるはずだから You don't have to ask her—she'll do it *as a matter of course*. (➤「当然のこととして」の意).

> 【文型】
> 物事(A)を当然だと思う
> take A for granted / take for granted A
> ～を当然のことだと思う
> take it for granted that S + V
> ➤ インフォーマルではしばしば that を, ときには it も省略する
>
> 〔解説〕 (1) A が長い場合は, 後者の形をとることが多い.
> (2)「(物事など)をもちろん当然のことと考える」という意味のほか,「(人・物事)の存在を当然視してありがたみを忘れる」という場合に用いられる.

▶私たちは健康であることを当然だと思っている We (tend to) *take* our health *for granted*. ‖ 彼は彼女が洗濯

してくれることを**当然だと思っている** He *takes it for granted that* his girlfriend will do his laundry. ‖ **対話**「私の財布を届けていただいてありがとうございます」「**当然のことをしただけです**」“Thank you for returning my lost wallet.” “(Don't mention it.) *Anyone would have done the same.*” (➤「誰だって同じことをしたでしょう」の意).

どうぜん 同然 ▶あの男は詐欺師も**同然**だ He is *little* [*no*] *better than* a con man. ‖ ここまできたら我々の仕事は終わったも**同然**だ Our work is *practically* finished now. (➤この practically は「実質的にはほとんど…と同じで」).

> **【文型】**
> A [B] も同然
> as good as A
> as much as B
> ➤ A は主に形容詞
> ➤ B は動詞

▶この車は新品**同然**だ This car is *as good as* new. ‖ きみは自分が間違っていることを認めたも**同然**だ You've *as much as* [*virtually*] admitted that you are wrong.

▶それではうそつき呼ばわりも**同然**ではないか That is *the same as* calling me a liar. ‖ 上司の頼みは命令も**同然**だ A request from your boss is, *in effect*, an order. (➤ in effect は「事実上」).

どうぞ

> **【解説】「どうぞ」と please**
> (1) 日本語の「どうぞ」は人にものを勧めるとき，要請するとき，丁寧に頼むとき，人の頼みを承知するときのいずれの場合にも用いるが，英語の please は要請・依頼などを丁寧にするために命令法の動詞とともに用いる．したがって，客に椅子などを勧めるときの「どうぞお座りください」は (Please) have a seat. がふつう．Please sit down. は「座ってほしい」という気持ちが強いときに用いる．また，丁寧な頼み事は Could you please do …? など疑問形を用いるのがふつう．→くれる．
> (2)「どうぞ，いいですよ」と人の頼みを受け入れる場合には please ではなく，Sure., Why not?, Go ahead., Of course., Certainly. (あとの 2 者はより丁寧) などを用いる．
> (3) 人に物を差し出す場合にも please は用いず，Here you are., Here it is., There you are. [《米また》There you go.], Here's your [some] … . などのように言う．
> (4) ステージで司会者が登場する歌手などを紹介するときの「…さん，どうぞ」にも please は用いない．英語では “Now, we present Madonna!” (マドンナさんをご紹介します！) のように言う．please を用いるのであれば Please welcome Madonna.

1【人に勧めたり要請したりして】**please** ▶**どうぞ**お座りください (*Please*) have a seat. / *Please* sit down. / Sit down, *please*. (● 第 1 文は please を言わないことが多いが，丁寧で友好的な表現．第 2 文は直接的で第 1 文ほど丁寧ではない．第 3 文は第 2 文よりも更に命令口調) ‖ **どうぞ**サンドイッチをつまんでください *Please* help yourself to the sandwiches. ‖ ジャスミンティーを**どうぞ** *Have* some jasmine tea. (➤ Tea, please. は「お茶をお願いします」の意) ‖ **どうぞ**楽しい夏休みを Have an enjoyable summer vacation. (➤ please は言わないのがふつう) ‖ **どうぞ**お構いなく *Please* don't bother.

2【人の頼みを承諾して】▶ **対話**「このボールペンをお借りしていいですか」「**どうぞ**」“Can I use this ballpoint pen?” “*Sure* [*Go ahead* / *Of course*].” (● “Yes, please.” では「どうぞお願いします」の意になり，ここでは使えない) ‖ **対話**「コピー機を使わせていただいていいですか」「**どうぞどうぞ**」“May I use the photocopier?” “*Certainly*.” (➤ May I …? は改まった言い方) ‖ **対話**「このオレンジ，頂いていいですか」「**どうぞ**(ご自由に)」“Can I have this orange?” “*Sure. Help yourself*.” ‖ **対話**「新聞取ってくれる？」「はい，**どうぞ**」“Can you get me the paper?” “*Here you are*.” ‖ **対話**「たばこを吸ってもかまいませんか」「ええ，**どうぞ**」“Do you mind if I smoke?” “*No, please go ahead*.” (● Do you mind … ? は「気にしますか，お嫌ですか」と聞いているので，かまわなければ，No や Not at all. などと否定形で答える．断るときには I'd rather you didn't. と言う).

[1]とうそう 逃走 (an) **escape** 一動 **逃走する escape, run away** ▶うまく**逃走する** *make* good one's *escape* (➤この make good は「(目的)を果たす」) ‖ 3 人組の男が現金 3 億3300万円を奪って**逃走した** Three men *escaped* with 333 million yen in cash. ‖ 死刑囚が 2 名刑務所から**逃走した** Two condemned criminals *ran away* [*escaped*] from prison. ‖ 殺人犯は依然**逃走中だ** The murderer *is* still *at large* [*on the loose*]. (➤ともに「捕まっていない」の意).

[2]とうそう 闘争 a **fight**, a **struggle** (闘い；後者が困難で激しいというニュアンスが強い)；a **strike** (ストライキ) ▶労使間の**闘争** the *struggle* between labor and management ‖ 従業員は賃上げ**闘争**に入った The workers have gone on (*a*) *strike for higher wages*. / The workers have walked out, demanding higher wages.
‖**闘争心** (a) fighting spirit.

どうそう 同窓 ▶**同窓**の先輩 an older graduate *from the same school* ‖ 私は健二とは**同窓**です Kenji and I *went to* [*studied at*] *the same school*.
‖**同窓会** (→見出語) ‖ **同窓生** a schoolmate, 《米》 a classmate; an alumnus /əlʌ́mnəs/ (➤女性は alumna /əlʌ́mnə/), 《英》 an old boy [girl] (卒業生).

どうぞう 銅像 a **bronze statue** ▶**銅像**を建てる erect *a bronze statue* ‖ 上野公園には西郷隆盛の**銅像**が立っている *A bronze statue* of Saigo Takamori stands in Ueno Park.

どうそうかい 同窓会 an **alumni reception**; a **class reunion** (同期生・同学年生の会) ▶きのうの**同窓会**で10年ぶりに森先生と再会した Yesterday I met Mr. Mori at our *alumni reception* [*class reunion* / *homecoming*] for the first time in ten years. (➤ homecoming はアメリカの大学や高校で毎年行うものをいう). 《参考》「同窓会」の組織は《米》では主に an alumni /əlʌ́mnaɪ/ [a graduates'] association, 《英》ではまた an old boys' [girls'] society という.

とうぞく 盗賊 a **bandit** (追い剝ぎ)；a **robber** (強盗).

どうぞく 同族 **the same family** (家族)；**the same tribe** (部族) ‖**同族会社** a family company ‖ **同族目的語** 《文法》 a cognate /kɑ́ːgneɪt/ object.

とうそつ 統率する lead +目 ▶中村主将はチームメートをよく**統率**している Captain Nakamura *leads* his teammates well. ‖ あいつは**統率力**がない He lacks the *qualities* [*abilities* / *skills*] *of a leader*. / He lacks *leadership abilities* [*qualities* / *skills*].

とうた 淘汰 ▶自然界では環境に適応できない生物は淘

汰される In the natural world, organisms that cannot adapt to their environment *die out*. (➤ die out は「滅亡する」).

‖自然淘汰 natural selection.

[1]**とうだい 灯台** a **lighthouse**; a **beacon**(浮標などを含めた標識) ▶《慣用表現》字のうまい人を探していたんだが, きみの姉さんが書道家だったとは. まさに**灯台もと暗し**だね I've been looking for someone who has good handwriting and it turns out your (older) sister is an expert in calligraphy. It goes to show how *often you miss something when it's right under your nose*. (➤「すぐ鼻先にあるとき, ものは見落とすことが多いことを証明している」の意).

[2]**とうだい 当代** ▶商才にかけてはビル・ゲイツは**当代**まれに見る人物だ Bill Gates is a man unparalleled *in the present age* for his business acumen. (➤ acumen /əkjúːmən ‖ ǽkjʊmən/ は「頭脳の鋭さ」の意) ‖彼女は**当代随一**の劇作家と言われている She is regarded as *the greatest contemporary* [*living*] dramatist. ‖**当代屈指**の日本画家 *one of the best* Japanese-style painters *of the day*.

[1]**どうたい 胴体** **the body**; **the trunk**(人・動物・魚の); a **torso** /tɔ́ːʳsoʊ/ (彫像・人の); **the fuselage** /fjúːsəlɑːʒ/ (飛行機の); **the hull**(船の) ▶そのセスナ機は軽井沢高原に**胴体着陸した** That Cessna *belly-landed* [*made a belly landing*] on the Karuizawa highlands.

[2]**どうたい 導体** a **conductor**

‖熱伝導体 a conductor of heat.

[3]**どうたい 動態**

‖動態経済学 dynamic economics ‖人口動態 a dynamic [fluid] population ‖人口動態調査 a demographic survey.

とうたつ 到達する **reach** +目 ▶目的地に**到達する** *reach* the destination ‖今月の売り上げは目標の半分にも**到達していない** This month we haven't even *reached* half of our sales target. ‖生徒たちにはきちんと彼らの**到達目標**を示してやるべきだ You should carefully give each student *an appropriately attainable goal* [*objective*].

とうだん 登壇する **mount** [**step onto**] **the podium**(➤ podium /póʊdiəm/ は「演台」).

[1]**とうち 当地** **here** ▶ご**当地**ソング a *local* song ‖ご**当地**キャラ(クター) a *local* mascot. ‖**当地**には3週間滞在します I'll be *here* for three weeks.

[2]**とうち 統治** **rule** 一動 **統治する** **rule**《over》, **govern** +目 ▶一国を**統治する** *govern* [*rule*] a nation ‖旧憲法においては天皇が日本を**統治していた** The Emperor *ruled over* Japan [*united* Japan *under his rule*] under the former Constitution. /天皇は君臨はするが, **統治しない** The Emperor reigns but does not *rule*.

[3]**とうち 倒置する** 《文法》**invert** +目

‖倒置構文《文法》inverted construction ‖倒置法《文法》inversion.

とうちゃく 到着 **arrival** 一動 (…に)**到着する** **arrive**《at, in》; **get**《to》; **reach** +目

> **語法** (1)**arrive at** は一点と感じられる場所(駅など)に, **arrive in** は広がりをもつ地域(都会・国など)のどこかに到着する場合にそれぞれ用い, 後者は特にそこでの滞在の意を含む.
> (2)**get to, reach** は「(努力の結果)たどりつく」のニュアンスをもつこともある.

▶我々は彼の飛行機の**到着**を待った We waited for the *arrival* of his plane. ‖この列車は何時に秋田駅に**到着しますか** What time will this train *arrive at* [*get to*] Akita Station? ‖列車は定刻に**到着した** The train *arrived* (*at* the station) [pulled in] on time. (➤ pull in は「(列車が)駅に入る」) ‖暗くなる前にホテルに**到着した** We *got to* [*arrived at*] the hotel before dark. ‖次の列車は3時に**到着する予定**だ The next train *is due* [*is scheduled to arrive*] at three. ‖警察が現場に**到着した** The police *arrived on* the scene. (➤ arrive on は事件の現場などに到着するときに用いる) ‖フランスからの支援物資が**到着した** Relief supplies from France *have arrived*.

✉ **ヒースロー空港には15時30分に到着の予定です. お会いするのを楽しみにしています** I *am arriving* at Heathrow Airport at 3:30 p.m. I'm looking forward to meeting you. ➤ arrive や leave など, 発着・往来を表す動詞の進行形は「…する予定だ」の意になる.

‖到着ゲート an arrival gate ‖到着時刻 the arrival time (➤「到着予定時刻」は the estimated time of arrival) ‖到着ホーム an arrival platform ‖到着ロビー an arrival lobby [lounge].

どうちゅう 道中 **while traveling, on** one's **way** ▶広島へ向かう**道中** *on my way* to Hiroshima ‖**道中ご無事で** *Have a safe trip*.

[1]**とうちょう 登頂** ▶5人の女性がエベレストの**登頂**を目指して出発した The five women set out to *reach the summit* of Mt. Everest.

[2]**とうちょう 盗聴** **wiretapping**(電話の); **bugging**(隠しマイクでの) 一動 **盗聴する** **wiretap** (+目), **tap** +目, **bug** +目 ▶電話の会話を**盗聴する** *tap* [*bug*] the telephone (wires).

‖盗聴器 a wiretap (電話の); a concealed microphone(隠しマイク).

[3]**とうちょう 登庁する** **go to** one's **government office** ▶新市長が初**登庁した** The new mayor *went to his* [*her*] *office* for the first time.

[1]**どうちょう 同調する** **go**《with》, **side**《with》; **tune in**《to》(放送などに) ▶どんなにとっぴな意見でも必ずそれに**同調する**人がいるものだ No matter how eccentric an opinion may be, there are always some who *side with* it. ‖この件では田中君に**同調します** I'll *go with* Tanaka on this issue.

‖同調圧力 peer pressure.

[2]**どうちょう 道庁** **the Hokkaido Prefectural Office.**

とうちょく 当直 ▶今夜は小山田君が**当直**だ Mr. Oyamada is *on duty* tonight.

‖当直医 a doctor on (night) duty.

どうつきながぐつ 胴付き長靴 a **chest wader** (➤通例複数形で) ▶**胴付き長靴**をはく put on *chest waders*.

とうてい 到底 ▶外国語を1年でマスターするのは**到底**(＝絶対)不可能だ It is *absolutely* impossible to master a foreign language in one year. ‖我々はあんな強いチームには**到底**勝てっこない There is *no way* for us to beat such a powerful team. ‖数学では佐々木さんには**到底かなわない** *I'm no match for* Sasaki in math.

[1]**どうてい 童貞** **virginity** /vəʳdʒínəṭi/ (童貞であること); a **virgin**(人) ▶《人生相談欄などで》ぼくは20歳の大学生で, まだ**童貞**です I am a 20-year-old college student and still *a virgin*. 《参考》(1) virgin は「処女」の意で使われることが多い. (2) 男どうしのくだけた

会話では，例えばI haven't had sex yet.（まだセックスの経験がない）のように言うことが多い．

[2]**どうてい 同定する** identify ＋⽬ ▶疾患の原因を同定する *identify* the cause of the disorder.

どうてき 動的な dynamic.

どうでもいい ▶（結婚相手は）顔はどうでもいいけど人柄はよくないと困る I *don't care* how she looks but I do care about her personality. ‖ 巨人が勝とうが阪神が勝とうがぼくはどうでもいい I *don't care* if the Giants or the Tigers win. ‖ そんなことどうでもいいじゃないか *What does that* [*it*] *matter?* ‖ 私にとってそんなことどうでもいい *It doesn't matter* to me. ／*It makes no difference* to me.

とうてん 当店 our [this] shop ▶当店のおすすめ *our specialty*.

[1]**どうてん 同点** a tie (score) ▶同点の試合 a *tie* game ‖ 同点だ！Now we're *even*!／Now we've *tied the score*! ‖ 日本は岡崎のゴールで1対1の同点とした Japan *tied the score* at 1 to 1 with Okazaki's goal.

‖**同点決勝戦** a play-off ‖ **同点ゴール** a (game-)tying goal,《英また》an equalizer ‖ **同点ホームラン** a (game-)tying homer.

[2]**どうてん 動転する** get [be] upset ▶彼女は恋人の急死の知らせで気が動転していた She *was upset* at the news of her lover's sudden death.

とうど 糖度 a sugar content ▶このリンゴは糖度が12%ある This apple has *a sugar content* of 12 percent.

とうとい 尊い・貴い sacred /séɪkrɪd/（神聖な）; precious（貴重な）; noble（気高い）▶仏教の尊い教え *sacred* teachings of Buddhism ‖ 限られた人生にあっては一日一日が貴い Each day in our short lives is *precious*. ‖ 無私の姿は誠に尊い Selflessness is indeed *noble*. →とうとさ.

[1]**とうとう 到頭** at (long) last, finally, in the end

> **語法** (1) at (long) last と finally は肯定文にのみ用い，否定文には用いない．at (long) last は「長期間の努力などのあとで，やっと」の意で，結果としてよいことや好ましいことが起こった場合に用いる．finally は「(予想外に) 長いことかかって」の意．
> (2) in the end は「結末としては，最終的には」の意で，肯定文に用いる．

▶とうとう彼は畢生(ひっせい)の大作を完成させた *At (long) last*, he has finished his masterpiece.／He has *finally* finished his masterpiece. ‖ 運転免許証がないので家中を捜し回ったあげく，とうとうげた箱の下に落ちているのを見つけた After I searched all over the house for my missing driver's license, I *finally* found it under the shoe cupboard. ‖ 彼女は働き過ぎてとうとう病気になった She overworked until she *finally* became ill. ‖ 逃げ回っていた誘拐犯人がとうとう捕まった The kidnapper, who had been running all over, was *finally* arrested [was arrested *in the end*]. ‖ 2時間待ったがとうとう彼女は姿を見せなかった Although I waited for two hours, she *never* showed up.（➤ 過去形とともに用いる never は「全然［結局］そういうことにはならなかった」で「とうとう」の意味が含まれる）.

[2]**とうとう 滔々** ▶とうとうと流れる四万十川 the *wide, fast-flowing* Shimanto River ‖ とうとうと自説を述べる express one's opinion *eloquently* [*fluently*].

どうとう 同等の equal /íːkwəl/, equivalent /ɪkwívələnt/（相当する）▶わが社では大卒も高卒も同等に扱われる In our company, university (graduates) and high school graduates are treated *equally*. ‖ 警察官になるには柔道の有段者であるか，有段者と同等の力がなくてはならない To become a police officer, one must have a black belt in judo or *its equivalent*.（➤ この equivalent は「同等のもの」の意の名詞）.

どうどう 堂々たる imposing（圧倒するような）; impressive（強い印象を与える）; confident（自信に満ちた）▶彼は180センチ90キロの堂々たる体格だ He is an *imposing* man, 180 centimeters tall and weighing 90 kilos. ‖ 彼女の堂々とした話しぶりには感服した Her *confident* speech impressed me. ‖ よく戦ったのだから堂々と胸を張って帰ればいい Since you put up a good fight, you should go home *holding your head high*.

どうどうめぐり 堂々巡り ▶どちらが悪いかという話をしたら議論はまた堂々巡りになるよ If you start talking about who is to blame, the argument will *go* [*run*] *around in circles* again.

どうとく 道徳 morals（社会的に認められた行動・個人の品行，モラル）; morality（道徳的であること，道徳律）; ethics（倫理）▶性［商］道徳の乱れ the corruption of *sexual morality* [*business ethics*] ‖ 武士道は日本において道徳心を形成するのに役立った Bushido helped mold the *sense of morality* in Japan. ‖ たばこの吸い殻を路上に投げ捨てるのは公衆道徳に反する Throwing away cigarette butts on the street goes against *public morality* [*morals*]. ‖ 彼は道徳を欠いている He *lacks morals* [*ethics*]. ‖ 一国の指導者には高い道徳基準が求められる The political leaders of a nation are expected to have high *moral standards*.

‖**道徳教育** moral education.

とうとさ 尊さ・貴さ preciousness; value（有用性・価値）▶人命の貴さ *the preciousness* of human life.

とうとつ 唐突な sudden（突然の）; unexpected（予想・予期しない）; abrupt（不意の）▶唐突な発言 an *unexpected* remark ‖ 唐突な終わり方をする come to an *abrupt* end ‖ 彼の辞職があまりに唐突だったので信じられなかった His resignation was too *sudden* for me to believe.

とうとぶ 尊ぶ・貴ぶ value ＋⽬（尊重する）; respect ＋⽬（尊敬する）▶真面目さを尊ぶ *value* seriousness ‖ 若い人たちは年配者の体験をもっと尊ぶべきだ Young people should *show* more *regard for* the experience of elderly people.

とうどり 頭取 the president (of a bank)

‖**副頭取** the executive vice-president.

どうなが 胴長 a long torso ▶父は胴長短足の典型だ My father is a typical example of a person with *a long torso and short legs*.

[1]**とうなん 東南** the southeast ▶東南アジアからの留学生たち students from *Southeast Asia*.

[2]**とうなん 盗難** (a) theft（盗む行為，盗難事件）; (a) robbery（強奪）▶《掲示》盗難に注意 Beware of Pickpockets [Muggers]／Beware of Purse [Bag／Luggage] Snatchers（➤ pickpocket は「すり」，mugger は「路上強盗」，snatcher は「ひったくり」）‖ イタリア旅行中に盗難に遭った I *had some of my things stolen* while traveling in Italy. ‖ この町では今まで一度も盗難事件はない There have been no *thefts* [*cases of theft*] in this town.

‖**盗難車** a stolen car.

とうに 疾うに **long ago, a long time ago**(ずっと前に); **already**(すでに) ▶彼, もうとうに出ましたけど, まだ着いてませんか? He left here *a long time ago*. Hasn't he gotten there yet? ‖ それはとうに承知だ I *already* know that.

どうにいる 堂に入る ▶彼女の生徒の扱いは堂に入ったものだ The way she handles her students is *outstanding*. ‖ その駐日大使の**日本語は堂に入ったもの**だ The ambassador to Japan *has a wonderful command of Japanese*.

どうにか **barely**(辛うじて); **somehow**(何とかして) ▶彼はどうにかテストに通った He *barely* passed the test. ／He *managed* to pass the test (*somehow*). ／He passed the test, *though with* (*great*) *difficulty*. ‖ 日常会話くらいならどうにか英語で話せます If you mean only daily conversation, I can *get by* in English. (➤ get by は「何とかやっていける」). ▶このごみの山, どうにかしてくれない? Can't you *do something* about this pile of trash? ‖ 彼は極めて楽観的で, いつもどうにかなるさと考えている He is very optimistic and always thinks that *things will work out somehow*. (➤ work out は「(うまく)いく」) ‖ 空港の周辺はものすごい爆音で, **耳がどうにかなりそうだ** The roar of the jet planes around the airport is so loud that I *feel I'm going deaf*. ‖ どうにかこうにか目標は達成した I (*somehow*) managed to achieve my goal.

どうにも ▶あいつの強情さにはどうにも我慢できない I *simply* can't stand his stubbornness. ‖ リンダの食欲はどうにも止まらない Linda *just* can't stop eating. ‖ 今となってはどうにも手の打ちようがない It is *too late* to do anything about it now. ‖ 迷惑メールはどうにもならない *We can't find any way* [*can't figure out how*] to get rid of (email) spam [spam email(s)]. ‖ こう暑くてはどうにもこうにもならない I just *can't do anything* in this heat.

[1]**とうにゅう 投入** ▶教育に全精力を投入する *put* one's whole heart *into* education ‖ このプロジェクトに巨費を投入したのは間違いだった It was a mistake to *invest* (such) a large amount of money in this project. (➤ invest は「(金・時間などを)つぎ込む」) ‖ デモを解散させるために機動隊が投入された The riot police *were sent in* to break up the demonstration.

[2]**とうにゅう 豆乳** **soy milk.**

どうにゅう 導入 **introduction** 一動 **導入する** **introduce** +目 ▶西洋文化の導入 the *introduction* of Western culture ‖ コンピュータを導入して事務の効率化を図る *introduce* computers to streamline office work.

とうにょうびょう 糖尿病 **diabetes** /dàɪəbíːṭəs/ 一形 **糖尿病の** **diabetic** ▶父は糖尿病だ My father suffers from *diabetes*. ／My father is (a) diabetic. (➤ a diabetic は「糖尿病患者」の意).

とうにん 当人 ▶振られるつらさは当人にしかわからないよ Only *someone* who has been dumped can know how painful it is. ‖ ほら, ご当人のお出ましだ Look, here comes *the person in question*. ／Well, here comes (*just*) *the person we were talking about*. (➤ Speaking of the devil (うわさをすれば)を使うこともできる).

どうねん 同年 ▶2010年3月T大卒, **同年**4月S社に入社 Graduated from T University in (the) March of 2010 and joined S Company in (the) April of *the same year*. (➤ 履歴書などの文).

どうねんぱい 同年配 ▶彼は若く見えるが私と**同年配**だろう He looks much younger, but is probably *about my age*.

どうのこうの ▶私はこの件についてどうのこうの言う資格はない I'm not qualified to say *anything* about this matter.

[1]**とうは 党派** a (**political**) **party**(政党); a **faction**(党内派閥) ▶党派の争い *factional* struggle.

[2]**とうは 踏破** ▶南アフリカを踏破する *travel the length and breadth of* South Africa ‖ 彼らは犬ぞりを使って北極を3か月で**踏破した** They *traversed* the Arctic Circle in three months riding on dog sleds. (➤ traverse /trəvə́ːʳs/ は「横断旅行する」).

とうば 塔婆 →そとば.

とうはつ 頭髪 **hair** (**on** one's **head**).

[1]**とうばん 当番** one's **duty**(任務); one's **turn**(順番) ▶きょうはきみが掃除**当番**だ It is *your turn* to sweep the room today. ‖ 彼はきょう**当番**だ[でない] He *is on* [*off*] *duty* today. ‖ 良太は**当番**をサボって先生に叱られた Ryota was scolded by our teacher for neglecting [skipping] *his assigned task*. ‖ 生徒たちは**当番**で教室の掃除をします Students *take turns* (*at*) cleaning their classroom. ／Students clean their classroom *by turns*.
‖**当番弁護士** a duty lawyer, 《英》 a duty solicitor.

[2]**とうばん 登板する** **take the mound** ▶きのうは山田が**登板した** Yamada *took the mound* yesterday.

どうはん 同伴する **go with, accompany** +目 (同行する) ▶夫人**同伴**でパーティーに行く日本人男性は少ない Few Japanese men go to parties *with* [*accompanied by*] their wives. ‖ 保護者**同伴**ならこの映画は見にいっていいんだって You can see this film if you *are accompanied by* an adult guardian.

どうはんが 銅版画 a **copperplate print.**

トウバンジャン 豆板醤 **doubanjiang**; fermented broad bean paste usually containing red chili peppers(説明的な訳).

[1]**とうひ 逃避** (an) **escape** 一動 (…から)**逃避する** **escape**《from》, **run away**《from》(逃げる) ▶現実から**逃避する**な Don't *escape from* reality. ‖ この問題から**逃避したら**きみは一生逃げ続けることになる If you *run away from* this problem, you'll have to keep running away from it for the rest of your life.

[2]**とうひ 当否** **right or wrong** (正誤); **propriety** /prəpráɪəṭi/ (妥当性) ▶その景気予測の**当否**は誰にもわからない No one knows *whether* that economic forecast *will prove* (*to be*) *correct* [*accurate*].

[3]**とうひ 頭皮** a **scalp** ▶汗をかくたびに**頭皮**がかゆくなる Whenever I sweat my *scalp* itches.
‖**頭皮マッサージ** a scalp [head] massage.

とうひょう 投票 **voting,** (a) **vote**(投票すること); a **vote,** a **ballot**(個々の票) 一動 **投票する** **vote**《for, against》 ▶保守[革新]系の候補に**投票する** *vote for* a conservative [reformist] candidate ‖ **投票で**決めよう Let's *take a vote*. ／Let's *vote* on it. ‖ 委員長は**投票**で決めることになっています The chairperson is to be elected [be decided] *by vote*. ‖ クラス代表は生徒たちの**投票**によって選出された The class representatives were elected by *a ballot* of the students [by student *ballot*]. ‖ その提案は**投票によって可決** [**否決**] **された** The proposal *was approved by vote* [*was voted down*]. ‖ その法案は**投票**の結果, 賛成290反対160で可決された The bill was approved through *a ballot* that resulted in 290 in favor and 160 opposed. ‖市長選挙の投票率は低かった The *voter turnout* was low in the mayoral election.

‖投票所《米》a polling place, the polls,《英》a polling station [place] ‖投票箱 a ballot box ‖投票日 an election day ‖投票用紙 a ballot, a voting card (➤これに記入するために用意されたボックスは《米》a voting booth,《英》a polling booth という) ‖国民投票 a plebiscite(国民の直接投票); a (national) referendum(議会の審議を経て行う).

とうびょう 闘病 ▶彼女の闘病生活は長い She's been *fighting the disease* for a long time.

どうひょう 道標 a **signpost**(案内標識); a **guidepost** (道しるべ).

どうびょう 同病 ▶同病相あわれむ People with the *same disease* empathize with each other.

とうひん 盗品 a **stolen article** [**item**]; **stolen goods** (➤複数扱い) ▶盗品を売買する traffic [deal] in *stolen goods*.

とうふ 豆腐 **tofu, bean curd** (➤前者は英語化している)
日本紹介 ✉ **豆腐はダイズから作った白くて軟らかい食べ物です. そのまましょうゆを掛けて食べたり, さいの目に切ってみそ汁に入れたりします. 低カロリーなので健康食品として人気があります** Tofu is a soft, white food made from soybeans. You pour soy sauce over it when you eat it, or cut it into cubes and put them in miso soup. It is low in calories and popular as a healthy food.

▶豆腐1丁 a block [cake] of *tofu*.

‖焼き豆腐 grilled [broiled] tofu.

[1]**とうぶ 東部** **the east side, the eastern part** ▶インド東部で大きな地震があった There was a big earthquake in *the eastern part* of India.

[2]**とうぶ 頭部** **the head** ▶彼女は自動車事故で頭部を負傷した She *suffered a head injury* [*an injury to the head*] in the car accident.

どうふう 同封する **enclose** +⊜
✉ **家族の写真を同封します** *I'm enclosing* a photo [some photos] of my family.
✉ **同封した写真は末の娘です** The photo I *have enclosed* is of my youngest daughter.
✉ **お支払いいただいた代金の領収証を同封いたしましたのでご査収ください** *Enclosed please find* a receipt for your payment. ●Enclosed please find ... は商用の書類などを送るときの形式ばった表現. 最近では please find を用いず Enclosed is a receipt ... や I have enclosed [am enclosing] a receipt ... のように書くことが多くなってきている.

どうぶつ 動物 an **animal**; a **beast**(獣) ▶野生の動物 a wild *animal* ‖私のおいは動物好きなので動物学を専攻している My nephew is majoring in *zoology* since he is fond of *animals* [he's an *animal* lover].

▶動物の世界は弱肉強食の法則が支配している *The animal kingdom* is a world where the law of the jungle prevails. ‖ケニアを旅行中珍しい動物を見ました I saw *rare animals* while I was traveling in Kenya.

▶動物的な勘が働いて間一髪のところで危険を逃れることができた Some *animal instinct* helped me (to) narrowly escape from danger. ‖きみはもう少し動物性たんぱく質をとったほうがいいよ I advise you to eat more *animal protein*.

‖動物園 a zoo /zuː/ (➤「上野動物園」は (the) Ueno Zoo) ‖動物実験 animal experiments ‖動物社会学 animal sociology ‖動物写真家 an animal photographer ‖動物的衝動 animal drive ‖動物的本能 (an) animal instinct ‖実験動物 animals used for experiments, experimental animals ‖ペット動物園 a petting zoo.

[1]**とうぶん 当分** **for some time, for a while**(しばらくの間); **for the present, for the time being**(今のところ, さしあたり) ▶私はここ当分は忙しいと思う I think I'll be busy *for a while*. ‖ここ当分天気は崩れないだろう This good weather will continue *for some time*. ‖当分電力復帰は望めない It will be *some time* before power is restored [returns]. ／We can't expect the return of (electric) power *for some time*.

[2]**とうぶん 等分** ▶ケーキを等分する *divide* a cake *equally* ‖彼女はリンゴを4等分した She *cut* the apple *into four equal pieces* [*segments*]. (➤segment は「1つのものを人為的に分けた部分・区分」) ‖線分ABを3等分しなさい *Divide* the line AB *into three equal parts*.

[3]**とうぶん 糖分** **sugar** ▶糖分の多い[少ない]食物 foods rich [low] in *sugar* ‖こちらのケーキは糖分が控えめです These cakes don't contain much *sugar*. 《参考》果糖は fructose, ブドウ糖は dextrose, しょ糖は sucrose, 乳糖は lactose.

とうへき 盗癖《心理学》 **kleptomania** /klèptəméɪniə/ ▶彼には盗癖がある He has *kleptomania* [*sticky fingers*].

‖盗癖者 a kleptomaniac.

とうべん 答弁 an **answer**, a **reply**(➤後者は堅い語)
一動 **答弁する** **answer**(+⊜), **reply to** ▶政治家はどんな質問にも答弁できなくては一流とは言えない First-rate politicians should be able to *answer* any question.

[1]**とうほう 当方** ▶大変申し訳ありません. 当方の手落ちでした We are very [terribly] sorry. The fault lies with *us*. ‖それは当方とは無関係です *We* have nothing to do with that. ‖当方にすべてお任せください Leave everything to *us*.

[2]**とうほう 東方** **the east** ▶台風20号は沖縄の東方20キロにあり, 東方に進んでいます Typhoon No. 20 is twenty kilometers (to the) *east* of Okinawa, and is moving *east* [*eastward*].

とうぼう 逃亡 (an) **escape** 一動 **逃亡する** **escape** ▶捕虜たちが逃亡を図った The captives attempted to make their *escape* [*getaway*].

どうほう 同胞 a **fellow countryman** [**citizen**], a **compatriot** /kəmpéɪtriət/ (➤最後は堅い語).

とうほく 東北 **the northeast** ▶山形市は長岡市の東北に当たる Yamagata lies to *the northeast* of Nagaoka. ‖東北地方は雪が多い They have a lot of snow in *the Tohoku district* [*area*].

とうぼく 倒木 a **fallen tree**.

とうほんせいそう 東奔西走 ▶社長は金策に東奔西走している Our president is *always on the go*, raising money *from all sources*.

どうまわり 胴回り **waist circumference**; one's **waistline**.

どうみても どう見ても ▶どう見ても彼女は10代とは思えない *Judging from her appearance*, there's no way she's (still) in her teens. ‖あの人はどう見ても学者とは思えない He is *anything but* a scholar. ／There is *no way* he could be a scholar. ‖《仮装

行列で）きみはどう見ても白雪姫というより魔法使いだね You look like the witch rather than Snow White *in every respect*. ‖ 彼はどう見ても50歳にはなっている He must be fifty *at least*. (「少なくとも50歳」と考える).

どうみゃく 動脈 an **artery** /ɑ́ːʳt̬əri/ ▶**動脈硬化**は老化の兆しだ *Hardening of the arteries* is a sign of aging.
▶《比喩的》ナイル川はアフリカ大陸の**大動脈**だ The Nile is *the main artery* of the African continent.
‖**大動脈** the main artery ; the aorta /eɪɔ́ːʳt̬ə/.

[1]**とうみん 冬眠** **hibernation**,《インフォーマル》**winter sleep** 一動 **冬眠する** **hibernate** /háɪbəʳneɪt/ ▶**冬眠する**リスもいる Some squirrels *hibernate*.

[2]**とうみん 島民** an **islander**, a **person living on an island** ▶佐渡島**島民** *an inhabitant* of Sado Island. (➤ inhabitant は「住民」)

とうめい 透明な **transparent** /trænspǽərənt/ ; **invisible**（見えない）; **clear**（水などが澄んだ）▶ガラスは**透明**だ Plain glass is *transparent*. ‖ 酸素は無色**透明**で無臭だ Oxygen is colorless, *invisible*, and odorless. ‖ 摩周湖は**透明度**では日本一だ Lake Mashu ranks first in Japan in (*water*) *transparency*. ▶行政の一層の**透明性**を求める demand more *transparency* in government.
☞ **不透明**（→見出語）

どうめい 同盟 (an) **alliance** /əláɪəns/（相互利益のための）; a **league**（特定の目的のための）; a **union**（全体が一体と見なされる強い結び付きの）▶日本はかつてドイツおよびイタリアと**同盟を結んで**いた Japan *was* once *allied* [*leagued*] *with* Germany and Italy. ‖ 米国は日本の最も重要な**同盟国**だ The United States is the most important *ally* of Japan.
‖**同盟国** an ally /ǽlaɪ, əláɪ/, an allied power.

どうめいし 動名詞《文法》a **gerund** /dʒérənd/.

とうめん 当面 ▶**当面の**問題から手をつけましょう Let's start with the *present* problem. ‖ うちの部署は**当面**3人でやっていくつもりだ The three of us will run the department *for the time being* [for the present].

どうも **1【どうしても, どういう訳か】** **somehow** ▶どうも彼は好きになれない *Somehow* I don't like him. ‖ あの2人はどうも仲がよくない Those two can't get along *for some reason or other*. ‖ このノートパソコンはどうも調子が悪い There is *something* wrong with this laptop. ‖ 彼女の話はどうもわからない I *just* can't figure out what she is talking about. ‖ どうもあいつの言うことはうそだと思えてしかたがない I cannot help thinking that what he says [said] is a lie. ‖ きみにはどうも困ったもんだね I *really* don't know what I'm going to do about [with] you!
2【どうやら…のようだ】 ▶どうも今夜は雪になりそうだ *I am afraid* it will (*probably*) snow tonight. ‖ 窓ガラスを割ったのはどうも健太らしい *It appears* [*seems*] *that* Kenta broke the windowpane. ‖ どうも困ったことになりそうだ *It looks like* we're in for (some) trouble.
3【本当に】 **very**（形容詞・副詞を修飾）; **very much**（動詞を修飾）▶この前は手伝ってくれてどうもありがとう Thank you *very much* for your help the other day. ‖ どうもすみません I'm *very* sorry.
▶ **対話**《人と出会って》「やあ！」「やあ, どうも. 元気かい？」"Hi!" "Oh, *hi*! How are you (doing)?"

> **解説**「どうも」について
> (1)「どうもありがとう」「どうもすみません」「どうもご苦労さま」のような感謝・謝罪・ねぎらいなどの挨拶ことばにつけられる強調副詞の「どうも」は, インフォーマルな日本語ではこれだけが残り, 気持ちを表す肝心なことばは省略されることが多いが, 英語では副詞だけが残ることはない. Thanks (a lot). ／ (I'm) (very [so]) sorry. ／Thank you (very [so] much) for your trouble. のようにきちんと言うか, 省略するならカッコに入れた部分を省略する.
> (2)「先日はどうも」「いや, こちらこそどうも」のような対話は英語にならない. 英語では先日の何が「どうも」なのか（例えば土産物へのお礼）を具体的に言い, それに反応するからである.

どうもう 獰猛な **fierce** /fɪəʳs/, **ferocious** /fəróʊʃəs/（➤ 後者がより強意）; **savage** /sǽvɪdʒ/（抑制の利かなさ・残忍さを強調する語）▶あの犬は見るからに**どう猛**そうだ That dog looks very *fierce*. ‖ 猫は怒ると**どう猛さ**をのぞかせる When they are angry, cats show their *ferocity*. ‖ 犬や猫も時には**どう猛**になる Dogs and cats can sometimes be very *savage*.

どうもく 瞠目 ▶中国はここ数十年で**瞠目**すべき経済成長を遂げた China has achieved *spectacular* economic growth over the past several decades.

とうもろこし 玉蜀黍《米》**corn**,《英》**maize** /meɪz/（➤ どちらも数えられない名詞）; **sweet corn**（甘味種のトウモロコシ）▶**トウモロコシ**を焼く[ゆでる] roast [boil] *corn* ‖ 私は昼に**焼きトウモロコシ**を2本食べた I ate *two ears of roasted corn on the cob* for lunch. (➤ corn on the cob は「軸付きのトウモロコシ」)《参考》《英》では corn は穀類の総称で, 特にイングランドでは「小麦」の意.

とうやく 投薬 ▶患者に**投薬する** *administer medication* [*drugs*] to a patient.

どうやって **how, in what way** ▶一発で合格するなんてすごい. どうやって勉強したの？ It's fantastic that you passed the test on your first try. *How* did you study for it? ‖ これはどうやって食べるのですか *What's the proper way* to eat this? ／*How* do I eat this? ／*How* is this eaten?

どうやら **1【たぶん】** ▶どうやら午後は雨らしい *It looks like* we are going to have rain in the afternoon. ／*It is likely* to rain in the afternoon. ‖ どうやら嵐も収まったようだ The storm *seems* to have calmed down. ‖ どうやらかぜをひいたようだ I *seem* to have caught a cold. ‖ どうやら開いている店はここだけらしい *It would seem that* this store is the only one open. (It would seem that ... は「…のようだ」の意で, It seems that…よりも自信のない堅い言い方).
2【何とか, 辛うじて】 ▶彼らは僅かの収入でどうやら暮らしを立てている They are *just* [*barely*] getting along on their small income. ‖ 1か月20万円あればどうやら（こうやら）生活できます Two hundred thousand yen a month is (*just*) *barely enough* to live on. ‖ **対話**「おたくの景気はどうですか」「どうやらやってます」"How's your business?" "We're managing *somehow*."

とうゆ 灯油 **heating oil** ;《米》**kerosene** /kérəsiːn/,《英》**paraffin (oil)** ▶ストーブに**灯油**を入れる put *heating oil* in the heater.

とうよ 投与 ▶がん患者に抗生物質を**投与する** *administer* [*give*] antibiotics to a cancer patient.

[1]**とうよう 東洋** **the East**,《やや古》**the Orient** 一形 **東**

洋の **Eastern,** 《やや古》 **Oriental**

> 《解説》 (1)「東洋」は「西洋」と対立するもので, ほぼウラル山脈以東の地域を指す. 特に中国・韓国・日本などの「東アジア」「極東」をいう場合は East Asia あるいは the Far East となる.
> (2) Orient, Oriental はやや古めかしい呼び方で,「中近東」や「イスラム圏の北アフリカ」も含む. どちらも軽蔑的な含みをもつことがあり, 特に「人」を指すのに用いるのは《米》ではタブーに近い.

▶東洋と西洋 *the East* and the West ‖ 東洋一高いビル the tallest building in *East Asia* ‖ 東洋の文化に関心を持つ西洋人が増えてきている More and more Westerners have come to show interest in *Eastern* [*Asian*] cultures.
‖東洋史 East Asian [《古》 Oriental] history ‖ 東洋諸国 Eastern [Asian] countries ‖ 東洋人 an Asian, 《古》 an Oriental ‖ 東洋風 Eastern style.

2**とうよう 登用 promotion** 一動 **登用する promote** +目 ▶わが社では有能な人材はどんどん登用していきたい Our company is eager to *promote* persons of ability to higher positions.

3**とうよう 盗用 plagiarism** /pléɪdʒərìzəm/ 一動 **盗用する plagiarize** +目 ; **pirate** +目 (著作(製作)者に無許可で複製する) ▶この論文の書き手はほかの学者の説を盗用した The author of this paper *has plagiarized* the theories of other scholars.

1**どうよう 童謡** a **children's** [**nursery**] **song** ; a **nursery rhyme** /raɪm/, a **Mother Goose rhyme** (英米などに昔から伝わる子供向け詩歌, マザーグース)
‖童謡集 (a book of) nursery rhymes [songs] (➤ rhymes の場合, 詩だけで曲のないものも多い).

2**どうよう 同様の the same** (同一の) ; **similar** (類似の) ▶以下同様 *same* as above ‖ 鯨と魚は同様の形をしている Whales and fish are *similar* [Whales *are similar to* fish] in shape. ‖ 新品同様のテレビが捨ててあった Someone had thrown away a TV that was *as good as new*.
▶イギリスの失業率はこのところ高比率ですが, ほかの多くの国でも同様です Recently, the level of unemployment in Britain has been high, but many other countries *are in the same situation* [*in the same boat*]. ‖ 人間が病気にかかることがあるのと同様に, 植物も病気にかかることがある *Just as* humans can get sick, so can plants (get sick). ‖ 彼はその少年をわが子同様にかわいがっている He loves the boy *as if* he was his own son [*just like* his son]. ‖ 私たちの先生はどの生徒に対しても同様に温かく接してくれる Our teacher treats all the students with *equal* warmth and consideration.

3**どうよう 動揺 upset** (心の乱れ) ; **unrest** (不安) ; **disturbance** (社会を不安にさせる行動) 一動 **動揺する be disturbed, be upset,** 《インフォーマル》 **be shaken** (かき乱される) ▶その知らせを聞いて彼はひどく動揺した He *was* very much *upset* when he heard the news. ／ He *was* badly *shaken* at the news. ‖ 彼女は両親の離婚で気持ちが動揺していた She *was disturbed* [*was upset*] by her parents' divorce. ‖ 彼は危険に直面しても決して動揺しなかった He *never lost his composure* even in the face of danger. ‖ そういううわさは世間に動揺を与えるおそれがある Such a rumor is likely to *cause public unrest* [*disturb the people*].

とうらい 到来 coming, arrival (➤ 後者が日本語に近い) 一動 **到来する come, arrive** ▶誰もが春の到来を待ちわびている Everyone is waiting for the *coming* [*arrival* ／ *advent*] of spring. (➤ advent は arrival のさらに堅い語で厳粛さが感じられる) ‖ サッカーシーズンの到来だ The soccer season *has come*. ‖ チャンス到来だ! *Here's* my chance! ／ Opportunity knocks! (➤ 文字どおりには「チャンスがドアをノックしている」).

とうらく 当落 the results of an election (選挙の結果) ▶最終的な当落は午後11時までに判明するでしょう The final *results of the election* [*election results*] will be revealed by 11 : 00 p.m. ‖ 彼は今回の選挙では当落線上にいる *It is a toss-up whether* [*The odds are even that*] he will win this election. (➤ toss-up は「五分五分の見込み」).

どうらく 道楽 1【趣味】 a **hobby** ; a **pastime** (気晴らし) ▶道楽で時々つぼを作ります I sometimes do pottery as *a hobby*.
2【ばくち・女遊びなど】 ▶彼も若い頃は道楽をしたものだ He *sowed his wild oats* in his youth. (➤ sow one's wild oats で「若いときに遊び回る」).
‖道楽息子 a profligate [dissipated] son (➤ profligate /prɑ́:flɪgət/ は「不品行な, 身持ちの悪い」, dissipated は「放とうの」の意のともに堅い語).

どうらん 動乱 (an) **upheaval** (社会などの大変動) ; a **disturbance**, a **riot** (暴動 ; 前者は後者の婉曲(えんきょく)語).

どうり 道理 reason ▶きみの言うことも道理だ What you say *is reasonable*. ／You *have every reason* to say so. ‖ 私は自分を道理をわきまえた人間だと思っている I consider myself a *reasonable* person. ‖ 彼の要求は道理にかなっている [いない] His claim is *reasonable* [*unreasonable*]. ‖ あの男の言うことには道理も何もあったものではない What he says *doesn't make any sense* (*at all*).
▶デートなの? 道理でうれしそうな顔をしていると思ったよ Going out on a date? *No wonder* you look happy. (➤「道理でね!」なら No wonder!) ‖ 対話 「裕子, いやにうれしそうじゃない」「彼女, ゆうべのパーティーですてきな男性と知り合ったのよ」「道理で」 "Yuko looks so happy." "She met a cool guy at the party last night." "*That figures*." (➤ That figures. は「それでわかった」「なるほど」の意のインフォーマルな言い方).

とうりつ 倒立 a **handstand** 一動 **倒立する do a handstand, stand on** one's **hands** ▶倒立して歩く walk *on one's hands*.

どうりつ 道立 ▶道立高校 a *Hokkaido Prefectural* high school.

とうりゅう 逗留 a **stay** 一動 **逗留する stay.**

とうりゅうもん 登竜門 a **gateway to success** ▶このコンクールは音楽家の登竜門となっている This contest is *a gateway to success* in the world [field] of music.

とうりょう 棟梁 a **master carpenter.**

どうりょう 同僚 a **colleague** /kɑ́:li:g/ ; a **fellow worker**, a **co-worker** ; an **associate** /əsóʊʃiət/

> 《解説》 **「同僚」の言い方**
> (1) **colleague** は専門職の人や会社の役職者が用いることが多い. **associate** (business associate ともいう) はビジネス上何らかの関係を持つ人をいい, 同義で business friend を用いる人もいる. (2) **fellow worker, co-worker** [《英また》 **workmate**] はともに同じ職場で働く人をいうが, 後の2者からは親密さが感じられる.

▶彼は同僚たちとしっくりいっていないみたいだ He doesn't seem to get along with his *colleagues* [with his *fellow workers* / with *the people he works with*].
▶私たちは会社の同僚です We *work for the same company*.

どうりょく 動力 (motive) power ▶水車は水を動力にしている Water wheels *are driven by water (power)*.
‖動力装置 a power system, a power generator ‖動力炉 a power reactor.

とうるい 盗塁 a steal 一動 盗塁する steal (a base) ▶四球で出塁したイチローは次打者の1球目に二塁へ盗塁した After walking, Ichiro *stole second* on the pitcher's first pitch to the next batter.
‖盗塁王 a base-stealing king.

どうるい 同類 ▶シャチはイルカと同類だ Killer whales and dolphins belong to *the same family* [*species*].
▶おまえもあの不良どもと同類か Are you *one of* those punks?

とうれい 答礼 a return salute.

どうろ 道路 a road(道, 車道); a street(市街地を走り, 両側に家並みのある歩道付きの街路) ▶砂漠の中を一直線に道路が続いていた *A road* ran straight across the desert. ‖道路で遊んではいけません Don't play *on* [《英》*in*] *the street*. ‖この3月に新しい高速道路が開通する A new *expressway* will be opened this coming March.
‖道路情報 traffic information ‖道路地図 a road map ‖道路標識 a road [street] sign, a traffic sign.

> **逆引き熟語 ○○道路**
> 迂回(うかい)道路 a detour / 片側1[2]車線の道路 a single-[two-] lane road / 環状道路 a beltway, 《英》a ring road / 幹線道路 a highway, an arterial road / 高速道路 an expressway, a freeway, 《英》a motorway / 舗装道路 a paved road / 有料道路 a toll road

とうろう 灯籠 a (garden) lantern ▶庭の石灯籠 *a stone lantern* in the garden.

とうろうながし 灯籠流し a Buddhist ceremony in which paper lanterns are floated on a river (to send off the spirits of the dead) (➤ 説明的な訳).

とうろく 登録 registration 一動 登録する register /rédʒɪstəʳ/ +目 ▶授業の登録をする do one's *registration* for classes ‖車を登録する *register* one's car ‖車は私の名前で登録してある The car *is registered* in my name. ‖刀剣は教育委員会に登録しなければならない Any sword must *be registered* with the board of education.
▶当サイトは無料ですが, 内容閲覧には登録が必要です This (web)site is free, but you *are required to register* [but *registration is required*] to see the content.
▶履修科目はすべて登録すること You are required to *register for* all the subjects you are going to take. ‖きみの名前は私の講義には登録されていませんよ You *are* not *registered* for this class. / Your name *is* not *on my roll book*.
‖登録者 a registrant ‖登録証 a registration ‖登録商標 a registered trademark ‖登録番号 a registration number ‖登録料 a registration fee ‖会員登録 member(ship) registration ‖外国人登録証明書 an alien-registration card, a certificate of alien registration.

とうろん 討論 (a) discussion; (a) debate 一動 討論する discuss +目, debate +目

> **解説** (1) **discussion** は問題解決のために建設的な意見を出し合うことをいい, 友好的なニュアンスがある.
> (2) **debate** は公開の場で賛成側と反対側に分かれて行う討論をいう.

▶我々は臓器移植について長時間討論した We *had a* long *discussion* about [on] organ transplants. ‖その問題について彼と何時間も討論した I *discussed* the matter with him for hours. (discuss は他動詞なので (×)discuss about とはしない) ‖この問題は来週また討論します This subject will *be discussed* again next week.
‖討論会 a debate ‖公開討論会 an open forum [debate]; a panel discussion (パネルディスカッション) ‖テレビ討論会 a TV [televised] debate ‖党首討論 a party leader's debate.

どうわ 童話 a children's story; a fairy tale(おとぎ話); a nursery tale(伝承された)
‖童話作家 a writer of children's stories.

とうわく 当惑 embarrassment 一動 当惑する be embarrassed /ɪmbǽrəst/ (どぎまぎする); be perplexed [puzzled] (戸惑う); be annoyed(迷惑する, 困る); be bewildered(うろたえる); be confused(考えが混乱する) ▶その女優はレポーターの失礼な質問に当惑した The actress *was embarrassed* [*discomfited*] by the reporter's rude question. (➤ discomfited は堅い言い方) ‖あの人の身勝手な態度には皆当惑しています We *are* all *annoyed* at his selfishness. ‖「それ, どういう意味ですか」と彼女は少し当惑したような顔で私に言った "What do you mean by that?" she said to me with a slightly *perplexed* look (on her face).
▶京子は別れた彼に偶然会って当惑した Kyoko *felt uncomfortable* [*confused*] when she ran into her ex-boyfriend.

とえい 都営の metropolitan /mètrəpɑ́ːlətn/ (大都市の)
‖都営地下鉄 the Tokyo metropolitan subway.

どえらい ▶どえらい(= ひどい)目に遭った I've had a *terrible* [*an awful*] experience. ‖どえらいことをしてくれたね You've really *screwed* (*things*) *up*, haven't you?
▶スティーブはどえらくもうけた Steve made a *tremendous* profit.

とおあさ 遠浅 ▶湘南海岸は海が遠浅なので夏の週末には多くの人が泳ぎに集まる Because the sea by the Shonan beaches *is shallow far out from shore*, many people gather there to swim on weekends in summer.

とおい 遠い 1【距離が】far(➤ 単独では通例疑問文・否定文に用いる); distant(➤ 簡単には到達できないことを意味する); remote(➤ 不便・困難な所を連想させる) ▶遠い国 a *far-off* [*distant* / *remote*] country(➤ a far country は古風で文語的) ‖あなたの学校は家から遠いですか? Is your school *far* from your house? (➤ この場合 distant は不可) ‖ 対話「松江までどのくらい遠いの?」「そんなに遠くないよ」"*How far away* is Matsue? / *How far* is it to Matsue?" "*Not* so *far*."

【文型】
場所(A)は場所(B)から遠い
A **is a long way from** B.
A **is quite a distance from** B.

【解説】(1) **far** は「遠くに, 遠くへ」の意の副詞として使うことが多い. 主に疑問文・否定文で用い, ふつうの文のときは far away, too far などの形で使う. 「AはBから遠い」は a long way を使うほうが好まれる.
(2) It's a long way [quite a distance] from A to B. の形も使う.

▶私の学校は家から遠い My school *is a long way from* my home. ／My school *is distant from* my home. ‖ここからその滝まではとても遠い *It's a* very *long way from* here *to* the waterfall. ‖歩くと遠いですよ It's a *long* walk. ‖地図によるとその温泉地はまだ遠いようだ From the map, it looks like the hot spring resort is still *a long way off* [*away*].
▶遠いところをわざわざお越しいただき恐縮です Thank you for coming *all the way* to see me.
2【時間が】▶遠い将来何が起きるかなんて誰にもわからない Nobody knows what will happen *in the distant future*. ‖遠い将来のことまで考えて人生設計をしなさい Look *far ahead* into the future to plan (for) your life. ‖それは遠い昔の話である That is a *very old* story. ／That happened *a long time ago* [*ages ago*]. ‖父の退職の日も遠くない (The date of) my father's retirement is *not far off*.
3【関係・程度が】**distant** ▶彼女は遠い親類の男性と結婚した She married a *distant* relative (of hers).
4【感覚が】▶祖父は耳が遠い My grandfather *is hard of hearing*. ‖私は左の耳が遠い I *have hearing difficulties* in my left ear. ‖炎天下で3時間立っていたら気が遠くなってきた I *feel really light-headed and faint* after standing under the scorching sun for the past three hours. ‖電話が遠くてよく聞こえないんだ. もっと大きな声でしゃべってよ *I can't hear you very well*. Could you speak louder, please?
☞ 遠く (→見出語)

トーイック **TOEIC** (➤ Test of English for International Communication の頭文字).

とおえん 遠縁 ▶彼は私の遠縁に当たる He is *a distant relative* (of mine). ／I'm *distantly related to* him.

とおからず 遠からず **in the near future** ▶彼は遠からず一軍に昇格するだろう He'll be promoted to the first team *in the near future*.

とおく 遠く **1**【距離が】▶遠くまで行く go *a long way* ‖遠くまで行っちゃだめよ Don't go *far*. ‖たくさんの人がこの遺跡を見に遠くからやって来ます Many people come *a long way* to see these ruins. ‖遠くから見るとその岩はライオンのように見える If you look at it *from far away*, the rock looks like a lion. ／Seen *from afar* [*from far away*], the rock looks like a lion. (● 前者は会話的で, 後者はフォーマル) ‖遠くに町の明かりが見えた I saw the lights of the town *far away* [*a long way off* ／*in the distance*]. ‖地図によるとその村は思ったより遠くにある The map shows the village to be *farther* [*further*] than I thought. ‖もっと遠くまで行こう Let's go *farther* [*further*].
2【程度が】▶ぼくは走ることにかけては彼に遠く及びません He is *far* better than me in running. ／When it comes to running, I'm *nowhere near* a match for him. (➤ nowhere near は「…に程遠く」の意).

トーク a **talk** (「講演」または「演説」を意味することが多い); a **chat** (おしゃべり) ▶あの歌手のコンサートはトークも楽しい That singer also entertains us with his [her] *chat* at his [her] concert.
‖トーク番組 a talk show.

とおざかる 遠ざかる ▶彼女の乗った電車ははるかかなたへ遠ざかってしまった Her train *disappeared* [*faded*] into the distance. ‖その車は遠ざかっていった The car *drove away* [*off*].
▶きみはあの連中から遠ざかっていたほうがいい You'd better *stay away from* that group. ‖しばらくピアノから遠ざかっているのでうまく弾けるかどうかわかりません I *haven't practiced* (on) the piano *for a long time*, so I'm not sure if I can play (it) well.

とおざける 遠ざける ▶なぜか彼女は親友さえ遠ざけるようになった For some reason or other, she started *keeping* even her closest friends *at arm's length* [*at a distance*]. ‖お嬢さんをあの男から遠ざけたほうがいいですよ You should *keep* your daughter *away from* him.

とおし 通し ▶宝くじを10枚通しで買う buy ten *serially-numbered* lottery tickets.
‖(靴ひもなどの)通し穴 an eyelet, an eyehole ‖通し切符 a through ticket ‖通し稽古 a run-through ‖通し番号 a serial number (識別のための); consecutive [running] numbers (続き番号) ‖通しページ consecutive paging, continuous pagination.

-とおし -通し ‖ゴム [ひも] 通し a bodkin.

-どおし -通し ▶彼女は授業中しゃべり通しだ She *keeps talking* all through class. ／She *chatters all the time* [*nonstop*] in class. ‖赤ん坊はその間泣き通しだった The baby *kept crying* the whole time. ‖新幹線で名古屋まで立ち通しだった I *stood all the way* to Nagoya on the Shinkansen. ‖中学時代は親に心配のかけ通しだった I was *a constant worry* to my parents while (I was) in junior high school.

とおす 通す **1**【向こう側へ行かせる】**pass ... through** ▶このひもをその輪に通しなさい *Pass* this cord *through* the ring. ‖(人込みなどで)すみません, ちょっと通してください Excuse me, may I *get through*? ／Please *let* me *pass* (*through*). (● get through や pass through は「通り抜ける」. あとの文はエレベーターを降りる場合にも使える. エレベーターではほかに Can I get by, please? などの言い方も用いられる) ‖学生証を忘れたので校門を通してもらえなかった I couldn't *get through* the school gate because I didn't have my student ID. ‖許可された車以外通すことはできない We can't *allow* unauthorized cars *to go through* this way.
2【通過して成立させる】**pass** +目 ▶法案を通す *pass* a bill (*through* the Diet) ‖物理は追試を2回受けてやっと通してもらった I finally *passed* physics after taking two makeup exams. (→通る).
3【案内する】**show** +目 ▶お客さまを校長室へお通ししてください Please *show* our guest *to* the principal's office. ‖私は応接間へ通された I *was shown to* the drawing room.
4【光・熱などを】▶銅は電気を通す(＝伝導する) Copper *conducts* electricity. ‖この黒いガラスは光を通さない Light *does not pass through* this black glass. ‖豚肉はちゃんと火を通さなければいけない Pork

must *be* thoroughly *cooked*. ‖ 天気のいい日に物置に風を通した(＝入れた) On a sunny day, I opened the door of the storeroom and *let in some fresh air*. ‖ このコートは絶対に雨を通しません This coat is absolutely *rainproof* [*waterproof*].

5【媒介とする】through ▶就職課を通してその仕事に応募した I applied for the job *through* the employment section. ‖ 食物の研究を通して江戸時代の庶民の生活程度を知ることができる *Through* the study of their diet [*By* studying food], we can learn how ordinary people lived in the Edo period. ‖ テレビを通してわが社への謝罪を発表してほしい We want you to apologize to our company *on* TV. ‖ 女の子は窓ガラスを通して雨の街路を見つめていた The girl gazed out on the rainy street *through* the windowpane.

6【初めから終わりまで続ける】▶『マタイ受難曲』を全曲通して聴いた I listened to "St. Matthew's Passion" *from* (*the*) *beginning to* (*the*) *end*. ‖ ポールは世界中どこへ行っても英語だけで通す Wherever he travels around the world, Paul *speaks nothing but English*.

▶あの女優は生涯を独身で通した The actress *remained single* all her life. ‖ 私は冬じゅう手袋なしで通した I did*n't wear* gloves all winter. ‖ 私は中学の3年間を無遅刻・無欠席 [皆勤] で通した I *made it through* three years of junior high school without ever missing a day of school or being late.

▶《慣用表現》この原稿に一度目を通してください Could you *look over* this draft, please? (look over は「ざっと読む」にも,「詳しく調べる」にも用いられる) ‖ この本に目を通しておくといい You should *read* this book *through*. (➤ read through は「最後まで読む」) ‖ 私はその記事にざっと目を通した I *skimmed through* [*over*] the article.

7【強行する】▶彼はいつもわがままを通そうとする He always tries to *get his own way*. (➤ get one's own way は「思いどおりにふるまう」) ‖ 彼女はあくまでも自分の意見を通そうとした She tried to *stick to* [*persist in*] *her own opinion*. (➤ stick to は「(主義などに)執着する」).

8【「…通す」の形で】▶メロスは倒れそうになりながらも走り通した Melos *continued running to the finish* though he nearly collapsed along the way.

トースター a **toaster** ▶トースターでパンを焼く *toast* a slice of bread(➤ toast は「(トースターで)焼く」の意の動詞).

トースト toast ▶朝はトースト1枚とコーヒーで済ませます I have *a piece* [*a slice*, 《英また》*a round*] *of toast* and a cup of coffee for breakfast.

‖ **バタートースト** buttered toast ‖ **フレンチトースト** French toast.

とおせんぼ(う) 通せん坊 ▶私は家に帰る途中で男の子たちに通せんぼされた A group of boys *blocked* [*stood in*] *my way* home.

トータル the total ; the total amount(総額) ; **the sum total**(合計額) ▶現在のところ最終的なトータルの数字はまだ出ておりません As of now, *the final total* is still not available. ‖ 物事をトータルで捉える look at things *from all angles* ‖ トータルで考えると, きみにはその大学が一番だと思うよ *Taking everything into consideration*, that university is best for you.

とおで 遠出 ▶今度の連休にどこかへ遠出しようよ Let's *go on an outing* during the (coming) holidays. ‖ 週末には車で箱根まで遠出する予定だ We are *going for a long drive* to Hakone this weekend.

トーテムポール a **totem pole.**

トートバッグ a **tote bag.**

ドーナツ a **doughnut** /dóʊnʌt/, a **donut**

《参考》アメリカのドーナツは輪型だが, イギリスのものは穴がなく中にジャムの入ったものが多い.

doughnuts

(中央は cruller と呼ぶもの, 右は イギリスのもの)

トーナメント a **tournament** /tʊ́əʳnəmənt/ ▶ワールドカップの決勝トーナメント *the second round* [*stage*] of the World Cup ‖ 私は大学対抗のテニストーナメントで優勝した[に出場した] I won [competed in] the intercollegiate tennis *tournament*.

とおのく 遠退く ▶コツコツという足音が遠のいていった The footsteps *died away*. ‖ 津波の危険は遠のいた The danger of a tsunami *has receded*. ‖ ジャイアンツの優勝の可能性は次第に遠のいていった The Giants' hope of winning the pennant gradually *faded*. ‖ 不況のせいで人々の足は歓楽街から遠のき始めた People began to *stay away from* the entertainment districts because of the economic recession.

ドーバー Dover(イングランド南東部の市)

‖ **ドーバー海峡** the Strait(s) of Dover(イギリスとフランスの間にある海峡).

ドーピング doping ▶ドーピング検査に引っ掛かる fail to pass *a dope* [*drug*] *test* / be caught in *a drug check*.

トーフル TOEFL(➤ Test of English as a Foreign Language の頭文字).

☛ トーイック (→見出語)

とおぼえ 遠吠え howling /háʊlɪŋ/ ▶犬の遠ぼえ a dog *howling* ‖ あいつが何を言ったって, 所詮負け犬の遠ぼえさ Whatever he says is just *whining*. (➤「泣き言」の意).

とおまき 遠巻き ▶大勢のやじ馬が燃えているビルを遠巻きにしていた A large crowd of curious onlookers *surrounded* the burning building *at a distance*.

とおまわし 遠回しの roundabout ; indirect(間接的な) ▶遠回しに忠告する advise a person *in a roundabout way* ‖ 彼女は近く結婚するかもしれないと遠回しに言った She *hinted* [*said indirectly*] that she might get married soon. (➤ hint は「ほのめかす」) ‖ 彼はいつも遠回しに言うばかりで要領を得ない He always *beats around* [*about*] *the bush* and never gets to the point. (➤ beat around [about] the bush は文字どおりには「茂みの周りをたたいて獲物を追い出す」の意).

とおまわり 遠回り ▶遠回りして帰る *go around* [《英》*round*] *the long way* home ‖ そちらは遠回りで, こちらが近道です That's *the long way around*. This way is a shortcut. ‖ 道路工事のため遠回りしなければならなかった We had to *make a detour* to avoid the construction work. (➤ detour /díːtʊəʳ/ は「う回路, 回り道」).

ドーム a **dome** ▶ドーム形の体育館 a *dome-shaped* gymnasium ‖ 広島の原爆ドーム the Hiroshima (Atomic Bomb) *Dome*.

‖ **ドーム球場** a domed baseball stadium ‖ **東京ドーム** the Tokyo Dome.

とおめ 遠目 ▶背が高いので遠目にも高田先生だとすぐわ

かった *Even at a distance*, I recognized Mr. Takada at once because he is tall.

ドーラン **greasepaint**（➤「ドーラン」はドイツのメーカー Dohran から）.

とおり 通り 1【街路】a **street**; an **avenue**（大通り）; a **boulevard** /bóləvɑːrd ‖ búːl-/（通例並み木のある広い通り）▶200メートルほど行くとにぎやかな通りに出ます Walk 200 meters, and you will come to a busy *street*. ‖ 私の家は本通りに面している My house is on *the main street*. ‖ 元町通りにはたくさんの喫茶店がある There are many coffee shops on Motomachi *Street*.

2【通ること】▶アメリカでは何でも弁護士を通したほうが話の通りが早い In the United States, *everything goes smoother* if you go through a lawyer. ‖ 彼は（本名より）あだ名のほうが通りがいい He *is better known* by his nickname. ‖ この部屋は風の通りがよくない This room *is not well-ventilated* [*has poor ventilation* / *is stuffy*].

3【…のように】**as** →-どおり ▶あなたの言うとおりです Just [It's exactly] *as* you say. / You're right. / You got that right. / What you say is true. ‖ ほら, ぼくの言ったとおりだろ？ See? It's *as* I told you. / What did I say! ‖ そのホテルはガイドブックで読んだ記事のとおりではなかったのでがっかりした I was disappointed that the hotel did*n't live up to* the description I had read in a guidebook. ‖ 詳しいデータは次のとおりです The details are *as follows*. ‖ 言われた[言う]とおりにしなさい Do *as* you are told [*as* I told].

4【種類】▶この方程式を解くには2通りの方法がある There are *two* ways to solve this equation.

☞ 大通り（→見出語）

-どおり -通り ▶彼女は約束どおりやって来た She came *as* she had promised. ‖ 申し込みは申請どおり認可された The application has been approved *as* filed. ‖ 彼は時間どおりやって来たためしがない He never comes *on time*. ‖ 万事予定どおり進んでいます Things are going exactly *according to plan*. ‖ 葬儀は厳かに作法どおりに行われた The funeral was conducted with great solemnity and *in accordance with* proper etiquette.（➤ in accordance with は「…に従って」の意の堅い言い方）‖ 彼の言うことをことばどおりにとるべきではない You should not take him *at his word*.

とおりあめ 通り雨 a (**passing**) **shower** ▶通り雨だからすぐに上がるよ Just a (*passing*) *shower*. It will stop soon.

とおりいっぺん 通り一遍の **superficial**（皮相的な）; **perfunctory**（おざなりの）▶北欧文学については通りいっぺんの知識しか持ち合わせていない I have only a *superficial* knowledge of Scandinavian literature. ‖ 警官は2つ3つ通りいっぺんの質問をした The police officer asked a few *perfunctory* questions.

とおりがかり 通り掛かり ▶通りがかりに彼女の家の前に救急車が止まっているのを見かけた *As I passed by* her house, I noticed (there was) an ambulance out in front. ‖ 通りがかりの人が助けてくれなければきみは凍死していたよ If the *passer-by* hadn't helped you, you would have frozen to death.

とおりこす 通り越す **pass** +㊐ ▶目印のコンビニをうっかり通り越してしまった My thoughts were elsewhere, and I *accidentally passed* a convenience store which was my landmark.

▶驚いたのを通り越して肝を潰すほどだったよ This *goes beyond* surprised; I was astounded.

とおりすがり 通りすがり ▶道に迷ってしまい通りすがりの人に尋ねた I got lost, so I asked *a passer-by* (for directions).

とおりすぎる 通り過ぎる **go past**, **pass** +㊐ ▶目の前を赤い車が通り過ぎていった A red car *went past* me. ‖ 夕立が通り過ぎた The shower *has passed* [*has stopped*]. ‖ 気がついたときには曲がるべき交差点を通り過ぎていた Before I knew it, I *had passed* the intersection where I was supposed to turn.

とおりぬける 通り抜ける **go** [**pass**] **through** ▶森を通り抜ける *pass through* a wood ‖ この道は通り抜けることができない You can't *go through* on this road.

《参考》掲示の「通り抜け禁止」は No Thoroughfare /θɑ́ːroofeər/ または No Through Road.

とおりま 通り魔

> **解説 「通り魔」について**
> (1)「通り魔」にぴったりの対応語はないので someone who harms a passer-by for no reason（理由もなく通行人に危害を加える者）のように説明的に言ったり, phantom attacker [slasher]（お化けのように出没して人を襲う者）のように言ったりする.
> (2)特に性的な動機から女性や子供に重大な危害を加える通り魔や人を切りつける者なら slasher, 切り裂き魔なら ripper,（無差別に[お化けのように出没して]人を殺す）殺人者なら random [phantom] killer のような語を使うこともできる. →痴漢.

▶昨夜, 女子高生が通り魔に襲われた A female high school student was attacked by *a phantom slasher* last night.

とおりみち 通り道 a **way**; a **passage**（通路）▶倒れた木が通り道をふさいでいた A fallen tree blocked [obstructed] the *way* [*passage*]. ‖ 通り道に自転車を放置しないよう生徒たちに言ってくれませんか Could you please tell the students not to leave their bikes in the *passage*? ‖ 本屋さんなら通り道だから, その雑誌帰りに買って来るよ I'*ll be passing by* the bookstore, so I'll buy that magazine for you on my way home.

とおる 通る

> **訳語メニュー**
> 通過する →go through, pass 1
> 運行する → run 1
> 合格する →pass 3
> 通用する →pass 5

1【向こう側へ達する】**go through**; **pass** +㊐（通り過ぎる）▶（空港で）税関を通る *go through* customs inspections (at the airport) ‖ 家の前をパトカーが通った A police car *passed* our house. ‖ 東名高速道路は深夜でも車がたくさん通る Traffic *is heavy* on the Tomei Expressway even late at night. ‖ スーパーの前を通る？ 牛乳を買って来てもらいたいんだけど *Will* you *be passing by* the supermarket? I'd like you to buy some milk for me.（● I'd like you to ... を I want you to ... とすると命令口調になる）‖ ちょっと通らせてください *Let* me *pass*. / *Let* me *through*.（● 後者は無理やり通るときなどの言い方で, ふつうは Excuse me. と言う）.

▶この古い橋は今では誰も通らない（＝渡らない）Nobody *crosses* this old bridge now. ‖ この糸は太すぎて針の穴を通らない I *can't get* this thread *through* the

eye of the needle ; it's too thick.
▶竹田・国際会館間は地下鉄が通っている Subway trains *run* between Takeda and Kokusai-Kaikan. (この意味では進行形にしない) ‖ 大潟村へはバスが通っている *There is* bus service to Ogatamura. ‖ 対話「すみません, このバスは天神を通りますか」「はい, 通ります」"Excuse me, does this bus *go to* Tenjin ?" "Yes, it does."
2【経由する】▶中央高速を通って長野へ出よう Let's *take* the Chuo Expressway to Nagano. ‖ 私たちは熊本を通って(＝経由して)鹿児島へ行った We went to Kagoshima *by way of* [*via*] Kumamoto.
3【通過して成立する】pass +目 ▶真由美はミス日本の１次予選を通った Mayumi *passed* the first elimination for the Miss Japan Contest. ‖ 彼女は(運転免許の)筆記試験には通ったのに実技で落ちた She *passed* the written exam, but failed the road test. ‖ 教育法案は国会を通った The education bill *has passed* the Diet.
▶《慣用表現》心配しなくても先方に話は通っているよ Don't worry. I*'ve* (already) *made the necessary arrangements* with them.
4【十分に届く, 通じる】▶彼女の声はよく通る Her voice *carries* well. ‖ この大根はまだ火がよく通ってない This daikon isn't *cooked through*. ‖ この部屋は風がよく通って気持ちがいい I feel refreshed because this room is well *ventilated* [is (nice and) *airy*]. ‖ 医者で薬をスプレーしてもらったら詰まった鼻が通るようになった My nose was stuffed up, but it *cleared up* when the doctor put nose spray in it.
5【通用する】pass《for, as》▶あの人は(学者でもないのに)学者として通っている He *passes for* [*as*] a scholar. (➤ pass for [as] は「(誤って)…として通る」の意) ‖ ミニスカートをはいたら彼女はティーンエージャーでも通る She *can pass for* a teenager if she wears a miniskirt. ‖ そんな要求は通らない Such requests *are not* [*cannot be*] *accepted*. ‖ そんないいかげんな言い訳じゃ通らないよ I *can't accept* that sort of half-baked excuse.
▶二審では被告の主張が通って, 判決がひっくり返った The defendant's claim *was accepted* at the second trial, and the judgment was reversed. ‖ この文章には意味の通らないところがいくつかある This passage has some places that *don't make any sense*.

トーン (a) **tone** ▶寝室は明るいトーンでまとめてみた I've harmonized the colors of the bedroom in bright *tones*.

どーん ▶男たちは扉にドーンと体当たりした The men hurled themselves against the door *with a thud*. ‖ 谷間にドーンと発破の音がこだました The *boom* of the blast echoed in the gorge. ‖ その地震では数回ドーンと突き上げるような衝撃があった During the earthquake, the ground *heaved upward* several times.

トーンダウン ▶野党は政府批判をトーンダウンした The opposition *toned down* its criticism of the government.

トおんきごう ト音記号《音楽》a **G** [**treble**] **clef**.

-とか ▶私はコーヒーとか紅茶とかは飲みません I don't drink coffee, black tea, *or* drinks *like that*. ‖ 弟はウクレレとかギターなどの弦楽器が弾ける My (younger) brother can play stringed instruments, *such as* ukuleles *and* guitars. ‖ 豊川商事とか何とかいう会社の人が来たよ A man came to see you from Toyokawa Trading Company *or something like that*.

とかい 都会 a **city** 一形 **都会の urban** /ɜ́ːrbən/
《参考》city は行政上の単位としては「市」で, 人口的に下位の「町」は town,「村」は village である. ただ,「買い物に町に出かけて行く」に当たる go into town for shopping のような決まった表現では都会にも town を当てることがある. また「都会」の対比としての「田舎」は a rural area [region] で, 町ほどの規模ならば, a rural town となる. しばしば「田舎」に当てられる the country は, 田畑・牧場・森・里山など, 自然や緑が優勢で人家がまばらな地域を指す. 自然豊かな地域, 美しい田園地帯という意味では the countryside が好まれる.
▶大都会 *a* large [big] *city* ／ a metropolis /mətrɑ́ːpəlɪs/ ‖ 都会に住む人 an *urban* resident ／ a *city* dweller ／an urbanite /ɜ́ːrbənaɪt/ ‖ 仕事を求めて都会へ出る go to *a city* to find work ‖ 大都会のライフスタイル an *urban* [a *big city*] lifestyle ‖ ぼくはどちらかと言えば都会よりも田舎に住みたい I would rather live in a rural town than in *a city*. (➤ a small town (in the country [countryside] としてもよい)) ‖ 田舎に住んでいると時々都会の生活が恋しくなる Living in the country, I sometimes miss *city life* [*life in the big city*]. (➤ city life の代わりに urban life でもよい) ‖ 彼女は都会的なセンスの持ち主だ She has a *sophisticated* taste. (➤ sophisticated /səfístɪkeɪtɪd/ は「洗練された」).
ディベートルーム **「都会は田舎よりも住みやすい」**

どがいし 度外視 ▶費用を度外視して計画を実行する carry out a plan *regardless of* [*without regard to*] expense ‖ その農協は採算を度外視して地元野菜を安価で販売した The agricultural cooperative sold local vegetables at low prices, *without considering* making a profit.

とがき ト書き a **stage direction**.

とかく ▶とかく日本人は人前に出ると恥ずかしがる Japanese *tend to* be shy in public. (➤ tend to do は「…する傾向がある」) ‖ 人はとかく他人のことを悪く思いがちだ We *are apt to* think badly of others. (be apt to do は「習慣的に通例好ましくない言動をとりがちである」の意. 次例の be liable to do も同様) ‖ こんな不注意がとかく事故を起こすものだ Such carelessness *is liable to* cause an accident.

とかげ 蜥蜴《動物》a **lizard** /lízərd/.

[1]**とかす 解かす・溶かす melt** +目 (熱を加えて) ; **dissolve** /dɪzɑ́ːlv/ +目 (液体の中に入れて) ▶鉄を溶かす *melt* iron ‖ 雪にお湯を掛けて解かす *melt* snow by pouring hot water on it ‖ 砂糖を水に溶かす *dissolve* sugar in water.

[2]**とかす 梳かす・解かす comb** /koʊm/ +目 (くしで) ; **brush** +目 (ブラシで) ▶髪をとかす *comb* one's hair.

どかす 退かす move +目 (移す) ; **remove** (取り除く) ▶机をどかす *remove* a desk ‖ 津波被災地からがれきをどかす *clear* the debris from tsunami-stricken areas ‖ 通れないので荷物をどかしてください *Move* your luggage, please. It's blocking my way. ／ *Get* your luggage *out of my way*, will you ?

どかどか ▶突然数人の男たちがどかどかと部屋の中に入って来た Suddenly several men *pounded* [*thudded*] into the room.

とがめる 咎める reproach +目 (穏やかに叱る) ; **rebuke** +目 (厳しく叱る) ▶彼女の目が私をとがめていた Her eyes *reproached* me. ‖ 彼は約束を破ったことで私をとがめた He *rebuked* me *for* having broken

my promise. ‖ 授業中に漫画を読んでいたら先生にとがめられた The teacher *reprimanded* me *for* reading a comic in class. (☗reprimand は「けん責する」の意で, reproach が個人的感情でとがめることをいうのに対して, 公式にとがめるというニュアンス).
▶《慣用表現》キセルをしたあと, どうにも気がとがめてしかたがなかった I couldn't help but *feel guilty* [*feel pangs of guilt*] after cheating on the fare.

どかゆき どか雪 **a sudden and heavy snow** ▶東北地方はどか雪に見舞われた The Tohoku district was hit by *a sudden and heavy snow*.

とがらす 尖らす **sharpen** +目 (物を); **pout** /paʊt/ +目 (口を) ▶ナイフで鉛筆をとがらす *sharpen* a pencil with a knife ‖ そんなに口をとがらすなよ Don't *pout* like that. ‖ 彼女は近頃神経をとがらせてばかりいる She's always *on edge* these days. ‖ その国会議員は批判に神経をとがらせている The Diet member is so *sensitive* to criticism.

とがる 尖る 一形 とがった **sharp, pointed** 《参考》 sharp は先端がとがっていることを指す以外に「刃物の刃が鋭い」の意もあるので, 物の先端を明確にいうには pointed のほうがよい.
▶とがった鉛筆 a *sharp* pencil(➤「鋭くとがった鉛筆」なら a sharply pointed pencil という) ‖ とがった鼻 a *pointed* nose ‖ とがったガラスのかけら a *jagged* piece of glass(➤ jagged は「ぎざぎざの」) ‖「早く食事をしなさい」と彼女はとがった声で子供に命令した She said to her children *in a sharp voice*, "Eat your food quickly!"

1**どかん 土管** an **earthen pipe**, a **clay pipe**(➤ 後者には「(喫煙具としての)陶製のパイプ」の意味もある) ▶下水用の土管 a *clay* drain*pipe*.

2**どかん** ▶ドカンという爆発音に驚いてみんな外へ飛び出した Alarmed by the *boom* of an explosion, everyone ran outside. ‖ タクシーどうしがドカンと正面衝突した Two taxis *crashed head-on* (into each other).

1**とき 鴇・朱鷺** 《鳥》 a **Japanese crested ibis** /áɪbɪs/ (➤ crested は「冠羽のある」の意).
‖とき色 pale pink.

2**とき 時** **1【時の流れ】time** ▶時がたつにつれて昔の記憶は薄れてしまうものだ As *time* passes [goes by], our memories of the old days fade away. ‖ 時のたつのは早いものだ *Time* flies. / *Time* goes by fast. ‖ ロックを聴いていると時のたつのを忘れる When I listen to rock music, I tend to *forget the passing of time*.
ことわざ 時は金なり Time is money.

2【時期, 時刻, 時点】time; a **chance**(機会) ▶今こそ核兵器を廃絶する時だ Now is the *time* to [Now is the *time* when we must] do away with nuclear weapons. ‖ そういうことは時が来れば自然にわかるようになります You'll understand that sort of thing yourself when *time* comes. / Only *time* will tell. ‖ 中村はちょうどいい時にホームランを打った Nakamura's home run was *very timely* [came at *the right time*]. ‖ 時を見てきみとそのことを話し合おうと思っていた I've been waiting for *a chance* to talk it over with you. ‖ 時と場合によって服装を考える必要がある You need to choose your clothes according to the *time and occasion*. ‖ 時の首相, 田中氏 Mr. Tanaka, the prime minister *at that time* [the *then* prime minister] ‖ コーヒーを飲む時もあれば, 紅茶を飲む時もある *Sometimes* I drink coffee, and *sometimes* tea. ‖ この歌は初めて聞いた時から大好きになった This song has been one of my favorites *since* the first time I heard it.

3【…の頃】when ▶若いときはよくスキューバダイビングをした I did a lot of scuba diving *when* I was young. ‖ 私が15歳のとき父が死にました My father died *when* I was 15. ‖ 最初のデートのときはどこへ行ったの? Where did you go *on* your first date? (➤ この on は特定の時や機会を指す前置詞) ‖ 好きなとき(はいつでも)来てくれ Come *whenever* [*anytime*] you like. ‖ 来られるときは電話をくれよ Call me *if* you can come. ‖ かぜをひいたときは温かくして寝るのがいちばんだ *When* you have a cold, the best remedy is (to) go to bed and keep yourself warm.
☞ 時の人 (→見出語)

どき 土器 an **earthen vessel**(土器の容器); **earthenware**(➤ 総称) ▶弥生式土器 Yayoi *earthen vessels* ‖ 青森で1万6500年前の土器片が出土した Some *pieces of earthenware* that date back to 16,500 years ago were excavated in Aomori.

ときあかす 解き明かす **solve** +目 ▶1枚のメモが彼女の失踪の謎を解き明かしてくれた A note *solved* the mystery of her disappearance.

ときおり 時折 **occasionally** →時々 ▶彼は時折電話をしてくるが一度も家に来たことはない He *occasionally* calls me, but he has never come to my house.

とぎすます 研ぎ澄ます **sharpen** [**hone**] **to a fine finish** ▶研ぎ澄ました刃 a *well-sharpened* [*-honed*] blade ‖ 研ぎ澄まされた感覚 a *finely-* [*keenly-*] *honed* sense.

ときたま 時偶 **(every) once in a while, occasionally**(➤ 頻度的には両者とも30%程度).

-ときたら -と来たら ▶うちの夫ときたらきのうも午前さまなのよ *That* husband of mine came home after midnight again yesterday. (➤ この that は軽蔑, 非難, いらだちなどを表す) ‖ うちの課長ときたら, まるっきり役立たずだね *Speaking of* our section chief, he is a real good-for-nothing.

どぎつい ▶どぎつい色 a *loud* [*garish*] color(➤ 後者には非難の響きがある) ‖ そんなどぎつい化粧をしてどこへ行くつもりだ Where're you going with such *heavy* makeup? ‖ あの子はかわいい顔してどぎついことを言うよ That girl uses *harsh* [*coarse* / *vulgar*] language though she looks cute.

どきっと ▶車の前に子供が飛び出して来たときは, どきっとしたよ I *nearly jumped out of my skin* [My *heart jumped into my mouth*] when a child rushed out in front of my car.

ときどき 時々 **1【時折】sometimes**(➤ 頻度的には50%程度); **occasionally, (every) once in a while** (たまに, 時折)(➤ 頻度的には両者とも30%程度); **(every) now and then**(不定期に); **from time to time**(やや定期的に) ▶私は時々弟とテニスをする I *sometimes* play tennis with my brother. ‖ 哲也は時々学校に遅刻する Tetsuya is *sometimes* late for school. (➤ be 動詞のときは sometimes はそのあとにくる) ‖《天気予報》晴れ時々曇り Clear, *occasionally* cloudy. ‖ 彼女とは水泳クラブで時々会うわ I meet her *(every) once in a while* at the swimming club. (➤ every がつくほうが強調的) ‖ 祖母は時々電話をくれる My grandmother calls me *(every) now and then*. ‖ 時々かき混ぜながらシチューを5分ほど熱します Heat the stew for about five minutes, stirring it *from time to time*.

2【その時その時】 ▶その公園に行けば時々の草花が楽しめる You can enjoy *seasonal* flowers in the park. ‖ あの男はその時々で言うことが違う He says different things *on different occasions*.

どきどき ▶手紙の封を切るときどきどきして手が震えた My heart *pounded* [*thudded* / *beat fast*] and my hands shook as I opened the letter. ‖ 初めて彼女の手を握ったときは胸がどきどきした The first time I held her hand, *my heart pounded*.

ときとして 時として →時に.

ときならぬ 時ならぬ unseasonable(季節外れの), unexpected(予想外の) ▶時ならぬ雷雨で帰宅の足が乱れた Because of an *unexpected* thunderstorm, there was confusion in the evening rush-hour traffic.

ときに 時に sometimes(ときどき) ; by the way(ところで) ▶人は時にうそと知りつつだまされることがある People are *sometimes* knowingly deceived.

ときには 時には sometimes ▶人と居るのは確かに楽しいが, 時にはひとりになりたいこともある I do enjoy being with people but *sometimes* I feel like being alone.

ときのひと 時の人 ▶彼女はその権威ある文学賞をもらって一躍時の人になった When she won the prestigious literary prize, she became *the woman of the hour* [became famous] overnight. (➤ 男性なら the man of the hour) ‖ 彼は今や時の人だ He *is much in the news* now.

ときふせる 説き伏せる persuade +㊐ ▶父を説き伏せてアメリカ留学を認めさせた I *persuaded* [*talked*] my father *into* sending me to the United States to study.

どぎまぎ ▶予想外の質問をされてどぎまぎした I *got flustered* [*rattled*] when I was asked an unexpected question.

1**ときめく 時めく** ▶Tさんは今を時めく大女優だ Ms. T is a great actress who is *riding a crest of popularity*.

2**ときめく** ▶美人に会うと胸がときめくのは当然だ It's natural for your heart to *beat fast* when you see a beautiful woman.

どぎも 度肝・度胆 ▶どぎもを抜かれるような事件 an *astonishing* incident ‖ 田中選手の場外ホームランにはどぎもを抜かれた I *was astounded* by Tanaka's out-of-the-park homer.

ドキュメンタリー a documentary
‖ドキュメンタリー映画 a documentary film.

1**どきょう 度胸** courage(勇気) ; nerve(ずぶとさ) ; 《インフォーマル》guts(肝っ玉) ▶度胸のある女性 a *brave* young woman ‖ 男は度胸 *Courage* makes a man. ‖ この崖からダイビングするには相当の度胸が要る It will take a lot of *nerve* [lots of *guts*] to dive from this cliff. ‖ 彼は度胸がない He has no *guts*. / He is timid. / He's a coward. ‖ 彼, なかなかいい度胸してるじゃないか Isn't he *daring* [*gutsy*] ! ‖ あんな度胸のない男は嫌いだ I hate *gutless* [*cowardly*] men like him.
▶度胸を据えてやってごらん *Gather your courage* and give it a try. ‖ 子供たちは度胸試しに墓地へ行った The children went to the cemetery *to play chicken* [*to dare each other*]. (➤ play chicken は2人以上が同時に, dare each other は1人ずつが「度胸試しをする」の意).

2**どきょう 読経** ▶お坊さんが読経を始めた The priest began *chanting a sutra*.

ときょうそう 徒競走 a footrace ▶徒競走をする run *a footrace* ‖ 息子は徒競走でびりだった My son came in last in *the footrace*.

どきり ▶ぼんやり窓の外を見ていたら先生に指されてどきりとした I *was startled* when the teacher called on me while I was looking vacantly out of the window. →どきっと.

とぎれとぎれ 途切れ途切れの broken ▶途切れ途切れのすすり泣き *broken* sobs ‖ 隣の部屋から話し声が途切れ途切れに聞こえてきた I heard *short snatches* of conversation from the next room.

とぎれる 途切れる break (off) ▶やっと車の流れが途切れたので道路を横断した When *there was* at last *a break* in the flow of traffic, I crossed the street. ‖ 会話が途切れてお互いに顔を見合わせた *There was a lull* in the conversation and we stared at each other. (➤ lull /lʌl/ は「途絶え」) ‖ 祖父の日記はその日で途切れていた My grandfather's diary *broke off* from that day. ‖ 私たちの文通は10年間途切れることなく続いた We exchanged letters for ten years *without a break*. ‖ チームの連勝は5で途切れた The team's winning streak *ended* at five games.

1**とく 得** (a) profit(利益) ; advantage(有利) ▶その株を買ってもあまり得にはならないと思う I am afraid you won't make much *profit* out of that stock. ‖ そんなことをしたって何の得にもならないよ *There's no profit* in doing that. / Doing that *won't help you in the least*. ‖ お宅のこの土地は今売ったほうが絶対得ですよ It'd *be* very *profitable* to sell this property of yours now. ‖ 進学とプロ入りと彼にとってどちらが得だろうか Which *is* more *to his advantage* [more *advantageous to* him], to go on to college or to become a pro player?
▶スーツケースは買うより借りたほうが得(＝経済的)かもしれない It might *be* more *economical* to rent a suitcase than to buy one. ‖ 英語ができると, 今の時代何かと得だよ Being able to communicate in English will *give you an edge* in this day and age. (➤ give an edge は「優位性を与える」の意のインフォーマルな表現) ‖ 年間購読の場合は2000円のお得になります You *can save* 2,000 yen if you apply for a yearly subscription. (➤ save は「(金銭などの無駄を)省く」).
☛ 得する (→見出語)

2**とく 徳** (a) virtue ▶徳の高い人 a person *of* (*high*) *virtue* ‖ あの僧の徳を慕う人は多い Numerous people admire the priest for his many *virtues*.

3**とく 解く・溶く** **1【問題を】** solve +㊐ ▶謎[難問]を解く *solve* a riddle [a difficult problem] ‖ 方程式を解く *solve* an equation ‖ 《クロスワードパズルで》15のヨコ[タテ]を解く *work out* 15 across [down] ‖ 1日かかってもこの問題を解いてみせる I'll *find the solution* to this problem, even if it takes all day.
2【ほどく】 untie +㊐, undo +㊐ (➤ 後者は「(包みなど)を開く」の意でも用いる) ▶彼は靴ひもを解いてきつく締め直した He *untied* the shoelaces and retied them tightly. ‖ 私は包みを解いて贈り物を取り出した I *opened* [*undid*] the package and took out the present.
3【解除する】 ▶禁止令を解く *lift* the ban ‖ リーダーの命令でゲリラたちは警戒態勢を解いた The guerillas *called off* the alert at the command of their leader. ‖ 私は任期が切れたので委員長の任を解かれた I *was relieved* of the chairmanship when my term of office was over. ‖ その課長は汚職により職を解かれた The section chief *was dismissed from* his post [job] for corruption.

4【怒り・誤解などを】▶どうしたら父の怒りを解くことができるだろうか I wonder how I can *calm* [*soothe*] my father's anger. ‖ 彼女の誤解を解くのは大変だった I had a hard time (in) *clearing up* her misunderstanding. (➤ in は通例省略する).

5【薄める】 dissolve /dɪzɑ́ːlv/ ＋目 ▶かたくり粉を水で溶く *dissolve* potato starch in water.

4**とく 説く** preach ＋目 (説いて勧める) ; explain ＋目 (説明する) ▶アメリカの思想家ソーローは簡素な生活をせよと説いた The American thinker Henry D. Thoreau *preached* [*advocated*] a simple life. ‖ 小さい子をいじめてはだめだと息子に説いて聞かせた I *explained* to my son that he should not bully small children.

とぐ 研ぐ・磨ぐ sharpen ＋目 ; whet /hwet/ ＋目 (といしで) ▶包丁を研ぐ *sharpen* a kitchen knife ‖ といしでナイフを研ぐ *sharpen* a knife on a whetstone / *whet* a knife on a stone ‖ 猫が縁側で爪を研いでいる The cat *is sharpening* its claws [nails] on the *engawa* (porch).

▶米を研ぐ *rinse* rice (➤ すすぎ洗いするとき) / *wash* rice (➤ ごしごし洗うとき).

1**どく 毒 1【毒物】** (a) poison ; venom /vénəm/ (蛇・蜂などの出す) ▶クモの毒 spider *venom* ‖ そのキノコには毒があるよ That mushroom is *poisonous* [*toxic*]. ‖ 毒をあおる *drink poison in one gulp* ‖ 王は毒をあおって死んだ The king *poisoned himself*. (➤「毒を飲む」は take poison).

ことわざ 毒をもって毒を制す Meet [Fight] evil with evil.

ことわざ 毒を食らわば皿まで After you eat the poison lick the plate. / You might as well be hanged for a sheep as for a lamb. (➤「子羊で絞首刑なら羊を盗んだほうがいい」の意の英語のことわざ).

‖**毒ガス** poison gas ‖ **毒キノコ** a poisonous mushroom ‖ **毒蛇** a poisonous snake.

2【害悪】 harm ▶ポルノサイトは青少年には毒だ Pornographic web (sites) *poison* [*harm*] young minds. ‖ たばこは体に毒なのでやめた I gave up smoking because it is *bad* for my health.

▶《慣用表現》あいつは毒にも薬にもならない男だ He is a guy who does *neither good nor harm*. / That guy's a cipher [a nobody].

☛ **毒する** (→見出語)

2**どく 退く** ▶そこをどけ! *Get out of my way!* ‖ すみません, 脇へどいてください Excuse me, but please *step aside*.

1**とくい 得意 1【上手である】** be good at

> 【文型】
> A が得意だ
> be good at A
> ➤ A は名詞・動名詞

▶岡さんはゴルフが得意だ Mr. Oka *is good at* golf. / Mr. Oka is a *good* golf player. ‖ 裕子は数学が得意だ Yuko *is good at* [*strong in*] math. ‖ きみの得意な学科は何? Which subjects *are* you *strong in*? / What *are* you *good at* at school? (➤ at が 2 つになることに注意).

▶あのレポーターは海外取材が得意だ Overseas reporting is that reporter's *specialty*. ‖ 母の得意料理はシチューです My mother's *special dish* [*specialty*] is stew. ‖ 社長は新年会でお得意の歌を披露した The president sang his *favorite* song at the New Year's party. ‖ 暗算は彼の得意中の得意だ He *is strongest in* mental arithmetic. / Mental arithmetic is his *forte*.

2【自慢・満足している】 be proud ▶彼は水泳大会で優勝して得意になっている He *is proud* that he won [*proud* of winning] the swim meet. ‖ 彼女は息子がホームランを打ったので得意になっている She *is elated* with her son's home run. (➤ be elated with は「…で歓喜する」) ‖ 英語の試験で満点を取ったからって得意になるなよ You shouldn't *crow* just because you got a perfect score on the English exam. (➤ crow には「(他人が嘆いているときに)自分だけ大得意になる」という含みがある) ‖ あの選手は三冠王になって得意の絶頂だろう (I suppose) that player must *be extremely happy and proud* after getting the triple crown. ‖ 新曲がヒットしたので彼女は得意満面だ She *is beaming with triumph* since her new song is a hit. ‖ 彼女は得意になって(＝調子に乗って)もう1曲歌った She *got carried away* and sang another song.

3【顧客】 a regular customer (常客) ▶佐藤はただいま得意先回りに出ております Sato is now visiting our *regular customers*.

☛ **不得意** (→見出語)

2**とくい 特異な** peculiar ; unique (類のない) ; idiosyncratic /ìdiəsɪŋkrǽṭɪk/ (性質・体質などが) ▶特異な例 a *peculiar* case ‖ 特異な(＝前例のない)事件 an *unprecedented* case ‖ 特異な才能の持ち主 a person of *unique* talent.

‖**特異体質** idiosyncrasy.

とくいく 徳育 moral education.

どぐう 土偶 a *dogu* ; an earthen figurine from the Jomon period (➤ 説明的な訳).

どくえんかい 独演会 a solo performance, a (solo) recital, a solo [one-man] show (➤ one-man は男性を指す形容詞なので, 性差を表さない solo を用いる傾向がある) ▶落語家の独演会 the *solo* [*one-man*] *show* of a rakugo storyteller ‖ 討論会といっても, 例の調子で彼の独演会みたいなものさ Even if it is called a discussion [debate], it will be his usual *solo* [*one-man*] *show*.

どくがく 独学の self-taught [-educated] ▶独学の人 a *self-taught* person ‖ 独学で外国語を学ぶには忍耐力が必要だ It takes patience to learn a foreign language *without a teacher* [*by yourself*]. ‖ 彼は独学で経済学をものにした He learned economics *on his own*. (➤ on one's own は「自分ひとりで」) ‖ 兄はデザインの勉強を独学でやった My brother is a *self-taught* designer.

とくぎ 特技 one's specialty /spéʃəlti/, (a) special talent ▶彼の特技は人を1分以内に笑わせることである His *specialty* is to be able to make anyone laugh within one minute. ‖ 私にはこれといった特技がない I have no *special talent(s)* to speak of.

どくけ 毒気 →どっけ.

どくさい 独裁 dictatorship

‖**独裁者** a dictator, a despot /déspɑːt/ ‖ **独裁政治** dictatorship, despotism.

とくさく 得策 ▶あの件には触れないほうが得策だよ It's *better* (for you) not to say anything about the matter.

とくさつ 特撮 ▶特撮シーン a *special-effects* scene (➤ special effects は「特殊効果」).

‖**特撮映画** a special-effects movie.

どくさつ 毒殺する poison ＋目 ▶大統領を毒殺する

poison the president ‖ ナポレオンは**毒殺**されたと主張する人もいる Some people assert that Napoleon *was poisoned to death*.

とくさん 特産 ▶マスカットは岡山県の**特産**(＝特産物)です Muscat grapes are a *special product* of Okayama Prefecture.

‖特産品 a (local) specialty.

とくし 特使 a **special envoy** /énvɔɪ/.

どくじ 独自の **original**(独創的な)；**unique**(無類の)；**independent**(ほかの影響を受けない) ▶一流の作家は**独自**の文体をもっている First-rate writers have their *original* [*unique*] styles. ‖どの国にもそれぞれ**独自の**習慣がある Each country has *its own* customs. ‖レポートにはほかの人の説ではなく**自分独自**の意見を書いてください In your paper you should write down not other people's theories but opinions *of your own*. ‖彼らはその事故に関して**独自の**調査を行った They made an *independent* investigation into that accident. ／They investigated that accident *independently*.

‖独自性 originality.

とくしか 篤志家 a **volunteer** /vɑ̀ːləntíəʳ/；a **charitable person**(慈善家).

1**とくしつ 特質** a **characteristic** /kæ̀rəktərístɪk/ ▶この論文は日本経済の**特質**を論じている This paper deals with the *characteristics* of the Japanese economy.

2**とくしつ 得失** **gain and loss**(得ることと失うこと)；**profit and loss**(利益と損失) ▶独身生活の**得失** the *advantages and disadvantages* of (the) single life **‖得失点差** a goal difference(サッカーの).

とくしゃ 特赦 a **special amnesty.**

どくしゃ 読者 a **reader**；a **subscriber**(定期購読者) ▶この雑誌には約10万人の**読者**がいる This magazine has *a readership* of about 100,000. (➤ readership は「読者数［層］」) ‖その作家は幅広い**読者層**を持つ The author has a wide *readership*.

とくしゅ 特殊な **special**(特別な)；**unique**(無類の) ▶**特殊**訓練を受けた犬 a *specially* trained dog ‖彼は一年中各地の縁日を渡り歩くという**特殊な**仕事をしている He has a very *special* [*unique*] job that takes him from one festival to another all year round.

‖特殊部隊 a special force, a commando unit ‖**特殊法人** a governmental corporation.

とくじゅ 特需 **special procurement.**

とくしゅう 特集 a **feature** 一㊐ **特集する** **feature** +㊀ ▶今週の『タイム』誌は日本を**特集している** This week's "Time" *features* Japan. ‖『ティーンズ』の**特集号**が来週出るそうだ They say *a special issue* [*number*] of "Teens" will be published next week.

‖特集記事 a feature, a cover story ‖**特集番組** a special program.

どくしゅう 独習・独修する **practice** [**learn**] **by oneself** ▶ギターを**独習する** *practice* playing the guitar *by oneself* ‖福沢諭吉は英語を**独修した** Fukuzawa Yukichi *taught himself* English.

どくしょ 読書 **reading** 一㊐ **読書する** **read** (a **book**) ▶秋の夜は**読書**をするのによい Autumn evenings are best for *reading*. ‖若いうちに**読書**の習慣をつけなさい Get into the habit of *reading* (*books*) while you are young. ‖息子は大の**読書好き**だ My son is *a great reader* [quite *a bookworm*]. (➤ 後者は「本の虫」の意).

‖読書会 a reading circle ‖**読書感想文** a book report ‖**読書室** a reading room ‖**読書週間** Book Week.

とくしょう 特賞 **the grand** [**highest**] **prize** ▶**特賞**はペアで1週間のハワイ旅行が5組の人に当たります The five *grand-prize* winning couples will receive a one-week trip to Hawaii.

とくじょう 特上 ▶**特上**ローストビーフ *prime* [*choice*] roast beef.

どくしょう 独唱 a (**vocal**) **solo** /sóʊloʊ/ ▶彼女はピアノに合わせて『冬の夜』を**独唱した** She *sang* "Winter Night" (*in*) *solo* with piano accompaniment. ／She *sang a solo* of "Winter Night" accompanied by a pianist.

‖独唱会 a (vocal) recital ‖**独唱者** a soloist /sóʊloʊɪst/, a solo singer.

とくしょく 特色 a **characteristic** /kæ̀rəktərístɪk/ (ほかから区別される点)；a (**special** ／**distinctive**) **feature**(人目を引く顕著な点)；**uniqueness**(独特であること, 唯一無二) ▶日本語の**特色** *characteristics* of the Japanese language ‖川端作品の最大の**特色** the most striking *feature* of Kawabata's works ‖越後人の**特色**は勤勉さだと言われる It is said that diligence is (*a*) *characteristic* [*a trait*] of the people in Echigo. (➤ a がつかない場合の characteristic は形容詞) ‖ルノワールの**特色**は暖かみのある色だ Renoir *is characterized by* the warmth of his colors. ‖**特色のある**大学に入りたい I want to get into a university *with a unique character*. ‖これといった**特色のない**小さな町 a small town with *no* (*special*) *features* to speak of.

とくしん 得心 ▶あんな説明では**得心**できない I can't *be convinced* by an explanation like that.

どくしん 独身の **single**；**unmarried**(未婚の) ▶**独身の**女性 a *single* [*an unmarried*] woman ‖彼は**独身**だ He is *single*. ／He is *a bachelor*. (➤ bachelor は「独身男性」の意であるが, 時に結婚歴のある独身男性を指す；日常語は single [unmarried] man) ‖ぼくの姉はまだ**独身**です My sister is still *single* [*unmarried*]. ‖ **対話** 「なぜ結婚しないんだい？」「もう少し**独身**を楽しみたいんだ」 "Why don't you get married?" "I want to enjoy life as *a single* for a while longer."

▶彼は**独身時代**の自由を懐かしがっている He misses the freedom he had *before he was married*. ‖妻が実家に帰ったのでぼくは2週間**独身生活**をせざるを得なかった My wife went back to her parents' home and I had to *bach it* for two weeks. (➤ bach /bætʃ/ は bachelor から出たインフォーマルな語).

‖独身者 a single [an unmarried] person ‖**独身寮** a dormitory for single [unmarried] employees.

1**どくしんじゅつ 読心術** **mind reading.**

2**どくしんじゅつ 読唇術** **lip-reading.**

とくする 得する **gain profits** ▶あんな男を助けてやっても**得する**ことなんか何もないぞ You'll *gain nothing* by helping that man. ‖ 2万円のかばんを1万5000円で買って5000円**得した**よ I bought a 20,000-yen bag for 15,000 yen and *saved* 5,000 yen. →得.

どくする 毒する **poison** +㊀ ▶最近の子供たちは低俗なテレビ番組に**毒されている** These days, children's minds are *being poisoned* by vulgar TV programs.

1**とくせい 特製** ▶**特製**の靴 shoes *of special make* ‖このラーメンは当店**特製**のスープを使っております This ramen is made with our own *special* soup stock. ‖**特製品** a specially made article.

2**とくせい 特性** a **characteristic**（特徴）; an **attribute**（属性）; a **property**（特質）; a **trait**（生活・習慣から生まれた特色）▶このシャツは洗濯してもしわにならないという**特性**を持っている The *special characteristic* of this shirt is that it doesn't wrinkle after washing. ‖その物質の化学的**特性** the chemical *properties* of the substance.

どくせい 毒性 **toxicity** /tɑ:ksísəṭi/ ▶**毒性の強い**化学薬品 a *highly toxic* [*poisonous*] chemical.

とくせつ 特設 ▶**特設**電話 a *specially installed* telephone ‖ポップコンサートのための**特設**ステージ a stage *set up specially* for a pop concert.

どくぜつ 毒舌 a **sharp** [**bitter**] **tongue** /tʌŋ/ ▶その評論家は**毒舌**で有名だ That critic is well known for his *sharp* [*acerbic*] *tongue*. (➤ acerbic は「辛らつな」の意の堅い語)
‖**毒舌家** a person who has a sharp [bitter] tongue.

とくせん 特選 ▶彼の絵は県のコンクールで**特選**になった His picture won [was awarded] *the highest honors* in the prefectural contest.
‖**特選品** choice goods.

どくせん 独占 a **monopoly** /mənɑ́:pəli/ 一動 **独占する** **monopolize** /mənɑ́:pəlaɪz/ +㊐ ▶江戸時代，オランダは日本との貿易を**独占していた** In the Edo era, the Netherlands *monopolized* [*had a monopoly on*] (all) trade with Japan. ‖今度のテストでは上位 10 人を女子が**独占した** The top ten scorers on this test were all girls. ／Girls got the top ten scores on this test. ‖きみの愛を**独占したい** I want to *have* your love (*all*) *to myself*. ‖彼女は**独占欲が強い** She *is very possessive*. ／She *wants to have everything all to herself*. ‖**独占企業** a monopoly (firm) ‖**独占禁止法** (an) antitrust law.

どくぜんてき 独善的な **self-righteous** /sèlfráɪtʃəs/ ▶**独善的な**人 a *self-righteous* person ‖**独善的な**考え方をする think *self-righteously* ‖あの人は何事にもひどく**独善的**（＝独断的）だ He's very *dogmatic* about everything.

どくそ 毒素 a **poisonous substance**, a **toxin** /tɑ́:ksɪn/ (➤ 後者は専門用語).

とくそう 特捜 a **special investigation.**

1**どくそう 独創** ▶**独創的な**アイデア an *original* idea ‖あの小説家は模倣はうまいが，**独創性**に欠ける That novelist is good at imitating, but lacks *originality* [*creativity*]. (➤ creativity は他との違いより，これまでなかったものを作り出す「創造性」).

2**どくそう 独奏** a **solo** /sóʊloʊ/ ▶彼は多くの聴衆の前でピアノを**独奏した** He *played a* piano *solo* [gave a piano recital] before a large audience.
‖**独奏会** a recital ‖**独奏者** a soloist /sóʊloʊɪst/.

3**どくそう 独走** ▶そのマラソンは30キロ地点を過ぎて無名選手の**独走となった** An unknown runner *led the race* after the 30-kilometer point in the marathon.

とくそく 督促 ▶税務署から税金を払うよう**督促された** The tax office *ordered* me to pay my taxes. (➤ order は「命令する」) ‖ 3 か月家賃を滞納したら家主から**督促状**が来た After I didn't pay rent for three months, I received *a demand letter* from the landlord. (➤「(税金などの)督促状」は reminder という).

ドクター a **doctor**（博士，医者）▶彼は**ドクターストップ**でたばこをやめた He stopped smoking *on doctor's orders*.

> **危ないカタカナ語✸ドクター**
> **1** 大学院の博士課程を指す「ドクターコース」は doctoral program とか doctorate program といい，通例 course は用いない.
> **2** ボクシングで，負傷した選手に対して(医師の勧めで)試合を中止することを「ドクターストップ」というが，これも和製語. the doctor's order to stop the fight のように説明的にいう.

‖**ドクターヘリ** an air ambulance, a medical helicopter ‖**オーバードクター** an unemployed Ph.D.

とくだい 特大の **king-size(d)**; **outsize(d)**（衣服などが）▶**特大の**ベッド a *king-size(d)* bed ‖**特大の**ステーキ an *extra-large* [*extra-big*] steak.
‖**特大サイズコーナー** the outsize (clothing) department ‖(雑誌の)**新春特大号** the special enlarged New Year issue.

とくたいせい 特待生 a **scholarship student.**

とくだね 特種 a **scoop**, an **exclusive** (**news story**) ▶その新聞は汚職官僚に関する**特種で他紙を出し抜いた** The newspaper *scooped* the rival papers with a report on corrupt officials. ‖これはうちの社だけの**特種**だ This is our *exclusive news story*.

ドクダミ 《植物》(a) ***dokudami***.

どくだん 独断 an **arbitrary** /ɑ́:ʳbətreri/ **decision** ▶その問題は私の**独断では**決められません I can't decide the matter *on my own authority* [*at my own discretion*]. ‖彼の意見は**独断的**すぎる His opinion is too *dogmatic*.

どくだんじょう 独壇場 ▶腕相撲ならぼくの**独壇場だ** When it comes to arm wrestling, I *am unrivaled* [*am unchallenged*]. ‖(体操の)跳馬では彼女の**独壇場だった** She *had no rivals* in the long horse vault.

とぐち 戸口 a **doorway** ▶**戸口**にいつまでも立ち止まってるなよ. 寒いじゃないか Don't stay *in the doorway* [*at the door*] so long. Aren't you cold?

とくちゅう 特注 (a) **special order**
‖**特注品** a specially ordered item, a custom-made item.

1**とくちょう 特徴** a **characteristic** /kæ̀rəktərístɪk/（ほかから区別される点）; a **feature**（人目を引く顕著な特色）; a **peculiarity** /pɪkjù:liǽrəṭi/（独特な点）一形 **特徴的な** **characteristic** ▶日本人の**特徴**を１つ挙げなさい Name one *characteristic* [*trait*] of the Japanese people. ‖日本語の**特徴**の１つにその混合的な書き表し方(＝かなと漢字の交ぜ書き)がある One of the *features* of the Japanese language is its hybrid writing system. ‖その政治家は**特徴のない**顔をしている That politician has a *featureless* face. ‖迷子さんには何か目立つ**特徴**がありますか Does the lost child have any noticeable *characteristics*? ‖彼の字には**特徴がある** His penmanship [writing] is *distinctive*. (➤ distinctive は「ほかの人との区別の目安になる」) ‖彼は目が大きいのが**特徴だ** He's *distinguishable* by his large eyes. (➤「大きな目がほかの人と大きく違う」の意) ‖ああいう品の無い話し方があの人の**特徴**なんですよ That vulgar way of talking is *characteristic* of him. ‖(病気の)**特徴的な**症状 a *characteristic* symptom (of a disease) ‖祖父は**特徴のある**歩き方をする My grandfather has a *unique* way of walking. (➤ unique は他にない「独特の」) ‖盗まれた

かばんの特徴を言ってください Please *describe* the stolen bag. (➤ describe は「形などをことばで表す」).

[2]**とくちょう 特長** a **strong point** ▶カヤックの特長は安定性の良いことだ The *strong point* of a kayak is its stability.

どくづく 毒づく ▶怒った客は店員に毒づいた The angry shopper *swore* at the salesclerk.

とくてい 特定の **specific** /spəsífɪk/ (具体的な, 明確な) ; **particular**(ほかでもないその) 一動 特定する **specify** +目 (指定する) ; **identify** +目 (身元を確認する) ▶私の発言は特定の人を指したものではない My remarks were not aimed at any *particular* person [at anyone *in particular*]. ‖ 警察はまだ犯人を特定できないでいる The police are still unable to *identify* the culprit [*determine* who the culprit is]. ‖ 医師は私の頭痛の原因を特定できなかった The doctor wasn't able to *specify* [*pinpoint*] the cause of my headache.

‖特定外来生物 an invasive alien species (➤ 《略》IAS).

[1]**とくてん 得点** **1【スポーツ】** a **score**(総得点 ; どのスポーツにも使える) ; a **point**(バレーボール・テニス・ラグビーなどの) ; a **goal**(アイスホッケー・サッカーの) ; a **run**(野球・クリケットの) ▶得点はどうなっていますか What's the *score* (now)? ‖ その体操選手はつり輪で得点9.5をあげた The gymnast *earned* 9.5 on the rings. ‖ 相手のミスで日本代表チームは得点を重ねた The Japanese national team *racked up* [*piled up*] *points* because of the opponents' errors. ‖ 私たちは7回の表に3点得点した We *got* [*scored*] three *runs* in the top of the seventh inning. ‖ 私たちは相手投手に8回まで無得点に抑えられた We were kept *runless* [*scoreless*] by the opposing pitcher for eight innings.

‖得点王 the top [leading] scorer ‖ 得点表 a scorebook(ノート式の) ; a scorecard(カード式の) ‖ 得点表示板 a scoreboard.

2【成績】 a **score**(総得点) ; a **point**, a **mark**(テストの点数など) ▶英語の得点は70点だった I got *a score* of 70 [70 *points*] in English. ‖ 先生はテストの得点を高い順に発表した The teacher announced our *test scores* beginning with the highest.

☛ 無得点 (→見出語)

[2]**とくてん 特典** a **privilege** /prívəlɪdʒ/ (特権) ; an **advantage**(利点) ; a **perk** [**perquisite**] (職務上の ; perk は通例複数形 perks の形で用いる) ▶成績優秀者には授業料全額免除の特典があります Superior students can enjoy the *privilege* of total exemption from tuition. ‖ 正会員の特典は次のとおりです The *privileges* [*advantages*] of regular membership are as follows.

とくとう 特等 **the highest prize**

‖特等席 a special seat.

とくとく 得々と **proudly** ▶おじは自分が若い頃いかに女性にもてたかを得々としゃべった My uncle talked *proudly* about how popular he was among girls when he was young.

どくとく 独特の **distinctive** (ほかとの違いを示す) ; **unique**(無類の) ; **peculiar**(特有の) ▶彼は独特のしゃべり方をする He has a *distinctive* way of talking. ‖ この絵には独特の美しさがある This picture has a *unique* beauty. / This picture has a beauty *all its own*. ‖ 年末にベートーベンの第九を演奏することは日本独特の風習だ Performing Beethoven's Ninth Symphony at the end of the year is a custom *unique* [*peculiar*] to Japan. ‖ ジムはアメリカ人独特の親しみを込めた身ぶりで話しかけてきた Jim spoke to me with the friendly hand gestures (which are) so *characteristic of* Americans. (➤ characteristic of は「…の特性を示す」).

どくどく ▶ナイフで切った傷口から血がどくどくと出てきた Blood *gushed out* of the knife wound.

どくどくしい 毒々しい ▶毒々しい(=いかにも毒がありそうな)キノコ a *poisonous-looking* mushroom ‖ 彼女は毒々しい(=どぎつい)化粧をしている She wears *very heavy* make-up.

とくに 特に **especially, specially ; particularly**

語法 especially と specially は同義に用いることもあるが, 一般的に言えば, especially は「(同種の中で1つだけを強調して)特に」, specially は「(目的・用途に合わせて)特に」の意で用いられる. particularly は「顕著に」の意.

▶私はスペインの, 特にアンダルシア地方に行ってみたい I'd like to visit Spain, *especially* Andalusia. ‖ 中間テストでは特に理科が悪かった I did *especially* poorly in science in the midterm examinations. ‖ このアイスクリームは特においしい This ice cream is *particularly* good.

▶このミートパイは特にあなたのために作りました I made these meat pies *specially* for you. ‖ このブローチは主人が特に私にとタイで買って来てくれたものです My husband bought this brooch *specially* for me while he was in Thailand. ‖ 何か特に言いたいことはありませんか Do you have anything you want to tell us *in particular*? ‖ あすは特に予定はありませんから一日中家に居ます I have no *special* [*particular*] plans for tomorrow [have nothing *special* to do tomorrow], so I'll be home all day. ‖ 特に話すことは無いよ I have nothing *special* to tell you [talk to you] about.

とくにん 特任

‖特任教授 a specially appointed professor ‖ 特任研究員 a specially appointed researcher [research scholar].

とくは 特派する ▶大統領は女王への書簡を持たせて使者を特派した The President *dispatched* his messenger with a letter for the Queen.

どくは 読破する **read through** ▶私は全8巻の小説をとうとう読破した I at last *read through* the 8-volume novel.

とくばい 特売 a (**bargain**) **sale**(➤ bargain はつけないほうがふつう) ▶あの店ではメロンの特売をやっている They are having *a sale* on melons at that store. / That store is *selling* melons *at a special price*. ‖ このスーツは特売で買った I bought this suit *at a sale*.

‖特売場 a bargain floor ; a bargain basement (➤ 英米のデパートでは地階にあることから) ; a bargain counter(売り台) ‖ 特売日 a special bargain day ‖ 特売品 a bargain, a sale item.

とくはいん 特派員 a (**special**) **correspondent** ▶父は朝日新聞の特派員としてニューヨークに駐在しています My father is stationed in New York as *a correspondent* for the "Asahi."

どくはく 独白 a **monologue**.

とくひつ 特筆 ▶2人の日本人化学者のノーベル賞受賞はその年の特筆すべき出来事であった Two Japanese chemists' winning the Nobel Prizes was a *memorable* event of that year.

とくひょう 得票 **the number of votes polled** ▶彼女は2万票を得票した She *polled* twenty thousand votes. ‖ 田中氏の得票数は予想より5000票少なかった Mr. Tanaka got 5,000 fewer votes than he had counted on.

どくぶつ 毒物 a **poisonous** [**toxic**] **substance**
‖**毒物劇薬取扱者** an authorized handler of toxic substances.

とくべつ 特別な special ; particular (ふつう以上の) ; **exceptional** (例外的な) **━副 特別に specially, especially, exceptionally ; particularly** ⇀特に ▶**特別な**友達 a *special* friend ‖ **特別に**デザインしたかばん a *specially* designed bag ‖ 7月6日は私にとって**特別な**日です July 6 is a (very) *special* day for me. ‖ この書類には**特別な**注意を払ってください Please handle these documents with *special* care.
▶ことしの夏は**特別**暑い It is *exceptionally* [*unusually*] hot this summer. (➤ unusually は「いつになく」) ‖ **特別**あなたに言いたいことはありません I have nothing *particular* to tell you. ‖ 彼だけ**特別扱い**するわけにはいきません We can't give *special treatment* to just him.
‖**特別国会** an extraordinary /ɪkstrɔ́ːʳdneri/ session of the Diet ‖ **特別番組** a special program ‖ **特別養護老人ホーム** a special nursing home for the elderly ‖ **特別料金** an extra charge (余分に取られる) ; a specially reduced rate(割引).

どくぼう 独房 an **isolation cell**, a **single cell.**

とくほん 読本 a **reader.**

どくみ 毒見をする taste food to see if it contains poison.

1**とくめい 匿名 anonymity** /æ̀nənímət̬i/ **━形 匿名の anonymous** /ənɑ́ːnɪməs/ ▶**匿名**を条件に話す speak on condition of *anonymity* ‖ **匿名の**投書 an *anonymous* letter ‖ 《投稿などで》**匿名希望** *Wish to remain anonymous* ‖ インターネットの**匿名性**を利用して不法行為をする take advantage of *the anonymity* of the Internet for illegal purposes ‖ **匿名で**文句を言うのは卑劣だ It is cowardly to complain *anonymously.* ‖ **匿名の**方から100万円のご寄付を頂きました We've received one million yen from an *anonymous* person. **《参考》** (1)匿名で寄付をする人の中には A well-wisher (人々の幸福を願う者)とだけ書く人が少なくない. (2)寄付者が誰かわかっているが匿名にしておくという場合には Someone who shall remain nameless [who asked that his [her] name be withheld] donated one million yen. のようにいう.

2**とくめい 特命** a **special mission.**

とくやく 特約 a **special contract.**

どくやく 毒薬 poison ▶**毒薬**を飲んで自殺する commit suicide by taking *poison* / poison oneself.

とくやくてん 特約店 an **authorized dealership** [**distributor**].

とくゆう 特有の unique 《to》, **peculiar** 《to》(独特の), **distinctive** (ほかとの違いを示す) ; **characteristic** 《of》 (…の特性を示す)
▶てれると頭をかくのは日本人**特有の**癖だ The habit of scratching their heads when embarrassed is *unique to* Japanese people. ‖ これは青年期**特有の**現象だ This phenomenon is *peculiar* [*unique*] *to* young people. ‖ ニンニクには**特有の**匂いがある Garlic has a *distinctive* smell. / Garlic has a smell *of its own.* ‖ 若者たちは時々**彼ら特有の**ことばで話をする Young people sometimes talk in a language *all their own.*

とくよう 徳用の economical /ìːkənɑ́ːmɪkəl/ ▶これは(燃料が少なくて済む)**徳用の**ガス台だ This is an *economical* stove.
‖**徳用品** an economical product.

どくりつ 独立 independence ━形 独立の independent ━動 (…から) **独立する become independent** 《of》 ▶1960年代にアフリカでは多くの国が**独立**を勝ち取った In the 1960s many African countries won [gained] their *independence.*
▶姉は親から**独立して**生計を立てている My sister *is* (*financially*) *independent of* our parents and supports herself. / My sister lives on her own. (➤ on one's own は「(他人に頼らず)ひとりで」) ‖ 彼は**独立心が旺盛**で, 親から**独立して**事業を始めた He is so *independent* that he left his parents and started a business *on his own.* ‖ きみたちは大学を卒業したら**経済的に独立**すべきだ You should *become financially independent* as soon as you graduate from college.
▶わが社は各部門の**独立採算制**を採用している Our company has a system in which each department has *an independent accounting system.*
‖**独立運動** an independence movement ‖ **独立記念日** Independence Day ‖ **独立国(家)** an independent state [country] ‖ **独立戦争** a war of independence.

どくりょく 独力で on one's own (自力で) ; **by oneself** (一人で) ▶遭難者数人が**独力で**浜辺に泳ぎ着いた Several victims swam to the shore *on their own.* ‖ この仕事は**独力で**やり遂げたい I want to do this work *on my own.* ‖ 母はその店を**独力で**経営している My mother runs the shop *by herself* [*alone*]. (➤ alone は「だれの助けもなく, 一人ぼっちで」でネガティブな響きがある) ‖ うちの社長は**独力で**今の地位を築いた人だよ Our boss is a *self-made man.* (➤ 俗に言う「たたき上げの人」) / Our boss *pulled himself up by his own bootstraps.* (➤ 文字どおりには「自分の靴のつまみ皮を引っ張って自分を持ち上げる」の意)

とくれい 特例 a **special case** ; an **exception** (例外) ▶今回は**特例**としましょう I'll make *an exception* in this case.

とぐろ ▶目の前に蛇が**とぐろ**を巻いていた I saw a snake *lying in a coil* [*coiling up*] in front of me.
▶《慣用表現》連中は朝からゲームセンターで**とぐろを巻いて**(＝たむろして)いる That bunch has been *hanging around* the amusement arcade since morning.

どくろ 髑髏 a **skull**
‖**どくろマーク**(毒薬の印の) a skull and crossbones.

とげ 棘・刺 a **thorn** (バラ・サンザシなどの) ; a **spine** (サボテン・硬骨魚などの) ; a **splinter** (木材などの) ; a **prickle** (動植物の表皮の)

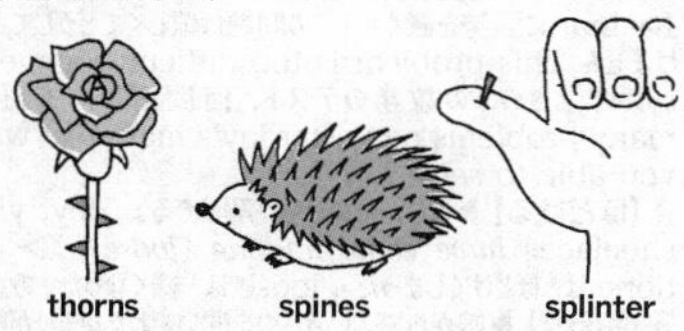

▶バラには**とげ**がある Roses have *thorns.* / There is no rose without *a thorn.* (➤ 後者は「楽あれば苦あり」の意の英語のことわざ) ‖ サボテンは**とげ**で覆われている Cactuses are covered with *spines.* ‖ このつるには**とげ**がいっぱいついている This vine is full of *prickles.* ‖

あら, 指にとげが刺さっちゃったわ Ah, I got *a splinter* in my finger.
▶《比喩的》あいつはとげのある言い方をする He has a *barbed* tongue. ／He always makes *acerbic* comments.（➤ acerbic /əsə́ːʳbɪk/ は「辛辣な」）.
‖とげ抜き (a pair of) tweezers.

とけあう 溶け合う ▶みんなの心が一つに溶け合ってすばらしい演奏になった The performers' hearts *merged* [*fused into one*] and they gave a stunning performance.

とけい 時計 a **watch**（腕時計, 懐中時計）; a **clock**（置き時計, 掛け時計）▶時計を進める［遅らせる］put a *watch* forward [backward] ‖私の時計は時刻がGPS 信号で自動的に合うようになっている My *watch* is automatically set by a GPS time signal. ‖鍵のダイヤルを左上から時計回りに回しなさい Rotate the dial of the lock *clockwise* from top left. ‖このはと時計は正確だ［よく狂う］This *cuckoo clock* keeps good [bad] time. ‖この時計は1日に数秒進む［遅れる］This *watch* gains [loses] a few seconds each day. ‖ 対話「その時計は合ってるの？」「いや, 2分遅れてる［進んでる］」"Is that *watch* accurate?" "No. It's two minutes slow [fast]."
‖時計台 a clock tower.

> **逆引き熟語 ○○時計**
> アナログ時計 an analog watch [clock] ／腕時計 a wristwatch ／置き時計 a table clock ／懐中時計 a pocket [fob] watch ／掛け時計 a hanging clock, a wall clock ／原子時計 an atomic clock ／水中時計 an underwater watch ／砂時計 a sandglass, an hourglass（➤ 前者がふつう）／体内時計 one's body clock ／デジタル時計 a digital watch [clock] ／電波時計 a radio [radio-controlled] clock ／柱時計 a wall clock ／日時計 a solar [sun] clock, sundial ／振り子時計 a pendulum clock ／目覚まし時計 an alarm clock ／ラジオ時計 a clock radio

とけこむ 溶け込む ▶きみならきっとチームに溶け込めるさ I'm sure you will *fit* in with our team *very nicely*.

どげざ 土下座 ▶あいつが土下座して謝ってもやつの罪は許せない His crime is unforgivable even if he *falls* [*goes down*] *on his knees* to ask for forgiveness.

とげとげしい ▶とげとげしい雰囲気が彼のユーモラスなジョークで和んだ The *hostile* atmosphere was relieved by his humorous joke.（➤ hostile /hɑ́ːstl/ は「敵意のある」）.

とける 解ける・溶ける **1【問題などが解決する】be solved** ▶それで謎が解けたぞ That *solves* the riddle!（➤ that に強勢を置く）‖この問題は難しくてどうしても解けません This problem is too difficult for me to *solve*. ‖きのうの数学のテスト, 何問解けた？ How many problems on yesterday's math test were you able to *solve*?
2【ほどける】▶ほら, 靴のひもが解けてるよ Hey, your shoelaces *have come undone* [*loose*].（➤ undone は「ほどけてしまった」, loose は「緩くなった」の意）.
3【和らぐ】▶娘から事のいきさつを聞いてわだかまりが解けた My hard feelings *disappeared* [*vanished* ／ *melted away*] when I learned from my daughter how it had happened. ‖彼のジョークでその場の緊張が解けた His joke *broke the ice*.（➤ break the ice は「緊張をほぐす」）‖彼の誠意ある謝罪に友人の怒りも解けた His friend's *anger was calmed* by his sincere apology.
4【液状になる】melt（固体が熱などによって）; **thaw** /θɔː/（陽気がよくなって徐々に）▶雪はまもなく解ける The snow will soon *melt* away [off]. ‖北海道では雪や氷は4月になって解ける In Hokkaido the snow and ice *melt* [the ground *thaws*] in April. ‖スズは熱で簡単に溶ける Tin *melts* easily with heat. ‖猛暑で道路のアスファルトが溶けている The asphalt on the road *became soft and sticky* in the blazing heat.
5【液体中に混じり合う】dissolve /dɪzɑ́ːlv/ ▶砂糖は水に溶ける Sugar *dissolves* in water.

とげる 遂げる **achieve** +目, **attain** +目（努力の末に; 後者には「成功するかどうかはわからないが」という含みがある）; **accomplish** +目（成し遂げる）▶何としても目的を遂げるつもりだ I will *achieve* [*attain*] my goal no matter what. ／I will *accomplish* my objective at any cost.
▶20世紀後半, 宇宙科学は驚くべき発展を遂げた Space science *achieved* wonderful developments in the latter half of the 20th century. ／Space science *made* remarkable advances [progress] in the latter half of the 20th century. ‖横綱は3場所連続優勝を遂げた The yokozuna *succeeded in* winning the championship three tournaments running.

どける 退ける **take away** ▶それ, どけてよ *Take* that *away*, please. ‖きみの車をどけてくれないか Could you *move* your car, please? ‖私の足を踏んでるんですけど, どけてくださる？ Would you please *get* your foot *off* my toe? ‖歩道の雪をどける *clear* [*get rid of*] the snow from the sidewalk.

どけん 土建
‖土建会社 a construction company ‖土建業 the construction industry ‖土建屋 a constructor; a building contractor /kɑ́ːntræktəʳ/（請負業者）.

とこ 床 a **bed**; **futon**（布団）▶床に就く *go to bed* ‖父はもう床に就いています Father *has* already *gone to bed*. ‖床に入って本を読むのは目に悪い Reading *in bed* is bad for the eyes. ‖けさはとても寒くてすぐには床を離れられなかった This morning it was so cold that it was hard to *get out of bed*.
▶彼女は3日前からかぜで床に就いている She *has been* (*ill*) *in bed* with a cold for three days. ‖母は来月には床を離れることができるでしょう My mother should be able to *leave her* (*sick*) *bed* next month.

どこ **1【場所】where** ▶《待ち合わせのときに》きみはどこに居る？ *Where* will I find [see] you? ／*Where* will you be? ‖案内所はどこですか *Where's* the information desk? ‖この道はどこに出ますか *Where* does this road lead (*to*)? ‖ぼくの辞書, どこに行ったかな？ *Where* did my dictionary go? ‖ 対話「ここはどこですか」「青山通りです」"*Where am I* [*are we*] (now)?" "You are on Aoyama Avenue."（➤（×）Where is here? とは言わない）‖ 対話「どこでお会いしましょうか」「どこでも結構です」"*Where* shall we meet?" "*Any place* that's convenient for you. ／*Anywhere* is fine with me."
▶この夏はどこへ行くつもり？ *Where* are you going this summer? ‖どこへ行っても日本の道路は混んでいる The roads in Japan are crowded *no matter*

where you go. ‖ 今度の夏休みはどこへでも好きな所へ連れていくよ I'll take you *wherever* you like during the summer vacation.

▶祖父は今年90歳になりますが，**別にどこといって悪いところはありません** My grandfather will be 90 years old this year, but *he's still in good health*.

2【特定の箇所・点】what ▶このブラウス，**どこの**お店で買ったの？ At *which* [*what*] store did you buy this blouse？（➤ which は「(複数ある店の)どこの」, what は「何という名の」）／*Where* did you buy this blouse？‖ **どこの会社**にお勤めですか *What company* do you work for？／*Who* do you work for？（● 後者は「誰の下で働いているのですか」の意にもなる.「どこにお勤めですか」なら Where do you work？）‖ あなたは**どこの国**からいらしたのですか *What* country are you from？‖ **どこの**高校を出たんですか *Which* [*What*] high school did you go to？‖ きみのデジカメ，**どこの**？ *What make is* your digital camera？／*Who made* [*makes*] your digital camera？‖ この学校の**どこが**いいのですか *What* do you like about this school？／*What*'s good about this school？‖ 就職は**どこに**決まりましたか *Where* did you get a job？‖ **対話**「どこの学校［大学］に行ってるの？」「平成高校［大学］です」"*Where* do you go to school [college]？" "Heisei High School [University]." ‖ タイの首都は**どこ**ですか *What* is the capital of Thailand？（● Where is ...? とすると「タイの首都はどこにありますか」という地理的な位置を聞く文になる）.‖「メイド・イン・P.R.C.」の P.R.C. って**どこ**ですか *What* is this P.R.C. in "Made in P.R.C."？

▶あんな男の**どこが**いいのよ *What*'s so good about him？‖ **対話**「どこが具合が悪いですか」「頭が痛いんです」"*What* seems to be the problem？" "I have a headache."

☞ どことなく，どこにでも，どこにも，どこまで，どこもかしこも（→見出語）

とこう 渡航する go overseas [abroad] ▶渡航手続きを済ませる go through the *formalities for one's travel overseas* [*abroad*] ‖ **海外渡航者**は年々増加している The number of *people traveling overseas* [*abroad*] is increasing every year.

どごう 怒号 angry shouts, a roar ▶怒号が飛び交った *Angry shouts* flew back and forth. ‖ 観客のやじと**怒号** the heckling and *shouting* of the audience.

どこか 1【場所】somewhere, someplace; anywhere, anyplace

語法 前の２語は主に肯定文・命令文で，あとの２語は主に否定文・疑問文で用いる. someplace, anyplace はいずれも《米・インフォーマル》の用法.

▶あの人には**どこか**で会ったような気がする I know I've met him *somewhere* before.（➤ この I know は「確かではないけど」の意）‖ 彼は郊外の**どこか**に家を買ったそうだ I hear he has bought a house *somewhere* in the suburbs. ‖ **どこか**暖かい国へ行きたいなあ I'd like to go to *some* warmer country. ‖ **どこか**近くの喫茶店でおしゃべりしましょう Let's have a chat at a coffee shop near here.（➤ a coffee shop で不特定の喫茶店を表す）‖ そのかばん，**どこかに**（＝どこでもいいから）置いておいてもいいよ You can put that bag *anyplace*. ‖ **対話**「きのう，どこかへ行ったの？」「いや，どこへも行かなかった」"Did you go *anywhere* yesterday？" "No, I didn't go anywhere."（➤ Yes か No かわからない疑問文では anywhere を使う）.

2【どことなく】 ▶彼女には**どこか**人を引き付けるところがある There is *something* about her that attracts people. ‖ あの人の服装は**どこか**だらしがない *Somehow* he always looks sloppy [scruffy]. ‖ 彼には**どこか**卑劣なところがある He has *a* mean *streak* in him.（➤ streak /striːk/ は「(性格の一部を成す)特質」）.

どこから from where ▶《授業で》えーと，きょうは**どこから**でしたっけ Well, *where* are we supposed to start today？／*How far* did we get？（➤ 後者は「(前回)どこまでやったっけ？」の意）‖《出身地を聞いて》きみ，九州の**どこから**来たの？ *What* [*Which*] *part of* Kyushu are you *from*？／*Where* in Kyushu do you come *from*？‖ この猫，一体**どこから**来たんだろう *Where* on earth did this cat come *from*？‖ 部屋は**どこから**手をつけたらいいのかわからないほど散らかっている The room is in such a mess that I don't know *where* to start (cleaning). ‖ あの人はもう70だけど，**どこから見ても**50代にしか見えない He looks like he's in his fifties *in every way*, though he's actually seventy.

どこからともなく ▶**どこからともなく**大勢の人が集まって来た A crowd gathered *out of* [gathered *from*] *nowhere*.

とこずれ 床擦れ a bedsore ▶寝たきりのお年寄りに**床擦れ**ができてしまった The bed-ridden elderly man developed *bedsores*.

とことこ ▶知らない子供が**とことこ**あとをついて来る Some child I don't know is *toddling* after me.

どことなく ▶彼女には**どことなく**上品なところがある There is *something* graceful about her. ‖ 彼は**どことなく**（＝どういう訳か）憎めない *Somehow* I can't dislike him.

とことん ▶彼らは**とことん**（＝最後まで）戦う決心をした They made up their minds to fight *to the last* [*end*]. ‖ 彼らはその問題についてお互いに**とことん**（＝徹底的に）話し合うつもりでいる They are going to discuss the problem *thoroughly* with each other. ‖ 彼は１つのことを**とことんやり抜く**というタイプではない He is not the type that *sticks to something and does it thoroughly*.

とこなつ 常夏 ▶**常夏**の国ハワイ Hawaii, the land of *perpetual summer* ‖ タヒチは**常夏**の島として知られる Tahiti is known as an island of *everlasting summer*.

どこにでも anywhere,《主に米・インフォーマル》**anyplace; everywhere**（あらゆる所に）▶そんなの今買わなくても，ハワイへ行けば**どこにでも**売ってるよ You don't need to buy a thing like that now. You can find one *anywhere* in Hawaii. ‖ 私の犬は私の行く所は**どこにでも**ついて来る My dog follows me *wherever* I go.

→どこにも.

どこにも anywhere,《主に米・インフォーマル》**anyplace** ▶財布が**どこにも**無いんだけど，見なかった？ I can't find my wallet *anywhere*. Have you seen it？‖ 私の自転車は**どこにも**見当たらなかった I couldn't find my bicycle *anywhere*. ‖《レストランの店主が》うちの野菜スープは**どこにもない**味だよ You *can't find* (tasty) vegetable soup like ours *anywhere else*.

とこのま 床の間 a *tokonoma*

日本紹介 ✉ **床の間は alcove のように日本間の一部が引っ込んだ所で，畳の面より一段高く作り，四季折々の掛け軸を掛けたり，生け花を飾ったりする場所です** A *tokonoma* is a place like an alcove set back and built a step higher than the tatami floor in a Japanese-style room. People hang a scroll that suits the season and

/or place a vase with fresh flowers there.

どこまで **1【場所, 距離】how far**
▶(教室で)先週はどこまで進みましたか *How far* did we get last week?／*Where* were we last week?‖これだけのガソリンでどこまで走れるだろうか I wonder *how far* I can go on [with] this much gas.‖切符どこまで買った? *How far* does your ticket take you?‖対話「このバスはどこまで行きますか」「藤沢までです」"*How far* does this bus go?" "(To) Fujisawa."‖あの本, どこまで読んだ? *How much* of the book have you read?‖どこまで話したっけ? Now, *where* were we?‖どこまでも青い海が続いていた The *endless* blue sea stretched before us.‖忠実な犬はどこまでも主人についていく A faithful dog will follow his [her] owner *anywhere*.
2【程度, 範囲】▶彼の話はどこまで本当なのかわからない I can hardly tell *how much* truth there is to his story.‖物価はどこまで高騰を続けるのだろう I wonder *how far* prices will continue to rise.‖どこまでも(＝最後まで)争うつもりよ I will fight *to the bitter end*.‖きみはどこまでお人よしなんだ *How* gullible can you get? (➤ gullible は「だまされやすい」).

どこもかしこも ▶行楽地はどこもかしこも家族連れでいっぱいだった *All* the vacation spots were crowded with family groups.

とこや 床屋 a **barbershop**(店); a **barber**, a **hairdresser**(人) ▶彼は月に2回床屋に行く He *goes to the barber* [*goes to the barber's*] twice a month.‖ぼくはきのう床屋に行った I *had a haircut* yesterday. ／I *had my hair cut* yesterday. (➤ 両方とも「髪を切ってもらった」の意. I cut my hair ... は「自分で切った」の意).

ところ 所・処 **1【場所】a place** ▶ここが金の鉱脈の発見された所です This is (the *place*) where a gold vein was discovered. (the place は入れないほうがふつう)‖こんな所で会うなんて思いがけないなあ I never expected to see you in such *a place*.‖体育館の入り口の所で(＝入り口で)10時に会おう Let's meet *at the entrance* to the gym at ten.‖あいつの居る所で彼女の話をするなよ You must not mention her *in his presence*.‖彼はきみの居ない所では(＝ときには)自分がボスのようにふるまっている *When* you are not around, he always acts like a big shot.
▶うちの猫は所かまわずおしっこをする Our cat pees *anywhere and everywhere*.‖きょうは所によりにわか雨が降るでしょう There'll be scattered showers *in some places* today.
ことわざ 所変われば品変わる Every place has its own customs.／Different places, different customs.
2【家, 組織】one's **place**; one's **address**(所番地) ▶今度彼のところへ集まって飲もうよ How about getting together at *his place* to have a drink?‖ここにおところとお名前をご記入ください Please write your name and *address* here. (英語では name and address の語順)‖今晩は小林さんのところに泊まります I'm staying *with* Kobayashi [*at* the Kobayashis'] tonight.
3【箇所, 部分, 点】a **part** ▶この話の中でいちばんおもしろいと思ったところはどこでしたか What did you think was the most interesting *part* in the story?‖この彫刻でいちばん苦労されたところはどこですか What was the hardest *part* of making this sculpture?‖彼女には片意地なところがある She's got a stubborn *streak* in her. (➤ streak は「(性格の)一傾向」)‖きみの文章には文法的におかしなところが多い There are a lot of grammatical *mistakes* in your sentences.‖対話「西郷さんのどんなところが好きですか」「積極果敢なところです」"*What* do you like about Saigo-san?" "I like his boldness."
▶私のどんなところが悪いのか言ってよ Tell me *what* it is you don't like about me [*what's* wrong with me].‖彼は利かん気なところが兄貴にそっくりだ He resembles his brother *in* his unyielding spirit.‖この芝居の悪いところはせりふが冗長な点だ The *bad thing* about this play is that there are dragged-out speeches.
4【範囲】▶私の知るところでは彼らの民主主義への熱望は強い *As far as* I know, they strongly hope for democracy.‖見たところ, 彼は新しい職場が気に入っていないようだ *Apparently* [*It seems that*] he isn't happy with his new workplace.‖聞くところによると雪崩で13人が亡くなったそうだ *I heard that* thirteen people were killed in an avalanche.‖新聞の伝えるところによるとイエメンで内戦が始まったようだ The newspapers *have reported* that a civil war broke out in Yemen. ／*According to* the newspapers, a civil war broke out in Yemen.
5【場合, 際】▶坂本はいいところで(＝タイムリーな)二塁打を打った Sakamoto hit a *timely* double. ／Sakamoto's double came *at the right moment*.‖ちょうどいいところへ来てくれた. きみに電話しようとしてたんだよ You've come *at* (*just*) *the right moment*. I was just going to call you.
▶ロッテはこのところ(＝最近)調子がいい The Marines have been in good shape *recently*.‖きょうのところは許してやる I'll forgive you *this time only*.‖お忙しいところをお越しいただいてありがとうございました Thank you for finding time (*in your busy schedule*) to come.
▶あの2人が腕を組んで歩いているところを見たことがあるよ I once saw the two of them walking arm in arm.‖ぼくがきみだったらとっくの昔にそんな会社は辞めているところだ If I were you, I *would* have quit (working for) that company long ago. (➤ 主節が仮定法の過去完了なので, 文法的には If I had been you となるはずだが, ネイティブスピーカーでも If I were you で済ますことが多い)‖彼女がその小さな箱を開けたところ, 中には砂時計が入っていた *When* she opened the small box, she saw an hourglass.
6【…するところ】be (just) about to do, **be just going to** do(今から…するところ); **have (just)** done(ちょうど…したところ)

> **【文型】**
> **(今から)…しようとするところだ**
> **be about to** do
> **(ちょうど)…したところだ**
> **have (just)** done
>
> **《解説》**(1)「今ちょうど…しようとするところだ」は **be about to** *do* で表す. これと同じことを be just going to *do* (今ちょうど決めて…するところ)で表すこともできる. しかし, 単に be going to *do* では「…するつもり」の意になるのがふつう.
> (2)「…したところだ」は現在完了形に just をつけたり, 過去形に just now をつけたりしたりして表すことができる.

▶ちょうど学校[仕事]に出かけるところだ I'*m just about*

to go to school [work]. ‖ 私が説明しようとしているところへ彼が口を挟んだ I *was just about to* explain (the situation), when he interrupted me. ‖ ちょうど高校[大学]を卒業したところです I *have just* graduated from high school [college]. ‖ ちょうどケーキが焼き上がったところよ The cake *has just* come out of the oven. ‖ 今ちょうど帰って来たところなんだ I *just* got home. ‖ やあ, 今きみのこと話していたところだ Hi! We *were just talking* about you. ‖ ちょうどきみに電話をしようとしていたところだ I *was just going to* call you. (● この場合の just を省略すれば「電話をするつもりだった」の意になる).
▶もう少しで忘れるところだった I *almost* forgot it. ‖ 私, もう少しで救急車を呼ぶところだったのよ I *came very near to* call*ing* an ambulance.

-どころ ▶彼女はうれしいどころではなかった(＝むしろ悲しかった) She *was far from* happy. ‖ 私たち, 来週は期末試験だから遊ぶどころじゃないんだ Since the finals are next week, we*'re in no position to* be goofing off.

ところが **but** ▶ドッグフードに牛肉を入れてやったんです. ところがうちの犬, 全然食べようとしないんです I put some beef in the dog food, *but* our dog wouldn't eat it. ‖ その映画は批評家たちからは賞賛された. ところが, 興行的には振るわなかった The film was praised by the critics ; *however* it didn't do well at the box office. ‖ **対話** 「酒もたばこもやらないんじゃ金が残るだろう」「ところがこれが全然残らないんだ」"You must save a lot of money since you don't drink or smoke." "*Actually* [*In fact*], I haven't saved any at all."

-どころか **1【反対に】**▶コンサートを楽しむどころか彼は途中で眠ってしまった *Far from* enjoying the concert, he fell asleep in the middle.
2【…は言うまでもなく】▶私は英語が書けるどころか, まだろくに読むこともできません I cannot read English well enough yet, *let alone* [*much less*] write it. (➤ let alone, much less はともに通例否定的語句のあとに用いて「まして…ではない」; 後者のほうが堅い言い方) ‖ 男は不潔どころか, 臭いさえ発していた The man was dirty, *and what was worse* he smelled (bad). (➤「なお悪いことに, おまけに」の意).

ところせましと 所狭しと ▶その芸術家のアトリエには彫像が所狭しと置かれている The artist studio *is filled with* sculptures *and there's little room to move around*.

ところで **1【…しても】**▶今頃出かけたところで彼女には会えないよ *Even if* you go now, you won't be able to see her.
2【話の続行を示して】 **so, well, now** ▶ところで何の用だい? *So*, did you want something? ／ *Well*, what do you want? ‖ ところで, きみの意見は? *Well*, what's your opinion? ‖ ところで私の話, 聞いてよ *Now*, you listen to me.
3【話題を変えて】 **by the way, incidentally** (➤ 前者がふつう.「そう言えば」「ついでながら」にも相当する) ▶ところで, この辺りで英字新聞が手に入る所をご存じありませんか *By the way*, do you (happen to) know where I can get an English newspaper around here? ‖ ところで, お父さんお元気? *By the way*, how's your father (doing)?
✉ **ところで, 水泳はまだ続けていますか** *By the way* [*Incidentally*], do you still swim regularly?

ところてん 心太 ***tokoroten*** ; a jelly-like snack food made from seaweed called '*tengusa*' (➤ 説明的な訳) ▶《慣用表現》3月になると生徒たちはどれほど怠けていたとしてもところてん式に高校を卒業していく In March, students graduate from high schools *in a conveyor-belt fashion*, no matter how much they have neglected their studies. (➤「ベルトコンベヤー式に」の意).

ところどころ 所々・処々 ▶通りにはところどころに雪が残っていた There were patches of snow *here and there* on the street. ‖ この記事にはところどころ間違いがある This article has *some* [*several*] mistakes. (➤「いくつか間違いがある」の意).

どこんじょう ど根性 **guts** →根性.

どざえもん 土左衛門 a **drowned, bloated body** 《参考》古いアメリカ俗語に bloat があり, この語が日本語のニュアンスに近い.

とさか 鶏冠 a **comb** /kóʊm/ ; a **cockscomb** (オンドリの) ; a **crest** (とさか, 冠毛).

どさくさ ▶引っ越しのどさくさでその本はどこかに行ってしまった I lost the book in the *hustle* (*and bustle*) [*confusion*] of moving. (➤ bustle /bʌ́səl/ は「騒ぎ」, confusion は「混乱」) ‖ 彼はどさくさに紛れて金を持ち逃げした He *took advantage of the confusion* to run away with the money. (➤ take advantage of は「…につけ込む」).

とざす 閉ざす **1【閉める】** **close** +㊐, **shut** +㊐ ▶この寺は午後6時以降は門を閉ざして人を入れない This temple *closes* [*shuts*] its gate to visitors after 6 p.m. ‖ 彼女はそのことについては固く口を閉ざした She *kept her mouth* (tightly) *shut* about the matter. ／She *kept quiet* [*mum*] about the matter. ‖ その女の子は誰に対しても心を閉ざしてしまった The girl *closed her heart* to everyone.
2【通れなくする】▶この山小屋は冬中雪に閉ざされる This mountain hut *is snowed in* through the winter.

どさっと ▶木から雪がどさっと落ちた The snow fell from the trees *with a thud*.
▶注文がどさっと舞い込んだ Orders *flooded in*.

とざま 外様 an **outsider** ▶《比喩的に》彼らは外様だ They are *not in the favored group*. ／They are *outsiders*. ‖ **外様大名** a *tozama daimyo* ; a feudal lord who was not a hereditary vassal of the Tokugawa family (➤ 説明的な訳).

どさまわり どさ回り ▶あの劇団はどさ回り専門だ That troupe is always *on the road* [*barnstorming*]. (➤「どさ回りの役者」は barnstormer).

とざん 登山 **(mountain) climbing, mountaineering** /màʊntníərɪŋ/ ▶登山には絶好の季節になった It is now the best *climbing* season. ‖ この夏, 乗鞍登山をしました I *climbed* Mount Norikura this summer. ‖ **登山家** a mountaineer, an alpinist ‖ **登山者** a (mountain) climber.

[1]とし 年・歳

訳語メニュー
年月 →year **1**
年齢 →age **2**

1【年月】 a **year** ▶年の始めに at the beginning of the *year* ‖ 年が明けたらすぐ練習を始めよう Let's start practicing as soon as *the new year begins*. ‖ 年とともに(＝年がたつにつれて)大気汚染は悪化していく Air pollution gets worse *as the years go by*. ‖ 高校中退者の数は年ごとに増えている The number of high

school dropouts is increasing *year by year*.
▶よいお年を！ *Happy New Year!*／*I wish you a Happy New Year!*
語法 (1)後者はカードなどに書く改まった言い方. (2)日本語の場合と異なり, 両方とも年内または元日に言うことが多い. (3)返事は (The) same to you. と言う.
2【年齢】age ▶広瀬さんと私は同い年です Ms. Hirose and I are *the same age*. ‖女性の年を聞くのは失礼です It's rude to ask a woman's *age*. ‖たかしは年に似合わず(＝まだ若いのに)博識だ Takashi is very knowledgeable *for his age*. ‖あなた方が愛し合っているなら年の差は何でもありません *The age difference* doesn't matter if you love each other. ‖私の年を当ててみて Guess *how old I am*. ‖私は年より若く見られるのは嫌だ. 年相応に見られたいんだ I don't want to *look younger*. I want to look my *age*.
▶年を取る *get old*, *age* ‖私も年を取った I *have gotten old*. ／I *am feeling my age*. (➤後者は「年だと感じる」の意) ‖品よく年を取りたいものだ I hope I'll *age* gracefully.
▶おまえも独り立ちしていい年だ You *are old enough to* be independent. ‖「スリップ」を「シュミーズ」と言うなんて, 年がわかるね Your referring to a slip as a chemise *really dates you* [*shows your age*]. (➤ A date B で「A で B(人)の年齢がわかる」の意) ‖彼女は若く見えるけど実はだいぶ年を食っている She looks young, but *is* actually *getting on in years*. (➤ be getting on (in years) で「年を取っている」の意).
3【老齢】▶もう年だなあ I feel like *I'm getting old*. ／I can really *feel my age*. (人に向かって「きみも年だなあ」と言う場合は You're getting old. でよい) ‖彼はまだ若いつもりだが年には勝てない Though he thinks he is still young, *his age is telling on* him. (➤ tell on は「…に影響を与える, こたえる」) ‖いい年をして親に金の苦労はかけられないよ I'*m too old to* be going to my parents with money problems.
4【「…年」の形で】▶ 対話「あなた, 何年生まれ？」「さる年よ」"*What year of the* (*Chinese*) *zodiac* were you born in?" "I was born in *the year of the Monkey*." →十二支.
☛ いい年, 年の差婚 (→見出語)

²**とし 都市** a **city**, a **town** (➤後者は前者より規模が小さいが, インフォーマルでは区別なく用いることもある；→都会)
一形 **都市の urban** ▶シンガポールは東南アジアを代表する国際都市の1つだ Singapore is one of the foremost *cosmopolitan cities* in Southeast Asia. ‖中小都市からマンモス都市に至るまでいろいろの問題を抱えているものだ Municipalities ranging from *small and medium size cities* to *huge metropolises* have many different problems. ‖ニューヨーク都市圏 the New York *metropolitan* area. ‖**都市化** urbanization ‖**都市銀行** a city bank ‖**都市行政** municipal administration ‖**都市計画** city planning ‖**都市国家** a city-state ‖**都市伝説** an urban legend [myth] ‖**主要[大]都市** a metropolis.

どじ ▶どじな探偵 a *bumbling* [*klutzy*] detective(➤ bumbling /bʌ́mblɪŋ/ は「へまばかりしている」, klutzy /klʌ́tsi/ は「不器用な」の意) ‖おまえもどじだなあ You're *an idiot*, you know? ‖あのばかめ, どじばかり踏みやがって That blockhead *cannot keep out of trouble*. (➤「面倒事を起こさないでいることができない」の意) ‖彼女とデートか. どじ踏むなよ You're going out with her? I hope you don't *blow it*. →どじる.

としうえ 年上の older；**senior**(先輩の) ▶彼女はきみよりいくつ年上なんだい？ How much *older* [How many years *older*] is she than you? ‖池田さんは私よりずっと年上です Mr. Ikeda is *many years my senior*. ‖年上の人には丁寧なことばを使いなさい You should speak politely to your *elders* [*seniors*]. ‖ 対話「あなたと彼, どっちが年上なの？」「彼のほうが2つ年上です」"Who *is older*, you or he?" "He's two years *older than* me. ／He's two years *senior to* me."

としおいた 年老いた elderly ▶彼は年老いた両親の介護で忙しい He is busy taking care of his *elderly* parents.

としおとこ 年男 a man who was born in a year with the same sign of the Chinese zodiac as the current year(➤説明的な訳；sign of the Chinese zodiac は「十二支」. なお「年女」は man を woman にする) ▶彼は来年年男だ His *Chinese zodiac sign will return* next year.

としがい 年甲斐 ▶年がいもなく薄着をするからかぜをひくのよ You dress too lightly *for your age*, and that's why you've caught a cold. (➤ for one's age は「年の割に」) ‖あんなことで大騒ぎして, 何よ. 年がいもない Why are you making a fuss over such a thing? *Act your age*. (➤「年相応にふるまいなさい」の意).

としご 年子 ▶兄と私とは年子です I am *only one year younger* than my brother. ／My brother and I *were born in consecutive years*. (➤ consecutive /kənsékjətɪv/ は「連続の」).

としこし 年越し ▶ことしは箱根で年越しをした I *greeted the New Year* at Hakone. (「新年を迎えた」と考える).

としこしそば 年越し蕎麦 ***toshikoshi-soba***
日本紹介 ✉ **年越しそばは大みそかの夜に食べるそばです. (短く情熱的にではなく)そばのように細く長く生きようという願いを込めて食べるのです** *Toshikoshi-soba* are buckwheat noodles eaten on New Year's Eve. People eat them wishing for a long and simple life (which is) symbolized by the noodles (as opposed to a short and passionate life).

とじこみ 綴じ込み a **bound in supplement** ⟪to⟫.

とじこむ 綴じ込む file ＋目 ▶この新聞記事を切り抜いてファイルにとじ込んでおいてくれる？ Could you clip out these articles from the newspaper and *file* them [*keep* them *on file*], please?

とじこめる 閉じ込める shut [**lock**] **up**；**coop up** (人・動物などを狭い所に) ▶母親は彼が宿題をやってしまうまで彼を部屋に閉じ込めた His mother *shut* [*locked*] him *up* in his room until he finished his homework. (➤ shut up は「戸を閉め切って出られないようにする」, lock up は「鍵を掛けて出られないようにする」) ‖犬たちを一日中狭い所に閉じ込めてはいけない You shouldn't *coop up* your dogs all day. ‖大雪のために3時間車の中に閉じ込められた I *was confined* in my car for three hours because of the heavy snow. (➤ confine は堅い語) ／I *was snowbound* in my car for three hours.

とじこもる 閉じ籠もる shut [**coop**] **oneself up** (➤ coop は狭い所に閉じ籠もる場合を強調する) ▶うちの娘は落ち込むと自分の部屋に閉じ籠もってしまう When my daughter becomes depressed, she *shuts herself up* [*confines herself*／*holes up*] in her room. ‖こんな狭い部屋に1週間閉じ籠もってなんかいられない I can't *coop myself up* in a small room like this for a week. ‖こんな天気のいい日に家に閉じ籠もってい

たくない I don't like to *stay indoors* on fine days like this.

としごろ 年頃 **1【年齢】**▶あの子は遊びたい年頃だ He [She] *is about the age* when he [she] wants to have fun. ‖きみはもう自分の面倒は自分で見てもよい年頃だ You *are old enough to* take care of yourself. ‖私はきみぐらいの年頃には自活しなければならなかった When I was *about your age*, I had to support myself. ‖子供は同じ年頃の子供と遊ばせなさい Have your child play with children *about the same age*. (● have の代わりに let を用いると「許可を与える」という意味になる).

2【適齢期】▶彼には年頃の娘が2人いる He has two daughters *of marriageable age*. →適齢期.

としした 年下の **younger** ; **junior**(後輩の) ▶私より年下の女性 a woman *younger than* me ‖彼は私より年下だ He *is younger than* I am [*than* me]. (● インフォーマルでは than me が一般的) ‖彼の妻は彼より2歳年下だ His wife *is* two years *younger than* him. ／His wife *is* two years *his junior*. (➤ His wife is two years junior to him. は堅い言い方).

としつき 年月 **years** ▶あの映画は5年の年月を経て完成された It took five *years* to make the film. ‖学校を卒業してから10年の年月がたった *It has been ten years since* I graduated from school.

-として **as** ▶彼は音楽家として大成した He achieved fame *as* a (great) musician. ‖彼女は作家としてより批評家としてのほうが有名だ She is better known *as* a critic than *as* a writer. ‖彼はルーキーとしてはピッチングがうまい He pitches well *for* a rookie. ‖報酬としては悪くない仕事だ The job is not bad *in terms of* pay. (➤ in terms of は「…の点では」).

-としても ▶尼僧の瀬戸内さんは小説家としても有名だ The nun Setouchi is also known *as* a novelist. ‖このソファーは夜はベッドとしても使える This couch *doubles as* a bed at night. (➤ double as は「…として二役を務める」の意).

▶きみは勉強が好きでないとしても義務教育は終えないといけない *Even if* you do not like to study, you must finish compulsory education.

どしどし ▶どしどし(＝遠慮なく)ご応募ください Please *don't hesitate* to apply. ‖わが社では男性化粧品をどしどし(＝次々に)発売する予定です We are planning to hit the market with *a series of* cosmetics for men.

▶マイクは廊下をどしどし歩いて通り過ぎていった Mike *tromped* down the hallway.

としなみ 年波 ▶寄る年波には勝てない You can't win out against *old age*.

としのこう 年の功 →功.

としのさこん 年の差婚 **a marriage with a significant age difference** ; **a May-December marriage**(➤ 5月を若い妻または夫に, 12月を年齢の高い妻あるいは夫になぞらえたもの).

としのせ 年の瀬 **the end of the year**(年末) ; **the last days of the year**(年の暮れの日々) ▶年の瀬は町の雰囲気も何となく慌ただしい The town feels (somehow) busier toward *the end of the year*.

としま 年増 **a middle-aged woman.**

とじまり 戸締まり ▶戸締まりをする *lock the door* ‖寝る前にもう一度戸締まりを確認しなさい Before going to bed, make sure once again that you *have locked* all the doors. ‖きのう戸締まりをしないで出かけて空き巣にやられた I didn't *lock up* when I left yesterday, and my house was broken into.

どしゃ 土砂 **earth and rocks** [**gravel**] ▶土砂崩れがあって国道が土砂に埋まった There was *a landslide* and the highway was buried under *earth and rocks*.

どしゃぶり 土砂降り **a heavy rain, a downpour**(➤ 後者は「突然の」というニュアンスがある) ; **a drencher**(➤「ずぶぬれにするもの[雨]」というインフォーマルな語) ▶外はどしゃ降りだよ *It's raining heavily* [*hard* ／ *buckets* ／ *cats and dogs*] outside. (● rain cats and dogs は 慣用表現だが, 滑稽味を出す狙いがある場合以外はあまり使われていない) ／*It's* (really) *pouring* outside.

としょ 図書 **a book** ▶その資料室には膨大な図書がある That reference library has a vast number of *books*. ‖**図書閲覧室** a reading room ‖**図書券** a book coupon [《英》 token] ‖**図書室** a library ‖**図書目録** a catalog of books ‖**参考図書** a reference book (参考書) ; a bibliography /bìbliá:grəfi/ (参考書目).

☞ 図書館 (→見出語)

とじょう 途上 ▶帰宅途上の出来事だった It happened *on my way home*. ‖リニアモーターカーはまだ研究開発の途上にある Linear motor trains are still *under development* [*in the R & D stage*]. (➤ R & D は research and development の略).

‖**発展途上国** a developing country [nation].

¹**どじょう 土壌** **soil** ▶この辺の土壌は米作に適している The *soil* around here is good for growing rice. ‖レンゲソウの栽培は土壌改良に役立つ Growing Chinese milk vetches helps *improve the soil*.

²**どじょう 泥鰌 (魚)** **a loach** /loʊtʃ/

‖**どじょうすくい** a loach-scooping dance ‖**ドジョウ鍋** loaches cooked in a pottery casserole ‖**ドジョウひげ** a thin mustache.

としょかん 図書館 **a library** ▶学校の図書館から本を借りる borrow [check out] a book from the *school library*(● check out は正式な手続きをして借り出すことを明確にいう場合 ; 「返す」は return または check in).

‖**図書館員** a librarian /laɪbréəriən/ ‖**図書館長** the director [curator /kjóreɪtəʳ/] of a library ‖**移動図書館** a traveling library, 《米また》 a bookmobile, 《英また》 a mobile library.

としより 年寄り **an elderly person** [**man** ／ **woman**], **a senior, a senior citizen**(➤ 最後の2つの言い方は婉曲(えんきょく)表現で, 特に定年退職したり年金で生活したりしている人を指す).

語法 old person や old man, old lady というと, 日本語の「老人」と同様マイナスイメージがあるので, 「お年寄り」に当たる言い方としては elderly [older] person や senior citizen を用いる.

▶お年寄りを大切に Be kind to *elderly* [*older*] *people*. ‖お年寄りは若者よりも寒さに弱い *Elderly people* [*The elderly*] are more sensitive to cold than young people [the young]. ‖年寄りの言うことは聞くものだ[ものよ] Better heed an *old man's* [an *old lady's*] advice. ‖私を年寄り扱いしないでちょうだい Don't *treat* me *like an old lady* [*an old woman*]. ‖年寄り臭いことをするな Don't *act like an old man*. ‖彼女は年寄りじみた歩き方[しゃべり方]をする She walks [talks] *like an old lady*.

¹**とじる 閉じる** **1【閉める】** **close** +目, **shut** +目 (➤ 前者は閉じた状態, 後者は閉じる動作に重点がある) ▶口を閉じる *close* one's mouth ‖ハスの花は夕方になると(花びらを)閉じる Lotus flowers *close* (their petals) in the evening. ‖しばらく本を閉じておきなさい

Close your books for a while. ‖ 彼女は目を閉じたままベッドの上に横たわっていた She lay down on the bed *with her eyes closed* [*shut*]. ‖ 傘はきちんと閉じてから傘立てに入れてください Please *close* your umbrella properly and put it in the stand.

2【終わる】▶会を閉じる *close* a meeting ‖ 店を閉じる *shut up* shop (for good) (➤「廃業する」の意) ／ *close* (the) store (➤「営業時間を終える」の意) ／ *close* a store (➤ 両義に用いる) ‖ 3年間続いたそのミュージカルもついに幕を閉じた The musical which had run for three years *dropped its final curtain*.

²とじる 綴じる file +目 ; **staple** +目 (ホッチキスで) ▶この手紙をファイルにとじておいてください *File* (*away*) these letters, please. ／Please *keep* these letters *on file*. ‖ ホチキスで書類をとじる *staple* a document.

どじる blow it (大失敗をする) ; **blunder** (失態を演じる) ▶名刺を忘れたり書類を忘れてきたり, きょうはどじってばかりだ I forgot to bring my business cards, and I left the papers at home. (It seems that) I *can't do anything right* [I *blew everything*] today.

としわすれ 年忘れ a **year-end party** (忘年会).

としん 都心 the center [**heart**] **of a city** ▶彼は東京の都心にある銀行に勤めている He works at a bank in *the center* [*heart*] *of Tokyo*. ／He works at a bank in *central* [*downtown*] *Tokyo*.

どしん ▶2階でドシンという音がした *A bump* was heard from upstairs. ‖ 彼女は凍った道で滑ってどしんと尻餅をついた She slipped on the icy road and fell on her bottom *with a thump*. ‖ 自転車で塀にどしんとぶつかった My bicycle *smashed against* the wall.

トス a **toss** 一動 **トスする toss** +目 ▶セッターは絶好のトスを上げた The setter gave a nice *toss*. ‖ 鳥谷がセカンドにトスをした Toritani *tossed* the ball to the second baseman.

どす ▶「金庫はどこだ」と強盗はどすの利いた声で言った "Where's the safe?" said the robber in *a deep threatening voice*.

どすう 度数 frequency /fríːkwənsi/ (頻度) ; **the number of times** (回数) ; a **degree** (角度, 温度) ; a **unit** (テレホンカードの).

どすぐろい どす黒い dark ▶その川は工場の廃液でどす黒く汚れている The river water is *ominously dark* because of waste water from factories.

-とすれば if ▶結婚するとすれば, どんな男性がいいですか *If* you were to get married, what type of man would you choose?

どすん ▶彼は地面にどすんと尻餅をついた His bottom hit the ground *with a thud* [*a thump*].

どせい 土星 Saturn /sǽṭəʳn/ ▶土星の輪 *Saturn's* rings (➤ 通例複数形).

どせきりゅう 土石流 an **avalanche** /ǽvəlæntʃ ‖ -lɑːntʃ/ **of rocks and earth**, a **mudslide** ▶家が土石流で押し流された A house was carried away by the *avalanche of rocks and earth*.

とぜつ 途絶・杜絶 ▶濃霧のため交通が一時途絶した Traffic *was* temporarily *disrupted* [*paralyzed*] by the thick fog. ‖ その地方との電話連絡は全く途絶している Telephone communication with that area *has been* entirely *cut off* [*interrupted*].

とせん 渡船 a (**small**) **ferry**, a (**small**) **ferryboat**, a **taxi boat**, a **boat taxi** →渡し船.

とそ 屠蘇 *toso*

日本紹介 ✉ **とそは元日の朝に飲むお酒です. 伝統的にはとそ散という薬草の入った絹の袋を浸した酒またはみりんをいいます. 悪霊 [邪気] を払うと言われています** *Toso* is a kind of sake served on the morning of New Year's Day. Traditionally, it is made by putting a silk bag containing a mixture of herbs called '*tososan*' into sake or *mirin* (sweet rice wine). The drink is said to drive away evil spirits [evil influences].

とそう 塗装 painting (塗ること) ; **paint** (塗られたペンキ) ▶壁の塗装がところどころ剝げ落ちている The *paint* on the wall has flaked off here and there. ‖ うちの屋根は塗装が必要だ Our roof needs a new *paint job* [*coat of paint*].

‖ **塗装工** a painter ‖ **塗装工事** painting.

どそう 土葬 burial /bériəl/ (埋葬) 一動 **土葬する bury** /béri/ +目 ▶遺体を土葬にする *bury* a person's body.

どそく 土足 ▶畳の上に土足で上がらないでください Don't step onto the tatami *with your shoes on* [*without removing your shoes*]. ‖ 《掲示》土足厳禁 Remove your shoes before entering. ／ Shoes Off.

どだい 土台 1【基礎】 a **base** (物理的な意味での) ; a **foundation** (堅固でしっかりした ; 比喩的にも用いる), a **basis** /béɪsɪs/ (理論などの基礎) ▶立像の土台 the *base* of a statue ‖ この家は土台がしっかりしている This house is built on a firm *foundation*. ‖ 私は自分の海外での4年間の経験を土台にしてこの本を書いた I wrote this book *based on* my four years of experience abroad.

2【もともと】▶オール5を取ろうなんて, ぼくにはどだい無理な話だった It was *basically* impossible for me to get straight A's. ‖ 首都移転など, どだい無理な話だ The relocation of the capital is *almost* impossible *to begin with* [*from the start*].

とだえる 途絶える・跡絶える stop ▶私たちの文通は最近途絶えている Our correspondence *has stopped* recently. ‖ 会話が一瞬途絶えた *There was a pause* [*lull*] in our conversation for a moment. ‖ アメリカの友人から3年間音信が途絶えている I *haven't heard from* my friend in America for three years. ‖ 会葬者の列が途絶えることなく続いた The procession of mourners continued *without a break*.

どたキャン a **sudden cancellation** ▶彼女は約束をよくどたキャンする She often *cancels* her appointments *at the last minute*.

どたどた ▶のぶ子はどたどた歩く Nobuko walks *heavily* [*noisily*]. ‖ 階段をドタドタ上り下りする音がうるさくてしようがない The noise of people *clumping* [《米また》*clomping*] up and down the stairs is annoying. (➤ clump, clomp は「どしんどしん歩く」).

とだな 戸棚 a **cupboard** /kʌ́bəʳd/, 《米》 a **closet** (食器・食料・衣類用の) ; a **cabinet** (流し台上方の食器戸棚 ; ガラス戸棚 ; 書類戸棚) ; a **sideboard** (サイドボード).

どたばた ▶家の中でどたばたするな Don't *run about noisily* [*romp about*] in the house.

‖ **どたばた喜劇** a slapstick (comedy).

とたん 途端 1【ちょうどそのとき】as soon as, the moment (that) (➤ 後者は前者より強意的) ▶太陽が沈んだとたん気温が下がり出した *As soon as* the sun went down, the temperature began to drop. ‖ その人を見たとたん恩師だとわかった *The moment* I saw him, I recognized him as my former teacher. ‖ バスを降りたとたんにかばんを置き忘れたことに気がついた

Just as I got off the bus, I realized that I had left my bag on it.
2【急に】▶**学校を卒業するととたんに勉強をやめてしまう人が多い** Many people stop studying *soon* [*right*] *after* they leave school.

トタン **galvanized iron** /gǽlvənaɪzd áɪəʳn/ (亜鉛びき鉄板)
‖**トタン屋根** a galvanized sheet iron roof, a tin roof(➤ 前者は専門用語で, 一般には後者が用いられる).

どたんば 土壇場 **the last minute** [**moment**] ▶**彼女は土壇場になって彼との婚約を破棄した** She broke her engagement with him *at the last minute* [*at the eleventh hour*]. (➤ 後者はインフォーマルな表現) ‖ **彼らは土壇場に追い込まれた** They *were driven into a corner* [*to bay*]. (➤ この bay は「窮地, 追い詰められた状態」の意の数えられない名詞).

どたんばたん ▶**彼らはさっきから2階でどたんばたんやっている** They've been *making a lot of noise* upstairs for some time.

とち 土地 **1【土壌】** **soil** ▶**この辺の土地は肥えて[痩せて]いる** The *soil* of this area is fertile [barren]. ‖ **この土地はトウモロコシの栽培に適している** This *soil* is good for growing corn.
2【地所】 (**a piece of**) **land** ; **a property**(建物を含む所有地) ▶**土地を買う** buy (a piece of) *land* ‖ **その土地を区画で売る** sell the *land* by lots / subdivide and sell the *land* ‖ **この土地の価格は1平方メートル当たり50万円です** The price of *land* here is half a million yen per square meter. ‖ **新宿には遊んでいる土地は無い** There's no *idle land* in Shinjuku. ‖ **今では都心で土地付きの家を持つのは不可能に近い** Now it's almost impossible to buy *a house with land* in the center of Tokyo. ‖ **父は那須にちょっとした土地を持っている** My father has *a bit of land* in Nasu. ‖ **この土地は祖父母のものだ** This *property* [This *piece of land*] belongs to my grandparents.
‖**土地改革** land reform ‖ **土地所有者** a landowner ‖ **土地台帳** a land ledger.
3【地方】 a **region**, an **area** /éəriə/ (➤ 前者のほうが広い地方を指す) **一形** **土地の** **local** ▶**私はこの土地の(=ここで生まれ育った)者です** I was born and raised *here*. ‖ **沖縄へ行ったら土地の人と話をしてみることですね** If you go to Okinawa, you should talk to *the local people*. ‖ **避難民たちは慣れない土地で新生活を始めねばならなかった** The evacuees had to start new lives in *unfamiliar surroundings*. ‖ **この土地の酒です. 一杯どうぞ** This sake was produced in this *area*. Won't you try some? ‖ **その容疑者は土地勘がある(=その場所をよく知っている)ようだ** The suspect seems to *know the place well*.
‖**土地ことば** the local dialect /dáɪəlekt/ ‖ **土地転がし** land flipping, quick land turnovers ‖ **土地っ子** a native.

トチノキ 《植物》 a **horse chestnut** /tʃésnʌt/.

どちゃく 土着の **native**(その土地で生まれた; この語に差別的ニュアンスを感じる人もいる) ; **indigenous** /ɪndídʒənəs/ (その土地固有の) ▶**ジャガイモは日本土着のものではない** Potatoes are not *native* [*indigenous*] *to* Japan.
‖**土着民** the natives.

とちゅう 途中 **1【道の】**▶**会社へ行く途中この手紙を出してちょうだい** Please mail this letter *on your* [*the*] *way to* work. ‖ **駅へ行く途中で財布が無いことに気づいた** *On my way to* the train station, I noticed I didn't have my wallet (with me). ‖ **道路が閉鎖されていたので, 私たちは途中で引き返さざるを得なかった** Since the road was closed, we had to turn back *halfway* [*partway*]. ‖ **途中までお供します** I'll go with you *part of the way*. ‖ **この切符は途中下車できますか** Does this ticket allow me to *make stopovers*? / Can I *break* my *journey* with this ticket?
2【物事の】▶**話の途中で電話が掛かってきた** I got a phone call *in the middle of* the conversation. ‖ **何かの途中だった?** Are you *in the middle of* something? ‖ **お話の途中ですが, あなたに急ぎの電話が入っています** *Excuse me for interrupting*, but you've got an urgent call. ‖ **恵子と私は宿題を途中まで終えた** Keiko and I are *partway* [*halfway*] through our homework.

どちら **1【どこ】** **where** →どこ ▶**この夏はどちらへいらっしゃいますか** *Where* are you going this summer? ‖ **対話**「**どちらの会社にお勤めですか?**」「**横浜の携帯電話会社です**」"*What company* [*Who*] *do you work for?*" "A cellphone company in Yokohama." (● Who ... ? は会社名を尋ねるのに用いるほか, 雇い主または上司を尋ねるのに用いる場合もある) ‖ **対話**「**どちらの国からおいでですか?**」「**ブラジルです**」"*What country are you from?*" "(I'm from) Brazil."

> **あなたの英語はどう響く?**
> 日本では隣人や知人に会ったとき, よく「ビルさん, こんにちは. (きょうは)これからどちらへ?」などと聞く. これを直訳して, "Hi, Bill. Where are you going (today)?" というと, 非難を込めて相手に詰問しているように響く. 英米人は軽い挨拶として他人の行き先を聞く習慣がないので, 相当する決まった表現を持たない. 日本語もしばしば単なる挨拶であることは, 返答で「ちょっとそこまで」と言われれば, それ以上詮索せず, 了解することからもわかる. ただし, 英米でも, 相手がゴルフやハイキングのいでたちであれば, Where are you going to golf [go hiking] today? あるいは, Where are you off to [Where are you headed] (today)? などと尋ねることはごく自然である.

2【いずれの】 **which** →どっち ▶**パンとライス, どちらになさいますか** *Which* would you like, bread or rice? ‖ **目黒君ときみとどちらが背が高い?** *Who* is taller, you or Meguro? (● which を使う場合は Which one of you ...? とする) ‖ **この2枚の1万円札はどちらが偽物なのか見分けがつかない** I can't tell *which* of these two 10,000-yen bills is (a) fake. ‖ **赤い車はどちらの方向へ行きましたか** *In what direction* was the red car going? ‖ **どちらの道を行っても河口湖には出られます** *Whichever* road you take, you'll be able to get to Lake Kawaguchi. ‖ **対話**「**麗子にはどちらのブラウスが似合うと思う?**」「**ぼくにはどちらとも言えないな**」"*Which* blouse do you think looks better on Reiko?" "I *can't say which*."
▶ **(褒めているともけなしているとも)どちらにもとれるお世辞** *double-barreled* compliments ‖ **どちらの話も怪しいものだ** *Both* stories are incredible. ‖ **静かにしているか出ていくかどちらかにしてくれ** *Either* keep quiet *or* get out. ‖ **その計画はどちらも実行不可能だ** *Neither of* those plans is workable. ‖ **佐藤も高橋もどちらもホームランを打てなかった** *Neither* Sato *nor* Takahashi hit a home run. ‖ **私か兄のどちらかが参ります** *Either* my

と

brother *or* I am coming. (neither A nor B, either A or B が主語の場合, あとにくる動詞はどちらも B に一致する) ‖ あの2人, どちらかが本当のことを言っていない *One* of the two is not telling the truth.

▶恵美はどちらかと言うと男の子に人気がある Emi, *if anything*, is popular with boys. ‖ 彼女はどちらかと言うと引っ込み思案のほうだ She is *rather* shy. ‖ 観客はどちらかと言うとその映画に失望したようだ It seemed that the audience was *more or less* disappointed in the movie. (more or less は否定的意味合いで用いられることが多い) ‖ どちらでもお好きなほうを選んでください Choose *whichever* you want. ‖ どちらにしても悪いのはきみのほうだ *In any case* [*Either way*], you're wrong.

あなたの英語はどう響く?

外国人から Would you like coffee or tea? (コーヒーにしますか, 紅茶にしますか) と聞かれて, It doesn't matter. (どちらでも結構です) とだけ答える日本人がいるが, これはいかにもぶっきらぼうな感じがする. Either would be fine. か Either would be fine. It doesn't matter. のような言い方のほうが丁寧.

3【どなた】**who** ▶ 対話 「失礼ですがどちらさまでしょうか」「阿部と申します」"(May I ask) *who*'s calling, please?" "This is Abe." (➤電話での場合) / "May I have [ask] *your name*, please?" "My name is Abe." (➤会社の受付で).

とちる **fluff** +目, ((米また)) **flub** +目; **blow it** (しくじる) ▶試験でとちる *fluff* a test ‖ 今度はとちらないでよ Please don't *blow it* this time. ‖ あの若い俳優はせりふをとちってばかりいる That young actor always *fluffs* [*blows*] *his lines*.

1**とっか 特価** **a bargain price** (安売り価格) ▶このデジタルカメラは特価で手に入れた I got this digital camera *at a bargain* (*price*).

‖**特価売り出し** a (bargain) sale ‖ **特価品** a bargain article [item] ‖ **特価品売り場** a bargain counter.

2**とっか 特化する** **specialize in** ▶当社は高級オーディオシステムに特化しています We *specialize in* high-end audio systems.

どっか ▶相撲取りはソファーにどっかと腰を下ろした The sumo wrestler flopped *heavily* onto the sofa.

どっかいりょく 読解力 **reading comprehension, ability to read and understand** ▶読解力をつけるには, やはりたくさんの本を読むしかない The only way to improve *reading comprehension* is to read a lot (of books).

とっかえひっかえ 取っ換え引っ換え ▶ぼくは3足の靴を毎日取っ換え引っ換え履いている I wear these three pairs of shoes *in rotation*. (➤rotate /róʊteɪt/ は「交代させる」).

とっかかり 取っ掛かり a **clue** /kluː/ ((to)) (糸口) ▶この事件には取っ掛かりが全くない There are no *clues* [*keys*] to solving this case.

とつがせる 嫁がせる **marry (off)** ((to)) ▶彼は娘を銀行員に嫁がせた He *has married* (*off*) his daughter *to* a bank clerk. ‖ 娘をようやく嫁がせました We've finally *married* our daughter *off*.

とっかんこうじ 突貫工事 a **crash job** ▶突貫工事でホテルを半年で完成させる complete a hotel in half a year *by working around the clock* (➤「昼夜休みなしに働いて」の意).

とっき 突起 a **protrusion**, a **projection** (➤両語とも表面からの突出物をいうが, 後者は鋭角をなして突出している点を強調する) ▶カタツムリの頭部には目や触角など突起が多い There are many *protrusions* on the head of a snail, such as the eyes and antennae.

どつき 度付き →度.

1**とっきゅう 特急** a **limited** [**special**] **express** ‖ **特急券** a ticket for a limited [special] express (train) ‖ **超特急** (→見出語).

2**とっきゅう 特級** **the highest quality**.

とっきょ 特許 a **patent** /pǽtnt/ (専売の) ▶特許を申請する file an application for *a patent* ‖ 家庭用品の発明で特許を取る obtain *a patent* for [on] the invention of a household article ‖ ((表示)) 特許出願中 Patent Pending.

‖**特許権** a patent (right) ‖ **特許庁** the Patent Office.

どっきょ 独居 ▶独居老人 an elderly person *living alone*.

どっきりカメラ a **candid camera** ▶(相手を驚かせるなどしておいて)「どっきりカメラです」*You're on a candid camera*.

ドッキング **docking** (宇宙船の) ▶2つの宇宙船はドッキングに成功した The two spaceships succeeded in *docking*.

とっく ▶2人はとっくの昔に別れた The couple broke up *a long time ago*. ‖ そんなことはとっくに知ってるよ I know that *already*. / I heard about that *long ago*. ‖ ぼた餅? とっくに食べちゃったわよ The botamochi? I've *already* eaten it. ‖ (高校で)暗記した数学の公式なんかとっくに全部忘れちゃってるよ I've *long since* forgotten all the math formulas I memorized (in high school). (long since は「ずっと前に」の意で, 完了形とともに用いる) ‖ 約束の時間はとっくに過ぎているのに由美はまだ来ない It's *well* past the time we agreed to meet, but Yumi hasn't turned up yet.

とつぐ 嫁ぐ **marry** +目, **get married to** ▶娘は画家に嫁いだ My daughter *married* [*got married to*] an artist. ‖ 姉は高田家に嫁いだ My sister *married into* the Takada family.

ドック a **dock** ▶その船は長い航海のあとドックに入った The ship *was put into dock* after a long voyage. ▶父は年に1度(人間)ドックに入る My father goes to the hospital once a year for *a comprehensive medical examination* [*a complete medical checkup*].

ドッグフード **dog food**.

とっくみあい 取っ組み合い a **grapple** /grǽpəl/ ▶ガードマンと泥棒は取っ組み合いになった The guard *grappled with* the burglar.

1**とっくり 徳利** a **sake bottle** [**flask** / **decanter**] ‖**とっくりセーター** a turtleneck [((英また)) poloneck] (sweater).

2**とっくり** **thoroughly** /θə́ːroʊli ‖ θʌ́rəli/ (徹底的に); **hard** (しっかり); **carefully** (注意深く) ▶事故の原因は何だったのか, みんなでとっくり考えてみようよ Let's try *hard* to figure out the cause of the accident.

とっくん 特訓 **special training** (特別な訓練); **intensive training** (集中訓練) ▶妹に英語の特訓をする give my (younger) sister *a special* [*an intensive*] *lesson* in English (「特訓を受ける」なら動詞は take または receive) ‖ あすの早朝柔道部の特訓がある The judo club will have *a special training session* [*a special workout*] early tomorrow morning.

どっけ 毒気 **poisonous air** ▶彼の失言に**毒気**を抜かれた I *was dumbfounded* by his gaffe.

とつげき 突撃 a **charge** 一動 (…に向かって)**突撃する** **charge** (at) ▶敵に向かって**突撃する** *charge* (*at*) [*make a charge upon*] the enemy.

とっけん 特権 a **privilege** /prívəlɪdʒ/ ▶**特権**を乱用する abuse one's *privileges* ‖ 1度や2度の失敗は許されるのが若者の**特権**だ It is the *privilege* of young people to be pardoned for a failure or two. ‖ 彼女は名家の出なので**特権意識が強い** She comes from a prestigious family and *is strongly conscious of social privilege*.

どっこい **1**【ちょっと待て】▶どっこい, そうはいかないよ *But wait a minute* [*hold on*]. You can't do that. **2**【五分五分】▶両者は力の点ではどっこいどっこいだ Both are *about the same* in power.

どっこいしょ ▶おばあさんはどっこいしょとソファーに腰を下ろした The old lady *plumped herself* on the sofa. (➤ plump oneself は「どすんと体を投げ出す」の意).

とっこうやく 特効薬 a **specific cure**, a **special remedy** (➤ 後者のほうが堅い言い方) ▶その病気にはまだ**特効薬**がない We have no *effective medicine* [*wonder drug* / *silver bullet*] for that disease yet. (➤ silver bullet はオオカミ男を撃つのに有効な「銀製の弾丸」という意味で, 言い伝えに由来).

とっさ 咄嗟 ▶とっさの(＝即席の)冗談 an *offhand* joke ‖ 突っ込んできた自転車をとっさによけた I *instinctively* [*reflexively*] moved out of the way of a speeding bicycle. (➤ 前者は「本能的に」, 後者は「反射的に」) ‖ とっさにはその人の名前を思い出せなかった I could not recall his name *on the spot* [*promptly*].

どっさり ▶私たちの先生はいつも宿題をどっさり出す Our teacher always gives us *lots of* [*a lot of*] homework. ‖ きょうは洗濯物がどっさりある I have a *huge* wash today. / I have *heaps of* washing to do today. ‖ 父のところには毎年年賀状がどっさり来る My father gets *stacks of* New Year's cards every year. (➤ stacks は「多量」の意のインフォーマルな語).

ドッジボール **dodge ball** ▶ドッジボールをして遊ぶ play *dodge ball*.

とっしゅつ 突出 ▶今大会ではジョコビッチの力が**突出**していた Djokovic *was far better than* any other players in this tournament.

とつじょ 突如 **all of a sudden, suddenly** (➤ 前者が日本語により近く, 物語などで好まれる) ▶**突如**明かりが消えた *All of a sudden* [*Suddenly*], the lights went out. →**突然**.

どっしり ▶どっしりした家具 *imposing* furniture ‖ あなたはもう社長なんですから, いつもどっしり構えて行動してください You're the president now, so always try to behave *with dignity*.

とっしん 突進 a **rush**, a **dash** ; a **charge**(突撃) 一動 **突進する** **dash, rush** (➤ 前者のほうが勢いが強い感じ) ▶ゴールに向かって**突進せよ** *Dash* [*Rush* / *Make a dash*] toward the goal. ‖ その牛は赤い布に向かって**突進した** The bull *charged* toward the red cloth.

とつぜん 突然 **suddenly, all of a sudden** (➤ 後者のほうが強意的) ; **abruptly** (出し抜けに) ▶**突然**銃声が聞こえた *Suddenly* [*All of a sudden*] a gunshot was heard. ‖ 彼は**突然**話題を変えた He *abruptly* changed the subject. ‖ 地震は**突然**(＝予告なしに)やって来る Earthquakes come *without warning* [*notice*]. ‖ **突然**知らない外国人から電話が掛かってきた *Out of the blue*, I got a phone call from a foreigner I didn't know. (➤ out of the blue は「青天のへきれきのように, 出し抜けに」).
▶加藤さんの**突然の**死は家族にとって大きな衝撃だった Mr. Kato's *sudden* death was a great shock to his family. ‖ **突然の**(＝予期せぬ)来客があってとても忙しかった I was very busy because of an *unexpected* guest.
‖**突然変異** (a) mutation.

とったん 突端 **the point** ▶島の北の**突端** the northern *point* of an island ‖ 桟橋の**突端** the *far end* of a pier.

どっち **which** →どちら ▶駅はどっち? *Which way* is the train station? / *Which way* to the station? (➤ Which way leads to … の leads が省略されている) ‖ どっちかにしなさい Choose *one or the other*. ‖ どっちがどっちだかわからないよ I can't tell *which is which*. ‖ どっちに転んでも損はない I've got nothing to lose *either way*. ‖ 対話「水泳とドライブ, どっち行きたい?」「ああ, どっちでもいいよ」"Do you want to go swimming, or for a drive?" "*Either is O.K.*" ‖ 対話「あのけんか, どっち(＝誰)が悪いの?」「そうだね, ぼくはどっちもどっちだと思うよ」"*Who* do you think is to blame for that fight?" "Well, I think *they both are*." (● 人について「どっち」と聞く場合には通例 which ではなく who を用いる. 返事には It seems to me it was (*a case of*) *six of one and half a dozen of the other*. (6個と言うか12の半分と言うか) という言い方もある).

どっちつかず ▶どっちつかずの返事 an *indecisive* [*a noncommittal*] answer (➤ indecisive は「優柔不断な」, noncommittal は「言質(げんち)を与えない」の意) ‖ **どっちつかずの態度をとる** *sit* [*stand*] *on the fence* (➤「塀に腰掛けて形勢を見る」の意) ‖ その大臣は日中経済問題では**どっちつかずの態度をとった** The minister *refused to clarify* [*make clear*] *his position* on the economic issues between Japan and China. (➤「自分の態度を明らかにするのを拒否した」の意).

どっちみち どっち道 ▶俺が行っても行かなくてもどっち道同じだよ *What difference does it make* whether I go or not? (➤「同じことじゃないか」の意) ‖ **どっち道**(＝遅かれ早かれ)やらなければならないのだから早く片づけようよ Since we have to do it *sooner or later*, let's start right now and get it over with. ‖ **どっち道**(＝いずれにせよ)きみは行かなきゃなんないよ *In any case*, you have to go.

とっちめる ▶あいつ生意気だからとっちめてやる He's such a smart aleck. I'm going to *teach* him *a lesson*. ‖ 彼はテストでカンニングをして先生にとっちめられちゃったよ My teacher *gave it to* him for cheating on the test. (➤ give it to … は「…をひどく叱る」).

とっつき 取っ付き ▶とっつきの悪い人 an *unapproachable* person ‖ 彼女はとっつきやすい She is *friendly*. ‖ とっつきにくい(＝やっかいな)問題は後回しにしよう Let's tackle the *thorny* problems later.

とって 取っ手・把手 a **handle**(つかむ部分) ; a **knob**(ノブ) ▶ドアの取っ手を回す turn a *doorknob* ‖ コーヒーカップの取っ手が欠けている The *handle* of the coffee cup has chipped off. ‖ ドアの取っ手が外れた The *doorknob* came off.

-とって **to** (「…にとって(の), …に対して(の)」の意で, 適用範囲を示す) ; **for** (「…のためになる」の意で, 利益を受ける対象を示す) ▶私にとってこのトロフィーは一生の宝物だ *To* me, this trophy is a lifetime treasure. ‖ それはきみにとっていい教訓になるよ That will be a good lesson *to* [*for*] you. ‖ 彼の死は学界にとって一大損失だ

His death is a great loss *to* the academic world. ‖ 子供の教育にとって(＝おいて)いちばん大切なものは何だと思いますか？ What do you think is the most important thing *in* children's education？ ‖ ドイツ人にとってのジャガイモは日本人にとってのお米みたいなものだ Potatoes are *to* the Germans *what* rice is *to* the Japanese. (➤ A is to B what X is to Y で「AのBに対する関係はXのYに対する関係と同じである」の意).

とっておき 取って置きの **best**(いちばん良い) ▶彼女は取って置きの靴を履いて彼とのデートに出かけた She went (out) on a date with him wearing her *best* shoes. ‖ 彼は客たちに取って置きのワインをふるまった He entertained his guests with the wine *kept* [*reserved*] *for special occasions*.

とっておく 取って置く **1**【蓄える】**save** +㊐(人や将来のために), **set aside**(予備に)(インフォーマルな言い方); **keep** +㊐(確保しておく) ▶これはあすのおやつに取っておきなさい *Save* this for your snack tomorrow. ‖ いざというときのために毎週一定額を取っておく *set aside* a certain amount of money each week for emergencies.

▶この席, 取っておいていただけますか Could you *save* this seat for me, please？(➤この意味では take は使わない) ‖ 《店で》このセーター, あすまで取っておいてくださる？ Could you please *keep* [*reserve*] this sweater *for me* until tomorrow？

2【受け取る】▶いいからそれは取っておきなさい(＝きみにあげる) It's OK. *You can have* [*keep*] it. ‖ 《タクシーの運転手に》お釣りは取っておいていいよ *Keep* the change.

とってかえす 取って返す **hurry back** ▶父の病気の知らせに私は旅先から取って返した As soon as I heard about my father's illness, I *hurried back home* from my trip.

とってかわる 取って代わる **replace** +㊐ ▶携帯音楽プレーヤーがヘッドホンステレオに取って代わった The portable music player *has replaced* the personal stereo. ‖ 社長が亡くなって副社長が取って代わった The vice-president *took the place of* the president who had passed away.

とってくる 取って来る **go (and) get**, 《英また》**fetch**

> 【文型】
> 人(A)に物(B)を取って来る
> **go (and) get** A B
> **go (and) get** B **for** A

▶私の部屋から帽子を取って来てくれ *Go* (*and*) *get* me the hat from my room. ／Please *get* [*fetch*] me the hat from my room.

とってつけた 取って付けた ▶彼女は面接のとき取ってつけたような愛想笑いをした She wore a *forced* [an *artificial*] smile during the interview. (➤ forced は「無理に作った」, artificial は「人工的な」).

どっと ▶ロッカールームに戻ったらどっと汗が出た When I returned to the locker room, I *broke into a sweat*. ‖ 先生の冗談に学生たちはどっと笑った The students *burst into laughter* [*burst out laughing*] at the teacher's joke. (➤ burst out laughing のほうがよりインフォーマル) ‖ コメディアンは観客をどっと笑わせた The comedian *set* the audience *off laughing*. (➤ set A off doing で「A(人)に…し始めさせる」) ‖ 開店と同時に客が店内にどっと流れ込んだ Just as the store opened, customers *rushed* [*poured*] *inside*. ‖ スタジアムが開門されると, ファンたちがどっと入場した As soon as the stadium opened, the fans *piled in*.

ドット a **dot**(.).

ドットコム a **dot-com**, a **dotcom** ▶2000年から2001年にかけてドットコムバブルがはじけた *The dot-com bubble* burst during 2000 and 2001.

とつとつ 訥々と・吶々と **falteringly** ▶彼女はとつとつと英語で身の上話を始めた She began to *falteringly* tell the story of her life in English.

とっとと ▶とっととうせろ！ *Scram*！／*Beat it*！ ‖ 子供はとっとと帰れ Get out of here *right now*, you little kids！

とつにゅう 突入する **1**【勢いよく突っ込む】**rush** [**charge** ／**dash**] **into** ▶1人の勇敢な兵士が敵陣に突入した One brave soldier *charged* [*rushed*] *into* the enemy's line. ‖ 警察は容疑者の家に突入した The police *broke into* the suspect's house.

2【ある状態になる】▶両国はついに戦争に突入した At last, war between the two countries *broke out*.

とっぱ 突破する **1**(突き破る) **break through** ▶強盗は非常線を突破して逃げた The robbers *broke through* the cordon and got away. ‖ 入試の難関を突破されるよう祈っています I hope you *clear* the entrance examination hurdle. ‖ 初戦突破が第一目標です Our primary aim is to *win the first game*. ‖ ラジウムの発見ががん研究の突破口となった The discovery of radium was *a breakthrough* in cancer research.

2【数量が超える】**exceed** +㊐ ▶志願者は1000人を突破する見込みだ The number of applicants is expected to *exceed* one thousand. ‖ きょうは気温がついに35度を突破した Today the temperature *has* finally *risen* [*gone*] *above* 35 degrees. ‖ 世界の人口が78億を突破した The population of the world *has topped* 7.8 billion. (➤このtopは「上回る」).

とっぱつ 突発 ▶突発的な事件 an *unexpected* [*unforeseen*] incident ‖ その静かな村に殺人事件が突発した A murder *suddenly occurred* in that quiet village.

とっぴ 突飛な **eccentric**(奇抜な); **reckless**(無謀な); **insane**(正気でない); **off-the-wall**(ばかげた) ▶とっぴな行動をとる人 a person who behaves in an *eccentric* way ‖ とっぴな計画 a *harebrained* plan (➤ harebrained /héəʳbreɪnd/ は「向こう見ずな」) ／an *insane* [*a wild*] scheme ‖ とっぴな考え *an off-the-wall* idea ‖ とっぴな服装をする wear *weird* clothes (➤ weird /wɪəʳd/ は「異様な」) ‖ あの男は時々とっぴな行動に出る He sometimes acts *recklessly* [*rashly*].

とっぴょうしもない 突拍子も無い **extraordinary** /ɪkstrɔ́ːʳdneri/ (異常な) ▶実に突拍子もない話 a most *extraordinary* story ‖ 彼は時々突拍子もないことを言う He sometimes says *ridiculous* [*absurd*] things. (➤ともに「ばかげた, 滑稽な」の意).

トッピング a **topping** ▶ヨーグルトに新鮮な果物をトッピングする *top* the yogurt with fresh fruit.

トップ **1**【一番】**the top** ▶トップクラスの出版社 a *top-class* [*first-rate*] publishing company ‖ (塾で)トップクラスの子供たち the *top* students (at a *juku*) ‖ 彼女はトップクラスの生徒だ She's *one of the brightest* [*best*] students.

▶彼は勉強家だからいつもクラスのトップだ He studies hard and is always at the *top* [*head*] of his class. ‖ ぼくの弟は大した勉強もしなかったが, 成績はいつもトップだった My (younger) brother didn't study

hard, but he always got *top* grades. ‖ 彼女は期末試験でトップになった She *came out top* in her final exams.
▶ミスターチルドレンはいまだ日本のロックシーンのトップにいる Mr. Children is still one of *the top* Japanese rock groups. ‖ その本はベストセラーのトップを占めている That book *tops* the best-seller list. ‖ 彼はマラソンで終始トップを守って１着でゴールインした He breasted the tape after *holding the lead* throughout the marathon.
▶世界トップレベルの技術のいくつかが大田区の町工場にある Some *top-level* global technology can be found in small-scale factories in Ota-Ward. ‖ 新システムの導入はトップダウンで決まった The introduction of the new system was decided *in a top-down way*.
‖**トップ記事** the lead story (新聞の) ; a feature (雑誌などの特集) ‖**トップニュース** top news ‖**トップバッター** a leadoff (man／batter).
2【上層部】▶トップレベルの会談 a *top-level* [*summit*] meeting ‖ うちの会社ではこの間トップの１人が突然辞任した One of the *top executives* of our company suddenly resigned the other day.

> **危ないカタカナ語✺トップ**
> **1**「最上位の」「最初の」の意味では top も使えるが, first, best, leading, head などのほうが適切な場合も多い. 例えば野球の「トップバッター」は top (of the order) ともいうが, ふつうは leadoff (man) または the first batter という. top batter では「最優秀打者」ととられる可能性がある. また,「トップメーカー」は leading manufacturer がよい.
> **2** 車の「トップギア」は《英》では top (gear) だが,《米》では high (gear)という.「ギアをトップに入れる」は shift [change] into high (gear)となる.

とっぷう 突風 a **gust** (**of wind**), a **blast** (**of wind**) (➤後者のほうが前者よりも強く長く吹く) ▶看板が突風にあおられた The signboard was hit by *a gust of wind*.
とっぷり ▶もうとっぷりと日が暮れた It has already become *quite* dark.
どっぷり ▶お湯にどっぷりつかって一日の疲れを癒やした I *soaked* (*myself*) in hot water to relieve the day's fatigue.
トップレス トップレスの topless.
とつべん 訥弁 ▶彼はとつ弁だ He *is an awkward speaker*.
とつめんきょう 凸面鏡 a **convex mirror.**
とつレンズ 凸レンズ a **convex lens.**
どて 土手 a **bank** (自然に近い) ; a **dike** (人為的な) ; a **levee**, an **embankment** (➤ともに「堤防」の意であるが, 後者はハイウェーの土手を指すことが多い) ▶江戸川の土手に立つ stand on the *bank* of the Edo River.
とてい 徒弟 an **apprentice** /əpréntɪs/
‖**徒弟制度** an apprenticeship system.
どでかい big, huge ▶何かどでかいことをやってやろうという気概のある若者が少なくなった Nowadays, there are fewer young men who have the (fighting) spirit [grit] to do something *big*.
どてっと ▶うちの夫ときたら,休みの日は一日中どてっと寝そべっているばかり My husband just *lies flat on his back* [*sprawls around*] all day long on his days off.
とてつもない 途轍も無い incredible (途方もない) ; **unreasonable** (法外な) ▶とてつもなく大きなくしゃみ an *incredibly* big sneeze ‖ 彼らは私にとてつもない額を要求した They charged me an *outrageous* [*unreasonable*] price. ‖ 彼は何かとてつもないことをたくらんでいるらしい I'm told he is planning something *wild* [*absurd*]. (➤ wild は「無謀な」, absurd は「ばかげた」).
とても 1【非常に】**very, so** (➤後者は女性に好まれる) ; **quite** (➤ very の意で用いるのは《米》用法で,《英》では「まあまあ」の意になることが多い) ; **really** (ほんとうに) ▶この１週間とても暑い日が続いている It has been *very* [*awfully／terribly／extremely*] hot for the past week. (➤カッコ内の副詞は very の強意語) ‖ 私今とても幸せなの I'm *so* happy now. ‖ この学校はとても気に入っています I like this school *very much* [*a lot*]. ‖ ２人はポールがいないのをとても寂しく思っています Both of them feel *very* lonely without Paul [miss Paul *deeply*]. ‖ 彼女の英語の発音はとてもいい Her English pronunciation is *quite* good. ‖ 私はガーデニングにとても興味があります I'm *really* interested in gardening. ‖ あなたの歌, とてもすてきでしたよ Your song was *just* great. (➤この just はインフォーマルで「全く」の意).

> **あなたの英語はどう響く?**
> (1)「あのレストランは値段がとても高い」は, That restaurant is *very* [*really*] expensive. とするのが最も一般的. ただし, really とすると「自分は行けないほど(高い)」という含みの文になるという人もいる. ちなみに, too とすれば「あまりにも(高い)」, pretty とすれば「まあまあ(高い)」という含みが生じる.
> (2) Thank you *so* much.／I'm *so* tired.／I went there *so* often. のように,「とても」の意で副詞の so を用いるのは主に女性の言い方. ただし, I'm *not so* tired.／I did*n't* go there *so* often. のように, 否定語とともに用いる場合は性差はない. very は男女の別なく使う.

2【到底…ない】**hardly** ▶そんなこと彼にはとても言えません I can *hardly* bring myself to tell him that. (➤ bring oneself to do は否定語を伴って「…する気になれない」) ‖ 彼女はきれいな肌をしているので, とても40歳には見えない With her beautiful skin, she *hardly* looks forty [you *could never* guess she's forty]. ‖ あの野郎がここに来ないことを願うよ. とてもじゃないが我慢できないやつだから I hope he won't be here. I *just* can't stand him. ‖ この仕事は５月までにはとてもできない I *can't possibly* get this work done by May. (➤ can't possibly ... は「とても…できない」) ‖ 数学ではとても彼にかなわない I am *nowhere near* as good as he in math. (➤ nowhere near は「…に程遠く」の意) ‖ **対話**「お嬢さんのピアノ, すばらしいですね. コンクールに出てみたらどうですか」「いやあ, うちの子なんてとてもとても」"Your daughter is an outstanding piano player. Why don't you have her take part in the contest ?" "Oh, no. She's *not in the same league as the others* !"
トド《動物》a **sea lion.**
ととう 徒党 ▶何だ, きみたちは徒党を組んで. ひきょうだぞ You've all *ganged up* against me. It's not fair.
どとう 怒濤 surging [**violent**] **waves.**
とどうふけん 都道府県 Tokyo and all the prefectures (➤北海道も prefecture の１つ).
とどく 届く 1【着く】**reach** (+目) ; **arrive** 《at》 (到着する) ▶私の E メールは届きましたか Has my email *reached* you ?／Have you *gotten* [*received*] my email ? ‖ きょう手紙を出してくだされば, あさってには私のところに届きます The letter

will *arrive* [*be delivered*] to me the day after tomorrow if you mail it today. (➤ be delivered は「配達される」).

✉ **品物が届き次第，代金を振り込みます** I will pay the money into your bank account by electronic transfer as soon as I *receive* the merchandise. ➤ electronic transfer は「コンピュータによる現金振り込み」の意.

✉ **先月注文した下記の品がまだ届きません** The following items I ordered last month have not yet *arrived*.

2【達する】reach（+目）▶深海は太陽の光の**届かない**暗黒の世界である Deep below the surface of the sea lies a dark world that sunlight never *reaches*. ‖ 洗剤は幼児の**手の届かない所**に置いてください Keep detergents *out of the reach of* young children. ‖ 屋根に居る父にロープを投げたが**届かなかった** I threw the rope to my father on the roof, but it *fell short* (of him). ‖ 学生が騒いでいたので先生の声は教室の後ろまで**届かなかった** The students were so noisy that the teacher's voice *didn't carry to* the back of the classroom. ‖ 彼女の髪は腰まで**届く** Her hair *hangs down to* her waist.

▶こんな高い指輪，私には**手が届かない**（＝買えない）わ I *can't afford to buy* such an expensive ring as this. ‖ 父は50に**手が届く** My father is *nearly* [*close to*] fifty. ‖ 彼はその歌手に毎日ファンレターを出し続けたが，結局**思いは届かなかった** He wrote a fan letter to the singer every day, but *failed to touch her heart*.

とどけ 届け a **notice**（通知）; a **report**（報告）▶彼は**届けを出さないで**学校を休んだ He was absent from school *without notice*. ‖ 赤ん坊が生まれたら14日以内に**届けを出さなければいけない** You must *register* the birth of a child within fourteen days. (➤ register は「登録する」).

‖転入[転出]届 a moving-in[-out] notification.

☛ 無届け（→見出語）

とどけでる 届け出る **report**《to》▶窃盗事件を警察に**届け出る** *report* a burglary *to* the police ‖ 現住所を区役所に**届け出る**（＝通知する）*give notice of* one's new address to the ward office.

とどける 届ける 1【届くようにする】take +目（持っていく）; **bring** +目（話し手のところに持って来る）; **deliver** +目（配達する）; **send** +目（送る）▶この書類を山田さんに**届けてください** Please *take* this document to Mr. Yamada. ‖ 花屋にランの鉢植えを**届けてもらった** I *had* the florist *deliver* a potted orchid. ‖ ビールを1ダース**届けてください** Could you *bring* us a dozen bottles of beer?／I'd like to have a dozen bottles of beer *delivered*, please. ‖ 彼女は私の誕生日に花を**届けてくれた** She *sent* me flowers for my birthday.

2【知らせる】inform《of》（通知する）; **report** +目; **hand** [**turn**]《in》（差し出す）▶泥棒に入られたので警察に**届けた** I *informed* the police *of* the burglary. ‖ 駅でICカードを拾ったので遺失物係へ**届けた** I picked up a commuter IC card [pass] at the train station and *handed* [*turned*] it *in* at the lost-and-found office. ‖ 無くしたかばんのことをどこに**届けたらいいのだろう** Where can I *report* a missing bag?

とどこおり 滞り ▶家賃[給料]の**滞り** *back* rent [pay] (➤ back は「未払いの」) ‖ 卒業式は**滞りなく済んだ** The graduation ceremony went off *smoothly* [*without a hitch*]. (➤ a hitch は「思いがけない障害」).

とどこおる 滞る 1【つかえて進まない】▶ひと月病気で寝ていたので仕事が山のように**滞っている** Since I was sick in bed for a month, a lot of work has been *left undone*.／I*'ve got a backlog* of work [Work *has piled up*] since I was sick in bed for a month. (➤ backlog は「未処理の仕事などの山」).

2【勘定がたまる】▶あなたは家賃が3か月**滞っています**よ You are three months *overdue* on your rent.／You are *in arrears* with your rent for three months.(➤ in arrears /əríəˊz/ は「(支払いが)滞って」).

ととのう 整う・調う **be ready** ▶夕食の**用意が整った** Supper *is ready*. ‖ さあ，これで出発の**準備が整った**わ Now we*'re ready to* leave. ‖ 田中・鈴木両家の間に縁談が**調った** A marriage *has been arranged* between the Tanakas and the Suzukis.

▶**整った服装**を心がけなさい Try to be *neatly* [*properly*] dressed. ‖ 彼は**目鼻だちが整っている** He *has regular features*.／He *is good-looking*.

ととのえる 整える・調える 1【きちんとした状態にする】▶身なりを**整える** *make* oneself *tidy*／*tidy* oneself *up* ‖ 部屋を**整える** *put* one's room *in order*／*tidy up* one's room ‖ 姉は髪をさっと**整えた** My (older) sister *arranged* her hair quickly. ‖ スピーチコンテストに備えて**体調を整えて**おこう I think I'd better *get in shape* for the speech contest.

2【用意する】prepare, get ready ▶ローンの申し込みに必要な書類を**調えた** I *prepared* [*got ready*] all the necessary documents to apply for a loan.

とどのつまり **in the end**（最後には）; **after all**（結局は）; **the upshot**（経過をたどって行き着いたところ）▶好景気のときに不動産を買いあさって，**とどのつまりが**倒産だ They bought up properties during an economic boom, but went bankrupt *in the end* [*ended in* bankruptcy].

とどまる 止まる・留まる 1【動かないでいる】remain, stay（人が; 前者より堅い語）; **hover**（ヘリコプター・鳥などが空中に）▶彼はたぶん現職[この町]に**とどまるだろう** He will probably *remain* in his present post [in this town]. ‖ 私はここに**とどまって**彼を待ちます I'll *stay* here waiting for him. ‖ ヘリコプターは空中に**とどまることができる** Helicopters can *hover* over the ground.

2【限られる】▶校則違反者は彼だけに**とどまらなかった** He was *not the only* student who violated (the) school regulations. ‖ 彼の野心は**とどまるところを知らない** His ambition *knows no bounds* [*no limits*].

とどめ 止め・留め ▶**とどめの一撃**を加える deliver *a coup de grâce* /kùː də gráːs/ (➤ フランス語からきた表現) ‖ 巨人は8回裏村上に満塁ホームランを打たれて，完全に**とどめを刺された** Murakami hit a grand slam in the bottom of the eighth inning to *put* the game *out of* the Giants' *reach*.

▶《慣用表現》サクランボは山形産に**とどめを刺す**（＝が最高だ）Cherries produced in Yamagata *are the best*.

どどめ 土留め a **retaining wall**.

とどめる 止める・留める 1【残す】retain ▶萩の町は今なお昔の面影を**とどめている** The city of Hagi still *retains* some traces of its former self. ‖ これこそまさにあなたが**心にとどめておく**べき忠告です This is a piece of advice that you should really *keep in mind*. ‖ 爆撃でその町は**原形をとどめぬほど**破壊された The town was bombed *beyond recognition*.

2【それだけに限る】▶きょうは問題点をいくつか指摘するだけにとどめた Today I *simply* pointed out several problems. ‖ 被害は最小限にとどめたい We'd like to *keep* the damage *to a minimum* [*minimize* the damage].

とどろかす 轟かす ▶レーシングカーは大きな音をとどろかせて走り去った The race car *roared* off.

とどろき 轟き a **roar**(太く響き渡る大きな音); a **rumble**(籠もったゴロゴロ・ガラガラいう音) ▶雷のとどろき *roars* of (the) thunder.

とどろく 轟く **roar**; **rumble**(ゴロゴロ鳴る); **resound**(響き渡る) ▶雷が辺りにとどろいた Thunder *roared* [*rumbled* / *resounded*].

▶彼のデザイナーとしての名声は今や世界中にとどろいている His fame as a designer *has spread worldwide*.

トナー **toner** /tóʊnəʳ/.

ドナー a **donor** /dóʊnəʳ/ (提供者) ▶臓器のドナー an organ *donor* (➤「臓器の被移植者」は donee /dòʊníː/) ‖ **ドナーカード** a donor card.

となし 都内 ▶家は浦和ですが都内の高校に通っています I live in Urawa, but go to a high school *in Tokyo*.

ドナウ ドナウ川 **the Danube** /dǽnjuːb/ (南西ドイツに発し, 黒海に注ぐ大河; Donau はドイツ名).

となえる 唱える 1【祈りなどを】**chant** +目 ▶僧侶たちは念仏を唱えた Buddhist priests *chanted* [*said*] the prayer to Amida Buddha. (➤ prayer は /preəʳ/ と発音) ‖ アリババは「開けごま」と呪文を唱えた Ali Baba *uttered* the magic spell "Open, Sesame!"

2【主張する】**advocate** +目 (公に); **advance** +目 (意見などを出す); **propose** +目 (提案する) ▶彼は熱心に原子力発電所の閉鎖を唱えている He keenly *advocates* the closing of nuclear power plants. ‖ 新説を唱える *advance* [*propose*] a new theory ‖ 計画に異議を唱える *raise* an objection to the plan ‖ 彼は内閣改造を唱えた He *advanced* the idea of a Cabinet reshuffle.

トナカイ 《動物》 a **reindeer** [複 **reindeer**].

どなた **who** ▶どなたですか May I have [ask] your name, please? / What's your name, please? (● Who are you? は「おまえは誰だ」に近く, 失礼に響く; ドアをたたく音に応じるときは Who is it? と言う) ‖ 対話「お母さんと話してらっしゃる女の方, どなた?」「九州のおばです」"*Who*'s that woman talking with your mother?" "My aunt from Kyushu." ‖ 《店などで》すみません, どなたかいらっしゃいませんか Excuse me. Is *anyone* there? / Excuse me. *Anybody* here? ‖ あの赤い車はどなたのですか *Whose* is that red car? ‖ どなたかペンを落としませんでしたか[どなたのペンですか] Did *somebody* drop a pen? / Is this *anybody's* pen? (➤ ともに落とし物などを拾って皆に聞くとき).

どなべ 土鍋 an **earthenware casserole** [**cooking pot**].

となり 隣 a **next-door house**(隣家); a (**next-door**) **neighbor** /néɪbəʳ/ (隣人) ― 形 **隣の** **next, neighboring**; **next-door**(隣家の); 《フォーマル》 **adjacent**(隣接の; 接触しているとは限らない) ▶隣の家 the house *next door* ‖ 警察署は消防署の隣に在ります The police station is *next* [*adjacent*] *to* the fire station. ‖ 夫の両親は私たちの隣に住んでいます My husband's parents live *next door* (*to* us). ‖ あなたの隣に座ってもいいですか Can I sit *beside* [*next to*] you? ‖ 私たちはお隣どうしです We're *next-door neighbors*. ‖ お隣さんとは引っ越して来てからずっと親しくしています We have been on close terms with our *next-door neighbor*(*s*) since we moved here. ‖ 隣の家の子はオリンピック選手だ The boy *next door* is an Olympic athlete. ‖ 私たちは隣町の朝市によく出かけます We often go to the morning market in *the neighboring town*.

どなりあい 怒鳴り合い a **yelling** [**shouting**] **match** ▶労使間の交渉はどなり合いに終わった The negotiations between labor and management ended in *a yelling* [*shouting*] *match*.

となりあわせ 隣り合わせ ▶その2つの教会は隣り合わせに立っていた Those two churches stood *side by side* [were *adjacent*]. ‖ 彼女の家とうちとは隣り合わせだ She and I *live next door to* each other. ‖ 教室ではいつも彼と隣り合わせに座る I always sit *next to* him in class.

どなりこむ 怒鳴り込む ▶ストに怒った数人の乗客が駅長室にどなり込んだ Several passengers *stormed into* the stationmaster's office *to make* (*a*) *protest* against the strike.

どなりつける 怒鳴り付ける **yell** 《at》 (声を限りに大声で); **shout** 《at》 (大声で); 《米・インフォーマル》 **chew out**(厳しく叱る) ▶私がウエーターをどなりつけると, 店主が飛んで来た The owner came running when I *yelled at* the waiter. ‖ 荒井先生は騒々しい生徒たちをどなりつけた Mr. Arai *yelled at* the noisy students. ‖ 彼女の父は怒って彼女をどなりつけてしまった Her father *shouted at* her in anger. ‖ 彼は仕事中に居眠りをしたその使用人をどなりつけた He *chewed out* the employee for dozing on the job.

どなる 怒鳴る **yell** 《at》 (どなりつける); **shout** (叫ぶ); **bellow**(大きく太い声で) ▶彼はドアのチャイムをいたずらした子供たちをどなった He *yelled at* the kids for playing with the doorbell. ‖ そんなにどならなくたって聞こえるよ You don't have to *shout* like that. I can hear you. ‖「早く自分の部屋を掃除しなさい!」と父はどなった "Hurry up and clean your room," Dad *bellowed*.

とにかく 1【いずれにしても】**anyway, anyhow** (➤ 後者はインフォーマル); **at any rate**(どんな場合にも); **in any case**(どんなことが起こるにしても) ▶とにかく行って見てみましょうか Well, let's go (and) take a look *anyway*. ‖ とにかくやってみることだよ *Anyhow*, try it. ‖ とにかくやってみなければわからない *At any rate*, you should at least give it a try. ‖ とにかく, これはきみの知ったことではない *In any case*, this is none of your business. →ともかく.

2【実に】▶とにかくとても楽しいミュージカルだった It was a *most* enjoyable musical. ‖ 大リーガーたちのパワーはとにかくすごい Those major leaguers are *really* powerful.

とにもかくにも ▶とにもかくにも我々はラーメン店の開店にこぎ着けた *At any rate*, we managed to open our ramen shop. ‖ とにもかくにも皆無事でよかった *Anyway*, I'm happy to know everybody is safe.

どの 1【疑問を表して】**which**(選ぶ物の数が限られている場合); **what**(選ぶ物の数が限られていない場合) ▶きょうはどのスカートをはいて行こうかしら *Which* skirt should I wear today? ‖ さあ, きょうはどの子がお皿洗いを手伝ってくれるかな? Well, *which* of you (kids) wants to help with the dishes today? ‖ どの人が森さんですか *Which* gentleman is Mr. Mori? ‖ 芝公園へ行くにはどの駅で降りたらいいですか At *what* station should I get off for Shiba Park? ‖

と

学校は東京のどの辺に在るんですか *Where* in Tokyo [*In which part* of Tokyo] is your school located? (→どの辺) ‖ 皆さんは地球や地球上の生物がどのように進化したか知っていますか Do you know *how* the earth and the living things on it evolved?
2【すべての】every(どの…も皆); **each**(それぞれの); **all**(すべての) ▶どのチャンネルも同じ事件を放送している The same event is being aired on *every* channel. / *Each* channel is covering the same incident. ‖ どの道を行っても駅へ出ます You can get to the train station *whichever* street you take. ‖ 私はどの質問にも答えられなかった I could*n't* answer *any* (of the) questions. ‖ どの生徒もその質問に答えられなかった *None* of the students were [was] able to answer the question. (◎ none of A の A が複数形のとき動詞は本来単数で応じるのが正しいとされたが, 現在は複数形で応じるのがふつう) ‖ 彼はチームのどの選手よりも足が速い He can run faster than *any other* member of his team. ‖ そのコンサートはどの席も売り切れています *All* tickets for the concert have been sold out. ‖ 彼の演奏はどの点から見ても非の打ちどころがない His performance is faultless *in every respect*.

-どの -殿 《解説》英語には「-殿」に当たる1語はないので,「-様」の項の説明に従って, Mr., Mrs., Ms. などを適宜使い分けるとよい. →-さま.

どのう 土嚢 a **sandbag**(砂袋) ▶土嚢を積んで台風に備える prepare for a typhoon by piling up *sandbags*.

どのくらい どの位 **1【距離】how far**(遠さを尋ねて); **how long**(長さを尋ねて) ▶ 対話「東京から大阪までどのくらいありますか」「約500キロです」"*How far* is it from Tokyo to Osaka?" "About 500 kilometers." ‖ 対話「大鳴門橋の長さはどのくらいですか」「約1600メートルです」"*How long* is the Ōnaruto Bridge?" "About 1,600 meters."
2【時間】how long ▶ 対話「東京から那覇まで飛行機でどのくらいかかりますか」「2時間半くらいだと思います」"*How long* does it take to fly to Naha from Tokyo?" "About two and a half hours, I suppose." ‖ 対話「静岡へ来られてどのくらいになりますか」「まだ3か月です」"*How long* have you been in Shizuoka?" "Only three months." ‖ 対話「トルコへはどのくらい行ってらっしゃるの?」「2か月です」"*How long* will you be in Turkey?" "Two months."
3【回数・量・広さ・高さなど】 ▶ 対話「1年にどのくらい(=何回)温泉に行きますか」「1, 2度ですよ」"*How many times* a year do you go to hot spring resorts?" "Just once or twice." (◎ How often ...? はより漠然とした頻度を聞くので a year をつけない) ‖ 対話「ロックコンサートにはどのくらいの人が集まりましたか」「数えたわけではありませんが1万人は超えていました」"*How many* people went to the rock concert?" "I didn't count how many, but there were more than ten thousand." ‖ 対話「コーヒーは1日にどのくらい飲みますか」「4, 5杯飲みます」"*How many* cups of coffee do you drink a day?" "Four or five." ‖ 対話「きみの勉強部屋はどのくらいの広さがありますか」「4畳半です」"*How large* [*big*] is your study room?" "Four and a half (tatami) mats." ‖ 対話「東京スカイツリーは東京都庁舎よりどのくらい高いの?」「知らないね」"*How much higher* is the Tokyo Skytree than the Tokyo Metropolitan Government Office Building?" "I don't know."
4【金額】how much ▶ 対話「ジェット機って一体どのくらいするものなの?」「ボーイング社に聞いたら?」"*How much* does a jet aircraft cost?" "How about asking Boeing?" ‖ 対話「東京でアパートに住んだら月にどのくらいかかるだろう」「10万円は要ると思うよ」"I wonder *how much* it costs a month to live in an apartment in Tokyo." "At least one hundred thousand yen, I suppose."
5【程度】 ▶私がどのくらい心配したか, 口では言えないほどよ I can't tell you *how much* I worried about you. ‖ 地震の被害[規模]がどのくらいか, 現在はまだ不明です It is not known yet *how much* damage there was from the earthquake [*how strong* the earthquake was]. ‖ 対話「輝夫のこと, どのくらい好きなの?」「死ぬほど」"*How much* do you love Teruo?" "I'm madly in love with him." (➤ madly は「狂おしいほど」の意. Enough to die for him. とすると「彼のためなら死んでもいいほど」の意となる) ‖ 対話「ギターはどのくらい(うまく)できる?」「まだ初心者レベルなんだ」"*How well* can you play the guitar?" "I'm still at a beginning level."

とのさま 殿様 a **(feudal) lord** (➤ 呼びかけは My lord /maɪ lɔ́ːʳd, mɪ lɔ́ːʳd/); a **prince**(小国の王, 領主) ▶この退職金を持って外国へ行けば殿様のような暮らしができる If I go abroad with this retirement pay, I can live *like a prince*.
‖トノサマガエル a (black-spotted) pond frog ‖ 殿様商法 an amateurish way of doing business.

どのへん どの辺 ▶きみ, 神戸のどの辺に住んでたの? *Where* in Kobe did you use(d) to live? / *What part of* Kobe did you use(d) to live in? ‖ 背中のどの辺が痛みますか? *Where* on your back does it hurt? ▶首相の真意がどの辺にあるのかわからない I don't know *what* the Prime Minister's real intention is.

どのみち どの道 →どっち道.

-とは **1【何かを殊更に説明して】** ▶『友情とは何か』という本を読んだ I read a book entitled "*What is Friendship?*" ▶あの人は芸術家とは言えない You *can't call* him an artist. / He *doesn't deserve to be called* an artist.
2【意外な気持ちを表して】 ▶こんな所でお目に掛かるとは思いませんでした I *never expected* to meet you in a place like this. ‖ おばは50歳とは思えないほど若い My aunt *hardly looks* fifty. ‖ 彼女がそんなことを言うとは思えない She *would be the last person to* say something like that. ‖ あの歌手がそんなに優秀な大学を卒業しているとは思ってもみなかった I *never dreamed* that singer could have graduated from such a prestigious college. (➤ 接続詞の that が dreamed のあとに省略されている).
3【…ほども】 ▶いちばん近いバス停まで5分とはかかりません It doesn't take *more than* five minutes to (get to) the nearest bus stop.

トパーズ (a) **topaz** /tóʊpæz/.

-とはいうものの -とは言うものの **but**(しかし); **(al)though**(…だけれども); **nevertheless, however**(➤ 前者が強意) ▶車は大気汚染のもととは言うものの, やはり便利さで使ってしまう *Though* we know cars cause air pollution, we use them because they are convenient.

-とはいえ -とは言え ▶事情を知らなかったとは言え, 彼の行為はやはり不適当だった *Even though* [*Granted*] he wasn't aware of the situation, his conduct was without doubt improper.

とばく 賭博 gambling ▶あの人は賭博で一文無しになったらしい They say that the man *has gambled away all his money*. ‖**賭博師** a gambler ‖**賭博場** a gambling den [house].

とばす 飛ばす 1【空中に飛ぶようにする】fly +㊐ ▶子供たちは模型飛行機を飛ばしていた The children *were flying* model planes. ‖どこまで紙飛行機を飛ばせるか競争しよう Let's compete to see how far we *can fly* our paper planes. ‖風で帽子が飛ばされた The wind *blew* my hat *off*. / My hat *blew off*.

2【勢いよく働かせる】hurry ▶電車に乗り遅れそうだったので，駅までタクシーを飛ばした I thought I would be late for the train, so I *rushed* to the station in a taxi. ‖この運転では遅すぎる. もっと飛ばせよ You're driving too slow. *Step on it* [*Speed up*].
▶今からそんなに飛ばすとあとでばてるぞ If you*'re going at it* so much now, you'll be worn out.

3【ことばを放つ】▶冗談を飛ばす *crack* a joke ‖『ドン・ジョバンニ』の主役が下手だったので観客はやじを飛ばした The audience *booed* the title-role player of "Don Giovanni" for his poor singing [performance].

4【省く】skip +㊐ ; leave out (抜かす) ▶私たちは教科書の最初の2課を飛ばして3課から始めた We *skipped* the first two lessons of the textbook and began with Lesson 3. ‖外国語を読むときは，わからない単語は飛ばしてまず大体の意味をつかむことだ When you read a foreign language, you should first *skip* unfamiliar words to grasp the general idea. ‖彼女はその歌の2番を飛ばした She *left out* the second verse of that song.

5【左遷する】▶父は地方の支店に飛ばされた My father *was relegated* [*was packed off*] to a local branch office. (➤ relegate /rélɪgeɪt/ は「格下げする」) ‖部長は気に入らない部下を地方支店に飛ばすので有名だ The department head is notorious for *transferring* his people to local offices if he is not pleased with them.

とばっちり ▶彼はその事件のとばっちりを受けた (＝に巻き込まれた) He *got dragged into* the affair. ‖私は彼らのけんかのとばっちりを受けてけがをした I *got caught in* their fight and was injured.

どばと 土鳩 《鳥》 a (common) pigeon.

とび 鳶 1【鳥】a (black) kite ▶まさに鳶が鷹(たか)を生んだかのようだ It's really a case of so-called *a kite breeding a hawk*.
‖**鳶色(の)** reddish brown, auburn.
2【職業】a steeplejack.

とびあがる 跳び上がる・飛び上がる jump 《up》 ▶足もとにムカデがいるのを見て少女は驚いて飛び上がった The little girl *jumped* [*sprang*] *to her feet* in surprise when she saw a centipede at her feet. ‖彼は合格の知らせを聞いて飛び上がって喜んだ He *jumped* [*danced*] *for joy* when he heard the news of his success. ‖弟に手の傷口を触られたときは飛び上がるほど痛かった I *almost jumped with pain* [*leaped out of my skin*] when my (younger) brother touched the cut on my hand.

とびあるく 飛び歩く ▶彼女はいつも仕事で飛び歩いている She *is* always *on the run* in her job. / Her job keeps her *on the run*. (➤ on the run は「せかせかと忙しそうにして」の意) ‖彼は毎日セールスに飛び歩いている Every day, he *is* always *running around* trying to make sales. (➤ run around は「活発に動き回る」).

とびいし 飛び石 stepping-stones (日本庭園などの踏み石) ▶飛び石伝いに歩く step *from stone to stone*.
‖**飛び石連休** on-and-off holidays ; a series of holidays separated by one or two workdays.

とびいた 飛び板 a diving board, a springboard.

とびいり 飛び入り ▶彼は飛び入りでその相撲大会に参加した He took part in that sumo tournament *though he had not submitted his entry beforehand*. (➤「前もって出場を申し込んでいなかったが」の意).

とびうお 飛び魚 《魚》 a flying fish.

とびうつる 飛び移る ▶猿は枝から枝へ飛び移った The monkey *jumped* [*moved*] from branch to branch.

とびおきる 飛び起きる ▶けさの地震でベッドから飛び起きた I *jumped* [*shot*] *out of bed* (frightened) by the earthquake this morning.

とびおりる 飛び降りる jump down ▶屋根から飛び降りる *jump down* from a roof ‖バスが止まると彼は慌てて飛び降りた The bus stopped and he rushed to *leap off*. ‖17歳の女子高生がアパートの9階から飛び降りて自殺した A 17-year-old high school girl *killed herself* [*committed suicide*] *by jumping* from the ninth floor of an apartment building.

とびかう 飛び交う ▶怒号が飛び交う中で法案の強行採決が行われた The bill was forced through while angry shouts *flew back and forth*.

とびかかる 飛び掛かる jump [leap] 《at》 (➤ leap はフォーマルで「大きく飛び越える」という含みがある) ▶黒い犬が急に私に飛びかかって来た A black dog *jumped at* [*on*] me suddenly. (● at は「目がけて」のニュアンス. on は接触を表し，飛びつかれたことをはっきりさせる) ‖猫はトカゲに飛びかかった The cat *pounced on* the lizard. (➤ pounce /paʊns/ は「飛びかかって爪などで勢いよくつかむ」) ‖タカがウサギに飛びかかろうとしている The hawk is about to *swoop upon* a hare. (➤ swoop は「突然舞い降りて飛びかかる」) ‖女性警察官が泥棒に飛びかかって捕まえた A female police officer caught the thief *by hurling herself on* top of him. (➤hurl oneself on は「体ごと猛然と飛びかかる」).

とびきゅう 飛び級 (grade-)skipping 一動 **飛び級する** skip grades ▶リンダは4年生から6年生に飛び級した Linda *skipped from grade 4 to grade 6*.
‖**飛び級制度** a fast-track program.

とびきり 飛び切り ▶このレストランの料理は飛び切りうまい The food at this restaurant is the *very* best [is *outstanding* / is *superb*]. ‖彼のお姉さんは飛びきりの美人だ His (older) sister is *quite* a looker [is a *real* knockout].

とびこえる 飛び越える・跳び越える jump [leap] over (➤ leap はフォーマルで「大きく飛び越える」という含みがある) ▶垣根を飛び越える *jump over* a fence / *clear* a fence ‖《飛行機などが》アルプス山脈を飛び越える *fly over* the Alps ‖少年は小川を飛び越えた The boy *jumped* [*leaped*] *across* the stream. ▶彼は期末テストで5人飛び越えて1番になった In the finals, he *passed over* five other students to reach the top of the class.

とびこす 飛び越す・跳び越す jump over ▶塀を飛び越す *jump over* a wall ‖彼女は先輩たちを飛び越して課長になった She was promoted to section chief *over the heads of* her seniors.

とびこみ 飛び込み 1【飛び込むこと】▶その男は列車に飛び込み自殺をした The man *killed himself by* *throwing himself* [*by jumping*] *in front of a train*.

2【ダイビング】diving

‖**飛び込み競技** a diving event ‖ **飛び込み台** a diving platform(固定した) ; a springboard(飛び板) ‖ **飛び板飛び込み** springboard diving.

3【予約がないこと】▶**飛び込み**だけど部屋は空いていますか I *don't have a reservation*, but do you have a room I could stay in tonight?

‖**飛び込み営業** door-to-door sales.

とびこむ 飛び込む jump into(空中に身を投げるようにして) ; **dive** [**plunge**] **into**(頭から水中へ) ▶子供を救おうと私は橋の上から川に**飛び込んだ** I *jumped* [*dived* / *plunged*] from the bridge *into* the river to save the child. (➤《米・インフォーマル》では dive の過去形に dove /doʊv/ も用いる) ‖ トラックが角の店に**飛び込んだ** A truck *crashed into* the store on the corner. ‖ 窓を開けたとたん何か黒いものが**飛び込んできた** The moment I opened the window, something black *flew in*.

▶急に雨が降り出したので近くの喫茶店に**飛び込んだ** Since it had begun to rain suddenly, I *rushed into* a nearby coffee shop.

▶《比喩的》彼女は19歳のとき映画の世界に**飛び込んだ** She *ventured into* the movie business at the age of nineteen. ‖ 朝刊を開けると「自民党, 惨敗」の大見出しが目に**飛び込んできた** The instant I opened the morning paper, the headline "LDP Routed" *caught my eye*.

とびさる 飛び去る fly away ▶捕まえる寸前にチョウは**飛び去ってしまった** The butterfly *flew away* just before I could catch it.

とびだし 飛び出し ▶《掲示》子供の**飛び出し**注意 *Watch out for* Children.

‖**飛び出しナイフ** a switchblade knife.

とびだす 飛び出す 1【勢いよく外に出る】jump out (of) ▶籠からバッタが**飛び出した** A grasshopper *jumped out of* the cage. ‖ 《標語》**飛び出すな**. 車は急には止まれない Don't *rush out*. Cars can't stop suddenly. ‖ 大きな揺れが来たとたん, 皆外へ**飛び出した** Everybody *rushed outside* the moment a big tremor occurred. ‖ (幼児向けの)**飛び出す絵本** a pop-out [pop-up] book.

2【リードする】▶《マラソンで》藤田はスタート直後から**飛び出して**先頭に立った Fujita *made a quick dash* and immediately took the lead in the marathon.

3【突出する】▶くぎが床から**飛び出している** A nail *is sticking out* from the floor. ‖ 大きな岩が頭上に**飛び出している** A big rock *projects* [*juts out*] over the road.

4【出ていく】▶彼は事件のあと郷里を**飛び出した** After the incident, he *ran away from* his hometown. ‖ その助手は大学を**飛び出して**企業の研究員になった The assistant *quit* (*his* [*her*] *job at*) a university and joined the company as a researcher.

とびたつ 飛び立つ fly away(鳥などが) ; **take off**(飛行機が) ▶飛行機は成田を定刻より10分遅れて**飛び立った** The plane *took* [*flew*] *off* from Narita Airport ten minutes behind schedule.

とびち 飛び地 an **enclave**.

とびちる 飛び散る ▶ガラスの破片が床一面に**飛び散った** Fragments of broken glass *flew* all over the floor. ‖ 泥水が壁まで**飛び散った** The dirty water *splashed* against the wall.

とびつく 飛び付く jump [**leap**] **at** ▶《犬などに向かって》**飛びつくな**! Don't *jump at* me! ‖ 彼は電話が鳴るとすぐにそれに**飛びついた** He *grabbed for* the phone the instant it rang. (➤ grab は「ぐいとつかむ」).

▶彼はきっとこの計画に**飛びつく** He is sure to *jump at* this plan. ‖ そのスウェットスーツは市価の半値だったので, みんな**飛びついた** We all *snapped up* the sweat suits because they were at half the normal retail price. (➤ snap up は「我先に買う」).

トピック a **topic** ▶今週の**トピック** the *topics* of this week ‖ **トピック**になるようなニュース a *topical* news item.

とびでる 飛び出る 1【勢いよく外に出る】spring out ▶手品師が帽子をステッキでぽんとたたくとウサギが**飛び出た** The magician tapped the hat with a stick, and *out* (*of it*) *sprang* a rabbit. ‖ あんまりびっくりしたんで, 心臓が口から**飛び出る**かと思ったよ I was so surprised I *almost jumped out of my skin*.

2【突出する】stick out ▶靴の中にくぎが**飛び出ていて**痛い A nail is *sticking out through* the sole of my shoe and it really hurts.

▶《慣用表現》その毛皮は目の玉が**飛び出る**ほど高い The fur (coat) is *exorbitantly* [*ridiculously*] high-priced. (➤ exorbitantly は「法外に」) / The price of the fur (coat) is simply *eye-popping*.

とびとび 飛び飛び ▶庭には石が**とびとび**に置かれている The rocks are placed *at intervals* [*here and there*] in the garden. (➤ at intervals は「間隔を置いて」) ‖ その連続ドラマは**とびとび**にしか見ていないが, 話はおおよそわかっている I see the serial only *on and off*, but I think I'm following the story fairly well.

とびにゅうがく 飛び入学 ▶大学への**飛び入学**制度 *an early* college *admission program* ‖ 3人の優秀な高校生がその大学に**飛び入学した** Three gifted high school students *skipped the last year of high school and went directly into* the university.

とびぬけて 飛び抜けて ▶彼女は暗算が**飛び抜けて**速い She is *outstandingly* [*amazingly*] quick at mental arithmetic. ‖ 今回のテストでは**飛び抜けて**成績のいい者はいなかった No student *distinguished himself* [*herself*] in this examination.

とびのく 飛び退く ▶彼は頭上から鉄骨が落ちてくるのを見ると同時に**飛びのいた** The instant he saw the steel girder dropping, he *jumped aside* [*back*].

とびのる 飛び乗る jump on [**into**] ; **hop on**(ひょいと飛び乗る) ▶記者は知らせを受けると同時にバイク[車]に**飛び乗った** The reporter *jumped on* his motorbike [*into* his car] as soon as he received the news.

とびばこ 跳び箱 a (**vaulting**) **horse** ▶**とび箱**を跳ぶ vault (over) *a horse*.

とびはねる 跳び跳ねる・飛び跳ねる ▶子犬が部屋の中で**跳びはねている** A puppy *is romping around* in the room. (➤ romp は「はしゃぎ回る」).

▶水が周りに**跳びはねた** Water *splashed* around.

とびひ 飛び火 flying sparks ▶**飛び火**で川向こうの家も焼けた Due to *flying sparks*, the houses on the other side of the river also caught fire. ‖ 《比喩的》アメリカの経済不況は日本にも**飛び火した** America's recession *had repercussions* in Japan. (➤ repercussions は「(間接的)影響, 余波」).

とびまわる 飛び回る fly around [**about**] ▶チョウがヒマワリの周りを**飛び回っている** A butterfly *is flying* [*fluttering*] *around* the sunflower. ‖ 子供たちが雪

の上を飛び回っていた Children were *running around* [*about*] in the snow. ▶《比喩的》ジャーナリストの彼はいつも仕事で飛び回っている He *gets about* [*around*] *quite a lot* in his job as a journalist.

どひょう 土俵 a **sumo ring** ▶力士は押されて土俵を割った The sumo wrestler was pushed out of the *ring*. ‖ほら, 横綱の土俵入りが始まるよ Look, the yokozuna's just starting to perform *the dohyo-iri* [*ring-entering*] *ceremony*.

▶土俵際でようやく交渉が妥結した *At the* (*very*) *last moment*, an agreement was finally reached in the negotiations.

▶《慣用表現》社会人になって, ようやく兄と同じ土俵に立てた After I began working full-time, I felt that I *was* finally *on an equal footing* with my elder brother.

とびら 扉 a **door**(ドア) ; a **title page**(本の) ▶鉄の扉 an iron *door*.

どびん 土瓶 an **earthenware teapot.**

とぶ 飛ぶ·跳ぶ

> 訳語メニュー
> 空中を進む →fly **1**
> 跳ねる →jump, leap **2**
> 急行する →fly, hurry **3**

1【空中に浮かんで移動する】**fly** ▶高く[低く]飛ぶ *fly* high [low] ‖カモメが飛んでいる There are seagulls *flying*. ‖ＵＦＯが西の方へ飛んでいくのを見た I saw a UFO *flying off* toward the west. ‖チョウがひらひら飛んでいる Butterflies *are fluttering* about. ‖どこからともなくタンポポの綿毛が飛んで来た Fluffy dandelion tufts *came floating in the air* from somewhere. ‖シャボン玉が空に飛んだ Soap bubbles *drifted* [*floated*] *up* into the air. ‖風で洗濯物が物干しざおから飛んでしまった The wind *blew* the laundry *off* the pole. (➤「風が吹き飛ばした」の意) ‖担当記者はあすニューヨークへ飛びます The reporter on assignment will *fly to* New York tomorrow. ‖ことわざ 飛んで火に入る夏の虫 A summer bug flies into the fire. (➤日本語からの直訳) ／A fool hunts for misfortune. (➤「愚か者は自ら不幸を探す」の意).

▶《慣用表現》このジーンズは飛ぶように売れている These jeans *are selling like crazy* [*mad*]. (● sell like hot cakes ともいうが陳腐) ‖彼は今や飛ぶ鳥を落とす勢いだ He'*s going great guns* at this stage of his life. (➤ go great guns は「急速に大成功する」の意のインフォーマルな表現).

2【跳ね上がる】**jump** ; **leap**(かなりの距離を) ▶彼は三段跳びで16メートル跳んだ He *leaped* [*jumped*] 16 meters in the triple jump. ‖その女の子は片足で石から石へぴょんぴょん跳んだ The girl *hopped* on one foot from stone to stone. ‖選手が飛び込むと水しぶきが観客席まで飛んだ The swimmer(s) dove into the pool, *splashing* water onto the stands. (➤ splash は「はね散らす」).

3【直行する】**hurry**(急ぐ) ; **rush**(大慌てで) ▶家に飛んで帰る *hurry* home ‖父が脳卒中で倒れたという電話が入ったので, 私は病院へ飛んでいった(＝駆けつけた) I *flew* [*rushed* ／*ran*] *to* the hospital as soon as I got the phone call saying that my father had had a stroke. (➤ flew は fly の過去形).

▶容疑者は長崎へ飛んだらしい The suspect appears to *have fled to* Nagasaki. (➤ fled は flee(逃げる)の過去分詞形).

4【途中が抜ける】▶この本は16ページ飛んでいる Sixteen (continuous) pages *are missing* from this book. ‖おばあちゃんの話はあちこち飛ぶのでついていくのが大変だ I find it difficult to follow what my grandmother says since she *jumps* from one subject to another.

5【つながっていたものが切れる】▶ヒューズが飛んだ The fuse *has blown*. ‖会社の金を使い込んだら首が飛ぶよ You'll *be fired* if you start pocketing money from your company.

6【消失する】▶借金を返したら給料の半分が飛んでしまった Half of my salary is *gone* after paying (off) the debt. ‖《親が子に》痛いの, 痛いの, 飛んでけ！*Out, out* with the pain!

どぶ 溝 a (**muddy**) **ditch**(排水溝) ; a **gutter**(側溝) ▶どぶさらいをする clear (out) *a ditch*.

‖どぶ板 a board cover for a ditch ‖どぶ川 a river with muddy [stagnant] water.

とぶくろ 戸袋 a **door** [**shutter**] **case.**

どぶねずみ 溝鼠《動物》a **Norway rat**, a **brown rat** ▶どぶねずみ色のスーツ a *drab, gray* suit (➤ drab は「くすんだ」).

どぶろく 濁酒 ***doburoku*** ; unrefined homebrewed sake(➤説明的な訳).

とべい 渡米 ▶首相は近く渡米して大統領と会談する予定だ Before long, the Prime Minister will *visit the United States* and have talks with the President.

どべい 土塀 an **earthen wall.**

とほ 徒歩で on foot (➤しばしば by car などと対比して用いる) ▶私は毎朝徒歩で学校へ通っています I walk to school every morning. ／I go to school *on foot* every morning. (●前者のほうが英語として自然) ‖ここから駅まで徒歩20分です It takes twenty minutes *to walk* from here to the train station. ／It's a twenty-minute *walk* from here to the train station.

‖徒歩旅行 a walking tour, a hike.

とほう 途方 ▶彼は３つの大学に全部落ちて途方に暮れた After failing the entrance exams for all three universities, he *was at a* (*total*) *loss*. ‖スリランカではことばが通じなくて途方に暮れた I *felt completely lost* in Sri Lanka because I did not understand the local languages.

とほうもない 途方も無い absurd(ばかばかしい) ; **wild**(法外な, でたらめの) ▶彼は時々途方もないことを言う Sometimes he says *absurd* things. ‖砂漠緑化は途方もない計画だ The greening of the desert is a *wild* plan. (➤プラスのイメージなら a far-reaching plan) ‖アマゾンは途方もなく大きな川だ The Amazon is an *extraordinarily* big river. (➤ extraordinarily /ɪkstrɔ́ːʳdnèrəli/ は「並外れて」) ‖その骨とう屋は, 途方もなく高い値段をつけている That antique shop owner is asking a *ridiculously* [an *exorbitantly* ／an *incredibly*] high price.

どぼく 土木 ▶土木工事には金が湯水のように使われる Money is being spent like water on *construction projects*.

‖土木技師 a civil engineer ‖土木工学 civil engineering.

とぼける 恍ける 1【知らないふりをする】▶とぼけるな！おまえが俺のカメラ取ったの知ってるんだぞ Don't *play innocent* [*dumb*]! I know you took my camera. (➤ play dumb /dʌm/ は「知っているのに知らん顔をする」)(→おとぼけ).

2【間の抜けたまねをする】▶彼はとぼけた演技でいつも観客を笑わせる He *plays the fool* and always makes the audience laugh.

とぼしい 乏しい **scant**(辛うじて足りる); **little**(ほとんどない); **scanty**(特に量が不足している); **scarce**(豊富でない・十分でない; 名詞の前では用いない) ▶乏しい証拠 *scant* evidence ‖ 科学に興味の乏しい学生 a student with *little* interest in science ‖ 乏しい情報 *scanty* information ‖ 乏しい収入 a *scanty* income ‖ 資金が乏しくなってきた Our funds have *become scarce*. ‖ こちらでは食糧は乏しく, 職は更に乏しい状態です Food is *scarce* and jobs are *scarcer* here. ‖ 日本は鉱物資源の乏しい国である Japan is a country with *few* mineral resources. ‖ 天体の知識に乏しいので, 星の名前は少しもわかりません I have *little* knowledge of astronomy, so I don't know the names of any of the stars.

とぼとぼ ▶お年寄りがとぼとぼと暗い道を歩いていた An elderly man was *plodding* along the dark road. ‖ 彼女に会えなくて, 彼はとぼとぼと帰っていった He *trudged* home after he failed to see her. (➤ trudge は「足取り重く歩く」).

どぼん ▶持っていたスーツケースがドボンと海に落ちてしまった The suitcase I was carrying fell into the ocean *with a big* [*huge*] *splash*. (➤ splash は「バシャッ」「ザブン」などとはねる音).

どま 土間 an **earth floor**, 《米また》 a **dirt floor**.

トマト a **tomato** /təméɪṭoʊ ‖ -máːt-/
‖**トマトケチャップ** (tomato) ketchup ‖ **トマトジュース** tomato juice ‖ **トマトソース** tomato sauce ‖ **トマトピューレ** tomato purée ‖ **ミニトマト** a cherry tomato.

とまどい 戸惑い **perplexity**(困惑); **embarrassment**(まごつき) ▶ぼくの姿を見ると彼女は戸惑いの表情を見せた She *looked embarrassed* [*perplexed*] when she saw me.

とまどう 戸惑う **be puzzled** ▶この島へ来た当初は生活習慣の違いに戸惑ったものです When I first came to this island, I *was puzzled* by the differences in lifestyle. ‖ 話したこともない岡田君からコンサートに行かないかと誘われて戸惑っちゃった *I didn't know what to say* [*I didn't know how to answer* / *I was at a loss*] when Okada, whom I've never spoken to, asked me to go to a concert with him. ‖ 彼が急に黙り込んでしまったので私は戸惑った His sudden silence *perplexed* me.

とまり 泊まり a **stay**(滞在); **night duty**(宿直) ▶1晩泊まりの客 an *overnight* guest ‖ 今夜は泊まりだ I am *on duty* tonight. (➤「泊まり勤務」は overnight shift という).
‖**泊まり客** a guest (at a hotel)(ホテルなどの).

-どまり -止まり ▶次のこだま号は名古屋止まりです The next Kodama will *go only as far as* Nagoya [will *not go beyond* Nagoya]. ‖ どんなに頑張っても彼はせいぜい課長止まりだ No matter how hard he works, he'll *make* section chief *at best*. ‖ この電車は当駅止まりです This train service *terminates* at this station. / This train *terminates* here.

とまりがけ 泊まり掛け ▶泊まりがけでいらっしゃいよ *Come and spend* the night with us. ‖ 泊まりがけで金沢へ旅行に行った I went on an *overnight* trip to Kanazawa. (➤ overnight は「1泊の」).

とまりぎ 止まり木 a **perch**; a **high stool**(バーなどの) ▶カナリアが止まり木に止まっていた A canary was on the *perch*.

とまりこむ 泊まり込む ▶記者たちは現地に泊まり込んで事件の取材を続けている Reporters are *staying overnight at* the site to cover the incident.

[1]とまる 止まる・留まる・停まる

📖 **訳語メニュー**
停止する →stop **1**
やむ →stop **2**
鳥などが枝で休む →perch **3**

1【動いているものが停止する】 **stop, make a stop** ▶《停車する》車はホテルの前で止まった The car *stopped* [*pulled up*] in front of the hotel. (➤「止まりかけていた」なら The car was stopping [was pulling up] ...) ‖《新幹線のアナウンス》まもなく小郡に止まります. 小郡を出ますと次は新下関に止まります Ladies and gentlemen, we'll soon *make a* brief *stop* at Ogori. After leaving Ogori, we will *stop* at Shin-Shimonoseki. ‖ あそこにバスが止まっている There is a bus *waiting* [*standing*] over there. (🔔 この文では stopping は使えない) ‖ 救急車が校舎の前に止まっていた *There was* an ambulance in front of the school building.
▶《アナウンス》飛行機が完全に止まるまで座席でお待ちください Please remain seated until the airplane *comes to a complete stop*. ‖《アナウンス》現在, 総武線は車両故障のために止まっています The Sobu Line trains *are not running* now due to mechanical failure. ‖ 止まれ! *Halt!* / *Freeze!* (🔔 前者は号令. 後者は警官などが逃げる者に向かって言う).

2【連続していたものがやむ】 **stop** ▶ばんそうこうを貼ったら指の切り傷の出血が止まった My finger *stopped* bleeding when I put a Band-Aid on the cut. ‖ この整腸剤を飲んだら腹痛が止まった My abdominal pain *went away* after I took this medicine for intestinal disorders. ‖ おかしくて笑いが止まらなかった I *couldn't stop laughing* because it was so funny. ‖ 爬虫(はちゅう)類や魚類は死ぬまで成長が止まらない Reptiles and fish *keep* growing until they die. ‖ 工事のため電気と水道が午前10時から正午まで止まります The electricity and the water supply will *be cut off* from 10 a.m. till noon due to the construction work. (➤ cut off は「(水道・電気・電話を)止める」) ‖《ホテルで》トイレの水が止まりません The toilet won't *stop flushing*.

3【動物が枝などに】 **perch** 《on》 ▶ワシが木の枝に止まった An eagle *perched* on the branch. ‖ スズメが電線に止まっている There are sparrows *perched* on the electric wire. ‖ 指先に赤トンボが止まった A red dragonfly *came to rest* on my fingertip.

4【固定される】▶太ってしまったのでスカートのホックが留まらなくなった I've gotten so fat I *can't get* this skirt *fastened* any more. ‖ カレンダーが画びょうで壁に留まっている A calendar *is tacked* on the wall.

[2]とまる 泊まる

stay 《at, with》 ▶私は今ヒルトンホテルに泊まっています I'*m* now *staying at* the Hilton Hotel. ‖ いとこは1週間うちに泊まった My cousin *stayed with us* for a week. (🔔「場所」のときは at, in,「人」のときは with) ‖ 奈良旅行のときはホテルに2日泊まった I *stayed at* a hotel in Nara for two days when I was sightseeing there. ‖ 息子は友だちのところへ行って泊まってくると言っていた My son said (that) he would visit a friend and *stay overnight with* him. ‖ このホテルは600人泊まれる This hotel *accommodates* six hundred

(people). ‖ このテントは大人 4 人が泊まれる This tent *sleeps* four adults.
▶大型タンカーが横浜港に泊まっている A supertanker *is anchored* [*is at anchor*] in Yokohama Port.

どまんなか ど真ん中 ▶私は名古屋のど真ん中で生まれました I was born in *the center* of Nagoya. ‖ 交差点のど真ん中でエンストしてしまった My car stalled *right in the middle* of the intersection.

とみ 富 wealth, riches (財産；後者は主に文語) a fortune (ばく大な財産) ▶富を蓄積する accumulate *wealth* ‖ ジョン・D・ロックフェラーは一代で巨万の富を築いた John D. Rockefeller made *a fortune* during his lifetime. ‖ 健康は富に勝る Health is better than *wealth*. (➤ 英語のことわざ).

とみに 頓に ▶私は最近とみに物覚えが悪くなった My memory is failing *quickly* these days.

ドミニカ Dominica (カリブ海の島国)
‖ドミニカ共和国 the Dominican Republic (ハイチの東隣の国).

ドミノ a domino ▶ドミノをする play *dominoes*.
‖ドミノ倒し domino toppling.

とみん 都民 a resident [a citizen] of Tokyo, a Tokyoite ; people in Tokyo (➤ 総称) ▶東京都民は政治に無関心なのだろうか Are *Tokyo residents* [*the people* (*living*) *in Tokyo* / *Tokyoites*] indifferent to politics ?

とむ 富む be rich 《in》 ▶大豆はたんぱく質に富む Soybeans *are rich in* protein. ‖ オーストラリアは地下資源に富んでいる Australia *abounds in* [*is rich in*] underground resources. / Australia has *abundant* [*plentiful*] underground resources. ‖ 経験に富んだ人の意見を聞いたほうがよい It would be better to ask someone who *has a lot of experience*.

とむらう 弔う hold a funeral (葬儀をする) ▶死者を弔う hold a funeral (for a deceased person) ‖ 我々は犠牲者の霊を弔った We *prayed for* the repose of the victims' souls. (➤ repose は「安らかな眠り」).

ドメイン 《コンピュータ》 a domain
‖ドメイン名 a domain name.

とめがね 止め金・留め金 a clasp (ベルト・ネックレス・バッグの) ▶バッグの留め金が壊れてしまった The *clasp* on my bag has broken. ‖ ネックレスの留め金を掛けてくれる? Could you *fasten* my necklace for me ?

ドメスティック domestic
‖ドメスティックバイオレンス domestic violence.

とめどなく 留め処無く・止め処無く endlessly ▶彼は酔っ払うととめどなくしゃべり続ける When he is drunk, he talks *endlessly* [*interminably* / *on and on*]. ‖ 母子の30年ぶりの対面シーンをテレビで見ていて, 涙がとめどなくあふれてきた When I saw on TV a mother meet her child for the first time in 30 years, I *couldn't hold back my tears*.

[1]とめる 止める・留める・停める

> **訳語メニュー**
> 停車させる →stop **1**
> スイッチを切る →turn off **2**
> 中断する →stop **3**
> 制止する →stop **4**
> 固定する →fasten **5**

1【停車させる】 stop +㊀ ; park +㊀ (駐車する) ▶次の信号の手前で車を止めてください Please *stop* the car just before the next signal. ‖ 警官たちは成田空港へ向かう車を全部止めて調べた The police officers *stopped* and checked all the cars heading for Narita Airport. ‖ 対話 「きみ, 車はどこに止めてきたの?」「路上です」"Where did you *park* your car ?" "On the street." ‖ 前の車にもう少し寄せて車を止めてください *Pull up* a little closer to the car in front.
▶警官はスピード違反のドライバーに車を止めるよう命じた The police officer ordered the speeding driver to *pull over*. ‖ 彼は手で合図してタクシーを止めた He *flagged down* a taxi. / He *hailed* a taxi. (➤ 後者の言い方がふつう).

2【停止させる】 turn off (スイッチを切る) ▶寝る前にエアコンは止めなさい *Turn off* the air conditioner before you go to bed. ‖ 女の子はショーウインドーの前で足を止めた The girl *stopped* in front of the show window. ‖ 《レントゲン撮影で》大きく息を吸って, はいそこで止めて Take a deep breath, (now) *hold it*. (➤ hold it は「そのままの状態でいる」).

3【連続しているものを中断する】 stop +㊀ ▶切り傷の出血を止めるためにばんそうこうを貼った I put a Band-Aid on the cut to *stop* the bleeding. ‖ 彼は電気料金を滞納して電気を止められた His electricity *was cut off* because he was behind in (paying) his electric bills. ‖ 温湯シロップはせきを止めるのに効果がある Lukewarm syrup is effective for *suppressing* a cough.

4【制止する, 禁止する】 stop +㊀ ▶誰も学生たちのけんかを止めようとはしなかった Nobody *tried to stop* the students' fight. ‖ 彼は私が止めるのも聞かず会社を辞めた He quit the company even though I tried to *stop* [*dissuade*] him. (● I stopped him とすると「彼を制止できた」ことになるので, try to を用いて説得がうまくいかなかったことを示す必要がある. dissuade (思いとどまらせる) も同様).

> **【文型】**
> 人(A)が…するのを止める
> stop A from doing

▶父は私がその指輪を買おうとするのを止めた My father *stopped* me *from* buy*ing* the ring.
▶私は親に外泊を止められた (=許可されなかった) I *was not allowed to* stay out overnight by my parents. ‖ 父はたばこと酒を医者に止められている The doctor has *told* my father *not to* smoke or drink.

5【固定する】 fasten /fǽsən/ +㊀ ▶彼女はマイケル・ジャクソンの写真を壁にピン[テープ]で留めた She *pinned up* [*taped*] a picture of Michael Jackson on the wall. ‖ レポートはホチキス[クリップ]で留めて提出しなさい *Staple* your term paper [*Fasten* your term paper *with a clip*] before handing it in. (➤ staple は「ホッチキスで留める」の意の動詞) ‖ 名札を胸に留めなさい *Stick* [*Fasten*] your name tag on your chest.
▶彼女は髪をバレッタで留めた She *held* her hair *in place* with a barrette. ‖ もう幼稚園児なんだから, ボタンはひとりで留められるね You're a kindergartener now, so you can *button* yourself *up*, can't you ?

[2]とめる 泊める ▶雨がひどく降っていたので, 私たちは彼を一晩泊めた Because it was raining hard, we *put* him *up* for the night. ‖ このホテルは客を50人しか泊める (=収容する) ことができない This hotel can *accom-*

modate only fifty guests.

▶船長は船を沖合に泊めた The captain *anchored* [*moored*] his ship off the coast.

1とも 友 a **friend** ▶心の友 one's *bosom* [*intimate*] *friend*(bosom は /bózəm/ と発音. intimate は異性の場合,「肉体[性的]関係のある」の意味になりえるので使用に注意) ‖ 生涯の友 one's *lifelong friend* ‖ 無二の友 one's *best friend* ‖ 酒を友とする have sake for *a companion*. →友だち.

2とも 供 an **attendant**(随行員) ; a **follower**(従者) ▶王様は大勢の供を連れていった The king went with many *attendants*. ‖ お供させてください Let me *go with* you.

▶喜んでお供しましょう I will be glad to *accompany* [*go with*] you. (➤ accompany も go with も対等の立場でともに行動すること). →お供.

3とも 艫 a **stern**(船尾).

1-とも -共 ▶2人とも私の友だちです *Both* (*of them*) are my friends. ‖ 2人とも正しいわけではない *Both of them* aren't right. ‖ 母子ともに元気です *Both mother and baby* are (doing) well. ‖ 2つの色とも気に入らない I do*n't* like *either* color. ／I like *neither* color. (➤ 前者のほうがふつう) ‖ きのう買った漫画本は5冊とも読んでしまった I finished reading *all of* the five comic books I bought yesterday. ‖ この切符は発売日とも1週間有効です This ticket is good for one week *including* [*inclusive of*] the day of issue. (➤ inclusive of のほうが形式ばった言い方).

2-とも **1【たとえ…でも】**▶独りのときは誰が来ようとも玄関の戸を開けてはいけないよ When you are alone at home, keep the front door closed *no matter* who comes.

2【見積もり】▶レポートを片づけるのにいくら長くともあと3日はかからないだろう It shouldn't take me more than three days *at the most* to complete my (term) paper.

3【強め】▶そんな雑誌は読みたいとも思いません I am not interested *at all* in reading that sort of magazine. ‖ 対話「代わりに行ってくれるかい？」「いいとも」"Will you go for me ?" "*Certainly.* ／*No problem.*"

ともあれ **anyway** ▶理由はともあれ, きみの行為は許し難い *Whatever the reasons*, your actions are unpardonable.

-ともあろうものが ▶三浦君ともあろうものがカンニングをするなんて信じられない I can't believe that Miura, *of all people*, cheated on the exam. (➤ of all people は「人もあろうに, よりによって」) ‖ 警官ともあろうものが賄賂を受け取るとはけしからん It is a shame that a police officer should take a bribe. (➤ この should は驚きや腹立ちを表す).

ともかく **1【どちらにしても】** **anyway** ▶ともかく10時までには家に帰りなさい *Anyway*, be sure to be home by ten. →とにかく.

2【…は別にして】▶冗談はともかく, たまには電話でもくれよ *Joking aside*, give me a phone call once in a while. ‖ 急用があるんならともかく, やたらに会社へ電話を掛けてくるなよ Don't call me at the office so often, *unless* you have urgent business. ‖ お父さんがどう言うかはともかくとして, 私はその計画に反対ですよ I am not for the plan, *whatever* your father may say about it.

ともかせぎ 共稼ぎ →共働き.

ともぐい 共食い **cannibalism** 一動 共食いをする **cannibalize** +目 ▶カマキリは共食いをする Mantises *cannibalize* each other.

▶《比喩的》その2つの商店は共食いして両方とも潰れた The two stores *preyed on each other's business* [*cannibalized* each other] until both went down.

ともしび 灯火 a **light**, a **lamplight**.

ともす 点す･灯す **light (up)** ▶ランプをともす *light* (*up*) a lamp ‖ ろうそくをともす *light* a candle.

ともすると[すれば] ▶ともすると一人っ子はわがままになる An only child *is apt to* [*is liable to*] become selfish. (「わがままになりがちだ」の意 ; be liable to do は特に好ましくない状態に陥りやすい場合に用いる).

ともだおれ 共倒れ ▶こう値下げ競争が続いては商店は共倒れしてしまう If the price war continues like this, many stores will end up *going under together*.

ともだち 友達 a **friend** ; **company**

語法 company は集合的に「仲間, 連れ」を指すが, 個人を指すこともある. したがって He is good company. (彼はおもしろい話し相手だ)ということができる.

▶親しい友だち one's *close friend* ‖ 新しい友だちを作る make *new friends* ‖ 私の何人かの男[女]友だち some *male* [*female*] *friends* of mine ‖ ビルとトムは友だちです Bill and Tom are *friends*. ／Bill is *friends* with Tom. (➤ friends と複数形になることに注意) ‖ 靖男は私の友だちです Yasuo is *a friend of mine*. (初めて話題になる友を指すときは a friend of mine とする. my friend はすでに話の中に出てきた友を指すとき).

> **あなたの英語はどう響く?**
> 「きのううちに友だちが来た」という日本語を Yesterday *my friend* came to my house. とすると, この話者には, 友だちはたった1人しかいないというように響く. Yesterday *a friend* (*of mine*) came to my house. とする.

▶彼女にはSNS上の友だちがいっぱいいる She has a lot of *friends* on social networking sites. ‖ 彼女と友だちになりたいんだ I hope I can *make friends with* her. ‖ 誕生会に学校の友だちを数人招待した I invited some of my *school friends* to my birthday party. (類語の schoolmate は「学友」に近いやや古風なことば) ‖ 悪い友だちはすぐできるが本当の友だちはなかなかできないものだ It is easy to get into *bad company*, but it is hard to make *true friends*. ‖ 彼は幼稚園時代の遊び友だちだ He was my *playmate* when we both were in kindergarten.

▶ 対話「いろいろ頼み事して悪いわね」「ばかね, 友だちじゃないの」"I'm sorry for asking so many favors (of you)." "Don't be silly. *That's what friends are for.*"

✉ **私と友だちになっていただけませんか** Will you *be friends with* me ?

✉ **文通[メール]を通じてお友だちになれたらどんなにすてきでしょう** It would be wonderful if you and I *could become friends* by writing [exchanging email(s)] with each other.

ともども 共々 ▶スタッフともども皆様のご利用をお待ちしております I'm looking forward to serving you *together with* my staff.

ともなう 伴う **1【連れていく】** **take** +目 ▶首相は夫人を伴ってそのパーティーに出席した The Prime Minister *took* his wife to the party. ／The Prime Minister attended the party *with* his wife. ‖ 芭蕉は曽良を伴って旅に出た Basho went on a journey *with* [*accompanied by*] Sora.

2【付随する】involve ＋㊀ ▶冬山登山はしばしば危険を伴う Climbing mountains in winter often *involves* risks. ‖ 戦争には多くの悲劇が伴う War *brings* many tragedies. ‖ 航空料金の変更に伴い，ツアー代金も変更になります The tour price will be revised *in accordance with* the change in airfare. ‖ 台風の接近に伴って風雨が強まるでしょう *As* the typhoon approaches, the rain and wind will become stronger.

3【釣り合う】▶人気の割に実力が伴わない芸能人がいる Some entertainers *don't have* the talent to match their popularity.

-ともなく ▶聞くともなく listen *idly*.

ともに 共に 1【両方とも】▶そのインスタント食品は老人にも子供にもともに好評です That instant food is popular with old folks and children *alike*.

2【一緒に】▶会社の倒産とともに失職した I lost my job *when* the company I worked for went bankrupt.

3【…につれて】as ; with（…とともに）▶祖父は年とともに体が弱くなってきた My grandfather became weak *as he grew older* [*with age*]. ‖ 昇進とともに給料が増えた I got a raise in pay *along with* my promotion.

ともばたらき 共働きの double-income ▶共働きの家庭 a *double-income* [*two-income* ／ *two-earner* ／ *two-career*] family ‖ 共働きの夫婦 a *working* couple.

▶うちは両親が共働きです *Both* (*of*) my parents *work*. ‖ 結婚後も共働きをし（＝仕事を続け）たいと思っています I'd like to continue to work after getting married.

ともびき 友引 *tomobiki*

✉ **友引は日本に古くからある暦上の６種類の日の分け方の１つです. この日には葬式を行うのを避けるのが一般的です.** *Tomobiki* is one of the six classification names of days on the old Japanese lunar calendar. Funerals are generally avoided on this day.

どもり 吃り stammering, stuttering（どもること；後者は（一時的でなく）どもりのある人の場合に用いることが多い）；a **stammerer**, a **stutterer**（どもる人）▶どもりは訓練によってある程度治すことができる You can cure yourself of *stammering* [*stuttering*] to some extent by (special) exercises.

ともる 点る・灯る be lit ▶ここの街灯は暗くなると自動的に灯がともる These street lamps *are* automatically *lit* [*turned on*] at dusk. ‖ クリスマスツリーにろうそくがともっていた The candles on the Christmas tree *were alight*.

どもる 吃る stammer, stutter ▶ぼくは緊張するとどもる I *stammer* [*stutter*] when I feel nervous. ‖ 彼はどもりながら礼を言った［言い訳した］He *stammered out* his thanks [excuses].

どやがい どや街 skid row ▶どや街に暮らす live on *skid row*.

とやかく ▶他人の生き方についてとやかく言うな Don't *be* so *critical about* other people's lives. ／Live and let live.（➤「己も生き他も生かせ」の意の英語のことわざ）‖ 今頃とやかく言ってももう遅い It is too late now to *quibble* about the matter.（➤ quibble は「ぐずぐず言う」）.

どやす ▶遅刻して上司にどやされた（＝叱りつけられた）よ The boss *chewed* me *out* [*came down hard on* me] for being late. ▶通りすがりにいきなり背中をどやされた（＝殴られた）As I passed by, I *received a* sudden *blow* on my back.

どやどや ▶数人の男がどやどやと部屋に押しかけてきた Several men barged into the room *noisily*. ‖ 兵士たちは輸送トラックにどやどやと乗り込んだ［輸送トラックからどやどやと降りた］The soldiers *piled into* [*off*] their transport trucks.

どよう 土用 *doyo* ; the period from July 20 or 21 to August 6 or 7 that connotes the very hot weather in midsummer（➤ 説明的な訳）《参考》英語の the dog days が「土用」に相当するが，こちらは７月３日頃から８月11日頃までを指す.

‖土用波 high waves in midsummer.

どよう(び) 土曜(日) Saturday《略 Sat.》▶おたくの会社は土曜日は休みですか Do you have *Saturdays* off at your company？ ⇀曜日.

どよめき a **stir** /stəːʳ/（ざわめき，興奮），**excitement** ▶中田がホームランを打つと札幌ドームにどよめきが起こった The moment Nakata hit a home run, *a stir* [*excitement*] swept through the Sapporo Dome.

どよめく stir ▶実験失敗の知らせにその場に居た人々はどよめいた *There was a stir* among those present when they heard that the experiment had failed.

とら 虎 1【動物の】a **tiger**（雄）; a **tigress** /táɪgrəs/（雌）▶トラはネコ科の哺乳動物だ *Tigers* are feline mammals.（➤ feline /fíːlaɪn/ は「ネコ科の」）‖ 去年はとら年だった Last year was *the year of the Tiger*. ▶《慣用表現》あれはとらの威を借るきつねというやつだ That's a case of *an ass in a lion's skin* [*a fox borrowing a tiger's authority*].（➤ 前者は「ライオンの皮をかぶったロバ」の意の熟語，後者は日本語からの直訳）.

2【酔っ払い】a **drunk** ▶年末には大とらが多い There are a lot of *loud drunks* at the end of the year. ‖ あいつは飲ませるとすぐとらになる When you get him to drink, he *gets drunk* right away.

どら 銅鑼 a **gong**.

とらい 渡来 ▶白鳥がいつもの年より早く北海道に渡来した（＝飛来した）Swans *flew over* [*across*] *the sea to* Hokkaido earlier than usual.

▶日本文化は仏教の渡来（＝伝来）によって大きな影響を受けた Japanese culture was deeply influenced by the *introduction* of Buddhism.

☛ **渡来人**（⇀見出語）

トライ a **try** ▶《ラグビーで》トライをあげる score *a try*. ▶T大にトライ（＝挑戦）してみたら？ Why don't you just *try* and take the entrance exam(s) for T University？

ドライ ▶彼はお金に対してドライな考え方をする He's *pragmatic* [*hard-nosed*] in financial matters. ‖ 近頃は物事をドライに割り切る若者が多い Nowadays, many young people *think* of everything *in a practical* [*unemotional* ／ *cut-and-dry*] *manner*.

‖ドライアイ《医学》dry eye ‖ ドライアイス dry ice ‖ ドライカレー curry-flavored fried rice with vegetables ‖ ドライフラワー a dried flower ‖ ドライフルーツ dried fruit ‖ ドライミルク dried [dry ／ powdered] milk ‖ ドライワイン dry wine.

危ないカタカナ語✸ドライ
英語の dry は「乾燥した, 無味乾燥な, そっけない」の意味であって, 日本語の「ドライ」の用法とは一致しない.「ドライに処理する」は deal with things in a pragmatic manner,「ドライな態度」は pragmatic [unemotional / businesslike] attitude,「彼女はドライだ」は She's all too practical. などとなる.

トライアスロン **triathlon** /traɪǽθlən/ ▶トライアスロンは鉄人レースと言われる The *triathlon* is called the iron man race.

トライアングル a **triangle** /tráɪæŋgəl/ ▶トライアングルを鳴らす play the *triangle*.

ドライクリーニング **dry cleaning** ▶このブラウスをドライクリーニングにしてください I'd like to have this blouse *dry-cleaned*.

とらいじん 渡来人 a ***toraijin***; the Chinese and Koreans who settled in Japan from the late fourth century to the early eighth century(➤説明的な訳).

ドライバー **1【運転者】** a **driver**; a **motorist**(自家用車の利用者) ▶ドライバーの皆さん, シートベルトを締めましょう Fasten your seat belts. / Please fasten your seat belts. (● ふつう, 英語で Drivers ...! と呼びかけることはあまりしない).
2【ねじ回し】 a **screwdriver**, a **driver** ▶ねじをドライバーで締める tighten a screw with *a driver*.
3【その他】 a **driver**(ゴルフのクラブ; コンピュータのプログラム).

ドライブ a **drive** 一動 **ドライブする go for a drive, take a drive** ▶きのう家族を箱根にドライブに連れていった I took my family to Hakone for *a drive* yesterday. / I *drove* my family (down) to Hakone. ‖ この新車でちょっとドライブしよう Let's *go for a drive* [*a spin*] in this new car. (➤ spin は「ひと走り」の意のインフォーマルな語) ‖ 私たちはあす伊豆にドライブに行く予定です We are going to *go for a drive* to Izu tomorrow.

あなたの英語はどう響く?
「私たちはあす, 箱根にドライブに行く予定です」を英訳すると, We are going to *go for a drive* to Hakone tomorrow. となるが, これを We are going to Hakone for a drive ... とすると,「まず箱根まで行って, そこで(例えばレンタカーを借りて)ドライブをする」という意味にも解釈される. We are going to drive to Hakone tomorrow. なら, 最初の日本語と同じ意味になる.

ドライブイン a **roadside restaurant**
〖解説〗英語の drive-in は車に乗ったまま食事ができる drive-in restaurant や, 乗ったまま映画を見られる drive-in theater を指す. したがって, 日本で見かける, 車を降りて入るレストランは roadside restaurant というほうが正確.

ドライブウェー a **scenic** /síːnɪk/ **highway** [**road**]; a **parkway**(樹木をたくさん植えたきれいな道).

危ないカタカナ語✸ドライブウェー
英語の driveway は表通りから私邸の車庫や玄関までの道, あるいはホテルなどの車回しを指す.

ドライブスルー a **drive-thru**, a **drive-through**(➤日常的には前者のつづりがふつう).

ドライブマップ a **road map**(➤ (×)drive map とはいわない).

ドライヤー a **dryer**, a **drier**, a **blower** ▶ドライヤーで髪を乾かす dry one's hair with *a blower* / blow-dry one's hair《参考》英語の dryer, drier は「ヘアドライヤー」に限らず「乾燥機」一般を指す.

トラウマ (a) **trauma**(➤医学用語としては trauma は「(重い)外傷」も指す) ▶長時間エレベーターに閉じ込められたトラウマで, 美香はエレベーターに乗るのが苦痛になっている Taking an elevator is very stressful for Mika because of her *traumatic experience* of being stuck in one for many hours.

とらえどころ 捕らえ所 ▶彼は何とも捕らえどころのない人物だ He has a rather *vague* personality. ‖ 彼の話は捕らえどころがなかった What he said *was ambiguous* [*fuzzy*]. (➤ ambiguous は「2つ以上の意味にとれる」の意) / He made a *vague* speech.

とらえる 捕らえる・捉える **1【捕まえる】** **catch** +⑪, **capture** +⑪; **arrest** +⑪ (逮捕する) ▶泥棒を捕らえる *capture* a burglar ‖ 殺人犯は警察に捕らえられた The murderer *was arrested* by the police.
▶レーダーが敵の機影を捉えた The radar *detected* an enemy plane. (➤ detect は「感知する」) / We *picked up* an enemy plane on the radar (screen).
2【心・意味・機会などを】 **capture** +⑪, **seize** /siːz/ +⑪; **grasp** +⑪ (把握する) ▶ビートルズの音楽は当時の若者の心を捉えた The music by the Beatles *captured* [*won*] the hearts of young people at that time. ‖ 警察はやっとその汚職事件の真相を捉えた The police *have* finally *gotten hold of* the facts behind that graft case. ‖ 読解問題では文章の要旨を捉えることが大切だ It is important to *grasp* the main point of passages on the reading comprehension test.

ドラキュラ **Dracula**.

トラクター a **tractor** ▶トラクターで畑を耕す cultivate [plow] field with *a tractor*.

トラスト a **trust**(企業合同).

[1]**トラック**《貨物自動車》a **truck**,《英また》a **lorry**《参考》「軽トラック」は light truck,「小型トラック」は pickup (truck) という.

[2]**トラック**《陸上競技》a **track**(走路) ▶トラック競技 *track* events.

ドラッグ **drugs**(麻薬) ▶ドラッグをやる do [shoot] *drugs*.

ドラッグストア a **drugstore**, a **chemist's (shop)**.

ドラッグバント《野球》a **drag bunt**
《参考》日本では「セーフティーバント」ともいうが, これは和製語.

どらねこ どら猫 a **stray cat**(迷い猫).

とらのこ 虎の子 ▶そのおばあさんはとらの子の貯金を取られてしまった The elderly woman had her *nest egg* stolen. (➤ nest egg は「(結婚・老後などに備えての)貯金」).

とらのまき 虎の巻 **the bible**(必携書, 必読書); a **key**(手引き, 解答集); a **crib**, a **pony**(あんちょこ) ▶ゴルフとらの巻 the *bible* of golf ‖ 英語問題集とらの巻 *a key* to an English exercise book ‖ とらの巻で答えを見てはいけない Don't use *a crib* (*sheet*) [*a pony*] to get the answers.

ドラフト ▶彼は2020年にドラフト1位でヤクルトに入団した He entered the Swallows in 2020 as the club's first *draft* choice. (➤「ドラフト1位」は top

draft pick とも, No.1 draft pick ともいう).
‖**ドラフト会議** a drafting session ‖**ドラフト制** the draft system.

トラブル **trouble** ▶彼女の家ではトラブルが絶えない There is no end of *trouble* [*problems*] in her family. ‖彼は会社でよく**トラブルを起こす** He often *makes trouble* in his office. ／He is a troublemaker in his office. (➤「トラブルを解決する人」は troubleshooter という) ‖彼女はしょっちゅうしゅうとめと**トラブルを起こす** She *is* always *causing problems* with her mother-in-law. (● with を for にすると,「しゅうとめに迷惑をかけている」というニュアンスになる. また,「トラブルを起こす」に get into trouble を当てることもできるが, こちらは警察や学校などの組織を連想させることもあるので, 訳例のような言い方が無難).

ドラマ a **drama**; a **play**(芝居) ▶テレビで**連続ドラマ**を見る watch *a serial drama* on TV ‖この夏の甲子園球場は数々の**ドラマ**を生んだ There were many *dramatic plays* [*scenes*] at Koshien Stadium this summer. ‖その事件は**ドラマ化された** The affair *was dramatized*. ‖彼のブラジルでの体験談は実に**ドラマチック**だった The story of his personal experiences in Brazil was really *dramatic* [*was full of drama*].
‖**テレビドラマ** a TV drama.

ドラマー a **drummer**.

ドラム a **drum**(太鼓; ドラム缶) ▶**ドラムをたたく** play [beat] the *drum* ‖石油の入った**ドラム缶** an oil *drum*. ‖**ドラムメジャー**(マーチングバンドの指揮者) a drum major; a drum majorette(女子).

どらむすこ どら息子 a **pleasure-loving son**(遊び好きな); a **son who has been spoiled rotten**(甘やかされてどうしようもなくなった); a **loose-living son**(生活態度のだらしない).

とられる 取[採・撮]られる **1**【奪われる】▶彼は電車の中で財布を**取られた** He *had* his wallet *stolen* on the train. (➤「盗まれた」の意) ／He *was robbed of* his wallet on the train. (➤「強奪された」の意) ‖駅前にスーパーができて, うちの店の客の大半を**取られた** The new supermarket in front of the train station has *taken* (*away*) most of our customers. ‖澤村投手は1回裏に2点**取られた** The pitcher Sawamura *yielded* [*gave up*] two runs in the bottom of the first inning.
2【採集される】▶この辺一帯の高山植物は心ない登山者たちに**採られてしまった** The alpine plants in this area have *been uprooted* by thoughtless climbers.
3【採取される】▶健康診断で尿と血を**採られた** I *had* urine and blood samples *taken* for the medical checkup.
4【写される】▶変な顔をしているところを偶然写真に**撮られた** I *was* accidentally *photographed* while making a funny face.
5【時間を要する】▶朝の時間の大半を洗濯に**取られる** My time in the morning *is* mostly *taken up* by doing the laundry.
6【要求される, 払わされる】▶壊れたバックミラーを新品と交換したら24000円(の**料金を**)**取られた** They *charged* twenty-four thousand yen for replacing the broken rearview mirror with a new one. ‖スピード違反で12000円の**罰金を取られた** I *was fined* twelve thousand yen for speeding. ‖父親の土地を相続してものすごい税金を**取られた** Whopping taxes *were imposed* [I had to pay whopping taxes] when I inherited my father's property.
7【制御できなくなる】▶自転車の荷台の荷物が重すぎて私はハンドルを**とられた** I *couldn't hold onto* the handlebars because the load on the rack was too heavy.
8【解釈される】▶彼の言動は**悪くとられがちだ** His words and actions tend to *be misinterpreted*.

とらわれる 捕らわれる **1**【捕らえられる】**be caught, be captured** →捕らえる.
2【こだわる】▶あまり外見に**とらわれるな** Don't *be overly influenced by* appearances. ‖村の人々は古いしきたりに**とらわれて**(＝縛られて)いた The village people *were bound by* [*tied to*] old traditions. ‖彼は誤った先入観に**とらわれている** He *is seized by* a false preconception.

トランク a **suitcase**(かばん); 《米》a **trunk**, 《英》a **boot**(車の) 《参考》trunk が「かばん」の意で用いられる場合, 通例日本語のトランクより大型のものを指す.

トランクス (a pair of) **trunks**.

トランシーバー a **transceiver**, 《インフォーマル》a **walkie-talkie**(携帯用).

トランジスター a **transistor**.

1**トランス** 《変圧器》a **transformer**.

2**トランス** 《恍惚》a **trance**.

トランプ a **card**(1枚の); (a **pack of**) **cards**(1組みの) ▶**トランプをする** *play cards* ‖**トランプ占いをする** *tell one's fortune with cards* ‖**トランプを切って**[**配って**]ください Please shuffle [deal] the *cards*.

> **危ないカタカナ語✹トランプ**
> 「トランプ」は英語の trump からきているが, この語は「切り札」の意味しかない.「トランプ遊び」は card playing といい,「トランプ1組み」は a pack [《米また》deck] of cards である. 1枚のカードは a (playing) card という.

トランペット a **trumpet** ▶**トランペットを吹く** play [blow] the *trumpet*.
‖**トランペット奏者** a trumpeter.

トランポリン a **trampoline** /trǽmpəli:n/ ▶**トランポリンをする** jump on *a trampoline*.

とり 鳥 **1**【鳥】a **bird**; **fowl** /faʊl/ (集合的に鳥類); **poultry** /póʊltri/ (鶏・ガチョウなど, 肉・卵が食用になる家きん一般) ▶**一群の水鳥** a flock of *water fowl*.
2【鶏】a **chicken**; a **hen**(雌); a **rooster**, 《英また》a **cock**(雄)(● cock にはタブー語としての penis の意があるので前者を用いることが多い) ▶父は**鶏(肉)**を食べない My father doesn't eat *chicken*. (➤「鶏肉」の意では Ⓤ 扱い).
‖**鳥インフルエンザ** bird flu(➤ 正式名称は avian influenza) ‖**鳥籠** a (bird) cage, a cage for birds ‖**鳥小屋** a birdhouse(小鳥用の); a henhouse(鶏用の) ‖**とり年** the year of the rooster.

> 「鳥」のいろいろ **アヒル** duck ／**アホウドリ** albatross ／**インコ** parakeet ／**ウ** cormorant ／**ウグイス** bush warbler ／**ウズラ** quail ／**ウミネコ** black-tailed gull ／**オウム** parrot ／**オシドリ** mandarin duck ／**オジロワシ** white-tailed eagle ／**オナガ** blue magpie ／**カケス** jay ／**カササギ** magpie ／**ガチョウ** goose ／**カッコウ** cuckoo ／**カナリア** canary ／**カモメ** (sea)gull ／**カラス** crow ／**カルガモ** spot-billed duck ／**カワセミ** kingfisher ／**キジ** pheasant ／**キツツキ** woodpecker ／**クジャク** peafowl; peacock(雄), peahen(雌) ／**コウノトリ** white

stork／コマドリ Japanese robin／コンドル condor／サギ heron／シジュウカラ great tit／シチメンチョウ turkey／シラサギ egret／スズメ sparrow／セキセイインコ budgerigar／セキレイ wagtail／タカ hawk／ダチョウ ostrich／タンチョウ Japanese crane／ツグミ thrush／ツバメ swallow／トキ Japanese crested ibis／トビ black kite／ハクチョウ swan／ハゲタカ vulture／ハチドリ hummingbird／ハト pigeon, dove／ヒバリ (sky) lark／ヒヨドリ brown-eared bulbul／フクロウ owl／フラミンゴ flamingo／ブンチョウ Java sparrow／ペリカン pelican／ペンギン penguin／ホオジロ meadow bunting／ホトトギス little cuckoo／ミヤコドリ oyster catcher／ムクドリ starling／メジロ white-eye／モズ shrike／ユリカモメ black-headed gull／ライチョウ ptarmigan／ワシ eagle／ワライカワセミ kookaburra, laughing jackass

ドリア ***doria***; rice gratin topped with white sauce or tomato sauce and lightly browned in an oven (➤ 説明的な訳).

とりあい 取り合い a **scramble**《for》▶席の取り合い *a scramble for* [to get] seats ‖ 進君とトモ子ちゃん, おもちゃの取り合いはやめなさい! Susumu and Tomoko, stop *fighting* over those toys!

とりあう 取り合う **1**【互いの手を取る】▶試験に合格したのを知って, 私は母と手を取り合って喜んだ My mother and I *took* [*clasped*] *each other's hands* with joy when we learned that I had passed the exam.
2【奪い合う】**scramble**《for》▶席を取り合うのはみっともない It is shameful to *scramble for* a seat. ‖ 兄弟は1つのおもちゃを取り合った The brothers *fought over* a toy. (➤「1つのおもちゃを巡ってけんかした」の意).
3【相手にする】▶彼が何と言ってきても取り合うな *Take no notice of* [*Pay no attention to*] anything he says. ‖ 夫は私のことなどまるで取り合ってくれない My husband doesn't *take* me *seriously* at all.

とりあえず 取り敢えず ▶とりあえずこれで間に合わせよう I will manage with this *for the time being* [*for the present*]. (➤ 前者は「しばらくの間」, 後者は「さしあたり, 今は」) ‖ 対話 (レストランで)「(ご注文は)これでよろしいでしょうか」「とりあえず, それで」"Will that be all?" "For now, *anyway*."

とりあげる 取り上げる・採り上げる **1**【手に取る】**pick** [**take**] **up** ▶受話器を取り上げる *pick up* the receiver／*lift* the receiver.
2【奪い取る】**take away** ▶いじめっ子が男の子の水鉄砲を取り上げた The bully *took* the water pistol *away* from the boy. ‖ 曽祖父は農地改革で土地を取り上げられた(=没収された) My great-grandfather *had* his land *confiscated* when the land reform took effect. ‖ 私は事故を起こして運転免許を取り上げられた(=停止された) My driver's license *was suspended* because of the car accident I caused.
3【採用する】**take up** ▶この議題は次の会議で採り上げます We will *discuss* this matter at the next meeting.／This agenda item will *be taken up* at the next meeting. ‖ 上司は私の苦情をなかなか採り上げて(=聞き入れて)くれそうもない My boss won't *listen to* my complaints. ‖ 私の提案は採り上げられなかった My proposal *was put aside*. (➤ put ... aside は「…を脇に置く」が原義).

とりあつかい 取り扱い ▶この耕うん機は取り扱いが簡単だ This cultivator is easy to *operate* [*run*]. ‖ 精巧なカメラですから, 取り扱いには注意してください The camera is very sophisticated, so you must be careful when *handling* it [you must *handle* it carefully]. ‖《表示》取り扱い注意 Handle with Care／Fragile(➤ 後者は「壊れやすい」の意).
‖取り扱い説明書 an instruction manual.

とりあつかう 取り扱う **1**【人を】**treat** ＋目 ▶人をぞんざいに取り扱う *treat* a person badly ‖ あなたは彼女をもっと丁重に取り扱うべきだ You should *treat* her more politely.
2【物を】**handle** ＋目, **operate** /ɑ́ːpəreɪt/ ＋目 ▶このリモコンは子供でも取り扱うことができる Even a child can *operate* [*use*] this remote control. ‖ この本は重要な問題を取り扱っている This book *deals with* an important subject. ‖ このテーマに関しては, 次章で取り扱います This topic *will be discussed* (in the next chapter). (➤ この discuss は「(テーマなど)を詳しく論じる」の意) ‖ うちでは酒類は取り扱っておりません We don't *carry* [*sell*] liquor. (➤ carry は「(店が品物を)置いている」) ‖ この事件は刑事事件として取り扱われることになった The case is going to *be treated* as a criminal case.

とりあわせ 取り合わせ **combination** (組み合わせ); **arrangement**(配列) ▶私は青と白の取り合わせが好きだ I like the *combination* of blue and white. ‖ 古城と月には取り合わせの妙がある *The combination* of an old castle and the moon is exquisite.

ドリアン a **durian** /dʊ́əriən/.

とりい 鳥居 a **torii**(➤ 英語化している)
日本紹介 ✉ **鳥居は神社の参道入り口にある大きな門です. 2本の柱の上部に2本の横木を渡した形で, 神域への入り口であることを示しています. 朱色に塗られていることもあります** Torii are large gates that stand at the start of the front approach to a Shinto shrine. They are made up of two pillars and two crossbars on the upper part to designate the entrance to a sanctuary. They are sometimes painted vermilion.
▶海に影を映す厳島神社の赤い鳥居は幻想的だ The sight of the red *torii* of (the) Itsukushima Shrine mirrored in the sea is like a dream.

とりいそぎ 取り急ぎ ▶取り急ぎ会議の中止をお知らせいたします We *hasten to* inform you that the meeting has been canceled.
✉ **取り急ぎお見舞い[お悔やみ]申し上げます** I am writing *immediately* to offer my deepest sympathy.

とりいる 取り入る ▶彼は上役に取り入ることばかり考えている He's always thinking of how to *play* [*suck*] *up to* his superiors. ‖ 見てごらんなさいよ. 彼女ったら部長に取り入っちゃってさ Look at her *buttering up* the department head. (➤ butter up は「おべっかを使う」の意).

とりいれ 取り入れ・穫り入れ **harvesting**(取り入れること); a **harvest**(1回の) ▶秋は取り入れの季節です Fall is *the harvest season*. ‖ ジャガイモの取り入れが行われている Potatoes *are* currently *being harvested*. ‖ 米の取り入れが終わった The rice crop *has been harvested* [*has been gathered in*].

とりいれる 取り入れる・採り入れる・穫り入れる
1【受け入れる, 採用する】**absorb** ＋目; **adopt** ＋目 ▶植物は太陽からエネルギーを取り入れる Plants *absorb*

[*take in*] energy from the sun. ‖ 明治維新以来, 日本人は西洋の文化を**採り入れてきた** The Japanese *have been absorbing* Western culture since the Meiji Restoration. ‖ きみの考えを我々の計画に**採り入れよう** I'd like to *use* [*adopt*] your idea(s) for our project. ／I'd like to *incorporate* your idea(s) *into* our project. (➤ incorporate は「組み込む」).

2【収穫する】harvest +㊐ ▶麦はいつ**取り入れる**のですか When *is* the wheat *harvested*?

とりえ 取り柄 a **strong** [**good**] **point**(強み) ; a **merit**(長所) ; an **asset**(プラスになるもの,「宝」) ▶私にはこれといった**取り柄**がない I have no *strong points* to speak of. ／I have no particular *talent*(*s*). ‖ この布は安くて丈夫なのが**取り柄**だ This cloth has the *merit* of being cheap and strong. ‖ 私は丈夫なだけが**取り柄**です Health is my only *asset*. ／My *strong point* is that I'm healthy.

トリオ a **trio** /tríːoʊ/ ▶ピアノ**トリオ** a piano *trio* ‖ クリーンアップ**トリオ** *a trio* of sluggers (➤ (×) cleanup trio とはしない. cleanup は 4 番打者のみを指す).

とりおこなう 執り行う hold (a ceremony) ▶当日はJR のストが予想されますが, 式は予定どおり**執り行われます** A JR strike is expected on that day, but the ceremony will *be held* as planned.

とりおさえる 取り押さえる catch +㊐ ; **arrest** +㊐ (逮捕する) ▶警官はすりを現行犯で**取り押さえた** The police officer *caught* [*arrested*] the pickpocket in the act.

とりおろし 撮り下ろし ▶**撮り下ろし**の授業用ＤＶＤ DVDs *especially edited* for classroom use ‖ 写真はすべてこのアルバムのための**撮り下ろし**です All the photos *have been taken specially* for this album.

とりかえ 取り替［換］え (a) **replacement** ; (an) **exchange**(交換) ▶このＴシャツ, もっと小さいのと**取り替え**できますか May I *exchange* this T-shirt for one in a smaller size? →**取り替える**.

とりかえし 取り返し ▶済んでしまったことは**取り返しがつかない** What is done *cannot be undone*. (➤ 英語のことわざ) ‖ 彼女は**取り返しのつかない**間違いをした She made an *irreparable* [*a fatal*] mistake. (➤ irreparable は「元に戻せない」, fatal は「致命的な」).

とりかえす 取り返す take [**get**] **back**(➤ take back のほうがより強引) ▶できることなら彼女にやった指輪を**取り返したい** If possible, I'd like to *get back* the ring I gave her. ‖ 若いうちにやりたいことをやっておきなさい. 若さは二度と**取り返せない**のだから Do what you want to while young. You *can't get back* your youth [you're only young once].

とりかえる 取り替［換］える 1【新しいものに替える】change +㊐, **replace**《A with B》▶ (赤ん坊の)おむつを**取り替える** *change* a baby's diaper／*change* a baby(➤ 後者は決まった言い方) ‖ 電池を**取り替える** *change* a battery ‖ 古い机を新しい机と**取り替える** *replace* an old desk *with* a new one ‖ この靴の底を**取り替えてください** Can you *resole* these shoes, please? ‖ 彼女はたくさんの恋人を**次々と取り替えている** She *has run through* a lot of boyfriends.

2【交換する】exchange《for》▶しわくちゃの1000円札を新しいのと**取り替えてもらった** I *had* my crumpled thousand-yen note *exchanged for* a new one. ‖《ホテルなどで》部屋を**取り替えて**もらえませんか Could you *give* me a *different* room? ‖ ぼくのＤＶＤときみのビデオゲームソフトを**取り替えないか** How about *trading* my DVD *for* your video game software? (➤ trade A for B で「AとBを交換する」) ‖ この品のお**取り替えはご容赦ください** This article *is not exchangeable*. ‖ バーゲン品の返品, および, **お取り替えはできません** Sale items cannot be refunded or *exchanged*.

とりかかる 取り掛かる set about ; **begin, start**《on》▶彼は会社に着くとすぐに仕事に**取りかかった** He *got down* to work as soon as he arrived at the office. ‖ 彼は 9 時に仕事に**取りかかった** He *began* [*started*] work at nine. ‖ 彼は先月から新しい小説の執筆に**取りかかっている** He *has been engaged in* writing a new novel since last month. (➤ be engaged in doing で「…に従事している」) ‖ 今**取りかかっている**仕事はことしいっぱいかかる予定だ The job (that) I *am working on* will end at the end of this year. ‖ あの人は仕事に**取りかかれば**早いんだが, **取りかかる**までがなかなかだ He doesn't take much time to finish a job once he *starts on* it, but it takes him a while to *get around to starting*.

とりかこむ 取り囲む surround +㊐ ▶大勢の少女たちがその歌手を**取り囲んだ** A crowd of girls *surrounded* [*gathered around*] the singer.

トリカブト《植物》an **aconite** /ǽkənaɪt/.

とりかわす 取り交わす exchange +㊐ ▶契約書を**取り交わす** *exchange* contracts ‖ 彼はローリーと 3 年間ずっと手紙を**取り交わしている** He *has exchanged* letters *with* Lori for three years.

とりきめ 取り決め an **agreement**(合意, 協定) ▶職員間の**取り決め**によりお中元やお歳暮は受け取らないことになっています We staff members *have agreed that* we will not accept midyear or year-end gifts.

とりきめる 取り決める fix +㊐, **settle** +㊐ (決める ; 前者が一般的) ; **arrange** +㊐ (段取りをつける) ▶委員会は競技会の日程を**取り決めた** The committee *set* [*fixed*] the date for the athletic meet.

とりくみ 取組 a **bout** /baʊt/ (相撲のひと勝負) ▶きょうは好**取組**が多い There are a lot of *interesting bouts* today.

とりくむ 取り組む wrestle /résəl/ **with, tackle** +㊐ (格闘する) ; **work on**(せっせと頑張る) ; **struggle** +㊐ (苦闘する) ▶困難な問題と**取り組む** *wrestle with* [*tackle*] a difficult problem ‖ 彼は卒論で公害問題と**取り組んだ** He *dealt with* [*took up*] the pollution problem in his graduation thesis. ‖ 弟は今新しいジグソーパズルに**取り組んでいる** My brother is now *working on* a new jigsaw puzzle. ‖ ＥＳＳのメンバーは全員英語力向上に**一生懸命取り組んでいる** All the ESS members *are struggling* [*striving hard*] to improve their English ability.

とりけし 取り消し (a) **cancellation** ▶彼らは契約の**取り消し**を一方的に要求してきた They demanded the unilateral *cancellation* of the contract. ‖ 彼女は注文を全部**取り消しにした** She *canceled* all of her orders.

とりけす 取り消す cancel +㊐ (約束・決定したことなどを) ; **revoke** +㊐ (許可などを無効にする) ; **take back**(言ったことを) ▶注文[予約]を**取り消す** *cancel* one's order [reservation] ‖ 婚約を**取り消す** *break off* one's engagement to a person ‖ さっきの発言は**取り消せ**. かず子さんはうそつきなんかじゃない! *Take back* what you just said. Kazuko is no liar! ‖ その医師は禁じられた薬品を売って免許を**取り消された** The doctor *had* his license *revoked* for selling banned drugs.

とりこ 虜・擒 a **prisoner**(捕虜) ; a **captive**(監禁されて

と

いる人；比喩的に「(美などに)魅(み)せられた人」) ▶《比喩的》私はその美しいタヒチの少女のとりこになって(＝に魅せられて)しまった I *was completely enthralled* [*captivated*] by the beauty of that Tahitian girl.

とりこしぐろう 取り越し苦労 ▶取り越し苦労はやめなさい Don't *worry too much about future problems*.

とりこみ 取り込み ▶ただいま取り込み中ですので，のちほどお電話いたします I'm sorry, but I *am engaged* [*tied up* ／*busy*] right now. Can I call you back later？‖お取り込み中失礼いたします I'm sorry to interrupt [bother] you (*when you are so busy*).

とりこむ 取り込む **bring** [**take**] **in** ▶雨が降り出しそうだから洗濯物を取り込んでよ It looks like rain. Could you *bring* [*take*] *in* the laundry？
▶テキストデータをエクセルに取り込む *import* text data into Excel.

とりこわし 取り壊し **demolition** ▶橋［建物］の取り壊し the *demolition* of a bridge [building].

とりこわす 取り壊す **demolish** ＋目, **pull** [**tear** /teəʳ/] **down**（➤ demolish は跡地に新しく建てる目的で計画的に取り壊すことをいう）▶彼らは古い工場を取り壊してマンションを建てた They *demolished* the old factory and built a condominium. ‖この通りの家屋は来年にはすべて取り壊される予定です All the houses on this street are due to *be pulled down* [*be torn down* ／*be demolished*] next year.

とりさげる 取り下げる **withdraw** ＋目 ▶彼女は夫に対する告訴を取り下げた She *withdrew* [*dropped*] the charges against her husband.

とりざた 取り沙汰 ▶あの家のことは近所でもいろいろと取り沙汰されていたようだ That family seems to have *been the subject of a rumor*.

とりざら 取り皿 a **plate**.

とりしきる 取り仕切る **manage** /mǽnɪdʒ/ ＋目（管理する）▶彼女はその花屋を取りしきっている She *manages* that flower shop. ／She *runs* that flower shop *by herself*. ‖あの町内会を取りしきってるのは森山さんだ Mr. Moriyama *runs the show* in that neighborhood association.（➤ run the show は「(組織などの)責任者である」の意).

とりしまり 取り締まり **control**（統制）; **regulation**（規則による）; a **crackdown**, a **clampdown**（締めつけ；後者には「突然の」という含みが強い）▶政府は賭博の取り締まりを強化した The Government reinforced *control* over [the *regulation* on] gambling. ‖警察は酒酔い運転に対する取り締まりを厳しくした The police *have cracked down on* [*have become harder on*] drunk drivers. ‖不法滞在者取り締まり期間 *open season* on illegal immigrants.
‖取締役 a director ‖取締役会長 the chair [chairperson ／ chairman ／ chairwoman] of the board of directors ‖取締役社長 a president, 《英》a managing director《参考》(1)《米》では chair は名目上の「会長」であることが多いが，《英》では managing director よりも chair(会長)のほうが実権が大きく，同一人物が２つの役職を兼ねている場合が少なくない. (2)《米》では社内の最高位の役職に就いている人を chief executive officer, 《略》CEO(最高経営責任者)と呼ぶことも多い ‖社外取締役 an outside director (→会社).

とりしまる 取り締まる **regulate** /régjəleɪt/ ＋目（規則に基づいて）; **control** ＋目（規制する），《インフォーマル》**crack down on**（違法行為などに対し厳しく）▶組織犯罪を取り締まる *control* [*crack down on*] organized crime ‖駐車違反をもっと厳しく取り締まってほしいものだ They [The police] should *exercise stricter control over* illegal parking. ／ Illegal parking should *be more strictly controlled*. ‖ああいう暴走族は厳しく取り締まったほうがよい They [The police] should *crack* [*clamp*] *down on* those hot-rodders.

とりしらべ 取り調べ **investigation**, **interrogation**（➤後者には威嚇的尋問や長時間という含みがあることが多い）▶彼は警察でその事件に関連して取り調べを受けた He *was investigated* [*was interrogated* ／*was questioned*] by the police about his possible involvement in the case. ‖容疑者は警察の取り調べで自白した The suspect confessed during the police *interrogation*. ‖火事の原因については目下取り調べ中です The cause of the fire is *under investigation* [is now *being investigated*].
‖取り調べ室 an interrogation room.

とりしらべる 取り調べる **investigate** ＋目 ▶彼は横領の疑いで警察に取り調べられた He *was investigated* [*was questioned* ／*was grilled*] by the police for suspected embezzlement.（➤grillは「厳しく調べる」).

とりそろえる 取り揃える ▶当店では夏物を豊富に取りそろえております We *have a* wide *selection* [*a* large *assortment*] *of* summer clothes. ‖体育館にはいろいろな運動器具が一とおり取りそろえてある The gymnasium *is equipped with* a full line of athletic gear.（➤ equip は「備え付ける」).

とりだす 取り出す **1**【中から出す】**take out** ▶彼女はハンドバッグから口紅を取り出した She *took* a lipstick *out of* her purse.
2【抽出する】▶（文脈から）その部分だけを取り出したのでは意味は通じない If you *take* that part *out of* context, it doesn't make any sense.

とりたて 取り立て **1**【徴収】▶彼は毎月滞った家賃の取り立てに回っている He goes around *pressing* tenants *to pay* their late rent [*dunning* tenants for late rent payment] every month. ‖彼は今借金の取り立て屋に悩まされている He is currently being harassed by *a debt collector*.（➤「借金の取り立て」は debt collection).
2【取ったばかり】▶私は免許取りたてです I *got* my driver's license *only very recently*. ‖このサクランボは取りたてだ These cherries *are fresh from the orchard* [*are freshly picked*].（→取れたて).

とりたてて 取り立てて ▶彼には取り立てて言うほどの長所もない He has no strong points *worth mentioning*. ／He has no strong points *to speak of*. ‖まずまずの映画で，取り立てて言うほどのものではなかった The movie was okay, but (it was) *nothing to write home about*.

とりたてる 取り立てる **1**【徴収する】**collect** ＋目 ▶あの借家人は行って取り立てないと家賃を払ってくれない That tenant won't pay his rent if I don't go and *collect* it.
2【起用する】▶販売促進計画がうまくいって彼は課長に取り立てられた The sales promotion plan worked well and he *was given* [*was appointed to*] *the position* of section chief.

とりちがえる 取り違える **misunderstand** ＋目（誤解する）▶文の意味を取り違える *misinterpret* a sentence ‖私は彼のことばを取り違えた I *misunderstood* the meaning of his remark. ‖彼は自由と無責任とを取り違えている He *confuses* liberty *with* irresponsibility.（➤ confuse は「混同する」）‖その病院

は2人の患者を取り違え，誤った手術を行った That hospital *mistakenly switched* the two patients and conducted the wrong operations on them.

とりちらかす 取り散らかす ▶小さい子がおりますので取り散らかしていますがどうぞお上がりください The house *is a mess* thanks to the kids. But come on in anyway.

とりつ 都立の **metropolitan** /mètrəpá:lətn/ ▶私は都立小山台高校の2年生です I'm a junior at Koyamadai *Metropolitan* High (School).
‖**都立病院** a metropolitan hospital.

とりつぎ 取り次ぎ ▶来客の取り次ぎをする *usher in* a visitor ‖ 彼は取り次ぎの案内もなく私の部屋に入って来た He entered my room *unannounced*.
‖**取次業者** a distributor ‖ **取次店** a wholesale distributing agent.

とりつく 取り付く・取り憑く **possess** +㊐, **obsess** +㊐ (➤前者がより堅い語) ▶少女には悪魔が取りついていた The girl *was possessed*. ‖ 彼は日本が近い将来沈没するという考えに取りつかれていた He *was obsessed by* the idea that the islands of Japan would sink into the sea in the near future. ‖ 彼は取りつかれたようにその絵の完成に情熱を燃やした He worked feverishly to finish the picture *as though obsessed* [*like a man possessed*].
▶《慣用表現》父は私のボーイフレンドに会おうともせず，全く取り付く島もなかった(＝全くどうしようもなかった) My father would not even meet my boyfriend, and I *felt completely helpless*.

トリック a **trick** ▶奇術のトリックを行う perform magic *tricks*.
‖**トリック撮影** a trick shot.

とりつぐ 取り次ぐ ▶彼女は部長に来客を取り次いだ She *told* the manager that his guest(s) had arrived. ‖ 吉田社長に取り次いでいただきたいのですが Please *tell* Mr. Yoshida that I am here to see him. (● 英語では社長であってもその人の名を言うのがふつう).

とりつくろう 取り繕う **gloss over** (失策などを) ▶失敗を取り繕う *gloss over* one's mistake ‖ 彼は問い詰められたが何とかその場を取り繕った Though he was pressed for an answer, he managed to *smooth things over for the moment*.

とりつけ 取り付け **1【設置】installation** ▶エアコンの取り付けには1時間かかります The *installation* of an air conditioner requires one hour.
2【預金の一斉引き出し】a run (on the bank) ▶その銀行の信用不安で取り付け騒ぎが起きた The credit worries of the bank prompted *a run*.

とりつける 取り付ける **install** +㊐; **fit up** (設備する) ▶彼は部屋にエアコンを取り付けた He *installed* an air conditioner [He *had* an air conditioner *installed*] in his room. (➤後者は「取り付けてもらった」) ‖ このブラインドは取り付けるのが簡単です You can *install* these window blinds quite easily. ‖ 大工さんは壁掛け式の食器戸棚を取り付けた The carpenter *fitted up* the wall cupboards.

ドリップコーヒー **drip coffee.**

とりで 砦 a **fort** (堡塁(ほうるい)); a **stronghold** (城塞) ▶ララミーとりで *Fort* Laramie.

とりとめ 取り留め ▶きのうの校長先生の話，全く取りとめがなかったわね The principal's speech yesterday was just *rambling*, wasn't it?

とりとめる 取り留める ▶子供の頃海で溺れかけて危うく一命を取り留めたことがある When I was a child, I *had a narrow escape* from [I *narrowly escaped*] drowning in the sea.

とりなおす 取り直す ▶彼は気を取り直して最初からやり直した He *pulled himself together* and started again from the beginning. ‖ 彼女は彼のはげましのことばを聞いて気を取り直した She *took heart* when she heard his words of encouragement.

とりなす 取り成す **intercede** 《with》(仲裁に入る) ▶母がとりなしてくれたおかげで父に怒られずに済んだ Since Mom *interceded with* Dad *for* me, I got off without a scolding. ‖ 部長が先方との間をとりなしてくれた The department head *mediated* between the other party and me. (➤ mediate /mí:dieɪt/ は「間に立って和解させる」).

とりにいく 取りに行く **pick up** ▶郵便局まで小包を取りにいってくれない? Could you please *pick up* a parcel for me at the post office?

とりにがす 取り逃がす **miss** +㊐ ▶無料の台湾旅行の機会を取り逃がす *miss* the chance for a free trip to Taiwan ‖ 警官は泥棒を取り逃がした The police officer *failed to catch* the thief.

とりのける 取り除ける **remove** +㊐, **take away** (➤前者は堅い語)

> **【文型】**
> **場所(A)から物(B)を取りのける**
> **remove** [**clear**] B **from** A
> **clear** A **of** B

▶衝突した事故車を道路から取りのけるにはかなりの時間がかかるだろう It will take quite a long time to *remove* [*clear* / *take away*] the wreckage of the car crash *from* the road. ‖ 津波被災地からがれきを取りのけるのが急務だ The most urgent task is to *clear* the tsunami-stricken areas *of* rubble [debris]. ‖ 勝男は茶わん蒸しからギンナンだけ取りのけた Katsuo *took* all the gingko nuts *out* of the *chawan-mushi*.

とりのこされる 取り残される ▶彼女はたったひとり教室に取り残された She *was left* all alone in the classroom. ‖ そんな考えじゃ時代に取り残される(＝ついていけない)ぞ If you're going to think like that, you *won't be able to keep up with the times*.

とりのぞく 取り除く **remove** +㊐, **take out, take away** (➤最初の訳語は堅い語) ▶魚のうろこを取り除く *remove* scales from fish ‖ 彼女は胃の腫瘍を取り除く手術をした She had an operation to *remove* a stomach tumor. ‖ 傷のあるリンゴは取り除きなさい *Take out* [*Remove*] any bad apples.

とりはからう 取り計らう ▶皆さんに必要なものは準備しておくよう取り計らいましょう I'll *see to it that* everything you want is provided. (➤ see to it (that) ... で「…するように配慮する」の意) ‖ 友人がコンサートのチケットが手に入るように取り計らってくれた A friend of mine *arranged for* me *to* get a ticket for the concert.

とりはずし 取り外し ▶このフードは取り外しできますか Is this hood *detachable*? ‖ この部屋の棚は取り外しができない The shelves in this room *are fixed*. (➤「固定されている」の意).

とりはずす 取り外す **take out, remove** +㊐ ▶祖父は口から入れ歯を取り外した My grandfather *took out* his dentures. ‖ そのポスターを壁から取り外してちょうだい Please *take* that poster *down* [*remove* that poster] from the wall. ‖ この蛍光灯を天井から取り外してください Please *detach* this fluorescent light

と

from the ceiling.

とりはだ 鳥肌･鳥膚 goose bumps, goose pimples, gooseflesh ▶そのホラー映画を見たらぞっとして鳥肌が立った That horror film gave me *goose bumps*.

とりはらう 取り払う remove +目, take away, get rid of ▶仕切りを取り払う *remove* a partition ‖ 祭り用に張られたテントもすっかり取り払われた The tents that had been pitched for the festival *were* all *taken away*.

とりひき 取り引き business(商売); a deal, a transaction(取引契約; 後者は堅い語); dealings(取引売買) 一動 取り引きをする deal with ▶取引契約を結ぶ close *a deal* ‖ おじの会社では昨年からフランスの会社と取り引きを始めました My uncle's company started doing *business* with a French company last year. ‖ わが社はあの会社とは取り引きがない We have no *dealings* [no *business connections*] with that company. ‖ わが社は信用のある会社とは手形で取り引きをするが, そうでない会社とは現金取り引きだ We *deal with* reputable companies on a draft basis, but with others on a cash basis. ‖ 先月の取引高はその前の月より多かった Our *turnover* last month was larger than that of the previous month.

▶裏で何か取り引き(＝密約)があったに違いない They must have made *a deal* with each other (behind the scenes).

‖取引価格 a market price ‖ 取引先 a customer (顧客); a business acquaintance, a business contact(関係者) ‖ 現金取引 a cash transaction.

トリプル triple ‖トリプルプレー a triple play ‖ トリプルボギー a triple bogey /bóʊgi/.

ドリブル a dribble 一動 ドリブルする dribble ▶宇佐美選手は５人をドリブルで抜いた Usami *dribbled* (the ball) *past* five opposition players.

とりぶん 取り分 a [one's] share ▶私は利益の自分の取り分を手にした I got *my share* in [of] the profits. ‖ 俺の取り分はいくらになるんだ？ What's *my share* [*cut*]?

トリマー a trimmer.

とりまき 取り巻き an admirer(ファン); a hanger-on (利益を狙う人).

とりまぎれる 取り紛れる ▶忙しさに取り紛れて彼に礼状を書くのを忘れた I was *so busy* (*that*) I forgot to write him a thank-you letter.

とりまく 取り巻く surround +目, encircle +目 ▶たくさんのファンが殺到して阿部選手を取り巻いた Lots of fans rushed toward Abe and *surrounded* [*encircled*] him.

とりまぜる 取り混ぜる ▶クッキーをいろいろ取り混ぜて袋に詰めてください Could you put *an assortment* of cookies together in a bag? (➤ assortment は「各種取り混ぜたもの」) ‖ 大小取り混ぜて５個の鍋を買った I bought five pans *of various sizes*, *from large to small*.

とりまとめる 取り纏める ▶山田はクラス委員として, クラスメートのさまざまな意見を取りまとめている As a class committee member, Yamada *brings together and harmonizes* the diverse opinions of his classmates. ‖ 紛争を取りまとめる *settle* a dispute.

とりみだす 取り乱す get [be] upset ▶あのとき父がどうしてあんなに取り乱したのかわからない I don't know why my father *was* so *upset* then. ‖ 彼女は父親の急死の知らせにも全く取り乱さなかった She *remained* quite *unruffled* [*remained calm*] even when she heard the news of her father's sudden death. ‖ 取り乱すな *Don't lose your head.*／*Keep your cool.*／*Don't get flustered.*

トリミング trimming.

とりめ 鳥目 night blindness.

とりもち 取り持ち a go-between; an intermediary.

とりもつ 取り持つ ▶親友が私たちの縁を取り持ってくれた One of my best friends *acted as a matchmaker* for our marriage. (➤ matchmaker は「結婚の仲介者」) ‖ スキーが取り持つ縁で(＝スキーを通して)彼らは親友になった They became good friends *through* skiing.

とりもどす 取り戻す get back, take back, recover +目 (➤ recover はやや堅い語) ▶私は彼に貸した金を取り戻した I *got* my money *back* from him. ‖ 盗難に遭った美術品はひとつも取り戻されなかった None of the stolen objects of art *were* [*was*] ever *recovered*. ‖ １週間自宅で静養して, すっかり健康を取り戻した I completely *regained my health* after resting at home for a week. (● regain は失ったものを自力で取り戻すことで, recover より意味が強い) ‖ 彼女は後れを取り戻すために夜遅くまで勉強した She studied till late at night to *catch up on* her studies. (➤ catch up on は「後れ[不足]を取り戻す」の意).

とりもなおさず 取りも直さず ▶日記をつけるということはとりもなおさず自分や自分の行動を見つめ直すことである Keeping a journal *involves* reflecting on oneself and one's behavior.

とりやめ 取り止め ▶その試合は雨で取りやめになった The game *was canceled* [*was called off*] because of the rain.

とりやめる 取り止める cancel +目, call off ▶あすの会合は取りやめます We are going to *cancel* [*call off*] tomorrow's meeting.

トリュフ a truffle /trʌ́fəl/.

とりょう 塗料 paint ▶塀を黒い塗料で塗る coat the wall with black *paint*／paint the wall black.

どりょう 度量 ▶あの男は度量が狭いので大成しそうにない He is too *narrow-minded* [*small-minded*] to be a (big) success. ‖ 独裁者は政敵を釈放して度量の大きいところを見せようとした The dictator tried to show *magnanimity* by releasing his political enemy. (➤ 発音は /mæ̀gnənɪ́məṭi/).

どりょうこう 度量衡 weights and measures ‖度量衡(換算)表 a (conversion) table of weights and measures.

どりょく 努力 (an) effort; an endeavor /ɪndévəʳ/ (持続的な); perseverance(地道な) 一動 努力する make an effort [efforts], strive《to do》▶努力しないで成功しようと思っても無理だ You can never succeed without *making efforts*. ‖ ご要望に応えるようできる限り努力しました I *made every effort* [*endeavor*] *to* meet your request. (● I did my best ... といってもよい) ‖ 一生懸命努力したおかげで大学に入学することができた I *worked very hard* and was successful in getting into the university. ‖ 我々は労働条件の改善に努力している We *are striving to* improve our working conditions. ‖ きょう中に仕上げるよう努力しなさい *Try to* finish it today. ‖ たゆまず努力すればきっと報われるよ Your *constant efforts* will surely pay off [bear fruit]. ‖ あすの水泳大会で諸君の努力の成果が見られることを楽しみにしています I'm looking forward to seeing *the fruit of your effort(s)* at the swimming meet tomorrow. ‖ 彼は大変な努力家で

独学で司法試験に合格した He is *a hard worker* who taught himself law and passed the bar exam. (➤「努力家」は《インフォーマル》では trier ともいう).

‖努力賞 an award [a prize] for effort.

とりよせる 取り寄せる order +目 (注文して) ▶この医療機器はドイツから取り寄せたものだ We *ordered* this medical instrument *from* Germany. ‖それはX社から取り寄せないといけないだろう We'll have to *put in a special order* for it [*order* it *specially*] *from* X Co.

ドリル 1【工具】a drill ▶厚い板にドリルで穴をあける make a hole through a thick board with *a drill* ／drill a hole through a thick board (➤ 後者の drill は動詞). ‖電気[電動]ドリル an electric drill.
2【繰り返しの練習】a drill ▶生徒たちは数学のドリルを行った The students did math *drills*. (➤「練習問題」には an exercise を用いる).

とりわけ 取り分け especially, in particular →特に ▶私はビートルズの歌, とりわけ,「イエスタデイ」や「レット・イット・ビー」が好きです I like the Beatles songs, *especially* [*in particular*] "Yesterday" and "Let It Be."

とりわける 取り分ける serve (food) ▶食べ物を取り分けてくれない？ Would you please *serve each of the guests* [*dish out* the food]？(➤ dish out はくだけた言い方).

ドリンクざい ドリンク剤 a health drink, an energy drink.

とる 取る・採る・捕る・執る・撮る

📖 **訳語メニュー**
- 手に持つ →take, get 1
- 撮影する →take 4
- 捕まえる →catch 5
- 奪う →take, rob 6
- 獲得する →get, win 7

1【手に持つ】take +目, get +目 (➤ 後者はややインフォーマル)；pick up (手に取る)；reach +目 (手を伸ばして) ▶どうぞお好きな品をお手に取ってご覧ください Please *take* [*pick up*] anything you like (in your hand) and have a look at it. (➤ 文意から自明なので in your hand は付けないのが普通) ‖彼女は病床の母親の手を取った She *took* her bedridden mother's hand (in hers). ‖そこの手袋を取ってもらえますか Can you *get* those gloves for me？‖その辞書を取ってください Please *pass* [*hand*] me the dictionary. (➤ 相手に手をのばして取ってもらう場合は動詞に reach を用いる) ‖《食卓で》おしょうゆを取ってちょうだい *Pass* me the soy sauce, please. (● 食卓で物を取ってもらうときは pass を用いる).
2【取りにいく】get +目 ▶郵便受けから郵便物取った？ Did you *get* the mail from the mailbox？‖ドライクリーニング店に頼んでおいたスーツを取って来てくれない？ Could you go to the dry cleaner's to *pick up* my suit. (→取りにいく).
▶うちでは『ジャパンタイムズ』を取っている We *get* [*take* ／《米また》*subscribe to*] "The Japan Times." ‖たまにはすしでも取ろうよ Let's *have* sushi *delivered* once in a while. ／Why don't we *order out for* sushi for a change？(➤ for a change は「気分を変えて」).
3【処理する】▶事務を執る *do* office work ‖数人の恩師とは今でも連絡をとっている I still *keep in touch with* some of my former teachers. ‖営業部員は外回りをして注文を取る Salespeople make their rounds to *take* orders. ▶彼女は講義を聴きながら熱心にノートをとった She *took notes* carefully while listening to the lecture.
4【撮影する, 録音する】take +目 ▶写真を撮る *take* a picture ‖子供の成長の過程をビデオに撮る *videotape* the stages of one's child's growth ‖すみませんが, 写真を撮っていただけますか Excuse me, but would you mind *taking* a picture of us？(➤ 通りがかりの人などにシャッターを押してもらう場合) ‖きのう銀座の写真館で写真を撮ってもらった Yesterday I *had* my picture *taken* at a photo studio in Ginza. ‖はい(写真を)撮るよ. カメラを見て I'll *shoot* [*take*] the picture now. Look at the camera. ‖きれいに撮ってよ *Take a good picture* of me. ／Make me look good. ‖念のため, 胸のレントゲン写真を撮ってみましょう We'll *take* an X ray of your lungs just in case. ‖これコピーとってくれない？ Could you *photocopy* this for me？
5【収穫する, 捕まえる】pick +目 (摘む, もぐ)；catch +目 (捕まえる)；fish +目 (魚を) ▶山へキノコを採りに行こう Let's go to the mountains to *pick* mushrooms. ‖当ブドウ園では自由にブドウを採って食べることができます If you come to our vineyard, you can *pick* and eat grapes freely.
▶この頃の猫はネズミを捕らない These days cats don't *catch* rats. ‖子供の頃はこの原っぱでバッタをたくさん捕った I *caught* many grasshoppers in this field when I was a child. ‖河口湖でたくさんのワカサギを捕った We *caught* a lot of smelt(s) on Lake Kawaguchi.
6【奪う】take +目；rob +目 (強奪する) ▶人の物を取ってはいけません Don't *take* things that don't belong to you. ‖強盗に入られて2万円取られた I *was robbed of* 20,000 yen. (➤ rob A of B で「A(人)からB(物)を強奪する」. ここはその受け身形；→取られる) ‖若い男が女性のハンドバッグを取って逃げた A young man *snatched* a woman's purse and fled. (➤ snatch は「ひったくる」) ‖ぼくは木村に彼女を取られた Kimura *took* my girlfriend *away*.
7【獲得する, 取得する】get +目, win +目 (➤ 後者には努力・競争などによって手に入れるという含みがある) ▶吉田君は期末試験で3教科満点を取った Yoshida *got* perfect scores on three subjects in the final exams. ‖この夏は運転免許を取りたい I want to *get* a driver's license this summer. ‖杉本さんはロシア語弁論大会で1等賞を取った Sugimoto *won* first prize in the Russian speech contest. ‖5回の裏, 阪神は5点を取った The Tigers *scored* five runs in the bottom of the fifth inning. (➤ score は「得点する」) ‖いつか俺が天下を取ってやる I'll *conquer* the whole country someday. (➤ conquer は「征服する」) ／I'll *be famous throughout Japan* someday.
8【確保する】keep +目 ▶おやつはちゃんと取ってありますよ We *have kept* [*have saved*] some snacks for you. ‖この席は取ってあるんです (I'm afraid) this seat *is taken* [*is occupied*]. ‖私は小学校時代の作文は全部取ってある I *have kept* all the compositions I wrote in elementary school. ‖せめて2週間は夏休みを取りたいものだ I'd like to *take* at least a two-week summer vacation. ‖森はきょう休みを取っています Mr. Mori *is taking* a day off today. ‖この授業は英作文(の授業)を取った人だけが取れる This class is *open* only to people who *have taken* English Composition. ‖その大学はことし(入試で)

2000人採った The university *admitted* 2,000 students this year.

9【採取する】▶ヒマワリの種から油を採る *extract* oil from the seeds of sunflowers ‖ 天窓から光を採る *let in light* through a skylight ‖ 警察は凶器から指紋を採った The police *lifted* fingerprints off the murder weapon.

10【必要とする】take (up) ▶この仕事は時間を取り過ぎる This work *takes up* too much of my time. ‖ この椅子は折り畳めるので場所を取りません This chair folds up, so it *doesn't take (up)* much space.

11【体内に取り込む】have, take ▶朝食をとる *have* [*eat*] breakfast ‖ 糖分をとる *eat* sugar ‖ 栄養をとる *take* nourishment ‖ あなた, 塩分のとり過ぎよ You'*re getting* too much salt. ‖ 私が元気なのは睡眠を十分にとっているからです The reason I am healthy is that I sleep well.

12【雇う】hire +目 ▶当社はことし100名の社員を採る予定です We are planning to *hire* 100 employees this year. ‖ うちの工場は忙しいシーズンは臨時工員を採る Our factory *takes on* extra workers during the busy season. (take on は「雇う」の意のインフォーマルな言い方).

13【選択する】take +目 ; **adopt** +目 (採用する) ▶交渉の場ではきぜんとした態度をとるべきだ You should *take* a firm stand at the bargaining table. ‖ こうなっては強硬［厳しい］手段をとるしかなさそうだ At this stage we have no choice but to *take* strong [strict] measures. ‖ 市議会はA案でなくB案を採った The city assembly *adopted* proposition B, not A. ‖ ぼくは名誉よりも愛をとる I *prefer* love *to* honor.

14【金を請求する】charge +目 ▶あの店, きみの自転車の修理にいくら取った? How much did they *charge* you for repairing [fixing] your bicycle at that shop? ‖ 彼は能力の割に高給を取っている He *gets* [*makes*] a very high salary considering his ability.

15【取り除く】take off (脱ぐ) ; **remove** +目 (除去する) ▶瓶の蓋を取る *take off* the cap of a bottle ‖ 室内では帽子をお取りください *Take off* your hat indoors.

▶顔の染みをとるクリームはないかしら Do you have a cream to *remove* facial blemishes? ‖ ズボンの裾についた汚れがとれない I can't *remove* the stains from the hem of my pants.

▶日曜日に庭の草を取った I *weeded* my garden on Sunday. ‖ あの人は胃を3分の2も取ったんだって I heard he had two-thirds of his stomach *taken out* [*removed*].

16【解釈する】take +目 ▶私の言うことを悪くとらないでよ (＝誤解しないで) Please don't *get* [*take*] me *wrong*. ‖ 彼女は私の冗談をひどく深刻にとってしまった She *took* my joke too seriously. ‖ この文はほかの意味にもとれる You can *take* [*interpret*] this sentence another way.

17【年を重ねる】▶年を取る *grow* older [in years] (➤「年齢を重ねる」の意) ／*grow* [*become*] old (➤「老人になる」の意) ‖ 1つ年を取る *grow* a year older ／*add* a year.

☛ 取られる (→見出語)

ドル a dollar ▶30ドル thirty *dollars* 《参考》「…ドル」という場合, 書きことばでは数字の前に＄または＄の記号をつけて, 例えば30ドルは ＄30 とすることが多い ‖ 1ドル札(さつ) a one-*dollar* bill ‖ 今1ドルは何円してますか How much is *a dollar* (worth) in yen now? ‖ ここ数か月ドル安［高］が続いている The *dollar* has been on the decline [on the rise] for some months now. ▶《慣用表現》彼女の新しい小説がわが社のドル箱になっている Her new novel has been *a big moneymaker* [*a real gold mine*] for our company. (➤ 本来 gold mine は「金鉱」).

トルコ Turkey 一形 **トルコの Turkish**
‖ **トルコ石** turquoise /tə́ːrkwɔɪz/ ‖ **トルコ語** Turkish ‖ **トルコ人** a Turk.

とるにたりない 取るに足りない trivial (注意・考慮に値しない) ; **insignificant** /ìnsɪgnífɪkənt/ (意味のない, 重要でない) ; **petty** (ちんけな) ▶取るに足りない問題 a *trivial* matter ‖ 取るに足りない金額 an *insignificant* [a *small*] amount of money (➤ 後者は「小額の」) ‖ 彼は取るに足りない絵描きだ He is *not much of* a painter. ／He is a painter of *little importance*. (➤前者のnot much of a…は「大した…ではない」の意).

とるものもとりあえず 取る物も取り敢えず ▶父が卒中で倒れたと聞いて取るものもとりあえず病院に駆けつけた I rushed to the hospital *as soon as* I heard that my father had suffered a stroke.

どれ 1【いずれ】which, what

> 語法 which は範囲を限定したものの中から選択を求める場合に, what は広く不特定のものの中から選択を求める場合に用いる.

▶どれを選んでよいのか決めかねている I can't decide *which* [*what*] to choose. ‖ どれでもお好きなものをお取りください Please take *whatever* [*whichever*] you like. ‖ その中の色ならどれでもよい *Any one* of those colors will do. ‖ この中のどれか1つください Give me *any one* of these. ‖ 対話「きみの好きなのどれ?」「黒いほう」"*Which* one do you like?" "The black one." ‖ 対話「どれが正しいのですか」「たぶんこっちでしょう」"*Which* is correct?" "Probably this one." ‖ 対話「あれを見てごらん」「どれ?」"Look at that." "*What?*" ‖ 対話「きょうはいていくスカート, どれ?」「先月買ったの」"*Which* [*What*] skirt will you wear today?" "The one I bought last month."

▶リンゴはどれも腐っていた *All* the apples were spoiled. ‖ どれもきれいに撮れている *Every* picture came out well [is well taken]. ‖ このドレス, どれも気に入らないわ I like *none* of these dresses. ／I *don't like any* of these dresses.

2【掛け声】▶ 対話「足をぶつけてあざを作っちゃった」「どれ, 見せてごらん」"I bumped my leg and got a bruise (on it)." "*Well*, let me have a look."

どれい 奴隷 a slave ▶奴隷制度を廃止する abolish *slavery* ‖ あの男は金の奴隷だ That man is *a slave* to [of] money.

トレー a tray.

トレーサビリティー traceability.

トレーシングペーパー tracing paper.

トレード a trade 一動 **トレードする trade** +目 ▶西武は2人の外野手と引き換えにベテランピッチャーを巨人にトレードに出した The Lions *traded* a veteran pitcher to the Giants for two outfielders.
‖ トレードマネー a transfer fee.

トレードマーク a trademark ▶ベレー帽と眼鏡があの漫画家のトレードマークだ A beret and glasses are that cartoonist's *trademarks*.

トレーナー a **trainer**(訓練する人); a **massage therapist**(マッサージ師); an **athletic trainer**(けがの処置や予防を指導する人); a **sweat suit**(スポーツウエア; 上着は sweat shirt, ズボンは sweat pants).

危ないカタカナ語✹ トレーナー
1 英語の trainer は「(馬・犬などを)訓練する人, 調教師」のことで, 衣服は意味しない. 日本でいう「トレーナー」に当たるのは sweatshirt.
2 training pants もいわゆる「トレパン」ではなく, 幼児の排便のしつけ(toilet training)のパンツを指す. 日本語の「トレーニングパンツ」に当たるのは sweat pants または gym pants である.

トレーニング **training** ▶厳しいトレーニング rigorous *training* ‖トレーニングに入る go into *training* ‖彼らはその試合に備えて毎日トレーニングに励んでいる They *are training* hard every day for the game.
‖**トレーニングウエア** a sweat suit, a warm-up suit ‖**トレーニングシャツ** a sweat shirt ‖**トレーニングパンツ** sweat pants, gym slacks.

トレーラー a **trailer** ‖**トレーラーキャンプ** a trailer camp [park] ‖**トレーラーハウス** 《米》 a trailer (house), a house trailer, 《英》 a caravan.

どれくらい ▶駅までどれくらい(の距離が)ありますか *How far* is it to the train station? ‖この池, (深さは)どれくらいだろう I wonder *how deep* this pond is. ‖この仕事を始めて(期間は)どれくらいですか *How long* have you been working on this job? →どのくらい.

ドレス a **dress** ▶ドレスアップして外出する *dress up* [*put on one's best dress*] and go out.
‖**ドレスコード**(服装規定) a dress code ‖**ドレスメーカー** a dressmaker.

とれだか 取れ高 a **catch**(魚の); a **crop**(農作物の).

どれだけ ▶オイル, どれだけ残ってる? *How much* oil is left? ‖幼い息子は母を亡くしてどれだけ悲しい思いをしていることだろう I can't tell you *how* sad my young son has felt since his mother passed away. ‖たばこはやめなさいと言っているのに, どれだけ言えばわかるの? *How many times do I have to tell you* that you should stop [quit] smoking? →どれほど.

とれたて 取れ立ての **fresh** ▶取れたての魚 a *fresh-caught* fish ‖田舎の両親が取れたてのキュウリを送ってきた My parents back home sent me *fresh* (-*picked*) cucumbers.

ドレッサー a **dresser**.

ドレッシング (a) **salad dressing** ▶サラダにドレッシングを掛ける *dress* a salad / *put dressing on* a salad.
‖**フレンチドレッシング** French dressing, vinegar-and-oil dressing.

どれどれ ▶どれどれ, ちょっとその写真見せてよ *Now*, let me have a look at the picture.

トレパン →トレーニング(パンツ).

どれほど 何れ程 ▶彼がどれほど偉い政治家かは知らないが人間的には尊敬できない *No matter how* great a politician he is, I cannot respect him as a human being. ‖あなたにはどれほど感謝してもし足りない I feel I *cannot* thank you *enough*. ‖私はあなたのことをどれほど心配したことか Do you know *how* worried I was about you?

ドレミ(ファ) (the **musical**) **scale**(音階); **sol-fa** /sòulfá:/ (ドレミファ音階) ▶ピアノでドレミ(ファ)を練習する practice *scales* on the piano ‖ドレミ(ファ)で歌を歌う sing *scales* 《参考》「ドレミ(ファ)」はイタリア語の *do*, *re*, *mi*, (*fa*)から.

どれもこれも **every**(どの…も皆); **any**(どんな…でも); **all**(すべての…) ▶どれもこれもおいしそうな料理で, 目移りしてしまうな *All* the dishes look so delicious (that) I can't decide which to eat first.

トレモロ 《音楽》 a **tremolo**.

とれる 取れる・採れる・撮れる **1**【離れる, 無くなる】**come off** ▶上着のボタンが取れた A button *has come off* my jacket. (●「取れかかっている」なら is coming off または is loose /lu:s/ を用いる) ‖染みは簡単にとれた The stain *came out* easily.
▶ちょっと横になったら疲れがとれた My fatigue *disappeared* [*was gone*] after lying down for some time. ‖痛みがとれるまでこの薬を食後に2錠ずつのみなさい Take two tablets of this medicine after each meal until the pain *goes away*.
2【収穫がある】▶ことしは柿がたくさん採れた We *had a good crop* of persimmons this year. ‖わが家の菜園からこんなにトマトが採れた We *gathered* [*harvested*] all these tomatoes from our backyard garden. ‖北海では毎年タラがたくさん捕れる They *have a big catch* of cod in the North Sea every year. (➤ every year, always, usually などがない英文は今年のことだけを言っているように響く)
3【得ることができる】▶ビザが取れたらすぐに出発だ I'll leave as soon as I *have* a visa *stamped* on my passport [I'*ve got* a visa]. ‖相手が前田では中日は1点も取れないだろう The Dragons will *not be able to score* even one run off Maeda. ‖うちの会社は有給を年に20日取れる We *can take* 20 days off with pay each year in our company. ‖最近忙しくて本を読む時間がとれない These days, I am so busy that I *cannot find* [*spare*] (any) time to read (books). ‖綿花から綿が採れる Cotton *is produced* from the cotton plant. ‖はちみつはミツバチから採れる Honey *comes from* bees.
4【外す】▶この瓶の蓋は固くてどうしても取れない I *can't open* this bottle because the cap is screwed on too tight.
5【写る, 写せる】▶彼女の写真はなかなかよく撮れている Her photograph *turned out* well. (➤ 彼女が撮った写真を指す場合も, 彼女のことを撮影した写真を指す場合もある) / She is photogenic. (➤「彼女は写真映りがいい」の意) ‖うまく撮れるといいんですが I hope this shot will *come* [*turn*] *out well*.
6【解釈できる】▶彼のことばは曖昧だったので, 幾とおりにもとれた What he said was so obscure that it *could be interpreted* [*taken*] in a number of ways.

トレンチコート a **trench coat** ▶トレンチコート姿の刑事 a detective in *a trench coat*.

トレンディー トレンディーな **trendy** ▶トレンディーなテレビドラマ a *trendy* TV drama.

トレンド a **trend** ▶遠出を控えて, 都心探訪が昨今のトレンドのようである It seems that exploring downtown Tokyo rather than traveling far away is a current *trend*.

とろ **fatty tuna** (**meat**)(マグロの脂身).

どろ 泥 **mud**(泥土); **dirt**(土, 土ぼこり) ▶私は車にばしゃんと泥を引っ掛けられた A car splashed *mud* on me. ‖マットで靴の泥を落としてからお入りください Wipe the *mud* off your shoes on the mat before entering. ‖雨中のラグビーでぼくたちは泥だらけになった Playing rugby in the rain, we *got muddy* [*were covered with mud*]. ‖床は泥だらけだった The floor

と

was covered with dirt.
▶《慣用表現》親の顔に泥を塗るようなことをしてはいけないよ You must not do anything that will *shame* your parents. ‖ 盗みの証拠は挙がっているんだ. いいかげんに泥を吐いたらどうだ We've got the evidence. Just *come clean and admit to* the theft. ‖ 社長はその汚職事件の泥をかぶって(＝責任を取って)辞任した *Taking the rap for* the scandal, the president stepped down.

とろい ▶あいつの仕事はとろくて見ているといらいらする His *stupid* [*slow*] way of working irritates me. ‖ あの２人の関係に気がつかなかったとはとろい(＝鈍い)やつだ You must be *slow* [*dull*] not to have noticed how close those two are.

トロイカ a **troika.**

とろう 徒労 ▶いろいろ手を尽くしたがすべては徒労に終わった I tried every possible means but all *my efforts were in vain* [*ended in failure*].

ドロー a **draw.**

トローチ **troche** /tróʊki:/ (➤専門用語)；a (**sore-throat) lozenge** /lá:zɪndʒ/, a **medicated drop.**

トロール a **trawl**(網)
‖トロール船 a trawler.

どろくさい 泥臭い **unrefined** (洗練されていない)；**crude**(粗野な) ▶あの歌手はデビューして何年もたつのにいまだに泥臭い That singer is still *unrefined* [*countrified* ／ *unpolished*] though she started her singing career several years ago. (➤それぞれ「洗練されていない」「田舎じみた」「磨かれていない」の意).

とろける **1**【溶ける】**melt** ▶このメロンはとろけるようにおいしい This melon really *melts* in your mouth.
2【うっとりする】▶私の心はその妖しいバイオリンの音色にとろけた I *was* totally *carried away* by the ravishing sound of the violin. (➤ ravishing は「うっとりさせる」).

どろじあい 泥仕合 **mudslinging** ▶知事選では両候補者が泥仕合を演じている Both candidates for governor *are throwing* [*slinging*] *mud at* each other. (➤ throw [sling] mud at は「…を中傷する」).

トロッコ a **truck**；a **handcar**(２人が向かい合ってハンドルを押し合いながら動かすタイプ).

どろっと ▶彼はどろっとしたその液体を容器に移した He put the *thick* liquid into a container.

ドロップ a **drop**(あめ) ▶ペパーミントドロップをしゃぶる suck (on) a peppermint *drop.*

ドロップアウト a **dropout.**

とろとろ ▶とろとろのコーンスープ *creamy* corn soup ‖ 煮立ったら弱火にしてとろとろになるまで30分ほど煮ます After it comes to a boil, simmer it over a low flame for about thirty minutes *until it becomes a pulp.*
▶机に向かっている間に, いつの間にかとろとろして(＝居眠りをして)いたようだ It looks like I began to *doze off* at the desk before I knew it.

どろどろ ▶どろどろの液体 *thick* liquid ‖ どろどろにぬかった道 a *muddy* [*slushy*] road(➤ slushy は「雪解けのためにぬかった」) ‖ この暑さで道路のアスファルトがどろどろに溶けてしまった The asphalt on the road *has melted* because of this heat.

どろなわ 泥縄 ▶政府の対応は後手後手に回って泥縄式のやり方に終始している The government is too slow in responding and continues to take only *stopgap* [*quick-fix* ／ *band-aid*] measures.

どろぬま 泥沼 a **bog,** a **morass** /mərǽs/ (➤後者はやや文語的) ▶《比喩的》彼はようやく借金の泥沼から抜け出した He has finally emerged from *a morass* of debt. ‖ その会社は借金の泥沼から抜け出せなくなった The company *was mired* in debt. ‖ 戦争は少しずつ泥沼化していった The war got *bogged down* [became *a quagmire* ／was *dragging on*].

とろび とろ火 (a) **low heat**(熱)；a **low flame**(炎) ▶とろ火で大豆を煮る simmer soybeans *over a low heat* [*over a low flame*].

トロピカル トロピカルな **tropical.**

トロフィー a **trophy** /tróʊfi/ ▶トロフィーを獲得する win *a trophy.*

どろぼう 泥棒 a **thief**；a **robber** (強盗)；a **burglar**(夜家に忍び込む)；**stealing,** (a) **theft** (行為) ▶留守中に家に泥棒が入った *A burglar* broke into my house in my absence. ‖ 泥棒だ(捕まえてくれ)！*Stop the thief!* ‖《路上の物売りなどが》持ってけ泥棒！ *You're robbing me!*

どろまみれ 泥まみれの **muddy** ▶泥まみれの靴 *muddy* shoes ‖ 泥まみれのジャージー a jersey *stained with mud* ‖ 男の子たちは泥まみれになって帰って来た The boys came home *covered with mud.*

どろみず 泥水 **muddy water.**

どろよけ 泥除け 《米》a **splashguard,** 《英》a **mud flap.**

とろり ▶とろりとしたソース *creamy* sauce ‖ お口の中でとろりとろけるチョコレートです This chocolate *melts* in your mouth.

トロリーバス a **trolly (bus).**

とろろ **grated yam** /jæm/
‖とろろ芋 a yam ‖ とろろそば buckwheat noodles topped with grated yam.

とろん ▶幼い息子はもう眠いらしく, 目がとろんとしていた My little son looked sleepy and his eyes [eyelids] were *drooping heavily.*

どろん ▶店員が売上金を持ってどろんした(＝姿を消した) The salesclerk *made off* [*disappeared*] with the sales proceeds.

どろんこ 泥んこの **muddy** ▶前の晩の雨で道は泥んこだった The roads were *muddy* because it had rained (during) the previous night. ‖ 子供は泥んこ遊びが好きだ Children like *playing with* [*in*] *mud.* ‖泥んこ道 a muddy road.

トロント **Toronto**(カナダ南東部の都市).

トロンボーン a **trombone** ▶トロンボーンを演奏する play the *trombone.*
‖トロンボーン奏者 a trombonist.

とわ 常の・永久の **eternal** ▶２人はとわの愛を誓った The couple swore *eternal* love.

どわすれ 度忘れ ▶その作家の名前を度忘れしてしまった I*'ve just forgotten* the writer's name *for the moment.* (➤「一瞬忘れてしまった」の意) ／I can't remember [think of] the writer's name right now. ／The writer's name *has slipped my mind.*

トン a **ton** /tʌn/ ▶５トントラック a five-*ton* truck ‖ 石炭を２トン買う buy two *tons* of coal ‖ この船のトン数はどのくらいですか What is the *tonnage* of this ship? (➤ tonnage /tʌ́nɪdʒ/ は「(船舶の)トン数」).

どん ▶太鼓がドンと鳴った The *bang* of a drum could be heard. ‖ 彼は拳でテーブルをドンとたたいた He *pounded* the table with his fist. ‖ 彼女の車はその立ち木にどんとぶつかった Her car bumped into the tree *with a thud.* ‖ 位置に着いて, 用意, ドン！ On your mark(s), Get set, *Go!*

ドン a **boss,** a **powerful leader**(組織の) ▶政界のドンと言われた男 the man who was dubbed *a political boss.*

どんかく 鈍角 an **obtuse** /əbtjúːs/ **angle.**

とんカツ 豚カツ a **pork cutlet.**

どんかん 鈍感な **clueless**(ヒントに気づかない, 空気が読めない) ; **insensitive**(他人の感情に無神経な) ; **dull**(他人への理解・想像力に欠ける) ; **dense, slow (on the uptake)**(頭の働きが鈍い) ▶この鈍感! 彼女の気持ちがわからないのか! How *clueless* [*insensitive*] you are! Don't you realize how she feels about you? ‖ プライバシーを求める患者の気持ちに鈍感な医者がいる Some doctors are *insensitive* to their patients' need for privacy. ‖ いじめや差別に鈍感であってはならない You shouldn't be *slow* to perceive bullying or discrimination.

どんき 鈍器 a **blunt instrument** [**object**].

ドンキホーテ **Don Quixote** /dὰːn kɪhóʊt̬i ‖ dɔ̀n kwíksət/.

どんぐり 団栗 an **acorn** /éɪkɔːrn/ ▶《慣用表現》服部君はどんぐり眼にへの字口だ Hattori has got *big, round eyes* and pursed lips. ‖ うちの息子のクラスはどの子もどんぐりの背比べで, 特別できる子はいない All the students in my son's class *are more or less the same in ability*, and nobody stands out.

どんこう 鈍行 a **local train,** 《米また》 a **way train** (各駅停車の列車) ▶札幌で鈍行に乗り換える transfer to *a local train* at Sapporo.

とんざ 頓挫する ▶計画は資金不足で頓挫した The plan *went awry* due to the shortage of funds.

どんじゅう 鈍重な ▶鈍重な男 a *plodding* man.

どんじり どん尻 **the tail end** ▶行列のどん尻 *the tail end* of a procession ‖ かけっこではいつもどん尻だった When running a race, I was always *the last* to reach the goal.

とんじる 豚汁 ***tonjiru*** ; miso soup with pork and vegetables(➤ 説明的な訳).

とんずら ▶制服でゲームセンターに入ろうとしたところを先生に見つかって(慌てて)とんずらした When I was caught [seen] entering an amusement arcade in school uniform by one of my teachers, I *ran away* (flustered).

どんぞこ どん底 **the depth(s)** ▶どん底の生活からはい上がる claw one's way up from *extreme poverty* ‖ 今日本は不景気のどん底にある At present Japan is at *the bottom* of a recession. ‖ 彼は絶望のどん底にあった He was in *the depth*(*s*) of *despair*.

とんだ ▶とんだ失礼をいたしました I'm *terribly* sorry (for what I have done). ‖ とんだ人違いをしてしまった I *completely* took him [her] for somebody else. ‖ 旅先で台風に見舞われるなんてとんだ目に遭ったね What *awful* luck you had to encounter a typhoon while traveling! ‖ とんだ災難でしたね This was *certainly* an unexpected misfortune.

とんち 頓智 **wit** ▶一休さんはとんちが利く Ikkyu-san is *ready-witted* [*quick-witted*]. (●「とんちが利かない」は dull-witted または slow-witted) ‖ 彼はとんちで窮地を切り抜けた He got through the crisis with his *quick* [*ready*] *wit*.

とんちゃく 頓着 ▶彼は金に頓着しない He *cares nothing for* money. (➤「金に対して無関心である」の意) ‖ 彼は他人が何と言おうと頓着しない He *doesn't care* what others say. →**無頓着**.

どんちゃんさわぎ どんちゃん騒ぎ **whoopee** /hwópiː/ ▶きのうの晩は友だちを連れて行きつけの飲み屋へ行き, どんちゃん騒ぎをやった Yesterday evening, I took my friends to my favorite bar and we *whooped it up*. (● whoop it up で「どんちゃん騒ぎをする」; raise the roof ともいう).

どんちょう 緞帳 a **stage curtain.**

とんちんかん 頓珍漢 ▶とんちんかんな(=的外れの)意見 an *irrelevant* remark ‖ 互いにとんちんかんなことを言い合う(=話が食い違う) *talk at cross-purposes* ‖ とんちんかんな答え an *off-base* answer(➤「ずっこけた」に近い) ‖ あの男は時々とんちんかんなことを言う He sometimes *talks nonsense*.

どんつう 鈍痛 a **dull pain** ▶胃に鈍痛がある I feel *a dull pain* in my stomach.

どんづまり どん詰まり ▶わが家は狭い路地のどん詰まりに在る My house is located at *the* (*dead*) *end* [《英》 at *the bottom*] of a narrow lane.

とんでもない **1【思いもかけない, ひどい】** **outrageous** (法外な) ; **terrible, horrible, horrendous**(➤ いずれも「ひどく悪い」の意のインフォーマルな語) ▶とんでもない要求[意見] an *outrageous* demand [opinion] ‖ とんでもない間違い a *horrible* [*horrendous*] mistake ‖ 3人もの女性に気を持たせてだますなんてとんでもない男だ What a *terrible* man he is to string along three women! ‖ それは彼のとんでもない誤解だ That's a *gross* misunderstanding on his part. ‖ 帰り道が渋滞していてとんでもない目に遭ったよ I *had quite an* (*awful*) [*quite a terrible*] *experience* on my way back because the street was so congested.

2【強い否定】 ▶1分だって無駄にしたくないのに1時間だなんてとんでもない(=もってのほかだ) I don't have a minute to spare, *let alone* an hour. ‖ 対話「面倒かけて悪かったね」「とんでもない」"Sorry to have troubled you." "*Not at all.*／*No problem.*" ‖ 対話「神戸の町を案内してくださってありがとうございます」「いえ, とんでもないです」"Thank you for showing us the sights of Kobe." "*Not at all. It was my pleasure.*" (➤「こちらこそ楽しかったです」の意).

どんてん 曇天 **cloudy** [**dull**] **weather**(➤ dull はうっとうしい感じを含む) ▶ここ数日曇天続きだ We've had *cloudy weather* for the past few days.

どんでんがえし どんでん返し ▶あの人が当選するなんて, 大方の予想とは逆の大どんでん返しだ His winning the election was *an unexpected upset*. (➤「予想外の番狂わせ」の意) ‖ このドラマの最終回にはあっというようなどんでん返しがある This drama has a marvelous *unexpected twist* in the last installment.

とんとん **1【たたく音】** ▶ドアをトントンたたく音がした There was *a knock* on the door.

2【釣り合っていること】 ▶(賭け事で)これでとんとんだな This makes us *even*. ‖ わが社の収支は昨年はとんとんだった Our company *broke even* last year. (➤ break even は「(商売で)損得なしに終わる」).

3【順調であること】 ▶両家の縁談はとんとんと運んだ The marriage talks between the two families went *smoothly*.

どんどん **1【音】** ▶少年は太鼓をドンドンと打ち鳴らしていた The boy was *beating* a drum *loudly*. (➤ beat は「繰り返したたく」).

2【勢いがよい様子】 ▶その国は人口がどんどん増えている That nation's population is increasing *rapidly*. ‖ 雪がどんどん降ってくる The snow is coming down *heavy and fast*. ‖ その国では物価がどんどん上がっている Prices *are skyrocketing* in that country. ‖ (料理を客に勧めて)さあ, どんどんやって(=食べて)ください Please *help yourself* to the food. ‖ どんどん質問してください Please (*feel free to*) ask *any* questions (you may have).

とんとんびょうし とんとん拍子 ▶彼はとんとん拍子

に出世した He got a *quick* [*speedy*] promotion. ‖ 事はとんとん拍子に運んだ Things went *smoothly and rapidly*. (➤「順調に速く運んだ」の意).

どんな 1【どのような】**what** ▶その手紙にはどんなことが書いてありますか *What* does that letter say? ‖ 監督は選手にどんなことを言いましたか *What* did the manager say to the players?

【文型】
A **はどんなふうですか**(性質・様子)
What is A **like?**

▶アイスランドってどんな所だろう I wonder *what* Iceland is *like*. ‖ 強盗はどんな人相だったか言ってください Please tell us *what* the robber looked like.
▶きみが仕事を辞めたら家族がどんなことになるか考えてみろ You should think about *what* will happen to your family if you quit your job.
▶どんな方法でその金を手に入れたんだい? Tell me *how* you got the money. ‖ それ, どんな味ですか *How* does it taste?
▶ 対話「あなたはどんな音楽が好きですか」「ラテン音楽です」"*What kind of* music do you like?" "(I like) Latin music." ‖ 対話「江田教授はどんな先生ですか」「とても頑固です」"*What kind* [*sort*] *of* teacher is Professor Eda?" "He is pretty hard-nosed."
✉ **オーストラリアのティーンエージャーの生活ってどんなふうなんですか** *What* is the life of a teenager in Australia *like*?
2【いかなる】**any** ▶どんな選手だってエラーはする *Any* player can commit an error. ‖ 対話「どんな紙が要りますか」「どんなものでも結構です」"What kind of paper do you need?" "*Any* type will do." ‖ 彼女のためならぼくはどんなことでもする I would do *anything* for her. ‖ どんなことをしても彼女と結婚したい I want to marry her, *no matter what* (*happens*). ‖ たとえどんなことがあっても部活はやめない *No matter what* (*happens*), I will never quit the club. ‖ どんなことがあっても彼女の心は変わらないだろう *Nothing in the world* will change her mind. ‖ どんなことをしてでも殺人犯は挙げてみせる I'll arrest the murderer *no matter what* [*how long*] *it takes*. ‖ どんなことがあっても私はあなたを許すことができない I can *never* forgive you. / *There's no way* I can forgive you.
3【慣用表現】▶大宮に支店を出すのはどんなものだろう I'*m not sure about the advisability* of opening a branch office in Omiya. (➤「自分の意見としては勧められない」の意).

どんなに ▶私がおまえのことをどんなに心配したか(考えてみろ) Just imagine *how much* I worried about you [*how* worried I was about you].

【文型】
どんなに…ても
no matter A
➤ A は how, what など疑問詞の文

▶どんなに難しそうに見えてもたいがいの問題には解決法があるはずだ *No matter how* difficult they may appear, there should be a solution to most problems. ‖ 彼がどんなに頑張っても3日間でそれを終わらせるのは無理だろう *No matter how* [*However*] hard he tries, he won't be able to finish it in three days. ‖ 夢がかなったらどんなにうれしいことか If I can make my dreams come true, *how* happy I'll be.

トンネル 1【鉄道などの】a **tunnel** /tʌ́nl/ ▶英仏海峡海底トンネル the Anglo-French Channel *Undersea Tunnel* (➤ the Channel Tunnel や the Chunnel ともいう) ‖ 桜のトンネル *a tunnel* [*an arch*] of cherry trees ‖ 青函トンネルは北海道と本州を結んでいる The Seikan *Tunnel* links Hokkaido with Honshu. ‖ 列車はトンネルを抜けた The train passed through the *tunnel*.
‖ **トンネル会社** a dummy company.
2【野球】▶三塁手はランナーが二塁の状況で打者のゴロをトンネルした With a runner on a second base, the third baseman *let* the batter's grounder *go through his legs*.

とんび 鳶《鳥》a (**black**) **kite**. →とび.

ドンびき ドン引き ▶あのタレントの新しいギャグにはドン引きしたよ That TV personality's new comic routine *was a* (*real*) *turnoff*.

どんぴしゃり ▶私の予想がどんぴしゃりだった My prediction *hit the bull's-eye*. / I *hit the nail on the head*.

ドンファン a **Don Juan** /dὰːn *h*wáːn/.

どんぶり 丼 a **big bowl** ▶丼1杯のご飯 *a big bowl* of rice ‖ 私は昼食に親子丼を食べた I had *a bowl of rice topped with chicken and eggs* for lunch.
▶《慣用表現》全くのどんぶり勘定なので, もうかっているのかどうかもわからない Because I'm *doing business without keeping accounts* [*books*], I don't know whether or not I'm making a profit.

とんぼ 蜻蛉 a **dragonfly**《参考》トンボは英米人にはむしろ嫌われ, 日本におけるような親しみや詩情は感じられない ▶網でトンボを捕まえる catch *a dragonfly* with a net.

とんぼがえり 蜻蛉返り・筋斗返り a **somersault** /sʌ́məʳsɔːlt/ ▶ピエロがとんぼ返り(=宙返り)をした A clown turned *a somersault*.
▶私はよく仕事で東京・札幌間をとんぼ返りする I often *shuttle back and forth* between Tokyo and Sapporo on business.

とんま 頓馬 a **dim-witted person**, a **turkey** ▶とんまだなあ! また車の鍵無くしちゃったのか You *turkey* [*dummy*]! You've lost the car keys again.《参考》You turkey [dummy]! は軽いけなしことばで, よく冗談に使う. 軽蔑して本気で言う場合は You jerk! と言う.

ドンマイ **Don't worry.**, **Never mind.** (日本語は (×) Don't mind. からだが, 英語では通例このような言い方はしない).

とんや 問屋 a **wholesaler**(人); a **wholesale store** (店)
▶《慣用表現》俺の借金を踏み倒そうだなんて, そうは問屋が卸さないぞ So you intend to weasel out of paying me the money you owe me! Well, *I won't let you get away with it* [*it isn't going to be like that*].
‖ **問屋街** a wholesale district.

どんよく 貪欲な **greedy** ▶ピラニアは貪欲な魚だ The piranha is a *greedy* fish. ‖ パリに居たとき, 彼女はさまざまなブランド品を貪欲に見て回った While in Paris, she went around looking *hungrily* at many (kinds of) brand-name products.

どんより ▶空はどんより曇っている The sky is *gray with clouds*. ‖ ここ2, 3日どんよりした空模様が続いている We've had *gloomy* skies for the last two or three days. ‖ きょうは一日どんよりとした天気だった *It was overcast* all day long today.
▶その酔っ払いはどんよりと濁った目で私を見た The drunk man looked at me with *dull* eyes.

な・ナ

な 名 **1【名前】** a **name** ⇀名前 ▶誰かが私の名を呼んだ Someone called my *name*. ‖あなたの学校に山中という名の先生はいますか Is there a teacher *named* Yamanaka at your school? ‖生まれた子犬にモモという名をつけた We *named* the new puppy Momo. ‖サンフランシスコは聖フランシスの名にちなんだものだ San Francisco *was named for* [*after*] Saint Francis. (➤ name A for [after] B で「AにBの名をとって命名する」). ☛ **またの名** (⇀見出し語).
2【名声】 (a) **name, fame** ▶松本さんは名の売れた作詞家です Mr. Matsumoto is a *famous* songwriter. ‖彼女はニュースキャスターとして名をあげた She *made a name for herself* [*became famous* / *won fame*] as a newscaster. ‖きみたちは万引きをして本校の名を汚した You shoplifted and, as a result, *disgraced* our school. ‖沢村は名投手として球史に名を残した(＝記憶されている) Sawamura *is remembered* as one of the best pitchers in baseball history.
3【名目】 **name**; a **pretext** (口実) ▶彼は会長といっても名ばかりで, 実際の仕事はほとんどしない He is chairman *in name only*, and seldom does any actual work. ‖防衛の名のもとに他国を侵略した国は数多くある Many countries have invaded other countries *under the pretext of* defending themselves [*in the name of* self-defense]. (➤ 後者のほうがインフォーマル).

-な **1【禁止を示して】** ▶そんなに泣くな *Don't* cry like that [so much]. ‖ばかなことを言うな *Don't* be silly. ‖《掲示》渡るな *No* Crossing.
2【くだけた命令を示して】 ▶早く行きな *Go* at once [right away].
3【確認を示して】 ▶とにかく行って謝って来い. わかったな Just go and apologize, *all right* [*O.K.*]? ‖おまえがこの窓ガラスを割ったんだな You broke this windowpane, *didn't you*?

なあ ▶なあ, ちょっとこれを見ろよ *Say* [*Hey* / 《英》 *I say*], look at this.

-なあ **1【感嘆を示して】** ▶あの女の人は背が高いなあ That woman is really tall. / *How* tall that woman is! (➤ How の感嘆文は会話で使うことは少ない) ‖かっこいい車だなあ *What* a cool car it is! ‖きれいだなあ *How* beautiful!
2【願望を示して】 **I wish** (➤ 不可能なことを願望する場合); **I hope** (➤ 未来への希望をいう場合) ▶今お金があればなあ *I wish* I had (some) money now. (● 現在の仮定は仮定法過去で表す) ‖あのときすべて話してくれていたらなあ *I wish* you had told me everything then. (● 過去の仮定は仮定法過去完了で表す) ‖あした晴れてくれたらいいなあ *I hope* it will be sunny tomorrow.
3【推測を示して】 ▶あのうわさって本当かなあ *I wonder* if that rumor is true.

ナース a **nurse**(➤ nurse は男女の別なく用いる)
‖ナースステーション a nurses' station.

なあなあ ▶なあなあの関係 a *collusive* [*cozy*] relationship ‖なあなあで決めた decide *collusively*.

なあに ▶なあに, 大したことはない It's nothing serious. / It's no big deal. ‖ 対話「今, 彼女にそれを言ったらまずいんじゃないかい?」「なあに, 構うもんか」"Isn't this a bad time to tell her about it?" "*Who cares?*"

ナーバス **nervous** ▶兄は大学受験が迫ってナーバスになっている My brother *is nervous* because the college entrance exams are approaching.

ない 無い・亡い **1【見当たらない, 存在しない】** **be gone, be missing** (なくなっている); **no** (➤ 名詞につく) ▶あれ, 傘がない Oh, no! My umbrella *is gone*. ‖ここへ置いておいた書類がない The paper that I left here is *missing*. (➤ missing は「行方不明で」) ‖ぼくのグローブがどこにもないんだよ I *can't find* my glove *anywhere*. ‖きょうは創立記念日で学校(＝授業)がない Today is Founder's Day, so *there's no* school. ‖いけない, 1時だ. もう電車がないよ Oh, no. It's one o'clock. *There's no* train service now [*There are no* more trains]. ‖ 対話「パイは残っている?」「全然残っていないよ」"Is there any pie left?" "No, there *isn't*." (● (×)There is nothing. としない).
▶お母さん, おしょうゆがない(＝切らしている)よ We've *run out of* soy sauce, Mom. ‖スケートとなると長島にかなう者はない *Nobody* can beat Nagashima when it comes to skating. ‖こんなおんぼろ車でもないよりはましだ Even a jalopy like this *is better than nothing*. ‖オリンピックまであと1年しかない *There's only* a year (left) until the Olympics.
☛ **なかったら, なければ** (⇀見出語)
2【所有していない】 **no** (➤ 名詞につく) ▶彼にはきょうだいがない He has *no* brothers or sisters. (➤ no のあとの可算名詞は複数形になることが多い) ‖今, 金が一銭も無いんだ I *don't have any* money (with me). / I'm broke now. ‖きょうは時間がないので来週にしてください I *don't have* time today, so please wait until next week. ‖きみには常識というものが無いのか Don't you *have* any common sense at all? (➤ 否定の疑問文は日本語と同様, 非難や驚きを表すことが多い) ‖彼はユーモアのセンスが無い He *lacks* a sense of humor.

> **あなたの英語はどう響く?**
> 「〜がない」「〜を持っていない」という場合, 時間・金など不可算名詞に関しては, I have *no* time [*no* money]. / I do*n't* have *any* time [*any* money]. のいずれの言い方でもよいが, 車・本など可算名詞に関しては, I have *no* car [*no* books]. よりも, I do*n't* have a car [*any* books]. のような言い方が好まれる.

3【死んでいる】 ▶この映画に出てくる人の多くはもうこの世には亡い Many of the actors in this film have already *passed away* [*gone*]. (➤ pass away は die の婉曲表現) ‖優しかった祖母も今はもう亡い My loving grandmother *is no longer with us*.
4【慣用表現】 ▶あることないこと(＝うそばかり)言いふらされたんじゃ黙ってはいられない I can't keep quiet after all *those lies* were told about me. ‖自転車通学は禁止だなんて, そんなのないよ *It's not fair that* we can't go to school by bike. (➤「公平じゃないよ」の意) ‖

な

おまえ，そういう言い方はないだろ？ *Don't talk* (*to me*) *like that.* ／*Watch your mouth.* (➤後者は「口のきき方に気をつけろ」の意で，ぞんざいな言い方) ‖ 金を貸してくれといわれてもない袖は振れないよ You're asking me for money, but *I can't give you what I haven't got.* (➤「持っていないものはあげられない」の意).

1**-ない** -無い **1**【打ち消し】**not** ▶あの男は真の政治家ではない He *is not* a real politician. ‖ ぼくはそんな事は知らない I do*n't* know about that. ‖ 高校生がたばこなんか吸うもんじゃない High school students should*n't* smoke. ‖ 彼に才能が無いと言っているわけではない I'm *not* saying he has no talent.

2【否定の疑問文】▶《レストランで》この店，どれも安いと思わない？ Everything at this restaurant is (really) inexpensive, *don't you think*？(➤相手が同意してくれることを期待する場合) ‖ きみ，自転車に乗れないの？ *Can't you* ride a bicycle？(➤否定形の質問はしばしば，「できなければおかしいでしょ」や「(えっ,)できないの？」という皮肉を表す．単にできるかできないかを聞くのならば，肯定形で Can you ...? (…できますか)を用いるのが無難(→-ませんか)) ‖ 近所でよい歯医者さんを知らないですか *Do you know* (*of*) a good dentist in this neighborhood？(➤ know of は口コミなどで知っている場合，know は体験的に直接知っている場合) ‖ この近くで公衆電話がどこにあるかを知らないですか *Do you* (*happen to*) *know* where I can find a pay phone near here? ‖ こんな単純なこともわからないの？ *You can't understand* something simple like this？／*Can't you understand* such a simple thing as this？

3【確認を示して】▶やあ，古賀君じゃない！ Well, *if it isn't* (my old friend) Koga！(➤「古賀君じゃない？」なら Aren't you Koga？／Isn't it Koga？).

4【勧誘・依頼を示して】▶どこか喫茶店に寄っておしゃべりでもしない？ *What do you say* we stop in at a coffee shop for a chat？‖ このCD，2，3日貸してくれない？ *Can* you lend me this CD for a couple of days？‖ **対話**「スキーに行かないか？」「それはいいね」"*How about* going skiing？" "That's a good idea."

5【禁止を示して】▶泣くんじゃない！ *Don't* cry！／*This is no time* to cry！(➤「泣いてる場合じゃないぞ」の意).

2**-ない** -内 ▶園［遊園地］内でのボール遊びはおやめください Don't play ball *in* the park. ‖ 部内でそれを検討しました We discussed it *in* our department [*among* our department staff]. ‖ 期限内にそれを終えてください Please finish it *within* the specified period.

ナイアガラ ナイアガラの滝 **Niagara Falls** (アメリカとカナダの国境にある滝).

ナイーブ **innocent**

> **危ないカタカナ語✹ ナイーブ**
> **1** 日本語の「ナイーブ」は「繊細で感じやすい」という意味で使われるが，英語の naive は「世間知らずでだまされやすい，幼稚な，単純で無知な」といった否定的ニュアンスで使われることが多い．Don't be so naive！と言えば「あんまり幼稚なことを言う［する］んじゃないよ」の意である．
> **2** したがって，繊細なナイーブさをいう場合は innocent (純粋無垢(ᵏ)な)，sensitive (感じやすい)，pure-hearted (純な心の)などを用いるほうがよい．

▶きみって，ナイーブだね You're so *pure-hearted.*

ないえん 内縁 **common-law marriage, putative marriage** 《解説》(1)前者は英語国の場合で，宗教上または民法上の手続きを経てはいないが，実質的な夫婦生活をしており，一定期間を経過すれば法的にも認められるもの．(2)後者は日本の場合のような民法上の手続きを経ていない関係をいう(putative は「世間で…で通っている」の意)．(3)後者は英語国では一般的な語ではないので，前者を用いるとよい ▶内縁の妻 a *common-law* [*putative*] wife.

ないか 内科 **internal medicine** (内科学)；**the department of internal medicine** (病院の部門) ▶内科専門の医師 a physician specializing in *internal medicine* ‖ 息子がかぜをひいたので内科で診てもらった I took my son to *a doctor* because he had a cold. 《参考》(1)《米》では内科医のことを internist /íntəːˈnɪst/ というが主に専門用語．ふつうは doctor または physician という．(2)専門医でない医者を primary care doctor [physician]／general practitioner などという．

ないがい 内外 **1**【内と外】▶生徒たちは校舎の内外を掃除した The students cleaned the school building *inside and out.*／社の内外から優秀な人材を集めてそのチームが編成された The team was formed with excellent people gathered from *inside* [*within*] *and outside* the company.

2【国内と国外】▶あの映画監督は内外に知られている That movie director is known both *at home and abroad* [*overseas*]. ‖ 丸山氏は内外の情勢に詳しい Mr. Maruyama is familiar with *domestic and foreign* affairs.

3【約】▶値段は1万円内外です The price is *about* ten thousand yen [*around* ten thousand yen／*in the neighborhood of* ten thousand yen].

1**ないかく** 内閣 **a cabinet** (➤現内閣や特定の国の内閣を指す場合はしばしば the Cabinet となる) ▶吉田内閣 the Yoshida *Cabinet* ‖ 新内閣を組織する form [organize] a new *cabinet* ‖ 内閣不信任案を提出する call for a nonconfidence vote in the *Cabinet.* ‖内閣総理大臣 the Prime Minister ‖ 内閣府 the Cabinet Office ‖ 連立内閣 a coalition cabinet.

2**ないかく** 内角 **1**【数学】an **interior angle** ▶三角形の内角の和は180度だ The sum of a triangle's *interior angles* always equals 180 degrees.

2【野球】**inside** ▶内角低めのストレート a fastball low and *inside*／a low, *inside* fastball.

ないがしろ 蔑ろ ▶学業をないがしろにしてはいけない You shouldn't *neglect* your studies. ‖ 彼は長い間妻をないがしろにしていたことを悔いた He regretted that he *had been taking* his wife *for granted* for a long time. (➤ take A for granted は「なれっこになって A のありがたみを感じない」).

ないき 内規 **a regulation,** 《米また》**a bylaw** (➤ bylaw は《英》では「地方条例」の意がふつう) ▶会社の内規では社内は禁煙です According to *bylaws* of the company, smoking is prohibited in the conference room.

ないけい 内径 (an) **inside** [**internal**] **diameter.**

ないこうてき 内向的な **introverted, shy** (内気な) ▶彼は内向的で女の子とろくに口もきけない He is such *an introvert* [*introverted* person] that he can hardly talk with girls.

ないし 乃至 **or** (または) ▶手紙は2日ないし3日で届くでしょう The letter will reach you in two *or* three days. ‖ 本学では英文科の教授ないし准教授1名を求めている Our university is looking for *either* a professor *or* an associate professor of English Literature. ‖ 道路の復旧には半年ないし1年かかる It will be six months *to* one year before the road is restored.

ないじ 内示 ▶成田先生は新しい高校の校長就任の内示を受けた Mr. Narita *was told* [*was notified*] *unofficially* that he would be appointed principal of the new high school.

ナイジェリア Nigeria(アフリカ中西部の国).

ないじえん 内耳炎 《医学》 otitis interna /oʊtàɪṭəs ɪntə́ːʳnə/, inflammation of the inner ear 《参考》日常的には単に an ear infection ということが多い.

ないしきょう 内視鏡 《医学》 an endoscope /éndəskoʊp/ ▶私はきょう胃の内視鏡検査を受けた Today I had *an endoscopic examination* of my stomach [a gastro*endoscopic examination*].

ないじつ 内実 ▶彼女は景気のよさそうなことを言っているが, 内実は火の車らしい She talks like she's doing well financially, but *in reality* [*the truth is*] she's hard up for money.

ないじゅ 内需 domestic [internal] demand ▶政府は内需拡大を呼びかけている The government is calling for measures to *increase domestic demand*.

ないしゅっけつ 内出血 internal bleeding [hemorrhage] (➤ 後者は医学用語で大出血をいう) ▶壁におでこをぶつけたら内出血した I hit my forehead on the wall and had some *internal bleeding*. (➤ 頭の場合はふつう intracranial bleeding という).

ないしょ 内緒 a secret (秘密); secrecy /síːkrəsi/ (秘密にする[である]こと) 一形 ないしょの secret ▶まだないしょだけどあの二人はことしの秋に結婚するそうよ This is still *a secret*, but they are going to marry this fall.

> 【文型】
> **あること(A)をないしょにする**
> keep A (a) secret
> keep A to oneself
>
> ◀解説▶ (1)上の型は「秘密にする」, 下の型は「自分の胸にしまって人に話さない」の意.「人(B)に」が必要なときは **keep** A (a) **secret from** B の型になる.
> (2) **keep ... secret** のときは secret は形容詞. 口調で選ばれることが多いが, **keep ... a secret** のほうが若干多い.

▶献金者は身元をないしょにしてほしいと望んだ The donor wished to *keep* his [her] identity *a secret*. ‖ このことはお父さんにはないしょにしておいてね Please *keep* this (matter) (*a*) *secret from* my father. ‖ そのことはないしょにしておくつもりだったんだ I was thinking of *keeping* it *to myself*.

▶おばあちゃんがないしょで(=こっそり)少しお小遣いをくれた My grandma *secretly* gave me some spending money. ‖ 彼らはその計画をないしょで実行した They carried out the plan *in secret* [*in* (*total*) *secrecy*]. ‖ 彼は事の一部始終をないしょで教えてくれた He told me the whole story *in confidence*. (➤ in confidence は「打ち明け話で」の意).

▶この話はないしょだよ This is just *between ourselves* [*between you and me*]. ‖ 彼女は親にないしょでバーで働いている She is working in a bar *without telling* her parents. ‖ ちょっと(きみと)ないしょの話があるんだ I have a little *secret* matter that I want to talk over with you. ‖ ないしょ話はよしてくれ Don't talk *in whispers*. / Stop *whispering*. ‖ 対話「ねえ, あなたたち何話してるの?」「ナイショ」"What are you talking about?" "*I'm not telling you.* / *It's a secret.*"

‖ないしょ事 a secret, a private [confidential] matter.

ないじょう 内情 ▶あの会社ははでな宣伝をしているが内情はあまりよくない That company has some showy advertising, but *inside the company, things aren't going so well*. ‖ ゆうべの盗難事件は会社の内情をよく知る者のしわざに違いない Last night's burglary must have been committed by someone *with inside knowledge* [must have been *an inside job*].

ないしょく 内職 a side job (副業); piecework (出来高払いの仕事) ⇀アルバイト ▶家で内職をする *do piecework* at home ‖ 彼は内職にシナリオを書いている He writes scenarios *on the side*.

▶《比喩的》社会の時間に英語の内職をした I *prepared for* the English class *secretly* during the social studies class.

ないじょのこう 内助の功 one's wife's help [support] ▶その候補者が当選できたのは内助の功によるところが大きい The candidate has won the election largely due to *his wife's help* [*support*].

ないしん 内心 ▶私は内心不安だったが強がってみせた I put on a brave front, although I felt uneasy *inside* [*deep down* / *in my heart*]. (➤ deep down は「心の底では」の意の副詞句) ‖ 彼に反対などできるものかと私は内心で思っていた I *thought to myself* that he wouldn't be able to raise any objections. ‖ 彼はその試験が中止になって内心ほっとした He was *secretly* [*inwardly*] relieved that the test was canceled.

ないしんしょ 内申書 a school report (on a student's grades and conduct); school recommendations (推薦文を中心とした) ▶入学願書に内申書を添えて出す submit an application for admission (to a school) with *school recommendations*.

ないしんのう 内親王 a princess ▶愛子内親王 *Her Imperial Highness Princess* Aiko, *Princess* Aiko.

ナイス nice ▶《ゴルフ》ナイスショット! *Good shot!* (➤ Nice shot! はあまり使われない).

ないせい 内政 domestic [home] administration (国内政治); domestic [internal] affairs (国内の政治業務) ▶日本の内政への不当な干渉 unjustified interference in Japan's *internal affairs* ‖ 新内閣は内政・外交とも問題が山積している The new cabinet has a lot of problems in both *domestic* and foreign *affairs*.

1ないせん 内線 an extension 《略 ext.》 ▶内線3939番をお願いします (Give me) *extension* 3939, please. / May I have *extension* 3939, please?

‖内線番号 an extension number.

2ないせん 内戦 (a) civil war ▶内戦状態にある国 a country in a state of *civil war* ‖ (アメリカの)「南北戦争」は内戦だ The Civil War was *an internal war* between the North and the South (of the United States).

ないそう 内装 interior /ɪntíəriəʳ/ decoration [furnishings]; décor /deɪkɔ́ːʳ/ (様式, デザイン) ▶きれいに内装された部屋 a nicely *decorated* room ‖ しゃれた内装のレストラン a restaurant *with* tasteful *décor* [*interior decoration*].

1ないぞう 内臓 internal organs

‖内臓疾患 an internal disease ‖ 内臓脂肪 visceral [(intra-)abdominal / central] fat.

[2]**ないぞう 内蔵** ▶このノートパソコンは DVD ドライブを内蔵している This laptop computer has a *built-in* DVD drive. (➤ built-in は「組み込まれた」).

ナイター a **night game**, a **nighttime baseball game** (➤ nighter は一般的ではない) ▶日本では多くのプロ野球試合がナイターだ Most pro baseball games *are played at night* in Japan. ‖ ナイターでも見に行こうか? How about going to see *a night game*?
‖**ナイタースキー** night skiing.

ないだく 内諾 **informal consent** [**agreement**] ▶その件については部長の内諾を得ておいたから安心していいよ I have received the manager's *informal consent* about the matter, so there's nothing to worry about.

ないち 内地 **the interior.**

ないちまい 内地米 **homegrown rice.**

ナイチンゲール (鳥) a **nightingale.**

ないつう 内通 **betrayal.**

[1]**ないてい 内定** ▶M銀行から就職内定の通知をもらった M Bank *unofficially* informed me that they would employ me. ‖ 対話「就職口見つかった?」「ええ, まだ内定だけど, N証券に」"Did you get a job?" "Yeah. N Securities Company, though (it's) still *unofficial*."

[2]**ないてい 内偵** a **secret investigation.**

ないてもわらっても 泣いても笑っても ▶泣いても笑っても(=好むと好まざるとにかかわらず)ことしもあと3日で終わりだ (*Whether you*) *like it or not*, this year has only three days left.

ナイトクラブ a **nightclub.**

ないない 内々 ▶内々の情報 *unofficial* information ‖ この件は内々に処理したいと思います I would like to deal with the matter *privately* [*just between you and me*].

ないねんきかん 内燃機関 **the internal combustion engine.**

ナイフ a **knife** ▶といしでナイフを研ぐ sharpen [hone] *a knife* on a whetstone ‖ このナイフはよく切れる This *knife* cuts well. ‖ ナイフとフォークを使って食事をするのはどうも苦手だ I am not good at eating with (*a*) *knife and fork*. (🏺 このように対になる場合は通例 a を省略する).
‖**カッターナイフ** a box cutter, a utility knife → **カッター** ‖ **ジャックナイフ** a jackknife ‖ **登山ナイフ** a hunting knife ‖ **ペンナイフ** a penknife ‖ **ポケットナイフ** a pocket knife.

ないぶ 内部 **the inside, the interior** /ɪntíərɪər/ ▶このホテルは内部も外部同様に豪華だ *The inside* of this hotel is as luxurious as the outside. / *The interior* of this hotel looks as magnificent as its exterior. ‖ 彼はファッション業界の内部事情に詳しい He has a lot of *inside* information about the fashion world. ‖ この窃盗は内部の者の犯行のようだ This burglary seems to be *an inside job*. ‖ 元社員が会社幹部の不正を内部告発した An ex-employee *blew the whistle* on the executives' irregular practices. (➤ blow the whistle は「人の秘密を暴露する」の意のインフォーマルな言い方.「内部告発」は insider's accusation).
‖**内部抗争** an internal struggle [strife].

ないふくやく 内服薬 a **medicine taken internally**, an **oral medicine** [**medication**] ▶かぜの内服薬 cold *medicine*.

ないふん 内紛 **internal strife** ▶その会社の上層部では内紛が絶えない There is endless *strife within* [*inside*] the management of the company.

ないぶんぴつ 内分泌 **internal secretion**
‖**内分泌かく乱物質** an endocrine disruptor (➤ ふつう「環境ホルモン」という).

ないみつ 内密の **secret** ▶交渉は内密に行われた The negotiations were conducted *secretly* [*clandestinely*].

ないめん 内面 ▶彼女の内面の美しさはふるまいに表れている Her behavior reveals her *inner* beauty. ‖ 外観から人の内面を伺うことは難しい It's difficult to tell *what a person's personality is like* just from his or her appearance.

ないものねだり 無い物ねだり ▶ 対話「もう少し絵心があったらなあ」「それは無い物ねだりよ」"How I wish I had a little more talent for painting!" "That's just like *asking for the moon*. / That's *asking the impossible*."

ないや 内野 **the infield** ▶内野安打を放つ beat out *an infield hit* ‖ 川崎は内野ならどこでも守れる Kawasaki can play any *infield position*.
‖**内野ゴロ** an infield grounder (➤ ふつうは単に grounder でよい) ‖ **内野手** an infielder ‖ **内野フライ** an infield fly.

ないよう 内容 **content** /kɑ́:ntent/ (書物・演説などの要旨・趣旨); **contents** (具体的な中身); **substance** (実質) ▶手紙の内容 *the contents* of a letter (➤ 実際に書かれている中身は contents) ‖ 本の内容 the *content* of a book (➤ 本の趣旨や述べられている考えは Ⓤ) ‖ 胃の内容物 stomach *contents* ‖ 大事なのは外見ではなく内容だ What's important is not the appearance, but the *content*. ‖ このサイトは内容が豊富 [貧弱] だ This site is rich [poor] *in content*. ‖ 彼女の話には内容がない There is no *content* [*substance*] in her speech.
▶会談の内容(=どんなことが議論されたか)は公表されなかった *What was discussed at the conference* was not made public. ‖ あの映画は昔見たことがあるが内容はよく覚えていない I have seen the film once but I don't remember very well *what it was all about*. ‖ (会社訪問の学生などが) 仕事の内容をお教えいただけませんか Could you tell me *what the job involves*? 《参考》アメリカでは雇用契約の際に職務の内容を明記した書類にサインするのがふつうで, これを job description という.

ないらん 内乱 (a) **civil war** (内戦); a **rebellion** (反乱) ▶内乱は鎮圧された The *rebellion* was suppressed.

ないらんかい 内覧会 a **sneak preview**, a **private showing** ▶彼は新築マンションの内覧会に行った He went to *a private showing* of the new condominium.

ないりく 内陸 an **inland** ▶アジアの内陸を旅する travel in *the inland areas* of Asia.
‖**内陸性気候** a continental climate ‖ **内陸地方** an inland area.

ナイル ナイル川 **the Nile** (エジプトの川).

ナイロン **nylon** ▶このコートの生地はナイロンです This coat is made of *nylon* cloth.

なえ 苗 a **seedling** (種から育てた); a **young plant**, a **sapling** (苗木) ▶トマトの苗 a tomato *seedling*.

なえる 萎える **wither** (花などがしぼむ); **become weak** (弱まる); **lose strength** (体力が弱まる) ▶なえたペニス a *flaccid* penis ‖ もう気力がなえてしまった My strength has already *withered*.

なお 猶・尚 **1** 【**依然として**】 **still** ▶乗客3名がなお行方不明です Three passengers are *still* missing.

2【なおいっそう】much, a lot, far（はるかに, ずっと）; **even, still**（さらに, いっそう）（➤ いずれも比較級を強める；前の3つは程度などの開きや差が大きいことを, あとの2つは形容詞・副詞が表す状況・性質などにおいては同じことが言えるが「さらに」「よりいっそう」と程度に違いがあることをいう）▶塩をあとひとつまみ入れるとスープはなおおいしくなる The soup would taste *much* [*a lot*] better with another pinch of salt. ‖ 彼女は髪を短くしたほうがなおすてきだ She'd look *much* nicer if she had her hair cut short. ‖ そのルートは（こちらより）なお危険だ That route is *even* more dangerous (than this one). (➤ どちらも危険だが, そのルートのほうが危険度が高いことをいう. much や a lot は差の大きさを強調する) ‖ それも難しいがこっちはなお難しい That's hard, but this is *even* [*still*] harder. ‖ なお悪いことに雨が降り出した *To make matters worse*, it began to rain.

3【付け加えれば】▶なお, 彼は独身です *Let me add that* [*Incidentally*,] he is single.

☞ なおも（→見出語）

なおさら 尚更 all the more（その分ますます）▶朝6時起きはつらい. 寒いときはなおさらだ It's hard for me to get up at six, and *all the more* so when it's cold. ‖ きみも行ってくれるならなおさら楽しくなる If you come along with us, it would be *much* [*even* / *still*] *more* fun.

なおざり ▶毎日の練習をなおざりにする *neglect* one's daily practice ‖ 彼は仕事にかまけて家庭をなおざりにした He was so engrossed in his work (that) he *thought little of* [*gave no thought to*] his family.

なおし 直し repair, mending（修繕）; **correction**（修正）▶このオートバイはもう直しがきかないよ There's no way to *repair* this motorbike. (➤ この repair は「直す」の意の動詞) ‖ その服は洋服屋に寸法直しに出した I took that suit to the tailor for *alterations*.

なおす 直す・治す

> 📖 訳語メニュー
> 修理する →repair **1**
> 病気を治す →cure **2**
> 訂正する →correct **3**
> 調整する →adjust **3**

1【修理する】repair +目, **mend** +目,《インフォーマル》**fix** +目

語法 (1) **repair** は比較的な大きな, または複雑なものを修理する場合に, **mend** は構造の比較的簡単なもの（《米》では特に布製品,《英》では屋根・垣根・衣服などの穴）を修理する場合に用いることが多い. (2) **fix** は repair, mend のいずれにも用いるインフォーマルな語.

▶時計を直してもらう *have* one's watch *repaired* ‖ このテレビを直してください Could you *repair* this television? ‖ 私は妹の壊れた椅子を直してやった I *fixed* my sister's broken chair. ‖ エンジンを直してもらうのに2万円も掛かったのよ It cost me 20,000 yen to *have* the engine *fixed*.

2【健康な状態にする】cure +目（完治させる）

> 【文型】
> 人(A)の病気(B)を治す
> **cure** A of B

▶医師は彼女の不眠症を治すのに全力を尽くした The doctor tried everything to *cure* her insomnia [her *of* her insomnia]. ‖ 息子のぜん息を治してやりたい I want my son to *be cured of* asthma.

▶二日酔い［頭痛］を寝て治す *sleep off* a hangover [headache] ‖ 父は肝炎を治すため3か月入院した My father was hospitalized for three months for *treatment* of hepatitis. (➤ treatment は「治療」) ‖ このかぜを早く治したいよ I want to *get over* this cold as soon as possible. ‖《患者が医者に》治せるでしょうか Is it *curable*? / Can it *be cured*?

3【修正する, 矯正する】correct +目（訂正する）; **adjust** +目（調整する）▶ライトさんは私のつづりの間違いを直してくれた Mr. Wright *corrected* my spelling mistakes. ‖ 壁にかかっている時計が2分遅れているから直して Please *adjust* the clock on the wall since it is two minutes slow. ‖ この計画書は一部直す（＝変更する）必要がある We need to *alter* part of the plan. ‖ このズボンの丈を直してもらえますか Could you *adjust* the length of these pants?

▶ネクタイを直す *straighten* one's tie ‖ つめをかむ悪いくせを直す *break* [*get rid of*] one's bad habit of biting one's nails ‖ 歌手はステージに上がる前に化粧を直した The singer *touched up* [*reapplied*] her make-up before coming out on stage.

4【換算する】▶150平米は坪に直すとどれくらいだろう？ How much is 150 square meters *in* tsubo? / How many tsubo is 150 square meters? ‖ 今, 1ポンドは円に直すとどれくらいですか How much do you get if you *convert* one pound *into* yen? / How much is one pound worth *in* yen now?

5【翻訳する】translate +目, **interpret** +目（通訳する）▶通訳者は市長の演説を同時通訳で中国語に直した The interpreter simultaneously *interpreted* [*translated*] the mayor's speech into Chinese. ‖ 次の英文を日本語に直しなさい *Put* the following English passage *into* Japanese.

6【「…し直す」の形で】▶文を書き直す *rewrite* a sentence ‖ 帯を締め直す *retie* the obi ‖ 問題を考え直す *reconsider* a question / *give* the question *further thought* ‖ 彼女は手紙を（何度も）読み直した She *read* the letter (over and over) *again*. ‖《電話で》30分したらこちらからかけ直します I'll *call* you (*back*) in half an hour.

なおのこと ▶ロンドン暮らしの鈴木さん一家はすしを食べに出かけると, なおのこと日本恋しさが募る When the Suzukis, who are living in London, go out for sushi, they miss Japan *all the more*. (● ふつうに「ますます」は more and more であるが, 特別な理由やきっかけを述べた文では「その分ますます」の意の all the more を用いる).

なおも 尚も ▶前半で大差でリードしていたにもかかわらず, ブラジルは後半でなおも攻撃の手を緩めなかった Though they had taken a big lead in the first half, the Brazilian team *didn't let up on their offense* [*kept up a strong offense*] in the second half.

なおる 直る・治る

1【物が修理される】be repaired, be mended; be fixed（➤ インフォーマルな語）▶修理工場へ行ったらうちの車はもう直っていた At the garage, I found that my car had already *been repaired* [*fixed*]. ‖ **対話**「この冷蔵庫は直るでしょうか」「だめですねえ」"Is this refrigerator *repairable*?" "I'm afraid it is beyond repair."

2【体が健康状態に戻る】get well（よくなる）; **heal**（傷がよくなる）; **recover**（回復する）▶彼女の病気じきに治るといいね I hope she'll *get* [she *gets*] *well* soon. / I hope she'll *recover* from her illness soon. ‖ ひざのけがは1週間で治った My knee injury *healed* in a week. ‖ かぜ, 治った？ *Is* your cold *gone*? /

Are you *over* your cold yet ? ‖ かぜがなかなか治らなくてね I can't seem to *get over* [*get rid of* ／*kick*] this cold. (➤ get over は「克服する」, get rid of は「取り除く」) ‖ この軟こうを塗れば湿しんはすぐ治ります This ointment will soon *cure* [*clear up*] your eczema. (➤ cure は「完治させる」) ‖ 病気が治ったら, また海外旅行に行きたい I'd like to take a trip overseas again when I'*m cured* (of this disease).

3【修正される】▶プレゼントをあげたら, とたんに彼の**機嫌が直った** After I gave him a present, his *mood* suddenly *improved.* ‖ 自分で働くようになればあの怠け**癖も直る**さ He'll *snap out of* his laziness once he gets a job. ‖ ここの誤植がまだ**直っていない** This typographical error hasn't *been corrected.* ‖ 彼女は大人になってもまだつめをかむ(悪い)**癖が直らない** She hasn't been able to *break* [*get rid of*] her bad *habit* of biting her nails, even though she's a grown woman now. ‖ **対話**「(北野)先生, 息子の**非行は直る**でしょうか」「もちろんです」"Mr. Kitano, will my son ever *reform himself* [*grow out of his delinquent behavior*] ?" "Of course he will."

4【元の状態に戻る】▶ (号令) 前へならえ, **直れ** Forward, dress ! *As you were !*

[1]**なか 中** **1【空間の内部】the inside ; in** (…の中に) ▶人間の**体の中** *the inside* of the human body ‖ このメロン, **中が腐ってる**わ This melon is rotten *inside.* ‖ **箱の中**はからっぽだった There was nothing *in* the box. ／The box was (completely) empty. ‖ スーツケースの**中**(＝中身)を見せてください Show me the *contents* of your suitcase. ‖ 彼はかばんの**中から**携帯電話を取り出した He took a cellphone *out of* his bag.

▶**講堂の中では**静かにしなさい Keep quiet *in* the auditorium. ‖ 振り向くと彼女は**人込みの中に消えて**いた When I glanced back, she had disappeared *into the crowd.* ‖ こんな天気のいい日は**家の中にいたく**ない I don't want to *stay home* on such a beautiful day. ‖ ジェット機は**雲の中に入った** The jet went *into* the cloud(s). ‖ どうぞ**中へお入りください** Please *come in.*

2【抽象的なものの内部】▶秘密は自分の**心の中だけに**しまっておくことにした I decided to keep the secret *to myself.*

3【範囲内】among ; of ; in ▶彼女は大勢の応募者の**中から選ばれた** She was chosen *from among* [*out of*] many applicants. ‖ 私たち3人の**中で**誰が最初に結婚するかしら I wonder who of the three *of* us will get married first. ‖ 土星の衛星の**中では**タイタンがいちばん大きい *Of* all Saturn's moons, Titan is the largest. ‖ これまで生きてきた**中で**こんなうれしいことはない I have never been happier *in* all my life. ‖ この生徒たちの**中には**エジソンのような大発明家がいるかもしれない *Among* these students, there could be another great inventor like Edison. (⇀**中には**) ‖ 若い人の**中にも**ハンバーガーが嫌いな人はいる *Some* young people don't like hamburgers. ‖ 彼はまさに**男の中の男**だ He is *a real man.* ／He is *a man among men.*

4【間隔, 中間】▶**中をとって**5500円で手を打ってはどうでしょう How about *splitting the difference* and settling for 5,500 yen ? ‖ 先発の田中は**中5日おいて**の登板です The starter Tanaka is pitching *after a five-day rest.*

5【最中】▶**お忙しい中を**よくおいでくださいました I am glad you could come *despite your busy schedule.* ‖ 救助隊は**吹雪の中を**行方不明者の捜索に向かった The rescue team went out *in* the snowstorm to search for the missing persons.

[2]**なか 仲** **terms** (間がら) ; **relation(ship)** (関係) ▶私と彼女は(すごく)**仲がいい** I'*m* (*good*) *friends with* her. (➤ 主語が単数でも friends となることに注意 ; ⇀**仲よし**) ‖ 姉と私はとても**仲がいい** My sister and I *are* very *close.* ‖ 田中さんのところは**夫婦仲がいい** The Tanakas *are happily married* [*are a happily married couple*]. ‖ あの兄弟はなぜか**仲が悪い** Those brothers *don't get along* (*with each other*) for some reason. ‖ 倉田さん一家とは**互いに行き来する仲**です We are *on visiting terms* with the Kuratas. ‖ 彼らは会えば挨拶を交わす**仲**だ They know each other well enough to greet each other. ‖ あの人とはどういう**仲**ですか What kind of *relation* [*relationship*] do you have with him ? ‖ **二人の仲**は公然の秘密だ *Their relationship* is an open secret. ‖ おしゅうとめさんとの**仲はうまくいって**ますか How are you *getting along with* your mother-in-law ? ‖ 二人は**仲むつまじく**暮らしている The couple is living *happily* together. ‖ 親が**二人の仲を裂いた** [**取り持った**] The parents *broke the pair up* [*fixed the pair up*].

☛ **犬猿の仲, 仲よく, 仲よし, 不仲** (⇀見出語)

ながあめ 長雨 a **long rain** ▶作物に水をやるには**長雨**が必要だ We need *a long rain* to water the crops. ‖ **長雨**で農作物への悪影響が心配される We are concerned about the crops because this *long rain* may cause a lot of damage.

なかい 仲居 a ***nakai***, a **room maid in a Japanese inn** (宿の) ; a **food server**(料亭の) 《参考》日本通の外国人の中には nakai-san と呼び掛ける人もいる.

[1]**ながい 長居** ▶どうやらすっかり**長居した**ようです I'm afraid I've *stayed too long.* ‖ **長居**は嫌われますよ. 気をつけなさい Do not *outstay* [*overstay*] your welcome. ／Be careful not to *outstay* [*overstay*]. 《参考》英語には Do not wear out your welcome. (長居をして飽きられるな)ということわざがある.

[2]**ながい 長い・永い** **1【距離や寸法が】long** ▶キリンは**首が長い** Giraffes have *long* necks. ‖ 桃子は**長い髪**をしている Momoko has *long* hair. ／Momoko *wears* her hair *long.* ‖ 世界でいちばん**長い橋**はどのくらい**長い**の？ How *long* is the *longest* bridge in the world ?

2【時間が】long ▶**長い夏休み** a *long* summer vacation ‖ 私は**長い間**彼女を待った I waited for her (*for*) *a long time.* ／I have *long* waited for her. ‖ 彼女は**長い間**口をきかなかった *For a long time*, she didn't speak. (● She didn't speak for a long time. とすると「彼女は長くは話さなかった(少しの間だけ話した)」の意になる) ‖ 父はトイレが**長い** My father always takes *a long time* in the bathroom. ‖ 金沢へは**長いこと**行ってない I haven't been to Kanazawa *in* [*for*] *a long time.* ‖ **長いこと**お会いしてませんね I haven't seen you *for ages*, have I ? ‖ **長い**1日だった It was a *long* day. ／I thought the day would *never end.* ／I felt as if the day would *last forever.* ‖ 彼女はもう**長いことあるまい**(＝死が間近だ) I'm afraid she does*n't have much time left* [will *not live much longer*]. ‖ 日本に来てまだそう**長くはありません** I haven't been here in Japan for very *long.*

▶学長は教育理念について**長いスピーチ**をした The president made a *lengthy* speech on his idea of what education ought to be like. (➤ lengthy

/léŋkθi/ は「長たらしい」).

3【慣用表現】▶長い目で見れば, 大学へ入るのが1年や2年遅れても何でもない *If you take a long view of it* [*In the long run*], it doesn't matter if you are a year or two late (in) entering a university. ‖ ことわざ 長い物には巻かれろ Be ruled by the stronger. (➤日本語からの意訳) ／If the master says the crow is white, the servant must not say it's black. (➤「主人がカラスは白いと言ったら, 召使いはそれを黒いと言ってはいけない」の意の英語のことわざ).

ながいき 長生き (a) **long life, longevity** /lɑːndʒévəṭi/ (長寿) 一動 **長生きする live long, live a long life ; live to be a grand old age** (➤「たいへんな長生きをする」の意でおどけた言い方) ▶祖父は95歳まで長生きしました My grandfather *lived to the great age of* 95. ‖ 一般的に言って男より女のほうが長生きする Generally, women *live longer* than men. ‖ 祖母は祖父よりも長生きをした My grandmother *outlived* her husband. ‖ 長生きの秘訣はバランスのとれた食事, 適度な運動, そしてストレスのない生活などと言われる It is often said that the keys to (*a*) *long life* [*longevity*] are a well-balanced diet, getting moderate exercise, and leading a stress-free life. ‖ 今や100歳以上の長生きは珍しくない Nowadays, *longevity* of over one hundred years is not uncommon.

ながいす 長椅子 a **couch** /kaʊtʃ/, a **sofa** /sóʊfə/ ; a **bench** (ベンチ) ▶長椅子に座る sit on *a couch* [*sofa* ／*divan*].

ながいも 長芋 a ***nagaimo*** ; a **Chinese yam.**

ながおし 長押し ▶ (携帯電話の) #ボタンを2秒間長押しする *press and hold* the pound key *down* for two seconds.

なかがい 仲買い brokerage
‖ 仲買人 a broker ／a middleperson.

なかがわ 中側 the inside.

ながく 長く 1【寸法などが】一動 **長くする lengthen** /léŋkθən/ ＋目 ▶スカートを長くしてもらう *have* one's skirt *lengthened* ‖ この釣りざおは伸ばせばもっと長くなる This fishing rod can be extended to make it even *longer*.

2【時間が】in [**for**] **a long time ; long** (➤主に否定文で) ▶彼女には長く会っていない I haven't seen her *for ages* [*in a long time*]. ‖ 病院が混んでいるから診てもらうのに長くかかりそうだよ The hospital is crowded, so it will *be* (*quite*) *a while* before you can see a doctor. ‖ 彼の人気は長く続かなかった His popularity didn't *last long*. ‖ 例によって会議が長くなった(＝長引いた) The meeting *dragged on* as usual. ‖ だんだん日が長くなってきた The days are *getting* [*growing*] *longer*. ‖ 最初から話せば話が長くなる *It is a long story* if I tell it from the beginning. ‖ ちょっと時間いいですか. 長くは取らせません Can you spare me a few minutes ? I won't keep you *long* [I'll be *brief* ／It won't take *long*]. ‖ 出かけてくるけど長くはかからないから I'm going out, but I *won't be long*. ‖ この陽気ではおにぎりは長くもたない Rice balls won't keep *long* in this warm weather. ‖ このいい天気は長くもつまい This fine weather won't *last* [*hold*] *long*.

ながぐつ 長靴 boots ; rain boots (雨靴) ; **hip boots** (腰まである) ; **snow boots** (雪用) 《参考》渓流釣りなどではく胸元までの防水長靴は chest waders という.
‖ ゴム長靴 rubber boots, 《英また》 wellingtons /wélɪŋtənz/.

なかぐろ 中黒 《印刷》 a **bullet.**

なかごろ 中頃 ▶70年代中頃に in the *mid*-70s [seventies] ‖ 月の中頃になるとたいてい懐が寂しくなる I usually run short of money *around* [*about*] *the middle of* the month.

ながさ 長さ (a) **length** (➤寸法にも時間の長さにも言う) ▶この川の長さはどのくらいですか What is the *length* of this river ? ／How *long* is this river ? ‖ 万里の長城は2400キロ以上の長さがある The Great Wall of China is over 2,400km *long* [*in length*]. ‖ このきれは長さが5センチ足りない This cloth is five centimeters *too short*. ／This cloth is *too short* by five centimeters. ‖ そのひもを30センチの長さに切ってください Please cut the string to *a length* of thirty centimeters.

なかされる 泣かされる ▶あの映画には泣かされたね That movie *made me cry*. ／I *was moved to tears* by that movie. ‖ 店をやっていると, たちの悪い客に泣かされることもありますよ When you're running a store [restaurant], you'll sometimes *have a lot of trouble* from bad customers.

ながし 流し 1【台所の】a (**kitchen**) **sink** ▶この流しは水がよく流れない This *sink* does not drain well.

2【タクシーなどの】▶流しのタクシーを拾う catch a *cruising* taxi ‖ 流しの演歌師 a *wandering* street enka singer.

ながしうち 流し打ち ▶イチローは外角のカーブをレフトへ流し打ちした Ichiro *sliced* [*pushed*] an outside curve to right. (➤slice は「カット打ちする」, push は「押し出す」).

ながしこむ 流し込む pour 《into》(型に) ; **wash down** (食物をのどに) ▶ろうを型に流し込む *pour* wax *into* a mold ‖ ミルクで食べかけのピザを流し込む *wash down* a mouthful of pizza with milk.

ながしどり 流し撮り ▶レーシングカーを流し撮りする *take a panning shot* of a racing car.

なかじめ 中締め ▶中締めとまいりたいと思います Now we'd like to *conclude the first session of the party*.

ながしめ 流し目 ▶おい, 今きみに流し目をした人は誰だよ Hey, who is that lady who *made eyes at* you ?

なかす 中洲 an island in the middle of a river (川の中の島) ; a **sandbank** (砂がたまった所).

ながす 流す

1【水などを】pour /pɔːʳ/ ＋目 ; **flush** ＋目 (水洗トイレの水などを勢いよく) ; **drain** ＋目 (排水する) ▶かめにたまった汚水を流した I *poured out* the dirty water in the pot. ‖ 残った水は流していいですね May I *drain* [*let out*] the remaining water ? ‖ トイレを使ったらちゃんと水を流すのよ Don't forget to *flush* the toilet. (●「使用後は水を流してください」のような掲示は Please be sure to flush after use.).

2【血や涙を】shed ＋目 ▶息子の無事がわかって彼女はうれし涙を流した She *shed tears of joy* when she learned (that) her son was safe. ‖ 彼は額から血を流していた He was *bleeding* from his forehead.

3【液体によって物を】wash away [**off**] ; **sweep away** (さっと押し流す) ▶橋は大水で流された The bridge *was washed away* by the flood. ‖ やだあ, コンタクトレンズを排水口に流しちゃった Oh, no ! I *let* my contact lens *go down* the drain. ‖ 風呂に入ってあかを流した I took a bath to *wash off* the grime. ‖ 5歳になる娘が背中を流してくれました My five-year-old daughter *scrubbed my back* for me. (➤scrub は「ごしごし洗う」).

な

▶アドバルーンが強い風に流されて飛んで行った An advertising balloon *was carried away* by the strong wind. ‖こんな流れの速い川で泳いだら流されちゃうよ You'll *be washed away* if you swim in a river with such a fast current. ‖幼い子供が川で流された A small child *was swept away* by the river.
▶《慣用表現》彼は過去のわだかまりをすべて水に流してくれた He *has forgotten* all the bad feelings (he had) toward me.
4【伝え広げる】▶電気回路に電流を流す *run* electricity through a circuit ‖久美がそのうわさを流したに違いない There's no doubt that Kumi *spread* the rumor. ‖あの喫茶店はいつもモーツァルトを流している The coffee shop always *plays* [*has*] Mozart *as background music*. ‖そのテレビ番組はきのう全国に流された That TV program *was broadcast* [*was aired*] nationwide yesterday.

な

ナガスクジラ 《動物》 a **finback whale**, a **razorback whale**.

なかずとばず 鳴かず飛ばず ▶あの新人投手は入団以来鳴かず飛ばずだ That rookie pitcher *hasn't shown his stuff* [*hasn't done a thing*] since he joined the club. (➤ show one's stuff は「本領を発揮する」の意).

-なかせ -泣かせ ⚠「…泣かせ」は「…にとって迷惑や悲しみの原因となるもの」と考え, **trouble, problem, headache, nuisance, grief** などを適宜使い分ける.
▶彼女は問題ばかり起こして親泣かせの娘だ She is always into trouble and *causing* her parents *a lot of grief*. ‖この文章は翻訳者泣かせだ This passage *is a real headache* for a [the] translator.

なかせる 泣かせる ▶この男の子をいじめて泣かせたのは誰だ Who picked on the boy and *made* him *cry*?
▶なんと泣かせる話じゃありませんか (It's) quite a *touching* [*moving*] story, isn't it? ‖(パパと)いつまでも一緒にいたいから, 私, お嫁に行かないなんて, あの子も泣かせるねえ My daughter *moved* me *to tears* when she told me she wouldn't get married because she wanted to stay with me forever. (英米人の中にはこの英文から「うれし涙」を連想しないで, あきれてくやしくて出す涙を思い浮かべる人がいるかもしれない).

ながそで 長袖 **long sleeves** ▶長袖のワイシャツ a *long-sleeved* shirt.

なかたがい 仲違い a **quarrel**, a **falling-out** (口論) ▶つまらぬことで友人と仲たがいをした I *quarreled* [*fell out*] *with* a friend over a trivial matter. (➤ fall out はくだけた言い方).

なかだち 仲立ち **mediation** (仲介) ; a **mediator**, a **go-between** (仲介者) 一動 仲立ちする **mediate** (+目)
▶もめごとの仲立ちをする *mediate* a dispute ‖イスラエルとパレスチナの仲立ちをする *mediate* between the Israelis and Palestinians. ‖この花はハチの仲立ちで花粉を運んでもらう These flowers have pollen brought to them *by* bees. / Bees act as *go-betweens* in bringing pollen to these flowers.

ながたらしい 長たらしい **lengthy** /léŋkθi/ ▶長たらしいスピーチ a *lengthy* [*long-winded*] speech ‖長たらしいタイトルだね What a *lengthy* title!

なかだるみ 中だるみ a **sag (in the middle)** (ひもなどの; 比喩的にも用いる) ; a **slump** (スランプ) ▶中だるみの市場 a *sagging* market ‖彼は初めは張り切っていたがこのところ中だるみで怠けている He was full of spirit at the beginning, but he *has fallen into a slump* [*has gotten lazy*] recently.

ながちょうば 長丁場 a **long way (to go)** ▶交渉がまとまるまでには長丁場が予想される It is expected that we have *a long way to go* before a deal is reached. ‖講演会は3時間に及ぶ長丁場だった The public lecture *stretched out* [*dragged on*] for three hours.

なかつぎ 中継ぎ 《野球》 a **middle reliever**, a **middle relief pitcher** ; a **relay** (交代) ▶私は彼の伝言を中継ぎして彼女に伝えた I *relayed* his message to her.

なかったら

> 【文型】
> (もし)A がなかったら
> **If it were not for** A
> **Without** A
>
> 《解説》最初の文型は文章で用いるやや堅い言い方で, 現在の事実と違う仮定をする場合に用いる. 過去の事実と違う仮定には if it had not been for ～ を用いる. 会話では, **if ... not** や **without** で表現するのがふつう. →なければ.

1【現在の事実に反する仮定】▶あなたの援助が(今)なかったら今ごろはさぞ苦労していることだろう *If it weren't for* [*Without*] your help, I'd be having a really hard time now. ‖空気や水がなかったら何も生存できない *If there were* [*was*] *no* air or water, life could not exist. / Life could not exist *without* air or water. ‖試験さえなかったら学校も楽しいのに School would be fun *if only* we *didn't have* tests. (➤ if only は「ただ…でありさえすれば」).
2【過去の事実に反する仮定】▶あなたが一緒じゃなかったら, 私, あの男に襲われてたわ *If* you *hadn't* been with me, I would have been mugged by that man. ‖彼のとりなしがなかったら, ぼくたちはけんか別れしていただろう *If it had not been for* [*Without*] his mediation, we would have quarreled and broken up (with each other). ‖あの原発事故さえなかったら *If only* that nuclear plant accident *had never happened*.

ながつづき 長続きする **last long** ▶この天気は長続きしないだろう This weather will not *last long*. ‖私たちの仲は長続きしないような気がする I don't think our relationship will *last long*. ‖私はあのテレビ番組に長続きしてほしいと思う I hope that TV program *continues for a long time*. ‖彼は何をやっても長続きしない He *can't stick with* [*to*] anything *for long*.

なかづり 中吊り ▶電車の中吊り広告 *an advertising poster hung* in a train.

なかでも 中でも **above all, among other things** (とりわけ) ; **especially, particularly** (特に) ▶私はどのスポーツも好きだけど, 中でもサッカーが好きだ I like all sports, *above all* [*in particular*], soccer. ‖卵は嫌いよ, 中でも半熟のはね I don't like eggs, *especially* soft-boiled ones.

ながでんわ 長電話 a **long** [**lengthy**] **phone call** ▶弟はゆうべ誰かと長電話をしていた My brother *was talking* with somebody *for a long time on the phone* last night. ‖由佳, 長電話はやめなさい Don't *talk so long on the phone*, Yuka.

なかなおり 仲直りする **make up** 《with》 ▶仲直りしよう Let's *make up*. / Let's (shake hands and) *be friends again*! (make up は男女間で用いることが多い. Let's kiss and ... と言うこともある) ‖チエミとはもう仲直りしたの? Have you *made up* [*come to* *terms*] with Chiemi yet? ‖ 彼らは3年間というもの一言も口をきかなかったが，ついに**仲直りした** After three years of not speaking to each other, they finally *buried the hatchet* [*patched up their quarrel*]. (● いずれもインフォーマルな表現で，前者は「矛(ほこ)を収める」が原義) ‖ あの二人を**仲直りさせる**ことは難しい It will be hard to *get* the two *back together*.

なかなか **1【簡単には，すぐには】**▶この問題は**なかなか解けない** This problem can*not* be solved *easily* [*isn't so easy* to solve]. ‖ この窓は**なかなか開かない** This window *won't* open. (➤ won't は「(思うようには)…しようとしない」の意) ／This window is *hard* to open. ‖ ゆり子をデートに誘っているが，**なかなかうんと言ってくれない** I have asked Yuriko out many times, but she *just won't* say yes. (➤ just は強調) ‖ 猫にひっかかれた傷が**なかなか治らない** The scratch the cat gave me *just won't* heal. ‖ 彼のアパートが**なかなか見つからないで困った** I *had trouble* finding his apartment.
▶バスが**なかなか**(＝長い間)来ないので，タクシーを拾った The bus did*n't* come *for a long time*, so we ended up taking a taxi. ‖ ゆうべは**なかなか寝つけなかった** *It was a long time before* I could get to sleep last night. ‖ 悪い癖は**なかなか直らない** Bad habits *are hard to break*. ／Bad habits *die hard*.
2【とても，かなり】really, quite ; some (➤ some はこの意味ではインフォーマルな用法) ▶彼女は**なかなか料理が上手だ** She cooks *really* [*quite*] well. ／She is *quite* a (good) cook. ／She is a *really* good cook. ‖ **対話**「彼は**なかなかの**ギタリストだね」「そうだね」 "He is *some* guitarist, isn't he?" "Yes, he is." (● この some は強く発音する；皮肉を込めて用いる場合がある) ‖ **対話**「きょうの講演，どうだった？」「うん，**なかなかのものだったよ**」 "How was today's lecture?" "Oh, it was *really something*!" (➤ something を強めるといい意味になる. really を強めると皮肉になることがある) ‖ **対話**「あの新入生をどう思う？」「**なかなかじゃない**」 "What do you think about that new student?" "She's [He's] *pretty good*. ／ She's [He's] *not bad*." (➤ not BAD と bad を強めると積極的な評価になる).

ながなが 長々と at (great) length (➤ great があるほうが強意；「懇切ていねいに」という意味になることもある)；**endlessly** (際限なく) ▶社長はなぜB社との契約が結べなかったのかを**長々と**説明した The president explained *at* (*great*) *length* why he couldn't sign the contract with B Company. ‖ 彼は**長々と**ゴルフの自慢話をした He bragged *endlessly* about his golf. ‖ 彼女は**長々と**言い訳をした She gave a *long* excuse. ‖ 校長は**長々と**2時間もしゃべった The principal's *speech went on* [*dragged on*] for two hours.
▶彼女は**長々と**ソファーの上に**寝そべっていた** She *stretched herself* (*out*) on the sofa.

なかには 中には▶バラには数千種の種類がある. **中には**紫色をしたものもある There are thousands of varieties of roses. *Some* of them are purple. ‖ あれだけ生徒がいれば，**中には**どうしようもない者もいるよ With so many students, there are bound to be *some* who are problem students. ⇀**中**.

なかにわ 中庭 a [an inner] **court**, a **courtyard** (建物や塀で囲まれた)；a **patio** /pǽt̬ioʊ/ (スペイン風家屋の).

ながねぎ 長ねぎ《植物》a **leek**, a **green onion**. ⇀**ねぎ**.

ながねん 長年 for (many) years▶朝食にコーヒーを飲むのは**長年の**習慣だ It's been my habit [custom] *for many years* to have coffee for breakfast. ‖ この発見は彼の**長年の**研究のたまものだ The discovery is the fruit of his *many years of* research. ‖ とうとう**長年の夢**がかなった My *long-cherished dream* has finally come true.

なかば 半ば **1【中間】the middle ; half**▶こちらでは10月**半ばには**もう雪がちらつき始めます It begins to snow here *in the middle of* October [in *mid*-October]. ‖ 8月も**半ばを過ぎて**夏休みも終わりに近づいた It is *halfway through* August and the summer vacation is drawing to an end. ‖ 父は**30代半ばで**会社を設立した My father established a company *in his mid-thirties*.
2【中途】▶彼は父親が急死したため，**学業半ばで**高校をやめて働かざるをえなくなった Because his father died suddenly, he had to quit *halfway* through high school and go to work. ‖ その科学者は**道半ばで**病に倒れた The scientist was taken ill *on the way to achieving his lifelong goal*.
3【半分】half ; partly, partially, in part (部分的に)▶宿題は**半ば**終わった My homework is *half* finished. ‖ 落とした財布は(戻ってこないと)**半ば**諦めていた I had *half* given up on getting back my lost wallet. ‖ この子のけがは**半ば**私の責任だ I am *partly* [*partially*] responsible for the boy's injury. ／I am responsible, *in part*, for the boy's injury.

ながばなし 長話 a long chat▶お姉さんの**長話**には困ったものだ *The way* my sister *talks on and on* really annoys me.

ながびかせる 長引かせる prolong +㊐, **drag out** (➤後者は「だらだらと」というニュアンスが濃い) ▶消費意欲の冷え込みが不況を**長引かせる**一因になっている A decline in consumer confidence is one of the causes of the *prolonged* recession. ‖ これ以上この議論を**長引かせても**意味が無い There is no reason to *drag out* this discussion any longer.

ながびく 長引く drag on (会議などがだらだらと) ▶不況が**長引いている** The economic slump *is dragging on*. (➤「長引く不況」は a prolonged [long] business slump) ‖ 当初の滞在予定が3日も**長引いた** Our original(ly) scheduled stay *was extended* by three days. ‖ かぜが**長引いた** It *took* me *a long time* to get over the cold. ‖ 労使の交渉は**長引きそうだ** The negotiations between labor and management seem likely to *go on for a long time*. (➤「長く続く」の意) ‖ 遅くなって申し訳ありません. 前の会議が思ったより**長引いてしまった**ものですから I'm sorry I'm late. The previous meeting *took longer* than I thought it would.

なかほど 中程▶広島は岡山と下関のちょうど**中ほどに**ある Hiroshima is located *halfway* between Okayama and Shimonoseki.
▶バスが込んできましたので**中ほど**(＝奥)までお詰めください The bus is getting crowded, so please move toward *the back*.

なかま 仲間 a **friend** (友人)；a **companion** (親友または行動をともにする人)；a **colleague** /kɑ́ːliːɡ/ (同僚；⇀**同僚**)；a **mate** (遊びなどの；主に複合語として用いる)；**buddy** (相棒，親友；インフォーマルな語) ▶雑踏の中で**仲間**と別れ別れになってしまった I got separated from my *friends* in the crowd. ‖ あんなわがままなやつを**仲間**にするのは反対だ I'm against including such a selfish guy in *our group*. ‖ **仲間に入らないか** Will you *join us*? ‖ きょうからこの2人が新しく**仲間に入る**ことになったので，よくめんどうを見てやって

な

くれ These two have *joined our club* today. So please take good care. (➤ 後半を「仕事や要領を具体的に手ほどきする」の意の熟語である show ... the ropes を使って, So please show them the ropes. とすることもできる) ‖ あの女の子はいつも**仲間外れにされている** That girl is always *left out* (*of the group*). ‖ 友だちはみんなカップルになり, ぼくは**仲間外れだ** All my friends have gotten paired off, and I am *the odd man out* [*I feel left out*]. (➤ 女性の場合は the odd woman out) ‖ **仲間割れ**はよせ! Don't *quarrel among yourselves*!

▶あの人たちは私の**遊び仲間**です They are my *friends* [*buddies*] *I hang out with*. (➤ buddy は「親友, 仲間」のくだけた言い方で, 短く bud ともいう. 主に男性を指す. hang out は「ある場所に集まっていっしょに時を過ごす」) ‖ 彼は私の**仕事仲間**です He's my *co-worker* [*fellow worker*]. (➤「同僚」の意.「仕事上の友人」ならば a friend from work) ／He and I often work together. ‖ この頃, 私は**商売仲間**とうまくいっていない Recently, I have not been on good terms with *my business associates*. ‖ あの人は父の**釣り仲間**だ That man is one of my father's *fishing buddies*. ‖ イルカは鯨の**仲間**(＝一種)だ Dolphins are *a species* of whale. ‖ **仲間意識** a fellow feeling, a feeling of fellowship.

なかみ 中身 **the contents** /kɑ́:ntents/ (内容物) ; **substance** (実質) ; a **filling** (パイやクッションなどの詰め物) ▶かばんの**中身** *the contents* of a bag ‖ この小包の**中身**は何ですか What are *the contents* of this package?／What's in this package? ‖ 娘は箱の**中身**を見てがっかりした顔をした When my daughter saw *what was inside the box*, she looked disappointed. ‖ 校長の話はいつも**中身が薄い** What the principal says never has much *substance*. ／The principal never says anything very substantial. ‖ 見かけよりも**中身**が大切だ It is not appearance, but *substance*, that counts.

[1]**ながめ 眺め** a **view** ▶いい**眺め**だ! What *a fantastic view*! ‖ ほら見て! 窓からの**眺め**がすてきよ Oh, look! The *view* from the window is fantastic. ‖ 《旅館などで》**眺めのいい**部屋がいいんですが I prefer a room *with a* (*good*) *view*. ‖ ホテルからの海の**眺め**は実にすばらしかった The *view* of the ocean from the hotel was simply magnificent. ／We had a fine *view* of the sea from the hotel.

[2]**ながめ 長め** ▶ぼくは**長め**のズボンが好きだ I like my pants *a bit long*. ‖ 髪は少し**長め**に切ってください Please don't cut it too short.

ながめる 眺める **1**【距離をおいて見渡す】**look**; **watch** (＋目) (動く物を) ; **gaze at** (じっと見る) ▶私は丘の上に立って沈みゆく太陽を**眺めた** Standing on the top of the hill, I *watched* [*gazed at*] the setting sun. ‖ 賢二はもの思いにふけりながら窓の外をぼんやり**眺めていた** Kenji stood *looking* out (of) the window, lost in thought. ‖ 晴れた日にはこの展望台からオホーツク海が**眺められます** On a clear day you *can see* the Sea of Okhotsk from this observation tower.

2【長時間見る】▶鏡に映った自分の姿をじっと**眺める** *look at* oneself in the mirror ‖ 黙って**眺めて**ないで手伝ってよ Give me a hand. Don't just stand by and *watch*.

ながもち 長持ちする **last** (**for**) **a long time** ; **keep** (**long**) (食物がもつ) ▶このドライヤーは**長もちしている** This hair dryer *has lasted a long time*. ‖ 牛乳は冷蔵庫に入れておかないと**長もちしない** Milk does*n't keep* (*long*) unless you put it in the fridge. ‖ この上着はずいぶん**長もちしている** This jacket *has worn* quite *well*. ‖ 木綿物は絹物よりも**長もちする** Cotton cloth *outlasts* silk.

ながや 長屋 《米》a **row house**, 《英》a **terraced house** (連棟式の住居).

なかやすみ 中休み a **break** ▶**中休み**する have a *break*.

ながゆ 長湯 ▶**長湯**をしたらのぼせてしまった I *stayed in the bathtub too long* and got dizzy.

なかゆび 中指 a **middle finger** ; a **middle toe** (足の). ⇀指.

なかよく 仲良く ▶《親が子供に》兄弟どうし**仲よくする**んですよ Try to *get along* (*well*) with your brothers. ‖ 彼らはみんな**仲よく**暮らしている They are all living together *happily* [*in harmony*]. ‖ 二人はすぐ**仲よくなった** The two *made friends* [*hit it off*] with each other immediately. ‖ 達也は同僚たちと**仲よくやってゆけない** Tatsuya cannot *get along* [*on*] *well* with his colleagues.

なかよし 仲良し a **good friend** ▶ジョンとポールは**仲よしだ** John and Paul *are good friends*. ‖ ヒロシはぼくの**大の仲よし**だ Hiroshi is my *best friend*.

-ながら **1**【…と同時に】**as** ; **while** (…する間に) ▶彼は字を書き**ながら**ぶつぶつ言う癖がある He has a habit of mumbling (something) *as* he writes. ‖ 私はよく音楽を聞き**ながら**勉強する I often study *while* listening to music. ‖ 涼子はにこにこ笑い**ながら**ぼくに手を振った Smil*ing* [*With* a smile on her face], Ryoko waved to me. ‖ 食べ物を口にほおばり**ながら**話してはいけません Don't talk *with* your mouth full. ‖ お茶を飲み**ながら**おしゃべりしましょう Let's have a chat *over* (a cup of) tea.

2【…だけれど】**though** ▶悪いとは知り**ながら**彼の自転車を黙って借りた I used his bicycle without (his) permission *though* I knew it was wrong. ‖ **残念ながら**今夜はお宅のパーティーに行けません *I'm sorry, but* I can't come to your party tonight. ‖ **残念ながら** (＝認めたくないが) 彼の言うとおりだ *I hate to admit it*, but what he said is true. ‖ **われながら**, よくできた I did a good job, *if I do say so myself*.

ながらうんてん ながら運転 **distracted driving**.

ながらく 長らく ▶皆さま, たいへん**長らく**お待たせいたしました Ladies and gentlemen, I am sorry to have kept you waiting so *long*. (● 日本文のほうはそれほど待たせていない場合にも用いるが, 英文のほうは実際に想定された時間以上に長い間待たせた場合に用いる).

ながれ 流れ **1**【水・電気などの】a **flow** (絶え間ない液体の) ; a **stream** (川・潮・空気などの) ; a **current** (水・空気・ガス・電気などの) ▶川の**流れ** the *flow* of a river ‖ 利根川もこの辺は**流れ**が急だ The *current* is rapid in this part of the Tone (River). ‖ フランクリンは電気は**流れ**であると考えた Franklin considered electricity (to be) *a current*. ‖ **流れにさからって**泳ぐのは大変だ It's hard to swim *against the current*. (● 比喩的に「流れにさからう」という場合は go against the flow).

2【人・自動車などの】▶車の**流れ**がよくなった Traffic began to flow smoothly. ‖ この通りは一日中人の**流れ**が絶えない There is always *a stream* [*flow*] of people on this street.

3【物事の移り変わり】▶時の**流れ** (＝時流) には逆らえない We can't swim against *the tide* [*the current of the times*]. ‖ (あのとき) 彼がヒットを1本打っていたら, 試合の**流れ**はすっかり変わっていただろう If only he had gotten a hit, it would have turned the *tide* in the game [would have changed the *course* of the game].

4【系統】▶彼の家は徳川家の流れをくんでいる He *is descended from* the Tokugawa family. ‖(奈良の)唐招提寺はギリシャ神殿の流れをくんでいる(＝影響を受けている) The design of Toshodaiji Temple *was* [*is*] *influenced by* Greek temples.

‖**流れ弾** a stray bullet(➤「流れ弾に当たる」は be hit by a stray bullet) ‖**流れ者** a drifter.

☞ お流れ, 流れ作業, 流れ星 (→見出語)

ながれこむ (…に)**流れ込む** **flow**《in, into》▶石狩川は日本海に流れ込む The Ishikari River *flows* [*runs* / *pours*] *into* the Sea of Japan. ‖冷気が窓から流れ込んだ Chilly air *came in* through the window.

ながれさぎょう 流れ作業 an **assembly** /əsémbli/ **line** ▶今日たいていの電気器具は大規模な流れ作業で製造されている Nowadays, most electrical appliances are produced *on* large-scale *assembly lines*.

ながれだす 流れ出す

1【流れて外へ出る】 **flow out** ▶汚染水が海に流れ出すのを防ぐ prevent contaminated water from *flowing out* into the sea.

2【流れ始める】 **begin to flow** ▶車はふたたび流れ出した The traffic *began to flow* again.

ながれつく 流れ着く ▶岸に流れ着く *drift* ashore.

ながれぼし 流れ星 a **shooting** [**falling**] **star.**

ながれる 流れる **1【液体や気体などが】** **flow, run**(➤ 前者は「ゆったりと[とうとうと]」という含みのことが多い); **drain**((水が)はける) ▶鴨(かも)川は京都の町を流れる The Kamo River *flows through* Kyoto. ‖セーヌ川はミラボー橋の下を流れる The Seine *flows* [*runs*] under the Mirabeau Bridge. ‖傷口から血が流れた Blood *flowed* from the wound. ‖涙が彼女のほおを流れ落ちた Tears *ran* [*rained*] *down* her cheeks. ‖バスタブの水がよく流れない The water in the bathtub does*n't drain well*. ‖このトイレは詰まっていて水が流れません This toilet is clogged up and *won't flush*. (➤ flush はトイレや排水管の水が「どっと流れる」の意).

2【時などが】 **pass** ▶高校を卒業して10年の歳月が流れた Ten years *have passed* since I graduated from senior high school. ‖時の流れるのは早いものだ Time really *flies*. / Time *goes by* [*passes*] quickly.

3【運行・仕事などが順調に行く】▶車は通りをスムーズに流れていた The traffic *was flowing* steadily (down the street). ‖作業はスムーズに流れている Our work *is going* smoothly.

4【流体によって物が動く】 **be washed away** ▶ゆうべの大雨で橋が流れた The bridge *was washed away* by the heavy rain last night. ‖川上から大きな桃が流れて来ました A large peach *came floating* from upstream.

5【一方に傾く】▶スーパーが開店して客足はそっちへ流れた The newly-opened supermarket *took away* most of the customers. ‖我々はともすると怠惰に流れがちだ Everyone *tends to* [*is prone to*] *give into* laziness.

6【物事が伝わり広がる】▶この有刺鉄線には電流が流れている Electricity *runs through* the barbed wire. /This barbed wire is live. (➤ live の発音は /laɪv/) ‖スピーカーから軽快な音楽が流れて来た Lively music *came* from the speakers. ‖会議室に気まずい沈黙が流れた An uncomfortable silence *spread* throughout the meeting room.

▶あの政治家には黒いうわさが流れている Dark rumors *are circulating* about that politician. ‖近く衆議院が解散するらしいというデマが流れた A false rumor *has spread* that the House of Representatives will be dissolved soon.

▶その男は流れ流れて北海道へやって来た The man *drifted from one place to another* until he reached Hokkaido.

7【不成立になる】 **be called off** (中止になる) ▶メンバーがそろわずに会は流れた The meeting *was called off* because of poor attendance. ‖みどりの誕生日パーティーは肝心の本人が病気のため流れた Due to her own illness, Midori's birthday party *was canceled*. ‖きのうの試合は雨で流れた Yesterday's game *was rained out* [*was called because of rain*].

ながわずらい 長患い a **long** [**protracted**] **illness.**

[1]**なき 亡き** **the late**; **deceased** /dɪsíːst/ (➤ 特に最近死亡した人に用いる堅い語; dec. とも略す) ▶(今は)亡き中田氏 *the late* Mr. Nakata ‖亡き母にささぐ *To the memory of my mother* (➤ 著者の献辞) (●「亡き母」の「亡き」に形容詞の dead を当てると死体を連想させることが多いので注意) ‖今は亡き松本氏をしのんで銅像が建てられた A statue was erected *in memory of* Mr. Matsumoto.

[2]**なき 泣き** ▶安いからといって飛びつくとあとで泣きを見る(＝後悔する)ぞ If you snap up items just because they are cheap, you'll *regret* it (later).

なぎ 凪 a **calm** /kɑːm/ ▶嵐のあとになぎがくる After a storm comes *a calm*. (➤「嫌なことがあったあとはよいことがある」の意の英語のことわざ).

‖**朝なぎ** a morning calm.

なきあかす 泣き明かす **cry** [**weep**] **all night (long)** ▶祖母が死んだとき私は一晩中泣き明かした When my grandmother died, I *cried* [*wept*] *all night* (*long*).

なきがお 泣き顔 a **tearful face** (涙ぐんでいる顔); a **tear-stained face** (涙に汚れた顔) ▶きみの泣き顔(＝涙)なんか見たくないよ I don't want to see your *tears*.

なきがら 亡きがら **the body of a deceased person.**

なきくずれる 泣き崩れる ▶子供の病気が治らないと聞かされて, 母親は泣きくずれた The mother *broke down in tears* [*burst into tears*] when she heard her child's disease was incurable.

[1]**なきごえ 泣き声** a **cry** ▶赤ん坊の泣き声はまもなくおさまった The baby's *crying* soon died down.

[2]**なきごえ 鳴き声** a **cry**(鳥獣の); a **song, singing** (鳥の); a **chirp** (虫や小鳥の) ▶ゆうべは隣の犬の鳴き声がうるさかった The neighbor's dog kept on *barking* noisily last night. ‖鳥の中には他の鳥の鳴き声を上手にまねるものがいる Some birds skillfully imitate the *songs* of other birds.

「鳴き声」のいろいろ (カラスの)**カーカー** caw / (アヒルの)**ガーガー** quack / (犬の)**キャンキャン** yelp, yip / (ハトの)**クークー** coo / (カエルの)**ケロケロ** croak / (鶏の)**コケコッコー** cock-a-doodle-doo / (ネズミの)**チュー** squeak / (小鳥の)**チュンチュン** chirp, cheep / (馬の)**ヒヒーン** neigh / (ヒヨコの)**ピヨピヨ** peep / (ブタの)**ブーブー** oink, grunt / (フクロウの)**ホーホー** hoot / (猫の)**ニャオ** meow / (羊の)**メー** bleat / (牛の)**モー** moo / (犬の)**ワンワン** bow-wow

なきごと 泣き言 a **complaint**, a **whine** /hwaɪn/ (➤後者には子供っぽい印象がある) ▶どんなに仕事がつらくても決して泣き言を言うなよ Don't *complain* [*whine*] about your job, no matter how hard it may be.

なぎさ 渚 a **beach** ▶なぎさに千鳥が群れていた Plovers gathered on the *beach*.

なきさけぶ 泣き叫ぶ **cry**; **scream** (悲鳴をあげる); **wail** (悲しみや苦痛で) ▶多くの子供たちが空腹のために泣き叫んでいた Many children were *crying* with hunger. ‖ 母親は死んだ息子を抱きかかえたまま泣き叫んでいた The mother *wailed* [*sobbed*] as she held her dead son in her arms. (💰形容詞の dead は死体を連想させるので避けられることが多いが(→亡き), この場合は死体を抱きかかえているので適切な用法).

な

なきじゃくる 泣きじゃくる **sob** ▶その男の子は泣きじゃくりながら「ママ!」と叫んだ *Between his sobs* the boy cried, "Mommy!"

なきじょうご 泣き上戸 a **maudlin** /mɔ́:dlɪn/ **drinker** ▶あの人は泣き上戸で閉口するよ He's such *a maudlin drinker* (that) I can't put up with him.

なぎたおす なぎ倒す ▶大風で公園の立木が数本なぎ倒された The storm *blew down* several trees in the park.

なきだす 泣き出す **begin** [**start**] **to cry** ▶彼の悲しい話を聞いてみんな泣き出した Everybody *began to cry* while they were listening to his sad story. ‖ 風船が割れると女の子はわっと泣き出した The little girl *burst into tears* when her balloon popped.
▶《比喩的》今にも泣き出しそうな空だ It is *threatening to rain*.

なきつく 泣きつく **beg** +㊐; **implore** +㊐, **entreat** +㊐ (哀願する) ▶その子は先生に許してほしいと泣きついた The child *begged* the teacher (*tearfully*) to please forgive him. ‖ 家を買う頭金が100万円足りなくて親に泣きついた We were short one million yen on the down payment for the house, so I *fell back on* my parents. (➤ fall back on は「最後に…に頼る」).

なきっつら 泣きっ面 ▶仕事は無くすし, 恋人にはふられるし, これでは泣きっ面に蜂(はち)だ I've lost my job and my girlfriend has left me. *Misfortunes never come singly*. (💰 When it rains, it pours. (降ればどしゃ降り)や, This is really rubbing salt into the wound. (傷口に塩をすり込まれている)を当てることもできる).

なきどころ 泣き所 a **weak point** ▶私の愛車の泣き所はガソリンを食い過ぎることだ *The problem* with my car is that it uses too much gasoline. ‖ チャンピオンは確かに強い. が, どこかに泣き所はあるはずだ The champion is really strong, but he must have *a weak point* [*a chink in his armor* / *an Achilles' heel*] somewhere. (➤ a chink in one's armor は文字どおりには「よろいの割れ目」; Achilles' /əkíli:z/ heel は「(英雄)アキレスのかかと」).

なきなき 泣き泣き ▶うちの子は幼稚園が嫌いで, 毎日泣き泣き行くのよ My son hates kindergarten so much (that) he leaves home *with tears in his eyes* every day.

なぎなた a ***naginata***; a pole weapon with a curved blade on the end (➤説明的な訳).

なきにしも ▶勝つ可能性はなきにしもあらずだ *There is* a possibility of winning, *though it is very small*.

なきねいり 泣き寝入り ▶あんなひどい仕打ちを受けて泣き寝入りする手はない You don't have to *bear* [*put up with*] such bad treatment *silently*. ‖ 被害を受けた女性の多くは泣き寝入りした Most of the women who were victims *suffered in silence*.

なきはらす 泣き腫らす ▶目を赤く泣きはらした男の子 a boy whose eyes *were red from crying*.

なきふす 泣き伏す ▶我が子の変わり果てた姿に母親はわっと泣き伏した The mother *broke down* (*and wept*) when she saw her child's dead body.

なきべそ 泣きべそ ▶転んだくらいで泣きべそをかくんじゃない Don't *cry* just because you fell down. ‖ 偉そうなことを言って, あとで泣きべそをかくなよ Stop acting so high and mighty, or you'll be *eating crow* later for sure! (➤ eat crow は「(誤りを認めて)屈辱を味わう」).

なきまね 泣き真似 ▶泣きまねをする *pretend to cry* / *shed crocodile* [*false*] *tears* (➤ crocodile tears は「ワニのそら涙」の意の熟語).

なきむし 泣き虫 a **crybaby**.

なきやむ 泣き止む ▶赤ん坊が泣き止んだ The baby *stopped crying*.

なきわかれる 泣き別れる **part in tears**.

なきわらい 泣き笑い ▶その俳優の一生は泣き笑いの連続だった In that actor's life, *laughter and tears followed one upon the other* (*in succession*).

[1]**なく 泣く** **1【涙を流す】cry** (しばしば声を出して泣く); **sob** (自制できなくて泣きじゃくる); **weep** (深い悲しみなどで静かに; 文語的な語)

▶赤ん坊が(乳を欲しがって)泣いている The baby is *crying* (for milk). ‖ 泣かないで Don't *cry*. ‖《子供に向かって》そんなに泣くんじゃないの! Don't be such a crybaby! (➤ crybaby は「泣き虫」の意) / Stop *crying*. ‖ 奈美恵はその知らせを聞いて声をあげて泣いた Namie *cried out loud* [*broke into sobs*] at the news. ‖ 彼は思いっ切り泣いた He *cried his heart* [*eyes*] *out*. ‖ 彼女は私の胸に顔を押しつけて泣いた She *wept* with her face pressed against my chest. (➤ wept は weep の過去形) ‖ 彼が亡くなったと聞いてみんなが泣いた Everybody *shed tears* when they heard that he had died. (➤「涙を流した」の意) ‖ 兄は悲しいドラマを見るとすぐ泣く My brother *is* easily *moved to tears* whenever he watches sad dramas.

> 「泣く」のいろいろ 大声を上げて泣く bawl / ぎゃあぎゃあ [わんわん] 泣く wail / 泣きじゃくる sob / 涙を流して静かに泣く weep / 鼻をすすりながら泣く snivel / めそめそ泣く whimper

▶数学で 0 点を取って泣きたい気持ちだった I *felt like crying* because I got a zero on the math test. ‖ 泣くだけ泣いたら気分が晴れた I felt a lot better *after a good cry*. ‖ 彼女は泣きながら事故の説明をした She *sobbed out* her account of the accident. (➤ sob out は「泣きながら言う」の意) ‖ その少年は泣きながら眠ってしまった The boy *cried* [*sobbed*] *himself to sleep*.

2【苦しむ】▶落選したB候補はわずか50票の差に泣いた Candidate B *unfortunately lost the election* by only fifty votes. ‖ ふだんからちゃんと勉強しておかないと

試験のとき泣く(＝後悔する)はめになるよ If you don't study hard regularly, you'll *regret it* at exam time.
3【面目を失う】▶こんないい加減な仕事をしたんではお宅の看板が泣きますよ Your reputation will *be tarnished* if you do such sloppy work. (➤「評判が傷つく」の意).
4【やむなく承知する】▶ここはひとつ泣いてもらえないだろうか I know it's asking a lot of you, but could you do it for me just this once?
☞ **泣いても笑っても, 泣かせる, 泣く泣く** (→見出語)

2**なく 鳴く** **cry**; **sing** (特に鳥が); **chirp** (特に鳥・虫が) ▶犬が鳴いている A dog *is barking*. (➤ bark は「ワンワン鳴く」) ‖ 猫がニャーと鳴いた A cat *mewed* [《米》*meowed*]. ‖ 木立の中で小鳥が鳴いている Birds are *singing* [*chirping* / *twittering*] in the trees. (➤ chirp は「チュンチュン鳴く」, twitter は「さえずる」) ‖ 庭で虫が鳴き始めた Insects began to *chirp* in the garden. →鳴き声.

なぐ 凪ぐ **become calm** /kɑːm/ (海が); **die away** (風が) ▶風がないだ The wind *died down*. ‖ 海がなぐまで船を出すのを見合わせよう We had better put off setting sail until the sea *calms down* [the waves *calm down*].

なぐさみ 慰み **fun** (楽しみ); **pleasure** (喜び); (an) **entertainment** (娯楽); **pastime** (気晴らし) ▶私はバイオリンをほんの慰みで弾いています I play the violin *just for fun*. ‖ カラオケが私の唯一の慰みだ Karaoke is my only *pleasure*.

なぐさめ 慰め (a) **comfort** /kʌ́mfəʳt/, (a) **consolation**, (a) **solace** /sɑ́ːləs/ (➤ 後2者は堅い語) ▶ペットはお年寄りには慰めになる Pets can be a real *comfort* to elderly people. ‖ モーツァルトを聴くことは私にとって大きな慰めだ Listening to Mozart *gives* me great *comfort* [*solace*].
▶被災された方々には全く慰めのことばもありません I have no words to *comfort* [*console*] the disaster victims. ‖ 被災地に咲いた桜は避難民にとってわずかな慰めであった The cherry trees that bloomed in the disaster area were a small *comfort* [*consolation*] for the evacuees.

なぐさめる 慰める **comfort** /kʌ́mfəʳt/ +㊐, **console** /kənsóʊl/ +㊐ (➤ 後者のほうが堅い語) ▶死者の魂を慰める *comfort* the spirits of the dead ‖ 彼は試験に失敗した友人を慰めようとした He tried to *comfort* [*console*] his friend who had failed the exam. ‖ みずえを慰めてやろうよ. 彼女, 大輔に振られて落ち込んでるから Let's try to *cheer* Mizue *up*. She's (all) depressed because Daisuke dumped her. (➤ cheer up は「元気づける」) ‖ エンヤの歌はぼくの心を慰めて(＝静めて)くれる Enya's songs *soothe* me.

なくす 無くす・亡くす **1【存在しなくする】** **get rid of, rid ... of** ▶私は地球上から戦争と貧困をなくす手助けをしたい I want to help *rid* the world *of* war and poverty. ‖ 経営改善のためにはできるだけ経費のむだをなくすことが大切だ You should *cut down on* expenses as much as possible if you hope to improve the company's performance. (➤ cut down on は「切り詰める」の意).
2【失う】 **lose** +㊐ ▶大事な鍵だから無くさないでね This key is very important. Be sure not to *lose* it. ‖ 彼は会社の重要書類の入ったかばんを無くした He *lost* his briefcase which contained important company papers. (➤ lost は lose の過去形) ‖ 車のキーを無くしたみたい It looks like I *lost* my car key. ‖ 三木君はテストの点が悪くて自信を無くしている Miki *has lost* confidence because of his poor test results.
3【死なせる】 **lose** +㊐ ▶彼女は父親を車の事故 [心臓病] で亡くした She *lost* her father in a car accident [to heart disease]. ‖ 《葬儀で》 惜しい人を亡くしました This is *a great loss* for us all.

-なくっちゃ ▶遅いからもう行かなくっちゃ It's late, so *I've got to go* [*run*]. ‖ 対話「しかたないなあ. じゃあ, 一杯おごるか」「そうこなくっちゃ」"Since you're begging, I guess I'll buy you a drink." "*That's great!*"

-なくて ▶コンピュータゲームばかりやっているのでなくて, 外でスポーツしなさい Go outside and play sports *instead of* just playing computer games.

なくてはならない **indispensable** 《to, for》 (不可欠な) ▶英文を書くとき和英辞典は無くてはならない A Japanese-English dictionary is *a must* for writing English. (➤ a must は「必需品」) ‖ 川上君はわが野球部にとっては無くてはならない人だ Our baseball club *wouldn't be complete without* Kawakami. / Kawakami *is indispensable* to our baseball team.

なくなく 泣く泣く ▶彼は泣く泣く(＝不承不承)その条件を受け入れた He accepted the terms *reluctantly* [*against his will*].

なくなる 無くなる・亡くなる **1【見当たらなくなる】** **be gone, be missing** ▶私の計算機が無くなった My calculator *is gone* [*missing*]. / I *can't find* my calculator *anywhere*. ‖ 戻ってみるとかばんが無くなっていた When I came back, my bag *was gone* [*had disappeared*].
2【尽きる】 **run out** 《of》 ▶ガソリン [金] が無くなった We *ran out of* gas [money]. ‖ 予算が無くなった The budget *has run out*. / The budget *has been used up*. ‖ 食料が無くなりかけている (Our) food *is running short*. / We're *running out of* food. ‖ 時間が無くなってきましたので, この辺で終わりにしたいと思います Since I'*m running out of* time [Since my time *is about up*], I guess I'll finish up now. ‖ 夜の12時半を過ぎると電車が無くなる *There is no* train service after twelve thirty at night. ‖ やっと心配事が無くなった At last I'*m free from* worries.
3【消える】 **disappear** ▶彼の仕事ぶりにはひところの熱が無くなった His initial enthusiasm for his job *has disappeared*. ‖ 最近はロックに興味が無くなった I'*ve lost* (my) interest in rock music recently. ‖ 地球上から戦争の無くなる日は来るのだろうか Will the day come when war *disappears* from (this) earth?
4【死ぬ】 **pass away** [**on, over**] (➤ die のえん曲な言い方で, on, over には来世や別の世界への連想がある) ▶彼の父親は先月の10日に亡くなった His father *passed away* on the tenth of last month. →死ぬ.

なぐりあい 殴り合い a (**fist**) **fight** (けんか); an **exchange of blows** (殴打の応酬) ▶きのう, その2つの応援団がひどい殴り合いをした There was a big *fight* between the two cheering squads yesterday. ‖ 太郎と次郎はささいなことから殴り合いを始めた Taro and Jiro *came to blows* about a trivial matter. / Taro and Jiro *began to fight* (with each other) about a minor thing.

なぐりがき 殴り書き a **scrawl** /skrɔːl/; (a) **scribble**

(走り書き) 一動 なぐり書きする **scrawl, scribble** ▶彼の手紙はなぐり書きで読みにくい His letter is *scrawled* [*scribbled*] and hard to read.

なぐりこみ 殴り込み a **raid** /reɪd/ ▶殴り込みをかける make *a raid*.
▶《比喩的》外国のハイテク産業は日本市場へ殴り込みをかけようとしている Foreign high-tech industries are trying to *make their way* [*make inroads*] into the Japanese market. (➤ make inroads into は「…に侵入する, 食い込む」).

なぐる 殴る **hit** +目, **strike** +目; **beat (up)** (続けざまに); **slug** +目 (こぶし・棒などで強く); **punch** +目 (ボクサーがするようにこぶしで); **slap** +目 (平手で)
▶彼はぼくの顔を殴った He *hit* [*struck*] me in the face. (● hit my face とすると「顔」を強調した表現になる) ‖ 妻が夫のほおを平手で殴った The wife *slapped* her husband on the cheek. ／The wife *gave* her husband *a slap* on the cheek. ‖ 私は彼のあごを思いきり殴ってやった I *punched* him *hard* on the jaw. ／I *gave* him a *hard punch* on the jaw. ‖ 暴徒が寄ってたかってその警官を殴った Some rioters ganged up and *beat* the policeman *up*.
▶ぼくはその男に殴りかかったが, 逆に殴り倒された I *tried to hit* the man but instead *was knocked down* myself. ‖ あいつを殴り倒してやる I'll *knock* him *flat*.
→たたく.

なげいれる 投げ入れる ▶洗濯機に衣類を投げ入れる *throw* clothes *into* the washing machine.

なげうつ 擲つ **give up** (放棄する); **quit** +目 (やめる); **resign** +目 (辞職する) ▶彼女は教職をなげうって難民キャンプで働くことにした She *gave up* [*resigned*] *her position as a teacher* and decided to work in the refugee camp. ‖ 彼は仕事をなげうってアフリカに渡った He *quit* his job and went to Africa. ‖ 吉田氏は私財をなげうって病院建設に尽くした Mr. Yoshida *spent all his private funds* [*his entire fortune*] to build a hospital.

なげうり 投げ売り a **sacrifice**; a **clearance sale** (蔵ざらえセール) ▶その靴屋はすべての商品を投げ売りしている The shoe store is *selling* everything *at a sacrifice* [*at a loss*]. ／The shoe store is *having a clearance sale*.

なげかける 投げ掛ける ▶相次ぐいじめによる事件は日本の教育制度に疑問を投げかけた The series of bullying incidents *cast some doubt on* the Japanese educational system.

なげかわしい 嘆かわしい **deplorable** (遺憾な); **regrettable** (残念な) ▶老人に席を譲らない若者が多いのは嘆かわしいことだ It's *deplorable* that many young people don't give (up) their seats to elderly people. ‖ 約束の時間に遅れることを何とも思わない人が多いのは実に嘆かわしい It is really *regrettable* that many people (should) think nothing of being late for appointments.

なげき 嘆き **sorrow**; **grief** (➤ 後者は特定の原因による一時的な激しい心の痛み) ▶両親をその飛行機墜落事故で失った少女の嘆きは想像もつかない It is impossible to imagine the *grief* of the little girl who lost her parents in that plane crash.

なげキス 投げキス ▶彼ったら, 向こうのホームから投げキスするんだもの, 恥ずかしくって When he *blew* me *a kiss* from the opposite platform, I felt so embarrassed. (● 日本語に近いのは throw a kiss であるが, 英語では blow a kiss がふつう. 唇に指を当て, 息を吹きかけるように離すことから blow という).

なげく (…を)嘆く **grieve** 《about, for》; **deplore** +目 /dɪplɔ́ːr/ (嘆き悲しむ) ▶現代の世相を嘆く人は多い There are many people who *deplore* present social conditions. ‖ 美津子はボーイフレンドの心変わりを嘆いた Mitsuko *grieved about* her boyfriend's change of heart. ‖ 彼女は死んだ息子のことを今でも嘆いている She still *grieves for* her son.

なげこむ 投げ込む **throw into** ▶キャッチャーのミット目がけて速球を投げ込む *pitch* a fastball *into* the catcher's mitt ‖ 澤村投手はウイニングボールをスタンドに投げ込んだ Pitcher Sawamura *threw* the winning ball *into* the stands. (➤ threw は throw の過去形) ‖ 新聞配達の少年が夕刊を玄関先に投げ込んで行った The newsboy *threw* the evening paper *on* (*to*) the porch.

なげし 長押 a ***nageshi***; a beam that connects the pillars (➤ 説明的な訳).

なげすてる 投げ捨てる **throw** +目 ▶空き缶を道端に投げ捨ててはいけない Don't *throw* empty cans on (to) the roadside. ‖ 彼は恋のために国王の地位を投げ捨てた He *gave up* [*abandoned*] his throne for love. (● his throne を his position as King としてもよい).

なげだす 投げ出す **1【放り出す】**▶たたみに両足を投げ出す *stretch out* one's legs on the tatami ‖ 清は通学かばんを玄関に投げ出して友だちの家に行った Kiyoshi *threw down* his schoolbag on the floor in the *genkan* and went to his friend's home.
2【途中でやめる】 **give up** ▶妹はジグソーパズルがどうしてもできなくて途中で投げ出した(＝放棄した) My sister found the jigsaw puzzle too difficult and *gave up on* it halfway through. ‖ この仕事は単調で, ときどき投げ出したくなることがあります This work is so monotonous I sometimes feel like *throwing* it *out the window*.
3【差し出す】▶会長は全財産を投げ出して会社の危機を救った The chairman *offered* [*gave*] all his property to save his company. ‖ 彼女は見ず知らずの子供を助けるために命を投げ出した(＝犠牲にした) She *sacrificed her life* to save a child that she didn't know.

なげつける 投げつける **throw at**; **hurl at** (乱暴に) ▶弟は腹を立てて手当たりしだいに私に物を投げつけた My (younger) brother, in his anger, started to *throw* everything in sight *at* me. ‖ 機動隊に石を投げつける *hurl* rocks *at* the riot police.

なげつり 投げ釣り **surf casting**.

なげとばす 投げ飛ばす ▶その青年はその力士を土俵の外に投げ飛ばした The young man *threw* the sumo wrestler *out* of the ring.

なけなし ▶なけなしの金をはたいてそのつぼを買った I spent *what little money I had* on the vase. ‖ なけなしの知恵をしぼって考えたが名案は思い浮かばなかった I *racked my brains*, but couldn't come up with a good idea.

なげやり 投げやりな **sloppy** ▶あの若者は仕事が投げやりだ That young man always does a *sloppy* job [does *slipshod* work]. ‖ きみのその投げやりな態度が気に入らないのだ It's your *apathetic* [*what-the-hell*] *attitude* that annoys me. (➤「くそくらえと言わんばかりの態度」の意).

なける 泣ける ▶そのドキュメンタリーを見て泣けてしまった I *was moved to tears* by the documentary.

なげる 投げる

1【ほうる】 **throw** +目; **hurl** +目 (乱暴に投げつける); **pitch** +目 (的

を定めて)；**toss** ＋⊕（軽く）▶フリスビーを投げる *throw* a Frisbee ‖車の窓から空き缶を投げるな Don't *throw* empty cans out of the car window. ‖ひろし，そのＣＤ取ってちょうだい. 投げないで！ Hiroshi, hand me that CD. Please don't *throw* [*toss*] it. ‖調教師はイルカにボールを投げてやった The trainer *threw* the dolphin a ball. ／The trainer *threw* a ball *to* the dolphin.

▶松坂は打者の胸元に快速球を投げた Matsuzaka *pitched* a fastball high inside. ‖彼女は海に身を投げた She *threw herself* into the sea (and drowned). (➤ drown は「水死する」).

2【あきらめる】give up ▶最後まで試合を投げるな Don't *give up* (hope of winning) a game until the very end.

なければ

〔文型〕
(もし)A がなければ
If it were not for A
Without A

〔解説〕A は名詞. 最初の文型は現在の事実と異なる仮定(仮定法過去)を述べるやや改まった表現. インフォーマルでは without を使うことが多い.

▶祖母はつえがなければ歩けない My grandmother can't walk *without* [*unless* she uses] a cane. ‖太陽がなければ生きられない *If it were not for* the sun, we could not live. (●現在の事実の反対を仮定した言い方) ‖弟は強力なコネがなければあの会社には入れなかっただろう *Without* [*If it had not been for*] strong connections, my younger brother couldn't have gotten a job with that company. (●過去の事実の反対を仮定した言い方. If it had not been for となる).

▶イーサン・ハントでなければこの任務は遂行できない *Nobody* can carry out this mission *but* [*except*] Ethan Hunt.

-なければならない ⇀-ねばならない.

なこうど 仲人 a ***nakodo***, a **matchmaker**（結婚の世話人）; a **go-between**（仲介者）

《参考》英米には日本のような仲人は存在しない.

日本紹介 ✉ **仲人は男女の間に立って正式に縁談をまとめる人のことです. 以前は未知の男女を引きあわせて縁談をまとめることが多かったのですが, 現在では結婚を決めた男女が結婚式のために, 形だけの仲立ちとして, これを職業としている人や尊敬する人に依頼するほうが多くなっています** A *nakodo* (also called matchmaker or go-between) is a person who goes between a man and a woman and formally arranges their marriage. Formerly, the *nakodo* often brought together people who had been strangers to each other and arranged their marriage. But nowadays, it is common for couples who have decided to get married to ask a professional *nakodo* or some respected person to act as pro forma matchmaker at their wedding receptions.

▶太郎と花子が結婚したとき森夫妻が仲人を務めた Mr. and Mrs. Mori acted as (the) *nakodo* [(the) *matchmakers*] when Taro and Hanako got married. ／Mr. and Mrs. Mori arranged a marriage between Taro and Hanako.

‖**頼まれ仲人** an honorary go-between.

なごむ 和む soften（和らぐ, 和らげる）; **relax**（緊張などが解ける）; **be soothed**（苦痛などが和らげられる）▶先生の温かい思いやりのあることばにすさんでいる少年の心は和んだ The teacher's warm, comforting words *softened* the heart of the unruly boy. ‖私はその場の雰囲気をなごませようと冗談を言った I told a joke to *lighten the mood* [*relax the atmosphere* ／ *break the ice*]. (➤ break the ice は「緊張をほぐす」) ‖この音楽を聞くと気持ちが和む My feelings *are soothed* when I listen to this music. ／This music soothes me.

なごやか 和やかな friendly（友好的な）; **peaceful**（平和な）▶記者会見は和やかな雰囲気のうちに終わった The press conference ended in a *friendly* atmosphere. ‖試合が終わると選手たちは和やかに談笑した The players chatted *amicably* after the match.

なごり 名残 1【跡】 a **trace**（形跡）▶このあたりはまだ昔の城下町のなごりをとどめている This neighborhood still retains *traces* of the former castle town.

2【惜別の気持ち】▶すばらしいパーティーでなごりは尽きませんが, これでお開きにします Though it's been such a wonderful party and *we'd like it to go on longer*, we have to end it now. ‖お別れするのはなごり惜しい *I'm sorry* [*It's sad*] to leave you. ／I hate to (have to) part from you. ‖その少女はなごり惜しそうに何度も後ろを振り返った That little girl looked back again and again *as if she hated to leave.*

‖**名残雪** lingering snow（消え残っている雪）; snow [a snowfall] at the beginning of spring（春先の雪[降雪]; early spring snow または an early spring snowfall としてもよい).

ナサ NASA /nǽsə/ (➤ the National Aeronautical and Space Agency（アメリカ(国立)航空宇宙局）の略).

-なさい ▶もう家に帰りなさい *Go back* home now. (●強い口調で言えば「帰れ」の意にもなる) ‖静かにしなさい *Be* quiet(, please). (➤ please を強くゆっくり発音すると, より強い命令になる).

▶初めてヨーロッパへ行くんだったら, 滞在はパリになさい If you are taking your first trip to Europe, *I'd advise you to* stay in Paris.

なさけ 情け sympathy（同等の人への共感）; **pity**（目下の者に対する哀れみ）; **compassion**（強い哀れみの気持ち）; **mercy**（慈悲）; **kindness**（優しさ）▶彼はかわいそうなその老婦人に何の情けもかけなかった He felt no *sympathy* [*pity* ／ *compassion*] for the poor old woman. ‖どうかお情けを Please have *mercy* on me.

▶その老人は人の情けで生きていくことを嫌った That old man was unwilling to live on *the kindness* of others [on *charity*]. (➤ charity は「慈善」) ‖被災して初めて人の情けのありがたみを知った I couldn't appreciate human *kindness* until I became a disaster victim.

▶《慣用表現》彼は情け容赦のない批評家だ He is a *merciless* [*ruthless*] critic. ‖監督は成績の悪い選手を情け容赦なく放出した The manager *mercilessly* threw the poor players off the team.

ことわざ 情けは人のためならず One who is kind to others is bound [sure] to be rewarded. ／Charity is a good investment. (➤「慈悲はよい投資だ」の意).

☛ **お情け**（⇀見出語）

なさけしらず 情け知らずな heartless（薄情な）▶あ

いつは自分の親に対して何という**情け知らずな**仕打ちをするのだろう How *heartlessly* he treats his own parents！‖この**情け知らずめ**！You *heartless* bastard！

なさけない 情けない miserable（みじめな）；shameful（恥ずかしい）▶**情けない**世の中になったものだ．人間が自分の生み出した機械に使われている What a *miserable* [*sad*] state the world is in now！People are being used by the very machines they have created.‖私の真意がわからないとは全く**情けない** *It's a shame* (that) you don't understand what I really mean.‖きみは自転車にも乗れないのか．**情けないね** Can't you even ride a bicycle？*How pathetic！*

▶試験でカンニングをするなんて**情けない**（＝恥ずべきだ）ぞ You *should be ashamed* of yourself for cheating on the exam. ／How *shameful* of you to cheat on the exam！‖**情けない**話だが，腕ずもうでは息子にかなわない It's rather *humiliating* [*I hate to admit it*], but I'm no match for my son in arm wrestling.

なさけぶかい 情け深い kindhearted（親切心のある）；sympathetic /sìmpəθétɪk/（同情的な）；merciful（慈悲深い）▶**情け深い**人 a *kindhearted* [*benevolent*] person（➤後者は「善意に満ちた」）.

なざし 名指し ▶首相はその野党議員を**名指しで**非難した The Prime Minister criticized the member of the opposition *by name*.

なし 梨《植物》a Japanese pear /peəʳ/《参考》pear は「洋ナシ」で，日本のナシとは形が違う．

なしくずし なし崩し ▶研究予算は最近**なし崩しに**削減されている The research budget has been *gradually* whittled down in recent years.（➤ whittle down は「（木など）をナイフで削る」の比喩的用法）‖天下りはすべて禁止すべきで，**なし崩しにしてはいけない** *Amakudari* should be totally banned. It should not *be dismissed* [*glossed over*] without discussion.（➤ dismiss, gloss over はそれぞれ「…を重要でないと捨てる」，「…を体裁よくごまかす」）.

▶借金を**なし崩しに**返済する pay one's debts *little by little* [*bit by bit*].

-なしで -無しで without

> 【文型】
> 物(A)無しで済ます
> do without A
> go without A
> ➤ A は名詞・動名詞
>
> 《解説》(1)**do without** は「～無しで困らないようにやっていく」の意で，can, can't または have to の後で用いることが多い．
> (2)**go without** は「～無しで我慢する，必要な物をぬかす」の意．→済ます．

▶（コーヒーに）砂糖がないんなら，**無しでいいよ** If there's no sugar for our coffee, we'll do *without* it.‖現状ではこの冬のボーナス**無しでいく**ことを覚悟しないといけない As things stand, we should be prepared to *go without* a bonus this winter.‖若者の多くが数時間でも携帯電話**無しではやっていけない** Many young people *can't go without* their cellphones even for a few hours.

▶このところ父は休み**無しで**働いている My father has been working hard recently *without* any time off.‖現代社会はコンピュータ**無しでは**成り立たない Modern society cannot function *without* computers.‖銀行の融資**無しでは**彼の会社は倒産するだろう *Unless* he gets a bank loan, his company will go bankrupt.

なしとげる 成し遂げる accomplish ＋㊐；achieve ＋㊐（困難なことを）▶偉業を**成し遂げる** *accomplish* a feat‖レスリングの吉田沙保里選手はオリンピックで３連覇を**成し遂げた** Yoshida Saori *won* three successive Olympic championships in wrestling.‖大きなことを**成し遂げる**には粘り強さが必要だ You need perseverance to *accomplish* something big.

なしのつぶて 梨のつぶて ▶あれっきり，彼からは**なしのつぶて**さ I*'ve heard nothing from* him since then. ／*Nothing's been heard from* him since then.

なじみ 馴染みの familiar（よく知っている）；favorite（お気に入りの）▶**なじみの**客 a *regular* customer‖**なじみの**バー one's *favorite* bar‖中米の国々は私には**なじみが薄い** I*'m unfamiliar with* Central American countries.‖上田さんはテレビで**おなじみの**司会者だ Mr. Ueda is a *familiar* emcee on TV.

☛ おなじみ，昔なじみ（→見出語）

なじむ 馴染む **1**【慣れる】get used [accustomed]《to》▶この種の宗教音楽は日本人には**なじみにくい** It's hard for Japanese to *get* [*become*] *used to* this type of religious music.

▶子供たちは新しい環境にすぐ**なじんだ**（＝順応した）The children *adapted* [*adjusted*] (*themselves*) quickly to their new surroundings.‖新しいシューズがようやく足に**なじんできた** I've finally *broken in* these new shoes.

2【しっくりする】▶はでなじゅうたんはこの部屋には**なじまない** A loud carpet won't *go well with* this room.‖家庭でパーティーをするのは日本人の生活様式にまだ**なじんでいない** Giving parties at home still *remains a foreign custom* to (most) Japanese people.

ナショナリズム nationalism.

なじる blame ＋㊐（非難する）；reproach ＋㊐（悲しげに責める）▶どうして本当のことを言ってくれなかったのと娘は母親を**なじった** The daughter *reproached* her mother for not telling her the truth.

¹なす 茄子《植物》《米》an eggplant,《英》an aubergine /óʊbəʳʒiːn/ ▶ナスの漬物 pickled *eggplant*.

²なす 成す・為す ▶益田さんは若くしてその分野で**名を成した** Masuda *made a name for himself* [*won fame*] in that field while young.‖彼女の言うことは**意味を成さない** What she says doesn't *make sense*.

▶事故は一瞬の出来事でどうにも**なすすべがなかった** The accident occurred in a flash, so *there was nothing* I *could do to avoid it*.

なすび →なす．

なすりあい なすり合い ▶二人は最初から最後まで責任の**なすり合いをした** The two never stopped trying to *pin the blame on each other*.（➤ pin the blame on は「責任を（人）にかぶせる」）.

なすりつける **1**【塗る】▶その子は手についた絵の具を壁に**なすりつけた** That boy *rubbed* the paint on his hand *off onto* the wall.

2【罪・責任などを】lay《on》▶私に罪を**なすりつける**なんてあいつは卑劣な男だ What a mean man he is to *put* [*lay*] *the blame on* me！‖彼は失敗の責任を他人に**なすりつけようとした** He tried to *blame* [*lay*] the failure *on* someone else.

なぜ why,《インフォーマル》how come ▶**なぜ**そんなに悲しいんですか？*Why* are you so sad (about it)？／*What makes* you so sad？‖**なぜ**テレビのリポーターになりたいの？*Why* do you want to be a TV reporter? ／*Why is it that* you wish to be a TV reporter?

▶彼女はなぜあんなうそをついたんだろう I wonder *why* she told such a lie. ‖エヴリンさん, なぜ日本に来ることになったんですか *What* (has) brought you to Japan, Evelyn? (● (1)動詞は来日したのがかなり以前なら過去形が, (比較的)最近なら現在完了形がそれぞれ適当. (2)Why did you come to Japan? ではあからさまに理由を聞いていて, 尋問のように響く) ‖あれぇ, なぜこんなところにいるの? Well, well. *What* are you doing here?

▶ 対話「なぜ早く帰ったの?」「歯医者に行かないといけなかったからさ」"*Why* did you leave early?" "Because I had to go to the dentist." ‖ 対話「なぜタクシーに乗ったんだい?」「時間どおりに着くためにね」"*Why* did you take a taxi?" "To get there on time." (● to ... で答えるのは目的を表すとき) ‖ 対話「なぜきのう来なかったんですか?」「気分がすぐれなかったものですから」"*How come* you didn't come yesterday?" "Because I didn't feel well." (● How come のあとはふつうの文の語順になることに注意) ‖ 対話「あの人と一緒に行ってはだめよ」「なぜ(＝なぜだめなの)?」"You mustn't go with him [her]." "*Why not?*" ‖ 対話「毎朝ジョギングを始めています」「なぜ?」「体調を整えたいので」"I've started to jog every morning." "*What for?*" "To get in shape."

なぜか somehow ▶春が来るとなぜか幸せな気分になるのです When spring comes, *somehow* I feel happy. ‖彼女はなぜか私とデートするのを嫌がった I do*n't know why*, but she didn't want to go out with me.

なぜなら(ば) because (➤ある事柄の直接の原因・理由を表す); since (➤相手も知っていると思われる事実に言及する場合に用いる) ▶あの二人は姉妹かもしれない. なぜなら(ば)とてもよく似ているから The two may be sisters *because* [*since*] they look very much alike.

なぞ 謎 **1**【なぞなぞ】a riddle ▶謎を解く solve *a riddle* ‖スフィンクスは人々に謎をかけて, 解けない者を殺した The Sphinx asked people *a riddle* and killed those who could not come up with the right answer.

2【不思議】a mystery ▶謎の人物 a *mystery* person (➤ mysterious person は正体はわかっていても「謎めいた人」) ‖テレサ・テンは42歳で謎の死を遂げた Teresa Teng died a *mysterious* death [died mysteriously] at the age of forty-two. ‖ウナギの生態には謎の部分が多い There are many *mysteries* about the life and habits of eels. ‖その殺人事件は依然謎に包まれている The murder case is still shrouded in *mystery*. ／The murder case still remains *a mystery*.

3【暗示】a hint ▶私は彼女に謎をかけてみたが通じなかった I dropped her *a hint*, but she didn't take it.

なぞなぞ 謎々 a riddle ▶そのなぞなぞはわけもなく解けた The *riddle* was very easy to solve [guess／work out]. ‖なぞなぞ遊びをしよう Do you want to hear *a riddle*? ‖きみになぞなぞ出すよ I'll ask you *a riddle*. ／I have *a riddle* for you.

なぞらえる compare《to》▶今日では地球はよく宇宙船になぞらえられる Today the earth *is* often *compared* [*likened*] *to* a spaceship.

なぞる trace ▶私は先生の書いた手本をなぞって習字の練習をした I practiced handwriting by *tracing* the master's model.

なた 鉈 a chopper《参考》hatchet は「手おの」.
▶なたでまきを割る split wood with *a chopper*.

なだかい 名高い famous, well-known (➤前者のほうが意味が強い) ▶山梨県はブドウの産地として名高い Yamanashi Prefecture is *famous* for its grapes.

なだたる 名立たる eminent ▶名立たる科学者たち *eminent* scientists ‖世界に名立たる音楽家 a *world-famous* musician.

なたね 菜種 rapeseed ▶菜種油 *rapeseed* oil.

なだめる 宥める appease ＋目 (要求を満たすことによって); calm (down) (落ち着かせる); coax /kóʊks/ ＋目 (子供などを優しく説得する); soothe ＋目 (悲しみなどを) ▶怒っている人をなだめる *appease* an angry person ／*calm* an angry person (*down*) ‖子供をなだめたりすかしたりして歯医者へ連れて行った I *coaxed* my son into going to the dentist with me. ‖赤ん坊は母親になだめられて泣きやんだ *Soothed* by its mother, the baby stopped crying.

なだらかな gentle ▶なだらかな坂[丘] a *gentle* slope [hill] ‖その山は5合目まではわりあいなだらかだった That mountain *sloped* quite *gently up* to the halfway point.

なだれ 雪崩 an avalanche /ǽvəlæntʃ/ (雪・氷などの大規模な); a snowslide (雪の) ▶春山登山で雪崩にあう be struck by *an avalanche* while climbing a mountain in the spring ‖春先には雪がゆるんで雪崩が起きやすい In early spring the snow begins to melt, so *an avalanche* could easily happen.

なだれこむ なだれ込む ▶自国チームの勝利に興奮したファンがフィールド内になだれ込んだ The fans who were excited over the victory of their home country team *rushed* [*surged*] *onto* the field.

ナチス the Nazis /nɑ́ːtsis/
‖ナチスドイツ Nazi Germany ‖ナチズム Nazism.

なつ 夏 summer ▶高原の夏はさわやかだ *Summer* is refreshing in the highlands. ‖キョウチクトウは夏に花を咲かせる Oleanders bloom *in* (*the*) *summer*. ‖ことしの夏の何日かは耐えがたい暑さだった It was unbearably hot on several days *this summer*. ‖夏の軽井沢は若者たちでいっぱいだ Karuizawa is crowded with young people *during the summer*. ‖それはある夏の日に起こった It happened *on a summer day*. ／It happened *one summer day* [*one day in summer*]. (● a を使えば第1文のように前置詞の on が必要となるが, one を使えば on は不要になる点に注意).

▶夏かぜをひいて, なかなか治らない I have caught *a summer cold* and can't seem to get over it. ‖私は夏負けしやすい体質です I just *can't take the summer heat*.

✉ **まだしばらくは暑い夏が続きます. どうぞお体にはお気をつけください** *Hot summer days* will continue for a while, so please take good care of yourself.

‖夏枯れ(時) the slack summer season ‖夏祭り a summer festival ‖夏物 summer wear [clothes]; a summer suit (スーツ).

☛ 夏ばて, 夏休み, 夏やせ (→見出語)

なついん 捺印 ▶契約書に署名となつ印をお願いします Would you please sign and put your *hanko* on the contract?《参考》欧米には日本の印鑑に相当するものはなく, 署名(signature)するのがふつう. →判.

なつかしい 懐かしい ⚠ **この語にぴったりの対応語はないので, miss ＝「ある人がいない[物などがない]ことを寂しく思う」とか, be good to see ＝「ある人[物など]にまた出会えてうれしい」などのよ**

うに文脈によって意訳する必要がある.

▶懐かしい思い出 *sweet* [*fond*] memories (➤この sweet は「快い」, fond は「楽しい」の意) ‖おふくろがよく作ってくれたじゃがいもの煮っころがしの味が懐かしい How I *miss* the taste of potatoes simmered in broth which my mom cooked for me so often! (➤ miss は「(物が)ないのを寂しく思う」) ‖懐かしい友人(=旧友)が20年ぶりに訪ねてきた An *old* friend came to visit me after 20 years. ‖《旧友に出会って》木村君か? 懐かしいなあ! Hey, is this Kimura? It's *really good to see* you *again* after so many years! ‖《何かを見ながら》これ [それ] は懐かしい This [That] *brings back memories*. ‖《昔を思い出しながら》ああ, あのころが懐かしい Ah, those *were the good old days*.

▶私は30年前に離れた故郷をときどき懐かしく思い出す I sometimes *think fondly of* my old home which I left 30 years ago. 《参考》「懐かしい故郷」は「親愛なる」の意の dear を用いて my dear old home ということができる.

なつかしむ 懐かしむ speak nostalgically 《about》, reminisce 《about》 ▶祖父は昭和をしきりに懐かしんでいる My grandfather often *speaks* [*talks*] *nostalgically about* the Showa era. (➤ やや文学的表現の wax nostalgic を使ってもよい. なお, remember は心の中で起きることで, それを他の人に伝えることまでは表さない) ‖旧友たちと会うたび, 大学時代を懐かしんで話に花が咲く Whenever I get together with my old friends, we *reminisce* (*fondly*) *about* our college days.

なつく 懐く take to; come to like (好きになる) ▶生徒たちは新しい先生にすぐになついた The students soon *took to* [*took a liking to* / *came to like*] their new teacher. ‖この犬はよくなついている This dog is really *friendly*.

ナックルボール 《野球》 a knuckleball /nʌ́klbɔːl/.

なづけおや 名付け親

《解説》(1)日本語の「名付け親」は, 新生児に名前を付ける親以外の人を指すのが一般的で, 昔は母方の祖父がその任に就くことが多かった. (2)しばしば, 英語の godparent がこの語の訳語とされるが, これはキリスト教国のものであり, しかも名付け親にはならない. あくまでも新生児の洗礼式に立ち会い, その子を保護し, 人生の良き道案内人となることを誓う. したがって, 日本人の場合は例文のように説明的に訳すほうがよい

▶息子が生まれたとき, 父に名づけ親になってもらった When our son was born, we *asked* my father *to choose a name for* him. ‖鍛治氏はパズル「数独」の名付け親だ Mr. Kaji is *the person who named* the puzzle 'Sudoku.' / Mr. Kaji is the person who gave (the puzzle) 'Sudoku' its name.

なづける 名付ける name +㊐ ▶ぼくはその犬を「クロ」と名づけた I *named* the dog "Kuro." ‖赤ん坊は祖父の名を取って玄太郎と名づけられた The baby *was named* Gentaro after his grandfather.

ナッツ a nut ▶ナッツ入りアイスクリーム ice cream *with nuts*.

> 「ナッツ」のいろいろ アーモンド almonds / カシューナッツ cashew nuts, cashews / クルミ walnuts / ピーナッツ peanuts / ピスタチオ pistachios / ヘーゼルナッツ hazelnuts / ペカン pecans / マカデミアナッツ macadamia nuts

なっている

> 【文型】
> …することになっている
> be to do
> be supposed to do
> be doing (進行形)
>
> 《解説》(1) **be to** *do* は公式に決められた予定や合意事項を表す, 改まった言い方. 特に新聞の見出しでは単に to *do* で「…する予定」を表す. なお, be to *do* は「…しなくてはならない」の must や have to に近い, 命令や強い期待を表すこともある.
> (2) **be supposed to** /səpóustə/ *do* は当然実現される予定や should *do* (…すべき)に近い, 他の人からの期待や要求を表す.
> (3) 人とすることにしている約束や手はずをすませた予定は進行形 **be doing** で表す. 「…するつもり」という意思は be going to *do* を使う. また, 日程上の予定は be scheduled to *do*, 計画は plan to *do* で表す.
> →つもり, 予定.

▶首相は来月ワシントンで米大統領と会談することになっている The Prime Minister *is to* [*is scheduled to*] meet with the US president in Washington next month. ‖最終退出者が戸締まりを確認することになっている The last person to leave the office *is supposed to* make sure that all the doors and windows have been locked. ‖館内は禁煙になっている We'*re not supposed to* smoke in the building. / We *must not* smoke in the building. / Smoking is not permitted [allowed] in the building. ‖私は車を運転するときは眼鏡を着用することになっている I *have to* wear glasses when driving. ‖朝一で打ち合わせすることになっている We'*re scheduled to* meet first thing in the morning. ‖夕方, 友子と渋谷で落ち合うことになっている I'*m meeting* Tomoko in Shibuya this evening. (● in Shibuya を at Shibuya とすると at Shibuya Station の意になる) ‖わが家では交替で夕食後の後片づけをすることになっている In my family we have *arranged for* all members *to* take turns doing the dishes after supper.

なってない ▶彼女はキャプテンとしてなってない She is *no good* as a captain. ‖あの男の子はしつけが全くなってない That boy has *very bad* manners. / That boy is *badly* disciplined. ‖彼女の運転技術はまるでなってない Her driving skills are *awful*. / Her driving is *awful*. (➤ awful は「ひどい」).

ナット a nut.

なっとう 納豆 *natto*

日本紹介 ✉ **納豆は大豆を発酵させて作る食品で, ねばねばしています. たんぱく質が豊富に含まれていますが, 特有のにおいがあるため嫌う人もいます** *Natto* is a sticky food made of fermented soybeans. Although it is rich in protein, some people dislike it because of its distinctive smell.

なっとく 納得する understand +㊐ (理解する); consent 《to》 (同意する); be convinced (確信する); be satisfied 《with》 (満足する) ▶彼のやり方は納得できない I cannot *understand* [*consent to*] his way of doing things. ‖あなたの説明では納得できません I'm not *convinced by* your explanation. / I don't *buy* your explanation. (● この buy は「信じがたいが(とりあえず)受け入れる」で, 否定文で使うことが多い) ‖私がいくら釈明しても先生に納得してもらうことができなかっ

た No matter how much I explained, I couldn't *get* the teacher *to accept* my explanation. ‖これっぽっちの賃上げでは社員は納得しないだろう The workers will not *be satisfied with* such a tiny pay raise. ‖そのピアニストは納得できるまで練習を繰り返す The pianist practices over and over again until he can play a piece *to his satisfaction*. ‖それで納得がいったよ *Now I get it*.

なつどり 夏鳥 a summer bird [visitor].

なつば 夏場 summer ▶その患者は夏場を越えられないだろう The patient will not survive the *summer*. ‖この静かな湖畔も夏場はキャンパーたちでにぎわう This quiet lakeside becomes lively with campers *in* (*the*) *summer*.

なっぱ 菜っ葉 greens, green vegetables.

なつばて 夏ばて ▶私はすぐ夏ばてするたちだ *The summer heat gets to* me immediately. ‖このところ夏ばてぎみです I'*m suffering from* (the effects of) *the summer heat* [*from summer lethargy*] these days. 《参考》「夏ばて」のことを堅い言い方で summer lethargy という.

ナップザック a knapsack /nǽpsæk/ ▶ナップザックを背負う carry *a knapsack* on one's back.

なつみかん 夏蜜柑《植物》a (large, thick-rinded) summer orange 《参考》夏ミカンは Chinese citron と訳されることが多いが, これは「中国産のシトロン」と解釈できるうえ, citron は皮を食用とする果物であるので不適切な訳語である.

ナツメグ nutmeg.

ナツメヤシ《植物》a date palm ▶ナツメヤシの実 *a date*.

なつメロ 懐メロ a hit song of the good old days,《インフォーマル》an oldie /óʊldi/ 《参考》特にたびたびリバイバルする名曲は golden oldie という.

なつもの 夏物(衣類) summer clothes.

なつやすみ 夏休み (the) summer vacation,《英》(the) summer holidays ▶学校は夏休みに入っている The school *is on summer vacation*. ‖ことしの夏休みはモルディブへ行く予定です I plan to go to the Maldives *during this summer vacation*. ‖夏休みの宿題がどっさり出た We were given lots of *homework to do during the summer vacation* [*summer vacation assignments*].

なつやせ 夏痩せ ▶私はことし 2 キロ夏やせした I *lost* two kilograms *this summer*. (●「夏やせ」という考え方は英米にはない).

なつやま 夏山 ▶夏山のシーズンがやって来た The *summer mountain* season has come.

なでおろす 撫で下ろす ▶遠足のバスが事故にあったが, けが人はなく親たちはほっと胸をなでおろした The school excursion bus was involved in an accident, but the parents *were greatly relieved* [*felt* (*greatly*) *relieved*] to find out that nobody was hurt.

なでがた 撫で肩 sloping [round] shoulders ▶なで肩の女性は着物が似合う A kimono looks good on a woman with *sloping* [*round*] *shoulders*.

なでしこ 撫子《植物》a pink.

なでつける 撫で付ける ▶授業中に髪をなでつけるのはやめなさい Stop *smoothing down your hair* in class.

なでる 撫でる stroke +⊞ (一方向にそっと) ; pet +⊞ (かわいがる) ▶その子は珍しそうに象の鼻をなでた The child *stroked* the elephant's trunk in wonder. ‖彼女はひざの上の猫をなでていた She was *petting* the cat on her lap.

▶《比喩的》夜風が優しくほおをなでた The night breeze gently *touched* [*brushed* (*against*)] my cheeks.

-など **1【例を示して】** and other ..., such as ... (…などの)

> **《解説》「…など」の言い方**
> (1)「…など」を表すのにいちばん多く使われるのは **and other ...** や **such as ...** の形で,「野球, サッカーなどに興味をもっています」は I'm interested in baseball, soccer *and other* sports. のようにいう. この場合, 英語では baseball と soccer をくくる共通の要素である sports を補う必要がある. これを and others とするのはまちがい.
> (2) 上の例文を I'm interested in (various) sports *such as* [*including*] baseball and soccer. と表現することもできる.
> (3) **and so on** や **and so forth** は「…などなど」の意でうんざりというニュアンスを込めて用いられることがあるが, ふつうの文には使わないほうがよい.
> (4) 書きことばでは **etc.** も用いられる. /et sétərə/ と読むが, etc. と書いたものを and so on あるいは and so forth と読むこともある.

▶茶わんやコップなどは戸棚にしまってください Please put the cups, glasses, *and the other things* back in the cupboard. ‖ライオンやトラなどはネコ科に属する Animals *such as* [*like*] the lion and the tiger belong to the cat family. ‖彼女のハンドバッグにはメモ帳や財布などが入っている She has a little notebook, a wallet *and other stuff* [*and what not*] in her purse. (● and what not は「…やなんか」の意のインフォーマルな言い方).

2【けんそん, または軽べつして】 ▶そんな高価な衣装は私などにはもったいない Such a costly dress is too good for *someone like me* [*the likes of* me]. ‖もうぼくのことなど忘れたの? Have you forgotten *me* already?

3【打ち消す気持ちを強めて】 ▶完璧な親など, どこにもいない There's no *such thing as* a perfect parent. ‖辞書など引かなくてもこの手紙の意味くらいわかる I can understand what the letter says without going to the trouble of consulting a dictionary.

4【婉曲に示して】 ▶コーヒーなどいかがですか How about coffee *or something*?

ナトー NATO /néɪt̬oʊ/ (➤ the North Atlantic Treaty Organization (北大西洋条約機構) の略).

ナトリウム《化学》sodium /sóʊdiəm/, natrium (➤ 後者は旧称).

なな 七 →しち.

ナナカマド《植物》a mountain ash.

ななくさ 七草 seven herbs
‖春の七草 the seven herbs of spring ‖秋の七草 the seven flowers of fall ‖七草がゆ seven-herb rice porridge.

ななころびやおき 七転び八起き ▶くじけるな, 人生は七転び八起きさ Don't be discouraged. Life is full of *ups and downs*.

ななつどうぐ 七つ道具 the (seven) basic [essential] tools (➤ 職業・商売に欠かせないという意味では, of (one's) trade をつけてもよい).

ナナハン 七半 a 750cc motorcycle.

ななひかり 七光り ▶彼女は父親の七光りで芸能界で幅をきかせている She is making her way in the show business world *through the influence of her father*.

ななふしぎ 七不思議 ▶エジプトのピラミッドは**古代の七不思議**の１つだ The pyramids in Egypt are one of *the Seven Wonders of the Ancient World*.

ななめ 斜めの **diagonal** /daɪǽgənəl/, **oblique** /əblíːk/ ▶**斜め**の線を引く draw a *diagonal* [an *oblique*] line ‖ 彼の**斜め後ろ**に座る sit *diagonally behind* him ‖ スクランブル交差点では**斜めに**横断することができる At a pedestrian scramble you can cross *diagonally*. ‖ 交番はそのデパートの（道をはさんで）**斜め前**にある The police box is *diagonally across* [is *kitty-corner*] from the department store. ‖ 壁の絵が少し**斜めに**なっている The painting on the wall is hanging *at a slant*. ‖ 立ち上がった瞬間，ボートが**斜めに傾いた** The moment I stood up, the rowboat *canted to one side*. (➤ cant は「傾く」).
▶《慣用表現》父は今ごきげん**斜めだ** My father is now *in a bad mood* [*humor*／*temper*]. ‖ **斜め読み**する read *cursorily*, read *diagonally*.

なに 何 **1【疑問を示して】what** ⇀なん ▶**何**してるの？ *What* are you doing？‖ **何が**起こったんですか？ *What* happened？‖ そんな空き缶を集めて**何になるの**？ *What's the use of* collecting those empty cans？‖ 朝食は**何を**食べましたか？ *What* did you have for breakfast？‖ **何が**そんなにおかしいの？ *What* are you chuckling *about*？‖ 彼女，**何を**泣いてるの？ *What* is she crying *about*？‖ 今，**何**言ってたの？ *What* were you saying just now？‖ 彼女が**何を**しようと私には関係ないね I don't care *what* she does.
▶ルクセンブルクでは**何語**を話しますか？ *What languages* do they speak [are spoken] in Luxembourg？(➤その地の出身者に尋ねる場合は they を you に代える) ‖ ウィンブルドンに行くのは**何線**ですか *Which* (*train*) *line* goes to Wimbledon？‖ (人の話などに興味を示して) **何，何？** *What's going on？*
▶ **対話**「きみのおじいさんは**何を**しておられたの？」「警察官でした」"*What* (kind of work) did your grandfather do？" "He was a police officer." ‖ **対話**「将来**何に**なりたいの？」「レーサーになりたいんだ」"*What* do you want to be (in the future)？" "A car racer." ‖ **対話**「きょうは**何で**（＝どうやって）来ましたか」「バスで来ました」"*How* did you come today？" "(I came) by bus." ‖ **対話**（レストランで）「**何に**しますか」「まだ決まってないんです」"*What* are you going to have？" "I haven't decided yet."
2【反問して】 ▶**なに**，もういっぺん言ってみろ *What？* Say that again！
3【慣用表現】 ▶**何が何だか**さっぱりわからなかった I *couldn't make heads or tails of* the whole thing. (➤《英》では not make head or tail of ともいう) ‖ 彼女は裕福な家で**何不自由なく暮らしている** She leads *a comfortable life* [lives *comfortably*] as a member of a rich family. ‖ 彼には**何から何まで**世話になった I owe him *everything*. ‖ あの新しいバイトの子は**何一つまともにできない** That new part-timer can't do *a single thing* right.

なにか 何か **1【不定の物事を示して】something, anything**
語法 something は通例肯定平叙文に用いるが，人に物を勧めたり，十分に肯定の答えが予想される場合には疑問文にも用いる．また，anything は通例否定文・疑問文・if 節に用いる．
▶**何か**食べなさい Eat *something*. (🔘 Eat anything. とすると「何でもいいから食べなさい」の意になる) ‖ 今**何か**言っただろう？ Did you just say *something*？(🔘 Did you say anything？は「何か言った？」の意) ‖ 彼の留守中に**何か**あったに違いない *Something* must have happened while he was away. ‖ わあ，**何か**おいしそうなにおいがするな！ Wow！*Something* really smells good！‖ **何か**おいしいものを食べに行きたいわね I could go for *something* good to eat right now. (🔘 -thing が形容詞を伴う場合，その形容詞は -thing の後ろ) ‖ **何か**書くものを貸してください Could you please lend me *something* to write with？(➤something to write with で「筆記用具」の意) ‖ 彼女は**何か**訳があって遅れて来たんだ She came late for *some* reason (*or other*).
▶**何か**なくなったの？ Was *anything* lost？‖ **何か**大きな病気をしたことがありますか Have you suffered from *any* major disease？‖ **何か**質問はありますか Do you have *any* questions？‖ **対話**「**何か**いいことあったの？うれしそうな顔して」「うん．オートバイ買ったんだ」"Did *something* good happen？You look so happy." "Yeah. I bought a motorcycle." ‖ **対話**（デパートで）「**何か**おさがしですか」「父にあげるプレゼントをさがしてるんです」"*May I help you？*" "I'm looking for a gift for my father."
2【同類の物事を示して】 ▶あの人はたしか医者か**なにか**ですよ He is a doctor *or something like that*, I'm sure. ‖ その話はテレビか**なにか**でやっていましたね I heard the story on TV *or somewhere* [*someplace*]. ⇀-なんか.

なにがし ▶鈴木**なにがし**と名乗る人から電話があったよ There was a phone call for you from *a* Mr. Suzuki. ‖ 神社にお参りをするときには**なにがしか**のおさい銭をあげるのが通例だ People usually make an offering of *some* money when they visit and pray at a Shinto shrine.

なにかしら 何かしら ▶**何かしら**手に職を持っていると強い You can get along in life if you have *some* (manual) skill *or other*.

なにかと 何かと ▶この１週間は**何かと**忙しかった I have been busy *with one thing or another* for the past week. ‖ 都心に住んでいると**何かと**好都合だ It is convenient *in many ways* to live in the center of Tokyo. ‖ あの男，**何かと**自分を売り込もうとする He turns *everything* into an opportunity to promote himself.

なにがなし 何がなし ▶晩秋は**何がなし**（＝何となく）さびしい気持ちになる You feel lonely *for some reason or other* in late fall.

なにがなんでも 何が何でも **at any cost, at all costs** [**cost**] ▶**何が何でも**栄冠を勝ち取るぞ We'll capture the crown of victory *at any cost* [*no matter what it takes*]. ‖ **何が何でも**スペインに行きたい I want to go to Spain, *no matter what*. (➤no matter what はあとに may happen が略されたインフォーマルな言い方).

なにかにつけ(て) 何かにつけ(て) ▶娘は結婚したのに**何かにつけて**家にやって来る Although my daughter got married, she often comes back (to our) home *for one reason or another*.

なにくそ 何糞 ▶**何くそ**，あんなやつに負けるものか *Damn* [*Darn*] *it！* I refuse to be defeated by a guy like that.

なにくれとなく 何くれとなく ▶近くにいるおばが**何くれとなく**世話を焼いてくれる My aunt who lives nearby takes care of me *in all sorts of ways* [does *all sorts of* things for me].

なにくわぬかお 何食わぬ顔 ▶放火犯は何食わぬ顔で現場に戻って来た The arsonist returned to the scene of the crime *with a look of feigned innocence*.(➤「悪いことはしていないという顔つきで」の意).

なにげない 何気ない casual(不用意な); unintentional(故意でない) ▶彼女の何げない一言からけんかになった Her *casual* remark caused a quarrel. ／What she said *unintentionally* caused a quarrel. ‖ 彼女の何げない動作にも色気が感じられる Every *little* way she moves is sexy. ‖ 何げなく新聞を見ていたら1枚の写真が目に留まった When I was *just* glancing through the paper, a picture caught my eye.

なにごと 何事 **1**【どんなこと】▶何事も最初が肝心だ Getting off to a good start is important in *everything*. ‖ いったい何事が起こったんだい? *Whatever* [*What ever*] has happened? ‖ 白井先生が真っ赤になって教室へ飛び込んで来たんで何事かと思ったよ Mr. Shirai came rushing into the room red-faced, so we wondered *what had happened*. ‖ 何事もなく半年が過ぎた Six months have passed *quietly* [*without any incident*].

2【非難して】▶小さな子をいじめるとは何事だ It'*s inexcusable* to bully a little child!

なにさま 何様 ▶きみは何様のつもり? *Who* do you think you are? ／What makes you so special? ‖ 自分の仕事を人に押しつけるなんて, 何様のつもりだろう He tried to force me to do his job. *Who does he think he is?*

なにしろ 何しろ ⚠ **この日本語には,「というのは」の意味で前文を補足する場合と,「(いちいち詳細は言わないが)要するにこうだ」と自分の意見や気持ちをかなり一方的に相手に伝えるのに用いる場合の2通りの用法があり, 前者には after all や because などを, 後者には in any case や anyhow などを当てる.**

▶彼は英語がうまいに決まってるよ. なにしろ5年もロンドンにいたんだから Of course his English is good. *After all*, he was in London for five years.

▶なにしろやってみないことには始まりません *In any case* [*Anyhow*], you should give it a try.

なにせ ▶なにせすごい人出で身動きがとれなかった The streets were *incredibly* crowded and I couldn't move an inch.

なにとぞ 何とぞ please(どうか) ▶なにとぞご許可くださいますようお願い申し上げます *Please* grant us your permission. ‖ なにとぞこの悲しい知らせがほんとうのことではありませんように *May* this sad news prove to be untrue! (● May ...!は「…でありますように!」と祈願する言い方) ‖ なにとぞお座りください *Pray* be seated. (➤形式ばった古風な表現).

なにはさておき 何はさておき ▶何はさておき, まずビール! *First of all*, I'll have beer.

なにはともあれ 何はともあれ ▶何はともあれ全員無事で安心したよ *At any rate* [*In any case*], I am relieved that everyone is safe and sound.

なにはなくとも 何は無くとも ▶何は無くとも健康が一番 *Nothing* is as important as health. ／*Even though I have nothing else*, I want to be healthy. (●後者が日本語に近い).

なにひとつ 何一つ ▶今の生活に何一つ不満はありません I *have nothing to complain about* [I *have no complaints*] in my present life. ‖ 火事にあったから小さいころの物は何一つ残っていないんだ Because my house was burned down in a fire, I *have no possessions* (*left*) from my childhood.

なにふじゆうなく 何不自由なく ▶彼女は何不自由なく育ったお嬢様だ She is a young lady brought up *in luxury* [*in ease and comfort*].

なにぶん 何分 ⚠ **相手の適当な判断や処置などを期待する気持ちを漠然と表す日本的表現で, ぴったり対応する英語はない. 英語では相手に依頼したい事がらを具体的に伝える必要がある.**

▶先に帰るからあとはなにぶんよろしく頼みます I must be leaving now. Please take care of the rest (of the work). ‖ なにぶん不慣れなものでご迷惑をおかけするかもしれません Since I'm not used to the job, I'm afraid I may put you to some trouble.

なにも 何も **1**【1つも…ない】not ... anything, nothing ▶私はけさ何も食べなかった I *didn't* eat *anything* this morning. ／I ate *nothing* this morning. ‖ 何も心配することはない There's *nothing* to worry about. ‖ ほんとうに何も覚えていません I really *don't* remember *a thing*. →何にも.

2【抗議の気持ちを示して】▶何もそんなにむきになることはないだろう There's *no* reason for you to get that uptight.

なにもかも 何もかも everything(1つ1つ皆); all(全部) ▶彼女はほかのことは何もかも忘れて仕事に没頭した She buried herself in her work, forgetting *everything* [*all*] else. ‖ 何もかも白状したらどうだい? Why not *come clean* about what you did?

なにもの 何者 who(だれ) ▶その岡田って男は何者ですか? *Who*'s this guy Okada?

▶留守中に何者かが私の部屋に忍び込んだ *Somebody* [*Someone*] sneaked into my room while I was out. (➤ someone は somebody よりやや堅い語).

なにやかや 何や彼や ▶マンションを買ったら税金や何やかやで1割余分にかかった When I bought a condominium, I found I had to pay 10 percent more for taxes *and other things*.

なにやら 何やら **1**【何か】something ▶子供たちが何やらロッカーの中に隠していた The children were hiding *something* in the locker.

2【など】▶夏休みといっても夏期講習やら何やらで結構忙しい I'm busy during summer vacation with summer school *and lots of other things*.

3【何となく】▶先生たちが何やら心配そうに顔を見合わせている The teachers are anxiously looking at each other *for some reason*.

なにより 何より **1**【何よりも, いちばん】▶何より大事なことはいつも健康でいることだ The *most* important thing is to stay healthy. ‖ 彼女はチーズケーキが何よりも好きだ She likes cheesecake *better* [*more*] *than anything else*. ‖ きみは何よりもまず体重を減らすことだ *The first thing you have to do* is (to) lose weight. (● to はふつう省略する) ／*Above all* you have to lose weight.

▶寒い冬の夜には熱いうどんは何よりのごちそうだ On a cold winter evening, *nothing is better than* a bowl of hot *udon* noodles.

✉ **何よりの贈り物をありがとう** Thank you very much for your [the] wonderful present. It is just what I wanted. (➤ your でも通じるが, ネイティブは the を用いるのがふつう)

✉ **きみの手紙が何よりの励ましだったよ** *Nothing* gave me *greater* encouragement *than* your letter.

2【最もよいもの[こと]】▶お元気で何よりです I am very glad (to hear) that you are well.

ナノ nano-(「10億分の1」を表す接頭辞).
‖**ナノセカンド** a nanosecond /nǽnəsèkənd/ ‖**ナノチューブ** a nanotube ‖**ナノテクノロジー** nanotechnology /nænoʊtekná:lədʒi/ ‖**ナノメーター** a nanometer /nǽnəmì:ţəʳ/.
-なので because, since(➤前者のほうが意味が強い)▶雨降りなので家にいました I stayed at home *because* [*since*] it was raining. (英語では「結果＋理由」の順にするほうがよい). →-ので.
-なのに →-のに.
なのはな 菜の花 ((植物)) rape blossoms ((参考))ヨーロッパには多いが英米人にはなじみが薄い. rape は「暴行, レイプ」の意のほうにとられやすいため, 人によっては mustard flower, canola /kənóʊlə/ flower などで言い換える.
なのり 名乗り ▶その選挙には多数の新人が名乗りをあげた Many new faces *announced* their candidacy in the election.
なのる 名乗る say [state, give] one's name (➤ state は形式ばった語) ▶何者だ, 名を名乗れ! Who's there? *State your name.* ‖彼は妻の姓を名乗っている He *has taken* his wife's family *name*. ‖彼女はその孤児と思われていた少年の母親だと関係者に名乗り出た She *presented herself* to the people concerned as the mother of a boy who had been considered an orphan. (➤ present oneself to は「(公の場に)姿を現す」の意).
なびかせる ▶順子は長い髪をなびかせて自転車を走らせた Junko rode her bicycle with her long hair *waving* [*streaming*/*blowing*] *in the wind*.
なびく 1【ひるがえる】 wave, stream ▶オリンピック旗が風になびいている The Olympic flag *is streaming* in the breeze.
2【屈服する】▶あの人は決して金になびく(=わいろがきく)ようなことはない He is the last man to *yield to a bribe*.
ナビゲーション navigation
‖**ナビゲーター** a (television) presenter (特集番組などの「案内役」; 有名人が務めるときは special guest presenter ともいう; ナレーターも兼ねるときは presenter and narrator) (➤ navigator は「航路や進路を決めたり, 案内する人あるいは装置」).
ナプキン a (table) napkin ▶ナプキンをひざにかける lay [put] *a napkin* on one's lap.
((参考))((米))では sanitary napkin(生理用ナプキン)を napkin ということもあるが, 単に napkin といえばふつうは table napkin のことである.
ナフサ ((化学)) naphtha /nǽfθə/ (ガソリンと灯油との中間の粗製ガソリン).
なふだ 名札 a name card [badge]; a name tag(荷物などに付ける); a nameplate(表札) ▶スーツケースに名札を付ける attach *a name tag* to one's suitcase ‖パーティーの出席者は全員胸に名札を付けていた Everybody at the party wore *a name card* on his or her chest. (インフォーマルでは his or her chest の代わりに their chest を用いる).
ナフタリン ((化学)) naphthalene /nǽfθəli:n/; mothballs (防虫剤の玉; 通例複数形で).
なべ 鍋 a pan(浅い); a pot(深い); a saucepan(片手なべ); a casserole (ふた付きの); a wok (中華なべ); an earthenware cooking pot (土なべ)
▶シチュー用のなべ a stew*pot* ‖なべを火にかける put *a pot* on the stove ‖私はお昼になべ焼きうどんを食べた I ate *noodles served hot in the pot* for lunch.
‖**なべつかみ** a pot holder, an oven mitten ‖**土なべ** an earthenware cooking pot.

ナベヅル ((鳥)) a hooded crane.
なべもの 鍋物 *nabemono*, a hot pot
日本紹介 **なべ物は食卓でなべに入れた素材をぐつぐつ煮ながらみんなで食べる冬の料理です. 魚介類や野菜を入れてたっぷりの汁で煮る寄せ鍋や, 骨付きの鶏肉や野菜を水で煮る水炊きなどがあります** *Nabemono* refers to a hot pot dish cooked at the table in the winter. The ingredients and soup stock are put in a pot and heated. The people around the table eat the dish as it simmers in the pot. One kind is called '*yosenabe*,' which is seafood and vegetables cooked in ample stock. Another is '*mizutaki*,' which is unboned chicken and vegetables cooked in water.
▶私はなべ物が好きだ I like *food cooked at the table*.
ナポリ Naples /néɪpəlz/ (イタリア南西部の都市; イタリア名 Napoli).
なま 生の 1【加熱していない】 raw /rɔ:/; uncooked (調理していない) ▶カキは生で食べるとあたる可能性がある There's a possibility of getting food poisoning if you eat oysters *raw*. ‖東南アジアでは生水は飲まないほうがよい It's better not to drink *unboiled water* in Southeast Asia.
2【生放送の】 live /laɪv/ ▶試合の模様は競技場から生中継される予定です The game will *be broadcast* [*be broadcasted*/*be aired*] *live* from the stadium. (➤この live は「生放送で」の意の副詞).
3【ありのままの】▶住民から生の声を聞けるいい機会だ This is a good opportunity to hear *frank* [*candid*] opinions from the residents.
‖**生演奏** a live performance ‖**生クリーム** ((米)) (heavy) cream, ((英)) double cream; whipping cream (ホイップ用の; ホイップしたクリームは whipped cream という) ‖**生コン** fresh concrete ‖**生魚** raw fish ‖**生卵** a raw egg ‖**生ハム** prosciutto, uncured ham ‖**生番組** a live program ‖**生バンド** a live band ‖**生バンド演奏** a live-band performance ‖**生ビール** draft [((英)) draught] beer ‖**生野菜** fresh [raw] vegetables ‖**生ワクチン** live [live-virus] vaccine /væksí:n/.
なまあくび 生欠伸 a small yawn /jɔ:n/ ▶生あくびをかみ殺す stifle *a small yawn* ‖きょうはどうも生あくびが出てしょうがない I can't stop *yawning* today.
なまあたたかい 生暖かい uncomfortably warm; lukewarm /lù:kwɔ́:ʳm/ (ぬるい) ▶エアコンのスイッチを入れるとなま暖かい風が出てきた When I turned [switched] on the air conditioner, *moist*, *warm* air blew out (of it).
なまいき 生意気な impudent(年長者に敬意を示さない); ((英)) cheeky(態度や言うことが); cocky(自信を態度やことばに出していて); ((米)) sassy, ((英)) saucy (人をばかにするようなところがあって）; **rude**（無礼な）▶**生意気**な子供 a *saucy* child ‖ あいつ新人のくせに**生意気**だから，一発かませてやれ He's really *cocky* [*forward*／*impudent*] for a newcomer. Let him have it. ‖ **生意気言うな** *None of your lip* [*cheek*]！／*Don't be such a smart-aleck* [*smart-ass*]. ‖ 彼の**生意気な**態度には我慢できない I can't stand his *cocky* attitude. ‖ おれに向かって**生意気な**口をきくんじゃないよ How dare you be so *impertinent* [*impudent*] to me！‖ 彼は**生意気**にも私に口答えした He *had the nerve* [*was rude enough*／*was impertinent enough*] to answer me back.（➤ nerveは「あつかましさ」，impertinentは「年上の者をうやまわず，ずうずうしい」）.

なまえ 名前 a **name**（→名，名づける）

〘解説〙名前について
(1)「姓名」のうち「姓」は family name または surname といい，「名」は given name という．欧米人の名前は「名＋姓」の順になっているので，「名」を first name，「姓」を last name ともいう．
(2)「お名前は？」（May I ask [have] your name, please？）に対して「山田太郎です」と答える場合，英語式には My name's [I'm] Taro Yamada. であるが，My name's [I'm] Yamada Taro. のように日本式に答えてもよい．その場合，Yamada is my family name and Taro is my given name. と付け加えるとよい．
(3) 表記する場合には Yamada, Taro または YAMADA, Taro とするとよい．

▶この山の猿には全部**名前がついている** All the monkeys on this mountain *are named* [*have names*]. ‖ きみ，**名前何ていうの？** What's your *name*？（●ぶっきらぼうな聞き方）‖ この花は何という**名前ですか** What is the *name* of this flower？／What do you call this flower？‖ 鈴木さん，**下の名前**のほうは何といいますか Miss Suzuki, may I have your *given name*？‖ 彼女の**名前だけは**知ってます I know her only *by name*. ‖ 私には友恵という**名前の**いとこがいます I have a cousin *named* [*called*] Tomoe.（● whose name is Tomoe よりこのほうが自然）‖ この子猫に**名前をつけて**くれませんか Would you please *name* the kitten [*give* the kitten *a name*]？‖ ぼくの**名前**は東郷隆盛といいますが，人からよく**名前負けしている**と言われます My *name* is Togo Takamori, and people often say that I *don't live up to* my *name*.（➤ live up to one's name は「名前に恥じないようにする」の意）.

あなたの英語はどう響く？
(1) 日本人の中には，自己紹介の際，My name is Suzuki. とか I am Suzuki. のように名字だけを言う人がいるが，英語を母語とする人々の耳には横柄に響くことが少なくない．My name is Taro Suzuki. とか I'm Taro Suzuki. のようにフルネームで言う．
(2) また，友人になれば first name（姓でなく名）で呼び合うのがふつうであるから，いつまでも日本流に「姓」で呼び合っていると非友好的な人間だと思われてしまう．したがって，付き合いをしたい相手には，最初から My name's [I'm] Hideo Noguchi. Just call me Hide.（私はヒデオ・ノグチです．ヒデと呼んでください）のように言うのが好感を持たれる．

直訳の落とし穴「（私は）…です」
名前を言うときにはいつでも I am ... でよいと思って，間違えて使っている人が多い．すなわち，I am Taro.（私は太郎です）はこちらの名前を知らない相手に最初に名乗るときの言い方．電話やメールの書き出しなどで，友人や家族に「太郎です」と告げるには I am ... ではなく，This is Taro.（こちらは［こちらで話しているのは］太郎です）という．人を紹介するときに「こちらはだれだれさんです」というときと同じ言い方で，それを本人が言っているだけである．電話の場合は This is Taro speaking. ということも多い．

なまかじり 生かじり ▶彼女の医学の知識は**なまかじり**（＝表面的）だ Her knowledge of medicine is *superficial*.
▶**なまかじり**のフランス語を振り回すな Don't show off your *smattering* [*small stock*] *of* French.（➤ stock は「蓄え」）.

なまがわき 生乾き **half dried** ▶（部屋干しの）**生乾きの臭い**の原因は菌である The (musty) *damp-dry smell* [*odor*] (of clothes dried indoors) is caused by bacteria.（➤ damp-dry は「（洗濯物が）生乾きの」の意）.

なまきず 生傷 a **cut**（切り傷）; a **bruise** /bru:z/（打撲傷）
▶弟は大変なわんぱくで**生傷が絶えない** My (younger) brother's a really mischievous boy and is always covered with *cuts and bruises*.

なまぐさい 生臭い **fishy**（魚が）▶**魚の生臭いにおい**が漂っていた *The smell of raw fish* was in the air.

なまけもの 怠け者 a **lazy person**,《インフォーマル》a **lazybones**, a **slacker** ▶この子はどうしようもない**怠け者**だ He [She] is hopelessly *lazy*. ‖ こら**怠け者**！いつまでごろごろしている気だ You *lazybones*！How long are you going to loaf around？‖ お父さん，ナマケモノっていう動物は本当に**怠け者**なの？Dad, is the sloth really a *slothful* animal？（➤ slothful は lazy の意の堅い語）.

なまける 怠ける **neglect** ＋㊐（なおざりにする）; **idle away** (one's) **time**, **goof off**（怠けて過ごす）; **be lazy**（怠けている）▶仕事を**怠ける**な Don't *neglect* your work.
▶忙しくて**怠けている**暇などない I am busy and don't have time to *be idle* [to *idle away*].
▶夏休みの間に**怠け癖**がついてしまった I've gotten into *a bad habit of goofing off* [*loafing around*] during the summer vacation.（➤ goof off, loaf around は「のらくらする」の意）.
▶私は中学時代に勉強を**怠けた**ことを後悔している I regret that I *slacked off* in [on] my studies in junior high school.（➤ slack off は一生懸命やらないで「いい加減にする」）.

なまこ《動物》a **sea cucumber** [**slug**].

なまごみ 生ごみ **(kitchen) garbage, garbage (from the kitchen)**.

なまじっか ▶**なまじっか**彼に結果を知らせなければよかった I wish I had never told him the results.
▶**なまじっかな**（＝生はんかな）練習では上達しませんよ If you practice *halfheartedly*, you will never make good progress.

なましょく 生食 ▶**生食用の**カキ oysters *to be eaten raw* ‖ **生食できない** be *inedible raw*.

なまず 鯰《魚》a **catfish**.

なまっちょろい →生ぬるい.

なまつば 生唾 ▶ショーウインドーの七面鳥の丸焼きを見て, 思わず生つばをごくんと飲み込んだ When I saw a roasted turkey in the shop window, *my mouth watered*. (➤「よだれが出た」の意) ‖ なまつばごっくんの彼女のプロポーション her *mouth-watering* figure.

なまなましい 生々しい vivid(目に見えるような) ; fresh (新しい) ▶その事件は今もなお記憶に生々しい The event is still *vivid* [*fresh*] in my memory.

なまにえ 生煮えの half-cooked, underdone ▶お母さん, このサトイモ生煮えで, しんがあるよ Mother, these taros are only *half-cooked* [are *underdone*] and the center's still hard.

なまぬるい 生ぬるい 1【中途半端に温かい】 lukewarm, tepid(➤ともに湯や料理などが「ぬるい」, 後者は前者より堅い語) ▶生ぬるい風 an *uncomfortably warm* wind.

▶生ぬるいビールなど飲みたくない I don't want to drink *lukewarm* beer. ‖ このビール, 生ぬるいよ This beer *isn't cold enough*. ‖ ふろの湯が生ぬるくて気持ち悪かった I felt uncomfortable in the bath because the water was *tepid*.

2【手ぬるい】 soft (甘い) ; halfhearted (気乗りしない) ▶そんな生ぬるい処置ではだめだ Such *halfhearted* [*lukewarm*] measures are no good.

なまはんか 生半可な halfhearted (気乗りのしない) ; superficial (浅薄な) ▶生はんかな勉強では試験に合格できませんよ *Halfhearted* studying will not bring you success in the examination. ‖ 生はんかな知識はときに有害である *Superficial* knowledge is sometimes harmful.

なまびょうほう 生兵法 ▶ ことわざ 生兵法は大けがのもと A little learning is a dangerous thing.

なまへんじ 生返事 a half-hearted answer (気のない, 半分上の空の) ; a noncommittal answer (煮えきらない, 関わろうとしない) ▶哲夫はテレビに夢中で,「ああ」とか「いや」とかの生返事しかしなかった Tetsuo was absorbed in watching TV, and answered only with a *half-hearted* [*vague* / *noncommittal*] "Yeah" or "Nope."

なまほうそう 生放送 live /laɪv/ broadcasting(放送すること) ; a live broadcast(1回1回の放送) ▶その番組は生放送だったの, 録画だったの? Was the program *live* or recorded? ‖ 球場からの生放送 *a live broadcast* from the stadium.

なまみ 生身 flesh and blood(人間) ▶プロレスラーだって悲しいときには泣くさ. 生身の人間だからね Even a pro-wrestler cries when he's sad—after all *he's only flesh and blood* [*he's only human*].

なまみず 生水 unboiled water.

なまめかしい 艶めかしい sexy (性的魅力のある) ; sultry (官能的な) ▶なまめかしい女 a *sexy* woman ‖ なまめかしい口元 *sultry* lips.

なまもの 生物 uncooked food(料理していない) ; perishables (傷みやすい食品) ; raw fish (生魚) ▶この和菓子はなま物ですので, できるだけお早めにお召し上がりください These Japanese sweets are *perishable*, so please eat them as soon as possible.

なまやけ 生焼けの underdone ; half-baked (パンなどが) ▶生焼けのステーキ an *underdone* steak ‖ 生焼けのパン *half-baked* bread.

なまやさしい 生易しい ▶人気歌手になるのはなまやさしい事ではない It is no *easy* thing [It isn't all that *easy*] to be a popular singer. ‖ 売り上げを伸ばすために彼のした努力はなまやさしいものではなかった His efforts to increase sales *were extraordinary*.

¹なまり 訛 an accent ; a dialect(方言) ▶工藤さんは東北なまりが強い Mr. Kudo has [speaks with] a strong Tohoku *accent*. ‖ あのテレビレポーターはなまりがある That TV reporter *speaks with a provincial* [*local*] *accent*. ‖ 彼女の英語には少しドイツ語なまりがある She speaks English with a slight German *accent*. / There is a trace of (a) German *accent* in her English.

²なまり 鉛 lead /led/ ▶鉛色の空 a *leaden* [*lead-colored*] sky ‖ 鉛中毒 *lead* poisoning.

¹なまる 鈍る ▶勉強ばかりしていると体がなまってしまうよ If you do nothing but study, your body is going to *weaken* [*get soft*].

²なまる 訛る ▶彼女の英語は少しフランス語風になまっている She *speaks* English *with* a slight French *accent*. ‖ 東京の地名「八重洲」は「ヤン・ヨーステン」がなまったものだ The place name Yaesu in Tokyo is *a corruption* of the "Jan Joosten."

¹なみ 波 1【水面の】 a wave ; a ripple(さざ波) ; surf (海岸などに打ち寄せる) ▶サーフボードで波に乗る ride *a wave* [*surf*] on a surfboard ‖ きょうは波が高い [荒い] The *waves* are high [rough] today. / The *sea* is high [rough] today. ‖ なぎさに波が寄せては返していた The *waves* were lapping on the shore.

▶釣り人が波にさらわれた An angler was washed away by the *waves*. ‖ サーフィンはうまく波に乗るのがポイントだ The key to surfing is to skillfully catch the *waves*. ‖ 湖には波一つない There isn't *a ripple* on the lake. ‖ 釣り舟が大波に飲まれた A fishing boat was swallowed up in *a huge wave*.

▶《比喩的》あの接戦をものにして以来うちのチームは波に乗っている Our team *has been going strong* [*great guns*] after winning that close game. (➤ go great guns は「快進撃する」の意のインフォーマルな表現).

‖波しぶき sea spray ‖ 波線 a wavy line ‖ 波乗り surfing.

2【流れるように動くもの】 ▶元日の明治神宮の参道は人の波で埋まる On New Year's Day the approach to Meiji Shrine *is inundated* [*swamped*] *with visitors*. ‖ 彼女の作品(の出来)には波がある Her works *vary* [*range*] *from good to bad*. ‖ あなたのお子さんは成績に波がありますね Your child's grades *fluctuate* (*from good to bad*). (➤ fluctuate は「変動する」の意) ‖ 彼のピッチングは好不調の波が大きい His pitching is *erratic* [*inconsistent*]. (➤ erratic は「一定しない, 不安定な」, inconsistent は「出来不出来がある」) ‖ あの電機会社は景気の波に乗っている That electrical company *is riding on a wave* of prosperity.

3【寄せてくるもの】 ▶静かな田舎町にも都市化の波が押し寄せてきた The *wave* of urbanization has finally reached the sleepy country town. ‖ わが社は円高の波をまともにかぶって倒産した Our company went bankrupt *after being heavily damaged* by the yen's appreciation.

²なみ 並の ordinary(ふつうの) ; average (平均的な) ▶並の人間じゃあ, あんなアイデアは出ないね No *ordinary* person would be able to come up with an idea like that. ‖ 並の成績じゃあ, 開明大には入れないよ You can't get into Kaimei University with *just average* grades.

▶漢字を6000字も記憶しているなんて並の子供じゃない The child is *quite extraordinary* to have memorized six thousand kanji characters. ‖ 天どんの並を１つお願いします One *regular* tendon [tempura bowl], please.

-なみ -並み ▶あの会社は世間並み以上の給料は払ってくれないだろう That company will not pay (you) above an *average* salary. ‖ 彼のゴルフはプロ並みの腕まえだ His skill in golf is at *a professional level*.
☞ 人並み (→見出語)

なみうちぎわ 波打ち際 the water's edge (水際); a shoreline (海岸線).

なみうつ 波打つ ▶地震で道路が波打ったようになった The roads *were warped* by the earthquake.

なみかぜ 波風 ▶彼は新しい職場で波風を立てないようにしばらくは目立たないようにしていた He kept a low profile at his new workplace for some time and tried *not to make (any) waves*. ‖ 多くの日本人は自分のまわりに波風を立てないように(＝他人との対立を避けようと)努めている Many Japanese try to *avoid conflict* [*confrontation*] *with others*.

なみき 並木 a row of trees ▶マロニエの並木道 *an avenue lined with* horse chestnut *trees*.

なみだ 涙 tears /tɪəʳz/ (➤「１粒の涙」は a tear) ▶優勝が決まって選手たちの目には涙が浮かんだ *Tears* came to the players' eyes when they won the championship. ‖ 大粒の涙が彼女のほおを伝って落ちた *Big tears* ran [fell] down her cheeks. ‖ かぐや姫は月を見上げて涙を流した Kaguya-hime *wept* [*shed tears*] as she looked up at the moon. (➤ wept は weep (泣く)の過去形) ‖ このハンカチで涙を拭きな *Wipe away your tears* with this handkerchief. ‖ 女優は記者会見で離婚の理由を涙ながらに[目に涙を浮かべて]語った *In tears* [*With tears in her eyes*], the actress talked about the reasons for her divorce at the press conference. ‖ 「涙無しでは見られない」というのがこの芝居のうたい文句だ The promotion for this play says, "You can't see the play *without tears* in your eyes." ‖ 彼は涙声でさよならと言った He said good-bye *in a tearful voice*. ‖ タマネギのせいで涙が出た The onion made me *tear up*.

▶《慣用表現》
お涙ちょうだい (→見出語). **すずめの涙** ▶ことしのボーナスはすずめの涙ほどだった I got a *very small* bonus [got *chicken feed* for a bonus] this year. ／ My bonus was *peanuts* this year. **血も涙もない** ▶「血も涙もない」とはあの男のようなやつのことだ The word "*cold-hearted*" was made for a man like him. **涙に暮れる** ▶事故で死んだ学生の両親は涙に暮れた(＝ただ泣くだけだった) The parents of the student who was killed in the accident *could do nothing but cry*.
涙を誘う ▶その孤児の身の上話は人々の涙を誘った The story of the orphan's life *moved people to tears*. (➤ move A to tears は「A (人)を泣かせる」).
涙を飲む ▶日本チームは１点差で涙を飲んだ (＝敗れた) To their bitter disappointment, the Japanese team *lost* by only one point. (➤ To their bitter disappointment は「悔しいことに」) ‖ 父は涙を飲んでその骨董品を手放した My father *reluctantly* [*unwillingly*] parted with that antique. (➤ ともに「気は進まないが, いやいやながら」の意).

なみたいてい 並大抵 ▶司法試験に合格するには並たいていの努力ではできない To pass the bar examination is *no easy* task. ／You aren't going to pass the bar examination by *just ordinary* efforts.

なみだきん 涙金 a pittance (ごくわずかな金) ▶勤めをやめたら涙金ほどの退職金しかもらえなかった When I retired, I received just *a pittance* as my lump-sum retirement payment. (➤ lump-sum は「一括の」).

なみだぐましい 涙ぐましい ▶母は何とか痩せようと涙ぐましい努力をしている My mother *is making painful efforts* [*struggling* (*painfully*)] to lose weight.

なみだぐむ 涙ぐむ ▶ちょっと小言を言われるとこの子はすぐ涙ぐむ The slightest complaint is enough to put her *in tears*. ‖ 彼女は涙ぐんでぼくに秘密を打ち明けた She told me the secret *tearfully* [*with tears in her eyes*].

なみだつ 波立つ ▶日没後しばらくすると湖は波立ってきた On the lake, *waves began to rise* soon after the sun set. ‖ 海は波立っていた The sea *was choppy*.

なみだもろい 涙もろい ▶父は酔うと涙もろくなる When my father gets tipsy, he *is easily moved to tears*. ‖ 彼は涙もろい He is *maudlin*. (➤ maudlin /mɔ́:dlɪn/ は「感傷的な」の意の堅い語).

なみなみと to the brim (縁まで) ▶父はビールをジョッキになみなみとつぎ, それを一気に飲み干した My father filled the mug *to the brim* with beer and gulped it down.

なみなみならぬ 並々ならぬ extraordinary /ɪkstrɔ́:ʳdneri/ (並外れた) ▶一流の同時通訳者になるには並々ならぬ努力が必要だ To become a first-rate simultaneous interpreter requires *extraordinary* effort(s).

なみはずれた 並外れた ▶彼は並外れた才能の持ち主だ He is *exceptionally* talented. ‖ 私たちの先生は並外れて記憶力がいい Our teacher has an *uncommonly* [*extremely*] good memory.

なみま 波間 ▶１そうの船が波間を漂っていた A boat was drifting on *the waves*.

なめくじ 《動物》 a slug.

ナメコ a *nameko* mushroom.

なめしがわ なめし革 leather.

なめす 鞣す tan ＋目 ▶皮をなめす *tan* leather.

なめらか 滑らかな smooth /smu:ð/; velvet (ビロードのような) ▶滑らかな声 a *velvet* voice ‖ この布地は滑らかで手触りがいい This cloth is *smooth* and feels very soft to the touch. ‖ 少し酒が入ると彼の舌は滑らかになる A drink will *loosen his tongue*.

なめる 舐める **1**【舌で】 lick ＋目 (ぺろりと); lap ＋目 (液体をぺちゃぺちゃと); suck on (あめ・アイスキャンディーなどをしゃぶる) ▶コロは生まれた子犬の全身をなめてきれいにしてやった Koro *licked* the new born puppies clean. ‖ 犬は皿のミルクを全部なめた The dog *lapped* up all the milk in the saucer.
▶キャンディーをなめる *suck on* a candy ‖ 彼女はホイップクリームを少し指先につけてなめて(＝味わって)みた She scooped up the whipped cream with her finger to *taste* it.
2【経験する】 experience ＋目, undergo ＋目 (➤ 後者は堅い語) ▶彼は若い頃多くの辛酸をなめた He *experienced* [*underwent*] many hardships in his youth.
3【あなどる】 make light of (軽んじる); make a fool of (ばかにする) ▶彼女は私が若いのでなめている She *looks down on* [*underestimates*] me because I am young. ‖ なめんなよ！ Don't take me for a fool.

なや 納屋 a shed (物置); a (storage) barn (特に農家

の).

なやましい 悩ましい **1【官能を刺激する】seductive**(誘惑するような); **sexy**(性的魅力のある) ▶彼女は悩ましい目つきでぼくを見た She looked at me *seductively*. ‖ そのドレスを着ると彼女はとても悩ましく見える She looks very *sexy* in that dress.

2【判断·理解に苦しむ】troubling(やっかいな); **worrying**(気にかかる) ▶悩ましい問題 a *troubling* question ‖ 悩ましい状況 a *worrying* situation ‖ 放射性廃棄物をどう処理するかは人類にとって悩ましい問題である How to deal with radioactive waste is a *thorny* issue for humanity. (➤ thorny は「困難な, やっかいな」).

なやます 悩ます **worry** (+目) (心配させる); **trouble** +目 (苦しめる); **pester** +目 (繰り返しいらいらさせる); **bother** +目 (煩わす); **annoy** +目 (いらいらさせる) ▶簡単さ, そんなに頭を悩ますことは無い It's quite easy. Don't *worry* so much. ‖ 彼女をどう扱ってよいか頭を悩ましている I have *been worried* [*been troubled*] *about* how to deal with [handle] her. (➤ handle には「(人)を制御 [コントロール] する」の含みがある) ‖ 我々はひどい(車の)騒音に悩まされている We *are bothered* by terrible (traffic) noise. ‖ そんなつまらないことで私を悩ませないでくれ Don't *bother* me with such a small matter.

▶その島では蚊に悩まされた I *was annoyed* [*was pestered*] by mosquitoes on the island. ‖ ゆうべは歯痛に悩まされた(=歯痛がした) I *had* a toothache last night. (➤ 慢性的な病気で苦しむ場合は suffer from を使う).

なやみ 悩み (a) **worry**(心配); (a) **trouble**(苦しめること); a **problem**(難問) ▶青春時代は悩み多き時代だ One's youth is full of *worries* [*troubles*]. ‖ 我々の現在の悩みは有能な販売外交員が足りないということだ Our current *problem* is that we are short of able salespeople. ‖ あなたの悩みは何ですか What's *troubling* you? / What are you *troubled about*? ‖ 悩み事があったらいつでも相談にのるよ I'm willing to listen to your *troubles* any time. ‖ 背が低いのが私の悩みの種だ My short stature is *a source of trouble* [*worry*] to me.

なやむ 悩む **worry** ⦅about⦆ (無益なことを思いわずらう); **be worried** ⦅**about**⦆ (はっきりした理由や原因があって不安や悩みを抱いている); **be troubled**(不安になっている) →心配.

▶あんまり悩むなよ Don't *worry* too much! ‖ 兄は仕事に行き詰まって悩んでいる My brother *is worried* [*troubled*] because he can't get anywhere in his job. ‖ 一人で悩んでいないで先生に相談しなさい Don't *keep your worries to yourself* [Stop *worrying by yourself*]. Go talk with your teacher (about them).

> 【文型】
> あること(A)で悩む
> **worry about** A
> あること(A)で悩んでいる
> **be worried about** A

▶彼女は彼と付き合うべきかどうか悩んでいる She'*s worrying* (*about*) whether or not she should go out with him. ‖ 何を悩んでるの? What's *bothering* [*worrying* / *troubling* / *bugging*] you? (➤ bugging が一番インフォーマル) / What *are* you *worrying about*? (この文はしばしば「悩むのはよしなさい」と励ますときにも使う) ‖ 彼は将来の事で悩んでいる He'*s worried about* his future. ‖ 彼はどういう道に進むかで悩んでいる He'*s worried about* what career path to take.

▶ゆき子は達夫との恋に深刻に悩んでいる Yukiko *is agonizing over* her love for Tatsuo. (➤ agonize は「苦しみもだえる」) ‖ うちの娘はにきびに悩んでいる Our daughter *agonizes over* her acne.

なよなよ ▶彼はどことなくなよなよしている There is something *weak and effeminate* [*feminine*] about him. (➤ effeminate は軽蔑的, feminine は「女性的な」).

なら 楢 ⦅植物⦆ a **Japanese oak.**

-なら **1【そういうことであれば】if** ▶欲しいならそのポスターあげるよ You can have that poster *if* you want it. ‖ まだ花屋が開いているようなら妻に花を買って帰ってやろうかな I think I'll buy my wife some flowers on my way home, *provided* the flower shop is still open. ‖ お礼が十分もらえるならその仕事を引き受けましょう I will take on that job *on* (*the*) *condition that* I am well paid. ‖ 私ならそんなことはしない I *would*n't do that. (➤ would で仮定の気持ちが裏にあることを表す).

2【…について言えば】▶来週の火曜なら空いてる I'll be free next Tuesday. ‖ その話なら, ぼくに任せとけ You can depend on me when it comes to that. / Leave that to me. ‖ 西田さんちなら, この先だよ Mr. Nishida's house? It's just ahead.

ならいごと 習い事 a **lesson**(➤ しばしば複数形で) ▶何か習い事でも始めようかな I'm thinking of taking *lessons* in something or other.

¹ならう 習う **learn** +目 (学んで身につける); **study** +目 (学習·研究する); **take lessons** (レッスンを受ける); **practice** +目 (練習する) ▶水泳を習う *learn* how to swim ‖ 自動車の運転を習う *take lessons* in driving / *take* driving *lessons* ‖ 私は高橋先生に英語を習いました I *learned* English from Mr. Takahashi. (➤「勉強した」ではなく「習得した」を意味する) ‖ 私はギターを習いたい I want to *take* guitar *lessons*.

▶きみはだれに習字を習いましたか Who *taught you* calligraphy? (➤「だれがあなたに習字を教えたか」の意) ‖ 学校では週4時間英語を習う We *study* English four hours a week at school. ‖ 私はアメリカ人から英語の発音を習っています I'*m practicing* [*getting training in*] English pronunciation under an American teacher.

[ことわざ] 習うより慣れよ Practice makes perfect. (➤「練習が完全にする」の意の英語のことわざで, 日本語の場合と異なり「習うこと」を否定してはいない).

²ならう 倣う **copy** +目 (そっくり同じに作る); **imitate** /ímɪteɪt/ +目 (まねる); **follow** +目 (先例に従う) ▶お手本にならって書きなさい Write it *copying* [*after*] the model. (➤ after は「…にならって, …をまねて」の意) ‖ お姉さんにならってショートカットにした I had my hair cut short *like* my sister. ‖ カモの子供はお母さんガモにならって次々と池にとび降りた When the mother duck jumped into the pond, her ducklings *followed suit*. (➤ follow suit は「(人や前例の)まねをする」) ‖ ⦅号令⦆ 右 [前] へならえ *Dress*, right! [Forward, *dress*!]

ならく 奈落 **hell**(地獄) ▶奈落のふち the edge of an *abyss* ‖ 奈落の底 an *abyss* ‖ 舞台の奈落 a *trap cellar* in a theater.

¹ならす 鳴らす **1【音を出す】sound** +目; **ring** +目 (鐘やベルを); **honk** +目, **blow** +目 (警笛などを) ▶何度もクラクションを鳴らしたがその牛はどこうとしなかった I

honked [*sounded* / *blew*] the horn a dozen times, but the cow wouldn't move. ‖ 赤ん坊が寝ていますのでチャイムを鳴らさないでください Please don't *ring* the doorbell. Our baby's sleeping. ‖ 新しいスピーカーを早く鳴らしてみたい I'd like to *listen to* the new loudspeakers as soon as possible.
▶猫が喉を鳴らしている The cat is *purring*. ‖ 子犬がくんくん鼻を鳴らしながら近づいてきた A puppy came up to me *whining*.
2【名を高める】▶岩隈はかつては速球投手として鳴らした Iwakuma was once a *famous* fastball pitcher.

[2]**ならす 均す level** +他 (平らにする); **average** /ǽvərɪdʒ/ +他 (平均する) ▶テニスコートをローラーでならす *level* a tennis court with a roller ‖ その土地をならすのにブルドーザーが使われた A bulldozer was employed for *leveling* [to *level*] the land.
▶私の収入は月にならして20万円だ My income is 200,000 yen a month *on* (*the*) *average*. / My income *averages* 200,000 yen a month.

[3]**ならす 慣らす accustom** /əkʌ́stəm/ +他 (慣れさせる) ▶英語の音に耳を慣らすことが大切だ It is important to *accustom* your ears to the sound of English. ‖ いきなりプールに飛び込まないで, 少しずつ体を水に慣らすようにしなさい Don't jump into the pool so quickly. *Get accustomed* [*used*] *to* the water little by little. ‖ 来月は遠足だから, 新しいスニーカーをよく足に慣らしておきなさい The field trip is next month, so *break in* your new sneakers *well* [*get* your new sneakers *broken in*]. (➤ break in は「(靴を)はき慣らす」).

ならずもの ならず者 a **rogue**, a **hoodlum** (➤ 後者には「若い」という含みがあることが多い).

-ならでは ▶この住宅には女性建築家ならではの心くばりがある This house incorporates thoughtful features that *only* a female architect could *come up with*.

-ならない **1【禁止】Don't ..., must not ...** ▶ここにごみを散らかしてはならない *Don't* litter here. / 《掲示》*No* littering. ‖ 酒を飲んだら運転してはならない You *must not* drink and drive. (➤ must not は強い禁止を表す) ‖ ここに停車してはならない You *can't* stop [pull over] your car here. (➤ can't は不許可を表す).
2【義務・必要】must (義務として…しなければならない); **have (got) to** do (客観的情勢から見て…しなければならない); **should** (当然…すべき) ▶約束は守らねばならない We *must* keep our promise. ‖ そろそろ失礼しなくちゃならないな I *have to* be leaving now. (➤ 用事があるか, だれかと決めた時間になったので) ‖ 10時に彼女に電話しなくちゃならないんだ I*'ve got* [I *have*] *to* call her at ten. (● have got to do は主に話しことばで使う) ‖ 彼女はかぜがひどくなるようなら医者に診てもらわなくてはならない She *should* go to see a doctor if her cold gets worse.
▶我々は資源をもっと大切に使わなくてはならない We *ought to* use natural resources more carefully. (● ought to は should よりも強い義務を表すが, must よりは弱い) ‖ このレポートはきのうまでに終えていなくてはならないはずだ You *should have* finished this report by yesterday. / You *were supposed to* have finished this report by yesterday. (● be supposed to do は「…することになっている」の意で, 穏やかだが皮肉っぽい言い方にもなる).
→いけない, -ねばならない, なくてはならない.
3【たまらない, しかたがない】▶山中湖へのスケート旅行が待ち遠しくてならない I *can hardly* wait to go skating at Lake Yamanaka. ‖ 彼はどうも無実のように思えてならない I *can't help* think*ing* that he is innocent. (➤ can't help doing は「…せざるをえない」) ‖ 入試の結果が心配でならない I*'m beside myself with worry* [I*'m deeply worried*] about the results of the entrance exams. ‖ 彼の辞職が残念でならない His resignation is *extremely regrettable*. / *Nothing* is *more regrettable than* his resignation. (➤「彼の辞職以上に残念なことはない」の意).
4【できない】▶あの人の自分勝手にはもう我慢がならない I *can't* put up with his selfishness anymore. ‖ できてしまったことは今さらどうにもならない What's done *can't be undone*. (➤ undo は「元に戻す」).

ならびに 並びに and (…と); **both** A **and** B (AもBも); B **as well as** A (Aと同じくBも) ▶ご来賓ならびに保護者の皆さま, … To our guests *and* parents of our students, ... ‖ 岸田さんは物理ならびに化学を専攻されました Mr. Kishida majored in chemistry *as well as* physics.

ならぶ 並ぶ **1【一列になる】line up, stand in (a) line**; **form a line** [《英》**queue**] (列を作る) ▶2列に並びなさい *Stand in two lines*. ‖ 2列に並んでお待ちください Please wait *in two lines*. ‖ 走者たちはスタートラインに並んだ The runners *are lined up* at the starting line. ‖ あのう, 私のほうが先に並んでいたんですよ Excuse me, but I *was in line* ahead of you. ‖ 生徒たちはパレード行進の開始を待って1列に並んでいた The students *stood in a row* waiting for the parade to start. (➤ row は「横の列」) ‖ 彼らは1列に並んでバスを待っていた They were waiting *in single file* for the bus. (➤ file は「縦の列」) ‖ 整理券の欲しい人はこちらに並んでください Anyone wanting a numbered ticket, please *form a line* here.
2【隣り合う】▶彼の家は私の家と並んでいる His house *stands* [*is*] *next to* mine. ‖ 私は彼女と並んで(=の横に)座った I sat *next to* [*beside*] her. / I sat *by her side*. / She and I sat *side by side*. ‖ 彼女と並んで立っている女の子は誰ですか Who is the girl standing *beside* her? ‖ 川内選手は30キロ付近でスパート, ついに先頭に並んだ(=追いついた) Kawauchi spurted at around the 30 kilometer mark and *caught up with* the front runner.
3【位置を占める】▶チャリティーバザーにはたくさんの骨董品が並んでいた A lot of antiques *were displayed* at the charity bazaar. ‖ 食卓にごちそうが並んでいる Many delicious-looking dishes *have been put* [*placed* / *arranged*] on the table. ‖ 今週はどの球場も好カードが並んでいる We *have* some exciting games at each ballpark this week.
4【匹敵する】equal; **rank** 《with》 (…と同列に位する) ▶歌唱力では彼女に並ぶ者はいない No one can *equal* [*rank with*] her in singing ability. / She has no equal in singing. ‖『カラマーゾフの兄弟』は『戦争と平和』と並んでロシア文学の頂点にある "The Brothers Karamazov" *ranks* at the top of Russian literature, *together with* "War and Peace." ‖ ヘンデルはバッハと並び称される Handel *ranks with* Bach (as a great composer).

ならべたてる 並べ立てる enumerate /ɪnjúːməreɪt/ +他 (列挙する) ▶彼は反対理由を並べ立てた He *enumerated* the reasons why he objected. ‖ あいつは会うといつも上司の悪口ばかり並べ立てる Every time I meet him, he *complains incessantly* about his boss. (➤ incessantly は「途切れることなく, ずっと」).

ならべる 並べる

📖 訳語メニュー
1列に並べる →line up **1**
配列する →arrange **1,3**
2つを隣り合わせる →put side by side **2**
展示する →display **3**

1【1列に】**line up**; **arrange** +⊜(配列する) ▶先生は子供たちを背の高い順に並べた The teacher *lined* the children *up* in order of height. ‖ 司令官は兵士を1列に並べた The commander *lined up* his soldiers (*in a row*). ‖ このカードを番号順［アルファベット順］に並べてください Could you *arrange* these cards in numerical [alphabetical] order?

2【隣り合わせる】**place** [**put**] **... side by side** ▶2つの絵をこうやって並べてみるとよく似ている The two pictures look quite alike when we *place* [*put*] them *side by side* like this. ‖ 二人は同じ大学で机を並べて勉強した仲です They *studied together* in college.

3【所定の位置に置く】▶彼女はテーブルに料理を並べた She *arranged* the food [*set* the food *out*] on the table. ‖ 展示室にはいろいろな形の埴輪(はにわ)や土器が並べて(＝展示して)あった There were many types of *haniwa* dolls and earthenware *displayed* in the exhibit room.

4【言いたてる】▶いつまでも文句を並べてないで, さっさと仕事をしなさい Stop *rattling off complaints* and get to work.

ならわし 習わし a **custom**(風習); (a) **tradition** (伝統) ▶正月を雑煮で祝うのが日本の習わしです Celebrating the New Year with a bowl of *zōni* is a Japanese *custom*. ‖ 元日に写真を撮るのがわが家の習わしです Taking family photos on New Year's Day is *a tradition* in our family. ‖ それが世間の習わしだ It is *the way of the world*. ／That's *the way things are done*.

¹なり ▶彼はなり(＝服装, 格好)を構わない He doesn't care about his *personal appearance* [*how he looks*]. ‖ 大きななりしてまだお人形が欲しいの? *You're so big* and yet you want a rag doll?

²なり 鳴り ▶あの歯に衣着せぬ政治家もこのところ鳴りを潜めている That outspoken politician *has been keeping a low profile* these days.

-なり **1**【例を挙げて】▶ドイツ語なりフランス語なり好きなほうを選んで学習してください You may choose to study *either* German *or* French. ‖ どこへなりと好きな所へ行っちまえ Go *wherever* you like.

2【…するとすぐ】**as soon as ...**, **scarcely ... when** [**before**] (➤ as soon as のほうがふつうの言い方) ▶男は警官を見るなり逃げ去った *As soon as* he saw the police officer, he ran away. ／The man had *scarcely* spotted the police officer *when* he ran away.

☞ -なりに, -なりの (→見出語)

なりあがり 成り上がり an **upstart** ▶成り上がりの政治家 an *upstart* politician.

なりあがる 成り上がる **rise to power suddenly**(権力を握る); **become suddenly rich**(成金になる) ▶きみは成り上がることができたら何をする? What would you do if you *rose to power* [*became rich*] *suddenly*?

なりかわる 成り代わる ▶息子に成り代わりまして, 事故で負傷された方々に心よりおわび申し上げます I offer my sincere apologies to those who were injured in the accident *on behalf of* my son.

なりきる 成りきる **get into** one's **role** ▶娘はAKB48に成りきって踊る My daughter dances *just as if she were* a member of AKB 48.

なりきん 成り金 a **parvenu** /pá:ʳvənju:/, a **nouveau riche** /nù:voʊ rí:ʃ/ (➤両者ともしばしば軽蔑的); **the new-rich**, **new money**(成り金たち; 後者は一人を指すこともある) ▶あの人の服装はいかにも成り金趣味だ You can tell he's one of *the nouveau riche* by the way he dresses. ‖ 彼は(新興)成り金だ He's *new money*.

‖土地成り金 a land profiteer /prɑ̀:fətíəʳ/.

なりさがる 成り下がる ▶人の物を盗むほど成り下がってはいない I *haven't sunk so low* as to steal someone else's things.

なりすまし an **identity theft**.

なりすます 成り済ます **pose**《as》; **pretend to be**(ふりをする) ▶彼は医者に成り済ました He *posed* [*passed himself off*] *as* a doctor. ‖ 彼女は東大生に成り済ましてその講義に出席した She attended the lectures, *pretending to be* a student at Tokyo University.

なりたち 成り立ち (a) **history**(歴史); an **origin**(起源); **structure**(仕組み) ▶私たちは市役所で自分たちの住む町の成り立ちを調べた We inquired about our town's *history* at the town hall. ‖ 私は宇宙の成り立ちに興味をもっています I'm interested in the *origin* of the universe.

▶生徒会長が生徒会のなりたちを新入生に説明した The student council president explained to the new students the *structure* [*background*] of the student council.

なりたつ 成り立つ **1**【できあがる】**consist**《of》, **be made up**《of》 ▶水は酸素と水素から成り立っている Water *consists of* [*is made up of*] oxygen and hydrogen. ‖ そのアイデアは商売として成り立たない The idea *isn't* commercially *viable*. (➤ viable は「(計画などが)存立できる」).

2【まとまる】▶xに1, yに3を代入すると, この連立方程式は成り立つ A simultaneous equation will *be established* if you substitute one for x and three for y.

3【採算がとれる】▶これ以上値引きをしたら商売が成り立ちません If I give you a further discount, I won't *make any money* [*profit*].

4【正しいと言える】▶そういう考えも成り立つ That kind of interpretation [That idea] is also *possible*. ‖ そんな理屈は成り立たない That reasoning *won't hold water*. (🏺 hold water は通例否定文で用いる).

なりて 成り手 ▶応援団長のなり手がなくて困ったなあ What shall we do? *Nobody wants to be* head of the cheering squad.

-なりに ▶彼女は自分なりに精いっぱいの努力をしているんだから, 大目に見てやれよ She is doing her best *in her own way*, so be lenient with her [go easy on her]. ‖ お父さんはお父さんなりにあなたの将来を心配しているのよ Your father is worrying about your future *in his own way*.

▶この路地を道なりに行けば, やがて駅に着きますよ If you just *go down* [*follow*] this alley, you will eventually arrive at the train station.

-なりの ▶その件に関しては私は私なりの考えを持っている I have *my own* ideas on that matter.

なりはてる 成り果てる ▶あの人も昔は肩で風を切っていたが, 哀れな姿になり果てたもんだ He used to walk around as if he owned the world, but he has *ended up* looking (pretty) pathetic [miserable].

なりひびく 鳴り響く ring out ▶1発の銃声が鳴り響いた A shot *rang out*. ‖ 深夜サイレンの音があたりに鳴り響いた A siren *went off* at midnight.
▶指揮者としての彼の名声は世界中に鳴り響いている His fame as a conductor *has spread* throughout the world.

なりふり ▶結婚したとたん彼はなりふりを構わなくなった Since he got married, he has *let himself go*. (➤ let oneself go は「身なりを気にしない」の意のインフォーマルな表現) ‖ その販売外交員はなりふり構わずノルマを達成しようとした The salesperson *fought tooth and claw* to make his sales quota. ／The salesperson tried to make his sales quota, *not caring what other people may think*. ‖ 彼はなりふり構わず親戚に借金を申し込んだ He *threw his pride to the wind* and asked his relatives to lend him money.

なりものいり 鳴り物入り ▶ダルビッシュ投手は鳴り物入りでレンジャーズに入団した Darvish joined the Rangers *with great* [*much*] *fanfare*.

なりゆき 成り行き course (自然の); **progress** (進展); an **outcome**(結果) ▶今後のなりゆきを見守るしかないだろう We'll just have to wait and see *how things turn out*. ‖ 多くの人が両国の会談のなりゆきを見守っている Many people are following the *progress* of the talks between the two countries. ‖ 話のなりゆきは予想できるものだった The *outcome* of the story could be predicted. ‖ 彼らは事態をなりゆきに任せることにした They decided to *let* things *take their own course* [*take care of themselves*]. ‖ しばらくはなりゆきに任せよう *Let things ride* for the time being. ‖ 自然のなりゆきに任せなさい *Let nature take its course*. ／*Let's things take their* (*natural*) *course*.

なりわい 生業 ▶彼は物書きを生業とする He *makes his living* as a writer.

[1]**なる 成る·為る·生る** **1【人がある役割·身分に変わる】become, be**(➤ 未来のことについては通例後者を用いる)

> **【文型】**
> **ある職業·物(A)になる**
> **become** [**be**] A
> **make** A
> ➤ A は名詞
>
> **【解説】** **become** がふつうの語だが, be going to や want to などの後で未来を表す場合は **be** のほうが好まれる. **make** はもともと備えた特質から望ましいものになるときに使う.

▶パイロットになるのが子供の頃からのぼくの夢だった It was my dream since childhood to *become* [*be*] a pilot. ‖ 大きくなったら何になりたい? What do you want to *be* when you grow up? ‖ 彼女ならいい奥さんになるだろう She will *be* a good wife. (➤ be の代わりに become を用いると,「今はよくないが, そのうちに」という含みになる) ／She will *make* a good wife. (➤ この make は「(変化·発達して)…になる」の意で, 素質があるという含みがある) ‖ 二人は理想的な夫婦になるだろう The two will *make* an ideal couple. ／I think they are a perfect match. ‖ この子とお友だちになってね Please *be* good friends with this boy.
▶今度, チームの主将になった I *was chosen* captain of our team recently. ‖ 息子はこの4月, 大学生になった My son *started* college this April.

2【ある状態に変わる】get, become (➤ get は become よりくだけた語); **go, turn**(➤ go は通例好ましくないことに用いる)

> **【文型】**
> **ある状態(A)になる**
> **become** A
> **get** A
> **grow** A
> **go** [**turn**] A
> ➤ A は形容詞
>
> **【解説】** (1) **become** が少し改まった表現なのに対し, **get** は口語的なくだけた言い方. 永続的な安定した状態には become を, 一時的な状態には get を使うことが多い.
> (2) **grow** は多少改まった語だが,「しだいに」というゆるやかな変化を表すのに使われる.
> (3) **go** と **turn** は色の変化や好ましくない状態になる場合に使われる.

▶最近, しのぶはずいぶんおしとやかになった Shinobu *has become* quite ladylike recently. ‖ 彼のすい臓炎は重くなった His pancreatitis *has become* serious. ‖ いじめが騒がれるようになったのはいつごろからだろう When did bullying *become* a social problem? ‖ 空が暗くなってきた The sky *is getting* dark. ‖ 試合はだんだんおもしろくなってきた The game *is getting* more (and more) exciting. ‖ 彼は働き過ぎて病気になった He *got* sick from overwork. ‖ 彼女は手紙を読むうちみるみる青くなった She visibly *turned* pale as she read the letter. ‖ 肉が悪くなった The meat *went* bad. ‖ なかなか思うようにはならないものだ Things *rarely go* as we wish [have planned].

> **【文型】**
> **…するようになる**(＝…し始める)
> **start** [**begin**] **to** do
> **…するようになる**(＝徐々に…の状態になる)
> **come** [**grow, get**] **to** do
> ➤ あとには like, know, love, realize などの知覚·感覚動詞が続く
> **(習熟·経験により)…するようになる**(＝習得する)
> **learn to** do

▶セーターを編んでいる間に雪になった It *started to* snow while I was knitting a sweater. ‖ 日本では明治時代に牛肉を食べるようになった People in Japan *began to* eat beef in the Meiji era. ‖ ラグビー部員たちは最近熱心に練習するようになってきた Recently, the members of the rugby team *have begun to* practice harder [more eagerly]. ‖ 友達の彼女を好きになっちゃったんだ I'*ve come* [*grown* ／*gotten*] to like my friend's girl. (● (×)become to do は不可; I've started to like ... とすると感情のこもった表現になる) ‖ いつ自転車に乗れるようになったの? When did you *learn* (*how*) *to* ride a bicycle?
▶じきに基礎的な英語はわかるようになるよ You'*ll* soon *be able to* understand basic English. ‖ 東京に何年か住んで, 納豆が食べられるようになった After living for several years in Tokyo, I *became able to* eat natto. (●「私は東京に住むようになって, 納豆が好きにな

った」だと After I began living in Tokyo, I came [grew, got] to like natto.).
▶彼は高校に入って遅刻しなくなった Now that he is in high school, he is *no longer* late for school [class].
▶野球中継が雨で中止になった The live baseball broadcast *was canceled* due to rain. ‖ 対話「ボスは君の提案にオーケーを出してくれるだろうか」「なるようになるさ」"Do you think the boss will accept your proposal?" "*Whatever happens, happens.*" (➤「成り行きに任せる以外にどうしようもない」の意).
3【他のものに変わる】change [**turn**]《into, to》▶王子は白鳥になった The prince *changed* [*turned*] *into* a swan. ‖ 水槽で飼っていたオタマジャクシがカエルになった The tadpoles in the aquarium *have turned* into frogs. ‖ 雨が雪になった The rain *turned to* snow. (● turn to は過程に, turn into は結果に力点がある).
4【ある時・数値に達する】be(➤ 経過よりも「なっている(だろう)」という状態を強調する) ; **turn** ((年齢・時刻などが)…に達する) ▶《年齢》私は来月17歳になる I*'ll be* [I*'m going to be*] 17 next month. ‖ 息子もやっと20歳になった My son *has* just *turned* twenty.
▶《時間》6時になったら生徒は全員下校すること The students are supposed to leave school *at* six. ‖ この建物はできてから100年になる This building was built one hundred years ago. ／This building is one hundred years old. ‖ 対話「東京へ出て来てどれくらいになりますか」「6年です」"How long *have* you *been* in Tokyo?" "(For) six years." ‖ 来年になれば景気も上向くだろう Next year, business should pick up. ‖ もう10日ほどで梅雨になる The rainy season will *come* [*set in*] in (another) ten days. ‖ 早く春にならないかなあ I wish spring would *come* soon. ‖ 冬になった Winter *has come*. ／Winter *is here*. (➤ この2つは「冬になったばかりだ」) ／It*'s* winter. (➤「冬だ」) ‖ 朝になった Morning *came*. (➤ 過去) ／It *is* morning. (➤「今, 朝だ」) ‖ すぐお昼になる It will soon *be* noon. ‖ 9時になった It*'s* nine o'clock.

> 【文型】
> …してから期間(A)になる
> **It has been** [《主に英》**is**] A **since ....**

▶結婚して5年になります *It has been* [*It is*] five years since we got married. (➤カッコ内は主に《英》) ／We*'ve been* married (for) five years.
▶《数値》8と18では26になる 8 and 18 *make* 26. ‖ 4に25を掛けると100になる 4 times 25 *is* 100. ‖ 60を5で割ると12になる 60 divided by 5 *equals* 12. ‖ 今月の売上は計100万円になった[いくらにもならなかった] Sales *amounted to* one million yen [*didn't amount to* anything] this month. (➤ amount to は「(金額が)合計…になる」) ‖ 対話「いくらになりますか」「税込みで合計9660円になります」"*How much do I owe you?*" "(The bill *comes to*) 9,660 yen, including tax."
5【ある機能・効果を果たす】▶来客用のソファーはふだんは猫のベッドになっている The sofas *are used* by our cats as beds when there are no guests.
▶この失敗は彼にはいい薬になったろう I think this failure *turned out to be* a good lesson for him. ‖ 専門家のアドバイスは大いに参考になる Advice from experts *is a* great *help*. ‖ 息子もときには助けになる My son sometimes *proves to be* a great help to me.
6【決定する】▶来月アメリカへ出張することになりました I *was told to* [I *have to*] make a business trip to the U.S. next month. (➤ was told は「指示された」の意) ‖ このままではきみが損をすることになる If things continue like this, you'll *end up* losing (money).
7【植物の実ができる】bear (木が実をつける) ; **grow**《on》(実が木に) ▶この柿(かき)の木はよくなる This persimmon tree *bears* [*fruits*] well. ‖ この木には何か実がなるんですか Does this tree *bear* any *fruit*? ‖ 庭の梅の木に実がなっている The ume tree in the garden *is bearing fruit* [*is fruiting*]. ‖ オレンジがたくさんなっている *There are* a lot of oranges on the tree. ／The orange tree *is bearing* a lot of fruit. ‖ ブドウが鈴なりになっている The grapes *are growing* in clusters. ‖ 金のなる木なんてないよ Money doesn't *grow on* trees.
8【できあがる】▶この陶器は人間国宝の手になるものだ This piece of pottery *was made by* an artist who has been designated as a human national treasure.
ことわざ ローマは1日にして成らず Rome was not built in a day.
9【構成される】consist《of》; **be made up**《of》▶理事会は30人のメンバーから成る The board of trustees *is made up of* thirty members. ‖ セ・パ両リーグともに6球団から成る Both the Central and Pacific Leagues *consist of* six club teams. ‖ フィリピンはおよそ7000の島から成る *There are* some 7,000 islands in the Philippines.
☛ なってない (→見出語)

²なる 鳴る **sound** ; **ring**(鐘・鈴・ベルなどが) ; **go off** (警報器・目覚まし時計などが突然) ▶学校のチャイムが鳴るのが聞こえた I heard the school chime *ring* [*sound*]. ‖ 電話が鳴ってるわよ. 出て The phone*'s ringing*. Please get [answer] it. ‖「ズドン!」と大砲が鳴った The gun *went*, "Bang!" ‖ 目覚まし時計が鳴り出した The alarm clock *went off*. ‖ 火災報知器は鳴らなかった The fire alarm *didn't go off*. ‖ 授業中に携帯(電話)が鳴った A cellphone *beeped* during class. ‖ 遠くで雷が鳴っている Thunder *is rumbling* [There is thunder] in the distance. ‖ 12時になったらグーッとおなかが鳴った At noon, my stomach began to *growl* [*rumble*].

ナルシスト a **narcissist** /ná:ʳsəsɪst/.

ナルシズム **narcissism** /ná:ʳsəsìzəm/.

なるべく **as ... as possible, as ... as** one **can** ▶あすはなるべく早く来てください (Please) come *as* early *as possible* tomorrow. ‖ なるべく両親には言わないようにしてください Please don't tell my parents *if you can help it*. (➤ if one can help it は「せずに済むものならば」) ‖ なるべくなら寒冷地には転勤したくない *Unless it's absolutely necessary*, I don't want to be transferred to a cold place. ‖ なるべくなら暖かい土地に転勤したい *If circumstances allow* [*If it is at all possible*], I would like to be transferred to a warm place.

なるほど **I see, indeed** ▶なるほどきみの言うとおりだ *Indeed*, you're right [it's just as you say]. ‖ なるほどこの店のコーヒーはおいしい This coffee shop *really* [*indeed*] serves good coffee. ‖ 対話「このボタンで安全装置が作動します」「なるほど」"This button activates the safety device." "*I see.*" ‖ 対話「海外旅行は体が楽に動くうちにしたほうがいいと思う」「なるほど」"It's best to travel abroad before you get too

old to move around easily." "*That's a good point*." (➤「的を得た発言だ」の意).
▶なるほど勝彦はりこうだがちょっと身勝手過ぎる *It is true that* Katsuhiko is smart, *but* he is too selfish. ／ Katsuhiko is smart, *to be sure*, *but* he is too selfish. (● to be sure を省いて is smart の is を強く発音してもよい) ‖ 彼らの主張はなるほどと思える Their argument is *quite convincing*.

なれ 慣れ practice ▶英会話は慣れが大事だからできるだけ話すようにしなさい *Practice* is important to improve your English conversational skills, so try to speak as often as possible.

なれあい 馴れ合い ▶なれ合いの試合 a *fixed* game [match] ／a *put-up* job (➤ ともにインフォーマルな言い方) ‖ 値上げは業界と役所のなれ合いの結果だった The price hike was the result of *collusion* [*a cozy relationship*] between industry and government figures.

ナレーション narration.

ナレーター a narrator /nǽreɪt̬ər/.

なれそめ 馴れ初め ▶きみたちのなれそめを聞かせてくれないか Tell us *how you first got to know each other*.

なれっこ 慣れっこ ▶おやじとおふくろのけんかには慣れっこになっている I'*m accustomed* [*used*] *to* Mom and Dad's quarrels.

なれなれしい 馴れ馴れしい (over) familiar, overfriendly ▶彼は誰とでもなれなれしい調子で話す He talks to anyone in an *overfamiliar* way. ‖ お客様になれなれしい口をきいてはいけません Don't go talking to our customers *in that overfriendly way*. ‖ 彼女になれなれしくするな Don't *get* [*be*] *fresh* with her. ‖ あの男はうちの娘といやになれなれしい口をきく The way that man talks to my daughter is unpleasantly *familiar*.

なれのはて 成れの果て ▶あれがぜいたくの限りを尽くした男のなれの果てだ This is *what has become* of the man who lived in such extreme luxury.

なれる 慣れる・馴れる

1【違和感を抱かなくなる】 get [become] used /juːst/ to, get [become] accustomed to

【文型】
あること(A)に慣れる
get used to A ➤ A は名詞
get accustomed to A
…することに慣れる
get used to doing
get accustomed to doing

【解説】「慣れる」の意では get がふつうだが, become や grow も使う.「慣れている」と状態を表すには be を使う.

▶粗食に慣れる *get* [*become*] *used to* a simple diet ‖ 電車での長距離通学には慣れています I'*m* quite *used* [*accustomed*] *to* the long train rides to school. ‖ 私, 育児にはまだ慣れてないの I'*m not used* [*accustomed*] *to* taking care of a child. ‖ 慣れない子守りで疲れた I'*m not used to* babysitting, so it really tired me out.
▶おばあちゃんはパソコンの扱いには慣れていない My grandma *is unfamiliar with* computers. ‖ 彼女はまだ仕事に慣れていないので作業が遅い She'*s new to* [*on*] the job, so she works slowly. ‖《外国人留学生に》日本語でレポートを書くのにずいぶん慣れてきたね You'*ve* really *gotten* the hang of writing papers in Japanese.
▶目が明るい日ざしに慣れる(＝適応する)のにしばらくかかった It took my eyes a short while to *adjust to* the bright sunlight. ‖ 彼女は慣れた手つきでおせんべいを焼いた She toasted the rice crackers *with a skilled hand*.

2【「…慣れる」の形で】 ▶あすのハイキングにははき慣れた靴をはいていらっしゃい For tomorrow's hike, wear shoes which you *have broken in*. (➤ break in は「(靴を)はき慣らす」) ‖ 映画での男女のキスシーンなど最近は見慣れてしまった We'*re not surprised when we see* [We'*re used to seeing*] men and women kissing in movies.

3【親しくなる, なつく】 become friendly《with》; become tame (動物が) ▶生徒たちは新任の先生になかなかなれない It takes time for the students to *become friendly with* [*warm up to*] a new teacher. ‖ どんなになれているように見えてもライオンなどの野獣は危険だ No matter how *tame* they look, wild animals such as lions are dangerous. ‖ アシカは人になれやすい Seals *are easily tamed*.

なわ 縄 a rope ▶麻縄 a hemp *rope* ‖ わらで縄をなう make *a* straw *rope* ‖ やじ馬が入らないように現場に縄が張られた *A rope* was stretched across the site to keep nosy onlookers out.
‖縄ばしご a rope ladder.

なわしろ 苗代 a bed for rice seedlings, a rice nursery.

なわとび 縄跳び jump(ing) rope, rope skipping ▶私は1日100回縄跳びをする I *jump* [*skip*] *rope* a hundred times a day. 《参考》「縄跳び用の縄」は a jump(ing) rope または a skip(ping) rope で,《英》では主に後者を用いる.

なわのれん 縄暖簾 a ***nawa-noren***; a straw-rope curtain hung at the entrance of an *izakaya* [a Japanese-style pub] (➤ 説明的な訳).

なわばり 縄張り a territory(動物の); turf(やくざなどの) ▶縄張り意識の強い犬 a *territorial* dog ‖ コマドリは自分の縄張りに入って来る他のコマドリを激しく攻撃する A robin fiercely attacks other robins that happen to fly into its *territory*. ‖ 俺たちの縄張りを荒らす気か? Are you out to [looking to] invade our *turf*? (➤ be out to do は「何としても…しようとする」, be looking to do は「…しようと思っている, …することをめざしている」) ‖ (東京の)池袋はぼくの縄張り(＝行きつけの場所)だ Ikebukuro is my *stomping ground*. ‖ あいつは縄張り意識の強い男だ He has a strong *sense of territory*.
‖(ギャングなどの)縄張り争い a turf war [battle].

[1]なん 難 **1【災難】** ▶私は事故機に乗り遅れて危うく難を逃れた I missed the flight and thereby *had a narrow* [*hairbreadth*] *escape* (*from death*).
ことわざ 一難去ってまた一難 Misfortunes never come singly [single]. ／When it rains, it pours.

2【困難】 (a) difficulty ▶ことし卒業する大学生は就職難だ *It's difficult* for college graduates *to get jobs* this year. ／The *shortage of jobs* is a serious problem to women graduates this year. ‖ 多くの人たちは住宅難で苦しんでいる Many people are suffering from *a housing shortage*.

3【欠点】 a defect ▶難を言えば彼は少し神経質だ His only *defect* is that he has a slightly nervous temperament.

☛ 難なく (→見出語)

[2]**なん** 何 **1【疑問を示して】what** ▶警察はホテル火災の原因が何であるか，まだつかんでいない The police haven't found *what* caused the hotel fire yet. ‖ これはいったい何だろう *What* could this be ? ‖ 対話「Y 高校が強い理由は何でしょう」「たぶんいい投手がいるからでしょう」"*What* do you think makes Y High School so strong ?" "Probably the fact that they have an outstanding pitcher." ‖ 対話「田中君，ちょっと」「何でしょうか？お呼びになりました？」"Mr. Tanaka." "*Yes ?* Did you call me ?"

▶ 対話「おもちゃ売り場は何階ですか」「5 階です」"*What floor* is the toy department (on) ?" "The fifth floor." ‖ 対話「富士山には何回登りましたか」「2 回です」"*How many times* have you climbed Mt. Fuji ?" "Twice." (→何回) ‖ 対話「こちらへ越して来たのは何歳のときだったの？」「5 歳のときです」"*How old* were you when you moved here ?" "I was five." ‖ 対話「このマンションには何世帯住んでいますか」「90世帯です」"*How many households* live in this condominium ?" "Ninety families (do)." ‖ 対話「きょうは何日だったっけ？」「6 月10日よ」"*What*'s today's *date* ? ／ *What*'s *the date* today ?" "(It's) June 10." (→何日) ‖ 対話「この学校の創立は何年ですか」「明治10年です」"*When* was this school founded ?" "In the tenth year of the Meiji period." (→何年).

2【不特定の数を示して】▶そのデモには何千人［何百人／何十人］もの主婦が参加した *Thousands of* [*Hundreds of* ／ *Dozens of*] housewives joined (in) the demonstration. (「何十もの」の意では tens of ... は用いない) ‖ 生態学者は何十日も島にこもって調査を続けた The ecologist spent *many days* on the island continuing his surveys. ‖ N 大学には何万人もの学生がいる N University has *tens of thousands of* students [*many thousands of* students]. (➤ 後者のほうがややインフォーマル) ‖ 同じ漢字を何百回も書いた I wrote the same kanji *hundreds of times*. ‖ あの画家はたしか90何歳まで生きたはずです I'm sure that painter lived *into his nineties*.

3【婉曲にぼかして】▶玄関で立ち話もなんだからまあ上がってください *It's not proper to* stand talking at the entrance, so please come on in. ‖ 母親の私が言うのもなんですけど，うちの子，勉強はできるんです I *might sound* like a proud mother, but our son is pretty smart. (➤「…のように聞こえるかもしれないが」の意) ／ I *don't mean to brag*, but my son is pretty bright. (➤「自慢話をするつもりはないが」の意) ‖ こう言っちゃなんだが，きみは少し部下に対する思いやりが欠けてるんじゃないかな *I don't want to offend you, but* I think you might be a bit inconsiderate of your staff members. (➤「きみを怒らせたくはないが」の意).

4【慣用表現】▶彼は自分の失敗にいつも何のかのと言い訳ばかりする He makes *all kinds of* excuses for his failures. ‖ 何の気なしに言ったことばが彼女を傷つけてしまった She was deeply hurt by something I *just* said *lightly*. ‖ ご用の折は何なりと［遠慮なく］お申しつけください If there's anything I can do, please *feel free to* ask [*don't hesitate to* ask].

☞ **何か，何だ，何だか，何て，何でもない，何と，何という，何と言っても，何ら** (→見出語)

[1]**なんい 南緯 the south latitude** ▶南緯10度15分，東経60度20分の地点でタンカーが沈没した A tanker sank at *lat*. 10° 15′ *S*., long. 60° 20′ E. (➤ at latitude ten degrees fifteen minutes south, longitude sixty degrees twenty minutes east と読む).

[2]**なんい 難易** ▶その 2 つの仕事の難易は決められない It's impossible to say *which* of the two jobs *is more difficult*. ‖ これらの問題は難易度によって分類されている These problems are classified according to [based on] their *difficulty*. ‖ T 大は入試難易度で日本のトップにランクされている The entrance examination of T University is ranked among *the most difficult* [is one of *the most difficult*] in Japan.

[3]**なんい 何位** ▶鈴木選手は100メートル背泳ぎで何位でしたか *How did* Suzuki *place* [*finish*] in the 100-meter backstroke ?

なんおう 南欧 Southern Europe.

[1]**なんか 軟化する soften** /sɔ́:fən/ ▶父は最初は憤慨していたが私が何度も謝るのでいくらか態度を軟化させた At first my father was furious with me, but his *attitude softened* a little after I had apologized many times.

[2]**なんか 何か** ▶なんか寒いなあ It's *a bit* cold. ‖ なんか忙しいよ I'm *kind of* busy. ‖ その企画，なんかだめみたいよ It seems the project won't go anywhere. ‖ 彼のこと，なんか好きになっちゃった I've *sort of* come to like him.

▶何かいいことないかなあ I wish *something* exciting would happen (to me).

[3]**なんか 南下する go south [southward].**

-なんか (この日本語は「…のようなもの」の意でけんそんや軽べつを表したり，断定をせず表現を和らげたりするときなどに用いるが，対応する英語はない.「なんか」を無視して訳すか，他の語を用いて全体の意味を表すしかない).

1【同類のものを示して】▶ 対話「玲子たちの結婚祝い，何にしようかしら」「時計なんかどうかな」"What should we give Reiko and her fiancé as a wedding gift ?" "How about a clock ?"

2【けんそんや軽べつを示して】▶私なんかいないほうがせいせいするでしょ You feel (more) relaxed when I'm not with you, don't you ? ‖ 彼は大作曲家なんかではない He is *no* great composer. ‖ それはダイヤモンドなんかじゃないよ It *can't* be a diamond. (➤ この can't は「…のはずがない」の意) ‖ きみなんかに期待するものか I don't expect anything from you.

[1]**なんかい 何回 how many times, how often**

> **【文型】**
> **何回…ですか？**
> **How many times ... ?**
> **How often ... ?**
>
> **《解説》** (1)**How many times ...** ? は回数を聞くときに使う. すぐ後に a day（1 日につき), a week（1 週間につき）などを付けると頻度を聞く言い方になる.
> (2)**How often ...** ? はふつう，現在形の動詞とともに用いて，習慣的または定期的に行うことの頻度を聞く. すぐ後に a day や a week などを付けない.

▶一夏に何回ぐらい海に泳ぎに行きますか *How many times* [*How often*] do you go swimming in the sea each summer ? ‖ 何回言ったらわかるの？ *How many times* do I have to tell you ? (➤「何回言わなきゃいけないの」の意) ‖ 対話「海外旅行は(これで)何回目ですか」「3 回目です」"(Including this trip,) *How many times* have you been abroad ?" "Three times."

▶光夫さんとは何回かデートしたことがあるわ I've gone out with Mitsuo *several times*. ‖『ローマの休日』は何回も見た I have seen "Roman Holiday" many times. ‖ 何回電話しても浩美は不在だった *Every time* I phoned, Hiromi was out. ‖ 彼は何回も何回もそれをやってみたがうまくいかなかった He tried it *again and again* [*over and over again*], but it didn't work. ▶《野球で》今, 何回? *What inning* is it?

2**なんかい 難解な** **difficult**; **recondite**(一般人には理解しにくい) ▶難解な詩 a poem *difficult to understand* ‖ 彼の難解な地球物理学の研究 his *recondite* studies of geophysics ‖ この小説の英語は難解過ぎて高校生向きではない The English in this novel is *too difficult* for high school students *to understand*.

なんかん 難関 (a) **difficulty**(困難); a **hurdle** (障害) ▶難関を切り抜ける overcome the *difficulty* / get over the *hurdle* ‖ 彼は現役で入試の難関を突破した He cleared [got over] the entrance exam *hurdle* on his first try. ‖ M大学は難関だ Admissions to M University *are highly competitive*. (➤「競争が激しい」の意).

なんぎ 難儀 ▶旅行中病気になって難儀した I *had a hard time* because I fell ill during my trip. ‖ その力士は正座するのが難儀のようだ It seems *difficult* for the sumo wrestler to sit in seiza.

なんきゅう 軟球 →軟式.

1**なんきょく 南極** **the South Pole**(南極点); **the Antarctic** (南極地方) 一形 **南極の** **Antarctic**
‖南極海 the Southern Ocean ‖ 南極圏 the Antarctic Circle ‖ 南極大陸 Antarctica, the Antarctic continent ‖ 南極探検 an Antarctic exploration.

2**なんきょく 難局** **a difficult situation, a difficulty**(困難な事態); a **crisis**(危機) ▶難局にうまく対処する cope with *a difficult situation* ‖ 難局を乗り切る overcome a *crisis* [*difficult situation*].

なんきん 軟禁 **house arrest** ▶その反体制学者は2か月間自宅に軟禁されていた The dissident scholar *was under house arrest* [*was confined to his house*] for two months.

なんきんじょう 南京錠 a **padlock**.

なんくせ 難癖 ▶運転がへたなくせに彼は車に難癖をつけた Although it's obvious that his driving was at fault, he *blamed everything on* his car. ‖ 彼女はいつも人に難癖をつけてばかりいる She's always *nitpicking*. ‖ 島課長はきまって部下に難癖をつける Section Chief Shima *is* always *too critical of* his subordinates.

1**なんこう 軟膏** (an) **ointment** /ɔ́intmənt/ ▶傷口にペニシリン軟こうを塗る apply penicillin *ointment* to a cut.

2**なんこう 難航** ▶参加者が皆優秀だったのでチャンピオンの決定は難航した It *was difficult* to pick a champion because the other participants were all excellent. ‖ 組閣は難航している The formation of the new cabinet *is making slow progress*. / The formation of the new cabinet *is proceeding with difficulty* [*slowly*].

なんこうふらく 難攻不落 ▶難攻不落の城 an *impregnable* [*indestructible*] castle (➤前者が日本語に近い; 後者は「破壊できない」)

なんごく 南国 a **southern country** ▶彼女は南国育ちなので, 北海道の寒さはこたえるようだ She was brought up in *the south*, so Hokkaido's cold (climate) seems to be hard on her.

なんこつ 軟骨 《解剖学》 **cartilage** /kɑ́:ʳṭəlɪdʒ/.

なんさい 何歳 →いくつ.

なんざん 難産 a **difficult** [**hard**] **delivery** ▶長男が生まれたときには難産だった My wife had *a difficult delivery* when our first son was born.

なんじ 何時 **what time**; **when** (いつ) ▶目覚まし何時にセットしておくの? *What time* do you want me to set the alarm clock for? ‖ 対話「今何時ですか」「4時50分です」"*What time* is it? / *What's the time*? / *What time* do you have?" "It's 4:50." (➤ four fifty と読む) ‖ 対話「すみません, 今何時でしょうか」「私の時計では4時53分です」"Excuse me. Do you have *the time*? / Could you tell me *the time*?" "Yes. It's 4:53 according to my watch [by my watch]." (● (1)Do you have the time? は「時計をお持ちですか」の意. (2)Yes をつけるとていねいに響く).
▶あすは何時から何時までご在宅ですか? *From when to when* [*From what time to what time* / *When*] will you be at home tomorrow? ‖ あした何時に車で迎えに行こうか *When* [*What time*] do you want me to come to pick you up tomorrow? (● 日本語に近いのは what time だが, 英語では when で聞くことが多い) ‖ この店は何時まで開いていますか *How late* is this store open? (● 視点を変えて「何時に閉店ですか」と考えれば What time do you close? とか When do you close? のようにも訳せる) ‖ 何時になっても彼女は現れなかった *Though it got later and later*, she never did show up.

なんしき 軟式 ‖軟式テニス soft tennis ‖ 軟式野球 rubberball baseball.
《参考》軟式テニスも軟式野球もともに日本で生まれて発達したスポーツ.

なんじゃく 軟弱な **soft**(やわらかい); **weak**(弱い) ▶この辺は地盤が軟弱で高層ビルは建たない A high-rise building cannot be built here because the ground is *not hard enough* [*is too soft*]. ‖ 日本の外交は軟弱(=弱腰)だと批判された Japanese diplomacy was criticized as being *too weak-kneed*.

なんじゅう 難渋 ▶思わぬ台風にぶつかって, 予定どおり目的地にたどり着くのに難渋したよ Being hit by an unexpected typhoon, we *had great difficulty* reaching the destination on schedule.

なんしょ 難所 a **dangerous place**(危険な所); a **difficult place to pass**(山道の) ▶駅伝選手たちは箱根越えの難所にさしかかった The ekiden [long distance relay] runners were approaching Hakone Pass, which is *the most difficult part* of the course.

なんしょく 難色 ▶幹事長の提案に総理は難色を示した The Prime Minister *expressed reservations about* the secretary general's plan. (➤ reservations は「全面的には同意できない気持ち, 懸念」).

なんすい 軟水 **soft water**. →硬水.

なんせい 南西 **the southwest** 《略 SW》 ▶南西の風が吹いている The wind is blowing *from the southwest*. ‖ 伊豆半島は東京の南西の方角にある The Izu Peninsula is (to *the*) *southwest* of Tokyo.
‖南南西 south-southwest (➤ SSW と略す).

ナンセンス **nonsense** 一形 **ナンセンスな** **nonsensical** /nɑ̀:nsénsɪkəl/ ▶砂漠で野菜を作ろうなんてナンセンスだよ To try to grow vegetables in the desert is *nonsense*. ‖ 彼女の発言は全くナンセンスだ Her remarks *don't make any sense* at all. ‖『不思議の

国のアリス』はナンセンスなところがおもしろい The *nonsensical* parts of "Alice in Wonderland" are interesting.

‖ナンセンス漫画 nonsensical comic strips.

なんだ 何だ 1【いらだち・挑戦の気持ちを示して】▶社長が何だ！*To hell with* the president！(➤ to hell with は「…なんかくそくらえだ」の意の俗語) ‖このくらいの寒さが何だ！*I don't give a damn about* this cold weather. (➤ not give a damn about は「…はちっとも気にしない」の意の俗語) ‖10キロ走るくらい何だ！Running ten kilometers — *it's nothing* [*a piece of cake*]！

▶何だ，それが親に向かって言うことばか！*What!* How dare you say such a thing to your parents！‖だから何だと言うんだ！*So what?* ‖何だと？もういっぺん言ってみろ！*What did you say?* Say that again！

2【意外な気持ちを示して】▶なんだ，おまえか *Oh,* it's you！‖なんだ，簡単じゃないか *Why,* it's easy！‖なんだ，彼女もう帰っちゃったの？*What* [*Oh, my*]*!* Has she gone home already？(🔊 Oh, my！は主に女性が用いる).

なんだい 難題 ▶それは難題だねえ That's *a tough question* [*a difficult problem*].

なんたいどうぶつ 軟体動物《動物学》a **mollusk** /mɑ́ːləsk/.

なんだか 何だか 1【なんのことか】▶何だか知らないけど，おもしろそうね It sounds interesting, although I don't know *exactly what it is*.

2【なんとなく】**somehow, for some reason (or other)** →何となく ▶部屋は何だか様子が違うように見えた The room *somehow* looked different. ‖彼女は何だかうれしそうな顔をしている She looks happy *for some reason or other*. ‖あなたが行ってしまって，私は何だか悲しいわ I feel *sort of* sad because you've gone. (➤ sort of は「ちょっと」の意のインフォーマルな言い方) ‖あなた，きょうは何だか変よ (=あなたらしくない) You're not yourself [your usual self] today. ‖何だか夢のようだ This is (*just*) *like* a dream.

なんだかんだ 何だかんだ ▶彼女，何だかんだとうるさいね She *always finds fault*. It's really annoying. (➤ find fault は「あら探しする」) ‖何だかんだ言っても横綱は強い The yokozuna is strong *no matter what people say* about him.

なんだったら 何だったら if you like (お望みならば) ▶何だったら宿題を手伝ってあげてもいいよ I can help you with your homework *if you like*.

なんだって 何だって 1【疑問を示して】▶何だって，バスはもう出ちゃったって？*What?* Has the bus left already？

▶何だってこんな遅くに人の家に電話をかけてくるんだ *Why on earth* did you call me this late at night？(🔊 on earth を the hell とすると，乱暴で下品な言い方になる) ‖何だって彼女はあんなことをしたんだろう *What* made her do such a thing, *I wonder*？

2【何でも】**anything** ▶ 対話「今夜，何が食べたい？」「何だっていいよ」"What would you like for dinner?" "*Anything* will be fine."

▶その気になりさえすれば何だってやれるさ You can do *anything* if you really put your mind to it.

なんたん 南端 the southernmost point [**tip**／**end**] ▶佐多岬は九州の最南端にある Cape Sata is at *the southernmost point* [*tip*] of Kyushu.

なんちゃくりく 軟着陸 a soft landing ▶月に軟着陸する *make a soft landing* on the moon.

なんちゅうする 南中する《天文学》**culminate** /kʌ́lmɪneɪt/ ‖**太陽の南中時刻** solar noon.

なんちょう 難聴 hearing impairment ▶うちの子は難聴です My son [daughter] is *hard of hearing*.

なんて 何て how, what

> 〈文型〉
> **なんて…だろう！**
> **How** ＋形容詞［副詞］(＋ S ＋ V)！
> **What** (a)＋(形容詞)＋名詞(＋ S ＋ V)！
> 《解説》(1)日常会話では文尾の S＋V はしばしば省略される.
> (2)この2つは日本人が思っているほど頻繁には使わない. 特に，How ...！はやや形式ばった表現で，古風な印象を与える.

▶なんてきれいなんだろう *How* beautiful！(🔊 It's really beautiful, isn't it？がふつうの表現) ‖なんてかわいい子犬だろう *What* a cute puppy！(🔊 子犬が複数いれば What cute puppies！となる) ‖なんてひどい天気だ *What* awful weather！(🔊 what のあとの名詞が不可算名詞の場合は a [an] はつかない) ‖なんておっちょこちょいなんだ，おまえは！*What* a scatterbrain you are！‖なんてことをしてくれたんだ Look *what* you've done. ‖なんてばかなことをしてしまったんだろう *What* a stupid thing I've done！

▶なんて父親なの，あなたは！恥ずかしいと思いなさいよ *What kind of* father are you？／*Some* father you are！You should be ashamed of yourself.

-なんて ▶幽霊なんて信じないね I (simply) don't believe in *such things as* ghosts. ‖学校をやめるなんて何かあったの？What happened *to* make you quit school？‖トムに金を貸すなんて，きみはなんて愚かなんだ How silly of you *to* lend Tom money！‖きみにこんな所で会うなんて！*What a surprise to* meet you here！‖あんないんちきな男が医者だなんて聞いてあきれる That creep is a doctor？You must be kidding. ‖あのけちが施設に毎年寄付してたなんて驚くね Did that cheapskate donate money annually to the institution？I can't believe it. ‖「だめ」なんて言わないで Don't say no (to that).

なんで 何で why. →なぜ.

なんてったって 何てったって →何と言っても.

なんでも 何でも

1【どんな物でも】**anything** (どんな物も)；**everything** (どれもこれも)；**whatever** (どんな…でも)；**what it takes** (必要なこと) ▶うちの犬は何でも食べる Our dog eats *anything*. ‖あいつは何でも金で片がつくと思っている He thinks he can settle *anything* with money.／He thinks money solves *everything*. ‖彼はプロレスのことならほとんど何でも知っている He knows *almost everything* about pro wrestling. ‖次の時間は何でも好きなことをしてよろしい You may do *whatever* you like during the next period. ‖家族を守るために必要なことは何でもする I'll do *whatever it takes* to protect my family.

▶ 対話「夕食ですが，お好きなものありますか」「何でもかまいません. あなたがお決めになるものでけっこうです」"Do you have any preferences for dinner？" "*Anything is okay*. Whatever you decide will be fine." ‖ 対話「おなかすいちゃった，お母さん」「何が食べたい？」「食べ物なら何でもいいよ」"I'm hungry, Mom." "What do you want to eat？" "*Anything will be fine* as long as it is food."

‖**何でも屋** a jack-of-all-trades.

2【人から聞いて】▶なんでも中川のやつ，恵子に振られた

ってうわさだ *I don't know for sure*, but there's a rumor that Keiko dumped Nakagawa. (➤「確かなことはわからないが」の意).

なんでもない 何でもない ▶そのくらいの金は彼にとって何でもない That sum of money is *nothing* at all to him. ‖ 彼は親類でも何でもない He is *no* relation to me *whatsoever*. (➤ whatsoever は whatever の強調語で否定を強めている) ‖ 二人は何でもないことでよくけんかする The couple often quarrel over *small things*. ‖ やってみなさいよ, 何でもないわよ Give it a try. *There's nothing to it!* ‖ 対話「どうかしたの？」「何でもないよ」"What's the matter?" "*Nothing*."

1**なんてん 難点** a **weakness**, a **weak point** (弱点); a **drawback** (好ましくない点); **trouble** (困ること) ▶ビニールは熱に弱いのが難点だ The *weakness* [*drawback*] of plastic is that it is easily affected by heat. ‖ この薬の難点は人によって副作用があることだ The *trouble* with this medicine is that it has side effects for some people.

2**なんてん 何点** ▶《野球で》今何点なの？ *What's the score* now? ‖ 対話「テスト, 何点だった？」「72点だった」"*What* (*score*) did you get on the test?" "I got a (score of) 72." ／《英また》"*How many points* did you get in the test?" "I got 72."

ナンテン 《植物》 a **nandina**, a **celestial bamboo**.

なんと 何と 1【疑問を示して】**what** (何); **how** (どのように) ▶「天の川」は英語で何と言いますか *How do you say* 'Amanogawa' in English? ／*What do you call* 'Amanogawa' in English? ／*What is* the English (word) for 'Amanogawa'? (➤ 最後はやや改まった言い方) ‖ 今, 何とおっしゃいました？ Excuse me. *Could you repeat that?* ／*What* did you say just now? ／I beg your pardon? (● 決まり文句; 最後を上昇調で言う) ‖ 彼女がやって来たら何と言いましょうか *What* shall I say when she comes?
▶私は何と答えたらよいのかわからなかった I didn't know *what* [*how*] to answer. ‖ 何とお礼を申し上げてよいかわかりません I don't know *how* to express my gratitude. ／I *cannot* thank you *enough*. ‖ きみが何と言おうとあの車を買うことをあきらめないよ *No matter what you* (*may*) *say*, I won't give up on buying the car. ‖ 人が何と言おうが構わない I don't care [mind] *what people* (*may*) *say*.
2【感嘆を示して】▶彼はなんとご飯を5杯もお代わりした He had an *unbelievable* five extra helpings of rice. (➤ unbelievable は「考えられない, 信じられない」の意) ‖ 彼女はなんとはだしで追いかけてきた *To my amazement*, she ran after me barefooted. (➤「驚いたことには」の意でかなり堅い言い方. ふつうは I was amazed that she ... のような言い方をする) ‖ なんとみごとな桜だろう！ *What* beautiful cherry blossoms! (→何て, 何という) ‖ 時間のたつのはなんと速いこと！ Time *really* flies! ／*How* fast time flies! (➤ How の感嘆文は会話ではあまり使わない; →何て).

1**なんど 何度** 1【温度, 角度】▶この部屋［温泉］の温度は何度ですか *What's the temperature* in this room [of this hot spring]? ‖ この角は何度ですか *How many degrees* is this angle?
2【回数】▶私たちはその温泉が気に入って何度も出かけた We took a liking to that hot spring resort and went there *many times* [*over and over again*]. ‖ 運転免許試験は何度受けてもよい You can take the driving test *any number of times*. ‖ 何度言ったらわかるんだ？ *How many times* do I have to tell you before you understand? →何回.

2**なんど 納戸**

> 《解説》(1)これに相当するものに **utility room** (掃除機・暖房器具などをしまっておく), **storeroom**, **storage room** (ともに物置), **closet** (食料・台所用具・陶器, または衣類などをしまっておく) などがあるが, 《英》の **boxroom** (スーツケース・家具・衣類などをしまっておく) がその用途からいって最も「納戸」に近い.
> (2)わが国のマンションで「納戸」と呼んでいる場所のほとんどは storeroom, storage room である.

なんという 何という 1【疑問を示して】**what** ▶それは何という会社ですか *What is the name* of that company? ‖ 何という題だったか忘れたが, その話は一度読んだことがある I have read the story before, although I can't remember *what* the title is. (➤ 後半を簡略に although I can't remember the title. とすることもできる).
2【感嘆を示して】**how**, **what** →何て ▶何という寒さだ It *really* is cold! (➤ How cold it is! は形式ばった表現でふつう言わない; →何て) ‖ 何というすばらしい眺めだ *What* a splendid view! ‖ 何といういいお天気！ *What* lovely weather! ／*Isn't* the weather lovely! (● 後者のように否定疑問文や普通の疑問文の語順のまま, 感嘆文にすることも多い).

なんといっても 何と言っても ▶彼は失敗したが, 何と言ってもまだ仕事に慣れていないからしかたがない He didn't succeed, but, *after all*, he is new at the job. ‖ イギリスではのどが渇いたときには何と言ってもシャンディーだ In England, *there is nothing like* a shandy when you are thirsty.

なんとう 南東 **the southeast** 《略 SE》
‖南南東 south-southeast (➤ SSE と略す).

なんとか 何とか 1【不定の内容に言及して】▶さっきから黙ってばかりいるけど, 何とか言ったらどうだ You have kept silent the whole time. *Why don't you speak up?* ‖ あいつは何とかかんとか口実を見つけて仕事をサボる He is always getting out of work *on some pretext or other*.
2【不明の人・物を指して】▶何とかさん Mr. [Mrs. ／ Miss ／ Ms.] *So-and-so* ‖ 山何とかさん *Yama-something-or-other* (➤ Yama what's-her [his]-name でもよい) ‖ 何とか工務店の佐藤さんから電話がありました Mr. Sato of *such and such* construction company called.
3【現状より好ましい状態を示して】▶いざとなれば何とかなるものさ When the time comes you'll *find a way*. ‖ 駅前の放置自転車を何とかしてほしい Please *do something about* [*with*] the bicycles left in front of the station. (● about は問題解決を, with はものの処分を表す) ‖ この臭い何とかならない *Can't you do something about* this smell?
4【やりくりして】**somehow** ▶彼は何とかその仕事を終えた *Somehow* he finished [He *managed to* finish] the job. ‖ 留学費用は自分で何とかする I'll *somehow come up with* the money for my overseas study program. ‖ これだけあれば今月は何とかやっていけそうだ With this much money, I think I can *manage to* get by this month. ‖ 自分の力で何とかやってみようと思います I think I will *manage* by myself.

なんとかして 何とかして ▶何とかして夏休み中に運転免許を取りたいんだ I want to get a driver's license during the summer vacation, *no matter what*. ‖ 我々は何とかしてきみをバックアップしたい We

な

want to support you *one way or another* [*somehow or other*].

なんとしても 何としても at all cost, at any cost(是が非でも) ▶今度の試合は何としても勝ちたい I *would give anything* to win this game. ‖ 彼は転勤の話を何としても承知しない He *just won't accept* the company order to transfer.

なんとでも 何とでも ▶何とでも言えよ. 俺は行かないと言ったら行かないんだ Say *what(ever) you like*. I said I won't go, so I won't go. ‖ 買うなら今だ. 金はあとから何とでもなるさ If you are going to buy it, now is the time. You can *manage* the money *somehow* later.

なんとなく 何となく somehow, for some reason (or other) ▶きょうは何となく体がだるい *Somehow* I feel sluggish today. / *I don't know why*, but I feel sluggish today. ‖ あの人は何となくおかしな人だ There is *something* funny about her [him]. ‖ ぼくは何となく彼女にひかれた I was drawn to her *for some reason* (*or other*). ‖ 何となく彼は来ないような気がする *Something tells me* that he may not show up. ▶グループで話しているうちに, 何となく木村がリーダー役みたいなことになった While we were discussing it in our group, Kimura *emerged as* the leader. ‖ 毎日をただ何となく過ごす若者が多くなった More and more young people live *aimlessly* these days. ‖ 対話「どうして吉田が嫌いなんだい?」「何となく」"How come you don't like Yoshida?" "*I don't know exactly why*."

なんとも 何とも 1【下に打ち消しの語を伴って「どのようにも」】▶痛くも何ともありません I feel [have] *no* pain *at all*. ‖ 医者の診断では何ともないということだった The doctor said there was *nothing the matter* with me. ‖ この子はうそをつくのを何とも思っていない This boy [girl] *thinks nothing of* lying. ▶母と離婚した理由を何度も尋ねたが, 父は何とも答えてくれなかった Although I asked my father repeatedly why he divorced my mother, he *wouldn't* answer. ‖ 彼の命が助かるかどうかは何とも言えない I *can't say anything definite* as to whether he will survive. (➤「明確なことは言えない」の意).

2【全く】▶何ともお粗末な映画だった I found the film *quite awful*. ‖ 何とも申しわけありません *I don't know how* to apologize to you. / I'm *awfully* sorry. ‖ 何ともお礼の申し上げようもありません I have *no* words to thank you. / I *can't* thank you *enough*.

なんなく 難なく without difficulty, with ease ▶テーセウスは難なく迷宮から脱出した Theseus found his way out of the labyrinth *without difficulty* [*with ease*]. ‖ 法案は衆議院を難なく通過した The bill *sailed through* the House of Representatives.

なんなら 何なら ▶なんならあした彼女に会ってみるよ I'll see her tomorrow, *if you like*. (➤「きみが希望するなら」の意) ‖ なんなら私が行きましょう *If necessary*, I'll go instead. (➤「必要なら」の意) ‖ きみ1人で行くのがなんなら, ぼくも一緒に行ってあげるよ *If* you *feel uncomfortable* going alone, I'll go with you. (➤「不安なら」の意).

なんなりと 何なりと ▶おわかりにならないことがありましたら何なりとお聞きください If there is anything you don't understand, please *feel free* to ask.

なんにち 何日 ▶バレエの発表会は何日なの? *When* is your ballet recital? ‖ 対話「きょうは何日だっけ?」「23日」"*What's* today's *date*? / *What's the date* today?" "It's the twenty-third." (◉序数で言う) ‖ 対話「島根には何日行っているの?」「9日だよ」"*How many days* will you be gone to Shimane?" "(For) nine days."

なんにも 何にも 1【何も】▶暗くて何にも見えない It's so dark I can't see *a thing* [see *anything*]. ‖ 私はそんなことは何にも知りません I don't know *anything* about it. / I know *nothing* about it. ‖ 冷蔵庫には何も残っていない There is *nothing* left in the fridge. ‖ 何にもありませんが, 遠慮なく召し上がってください *This is nothing special* [*fancy*], but please help yourself to what's here. (➤「ごちそうではありませんが」の意; ◉「何にもありませんが」はきわめて日本的な表現で, 文字どおり There is nothing. では意味をなさない.「大したごちそうはありませんが」ぐらいに考えて英訳する).

2【「何にもならない」の形で】▶せっかくの彼の苦労も何にもならなかった His best efforts *came to nothing* [*went down the drain*]. (➤後者はインフォーマルな表現).

なんにん 何人 ▶あなたの会社の従業員は何人ですか *How many* employees are there in your company? ‖ 友だちの何人かがピアスをしている *Some* of my friends have had their ears pierced. ‖ そう考える人は何人もいる There are *many people* who think so. ‖ 対話「家族は何人?」「5人です」"*How many people* are there in your family?" "Five."

なんねん 何年 1【年度】▶ことしは何年ですか *What year* is this? ‖ きみは高校の何年ですか *What grade* [(英) *form*] are you in at (senior) high school? (◉大学なら What year とする) ‖ メキシコにおられたのは何年から何年までですか *When* [*What years*] were you in Mexico? ‖ 対話「あなたは平成何年生まれ?」「7年です」"*In what year* of Heisei were you born?" "In the 7th year."

2【年数】▶それは何年前の出来事ですか *How many years ago* did that occur? ‖ 私は何年も帰省していません I haven't returned home *for years*. ‖ 何年もお会いしていませんでしたね I haven't seen you *for ages*. ‖ 対話「結婚なさって何年ですか」「3年です」"*How many years* have you been married?" "(For) three years." / "*When* [*What year*] did you get married?" "Three years ago." (➤後者の答えは, "In 2008." のように言ってもよい).

なんの 何の 1【疑問を示して】what ▶いったい何の騒ぎだ *What's this fuss* (*all*) *about*? ‖ きょうは何の日? *What's special* about today? / *What day is it* today? (◉後者は曜日を聞く場合にも用いる) ‖ いったい何のことですか *What* in the world are you talking about? / *What* are you trying to say? ‖ きみは何の用でここへ来たの? *What*'s brought you here? ‖ 数学を勉強して何の役にたつのですか *What use* is studying mathematics (to me)? / *What's the use of* studying mathematics? ‖ きみは何のために大学へ行くのか *What* do you want to go to college *for*?

2【少しも…ない】▶この切手はコレクターにとって何の価値もない This postage stamp has *no* value *at all* for collectors. ‖ その後宏美からは何の連絡もない I have heard *nothing* [haven't heard *a thing*] from Hiromi since then. ‖ 彼女は何のためらいもなくデザイナーの仕事をやめた She gave up her career as a designer *without any* hesitation.

3【感嘆を示して】▶うれしかったのなんのって *You can't imagine how* happy I was. (➤ happy に強勢を置く) ‖ こわかったのなんのって *Was I* scared! (◉強調の

ために倒置構文になっている. 疑問文と区別するために I に強勢を置く) ／I was scared *to death.* ／I was *really* scared.

4【さまざまの内容を示して】▶博はちょっと成績が下がったら, 進学はあきらめるのなんのと言い出した Hiroshi began to say he would give up on going on to college *and stuff like that* when he saw his grades began to slip a bit.

5【慣用表現】 **何のかの** ▶嫁に行った娘は何のかの言ってはしょっちゅう帰って来る Our daughter, who got married and moved out, frequently returns *on some pretext or other.* **何のことはない** ▶頭が割れるように痛かったので医者へ行ったら, 何のことはない, ただのかぜだった I went to see the doctor because I had a splitting headache. However, it *turned out to be nothing* but a common cold. ‖電球が切れているのかと思ったが, 何のことはない, コンセントが抜けていた I thought the light bulb had burned out, but *the truth was just that* it had been unplugged. **何のその** ▶不況も何のその, その会社は急成長している That company is growing rapidly *despite* [*in the face of*] the recession.

¹なんぱ 難破 a **shipwreck** /ʃíprek/ **━動 難破する be wrecked** /rekt/ ▶その船は沖合い10キロのところで暗礁に乗り上げ難破した The ship *was wrecked* on a submerged rock ten kilometers offshore. ‖台風で多くの船が難破した The typhoon *caused* many *shipwrecks*. ‖**難破船** a wreck, a wrecked ship.

²なんぱ 軟派 ▶彼らは六本木の街角で女の子たちをナンパした They *picked up* girls on the street in Roppongi. (➤ pick up は「ひっかける」の意) ‖あいつはナンパしやすい女だ She's *an easy pick-up*.

ナンバー a **number**(番号) ; a **registration number**(自動車の登録番号) ▶その書類に1つ1つナンバーを打ってください Give *a number* to each of those documents. ／*Number* each of those documents. (➤ 動詞用法) ‖あれは大阪ナンバーの車だ That car bears an Osaka *license plate* [《英》 *number plate*]. ‖**ナンバープレート** 《米》 a license plate, 《英》 a number plate.

ナンバーワン number one 《略 No. 1》 ▶歌のうまさでは美空ひばりはナンバーワンだった In terms of singing ability, Misora Hibari was *number one*. ‖彼は日本野球界のナンバーワンピッチャーだ He is the *number one* [*top*] pitcher in Japan.

なんばん 何番

1【番号】▶《まちがい電話に対して》何番におかけですか *What number* are you calling? ‖一郎おじさんのところの電話番号, 何番? *What is* Uncle Ichiro's phone *number*? ‖高橋選手の背番号は何番ですか *What's* Takahashi's uniform *number*?

▶《試験などで》何番の問題が難しかった? *Which* problems were difficult (for you)? ‖彼女(の成績)はクラスで何番? *Where* does she *stand* in her class? ／*What's her class rank?* ／*What's her rank in class?* ‖《野球で》鈴木は何番を打っていますか *What*'s Suzuki's batting *order*? ／*Where* does Suzuki bat [*stand* in the batting order]?

2【番目, いくつ目】▶桜町は何番目の駅ですか *How many* stops *away* is Sakura-machi? ‖あなたはきょうだいの何番目? *Which* (*number*) child are you in your family? ‖**対話**「大阪市は日本で何番目に人口の多い都市ですか」「3番目です」"*Where* does the city of Osaka *rank* in population in Japan?" "Third." ‖**対話**「ケネディーは何番目の大統領ですか」「35番目です」"*How many* presidents were there *before* Kennedy?" "There were thirty-four." (● What number president was Kennedy? と聞いてもよいが一般的ではない).

なんびょう 難病 an **intractable disease**(治療の難しい ; /ɪntrǽktəbəl/ と発音) ; an **incurable disease** (不治の).

なんぴょうよう 南氷洋 the Antarctic /æntɑ́ːrktɪk/ **Ocean** (➤ 2000年に the Southern Ocean (南極海) に呼称変更された).

なんぶ 南部 the southern part, the south ; the South (米国の) ▶昨夜関東南部に大雨が降った There was a heavy rain in *the southern part* of the Kanto district last night. ‖彼は米国南部の生まれだ He was born in *the South* of the U. S. ／He is a Southerner by birth. ／He is from *the South* (of the U.S.). ‖(米国の)**南部諸州** the Southern States(➤ そのうちの最南部を the Deep South という).

なんぶつ 難物 a **person hard to deal with,** 《インフォーマル》 a **hard nut to crack**(人) ; a **difficult** [**hard**] **problem** (難問)

なんべい 南米 South America ━形 南米の South American ‖**南米諸国** South American countries ‖**南米大陸** South America, the South American continent.

¹なんべん 軟便 a **loose stool, soft feces.**

²なんべん →**何回.**

なんぽう 南方 the south ▶大島は東京の南方にある Oshima is *to the south* of Tokyo. ‖彼女は南方系の顔だちだ Her features are typical of those of *southern* Japan.

なんぼく 南北 north and south(➤ 語順に注意) ▶日本は南北に長い島国だ Japan is an island country stretching [extending] *from north to south.*
‖**南北アメリカ** North and South America ; the Americas (中央アメリカを含む) ‖(合衆国の)**南北戦争** the Civil War ‖**南北問題** the North-South problem.

なんみん 難民 refugees /rèfjʊdʒíːz/ (国外に保護を求めた人々) ; **displaced people** (戦争などで国を追われた人々 ; その一人は displaced person) ; an **evacuee** (避難者) ▶難民申請をする apply for *refugee* status (➤「難民申請」は refugee application) 《参考》小船で自国を脱出する難民を boat people と呼ぶ. ‖**難民キャンプ** a refugee camp ‖**難民救済** refugee aid, aid to refugees.

なんめい 何名 ▶《レストランなどで店員が》何名様ですか *How many of you are there?* ／*How many in your party?*

なんもん 難問 a **difficult** [**hard**] **problem** ▶難問を抱える have *a difficult problem* to tackle [wrestle with] ‖数学の難問を解く solve *a difficult* [*hard*] math *problem* ‖いじめの問題は教育上の難問だ Bullying is *a thorny problem* in education. (➤ thorny は「扱いがやっかいな」).

なんら 何ら ▶彼女はその事件と何ら関係ありません She has *nothing* to do with that incident. ‖彼が失敗しても何ら不思議ではない It is *no* wonder (that) he failed.

なんらか 何らか ▶手をこまねいて見ていないで今すぐ何らかの手を打つべきだ Instead of just standing there with your arms folded, you should *do something* immediately. ‖彼女は何らかの理由で退学処分になった She was expelled from school *for some reason or other*.

に・ニ

[1]**に 二** **two**（２つ）; **the second**（２番目）▶そのメロンを２個ください Give me *two* of the melons, please. ‖ ２分の１ *a* [*one*] *half* ‖ 横浜は日本で**第２の**大都市である Yokohama is *the second* largest city in Japan.

[2]**に 荷** a **load**（積み荷）; **freight**（貨物）; (a) **cargo**（１便分の荷）; a **pack**（背負える程度の）; a **package**（箱などに詰めた）▶彼らはトラックに**荷を積んだ**［から荷を下ろした］They *loaded* [*unloaded*] the truck. ‖ その船は堺で**荷を積んだ** The ship *was loaded* [*took on cargo*] at Sakai.

▶《慣用表現》この仕事は私には**荷が重い** This task *is a burden* to me. ／This task *is too much* for me.（➤ 後者はインフォーマルな言い方）‖ 息子が入試に合格して**肩の荷が下りた** My son's passing the entrance examination *took a load off my mind*.

[1]**-に** **1**【場所を示して】**in, at, on, to, into**

> **語法** (1)**in** は広がりのある場所の中やある範囲の内側を指す場合に, **at** は地図上の一点と感じられるような場所を指す場合に用いる.
> (2)**on** は「接触して…の上に」の意を表す場合に, **to** は到着点を意識して「…に」の意を表す場合に, **into** は in よりも動きを意識して「…(の中)へ」の意を表す場合にそれぞれ用いる. →-で.

▶《存在する場所》私は三重県の津市に住んでいます I live *in* Tsu, Mie Prefecture.（◉ live のあとでは都市名や建物がくることが多いのでふつうは「中」を表す in を用いる. at は at 1000 West Street, at 1-1-1 Kitamachi のように番地をいう場合, on は番地のない… Street, … Avenue（…通り）や建物の何階, あるいは半島, 島などに用いる. なお, I'm living と進行形にするのは, 定住でなく「現在一時的に住んでいる」を表す場合）‖ この空き地にごみを捨てないでください Don't dump trash *in* this vacant lot. ‖ 玄関に誰か来ている Somebody is *at* the door. ‖ 学校の南に［南側に］公園がある There is a park *to* the south [*on* the south side] of our school.（◉ to は「(学校の)南の方向に」）‖ 彼は部屋の壁に今日子の写真をはっている He has a picture of Kyoko pinned up *on* the wall of his room. ‖ 私の故郷は帯広の近くにある My hometown is *near* Obihiro. ‖ パトカーがバーの前に止まっている A police car is parked *in front of* the bar.

▶《到達する場所》私たちはゆうべ広島に着いたばかりです We arrived *in* Hiroshima (just) last night. ‖ 《新幹線のアナウンス》まもなく名古屋に短時間停車します We will soon make a brief stop *at* Nagoya.（◉ ここでは「名古屋駅」の意味なので at となる）‖ 彼はドアのところに行った He went *to* the door. ‖ 私は彼女が校長室に入るのを見た I saw her go *into* the principal's room. ‖ 次の列車は３番ホームに到着します The next train will pull *into* Track 3. ‖ あすの朝マニラにたちます I'm leaving *for* Manila tomorrow morning.

▶《表現する場所》この紙にご住所とお名前を書いてください Please write your name and address *on* this paper. ‖ 彼女は怒るとすぐ顔に出る She easily shows her anger *on* her face. ／Her anger quickly shows *on* her face.

2【時を示して】**at**（主に時刻）; **on**（日, 曜日）; **in**（月・年・季節など）

> 【文型】
> at ＋時刻, 時 ／年齢
> on ＋日付, 曜日 ／特定の朝・夜
> in ＋月, 年, 季節 ／朝・午後・夕方
>
> **解説** (1)**at** は時点を表す. 何時何分に, という時刻のほか, at noon（正午に）, at recess（休み時間に）, at night（夜に）, at midnight（真夜中に）, at Christmas（クリスマスに）や年齢を表すときに使う.
> (2)**on** は日付, 曜日と on Monday morning（月曜日の朝に）など, 特定の日の朝・午後・夕方・夜を表すときに使う.
> (3)**in** は期間を表す. 何月, 何年, 季節のほか, 一日のうちで night（夜）を除いて, in the morning（午前中に）, in the afternoon（午後に）などに用いる.
> (4)英語では, 時刻→日付→年などのように, 細かなものから順に表記する.

▶コンサートは午後６時に始まります The concert begins *at* 6 p.m. ‖ 彼女は二十歳のときに結婚した She got married *at* (the age of) twenty.（◉ かっこ内を言うのは改まった場合）／She got married *when* she was twenty.

▶卒業式は３月15日に［３月に］行われます The graduation ceremony will be held *on* March 15 [*in* March]. ‖ 音楽の授業は金曜日にあります We have music class *on* Fridays. ‖ ５月５日の午後にまたお会いします I'll see you again *on* the afternoon of May 5. ‖ じゃまた月曜日の朝にね See you (*on*) Monday morning. ‖ 私は1998年３月１日の朝５時半に生まれた I was born *at* 5 : 30 *on* the morning of March (the) first *in* 1998.

> **語法** (1)「何月何日の午前［午後／夕方］に」といった特定の時を表す場合には *on* the morning [the afternoon ／the evening] of … のように, 単に「一日のうちの午前［午後／夕方］に」の場合には *in* the morning [the afternoon ／the evening] という.
> (2)at, on, in の順に細かなものから大きなものへと並べる. つまり日本語と逆になる.

▶チューリップは春に咲く Tulips bloom *in* (the) spring. ‖ 父は来年の夏に香港から帰って来ます My father will return from Hong Kong next summer.（➤ (1)in next summer とはしない. (2)特定の年の夏をいう場合は in the summer of 2012 のように the が必要）‖ 私たちは１月に［１月の初めに］静岡に引っ越します We are moving to Shizuoka *in* January [*at* the beginning of January]. ‖ 山村さん一家は2005年に［10年前に］カナダへ移住した The Yamamuras moved to Canada *in* 2005 [ten years ago]. ‖ 私は令和元年に高校に入った I entered high school *in* the 1st year of Reiwa. (● 英語的に in 2019と表現するほうがよい) ‖ 英語の時間にＤＶＤを見た We watched a DVD *in* [*during*] English class. ‖ 冬休みに志賀高原へスキーに行った *During* the winter break I went skiing at Shiga Kogen. ‖『源氏物語』は平安時代に書かれた有名な長編小説だ "The Tale of Genji" is a famous long novel written *during* the Heian period.

3【動作・作用の対象を示して】to, for, by ▶鳥にえさをやる feed the birds ‖ 悩みをカウンセラーに相談する consult a counselor about one's problems ‖ できたら毎日でも彼女に会いたい I wish I could see her every day. ‖ 田中さんにすぐ電話しなさい Call Mr. Tanaka right away. (➤ 以上は前置詞を用いず, 他動詞の目的語になる場合) ‖ 彼はテニスに熱中している He's crazy *about* tennis.

▶《作用の対象》たばこは体に悪いぞ Smoking is bad *for* your health. ‖ 彼は自分に甘く, 他人に厳しい He's easy *on* himself but strict *with* [hard *on*] others.

▶《受け身・使役の対象》その老婦人は若い男にバッグをひったくられた The old woman had her purse snatched *by* a young man. ‖ 子供の頃はきみによくいじめられたっけ I remember being picked on *by* you a lot when we were kids. ‖ 宿題を兄に教わった My older brother helped me with my homework. ‖ 体の調子が悪いので医者に診てもらった I saw a doctor because I didn't feel well.

4【動作・作用が行われる状況・状態を示して】for ▶小百合ちゃん, サンタさんはクリスマスに何を持って来てくれたの? What did Santa bring you *for Christmas*, Sayuri?

5【変化の結果を示して】to ▶雨が雪になった The rain turned *to* snow. ‖ 弟はことし10歳になった My younger brother *turned* [*became*] ten (years old) this year. ‖ この市の人口は30万から35万に増えた The population of this city has increased from 300,000 *to* 350,000.

6【比較や程度の基準を示して】(● この意味では訳文に現れないことが多い) ▶この問題, きみにできるかな Do you think you can solve this problem? ‖ その車はとてもぼくに買える値段ではなかった That car was priced so high that I couldn't even think of buying it. ‖ 詩人はよく死を眠りにたとえる Poets often compare death *to* sleep. ‖ ここでの生活は東京に比べて安く済む Living here is cheap in comparison *with* Tokyo. ／The cost of living here is cheaper than in Tokyo. ‖ この病気は中年女性に多い This disease often strikes middle-aged women. ／This disease is common *among* middle-aged women.

7【割合を示して】▶父は年に２, ３度は外国へ出張します My father goes abroad on business two or three times *a year*.

> **【文型】**
> **3人に1人の** A
> **one** A **in** three
> **one in** three As
> **one out of** (**every**) three As
>
> **《解説》**「何人に１人」に応じて three を適当な数に変える. in はふつう **one in ～** (何人に１人)の場合に使う.「何人に２人」のような場合には主に two out of ～を使う. two in ～も使われるが, 少し堅い言い方になる.

▶厳しいな. 20人に１人しか合格していないのか What a tough exam! Only *one out of twenty* has passed it. ‖ 私たちの大学では３人に１人の学生がバイトをしている At our college, *one* student *in three* [*one out of* (*every*) *three* students] has a part-time job.

8【状態や内容を示して】in ▶きみは古典の理解に欠ける所があるね You are lacking *in* your understanding of the classics. ／Your understanding *of* the classics is deficient. ‖ 牛乳はカルシウムと鉄分に富む Milk is high *in* calcium and iron. ／Milk has a high calcium and iron content. ‖ その批評家の批評は偏見に満ちていた That critic's review was filled *with* [was full *of*] bias.

9【目的を示して】on, to do ▶使い［旅行］に行く go *on* an errand [a trip] ‖ 週末は友人たちとスケート(をし)に［映画(を見)に］行った I *went skating* [*went to the movies*] with my friends last weekend. ‖ 村松君は忘れ物を取りに家へ帰りました Muramatsu went back *to* get something he had left at home.

10【原因を示して】at, because 《of》 ▶誰もがそのニュースに驚いた Everybody was surprised *at* the news. ‖ この暑さに電力の消費量もうなぎ昇りだ Electricity consumption is skyrocketing *because of* this heat. ‖ その奇術のあまりの不思議さに観客は拍手も忘れていた The audience forgot to clap *because* the magic was so amazing.

11【資格・名目を示して】as ▶ごほうびにこのチョコをあげよう Let me give you this box of chocolate *as* a reward. ‖ 福引の賞品におしょうゆを１本もらった I won a bottle of soy sauce *as* a prize in a drawing.

12【取り合わせを示して】▶赤い洋服に黄色いリボンだなんて合わないよ The yellow ribbon doesn't match [suit] the red dress. ／A yellow ribbon *with* a red dress is a mismatch. (● 前者は目の前の具体的な例, 後者は一般的な例についての文).

13【残念がる気持ちを示して】▶ぼくが彼女の立場だったら, 相手に殴りかかっていただろうに If I had been in her position, I *would* have hit the person.

²-に -似 ▶彼女は母親似だ She *looks just like* her mother. ／She *is just like* [*takes after*] her mother. (● 前者は見た目, 後者は性格. take after は「(親や親族)に似ている」で見た目にも性格にも用いるが, 性格を表すことが多い).

にあい 似合い ▶白がお似合いですね You *look good* in white. ‖ その髪型とてもお似合いよ You *look great* with that hairstyle. ／That hairstyle *really becomes* you. (➤ 後者はやや古風な言い方) ‖ 二郎と恵美は似合いのカップルだ Jiro and Emi are a *well-matched* [*nice*] couple. ／Jiro and Emi make a *fine* pair [an *ideal* match].

✉ **《結婚のお祝い状》お二人はきっとお似合いのご夫婦になられるでしょう** I'm sure the two of you will make [be] a *perfect* couple.

☛ **不似合い** (→見出語)

にあう 似合う suit +㊐ (物が人に) ; **look good on** (➤「服などが人に」; 人を主語にすると in (…を着て)を用いるので look good in となる) ▶そのセーターはあなたによく似合う That sweater *suits* you *very well*. ／That sweater *looks good* [*nice*] *on* you. ／You *look nice* in that sweater. (➤ 後２者は第１例よりもインフォーマル) ‖ お姉さん, 和服がとても似合うね Your sister *looks* really *good* [*nice*] *in* a kimono.

に

▶あなたに**似合わない**(＝あなたらしくない)ことを言うわね That *doesn't sound like* you. ‖ 祖母は年に**似合わず**歯が丈夫だ Grandma has strong teeth *for* her age. (➤ for one's age は「年の割には」).

ニアミス a **near miss** ▶日航機と自衛隊機の間で**ニアミス**があった There was *a near miss* between a Japan Airlines jet and a Japan Self-Defense Forces plane. ／A Japan Airlines jet nearly collided with a Japan Self-Defense Forces plane.

にい 二位 **second place** ▶入江選手は**2位**に入賞した Irie *won second prize* [*came in second*]. ‖ 巨人はこのところ**2位**を守っている The Giants are keeping in *second place* these days.

にいさん 兄さん one's **older** [**big**／**elder**] **brother**

> **《解説》** (1)英語では年上か年下かをあまり区別しない. したがって older [big／elder] をつけないことが多い.
> (2)「兄さん, 外でガールフレンドが待ってるよ」のような自分の兄に対する呼びかけの場合, 英語では相手の名を用いて, 例えば David, Julia is waiting outside. のようにいう.

▶きみのほうが**お兄さん**よりふけて見えるね You look older than *your brother*. ‖ あなた, **お兄さん**でしょ. もっと優しくしてあげなさい You'*re older* than your brother [sister]. You should be kind to him [her]. ‖ 隣の**お兄さん**にギターの弾き方を教わってるんだ I'm learning how to play the guitar from *the boy* next door. (この場合 brother は使えない).

▶**兄さん**, これ安いよ. 持ってきな *Hey, mister*. This is cheap. How about buying one?

ニーズ (a) **need**(必要性); **demand** (需要) ▶若者の**ニーズ**に合った商品を開発していかねばならない We have to develop products which meet the *needs* of young people.

▶この種の品は**ニーズ**が大きい There is a great *demand* for this type of product. ‖ 市当局は市民の**ニーズ**にこたえねばならない The city (authority) has to respond to the citizens' *needs*.

> **危ないカタカナ語✷ ニーズ**
> 需要とか要求の意味で「ニーズ」というが, これは英語の need(必要性)の複数形の発音からきている. 英語でも the needs of the age(時代の要求するもの)という言い方はするが, demand や request を使ったほうがいい場合もある. 特に demand は great, high, strong, weak などの形容詞を伴う場合に多く用いられる.

にいづま 新妻 a **recently-married wife**.

ニート a **young jobless** [**unemployed**] **person** (**not in training**); a **NEET**(➤ 後者はイギリスで作られた造語で Not in Education, Employment or Training (教育, 労働, 職業訓練のいずれにも参加していない)を表し, 義務教育修了後の16～18歳(もしくは19歳)までの者と定義されている).

にいぼん 新盆 **the first Bon after someone's death** (Bon is a Buddhist celebration held in mid-July or mid-August (depending on the region) to honor the departed spirits of one's ancestors).

にいんせいど 二院制度 a **bicameral** /baɪkǽmərəl/ [**two chamber**] **system**.

にうけにん 荷受け人 a **consignee** /kɑ̀:nsaɪní:/ (➤荷送り人は consignor).

にえきらない 煮え切らない **irresolute** /ɪrézəlu:t/ (優柔不断な); **noncommittal** /nɑ̀:nkəmíṭl/ (あいまいな) ▶決断を迫られても彼は**煮えきらない**態度をとっていた Even when pressed for a decision, he remained *irresolute* [maintained a *noncommittal* attitude]. ‖ **煮えきらない**やつだな, おまえも. 彼女が好きならちゃんと彼女にそう言えよ Don't be so *wishy-washy* [*wimpy*]. If you love her, tell her so. (➤ wishy-washy は「うじうじした」に相当するインフォーマルな語).

にえくりかえる 煮えくり返る ▶彼にあんなひどいことをされてはらわたが**煮えくり返っている** He did such a terrible thing to me. *It really made my blood boil*. [*I'm absolutely furious about* that.]

にえたぎる 煮えたぎる ▶ポットのコーヒーが**煮えたぎっている** The coffee in the pot *is boiling* [*is hissing hot*].

にえゆ 煮え湯 **boiling water** ▶《慣用表現》彼には何度か**煮え湯を飲まされている** I *have had* several *terrible experiences* because of him. ／I *have been betrayed* by him several times. (➤ betray は「(人を)裏切る」).

にえる 煮える **cook**; **boil**(沸騰した湯の中で); **simmer** (コトコト煮える) ▶おでんが**煮えている** The oden *is cooking* [*simmering*]. ‖ じゃがいもが**煮えた**よ The potatoes *are cooked* [*are done*]. (➤ ともに「(料理が)できあがっている」の意).

におい 匂い・臭い (a) **smell**, (a) **scent**, (an) **odor** /óʊdəʳ/

> **《解説》** (1)**smell**, **scent** は鼻に感じられるにおいに, **odor** は物自体がもっている [発散している] においに言及する場合にそれぞれ用いる. →**かおり**.
> (2)scent は主に心地よい香り, odor はしばしば悪いにおいの含み. smell はどちらにも用いるが, 形容詞がつかないと「悪臭」の意味になることが多い.

1【物・人が発散する】▶バラはいい**においがする** Roses *have a nice smell* [*scent*]. ／Roses *smell sweet*. ‖ いやな**においのする**花もある Some flowers give off an unpleasant [a foul] *odor*. ‖ 腐った卵はいやな**においがする** A rotten egg *stinks* [*smells awful*]. (➤ stink は「鼻を刺すように強くにおう」) ‖ 台所から(生臭い)魚の**においがしてきた** An *odor* of fish [A fishy *smell*] came from the kitchen.

> **【文型】**
> A が B, C の**においがする**
> A **smells of** B. ➤ B は名詞
> A **smells** C. ➤ C は形容詞
>
> **《解説》** (1)においの発生源や場所を主語にして, 「…のにおいがする」という場合, 「**smell of** ＋名詞」を用いる.
> (2)においの良し悪しをいう場合は形容詞を用いて後者の文型になる.
> (3)においを感じる人(D)を主語にして「E のにおいを感じる, E のにおいをかぐ」のときには, D smells E. の形になる.

▶この家はまだ塗り立てのペンキの**においがする** This house still *smells of* fresh paint. ‖ 日に干した洗濯物の**においをかいだら**お日さまの**においがした** When I *smelled* the laundry drying in the sun, it *smelled of* sunshine. ‖ この魚, 少し変な**においがしない**? Does this fish *smell* a little *off*？（● この off は「悪くなりかけて」の意の形容詞. funny を用いてもよい）‖ 硫黄は腐った卵のようなにおいがする Sulfur *smells like* rotten eggs.（● においを別のもののにおいに例えるときは smell like を用いる）.

▶その男は強烈なたばこのにおいがした That man *reeked of* cigarettes.（➤ reek of は「…のひどい悪臭を放つ」）.

2【人が感覚でとらえる】▶何か燃えているにおいがする I *smell* something burning. ‖ 風呂場でガスのにおいがする I *smell* gas in the bathroom. ‖ このにおいは何なの？ What do I *smell*？‖ ちょっとこの肉のにおいをかいでみて Just *smell* this meat. ‖ その犬はぼくのソックスのにおいをくんくんかいだ The dog *sniffed* my socks. ‖ ああ, いいにおい！ What a nice [sweet] *smell*！

‖**におい消し** a deodorant /dióʊdərənt/（人体用の）; a deodorizer, (an) air freshener（トイレ用などの）‖ **におい袋** a sachet, a scent bag.

1**におう 匂う・臭う** **1【においがする】smell**《of》▶何かにおう I can *smell* something. ‖ また酔っているのね. お酒がにおうわよ You're drunk again—you *smell* [*reek*] *of* booze.（● 進行形にしない）‖ 生ごみがあるので台所がにおう The kitchen *smells bad* [*stinks*] because of the garbage.（➤ stink は「鼻を刺すように強くにおう」の意）.

▶彼女は口がにおう（＝口臭がある） Her breath *smells*. ／She has bad breath.

2【怪しい】▶二人の関係はにおう *There's something suspicious* about their relationship. ‖ 彼のアリバイはどうもにおう His alibi *sounds fishy*.

2**におう 仁王** ***Nio***; a **temple guardian deity.**

におわせる 匂わせる ▶容疑者は一連の犯行をにおわせる供述を始めた The suspect has begun revealing information that *suggests* [*implies*] that he committed the series of crimes.

1**にかい 二階**《米》**the second floor,**《英》**the first floor**（→階）**一副 2階に**［へ］**upstairs**（上の階に）▶私の部屋は2階にある My room is *upstairs*. ‖ どうぞ2階へ上がってください Please go *upstairs*.（➤ 2階建ての家の場合は upstairs で「2階に」の意）‖ 彼は2階から下りて来た He came *downstairs*.（➤ downstairs は「階下へ」の意）‖ わが家は5階建てのアパートの2階です My home is on *the second floor* of a five-story apartment building. ／《英》My home is on *the first floor* of a five-storey block of flats.（➤《英》では1階は the ground floor という）‖ うちは2階建てです My house *has two stories*. ／We live in *a two-story house*.

‖**2階建てバス** a double-decker (bus) ‖ **中二階** a mezzanine /mézəni:n/.

2**にかい 二回** →二度.

にがい 苦い

1【味が】bitter ▶苦い味 a *bitter* taste ‖ ニガウリは苦い Bitter gourds *taste bitter*. ‖ ことわざ 良薬は口に苦し Good medicine tastes *bitter*. ／Good advice is usually *unpleasant to the ears*.（➤「ためになる忠告は耳が痛いものだ」）

2【不快な】bitter, hard ▶苦い思い出 a *bitter* memory ‖ 私は苦い経験をした I've had a *bitter* [*hard*] experience. ／I've had a *hard* time (of it). ‖ 彼女は自分についてのそのうわさを聞いて苦い（＝不機嫌な）顔をした When she heard the rumor about herself, she *made a* (*sour*) *face*.（➤ make a (sour) face で「不機嫌な顔をする」の意）.

にがおえ 似顔絵 a **portrait** /pɔ́ːʳtrət/; a **caricature**（風刺の利いた）; a **composite drawing** [**sketch**]（容疑者の）▶私たちの先生は生徒の似顔絵をかくのが上手です Our teacher is good at drawing *portraits* of her students.

‖**似顔絵師** a portrait painter; a sidewalk [pavement] artist（街頭の）.

にかこくご 二か国語 **two languages** ▶彼女は（英語とドイツ語の）2か国語を話す She speaks *two languages*(—English and German). ／She is *bilingual* (in English and German).（➤ 発音は /baılíŋgwəl/ で, 2か国語を「自在に」使えることをいう）‖ そのテレビ番組は2か国語放送だ That TV program is *televised in multiplex*. ／That TV program is *broadcast bilingually*.（➤ multiplex は「多重放送（システム）」）.

にがす 逃がす **1【放す】set ... free** ▶彼女はその小鳥を逃がしてやった She *set* the bird *free*. ／She *let* the bird *go*.

2【捕まえそこなう】miss ＋目; **let ... escape**（逃げるにまかせる）▶容疑者を逃がすな Don't *let* the suspect *escape*. ‖ 大きな魚だ. 逃がすなよ That's a big fish—don't *lose* it. ‖ 私はせっかくのチャンスを逃がした I *missed* a good opportunity.

にがつ 二月 **February**《略 Feb.》▶うるう年には2月は29日まである There are 29 days in *February* in a leap year.

にがて 苦手 ⚠ **一口に「苦手」といっても,「得意でない」という意味のほかに,「きらいだ」「扱いにくい」「いやだ」「こわい」など, さまざまなニュアンスがある. したがって, 文の内容によって訳し方を考える必要がある.**

▶私は英語は苦手だ English *is my weak subject*. ／I'*m very weak in* English. ／I'*m not good* [*I'm poor*] *at* English.（➤ be good at は「…が得意である」の意）‖ 私は甘いものは苦手です（＝好きじゃない） I *don't care for* sweets. ／I don't have a sweet tooth.（➤ have a sweet tooth は「甘いものが好きだ」の意の熟語）. ‖ 苦手な食べ物は何ですか What are your *least favorite* foods？

▶田辺さんの奥さんはどうも苦手だ Mrs. Tanabe *is hard* (for me) *to deal with*.（➤「扱いにくい」の意）‖ 青木先生は苦手だ I *can't get along well with* Mr. Aoki.（➤「仲よくやっていけない」の意）‖ 私は赤ん坊が苦手だ I'*m not good with* babies.（➤「扱うのが得意でない」の意）‖ 私は堅苦しいパーティーは苦手です I'*m allergic to* [*I have an aversion to*] formal parties. ‖ どうも飛行機は苦手だ I just *don't like* to fly. ‖ 実はぼくは高い所が苦手なんだ Actually, I'*m afraid of* heights. ‖ カラオケは苦手です Karaoke *isn't my cup of tea*.（➤ one's cup of tea は「好きなこと, 得意なこと」）.

にがていしき 苦手意識 a **mental block** ▶数学に対して苦手意識がある have *a mental block* about math.

にがにがしい 苦々しい **bitter** ▶市長は政府の発表を苦々しい表情で聞いていた The mayor listened to the (central) government's announcement with a *bitter* expression on his face. ‖ その老人は電車内を走り回る子供を苦々しげに見ていた The old man was looking *with disgust* at the children running around in the train.

にがみ 苦み **bitterness** ▶ホウレンソウを湯がいて苦みを取る parboil spinach to get rid of the *bitterness* ‖ このチーズは苦みが強くて私には食べられない This cheese is too *bitter* for me to eat.

にがむし 苦虫 ▶《慣用表現》あの人はいつも苦虫をかみつぶしたような顔をしている He always looks *grumpy* [*sullen*]. ／He always wears a *sour* face.

にかよう 似通う ▶この 2 つの話はとても似通っている These two stories *are* very much *alike* [*resemble each other* very much].

ニカラグア **Nicaragua**(中央アメリカの国).

にがり 苦汁 **bittern.**

にかわ 膠 **gelatinous** /dʒəlǽtnəs/ **glue.**

にがわらい 苦笑い ▶プロスケーターの小田は氷の上でころんで苦笑いをした When Oda, a professional skater, fell on the ice, he *gave an embarrassed* [*bitter*] *smile*.

にき 二期 **two terms, two periods.**

にきさく 二期作 **double cropping**; a **second crop**(2番めの収穫).

にきび a **pimple**, **acne** /ǽkni/ (➤ 後者は医学用語でⓊ扱い) ▶にきびをつぶす squeeze *a pimple* ‖ にきび面の少年 a *pimply-faced* boy ／a boy with a *pimply* [*pimpled*] face ‖ 額ににきびができた A *pimple* has come out [*Pimples* have broken out] on my forehead.

▶チョコレートを食べるとにきびができるというのは神話らしい It seems to be a myth that (eating) chocolate causes *acne*. ‖ にきびは青春のシンボルだ *Pimples* are the symbol of youth.

にぎやか 賑やか **1【活気がある】** **lively** /láɪvli/ ▶にぎやかな音楽 *lively* music ‖ にぎやかな(＝人通りの多い)通り a *busy* [*crowded*] street ‖ 女の子たちが集まるとにぎやかだ When girls gather, things get *lively*. ‖ パーティーは歌や踊りが出てにぎやかになった The party *was enlivened* with singing and dancing. (➤ enliven /ɪnláɪvən/ は「活気づける」) ‖ にぎやかな(＝よくしゃべる)人 a *talkative* person.

2【豊かではでな】 ▶パーティー会場は花やテープでにぎやかに飾りたててあった That party hall was *festively* [*lavishly*] decorated with flowers and ribbons.

にぎり 握り a **grip** ▶握りの太い[細い]ラケット a racket with a thick [thin] *grip* ‖ アメリカ人の握手は握り方が強いとよくいわれる I often hear that Americans *grip strongly* when they shake hands.

▶握り(ずし) 2 人前お願いします Two *nigiri*(*zushi*), please.

☛ **おにぎり** (→見出語)

にぎりこぶし 握り拳 a **clenched fist** ▶握りこぶしを固める clench one's *fist* ／make *a fist* ‖ 握りこぶし大の石が屋根から落ちてきた Rocks *the size of my fist* came rolling off the roof.

にぎりしめる 握り締める **hold firmly**(しっかり持っている); **clasp** +㊐, **grip** +㊐ (しっかりと物を握る; 前者は堅い語) ▶彼は旧友の手を握りしめた He *clasped* his old friend's hands. ／He *held* his old friend's hands *firmly*. ‖ 男の子は500円玉を握りしめてお菓子屋に行った The boy went to the candy shop *holding* a five-hundred yen coin *firmly in his hand*.

にぎりつぶす 握り潰す **crush ... in** one's **hand** ▶試合に興奮して手にしていた紙コップを握りつぶしてしまった I got so excited over the game I *crushed* the paper cup *in my hand*.

▶独裁者は不利になる報道を握りつぶした The dictator *squashed* any news unfavorable to him.

にぎりめし 握り飯 →おにぎり.

にぎる 握る **1【手でつかむ】** **hold** +㊐, **grasp** +㊐, **grip** +㊐ (➤ この順に握り方が強くなる) ▶鉄棒はしっかり握りなさい *Grasp* the iron bar firmly. ‖ クラブはあまりきつく握らないこと Don't *hold* the club too firmly.

▶ぼくは彼女の手を握った I *held* her hand(s). ／I *held* hands with her. (➤ 後者は愛情表現としての「手を握る」) ‖ クライマーはロープをしっかり握った The climber firmly *gripped* the rope.

▶週末はよくマイカーのハンドルを握ります(＝運転する) I often *drive* (*my car*) on weekends. (➤ そのものずばりの「ハンドルを握る」は hold [grip, take] the wheel, 「運転席に着く」は get [sit] behind the wheel; 「行楽のドライブに行く」は go for a drive) ‖ 私はときどき自分ですしを握ります I sometimes *make* sushi myself. (→握り).

2【支配する】 ▶全権を握る *have* [*hold*] all the power ‖ その将軍が政権を握ってから 3 年になる It has been three years since that general *came to* [*into*] *power*. ‖ 目下, 保守党が政権を握っている The Conservatives *are* now *in power*. ‖ わが家では母が実権を握っています My mother *wears the pants* in the family. (➤ wear the pants は文字どおりには「ズボンをはいている」で, 「(女房が)夫をしりに敷く」の意のインフォーマルな言い方) ‖ 由利子の所はだんなが財布を握っている Yuriko's husband *controls* the household budget. ／Yuriko's husband *holds* [*controls*] the purse strings. (➤ あとの文はくだけた表現) ‖ ぼくは姉さんの弱みを握っている I *have something on* my sister. (➤ この something は「不利な証拠[情報, 秘密]」).

にぎわい 賑わい ▶祭りは大変なにぎわいだった There was a great *crowd* [a large *turnout*] at the festival. (➤ turnout は「繰り出した人出」) ‖ 大都市のにぎわいの中でも人々は孤独を感じることがある People sometimes feel lonely even amid *the hustle and bustle* of a big city. (➤ hustle and bustle /hʌ́səl ənd bʌ́səl/ は「押し合いへし合い, 雑踏」).

にぎわう 賑わう **be crowded** ▶年の暮れになるとその商店街は買い物客でにぎわう At the end of the year, that shopping street *is crowded* with shoppers. ‖ あの市場はいつもにぎわっている That market *is* always *bustling* (with people).

にぎわす 賑わす ▶その問題は最近ずいぶんと新聞をにぎわしている That problem has *been in the newspaper* a lot lately.

にく 肉

◀解説▶「肉」について

(1)一般語の **meat** は通例食用にする獣肉を指す. 食用にしない肉は **flesh** という. flesh はまた, 骨や皮に対して「肉」の意でも用いる.

(2)食用の肉でも「魚肉」は **fish**, 「鳥肉」は **poultry** または **fowl** と区別するのがふつう.

(3)meat については, **beef** (牛肉), **veal** (子牛肉), **pork** (豚肉), **mutton** (羊肉)のように使い分ける. また, poultry についても chicken(鶏肉), duck(アヒルの肉), turkey(七面鳥の肉)のように使い分ける.

1【食用の肉】 **meat** ▶肉 1 切れ a piece of *meat* ‖ やわらかい[かたい]肉 tender [tough] *meat* (● soft, hard は用いないことに注意) ‖ 今のたいていの若い人は魚より肉を好む Most young people today prefer *meat* to fish. ‖ 脂の多い肉は食べないほうがいい You should avoid fatty *meats*. (● いろいろな種類の肉の意味では複数形になる)

‖肉料理 meat dish ‖精肉店 a butcher (人) ; 《米》a meat [butcher] shop, 《英》a butcher's (店) (➤ 大型スーパーなどの中にあるものは meat department [section ／counter] でよい).
2【骨に対して】flesh ▶ライオンは口にシマウマの肉をくわえていた The lion had the *flesh* of a zebra in its mouth. ‖彼は近頃肉がついて［落ちて］きた He *has put on* [*has lost*] *weight* lately. ‖ほおの肉が落ちた My cheeks have *become sunken*. (➤「ほおがこけた」) ／I have *lost cheek fat* and my cheeks are slimmer. (➤「ぜい肉が落ちて, ほおがほっそりした」).

逆引き熟語 ○○肉
あばら肉 ribs ／牛ひれ肉 beef tenderloin ／牛もも肉 a round of beef ／霜降り肉 marbled meat [beef] ／ひき肉 ground beef

にくあつ 肉厚な thick, meaty, fleshy, plump ▶肉厚なしいたけ a *meaty* [*plump* ／*fleshy*] shiitake mushroom.

にくい 憎い ▶俺から金をだまし取ったあいつが憎い I *hate* him because he swindled money out of me.
▶なかなか憎い(＝気のきいた)ことを言うねえ You say some *neat* things. ‖太郎と花子は互いに憎からず思っているようだ It seems that Taro and Hanako *have tender feelings for* [*care for*] each other.
ことわざ 坊主憎けりゃけさまで憎い Once you hate a bonze, you tend to hate his surplice. (➤ 日本語からの直訳) ／Love me, love my dog. (➤「私が好きなら, 私の犬も好きになれ」の意の英語のことわざ ; 日本語とは発想が逆).
《参考》「殺人犯が憎い」は一応, I hate [detest ／loathe] the murderer. と訳せるが, 特に, 行為でなく, 人を hate することはキリスト教ではそれ自体が罪とされているので, 大人はあまり使わない(⇀憎む). 裁判で犯人の残虐さや罪の重さを訴える場合, 英語圏の人々はこういう主情的な表現はふつうしない. むしろ, 逆になるべく客観的に言うことで, 単に個人的な感情でないと訴えようとする. たとえば, I want justice. He deserves the death penalty. (正義を望みます. 死刑が相当です), I want him to get the death penalty. He deserves no less ! (死刑を宣告してください. それ以下ではだめです)などと言うと思われる.

-にくい ▶治り［治し］にくい病気 a disease (that is) *difficult to* cure ‖そのＣＤは今では手に入りにくい That CD *is difficult to* obtain these days. ‖あの人は扱いにくい人だ That man *is hard* (for me) *to deal with*. ‖黒板が光って見にくい I find it *hard to read* the blackboard because of the glare. ‖言いにくいんですが, お金を少し貸してください *I hate to ask, but* could you lend me a little money ? (⇀言いにくい).
▶今の私の気分は説明しにくい I *can't explain well* how I feel now. ‖このボールペンは書きにくい This ballpoint pen *doesn't write well*. ‖この大きな部屋は暖まりにくい It *takes a long time to warm up* this big room. (➤「暖まるのに長い時間がかかる」の意).

にくがん 肉眼 the naked /néɪkɪd/ eye ▶その虫は小さ過ぎて肉眼では見えない Those insects are too small to be seen *with the naked eye*. (➤ 決まった言い方で eyes としない).

にくきゅう 肉球 a pad.

にくぎゅう 肉牛 beef cattle(➤ 複数扱い).

にくしつ 肉質 the quality [consistency] of meat ; pulpy substance(果肉) ▶肉質の葉 a *fleshy* leaf ‖多肉質の果物 a *fleshy* fruit.

にくしみ 憎しみ hatred /héɪtrɪd/ ▶その殺人犯に対する憎しみはいつまでも消えないだろう *The hatred* toward that murderer will not disappear for a long time.

にくじゃが 肉じゃが *nikujaga* ; meat, potatoes, onions and carrots simmered in sweetened soy sauce (➤ 説明的な訳).

にくしゅ 肉腫《医学》a **sarcoma** /sɑːʳkóʊmə/.

にくじゅう 肉汁 (a) **meat juice, jus ; gravy**(肉汁ソース) ▶肉汁の多いステーキ (a) *juicy* steak.

にくしょく 肉食 ▶日本では明治になるまで肉食は一般的ではなかった In Japan, *eating meat* was not common until the Meiji period. ‖カバは草食性で, 肉食性ではない Hippos are herbivorous, not *carnivorous*.
▶あの女優は肉食系だ That actress is rather *aggressive toward men and dating*.
‖肉食動物 a carnivorous animal, a carnivore /kɑ́ːʳnəvɔːʳ/.

にくしん 肉親 a **blood relation [relative]** ; one's **family**(家族) ▶中国残留日本人孤児の人々が肉親をさがしに日本を訪れた The Japanese war orphans left in China came to Japan to search for their *relatives*.

にくずれ 荷崩れ ▶荷くずれが起きた *Packages collapsed*.

にくせい 肉声 one's **(natural) voice** ▶(マイクを使わず)肉声で講演する speak without a microphone.

にくたい 肉体 a **body** ━形 **肉体の bodily**(心・精神に対して) ; **physical**(肉体に関する) ▶父は60歳だが肉体は40代の若さだ My father is sixty years old, but he has *the body* [*physical strength*] of someone in his forties. ‖病気をすると肉体的にも精神的にも苦痛を味わう When we fall sick, we suffer both *physically* and mentally. ‖あの二人は肉体関係があるといううわさだ Rumor has it that those two have had (*physical*) *relations*. ‖彼は肉体の復活を信じている He believes in *bodily* resurrection. ‖肉体は滅びても魂は生き続けるとよく言われる It's often said that although we must perish *physically*, our souls live on.
‖肉体美 physical beauty ‖肉体労働 manual [physical] labor.

にくたらしい 憎たらしい spiteful(悪意に満ちた) ; **mean, nasty**(意地悪な ; 前者には「品性が下劣な」という含みがある) ; **impudent,**《英》**cheeky, sassy**(生意気な), **obnoxious**(気に障る) ▶私と彼女の友情を壊そうとするなんて彼って憎たらしい人ね It is *spiteful* [*mean*] of him to try to destroy my friendship with her. ‖なんて憎たらしい子だろう What an *annoying* [*obnoxious*] kid ! ‖あの子は憎たらしい口をきく That boy [girl] speaks *disrespectfully*. (●「憎たらしい口をきく」に say nasty things を当てると, 意味が異なるので要注意. その場合「いやらしい［ひわいな］ことを言う」とか(英語なら)「4文字語を用いる」の意味になる) ‖チャンピオンは憎たらしいほど強い The champion is *disgustingly* strong.

にくだんご 肉団子 a **meatball**.

にくづき 肉付き ▶(力士の)白鵬は胸のあたりの肉付きがいい Hakuho *is well built* around the chest.

にくづけ 肉付け ▶登場人物をもう少し肉付けすればドラマがもっと生き生きしてくる You'll be able to make the play better if you *flesh out* the characters. ‖これはまだ素案で肉付けはこれからだ This is just a basic proposal which has to *be elaborated on*. (➤

elaborate on は「…についてさらに詳しく述べる」).

にくにくしい 憎々しい ▶昔の映画の悪役は見るからに憎々しい顔つきをしていた In old films, every bad guy had an obviously *malicious* look. ‖ その男は殴った男を憎々しげににらみ返した He stared back *with hatred* at the man who hit him.

にくはく 肉薄 ▶広島は3連勝で首位のヤクルトに肉薄してきた The Carp *are coming close* [*edging up*] behind the leading Swallows by winning three games in a row.

にくばなれ 肉離れ a **pulled** [**torn**] **muscle** /mʌ́səl/ ▶左の太ももに肉離れを起こした I *pulled a muscle* in my left thigh. ／I *had a torn muscle* in my left thigh.

にくひつ 肉筆 one's **own handwriting** ▶これは太宰治の肉筆の手紙だ This is a letter of Dazai Osamu's *in his own handwriting*.

にくぶと 肉太の bold, **bold-face(d)** ▶壁の張り紙には大きな肉太の文字で「目ざせ東大」と書いてあった A poster on the wall proclaimed "Aim for Todai" in big, *bold* letters. (➤「肉細の」は light-face(d)).

にくまれぐち 憎まれ口 ▶そんな憎まれ口をきくんじゃないよ Don't *say spiteful things* like that.

にくまれっこ 憎まれっ子 ▶ [ことわざ] 憎まれっ子世にはばかる Hated children grow vigorously. (➤日本語からの直訳) ／ Ill weeds grow apace. (➤「雑草はよく茂る」の意).

にくまれやく 憎まれ役 ▶パパはいつも憎まれ役だ Dad always has to *play the bad guy*.

にくまん(じゅう) 肉饅(頭) a **meat bun**.

にくむ 憎む hate +㊐, **detest** +㊐ (➤後者がより強意) ▶憎み合う *hate* each other ‖ 憎むべき敵 a *hateful* enemy ‖ 憎むべき犯罪 a *detestable* crime ‖ 彼は困っているとき助けなかった私の事を憎んでいるに違いない He must *have resentment* towards me because I didn't help him when he was in trouble. (➤ resentment は「憤慨, 恨み」) ‖ 我々を裏切ったあの男を憎まずにはいられない It is hard not to *hate* that man who has betrayed us.

> **《解説》hate は love の対語で罪とされる**
> Love your enemies. (汝の敵を愛せよ), Hate the sin, love the sinner. (罪を憎め, 罪びとは愛せよ) と教えるキリスト教では, 人を hate すること自体が罪 (sin) とされる. 従って, 特定の個人名を挙げて, hate を使うことには裏切りやだましなど, 余程ひどいことをされた相手に対して以外は, ためらいがあることが多い. キリスト教徒はふつう, hate を避けて, detest, loathe, despise, have contempt for などの言い方を使う. 憎むべき相手に対しても, I despise him, but I don't hate him. (軽蔑するが憎みはしない) と言ったりする. なお, 一般論として言う, I hate liars. (うそつきは嫌いだ) のような文には抵抗感は少ない(→憎い).

にくめない 憎めない ▶彼は欠点だらけだがどこか憎めないところがある He has many faults, but there is *something charming* about him. ‖ あなたって憎めない人ね You're *a person who's hard not to like*.

にくよく 肉欲 carnal desire(s) ; **lust**(過度の色欲).

にくらしい 憎らしい mean, spiteful (➤後者は「つまらないことで人をいじめたり仕返しをしたりする」という含みがある) →憎たらしい ▶わざと私の靴を隠すなんて憎らしいったらないわ, あの子! How *mean* [*spiteful*] of him to have hidden my shoes on purpose! ‖ 彼女はライバルの美貌が憎らしかった She *was painfully jealous of* her rival's beauty.

にぐるま 荷車 a **cart** ; a **wagon** (大型の) ▶荷車を引く pull *a cart* ‖ 荷車に野菜を積む load vegetables on *a cart* [*wagon*].

にぐん 二軍 《野球》a **farm**, a **farm team** [**club**] ; **the minors** (マイナーリーグ) ▶その内野手は二軍に落とされた The infielder was demoted [was sent] to the *farm*.

にげおくれる 逃げ遅れる ▶うちが火事になったとき祖父母は危うく逃げ遅れるところだった Once when a fire broke out in our house, my grandparents almost *failed to escape*.

にげこうじょう 逃げ口上 an **excuse**(言いわけ) ; an **evasion** /ɪvéɪʒən/ (あいまいな返答) ▶その男は逃げ口上を並べて責任を回避しようとした He tried to shirk his (own) responsibility by giving *poor excuses*.

にげごし 逃げ腰 ▶警官を見ると彼は逃げ腰になった When he saw the policeman, he *got ready to run away*.
▶そんな逃げ腰では問題はいつまでたっても解決しないよ The problem will never be solved if you *don't face up to* it. (➤ face up to は「…に敢然と立ち向かう」).

にげこむ 逃げ込む ▶犯人はその別荘に逃げ込んだ The criminal *ran* [*fled*] *into* that summer house for refuge. (➤ fled は flee(逃げる)の過去形) ／The criminal *escaped to* that summer house.

にげだす 逃げ出す run away, escape →逃げる ▶練習がきついので3人の部員が合宿所から逃げ出した Three members *ran away* [*escaped*] from the training camp because of the hard workout. ‖ 「こらっ」という声に子供たちはいっせいに逃げ出した When someone yelled "Hey!", the children *took to their heels* all at once. (➤ take to one's heels は「さっと逃げる」).

にげのびる 逃げ延びる ▶これ以上逃げ延びられないとわかって泥棒は自首した When the robber realized he couldn't *run away any more*, he turned himself in to the police.

にげば 逃げ場 ▶4階全体が炎に包まれて, 5階から上のホテルの泊まり客は逃げ場を失った The whole fourth floor was enveloped in flames, *blocking off all means of escape* for the guests on the upper floors of the hotel.

にげまどう 逃げ惑う run about trying to escape.

にげまわる 逃げ回る ▶その容疑者は世界中を逃げ回っていた The suspect *ran around* the world trying to avoid getting caught.
▶寺山さんは旅行の幹事になるのがいやで逃げ回っている Mr. Terayama *is trying to avoid* taking charge of the arrangements for the trip.

にげみち 逃げ道 an **escape route** ▶亡くなった人たちは煙に追われて逃げ道を失ったらしい The victims seem to *have lost their way out* in the smoke. (➤ way out は「出口」).

にげる 逃げる **1【のがれる】run** [**get**] **away** ; **escape** (拘束・危険などから脱出する) 《文》**flee**(危険・災害などから) ▶安全な場所へ逃げる *run* [*get*] *away* to a safe place ／*run for* shelter ‖ 彼は店にあった金を全部持って逃げた He *made away with* all the money in the store. (➤ make away with は「…を持ち逃げする」) ‖ 待て! 逃げるな *Freeze!* (➤ freeze は「(一歩も)動くな」の意) ‖ その馬は先頭に

立つとそのまま逃げ切った Once that horse took the lead, it kept that position all the way to the finish.

▶囚人が2人逃げた Two prisoners *have escaped*. ‖ライオンがおりから逃げた A lion *broke out of* [*escaped from*] its cage. ‖鳥がかごから逃げた The bird *flew out* of the cage.

▶ ことわざ 逃げるが勝ち Running away is the better part of valor. (➤ Discretion is the better part of valor. (慎重さは勇気の大半を占める) という英語のことわざのもじり).

2【かわす, 避ける】**dodge** +目, **evade** +目 (➤後者には「ずるいことをするなどして」という含みがある) ▶彼女は私の質問からうまく逃げた She *dodged* [*evaded*] my question. ‖彼はいつでも難しい仕事から逃げる He always *gets out of* doing difficult work. ‖山本はどんな強打者に対しても逃げずに立ち向かう No matter how good the batter is, Yamamoto pitches *bravely*. ／Yamamoto pitches *bravely* against any slugger.

にげん 二元の **dual, binary** ▶二元構造 a *binary* structure

‖二元論 dualism.

にこごり 煮凝り 《料理》**aspic.**

にごす 濁す **1**【濁らせる】**make ... muddy** ▶子供が水をばしゃばしゃやって泉を濁した Some children splashed in the spring and *made the water muddy*. ‖ ことわざ 立つ鳥後を濁さず A water bird taking wing does not stir up the mud. ／An outgoing person should put his [her] affairs in order before leaving. (➤前者は日本語からの直訳, 後者は意訳).

2【あいまいにする】▶理由を聞かれて彼はことばを濁した When asked the reason, he *gave an evasive* [*a vague*] answer.

ニコチン 《化学》**nicotine** /níkəti:n/ ▶彼はニコチン中毒だ He *is addicted to* [He's *hooked on*] *nicotine*. ／He *is a nicotine* [*tobacco*] *addict*.

にこにこ ▶彼女はいつもにこにこしてうれしそうだ She *is* always *smiling* and seems happy. ‖母はにこにこしながら私の成績表を受け取った My mother took my report card *with a smile*.

にこみ 煮込み a **stewed dish** ▶牛の煮込み *stewed* beef ‖(みそ)煮込みうどん *udon* noodles *in a hot* (*miso*) *soup with meat and vegetables*.

にこむ 煮込む **cook** [**boil**] **well** (よく煮る); **stew, simmer** (弱火で); **cook together** (いろいろな材料を一緒に煮る) ▶煮込みハンバーグ a *stewed* [*simmered*] hamburger ‖牛すじを煮込む *cook* the beef tendon *well* ／*simmer* the beef tendon.

にこやか ▶にこやかな顔 a *beaming* face ‖山小屋の主人は我々をにこやかに迎えてくれた The owner of the lodge welcomed us *with a* (*broad, hearty*) *smile*.

にこり ▶あの人は道で近所の人に会ってもにこりともしない He *won't even smile* when he meets a neighbor on the street.

にごり 濁り ▶濁りのない声 a *clear* voice ‖濁りが消えるまでこの水を飲んではいけない Don't drink this water until the *mud* in it settles.

にごる 濁る **get muddy** [**cloudy**] 一形 濁った **muddy** (泥で); **cloudy** (澄んでいない) ▶この川の水は濁っている The water of this river *is muddy* [*isn't clear*]. ‖伊香保温泉の湯は赤く濁っている The water in the baths at Ikaho Hot Spring *is cloudy*, with a reddish tinge.

▶配水管を取り替えたのに水がまだ濁っている Even though the pipes were replaced, the water is still *dirty* [*cloudy*]. ‖濁った目には真理は見えない *Corrupt* eyes cannot see the truth.

▶関東の人はふつう「3階」を「さんがい」と濁って発音する Most people in Kanto *voice* the second syllable of the word "san-kai" so that it sounds like "san-gai." (➤ voice は「有声音で発音する」の意の動詞).

にころがし 煮ころがし ▶サトイモ [ジャガイモ] の煮ころがし *taros* [*potatoes*] *simmered in broth*.

にごん 二言 ▶武士に二言はない *A samurai never retracts his words*. (➤ retract は「(ことば)を撤回する」).

にざかな 煮魚 **fish cooked in broth.**

にさん 二, 三の **two or three, a couple of** (➤後者は《英》では通例「2つの」を意味する) ▶まだ問題が二, 三残っている There are *two or three* problems still remaining. ‖きみに二, 三聞きたいことがある I'd like to ask you *a few* questions. ‖私は週に二, 三度図書館へ行く I go to the library *two or three times* a week.

にさんかたんそ 二酸化炭素 《化学》**carbon dioxide** /daɪɑ́:ksaɪd/

‖二酸化炭素排出規制 control of carbon dioxide emissions.

にし 西 **the west** 一形 西の **west, western** ▶太陽は西に沈もうとしている The sun is about to set in *the west*. ‖日本海は日本列島の西にある The Sea of Japan lies *to the west of* the Japanese Archipelago. ‖わが家は西向きだ My house *faces west*. ／My house has a western exposure. (➤後者は堅い言い方).

▶《慣用表現》この町は初めてで西も東もわからない I'*m a* (*complete*) *stranger* in this city.

‖西海岸 (アメリカの) the West Coast (of the United States) ‖西風 the west wind ‖西側諸国 the West, the Western nations ‖西側陣営 the Western bloc ‖西日本 Western Japan, the western part of Japan ‖西半球 the Western Hemisphere.

☛ 西日 (→見出語)

[1]にじ 虹 **a rainbow** ▶あ, にじが出てるよ Look, there's *a rainbow*. ‖空 [谷] ににじが掛かっている There's *a rainbow* in the sky [over the valley]. ‖にじ色のソックス a pair of *rainbow-colored* socks.

[2]にじ 二次の (**the**) **second**; **secondary** (二次的な) ▶第二次世界大戦 World War II (➤ II は two と読む; この言い方では the を付けない) ／*the Second* World War ‖インフルエンザ(後)の二次感染を防ぐ必要がある It's necessary to prevent (*a*) *secondary infection* after influenza. ‖S大学の入学試験は二次試験まである S University has two entrance exams, a preliminary and *a final*. (➤ final は「最終試験」).

▶頭の良し悪しは二次的な問題で, 大事なのは人柄だ Intelligence is *subordinate to* character. (➤ subordinate to は「…より下位の」) ／Intelligence is less important than character.

‖二次方程式 a quadratic equation.

にしインド 西インド諸島 **the West Indies** (アメリカの南方, カリブ海を囲む島々).

にじかい 二次会 a **party after the party**, an **after-party party**, a **post-party party.**

あなたの英語はどう響く?

「二次会」にぴったりの英語はない. あえて訳せば a party after the party, または an after-party party となるが, ふつうの言い方ではない. また直訳して second party とすると「2番目の政党」などととられる可能性もある. 一般には Let's continue our party at a karaoke bar. (二次会はカラオケバーでやろう) などという.

にしき 錦 ▶《慣用表現》その作家は芥川賞受賞というみやげをもって**故郷に錦を飾った** That writer *returned home in glory* with the Akutagawa Prize.

にしきごい 錦鯉 a *nishikigoi*, a varicolored carp.

にじげん 二次元 two dimensions ; the second dimension (第二次元) **一形 二次元の** two dimensional.

-にしては for ▶ 7月にしてはきょうは涼しい It's cool today *for* July. ‖ この店のカレーライスはこの値段にしてはおいしい The curry and rice at this restaurant is good *for* the price [*considering* the price]. ‖ 彼は20歳にしては子供っぽく見える He looks quite boyish *for* a twenty-year-old. ‖ カーリングはオリンピックの競技としてはいささか地味だ Curling is rather unexciting *for* an Olympic sport [*as* Olympic sports *go*]. (➤ as ... go で「一般的な…としては」の意 ; …には通例複数名詞がくる) ‖ けちなあいつにしてはきょうはやけに気前がいい *Even though* [*Although*] he is usually stingy, he is quite generous today. (➤「ふだんはけちなのに」の意).

にしび 西日 the afternoon sun, the setting sun ▶私の部屋は**西日が入る** My room *gets the afternoon sun*.

にじます 虹鱒 《魚》 a rainbow trout /traʊt/.

にじみでる 滲み出る ooze /uːz/ (血などが) ▶傷口から血がにじみ出ていた Blood *was oozing* from the wound. ‖ 父の顔には苦労がにじみ出ている The hardships my father has experienced in life *are etched* on his face. (➤「刻み込まれている」の意) ‖ 彼女の演技には役者としての年輪がにじみ出ている (=反映されている) Her long career as an actress *is reflected* in her performance.

にじむ 滲む blot (紙などが汚れる) ; run (色・インクなどが広がる) ▶この種の紙はインクがにじみやすい This kind of paper *blots easily* with ink. ／ Ink *runs* [*spreads*] *easily* on this kind of paper. ‖ けんかのあと彼のシャツに**血がにじんでいた** His shirt *was stained with blood* after the fight.

▶《慣用表現》研究者たちは**血のにじむ思い**でその病気の原因を突き止めた The researchers *worked strenuously* and succeeded in tracing the cause of the disease.

にしゃたくいつ 二者択一 a choice between two alternatives /ɔːltə́ːʳnət̬ɪvz/ ▶首相は内閣総辞職か衆議院の解散かの二者択一を迫られている The Prime Minister has to *choose between two alternatives* [*options*] ; the resignation of the whole Cabinet and the dissolution of the House of Representatives.

1にじゅう 二十 twenty ; the twentieth (20番目) ▶怪人**20面相** the *20-faced* mystery man ‖ 姉は来年**20歳**になります My sister will be *twenty years old* next year. ‖ 彼女はまだ**20代**だ She is still *in her twenties*. ‖ **20[21]世紀** the twentieth [twenty-first] century.

2にじゅう 二重の double /dʌ́bəl/ **一副 二重に** double ; twice (二度) ▶**二重**生活をする lead a *double* life ‖ 物が**二重に見える** I see things *double*. ‖ それ, **二重に包んでくれませんか** Could you please *double wrap* it [*wrap* it *with a double layer of paper*]? ‖ 水道料金を**二重に**支払ったようだ It seems that I paid the water bill *twice*.

▶このタイトルは**二重の**意味を持っている This title has a *double* meaning. ‖ それは**二重の**手間だ That would *double* the trouble. (➤ この double は「2倍[二重]にする」の意の動詞) ‖ 先生はその答えに**二重丸**をつけた The teacher marked the answer with *a double circle*.

‖**二重あご** a double chin ‖ **二重国籍** dual nationality ‖ **二重唱[奏]** a duet, a duo ‖ **二重人格者** a person with a dual [double ／split] personality, a Jekyll and Hyde /dʒèkəl ənd háɪd/ ‖ **二重スパイ** a double agent ‖ (皇居の)**二重橋** the Double Bridge ‖ 《文法》**二重否定** a double negative ‖ 《音声学》**二重母音** a diphthong /dífθɔːŋ/ ‖ **二重窓** a double window.

にじゅうよじかん 二十四時間 24 hours ▶コンビニの多くは**24時間営業している** Most convenience stores are open *24 hours a day* [*around the clock*]. (➤「週7日[年中無休], 24時間営業」を24/7 [twenty-four seven] という).

にじょう 二乗 《数学》 a square ▶ 5の2乗は25だ 5 to *the 2nd power* is 25. ／The *square* of 5 is 25. ／ Five squared is 25. →自乗.

にじりよる にじり寄る sidle over 《to》.

にじる 煮汁 broth /brɔːθ ‖ brɒθ/.

-にしろ ▶春夫にしろ秋夫にしろ当てにならない We can't rely on *either* Haruo *or* Akio. ‖ 海外にしろ国内にしろ旅行するにはちゃんと計画をしなければならない *Whether* you travel abroad *or* domestically, you need to plan (your trip) properly.

にしん 鰊 《魚》 a herring

‖**燻製にしん** a kipper, a kippered herring.

にしんほう 二進法 《数学》 the binary /báɪnəri/ system, the base-two system, base 2.

ニス varnish ▶いすに**ニスを塗る** *varnish* [*put varnish on*] a chair ‖ この箱は**ニスが塗ってある** This box *is varnished*.

にせ 偽の false (真実でない; うその) ; sham (いんちきの) ; imitation (模造の) ; counterfeit /káʊnt̬əʳfɪt/, fake, bogus /bóʊgəs/ (人をだます目的で偽造した ; あとの2者はくだけた語) ▶**にせの証明書** a *false* [*fake*] certificate ‖ **にせのルビー** an *imitation* [a *sham* ／a *fake*] ruby.

▶そのサイン[絵]は**にせとわかった** The signature [painting] was found to be a *forgery*. (➤ forgery は「署名・絵画などのにせ物」) ‖ あの人は本物の医者じゃない. **にせ医者**だよ He's not a real doctor. He's a *phon(e)y*. (➤ phon(e)y は「にせ(者)」; phon(e)y doctor ともいう).

‖**にせ学生** a bogus student ‖ **にせ金** bogus [counterfeit] money ‖ **にせ札** a counterfeit bill [note]. →イミテーション.

にせい 二世 ▶エリザベス2世 Queen Elizabeth *II* (➤ the second と読む) ‖ 日系**二世** *a nisei* (➤ 英語化している) ／a second generation Japanese-American (アメリカ人の場合 ; 日本から見れば最初の世代の移民の子なので second generation となり, アメリカ側から見れば, 現地生まれの最初の世代なので first generation と呼ぶことになる) ‖ 兄夫婦に**二世が誕生した** *A first son* [*daughter*] was born to my brother and his wife. ‖ 彼女はデビューしたとき，シャラポワ二世と騒がれた When she came out, she was touted as a *second* Sharapova. (➤「第二のシャラポワとほめちぎられた」の意).

‖**二世議員** a second-generation Diet member.

にせたいじゅうたく 二世帯住宅 a house designed for two generations [households] of the (same) family.

1**にせもの 偽物** an **imitation** (模造品) ; a **counterfeit** /káʊnṭəʳfɪt/ (主に貨幣の), a **fake** (偽造品) ; a **forgery** /fɔ́ːʳdʒəri/ (主に署名・絵などの) ▶この身分証明書は偽物だ This ID card is *a counterfeit*. ‖ そのシャガールの絵は実は偽物だった The Chagall proved to be *a forgery* [*a fake*]. ‖ 偽物のダイヤをつかまされてしまった I had an *imitation* [a *sham*／a *fake*] diamond palmed off on me. ／I was tricked into buying a *false* diamond.

2**にせもの 偽者** a **fake** ; an **impostor** (詐欺師).

-にせよ →-にしろ.

にせる 似せる **imitate** /ímɪteɪt/ +㊐, **copy** +㊐ ▶彼に姿形は似せられても人柄までは無理だよ You can *imitate* his appearance but not his personality. ‖ この建物は金閣寺に似せて造ってある This building is modeled *after* (the) Kinkakuji Temple.

にそう 尼僧 a **nun** ‖**尼僧院** a convent.

にそくさんもん 二束三文 ▶彼は外国へ移住するため車を二束三文で手放した He sold his car *dirt-cheap* [*for a song*] because he was moving to a foreign country. (●ともに「ばか安で」の意のインフォーマルな言い方. 買う場合にも用いる).

にそくのわらじ 二足の草鞋 ▶彼女は教師と画家という二足のわらじをはく生活をしている She *is wearing two hats* as a teacher and an artist. (● 英語では「2つの帽子をかぶる」という).

にだい 荷台 a **carrier** (自転車・オートバイの) ; a **load-carrying platform** (トラックなどの) ; a **roof-rack** (自動車などの屋根上の).

にたき 煮炊き **cooking.**

にたつ 煮立つ **boil (up), come to the boil** ▶スープが煮立っている The soup *is boiling*. ‖ お湯がぐらぐら煮立ってからスパゲティを入れなさい Put the spaghetti into the water after it *comes to a rolling boil*.

にたてる 煮立てる **boil (up) ; bring ... to a boil** ▶大豆を15分間煮立ててください *Boil* the soybeans for 15 minutes.

にたにた ▶あいつは何をあんなににたにたしてるのだろう I wonder what that guy *is snickering* about [*is smirking* at]. (snicker は「せせら笑う」, smirk は「うすら笑いをする」).

にたもの 似た者 ▶ふたりは似た者どうしだ They *are a lot alike*. ／They *have a lot in common*. ／They *resemble each other a lot*.

にたり ▶泥棒は金庫の金塊を見てにたりとした The burglars *grinned* when they saw the pile of gold ingots in the safe.

にたりよったり 似たり寄ったり ▶朝のテレビ番組はどれも似たり寄ったりだ All the morning shows on TV *are almost the same* [*pretty much alike*].

にだんベッド 二段ベッド a **bunk bed.**

-にち -日 ▶ 対話「きょうは何日ですか」「(7月)23日です」"*What's the date* today?" "It's (July) the twenty-third."

▶彼は1日に1度しか食事をとらない He eats only one meal *a day*.

にちえい 日英 **Japan and Britain, Japan and the United Kingdom** ▶日英の友好関係を維持する maintain friendly relations between *Japan and Britain*.

‖**日英関係** Japan-U.K. relations.

にちぎん 日銀 **the Bank of Japan**

‖**日銀総裁** the governor of the Bank of Japan.

にちじ 日時 **the time and date** ▶日時は追ってお知らせします You will be notified of *the time and date* later. ‖ 日時を間違えないようにしてください Make sure (that) you do not make mistake *the time and date*.

にちじょう 日常 **every day** —形 **日常の** **everyday, daily** ▶大震災で何十万という人の平穏な日常が崩れてしまった The peaceful *everyday lives* of hundreds of thousands of people were gone due to the great earthquake. ‖ 日常を失って日常のありがたみが身にしみた I learned to appreciate the blessings of our *normal*, *everyday life* after I was deprived of them.

▶清潔は日常(＝常日ごろ)心がけねばならないことです Cleanliness is something you have to pay attention to *every day*. ‖ この辞書は日常生活で使うことばを重視している This dictionary focuses on words used *in daily* [*everyday*] *life*. ‖ フランス語は日常会話程度ならできます I can speak French at a *daily conversation* level. (●「フランス語の日常会話」は everyday French (conversation) のようにもいう) ‖ 交通事故など日常茶飯事だ Traffic accidents are *everyday occurrences* [*happen all the time*].

にちどく 日独 **Japan and Germany** ▶日独の経済関係 *Japanese-German* economic relations.

にちぶ 日舞 **(traditional) Japanese dance.**

にちふつ 日仏 **Japan and France** ▶日仏の文化交流 *Japanese-French* cultural exchanges ／cultural exchanges *between Japan and France*.

にちべい 日米 **Japan and the United States** ▶日米関係 *Japan-U.S.* [*Japanese-U.S.*] relations ‖ 日米間の貿易収支は不均衡だ There is a trade imbalance between *Japan and the United States*.

‖**日米安全保障条約** the Japan-U.S. Security Treaty.

にちぼつ 日没 **(a) sunset** ▶エーゲ海の日没は実に美しい *Sunsets* in the Aegean Sea are really beautiful. ‖ 日没とともにあたりの家々に次々と灯がともった *As the sun set*, lights went on in the surrounding houses one after another.

にちや 日夜 **day and night, night and day** ▶試合まであとひと月，私たちは日夜練習に励んでいます There is only one month to go before the match and we are practicing very hard, *day and night*.

にちよう(び) 日曜(日) **Sunday** 《略 Sun., S.》 →曜日 ▶私は日曜日は朝寝をする I get up late *on Sunday*(*s*). ／I sleep in *on Sunday*(*s*). ‖ 私は先週の日曜日に友人の結婚披露宴に出席した I attended my friend's wedding reception *last Sunday*. ‖ きのうは日曜大工で本棚を作った I did some *home carpentry* and made a bookshelf yesterday.

《参考》日曜大工をする人のことを do-it-yourselfer という.

‖**日曜画家** an amateur painter, a Sunday painter ‖**日曜学校** a Sunday school.

にちようひん 日用品 **daily necessities** [**goods**／**commodities**].

にちロ 日ロ **Japan and Russia** ▶日ロ関係 *Japan-Russia* [*Japanese-Russian*] relations

‖日露戦争 the Russo-Japanese War.

にっか 日課 a **(daily) routine** /rùːtíːn/ ▶日課として on a *daily basis* ‖ 早朝に芝に水をやるのが彼の日課だ Watering the lawn in the early morning is (*part of*) *his daily routine*.
▶毎朝ジョギングするのが私の日課だ I'*m in the habit* of jogging every morning. ／I jog every morning.

ニッカーボッカー knickerbockers.

につかわしい 似つかわしい suitable ▶夜のパーティーならこちらの豪華なドレスのほうが似つかわしい This fancy dress would *be* more *suitable* [*fitting*] for an evening party. ‖ そんな仕事はきみには似つかわしくない It's not the *right* job for you.

1**にっかん 日韓 Japan and South Korea** ▶日韓政府代表者会議 a meeting between *Japanese and South Korean* officials.

2**にっかん 日刊の daily** ▶家では2種類の日刊新聞を取っている We take two *daily newspapers* [two *dailies*].

-につき 1【…ごとに】**a, per** (➤ 後者は主にビジネス用語) ▶1人につき500円頂きます We charge 500 yen *per person*. ‖ このコンピュータのリース料金は1か月につき5万円です This computer leases for 50,000 yen *a* [*per*] *month*.
2【…の理由で】**because of, due to** ▶荒天につき本日のフェリーの運航は中止させていただきます *Due to* [*Because of*] bad weather, ferry service will be suspended today.

にっき 日記 a **diary** (出来事などを簡潔に記した); a **journal** (日々の思いを記した) ▶英語で日記をつけ(続け)る keep *a diary* in English (「日記をつける」という1回1回の動作は write in a diary) ‖ 私は小学校時代から日記をつけています I have been *keeping a diary* since elementary school.
▶先生にののしられたことを日記につけておこう I'm going to *write in my diary* that my teacher swore at me.
‖日記帳 a diary ‖ 絵日記 a picture diary ‖ 交換日記 an exchange diary.

にっきゅう 日給 daily wages ▶この仕事は日給1万円です This job *pays* 10,000 yen *a day*. ／*Daily wages* on [for] this job are 10,000 yen. ‖ 日給で働く人の生活は不安定だ The livelihood of *those who work by the day* [The livelihood of *day laborers*] is unstable.

にっきょうそ 日教組 the Japan Teachers' Union.

ニックネーム a **nickname** ▶ロバートのニックネームはボブだ Robert's *nickname* is Bob.

にづくり 荷造り packing 一動 荷造りする pack (＋㊐) ▶家財道具を荷造りする *pack* one's household effects.

につけ 煮付け ▶魚の煮付け *fish boiled and seasoned with sugar and soy sauce*.

にっけい 日系 ▶日系ブラジル人 *a Japanese-Brazilian* ‖ 日系3世 a *sansei*, a third generation *Japanese-American* (➤ アメリカ人の場合) ‖ ハヤカワ博士は日系アメリカ人です Dr. Hayakawa is a *Japanese-American* [*an American of Japanese descent*]. (descent の代わりに ancestry でもよい) ‖ メアリーさんはロサンゼルスにある日系企業で働いている Mary works for *a Japanese company* in Los Angeles.

ニッケイ 肉桂《植物》**cinnamon.**

ニッケル nickel /níkəl/ ▶その製品はニッケルめっきがしてある The product is coated [plated] with *nickel*. ‖ ニッケルめっきのフォーク a *nickel-plated* fork.

にっこう 日光 sunlight, (the) sun ; sunshine (心地よいひなた) ▶夏の浜辺は日光が強い The *sunlight* on summer beaches is strong. ‖ この部屋は日光がよく入る This room gets plenty of *sun* [a lot of *sunshine*]. ‖ 布団はときどき日光に当てる必要がある It's necessary to *air* futon(s) *in the sun* occasionally.
▶この植物は日光の十分当たる所に置いてください Please place this plant where it will get plenty of *sunlight* [*sunshine*]. (「(直射)日光の当たらない所に」なら Please place this plant out of (the) direct sunlight. あるいは Please place this plant in the shade とする).

にっこうよく 日光浴 sunbathing 一動 日光浴する sunbathe /sʌ́nbeɪð/ ▶我々は海辺で日光浴した We *sunbathed* on the beach.

にっこり ▶赤ちゃんは母親の顔を見るとにっこり笑った The baby *smiled* when he [she] saw his [her] mother. ‖ 彼女はにっこり笑いながら玄関に出て来た She came to the door *with a* (*sweet*) *smile*.
《参考》日本語ではさまざまな副詞をつけて笑い方を表現するが, 英語では smile (にっこり笑う), grin (声を立てずに歯を見せて笑う), giggle (くすくす笑う), laugh (わっはっはと笑う) などと動詞1語で表すことができる. →笑う.

1**にっさん 日参** ▶父は母との結婚の許しをもらうために母の両親のもとに日参したという My father says (that) he *visited* my mother's parents *daily* to get their consent to marry her.

2**にっさん 日産 daily production** [**output**].

にっし 日誌 a **diary** (私的な) ; a **journal** (公的な) ▶日誌をつける keep *a diary* [*journal*] ‖ 私たちは学級日誌をつけている We keep *a daily record of class activities*. ‖航海日誌 a log(book).

にっしゃびょう 日射病 sunstroke ▶外で遊ぶときは帽子をかぶらないと日射病になりますよ You'll get [have] *sunstroke* if you play outdoors without a hat on. →熱中症.

にっしょう 日照 ▶先月は異常なほど日照時間が少なかった We had an unusually small *amount of sunlight* last month. ‖ わが家の前にビルが建ったために日照権が奪われた They constructed a building in front of my house and infringed on our *right to sunshine*.

にっしょうき 日章旗 the Rising Sun flag.

にっしょく 日食 a **solar eclipse** /ɪklíps/, **the eclipse of the sun** ‖皆既[部分]日食 a total [partial] eclipse of the sun.

にっしんげっぽ 日進月歩 ▶科学技術は日進月歩だ Technology *is advancing in* [*by*] *leaps and bounds*. ／Technology *is rapidly advancing*. ‖ 現代医学の日進月歩にもかかわらずがん制圧の日はまだ遠いだろう Despite *the steady progress* of modern medical science, the day when cancer is defeated is (still) far off.

にっすう 日数 ▶この家を建てるのにどれくらい日数が掛かりますか *How many days* [*How long*] will it take to build this house ?
▶きみは出席日数が足りないから, もう1年やり直しだ Because your *attendance was* so *bad* [you *missed too many days of school*], you'll have to repeat the year.

ニッチ a **niche** /nɪtʃ ‖ niːʃ/
‖ニッチ市場 a niche market.

にっちもさっちもいかない ▶仕事を失い, 貯金を使い果たした彼はにっちもさっちもいかなくなった Having lost his job and spent all his savings, he *found himself in a tight corner* [*in a fix*]. (➤ tight corner, fix はともに「窮地」の意).

1**にっちゅう 日中 the daytime, day** ▶ここは日中はとても暑いが夜は涼しい In this district it is very hot *in the daytime*, but cool at night. ‖ 日中は雨, 夜は山沿いで雪となるでしょう Rain *during the day* will turn into snow at night in the mountains.

2**にっちゅう 日中 Japan and China** (日本と中国) ▶その番組は日中のテレビ局が共同制作した The TV program was jointly produced by TV stations from both *Japan and China*.

にっちょく 日直 day duty ▶私は今度の日曜日は日直です I am *on* (*day*) *duty* this coming Sunday.

にってい 日程 a schedule /skédʒuːl ‖ ʃédjuːl/ (時間ごとに区切られた) ; **a program** (ある目的を達成するための) ▶今月の日程はどうなっていますか What's the *schedule* [*program*] for this month? ‖ 今週は日程が詰まっている I *have a full schedule* this week. ／I'*m tied up* all this week. ‖ 航空会社のストで旅行の日程を変更しなければならなかった We had to change our *travel plans* [our *itinerary*] due to the airline strike. (➤ itinerary /aɪtínəreri/ は「旅程」).

✉ **日程が決まりしだいお知らせください** Please let me know as soon as your *schedule* [*itinerary*] is set. (➤ 最後の set は fixed や decided としてもよい).

‖**日程表** a schedule.

にっと にっと笑う grin.

ニット knitwear /nítweəʳ/ ━ 形 **ニットの knitted** /nítɪd/ ▶ニットのドレス a *knitted* dress ‖ ニット製品 *knitted* goods ‖ ニット専門店 a *knitwear* specialty store ‖ ニット帽 a *knit* cap.

にっとう 日当 a daily allowance /əláʊəns/ (1日ごとの手当) ; **daily wages** (日給) ; **a per diem** /pəʳ díːem/ (出張時などの) ▶出張には日当が出るのでしょうか Do I get *a per diem* for business trips? ‖ みんなで海岸をきれいにして, わずかばかりの日当をもらった We all went out to clean the beach and got *a small sum* (*of money*) *for the day*.

にっぽん 日本 Japan, Nippon ▶日本, がんばれ! Give it your best [Don't give up], *Japan*! →にほん.

につまる 煮詰まる boil down ▶友達と長電話をしているうちにスープが煮詰まってしまった During a long phone conversation with my friend, the soup *boiled down*.

▶《比喩的》私たちの海外公演の話はだいぶ煮詰まってきた The plans for our overseas performance have begun to *take shape*. (➤ take shape は「具体化する」).

につめる 煮詰める boil down ▶リンゴの果汁を量が半分になるまで煮詰めてください *Boil down* the apple juice to half the original amount.

▶《比喩的》実行に移す前に計画は十分煮詰めておかなければならない Before we put the plan into action, it has to *be fully discussed*.

にている 似ている →似る.

にてもにつかない 似ても似つかない ▶彼女は姉とは似ても似つかない She *is quite unlike* her sister. ／*There is no resemblance* between her and her sister.

▶その映画は原作とは似ても似つかぬ駄作だ It is a third-rate movie that *is entirely different from* the book it was based on.

にてんさんてん 二転三転 ▶得点は二転三転した The score *seesawed back and forth*. ‖ 状況は二転三転した The situation *changed again and again*.

にと 二兎 ▶2人の女の子を追い回していると「二兎を追う者は」ということになりかねないよ If you continue running after two girls, you'll end up with neither (one). (➤「どちらも結局つかまえ損ねて」の意) ‖ [ことわざ] **二兎を追う者は一兎をも得ず** He who runs after two hares will catch neither. (➤ 日本語からの直訳).

にど 二度 twice /twaɪs/, **two times** (2回 ; 前者がふつう) ; **again** (再び) ▶この映画は2度見た I've seen this movie *twice* [*two times*]. (● two times は強調するときなどに用いられる) ‖ 私は週に2度彼にポルトガル語を教えている I teach him Portuguese *twice* a week.

▶もう二度といたしません I won't do it [let it happen] *again*. ／It won't happen *again*. ‖ おまえの顔なんか二度と見たくない I do*n't* want to see your face *ever again* [*any more*].

[ことわざ] **二度あることは三度ある** What happens twice will happen thrice. (➤ 日本語からの直訳) ／When it rains, it pours. ／It never rains but it pours. (● あとの二文は「降れば必ずどしゃ降り」の意の英語のことわざで, どちらかといえば悪い意味で用いられることが多い).

▶京都に来たのはこれで2度目だ This is my *second* visit to Kyoto. ‖ あなたに電話するのはこれが2度目です This is *the second time* (that) I've called you. (➤ that 以下の文はふつう完了形になる).

にとう 二等 (the) second place (2位) ; **(the) second prize** (2等賞) ▶二等になる get [win] (*the*) *second prize* ‖ 彼女はスピーチコンテストで二等だった She won *the second prize* in the speech contest.

‖**二等船室** [**客室**] a second-class cabin [《英》carriage].

にとうぶん 二等分する halve /hæv/ +㊐ (半分にする) ▶ケーキを二等分する *cut* a cake *in half* ／*halve* a cake.

にとうへんさんかっけい 二等辺三角形 《数学》 an **isosceles** /aɪsɑ́ːsəliːz/ **triangle.**

にとうりゅう 二刀流 a two-way player (➤ アメリカンフットボール, バスケットボール, 野球などで, 攻守両方のプレーができる選手を指す. 両手に刀を持って闘う剣術は dual wielding という).

にどでま 二度手間 ▶区役所にはんこを持って行かなかったために家に取りに戻らねばならず, 結局は二度手間になった Since I didn't take my *hanko* when I went to the ward office, I had to return home to get it. It ended up being *double* (*the*) *work* for me [being *an unnecessary duplication of effort*].

にどね 二度寝する go back to sleep.

ニトログリセリン 《化学》 **nitroglycerin** (e) /nàɪtrəglísərɪn/.

にないて 担い手 a bearer ▶佐々木や石川は球界の次世代の担い手になるだろう Sasaki and Ishikawa will *lead the next generation* of baseball players. ／Sasaki and Ishikawa will *shoulder the future* of baseball in Japan. ‖ 皆さんにはわが社の将来の担い手として頑張ってもらわなければなりません The future of our company depends on you [is on your shoulders], so you need to do your best. (➤「将来を背負っている」の意).

になう 担う ▶その政治家は日本の政界のあすを担うと言われている It is said that the future of Japanese politics *rests on him* [*on his shoulders*]. ‖ 次代を担うのはきみたちだ The coming era *rests on your shoulders*.
▶中央自動車道は東名のバイパスとしての役割を担っている The Chuo Expressway *serves as* a bypass for the Tomei Expressway.

ににんさんきゃく 二人三脚 a **three-legged race** ▶二人三脚のレースをする run a *three-legged* race
▶《比喩的》おばあちゃんはおじいちゃんと二人三脚で(＝二人で力を合わせて)しにせののれんを守ってきた Grandma and grandpa worked *hand in hand* to keep their long-established store.

ににんしょう 二人称 《文法》**the second person.**

にぬし 荷主 a **consignor** /kənsáɪnəʳ/ (送り主).

にねんせい 二年生 ▶来年は高校2年生になります Next year I'll be in my *second year of* (*senior*) *high school*.

> 【解説】(1)アメリカでは小・中学校の2年生はそれぞれ **second grader, eighth grader** といい, 3年制の高校では **junior**, 4年制の高校・大学では **sophomore** /sɑ́:fəmɔ:ʳ/ を用いる. 両者の代わりに, eleventh grader ともいう.
> (2)日本の小・中学校の2年生は **second-year student** [**pupil**] とするか, 《米》式の言い方を用いる. 大学2年生は second-year student, または《米》の sophomore がよい.

にのあし 二の足 ▶兄にいい仕事の話が来たが本人は二の足を踏んでいる Though my (older) brother has been offered a good job, he'*s hesitating about whether to take it*.

にのうで 二の腕 **the upper arm.**

にのく 二の句 ▶彼の返答にはあきれて二の句が継げなかったよ When we heard his answer, we *were dumbfounded* [*were speechless*].

にのつぎ 二の次 ▶父はいわゆる「仕事中毒」で家庭のことなど二の次だ My father is what you call a workaholic and always *puts* the family *second*.

にのまい 二の舞 ▶去年の私の二の舞を演ずることだけは避けなさいよ Just try to avoid *making the same mistake* I made [did] last year.

-には ⚠ **in, to, by, for などの前置詞が対応するケースと, 主語などの中に「-には」の意味が含まれていて訳文に出ないケースとがある.**

1【特定して】▶日本語には漢字・平がな・片かなの3種類の文字がある There are three types of symbols used *in* writing Japanese—they are kanji, hiragana and katakana. ‖ この新しいホテルには500の客室がある This new hotel has five hundred rooms. ‖ そこには誰も居なかった There was nobody *there*. ‖ 私にはたくさんの友人がいます I have lots of friends.
▶荷物はあす[5時]までには着くでしょう The parcel should reach you *by* tomorrow [five]. ‖ 父は来年の春には海外勤務を終えて帰って来る My father will return from his overseas assignment next spring. ‖ 翌朝には雪はすっかり消えていた The next morning, the snow had completely disappeared. (🔔 過去の一時点を基準にして, そこから「次の朝」というときには next morning に the をつける).
▶由利子には会いたくないんだ I don't want to see Yuriko. ‖ 政治家には失望している I'm disappointed *in* [*with*] politicians. ‖ 社長さんには礼儀正しくするんですよ You should be courteous *to* the president. ‖ その私大の名前は高校生たちにはよく知られている The name of that private university is well known *to* high school students.
▶この本は私には難し過ぎる This book is too difficult *for* me. ‖ 私には何も見えない I can't see anything. ‖ きみが何と言おうとぼくにはぼくの考えがあるんだ Whatever you say [No matter what you say], I have my own ideas. ‖ グリーンはきみには似合わない Green doesn't look good *on* you. ‖ 肉料理には赤ワインがよく合う Red wine goes well *with* meat dishes.
▶この機械を動かすにはどうすればいいのですか What should I do *to* start this machine? ‖ ドイツに留学するにはもっとドイツ語を勉強する必要がある *To* study abroad in Germany, you must study German harder. ‖ 鉛筆書きを消すには消しゴムがいる You need an eraser *for* erasing pencil marks.
▶彼女のずうずうしさにはあきれてしまう I'm astonished *at* her audacity. ‖ 大変うれしいことには, 彼らはみな無事だった I found, *to* my great joy, that they were all safe.

2【「…するにはしたが」の形で】▶答案を書くには書いたが自信がない I *did answer* all the questions, *but* I don't know whether (or not) my answers were right. (🔔 did answer は answered を強調した形で did に強勢を置く. 次例も同じ) ‖ B大に願書を出すには出したが, 受験はしなかった I *did send in* an application to B University, *but* I didn't take the entrance exam.

にばい 二倍 **double ; twice, two times** (➤ 前者がふつう) **━形 二倍の double** (➤ the や所有格などの前に置く) ▶8は4の2倍だ Eight is the *double* of four. ‖ 5の2倍は10だ *Twice* [*Two times*] five makes ten. ‖ 家賃は6年で2倍になった The rent *doubled* in six years. ‖ 原料費は以前の2倍に上がっている Raw material prices are *two times as* high *as* they used to be. ‖ ぼくは彼の2倍の努力をした I worked *twice as* hard *as* he did. ‖ B4判はB5判の2倍の大きさです A sheet of B4 paper is *twice* the size of B5 [*twice as* large *as* B 5]. (🔔 twice of the size としない) ‖ アメリカの人口は日本の2倍以上だ The population of the U.S. is *over twice* that of Japan.

にばん 二番 **the second, number two** (➤ No. 2と略す) ▶数学の試験はクラスで2番の成績だった On the math test I *scored* (*the*) *second highest* [*best*] in my class.
▶2番の問題が解けなかった I couldn't solve problem *No.2*. ‖ 私はクラスで小さいほうから2番目です I'm *the second shortest* in my class. ‖ 彼女は2番目に到着した She was *the second* to arrive.
▶《慣用表現》彼の新しい小説は旧作の二番せんじだ His new novel is simply *a rehash* of a former one. (➤ rehash は「焼き直し」).

ニヒリスト a **nihilist** /náɪɪlɪst/.

ニヒリズム 《哲学》**nihilism** /náɪɪlɪzm/.

ニヒル **nihilistic** /nàɪɪlístɪk/ (ニヒルな) ▶ニヒルな(雰囲気の)男 a man who has a *nihilistic* air.

にぶ 二部 ▶きょうの番組は2部に分かれている Today's program has *two segments* [*parts*]. ‖ 第2部 the second part / Part Two.
▶プログラムを2部(＝2冊)ください Give me *two copies* of the program. / *Two* programs, please.
▶大学の二部(＝夜間部) the *night division* of a

university.

‖二分音符《音楽》a half note,《英》a minim ‖二部合唱 a chorus in two parts (☛「二部合唱する」は sing in two parts).

にぶい 鈍い **1【刃物などがよく切れない】dull ; blunt** (なまくらの) ▶このナイフは切れ味が鈍い This knife *is dull* [*blunt*].

2【光・音がぼんやりとした】dull ; dim(うす暗い) ▶ガス灯が鈍い光を放っている The gaslight is emitting (a) *dim* light. ‖ 2 階で何かが鈍い音を立てて倒れた Something fell upstairs with *a thud* [*a dull sound*]. (➤ thud は「ドスンという音」).

3【遅い, のろい】slow ▶この子は動作が鈍い This child moves *slowly* [*is slow-moving*]. ‖ 彼女はちょっと頭が鈍い She *is* a bit *slow on the uptake.* ／ She *is* a bit *dull-witted*. ‖ 彼女はおまえのことが好きなんだぞ. 鈍いなあ(＝ばかだ) She's in love with you. What *a numbskull* [*dimwit*] you are (not to have noticed)!

にふくめる 煮含める simmer until the flavor has been absorbed.

にふだ 荷札 a **tag**(下げ札) ; a **label** /léɪbəl/ (張り札) ▶荷物にこの荷札をつけてください Please put this *tag* on your baggage.

にぶる 鈍る **1【よく切れなくなる】become dull** ▶このナイフは切れ味が鈍ってきた This knife *has become dull* [*blunt*].

2【弱くなる, のろくなる】▶多くの動物が冬の間は活動が鈍る Many animals are *inactive* during the winter. ‖ 寒さで足の感覚が鈍ってしまった My legs *have become numb* with cold. (➤ numb /nʌm/ は「無感覚な」) ‖ 私のゴルフの腕前は鈍った I've *lost my touch* at golf. (➤ lose one's touch で「腕が落ちる, 勘が鈍る」).

▶彼女に別れようと言うつもりだったが, 彼女の顔を見たら決心が鈍った I was going to tell her I would stop seeing her, but my resolution *wavered* [*was shaken*] when I saw her. (➤ waver は「(決心が)ぐらつく」).

にぶん 二分 ▶松田聖子と中森明菜は1980年代の女性アイドル界の人気を二分していた Matsuda Seiko and Nakamori Akina were *the two top singing idols* in 1980s.

にべもない ▶彼の所に頼みに行ったが, にべもない返事でね I went to him for help, but he *flatly refused* my request [but he (only) *gave* me *a curt refusal*]. (➤ curt は「ぶっきらぼうな」) ‖ にべもなく断られたよ I was given a flat refusal. ／I was *flatly* refused.

にぼし 煮干し ***niboshi*** ; small sardines boiled and dried (➤ 説明的な訳).

にほん 日本

Japan(➤ 場合により Nippon を用いてもよい) **一形 日本の Japanese** ▶日本の文化 *Japanese* culture ‖ 日本一長い橋 *the longest* bridge *in Japan* ‖ 日本風の庭園 a *Japanese-style* garden ‖ 私は日本から来た村上由佳です I'm Murakami Yuka from *Japan*. ‖ 日本の経済は今や危機に直面している The *Japanese* economy [*Japan's* economy ／The economy *of Japan*] is now facing a serious crisis. ‖ うちの会社は日本中に支店を持っている Our company has branches *all over Japan* [*throughout Japan* ／ *across the country* ／ *nationwide*].

▶とても日本的なデザイン a very *Japanese-looking* design ‖ 水はただという考え方はきわめて日本的だ It's very *Japanese* to think that water is free. ‖ 加納さんは日本的な顔だちの美人だ Kano-san is a *typical Japanese* beauty. ‖ 彼女は日本びいき［嫌い］だ She is *pro-Japanese* [*anti-Japanese*].

✉ **日本は東アジアに位置する山の多い島国です** *Japan* is a mountainous island country located in Eastern Asia.

✉ **日本でいちばん高い山は富士山です** The highest mountain *in Japan* is Mt. Fuji.

✉ **松島, 宮島, 天の橋立は日本三景と呼ばれています** Matsushima, Miyajima and Amanohashidate are called *Nihon-sankei* (*Japan's three most scenic spots*).

✉ **日本の人口は 1 億2500万人以上です** *Japan's population* is over 125 million.

✉ **夏の夕方, 日本各地で花火大会が開かれます** On summer evenings, fireworks festivals are held *in many places all over Japan*.

✉ **日本においでのときは, ぜひわが家にも泊まってください** When you visit *Japan*, do stay with us [at our home].

‖日本アルプス the Japan Alps ‖ 日本画 a Japanese painting ‖ 日本髪 the traditional Japanese hairstyle ‖ 日本研究 Japanology /dʒæ̀pənɑ́:lədʒi/ ‖ 日本研究家 a Japanologist ‖ 日本史 Japanese history ‖ 日本時間 Japan time ‖ 日本酒 sake /sɑ́:ki/ ‖ 日本食 Japanese food ‖ 日本シリーズ the Japan Series ‖ 日本製品 Japanese products [goods] ‖ 日本庭園 a Japanese garden ‖ 日本刀 a Japanese sword ‖ 日本舞踊 Japanese traditional dance ‖ 日本文学 Japanese literature ‖ 日本間 a Japanese-style room ‖ 日本料理 Japanese cuisine /kwɪzí:n/, Japanese food [dish] ‖ 日本料理店 a Japanese restaurant ‖ 日本列島 the Japanese Archipelago /ɑ̀:ˈkəpéləgoʊ/ [Islands].

☞ 全日本 (→見出語)

にほんかい 日本海 the Sea of Japan ▶日本海側は大雪だった *The Japan Sea* coast was [The regions along *the Sea of Japan* were] covered with [in] heavy snow.

にほんご 日本語 Japanese, the Japanese language(➤ 後者は堅い言い方) ; a **Japanese word**(日本語の単語) ▶アキラさん, bribery は日本語では何といいますか How do you say 'bribery' in *Japanese*, Akira? ／ What's the *Japanese* (word) for 'bribery,' Akira? (☛ 後者の文では「(相当する)日本語の単語」の意なので the が必要) ‖ モニカさん, 日本語はいくつ知っていますか Monica, how many *Japanese words* do you know?

にほんじん 日本人

a **Japanese (person)** (1 人) ; **Japanese (people)**, **the Japanese 一形 日本人の Japanese**

> **解説** (1) the Japanese は「日本人全体」を他の国民と対比して客観的にいうような場合に使われ, Japanese(複数形)または Japanese people は日本人の一面を一般化して表現する場合に使う. しかし, 両者の違いは微妙でどちらでも意味に変化のないこともある. なお, the Japanese people とすると「日本民族」「日本国民」の意になる.
> (2)「我々日本人は」の意味の We Japanese はしばしば排他的に響く. We または Japanese を文脈に応じて使い分けるほうがよい.

▶平均的日本人 an average *Japanese* (*person*) ‖

私が知っている**日本人たち** *the Japanese people* I know ‖ **日本人**観光客 *Japanese* tourists ‖ 第２次大戦後**日本人**の食生活はずいぶん変わった The eating habits of *the Japanese* changed a lot after World War II. ‖ **日本人**は平和を愛する国民です *Japanese people* love peace. ‖ ジョンソンさんの家に**日本人**の学生がホームステイしている A *Japanese* student is homestaying with the Johnsons. ‖ ほとんどの**日本人**は６年間あるいはそれ以上, 学校で英語を勉強している Most *Japanese* (*people*) study English at school for six years or more. ‖ その飛行機には５人の**日本人**が乗っていた模様です It seems that there were five *Japanese* (*people*) on board (the plane).

▶ 対話「あなたは中国人ですか」「いいえ, **日本人**です」"Are you Chinese?" "No, (I'm) *Japanese*." (国籍をいうときは a Chinese, a Japanese と名詞でいうより, 形容詞でいうほうがふつう).

に

にほんだて 二本立て a **double feature** ▶この映画館はいつも洋画の**２本立て**だ They are always showing *a double feature* of foreign movies at this theater.

にほんばれ 日本晴れ a **cloudless sky** ▶きょうは雲一つない**日本晴れ**だ Today is *a perfect day*, without a (speck of) cloud in the sky.

にまいがい 二枚貝 《生物学》 a **bivalve** /báɪvæ̀lv/.

にまいじた 二枚舌 ▶**二枚舌**を使う人 a *double dealing* person [《インフォーマル》 a *double-dealer*], a person *with a forked* [*double*] *tongue*.

にまいめ 二枚目 a **handsome** [**good-looking**] **man** ▶彼女のボーイフレンド, なかなかの**二枚目**よ Her boyfriend is quite *handsome*. ‖ 彼は**二枚目半**だ He'*s good-looking and funny*.

-にも **1**【同様であることを示して】▶ライオンはアフリカだけでなくインド**にも**すんでいる Lions live not only in Africa, but (*also*) *in* India. ／Lions live in India *as well as* in Africa. ‖ きみ**にも**いずれわかる時が来る The time will come when *you* can understand it, *too*. (➤ you と too に強勢を置く) ‖ 俺**にも**やらせろ Let *me* have a try, *too*. (➤ me と too に強勢を置く).

▶ 対話「私にいい考えがあります」「私**にも**」"I've got a good idea." "*Me too!*" ‖ 私**にも**わからない I don't understand it, *either*. (➤ 否定文では either を使う).

2【強調して】▶東京**にも**こんな静かな所があったのか I'm amazed to find such a quiet place as this in Tokyo. ‖ ベイスターズはきょう**にも**胴上げです The BayStars could clinch the pennant *as early as* today.

▶予算案は今月末［今週中］**にも**衆議院を通過する予定だ The budget bill is scheduled to be approved by the House of Representatives *by* the end of this month [*within* this week] *at the latest*. (➤「遅くても今月末までに」の意).

▶私**にも**車の運転くらいできます *Even* I can drive a car. ‖ 冗談**にも**そんなことを言ってはだめだ Don't say such a thing, *even* just for fun. ／You shouldn't say thing like that, *even* in jest. ‖ 何をやる**にも**中途はんぱはいけない *Whatever you do* [*No matter what you do*], you must not leave it half-done.

▶少年は親切**にも**私を駅まで連れて行ってくれた The boy *was so kind as to* [*was kind enough to* ／*had the kindness to*] take me to the train station.

にもうさく 二毛作 **double cropping**.

-にもかかわらず ➡かかわらず.

にもつ 荷物 **baggage**, **luggage** (旅行の際の手荷物；ともに Ⓤ で, ２つ以上の荷物を総称的に指す)；**belongings** (身の回りの品；複数扱い)；a **load** (積み荷)

> **語法** (1) baggage, luggage は複数形をとらず, 多い少ないを表すときは **much** [**a lot of**] **baggage, little baggage** のようにいう. また数えるときは a piece [two pieces] of baggage のようにいう.
> (2) 《米》では「手荷物」は baggage,「かばん類など入れ物」は luggage と使い分けることがある. 《英》では luggage がふつう.
> (3) baggage や luggage は２個以上の荷物を指す総称なので, １つの荷物をいう場合は具体的に suitcase, shopping bag などとしなければならない.
> (4)「荷物を詰める」も (×) pack one's baggage [luggage] ではなく, pack one's bag [suitcase], pack clothes into a suitcase, pack a suitcase with clothes などのように具体的にいうのがふつう.

▶あなたは**荷物**はおいくつあるのですか How many pieces of *baggage* do you have? ‖ 私は旅行のときはあまり**荷物**を持っていかない I don't take much *baggage* with me on trips. ‖ 網棚の**荷物**を忘れないように Make sure you don't leave your *luggage* on the rack. ／Make sure you don't forget to take *your things* down from the rack. (➤ one's things は「手回り品」) ‖ すぐに自分の**荷物**をまとめなさい Get *your things* ready quickly. ‖ **荷物**をお持ちしましょうか Can I carry your *bag* [*suitcase*]? ‖ 彼はフロントに**荷物**を預けた He checked his *bag* [*briefcase*] at the front desk.

▶ 対話「**荷物**はどこへ預けたらいいですか」「そこの**荷物**預かり所に預けられますよ」"Where can I leave my *baggage*?" "You can leave it at the *baggage office* over there."

☛ お荷物 (➡見出語)

にもの 煮物 **food simmered in broth** ▶野菜の**煮物** *vegetables simmered in broth* ‖ 夕食にはタケノコとレンコンとゴボウの**煮物**が出た *A dish* of *simmered* bamboo shoots, lotus root and burdock was served at supper.

にゃあ ▶猫が**ニャア**と鳴いた A cat *mewed* [*meowed*]. (➤ mew, meow の発音はそれぞれ /mjuː/, /miáʊ/).

にやけた **foppish** (きざな)；**sissy** (女々しい)；**effeminate** /ɪféməneɪt/ (なよなよした) ▶あんな**にやけた男**は嫌いよ I don't like *effeminate men* like him.

にやにや ▶彼はしかられても**にやにや**している He *smirks* even when he is getting a scolding. ‖ **にやにや**するな Take [Wipe] *the smile* off your face.

にやり ▶彼らは意味ありげに**にやり**と顔を見合わせた They looked at each other *with* a meaningful *smile*.

ニュアンス (a) **nuance** /njúːɑːns/, a **shade** ▶ことばの**ニュアンス**にむとんちゃくでは詩は理解できない You can't appreciate poetry if you are indifferent to the *shades* [*nuances*] of meaning in words. ‖ 彼女の考えと私の考えでは少し**ニュアンス**が違う (＝わずかな違いがある) *There's a slight difference* between her thinking and mine.

にゅういん 入院 **hospitalization** 一動 **入院する** **be hospitalized** /hɑ́ːspɪṭəlaɪzd/ ▶彼の病状は深刻で**入院**が必要であった His illness was serious enough to require *hospitalization*. ‖ **入院の手続きをする** *go* *through the procedures for hospitalization* ‖ **入院中の友人を見舞う** visit a friend *in* (*the*) *hospital* (➤ the を省くのは《英》).

【文型】
人(A)が病気(B)で入院している
A is hospitalized with [**for**] B.

▶父が肝炎で**入院した** My father *was hospitalized with* [*for*] hepatitis.
▶彼女はゆうべ発作を起こして**入院した** She had a seizure and *was sent to* (*the*) *hospital* last night. ‖ きみは**入院して**治療を受けるべきだ You should receive treatment *in a hospital* [《英》*in hospital*]. ‖ あと2, 3週間**入院して**なくちゃだめだよ You'd better *stay in* (*the*) *hospital* for another couple of weeks. ‖ 祖父は**入院させる**必要がある My grandfather has to *be hospitalized* [*be admitted to the hospital*]. ／ My grandfather needs to *go into* [to *be put in*] *the hospital*.
▶母はまだ**入院中**です My mother *is* still *in* (*the*) *hospital*.
‖**入院患者** an inpatient /ínpèɪʃənt/ (➤「外来患者」は outpatient という) ‖ **入院料** hospital charges.

ニューイングランド New England (アメリカの北東部の, メーン, コネチカットなど6州から成る地域).

にゅうえき 乳液 milky lotion, skin milk.

にゅうえん 入園 entrance ▶幼稚園［保育園］に**入園する** *enter* kindergarten [nursery school] (● enter が日本語に近いが, 英語では start を用いることが多い). ‖**入園式** an entrance ceremony (at a kindergarten) ‖ **入園料** admission, an admission fee (遊園地・動物園などの) ; an entrance fee (幼稚園などの).

ニューオーリンズ New Orleans (アメリカ南部, ミシシッピー川河口の都市).

にゅうか 入荷する arrive (到着する) ; **come in** (入って来る) ▶初がつおは明朝**入荷します** The first bonito of the season will *come in* tomorrow morning.

にゅうかい 入会 admission (入会許可) ; **entrance** (入ること) **一動 入会する join** +㊐ ▶彼女は演劇クラブに**入会**を申し込んだ She applied for *membership* in [*admission* to] the drama club. ‖ その作家はペンクラブへの**入会**が許された The writer *was admitted* into the PEN Club.
▶私はその歌手のファンクラブに**入会した** I *have joined* the singer's fan club. ／I *have become a member* of the singer's fan club.
‖**入会金** an entrance fee, a sign-up fee ‖ **入会者** a member, an entrant.

にゅうかく 入閣 ▶鈴木氏は初めて**入閣した** Mr. Suzuki *joined the Cabinet* [*became a Cabinet Minister*] for the first time.

にゅうがく 入学

entrance ; admission (to school) (入学許可) **一動 入学する enter (school) ; start school** (小学校に) ; **be admitted** 《**to**》, **be accepted** 《**by**》 (入学を許される) ▶大学に**入学する** *enter* college ／*get into* (a) college [university] (➤ 後者のほうがふつう) ‖ 妹はこの4月**小学校に入学する** My younger sister will *start school* this April. ‖ ことしはT大学に約3000人が**入学した** About 3,000 students *were admitted to* [*were accepted by*] T University this year. ／ About 3,000 students *were newly enrolled in* T University this year. (➤ enroll は「(学生)名簿に載せる」) ‖ 娘は私立中学に**入学させたい**と思っています I want to *send* my daughter to a private junior high school.
▶これ, ワカメちゃんへの(小学校)**入学祝い**よ Wakame, this is *a* (monetary) *gift to celebrate your starting* (*elementary*) *school*. ‖ おかげさまでP大の**入学試験**に合格しました Thank goodness, I passed *the entrance examination* for P University. ‖ **入学式**は4月10日に行われた *The start-of-school ceremony* was held on April 10. 《参考》この言い方は主に小学校の場合. 中学校以上は enrollment [entrance ／admission] ceremony のような言い方がよいが, 英米の学校では日本の学校の場合のような入学式がないので, enrollment [entrance ／admission] ceremony という表現は一般には用いない.
✉ **スタンフォード大学に入学されるとのこと, おめでとう!** Congratulations on your *being accepted by* Stanford University. →**合格**.
‖**入学案内** a guidebook [pamphlet] for applicants ; a university catalogue (大学の) ‖ **入学願書** an application form for admission (用紙) (●「K大へ入学願書を出す」は send in an application for admission to K University) ‖ **入学金** an admission [entrance] fee ‖ **入学手続き** admission [enrollment] procedures.

にゅうがん 乳癌 breast cancer, cancer of the breast ▶乳がんを発症する develop *breast cancer* ‖ 彼女は乳がんにかかっている She has *breast cancer*.

ニューギニア New Guinea (オーストラリア北方の大きな島).

にゅうぎゅう 乳牛 a **milk** [**milch** /mɪltʃ/] **cow ; dairy** /déəri/ **cattle** (➤ 総称).

にゅうきょ 入居 ▶新居にはいつ**入居するの**? When do you *move into* your new home? ‖ このアパートには20世帯が**入居している** Twenty families *live in* this apartment house. ‖ 新しいオフィスビルが**入居者**を募集している The new office building is seeking *tenants*.

にゅうぎょう 乳業 the dairy business.

にゅうきん 入金 ▶今月末にG社から100万円の**入金が**あるはずだ We will *be paid* one million yen from G Company at the end of this month. ‖ 自分の預金口座に5万円**入金した** (＝預金した) I *deposited* fifty thousand yen in my bank account.
‖**入金伝票** a deposit /dɪpɑ́:zət/ slip.

にゅうこう 入港 ▶豪華客船が横浜港に**入港した** A luxury liner *arrived* at Yokohama Port. ‖ 町の人々は原子力船の**入港**に反対している People in town are against nuclear-powered vessels *visiting the harbor*.

にゅうこく 入国 (an) **entry,** (an) **entrance 一動 入国する enter** (+㊐) ▶アメリカへ**入国する**にはビザが必要です You need a visa to *enter* the U.S. ‖ その外交官はアメリカへの**入国を許可された**［**拒絶された**］The diplomat *was admitted* [*was refused entry*] *into* the United States. (➤ admit は人の「入室・入場・入学・入国などを許す」) ‖ **入国手続き**は済みましたか Have you gone through *entry procedures* [*entry formalities*] to this country? ／Have you gone through *immigration*? ‖ **対話** 《入国審査で》「**入国の目的は?**」「観光［仕事］です」"*What's the purpose of your visit?*" "Sightseeing [Business]." ‖ 最近日本への**不法入国者**は減っている The number of *people who enter* Japan *illegally* is decreasing these days. (➤「不法入国者」は illegal en-

に

trant).
‖**入国カード** a disembarkation card, a landing card ‖**入国管理局** the immigration bureau /bjóʊroʊ/ ‖**入国許可証** an entry permit ‖**入国審査** immigration ‖**入国審査官** an immigration officer.

にゅうこん 入魂 ▶ダビデはミケランジェロ入魂の像だ David is a statue Michelangelo *put his whole heart and soul into*.

にゅうさつ 入札 bidding 一動 (…に) **入札する bid** 《for, on》▶その事業に入札する *bid for* [*on*] the project ‖研究所の跡地は入札によって売却される予定だ The site of the former laboratory will be put up for *bid*. (➤ put up は「売りに出す」).

にゅうさん 乳酸 《化学》 **lactic acid**
‖**乳酸飲料** a lactic acid beverage ‖**乳酸菌** lactic acid bacteria.

1**にゅうし 入試** an **entrance examination** ▶高校入試 *an entrance examination* for high school ‖X大の入試に受かる[落ちる] pass [fail] *the entrance exam* for X University ‖私は大学入試に備えて猛勉強中です I'm studying hard to prepare myself for *my university entrance exams*. ‖日本の大学入試制度は大いに改善の余地がある Japan's university *entrance examination system* leaves plenty of room for improvement.

2**にゅうし 乳歯 baby teeth, milk teeth** (➤ ともに複数形でいうことが多い).

にゅうじ 乳児 a baby, a suckling
‖**乳児食** baby food.

ニュージーランド New Zealand /njù: zí:lənd/
‖**ニュージーランド人** a New Zealander.

にゅうしつ 入室する enter a room ▶《掲示》期末試験中, 入室禁止 *Do Not Enter* During the Final Exams.

にゅうしゃ 入社する join a company [**corporation**] → 会社 ▶兄は昨年T社に入社した My (older) brother *joined* T Corporation last year. ／My (older) brother *got a job with* T Corporation last year.
‖**入社式** an entrance ceremony for new employees ‖**入社試験** an employment [entrance] examination, a test for employment.

ニュージャージー New Jersey (アメリカ東部の州; 略 NJ, N.J.).

にゅうじゃく 柔弱な weak ▶この頃の若者は精神的に柔弱になってきているようだ Young people today seem to have *become weak-willed*.

にゅうしゅ 入手する obtain +⑥ (苦労して); **gain** +⑥ (大きな努力の末, 望みのものを) ▶土地を入手する *gain possession of* land ‖一般の人が相撲の桟敷席の切符を入手するのは難しい It's hard for ordinary people to *obtain* a box seat ticket at a sumo tournament. ‖こんな秘密書類をどうやって入手したんだい？ How did you *come to possess* such classified papers?

にゅうしょ 入所する enter (+⑥) ▶老人ホームに入所する *enter* a nursing home.
‖**入所者** an inmate (刑務所の受刑者).

にゅうしょう 入賞する win a prize ▶目標は入賞です My goal is to *win* [*get*] *a prize*. ‖川内選手はマラソンで6位に入賞した Kawauchi *won sixth prize* [*took sixth place*] in the marathon.
‖**入賞者** a prizewinner.

にゅうじょう 入場 (an) **entrance; admission** (入場許可) **一動 入場する enter** (+⑥); **be admitted to** (観客として) ▶参加チームがグラウンドに入場した The participating teams *entered* the playing field. ‖この券で2名入場できます This ticket *admits* two persons. (➤ admit は「…の入場を許可する」) ‖皇居東御苑は一般の入場が許されている The Imperial Eastern Gardens *are open to the public*. ‖参加チームの入場行進が始まった The participating teams have begun to *march in*.
▶そのコンサートの入場料はいくらですか What is the *admission* (*fee*) to the concert? ‖ことしの日本シリーズの入場者数は約25万人でした This year's *attendance* at the Japan Series was approximately 250,000.
▶《掲示》子供は入場できません No children allowed. ／Adults only. ‖《掲示》入場無料 Admission Free ‖《掲示》券をお持ちの方に限り入場できます *Admission* (will be) by ticket only.
‖**入場券** an admission ticket; a platform ticket (駅の) ‖**入場券売り場** 《米》 a ticket office, a box office (劇場の), 《英》 a booking office ‖**入場者** visitors; an attendance (➤ 集合的).

にゅうしょく 入植 settlement 一動 入植する settle (+⑥) ‖**入植者** a settler ‖**入植地** a settlement.

にゅうしん 入信する join [**become a believer in**] **a religion** ▶キリスト教に入信する *become a Christian*.

ニュース news /nju:z/
語法 「1つのニュース」は (×)a news ではなく, a piece [an item] of news または a news item あるいは a news story とする.
▶最新のニュース the latest *news* ‖(締め切り間際の)飛び込みのニュース (late) breaking *news* ‖そのニュースを聞いて驚いた I was surprised at the *news*. ‖きみに聞かせたいすばらしいニュースがあるんだ I have (some) wonderful *news* for you.
▶首相が入院したというニュースが入った *News* came in [We received *word*] that the Prime Minister had been hospitalized. (➤ この word は「知らせ」「うわさ」の意).
▶《アナウンサーが》ただ今新しいニュースが入りました We have *breaking news*. ／*Another news item* [*story*] has arrived. (➤ 2例とも放送中のニュースと別件のニュースの場合) ／*More news* has arrived. (➤ 同じ件の新情報の場合) ‖犬が人をかんでもニュースにならないが, 人が犬をかめばニュースだ When a dog bites a man that is not *news*, but when a man bites a dog that is *news*. (➤ アメリカのジャーナリスト, デイナのことば).
▶何かいいニュースはありませんか Is there [Do you have] any good *news*? ‖事故のことは7時のラジオニュースで聞いた I heard about the accident on the seven o'clock radio *news*. ‖その種の事件はニュースバリューが高い That sort of incident *has high news value*. ／That sort of incident *is quite newsworthy*. ‖これはビッグニュースになる This will make *big news*.
‖**ニュース映画** a news film, a newsreel ‖**ニュース解説** a news commentary ‖**ニュース解説者** a news commentator ‖**ニュースキャスター** a newscaster (➤「総合司会」するキャスターは anchor) ‖**ニュース速報** a news flash, breaking news ‖**ニュース番組** a news program ‖**海外** [**国内**] **ニュース** foreign [home] news ‖**経済** [**スポーツ**] **ニュース** financial [sports] news ‖**ローカルニュース** local news.

危ないカタカナ語✸ ニュース
1「ニュース」は英語の news からだが, 発音は /njúːz/ となることに注意.
2 ニュース番組のまとめ役の総合司会者は anchorman (女性は anchorwoman)と呼ばれるが, 最近は男女差のない anchor, anchorperson という言い方が好まれる.

にゅうせいひん 乳製品 dairy products [goods].
にゅうせき 入籍 registration ▶私たちは長年連れ添っているが, まだ入籍していない Although we have been (living) together for years, we haven't *registered our marriage* yet.
1**にゅうせん 入選** ▶彼の絵は二科展に入選した His picture *was accepted* for the Nika Exhibition. ‖**入選作品** a winning piece of work ‖ **入選者** a winner.
2**にゅうせん 乳腺** 《解剖学》 a mammary gland ‖**乳腺炎** 《医学》 mastitis /mæstáɪṭɪs/ ‖ **乳腺科** the department of breast surgery, the department of breast oncology (乳がんの).
にゅうたい 入隊 enlistment 一動 **入隊する** join, enlist in ▶自衛隊に入隊する *join* [*enlist in*] the Self-Defense Forces.
にゅうたいいん 入退院 ▶彼女は入退院を繰り返した She *went in and out of the hospital repeatedly*.
にゅうだん 入団 ▶斉藤は2010年, ファイターズに入団した Saito *joined* the Fighters in 2010.
ニューデリー New Delhi (インドの首都).
にゅうとう 入党 ▶労働党に入党する *join* [*become a member of*] the Labour Party.
にゅうどうぐも 入道雲 a thunderhead, huge columns of clouds ▶入道雲が出てきた *Thunderheads* are forming.
ニュートラル neutral ▶ギヤをニュートラルに入れる shift (the gear) into *neutral* ‖ ニュートラルな立場をとる take a *neutral* position / remain *neutral*.
ニュートリノ 《物理学》 neutrino /njuːtríːnoʊ/.
にゅうねん 入念な elaborate /ɪlǽbərət/ ; thorough /θə́ːroʊ ‖ θʌ́rə/ (徹底的な) ▶その女優は入念なメークをした The actress put on *elaborate* make-up. ‖ 選手たちはレース前に入念なウォーミングアップをした The athletes had a *thorough* warm-up before the race.
ニューハーフ a transgender male ; a male cross-dresser (女装する).
にゅうばい 入梅 the start [onset] of the rainy season.
にゅうはくしょく 乳白色 milky white 一形 **乳白色の** milky-white, milk-white ; opalescent /òʊpəlésənt/ (➤「オパールのような」の意).
にゅうばち 乳鉢 a mortar.
ニューハンプシャー New Hampshire (アメリカ北東部の州 ; 略 NH, N.H.).
にゅうぶ 入部する join a club, become a member 《of》 ▶ヨットクラブに入部しませんか How would you like to *join* the yacht *club*?
ニューフェース a new face.
にゅうぼう 乳棒 a pestle /pésəl/.
にゅうまく 入幕する be promoted to the top division of sumo.
ニューメキシコ New Mexico (アメリカ南西部の州 ; 略 NM, N.Mex., N.M.).
ニューメディア the new media.
にゅうもん 入門 1【弟子入り】▶こちらに入門させてください I'd like to *become* one of your *students*. / I'd like to *study* under you. (● 相撲部屋なら I'd like to be admitted into this stable. のようにいう).
2【初歩】▶《書名》コンピュータ入門 *An Introduction to Computers* ‖ もう一度最初からお始めになりたいのなら入門コースをお勧めします I recommend that you take *the beginners'* [*introductory*] *course* if you want to begin all over again. ‖ 《書店で》チェスの入門書はありますか Do you have *a beginner's book* on chess?
にゅうようじ 乳幼児 infants.
ニューヨーク 1【市】New York (アメリカ第一の都市 ; 州名と区別するために, New York City または New York, N.Y. と書くことがある ; 略 NYC)
‖**ニューヨーク市民** a New Yorker.
2【州】New York (市の名と区別するために New York State ともいう ; 略 NY, N.Y.).
にゅうよく 入浴 a bath, bathing /béɪðɪŋ/ 一動 **入浴する** take [(英また) have] a bath ▶おまえの入浴中に電話が掛かってきたよ You got a telephone call *while you were in the bath* [*while you were taking a bath*]. ‖**入浴剤** bath salts (水質をやわらげ香気を発する) ; bath powder (粉末の) ; a bath bomb (発泡性の).
にゅうりょく 入力 input 一動 **入力する** input +目, enter +目 ▶データを入力する *input* data ‖ この数字を入力してエンターキーを押してください Please *input* [*enter*] these figures and push the Enter key.
にゅうわ 柔和な mild (生まれつき優しい) ; gentle (穏やかで感じの良い) ; meek (柔順でおとなしい) ▶担任の先生はとても柔和な人です Our homeroom teacher is very *mild* [*gentle*].
にゅっと ▶暗やみからにゅっと手が出て来たときは飛び上がるほど驚いた I nearly jumped out of my skin when a hand *suddenly* reached out of the darkness.
にょう 尿 urine /jóərɪn/ 一動 **尿をする** urinate, make [pass] water ▶尿の検査を受ける have *a urine test* ‖ 尿の回数は多いですか Do you *urinate* frequently? ‖**尿酸** 《生化学》 uric acid ‖ **尿素** 《化学》 urea /juəríːə/ ‖ **尿道** 《解剖学》 a urethra /juríːθrə/ →おしっこ.
にょうい 尿意 ▶急に尿意を催した I felt a sudden *need to urinate*.
にょうぼう 女房 one's wife, one's old lady (➤ 後者を old woman とすると軽蔑的に響く).
にょきにょき ▶この2, 3年間に高いビルがにょきにょき建ち始めた In the last two or three years, tall buildings have begun *springing up* [*sprouting up* / *mushrooming*]. (➤ mushroom は「(キノコのように)どんどんできる」).
にょじつ 如実に vividly ▶彼女の話は戦争の恐ろしさを如実に表していた Her story *vividly* expressed the horrors of war.
にょたい 女体 a woman's body.
にょろにょろ ▶蛇がやぶからにょろにょろっと出て来た A snake came *wriggling* out of the bushes. (➤ wriggle /rígəl/ は「のたくる」).
にら 韮 《植物》 a *nira* scallion /skǽljən/.
‖**にらレバーいため** slices of pork liver sautéed with *nira* scallions.
にらみ 睨み ▶うちではいまだに祖父がにらみをきかせている (＝権威をもっている) My grandfather still *has a lot of authority* [*influence* / *clout*] *in* my family.
にらみあい 睨み合い ▶《比喩的》この町では原発賛

成派と反対派が3年越しのにらみ合いをしている(＝もめている) In this town, people for and against the nuclear power plant *have been at odds* [*at loggerheads*] for three full years.

にらみつける 睨みつける **glare at** ▶先生はいたずらをしている生徒をにらみつけた The teacher *glared at* the boy who was fooling around.

にらむ 睨む **1**【憎悪の気持ちでじっと見る】**glare** 《at》▶彼女はすごい目で私をにらんだ She *glared at* me. ／She *looked sharply* [*angrily*] *at* me.

2【考えながらじっと見る】▶父は腕組みをして将棋の盤面を長い間にらんでいた My father sat *watching* [*gazing*] *over* the shogi board with his arms crossed for a long time.

3【警戒する, 嫌う】▶あの数学の先生ににらまれたらおしまいだよ You'll be finished if you *get in bad with* that math teacher. It's all over if you *get on* that math teacher's *blacklist* [*black books*].

4【見当をつける】**suspect** ▶私はあの男が親玉に違いないとにらんだ I *suspected* he was the ringleader. ‖彼は小物だと私はにらんだ I *sized* him *up* as someone of little importance. (➤ size up は「(人物を)品定めする」).

にらめっこ 睨めっこ a **stare-down**, a **staring contest** ▶にらめっこしよう Let's have *a staring contest*. ▶彼は時計とにらめっこで働いている He is working *against* the clock.

にりゅう 二流の **second-class, second-rate** ▶このチームは二流の選手ばかりだ This team consists of only *second-class* [*second-rate*] players.

にりんしゃ 二輪車 a **two-wheeler**, a **two-wheeled vehicle**; a **bicycle**,《インフォーマル》a **bike**(自転車).

[1]**にる 似る** **look alike, look like**(見た目が); **be alike, be like**(性格や行動などが); **resemble** +⊕(見た目, あるいは性格などが); **take after**(主に性格など, 時に見た目が; 同一の血統の者に用いる)

【文型】
人・物(A)に似ている
look like A
be like A
resemble A

《解説》**look like** は見かけの類似をいい, **be like** は性格・性質を含めた類似をさす. あとに A がこないときは, それぞれ, **look alike, be alike** を用いる. **resemble** は見かけ・性質のどちらにも使う. いずれも進行形にしない.

▶彼は父親によく似ている He *looks* very (much) *like* his father. ／He *is* very (much) *like* his father. ‖雄作は容貌は父親に, 性格は母親に似ている Yusaku *resembles* [*takes after*] his father in appearance, and his mother in personality. ／Yusaku *looks like* his father and *takes after* his mother (in temperament). ‖この男の子たちはよく似ているけれども兄弟ではない These boys *look* much *alike*, but they are not brothers. ‖私たちは似たものどうしだ We'*re a lot alike*.

▶真ちゅうは色が金に似ている Brass *is similar to* gold in color. (➤ be similar to は「…に類似している」) ‖私, ウナギとか蛇とか, それに似たのが嫌いなの I hate eels, snakes, and *things like that* [and *the like*]. ‖彼は父親に似て(＝と同様に)ひょうきんだ He is funny *like* his father. ‖親に似ず, 彼女はとても背が高い *Unlike* her parents, she is very tall. ‖彼らは似た者どうしで仲がいい They are good friends since they *have a lot in common*. (➤「共通点が多い」の意).

▶鳥と烏は似て非なる漢字だ 鳥 and 烏 are (very) *similar at first glance*, but they *are completely different* kanji.

✉ **写真を送ってくださってありがとう. 目もとがお父さんに似ていますね** Thank you for the picture you sent. *You have your father's eyes*, don't you? 《参考》自分は自分という意識の強い英米人はこういう指摘を喜ばないことも多いので注意が必要.

☛ **似たり寄ったり, 似ても似つかない** (→見出語)

[2]**にる 煮る** **cook** +⊕(熱を加えて料理する); **simmer** /símər/ +⊕(とろ火でぐつぐつ[ことこと]と); **boil** +⊕(ゆでる) ▶なべでニンジンを煮る *cook* carrots in a pan ‖豆をとろ火で2時間ぐつぐつ[ことこと]煮た I *simmered* the beans for a couple of hours. ‖芋はやわらかく煮てほしいな Please *boil* the potatoes until they are tender.

▶《慣用表現》あいつは煮ても焼いても食えない男だ I just *can't stomach* that man. (➤ stomach /stʌ́mək/ は否定文で用いて「…に耐えられない」の意) ／He is a *tough nut* (*to crack*). (➤ tough nut (to crack) は「付き合いにくい人間, がんこ者」の意のインフォーマルな表現).

にるい 二塁 **second** (**base**) ▶二塁を守る play *second* (*base*). ‖**二塁手** a second baseman ‖**二塁打** a double, a two-base hit.

にれ 楡 《植物》an **elm** (**tree**).

にわ 庭 a **garden**, a **yard**

《解説》**garden と yard**
(1)花木の有無や舗装・未舗装に関係なく, 家の周辺の庭や中庭は《米》では **yard** という.《米》では **garden** は「庭園」「花園」「菜園」の意になるのがふつう.
(2)《英》では yard は舗装された庭をいい, 花木が植えられていれば garden という.

yard

garden

▶彼のところは裏に広い庭がある He has a large *yard* at the back of his house. ／He has a large *backyard* [《英》*back garden*]. (➤ backyard, back garden は「裏庭」) ‖誰が庭の手入れをするのですか Who takes care of the *yard* [*garden*]? ‖趣味は庭いじりです My favorite pastime is *gardening*. ‖大都会では庭付きの一戸建てはふつうのサラリーマンには手が届かなくなった In big cities, *a house with a yard* [*garden*] has gone beyond the reach of the ordinary office worker.

‖**庭石** a garden rock ‖**庭木** a garden tree ‖**庭師** a gardener ‖**庭づくり** landscaping,《英》landscape gardening.

にわか ▶日が暮れたと思ったらにわかに風が冷たくなった The breeze became cooler *all of a sudden* after it got dark. ‖武はあすのテストのにわか勉強を始めた Takeshi has begun to *cram* for the test tomorrow. (➤ cram は「詰め込み勉強をする」の意のインフォーマルな語).

にわかあめ にわか雨 a **shower** ▶学校の帰り道ににわか雨に降られた I was caught in *a shower* on my way back from school.

ニワトコ 《植物》 a **Japanese red elder.**

にわとり 鶏 a **chicken**; a **hen** (めんどり); a **rooster,** 《英また》 a **cock** (おんどり; この語には「ペニス」の意があるので, 《米》ではこの連想を避けるため rooster を用いる)
▶うちでは**鶏**を飼っています We raise *chickens.* (➤ raise は事業として「飼育する」の意) ‖ これは**鶏が先か卵が先かという問題**と同じだ This is like *the problem of which comes first, the chicken or the egg.* (➤ 簡単に, This is a chicken or egg problem. ともいう).
‖**鶏小屋** a henhouse, a chicken coop.

にん 任 a **post**(主に軍隊・警察の地位); (a) **duty**(役目, 本分); (a) **responsibility**(責任) ▶外交官は新しい**任**に赴いた The diplomat took up his new *post.* ‖ ホテルの支配人の**任**は私には重過ぎる The *responsibility* of being a hotel manager would be too great for me.
▶加藤さんは校長の**任**を解かれた Mr. Kato was relieved of his *duties* as school principal. ‖ **私はその任ではない** The job *is beyond my ability.* / I'm *not up to the job.*

-にん -人 a **person**; **people** (2人以上) ▶その事故で**17人**がけがをした *Seventeen people* [*persons*] were injured in that accident. (● people のほうがふつう) ‖ **対話** 「結婚披露宴には**何人**(の客を)招待するのですか」「**70人**ほどです」 "*How many guests* will you invite to your wedding reception?" "About *seventy* (*people*)." ‖ **我々3人**は1つテントに寝た The *three* of us [*Three* of us] slept in a tent. (● 前者は我々は全部で3人, 後者は「我々のうち3人」を意味する) ‖ **5人に1人の生徒**がインフルエンザにかかっている *One student in five* has [*A fifth of the students* have] the flu.

にんい 任意の **optional** (随意の); **voluntary** /vɑ́ːləntèri/ (自発的な); **arbitrary** /ɑ́ːrbətrèri/ (不定の) ▶この企画への参加, 不参加は**任意**です You have the *option* of participating in this project or not. ‖ ご寄付は全くの**任意**になっております Donations are entirely *voluntary.* ‖ 伊藤氏は取り調べを受けるため**任意**で警察に出頭した Mr. Ito *voluntarily* showed up at the police station for questioning. ‖ 円外の**任意**の1点から円に接線を引きなさい Draw a tangent along the circle from an *arbitrary* point outside (of) the circle.
‖**任意保険** optional [voluntary] insurance.

にんか 認可 **approval** /əprúːvəl/ **一動 認可する approve** +◉ (是認する, 賛成する); **authorize** /ɔ́ːθəraɪz/ +◉ (権限を持って認定する) ▶**無認可の**保育所 an *unauthorized* day-care center ‖ この地区に店を開くには県の**認可**が必要だ The prefectural government's *approval* is required to open a shop in this area.
▶大学新設の**認可**を文部科学省に申請した We applied to the Ministry of Education for *approval* to establish a college.

¹**にんき 人気** **popularity 一形 人気の popular** ▶**人気のある**スポーツ a *popular* sport ‖ **人気を得る** [**失う**] win [lose] *popularity*

> **【文型】**
> **人(A)に人気がある**
> **be popular with** [**among**] A

▶彼女はみんなに**人気がある** She *is popular with* everybody. / Everybody *likes* her. ‖ 浅草は外国人観光客に**人気がある** Asakusa *is popular with* foreign tourists. ‖ このウェブサイトは大学生に**人気だ** This website *is popular with* [*among*] college students. (● among は「漠然と多くの人に」というニュアンスで用いる).
▶秋山先生はなぜか**人気がない** For some reason, Mr. Akiyama is an *unpopular* teacher. ‖ この小説は今非常に**人気がある** This novel is now enjoying great *popularity.* / This novel is now very widely read.
▶あの歌手は最近**人気が出て** [**落ちて**] **きた** That singer *is becoming popular* [*losing popularity*] these days. ‖ そのテレビ番組は**今人気を集めている** The TV show *is catching on* now. (➤ catch on は「受ける」) ‖ 彼はクラスの**人気者**です He is *a favorite* [*a popular person*] in our class.
‖**人気歌手** a popular singer ‖ **人気投票** a popularity vote ‖ **人気取り政策** (a) vote-catching policy ‖ **人気番組** a popular [hit] program.
☞ 不人気 (→見出語)

²**にんき 任期** a **term of office** ▶その大統領の**任期**は来年切れる The president's *term of office* will expire next year. ‖ 参議院議員の**任期**は6年だ The *term of office* for a member of the House of Councilors is six years. ‖ その市長は**任期半ばで**死亡した The mayor passed away *midterm* [*in the middle of his term*]. ‖ 大統領は**任期中は**ホワイトハウスに住む The President resides in the White House *during his term in office.*

にんぎょ 人魚 a **mermaid**; a **merman** /mə́ːrmæn/ (男の).

にんぎょう 人形 a **doll**; a **rag doll**(縫いぐるみの) ▶人形で遊ぶ play with *a doll.*
‖**人形劇** a puppet show [play] ‖ **操り人形** a puppet, a marionette ‖ **からくり人形** a windup [mechanical] doll ‖ **着せ替え人形** a dress-up doll ‖ **フランス人形** a French doll ‖ **指人形** a hand puppet.

にんげん 人間 **1 【ひと】** (a) **man,** a **human** (**being**) **一形 人間の human**

> **【解説】「人間」の言い方**
> (1)抽象的に「ひと, 人類」の意味では **man** またはその堅い語である **mankind** が用いられ, 人類を他の動物と対比するような場合には **human** またはその堅い語である **human being** が用いられる. (2)最近では「男性」を暗示する man, mankind は避けられ, 代わりに a human (being), the human race, humankind, people などが好まれる.

▶**人間の**歴史 the history of *the human race* [*humanity* / *mankind*] ‖ **人間**は多くのすばらしい発見をしてきた. *Man* has discovered many wonderful things. ‖ そんな仕事なら**人間**よりもロボットのほうが効率よくやるだろう That kind of job could be done more efficiently by a robot than by *a human* (*being*). ‖ 地球上には現在70億以上の**人間**がいる Over seven billion *people* live on the earth at present. ‖ 信頼される**人間**になりたい I want to become *a person* [*someone*] who is trusted. (●「信頼される人間」を a human who is trusted とはふつう言わない. a human being who ... とはまれに言う) ‖ 祖父はすばらしい**人間**だと思う I think my grandfather is a wonderful *person* [a wonderful *human being*].

直訳の落とし穴「人間［人］の一生」
「人間」には a human being, a human や総称的には humankind, humanity などが当てられるが, これらはふつう, いずれも他の動物やロボットなどと対比して,「人類」に近い感覚で用いる. 人間だけを話題にして, つまり,「私たち」を一般化して「人間」や「人」というときには, a person や people, あるいはそのまま we を用いるのが一般的. たとえば,「人間の欲望には切りがない」は There are no limits to people's desires. で, (×)to humans' desires とは言わない. (ただし, 形容詞 human (人間のもつ) を用いて, to human desire という言い方にすればごく自然. ⇀**黒人**) また,「人間［人］の一生にはよいこと, 悪いこと, いろいろなことがある」は A lot of things, both positive and negative, happen during a person's life. といい, (×)during a human's life とは言わない.

▶世の中にはいろいろな人間がいる *It takes all sorts* to make a world. (➤ 英語のことわざ ;「人によっていろいろな考え方がある」の意で使うことが多い. to 以下を省略することもある) ‖ 先生だって**人間**だ. ときには間違えるさ Teachers are *human*. They sometimes make mistakes. (➤ この human は形容詞で「神と違って完璧ではない, 人間特有の弱みがある」の意) ‖ 捕虜たちはだれも**人間的な**扱いを受けなかった None of the war prisoners received *humane* treatment. (➤ humane /hju(ː)méɪn/ は「人道的な」) ‖ 勉強に追われずにもっと**人間らしい**生活がしたい I'd like to live *like a normal human being* [have a *decent* life] instead of being pressured into studying (all the time).

▶寮での**人間関係**はどうもうまくいかない It's really hard to keep up good (*human*) *relationships* in the dorm. ‖ シリルの技はとても**人間わざとは思えない** Cyril's prowess *is* almost *inhuman*. ‖ すぐれた芸術に親しむことは**人間形成**に役立つと信じます I believe that the appreciation of outstanding art serves to *build our character*.

▶私って**ご飯大好き人間**なのよ I'm *a rice person*. (➤「名詞 + person」で「…タイプの人, …が好きな人」の意).

‖ **人間嫌い** misanthropy /mɪsǽnθrəpi/ ; a misanthrope /mísənθroʊp/ (人) ‖ **人間工学** human engineering ‖ **人間国宝** a living national treasure ‖ **人間味** a human touch.

2【人柄】▶田中さんはあれ以来**人間が変わった** Ms. Tanaka *has completely changed* since then. ‖ 山本さんは**人間ができている**［いない］Mr. Yamamoto *is a man of character* [*a man of no character*].

逆引き熟語 ○○人間
朝型人間 a morning person, an early riser [bird] ／**会社人間** a company person ／**クローン人間** a human clone ／**仕事人間** a work-oriented person, a workaholic ／**だめ人間** a good-for-nothing, an incompetent (person) ／**透明人間** an invisible person ／**真面目人間** a serious person ／**夜型人間** a night person, a night owl

にんげんせい 人間性 humanity (人間的な性質) ; human nature (人間が本来持っている感情, 人間の本性)
▶奴隷制度は**人間性**の否定だ Slavery is a denial of *humanity*. ‖ 平気で動物を殺すなんてあの人の**人間性**を疑うね I can't help questioning his *sense of humanity* when I see him kill animals without the least remorse.

にんげんドック 人間ドック a complete physical checkup [examination] ▶ 30歳以上の人は年１回は**人間ドック**に入ったほうがいい It is best for all people over thirty to have *a complete physical* (*checkup*) at least once a year. (➤ checkup を省略するのは主に《米・インフォーマル》).

危ないカタカナ語 人間ドック
体の検査のために病院に入ることを船が修理のためにドックに入ることにたとえて「人間ドック」というが, これは日本的. 英語では dock は使わず, (complete) physical checkup や (complete) medical examination を用いる.

にんげんみ 人間味 humanity ▶**人間味のある**医者 a *warm-hearted* doctor.

にんさんぷ 妊産婦 a woman who is pregnant or has recently given birth.

にんしき 認識 understanding (理解) ; awareness (気づいていること) ; knowledge (知識) ━動 **認識する** understand +目, be aware of ▶この40年で脳に対する我々の**認識**は急速に深まった Our *understanding* of the brain has advanced very rapidly in the last forty years. ‖ HIV /エイズに対する誤った**認識**がいまだ世間には存在している An incorrect *understanding* of HIV /AIDS still exists in society. ‖ 彼は社会人としての**認識**が欠けている He lacks proper *awareness* of his place in society.

▶総理のあの発言は減税を約束されたと**認識しております** It is *my understanding* [I *understand*] that the Prime Minister promised tax reductions in his [her] comments. ‖ 彼が尺八の名手だなんて私の**認識不足だった** I *wasn't aware* that he was a master of the shakuhachi. ‖ 東日本大震災のあと, われわれは防災に対する**認識を新たにした** Following the Great East Japan Earthquake and Tsunami, we *came to see* disaster preparedness *in a new* [*fresh*] *light*.

☛ **再認識** (⇀見出語)

にんじゃ 忍者 a *ninja* ; a professional spy in the Japanese feudal times (➤ 説明的な訳) ▶**忍者**ごっこ playing *ninja*.

にんじゅう 忍従 submission ; resignation (あきらめ).

にんじゅつ 忍術 (the art of) *ninjutsu*, the art of *ninja*.

¹にんしょう 人称 《文法》(grammatical) person ▶**一人称**の "I" は話している人を指している *The first person* "I" refers to the person speaking.
‖ **二［三］人称** the second [third] person ‖ **人称代名詞** a personal pronoun.

²にんしょう 認証 authentication, verification
‖ **カード認証** credit card verification ‖ **顔認証システム** a facial recognition [authentication] system ‖ **個人認証システム** a personal authentication [verification] system ‖ **生体認証** biometric identification ‖ **電子認証** a digital [electronic] authentication [verification] system.

にんじょう 人情 human nature 《参考》human nature は「人間が本来持っている感情, 人間性」の意味であって, 日本語で「義理と人情」というようなときの「なさけ」のニュアンスはない ▶体の不自由な人がいたら手をさしのべるのが**人情**だ It is *human nature* to offer a helping hand to a physically disabled person. ‖ できれば安楽に暮らしたいと願うのが**人情だ** It is *natural for a human* [It's only *human*] to wish to lead an easy life, if possible. (●前者は「人間として当然」, 後者は「人間(の弱点)としてありがち」の意) ‖ おじ, おばたちは皆**人情味のある** [**人情に厚い**] 人たちだ My uncles and aunts are all very *kind* [*warm-hearted*].
☛ 不人情 (→見出語)

にんじる 任じる appoint +目 (任命する) ; profess +目 (自称する) ▶国連大使に**任じられる** *be appointed* ambassador to the United Nations ‖ 彼は自ら世界的な言語学者をもって**任じている** He *professes* [*claims*] to be a world-famous linguistic scholar.

にんしん 妊娠 pregnancy /prégnənsi/ ━動 **妊娠する** become [get] pregnant ▶**妊娠している**女性 a *pregnant* woman ‖ 女の子を**妊娠させる** *make* [*get*] a girl *pregnant* ‖ 彼女は**妊娠している** She's *pregnant*. (➤えん曲に She is going to have a baby. とか She is expecting (a child). ともいう) ‖ 彼女は**妊娠**3か月だ She is two months [eight weeks] *pregnant*. ／She's been *pregnant* for two months [eight weeks]. ／She's in her second month of *pregnancy*. (➤「妊娠3か月の女性」なら a two-month-pregnant woman のようにいう) ‖ **妊娠中の**喫煙は危険を伴う It's risky to smoke *during pregnancy*.
‖**妊娠中絶** an abortion.
《参考》日本では妊娠期間を最終月経の第1日目から約280日間, すなわち10か月または10月(とつき)10日と考えるのに対して, 英米では排卵日から数えて266日間, すなわち9か月と考える. これに伴い, 英米人は日本人が妊娠2か月目, 3か月目ととらえるところを1か月目, 2か月目ととらえる. 週で表すことも多い.

にんじん 人参 《植物》 a carrot
‖**朝鮮ニンジン** a ginseng /dʒínseŋ/ (➤薬剤としては Ⓤ 扱い).

にんずう 人数 ▶旅行参加者の**人数**を確認してください Please confirm the *number* of applicants for the trip. ‖ きみのクラスの**人数は?** *How many students* are there in your class? ‖ **人数が足りなくて**サッカーの試合ができなかった We were unable to play a soccer game because we *were short of players*.
☛ 少人数, 多人数 (→見出語)

にんそう 人相 looks (顔の美醜) ; features (顔だち)
《参考》日本語の「人相」はどちらかと言えばマイナスイメージの濃い語であるが, 英語はいずれも中立的. ▶**人相の悪い**男 an *evil-looking* man ‖ 眼鏡を取ると人は**人相がらりと変わる** People *look* quite *different* without their glasses on.
▶犯人の**人相**を教えてください Describe the *features* of the suspect. ／Tell me *what* the suspect *looks like*. ‖ 新聞の**人相書き**に一致する男が公園にいた A man answering to the *description* in the paper was seen in the park.
‖**人相見** a physiognomist /fìziágnəmɪst/.

にんたい 忍耐 endurance (継続的な頑張り・持久力) ; perseverance /pə̀ːrsəvíərəns/ (積極的な不屈の努力) ; patience (がまん) ▶**忍耐強い** [**強くない**] 人 a *patient* [*an impatient*] person ‖ 登山は**忍耐がいる** You need *endurance* to climb a mountain. ／Mountain climbing requires *endurance*. ‖ マラソンは**忍耐力を養う**のによいスポーツだ Marathon running is a sport which nurtures *perseverance* [*endurance*].

[1]**にんち 認知** **1【見て[聞いて]それとわかること】** recognition, (legal) acknowledgement (事実などの) ━動 **認知する** recognize +目, acknowledge +目 ▶日本のアニメーションは海外でも広く**認知されている** Japanese animation *is* widely *recognized* abroad. ‖ 彼女は相手の男性に子供の**認知**を求めた She asked the man to *acknowledge* her child as his own. ／She sought the man's *legal acknowledgement* of paternity.
2【外界を認識すること】 (心理学) cognition ━形 **認知に関する** cognitive
‖**認知言語学** cognitive linguistics ‖ **認知行動療法** cognitive behavioral therapy (➤CBT と略す) ‖ **認知障害** a cognitive disorder ‖ **認知心理学** cognitive psychology.

[2]**にんち 任地** one's new post [posting].

にんちしょう 認知症 《医学》 dementia /dɪménʃə/ ▶彼は**認知症**にかかっている He suffers from *dementia*.
‖**若年性認知症** early-onset dementia ‖ **認知症ケア専門士** a qualified dementia care specialist [caregiver] ‖ **老年性認知症** senile dementia.

にんてい 認定 recognition ; authorization (正式な認可) ━動 **認定する** recognize +目 ; certify +目 (証明する) ; authorize +目 (認可する) ▶水俣病**認定**患者 a *recognized* patient of Minamata disease ‖ その女性は要介護1と**認定された** The woman *was certified* as requiring long-term care level 1.
‖**認定書** a certificate /səˈtífɪkət/.

にんにく 大蒜 《植物》 garlic.

にんぷ 妊婦 a pregnant woman
‖**妊婦服** a maternity dress.

にんまり ▶すりはすった財布の中身を確かめて**にんまりした** The pickpocket checked the contents of the wallet he had stolen and *chuckled to himself*. (➤chuckle は「(声をひそめて)くっくっと笑う」).

にんむ 任務 a duty (義務) ; a task (課せられた職務) ; an assignment (上役から命ぜられた) ▶**任務**を遂行する accomplish [carry out] one's *duty* (● accomplish は carry out よりも堅い語) ‖ この**任務**を終えたら私は辞職するつもりだ I'm going to resign after I complete this *task*.
▶その刑事にはたえず**任務があった** The police detective was constantly on *assignment* [was *assigned* to one case after another]. (➤on assignment は「任務に就いて」).

にんめい 任命 appointment, designation (➤ともに堅い語であるが, 前者がより堅い) ━動 **任命する** designate +目, appoint +目 ; name +目 (➤name はほかの語よりもくだけており, 「名指しで決める」の意) ▶私は課長に**任命された** I *was appointed* (to the post of) section chief. ‖ 彼女は駐デンマーク大使に**任命された** She *was named* ambassador to Denmark. ‖ 大臣の**任命権**は総理大臣にある The Prime Minister has *the power to appoint* [*designate*] ministers.

にんめん 任免 ▶首相の国務大臣**任免権** the prime minister's *power to appoint and dismiss* cabinet ministers.

ぬ・ヌ

ぬいあわせる 縫い合わせる ▶2枚の布を縫い合わせる *sew* two pieces of cloth *together* ‖ 傷口を縫い合わせる *suture* [*sew up*] a wound.

ぬいいと 縫い糸 **sewing thread.**

ぬいぐるみ 縫いぐるみ a **stuffed** (**toy**) **animal** (➤ toy がないと「はく製の動物」の意にもなる) ▶縫いぐるみの犬 a *stuffed toy* dog ‖ 縫いぐるみのクマ a *stuffed toy* bear／a teddy bear ‖ 女の子は縫いぐるみの怪獣を見て泣きだした The little girl began to cry when she saw a *stuffed* monster [someone *in a* monster *costume*]. (後者は中に人が入っているもの).

ぬいとり 縫い取り **embroidery.**

ぬいめ 縫い目 a **seam**(合わせ目) ; a **stitch** (一針分の) ▶縫い目のない靴下 *seamless* stockings ‖ スカートの縫い目がほころびてしまった The *seam* of my skirt has come apart.

ぬいもの 縫い物 **sewing** /sóʊɪŋ/, **needlework** ▶あとで少し縫い物をしなくっちゃ I have a little *sewing* to do later.

ぬう 縫う **1【とじ合わせる】sew** /soʊ/ +㊐, **stitch** +㊐ (一針ずつ) ▶ズボンのほころびを縫う *sew* [*stitch*] *up* the rip in one's trousers ‖ (上着に)ボタンを縫いつける *sew* a button *on* (a coat) ‖ 彼女は子供の服はほとんど自分で縫う She *sews* almost all her children's clothes. ‖ 医者は傷口を3針縫った The doctor *sewed up* [*sutured*] the cut with three stitches. ‖ 腕を5針縫った I *had* five *stitches* in my arm.

2【すり抜ける】 ▶男は人ごみを縫うようにして逃げた The man *threaded his way through* the crowd and escaped.

ヌード a **nude** 一㊋ ヌードの **nude** ▶ヌードの女性 a *nude* woman／a woman *in the nude* ‖ 画学生たちはプロのヌードモデルを使ってデッサンしていた The art students were sketching a professional *nude model*.

‖ヌード雑誌 a nude [nudie] magazine (➤ porn(o) [girlie／cheesecake] magazine などともいう) ‖ ヌードシーン a nude scene ‖ ヌード写真 a nude picture [photo].

> **危ないカタカナ語✸ ヌード**
> **1** nude は naked ほどどぎつさがなく, 芸術用語としても用いる. 赤ん坊や子供に関しては通例 naked を使い, 例えば子供が裸で泳ぐような場合は swim naked と表現する. 思春期以降のおとなの場合には, 強い性的連想がある naked を避けて, swim in the nude とすることが多い.
> **2**「ヌードショー」は和製語で, 英語では strip show, または striptease という. 「ヌードダンサー」は stripper または stripteaser.

ヌードル **noodles**

‖カップヌードル Cup Noodles (➤ 商標) ; noodles in a cup.

ぬか 糠 **rice bran** ▶《慣用表現》彼女への忠告もぬかにくぎだった My advice *slid off her like water off a duck's back*. (文字どおりには「アヒルの背中の水のようにすべり落ちた」の意)／My advice to her *went in one ear and out the other*. (文字どおりには「右の耳から入って左の耳に抜けた」の意).

1**ぬかす 抜かす** **omit** +㊐, **skip** +㊐ (省略する, 飛ばす ; 後者はインフォーマルな語) ; **leave out**(除外する)

▶私はときどき寝坊して朝食を抜かす I sometimes oversleep and *skip* [*go without*] breakfast. ‖ 先生は私を抜かして次の生徒を当てた The teacher *skipped* me and called on the next student. ‖ friend の i を抜かさないように Don't *omit* the i in (the word) 'friend.'

▶うっかりリストからその商品名を抜かしてしまった I carelessly *omitted* the item from the list.／I carelessly *left* the item *off* the list.

2**ぬかす 吐かす** ▶何をぬかすか What's that you *said*?

ぬがせる 脱がせる ▶赤ん坊の服を脱がせる *undress* a baby ‖ あなた, ユミのセーター脱がしてやって. Honey, will you *help* Yumi *take off* her sweater? (➤「ユミが脱ぐのを手伝って」の意).

ぬかづけ 糠漬け **vegetables pickled in salted ricebran paste.**

ぬかみそ 糠味噌 salted rice-bran paste for pickling ▶ナスのぬかみそ漬け eggplants seasoned in *salted rice-bran paste*.

▶《慣用表現》私はぬかみそ臭い女にはなりたくない I don't want to be *a woman with dishpan hands*. (➤ dishpan hands は「炊事・洗濯で荒れた手」).

ぬかよろこび 糠喜び ▶大もうけしたと思ったのに株がその後急落したのでぬか喜びとなった Although I thought I'd made a lot of money, the stock price later plummeted, so *I wasn't happy for long*.

ぬかり 抜かり ▶あいつは何をやらせても抜かりがない Everything he does is *perfect*.

1**ぬかる 抜かる** ▶ぬかるなよ *Look sharp!*／*Be alert!* ‖ 相手が子供だと思ってぬかるな *Don't be too* [*overly*] *confident*, thinking your opponents are just kids!

2**ぬかる** ▶道がぬかっているから足元に気をつけて! The road *is muddy* [*slushy*], so watch your step! (➤ muddy は「泥でぬかって」, slushy は「雪解けでぬかって」).

ぬかるみ **mud** ▶私はぬかるみで足を滑らせてころんだ I slipped in the *mud* and fell.

ぬき 抜き ▶きょうは堅苦しいことは抜きにしよう Let's *skip* (the) formalities today. ‖ 姉はけさは朝食抜きで仕事に出かけた My sister went to work *without* breakfast this morning. ‖ 今夜のカラオケは細川抜きでやろう Let's do karaoke tonight *without* Hosokawa.

ぬきあし 抜き足 ▶抜き足差し足で部屋に入る enter a room *stealthily*／*tiptoe into* a room.

ぬきうち 抜き打ちの **surprise** ; **snap**(不意の) ▶きのうその工場で役人による抜き打ち監査が行われた Yesterday several officials carried out *a surprise inspection* of the factory. ‖ きょう数学の抜き打ちテストがあった We had *a pop quiz* [*a pop test*／*a surprise test*] in math today.

ぬきがき 抜き書き an **extract** /ékstrækt/ ; an **excerpt** /éksəːrpt/ (特に主要な部分の抜粋) ▶教科書から大事な文章だけを**抜き書きにした** I *excerpted* the important passages from the textbook.

ぬきさしならない 抜き差しならない ▶**抜き差しならない状態に陥る** *get oneself into a fix* [*a difficult situation*].

ぬきさる 抜き去る ▶設楽選手, ここでスパートをかけて, 一気に3人を**抜き去りました** Shitara put on a spurt, *overtook* three runners in a moment and *left* them (*far*) *behind*.

ぬぎすてる 脱ぎ捨てる **throw off** ; **kick off**(靴をけって脱ぐ) ▶子供たちは服を**脱ぎ捨てて**海に飛び込んだ The children *threw off* their clothes and plunged into the sea. ‖ 玄関に息子の靴が**脱ぎ捨てたまま**になっている My son's shoes are still in the genkan [entrance hall] where he *kicked* them *off*.

ぬきずり 抜き刷り an **offprint**.

ぬきだす 抜き出す **pick out**(選ぶ) ; **extract**(情報などを) ▶電話帳を調べて変わった名前の人を**抜き出した** I looked in the phone directory to *pick out* people with unusual names. ‖ 私はテキストから重要なフレーズを**抜き出した** I *extracted* important phrases from the text.

ぬきとり 抜き取り ▶**抜き取り検査を行う** *spot-check* ／*carry out* [*conduct*] *a spot* [*random*] *inspection*.

ぬきとる 抜き取る ▶とげを**抜き取る** *pull out* a splinter ‖ その男はレジから1万円札を2枚そっと**抜き取った**(＝盗んだ) The man stealthily *lifted* two ten-thousand-yen bills *from* the cash register. (➤ lift は「盗む」の意のインフォーマルな語).

ぬきんでる 抜きん出る ▶ビジネスの世界で**抜きん出る** *excel* in the business world ‖ 数子さんは暗算ではクラスの中で**抜きん出ている** Kazuko *stands out from* the rest of her class in her ability to do mental arithmetic. ／Kazuko *surpasses* [*is head and shoulders above*] everyone in class in mental arithmetic.

ぬく 抜く

📖 **訳語メニュー**
引き抜く →pull out **1**
武器などを取り出す →draw **2**
省く →skip **3**
追い越す →pass, overtake **4**

1【引っぱって取り出す】 **pull out** ▶くぎを**抜く** *pull out* a nail ‖ ビール(の栓)を**抜く** *open* a bottle of beer ‖ 彼女はユリを根元から**抜いた** She *pulled out* the lily by the roots. ‖ 私は上の歯を1本**抜いてもらった** I *had* an upper tooth *pulled* (*out*) [*extracted*]. ‖ 指にとげが刺さっちゃった. **抜いてちょうだい** I've got a splinter in my finger. Please *take it out*.

2【取り出す】 **draw** +㊐ (滑らかに) ; **pick** +㊐ (注意して) ▶警官はけん銃を**抜いて**空砲を1発撃った The police officer *drew* his pistol and fired a blank. ‖ 彼は本棚から本を1冊**抜いて**よこした He *took* a book from the shelf and handed it to me. ‖《手品》お好きなカードを1枚**抜いて**覚えてください *Pick* your favorite card and remember it.

▶ハンバーガーください. タマネギは**抜いて** I'll have a hamburger *with no* onions [*and hold* the onions], please. (➤ hold は注文で「入れない」) ‖ 誰かがタイヤの**空気を抜いた**に違いない Someone must *have deflated* the tire [*let the air out of* the tire]. ‖ 肩の**力を抜いて**ごらん *Relax* your shoulders. ‖ クリーニング店でズボンのしみを**抜いてもらった** I *had* a stain *dry-cleaned out of* my pants. ／I *had* a spot *removed* from my pants at the dry cleaners.

3【必要な物を省略する】 **skip** +㊐ ▶彼は忙しいのでよく昼食を**抜く** He is so busy he often *skips* [*goes without*] lunch. ‖ その作業員は監督が見ていないと**手を抜く** The worker *slacks* [*goofs*] *off* when his boss isn't watching. ‖ 途中で**気を抜くな** Don't *let up* on your effort [Keep up your concentration] when you are working.

4【あとから追い越す, 負かす】 **pass** +㊐, 《主に英》 **overtake** +㊐ ; **beat** +㊐ (負かす) ▶スポーツカーが我々の車を**抜いて行った** A sports car *passed* us. (● 「スポーツカーに追い抜かれた」なら We were passed by a sports car.) ‖ カナダの選手がアメリカの選手を**抜いて**先頭に立った The Canadian runner *overtook* the American runner and took the lead. ‖ 優子は中間試験で麻里子を**抜いた** Yuko *did better* than Mariko in the midterm exam. (➤ do better は「より良い成績をあげる」).

▶《慣用表現》二人の走者は**抜きつ抜かれつの大接戦**を**演じた** The two runners *ran a close race* [*were in a dead heat*] from the start to the finish. ‖ 彼の絵は出品された作品の中で**群を抜いて優れていた** Among all the paintings exhibited, his was *by far the best*.

5【間を貫く】 ▶イチローの打球はピッチャーの足元を**抜き**センターに達した Ichiro hit *past* the mound for a single to center. ‖ 内川は三遊 [二遊] **間を抜く**ヒットを放った Uchikawa hit a single *through* third and short [*through* the middle].

▶校旗は紺地に校章を**白く抜いた**デザインだ The design of our school flag consists of our school emblem *in white against* a navy-blue background.

-ぬく -抜く **1【向こう側へ貫く】** ▶矢は的の真ん中を**射抜いた** The arrow *shot through* the center of the target. ‖ そのテロリストは頭を**撃ち抜かれて**即死した The terrorist was killed instantly by a bullet that *went* [*passed*] *through* his [her] head.

2【完全に…する】 ▶ 20キロを**走りぬいた**ことは私にとって大きな自信となった *Running the entire* 20 kilometers has given me considerable confidence.

ぬぐ 脱ぐ **take off** ; **remove** +㊐ (➤ 堅い語) ▶ズボンを**脱ぐ** *take off* one's trousers [pants] ‖ 彼は帽子を**脱いで**その婦人に深々とおじぎをした He *took off* his hat and bowed deeply to the lady. ‖ 靴を**脱いで**上がってください Please *remove* [*take off*] your shoes before entering. ‖ 上半身**服を脱いで**この椅子にお座りください Please *undress* to the waist and be seated on this chair.

▶彼は靴を**脱いで**立っていた He was standing *with* his shoes *off*. ‖ コートは**脱がないで**結構です You may *keep* your coat *on*.

▶《慣用表現》きみのために**一肌脱ごう** I'll *lend* [*offer*] you *a helping hand*. (➤「手を貸そう」の意).

ぬぐう 拭う **wipe** 《off, away》 ▶汗を**拭う** *wipe off* [*away*] the sweat ‖ 私はティッシュで口のまわりを**拭った** I *wiped* my mouth with a tissue. ‖ 彼女はハンカチでそっと目がしらを**拭った** She *dabbed* at her eyes with her handkerchief. (➤ dab は「軽く押さえる」).

▶《比喩的》不安な気持ちを**拭いきれない** I *can't free*

myself of this anxiety.

ぬくぬく ▶猫はストーブの前でぬくぬくと(＝暖かそうに)寝ていた The cat was lying *snugly* [*cozily*] in front of the heater.

▶ぬくぬくした環境に育ったせいかどうも彼はのんびりし過ぎている He is entirely too easygoing. It may be because he was raised in such a *comfortable* [*comfy*] environment.

ぬくもり **warmth** ▶干した布団にはまだ日のぬくもりが残っていた One could still feel the *warmth* of the sun in the aired futon.

▶ごく幼い頃母に死なれたので私は母親のぬくもりというものを知らない My mother died when I was very little, so I have never known the *warmth* of a mother.

ぬ

ぬけあな 抜け穴 a **secret passage**(秘密の通路)；a **loophole** (➤「(城壁・とりでなどの)銃眼；明かり穴」が原義で，今は「抜け穴」の意で比喩的に用いるのがふつう)

▶悪賢いやつらはどんな法律にもすぐに**抜け穴**を見つけてしまう Shrewd people can easily find *a loophole* in any law.

ぬけがけ 抜け駆けをする **steal a march on** (one's enemy)；**outsmart** ＋目，**outwit** ＋目 (➤ともに「人を出し抜く」) ▶**抜けがけ**は許さんぞ I won't let you *outsmart* me.

ぬけがら 抜け殻 a **shell**(セミなどの) ▶木の根元にセミの**抜け殻**があった I found a cicada's *shell* at the base of the tree.

▶去年奥さんを亡くしてから彼は**抜け殻**のようになってしまった Last year he lost his wife. Since then he has been *a* (*mere*) *shadow of* his former self.

ぬけげ 抜け毛 (a) **fallen hair** ▶最近**抜け毛**がひどい I'*m losing* a lot of *hair* these days. ／My *hair* is *falling out* terribly these days.

ぬけだす 抜け出す ▶象が1頭おりから**抜け出した** An elephant *has escaped from* its cage. ‖ 学生が2名，講義の途中で教室からそっと**抜け出した** Two students *slipped* [*sneaked*] *out of* the room during the lecture. ‖ 早く都会を**抜け出したい** I want to *get out of* the city as soon as possible.

▶第3レーンの選手がプールの中央で頭1つ**抜け出した** The swimmer in the third lane *took the lead* by a head at the halfway point of the swimming pool.

ぬけぬけと ▶よくもぬけぬけと私の前に顔を出せたものだ *How dare* you show yourself in front of me! (● 憤りを表す言い方).

ぬけみち 抜け道 a **byroad**, a **byway**；a **secret passage** (秘密の通路)；a **shortcut**(近道)；a **loophole** (➤比喩的な意味での「抜け穴」)

▶この**抜け道**を行けば渋滞に巻き込まれずに済むよ If you take this *byroad* [*byway*], you won't get caught in a traffic jam.

▶《比喩的》税金を払わないで済むうまい**抜け道**を知っている I know *a* tax *loophole* [a good way to evade taxes]. (● 前者は合法，後者は違法).

ぬけめ(の)ない 抜け目(の)ない **shrewd**, **sharp** (➤ともに「鋭敏な，賢い」という良い意味もある)；**clever** (➤悪い意味合いは少ない) ▶**抜け目のない**実業家 a *shrewd* [*sharp*] businessperson ‖ 彼は賢いと言うよりも**抜け目がない**といったほうがいい He's more *shrewd* [*clever*] than wise. ‖ あいつは先生の前ではいつも**抜け目なく**立ち回る He always acts *tactfully* in the presence of his teacher. (➤ tactfully は「如才なく」).

ぬける 抜ける

訳語メニュー
引っぱると取れる →come out **1**
通り抜ける →go [pass] through **3**
底が落ちる →drop out **3**
脱落している →be missing **4**

1【引っぱると取れる】come out ▶このコルクの栓[くぎ]はなかなか**抜けない** This cork [nail] will not *come out*. ‖ かぎがかぎ穴から**抜けない** The key won't *come out of* [*come off*] the keyhole. ‖ 最近よく髪の毛が**抜ける** I'*m losing* a lot of hair these days. ／My hair is *falling out* a lot these days. ‖ 歯が1本**抜けた** One of my teeth *came out*. ‖ みんなでその切り株を引っぱったらやっと**抜けた** Everybody worked together to *pull out* the stump. (➤ pull out は「抜く」).

2【取れて失われる】 ▶力が全部**抜けてしまった** I'*ve lost* all my strength. ／I'*m* completely *drained* (*of strength*). ‖ 風船の空気が**抜けて**落ちてきた The balloon *lost* air and started to descend. ‖ このコーラ，気が**抜けてる**よ This cola *tastes* [*has gone*] *flat*. ／This cola *lost its fizz*. (➤ fizz は「シュワッという音」) ‖ のりがしけって香りが**抜けた** The nori [pressed laver] has gotten damp and *lost* most of its flavor [most of its flavor *was lost*].

▶かぜが**抜けない** I cannot *get over* [*get rid of* ／*shake* (*off*)] my cold. ‖ 年を取るとなかなか疲れが**抜けない** It becomes harder to *get rid of* your tiredness [fatigue] as you get older. ‖ 悪い習慣はなかなか**抜けない**ものだ A bad habit is hard to *get rid of* [*to break* ／to *quit* ／to *kick*]. (➤ quit は「(意図的に)きっぱりやめる」の意のインフォーマルな語；kick は「(悪い習慣など)をやめる」の意のインフォーマルな語).

3【向こう側へ通る】go [pass] through ▶商店街を**抜ける**と大きな公園に出た I *went through* the shopping mall and came to a big park. ‖ **対話**「この路地は**抜けられ**ますか」「いいえ，**抜けられ**ません」"Can I *pass through* this alley?" "No, it's a blind alley." (➤ blind alley は「袋小路」) ‖ 鹿児島に上陸した台風は九州を横断してけさ日本海へ**抜けた** The typhoon hit Kagoshima, and then *blew* [*blasted*] *through* Kyushu *into* the Japan Sea this morning. ‖ 《野球》ボールはファーストの股間を**抜けた** The ball *passed between* the legs of the first baseman.

▶ダンボールの底が**抜けた** The bottom of the cardboard box *dropped out*. ‖ 20人の重みで床が**抜けた** The floor *gave way* under the weight of 20 people.

4【脱落している】be missing ▶この文章には句読点がいくつか**抜けている** There are some punctuation marks *missing* in these sentences. ‖ 5ページ目が**抜けている** The fifth page *is missing*.

▶彼はほんとうにいい男だが，ちょっとばかり**抜けた**ところがある He's really a good guy, but he's a bit *dimwitted* [*missing a few screws*].

5【組織から離れる】leave, quit ▶会議を**抜ける**ことはできないの？ Can you *get out of* the meeting? ‖ メンバーの半数がクラブを**抜けた**(＝やめた) Half the members *left* [*quit*] the club.

6【透明に見える】 ▶つゆが明けて**抜ける**ような青空が広がっている The rainy season is over and a *clear* blue sky is [has] spread out. ‖ 北欧の人は**抜ける**よ

うな白い肌をしている People in Northern Europe have very *fair* skin.

ぬげる 脱げる come off ▶川底の泥にはまって長靴が脱げてしまった My boots got stuck in the muddy riverbed and *came off*. ‖ ぴったりのTシャツを試しに着たのはいいけどなかなか脱げなくて困った I tried on a tight-fitting T-shirt, but I had a terrible time *getting* it *off*.

ぬし 主 one's master（主人）; the proprietor /prəpráɪəṭəʳ/, the owner（持ち主）▶その老人はアパートの主のような存在だった The old man seemed to *have been living* in the apartment house *forever*.

ぬすみ 盗み (a) theft /θeft/ ▶A氏は盗みを働いて捕まった Mr. A was arrested for *theft* [*stealing*]. ‖ あんなかわいい子が盗みを働いたとは信じられない I can't believe such a cute girl could *have stolen* (something).

ぬすみぎき 盗み聞き eavesdropping 一動（…を）盗み聞きする eavesdrop /íːvzdrɑːp/ 《on》（立ち聞きする）; overhear +自（聞こえてくる話をそれとなく聞く）; bug +自（盗聴する）▶人の話を盗み聞きしたいという心理は誰にでもある Everybody has a tendency to want to *eavesdrop on* other people [*listen in on* other people's conversations].

ぬすみぐい 盗み食い ▶ケーキを盗み食いする *eat* some cake *while no one is looking* / *sneak* some cake.

ぬすみみる 盗み見る sneak a look 《at》, steal a glance 《at》（ちらりと）▶少女は怒っている父親の顔を盗み見た The little girl *stole a glance at* her angry father.

ぬすむ 盗む steal +自（他人の物を）; rob 《A of B》（A（人・場所）からB（物）を盗む）; snatch +自（ひったくる）▶少年はその本屋で漫画本を盗もうとした The boy tried to *steal* a comic book from the bookstore. ‖ 誰かが私の時計を盗んだ Somebody *stole* my watch.（➤ stole は steal の過去形）‖ 人込みの中で財布を盗まれた I *had* my wallet *stolen* in the crowd.（● I was stolen ... とはしない）‖ 外国に行ったらかばんを盗まれないよう注意しなさい When traveling abroad, you should be careful not to *have* your bag *snatched*.

▶泥棒が入って店から500万円を盗んだ A thief *robbed* the shop *of* five million yen.（● 文型に注意）/ A thief broke into the shop and *took* five million yen. ‖ 彼は雇い主の金を盗んで逃げた He *ran away* [*made off*] *with* his employer's money.

▶博士は他の研究者の論文から研究成果を盗んだ（＝盗用した）The doctor *lifted* [*took*] the findings from another researcher's paper.

▶《慣用表現》彼は授業中, 先生の目を盗んで漫画本を読んだ He read a comic book during class *while the teacher wasn't looking*.（➤このような状況を He sneaked [snuck] and read a comic book in class. とも表現できる）.

ぬっと ▶目の前に人の顔がぬっと現れたのでびっくりした I was startled when a person's face *suddenly* loomed before my eyes.

ぬの 布 cloth, fabric（➤後者は堅い語）▶布の袋 a *cloth* bag ‖ 布きれ a piece of *cloth* ‖ このかばんは革でなく布製です This bag is *made of cloth*, not leather.

ぬのじ 布地 (a) fabric, cloth.

ぬま 沼 a shallow pond in a marsh（湿地にある浅い池）

> **●解説●「沼」について**
> (1)「沼」の訳語にしばしば swamp や marsh があてられるが, swamp は「(常時水におおわれた)湿原」のことであり, marsh は swamp と同義に使われることもあるが, 日本語の「湿地, 沼地」に相当する語である. 日本の「沼」は比較的小規模なものを指すことが多いので, 上記のような説明訳にする.
> (2)「印旛沼」「尾瀬沼」などの沼は「湖」と同義なので, Lake Imba, Lake Oze でよい.

ぬまち 沼地 a marsh, a swamp; marshland, wetlands（湿地帯）▶一面に沼地が広がっている There is *marshland* all around.

ぬめぬめ ▶ナメクジがはった所がぬめぬめしている It is *slimy* where the slug crawled.

ぬめり slime.

ぬらす 濡らす wet +自 ▶ぬらしたタオル a *wetted* towel（● wet towel とすると「湿ったタオル」の意味にもなる）‖ 彼は冷たい水でタオルをぬらして顔を拭いた He *wet* [*wetted*] a towel with cold water and wiped his face with it. ‖ にわか雨で新しい帽子をぬらしてしまった I *got* my new hat *wet* in a shower.

ぬらぬら ▶ドアの取っ手がぬらぬらして気持ち悪い The doorknob is disgustingly *slimy*.

ぬらりくらり →のらりくらり.

ぬり 塗り a coat (of paint)（ペンキやワックスの）▶ワックスの2度塗り two *coats* of wax ‖ 黒塗りのお盆 a *black lacquer* tray ‖ 会津塗り Aizu *lacquer ware* ‖ 塗りが乾くまで手すりに手を触れないでください Please do not touch the handrail until the *lacquer* [*paint* / *varnish*] has dried. /《掲示》Wet Paint.

‖下塗り undercoating; (an) undercoat（➤「下塗り用ペンキ」の意もある）.

ぬりえ 塗り絵 a line drawing for coloring-in; a coloring book（塗り絵帳）▶人形の塗り絵をする *color a picture* of a doll.

ぬりかえる 塗り替える repaint +自 ▶わが家もそろそろ外壁を塗り替えないと It's about time we *repainted* the outer walls.（➤ repainted は仮定法過去形）‖《比喩的》彼は走り高跳びの世界記録を2度塗り替えた He *broke* the world high jump record twice. ‖ 羽生結弦はフィギュアスケートの歴史を塗り替えた（＝書き換えた）Hanyu Yuzuru *rewrote* the history of figure skating.

ぬりかためる 塗り固める ▶壁にしっくいを塗り固める *cover* a wall *with plaster* / *plaster* a wall.

ぬりぐすり 塗り薬 (an) ointment ▶顔のおできに塗り薬をつけた I applied some *ointment* to a sore on my face.

ぬりたくる 塗りたくる ▶そのいたずらっ子は校舎の壁にペンキを塗りたくった That naughty boy *smeared* [*daubed*] paint *all over* the walls of the school building.

ぬりたて 塗り立て ▶ドアはペンキの塗りたてですから, 触らないように Be careful not to touch the door because it's *been just* [*freshly*] *painted*. ‖《掲示》ペンキ塗りたて Wet [《英》Fresh] Paint.

ぬりつぶす 塗りつぶす paint [smear] out ▶我々はその落書きを白いペンキで塗りつぶした We *painted* [*smeared*] *out* the graffiti with white paint. ‖ 該当する□を鉛筆で塗りつぶしてください *Blacken* [*Black out*] the applicable boxes with a pencil.

ぬりもの 塗り物 lacquerware ▶塗り物のお椀(わん) a *lacquerware* bowl ‖塗り物師 a lacquer craftsperson [artist], a lacquerer.

ぬる 塗る **paint** +目 (塗料を) ; **color** +目 (色を) ; **plaster** +目 (しっくいなどを) ; **spread** +目 (バターなどを) ; **apply** +目 (薬などを) ▶父は犬小屋を白く塗った My father *painted* the doghouse white. ‖ 彼の家は緑色のペンキが塗ってある His house *is painted* green. ‖ 彼はその地図に色を塗った He *colored* that map. ‖ 私はパンにバターを塗った I *spread* butter on the bread. ／I *buttered* the bread.

▶日焼け止めクリームを塗る *apply* sunscreen ‖ 傷口に消毒薬を塗った I *applied* some disinfectant *to* the cut. ／I *put* some disinfectant *on* the cut. ‖ 彼は机にニスを薄く塗った He *gave* the desk *a thin coat* of varnish. ‖ この菓子盆は黒と朱の漆が塗ってある This dessert tray *is lacquered* in black and vermilion. (「漆を塗る」は cover [varnish] ... with lacquer といってもいい).

▶《慣用表現》あいつは俺の顔に泥を塗りやがった I *lost face* because of his bad behavior.

ぬるい **lukewarm** /lù:kwɔ́:ʳm/, **tepid** (➤ 後者には不快なイメージがあることが少なくない) ▶ぬるい湯 *lukewarm* [*tepid*] water ‖ コーヒーは熱いのがいい. ぬるいのはいやだ I like my coffee hot, not *lukewarm* [*tepid*]. ‖ 風呂がぬるくて入った気がしなかった The bath was*n't hot enough* so I was unable to enjoy it. ‖ ビールがぬるくなってしまった The beer became *slightly warm*.

☛ **生ぬるい** (→見出語)

ぬるぬる ▶浴槽のタイルがぬるぬるしている The tiles of the bathtub are *slimy*. (➤ slimy /sláɪmi/ は汚れてぬるぬるするとき, 油でなら greasy を用いる) ‖ ウナギはぬるぬるしてつかみにくい Eels are hard to get hold of because they are *slippery*.

ぬるまゆ ぬるま湯 **lukewarm** [**tepid**] **water** ▶ウールのセーターはぬるま湯で洗いなさい You should wash your woolen sweaters in *lukewarm water*. ‖ いつまでもぬるま湯につかった生活をしていてはだめだ You shouldn't keep leading *an easy, sheltered life*.

ぬるむ 温む ▶氷が解けて川の水もぬるんできた The ice has melted and the water of the river *has become a bit warmer*.

ぬれぎぬ 濡れ衣 ▶私はやってない! ぬれぎぬだ! I didn't do it! *It's a frame-up!* (➤ frame-up は「計画的なでっちあげ」) ‖ 彼女は万引きのぬれぎぬを着せられた She *was falsely* [*unjustly*] *accused of* shoplifting. ‖ その男はぬれぎぬを晴らすことができずに獄死した He failed to clear himself of the *false charge* and died in prison.

ぬれてであわ 濡れ手で粟 ▶土地ころがしでぬれ手であわの大もうけをする *get easy money* [*get rich quick*] through land flipping.

ぬれねずみ 濡れ鼠 ▶夕立にあってぬれねずみになった I was caught in a shower and *got drenched* [*got soaked*] *to the skin*. ／I *got sopping* [*dripping*] *wet* in a shower. (いずれも「ずぶぬれになった」の意) ‖ 家にたどり着いたとき彼女はぬれねずみだった When she got home, she looked (just) like *a drowned rat*. (「おぼれ死んだネズミのよう」の意).

ぬれる 濡れる **get wet** 一形 **ぬれた wet** ▶傘をささないとぬれるわよ Put up your umbrella or you'll *get wet* [*get rained on*]. ‖ 彼らはひどい雨でびしょびしょにぬれてしまった They *got dripping* [*soaking* ／ *sopping*] *wet* in the heavy rain. ／They *got drenched* [*soaked*] in the heavy rain.

▶赤ちゃんのおむつがぬれてるみたい The baby's diaper seems (to be) *wet*. ‖ 彼女は髪をぬれたままにしておいたのでひどいかぜをひいた She went around with her hair *wet*, and caught a bad cold. ‖ 彼はぬれたタオルで車のフロントガラスをふいた He wiped the windshield of his car with a *wet* towel. ‖ ぬれた手で電気コードに触るな Don't touch an electric cord with *wet* hands. ‖ 雨にぬれた街路樹が美しかった The trees *glistening with rain* along the roadside were beautiful. (➤ glisten /glísən/ は「(水滴や氷雪が光を受けて)きらきら輝く」).

ね・ネ

1**ね** 根 **1【植物の】a root** ▶桜の木の根がついた The cherry tree *took root*. ‖ その木は深く根を張っていた The tree *was* deeply *rooted*.

2【本質, 根源】▶根がいい人 a good person *at heart* ‖ 彼は根が正直だ He is *naturally* honest. ／He is honest *by nature*. ‖ うちの店長は口は悪いが根はとても親切だ Our store manager is rough-spoken, but he is very kind *at heart*. ‖ M専務とY部長の対立は根が深い The conflict between senior managing director M and department manager Y *is deeply rooted* [*has strong roots*]. ‖ すべての悪の根を断つことはできない You can't *root out* every evil (in the world).

3【慣用表現】根に持つ ▶彼は私が会議で言った事を根に持っているようだ Apparently, he *has* [*holds*] *a grudge* against me over what I said at the meeting. **根も葉もない** ▶彼がすぐ引退するというのは根も葉もないうわさだ It is a *groundless* [*baseless*] rumor that he will retire immediately. **根を下ろす** ▶民主主義が日本にしっかり根を下ろした Democracy *has taken* firm *root* in Japanese soil. (➤ take root は「(思想・文化などが)定着する」).

☛ **根っから, 根詰まり, 根掘り葉掘り** (→見出語)

2**ね 音** (a) **sound** ; a **chirp** (虫の) ▶遠くのお寺から鐘の音が聞こえてきた We heard the *sound* of a bell from a distant temple. ‖ 秋の夜に虫の音に耳を傾けるのが好きだ On autumn evenings, I like to listen to the *chirps* [*chirping*] of insects.

▶《慣用表現》彼はその問題と1週間格闘したが, 結局音を上げてしまった He wrestled with that problem the whole week, and finally had to *give up* [*throw in the towel*]. (➤ 後者はボクシングで「(負けを認めて)タオルを投げ入れる」ことから出たインフォーマルな表現).

3**ね 値** a **price** ▶値がつけられないほどの(貴重な)花びん a *priceless* vase ‖ 私はその携帯音楽プレーヤーを安い値で手に入れた I got the portable music player *at a low* [*reasonable*] *price*. (➤ reasonable は「妥当な」) ‖ これはきわめて珍しい品でとても値がつけられない This is such an extremely rare item that I can hardly *put a price* on it. ‖ このサイン入りのＴシャツは将来いい値がつくかもしれないよ You may *get a good price* for this autographed T-shirt in the future. ‖ カシミヤのセーターは値が張る Cashmere sweaters *cost* (you) *a lot*.

4**ね 1【呼びかけ】say,（英）I say ; hey, hi** ▶ね, 文太さん, あれ見て！ *Say* [*I say*], Bunta. Look at that ! ‖ ね, ちょっと！ *Now*, listen ! ‖ ね, 言ったとおりでしょ *See*, I told you so. ／ *There !* You see ? (➤ (You) see ? は「わかったでしょ」の意). ⇀ねえ.

2【念を押して】

> 【文型】
> A さんは…だね
> A **is** ..., **isn't he** [**she**] ?
> A **does** ..., **doesn't he** [**she**] ?
> B さんは…じゃないよね
> B **isn't** ..., **is he** [**she**] ?
> B **doesn't** ..., **does he** [**she**] ?
> 【解説】(1) 相手に同意を求めたり, 念を押す「-ね」は上にあるような付加疑問を用いる. 前半が肯定文のときは否定疑問文の「(助) 動詞＋代名詞」の部分, 前半が否定文のときは肯定疑問文の同じ部分を付ける. Yes か No かわからずに聞くときには最後を上昇調で言うが, ふつうは下げて言う.
> (2)「-ね」はほかに調子を和らげる役目もし, はるかに使い方が広く, 付加疑問になるとはかぎらない.

▶佐藤さんは本当に紳士ですね Mr. Sato is a real gentleman, *isn't he* ? ‖ 彼女は本当に手際がいいですね She's really efficient, *isn't she* ? ‖ 対話「きみ, 松田君ですね」「ええ, そうです」"You are Matsuda, *aren't you*?" "Yes, I am. ／ (Yes.) That's right." ‖ 対話「これやったの, きみだね」「違いますよ」"You did it, *didn't you ?*" "No, I didn't." ‖ きみはあまり納豆が好きじゃないよね You're not very fond of natto, *are you* [*right*] ? ‖ 本当に絵が上手ですね You draw really well. (● 相手をほめるのだから付加疑問をつけないで, これで十分) ‖ 対話「いやなお天気ですね」「そうですね」"The weather is lousy, *isn't it* ?" "(Yes,) isn't it." (● 返事の isn't it は Yes, it is. や It sure is. などよりくだけた言い方で, 軽く相づちを打つ場合に使う) ‖ ぜひ遊びに来てね Be sure and come to see us. ／ (You'll) come and see us, *won't you* ? (● 後者は大いに期待していることを表す).

> **直訳の落とし穴「疲れたね」**
> (1)「察し」の文化を背景に持つ日本語では, 自分だけでなく, 様子から判断して相手も同じだろうと推測して, Yes を予測しながら,「疲れたね」とか,「おなかが空いたね」などと言うが, これをそのまま, We're tired, aren't we ?, We're hungry, aren't we ? などとしても通じない. この we の使い方は文法で patronizing 'we' (上から目線の we) と呼ばれるもので, 実質的には you を意味していて, 相手を子供扱いして,「(あなたは) 疲れたんでしょう？」と聞く言い方になる. 英米文化圏では自分は自分, あなたはあなた, という個人主義が徹底しているので, 自分とあなたを同一視する, aren't we ? というような表現はふつう用いない. お節介なことだが, 無理に訳せば, I'm tired. You must be tired, too. または It looks like we're both tired. などとするしかない.
> (2) 相手の様子から「(ずいぶんと) 忙しそうだね」は You look (really) busy. が自然で,「-ね」にとらわれて, 付加疑問を足すとおかしな文になる.

3【感動を強調して】▶きみは料理がうまいね！ *What* a great cook you are ! ／ You are a wonderful cook !

5**ね 子 the Rat**(十二支の1つ, ネズミ)
‖ 子年 the year of the Rat.

ねあか ▶私, ネアカだからあまり悩まないの I'm *the cheerful type* [I'm *cheerful by nature*], so nothing worries me much. ⇀ねくら.

ねあがり 値上がり a rise [**an increase**] **in price** ▶食料品の値上がりは消費者にとって深刻な問題だ The *rise in* food *prices* is a serious matter for consumers. ‖ 米が5パーセント値上がりした The *price* of rice *has gone up* [*has risen*] by 5 percent. ‖ バブル経済の間, 土地は急激に値上がりした During the 'bubble economy,' land *prices skyrocketed*.

ねあげ 値上げ a price increase, a raise [**an increase**] **in price, a price markup** 一動 **値上げする raise (a price), increase (a price), mark up (a price)** ▶全商品は平均1割値上げされた The *prices* of all the items *were raised* (by) ten percent on average. ／ All the items *were marked up* (by) ten percent on average. ‖ 鉄道料金が5パーセント値上げされた Railroad fares *have been raised* by 5 percent. ‖ また運賃の値上げだって！ (Train) fares are *going up* again !

ねあせ 寝汗 ▶私は最近よく寝汗をかく These days I *sweat* a lot *in my sleep*.

ネアンデルタールじん ネアンデルタール人 a Neanderthal.

ねいき 寝息 ▶妹の安らかな寝息が聞こえる I can hear the quiet *breathing of* my sister *sleeping*.

ネイティブ(スピーカー) a native speaker (➤ a native は「(ある土地の) 生まれの人」) ▶ボブは英語のネイティブだ Bob is *a native speaker* of English.

ネイリスト a manicurist, a nail artist.

ねいりばな 寝入りばな ▶寝入りばなに起こされて, 赤ん坊がぐずっている The baby is fussy because he was awakened *just after he had gone to sleep*.

ねいる 寝入る fall asleep, go to sleep ▶12時頃帰宅したときには妻と子供たちはもうぐっすりと寝入っていた When I got home around midnight, my wife and children *had* already *fallen asleep*.

ねいろ 音色 a tone ▶私はパンパイプやオカリナのような素朴な音色が好きです I like simple *tones*, like those of a panpipe or an ocarina.

ねうち 値打ち value, worth (➤ 実際的な有用性や金銭的価値については前者が, また, 精神的・道徳的価値については後者が使われるが, 同義に用いる場合も少なくない) ⇀価値 ▶この刀は大変な値打ちがある This sword *has a great value* [*is very valuable*]. ／ This sword *is of great value* [*is worth a lot* (*of money*)].

> 【文型】
> …円(金額)の値打ちがある
> **be worth** ... **yen**
> …するだけの値打ちがある
> **be worth** doing ➤ doing の代わりに名詞もくる

▶このつぼは800万円の値打ちがある This vase *is worth* eight million *yen*. ‖ この家はどのくらいの値打ちがありますか *How much is* this house *worth* ? ／ *What is the value* of this house ? ‖ 彼の家は買った額の倍の値打ちがある His house *is worth twice as much as* he paid for it. ‖ 彼の提案はやってみる値打ちがあると思う I think his proposal *is worth a try*. ‖ その寺の庭は一見する値打ちがある The garden of the temple *is worth visiting*.（● worth のあとの doing は「…されること」という受け身の意になる）‖ **この洗濯機は修理する値打ちがない** This washing machine *isn't worth repairing*. ‖ その修理は**費用をかけるだけの値打ちがない** The repairs *aren't worth the cost*.

▶彼女の絵は**値打ち**が出てきた［下がった］Her paintings have risen［fallen］in *value*. ‖ こんな切手は**全く値打ちがない** These stamps *are worthless*［*are of no value*］.（➤「大いに値打ちがある」なら are highly-valued）.

▶人間の**値打ち**は容ぼうや財産にではなく，人柄や何をしてきたかにある A person's *worth* doesn't lie in their appearance or assets, but in their character and what they have accomplished.

ねえ 1【呼びかけ】**say**；**look**；**hi, hey**《参考》夫婦・恋人など親しい間では，dear, darling, honey などもよく使われる ▶**ねえ**，どうしたの？ *Hey*, what's the matter？‖ **ねえ**，相談があるんだけど *Hey*, I've got something to discuss with you. ‖ **ねえ**，何かあったの？ *Hi*, is something wrong？‖ **ねえ**，起きてちょうだい Wake up, *dear*［*darling*／*honey*］. ‖ **ねえねえ**，大ニュースよ *Guess what？* I've got big news for you.（● You know what？とか You know something？などともいう）.

2【感嘆】▶すばらしい**ねえ** *How* wonderful！‖ いい天気です**ねえ** Beautiful day, *isn't it*？‖ よく降る**ねえ** It's really been raining a lot, *hasn't it*？

ねえさん 姉さん one's **older**［**big**／**elder**］**sister**

> 【解説】(1) 英語では年上か年下かをあまり区別せず，older［big／elder］もつけないことが多い．(2)「お姉さん！」と呼びかけるときも "Mary", "Lucy" などとファーストネームで呼ぶのがふつう．→**姉，兄さん**．

▶**お姉さん**によろしく Please say hello to your *sister* for me. ‖ **姉さん**，ちょっと教えて *Sis*, will you tell me something？（➤ sis は自分の姉（または妹）に対する呼びかけに用いる．また，姉妹関係にない女性に対しても用いることがある）.

ネーブル《植物》a **navel** /néivəl/ **orange**（➤ 果頂部にへそのようなくぼみがある；navel だけでは「へそ」の意味にしかならない）.

ネーム a **name** ▶学校の**ネーム**入りのかばん a bag with the school *name* printed on it.

ネームバリュー **fame, a name** ▶テニス選手としての**ネームバリュー**を生かして彼は新事業を始めた Capitalizing on his *fame*［*name*］as a tennis player, he started a new business.

▶芸術院会員といえば大変な**ネームバリュー**がある To be a member of the Japan Academy of Arts adds great *value to* an artist's *name*［is of great *value to* the artist's *name*］.

> **危ないカタカナ語 ネームバリュー**
> 英語の name（名前）と value（値打ち）を組み合わせた和製語．name value では通じないので fame（名声）を使って表す．また，英語の name そのものに「名声，評判」の意味があるので，have a name でも「ネームバリューがある」の意味を出すことができる．

ねおき 寝起き ▶息子はいつも**寝起きが悪い** My son *is* always *in a bad mood when he wakes up*.

ネオコン a **neoconservative**, a **neocon**（人）.

ネオン a **neon** /níːɑːn/, a **neon sign**（ネオンサイン）；a **neon light**（ネオン灯）▶歌舞伎町一帯は毎晩**ネオン**でこうこうと輝いている The Kabukicho area is ablaze with *neon signs* every night.

ネガ a **negative**.

ねがい 願い 1【望むこと】**hope**（望み）；a **wish**（実現がかなり難しい希望）；a **desire**（強い望み）；a **request**（依頼）▶人の**願い**を聞き届ける grant *a wish* ‖ 星に**願いをかける** *wish on*［*upon*］a star ‖ **願い事をしてからろうそくを吹き消す** *make a wish* and blow out the candles ‖《神社で》お札に**願い事**を書く write one's *wish* on a tablet ‖ **願いがかないます**ように I hope my *wish* will come true. ‖ この辞書には，高校生の皆さんに英作文が好きになっていただきたいという**願い**が込められています This dictionary is made with the *hope* that you, high school students, will learn to enjoy writing English. ‖ 平和はみんなの**願い**だ Peace is everybody's *wish*.／All people *hope for*［*desire*］peace. ‖ 彼のたっての**願い**でもう１日滞在した I stayed another day at his earnest *request*. ‖ 私は彼の**願い**を聞いてやった I granted him his *request*.

▶**お願いだからその子をぶつのはやめてください** Stop beating［hitting］the boy. *I beg you*. ‖ **お願いですからあ**の騒ぎをやめさせてください Stop making so much noise, *please*.

▶ 対話「**お願いがあるのですが**」「はい，何でしょう」"*Would you do me a favor？*" "(Sure.) What is it？"（● May I ask a favor of you？はより堅い言い方．なお，日本語の「はい」は単なる相づちだが，Sure. は「もちろん，いいとも」という受け入れを表すので願いごとの中身を聞くまでは言うのをためらうこともある）.

2【申し込み】▶私は大学に１年間の**休学願い**を出した I sent in *an application for* a year's *leave of absence from college*.

☛ **お願い**（→見出語）

ねがいさげ 願い下げ ▶私はそういう種類の仕事は**願い下げだ** I *don't want* to take such a job.

ねがいでる 願い出る ▶彼女は上司に10日間の休暇を**願い出た** She *asked* her boss for a ten-day leave.

ねがう 願う 1【望む】**hope**（期待・希望する）；**wish**（実現がかなり難しいことを望む）；**desire**（強く望む）

> 【文型】
> …であることを願っている
> **I hope**（**that**）S＋V.
> ➤ 未来のことは V を未来形にすることもある

▶早くお元気になられる**ように願っています** *I hope*（*that*）you('ll) get well soon. ‖ 娘が心優しい子に育つ**ように願っています** *I hope*（*that*）my daughter grows up to be a kind-hearted person.

> **直訳の落とし穴「…と願っております」**
> 「願う」＝wish と考えて，「(お二人の)幸せを願っております」を（×）I wish you'll be happy. と間違えた言い方をする学習者が多い．〈I wish ＋文〉の形はあとに未来形がくることはない．あとは過去形の文にして，I wish you were happy. のようにするのが正しい使い方．ただし，この文が意味するところは「あなた(がた)が現在幸せでないので，幸せになればいいのになあ」である．日本語の期待をこめた希望を表すのは I hope を使って，I hope you'll be happy. という．なお，日本人学習者の場合なかなか口をついて出ないが，wish を用いて，I wish you happiness. という言い方をしてもよい．

▶誰もが世界の平和を**願っている** Everybody *wishes*

for [desires] world peace. ／Everyone *wants* peace in the world. ‖我々はこの町がもっと住みよくなるよう願っている We *wish* [*desire*] *to* make our town a more comfortable place to live (in).

2【「お願いします」の形で】▶《タクシーで》赤坂までお願いします Akasaka, *please*. ‖明朝は7時集合ですから, 遅れないようお願いします We are meeting at seven tomorrow morning. So *please* be careful [make sure] not to be late. ‖**対話**「モロッコの話をしましょうか」「お願いします」"Would you like me to tell you about Morocco?" "Yes, *please*." ‖**対話**《電話で》「佐藤さんをお願いします」「私です」"*May I speak with* [*to*] Mr. Sato, *please*? ／*I'd like to speak with* Mr. Sato, *please*." "Speaking." (● Speaking. は This is he speaking. の略) ‖**対話**「お席はどこがよろしいですか」「禁煙席の窓側をお願いします」"Where would you like to sit?" "*I'd like to* have a window seat in the nonsmoking section." ‖皆さんのご理解とご協力をお願いします We *ask for* your understanding and cooperation.

3【…してください】▶ここにお名前をお書き願います *Please* write [sign] your name here. ‖どうかお静かに願います *Please* be quiet.

☛ 願ったりかなったり, 願ってもない(→見出語)

ねがえり 寝返り ▶ゆうべは眠れなくて一晩中寝返りをうっていた Last night I couldn't sleep at all. I *kept tossing and turning* all night.

ねがえる (…に)**寝返る** **sell out** 《to》(内通する, 売る) ; **defect** 《to》(国・主義・党などを捨てて敵方に売る) ▶敵側に寝返る *sell out* [*defect*] *to* the enemy.

ねがお 寝顔 one's **sleeping face** ▶夫は帰って来ると娘の寝顔をしばらくじっと眺めていた When my husband came home, he gazed down at his daughter's *sleeping face* for a while.

ねかせる 寝かせる **1【眠らせる】put ... to sleep** [**bed**] ▶子供たちを寝かせなさい *Put* the children *to bed*. ‖本を読んで[子守歌を歌って]子供を寝かせた I read [lullabied] the child *to sleep*. ‖もう少し寝かせてよ *Let* me *sleep* a little bit longer.

2【横にする】lay (down) ▶酒瓶を寝かせる *lay* a sake bottle ‖はしごを寝かせたままにしておく *leave* a ladder *on its side* ‖動かさないで寝かせたまま病院へ運んだほうがいい Don't move him. You'd better take him to the hospital *lying down*.

▶これは20年寝かせたウイスキーです This whisky *has been aged* for twenty years.

3【使わないでそのまま置く】▶そんな大金をねかせておくのはもったいない It's a waste to *let* such a large sum of money *lie idle*.

ねがったりかなったり 願ったり叶ったり ▶大学院に, それも奨学生として受かるなんて, まさに願ったりかなったりだ I have been accepted by the graduate school, and what is (even) better, as a scholarship student. *This is like a dream come true* [*more than I could ever hope for*]!

ねがってもない 願ってもない ▶柴田さんが協力を申し出てくれているって? それは願ってもないことだ Mr. Shibata has offered to help us? *Nothing could please me more* [*make me happier*]. (➤ please は「人を喜ばせる」).

ネガティブ **negative** ▶ネガティブな態度 a *negative* attitude.

ねがわくは 願わくは ▶願わくは息子に司法試験に合格してほしいが, だめならだめでそれもしかたがないことだ I *hope* my son will pass the bar exam, but it can't be helped if he fails.

ねぎ 葱 《植物》a **leek** **解説** (1)日本のネギは東洋原産のもので, 欧米にはなく, 近縁の leek も日本のものより太い. (2)scallion や spring onion はワケギに近い.

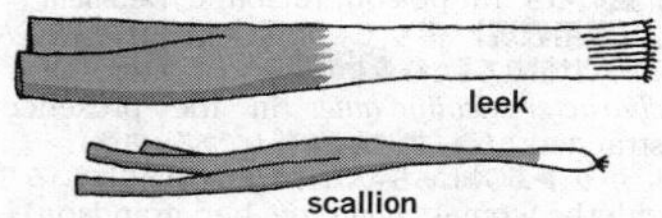

‖**ネギトロ** a type of sushi with minced fatty tuna and negi [Welsh onion] on top.

ねぎらう 労う **thank** +目 (礼を言う) ▶我々は木村さんの長年の労をねぎらった We *thanked* Mr. Kimura for his long years of service (to the company).

ねぎる 値切る **get** [**beat**／**knock**] **the price down, bargain** +目 ▶私はその中古のゲーム機を6000円に値切った I *got* [*beat*] *the price* of the secondhand game machine *down* to six thousand yen. ‖バザールで買い物をするときは値切るのも楽しみのうちだ *Bargaining* is among the pleasures of shopping at a bazaar.

ねくずれ 値崩れ a (**sharp**) **drop in price**, a **price collapse** (➤ 後者のほうが突然であることを強調) ▶ことしはサンマが豊漁で値崩れを起こしている There has been *a drop in the price* of sauries this year because of a huge catch.

ねぐせ 寝癖 ▶髪の毛に寝癖がついちゃった My hair got *messed* [*tangled*] *up while* I was *sleeping*.

ネクタイ a **necktie**, a **tie** (➤ インフォーマルでは後者がふつう) ; a **bow** /boʊ/ **tie** (ちょうネクタイ) ▶ネクタイを締める[外す] put on [take off] *a tie* ‖ネクタイを直す straighten one's *tie* ‖私はふだんはネクタイはしません I usually don't wear *a tie*. ‖そのパーティーはネクタイをしていったほうがいいですか Should I *wear a tie to* the party?

> **危ないカタカナ語✹ ネクタイピン**
> 日本語の「ネクタイピン」は上から刺して留めるタイプと横からはさんで留めるタイプの両方に使われるが, 英語では前者は tiepin, tie tac(k), 後者は tie bar, tie clip, tie clasp と区別する.

ねくび 寝首 ▶寝首をかく *behead a person in their sleep* ; *catch a person off guard* (➤ 比喩的に「虚をつく」) ‖寝首をかかれる *be caught off guard*.

ねくら ▶ネクラな感じのする映画俳優 a *dark*, *moody* movie actor ‖ネクラなタイプは嫌いだ I don't like the *gloomy* type. →ねあか.

ねぐら a **roost**, a **roosting place** (鳥の) ; (a) **home** (家) ▶(鳥が)ねぐらに帰る *fly home to roost* ‖ホームレスの人たちは公園をねぐらにしていた The homeless people gathered in *makeshift lodgings* in the park. (➤「間に合わせの宿」の意).

ネグリジェ a **nightgown**, a **nightdress**, 《インフォーマル》 a **nightie** (ワンピース型の寝巻き) 《**参考**》 negligee /nèɡləʒéɪ/ (フランス語から)は「レース飾りのついた部屋着, 化粧着」の意.

ねぐるしい 寝苦しい ▶このところ暑くて寝苦しい夜が続いている Because it's been hot lately, I have*n't* been *sleeping well*.

ねこ 猫

1【動物】a **cat** ; a **kitten** (子猫) ▶猫がニャーニャー鳴いている *A cat* is meowing [mewing]. ‖うちの猫が子猫を3匹生んだ Our *cat* gave birth to three *kittens*.

✉ **うちには猫が2匹います. 1匹は雄, 1匹は雌です** We have two *cats*—one is male and the other is female.

‖**猫いらず** rat poison, ratsbane /rǽtsbèin/.

2【慣用表現】 借りてきた猫 ▶息子は知らない人のいる所では借りてきた猫のようにおとなしい Our son *is uncharacteristically quiet* in the presence of strangers. (「柄にもなく静かである」の意). **猫かわいがり** ▶あのおばあちゃんは孫を猫かわいがりしている That elderly woman *dotes on* her grandson [*is a doting grandmother*]. (➤ dote on は「でき愛する」). **猫に小判** ▶あんなやつにそんな高級なゴルフクラブなんて, 猫に小判だよ A guy like that with expensive golf clubs! *What a waste of money!* (「何という金のむだづかいだ」の意). **猫の手も借りたい** ▶忙しくて猫の手も借りたいほどだ I am so busy (that) *I'd appreciate any help I can get*. **猫の額** ▶うちには猫の額ほどの庭しかない We have a piece of yard *the size of a postcard*. (「はがきのサイズの庭」の意). **猫の目** ▶彼の意見は猫の目のように変わるのでまるで信用できない Since he *is forever blowing hot and cold*, he can't be trusted. (➤ blow hot and cold は「(意見や態度を)ころころ変える」). **猫もしゃくしも** ▶猫もしゃくしもタブレット型コンピュータに飛びついている *Everybody and his brother* [*Every Tom, Dick and Harry*] has bought a tablet computer. (「誰もかれも」なら Everybody is … がよい). **猫をかぶる** ▶彼は先生の前ではいつも猫をかぶっている He always *acts innocent* around the teacher.

「猫」のいろいろ アビシニアン Abyssinian /アメリカンショートヘア American Shorthair /シャム Siamese /スコティッシュフォールド Scottish Fold /ソマリ Somali /とら猫 tabby /ヒマラヤン Himalayan /ペルシャ Persian /マンクス Manx /三毛猫 tortoiseshell /メインクーン Maine coon /山猫 lynx /ラグドール Ragdoll /ロシアンブルー Russian blue

☞ 猫舌, 猫背, 猫なで声, 猫ばば (→見出語)

ねごこち 寝心地 ▶このベッドは寝心地がいい[悪い] This is a *comfortable* [an *uncomfortable*] bed *to sleep in*.

ねこじた 猫舌 ▶猫舌だからこのスープは冷ましてからでないと飲めないよ Since my *tongue is sensitive to heat*, I have to let this soup cool before eating it.

ねこぜ 猫背 stoop shoulders ▶猫背の老人 a *stoop-shouldered* old man.

ねこそぎ 根こそぎ ▶雑草を根こそぎ抜く pull a weed *by the roots* /root up [out] a weed ▶組織犯罪は根こそぎにされた Organized crime *was eliminated root and branch*. (➤ root and branch は「徹底的に」) /The gangsters *were arrested to the last man*.

ねごと 寝言 ▶まみちゃん, あなたゆうべ寝言を言ってたわよ You *were talking in your sleep* last night, Mami.
▶寝言を言ってるんじゃないよ Stop *talking nonsense*. /Stop *saying absurd things*.

ねこなでごえ 猫撫で声 a **coaxing** /kóuksiŋ/ **voice** ▶彼女は急に猫なで声になって父親に「パパ, あのドレス買って」とねだった She suddenly said to her father *in a coaxing* [*silky*] *voice*, "Daddy, could you buy me that dress?" (➤ coaxing は「言いくるめるような」, silky は「甘く説き伏せるような」).

ねこばば 猫ばばする pocket +㊐ ▶そばに誰もいなかったのをさいわいに, 彼は道で拾った1万円札をそのまま猫ばばした He *pocketed* the ten-thousand-yen bill he found on the street since there was no one around.

ねこみ 寝込み ▶奇襲部隊はテロリストたちの寝込みを襲った The commandos made an attack on the *sleeping* [*slumbering*] terrorists.

ねこむ 寝込む sleep soundly (熟睡する) ; **be laid up, be (sick) in bed** (病床につく) ▶父は(1日がんばって)今はぐっすり寝込んでいる My father *is sleeping soundly* [*is fast asleep*] (after a hard day's work).
▶母はかぜで寝込んでいます My mother has *been in bed* with a cold. ‖私は流感で1週間寝込んでしまった I *was laid up* with the flu for a week.

ねこやなぎ 猫柳 《植物》 a **pussy willow**.

ねごろ 値頃 a **reasonable price**.

ねころぶ 寝転ぶ lie down ▶草の上に寝ころんで話をしよう Let's *lie down* on the grass and talk. ‖そんな所に寝ころんでいたら邪魔よ You're in the way *sprawled out* there.

ねさがり 値下がり a **fall** [**drop**] **in price** ▶野菜の値下がり *a fall in* vegetable *prices* ‖株はこのところ値下がりしている Stocks *have been dropping* [*falling*] recently.

ねさげ 値下げ a **price cut** [**reduction**], a **reduction** [**cut**] **in price** 一㊐ **値下げする reduce** +㊐, **mark down** ▶お米が値下げになった The *price* of rice *was cut*. ‖電気料金やガス料金が値下げになった Electric and gas rates *have been reduced*. ‖あの店では全品を値下げする They are going to *mark down* all the items at that store.

ねざけ 寝酒 a **nightcap**.

ねざす (…に)**根差す be rooted** 《in》 ▶演歌は大衆の心に深く根差している *Enka* music *is* deeply *rooted in* the hearts of the people. ‖社会悪は貧困に根差している(=からきている) Social evils *have their origins in* poverty. /Poverty *is the root of* social evils.

ねざめ 寝覚め ▶けさは寝覚めが悪かった I *didn't feel refreshed when I got up* this morning.
▶《慣用表現》うそをつくと寝覚めが悪い(=気がとがめる) You will *feel guilty* if you tell a lie.

ねじ a **screw** /skruː/ ▶ねじ回しでねじを締める[ゆるめる] tighten [loosen] *a screw* with *a screwdriver* ‖ねじがゆるんでいる The *screw* is loose. ‖部品をシャシーにねじで留める *screw* a part to the chassis.
▶《慣用表現》販売員たちは近頃たるんでいる. ここら辺でねじを巻いておかなきゃあ The salespeople seem to be slacking off these days, and I think it's time to *light a fire under them* [*get them on the ball*]. (前者は「やる気を起こさせる」, 後者は「気を引き締める」).

‖**ねじ山** a (screw) thread.

ねじける become warped [**twisted**] ▶逆境に育って彼は性格がねじけてしまった Adversity *warped* [*twisted*] his personality.

ねじこむ ねじ込む 1【はめ込む, 押し込む】 ▶裏木戸の隙間に折れた糸のこをねじ込んで掛け金を外した I *forced* a piece of a broken coping saw *into* the slit at the back door and lifted the latch. ‖彼女は私のポケットにお金をねじ込もうとした She tried to *thrust* the money *into* my pocket.

2【押しかけて抗議する】▶ピアノの音がうるさいと近所の人がねじ込んできた A neighbor *came to complain* that our piano was too loud.

ねしずまる 寝静まる ▶子供たちが寝静まってからでないとゆっくり新聞も読めない I can't relax and read the paper until after the children *have fallen asleep*.

ねしな 寝しな ▶寝しなに甘いものを食べると太るよ You'll get fat if you eat sweets *at bedtime*.

ねじふせる ねじ伏せる ▶和夫は暴漢の腕をつかんでねじ伏せた Kazuo *twisted* the thug's arm and *held* [*forced*] him *down*.

ねじまげる ねじ曲げる **bend** +目 (曲げたりひねったりして) ; **twist** +目 (ねじる) ; **distort** +目 (ゆがめる) ▶針金をねじ曲げる *twist* a wire / *bend* a wire *by twisting* ‖ 彼は素手で鉄の棒をねじ曲げた He *bent* the iron bar with his bare hands.

▶我々新聞記者は事実をねじ曲げてはならない We newspaper reporters must not *distort* [*twist*] *the facts*.

ねしょうべん 寝小便 **bed-wetting** 一動 寝小便をする **wet** one's **bed**. →おねしょ.

ねじりはちまき ねじり鉢巻き

> 《解説》(1)日本人(特に男性)は真剣であることを示したり, 気を引き締めるためにねじり鉢巻きをすることがあるが, これは日本的習慣なので直訳しても英米人には通じない. (2)比喩的に言う「ねじり鉢巻きでがんばる」は work intently [(very) hard] とするか, stick to などを用いる.

▶その魚屋さんはねじり鉢巻きをしていた The fishmonger wore *a twisted towel* like a headband. ‖ 兄は毎晩遅くまで, ねじり鉢巻きでがんばっている My (older) brother *works intently* till late every night.

ねじる 捩る **twist** +目 ; **wrench** /rentʃ/ +目 (急に力を入れて) ▶リンゴをねじって枝からもぐ *twist* [*wrench*] an apple off a branch ‖ 階段を踏み違えて足首をねじった I *twisted* my ankle when I took a wrong step on the stairs. ‖ 瓶のふたをねじって開けた I *screwed open* the bottle.

ねじれ 捩れ a **twist** (ねじ曲げ) ; a **distortion** (ゆがみ) ▶イヤホンのコードのねじれ a *twist* in the earphone cord.

‖ねじれ国会 a divided Diet (in which the ruling party controls only the lower house).

ねじれる 捩れる **be twisted** ; **be warped** (ゆがんでいる) ▶電気コードがねじれている The electric cord *is twisted*.

▶ねじれた根性 a *warped* mind ‖ 彼の性格はすっかりねじれている His character *is* completely *warped*.

ねじろ 根城 a **home** (根拠地) ; a **hideout** (隠れ家) ▶上野一帯を根城とするすりの一団がきのう捕まった A group of pickpockets *based in* the Ueno area were arrested yesterday.

ねすごす 寝過ごす **oversleep** ▶目覚まし(時計)の音に気づかず寝過ごす *sleep through* one's alarm ‖ けさは寝過ごして学校に遅れた I *overslept* this morning and was late for school.

ねずのばん 寝ずの番 **vigil** /vídʒɪl/ ▶多くのテレビレポーターが彼女の家の外で寝ずの番を続けた Many TV reporters *kept vigil* outside her house.

ねずみ 鼠 a **rat** (ドブネズミなど大きいもの) ; a **mouse** [複 **mice**] (ハツカネズミなど小さいもの) ▶ネズミが天井裏で走り回っている *Mice* [*Rats*] are running about in the attic.

▶《慣用表現》最近ではスマートフォンを持つ人の数がねずみ算式に増えている These days the number of people who have smartphones is increasing *exponentially* [*in geometric progression*]. (➤ それぞれ「幾何級数的に」「等比級数的に」の意).

‖ネズミ捕り a mousetrap, a rattrap (捕獲器) ; a speed trap (スピード違反の).

ねずみいろ 鼠色 (**dark**) **gray** [《英》 **grey**] ▶ねずみ色のコート a *gray* coat.

ねぞう 寝相 ▶ずいぶん寝相が悪いのね You sure *toss and turn in your sleep* a lot. (➤ toss and turn は「寝返りをうつ」).

ねそびれる 寝そびれる ▶ゆうべは妻のぐちを遅くまで聞いて寝そびれてしまった I listened to my wife's complaints until late last night, and *never got to bed*.

ねそべる 寝そべる **lie down** (横たわる) ; **sprawl** (だらしなく手足を伸ばす) ▶父は寝そべって新聞を読んでいた My father was *lying on his stomach* reading the paper. (➤ lie on one's stomach は「腹ばいになる」) ‖ 姉はじゅうたんの上に寝そべってクッキーをポリポリやっている My (older) sister is munching cookies while *sprawled out* on the carpet.

ネタ **1**【情報, 証拠】**info** (➤ information の略) ; a **tip** (秘密情報) ; **material** (材料) ▶人にネタを提供する give a person a piece of *info* / give a person a (hot) *tip* ‖ 小説のネタを集める gather *material* for a novel ‖ もうブログに書き込むこともネタ切れだ I've *run out of topics* to write about in my blog. ‖ ネタばれ注意 *Spoiler* alert. ‖ もうネタは挙がっているんだぞ We've got *the goods* on you. (➤ the goods は「(有罪にするための)証拠」).

2【すしの】**ingredients** /ɪngríːdiənts/ (材料) ; a **topping** (上に載せるもの).

ねだ 根太 《建築》 a **joist**.

ねたきり 寝たきりの **bedridden** ▶寝たきりのお年寄り a *bedridden* elderly man [woman] ‖ 妻は二度目の出産以来, ほとんど寝たきりの状態になっている My wife *has been* mainly *confined to bed* since the birth of our second child.

ねたばこ 寝たばこ ▶火事の原因は泊まり客の寝たばこだった The fire was caused by a guest *smoking in bed*. ‖《掲示》寝たばこはおやめください Please refrain from smoking in bed.

ねたましい (…が)**妬ましい** **be jealous** 《of》 (嫉妬する), **be envious** 《of》 (うらやましい) ▶彼女は姉の美貌がねたましかった She *felt* [*was*] *jealous of* her sister's good looks.

ねたみ 妬み **jealousy** (憎しみなどのこもった) ; **envy** /énvi/ (うらやましさ) ▶彼はねたみから友人のバイクを盗んだ He stole his friend's motorbike *out of jealousy* [*envy*]. ‖ あいつの人気にはねたみを感じる I *feel jealous* [*envious*] *of* his popularity.

ねたむ 妬む **feel jealous of** ; **envy** +目 (うらやむ) ▶人の幸せをねたんでもしかたがない It's no use *feeling jeal-*

ous of other people's happiness. ‖ 人にねたまれるほど裕福じゃありませんよ I am not so wealthy that people *feel jealous of* me.

ねだめ 寝溜めする store up sleep (➤ catch up on one's sleep（寝不足を取り戻す）という発想のほうがふつう).

ねだやし 根絶やし eradication（好ましくないものの撲滅）; extermination（皆殺し）▶この除草剤を使えば雑草を根絶やしにできます You can *eradicate* weeds with this weed killer.

▶この町から暴力［風俗犯罪］を根絶やしにしてほしい We want violence [vice] to *be eradicated* from this town.

ねだる coax /koʊks/ ＋目; wheedle ＋目（心にもないことを言って）; ask《for》（頼む）▶その息子は両親にねだって車を買ってもらった The son *coaxed* his parents *into* buying him a car. (➤ coax A into doing は「A（人）にねだって…させる」の意) ／The son *wheedled* a car *out of* his parents. (➤ wheedle A out of B で「心にもないことを言ってB（人）からA（物）をせしめる」の意) ‖ 彼は母親にこづかいをねだった He *asked* his mother *for* spending money. ‖ 勇太はお父さんに遊園地に連れて行ってとねだった Yuta *got* Daddy *to* take him to the amusement park. (get A to do は「A（人）に…してほしいと説き伏せるなど工作する」. この例のように過去形の場合は成功したことを意味する).

ねだん 値段 a price →値 ▶この食事で3000円ならまあまあの（＝相応の）値段だ Three thousand yen is a reasonable *price* for this dinner. ‖ 日本の牛肉の値段はまだちょっと高いと思う I think the *price* of beef is still a little too high in Japan. ‖ 対話「このダイヤのお値段はおいくらですか？」「85万円です」"*What's the price* of this diamond?" "Eight hundred (and) fifty thousand yen." ((1)質問文はほかに How much [What] does this diamond cost?／How much is this diamond?／How much are you asking for this diamond? のような言い方もできる. (2)「…の値段はいくらですか」を How much is the price of ...? のようには言わない).

▶あのレストランは値段が高い［安い］*The prices are high* [*low*] at that restaurant. (「高い［安い］値段」は a high [low] price といい, (×)an expensive [a cheap] price とはいわない) ／That restaurant *is expensive* [*inexpensive*]. ‖ 私はこれを非常に安い値段で買った I bought this *at a* very *low price*. ‖ もう少し値段の安いのはありませんか Do you have a *cheaper* one?

▶このつぼに値段をつけるとすれば最低でも200万円はする If I were to *put a price* on this pot, it would be at least two million yen. ‖ その絵には50万円の値段がついていた That picture *was priced* at half a million yen. ‖ この黒テンのコートは値段がつけられないほど高価だ This sable coat is *priceless*.

▶当店ではお値段以上の（価値ある）もの（＝支払う金以上のもの）をお求めいただけます At our store you get *more than your money's worth* [get *excellent value* (for *your money*)].

ねちがえる 寝違える ▶どうも寝違えたようだ I must *have got a crick in my neck while I was sleeping*. ／I must *have twisted my neck in my sleep*.

ねちっこい ▶酒が入ると彼はいよいよねちっこくなる The more he drinks, the more *persistent* [*insistent*] he becomes. ‖ 不意に誰かのねちっこい視線を感じてぞっとした I suddenly got the feeling someone was *staring* at me *persistently* [*had his eyes glued on* me] and got the creeps.

ねちねち ▶しゅうとめは嫁にねちねち小言を言った The mother-in-law *persistently* nagged at her daughter-in-law.

ねつ 熱

> 📖 訳語メニュー
> 熱する力 →heat **1**
> 体温 →temperature, fever **2**
> 熱意 →enthusiasm **3**

1【熱する力・エネルギー】 heat ━形 熱の thermal /θə́ːrməl/ ▶太陽はものすごい熱を発している The sun emits tremendous *heat*. ‖ この薬品に熱を加えて（＝熱して）みましょう Let's *heat* this chemical.

‖熱エネルギー thermal energy ‖太陽熱 solar heat. (→太陽).

2【体温】 a temperature /témprətʃər/; (a) fever（発熱したときの熱）▶きみは少し熱がある［熱が高い］ね You *have a slight* [*high*] *fever*. ‖ 38度も熱があるよ Your *temperature* is 38° C.／You have *a fever* of 38° C. ‖ きょうは熱があるようだ I feel I *have a fever* [I feel *feverish*] today. ‖ また熱が上がった My *fever* has gone up again. ‖ やっと熱が下がった［引いた］My *fever* has finally come down.

▶熱（＝体温）を計ってみましょう Let me take your *temperature*. ‖ 注射のあとで息子が熱を出した My son *ran a fever* after getting a shot. ‖ 熱で体がぞくぞくする I am shivering because of [with] (*a*) *fever*. ‖ 彼女はひどい熱に浮かされている She *is in delirium with a high fever*. (➤ delirium /dɪlíəriəm/ は「（高熱などによる）うわごとを言う状態」).

‖熱冷まし a medicine to reduce fever.

3【熱意, 情熱】 enthusiasm /ɪnθjúːziæzəm/, passion ▶このところ彼はどうも仕事に熱が入ってないようだ These days, he doesn't seem to *be enthusiastic about* his job. ‖ 国会では熱のこもった討論が行われた There was a *heated* discussion in the Diet. ‖ 拓也への熱はもう冷めてしまった My *passion* for Takuya has cooled (down). ／I'm no longer interested in Takuya.

▶敏雄はこのところ美幸に熱を上げている（＝夢中だ）Toshio *is crazy* [*nuts*] *about* Miyuki now. (➤ nuts は俗っぽい語) ／Toshio *has a crush on* Miyuki now. (➤ crush は「一時的なほれ込み」) ‖ 彼らの討論はしだいに熱を帯びてきた Their debate *became more and more heated*. ‖ サッカー熱が再び高まっている There's been another surge in the *popularity* of soccer. (➤ surge は「大波, うねり」).

ねつあい 熱愛する love passionately ▶彼はオーストラリアから来たその女子留学生を熱愛していた He *was passionately in love with* that female student from Australia.

ねつい 熱意 eagerness（内に秘めた熱心さ, 本当のやる気）; enthusiasm /ɪnθjúːziæzəm/（表情に表れる熱中や強い興味,「熱く」なること）; zeal（強い興味; 堅い語）▶彼は英語を身につけたいという生徒たちの熱意をかきたてるすべを知っている He knows how to increase his students' *eagerness* [*enthusiasm*] to learn English. ‖ 娘の熱意に動かされてフランス留学を許しました Moved by our daughter's *eagerness* [*enthusiasm*], we decided to allow her to study in France. ‖ 彼は何事にも熱意がない He lacks *enthusi-*

asm [*zeal*] in everything he does. ／He *is* not *enthusiastic about* anything. ‖彼の熱意に圧倒された I was overwhelmed by his *enthusiasm*.

ねつえん 熱演 an **impassioned performance** ▶彼はハムレットの役を熱演した He *gave an enthusiastic* [*impassioned*] *performance* of Hamlet.

ネッカチーフ a **neckerchief.**

ねっから 根っから ▶彼は根っからの食いしん坊だ He is a *complete* [*total*] glutton. ‖彼は根っからのうそつきだ He's an *inveterate* [a *congenital*] liar. (➤ inveterate は性格・性質などが「根深い」,congenital は「生まれつきの, 元から備わった」) ‖彼は根っからの商売人だ He is a *born* [*dyed-in-the-wool*] merchant. (➤ born は「生まれつきの」).

ねつき 寝付き ▶母は寝つきがいい. 横になったと思ったらもういびきをかいている My mother *is a good sleeper*. She starts to snore as soon as her head hits the pillow. ‖運動不足だと寝つきが悪くなる Insufficient exercise *causes difficulty in falling asleep*. ／If you don't get enough exercise, you *won't fall asleep easily*.

ねっき 熱気 **heat** (熱) ; **enthusiasm** (熱狂) ; **excitement** (興奮) ▶コンサート会場は熱気でむんむんしていた The concert hall was filled with *feverish excitement*.

ねつききゅう 熱気球 a **hot-air balloon** ▶熱気球に乗る ride (in) *a hot-air balloon*.

ねっきょう 熱狂 **enthusiasm** ; **excitement** (興奮) ━形 **熱狂的な enthusiastic** ━動 (…に) **熱狂する get excited** 《at, about, over》 (興奮する) ; 《インフォーマル》 **be crazy** 《about》 (夢中になる) ▶観衆は彼のファインプレーに熱狂した The spectators *were excited about* [*over*] his spectacular play in the game. ‖私はかつてロックに熱狂したものだ I used to *be crazy* [*wild*] *about* rock music. ‖彼はホラー映画の熱狂的なファンだ He is an *enthusiastic* fan of horror movies. ‖国民は熱狂的に新大統領を歓迎した The whole nation welcomed the new president *enthusiastically*.

ねつく 寝付く **get to sleep** (➤ 主に否定文で使う) ▶この頃なかなか寝つけない I *have trouble falling asleep* [*getting to sleep*] these days.

ネック a **bottleneck** (通路障害) ▶あの橋の近くがネックになっていて交通渋滞が起こっている There is *a bottleneck* [*an obstruction*] near the bridge and traffic jams often occur there. ‖どうも彼がネックだ. 彼のところにすぐ仕事がたまる That guy *holds up* [*slows up*] *everything*; all the work just piles up on his desk. (➤「すべてを滞らせる」の意).

> **危ないカタカナ語✹ ネック**
> 進行の障害になるものを指す「ネック」は英語の bottleneck の前半を省略したもの. bottleneck は文字どおり「びんの首」であり, 転じて「狭い通路障害」を意味する. 「…がネックだ」に当たるのは be a bottleneck である.

ねづく 根付く **take root** ▶サツキの挿し木は容易に根づく Azalea cuttings *take root* easily.
▶《比喩的》イースターは(まだ)日本に根づいていない Easter hasn't *taken root* in Japan (yet).

ネックレス a **necklace** ▶金 [真珠] のネックレスを身に付ける wear a gold [pearl] *necklace*.

ねっけつかん 熱血漢 a **passionate** [**hot-blooded**] **man** (● hot-blooded は「血気にはやる」の意で, マイナスイメージになることが多い).

ねっこ 根っこ a **root** (根) ; a **stump** (切り株).

ねっしゃびょう 熱射病 **heatstroke.** →熱中症.

ねっしょう 熱唱 ▶彼女は『舟唄』を熱唱した She *sang* "Funauta" *with all her heart* [*enthusiastically*].

ねつじょう 熱情 **ardor, passion** (➤ 前者は文語) ▶その若き研究者は古代エジプトへのあこがれを熱情を込めて語った The young researcher *ardently* [*passionately*] talked about his fascination with ancient Egypt.

ねっしん 熱心

━形 **熱心な eager, avid** (本当にやる気のある; 後者がより強意) ; **keen** (意欲的な) ; **enthusiastic** /ɪnθjùːziǽstɪk/ (熱狂的な) ; **hard** (一生懸命な) ; **diligent** (仕事・勉強に手抜きしない) ; **dedicated** (献身的な) ━副 **熱心に eagerly, enthusiastically** ▶熱心な生徒 an *eager* [*earnest*] student, a *diligent* student (➤ earnest は「まじめな, 真剣な」) ‖熱心な教師 a *dedicated* teacher ‖熱心な読者 an *avid* reader ‖きみは何事にも熱心さが足りないね You lack *eagerness* [*zeal*] in everything you do.
▶彼は記念乗車券の収集に熱心だ He *is keen on* [*avid about*] collecting commemorative tickets. ‖彼女は熱心な西武ファンだ She is an *enthusiastic* Lions fan. ‖彼女は仕事に熱心だ She *is diligent in* her work. ‖山田先生は熱心な先生だ Mr. Yamada is a *dedicated* teacher. (➤ dedicated は「打ち込んでいる, ひたむきな」) ‖タイには熱心な(＝信心深い)仏教徒が多い There are many *devout* Buddhists in Thailand.
▶彼は熱心に勉強している He is studying *hard* [*eagerly* ／*diligently* ／*intently*]. ‖視察団は自動車工場を熱心に見学した The inspection party observed the car factory *attentively*. (➤ attentively は「注意深く」) ‖授業はもっと熱心に聞きなさい You must be more *attentive* in class.

ねっする 熱する **1【加熱する】heat** +目 ▶その液体が気化するまで熱する *heat* the liquid until it evaporates ‖フライパンを熱してバターを入れなさい *Heat* the pan and put some butter in it.
2【熱くなる】▶彼は熱しやすく冷めやすい性質です He *easily gets excited* and easily cools off. (● and doesn't stick with anything. と言ってもよい).

ねっせん 熱戦 **heated competition** (熱い戦い) ; an **exciting game** (手に汗握る試合) ▶国立競技場で連日熱戦が展開されている The National Stadium is the site of *heated competition* every day. ‖きょうのラグビー明慶戦はすごい熱戦だった Today's Meiji-Keio rugby game *was* very *exciting*.

ねつぞう 捏造 (a) **fabrication** ━動 **ねつ造する fabricate** +目 (人をだますために), **concoct** +目 (いろいろと仕組んで) ; **manufacture** +目 (うその証拠などをでっち上げる) →でっちあげる ▶ねつ造データ *fabricated* data ‖ねつ造された(人をだますための)情報 *hoax* information ‖その話はねつ造されたものだった The story was *a fabrication*. ‖記者がその雑誌記事をねつ造したに違いない The reporter must *have fabricated* [*have concocted*] the magazine article.

ねったい 熱帯 **the tropics** ━形 **熱帯の tropical** ▶台風は熱帯で発生する Typhoons are born *in the tropics*. ‖アンスリュームは熱帯植物だ Anthuriums are *tropical plants*.
‖**熱帯雨林** a tropical rain forest ‖**熱帯魚** a tropical fish ‖**熱帯性低気圧** a tropical low

ね

(pressure) ‖ **熱帯地方** the tropics

ねったいや 熱帯夜 ▶ゆうべは**熱帯夜**だった We had a "*tropical night*" yesterday.

あなたの英語はどう響く?
夜になっても屋外の気温がセ氏25度以下に下がらない暑い夜を「熱帯夜」というが, これに相当する英語はない. tropical night と直訳すると「熱帯地方の夜」または「南国式のパーティー」と解釈されるおそれがある. したがって, It was a hot and humid [a muggy] evening. (蒸し暑い夜だった)などと説明的に言うか, 引用符をつけて "tropical night" とする.

ねっちゅう (…に)熱中する **be enthusiastic** /mθjùːziǽstɪk/ 《about》, 《インフォーマル》 **be crazy** 《about》, 《インフォーマル》 **be hooked** 《on》 ; **be absorbed** 《in》 (➤「没頭する」に相当する堅い言い方) ▶彼は若い頃ハワイアンに**熱中した** When he was young, he *was enthusiastic about* [*was hooked on*] Hawaiian music. ‖ 私はこのところ陶芸に**熱中している** These days I *am into* [*am absorbed in*] pottery making. ‖ 彼はスカイダイビング[バラ作り]に**熱中している** He *goes in for* skydiving [growing roses]. (➤ go in for は「(スポーツ・趣味などに)打ち込む, 熱中する」の意のインフォーマルな表現) ‖ 弟は物事に**熱中する**たちだ My (younger) brother is the type who *gets crazy about* anything [who *throws himself into* anything he does].

ねっちゅうしょう 熱中症 (a) **heat illness** 《参考》この下位区分に熱射病(heatstroke), 熱疲労(heat exhaustion, heat prostration)などがある.

ねっぽい 熱っぽい **feverish** /fíːvərɪʃ/ (熱のある) ▶熱っぽかったのできょうは学校を休んだ I didn't go to school today because I *was feverish* [I *had a bit of a fever*].
▶彼は自分の理想を**熱っぽく**語った He made an *enthusiastic* speech about his ideals. / He talked about his ideals *excitedly* [*fervently*].

ネット 1【網】 a **net** ; a **hairnet** (ヘアネット) ▶テニスコートに**ネット**を張る put up *a net* on a tennis court ‖ **ネット裏**から野球を観戦する watch a ball game from the seats *behind the backstop* (➤ backstop は「バックネット」) ‖ 彼女のラストボールは**ネットインした** Her last ball *hit the net and fell in*. ‖ あの選手は**ネットプレー**に強い That player is strong at *net play* [is good at *playing close to the net*].
2【通信網】 **the Net, the Internet** (インターネット ; 小文字で net, internet とも書く) ; a **network** (通信網) ▶**ネット**に接続する connect to *the Internet* ‖ **ネット**で情報を検索する *search the Internet* for information ‖ **ネット上**で商売をする do business *online* [*on the Internet* / *on the Net*] ‖ **ネットオークション**を見て回る troll through *online auction sites* ‖ 50点の品を**ネットオークション**にかける put up 50 items for *online auction* ‖ 野菜を**ネット販売する** *sell* vegetables *on the Net* [*over the Internet*] / *use the Internet for direct sales* of vegetables ‖ このパソコンは**ネット**につながっていますか Is this computer *connected to the Internet*? ‖ 当社の製品はすべて**ネット**で入手可能です All our products are available *online* [*on the Internet*]. ‖ この番組は**全国ネット**で放映中です This program is being aired [broadcast] *on the national networks*.
‖ **ネットカフェ難民** an Internet cafe refugee ‖ **ネット広告** online advertising ‖ **ネットサーフィン** net surfing (➤「ネットサーフィンする」は surf the Net) ‖ **ネットショッピング** Net shopping (➤ online shopping または, Internet shopping というのがふつう) ‖ **ネット取り引き** online [Internet] trading ‖ **ネットバンキング** Internet [online] banking ‖ **ネット犯罪** (a) cybercrime.

危ないカタカナ語 ネット
1「網」の意味では net でよいが, スポーツで使われる「ネット」は和製語が多いので注意が必要. 例えば, テニスや卓球の「ネットイン」は touch [hit] the net and fall in (ネットに触れて相手コートに入る), バレーボールの「ネットタッチ」は touch [hit] the net のように動詞で表現する. (→**バックネット**).
2 放送用語の「ネット」は「放送網」の意味の英語 network を略したもので,「全国ネット」は national network となる.
3「インターネット」の意の「ネット」は the Net であるが, もとの the Internet を使うことも多い.「ネット上の」は通常 online で表せる.

ねっとう 熱湯 **boiling water** ▶**熱湯**を注いでふたをしてください Pour in *boiling water* and put the lid on.
‖ **熱湯消毒** sterilization by boiling.

ねっとり ▶ねっとりしたクリーム *thick* [*sticky*] cream ‖ ねっとりとした視線 a *persistent* stare (➤ persistent は「しつこい」の意).

ネットワーク a **network** ▶テレビの**全国ネットワーク** a national television *network* ‖ 彼女には**ソーシャルネットワーキング(サイト)**で知り合った友だちがたくさんいる She has a lot of friends she met on a *social networking* (site).

ねっぱ 熱波 a **heat wave**.

ねつびょう 熱病 (a) **fever** ▶**熱病**にかかる suffer from *a fever* ‖ 彼はまるで**熱病**に浮かされたように夜の街をさまよい歩いた He wandered around the town at night *as though he were delirious with fever*.

ねっぷう 熱風 a **hot wind** ▶火事の**熱風**でやけどをする get scorched by [with] *hot air* from the fire.

ねつべん 熱弁 an **impassioned** [a **fiery** /fáɪəri/] **speech** ▶彼は聴衆を集めて**熱弁**を振るった He gathered an audience and made [delivered] *an impassioned speech*.

ねつぼう 熱望 an **earnest desire** [**request**] 一動 **熱望する** **be eager** 《for, to do》 ▶市民の**熱望**にこたえてジョギングコースが整備された A jogging course was constructed in response to the *earnest requests* of the citizens. ‖ 彼女は音楽の勉強のためにイタリアへ行くことを**熱望している** She *is eager to* go to Italy to study music. ‖ 人々は平和を**熱望している** People *long* for peace.

ねづまり 根詰まり ▶ (鉢植えの)ポトスが**根詰まり**をおこしている The (potted) pothos *is almost chocked by its roots*.

ねづよい 根強い **deep-rooted** ▶一部の日本人は外国人に対して**根強い**偏見を持っている Some Japanese have a *deep-rooted* [*deep-seated*] prejudice against foreigners. ‖ その政治家は地元で**根強い人気**がある That politician has *solid* local *support*.

ねつりょう 熱量 《物理学》 a **calorie** 《略 Cal.》.

ねつれつ 熱烈な **ardent, passionate** (➤ 前者は文語) ; **enthusiastic** (熱狂的な) ; **fervent** (誠実で燃えるような) 一副 **熱烈に** **ardently, passionately, enthusiastically, fervently** ▶**熱烈な**支持者 an *enthusiastic* supporter ‖ 彼は美佐子に**熱烈な**愛の告白をした He declared his *ardent* love for Misako. ‖ 夏子は熱烈な恋愛を夢見ている Natsuko is dreaming of (a) *passionate* love. ‖ 夢子はロマンス小説の熱烈なファンだ Yumeko is an *avid* reader of romance novels. ‖ サッカー選手たちはサポーターの熱烈な歓迎を受けた The soccer players received an *enthusiastic* welcome from their supporters. ‖ 彼は裕美を熱烈に愛している He is *passionately* in love with Hiromi. ／ He *passionately* [*ardently* ／ *fervently*] loves Hiromi.

ねてもさめても 寝ても覚めても awake and asleep (➤ 日本語と順序が逆になることに注意) ▶寝ても覚めてもきみのことばかり考えているよ I'm thinking of you *day and night*. ‖ 息子は寝ても覚めてもサッカーだ My son *eats, drinks and sleeps* soccer. (➤ 慣用的な言い方).

ねどこ 寝床 a bed ▶寝床で本を読む read *in bed* ‖ 寝床に入る *go to bed* ‖ 寝床を敷く spread out one's *futon* [*bedding*] ‖ 寝床をたたむ fold up one's *futon* [*bedding*] ‖ 冬の寒い朝は寝床を離れるのがつらい On cold winter mornings, it's hard to *get out of bed*.

ねとねと ▶このねとねとしたもの何？ What is this *slimy* stuff？‖ このあめ，いやにねとねとするね This candy is awfully *sticky*, isn't it？(➤ sticky は「粘つく」).

ねとまり 寝泊まり ▶調査が終わるまではここで寝泊まりするつもりだ I plan to *stay* here till I have completed my survey. ‖ この学生会館には学生が寝泊まりできる部屋がある This student union has rooms where students can *stay* [*spend*] *the night*.

ねなしぐさ 根無し草 duckweed(浮き草)；a drifter, a rootless wanderer [vagabond] (落ち着く先を持たない人) ▶根無し草の暮らし a *rootless* life ／a *wandering* life.

ネパール Nepal ‖ネパール語 Nepalese ‖ ネパール人 a Nepalese, a Nepali.

ネバダ Nevada(アメリカ西部の州；略 NV, Nev.).

ねばつく 粘つく be sticky, be gluey (➤ 前者はジャム・はちみつ・汗などを，後者は接着剤・のり・にかわなどを連想させる).

ねばっこい 粘っこい sticky；《インフォーマル》gooey ▶私は納豆のような粘っこい食べ物は嫌いだ I don't like *sticky* foods like natto.
▶雪国の人は概して粘っこい(＝粘り強い)性格だ Generally, people in snowy areas have a *tenacious* character.

-ねばならない must, have (got) to do

> **語法** (1) 日本語と同様，**must** は文語的な語だが，人に命令したり人の義務や守るべき事がらなどを問題とする場合には日常会話でも用いられる. (2) 日常会話では，近い未来に起こさなければならない行動をいう場合には，must よりも **have (got) to** が用いられる. →いけない，-ならない.

▶社員は会社の規定に従わねばならない Employees *must* observe the company regulations. ‖ ここに道路ができるので私たちは立ち退かねばなりません We'*ve got to* move somewhere since they are building a road here. ‖ 友達どうしお互いにいたわり合わねばなりません Friends *should* take good care of each other. (● should は「義務」より「必要」に重点がある).

ねばねば ▶接着剤が手についてまだあちこちねばねばしている I got glue on my hands and they are *sticky* [*gooey*] all over. (➤ 後者はインフォーマルな語で sticky より粘り気が弱い)

ねばり 粘り **1【ねばねばすること】** stickiness ▶粘り気がある *be gluey* [*sticky*] (➤ 前者は「接着剤・のりなどのような」の意) ‖ 機械でついたもちには粘りが足りない Mochi made by machine *isn't sticky enough*. ‖ 粘りが出るまで材料をかきまぜてください Please stir the ingredients until they *begin to thicken*.
2【根気】 tenacity /tɪnǽsəṭi/ (がんこなまでの決心の固さ)；perseverance /pə̀ːˈsəvíərəns/ (困難にもめげないがんばり) ▶彼は何をやっても粘りがない He lacks *tenacity* in whatever he does. ‖ 彼女の粘りには感心した I'm impressed with her *perseverance* [*stick-to-it-iveness*]. (➤ stick-to-it-iveness は「最後までがんばる根性」の意).

ねばりがち 粘り勝ち ▶石川遼はその大会で粘り勝ちした Ishikawa Ryo *hung in there* [*never gave up*] *and finally won* the tournament.

ねばりづよい 粘り強い persistent (くじけずに耐える)；persevering /pə̀ːˈsəvíərɪŋ/ (困難にもめげずがんばり続ける)；tenacious /tɪnéɪʃəs/ (がんこなまでに決心の固い) ▶粘り強く努力する *be persevering* in one's efforts ‖ 警察の粘り強い捜査で被害者の身元が判明した The victim's identity was established thanks to the *persistent* investigation by the police. ‖ 粘り強く交渉した結果，会社の休日が増えた After *persistent* negotiations with the company, we were given more days off. ‖ 粘り強いのが彼のいいところだ *Tenacity* [*Perseverance*] is his strong point. ‖ 私は今の仕事を粘り強く続けるつもりだ I intend to *stick it out* in my current job.

ねばる 粘る **1【粘着性がある】** stick《to》, be sticky ▶この納豆はよく糸を引いて粘る This *natto is* very thready and *sticky*.
2【根気よくがんばる】 ▶もう少し粘れば契約は取れると思う I think if you just *persevere* a little more, you'll get the contract. ‖ 彼女は私がオーケーを出すまで事務所で粘った She *didn't budge* from my office until I gave her my OK. (➤ don't budge は「少しも動かない」).
▶きょうはコーヒー1杯で喫茶店に2時間粘った Today I *lingered* in a coffee shop for two hours over a cup of coffee. ‖ 最後まで粘れ！*Stick to it!* ／*Hang in there!*

ねはん 涅槃 《仏教》nirvana /nɪəˈvɑ́ːnə/ (➤ Nirvana ともつづる).

ねびえ 寝冷え ▶そんな所でうたた寝していると，寝冷えするわよ If you doze off there, you'll *get a chill*.

ねびき 値引き (a) discount /dískaʊnt/ **一動** 値引きする give a discount, discount /dískaʊnt/ ＋目 ▶5パーセント値引きする *take* 5% *off the price* ‖ 値引きしてもらえますか Could you *give* me *a discount*？‖ コート類が30パーセントの値引きになっております Thirty percent *off* on all coats. ‖ スーパーどうしが値引き競争をしている The two supermarkets are competing in *a price war*.
‖値引き価格 a discount [reduced] price.

ねぶかい 根深い deep-rooted ▶根深い偏見 a *deep-seated* [*deep-rooted*] prejudice ‖ 彼らの対立は思っていたよりもかなり根深いもののようだ It seems that the conflict between them is far more *deep-rooted* than we had thought.

ねぶくろ 寝袋 a sleeping bag ▶寝袋で寝る sleep in *a sleeping bag*.

ね

ねぶそく 寝不足 lack of sleep ▶母さんは寝不足で機嫌が悪い My mother is cross [in a bad mood] from *lack of sleep*. ‖ 最近寝不足だ I *haven't gotten enough sleep* recently. ‖ きょうは少し寝不足ぎみだ I'*m* a little *short of sleep* today. ／I di*dn't get enough sleep* last night. ‖ 日曜日にはよく寝不足を取り戻す I often *catch up on my sleep* on Sundays.

ねふだ 値札 a price tag, a price label /léɪbəl/. ‖値札シール a price sticker.

ねぶみ 値踏み (an) appraisal (金銭的価値を判断すること) ; (an) evaluation (価値を判断して決めること) ; estimation (評価・判断すること) ▶一度家にある茶道具を値踏みしてもらえませんか I wonder if you could *appraise* [*set a price on*] the tea ceremony items we have at home. ‖ 人の持ち物を値踏みするのはやめなさい Stop *estimating the value* of people's belongings.

ネブラスカ Nebraska (アメリカ中部の州 ; 略 NE, Nebr., Neb.).

ねぼう 寝坊する oversleep (寝過ごす) ; get up late, sleep late (遅くまで寝ている) ▶私はけさ寝坊した I *overslept* this morning. ‖ 日曜の朝はたいがい寝坊する I usually *sleep late* [*sleep in*] on Sunday mornings.
▶さあさあお寝坊さん, 起きなさいよ ! Come on, (you) *sleepyhead*, it's time to wake up !
☞ 朝寝(坊) (→見出語)

ねぼけ 寝惚け ▶寝ぼけ顔 a *sleepy* face ‖ 寝ぼけまなこ *sleepy* eyes.

ねぼける 寝惚ける ▶彼女は寝ぼけた顔で朝食の席についた She sat at (the) table for breakfast with a *sleepy* look [face]. ／She came to the breakfast table *still half asleep*. ‖ 彼はよく寝ぼけて部屋の中を歩き回る He often walks around the room *in his sleep*.
▶《比喩的》やっこさんが来たって ? 何寝ぼけているんだろ. 約束はあしたじゃないか He came here ? How *absent-minded* of him ! [He must *be daydreaming*.] Our appointment is for tomorrow. ‖ 寝ぼけたこと(＝たわごと)を言うな ! Stop talking *nonsense* !

ねほりはほり 根掘り葉掘り ▶学生たちはハリソンさんに家族のことを根掘り葉掘り聞いた The students *asked* Mr. Harrison *all sorts of questions* about his family. ‖ 他人の個人的事柄についてそう根掘り葉掘り聞くものじゃないよ Don't *be* so *inquisitive* about the personal affairs of other people. (➤ inquisitive /ɪnkwízəṭɪv/ は「むやみに知りたがる」).

ねまき 寝巻き nightwear, night clothes (➤ 総称) ; (a pair of) pajamas /pədʒɑ́:məz/, 《英》 pyjamas (パジャマ) ; a nightgown, 《インフォーマル》 a nightie (ワンピース型の) ; a nightshirt (長いシャツ型で男子用).

ねまわし 根回し *nemawashi*

> **解説 「根回し」の訳し方**
> (1) 会議などの前に, 関係者に前もって企画の意図などを説明し, ある程度の了解を得ておくことを「根回し」というが, これにぴったりの英語はない. 欧米では企業の意思決定は組織のトップまたはその周辺のごく一部の人々によって, かなり短時間でなされるからである.
> (2) したがって「根回し」は preliminary negotiations aimed at consensus-building (コンセンサス作りのための予備交渉) のようにいうか, 日本通の外国人に知られている *nemawashi* をそのまま用いるのがよい.

▶根回しのうまい人 a person who is good at *nemawashi* tactics ‖ 彼は会議に先だって出席者に根回しをしておいた He had *worked on* those present before the conference began. (➤ work on は「…に働きかける」) ‖ もう根回しは済ませてあるよ I'*ve laid the groundwork* [*done the spadework*] (for the meeting) already. (➤ groundwork, spadework はともに「基礎工事」の意).

ねみみにみず 寝耳に水 ▶彼の辞任は寝耳に水だった His resignation was *a bolt from* [*out of*] *the blue*. (◉「(青空から突然雷が落ちたように) 降ってわいた出来事」の意).

ねむい 眠い sleepy ; drowsy /dráʊzi/ (眠い ; 眠けを誘う) ▶あー, 眠い Ah, I'*m sleepy*. ‖ 眠くなってきた I'm *getting sleepy*. ‖ このかぜ薬を飲むと眠くなることがあります This cold medicine can *make you drowsy*. ‖ あの老教授の講義は眠い That old professor's lecture *puts* [*sends*] me *to sleep*. ‖ きみ, 眠そうな顔してるね You look *sleepy* [*drowsy*]. ‖ 弟は眠い目をこすりながら二階から下りて来た My brother came downstairs, rubbing his *drowsy* eyes.

ねむけ 眠気 sleepiness ▶眠けを催させるような音楽 *soporific* music ‖ 彼の話がつまらないので眠けがさした What he was talking about was so boring (that) I *became sleepy* [*drowsy*]. ‖ 眠け覚ましにコーヒーでもいかが ? How about a cup of coffee to *keep* yourself *awake* ? (➤ keep ... awake は「…を眠らせないでおく」). →睡魔.

ネムノキ 《植物》 a Persian silk tree.

ねむり 眠り (a) sleep (➤ 形容詞がつくと a をつける) ▶眠りに落ちる *fall asleep* ‖ 深い眠りに落ちる fall into *a deep sleep* ‖ 私は眠りが深い [浅い] I *am a heavy* [*light*] *sleeper*. ‖ みんなは眠りについた Everyone *went to sleep*. ‖ このところ眠りが浅いようだ I seem to be *sleeping lightly* these days.
▶その偉大な音楽家は永遠の眠り(＝死)についた The great musician *took his last breath* [*breathed his last* (*breath*)]. ‖ 小沢さん, 安らかにお眠りください *May you rest in peace*, Mr. Ozawa. (➤ you はさす相手や場合により, he や she に変える ; 日本語で「眠り」と表現するところをキリスト教の影響を受けた欧米では一般に rest を当てる. 眠りのように (目を閉じた) 没意識的なものととらえるのではなく, キリストの統べる天国での魂の永遠の休息 (で魂が目を開けた状態—beatific vision (至福の視覚)—という) と考えるからである).
‖眠り薬 a sleeping pill, a sleeping tablet.

ねむりこける 眠りこける ▶彼女はよほど疲れているとみえて正体なく眠りこけている She must be very tired because she *is sleeping like a log*. (➤ sleep like a log は「ぐっすり眠る」).

ねむりこむ 眠り込む drop off (うとうとと) ; doze off (こっくりこっくりと) ▶私はひどく疲れていたのでソファーで眠り込んでしまった I was so tired I *dropped* [*nodded*／*dozed*] *off* on the sofa.

ねむる 眠る

1【睡眠をとる】 sleep ; fall asleep (寝入る) ; take a nap, doze (居眠りする)

> **語法** **sleep** は「眠る, 眠っている」の意で, 主に状態を表す語. **go to sleep** は「眠りにつく, 眠り始める」の意. **get to sleep** は「何とか寝つく」の意で, 否定文・疑問文で使うことが多い. **fall asleep** は「寝入る」で, ベッドでない所で, または寝る時間でないのに, という状況で使われることが多い.

▶8時間眠る *sleep* (for) eight hours／*get* eight hours' *sleep* ‖ 眠らずにいる *stay awake* ‖ お休み，モモちゃん．よく眠るのよ Good night, Momo-chan. *Sleep tight!* ‖ 赤ちゃんを眠らせる *put* one's baby *to sleep* ‖ 私はいつのまにか眠ってしまった I *fell asleep* [*went to sleep*] before I knew it. ‖ 彼女はけさ5時にようやく眠った She finally *got to sleep* at five o'clock this morning. ‖ 対話「よく眠れましたか」「ええ，ぐっすり」"Did you *sleep* well?／Did you *have* [*get*] a good night's *sleep*?" "Yes, I slept like a log [soundly]." (● Could you ...? とはしない) ‖ よく眠れていない気がする I guess I *don't get enough sleep*. ‖ 今夜はなぜか興奮して眠れない I don't know why, but I'm so excited I *can't get to sleep* tonight.

▶ゆうべは弟のいびきでよく眠れなかった I *couldn't sleep well* [*I slept badly*] last night because of my brother's snoring. ‖ 最近はよく眠れない I *haven't been sleeping well* lately. ‖ 検診の結果が心配で眠れない日が続いた I had a series of *sleepless* nights, worrying about the results of the checkup. ‖ 赤ん坊は泣きながら眠ってしまった The baby *cried* himself *to sleep*. ‖ 私はコーヒーを飲むと眠れなくなる Coffee *keeps* me *awake*.

▶私は机にもたれてちょっと眠った I *took a nap* at my desk. ‖ 彼は会議の間ずっと眠っていた He *dozed* through the whole meeting. ‖ 電車の座席で眠っている人をよく見かける I often see people *nodding off* in their seats in the train. (➤ nod off は「こっくりする」).

▶《比喩的》おばあさんはおじいさんと一緒にこの墓に眠っている My grandma *lies* beside my grandpa in this grave.

2【活動していない】▶米倉には市場に出ることのない米が大量に眠っていた A large amount of unsold rice *was stored* [*was stocked*] in the warehouse. ‖ この土の中には大量の鉄鉱石が眠っている A large quantity of iron ore *lies untapped* [*idle*] under this soil. (➤ untapped は「未開発の」, idle は「利用されないまま」).

ねもと 根元 a **foot**; a **base** (土台の部分) ▶この柱は根元が腐っている The pillar is decaying at its *foot* [*base*].

ねゆき 根雪 ▶この雪は根雪になりそうだ It looks like this *snow* will *stay* till spring.

ねらい 狙い 1【目的，目標】a **purpose**, an **aim**; an **intention** (意図) ▶今回の彼の日本滞在のねらいは自動車工場を見学することです The *purpose* [*aim*] of his stay in Japan this time is to visit some car factories. ‖ 彼の(本当の)ねらいは別の所にあると思う I think his (true) *aim* lies elsewhere. ‖ 彼女のねらいは何だろう I wonder what her *intention* is. ‖ この作者のねらい(＝言おうとしていること)がわからない I don't understand *what* this author *is trying to say* [*has in mind*]. ‖ この雑誌は高校生にねらいを絞っている This magazine *is* (*solely*) *targeted* [*aimed*] *at* high school readers.

2【標的】a **mark**, (an) **aim** ▶その矢はねらいが外れた The arrow missed the *mark*. ‖ 的にねらいを定めて矢を放ちなさい Take *aim* at the target and release the arrow.

ねらいめ 狙い目 ▶あの店へ行くなら平日のお昼が狙い目だ *The best time* to go to that store is at noon on weekdays. ‖ 今は新築マンションが狙い目だ Now newly-built condominiums are *a good investment*.／Now is *a good time to buy* new condominiums.

ねらう 狙う 1【射撃で】aim《at》, **take aim**《at》

> **【文型】**
> 目標(A)をねらう
> **aim at** A

▶彼はその的の黒い点をねらった He *aimed* [*took aim*] *at* the black spot on the target.

▶よくねらって撃つんだ *Take good aim* and fire. ‖ 彼はその鳥をねらって撃った He *shot at* the bird. (● この英文は「ねらって撃った」というだけで必ずしも「当たった」ことを意味しない．撃って当たったことを明確にする場合は He shot the bird. とする).

2【手に入れようとする】seek ＋目 (得ようと努力する); **watch for** (待ち構える) ▶彼はもっと良い地位をねらっている He *is seeking* a better position.／He's *watching for* a chance to move up the corporate ladder.／He *is after* [*is out for*] a better position. (➤ be out for は「…を得ようとやっきになっている」の意のインフォーマルな表現) ‖ 自爆犯が大統領の命をねらっていた A suicide bomber *was after* [*seeking*] the president's life.

▶俺はK大の法学部をねらってるんだ I'*m aiming at* [*for*] the Law Department of K University. (● at は「…を目標として」, for は「…(の合格)を得ようとして」) ‖ 私は部屋を抜け出る機会をねらって(＝うかがって)いた I *was watching* [*looking out*] *for* a chance to slip out of the room. ‖ 泥棒は警備員のすきをねらって侵入した The burglar broke in after sneaking past the guard.

ねりあげる 練り上げる work out (考え出す) ▶私は1か月かけてこの計画を練りあげた I have spent a whole month *working out* this plan.

ねりあるく 練り歩く parade; **march** (行進する) ▶学生たちは仮装して街を練り歩いた The students *paraded* through the street wearing wild costumes. ‖ デモ隊は国会の周辺を練り歩いた The demonstrators *marched* around the Diet Building.

ねりなおす 練り直す reconsider ＋目 ▶そのプランはもう一度練り直してこい You'd better *reconsider* the plan again.

ねりはみがき 練り歯磨き toothpaste.

ねりもの 練り物 a **product made from boiled fish paste** (魚肉で作る食品).

[1]ねる 寝る

> 訳語メニュー
> 床につく →go to bed **1**
> 眠る →sleep **2**
> 横たわる →lie down **3**

1【床につく】go to bed ▶私はたいてい11時に寝る I usually *go to bed* at eleven. ‖ もう寝る時間ですよ It's time to *go to bed*.／It's bedtime. (➤ 後者はややくだけた言い方) ‖ 寝る時刻が過ぎてますよ It's past your *bedtime*. ‖ 父はもう寝ています My father *is* already *in bed*. ‖ かぜで1週間も寝ていた I *was in bed* for a whole week with a cold.／A cold kept me in bed for a whole week. ‖ 彼は何年も病気で寝ている He has *been sick in bed* for years. ‖ もう8時よ．いつまで寝ているつもり？ It's eight o'clock. Are you going to *stay in bed* all day? ‖ 私は日曜日は10時まで寝ている I *stay in bed* till ten on Sundays.

▶日曜日の朝くらいのんびりと寝ていたい I'd like to *sleep in* at least on Sunday mornings. (➤ sleep in は「朝遅くまで寝ている」) ‖ 彼は退院後しばらくは寝たり起きたりの生活をしていた For some time after he left the hospital, he *was partially confined to bed*. ‖ 母は父の帰りをたいがい寝ないで待っています My mother usually *waits up* [*stays up*] *for* my father. ‖ きのうは一晩中寝ないでマージャンをした We played mahjong *all night* last night.

2【眠る】sleep ; go to sleep (寝入る) ▶私は毎日9時間は寝ます I always *sleep* (for) nine hours a night. ‖ ああよく寝た. もう10時か I *had a* (*really*) *good sleep*. Is it ten already? ‖ 往来する車の音がうるさくて寝られない(＝寝つかれない) I *can't go to sleep* ; traffic is too noisy. ‖ ゆうべはぐっすり寝られ(＝眠れ)ましたか Did you *sleep* well last night? (Could you ...? とはしない) ‖ 入試前はそれこそ寝る間も惜しんで勉強した I cut down on (my) *sleeping time* so that I could study harder for the entrance exam. (➤ cut down on は「…を切り詰める」) ‖ 進学か就職か一晩寝て考えてみなさい *Sleep on* the question of whether to go to college or to get a job. (➤ sleep on は「…を一晩寝て考える」) ‖ ことわざ 寝る子は育つ Children who sleep well grow well. (➤ 日本語からの直訳).

3【横たわる】lie down ▶診察台の上にあおむけに [うつぶせに] 寝てください *Lie down* on your back [on your stomach] on the examination table. ‖ 寝ながら本を読むと目に悪い It's bad for your eyes to read *lying down*.

▶日曜日はかぜで一日寝ていた I *lay in bed* all day Sunday with a cold. (slept にすると「目を覚まさずに眠っていた」の意になる) ‖ 気分が悪いならベッドで少し寝てなさい If you feel out of sorts, *stay* [*take a rest*] in bed for a while.

4【セックスする】sleep with ▶彼は彼女と寝ていない He hasn't *slept with* his girlfriend.

5【慣用表現】▶どうして彼女の前でひろしさんの名前を言うの? やっと忘れかけているのに. 寝た子を起こすようなことをしないでよ Why mention Hiroshi's name in front of her? She's at last beginning to forget him. *Let sleeping dogs lie*. (➤「眠っている犬はそのままにしておけ」が文字どおりの意).

☛ 寝ても覚めても (→見出語)

[2]**ねる 練る 1【こねる】knead** /niːd/ +目 ▶パン生地を練る *knead* the dough.

2【十分に考える】▶文章を練る *polish* one's writing ‖ 我々は販売作戦を練った We *worked out* [*elaborated*] our plan for the sales campaign. ‖ その計画はもう少し練る必要がある We should *consider* the plan more *carefully*.

ねれる 練れる ▶練れた人 a person *with a* (*well-*)*rounded character and personality*.

ねわざ 寝技 a **groundwork** [**pinning**] **technique in judo** (柔道の).

[1]**ねん 年 1【とし】a year** ▶その島は暖かいので年に2回米が取れます They have rice crops *twice a year* because of the island's mild climate. ‖ 対話「関西へは年に何回くらい行きますか」「4, 5回です」"How many times *a year* do you go to Kansai?" "Four or five (times)." ‖ 対話「こちらへ引っ越してこられて何年になりますか」「まる5年です」"*How long* have you been here?" "Five whole *years*." (➤「ここにどのくらい長くいるか」の意) / "*How long* has it been since you moved here?" "It's been a full five *years*." →何年. ‖ 対話「きみは何年の卒業ですか」「2021年です」"*When* did you graduate?" "In 2021." ‖ 年に1度の文化祭が待ち遠しい I can hardly wait for the *annual* school festival. ‖ この計画は2025年に完成する予定だ This project is scheduled to be completed *in 2025* [*in the year 2025*]. (➤ twenty twenty-five と読む).

2【学年】a year ; 《米》 **a grade,** 《英》 **a form** (➤ form は主に中等学校で用いる) (→学年, -年生) ▶3年C組 Third *Year*, Homeroom C ‖ あの人は私の小学校3年のときの先生です The man over there was my *third-grade* teacher. ‖ この委員会は大学1, 2年の学生で構成されている This committee is made up of *college freshmen and sophomores*.

[2]**ねん 念 1【観念, 気持ち】a sense, a feeling** ▶今時の人は祖先に対する感謝の念がない Many people today have no *sense of gratitude* to [toward] their ancestors. ‖ 彼には尊敬の念を抱いている I have *a feeling of respect* for him. / I hold him in *high regard*.

2【心づかい, 注意】care ▶彼は何事でも念を入れてやる He does everything *with great care* [*thoroughly*]. ‖ 仕事はできるだけ念を入れてやりなさい Do your work *with the utmost care*. ‖ 念には念を入れて彼は窓にも鍵をかけた *To make doubly sure*, he locked the windows. ‖ 爆薬を扱うときは念には念を入れてください You *can't be too careful* in handling explosives. (「いくら注意してもし過ぎることはない」の意).

【文型】
人(A)に…するよう念を押す
remind A **to** do

▶校門の所で待っていてくれるように彼女に念を押した I *reminded* her *to* wait for me at the school gate. (➤ remind は「(忘れないように)思い出させる」).

☛ 念のため (→見出語)

ねんいり 念入りな careful (注意深い) ; **elaborate** /ɪlǽbərət/ (手の込んだ) ▶念入りな仕事をする do a *careful* job / do a job *carefully* ‖ 父は念入りに盆栽の手入れをしていた My father was tending his bonsai *meticulously* [*carefully*]. ‖ 彼女は衣装に念入りにししゅうを施した She embroidered her costume *elaborately*. ‖ 警察は彼の部屋を念入りに捜索した The police searched his room *thoroughly* [went through his room *with a fine-tooth*(*ed*) *comb*]. (➤ with a fine-tooth(ed) comb は「目の細かいくしで」が原義で, ややインフォーマルな表現).

ねんえき 粘液 viscous /vískəs/ **liquid, mucus** /mjúːkəs/ (動植物の) ; **mucilage** /mjúːsɪlɪdʒ/ (植物の).

ねんが 年賀 New Year's greetings ▶私たちは電話で年賀(の挨拶)を交わした We exchanged *New Year's greetings* on the phone. / We *wished* each other *a happy New Year* over the phone. ‖ きのう親せきの家に年賀に行った Yesterday I *paid a New Year's visit* to my relatives.

▶先生に年賀状出した? Did you send your teacher *a New Year's card*? 《参考》英米ではクリスマスを盛大に祝い, そのときに I wish you a Merry Christmas and a Happy New Year. とか Greetings and good wishes for Christmas and the New Year などのような新年を祝賀する挨拶状を縁者・友人などに出すことが多い.

日本紹介 ✉ **年賀状は新年を祝うことばに近況報告などを添えたはがきです. 多くの日本人は友人, 親類, 恩師などにあてて数十枚から数百枚の年賀状を書きます. 近年は年賀状の代わりにパソコンや携帯電話の年賀メールを利用する人が増えています** A New Year's card is a postcard on which New Year's greetings are written along with some news about the sender's recent events and activities. Many Japanese write and send them to their friends, relatives and (former) teachers. The number sent ranges from a few dozen to several hundred. In recent years, a growing number of people have replaced them with e-mail or text messages.
‖**年賀郵便** New Year's mail.

ねんがく 年額 ▶この会の会費は**年額**5000円です The *annual* membership *fee* for this society is five thousand yen.

ねんがっぴ 年月日 **the date** ▶瓶に書かれた**年月日**は品質保証期限です *The date* on the bottle shows when you should drink it by.
‖**製造年月日** the date of production ‖ **生年月日** the date of birth.

ねんがらねんじゅう 年がら年中 **year in and year out** ▶あの先生は**年がら年中**同じことばかり言っている That teacher says the same thing(s) *year in and year out*. ‖彼は仕事で**年がら年中**忙しくしている His job keeps him *constantly* busy.

1**ねんかん 年鑑** a **yearbook,** an **almanac** /ɔ́:lmənæk/ ▶科学**年鑑** a scientific *yearbook*.

2**ねんかん 年刊** an **annual publication** ▶この会報は**年刊**です This bulletin *is published annually* [*yearly*]. ／This is an *annual* [*a yearly*] bulletin.

3**ねんかん 年間の** **annual, yearly** (1年の; 前者は後者より堅い語) ▶**年間**所得 an *annual* [*a yearly*] income ‖ 半導体の**年間**生産高 the *annual* output of chips ‖ 海外旅行者の数は**年間**どのくらいですか How many people go abroad *a* [*per*] *year*? (● a [per] year は「1年につき」; per は主にビジネス用語) ‖ 小豆島は**年間**を通じて気候が温暖だ Shodo Island has a mild climate *all* (*the*) *year round*. ‖ 彼とは3**年間**会っていない I haven't seen him *for three years*.
▶法隆寺は白鳳**年間**(=時代)に創建された (The) Horyuji Temple was founded in the Hakuho *period* [*era*].

ねんがん 念願 a **dream**(夢); a **wish** (実現がかなり難しい); a **desire** (強い望み) ▶**念願**を果たす realize one's *dream* ‖ 父は長年の**念願**だった中国旅行に行った My father went on a trip to China, which had been his *long-cherished dream* [*wish*]. ／My father went on a *long-dreamed-of* trip to China. ‖ 長年の**念願**がついにかなった My *long-cherished desire* has at last been fulfilled. ‖ 彼らは**念願**のマイホームを手に入れた They bought their dream home. ／They bought the home *of their dreams*. (●「念願の[あこがれの]…」は one's dream ... または複数形で ... of one's dreams ということが多い).

ねんき 年季 ▶彼女のフラメンコは**年季**が入っている She's had *many years of experience* in flamenco dancing. ／ She's an *experienced* flamenco dancer.

ねんきん 年金 a **pension** (恩給); an **annuity** /ənjú:əṭi/ (積み立ててあとでもらう年金) ▶祖父は**年金**で暮らしている My grandfather lives *on a pension*. ‖ 彼は**年金**をもらう年齢に達した He is now old enough to receive *an annuity*.
‖**年金受給者** [**生活者**] a pensioner ‖ **企業年金** a corporate [company] pension ‖ **厚生年金** a welfare pension ‖ **公的年金** a public pension ‖ **国民年金** a national pension ‖ **終身年金** a lifetime pension ‖ **障害年金** a disability pension ‖ **退職年金** a retirement pension ‖ **老齢年金** an old-age pension ‖ **日本年金機構** the Japan Pension Service ‖ **年金制度改革** a reform of the pension system.

ねんぐ 年貢 **(annual) land tax** (地租); an **annual tribute** (みつぎ物, 上納金) ▶高い**年貢**を取り立てる collect very high *land tax*.
▶《慣用表現》もう**年貢の納めどきだ** The game [jig] is up [over]. (➤「万事休す」の意).

ねんげつ 年月 **years; time** (時) ▶あれから15年の**年月**がたった It has been fifteen *years* since then. ／Fifteen *years* have passed since then. (➤ 後者はやや堅い表現) ‖ 彼女の心の痛手が消えるまでには長い**年月**がかかるだろう It will take *many years* [*a long* (*period of*) *time*] to heal her broken heart.

ねんこう 年功 **years of experience** (経験年数); **seniority** (先任, 先輩であること) ▶わが社では昇進は**年功**で決まる Promotion in our company goes by *seniority* [depends on *how many years you've been working*].
☛ 年功序列 (→見出語)

ねんごう 年号 **the name of an era** /íərə/ ▶1944年は日本の**年号**で言うと何年ですか What year does 1944 correspond to in the Japanese system of *era names*? ‖ 2012年は日本の**年号**では平成24年です The year 2012 is the twenty-fourth year of Heisei, which is the current *era name* in Japan.

ねんこうじょれつ 年功序列 a **seniority** /si:njɔ́:rəṭi/ **system** ▶多くの日本の企業では**年功序列**は崩れ始めている *The seniority system* has begun to break down in many Japanese companies.

ねんごろ 懇ろ ▶犬が死んだのでお寺で**ねんごろ**に弔ってもらった When my dog died, I had a *reverent* memorial service held for him at the temple. ‖ あの家の人たちとは**ねんごろ**(=懇意)にしています We *are on very friendly terms with* that family.

ねんざ 捻挫 a **sprain** 一動 **ねんざする** **sprain** +目, **twist** +目 ▶きのうアイススケートをしていて足首を**ねんざした** I *sprained* [*twisted*] my ankle (while) ice-skating yesterday.

-ねんさい -年祭 an **anniversary** ▶黒澤明生誕100**年祭** *the centennial* (*anniversary*) of the birth of Kurosawa Akira ‖ きのうわが社の創立25[50]**年祭**を祝った Yesterday we celebrated *the 25th* [*50th*] *anniversary* of the founding of our company. (●「25年祭」は silver jubilee /dʒú:bɪli:/,「50年祭」は golden jubilee ともいう).

ねんさん 年産 **annual production** [**output**].

ねんし 年始 **the beginning of the year; New Year's Day** (元日) ▶おじの所へ**年始のあいさつ**(=年始回り)に行こうと思う I'm going to make *a New Year's visit* to my uncle's (house). ‖ **年始の客**が次々とやって来た People came one after another to *wish* us *a Happy New Year*.

ねんじ 年次 ▶H大学3**年次**の学生 a student in his or her *third year* at H University ／《米また》a

junior at H University ‖ 彼とは大学の入学年次は同じだが，卒業年次は彼のほうが１年早い He and I entered college in the same *year*, but he graduated a year earlier than I (did).
‖年次休暇 an annual paid leave [《米また》vacation／《英また》holiday] ‖ 年次計画 an annual [a yearly] program ‖ 年次総会 an annual [a yearly] meeting ‖ 年次報告(書) an annual [a yearly] report.

ねんしき 年式 the model year (of a car) ▶年式の古いポルシェ an *old-model* Porsche ‖ 2009年式のアウディ a 2009 *model* Audi.

ねんしゅう 年収 an annual [a yearly] income ▶彼の年収は500万円だ His *annual income* is five million yen. ／He *earns* [*gets*] five million yen *a year*. (➤ get はややインフォーマルな語).

ねんじゅう 年中 all (the) year round, throughout the year ▶ディズニーランドは年中込み合っている Disneyland is crowded *all (the) year round*. ‖ このレストランは年中無休だ This restaurant is *open throughout the year*.
▶彼女は年中(＝しょっちゅう)計算間違いをしている She's *forever* [*always*] making calculation errors.

ねんしゅつ 捻出 ▶どうにかして旅費を捻出しなければ I have to *raise the money* for my trip somehow.

ねんしょ 念書 a signed memorandum, a letter of awareness.

1**ねんしょう 燃焼** combustion /kəmbʌ́stʃən/ 一動 燃焼する burn ▶ガス給湯器の不完全燃焼で一酸化炭素が発生した Carbon monoxide was released due to *incomplete combustion* in the gas water heater. ‖ 物は酸素なしでは燃焼しない Nothing *burns* without oxygen.
▶《比喩的》「私はもう燃焼し尽くした」と言ってその選手は引退した The player retired saying, "I *have* simply *burned out*."

2**ねんしょう 年商** annual sales [turnover].

ねんしょうしゃ 年少者 young people(若い人たち)；a younger person (年下の人)；a juvenile /dʒúːvənəl/ (青少年) ▶年少者の方からお先にどうぞ *Younger ones* go first, please. ‖ 最近年少者の犯罪が増えた In recent years the number of crimes committed by *juveniles* has increased.
☛ 最年少 (→見出語)

ねんじる 念じる will +目；wish for ▶念じれば通じる What you *strongly will* will be realized.

ねんすう 年数 the number of years.

-ねんせい -年生 → 学年 ▶ 対話「きみ，何年生？」「５年生です」"*What grade* [*year*] *are* you *in*?" "I'm *a fifth grader*. ／I'*m in the fifth grade* [*year*]."

ねんだい 年代 1【世代】a generation ▶親と私たちとでは年代が違うように考え方も違う (Just) as we belong to a different *generation* from our parents, so our way of thinking is different from theirs. ‖ 私たちの年代は無気力だと言われる People criticize our *age group* for being spiritless. (➤ age-group は「年齢層」).
2【時代】▶この仏像の制作年代は特定できない We cannot pinpoint the *date* when this Buddhist statue was made. ‖ この歌は1990年代前半に流行した This song was popular in the early *1990s*. (➤ nineteen nineties と読む) ‖ これらの古時計は年代順に陳列してあります These antique clocks are displayed *in chronological order*.
‖年代記 a chronicle.

ねんちゃく 粘着 adhesion /ədhíːʒən/
‖粘着テープ adhesive tape ‖ 粘着のり powerful glue.

ねんちゅうぎょうじ 年中行事 an annual event ▶本校では運動会は重要な年中行事です The athletic meet at our school is an important *annual* [*yearly*] school *event*.
▶《比喩的》その国では交通ストは年中行事のようなものだ The traffic strike is *a yearly event* in that country.

> 「年中行事」のいろいろ **正月休み** New Year's holidays ／**豆まき** bean-scattering ceremony ／**バレンタインデー** (St.) Valentine's Day ／**ひな祭り** Doll Festival ／**こどもの日** Children's Day ／**母の日** Mother's Day ／**父の日** Father's Day ／**七夕** the Tanabata [Star] Festival ／**夏休み** summer vacation ／**全国高校野球大会** the National High School Baseball Tournament ／**お盆** the Bon Festival ／**七五三** *shichi-go-san* ／**クリスマス** Christmas ／**おおみそか** New Year's Eve

ねんちょう 年長の older, senior (➤ 前者がよりふつう) ▶永井さんは私よりも５つ年長です Mr. Nagai is five years *older than* I [me]. (➤ than me はインフォーマルな言い方) ／Mr. Nagai is five years *senior to* me. ‖ 年長者の忠告を聞くべきだ You should take the advice of your *elders* [*seniors*].
‖(幼稚園の)年長組 a senior class.
☛ 最年長 (→見出語)

1**ねんど 年度** the school year(学校の)；the fiscal year (会計年度) ▶来年度 [2012年度] の予算 the budget *for next year* [*fiscal* 2012] ‖ 2012年度ノーベル賞受賞者 a winner of a 2012 Nobel Prize ‖ 2011年度のM大学卒業生 the class of 2011 of M University ‖ 本年度の営業状態はかなり安定していた Sales were quite stable *this year*. ‖ 年度末に支払いを清算した We cleared off our debts at *the end of the fiscal year*.

2**ねんど 粘土** clay；《米》play dough /doʊ/，《主に英》plasticine /plǽstəsiːn/ (工作用の) ▶粘土で人形を作る shape *clay* into a doll／make a doll of *clay*
‖粘土細工 (a piece of) clay work ‖ 紙粘土 papier-mâché /pèɪpəˈməʃéɪ/.

1**ねんとう 年頭** the beginning of the year(年の初め)；the new year (新年) ▶校長先生が年頭の挨拶をされた The principal gave *a New Year's speech*.

2**ねんとう 念頭** ▶今は入試のことしか念頭にない I have nothing but the entrance exams *on my mind* now. ‖ 今言ったことを念頭に置いておきなさい *Keep* [*Bear*] *in mind* what I have just said. ‖ 彼は私の事なんかまるで念頭にないみたい It seems he *doesn't think about* me at all.

ねんない 年内 within the year, before the end of the year ▶年内に(＝ことし中に)引っ越そうと思っている I'm thinking of moving (*sometime*) *this year*. (⚠ within this year とはしない) ‖ 年内にもう一度集まりましょう Let's get together again *sometime this year* [*before this year is over*].
▶あの殺人事件は年内には解決しそうにないね That murder case won't be solved *before the end of the year*, I'm afraid.

ねんね 1【眠ること】▶いい子だからねんねしなさいね Now

be a good girl [boy] and *go beddy-bye*.
2【世間知らず】▶彼女はいつまでたってもねんねなんだね She *hasn't grown up* enough to join the real world.

ねんねん 年々 every year(毎年); year by year(年ごとに) ▶大学の授業料は年々高くなっている College tuition is going up *every year* [*year by year*].

ねんのため 念の為 just to make sure(確認のため); just in case(万一に備えて); just to be safe(安全のため) ▶念のためもう一度電話番号を言ってください Please give me your phone number again, *just to make (doubly) sure* [*just to be sure*]. ‖雨は降らないかもしれないけど念のため傘を持って行きなさい It may not rain, but take an umbrella *just in case*. ‖念のため予約をしたほうがいいですよ *Just to be safe*, you had better make a reservation. ‖問題は無いと思うけど, 念のために警察に届けておいたほうがいいね It's probably nothing, but maybe you should report it to the police *as a precaution*. (● as a precaution は just in case より強意).

ねんぱい 年配 ▶50年配の人 a person *about* [*around*] fifty (*years of age*) ‖私たちの先生は母と同年配だ Our teacher is *about* my mother's *age*. ‖あのシルバーシートは年配の方々のためのものです Those "silver seats" are put there especially for *elderly people* [*senior citizens*].
‖年輩市民 a senior citizen(高齢者).
☞ 同年配(→見出語)

ねんぴ 燃費 fuel [gas] mileage /máɪlɪdʒ/ ▶燃費のいい車 a *gas-*[*fuel-*]*efficient* car ‖この車の燃費はどれくらいですか What is *the fuel* [*gas*] *mileage* of this car?
▶私のこの新車は前の車よりも燃費がいい My new car gets better *mileage* than the old one. ‖日本車は燃費がよいことで知られる Japanese cars are known for (their) *efficient use of gas*.

ねんぴょう 年表 a chronological table, a chronology /krənɑ́ːlədʒi/ (日付順に列記したもの) ▶日本史の年表 *a chronological table* of Japanese history.

ねんぷ 年譜 a chronological list of the main events, a chronological résumé (➤ chronological は「年代順の」) ▶作家の年譜を見ると, 昭和8年に東北地方へ旅行したとある According to the *chronology of* the author's *life*, he traveled to the Tohoku region in the eighth year of Showa.

ねんぶつ 念仏 ▶念仏を唱える recite the (*holy*) *name of Amida* [*Amitabha*] *Buddha* (*with faith*).

ねんぽう 年俸 an annual salary ▶彼は年俸1億円で契約した He signed an employment contract with *an annual salary* of one hundred million yen.

ねんまく 粘膜 《解剖学》 a mucous membrane /mémbreɪn/ ▶スギ花粉は鼻[のど]の粘膜を刺激する Cedar pollen stimulates the *mucous membranes* of the nose [throat].

ねんまつ 年末 the end of the year ▶去年の年末は伊豆で過ごした I spent *the end of* last *year* in Izu. ‖多くの日本人が年末には忘年会を開く Many Japanese hold year-end parties *at the end of the year*.
‖年末大売り出し a year-end sale ‖年末賞与 a year-end bonus ‖年末調整 a year-end tax adjustment.

ねんらい 年来 ▶80年来の大地震 the biggest earthquake *in 80 years* ‖年来の夢がかなった My *long-cherished dream* has come true. ‖やっと年来の課題が解決した We have finally solved a *long-pending* problem. ‖佐藤君とは10年来の友人です Sato and I have been friends *for ten years*.

ねんり 年利 (an) annual interest rate ▶年利15%で消費者金融から金を借りる borrow money from a consumer finance company at *an annual interest rate* of 15 percent.

ねんりき 念力 psychokinesis /sàɪkoʊkəɪníːsɪs/ ▶念力でスプーンを曲げる bend a spoon *by psychokinesis* ‖彼は念力で車を動かすことができる He can move a car *with his mind*. /He can move a car *by psychokinesis* [*the power of his will*].

ねんりつ 年率 an annual rate.

ねんりょう 燃料 fuel ▶この車は燃料を食う[食わない] This car is *a gas guzzler* [is *fuel-efficient*]. ‖燃料が乏しくなってきた We are running short of *fuel*. / (Our) *fuel* is running short [out]. ‖戦闘機は燃料補給のため空母に帰艦した The fighter flew back to the aircraft carrier to *refuel*.
‖燃料計 a fuel gauge /geɪdʒ/ ‖燃料タンク a fuel tank ‖燃料電池 a fuel cell ‖燃料電池車 a fuel-cell car [vehicle] ‖燃料費 the cost of fuel, fuel expenses ‖液体燃料 (a) liquid fuel ‖核燃料 nuclear fuel ‖化石燃料 (a) fossil fuel ‖固形燃料 (a) solid fuel ‖代替燃料 an alternative fuel.

ねんりん 年輪 annual rings, tree rings ▶年輪から計算するとこの木の樹齢は250年です By counting the tree's *annual rings*, we can determine that it is 250 years old.

ねんれい 年齢

(an) age ▶このクラブにはいろいろな年齢の人がいる This club has members of all *ages*. ‖彼女は年齢の割には若く見える She looks young for her *age*. ‖私は年齢の隔たりなど気にしません I don't care about our *age difference*. ‖その少年は自分のことは自分でやれる年齢だ That boy is *old enough* to take care of himself.
▶申込書には住所と年齢を明記してください Write your address and *age* clearly on the application form. ‖この仕事には年齢制限がない There is no *age requirement* for this job. ‖焼酎は若い年齢層に人気があるようだ Shochu seems to be popular with the younger *age group*. ‖あの歌手は年齢不詳だ That singer's *age is unknown*. /*No one knows how old* that singer is. ‖参加者を年齢別に分類してください Please classify the participants *by age*. ‖母は実年齢よりも若く[年取って]見える My mother looks younger [older] than her *actual age*. ‖社員の平均年齢は29歳です The *average age* of the employees of [at] this company is twenty-nine.

の・ノ

の 野 a **field**(野原) ; a **plain**（平原）▶野の花 a *wild* flower(➤「野生の花」の意).

ことわざ あとは野となれ山となれ After me [us] the deluge. (➤ フランスのことわざからで,「われ亡きあとに洪水よ来たれ」の意 ; deluge は /délju:dʒ/ と発音).

-の 1【所有・帰属を示して】of, 's

> **語法「-の」の訳し方**
> (1)「-の」は人称代名詞の所有格 (my, your, our, his, her, their, its), 疑問代名詞および関係代名詞の所有格 (whose) を用いて表せることが多いが, このほか, 帰属・所属・職種・身分に関連した表現には the handle *of* a cup, a member *of* the tennis club, a professor *of* physics のように of を使うことが多い. これらは a cup handle, a tennis club member, a physics professor のような表現もできる.
> (2)a son *of* a teacher の場合のような「A of B」の形は a teacher's son のように「B's A」の形にすることができ, 特に所有の意味が強い場合は the girl's toy のように「B's A」の形のみを用いる.

▶私[彼／彼女／由佳]の自転車 *my* [*his*／*her*／*Yuka's*] bicycle ‖ 私の友人の1人 a friend (*of mine*)／one of *my* friends ‖ 日本の首都 the capital *of* Japan ‖ カップの取っ手 the handle *of* a cup ‖ その傘は私[彼／彼女／由佳]の(もの)です The umbrella is *mine* [*his*／*hers*／*Yuka's*]. ‖ 私の経験からきみに忠告しているんだ I'm advising you from *my* (*own*) experience. ‖ これはだれの辞書ですか *Whose* dictionary is this?

> **直訳の落とし穴「-の」**
> 学習者は「-の」='s と考えて, 's を多用しすぎる傾向がある. 's は基本的に所有を表し, 無生物には通例用いない. よくあるミスは次の通り.
> 「リビングの天井」
> (×)the living room's ceiling
> (○)the ceiling **of** the living room
> 「姉の写真」
> my sister**'s** photos(姉が写した, 姉がもっている)
> photos **of** my sister(姉を写した)
> 「名古屋の私の住所」
> (×)my Nagoya's address
> (○)my address **in** Nagoya
> 「北海道の土産です」
> (×)Here's a Hokkaido's gift.
> (○)Here's a gift **from** Hokkaido.

2【所属を示して】at, of, with, for ▶私はB大学の学生です I'm a student *at* B University. (➤ 多数の中の1人という場合は at を用いる) ‖ 関氏はN大学の教授[学長]です Mr. Seki is a professor *at* [(the) president *of*] N University. (1人しかいない役職の場合は of) ‖ 私はバスケット部のメンバーだ I'm a member *of* the basketball club. ‖ 《電話で》国際電機の小山です This is Koyama *of* [*from*] Kokusai Electric Company. ‖ 彼はフジテレビのプロデューサーだ He is a producer *for* [*at*／*with*] Fuji Television.

3【身分・職種などを示して】of ▶オーケストラの指揮者 the conductor *of* an orchestra ‖ おじはO大学の物理学の教授[講師]だ My uncle is a professor *of* [a lecturer *in*] physics at O University. (前置詞の違いに注意) ‖ 富田氏は化学の先生だ Mr. Tomita is *a chemistry teacher*.／Mr. Tomita teaches chemistry.

4【同格を示して】▶歴史家のトインビー Toynbee, the historian ‖ ゴールキーパーの川島がスパイクされた Goalkeeper Kawashima got spiked. (役職名, ポジション名などが名前の前にくるときには the や a は省略される) ‖ これは次女の裕子です This is my second daughter Yuko. ‖ 弁護士の小林氏がちょうどそこにいた Mr. Kobayashi, a lawyer, was right there.

5【行為者・作者などを示して】by, of ▶ピカソの(描いた)絵 a painting *by* Picasso／a Picasso (「a＋芸術家の姓」でその人の「作品」の意. 絵・彫刻・楽曲を表すことが多い) ‖ 芥川龍之介の作品 the works *of* Akutagawa Ryunosuke／Akutagawa Ryunosuke*'s* works ‖ AKB48のCD a CD *of* AKB48／an AKB48 CD ‖ 神の愛 God*'s* love (➤ the love of God は「神への愛」).

6【時を示して】of, in ▶去年の5月に in May (*of*) last year ‖ 2013年の3月に in March, 2013 ‖ 当時の人々 people *in* those days／people *of* that time ‖ 5月の第2日曜日は母の日です The second Sunday *in* [*of*] May is Mother's Day. ‖ 7時のニュースは必ず見る I never miss the seven o'clock news.

▶きょうの新聞 today*'s* newspaper ‖ あすの天気 tomorrow*'s* weather ‖ 今晩のテレビ番組 this evening*'s* TV programs (これらでは 's が使われる).

7【所在地・産地などを示して】at, in, from

> **語法 場所を表す in, at, from**
> 所在地・産地などに関連した表現を訳す場合, 活動する場所や空間内部を意識すれば in, 1地点を意識すれば at,「どこどこから」という意味であれば from を用いればよいことが多い.

▶交差点の信号 traffic signals *at* the intersection ‖ 私の北海道のおじ my uncle *in* [*from*] Hokkaido (前者は「…にいる」, 後者は「…から(訪ねて／遊びに)来ている」) ‖ 横浜(市)の人たち the people *in* [*of*] Yokohama (of は堅い言い方) ‖ 中山さん(から)の手紙 a letter *from* Mr. Nakayama ‖ 東京のホテルにいるヘンリーさんを訪ねた I visited Henry at a hotel *in* Tokyo [at a Tokyo hotel]. ‖ 宮城の米はうまい Rice *from* Miyagi [Miyagi rice] tastes good. ‖ ゆうべ遅く近所[隣]の家が火事にあった There was a fire in a *neighbor's* house [the house *next door*] late last night. ‖ 私はニュージーランドの出身です I'm [I *come*] *from* New Zealand.

8【対象・関連などを示して】for, of, to ▶子供(向け)の本 books *for* children／children*'s* books ‖ 大

阪の地図 a map *of* Osaka ‖ 日本の歴史 *Japanese* history／*Japan's* history／the history *of Japan*（● この順に堅い表現となる）‖ 南極大陸の発見 the discovery *of* Antarctica ‖ 英語のテスト a test *in English*／an *English* test ‖ 子供への母親の愛 the mother's love *for* her child(ren) ‖ 私の写真（＝私が写った写真）a photo *of* me（● my photo はふつう「私が写した写真；私が持っている写真」の意）.
▶第1問の正解 the correct answer *to* Question 1 ‖ 玄関の鍵 a key *to* the front door ‖ その博物館の入り口 the entrance *to* the museum ‖ 社長の秘書 the secretary *to* the president.
▶私は方言の調査で東北に行った I went to Tohoku to study the dialects there. ‖ 練習試合の申し込みはどうすればいいのですか How can we request a practice match? ‖ 体育館の建築が始まった The construction *of* the gymnasium has begun. ‖ あのサングラスの少年を見て. あの赤い服の女の子も Look at that boy *wearing* [*with*] sunglasses and that girl dressed *in* red.

9【材料・手段などを示して】of ▶プラスチックの箱 a box (*made*) *of plastic*／a *plastic* box ‖ れんが造りの家 a house (*built*) *of bricks* ‖ イタリア語の手紙 a letter (*written*) *in Italian*／an *Italian* letter ‖ 毛皮のコートが欲しい I'm dying for a *fur* coat.

10【値段・数量などを示して】of ▶1枚の紙 *a sheet of* paper ‖ 5000円の本 a *five-thousand-yen* book ‖ 500円分の切手 five hundred yen's *worth of* stamps ‖ 10キロの米 *ten kilograms of* rice ‖ 10歳の少女 a girl *of ten* (*years*)／a *ten-year-old* girl ‖ 歩いて30分の道のり a *30-minute* walk [*30 minutes'* walk] from here（➤ 前者のほうがよく使われる）‖ 彼は5日間の休みを取った He took five days off.／He took a five-day [five days'] vacation.

11【部分を示して】of ▶私の友人の何人か［多く］some [many] *of* my friends ‖ 生徒の半数はかぜをひいていた *Half of* the students were sick with flu. ‖ 収益金の一部は慈善団体に寄付します We're planning to donate part *of* the proceeds to a charity. ‖ 我々はふつう, 読んだものの1割も覚えていない Normally, we remember less than 10 percent *of* what we've read.

12【名詞の代わりに使って】one ▶私が編んだのはこのセーターです The sweater I knitted is this *one*. ‖ このジーパン, きついな. もっと大きいサイズのはありませんか？ These jeans are tight. Do you have (*any* in) a bigger size? ‖ 対話「どんなケーキがいいですか」「あまり甘くないのがいいな」"What kind of cake(s) do you like?" "I like *ones* that are not too sweet."（● ones は cakes を繰り返す代わりに使われた代名詞）.

13【「こと」の意の名詞節を作って】 ▶こんな暑い日に満員電車に乗るのは嫌だ I hate riding on crowded trains on hot days like today. ‖ この学校は校庭が狭いのが欠点だ One drawback of this school is the small size of the playground.

14【疑問を示して】 ▶こんな漢字も読めないの？ Can't you read this kanji? ‖ 対話「その手, どうしたの？」「やけど」"What's wrong with your hand?" "I burned it."

15【複数のことを並べて】 ▶生徒たちは校庭が狭いの, 校舎が古いのと不平を並べている The students are complaining about the small playground, old school buildings, *and things like that*.

ノイズ (a) **noise**（一般に雑音）; **static**（ラジオの）▶ここの局に合わせるとノイズが入るんだ If you tune in to this station, you'll just get *static*.

ノイローゼ a **nervous breakdown**,《インフォーマル》a **crackup**（一時的状態）; (a) **neurosis** /njuróʊsɪs/（神経症）▶うちの息子はノイローゼだ Our son has had *a nervous breakdown*.／Our son suffers from (*a*) *neurosis*.（● 後者は堅い言い方）‖ その母親は育児ノイローゼになった The mother *had a nervous breakdown* [*cracked up*] under the strain of child care.（➤ 後者は俗語）‖ そんなに心配ばかりしているとノイローゼになっちゃうぞ If you worry so much, you will develop *a neurosis*. ‖ もうノイローゼになりそう I'll *go crazy* [*crack* (*up*)].

> **危ないカタカナ語 ノイローゼ**
> 「ノイローゼ」はドイツ語の *Neurose*（神経症）が語源. 英語では neurosis であるが, 一般には nervous breakdown（神経衰弱）という. neurosis はかつて「神経症」の意で医学用語として用いられていたが, 現在の医学では anxiety disorder または mood disorder が用いられる.

の

[1]**のう 脳** **the brain** 一形 脳の **cerebral** /sérəbrəl/ ▶脳の手術を受ける have an operation on one's *brain* ‖（人の）脳の仕組みは完全にはわかっていない The mechanism of the (human) *brain* is not completely understood.
‖**脳下垂体** the pituitary gland ‖ **脳外科** brain surgery ‖ **脳外科医** a brain surgeon ‖ **脳血栓** cerebral thrombosis /θrɑːmbóʊsɪs/ ‖ **脳こうそく** cerebral infarction ‖ **脳軟化(症)** encephalomalacia, softening of the brain（➤ 前者は専門用語）
☛ **脳死, 脳出血, 脳腫瘍(しゅよう), 脳しんとう, 脳性まひ, 脳卒中, 脳貧血**（→見出語）

[2]**のう 能** ▶彼は食べるほかに能がない *All he can do* is (to) eat. ‖ 学校の勉強ばかりが能じゃない. 少しは社会勉強もしろよ Schoolwork *is not everything*. You should learn a little more about real life. ‖ ことわざ 能あるタカはつめを隠す A wise hawk hides [never shows (off)] its talons.（➤ 日本語からの直訳）／Still waters run deep.（➤「静かな流れは深い, 思慮のある人はあまりしゃべらない」の意の英語のことわざ）.
☛ **能無し**（→見出語）

[3]**のう 能** a **Noh** (**play**)（➤ 英語化している）
日本紹介 ✉ **能は600年ほど前に観阿弥, 世阿弥の親子によって大成された仮面舞踏劇で, 主役を演じるシテ, 相手役のワキ, 楽器を演奏する囃子(はやし)方などによって演じられます** Noh is a masked dance-drama, developed by the father-and-son team of Kan-ami and Zeami some 600 years ago. It is performed by a '*shite*,' who is the protagonist, a '*waki*' the antagonist, and a team of musicians called '*hayashikata*.'
▶能を舞う perform *a Noh play* ‖ 能を見る［見に行く］see [go to] *a Noh play*.
‖**能舞台** a Noh stage ‖ **能面** a Noh mask ‖ **能役者** a Noh player [dancer].

のういっけつ 脳溢血 →脳出血.

のうえん 農園 a **farm**; a **plantation**（大規模農園）
‖**農園主** a farmer ‖ **市民農園** a municipal /mjunísɪpəl/ farm,《英また》a municipal [town council] allotment.

のうか 農家 a **farming family**; a **farmhouse**（建物）▶うちは農家です My family are *farmers*. ‖ 彼は農家の

次男だ He is the second son of *a farming family*. ‖ 今農家は田植えで忙しい *Farmers* are now busy planting rice seedlings.

のうかい 納会 a year-end meeting.

のうがき 能書き a statement of the effects (of a medicine) (薬の効能説明) ▶能書きはそれくらいにして, 実際にその包丁で切ってみてよ *I've heard enough about how good* the knife *is*. Now let's see how well it cuts.

のうがく 農学 agriculture /ǽgrɪkʌ̀ltʃəʳ/
‖ **農学部** the school [college] of agriculture.

のうかん 納棺 (an) encoffining
‖ **納棺師** a *nokanshi*, an encoffining master ‖ **納棺式** the rites of placing a body in a casket.

のうかんき 農閑期 an off-season for farmers, the agricultural off-season.

のうき 納期 a deadline ; the (agreed-upon) date of delivery (物品の配送日) ; a delivery schedule (配送予定) ; the (due) date of payment (金銭の) ▶ (きちんと)納期を守る keep to *the agreed-upon date of delivery* ／meet *a promised delivery deadline* ‖ 納期には何とか間に合わせます Somehow, we will manage to deliver the goods by *the deadline* [*the date agreed upon*].

のうきぐ 農機具 farm machines [implements].

のうぎょう 農業 agriculture /ǽgrɪkʌ̀ltʃəʳ/ ; farming (農耕) 一形 **農業の** agricultural /æ̀grɪkʌ́ltʃərəl/ ▶うちは農業です We *run a farm*. ／We *are farmers*. ‖ 昔は農業をやっていましたが, 今は勤めています We used to *be engaged in farming*, but now we've got jobs in town.
‖ **農業学校** an agricultural school ‖ **農業協同組合** an agricultural cooperative association (➤「日本農業協同組合」は Japan Agricultural Cooperatives) ‖ **農業国** an agricultural country, a farming nation.

のうぐ 農具 a farming tool [implement].

1**のうこう 農耕** farming, agriculture
‖ **農耕生活** an agricultural life ‖ **農耕民族** an agricultural people.

2**のうこう 濃厚な** rich ▶濃厚な牛乳 *rich* milk ‖ 濃厚なバラの香り the *strong* fragrance of roses ‖ このコーンスープは少し濃厚過ぎる This corn soup is a little too *thick*. (➤ thick は「どろどろしている」の意) ‖ その映画には濃厚なラブシーンが多かった There were a lot of *hot* [*steamy*] love scenes in the movie. ‖ 彼が再選される公算が濃厚になってきた The prospects for his winning the re-election have become *stronger*. ／There is a greater possibility that he will be re-elected. (● 明確に「濃厚だ」という場合, 後者の文型を用いて There is a strong possibility that ... のようにいう).

のうこつ 納骨する put someone's ashes in his [her] grave, place someone's cremated remains in a columbarium (➤いずれも説明的な訳)
‖ **納骨堂** a columbarium /kɑ̀:ləmbéəriəm/.

のうこん 濃紺 dark blue, navy blue ▶濃紺のスーツ a *dark blue* suit.

のうさぎ 野兎 《動物》 a wild rabbit.

のうさぎょう 農作業 farming, farm work ▶農作業をしていた女性が毒蛇にかまれた A woman *working on the farm* was bitten by a poisonous snake.

のうさくぶつ 農作物 crops ; agricultural products [produce].

のうさつ 悩殺 ▶悩殺ポーズ a *bewitching* [an *enchanting* ／a *captivating*] pose.

のうさんぶつ 農産物 (farm) produce (野菜・果物など) ; farm [agricultural] products (広く生産物) ▶有機農産物 organic *produce* ‖ 北海道の主要な農産物は何ですか What are the principal *farm products* in [of] Hokkaido ?

のうし 脳死 brain death 一形 **脳死の** brain-dead ▶患者は脳死の状態だ The patient *is brain-dead*. (➤「脳死の患者」は brain-dead patient) ‖ 脳死を人の死と考えている医師も多い Many doctors regard *brain death* as the (true) death of a person.

のうじ 農事 agriculture
‖ **農事試験場** an agricultural experimental [testing] station.

のうしゅく 濃縮 concentration, enrichment 一動 **濃縮する** concentrate +目
‖ **濃縮ウラン** enriched uranium ‖ **濃縮ジュース** concentrated juice, juice concentrate.

のうしゅっけつ 脳出血 (a) cerebral hemorrhage /hémərɪdʒ/ ▶脳出血で倒れる have *a cerebral* [*brain*] *hemorrhage*.

のうしゅよう 脳腫瘍 《医学》 a brain tumor /tjú:məʳ/ ▶脳腫瘍ができる have *a brain tumor*.
‖ **悪性脳腫瘍** brain cancer.

のうじょう 農場 a farm ; a plantation (大規模コーヒー農場など) ‖ **農場主** the owner of a farm [a plantation], a farmer, a plantation owner ‖ **実験農場** an experimental farm.

のうしんとう 脳震盪 《医学》 (a) (brain) concussion /kənkʌ́ʃən/ ▶彼女は氷の張った道路で滑って脳しんとうを起こした She suffered *a concussion* after slipping on the icy street.

のうすいしょう 農水省 the Agriculture Ministry, the Ministry of Agriculture. →農林.

のうぜい 納税 tax payment, payment of taxes 一動 **納税する** pay one's taxes ▶国民には納税の義務がある Every citizen has the obligation to *pay taxes*.
‖ **納税額** the amount of one's taxes ‖ **納税者** a taxpayer ‖ **高額納税者** a large taxpayer.

のうせいまひ 脳性麻痺 《医学》 cerebral palsy /sèrəbrəl pɔ́:lzi/ ▶脳性まひにかかる have *cerebral palsy*.

ノウゼンカズラ 《植物》 a trumpet vine [creeper].

のうそっちゅう 脳卒中 《医学》 a stroke ▶脳卒中で倒れる have *a stroke*.

のうそん 農村 a farm(ing) village, an agricultural village ‖ **農村地帯** an agricultural area.

のうたん 濃淡 light and shade (明るい部分と影の部分) ; shades (陰影).

のうち 農地 farmland, agricultural land
‖ **農地改革** (an) agricultural reform.

のうてんき 脳天気な blithe /blaɪð/ ▶寅さんは脳天気な男だ Tora-san is *a ridiculously easygoing man* [is *an eternal optimist*].

のうど 濃度 concentration (液体などの) ; density (密度, 比重) ▶ビールのアルコール濃度 the *concentration* [*strength*] of alcohol in beer ‖ 濃度0.6パーセントの食塩水 water with a salt *density* of 0.6 percent ‖ このしょうゆは塩分の濃度が高い This soy sauce *contains a lot of salt* [*is high in salt*].

のうどう 農道 a farm road.

のうどうてき 能動的な active ▶核廃絶を目指して各国に能動的な働きかけをする make an *active* appeal to various countries for the abolition of nuclear weapons.

のうなし 能無し a **good-for-nothing** ▶この能無しめ！ You *good-for-nothing*!

のうにゅう 納入 **payment**（支払い）; **delivery**（配達） **一動 納入する pay** +目, **deliver** +目 ▶授業料を納入する *pay* one's school fees ‖ 入学金の**納入期限**は3月20日です The school admission fee is *due* March 20. ／*The deadline for payment* of your admission fee is March 20.

‖**納入金** the amount [money] paid（納めた）; the amount [money] due（納めるべき）‖**納入品** supplies.

のうのうと ▶のうのうと暮らす live a *carefree* [an *easy*] life／live *without a care in the world*.

のうは 脳波 **brain waves**（➤ 通例複数形で）▶サルの脳波を調べる *check* a monkey's *brain waves*／*give* a monkey *an electroencephalogram* [*an EEG*]／*do an electroencephalogram* [*an EEG*] on a monkey（➤ electroencephalogram は「脳波図, 脳電図」).

ノウハウ →ノーハウ.

のうはんき 農繁期 a **busy season for farmers** ▶今はいちばんの農繁期です It's *the busiest season* for farmers.

のうひん 納品 **delivery of goods**（納品すること）; **delivered goods**（納品された物）**一動 納品する deliver goods** ‖**納品書** a statement of delivery.

のうひんけつ 脳貧血《医 学》 **cerebral anemia** /əníːmiə/ ▶脳貧血を起こす suffer from *cerebral anemia*（● 日常会話では faint とか pass out という. ともに「失神する」の意).

1**のうふ 農夫** →農民.

2**のうふ 納付** **payment 一動 納付する pay** +目 ▶10月1日に納付期限が来る *Payment* is due on October 1. ‖**納付期限** the payment deadline, the due date for payment.

のうべん 能弁 **eloquence** /éləkwəns/（説得力のある弁舌）; **fluency**（流ちょうさ）

‖**能弁家** an eloquent speaker.

のうみそ 脳味噌 **brains,**《インフォーマル》**gray matter** ▶もう少し, 脳みそを絞って考えろ Use your *brain* more. ／Work your *brain* harder.

のうみん 農民 a **farmer,** a **farm worker**

> 《解説》(1) farmer は「相当な規模の耕作地を所有している人」「(大) 農場主」の意で, farm worker [laborer], farmhand は farmer に雇用されている人を指す. (2) したがって,「農民」「農夫」は farmer あるいは farm worker [farm laborer／farmhand] を適宜使い分けるか,《英》の smallholder (50エーカー以下の耕地を所有する自作農) を用いる.

のうむ 濃霧 a **dense** [**thick**] **fog** ▶濃霧のため電車は徐行しています The train is going at a slow speed because of the *dense fog*.

‖**濃霧警報** a dense fog warning.

のうやく 農薬 **agricultural chemicals,**《インフォーマル》**agro-chemicals**; **pesticide**（殺虫剤, 除草剤を含む総称）▶作物に農薬を散布する spray crops with *pesticides* [*chemicals*] ‖ 農薬に汚染された土地 soil contaminated with *pesticides* [*agricultural chemicals*].

‖**無農薬野菜** chemical-free [pesticide-free] vegetables.

のうり 脳裏 one's **mind** ▶脳裏をかすめる cross *one's mind* ‖ 彼女のことが彼の脳裏に焼きついていた She was always on *his mind*.

のうりつ 能率 **efficiency** /ɪfíʃənsi/ **一形 能率的な efficient** ▶仕事の能率を上げる improve *efficiency* ‖ 能率の面では人は機械にかなわない In terms of *efficiency*, humans are no match for machines. ‖ 早朝の勉強は**能率が上がる** Studying early in the morning *is* very *efficient*. ／You can *get more done* if you study early in the morning. ‖ このやり方のほうが**能率的**だ This (way) is *more efficient*. ‖ あの方法は**非能率的**だ That method is *inefficient*. ‖ この仕事はもっと**能率よく**できたはずだ This job could surely have been done more *efficiently*.

‖**能率給** efficiency wages.

のうりょう 納涼 ‖**納涼船** a summer pleasure boat ‖ **納涼花火大会** a display of fireworks on a summer evening.

のうりょく 能力

(an) **ability,** (a) **capacity** /kəpǽsəṭi/, a **faculty** /fǽkəlṭi/; (a) **capability**

> 《解説》**ability** は努力によって伸ばすことのできる才能や伸び育った能力を, **capacity** は主に潜在的な能力や特定分野の優れた才能を, **faculty** は人間の心身に備わった能力を, **capability** は主に実務能力をいう.

▶運動**能力** athletic *ability* ‖ 経営**能力** management *ability* ‖ ほとんどの鳥には飛ぶ**能力がある** Most birds have the *ability* to fly. ‖ ある種の動物には地震を予知する**能力がある**と考えられている Some animals are thought to have the *ability* to predict earthquakes.

▶他の動物と違って人間には話す**能力**（＝機能）がある Unlike other animals, human beings have the *faculty* of speech. ‖ あの先生には数学を教える**能力はない** That teacher *is incompetent* at teaching mathematics. ‖ 数学は考える**能力**を養う Mathematics develops our *thinking faculties* [*abilities*]. ‖ 工場は**生産能力**を倍増させた The plant doubled its *production capacity*.

▶それは私の**能力**を超えた仕事だ It is a job beyond my *capacity* [*ability*]. ／I'm not equal [not up] to the task.（➤ be equal to は「…に耐える力量がある」）‖ 彼は**能力**以上の仕事をしている He has a job that is beyond his *ability* [*capability*].

▶生徒は**能力**別に3クラスに編成してある Students are grouped into three classes *according to* their *ability*. 《参考》「能力別クラス編成」を ability grouping,《主に米》tracking,《主に英》streaming などという.

‖(会社などの) **能力開発部** a human resource [personnel] development department ‖ **能力主義** meritocracy /mèrɪtɑ́ːkrəsi/.

のうりん 農林 **agriculture** /ǽgrɪkʌ̀ltʃəʳ/ **and forestry**

‖**農林水産省** the Ministry of Agriculture, Forestry and Fisheries ‖ **農林水産大臣** the Minister of Agriculture, Forestry and Fisheries.

ノー

1【ゼロの】▶ぬれたまま干せる**ノーアイロン**のシャツ a drip-dry, *no-iron* [《英》*non-iron*] shirt ／a *wash-and-wear* shirt（● 後者の言い方が日常的）‖ **ノーアウト**, ランナー一・二塁で鳥谷が打席に立った Toritani came to bat with runners at first and second and *no outs*. ‖ そのパーティーは**ノーネクタイ**では行けない You can't attend the party *without a tie*. ‖ 彼女はいつも**ノーブラ**だ She *never wears a bra*. ／She always goes *braless*.（➤ この go は「…で通

す」) ‖ 警察はその男にノーマークだった The police were *not on the alert for* the man.

2【否定】 **no** ▶キムチは好きかと聞かれたら, 私はノーと答える If I were asked whether or not I liked kimchi, I would answer *no* [I would say *no*].

> **危ないカタカナ語✸ ノー**
> あることばの頭につけて「…のない」の意味で使う「ノー…」は和製語が多い. 以下に例を挙げる.
> **ノーカット**「ノーカットの映画」は uncut movie (短くされていない) という.
> **ノークラッチ** クラッチ (clutch) がないことから「ノークラッチ」というが, 正しくは automatic transmission [drive] という.
> **ノースリーブ** sleeveless という形容詞がこれに相当する.「ノースリーブのブラウス」なら sleeveless blouse である.
> **ノーブラ** 英語では braless という.「ノーブラでいる」は don't wear a bra でよい.
> **ノーメイク** 文脈により no make-up (例えば She wears no make-up.) のようには言う.

ノーカウント ▶今の投球はノーカウントだ That pitch does*n't count*. (ノーカウントは和製語).

ノーゲーム ▶突然の豪雨で3回を終わったところでノーゲームになった Because of the sudden downpour, *the game was called off* after the third inning. ‖ 雨でノーゲームになった *The game was rained out*.

ノーコメント **no comment** ▶その男はノーコメントを続けている The man is still *refusing* (*to*) *comment*.

ノーコン 《野球》 ▶あのピッチャーはきょうはノーコンだ The pitcher has *no control* today. / The pitcher is *wild* today.
‖ **ノーコンピッチャー** a wild pitcher, a pitcher with poor control.

ノースカロライナ **North Carolina** (アメリカ南東部の州 ; 略 NC, N.C.).

ノースダコタ **North Dakota** (アメリカ中北部の州 ; 略 ND, N.Dak., N.D.).

ノータッチ ▶夫は子供たちの教育にはノータッチです My husband *doesn't involve himself* [*doesn't get involved*] *in* our children's education. ‖ 私はこの件に関してはノータッチ (＝無関係) だ I *have nothing to do with* the matter.

ノート **1【帳面】** a **notebook** ▶けいの引いてない [引いてある] ノート a blank [ruled] *notebook* ‖ これから言うことをノートに書き留めておくように Please write down what I'm about to say in your *notebooks*.
‖ **ノートパソコン** a notebook computer 《参考》 日本では和製語の「ノートパソコン」が広く使われるが, 英語では膝の上に置けるサイズのものは laptop computer または単に laptop ということが多い.
2【メモ】 **notes** ▶聴衆は講演者の言うことを克明にノートした The audience *took* [*made*] *notes of* everything the lecturer said. ‖ ノートを取ることに夢中で講義をよく理解していない学生がいる Some students are so engrossed in *taking notes* they fail to understand the lecture.

ノートルダム **Notre Dame** /nòutrə déim/ (聖母マリアに捧げられた大聖堂).

ノーハウ **know-how** ▶経営のノーハウ management *know-how* ‖ 彼はペンション経営の基本的ノーハウを知りたがっている He wants to get (the) basic *know-how* on running a resort inn.

ノーヒットノーラン 《野球》 ▶ノーヒットノーランを達成する pitch *a no-hitter* / pitch a *no-hit, no-run* game.

ノーブランド a **generic brand** 一形 ノーブランドの **generic** ▶ノーブランドのワイン *generic* (*brand* of) wine ‖ **ノーブランド商品** a generic product.

ノーベルしょう ノーベル賞 a **Nobel prize** ▶アウン・サン・スー・チーは1991年ノーベル平和賞を受賞した Aung San Suu Kyi won [was awarded] *the Nobel Peace Prize* [*the Nobel Prize for Peace*] in 1991.
‖ **ノーベル賞受賞者** a Nobel prize winner.

ノーマーク ▶ノーマークだった服部がゴールを決めた Hattori, who *was unmarked*, scored a goal. ‖ 我々はその1年生投手をノーマークだった We *haven't paid any special attention* to that freshman pitcher.

ノーマル **normal** ▶ノーマルな考え方 a *normal* way of thinking ‖ 体重60キロは私にはノーマルです My *normal* weight is 60 kilograms. ‖ この凍りついた道路ではノーマルタイヤは滑るかもしれない *Ordinary tires* may skid on this icy road.

のがす 逃す **miss** ＋目 ▶このチャンスを逃すな Don't *let* this chance *slip by*. / Don't *miss* this chance. ‖ 彼は惜しいチャンスを逃した It was a pity that he *missed* [*lost*] such a good chance.

のがれる 逃れる **escape** (from, out of) (危険などから) ; **evade** ＋目, **dodge** ＋目 (困難・責任などから) ; **avoid** ＋目 (ずるいことをして義務などから) ▶燃えている家から逃れる *escape from* [*out of*] a burning house ‖ 税金の支払いを逃れる *avoid* paying taxes ‖ 夏休み中は蒸し暑い東京を逃れて那須で過ごす予定です I'm planning to stay at Nasu during the summer vacation to *get away from* the heat and humidity of Tokyo. ‖ 彼女はその生徒のけがの責任を逃れ (＝避け) ようとしている She is trying to *evade* [*dodge*] her responsibility for the student's injury.
▶《慣用表現》その大地震の日, わが家は旅行に出ていて難を逃れることができた On the day the big earthquake hit, our family *escaped tragedy* because we were away on a trip.

のき 軒 **the eaves** (➤ 通常複数形で) ▶私たちは軒先で雨宿りした We took shelter from the rain *under the eaves*. ‖ 軒下にツバメが巣を作った Some swallows built their nests *under our eaves*. ‖ その通りにはみやげ物屋が軒を並べている Souvenir shops *stand side by side* along the street. / The street *is lined with* souvenir shops.

のぎく 野菊 《植物》 a **wild chrysanthemum**.

のきなみ 軒並み ▶2回戦で有力チームが軒並み (＝続けざまに) 敗退した The favorites were defeated *back to back* [*one after another*] in the round two games. ‖ 台風のため午後の便は軒並み欠航となった *All* (the) afternoon flights [Afternoon flights *across the board*] were canceled due to the typhoon.

のく 退く →どく.

ノクターン 《音楽》 a **nocturne** /nɑ́:ktəːrn/.

のけぞる のけ反る **bend backward** ▶野間先生は巨体をのけぞらせて大笑いした Mr. Noma roared with laughter, *bending* his big body *backward*. ‖ 打者は内角の速球にのけぞった An inside fastball made the batter *arch his back*. (「背中を弓形に曲げた」の意).

のけもの 除け者 an **odd one out** (仲間はずれの人) ; an **outcast** (社会から追放された人物) ▶クラスのみんながその子をのけ者にした (＝遠ざけた) His classmates *treated* him *like an outsider* [*ostracized* him]. ‖

私は将棋がへたなのでゲームのたびにのけ者にされる Since I'm a poor shogi player, I *am left out in the cold* every time they play. (●「全く無視される」の意).

のける 除ける remove +目 (取り除く) ▶不良品をのける *remove* defective products ‖ 私の分はのけといてよ *Keep* [*Save*] some for me, OK?

-のける ▶彼女は私が部長に言えなかったことをいとも簡単に言ってのけた She *told* the manager *without any hesitation* what I had been unable to say. ‖ 学生たちはその企画を見事にやってのけた The students *pulled* that plan *off* beautifully. (➤ pull off は「困難なことをやってのける」).

のこぎり 鋸 a saw /sɔː/ ▶のこぎりで丸太を切る cut a log with *a saw* / saw a log (➤ この saw は「のこぎりを引く」という動詞; ただし, 欧米ののこぎりは押して使う) ‖ 糸のこ(ぎり) a coping saw.

のこす 残す 1【余す】leave +目; save +目 (節約して) ▶お姉ちゃんにも少しおやつを残しておきなさいよ *Leave* some of the snacks for your sister. ‖ 私にもおやつ残しといてね *Leave* [*Save*] me some snacks. ‖ 彼は仕事を半分残した He *left* his work half-done. (➤ left は leave の過去形) ‖ ポチにやろうと肉を半分残した I *saved* half of the meat to give to Pochi.

▶卒業まであと一月を残すばかりだ There is only one month *left* [*to go*] before graduation. (➤ to go は「残っている」の意).

✉《お悔やみ状で》残されたご家族の皆さまに何と申し上げてよいかわかりません I don't know what to say to console you *who have been left behind*.

2【あとにとどめる】leave (behind) ▶子供たちにばく大な財産を残す *leave* a large fortune to one's children ‖ (与謝)蕪村は画家としても後世に名を残した Buson *left* his name to posterity as a painter as well. ‖ アンデルセンは多くのすぐれた童話を残した Andersen *left behind* him many wonderful (children's) stories.

▶彼女は幼い子供をたった1人残して買い物に出かけた She went shopping, *leaving* her little child all alone. ‖ 私は放課後学校に残された I *was kept* after school. (➤ keep は「(人を)引き留める」) / I *was told to stay* after school. ‖ 犯人は凶器に指紋を残していた The murderer *left* his fingerprint(s) on the weapon.

のこのこ shamelessly (あつかましく); nonchalantly /nàːnʃəláːntli/ (平気で) ▶呼ばれもしないパーティーにのこのこ出掛けるものではありません It would be *shameless* [*brazen*] of you to crash the party. ‖ 会議が始まって1時間もした頃彼はのこのこやって来た He showed up at the meeting *nonchalantly* one hour after it started.

のこらず 残らず all (全部); everything (1つ1つ皆) ▶きみの知っていることを残らず(=すべて)警察に話したらどうだい? Why don't you tell the police *everything* you know? ‖ 容疑者は一人残らず捕らえられた *Every one of* the suspects was arrested. / *All of* the suspects were arrested.

のこり 残り the rest, the remainder (残りの人・物); the remains (残りの物, 残がい); the leftovers (料理の残り) ▶このクラスの生徒のうち20人は福岡出身で, 残りは他県から来ている Twenty students in this class are from Fukuoka, and *the rest* [*the others* / *the remainder*] are from other prefectures. ‖ 食事の残りを犬にやった I gave *the leftovers* [*the remains* of the meal] to my dog. ‖ 支払いを済ませたら残りは500円硬貨1枚だった After paying (the bill), I *was left with* a single 500-yen coin. ‖ 10から2を引くと残りは8だ Two from ten *leaves* eight. ‖ 残り2日しかない I have only two days *left*. ‖ ことわざ 残り物には福がある There is luck in the last piece. / There is still good fortune to be found in what's left over. (➤ ともに日本語からの直訳).

のこりすくない 残り少ない ▶時間[砂糖]が残り少なくなってきた Time [Sugar] *is running short*. / We *are running out of* time [sugar]. ‖ 私の人生も残り少なくなってきた I *don't have much time left* (to live). ‖ ことしも残り少なくなった There *aren't many* days *left* before the end of the year. ‖ 夏休みも残り少なくなってきた The summer vacation *is coming to an end*.

のこる 残る 1【余る】be left ▶20から15を引くと5残る If you take 15 away from 20, 5 *is left*. / 15 from 20 *leaves* 5. ‖ グラスにまだワインが少し残ってるよ There's a little wine *left* in your glass. ‖ 対話「お金いくら残ってる?」「全然」"How much money *is left*?" "None." ‖ まだ仕事が残っている I *still have* (some) work to do.

2【消えないで存在する】remain ▶小田原城は現在では石垣だけが残っている At present, only the stonewall of Odawara Castle *remains*. ‖ 妻籠(つまご)には昔の古い町並みがそのまま残っている In Tsumago, the old houses and streets *remain* unchanged [as they were built a long time ago]. ‖ このイギリス旅行は私の記憶にいつまでも残ることだろう This trip to Britain will always *remain* in my memory. ‖ その風習は今でも各地に残っている That custom still *survives* in many parts of the country. (➤ survive は「生き残る」).

▶彼の最後のことばはまだ私の耳に残っている His last words still *linger* in my ears. (➤ linger は「なかなか消えない」) ‖ この試合は悔いの残る試合になった This game *left a lot to be desired*. / This game turned out to be a *regrettable* one. ‖ 地面にはまだ雪が残っていた *There was still* snow on the ground. ‖ あれだけけちに徹すれば金が残るはずだよ He's a real tightwad. It is no wonder he *saved* so much money. ‖ 第一印象がいつまでも残るとは限らない First impressions are not always *lasting*.

3【そのままそこにいる】stay 《behind》 ▶《先生が》きみたちは放課後残れ! You *stay* (*behind*) after school. ‖ 兄は大学卒業後も研究室に残って助手になった After graduation from his university, my older brother worked in a laboratory and became the assistant to the professor.

のさばる ▶彼はクラブの監督になってからのさばっている(=いばっている) He *has been acting important* (ever) since he became the club manager. ‖ いじめっ子をのさばらせておくな Don't *let* the bullies *have their own way*. (➤「いじめっ子に勝手放題をさせるな」の意).

のざらし 野晒し ▶売れ残った中古車が野ざらしになっていた Some unsold used cars *were left exposed to the weather*.

のし 熨斗 *noshi*; a red-and-white folded paper decoration used on a formal gift (➤ 説明的な訳) ▶御礼ののし紙をかけて包んでください Could you please wrap it with *a noshi paper* expressing gratitude? ‖ のしをおかけしましょうか Shall I use *a*

noshi cover?
‖のし袋 a *noshi* envelope.
のしあがる のし上がる ▶彼は会長の権力をバックにして副社長にのし上がった With the backing of a company chairman, he *climbed* (*over others*) to the position of company vice-president.
のしかかる のし掛かる lean on [over] (もたれる); weigh on (重荷となる) ▶私にのしかからないでよ! Don't *lean over* me! ‖電車が急停車したので隣の人がのしかかってきた When the train stopped suddenly, the person next to me *fell against* me.
▶いちどきに彼の上に責任がのしかかった The responsibility *fell on* him all at once.
のじゅく 野宿する sleep outdoors; camp out (テントを張って) ▶彼は野宿しながら北海道へ行った He went to Hokkaido *camping out* [*sleeping outdoors*] the whole way. ‖ゆうべ彼はぐでんぐでんに酔っぱらって公園で野宿した He got dead drunk and *slept in the park* last night.
のす 1【勢力などが増す】rise in power, gain influence ▶彼女はグループの中でのしてきている She *is gaining influence* within the group.
2【殴り倒す】knock down [out], beat up (➤後者がより日本語に近い).
ノスタルジア nostalgia /nɑːstǽldʒə/ ▶ノスタルジアにひたる indulge oneself in *nostalgia*. →郷愁.
ノズル a nozzle.
のせる 乗せる・載せる 1【人を乗り物に】give ... a ride; carry +⊜ (運ぶ) ▶駅まで乗せてってやるよ I'll *give* you *a ride* [*a lift*] to the station. / I'll *drive* you to the station. ‖(ここへ来るのに)小沢君に乗せて来てもらったのよ I *got a ride* here from Ozawa. ‖途中で大沢君が乗せてくれた Osawa *picked* me *up* on the way. (➤pick up は「(途中で)車に乗せる, 拾う」).
▶飛行機は200人の乗客を乗せてホノルルへ向かった The plane left for Honolulu *carrying* two hundred passengers. ‖その船は1000人の乗客と100人の乗務員を乗せていた There were one thousand passengers and a crew of one hundred people *on board* the ship.
▶娘を自転車(の後ろ)に乗せて幼稚園まで送って行った I took my daughter to kindergarten *on* the back of my bicycle.
2【物の上に】put ... on; load (荷物を) ▶こんろの上にシチューなべを載せる *put* a stewpot *on* the stove ‖《提示》この上に物を載せないでください Don't *put* anything *on* top of this. ‖彼は積み荷をトラックに載せた He *loaded* (the) cargo onto the truck. ‖彼は人込みで息子を自分の肩に乗せて歩いた He *carried* his son *on* his shoulders through the crowd.
3【掲載する】carry +⊜ ▶その雑誌はおもしろい連載小説を載せていた The magazine *carried* an interesting serial novel. ‖わが社は地元の新聞に事務員募集の広告を載せている Our company *is advertising* [*running an ad*] for clerical staff in the local paper.
4【勢いづかせる】▶あんまり村木を乗せる(=おだてる)なよ. 手がつけられなくなるから Don't *flatter* Muraki too much, because he'll soon get a swelled [swollen] head. ‖そのもうけ話, 俺も一口乗せてもらいたいなあ I'd like to *participate in* [*join in*] that lucrative deal. / I'd like to *get a piece of the action*. (➤後者は俗語表現) ‖姉は販売員の口車にすっかり乗せられて化粧品をごっそり買い込んだ My (older) sister *was* completely *taken in* by the saleslady's honeyed words and bought a lot of cosmetics. (➤take in は「(人を)だます」の意のインフォーマルな表現).
のぞかせる 覗かせる ▶彼は自信をのぞかせた He *showed* self-confidence. ‖太陽が雲間から顔をのぞかせた The sun *peeked through* the clouds.
のぞき 覗き a peep (のぞき見) ▶あいつはのぞきの常習犯なんだ He is *a Peeping Tom*. ‖のぞき穴 a peephole (ドアの) ‖のぞき趣味 voyeurism /vwɑːjɔ́ːrìzəm ‖ vwaɪə́ːr-/.
のぞきこむ 覗き込む peer into (目をこらして); peep into (穴からこっそりと) ▶顕微鏡をのぞき込む *peer into* a microscope ‖医者は私の目をのぞき込んで「緑内障の気味がありますね」と言った The doctor *peered into* my eyes and said, "You have a touch of glaucoma." ‖彼は隣の乗客のスポーツ紙を肩越しにのぞき込んだ He *sneaked a look at* a sports paper over the shoulder of the man next to him (on the train).
のぞきみ 覗き見 a peep 一動 (…を)のぞき見する peep《at, into》▶少年たちは垣根の後ろから泳いでいる女の子たちをのぞき見した The boys hid behind the hedge and *peeped at* the girls swimming.
¹のぞく 覗く 1【のぞき見する, ちょっと見る】look [peep] into (中を; peep は悪い行為のニュアンスが強い); look out of (外を) ▶少年は鍵穴から部屋の中をのぞいた The boy *looked* [*peeped*] *into* the room through the keyhole. ‖ドアを開けて中をのぞいてごらん Open the door and *look inside*. ‖誰かが家の中をのぞいている Somebody *is looking inside* our house. ‖その入院患者は窓の外をのぞいた The hospital patient *looked out* the window.
2【ちょっと立ち寄る】▶ちょっとこのリサイクルショップをのぞいてみない? Why don't we *have a look in* [*drop in at*] this recycled-goods store? ‖帰りにおじの会社をのぞいてみよう I think I'll *look in on* my uncle at his office on my way home. (➤look in on は「(人を)ちょっと訪ねる」).
3【一部分だけが見える】▶雲間からまた太陽がのぞいた The sun *peeped out* from behind the clouds again. ‖トシちゃん, おへそがのぞいてるよ! Hey, Toshi-chan, your belly button's *showing*!
²のぞく 除く 1【除去する】remove +⊜; get rid of (いやなものを) ▶我々は彼の名前を名簿から除いた We *removed* his name from the list. / We *struck* his name *from* [*off*] the list. ‖邪魔者は除け *Get rid of* [*Weed out*] those who stand in our way.
2【除外する】exclude +⊜
語法 「…を除いて」の意を表すには, excluding ... (…を含めないで), except ..., except for ... (…を例外として; 前者は文頭に置かないが, 後者は可能), but ... (…以外; 堅い言い方)のような言い方がある.
▶17歳未満の若者を除く *exclude* young people under seventeen ‖搭乗員を除いて300名がその飛行機に乗っていた *Excluding* the crew, there were 300 people on the plane. ‖トムを除いてクラスの全員がそのテストに通った The whole class passed the test *except* (*for*) Tom. ‖少し頭痛がするのを除けばきょうは元気です *Except for* [*Aside from*] a slight headache, I feel fine today. ‖乗客は私たち二人を除いて全員ヨーロッパ人だった All the passengers *except* us two were Europeans. ‖日曜日を除いてくれればいつでもいいよ Any time will be okay *except* Sunday. ‖石田君を除いて全員出席した Everyone *but* Ishida was present. ‖「微分」は今回の出題範

囲から除く Differential calculus is *not* going to *be on* the test.

のそのそ ▶末っ子の男の子は後ろからのそのそついて行った The youngest boy tagged along after them *slowly*. ‖ クマがおりの中をのそのそ歩き回っている The bear *is ambling around* in the cage *slowly*.

のぞましい 望ましい **desirable**（好ましい）; **advisable** /ədváɪzəbəl/（勧められる）▶望ましい人間関係 *desirable* interpersonal relationships [relations] ‖ 健康を維持したいのなら半年に１度は健康診断を受けることが望ましい If you want to maintain good health, *it is desirable* [*advisable*] to get a physical examination at least every six months. ‖ 彼はきみたちにとって望ましくない人物だ He is an *undesirable* person for you.

のぞみ 望み **1【願望, 希望】**(a) **hope**; a **wish**（すぐにはかなえられそうにない願いごと）; a **dream**（理想, 夢）; (a) **desire**（強い願い）→希望 ▶望みは高くもて Have high *hopes*. ／Aim high. ‖ 私の望みは自分のブティックを持つことです My *dream* is to have my own boutique. ‖ 私の望みはかなった My *wish* was fulfilled.

▶安藤さん一家は長年の望みがかなってニュージーランドへ移住した The Andos' *long-cherished dream* of living in New Zealand came true when they moved there. ‖ どんなときでも望みを捨ててはいけない No matter what happens, you must keep your *hope(s)* up [you must not give up *hope*]. ‖ 子供に望みをかけ過ぎてはいけない You shouldn't *expect* too much *of* your child(ren). ‖ 物事はそうそう自分の望みどおりにはいかないよ Things don't always go *as you expect*.

2【見込み, 可能性】hope; a **chance**（有望な見込み）; (a) **prospect**（予想）▶飛行機墜落後も彼女が生存している望みはまだある [ほとんどない] There is still some [is little] *hope* that she has survived the plane crash. ‖ 彼には成功の望みは全くない He has no *chance* of succeeding [success]. ‖ この１勝で横綱は優勝に望みをつないだ Winning this bout has kept the yokozuna's *hope* of victory alive. (➤ keep ... alive は「…を消さないで残す」) ‖ 近いうちに平和になるという望みはない There is no immediate *prospect* of peace.

のぞむ 望む･臨む **1【将来のことを希望する】hope** +目; **want** +目（…したい, ほしい）; **wish** +目（すぐには実現できないことを）▶彼は青森支店への転勤を望んでいる He *hopes* he will be transferred to the Aomori branch office. ‖ どの親も子供の幸福を望んでいる All parents *wish* their children happiness. (● (×) wish (that) their children will be happy はあやまり. that のあとは仮定法になる. この場合は次例のように hope を用いる →願う, いい) ／All parents *hope* their children will be happy.

> 【文型】
> (自分が)…することを望む
> **want to** do
> **hope to** do
>
> ◀解説▶ **want to** do が可能性に関係なく言う「…したい」という強い欲求なのに対して, **hope to** do は「…できたらいいな」という可能性のある望みをいう.

▶彼女は海外留学を望んでいる She *hopes* [*wants* ／ *wishes*] *to* study overseas. (● wish to do は want to do の堅い言い方) ‖ 父は田舎暮らしを望んでいる My father *wants to* live in the country. ‖ ガールフレンドとの結婚を望んでいるのですか Do you *want* [Are you *hoping*] *to* marry your girlfriend?

▶彼女は自分から望んで青年海外協力隊に加わった She joined the Japan Overseas Cooperation Volunteers *of her own choice*. (➤ of one's own choice は「自分で選んで, 自分の好きで」) ‖ 望もうと望むまいときみは彼と仕事をしなければならない *Whether you like it or not*, you must work with him.

2【相手に期待する】want +目, **hope** +目; **expect** +目

> 【文型】
> 人(A)が…することを望む
> **want** A **to** do
> **wish** A **to** do
> ➤ hope にはこの文型がない
>
> ◀解説▶ **wish** は堅い語で, すぐにはかなえられそうにない望みを指すことが多い.

▶彼らは我々の援助を望んでいる They *want* us to help them. ／They *are hoping* for our help. ／They *hope* (that) we (will) help them.

▶一般に親は子供に多くを望み過ぎる Generally, parents tend to *expect* too much of their children. ‖ きみが望むなら, レポートを手伝ってあげる *If you want* [*wish*], I'll help you with your report.

3【得たいと思う】want +目; **desire** +目（切望する）▶すべての人が平和を望んでいる All people *want* [*desire*] peace. ‖ 恵子さんは社長の息子の嫁にと望まれている Keiko *is wanted as* a bride for the president's son. ‖ 彼女は(首相に)望まれて駐スウェーデン大使になった She accepted the (Prime Minister's) *request* to become ambassador to Sweden.

4【遠くを見渡す】can see（人が）; **command**（場所・景色などが）▶この天守閣からは松本市を一望に望める From this castle tower, you *can see* the entire city of Matsumoto. ‖ 私の家は城ケ島を望む高台に建っている My house stands on a hill *commanding a view of* Jogashima.

5【開けた場所に面する】face +目 ▶そのホテルは海に臨んでいる The hotel *looks over* [*looks out over*, *faces*] the sea.

6【直面する, 出席する】▶私たちは決意も新たに試合に臨んだ We *participated in* the match with renewed determination. ‖ 首相は期待を込めて日米首脳会談に臨んだ The Prime Minister *attended* the Japan-U.S. Summit with high expectations.

7【対処する】▶違反者には厳罰をもって臨むつもりだ Anyone who breaks these rules *will be* severely punished.

のたうちまわる **writhe** /raɪð/ ▶夜中に虫歯が痛くて痛くて, のたうちまわっちゃったよ I *writhed* in agony with an unbearable toothache which started in the middle of the night.

のだて 野点 *nodate*; an **open-air tea ceremony**.

のたれじに 野垂れ死に ▶昔は旅の途中で野たれ死にする人も多かった In former times, many travelers *collapsed and died by the roadside* during their journey. (●「みじめな死に方をする」の意なら die like a dog, die a dog's death, come to a miserable end のように訳してもよい).

のち 後 **later**（あとで）; **afterward**（その後）▶晴れ, 後曇

り Fair, *later* cloudy. ‖ 後に彼は有名な彫刻家になった He *later* became a famous sculptor. ‖ 後になって彼が亡くなっていたことがわかった I found out *afterward* that he had died. ‖ 彼は(それから)10年の後彼女とばったり再会した He ran into her again *after* ten years [ten years *later*].

のちのち 後々 the future ▶後々の参考に事故の詳細な記録を残す leave a detailed record of the accident for *future* reference.

のちほど 後程 later (on) ▶では, 後ほど(お会いしましょう) See you *later*. ‖ 後ほどお電話いたします I'll call you *later* (*on*).

ノック 1【たたくこと】a **knock** ▶部屋に入るときはノックしなさい, 横山君 *Knock on* [*at*] the door before you come in, Yokoyama. ‖ ドアをノックする音が聞こえた I heard someone *knock on* the door. / There was a knock at the door. 《参考》ノックの「トントン」「コツコツ」は knock knock という.

2【野球】**hitting grounders and flies for practice**

‖ **ノックバット** a fungo bat [stick].

危ないカタカナ語✹ ノック

ドアの「ノック」や,「ノックアウト」の「ノック」はそれぞれ knock, knockout でよいが, 野球の「ノック」は knock とはいわない.「練習のためにゴロやフライを打つこと」と説明的にいうしかない.「ノック用の長いバット」のことを fungo bat [stick] というが, この fungo /fʌ́ŋgoʊ/ は「ノックしたフライ」のこと.

ノックアウト a **knockout** 《略 K.O. または KO》 **一動 ノックアウトする knock out** ▶彼は第 3 ラウンドに頭に一撃を受けてノックアウトされた He *was knocked out* [*was KO'd*] by a blow to the head in the third round. ‖ 我々は 3 連打でそのピッチャーをノックアウトした We *knocked* the pitcher *out of the box* by hitting 3 back-to-back singles. (➤ この box は「ピッチャーズマウンド」).

ノックダウン a **knockdown 一動 ノックダウンする knock down** ▶チャンピオンは第10ラウンドに相手に 2 度ノックダウンを与えた The champion *knocked* his opponent *down* twice in the tenth round.

のっけから from the start [beginning] ▶あの天気予報のお姉さん, のっけからとちったよ That weather girl blew her lines *from the very start*.

のっしのっし ▶お相撲さんがのっしのっしと現れた A sumo wrestler came *lumbering* along. (➤ lumber は「重そうに歩く」).

のっそり ▶セントバーナードがのっそり起き上がった The Saint Bernard *slowly* [*heavily*] got up. / The Saint Bernard *lumbered* to its feet. (➤ lumber は「重々しく動く」).

ノット 《海事》a **knot** /nɑːt/ ▶この船は時速20ノット出る This ship goes [has a speed of] 20 *knots* an hour.

のっとり 乗っ取り a **takeover**(会社などの) ; **hijacking**, a **hijack** (飛行機・客船などの)

‖ **乗っ取り犯人** a hijacker.

¹のっとる 乗っ取る take over(会社などを) ; **hijack** +㊐ (飛行機・客船などを) ; **annex** +㊐ (領土などを併合する) ▶その実業家は株を買い占めて会社を乗っ取った That businessman *took over* the company by buying up a majority of the shares.

▶武装ゲリラがその旅客機を乗っ取った The armed guerrillas *hijacked* the passenger plane. ‖ 領土を乗っ取る国もある Some countries *annex* territory. →ハイジャック.

²のっとる 則る observe +㊐ (遵守する) ▶スポーツマンシップにのっとって正々堂々と戦います We promise to play fair and square and *observe* sportsmanship at all times. ‖ 宮中の儀式は古式にのっとって行われる The ceremonies in the Imperial Court are held *in accordance with* the forms prescribed by tradition.

のっぴきならない ▶きのうはのっぴきならない事情があって会合を欠席しました I was absent from the meeting yesterday due to *unavoidable* circumstances. ‖ 彼はのっぴきならない立場に追い込まれている He's *in big trouble* [*in hot water*] now. (➤ be in hot water は「(自分がへまをやって)苦境にある」の意のインフォーマルな表現).

▶彼女はあとでのっぴきならないことになるようなことはけっして言わない She never *commits herself*. (➤ commit oneself は「深くかかわる」).

のっぺらぼう a **flat and smooth** [**monotonous**] **face**.

のっぺり ▶彼女はのっぺりした顔をしている She has a *smooth, blank* [*expressionless*] face.

のっぽ a **beanpole** ▶彼は大変なのっぽだ He is a real *beanpole* [《米また》*string bean*].

-ので **because, since** (➤ 節が続く) ; **because of, due to** (➤ 名詞(句)が続く)

語法 (1) **because** は I'm angry at him *because* he lied to me. (私にうそをついたので, 私は彼に対して腹を立てている) のように, 原因・理由と結果・行動が直接結びついて, 原因・理由を強く言いたいときに用いる語で, 日本語の「…ので」よりも意味が強い. Why...? (なぜ…か) と原因・理由を問われて答えるときに用いることが多い.

(2) **since** は Many parts are made of aluminum *since* aluminum is lighter than steel. (アルミニウムは鋼より軽いので, 多くの部品はアルミニウム製である) のように, 理由が明らかか, または, because ほど原因・理由と結果の結びつきが強くない場合に用いる. しばしば, 文頭に置かれる.

(3) 学習者は「-ので」や「-(だ)から」=because あるいは=since と覚えているので, これらを使いすぎる傾向がある. 因果関係を強調しない場合は because や since を使わず, **..., so** のほうが自然なことも多い. ..., so は＜原因・理由＞＋, **so** ＋＜結果・行動＞と, 原因や理由より後半の結果・行動に焦点を当てた言い方になる.「眠かったので昼寝をした」は, I was sleepy, *so* I took a nap. (眠くなった, それで昼寝をした)のように, 物事が起きた順に, 原因や理由をことさら強調しないで言うのが普通. I took a nap *because* I was sleepy. とすると, 理由を聞かれての答えならともかく, この英語だけではどうして理由を強調するのかわからない, やや不自然な文になる. 事実を時間順にさらりと言うのなら, I was sleepy *and* took a nap. (眠くなって昼寝をした) でもよい.「あすは出るのが早いから [ので] 早く寝よう」も, because を使いたくなるのをぐっと抑えて,「早く寝よう」のほうを主にして, I have to leave early tomorrow, so I think I'll go to bed early. とする.

▶バスに乗り損ねたので遅れた I was late *because* [*since*] I missed the bus. (🔔 文の主眼は because [since] I missed the bus という理由にある. 普通に事実を述べるなら I missed the bus, *so* I was late. がよい) ‖ 雨が降ったので試合は延期された The game was postponed *because of* rain [*because* it rained].

(➤ due to rain (雨のために) でもよい) ‖ もう遅いので家に帰ります It's getting late, *so* I'd better head (on) home. (● 日本人は後半を I'll go home now. と言いがちだが, これは極めて無愛想で, 失礼な言い方になる. それは will が今急に思い立って決めたことを表し, 何か不愉快なことがあったせいではないか, と思わせるからである).

【文型】
非常に A, [B] なので～である
so A **that** S + V
➤ A は形容詞・副詞
such a B **that** S + V
➤ B は名詞

▶科学技術の進歩が激しいので, コンピュータは数年で時代遅れになってしまう Technology advances *so* fast *that* computers become outdated in a few years. ‖ ケーキがひどく甘かったので私は気持ちが悪くなった The cake was *so* sweet (*that*) it made me feel sick. (● that はしばしば省略する) ‖ とても難しいパズルだったのでいくら頑張っても解けなかった It was *such* a difficult puzzle *that* I couldn't solve it no matter how hard I tried. (● 学習者はよく, (×)It was such a difficult puzzle (that) I couldn't solve it. (そのパズルはあまりに難しくて解けなかった) というような英文を作るが, ネイティブはこうは言わない. 難しさとそれが解けない事に必然性が無いからである. It was such a difficult puzzle that it took me a week to solve it. (あまりに難しくて解くのに1週間かかった) ならOK. →直訳の落とし穴).

▶とても喉が渇いたので水を1杯飲んだ I was very thirsty, *so* I drank a glass of water. (● この so は「それで」の意 ; この文を so thirsty that とするのは不自然).

直訳の落とし穴「とても眠かったので寝た」

「とても [非常に] …なので～した」というと so … that の構文を思い出す人が多いが, 使い方には注意が必要. so … that は原因 [理由] と結果としての行動の間に明確な因果関係や必然性があることを表す言い方で, その行動が"どうしようもなく～した」「そうせざるを得なかった」というような, 選択の余地のないものであることを示す. 具体的には「とても眠かったので寝た」では因果関係は希薄で, 例えば,「眠かったので眠気覚ましに濃いコーヒーを飲んだ [二, 三度深呼吸をして眠気を飛ばした]」もありうる. したがって, (×)I was so sleepy (that) I went to bed. は不可で, 結果としての行動を示すだけの so (そこで) を用いて, I was very sleepy, *so* I went to bed. とする.「眠くて眠くてとても目をあけていられなかった」は因果関係が明確で, 両者が強く結びついているので, I was so sleepy that I could hardly keep my eyes open. でよい.「彼はひどく汗をかいたのでシャワーを浴びた」も, 例えばタオルで拭くことでもよいのだから, (×)He sweated so much that he took a shower. は不可で, He sweated a lot, *so* he took a shower. とする. また, He had sweated *so* much *that* he needed a shower. (たくさん汗をかいたのでシャワーを浴びる必要があった) であれば, 必然性が示されているので何の問題もない文となる.

のてん 野天 →露天風呂.

のど 喉 **1**【器官の】**the throat** ▶喉をうるおす *quench one's thirst* ‖ かぜを引いて喉が痛いよ I've got a sore *throat* from a cold. ‖ そんなにおしんこを食べると喉が渇くよ You'll *get thirsty* if you eat so many pickles. ‖ 彼女は心配のあまり食事が喉を通らないほどだった She was so worried that she *could hardly eat*. ／She *lost her appetite* from anxiety. ‖ その猫はゴロゴロと喉を鳴らしていた The cat was *purring* loudly.

▶《慣用表現》彼は喉から手が出るほどそのクラシックカメラを欲しがっている He *is dying to have* that classic camera. ／He *wants* that classic camera *bad*. (➤ bad は「ひどく」) ‖ そのことばは喉まで出かかっていたが, どうしても思い出せなかった I just could not recall the word, though it *was on the tip of my tongue*.

‖**喉あめ** a cough drop ‖**喉仏** the Adam's apple.

2【声】▶彼女はいい喉をしている She has a good *singing voice*. ‖**しろうと喉自慢大会** an amateur singing contest.

のどかな **peaceful, calm** ▶のどかな春の一日 a *peaceful* [*calm*] spring day ‖ 牧場では牛がのどかに草を食べていた Cattle were grazing *peacefully* in the pasture.

のどごし のど越し ▶ビールののど越し *a soothing sensation experienced as beer goes down* (*one's throat*) ‖ このそばはのど越しがいい These buckwheat noodles *are nice and smooth as they go down the throat*.

のどちんこ 《解剖学》**the uvula** /júːvjələ/.

のどもと 喉元 ▶ ことわざ 喉元過ぎれば熱さを忘れる Once past your throat, heat is forgotten. (➤ 日本語からの直訳) ／A hardship is forgotten after it has been overcome. (➤ 意訳).

-のに **1**【…にもかかわらず】**although, though** (➤ 節が続く ; 前者が後者より堅い語) ; **in spite of, despite** (➤ 名詞(句)が続く) ▶きのう雨が降っていたのに子供たちは野球をやった The children played baseball yesterday *though* it was raining. ／The children played baseball yesterday *despite* [*in spite of*] the rain. ‖ 一生懸命走ったのに終バスに間に合わなかった *Although* I ran for all I was worth, I couldn't catch the last bus. ‖ これらの輸入車は1000万円以上するのによく売れる These imported cars sell well, *even though* they cost more than ten million yen. (● even though は although より強意で, 前後の対比が際だつときに用いる) ‖ よせと言ったのに *I told you* not to do it.

2【一方】**while ; when** (…なのに) ▶お兄さんは勉強なのに彼は怠け者だ His (older) brother is diligent, *while* he is lazy. ‖ バスのほうが安いのにどうしてあなたはそこへ電車で行くんですか Why are you going there by train *when* the bus is cheaper?

3【願望, 不満, 仮定】

【文型】
人・もの(A)が…だといいのに
I wish (**that**) A + **did.**
➤ 現在の不満は過去形 did や were で表す. 意思を表して would を, 可能性を表して could を用いる
…すればいいのに
should do
…しさえすればよいのに
if only S + V
➤「ただ…しさえ[…でありさえ]すれば」と一事を強調する. 後悔や心残りなどを表すことが多い.「もし…ならば, …なのに」は仮定法 if の文で表せる. →[2]もし

▶娘がもう少し勉強を頑張ってくれるといいのに I *wish* my daughter *would* study harder. ‖ 夫がもう少し心遣いを見せてくれればいいのに *I wish* my husband *would* be more considerate. ‖ あと5センチ背が高かったらよかったのに *I wish* I *were* [*was*] five centimeters taller. (一人称および三人称単数でも文法的には were だが, was を使う人も多い) ‖ おじいちゃん, おばあちゃんが今も元気で, もっと孝行できるとよかったのに *I wish* my grandpa and grandma were (still) alive, and *that* I *could* be a better grandson [granddaughter] (to them).

▶晴れていれば富士山が見えたのに If it were a clear day today, *I would be able to see* Mt. Fuji. ‖ 地下鉄で来ればもっと早く来られたのに If you had taken the subway, *you could have arrived* earlier. ‖ 声を掛けてくれれば喜んで手を貸してあげたのに If you had asked me, *I would have been* willing to give you a hand.

▶嫌なら断ればいいのに You *should* turn it down if you don't want to do it. ‖ よせばいいのに *You shouldn't do that.* ‖ どうせ言っても聞かないんだから, ほっとけばよいのに She [He] never listens to what you want to say, so you *should leave her* [*him*] *alone.* ‖ お互いにもっと早く知り合っていたらよかったのに *If only* we had met (each other) earlier. ／*I wish* we *had* met (each other) earlier.

▶せめて「ありがとう」ぐらい言ってくれてもいいのに You *might* at least say, "Thank you." (すべきなのにしないことに対して, いらだちや非難を表す).

4【強調して】▶一緒に来いと言うのに *I'm telling you* to come with me. ‖ だめだと言うのに When I say no, I mean it!

5【…のために】to do, for ▶辞書はことばの意味を調べるのに使う We use a dictionary *to* look up the meaning of words.

ののしる 罵る abuse /əbjúːz/ +目 (汚いことばを乱用する); **swear at, curse** +目 (➤ ともに人をのろうことばを吐くことをいうが, 前者は宗教上不敬に当たることばを使う場合を指す); **call ... names** (…を「ばか」「とんま」などと言ってののしる) ▶彼女は私を口汚くののしった She *abused* me with foul language. ‖ 彼は彼女を愚かだと言ってひどくののしった He *cursed* (*and swore at*) her for stupidity. ‖ 男は妻にののしられてかっとなった The man got mad when his wife *called* him *names*.

-のは

> **【文型】**
> **～なのは A だ**
> **It is** A **that** ～.
> **～なのは人(B)だ**
> **It is** B **who** ～.
> B **is the one who** ～.
>
> **《解説》** (1)**It is A that ～.** はふつう強調構文と呼ばれる改まった文型で, 強調するものをAの位置に出す. It is と that を消しても文章としての形はくずれないのがふつう.
> (2)強調されるのが人のときには that はしばしば who になる.

▶私たちがネパール旅行に行ったのは一昨年の夏だった *It was* the summer before last *that* we took a trip to Nepal. (「一昨年の夏」を特に強調しないのであればふつうに We took a trip to Nepal the summer before last. でよい) ‖ 金メダルを獲得したのはアメリカ人選手だった *It was* an American athlete *who* won the gold medal. ‖ きのう最後に退社したのは私です I *was the one who* left the office last. (「我々です」のときは We were the ones who ... となる).

> **【文型】**
> **～なのは A だ**
> **It is** A **that** S + V.
> **…するのは A だ**
> **It is** A **to** do.
> ➤ A は形容詞・名詞
>
> **《解説》** 英語は主語が長くなるのを避ける傾向があり, that の文や to do を文の頭に出す代わりに, it を主語にして, **It is ... that** [**to do**] ～. という言い方をする.

▶彼女がきみに腹を立てるのは当然だ *It's* (quite / only) natural *that* she should get [be] angry with you. (be angry は現在も怒っていることを表す) ‖ 外でバーベキューパーティーをするのは楽しい *It's* fun *to* have a barbecue outside. ／Hav*ing* an outdoor barbecue is fun. ‖ すべてを覚えているのは不可能だ *It is* impossible *to* remember everything.

> **【文型】**
> **人・物(A)が…するのは B だ**
> **It is** B **for** A **to** do.
> **人(A)が…するのは C だ**
> **It is** C **of** A **to** do.
> ➤ B, C は形容詞
>
> **《解説》** (1)to do の主語は for A の形でその前に置く. このとき A ≠ B の関係にある.
> (2)A ＝ C の関係が成り立つときには of A の形で主語を示す. この C には good, kind, nice(親切な); foolish(ばかな); rude(乱暴な); sensible(気がきく)など, 人をほめたり, けなす語が多い.

▶幼児にとってじっとしているのはたやすくない *It's* not easy *for* little children *to* keep still. ‖ 彼のプロポーズを断ったのは私がばかだった *It was* foolish *of* me *to* turn down his (marriage) proposal (of marriage). ／I was foolish to turn down his proposal (of marriage). (前者は行為が愚か, といっているのに対し, 後者は私が愚かといっている).

▶知りたいのは(＝ことは)どうしてきみがそんなことをしたかだ *What* I want to know is why you did that. ‖ あなたに必要なのは自分に自信をもつことだ *What* you need is (to have) confidence in yourself. ‖ 動物をいじめるのはやめなさい Stop abus*ing* [tortur*ing*] animals.

のばす 伸ばす・延ばす

> **訳語メニュー**
> 長さを長くする →lengthen, extend **1**
> 髪やひげを伸ばす →grow (long) **1**
> まっすぐにする →straighten **2**
> 伸縮するものを伸ばす →stretch **2**
> 能力を伸ばす →develop **4**
> 延期する →put off **6**

1【長さを長くする】lengthen /léŋkθən/ +目, **make ... longer**; **extend** +目 (延長する) ▶洋服屋にジャケットの袖を2センチ伸ばしてくれるように頼んだ I asked the tailor to *lengthen* my coat sleeves by two centimeters. ‖ 流行に合わせてスカートの丈を伸ばした(＝すそをおろした) I *let* the hems of my skirts *down* to keep in style. ‖ 最後のドの音はもっと伸ばして歌ってください Please *make* the last 'doh' (note) *lon-*

ger. ／Please *lengthen* the last 'doh' (note).
▶つめを伸ばしておくんじゃありません Don't let your nails *grow out*. ／Don't *wear* your nails *long*. ‖兄はあごひげを伸ばし始めた My (older) brother began to *grow* a beard. ‖隣の桜の木がうちの屋根の上に枝を伸ばしている My neighbor's cherry tree *extends* over the roof of my house.
▶市当局は地下鉄を30キロ延ばす計画だ The city government plans to *extend* the subway another thirty kilometers.
2【まっすぐに，または平らにする】straighten ＋㊐，**stretch** ＋㊐；**smooth (out)**（平らにする）▶曲がったピンを伸ばす *straighten* a bent pin ‖思い切り手足［背筋］を伸ばしてごらん *Stretch* your arms and legs [spine] fully. ‖ストレートパーマをかけて縮れた髪を伸ばした I had my frizzy hair *straightened* with a straight permanent. ‖マラソンランナーたちはドリンクを取ろうと手を伸ばした The marathon runners *reached for* their drinks. ‖イソギンチャクが触手を伸ばして獲物を待っている A sea anemone is waiting with its antennae *extended* to catch its prey.
▶彼女はくしゃくしゃになった手紙を伸ばした She *smoothed out* a crumpled letter. ‖ズボンにアイロンをかけてしわを伸ばした I *ironed* the wrinkles *out of* my pants. ‖彼女は顔のしわを伸ばす（＝取り除く）ために整形手術した She had a facelift to *remove* wrinkles from her face.
3【面積を広げる】▶写真を四ツ切りに伸ばす *have* a picture *enlarged* to a 10″ ×12″ print ‖（パン）生地をこねて綿棒で延ばす knead the bread dough, and *roll it out* with the rolling pin ‖乳液を指先に少し取り，お顔にのばして十分マッサージします Take a small amount of milky lotion on your fingertips, *apply* [*spread*] it over your face, and massage it into the skin.
4【発展させる】develop ＋㊐（能力を）；**increase** ＋㊐（売り上げなどを）▶息子の演技力を伸ばしてやりたい I want to help my son (to) *develop* his acting skills. ‖今月こそ売り上げを伸ばそう This is the month we should *increase* our sales. ‖P社は創業以来順調に業績を伸ばしてきた P Company has steadily *increased* its sales since it was established.
5【時間を延長する】extend ＋㊐ ▶宿泊を2日間延ばしたいのですが Could I *extend* my stay for two more nights? ‖奈良での滞在を少し延ばしませんか Why don't you *stay* in Nara a little *longer*?
6【締め切りなどをずらす】put off；delay ＋㊐（やむを得ない事情で当初の予定［開始時刻］を遅らせる）▶家賃の支払いを来週まで延ばしてもらえませんか Can I *put off* [*defer*] payment of my rent until next week?（● defer payment は「延納する」に近い堅い言い方）‖彼女は旅行を1週間延ばした（＝遅らせた）She *delayed* her trip for a week. ‖母は販売店に洗濯機を修理してくれるまで支払いを延ばすと言った My mother told the dealer that she would *hold off* paying for the washing machine until they fixed it.（● hold off は「…するまで［してくれるまで］～を延ばす」というニュアンス）‖ことわざ きょうできることをあすに延ばすな Don't [Never] put off until tomorrow what you can do today.
7【殴って気絶させる】▶一発でやつをのばしてやった I *floored* him [*stretched* him *out*] with one blow.

のばなし 野放し ▶犬を野放しにする *leave* one's dog *loose* [*free*] ‖悪徳業者を野放しにするな Fraudulent [Crooked] businesses should not *be left uncontrolled*. ‖その国ではソフトウェアの複製行為は野放し状態である（＝はびこっている）Software piracy is *rampant* in that country.

のはら 野原 a **field** ▶あちこちにタンポポの咲いている野原 *a field* with blooming dandelions here and there.

のばら 野薔薇《植物》a **wild rose**.

のび 伸び 1【手足を伸ばすこと】▶少年は思い切り伸びをした The boy *stretched himself* to his full length.
2【伸びぐあい】▶この塗料はとてものびがよい This paint *goes on* [*spreads*] very easily.
3【成長】growth；development（発展）▶ことし，この商品の売り上げの大きな伸びは期待できない No sizable *growth* in the sales of this product can be expected this year.

のびあがる 伸び上がる ▶彼は人込みの中で伸び上がって前方を見た He *stood on tiptoe* [*craned his neck*] in the crowd to see ahead (of him).（➤ crane one's neck は「（よく見えるように）首を伸ばす」）.

のびざかり 伸び盛り ▶伸び盛りの子供にとってカルシウム不足はよくない A calcium deficiency is bad for *growing* children.

のびちぢみ 伸び縮み ▶伸び縮みするベルト an *elastic* belt ‖伸び縮みする（＝繰り出し式の）はしご an *extension* ladder ‖この生地は伸び縮みします This material *is elastic* [*stretchable*]. ‖イモムシは伸び縮みしながら進む Caterpillars move forward *by alternately stretching and contracting*.

のびなやむ 伸び悩む ▶最近パソコンの売り上げは伸び悩んでいる Recently, personal computer sales have *been sluggish* [have *plateaued*]. ‖うちの息子の成績は最近伸び悩んでいる These days our son's grades have *stopped improving* recently.

¹のびのび 延び延び ▶運動会は延び延びになった末，とうとう取りやめになった The athletic meet kept on being *put off from day to day*, and was finally called off. ‖台風で飛行機の出航が延び延びになった The plane's departure *was repeatedly postponed* due to the typhoon.
✉ **返事が延び延びになり申しわけありません** I am terribly sorry I *have delayed* my reply to you *for a long time*.

²のびのび 伸び伸び ▶子供たちにはできるだけのびのびと育ってもらいたいと思います I hope my children will grow up as *carefree* as possible. ‖大学受験さえなければもっとのびのびした高校生活を送れるのに Life in high school would be much more *relaxed* if it were not for the university entrance examinations. ‖ああ，田舎はのびのびできるなあ Ah, you can really *relax* [*take it easy*] in the country.

のびやかな 伸びやかな ▶サラ・ブライトマンの伸びやかな歌声 Sarah Brightman's *smooth and silky* (singing) voice.

のびる 伸びる・延びる

📖 訳語メニュー
成長する →grow **1**
延長される →be extended **1, 5**
まっすぐになる →stretch **2**
進歩する →improve **4**
延期される →be put off **6**

1【長さが長くなる】grow（成長する）；**be extended**

(延長される) ▶キリの木は伸びるのが早い Paulownia trees *grow* quickly. ‖ アサガオのつるが伸びてきた The morning glory vine started to *grow*. ‖ 私はことし背が5センチ伸びた I'*ve grown* (by) 5 centimeters this year. ‖ 髪が伸びているから床屋へ行きなさい Your hair has *grown too long*. Get a haircut at the barbershop.

▶ (掃除機の)コード, これ以上伸びないの？ This cord doesn't *extend* (any) further? ／Doesn't the cord *get longer*? ‖ 打球は意外に伸びなかった The ball *didn't go* as *far* as I thought (it would).

2【伸び縮みするものが長くなる】stretch ▶パンツのゴムが伸びてしまった The elastic in my briefs *has lost its stretch*. ‖ ラーメンが伸びちゃった The ramen noodles *have become* too *soft*.

▶《慣用表現》ついに財務省の高官に捜査の手が延びた The investigation at last *reached* a high-ranking official in the Ministry of Finance.

3【広がる】extend (範囲などが及ぶ); **stretch** (両脇に広がって続く); **range** (山などが連なる) ▶この道路は宗谷岬まで延びている This road *extends* to [as far as] Cape Soya.

▶ニューヨークでは, 多くのビルが垂直に伸びている Many buildings *stretch* upward [*expand* vertically] in New York. ‖ 奥羽山脈は青森県から福島県まで延びている The Ou Mountains *range* from Aomori to Fukushima.

▶この乳液はよくのびる This milky lotion *smoothes on* very well.

4【発展する】improve ▶彼女の数学の力はぐんと伸びた Her ability in math *has improved* considerably. ‖ その選手の記録は今年に入ってから飛躍的に伸びた That athlete's record *improved* drastically this year. ‖ 円高にもかかわらず輸入はそれほど伸びていない Despite the yen's appreciation, imports did not *increase*.

5【延長される】be extended ▶野球中継が30分延びた The live broadcast of the baseball game *was extended* by [for] thirty minutes. ‖ 日本人の平均寿命はまた延びた(＝長くなった) The average life expectancy of Japanese people *has increased*. ‖ 春分の日を過ぎると一日一日と日が延びてくる After the spring equinox, the days *become longer*.

6【延期される】be put off ▶レディ・ガガの来日は1か月[来月に]延びた Lady Gaga's visit to Japan *has been put off* for a month [till next month]. ‖ 教授が入院したので試験の日程が延びた The examination date *was postponed* [*was put off*] because the professor was hospitalized.

7【体が参る】▶アッパーカットをくらってそのボクサーはリングにのびた That boxer took an uppercut and *was floored* [*was knocked down* to the canvas]. ‖ このところの猛暑でみんなのびている We *are* all *worn out* from this constant intense heat.

ノブ a **knob** ‖ ドアノブ a doorknob.

のべ 延べ ▶この家の延べ床面積は200平方メートルです The *total* floor space of this house is 200 square meters. ‖ 延べ100人の研究者がその治療薬の開発に携わった A *total* of 100 researchers were involved in developing the cure. ‖ その工事は延べ日数で70日かかるだろう The construction work will require 70 *workdays*.

のべつ ▶妹はのべつ何か食べている My (younger) sister is eating something *all the time*. ‖ 彼女はのべつ幕なしにしゃべりまくった She talked *nonstop*. ／She talked *a mile a minute*.

のべぼう 延べ棒 a **bar, bullion** (➤ 後者は数えられない名詞) ▶金の延べ棒 a gold *bar*, gold *bullion*.

のべる 述べる speak +㊂ (話す); **express** +㊂ (表明する); **state** +㊂ (➤ 形式ばった場合の発言・書き物について用いる)

▶真実のみを述べてください *Speak* only the truth. ‖ 彼女は彼らの暖かいもてなしに謝辞を述べた She *expressed her gratitude* [*thanked them*] for their warm hospitality. ‖ 著者は最新作の中で自分の政治的見解を述べている The author *states* his political views in his latest work. ‖ 次の文を読んで大意を述べよ Read the following passage and *make a brief summary* of it.

のほうず 野放図 ▶セイタカアワダチソウはいったん根をおろすと野放図に広がってしまう Goldenrod spreads *rampantly* once it takes root.

のぼせあがる のぼせ上がる ▶一度くらい勝ったからってのぼせ上がるなよ Don't let this one victory *go to your head*! ‖ 三郎は礼子にのぼせ上がっている Saburo *has fallen head over heels for* Reiko. (➤ fall head over heels for は「…に夢中になる」の意のインフォーマルな表現).

のぼせる 1【ぼーっとなる】feel dizzy ▶長い間風呂に入っていてのぼせた I *felt dizzy* after staying in the hot bath too long.

2【夢中になる】be crazy《about》▶彼はクラスの女の子にのぼせている He *is crazy about* [*has a crush on*] a girl in his class.

のほほん ▶あした試験だというのに, そんなにのほほんとしていていいの？ Is it OK for you to *be goofing off* [*taking it easy*] like that with an exam tomorrow?

¹のぼり 上り 1【上昇】(an) **ascent** 一形 **上りの up**; **uphill** (上り坂の) ▶上りのエスカレーター an *up* escalator ‖ 駅から彼女の家まで道はずっと急な[ゆるやかな]上りだった The road made a steep [gentle] *ascent* all the way from the station to her house. ‖ さあ, ここからずっと上りだぞ Ah, the road is *uphill* all the way from here. ‖ この道は丘の頂上まで上りになっている This road *ascends* [*goes up* all the way] to the top of the hill.

2【列車の】▶上りの列車 an *up* train ／an *inbound* train《参考》イギリスでは up train というが, アメリカでは「上り」「下り」という分け方はしない. アメリカで up train といえば「北に向かう列車 (northbound train)」と解釈されるであろう. 反対の down train は「南へ向かう列車 (southbound train)」の意となる. なお, inbound train は「市内へ向かう列車」の意.

²のぼり 幟 a **streamer**(吹き流し); a **flag** (旗).

のぼりおり 上り下り ▶妊娠すると階段の上り下りが大変です It's tough to *go up and down* the stairs when you're pregnant.

のぼりざか 上り坂 an **uphill road** [**path**] ▶この道は上り坂になっている This is *an uphill road*. ／This road goes *uphill*. (➤ 後者の uphill は副詞) ‖ 我々は上り坂にさしかかった We came to *an upward slope* [*a rise in the road*].

▶《比喩的》わが社は今上り坂だ Our company *is on the way up*.

のぼりつめる 上り詰める ▶とうとう彼は官僚の世界で最高の地位にまで上り詰めた He finally *reached* the highest post in the bureaucracy.

のぼる 上る・登る・昇る 1【上へ行く】go up; **climb** (+㊂) (よじ登る);

scale ＋目（切り立ったがけや高峰を）; rise（太陽などが）▶マッターホルンに登る *climb* [*scale*] the Matterhorn ‖ この階段を上ると自由の女神の頭部に出られます If you *go up* this stairway, you can reach the head of the Statue of Liberty.
▶冬の谷川岳に登るのはかなり危険だ It is quite dangerous to *climb* Mt. Tanigawa in wintertime. ‖ ロープウェーで白根山に登った We *went up* Mount Shirane on the ropeway.（● 乗り物を使って登るときは climb は使えない）.
▶東京スカイツリーの展望台に上ったことがありますか Have you ever *been up* [*gone up*] to the observation deck of (the) Tokyo Sky Tree？‖ 私たちの学校はこの坂を上ったところです Our school is at *the top* of the hill.
▶たくさんのサケが石狩川を上ってきた Quite a few salmon *came up* the Ishikari River. ‖ 地平線から朝日が昇った The morning sun *rose* above the horizon. ‖ 気球はゆっくりと上空へ昇っていった The balloon slowly *rose* [*went up*] into the sky. ‖ 学長が演壇に登った The president *took* [*mounted*] *the platform*.
2【数量が達する】reach ＋目 ▶台風による被害は10億円に上った The damage caused by the typhoon *amounted to* [*reached*] a billion yen.（➤ amount to は「(合計で)…の金額になる」）‖ 日本で運転免許を持つ人は8000万人に上っている *As many as* 80 million Japanese have driver's licenses.（●「8000万もの人が持っている」と考える）.
3【取り上げられる】▶宴会できみのことが話に上ったよ (Things about) you *came up* (in our conversation) at the party. ‖ 最近彼女のことが我々の間でよく話題に上る Her name *is* often *on our lips* these days. ／We *talk about* her often these days.

のませる 飲ませる ▶子供に薬を飲ませる *give* medicine to a child ‖ ちょっと１杯水を飲ませてくれ Just *let me have* a glass of water. ‖ 赤ん坊にミルクを飲ませる時間だ It's time to *feed* the baby. ‖ 猫が子猫に乳を飲ませている The cat *is nursing* its kitten(s).

のまれる 飲まれる・呑まれる ▶その小舟は濁流にのまれてしまった The small boat *was swallowed up* in the muddy stream. ‖ 彼女は聴衆にのまれて（＝圧倒されて）しまい，うまく演奏ができなかった She failed to give a good performance because she *was overwhelmed* by the audience. ‖ 酒は飲んでも飲まれるな Drink, but don't *get drunk*.（➤ get drunk は「酔っぱらう」）.

¹のみ 蚤 a flea ▶猫にたかったノミ *fleas* on a cat ‖ 犬のノミを取る rid a dog of *fleas* ‖ ノミの食った跡 a flea-bite
▶《慣用表現》野田さんの所はのみの夫婦だ（＝ご主人が小さく奥さんが大きい）Mr. Noda is a small man with a big wife.
‖のみの市 a flea market.

²のみ 鑿 a **chisel** /tʃízəl/（道具）▶のみで木を彫る carve a piece of wood with *a chisel*.

-のみ only ▶市長は同じ返事を繰り返すのみだった The mayor *only* repeated the same reply. ‖ あとは社長のオーケーを待つのみだ *There's nothing to do but* wait for the green light from the president. ‖ あとは幸運を祈るのみだ *All I can do* is hope [pray] to be lucky.（● is のあとは本来 to- 不定詞だが，インフォーマルでは原形動詞を続けることが多い）.

のみあかす 飲み明かす ▶きょうは一晩飲み明かそうぜ Let's *drink the night away*. ‖ 差しつ差されつ，彼と一晩飲み明かした He and I *drank all night*, taking turns pouring drinks for each other.

のみあるく 飲み歩く ▶独身の頃はよく飲み歩いた I often *went barhopping* [《英》*went on a pub-crawl*] when I was single.

のみかい 飲み会 a ***nomikai***; a **get-together (for drinks) at a restaurant or pub**（➤ 直訳すれば a drinking party だが，これは響きがよくないし，酔っ払うのが目的のパーティーと解釈されかねない）▶今度の金曜日に飲み会がある We're *getting together for drinks* this Friday.

のみくい 飲み食い eating and drinking（➤ 日本語と語順が逆になる）▶その力士は飲み食いの代金をすべて後援者に払わせた The sumo wrestler charged all his *food* [*restaurant*] *bills* to his supporter's account.（● bill は「勘定書」. food の中には飲むことも含まれる）‖ 今夜は大いに飲み食いしよう Let's *eat and drink* our fill this evening, shall we？

のみぐすり 飲み薬 (a) **medicine.**

のみくだす 飲み下す swallow ＋目 ▶その錠剤を水と一緒に飲み下しなさい *Swallow* the pill with water.

のみこみ 飲み込み・呑み込み ▶彼女はのみ込みがいい[悪い] She's *quick* [*slow*] *to understand things*. ／She *is quick* [*slow*] *on the uptake*.（● 後者は「理解が早い[遅い]」のくだけた言い方）‖ 私の上司はいつものみ込みが早い My boss always *gets the point quickly*.

のみこむ 飲み込む・呑み込む swallow ＋目（物を）; **figure out, understand** ＋目（理解する）▶大変！赤ちゃんがコインをのみ込んじゃった Oh, no！The baby has *swallowed* a coin. ‖ 大波があっという間に漁船をのみ込んだ The big wave(s) *swallowed* the fishing boat instantly.
▶先生の言うことがよくのみ込めなかった I *could not understand* [*figure out*] what our teacher was saying. ‖ ようやくこつがのみ込めた I managed to *get the hang of* it. ‖ この会社に入って２年になるのにまだよく事情がのみ込めていない I've been with this company for two years, but I still don't *know all the ropes*.（➤ know the ropes は「帆船のかじ取りロープの扱い方を知っている」が原義）.

のみともだち 飲み友達 a drinking friend.

-のみならず not only A **but (also)** B（単にAだけでなくBもまた）; B **as well as** A（Aはもちろん B も）▶リチャーズ氏は俳句を理解するのみならず，みずからも作る Mr. Richards *not only* understands *but* (*also*) writes haiku. ‖ 私のみならず皆さんも彼女のことを誤解していたのかもしれませんよ You *as well as* I may have misunderstood her.

ノミネート nominate ＋目 ▶菊地凛子がアカデミー助演女優賞にノミネートされた Kikuchi Rinko *was nominated* for the Academy Award for Best Actress in a Supporting Role.

のみほうだい 飲み放題 ▶本日は2000円で飲み放題です Today you *can drink as much as you like* for 2,000 yen！‖ 3000円で飲み放題 *All you can drink* for 3,000 yen.

のみほす 飲み干す drain ＋目（容器をからにする）▶彼はジョッキのビールを一息に飲み干した He *drained* a mug of beer in one gulp. ‖ ぐっと飲み干してください *Drink* (*it*) *up*, please.

のみみず 飲み水 drinking water ▶雨不足で飲み水にも不自由している We are short of *drinking water* due to little rainfall. ‖ これは飲み水になります This water *is good to drink*.

のみもの 飲み物 a **drink**, a **beverage** /bévərɪdʒ/ (➤後者は堅い語で, 水は含まない) ▶温かい飲み物 *a* hot *drink* ‖ 何か冷たい飲み物が欲しい I want (to have) *something* cold *to drink*. ‖ お飲み物は何になさいますか What would you like *to drink* [*for a drink*]? (➤レストランなどでウエーターが客に尋ねる言い方) ‖ うちにはアルコールの入った飲み物はいっさい置いてありません We don't serve any alcoholic *drinks* [*beverages*]. ‖ 山に登るときは食べ物と飲み物を十分に持っていったほうがいい When you go mountain climbing, you had better take plenty of *food and drink* with you. (➤決まった言い方).

‖飲み物売り場 a drink counter.

> 「飲み物」のいろいろ ウーロン茶 oolong tea ／オレンジエード orangeade ／カフェオレ café au lait ／クリームソーダ ice-cream float ／紅茶 tea ／コーヒー coffee ／コーヒーフロート coffee float ／コーラ cola ／ココア hot chocolate, cocoa ／サイダー soda (pop) ／酒 alcohol ／ジュース juice ／ジンジャーエール ginger ale ／ソーダ水 soda water ／ハーブティー herbal tea ／ビール beer ／フルーツジュース fruit juice ／ミネラルウォーター mineral water ／ミルクセーキ milk shake ／ミルクティー tea with milk ／麦茶 barley tea ／緑茶 green tea ／レモネード《米》lemonade,《英》lemon squash ／レモンスカッシュ《米》lemon soda,《英》lemonade ／レモンティー tea with lemon

のみや 飲み屋 a **bar**; a **tavern** /tǽvəʳn/ (居酒屋).

のむ 飲む·呑む

> 訳語メニュー
> 飲み物を飲む →drink **1**
> 薬を飲む →take **2**
> 条件をのむ →accept **4**

1【飲み物を】**drink** +目, **have** +目 (➤後者は飲食行為(eat, drink)をあからさまにいうのをはばかって用いる語); **sip** +目 (少しずつ)

▶水を(少し)飲む *drink* (some) water ‖ お茶[コーヒー]でも飲みましょう Let's *have* some tea [coffee]. ‖ 彼は熱いコーヒーを少しずつ飲んだ He *sipped* his hot coffee. ／He *drank* his hot coffee *in sips*. ‖ 少年は水をごくごく飲んだ The boy *gulped* the water. ‖ 彼は飲まず食わずで3日間山中で過ごした He spent three days in the mountains *without eating or drinking* [*with nothing to eat or to drink*]. ‖ 我々はお茶を飲みながら話をした We talked *over* (our) tea.

▶この水は飲めますか Is this water *safe* [*good*] *to drink*? ‖ (酒を)飲み過ぎないように Be careful not to *drink* too much. ‖ 一杯飲まないか How about *a drink*? ‖ 対話「何を飲みますか?」「ウーロン茶をお願いします」"What would you like to *drink*?" "Oolong tea, please."

2【薬などを】**take** +目;《インフォーマル》**get down** (飲み下す) ▶私はこの薬を日に3度飲まなければならない I have to *take* this medicine three times a day. ‖ その薬はとても苦くて飲めなかった The medicine was so bitter I couldn't *get* it *down*.

3【軽く見る】▶舞台に立ったら聴衆をのんでかかることが大事だ When you're on the stage, it is important not to think about the audience so you can stay calm.

4【受け入れる】**accept** +目 ▶日本側はその条件をのんだ Japan *accepted* [*agreed to*] the terms. ‖ 組合側の要求はのめないね We *cannot accept* [*agree to*] the labor union's demands.

のめりこむ のめり込む ▶悪の道にのめり込む *fall into* a life of vice ‖ 彼はコンピュータゲームにのめり込んでいる He *is into* computer games. ‖ お隣は最近新しい宗教にのめり込んでいる My next-door neighbors *are into* a new religion lately.

のめる →つんのめる.

のやき 野焼きをする **burn dead grass (off a field)**.

のやま 野山 **fields and hills** [**mountains**].

のら 野良 a **field** (畑); a **rice paddy** (田)

‖野良仕事 farm work, work in the field.

のらいぬ 野良犬 a **homeless** [an **ownerless**] **dog** 《参考》stray dog は「迷い犬」に近い.

のらくら ▶いい年をして彼はまだのらくら暮らしている Even at that age, he is still *loafing around* [*idling away his time*].

のらねこ 野良猫 a **homeless** [an **ownerless**] **cat**; an **alley cat** (都会の裏通りにいるような) 《参考》stray cat は「迷い猫」に近い.

のらりくらり ▶彼は何を聞いてものらりくらりとした返事しかしないのでらちがあかない I can't get anywhere with him because no matter what I ask, he comes back with a *noncommittal* answer.

¹のり 糊 **glue**, (a) **paste** (接着用の); **starch** (洗濯用の) ▶紙をのりではり合わせる stick paper together with *glue* ／glue two pieces of paper ‖ のりのきいたワイシャツ a *well-starched* shirt ‖ このシーツはのりがきき過ぎている This sheet is too stiff with *starch*. ／This sheet is too starchy.

‖のりしろ an edge of paper onto which paste is applied.

²のり 海苔 ***nori***, **laver** /lɑ́ːvəʳ/

日本紹介 ✉ **のりは海草を薄く紙のように広げて乾燥させた食品です. 濃い緑や黒紫色をしています. おにぎりを包んだり, 巻きずしを巻いたりするのに使います** *Nori* is a food made from laver, a type of seaweed, that has been pressed into paper-thin sheets and dried. It is deep green or deep purple. You can wrap an *onigiri* (rice ball) or make a *makizushi* (*nori*-wrapped sushi) with it.

▶のり1枚 a sheet of *nori* [*(dried) laver*].

‖のり巻き sushi rolled in *nori* [dried laver] ‖ 味つけのり seasoned *nori* [(dried) laver] ‖ 焼きのり toasted *nori* [laver].

³のり 乗り ▶のりのいい曲 a *rhythmic* [*danceable*] tune ‖ この曲はのりがいいからヒット間違いなしね This is a *catchy* tune. I bet it'll make a great hit. (➤catchy は「覚えやすい」) ‖ あのDJはおしゃべりののりが最高だな That DJ really keeps up a steady stream of patter. (➤patter は「軽妙なおしゃべり」) ‖ あの俳優は今のりに乗っている That actor *is riding the crest of popularity*.

▶きょうは寝不足でお化粧ののりが悪い This make-up *doesn't go on well* [*evenly* ／ *smoothly*] today because I didn't get enough sleep last night.

-のり -乗り ▶2人乗りの自転車 a bicycle *for* two ／a tandem (bicycle) ‖ 62人乗りのバス a 62-*passenger* bus ‖ 4人乗りカプセル(ロケット) a four-*person* capsule ‖ このスポーツカーは2人乗りだ This sports car *seats two*. ／This is a *two-seater* sports car.

のりあげる 乗り上げる **run (up) onto**; **run aground**

（浅瀬に）; **run ashore**（岸に）▶**漁船が浅瀬に乗り上げた** A fishing boat *ran aground*. ‖ **車が安全地帯に乗り上げた** A car *ran* (*up*) *onto* the safety zone. ▶《慣用表現》2国間の交渉は**暗礁に乗り上げた** The negotiation between the two countries *has reached* [*has come to*] *a deadlock*. (➤ deadlock の代わりに impasse や stalemate を用いてもよい; →デッドロック).

のりあわせる 乗り合わせる ▶**学校の帰りに父とたまたま同じバスに乗り合わせた** On my way home from school I happened to *be on the same bus as* my father (was). ／On my way back from school I *took* [*rode* ／ *got on*] *the same bus* my father did.

のりいれる 乗り入れる ▶**河川敷に車を乗り入れないように** Don't *drive* your car *onto* the riverbed.
▶**この区間では2つの私鉄が相互に乗り入れている** Two private railroad companies use the same rail lines in this section.

のりうつる 乗り移る ▶**やがて, 巫女(みこ)に神の霊が乗り移った** Soon the medium *was possessed* with the spirit of the god. (➤ possess は「(霊などが)取りつく」).

のりおくれる 乗り遅れる **miss** +目 ▶**終バスに乗り遅れないよう, バス停に急いだ** I hurried to the bus stop so I would not *miss* the last bus. ‖ **けさはいつものバスに乗り遅れた** This morning I *missed* [*couldn't catch*] my bus.
▶**流行に乗り遅れまいとする若者が多い** Many young people are keen on *keeping up with* fashions.

のりおり 乗り降り ▶**ホームは乗り降りする客でいっぱいだった** The platform was filled with people *getting on and off the train*.

のりかえ 乗り換え (a) **transfer** ▶《構内アナウンス》**西鉄大牟田線は当駅でお乗り換えです** *Transfer* [*Change*] here to the Nishitetsu Omuta Line.
‖**乗り換え駅** a transfer [junction] (station) ‖ **乗り換え切符** a transfer ticket.

のりかえる 乗り換える **change** (**trains**); **transfer** /trænsfə́ːr/《to》, **change**《to》(➤ 交通機関の用語としては transfer がより一般的) ▶**彼は新宿に行くために東京駅で電車を乗り換えた** He *changed trains* at Tokyo Station for Shinjuku. (● trains と複数形になることに注意).

【文型】
A から B に乗り換える
change from A to B
transfer from A to B

▶**松江駅でバスに乗り換えてください** Please *transfer* from the train *to* a bus at Matsue Station. ‖ **品川に着いたら京浜急行線の三崎口行きに乗り換えてください** When you get to Shinagawa, please *transfer* [*change*] *to* the Keihin Kyuko Line for Misakiguchi.
▶《比喩的》**A子からB子に乗り換える** *dump* Girl A for Girl B.

のりかかる 乗りかかる ▶**乗りかかった船だ, 最後まで付き合うよ** *Now that I've gotten involved* [*committed myself*] (*to* the project), I'll stick with it to the end.

のりき 乗り気 ▶**社長は事業を拡張する計画に乗り気だった** The president *was very interested in* [*showed great enthusiasm for*] the plans for expanding the business. ‖ **父は私の結婚にあまり乗り気じゃないようだ** My father doesn't seem to *be* very *enthusiastic about* [*keen on*] my marriage.

のりきる 乗り切る **ride out**; **get over**（越える）▶**あらしを乗り切る** *ride out* a storm ／*weather* a storm.
▶**酷暑を乗り切る** *beat* the heat of summer ‖ **不況を乗り切る** *ride out* [*get through*] a recession ‖ **この危機を乗り切れば前途は明るい** Our future will be bright if we can *ride out* [*overcome*] this crisis. ‖ **我々は力を合わせて幾多の困難を乗り切った** We combined our efforts to *overcome* many difficulties.

のりくみいん 乗組員 a **crew** /kruː/（全員）; a **crewman**, a **crew member**, a **member of the crew**（1人; あとの2つは性差のない言い方）▶**乗組員は全員無事だった** All the *crew* was [were] found safe. (● 全体として扱えば単数扱い, 一人一人を考えていえば複数扱い) ‖ **その船には少数の乗組員しかいなかった** The ship had only a small *crew* [a few *crewmen*] on board.

のりくむ 乗り組む **board** +目, **get on board**（乗船する）▶**スペースシャトルには宇宙飛行士5人が乗り組んだ** Five astronauts *boarded* the space shuttle.

のりこえる 乗り越える **get over**; **overcome** +目（打ち勝つ）; **put** A **behind** B（B(人)が A(悪いことなど)を過去のものとする）▶**塀を乗り越える** *climb* [*get*] *over* a fence.
▶**先生を乗り越える** *outdo* one's teacher ‖ **両親を失った悲しみを乗り越えて少年は高校に進学した** The boy *overcame* his grief over the loss of his parents and went on to high school. ‖ **彼は倒産を乗り越えて新たな道に進もうと決意した** He decided to *put* his bankruptcy *behind* him and start a new career.

のりごこち 乗り心地 ▶**乗り心地のいい車** a *comfortable* car. ‖ 対話「**新車の乗り心地はどうですか**」「**とてもいい乗り心地ですよ**」"*How do you like* your new car?" "*It's comfortable to drive* [*ride in*]. ／It *rides comfortably*."

のりこし 乗り越し ▶**乗り越しの方はご精算ください** *Anyone who does not have the exact fare*, please adjust your ticket now. (●「(乗り越して)運賃が足りない人」の意).
‖**乗り越し料金** an extra [excess] fare, a fare for excess distance traveled.

のりこす 乗り越す ▶**お客さん, 2駅乗り越してますよ** Excuse me. You'*ve come* [You'*re*] two stops *too far*. →乗り過ごす.

のりこむ 乗り込む **get on**（電車・バスなどにそのまま歩いて）; **get in** [**into**]（タクシーなどに身体をかがめたりして）▶**発車のベルが鳴り始めたので彼らはあわてて列車に乗り込んだ** When the (starting) chime began ringing, they *got on* the train in a hurry. ‖ **救助隊は飛行機に乗り込んだ** The rescue team *got* [*went*] *on board* the plane. (➤ get [go] on board は「(飛行機や船に)乗り込む」) ‖ **二人はタクシーに乗り込んだ** The couple *got in* [*into*] a taxi. ‖ **学生たちがエレベーターにどやどやと乗り込んできた** The students *piled into* the elevator.

のりすごす 乗り過ごす ▶**電車でうとうとして降りる駅を乗り過ごした** I dozed off on the train and *went past* [*went beyond* ／*missed*] my stop. →乗り越す.

のりすてる 乗り捨てる **abandon** +目（捨てる）; **get off**（降りる）▶**犯人はここで車[タクシー]を乗り捨てたようだ** It seems that the culprit *abandoned* his car [*got off* the taxi] here.

の

のりそこなう 乗り損なう miss +目 ▶7時の岡山行きよ．乗り損なわないでね Take the seven o'clock train for Okayama, and be sure you don't *miss* it.

のりだす 乗り出す 1【乗って出て行く】sail out ▶漁船の一団が北洋の荒海に乗り出した A team of fishing boats *sailed* [*ventured*] *out* on the rough north seas.

2【始める】start ▶彼の会社は新しい育毛剤の開発に乗り出した His company *started* developing new hair restorers. ‖ 彼は26歳で政界に乗り出した He *entered* [*went into*] politics when he was 26. ‖ その事件の捜査には国税庁も乗り出した The National Tax Administration Agency *joined* [*participated*] in the investigation of that case.

3【体を前に出す】lean forward ▶私はパレードを見ようと窓から身を乗り出した I *leaned forward* out of the window to see the parade. ‖ 弟は手すりから身を乗り出し過ぎて下へ落ちてしまった My (younger) brother *leaned* too *far* over the railing and fell.

の

のりつぎ 乗り継ぎ ‖(飛行機などの)乗り継ぎ客 a connecting [transit] passenger ‖ 乗り継ぎ券 a transit pass [card] ‖ 乗り継ぎ便 a connecting flight.

のりつぐ 乗り継ぐ ▶(飛行機で)ロンドンからノッティンガム行きに乗り継ぐ *have a connecting flight* from London to Nottingham ‖ 電車とタクシーを乗り継いで来ました I came here by train *and* taxi.

のりづけ ▶ノートにメモをのりづけする *glue* a note *into* a notebook.

▶このワイシャツに(軽く)のりづけしてもらいたいのですが I'd like to have this white shirt *starched* (lightly), please.

のりつける (…に)**乗り付ける drive up** 《to》 ▶彼は外車でガールフレンドの家に乗り付けた He *drove up to* his girlfriend's house in an import(ed) car.

のりつぶす 乗りつぶす drive a car until it's beyond repair(車を).

のりと 祝詞 (a) *norito*, a **Shinto prayer** ▶祝詞をあげる recite [read] *a norito prayer*.

のりにげ 乗り逃げ ▶その男はタクシーを乗り逃げした The man *ran away without paying* the taxi *fare*. ／The man *jumped* [*skipped*／*dodged*] the taxi *fare*.

のりば 乗り場 a **bus stop**(バス停)；《米》a **taxi stand**, 《英》a **taxi rank** (タクシーの)；a **platform** (列車の)；a **landing pier** (船の) ▶この近くにタクシー乗り場はありますか Is there *a taxi stand* near here? ‖ その列車の乗り場は10番ホームです The train leaves from *platform* 10.

のりまわす 乗り回す drive [**ride**] **around** ▶彼はベンツを得意になって乗り回した He *drove around* (town), showing off his Mercedes. (オートバイ・自転車なら動詞は ride).

のりもの 乗り物 a **vehicle** /víːəkəl/ (陸上の)；a **vessel** (海上の)；an **aircraft** (空の)；a **ride** (遊園地の) ▶1頭立ての馬車は19世紀にはごく一般的な乗り物だった Buggies were popular *vehicles* in the nineteenth century. ‖ ナイロビまでは乗り物は何で行くつもりですか What *means of transportation* are you going to take to Nairobi? (➤「交通手段は何を利用するのか」の意)／*How* are you going to go to Nairobi? (「どうやって[何を利用して]行くのか」の意の，ごくふつうの聞き方) ‖ この辺は乗り物の便が悪い *Public transportation* [*transport*] is very poor in this area. (➤ public transportation は「公共交通機関」) ‖ 私は乗り物酔いなどしたことがない I have never suffered from *motion* [*travel*] *sickness*. (➤ motion sickness は《米》, travel sickness は《英》)／I have never gotten *motion* [*travel*] *sick*. 《参考》乗り物の種類によって carsick (車酔い), seasick (船酔い), airsick (飛行機酔い) などのようにいう.

▶遊園地でいくつか乗り物に乗った I *went on* some *rides* at the amusement park.

のる 乗る・載る 1【乗り物に】ride +目 (乗って行く)；**drive** +目 (運転する)；**get on, get in** [**into**] (乗り込む)；**board** +目 (船・飛行機・電車などに)；**take** +目 (交通機関を利用する)

> **解説**「乗る」の言い方
> (1)**ride** はオートバイ・自転車・馬などに「自分で動かすために乗る」の意で用いる．**drive** は車を「運転する」，**take** は「交通機関を利用する」の意．(2)**ride in** は車・タクシーなどに「乗客として乗る」で，**ride on** は電車・バスなど大型の乗り物に乗るときに使う．(3)**get in** はタクシーなど小型の乗り物に「身をかがめるようにして乗り込む」で，「降りる」は get out (of) になる．**get on** は中で立っていられる大型の乗り物に歩いて乗り込むときで，「降りる」は get off.

▶ラクダ[自転車]に乗る *ride* a camel [a bicycle] (「乗って行く」の意)／*get on* a camel [a bicycle] (動作として「乗る，乗り込む」の意) ‖ 電車に乗る *take* a train (➤「利用する」の意) ‖ 飛行機に乗る *board* [*get on*／*go aboard*] an airplane ‖ 佐渡島行きの船に乗る *board* [*go aboard*] a ship going to [headed for] Sado Island.

▶羽田行きのバスに乗る *take* the bus to [for] Haneda／*take* the Haneda bus ‖ **対話**「鎌倉へ行くには何線に乗ればいいんですか」「横須賀線です」"Which line do I *take* to go to Kamakura?" "The Yokosuka Line."

▶我々は彼の車に乗った We *rode in* his car. ‖ ロンドンで2階建てバスに乗った We *rode on* a double-decker (bus) in London. ‖ エスカレーター[ボート]に乗るときは足元に気をつけなさい Watch your step when you *get on* the escalator [*get in* the rowboat]. ‖ 私たちは急いでバス[遊覧船]に乗った We *got on* the bus [pleasure boat] hurriedly. ‖ 乗れよ．駅まで送ってやるよ *Get in*. I'll take you to the station.

▶私はヘリコプターに乗ったことがある I have *flown* in a helicopter. (➤ flown は fly (飛行機で飛ぶ)の過去分詞形) ‖ 急がないと終電に乗れないぞ Hurry up, or we *won't catch* [*make*] the last train. ‖ この車は6人乗れる This car *holds* [*seats*] six people.

あなたの英語はどう響く?
電車などに「乗り込む」は get on が使われるが，目的語に代名詞 it がくる場合は語順に要注意．例えば，来た電車を指して Shall we take this train ?（この電車に乗りましょうか）と聞かれ，「ええ，乗りましょう」のつもりで Yes, let's get it on. などと言わないこと．正しくは Yes, let's get on it. である．この on は前置詞で，it はあとにくる．get it on とすると俗語で「セックスをする」という意味になってしまう．

2【物の上に】▶猫は少年の左肩に乗った The cat *got on* [*onto*] the boy's left shoulder. ‖ 体重計に乗ってください *Step on* the scales, please. ‖ 椅子に乗って（＝立って）この絵を壁に掛けてくれ *Stand on* the chair and hang this picture on the wall. ‖ うちの猫はすぐひざの上に乗ってくる Our cat always *climbs* (*up*) onto my lap. (➤ climb は「手足を使って登る」).
▶机の上に手紙が1通載っていた A letter *lay on* the table.
3【あるものといっしょになって動く】▶弟の紙飛行機は風に乗って飛んで行った My (younger) brother's paper plane was carried away *by* the wind. ‖ ディスコでは若い男女がリズムに乗って（＝音楽に合わせて）踊っていた Young people were dancing *to* music at the disco. ‖ 彼女はピアノの伴奏に乗って上手に歌った She sang very well *to* the piano *accompaniment*. ‖ 彼は景気の波に乗って（＝を利用して）大もうけした He *took advantage of* the economic boom and made a lot of money. ‖ 商売はどうやら軌道に乗ってきた My business finally seems to *be getting into gear*.
4【勢いづく】▶洋子ちゃん，今夜は乗ってるね！ You'*re* (really) *with it* [*in the groove*] tonight, aren't you, Yoko-chan ! ‖ 今気分が乗っているところだから，じゃましないでよ！ I'*m just getting into it* now, so don't bother me.
▶あの男はおだてられるとすぐ調子に乗る[図に乗る]タイプだ He is the type who *gets carried away* [whose *head swells*] when (he's) flattered. (➤ get carried away は「夢中になる」, one's head swells は「うぬぼれる」).
5【伸びて広がる】▶この紙はインクがよくのる This paper *takes* ink well. ‖ ゆうべは寝不足でファンデーションがのらない This foundation doesn't *spread well* over my face [*go on* easily] today because I didn't get enough sleep last night. ‖ このサンマは脂が乗っていておいしい This saury *has got lots of fat* and tastes good.
6【応じる】▶彼女は不動産屋の話にすぐ乗った（＝飛びついた）She *jumped at* the realtor's offer. ‖ 彼はこのもうけ話に乗ってきた[乗ってこなかった] He *showed an interest* [*didn't show any interest*] in the money-making scheme. ‖ 私もその話に一口乗りたいわ *Count me in* on the project. (➤ count in は「(仲間などに)入れる」) ‖ 悪いけど，その話には乗れないな Sorry, but *count me out*. (➤ count out は「(仲間などに)加えない」) ‖ ちょっと相談に乗ってほしいんだけど I would like to *ask your advice*. ／Could you *give me some advice* about a problem ? ‖ あの詐欺師の口車につい乗ってしまった I *fell for* the con man's glib talk [smooth story]. (➤ fall for は「…にだまされる」の意のインフォーマルな表現) ‖ ぼくはそんな手には乗らないよ I *won't be taken in* by an old trick like that.
7【掲載される】 appear ▶その事件は新聞に載った The incident *appeared* in the newspaper. ／The incident *was reported* [*was published*] in the newspaper(s). ‖ 私の記事が『文春』に載った My article *was printed* in "Bunshun." ‖ その熟語はこの辞書には載っていない The idiom *isn't given* [*isn't entered* ／*isn't listed*] in this dictionary. ‖ 最も大きな辞書でさえ英語のすべての単語や表現が載っているということはない Even the largest dictionary doesn't *cover* all the words and expressions used in English.
▶きみの名前はその名簿に載っていますか *Is* your name *on* the list ? ‖ そのことならこの本に載っている It *is mentioned* in this book. ‖ その温泉はこの地図には載っていない That hotspring resort *is not* (*found*) on this map.
8【基準以上になる】▶円はついに1ドル80円の大台にのった Finally [At long last], the yen *hit* the 80-yen-to-the-dollar mark.

ノルウェー Norway ―形 ノルウェーの Norwegian
‖ノルウェー語 Norwegian ‖ ノルウェー人 a Norwegian.

のるかそるか 伸るか反るか win or lose, sink or swim
▶伸るか反るかの勝負 a *life or death* battle [match] (➤ match はボクシング・テニスなどのスポーツの場合).

ノルディック Nordic
‖ノルディックスキー Nordic skiing.

ノルマ one's **assigned work**, one's **assignment**（割り当てられた仕事）; a **quota** /kwóʊṭə/（その量）▶ノルマを達成する finish the *assigned work* ／attain one's *quota* ‖ 販売ノルマをこなす meet one's sales *quota* ‖ 我々はセールスマンの能力に応じてノルマを決めている We set *quotas* for our sales staff based on their ability.

危ないカタカナ語 ノルマ
1「割り当てられた仕事」の意味で使う「ノルマ」はロシア語の *norma* からきている．英語では assignment または assigned work で，「自分のノルマ」は one's assignment となる．
2 数字や分量を指す場合の「ノルマ」は quota というが，これは，生産・販売，輸出入などの分野で用いられる語である．

のれん 暖簾 a ***noren*** (-curtain) ; a split half-curtain hung over the entrance of a shop, etc. (➤ 説明的な訳)
日本紹介 ✉ **のれんは商店，料理屋，飲み屋などの入り口や軒先にかけてある切れ目の入ったカーテンです．屋号や商品名が染め抜いてあって店の顔の役目をしています** A *noren* is a split curtain hung over the entrance or under the eaves of a store, a restaurant or a Japanese-style pub. It serves as an advertisement since the name of the store or brand name is dyed on it.
▶《慣用表現》粗悪品を売らないようにしなさい．でないとのれんに傷がつきますよ Let's not sell shoddy goods. If we do, *our reputation will be damaged*.
ことわざ **のれんに腕押し** It's no use, like pushing a *noren*-curtain. (➤ 日本語の直訳) ／It's like beating the air.
‖**のれん分け** *norenwake* ; a Japanese system where the employer gives a trusted employee permission to use the name of the store, company or restaurant to set up an independent

business, often with financial assistance from the employer (➤ 説明的な訳).

¹のろい 呪い a **curse** ▶その男にのろいをかける put *a curse* on that man.

²のろい 鈍い **slow**(遅い) ; **slow-witted, dull** (にぶい) ▶彼女は足がのろい She *is slow* of foot. ／She is a *slow* walker. ‖ のろいぞ, (もっと) 速く歩け You are too *slow* [You're a slowpoke]. Walk fast [faster]! (➤ slowpoke は「のろま」) ‖ うちの息子は何をやらせてものろい My son *is slow* in everything. ‖ 彼は頭の働きはのろいが, 弁当を食べるのは速い He is *slow-witted* [*dull*] but is quick to eat his lunch.

のろう 呪う **curse** +目 ▶私は自分の運命をのろった I *cursed* my fate. ‖ 世の中をのろっても何にもならない You can't do anything by merely *cursing* the world.
▶おまえはのろわれているのだ! You*'re cursed*!

ノロウイルス 《医学》 (a) **norovirus** /nɔ́ːrəvàɪərəs/.

のろける ⚠ **妻･夫･恋人などのことをほめるのを自然な行為と考える英米人は, この語にぴったりの英語表現をもたない. したがって,「…のことをほめてばかりいる」とか「…のことを話してばかりいる」というように, 特定の人のことを過度に話題にしている事実に言及するしかない.** ▶けさ, 先週結婚した美奈子に会ったんだけど, だんなさんのことのろけっぱなしだったわ I met Minako this morning for the first time since she got married last week. She *did nothing but talk happily about* her (new) husband. (➤ 大げさにほめてばかりと言いたければ, sing a person's praises(人のことをほめちぎる)という熟語を用いて, All she did was *sing* her (new) husband's *praises*. または, She *went on* (*and on*) *about how great* her new husband is. としてもよい).

のろし 狼煙 a **smoke signal, smoke as a signal** (➤ 両者とも煙による合図) ; a **beacon** (火による合図)
▶《慣用表現》全国で新税反対ののろしが上がった They *started a* nationwide *campaign* against the new tax.

のろのろ **slowly** ▶のろのろするな. 遅れているじゃないか Don't *be slow*. [Don't *dawdle*.] You are falling behind (in your work). ‖ 渋滞が続き, 車はのろのろと進んだ The traffic jam continued and the cars could only *inch forward* [*move at a snail's pace*].
▶彼はのろのろと仕事をしていたので上司に怒られた He was scolded by his boss because he worked *sluggishly*. (➤ sluggishly は「不活発に」).
‖のろのろ運転 driving at a snail's pace.

のろま a **dull** [**slow**] **person,** 《インフォーマル》 a **slowpoke,** a **slowcoach** (ぐずぐずする人) (➤ slowcoach は《英》で好まれる) ; a **dimwit** (血のめぐりの悪い人) ▶早くしなさいよ, のろまなんだから! Hurry up, you *slowpoke* [*slowcoach*]!

のんき 暢気な **easygoing**(こせこせしない) ; **carefree** (心配事のない) ; **easy** (気楽な) ; **happy-go-lucky** (楽天的な, 運まかせの) ▶のんきな人 an *easygoing* [a *happy-go-lucky*] person ‖ 母さんはのんきな性格だ My mother is an *easygoing* type of person. ‖ 彼は田舎でのんきに暮らしている He is leading an *easy* [a *carefree*] life in the country. ‖ 来年は入試だというのに, のんきに構えてるときじゃないでしょ You can't (afford to) *take it easy* with the entrance exams coming up next year.

ノンストップ **nonstop** ▶新潟までノンストップのバスを利用する take a *nonstop* bus to Niigata ‖ この列車は(東京から)名古屋まではノンストップだ This train *goes* (from Tokyo) to Nagoya *nonstop*.

のんだくれ 飲んだくれ a **drunk,** a **drunkard,** a **problem drinker.**

のんでかかる 呑んでかかる ▶相手をのんでかかる *make light of* one's opponent.

ノンバンク a **nonbank** (**finance company**).

のんびり **leisurely** /líːʒərli/ (ゆったりと) **一動 のんびりする** **relax** ; 《インフォーマル》 **take it easy** (のんきに構える) ▶のんびりしようよ Let's *relax*. ／Let's *take it easy*. ‖ のんびりやりましょう Let's *take our time*. ‖ 子供たちの学校がまた始まったから, 少しはのんびりできるわ After the children go back to school, I'll be able to *take it easy* for a while.
▶たまにはのんびりと旅行をしたい I want to take a *leisurely* trip for a change. ‖ 妻はのんびり屋だ My wife is always *taking it easy*. ／My wife never rushes (herself). (「自分を急がせることをしない」の意) ／My wife takes her time in everything she does. (「何をするにも時間がかかる」の意).

ノンフィクション **nonfiction** (➤ 人生論や実用書のたぐいも含めることがある)
‖ノンフィクション映画 [作家] a nonfiction film [writer].

ノンブル a **page number**(ページ番号).

ノンプロ ‖ノンプロ選手 a nonprofessional player, 《英また》 an amateur ‖ ノンプロ野球 nonprofessional baseball 《参考》 社会人野球チームは a corporate team という.

のんべえ 飲ん兵衛 a **heavy drinker,** 《古風》 a **boozer.**

のんべんだらり ▶長い夏休みをのんべんだらりと過ごしてはいけない Don't *idle* [*fritter*] *your time away* during the long summer vacation. ‖ そんなふうにのんべんだらりとやっていたら, いつになったら終わるかわかりゃしない There is no telling when you will ever finish your work if you go on *halfheartedly* [*sluggishly* ／*lackadaisically*] like that. (いずれも「気乗りしない様子で」の意).

ノンポリ ▶ノンポリ学生 an *apolitical* student ／a student who *is not interested in politics*.

ノンレム ‖ノンレム睡眠 《生理学》 non-REM sleep. →睡眠.

は・ハ

[1]**は 歯** **1【人・動物の】** a **tooth**［複 **teeth**］━形 **歯の dental** ▶上の［下の］**歯** an upper［a lower］*tooth* ‖ 前［奥］**歯** a front［back］*tooth* ‖ **歯**を抜いて［治療して］もらう have *a tooth* pulled［treated］‖ **歯の治療**を受ける get *dental treatment* ‖ ママ，**歯が痛**いよ Mom, I *have a toothache.* ‖ おせんべいを食べてたら**歯**が欠けちゃった I chipped *a tooth* while I was eating rice crackers. ‖ 上の**前歯**がぐらぐらしてるんです This upper *front tooth* is loose. ‖ **歯が生え替わる**のはふつう 6 歳ごろだ We *lose our baby teeth and get permanent teeth* when we are about six.（➤「乳歯が抜け，永久歯が生える」と考える）‖ 赤ん坊の**歯が生え始め**ました The baby is *teething*［*cutting her teeth*］.（➤ teethe /tiːð/ は「(幼児が) 歯が生える」の意で通例進行形で用いる）‖ 甘いものを食べ過ぎると**歯が悪くなる** Eating too many sweets *causes tooth decay*［*will damage your teeth*／*will ruin your teeth*］. ‖ 冷たい水が**歯にしみる** My *teeth ache*［*hurt*］when I drink cold water. ‖ 寝る前には必ず**歯をみが**きなさい Be sure to *brush your teeth* before going to bed. ‖ 猿は**歯**をむき出して相手を威嚇(いかく)する Monkeys threaten their enemies by showing their *teeth.*

逆引き熟語 ○○歯
入れ歯 a false tooth（➤「総入れ歯」は a denture ; dentures）／**奥歯** a back tooth, a molar／**さし歯** a false tooth, a dental implant／**すき歯** gapped［spaced］teeth／**出っ歯** a bucktooth, a protruding tooth（➤後者は「突出歯(とつしゅつし)」に相当する専門用語）／**前歯** a front tooth／**虫歯** a cavity, a decayed［bad］tooth／**八重歯** an overlapping canine (tooth), a double tooth

2【器具・道具の】 a **tooth** ▶のこぎりの**歯** the *teeth* of a saw／a saw*tooth*（後者は「歯の1本」）‖ くしの**歯**が折れた *A tooth* broke off the comb. ‖ 歯車の**歯**が欠けている Some *teeth* of the gear are missing.（➤「歯車の歯」は cog ともいう）.

3【慣用表現】 **歯が浮く** ▶千田さんの奥さんは歯の浮くようなお世辞を言う Mrs. Senda's flattery is *nauseating*［*disgusting*］to us.（➤前者は「むかつくほど不快だ」の意）‖ 桂子のバイオリンの音を聞くと歯が浮く The sound of Keiko's violin *sets my teeth on edge.* **歯が立たない** ▶日本のラグビーチームはイギリスチームにまるで歯が立たなかった The Japanese rugby team *was no match for* its British counterpart.（➤「相手にならなかった」の意）. ‖ T大の入試問題をやってみたが全然歯が立たなかった I tried to solve some of the problems on the entrance examination of T University, but found they *were too hard for* me.
歯に衣(きぬ)を着せない ▶渡辺さんは歯に衣を着せずに物を言う人だ Mr. Watanabe is *outspoken.*（➤ outspoken は「言うことに遠慮がない」で日本語よりもプラスイメージをもつ）. **歯を食いしばる** ▶彼女は歯を食いしばって厳しいトレーニングに耐えた She *gritted her teeth* and endured the hard training.

[2]**は 葉** a **leaf**［複 **leaves**］; a **blade**（細長い葉）; a **needle**（細くてとがった）; **foliage** /fóʊliɪdʒ/（➤集合的）

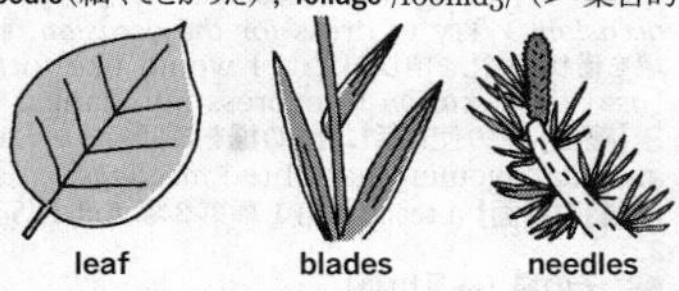

▶カエデの**葉** a maple *leaf* ‖ 草の**葉** *a blade* of grass ‖ **葉の多い**［**葉物**］野菜 *leafy* vegetables ‖ 秋になると落葉樹は**葉**を落とす Deciduous trees shed their *leaves* in autumn. ‖ 春には木々はまた**葉をつける** In spring, trees *come into leaf* again. ‖ 茂った**葉**の間から日の光が漏れている The sunlight is filtering through the thick *foliage.* ‖ **お茶の葉**はもう少し多めに入れたほうがおいしいですよ If you put more *tea leaves* into the pot, the tea will taste better.

[3]**は 派** a **faction**（派閥）; a **sect**（宗派）; a **denomination**（キリスト教の）a **school**（学問・思想などの流派）▶加藤派 the Kato *faction* ‖ 仏教はたくさんの**派**に分かれている Buddhism is divided into many *sects.* ‖ ゴッホは**印象派**に属する Van Gogh belongs to *the impressionistic school*［is one of *the impressionists*］. ‖ **反対派**の候補が市長に選ばれた The candidate from *the opposition group*［on *the opposition side*］was elected mayor. ‖ 私は犬［猫］**派**です I'm a dog［cat］*person.*

[4]**は 刃** an **edge**（刃先）; a **blade**（刃全体）▶鋭い［なまくらの］**刃** a sharp［blunt］*edge* ‖ この包丁は**刃がこぼれている** This kitchen knife *has a nicked edge.* ‖ このかみそりの**刃**は切れ味が悪い This razor *blade* is dull.

-は **1【主題・題目を提示して】** ▶私は吉田です I am (＝I'm) Yoshida. ‖ 彼は医者だ He is (＝He's) a doctor. ‖ ぼくの弟は頭がいい My brother is smart. ‖ 私の財布は机の上にある My wallet is on the desk.（➤主語に my や the がつくときは There is … の文は使えない）‖ きのうは楽しかった I had a good time yesterday.／I enjoyed myself yesterday.
▶通勤はつらい Commuting is hard for me. ‖ 海外旅行は楽しい It's fun to travel abroad.

2【強意・対比を示して】 ▶ロンドンは冬は寒い In London it is cold in winter.／London is cold in winter. ‖ 私は反対だ *As for* me, I'm against it. ‖ きみは若いが，私は年をとっている You're young, but I'm old. ‖ リンゴは好きだがナシは嫌いだ Though I like apples, I don't like pears. ‖ 私はテニスが好き．あなたは？ I like playing tennis. How about you? ‖ 私はいいけど，きみは？ It's okay with me. How about you?

3【限定して】 ▶秋田はどちら(のご出身)ですか What part of Akita do you come from?／Where in Akita were you born? ‖ あなたとはもう会いたくないわ I don't want to see you any more. ‖ ジーンズはリーバイスでなくちゃ If you want jeans, they've got to be Levi's.

ば 場 **1【場所】** a **place**; a **spot**（特定の場所）▶目の前で事故が起こり，彼女は**その場に**立ちすくんでしまった The accident occurred right before her eyes, and she froze *on the spot*. ‖私たちはたまたま**その場に**居合わせて事件を目撃した We happened to be *there* [*on the scene*] and witnessed the incident.

2【場合】 an **occasion** ▶**その場に**ふさわしい服装を心掛けなさい Try to wear clothes *suitable* [*fit*] *for the occasion*. ／Try to dress *for the occasion*. ‖**この場を借りて**お礼を申しあげたい I would like to *take* [*use*] *this occasion* to express my thanks.

3【機会】 ▶労使は話し合いの**場**を３回持った Labor and management had three *meetings*.

4【劇中場面】 a **scene** ▶第１幕第２**場** Act 1, *Scene* 2.

☛ **その場**（→見出語）

はあ ▶**はあ**，なるほど *Oh*, I see. ‖**はあ**，かしこまりました *Yes*, sir（➤女性に対しては madam，または ma'am《おもに米》という）．／Certainly. ‖《驚き・疑問などを表して》**はあ**？ *Huh*?

バー **1【酒場】** a **bar** ▶**バー**で酒を飲む drink at *a bar* ‖**バー**へ飲みに行く go to *a bar* to have a drink.

2【横棒】 a **bar**, a **crossbar** ▶《高跳び》**バー**を越える clear *a bar* ‖**バー**の高さを５センチ上げる raise the *bar* five centimeters.

[1]パー《おじゃん》▶おまえがうっかりしゃべるから計画が**パー**になってしまったじゃないか Our plan *went down the drain* when you let the secret out.（➤ go down the drain は「どぶに流れる」が原義）．

[2]パー《ゴルフ》a **par**.

ばあい 場合 a **case**（事例）；**time**（時）；an **occasion**（特別な時）；**circumstances**（事情）▶**その場合には** in that *case* ‖**こういう場合には**どうしたらよいでしょうか What should I do *in such a case*? ‖**雨の場合は**遠足は延期される *If* [*In case*] it rains, our outing will be postponed. ‖**火事の場合は**このはしごを使ってください *In case of* fire, use this ladder. ‖**私の場合**，英語を習得するのにテレビを使いました *In my case*, I used television to learn English. ‖**最悪の場合**，会社は倒産するかもしれない *In a worst case scenario*, our company could go bankrupt. ‖今はめそめそしている**場合**ではない This is no *time* for tears. ‖祭りや婚礼などの**特別の場合に**このすしを作ります We make this sushi *on special occasions* like festivals or weddings.

▶この契約を解約すると違約金を取られる**場合があります** If you cancel this contract, a penalty fee *may* be imposed. ‖**場合**（＝事情）**によっては**家を売らなければならないかもしれない *Under certain circumstances*, we may have to sell the house. ‖**場合によっては**１週間ばかりロンドンに滞在するかもしれない *Depending on how things go*, I may stay in London for a week or so. ‖**場合によっては**きみ自身が行かなければならないかもしれない You may have to go yourself *depending on the situation*. ‖ **対話**「本当に車を売るの？」「まだわからないけど，**場合によってはね**」"You say you're selling your car. Is that correct?" "I don't know yet. *It all depends*."（➤ It all depends. は後ろに on circumstances が略された形で，会話でよく用いられる）‖**それは場合によりけりだ** *That depends*.

パーカ a **parka**.

パーカッション《音楽》**percussion**.

パーキング **parking** ‖**パーキングチケット** a parking lot ticket ‖**パーキングビル**《米》a (multi-level) parking structure,《英》a multi-storey [multi-deck] car park. ‖**パーキングメーター** a parking meter.

パーキンソンびょう パーキンソン病《医学》**Parkinson's disease.**

はあく 把握 (a) **grasp** **一動** **把握する** **grasp** ＋㊐（つかむ）；**understand** ＋㊐（理解する）▶講演の要点を**把握する** *grasp* the main points of the speech ‖まず問題の意味を**把握**しなければいけない First of all, you have to *understand* [*get a grasp of*] the meaning of the question. ‖彼は状況をよく**把握している**とは思えない I don't think he *has a good grasp of* the situation.

バーゲン a (**bargain**) **sale** ▶このセーター，**バーゲン**で安く買ったの I got this sweater cheap *at a sale*. ‖原宿へ行きましょう．どこも**バーゲン中**よ Let's go shopping in Harajuku. All the stores *are having sales*. ‖角の店では今冬物の**バーゲンをやっている** Winter goods *are* now *on sale* at the store on the corner.

‖**バーゲン会場** a bargain counter; a bargain basement（➤英米では通例「地階」にあることから）．

> **危ないカタカナ語✸バーゲン**
> 日本語では「バーゲンセール」を略して「バーゲン」というが，英語では逆に bargain を略して単に sale という．英語の bargain は「掘り出し物，買い得品」の意であって，bargain だけでは「特価売り出し」の意味にはならないことに注意．

バーコード a **bar code** ‖**バーコード読み取り機** a bar code scanner.

パーサー a **purser** ‖**アシスタントパーサー** an assistant purser.

ばあさん 婆さん an **old woman.**

バージニア **Virginia**（アメリカ東部の州；略 VA, Va.）．

バージョン a **version** ▶iTunes の**最新バージョン**をダウンロードする download *the latest version* of iTunes.

バージョンアップ an **upgrade** ▶**バージョンアップ**したソフト *upgraded* software《**参考**》「バージョンアップ」は和製語．

バージン a **virgin** ▶私，まだ**バージン**よ I'm still *a virgin*. 《**参考**》英語の virgin は He's a virgin. のように「童貞」の意でも用いる．

バージンロード the center aisle of a church or chapel down which a bride walks（➤説明的な訳；「バージンロード」は和製語）．

バースコントロール **birth control.**

バースデー a **birthday**（誕生日）‖**バースデーケーキ** a birthday cake ‖**バースデーパーティー** a birthday party.

パーセンテージ **percentage.**

パーセント **percent, per cent**（➤「100につき」が原義なので複数形にはしない）▶人体の**70パーセント**は水分だ Seventy *percent* of the human body is water. ‖定期預金の利息は年**何パーセント**ですか What *percent* interest does the fixed deposit earn in a year? ‖当クラブの会員は女性が**約80パーセント**を占めています In our club, women make up about 80 *percent* of the membership.

▶ **対話**「男子高校生の**何パーセント**が就職しますか」「18**パーセント**くらいです」"*What percentage* of the high school boys get a job after graduation?" "About eighteen *percent*."（➤(1) percentage には疑問詞の what のほか，large, small, certain など

のような形容詞が先行することが多い．(2)動詞は of のあとの名詞に合わせる）‖彼の成功を100パーセント確信しています I'm *100 percent sure* that he will succeed.

パーソナリティー a **personality** ▶テレビのパーソナリティー a TV *personality*. →タレント
‖**パーソナリティー障害** a personality disorder.

パーソナル **personal**
‖**パーソナル・アイデンティティー・ナンバー** a personal identity number《略 PIN》‖**パーソナルトレーナー** a personal trainer.

ばあたりてきな 場当たり的な **haphazard** /hæphǽzəʳd/ **—副 場当たり的に** **haphazardly, in a disorganized way.**

バーチャル **virtual** ▶インターネットのバーチャルな世界 the *virtual* world of the Internet.
‖**バーチャルオフィス** a virtual office ‖**バーチャルコミュニティー** a virtual community ‖**バーチャルショッピング** virtual shopping ‖**バーチャル大学** a virtual university (➤インターネットを通じて受講する大学) ‖**バーチャルフレンド** a virtual friend ‖**バーチャルリアリティ** (a) virtual reality (略 VR).

パーツ **parts** (➤一個のパーツは one part).

ぱーっと ▶今夜はぱーっとやろう Let's *party* tonight!

バーディー《ゴルフ》a **birdie** ▶石川は5つのバーディーを決めた Ishikawa made five *birdies*. ‖彼女はショートパットを決められずバーディーを逃した She missed a short putt for *birdie*.

パーティー 1【集まり】 a **party** ▶パーティーを催す hold [have／give] *a party* ‖新入生の歓迎パーティーをやろう Let's throw *a welcome party* for the freshmen. (➤ throw a party はくだけた言い方) ‖あしたのパーティー，出る？ Are you going to tomorrow's *party*? ‖あすは竹田さんの結婚披露パーティーに招待されている I'm invited to Mr. Takeda's *wedding reception* tomorrow.
‖**卒業パーティー** a graduation party.

> **あなたの英語はどう響く？**
> 外国人に「今週末うちでパーティーをしますが，来ていただけますか」のつもりで We are having *a party at home* this weekend. Can you come? と言う人が少なくないが，英語国で party といえば「ホームパーティー」(これは和製語)に決まっているので at home は不要．

2【隊，一行】 a **party** ▶（登山の）女性だけのパーティー a women-only mountain climbing *party*.

バーテン《米》a **bartender** /bɑ́:ʳtèndəʳ/,《英》a **barman**; a **barmaid** (女性の) (➤ bartender が性差のない語).

ハート 1【心臓，心】 a **heart** ▶封筒にハートの印のシールをはる seal an envelope with *a heart* ‖女性のハートを射止める win a woman's *heart* ‖その歌はハートにじーんときた That song touched my *heart*.
2【トランプの】 a **heart** ▶ハートのエース[女王] the ace [queen] of *hearts* ‖ハート型のチョコレート a *heart-shaped* chocolate.

ハード 1【厳しい，強い】 **hard** ▶ハードな練習 *hard* training ‖ハードスケジュール a *tight* [*heavy*] schedule (➤ hard schedule は一般的ではない) ‖ハードパンチ a *strong* [*hard*] punch ‖スキーのハードトレーニングを受ける undergo *rigorous* training [receive *strict* training] in skiing ‖仕事はますますハードになりそうだ It looks like my job is going to get *harder*.
2【ハードウェア】 **hardware** (➤Ⓤ扱い).

バード a **bird**
‖**バードウォッチャー** a bird watcher ‖**バードウォッチング** bird watching ‖**バードストライク** a bird strike [hit] (➤鳥が構造物に衝突する事故).

パート 1【パートタイム】 a **part-time job** (仕事); a **part-time worker**, a **part-timer** (パートで働く人) ▶母はパートでスーパーに勤めている My mother is working *part-time* at a supermarket. ‖彼女は時給1000円のパートをさがしている She is looking for *a part-time job* which pays 1,000 yen an hour.

> **危ないカタカナ語✹ パート**
> 「パートタイム」を略して「パート」といっているが，part だけでは英語の part-time の意味にはならない．人を指す場合は part-time worker とか，インフォーマルで part-timer，仕事を指す場合は part-time job という．work part-time (パートで働く)のように副詞としても使う．時間給で働くパートであることをはっきりさせる場合は hourly worker と言えばよい．

2【音楽】 a **part** ▶私たちの合唱団はソプラノ・メゾソプラノ・アルトの3つのパートから成っている Our chorus is made of three *parts*: soprano, mezzo-soprano and alto.

ハードウェア **hardware** (➤Ⓤ扱い) ▶ハードウェアはコンピュータの機械そのものをいい，ソフトウェアはそれを動かすプログラムなどをいう *Hardware* refers to the computer machinery itself, while software means programs to operate it.

ハードカバー a **hardcover**, a **hardback**, a **hardbound book**.

ハードコピー a **hard copy** ▶文書のハードコピーをプリントアウトする print out a *hard copy* of a document.

パートタイマー →パート．

ハードディスク a **hard disk** ▶ハードディスクに番組を録画する record a TV program on *a hard disk* (➤そのような録画機を digital video recorder と呼ぶ).
‖**ハードディスクドライブ** a hard disk drive, an HDD.

パートナー a **partner**.

ハードボイルド ▶ハードボイルドの推理小説 a *hard-boiled* detective story.

ハードル a **hurdle** ▶100メートルハードル the 100-meter *hurdles* ‖ハードルを越す clear *a hurdle*
▶《比喩的》M大は私にはハードルが高い Getting into M University *is too hard* for me.
‖**ハードル競走** a hurdle race.

バーナー a **burner** ▶バーナーで焦げ目をつける scorch ... with *a burner*.

はあはあ ▶彼ははあはあ言いながら階段を駆け上がった He ran up the stairs *gasping for breath* [*panting*]. (➤ pant は「あえぐ」).

ハーフ

> **解説** 混血の人をいう場合の「ハーフ」は英語では half-breed であるが，この語には軽蔑的なニュアンスがあるので使わないほうがよい．一般的には She is half-Japanese and half-American. (彼女は日本人とアメリカ人のハーフだ)のようにいう．

‖**ハーフコート** a half-length coat.

ハーブ an [a] **herb** /əːʳb ‖ hə:b/ (薬草)
‖**ハーブ園** an [a] herb garden ‖**ハーブティー**

herbal tea.

> 「ハーブ」のいろいろ **ウイキョウ** fennel／**カモミール** chamomile／**セージ** sage／**タイム** thyme／**バジル** basil／**ヒメウイキョウ** cumin／**ペパーミント** peppermint／**ヘリオトロープ** heliotrope／**ベルガモット** bergamot／**マヨラナ** marjoram／**ラベンダー** lavender／**レモングラス** lemon grass／**ローズマリー** rosemary

ハープ a **harp** ‖**ハープ奏者** a harpist ‖ **グラスハープ** a glass harp(➤ その奏者は glass harpist).

ハープシコード a **harpsichord.**

ハーフスイング 《野球》 a **checked swing**, a **half swing.**

ハーフタイム **halftime** ▶アメフトの試合ではハーフタイムにショーが行われる During an American football game a show is staged at *halftime*.

ハーフミラー a **one-way mirror.**

バーベキュー a **barbecue** /báːʳbɪkjuː/ ▶今夜は家の庭でバーベキューをする予定だ We are going to have *a barbecue* in our yard this evening.

‖**バーベキューこんろ** a barbecue grill (脚のついた大型の) ; a hibachi (小型の).

バーベル a **barbell** ▶ 100キロのバーベルを持ち上げる lift a 100kg *barbell*.

バーボン **bourbon (whiskey).**

パーマ a **permanent (wave)**, 《インフォーマル》 a **perm** ▶私の髪はパーマがかかりやすい[にくい] My hair is easy [difficult] to *perm*. ‖ 私たちの学校ではパーマ(をかけること)は禁止されている We are not allowed to *have our hair permed* at our school. ‖ パーマをかけたいのですが I'd like to *get a perm*.

‖**パーマ店** a hairdresser's ; a beauty salon.

バーミンガム **Birmingham** /báːʳmɪŋəm/ (イギリス中部の工業都市).

パームボール 《野球》 a **palmball.**

パームゆ **パーム油** **palm oil.**

ハーモニー (a) **harmony** ▶音と光のハーモニー the *harmony* of sound and light ‖ ママさんコーラスは見事なハーモニーを聞かせた The mothers' chorus sang in beautiful *harmony*.

ハーモニカ a **harmonica** /hɑːʳmάːnɪkə/ ▶『ふるさと』をハーモニカで吹く play "Furusato" on the *harmonica*.

バーモント **Vermont** /vəːʳmάːnt/ (アメリカ北東部の州 ; 略 VT, Vt.).

パーラー a **parlor.**

バール a **crowbar** ▶バールでドアをこじ開ける pry open the door with a *crowbar*.

パール a **pearl** ▶パールのネックレス a *pearl* necklace.

パーレン a **parenthesis** /pərénθəsɪs/ [複 **parentheses**] (丸かっこ).

ばーん ▶石油タンクがバーンと音を立てて爆発した An oil tank exploded *with a bang*.

[1]**はい** **肺** a **lung** /lʌŋ/ (➤ 左右 2 つあるので通例 lungs の形で用いる)

‖**肺がん** lung cancer ‖ **肺気腫** pulmonary emphysema /èmfɪsíːmə, -zíːmə/ ‖ **肺結核** pulmonary tuberculosis (➤ ふつうは単に tuberculosis または T.B. という).

[2]**はい** **灰** **ashes** ▶家も家財道具も一瞬のうちに灰になってしまった The house and the furniture were burned to *ashes* in an instant. ‖ たばこの灰を落とさないでよ Don't *flick your cigarette*.

‖**死の灰** lethal ash, radioactive fallout.

[3]**はい** **1**【質問に対する返事】 **yes**

> 《解説》日本語の「はい」に常に yes が対応するわけではない. 英語では答えの内容が肯定ならば yes, 否定ならば no を用いるからである. 例えば,「泳げないのですか」「はい, だめなんです」は "Can't you swim ?" "*No*, I can't." となる. 答えの文が「いいえ, 泳げますよ」なら "Yes, I can." となる. この食い違いは質問文が否定疑問文や付加疑問文の場合に起こる. →うん.

▶ 【対話】「きみは彼の言うことを信じますか」「はい, もちろんです」"Do you believe him ?" "*Yes*, of course." ‖ 【対話】(電話で)「もしもし, 土井さんのお宅ですか」「はい, そうですが, どちら様でしょうか」"Hello, is this the Doi residence ?" "*Yes* (, it is). May I ask who's calling, please ?"

▶ 【対話】「きみはカラオケは好きじゃないんだろう」「はい, きらいです」"You don't like karaoke, do you ?" "*No*, I don't."

2【承諾して】 **certainly** (かしこまりました) ; **sure** (もちろん ; わかった) ; **all right** (いいですよ) ▶ 【対話】「タイヤも点検してもらえる?」「はい」"Could you check the tires, too ?" "*Sure* [*Certainly*]." ‖ 【対話】「お兄ちゃんの言うことをよく聞くのよ, いい?」「はい」"Do as your brother tells you, all right ?" "*Sure.*／*O.K.*" ‖ 【対話】「あす, うちへいらっしゃいませんか」「はい, 喜んでうかがいます」"Won't you come to see me tomorrow ?" "*Yes*, I'd be glad to.／*Yes*, with pleasure." (➤ with pleasure がより改まった言い方) ‖ 【対話】「ママ, 早くしてよ!」「はい, はい, はい. 今行きますよ!」"Mommy, hurry up !" "*All right*, *all right*, *all right*, I'm coming !"

3【点呼・呼びかけの返事】 **here**, **present** ; **Yes ?** (➤ 呼びかけに対して) ▶ 【対話】(出欠をとって)「伊藤さん」「はい」"Ito ?" "*Here.*／*Present.*" (➤ Yes とは言わない) ‖ 【対話】「佐藤君」「はい?」"Mr. Sato." "*Yes ?*" (➤ 上昇調で言い,「何でしょうか」の意. 店の客などに言うときには Yes, sir [ma'am] ? と言う).

4【注意を喚起して】 ▶はい, 黒板を見て *Now*, look at the blackboard. ‖ (赤ん坊に向かって) はい, はい, 太郎ちゃん. 泣いちゃだめよ *Now*, *now*, Taro. You mustn't cry.

5【物を見せたり手渡したりして】 ▶ 【対話】「ちょっとそのカードを見せてください」「はい, どうぞ」"Can I have a look at the card ?" "*Certainly* [*Yes*]. *Here you are* [*Here it is*]." ‖ 【対話】「はい, お茶」「ありがとう」"*Here's* your tea." "Thanks."

[4]**はい** **胚** 《動物》《植物》 an **embryo** /émbrioʊ/.

ハイー

> **危ないカタカナ語** ハイー
>
> 「ハイー」のつくカタカナ語は多いが, そのまま high ... とはできないものも多いので注意を要する.
>
> **ハイウェー** highway は「公道, 街道, 幹線道路」のことで,「高速道路」とは限らない.「高速道路」に相当する語には《米》 expressway, freeway, 《英》 motorway などがある.
>
> **ハイセンス** センスが高級であることを high sense といっても通じない. この場合の「センス」は「趣味, 好み」の意味であるから, taste を用いて good [excellent／refined] taste などとする. high taste は不可.
>
> **ハイソックス** 膝下までの寸法の丈の長い靴下を「ハイソックス」というのは和製語で, 英語では knee socks という.

ハイヒール かかとの高い婦人靴を「ハイヒール」というが，英語では high heels あるいは単に heels と複数形になる．high-heel(ed) shoes といってもよい．
ハイティーン（→見出語）

[1]**-はい -杯** ▶ご飯１杯 *a bowl* of rice ‖ ビール２杯 *two glasses* [*mugs*] of beer ‖ スプーン１杯の砂糖 *a spoonful of* sugar ‖ お茶をもう１杯もらえますか Could I have *another cup* of tea?

[2]**-はい -敗** ▶横綱はすでに３敗している The yokozuna has already suffered *three losses.* ‖《サッカーで》わがチームもあと１敗したら優勝は望めない If we *lose one more game*, there will be no hope of winning the championship.

ばい 倍

【文型】
A の～倍
～ times A
➤ A は数量を表す名詞
A の～倍 B の［で］
～ times B than A
➤ B は形容詞・副詞の比較級
～ times as B as A
➤ B は形容詞・副詞の原級など

【解説】(1)「２倍」は twice があるが，３倍以上は「３倍」なら three times,「８倍」なら eight times のように,「数詞＋ times」で表す．
(2)「～倍大きい」のように形容詞がポイントのときは通例，比較級を使う前者の ～ times bigger than ... を用いる．ただし，「2倍」に限っては（×）twice bigger とは言えず，後者の形で twice as big as という．また，「～倍の人口」のように名詞がくるときには ～ times the population of ... のようにする．

1【2倍】twice, two times ; double
▶３の倍は６だ *Twice* [*Two times*] three is six. ‖ 母はちょうど私の年の倍だ My mother is just *twice* my age.（➤ twice のあとに of などの前置詞はつけない）／My mother is *twice* as old as I am. ‖ 彼の収入は以前の倍になった His income *has become double* [*twice*] what it used to be. ‖ 彼女はぼくの倍の給料をかせぐ She earns *double* my salary. ‖ 倍の速度で at *double* the speed ‖ 赤ん坊は１年間で体重が倍になった The baby *doubled* its weight in a year.（➤この double は「倍加する」の意の動詞）‖ このビルの建築には当初の見込みの倍の金がかかった The construction of the building cost *twice as much as* expected.
▶彼は他の水泳部員の倍は練習する He practices at least *twice as much* as the other members on the swimming team.

2【…倍】... times ; -fold ▶このレンズを使うと物が10倍の大きさに見える This lens magnifies (an object) *ten times.*（➤ magnify は「拡大する」）‖ 対話「1000は10の何倍ですか」「100倍です」"*How many times* ten is one thousand?" "One hundred *times.*" ‖ オーストラリアは日本の約20倍の広さがある Australia is about *20 times* larger *than* Japan.／Australia is about *20 times* the size of Japan.（➤前の文がふつう. Australia is about 20 times as large as Japan. も頻度的には低くなるが可）‖ ６人分のパンを焼くにはこの３倍の小麦粉が必要だ In order to bake bread for six, you need *three times* more flour *than* this [*three times as much* flour *as* this]. ‖ 彼の家はうちの家より２，３倍広い His house is *two or three times* larger *than* ours [*two or three times* the size of ours]. ‖ こちらのほうがそれより何倍も大きい This is *several times* bigger *than* that.
✉ **日本の人口はあなたの国の人口の約10倍です** The population of Japan is about *10 times* larger *than* [*10 times as* large *as*] that of your country. ➤ 人口の多い，少ないは large, small で表す．
▶Ｋ大学理学部の今年度の入試競争率は12倍だ The competition to enter the Science School of K University is *12 to 1* this year.（➤「１人に対して12人の競争率」の意）‖ あの土地の値段は10年間で20倍になったそうだ I hear the value of that land has increased *20-fold* in ten years.／I hear the value of that land is *twenty times as much as* it was ten years ago.

[1]**パイ** a **pie** ▶カボチャ［ミート］パイ a pumpkin [meat] *pie* ‖ 今アップルパイを焼いているところなの I'm baking *an apple pie* now. ‖ **パイ皮** a pie crust.

[2]**パイ**《数学》**pi**（➤円周率；記号はπ）▶パイの値 the value of *pi* ‖ 円の面積はパイ掛ける半径の２乗である The area of a circle is *pi* times the radius squared.

[3]**パイ 牌** a **mah-jongg tile**（マージャンの）.

はいあがる 這い上がる crawl up ▶少年たちは土手をはい上がった The boys *clambered* [*crawled*] *up* the bank.
▶あの歌手はどん底からはい上がってスターの地位を築いた That singer *crawled up* from the pits to stardom.

バイアスロン the biathlon /baɪǽθlən/.

はいあん 廃案 ▶廃案にする *scrap a bill*（➤ scrap は「（計画など）を捨てる」）‖ 野党は政府提出の法案を廃案にした The opposition parties *blocked the bill* proposed by the government *from being passed.*／The opposition *forced the bill* proposed by the government *to be dropped.*

はいいろ 灰色 gray（➤《英》では通例 **grey** とつづる）― 形 **灰色の gray, grey** ▶ピンクは灰色系の地に映える Pink stands out on a *grayish* background.
▶《比喩的》私の大学時代は灰色だった Life in college *was gray* [*dull*／*depressing*] for me.

はいいん 敗因 the cause of one's **defeat** ▶敗因は何だと思いますか What do you think is *the cause of your defeat*? ‖ わがチームの敗因は練習のし過ぎだ *The cause of our defeat* is too much practice.

ばいう 梅雨 a **long spell of rainy weather (in June and July) ; the rainy season**（梅雨期）→つゆ ▶梅雨期には食中毒に特に注意しなさい Take special precautions against food poisoning during *the rainy season.*
‖ **梅雨前線** a seasonal rain front.

ハイウェー《米》an **expressway**, a **freeway,**《英》a **motorway**（➤英語の highway は「公道」の意）. →ハイー.

はいえい 背泳 the backstroke. →背泳ぎ.

はいえき 廃液 waste, waste water ▶化学工場から出る廃液 *waste* (*water*) from a chemical factory.

ハイエナ《動》a **hyena** /haɪíːnə/.

[1]**はいえん 肺炎**《医学》**pneumonia** /njumóunjə/ ▶肺炎にかかる contract [get] *pneumonia.*
‖ **急性肺炎** acute pneumonia.

²**はいえん 排煙する** **emit smoke**.

ばいえん 煤煙 **soot** /sʊt/（すす）; **smoke**（煙）▶ばい煙の多い大都市 a *sooty* [*smoky*] big city.

ハイオク ▶この車はハイオクで走る This car runs on *high-octane gas*.

‖ハイオクガソリン high-octane gas(oline).

バイオ(テクノロジー) **biotechnology** /bàɪoʊteknɑ́ːlədʒi/ ▶バイオの力で種を大量に作り出す produce a large number of seeds *utilizing biotechnology* 《参考》略語の bio は単独では通例 biography(伝記, 略歴紹介), または biology（生物学)の意.

‖バイオ燃料 a bio-fuel.

パイオニア a **pioneer** /pàɪəníər/ ▶彼は心臓移植のパイオニアの１人だ He is one of the *pioneers* in the field of heart transplantation.

バイオリズム **biorhythm** /báɪoʊrìðəm/.

バイオリン a **violin** /vàɪəlín/ ▶バイオリンを弾く play the *violin*.

‖バイオリン奏者 a violinist.

は

ばいおん 倍音《音楽》a **harmonic**, a **harmonic overtone**.

はいが 胚芽 (**rice**) **germ**

‖はい芽米 partially polished rice《参考》germ には「ばい菌」の意味もあるので,「はい芽米」を rice with germs とするのは好ましくない.

ばいか 倍加 ▶消費者のエコ意識の高まりで, ハイブリッド車や電気自動車の販売が倍加した Due to consumers' growing eco-consciousness, sales of hybrid and electric vehicles *have doubled*.

ハイカー a **hiker** ▶その山は秋になるとハイカーたちでにぎわう The mountain is thronged with groups of *hikers* every fall.

はいかい 徘徊する ▶その老人には夜中に徘徊する癖がある The old man has a tendency to *wander about* in the middle of the night.

ばいかい 媒介する **carry** +ⓐ; **transmit** +ⓐ(伝染病などをうつす) ▶昆虫の中には伝染病を媒介するものがいる Some insects *carry* contagious diseases. ‖この病気はシラミが媒介する This disease *is transmitted* by lice.

はいガス 排ガス →排気ガス.

はいかつりょう 肺活量 **lung capacity, breathing capacity** ▶水泳の選手は一般に肺活量が大きい Generally, swimmers have a large *lung* [*breathing*] *capacity*.

‖肺活量計 a spirometer, a pulmometer.

ハイカラ ハイカラな **stylish**;《英》**smart**(しゃれた); **fashionable**(流行の); **ritzy**(高級な).

¹**はいかん 配管** **plumbing** /plʌ́mɪŋ/, **piping** ▶配管工事のためこの道路は通行止めになっています This road is closed (to traffic) due to *water main construction* [*installation*] (*work*). (➤ water main は「水道本管」; plumbing は建物内での工事を指すので, この文では使えない).

‖配管工 a plumber /plʌ́məʳ/.

²**はいかん 廃刊** ▶その写真週刊誌はとうとう廃刊になった They finally *stopped the publication* of that weekly photo magazine. / That weekly photo magazine *was* finally *discontinued*.

³**はいかん 拝観** ▶東大寺を拝観する *visit* (the) Todaiji Temple ‖拝観料 an admission [entrance] fee.

¹**はいき 廃棄** ▶その工場は古い機械類を廃棄することにした The factory decided to *do away with* [*to scrap*] the old machinery.

‖産業廃棄物 industrial waste.

²**はいき 排気** ▶たばこの煙を排気する *vent* cigarette smoke.

‖排気ガス exhaust /ɪgzɔ́ːst/ (gas), (automobile) exhaust fumes.

ばいきゃく 売却 **sale** 一動 **売却する** **sell** +ⓐ; **dispose of**（処分する）▶彼は軽井沢の別荘を売却した He *sold* [*disposed of*] his vacation home in Karuizawa.

はいきゅう 配給 **distribution**（分配）; **rationing** /rǽʃənɪŋ/（物不足時の割り当て）一動 **配給する** **distribute** +ⓐ, **ration** +ⓐ ▶救援物資の配給 the *distribution* of relief supplies ‖難民に食料と毛布が配給された Food and blankets *were distributed* [*were given out*] to the refugees.

‖(映画の)配給会社 a film distributor ‖配給制 rationing.

はいきょ 廃虚 **ruins, remains** ▶長引く内戦で町は廃虚と化した The city *fell into ruins* [*was devastated*] because of the prolonged civil war.

はいぎょう 廃業 ▶彼は最近商売を廃業した He *closed down* his business recently. ‖おじは医者［弁護士］を廃業した My uncle *gave up* his practice.

はいきりょう 排気量 **displacement** ▶排気量1500ccの車 a car of [with a] 1,500cc *engine* (*capacity* / *displacement*).

はいきん 背筋 **back muscles**

‖背筋力 back muscle strength.

ばいきん 黴菌 a **germ**,《インフォーマル》a **bug**; a **microbe** /máɪkroʊb/, **bacteria** /bæktíəriə/（細菌）▶空気中にはばい菌がいっぱいいる The air is full of *germs*. ‖傷口からばい菌が入った(＝化のうした) The wound *became infected*.

ハイキング **hiking**(活動); a **hike**(１回１回の) ▶この前の日曜日に久美子と私はハイキングに行った Kumiko and I went on *a hike* last Sunday. ‖あす丹沢へハイキングに行きませんか How about going *hiking* in Tanzawa tomorrow? (➤ to Tanzawa とはしない) ‖このハイキングコースは初心者向きだ This *hiking trail* [*route*] is for beginners. (➤ hiking course は一般的ではない).

バイキング a **buffet** /bəféɪ ‖ bʊ́feɪ/, (a) **smorgasbord** /smɔ́ːʳgəsbɔːʳd/ (バイキング料理)

> **危ないカタカナ語✹ バイキング**
> テーブルに並べた各種の料理から好みに応じて自由に取って食べる形式の料理を「バイキング」と呼んでいるが, 英語では smorgasbord という. これはスウェーデン語から英語になった語で, 立食式のスカンジナビア料理(の店)を指す. ちなみに「バイキング」のもとになった Viking は８～10世紀にヨーロッパの海岸を荒らし回ったスカンジナビアの海賊である.

▶バイキングレストラン a *buffet*(*-style*) restaurant / a *smorgasbord* restaurant.

‖朝食バイキング a breakfast buffet [smorgasbord] (➤ 前者がふつう).

はいきんしゅぎ 拝金主義 **the worship of money**

‖拝金主義者 someone who worships money; a money-worshipper.

はいく 俳句 a **haiku** (➤ 英語化している) ▶俳句を作る write [compose] *a haiku*.

日本紹介 ✉ **俳句は５・７・５の17音をしばしば３行に並べたごく短い定型詩です. 伝統的な俳句**

では季節を表すことばである季語を入れます A haiku is a very short fixed verse form of 17 syllables often arranged in three lines of 5, 7, and 5 syllables. Traditional haiku contain a word or phrase called a '*kigo*' that indicates the season.

バイク a **motorcycle**, a **motorbike**, 《インフォーマル》a **bike** (➤ bike は「自転車」の意で用いられることのほうが多い) ▶バイクに乗る ride *a motorcycle* ‖ バイク便の配達員 a *motorcycle* [*motorbike*] messenger ‖ ひったくりはバイクで走り去った The purse snatcher sped away *on* his *motorcycle*.

はいぐうしゃ 配偶者 a **spouse** /spaʊs/
‖配偶者控除 a tax exemption for one's spouse.

ハイクラス ▶私たちはハイクラスのレストランで食事をした We ate at a *high-class* [*fancy*] restaurant.

ハイグレード **high-grade** ▶ハイグレード潤滑油 *high-grade* lubricating oil ‖ ハイグレードなカレールー *high-quality* curry roux.

1**はいけい 背景** **1【絵・写真などの】** a **background** ▶私たちは中国で万里の長城を背景に写真を撮った We had our photos taken *with* the Great Wall of China *in the background*. ‖ 富士山が夕空を背景にくっきりと見えた We could see Mt. Fuji clearly *against* the evening sky.

2【背後の事情】 a **background** ▶子供の自殺増加の背景にはコミュニケーションの欠如の問題がある *Behind* [*In the background of*] the increase in the number of children's suicide lies the problem of lack of communication. ‖ これは飛鳥時代を背景にした小説です This is a novel *set* in the Asuka period. ‖ 外国語を習うときはその文化背景も勉強しなければならない When you learn a foreign language, you should study its *cultural background* as well.

2**はいけい 拝啓**

> **《解説》「拝啓」の書き方**
> (1) 英語では相手の性別, 職業, 身分, 親しさの度合いなどによってそれぞれ違った呼びかけを用いる. 形式ばった手紙では Dear Sir [Madam], とするか, あるいは Dear Mr. [Mrs. ／Miss ／Ms.] Perkins, のように姓をつける. ビジネスレターでは Gentlemen : や《英》Dear Sirs : が一般的であったが, 最近では性差をなくす目的や, これらの言い方に人格が感じられないなどの理由で使われなくなりつつある.
> (2) 親しい間がらでは Dear Cathy, My dear Cathy, のように名前を使う. My をつけると《米》では形式ばった感じを与えるが, 《英》では親しみをこめた表現になる.

はいけつしょう 敗血症 《医学》 **blood poisoning**, **septicemia** /sèptɪsíːmiə/ (➤ 後者は医学用語).

はいけん 拝見する **see** +目 (見る) ▶ちょっとその書類を拝見させてください Please *let me see* [*let me have a look at*] those papers. ‖ 乗車券を拝見させていただきます *May I see* your tickets, please?
✉ **お手紙拝見しました** Thank you for your letter. ／I have received your letter. ➤ 冒頭のあいさつとしては I've read your letter. とは書かない.

1**はいご 背後** **1【後ろ】** **the back**, **the rear** ▶彼は背後から撃たれて肩に傷を負った He was shot *from behind* [*from the back* ／*from the rear*] and received a wound in his shoulder.

2【事件などの背景】 **the background** ▶警察はやくざが殺害された事件の背後関係を調べている The police are investigating *the background* of a case in which [where] a yakuza was killed.

2**はいご 廃語** an **obsolete word**
‖準廃語 an obsolescent word.

はいこう 廃校 **the closing of a school** ▶その学校は生徒不足でこの3月で廃校になる That school will *be closed* [*will close*] at the end of March due to a decline in enrollment.

はいごう 配合 (a) **combination** (取り合わせ) ; a **mixture** (混ぜたもの) 一動 **配合する** **mix** +目 ▶化学肥料は植物に必要な養分をバランスよく配合してある Chemical fertilizer is a well-balanced *combination* of essential plant nutrients.

ばいこく 売国 **treason**
‖売国行為 an act of treason ‖ 売国奴 a traitor.

はいざい 廃材 **scrap wood** ▶廃材でベンチを作る make a bench out of *scrap wood*.

はいさつ 拝察
✉ **お母さまがご病気の由, どんなにかご心配のことと拝察申し上げます** I'm sorry to hear of your mother's illness. I can *imagine* how worried you must be.

はいざら 灰皿 an **ashtray**.

はいし 廃止 **abolition** (制度・慣習などの) 一動 **廃止する** **abolish** +目, 《インフォーマル》**do away with** ; **discontinue** +目 (打ち切る) ▶ローカル線を廃止する *discontinue* services on the local line ‖ 韓国は死刑を廃止した South Korea has *abolished* the death penalty. ‖ わが校はことしから制服を廃止した Our school *did away with* uniforms at the beginning of the year.

1**はいしゃ 歯医者** a **dentist** ▶歯医者に行く see the *dentist* ／go to the *dentist* [*dentist's*] (➤ dentist's のあとには office が略されている) ‖ あす歯医者に予約がある I have an appointment with the *dentist* [a dental appointment] tomorrow.

2**はいしゃ 敗者** a **loser**, a **defeated person** [**team**]
‖敗者復活戦 a consolation match [game ／race].

3**はいしゃ 廃車** a **disused** [**scrapped**] **car** ▶廃車にする *scrap a vehicle* [*car*].

4**はいしゃ 配車** **vehicle dispatching** ▶タクシーを配車する *dispatch* [*send out*] taxicabs.

はいしゃく 拝借する **borrow** +目 ▶ **対話**「社内電話帳を拝借してよろしいですか」「どうぞ」"Could I *borrow* the office telephone directory?" "Certainly." ‖ ちょっとお手洗いを拝借したいのですが May I *use* the bathroom?

ばいしゃく 媒酌 ▶私たちは山下先生ご夫妻の媒酌で結婚しました Our marriage was arranged *through the good offices of* Mr. and Mrs. Yamashita. ‖媒酌人 a *baishakunin*, a matchmaker (→仲人).

ハイジャック a **hijack**, (a) **hijacking** 一動 **ハイジャックする** **hijack** +目 ▶イラン航空機がハイジャックされたらしい I hear that an Iranian airplane *was hijacked*. ‖ ハイジャック犯人は6人だ There are six *hijackers*.

ハイジャンプ **the high jump**.

ばいしゅう 買収 **1【買い取ること】** **purchase** /pə́ːʳtʃəs/ ; **acquisition** (企業の) 一動 **買収する** **purchase** +目, **buy up**, **acquire** +目 ▶会社を買収する *acquire* a company ‖ その店を丸ごと買収する *buy up* the whole shop ‖ 国はダムを建設するために広大な土地を買収した The government *purchased* [*bought* (*up*)] extensive land to build a dam.

2【賄賂を贈ること】bribery —動 買収する bribe +(目), 《インフォーマル》**buy off** ▶証人を買収する *bribe* [*buy off*] a witness ‖その立候補者は買収工作が明るみに出て市長選挙戦から脱落した The candidate for mayor dropped out of the race when his *bribery scheme* came to light.

1はいしゅつ 排出 (a) **discharge —動 排出する discharge** +(目) ▶下水はここから排出される Sewage *is discharged* here. ‖車の排気ガスの排出量を規制する limit permissible exhaust *emissions* of motor vehicles.

‖**排出口** an outlet.

2はいしゅつ 輩出する produce +(目) ▶元禄時代は近松門左衛門や井原西鶴など多くの文人を輩出した The Genroku period *produced* many authors such as Chikamatsu Monzaemon and Ihara Saikaku.

ばいしゅん 売春 prostitution ▶好奇心から売春をする女の子もいる Some girls *sell themselves* [*turn to prostitution*] out of curiosity.

‖**売春婦** a prostitute, a whore /hɔːʳ/ (➤ 後者には軽蔑的な響きがある) ; 《米・インフォーマル》a hooker 《参考》売春をする男性のことを male prostitute, 軽蔑的に gigolo という ‖**売春防止法** Anti-Prostitution Act.

はいじょ 排除する remove +(目), **eliminate** +(目) ▶障害物を排除する *remove* [*get rid of*] the obstacles ‖市民はここ数年暴力を排除するよう努めてきた Citizens have made efforts to *eliminate* violence for the past few years. ‖警察は路上から群衆を排除した The police *cleared* the crowd (*away*) *from* the street.

ばいしょう 賠償 compensation —動 賠償する compensate /kɑ́ːmpənseɪt/ 《for》 ▶我々はバス会社に損害賠償を要求した We demanded that the bus company *pay* [*make compensation*] *for the loss*. (➤ demand に続く節の動詞は原形) ‖福岡地方裁判所は住民の損害賠償要求の訴えを却下した The District Court of Fukuoka Prefecture dismissed the residents' *suit for damages*.

‖**賠償金** compensation ; reparations (戦争の).

1はいしょく 配色 a **color scheme** /skiːm/ ▶彼の絵は配色がすばらしい His paintings have a wonderful *color scheme* [*color harmony*].

2はいしょく 敗色 ▶わがチームの敗色が濃くなった It looks like *the odds are against* our team. (➤ odds は「勝ち目」の意).

1はいしん 配信する deliver +(目), **wire** +(目) ▶インターネットでゲームソフトを配信する *deliver* [*distribute*] game software over the Internet.

2はいしん 背信 a **betrayal of trust —動 背信する betray** someone's **trust**.

1はいじん 俳人 a **haiku poet**.

2はいじん 廃人 a **(human) wreck**.

ばいしん 陪審 the jury(陪審(員)団 ; 個々の成員を指すときは複数扱い) ▶陪審は(被告に)無罪の評決をした *The jury* reached a verdict of "not guilty" (for the defendant).

‖**陪審員** a juror, a jury member ‖**陪審制度** the jury system.

1はいすい 排水 drainage /dréɪnɪdʒ/ **—動 排水する drain** ▶その庭は排水が悪い The garden *drains badly* [*does not drain well*].

▶排水量1万トンの客船 a passenger liner with *a displacement* of 10,000 tons.

‖**排水管** a drainpipe ‖**排水口** a drain ‖**排水溝** a drain, a drainage ditch ‖**排水工事** drainage work(s) ‖**排水設備** drainage ‖**排水ポンプ** a drain [drainage] pump ‖**排水量** displacement ‖**排水路** a drainage canal.

2はいすい 配水する supply water ▶配水の設備 *water supply* facilities ‖作業員たちが配水工事のため道路を掘り起こしている Workers are digging up the road *to lay water pipes*.

‖**配水管** a water pipe.

3はいすい 廃水 wastewater ▶その川は工場の廃水で汚染されている The river is contaminated by *wastewater* from a factory.

はいすいしゅ 肺水腫 pulmonary edema.

はいすいのじん 背水の陣 ▶彼は今回の選挙は背水の陣で臨んだ He fought in this election *with his back to the wall*. (➤ 文字どおりには「背中を壁につけて」) ‖浪人3年目だから来年は背水の陣(＝最後のチャンス)だ I've spent three years preparing for college entrance examinations, so next year is my *last chance*.

ばいすう 倍数 《数学》a **multiple** ▶6や8は2の倍数だ Six and eight are *multiples* of two.

ハイスクール a **high school.** →高校.

ハイスピード ハイスピードの high-speed

‖**ハイスピードカメラ** a high-speed camera.

はいする 配する arrange +(目) (配置する) ▶青い地に水玉模様を配した柄 a pattern of polka dots (*arranged*) on a blue ground ‖適材を適所に配することが重要だ It's important to *put* the right person in the right place.

はいせき 排斥する exclude +(目) (中に入れない) ; **reject** +(目) (拒絶する) ▶会から未成年者を排斥する *exclude* minors from the association ‖欧米流の考え方を排斥する *reject* Western thinking ‖日本製品の排斥運動(＝不買運動)が各国に起こっていた There was *a movement against* Japanese goods in many countries. ／There was *a boycott against* Japanese goods in various countries.

はいせつ 排泄 excretion /ɪkskríːʃən/ (排出作用) **—動 排せつする excrete** +(目) ▶子供は好んで排せつ物を表す汚いことばを口にする Children love to use vulgar words having to do with *excretion* [*excrement* ／ *bodily waste*]. (➤ excrement は「大便」) ‖自分で排せつ物の始末をするのが困難な人 a person who can not dispose of his or her own *bodily waste*.

‖**排せつ器官** an excretory organ.

はいぜつ 廃絶 abolition —動 廃絶する abolish +(目) ▶原発の廃絶を求める運動 a movement for the *abolition* of nuclear power plants.

1はいせん 配線 wiring ▶配線を間違えないように注意してキットを組み立てた I built the kit taking care not to make mistakes in the *wiring*. ‖たこ足配線をしないでください Please do not *put many plugs in one outlet*.

‖**配線工事** wiring work ‖**配線図** a wiring diagram ‖(コンピュータの)**配線盤** a plugboard, a patchboard.

2はいせん 敗戦 a **defeat** ; a **loss** (勝負などの)

‖**敗戦国** a defeated nation ‖**敗戦投手** a losing pitcher, a loser.

3はいせん 廃船する take a ship out of service (使用しなくなる) ; **scrap a ship** (くずとして廃棄する).

4はいせん 廃線 a **discontinued railway line.**

ばいせん 焙煎 ▶コーヒー豆を焙煎する *roast* coffee beans.

ハイセンス →ハイ-.

はいそ 敗訴 a losing suit 一動 **敗訴する** lose a (law) suit [case] ▶その裁判は原告の敗訴となった The plaintiff *lost the suit* [*case*].

1**はいそう 配送** delivery 一動 **配送する** deliver +目 ▶品物の配送は1週間かかります *Delivery* (of the goods) will take a week. ‖《掲示》都内は無料で配送します *Free delivery* within Tokyo.
‖**配送センター** a delivery center ‖**配送先** the delivery address.

2**はいそう 敗走** a rout /raʊt/ 一動 **敗走させる** rout +目.

ばいぞう 倍増する double +目; redouble +目 (さらに倍加する) ▶この仕事につけばきみの収入は倍増するよ If you take this job, you can *double* your income.

はいぞく (…に)**配属する** assign /əsáɪn/ 《to》 ▶このたび私は国際部に配属になりました I have *been assigned* [*been attached*] *to* the International Division. (➤ attach は「一時的」の含み).

ハイソサエティー high society.

ハイソックス (a pair of) knee /niː/ socks.

はいた 歯痛 a toothache ▶歯痛に悩む suffer from (*a*) *toothache* (➤ a を省略するのは主に《英》) ‖歯痛がする I *have a toothache*. (➤《米》では a を省略しないのがふつうで, この表現では通例痛いのは1本と受け止める; 数本の歯が痛む場合は I have aching teeth. または, My teeth ache. と表現する) ‖最近歯痛がするようになった I have started *having* [*getting*] *toothaches* recently.

はいたい 敗退する be defeated ▶わがチームは2回戦で5対3で敗退した Our team *was defeated* in the second round by (a score of) 5 to 3.

ばいたい 媒体 a medium /míːdiəm/ [複 media] ▶テレビは宣伝媒体として最も効果があるものの1つだ Television is one of the most effective *advertising media*.

はいだす 這い出す crawl out ▶猫がテーブルの下からはい出した A cat *crawled out* from under the table.

はいたつ 配達

(a) delivery 一動 **配達する** deliver (+目) ▶彼は毎朝新聞配達をしている He *delivers* newspapers every morning. ‖これをもらうわ. 配達していただける? I think I'll take this one. Can it *be delivered*? ‖ 対話 「このパソコン, 配達してくれますか」「申しわけありません. うちは配達はしてないんですよ」"Could we *have* this PC *delivered*?" "I'm sorry. We *don't have a delivery service*." ‖お宅は配達してもらえるの? Do you *deliver*? ‖ビールを2ダース配達してもらった We *had* two dozen bottles of beer *delivered*.
‖**配達区域** a delivery area, 《米また》a route, 《英また》a round ‖**配達証明郵便**《米》certified mail, 《英》recorded delivery ‖**配達料** a delivery charge ‖**牛乳配達人** a milk deliverer ‖**再配達** redelivery ‖**新聞配達人** a newspaper deliverer ‖**即日** [**翌日**] **配達** a same-day [next-day] delivery ‖**郵便配達人** a mail [postal] carrier.
《参考》「…配達人」という場合, 従来は男性の働き手が多かったために milkman, mailman, postman など, -man をつけた言い方が一般的であったが, 最近では -man の代わりに性差のない deliverer, carrier のような言い方が好まれる傾向がある.

ハイタッチ a high five (スポーツ選手の) ▶2人はハイタッチを交わした The two *exchanged a high five*. / The two *high-fived*. ‖ハイタッチしよう Give me *five*.

はいたてき 排他的な exclusive ▶この地域の人々はひどく排他的でよそ者には冷たい The people in this region are very *unfriendly* and cold to strangers.
‖**排他的経済水域** an exclusive economic zone 《略 EEZ》.

バイタリティー vitality (生命力); vigor (元気) ▶新しく来た体育の先生はバイタリティーにあふれている Our new PE teacher is full of *vitality*.

はいち 配置 (an) arrangement 一動 **配置する** arrange +目 (並べる); station +目, post +目 (人を) ▶この部屋の家具はどう配置しましょうか How should we *arrange* the furniture in this room? ‖母は家具の配置替えが好きだ Mother is fond of *rearranging* the furniture. ‖警官が飛行場からホテルまでの沿道に配置された The police officers *were stationed* along the route from the airport to the hotel. ‖6月には社員の配置転換がある予定だ We are going to have *a personnel reshuffle* [*a shake-up*] in June. (➤ shake-up には「思い切った」という含みがある).

ハイチ Haiti /héɪṭi/ (西インド諸島の国)
‖**ハイチ人** a Haitian.

ハイツ heights ▶目黒ハイツ Meguro Heights.

ハイティーン late teens ▶ハイティーンの女の子たち girls *in their late teens* ‖母はハイティーンの頃ミスチルに夢中だったらしい My mother says she was crazy about Mr. Children *in her late teens*.

> **危ないカタカナ語✸ハイティーン**
> **1** ティーンエージャーのうちで年齢の高い者のことを日本語で「ハイティーン」といっているが, 英語では late teens (16～19歳) という. 一方「ローティーン」は early teens (13～15歳) という. teens となっているのは複数の年代を指すためである.
> **2** 10歳くらいから12歳くらいまでの子供を指して preteen ということもある.

ハイテク high tech, high technology 一形 **ハイテクの** high-tech ▶ハイテク機器 a *high-tech* device ‖ハイテク産業 a *high-tech* industry ‖ハイテク社会 *high-tech* society.

はいでる (…から)**這い出る** crawl [creep] out 《of》 ▶寝袋からはい出る *crawl out of* a sleeping bag.

1**はいてん 配点** the allotment of points [marks] ▶問3の配点は何点ですか How many *points* is Question 3 *worth*?

2**はいてん 配転** a personnel transfer.

はいでん 配電する supply (electric) power
‖**配電盤** a switchboard.

ばいてん 売店 a stand, a kiosk /kíːɑːsk/ (ともに駅や街頭の); a school store (学校の) ▶駅の売店 *a newsstand* at a railroad station.

1**バイト** a part-time job →アルバイト
‖**バイト学生** a working student, a student working part-time.

2**バイト** 《コンピュータ》a byte (情報の単位)
‖**ギガバイト** a gigabyte (➤ 2^{30}バイト) ‖**キロバイト** a kilobyte (➤ 2^{10}バイト) ‖**テラバイト** a terabyte (➤ 2^{40}バイト) ‖**メガバイト** a megabyte (➤ 2^{20}バイト).

はいとう 配当 a dividend (株の) ▶その株は高配当利回りだ That stock has a *high dividend* yield.

‖配当金 a dividend,《インフォーマル》a divvy.
はいとく 背徳 ▶背徳行為 an *immoral* act.
ばいどく 梅毒《医学》**syphilis** /sífəlɪs/
‖梅毒患者 a syphilitic /sɪfəlítɪk/.
ハイドパーク Hyde Park(ロンドンにある公園).
パイナップル (a) **pineapple** ▶パイナップルの缶詰 a can[《英また》tin] of *pineapple*.
‖パイナップルジュース pineapple juice(➤ pine juice とはしない).
はいにち 排日の anti-Japanese ▶排日運動 an *anti-Japanese* movement ‖ 排日感情をかきたてる stir up *anti-Japanese feelings*.
はいにょう 排尿 urination 一動 **排尿する urinate.**
はいにん 背任 ‖背任行為 a breach of trust; malpractice(医師の); malfeasance(公務員の).
ハイネック ハイネックの high-necked ▶ハイネックのセーター a *high-necked* sweater.
ハイパー hyper
‖ハイパーインフレ hyperinflation.
はいはい 這い這い ▶この子ははいはいができます The baby can *crawl*. ‖ はいはいがお上手だこと! He [She] can *crawl* so well! ‖ はいはいしてここまでいらっしゃい! Come on! *Crawl* (over) to me.
ばいばい 売買 buying and selling(➤ 語順は一般的には日本語と逆) ▶麻薬は多くの国で売買が禁じられている In most countries *buying or selling* drugs [*drug trafficking*] is prohibited. (➤ traffic は特に「不正に売買する」の意) ‖ 父は株の売買で大もうけした My father made a lot of money *buying and selling stocks*. /My father made a fortune in the *stock market*. /My father made large profits from *stock transactions*. (➤ transaction は「取り引き」の意の堅い語).
▶父は革製品の売買をしている My father *deals in* leather products. (➤ deal in は「商取り引きをする」) ‖ その会社はアメリカの一流メーカーと売買契約を結んだ The company made *a sales contract* with one of the leading manufacturers in America.
バイバイ bye-bye(➤ おとな同士は bye とだけ言うことが多い) ▶おじいちゃん, バイバイ *Bye-bye*, grandpa! ‖ バイバイ. またね *Bye* for now!
バイパス a **bypass.**
はいばん 廃盤 ▶ご注文のCDは廃盤になっております The CD you ordered is now *out of print* [*has been discontinued*].
はいび 配備 deployment 一動 **配備する deploy** +目 ▶隣国の国民を威嚇するためにミサイルを配備する *deploy* missiles to intimidate people in a neighboring country ‖ F-16戦闘機10機がその基地に配備された Ten F-16s *were deployed* at the base.
ハイヒール high-heeled shoes, high heels. →ハイ-.
ハイビジョン(テレビ) high-definition television《略 HDTV》▶この番組はハイビジョンでお送りします This program is brought to you in *HDTV*.
ハイビスカス《植物》a **hibiscus.**
はいびょう 肺病 lung disease.
はいひん 廃品 waste [**unwanted**/**disused**] **articles; rubbish, junk** (くず) ▶この辺りは2週間に1度廃品回収がある *Waste articles* are collected every two weeks here.
‖廃品置き場《米》a junkyard ‖ 廃品回収業者 a junk dealer,《英また》a rag-and-bone merchant.
はいふ 配布・配付 distribution 一動 **配布する distribute** /dɪstríbju:t/ +目; **hand** [**pass**] **out** (手渡す) ▶申込書はあす配布します The application forms will *be distributed* tomorrow. ‖ 運動員たちが群衆にビラを配布していた The campaigners *were handing out* fliers to the crowd. ‖ 先生がテスト用紙を全員に配付した The teacher *passed* [*handed*] *out* exam sheets to everybody.
‖配付資料 a handout.
パイプ 1【管】a pipe ▶パイプが詰まって流しに水があふれた The *pipe* was clogged (up) and the sink overflowed.
‖パイプオルガン a pipe organ, an organ ‖ パイプライン a pipeline.
2【たばこの】a pipe ▶彼はゆったりとソファーに腰をおろしパイプをふかしていた He was sitting comfortably on the sofa smoking *a pipe*. /He was sitting comfortably on the sofa, *pipe* in mouth.
3【仲介】▶賛成派と反対派のパイプ役を務める act as the *mediator* between the supporting group and the opposition ‖ PTA は生徒の父母と先生とのパイプである The PTA provides *a means of communication* between the students' parents and the teachers. (「コミュニケーションの手段を提供する」と考えて訳す).
ハイファイ hi-fi(➤ high fidelity の略) ▶ハイファイ装置 *hi-fi* equipment.
ハイファイブ →ハイタッチ.
はいふく 拝復 Dear ... →拝啓.
はいぶつ 廃物 refuse /réfju:s/, **rubbish** ▶廃物利用でクッションカバーを作った I utilized [recycled] *refuse material* to make a cushion cover.
パイプライン a **pipeline.**
ハイブリッド hybrid ▶このパソコンソフトはハイブリッド版だ This software is *a hybrid version*.
‖ハイブリッドカー a hybrid car.
バイブル the Bible(聖書); a **bible**(権威ある書物) ▶『ヴォーグ』誌はファッション界のバイブルと考えられている "Vogue" is considered the *bible* of the fashion world.
バイブレーション a **vibration.**
バイブレーター a **vibrator.**
ハイフン a **hyphen** /háɪfən/ ▶ハイフン付きの語 a *hyphenated* word.
はいぶん 配分する divide +目 (分ける); **allot** +目 (時間などを割り当てる) ▶遺産を配分する *divide* the inheritance ‖ まず仕事の配分を決めなければ First of all, we have to *decide how to divide* (*up*) the work among us. ‖ (テストで)私は各問題に5分を配分した I *allotted* five minutes for each question.
はいべん 排便 evacuation, bowel movements 一動 **排便する evacuate** /ɪvǽkjueɪt/, **defecate** ▶室内犬に排便のしつけをする *housetrain* a dog kept indoors.
ハイボール《米》**highball,**《英》**whisky and** [**with**] **soda.**
はいぼく 敗北 (a) **defeat** ▶敗北を喫する suffer *a defeat* / be defeated ‖ 潔く敗北を認める accept (one's) *defeat* gracefully [with good grace].
ばいめい 売名 self-advertisement(自己宣伝) ▶売名行為をする perform [do] *a publicity stunt*.
はいめん 背面 the back, the rear ▶背面からの写真 a back shot.
‖背面攻撃《軍事》a rear attack ‖ (走り高跳びの)背面跳び a backward jump ‖ 背面飛行 an inverted flight.
ハイヤー a **cab for hire** ▶私たちはハイヤーで市内観光に

出かけた We went to see the sights of the town in *a chauffeur-driven* [*chauffeured*] *car*.

危ないカタカナ語✸ ハイヤー
乗用車を hire する(借り切る)ことから「ハイヤー」というが，これは日本独特のもので，英米には存在しない. cab for hire, car with a chauffeur /ʃoʊfə́ːʳ/(運転手つきの車)，あるいは chauffeur-driven car(おかかえ運転手が運転する車)のように説明する必要がある.

バイヤー a **buyer**(➤ 英語では個人の「購入者，買い手」の意で用いることも多い).

はいやく 配役 **the cast**(役者全体)；**the casting** (役を振り分けること) ▶この映画は**配役**がいい This movie *is well cast*. ‖ 来年の連続テレビドラマの**配役**が発表された *The cast* [*casting*] of the serial TV drama for the next year was announced. →**キャスト**.

1**ばいやく 売約** ▶このソファーベッドは**売約済み**です This sofa bed *has been sold*. ‖ その品には**売約済みの札**がついていた The article had *a "Sold" sign* on it. ／ The article was labeled "Sold."

2**ばいやく 売薬** a **patent** [an **over-the-counter**] **medicine**.

はいゆう 俳優 an **actor**；an **actress** (女優) 《参考》現在では女性にも actor を用いることが多い.
‖**映画俳優** a movie actor [actress] ‖ **舞台俳優** a stage actor [actress].

ばいよう 培養 (a) **culture**, **cultivation** 一動 **培養する culture** +目, **cultivate** /kʌ́ltɪveɪt/ +目 ▶コレラ菌の**培養** *a culture* of cholera germs ‖ コレラ菌を**培養する** *cultivate* cholera germs.
‖**培養土** potting compost.

ハイライト a **highlight** ▶エーゲ海でのクルージングが旅行の**ハイライト**でした The Aegean Sea cruise was the *highlight* of our trip. ‖ きょうのスポーツの**ハイライト**をごらんください Let's look at the *highlights* of today's sports.

はいらん 排卵 《生理学》**ovulation** 一動 **排卵する ovulate**.

はいりこむ 入り込む **get in** [**into**] ▶ケンとヒロシは裏門から校舎に**入り込んだ** Ken and Hiroshi *got into* the school through the back gate.

ばいりつ 倍率 **1**【拡大率】**magnifying power**, **magnification** (➤ 後者は専門用語) ▶**倍率**の高いレンズ a high-*zoom* lens ‖ 望遠鏡の**倍率**を上げる increase the *magnification* of a telescope ‖ **倍率**20倍の望遠鏡 a twenty-*power* telescope ／ a telescope with *a magnification* [*a power*] of twenty ‖ この双眼鏡は**倍率**が6倍だ These binoculars have *a magnification* [*a power*] of six.
2【競争率】▶B大学法学部の**倍率**は4倍だ The *competition* to enter the Law School of B University is 4 to 1. (➤「競争は4対1だ」の意).

はいりょ 配慮 **attention**(注意・心くばり；通例修飾語を伴う)；**consideration** (考慮) 一動 **配慮する consider** +目 ▶このレストランはインテリアや照明にまで**配慮が行き届いている** They've *paid careful attention to* the decor and lighting in this restaurant. ‖ 彼女は栄養のバランスを**十分配慮して**食事を作る She prepares meals *paying full attention to* nutritional balance.
▶警察は彼が未成年であることを**配慮して**厳重注意だけで帰宅させた The police *took* his being a minor *into consideration* and let him go home after admonishing him severely.
✉ **ご配慮いただき深く感謝いたします** Thank you so much for your *thoughtfulness* [*trouble* ／ *kind consideration*]. ➤ trouble は「骨折り」の意. kind consideration は形式ばった表現.

バイリンガル a **bilingual** /baɪlíŋgwəl/ **person** (人) (➤ 2か国語を自在に話す人を指す) 一形 **バイリンガルの bilingual** ▶田中さんは日本語と中国語の**バイリンガル**だ Ms. Tanaka *is bilingual* in Japanese and Chinese.

はいる 入る **1**【外から中へ】**go in** [**into**], **come in** [**into**], **enter** +目；**get in** [**into**]

語法 (1)**go in, go into** は外にいる人がある場所に入って行く場合に用いる. **come in, come into** は中にいる人が別の人が入って来ることをいう場合，および，自分が入って行く行為を中にいる人の立場から表現するときに使う.
(2)**enter** は go in [into], come in [into] の両義を持つが，改まった語.
(3)**get in [into]** は単に歩いて入るのではなく，障害物をどかすなり，もぐり込むなりして，多少とも骨折って入るときに使う. また，「車に乗り込む」にも使う.

▶あの門から**入って**ください Please *enter* at that gate. ‖ 列車は清水トンネルに**入った** The train *went into* [*entered*] the Shimizu Tunnel. ‖ 列車が**入って来た** A train *pulled in*. (➤ pull in は「(列車・船などが)着く」の意) ‖ 出席簿を抱えて西田先生は教室に**入って来た** [**入って行った**] Holding her roll book in her hand, Ms. Nishida *came* [*went*] *into* the room. ‖ **対話**「中へ**入って**もよろしいですか」「どうぞ」"May I *come* [*go*] *in*?" "Please." ‖ そこにどうやって**入った**の How did you *get in* there? ‖ 路地を**入ると**突き当たりに先生の家があった As I *entered* [*went into*] the alley, I could see my teacher's house at the far end.
▶女王が議事堂に**入られた** The Queen *entered* the Houses of Parliament. (➤ enter in [into] としないことに注意) ‖《ドアなどの掲示》応募者は**お入りください** Applicants *walk in*. ‖《掲示》芝生に**入らないでください** *Keep Off* the Grass ‖ 私は遅刻して**こっそり教室に入った** I was late for school, so I *sneaked into* the classroom.
▶ここはいい風[すきま風]が**入って来る** A fresh breeze [A draft] *is blowing in* here. ‖ 突然ツバメが1羽窓から教室へ**入って来た** Suddenly a swallow *flew into* the classroom through the window. (➤ flew は fly(飛ぶ)の過去形) ‖ プールに**入る**と水が冷たかった I found the water (was) cold when I *got into* the swimming pool.
▶ゆうべ泥棒に**入られた** Last night a thief *broke into* our house. (➤ break into は「(家や店に)押し入る」) ‖ 左目にごみが**入って**痛い I'*ve got* some dust in my left eye and it hurts.
▶満月が雲の陰に**入った**(＝隠れた) The full moon *was hidden* by the clouds. ‖ 私たちは横浜インターで東名高速道路に**入った** We *got onto* [*entered*] the Tomei Expressway at the Yokohama Interchange. ‖ ファーストフード・レストランが日本に**入って来た**のは40数年前のことだ It was forty years or so ago that fast-food restaurants *were introduced* into Japan.
▶ **対話**「あしたの午後，時間あるかい？」「あいにく，あしたは予定が**入ってる**んだ」"Do you have any time to-

morrow afternoon?" "Sorry, I *have* a previous appointment."

2【加入する，位置する】join +目, **go** [**get**] **into** ▶テニスクラブに入る *join* a tennis club ‖ 芸能界に入る *go into* show business ‖ 兄はこの春銀行に入った My (older) brother *joined* [*got a job with*] a bank this spring. ‖ 高校生のときは放送部に入っていた When I was a high school student, I *was* (*active*) *in* the broadcast club. ‖ ぼくは野球部に入っている I *am on* the baseball team. ‖ この大学は入るのが大変だ It is hard to *get into* this university. ‖ 彼は鹿児島大学に入った He *was admitted to* Kagoshima University. (➤ be admitted は「入学を許可される」).

▶彼女の新曲がベストテンに入った Her new song *ranked in* the top ten. ‖ 彼女は1,000メートル走で3位に入った She *came in* third in the 1,000-meter race.

3【入手する】get +目 ▶給料は入った？ Did you *get* your salary？‖ バイト代が入ったら何買おうかな What shall I buy *with* the money from my part-time job？‖ ご注文の品が入りました The item you ordered *has come in*.

▶ただ今，新しいニュースが入りました Another news item *has arrived*. ／We *have* just *gotten* some late-breaking news. ‖ 8回，ヤクルトに一挙5点が入りました The Swallows *scored* five runs in a single sweep in the eighth inning. (➤ score は「得点する」).

4【収められる，含まれる】hold +目 ▶あの講堂には1000人は楽に入る(＝収容できる) That auditorium *accommodates* [*holds*] more than 1,000 people. ‖ このつぼが入るような袋が欲しい I want a bag that will *hold* this pot. ／I want a bag that this pot will *fit into*. ‖ この料金に消費税は入って(＝含まれて)いますか Does this price *include* the consumption tax？‖ このケーキにはアルコール分が入っております This cake *contains* liquor. (➤ contain は「成分として含有する」の意) ‖ きみのバッグ，何が入ってるの？ What do you *have* in your bag？／What's *in* the bag？

▶《慣用表現》赤ん坊の泣き声がうるさくて勉強していてもちっとも頭に入らない That baby is crying so loudly that I *can't concentrate on* my studies at all.

5【ある状態になる】▶交渉は新しい局面に入った The negotiations *have entered* a new phase. ‖ チームは来月長期合宿に入る予定だ We plan to *have* a long-term training camp starting from next month. ‖ 学校はあしたから夏休みに入る My school's summer vacation *begins* [*starts*] tomorrow. ／My school *breaks up* for the summer vacation tomorrow. (➤ break up は主に《英》で「(学校などが)休みになる」の意).

▶大学を出てすぐ家庭に入る(＝主婦になる)のはいやだわ I don't want to *become a housewife* right after graduation from college. ‖ 冗談はさておき本題に入りましょう Joking aside, *let's get down* to business.

6【その他】▶中に入ってけんかを止める *step in* and stop a fight ‖ 課長，電話が入ってますよ Chief, *you are wanted* on the phone. ／*There's* a phone call for you, Chief. ‖ お茶が入りましたからこちらへどうぞ I've *made* some tea. Come and have some if you like.

はいれつ 配列 (an) **arrangement**；《生化学》a **sequence** 一動 **配列する arrange** +目 ▶彼は出席者名をあいうえお［アルファベット］順に配列した He *arranged* [*put*] the participants' names *in* A-I-U-E-O [alphabetical] *order*. ‖ 机の配列を変えたら気分が変わった *Rearranging* the desks gave the room a different atmosphere [mood].

‖**遺伝子配列** a genetic sequence.

ハイレベル ハイレベルな high-level ▶今回のフィギュアスケート競技会はハイレベルな戦いが予想される The figure skating competition this time is expected to be *high-level*.

はいろ 廃炉 ▶(原子炉を)廃炉にする *decommission a* (*nuclear*) *reactor* ‖ 原発を廃炉にする *decommission* a nuclear power plant.

パイロット a **pilot**

‖**パイロットランプ** a pilot lamp [light] ‖ **テストパイロット** a test pilot.

パイン a **pineapple**(パイナップル)

‖**パインジュース** pineapple juice.

バインダー a **binder** ▶書類をバインダーにとじ込む file papers in *a binder*.

‖**リングバインダー** a ring binder.

はう 這う crawl, creep(➤ 同義の場合もあるが，後者には「音を立てずにゆっくりと」とか「蛇のような気味の悪いものが」といったニュアンスがある)；**slither**(蛇が) ▶うちの赤ん坊はようやくはい始めた Our baby has finally begun to *crawl*. ‖ 虫がテーブルの上をはっている A bug *is crawling* along the table.

▶蛇が庭をはっていた A snake *was slithering* along in the garden. ‖ 車はのろのろとはうように進んだ Traffic *crept forward*. ‖ そのれんが造りの家には壁一面にツタがはっている Ivy *has crept* all over the wall of that brick house.

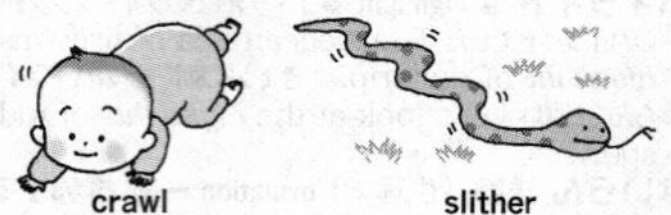

ハウス a **house**(家)；a **hothouse**, a **greenhouse**(温室) ▶ハウス栽培のイチゴ *hothouse* [*greenhouse*] strawberries.

‖**ハウス栽培** hothouse [greenhouse] cultivation ‖ **ハウスダスト** house dust.

ハウステンボス Huis Ten Bosch(長崎県佐世保市にあるオランダの村や街を再現したテーマパーク).

パウダー powder ▶彼女は顔にパウダーをはたいた She put *powder* on her face.

‖**ベビーパウダー** baby powder ‖ **ベーキングパウダー** baking powder.

ハウツー

> **危ないカタカナ語✸ ハウツー**
> **1**「…のやり方」の意味で「ハウツー…」というのは英語の how to からきているが，注意を要するのは to のあとに動詞の原形がくることである．したがって how to tennis は間違い．how to play tennis とする．
> **2**「ハウツーもの(の本)」は a how-to book でよい．

バウムクーヘン a **Baumkuchen**(➤ ドイツ語から).

バウンド a **bounce**, a **bound** (➤ 前者のほうが好まれる) 一動 **バウンドする bounce** ▶ワンバウンドで捕球する catch a ball *on the first bounce* ‖ ツーバウンドのゴロ a two-bouncer ／a two-hopper.

パウンドケーキ (a) **pound cake.**

はえ 蠅 a **fly** ▶皿の上の魚にハエがたかっている There are *flies* crawling on the fish on the plate.
▶《慣用表現》他人の世話を焼く前に自分の頭の上のハエを追え *Mind your* (*own*) *business* before you meddle in that of others.
‖ハエたたき a fly swatter.

はえかわる 生え替わる **get** one's **permanent teeth** (歯が); **molt**(鳥の羽毛が).

はえぎわ 生え際 a **hairline.**

はえぬき 生え抜き ▶彼の父親は生え抜きの外交官だった His father was a *career* diplomat. (➤ career /kəríəʳ/ は「専門職の」の意).

¹はえる 生える **grow** ▶うちの裏山にはキノコがたくさん生えている A lot of mushrooms *grow* on the hill at the back of my house. ‖むしってもむしっても雑草はすぐ生えてくる Weeds *grow* quickly no matter how often you pull them out. ‖牛の頭には角が生えている Cattle *have* horns on their heads.
▶息子のわきの下に毛が生えてきた My son has begun to *grow* underarm hair. ／Hair has begun to *grow* under my son's arms. ‖赤ん坊に歯が生えてきた The baby is beginning to *cut her* [*his*] *teeth.*

²はえる 映える **1【輝く】**▶山並みが夕日に映えている The mountains *are lit* by [*are glowing* in] (the rays of) the setting sun. (➤ lit は light(照らす)の過去分詞形).
2【目だつ, 引き立つ】▶彼女は和服の映える人だ She *looks* good in (a) kimono. (➤ 容姿に重点) ／A kimono *looks good* on her. (➤ 和服に重点) ‖せっかくの絵もここに掛けたのでは映えない The valuable picture *is not shown to advantage* here. (➤ to advantage は「引き立って」の意).

はおと 羽音 **the flutter of wings** (鳥の); **the buzz of bees**(ミツバチの).

はおり 羽織 a ***haori***, a ***haori* coat**
日本紹介 ✉ **羽織は和服の上に着る丈の短いコートです. 家紋を染め抜いた羽織を「紋付き」といいます. 日本の伝統的な男性の礼服は紋付きを着て, はかまと呼ばれるキュロットのようなズボンをはくものです** A *haori* is a short coat worn over kimono. A *haori* that has a dyed family crest is called a *'montsuki.'* When men dress in a traditional Japanese style for formal occasions, they put on a *montsuki* and culotte-like pants called *'hakama.'*

はおる 羽織る **throw** [**slip**] **on** ▶寒いのならこのカーディガンを羽織りなさい *Throw on* this cardigan [*Slip* this cardigan *over your shoulders*] if you feel chilly.

はか 墓 a **grave** (**plot**)(➤ plot は「一区画の土地」); a **tomb** /tuːm/ (特に大きな) ▶死んだ犬のために墓を掘って葬った We dug *a grave* for the dead dog and buried it. ‖古代エジプトのファラオは生前から自分の壮麗な墓を造営させた In ancient Egypt, Pharaohs had splendid *tombs* built during their lifetimes. ‖彼岸の中日に一家で墓参りに行った We all *visited our family grave* (*plot*) on the day of the spring [fall] equinox.
‖墓石 a gravestone, a tombstone ‖墓場(→見出語).

ばか 馬鹿 **1【愚かな人】** a **fool**, an **idiot**, 《インフォーマル》a **goof** 一形 **ばかな** **stupid**, **foolish**, **silly**, 《インフォーマル》**goofy**

> **《解説》** (1)「ばかな人」の意味では **fool** が一般的で, idiot はこれよりも意味が強い. goof はくだけた語.
> (2)形容詞の場合, 一般的には **foolish** は常識や分別を欠いていることを, **silly** は態度や動作がおかしくてばかばかしいことを, **stupid** は頭の働きが鈍いことや知能の低いことを指すのにそれぞれ用いる傾向があるが, 区別なく用いることもある.

▶こんな大事なことを忘れるなんて私はなんてばかなんだろう How *stupid* of me to forget such an important thing! ／What *an idiot* [*a fool*] I am to forget such an important thing! ／I must be *a real fool* to forget such an important thing. ‖こんな高価な絵を買うなんて, われながらばかなことをしたものだ It was *stupid* of me to have bought such an expensive painting. ‖こんな寒い日にセーターも着ないで出かけるなんて私もばかだった *It was silly of* me *to* go out without a sweater on such a cold day. (➤ silly はそれほど深刻でないことに使う).
▶彼の話をうのみにするほど私はばかじゃないよ I *know better than to* take him at his word. (➤ know better than to do は「経験・分別があるから…しない」の意).
▶ばかなことを言うんじゃない Don't be *silly*! ‖ばかも休み休み言え Don't be *stupid*. Enough is enough! (➤「ばかなことを言うな, もうたくさんだ」の意) ‖ばかみたい! 私ってガスをつけるの忘れてたわ *How stupid* [*Shoot*]*!* I didn't turn the gas on. ‖あんたって, ばかね! You're so *stupid*! ‖そんなばかなまねはやめろよ! Stop acting so *goofy*! ‖ 対話 「ディズニーランドで5万円使っちゃった」「おまえ, ばかか」"I spent fifty thousand yen at Disneyland." "*You must be crazy.*"
▶《慣用表現》あの人はちょっと新しいことばを覚えると, ばかの一つ覚えでそればかり使う Once he learns a new word, he tends to *run it into the ground.* (➤ run ... into the ground は「…をやり過ぎる」) ‖ばかは死ななきゃ治らない Fools never learn. (➤「ばかは学ぶことをしない」の意;「ばかにつける薬はない」に近いのは There is no cure for a fool.; 年寄りに対しては There's no fool like an old fool. (年寄りのばかほど困るものはない)をよく用いる).
2【失敗すること】▶こんな安物の革靴を買ってばかをみた I *could kick myself* for buying such cheap leather shoes as these. (➤ could kick oneself for doing は「…したことで自分をけ飛ばしたいくらいだ」で「自分に腹が立つ」の意のインフォーマルな表現) ‖あの男の言うことを信用すると最後にばかをみるぞ You're going to end up *making a fool of yourself* if you believe what he says. ‖きょうの日本史の試験ですごいばかをやっちゃった I *made a big mistake* [*I blew it*] on the Japanese history test today. (➤ blew は blow (しくじる) の過去形でインフォーマルな語).
3【軽くみること】▶毎月の余分な出費もほんとにばかにならないのよね The amount of money we waste each month *is* certainly *not to be sneezed at.* (➤ not to be sneezed at は「…を軽視できない」の意).
4【程度が過ぎること】▶彼女はばか丁寧な話し方をする She uses *ridiculously polite* (forms of) speech. ‖この子はばか正直で困ります I'm afraid he's *honest to a fault.* (➤ to a fault は「(本来の長所が)欠点となるほどに」) ／He's *painfully* [*embarrassingly*] *honest.* ‖彼はばか力があるから引っ越しにはもってこいだ He's

a great help when moving because he's got *enormous strength*. ‖ うちのバスケットボール・チームにはばかでかい選手が２人いる There are two *really huge* players on our basketball team. ‖ ホテルのロビーでばか笑いするんじゃない Don't *laugh* (*so*) *loudly* in the hotel lobby.

5【理屈に合わないこと】▶彼女が会社をやめるって？そんなばかな！ She's leaving the company？ *I can't believe it.*

6【役にたたなくなること】▶このねじはばかになっている This screw *is no good*. ‖ 鼻がばかになって全然においがわからない *My sense of smell has gotten so dull* that I can't distinguish between smells at all.

☛ ばかに, ばか野郎 (→見出語)

はかい 破壊 destruction **―動 破壊する** destroy ＋目 →こわす ▶住民は自動車専用道路の建設は自然環境の破壊につながるとして反対している The residents are opposing the expressway construction claiming that it will lead to *destruction* of the natural environment. (➤「環境破壊」は environmental destruction ともいう) ‖ 爆撃によって街は完全に破壊された The town *was* completely *destroyed* by (the) bombing.

▶核実験は環境に対する破壊的行為だ Nuclear tests are environmentally *destructive actions*. ‖ 原子爆弾は一瞬のうちに何十万人もの人間を殺す破壊力を持っている Atomic bombs have such *destructive power* that hundreds of thousands of people can be killed in a flash.

はがいじめ 羽交い締め ▶刑事はその男をはがい締めにした The detective *got a full nelson on* the man. (➤ nelson はレスリング用語で「首固め」) ／The detective *pinned* [*pinioned*] the man's arms *behind* him. (➤ pinion /pínjən/ は「両腕または両足を押さえたり縛ったりして動けなくする」の意；したがってこの英文は「後ろ手に押さえつけた」の意にもなる).

はがき 葉書 a postcard, a postal (card)
《参考》絵はがきを除き, 英米ではほとんどはがきを使わない. したがって postcard というと通例絵はがきを指す. 簡単な私信も封書にするのがふつう ▶このはがきを出してきてくれる？ Could you go and mail this *postcard*？

✉ **きれいな絵はがきを送っていただきありがとう** Thank you for the beautiful *postcard*.

‖ **往復はがき** a postcard with an attached reply card, a postcard with a (self-addressed) return portion (➤ 英米にはない).

はかく 破格の exceptional (例外的な) ▶彼は今度部長になったが破格の昇進だ He has become a general manager, which is an *exceptional* [*unprecedented*] promotion. (➤ 後者は「前例のない」) ‖ 真珠のネックレスを破格のお値段で提供しています We are offering pearl necklaces at *drastically reduced* prices.

ばかげた 馬鹿げた absurd (道理に合わない) ; ridiculous (こっけいな) ; foolish (常識・判断力を欠いた) ; stupid (頭の働きが鈍い, 愚かな) ▶そんなばかげた話, だれが信じるものか Who would believe such an *absurd* story？ ‖ ばかげたまねをするんじゃないよ Don't *be ridiculous*. ／Don't *be stupid*. ‖ そんなつまらないことでけんかするなんてばかげてるよ It is *foolish* of you to quarrel over such a little thing.

▶１枚の切符を手に入れるために徹夜で並ぶなんてばかげている It's *ridiculous* to line up all night to get a ticket.

ばかさわぎ 馬鹿騒ぎ ▶彼らはアパートでばか騒ぎをして追い出された They were kicked out of the apartment house for *wild* [*noisy*] *partying*. ‖ 隣の部屋の人たちがばか騒ぎしている The people in the next room *are really living it up*. (➤ live it up は「大いに騒ぐ[楽しむ]」の意).

はがす 剝がす peel off (引きはがす) ; tear /teəʳ/ off, rip off (破り取る) ▶箱のシールをはがす *peel* [*rip*] a seal *off* the box.

▶ 対話「この切手はがしてもいい？」「うん, でも上手にはがさないと破れちゃうよ」"May I *take* this postage stamp *off* the envelope？" "Yes, but *remove* it carefully or you'll tear it."

ばかす 化かす ▶日本の昔話ではキツネやタヌキは人を化かすことになっている In Japanese folktales, the fox and the *tanuki* are believed to *play tricks on* people.

ばかず 場数 ▶彼はニュースキャスターとして場数を踏んでいる (＝経験豊富である) As an anchorperson, he *has rich and varied experience*. ／He is a veteran anchorperson.

はかせ 博士 a doctor ▶小金井博士 *Dr.* Koganei ‖ 北さんは昆虫博士だ (＝何でも知っている) Mr. Kita *knows everything about* [*is an expert on*] *insects*. ‖ 彼はハーバードで博士号を取った He got his *doctorate* [Ph.D.] at Harvard. →はくし.

¹はがた 歯型 a dental impression.

²はがた 歯形 teeth marks.

はかどる make progress ▶テレビを見ながらでは勉強は少しもはかどりませんよ If you study while watching TV, you aren't going to *make a lot of progress*. ‖ 文化祭の準備は今のところ順調にはかどっている So far, our preparations for the school festival *have gone quite well*. ‖ 対話「仕事, はかどってる？」「それが, だいぶ遅れてててね」"*How are you getting along* with your work？" "I'm badly behind with [in] it, actually."

はかない empty (空虚な) ; vain (むなしい) ▶宝くじで一獲千金などというのははかない夢にすぎない Trying to hit the jackpot in a lottery is just *an empty* [*a vain*] *dream*. ‖ 彼のアメリカ留学の望みははかなく消え去った His hope of studying in America *went up in smoke*. (➤ go up in smoke は「(計画などが)煙のようにはかなく消える」).

ばかに 馬鹿に very (とても) ; awfully (ひどく) ▶あなた, きょうはばかに元気のようね You look *very* cheerful today. ‖ けさはばかに早起きじゃないか Why did you get up *so* early this morning？ ‖ ９月も末だというのにばかに暑いね It's *awfully* hot for the end of September.

はがね 鋼 steel ▶はがねのような強じんな肉体 a body (as) strong as *steel*.

はかば 墓場 a graveyard ; a cemetery /séməteri/ (共同墓地) ; a churchyard (教会に付属した) ▶結婚は人生の墓場であると言った人もいる Someone once said marriage is the *graveyard* of life.

ぱかぱか ▶馬の親子がパカパカ駆けて来た A mare and her colt came *clip-clopping along*.

はかばかしい ▶部長に新しいプランを提案してみたが, はかばかしい返事は得られなかった I proposed a new plan to the manager, but I didn't get any *positive* feedback. ‖ 彼の今度の試験の結果ははかばかしくなかった The results of his latest exam *were not satisfactory*. ‖ 母は回復がはかばかしくありません My mother's recovery *has been very slow*.

ばかばかしい 馬鹿馬鹿しい absurd (理屈に合わな

い)；ridiculous（こっけいなほどの）▶あの古切手が30万円もするって！ばかばかしい！That old stamp costs three hundred thousand yen！*That's outrageous*.（➤ outrageous /aʊtréɪdʒəs/ は「途方もない」）‖ 対話「美子がこの薬を飲めば肌がきれいになるって勧めてくれたのよ」「ばかばかしい」"Yoshiko recommended this medicine. She said it would make my skin beautiful." "*Ridiculous！／Idiotic！*"（➤ この場合 Nonsense！にすると堅い感じになるので合わない）‖ このクロスワードパズルはばかばかしいくらいやさしい This crossword puzzle is *ridiculously* easy.

はかま 袴 a ***hakama***；a pleated, skirt-like garment worn over a kimono (originally worn by men on formal occasions)（➤ 説明的な訳）▶卒業式にはかま姿で出席する女子学生が増えた More and more female college graduates are attending graduation ceremonies *wearing hakama*.

ばかやろう 馬鹿野郎 a **fool** ▶《相手を罵倒(ばとう)して》ばか野郎！*You idiot*［*moron*］*！*‖ あんな若い連中になんでわしがばか野郎呼ばわりされなきゃならんのだ Why should I have to be called *a fool* by those young kids？（➤「ばか野郎！」と罵声(ばせい)を浴びせる場合は You (stupid) idiot！などという）.

はがゆい 歯がゆい **feel irritated**（いらいらする）；**feel impatient**（がまんできなくなる）▶息子がパジャマを着るのがのろいので**歯がゆくなった** My son was putting on his pajamas so slowly that I *felt irritated and couldn't sit still*.（➤「いらいらしてじっとしていられなかった」の意）‖ 彼の仕事ぶりを見ていると**歯がゆくなる** I *feel impatient* with the way he works.

はからい 計らい ▶旅行会社の**計らい**で予定になかった島巡りが実現した *Through the good offices* of the travel agency, we were able to go around the islands, though we hadn't made plans ahead of time.

はからう 計らう ▶きみが来週休みが取れるよう**計らい**ましょう I will *see (to it) that* you get some time off next week.（➤ see (to it) that は「必ず…するよう取り計らう」；that 以下の節は現在形がふつう）.

ばからしい 馬鹿らしい **ridiculous**（ばかばかしい）；**useless**（むだな）▶こんな仕事，**ばからしく**てやってられないよ This job is just too *ridiculous* to bother with.

はからずも 図らずも **unexpectedly**（思いがけなく）▶このたびは**はからずも**委員長の大役を仰せつかりました I have been *unexpectedly* honored by being elected as chairperson.

はかり 秤 a **scale**（➤ しばしば複数形で）；a **balance**（天びんばかり）▶**はかり**に乗ってください Please step on the *scales*.‖ 荷物を**はかり**にかけてみてください *Weigh* the baggage *on the scale*［*on the balance*］.
‖**上皿天びんばかり** a trip balance ‖ **ばねばかり** a spring scale.

-ばかり 1【およそ】**about**,《米また》**around**；**or so**（…かそこら）▶100人**ばかり**の人がきょうのマラソンに参加した *About* 100 people participated in today's marathon.‖ 1週間**ばかり**バリ島へ行って来たい I want to go to Bali for a week *or so*.
▶2万円**ばかり**貸してくれよ Please lend me 20,000 yen.（➤ 数字をはっきり言うのをはばかって「…ばかり」と言うときには about などはつけないのがふつう）.
2【だけ】**only** ▶息子は野球**ばかり**でほかのスポーツはやらない The *only* sport my son plays is baseball.‖ 弟は家ではごろごろして**ばかり**いる My (younger) brother does *nothing but* lie around at home.（➤ nothing but は only と同じ意味）‖ どうして私に**ばかり**用を言いつけるの？Why do you *always* make me do all the errands？
▶おばあちゃんは眼鏡をどこかに置き忘れて**ばかり**いる Grandma is *always* forgetting where she put her glasses.（➤ 進行形に always をつけて「しじゅう…している」という非難の意を表す）‖ テレビ**ばかり**見てないで少しは勉強しなさいとよく母は言う My mother often tells me not to watch TV *all the time* but to study a little more.‖ 人生悪いこと**ばかりじゃない**よ Life is *not all* bad.
▶あの映画監督は国内**ばかりでなく**外国でも名が売れている That film director is well known abroad *as well as* in Japan.／That film director is well known *not only* in Japan *but* (*also*) abroad.
▶食事は温める**ばかりにしてあります** The meal is prepared so that *all you have to do is* (to) warm it up.（➤ インフォーマルでは to は省略するのがふつう）.
✉ **一日中あなたのことばかり考えています** I think *only* of you all day long.
3【それだけが理由で】**just**［**all**］**because** ▶私が注意していなかった**ばかりに**子供にけがをさせてしまった My child got injured *just*［*all*］*because* I wasn't paying attention (to him／to her).／My child got injured. It was *just*［*all*］*because* I wasn't paying attention (to him／to her).
4【たった今…したところ】**just** ▶私たちは盛岡に着いた**ばかりです** We *have just* arrived at Morioka.／We arrived at Morioka *just now*.（➤ just は現在完了形，just now は過去形で用いるのが原則だが，We just arrived ... のように過去形でもいう人もいる）‖ 対話「お母さん，2000円ちょうだい」「きのうあげた**ばかり**なのに．何に使うの？」"Mom, can you give me two thousand yen？" "I gave you money *only*［*just*］yesterday. What are you going to use it for？"
5【ほとんど…しそう】**almost** ▶冬山登山はやめるようにと母は泣かん**ばかり**だった My mother was *almost* crying, begging［imploring］me not to go mountain climbing in winter.‖ 彼は黙ってろ**と言わんばかりの顔**で私をにらみつけた He glared at me *as if to say*, "Keep quiet."‖ ぼくが万引きをしたとは誰も直接は言わなかったが，みんなそう**言わんばかり**だった I was not directly accused of shoplifting but *the implication*［*insinuation*］*was there*.（➤ implication, insinuation はともに「含み」の意だが，後者は特に「嫌な」）.

はかりうり 量り売り ▶こちらの惣菜は**量り売り**です These prepared foods *are sold by weight*［*by measure*］.（➤ by weight は「重さで」，by measure は「量で」）.

はかりごと a **plot**.

はかりしれない 計り知れない **immeasurable**；**incalculable**（数えきれない）▶人間はいざというとき**計り知れない**力を出すものだ People can summon *immeasurable* power in the face of difficulty.‖ 養父母には**計り知れない**ほど恩を感じている I owe my adoptive parents an *incalculable* debt of gratitude.

[1]**はかる 測る・量る・計る** **measure** ＋㊐（ものさし・カップなどで）；**weigh** /weɪ/ ＋㊐（重さを）；**time** ＋㊐（時間を）▶**雨量を測る** *measure* the rainfall ‖ **湖の水深を測る** *measure* the depth of the lake ‖ 姉は毎日**体重を量る** My (older) sister *weighs herself* every day.‖ 50メートル泳ぐから**タイムを計って**くれない？Please *time*［*clock*］me while I swim 50 meters.
‖ 看護師は患者の体温［脈］を**計った** The nurse *took*

the patient's temperature [pulse]. ‖ スーツを新調するので寸法を計ってもらった I *had my measurements taken* for a new suit.
▶私は彼の発言の真意を測りかねた I *couldn't understand* [*figure out*] what he really meant by that comment.

2**はかる 図る・謀る** 1【計画する】**attempt** +㊐ (企てる) ; **plot** +㊐ (特に悪事を) ▶彼女は自殺を図った She *attempted* (to commit) suicide. (➤ attempt はしばしば結果が失敗だったことを暗示する).
▶彼らは政府の転覆を謀った They *plotted* to overthrow the government.
2【だます】**trick** +㊐ ▶よくも謀ったな How dare you *trick* me!

3**はかる 諮る** **consult** 《with》 (相談する) ▶教員たちはその計画を校長にはかった (＝相談した) The teachers *consulted* [*conferred*] *with* the principal on the plan. ‖ その件は会議にはかられた (＝審議に付された) The matter *was submitted to* (a) conference for deliberation.

はがれる 剝がれる **come off** (取れてくる) ; **peel off** (むけてくる) ▶ポスターが風ではがれた The poster *came off* [*blew off*] in the wind.

バカンス 《主に米》(a) **vacation,** 《英》 **holiday(s)** ▶バカンスでスペインに出かける go to Spain *on vacation* [*holiday*].

1**はき 覇気** **spirit** (元気) ; **drive** (やる気, 積極性) ▶覇気のある男性 a man of *spirit* ‖ 彼は若者にしては覇気がない For a young man, he *lacks drive*.

2**はき 破棄する** **cancel** +㊐ (契約などを) ; **reverse** +㊐ (判決などを) ; **abrogate** +㊐ (条約などを) ▶二人は婚約を破棄した They *canceled* [*broke off*] the engagement. ‖ 原判決は破棄された The original judgment *was reversed*. ‖ その条約は破棄された The treaty *was abrogated*.

はぎ 萩 《植物》(a) **bush clover.**

はきけ 吐き気 **nausea** /nɔ́ːziə/ ▶吐き気がする. 変な物を食べたかな I *feel nauseous* [*feel sick*]. It must be something I ate. ‖ 私は船に乗るといつも少し吐き気がする I always *feel* [*get*] a little *queasy* on boats. (➤ queasy は「吐き気がする」の意の形容詞) ‖ 納豆のにおいで吐き気を催すという人もいる The smell of natto *is nauseating* to some people. ‖ あいつの顔を見ただけで吐き気がする The mere sight of his face *makes me sick* [*turns my stomach*].

はきごこち 履き心地 ▶はき心地のよい靴 *comfortable* shoes ‖ そのジーパン, はき心地はどう? *How do* those jeans *feel*?

はぎしり 歯ぎしり ▶私の弟は夜中によく歯ぎしりをする My (younger) brother often *grinds his teeth* in his sleep.
▶選抜テストに漏れたとき彼は歯ぎしりしてくやしがった He *ground his teeth in frustration* when he failed in the screening test for the competition. (➤ ground は grind の過去形).

パキスタン **Pakistan**
‖パキスタン人 a Pakistani [複 Pakistanis].

はきすてる 吐き捨てる **spit** +㊐ ▶「ただではおかないぞ」と彼は吐き捨てるように言った "You'll pay for this," he *said in disgust*. ／He *spat out* the words; "You'll pay for this."

はきだす 吐き出す **spit out** ▶変な味がしたので口に含んだ牛乳をすぐに吐き出した I *spat* [《米また》 *spit*] *out* the milk immediately because it tasted strange.
▶《比喩的》日ごろ胸につかえていたことをすべて吐き出して彼女はすっきりしたようだ She looked relieved after *giving vent to* [*after venting*] her pent-up frustration(s).

はきちがえる 履き違える 1【まちがえてはく】▶ゆうべ父はなじみの飲み屋から靴をはき違えて帰宅した Last night my father came home from his favorite drinking place, *wearing somebody else's shoes*. ‖ スリッパを右左はき違えたのではき直した I *had* my slippers *on the wrong feet*, so I took them off and put them (back) on again.
2【考え違いをする】**misunderstand** +㊐ ▶権利の意味をはき違えている人が少なくない Not a few people *misunderstand* the meaning of [*get the wrong idea of*] rights. ‖ 自由と勝手気ままとをはき違えている若者が多い Many young people *mistake* liberty *for* license.

はぎとる 剝ぎ取る **tear** /teəʳ/ [**strip**] **off** ▶壁にはったポスターをはぎ取る *tear* [*strip*] a poster *off* the wall ‖ 彼は強盗に身ぐるみはぎ取られた The thief *stripped* him *of* all his belongings.

はきはき ▶あの少年ははきはきしていて気持ちがよい He is such a *lively* boy and it's a pleasure to be with him. ‖ はきはきものを言いなさい Speak out *promptly and clearly*.

はきふるし 履き古しの **worn-out** (使い古した) ▶はき古しのスニーカー *worn-out* sneakers.

はきもの 履き物 **footwear, footgear** (➤ともに集合的) ; **shoes** (靴) (● footwear, footgear は「靴下」を含むので, 次の用例にこれらを用いると誤解が生じるおそれがある) ▶はき物はここで脱いでください Please take off your *shoes* here.

ばきゃく 馬脚 ▶やつもとうとう馬脚(＝本性)を現したか He finally *showed his true colors* [*revealed his true character*].

はきゅう 波及する **spread** /spred/ (広がる) ▶駅構内での禁煙の動きは全国に波及した The move to ban smoking in train stations *spread* throughout the country. ‖ そのスキャンダルは政府高官にまで波及した The scandal *spread to involve* even some high-ranking government officials.
‖波及効果 a ripple effect.

バキュームカー a **septic tank disposal truck** (➤ septic tank は「浄化槽」, a **honey wagon** (➤ honey wagon は前者を美化していったもの).

はきょく 破局 a **breakup** (仲たがい) ; a **catastrophe** /kətǽstrəfi/ (悲劇的な結末) ▶二人の仲は破局を迎えようとしていた The two were on the verge of *breaking up*. ‖ 社長の放漫経営がその会社を破局に導いた The president's loose management brought *catastrophe* [*disaster*] to the company.

1**はぎれ 歯切れ** ▶彼女の話, どうも歯切れがよくないわね She's *not* so *open and direct*. ‖ あの大臣は肝心なことを質問されると急に歯切れが悪くなる That minister suddenly becomes *evasive* [*inarticulate*] when he is asked about an important matter. (➤ evasive は「のらりくらりした」, inarticulate は「ことばがはっきりしない」の意).

2**はぎれ 端切れ** a **scrap of cloth,** a **remnant.**

1**はく 箔** 1【金・銀・アルミなどの】**foil, leaf** ▶金[銀]ぱく gold [silver] *foil* ‖ 金ぱくの文字 *gilded* [*gilt*] letters.
2【値打ち】▶勲章をもらうとはくがつくと思う人がいるらしい Some people seem to think that receiving a decoration will *make* them *more important*.

[2]**はく 吐く** **1【口から出す】throw up, vomit** +⑬(➤後者には生々しいイメージがある); **spit** +⑬(つばなどを); **exhale** /ekshéɪl/ +⑬, **breathe out**(息を) ▶吐きそうになったのでバスの窓を開けてもらった Since I *felt sick* [*felt like throwing up*], I got someone to open a bus window. ‖ 彼は食べた物をみな吐いてしまった He *threw up* [*vomited*] everything he had eaten. ‖ ホームにつばを吐かないでください Don't *spit* on the platform.

▶彼女は大量の血を吐いた She *spat* [*coughed*] *up* a lot of blood. (➤ spat は spit の過去形; cough up は「せき込んで吐く」の意) ‖ 寒い朝は吐く息が白く見える When you *breathe out* on cold mornings, your breath appears white.

2【言う】▶とうとう彼は本音を吐いた He finally *revealed* his true feelings. ‖ そう簡単に弱音を吐くもんじゃない Never *say die* so easily.

3【煙などを】send out [**up**]; **belch** +⑬(火山などが) ▶(工場の)煙突がもくもくと煙を吐いていた The smokestack *was sending up* [*was belching*] volumes of smoke.

[3]**はく 掃く** **sweep** +⑬ ▶部屋を掃きなさい *Sweep* the room. ‖ 窓の下の割れたガラスを掃いて捨てなさい *Sweep up* the pieces of broken glass under the window and throw them away. ‖ 私は庭の落ち葉を掃いた I *swept* [*raked*] *up* the fallen leaves in the garden. (➤ rake は「くまででかく」) 《参考》英米人は落ち葉はほうきで掃かないで, くまででかくのがふつう.

▶《慣用表現》彼女には金が掃いて捨てるほど(＝あり余るほど)ある She has *more than enough* money. ／ She has *money to burn*. (➤後者は「燃やすほどの金」の意) ‖ 彼程度の画家なら掃いて捨てるほどいる There are *lots of* painters like him. ／《米また》Painters like him are *a dime a dozen*. (➤ a dime a dozen は「ありふれた」の意のインフォーマルな表現).

[4]**はく 履く** **put on**(➤「はく」という動作); **wear** +⑬(➤「はいている」という状態) ▶靴をはきなさい *Put on* your shoes. ‖ 少女は白いスカートに白い靴をはいていた The girl *wore* [*was wearing*] a white skirt and white shoes. ‖ 彼はトレパンをはいていた He *had* sweat pants *on*. ／ He *wore* sweat pants. ‖ 多くのアメリカ人学生は学校にジーンズをはいて行く Many American students *wear* jeans *to* school. ‖ 妹は新しい靴をはいて出かけた My sister went out *in* her new shoes.

▶ちょっとこのジーンズをはいてみてごらん Just *try* these jeans *on*. ‖ 欧米では靴をはいたまま家に入る In Europe and America people go into houses *with* their shoes *on*.

-はく -泊 ▶最終便に乗り遅れて札幌で1泊した I *stayed overnight* in Sapporo since I missed the last plane. ‖ 1泊いくらですか? How much do you charge *for a night*? ／How much is it *a night* [*for overnight*]? ‖ ホテル代は1泊2食付きで1万5000円だ The hotel rate is 15,000 yen *a night, including dinner and breakfast* [15, 000 yen *a night with two meals*]. ‖ 我々は沖縄へ5泊6日の旅行に行く予定だ We are going to take *a six-day trip* to Okinawa. (➤「5泊6日の旅行」は厳密には a trip for six days and five nights となるが, ふつうは a six-day trip のように表す) ‖ **対話** (ホテルで)「何泊なさいますか」「2泊したいんです」"*How long* [*How many nights*] are you going to *stay*?" "I'd like to *stay for two nights*."

はぐ 剝ぐ **strip** +⑬(衣類・皮などを); **skin** +⑬(動物の皮を) ▶蛇の皮をはぐ *skin* a snake ‖ 木の皮をはぐ *bark* a tree ／*strip* the bark *off* a tree ‖ 俊夫はふとんをはがないと起きない Toshio won't get out of bed unless I *pull* the comforter [quilt] *off* him.

▶《慣用表現》いつかあいつの化けの皮をはいでやるぞ One of these days I'm going to *expose his true colors*. (→化けの皮).

ばく 貘《動物》a **tapir** /téɪpəʳ/; a **dream devouring Chinese chimera**(想像上の動物).

バグ《コンピュータ》a **bug**(プログラム上のミス) ▶何かのバグでシステムエラーが起きた A system error occurred due to *a bug*. ‖ バグをとる *debug*.

はくあ 白亜 ▶あの白亜の殿堂が最近完成した大学です That *gorgeous white building* is the recently built university.

‖ **白亜紀** the Cretaceous (Period).

はくあい 博愛 **philanthropy** /fɪlǽnθrəpi/ ▶マザー・テレサは博愛(＝人間愛)のために身をささげた Mother Teresa devoted herself to *loving humanity*.

‖ **博愛主義者** a philanthropist.

はくい 白衣 a **white robe**; a **white coat**(医者の); a **white lab coat**(実験する人の) ▶白衣の女 a woman *in white* ／a *white-robed* woman 《参考》女性看護師のことを「白衣の天使」ということがあるが, 英語でも an angel in white ということがある. また She is a (Florence) Nightingale. のような言い方をすることもある.

‖ **白衣高血圧症** white coat hypertension [syndrome].

ばくおん 爆音 a **roar**(飛行機などの); an **explosion**(爆発音) ▶白い機体が爆音をとどろかせて青い空へ消えていった The white airplane disappeared into the blue sky with *a* (*deafening*) *roar*.

ばくが 麦芽 **malt** /mɔːlt/.

はくがい 迫害 **persecution** 一動 **迫害する** **persecute** /pə́ːʳsɪkjuːt/ +⑬ ▶江戸時代の一時期, キリスト教徒たちは幕府から迫害された For a time during the Edo period, Christians *were persecuted* by the shogunate.

はくがく 博学な **learned** /lə́ːʳnɪd/(学問のある); **knowledgeable**(物知りの) ▶博学な人 a person *of great learning* ‖ モデルTのこと? 中川さんに聞いてみなさいよ. 車のことなら博学だから Model T? Ask Mr. Nakagawa. He's *knowledgeable* about automobiles.

はくがんし 白眼視 ▶最初のうち村人たちはその音楽家を白眼視した In the beginning, the villagers *looked askance at* the musician. (➤ look askance at は「…を横目でうさんくさそうに見る」).

はぐき 歯茎 **the gums**(➤通例複数形で) ▶歯をみがくと歯ぐきから血が出る My *gums* bleed when I brush my teeth.

はくぎん 白銀 **silver**(銀); **snow**(雪) ▶白銀の世界 a *winter wonderland*.

はぐくむ 育む **cultivate** +⑬(精神や才能を養う); **foster** +⑬(促進する); **nurse** +⑬(大事に守る) ▶地域の連帯感をはぐくむ *foster* a sense of community ‖ 北欧の雄大な自然がシベリウスの音楽をはぐくんだ The natural grandeur of Northern Europe *cultivated* Sibelius' music.

▶彼女の自主性はB学園ではぐくまれた B Gakuen *encouraged* her *to develop* an independent spirit. ‖ 二人の愛は時間をかけてはぐくまれた Their love *grew* over time.

ばくげき 爆撃 bombing, a bombing attack **一動 爆撃する** bomb +目, bombard /bɑːmbɑ́ːʳd/ +目 ▶タンカーはイラン機の**爆撃**を受けた The tanker *was bombed* [*was attacked*] by an Iranian bomber.
‖**爆撃機** a bomber /bɑ́ːməʳ/.

はくげきほう 迫撃砲 a trench mortar.

はくさい 白菜 (a) *hakusai*, a nap (p) a cabbage 《参考》(1)白菜は英米では nap(p)a cabbage の名でも店頭に並んでいる. (2)従来 Chinese cabbage と訳されてきたが, この訳語では「中国(産)のキャベツ」と解釈されるおそれがある.

1**はくし 白紙** blank paper **一形 白紙の** blank ▶彼は**白紙の答案**を提出した He handed [turned] in *a blank exam paper*.
▶《慣用表現》**白紙に戻して**やり直そう Let's start over *with a clean slate*. (➤ clean slate は「字の書いてないきれいな石盤」の意) ‖ その空き地をどう利用するかについては**白紙の状態である** We *haven't decided yet* how to make use of the vacant lot.
‖**白紙委任状** a carte blanche /kɑ̀ːʳt blɑ́ːnʃ/ ‖ **白紙撤回** cancellation, complete withdrawal.

2**はくし 博士** a doctor 《略 Dr.》 **一形 博士の** doctoral ▶医学**博士** *a Doctor* of Medicine 《略 M.D.》 ‖ 応用言語学**博士** a *Ph.D.* in applied linguistics ‖ 文学**博士** *a Doctor* of Letters 《略 D. Litt.》.
‖**博士課程** a doctoral [doctorate] program, a doctor's [Ph.D.] program (➤「博士後期課程」の訳語としても使える) ‖ **博士号** a doctor's degree, a doctorate, a Ph.D. ‖ **博士論文** a dissertation (for a doctor's degree), a doctoral dissertation ‖ **課程博士** a doctorate [Ph.D.] by way of advanced course ‖ **論文博士** a doctorate [Ph.D.] by way of dissertation.

はくしき 博識 ▶荒俣さんは**博識**で知られる Mr. Aramata is known for his *extensive* [*wide*] *knowledge*. ‖ 彼は**博識**だ He is *knowledgeable* [*well informed*] *about a wide range of subjects*. →博学.

はくしゃ 拍車 a spur (乗馬靴につける) ▶《慣用表現》車の増加が交通渋滞に**拍車をかけている** The increase in the number of cars *makes* traffic congestion *even worse* [*exacerbate* traffic congestion]. ‖ 社長のワンマン経営がわが社の衰退に**拍車をかけた**のだ The president's autocratic management *accelerated* the company's decline.

はくしゃく 伯爵 a count (イギリス以外の) ; an earl /əːʳl/ (イギリスの) ▶ウェセックス**伯爵** the *Earl* of Wessex (➤ 呼びかけは My Lord).
‖**伯爵夫人** a countess (➤「女伯爵」の意にもなる).

はくじゃく 薄弱な weak ; tenuous (関係・根拠などが) ▶**薄弱な**論拠 a *tenuous* argument ‖ 彼は意志**薄弱**だ He has *a weak will*. ‖ そんな**薄弱な**言いわけではきみの行為を正当化することはできない Such a *feeble* [*flimsy*] excuse does not justify your behavior [what you did].

はくしゅ 拍手 clapping (手をたたくこと) ; applause /əplɔ́ːz/ (賞賛の拍手) **一動 拍手する** clap (one's hands), applaud (+目) ▶彼の演説が終わるとぱらぱらと**拍手があった** A few people *clapped* their *hands* after his speech. ‖ 彼が現れると**嵐のような拍手が起こった** *A storm of applause* arose when he came in. ‖ 二人に**温かい拍手を送りましょう** Let's *give* the two *a big hand* [*a round of applause*]. (➤ ともに「拍手かっさい」) ‖ 聴衆はそのピアニストの演奏に熱狂的に**拍手した** The audience *applauded* the pianist's performance with enthusiasm.

はくじゅ 白寿 one's 99th birthday.

はくしょ 白書 a white paper ▶きのう政府は**経済白書**を発表した Yesterday the government released *an economic white paper*.

1**はくじょう 白状** (a) confession **一動 白状する** confess 《that, to》 ; admit +目 (認める) ; 《インフォーマル》 come clean (本当のことをいう) ; 《おもに米・インフォーマル》 fess up ; 《インフォーマル・やや古風》 own up (罪などを詰問されて) ▶男は盗んだピストルで強盗をはたらくつもりだったことを**白状した** The man *confessed* that he intended to commit robbery with the stolen gun. ‖ 彼はＤＶＤを万引きしたことを**白状した** He *confessed to* shoplift*ing* the DVDs. ‖ 彼は人妻に恋したことを**白状した** (＝打ち明けた) He *confessed* (*to*) hav*ing* loved a married woman. (➤「打ち明ける」の意では to は省略可能だが, 「万引き」のような犯罪行為の場合には confess to doing とする).
▶いいかげんに**白状したらどうだ** It's high time you *came clean*. ‖ 彼女が好きなんだろ? **白状しろよ** I know you like her. *Admit it* [*Fess up*] *!* ‖ 容疑者は(盗みを)**すっかり白状した** The suspect *owned up* (to the theft).

2**はくじょう 薄情な** heartless (優しさを欠いた, 心ない) ; cold-hearted (心の冷たい) ; unkind (不親切な) ▶彼女を追い返すなんて**薄情な**ことをするね You are *heartless* [*cold-hearted*] indeed to have turned her away. ‖ そんな**薄情な**ことを言わないでくれよ Don't say such *harsh* [*cruel* / *heartless*] things.

ばくしょう 爆笑 a burst [roar] of laughter (➤ burst はどっと笑うさまを, roar は大声で笑うさまを強調する) ▶期せずして聴衆の中から**爆笑が起こった** The audience unexpectedly *burst into laughter*.

はくしょん 《米》 atchoo /ətʃúː/, a (h) choo /ɑːtʃúː/, 《英》 atishoo /ətíʃuː/ ▶ハクション! どうもかぜをひいたらしい *Atchoo !* I'm afraid I'm catching cold. →くしゃみ.

はくしん 迫真の realistic ▶彼女の**迫真の**演技は観客を魅了した Her *realistic* performance enthralled the audience.

はくじん 白人 a white person (➤ 複数形は white people または単に whites. →黒人), a Caucasian /kɔːkéɪʒən/ (➤ 人類学用語の Caucasoid (白色人種) の形容詞および名詞で, 日常語としては前者よりも堅い語) **一形 白人の** white ▶**白人の男性** a *white* man, a *Caucasian* male.

ばくしん 驀進 ▶白鵬はただ一人全勝で優勝街道を**ばく進している** Hakuho alone *is making a straight run* [*is headed straight*] for the championship.

ばくしんち 爆心地 the epicenter of an explosion ; Ground Zero.

ばくすい 爆睡 ▶家に帰って**爆睡した** I came home and (*totally*) *crashed* (*out*).

はくする 博する earn +目 (獲得する) ; win +目 (勝ち取る) ▶**巨利を博する** *earn* [*make*] a big profit ‖ そのテレビのシリーズものは**人気を博した** The television series *won high ratings*. ‖ 小澤征爾は国際的指揮者として**名声を博した** Ozawa Seiji *won* international *fame* [*recognition*] as a conductor.

はくせい 剝製 a stuffed animal [bird] (➤ 文脈によって「縫いぐるみ」の意味にもなる) ▶**このはく製のクマ**はまるで生きているように見える This *stuffed* [*mounted*] *bear* looks as if it were alive.
‖**はく製師** a taxidermist ‖ **はく製術** taxidermy.

1**はくせん 白線** a white line ▶3番線に電車が到着いた

します. 白線の内側に下がってお待ちください The train is approaching Platform 3. Please step back and wait behind the *white line*. (➤ 英米では通例このようなアナウンスはしない).

2**はくせん 白癬**《医学》**ringworm.**

ばくぜん 漠然とした vague /veɪɡ/ (不明りょうな); **dim**(おぼろげな) ▶子供の頃のことは漠然とした記憶しかない I have only *dim* [*vague*] memories of my childhood. ‖ 将来何になりたいかは漠然とした考えしかない I've only a *vague* idea of what I want to be in the future.

ばくだい 莫大な vast; **huge**(ふつうより大きな); **enormous**(並はずれて大きな); **great**(巨大な) ▶ばく大な損害をこうむる suffer an *enormous* loss ‖ ばく大な金がその事業につぎ込まれた *A vast* [*huge*] *sum of* money was put into that project. ‖ ロックフェラーはばく大な富を蓄えた Rockefeller amassed a *great* fortune.

はくだつ 剝奪 deprivation 一動 (…を)**はく奪する deprive** /dɪpráɪv/ 《of》 ▶その選手はドーピングが発覚してアマチュア資格をはく奪された The athlete *was deprived* [*was stripped*] *of* his amateur status after the disclosure of his drug use.

バグダッド Baghdad /bæɡdæd/ (イラクの首都).

ばくだん 爆弾 a **bomb** /bɑːm/ ▶敵機は私たちの町に爆弾を投下した The enemy planes *bombed* [*dropped bombs on*] our town. ‖ 交番に時限爆弾が仕掛けられたらしい They say *a time bomb* was planted in the police box.

▶外務大臣が昨夜爆弾発言をした The Foreign Minister dropped *a bombshell* last night.

‖**爆弾テロ** terrorist bombing ‖ **原子爆弾** an A-bomb ‖ **自動車爆弾** a car bomb ‖ **中性子爆弾** a neutron bomb ‖ **汚い爆弾** a dirty bomb.

はくち 白痴 idiocy(症状); an **idiot**(人).

ばくち 博奕 gambling ▶ばくちで身を持ち崩す ruin oneself by *gambling* ‖ 彼はばくちで負けてすってんてんになった He lost his shirt (at) *gambling*. (➤ lose one's shirt は「すってんてんになる」) ‖ 彼はトランプでばくちをする He *gambles* on [at] cards.

▶《慣用表現》犯人は捜査のほこ先をかわすためいちかばちかの大ばくちを打った The criminal tried *an all-or-nothing gambit* to shake the police from the search. (➤ gambit はチェス用語で「作戦」).

‖**ばくち打ち** a gambler.

ばくちく 爆竹 a **firecracker.**

はくちず 白地図 a **blank map.**

1**はくちゅう 伯仲** ▶実力が伯仲したチームどうしの対戦なのでおもしろい試合になりそうだ Both teams *are well* [*evenly*] *matched* (*in strength*), so the game should be an interesting one. ‖ あの二人は実力が伯仲している The two *are nearly equal* in ability.

2**はくちゅう 白昼** ▶強盗は白昼堂々と郵便局を襲った The burglar broke into the post office *in broad* [*open*] *daylight*. ‖**白昼夢** a daydream.

はくちょう 白鳥 a **swan** ▶醜いアヒルの子は気がつくと美しい白鳥になっていた The ugly duckling found that he had turned into a beautiful *swan*.

‖**白鳥の歌** one's swan song (➤ 白鳥が死に際して歌うと信じられた美しい歌; 英語では意味合いが広く, 最後の演技や試合, 最後の作品や絶筆もさす).

ぱくつく take quick bites 《of》; **gobble** +⑪ (がつがつ食う) ▶ハンバーガーをぱくつく *take quick bites of* a hamburger ‖ 子供たちは学校から帰って来るとさっそくおやつをぱくついた As soon as the children got home from school, they *devoured* [*wolfed down* / *gobbled down*] their afternoon snack.

ぱくっと →ぱくり.

バクテリア bacteria /bæktíəriə/ (➤ 単数形の bacterium はほとんど用いない).

はくとうわし 白頭鷲《鳥》a **bald eagle.**

はくないしょう 白内障《医学》a **cataract** /kǽṭərækt/ ▶右目が白内障になる get *a cataract* in one's right eye. ‖**老人性白内障** a senile cataract.

はくねつ 白熱した heated ▶きょうの会議では白熱した議論が飛び交った There was a *heated* discussion at today's meeting. / A *heated* discussion took place at today's meeting. ‖ 試合はだんだん白熱してきた The game *has become* more and more *thrilling*. / The game *is getting hotter*.

‖**白熱電球** an incandescent bulb.

ばくは 爆破 blowing up; **blasting** (主に岩石の) 一動 **爆破する blast away** [**off**], **blow up** ▶ダイナマイトで爆破してトンネルを貫通させる *blast* a tunnel through with dynamite ‖ 敵は我々の列車が渡るのを止めようとその橋を爆破した The enemy *blew up* the bridge to stop our trains from crossing.

バグパイプ a **bagpipe** (➤ 通例, bagpipes) ▶バグパイプを演奏する play the *bagpipes*.

ぱくぱく ▶子供たちはハンバーガーをぱくぱく食べた The kids *munched on* hamburgers. ‖ 金魚が口をぱくぱくしている The goldfish *is opening and closing its mouth*.

はくはつ 白髪 white hair, gray [《英》**grey**] **hair** ▶白髪の紳士 a *white-haired* [*gray-haired*] gentleman.

ばくはつ 爆発 an **explosion**; (an) **eruption** (噴火) 一動 **爆発する explode, go off** (爆弾などが); **erupt** (火山が) ▶ゆうべ近所でガス爆発があった There was *a gas explosion* in my neighborhood last night. ‖ 石油タンクが爆発した An oil tank *exploded* [*blew up*]. (➤ 後者はややインフォーマルな言い方) ‖ 駅のトイレで時限爆弾が爆発した A time bomb *went off* in the restroom of the railway station. ‖ その火山は2年ぶりに爆発した The volcano *erupted* for the first time in two years.

▶ついに柴田先生の怒りが爆発した Mr. Shibata finally *exploded with anger*. ‖ 兄の日頃の不満が爆発した My brother *gave vent to* his accumulated anger. (➤ give vent to は「(抑えた感情を)発散する, ぶちまける」) ‖ ツイッターが爆発的人気だ Twitter *has become explosively popular*.

‖**爆発物** an explosive ‖ **爆発力** explosive force ‖ **核爆発** a nuclear explosion ‖ **鉱山爆発** a mine explosion ‖ **人口爆発** a population explosion.

はくはん 白斑 vitiligo /vìṭəláiɡəʊ/ ‖**尋常性白斑** vitiligo vulgaris.

1**はくひょう 白票** a **blank vote**(白紙のままの票) ▶白票を投じる cast *a blank vote*(➤ 国会での「賛成票」の意味では white ballot を用いる).

2**はくひょう 薄氷 thin ice** ▶薄氷を踏む *tread* [*skate*] *on thin ice*.

1**ばくふ 幕府 the shogunate** /ʃóʊɡəneɪt/

‖**徳川幕府** the Tokugawa shogunate.

2**ばくふ 瀑布** a **waterfall.**

ばくふう 爆風 a **blast** (**from an explosion**) ▶爆風で窓ガラスがすべて吹き飛んだ All the windowpanes were blown out by the *blast*.

はくぶつがく 博物学 natural history.

はくぶつかん 博物館 a **museum** ‖**科学博物館** a science museum ‖ **交通博物館** a transportation museum ‖ **民族博物館** an ethnographic museum ‖ **歴史博物館** a history museum.

はくぼ 薄暮 twilight.

はくぼく 白墨 (white) chalk ▶白墨１本 a piece of *chalk*.

はくまい 白米 polished rice.

ばくまつ 幕末 the last days of the Tokugawa shogunate /ʃóʊɡənèɪt/.

はくめい 薄命 a short life ▶佳人薄命 Beauties die young.

ばくやく 爆薬 gunpowder(火薬) ; an explosive (爆発物).

はくらい 舶来の imported(輸入された) ; foreign-made (外国製の)

‖**舶来品** an imported [a foreign-made] article ; imported goods (総称).

はぐらかす dodge +目 (質問などをひらりひらりとかわす ; インフォーマルな語) ; evade +目 (話題を変えたり, 無関係なことを言ったりして問題に立ち向かわない ; 堅い語) ▶政治家はめんどうな質問をはぐらかすのがうまい Politicians are very good at *dodging* [*evading*] tough questions.

はくらんかい 博覧会 an exhibition /èksɪbíʃən/, an exposition (➤後者のほうが規模が大きい ; インフォーマルでは an expo という) ‖**万国博覧会** an international exposition, a world('s) fair.

はくり 剥離する peel off ; exfoliate(皮膚・樹皮などが) ‖**網膜剥離** a detached retina.

ぱくり ▶魚はぱくりとえさに食いついた The fish caught the bait *with a snap*. ‖ワニが男の足にぱくりとかみついた A crocodile *snapped at* the man's leg. ‖先日の地震で地面がぱくりと口を開けた The ground *split* [*cracked*] *wide open* in the earthquake the other day.

パクリ a rip off(盗作) (➤フォーマルな言い方は plagiarism /pléɪdʒərìzəm/ (剽窃)).

はくりきこ 薄力粉 cake flour (➤強力粉は bread flour, 中力粉は all-purpose flour).

はくりたばい 薄利多売 high volume sales with small profit margins.

はくりょく 迫力 power(力強さ) ▶迫力のある演奏 a *powerful* performance ‖生の舞台はテレビで見るよりもはるかに迫力がある A live performance *is* far more *impressive* when you see it on the stage than when you watch it on TV. (➤ impressive は「印象的な」) ‖彼の演説は迫力があった His speech *was convincing* [*impressive*]. (➤ convincing は「説得力のある」の意).

ぱくる snitch +目 (盗む) ; lift +目 (盗用する) ; nab (捕まえる).

はぐるま 歯車 a cogwheel, a toothed wheel ; a cog (歯車の歯) ; a gear (wheel) (➤ gear は「伝動装置」) ▶大小の歯車がかみ合って動いている *A* big *gear* is meshing with a smaller one.

▶《比喩的》(組織の中では) 人間は歯車の１つの歯に徹しなければならない You are required to be just one of many *cogs in a big wheel*. ‖中日は投打の歯車がかみ合って破竹の連勝を続けている The Dragons are on a big winning streak, *with a balanced batting and pitching attack*.

はぐれる lose sight of(見失う) ; get separated 《from》 (別れ別れになる) ▶途中でみんなとはぐれてしまったので一人で帰って来た I came back alone since I *lost sight of* my companions. ／I *got separated from* the group and came back alone. ‖人込みの中ではぐれないようにしっかり手をつないでいなさい Hold hands tightly so that we don't *get separated* [*lose each other*] in the crowd. ‖人込みで母とはぐれた I *lost* my mother in the crowd. ‖ハイキングの途中私たち２人ははぐれてしまった During the hike, the two of us *wandered off* (*from* the party). (➤「一行と離れて迷子になる」の意).

ばくろ 暴露 (an) exposure(悪事・正体などの) ; revelation, (a) disclosure (秘密などの ; 前者は後者よりくだけた語) **一動** **暴露する** expose +目, reveal +目, disclose +目 ; unmask +目 (正体を) ▶偽善者の正体を暴露する *unmask* a hypocrite ‖その新聞記事で政界と財界の癒着が暴露された The close relationship between political and business circles *was exposed* by the newspaper report. ‖彼はその本の中で自分が刑務所にいたことがあるとみずから暴露した He himself *revealed* [*disclosed*] in the book that he had been in prison.

‖**暴露記事**[本] an exposé /èkspoʊzéɪ/.

[1]**はけ 刷毛** a brush.

[2]**はけ 捌け** ▶この新しいボールペンははけがいい(＝よく売れる) This new type of ball-point pen *sells quite well*. ／There is *strong demand* for this ball-point pen. ‖このグラウンドは砂が多く, 水はけがいい This field is sandy and *drains well*.

はげ 禿 baldness(はげていること) ; a bald spot (はげた箇所) ; a bald-headed person (はげの人) ▶はげの [はげ頭の] 男性 a *bald* man ‖ストレスが原因ではげになることがある Stress can cause *baldness*. ‖何時間も(ブレークダンスの)ヘッドスピンやってたら頭のてっぺんに丸いはげができちゃったよ I've got *a bald spot* on the top of my head from doing headspins so long.

‖**はげ頭** a bald head(頭) ; a baldhead(人) ‖**はげ山** a bare [treeless ／bald] mountain.

はげいとう 葉鶏頭 《植物》 amaranth /ǽmərænθ/.

はけぐち 捌け口 an outlet(水・感情・エネルギーの) ; a market(商品の) ▶このベランダには水のはけ口がない This balcony has no *outlet* for water [water *outlet*]. ‖和田さんはカラオケをストレスのはけ口にしている Mr. Wada sings karaoke as *an outlet* for stress [to relieve stress].

はげしい 激しい

severe (寒暑・苦痛などが) ; fierce (風・争いなどが) ; violent (感情・苦痛・風などが) ; intense(感情・性質などが) ▶激しい地震 a *severe* [*strong*] earthquake ‖激しい首位争い a *fierce* battle for first place ‖一晩中激しい嵐が吹き荒れた A *violent* storm raged all (through) the night. ‖風は私たちが立っていられないほど激しかった The wind was so *fierce* (that) we could hardly stand up. ‖雨はそのときがいちばん激しかった The rain was *heaviest* [*fiercest*] then. ‖彼女はその男性に激しい嫌悪感をもっていた She had an *intense* dislike of that man. ‖彼女は激しい頭痛を訴えた She complained of a *violent* [*severe*] headache. ‖背中に激しい痛みがあった I had a *severe* [*sharp*] pain in my back. ‖食後すぐに激しい運動をするのは体によくない It is bad for the health to exercise *hard* right after a meal. ／*Vigorous* exercise right after a meal is bad for the health. ‖アキ子は気性が激しい Akiko *has a violent* [*fiery* ／*hot*] *temper*. (➤ fiery /fáɪəri/ は「火のような」が原義 ; hot は「すぐにかっとなる」の意でインフォーマルな語).

▶彼は激しくドアをたたいた He knocked *hard* on the door. ‖雪はいっそう激しくなった It began to snow *even harder*. ‖ 彼女は激しく泣いた She cried *bitterly*. ‖ その賞を得ようと二人は激しく争った They competed *keenly* [*fiercely*] for the prize. ／There was *keen* competition between them for the prize. ‖ 彼は父親と激しく議論した He had a *hot* argument [*heated* discussion] with his father.

はげたか 禿鷹 《鳥》 a **vulture**.

バケツ a **bucket** ▶ポリバケツ *a plastic bucket* ‖ バケツ１杯の水 *a bucket*(*ful*) *of* water.

▶《慣用表現》北関東地方で昨夜バケツをひっくり返したような雨が降った In the northern Kanto area, it *rained* (*in*) *buckets* last night. (➤ rain (in) buckets で「雨が激しく降る」).

パケット a **packet**.

ばけのかわ 化けの皮 ▶そのうち，やつの化けの皮がはがれるさ His *true character will reveal itself* soon. ／Soon he will *show his true colors*. (➤ show one's true colors は「本性を現す」).

はげまし 励まし (an) **encouragement** ▶励ましの手紙 a letter of *encouragement* ‖ テニスの選手として私が今日あるのは両親の励ましのおかげです I owe what I am as a tennis player to the *encouragement* of my parents.

✉ **あなたのお手紙は大きな励ましとなりました** Your letter was *a* great *encouragement* to me. ／Your letter encouraged me a great deal.

¹**はげます 励ます** **encourage** /ɪnkə́ːrɪdʒ/ +㊐ (自信を与える) ; **cheer up** (元気づける) ▶子供は叱るのと同様励ますことも必要だ To *encourage* children is just as necessary as (it is) to scold them. ／Children need *encouragement* as well as scolding. ‖ 将来のことを思って憂鬱になっていたとき，おばが励ましてくれた Once when I was depressed about my future, my aunt *cheered* me *up*. (➤ cheer up は落ち込んでいる人を励ますときに用いる).

【文型】
人(A)を…するように励ます
encourage A **to** do

▶父は教師になるように私を励ましてくれた My father *encouraged* me *to* become a teacher. (➤ to do はこれからすることについていう) ‖ 両親は女優の道に進んだ私を励ましてくれている My parents *have encouraged* me in my career as an actress. (➤ encourage A in B は「人(A)に現在やっている行為(B)をもっとやるよう励ます」).

はげみ 励み (an) **encouragement**(激励) ; an **incentive** /ɪnsénṭɪv/ (刺激) ▶先生に褒められたのが励みになって英語が好きになりました My teacher's praise was (a) real *encouragement* that led me to like English. ‖ 良いライバルがいると勉強のよい励みになる Having a good rival is *an incentive* to study hard(er). ‖ 彼女の受賞は若い人たちにも励みとなるだろう Her winning the award will be *an inspiration* to young people. (➤ inspiration は「奮起させるもの」).

はげむ 励む ▶今後も学問にいっそう励む所存です From now on, I will *push* (*myself*) *to do my best* in (my) scholarly work. ‖ もっと野球の練習に励め *Practice* baseball *harder*.

ばけもの 化け物 a **monster** ▶この家には化け物が出るそうだ It is said that this house *is haunted*. (➤ be haunted /hɔ́ːnṭɪd/ で「(幽霊などが)出没する」) ‖ 化け物みたいなカボチャだ That pumpkin looks like *a monster*.

‖化け物屋敷 a haunted [spooky] house.

はける 捌ける ▶この辺りは水がよくはけない Water doesn't *drain* [*run off*] well here. ‖ そのおもちゃは１日ではけた(＝売れた) Those toys *sold* (*out*) in a day.

¹**はげる 禿げる** **go** [**get**] **bald** ▶あまり心配するとはげるよ Don't worry too much, or you'll *go bald*. ‖ 父さんは頭がはげてきた My father *is getting bald* [*is balding*]. ‖ あのおじさん，つるつるにはげているね That man *is as bald as an egg*.

²**はげる 剝げる** **come off** ; **peel off** (むけて) ▶壁のペンキがはげてしまった The paint *has come off* [*has peeled off*] the wall.

▶《慣用表現》初めはすごい選手だと思ったが，すぐメッキがはげてきた At first, he impressed us as a fabulous player, but he soon *showed his true colors*. (➤ show one's true colors は「正体を現す」).

ばける 化ける ▶(日本の)おとぎ話ではキツネやタヌキはよく人間に化ける In fairy tales, it often happens that a fox or a tanuki *takes* [*assumes*] *the shape of* a human being. ‖ キツネは花嫁に化けた The fox *changed into* a bride. ‖ 猫を殺すと化けて出るよ If you kill a cat, its *spirit will haunt* you.

▶宝くじの賞金は応接間の新しいソファーに化けた The money I won in the lottery *was spent on* [*went for*] a new couch for the living room.

はげわし 禿鷲 《鳥》 a **vulture**.

¹**はけん 派遣する** **send** +㊐ ; **delegate** +㊐ (代表として) ▶日本はオリンピックに大勢の代表選手を派遣した Japan *sent* many athletes to the Olympics. ／Japan *sent* a big delegation to the Olympics. (➤ delegation は「代表団」) ‖ 彼はその会議に代表として派遣された He *was sent* as a delegate to the conference. ‖ うちは200社以上に社員を派遣している We *provide* more than 200 companies *with* (working) staff.

‖派遣会社 a temp agency, a temporary (employment) agency ‖ 派遣社員 a temp, an employee from a temp agency ‖ 派遣労働者 a temp, a temporary worker.

²**はけん 覇権** **hegemony**.

ばけん 馬券 a **betting ticket** (**on a horse**)

‖馬券売り場 a betting ticket office, 《英また》 a betting shop (私設の) (➤ ここでは馬券以外のチケットも扱う).

はこ 箱 a **box** ; a **case** (容器) ▶木 [紙／プラスチック] の箱 a wooden [paper／plastic] *box* ‖ たばこ３箱 three *packs* [*packages*] of cigarettes ‖ その本はこの箱に入れてくれ Put the book in this *box*. ‖ 私は果物を箱に詰めた I *boxed* the fruit. ‖ 青森の祖母からリンゴを１箱送ってきた My grandmother sent me *a box* of apples from Aomori. ‖ 父は１週間にたばこを２箱吸う My father smokes *two packs of cigarettes* a week.

‖筆箱 a pencil case ‖ 宝石箱 a jewelry case.

はごいた 羽子板 a **battledore** /bǽṭldɔːr/ 《参考》「羽根」は shuttlecock. どちらも本来はバドミントンの用語. →羽根つき.

はこいりむすめ 箱入り娘 ▶あの娘は箱入り娘だ She *was brought up like a princess* [*in a sheltered home*]. (➤ 前者は「王女のように育った」の意 ; 後者は「(世間の荒波にもまれることのない) 保護の行き届いた家庭で育った」の意).

はごたえ 歯応え ▶パスタは少し歯ごたえがあるくらいがいちばんいい Pasta is best when it *is* slightly *firm to the bite* [when it is *al dente*]. (➤ al dente は「歯

ごたえのある」の意のイタリア語から) ‖ **この肉は歯ごたえがありそうだ** This meat looks *tough* [*firm*]. (➤ tough は「(肉などが)かたい」, firm は「締まっている」というよい意味).

はこづめ 箱詰め ▶**リンゴを箱詰めにする** *pack* apples *in a box* [*a case*] ‖ **箱詰めのミカン** tangerines *packed in a box* [*a case*] / *boxed* [*cased*] tangerines.

はこにわ 箱庭 a **miniature landscape garden.**

はこび 運び ▶**停戦協定はようやく調印の運びとなった** At last the cease-fire agreement *has reached the signing stage.*

はこびこむ 運び込む ▶**4人がかりでピアノを部屋に運び込んだ** It took four people to *carry* the piano *into* the room.

はこぶ 運ぶ 1【運搬する】**carry** +㊐; **transport** /trænspɔ́ːʳt/ +㊐ (特に長距離を) ▶**ボーイさんがスーツケースを部屋まで運んでくれた** A bellhop *carried* my suitcase to the room. ‖ **運送業者は家具を次々と外へ運び出した** The movers *carried out* the furniture one piece after another. ‖ **エアポートリムジンは乗客を空港まで運ぶ** Airport limousines *transport* passengers to the airport. ‖ **そこの荷物をこっちへ運んでくれない?** Could you *bring* that piece of luggage (over) here? (➤ bring は話し手のところへ「持って来る」, 相手のところへ「持って行く」) ‖ **救急車が男の子を病院へ運んできた** The ambulance *brought* a little boy to the hospital. ‖ **これを台所まで運んでくれませんか** Can you *take* this to the kitchen? (➤ take は話し手・相手から離れたところへ「持って行く」).

2【はかどる】**go on (well), progress** ▶**万事うまく運んでいる** Everything *is going* smoothly. ‖ **仕事は順調に運んでいる** The work *is progressing* satisfactorily.

はこぶね 方舟 an **ark** ‖ **ノアの方舟** Noah's ark.

はこべ (植物) **chickweed.**

はこぼれ 刃こぼれ a **nick on a blade** ▶**刃こぼれした包丁** a kitchen knife with *a nicked blade*.

バザー a **bazaar** /bəzɑ́ːʳ/ ▶**バザーを開く** hold *a bazaar* ‖ **不用品がありましたらバザーに出してください** If you have any things you aren't using, please contribute them to the *bazaar*.

ハザード a **hazard** ‖ **ハザードマップ** a hazard map ‖ **ハザードランプ** a hazard light [lamp].

はざかいき 端境期 **the lean period before the rice harvest** (収穫前の品薄期); a **changeover period** (切り替わる時期).

はさき 刃先 **the edge (of a blade).**

ばさばさ ▶**風に当たって髪がばさばさになった** My hair *became disheveled* after being blown about in the wind. (➤ disheveled /dɪʃévəld/ は「乱れた」). ▶**後ろのやぶでバサバサッと音がしたのでびっくりした** I was startled because something *rustled* in the bush behind me.

ぱさぱさ ▶**ぱさぱさの髪** *dry* hair ‖ **こんなぱさぱさのそばは食えないよ** I can't eat such *mealy* noodles.

はざま 狭間 a **narrow gap** ▶**雲のはざま** *a narrow gap* between the clouds / *an interstice* in the clouds (➤ interstice /ɪntə́ːʳstɪs/ は「狭い隙間」).

はさまる 挟まる **get caught** 《in, between》 ▶**野菜の繊維が歯にはさまった** A vegetable fiber *got caught* [*got stuck*] *between* my teeth.

はさまれる 挟まれる 1【間に入れられる】**get caught, get sandwiched** ▶**彼女はエレベーターのドアにはさまれた** She *got caught* [*got sandwiched*] *between* the doors of the elevator. ‖ **閉まるドアに手をはさまれないように気をつけてください** Take care not to *get* your hands *caught* [*pinched*] by the closing doors.

2【間に位置する】**be sandwiched** 《between》 ▶**ネパールは中国とインドにはさまれている** Nepal *lies* [*is sandwiched*] *between* China and India. ‖ **2つのビルにはさまれて小さな家があった** There was a small house *sandwiched between* two tall buildings. ‖ 《野球》 **坂本は一, 二塁間にはさまれアウトになった** Sakamoto *was run down between* first *and* second. (➤ run down は「(走者を)挟殺する」の意).

はさみ 鋏 **(a pair of) scissors** /sízəʳz/ (紙・布用の); **(a pair of) shears** /ʃɪəʳz/ (園芸・羊毛用の大ばさみ); a **claw** (カニなどの)

▶**このはさみはよく切れる** These *scissors* cut well [are sharp]. ‖ **彼女はテープをはさみでチョキンと半分に切った** She snipped the tape in half with her *scissors*. ‖ **車掌は検札のため切符にはさみを入れた** The conductor *punched* the tickets he was given for inspection. ‖ **庭師が庭木にはさみを入れている** A gardener *is trimming* the garden trees.

はさみうち 挟み撃ち ▶**敵を挟み撃ちにする** *attack* the enemy *on* [*from*] *both sides*.

はさむ 挟む 1【つまむ】**hold** 《between》 ▶**たばこを指にはさむ** *hold* a cigarette *between* one's fingers ‖ **本をわきにはさむ** *hold* a book *under* one's arm.

2【間に入れる】**put** 《between》 →**はさまれる** ▶**本(の間)にしおりをはさむ** *put* a bookmark *between* the pages of a book ‖ **大工さんは鉛筆を耳にはさんで仕事をする** Carpenters work with their pencils *stuck behind* their ears. ‖ **ドアに手をはさんでしまった** I *got* my hand *caught* [*pinched*] in the door.

3【割り込ませる】▶**番組の間にコマーシャルをはさむ** *insert* commercials during a program ‖ **人が話しているときに口をはさまないでくれ** Don't *interrupt* [*cut in* / *butt in*] while I'm speaking.

4【間に置く】▶**大通りをはさんで2軒のデパートがある** Two department stores stand *facing each other across* the boulevard.

はざわり 歯ざわり ▶**セロリはしゃきしゃきした歯ざわりだ** Celery is *crisp* [*crunchy*].

はさん 破産 **bankruptcy** /bǽŋkrʌptsi/ 一動 **破産する** **go bankrupt, fail** ▶**おじ[S社]は破産した** My uncle [S Company] *went bankrupt*. ‖ **こう学費がかさんだのではわが家は破産してしまう** We will *be financially ruined* if we have to spend so much money on the children's education.
‖ **自己破産** personal bankruptcy.

[1]**はし 橋** a **bridge** ▶**橋を渡る** cross *a bridge* ‖ **ボスポラス海峡に橋を架ける** build [throw] *a bridge* across the Bosporus ‖ **隅田川には23の橋が架かっている** There are 23 *bridges* over the Sumida River. ‖ 《駅の掲示》 **下関方面の方はこの橋をお渡りください** Passengers bound for Shimonoseki, take [cross] this *walkway*. (➤ walkway は「(駅・空港などの)渡り廊下, 通路」の意) 《参考》固有名詞で「…橋」という

ときには the Golden Gate Bridge(金門橋), the Bay Bridge(ベイブリッジ)のように the が付くことが多いが, London Bridge(ロンドン橋)のように付かないこともある.

▶《慣用表現》私は彼女に**危ない橋は渡らない**よう忠告した I advised her to *steer clear of anything risky*. (➤ steer clear of は「(危険・人・物に)近づかない」).

2**はし 箸** (a **pair of**) **chopsticks** (➤ 2本1組で用いるので複数形) ▶テーブルの上に**箸**が2ぜん並べてあった Two pairs of *chopsticks* were set on the table. ‖ 正しい**箸**の持ち方を知らない子が多い Many children don't know how to hold *chopsticks* correctly.

▶《慣用表現》あいつは**箸にも棒にもかからない** That guy is *a good-for-nothing*.

‖**箸置き** a chopstick rest ‖ **箸立て** a chopstick stand ‖ **割り箸** disposable chopsticks.

3**はし 端** an **end**(先端); a **corner** (隅); an **edge** (ふち); a **side** (わき) ▶このひもの**端**を持っててちょうだい Hold the *end* of this cord. ‖ このテーブルは**端**のところの塗料がはげてしまった Paint came off from the *corner* [*edge*] of the table. ‖ ほら, 自動車が来ますよ. **端に寄りなさい** Look, a car is coming. Move *to the side* of the road.

▶そのアーケードの**端から端まで**歩いた I walked *from one end* of the shopping mall *to the other*. / I walked *the length* of the shopping mall. ‖ 彼女はその小説を**端から端まで**読んだ She read the novel *from cover to cover*. ‖ 彼女は新聞の広告欄を**端から端まで**読んだ She read the paper's ad column *from beginning to end* [*from top to bottom*].

▶子供たちは母親が片づける**端から**おもちゃを散らかした *The moment* [*As soon as*] their mother put away the toys, the children got them out again.

はじ 恥 (a) **shame**, ***haji***(-**shame**)

> **《解説》「恥」と shame**
> (1) 日本人は「一家の恥」「身内の恥」「学校の恥」などのように,「恥」を集団と結びつけて考える傾向があり, 自分の属する集団に迷惑をかけたり, それを裏切ったりすることを「恥」として罪悪視することが多いが,「恥」の訳語とされる shame は(集団ではなく)自分個人に対する評価が損なわれたことから生じる不面目・不名誉な気持ち, またはエチケット違反などを目撃されたりしたときに感じる恥ずかしい思いをいうことが多く,「恥」とは正確には一致しない. → **恥ずかしい**.
> (2) したがって, 日本語の「恥」に対しては *haji*(-shame) または *haji*(-type) shame を適宜用いるのがよい. なお, humiliation(屈辱, 恥辱)や disgrace (不名誉, 不面目)が日本語の「恥」に相当することも少なくない. → **恥さらし**.

▶知らないことを聞くのは**恥**ではない There's no *shame* in asking about what you don't know. ‖ **恥を知れ** *Shame on you*. ‖ あの政治家は**恥を恥とも思わない** That politician is *completely shameless* [*has no sense of shame*]. ‖ 彼の行為は**一家の恥**(=不名誉)であった His conduct brought *disgrace on his family*.

▶彼らは彼女の前で私に**恥をかかせた** They *humiliated* me [*put* me *to shame*] in front of her. ‖ よくも内輪の**恥をさらして**くれたな How could you *have washed our dirty linen* [*laundry*] *in public*? (➤ 文字どおりには「人前で自分のところの汚れたリネン製品(下着, シーツなど)[洗濯物]を洗う」の意) **《参考》**「内輪の恥」をインフォーマルでは a skeleton in the closet という.

▶敬語の使い方を間違えて**恥をかいてしまった** I *embarrassed myself* when I made a mistake in using honorifics. ‖ **恥をしのんで**彼に借金を頼んだ I *swallowed* [*pocketed*] *my pride* and asked him to lend me some money.

▶おじは**恥も外聞もなく**自分の娘のような年の女の子と再婚した My uncle *shamelessly* [*brazenly*] *went and* remarried a girl young enough to be his daughter. (➤ go and do は「…するようなばかなまねをする」) ‖ あの人ったら, 全く**恥知らず**だわ She's completely *shameless*. / She *has no shame*. ‖ 度重なる釈明会見は**恥の上塗り**以外の何ものでもない Holding repeated interviews where they try to make excuses is nothing but *adding shame to their shameful behavior*.

ことわざ **聞くは一時の恥, 聞かぬは一生の恥** To ask may bring momentary shame, but not to ask and remain ignorant brings everlasting shame.

はしか 麻疹 measles /míːzəlz/ (➤ 通例単数扱い) ▶はしかにかかる catch (*the*) *measles* ‖ 彼女は学校で友だちからはしかをうつされた She caught *measles* from a friend at school.

はしがき 端書き a **foreword**(特に著者以外の人の); a **preface** /préfəs/ (序文).

はじきだす 弾き出す 1【算出する】figure out, calculate +Ⓞ ▶旅行の費用を**はじき出す** *calculate* [*figure out*] the travel expenses.

2【のけものにする】shun +Ⓞ (敬遠する); **ostracize** +Ⓞ (のけものにする); **keep ... at a distance**(…に近寄らない) ▶その子はうそつきなのでクラスの仲間から**はじき出された** He *was shunned* [*ostracized*] by his classmates because he was a liar.

はじく 弾く 1【指ではね飛ばす】flip +Ⓞ (親指の先を人さし指の腹で包むようにして); **flick** +Ⓞ (中指のつめを親指の先で押さえて) ▶硬貨を**はじく** *flip* a coin ‖ 彼は机の上のテントウ虫を人さし指で**はじいた** He *flicked* a ladybug *off* the desk with his forefinger. ‖《野球》中島は内川のゴロを**はじいた** Nakajima *fumbled* Uchikawa's grounder.

2【水などを】repel /rɪpél/ +Ⓞ ▶油は水を**はじく** Oil *repels* water. ‖ このレインコートはよく水を**はじく** This raincoat *sheds* [*repels*] water well.

3【計算して算定する】▶利益をざっと3000万と**はじいた** We *estimated* our profit at [to be] about thirty million yen.

はしくれ 端くれ ▶私だって音楽家の**端くれ**だ I'm *a bit of* a musician, too.

はしけ a **barge**.

はしげた 橋げた a **bridge girder**.

はじける 弾ける crack open(パンと音を立てて割れる); **burst open** (つぼみなどがぱっと開く) ▶ハシバミの実が**はじける**音がした I heard a hazel nut *crack open*.

▶若い女の子の**はじける**ような笑い声があがった The young girls' peals of (high-pitched) laughter filled the air.

はしご 梯子 1【道具】a **ladder**; a **stepladder** (脚立) ▶**はしご**を登る[降りる] go up [go down] *a ladder* / mount [descend] *a ladder* ‖ **はしご**を掛けて屋根に登った I put up *a ladder* and went onto the roof.

‖**はしご車** a ladder truck, a hook and ladder ‖

はしご段 a staircase ‖ **なわばしご** a rope ladder.

2【連続】▶きのうは喫茶店を4軒も**はしごして**しまった Yesterday I went *from* one coffee shop *to another*. I *dropped in* a total of four coffee shops. ‖ 彼は**はしご酒**をして明け方近く家に帰った He went back home at about daybreak after *bar-hopping* [《英》*a pub crawl*].

はじさらし 恥曝し ▶おまえはわが家の**恥さらし**だ You're *a disgrace* to our family.

はしたがね 端金 **chicken feed, peanuts,** a **paltry sum (of money)** ▶そんな**はした金**はいらないよ I refuse to accept such *chicken feed*.

はしたない **shameful**(恥ずべき); **vulgar**(下品な); **immodest** /ɪmɑ́:dɪst/(慎しみのない) ▶人の残したものを食べるなんて**はしたない** It is *shameful* [*bad manners*] to eat other people's leftovers. ‖ そういう**はしたない**口をきくものではない Don't use such *vulgar* language. ‖ ぼくのジョークに彼女は**はしたない**笑い声を出した She burst into *immodest* [*unrestrained*] laughter at my joke.

ばじとうふう 馬耳東風 ▶母親の説教も息子には**馬耳東風だった** The son *turned a deaf ear* [*paid no attention*] *to* his mother's preaching [nagging].

はじまらない 始まらない ▶今さらじたばたしても**始まらない** It's *no use* making [*too late* to make] a fuss over it. (➤ no use は「むだだ」, too late は「もう遅い」) ‖ 今さら単語帳を見たって**始まらない**わよ. テストはすぐに始まるんだから *There's no point* (in) looking at your word book. The test is about to begin. (➤ there's no point (in) doing は「…してもむだだ」).

はじまり 始まり **the beginning** ▶ほとんどの科学者はビッグバンが宇宙の**始まり**と考えている Almost all scientists think that the Big Bang was *the beginning* of the universe. ‖ くしゃみはかぜの**始まり**だ Sneezing is the *beginning* of a cold. / Sneezing means that you are starting to catch a cold. ‖ さあさあ, 人形芝居の**始まり始まり** Everyone come and watch the puppet show!

はじまる 始まる **begin, start**

語法 (1)両者はしばしば同義で用いられるが start のほうがくだけた語. (2)もともと begin は活動の開始に力点があり, 反意語は end(終わる). start は静止から動き始める運動性に力点があり, 反意語は stop(止まる).

▶コンサートは7時から**始まる** The concert *begins* [*starts*] at eight. ‖ 書道展は今度の日曜日から**始まる** A calligraphy exhibition *begins* this coming Sunday.

▶私たちがドームに着いたときには試合はもう**始まっていた** The game *had* already *begun* when we got to the dome. ‖ プロ野球が4月3日から**始まる** The professional baseball season is going to *start* [*open*] on April 3. (➤ season には open を使うことが多い) ‖ 授業はいつから**始まる**の? When do your classes *begin*? / When do you *get started with* your classes?

> **直訳の落とし穴「(日時)から始まる」**
> 日本語では「(日時)に始まる」とも「(日時)から始まる」ともいうが, 後者の場合「…から」につられて from を使ってしまいがち. 例えば,「打ち合わせは午後3時から始まります」は(×)The meeting will begin from 3 p.m. でなく, The meeting will begin at 3 p.m. が正しい. begin や start は瞬間動詞で, (×) begin from とはしない. 時刻の場合は at, 曜日は on, 月は in など, ふつうに「…に」に当たる前置詞を用いる. したがって,「大半の国では新学期は9月から始まる」は The school year begins [starts] in September in most countries. となる.

▶アルファベットは A で**始まる** The alphabet *begins with* A. ‖ この物語は回想場面で**始まる** This story *begins with* a flashback. ‖ 会は2人の新メンバー紹介で**始まった** The meeting *opened with* the introduction of two new members.

▶太平洋戦争は1941年に**始まった** The Pacific War *broke out* in 1941. (➤ break out は戦争や災害が「突然起こる」) ‖ 外が騒がしいな. **何が始まったんだろう** There's a lot of noise outside. *What's going on?*

▶**また始まった** *There you go again*. (➤ ぐち・説教・自慢などをまた聞かされるような場合に用いる. 相手によって適宜 he, she などに変える) ‖ ほら, また彼女の自慢話が**始まった** There she *goes* again boasting.

☛ **始まらない** (→見出語)

はじめ 初め **the beginning**; a **start**(競技・活動などの)

▶何事も**初め**が肝心だ In everything, *the beginning* is most important. ‖ この試合, **初めから**見たかったなあ I wanted to see the game *from the beginning*. ‖ その映画には**初めから終わりまで**笑いっぱなしだった The movie kept me laughing *from beginning to end* [*from start to finish*]. (➤ どちらも対になった慣用句) ‖ 計算が合わない. **もう一度初めからやり直してみよう** The calculation didn't come out right. I'll do it *all over again* [*from scratch*]. ‖ **初めっから**そう言ってるでしょ I've been telling you that *all along*.

▶**初めに**2, 3質問したい *First*, I'd like to ask you a couple of questions. ‖ 私たちは**6月の初めに**結婚しました We got married *in early June* [*early in June* / *at the beginning of June*]. (➤ in early June の語順がふつう) ‖ 教科書の**初めの**5ページをノートに写しなさい Copy the *first* five pages of the textbook in your notebook. ‖ キーツは**19世紀初めの**大詩人だ Keats was a great poet *in the early 19th century*.

▶監督は**初めは**やさしかったが, あとでとても厳しくなった *At first* [*Initially*], the manager was lenient but he became very strict later on. ‖ 結婚生活も**初めは**とても幸せでした We were extremely happy *in the early days* of our married life.

はじめて 初めて **first, for the first time** (➤ 後者は前者の強意形) ▶**初めて**会ったとき彼は学生だった When I *first* met him [*The first time* I met him], he was a student. (➤ 最初の文で first は動詞の前に置くことに注意) ‖ 沖縄生まれの絵理子はきのう**生まれて初めて**雪を見たそうだ I hear Eriko, who was born in Okinawa, saw snow yesterday *for the first time in her life*. ‖ この辺り(に来たの)は**初めてです** I'*m new* [I'*m a stranger*] around here. ‖ こんなにおいしいケーキは**初めてよ** I've *never* had such delicious cake *before*.

> **【文型】**
> **…するのはこれが初めてだ**
> **This is the first time (that)** S + V.

▶ハワイに来たのは**これが初めてです** *This is my first* visit to Hawaii. (➤ この言い方は visit や trip で用いること

が多い）／*This is the first time that* I've visited Hawaii.（➤（×）This is the first time for me to have visited Hawaii. とはしない）‖大リーグのチームが日本で開幕試合を行うのはこれが**初めて**ではない *This is not the first time that* Major League baseball teams have played an opening game in Japan.

✉ **実は外国の人と文通するのはこれが初めてです** Actually, *this is my first time* to correspond with someone who is not Japanese. ➤ This is the first time that I have corresponded ... よりも簡潔なくだけた言い方.

【文型】
A になって[A して]初めて…する
not ... until A
➤ A は時を表す語句, または文

▶彼女がいなくなって**初めて**彼女をどんなに好きだったか気がついた I did*n't* realize how much I loved her *until* she left me.（➤「彼女が去るまでは気がつかなかった」の意；この文が最も ふつうで, 以下の文は強調構文）／*It was not until* she left me *that* I realized how much I loved her. ／*Only after* she left me did I realize how much I loved her.（➤ 副詞節を文頭に出すと主語と動詞が逆の語順になる）.

はじめまして 初めまして ▶ 対話「はじめまして, 中山です」「はじめまして」"*How do you do?* I'm Nakayama." "*How do you do?*"（➤ 英語的発想では第1文は "How do you do? I'm Taro Nakayama." とフルネームで名乗るのがふつう）.

解説 「はじめまして」について
(1)「はじめまして」に相当する改まった表現は **How do you do?** で, 言われたほうも How do you do? と応じる.
(2) この応答に続けて,「お目にかかれて光栄です」や「どうぞよろしくお願いいたします」の意の (I'm) glad to meet you. や Nice [Pleased] to meet you. と言うことも多い(いずれの場合も meet を強く発音する). こう言われた人は The pleasure is mine. とか (It's) nice to meet you, too. などと答える（この場合, それぞれ mine, you を強く発音する）.
(3) 形式ばる必要のない場合には, How do you do? を抜きにして **How are you?, Hello!, Hi!** などのことばを交わすことが多く, 特に若い人たちの間にこの傾向が見られる.

はじめる 始める

begin +目, **start** +目（➤ あとに続く動詞は不定詞または動名詞）→はじまる ▶いつエアロビクスを**始め**たんですか When did you *begin* [*start*] doing aerobics? ‖井上さんは70歳を過ぎてから絵をかき**始めた** Mr. Inoue *began* painting after the age of 70. ‖父は抗がん剤の投与を受け**始めた** My father (has) *started* taking anti-cancer drugs. ‖健康のためにジョギングを**始めた** I *began* jogging [to jog] for my health. ‖両親は新しく商売を**始めた** My parents *started* a new business.

▶先生は前の週の続きからレッスンを**始めた** The teacher *took up* the lesson where she had left off the week before.（➤ take up は「(中断していたものを)また続ける」の意）.

▶彼は駅の近くで飲み屋を**始めた** He *opened* a pub near the train station. ‖きょうは35ページから**始め**ましょう Let's *begin* on [《主に英》at] page 35 today.（➤「35ページの20行目から始める」なら begin on [at] page 35, line 20 とするか begin with line 20, page 35とする）‖どの歌から**始め**ようか Which song shall we *begin with*? ‖そろそろ**始め**ようか Shall we *get started*? ／Well, I guess it's about time we *got started* [we *began*].（➤ It's about time に続く文の動詞は通例過去形）.

はしゃ 覇者 **1**【武力・権力による征服者】a **conqueror** /ká:ŋkərəʳ/.
2【優勝者】a **victor**; a **champion**（チャンピオン）; a **winner**（勝利者）▶ベイスターズが今シーズンの**覇者**だ The BayStars are this season's *champions*.

ばしゃ 馬車 a **carriage**（有蓋(がい)または無蓋の）; a **coach**（有蓋で大型の）▶4頭立ての**馬車** *a carriage* and four ‖**馬車**で宮殿に向かう go to the palace *by coach* ‖彼は**馬車馬**のように働いた He worked *like a dog* [*slave*].（➤「奴隷のように」の意；work like a horse という言い方もあるが, これは「元気いっぱい働く, 馬力がある」という好ましいニュアンス）.
‖**駅馬車** a stagecoach ‖**荷馬車** a cart（通例1頭立てで2輪の）; a wagon（通例2頭以上の馬が引く大型4輪の）‖**ほろ馬車** a covered wagon; a prairie schooner(大型の).

はしゃぐ ▶あすは遠足だというので子供たちが**はしゃいで**（＝興奮して）いる The children *are* all *excited* because they're going on an outing tomorrow. ‖子供たちが公園で**はしゃぎ回って**（＝跳ね回って）いる The children *are romping about* in the park.

はしやすめ 箸休め a ***hashiyasume***; a small side dish that serves as a palate cleanser between the main courses of a full-course Japanese meal（➤ 説明的な訳; palate cleanser は「お口直し」）.

ばしゃばしゃ ▶子供たちが水際でうれしそうに**ばしゃばしゃ**やっている The children *are* happily *splashing around* at the water's edge.

パジャマ 《米》**pajamas**, 《英》**pyjamas** /pədʒá:məz/ ▶**パジャマ**に着替えて早く寝なさい Change into your *pajamas* [*pj's*] and go to bed right away. ‖私は日曜日は1日中**パジャマ**で過ごす I always spend my Sundays *in my pajamas*.

危ないカタカナ語 パジャマ
「パジャマ」は英語では pajamas と複数形で使う. ただし a pajama coat（パジャマの上着）, pajama trousers(パジャマのズボン)のように形容詞的に使う場合は単数形. a pajama top, pajama bottoms という言い方もある.「パジャマ」は, インフォーマルでは PJs [PJ's ／pjs] /pí:dʒèɪz/ ともいう.

ばじゅつ 馬術 **equestrianism**, **horsemanship**（➤ 後者は性差を感じさせるために避けられる傾向がある）; **(horseback) riding**（➤「乗馬」に近い）▶彼は**馬術**が得意だ His *horseback riding skills* are remarkable. ／He is a good (horseback) rider [horseman].
‖**馬術競技** an equestrian event.

はしゅつじょ 派出所 a **police box**.

ばしょ 場所

1【所】a **place**; a **location**(位置); a **venue** /vénju:/（開催地・会合の場所）▶お弁当を広げるのにいい**場所**をさがさなくては We have to find a good *place* to eat our box lunches. ‖先に行って花見の**場所**を取っておいてくれ Would you go ahead and reserve *a place* for our cherry blossom viewing picnic? ‖その喫茶店は**場所**が悪くてつぶれてしまった The coffee shop has gone under because of its bad *location*. ‖ここが埴輪

(はにわ)がたくさん出てきた**場所**だ This is (the *place*) where a lot of *haniwa* dolls were excavated. ‖ その病院の**場所**を教えてください Can you tell me *where* the hospital *is*?
▶次の全国大会の**場所** the *venue* of the next national convention ‖ 対話「あしたは飲み会だ」「**場所**はどこなの?」"We're having a drinking party tomorrow." "*Where at?*"
2【余地】room; **space** (空間) ▶ロッキングチェアーを買いたいけど, 私のアパートには置く**場所**がない I'd like to buy a rocking chair but there's no *room* for one in my apartment. ‖ このピアノは**場所**を取る This piano occupies [takes up] a lot of *space*.
3【席】a **place**; a **seat** (座席) ▶**場所**を交換してくれますか Would you mind changing *places* with me? ‖ 映画館は満員で座る**場所**がなかった No *seats* were available at the theater.
4【すもうの興行】a **tournament** ▶日馬富士が夏[名古屋]**場所**で優勝するといいなあ I hope Harumafuji will win the Summer [Nagoya] Sumo *Tournament*.

はしょうふう 破傷風 **lockjaw**, **tetanus** /tétənəs/ (➤後者は医学用語) ▶**破傷風**にかかる contract *tetanus*.

ばしょがら 場所柄 ▶寅(とら)次郎君, **場所柄**をわきまえたまえ. きみは葬式に来てるんだよ *Think about where you are*, Torajiro. This is a funeral (service).

ばしょふさぎ 場所塞ぎ ▶このソファーは**場所ふさぎ**だから処分しようよ This sofa *takes up too much space*, so let's get rid of it.

はしょる 端折る **1【すそを折る】tuck up** ▶少女は水にぬれないようにゆかたのすそを**はしょった** The girl *tucked up* her yukata so that its hem would not get wet.
2【短くする】cut ... short ▶全部話せば長くなるのではし**ょって**話します Since it is a long story, I will *cut* [*make*] it *short*.

はしら 柱 a **post**; a **pillar** (屋根を支える柱); a **column** /kɑ́:ləm/ (円柱); a **pole** (電柱など) ▶おでこを**柱**にぶつけた I bumped my forehead against the *post*. ‖ この床の間の**柱**はヒノキです The *pillar* of this tokonoma is made of hinoki (Japanese cypress).
▶父が心臓病で倒れて以来, 兄が一家の**柱**となっている Since my father came down with heart disease, my (older) brother has become the (main) *breadwinner* [the *pillar*/*mainstay*] of our family. (➤ mainstay は「(船の)大檣(しょう)支索」, 転じて「頼みの綱」; pillar と mainstay は「精神的支柱」の意味合いが強い; ⇀**大黒柱**).
‖**柱時計** a wall clock.

はじらい 恥じらい ⚠「恥じらい」は日本語に特有の語でぴったりの英語はない. **demureness (慎ましさ), reserve (控え目), あるいは shyness, bashfulness (はにかみ)などを適宜使って表すしかない.**
▶日本の若い女性の多くは**恥じらい**というものを忘れてしまったかに見える It seems that many young Japanese women have quite forgotten (*modest*) *reticence* [(*demure*) *reserve*]. ‖ 日本文化においては**恥じらい**は美徳である In Japanese culture, *reticence* is (viewed as) a virtue.

はしらせる 走らせる
1【乗り物を】drive +目; **sail** +目 (人が船などを); **carry** +目 (風が船などを); **gallop** +目 (馬をギャロップで) ▶河川敷で車を**走らせる** *drive* one's car on the riverbed ‖ 1人でヨットを**走らせる** *sail* a yacht solo.

> **直訳の落とし穴「車を走らせる」**
> 「走らせる」というとすぐ run が思い浮かぶが, run a [one's] car だけでは「車のエンジンをかける」, つまり, 一般の機械と同じようにスイッチオフの状態から「(走行するために) 車を作動させる, 動かす」という意味である. また,「試しに走行させてみる」という意味の場合もある.「彼は夜通し車を走らせた」は「車を(ずっと)走行させた」という意味なので, He drove (his car) all night. とする.「彼はタクシーを走らせて病院に駆けつけた」は He rushed to the hospital in a taxi [by taxi]. でよい. また,「走っている車」を running car と直訳しないこと. それでは「エンジンがかかっている車」の意になってしまう. 英語ではその場合 moving car という.

2【急行させる】dispatch +目; **send quickly** ▶人を医者に**走らせる** *send quickly* for a doctor.
3【すばやく動かす】scan +目 (ざっと目を) ▶その書類にざっと目を**走らす** *scan* the document.

はしり 走り ▶**走り**のサンマ *the first* saury *to come on the market* ‖ **走り**のトマト *early* tomatoes ‖ 梅雨の**走り**の雨 rain that *heralds the start* of the rainy season.

はしりがき 走り書き (a) **scribble** 一動 **走り書きする scribble** (+目) ▶テーブルの上に私の妹の**走り書き**のメモが置いてあった There was a *scribbled* note from my (younger) sister on the table. ‖ **走り書き**ですみませんが, うちの住所と電話番号です Please excuse my *poor handwriting*. Here's my address and phone number.

はしりたかとび 走り高跳び **high jumping** (すること); **the high jump** (競技) ▶彼女は**走り高跳び**で1メートル70センチ**跳んだ** She *high-jumped* 170 centimeters.
《参考》「走り高跳びの選手」は high jumper という.

はしりづかい 走り使い ⇀**使い走り**.

はしりはばとび 走り幅跳び **broad jumping**, **long jumping** (すること; 《英》では後者を主に用いる); **the broad jump**, **the long jump** (競技; 後者が一般的) ▶彼は**走り幅跳び**で7メートル**跳んだ** He *long-jumped* seven meters. 《参考》「走り幅跳びの選手」は broad jumper または long jumper という.

はしりよみ 走り読みする **scan** +目, **skim over** [**through**] (➤前者には「自分が必要としている情報を得るために」という含みがあることが多い) ▶彼は(家に)たまっていた新聞を**走り読みした** He *scanned* [*skimmed over*] the papers which had piled up (at home).

はしる 走る

1【人や乗り物などが】run; **rush** (急ぐ); **dash** (突進する); **jog** (ゆっくり走る) ▶いてついた道は**走らない**ようにしなさい Don't *run* on an icy street. ‖ マラソンの参加者たちは今外堀通りを**走っている** The participants in the marathon *are running* along Sotobori Street. ‖ 雨が降りだしたので**走って帰った** It started raining so I *ran back*.
▶**走っている**車から空き缶を投げるな Don't throw empty cans out of a *moving* car. ‖ 車は時速80キロで**走っている** The car *is going* [*doing*] 80 kilometers an hour. ‖ 彼女の車は東名高速を**走っていた** Her car *was traveling on* [*along*] the Tomei Expressway. ‖ 船は気持ちよい速度で**走って行った** The ship *sailed* at a comfortable speed.
▶彼は音のした方へ**走った** He *rushed* [*dashed*] to where the sound had come from. ‖ 事故の第一報とともに記者たちは現場へ**走った** Upon hearing of

the accident, the reporters *rushed for* the site. ‖彼女は寄付集めに**走り回った** She *ran around* soliciting donations.

2【道路などが通じる】run；**extend**（伸びる）▶ベネチアは町の中を水路が縦横に**走っている** Canals *run* in all directions throughout Venice. ‖近鉄特急は名古屋・難波間を**走っている** Kintetsu express trains *run* between Nagoya and Nanba. ‖奥羽山脈は東北地方を南北に**走っている** The Ou Mountains *extend* from north to south through the Tohoku district.

3【好ましくない方向へ行く】▶敵側に**走る**（＝寝返る）*defect* to the enemy ‖何事も**極端に走るな** Don't *go to extremes* in anything. ‖その教師は**感情に走って**生徒たちを殴った The teacher *was carried away by his anger* and struck the students.（➤ be carried away は「我を失う，夢中になる」）‖貧困から悪事に**走る**というケースはしばしばある Poverty sometimes *drives* [*leads*] a person *to* crime. ‖彼は妻を**捨てて**別の女性に**走った** He *abandoned* [*walked out on*] his wife *for* another woman.

4【現れる】▶夕空に稲妻が**走った** Lightning *flashed* across the evening sky.

はじる 恥じる feel ashamed《of, that》▶きみは仕事がよくできるんだから大学中退であることを**恥じる**ことはない You do good work, so you don't have to *feel ashamed* that you dropped out of college. ‖松山商業は名門の**名に恥じない**（＝値する）活躍をした Matsuyama Commercial High played well, (in a manner) *worthy of* its illustrious name.

バジル《植物》**basil** /béɪzəl ‖ bǽzəl/.

はしわたし 橋渡し▶アメリカは両国間の紛争解決の**橋渡しをした** The U.S. *acted as a mediator* [*a bridge*] to settle the dispute between the two countries.

1**はす 蓮**《植物》a **lotus** /lóʊṭəs/.

2**はす 斜に diagonally** /daɪǽgənəli/（対角線に）；**slantwise**（傾斜して，斜めに）▶紙を**はすに切る** cut paper *diagonally* ‖気合いと同時に武士はわら人形を**はすに切り落とした** With a shout, the samurai cut the straw doll *slantwise*.

☛ **はす向かい**（→見出語）

-はず 1【当然】no wonder →当然 ▶あんなことをしたんだから先生も怒る**はずだ** *It is no wonder* (that) the teacher got angry after he did something like that.

2【確信】must, ought to, should（➤ この順で確信の度合いが低くなる）

> 【文型】
> …する[である]はずだ
> **must** do [be]
> …するはずだ
> **should** do ／**ought to** do
> 《解説》(1)現在のことについて，数％の不確かさを残した「…のはずだ」は，must または have to で表す.「…に違いない」とも訳す. →違いない.
> (2)これからのことについては，確信していることについては will や be bound to で表すが，幾分かの期待を込めた予測は should や ought to で表す. →-だろう.

▶きょうは図書館は開いている**はずだよ** The library *must* [*should*] be open today.（➤ should は多少確信度が下がる. be supposed to を用いてもよい）‖彼らは今頃はアテネに到着している**はずです** They *must* [*should*] have arrived in Athens by this time. ‖こんなやさしい問題を大半の生徒が間違える**はずがない** Most students *will never* answer the easy questions like these incorrectly. ‖スタジアムは来年春には完成している**はずだ** The stadium *is expected to* [*is supposed to*] be completed next spring. ‖高速道路の渋滞は夕方には解消される**はず**です Traffic on expressways *should* [*is expected to*] ease this evening.

3【予定】be going to do, **be to** do（➤ 後者は堅い言い方）▶きょうはナゴヤドームで2試合行われる**はずだ** Two games *are going to* be played at Nagoya Dome today. ‖あの俳優が主役を演じる**はずだった**が，急病でほかの人に代わった That actor *was to* play the lead role, but his sudden illness resulted in another person playing the part. ‖全日空148便は午後9時に**到着するはずだ** All Nippon Airways Flight No. 148 *is due* at 9 p.m.（➤ be due は「到着の予定で」）.

▶**こんなはずではなかった** *This wasn't how it was supposed to be.* ／*I didn't think things would turn out this way.* ／*I didn't want it to be* [*end*] *this way.*

☛ **-はずが[は]ない**（→見出語）

1**バス** a **bus**；《英また》a **coach**（長距離バス）▶**バス**に乗る get on *a bus*, board *a bus* ‖**バス**から降りる get off *a bus* ‖私は**バス**で通学しています I go to school *by bus* [*on a bus* ／*in a bus*]. ／I take [ride] *a bus* to school. ‖**9時23分のバスに乗り遅れた** I missed *the 9 : 23 bus*. ‖**このバス**は市民病院に行きますか[を通りますか] Does *this bus* [Do you] go to the city hospital？

▶**その**バス**に乗れば**河口湖に行けます The *bus* will take you to Lake Kawaguchi. ‖その温泉地へは鉄道の駅から**バス**に乗って45分です The hot spring resort is a 45-minute *bus ride* from the railway station. ‖その滝に行くなら**バス**を使いなさい If you are going to the waterfall, take *a bus*. ‖**バス**の中で先生に会った I saw our teacher *on the bus*. ‖新宿・博多間には**バスの便**がある There is *bus service* between Shinjuku and Hakata.

‖**バスガイド** a (bus) tour guide, a bus conductor, a guide on a sightseeing bus《参考》bus guide とすると「バス路線案内」の意になる ‖**バスターミナル** a bus terminal [depot] ‖**バス代** a bus fare ‖**バス停** a bus stop ‖**バス旅行** a bus tour ‖**バス路線** a bus route [line]；a bus lane(専用路) ‖**貸切バス** a chartered bus ‖**観光バス** a sightseeing bus ‖**高速バス** an express bus(急行バス)；an intercity bus(都市と都市を結ぶ) ‖**市内バス** a city bus ‖**深夜バス** a late-night bus ‖**スクールバス** a school bus ‖**低床バス** a low-floor bus ‖**二階建てバス** a double-decker (bus) ‖**ワンマンバス**(→ワンマン).

2**バス**《ふろ》a **bath** ▶バス・トイレ付きのアパート an apartment *with bath and toilet*.

‖**バスタオル** a bath towel ‖**バスタブ** a bathtub ‖**バスマット** a bath mat ‖**バスルーム** a bathroom ‖**バスローブ** a bathrobe.

3**バス**《音楽》**bass** /beɪs/ ‖**バス歌手** a bass.

パス 1【球技】a **pass** 一動 **パスする pass**（＋目），**throw a pass** ▶ロングパスをする make a long *pass* ‖《実況放送で》本田が香川に**パス**. 香川がシュート！ Honda *passes* the ball to Kagawa. Kagawa shoots !

2【トランプなどで】a **pass** 一動 **パスする pass** ▶（ダイエットしているので）私，デザートは**パス**するわ *No* des-

sert for me, please.／(I think) I'll *pass on* dessert. ‖ 対話「みどり, きみの番だよ」「パス」"Your turn, Midori." "*Pass*."
3【合格】▶筆記試験にパスする *pass* the written test.
4【通行券・入場券】a pass.

はすい 破水 ▶彼女は破水した Her *water* [*waters*] *broke*.

はすう 端数 a **fraction** ▶1万円未満の端数 *a fraction* less than ten thousand yen ‖ 端数を切り捨てると20になる If you round off *fractions*, you'll get 20.／Omit *fractions* and you'll get 20.

ばすえ 場末 a **back alley** ▶場末の酒場 a drinking place in a *back alley*.

はずかしい 恥ずかしい

訳語メニュー
恥である →be ashamed 1
きまりが悪い →feel embarrassed 2
(性格的に)引っ込み思案である →feel shy 2

1【不名誉に思う】**be ashamed** ((of))

【文型】
当人やその行為(A)が恥ずかしい
be ashamed of A
➤ A は名詞・動名詞
…して自分が恥ずかしい
be ashamed of oneself for doing
…することが恥ずかしい
be ashamed to do

▶彼はカンニングしたことがとても恥ずかしかった He *was* very *ashamed of* cheating on the exam.／He *was* very *ashamed of himself for* cheating on the exam. (➤後者はそういうことをしたことで「自分が恥ずかしい」という場合) ‖ そんなことして(自分が)恥ずかしくないの, 太郎ちゃん！Taro, *aren't you ashamed* (*of yourself*) *for* doing such a thing? ‖ 恥ずかしくて両親に合わせる顔がない I *am too ashamed to* look my parents in the face. ‖ 恥ずかしい話ですがコンピュータのことは少しもわかりません *I am ashamed* [*embarrassed*] *to say this*, but I don't know anything about computers. (➤ to do はこれからすることを表す. ashamed のほうがずっと強意で,「できて当然なのにできない, できなくて恥だ」という感じ).
▶江藤氏は大家といっても恥ずかしくない技術を持っている Mr. Eto is skilled enough [has enough skill] *to be called* a master (craftsman). ‖ 対話 (個展で)「すばらしい作品ですね」「いやあ, お恥ずかしい限りです」"You really have some excellent pieces of work here!" "Thank you. *I'm flattered* (*to hear that*).／They're *nothing to boast about*." (➤ I'm flattered. は「うれしい, 光栄です」の意. 英語国民は「ほめられて恥ずかしい」という考え方はしない. 後者は「自慢するほどのことではない」の意).
2【平静でいられない】**feel shy** (はにかむ) ; **feel embarrassed** (きまりが悪い) ▶好きな女の子の前では恥ずかしくて落ち着いて話せない I *feel* too *shy* in front of the girl I like to speak naturally. ‖ 左右違うソックスをはいていることに気づいたときには恥ずかしかった I *felt* [*was*] *embarrassed* when I noticed I was wearing mismatched socks. ‖ 恥ずかしいからそうじろじろ見ないで Don't stare at me like that. It's *embarrassing*. (➤恥ずかしく感じるのは embarrassed だが, 原因となることは embarrassing) ‖ 男の子は恥ずかしそうに花束を差し出した The boy held out a bunch of flowers *shyly* [*bashfully*]. ‖ 恥ずかしさのあまり少女はカーテンの陰に隠れた The girl hid behind the curtain *due to bashfulness*.

直訳の落とし穴「ほめられて恥ずかしい」
「みんなの前で先生にほめられて恥ずかしかった」を(×)I was shy when my teacher praised me ... とするのは誤り. shy は「(性格的に)恥ずかしがり屋の」という意味で, 一時的に「きまりが悪い」「照れ臭い」には embarrassed を用いて, I felt [was] embarrassed when my teacher praised me in front of everybody. という. また,「同じミスをくり返して自分が恥ずかしい」のような「恥じる」という意味の「恥ずかしい」には ashamed を用いて, I'm ashamed of myself for repeating the same mistake. のようにいう.

はずかしがる 恥ずかしがる **be shy** ▶恥ずかしがらないで, どしどし意見を述べてください *Don't be shy*. Please express your opinions freely [without hesitation]. ‖ 生徒の中には手を上げて答えを言うのを恥ずかしがる者もいる Some students are too *shy* to raise their hands to give their answers. ‖ 間違いをすることを恥ずかしがるな Don't *be ashamed of* making mistakes.
‖恥ずかしがり屋 a shy person.

はずかしめ 辱め **humiliation** ▶はずかしめを受ける *be humiliated*.

はずかしめる 辱める **disgrace** +㊐ (名を汚す) ▶母校の名をはずかしめないよう精一杯がんばります We are determined to play to the best of our ability so as not to *disgrace* our school name. ‖ はずかしめられて生きるくらいならむしろ死にたい I would rather die than live *in dishonor*.

-はずが[は]ない **cannot, can't**

語法 (1)「…はずが[は]ない」に相当するのは **cannot** で, 形式ばらない場合は話しことば・書きことばにかかわらず **can't** を用いることが多い.
(2)「…であった[…した]はずがない」のように過去の事柄についていう場合は cannot [could not] +完了形を用いる. この場合も形式ばらないときは can't, couldn't が好まれる.

▶この指輪が金のはずがないわ. 軽すぎるもの This ring *can't* be gold; it's too light. ‖ 彼女がこんな時間に勉強しているはずがない She *can't* be working at this hour.
▶誰かしら？ 玄関のベルを鳴らしてるの. お父さんがこんなに早いはずはないわね Who's ringing the doorbell? It *can't* be Dad this early. ‖ 電話番号が違う？ そんなはずはないんだけど The phone number's wrong? *That can't be*.
▶こんな小さな子に離婚のことを念入りに話してもわかるはずがない Such a young child *can't* understand divorce even if you talk to him [her] carefully. ‖ 彼は UCLA に留学したことがあるって言ってたが, そんなはずはないね He said that he had studied at UCLA, but he *can't* [*couldn't*] *have*. (➤ have のあとには studied ... が省略されている).
▶私の報告書が出てないって？ そんなはずないよ My report hasn't been turned in? *That's impossible*. (➤「あり得ない」の意).

ハスキー **husky** ▶ハスキーな声 a *husky* voice.

バスケットボール basketball ▶バスケットボールをする play *basketball*.

はずす 外す 1【取る】take off, remove +目 (➤後者は堅い語) ▶腕時計を外す *take off* one's watch ‖ シャツのボタンを外す *unbutton* one's shirt ‖ 犬を鎖から外す *unchain* [*unleash* / *set free*] a dog ‖ 祖父は眼鏡を外して私を見た My grandfather *removed* [*took off*] his glasses and looked at me.
▶泥棒は雨戸を外して侵入した The burglar *removed* the sliding (storm) shutters and entered the house.
2【当てない】miss (+目) ▶彼はライフルを10発撃ったが全部外した He shot 10 times with his rifle, but they all *missed* the target. ‖ 内海は2ストライクから1球アウトコースに外した Utsumi *threw* an outsider *as a waste pitch* after getting two strikes.
▶大野はスローカーブで打者のタイミングをはずした Ohno *threw* the batter's *timing off* with a slow curve.
3【除外する】exclude +目 ▶大学入試から英語をはずすべきだという声がある Some people claim that English should *be excluded* from the college entrance examinations. ‖ 《サッカーで》監督は本田選手を日本代表からはずした The coach *dropped* Honda from the Japanese national team. ‖ その選手はスターティングメンバーからはずされた The player *was left out of* the starting lineup.
4【避ける】avoid +目 ▶ラッシュ時間をはずして早く外出する leave early *to avoid* the rush hour.
5【離れる】leave +目 ▶すまないがちょっと席をはずしてくれないか Would you mind *leaving* the room for a while? ‖ 彼は会議中に席をはずした He *excused himself* [*left his seat*] during the conference. (➤前者は「中座した」, 後者は「退出して戻らなかった」) ‖ 《電話で》ただ今, 北野は席をはずしております Sorry, but Ms. Kitano *is not at* her desk now.
6【逃す】miss +目 ▶今度の連休をはずすと当分休みは取れない I won't be able to take days off for a while if I *miss* these consecutive holidays.

パスタ pasta ▶自家製パスタ homemade *pasta*.

パステル (a) pastel
‖パステル画 a pastel (drawing) ‖ パステルカラー a pastel color.

バスト the bust (measurement) ▶彼女はバストが大きい She's big around *the bust*. ‖ 久美子はバスト86, ウエスト59, ヒップ92だ Kumiko's measurements [vital statistics] are 86-59-92 (in centimeters). (➤vital statistics は「(女性の)スリーサイズ」の意のおどけた言い方).

パスポート a passport ▶パスポートの申請をする apply for *a passport* ‖ 対話「パスポートを拝見します」「はい」"May I see your *passport*, please?" "Sure."

パスボール 《野球》a passed ball ▶パスボールをする fail to catch a pitch / allow *a passed ball*.

はずみ 弾み 1【勢い】momentum ▶坂道を駆け降りたらはずみがついて止まらなくなった As I ran down the slope, I *gained* [*gathered*] *momentum* and found it difficult to stop.
2【その瞬間】▶彼は自転車をよけようとしたはずみに溝に落ちた *In* trying to dodge a bicycle, he fell into the ditch.

はずむ 弾む 1【はね返る】bounce ▶このボールはとてもよく弾む This ball *bounces* very well. ‖ このボールは全然弾まなくなってしまった This ball *has lost* all *its bounce*.
2【活気づく】▶これから始まる大学生活に対する期待で胸がはずんだ *My heart thrilled* at the thought of all the exciting things that were in store for me at college. ‖ 5年ぶりに会った私たちは大いに話がはずんだ When we met after five years, we *had a lively conversation*.
3【息が】▶6階まで階段を駆け上がったら息がはずんだ I bounded up the stairs to the sixth floor and found myself *out of breath*.
4【奮発する】▶タクシーの運転手にチップを弾む *tip* a taxi driver *generously* ‖ 大工の棟梁に祝儀を弾む *give* a master carpenter a *generous gift of money*.

はすむかい 斜向かい ▶M銀行のはす向かいにTデパートがある T Department Store is *diagonally opposite* M Bank. ‖ コンビニがうちのはす向かいにある A convenience store *is cater-corner across from* my house. (➤cater-corner は「対角線上に」の意の副詞で, cattycorner, kittycorner などいろいろにつづられる; across from は「…の向かい側に」の意).

バズる go viral /váɪrəl/ ▶彼女のツイートがバズった Her tweet *went viral*.

パズル a puzzle ▶パズルを解く solve *a puzzle* ‖ ジグソーパズルをする work on *a jigsaw puzzle*.
‖クロスワードパズル a crossword puzzle.

はずれ 外れ 1【当たっていないこと】▶私は福引きを15回やったのに全部外れだった I tried fifteen times at the chance games but *didn't win* anything. ‖ 私は外れくじを引いてしまった I have drawn *a blank*. 《参考》「外れくじ」や「外れ券」には No Prize と表記してあることが多い.
▶ 対話「おみやげ何だと思う?」「チョコレート!」「はずれ」"Guess what I have for you." "Chocolate." "*Wrong*."
2【中心から離れていること】the edge (端); the outskirts (郊外) ▶その町のいちばんはずれ the extreme *edge* of the town ‖ 村のはずれに古びた家が1軒ある There is an old house on the *edge* [*outskirts*] of the village.

はずれる 外れる 1【つけていたものが取れる】come off ▶このドアノブは外れそうだ This doorknob is about to *come off*. ‖ ボールが顔に当たって彼の眼鏡が外れた(=外れて落ちた) When a ball hit his face, his glasses *fell off*. ‖ 柔道の練習中に腕の関節が外れた My arm *went out of joint* while I was practicing judo.
▶きみ, 上着のボタンが外れているよ The button of your coat *is undone*.
2【当たらない】miss ▶5本の矢のうち3本が的を外れた Three out of five arrows *missed* the target. ‖ 宝くじが外れた I *didn't win* the lottery. / My lottery ticket was a loser. ‖ 天気予報は外れた The weather forecast *turned out to be wrong*. (➤「誤りとわかった」の意) ‖ 父に小遣いをもらえると思ってたのに期待が外れた I had thought that my father would give me some spending money, but I *was disappointed*.
3【基準をそれる】go out of, go off ▶人工衛星が軌道を外れることはまずない Artificial satellites rarely *go* [*stray*] *out of orbit*. ‖ その飛行機は航路から外れた The plane *went off* the regular route.
▶あの大臣の答弁はピントが外れていた The minister's answer *missed the point*. (➤「要点を外れて, 見当違いで」の意) ‖ この写真ピントが外れてない? Isn't this picture *out of focus*?

▶父の歌ときたら全く**調子が外れている** My father sings quite *out of tune*. ‖吉岡君は**人並みはずれた**体力を持っている Mr. Yoshioka has *extraordinary* physical strength.

4【職務などを解かれる】▶上野氏は役員から**はずれた** Mr. Ueno *lost his seat* on the board of directors.

5【中心から離れる】▶そのレストランは表通りを少し**はずれた**所にある That restaurant is just *off* the main street. ‖この町をちょっと**はずれた**所にゴルフ場があるんだ *Just outside* this town, there's a golf course.

パスワード a **password** ▶パスワードを入力してください Enter your *password*. ‖生年月日を**パスワード**に使うのは危険だ Using your birthdate as *a password* is risky.

はぜ《魚》a **goby** /góʊbi/ ▶**ハゼ釣り**に行く go *goby fishing* / go *fishing for goby*.

はせい（…から）**派生する derive**《from》▶多くの英単語がラテン語から**派生している** Many English words *derive from* Latin. ‖そこから思わぬ事態が**派生した** An unexpected situation *developed* from there.

‖**派生語** a derivative /dɪrívəṭɪv/.

ばせい 罵声 ▶酔っぱらいの**罵声** wild, drunken *yelling* ‖逮捕された汚職官僚に群衆から**罵声が浴びせられた** The crowd shouted [hurled] *abuse* at the corrupt bureaucrat who had been arrested.

パセリ《植物》**parsley** /pɑ́ːʳsli/ ▶ポテトサラダに**パセリ**を添える garnish potato salad with *parsley*.

はぜる ▶栗の実が**はぜた** The chestnut *popped out*. ‖ポップコーンが**はぜた** The popcorn *popped and crackled*.

はせん 破線 a **broken line.** ⇀実線.

パソコン a **personal computer**《略 PC》(➤ ふつうは単に computer という) ▶きみ, **パソコン**できる? Can you use [operate] *a computer*?

‖**パソコンゲーム** a video [computer] game ‖**パソコンソフト** computer software ‖**パソコン通信** computer communications.

はそん 破損 damage /dǽmɪdʒ/（損傷）; **breakage**（ばらばらに壊れること）**━動 破損する be damaged, be broken** ▶追突事故にあって後ろのバンパーを**破損した** When I was hit from behind, the rear bumper of my car *was damaged*. ‖引っ越し業者が乱暴に取り扱ったので, 皿が数枚**破損した** Several dishes *were broken* because the movers handled them roughly.

[1]はた 旗 a **flag**; a **banner**（横断幕など; 文語的な語）▶**旗**を掲揚する hoist [raise] *a flag* ‖山頂に**旗**を立てる put *a flag* on a summit ‖祭日にはうちでは**日の丸の旗**を揚げる We hang out *the Hinomaru* (*flag*) on national holidays.

▶生徒たちは**旗**を振って両陛下をお迎えした Schoolchildren waved *flags* to welcome the Emperor and Empress.

‖**旗ざお** a flagpole ‖**旗日** a national holiday.

[2]はた 機 a **loom** ▶**機**を織る weave on [at] *a loom*.

[3]はた 傍 ▶花屋の仕事は**はたから見るほど**楽ではない A florist's job is not as easy *as it looks*. ‖**はたの人**の迷惑になるようなことはやめなさい Don't make trouble for *others*.

はだ 肌 1【皮膚】skin ▶**肌の色**の異なったさまざまな人々 various people with different *colors of skin* ‖赤ん坊はすべすべした[やわらかい]**肌**をしている Babies have smooth [soft] *skin*. ‖冬になると**肌が荒れ**やすい I get dry *skin* easily in winter. ‖彼女は**肌が白い** She *is fair-skinned* [*light-skinned*]. / She *has a light complexion*. (➤ complexion は「肌の色」) ‖この(ハンド)クリームは私の**肌に合わない** This (hand) cream *doesn't suit my skin*. / This (hand) cream *doesn't suit* [*feel good*] *on my skin*. ‖石けんで**肌荒れ**を起こす人もいる Soaps cause *skin problems* for some people.

▶ボランティアたちは被災者の窮状を**肌で感じた** The volunteers felt the plight of the evacuees *firsthand*.

2【性質, 気質】▶あの男とは**肌が合わない** That man and I *don't have compatible personalities* [*similar temperaments*]. ‖長年一緒に働いているが, あいつとは**肌が合わない**（= 仲よくやっていけない） Though we've worked together (for) years, I *don't get along well with* him. ‖都会暮らしは**肌に合わない** Living in a big city *doesn't suit* [*agree with*] *me*. ‖彼は**芸術家肌**の男だ He has *an artistic temperament*. ‖彼は**天才肌**のバイオリニストだ He is a violinist *cast in a gifted mold*. (➤ mold は「(人の)タイプ」).

バター butter ▶パンに**バター**を塗る spread *butter* on bread / spread bread with *butter* (➤「バターを塗ったパン」は bread and butter /brèdnbʌ́ṭəʳ/) ‖彼女はヒラメを**バター**で焼いた She sautéed a flounder in *butter*.

‖**バター入れ** a butter dish ‖**バターナイフ** a butter knife ‖**バターロール** a butter roll ‖**無塩バター** unsalted butter.

パター《ゴルフ》a **putter.**

はたあげ 旗揚げ ▶昨日, 新しい政党が**旗揚げした**（= 発足した）A new political party *was organized* yesterday. ‖わが「大根座」はあす上野で**旗揚げ公演**をする Our troupe, Daikon-za, *is giving its first performance* in Ueno tomorrow.

ばたあし ばた足 a **flutter kick** ▶**ばた足**で10メートル泳ぐ travel 10 meters through the water *by kicking* [*by doing flutter kicks*] only.

パターン a **pattern** /pǽṭəʳn/ ▶イルカの**行動パターン** the *behavior patterns* of dolphins ‖このリボンはグレーの地にピンクと白のハート型の**パターン**の繰り返しだ This ribbon has *a pattern* of repeated pink and white hearts on a gray background. ‖私は日曜日は11時頃起きて昼兼用の朝食をとり, 夕方は外食と**パターン**が決まっている I get up around eleven and have brunch and eat out in the evening — that's my usual *pattern* [my (usual) *routine*] on Sundays.

☛ **ワンパターン**（⇀見出語）

はたいろ 旗色 the tide（形勢）; **odds**（勝算）▶その戦争では国連軍の**旗色が悪くなった** In the war, *the tide was turning against* the United Nations forces. / *The odds were piling up against* the United Nations forces in the war. ‖父は議論で**旗色が悪く**なるとすぐ書斎に逃げ込む When my father sees that he *is likely to lose an argument* [sees *an argument turning against* him], he escapes to his study.

はだか 裸 1【衣服を着ていない】━形 裸の nude, naked /néɪkɪd/ (➤ (1)部分を明示しない限り, どちらも全裸を意味する. (2)nude は意識的に着衣をまとっていないことを表すので, しばしば絵画・彫刻に用いる. やや品のよい語. naked は性的連想の強い語だが, 子供の裸には通例 naked を用いる) ⇀ヌード

▶**裸の女性** a *nude* [*naked*] woman / a woman

in the nude ‖ 裸になりなさい *Take* your *clothes off.* ／*Get undressed.* ‖ 彼は暖かい部屋の中で上半身裸になった He *stripped* to the waist in the warm room. ‖ お父さん，裸でその辺をうろうろしないでよ Dad, don't wander around *in the nude* [*in your underpants*]. (➤ 後者はパンツ姿の場合) ‖ 建設作業員たちは裸で作業をしていた The construction workers were working *with their shirts off* [*without their shirts*]. (● この場合，nude や naked は使えない).

▶《慣用表現》彼は裸一貫から始めて今では大会社の社長である He started a business *from scratch* and now is the president of a big company. (➤ from scratch は「ゼロから」).

2【包まれていない】 一形 裸の **bare** ▶裸電球 a *bare* lightbulb ‖ 冬になるとカエデやイチョウの木は裸になる Maple trees and ginkgoes *lose their leaves* [*become bare*] in winter. ‖ 木枯らしはイチョウの木を裸にしてしまった The cold winter wind *stripped* the ginkgo trees *of* their leaves. ‖ 裸馬に乗れるかい？ Can you *ride bareback*?

はたき a (**cloth**) **duster** ▶本棚にはたきをかける *dust* a bookshelf.

はだぎ 肌着 underwear, underclothes (➤ 特にシャツの場合には《米》an undershirt,《英》a vest という) ▶汗をかいたのなら肌着を取り替えたら？ If you are sweaty, how about changing your *underwear*?

はたく 叩く dust +目 (ほこりを)；**slap** +目 (平手で打つ) ▶花瓶のほこりをはたく *dust off* a vase ‖ 稀勢の里は突進してくる鶴竜をはたいた Kisenosato *slapped* Kakuryu, who was rushing at him, down to the ring floor.

▶《慣用表現》私は財布の底をはたいてその古本を買った I *used up all* (*the money*) *I had* to buy those old books.

バタくさい バタ臭い ▶バタ臭い男 an overly Westernized man(西洋かぶれした)；a man with Western features(顔立ちが).

はたけ 畑 1【栽培のための土地】 a **field**；a **garden** (特に野菜などの) ▶トウモロコシ畑 a corn*field* ‖ キャベツ畑 a cabbage *field* [*patch*] ‖ 畑を耕す plow [till] *a field* ‖ このトマトはうちの畑でとれたものです I harvested this tomato from our *garden.* ‖ 老人は朝早くから畑仕事をした The old man *worked in the fields* [*did farm work*] from early in the morning.

2【専門分野】 a **field** ▶彼は畑違いのこともよく知っている He knows a lot about things *outside his field.* ‖ 父は経理畑一筋の人です My father is a *career* accountant. (➤ career /kəríə'/ は「専門職の」の意).

はだける ▶胸をはだける *expose* one's chest ‖ 起きてみると寝巻きの前がはだけていた When I got up, I found the front of my nemaki had *come open.*

はださむい 肌寒い chilly ▶けさはいくらか肌寒い It's sort of *chilly* this morning. ‖ 春とはいえまだ風は肌寒い It's spring now but *there is* still *a chill* in the air.

はだざわり 肌触り the feel, the touch (➤ 前者は触ったときの感覚に，後者は触るという動作に力点がある) ▶この布は肌触りがなめらかだ [ごわごわしている] This cloth *feels* smooth [rough]. ／This cloth is smooth [rough] to *the touch.*

はだし 裸足 bare feet 一形 はだしの **barefoot(ed)** 一副 はだしで **barefoot(ed)** ▶はだしの少女 a *barefoot*(*ed*) girl ‖ 砂浜をはだしで歩くのは気持ちがいい It's pleasant to walk on a sandy beach *barefoot*(*ed*) [*with bare feet*]. ‖ 妹は強い地震にびっくりしてはだしで外に飛び出した My (younger) sister was so alarmed by the strong quake that she ran outside *barefoot*(*ed*).

☞ 玄人はだし (→玄人 (見出語))

はたしあい 果たし合い a duel.

はたしじょう 果たし状 a duel request.

はたして 果たして really(本当に)；**sure enough**(案の定) ▶はたしてそんなことがありうるか I wonder if such a thing could *really* happen. ‖ はたしてだれが彼女のハートを射止めるだろうか Who *in the world* [*on earth*] will win her heart? (➤ in the world, on earth は「いったい全体」).

▶彼の予想ははたして的中していた *Sure enough,* his prediction came true.

はたじるし 旗印 a banner.

はたす 果たす carry out(実行する)；**fulfill** +目 (要求されていることや期待されていることを)；**accomplish** +目 (実のあることを成し遂げる)；**realize** +目 (願望・夢を実現する) ▶義務を果たす *carry out* [*fulfill*] one's duty ‖ 目的を果たす *accomplish* [*attain*] one's purpose.

▶彼女は女優になりたいという長年の夢をついに果たした She finally *realized* her long-cherished dream of becoming an actress. ‖ 伊藤氏は苦戦の末，初当選を果たした Mr. Ito *managed to win an election for the first time* after (fighting) a tough campaign.

はたち 二十歳 twenty years old, twenty years of age ▶兄は二十歳になったばかりです My (older) brother has just turned *twenty.*

ばたっと ▶草むらにばたっと倒れる fall *flat* on the grass.

ぱたっと ▶本をぱたっと閉じる *snap* one's book *shut* ‖ さっきまでの強い風がぱたっとやんだ The strong wind that was blowing until a moment ago *abruptly* stopped.

はたと abruptly(不意に)；**suddenly**(突然) ▶忘れ物にはたと気づいた I *suddenly* realized that I'd forgotten something. ‖ 難問にはたと困った I *was stumped* by a question.

ハタハタ《魚》a (**sailfin**) **sandfish.**

ばたばた ▶子供たちが廊下をバタバタと走り回っている The children are running around the halls *noisily.* ‖ 国旗が強風でバタバタあおられている The national flag *is fluttering* in the strong wind.

▶まだ引っ越したばかりでばたばたしています We have just moved here and things are still *hectic.* (➤ hectic は「ひどく忙しい」の意).

▶難民キャンプでは伝染病のため人がばたばた(＝次々と)死んだ *One after another,* people died of an epidemic at the refugee camp.

ぱたぱた ▶うちわでぱたぱたあおぐ fan oneself with a round fan *noisily* ‖ 傷ついた小鳥は飛び立てずに羽をぱたぱたさせるばかりだった Unable to fly, the wounded bird could only *flap* its wings. ‖ 息子がスリッパをパタパタいわせながら廊下を歩いてきた My son came *pitter-pattering* in his slippers down the corridor.

バタフライ the butterfly (**stroke**) ▶バタフライで泳ぐ swim *the butterfly stroke* ／do *the butterfly.*

はだみ 肌身 ▶彼女はフィアンセの写真を肌身離さず持っている She *always* carries a photograph of her fiancé *with* [*on*] her.

はため 傍目 ▶冬子に振られてしょんぼりしている春夫の姿ははた目にも気の毒だった *We were really sorry to see* how depressed Haruo was after Fuyuko dumped him.

はためいわく 傍迷惑 ▶暴走族ははた迷惑(＝近所迷惑)だ Hot-rodders are *a nuisance to the neighborhood*. ‖ はた迷惑な音だ That noise is *a bother*. (➤ bother は「ちょっと迷惑なこと・もの」の意)／That noise *bothers* me. (➤ この bother は「悩ませる」の意).

はためく flutter ▶日本の国旗がオリンピックスタジアムにはためいていた The Japanese national flag *was fluttering* in the Olympic stadium.

はたらかせる 働かせる make ... work (人を) ; **use** ＋目 (能力などを) ▶頭を働かせろ！ *Use* your head [brains]!

▶想像力を働かせてもっとのびのびした絵をかきなさい *Use* your imagination and draw (your pictures) more freely.

はたらき 働き 1【働くこと】work ▶彼のめざましい働きは高く評価されるべきだ His marvelous *work* should be valued highly. ‖ この新しいロボットは10人分の働きをする This new robot does the *work* of ten people. ‖ きょうの試合では広瀬が良い働きをした Hirose *did a good job* in today's game.

▶私も働きに出ようかな Maybe I should *get a job*. ‖ 父は働き盛りだ My father is *in his prime* now. ‖ 母は働き者だ My mother is *a hard worker*. ／My mother works very hard.

‖ **働き口** a job ‖ **働き手** a breadwinner(稼ぎ手) ‖ **働きバチ** a worker bee.

2【機能, 作用】a function ▶神経の働きはきわめて複雑だ The *functions* of nerves are very complicated. ‖ この薬は食物の消化を助ける働きをする This medicine *works* to help digest food. ‖ 心臓はポンプのような働きをする The heart *acts* like a pump.

はたらきかける (…に)働きかける work 《**on**》 ▶監督は上田君をキャプテンに選ぶよう部員に働きかけた The manager *worked on* the club members to get them to pick Ueda as captain.

▶林さんは我々にそのチームを応援するよう働きかけた Mr. Hayashi *urged* [*appealed to*] us to support the team. (➤ urge A to do は「A(人)に…せよと説き勧める」, appeal to A to do は「A(人)に…してくださいと懇願する」の意).

はたらく 働く

1【仕事をする】work ▶父は朝から晩まで働いている My father *works* from morning to night. ‖ 母は工場で働いている My mother *works* at a factory. (➤「一時的に」の意味でなければ進行形にしない) ‖ 母は長年病院で働いている My mother *has worked* at [in／for] a hospital for many years. ‖ 彼女はこれからは自分で働いて生活していかなければならない She has to *support herself* [*work for her living*] from now on. ‖ 宮下君は働きながら大学を出た Miyashita *worked his way through* college. ‖ 母は働き過ぎて病気になった My mother *overworked herself* and got sick. ／My mother fell ill *from overwork*. ‖ 日本人は働き過ぎるとよく言われる Japanese are often referred to as *workaholics*. (➤ workaholic は「働き過ぎの人」).

2【作用する】work ; function(機能する) ▶サーモスタットがきちんと働かなかった The thermostat did not *work* [*function*] well enough. ‖ ぼうっとして思うように頭が働かない My brain is half asleep and I *can't think* as clearly as I would like to.

3【悪い事をする】commit ＋目 ▶盗みをはたらく *commit* a theft ‖ 悪事をはたらく *commit* a crime.

☛ 働かせる (→見出語)

はたん 破綻する break up(結婚生活・人間関係がだめになる) ; **come to an end**(終わりになる) ; **fall through**(事業・計画などが失敗に終わる) ▶彼らの結婚生活は半年で破たんした Their marriage *broke up* [*came to an end*] in half a year. ‖ その地下鉄建設計画は破たんをきたした The plans for building a subway *fell through*.

はだん 破談 ▶彼の婚約は破談になった His engagement *was called off*. (➤ call off は「取り消す」) ‖ 彼女は結婚式直前になって婚約を破談にした She *broke her engagement* just before the wedding.

ばたん ▶彼はドアをバタンと閉めて出て行った He *slammed* the door *shut* and left. ‖ 立て看板が風でバタンと倒れた Blown by the wind, the billboard fell *with a bang*.

▶彼は酔っ払って帰ってくるなりバタンキューだった He got back home drunk and *passed out* [*conked out*]. (➤ pass out は「酔って正体がなくなる」, conk out は「ぶっ倒れて寝る」の意のインフォーマルな言い方).

ぱたん ▶ふたをパタンと閉める *snap* a lid *shut* ‖ ドアがパタンと閉まった The door *snapped shut*. ‖ 授業が終わると学生たちはいっせいに教科書をパタンと閉じた When the class ended, the students all *snapped* their textbooks *shut* at once.

¹はち 八 eight ; the eighth /eɪtθ/ (8番目) ▶ジェット機が空に大きな8の字を書いた The jet plane wrote a big *figure eight* in the sky.

▶《慣用表現》先生は教室が騒がしくなると額に八の字を寄せた The teacher *frowned* [*knitted her brows*] when the classroom became noisy.

²はち 蜂 a bee, a honeybee (ミツバチ) ; **a wasp** (スズメバチ, ジガバチ) ; **a hornet** (スズメバチ) ▶ハチの群れ a swarm of *bees* ‖ 私はきのうスズメバチに刺された I was stung by *a wasp* yesterday.

ことわざ 泣き面にハチ Bees on a weeper's face. (➤日本語からの直訳)／Misfortunes seldom come singly. (➤「不幸は単独ではやって来ない」の意).

‖ **足長バチ** a long-legged wasp ‖ **雄バチ** a drone ‖ **女王バチ** a queen (bee) ‖ **働きバチ** a worker (bee).

☛ はちの巣 (→見出語)

³はち 鉢 a bowl(どんぶり鉢) ; **a dish** (深皿) ; **a flower pot** (植木鉢).

☛ お鉢 (→見出語)

¹ばち 罰 a judgment(裁き) ; **a punishment**(こらしめ)

> **《解説》「罰」と judgment**
> (1)「罰(ばち)」は英語では judgment とか punishment というが, これはキリスト教の God's judgment (神の裁き), a punishment from God (神のこらしめ) のことなので, 日本語の「神罰」「仏罰」を取り立てて言いたいときには, the *kami*'s judgment, a punishment from the *kami*, Buddha's judgment, a punishment from Buddha のように表現する.
> (2) divine judgment [punishment], divine retribution はキリスト教の場合にも日本の神道の場合にも用いることができる.
> (3) 日常的には, これらの語を使うよりも用例のような言い方をすることが多い.

▶おさい銭を失敬すると罰が当たるぞ *You're in for divine punishment* [You'll *pay the price* / *Heaven will punish you*] if you steal money from the offertory box. ‖ 食べ物を粗末にすると罰が当たるよと祖母はよく言う My grandmother often says that I'll *get it* [*pay for it*] if I waste food. (➤ ともに「その報いがある」の意のインフォーマルな言い方) ‖ なんて罰当たりなことをするんだ How can you do such an *outrageous* [*sinful* / *evil*] thing! ‖ いい気味だ. 罰が当たったんだよ *It serves you right*. (➤ 面と向かって言う場合 ; その場にいない人について言うのなら you を him, her などにする).

[2]**ばち 撥** a **plectrum**, 《インフォーマル》 a **pick** (三味線などの) ; a **drumstick** (太鼓の).

はちあわせ 鉢合わせ ▶恭子と原宿をふらついていたら前のガールフレンドと鉢合わせしてしまった While strolling in Harajuku with Kyoko, I *ran into* [*came across*] my ex-girlfriend.

はちうえ 鉢植え a **potted plant** ▶父はお祭りで鉢植えの朝顔を買った My father bought a *potted* morning glory at the festival.

ばちがい 場違い ▶彼の服装は場違いな感じがした His attire looked *out of place*.

はちがつ 八月 August 《略 Aug.》 ▶8月に家族で海へ行くつもりだ Our family has plans to go to the beach *in August*. ‖ 私は8月20日生まれだ I was born *on August 20*.

バチカン the Vatican (ローマ市内にあるローマ教皇庁, またその宮殿).

はちきれる はち切れる burst ▶はち切れそうな若さ *exuberant* youth ‖ 食べ過ぎておなかがはち切れそうだ I've eaten too much and my stomach is ready to *burst*. ‖ ひろみははち切れそうなバストをしている Hiromi has an *enormous* bust.

はちく 破竹 ▶ベイスターズは破竹の勢いで勝ち続けた The BayStars *overwhelmed* the other teams and were on a winning streak. (➤ on a winning streak は「連勝で」の意).

ぱちくり ▶子供は初めてカバを見て目をぱちくりさせた The child's *eyes were like saucers* when he [she] saw a hippo for the first time.

はちじゅう 八十 eighty ; the eightieth (80番目) ▶80年代の出来事 events in *the eighties* ‖ 祖父は80歳 [80代半ば] です My grandfather is *eighty* (*years old*) [*in his mid-eighties*].

はちのす 蜂の巣 a **honeycomb** (巣) ; a **(bee)hive** (巣箱) ▶《慣用表現》 地震で会場がガタガタ揺れると場内ははちの巣をつついたような騒ぎになった When the hall rattled with an earthquake, the audience was thrown into *utter confusion*.

ぱちぱち ▶竹がパチパチと音を立てて燃えている The bamboos *are cracking* [*crackling*] as they burn. ‖ 子供たちは小さな手でパチパチと拍手した The children *clapped their* little *hands*.

▶目をぱちぱちさせたらごみが取れた The dirt in my eye came out when I *blinked several times*.

はちぶどおり 八分通り ▶仕事は八分どおり終わった *About eighty percent* of the work is done. ‖ そのマンションは八分どおりできあがっている The condominium is *80 percent* completed.

はちまき 鉢巻き a **headband**, a ***hachimaki*** (**headband**) 《参考》 日本人は威勢のよさを示したり, 気持ちを引き締めるために鉢巻きをすることが多いが, 英米人の用いる headband は髪の乱れを防ぐため, または装飾用である.

headband

hachimaki

▶運動会では日本の子供たちは赤または白の鉢巻きを締める On (their school's) sports day, Japanese children tie *a* red or white *hachimaki* (*headband*) around their heads.

☛ ねじり鉢巻き (→見出語)

はちみつ 蜂蜜 honey ▶ホットケーキにはちみつをかける pour *honey* over a pancake.

ばちゃばちゃ ▶彼のボートはオールでバチャバチャ水をたたくばかりで全然前に進まなかった He was just *splashing* with his oars and not moving the boat forward at all.

はちゃめちゃ ▶ゆうべの宴会ははちゃめちゃだったよ Everybody *kicked up their heels* at last night's party. (➤「はめをはずして楽しんだ」の意) / Everybody *had a blast* at last night's party. (➤ blast は「はめをはずしたパーティー」の意の主にアメリカ俗語).

はちゅうるい 爬虫類 reptiles /réptlz/.

はちょう 波長 a **wavelength** ▶FM 東京に波長を合わせる *tune in* to FM Tokyo ‖ X線は波長の短い電磁波だ X rays are a type of electromagnetic radiation with short *wavelengths*.

▶《慣用表現》 あの先生とはどうも波長が合わない That teacher and I *are not on the same wavelength*.

ぱちん ▶指をパチンと鳴らす *snap* one's fingers ‖ 彼女はハンドバッグをパチンと閉めた She shut her purse *with a snap*.

パチンコ 1【ゲーム】 pachinko (➤ 英語化している)

日本紹介 ✉ **パチンコはピンボールに似た一種のかけ事ゲームです. つまみを回して鋼鉄製の小さな玉をはじいて, 盤面にある当たり穴に入れると新たな玉が出てきます. 取った玉は景品と交換することができます. 18歳未満の人は店に入ることが禁じられています** Pachinko is a kind of gambling game that resembles pinball. You turn a knob to flick small steel balls, trying to shoot them in the winning holes on the board and get more balls. You can exchange the balls you have won for prizes. Those under eighteen years old are prohibited from entering a pachinko parlor.

▶パチンコをする play *pachinko*.

‖パチンコ屋 a pachinko parlor [hall].

2【小石などを飛ばすおもちゃ】 《米》 a **slingshot**, 《英》 a **catapult** /kǽtəpʌlt/ ▶パチンコで石を飛ばす let fly a stone with *a slingshot*.

はつ 初の the first ▶日本人初の宇宙飛行士 *the first Japanese* astronaut ‖ ガガーリンは1961年, 人類初の宇宙飛行を成し遂げた In 1961 Gagarin became *the first man* to travel in space. ‖ これは音声入力できる世界初のワープロソフトでした This was *the first* word processing program *in the world* that enabled voice input. ‖ バンジージャンプは初体験なので少しどきどきしている I'm a little nervous because this is *the first time for me to experience* bungee jumping [this will be *my first experience* of bungee jumping].

☛ 初顔合わせ, 初舞台 (→見出語)

-はつ -発 ▶10時発の東京行きの列車 the 10:00 train to Tokyo／the train to Tokyo *leaving at* 10:00 (➤ 10:00 は ten (o'clock) と読む) ‖ 父は成田発の日航機でハワイに向かった My father took a JAL flight *from* Narita to Hawaii.

▶強盗が弾を３発撃った A burglar fired three *shots* [*rounds*].

1**ばつ 罰** (a) **punishment,** (a) **penalty** /pénlti/ ▶彼は罪を犯したのだから罰を受けるのは当然だ Since he committed a crime, it's only natural for him to receive the *punishment*. ‖ 彼は当然の罰を受けた He got his *just deserts*. (➤ deserts は「受けるべき罰」の意だが, まれに「受けるべき賞」の意になることもある).

2**ばつ 閥** a **clique** /kli:k/ (排他的な小集団); a **faction** (大きな組織の中のグループ, 派閥) ▶日本の大学の卒業生は閥を作る傾向がある Japanese college graduates tend to form *cliques*.

3**ばつ** an **x** /eks/ (ばつ印) ▶先生は私の答えにばつをつけた The teacher *put an x* on my answer. ／The teacher *crossed out* [*x-ed*] my answer. (➤ *x*-ed は /ekst/ と読む) ‖ 私の答案はほとんどばつだった Most of my answers *were marked as incorrect*. 《参考》英米では「ばつ」の場合は何もつけないのがふつう. ただし, アンケートなどでは該当する箇所に一般に○でなく×または✓をつける. →まるばつ式. ‖ 私はバツイチ[バツ２]です I *have been divorced once* [*twice*]. ／I have *one divorce* [*two divorces*] *behind me*.

4**ばつ** ▶パーティーで別れた妻と会ったときはばつの悪い思いをした I *felt ill at ease* [*felt awkward*] when I met my ex-wife at the party.

はつあん 発案 an **idea** (アイデア); a **plan** (計画); a **suggestion** (提案) ▶これは誰の発案ですか Whose *idea* [*plan*] was this? ‖ 我々は西条さんの発案で資金カンパを始めた We started a fund-raising campaign at Mr. Saijo's *suggestion*.

‖発案者 a proposer ／an originator ／a sponsor (法案の).

はついく 発育 **growth** (大きく, 強くなること), **development** (成長したり変わったりすること) 一動 **発育する** **grow, develop** ▶骨の発育にはカルシウムは欠かせない Calcium is indispensable for the *growth* of your bones. ‖ 最近の子供は発育がいい Most children *grow tall* [*grow fast*] nowadays. ‖ 読書は心の発育を促す Reading helps to *develop* your mind. ‖ 体の発育は20歳までにはだいたい完了する *Physical development* is almost complete by around the age of twenty. ‖ 発育盛りの子供はよく食べる *Growing* children eat a lot.

はつおん 発音 **pronunciation** /prənʌ̀nsiéɪʃən/ 一動 **発音する** **pronounce** (+目) ▶きみの英語の発音はすごくいいよ Your *pronunciation* of English [Your English *pronunciation*] is very good. ‖ San Jose はどう発音するの？ How do you *pronounce* "S-a-n J-o-s-e"? ‖ もっとはっきり発音してください Please *pronounce* more clearly.

‖発音記号 a phonetic /fənétɪk/ symbol [sign].

はつか 二十日 **the twentieth** (月の); **twenty days** (20日) ▶４月20日に on April *20th*.

‖二十日大根 a radish.

1**はっか 薄荷** 《植物》**peppermint, mint**; **menthol** (ハッカ脳) ▶ハッカ入りのガム *peppermint* gum ‖ ハッカ入りのたばこ a *mentholated* cigarette.

2**はっか 発火** **combustion** (燃焼); **ignition** (点火) 一動 **発火する** **catch fire, ignite**; **start burning** (燃え始める)

‖自然発火 spontaneous combustion ‖ 発火点 the ignition point.

はつが 発芽 **sprouting** (植物の); **germination** (種の) 一動 **発芽する** **sprout** /spraʊt/, **germinate** /dʒə́:ʳmɪneɪt/ ▶日光を遮断したほうが発芽は早まる *Sprouting* will be speeded up when sunlight is cut off. ‖ 大豆が今ちょうど発芽している The beans *are* now *germinating*.

ハッカー a **hacker** ▶ハッカーがそのウェブサイトに侵入する *break into* that website.

‖ハッカー対応プログラム antihacker [debugging] software.

はつかおあわせ 初顔合わせ ▶このドラマで二大女優が初顔合わせする Two of the most popular actresses *perform together* in this drama *for the first time*.

はっかく 発覚 **detection** (発見); **exposure** (暴露) 一動 **発覚する** **be found out, be discovered** ▶その男は事件の発覚を恐れて海外に高飛びした The man skipped the country for fear that the crime would *be discovered* [*found out*]. ‖ 彼らの陰謀はすぐに発覚した Their plot *was* soon *brought to light* [*was* soon *found out*].

はっかくけい 八角形 an **octagon** 一形 **八角形の** **octagonal** /ɑ:ktǽgənəl/ ▶法隆寺の夢殿は八角形をしている The Yumedono at the Horyuji (Temple) is *octagonal*.

はつかねずみ 《動物》a **mouse** [複 **mice**].

1**はっかん 発刊** **publication** (出版) 一動 **発刊する** **publish** +目 ▶新しい雑誌が来月発刊になる A new magazine will *be published* next month.

2**はっかん 発汗** **perspiration, sweating** (➤ 前者のほうが上品な語) 一動 **発汗する** **perspire, sweat** ▶唐辛子には発汗作用がある Hot pepper *causes* people *to perspire*.

はつがん 発癌 一形 **発がん性の** **carcinogenic** /kɑ̀:ʳsənoʊdʒénɪk/ ▶食物の焼け焦げは発がん性があると信じられている The scorched part of some foods is believed to *cause cancer* [to *be carcinogenic*].

‖発がん物質 a carcinogen, a carcinogenic [cancer-causing] substance.

はっき 発揮する **show** +目 ▶彼は経営者としての手腕を発揮した He *showed* his abilities as a manager. ‖ 体が弱くては実力を十分に発揮することはできない If you have poor health, you can't *make full use of* [*give full play to*] your abilities.

はつぎ 発議 a **proposal** ▶発議したいことがある have a *proposal* to make ‖発議者 a proposer.

はっきゅう 薄給 **small salary**; **low wages** (低賃金) ▶ぼくらのような薄給ではとてもこんな車は買えない There's no way for *low-wage* earners [*poorly paid* workers] like us to afford such a car.

はっきょう 発狂する **go mad** [**insane**] ▶工事の騒音がやかましくて発狂しそうだ The loud construction noise is (*nearly*) *driving me crazy*. ／The construction noise is so loud I *am nearly going mad*.

はっきり

訳語メニュー
- 鮮明な →clear 1
- 明確な →definite 2
- 正確な →exact 2
- 明白な →obvious 3

1【形や音が鮮明な】一形 **はっきりした** **clear** (あいま

いなところがない)；**distinct**(区別がきちんとついた，違いがよくわかる)；**vivid**(記憶・印象などが鮮やかな)(➤あとの2語はやや堅い語)；**pronounced**(著しい)

▶はっきりした声 a *clear* voice ‖ はっきりした記憶 a *vivid* memory ‖ はっきりした外国語なまり a *pronounced* foreign accent ‖ そのアナウンサーの発音は実にはっきりしている The announcer's pronunciation is very *clear*. ‖ きょうは学校の屋上から筑波山がはっきりと見えた Today I could see Mt. Tsukuba *clearly* from the roof of the school building. ‖ 祖父はその事件のことをはっきり覚えているという My grandfather says that he still remembers the incident *clearly*. ‖ はっきりした特長のない雑誌は売れない A magazine without a *distinct* character [personality] doesn't sell well. ‖ 写真に写っている彼の顔ははっきりしなかった His face in the photograph was *indistinct*.

2【明確な，正確な】一形 はっきりした clear；definite /défənət/ (明確な)；**exact** (正確な)；**straight**(率直な) ▶難しい文の意味をはっきりさせる *clarify* a difficult sentence ‖ きょうはきみからはっきりした(＝明確な／率直な)答えを聞きたい I want a *clear* [*definite* ／ *straight*] answer from you today. ‖ 校長はその問題に関してはっきりした意見を述べようとはしなかった The principal avoided expressing *definite* opinions on that question. ‖ その会議に出席していた人のはっきりした(＝正確な)数はわかりませんか Do you know the *exact* number of people who attended the meeting？‖ 彼ははっきり「ノー」とは言わなかった He didn't *exactly* say no. (➤「紛れもなくノーということばは言わなかった」の意. clearly を用いると「声がよく聞き取れなかった」, または「ノーをあいまいに言った」のどちらにもとれる).

▶あの人が何歳かはっきりとは知らない I don't know *for certain* [*for sure*] how old he is. ‖ 彼女がなぜそんなに急に引退を決意したのかはっきりわからない I'*m not sure* why she decided to retire so suddenly. ‖ (迷ってないで)はっきりしなさいよ *Be decisive*.

3【明白な】一形 はっきりした clear；obvious /á:bviəs/ (すぐわかる)；**evident**(状況などから判断してすぐそれとわかる) ▶やつが犯人だということははっきりしている *It is clear* [*obvious*] that he committed the crime. ‖ 彼女が試験に受かったことは彼女の笑顔ではっきりとわかった Her big smile *made it clear* that she had passed the examination.

▶彼の意図がどうもはっきりしない(＝理解できない) I still *don't understand* what he's up to. (➤「彼の意図ははっきりわかっている」なら I *clearly* understand what he's up to.).

4【頭・天気がすっきりした】▶濃いコーヒーを飲んだら頭がはっきりした A cup of strong coffee *cleared* my mind. ‖ このところ天気がはっきりしませんね The weather has been *unsettled* recently.

5【直接的な】▶はっきり言って彼は少しわがままだ *To tell the truth* [*To be frank*], he's a little selfish. ‖ 彼女はものをはっきり言う人だ She is an *outspoken* person.

[1]**はっきん 発禁** ▶その本は長い間発禁になっていた The book had *been banned* for a long time.

‖**発禁本** a prohibited book.

[2]**はっきん 白金**《化学》**platinum** /plǽtnəm/.

ばっきん 罰金 a **fine**(科料)；a **penalty** /pénlti/ (反則金) ▶彼は駐車違反で2万1千円の罰金を取られた He *was fined* 21,000 yen for a parking violation. ‖ 規則を破った場合の罰金は1万円です The *penalty* for violating the rule is 10,000 yen.

パッキン a **packing**, an **O-ring**, a **toric joint** ▶蛇口のパッキンを取り換える change the *O-ring* in a faucet.

バッキンガム バッキンガム宮殿 Buckingham Palace(ロンドンにあるイギリス国王の宮殿).

パッキング packing ▶パッキングは終わりましたか Have you finished *packing*？／Have you packed already？

バック 1【後退】一動 バックする move back；step back(歩いて) ▶車をバックさせる *back* one's car ‖ ちょっと(車を)バックしてください Please *back up* a little！‖ 《写真撮影で》少しバックしてください Please *step back* a little.

‖**バックコーラス** backup singers ‖ **バックライト** a backup light(自動車の)；backlight(液晶の).

2【背景】the background ▶お花畑をバックに写真を撮ってもらった We had a picture taken with a field of flowers *in the background*. ‖ オーケストラをバックに(＝伴奏してもらって)歌ったご感想は？ How did you feel when you sang *accompanied by* an orchestra [*with* orchestral *backing*]？

▶田中氏のバックには有力政治家がついているらしい I hear (that) an influential politician *is backing* [*is behind*] Mr. Tanaka.

> **危ないカタカナ語✸ バック**
> 1「バック」は「後部」,「背景」,「背泳ぎ」,「後退」などの意で用いるが，英語の back がこれらにそのまま当てはまる場合はむしろ少ない. 例えば「ギアをバックに入れる」は put the gear into reverse あるいは shift into reverse であるし,「富士山をバックに山中湖を描く」は paint Lake Yamanaka with Mt. Fuji in the background のようにいう. 水泳の「バック(＝背泳ぎ)」は backstroke である.
> 2「バック」にはまた「バックスクリーン」,「バックネット」などのような和製語があるので注意が必要. 英語では前者は center-field fence, 後者は backstop という.
> →バックホーム，バックミラー.

パック 1【包装】a pack；a carton (紙製の容器) ▶真空パックのお茶 *vacuum-packed* tea ‖ 牛乳2パック two *cartons* of milk ‖ トマトを1パック350円で買った I bought *a pack* of tomatoes for 350 yen.

2【美容の】a pack ▶美顔パック a face [facial] *pack* ‖ 彼女は寝る前に顔にどろパックをした She applied *a clay mud pack* to her face before going to bed.

3【旅行の】▶私たちはパック旅行でシンガポールへ行った We went to Singapore on *a package tour*. ／We joined *a tour group* to Singapore.

4【アイスホッケーの】a puck /pʌk/ ▶ゴールにパックを打ち込む fire *the puck* into the net.

バッグ a **bag**(袋)；a **handbag**,《米・古風》a **purse**(ハンドバッグ) ▶《店で》エルメスのバッグ，ありますか Do you have Hermes *handbags*？

バックアップ 1【支持，援助】support, backing (➤後者が日本語に近いややインフォーマルな語) **一動 バックアップする support ＋目, back ＋目** ▶多くの市民がその若い市長をバックアップした Many citizens *supported* the young mayor. ‖ 政府の資金面でのバックアップを受けてスーパーコンピュータが開発された Supercomputers were developed with financial *backing* from the government. ‖ A氏が我々の計画をバックアップしてくれている Mr. A *is behind* us on our plan. ／Mr. A *is supporting* [*is backing*] our

plan.
2【予備の複製】 a **backup** ▶ファイルのバックアップをとる *make a backup of* a file／*back up* a file.
バックグラウンド (a) **background**
‖**バックグラウンドミュージック** background music《略 BGM》.
バックスキン **buckskin** ▶バックスキンの靴 a pair of *buckskin* shoes.
バックスクリーン **the center-field fence, the batter's eye (screen)** 《参考》「バックスクリーン」は和製語.
バックストレッチ **the backstretch.**
バックストローク **the backstroke** ▶バックストロークで泳ぐ swim *the backstroke*.
はっくつ 発掘 (an) **excavation** 一動 **発掘する** **excavate** /ékskəveɪt/ +目; **dig up**(掘り出す) ▶彼らは古代都市の遺跡を発掘した They *excavated* [*unearthed*] the ruins of the ancient city.
▶スカウトたちは有望な人材を発掘しようと一生懸命だ The scouts are going all out to *dig up* promising talent.
バックナンバー a **back number,** a **back issue.**
バックネット a **backstop**(➤ backnet とはいわない).
バックホーム《野球》a **throw to home** [**to the (home) plate**] ▶森本の好バックホームでランナーはホーム寸前でタッチアウトとなった A good *throw* from Morimoto put the runner out at the plate.
バックボーン **the** [one's] **backbone** ▶武士道は日本の精神的バックボーンの1つです Bushido is one of the spiritual *backbones* of Japan.
バックミラー a **rearview mirror,**《英また》a **driving mirror** (➤ back mirror とはいわない) ▶バックミラーをのぞくとパトカーが近づいて来るのが見えた When I looked in *the rearview mirror*, I saw a police car approaching.
ぱっくり ▶傷口がぱっくり口を開けている The wound is *wide* open.
バックル a **buckle** ▶シートベルトをバックルで締める *buckle up* (a seat belt).
ばつぐん 抜群の **outstanding** ▶彼は抜群の成績で大学を卒業した He graduated from university with *outstanding* grades. ‖悦子は数学にかけてはクラスで抜群だ Etsuko is *at the top* of the class [*far ahead* of the others] in mathematics. ‖販売員として彼女はうちの会社では抜群だ As a salesperson, she'*s head and shoulders above the others* in our company. (➤「一頭飛び抜けている」の意).
パッケージ **packaging**(包装); a **package**(包み, 荷物) ▶かわいいパッケージのお菓子 sweets in cute *packaging*.
パッケージツアー a **package tour.**
はっけっきゅう 白血球《生理学》a **white blood cell,** a **white corpuscle** /kɔ́ːʳpʌsəl/.
はっけつびょう 白血病《医学》**leukemia** /lukíːmiə/ ▶白血病を発病する develop *leukemia*.
[1]**はっけん 発見** (a) **discovery** 一動 **発見する** **discover** +目 (今まであったのだが誰も知らなかったようなものを); **find** +目 (今まで知らなかったことやさがしていたものを); **detect** +目 (検査などで) ▶彼は科学上の偉大な発見をした He *made* a great scientific *discovery*. ‖アルキメデスは入浴中に浮力の原理を発見した Archimedes *discovered* the principle of buoyancy while taking a bath.
▶被害者は遺体で発見された The victim *was found* dead. ‖旅行者のスーツケースの底から大麻が発見された Marijuana *was discovered* in the bottom of the traveler's suitcase. ‖がんの治療には早期発見が欠かせない *Early detection* is essential to cure cancer.
‖**発見者** a discoverer(➤「死体の第一発見者」は the first person to discover the body [corpse]).
☛ 再発見 (→見出語)
[2]**はっけん 発券** **ticketing** ‖**発券カウンター** a ticketing counter.
はつげん 発言 an **opinion**(意見); a **comment**(コメント); a **remark**(ことば) 一動 **発言する** **speak** ▶私たちのクラスでは発言する人はいつも決まっている In our class, it's always the same people who *give their opinions* [*speak out*]. ‖ご発言をありがとうございました Thank you for your *comment*. ‖今の発言を取り消したい I'd like to take back *what I just said*. ‖彼は発言を求められた He was asked to *make a comment*. ‖発言してもよろしいですか May I *express* [*state*] *my opinion*? (➤ state のほうが改まった語) ‖会議で彼は一度も発言しなかった He *didn't say* [*utter*] *a word* during the meeting. ‖この件に関して彼らに発言権はない They have no *say* in this matter.
‖**発言者** a speaker.
はつこい 初恋 one's **first love** ▶初恋のほろ苦い思い出 a bittersweet memory of one's *first love* ‖礼子はぼくの初恋の人だ Reiko was my *first love*.
[1]**はっこう 発行** **publication**(出版物の); **issue**(公的機関による証書・切手などの) 一動 **発行する** **publish** +目 (書籍などを); **issue** +目 (各種証書・新聞・雑誌・通貨などを) ▶身分証明書を発行する *issue* an ID card ‖この雑誌は毎月5日に発行されます This magazine *is published* on the 5th of each month.
▶その新聞の発行部数は全国で100万部に達する The newspaper has a nationwide *circulation* of one million.
‖**発行者** a publisher ‖**発行所** a publishing house.
[2]**はっこう 発酵** **fermentation** 一動 **発酵する**[させる] **ferment** /fəʳmént/ (+目) ▶ウイスキーは大麦を発酵させて作る Whisky is made from *fermented* barley.
[3]**はっこう 発効する** **come into effect** ▶この法律はことしの4月から発効する This law *comes into effect* in April this year. ／This law *becomes effective* in April of this year.
[4]**はっこう 薄幸** **ill fortune** ▶久美子は薄幸の少女の役を演じた Kumiko played the role of an *unfortunate* girl.
[5]**はっこう 発光** ‖**発光ダイオード** a light-emitting diode《略 LED》‖**発光体** a photogen /fóʊtədʒən/.
はっこつ 白骨 a (**white**) **bone**; a **skeleton** (がい骨) ▶林の中から白骨死体が発見された *The remains of a body* were [*A skeleton* was] found in the woods.
ばっさい 伐採する **fell** +目; **cut down** (切り倒す) ▶この山の木をすべて伐採したら洪水が起こるだろう *Felling* [*Cutting down*] all the trees on these mountains may cause flooding.
ばっさり ▶智子は長い髪をばっさり切ってもらった Tomoko had her hair cut *drastically* short. (➤「思い切りよく」の意) ‖今年度は文教予算がばっさり削られてしまった There have been *drastic* cutbacks in the educational and cultural budgets this fiscal year.
はっさん 発散する **let off**; **give off**(ガスなどを発生す

る）▶子供たちは外で遊んでエネルギーを発散させた The children *let off* [*released*] their energy by playing outside.
▶コンサート会場の若者たちはむんむんするような熱気を発散していた The young people in the concert hall *were giving off* steamy heat. ‖ 彼は自分の部屋に掛けてあった通学かばんを殴って怒りを発散させた He *found an outlet for* his anger in punching the school bag hanging on the wall in his room.（➤ outlet は「はけ口」）.

1**ばっし 抜糸する** remove (the) stitches ▶きょう，手の傷の抜糸をした I *had the stitches removed* from my hand today.

2**ばっし 抜歯** extraction of a tooth ▶抜歯する *extract a tooth.*

バッジ a badge ▶日本の国会議員は金バッジをつけている Members of the Japanese Diet wear *a gold badge.* ‖ 私は学級委員のバッジをなくした I lost my class monitor's *badge.* 《参考》《米》では円形で比較的大きいものを button ともいう．またピンで襟につけるものを (lapel) pin ともいう．

はつしも 初霜 the first frost.

1**はっしゃ 発車** departure 一動 発車する leave, depart（➤ 後者は堅い語）▶発車まであとどのくらいありますか How much time do we have before *departure*? ‖ 次の電車は5時に発車します The next train *leaves* [*departs*] at five o'clock. ‖ 3時40分発の東京行き特急は3番線から発車します The 3 : 40 limited express for Tokyo *leaves* from Track 3. ‖ バスは定刻より3分遅れて発車した The bus *departed* three minutes behind schedule. ‖ 発車ベルが鳴り終わると電車は定刻どおり発車した When *the* (*starting*) *bell* stopped ringing, the train *left* [*started*／*pulled out*] on time.
‖ 発車時刻 the departure time.

2**はっしゃ 発射** firing（銃の）; launching /lɔ́:ntʃɪŋ/（発射台からの打ち上げ）一動 発射する fire ＋㊐; launch ＋㊐ ▶ミサイルを発射する *launch* a missile ‖ 3，2，1，0，発射！Three, two, one, zero. *Go!* ‖ 警官が空に向けてピストル［空砲］を発射した The police officer *fired* his gun [a blank] into the air.
‖ 発射場［台］a launch site [pad].

はっしゅつ 発出 an issuance 一動 発出する issue（公式に声明などを出す）; declare（宣言する）▶緊急事態宣言を発出する *declare* a state of emergency.

はつしゅつじょう 初出場 ▶わが校のチームは今年，甲子園に初出場した Our high school team *made its debut* [*its first appearance*] at Koshien Stadium this year.

1**はっしょう 発祥** ▶ニューオーリンズはジャズの発祥の地だと言われている New Orleans is said to be the *birthplace* of jazz.

2**はっしょう 発症する** develop ＋㊐ ▶がん［うつ病］を発症する *develop* cancer [depression].

はつじょう 発情 ▶発情する *go into heat* ‖ 発情している *be in* [《英また》*on*] *heat.*
‖ 発情期 the mating season.

1**はっしん 発信する** send ＋㊐; transmit ＋㊐（信号・情報を）▶信号を発信する *send* (*out*) [*transmit*] a signal ‖ この手紙はニューヨークから発信されている This letter *has been sent* [*was mailed*] from New York. ‖ 正確な情報を発信し続けることが重要だ It's important that we keep *providing* correct information.
‖ 発信音 a dial [《英》dialling] tone（➤「ピーという発信音のあとにメッセージをどうぞ」は Leave your message after the beep.）‖ 発信基地 a base for transmitting information ‖ 発信局 a sending office ‖ 発信装置 a transmitter ‖ 発信地 a place of dispatch ‖ 発信人 a sender.

2**はっしん 発進する** take off（航空機が）; start (to move)（車が）▶戦闘機数機が空母から発進した Several fighter planes *took off* from the aircraft carrier.
▶彼女はジャガーを急発進させた She *abruptly took off* in her Jaguar.

3**はっしん 発疹** a rash ▶発しんができた I came [broke] out in *a rash.* ‖ その合成洗剤を使うと手に発しんができる That synthetic detergent gives me *a rash* on my hands.
‖ 発しんチフス typhus (fever).

バッシング bashing ▶ジャパンバッシング Japan-*bashing* ‖ マスコミからのバッシングにあう *take a bashing* from the media.

はっすい 撥水 一形 はっ水性の water-repellent ▶はっ水性の［はっ水処理を施した］帽子 a *water-repellent* hat.

ばっすい 抜粋 an extract /ékstrækt/, an excerpt /éksə:rpt/ 一動 抜粋する extract /ɪkstrækt/ ＋㊐ ▶長い詩からの抜粋 *an extract* [*an excerpt*] from a long poem ‖ 書物からある文章を抜粋する *extract* some passages from a book.

はっする 発する 1【外に向かって出す】emit ＋㊐, give off（光・熱・においなどを）▶太陽は光と熱を発している The sun *emits* light and heat. ‖ ホタルが草むらで時折ほのかな光を発している Occasionally, fireflies *give off* a dim light amid the grasses. ‖ ガラガラヘビは敵が近づくとしっぽを振って警告を発する Rattlesnakes *warn off* their approaching enemies by rattling their tails.
2【始まる】▶木曽川は飛騨山脈に源を発する The Kiso River *originates* [*rises*／*has its source*] *in* the Hida Mountains. ‖ その戦争は2国間の不和に端を発している The war *started* [*originated*] *from* the discord between the two nations.

ハッスル ⚠ hustle が元であるが，英語は「急いで行く」「急いで［さっさと］やる」などの意味で，「張り切ってやる」の意味は伝わりにくい． ▶ハッスルして部屋の掃除をする *work hard* to clean one's own room ‖ 彼は宴会となるとハッスルする He *gets* really *enthusiastic* when it comes to parties.

ばっする（…のことで）**罰する** punish《for》▶川にごみを捨てると罰せられます Those who dump rubbish in the river should *be punished.* ‖ 彼は校則に違反して罰せられた He *was punished for* violating the school regulations.

1**はっせい 発生** occurrence /əkə́:rəns/; an outbreak（疫病・事件などの突発）一動 発生する occur, happen →起こる ▶インフルエンザの発生 a flu *outbreak* ‖ 非常事態が発生した An emergency *has occurred.* ‖ フィリピン東方に台風が発生した A typhoon *has appeared* [*has formed*] to the east of the Philippines. ‖ 台風は熱帯で発生する Typhoons *are born* in the tropics.
▶この町の犯罪発生率は最近高くなってる The *incidence* of crime [The *crime rate*] in this city is growing these days.

2**はっせい 発声** ▶発声練習をする do *vocal* [*singing*] *exercises.*

1**はっそう 発想** an idea（考え）; a concept（着想）; a

way of thinking（考え方）▶おもしろい**発想**だね It's an interesting *idea*. ‖ 彼女のデザインは草花から**発想**したものが多い She mainly *gets her ideas* for her designs from plants and flowers.

▶このおもちゃは**発想**がユニークだ The *concept* behind this toy is unique. ／This toy is unique in its *conception*. ‖ 家庭内の男女の役割分担についてそろそろ**発想の転換**が必要だ It's about time we *changed our way of thinking* on gender roles in the family.

2**はっそう 発送する** **send**《off, out》, **dispatch** ＋㊐（➤ 後者が「発送する」という日本語に近い）; **ship** ＋㊐（商品を）; **mail** ＋㊐,《英また》**post** ＋㊐（郵便物を）▶DM を**発送する** *send off* [*mail*] advertising letters ‖ 当校の入学願書は本日（中に）**発送いたします** Our application form will *be in the mail* today. ‖《掲示》地方**発送**承ります *Mailed* [*Shipped*] anywhere nationwide.

✉ **ご注文の品は一両日中に宅配便で発送します** Your order will *be shipped* [*be dispatched*] by a delivery service within a couple of days. ➤ ship は船以外で送る場合にも用いる.

ばっそく 罰則 **penal** /píːnl/ **regulations**, (a) **penalty** /pénlti/ ▶飲酒運転に対する**罰則** the *penalty* for drunken driving ‖ 悪質な反則には重い**罰則**が科せられる Heavy *penalties* will be imposed for serious offenses.

ばった《虫》a **grasshopper**; a **locust** /lóʊkəst/（特に大発生する）▶**バッタ**はよく跳ぶ *Grasshoppers* are great jumpers. ‖ **バッタ**の大群 a swarm of *locusts*.

バッター a **batter**, a **hitter** ⇀打者 ▶右[左]**バッター** a right-[left-] handed *batter* ‖ 高橋が**バッターボックス**に立った Takahashi *went to the plate* [*came to bat*].

‖**バッターボックス** the batter's box.

はったつ 発達 **development**（高度なものへの発展）; **progress**（進歩）; **growth**（徐々で自然な成長）**一動 発達する** **develop**, **make progress**, **grow** ▶ 20世紀の機械文明の**発達**はめざましかった The *development* of industrial civilization in the 20th century was remarkable. ‖ バイオテクノロジーは近年急速な**発達を遂げた** Biotechnology *has made* rapid *progress* in recent years. ‖ 東京は交通網が高度に**発達している** Tokyo has a *highly-developed* transportation network.

▶ 10代は心身ともに大いに**発達する**時期である People *develop* [*grow*] greatly both in mind and body in their teens. ／The teens are a time of rapid physical and mental *development*. ‖ 重量挙げをすると筋肉が**発達する** Weight lifting *develops* your muscles.（➤ この develop は「発達させる」）‖ 低気圧はオホーツク海で猛烈に**発達した** The low pressure area *expanded* enormously in the Sea of Okhotsk.

☛ **未発達**（⇀見出語）

ばったばった ▶松坂は打者を**ばったばった**と三振に切って取った Matsuzaka *struck out one* batter *after another*.

はったり **bluff** ▶挑戦者は絶対勝つと言っているが, **はったり**を利かしているだけだ The challenger says he is sure to win the match, but it's all *bluff*. ‖ 彼の言うことは**はったり**ばかりだ He's only *bluffing*. ‖ あいつは**はったり屋**だ He's *a big talker* [*a bluffer*].

ばったり ▶俺がさっと身をかわすとあいつは**ばったり**と倒れた When I abruptly stepped aside, he fell *flat* on the ground.

▶ワイキキで小学校のときの友だちに**ばったり会った** In Waikiki I *bumped into* [*ran into*] an old friend from elementary school.

ぱったり ▶**ぱったり倒れる** *collapse* ／*tumble over*（前者は「卒倒する」, 後者は「何かにつまずいて倒れる」の意）.

▶午後 9 時を過ぎると客足は**ぱったり**（＝急に）止まった After 9 : 00 p.m., customers *suddenly* stopped coming in. ‖ 彼は**ぱったり**教会に行かなくなった He *suddenly* stopped going to church.

ばっちい **yucky**,《英また》**yukky** ▶**ばっちい**お手々 *yucky* hands.

はっちゃく 発着 **arrival and departure** ▶管制官が飛行機の**発着**を管理している Air traffic controllers are in charge of the *arrival and departure* of the airplanes.

はっちゅう 発注する **place an order** ▶最新型ＤＶＤレコーダーを10台**発注する** *place* [*give*] *an order for* 10 latest-model DVD recorders.

‖**発注書** an order form.

ばっちり ▶きょうは（服装を）**ばっちりきめてるね** You'*re dressed to kill* today, aren't you?（➤ be dressed to kill は「めかし込んでいる」）／*Looks great!*（➤ That looks great on you. を縮めた言い方）.

▶ **対話**「数学の試験, どうだった？」「**ばっちり**だよ」"How did you do on your math test ?" "*Great.* ／*It was a breeze.*"（➤ a breeze は《米・インフォーマル》で「たやすいこと」の意）.

ぱっちり ▶目の**ぱっちり**したかわいい赤ちゃん a cute baby with *big bright* eyes ／an adorable baby with *sparkling* eyes.

パッチワーク (a) **patchwork** ▶**パッチワーク**をする do *patchwork*.

バッティング **batting**, **hitting** ▶**バッティング**の練習をする have *batting* practice ‖ ことしのマリーンズは**バッティング**がいい The Marines *are batting well* this year. ⇀打撃.

ばってき 抜擢する **select** ＋㊐, **pick** (**out**)（➤ 前者が日本語に近いやや堅い語）▶堀さんは副社長に**抜てきされた** Mr. Hori *was selected* [*was picked out*] as executive vice president. ‖ 駆け出しの女優が主役に**抜てきされた** They *picked* a budding starlet to take the leading role.

バッテリー **1【蓄電池】** a **battery** ▶（車の）**バッテリー**があがってしまった The (car) *battery* is dead. ‖ 私のスマホ, 新しい**バッテリー**が必要みたい I think my smartphone needs a new *battery*.

2【野球の】 a **battery** ▶澤村・阿部の**バッテリー** the Sawamura-Abe *battery* ‖ ぼくは高校時代彼と**バッテリーを組んだ** I *paired with* him *as a battery* [*formed a battery with* him] when we were in high school.

はってん 発展 (a) **development**（発達）; **growth**（成長）; (an) **expansion**（拡大）**一動 発展する** **develop**, **grow**, **expand** ▶経済の**発展** economic *development* ‖ 二人の友情は恋に**発展した** Their friendship *developed* [*grew*] into love.

▶その事件は政界を巻き込む汚職事件に**発展した** The incident *has developed into* a scandal involving political circles. ‖ 短編小説を長編小説に**発展させる** *expand* a short story into a novel（「その長編小説は短編小説を発展させたものだ」なら, The novel is an expansion of a short story. のようにいう）.

‖**発展途上国** a developing country.

はつでん 発電 (electric) power generation, generation of electricity **一動 発電する** generate electricity ▶原子力による発電 the *generation of electricity* by nuclear energy／nuclear *power generation* ‖水力［火力］で発電する *generate electricity* by water-power［thermal power］(➤「水力発電」は hydroelectric power generation,「火力発電」は thermal power generation がふつう).
‖**発電機** a generator, a dynamo ‖**原子力発電** nuclear power generation ‖**太陽光発電** solar［photovoltaic］power generation ‖**風力発電** wind power generation.
☛ 発電所（→見出語）

ばってん 罰点 an x, a black mark ▶つづりを間違えて罰点をもらった I misspelled the word and got *an x*. →ばつ.

はつでんしょ 発電所 a power plant［station］
‖**水力［火力］発電所** a hydroelectric［thermal］power plant ‖**原子力発電所** a nuclear power plant.

はっと ▶はっとするような美人 a *stunning*［*breathtaking*］beauty ‖驚いてはっと息をのむ *give*［*let out*］*a gasp* of surprise ‖かぎを掛けずに家を出てきたことをはっと(＝突然)思い出した I *suddenly* remembered that I had left home without locking up. ‖真夜中に物音ではっと目が覚めた I *was startled out of my sleep* by a noise in the middle of the night.

バット a bat ▶バットを鋭く振る swing *a bat* sharply.
‖**金属バット** a metal baseball bat.

ぱっと ▶彼女が部屋に入って来るとあたりがぱっと明るくなった As soon as she came in, the room *brightened*. ‖そのうわさは村中にぱっと広がった The rumor spread *quickly*［*like wildfire*］through the village.
▶彼は宝くじで当てた100万円をぱっと使ってしまった He spent the one million yen he won in the lottery *like water*. (➤ like water は「惜しげもなく, 湯水のように」).

ぱっとしない ▶彼女は小学校ではあまりぱっとしない児童だった She was quite an *ordinary* student in elementary school. ‖彼は大学時代はあまりぱっとしない男だった He *didn't stand out* in college. (➤ stand out は「目立つ」).

ハットトリック a hat trick ▶ハットトリックを達成する score *a hat trick*.

はつねつ 発熱する develop［run］a fever ▶彼女は発熱のため学校を休んだ She stayed home from school because of a (*high*) *temperature*［because she was *feverish*］.／*A fever* prevented her from coming to school.

はつのり 初乗り ‖**初乗り運賃** a starting［basic］fare.

はっぱ 発破 **1【爆破】**▶がけに発破をかける *dynamite* a cliff／*blow up* a cliff *with dynamite*.
2【激励】▶監督はタイムを取って選手にはっぱをかけた The manager called a timeout and *gave a pep talk to*［*encouraged*］the players.

はつばい 発売する sell ＋目; put on sale (初めて売り出す); come out《with》(出版物・製品を出す) ▶新製品を発売する *sell* a new product ‖その型のテレビはもう発売していません TV sets of that model *are not sold* any more. ‖本日, 記念切手を全国いっせいに発売します The commemorative stamp *goes on sale* today throughout the country. ‖新しいゲームソフトが来月発売になる A new game program will *be put on sale*［*be launched*］next month. ‖予約券は発売中です Reserved tickets are *now on sale*［*now available*］.
▶竹内まりやの新しいCDが発売された Takeuchi Mariya's new CD *has been released*［*has come out on the market*］. (➤ release は「(本やレコードなどを)発売する」) ‖あの会社は来月新しいテレビゲームを発売するんだって They are going to *come out with* a new video game next month.
▶その本［DVD］は発売禁止になった That book［DVD］*was banned*.／*Sale* of that book［DVD］*was prohibited*. ‖《掲示》本日発売 On Sale Today.
‖**発売元** a sales agency.

はつばしょ 初場所 the New Year's (grand) sumo tournament.

はっはっは Ha-ha! ▶彼ははっはっはと笑った He *laughed loudly*.／He *roared with laughter*.／He *guffawed*.

はつはる 初春 early spring, the beginning of spring (春の初め); the New Year (新年).

はっぴ 法被 a happi(-coat) (➤ happi は英語化している)
日本紹介 ✉ **はっぴは一部の職人が着用するうわっぱりで, えりや背中に屋号や着用者の通称などが染め抜いてあります. 一般の人がお祭りのときに着ることもあります** A happi(-coat) is an outer garment worn by some craftsmen. It often bears on its collar or back a dyed store logo or the wearer's nickname. Ordinary people also wear a happi(-coat) at festivals.

ハッピーエンド a happy ending ▶ロマンス小説の多くはハッピーエンドになっている Most romance novels have *happy endings*.／Most romance novels *end happily*.

はつひので 初日の出 the sunrise on New Year's Day ▶富士山頂で初日の出を拝んだ We reverently watched *the first sunrise of the year* from the top of Mt. Fuji. (➤ reverently は「敬けんな気持ちで」)

はつびょう 発病する be taken ill, fall ill ▶父は中国への旅行中発病した My father *was taken ill*［*fell ill*］during his trip to China. ‖HIVの感染者が必ずエイズを発病するとは限らない HIV carriers don't necessarily *come down with* AIDS.

はっぴょう 発表 (an) announcement (公表); (a) presentation (製品・成果などの); (a) release (ニュース・CDなどの); publication (出版物による公表) **一動 発表する** announce, present /prizént/, release, publish
▶審査の結果を発表いたします We will *announce* the results of the examination. ‖合格者名は来週の月曜日に発表される予定だ The names of successful candidates will *be announced* next Monday. ‖私は次回のゼミで発表することになっている I am supposed to *make*［*give*］*a presentation* at the next seminar.
▶首相は政見を発表した The Prime Minister *presented*［*stated*］his［her］political views. ‖彼は医学学会で［医学誌に］論文を発表した He *read* a paper at a medical conference［*published* a paper in a medical journal］. (➤この read は「(論文・詩などを)声を出して読む」) ‖彼はたびたび同人誌に詩を発表している He often *presents* his poetry in the literary (club) magazine. ‖そのニュースはけさ発表された The news *was released*［*was made*

public] this morning.
▶その俳優は婚約発表の記者会見を行った The actor held a press conference to *announce* his engagement. ‖ 共同声明の発表は2，3時間遅れるようだ It seems that the *release* of a joint statement will be delayed a few hours. ‖ 今度の日曜日に娘のピアノの発表会がある My daughter will take part in a piano *recital* this Sunday.
☛ **未発表**（⇀見出語）

はっぷ 発布 **promulgation** 一動 **発布する** **promulgate** +目 ▶新憲法の発布 the *promulgation* of a new constitution.

はつぶたい 初舞台 one's **first appearance on** (the) **stage**；one's **debut** /déɪbjuː/（デビュー）▶彼は浅草の演芸場で初舞台を踏んだ He *made his first appearance* [*his debut*] on the vaudeville stage in Asakusa.

はっぷん 発奮する **rouse** /raʊz/ **oneself** ▶負けてくやしかったら発奮してほしい If you feel bad about losing, I hope you will *rouse* [*stir*] *yourselves* to do better next time. ‖ 息子は先生のことばに発奮して（＝励まされて）熱心に勉強を始めた *Inspired* by his teacher's words, my son began to study hard.

1**はっぽう** （…に）**発砲する** **fire** 《at》 ▶機動隊はデモ参加者たちに発砲した The riot squad *fired at* [*on*] the demonstrators.
‖**発砲事件** a shooting incident.

2**はっぽう 八方** ▶八方手を尽くし（てさがし）たが猫の行方を突き止めることはできなかった We searched for our cat *far and wide* [*high and low*], but we couldn't find her. ‖ 会社の財政状態は今や八方ふさがりだ The company is *up against a wall* financially.
▶彼女は八方美人だ She tries to please everyone. ／She says whatever other people want to hear.

はっぽうスチロール 発泡スチロール **Styrofoam** /stáɪrəfoʊm/（➤商標名），**styrene** /stáɪəriːn/ **foam** 《英》**polystyrene** /pɑ̀ːlistáɪriːn ‖ pɔ̀l-/ ▶発泡スチロール製のカップ a *styrofoam* cup.

はつぼん 初盆 ⇀新盆(にいぼん).

ばっぽんてき 抜本的な **drastic**（思い切った）；**radical**（根本的な）▶日本の税制は抜本的な改革が必要だ *Drastic* reform is needed in the Japanese taxation system.

はつみみ 初耳 ▶そいつは初耳だ Oh, *that's news to me*. ／Oh, I *didn't know that*. ‖ 木登りする犬なんて初耳だね I'*ve never heard* of a dog that climbs a tree *before*.

はつめい 発明 (an) **invention**（➤「発明品」の意味では Ⓒ扱い）一動 **発明する** **invent** +目 ▶印刷機の発明は歴史を変えた The *invention* of the printing press changed history. ‖ ボールペンはすばらしい発明だと思う I think the ballpoint pen is *a* great *invention*. ‖ 電灯はいつ発明されたのか When *was* the electric light *invented*? ‖ 対話「電話を発明したのはだれですか」「アレクサンダー・グラハム・ベルです」"Who *invented* the telephone?" "Alexander Graham Bell did." ‖ 発明王エジソン Edison, the great inventor（➤ inventor は「発明家」）.

はつもう 発毛 **hair growth**（育毛）；**hair restoration**（毛髪の回復，育毛）‖**発毛剤** a hair restorer.

はつもうで 初詣 ***hatsumode***
日本紹介 ✉ 初もうでは新年最初に神社または寺院に参詣することです．新しい年の商売繁盛や家族と自分の無病息災を祈ります *Hatsumode* refers to the first New Year's visit to a Shinto shrine or a Buddhist temple. People pray for the prosperity of their businesses or for the health and safety of themselves and their families during the year.

はつもの 初物 ▶農家から直接初物の桃を買った I bought *the first peaches of the season* direct [directly] from a farmer.

はつゆき 初雪 **the first snow(fall of the season)** ▶昨夜札幌に初雪が降った Last night *it snowed* [*snow fell*] in Sapporo *for the first time this winter*.

はつゆめ 初夢 **the first dream of the New Year** (**that** one **has on the first or second night of January**) ▶ことしの初夢は富士山だった *My first dream of the New Year* was of Mt. Fuji.

はつらつ 溌剌 ▶はつらつとした女の子 a *lively* girl（➤ lively の発音は /láɪvli/）‖ 彼はいつも元気はつらつとしている He is always *full of life* [*vigor* ／*pep*].（➤ pep はインフォーマル）‖ 彼女，働きに出るようになってからますますはつらつとしてきたね She *has become* more *lively* [*energetic*] since she started to work.

はつれい 発令する **issue** +目；**announce** +目（公式に）▶人事異動を発令する *announce* personnel changes [movements of personnel] ‖ 津波警報が発令された A tsunami warning has *been issued*.

はて 果て **the end** ▶地の果てまで行く go to *the end* [*ends*] *of the earth* ‖ 私はヨーロッパを果てから果てまで旅行した I traveled *from one end* of Europe *to the other*. ‖ 彼らは口論の果てに殴り合いになった They quarreled and *finally* came to blows.

はで 派手な **showy**（人目を引く）；**bright**（色が鮮やかな）；**tacky**（けばけばしい）；**loud**（柄が大きい）；**flashy**（安ぴかの）；**gaudy** /gɔ́ːdi/（俗っぽい）▶彼女はいつもはでな服を着ている She always wears *showy* [*tacky*] clothing. ‖ そのシャツはきみには少しはで過ぎると思うよ I think that shirt is a little (too) *bright* [*loud*] for you.
▶彼女は生活がはでだ She *lives lavishly* [*luxuriously*].（➤ lavishly は「ぜいたくに」）‖ 彼ははでに金を使った He spent money *lavishly* [*prodigally*].（➤ prodigally は「惜しげもなく」）‖ 彼は万事にはで好みだ He's *fond of show* in everything. ‖ 忘年会はぱっとはでにやろう！Let's *make* the year-end party *a* real *blowout*!（➤ blowout は「はめをはずして飲み食いするパーティー」の意の俗語）.
▶M社は（ラジオやテレビで）はでに新製品の宣伝をしている M Company is plugging their new product *like mad*. ‖ ゆうべ父と兄ははでな（＝すごい）けんかをやった My father and brother had a *terrible* fight [*quite* a fight] last night.

パテ **pâté** /pɑːtéɪ ‖ pǽteɪ/（料理）；**putty** /pʌ́ţi/（充てん材）.

はてしない 果てしない **endless** ▶果てしなく続く砂漠 an *endless* desert ‖ 我々の論争は果てしなく続いた Our controversy went on *endlessly*. ／*There was no end to* the argument.

はてる 果てる **1**【終わる】▶パーティーはいつ果てるともなく続いた The party seemed to go on *endlessly*.（➤ endlessly には「うんざりした」のニュアンスがある）.
2【「…し果てる」の形で】▶重要な書類を紛失してしまい困り果てている I have lost some important documents and *am in big trouble*. ‖ きのうのハイキングは距離が長くてくたびれ果てた I hiked a long distance yesterday and *was totally exhausted*.

ばてる **be dead tired** ▶きょうは5時間も歩き通しでばててしまった I'*m dead tired* today since I walked for five hours. ‖ 俺, もうばてたよ I'*m* (*dead*) *beat*.

パテント a **patent** /pǽtnt/, a **patent right** ▶彼は新しいコンピュータソフトのパテントを持っている He has *a patent* for a new computer software program.

はと 鳩 a **pigeon**; a **dove** /dʌv/ (特に小型の; 文学的な語) ▶寺や神社にはたいていハトがたくさんいる There are often a lot of *pigeons* at temples and shrines. ‖ ハトは平和の象徴である The *dove* is a symbol of peace.

▶あの政治家はハト派として知られている That politician is known as *a dove*.

‖**ハト小屋** a dovecot(e), a dovehouse, a pigeon house ‖ **ハト時計** a cuckoo clock (➤ cuckoo /kúːkuː/ は「カッコウ」; pigeon [dove] clock は一般的でない) ‖ **伝書バト** a carrier [homing] pigeon.

はどう 波動 **undulation** /ʌ̀ndʒəléɪʃən/.

ばとう 罵倒 **abuse** /əbjúːs/ **一動 罵倒する** **abuse** /əbjúːz/ +㊐ ▶紀子は自分の夫を私の前で罵倒した Noriko *abused* her husband *loudly* in front of me. ‖ 群衆は殺人の容疑で逮捕された男を口々に罵倒した The crowd *showered abuse on* [*clamored abuse at*] the man arrested for murder.

パトカー a **police** [**patrol**] **car** 《参考》《米》では squad [prowl] car, cruiser /krúːzəʳ/, 《英》では panda car ともいう.

はとこ 再従兄弟[姉妹] a **second cousin**.

はとば 波止場 a **wharf** /hwɔːʳf/; a **pier** (大きな突堤) ▶波止場に数隻の船がつながれていた Several ships were moored to the *pier*.

バドミントン **badminton** /bǽdmɪntən/ ▶バドミントンをする play *badminton* 《参考》バドミントンの「羽根」は shuttlecock という.

はどめ 歯止め a **brake** ▶政府はインフレに歯止めをかけようとした The government tried to *put the brakes on* inflation. ‖ あの男はかけ事をやり出すと歯止めがきかなくなる Once he starts gambling, he *can't stop*.

バトル a **battle**.

パトロール **patrol** ▶私は無灯火で自転車に乗っていてパトロール中の巡査に尋問された I was questioned by *a policeman on patrol* [*on the beat*] when riding my bicycle without a (head) light.

‖**パトロールカー**(→パトカー).

パトロン a **patron** /péɪtrən/, a **patroness** (女性); a **sponsor** (後援者).

バトン a **baton** /bətáːn/ (リレーなどの) ▶彼はアンカーにバトンを渡した He passed the *baton* to the anchor (runner).

▶川崎氏は後任者にその仕事をバトンタッチした Mr. Kawasaki *passed* that job *on* [*handed* that job *over*] *to* his successor.

> **危ないカタカナ語✺ バトン**
> 「バトン」は baton でよいが, 「バトンタッチ」, 「バトンガール」は和製語. 「バトンタッチ」は baton pass, 「バトンガール」は baton twirler が正しい. なお, 楽隊の先頭に立ってバトンを回す女性は drum majorette /mèɪdʒərét/ と呼ばれる.

[1]**はな 花** **1**【草木の】a **flower**; (a) **blossom** (特に果樹の) ▶花を育てる grow *flowers* ‖ 花を摘む pick *flowers* ‖ 花が散った The *flowers* are gone. ‖ 温室にはいろいろな花が咲いている Various *flowers are in bloom* [*blooming*] in the greenhouse. (➤「花が咲く」に当たる動詞は bloom が一般的. ただし, 桜やハナミズキなど樹木の華やかな花には主に blossom を用いる; なお, be blooming は開花から咲きそろうまでの途中の段階で「咲きつつある」, 咲きそろった状態は in bloom, 満開は in full bloom) ‖ 桃の花が咲き始めた *Peach blossoms* are beginning to come out [to bloom]. / The peach trees are beginning to blossom [bloom]. ‖ 花(=桜)の見頃は来週の日曜辺りになりそうです The *cherry blossoms* will be in full bloom next Sunday. ‖ 花の生け方を教えてください Could you please teach me *how to arrange flowers*?

‖**花曇り** cloudy weather during the cherry blossom season ‖ **花ことば** the language of flowers ‖ **花園** a flower garden ‖ **花時計** a flower clock ‖ **花畑** a field of flowers, a flower garden ‖ **花冷え** a return of chilly weather during the cherry blossom season ‖ **花祭** a flower festival ‖ **花模様** a flower [floral] design ‖ **花屋** a flower shop (店); a florist (人).

2【美しいもの】▶吉田都はロイヤル・バレエ団の花だった Yoshida Miyako was *a star* of the Royal Ballet. ‖ 君たちは振り返ってみて学生時代が花(=生涯で最高の時代)だったと思うだろう You will look back on your school days as *the best days of your life*.

3【慣用表現】▶言わぬが花だよ Some things are better left unsaid. ‖ クラス会では青春時代の話に花が咲いた At the class reunion, we really *enjoyed talking* about our younger days. ‖ 夏の浜辺には色鮮やかな水着の花が咲く(=浜辺を飾る) Bathing suits in vivid colors *adorn* summer beaches. ‖ 彼は後輩に花を持たせた He *let* the younger man *take the credit*. ‖ もう一花咲かせたい I wish I could be successful one more time.

[2]**はな 鼻** **1**【顔の一部分】a **nose**; a **muzzle** (犬・馬などの); a **snout** /snaʊt/ (豚などの); a **trunk** (象の) ▶彼は鼻が高い[ぺちゃんこだ] He has a long [flat] *nose*. (➤「高い[低い]鼻」を(×)high [low] nose とはいわない) ‖ 彼女は鼻が上を向いて[あぐらをかいて]いる She has *an upturned* [*a pug*] *nose*. ‖ 鼻が詰まっていやな感じだ My *nose is stuffed up*, so I feel lousy. ‖ ぼくは鼻が悪い My *sense of smell* is not good. ‖ あの人は鼻にかかったようなしゃべり方をする He has a *nasal* voice. (➤ nasal /néɪzəl/ は「鼻の, 鼻にかかった」) / He speaks through his nose. ‖ 犬が鼻をくんくんさせている The dog *is sniffing*. ‖ あまりの臭さに鼻をつまんだ I *held my nose* because of the stink. ‖ こら, 鼻をほじくるんじゃない Don't *pick your nose*.

‖**鼻の穴** one's nostril(s) ‖ **鼻眼鏡** a pince-nez /pænsnéɪ/.

2【嗅覚】▶かぜひいてて鼻がきかないんだ I have a cold and *can't smell* now. ‖ この犬, あまり鼻がきかないみたい It looks like this dog *doesn't have a very good nose*. ‖ 実験室に入ると強い酸のにおいが鼻をついた When I entered the laboratory, a strong acidic odor *assailed my nostrils* [*nose*].

3【はなみず】**mucus** /mjúːkəs/ (➤ 医学用語) ▶赤ちゃんのはなが出てるわよ Your baby's *nose is running*. ‖ はなをかみなさい *Blow your nose*. ‖ あの子はいつもはなをすすっている The boy [girl] *is always sniffling*.

4【慣用表現】 **鼻が高い** ▶優秀な部下を持って私も鼻が高いよ I'*m very proud to* have excellent men

は

working for me in our office. **鼻であしらう** ▶彼は私の考えを鼻であしらった He *pooh-poohed* my idea. **鼻にかける** ▶彼女, 社長の娘だってことをすごく鼻にかけてるのよ She *brags* that her father is the president of a company. (➤ brag は「鼻もちならない」のニュアンス) ／She *boasts* about her father being the president of a company. **鼻につく** ▶あのキャスターも初めはよかったが, この頃鼻についてきた That newscaster was interesting at first, but he has begun to *get on my nerves* recently.

鼻もひっかけない ▶彼女は同級生の男の子なんかには鼻もひっかけない She *doesn't give* the boys in her class *the time of day*. (➤ not give ... the time of day で「…に見向きもしない」) ／She *turns up her nose at* the boys in her class. (➤ turn up one's nose at は「…を鼻先であしらう」). **鼻をあかす** ▶あの人より偉くなって鼻をあかしてやるわ I'll get ahead of her some day and (that will) *take the wind out of her sails* [*put her nose out of joint*]. **鼻をへし折る** ▶何とかしてあいつの鼻をへし折ってやりたい I want to *take* him *down a peg or two*. (➤「(人を)やり込める」の意).

3**はな** ▶あいつのことなんか, はなから相手にしていない I don't take him seriously *to begin with*.

はないき 鼻息 ▶あいつはいつも上役の**鼻息をうかがって**ばかりいる He's always trying to *curry favor with* his boss. (➤ curry favor with は「…のごきげんをとる」の意) ‖ その会社はゲーム機が売れに売れて**鼻息が荒い** That company *is riding high* because their game machines are selling like hotcakes. (➤ ride high は「絶好調である」の意).

はなうた 鼻歌 **humming** ▶父はお風呂に入りながら**鼻歌を歌っている** My father *is humming a song* in the bath(tub).

はなかぜ 鼻風邪 a **head cold**(➤ (×)nose cold とはいわない) ▶私は鼻かぜをひいている I have *a head cold*. ／I have *the sniffles*.

はながた 花形 a **star** ▶彼はわがチームの**花形選手**だ He is the *star player* in our team. (➤ 複数名いるうちの1人ならば one of the star players) ‖ ハイテク産業は時代の**花形**だ High-tech industries are the *new stars* of our age.

▶彼女はNHKの**花形**アナウンサーだ She is *the most popular* announcer at NHK.

はながみ 鼻紙 a **tissue**, a **Kleenex** /klíːneks/ (➤ 後者は商標名だが, 普通名詞として使われる) ▶**鼻紙**ではなをかむ blow one's nose with *a tissue* [*a Kleenex*].

はなくそ 鼻糞 **dried (nasal) mucus**,《米・インフォーマル》a **booger**

▶鼻くそをほじる *pick* one's *nose* ‖ 鼻くそがついてるよ You've got *a booger* on [in] your nose. (➤ 鼻の上ならば on, 中ならば in).

はなげ 鼻毛 (a) **nose** [**nostril**] **hair**.

はなごえ 鼻声 a **nasal** /néɪzəl/ **voice** ▶**鼻声**でしゃべる speak *with a nasal voice* ‖ かぜをひいたのか, 花田先生は**鼻声**だ Miss Hanada *is talking through her nose*. Maybe she has a cold.

はなざかり 花盛り ▶今が桜の**花盛り**だ The cherry blossoms *are* now *at their best*. ／The cherries *are* now *in full bloom*.

▶《比喩的》フィットネスブームでアスレチッククラブは**花盛り**だ The fitness craze *has spawned* many athletic clubs. (➤ spawn /spɔːn/ は「大量に生む」) ／Many athletic clubs *have sprung up* due to the fitness craze.

はなし 話

訳語メニュー
会話, 談話 →talk **1**
スピーチ →speech **1**
うわさ →rumor **2**
ニュース →news **6**
物語 →story **7**

1【話すこと, その内容】 a **talk** (会話, 談話) ; (a) **speech** (話すこと, スピーチ) ; a **subject**, a **topic** (話題 ; 後者は前者よりくだけた語) ▶彼は旧友と長いこと**話をした** He *had a* long *talk* with an old friend of his. ／He *talked* with an old friend of his for a long time. ‖ ホワイトさんに**お話ししたい**のですが Could I *speak* to Mr. White, please? ‖ きょうぼくたちの先生は江戸時代の**話をしてくれた** Today our teacher *talked* about the Edo period. ‖ きのうの社長の**話**, 聞いた? くだらないったらありゃしない Did you hear the president's *talk* yesterday? Nonsense is the word for it. ‖ 人の**話**は最後まで聞けよ Listen until I'm finished.

▶校長先生の**話**が始まった The principal's *speech* has begun. ‖ 彼は臓器移植について**話**(＝講演)をした He *gave* [*delivered*] *a lecture* on organ transplantation. ‖ 彼は**話がうまい** He *is a good speaker*. ‖ 私は**話が下手だ** I *am a poor speaker*. ‖ **話をそらさないでよ** Don't *change the subject* [*topic*]. ‖ アメリカの大学を出たという彼の**話**(＝主張)は本当のはずがない His *claim* about graduating from college in the U.S. is unlikely to be true. ‖ **彼女の話**はあまり信用しないほうがいいわよ You cannot trust *what she said* [*says*]. (➤ her talk とすると「彼女の演説」の意になる).

▶**父の話では**フィリピンでは物価が高騰しているそうだ *According to my father*, prices are skyrocketing in the Philippines. ‖《教室で教師が》はい, みんな. **話をやめて**! (Stop talking and) *listen up!*

▶ひどい**話**だね It *sounds awful*. (➤ sound のあとに形容詞がきて「話の内容や調子が…という印象だ」を表す) ‖ よくある**話**でしょ? *Sound familiar?*

直訳の落とし穴「彼女の話にはうんざり」
「彼女は夫への不満をよく言う. 彼女の話を聞くのにはうんざりしてきた」を (×) She often complains about her husband and I'm getting tired of listening to her story. などとする人がいる. story は物語性のある話や, 事件・事実をめぐる経過など, 話すその人の視点からの説明のことで, 不満やおしゃべりは story ではない. 英文の後半を I'm getting tired of listening to her complaining [complaints]., または I'm getting tired of listening to her complain about it. とする. なお, 「上司の長話にはうんざりだ」は I'm tired of (listening to) my boss's long-winded monologues [endless preaching]. などとする. 後者は「際限のないお説教」の場合である.

2【うわさ】 **talk**(話の種) ; a **rumor**(うわさ) ▶会長が辞任するという**話**が出ている There is some *talk* [There are some *rumors*] of the chairman resigning. ‖ 青木君が退学するって**話**, ほんとなの? Is *it* true *that* Aoki is going to quit school? ‖ 彼はブルガリアへ留学するという**話だ** I *heard* [*hear*] he is going to study in Bulgaria.

3【相談など】 ▶ 対話「加藤先生，ちょっとお話があるんですが」「どうぞ」"Mr. Kato, *may I talk to you* for a moment?" "Certainly." (➤ may I talk with you? とすると，やや重大な相談ごとのニュアンスになる).
4【提案，交渉】 ▶彼女の話(＝申し出)に乗ろうと思う I think I'll accept her *offer*. ‖ 話(＝交渉)はまだそこまで行っていないんだ The *negotiations* haven't gone that far.
▶めんどうな話を持ち出さないでよ Don't bring up *anything that will cause trouble*.
5【話題】 a **subject** ▶この話はなかったことにしよう Let's just forget that this *subject* ever came up.
6【ニュース】 **news** /njuːz/ ▶由美さん，いい話があるわよ Yumi, here's *good* [*great*] *news* for you.
7【物語】 a **story**; a **tale**(事実・架空・伝説に基づく；文語的な語) ▶この本にはおもしろい話がたくさん載っている This book contains a lot of interesting *stories*. ‖ 私は桃太郎の話［動物の出てくる話］が大好きだった I liked the *story* of Momotaro [*stories* about animals].
8【道理，事情】 ▶話のわからんことを言うなよ Don't be unreasonable. ‖ それはまた話が別だ That's a different *story*. ‖ きみには話(＝事実)が全然わかっていないね You don't understand *the facts* at all, do you?
9【慣用表現】 **ここだけの話** ▶ここだけの話だけど，正夫と友子は別れたんだって *Just between us* [*ourselves* / *you and me*], I hear that Masao and Tomoko broke up. **話が合う** ▶私は支店長とは話が合う I *get along well* [*great*] with the branch office manager. ‖ 岡田君と私は話が合う Okada and I *speak the same language*. (➤「趣味や考えが同じ」の意) / Okada and I *are on the same wavelength*. (➤「同じ波長だ」の意).
話がうま過ぎる ▶そりゃあ話がうま過ぎるよ That's *too good to be true*. **話が違う** ▶おい，それじゃあ話が違うじゃないか Hey, that *isn't what you told me* [*what you said before*]. **話がつく** ▶売買の条件については先方と話がついている(＝合意した) We *reached an agreement* on the terms of sale. ‖ 二人の間では話がついているようだ *There* seems to *be some* (*private*) *understanding* between the two. **話がはずむ** ▶ゆうべは話がはずんで気がついたら1時だった Last night we *talked and talked*, and it was one o'clock before we knew it. ‖ クラス会で昔の友だちと話がはずんだ I *had a lively conversation* with my old friends at the class reunion. **話がわかる** ▶あの部長はまるっきり話がわからない That manager *is not sensible* at all. (➤ sensible は「良識がある」) ‖ うちのおやじは話がわかる My father *is generous* [*understanding*]. (➤ 前者は「度量が大きい」，後者は「理解がある」).
話にならない ▶そんな契約条件では無理だ．話にならないよ With those contract terms, *it's impossible* [*it's* (*totally*) *out of the question*]. **話によっては** ▶話によっては，私も一口乗せてもらおう *Depending on the terms*, I may join the venture. **話の腰を折る** ▶人の話の腰を折るな Don't *spoil the story*. **話の種** ▶話の種にちょっとこれ食べてみないか *Just for the experience*, how about trying a bite of this? **話は変わる** ▶話は変わるけど，伊藤さんどうしてるか知ってる? *Changing the subject*, do you know anything about what Ito is doing now? (➤ 英語では Not to change the subject (話題を変えるわけではないが) と言うことも多い). **話をそらす** ▶私の尋ねたことが聞こえなかったふりをして，彼は話をそらした Pretending he didn't hear what I was asking, he *changed the subject*. **話をつける** ▶私が局長と話をつけてくる I will go to see the bureau chief and *settle the matter*.

> **逆引き熟語 ○○話**
> うまい［おいしい］話 a tempting [seductive] offer / うわさ話 (a) gossip, (a) rumor / おかしな(＝こっけいな)話 a funny tale [story] / おとぎ話 a fairy tale [story] / 怪談話 a ghost story / きわどい話 a highly suggestive story, an indecent story / 苦労話 a hard-luck story / 怖い話 a scary story / 自慢話 a boastful account / たとえ話 an allegory, a parable / つまらない［むだ］話 boring [idle] talk / 内緒話 a confidential talk / 泣かせる話 a moving [touching] story / ひそひそ話 a whispered talk [conversation] / よくある話 a familiar story / 耳寄りな話 good news

-ぱなし -放し ▶水道を出しっぱなしにしちゃあだめよ Don't *leave* the faucet *running*. ‖ その部屋のドアは開けっぱなしになっていた The door of that room was *left open*.
▶英夫ったら，またおもちゃを出しっぱなしだわ Hideo *left* his toys *out* again. ‖ きのうは鼻水が出っぱなしだった My nose *kept running* yesterday. ‖ もうへとへと．一日中立ちっぱなしよ I'm exhausted. I'*ve been on my feet* all day.

はなしあい 話し合い a **talk**; **talks** (会談); (a) **discussion**(討議) ▶話し合いを始める start *talks* / start *talking* [to *talk*] / begin *talking* [to *talk*] ‖ クラスの代表たちは校則問題について教員たちと話し合いの機会を持ちたがっている The class representatives want to have *a talk* with the teachers about the school regulations.
▶その問題は両首脳の話し合いで決着した The issue was settled in the *talks* between the two leaders.

はなしあいて 話し相手 ▶高齢者たちは話し相手を求めている Senior citizens need *somebody to talk to*. ‖ 孫はよく私の話し相手になってくれる My grandson often *keeps* me *company*.

はなしあう 話し合う **talk** 《about》; **discuss** +目 (論じ合う；他動詞なので about はつけない)

> **【文型】**
> 人(A)と B について話し合う
> **talk with** A **about** B
> **discuss** B **with** A

▶その件はあす話し合おう Let's *talk about* [*discuss*] it tomorrow. ‖ 私は彼女と将来について話し合った I *talked with* my girlfriend *about* our futures. ‖ 私たちはみんなで今度の文化祭について話し合った We all *discussed* the coming school festival. / We *exchanged* (*our*) *opinions* about the coming school festival.
▶そのことを彼女とよく話し合ってみます I'll *talk* it *over* with her. (➤ talk over は「…を子細に話し合う」の意) ‖ そのことはよく話し合って解決しようよ Let's *talk* it *out*. (➤ talk out は「徹底的に話し合う」の意で，その結果問題などを解決するという含みがある).

はなしがい 放し飼い ▶犬を放し飼いにしてはいけない Don't *let* your dog *run loose*. / Dogs must be on a leash. (➤「リードにつないでおかねばならない」の意).

はなしかける 話しかける talk [speak] to ▶本を読んでいるときに話しかけないでよ Don't *talk* [*speak*] *to* me when I'm reading. ‖ 私は通りで外国人に英語で話しかけられた A foreigner came up to me on the street and *said* something in English. (➤ I was spoken to ... も可能だが堅すぎる言い方で不自然).
▶彼女は真相を話しかけてふと口をつぐんだ She *almost started* [*was about to start*] *talking about* what had really happened, but the next moment she closed her mouth.

はなしごえ 話し声 a voice(声) ▶職員室から先生方の話し声が聞こえてきた We heard the teachers' *voices* coming from the faculty room. ‖ 隣の部屋で人の話し声がした I *heard* (some) people *talking* in the next room.

はなしことば 話し言葉 a spoken language.

はなしこむ 話し込む have a long talk ▶久しぶりに会った友人とすっかり話し込んでしまった I *had a long talk* with a friend of mine who(m) I had not seen for a long time. ‖ 話し込んでいて電車を乗り越してしまった We *were lost in conversation* and forgot to get off at our station.

はなしじょうず 話し上手 a good talker, a good conversationalist.

はなしずき 話し好きな talkative ▶母は話し好きで電話で１時間もしゃべっていることがある My mother is so *talkative* that she sometimes talks on the telephone for an hour.

はなしちゅう 話し中 ▶お話し中すみませんが，急ぎの電話が入っております *Excuse me for interrupting you*, but you have an urgent call. ‖ あら，(電話は)まだ話し中だわ Gosh, *the line is* still *busy* [《英また》*engaged*].

はなしはんぶん 話半分 ▶彼の言うことは話半分に聞いておいたほうがいい You should *take* what he says *with a grain of salt*. (➤ take ... with a grain of salt は「(人の話などを)割引して聞く」の意) ／Don't believe everything he says.

はなしぶり 話しぶり one's manner [way] of speaking.

はなしょうぶ 花菖蒲 《植物》an iris.

1 **はなす 話す** speak(＋目), talk, tell ＋目, say(＋目)

> **《解説》** speak は「しゃべる」という動作や話のしかたに重点をおく場合に，talk は「(人と)打ち解けて話す」ような場合に，tell は「(話の内容を人に)伝える」ような場合にそれぞれ多く用いる. say はことばを「言う」.

1【まとまった会話をする，伝える，相談する】 speak(＋目), talk《about》, tell ＋目

> **【文型】**
> 人(A)とあること(B)を話す
> speak to [with] A about B
> 人(A)にあること(B)を話す
> talk to [with] A about B
> 人(A)にあること(B)を話す
> tell A B ／tell B to A
> ➤ AB の B に that や wh- の文がくることも多い
> tell A about B

▶もっと大きな声で話してください. 聞こえませんので Please *speak* louder [*speak* up]! We cannot hear you. ‖ 私たちはコーヒーを飲みながら１時間話した We *talked* for an hour over coffee. ‖ 彼女は自分のことはあまり話さない She doesn't *talk* very much *about* herself. ‖ 何を話しているの？ What are you *talking about*? (➤ 口調によって，「何のことだ」「変なことを言うな」の意味にもなる).
▶その件は電話ではちょっと話せません I can'*t talk* to you about that over the phone. ‖ 監督はその負け試合については記者たちに何も話さず足早に立ち去った The manager walked away quickly *without speaking to* the reporters [*saying anything to* the reporters] about the lost game. ‖ どこまで話したっけ？ Where were we?
▶話したいことがあるんだけど時間ある？ I've got something to *talk* with you *about*. Do you have time [a minute]? ‖ 何もかも話してくれませんか Will you please *tell* me all (you know) about it? ‖ 泣いてばかりいないで訳を話してよ Stop crying and *tell* me why (you're crying). ‖ きみにアリバイがあることは俺が警察に話してやるよ I'll *tell* the police that you have an alibi.
▶そのことについては彼は何も話さなかった He didn't *mention* anything about it. (➤ mention は「ちょっと触れる」).

2【言語をあやつる】 speak(＋目)

> **【文型】**
> ある国語(A)を話す
> speak A

▶彼は英語とフランス語を話す He *speaks* English and French. ‖ 英語は世界の多くの国で話されている English *is spoken* in many countries around the world. ‖ 《外国人に》日本語をお話しになりますか *Do you speak* Japanese? (→話せる) ‖ 私は標準語を話すが，妻は少し関西なまりがある I *speak* standard Japanese, while my wife *speaks* with a slight Kansai accent.
☞ 話せる (→見出語)

2 **はなす 放す・離す** **1【自由にする】** set free, release ＋目 (➤ 後者は前者より堅い語)；let go《of》(手を放す) ▶少年は捕まえたトンボを放してやった The boy *set free* [*released*] the dragonfly he caught. ‖ 釣った魚は川に放してやりなさい *Release* the fish you've caught into the river. ‖ 公園で犬を放してはいけません You shouldn't *let* your dog *loose* [*unleash* your dog] in the park.

2【手を放す】 let go《of》 ▶放してよ *Let* me *go*! ／*Let go of* me. ‖ その手放してよ *Get* [*Take*] your hands *off* me. (➤ get のほうが一般的. take のほうが響きが穏やか) ‖ そのロープを放すなよ Don't *let go of* that rope.
▶彼女は手すりをつかんだ手を放さなかった She *kept hold of* the rail.

3【間をあける】 separate /sépəreɪt/ ＋目 ▶ゴングが鳴ると二人のボクサーは離されてそれぞれのコーナーに戻った At the bell, the boxers *were separated* and returned to their corners. ‖ 冷蔵庫は壁から10センチ離して置いてください Please set the refrigerator 10 centimeters *away from* the wall. ‖ 高橋は２位を大きく離してゴールインした Takahashi arrived at the goal [finish line] *far ahead of* the second place runner.

4【「…を離さない」の形で】 ▶スーツケースから目を離さないように *Keep an eye on* your suitcase. ‖ よちよち歩きの幼児は少しも目が離せない You *can't take* your *eyes off* a toddler for even a moment. ‖ 父はかばんをいつも手元から離さない My father always *keeps* his briefcase *with him*.

はなすじ 鼻筋 **the ridge of the nose** ▶彼女は父親に似て鼻筋が通っている With *a fine shapely nose*, she looks like her father. (➤ shapely は「格好のいい」).

はなせる 話せる **1**【話すことができる】▶あなたは日本語が話せますか *Do* [*Can*] *you speak* Japanese? (➤ Can you ...? は相手の能力を聞くような響きになるので前者の言い方が望ましい) ‖ ここに日本語を話せる人はいますか Is there anyone here who *can speak* Japanese? ‖ 英語がすらすら話せたらなあ I wish I *could speak* English fluently. ‖ 私はパーティーに何回か出席して, 以前よりも自由に話せるようになりました *I've learned to express myself* more freely by going to parties. (➤「自分の思っていることを言える」の意).

2【物わかりがいい】**understanding** ▶きみのお父さんは話せるね Your father is very *understanding*.

はなたかだか 鼻高々 ▶彼は息子のことで鼻高々だ He *is very proud of* his son. ／He *brags* [*boasts*] *about* his son.

はなたば 花束 a **bunch of flowers**; a **bouquet** /boʊkéɪ/ (贈答用にきれいに整えたもの) ▶バラの花束 *a bunch* [*bouquet*] of roses ‖ ファンから花束の贈呈があります There will be a presentation of *a flower bouquet* by the fans.

はなたれ 鼻たれ a **snotty child** (はな汁をたらしている子供); a **brat** (がき); a **whippersnapper**, a **greenhorn** (青二才) ▶あんなはなたれ小僧に政治がわかってたまるか How can such *a greenhorn* understand politics?

はなぢ 鼻血 a **nosebleed** ▶鼻血が出ているよ Your nose is bleeding. ／You have *a nosebleed*. ‖ 鼻血が止まらないんです My nose won't stop *bleeding*.

はなつ 放つ ▶矢を放つ *shoot* an arrow ‖ ホームランを放つ *hit* a home run ‖ ハトを空に放つ *let* a pigeon *loose* [*set* a pigeon *free*] in the air ‖ ごみの山が悪臭を放っている The pile of garbage *smells bad* [*is giving off a bad smell*]. ‖ その映画の脇役の中ではアンソニー・ホプキンズが異彩を放っていた Anthony Hopkins *cut a conspicuous figure* among the supporting actors in the film.

はなっぱしら 鼻っ柱 ▶誰かあの男の鼻っ柱を折ってやれ Somebody should *cut* him *down to size*. ‖ あいつは鼻っ柱の強い男で, 人の言うことには耳を傾けようとしない He's a very *arrogant* [*haughty*] man who never listens to others. (➤ arrogant は「高慢な」, haughty は「横柄な」).

はなつまみ 鼻つまみ ▶彼は全くの鼻つまみで誰も相手にしない He's *a real pest* [*jerk*], so nobody wants to have anything to do with him.

はなづまり 鼻詰まり ▶かぜをひいて鼻詰まりになってしまった I have a cold and *my nose is stuffed up* [*is stopped up*].

バナナ a **banana** /bənǽnə/ ▶1房のバナナ a bunch [cluster] of *bananas* ‖ バナナの皮をむく peel *a banana*.

はなはだ 甚だ **awfully**, **terribly** (ひどく; 後者は《米》では通例悪い意味に, 《英》ではよい意味にも用いる); **very much** (たいへん); **really** (本当に) ▶はなはだ申しわけございません I am *awfully* [*terribly* ／ *really*] sorry. ‖ 我々はこの決定にははなはだ不満だ We are *very* (*much*) dissatisfied with this decision.

はなはだしい 甚だしい **gross** (誤りなどが) ▶甚だしい誤解 a *gross* misunderstanding ‖ 甚だしい怠慢 *gross* negligence ‖ 急流を救命胴衣もつけずに泳ぐなんて無鉄砲も甚だしい It is *totally* reckless of you to swim in a fast-flowing river without a life jacket.

はなばなしい 華々しい **brilliant** (光り輝く); **splendid** (格別にりっぱな) ▶華々しい業績 a *brilliant* [*splendid*] achievement ‖ 彼女は芸能界で華々しい活躍をしている She is *remarkably* active in show business. ‖ 新人歌手が華々しくデビューした A new singer has made a *brilliant* [*splashy*] debut.

はなび 花火 **fireworks** ▶庭で花火をして遊ぶ play with *fireworks* in the yard ‖ 夏の夜空に花火がみごとに揚がった Spectacular *fireworks* were set off in the summer night sky.

▶今夜隅田川で花火大会がある There will be *a firework*(*s*) *display* [*a display of fireworks*] over the Sumida River this evening. (➤《米》では fireworks display がふつう).

‖仕掛け花火 set fireworks ‖線香花火 a sparkler.

はなびら 花びら a **petal** ▶バラの花びら a rose *petal* ‖ 桜の花びらが風に舞っている The *petals of cherry blossoms* are fluttering in the breeze.

はなふぶき 花吹雪 **a shower of cherry blossom petals.**

はなぺちゃ 鼻ぺちゃ ▶あの美人の景子も子供のころは鼻ぺちゃだったんだよ Keiko, now quite a beauty, used to have *a flat nose* as a child.

パナマ **Panama** (中米の国)

‖パナマ運河 the Panama Canal.

[1]はなみ 花見 ***hanami***

日本紹介 ✉ **花見は春に満開の桜の花を見に出かけることです. 木の下ではしばしば酒宴が開かれます. 桜の花は散りやすく, 満開は数日しか続きませんから, 桜の名所にはいちどきに多くの人々が押しかけます** *Hanami* refers to an outing in the spring to view cherry blossoms in full bloom. People often have a drinking party under the trees. Cherry blossoms fall easily after blooming and remain at the peak of their beauty for only a few days. During this time famous cherry blossom spots are thronged with people. →桜.

▶私たちはきのう吉野へ花見に行った We *went to see the cherry blossoms* in Yoshino yesterday. ／We *went on a picnic* to Yoshino *to see the cherry blossoms* (there) yesterday. ‖ 山は花見客でいっぱいだった The hill was full of *people enjoying the cherry blossoms* [*cherry blossom viewers*].

[2]はなみ 花実 ▶死んで花実が咲くものか If you're dead, you won't be able to bloom nor bear fruit. ／When you're dead, you're dead. (➤ 後者は「死ねばそれきり」の意).

はなみず 鼻水 **snot**; **mucus** /mjúːkəs/ (➤ 医学用語) ▶おまえ, 鼻水が出てるよ Your *nose's running*. ／You *have a runny nose*. (➤ 前者がふつう; 小さな子によく見られる, はなを垂らした状態は You've got (some) *snot* hanging (from your nose). ともいう) ‖ かぜで鼻水が出てしようがないんだ I've caught a cold and my *nose* just won't stop *running*.

はなみずき 花水木 《植物》 a **dogwood.**

はなみち 花道 a **runway** (客席に伸びた張り出し舞台) ▶その馬は有馬記念に勝って, 引退の花道を飾った The horse *retired gloriously* by winning the Arima Memorial Horse Race.

はなむけ ▶恩師は新郎新婦にはなむけのことばを述べた

は

The former teacher offered his *best wishes* [*kind words of encouragement*] to the bride and groom.

はなむこ 花婿 a **groom**, a **bridegroom**.

はなもちならない 鼻持ちならない **disgusting** (むかつく) ▶あの女はいつも自分がいちばん偉いと思っている**鼻持ちならない**やつだ She *is disgusting* because she always thinks she's better than anyone else. ‖ あいつはきざで**鼻持ちならない** His affected manner *makes* me *sick* [*is nauseating*].

はなやか 華やかな **gorgeous**; **showy** (はでな); **flamboyant** /flæmbɔ́ɪənt/ (色・生活などが) ▶彼女は**華やかな**装いで現れた She appeared in a *gorgeous* [*showy*] dress. ‖ 多くの少年少女が芸能界の**華やかな**生活にあこがれる A lot of boys and girls long for the *flamboyant* life of show business.

はなやぐ 華やぐ **become cheerful** [**bright**].

はなよめ 花嫁 a **bride** (➤ 式を挙げる前までは bride-to-be ともいい, 花婿も bridegroom-to-be ともいう) ▶姉は今**花嫁修業中**です My sister is now learning how to be a good homemaker. / My sister is now learning cooking and other things she needs to know to be a good housewife in the future.

‖**花嫁衣装** a wedding dress, bridal costume.

はならび 歯並び a **set of teeth** ▶あなた, 真っ白ないい**歯並び**してるわね My, you have such (lovely) white, *even teeth*. (➤ even は「凹凸のない」) ‖ 妹は**歯並びが悪い** My sister *has crooked teeth*. (➤ crooked /krʊ́kɪd/ は「曲がった」) ‖ 私は**歯並びを直す**のに矯正具を使っています I wear braces to *have my teeth straightened*. →**八重歯**.

はなれ 離れ ▶**離れ**を増築した We had a new *annex* built to our house. ‖ 祖父母はうちの**離れ**に住んでいます Our grandparents are living in *a small house* that is *detached from the main house*.

‖**離れ島** a remote island.

ばなれ 場慣れ ▶**場慣れ**した司会者 an *experienced* emcee.

▶土井さんは**場慣れ**しているので大勢の前でしゃべっても全然あがらない Mr. Doi doesn't get nervous at all because he *is used to speaking* in front of a great many people.

-ばなれ -離れ ⚠ **「-離れ」にぴったりの対応語はない. この語は文脈によって「疎遠になること」,「興味を失うこと」,「独立すること」,「並以上であること」などのような意味を表すので, 適宜意味をくんで訳す必要がある.**

▶若者の活字**離れ**が進んでいる The younger generation's *dislike for reading* is getting worse. / Young people are *less interested* than ever *in the printed word*. ‖ 最近は**子離れ**できない親が多い Nowadays there are many parents who cannot *detach themselves from their children*. ‖ あのピッチャーの度胸のよさは**新人離れ**している That pitcher's pluck is something *you don't see often in rookies*.

▶久美子は彫りの深い**日本人離れ**した顔だちをしている Kumiko's face has deeply chiseled features, *unlike those of most Japanese*.

はなればなれ 離れ離れ ▶兄弟は人込みの中で**離れ離れ**になった The brothers *got separated* (*from each other*) in the crowd. ‖ 彼は現在妻子と**離れ離れ**に暮らしている He now lives *apart* [*away* / *separately*] *from* his wife and children.

はなれる 離れる **1**【場所などを去る】**leave** +㊐ ▶客船が波止場を**離れた** The passenger ship *left* the harbor. ‖ 故郷を**離れて**から10年になる It has been ten years since I *left* home. ‖ 列を**離れない**でください Don't *fall* [*get*] *out of* line. ‖ 会長は3年前に第一線を**離れ**, 社長に経営の全てを任せている The chairman *left* the front line [*stepped down* from day-to-day management of the company] three years ago and let the president manage the entire company. ‖ ボートをつかんでいた彼女の手が**離れた** She *lost* (her) *hold of* the boat.

2【別々になる】**separate** /sépəreɪt/ ▶2枚の紙はぴったりくっついて**離れなかった** The two sheets of paper stuck fast together and wouldn't *separate* [*come apart*]. ‖ 父は家族と**離れて**大阪で暮らしている My father lives in Osaka *away from* my family. ‖ 私は一生父母の元を**離れ**たくない I don't want to *part from* my parents as long as I live. ‖ 子供たちは大きくなって私の手を**離れ**ました The children have grown up and are *off my hands* now.

3【距離・年齢などがあく】**be away** 《from》(離れている) ▶私の家は駅から500メートル**離れている** My house *is* 500 meters (*away*) *from* the train station. (➤away from の前に距離を示す数字がくると away は省略されることがある) ‖ 私の席は舞台から少し**離れて**いて, 演奏者の顔はよく見えなかった My seat *was* a little *far away from* the stage, so I couldn't see the performers' faces very well. ‖ その少年は3キロ**離れ**た学校に通っている The boy goes to a school three kilometers *away*.

▶駅はここから**遠く離れている** The railroad station *is a long way* (*off*) from here. ‖ ニューヨークとボストンはどのくらい**離れています**か *How far* is New York *from* Boston? ‖ もう少し**離れて**テレビを見なさい Don't watch TV from so close. / *Move back* from the TV (screen). / *Don't* sit *so close* to the TV. ‖ 《エレベーター内などの掲示》ドアから**離れて**お立ちください Stand *clear of* the door. (➤ 電車・列車なら doors と複数形) ‖ (危険物などから)**離れろ**! *Get back!* / *Back off!*

▶父と母は年がだいぶ**離れている** My father is much *older than* my mother. (➤ 英語ではどちらが年上かをはっきりさせるのがふつう. 上の訳例は父が年上の場合) ‖ 兄弟は3つ年が**離れている** These brothers are three years *apart* (in age).

4【関係が薄くなる】▶いつのまにか友人は皆彼から**離れて**(=去って)しまった All of his friends *deserted* him before he knew it. ‖ その代議士は汚職が発覚して支持者が**離れた** When the Dietman's corruption was made public, his supporters *deserted* him. ‖ 浩子の心はいつか道夫から**離れてしまった** Hiroko gradually *lost interest* in Michio.

▶明美のことが頭から**離れない** I *can't get* Akemi *out of my mind*.

はなれわざ 離れ業 a **feat**(偉業); a **stunt** (危険を伴う) ▶その野球選手は3年連続三冠王を取るという**離れ業**をやってのけた That ball player accomplished the *feat* of winning the triple crown for three straight years. ‖ 彼は鉄棒で**離れ業**を演じた He delivered *a spectacular performance* on the horizontal bar.

はなわ 花輪 a **wreath** /riːθ/ (葬儀や祝い事に用いる円形の); a **floral tribute** (日本の葬儀での献花); a **garland** (花冠); a **lei** (レイ) ▶戦没者の墓の前に**花輪**を

供えた We placed *a wreath* on the grave of the war victims.

はにかみや はにかみ屋 ▶私は小学生のころははにかみやだった I was a *shy* [*bashful*] boy when I was in elementary school.

はにかむ **be shy** [**bashful**] ▶由佳はその男の子の前でははにかんで一言も口がきけなかった Yuka *was* so *shy* [*bashful*] with that boy that she couldn't say a word. ‖博満はみんなにほめられてはにかんだ Hiromitsu *looked embarrassed* when he was praised by everyone.

ばにく 馬肉 **horse meat.**

パニック (a) **panic** ▶大地震が起こるといううわさで人々はパニック状態になった People *were thrown into a panic* by the rumor that a big earthquake would occur. ／People *were panicked* [*got panicky*] at the rumor that there would be a big earthquake. (➤ get panicky はインフォーマル).
‖**パニック障害** panic disorder.

バニラ (a) **vanilla** /vənílə/ ▶バニラアイスクリーム *vanilla* ice cream.

はにわ 埴輪 a ***haniwa***; a clay image of a human being or of an animal used in ancient graves, etc (➤ 説明的な訳).

[1]**はね 羽・翅** **1**【翼】a **wing** ▶コンドルは羽を広げると３メートル以上にもなる Condors are more than three meters wide when they spread their *wings*. ／Condors have a wingspan [wingspread] of over three meters. (➤ wingspan, wingspread は「翼幅」).
▶コオロギははねをこすり合わせて鳴き声を出す Crickets chirp by rubbing their *wings* together.
▶《慣用表現》ボーナスは羽が生えたようになくなってしまった My bonus disappeared as though it had *sprouted wings and taken off by itself*. ‖夏休みに実家へ帰省して思い切り羽を伸ばしてきた I went home for my summer vacation and *had a great time*. ‖親が留守だと子供は羽を伸ばすものだ When the parents are away, the children will *play*.
2【羽毛】a **feather**(１本の羽); **down** (柔毛) ▶クジャクが羽を広げたところを見たことがありますか Have you ever seen peacocks spreading their beautiful tail *feathers*?
‖**羽根飾り** a plume ‖**羽根ぶとん** a feather quilt; a down quilt (羽毛ぶとん).

[2]**はね 羽根** a **shuttlecock**(羽根つき・バドミントンの) ▶扇風機の羽根 the *blades* of a fan.
☛ 赤い羽根 (→見出語)

[3]**はね 跳ね** a **splash (of mud)**, a **(mud) spatter** ▶車にはねをかけられた A car *splashed* me *with mud* [*water*]. ‖ズボンにはねがあがった My trousers *were splashed* [*were spattered*] *with mud*.

ばね a **spring** ▶このおもちゃのカエルはばねで跳ぶ This toy frog jumps using *a spring*. ／*A spring* makes this toy frog jump. ‖彼は足腰のばねが強い He's got good *spring* in his legs.
‖**ばねばかり** a spring balance [scale].

はねあがる 跳ね上がる **jump** [**spring**] **up** (飛び上がる); **shoot up**, 《インフォーマル》**skyrocket**(価格・相場などが) ▶カカオの相場が跳ね上がった The cocoa market *has shot up* [*has skyrocketed*].

はねおきる 跳ね起きる ▶ベッドから跳ね起きる *spring out of* bed ‖非常ベルの音に私はベッドから跳ね起きた The sound of the alarm (bell) *made* me *jump out of* bed.

はねかえす 跳ね返す **bounce back** ▶劣勢をはね返す turn the tables／reverse the situation ‖ドラゴンズは５点差をはね返した The Dragons *bounced back from* a 5-run deficit.

はねかえる 跳ね返る **rebound** /rɪbáʊnd/ ▶跳ね返ってくるテニスボールを打つ hit a tennis ball *on the rebound* (➤ on the rebound /ríːbaʊnd/ は「跳ね返ってくるところを」) ‖ボールが左中間のフェンスに当たって跳ね返った The ball *bounced off* [*rebounded from*] the left-center fence.
▶悪いことをすると結局は自分の身に跳ね返ってくるよ If you do something wrong, it will *come back to* [*haunt*] you in the end.

はねつき 羽根つき **battledore and shuttlecock, Japanese badminton** ▶羽根つきをする play *battledore and shuttlecock*.

はねつける **reject** ＋㊐, **turn down**(➤ 後者はややインフォーマル) ▶彼は我々の申し出をはねつけた He *rejected* [*turned down*] our offer. ‖由美は淳のデートの誘いをはねつけた Yumi *gave* Jun *the brush-off* when he asked her (to go) out. (➤ the brush-off は「冷たい拒絶」の意のインフォーマルな言い方).

はねとばす はね飛ばす ▶その老婦人はタクシーにはね飛ばされた The old woman *was hit* [*was knocked down*] by a taxi.
▶横綱は全勝優勝して引退のうわさをはね飛ばした The yokozuna won the championship with a straight win record and *shook off* rumors of his retirement. (➤ shook off は shake off(振りはらう)の過去形).

はねのける **push aside, thrust aside** (➤ 後者がより強力) ▶我々は低木をはねのけながら進んだ We made our way, *pushing* the bushes *aside*. ／We *thrust* our way through the bush. (➤ この thrust は過去形).

はねばし 跳ね橋 a **drawbridge.**

はねまわる 跳ね回る **run and jump around, romp around** [**about**] ▶子供たちが楽しそうに庭で跳ね回っている The children *are* happily *running and jumping around* [*about*] in the garden.

ハネムーン a **honeymoon** /hʌ́nimuːn/ ▶ **対話** 「ハネムーンはどちらへ？」「モーリシャスです」"Where are you going on your *honeymoon*?" "Mauritius."

パネラー a **panelist**(➤「パネラー」は和製語).

パネリスト a **panelist.**

はねる 跳ねる・撥ねる

1【跳ぶ】**jump**(前方または上方へ); **leap** (前方に大きく); **hop** (人が片足で, または動物・鳥が足をそろえてぴょんぴょんと) ▶ときどきコイが池で跳ねた Carp *jumped* in the pond from time to time. ‖カエルが跳ねて池に飛び込んだ A frog *leapt* into the pond. (➤ leapt の発音は /lept/) ‖ウサギが野を跳ねて行った A rabbit *hopped* across the field.
2【飛び散る】**splash**(液体が空中にはね上がる); **spatter**(液体が物の上にはねかかる) ▶服に泥がはねた The mud *splashed* (against) my dress. ‖ペンキがカーペット一面にはねた The paint *spattered* all over the carpet.
3【下から上に勢いよく上がる】▶隣のおじさんのひげはぴんとはねている The man next door has a *pointed* mustache.
4【車ではね飛ばす】**hit** ＋㊐ (ぶつける); **knock down** (はね倒す) ▶うちの猫は車にはねられて死んだ Our cat *was hit* and killed by a car. ‖男はバイクで女の子をはねて逃げた The man on the motorbike *hit*

[*knocked down*] the girl and sped off.

5【首を切る】cut off ▶織田信長は敵方の大将の首をはねた Oda Nobunaga *cut off* the head of the enemy warload.

6【取り除く】▶欠陥製品は最終チェックではねられる Defective products will *be eliminated* in the final check. ‖ 彼は面接ではねられた He *was rejected* in the interview.

7【終わる】▶ショーは11時にはねた The show *ended* [*let out*] at eleven. ‖ 芝居はとっくにはねた The play has *been over* for a while now.

パネル a panel ▶人権問題についてのパネルディスカッションを行う hold *a panel discussion* about human rights problems ‖ **パネルヒーター** a panel heater ‖ **コントロールパネル** a control panel ‖ **ソーラーパネル** a solar panel.

ハノイ Hanoi /hænɔ́i/ (ベトナムの首都).

パノラマ a panorama /pænərǽmə/ ▶展望台からパノラマのような景色を楽しむことができた We enjoyed *a panoramic view* from the observation deck.

はは 母 a **mother** →お母さん ▶母は母らしいことは何もしてくれたことがなかった *My mother* did nothing for me *that a mother should* (do). ‖ 彼女は5年前に母親を亡くした She lost her *mother* five years ago. ‖ あの人は母方の祖父です He is my grandfather *on my mother's side*. ‖ 彼女は19歳で未婚の母となった She became *an unmarried mother* at the age of nineteen. (➤ a single mother ともいうが, この表現は離婚や夫との死別の場合も含む).

▶彼女も今や一児の母だ She's now *a mother of one*. / She now *has one child*. (➤ 後者のほうが英語として自然) ‖ 母は強し Mothers are strong.

[ことわざ] 必要は発明の母 Necessity is the mother of invention.

‖ **母の日** Mother's Day ‖ **生みの母** one's birth [biological] mother ‖ **育ての母** one's foster mother ‖ **まま母** one's stepmother.

はば 幅 width ▶幅の広い川 a *wide* [*broad*] river ‖ 幅の狭い道 a *narrow* road ‖ 幅90センチ長さ180センチのテーブル a table 90 centimeters *in width* and 180 (centimeters) in length / a 90 × 180cm table (➤ × は by と読む) ‖ この冷蔵庫は幅80cmです This refrigerator is 80 centimeters *wide* [*in width*]. (➤ 形容詞を使うのがふつう) ‖ きみの車が通るにはこの道は少し幅が狭いようだ I am afraid this road is a little too *narrow* for your car to pass. ‖ [対話]「この板の幅はどのくらいですか」「50センチです」"*How wide* is this board?" "It's 50 centimeters wide."

▶《慣用表現》あの俳優も結婚してから演技に幅が出てきた That actor *has a broader scope* in his acting since he got married. ‖ 彼はこの村ではなかなか幅をきかせている He is quite *influential* in this village.

☛ 幅広い (→見出語)

パパ a dad, a daddy, a papa ▶はい, パパ. 新聞 Here's the paper, *Dad* [*Daddy*].

> **危ないカタカナ語✸ パパ**
> **1** 英語の papa からだが, この語はイタリア系アメリカ人など一部の人を除いてはあまり使わない. ふつうは dad, daddy という. また呼びかけに使う場合は, 固有名詞扱いにして Dad, Daddy と大文字で始める.
> **2** 女性がパトロンのことを「パパ」と呼ぶことがあるが, 日本独特. ただし, 若い女性や愛人などに盛んに贈り物をする金持ちの, 特に年配の男性のことを sugar daddy というが, これは日本語の「パパ」に似ている.
> **3** 日本では妻が(子供の面前であるとないとにかかわらず)夫に「パパ」と呼びかけることがあるが, 英米では子供の面前を除いて妻が夫に Dad, Daddy と呼びかけることはふつうではない.

パパイア 《植物》 a **papaya**.

ははかた 母方の maternal ▶母方の祖母 a *maternal* grandmother.

はばかる ▶二人は人目もはばからず抱き合っていた They were embracing each other *without regard for* the people around them. ‖ 彼女があまりにも悲しみに沈んでいたので声をかけるのもはばかられた She was so overcome with grief that I *refrained from* speaking to her. (➤ refrain from doing は「遠慮して…するのをやめる」).

はばたき 羽ばたき a **flap**(比較的ゆっくりとした大きな音の); a **flutter**(比較的速い小さな音の) ▶タカは羽ばたきをした The hawk *flapped its wings*.

はばたく 羽ばたく flap [**flutter**] (one's **wings**) ▶ハチドリは1秒間に50〜70回羽ばたく Hummingbirds *flutter their wings* 50 to 70 times per second.

▶《比喩的》日本の多くの若き音楽家たちが世界に羽ばたいている Many young Japanese musicians *are spreading their wings* [*are active*] *around the world*.

はばつ 派閥 a **faction** ▶派閥を解消するのは難しい It is not easy to dissolve [disband] *factions*. ‖ 日本の政治家は派閥争いに明け暮れている Japanese politicians spend day in and day out in *factional strife*.

‖ **派閥政治** factional politics.

はばとび 幅跳び the long jump, 《米また》 **the broad jump** (➤ ともに競技名) ▶我々は砂浜で幅跳びの練習をした We practiced *broad jumping* on the sandy beach.

‖ **立ち幅跳び** the standing broad jump.

はばひろい 幅広い wide, broad ▶T 氏はコラムニストとして連載や講演など幅広い活動を行っている As a columnist, Mr. T is involved in *a wide range of activities* including writing serials and giving lectures. ‖ その政治家は地域の幅広い層から支持されている The politician has *a wide range* of supporters in the community.

はばむ 阻む prevent +㊐ (妨げる); **stop** +㊐, **check** +㊐ (阻止する) ▶デモ隊は機動隊に阻まれて前へ進むことができなかった The demonstrators *were prevented* by the riot police *from* going ahead. (➤ prevent A from doing で「A(人)が…するのを阻む」の意) ‖ その横綱の連勝を阻むのはだれだろう I wonder who will *end* [*stop*] the yokozuna's winning streak.

パパラッチ paparazzi /pɑ̀:pərɑ́:tsi ‖ pæpərǽtsi/ (➤ イタリア語から. 単数形は paparazzo だが通例複数形を用いる).

ババロア Bavarian cream.

はびこる 1【茂って広がる】overrun(草などが) ▶長い旅行から帰って来たら庭に雑草がはびこっていた When I came back from a long trip, the garden *was overgrown* [*was overrun*] *with weeds*.

2【一面に広がる, のさばる】be infested, be rife(病気・害虫など好ましくないものが; 後者は主に文語); **prevail**(流行している) ▶その家には多くのネズミがはびこっていた The house *was infested* with rats. ‖ 中世のヨーロッパにはペストがはびこっていた The plague *was rife* in Europe during the Middle Ages. ‖ あの学校ではいじめがはびこっている Bullying *prevails* in that school.
▶アルコール中毒や銃の存在が暴力をいつまでもはびこらせることになる Alcoholism and guns *perpetuate* violence. (➤ perpetuate は「(好ましくないもの)をいつまでも継続させる」).

パビリオン a **pavilion.**

パフ a (**powder**) **puff.**

パブ a **pub**, a **public house** ▶イギリス人にとってパブは社交の場である The *pub* is a social gathering place for the British.

パフェ a **parfait** /pɑːrféi/ (➤ フランス語から) ▶イチゴのパフェ a strawberry *parfait*.

パフォーマンス (a) **performance** (演奏・性能) (➤ performance は「演奏, 演技, 性能」などの意では「パフォーマンス」と一致するが,「人に注目されるための行動」は日本語独自の使い方) ▶あれはあの政治家得意のパフォーマンスだ That's the politician's favorite *ploy to impress people*.

はぶく 省く **omit** +㊐, **leave out** (削る) ; **save** +㊐ (節約する) ▶この部分を省いても文の意味はつながる If you *omit* [*leave out*] this part, the sentence will still make sense. ‖ ワープロソフトは清書の手間を省いてくれる A word processor program *saves* the trouble of typing a fair copy. ‖ エアコンを止めてエネルギーの無駄を省こう Let's turn off the air conditioner to *save* energy. ‖ 時間の無駄を省きなさい *Don't waste* (your) time.

ハプニング ▶卒業式の最中にハプニングが起こった *Something unexpected* happened during the graduation ceremony.

> **危ないカタカナ語✸ ハプニング**
> 1 計画的に進められている式や催し物などの最中に起こる思いがけない出来事のことを「ハプニング」といっているが, 英語の happening は単に「出来事, 事件」の意であり, 日本語の「ハプニング」に含まれる意外性のニュアンスはない.
> 2 演劇用語としての happening は劇の筋とは無関係な即興的演技(観客の飛び入り参加もある)をいう.

はブラシ 歯ブラシ a **toothbrush** ▶歯ブラシで歯を磨く brush [clean] one's teeth with *a toothbrush*(➤ 単に brush one's teeth でもよい).

はぶり 羽振り ▶おじは最近なかなかはぶりがいいようだ It looks like my uncle is quite *well off* [*prosperous* / *influential*] these days. ‖ 彼は財界ではぶりをきかせている He is a very *influential* figure in the business world.

パプリカ **paprika** /pəpríːkə ‖ pǽprɪkə/.

バブル 《経済学》a **bubble** ▶バブルがはじけて日本経済は大幅に縮小した Japan's economy shrank considerably after its *bubble* burst.
‖バブル経済 the bubble economy, the economic bubble.

はへい 派兵する **send troops** ▶日本は海外派兵を要請された Japan was requested to *send troops overseas*.

はへん 破片 a (**broken**) **piece**, a **fragment** ▶小石がぶつかって窓ガラスが割れ, 破片があたり一面に飛び散った A stone hit and broke the windowpane and *pieces* [*fragments*] of glass flew all over the place.

ハボタン 《植物》an **ornamental cabbage**, a **flowering kale.**

はまき 葉巻 a **cigar** /sɪgɑ́ːr/ ▶葉巻をくゆらす smoke *a cigar*.

はまぐり 蛤 a **clam** 《参考》clam はハマグリを含む食用となる二枚貝の総称.

ハマチ 《魚》a **young yellowtail.**

ハマナス 《植物》a **rugosa rose.**

はまべ 浜辺 **the beach** ; **the** (**sea**)**shore** (水に接する部分) ▶浜辺を散歩する walk along *the beach* ‖ 子供たちが浜辺で貝殻を拾って遊んでいた Some children were having fun picking up shells *on the beach* [*seashore*].

はまや 破魔矢 a ***hamaya*** ; an arrow you can get at a Shinto shrine or a Buddhist temple during the New Year holiday to ward off evil (➤ 説明的な訳).

はまりやく はまり役 **the best-suited role** ▶刑事コロンボはピーター・フォークのはまり役だった Peter Falk *was suited* [*was the right person*] *for the role* of Lieutenant Columbo.

はまる **1【ぴったり入る, 合う】fit** (+㊐) ▶コルク栓は瓶にぴったりはまった The cork *fit* the bottle perfectly. ‖ 指が太くなって指輪がはまらなくなった My finger has gotten fatter and the ring won't *fit*. ‖ ふすまを外したらはまらなくなった We took off the *fusuma* sliding doors, but couldn't *get* them back *on* again.
▶ブラウスのボタンがうまくはまらない The blouse won't *button* (up). (➤ この button は動詞).
2【条件・考え方などが合う】fit (+㊐) ▶この志望者はわが社の条件にぴったりはまる This candidate *fits* the needs of our company perfectly.
3【落ち込む】▶車がぬかるみにはまってしまった My car *got stuck* [*got caught*] *in* the mud. ‖ 敵はまんまと我々のわなにはまった The enemy *has fallen into the trap* [*for the trick*] easily.
▶《比喩的》このところ弟はラップにはまっている My (younger) brother *is into* [*is hooked on* / *is addicted to*] rap these days. (➤ be addicted は「中毒になっている」で, やや非難のニュアンス).

はみがき 歯磨き **tooth-brushing** (歯をみがくこと) ; **toothpaste** (練り歯みがき) ▶食べたあとは歯みがきを忘れずに Don't forget to *brush your teeth* after eating.

はみだす はみ出す **stick out** 《of, from》 ▶ふとんから息子の足がはみ出している My son's feet *are sticking out from* the bottom of the futon. ‖ 講演に聴衆が大勢押しかけてホールからはみ出す人たちもいた So many people gathered to hear the lecture that some *were pushed out of* the hall.

ハミング **humming** 一㊍ **ハミングする hum** /hʌm/ (+㊐) ▶歌詞を思い出せなかったのでハミングした The lyrics had slipped my memory, so I *hummed the tune*.

ハム **1【食品の】ham** ▶ハム1枚 a slice of *ham* ‖ 朝食にハムエッグを食べた I had *ham and eggs* for breakfast. (➤ ham eggs とはしない) ‖ ハムサンドはいかがですか Would you care for *a ham sandwich*?
2【アマチュア無線家】a **ham**, a **ham radio operator.**

はむかう 刃向かう **stand up** 《to, against》 ▶彼以外誰も上司には刃向かわなかった No one except him *stood up to* the boss. ‖ あんな乱暴者に刃向かうのはよしなさい You'd better not *get into a fight* with such a violent man. (➤「けんかを始める」の意).

は

ハムスター《動物》a **hamster**.

はめ 羽目 1【好ましくない事態】▶軽いうちに虫歯を治療しなかったばかりに長期間歯医者に通うはめになった Since I didn't get my cavities taken care of while they were small, I *had to* make regular trips to the dentist's office for a long time.

2【慣用表現】▶試験が終わった解放感から私たちははめをはずして騒ぎまくった Feeling free after the test, we *let ourselves go* and partied hardy. (➤ let oneself go は「思い切り自由にふるまう」, party hardy は「気を失うまで飲み騒ぐ」) ‖ 夏休みだからってあんまりはめをはずすとあとで後悔するよ You will regret it later if you *let yourself go* too much even if you're on summer vacation.

はめこむ はめ込む **inlay** /ìnléɪ/ +目 (象眼材料・模様などを); **set** +目 (宝石などを); **fit** +目 (ジグソーパズルなどを) ▶彼女はぬいぐるみの目にガラス玉をはめ込んだ She *inlaid* a couple of beads into the eyes of the stuffed animal. (➤ inlaid は inlay の過去形) ‖ 彼はそのジグソーパズルを簡単にはめ込んだ He *fitted together* the pieces of the jigsaw puzzle easily.

はめつ 破滅 **ruin** 一動 破滅する **be ruined, ruin oneself** ▶彼はギャンブルで身の破滅を招いた He *ruined himself* by gambling. ／Gambling was his ruin. (➤ 後者の ruin は「破滅の原因」の意) ‖ そんなぜいたくを続けていたら身の破滅だぞ You'll *be ruined* if you go on living so extravagantly.

はめる 嵌める 1【ぴったり入れる，取りつける】**put in** [**on**], **fit** +目 ▶窓にガラスをはめる *put* a pane of glass *in* a window ‖ 自転車(の車輪)に新しいタイヤをはめた I *put* [*fitted*] a new tire *on* my bicycle. ‖ 花婿は花嫁の指に金の指輪をはめた The groom *put* the gold ring *on* the finger of the bride. ‖ 背中のボタン，はめてくれる？ Would you *do up the buttons* at the back (of my dress)?

▶子供を一定の型にはめてしまう教育は間違っていると思う I think (that) education that *pushes* [*forces*] children *into a set mold* is wrong.

2【身につける】**put on**; **wear** +目 (つけている) ▶手袋をはめる *put* [*pull*] *on* one's gloves ‖ 花嫁は白い手袋をはめていた The bride *wore* [*was wearing*／*was in*] white gloves.

3【だます】**set up**; **frame** +目 (罪を着せる) ▶俺は悪くない. はめられたんだ I'm not to blame—I *was set up*. ‖ きみはやつらにはめられたんだよ You'*ve been framed* by them. ‖ ちきしょう，はめやがったな Damn it! *You cheated me!*

ばめん 場面 a **scene** (劇・映画の) ▶その映画の最後の場面に私は深く感動した I was deeply moved by the last *scene* of the movie. ‖ それは心に残る場面だった It was an unforgettable *scene*.

1**はもの 刃物** an **edged tool**, a **cutting tool** [**instrument**].

2**はもの 端物** an **odd piece**; **odds and ends** (がらくた類).

ハモる **harmonize** one's **voice** ▶ここで皆さんがハモってください Please *sing in harmony* here. ‖ 我々の歌声がきれいにハモった Our (singing) voices *harmonized* beautifully.

1**はもん 波紋** a **water ring**; a **ripple** (さざ波) ▶カエルが池に飛び込んで波紋が広がった A frog jumped into the pond and the *ripples* spread across the water.

▶《慣用表現》その裁判の結果は大きな波紋を巻き起こした The outcome of the trial *created a big stir* [*had great repercussions*].

2**はもん 破門** (an) **excommunication** (キリスト教会からの) 一動 破門する **oust** /aʊst/ +目, **expel** +目 (追放する); **excommunicate** +目 ▶師匠は彼を破門した The master *ousted* him as a disciple. ／The master *expelled* him from school. ‖ ルターは教会から破門された Luther *was excommunicated from* the church. ／Luther *was driven out* [*was expelled*] *from* the church.

はやあし 早足 a **brisk walk** ▶そんなに早足で歩かないで. あなたについていくのが大変よ Don't walk so *fast*. It's hard to keep up with you.

1**はやい 早い** **early** (➤「遅い」は late) 一副 早く **early** (時間・時期が); **quickly** (すばやく，すぐに); **soon** (ある時点からあまり時をおかないで) ▶(朝の)早い電車に乗る catch an *early* train ‖ 母はいつも朝が早い Mother always gets up *early* (in the morning). ‖ 寝るには[あきらめるのは]まだ早い It's still too *early* to go to bed [to give up]. ‖ 酒を始めるのはまだ早すぎるぞ You're still *too young* to drink. (➤ 未成年者に) ／It's *too soon* for you to drink. (➤ 病後の人などに) ‖ 早いとこ頼む Do it *quickly*.

▶ 対話「いつにしましょうか」「早ければ早いほどいいね」"When will it be convenient for you?" "*The sooner, the better*." ‖ 子供の悪習慣は早いうちに芽を摘んだほうがよい A bad habit in a child should *be nipped in the bud*. (➤ nip A in the bud は「Aをつぼみのうちに摘み取る」; 比喩的には「事(A)を未然に防ぐ」).

▶早いところ医者に見せたほうがいいよ You'd better see a doctor *as soon as possible* [*before it's too late*]. (➤ 後者は「手遅れにならないうちに」) ‖ 早い話が，私の提案は受け入れられなかったのだ *To make a long story short* [*In short*], my proposal was rejected.

✉ **早いものでヨーロッパから帰ってまもなく1年になります** *Time passes so quickly!* It'll soon be one year since I came back from Europe.

▶父は朝早く仕事に出かける My father leaves for work *early in the morning*. ‖ 早く帰って来なさい Come back *early*. ／Don't be long. ‖ 学校に早く着き過ぎた I got to school too *early*. ‖ きょうは当番なのでいつもより30分早く登校した I came to school *30 minutes earlier* than usual because I am on duty today. ‖ もっと早くに言ってくれればよかったのに You should have talked to me about it *earlier*.

▶《病気見舞いで》早くよくなってね Get well *soon*. ‖ 早く夏休みにならないかなあ I wish summer vacation would come *sooner*. ‖ 早く来い来いお正月！ *Roll in* the New Year! ‖ 早くしろ Hurry up. ／(Be) quick. ／Make it snappy. ‖ 早く来て！ Come *quick* [*quickly*]! (➤ くだけた話しことばでは quick を使うことが多い).

✉ **早くあなたにお会いしたいです** I *can hardly wait to* see you.

✉ **なるべく早くお返事ください** I am looking forward to hearing from you *soon*. ／I am waiting for your *prompt* reply. ➤ 後者は主に商用文で.

☛ 早くても，早くも (→見出語)

2**はやい 速い** **fast** (運動・速度が); **quick** (動作などがすばやい，機敏な); **rapid** (動作・流れの速さなどが) (➤「遅い」は slow) 一副 速く **fast, quickly, rapidly** ▶速い電車 a *fast* train ‖ 子供は覚える

のが速い Children learn *fast*. ／Children catch on *quickly*. ‖グリーンさんは足が速い Greene walks [runs] *fast*. ／Greene is a *fast* walker [runner]. ‖彼女は計算[飲み込み]が速い She is *quick* at figures [to understand]. ‖この川は流れが速い This river flows *swiftly* [*fast*／*rapidly*]. ‖彼はいつも仕事が速い He always gets his work done *speedily*. ‖チーターは地球上でいちばん足の速い動物だ Cheetahs are *the fastest* animals on earth. ‖きみは足が速過ぎてついていけないよ You walk *too fast* for me to keep up.

▶ジョギングは速く走る必要はない You don't have to run *fast* when you jog. ‖もっと(ピッチを)速く泳いでごらん Try to swim more *quickly*. ‖流れが速く，川を渡るのをあきらめた The river flowed so *rapidly* we gave up trying to cross it.

はやいものがち 早い者勝ち **First come, first served.** 《参考》「早く来た者が早くもてなしを受ける」という意味のことわざであるが，普通の英文に書き替えると He [The person] who comes first will be served first. となる ▶100台限定のデジカメです．早い者勝ちですので，今すぐご連絡ください We can offer the digital camera to the first 100 people. It's *first-come, first-served*. So please contact us immediately.

はやうまれ 早生まれ (● 4月から始まる日本の学制から生まれた表現なので，例文のように意味をくんで訳すしかない) ▶私は早生まれだ I *was born* (*early in the year*) *between January 1 and April 1*.

はやおき 早起き **early rising** 一動 **早起きする** **get up early** ▶祖父母は早起きだ My grandparents *get up early*. ／My grandparents *are* both *early risers*. ‖家族でいちばんの早起きは誰ですか Who *gets up earliest* in your family?

ことわざ 早起きは三文の得 The early riser gains three *mon*. (➤日本語からの直訳) ／The early bird catches the worm. 《参考》「早起きの人」をインフォーマルな英語ではおどけて early bird という．

はやおくり 早送り **fast-forward** 一動 **早送りする** **fast-forward** (+⑬) ▶早送りのボタンを押す push [press] the *fast-forward* (button) ‖DVD[テープ]を早送りする *fast-forward* a DVD [tape] ‖早送りでコマーシャルを飛ばす *fast-forward through* commercials.

はやがてん 早合点 ▶彼は早合点する傾向がある He tends to *jump to conclusions* [*make hasty decisions*]. ‖明夫は私が裏切ったと早合点した Akio *jumped to the* (*wrong*) *conclusion* that I had betrayed him.

はやく 端役 **a bit [small] part**; **a walk-on (part [role])** (➤せりふのない「通行人」の役) ▶彼女はその芝居で端役を演じた She played *a bit* [*small*] *part* in that play.

はやくち 早口 ▶伊藤さんは早口だ Mr. Ito *speaks* (too) *fast*. ‖そのアメリカ人は早口だったので言っていることがよくわからなかった The American *spoke* so *fast* that I could not understand him.

‖**早口ことば** a tongue twister.

はやくても 早くても **at (the) earliest** ▶出来上がりは早くても今月の末になります It will be completed at the end of this month *at the earliest*.

はやくも 早くも ▶1863年には早くもロンドンで地下鉄が営業を開始した *As early as* in 1863, the underground railway began service in London. ‖そのコンサートの入場券は発売後10分で早くも売り切れた Ten minutes after they went on sale, the concert tickets were *already* sold out.

はやげこう 早下校 **early dismissal [release]** ▶早下校の日 an *early dismissal* [*release*] day.

はやさ 速さ **speed** ▶ハチドリはすごい速さではばたく The humming bird flutters its wings at an incredible *speed*.

はやざき 早咲きの **early(-flowering)** ▶早咲きのグラジオラス an *early* gladiolus.

[1]**はやし 林** a **wood** (➤しばしば複数形で the woods); a **grove** (木立ち); a **forest** (広大な森林) ▶カラマツの林 a larch *grove* ‖家の裏手に松林がある There is *a pine wood* [*grove*] behind our house. (➤広大な松林は pine forest).

[2]**はやし 囃子** ***hayashi***; accompanying music in Japanese performing arts such as Noh and Kabuki (➤説明的な訳).

はやしたてる 囃し立てる **jeer, hoot**; **tease** +⑬ (善意で口笛を吹いたりして) ▶闘牛士がしくじるたびに観客は盛んにはやし立てた Each time the matador made a mistake, the spectators *jeered* [*hooted*／*hooted at*] him.

はやじに 早死に an **early death** ▶いとこの早死には働き過ぎのためだ My cousin's *early death* was brought on by overwork. ‖祖父は早死にしたとのことだ I'm told my grandfather *died young*.

ハヤシライス ***hayashi-raisu***; small pieces of sliced beef, onion and button mushrooms simmered in a demiglace sauce served with rice (➤説明的な訳).

[1]**はやす 生やす** **grow** +⑬ ▶彼は口ひげを生やし始めた He began to *grow* a mustache. 《参考》「生やしている」という状態を表す場合は grow でなく have を用いる. wear を用いると「つけひげをつけている」ともとれる.

[2]**はやす 囃す** **make fun of** (冷やかす); **cheer** +⑬ (声援する) ▶クラスメートから彼女との仲をはやされた My school friends *made fun of* my friendship [relationship] with her.

▶その年配の女性が歌を歌い始めると聴衆は手拍子ではやした When the elderly woman started to sing, the audience *urged* her *on* [the audience *encouraged* her] by keeping time by clapping their hands.

はやてまわし 早手回し ▶彼は早手回しに私のタクシーを手配してくれた He made arrangements for a taxi to pick me up *ahead of time*.

はやとちり 早とちり ▶彼はときどき早とちりしてへまをやる He sometimes *jumps the gun* [*jumps to conclusions*] and makes a mistake. (➤jump the gun は「(競技で)フライングする」が原義).

はやね 早寝する **go to bed early** ▶私は早寝早起きを心がけている I try to *go to bed and get up early* [*keep early hours*]. (➤keep early hours は一般的な表現ではない) 《参考》「早寝する人」のことを early-to-bed person という.

はやのみこみ 早呑み込み ▶彼は人の言うことを最後まで聞かないで早のみ込みしてしまう傾向がある He *jumps to conclusions* before you finish what you have to say.

はやばや 早々 ▶息子は早々と宿題を済ませて遊びに行ってしまった My son finished his homework *quickly* and went out to play. ‖早々と招待状をありがとう Thanks for such an *early* invitation.

はやばん 早番 ▶あすは早番ですから早く寝ようと思っています I'm *on the early shift* tomorrow, so I think I'll go to bed early. (➤shift は「(勤務の)交替」).

はやびけ 早引けする leave early ▶頭痛がひどいので早引けしてもいいでしょうか Could I *leave early*? I have a terrible headache.

ハヤブサ (鳥) a peregrine falcon.

はやまる 早まる·速まる 1【よく考えずに行動する】▶早まったことをするな! Don't *be hasty*! ‖ 結婚を早まるな Don't get married *hastily*. ／Don't *rush into* marriage. ‖ 早まった判断をすることは非常に危険だ It's very dangerous to *make a hasty* [*snap*] *judgment*. (➤ snap は「即座の」).

2【時期や速度が早くなる】▶この調子なら完成は2, 3日早まるだろう At this rate, we should finish two or three days *early* [*earlier than expected*]. ‖ ことしは修学旅行の日程が早まった The date of our school trip this year has *been moved up* [*been advanced*].

▶ 30キロ付近を過ぎてから先頭を行くランナーたちのペースはますます速まった After 30 kilometers, the lead runners *picked up* their pace. (➤ pick up は「(スピードを)上げる」).

はやみち 早道 ▶学校への早道(＝近道)を見つけたよ I've found *a shortcut* to school.

▶ゴルフに上達する早道はありませんか Isn't there *an easy way* to rapidly improve my golf game?

はやみみ 早耳 ▶彼女は早耳で, 会社の出来事は何でも知っている She is always *up on the latest news* and knows everything that's going on in the office.

はやめ 早めに early (早く) ▶私はきょう早めの昼食をとった I had an *early* lunch today. ‖ きょうは早めに切り上げよう Let's call it a day *earlier than usual*.

はやめる 早める·速める advance ＋㊐, move up (繰り上げる) ; quicken ＋㊐ (急がせる) ▶先生はレポート提出の締め切り日を2日早めた Our teacher *advanced* the deadline for the papers (to be turned in) by a couple of days. ‖ 来日をひと月早められますか Can you *move up* your visit to Japan by one month?

▶友達からの手紙が少女の病気回復を早めた(＝助けた) The letters from her friends *helped* the little girl get well faster.

▶雨が降り出したので彼女は足を速めた She *quickened* her pace because it had started raining. ‖ 列車は速度を速めた The train *speeded up* [*gathered speed*].

はやり 流行 (a) fashion; a fad (一時的な) 一形 はやりの fashionable ▶男性の短髪が今はやりである Short hair for men *is* now *in fashion* [*in style* now]. ／Short hair for men *is in* now. (➤ in を強く発音する) ‖ 服装にははやりすたりがある Clothes are subject to *changes in fashion*. ／Clothes *go in and out of fashion*. ／Fashions in clothes come and go.
‖ はやりことば a vogue word [phrase].

はやりめ はやり目 《医学》 conjunctivitis, pinkeye.

1**はやる 流行る 1【流行する】** come into fashion; catch on 《with》 (歌などが) ; be in fashion, be popular (はやっている) ▶来年はどんな水着がはやるのか見当がつかない I have no idea what kind of bathing suit will *come into fashion* next year. ‖ ことしは黒がはやっている Black *is popular* [*is in*] this year. (➤ ライフスタイルや小物などには単に be in を使うことが多い).

▶ルーズソックスはもうはやらない Loose [Baggy] socks are *out of style* now.

✉ あなたの国では今どんなファッションがはやっていますか What kind of fashions *are popular* in your country?

2【病気が流行する】▶この冬は悪性の流感がはやっている There's a bad flu *going around* this winter.

3【繁盛する】▶このレストランはこの頃はやっている This restaurant *is attracting a lot of customers* these days. (➤「多くの客をひきつけている」の意) ／This restaurant *is doing good business* these days. ‖ あの医者[弁護士]はよくはやる That doctor [lawyer] *has a large practice*. (● 医者の場合は has a lot of patients, 弁護士の場合は has a lot of clients としてもよい).

2**はやる 逸る** ▶はやる気持ちを抑える control one's *eagerness* ‖ 血気にはやる若者たちが取っ組み合いを始めた Some *hot-blooded* young men began to grapple.

はやわざ 早業·早技 ▶彼は目にもとまらぬ早業でトランプの手品をした He performed a card trick *as quickly as lightning* [*quicker than the eye could follow*].

はら 腹 1【腹部】 the stomach /stʌ́mək/ ; the belly (➤ 人間の腹部を指す場合, stomach に比べて下品な語とされる) ▶腹が痛い I have a stomachache. ‖ どうも腹が張る My *stomach* feels bloated [heavy]. ‖ 父は腹が出ている My father's *stomach* sticks out. ／My father has a *protruding belly* [*spare tire*]. (➤ spare tire (予備タイヤ)は腹の回りに脂肪がついている状態をおどけて言ったもの) ‖ 私は腹が出てきた I'm *getting big around the waist*. ‖ 腹いっぱい食べなさい Eat *as much as you want*. ／Eat your fill.

▶腹がいっぱいだ[減った] I'm full [hungry]. (➤ もっと強調して言えば I'm stuffed [starved].) ‖ さっきのケーキが腹にもたれている That cake *sits* [*lies*] *heavy* in my stomach. (➤ 固い文章表現. 日常的にはこのような状況を I'm still full from that cake. (あのケーキを食べてまだお腹がいっぱいだ) で表す).

▶食べ過ぎて腹をこわした I overate and *upset my stomach*. ‖ 腹が減っては軍ができぬ You can't fight (a battle) on an empty stomach. (➤ 日本語からの直訳) ／Have a meal before you get down to work. (➤「本腰を入れる前に食事をせよ」の意).

▶ (料理で) まず, サケの腹を開きます First, we will cut open the *belly* of the salmon.
‖ 下腹 the lower abdomen [belly] ‖ 横[脇]腹 the side, the flank.

2【本心, 心の中】▶やつらは金を受け取ったら逃げる腹だ They *are going to* run away after getting the money. ‖ 彼はにこにこ笑ってはいるが, 腹ではどう思っているか知れたものではない In spite of his smiling appearance, you can't tell what he is thinking *deep down* (*inside*). ‖ あの社長の腹の中はわからない I don't understand *what* the president *is thinking* [*has in mind*].

3【慣用表現】 腹が黒い ▶あいつは腹が黒い He is *evil-minded*. (→腹黒い). 腹がすわる ▶渋沢さんは腹のすわった人物だ Mr. Shibusawa is a *resolute* [*determined*] man. (➤ resolute は「決心の堅い」, determined は「意志の堅い」). 腹が立つ ▶深夜の自動車騒音には腹が立つ The traffic noise late at night *drives* me *crazy*. ‖ こんなばかげたミスをした自分に腹が立つ I'*m angry* at myself [I *could kick myself*] for making such a stupid mistake. (➤ could kick myself は「自分をけとばしたいくらいだ」) 腹が太い ▶木村君は腹が太い Mr. Kimura is *big-*

hearted [*broad-minded*]. ／Mr. Kimura isn't bothered by small things. (➤前者は「寛容だ」, 後者は「小さいことに思い悩まない」の意).
腹に一物 ▶彼は腹に一物といったタイプの男ではない He's not the type who *is* always *up to something* [who *has something up his sleeve*]. **腹におさめる** ▶この話は私だけの腹におさめておこう I'll *keep* what we talked about *to myself* [*under my hat*]. **腹にすえかねる** ▶不公平税制は腹にすえかねる(＝もうがまんできない) I *can't stand* [*can't stomach*] the unfair tax system. **腹の虫** ▶彼が間違っていることを証明するまでは腹の虫がおさまらない(＝満足できない) I *won't be satisfied* until I prove him wrong. ‖ あんなことを言われては腹の虫がおさまらない I *can't swallow* [*stomach*] such humiliation. (➤「そんな屈辱は我慢できない」の意).
腹を抱える ▶彼の冗談に私たちは腹を抱えて笑った We *laughed so hard* at his joke we had to *hold our sides*. (➤ side は「わき腹」). **腹を決める** ▶彼はシーズン途中で引退する腹を決めた He *made up his mind* to retire in the middle of the season. **腹を探る** ▶彼らはお互いに腹を探り合っている They are *sounding out* each other's *intentions*. **腹をすえる** ▶海賊版ＤＶＤの取り締まりは腹をすえてかからなくてはだめだ If you're going to crack down on pirated DVDs, you have to go about it *with determination*. **腹を立てる** ▶私たちの担任の先生はすぐに腹を立てる Our homeroom teacher *gets angry* [*upset*] easily. (➤前者は「かんかんに怒る」, 後者は「気を悪くする」の意). **腹を読む** ▶相手チームの監督の腹を読むのは難しい It is difficult to *know what* the other team's manager *is thinking*. **腹を割る** ▶腹を割って話そうじゃないか Let's talk *straight* with each other. (➤この straight は「率直に, ありのままに」の意)／Let's speak *frankly* with each other.

¹ばら 薔薇 《植物》a **rose** ▶バラにはとげがある *Roses* have thorns.
▶きみの将来はばら色だ(＝明るい) Your future *looks bright* [*rosy*]. ‖ 結婚生活はいつもばら色とは限らない Married life is not always *a bed of roses*. (➤ a bed of roses は「安楽な生活」).

²ばら ▶ぼくは小銭はいつもばらでポケットに入れている I always carry my small change *loose* in my pocket. ‖ 彼女は赤と緑の絵の具をばらで買った She bought red and green paints *separately* [*loose*]. ‖ すみません. このティーカップはばらではお売りできません Sorry. We don't sell these teacups *by the piece*.

バラード a **ballad** /bǽləd/ (感傷的なラブソング；物語詩)；**ballade** /bəlɑ́ːd/ (フランス起源の詩形；ピアノ曲) ▶ラブバラード a love *ballad*.

はらい 払い **payment** ▶現金払い cash *payment* ‖ 分割払い *payment* in installments ‖ あの客は払いが悪い That customer is bad about *paying*.

はらいおとす 払い落とす **shake ... off** (振って)；**brush ... off** [**away, down**] (ブラシ・手で) ▶カーペットのほこりを払い落とす *shake* the dirt *off* [*from*] the carpet ‖ 彼は上着の背中についたふけを手で払い落とした He *brushed* dandruff *off* the back of his jacket with his hands.

はらいこむ 払い込む **pay** ＋目；**deposit** ＋目 (銀行に) ▶税金を払い込む *pay* a tax ‖ 私の口座に１万円払い込んでください Please *deposit* ten thousand yen into my account. ‖ 通信販売で買った枕の代金を口座振替で払い込んだ I *paid* for the pillow that I had mail-ordered *by bank transfer*. (➤「買う」は buy だが, buy は支払いを含意するので, この文を that I had bought by mail order ... とすることはできない).

はらいさげる 払い下げる **sell off** (安く売り払う) ▶その国立病院は民間企業に払い下げられた The national hospital *has been sold off* to a private business.

はらいせ 腹いせ ▶彼女は父親にしかられた腹いせにいすをけ飛ばした After she was scolded by her father, she *took her frustration out on* the chair by kicking it. (➤ take one's frustration out on は「…に八つ当たりする」).

はらいのける 払いのける **brush aside** [**away**] ▶彼女はハエを手で払いのけた She *brushed away* a fly with her hand. ‖ 触ろうとしたら彼女はぼくの手を払いのけた When I tried to touch her, she *brushed* my hand *aside*.

はらいもどし 払い戻し (a) **refund** /ríːfʌnd/ (➤「払戻金」の意もある)；a **rebate** /ríːbeɪt/ (税金などの) ▶チケットの(全額)払い戻し *a* (*full*) *refund* of the price of a ticket ‖ 税金の払い戻しを受ける get a tax *refund* [*rebate*] ‖ このチケットは払い戻しができない This ticket is *nonrefundable*.

はらいもどす 払い戻す **pay back, refund** /rɪfʌ́nd/ ＋目 ▶このチケット(の代金), 払い戻してもらえます? Could you *refund* my payment on [for] this ticket? (➤ refund this ticket とはいえない)／Can I *get a refund* on [for] this ticket? (➤ get a refund /ríːfʌnd/ は「払い戻しを受ける」) ‖ 特急料金は請求により払い戻しいたします Express fares will *be refunded* on request.

はらう 払う **1【金を】pay** ＋目 ▶現金で払う *pay cash, pay in* [*by*] *cash* ‖ 小切手[カード]で払う *pay* by check [credit card]

> **【文型】**
> **人(A)に金額(B)を払う**
> **pay** A B／**pay** B **to** A
> **物(A)の代金を払う**
> **pay for** A
> **物(A)の代金(B)を払う**
> **pay** B **for** A

▶ベビーシッターに時間当たり2000円を払っています We *pay* our babysitter 2,000 yen an hour. ‖ 会費は井上君に払ってください Please *pay* your dues *to* Inoue. ‖ そのソファーにいくら払ったの? How much did you *pay for* that couch?
▶大学卒業までは子供の教育費を払うのは親の義務と思っています I think it's our duty to *pay for* our children's education until they graduate from college. ‖ 父はこのつぼに50万円も払った My father *paid* a whopping half a million yen for the vase. (➤ whopping は「目ん玉が飛び出るほどの途方もない(金額の)」).
▶お貸ししたお金, あすまでに払ってください Please *pay back* the money I lent you by tomorrow. (➤ pay back は「(借金などを)返す」) ‖ 勘定は私が払うよ *I'll pay.*／*I'll* [*Let me*] *take care of that.*
2【注意などを】pay ▶カロリーだけでなく栄養のバランスにももっと注意を払いなさい *Pay* more *attention to* nutritional balance as well as calories. ‖ 彼は細心の注意を払って彫刻の仕上げをした He completed the sculpture *with* scrupulous *attention* to detail.
3【取り除く】brush ... away [**off**] (ブラシなどで) ▶アブを手で払う *brush away* a horsefly with one's hand ‖ 枝をはらう *lop off* a branch ‖ 机のほこりを払い

は

なさい *Brush* [*Dust*] *off* your desk.

バラエティー variety /vəráɪəṭi/ ▶ことしの新入部員は個性的なのが多くバラエティーに富んでいる The new members this year *have* unique personalities and *a wide variety of experience and skills*.

‖**バラエティーショー** a variety show, 《米また》vaudeville /vɔ́:dəvɪl/.

はらぐあい 腹具合 ▶腹ぐあいが悪いのでケーキは食べたくない I don't feel like eating cake because I'*m having stomach trouble* [I *have an upset stomach*].

パラグアイ Paraguay(南米中部の国)

‖**パラグアイ人** a Paraguayan.

パラグライダー a paraglider /pǽrəglaɪdəʳ/ (器具); paragliding(飛ぶこと).

パラグラフ a paragraph(段落).

はらぐろい 腹黒い black-hearted; evil-minded (悪意のある); scheming /skí:mɪŋ/ (計略をめぐらす); insidious (人をだまそうとしている) ▶腹黒い人 a *black-hearted* [an *evil-minded* ／a *scheming* ／an *insidious*] person.

はらげい 腹芸 *haragei*; silent communications, implicit understanding(➤ 説明的な訳).

ばらける ▶ばらけた髪を束ねてまとめる tie up one's *disheveled* hair ‖ 古新聞がばらけないようにひもで縛る tie up old newspapers with string so that they do*n't come loose* ‖ マラソンの先頭集団がばらけた The leading group in the marathon *broke up*.

はらごしらえ 腹ごしらえ ▶本番の前に腹ごしらえをしておこう Let's *eat something* [*get some food in our stomachs*] to prepare ourselves for the big event.

はらごなし 腹ごなし ▶《昼食のあと》腹ごなしに散歩に行こう Let's take a walk to *walk off* our lunch.

パラサイト a parasite /pǽrəsaɪt/

‖**パラサイトシングル** a single person in their late 20s to early 40s who lives with his or her parents and is financially dependent on them while enjoying a comfortable lifestyle (➤「パラサイトシングル」は和製語).

パラシュート a parachute /pǽrəʃu:t/ ▶飛行機からパラシュートで降下する jump from an airplane with *a parachute* ／parachute from an airplane ‖ 救援物資をパラシュートで落とす drop relief supplies *by parachute*.

1**はらす 晴らす** clear +㊐ (疑いなどを) ▶私は友人にかけられた疑いを晴らすために一生懸命に説明した I did my best to explain things to help *clear* the suspicion laid on my friend.

▶真犯人が現れて那須さんは無実の罪を晴らすことができた The real culprit appeared, and Mr. Nasu succeeded in *clearing himself of* the false charge. ‖ 憂さを晴らしに海岸へドライブに出かけた We went for a spin in the car along the beach *to forget about our blues*. ／We went for a drive along the beach *to raise our spirits* [*to cheer ourselves up*].

2**はらす 腫らす** ▶顔をはらしたボクサーは見るも痛々しかった It was painful to see the boxer with *a swollen face*.

ばらす **1**【分解する】take ... apart ▶その子はおもちゃをばらして中を調べた The kid *took* the toy *apart* [*to pieces*] to see what was inside.

2【暴露する】blow the whistle 《on》 ▶言うとおりにしないとおまえの秘密をばらすぞ Do as I tell you, or I'll *blow the whistle on* you. ／If you don't do as I say, I'll *expose* your *secret*!

パラソル a parasol, a sunshade ▶パラソルを開く［閉じる］open [shut] *a sunshade*.

‖**ビーチパラソル** a beach umbrella.

パラダイス (a) paradise ▶この世のパラダイス an earthly *paradise* ／(a) *paradise* on earth ‖ ここはバードウォッチャーのパラダイスだ This place is *a paradise* for bird watchers.

パラダイム a paradigm(理論的枠組み).

はらだたしい 腹立たしい ▶腹立たしい事件 a *maddening* incident ‖ バスが時間どおりに来ないのは実に腹立たしい It is very *irritating* [*exasperating*] that the buses don't come on schedule. ‖ 自分の要領の悪さが腹立たしかった I *was angry with* myself for my (social) clumsiness.

はらだちまぎれ 腹立ちまぎれ ▶彼は腹立ちまぎれにテーブルをたたいた He pounded on the table *in a fit of anger*.

はらちがい 腹違い ▶兄とは腹違いの兄弟です My brother and I *have different mothers but the same father*. ／My brother and I are *half brothers*. (➤ half brother は父母の一方だけが同じ兄弟をいう).

ばらつき ▶このクラスの生徒は学力のばらつきが大きい *There is a wide range* of scholastic ability among the students in this class.

ばらつく ▶生徒たちの試験の点はばらついていた The students' test scores *were all over the map*.

バラック a temporary shelter, a shanty(➤ barracks は「兵舎」).

ぱらつく ▶朝方雨が少しぱらついた *It sprinkled* in the morning. (➤ sprinkle は「小雨」).

はらっぱ 原っぱ an open field ▶原っぱへ行ってキャッチボールをしよう Let's go to the *open field* and play catch.

はらづもり 腹づもり ▶父親は次男に家業を継がせる腹づもりだ The father *intends* [*has* it *in mind*] *to* have his second son take over the family business.

はらどけい 腹時計 an inner clock ▶ぼくの腹時計ではもう夕飯時だよ My *inner clock* [My *stomach*] *tells me* it's about dinnertime.

パラドックス a paradox ▶「急がば回れ」はパラドックスだ "More haste, less speed" is *a paradox*.

ばらにく ばら肉 ‖**豚ばら肉** pork belly, belly pork ‖ **牛ばら肉** beef belly, belly beef.

はらばい 腹這い 一動 **腹ばいになる** lie on one's stomach ▶一平は腹ばいになって漫画を読んでいる Ippei is reading a comic book, *lying on his stomach*. ‖ 子供たちがさくの下を腹ばいで抜けてきた The boys came *crawling* under the fence.

はらはちぶ 腹八分 ▶腹八分のほうが健康にはよい It's better for your health *not to eat too much* [*not to eat your fill*]. ／Moderate eating keeps the doctor away.

はらはら **1**【気がもめる様子】一動 **はらはらする** feel nervous ▶はらはらさせられる映画 an *exciting* [*a thrilling*] movie ‖ 彼はけんか早いので, ときどき私たちをはらはらさせる He often *makes* us *nervous* because of his short temper. ‖ 新米のアナウンサーがいつとちるかと周囲の者ははらはらした All the people around the new announcer *were on pins and needles* wondering when he would blow it. (➤ on pins and needles は「はらはら［ひやひや］して」の意のインフォ

ーマルな表現).
▶その試合はシーソーゲームで最後まではらはらしどおしだった It was a seesaw game that kept us *in suspense* to the end.
2【軽い物が落ちる様子】▶桜の花びらがはらはらと散った The petals of the cherry blossoms *fluttered* to the ground. (➤ flutter は「(葉などが)舞う」).

ばらばら 1【まとまりがこわれる様子】▶オルゴールをばらばらに分解した I *took* the music box *apart* [*to pieces*]. ‖ 一円玉がばらばらっと床に落ちた Some one-yen coins fell and *scattered* (*in all directions*) on the floor. ‖ 人形は棚から落ちてばらばらにこわれた The doll fell off the shelf and *broke into pieces*.
▶今うちのチームはばらばらだ The players on our team *are doing their own thing*. (➤「各自が好き勝手なことをしている」の意) ‖ 私たちのグループはクラス替えで全員ばらばらになってしまった The members of our group all *went their separate ways* after we were put in different homerooms. ‖ 行きは一緒だったが帰りはばらばらに帰った We went there together and came back *separately*. ‖ この付近でばらばら死体が発見された *A dismembered body* was found in this neighborhood.
‖ばらばら殺人事件 a mutilation murder case.
2【大粒で降る様子】▶ひょうがばらばらと降ってきた The hail came *pelting down*. (➤ pelt down は「激しく降る」).

ぱらぱら 1【雨などが少量に降る様子】▶ 対話「雨が降ってきたね」「うん, でもぱらぱら降ってるだけだよ」"It's starting to rain." "Yeah, but it's just *a sprinkle* [it's just *sprinkling*]."
2【まばらに離れる様子】▶本のページをぱらぱらとめくる *leaf through* the pages of a book ‖ 彼はスパゲッティにぱらぱらとこしょうを振りかけた He *sprinkled* pepper on the spaghetti.
▶彼女のデビューコンサートは聴衆がぱらぱらの状態だった There was (only) *a scattering of people* at her debut concert. (➤ a scattering of で「まばらな…」の意) /The attendance at her debut concert was *extremely small*.

はらぺこ 腹ぺこ ▶ 対話「おなかすいてる?」「腹ぺこ(で死にそう)だよ」"Are you hungry?" "Yes. I'*m starving* (*to death*)."

パラボラアンテナ a **parabola**, a **parabolic antenna**, 《インフォーマル》a **dish**.

はらまき 腹巻き ***haramaki***; a **stomach band** [**supporter**].

ばらまく **scatter** +㊐, **strew** /struː/ +㊐ (➤ 後者はやや文語的な語) ▶転んだ拍子に財布の小銭を路上にばらまいてしまった The coins in my wallet *were scattered* on the road when I fell.
▶その候補者は票集めのために相当金をばらまいたらしい The candidate seemed to *have thrown* a substantial sum of money *around* to collect [buy] votes.

はらむ 孕む 1【子を宿す】 **become pregnant** ▶この猫は子をはらんでいる This cat *is big* [*heavy*] *with* kittens.
2【中に含む】▶ヨットの帆は風をはらんでふくれあがった The sails of the yacht were *filled with* wind.
▶二国間の国境紛争は一応の決着を見たが, まだ多くの問題をはらんでいる The border conflicts between the two countries have been settled for the present, but the situation *is* still *highly problematic*.

はらもち 腹持ち ▶腹持ちのいい物 something that will *keep you going*.

バラライカ a **balalaika** /bæ̀ləláɪkə/.

ぱらり ▶彼女の額に前髪がぱらりと垂れた Her bangs fell *gently* on her forehead.

パラリンピック **the Paralympics**.

はらわた 腸 **the guts**; **the bowels** /báʊəlz/ (腸全体) ▶魚のはらわたを取る *gut* a fish /take *the guts* out of a fish
▶《慣用表現》あの男ははらわたの腐ったようなやつだ He is *corrupt to the core*. /He has *a corrupt* [*rotten*] *heart*. ‖ あいつのやったことを考えるとはらわたが煮えくり返る It *makes my blood boil* when I think of what he has done.

[1]はらん 波乱 **ups and downs** (浮き沈み); **trouble** (騒ぎ); (an) **uproar** (大騒動) ▶一波乱ありそうだ *Trouble* is brewing. ‖ 社長の突然の退陣は波乱を呼んだ The president's sudden resignation caused *an uproar*.
▶彼女は波乱万丈の生涯を送った She lived an *eventful* life. (➤ eventful は「出来事の多い」) /Her life was *full of ups and downs*. ‖ ペナントレースはまだ一波乱も二波乱もありそうだ It looks like the pennant race may still *have some upsets* (*in store*). (➤ upset は「番狂わせ」).

[2]はらん 葉蘭 《植物》a **cast-iron plant**, an **aspidistra** (**elatior**).

バランス **balance** ▶バランスのとれた食事 a *well-balanced* meal ‖ 私は自転車に乗っていてバランスを失って倒れた While riding my [a] bicycle, I *lost my balance* and fell. ‖ 彼は片足でバランスをとろうとした He tried to *balance himself* on one leg. ‖ 私たちは仕事と余暇とのバランスをうまくとらなければいけない時期に来ていると私は思う I think it is time for us to *strike a proper balance* between work and leisure.

バランスシート a **balance sheet**.

[1]はり 針 a **needle** (縫い針, 注射針, レコード針など); a **pin** (留め針, 待ち針); a **hook** (釣り針); a **hand** (時計の針); a **sting** (昆虫の) ▶針の穴 the eye of *a needle* ‖ 針に糸を通す thread *a needle* ‖ 針にえさをつける put bait on *a hook* /bait *a hook* (with a worm) ‖ 痛っ! 針で指を刺しちゃった Ouch! I stuck my finger *with a needle* [*a pin*]. ‖ 犬にかまれて足を5針縫った I was bitten by a dog and *got five stitches* in my leg. (➤ stitch は「1針, 1縫い」).
▶時計の針は1時半を指していた *The hands of the clock* showed 1 : 30. ‖ あの女の子は針仕事がうまい The girl is good at *needlework*.
‖針刺し a pincushion ‖ 針箱 a sewing /sóʊɪŋ/ box.

[2]はり 鍼 **acupuncture** /ǽkjupʌ̀ŋktʃəʳ/ (はり療法) ▶はりを打ってもらう undergo *acupuncture* (*treatment*).

[3]はり 張り **life** (活気) ▶張りのある声 a voice *full of life* ‖ 彼女の声は張りがある [ない] Her voice is full of *life* [is lifeless].
▶年配者も何か仕事を持ったほうが生活に張りが出るだろう Elderly people, too, will *enjoy life more* if they have some kind of work to do.

[4]はり 梁 a **beam** ▶コンクリート製 [オーク製] のはり a concrete [an oak] *beam*.

バリ バリ島 **Bali** (インドネシアの島).

-ばり -張り ▶白いタイル張りの浴室 a white-*tiled* bathroom /a bathroom *covered in* white *tile*

▶この絵はピカソ張り(＝風)だ This picture looks *just like it could have been done by Picasso*.

パリ **Paris** /pǽrɪs/ (フランスの首都).

はりあい 張り合い ▶張り合いのある(＝やりがいのある)仕事 a *challenging* job ‖ 張り合いのない(＝退屈な)生活 a *dull* life.

はりあう 張り合う **compete** 《with》 ▶クラスの男の子どうしが一等賞を張り合った The boys in the same class *competed* [*contended*] *with each other* for the first prize.

▶お隣どうしで張り合うなんてつまらない There's no point in trying to *keep up with the Joneses*. (➤「隣人に負けまいと見栄を張って同じ物を買ったりする」の意の熟語 ; There's no point in doing は「…しても意味がない」).

はりあげる 張り上げる **raise** /reɪz/ ＋目 (声などを上げる) ▶声を張りあげて自分たちのチームを応援した We cheered [rooted] for our team *at the top of our lungs* [*voices*]. (➤ at the top of one's lungs は「声を限りに, ありったけの声で」) ‖ そんなに大声を張りあげなくても聞こえています You don't have to *raise your voice* to be heard. ／Your voice is (perfectly) audible without *shouting*.

は

バリアフリー **barrier-free** ▶バリアフリーのトイレ a *barrier-free* bathroom 《参考》「障害者が使いやすい, 車いすで利用しやすい」を表す語の accessible を用いて, Our bathroom is (wheelchair) accessible. などとも言える.

▶わが家はバリアフリーの設計で新築した We had our new house built *barrier-free*.

ハリウッド **Hollywood** (アメリカのロサンゼルスにある映画製作の中心地).

バリウム 《化学》 **barium** ▶胃のX線検査のためにバリウムを飲む drink *barium* before a stomach X-ray.

はりえ 貼り絵 a **collage**.

バリエーション (a) **variation** ▶1枚のスカーフの使い方にもいろいろなバリエーションがある There are many *variations* in how you can use a scarf.

はりかえる 張り替える **repaper** ＋目 (紙で) ; **recover** ＋目 (おおっているものを) ▶障子を張り替える *repaper* a shoji (partition).

はりがね 針金 (a) **wire** (➤針金1本は a piece [length] of wire とか a wire という) ▶ペンチで針金を切る cut *wire* with pliers ‖ 折れた枝が針金で縛りつけてあった The broken part of the branch was tied to the rest of the branch with *wire*.

はりがみ 貼り紙 a **notice** (掲示) ; a **sticker** (のり付きの) ; a **bill** (ビラ) ▶掲示板にはり紙をする put up *a notice* on a bulletin board ‖ 店内の商品には「値下げ」のはり紙がしてあった The goods in the store had *stickers* saying "Price Slashed." ‖ (掲示) はり紙お断り Post [Stick] No Bills. ／No Posters.

バリカン **hair clippers** ▶父は電気バリカンでぼくの髪を刈ってくれた My father cut my hair with *electric clippers*.

ばりき 馬力 **1**【単位】**horsepower** (略 hp) ; **hauling** /hɔ́ːlɪŋ/ **power** (蒸気機関車などの牽引力) ▶このモーターは200馬力です This motor has a capacity of 200 *hp*. (➤ hp は horsepower と読む) ／This is a 200 *hp* motor. ‖ このエンジンは馬力が強い This engine has great *horsepower*.

2【勢い】▶彼は馬力があるので人一倍仕事をこなす Since he's *full of energy* [*very energetic*], he does twice as much work as others.

はりきゅう 鍼灸 **acupuncture and moxibustion**.

はりきる 張り切る **come to life** (活気づく) ▶弁当を食べる段になると彼らはがぜん張り切る They suddenly *come to life* when it's time to eat lunch. ‖ 彼はいつも張り切っている He's always *in high spirits*. ‖ 川田さんは張り切ってアフリカに向かった Mr. Kawada left for Africa *with hope and enthusiasm*.

▶けさはあんなに張り切ってたのに, どうしたんだい? Why were you so *peppy* this morning, but not now? (➤ peppy は「元気いっぱいの」の意のインフォーマルな語).

バリケード a **barricade** /bǽrəkeɪd/ ▶建物の入り口にバリケードが作られた *Barricades* were set up at the entrance to the building. ／The entrance to the building was barricaded.

ハリケーン a **hurricane** /hə́ːrəkeɪn/ ▶アメリカの東海岸が猛烈なハリケーンに襲われた The east coast of the U.S. was hit by a violent *hurricane*.

はりこ 張り子 **papier-mâché** /pèɪpəʳməʃéɪ ‖ pæpieɪmǽʃeɪ/ ▶張り子の虎 a *paper* tiger.

はりこみ 張り込み a **stakeout** ▶誘拐犯は張り込み中の警官に逮捕された The kidnapper was arrested by the policemen *on a stakeout*.

はりこむ 張り込む **1**【見張る】**stake out** ▶警官が密輸団のアジトに張り込んでいた Some police officers *were staking out* the smugglers' hideout.

2【奮発する】**splurge** 《on》 ▶おじが結婚祝いにうるし塗りのたんすを張り込んでくれたの My uncle *splurged on* a lacquerware chest as a present for my wedding.

はりさける 張り裂ける ▶友の死に胸が張り裂ける思いがした I thought *my heart would break* when my friend died.

はりす 鉤素 《釣り》 a **leader**.

バリスタ a **barista** ▶バリスタに私のラテに追加バニラを入れるように頼んだ I asked *the barista* to put extra vanilla in my latte.

はりたおす 張り倒す **knock down, floor** ＋目 ▶彼はそのいじめっ子を張り倒した He *knocked down* [*floored*] the bully.

はりだす 張り出す・貼り出す **1**【掲げる】**put up** ▶合格者の名前が掲示板にはり出されている The names of the successful applicants have *been put up* [*posted*] on the board.

2【出っ張る】▶高気圧が日本列島の上空に張り出してきている A high (atmospheric) pressure zone *is overlying* the Japanese archipelago. (➤ overlie は「…の上方に横たわる」).

はりつけ 磔 **crucifixion** /krùːsəfíkʃən/ (十字架上の) ▶イエス・キリストの磔 the *crucifixion* of Jesus Christ ‖ 聖ペテロは西暦67年にローマで磔になった St. Peter *was crucified* in Rome in A.D. 67.

はりつける 貼り付ける **stick** ＋目 ; **paste** ＋目 (のりで) ▶封筒に切手をはり付ける *stick* [*put*] a stamp on the envelope ‖ びんにラベルをはり付ける *paste* a label on a bottle.

ぱりっと ▶先生はいつになくぱりっとした格好で登校して来た The teacher came to school looking unusually *crisp and neat*.

はりつめる 張り詰める **1**【気持ちが】**become tense** ━形 **張り詰めた** **tense, strained** (➤後者は前者より堅い語) ▶そんなに四六時中気を張り詰めていたら体が参っちゃうよ If you stay *wound up* like that, you'll ruin your health. (➤ wound /waund/ up は「緊張して」) ‖ 入試が終わったとたんに張り詰めていた気持ちがいっぺんにゆるんだ When I finished all the entrance exams, *my strained nerves* immediately relaxed.

2【氷が】freeze over ▶湖には氷が一面に張り詰めている The lake *is frozen over*.

はりとばす 張り飛ばす →張り倒す.

バリトン《音楽》**baritone** /bǽrətoʊn/

‖**バリトン歌手** a baritone.

ハリネズミ《動物》a **hedgehog**.

はりのむしろ 針の筵 a **bed of nails** [**thorns**] (➤英語では「くぎ[とげ]のベッド」という) ▶封建的な旧家に嫁いだ彼女は毎日が針のむしろだった Having married into an old traditional family, she felt that every day was *like lying on a bed of nails*.

ばりばり ▶のりをきかせ過ぎてワイシャツがばりばりしている I put too much starch on the shirt and it is *stiff*.

▶彼は毎日ばりばり仕事をする He works *energetically* [*vigorously*] every day. ‖彼はばりばりのやり手ビジネスパーソンだ He's a go-getting, *high-powered* businessperson. ‖緒方さんはことし75歳になるが現役ばりばりの通訳である Although he will be 75 years old this year, Mr. Ogata is *an active, full-time* interpreter.

ぱりぱり ▶クラッカーをパリパリ食べる *crunch on* a cracker ‖水たまりに張った薄氷をパリパリ割った We *cracked* the thin ice that had frozen over the puddle.

▶当時, 小野先生はぱりぱりの新人教師だった At that time, Mr. Ono was a novice teacher, *fresh from college*. (➤「大学を出たての」の意).

はりぼて 張りぼて →張り子.

はりめぐらす 張り巡らす ▶家のまわりに垣根を張り巡らす *put up* a fence *around* the house ‖犯行現場にはロープが張り巡らされていた The scene of the crime *was roped off*.

▶わが社は世界中に情報網を張り巡らせてある Our company *has set up* a global information network.

[1]**はる 春** **spring**; **springtime** (春季) 一形 **春らしい springlike** ▶春が来た *Spring* [*Springtime*] has come. (➤「春が来たばかりだ」の意) / *Spring* is with us [is here]. (➤「今は春だ」の意) ‖春になったらピクニックに行こうよ Let's go on a picnic when *spring* comes. ‖姉はことしの春結婚した My sister got married *this* (*past*) *spring*. ‖春になると[春には]いろいろな花が咲きます Many kinds of flowers bloom *in* (*the*) *spring*. ‖2012年の春に兄は大学を卒業した My brother graduated from university in the *spring* of 2012.

▶食卓には春の花々が飾ってあった The table was decked with *spring flowers*. ‖だいぶ春らしくなってきたね It has become quite *springlike*, hasn't it? ‖川辺の桜も満開で, まさに春たけなわだ The cherry trees on the riverbank are in full bloom and now *spring is in full swing*.

▶《慣用表現》彼は今まさにわが世の春を謳歌(おうか)しているようだ He really appears to *be at the height of his prosperity* now.

‖**春がすみ** spring haze ‖**春の七草** the seven herbs of spring.

☛ **春一番, 春先, 春休み** (→見出語)

[2]**はる 張る・貼る** **1【ゆるみをなくす】stretch** +目 ▶もっとロープをぴんと張ってください *Stretch* the rope tighter. ‖テニスコートにネットを張った We *put up* the net on the tennis court. ‖兄さんは一人で上手にテントを張る My brother can *set up* [*put up* / *pitch*] a tent well by himself.

2【緊張する】 ▶肩が張っているときはこの塗り薬が効く This ointment is effective when your neck is *stiff*. ‖胸を張って歩こう *Hold your head high* when you walk.

▶気が張っているときは意外にかぜをひかないものだ When you *are on your toes*, you surprisingly don't catch (a) cold. (➤ on one's toes は「緊張して」).

▶そんなに意地を張るもんじゃない Don't be so *stubborn*. ‖彼は虚勢を張っているにすぎない He's only *bluffing*.

3【ある場所をおおう】 ▶神社のまわりにはぐるりと幕が張られていた Curtains *were hung* around the shrine. ‖ステージの前にはロープが張られていて, 近づけないようになっていた A rope had *been set up* around the stage [There *was* a rope *across* the stage], so we could not approach it. ‖天井にクモの巣が張っている *There is* a cobweb on the ceiling. ‖庭の池に初氷が張った A sheet of ice *formed* on the pond in our yard for the first time this year. / The pond in our yard froze for the first time this year.

4【取れないようにつける】put +目; **stick** +目 (くっつける) ▶ノートにシールをはる *put* a sticker on a notebook ‖家の外壁にタイルをはった We *had* the outer walls of our house *tiled*. ‖切手をはるのを忘れて手紙を出してしまった I forgot to *put* a stamp on the letter before mailing it.

▶願書には忘れずに写真をはってください Please be sure to *attach* a picture of yourself to the application form. (➤ attach は「添付する」) ‖このポスター, お宅の塀にはっていいでしょうか May I *put up* this poster on your wall?

5【出っぱらせる】 ▶ケヤキの木が大きく枝を張っている A zelkova tree stands (there), *extending* its branches widely *in all directions*. ‖ナイフとフォークを使うときはひじを張ってはいけません *Keep your elbows in* [*at your side*] while eating with a knife and fork.

6【値段が高い】 ▶この西陣織の着物はお値段が張りますが最高の品です This Nishijin kimono is rather *expensive*, but it is of excellent quality.

7【平手でなぐる】 ▶あんちくしょうの横っ面を一発張ってやった I *slapped* that stupid guy on the cheek.

-ばる ▶そんなに四角ばらないで Don't *be* so *formal*. / Don't *stand on formality*.

はるいちばん 春一番 **the first spring gale, the first strong south wind of the year.**

はるか 遥かな **far** (距離・時間が遠い) 一副 **はるかに much, by far, far and away** (➤最後の言い方は前2者の強意形) ▶はるか海上に船が見えた We saw a ship *far* out to sea. ‖はるか上空に飛行機の姿が見えた I spotted a plane *far* up in the sky. ‖はるかかなたに[前方に]島が見える I can see an island *far away* [*far ahead*].

▶はるか遠くに滝が見えた I could see a waterfall *in the distance*. ‖その話ははるか昔にさかのぼる The story goes *far* back into the past. ‖私がアメリカに留学したのははるか昔のことだ It was *a long time ago* that I went to America to study.

▶オーストラリアの面積はグリーンランドよりはるかに広い Australia is *much* greater in area than Greenland. ‖テクニックという点では弘より健のほうがはるかにすぐれている When it comes to technique, Ken is *far* (*and away*) better than Hiroshi [is better than

Hiroshi *by a long shot*].
バルカン バルカン半島 the Balkan Peninsula(ヨーロッパ南東部の半島).
バルコニー a balcony /bǽlkəni/ ▶バルコニーで日光浴をする take a sunbath on *a balcony*.
はるさき 春先 early spring ▶私は春先によくかぜをひきます I often catch a cold *in* (*the*) *early spring*.
バルサミコす バルサミコ酢 balsamic vinegar /bɔːlsǽmɪk vínɪgəʳ/.
はるさめ 春雨 1【雨】 a spring shower [rain] ▶丘の上の城が春雨に煙っていた The castle on the hill appeared hazy in the *spring rain*.
2【食品】 *harusame*; noodles made from potatoes or mung bean starch (➤ 説明的な訳).
バルセロナ Barcelona(スペイン北東部の都市).
パルテノン the Parthenon /pɑ́ːʳθənɑːn/.
バルトかい バルト海 the Baltic Sea(デンマーク, ポーランド, スウェーデンなどに囲まれた海).
バルトさんごく バルト三国 the (three) Baltic countries.
はるばる all the way ▶青木さんは2年前にはるばる北海道から沖縄へやってきた Aoki came to Okinawa *all the way* from Hokkaido two years ago. ‖ 雨の中を遠路はるばるお越しくださいましてありがとうございます Thank you for coming *all this way* [*such a long way*] in the rain. ‖ 彼ははるばるニュージーランドから私に会いにやって来た He came *over* from New Zealand to see me.
バルブ a valve ▶バルブを閉じる[開ける] close [open] *a valve*.
パルプ pulp, wood pulp.
はるまき 春巻 《米》an egg roll, 《英》a spring roll.
はるめく 春めく ▶池の氷も解けて春めいてきた It's *getting springlike* as the ice melts in the pond.
はるやすみ 春休み (the) spring vacation [《英》holidays]; (a) spring break(短めの) ▶うちの子供たちは春休み中です Our children are *on spring break*.

[1]**はれ 晴れ 1【天候】** fair, fine

> 《解説》(1)「晴れ」には sunny, fair, fine が使われるが, 厳密には **sunny** はよく日が差していることをいい, **fair** は雲一つない快晴を, また **fine** は多少雲があってもよい状態をいう.「晴天」の意で clear weather [skies] も用いる. (2)「晴れ」が「すばらしく天気がよい」という広い意味のときは **beautiful, nice, gorgeous** などの形容詞も使える.
> (3)天気予報では fair, sunny が好まれる.

▶あしたは晴れだろう It'll be *sunny* [*fair*] tomorrow. / Tomorrow will be a *sunny* [*fine*] day. (➤ fine はふつう day, weather のような名詞とともに用いられる) ‖ 《天気予報》あすは関東地方全域, 晴れでしょう The weather forecast for tomorrow calls for *sunny* [*clear*] weather throughout the Kanto area. (➤ weather の代わりに skies とすることもできる) ‖ 晴れ後曇り *Fair* [*Sunny*], *later cloudy* ‖ 《日記で》10月10日, 月曜日. 晴れ Mon., Oct. 10. *Fair*.
2【改まっていて華やかな場所】 ▶晴れの舞台に出るのだから正装していかなければ I must dress formally for such a *grand* occasion.
[2]**はれ 腫れ** a swelling ▶氷で冷やせばそのはれはひくでしょう An ice pack will relieve the *swelling*.
[1]**はれあがる 晴れ上がる** clear up ▶空はじきに晴れあがった The sky *cleared up* soon.
[2]**はれあがる 腫れ上がる** swell up ▶彼の額はスズメバチに刺されてはれあがった After the wasp stung him, his forehead *swelled up*.
バレエ (a) ballet /bæléɪ/ ▶バレエを踊る dance *a ballet* ‖ バレエを見に行く go to see *a ballet*.
‖バレエ団 a ballet company [troupe / group] ‖ バレエダンサー a ballet dancer, a ballerina(➤前者は男女, 後者は女性) ‖ クラシックバレエ classical ballet.
ハレーすいせい ハレー彗星 Halley's Comet.
ハレーション 《写真》a halation.
パレード a parade 一動 **パレードする** parade ▶優勝パレード a victory *parade* ‖ 優勝チームが市内をパレードした The champion team *paraded* through the city.
バレーボール volleyball /vɑ́ːlibɔːl/ ▶6人制バレーボール a six-member team *volleyball* ‖ バレーボールをする play *volleyball* ‖ バレーボールの試合をする play *a volleyball game*.
‖バレーボール選手 a volleyball player.
はれがましい 晴れがましい formal(改まった); grand (盛大な) ▶このような晴れがましいお席にお招きいただきまして光栄でございます It's a great honor to be invited to such a *grand* party.
はれぎ 晴れ着 one's best clothes, one's (Sunday) best ▶陽子は晴れ着姿でパーティーに来た Yoko came to the party (*dressed*) *in her best clothes* [*in her best*].
はれすがた 晴れ姿 1【晴れ着を着た姿】 ▶晴れ姿の卒業生 a *formally-dressed* graduating student.
2【晴れの場所でのりっぱな姿】 ▶彼女は柔道チャンピオンの娘の晴れ姿を見るために表彰式に臨んだ In order to see her daughter's *proudest moment* [*moment in the sun*] as a judo champion, she attended the award ceremony.
パレスチナ Palestine /pǽləstaɪn/ (西アジア西部, 地中海沿岸の地域)
‖パレスチナ人 a Palestinian.
はれつ 破裂 a burst(内部の圧力による); an explosion (爆弾などの爆発) 一動 **破裂する** burst, explode ▶水道管が凍結して破裂した The water pipe *burst* after freezing over. ‖ 風船が破裂した The balloon *burst*. ‖ 食べ過ぎておなかが破裂しそう I've eaten so much (that) my stomach *is about to burst*. ‖ 大きな破裂音がしたと思ったら松井のおならだった I thought I heard *a big explosion*, but it was just Matsui's fart.
▶《慣用表現》とうとうお父さんのかんしゃく玉が破裂した At last, my father *blew his top*. (➤ blow one's top は「怒りを爆発させる」の意のインフォーマルな言い方).
バレッタ a barrette.
パレット a palette /pǽlət/ ▶パレットで絵の具を混ぜる mix colors on *a palette*.
‖パレットナイフ a palette knife.
はれて 晴れて ▶長い苦難の末二人は晴れて(=正式に)夫婦となった After a long struggle, the two *officially* became man and wife.
はればれ 晴れ晴れ ▶姉は父に結婚を許してもらい晴れ晴れとした顔をしている My (older) sister looks *radiant* now that Dad has agreed to her getting married.
はれぼったい 腫れぼったい ▶何となく顔がはれぼったい My face *feels* somewhat *swollen*. ‖ 妹ははれぼったい目をしていた My sister was *puffy eyed*. / My sister's *eyes were puffy*.

はれま 晴れ間 a lull /lʌl/ in the rain（雨の小休止）; a patch of blue sky（雲間からのぞく青空）▶梅雨の**晴れ間**を見て急いで洗濯した We did the laundry quickly, taking advantage of the *lull* in the rainy season. ‖ 午後になったら**晴れ間**が見えてきた In the afternoon we saw *patches of blue sky* here and there.

はれもの 腫れ物 a swelling ; a boil（おでき）▶背中に**はれもの**ができた I got *a boil* on my back. ／*A boil* has come out on my back.

▶《慣用表現》入試が目前なので和男は家族から**はれもの**に触るような扱いを受けた With the entrance exam fast approaching, Kazuo *was treated with kid gloves* by his family. (➤ treat with kid gloves は「(人を)慎重に扱う」).

はれやか 晴れやかな radiant /réidiənt/ （輝く）; cheerful（快活な）▶**晴れやかな**5月の空 a *fair* May sky ‖ 彼は**晴れやかな**笑顔で私を迎えた He welcomed me with a *cheerful* [*beaming*] smile. ‖ 彼女はそのとき**晴れやかな**気分だった She was in a *cheerful* mood then.

▶花嫁は**晴れやかな**笑顔をしていた The bride smiled *radiantly*.

バレリーナ a ballerina /bæ̀lərí:nə/

‖**プリマバレリーナ** a prima ballerina.

1**はれる 晴れる** **1【天気が】** clear (up) 一形 **晴れた** fair, clear ▶あすは**晴れる**でしょう It will *be fair* tomorrow. ‖ 夕方ごろになって**晴れた** It [The sky] *cleared up* toward evening. ‖ こんなよく**晴れた**(＝天気のよい)日に家でごろごろしていてはいけません You shouldn't lie around at home on such a *beautiful* [*gorgeous*] day. ‖ 雲一つなく**晴れている** The sky is very *clear* and there's not a cloud in the sky.

▶ようやく霧が**晴れてきた** At last the fog began to *clear* [*lift* ／*let up*].

2【疑いが】 be cleared《of》▶あなたの話を聞いて私の疑念は**晴れました** After listening to you, my suspicions *have been cleared up*. ‖ 囚人は殺人の容疑が**晴れて**釈放された The prisoner was set free, since he *was cleared of* the murder charge.

3【気分が】 ▶思いっきり汗を流せば気分も**晴れる**よ A good sweat will make you *feel better*. ‖ どうも気分が**晴れない** I *can't shake off my bad* [*low*] *mood*.

2**はれる 腫れる** swell (up) ▶おでこをドアにぶつけたら**はれて**きた My forehead began to *swell* after hitting the door. ‖ 目が**はれてる**よ Your eyes *are swollen*.

ばれる come out（公になる）; leak out（漏れる）▶ぼくたちの秘密が**ばれた** Our secret *is out*. ／Our secret *has come* [*has leaked*] *out*. ‖ カンニングが**ばれて**停学になった I *got caught* cheating and was suspended. (➤ be [get] caught doing は「(悪いことをしているところを)見つかる」) ‖ 彼の浮気は奥さんに**ばれてしまった** His wife *found out* about his extramarital [illicit] affair.

バレル《容量の単位》a barrel.

ハレルヤ alleluia,hallelujah.

バレンタイン(デー) (St.) Valentine('s) Day(➤ St. はつけないのがふつう) ▶**バレンタイン(デー)**に何個チョコレートをもらったの? How many boxes [pieces] of chocolate did you receive on *(St.) Valentine's Day*? 《参考》(1)欧米では男女どちらから贈ってもよい. 贈り物は基本的にはカード. もちろん, ほかのものを添えてもよい. (2)英米のティーンエージャーはバレンタインカード(valentine)には送り主である自分の名は書かないか, "Guess Who"（誰だかわかる?）などと書く.

✉《カードで》**バレンタインデーおめでとう** *Happy Valentine's Day!*

バレンタインカードには次のように書きます.
(1) *Happy Valentine's Day!*
(2) *Thinking of You on Valentine's Day!*
(3) *Be My Valentine!* ➤ これは主に恋人になってほしいと望む場合に使う.

✉《カードで》**チョコレートを贈ります. バレンタインデーに愛を込めて** Here's a box of chocolates for you with much love and *Valentine's Day* wishes.

✉ **日本ではバレンタインデーに女の子が男の子にチョコレートを贈る習慣があります** In Japan, girls customarily give chocolates to boys on *Valentine's Day*.

は

はれんち 破廉恥な shameless（恥知らずの）; scandalous（恥ずべき）▶他人の研究成果をそのまま盗用するとは全くもって**破廉恥だ** It is absolutely *shameless* to steal the results of somebody else's research. ‖ 某教授は女子学生を研究室に呼んで**破廉恥な**ことをした A certain professor called a female student into his office and did a *scandalous* thing.

‖**破廉恥罪** an infamous offense [crime].

はろう 波浪 waves ▶**波浪**注意報が出された *A high-sea warning* has been issued.

ハロウィーン Halloween /hæ̀louí:n/ (➤ 10月31日の夜) ▶ハロウィーンのかぼちゃ a *Halloween* pumpkin (中をくりぬいて顔形のちょうちんにしたもの; jack-o'-lantern ともいう).

ハローワーク Hellowork ; a Public Employment Security Office（公共職業安定所）.

ハロゲンとう ハロゲン灯 a halogen bulb（電球）; a halogen light（明かり）.

バロック Baroque /bəróuk/

‖**バロック音楽** Baroque music ‖ **バロック建築** Baroque architecture.

パロディー a parody ▶この歌はアメリカの民謡の**パロディー**です This song is *a parody* of an American folk song.

バロメーター a barometer /bərɑ́:mɪṭəʳ/ ▶食欲は健康の**バロメーター**だ Your appetite is the *barometer* of your health.

パワー power ▶住民**パワー** people [citizen] *power* ‖ 老人**パワー** gray *power* ‖ 彼は中古車を買って自分で**パワーアップした** He bought an old car and *souped* it *up* himself. (➤ power up は「宇宙船の出力を上げる」の意で, 自動車には使えない) ‖ このエンジンは**パワーがある** This engine *is powerful* [*is high-powered*].

‖**パワーショベル** a power shovel ‖ **パワーステアリング** power steering ‖ **パワーハラスメント** → パワハラ.

ハワイ Hawaii /həwáɪ(:)/ (太平洋に浮かぶアメリカの州; 略 HI) 一形 **ハワイの** Hawaiian

‖**ハワイ語** Hawaiian ‖ **ハワイ人** a Hawaiian.

ハワイアン Hawaiian music（音楽）.

パワハラ supervisor harassment, (an) abuse of power in the workplace（職場の上司の職権乱用）.

パワフル powerful.

[1]**はん 半** (a) **half**(半分) ▶半年 *half a year* ／*a half year* ‖ 鉛筆を半ダース買った I bought *half a dozen* [*a half dozen*] pencils. (➤ 後者は half-dozen とつづることも多い).
▶彼の家から学校まで約２キロ半ある It is about *two kilometers and a half* [*two and a half kilometers*] from his house to his school. ‖ 私たちは彼女を１時間半ほど待っていた We waited for her for about *an hour and a half*. ‖ 彼が到着したのは３時半でした It was *half past three* [*three thirty*] when he arrived.
▶その会合は半月［半年］ごとに開かれる The meeting is held *every two weeks* [*every six months*]. ‖ ドバイのブルジュ・カリファタワーはエンパイアステート・ビルの１倍半の高さがある The Burj Khalifa Tower in Dubai is *one and a half times* as tall as the Empire State Building.

[2]**はん 判** **1**【はんこ】a ***hanko***, a **signature seal**, a **stamp**

> 《解説》(1)seal は紋章や字句などを金属や石などに彫ったもので，公式な権威を示すために使われるものをいう．欧米ではこれを文書に直接押したり，封蠟(ろう)の上から押すが，一般的なものではない．ふつうは署名だけで済ます．
> (2)stamp はゴム印を指す場合が多い．
> (3)日本の「はんこ」は *hanko* とするか，name seal, signature seal または personal(ized) seal などとするのがよい．

▶ここに署名をして判を押してください Please sign and *put your seal* [*hanko*] here. 《参考》英語で seal here というと「(封筒の)ここをのりづけする」の意になる．
▶《慣用表現》彼女は判で押したように毎朝８時に家を出る She leaves home at eight every morning *like clockwork*. (➤「(時計のように)正確に，規則正しく」の意).
2【判型】▶『坊っちゃん』なら小型の判でも出ています "Botchan" is also available in *a compact* [*pocket*] *size version*.

[3]**はん 版** an **edition** ▶これは初版の第５刷です This is the fifth printing of *the first edition*. ‖ その本の改訂版は先月出た *A new* [*revised*] *edition* of the book came out last month. ‖ この辞書は10版を重ねた This dictionary has gone through *ten editions*.
‖**重版** a second printing, a reprint (重刷)；a second edition (改訂版).

[4]**はん 班** a **group**(組)；a **squad** (特定の行動目的を持った)；a **team**(協力して何かをする) ▶救護班 a rescue *squad* [*team*] ‖ 先生は生徒を５班に分けた The teacher divided the students into five *groups*. ‖ 第１班と第２班，集合！ *Groups* 1 and 2, gather around.
▶大介は班長に選ばれた Daisuke was elected as *a group* [*squad*] *leader*.

[5]**はん 藩** a **fief**, a (daimyo) **domain**(領土)；a (**feudal**) **clan**(一族) ▶薩摩藩 the Satsuma *Fief* [*Domain*].

はん- 反- **anti-** ▶反核運動 an *antinuclear* movement ‖ 反作用《物理学》a reaction ‖ 反主流派 an *anti-mainstream* faction ‖ 反体制運動 an *anti-establishment* movement ‖ それは反社会的な行為だ It is an *antisocial* act. ‖ その国では反米感情がいまだに強い *Anti-American feelings* are still strong in that country.

[1]**ばん 番** **1**【順番】one's **turn** ▶西君，きみの番だよ It's *your turn*, Nishi. ‖ 次は誰の番ですか *Whose turn* is it next？‖ 次は森田君の番だ Morita is next. ‖ 私の番はまだしばらくは回ってこない My *turn* will not come for some time.
2【順序】▶私はクラスで１番だ I'm at *the top* of the class. ‖ 彼はマラソンで10番でゴールインした He came in *tenth* in the marathon.
▶立川はここから５番目の駅です Tachikawa is *the fifth* stop from here. ‖ 写真の向かって左から３番目が兄です My (older) brother is *third* from the left in the photo. ‖ 対話「あなたの背の順はクラスで前から何番目ですか」「前から４番目です」"How many classmates are there before you in order of height？" "There are three.／I am *the fourth* shortest." (➤ 後者の答え方は「４番目に背が低い」の意.「背の高い順」というのであれば shortest は tallest になる．→何番).
3【番号】a **number** (略 No.) ▶３番の問題を読みなさい Read Problem *No.* 3. ‖ 私の学籍番号は360番だ My ID card number is 360. ‖ お宅の電話番号は何番ですか May I have your telephone number？‖ 《電話で》何番におかけですか *What number* are you calling？(● May I ask what number you are calling？とすると，丁寧な聞き方になる).
4【見張り】**watch** ▶電話をかけてくるから荷物の番をしててね Can you *watch* [*keep an eye on*] my baggage while I go (and) make a telephone call？‖ あのたばこ屋ではおばあさんが店の番をしている An elderly woman *tends* that tobacco shop.
‖**番記者** a guard [watch] reporter.
5【試合】a **match** ▶《相撲のニュース》本日の取り組みからこの一番をご覧ください Please watch *this sumo match* from today's bouts.

[2]**ばん 晩** (an) **evening**；(a) **night**

> 《解説》evening は日没から就寝までの時間帯を，night は日没または就寝後から明け方までの時間帯を指す．

▶あすの晩外で食事しようよ How about eating out *tomorrow evening*？‖ 土曜日の晩は彼女と映画を見た I watched a movie with my girlfriend on *Saturday night*. ‖ その晩は疲れていたので早く床についた I was tired *that evening*, so I turned in early. ‖ 一晩中雨が降っていた It rained *all through the night*.
▶《慣用表現》彼は朝から晩までギターを弾いている He plays the guitar *from morning till* [*to*] *night*.
‖**晩ごはん** an evening meal, (a) supper, (a) dinner.

[3]**ばん 盤** a **board** ▶チェスの盤 a chess*board*.

バン a **van**
‖**ライトバン** a delivery truck [《英》van] (商用の)；《米》a station wagon, 《英》an estate car (乗用車兼用の) (➤ light van とはいわない).

パン **bread** (➤ パンの総称だが，しばしば食パンを指す)；a **roll**(小型パン) ▶食パン１個 a loaf of *bread* ‖ パンにバターを塗る spread [put] butter on *bread* ／spread a slice of *bread* with butter ‖ パンをオーブンで焼く bake *bread* in an oven ‖ 私は朝食はたいていパンだ I usually have *toast* for breakfast. (➤ 日本語ではパンをトーストにしても「パン」と呼べるが，英語ではトーストにしたパンは toast と呼ぶのがふつう) ‖ パン屋さんに行ってフランスパンとライムギパンを買って来てちょうだい

Please go to the *bakery* to get some *French* and *rye bread*.
▶ 対話 《レストランで》「パンになさいますか，ライスになさいますか」「ライスをください」“Which would you like, *rolls* or rice ?” “Rice, please.” ‖ 人はパンのみにて生きるにあらず Man shall not live on bread alone. (➤ 聖書のことば).
‖パン生地 (bread) dough ‖パン粉 bread crumbs /krʌmz/ ‖パン屋 a bakery (店); a baker (人).

「パン」のいろいろ あんパン bun stuffed with sweet bean paste／菓子パン bun／クロワッサン croissant／スコーン scone／デニッシュペストリー Danish pastry／バゲット baguette／バンズ bun／フランスパン French bread／ベーグル bagel／マフィン muffin／ライムギパン rye bread／レーズンブレッド raisin bread／ロールパン roll

はんい 範囲 a **range** (何かが及ぶ); **scope** (理解力・能力・活動などの); **sphere** (知識・勢力・興味などの); **area** (漠然と1つの) ▶知識の範囲を広げる widen one's *sphere* of knowledge ‖ 彼女の研究は広い範囲にわたっている Her field of study covers a wide *range* [*scope*]. ‖ 彼は交際範囲が広い He has a wide *range of acquaintances*.
▶火口から発生した有毒ガスは広い範囲に広がった Poisonous gas from the crater spread *to a wide area* [spread *far and wide*]. ‖ その現象は我々の理解の範囲を超えている The phenomenon is *beyond our comprehension*.
▶分詞構文は今度の試験の範囲内ですか Are the participial constructions going to *be on the test* ? (➤「試験に出るか」の意) ‖ みんなには各自ができる範囲内で彼女に協力してほしい I want you to cooperate with her *as much as possible*. ‖ パーティーの費用は10万円の範囲内におさえてください I want you to keep the cost of the party *under* 100,000 yen. ‖ 対話「試験の範囲はどこまでですか」「1ページから30ページまでです」“*What* does the exam *cover* ?” “It covers pages one to thirty.”
☛ 広範囲 (⇀見出語)

はんいご 反意語 an **antonym** ▶import の反意語は export だ The *antonym* of “import” is “export.”

1**はんえい 反映** a **reflection** 一動 **反映する reflect** +目 ▶国民の声を政治に十分反映させることのできる政治家は少ない There are few politicians who *reflect* public opinion adequately in their politics. ‖ 流行歌は世相を反映する Popular songs *are the mirror of* society.

2**はんえい 繁栄 prosperity** 一動 **繁栄する prosper** (物質的成功を遂げ，安楽になる); **thrive** (好条件に恵まれて成長・発展する) ▶国家の繁栄 the *prosperity* of a nation.
✉ 《年賀状で》ご家族のご多幸とご繁栄をお祈り申し上げます I wish your family happiness and *prosperity*.

はんえいきゅうてき 半永久的 ▶DVD の品質は半永久的に変わらない The quality of DVDs remains unchanged *almost permanently*.

はんえん 半円 a **semicircle**, a **half circle** 一形 **半円の semicircular** ▶半円のテーブル a *semicircular* table.

はんおし 半押し ▶シャッターを半押しする *press* the shutter button *halfway down* (to lock the auto focus).

はんおん 半音 《音楽》《米》a **halftone**, a **half step**, 《英》a **semitone** ▶半音下げる[上げる] lower [raise] (a note) by *a halftone* ／flat [sharp] (a note).
‖半音階 a chromatic scale ‖ 半音符 《米》a half note, 《英》a minim.

はんが 版画 a **woodblock print** (木版画); a **print**; an **etching** (銅版画); a **lithograph** /líθəgræf/ (石版画) ▶広重の版画を集める collect *woodblock prints* by Hiroshige ‖ 版画を彫る cut on wood ／engrave
‖版画家 a print artist.

1**ばんか 挽歌** a **dirge** (葬送歌); an **elegy** (哀歌).

2**ばんか 晩夏 late summer.**

ハンガー a **hanger**, a **coat** [**clothes**] **hanger** ▶ハンガーにコートを掛ける put a coat on *a hanger*.
‖ハンガーボード a pegboard.
☛ ハンガーストライキ ⇀ハンスト (見出語)

バンカー 《ゴルフ》a **bunker**, 《米また》a **sand trap** ▶ボールをバンカーに入れる[から出す] hit the ball into [out of] the *bunker*.
‖フェアウェーバンカー a fairway bunker.

はんかい 半壊 ▶昨夜の地震で3軒が全壊，10軒が半壊した Three houses *were* totally destroyed, and ten *partially destroyed*, in last night's earthquake.

ばんかい 挽回 recovery 一動 **ばん回する recover** +目 ▶勢力をばん回する *recover* [*regain*] one's power ‖ 名誉ばん回のために次回は頑張ろう Let's do our best next time to *recover our honor* [*reputation*]. ‖ わがチームは7回に1点をばん回した Our team *rallied for* a run in the seventh inning. ‖ 今から頑張れば期末テストでばん回できるよ If you start studying hard now, you'll *be able to make up for* your bad marks on the final exams. (➤ make up for は「…の埋め合わせをする」の意).

はんかがい 繁華街 a **busy street**; a **downtown** (中心街) ▶駅前の繁華街を過ぎれば住宅地だ After you pass the *busy area* in front of the train station, you will come to a residential area.

はんかく 半角 《コンピュータ》▶半角の文字 a *single-byte* character ‖ 半角英数字で名前をタイプする type one's name *in single-byte alphanumeric* (➤「全角英数字で」なら in two-byte alphanumeric).

はんがく 半額 half (the) price [**fare**] (➤ fare は運賃などの場合) ▶このセーターは半額で買った I bought this sweater *at half (the) price* [*at a fifty percent discount*]. ‖ 6歳未満の子供は半額です Children under six are charged *half the adult price* [*fare*].
‖半額セール a 50% discount sale (➤ 掲示では “Sale—Half Price” など).

ハンカチ a **handkerchief** /hǽŋkəʳtʃɪf/ ▶額の汗をハンカチでふく wipe the sweat from one's brow with *a handkerchief*.

ハンガリー Hungary (ヨーロッパ中部の国)
‖ハンガリー語 Hungarian ‖ハンガリー人 a Hungarian.

バンガロー a **cottage** /kɑ́:ṭɪdʒ/ ▶休暇を避暑地のバンガローで過ごす spend a vacation at *a cottage* in a summer resort.

危ないカタカナ語✸ **バンガロー**
1 英語の bungalow /bʌ́ŋgəloʊ/ からきているが，これはもともとインドのベンガル地方の住宅で，暑さと湿気を防ぐために作られた風通しのよい平屋を指す．今ではこれにならったベランダのある平屋住宅が bungalow と呼ばれる.
2 日本のキャンプ場などにある「バンガロー」は cottage のほうがふさわしく, もっと粗末なものは hut または cabin がよい.

はんかん 反感 **ill feelings**(悪感情); (an) **antipathy** /æntípəθi/(嫌悪感); (a) **revulsion**(激しい嫌悪感); (a) **resistance**(抵抗) ▶美津夫はなぜかぼくに**反感**をもっている Mitsuo has *ill feelings* toward me for some reason or other. ‖新しい考えはしばしば人に**反感**を抱かせる New ideas often arouse *resistance* (*s*).

ばんかん 万感 ▶30年ぶりにふるさとの山々と向かい合ったとき詩人には**万感胸迫るものがあった** The poet *was overwhelmed with emotion* when he [she] faced the mountains in his [her] homeland for the first time in thirty years.

はんかんはんみん 半官半民 ▶多くの日本人が NHK は**半官半民**の特殊法人だと誤解している Many Japanese misunderstand that NHK is a public corporation *partly controlled* [*supported*] *by the* Japanese *government*. (「半官半民の」を semi governmental と訳してはいけない. これは「半行政的な(機能・権限の)」「ある行政機能・権限を持つ」という意味であって,「政府と民間が共同出資して経営する」という日本語の意味を表す語ではない).

はんがんびいき 判官びいき →ほうがんびいき.

1**はんき 半期** a **half year** ▶上[下]**半期**の売り上げは良好だった Sales have been good during *the first* [*last*] *half year*. ‖バーゲンは**半期**に1度行います We have a sale *semiannually* [*every six months*]. (➤「半期に1度のバーゲン」は a semiannual sale).

2**はんき 半旗** ▶急死した大統領の喪に服して**半旗を掲げる** *fly a flag at half mast* in mourning for the president who has passed away suddenly.

3**はんき 反旗** ▶若手党員たちは党首に**反旗をひるがえした** Young party members *rose in revolt* against the chairman.

はんぎゃく 反逆 **treason** /tríːzən/ 一動(〜に)**反逆する** **rebel** /rɪbél/《against》▶外国に機密を売り渡すなどということは国家に対する**反逆**である It is *treason* against the nation to sell classified information to foreign countries. ‖光秀は主君に**反逆した** Mitsuhide *rose* [*rebelled*] *against* his lord.
‖**反逆罪** treason, a treasonable crime ‖**反逆者** a traitor /tréɪtəʳ/.

はんきゅう 半球 a **hemisphere** /hémɪsfɪəʳ/
‖**北**[**南**]**半球** the Northern [Southern] Hemisphere(➤ 小文字での表記も可).

はんきょう 反響 an **echo** /ékoʊ/(音の); (a) **response**(反応); (a) **sensation**(評判) 一動 **反響する** **echo** ▶洞穴の中で私たちの声が**反響した** Our voices *echoed* in the cave.
▶彼女の呼びかけには多くの**反響**があった There were many *responses* to her appeal. ‖一少女の作文が全国に**大反響**を呼んだ A girl's composition caused *a great sensation* throughout the country.

はんきょうらん 半狂乱 ▶交通事故で死んだ息子を見て母親は**半狂乱**になった The mother *was half-crazed* when she saw her son killed in a traffic accident.

ばんきんこう 板金工 a **sheet(-)metal worker**.

パンク a **blowout**, a **puncture**, a **flat** (**tire** [《英》**tyre**]) 一動 **パンクする** **go flat**; **blow out**(破裂する) ▶**パンク**を直す fix *a flat tire* / mend *a puncture*(➤ 後者は主に《英》) ‖フロントタイヤの1本が**パンクした** One of the front tires *has gone flat*. ‖タイヤが**パンクしちゃった**よ I've *got a blowout* [*a flat* (*tire*) / *a puncture*].
▶《比喩的》食べ過ぎておなかが**パンク**しそうだ My stomach is about to *burst*. ‖大地震のあと家族と連絡をとろうとする電話が殺到して**携帯ネットワークがパンクした** After the big earthquake, there were so many phone calls as people tried to reach their families (that) *the cellphone networks were overloaded and nobody could get through*.

危ないカタカナ語✸ **パンク**
1「パンク」は puncture の日本式省略形だが, この語は「(くぎなどで穴をあけて)パンクさせる」の意. したがって, 名詞としての意味も「穴あきパンク」である. 破裂によるパンクは blowout. なお, パンクしたタイヤは flat とか flat tire と呼ばれる.
2 音楽の「パンク(ロック)」は punk (rock) でよい.

バンクーバー **Vancouver**(カナダ西部の都市).

ハンググライダー a **hang glider**(器具); **hang gliding**(飛ぶこと) ▶**ハンググライダー**, やったことある? Have you ever tried *hang gliding*?

ばんぐみ 番組 a **program** ▶テレビ[ラジオ]の**番組** a TV [radio] *program* ‖**教育番組** an educational *program* (➤ education program は政府などの「教育施策」) ‖**スポーツ番組** a sports *program* ‖**料理番組** a cooking *program* ‖ 2時間**番組** a two-hour-long *program* ‖その**番組**は毎週日曜日午後7時から4チャンネルで放送される That *program* is broadcast [is aired] on Channel 4 at 7 p.m. every Sunday.
▶何か見たい[聞きたい]**番組**ある? Is there some *program* you want to watch [listen (in) to]? ‖今夜はおもしろそうな**番組**がない There are no good *programs* on tonight. (➤「放映されて」の意の on を落とさないこと) ‖ゆうべの6チャンネルの**特別番組**見た? Did you watch last night's *special* (*program*) on Channel 6?
‖(新聞の)**番組欄** TV [radio] program section (page).
☞ **裏番組**(→見出語)

バングラデシュ **Bangladesh**
‖**バングラデシュ人** a Bangladeshi.

ハングリー **hungry** ‖**ハングリー精神** strong ambition; hunger for success.

ハングル **hangul**(文字); **Korean**(言語) ▶**ハングルを話す** speak *Korean* (➤「ハングル」も hangul も韓国語[朝鮮語]の文字をいうので,「ハングル語」というものは存在しない. また,「ハングルを話す」も本来あやまった使い方. もちろん (×)speak hangul とは言えない).

はんぐれ 半グレ a **gang of petty hoodlums**(集団).

ばんくるわせ 番狂わせ an **upset** /ʌ́pset/ ▶**番狂わせの勝利** an *upset* victory ‖きょうの相撲の取組では**番狂わせ**が3番あった We had three *upsets* in today's sumo bouts. ‖優勝候補が1回戦で敗れるという**番狂わせ**があった The top favorite for the championship was beaten *unexpectedly* in the first round.

はんけい 半径 a **radius** /réɪdiəs/ ▶**半径**5センチの円をかきなさい Draw a circle with *a radius* of five centimeters. ‖台風の中心から**半径**300キロ以内は風速25メートル以上の暴風雨になっています The typhoon has a storm zone [belt] with winds of 25 or

more meters per second within a 300-kilometer *radius* from the eye.
▶《比喩的》野田さんは行動半径が広い Noda is involved in a wide *range of activities*.

はんげき 反撃 a **counterattack** 一動 **反撃する fight back** ▶敵は反撃に転じた The enemy made *a counterattack* on us. ‖ 我々は反撃の機会をうかがった We looked for a chance to *fight back*.
▶《野球》5対2とリードされた西武は6回に反撃，同点とした Trailing 5-2, the Lions *rallied* with three runs in the sixth inning to tie the score. (➤ rally は「盛り返す」).

はんけつ 判決 (a) **judgment**, a **ruling** ▶判決を言い渡す hand down *judgment* [*a ruling*] ‖ 判決は被告に有利[不利]だった The *ruling* was in favor of [against] the defendant. ‖ 彼は有罪[無罪]の判決を言い渡された He *was found guilty* [*not guilty*]. ‖ 彼は終身刑の判決を受けた He *was sentenced* to life imprisonment.
‖判決書 a sentence.

はんげつ 半月 a **half-moon**.

はんげつばん 半月板《解剖学》**semilunar cartilage**, a **meniscus** /mɪnískəs/.

1**はんけん 版権** (a) **copyright** ▶版権を侵害する infringe *a copyright* ‖ その本の版権は出版社が持っている The publisher owns the *copyright* on the book.
▶この本は版権が切れている The *copyright* on this book *has expired*. / This book *is in the public domain*. (➤ public domain は「著作権消滅状態」の意)《参考》「版権所有」の表示は Copyright [All rights] reserved.

2**はんけん 半券** a (**ticket**) **stub**.

はんげん 半減する decrease by half ▶悪天候で今月の売り上げは半減した This month's sales *are down* [*have decreased*] *by half* due to bad weather. ‖ 推理小説は結末がわかってしまっては興味が半減する If you know the ending to a mystery (novel), *half* the fun *is gone*.
▶セシウム137の半減期は約30年だ Cesium 137 has *a half-life* of about 30 years.

ばんけん 番犬 a **watchdog** ▶《掲示》番犬に注意 Beware of Dog.

はんこ 判こ a ***hanko*** (**stamp**), **a signature seal**《参考》日本語の「判こを押す」にあたるのは英語文化圏ではふつう「署名(signature)」で，「署名する」は sign を用いる．「契約書に判を押す」は日本語的には put a *hanko* on a contract だが，英語では sign a contract となる．
‖はんこ屋 a *hanko* shop, a seal shop. →判.

はんご 反語 irony /áɪərəni/ ; **sarcasm** /sɑ́ːˈkæzəm/ (皮肉) ; a **rhetorical question** (修辞疑問).

1**はんこう 反抗 resistance** (抵抗) ; (a) **rebellion** (権威などに対する公然とした) 一動 **反抗する resist** ＋目, **rebel** /rɪbél/《against》▶反抗的な子供 a *rebellious* child ‖ 子供たちは先生に反抗した The children *rebelled* [*stood* (*up*)] *against* their teacher. (➤ stand (up) against は「(反対して)立ち上がる」) ‖ 彼女は父親の命令に反抗した She *disobeyed* her father's order. (➤ disobey /dìsəbéɪ/ は「従わない」) ‖ 弟は最近両親に反抗的だ My brother has become *defiant* toward [*rebellious* against] our parents lately. (➤ defiant /dɪfáɪənt/ は「挑戦的な」) ‖ 彼は今反抗期なのです He is at *a rebellious age* now.
▶軍事政府に執ように反抗する tenaciously *resist* the military government.

2**はんこう 犯行** a **crime** ▶容疑者は犯行を認めた[否認した] The suspect confessed (to) [denied] his *crime*. ‖ 彼は捕まるまでに次々に犯行を重ねた He committed one *crime* after another before being arrested.
▶テロリストグループがその攻撃に対して犯行声明を出した A terrorist group *claimed responsibility for* the attack.
‖犯行現場 the scene of a crime.

はんごう 飯盒 a **mess kit** ▶飯ごうでご飯をたく boil rice in *a mess kit*.

ばんごう 番号 a **number** ▶《号令》番号! *Count off!* /《英》*Number off!* ‖《電話で》すみません，番号を間違えました I'm sorry. I dialed the wrong *number*. ‖ 番号順に並んでください Line up *in numerical order* [*in the order of your numbers*]. ‖ これらの学生証には番号が打ってある These students IDs *are assigned a number* [*are numbered*]. ‖《アナウンス》あなたのおかけになった電話番号は現在使われておりません The *number* you have dialed is no longer in service.
‖番号札 a numbered ticket [tag]

> **逆引き熟語 ○○番号**
> **暗証番号** a personal identification number [PIN], a code number, a password / **受付番号** a receipt number / **学籍番号** a student ID number / **クレジットカード番号** a (credit) card number / **口座番号** an account number / **受験番号** an examinee's [application] number / **製造番号** a serial number / **整理番号** a reference number / **背番号** a uniform number / **抽選番号** a lottery number / **通し番号** running [consecutive] numbers / **電話番号** a phone number / **当選番号** a lucky [winning] number / **郵便番号** a postal code (number), a zip code / **予約番号** a reservation number

ばんこく 万国 all nations [**countries**] ▶子を思う親の気持ちは万国共通だ The care parents give to their children is *common to all nations*. ‖ 環境汚染は万国共通の現象である Environmental pollution is a *universal* phenomenon.
‖万国旗 the flags of all nations ; bunting (装飾用の) ‖ 万国博覧会 an international exposition, a world('s) fair.

バンコク Bangkok (タイの首都).

はんこつ 反骨 ▶反骨精神 *rebellious* [*rebel*] *spirit* ‖ 金子光晴は反骨の詩人として名高い Kaneko Mitsuharu is a well-known *anti-establishment* poet.

はんごろし 半殺し ▶半殺しの目にあう *be half beaten to death*.

ばんこん 晩婚 a **late marriage** ▶母は晩婚で，私を37歳のときに産みました My mother *married late* and gave birth to me when she was thirty-seven. ‖ 日本では晩婚化がますます進んでいる There's a growing tendency to *get married late* in Japan.

はんざい 犯罪 (a) **crime** (➤ 具体的な犯罪を指す場合は Ⓒ 扱い) 一形 **犯罪の criminal** ▶犯罪を防ぐ prevent *crime* ‖ 犯罪を犯す commit *a crime* ‖ 彼には犯罪の前歴がある He has *a criminal record*. ‖ 犯罪捜査を開始する open *a criminal investigation*.
‖犯罪者 a criminal, an offender ‖ 犯罪心理学

criminal psychology ‖ **軽犯罪** a minor offense ; a misdemeanor /mìsdɪmíːnəʳ/ (➤ 法律用語) ‖ **国際犯罪** an international crime ‖ **少年犯罪** (a) juvenile crime ‖ **二国間犯罪人引渡条約** a bilateral extradition treaty.

「犯罪」のいろいろ **暗殺** assassination／**横領** embezzlement／**押し込み** burglary／**過失致死** manslaughter／**偽証** perjury／**金庫破り** safecracking／**強姦** rape／**強盗** robbery／**詐欺** swindling／**殺人** murder／**すり** pickpocketing／**窃盗** theft／**贈収賄** bribery／**脱税** tax evasion／**テロ** terrorism／**ハイジャック** hijacking／**売春** prostitution／**不法侵入** trespass／**放火** arson／**暴行** assault (and battery)／**万引き** shoplifting／**密輸** smuggling／**密漁** poaching／**名誉毀(き)損** libel, slander／**誘拐** kidnapping, abduction／**ゆすり** blackmailing, extortion／**略奪** looting

は

ばんざい 万歳 **hurray** /həréɪ/, **hurrah** /hərɑ́ː/ (➤ 後者はやや古風) ▶**万歳**！勝ったぞ *Hurrah* [*Hurray*] ! We won. ‖ 勝利を祝って「**万歳**」を三唱した We shouted "*Banzai !*" three times [gave three *cheers*] for our victory. (➤ three cheers は "Hip, hip, hurrah !" という文句を3度繰り返すこと) ‖ ジャイアンツ，**万歳**！ *Long live* the Giants !
▶この方法でだめだったらもう**万歳**（＝お手上げ）だ If I'm not successful with this method, it will *be all over* for me.

ばんさく 万策 ▶もう**万策**尽きた We have already *tried everything possible*.

はんざつ 煩雑な・繁雑な **complicated**/kɑ́ːmpləkeɪṭɪd/; **troublesome**（煩わしい）▶かつては外国に留学するには**煩雑**な手続きが必要だった Once you had to go through *complicated* procedures to study abroad.

ハンサム **handsome** /hǽnsəm/, **good-looking** 《参考》 handsome は女性に使うこともあり，その場合は，「(主に中年の女性が）上品できりっとした顔つきの」の意 ▶彼女は自分の彼氏が**ハンサム**なのを鼻にかけている She boasts of her boyfriend being *handsome* [her boyfriend's *good looks*]. ‖ 彼女の弟さん，背が高くてすごく**ハンサム**よ Her (younger) brother is tall and very *good-looking*.

ばんさんかい 晩餐会 a **dinner**, a **dinner party** ; a **banquet**（大がかりで正式な宴会）▶彼は首相主催の**晩さん会**に招かれた He was invited to the *dinner* (*party*) given [hosted] by the prime minister.

はんじ 判事 a **judge** ; **the bench**（➤ 総称）.

ばんじ 万事 **everything, all** ▶**万事**うまくいった *Everything* [*All*] went well. ‖ **万事**うまくいかない時がある Sometimes *everything* goes wrong. ‖ **万事休す** *It's all over for me* [*us*]. ／*The game's* [*jig's*] *up*. ／*There's no way out*. (➤ way out は「出口，解決法」).

パンジー 《植物》a **pansy**.

バンジージャンプ **bungee** [**bungy**] **jumping** 一動 **バンジージャンプをする** **bungee** [**bungy**] **jump**.

はんしはんしょう 半死半生 ▶山で遭難した登山者たちは**半死半生**で小屋にたどりついた The mountain climbers who had gotten lost (on the mountain) *were nearly dead* when they arrived at the hut. ‖ 彼はその災害で**半死半生**の目にあった He *almost died* in the disaster.

はんしゃ 反射 **1**【光・熱・音などの】**reflection** 一動 **反射する** **reflect** ＋目 ▶万華鏡は光の**反射**を利用したおもちゃだ A kaleidoscope is a toy that makes use of the *reflection* of light. ‖ 湖に張った氷が太陽の光を**反射している** The ice on the lake *is reflecting* the sunlight.
‖**反射鏡** a reflecting mirror ‖ **反射板** a reflector ‖ **反射望遠鏡** a reflecting telescope, a reflector.
2【生理学上の】**reflex** ▶銃声が鳴ると全員**反射的に**身を伏せた We all threw ourselves down on the ground *by reflex* [*out of reflex* ／*instinctively*] when a shot was heard. ‖ 車の運転にはすばやい**反射神経**が必要だ You need quick *reflexes* to drive a car.
‖**反射運動** reflex (movement) ‖ **反射作用** reflex action.

はんしゃかいてき 反社会的な **antisocial** ▶**反社会的**行動[集団] activities [a group] *destructive to society*（➤ antisocial activities は「社会に敵意を向けた行動」).

ばんしゃく 晩酌 ▶父は毎晩のように**晩酌**をする My father *has a drink with his dinner* almost every evening.

ばんじゃく 盤石 ▶**盤石**の守り (a) *rock-solid* defense.

はんしゅう 半周 ▶我々は自転車で湖のまわりを**半周し**た We *went halfway around* the lake by bicycle.

ばんしゅう 晩秋 **late autumn** [**fall**] ▶この辺りの景色は**晩秋**が美しい The scenery in this area is lovely in *late autumn*.

はんじゅく 半熟の **soft-boiled** ▶**半熟**の卵 a *soft-boiled* egg（➤ three-minute egg ともいう）‖ 卵は**半熟**にしてください Could you please *soft-boil* my egg (s) ?／I'd like my egg (s) *soft-boiled* [*half-boiled*].

はんしゅつ 搬出する **carry out** 《of》.

ばんしゅん 晩春 **late spring**.

ばんしょ 板書する **write on a blackboard** ▶数学の公式を**板書する** *write* mathematical formulas *on the blackboard*.

はんしょう 反証 **contrary evidence, counterevidence** ; **rebuttal**（反ばく，反論）一動 **反証する** **disprove** ＋目 ▶その学説に対する**反証**を挙げる give *contrary evidence* to that theory ／disprove that theory.

はんじょう 繁盛 **prosperity** 一動 **繁盛する** **prosper** ▶商売**繁盛**でけっこうじゃないですか It's great that your *business is going* so *well*. ‖ あのラーメン屋は**繁盛している** That ramen shop *is doing* (*a*) *good business*.
▶あの歯医者さんは**繁盛している** That dentist *has a large practice*. (➤「患者が多い」の意) ／That dentist *is very popular*.

ばんしょう 万障 ▶**万障**お繰り合わせのうえご出席ください We do hope you will attend. (➤ 英語は「切に望みます」の意).

バンジョー a **banjo**.

はんしょく 繁殖 **breeding** 一動 **繁殖する** **breed**（動物が）; **multiply, propagate** (one**self**)（動植物が；後者はより堅い語）
▶ウサギは**繁殖**が早い Rabbits *breed* [*multiply* ／*propagate*] rapidly. ‖ 梅雨時は雑菌が**繁殖しやすい** Various kinds of bacteria *multiply easily* in the rainy season. ‖ ネズミは**繁殖力の強い**動物だ The mouse is a *prolific* [*fertile*] animal. (➤ ともに「多産の」の意).
‖**繁殖期** the breeding season.

はんしん 半身 ▶上[下]半身 the upper [lower] *half of the body* ‖ 胸のレントゲンを撮りますので，上半身裸になってください I'm going to take an X-ray of your chest. Please *strip (yourself) to the waist*. (➤「腰まで」と考える).
▶右半身の神経中枢は左側の脳にある The nerve center for *the right side of the body* lies in the left side of the brain. ‖ 父は交通事故で半身[下半身]が不随になった My father had a traffic accident, and is paralyzed *on one side* [*from the waist down*].
‖半身像 a portrait of a person from the waist up (絵画の) ; a half-length statue (彫刻の) ; a bust(胸像).

はんしんはんぎ 半信半疑 ▶我々は彼の話を半信半疑で聞いていた We listened to his story *half in doubt* [*disbelief*]. ／We *took* his story *with a grain* [*pinch*] *of salt*. (➤ take ... with a grain [pinch] of salt は「…を割り引いて聞く」の意) ‖ 弟がくじで1等を当てたと聞いても私たちは半信半疑だった We *could not quite believe* (that) my brother won first prize in the lottery.

1**はんすう 半数** **half the number, half of the members** ▶国会議員の半数はその計画に反対している *Half of the members* of the Diet are against the plan. ‖ もし半数以上の得票がなければ上位2名で決選投票が行われる If any candidate fails to get *a majority*, a deciding vote will be taken between the top two.

2**はんすう 反芻** **rumination** 一動 **反すうする** **ruminate** /rúːmɪneɪt/ ▶牛が食べ物を反すうしている The cow *is ruminating* [*is chewing its cud*].
▶彼の提案を反すうする *ruminate over* his proposal.

ハンスト a **hunger strike** ▶ハンストをする go on (*a*) *hunger strike*.

パンスト **pantyhose** /pǽnṭihoʊz/ (➤ 複数扱いで1足でも a をつけない), 《英また》**tights** ▶パンストをはく wear *pantyhose* ‖ パンスト2足 two pairs of *pantyhose*.

はんズボン 半ズボン **shorts** (➤《米》では下着の「パンツ」の意にもなる).

はんする 反する **be opposed** [**contrary**] **to** (逆である) ; **be against** (背く) ▶それは事実に反する It *is contrary to* the fact(s). ‖ きみの行為は規則に反する Your act *is against* the rules. ‖ 金権政治は民主主義の精神に反する Money politics *goes against* the spirit of democracy.
▶私たちの期待に反して娘は大学に進学しなかった *Against* our expectations, my daughter didn't go to college.

1**はんせい 反省** **soul-searching** (内省，自己分析) ; **reflection** (熟考) 一動 **反省する** **do some soul-searching, reflect** 《on》, **think over** (➤ think over はややインフォーマルな言い方) ; **regret** (後悔する) ▶どうして失敗したのか反省してみなさい You'd better *reflect on* [*think over*] why you failed. ‖ あなたにひどいことを言ってしまったと反省しています I *regret* [*feel sorry*] I said awful things to you. ‖ 二人は離婚を決意する前にじっくり反省してみた They did a lot of *soul-searching* before they decided to get divorced. ‖ 私たちは毎日反省会をする We have *a review meeting* every day (to see what improvements can be made).

2**はんせい 半生** ▶彼は半生を難民救済にささげた He devoted *half his lifetime* to the relief of refugees [to the refugee relief]. ‖ 自分のこれまでの半生を振り返るとき何をしてきたのかと恥ずかしくなる When I look back on my *earlier life*, I feel ashamed of what I've done.

1**はんせん 帆船** a **sailing ship**, a **sailboat** 《参考》形態により clipper, schooner, dinghy, yacht, catamaran など個々の名がある.

2**はんせん 反戦の** **antiwar** ▶反戦を叫ぶ cry out *against war* ‖ 反戦デモ[集会]に加わる join *an antiwar demonstration* [*rally*].
‖反戦運動 an antiwar movement ‖ 反戦映画 an antiwar movie ‖ 反戦主義 pacifism ‖ 反戦主義者 a pacifist.

はんぜん 判然 ▶なぜ彼女が断ったのか理由は判然としない The reason why she refused *is not quite clear*.

-ばんせん -番線 ▶上野行きの電車が3番線に停車している The Ueno-bound train is now on *Track* [*Platform*] (*No.*) *3*. ‖ 次の列車は7番線から発車する The next train leaves from *Track 7*.

ばんぜん 万全 ▶試験準備は万全だ My preparation for the exam is *complete*. ‖ 地震に対して万全の策を講じる必要がある We have to take *all possible* [*necessary*] *measures* against quakes. ‖ 万全を期してもう一度数をチェックした *To be doubly* [*double*] *sure*, I checked the number again.

ハンセンびょう ハンセン病 《医学》 **Hansen's disease** (➤ 英語では通例，正式な用語である leprosy を用いる．また，その患者は差別的な leper でなく，a leprosy patient または a person with leprosy という).

1**はんそう 帆走する** **sail** ▶1そうのヨットが湖を帆走していた A yacht *was sailing* [*gliding*] over the lake.

2**はんそう 搬送する** **transport** +目 ▶救急車でけが人を病院へ搬送する *transport* the injured people to the hospital in ambulances.

1**ばんそう 伴奏** (an) **accompaniment** 一動 **伴奏をする** **accompany** +目 ▶ピアノの伴奏で歌う sing *to* (*the accompaniment of*) the piano ‖ 私はギターで姉の伴奏をした I *accompanied* my sister on the guitar. ‖ ジャネットが歌を歌い，ポールが伴奏した Janet sang, and Paul *accompanied* (her).
‖伴奏者 an accompanist.

2**ばんそう 伴走** ‖伴走者 an escort runner.

ばんそうこう 絆創膏 a [an **adhesive**] **plaster** ; an **adhesive tape** (テープ状の) ▶傷口にばんそうこうをはった I put *an adhesive tape* [*a* (*sticking*) *plaster* ／《米また》*a Band-Aid* ／《英また》*an Elastoplast*] on the cut. 《参考》Band-Aid, Elastoplast はともに商標名だが，普通名詞として扱うことが多い.

はんそく 反則 a **foul** /faʊl/ (競技の) 一動 **反則を犯す** **foul, commit a foul** ▶相撲では相手の力士のまげをつかむのは反則だ In sumo wrestling, it is *a foul* to take hold of the opponent's topknot. ‖ 彼はその試合で2度も反則を犯した He *committed* two *fouls* [*fouled* twice] in the game. ‖ 南野選手はハンドの反則をとられた Minamino *was charged with* handling. ‖ その選手は反則で退場を命じられた That player *fouled out of the game*. ‖ 松本はその試合で反則負けになった Matsumoto *lost* the match *on a foul*.

はんそで 半袖 **short sleeves** ▶暑くなってきたので半袖シャツが目立つ Now that it's getting hotter, there are more people wearing *short-sleeved shirts*.

はんだ **solder** /sɑ́ːdəʳ ‖ sɔ́ldə/ ▶IC チップを基盤にはんだ付けする *solder* an IC chip to the base.

‖はんだごて a soldering iron.

パンダ a (giant) panda ▶パンダの赤ちゃん a baby *panda* ‖パンダは垂れ目だ The *panda* has downturned eyes.

‖レッサーパンダ a lesser panda ‖パンダウサギ a checkered giant rabbit.

ハンター a hunter.

はんたい 反対 1【逆】the opposite /ά:pəzɪt/ ―形 反対の opposite, contrary /kά:ntreri/ (➤ contrary は opposite よりも対立の意味が強い) ▶「白」の反対は「黒」だ "Black" is *the opposite* of "white." (➤ the opposite *to* は誤用だが, これを用いる人もいる) ‖私の意見はあなたとは全く反対だ My opinion *is* completely *opposite to* yours. ‖調査結果は予想とはまるで反対だった The result of the investigation *was contrary to* our expectations.

▶ヘリは急に向きを変えて反対の方向へ飛んで行った The helicopter suddenly made a turn and flew in the *opposite* direction. ‖その靴下, 左右反対にはいてるんじゃない? You're wearing your socks *on the wrong feet*, aren't you? ‖道をはさんで家の反対側 (=向かい側)がアイスクリーム屋になった An ice cream shop opened *just across from* my home.

‖反対車線 the opposite lane ‖反対色 a complementary color.

2【不賛成】opposition ; (an) objection (異議申し立て) ; (a) resistance (抵抗) ―動 反対する oppose +目, object to ; be opposed to, be against (反対している)

【文型】
あること(A)に反対する
oppose A
object to A
あること(A)に反対である
be opposed to A
be against A
➤ Aは名詞・動名詞

【解説】(1) **oppose** は「受け入れない, 阻止のための行動を起こす」ことで, **object to** は「異論がある, 異議を唱える」の意. 後者はその理由なり, 根拠なりを述べるのが, あるいは, 聞き手から求められるのがふつうである.
(2)態度や考え方として「人(A)が…するのに反対である」という状態は **be opposed to** [**be against**] A **doing** で, その立場を表明することもしないこともある. Aの代わりに A's の形にすることもある. 代名詞は所有格 my, your, his, her などを使う.
(3)話をしている相手の意見に反対する場合は don't agree や disagree (=「意見が合わない」)が使われることが多い. それは, 意味の強い oppose や object と比べるとまだ穏やかな表現だからである.

▶法案に反対する *oppose* a bill (➤ 単に,「可」としない, 通過させない ; こちらを用いるのがふつう) ; *object to* a bill (➤ 法案に対して「異議がある」; 公正を欠く, 違憲である, などの理由や根拠がある) ‖増税に反対する *oppose* [*object to*] a tax increase ‖誰もが戦争に反対なはずなのに, 世界中でいくつもの戦争が続いている Despite the fact that almost everybody *opposes* war, many wars are continuing around the world. ‖市長は原子炉の再稼働に反対した[反対を表明した] The mayor *opposed* [expressed his *opposition* to] the restart of the nuclear reactor. ‖息子が夜更かしするのは反対だ I *am against* [*am opposed to*] my son staying up late. ‖住民たちは原子力発電所の建設に反対している The residents *are opposed to* the construction of a nuclear power plant.

▶この案に反対の方は挙手をお願いします Those (who *are*) *opposed to* the motion, please raise your hand. ‖ 対話「銀行は国によって守られるべきだと思います」「私は反対です」"I think banks should be protected by the government." "*I disagree with you.*" (➤ 面と向かって言うときにはかなり強い意味になる).

▶私は体罰には反対だ I *am against* [I *don't believe in*] corporal punishment. (➤ believe in は「価値[有効性]を信じる」の意) ‖お母さんは私のやりたいことにいつでも反対するじゃない? You'*re* always *against* what I want to do, aren't you, Mom? ‖彼らは職場でのパワハラ反対運動を組織した They organized *a movement against supervisor harassment* in the workplace.

▶彼らの反対で我々の計画はだめになった Their *resistance* spoiled our plans [project]. ‖核実験反対の声 an outcry *against* a nuclear test ‖《プラカードなどの文句》核兵器反対! *No Nukes!*

‖反対者 an opponent ‖反対尋問 a cross-examination ‖反対勢力 a counterforce ‖反対派 an opposition group [faction].

☛ 正反対 (→見出語)

はんたいせい 反体制の anti-establishment ; dissident (政府などの意見に従わない) ▶3人の反体制作家がその国から追放された Three *anti-establishment* [*dissident*] writers were expelled from the country.

‖反体制活動家 a dissident.

バンダナ a bandanna (➤ bandana ともつづる) ▶バンダナを首に巻く wear *a bandanna* around one's neck.

バンタムきゅう バンタム級 the bantamweight class [division] ▶バンタム級の選手 *a bantamweight*.

パンタロン pantaloons (➤ 19世紀ごろ流行した細い男性用ズボンを指したが, 今は一般に男性・女性用のズボンを指す)

‖パンタロンスーツ a pantsuit, a pants suit, a trouser suit.

はんだん 判断 (a) judgment ; (a) decision (決定) ―動 判断する judge (+目), decide (+目) ▶判断を誤る make an error in *judgment* ‖年齢・性別・容ぼうなどをもとに人を判断する *make judgments* on people based upon their age, sex, appearance, etc. ‖人を顔や身なりで判断するな Don't *judge* people by the way they look and dress.

▶父と母のどちらの言うことが正しいか判断に苦しんでいる I find it difficult to *judge* who is right, Mom or Dad. (➤「父と母」は Mom or Dad の語順が普通) ‖手元にある情報をもとに判断すると彼は過去に犯罪にかかわったことはないようだ *Judging from* the information at hand [the available information], he has not been involved in any crimes in the past.

▶それは自分で判断しなさい *Decide* for yourself. ‖どの辞書を買えばよいかはきみたちの判断に任せる Which dictionary to buy *is up to* you. (➤ be up to は「…しだい」) ‖彼にはしっかりした判断力がある He has *good judgment*.

‖姓名判断 fortune-telling [divination] using a person's name ‖夢判断 dream reading.

あなたの英語はどう響く?
日本人の好きな慣用句の１つに Judging from [by] ... があるが，これを用いて，例えば Judging from what you say, he must be a capable leader. のように言うと，日本語で「きみのことばから察すると，彼は有能なリーダーに違いないね」と言うのと同じで，やや，あるいはかなり気取った言い方に響くので要注意. From what you say, he must be a good leader. のような言い方が好ましい.

ばんち 番地 one's **address** /ǽdres/ ; a **house number** (家屋番号)

〘解説〙(1) 日本の番地は居住地の土地区画に対してつけられた番号であるが，英米では１軒１軒の家屋に番号がつけてあり，これを house number と呼ぶ. (2) 日本も都市によっては３丁目４番５号のようになっていて，５号が特定の一軒を指していることがあるが，この場合の５号が英語の house number の役をしている.

▶お宅は何番地ですか What is your *address* [*house number*]? ‖この手紙は番地が違っている The *address* on this letter is wrong. ／This letter is wrongly addressed. ／This letter has the wrong *house number* on it. ‖私は桜通り５番地に住んでいます I live *at* [*in*] *number 5*, Sakura Street. (● I live を I am living とすると，「一時的に」の意になる).

パンチ 1【げんこつ】 a **punch** ▶鼻にパンチを食らう get *a punch* on the nose ‖あごに一発，パンチを食らわしてやろうか Do you want me to *punch* [*sock*] you on the chin?
2【迫力】punch ▶パンチの効いたロック rock music *with a lot of punch* ‖彼女の歌はパンチが効いている[に欠ける] Her song has [lacks] *punch*.
3【穴】▶切符にパンチを入れる *punch* (a hole in) a ticket. ‖パンチカード a punch card.

ばんちゃ 番茶 ***bancha***; a variety of green tea, made from larger, tougher leaves which are picked along with stems(➤ 説明的な訳).

はんちゅう 範疇 a **category** /kǽṭəgɔ̀ːri/ ▶これらの現象は３つの範ちゅうに分けられる These phenomena are classified into three *categories*.

ばんちょう 番長 a **school gang leader**.

パンツ 1【下着】underpants ▶パンツ１枚になる strip to one's *underpants*.
‖海水パンツ bathing [swimming] trunks.
2【ズボン】pants ▶夏向きのパンツ *pants* for summer. ‖パンツスーツ a pantsuit, 《英》a trouser suit ‖ショートパンツ shorts ‖スエットパンツ sweat pants ‖美脚パンツ figure-flattering pants ; stretch pants (伸縮性のあるもの) ‖ホットパンツ hot pants.

危ないカタカナ語✸パンツ
1 pants は《英》では下着のパンツを指し，《米》ではズボンを指すことが多いが，最近では《米》の用法が《英》にも及んでいる. 日本で「パンツ」が「ズボン」の意味で使われるのも《米》用法の影響.
2 誤解を避けるためには下着のパンツは underpants といえばよい. 日常的には briefs とか shorts ともいうが，これらはすべて男性用のパンツで，女性用のものは panties という.

はんつき 半月 **half a month, a half month** ▶競技会まであと半月だ We have *two weeks* to go before the athletic meet. (➤ half a month を用いないで，このように two weeks とすることが多い).

ばんづけ 番付 a **list** ▶夏場所の相撲の番付 the *ranking list* of sumo wrestlers for the summer tournament ‖あの人はいつも長者番付に載る He is always on the *list of millionaire* taxpayers.

ハンデ 1【不利な条件】 a **handicap** ; an **obstacle** (障害物) ; a **disability** (身体の障害) ; a **disadvantage** (不利なこと[立場]) ▶肉体的なハンデを克服する overcome one's physical *disability* ‖英語を話せないことが彼にとって大きなハンデになっている His lack of English speaking ability is a great *handicap* for him.
▶辞書編さんには視力が弱いことはハンデになる Weak eyesight is *an obstacle* [*a disadvantage*] in compiling a dictionary.
2【ゴルフなどの】 a **handicap** ▶ゴルフのハンデは10です I'm a 10-*handicap* player. ／My (golf) *handicap* is 10. ‖プロとアマが試合をするんじゃ不公平だから，少しハンデをつけようか It's not fair for professionals to compete with amateurs, so shall we give a small *handicap* to the professionals?

危ないカタカナ語✸ハンデ
「不利な条件」の意味の「ハンデ」は「ハンディキャップ」の日本式省略形. 英語では必ず handicap とする. 「障害になるもの」という広い意味ならば obstacle を使うこともできる.

はんてい 判定 (a) **judgment** (公の判断) ; (a) **decision** (決定) ; a **call** (審判の) 一動 **判定する judge, decide**
▶選手は審判の判定に抗議できない A player is not allowed to protest an umpire's *judgment* [*decision* ／ *call*].
▶レフェリーは彼らに不利な判定を下した The referee *decided* against them. ‖渡辺は挑戦者に判定で勝った[負けた] Watanabe *won a decision over* [*lost a decision to*] the challenger. ‖その馬は写真判定でレースに勝った That racehorse won on *a photo finish*. ／That racehorse got a *photo-finish* victory.

ハンディー handy ▶ハンディーな案内書 a *handy* guidebook.

パンティー panties ‖パンティーストッキング pantyhose, 《英また》tights. (→パンスト).

ハンディキャップ →ハンデ.

パンデミック a **pandemic** (全国[全大陸, 全世界]的流行病). →エンデミック.

はんてん 斑点 a **spot** ; a **speck** (小さな) ▶はん点のある犬 a *spotted* dog ‖多くのシカには背にはん点がある Many deers have *spots* on their backs. ‖赤いはん点が体中にできた I got red *spots* all over my body. ‖セッター犬は白地に黒や赤茶色の小さなはん点がある A setter has a white coat with small *flecks* of black and Indian red.
▶犯人の衣服には返り血がはん点になってついていた The criminal's clothes *were spotted* with blood stains from the victim.

ハント ▶彼は女の子をハントするのがうまい He's good at *picking up* girls.

バント a **bunt** 一動 **バントする bunt** ▶稲葉は一塁線にバントを決めた Inaba *bunted successfully* down the first base line. ‖走者はバントで二塁へ進んだ The runner was sent to second base *on a bunt*.

‖スリーバント a two-strike bunt ‖ セーフティーバント a drag bunt.

バンド **1**【束ねたりするためのひも】a **band** ▶ゴムバンド a rubber *band* ‖ 時計のバンド a watch *strap*
‖ブックバンド a book band ‖ ヘアバンド a hair band.
2【楽団】a **band** ▶ジャズ［ブラス］バンド a jazz［brass］*band* ‖ 彼は大学のロックバンドのメンバーだ He is a member of the college *rock band*.
‖バンドマン a bandsman.

はんドア 半ドア a **half-open door** ▶左のドアが半ドアですよ Your left car door *isn't completely shut*.

ハンドアウト a **handout**. →プリント.

はんとう 半島 a **peninsula** /pənínsələ/ ▶能登半島 the Noto *Peninsula*.

はんどう 反動 (a) **reaction** ▶タクシーが急ブレーキをかけたので我々は反動で前のめりになった When the taxi stopped abruptly, we lurched forward *in reaction*. ‖ 厳しく育てた反動か, 娘は最近私の言うことを聞かなくなった It may be *a reaction* against my strict upbringing, but my daughter won't listen to me these days.
‖反動勢力 reactionary forces.

ばんとう 番頭 a **chief clerk** ‖大番頭 the head of the clerks and chief clerks.

はんどうたい 半導体 a **semiconductor**.

はんとうめい 半透明の **semitransparent, translucent**（➤ 後者は書き言葉に多い）▶オパールは半透明の鉱物だ The opal is a *semitransparent*［*translucent*］mineral.

バンドエイド a **Band-Aid**（➤ 商標名）▶指の傷にバンドエイドをはる put *a Band-Aid* over a cut on one's finger.

はんどく 判読 ▶その古文書は虫食いがひどく判読不能だった The old document was so moth-eaten we *couldn't figure*［*make*］it *out*.（➤ figure out は「理解する」）／The old document was so moth-eaten (that) it was *illegible*.
✉**なぐり書きで申しわけありませんがよろしくご判読ください** I apologize for the poor handwriting, but could you please *read* what I have written ?

はんとし 半年 **half a year**,《米また》a **half year, six months**（➤ 3番目の「6か月」という言い方のほうが好まれる）《参考》「1年半後」は a year and a half later,「2年半の間」は for two and a half years という言い方が多い.
▶私たちが新居に越して来てから半年になる It has been *half a year*［*a half year*／*six months*］since we moved into the new house. ‖ それは半年前の出来事だ It happened *six months ago*［*half a year ago*］. ‖ 私たちは半年ごとに例会を開く We hold a regular meeting *twice a year*［*every six months*／*semiannually*］.

ハンドタオル a **hand towel**.

ハンドバッグ a **handbag**;《米また》a **pocketbook**, a **purse**（➤ ともに肩ひものない小型のもの）.

ハンドブック a **handbook**(便覧); a **manual**(手引き) ▶海外旅行ハンドブック *a handbook* for overseas travel.

ハンドブレーキ《米》a **parking brake**,《米》an **emergency brake**,《英》a **handbrake**.

ハンドボール **(team) handball** ▶ハンドボールをする play *(team) handball*.
《参考》handball は《米》では, ゴムのボールを手で壁に打ち返して得点を競う競技を指すので, 7人制ハンドボールをいう場合は誤解を避けて team handball という.

ハンドマイク《米》a **bullhorn**,《英》a **loudhailer**.

パントマイム a **pantomime** /pǽntəmaɪm/, a **mime**

> 《解説》(1) 日本語の「パントマイム」は身ぶりや表情だけで行う演技・芝居を指すが,《米》ではこれを pantomime,《インフォーマル》mime という.
> (2)《英》の pantomime（《インフォーマル》panto）は子供向けのクリスマス演劇をいい, 無言劇ではない. 無言で行うのは mime という.

▶パントマイムを演じる act *a (panto)mime*.
‖パントマイム役者 a mime, a pantomimist, a pantomime artist.

パンドラのはこ パンドラの箱 **Pandora's box** ▶パンドラの箱を開ける open (up) *a Pandora's box*（➤ 比喩的に用いるときは a を付けることが多い）.

ハンドル **1**【乗り物の】a **steering wheel**（自動車の）; **handlebars**（自転車・オートバイの）

steering wheel
handlebars
handle

▶右ハンドルの車 a car *with a right-hand drive*／a *right-hand-drive* car／a *right drive* car ‖ ハンドルを取られる *lose directional control* ‖ ハンドルを握る(＝運転する) *take the steering wheel* ‖ ハンドルを握っているときは話しかけないで Don't talk to me when I'*m at*［*behind*］*the wheel*.（➤ when I'm driving としてもよい）‖ ハンドルを握って10年になります I have ten years(') *driving experience*.
▶彼女は犬をひくまいとしてすばやくハンドルを左へ切った She turned［swung］the *wheel* quickly to the left to avoid hitting a dog. ‖ 曲がるときハンドルを切り損ねて電柱に衝突した I *lost control of the car* when making a turn and crashed into a telephone pole. ‖ トムのハンドルさばきは危なっかしくて見ていられない Tom's *driving* (*technique*) is so dangerous I can't watch.
‖(自転車の)ドロップハンドル dropped handlebars.
2【取っ手】a **handle**; a **knob**(ノブ) ▶ハンドルを回してドアを開けた I turned the *knob* and opened the door.

> **危ないカタカナ語✸ ハンドル**
> **1**「ハンドル」は handle からきているが, 用法は全く異なる. 英語の handle は「持つところ」の意で, 具体的には握りの部分に限られる. 自転車やオートバイの「ハンドル」は handlebars といい, その両端の握りの部分が handle である. 車のハンドルは輪状になっているので steering wheel という.
> **2** ドアのハンドル は handle でよいが, 丸い取っ手は knob である.

‖ハンドルネーム《コンピュータ》a handle, a screen name（➤ handle name ということもある）.

はんドン 半ドン a **half-day off** ▶あすは半ドンだ We have *a half-day off*［*half-holiday*］tomorrow.

ばんなん 万難 ▶万難を排して目標を達成してほしい I

hope you'll attain your goals *in the face of* [*despite*] *all difficulties*. (➤ in the face of は「…をものともせず」).

[1]**はんにち 半日** **half a day,**《米また》a **half day** ▶きょうは会議，会議で**半日**つぶれた I've wasted *half the day* attending one meeting after another. ‖ 午後はPTAの会合があるので授業は**半日**(＝午前中だけ)です We have classes *only in the morning* because there is a PTA meeting in the afternoon.

[2]**はんにち 反日の** **anti-Japanese** ▶**反日**感情 *anti-Japanese* sentiment [feeling].

はんにゅう 搬入する **carry into** ▶展覧会場に絵画を**搬入する** *carry* paintings *into* the exhibition hall.

はんにん 犯人 a **criminal**(有罪となった罪人)；a **culprit** /kʌ́lprɪt/ (犯罪・悪事を行った者)；a **suspect**(容疑者)

> **解説** (1)「容疑者」を指す場合は suspect という.
> (2)「殺人犯(人)」は murderer,「誘拐犯(人)」は kidnapper,「強盗犯(人)」は robber,「万引犯(人)」は shoplifter,「放火犯(人)」は arsonist のように具体的にいうことが多い.

▶きのうの殺人事件の**犯人**はまだ捕まっていない The *suspect* of yesterday's murder case is still at large. ‖ 彼は窃盗(せっとう)の**犯人**として警察で取り調べを受けた He was examined by the police *on suspicion* of theft. ‖ **犯人**は誰だ Who did it? ／Who is the *culprit* [*perpetrator*]?

‖**真犯人** the real culprit.

[1]**ばんにん 万人** **everybody** ▶この清涼飲料は**万人**向きだ This soft drink suits *everybody*'s taste [pleases *all* tastes].

[2]**ばんにん 番人** a **guard**, a **watch**(見張り) ▶裁判所は「法の**番人**」といわれる The courts are called "*(the) guardians of the law.*"

はんにんまえ 半人前 ▶きみの仕事はまだ**半人前**だね Your work *fails to come up to scratch* [*to measure up to the standard*]. (➤ up to scratch は「一定の水準に達して」).

はんね 半値 a **half price, half the price** ▶商品を市価の**半値**で売る sell goods *at half the market price* ‖ その百科事典全巻を**半値**で買った I bought the whole set of encyclopedias *(for) half-price* [*at half (the) price*]. (➤ 前者は副詞用法).

ばんねん 晩年 one's **later years** ▶祖父母は幸せな**晩年**を送った My grandparents lived happily in *their later years*.

▶モーツァルトの**晩年**は悲惨だった *The last years* of Mozart's life were tragic.

はんのう 反応 (a) **reaction**(反射的・直接的な)；(a) **response**(答えとしての対応・行動)；**feedback**(消費者・利用者・視聴者などからの「声」) 一動 (…に)**反応する** **react**《to》, **respond**《to》▶市民の要望に対して市当局からは冷たい**反応**しか返ってこなかった The demands of the citizens have met with [have encountered] a cool *response* from city officials. ‖ 消費者の**反応**はいい We have received a positive *response* from consumers. ‖ 新製品の**反応**はいい Our new product is getting a favorable *response*.

▶読者からよい[芳しくない]**反応**が届く receive positive [negative] *feedback* from readers ‖ 新車についてディーラーから何か**反応**はありましたか Did you get any *feedback* from the dealers on our new cars? ‖ 少し**相手方の反応**を見たらどうだろうか How about watching *how they react* [*respond*] for a while? ‖ 国民はその政策に対して**拒否反応**を示した The people showed an *adverse reaction* to the policy.

‖**アレルギー反応** an allergic reaction ‖ **化学反応** a chemical reaction ‖ **連鎖反応** a chain reaction.

ばんのう 万能の **almighty**(全能の)；**all-around** [**all-round**](多方面の) ▶**万能の神** *almighty* God ／God *Almighty* ‖ インターネットは**万能**ではない The Internet is not *everything*.

▶今は科学**万能**(の世の中)だ Science *is everything* [*rules the world*] nowadays. ‖ 彼はスポーツ**万能**だ He is an *all-around* athlete. ／He is good at *all* sports. (➤ 後者はやや文語的な言い方)《参考》野球などで，どのポジションでもこなせる万能選手のことを utility player という.

‖**万能薬** a cure-all, a panacea.

はんぱ 半端な **odd** ▶**はんぱ物**(＝がらくた) odds and ends ‖ **はんぱな**布(＝端切れ)でぞうきんを作った I stitched together some cleaning cloths from cloth *remnants*. (➤ remnants は「残り物」) ‖ **はんぱな**気持ちなら和子さんとデートするのはやめなさい If you are *halfhearted*, stop seeing Kazuko. ‖ 100円未満の**はんぱな**数字は切り捨てて結構です You can drop any *fractional* sum less than 100 yen. (➤「半端な数字」に当たる表現は一般的でないので，趣旨は If the last two digits are less than 100, change them to 00. などと伝えるしかない) ‖ 昨日の雨は**半端じゃなかった** It rained *unbelievably* hard yesterday. ‖ 彼のテクニックは**半端じゃない** [**ハンパない**] His technique is *incredible* [*amazing*].

‖**はんぱ仕事** an odd job.

バンパー a **bumper** ▶門柱に**バンパー**をぶつけた I hit the *bumper* against the gatepost.

ハンバーガー a **hamburger** /hǽmbəːʳgəʳ/ ▶お昼に**ハンバーガー**を食べる eat *a hamburger* for lunch.

‖**ハンバーガーショップ** a hamburger stand [restaurant].

ハンバーグ a **hamburger** /hǽmbəːʳgəʳ/ **steak** (➤ hamburg とは言わない) ▶子供たちはたいてい**ハンバーグ**が大好きだ Most children love to eat *hamburger steaks*. (➤「ハンバーグ」は《米》の a Salisbury /sɑ́ːlzberi/ steak や meatloaf に似ているが独自の発展を遂げているので，a hamburger steak とするのがよい. a hamburger だけではパンにはさんだ「ハンバーガー」の意になるのがふつう).

はんばい 販売 (a) **sale** 一動 **販売する** **sell** ＋目 ▶現金**販売** a cash *sale* ‖ このコンビニでは酒類を**販売**している They *sell* alcoholic drinks in this convenience store. ‖ この型のステレオはもう**販売されていない** This type of stereo set *isn't on the market* [*isn't available*] any more. ‖ この薬はやがて**販売禁止になる**だろう The *sale* of this medicine will *be banned* soon.

▶あの会社は**販売力がある** That company *has strong sales channels*. ‖ 自動車メーカー各社は新車の活発な**販売合戦**を始めた The car manufacturers have started [launched] vigorous *sales campaigns* for their new models.

‖**販売員** a salesperson, salespeople, a sales representative (販売外交員)；a salesman(男性), a saleswoman (女性) ‖ **販売促進(活動)** sales promotion ‖ **販売代理店** a sales agency ‖ **販売部** the sales department ‖ **販売部長** a sales manager ‖ **販売網** a sales network ‖ **販売予測** sales projections ‖ **販売ルート** a marketing route ‖ **自動販売機** a vending machine ‖ **直販** direct sales.

はんばく 反駁 refutation **一動 反ばくする** refute +㊐ ▶社長の発言に**反ばくする**勇気のある役員は1人もいない No other executive is courageous enough to *refute* the president's statement.

ばんぱく 万博 an **international exposition**, an **Expo** /ékspoʊ/ ▶エッフェル塔はパリ**万博**のときに建てられた The Eiffel Tower was built on the occasion of *the Paris Exposition*.

はんぱつ 反発 repulsion /rɪpʌ́lʃən/ **一動 反発する** react against, repel +㊐ ▶リニアモーターカーは磁石の**反発**力を利用している Maglev trains make use of magnetic *repulsion*.
▶税制改革には国民の**反発**(＝抵抗)が強い The people's *resistance* against the revision of the tax system is great. ‖ 少年は父親のことばに強く**反発した** The boy *reacted* strongly *against* his father's words.

はんはん 半々に half-and-half, fifty-fifty ; equally (平等に) ▶会員は男性と女性が**半々**だ We have male and female members *half-and-half* [*fifty-fifty*]. ‖ 彼らは利益を**半々に**分けた They divided the profit *equally* [*evenly*]. ／They split the profit *fifty-fifty*. ‖ 酢とサラダ油を**半々に**入れてよくかき混ぜなさい Add *equal parts* [*quantities*] of vinegar and salad oil and mix well.
▶アメリカでの学生生活を考えると期待と不安が**半々**です When I think about being a student in America, I *feel a mixture* of expectation and anxiety.

ばんばん ▶誰かがドアを**バンバン**たたいた Someone *banged* on the door.
▶**ばんばん**食べてよ *Go right ahead and* eat (up).

ぱんぱん ▶おなかが**ぱんぱん**です My stomach's *ready to burst*. (➤「破裂しそう」の意).

はんびょうにん 半病人 a semi-invalid ▶きみは**半病人**のような顔をしているね You do*n't look very well*. ／You *seem to be in poor health*.

はんびらき 半開きの half-open ▶猫が入れるようにドアを**半開き**にしておいてね Please leave the door *half open* [*ajar*] so the cat can get in. (➤ ajar は「少し開いて」).
▶玉美はいつも口が**半開き**だ Tamami always has her mouth (*hanging*) *half open*.

はんぴれい 反比例《数学》inverse proportion ▶Xは Yに**反比例する** X *is in inverse proportion to* Y. ／X *is inversely proportional to* Y.

はんぷ 頒布する distribute +㊐ ; pass out(配る) ▶大学案内は無料で**頒布して**おります We are *passing out* free college guides [free guides to our college].

はんぷく 反復 repetition /rèpətíʃən/ **一動 反復する** repeat(+㊐) ▶CDを**反復して**聞く listen to a CD *repeatedly* [*over* (*and over*) *again*] ‖ 語学を習得するには**反復練習**しかない *Repeated practice* is the only way to learn a foreign language.

パンプス (a pair of) pumps.

ばんぶつ 万物 all things ; creation(神の創造物) ; all nature(宇宙の全て) ▶**万物の霊長** the lord of *creation*.

はんぶっしつ 反物質《物理学》antimatter.

パンフレット a pamphlet ; a brochure /broʊʃóəʳ/ (営業用の) ; literature(広報・宣伝用印刷物) ▶安全なセックスについての**パンフレット**を配る distribute *pamphlets* on safe sex ‖ 販売促進**パンフレット** promotional *literature*.
▶彼は通りで会社案内の**パンフレット**を配っていた He was distributing *brochures* explaining his company on the street. ‖ **パンフレット**頂けますか May I have *a brochure*? ‖ ツアーの**パンフレット**はありますか Do you have any tour *brochures*?

> **危ないカタカナ語✹ パンフレット**
> **1** 日本では宣伝用の一枚刷りの紙から, 数ページ, あるいは十数ページの小冊子までを含めて「パンフレット」と呼んでいるが, 英語の pamphlet は数ページの小冊子を指し, 一枚刷りのものは leaflet という.
> **2** パンフレットの中でも, 営業用に写真・イラストなどを掲載した商品カタログや旅行の案内書などは brochure という.

はんぶん 半分 (a) half

> 【文型】
> **A の半分**
> **half (of) A**
> ❰解説❱ (1) A が「my, the, this ＋名詞」のときには正式には **half of** A という. 話しことばやくだけた文ではしばしば単に **half** A ともいう. 全体を強く意識するときは **half of** A を用いる.
> (2) A が us, you, them など代名詞のときは **half of** us [you] とする.
> (3) A が a kilometer, a mile, a dozen など, 数量を表す単位のときは **half** a kilometer (こちらがふつう)または a **half** kilometer とする.

▶人類の**半分**は女性です *Half of* humanity are women. ‖ クラスの [私たちの] **半分**は数学の授業についていけない *Half of* the class [*Half of* us] can't keep up in math. ‖ 私はその小説を**半分**読んだ I have read *the first half* of the novel. ／I am *halfway* through the novel. ‖ この伝記はまだ**半分**しか読んでいない I have read only *half of* this biography. ‖ やっと仕事が**半分**終わった At last, I've finished *half* the job. ／At last, the job is *half* finished. ‖ 彼は月の**半分**は出張です He's away on business trips *half the month*.

> 【文型】
> **A の半分の〜**
> **half as 〜 as** A
> ➤ 〜は形容詞・副詞
> **数が A の半分の〜**
> **half as many (〜) as** A
> ➤ 量のときは much

▶フランスの人口は日本の約**半分**だ The population of France is about *half as* large *as* that of Japan. ‖ せめてきみの**半分**でもうまく英語が話せたらなあ I wish I could speak English even *half as* well *as* you (do).
▶その建設業者には去年の**半分**しか仕事がない That building contractor only has *half as many* jobs *as* he [her] had last year. ‖ こちらの再生品は約**半分**のお値段です These recycled items cost about *half the original prices*.
▶鍋に**半分**水を入れなさい Fill the pan *halfway* with water. ‖ このケーキ, **半分**に切ってちょうだい Please cut

the cake *in half*. ‖ 半分こしようよ *Let's split it*. ‖ 冗談半分に言ったことが本当になった What I said *half jokingly* [*half in jest*] came true.

ばんぺい 番兵 a **sentry** ▶番兵に立つ *stand sentry*.

はんべそ 半べそ ▶息子が半べそをかきながら帰って来た My son came home *sobbing*.

はんべつ 判別する **distinguish** +⊞ ▶しろうと目にはどちらが偽物でどちらが本物か判別できない An amateur cannot *tell* which is the imitation and which is the real thing. ／An amateur cannot *distinguish* the imitation *from* the real one.

はんぼいん 半母音《音声学》a **semivowel**.

はんぼうき 繁忙期 **the busiest time (of the year)**.

ハンマー a **hammer** ▶ハンマーで板にくぎを打ち込む *hammer* a nail *into* a board.

‖ハンマー投げ the hammer throw.

はんめい 判明する **become clear**(明らかになる); **turn out**《that, to be》(…とわかる) ▶彼の証言によって事故の原因が判明した The cause of the accident *became clear* from his testimony. ‖ 調査の結果，その絵は偽物であることが判明した As a result of the investigation, it *turned out* that the picture was bogus [the picture *proved* to be a fake]. (➤ turn out, prove はともに「結局…であるとわかる」の意) ‖ 遭難者の身元が判明した The victim *was identified*.

ばんめし 晩飯 (a) **supper**; **the evening meal**(夕食); (a) **dinner**(1日のうちの主要な食事).

1**はんめん 反面** ▶この道具はとても便利な反面，壊れやすい This tool is very useful, but *on the other hand*, it is fragile. ／*While* this tool is very useful, it is fragile.

▶あのひどいおばさんたちを私たちの反面教師(＝悪い見本)としましょう Let's use those awful women as *negative examples*.

2**はんめん 半面** **one side, the other side** (➤ 両面あるもののいずれか片方を one side で表せば，もう片方は the other side で表す) ▶彼は真面目だが，ひょうきんな半面もある He is serious [earnest], and yet he has a humorous *side* to him.

はんも 繁茂する **grow thick** ▶空き地に雑草が繁茂していた The weeds *grew thick* in the vacant lot.

はんもく 反目 ▶両家は長年にわたって反目し合っている The two families have been *on hostile terms* for years.

▶彼らはつまらないことで互いに反目している They *are at odds* [*at loggerheads*] with each other over a trivial matter.

ハンモック a **hammock** ▶ハンモックをつる sling [put up／hang up] *a hammock* ‖ ハンモックで寝る sleep in *a hammock*.

1**はんもん 反問する** **ask back (without answering the other person's question)**.

2**はんもん 煩悶** **agony, anguish**(➤ 前者がより激しい苦しみを指し，肉体的苦痛にも用いる) ▶子供ががんであることをどう告げたらよいか母親は煩悶した The mother *agonized over* how to tell her child that he had cancer.

ばんゆういんりょく 万有引力《物理学》**universal gravitation** ▶万有引力の法則 the Law of *Gravitation*.

はんよう 汎用 a **general purpose** ▶汎用コンピュータ a *general-purpose* computer ‖ 汎用性の高い製品 a *versatile* product.

はんら 半裸の **half-naked, seminude** ▶半裸の死体 a *half-naked* dead body.

ばんらい 万雷 ▶演説者は聴衆から万雷の拍手を浴びた The speaker received *thunderous applause* from the audience.

1**はんらん 反乱** (a) **rebellion** (➤ revolution(革命)と異なり，根本的変革をもたらさないものをいう); an **uprising** (民間人による通例小規模の; 失敗に終わったものをいう); (a) **revolt**(圧制に対する)

▶軍が反乱を鎮圧した The army suppressed [put down] the *rebellion*. ‖ 彼らは独裁者に対して反乱を起こした They *revolted* [*rebelled*] *against* the dictator.

‖反乱軍 a rebel army.

2**はんらん 氾濫** **flooding**; a **flood**(1回の) 一動 **はんらんする** **overflow, flood**; **be flooded**《with》▶台風で利根川がはんらんした The typhoon caused the Tone River to *flood over* [to *overflow*].

▶日本の家庭には韓国製の電気製品がはんらんしている Japanese homes *are flooded with* Korean electrical appliances.

ばんりのちょうじょう 万里の長城 **the Great Wall of China**.

はんりゅう 韓流の **Korean**(韓国の) ▶韓流ドラマ a *Korean drama*.

はんりょ 伴侶 a **companion**(連れ); a **spouse** /spaʊs/ (配偶者); a **life partner**(人生のパートナー; 夫または妻のこと) ▶その犬は老人にとって終生の伴りょだった The dog was the old man's *companion* until the end of his life.

▶良き伴りょが見つかりますように I hope I can find a good *husband* [*wife*].

1**はんれい 凡例** **explanatory notes** (辞書などの); a **legend**(地図・図表の).

2**はんれい 判例** a **(legal) precedent** /présɪdənt/ ▶最高裁の判例 (a) Supreme Court *precedent*.

はんろ 販路 a **market**(市場) ▶自動車メーカーはインドに販路を開拓しようとしている The car manufacturers are trying to find [open] a new *market* in India.

はんろん 反論 (an) **objection**(異議) 一動 (…に)**反論する** **argue**《against》▶彼の言うことには反論の余地がない What he says leaves no room for *objection*. ／What he says is irrefutable. ‖ 気に入らないなら反論してみろ If you don't like it, *tell me* (*the reasons*) *why*.

▶彼は彼らの提案に反論した He *argued against* their proposal.

ひ・ヒ

1**ひ** 日

> 📖 **訳語メニュー**
> 太陽 →the sun **1**
> 日光 →sunshine **1**
> 1日 →day **2**
> 昼間 →day **4**

1【太陽】the sun ; sunshine（心地よい日の光）▶**日が差してきた** *The sun* began to shine. ／*The sun* came out. ‖ **日がかげった** *The sun* was covered with clouds. ／*The sun* hid behind the clouds. ‖ **日が昇った** *The sun* has risen. ‖ **日が沈む**と温度はぐっと下がった The temperature dropped sharply after *the sun* set. ‖ 私の部屋は**日がよく当たる**［全く当たらない］ My room gets plenty of *sunshine* ［never gets (any) *sunshine*］. (➤「日の当たる部屋」は sunny room) ‖ 強烈な夏の**日に当たって**百日草はしおれてしまった The zinnias wilted under the strong summer *sunshine*. ‖ 子供たちは真っ黒に**日に焼けた** My children have *got* good *suntans*.
▶《慣用表現》彼は官僚として**日の当たる場所**ばかりを歩いてきた He has always had *a comfortable spot* ［*a place in the sun*］ in the bureaucracy.
2【1日】a day ; a date（日取り）▶**雨の日に**外出する go out on a rainy *day* ‖ 天気のいい**日は**うちから阿蘇山が見える On a clear *day*, you can see Mt. Aso from my house. ‖ とうとう入試の**日が**やって来た The *day* of the entrance exam has finally arrived. ‖ 今度集まる**日を決めよう** Let's set ［fix］ the *date* for our next meeting. ‖ 東京では**雪の日は**交通機関がすぐ止まってしまう Transportation often comes to a halt *when* it snows in Tokyo. ‖ きょうは**ゴミの日だ**. The garbage collector will come to collect the garbage today. ‖ **対話**「あした何の日か知ってる?」「ぼくたちが初めてキスした記念日だろ?」"Do you know *what day* tomorrow is ?" "It's the anniversary of when we kissed for the first time, right ?"
▶**ある日**トムは塀のペンキ塗りを頼まれた *One day*, Tom was asked to paint the fence. ‖ 市長選の投票結果は**その日のうちに**わかる The results of the mayoral election will be announced *before the day is over*. ‖ また**日を改めて**うかがいます I'll come again *another time* ［*some other day*］. ‖ その病気が克服される**日が**やがて来るだろう *The day* will come soon when that disease is conquered. ‖ 今度の日曜日は結婚式には**日が悪い** This coming Sunday is *not a lucky* ［*not an auspicious*］ *day* for weddings. ‖ この写真は**若き日の**島崎藤村です This picture shows Shimazaki Toson *in his youth* ［*younger days*］.
✉ **ロンドンへの出発の日が近づいてきたのでわくわくしています** It's getting close to *the day of my departure* for London and I'm really excited.
3【日数】▶ピアノの発表会までもうあまり**日がない**［まだ**日がある**］ We have only a few *days* ［still a lot of *days*］ before the piano recital. ‖ **日がたつにつれて**彼の記憶は薄らいだ *As time went by*, his memory faded. ‖ 彼が一緒に働くようになってまだ**日が浅い** *It hasn't been long since* he began working with us. ‖ うちの猫は**日を追って**衰弱している Our cat is getting weaker *day by day*.
4【昼間】a day ▶今頃が1年でいちばん**日が短くなる** The *days* are shortest at this time of (the) year. (➤ the は省略するほうが多い) ‖ 春分を過ぎるとどんどん**日が長くなる** The *days* become longer and longer after the spring equinox. ‖ **日が暮れないうちに**テントを張ろう Let's pitch the tent *before* (*it gets*) *dark* ［*while it's still light*］.
5【好ましくないことの仮定】▶あいつが議長になった**日には**, 会議がめちゃくちゃになること請け合いだ *If* he ever became the chairperson, the meetings would surely end up in chaos.
☛ **日一日と, 日毎に, 日に日に**（→見出語）

2**ひ** 火 **1【火】(a) fire**(➤ たき火や暖炉の火には a をつける) ; (a) **flame**（炎）; a **light**（マッチなどの）▶**火をおこす** make ［build ／start］ *a fire* ‖ なべを**火にかける** put the pot on the *fire* ‖ **火**（＝ガス）を弱くしなさい Turn down the *gas*. ‖ 落ち葉の山に**火をつける** *set fire* to a pile of fallen leaves ‖ 彼女はバースデーケーキのろうそくに**火をつけた** She *lit* the candles on the birthday cake. (➤ lit は light（火をつける）の過去形) ‖ 枯れ草に**火がついた** The dead grass *caught fire*. ‖ 寒そうだね. **火にあたれよ** You look cold. Warm yourself by the *fire*. ‖ 早く**火を消せ** Put out the *fire* quickly.
▶暗闇の中でろうそくの**火が**揺れていた The *candle flame* flickered in the darkness. ‖ ガスタンクの爆発であたり一面**火の海**となった The whole area was *in flames* after the explosion of the gas tank.
▶すみません. たばこの**火**もらえますか Excuse me. Could you give me *a light* ? (➤ この場合 fire は使えない).
ことわざ **火のない所に煙は立たぬ** Where there is smoke, there is fire. ／There is no smoke without fire.
2【火事】a fire ▶**火は**台所から出た The *fire* started in the kitchen. ‖ **火は**夕方までかかってやっと消えた The *fire* was finally brought under control by evening. ‖《標語》**火の用心** Prevent fires.
3【熱】▶このカレーは食べる前に**火にかけた**（＝温めた）ほうがいい It's better to *heat up* the curry (*on the stove*) before eating it. ‖ このカツはよく**火が通ってない**よ This cutlet *is not done* yet.
4【慣用表現】
顔から火が出る ▶あのときのばかげた失敗を思い出すだけで顔から火が出るようだ Just thinking of that stupid mistake *makes me blush* ［*makes my face turn red*］ (*with embarrassment*). **火が消えたよう** ▶鉱山の閉山で町は火が消えたような寂しさだ The closure of the mine made the town *look like a deserted place* ［*a ghost town*］. ‖ 2人の息子が海外留学したのでわが家は火が消えたみたいだ Our house *feels empty* now that our two sons have gone overseas to study. **火に油を注ぐ** ▶警察のデモ取り締まりはかえって火に油を注ぐ結果になった The police crackdown on the demonstration only *added*

fuel to the flames [*made the situation worse*].
火を見るより明らか ▶このままではこの辺の渋滞がさらにひどくなるのは火を見るより明らかだ It is *clear as daylight* [It is *obvious*] that if things go on like this the traffic congestion around here will only get worse.
☛ **火だるま, 火の車, 火の気, 火の手** (→見出語)

3ひ 灯 a **light** ▶灯をともす turn [switch] the *light* on ‖ 眼下に**街の灯**が広がっている The *city lights* are spread out below (me).

4ひ 比 1【割合】 a **ratio** /réɪʃoʊ/ (比率) ; a **rate** (割合) ▶65歳以上の男性と女性の**比**は2対3だ Men and women over 65 have a *ratio* of 2 : 3. (➤ two to three と読む) ／Among those over 65, the *ratio* of men to women is two to three.
2【比較】 ▶アメリカの農場の広さは日本の**比ではない** American farms *are beyond comparison with* Japanese farms in size. ／*There is no comparing* the size of American *and* Japanese farms.

5ひ 碑 a **monument** (記念碑) ; a **tombstone** /tú:mstoʊn/ (墓碑) ▶碑を建てる set up [erect] *a monument* ‖ **戦没者慰霊の碑** a war *memorial*.

6ひ 非 a **mistake** (誤り) ; a **fault** (過失) ▶彼は頑として自分の**非**を認めようとしなかった He would not admit his *mistake* [*that he was at fault*]. (➤「すなおに認めた」なら He frankly admitted ...).
▶《慣用表現》彼は**非の打ちどころのない**英語を書く He writes *impeccable* English. ‖ 彼女は**非の打ちどころのない**装いをしていた She was *impeccably* dressed. ‖ 彼女の原稿は**非の打ちどころがなかった** Her manuscripts *left nothing to be desired*.

7ひ 妃 a **princess**. →**妃殿下**.

1ひ- 非- **un-, non-, in-**
語法 un- は「反対」「逆」を意味するのに対して, non- は「(消極的)否定」を意味する. また, in- はラテン語起源の語に用いられ, l の前では il- に, r の前では ir- に, b, m, p の前では im- に変化する.
▶**非**現実性 *un*reality ‖ **非**協力的な人 an *unco*operative person ‖ **非**教育的な番組 a *non*educational program ‖ **非合法**ドラッグ an *illegal* drug ‖ **非**日本人 a *non*-Japanese ‖ **非**物質主義 *im*materialism.
▶この民間療法は一見**非**科学的に見えるが, 実際はそうではない This folk remedy seems *un*scientific at first glance, but actually it isn't. ‖ あいつの言うことは**非**論理的だ What he says is *il*logical [*ir*rational].

2ひ- 被- ‖**被選挙人** a person eligible for elective office ‖ **被相続人** a decedent /dɪsí:dnt/ (➤「死者」の意の法律用語) ‖ **被扶養者** a dependent ‖ **被保険者** an insured person.

-ひ -費 **expenses** (支出する経費) ; (a) **cost** (費用) ; a **fee** (専門職の人への謝礼 ; 会員資格など, ある権利を得るための料金) ; **dues** (会費など) ▶**生活費** living *expenses* [*costs*] ‖ **医療費** medical *expenses* [*fees*] ‖ **教育費** educational *expenses* ‖ **交通費** transportation *expenses* ‖ **建築費** the *cost* of building a (new) house ‖ **制作費** production *costs* ‖ **年会費** the annual membership *fee* [*dues*] ‖ **給食費** a school lunch *charge* [*fee*].

び 美 **beauty** ▶**自然の美** natural *beauty* ／ the *beauty* of nature ‖ 芸術家は生涯, **美**を追い求める Artists devote their lives to the pursuit of *beauty*.
☛ **美意識** (→見出語)

ひあい 悲哀 **sorrow** (心の痛み) ; **sadness** (失望した気持ち) ; **misery** (みじめさ) ▶転勤を命じられたときはサラリーマンの**悲哀**を痛感した When I was assigned to a new position in another city, I felt the *misery* of being a company employee.

ビアガーデン a **beer garden** 《参考》日本のビアガーデンはビルの屋上を利用した夏用のものをいうことが多いが, イギリスではパブの庭を指し, 夏はここで飲食ができる.

ひあがる 干上がる **run dry, dry up** ▶学校の池は暑い夏の間に**干上がって**しまった Our school pond *ran dry* during the hot summer. ‖ 田んぼが日照りで**干上がった** The rice paddies *dried up* during the drought.
▶《比喩的》これ以上注文が減ればうちみたいな小さな会社は**干上がって** (＝倒産して) しまう If orders fall off any further, a small company like ours may *go under* [*go bankrupt*].

ピアス **pierced earrings** (➤ 通例複数形. pierce は「突き通す」の意) ▶彼女は耳に**ピアス**をしている She wears *pierced earrings*. 《参考》ピアスでないクリップ式のイヤリングは clip-ons とか clip-on earrings, ねじ式のは screw(-back) earrings という.

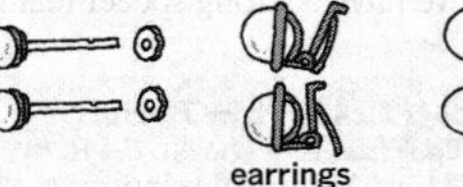

ひあそび 火遊び ▶**火遊びをする** *play with fire* [*matches* ／*a lighter*] 《参考》比喩的な用法の play with fire は「(自分に危害が及ぶような)危険なかけをする」の意. また,「その場限りの情事をする」の意での「火遊びをする」は play with love という.

ひあたり 日当たり ▶この日本間は**日当たりがいい** [**悪い**] This Japanese-style room *is* [*isn't*] *sunny*. ／This tatami room *gets a lot of* [*gets little*] *sunshine*. ‖ 《広告で》交通至便, **日当たり良好** Convenient (to) transportation, lots of [good] *sunlight*.

ピアニスト a **pianist** /piǽnɪst/ ▶新進**ピアニスト** an up-and-coming *pianist*.

ピアノ a **piano** /piǽnoʊ/ ▶アップライト**ピアノ** an upright *piano* ‖ グランド**ピアノ** a grand *piano* ‖ **ピアノ**の練習をする practice the *piano* ‖ **ピアノ**を弾く play the *piano* ‖ 彼女のお姉さんは**ピアノ**が上手だ Her (older) sister plays the *piano* well. (● プロ並みに上手ならば Her sister is a good pianist. と訳してもよい) ‖ 小野先生は『エリーゼのために』を**ピアノ**で弾いた Mr. Ono played "Für Elise" *on the piano*. ‖ 彼女はその歌手の**ピアノ**伴奏をした She *accompanied* the singer *on the piano*. ‖ 私は毎週**ピアノのレッスンを受けています** I *take piano lessons* every week. ‖ 京子は5つのときから**ピアノを習っている** Kyoko *has studied piano* since she was five.
‖**ピアノ独奏** a piano solo /sóʊloʊ/.

ビアホール a **beer hall**.

ひあり 火蟻 a **fire ant**, a (**red**) **imported fire ant**.

ヒアリング 1【聞き取り】 **listening comprehension** [**ability**] (➤ comprehension は「理解力」, ability は「能力」) ▶うちの学校の生徒は英語の**ヒアリング**の力が著しく不足している Students at this school have very poor *listening comprehension* [*ability*] *in English*. ／Students at this school have a great deal of difficulty (in) *understanding spoken*

English. ‖ S 大の入試には英語のヒアリングテストがある *A listening comprehension test* is included in the entrance exams for S University. (➤ hearing test とすると「聴力検査」になる). ⇀リスニング.
2【公聴会】a **hearing** ▶政府はその原発の安全性についてヒアリングを実施した The government held *a* (*public*) *hearing* on the safety of the nuclear power plant.

ヒアルロンさん ヒアルロン酸《生化学》**hyaluronic** /hàɪəluróʊnɪk/ **acid.**

ひい- ▶ひいおじいさん a *great*-grandfather ‖ ひい孫 a *great*-grandchild (⇀ひまご).

ピーアール PR, P.R. (➤ public relations の略語) ; **publicity** 一動 **ピーアールする publicize** +目 ; **advertise** +目 (広告を出す) ▶ピーアール合戦 a *publicity* war ‖ 自己ピーアール *self promotion* (➤「自己ピーアールする」は promote oneself) ‖ うちの社はもっとピーアールが必要だ Our company needs more *publicity*. ‖ この新製品を大いにピーアールしよう Let's give this new product a big *buildup* [a big *publicity campaign* / a lot of *PR*]. ‖ わが校のサッカー部が強いことを大いにピーアールしてください Please *spread the word* that we have a strong soccer team at our school.

> **危ないカタカナ語✹ ピーアール**
> **1** 日本語では宣伝広告全般に関して PR といっているが, この略語の元である public relations は本来「広報宣伝活動」をひっくるめた言い方なので,「宣伝」には publicity,「広告」には advertisement と区別するほうがよい.
> **2** 新製品や新人などの「組織的・集中的ピーアール, ふれこみ」の意味では buildup という語も使える.

ピーエイチディー Ph.D., PhD /pìːeɪtʃdíː/ (➤ Doctor of Philosophy に当たるラテン語 Philosophiae Doctor の略語で, 日本の博士号(doctorate)に相当するもの) ▶彼は応用言語学の Ph.D. を M 大でとった He got his *Ph.D.* in applied linguistics at M University.

ビーカー a **beaker.**

ひいき 贔屓 1【偏愛】**favor** 一形 **ひいきの favorite** 一動 **ひいきする favor** +目 ▶ひいきの役者 one's *favorite* actor ‖ あの先生は女生徒をひいきする That teacher *favors* [*is partial to*] girl students. (➤ be partial to は「…をえこひいきする」) ‖ 彼は中国びいきだ He is *pro*-China. (➤ pro- は「賛成の, 味方の」の意味の接頭辞. 反対は anti-) ‖ 父は大の巨人びいきだ My father is a great *fan* of the Giants. ‖ どうひいき目に見ても彼は二流画家だ *I'd like to make a favorable comment about* him [*to say something nice about* him], but he is a second-rate painter at best. (➤「ほめてあげたいのだが, せいぜい」の意).
2【愛顧】**patronage** /pǽtrənɪdʒ/,《主に英》**custom** ▶彼女はそのブティックをひいきにしている She *is a regular customer* of that boutique. / She *is a patron* of that boutique. (➤ ともに「常連だ」の意) ‖ 毎度ごひいきいただき, ありがとう存じます Thank you very much for your (*continued*) *patronage* [*favor*].

ビーきゅうグルメ B 級グルメ B-grade gourmet food.

ピーク a **peak** ▶ラッシュアワーのピーク the *peak* of rush hour / the rush-hour *peak* ‖ ゴールデンウィークの人出はきょうがピークだ The number of Golden Week holidaymakers has reached its *peak* today. ‖ あのレスラーは今がピークだ[ピークを越えた] That wrestler *is at his peak now* [*has passed his peak*]. ‖ 暑さもここ2, 3日がピークだろう The heat should *peak* during these next few days. (➤ この peak は「最高に達する」の意の動詞) ‖ 11月が忙しさのピークだった We *were busiest* in November.

ビーグル《動物》a **beagle.**

ピーケー《サッカー》a **PK**, a **penalty kick**
‖ **PK 戦** a (penalty-kick) shoot-out, a penalty shoot-out.

ピーシー a **PC** (＝personal computer).

ビージーエム background music (➤ 略語の B G M は一般に使われていない), **elevator music, Muzak** /mjúːzæk/ (➤ 商標名).

びいしき 美意識 a **sense of beauty**, an **aesthetic** /esθéṭɪk/ **sense** ▶日本人の美意識を知るには百人一首を読むのもいい Reading the *Hyakunin Isshu* is a good way to understand the *aesthetic sense* of the Japanese.

ビーズ a **bead** ▶ビーズのネックレス a string of *beads* ‖ ビーズのハンドバッグ a *beaded* handbag.
‖ **ビーズ細工** beadwork.

ピースサイン the peace [**V-**] **sign** ▶ピースサインを出す flash *the peace* [*V-*]*sign*.

ヒーター a **heater** ▶ヒーターで部屋を暖める use *a heater* to heat one's room.
‖ **ガスヒーター** a gas heater,《英また》a gas fire ‖ **電気ヒーター** an electric heater ‖ **ファンヒーター** a fan heater.

ビーだま ビー玉 a **marble** (玉) ; **marbles** (遊び) ▶ビー玉遊びをする play *marbles*.

ビーチ a **beach** ▶ワイキキビーチ Waikiki *Beach*.
‖ **ビーチウエア** beachwear ‖ **ビーチサンダル** (a pair of) beach sandals / (a pair of) flip-flops ‖ **ビーチパラソル** a beach umbrella ‖ **ビーチバレー** beach volleyball ‖ **ビーチボール** a beach ball ‖ **ビーチリゾート** a beach resort.

ひいちにちと 日一日と day by day ▶日一日と暖かくなっている It is getting warmer *day by day*. ‖ 日一日と彼女は健康を取り戻した *Day by day*, she was recovering her health.

ピーティーエー a **PTA** (➤ a Parent-Teacher Association の略) ▶きょう P T A の会合が 2 時からあります There will be a *PTA meeting* from 2 o'clock today.
‖ **P T A 会長** a PTA president.

ピーティーエスディー PTSD (➤ post-traumatic stress disorder (心的外傷後ストレス障害)の略).

ひいては ▶節電は自分のため, 社会のため, ひいては次世代のためになる Saving electricity will benefit yourself, society, *and even* the next generation.

ひいでる 秀でる excel /ɪksél/《in, at》▶彼は英語だけでなく数学にも秀でている He *excels* not only *in* English, but also *in* mathematics. ‖ 一芸に秀でるのはなまやさしいことではない *Mastering an art* is not an easy thing.

ヒート ▶彼らの討論はだんだんにヒート(アップ)した Their debate *became* more and more *heated*. ‖ うちの犬は今ヒート(＝発情)している Our dog *is in heat* now.

ビート a **beat** ▶ビートのきいた音楽 music with a powerful *beat*.
‖ (水泳の) **ビート板**《米》a kickboard, a flutterboard,《英》a float.

ヒートアイランド a **heat island** (大都市の高温域現

象).
ビーナス Venus /víːnəs/ ▶ミロのビーナス the *Venus* de Milo.
ピーナツ a **peanut**,《英また》a **groundnut** ▶ピーナツの殻を取る shell *a peanut*.
‖**ピーナツバター** peanut butter ‖ **バターピーナツ** fried and salted peanuts.
ビーバー《動物》a **beaver**.
ひーひー ▶やけどした人が病院のベッドの上でひーひーうめいていた The burn victim lay on the hospital bed *groaning in pain*.
ぴーぴー ▶子供がピーピー笛を鳴らして遊んでいる The child is *tooting a whistle* as he plays.
▶彼はしょっちゅうぴーぴーして(＝金に困って)いる He's always *hard up for money*.
ピーピーエム《単位》**PPM**(➤ parts per million(百万分率)の略).
ビーフ beef ‖**ビーフシチュー** beef stew ‖ **ビーフジャーキー** beef jerky.
ビーフン rice vermicelli /vəːʳmɪtʃéli, -séli/ (米粉).
ピーマン a **green pepper**,《米》a **bell pepper**, a **pim(i)ento** /pɪmjénṭoʊ/ ▶ピーマンの肉詰め a stuffed *green pepper*.
ビーム a **beam**.
ひいらぎ 柊《植物》a **holly**.
ヒール a **heel** ▶ヒールの低い靴 *low heel* shoes.
ビール beer /bɪəʳ/

> **語法** (1)「ビール1本」は a bottle of beer,「ビール1杯」は a glass of beer という。
> (2)ビアガーデンなどでジョッキで出されるビールを注文する場合は One [A] beer, please! とか Two beers, please! のように言う。

▶このところ父はビール腹になってきた Recently my father has been developing *a beer belly* [*potbelly*].
‖**缶ビール** canned beer; a can of beer (1缶) ‖ **黒ビール** dark [black] beer, stout ‖ **生ビール** draft [draught] beer ‖ **ラガービール** lager (beer).
ビールス →ウイルス.
ヒーロー a **hero** /híːroʊ/ ▶きょうの試合のヒーローは野口投手だ Pitcher Noguchi is the *hero* of tonight's game. ‖(宇宙飛行士の)ジョン・グレンはアメリカの国民的ヒーローだ John Glenn is *a national hero* in the U.S.
ひうちいし 火打ち石 a **flint**.
ひうん 悲運 (a) **misfortune** ▶悲運を嘆くな Don't complain about [of] your *misfortunes*. ‖義経はよく悲運の英雄と呼ばれる Yoshitsune is often referred to as the *unfortunate* hero.
ひえいせい 非衛生な unsanitary, unhygienic /ʌ̀nhaɪdʒiénɪk ‖ ʌ̀nhaɪdʒíːnɪk/ ▶この調理場は非衛生的だ This kitchen is *unsanitary* [*not hygienic*].
ひえいりの 非営利の nonprofit
‖**非営利団体** a nonprofit organization (略 NPO).
ひえきる 冷え切る ▶彼女は体のしんまで冷え切っていた She *was chilled to the bone*.
▶《比喩的》二人の仲はすっかり冷え切っていた Their love had *turned cold* [*cooled off*].
ひえこみ 冷え込み ▶《アナウンサー》けさはこの冬いちばんの冷え込みとなりました This morning was *the coldest* (so far) this winter.
ひえこむ 冷え込む ▶あすは一段と冷え込むでしょう It will *be* much *colder* tomorrow.
ひえしょう 冷え性 ▶私は冷え性です I *have poor* (*blood*) *circulation*. (➤「血行が悪い」の意).
ひえびえ 冷え冷え ▶廊下は冷え冷えとしていた *There was a chill* in the corridor. ／The corridor was *like an icebox*.
ヒエラルキー a **hierarchy** /háɪərɑːʳki/.

ひえる 冷える

1【冷たくなる】cool (**down**) ▶スイカが冷蔵庫で冷えている The watermelon *has cooled* (*down*) in the refrigerator. ‖このビール冷えてないよ This beer is not *cold* enough. ‖ビールは冷えてる? *Have* you *chilled* the beer(s)? (➤「冷やしたか」の意).
2【寒くなる】get [**become**] **cold, be chilled** ▶冷えてきたね It's *getting cold*, isn't it? ‖雪の降る中を歩いて, 体のしんまで冷えてしまった After walking in the snow, I *was chilled to the bone*. ‖ **対話**「きょうは外は少し冷えるわね」「冷えるなんてもんじゃないわよ」"It's kind of *chilly* out today." "*Chilly* is not the word for it!"
ピエロ a **clown** /klaʊn/ (サーカスなどの); a **pierrot** /píːəroʊ/ (パントマイムの; フランス語から).
びえん 鼻炎《医学》(a) **nasal inflammation**; **rhinitis** /raɪnáɪṭɪs/.
‖**アレルギー性鼻炎** allergic rhinitis (➤ 日常的には chronic runny nose (慢性はなみず)といってもよい).
ビエンナーレ a **biennial** /baɪéniəl/ (**exhibition**) (➤ 2年に一度開催される展示会・美術展).
ビオトープ《生態学》a **biotope**.
ビオラ a **viola** /vióʊlə/ ▶ビオラを弾く play the *viola*.
‖**ビオラ奏者** a violist.
ひか 皮下 ▶最近おなかに皮下脂肪がついてきた Recently I've been putting on some *fat* around my tummy. (➤「皮下脂肪」は subcutaneous fat だが専門用語).
‖**皮下注射** a hypodermic injection.
びか 美化する beautify +⽬ (飾る); **glorify** +⽬ (実際以上によく見せる) ▶校内美化運動 a campaign to *beautify* [*clean* (*up*)] the school ‖若者はともすれば死を美化して考えがちだ Young people are apt to *glorify* [*idealize*] death.

ひがい 被害

damage /dǽmɪdʒ/ (損害); a **loss** (損失) ▶先月の洪水でこの地方は大きな被害を受けた We *had* a lot of flood *damage* in this area last month. ‖先日の台風で農作物は多大の被害をこうむった The crops *were* badly *damaged* by the typhoon the other day. ‖この地方はその地震の被害を受けなかった This district suffered no *damage* from the earthquake. ‖台風18号は日本各地に大きな被害を与えた Typhoon No.18 *caused* [*did*] great *damage* to many places in Japan. (➤ (×) give damage としない) ‖被害額はどのくらいだったんですか How much was the *loss*?
▶彼女はひどい被害妄想で, クラスのみんなが自分をのけ者にしていると思い込んでいる She's so *paranoid* she thinks her classmates are avoiding her. (➤「被害妄想症」は paranoia).
✉ **南部をハリケーンが通過したというニュースを聞きましたが, 被害はありませんでしたか** I heard a hurricane went through the South. Have you suffered any *damage*? ➤ Haven't you ...? とすると「被害がありましたでしょう」というニュアンスになるので注意.
‖**被害者** a victim, a sufferer; an injured

ひ

person（負傷者）‖**被害地** the stricken district, the damaged area ‖**被害報告** a damage report.

ぴかいち ぴかー ▶彼は同期入社のセールスマンの中ではぴかーだ He is the *number one* salesman among those hired that same year. ／Of all the people who joined the company at that time, he turned out to be *the best* salesman.

ひかえ 控え a **copy**（写し）; a **duplicate** /djúːplɪkət/（副）; a **reserve**（選手）▶契約書の控え *a copy* [*a duplicate*] of the contract ‖控えの内野手 a *reserve* infielder.

‖**控え室** a waiting room.

ひかえめ 控え目な **modest**（謙虚な）; **moderate**（適度の節度がある）; **reserved**（自分のことや本心を語りたがらない）▶彼は少し控えめだ He's a little *reserved*.（➤ modest はほめことばで, He's very modest. とはいうが,（×）a little modest とはいわない）‖彼女は夫を立てて控えめにふるまった She treated her husband with respect, and she herself acted *modestly*. ‖彼女の要求は控えめだった Her demands were *moderate*. ‖それはイギリス人特有の控えめな言い方だよ It's a kind of *understatement* peculiar to the British. ‖控えめに言ってもおじの財産は10億はある *To put it conservatively* [*Even conservatively estimated*], my uncle has a fortune worth at least one billion yen.

▶塩分の摂取は控えめにしなさい *Be moderate* in your intake of salt [sodium]. ‖脂っぽいものは控えめにしています I'm *going easy on* greasy food.

ひがえり 日帰り ▶今では東京から新潟へ日帰りができる We can now *travel from* Tokyo *to* Niigata *and back in a day*. ‖この前の日曜日に私たちは白浜へ日帰り旅行をした We took *a day trip* to Shirahama last Sunday.

‖**日帰り手術** day surgery.

ひかえる 控える **1【書き留める】write** [**put** ／ **jot**] **down** ▶彼の電話番号を聞いてノートに控えた I asked (for) his telephone number and *wrote* [*put* ／ *jotted*] it *down* in my notebook.

2【やめる】refrain from ; **avoid** +目（避ける）

> **【文型】**
> …するのを控える
> **refrain from doing**
> **abstain from doing**
>
> **《解説》**(1)ともに「…するのを全くやめる, たしなむ量をゼロにする」の意である. **refrain** は「一時的に」, **abstain** はより強意で「自制して断つ」こと.
> (2)「ほどほどにする」ならば do **in moderation**,「量を減らす」ならば **cut down on** を使って表す.

▶私はその問題についてのコメントを控えた I *refrained from* making any comment on the issue. ‖イスラム教徒は豚肉を食べるのを控える（＝食べない）Muslims *abstain from* eating pork.（➤ たとえ, 食べたいという欲求があっても抑える, という含み）‖携帯電話の使用は控えてください Please *avoid* using mobile phones. ‖医者は彼にアルコールを控えるようにと忠告した The doctor advised him to *cut down on* alcohol [to drink *in moderation*].（➤ abstain from alcohol とすると「禁酒する」の意）‖コレステロールの多い物は控えてください *Go easy on* food rich in cholesterol.（➤「ほどほどにする」の意）‖体調が悪いのならハイキングに参加するのは控えたほうがいい If you are not feeling well, you should *not* take part in the hike.（➤ should refrain from taking part ... も可）.

3【すぐ近くにある】▶彼は入試を3か月後に控えて猛勉強している He's hitting the books *with* the entrance examination *three months away*. ‖年度末を控えて銀行の職員たちは多忙だ *With* the end of the fiscal year *coming up*, bank employees are all very busy.

▶その村は背後に中国山地を控えていた *Behind* the village was the mountainous region of the Chugoku district.

4【そばで待つ】▶名前を呼ばれるまでこちらで控えていてください Please *wait* here until your name is called. ‖彼は初戦を突破したが, そのあとには強豪がずらりと控えていた He won (in) the first round, but still *had* many strong opponents to contend with.

1**ひかく 比較** (a) **comparison** /kəmpǽrɪsən/ 一形 **比較の** **comparative** /kəmpǽrətɪv/ 一動 **比較する** **compare**《A with [to] B》

> **【文型】**
> A と B を比較する
> **compare** A **with** [**to**] B

▶この2枚の写真を比較してみよう Let's *compare* these two photographs. ‖両親は何かというと私と兄を比較する My parents *compare* me *with* [*to*] my big brother in everything. ‖きみと比較すると, 彼女はまるで子供だね *Compared with* [*to*] you, she is a mere child. ‖日本のロケット打ち上げの技術はアメリカのそれとは比較にならない Japanese rocket-launching technology *does not compare with* that of the United States.（➤「非常に劣る」の意で使う）.

▶ことしの夏は比較的涼しかった We had a *comparatively* cool summer this year. ‖健康には比較的恵まれています I enjoy *relatively* good health.（➤ relatively は「わりあいに」）.

‖**比較級**《文法》the comparative degree ‖**比較文学** comparative literature.

2**ひかく 非核の** **nonnuclear** /nɑ̀ːnnjúːkliəʳ/

‖**非核国** a nonnuclear nation ‖**非核三原則** the three nonnuclear principles ‖**非核武装** nonnuclear armament.

3**ひかく 皮革** **leather**.

びがく 美学 **esthetics**,《英》**aesthetics**.

ひかげ 日陰 **the shade** ▶高原は日差しは強いが日陰に入るとひんやりする On the plateau, the sun is strong, but it is chilly in *the shade*.

ひかげん 火加減 ▶そばをゆでるときは火加減に注意しなさい When you boil *soba* noodles, pay attention to the *level of heat* [to the *flame*].

ひがさ 日傘 **a parasol**.

1**ひがし 東** **the east** 一形 **東の** **east**, **eastern** ▶道の東側 the *east* side of a street ‖風は東から吹いている The wind is blowing *from the east*.（➤「東風」は an east [easterly] wind）‖太陽は東から昇る The sun rises *in the east*.（➤ この場合, 出発点でなく方角をいい, from the east とはしない）‖東の空が白んできた The *eastern* sky began to brighten. ‖日本はアジアの東（＝東部）にある Japan is in *East* Asia [in *eastern* Asia]. ‖その町は東京から20キロ東（＝東方）にある The town is 20 kilometers (*to the*) *east of* Tokyo.（➤「その町は東京の東にある」なら The town is (to the) east of Tokyo.）‖こ

の窓は東向きなので部屋に朝日が差し込む Since this window *faces east*, the room gets the morning sun.
‖東アジア East Asia ‖東側陣営 the Eastern bloc ‖東シナ海 the East China Sea ‖東日本 eastern Japan ‖東半球 the Eastern Hemisphere.

²**ひがし 干菓子** a dry (Japanese) confection, (a) higashi.

ひかぜい 非課税の tax-free, tax-exempt
‖非課税所得 tax-free [-exempt] income.

ひがた 干潟 tidal flats, mudflats.

ぴかっと ▶遠くで稲妻がぴかっと光った Lightning *flashed* in the distance.

ピカデリー Piccadilly /pìkədíli/ (ロンドンの繁華街).

ぴかぴか ▶ぴかぴかの新車 a *brand-new* [*shiny* new] car ‖ぴかぴかにみがいた靴 a pair of (*highly*) *polished* shoes ‖ライトがぴかぴかしている The light *is flickering* [*blinking*]. ‖掃除したバスタブはぴかぴかだ The bathtub is *spick-and-span* after being cleaned. ‖冬の夜空に星がぴかぴか輝いている Stars *are twinkling* in the winter sky.

ひがみ 僻み ⚠「ひがみ」にぴったりの英語はないので, 以下の例のように説明的にいうしかない.
▶そりゃあきみにひがみがあるからだよ That's because you *are prejudiced* [*feel a grudge*]. (➤前者は「偏見がある」, 後者は「恨みをもっている」の意) ‖私って, ひがみっぽい性格なの I'm *jealous* by nature. / I have a *jealous* nature. (➤ともに「嫉妬(しっと)深い」の意).

ひがむ 僻む ⚠ぴったりの英語はない. →ひがみ
▶ 対話「明子姉さんには欲しいものは何でも買ってあげるんだから!」「そうひがむな. 同じようにしてやってるじゃないか」 "You buy Akiko everything she (ever) wants." "Don't *feel bad*. I always treat you the same way, don't I?" (➤feel bad は「気を悪くする」の意).

ひからす 光らす ▶試験監督官たちがカンニングが行われないように生徒たちに目を光らせていた The proctors *were keeping close watch over* the students to prevent them from cheating.

ひからびる 干からびる shrivel (up); dry up (乾燥する) ▶この花, みんなかさかさに干からびちゃってるわ The flowers *have* all *shriveled up*.

ひかり 光 (a) light; a ray (一筋の光); a beam (光の束); a gleam (弱々しい光) ▶月の光 the *light* of the moon / moon*light* ‖フィルムを直接光に当てるな Don't expose the film to (the) *light*. ‖光は秒速約30万キロで進む *Light* travels at about three hundred thousand kilometers per second. ‖カーテンを通して日の光が差し込んだ *A ray* [*A beam*] of sunlight came in through the curtains. ‖満月がこうこうと光を放っていた The full moon *was shining* brightly.
▶《比喩的》この実験の成功で前途に希望の光が見えてきた The success of the experiment shed *a ray of hope* on our (future) prospects.
‖光通信 optical (-fiber) communications [transmission] ‖光ディスク an optical disk ‖光ファイバー optical fiber.

ひかりかがやく 光り輝く glitter, shine brightly.

ひかりもの 光り物 (shiny) fish with silver-blue scale (eaten as a sushi) (such as kohada (gizzard shad) and horse mackerel) (➤説明的な訳. 寿司ネタとしての青魚のこと).

ひかる 光る **1【光を発する】** shine; flash (稲妻などがぴかっと); sparkle (火花のようにきらっと); twinkle (星などがぴかぴかと) ▶彼女の指に婚約指輪が光っていた An engagement ring *shone* on her finger. (➤shone は shine の過去形) ‖けさよくみがいたので靴がぴかぴかに光っている My shoes *are shiny* because I gave them a good polishing this morning. ‖稲妻が夜の闇にぴかっと光った Lightning *flashed* in the night. ‖ダイヤモンドがきらっと光った The diamond *sparkled*.
▶星は空で光っていた The stars *were twinkling* in the sky. ‖ほら, 遠くに何か光るものがあるわ Look! There is something *gleaming* in the distance. (➤gleam は「かすかに光る」).
ことわざ 光るもの必ずしも金ならず All that glitters is not gold. / All is not gold that glitters. (➤glitter は宝石などが「きらきら輝く」).
2【抜きんでる】 shine; stand out (際だつ) ▶彼はクラスの中で光っている He *shines* [*stands out*] in his class. ‖応募原稿の中では彼女のエッセーが光っている Her essay *is outstanding* [*stands out*] among the manuscripts submitted. ‖ことし(の音楽シーンで)は乃木坂46の活躍が光った The activities of Nogizaka46 (in the Japanese music scene) *were outstanding* this year.

¹**ひかれる 引かれる** be attracted 《to》(引き寄せられる); be charmed 《by》(魅了される) ▶初めて会ったときから守にひかれた I've *been attracted to* Mamoru since the first time I met him. ‖彼の人柄にひかれました I *was charmed by* his personality. ‖小百合はほんとうの美人だからな. どんな男だって, あんな女性にはひかれるよ Sayuri is a real beauty. Any man who saw her would *be attracted* to her.

²**ひかれる 轢かれる** →³轢く.

ひがわり 日替わり ▶ランチは日替わりの3種から選べます There are three *daily* lunch specials to choose from.

ひかん (…に)悲観する be pessimistic /pèsəmístɪk/ 《about》 ▶そう悲観するなよ. 人生楽しいこともあるさ Don't *be* so *pessimistic*. Life isn't all bad. (➤英語では最初の文をしばしば, Look on the bright side. (明るい面を見ろよ) と言って励ます) ‖彼女は恋人にふられてから人生を悲観している She *has taken a pessimistic view of life* ever since she was dumped by her lover. ‖彼は前途を悲観して自殺した *Having lost all hope* for the future, he killed himself.
‖悲観論 pessimism ‖悲観論者 a pessimist.

¹**ひがん 悲願** one's long-cherished dream [hope / wish] ▶オリンピックに出場するのは我々のかねてからの悲願であった To participate in the Olympic Games has been our *long-cherished dream*. ‖わが校野球部は甲子園大会出場5回目にして悲願の初優勝を果たした Our school's baseball team won a *long-coveted* first championship on its fifth attempt at the Koshien tournament.

²**ひがん 彼岸** *higan*
日本紹介 ✉ **彼岸はふつうはお彼岸といい, 春分の日または秋分の日を中日とした7日間のことです. 人々はこの期間に墓参りをして死者をしのびます** *Higan*, or more commonly *ohigan*, refers to a seven-day period with the spring or autumnal equinox falling on the middle day. During this period, people visit their family graves and remember those who have passed away. →ぼたもち.

ことわざ 暑さ寒さも彼岸まで No heat or cold lasts over the equinox.

‖彼岸の中日 the spring [autumn(al)] equinox (day).

びかん 美観 **beauty** ▶あの建物が湖の美観を損ねている That building spoils the *beauty* [the *fine sight*] of the lake. ／That building by the lake is an eyesore. (➤ eyesore は「目ざわりな物」).

びがんじゅつ 美顔術 a **facial** ▶美顔術を受ける have *a facial.*

ひがんばな 彼岸花《植物》a (**red**) **spider lily.**

ひき 引き **pull, connections**(縁故, コネ) ▶彼のような人物は引きがなくても出世するよ A person like him will be promoted even if he has no *pull* [*connections*].

-ひき -匹 ▶子犬5匹 five puppies ‖こんなどぶ川には魚1匹いない Not a fish can be found in this muddy river.

-びき -引き ▶2割引きでビデオカメラを買った I bought a camcorder *at a* twenty percent *discount* [*at* twenty percent *off*]. ‖《広告文で》3割[100円]引き 30% [100 yen] *off* !

ひきあい 引き合い **1【言及】** ▶あわてんぼうというと, きまって小川君が引き合いに出される When the subject of scatterbrains comes up, Ogawa's name is always the first to *be mentioned.*

2【問い合わせ】 an **inquiry** ▶わが社の新製品には多くの引き合いがあった We received many *inquiries* about our new product.

ひきあう 引き合う **pay** ▶あの商売は引き合わない That business does*n't pay*. ‖そんなに値切られたのでは引き合いませんよ If you beat me down that much, I won't be able to *make* any *profit.*

ひきあげ 引き上[揚]げ a **raise** /reɪz/ (給料などの); (an) **increase** /íŋkriːs/ (増加); **salvage** /sǽlvɪdʒ/ (沈没船などの) ▶我々は賃金の引き上げを要求した We demanded *a wage increase* [*a pay raise* ／《英》*a pay rise*]. ‖タイタニック号の引き揚げ作業 the *salvage operations* on the Titanic.

ひきあげる 引き上げる・引き揚げる

> 訳語メニュー
> 引っぱり上げる →pull [draw] up **1**
> 回収する →recover **1**
> 高くする →raise, increase **2**
> 撤退する →leave, withdraw **3**

1【引っぱり上げる】 **pull up, draw up** (➤ 後者には「ゆっくり滑らかに」の含みがある); **recover** +目 (回収する); **salvage** /sǽlvɪdʒ/ +目 (沈没船を) ▶ブラインドを引き上げる *pull* [*draw*] *up* the blind ‖あの海域から沈没船を引き揚げるのは不可能だ It is impossible to *recover* [*salvage*] a sunken ship from that part of the ocean.

▶うちの会社は社歴の浅い社員でも能力しだいでどんどん管理職に引き上げる(＝昇進させる) This company *promotes* even recently-hired employees *to* managerial positions, depending on their ability.

2【高くする】 **raise** /reɪz/ +目; **increase** /ɪnkríːs/ +目 (増やす) ▶定年を65歳に引き上げる *raise* the retirement age to sixty-five ‖賃金が5パーセント引き上げられた Our wages *were raised* [*were increased*] by 5 percent.

3【撤退する】 **withdraw**《from》; **leave** (去る) ▶軍隊はその国から引き上げた The troops *withdrew from* that country. ‖家を荒し回って, 泥棒は引き上げて行った The burglar *left* after he had ransacked the house. (➤ left は leave の過去形).

4【外地から帰る】 **be repatriated** ▶終戦後中国から引き揚げてきた人々もたくさんいる There are many people who *were repatriated* from China after the war.

ひきあわせる 引き合わせる **introduce** +目 (紹介する); **check** +目 (照合する) ▶藤井君をきみに引き合わせるよ I'll *introduce* Fujii *to* you.

▶伝票を帳簿と引き合わせてみてくれないか Will you *check* the slips *with* [*against*] the books?

ひきいる 率いる **lead** +目; **head** +目 (頭となる) ▶救助隊を率いる *lead* a rescue team ‖部隊を率いる *command* a unit ‖EXILE(エグザイル)は HIRO が率いていた EXILE *was led* by HIRO. (➤ led は lead の過去分詞形) ‖内閣を率いるのは首相である The Cabinet *is headed* by the prime minister.

ひきいれる 引き入れる ▶地元の人を味方に引き入れるように努める make an effort to *win over* the local people ‖自分の意見に引き入れる *attract* someone [*bring* someone *around*] to one's view.

ひきうける 引き受ける **take on, undertake** +目 (➤ 後者は責任の重い仕事を引き受けるという含み); **shoulder** +目 (肩代わりする) ▶任務を引き受ける *undertake* a mission ‖政策の再点検を引き受ける *undertake* an reexamination of the policy ‖あとの仕事は私が引き受けるよ I'll *take on* [*take over*] the rest of the work. ‖きみは仕事をたくさん引き受け過ぎている You have *taken on* too much work.

▶彼女は弟の子供たちを育てる仕事を引き受けた She *shouldered* the job of bringing up her brother's children. ‖あなたが買い物をしている間, 子供さんは私が引き受けるわ(＝めんどうをみてあげる) I'll *take care of* [*look after*] your child while you go shopping. ‖彼は理事の役を引き受けた He *assumed* the position of director. (➤ assume は「(責務などを)引き受ける」).

▶彼女の身元は私が引き受けるよ I will *vouch for* her. (➤ vouch /vaʊtʃ/ for は「…の保証人になる」).

ひきうつす 引き写す **copy** +目 ▶彼は黒板の答えを急いで引き写した He hastily *copied* the answers from the blackboard.

ひきおこす 引き起こす **cause** +目 (原因となる); **bring about** (結果としてもたらす; ややインフォーマル) ▶彼は学生時代によく問題を引き起こした He used to *cause* trouble when he was a student. ‖何が現在の景気後退を引き起こしたのか What *caused* [*brought about*] the current recession?

▶大統領の不正行為がその国のクーデターを引き起こした The president's corruption *led to* a coup d'état in that country. (➤ lead to は「(ある結果に)つながる」) ‖運転者の一瞬の不注意が大事故を引き起こした The driver's momentary carelessness *triggered* the disaster. (➤ trigger は「(事件などの)引き金となる」).

ひきおとす 引き落とす ▶公共料金は毎月私の銀行口座から(自動的に)引き落とされている My utility bills *are paid by automatic withdrawal* [*transfer*] from my bank account every month.

ひきかえ 引き換え ▶配達人は預かり証と引き換えに彼女に品物を渡した The delivery person handed her the goods *in exchange for* the receipt. ‖当選券と賞品との引き換えは7月15日までに行ってください Please *exchange* your winning ticket *for* your prize by July 15. ‖ 品物は代金引き換えでお渡しします We collect [take] *cash on delivery*. (➤ cash on delivery は「着払いで」)

‖引き換え券 a claim check [tag ／ticket] (荷物などの預かり証) ; a voucher /váʊtʃəʳ/ (商品・サービスの).

ひきかえす 引き返す **turn back** (向きを変えて戻る) ; **return** (戻る) ▶この天気では山小屋へ引き返したほうが賢明だ With this weather, it would be wiser to *turn back* to the hut. ‖ 同じ道を引き返すのも知恵がない There's no sense in *going back* the same way we came [in *taking* the same route *back*].

ひきかえる 引き換える **1**【(…と) 交換する】**exchange**《for》▶予約券を商品と引き換える *exchange* the reservation ticket *for* the goods.

2【反対に】**unlike** (…と違って) ▶兄にひきかえ, 弟は勉強ができない *Unlike* his older brother, he doesn't do well at school. ‖ 去年にひきかえ, ことしは豊作のようだ This year it seems we'll have a good harvest *unlike* last year.

☛ **それにひきかえ** (→見出語)

ひきがえる《動物》a **toad**.

ひきがたり 弾き語り ▶彼はギターの弾き語りがうまい He is good at *singing to his own guitar accompaniment*.

ひきがね 引き金 a **trigger** ▶彼女は男の方を向くと引き金を引いた She turned to the man and pulled the *trigger*.

▶《比喩的》心臓発作の引き金となる *trigger* a heart attack ‖ 小学生のちょっとしたいたずらが事故の引き金(=きっかけ)になった A schoolboy's playful trick *triggered* the accident.

ひきぎわ 引き際 ▶日本人はよく引き際が肝心だという The Japanese often say you have to know *when to retire* [*quit* ／*leave*].

ひきくらべる 引き比べる **compare** +⊞ ▶わがチームの力と彼らの力とを引き比べてみよう Let us *compare* our team's strength *with* theirs.

ひきげき 悲喜劇 (a) **tragicomedy**.

ひきこむ 引き込む **draw**《into》▶私はいつのまにかその議論に引き込まれた I *was drawn into* the argument before I knew what was happening. ‖ 聴衆は彼女のピアノ演奏にしだいに引き込まれていった The audience was gradually *captivated* by [*drawn* into] her piano performance.

ひきこもごも 悲喜交々 ▶人生は悲喜こもごもだ In life, *joys and sorrows are mingled together*.

ひきこもり 引き籠り **social withdrawal, *hikikomori*** ▶ひきこもりは思春期における深刻な問題である *Social withdrawal* is a serious problem in adolescence.

ひきこもる 引き籠る ▶彼は一日中家に引きこもっている He *stays indoors* [*stays* (*at*) *home*] all day. ‖ 彼女はかぜで1週間家に引きこもったままだ She has *been laid up* with a cold for a week.

ひきころす 轢き殺す ▶愛犬がスポーツカーにひき殺された My pet dog *was run over and killed* by a sports car.

ひきさがる 引き下がる ▶彼は一度決めたら簡単には引き下がらない Once he has decided on something, it's not easy to make him *back down*. (➤「彼を引き下がらせるのは容易ではない」の意).

▶娘は夕飯を食べると早々に自分の部屋に引き下がる My daughter *goes into* [*retires to*] her room as soon as she finishes her supper. (➤ 後者は堅い言い方).

ひきさく 引き裂く **tear** /teəʳ/ +⊞ ▶彼はその書類を手に取るや, ずたずたに引き裂いてしまった As soon as he picked up the document, he *tore* it to pieces. (➤ tore は tear の過去形).

▶《比喩的》親が二人の仲を引き裂いた The parents *separated* [*broke up*] the two.

ひきさげる 引き下げる **lower** +⊞ ; **reduce** +⊞ (減じる) ▶4月には電気料金が引き下げられる Electricity rates will *be lowered* [*be reduced*] in April.

ひきざん 引き算 (a) **subtraction** 一動 **引き算する** **subtract** /səbtrǽkt/ ▶35から15を引き算するといくつですか If you *subtract* 15 *from* 35, how much do you have?

ひきしお 引き潮 **the ebb tide** ▶引き潮だ *The tide is on the ebb*. ‖ あすの朝は5時に引き潮になる The *tide will go out* at five tomorrow morning.

ひきしまる 引き締まる ▶引き締まった筋肉 *firm* muscles ‖ 彼は引き締まった体つきをしている He has a *firm* [*lean*] build. ‖ この一文で文章全体が引き締まった This one sentence *tightened up* the whole paragraph.

ひきしめ 引き締め a **tightening**.

ひきしめる 引き締める ▶相手を甘く見ないで, 気持ちを引き締めていこう Let's *pull ourselves together* [*brace ourselves*] and not underestimate our opponents. ‖ 彼は部下をきちっと引き締めている He *keeps* his subordinates *on their toes*.

ひぎしゃ 被疑者 a **suspect** /sʌ́spekt/, a **suspected person**.

ひきずりおろす 引きずり下ろす ▶若手議員の造反で彼は党総裁のいすから引きずり下ろされた He *was forced to step down* from the post of party president when young Diet members rose (up) against him.

ひきずりこむ 引きずり込む ▶野犬は子ヤギを襲って草むらに引きずり込んだ A stray dog attacked the kid and *dragged* [*pulled*] it *into* the thicket.

ひきずりだす 引きずり出す ▶彼は納戸からトランクを引きずり出した He *dragged* a trunk *out of* the utility room.

ひきずりまわす 引きずり回す **drag ... around, take ... around**.

ひきずる 引きずる **1**【引っ張って行く】**drag** +⊞ (重い物や疲れた足などを) ; **shuffle** (足を引きずるような歩き方をする ; 老人を連想させる) ; **hobble**《along》(不自由な片足を引きずりながら歩く) ; **trail** +⊞ (着物・ドレスなど比較的軽い物を) ▶そのトランクを部屋の端から端まで引きずって運ぶ *drag* the trunk across the room ‖ 足を引きずってるけどどうしたの? You'*re dragging* your foot. What's wrong? ‖《けがや体が不自由で》彼女は少し足を引きずって歩く She *has a* slight *limp*. ‖ 彼女は着物のすそを引きずって歩いた She walked with her kimono *trailing*. ‖《綱引きで》わあ, 引きずられる! Oh, no! We'*re slipping*! (➤「滑っている」の意).

2【残っている】▶その地方ではいまだに封建的な慣習を引きずっている In that region, feudal customs still *linger on*. ‖ 道夫は菜々子への恋心を今も引きずっている Michio still *hasn't gotten over* (*his love for*) Nanako. ／Michio's affection for Nanako *lingers*. ‖ 彼は今なお罪悪感を引きずっている He is still *haunted by guilt*.

ひきだし 引き出し **1**【机などの】a **drawer** /drɔːʳ/ ▶いちばん上[下]の引き出し the top [bottom] *drawer*

‖引き出しを開ける pull open *a drawer*.
2【金を下ろすこと】(a) **withdrawal** /wɪðdrɔ́:əl/ ▶1回のお引き出しは50万円までです You can *withdraw* as much as 500,000 yen at a time (from your account).

ひきだす 引き出す **withdraw** +⃝目 (金を下ろす); **bring out** (引っ張り出す) ▶銀行から金を引き出す *withdraw* (some) money from a bank.
▶味を引き出す *bring out* the flavor ‖子供の音楽の才能を引き出す *bring out* [*develop*] a child's talent for music ‖彼からは何の情報も引き出せなかった I couldn't *extract* any information from him.

ひきたつ 引き立つ ▶女性の美しさは着る物や装身具で引き立ってくる A woman's beauty *is often enhanced* [*is often set off*] by her clothes and accessories. ‖青を着ると彼女は引き立つ Blue *flatters* her. (➤ flatter は「いっそう魅力的に見せる」).

ひきたて 引き立て ▶毎度お引き立て(=ごひいき)ありがとうございます Thank you for your *business* [*patronage*].

ひきたてる 引き立てる **set off** ▶その絵は居間を一段と引き立てていた The picture *set off* [*enhanced*] the living room all the more.
▶あの先輩はいつも私を引き立ててくれる That sempai always tries to *look after* [*support*／*take care of*] me.／That sempai does everything to *help me succeed* [*get ahead*].

ひきちぎる 引きちぎる **tear off** [**out**].

ひきつぎ 引き継ぎ ▶後任者への引き継ぎを行う *transfer* [*hand over*] (one's) work to one's successor (➤ hand over は「後任者に引き渡す」;「前任者から引き継ぐ」の場合は take over work from one's predecessor という).

ひきつぐ 引き継ぐ **take over** (仕事などを); **inherit** +⃝目 (財産・権利などを) ▶私は来月転勤になるが, 林さんがあとを引き継いでくれる I'll be transferred next month and Mr. Hayashi will *take over* (my job). ‖父親が死ぬと彼女がすべての財産を引き継いだ When her father died, she *inherited* his entire estate.

ひきつけ 引き付け a **fit**; **convulsions** (けいれん) ▶うちの長男は時々引きつけを起こす My oldest son sometimes has *fits* [*convulsions*].

ひきつける 引き付ける **draw** +⃝目; **attract** +⃝目 (魅了する) ▶都会は若者たちを引き付ける Big cities *draw* [*attract*] young people. ‖彼女は話し方はうまくないが何か人を引き付ける魅力をもっている Though she is not a good speaker, there is something about her that *attracts* people. ‖彼にはどこか人を引き付ける(=魅力的な)ところがある There's something *attractive* about him.

ひきつづき 引き続き ▶あと1年引き続きこの仕事をするつもりだ I'm going to *continue* this work for another year.
▶私は2学期も引き続き学級委員になった I was elected as a class monitor for the second *straight* term. ‖引き続き5チャンネルをご覧ください *Stay tuned* to Channel 5.

ひきつづく 引き続く ▶卒業式に引き続いて謝恩会が開かれた The graduation ceremony *was followed* by a thank-you party for the teachers (held by the students). ／*Following* the graduation ceremony, a thank-you party for the teachers was held by the students.

ひきつる 引きつる **twitch** ▶彼の顔は恐怖で引きつっていた His face *twitched* [*convulsed*] with fear.

ひきつれる 引き連れる ▶家族を引き連れて東京見物に行った I *took* my family sightseeing in Tokyo. ／I went sightseeing in Tokyo *with* my family *in tow*. (➤ in tow は「綱で引いて」が原義).

ひきて 引き手 a **handle** (ハンドル); a **knob** (球状のノブ).

ひきでもの 引き出物 a **gift given to guests at a banquet**.

ひきど 引き戸 a **sliding door**.

ひきとめる 引き止める **stop** +⃝目; **hold back** (制止する) ▶勝子が家出した? なぜ引き止めなかったんだ Katsuko ran away from home? Why didn't you *stop* her? ‖できるだけ彼を引き止めておいてくれ Please *hold* him *back* as long as possible. ‖長くはお引き止めいたしません I won't *keep* you long. ‖長時間お引き止めして申しわけありません I'm sorry to *have kept* you so long.

ひきとる 引き取る **take back** (返品に応じる) ▶特売品はお引き取りいたしかねます I'm sorry, but we can't *take back* sale items. ‖彼女はその子供を引き取るつもりでいる She is going to *take custody of* the child. (➤ custody /kʌ́stədi/ は「(特に未成年者の)保護・監督」).
▶この忘れ物は誰も引き取りに来ない No one has come to *claim* this lost article. (➤ claim は「自分の物だと名乗り出る」).
▶どうぞお引き取りください I *have to ask you to leave*.
▶彼は穏やかに息を引き取った(=死んだ) He *breathed his last* (*breath*) peacefully.

ひきなみ 引き波 an **undertow**; a **rip current** ▶引き波に(さらわれないように)注意してください Watch out for *the undertow*.

ビキニ a **bikini** /bɪkí:ni/ ▶ビキニ姿の女の子 a girl *in a bikini*.

ひきにく 挽き肉 **(米) ground meat** (➤ ground は grind(ひく)の過去分詞形), **(英) mince, minced meat** ▶牛のひき肉 *ground* [*minced*] beef (➤ ハンバーグ用の牛のひき肉は特に hamburger /hǽmbɚ:ɡəʳ/ とか hamburger meat という).

ひきにげ 轢き逃げの **hit-and-run** ▶ひき逃げした運転手 a *hit-and-run* driver ‖ひき逃げ事件で死亡した女の子 a little girl who was killed in *a hit-and-run accident* ‖どこかの車がそのお年寄りをひき逃げした A car *knocked down* the elderly man *and sped away*. (➤ sped は speed の過去形).

ひきぬき 引き抜き **headhunting** (幹部人材の).

ひきぬく 引き抜く **pull** +⃝目 (草などを); **headhunt** +⃝目 (人材を) ▶雑草を引き抜く *pull* [*take out*] weeds ‖彼は他社に引き抜かれた He *was headhunted away to* another company. **《参考》** headhunt は特に「幹部を引き抜く」の意. 人材の引き抜きを専門とする会社を headhunting firm という.

¹ひきのばす 引き伸ばす **enlarge** +⃝目, **blow up** (➤ 後者はややインフォーマルな言い方) ▶その写真はよく撮れていたので(3倍に)引き伸ばしてもらった I had the picture *enlarged* [*blown up*] (to three times the size of the original) since it had come out well. (➤「引き伸ばし写真」は an enlargement,《インフォーマル》a blowup).

²ひきのばす 引き延ばす **drag out** (長引かす); **delay** +⃝目, **put off** (遅らせる; 後者はややくだけた言い方) ▶野党は審議を引き延ばす作戦に出た The opposition used tactics to *drag out* the discussion. ‖社員のボーナスの支払いをこれ以上引き延ばせない We can't *put* *off* paying bonuses to our employees any longer.

ひきはなす 引き離す ▶彼の車はぐんぐんほかの車を引き離した His car *pulled away from* [*outdistanced*] the others. ‖ 清は実に頭のよい子で, テストではクラスのほかの生徒をいつも引き離していた Kiyoshi was an extremely intelligent boy who always *did far better* on tests *than* the others in his class.
▶彼は二人の仲を無理やり引き離した He *separated* the two lovers by force.

ひきはらう 引き払う move (away)（引っ越す）▶彼のアパートを探し当てたときは, 彼はすでに引き払っていた When I found his apartment, he had already *moved* (*away*). ‖ 彼は東京を引き払っていなかに引っ込んだ He *pulled up stakes* and moved from Tokyo into the country. (➤ pull up stakes はかなり長い年月にわたって住んだ場所を引き払う場合に用いるインフォーマルな言い方).

ひきもきらず 引きも切らず ▶この新製品に関するお問い合わせの電話が引きも切らず入っております We're getting *an endless stream of* inquiry phone calls about this new product.

ひきもどす 引き戻す ▶両親は彼をアパートから引き戻した His parents *made* him *give up his apartment and move back home*.

ひきゅう 飛球《野球》a fly (ball) ▶大きな飛球 a long *fly*.

1**ひきょう 秘境** ▶ヒマラヤの秘境を探る explore *the untrodden regions* of the Himalayas ‖ その村は日本の秘境の1つだ That village is in one of *the most remote, inaccessible regions* in Japan.

2**ひきょう 卑怯な** dirty（汚い）; cowardly /káʊərdli/（臆病な）▶ひきょうな手は使うなよ Don't play *dirty* tricks on me! ‖ 大勢でかかってくるなんてひきょうだよ（＝フェアじゃない）It is*n't fair* to gang up on us.
▶ひきょう者め! *You coward!* ／*You traitor!*（➤ 後者は「裏切り者め」の意）‖ 今になってそんなことを言うなんてひきょうだ I don't think you ought to say things like that now. *That's hitting below the belt.*（➤ hit below the belt は文字どおりには「ベルトより下を打つ」で, ボクシングの試合での反則行為）／*It's not fair* [*It's mean*] *of you to* say such a thing this late in the game.

ひきよせる 引き寄せる pull near, pull close to ▶彼はなべを手元に引き寄せた He *pulled* the pan *near* him. ‖ もっと机に椅子を引き寄せなさい *Pull* the chair *closer to* the desk.

ひきょり 飛距離 flying distance ▶ものすごい飛距離のティーショット an *amazing* tee shot.

ひきわけ 引き分け a draw; a tie（同点）《参考》日本語で「引き分け試合」のことを「ドロー」とか「ドローゲーム」ともいうが, これは英語の drawn game からきたもの ▶試合は時間切れで引き分けに終わった The game ended in *a draw* [*a tie*] due to the time limit.

ひきわける 引き分ける draw ▶オリックスとソフトバンクは5対5で引き分けた The Buffaloes *tied* [*drew*] 5－5 with the Hawks. ／The Buffaloes and the Hawks *tied* [*drew*] 5－5.（➤ 5－5 は five to five と読む).

ひきわたす 引き渡す turn [hand] over ▶その逃亡者は警察に引き渡された The fugitive *was turned* [*handed*] *over* to the police.

ひきん 卑近な familiar（身近な）; common（ありふれた）▶卑近な例を挙げますと… To take a *familiar* example, ... ‖ そのラジオ番組では卑近な話題がよく取り上げられる On that radio program, they discuss *common* [*everyday*] topics.

1**ひきんぞく 非金属** (a) nonmetal
‖非金属元素 a nonmetallic element.

2**ひきんぞく 卑金属** a base metal.

1**ひく 引く**

訳語メニュー
引っ張る →pull, draw **1**
引用する →quote **3**
注意や同情を →draw, attract **5**
引き算する →subtract **6**
線を →draw **7**

1【引っ張る】 pull ＋目（手前に引く）; draw ＋目（なめらかに動かす）; drag ＋目（重い物を引きずる）; jerk ＋目（急にぐいと引っ張る）; tow ＋目（綱をつけて引く）▶このドアは引くと開きます *Pull* this door and it will open. ‖ 押してだめなら引いてみなさい If pushing doesn't work, why don't you *pull* it? ‖ 緊急の際はこのレバーを手前に引いてください *Pull* this lever in case of emergency.
▶日本ののこぎりは引くと切れる A Japanese saw cuts *on the pull stroke*. ‖ 初めて銃の引き金を引いたときは興奮した I was excited when I first *pulled* the trigger of a gun.
▶ハスキー犬はそりを引く犬だ Huskies are dogs that *draw* [*pull*] sleds. ‖ 姿勢をよくしてあごを引いて Straighten your back and *draw in* your chin. ‖ 日がまぶしいのでカーテンを引いてくれる? The sunlight is too bright. Would you *close* [*draw*] the curtain?（➤ draw はカーテンを「開ける」にも「引いて閉める」にも使う）‖ レッカー車が違法駐車の車を引いて行った A tow truck *towed away* the illegally parked car.
▶横断歩道を渡るときは子供の手を引いてください Please *lead* your child *by the hand* when you cross a pedestrian crossing.（➤ lead ... by the hand で「…の手を引いて導く」).

2【内部に引き込む】 ▶家に電話を引く *have* a telephone *installed* in one's house（➤ install は「電話・電気などを設置する」）‖ この家はガスはもう引いてあります This house already *has* gas. ‖ 檜枝岐村では全戸に温泉が引かれている In Hinoemata, the hot spring *is piped to* every household. ‖ この水田は多摩川から水を引いている This paddy field *takes* [*draws*] water from the Tama River.
▶かぜをひいてしまった I *caught* (*a*) *cold*. ／I *have a cold*.（➤ 後者は「かぜをひいている」という状態).

3【引用する】 quote ＋目（一節をそのままの形で）; cite ＋目（例証として）▶その論文には小林秀雄の一節が引いてある The dissertation *quotes* from Kobayashi Hideo. ‖ 先生は例をいろいろ引いてその理論を説明した The teacher explained the theory *citing* [*giving*] many examples.

4【選択して取り上げる】 pick ＋目（選び取る）; draw ＋目（くじを）; consult ＋目（辞書で調べる）▶このトランプの中から1枚引いてください *Pick* [*Draw*] a card from among these. ‖ 1000円以上お買い上げの方はくじを引くことができます Those who make purchases of over 1,000 yen get a chance in the *drawing*.
▶辞書を引く *consult* [*use*] a dictionary（➤ consult は書きことばで, use は話しことばで用いられることが多い）‖ その語の読み方がわからなければ辞書を引きなさい If you don't know how to read the word, *look* it

up in your dictionary.（➤ look up は「（ことばを）さがす, 調べる」）.

5【注目させる】draw +㊐ ; **attract** +㊐（引き寄せる）▶彼女はいつも人の**注意を引こう**としている She is always trying to *attract* [*draw*] *attention*. ‖ 彼は私の同情を**引こう**として泣き言を言った He grumbled to *attract* [*get*] my sympathy. ‖ けばけばしい広告が人目を**引いた** The showy ad *drew* [*attracted*] people's attention.

6【減らす】subtract +㊐（引き算する）; **take away**（取り去る）; **give a discount**（割り引く）▶100**引く**78は22 100 *minus* 78 is 22. ／78 *from* 100 is 22. ‖ 100から78を**引く**といくつになりますか If you *take* 78 *away* from 100 [If you *subtract* 78 from 100], what do you get?（➤ 引き算の記号（−）は take-away sign という）‖ 小遣いから昼食代を**引く**といくらも残らない After I *deduct* [*subtract*] lunch expenses from my monthly allowance, not much money is left.（➤ deduct は「差し引く」）.
▶少し**引いて**くれませんか Can you *give me* [Can I *get*] *a discount* on this? ‖ 今, あの店では化粧品を2割**引いて**くれる They are selling cosmetics 20 percent *off* at that store now. ‖ 10個以上お買い上げいただければ100円お**引き**いたします If you buy ten or more, we will *knock* 100 yen *off* the price.

7【線を】draw +㊐ ; **underline** +㊐（下線を）▶直線を**引く** *draw* a straight line ‖ 語に線を**引いて消す** *cross out* a word（➤ 訂正のために）／*draw* a line through a word ‖ 大事な部分に**下線を引き**なさい *Underline* important points.

8【受け継ぐ】▶姉の日本舞踊は藤間流の系統を**引いている** My sister's style of Japanese dancing *is derived from* the Fujima school. ‖ 海老蔵は父親の**血を引いて**演技がうまい Ebizo *has* his father's *blood in him* and is an excellent actor. ／Like his father, Ebizo is a great actor.

9【一面に塗る】▶床にワックスを**引く** *wax* the floor ‖ フライパンに油を**引いて**肉を焼く *oil* the frying pan and fry the meat in it.

10【現場から下がる】retire（引退する）; **resign**（自分の意志で辞任する）▶そろそろ身を**引く**時期だ It is almost time I *retired*. ‖ 彼は責任を取って**身を引いた** He took the responsibility and *resigned*. ‖ 私はもうこのプロジェクトから**手を引きたい** I'd like to *withdraw* from this project. ‖ 彼はその計画を提案しただけに, 担当者に指名されたとき**引くに引けなくなった** Since he himself proposed the project, he *had no choice but to accept* [he *was obliged to accept*] his appointment as the person in charge.（➤「引き受けざるを得なかった」の意）.

11【向こうへ去る】▶もうすぐ潮が**引く** The tide will soon *go out*. ‖ ようやく洪水が**引き始めた** At last the flood water began *receding*. ‖ やっと熱［はれ］が**引いた** My fever [swelling] has *gone down* at last. ‖ 木陰に入ると汗がすっと**引いた** Once I got into the shade of the trees, my sweating *stopped* (immediately). ‖《時代劇・戦争映画などで》**引け！**（＝退却せよ）*Fall back!*

12【興ざめである】▶部長の古臭い冗談にみな**引いた** We *were* all *put off* by our manager's corny joke. ‖ そんなださい格好では若い女の子は**引いちゃう**わよ Those ugly clothes of yours will surely *put* young girls *off*.

²ひく 弾く play +㊐ ▶バンジョーを**弾く** *play* the banjo（➤ プロの演奏者の場合は通例 the を省略する）‖ ピアノでショパンの曲を**弾く** *play* a Chopin piece on the piano ‖ ギターで何か**弾いて**ちょうだい Please *play* me something on your guitar.

³ひく 轢く run over, run down（➤ 後者には「はねる」の意もある）▶歩行者を**ひく** *run over* [*down*] a pedestrian ‖ 彼は交差点でトラックに**ひかれた** He *was run over* [*down*] by a truck at the intersection.

⁴ひく 碾く・挽く grind /graɪnd/ +㊐（うす・機械などで）; **saw** +㊐（のこぎりで）▶小麦を**ひいて**粉にする *grind* wheat into flour ‖ 肉を**ひく** *grind* meat ‖ 彼はコーヒー豆はいつも自分で**ひく** He always *grinds* his coffee beans himself. ／He always *grinds* his own coffee.
▶きこりが木を**ひいている** A woodcutter *is sawing* (wood).

びく a fishing basket, a creel.

ひくい 低い 1【高さが】low（高さ・位置が）; **short**（背が）▶うちの裏手には**低い**山がある There is a *low* hill behind our house. ‖ このマンションは天井が**低い**ね This condominium has a *low* ceiling, doesn't it? ‖ 月は空の**低い**ところに出ている The moon is *low* in the sky. ‖ ぼくは背が**低い**けど, 兄貴はもっと**低い**んだよ I'm *short*, but my (older) brother's (*even*) *shorter*. ‖ 彼女, 鼻が**低い**ね She's got a *flat* [*small*] nose.
▶《慣用表現》部長は**腰の低い**人だ Our manager is a *modest* [an *unassuming*] man.（➤ unassuming は「偉ぶらない」「気取りのない」）.
✉ **この写真で背の低いほうが姉の貴子です** In this picture, *the shorter one* is my older sister Takako.

2【声・音が】low ▶**低い**声で話す speak in a *low* voice ‖ 彼は突然声を**低くした** He suddenly *lowered* [*dropped*] his voice.

3【地位・程度などが】low ▶彼はまだ会社での地位が**低い** His position in the company is still *low*. ‖ 普通のサラリーマンになるのが夢だなんて, **望みが低い**な You say your dream is to be an ordinary company employee? You *have no ambition* at all. ‖ きみはいつも**次元の低い**話しかしないね Your conversation [Your mouth] is always *in the gutter*.（➤ gutter は「低俗なレベル」の意 ; Your mind is always in the gutter. ともいう）.

4【数量・割合が少ない】low ▶起きぬけは体温が**低い** Your body temperature is *low* right after rising in the morning. ‖ きょうはきのうよりも最低気温が3度**低い** Today's low is three degrees *lower* than yesterday's. ‖ 最近, **低い**年齢層にも喫煙が広がっている Smoking is spreading among the *younger* generations.

ピクセル《コンピュータ》a **pixel**（画素）▶640×480**ピクセル**の画像 a 640×480-*pixel* image（➤ 形容詞のように用いるときは pixels としない）.

ひくつ 卑屈な subservient /səbsə́ːrviənt/（追従（ついしょう）する）; **obsequious** /əbsíːkwiəs/（必要以上にへりくだった）; **servile** /sə́ːrvəl/（奴隷根性の）▶**卑屈**になるな! Don't be *subservient*. ‖ 私は彼が嫌いだ. 上役に**卑屈**な態度をとってばかりいるから I hate him. He's always so *obsequious* to his superiors.

びくつく be jumpy →びくびく ▶ **対話**「あの大きいブルドッグを見てよ」「**びくつく**なよ. かまないから」"Look at that big bulldog." "Don't *be jumpy* [*nervous*]. It won't bite."

びくっと ▶私は**びくっと**してそこで立ち止まった I stopped there *with a start*. ‖ あのことを聞かれるかと思い, 一瞬びくっとした For a minute, I *had quite a start* as I thought they were going to ask me about that matter.

ぴくっと ▶魚は1度ぴくっと動いただけでそのまま動かなくなった The fish *twitched* just once and didn't move again.

ひくて 引く手 ▶ゲームのプログラマーは今引く手あまたである Currently, video game programmers *are much sought after* [*are in great demand*].

びくとも ▶たんすを動かそうとしてみたがびくともしなかった I tried to move a chest of drawers, but it *wouldn't budge an inch*. (➤「1インチも動かなかった」の意).

▶おじはがんを宣告されてもびくともしなかった My uncle *didn't flinch* when he was told he had cancer. (➤ flinch は「たじろぐ」).

ビクトリー (a) **victory**

‖ビクトリーラン《米》a victory lap ;《英》a lap of honor.

ピクニック a **picnic** ▶森へピクニックに行く *go on a picnic* in the woods / *go* to the woods *for a picnic* / *go picnicking* in the woods (➤ -ing をつけるときにはその前に k が必要になることに注意)《参考》picnic は遠出しない単なる「戸外での食事」を指すこともある.

ひくひく ▶右腕がひくひくするのを感じた I felt my right arm *twitch*. ‖ 犬はその箱のにおいをひくひくかいだ The dog *sniffed* at the box.

びくびく ▶なぜそんなにびくびくしてるの？Why *are* you so *jumpy* [*nervous*]? ‖ びくびくするなよ Don't *be afraid*. ‖ 数学の時間, 私は当てられるのではないかとびくびくしていた I *was nervous* about being called on during math class.

▶彼はびくびくしながら, はしごに登った He climbed the ladder *cautiously* [*timidly*].

ぴくぴく ▶フナがおけの中でまだぴくぴく生きている The crucian carp in the wooden bucket are still alive and *twitching*. ‖ 彼は鼻をぴくぴくさせた He *twitched* his nose.

ひぐま 羆《動物》a **brown bear**.

ひくめ 低め ▶低めの球 a *low* pitch ‖ アメリカのバッターは概して低めの球に強い American batters generally go for *low* balls. (➤ go for は「…を好む」) / Americans are generally *low* ball hitters.

ひぐらし 蜩《虫》a **clear-toned cicada** /sɪkéɪdə/. → せみ.

ピクルス a **pickle** (➤しばしば複数形で) ▶キュウリのピクルス cucumber *pickles* / pickled cucumbers (➤ pickled は「ピクルスにした」).

ひぐれ 日暮れ (an) **evening** (夕方) ; (a) **sunset** (日没) ; **dusk, nightfall** (夕暮れ, たそがれ) ▶子供たちは日暮れには帰って来ます The children will be back *by evening* [*nightfall*]. ‖ 日暮れまでにふもとに着けるだろうか I wonder if we'll be able to reach the foot of the mountain *before sunset*. ‖ 冬は日暮れが早い *Dusk* falls early in (the) winter.

ひけ 引け ▶私は数学と物理は弱いが英語なら誰にも引けはとらない I'm weak in math and physics, but I *can hold* my *own* [*I'm second to none*] in English. (➤ hold one's own は「負けない」, second to none は「誰にも劣らない」).

¹**ひげ 髭** a **beard** /bɪəʳd/ (あごひげ) ; a **goatee** /gòʊtí:/ (あごひげ, やぎひげ) ; a **mustache** /mʌ́stæʃ/,《英》a **moustache** /məstɑ́:ʃ/ (口ひげ) ; **whiskers** (ほおひげ ; 猫やネズミのひげ) ; **stubble** (無精ひげ) (➤単に「ひげ」という場合は beard を用いる)

▶ひげもじゃの男 a man *with a stubbly beard* ‖ 父はひげが濃い[薄い] My father has a heavy [sparse] *beard*. ‖ ぼくはひげが早く伸びるので朝晩そらなければならない My *beard* grows quickly, so I have to shave every morning and evening. ‖ あごにひげが生えてきた *Hair* has begun to grow on my chin. ‖ 祖父は口ひげを生やしている My grandfather has *a mustache*. (➤動詞に wear を用いると「つけひげをしている」という響きが出る).

‖ひげそり道具 shaving things [gear], a shaving set ‖ ひげづら an unshaven face (無精ひげの) ; a bearded face (ひげの多い).

²**ひげ 卑下する** **humble** one**self** ▶そんなに卑下することはない You don't have to *humble yourself* that way.

びけい 美形 **good looks** (美貌).

ひげき 悲劇 a **tragedy** /trǽdʒədi/ 一形 悲劇の **tragic** ▶『オセロ』はシェークスピアの4大悲劇の1つだ "Othello" is one of Shakespeare's four great *tragedies*. ‖ このような悲劇を二度と起こしてはいけない We must not repeat *a tragic accident* like this. / We must not allow *a tragic accident* like this to happen again. ‖ 彼女の一人息子はカナダで悲劇的な死を遂げた Her only son died *tragically* in Canada.

¹**ひけつ 秘訣** **the secret** ; a **tip** (ちょっとしたヒント) ▶成功の秘けつは失敗を考えないことだ *The secret* of success is not to think of failure. ‖ おいしいアップルパイを作る秘けつを教えてよ Can you give me *tips* on how to make a good apple pie? / Can you give me your *secret recipe* for a good apple pie?

²**ひけつ 否決** **rejection** 一動 否決する **reject** +目 ; **vote down** (投票で)

▶その議案は議会で否決された The bill *was voted down* [*was rejected*] at the council.

ひけめ 引け目 ▶彼女は秀才なので私はいつも引け目を感じている I always *feel inferior to* her because she is extremely bright. ‖ 何か彼に引け目でもあるのかい？Do you have some reason to *feel small* in his presence? (➤ feel small は「肩身の狭い思いをする」).

ひけらかす **show off** ▶彼はいつも外国語の知識をひけらかしている He's always *showing off* his knowledge of foreign languages.

ひける 引ける ▶学校は3時に引ける School *is over*

at three. ‖ うちの会社は5時に**引ける** Our office *closes* at five. ‖ **仕事が引けるの**は何時ですか What time do you *get off work*? ‖ **学校が引けてから**テニスをした We played tennis *after school*.

▶株価は2500円で**引けた** The stock *closed* at 2500 yen. (➤「2500円で寄り付いた」の「寄りつく」は open).

ひげんじつてき 非現実的な unrealistic; impractical (実際的でない) ▶彼女の人生観は少々**非現実的だ** Her view of life is a bit *unrealistic*.

ひけんしゃ 被験者 a subject ▶実験は50人の**被験者**に対して行われた The experiment was conducted on 50 *subjects*.

[1]ひご 庇護 protection ▶子供は親の**庇護**の下に育つ Children grow up under the *protection* [*care*] of their parents. ‖ 政治的**庇護**を求める seek political *asylum*.

[2]ひご 卑語 a vulgar word, a vulgarism ▶ 'fuck' は**卑語**です 'Fuck' is a *vulgar word* [*vulgarism*].

ひ

[1]ひこう 非行 delinquency /dɪlíŋkwənsi/ (➤ 窃盗・麻薬使用などの違法行為を連想させる); antisocial behavior (反社会的行為) ▶その少年はぐれて**非行に走った** That boy went wrong and *became involved in delinquent behavior*. ‖ 彼は**非行少年**だったが, 大きくなって立派な音楽家になった Though he had been *a juvenile delinquent* [*a delinquent boy*], he grew up to be a great musician. (➤ juvenile delinquent は非行少女についてもいう).

▶ここ数年間に**青少年の非行**は急増してきた There has been a sudden increase in *juvenile delinquency* over the last few years.

[2]ひこう 飛行 a flight (1回の); flying (飛ぶこと) 一動 **飛行する** fly ▶リンドバーグはニューヨークからパリまで無着陸**飛行をした** Lindbergh *made a* nonstop *flight* from New York to Paris. / Lindbergh *flew* nonstop from New York to Paris. (➤ flew は fly の過去形) ‖ ホノルルまでの**飛行時間**は約6時間半です Our *flight time* to Honolulu is about six and a half hours.

‖**飛行場** an airfield (設備の少ない); an airport (空港) ‖ **夜間飛行** a night flight.

ひごう 非業 ▶**非業の死を遂げる** die an *accidental* [*unexpected*] death (➤ 前者は「事故死」, 後者は「不慮の死」) / die a *tragic* death (➤「悲劇的な死」).

[1]びこう 尾行する shadow +⑪; follow +⑪ (跡をつける) ▶ 2人の刑事が容疑者を**尾行した** Two detectives *followed* [*shadowed* / *tailed*] the suspect. (➤ tail はインフォーマル) ‖ 私は**尾行されている**ような気がした I felt as though I was *being followed*. ‖ 彼は**尾行を振り切った** He shook off the *tail*.

[2]びこう 備考 a note ‖ **備考欄** notes.

[3]びこう 鼻孔 a nostril /nɑ́:strəl/.

[4]びこう 鼻腔 《解剖学》 the nasal cavity.

ひこうかい 非公開の closed ▶その会議は**非公開で**行われた That meeting was held *behind closed doors*. ‖ その庭園は現在は一般には**非公開となっている** The garden *is not open* to the public now.

ひこうき 飛行機

an airplane, a plane, 《英また》 an aeroplane /éərəpleɪn/ ▶初めて**飛行機に乗った**のは大学生のときだ The first time I *flew on an airplane* was when I was a college student. ‖ 首相一行が**飛行機に乗り込みました** [乗るところです] The Prime Minister and his party *went on board* [*are boarding*] *the plane*. (➤ go on board は「(飛行機・船に)乗る」) ‖ ソウルまでは**飛行機**でわずか2時間です You can *fly* to Seoul in just two hours. (➤「飛行機で行く」は go by plane より fly のほうがふつう. ただし, 対比的にいう場合は by plane, by air も使う; 次の対話例参照) ‖ 対話「札幌までは列車で行くの?」「いいえ, **飛行機**です」"Are you going to Sapporo by train?" "No, I'm going *by plane* [I'*m flying*]."

▶父は**飛行機の免許**を持っています My father has *a pilot's license*. ‖ 《機長のアナウンス》ただ今**この飛行機**は高度1万メートルを時速960キロで飛行中です *We* are now cruising at an altitude of 10,000 meters and at a speed of 960 kilometers per hour. ‖ 長い**飛行機雲**が空にできた There's a long *contrail* in the sky. (➤「飛行機雲」は vapor trail とも condensation trail ともいうが, 一般には後者の短縮語 contrail が用いられる) ‖ あの**飛行機墜落事故**では520人の乗客が死亡した Five hundred (and) twenty people were killed in the *plane crash*. ‖ 少し**飛行機酔いをした**ようだ I *feel* a little *airsick*. (➤「飛行機酔い」は airsickness).

‖**軽飛行機** a light aircraft ‖ **水上飛行機** a seaplane.

ひこうしき 非公式の unofficial (公式でない); informal (略式の) ▶**非公式の訪問** an *informal* [*unofficial*] visit ‖ **非公式な見解** one's *private* opinion ‖ 彼は**非公式ながら**日本新記録を出した He set a new Japanese record, *though unofficially*.

ひこうせん 飛行船 an airship, a dirigible /dírɪdʒəbəl/, a blimp (➤ blimp は宣伝または観測用の小型飛行船をいう) ▶都心上空に**飛行船が飛んでいる** *A blimp* is flying over downtown Tokyo.

ひごうほう 非合法の illegal /ɪlí:gəl/ ▶**非合法**活動 an *illegal* activity.

ひごうり 非合理な irrational (理にかなわない); unreasonable (筋の通らない).

ひこく 被告 a defendant (民事上の); the accused (刑事上の被告人; 単独の被告人を指す場合も集合的に用いる場合もある) ‖ **被告席** the dock.

ピコグラム 《単位》 a picogram (1兆分の1グラム).

ひごとに 日毎に by the day (日に日に); day by day (毎日少しずつ, 徐々に) ▶父は**日ごとに**健康を回復してきている My father is getting better *by the day*.

ひごろ 日頃の everyday ▶最後には**日ごろの**勉強がものを言う In the end, your *everyday* [*daily*] work is what will make the difference. ‖ **日ごろから**健康には気をつけなさい *Always* take care of your health.

ひざ 膝 1【ひざがしら】 a knee /ni:/ ▶**ひざをすりむく** scrape one's *knee* ‖ **ひざを抱えて座る** sit hugging one's *knees* ‖ **ひざを組む** cross one's *legs* (➤ sit with one's legs crossed は「ひざを組んで座る」, sit cross-legged は「あぐらをかく」の意) ‖ 金毘羅(こんぴら)さんの石段を上ったら**ひざがが**くがくした My *knees* were shaking when I climbed the stone steps to (the) Konpira Shrine. ‖ 雪は**ひざの深さ**まで積もっていた The snow lay *knee-high*. (➤ 本人が雪の中にいるときは knee-deep ともいう) ‖ 裏庭の草は**ひざのたけくらい**まで伸びている The weeds in the backyard are *knee-high*.

▶彼女はミニスカートをはいているので**ひざこぞう**が丸見えだ She wears a miniskirt, so her *knees* are completely exposed.

‖**ひざ当て** a kneepad.

2【ももの上】 one's lap (➤ knee と違い lap は複数にしない; lap は体の部位名ではなく, 座ったときにできる場所) ▶猫が私のひざに乗ってきた The cat climbed onto my *lap*. ‖ 彼はかばんをひざの上に載せていた He had a bag on his *lap*.

‖ひざ掛け《米》a lap robe, a wrap, a lap warmer, a lap blanket《英》a rug.

3【慣用表現】 ▶どうぞひざを崩して(=楽にして)ください Please make yourself at home. ‖ 先生は生徒とひざを交えて語り合った The teacher had a heart-to-heart talk with the student.

ビザ a **visa** /víːzə/ ▶ビザを延長する extend one's *visa* ‖ 中国へのビザを申請する apply for *a visa* to China ‖ その国へ入国するにはビザが必要だ You need *a visa* to enter that country. ‖ 日本はビザ免除プログラムに参加しているので, 米国への渡航ではビザが免除されている Japan is part of *the Visa Waiver Program*, which enables Japanese citizens to travel to the United States without *a visa*. ‖ ビザがまだ下りないんです I haven't gotten my *visa* yet. ／My *visa* hasn't come through yet. ‖ ビザが切れた My *visa* has run out [has expired].

‖ビザなしでの旅行 visa-free travel ‖ 観光ビザ a tourist visa ‖ 就労ビザ a work [working] visa.

ピサ Pisa /píːzə/ (イタリア北西部の都市)

‖ピサの斜塔 the Leaning Tower of Pisa.

ピザ (a) **pizza** /píːtsə/ ▶ピザ1切れ a slice of *pizza* ‖ 夕食にピザを注文する order *(a) pizza* for dinner ‖ ピザパイを焼く bake *a pizza (pie)* (➤ pizza pie という言い方もあるが, 単に pizza がふつう) ‖ ピザを宅配してもらった We had *a pizza* delivered.

‖ピザ専門店 a pizzeria /pìːtsəríːə/, a pizza parlor.

ひさい 被災 ▶その地震で何千人もの人が被災した Thousands of people *became victims* of the earthquake. ‖ 津波被災者を支援する aid tsunami *victims* ‖ 地震の被災者たちに食糧[救援物資]を送る send provisions [relief supplies] to the *victims* of an earthquake.

‖被災地 the (disaster-) stricken area(s); the disaster area(s).

びさい 微細な minute /maɪnjúːt/.

びざい 微罪 a **minor offense**.

ひさく 秘策 a **secret plan, secret measures** (➤ 後者は複数形がふつう).

ひさし 庇 eaves (家の); a **peak**, a **visor** /váɪzəʳ/ (帽子の) ▶ひさしのついた帽子 a *peaked* cap.

ひざし 日差し sunshine, sunlight ▶日ざしが強くなってきた The *sunshine* [*sunlight*] is getting stronger.

ひさしい 久しい ▶クリスマスが日本の大事な行事になってからすでに久しい Christmas has *for many years* been an important event in Japan. ‖ 久保先生には久しくお会いしていない I haven't seen Mr. Kubo *for ages* [*for years*].

✉ **久しくごぶさたいたしております** Excuse me for not getting in touch *for so long*.

ひさしぶり 久し振り ⚠「久しぶり」に相当する1語の英語はない. 第1用例のように「長い間で初めての…だ」と考えて訳すか,「最後に…してから長い時間がたった」, あるいは「長い間…していない」と考える.

▶久しぶりに理恵から手紙をもらった I got a letter from Rie *for the first time in ages* [*in years*／*in a long time*／*in a long while*]. ‖ 久しぶりの青空だ It's *the first* blue sky *in a while* [*in days*]. ／It's *the first* blue sky *we've seen in a while*. ‖ おやじの背中を流すのも久しぶりだ *It's been a long time since* I last washed my father's back for him. ／I *haven't* scrubbed my father's back *for a long time*. ‖ 久しぶりだね *It's been a long time* [*years*／*ages*] *since I saw you last*. (➤ years は何年かぶり, ages はあいまいで, おどけて数か月ぶりでも用いる. かなりくだけた言い方) ／*Long time no see*. (➤ くだけた言い方; 1か月など, それほど長い期間でないとき) ／*It's good to see you again*. (➤「また会えてうれしい」の意) ‖ やあ, 久しぶり! *Hello, stranger!* (➤ stranger は「見知らぬ人」の意で, 親しい人におどけて言う).

▶きのう久しぶりにいとこが訪ねて来た My cousin who(m) we had*n't seen in a long time* visited us yesterday. ‖ 久しぶりにポールに会った I met Paul who(m) *I hadn't seen for ages* [*years*].

✉ **久しぶりにお便りします** *It's been a long time* [*It's been ages*] *since* I wrote (to) you last.

ひざづめ 膝詰め ▶社長とひざづめ談判をする *negotiate face to face* with the president.

ひさびさ 久々 →久し振り.

ひざまくら 膝枕 ▶弟は母のひざまくらで寝てしまった My little brother fell asleep *with his head on his mother's lap*.

ひざまずく 跪く kneel /niːl/ **(down)** ▶ひざまずいて彼の許しを請う ask for his forgiveness *on one's knees* ‖ クリスチャンは祈りをささげるためによくひざまずく Christians often *kneel (down)* to say their prayers.

ひさめ 氷雨 a **cold autumn rain**.

ひざもと 膝元 ▶親のひざ元を離れて東京に出る leave (the) *home* (*of his* [*her*] *youth*) and go to live in Tokyo. (➤「親元を離れて独り立ちする」は leave the nest (巣立つ)という比喩的な表現もよく用いる).

[1]**ひさん 悲惨 misery** /mízəri/; **distress** (困窮) **一形 悲惨な miserable** (人をみじめにさせる); **terrible** (恐ろしい); **tragic** (悲劇的な) ▶悲惨な貧民街 a *miserable* slum ‖ 悲惨な事故 a *terrible* [*tragic*] accident ‖ 洪水による悲惨な状態 *distress* caused by floods ‖ この子供たちに戦争の悲惨さを味わわせたくない We don't want these children to experience the *misery* of war. ‖ 彼の最期は悲惨だった He died *miserably*. ／He met a *tragic* end.

[2]**ひさん 飛散 dispersal; scattering** (まき散らし) ▶花粉の飛散 pollen *dispersal* ‖ 放射性物質の飛散 *dispersal* of radioactive materials ‖ 風で飛散した花粉 pollen *carried* [*blown*] *by the wind*／*wind-carried* [*-blown*] pollen／*windborne* pollen ‖ 花粉が空中に飛散した Pollen *was blown about* in the air. ‖ 床一面に血が飛散していた There was blood *splattered* all over the floor.

ひし 皮脂《生理学》**sebum** /síːbəm/

‖皮脂腺 the sebaceous /səbéɪʃəs/ gland.

ひじ 肘 an **elbow** ▶ひじを曲げる[伸ばす] bend [stretch] one's *elbow(s)* ‖ ひじをついて食事をしてはだめよ Don't put your *elbow(s)* on the table while you eat. ‖ そのおばあさんはひじで人を押し分けて込んだバスに乗り込んだ The elderly woman *elbowed her way* onto the crowded bus.

‖ひじかけいす an armchair
ひしがた 菱形 a **diamond**, a **lozenge** /lɑ́:zɪndʒ/, a **rhombus** /rɑ́:mbəs/ (➤ rhombus は専門用語) ▶ひし(形をした)もち a *diamond-shaped* [*lozenge-shaped*] rice cake.
ひじき 《植物》 ***hijiki***; a kind of edible seaweed that grows in clusters on rocky coastlines (➤説明的な訳).
ひしきじ 非識字 illiteracy /ɪlɪ́t̬ərəsi/ 一形 **非識字の illiterate** /ɪlɪ́t̬ərət/.
びしっと ▶きょうはびしっと決めてるじゃないか What a *sharp-looking* suit!
▶一度彼にびしっと注意してやるよ I'll *let* him *know what's what* [*teach* him *a lesson*].
ぴしっと ▶彼は馬のしりにピシッとむちを当てた He *cracked* the whip on the horse's rump. ‖熱湯を注ぐとガラスのコップがピシッと音を立てて割れた When I poured boiling water into the glass, it broke with a loud "*crack*."
ひじてつ 肘鉄 the brush-off(冷たい拒絶) ▶正彦は直美をくどきにかかったが, ひじ鉄を食った Masahiko *got the brush-off* from Naomi when he tried to smooth-talk her. ／Masahiko tried to win Naomi's heart, but she just *gave him the brush-off*.
ビジネス business ▶ビジネスで仙台に行く go to Sendai *on business* ‖彼は何事もビジネス優先だ With him, it is always *business first*. ‖彼はやることがいつもビジネスライクだ He always does things in an *overly businesslike* manner. (日本語のもつ否定的な含みを出すために overly を添える).

> **危ないカタカナ語✸ ビジネスライク**
> 日本語の「ビジネスライク」には「私情をはさまない, 冷たい」というニュアンスが含まれることがあるが, 英語の businesslike は「てきぱきした, きちょうめんな」の意で, 否定的なニュアンスはない. したがって, この日本語を英訳するときにはことばを補うか hard-headed (実際的な)を用いるのがよい.

‖ビジネス英語 business English ‖ビジネス街 a business district ‖《飛行機の》ビジネスクラス business class (➤「ビジネスクラスで旅行する」は travel business class) ‖ビジネススクール a business college, a business school (➤後者は《米》では「経営学大学院」の意) ‖ビジネスホテル a no-frills hotel for business people (➤no-frills は「余分なサービスのつかない」の意.「手ごろな値段のホテル」の意で economy [cheap] hotel for business people を用いることもある.「ビジネスホテル」は和製語).
ビジネスマン a **businessman** (実業家); an **office worker** (会社員) ▶手島氏は第一線のビジネスマンだ Mr. Tejima is a front-line *businessman*.

> **危ないカタカナ語✸ ビジネスマン**
> **1** 英語の businessman は「実業家」または「会社での地位の高い人, 経営に携わる地位の人」を指すことが多いが, 日本語と同様「会社員」の意味で用いられることもある.
> **2** 最近ではビジネスの世界に女性も多く進出しているので, businessman は男性について用い, 女性には businesswoman を用いるほうがよい. なお, 性差のない言い方として businessperson も好まれる. 総称としては businesspeople を用いるのがよい.

ひしひし ▶最近は自分の老いをひしひしと感じます These days I *clearly feel* myself growing old. ‖その映画を見ていると主人公の喜びや悲しみがひしひしと伝わってきた I *keenly* felt the joys and sorrows of the protagonist as I watched the movie.
びしびし ▶コーチは選手をびしびし鍛えた The coach trained the players *rigorously*.
ひしめく jostle /dʒɑ́:səl/ (押し合う) ▶パレードを一目見ようとする群衆が沿道にひしめいていた The crowd along the street *jostled* (*against each other*) to get a glimpse of the parade.
ひしゃく 柄杓 a **dipper**.
びじゃく 微弱な weak(弱い); **faint**(かすかな) ▶微弱な電流 a *weak* electric current ‖微弱な脈 a *faint* pulse.
ひしゃたい 被写体 an **object** /ɑ́:bdʒekt/ (写す対象); a **subject** (写したいテーマ) ▶ 対話「この写真, きれいに撮れてるね」「被写体がいいからよ」"These pictures (of you) look good." "That is because the *subject* (of the pictures) is good (-looking)."
ぴしゃり ▶いつまでもいたずらをやめないので母親は子供の手をピシャリとぶった The mother *slapped* [*smacked*] the child's hand because he would not stop his misbehavior. (➤slap, smack はともに「平手で打つ」).
▶彼女は強引な販売員の鼻先で扉をピシャリと閉めた She *slammed* the door in the face of the aggressive salesperson.
▶我々は彼らの申し出をぴしゃりと断った We *flatly* rejected their proposal.
ビジュアル visual ▶ビジュアル系ロックバンド a "*visual kei*" rock band.
‖ビジュアルデザイン visual design.
ひじゅう 比重 1【重要性】priority(優先度); **importance**(重要性) ▶最近はテニスよりもゴルフに比重を置いています Recently I've been giving more *priority* [*importance*] to golf than (to) tennis. ‖彼女の生活では演奏活動が大きな比重を占めている Performing (music) on stage occupies a great *part* [*portion*] of her life.
2【物理的な】specific gravity.
ひじゅつ 秘術 a **secret plan.**
びじゅつ 美術 art, the fine arts
《解説》art は絵画・彫刻などのほかに, 文学や音楽も含む芸術全般を指す. また fine arts は音楽も含むが, 特に絵画・彫刻・建築などの視覚・造形美術を指す.
▶美術の時間にリンゴのデッサンをした I sketched an apple during *art class*. ‖趣味は美術鑑賞です I enjoy *looking at works of art* (in my spare time).
‖美術愛好家 an art lover, a lover of art ‖美術家 an artist ‖美術学校 an art school ‖美術館 a gallery, an art gallery [museum] ‖美術史 art history ‖美術室 an art room ‖美術商 an art dealer ‖美術展 an art exhibition ‖美術評論家 an art critic ‖美術品[作品] a work of art ‖美術部(学校の) an art club.
ひじゅん 批准 (a) **ratification** 一動 **批准する ratify** /rǽt̬əfaɪ/ ＋目 ▶条約を批准する *ratify* a treaty
‖批准書 an instrument of ratification.
[1]**ひしょ 避暑** ▶私たちは軽井沢へ避暑に出かける予定です We're going to Karuizawa to *escape the summer heat*.
‖避暑客 a summer visitor ‖避暑地 a summer

resort.

[2]**ひしょ 秘書** a **secretary** /sékrəteri/《to》▶彼女は学長の**秘書**です She is (*a*) *secretary to* the president.

語法 (1) a は秘書が何名かいる場合の1人を, a の省略は1人の場合のその人を指す. (2) 1人の場合は the secretary とすることも可. (3)「…の秘書」の「の」に引かれて secretary *of* としないこと ‖ 私は**秘書課**勤務です I work in the *secretarial section*.

‖**秘書官** a minister's secretary ‖ **秘書室** the secretariat /sèkrətéəriət/.

びじょ 美女 a **beautiful woman**, a **beauty** ▶絶世の**美女** *a woman of* incredible *beauty* ‖ 二人は美男美女のカップルだ They are a *very good-looking* couple.

[1]**ひじょう 非常** (an) **emergency**(非常時) ▶**非常**ブレーキをかける apply the *emergency brake* ‖ **非常**の際はこの(**非常**)階段をご利用ください In case of (*an*) *emergency*, please use this *emergency staircase*. (➤ 火災のときの「非常階段［ばしご］」は a fire escape).

▶**非常**ベルが鳴った The *fire* ［*burglar*］ *alarm* went off. (➤ fire alarm は火災用の, burglar alarm は防犯用のもの) ‖《掲示》**非常**持ち出し To Be Taken Out in Case of Emergency.

‖**非常口** an emergency exit ［door］ ‖ **非常コック** an emergency handle ‖ **非常手段** emergency measures (➤ 通例複数形で) ‖ **非常招集** an emergency summons ‖ **非常食** emergency food ‖ **非常停止ボタン** an emergency stop.

☛ **非常事態, 非常線, 非常な, 非常に** (→見出語)

[2]**ひじょう 非情** ▶**非情**な男 a *cold-hearted* man.

[1]**びしょう 微笑** a **smile** ━動 **微笑する smile** ▶モナリザは口もとに謎めいた**微笑**を浮かべている (The) Mona Lisa has a mysterious *smile* on her lips.

[2]**びしょう 微小** ‖**微小植物** a microphyte ‖ **微小生物** a microcyte.

ひじょうきん 非常勤の **part-time** ▶**非常勤**で働く work *part-time* ‖ 私はS大学で物理学の**非常勤講師**をしています I'm *a part-time lecturer* ［*instructor*］ in physics at S University. ／I teach physics *part-time* at S University.

ひじょうしき 非常識な **absurd**(ばかげた) ; **thoughtless**(思慮のない) ▶彼の要求は全く**非常識**だ His demands are absolutely *absurd*. ‖ 病人にそんなことを言うなんて**非常識**だよ It's *thoughtless* of you to say such a thing to a sick person.

ひじょうじたい 非常事態 a **state of emergency**, an **emergency** ▶首都圏に**非常事態**宣言が出された The government declared *a state of emergency* in the Tokyo metropolitan area. (➤「非常事態宣言」を an emergency declaration ということもある) ‖ 宇宙ステーションで**非常事態**が発生した An *emergency situation* has arisen inside the space station.

びしょうじょ 美少女 a **beautiful girl**.

ひじょうせん 非常線 a (**police**) **cordon** ▶**非常線**を張る set ［throw］ up *a cordon* ‖ 誘拐犯は**非常線**を突破して逃走した The kidnapper broke through the *police cordon* and made his escape. ‖ 警察は直ちに一帯に**非常線**を張った The police immediately *cordoned off the area*.

ひじょうな 非常な **great**(大いなる) ; **extreme**(極度の) ▶**非常な**貧しさの中に生きている live in *extreme* poverty ‖ 彼の成功は我々にとっても**非常な**喜びです His success is also a source of *great* joy for us. ‖ その男の子は昆虫に**非常な**興味をもっている The boy is *very much* ［*extremely*］ interested in insects.

ひじょうに 非常に very, extremely ; much, very much

語法 (1) **very** は原級の形容詞・副詞および現在分詞形の形容詞を修飾する.
(2) very の同義語として **extremely**, **greatly**, **awfully** などが用いられることも多い(この3語の中では awfully が最もくだけた語).
(3) 過去分詞形の形容詞も very で修飾することが多いが, 過去分詞形がはっきり受け身形と思われる場合は very は避けられ, **much** または **very much** が用いられる.

▶きのうは**非常に**寒かった It was *very* ［*extremely* ／ *awfully*］ cold yesterday. ‖ 私はその報告に**非常に**失望している I'm *very* disappointed by the report. ‖ ウィーンフィルの演奏は**非常に**すばらしかった The performance of the Vienna Philharmonic Orchestra was *extremely* good. ‖ ご親切には**非常に**感謝しております Thank you *very much* for your kindness. ／I *truly* ［*deeply*］ appreciate your kindness. ／Your kindness is *much* ［*very much*］ appreciated. (➤ 第3文は事務的で冷たい印象を与える).

▶この辺は違法駐車が**非常に**多い There is *a great number of* ［There are *a great many*］ illegally parked cars around here. ‖ その箱は**非常に**重くて, 私には持ち上げられなかった The box was *too* heavy for me *to* lift. ／The box was *so* heavy (*that*) I could not lift it.

びしょうねん 美少年 a **handsome boy** ［**young man**］ (➤ handsome の代わりに good-looking でもよい).

びしょく 美食 (a) **gourmet** /gʊ́əʳmeɪ/ **food**(高級な料理) ▶**美食**しすぎは健康によくない Eating too much *rich food* is not good for the health. (➤ rich は「脂肪分の多い, こってりした」) ‖ 彼は**美食家**だ He is *a gourmet* ［*an epicure*］. (➤ epicure /épɪkjuəʳ/ は文学的な語).

びしょぬれ びしょ濡れ ▶夕立にあい**びしょぬれ**になった I was caught in a downpour and *got wet* ［*was drenched*］ *to the skin*.

びしょびしょ **drenched**, **soaked**(➤ 前者がぬれ方がひどい) ▶彼は頭のてっぺんから足の先まで**びしょびしょ**だった He *was drenched* ［*was soaked*］ from head to toe.

ビジョン **vision** ▶国民は**ビジョン**のある政治家を求めている The people want politicians of *vision*. ‖ 地域開発は長期的**ビジョン**で行うべきだ Regional development ought to be carried out as part of *a long-range vision*.

びじれいく 美辞麗句 **flowery language** ; **rhetoric** /rétərɪk/ (きれいごと)
▶彼のあいさつは**美辞麗句**を連ねたものだった His speech was full of *flowery language* ［*phrases* ／*words*］.

びじん 美人 a **beauty**, a **good looker**, a **good-looking woman** ▶彼女は**美人**だ She is *beautiful*. ／She is *a beauty*. (➤ 後者はジャーナリズムで好まれる言い方) ‖ きみの彼女, すっごい**美人**だね！ Your girlfriend's *a real knockout*! (➤ knockout は「すごい美人」の意のインフォーマルな語) ‖ クレオパトラ, 楊貴妃, 小野小町は世界の三大**美人**といわれる Cleopatra, Yang Guifei, and Ono-no Komachi are said to be the three

greatest *beauties* in (world) history.
‖美人コンテスト a beauty contest [pageant].

ひすい 翡翠《鉱物》**jade** /dʒeɪd/.

ビスケット《米》a **cookie**, a **cracker**;《英》a **biscuit** /bískɪt/.

危ないカタカナ語✹ **ビスケット**
1 biscuit は《英》と《米》では別物.《英》の biscuit は日本でいう「ビスケット」と同じだが,《米》では小型のやわらかいパンを指す.
2《米》では cookie または cracker が日本語の「ビスケット」に当たる.

ピスタチオ a **pistachio** /pɪstǽʃioʊ/ [複 **pistachios**].

ヒステリー **hysteria** /hɪstíəriə/ (病気としての); **hysterics**, an **emotional outburst** (発作) ━形 **ヒステリーの hysterical** ▶彼女はときどきヒステリーを起こす She sometimes *gets hysterical* [*reacts hysterically*]. (➤全く自制が効かない状態を言う) ／She sometimes *has emotional outbursts* [*makes a scene*]. (➤「感情を爆発させる」).

ヒステリック **hysterical** ▶ヒステリックな叫び a *hysterical* cry ‖娘さんに彼氏がいたからって, そうヒステリックになるなよ Don't *get hysterical* [*so emotional*] simply because your daughter has a boyfriend.

ピスト(バイク) a **piste bike** (**without brakes on**), a **brakeless bicycle**,《インフォーマル》a **fixie**.

ピストル a **pistol**, a **gun**; a **revolver** (連発式の) ▶警官はその男に向かってピストルを撃った The policeman fired his *pistol* at the man.

ビストロ a **bistro**.

ピストン a **piston** ▶《慣用表現》博覧会場と駅の間をバスがピストン輸送している Buses *shuttle between* the exhibition site *and* the station. (➤ shuttle は「往復する」).

ヒスパニック a **Hispanic**.

ひずみ 歪み (a) **distortion** (音のゆがみ); a **strain** (強く引く力) ▶ひずみのないきれいな音 a clear sound without *distortion* ‖プレートのひずみが巨大地震を引き起こす *The strains* in the plates trigger massive earthquakes. ‖ＣＤは音のひずみがほとんどないと言ってもよい On CDs, sound *distortion* is (reduced to) virtually zero.
▶《比喩的》彼らは教育のひずみをなくそうと努力している They are trying to eliminate the *distortions* in education.

びせい 美声 a **beautiful voice**.

びせいぶつ 微生物 a **microbe**, a **microorganism** (➤前者は特に「病原菌」を指す)
‖微生物学 microbiology.

びせきぶん 微積分《数学》(**differential and integral**) **calculus**.

ひぜに 日銭 ▶日銭をかせぐ earn *daily cash income*.

ひせんきょけん 被選挙権 **eligibility for election** [**to hold** (**public**) **office**] (➤ hold (public) office は「公職に就く」) ▶市長の被選挙権は25歳以上の者に与えられる You must be 25 or older to run for mayor. ／Those who are 25 or older are eligible to be candidates for mayor.

ひせんとう 非戦闘 ‖非戦闘員 a non-combatant.

ひせんろん 非戦論 **pacifism**.

ひそ 砒素《化学》**arsenic** /ɑ́:ʳsənɪk/.

1**ひそう 悲壮な** **tragic** (悲劇的な); **heroic** /hərόʊɪk/ (勇ましい) ▶悲壮な決意をする make a *tragic but brave* resolution ‖悲壮な最期を遂げる die a *tragic* death ／meet a *heroic* end ‖戦艦大和の最期は実に悲壮だった The end of the battleship Yamato was very *tragic*.

2**ひそう 悲愴** ▶悲そうな顔つき a *mournful* look.

3**ひそう 皮相な** **superficial** /sù:pəʳfíʃəl/ ▶彼の観察は皮相的で説得力に欠ける His observations are only *superficial* and lack persuasive power.

1**ひぞう 秘蔵の** **treasured** ▶秘蔵の品 one's *treasure* ‖わが家では良寛の書を秘蔵している Our family's *treasure* [*prized possession*] is a piece of calligraphy [writing] by Ryokan.

2**ひぞう 脾臓**《解剖学》**the spleen**.

ひそか 密かに **secretly** ▶ぼくは中学時代ひそかに彼女にあこがれていた I had a *secret* crush on her when I was in junior high school. ‖私はひそかに彼女と会った I met her *in private*. (➤ in private は「こっそりと」) ‖彼はひそかに転職の決心をした He *inwardly* made up his mind to change his job. (➤ inwardly は「心の中で」) ‖科学者たちは衛星打ち上げは成功するとひそかに自信をのぞかせていた The scientists were *quietly* confident that they could successfully launch the satellite. (➤ quietly は「様子が控えめで」).

ひぞく 卑俗な **vulgar**.

ひぞっこ 秘蔵っ子 ▶彼は陶芸家のおじの秘蔵っ子だ He is *the favorite disciple* of his uncle, who is a potter. ／He is *the object of all the hopes and love* of his uncle, a potter.

ひそひそ ▶２人は部屋の隅っこでひそひそ話をしていた The two *were whispering* in a corner of the room.

ひそむ 潜む **hide** (隠れる) ▶殺人犯はこの建物のどこかに潜んでいるに違いない The murderer must *be hiding* somewhere in this building.

1**ひそめる 潜める** **conceal** [**hide**] **oneself** (隠れる) ▶彼はソファーのかげに身を潜めた He *concealed himself* behind the sofa. ‖きみたちみたいに声を潜めて話をするのはよくないよ It's really not good manners to *mutter* [*speak under your breath*] like you're doing now. (➤ mutter は「(不満などを)ぼそぼそ言う」).

2**ひそめる 顰める** ▶まゆをひそめる *knit* [*bend*] one's brows ‖中年の婦人たちは少女たちの格好にまゆをひそめた The middle-aged women *frowned* at the girls for what they were wearing. (➤不愉快を表すしぐさ).

ひだ 襞 a **fold** (折り目); a **pleat** (スカートなどの) ▶カーテンのひだ *a fold* in a curtain.
‖ひだスカート a pleated skirt.

ひたい 額 a **forehead** /fɔ́:ʳhed, fɔ́(:)rɪd/, a **brow** /braʊ/ (➤後者は文語的)

《解説》 brow は感情や知性の表れる場所ととらえられることも多い. 例えば「困った顔つき[表情]」を troubled brow というが, これは, 額を感情の表れる場所としてとらえている. また, highbrow (インテリぶる人), lowbrow (俗物趣味の人) のような言い方は brow が知性の表れる場所としてとらえられていることを示している.

▶広い[狭い]額 a broad [narrow] *forehead* ‖熱があるかどうか額に触ってみて Touch my *forehead* to see if I have a fever. ‖彼女は考え込んでいるときには額にしわを寄せる She *wrinkles her forehead* [*brow*] when she is thinking hard about something.

▶《慣用表現》ささやかだが，これは私が額に汗して建てた家だ It may not be much, but this is a house that I built *by the sweat of my brow.* ‖ 彼らは額を集めてその問題の解決方法を話し合った They *put their heads together* to solve the problem.

ひだい 肥大 enlargement
‖前立腺肥大 prostate enlargement, prostatic hyperplasia(➤ 後者は医学用語).

びたいちもん びた一文 ▶びた一文負けられないね I won't take off *one cent.*

ひたかくし 直隠し ▶銀行幹部は悪行をひた隠しにした The bank executives *thought only of concealing* their misdeeds.

ピタゴラス Pythagoras /pəθǽgərəs/
‖ピタゴラスの定理 the Pythagorean theorem.

ひたす 浸す dip +⊞ (ちょっと), soak +⊞ (十分に); steep +⊞ (食材や布などを) ▶手を冷たい谷川の水に浸した I *dipped* my hands in the water of the cold valley stream. ‖ 汚れ物は石けん水に浸しておきなさい Let your dirty clothes *soak* in soapy water.

ひたすら ▶店員はひたすら謝罪するのみであった The clerk did *nothing but* apologize. ‖ 彼はひたすらバイオテクノロジーの研究に専念した He devoted himself *whole-heartedly* [*earnestly*] to the study of biotechnology.

ひだち 肥立ち ▶母は産後の肥立ちがよくなかったそうだ I hear my mother *didn't have an easy recovery* after she gave birth to me.

ぴたっと →ぴたり.

ひだね 火種 a live charcoal used to build a fire; a cause, a flashpoint(紛争の元).

ひたひた ▶濁流がひたひたと押し寄せて来た The muddy water *lapped* higher and higher.

ひだまり 日だまり a warm sunny spot [place].

ビタミン a vitamin /váɪţəmɪn/ ▶もっとビタミン類をとりなさい Take more *vitamins.* ‖ キウイフルーツはビタミンCが多い A kiwi (fruit) contains a lot of *vitamin C.* ／A kiwi (fruit) is rich in *vitamin C.*
‖ビタミン剤 a vitamin tablet [pill].

ひたむきな earnest(真剣な); whole-hearted (いちずな) ▶彼女のひたむきな努力 her *earnest* efforts ‖ 彼女は徹夫をひたむきに愛している She loves Tetsuo *whole-heartedly* [*single-heartedly*]. ‖ 球児たちのひたむきな姿に深く感動した The young players' *devotion* to baseball moved me deeply.

ひだり 左 1【左側】the left 一形 左の left ▶次の角を左に曲がると左手にその神社があります Turn (*to the*) *left* at the next corner and you will find the shrine *on the left.* ‖ 左から4つ目の時計を見せてくれますか Could you show me the *fourth* watch *from the left*? ‖ 左から右へ読みなさい Read (it) *from left to right.* ‖ 《コの字型に並んだ人に》左まわりに自己紹介してください Would you please introduce yourselves *going counterclockwise*? (➤「時計の針と逆回りに」の意) ‖ 左向け左! Left turn [face]!
✉ **同封の写真は日本の代表的な食べ物を写したものです. いちばん左が「すし」, その右が「うどん」です** The enclosed photo shows some typical Japanese foods. *On the far left* is sushi and to the right of that is udon [*First from the left* is sushi and next is udon].
2【左翼】▶あの政治家は左寄りと見られている That politician is regarded as *leaning toward the left* [*as a left-winger*].

ぴたり right(正しく); exactly (正確に) ▶私の予想がぴたりと当たった I guessed *right.* ‖ 彼の計算はぴたりと合っていた His calculations were *exact* [*spot on*]. ‖ 彼女の説明は事実とぴたり一致する Her explanation corresponds *exactly* to [with] the facts. ‖ 私の試験の予想がぴたりと当たった My guess about the exam questions *hit the nail on the head.* (➤「くぎの頭を打つ」が原義) ‖ 足音はドアの前でぴたりと止まった The footsteps stopped *dead* in front of my door.
▶シールがぴたりとくっついていて取れない The sticker is stuck so *fast* it won't come off. →ぴったり.

ひだりうえ 左上 upper left.

ひだりうちわ 左団扇 ▶あいつは父親の遺産をもらって, 左うちわで暮らしている He *has been living on easy street* after inheriting his father's estate.

ひだりがわ 左側 the left side ▶彼は私の左側に座った He sat *on* [*to*] *my left.* ‖《掲示》左側通行 Keep (to the) left. ‖ 日本では車は左側通行です Vehicles *travel on the left side of the road* in Japan.

ひだりきき 左利きの left-handed ▶マギーは左ききだ Maggie is *left-handed.* ‖ 私はものを書くときは左ききで, 食事をするときは右ききだ I write *left-handed* but eat right-handed. ‖ 石井は左ききの投手だ Ishii is *a southpaw* (*pitcher*). 《参考》英米では一般に左ききは無器用だと考えられている.

ひだりした 左下 lower left.

ひだりづめ 左詰め →左寄せ.

ひだりて 左手 the left hand ▶右手がふさがっていたら左手を使えばいい You can use your *left hand* if your right one is full.
▶左手に(＝左の方に)見えるのが皇居です *On* [*To*] *the left,* you can see the Imperial Palace. (➤ on [to] your left としてもよい).

ひだりまえ 左前 1【着物の】▶ジョンはゆかたを左前に着ている John is wearing his yukata *with the left side* (*tucked*) *under the right.* (➤「左前」とは左身ごろを右身ごろの下に着ること).
2【調子が悪い】▶あの店も左前になった That store *has run into financial trouble.*

ひだりよせ 左寄せ a left-justify ▶そのテキストを左寄せにする *left-justify* the text.

ひたる 浸る 1【つかる】soak ▶温泉の湯に肩まで浸った I *soaked* in the hot water (of the hot spring) up to my shoulders.
2【ふける】▶我々はしばし思い出に浸った We *indulged ourselves in* fond memories for some time.

ひだるま 火だるま ▶車は塀に激突し, あっという間に火だるまになった The car smashed into a wall and *was enveloped in flames* in an instant.

ひたん 悲嘆 ▶息子の自殺の知らせを聞いて両親は悲嘆に暮れた At the news of their son's suicide, the parents *were crushed with grief* [*were grief-stricken*].

びだん 美談 ▶それは美談だね That's *a lovely story.* ／That's *a lovely thing to hear.* ／That's truly *admirable.*

びだんし 美男子 a handsome [good-looking] man.

びちく 備蓄 (a) stock, a stockpile ▶石油の備蓄 oil *stock* ‖ 非常用に水と乾燥食品を備蓄しておかなくてはいけない You must *keep an emergency stock* of water and dried food.
‖備蓄米 rice stockpiled by the government.

ぴちっと ▶蓋はぴちっとしなさい Close the lid *firmly.*

ぴちぴち ▶ぴちぴちした女の子たち *fresh*, *young* [*young and lively*] girls ‖ 5キロ太ったらスカートがぴちぴちになってしまった Since I've put on five kilos, my skirts have become *too tight*.

▶びくの魚がぴちぴちはねた The fish in the creel jumped *vigorously*.

びちゃびちゃ soaking wet, slushy.

ぴちゃぴちゃ ▶水たまりをぴちゃぴちゃ歩かないで Don't *splash* [*slosh*] through puddles (like that).

びちょうせい 微調整 a minor adjustment 一動 微調整する make a minor adjustment ; fine-tune ＋目 (より完璧にする)

▶タイトルの位置を微調整する *make a minor adjustment* to the position of the title ‖ デザインを微調整する *fine-tune* a design.

ひつあつ 筆圧 pressure a writer puts on a calligraphic brush, pressure of a pen on paper.

ひつう 悲痛な sad (悲しい) ; anguished (苦悩に満ちた)

▶彼は悲痛な面もちで会議室に入って来た He came in the meeting room with a *sad* face. ‖ 政府は被災者たちの悲痛な叫びにもっと真剣に耳を傾けるべきだ The government should listen more sincerely [earnestly] to the *anguished* cries of the victims.

ひつうち 非通知 ▶非通知の電話番号 a *restricted* [《主に英》 *withheld*] phone number ‖ 非通知の電話がかかってくる get a *restricted* [*withheld*] phone call.

ひっかかる 引っ掛かる 1【突き出ている物などに】catch [be caught] 《on, in》 ▶セーターが木の枝に引っかかった My sweater *caught on* [*in*] a twig. (➤ in は物にからみついているような状態の場合).

2【やっかいなものなどに】▶その車は検問に引っかかった The car *was caught* [*was stopped*] at the checkpoint. ‖ 彼の映画は検閲に引っかかった His movie *failed to pass* censorship. (「パスしなかった」と考えて訳す).

▶彼は人妻に引っかかっている He *is involved with* a married woman.

3【気になる】▶何か引っかかることでもあるの？ Is there something that is *giving* you *trouble*? ‖ 彼女のことばがさっきから引っかかっている I *can't get* what she said a little while ago *off my mind*.

ひっかきまわす 引っ掻き回す rummage /rʌ́mɪdʒ/ 《through, in》 ▶彼女はホッチキスを見つけようと引き出しの中を引っかき回した She *rummaged through* (the things in) the drawer looking for a stapler.

▶《比喩的》ときどき彼はクラスを引っかき回す (＝混乱させる) He often *disrupts* the class.

ひっかく 引っ掻く scratch ＋目 ▶猫がふすまを引っかいた The cat *scratched* the paper sliding door with her claws. ‖引っかき傷 a scratch.

ひっかける 引っ掛ける 1【突き出ている物などに】catch 《on, in》; hang (つるす) ▶セーターをくぎに引っかけた I *caught* my sweater *on* a nail. (➤「引っかけて破いた」なら caught を tore にする) ／A nail *caught* my sweater.

▶彼はオートバイに引っかけられて腕を骨折した He *was hit* [*was scraped*] by a motorcycle and broke his arm. (➤ scrape は「接触してこする」).

2【無造作に着る】throw [slip] on ▶彼はパジャマの上にコートを引っかけてコンビニに行った He *threw* [*slipped*] *on* a coat *over* his pajamas and went out to a convenience store.

3【だます】▶男を引っかけては金をしぼり取っていた女が捕まった A woman, who had *tricked* men out of their money, was arrested. (➤ trick のかわりに「だまし取る」の意の swindle を用いてもよい) ‖ また女の子を引っかけようってのか Are you trying to *pick up* a girl again?

4【酒を軽く飲む】▶ちょっと1杯ひっかけて来たんだ I've just *had a quick one*.

ひっき 筆記する write down ▶私の言うことを筆記しなさい *Write down* what I say. ／*Take notes on* what I say. ‖ 筆記用具をご持参ください You're supposed to bring *writing implements* [*tools*]. ／Please bring *something to write with*. (➤ 後者はややインフォーマルな言い方).

‖筆記試験 a written examination [test] ‖ 筆記体 cursive /kɑ́ːˈsɪv/, script (➤ 後者は主に印刷用語. 「筆記体で書く」は write in cursive letters [in script]).

ひつぎ 柩 a casket, a coffin 《解説》前者は後者の婉曲(えんきょく)語として用いられることが多いが, 厳密には前者は長方形のもの, 後者は六角形のもの(ドラキュラから連想されるタイプ)をいう.

ひっきりなしに constantly (絶えず) ; continuously (止むことなく) ; one after another (次々に)

▶この通りはひっきりなしに人が往来する People come and go *constantly* on this street. ／This street is *always* busy with pedestrians. ‖ 3日間ひっきりなしに雨が降った It rained *continuously* for three days. ‖ きのうはひっきりなしに来客があった We had *one* visitor *after another* yesterday. ‖ 彼女はひっきりなしにしゃべった She talked *nonstop* [*without stopping*].

ピッキング lock-picking ▶逮捕された男性はピッキング用の道具と共犯者の連絡先が記されたノートを保持していたことがわかった The arrested man was found to be carrying *lock-picking* equipment, and a notebook with the names and addresses of accomplices.

ピックアップ 一動 ピックアップする pick out ; choose ＋目 (選ぶ) ▶好きなのをピックアップしてくれ *Pick out* anything you like. ‖ 彼はそのリストの中から数冊の本をピックアップした He *chose* several books from the list.

> **危ないカタカナ語✸ ピックアップ**
> 1 日本語の「ピックアップ」と英語の pick up には意味のずれがあるので注意を要する. 日本語の「ピックアップ」は「選ぶ, えり抜く」の意味なので, これには pick out や choose を用いるのがよい.
> 2 英語の pick up は「(物を)拾い上げる」,「(人を)車に乗せる ; ナンパする」の意味で用いることが多い.

ビッグバン 《天文学》 the Big Bang.

びっくり 一動 びっくりする be surprised (思いがけないことに) ; be astonished (仰天する) ; be amazed (目を見張るほど驚く) ; be startled (ぎょっとする) ; be shocked (ショックを受ける) ; be flabbergasted /flæbəˈgæstɪd/ (あっけにとられて口がきけない) →驚く

> 【文型】
> 人・物(A)にびっくりする
> be surprised by [at] A
> …してびっくりする
> be surprised to do
> ～ということにびっくりする
> be surprised that S ＋ V

《解説》(1)「びっくりする」は形容詞 surprised(人が驚く)を用いて, **be surprised** の形で表現するのが一般的.「人が驚く」は surprised であるが, 原因となるものが「びっくりするような」は surprising, また, 動詞 surprise は「人をびっくりさせる」の意の他動詞.
(2)「瞬間的に飛び上がるほどびっくりする, ぎょっとする」は **be startled**,「びっくり仰天する」は **be astonished**, さらに「ショックを受けるほどびっくりする」は **be astounded** や **be shocked**,「ぼう然とする」は **be stunned** /stʌnd/,「あきれるほどびっくりする, あ然とする」は **be flabbergasted** や **be dumbfounded** /dʌmfáʊndɪd/,「驚き, 当惑する」やしばしばよい意味で「信じられないことにびっくりする」は **be amazed** を使う.

▶その知らせを聞いて本当にびっくりしました I *was* really *surprised by* [*at*] the news. (➤ by は原因となるものを指し, at は「知らせに接して」の意) ‖ 朝方の大きな地震には本当にびっくりしました I *was startled* [*shocked* / *stunned*] *by* the severe earthquake early in the morning. (➤ 地震を主語にして The severe earthquake early in the morning really startled me. としてもよい) ‖ その発見は世界をびっくりさせた The discovery *amazed* [*stunned*] the world. ‖ その遊園地の乗り物の多さにびっくりした I *was amazed at* the number of rides at the amusement park. ‖ 彼女に逮捕状が出ていると聞いてびっくりしている I*'m surprised* [*shocked*] *to* hear that there's a warrant out for her arrest. ‖ 彼女がその事故で亡くなったと聞いてただもうびっくりした I *was shocked to* learn that she was killed in the accident. ‖ 宝くじでこんな大金が当たるなんてただもうびっくりです I *was stunned at* winning [*It was a tremendous surprise to* have won] such a large amount of money in the public lottery. ‖ びっくり仰天して私は口もきけなかった I *was flabbergasted*.

▶自由の女神の前で彼女に会ってびっくりしたわ *What a surprise to* meet her in front of the Statue of Liberty! ‖ びっくりするじゃないか! You *scared* me! ‖ ぼくはびっくりして彼女を見つめた I stared at her *in surprise* [*in astonishment*]. ‖ 隣に知らない人が寝ていたのでびっくりして飛び上がった I (immediately) *jumped out of bed* when I found a stranger sleeping beside me. ‖ あなたをびっくりさせることがあるのよ I *have a big surprise* for you. ‖ 彼女の指はびっくりするほど細かった Her fingers were *surprisingly* thin. ‖ きのうはびっくりするような出来事があった There was a *surprising* [*shocking*] incident yesterday. / Something *surprising* [*shocking*] happened yesterday.

‖びっくり箱 a jack-in-the-box.

ひっくりかえす 引っくり返す upset +目 (転覆させる); turn over, overturn +目 (横倒しにする) ▶湯飲み茶わんを引っくり返す *upset* [*knock over*] a cup of tea ‖ 彼は修繕するためにテーブルを引っくり返した He *turned* the table *upside down* to repair it. / He *overturned* the table to repair it. ‖《お好み焼き屋などで》下がこんがりしてきたら引っくり返してね *Turn* [*Flip*] it *over* when the bottom side has browned. (➤ flip は「すばやく裏返す」).

ひっくりかえる 引っくり返る turn over, overturn
▶事故でトラックが引っくり返った A truck *turned over* in an accident. ‖ 突風で漁船が引っくり返った A fishing boat *was overturned* [*was capsized*] by a sudden wind. (➤ capsize /kǽpsaɪz/ は「(船を)転覆させる」) ‖ 彼は氷の上で滑って引っくり返った He slipped on the ice and *fell* (*down*) *on his back*.
▶《比喩的》畠山のスリーランで試合が引っくり返った Hatakeyama's three-run homer *turned the tables*. (➤ turn the tables は「形勢を逆転させる」) ‖ 一審の判決が高裁で引っくり返った The ruling of the first trial *was overturned* [*reversed*] by the high court.

ひっくるめる ▶家賃は管理費その他ひっくるめて 8 万 3000円です The rent is 83,000 yen, *including* upkeep and other expenses. (● この場合の「その他」を others と訳すと,「その他の人たち」と解釈されるおそれがあるので, 訳例のように「その他の費用」ときちんと言うこと) ‖ 全部ひっくるめておいくらですか How much is it *altogether* [*in all*]?

ひづけ 日付 a date ▶新しい日付の牛乳パック a carton of milk with a recent *date* on it ‖ この手紙には日付がない The letter has *no date* (on it). / The letter is *undated*. ‖ その手紙は 5 月 5 日の日付になっている The letter *is dated* May 5. (➤ 日付はふつう May (the) fifth のように序数で読む.《米》では the を省くことが多い).

‖国際日付変更線 the International Date Line.

ひっけい 必携 ▶受験生必携の書 an *indispensable* book for students preparing for entrance examinations.

ひつけやく 火付け役 a troublemaker (トラブルメーカー); an agitator (扇動者); an originator (創始者) ▶日本の釣りブームの火付け役 *the originator* of the fishing boom in Japan ‖ その会社は男性化粧品ブームの火付け役だといわれている That company is credited with *triggering* the men's cosmetics boom.

ピッケル an ice ax [《英》axe] (➤「ピッケル」はドイツ語の *Pickel* から) ▶ピッケルで氷を砕く break ice with *an ice ax*.

ひっけん 必見 ▶必見の映画 a movie you *can't miss* / a *must-see* [*must*] film 《参考》不動産屋の物件紹介などにしばしば This is a must-see [a must]. のような表示がある.

ひっこし 引っ越し a move (1 回の); moving (引っ越すこと) ▶引っ越しを手伝ってくれますか Could you help me *move*? (➤ この move は「引っ越す」の意の動詞) ‖ ベートーベンはウィーン時代80回以上の引っ越しをした Beethoven *moved* more than 80 times during his days in Vienna. ‖ 引っ越しは来週の日曜の予定です We're *moving* next Sunday.

‖引っ越し先 (=新しい住所) a new address ‖ 引っ越しのトラック《米》a moving van,《英》a removal van ‖ 引っ越し業者 a moving company, a mover (➤ 前者は店の規模に無関係, 後者は小規模).

ひっこす 引っ越す move《to, into》

【文型】
場所(A)から場所(B)に引っ越す
move from A **to** [**into**] B
➤「(建物)の中へ」という意識では into を用いる.「越して(建物を)出ていく」は move out《of》となる

▶新しい家へ引っ越す *move to* a new house ‖ 小田さん一家は先週東京から博多に引っ越した The Odas *moved from* Tokyo *to* Hakata last week. ‖ 私たちはこの家へ最近引っ越してきたばかりです We've just *moved into* this house recently. ‖ きのう引っ越してきた本田です I'm Honda. I *moved here* [*moved in*] yesterday. ‖ 私たち，あす(このアパートを)引っ越すんです Tomorrow we are *moving out* (of this apartment).

✉ **先月ワンルームマンションに引っ越しました．遊びに来てね** I *moved into* a studio apartment last month. Come and see my new place !

ひっこぬく 引っこ抜く ▶庭の雑草を根こそぎ引っこ抜いた I *have pulled out* the weeds in the garden.

ひっこみ 引っ込み ▶ここまできたらもう引っ込みがつかない Now that we've come this far, there's no way we can *back out* [*pull out*].

ひっこみじあん 引っ込み思案の **shy**(恥ずかしがり屋の)；**retiring**(付き合いを避けて内に閉じこもりがちの) ▶引っ込み思案な少女 a *shy* [*quiet* ／*retiring*] girl ／a *reserved* [an *introverted*] girl (➤ introverted は「内向的な」) ‖ 剛志，そんなに引っ込み思案じゃだめだよ Don't be *shy*, Tsuyoshi !

ひっこむ 引っ込む **retire** 《to, into》(引退する) ▶いなかへ引っ込む *retire into* the country ‖ カタツムリが殻の中に引っ込んだ The snail *drew back into* its shell.

▶うちは商店街からちょっと引っ込んだ所にあります My house is just *off* the shopping street. ‖ その店は引っ込んだ所にあるからさがしにくい The store *is tucked away in* a hard-to-find place. ‖ 口を出すな，引っ込んでろ！ Keep your nose out of this !

ひっこめる 引っ込める **withdraw** ＋㊐；**draw back** (足を) ▶猫はつめを引っ込めることができる A cat can *withdraw* its claws. ‖ カメは首を引っ込めた The tortoise *pulled in* its head. ‖ 手を引っ込めなさい *Put* [*Pull*] *back* your hands.

▶彼女はしぶしぶ自分の提案を引っ込めた She *withdrew* her proposal reluctantly.

ピッコロ a **piccolo** /píkəloʊ/ ▶ピッコロを吹く play the *piccolo*.

ひっさつ 必殺 ▶《プロレス》必殺のドロップキック a *deadly* dropkick ‖ スカンクの必殺の武器は強烈な悪臭がする分泌液だ The *fatal* weapon of a skunk is its highly offensive discharge.

‖**必殺技** a deadly [lethal] technique (相手を殺す技)；a killer technique (効果のある見事な技).

[1]**ひっし 必死の** **desperate** /déspərət/ 一副 **必死に** **desperately** ▶我々の必死の努力も実らなかった Our *desperate* efforts came to nothing. ‖ たけしは彼女の気を引こうと必死だ Takeshi *is* trying *desperately* to get her attention. ‖ 彼は必死になって自己弁護した He *desperately* defended himself. ‖ こそどろは必死になって逃げた The thief ran *for his life*. (➤ for one's life は「命がけで」).

▶彼はノルマを達成しようと必死だ He'*s* (*all*) *out to* reach his quota. (➤ be out to do は「…しようとやっきになっている」).

[2]**ひっし 必至の** **inevitable**(避けられない) ▶校長と教員との意見の衝突は必至だ A clash of opinion between the principal and the teachers is *inevitable* [*unavoidable*].

ひつじ 羊・未 a **sheep** [複 **sheep**]；a **ram** (雄羊)；an **ewe** /juː/ (雌羊)；a **lamb** /læm/ (子羊) ▶羊の群れ a flock of *sheep* ‖ 羊の肉 mutton ‖ 羊の毛を刈る shear *a sheep*.

‖**羊飼い** a shepherd /ʃépərd/ ‖ **未**(ひつじ)**年** the Year of the Sheep.

ひっしゃ 筆者 **the writer**(その文章を書いた人，執筆者)；**the present writer** (➤ 論文中で自分を指して使うが，最近では I, We が好まれる).

ひっしゅう 必修の **required**, 《英》 **compulsory** /kəmpʌ́lsəri/ ▶英語は必修科目ですが，フランス語は選択科目です English is *a required subject*, but French is an elective [《英》 optional] subject.

ひつじゅひん 必需品 a **necessity**, 《主に英》 **necessaries**, 《インフォーマル》 a **must**, a **must-have** ▶生活必需品 the *necessities* of life ‖ 今やパソコンはオフィスの必需品になった Computers [Personal computers] have become *a necessity* in offices. ‖ トイレットペーパーは日常必需品です Toilet paper is *a daily necessity*. ‖ パスポートは海外旅行をする人にとって必需品だ A passport is *a must* [*a must-have*] for a person who travels overseas.

ひつじゅん 筆順 a **stroke order** ▶右と左は最初の２画の筆順が違う The first two *strokes* of the kanji 'migi' and 'hidari' are different in their *order*.

ひっしょう 必勝 ▶必勝を期して戦う fight *with a firm expectation of victory* ‖ 必勝！ Ｙ商業高校 *Victory* for Y Commercial High School ! ／May Y Commercial High School *be victorious* !

びっしょり ▶にわか雨にあって下着までびっしょりぬれた I was caught in a shower and *got soaked through* to my underwear. ‖ 私はびっしょり汗をかいた I *was drenched with sweat*.

びっしり ▶箱を開けたら札束がびっしり詰まっていた I opened the box to find it was *packed with* stacks of bills. ‖ 10月末までは予定がびっしりです My schedule is *packed full* [*very tight*] until the end of October.

ひっす 必須の **essential** ▶体力は探検家になるための必須条件だ Physical strength is *an essential condition* [*requirement*] to become an explorer. (➤ １語で a prerequisite としてもよい) ‖ 鶏卵は８種類の必須アミノ酸を含んでいる Chicken eggs contain eight kinds of *essential amino acids*.

☛ **必須科目** →必修

ひっせき 筆跡 **handwriting** ▶他人の筆跡をまねる imitate another person's *handwriting* [*hand*] ‖ この筆跡は間違いなく男性のものだ This *handwriting* is certainly that of a man.

‖**筆跡鑑定** handwriting analysis.

ひつぜつ 筆舌 ▶グランドキャニオンの美しさは筆舌に尽くしがたい The beauty of the Grand Canyon *is beyond description* [*is indescribable*].

ひつぜん 必然の **inevitable**

▶彼が食べ過ぎて肥満になったのは必然の結果だ Obesity was an *inevitable* result of his overeating. ‖ 不景気は必然的に失業につながる A recession *inevitably* leads to unemployment. ‖ １位が失格になれば２位が必然的に優勝となる The runner-up will become the winner *as a matter of course* if the first-in runner is disqualified. (➤ as a matter of course は「当然のこととして」の意) ‖ その女優は必然性のない場面では裸にならないと宣言した The actress declared that she would not appear nude unless there was *an absolute need* to do so in the scene.

ひっそり ▶家の中はひっそりしていた The house was *still*. ‖ ご主人を亡くしてからあの人は娘さんと２人でひっそりと暮らしている Since her husband died, she and her daughter have been leading a *quiet* life together.

ひったくり a **snatch**(行為)；a **snatcher** (人) ▶あいつがひったくりの犯人に違いない That man must be the bag *snatcher*. ／That man must be the *one who snatched* the bag. ‖ 私はイタリアでひったくりにあった I *had* [*got*] my purse *snatched* in Italy. (➤ (×)I was snatched ... としないこと).

ひったくる **snatch** +目 ▶自転車に乗った男が彼女のハンドバッグをひったくって逃げた A man on a bicycle *snatched* her purse out of [from] her hand and fled.

ぴったり 1【適切に】**perfectly** 一形 **ぴったりの** **right**(最適な) ; **suitable**(適切な) ; **perfect**(申し分のない) ▶体にぴったりのドレス a *tight-fitting* dress ‖ その服あなたにぴったりよ That dress *fits* [*suits*] you *perfectly*. (➤ fit はサイズや型が「合う」, suit は「似合う」) ／That dress *fits* you *to a T*. (➤ to a T は「ぴったり」の意のインフォーマルな言い方) ‖ ガラスの靴はシンデレラにぴったりだった The glass slipper *fitted* Cinderella *perfectly*. ‖ この辞書は初心者にはぴったりだ This dictionary *is just right for* beginners. ‖ 彼女は会計係に(まさに)ぴったりだ She is (*exactly*) the *right* person *for* accounting. ‖ 彼のシャツとネクタイはぴったり合っている His shirt and tie are *a perfect match*. ‖ 対話「いいホテルみたいね」「若いカップルにぴったりだね」"It sounds like a nice hotel." "It's *perfect* [*just right*] *for* a young couple." ‖ ここは新工場を建設するのにぴったりの場所だ This is a *perfect* place to build a new factory. ‖ ドアをぴったり閉めなさい Shut the door *completely* [*all the way*].

2【正確に】**exactly** ▶日本語の「いただきます」にぴったりの英語表現はない An *exact* one-word English equivalent for the Japanese "itadakimasu" doesn't exist. ‖ 時刻は3時ぴったりです The time is *exactly* three. ‖ 8時ぴったりにそこへ着いた I got there *exactly* at eight [at eight *sharp*].

3【くっついて】**closely** ▶二人はぴったり寄り添って座っていた The two sat *close* [*closely*] together. ‖ 刑事は男をぴったり尾行した The detective followed the man *closely*. ‖ この瓶の蓋はぴったりはまっていない The lid of this jar isn't (on) *tight*. ‖ ぬれたシャツが肌にぴったりくっついて気持ちが悪い I feel uncomfortable because my shirt is wet and *clinging* [*sticking*] *to* my body.

4【急に全く】▶彼はギャンブルをぴったりやめた He quit gambling *cold turkey*. (➤ cold turkey は「ぴたりと(断つ)」に相当するインフォーマルな言い方).

ひつだん 筆談する **communicate by** [**in**] **writing**.

ひっち 筆致 **handwriting style**.

ピッチ 1【速度】a **pace**, (a) **speed** ▶工事は急ピッチで進んだ The construction progressed *at a rapid pace*. ‖ クルーはさらにピッチを上げた The crew *picked up speed*.

2【音の高さ】a **pitch** ▶オーケストラのピッチはラ音が440ヘルツ前後だ An orchestra's *pitch* is at about A = 440 Hz.

3【試合を行う所】《英》a [**the**] **pitch**(サッカー・ホッケーなどの) ▶ピッチ上の彼のプレーは知的である His play on *the pitch* shows intelligence.

> **危ないカタカナ語✸ ピッチ**
> 1「ピッチが早い」とか「ピッチを上げる」という場合の「ピッチ」は「速度」の意味だが, 英語の pitch にはこの意味はない. pitch は主に「音の高低」の意である.
> 2 日本語の「ピッチ」の意味を表すには pace や speed を用いる必要がある. またボートの「一こぎ」や水泳の「一かき」の意味では stroke を用いる.

ヒッチハイク **hitchhiking** 一動 **ヒッチハイクする** **hitchhike** ▶彼は北海道までヒッチハイクした He *hitchhiked* to Hokkaido. ／He *thumbed a ride* [《英》*a lift*] to Hokkaido. (➤ thumb a ride は「親指を立てて便乗を頼む」の意).

ピッチャー a **pitcher** ▶試合でピッチャーをやる *pitch* in a game ／take the mound.

ひっちゃく 必着 ▶応募原稿は10月31日までに必着のこと Manuscripts *must reach us* [*must arrive*] by October 31.

ぴっちり ▶体にぴっちりの服 *tight-fitting* clothes ‖ 蓋がぴっちりし過ぎて瓶が開けられない The lid is on too *tight* and I can't get the jar open.

ピッチング 《野球》**pitching**
‖ピッチングフォーム pitching form ‖ ピッチングマシーン a pitching machine.

ピッツバーグ **Pittsburgh** /pítsbəːrg/ (アメリカ, ペンシルベニア州の都市).

ひってき 匹敵する **be equal to**(…に等しい) ; **compare with** (…と比べられる) ▶アマチュアながら彼のゴルフの腕前はプロに匹敵する Though an amateur, his golf skills *are equal to* those of a pro. ‖ 日本のゴルファーで彼に匹敵する人はほとんどいない Among Japanese golfers, he *has few equals* [*is almost unrivaled*]. ‖ 歌のうまさで彼女に匹敵する歌手はいない There is no other singer who *can hold a candle to* her in singing ability. (➤ cannot hold a candle to は「…にはとても及ばない」).

ヒット 1【安打】a **single** (**hit**), a **base hit** ▶ヒットを打つ hit *a single* ／single ‖ 阿部のライト前ヒットで, 村田は三塁に進んだ Murata advanced to third on Abe's *single* to right.

2【大当たり】a **hit** ; a **great success** (大成功) ▶あのミュージカルはヒット間違いなしだろうな That musical will be *a hit* for sure. ‖ その映画は大ヒットした The movie *was a great hit* [*a smash hit* ／*a great success*]. ‖ この歌は現在ヒット中だ The song *is a great hit*. ‖ その歌は何週間もヒットチャートのトップの座を占めている The song has been at the top of the *charts* for weeks. ‖ヒット曲 a hit song.

3【該当数】《コンピュータ》a **hit** ▶そのキーワードで探したら, 1000件を超えるヒットがあった When I did a search using that keyword, I got more than one thousand *hits*.

ビット 《コンピュータ》a **bit** (情報量の単位).

ひっとう 筆頭 ▶T高校は優勝候補の筆頭だ T High School *heads the list* of likely winners [is the *top* favorite].

ヒットエンドラン 《野球》a **hit and run** ▶ヒットエンドランをする hit-and-run ／execute *a hit-and-run play*.

ひつどく 必読 ▶これは学生の必読書だ This is *a book* which every student *should* [*must*] *read*. ／This is *a must-read* for students.

ビットコイン a **Bitcoin**(登録商標), **bitcoin**(ビットコインの単位).

ひっぱく 逼迫 ▶その会社は財政的にかなりひっ迫していた The company was pretty *tight* for funds. ‖ 情勢はひっ迫している The situation is *urgent* [is *pressing*].

ひっぱたく **slap** +目, **smack** +目 (➤ ともに「平手で打つ」の意だが, 後者のほうが打ち方が激しい) ▶女主人公はその無礼な男をひっぱたいた The heroine *gave* the rude man *a slap* [*a smack*]. ／The heroine *slapped* [*smacked*] the rude man.

ひっぱりこむ 引っ張り込む **draw** [**drag**] **into** ▶きみ

ひ

の個人的問題に私を引っ張り込まないでくれ Don't *drag* me *into* your personal affairs.

ひっぱりだこ 引っ張りだこの **sought-after** ▶彼女は引っ張りだこのテレビタレントだ She is a much *sought-after* TV personality. ‖ その学部出身の学生は各会社から引っ張りだこです Graduates of that department *are in great demand* by employers.

ひっぱりだす 引っ張り出す ▶ガムを1枚引っ張り出す *pull* [*take*] *out* a stick of gum.

ひっぱる 引っ張る **1【引く】pull** +⊕；**draw** +⊕（一定速度で力を入れて）；**tug**（+⊕）（何回か続けて強く）；**tow** +⊕（けん引する）；**pluck at**（ぐいと）▶赤ん坊は母親の髪を引っ張った The baby *pulled* its mother's hair. ‖ 女の子は父親の左腕を引っ張った The little girl *pulled* her father by the left arm.（➤ この by は動作の対象となる体の部位を示す前置詞）‖ ぼくは荷車を後ろから押すから，きみは前から引っ張ってくれ I'll push the cart from behind, so please *pull* [*draw*] it from the front. ‖ 彼女は戸を強く引っ張ったが，引っ張っても引っ張っても開かなかった She *tugged at* the door, but *no matter how hard* she *tugged at* it, it wouldn't open. ‖ タグボートは貨物船を桟橋まで引っ張った The tugboat *towed* the cargo ship to the dock. ‖ 彼女はひもをぐいと引っ張った She *jerked* the cord. ／She *gave a jerk on* the cord.（➤ jerk は「引く」だけでなく「ぐいと動かす」の意）‖ その子は母親のスカートを引っ張った The child *pulled at* his [her] mother's skirt. ‖ 犬はリードを強く引っ張った The dog *strained at* the lead. ‖ 弟たちはおもちゃを引っ張り合った My little brothers tried to *pull* the toy *away* from each other. ‖《慣用表現》他人の足を引っ張るのはやめなさい Stop trying to *hold* other people *back* [*trip* other people *up*].（➤ ともに「人を妨害する」の意）‖ きみはキャプテンなのだから，チームをしっかり引っ張っていくのが仕事だ Since you're captain, it's your job to *lead* the team.

2【連行する】take +⊕（連れて行く）；**bring** +⊕（連れて来る）→連れる ▶彼女は警察へ引っ張られた She *was taken* to the police station. ‖ パトロール中の警官がすりを交番に引っ張って来た A police officer on patrol *brought* a pickpocket into the police box.

3【誘う】▶あの有名な建築家をわが社に引っ張ったのは社長だ It was our president that *persuaded* the famous architect *to join* our company.

4【野球】pull +⊕ ▶イチローは初球を引っ張って2塁打とした Ichiro *pulled* the first pitch for a double.

ヒッピー a **hippie**, a **hippy**.

ヒップ **hips**（腰；通例複数形で）；a **bottom**（しり）▶私はヒップが大きい I have *a big bottom* [*butt*].（➤「腰回りが太い」なら I have wide hips.）.

> **危ないカタカナ語✸ ヒップ**
> **1** 英語の hip はおしりではなく，腰から下の左右に張り出した部分のどちらか一方を指す．したがって，「ヒップ…センチ」というときのヒップはその両方を含むから hips と複数形になる．→腰．
> **2** 座ったとき体の下にくる部分は buttock または bottom（後者はくだけた語）というが，buttock は左右に分かれた一方を指すことばなので，buttocks と複数形でいう．《米・インフォーマル》ではこれを butt という．

ビップ a **VIP**（➤ very important person のこと．英語ではふつう /víːaɪpìː/ のように発音する）．

ヒップホップ《音楽》**hip-hop**.

ひづめ 蹄 a **hoof**.

ひつめい 筆名 a **pen name** ▶サミュエル・クレメンスはマーク・トウェーンの筆名で小説を書いた Samuel Clemens wrote novels *under the name of* Mark Twain.（文脈からここでは pen は不要）．

ひつよう 必要 **necessity** /nəsésəṭi/, **need**（必要性）**一形 必要な necessary**；**mandatory**（義務的な）**一動 必要とする need** +⊕（➤ 主に人が主語になる）；**require** +⊕（➤ 主に物・事が主語になる）▶ぼくにはきみが必要なんだ I *need* you. ‖ 卒業には124単位が必要だ 124 credits are *mandatory* [*required*／*necessary*] for graduation. ‖ あの子にはもっと母親の愛情が必要だ That child *needs* more motherly affection. ‖ きみの会社じゃ英語は必要なのかい？Do you *need* English at your office？／Is English *necessary* at your office？‖ 子供たちを守るために必要なことは何でもします We'll do whatever is *necessary* to protect our children. ‖ 私は銀行ローンを返すのにどうしても30万円必要なのです I'*m* badly *in need of* 300,000 yen to pay back the bank loan. ‖ 食べ物は生きていくには必要なものだ Food is *a necessity* of life. ‖ 石油は現代人の生活にどうしても必要なものだ Oil is *indispensable* to modern life.

> **【文型】**
> **人・物(A)が…することが必要だ**
> **It is necessary for** A **to** do.
> **It is necessary that** A do.
> ➤ 下は堅い言い方．動詞は《米》では原形．《英》では should do または直接法

▶きみはあすまでにレポートを仕上げる必要がある *It's necessary for* you to finish the report by tomorrow.（➤ 必要なのはものごと・条件・行為で，人ではないので，(×)You are necessary … は不可）／*It's necessary that* you finish the report by tomorrow. ‖ 車を運転するには運転免許が必要だ *It is necessary to* have a license to drive a car. ／A driver's license *is necessary to* drive [for driving] a car. ‖ 前大統領は裁判を受ける必要がある *It is necessary that* the former president (should) stand trial. ‖ **対話**「翻訳家になるにはどんな資格が必要ですか」「何もいりません」"What kind of qualification *is necessary to* become a translator？" "None."

> **【文型】**
> **…する必要がある**
> **need to** do
> **have to** do ／**must** do
> **…する必要がない**
> **don't need to** do ／**needn't** do
> **don't have to** do
>
> **《解説》**(1)**need to** do は必要を，**have to** do と **must** do は必要や強意の義務を表す．**have to** do と **need to** do では前者のほうが強い必要度を表すが違いはわずかである．
> (2)否定形は **don't need to** do や **don't have to** do がふつうで，**needn't** do は改まった堅い言い方．また過去形は needed は使われず，had to do がふつう．
> (3)**don't have to** do は「…する必要がない」を表すが，**must not** do は「…してはいけない」という強い禁止を表す．

▶きみたちにはハードトレーニングが**必要だ** You *need* hard workouts. ／You *need to* train hard. ‖ ワールドカップに進むには日本チームはあと２つ勝つ**必要がある** The Japanese team *needs* two more wins [*needs to* win two more games] to make it into the World Cup. ‖ 我々は初心に立ち返る**必要がある** We *need to* get back to our original objective(s). ‖ この時計は**修理する必要がある** This watch *needs to be repaired* [*needs repairing*]. ‖ 海外に渡航する人はパスポートを携帯する**必要がある** People who are going abroad *must* carry their passports (with them). ‖ お金のことを心配する**必要はありません** You *don't need to* worry about money (matters). ‖ きみが辞任する**必要はない** You *don't have to* resign. ／*There's no need* for you to resign. (➤ 前者は「やめなくていい」, 後者はより強い否定で「やめる必要など全くない」).

▶この仕事をするには大卒の資格が**必要だ** This job *requires* a college degree. ‖ 外国語を学ぶには根気が**必要だ** It *takes* patience to learn a foreign language.

▶**必要なら**この辞書は持っていていいよ You can keep this dictionary *if necessary* [*if you need it*]. ‖ **必要に迫られて**中国語を勉強しています I'm studying Chinese *out of necessity*. ‖ 修学旅行には**必要以上**のお金は持って来ないこと Do not bring *more* money *than is necessary* for the school excursion. ‖ 核兵器は平和を維持するための**必要悪**だろうか I wonder if nuclear weapons are *a necessary evil* to preserve peace.

▶相撲部屋を持つには日本人であることが**必要条件だ** You *are required* to be a Japanese citizen to own a sumo stable. (➤「要求される」の意) ／Japanese citizenship is *a requirement* [*a prerequisite*] for having a sumo stable. (➤ prerequisite /priːrékwəzɪt/ は「前提条件」).

[ことわざ] **必要は発明の母** Necessity is the mother of invention.

‖**必要経費** necessary expenses.

☛ **不必要** (→見出語)

ビデ a **bidet** /bɪdéɪ ‖ bíːdeɪ/ (➤ フランス語から).

ひてい 否定 a **denial** /dɪnáɪəl/ 一形 **否定の negative** 一動 **否定する deny** /dɪnáɪ/ ＋目 ▶学長は辞任のうわさを**否定した** The president *denied* the rumor of his resignation. ‖ 大臣はそのやくざとの関係をはっきりと**否定した** The minister firmly *denied* involvement with the yakuza. ‖ 地球の温暖化は**否定できない事実だ** Global warming is *an undeniable fact*. ‖ 彼女はそのうわさを**肯定も否定もしなかった** She didn't *confirm or deny* the rumor. ‖ 法王は女性司祭の可能性を**否定した** The pope *ruled out* the possibility of women priests. (➤ rule out は「排除する, 認めない」の意).

▶その案に対して彼(の態度)は**否定的**だった His attitude toward the plan was *negative*. ／He took a *negative* attitude toward the plan. ‖ 物事をそんなに**否定的に**ばかり見てはいけない Don't always look at things so *negatively*.

‖**否定文** a negative sentence.

びていこつ 尾てい骨《解剖学》**the coccyx** /kɑ́ːksɪks/, **the tailbone**.

ビデオ (a) **video** /vídioʊ/ ; a **videocassette recorder**(機器, デッキ ; 略 VCR)

《参考》video は本来 audio(オーディオ)に対する語で「(テレビの)映像」を指すが, インフォーマルな英語では「ビデオ装置」や「ビデオテープ」をもいう.

▶ビデオを見る watch *a video* on one's VCR ‖ 結婚式の模様を**ビデオに撮った** I *got a videotape recording* of the wedding. ／I *recorded* the wedding *on video*(*tape*). ／I *videotaped* the wedding.

‖**ビデオ・オン・デマンド** video on demand ‖ **ビデオカセット** a videocassette ‖ **ビデオカセットレコーダー** a videocassette recorder《略 VCR》‖ **ビデオカメラ** a video camera ; a camcorder (軽量の) ‖ **ビデオゲーム** a video game ‖ **ビデオショップ** a video (rental) shop ‖ **ビデオソフト** a video ‖ **ビデオディスク** a videodisc ‖ **ビデオテープ** a videotape ‖ **ミュージックビデオ** a music video.

びてき 美的な aesthetic /esθétɪk/ ▶**美的価値** *aesthetic* value ‖ **美的感覚** (an) *aesthetic* sense ／a sense of beauty.

ひでり 日照り a **drought** /draʊt/ (干ばつ); **dry weather** (雨の降らない天気) ▶**日照り**のため作物がだめになった Because of the *drought* [the *dry weather*], the crops (have) failed. (● 日照りを昨年や一昨年など, 過去のものとして言及する場合は failed を, (比較的)最近のものとして言及する場合は have failed を用いる).

ひでん 秘伝 secret teaching(s)

▶**秘伝の技** a technique *that has been handed down* (*from generation to generation*) ‖ **秘伝のたれ** *secret* sauce.

びてん 美点 a **virtue**(賞賛に値する点) ; an **advantage** (利点) ▶人の**美点**に学ぶ learn from the *virtues* [*good points*] of others ‖ 人にやさしいところが彼の**美点**でもあり, 欠点でもある His kindness to others is both *a virtue* and a fault. →メリット.

びでん 美田 a **rich paddy field** ▶子孫に**美田**を残さず Don't leave *rich paddy fields* to your descendants.

ひでんか 妃殿下 a **princess** ; **Her Imperial Highness** (➤ 日本の場合 ; イギリスなどの王室に対しては Imperial の代わりに Royal を用いる) ▶秋篠宮**妃殿下** *Princess* Akishino.

ひと 人 1【人間全体】man, humans 一形 **人の human**

> **《解説》「人」の言い方**
> (1)抽象的に「人間, 人類」の意味では **man** またはその堅い語である **mankind** が用いられ,「人」をほかの動物と対比する場合は **humans** またはその堅い語である **human beings** が用いられる.
> (2)ただし, 最近では男(性)の意味をもつ man, mankind は避けられ, 代わりに **humans, people** など性差のない語が好まれる傾向がある.
> (3)単数の場合は a human (being) となる.

▶**人の**脳 the *human* brain ‖ **人は**ものを考えるという点で動物とは異なる *Humans* [*Human beings*] differ from animals in that they think. ‖ 困った人を助けるのが**人の道だ** Helping a person in need is *the right thing to do*. ／A decent [An ethical] person is expected to help a person in need. ‖ **人は**みな平等だ All *men* are equal. ／All *people* are equal. (➤ 前者は男性を連想させるので, 後者の言い方が望ましい) ‖ たいていの鳥や動物は**人を**こわがる Most birds and animals are afraid of *humans* [*people*].

▶ヒト免疫不全ウイルス *Human* Immunodeficiency

Virus(➤ HIV と略す).
2【個々の人】 a **person** [複 **people, persons**]; a **man** [複 **men**](男), a **woman** [複 **women**](女); **people**(人々); **somebody, someone**(ある人; 前者がややくだけた語) ▶この人 this *person* [*man*/*woman*/*one*] ‖ 村田という人 *a person* called Murata/*a person* by the name of Murata/a Mr. [Mrs./Miss/Ms.] Murata ‖ きのう一緒に歩いていた男の人は誰? Who is the *man* you were walking with yesterday?
▶私って朝弱い人なの I am *not a morning person*. ‖ 今名前を呼ばれた人は前に出てください Would *the people* I have just called please come to the front? ‖ 彼女は青森の人です(=青森出身です) She is [comes] from Aomori. ‖ 彼女は絶対に約束を守る人だ She never breaks her promises. /She is *a woman of her word*. ‖ ねえ, うちの人見なかった? (Excuse me, but) have you seen *my husband*?
▶あしたは人(=客)が2, 3人来ることになっている We are expecting a few *guests* tomorrow. ‖ きょうは午後, 人と会う約束がある I have *an appointment* this afternoon. (➤ appointment は「会合や訪問の約束」) ‖ 誰かきみに会いたいって人が来てるよ There's *someone* who says they want to see you. /*Someone* has come to see you.
▶この問題のわかる人は(だれでも)手を挙げて *Anybody* [*Anyone*] who can solve this problem, please raise your hand. ‖ 知らない人から誘われてもついて行ってはだめよ Don't go with *strangers* who talk to you.
3【世間の人, 他人】people(人); **other people, others**(ほかの人たち) ▶人はうわさ話が好きだ *People* like gossiping. ‖ 困っているときほど人の情けのありがたさを感じるときはない It's when you are in need that you truly appreciate *people's kindness*. ‖ 自由が丘は若い人に人気の町だ Jiyugaoka is a popular area with young *people*. ‖ 人には親切にしなさい Be kind to *others*. ‖ 最近は人のことはどうでもいいと考える人が多い These days, many people don't care about what happens to *others*.
▶彼は人が自分をどう見ているかをいつも気にしている He is always anxious about how *other people* see him. ‖ 人に頼るな Don't depend on *others*! /Be independent! ‖ 身軽に旅行する人もいるし, 荷物をたくさん持って行く人もいる *Some people* travel light, and *others* take a lot of baggage. ‖ 人は人, 自分は自分 I do*n't care* (*about*) *what others think* [*say*]. /I do things my (own) way. ‖ 人の道を踏み外す *go astray*.
4【人材】▶企業は人である A company's most valuable asset is its *employees*. ‖ 今, 人(=従業員)が足りなくて困っています The shortage of *workers* is a headache right now.
5【性質, 人柄】▶彼女は人がいい She is a *good-natured* person [woman]. ‖ 彼女はアメリカに数年間いたらすっかり人が変わって積極的になった After staying in the U.S. for several years, she *has become* quite *a different woman* and is much more assertive.
6【自分を指して】▶人をばかにするな Don't look down on *me*! ‖ 人を何だと思ってるんだ What do you think *I* am?
7【慣用表現】▶ずっとぼくをだましていたとは, きみも人が悪いね It's *mean* [*spiteful*] of you to have deceived me so long. ‖ 人の気も知らないでよくそんなことが言えたもんだ How dare you say that? *Don't you care how I feel*? (🔘 この場合の「人」は話し手を指す.「私がどう思っているか気にならないのか」という言い方) ‖ 裁判官も人の子. ときには感情的になることもある Judges are only *human*. Sometimes they get emotional. (➤ human は「人としての弱みをもつ」) ‖ 人もあろうに, 宮本さんがあんなことをするなんて! (What a shock it is) to find out that Mr. Miyamoto, *of all people*, did such a thing! (➤ of all people は「すべての人の中で, よりによって」の意) ‖ 彼はいつも人を食ったような(=ばかにした)態度をとる He is always *making fools of people*.
☛ いい人, 人々 (→見出語)

ひとあし 一足 a **step**
▶おばの家まではほんの一足だ My aunt's house is only *a hop, skip and* (*a*) *jump* [is only *a short distance*] from here. ‖ 一足お先に失礼します Excuse me, but I'm going to leave *a little ahead of you*.
▶一足違いで電車に間に合わなかった I missed the train *by a second*. (➤ by a second は「(時間的に)わずかのところで」).

ひとあじ 一味 ▶母さんの漬けた漬物は一味違う Mom's pickles *taste special*. /Mom's pickles *have a taste like no* one else's.

ひとあせ 一汗 ▶花壇の手入れをして一汗かくか Now I think I'll tend the flower beds and *work up a* (*little*) *sweat*.

ひとあたり 人当たり ▶池田さんは人当たりがやわらかい Mr. Ikeda is a *friendly* [an *affable*] person. /Mr. Ikeda *has a gentle* [*personable*] *manner*.

ひとあめ 一雨 a **shower**(にわか雨)
▶一雨来そうな空模様だ It looks like we're going to have *a shower*. ‖ 一雨ごとに暖かくなってきた It's getting warmer *every time rain falls* [*with every rainfall*].

ひとあわ 一泡 ▶三者凡退ばかりしていないで, たまにはホームランをかっ飛ばして, 相手ピッチャーに一泡吹かせてやれ How about belting a home run once in a while and *give* the opposing pitcher *a big surprise*, instead of letting one batter after another be put out so easily?

ひとあんしん 一安心 ▶ああ, これで一安心だ What *a relief*! ‖ 娘が無事ロンドンに着いたとわかり, 一安心した I *felt relieved* when I learned that my daughter had arrived in London safely.

ひどい

訳語メニュー
恐ろしい →terrible **1**
つらい →hard **2**
悪い →bad, awful, terrible **3**
すさまじい →violent, fierce **4**

1【恐ろしい】terrible; **cruel**(冷酷な) ▶妻に保険金をかけて殺すなんてひどい男だ What a *terrible* [*cruel*] man! He killed his wife for the insurance money. ‖ あんなひどいことをして, あなたそれでも人間ですか! Do you still call yourself human after doing such a *terrible* thing?
2【つらい】hard ▶大酒飲みと結婚するとひどい目にあうわよ You'll *have a hard time of it* if you marry a heavy drinker. ‖ あす金を持って来ないと, ひどい目にあうぞ If you don't bring the money tomorrow, you'll *be in big trouble*.

3【悪い】bad ; awful, terrible (ひどく悪い；後者が意味が強い) ▶ひどい成績を取る get *bad* grades ‖ ひどい間違い a *terrible* [*horrible*] mistake ‖ 雪で道路はひどい状態だ The road is *bad* [*terrible*] because of the snow. ‖ なんてひどいにおいだ What an *awful* smell!

▶どうしたの？ひどい顔色だよ What's wrong? You look *awful*. ‖ なんてひどい人たちだ What *awful* [*rotten*] people! (➤ rotten (いやな) はかなり強い語) ‖ 彼の字はひどい His handwriting is *awful* [*very poor*]. ‖ 彼の英語はひどいものだ His English is *terrible* [*awful*]. ‖ 私のテニスはそれはひどいの I'm a *terrible* tennis player.

▶今度の試験はひどかった I *did very badly* on the last exam. ‖ 対話「待たせてごめん」「ひどいじゃないの. 1時間も待ったのよ」"Sorry to have kept you waiting." "*You're really inconsiderate*. I've been waiting an hour."

4【すさまじい】violent (激しくて破壊的な), **fierce** /fɪəʳs/ (激しい) ▶ひどい風が吹いている The wind is blowing *violently*. ‖ ひどい風だな What a *terrible* wind! / The wind is really blowing *fiercely*. ‖ ひどい雨で試合は中止になった The game was called off because of the *heavy* rain. (➤ heavy は「(雨やあらしが)強い」) ‖ ひどい熱だ. すぐ医者へ連れて行こう He has a *terrible* [*very high*] fever. Let's take him to the doctor right now. ‖ 外はひどい寒さだ It's *freezing* outside.

▶道路工事の騒音がひどくていらいらする The noise from the road construction is *so loud* that it's driving me crazy.

☛ ひどく (→見出語)

ひといき 一息 1【息】a breath ▶彼女はバースデーケーキのろうそくを一息で吹き消した She blew out the candles on her birthday cake *in one breath*.

2【休息】a (short) rest, a (short) break ▶ここに座って一息入れよう Let's sit down here and *take a short rest*. ‖ ここらで一息入れようじゃないか Why don't we *take a short break*? / How about *taking a break* now?

3【もう少しの努力】▶さあ, あと一息で仕事も終わりだ. 頑張ろう！ Okay, just *one more go* [*push*] and we'll be finished. Let's get busy [get down to work]. ‖ 頂上までもう一息だ Just *one more push* will get us to the summit.

ひといきれ 人いきれ ▶会場はむっとするような人いきれだ The hall is so *crowded and stuffy*.

ひといちばい 人一倍 ▶弟は家でぶらぶらしているくせに人一倍食べる My (younger) brother spends his days loafing around the house, but he still eats *twice as much as anyone else*. ‖ 事業を起こし, 成功させるには人一倍の努力が必要だ It takes *extraordinary effort* to start a business and make a success of it.

▶父は人一倍気が短い My father is *extremely* short-tempered.

ひとう 秘湯 an **out-of-the-way** [a **secluded**] **hot spring**.

びとう 尾灯 a **taillight**, 《英》a **tail lamp**.

びどう 微動 ▶彼はもてる力をふりしぼったが, その岩は微動だにしなかった He used all the force he had, but the rock *didn't move an inch* [*didn't budge*].

ひとえ 一重の single-petal ▶一重のアジサイ a *single-petal* hydrangea.

‖一重まぶた a single eyelid (➤ アジア人特有のもの. →二重).

ひとえに 偏に ▶私の成功はひとえに皆さまのおかげです I owe *all* my success to you.

ひとおもいに 一思いに ▶いっそひと思いに死んでしまいたいと思ったこともありました There've been times when I thought that it would be better to die and get it over with. (➤ get it over with は「(めんどうなことに)けりをつける」).

ひとがき 人垣 ▶店の前には人垣ができていた The front of the store *was crowded with people*. ‖ 大通りにパレードの見物人が(三重の)人垣を作っていた *Crowds of people lined* the main street (three deep) to see the parade.

ひとかげ 人影 a **figure** (人の姿) ▶私は庭に怪しい人影を見た I saw a suspicious *figure* in the garden. ‖ 夜8時を過ぎればこの通りは人影もまばらだ After 8 p.m., this street *is almost deserted* [*only a few people are to be seen* on this street]. ‖ 通りに人影はなかった The street was *empty* [*dead*].

ひとかたならぬ 一方ならぬ

✉ **在米中はひとかたならぬお世話になり, ありがとうございました** Thank you for the wonderful hospitality you showed me while I was in the U.S.

ひとかど ▶ひとかどの人物になるには大変な努力がいる It takes a lot of hard work to become *somebody* [*a respected person* / *a person to be reckoned with*].

ひとがら 人柄 (a) **character** /kǽrəktəʳ/ (人格) ; (a) **personality** (性格) ▶彼はすばらしい人柄だ He has a fine *character*. (➤「人格的に尊敬できる」の意) / He has a wonderful [pleasant] *personality*. (➤「好かれる性格だ」の意) ‖ 彼の書いたものには人柄がにじみ出ている His *personality* emanates from what he has written. / His writings reveal his *true self* [*his character*].

ひとかわ 一皮 ▶いくら善人ぶっていても人間なんて一皮むけばみな欲のかたまりだ However good-natured people may try to appear, *beneath the surface* everyone is full of selfish desires.

ひとぎき 人聞き ▶ぼくが浮気しているって？あんまり人聞きの悪いことを言わないでくれよ I'm cheating on my wife? Don't say *scandalous* [*embarrassing*] things like that.

ひとぎらい 人嫌い a **misanthrope** /mísənθroʊp/.

ひときれ 一切れ a **slice** (薄切りの一切れ) ; a **piece** (1片, 1個) ▶チーズ[ケーキ], もう一切れちょうだい Please give me another *slice* of cheese [another *piece* of cake].

ひときわ 一際 remarkably

▶彼女の歌はひときわうまかった She sang *remarkably* well. ‖ 伸夫はのっぽなのでクラスメートの中でひときわ目だつ Nobuo *stands out* among his classmates because he is very tall.

ひどく 1【たいへん, とても】very ; terribly, awfully (➤ 前者が意味が強い) ; **badly** (➤ 通例 need, want などの動詞を修飾する)

▶ひどく疲れた I am *very* tired. ‖ 彼の態度がひどくしゃくにさわった I was *very much* annoyed with his attitude.

▶きょうはひどく寒いねえ It's *terribly* [*awfully*] cold today, isn't it? ‖ 彼女は今ひどく金に困っている She *badly* needs money now. / She is *really* hard up (for money). ‖ このことでは母にひどくしかられました I got a *good* scolding from my mother for this.

2【激しく，きつく】hard, heavily ▶彼は私の背中をひどく殴った He hit me *hard* on the back. ‖ かぜがひどくなってきた My cold is getting *worse*.

びとく 美徳 (a) **virtue** ▶勤勉は美徳か？Is diligence *a virtue*? ‖ 日本人にとって謙譲は美徳だ For Japanese people modesty is *a virtue*.

ひとくぎり 一区切り ▶今の仕事が一区切りついたら温泉にでも行こうと思っている I'm thinking of going to a hot spring resort or somewhere *when I'm over the hump* with my current job. ‖ ここで一区切りつけて，お茶を飲もう Let's *take a break* for tea.

ひとくせ 一癖 ▶あの学生は一癖ありそうだ (It) looks like that student will *be hard to get along with*. (➤「付き合いにくい」の意).

ひとくち 一口 1【飲食物の】a **mouthful** (口いっぱい)；a **bite** (一かじり；インフォーマルな語)；a **sip** (一すすり) ▶彼女はそのケーキを一口で食べてしまった She ate the whole slice of cake *in one mouthful*. ‖ そのリンゴ，一口かじらせてよ Give me *a bite* of that apple. ‖ 彼女はコーヒーを一口すすった She took *a sip* of the coffee.

▶彼は激辛カレーを一口食べて吐き出した After putting *a spoonful of* the extra hot curry and rice in his mouth, he spat it out. (➤ 口に入れただけで飲み込んでいないので eat は使えない).

2【ひと言】a **word** ▶一口に言えば日本人はせかせかしている *In a word*, Japanese are always in a rush. ‖ 一口に芸術家といってもさまざまだ There are all sorts of artists.

3【一単位】▶卒業生は２口以上の寄付をお願いします Graduates are asked to contribute *at least twice the standard* [*fair share*] *amount*. ‖ うまい話があるんだけど一口乗らないか I've got a surefire business proposal. How about getting *a piece of the action*? (➤ a piece of the action は「(もうけの)分け前，分担」).

ひとくろう 一苦労 ▶彼の家を見つけるのに一苦労だった It *was a real job* to find his house.

ひとけ 人気 ▶その建物の中は全く人けがなかった There were no *signs of life* in that building. ‖ 彼は人けのない街を歩いて行った He walked up the *deserted* street.

▶この辺りは夜８時を過ぎると人けがなくなる The streets in this neighborhood are *nearly deserted* after eight o'clock.

ひどけい 日時計 a **sundial** /sʌ́ndàɪəl/.

ひとけた 一桁 ▶昭和一けた生まれの人 a person born *during the first nine years of the Showa era* ‖ 社長の年収と私の年収では一けた違う The president's annual salary is *one digit larger* than mine.

ヒトゲノム《生化学》the **human genome**.

ひとこいしい 人恋しい ▶秋の夕べは人恋しくなる We feel lonely and *want someone to keep us company* on a fall evening.

ひとこえ 一声 ▶パンフレットをご希望の方は一声かけてください Anybody who wants a brochure, *please let me know*. ‖ お出かけは一声かけて鍵かけて When you go out, *let* your neighbors *know* and don't forget to lock the front door [lock the doors and *give* your neighbors *a shout*].

ひとごえ 人声 a (**human**) **voice** ▶廊下で人声がした I heard *a voice* from the corridor.

ひとごこち 人心地 ▶きょう１日忙しかったが，これでやっと人心地がついた I've had a very busy day today. Now at last I *can breathe again*.

ひとこと 一言 a **word** ▶その外国人の言ったことはひと言もわからなかった I couldn't understand *a word* the foreigner said. ／I couldn't make out *a single word* the foreigner said. (➤ make out は「理解する」; a single word は a word の強調) ‖ ひと言ご挨拶いただけますか Would you *say a few words* (*of welcome*)? ‖ きみにひと言言いたい[忠告したい]ことがある I have *something to say* to you [*a few words of advice* to give you]. ‖ 彼女にひと言言ってやりなさいよ Give her *a piece* [*bit*] *of your mind*. ‖ 対話「彼女って，最後に何かひと言言わないと気がすまないのね」「いつもひと言多いのよね」"She always has to have *the last word*, doesn't she?" "It's usually *one word too many*." (➤ the last word は「最後の決定的なことば」).

▶料理はすばらしいのひと言だった The food was *just* [*simply*] wonderful. ‖ ひと言で言えば夫は利己的だ *In a word* [*To put it simply*], my husband is self-centered.

✉ **昨夜のディナーがどんなに楽しかったかひと言お礼を申し上げたくて筆をとりました** *Just a line* [*a note*] to tell you how much we enjoyed your dinner last night. ➤「ほんの１行」の意. This is just a line to tell you ... としてもよい.

ひとごと 他人事 a **someone else's problem, other people's affairs** ▶この不況下では倒産はひと事ではない In this recession, bankruptcies are not just *other people's affairs* [bankruptcies *can happen to anyone*]. ‖ ひと事だと思って笑うなよ Don't laugh *as if it had nothing to do with you*. ‖ ひと事じゃあないぞ(きみにも関係している) It's *something that concerns you, too*. ‖ ひと事ながら，彼はあんなにたばこを吸わないほうがいいのにと思う *Although it's none of my business*, I really wish he wouldn't smoke so much.

ひとこま 一齣 a **scene** (映画などのシーン) ▶その戦争映画の残酷なひとこまが忘れられない I cannot forget that horrible *scene* in that war movie.

ひとごみ 人込み a **crowd** (**of people**) ▶その神社の縁日はたいへんな人込みだった *There was a great crowd of people* at the shrine festival. ／The shrine *was thronged with people* during the festival.

ひところ 一頃 once ▶あの商業地区はひところ栄えた That business district prospered *for a time*. ‖ 父もひところのような元気はなくなった My father isn't as energetic as he *once* was.

ひとごろし 人殺し (a) **murder** (殺人行為；「殺人事件」の意では a をつける)；a **murderer** (殺人犯) ▶彼は「人殺し！」と叫んだ He shouted, "*Murder*!" ⇀殺人.

ひとさしゆび 人差し指 a **forefinger**, an **index finger**. ⇀指.

ひとざと 人里 ▶彼は人里離れた所に住んでいる He lives in *a lonely place remote from any town or city*. ／He lives *off the beaten track*. (➤ off the beaten track は「人が行かない」の意) ／He lives *in the middle of nowhere*. (➤ in the middle of nowhere は「どこともわからない場所の真っただ中」).

ひとさらい 人さらい kidnapping (行為)；a **kidnapper** (人)；**abduction** (拉致行為).

ひとさわがせ 人騒がせ ▶ゴキブリ１匹に大騒ぎをしてみんなを起こすなんて全く人騒がせな母さんだ My mother is such *a scaremonger* that she made a fuss over one (little) cockroach and woke everybody up. ‖ **人騒がせなことを言う**な Don't *cry wolf*. (➤ cry wolf は『イソップ物語』の「オオカミが来たぞ」とうそを言って騒ぎたてた少年の話から).

ひとしい 等しい **be equal** /íːkwəl/《to》▶ 125は5の3乗に等しい 125 *is equal to* 5 cubed. ‖ 彼らは別々の道を行ったが, 目的地に着くまでの走行距離は等しかった Although they took different roads, they had to drive *the same* distance to reach the destination.

▶塀を作る費用は両家で等しく分担した The two families shared the expenses of building the wall *equally*. ‖ **皆等しく**幸福を願っている *Everyone without exception* longs for happiness.

▶うちのネコは5年前から蒸発していて死んだに等しい(=同然だ) My cat *is as good as* dead after disappearing five years ago. ‖ (多忙で)ことしの夏休みはほとんどないに等しかった(=実質上なかった) I had *practically* no summer vacation this year.

ひとしお ▶雨に洗われて若葉がひとしお(=いっそう)美しかった The rain made the new leaves *all the more* fresh and beautiful. ‖ ふたりとも子供は授からないと思い始めていたので, 妻が妊娠したと知ったときは**喜びもひとしお**でした Since we had begun to accept that we wouldn't be able to have a baby, my wife and I *felt all the happier* when we learned that she had become pregnant.

ひとしきり **for some** [a] **time** (しばらくの間)
▶番犬がひとしきり激しくほえていた The watchdog was barking ferociously *for some time*.

ひとしごと 一仕事 ▶では一仕事するか Now, let's *get to work*. ‖ 10人分の食事を作るのは**一仕事**よ It's *quite a job* to fix meals for ten people.

ひとじち 人質 a **hostage** /hɑ́ːstɪdʒ/ ▶人質を解放する release *a hostage* ‖ 男は店の主人夫婦を**人質に取った** The man *took* the storekeeper and his wife *hostage* [*as hostages*]. (➤ take a person hostage は「人を人質に取る」の意の熟語) ‖ 機長は**人質に取られた** The captain *was taken* [*held*] *hostage*.

ひとしれず 人知れず **secretly, in private** /práɪvət/ (ひそかに) ▶彼は濃い胸毛に人知れず悩んでいた He was *secretly* worried about his abundant chest hair.

ひとしれぬ 人知れぬ ▶彼は人知れぬ苦労をしたらしい I hear that he had to go through many hardships *unknown to others*.

ひとずき 人好き ▶彼女は人好きのするタイプだ She is *likable* [*attractive*]. ‖ 彼はどことなく**人好きがする** There's something *likable* about him.

ひとすじ 一筋(の) a **trickle**《of》(細い流れ); a **streak**《of》(細いしま) ▶一筋の涙が彼女のほおを伝わった *A trickle of* tears ran down her cheek. ‖ **一筋の道**が野原に続いていた A *single* road led [continued] through the fields.

▶師匠はこの道一筋60年だ The master has *devoted himself single-mindedly to his craft* for the past 60 years. ‖ 故郷を出てからというもの, 彼は**仕事一筋**にやってきた He has lived *only for his work* ever since leaving his hometown.

ひとすじなわ 一筋縄 ▶一筋縄ではいかない問題 a problem *that cannot be solved by a usual method* ‖ 彼は**一筋縄ではいかない男**だ He *is a very difficult man* to deal with. / He *is a tough* [*a difficult*] *customer*.

ひとそろい 一揃い a **set** (道具の); a **suit** (衣服の) ▶百科事典一そろい *a set of* encyclopedias ‖ 一そろいのゴルフ道具 *a set of* golf clubs / a golf *set* ‖ 一そろいの服 *a suit of* clothes.

▶このティーカップは12個で一そろいなのですか? Do these teacups come in *a set* of 12? / Do 12 of these teacups make *a set*?

ひとだかり 人だかり a **crowd of people** ▶バーゲン会場は黒山のような人だかりだった There was *a large crowd of people* at the bargain counter. / *People were swarming* around the bargain counter.

ひとだすけ 人助け ▶人助けだと思って5万円貸してくれ Could you lend me fifty thousand yen and *help out a person in need*?

ひとたび 一度 **once** ▶ひとたび大地震が来ればこの辺は壊滅状態になるだろう *Once* a big earthquake hits, this neighborhood will be completely destroyed.

ひとたまりもなく ▶土手が決壊すると, 川沿いの民家はひとたまりもなく濁流に飲み込まれてしまった As soon as the bank collapsed, the houses by the river were *easily* engulfed [were swallowed up] by the muddy waters of the river. (➤「簡単に」の意).

ひとちがい 人違い ▶ 対話「あら, 松村さん!」「人違いでしょう」"Hi, Mr. Matsumura!" "You must *be mistaking* me *for someone else*."

ひとつ 一つ

訳語メニュー
1個, 1歳 →one 1
たった1つの →only, single 1
もう1つの →another 1
同じこと →the same 2

1【数】one 一形 1つの one, a ▶角砂糖1つ *a lump of* sugar ‖ 忠告1つ *a piece of* advice ‖ 父が大事にしている骨董品の1つ *one of* the antiques my father treasures ‖ うちの娘(の年)は1つ[1つ半]です My daughter is *one year old* [*one and a half years old*].

▶あの力士の勝ち星はわずかに1つだ[まだ1つもない] That sumo wrestler has earned only *one* win [*no* wins yet]. ‖《レストランで》コーヒー1つと紅茶2つください *One* coffee and two teas, please. (➤「1杯のコーヒー」は a cup of coffee だが, 店で注文するときは one coffee がふつう).

▶これは世界にたった1つしかない古代の楽器です This ancient musical instrument is *the only one* of its kind (remaining in the world). ‖ この大学は県内ただ1つの国立大学だ This university is *the only* national university in the prefecture. ‖ 彼女はたった1つのミスも見逃さなかった She didn't overlook a *single* mistake.

▶部屋がもう1つ欲しいところだ We would like *another* room. (→もう1つ) ‖ 盗難にあった美術品は1つも回収されなかった *None* of the stolen works of art were ever returned.

ことわざ 親の意見とナスビの花は千に1つの無駄がない Your parents' (pieces of) advice and the flowers of an eggplant—not *one in a thousand* of them is fruitless.

▶このリンゴは1ついくらですか How much are these apples *each* [*apiece*]? ‖ みんなの考えを一つにまとめる(=全員を同意させる)ことは不可能だ It is impossible to *get everyone to agree*. ‖ イエスかノーか, 返事は2

つに1つだ Yes or no. Answer *one or the other*.
▶私は腕時計を2つ持っています．1つは日本製で，もう1つは中国製です I have two wrist watches—*one* is Japanese, and *the other* (is) Chinese.
▶皆の思いは1つ，被災地の復興です *Our wishes are one*—to reconstruct the disaster-stricken area.
2【同じこと】**the same (thing)** ▶高齢者は一つのことを繰り返し言う傾向がある Elderly people tend to repeat *the same thing*.
3【一面】▶今の若者があまり本を読まないのは，一つにはやることが多過ぎるからだ Young people today don't read much because, *for one thing*, they have too many other things to do.
4【さえも，だけ】**even** ▶息子は大学は出ているが手紙ひとつ満足に書けない My son can't *even* write a letter properly, even though he graduated from college. ‖空には雲ひとつなかった There was *not a* cloud in the sky. ‖この冬はかぜひとつひかなかった I didn't catch (a) cold *even once* this winter.
▶母は女手ひとつで4人の子供を大学まで出した My mother *single-handedly* sent her four children to college.
5【…しだい】**be up to**（➤ to のあとは名詞）▶進学するかしないか，あなたの気持ちひとつよ It'*s entirely up to* you to decide whether to go to college or not. ‖ものになるかどうかはきみの努力ひとつだ Whether you make it or not *depends solely on* your effort. (➤ solely は「ひとえに」).
6【ちょっと】▶ひとつお願いがあるのですが May I ask you *a favor*？（➤ 決まった言い方）‖ひとつみんなで彼を助けようじゃないか *Let's* combine our efforts to help him. ‖ひとつ私の話を聞いてください *Just* listen to me.
▶ **対話**「なんとかやってみましょう」「ひとつよろしく頼みます」"Let's see what I can do for you." "*Thank you.* [*I appreciate it.*]"

ひとつおき 一つ置きの **every other**（➤ 単数名詞を修飾する）; **alternate** /ɔ́:ltərnət/（➤ 複数名詞を修飾する）▶一つ置きに丸に色を塗ってください Color *every other* [*second*] circle. ／Color the circles *alternately*.

ひとつおぼえ ひとつ覚え ▶ばかのひとつ覚え *A fool repeats the same thing.* ／*A fool has a one-track mind.*

ひとづかい 人使い ▶今度の支店長は人使いが荒いんだって？そりゃとんでもない誤解だよ．実に人使いのうまい人だよ (You heard) the new branch manager is *a slave driver*? That's a ridiculous misunderstanding—he's really good at *managing people* [*getting people to work well*].

ひとつかみ 一掴み a **handful** 《of》▶一つかみの塩 *a handful of* salt.

ひとづきあい 人付き合い ▶人付き合いのよい人 a *sociable* person ／a *good* mixer（➤ 後者はインフォーマル）‖人付き合いの悪い人 an *unsociable* person ／a *bad* mixer（➤ 後者はインフォーマル）‖私は人付き合いが苦手だ I'm *not very outgoing*. (➤ outgoing は「社交的な」) ‖あいつ，人付き合いはいいよ He's easy to *get along with*. ／He *gets along with people* easily.
▶少しは人付き合いも必要だよ *Spending time with other people* [*Socializing*] is necessary to some extent.

ひとっこ 人っ子 ▶通りには人っ子一人いなかった *No one was* (*seen*) on the street. ／*There was not a soul* on the street. ／The street *was deserted*.

ひとつずつ 一つずつ **one by one**; **one at a time**（一度に1つ）▶首相は難問を1つずつ処理した The Prime Minister dealt with the difficult problems (facing him) *one by one*.

ひとづて 人伝て ▶ **対話**「彼女が婚約したってどうして知ってるの？」「人づてに聞いたのさ」"How do you know she's engaged?" "Oh, *someone* told me. ／I heard it *through* [*on*] *the grapevine*." (➤ through [on] the grapevine は「うわさで」の意).

ひとつとして 一つとして ▶山口監督の作戦は一つとして失敗がない *Not a single one* of Manager Yamaguchi's strategies has failed.

ひとつひとつ 一つ一つ **individually**（個々に）; **one by one**（1つずつ）▶父はこの骨董品を1つ1つ買い集めました My father bought all these antiques *individually* [*one by one*]. ‖箱には1つ1つ番号が振ってある *Each* box has a number.

ひとつぶ 一粒 a **grain**（穀類の）; a **drop**（液体の）
▶お米は1粒も無駄にしてはいけません You should not waste even *a single grain* of rice. ‖空を見上げたとき，1粒の雨が目に入った *A drop* of rain fell in my eye when I looked up at the sky.

ひとつぶだね 一粒種 one's **only child**
▶あの子は黒田夫妻の一粒種だ He is the Kurodas' *only child*.

ひとづま 人妻 a **married woman**（結婚している女性）; **someone else's wife**（他人の妻）.

ひとつまみ 一つまみ a **pinch** ▶塩を一つまみ加える add *a pinch* of salt.

ひとつめこぞう 一つ目小僧 a **one-eyed goblin.**

[1]**ひとで 人手** **1**【働き手】a **hand**; **help**（助力）▶もっと人手をかけなければこの仕事は期限内に終わらないだろう Without more *help*, this job won't be finished by the deadline. ‖人手を借りなくても（＝独力で）なんとかやれます I can manage it *by myself*. ‖うちの工場は今人手不足です We are *shorthanded* [We *have a labor shortage*] at our factory.
2【他人の手】▶その邸宅は借金のかたに人手に渡った The house *has passed into other hands* [*has changed hands*] because they could not pay off the loan.
3【人間の加工】▶この森には人手が加えられた跡がない This forest appears untouched by *human hands*.

[2]**ひとで 人出** a **turnout**
▶その神社の初もうでの人出は100万人を超えた The *turnout* of New Year well-wishers at the shrine topped one million. ‖夏祭りにはいつも大変な人出です *Lots of people turn out* for the summer festival. ‖動物園は大変な人出だった The zoo *was extremely crowded* (*with people*). (● turnout は「(特定のイベントの)出席者数，観客」の意だから，ここでは不適当．「動物園は(人で)混雑していた」と考える).

[3]**ひとで** 《動物》a **starfish.**

ひとでなし 人でなし a **brute**, a **beast**（けだもののような人）; a **cold-blooded beast**（情のない人）▶この人でなし！You *cold-blooded beast*!

ひとてま 一手間 **a little extra effort, one small touch**
▶インスタント食品に一手間加えるだけでおいしくなる Just *a little extra effort* makes instant food delicious.

ひととおり 一通り ▶事件の概要を一通り（要点を省かずに）ご説明します I'll give you a *brief* rundown on the incident. (➤ brief は「手短な」) ‖車のメカについても一通り知っておくべきだ You should also have some *general* knowledge of how a car works. ‖ 娘はお茶とお花を一通り習っております My daughter has learned *the basics* of tea ceremony and flower arrangement. (➤ the basics は「基本」) ‖ スキー道具を一通りそろえるには10万円以上かかる More than 100,000 yen is necessary to get *completely* outfitted for skiing.

▶その書類に一通り目を通して意見を聞かせてください Let me know your opinion after you *look through* the papers.

ひとどおり 人通り (**pedestrian** [**foot**]) **traffic** ▶人通りの絶えた街 a *deserted* street ‖ この通りは日中は人通りが多い This street *is very busy* in the daytime. ‖ 最近この商店街は夜は人通りが少ない These days *few people pass* along this shopping street at night. ／This shopping street *is quite empty* at night.

ひととき 一時 ▶一家だんらんのひととき a happy *hour* at home ‖ 《司会者》夕食後のひとときをクイズ番組でおくつろぎください *Sit back and relax* with our after-dinner quiz show.

ひととなり 人となり one's **personality** (人, 人柄); one's **character** (人格) ▶K教授の人となりを慕って多くの学生が受講を申し込んだ Many students signed up for Professor K's lecture course because they *admire* him *as a person* [they *like his personality*]. (➤ personality の代わりに character でもよい).

ひとなつっこい 人懐っこい friendly; **amiable** /éɪmiəbl/ (愛想のよい) ▶人なつっこい少年[子犬] a *friendly* boy [puppy] ‖ 人なつっこい笑顔 a *friendly* [an *amiable*] smile ‖ うちの猫, みんなから人なつっこいねって言われるのよ Everybody says our cat *likes people* [*is friendly*].

ひとなみ 人並みの average /ǽvərɪdʒ/ (平均的な); **decent** /díːsənt/ (恥ずかしくない) ▶人並みの能力 *average* ability ‖ 人並みの生活をする make a *decent* living ‖ 人並みにかぜをひいた I caught a cold *just like everyone else*. (➤「他の人たちと同じように」の意).

▶ 対話「酒は飲むんだろ?」「ええ, 人並みに」"You drink, don't you?" "Yes. I drink *as much as the next guy*." ‖ レギュラーになるには人並み以上に練習しなくてはだめだ You'll have to practice harder *than others* to make the regular team. ‖ 彼は人並みはずれたよい体格をしている He is an *extraordinarily* well-built man.

ひとにぎり 一握り a **handful**

▶一握りの砂 *a handful of* sand ‖ この事実を知っているのはほんの一握りの(=少数の)人だけだ Only *a handful of* people know the facts. ‖ 一握りの人々が権力を牛耳っていた *A handful of* people held power.

ひとねむり 一眠り a **short sleep**; a **nap** (うたた寝) ▶一眠りしたらすっきりした I felt refreshed after *a nap*.

ひとはしり 一走り ▶ぼくの新車で一走りしない? Would you like to go for *a spin* in my new car? ‖ 一走り行ってバターを買って来てくれない? Could you *run* to the store and get some butter?

ひとはた 一旗 ▶俺も今に一旗揚げてみせると秀吉は言った Hideyoshi said, "I'll *make a name* (*for myself*) in the world some day."

[1]**ひとはだ 一肌** ▶きみのためなら一肌脱ぐよ I'm always ready to *go the extra mile* (for you). (➤ go the extra mile は文字どおりには「(自分から進んで)もう1マイルを行く」の意) (●「一肌でも二肌でも脱ぐよ」なら to give you the shirt off my back (「きみのためなら着ているシャツを脱いできみにあげる」の意)のように言えばよい).

[2]**ひとはだ 人肌** ▶人肌にかんした酒 sake warmed to *body temperature*.

ひとはな 一花 ▶おじはもう一花咲かせたいと50を過ぎて事業を起こした My uncle started a business after he turned fifty, wishing to *be successful* [to *achieve something worthwhile*] one more time.

ひとばん 一晩 a **night** ▶一晩泊めてくれますか Can you put me up for the *night*? ‖ おじの家に一晩泊まった I *stayed overnight* at my uncle's. ‖ 若者たちは一晩中騒いでいた The young people were partying hearty [noisily] *all night* (*long*). (➤ party hearty はパーティーで騒ぐこと).

▶一晩考えさせてください *Let me sleep on it*. (➤ 決まった言い方; 断りの文句として使われる場合もある).

ひとびと 人々 people ▶貧しい人々 poor *people* ／ the poor ‖ この島では人々はもっぱら観光で生活している The *people* of this island mainly live on tourism.

▶その村の人々はみな集会所の建設を望んだ *Everyone in the village* wanted to build a meeting place. ／*All the villagers* wanted to build a meeting place.

ひとひねり ▶このタイトルはパンチがない. もうひとひねり工夫がほしい This title doesn't have enough impact. We should give it *a new twist*. (➤ twist は「奇抜な工夫」).

ひとひら ▶ひとひらの雲 *a wisp of* cloud.

ひとふで 一筆 ▶一筆書きの図形 a figure *drawn with one stroke* ‖ 一筆便りを頼む *Drop me a line*.

ひとべらし 人減らし a **reduction in work force**

▶多くの会社が業績不振で人減らしを行っている Many companies *have been reducing* [*downsizing*] *their work force* due to slow business.

ひとまえ 人前で in public ▶人前で話をする speak *in public* ‖ 人前で話すのをこわがる[こわがらない] have [don't have] *stage* fright ‖ 妹は人前に出たがらない My (younger) sister avoids meeting *people*. ‖ 私, 人前に出るだけで心臓がどきどきするの Just *being in front of people* makes my heart pound.

ひとまかせ 人任せ ▶人任せにしないで自分で決めなさい Don't *leave* it (up) *to others*. Decide for yourself.

ひとまず ▶ひとまずぼくの家に行こうよ Why not go to my home *first*? ‖ では, パーティーはここでひとまずお開きにしましょう Well, let's wrap up the party *first*.

ひとまとめ 一まとめ ▶持ち物をひとまとめにしておきなさい *Get* your things *together*. ／ *Gather* your things. ‖ 古新聞はひとまとめにして物置きに入れておくよ I'll *bundle* the old newspapers *together* and put them in the storeroom.

ひとまね 人真似 mimicry /mímɪkri/ (人のしぐさや癖をふざけてまねること); (an) **imitation** (誰かを手本にしてその人に似せようとすること) ▶彼はよく先生たちの人まねをしては友だちを笑わす He often does *imitations* of his teachers to make his friends laugh. ‖ 彼女はとても人まねがうまい She's a great *mimic*. (➤ mimic は「まねをする人」).

▶人まねはやめて自分の絵をかきなさい Stop being *a copycat* and draw your own picture. (➤ copycat は「他人の作品・行動をまねる人」).

ひとまわり 一回り 1【1周】a **round** ▶展覧会場を一回りしたところです I've just *made a round* of the

ひ

exhibition galleries. ‖ ボートに乗って湖を一回りした We *went around* the lake in a rowboat. (→一周).

2【1ランク】▶これより一回り大きなかばんはありますか Do you have a bag *one* [*a*] *size* bigger than this?

▶兄とは一回り(＝12年)年が違います I'm *twelve years* younger than my brother. (英米には「十二支の一回り」という考え方はないから, 場合によっては「十二支」(one cycle of the twelve years of the zodiac)を説明する必要がある). (→えと).

ひとみ 瞳 an **eye**(目); **the pupil** (どう孔)

▶つぶらなひとみの女の子 a girl with lovely round *eyes* ‖ 暗やみにひとみをこらしたが何も見えなかった I *strained my eyes* in the dark, but couldn't see anything.

ひとみしり 人見知り ▶この子は人見知りをする She [He] *is timid with strangers*. ／She [He] is *shy*. ‖ 妹はちょっと人見知りをする My (younger) sister is a bit *uncomfortable around people she doesn't know*. (「周りに知らない人がいると落ち着かない」と考えて訳す).

ひとむかし 一昔 **ages** (長い間); a **decade** /dékeɪd/ (十年) ▶それはもう一昔前の話だ It's an *old* story.

1**ひとめ 人目** ▶彼女の特異なヘアスタイルは人目を引いた Her unique hairstyle *drew* [*attracted*] *people's attention*. ‖ このポスターは人目を引く This poster *is eye-catching* [*is an attention getter*]. ‖ その女優は人目につかないように裏口から出た The actress went out (of) the back door *to escape notice*. ‖ 人目を気にしないでやりたいようにやったらいい Just do what you want, and *never mind what people think* [*don't worry about how others view you*]. ‖ 彼らは人目を忍んでデートを重ねている They have been dating *secretly*. ‖ 二人は人目をはばからずに抱き合ったりキスをしたりした The two hugged and kissed *in public* [*openly*].

2**ひとめ 一目** a **glance**(ちらっと見ること)

▶一目で馬場君とわかった I recognized Baba *at a glance* [*at first glance*]. ‖ お城の上から街並みが一目で見渡せる From the top of the castle, we can get a view of the whole city.

▶豪華客船を一目見ようとケイコと私は港へやって来た Keiko and I came to the harbor *to see* the luxurious passenger ship.

ひとめぐり 一巡り ▶季節が一巡りした The seasons *have come* [*gone*] *around* (*again*).

ひとめぼれ 一目惚れ ▶ぼくは夏子に一目ぼれした I *fell in love* with Natsuko *at first sight*.

ひともうけ 一儲け ▶競馬で[新製品で]ひともうけする *make a killing* [*a fortune*] at a horserace [with a new product] ‖ 彼はまたひともうけをたくらんでいるようだ He seems to be planning a *big money-making* scheme again.

ひともじ 人文字 **letters, numbers, kana or kanji formed by groups of people.**

ひともんちゃく 一悶着 ▶新社長が決まるまでにはひと悶着ありそうだ There will probably be *some dispute* [*wrangling*] before a new president is chosen.

ひとやく 一役 ▶我々の計画に一役買ってくれないか Won't you *be a part* of our project?

ひとやすみ 一休み **a rest; a break** (特に仕事中などの) ▶我々は山腹で一休みした We *took a rest* [*a break*] halfway up the mountain.

ひとやま 一山 **a pile** ▶キュウリ一山 *a pile* of cucumbers ‖ そのリンゴは一山500円です The apples are 500 yen *a pile* [*a trayful*]. (➤ trayful は「(皿の)一盛り」).

▶《慣用表現》彼は株で一山当てた He *hit the jackpot* in the stock market.

ひとり 一人・独り **1**【1人】**one, one person** 一形 **1人の one, a** ▶女の子1人に対し男の子5人 five boys to *one* girl ‖ 彼はわが社の成長株の1人だ He is *one* of the most promising people in our company. ‖ うちの大学にはタンザニアの学生が1人います There is *a* Tanzanian student at our college. ‖ 1人の男が捜査線上に浮かんだ *A man* emerged (as a possible suspect) in the course of the police search. ‖ 全問正解はクラスに1人もいなかった[彼1人だった] *No one* in the class was able to [*He was the only one* in the class who was able to] answer all of the questions correctly. ‖ 乗客は1人も危険に気がつかなかった *None* of the passengers was [were] aware of the danger.

▶面接会場には1人ずつ入って来てください Please enter the interview room *one by one*. ‖ うちのチームには左打者がもう1人欲しい We need *another* left-handed batter. ‖ 詐欺グループは一人残らず検挙された *All* the swindlers were arrested.

▶《レストランなどで》お一人様ですか Table for *one*? ／Are you *by yourself*?

‖一人息子[娘] one's only son [daughter] (➤「私は一人息子[一人娘]です」なら I'm the only son [daughter].).

2【単独で】**alone, by oneself; on one's own** (独力で; インフォーマルな言い方) ▶彼はひとりが好きだ He likes to be *alone*. ‖ ひとりにさせてくれ Leave me *alone*. ‖ 少しひとりになる時間がほしい I need some time *alone*. ‖ 彼は(たった)ひとりで大家族を養っている He supports a big family *all by himself*. ‖ それ, きみひとりで考えたの? Did you think it up *by yourself* [*on your own*]?

3【独身の】**single** ▶生涯ひとりで暮らすつもりはありません I don't intend to *remain single* [*remain unmarried*] all my life. ‖ **対話**「あなたは結婚していますか」「まだひとりです」"Are you married?" "No, I'm still *single*." (➤ 既婚か未婚かのようなプライバシーに関する質問はよほど親しい間がらの人以外にはしないほうがよい).

ひどり 日取り **the day, the date** (➤ 前者は特定の日を, 後者は通例月と日, ときに年月日を指す) ▶結婚式の日取りを決める *set the date* for the wedding.

ひとりあたま 一人頭 **per head.**

ひとりあたり 一人当たり **per capita** ▶一人当たりのＧＮＰ *per capita* GNP.

ひとりあるき 独り歩き ▶その都市[地域]では女性の夜のひとり歩きは危険です It's dangerous for a woman to *go out alone* at night in that city [that area]. ‖ 赤ん坊がひとり歩きできるようになった The baby can *walk by himself* [*herself*] now.

ひとりがち 一人勝ち ▶彼は一人勝ちをした He was *the only winner*.

ひとりがてん 独り合点 ▶彼はよくひとり合点する He tends to *jump to conclusions*. ‖ ひとり合点は困るよ Don't try to *decide things all by yourself*.

ひとりぐらし 独り暮らし ▶彼はニューヨークでひとり暮らしを始めた He started *living alone* [started *life on his own*] in New York (City). ‖ この辺にはひと

り暮らしの老人が多い There are a lot of elderly people around here who *live alone*.

ひとりごと 独り言 ▶彼はひとり言を言いながら何かを書いていた He was writing something while *talking to himself*. ‖ あの女の子は一人になるとよくぶつぶつひとり言を言う That little girl often *mutters to herself* when she is alone.

▶彼女は考えごとをしながらひとり言を言っている She's *thinking aloud*. ‖ 対話「何か言った？」「いや, ひとり言」"Did you say something?" "No. I *was* (just) *talking to myself*."

ひとりしばい 一人芝居 a **one man** [**woman**] **show**.

ひとりじめ 独り占めする monopolize /mənɑ́:pəlaɪz/ +目, **hog** +目 (➤ 後者はインフォーマルな語) ▶会話をひとり占めする *monopolize* a conversation ‖ お菓子をひとり占めしないでお兄ちゃんにも少しあげなさい Don't *hog* all the cookies. Give some to your brother. ‖ うちの部長は手柄をひとり占めしたがる Our department head likes to *take all the credit for himself*.

ひとりずもう 独り相撲 ▶きみはひとり相撲をとっていることに気づくべきだ You should know you're just *fighting* [*tilting at*] *windmills*. (➤ fight [tilt at] windmills は「実在しない敵 [相手] と戦う」の意).

ひとりだち 独り立ち ▶彼がひとり立ちするのはまだ早すぎる It's too early for him to *stand on his own feet*. →独立.

ひとりっこ 一人っ子 an **only child** (➤ only も child もどちらも強めず, 1語のように発音する), a **single child** ▶私はひとりっ子です I'm *an only* [*a single*] *child*. ‖ ひとりっ子は過保護になりやすい *Only children* [*Single children*] are often overprotected.

ひとりでに 独りでに (all) by itself ▶ドアがひとりでに開いた The door opened *all by itself*. ‖ 車がひとりでに動き出した The car began to move *on its own*.

ひとりひとり 一人一人 each (めいめい) ▶一人一人顔が違うように考え方も違う *Each person* has their own ideas just as they have their own unique faces.

▶学校をきれいにするのは私たち一人一人の責任だ It's the duty of *each and every one* of us to keep the school clean.

ひとりぶたい 独り舞台 ▶決勝戦は彼のひとり舞台だった He *carried the game* in the finals. (➤ carry a game は「試合の主導権を得る」の意のインフォーマルな言い方).

ひとりぼっち 独りぼっちの alone

▶どんなことがあってもきみをひとりぼっちにはさせないからね No matter what happens, I won't leave you *alone* [I won't *abandon* you]. ‖ 大都会にはひとりぼっち (= 孤独) で悲しんでいる人がたくさんいる There are many sad and *lonely* people in big cities.

▶ひとりぼっちになってどうしてよいかわからなかった When I *was left to myself*, I was at a loss about what to do.

ひとりよがり 独り善がりの self-satisfied (自己満足の) ; **self-righteous** /sèlfráɪtʃəs/ (独善的な)

▶あいつのひとりよがりにはあきれるね I'm disgusted with his *self-satisfied* [*self-righteous*] *attitude*.

ひとわたり 一わたり ▶学生のレポートに一わたり目を通したところです I have just *looked over* the students' reports.

ひな 雛 a **chick** (ひよこ) ; a **nestling** /nésl̩ɪŋ/ (巣立ち前の) ; a **fledgling** (巣立ちしたばかりの)

▶ひなが5羽かえった Five *chicks* have hatched.

ひながた 雛形 a **form** (書式見本) ; a **template** (コンピュータ用の) ▶履歴書のひな型 a résumé *form*.

ひなぎく 雛菊 《植物》 a **daisy**.

ひなげし 雛げし 《植物》 a **corn** [**red**] **poppy**.

ひなた 日向 the sun(shine)

▶子猫がひなたで遊んでいた A kitten was playing *in the sun*. ‖ ひなたで本を読むのはやめなさい. 目を悪くするわよ Don't read *in the bright sunlight*. You'll hurt your eyes.

▶おじいちゃんは裏庭でひなたぼっこをしている Grandpa is *sunning* (*himself*) in the backyard.

ひなにんぎょう 雛人形 a **doll displayed on *Hinamatsuri***.

ひなびた rural, **rustic** (➤ 後者は粗野・素朴さを強調する) ▶ひなびた農家 a *rustic* farmhouse ‖ この夏はひなびた温泉にでも行こうかと思っている I'm thinking of going to a *rural* hot spring this summer.

ひなまつり 雛祭り *Hinamatsuri*, the Doll Festival

日本紹介 ✉ **ひな祭りは3月3日に行われる女の子の祭りです. 桃の節句ともいいます. 女の子のいる家ではひな壇にひな人形を飾り, 健やかな成長と幸せを祈ります** *Hinamatsuri* (the Doll Festival) is a festival for girls held on March 3. It is also called '*momo-no-sekku*' (the Peach Festival). People display *hina* dolls on a tiered stand at home, and wish for the healthy growth and happiness of their daughter(s).

ひなわじゅう 火縄銃 a **matchlock**.

1**ひなん 非難 criticism** (批判) ; **attack**, **censure** (厳しい) 一動 **非難する criticize** +目, **attack** +目 《参考》 日本人学習者は「非難する」に blame を当てることがあるが, これは「…のせいにする」の意であって, 非難は含まない

▶市長の声明は非難の的となった The mayor's statement became the target [focus] of *criticism*. ‖ 彼はおぼれかけた友を見捨てたために非難を浴びた He drew *criticism* for forsaking his drowning friend.

▶その新聞は警察が容疑者を取り逃がしたことを強く非難した The newspaper strongly *criticized* the police for failing to arrest the suspect. ‖ 監督はチームが負けたことで非難された The coach *was attacked for* the team's defeat.

2**ひなん 避難 shelter**, **refuge** /réfju:dʒ/ (➤ 前者は風雨などを, 後者は危険などを避けるのに用いる傾向があるが, 同義にも用いる) ; **evacuation** (立ち退き) 一動 **避難する take shelter** [**refuge**] 《from》 ; **evacuate** /ɪvǽkjueɪt/ +目 (場所を立ち退く) ▶ゴルファーたちは雷を避けてクラブハウスに避難した The golfers *took shelter* [*refuge*] *from* the lightning in the clubhouse. ‖ 村民たちは洪水になる前に自主避難した The villagers voluntarily *evacuated* their homes before the flood arrived.

▶あす学校で避難訓練がある *An evacuation drill* will be conducted at school tomorrow. (➤ 火災の場合は fire drill, 地震の場合は earthquake drill) ‖ 大地震のときの避難場所はこの辺では多摩川の河川敷だ In case a big earthquake hits, the regional *evacuation area* around here is the dry riverbed of the Tama River.

‖ **避難勧告** an evacuation advisory ‖ **避難区域** an evacuation area [zone], a refuge area ‖ **避難指示** an evacuation directive ‖ **避難者** an evacuee /ɪvǽkjuí:/ (災害などからの) ‖ **避難所** a shelter, a place of refuge ‖ **避難センター** an evacuation center ‖ **避難命令** an evacuation order ‖ **避難路** an escape [evacuation] route ‖ **緊急避難** an emergency evacuation ‖ **自主避難** a voluntary evacuation.

びなん 美男 a **handsome man**
▶まさに**美男**美女の取り合わせだ They are a perfect match of *a handsome man* and a beautiful woman.

びにいりさいにわたって 微に入り細にわたって **in extreme detail** ▶彼はその計画について**微に入り細にわたって**説明した He explained the project *in extreme detail*.

ビニール vinyl /váɪnl/ ; **plastics** 一形 **ビニールの plastic** ▶**ビニール**のレインコート a *vinyl* [*plastic*] raincoat ‖ **ビニール**のごみ袋 a *plastic* garbage bag
‖ **ビニールハウス** a plastic greenhouse.

危ないカタカナ語 ビニール
「ビニール」は英語の vinyl からきているが, この語は「ビニール樹脂」の意の化学用語で, 一般にはあまり用いられない. 英語ではビニール樹脂をはじめとする合成樹脂で作られたものをひとまとめにして plastic と呼ぶのがふつう. したがって「ビニール袋」は plastic bag となる. ただし, vinyl bag と言う人もいる.

ひにく 皮肉 (an) **irony** /áɪrəni/ (当てこすり ; 意外な結果) ; **sarcasm** (悪意のある皮肉) ; **cynicism** (冷笑) 一形 **皮肉な ironic(al), cynical** ▶医者が自分のがんに気づかなかったとは**皮肉だね** It is *ironic* [*ironical*] that the doctor wasn't aware of his own cancer. ‖ 兄弟が同じ人を好きになるなんて**運命の皮肉だ** It is *an irony of fate* that the brothers fell in love with the same woman.
▶**皮肉にも**ハイキングの中止を決めたとたん雨があがった *Ironically*, as soon as we decided to cancel our hike, the rain stopped.
▶「どうせ私なんかいないほうがいいんでしょ」と祖母は**皮肉たっぷりに**言った "You would rather have me out of the way, wouldn't you?" said my grandmother *with evident sarcasm*. ‖ 彼は**皮肉っぽい**笑いを浮かべた He gave me a *cynical* smile. ／He smiled at me cynically.
▶彼女はよく私の手際の悪さを**皮肉る** She often *makes sarcastic* [*cynical*] *remarks* about my inefficiency.
‖ **皮肉屋** a cynic, a sarcastic person.

ひにち 日にち a **date** (日付) ; **days** (日数) ▶やっと退院の**日にち**が決まった The *date* for my release from the hospital has finally been set [decided]. ‖ 締め切りまであまり**日にち**がない I don't have many *days* before the deadline.

ひにひに 日に日に day by day ▶谷間の木々が**日に日に**色づいてくる The trees in the gorge are turning redder *day by day*.

ひにょうき 泌尿器 《解剖学》**the urinary** /jʊ́ərəneri/ **organs**
‖ **泌尿器科** the urology department.

[1]**ひにん 否認** (a) **denial** /dɪnáɪəl/ 一動 **否認する deny** +目 ▶容疑者は容疑を**否認した** The suspect *denied* [*made a denial of*] the charge.

[2]**ひにん 避妊 contraception ; birth control** (産児制限) ▶**避妊する**ために経口**避妊薬**を飲む take *oral contraceptives* to *prevent pregnancy* (➤ pregnancy は「妊娠」) ‖ ピルは非常に有効な**避妊法**である The pill is a very effective *means of birth control*.
‖ **避妊具** a contraceptive (device).

ひねくりまわす 捻くり回す toy 《with》, **play** 《with》(おもちゃにする) ; **tinker** 《at, with》(直そうとへたな修繕をする)
▶弟は私の顕微鏡を**ひねくり回して**こわしてしまった My (younger) brother *fiddled* [*messed*] *around with* my microscope and broke it.

ひねくれもの ひねくれ者 a **contrary** [**perverse**] **person** (➤ contrary は「へそ曲がりの」).

ひねくれる get [**be**] **warped**
▶**ひねくれた**人 a person with *a warped* [*distorted*] *nature* (➤「性格のゆがんだ人」の意) ‖ 子供は叱られてばかりいると**ひねくれてしまう** Children's personalities will *be warped* by constant scolding. ‖ 彼女は**ひねくれた**見方しかできない人だよ She just can't see things straight. (➤「物ごとをまっすぐには見られない」の意).

ひねつ 比熱 《物理学》**specific heat.**

びねつ 微熱 a **slight fever** ▶**微熱**がありますね You have *a slight fever*. ‖ ここ 2, 3 日**微熱が続いている** I've been *a little feverish* for the past few days.

ひねりだす 捻り出す ▶旅費を**ひねり出す** *scrape together* one's travel expenses ‖ 答えを**ひねり出す** *extract* an answer.

ひねる 捻る 1【ねじる】twist +目, **turn** +目 ▶その栓は引っぱらないで左に**ひねりなさい** Don't pull the top. *Turn* [*Twist*] it counterclockwise. (➤ counterclockwise は「時計の針と反対回りに」の意) ‖ ガス栓を**ひねって**ガスを出す[止める] *turn on* [*off*] the gas.
2【曲げる】twist +目 ▶体を**ひねる** *twist* one's body ‖ 腰を**ひねる** *twist* (one's body) at the waist ‖ 彼はつまずいて足首を**ひねった** (＝くじいた) He stumbled and *twisted* [*sprained*] his ankle.
3【考えたりくふうしたりする】▶いくら頭を**ひねっても**私にはその問題は解けない No matter how long I *puzzle over* the problem, I cannot solve it. ‖ 学生たちはみな大学側の方針に**首をひねっている** The students *are* all *puzzled by* the policy of the university administration. ‖ あの先生は**ひねった**問題ばかり出す That teacher always gives us *tricky* [*trick*] questions.
4【やっつける】▶あいつなんか簡単に**ひねってやる** I can *beat* him easily. ／I'll *make mincemeat out of* him. (➤ make mincemeat (out) of は「…をこてんぱんにやっつける」の意のインフォーマルな言い方).

ひのいり 日の入り sunset.

ひのえうま 丙午 ***hinoeuma***
日本紹介 **丙午は中国の暦に基づいて60年に1度やってくる火と午の年です. 迷信からこの年に女の子を産むのを避ける人がたくさんいます** According to the Chinese calendar [astrology], *Hinoeuma* is the Year of the Fire Horse, which comes around every sixty years. Many people avoid having a baby girl during this year because of superstition.

ひのき 檜 《植物》a **Japanese cypress.**

ひのきぶたい 檜舞台 ▶武道館の**ひのき舞台を踏む**のがミュージシャンたちの夢だ The dream of musicians is *playing on the big stage* of the Budokan.

ひのくるま 火の車 ▶うちは年中**火の車だ** (＝金に困っている) We *are* always *hard up for money*. ／We *are* always *very badly off* (*financially*).

ひのけ 火の気 ▶部屋は**火の気**がなく寒々としていた The room was *fireless* [*unheated*] and chilly. ／The room was chilly because there was *no fire* in it.

ひのこ 火の粉 a **spark** ▶燃え盛る家から火の粉が飛んでいた *Sparks* were flying from the burning house.

ひのて 火の手 ▶暗い住宅街から次々に火の手が上がった *Fires* broke out one after another within the residential area in the dead of night.
▶《比喩的》その市では市長リコール運動の火の手が上がった A movement *was started* in the city to recall the mayor.

ひので 日の出 **sunrise** ▶日の出前に before *sunrise* ‖ 夏は日の出が早い *The sun rises early* in (the) summer. ‖ 私たちは初日の出を拝むために早起きした We got up early to reverently watch *the first sunrise of the year*.
▶《慣用表現》あの歌手は新曲が次々にヒットして, まさに日の出の勢いだ That singer *is going great guns* with one new song after another of his becoming a hit. (➤ go great guns は「とんとん拍子にいく」の意のインフォーマルな言い方).

ひのべ 日延べ ▶台風の影響で陸上大会は2週間日延べになった Due to the typhoon, the track meet *was postponed* for two weeks.

ひのまる 日の丸 **the *Hinomaru*, the Rising Sun flag** ▶人々は日の丸を振ってマラソン選手を応援した People cheered the marathon runners, waving *the Rising Sun flags*.

ひのみやぐら 火の見やぐら a **fire tower**.

ひのめ 日の目 ▶彼の長年にわたる研究成果はついに日の目を見ることがなかった The fruit of his long years of study *never saw the light of day*. ‖ その学者が生前書いた本がついに日の目を見る(＝出版される)ことになった The book the scholar spent a lifetime writing will *be published* at (long) last.

ひのもと 火の元 ▶寝る前には火の元を確かめなさい Make sure to *turn off the gas* (*at the main*) *and the heater* before you go to bed. (●「ガスの元栓や暖房具を止める」と考えて訳す).

ひばいひん 非売品 an **article not for sale** ▶《表示》非売品 *Not For Sale*.

ひばく 被爆・被曝 ▶彼の祖父は若い頃広島で被爆した When his grandfather was young, he *was exposed to radiation* from the atomic bomb that was dropped on Hiroshima. (➤ radiation は「放射線」) ‖ その原子力発電所で2人の作業員が被曝した Two workers *were exposed to radiation* at the nuclear power plant.
‖**被爆者** an atomic bomb victim ; a hibakusha (➤ 英語化している) ; a person exposed to radiation(被曝者, 放射線を浴びた人) ‖ **被曝線量** a radiation dose, an exposure dose ‖ **被爆地** a bombed area.

ひばし 火箸 ***hibashi*** ; a pair of iron chopstick-like tools that is used to grasp (burning) charcoal (➤ 説明的な訳).

ひばしら 火柱 a **pillar** [**column**] **of fire**.

びはだ 美肌 **beautiful skin**.

ひばち 火鉢 a ***hibachi***
日本紹介 ✉ **火鉢は灰の上に炭火を入れた, 昔広く使われていた陶器や金属製の暖房器具です. やかんで湯をわかしたり, 長時間の煮込み料理を作ったりしました** A *hibachi* is a ceramic or metal heating device containing burning charcoal on ashes that was commonly used in the past. *Hibachi* were also used to heat water in a kettle or cook and simmer food for a long time.

ひばな 火花 a **spark** ▶古くなったヘアドライヤーから火花が出た *Sparks flew* from my old hair drier. ／My old hair drier *sparked*.
▶《比喩的》彼らは論戦に火花を散らした They had a *heated* discussion [argument]. ‖ 両チームは決勝進出をかけて火花を散らした Both teams *fought fiercely* for a berth in the finals. (➤ berth は「出場権」).

ひばらい 日払い ▶日払いをする *pay by the day*.
‖**日払い賃金** daily wages.

ひばり 雲雀 《鳥》 a **lark**, a (**Japanese**) **skylark**
▶揚げヒバリ an ascending *lark* ‖ ヒバリが空高く舞い上がった *A lark* flew high into the sky. 《参考》(1) lark は旧大陸の鳥でイギリスには多いが, アメリカにはいない. (2) lark はアメリカではしばしば meadowlark (マキバドリ) を指すが, この鳥はヒバリとは縁が遠い.

ひはん 批判 **criticism** 一動 **批判する** **criticize** ＋㊐
▶痛烈な批判 severe *criticism* ‖ 批判的な意見 *critical* remarks ‖ 専門家なら冷静に他人の批判を受け入れるべきだ A professional should take others' *criticism* calmly. ‖ 外国人は日本人が働き過ぎだと批判する Foreigners *criticize* the Japanese for overworking.
▶父は私の留学に批判的だ(＝いい顔をしない) My father *takes a critical* [*dim*] *view of* my studying abroad. ‖ 人の意見をやみくもに受け入れるのではなく批判精神をもつ必要がある You need to have *a critical mind*, instead of blindly accepting the opinions of others.
☛ 無批判 (→見出語)

ひばん 非番の **off-duty** ▶父はきのうが非番だった My father *was off-duty* yesterday.

ひひ 《動物》 a **baboon**.

[1]**ひび 1【割れ目】** a **crack** ; a **split** (裂け目)
▶この湯飲み, ひびが入ってるわ There's *a crack* in this teacup. ‖ コーヒーカップをテーブルから落としたらひびが入ってしまった The coffee cup *cracked* when I knocked it off the table. ‖ 骨にひびが入ってますね There's *a fracture* in the bone.
▶《比喩的》二人の友情にひびが入った *Cracks* appeared in their friendship. ‖ その事件のために両社の協力関係にひびが入った The incident caused *a split* [*a rift*] in the cooperative relationship of the two companies.
2【皮膚の】 **chaps** ▶母の手はひびだらけだ My mother's hands *are chapped all over*. ‖ 冬になると手にひびが切れる My hands always *get chapped* in (the) winter.

[2]**ひび 日々** **every day**(毎日) ; **day after day** (来る日も来る日も) ▶日々の暮らし one's *daily* life ‖ 忙しい日々を送る *lead* a busy *life* ‖ あなたとともに過ごした日々をしばしば懐かしく思い起こします I sometimes think back fondly on *the days* I spent with you. ‖ 日々努力することが大切だ It is important to make an effort (to do something useful) *every day*.
‖**日々是好日** Every day is a good day.

ひひーん ▶馬小屋に入ると馬たちがいっせいにヒヒーンと鳴いた When I entered the stable, all the horses began *neighing* at once. (➤ neigh /neɪ/ は「(馬が)いななく」).

ひびき 響き a **sound** ; a **ring** (ことばの音(おん)の感じ) ▶ホルンの温かみのある響き the mellow *sound* of a horn ‖ 「いろり」ということばには懐かしい響きがある The word 'irori' (fireplace set in the floor) has a nostalgic *ring* to it.

ひ

ひびきわたる 響き渡る **resound**(音でいっぱいになる); **echo**(反響する) ▶響き渡る声 a *resonant* voice.

ひびく 響く **1【音がする】sound; echo** /ékoʊ/, **reverberate**(反響する); **resound** /rɪzáʊnd/ (反響する; 共鳴する) ▶救急車のサイレンが響いた The siren of an ambulance *sounded*. ‖生徒たちの笑い声が教室に響いた The students' laughter *reverberated* [*echoed*] through the classroom. ‖風呂場では声がよく響く A voice *resounds* well in the bathroom. ‖夜になると隣の話し声が響いてくる(＝聞こえてくる) At night the sound of people talking next door *can be heard* in my house.

2【影響する】affect ＋目 ▶暴飲暴食は健康に響く Excessive eating and drinking will *affect* [*tell on*] your health. (➤ tell on は「響く, こたえる」の意) ‖交通費の値上げは日常生活に大きく響く A rise in transportation expenses seriously *affects* our everyday life.

▶たびたび出かける韓国への買い物旅行が彼女の貯金には響いた Her frequent shopping trips to Korea *made inroads on* [*made a dent in*] her savings. (➤ make inroads on は「…を侵食する」, make a dent は「減らす」).

ひ

びびたる 微々たる **very little**

▶今その株を売ってももうけは微々たるものだ There's *very little* profit in selling those stocks at present.

▶一人一人がやれることは微々たるものだが, 100人, 1000人集まれば大きな力になる Although what a single person can do *is very small* [*not much*], if 100 or 1,000 people gather, they can have a big impact.

びびっと ▶私たちは初めて会ったとき, びびっとくるものがあった We just *clicked* the first time we met.

ひひょう 批評 (a) **review** /rɪvjúː/ (新聞・雑誌などに発表する書評など); a **critique**(文学・芸術などの建設的な); (a) **criticism**(しばしば, 欠点などの批判); (a) **comment**(短い論評); a **remark**(意見) **一動 批評する review** ＋目, **criticize** ＋目, **critique** ＋目, **comment on**; **evaluate** ＋目(評価する)

▶小説の批評を書く *review* [make a *review* of] a novel／write a *critique* on a novel(➤ 具体的な「批評文」の意では a をつける) ‖人の演奏 [絵] を批評する *criticize* a person's playing [painting] ‖人のことばかり批評しないで自分のことも反省しなさい Don't *criticize* others too much. You should reflect on your own behavior, too.

▶私たちの詩を批評してください Please *comment on* our poems.

✉ **これらは私の作った英語の俳句です. あなたの批評をお聞かせください** These are some English haiku which I composed. I'd appreciate [like to hear] your *comments*.

‖**批評家** a critic; a reviewer (書評の).

びびる ▶相手が強そうなんでびびっちゃったよ I *got cold feet* because my opponent looked very strong. (➤ get cold feet は「おじけづく」の意のインフォーマルな言い方).

びひん 備品 **equipment**(ある目的に必要なもの); **fixtures** (浴槽など作りつけのもの); **fittings** (ロッカーなど移動可能なもの); **furnishings** (家具調度品) ▶会社の備品には通し番号がつけてある All the pieces of office *equipment* are numbered consecutively.

ひふ 皮膚 **skin** ▶彼女は皮膚が荒れている[弱い] She has rough [delicate] *skin*. ‖冬にかぜをひかないよう, 今から皮膚を鍛えておきなさい *Build up your resistance* [*strength*] now (by brushing your skin or rubbing your skin with a dry towel) so as not to catch cold in winter. (➤ かっこ内は「乾布摩擦」の場合. 「薄着」の場合は by wearing light clothing).

‖**皮膚炎** dermatitis /dəːrmətáɪṭəs/ ‖**皮膚科** dermatology /dəːrmətɑ́ːlədʒi/ ‖**皮膚科医** a dermatologist ‖**皮膚がん** skin cancer ‖**皮膚病** (a) skin disease.

ひぶ 日歩 **daily interest.**

ビフィズスきん ビフィズス菌《生物学》**bifidus (bacteria).**

[1]**びふう 微風** a **breeze.**

[2]**びふう 美風** a **good custom.**

ビフォー・アンド・アフター **before and after.**

ひぶくれ 火ぶくれ a **blister.**

ひぶそう 非武装 **demilitarization**(地域の); **disarmament**(武装解除)

‖**非武装地帯** a demilitarized zone《略 DMZ》‖**非武装中立** unarmed neutrality.

ひぶた 火蓋 ▶甲子園球場で夏の高校野球の熱戦の火ぶたが切って落とされた The *exciting* summer high-school baseball *games have just started* at Koshien Stadium. ‖彼らは臓器移植について論争の火ぶたを切った They *started* a heated discussion on organ transplantation.

ビフテキ (a) **beefsteak**, (a) **steak**(➤ 後者のほうがふつう) ▶たまにはビフテキを食べないか How about having *steak*(*s*) for a change?

ビブラート《音楽》**vibrato** ▶ノンビブラートで演奏する play *non-vibrato* [*vibrato-free*].

ひぶん 碑文 an **inscription on a monument** [**tomb**]; an **epitaph**(墓碑銘).

びぶん 微分《数学》**differential calculus** **一動 微分する differentiate** ＋目

‖**微分法** differentiation ‖**微分方程式** a differentiation equation.

[1]**ひほう 悲報** **(a piece of) sad news**

▶けさ早くおばが急死したという悲報が届いた I received the *sad news* of my aunt's sudden death early this morning.

[2]**ひほう 秘宝** a **hidden** [**cherished**] **treasure.**

ひぼう 誹謗 (a) **slander**(口頭による); (a) **libel** /láɪbəl/ (文書による) **一動 ひぼうする slander** ＋目, **libel** ＋目 ▶ある候補者をひぼうする *slander* [*libel*] a candidate.

びぼう 美貌 **good looks, beauty** **一形 美貌の beautiful, good-looking** ▶美貌の映画スター a *good-looking* [*beautiful*] movie star (➤ beautiful は主に女性に用いる) ‖美貌はほんのうわべのもの *Beauty* is only skin-deep. (➤ 英語のことわざ).

ひぼうりょく 非暴力 **nonviolence.**

ひぼし 日干し ▶魚を日干しにする *dry* fish *in the sun*

‖**日干しれんが** adobe.

ひぼん 非凡な **unusual, uncommon** ▶彼には非凡な才能がある He has *an unusual talent*. ／He is a man of *rare ability*.

ひま 暇 **1【何もしていない時間】free** [**spare**] **time** (余暇) **一形 暇な free** ▶暇なときはいつも何をしているの? What do you usually do in your *free* [*spare*] *time*? ‖弟は暇があればだいたいテレビゲームをしている My brother spends much of his *free* [*spare*] *time* playing video games. ‖あしたは暇だから遊びに来なよ I'm free tomorrow so come (on)

over to my place.

▶ 対話「きょうの午後は暇？」「忙しいんだ. あしたはどう？」"Are you *free* this afternoon?" "No, I'm busy. How about tomorrow?" ‖ たけし, 暇だったら(＝することがなければ)そこの皿を洗ってよ Takeshi, could you wash the dishes *if you have nothing else to do*? →暇つぶし.

▶彼はいつも暇がないとこぼしている He's always complaining that he has no *leisure time*. ‖ 弟は暇さえあれば飛行機のプラモデルを作っている My (younger) brother builds plastic model planes *whenever he has time to spare*.

▶家事が楽になって暇を持て余している主婦もいる Some housewives *don't know what to do with* [*how to spend*] *their free time* now that housework has become so much easier. ‖ このベッドカバーは姉が暇にあかせて編んだものだ My (older) sister knitted this bedspread *when she had* (*a lot of*) *time on her hands*.

▶このところ注文が減って商売は暇です Business is *slow* [*dull*] these days due to decreasing orders. (➤ slow, dull は商売が「不景気な」).

2【特定のことをする時間】**time** ▶忙し過ぎて寝る暇がない I'm so busy I don't have enough *time* to sleep. ‖ ゲームセンターで遊んでる暇なんかないよ I have no *time* to play games at the video arcade. ‖ 暇をみて少し庭の手入れをしなくちゃ I have to *find time* to do some work in the garden. ‖ 妻は帰宅すると休む暇もなく夕食の準備にかかる As soon as my wife comes home, she starts preparing dinner without taking any *time* to relax.

ひまご 曾孫 a **great-grandchild** [複 **great-grandchildren**]; a **great-granddaughter** (女の); a **great-grandson** (男の).

ひましに 日増しに day by day(日ごとに) ▶母の病状は日増しに悪化していった My mother was getting worse *day by day*. ‖ 日増しに暖かくなってきた It is getting warmer and warmer *every day*.

ひまじん 暇人 an **idle person**(のらくらしている人)

▶あなたってよほどの暇人ね You sure *have a lot of free time* [*a lot of time on your hands*].

ひまつぶし 暇つぶし ▶暇つぶしにパチンコをしよう Let's *kill time* playing pachinko. ‖ きみが戻って来るまでなんとか暇つぶしをしてるよ I'll *while away the time* somehow till you come back. (➤ while away は「(気を紛らして)時間を過ごす」).

ヒマラヤ ‖ヒマラヤ山脈 the Himalayas /hìməléɪəz, hɪmɑ́:liəz/ (インドの北部, チベットとの間を走る大山脈) ‖ **ヒマラヤ杉**《植物》a Himalayan deodar cedar.

ひまわり 向日葵《植物》a **sunflower.**

ひまん 肥満 obesity /oʊbí:səṭi/ (病的肥満), **fatness** ▶肥満は生活習慣病のもと *Obesity* is a cause [one of the causes] of lifestyle-related diseases. ‖ 彼女は肥満体質だ She has a predisposition to *obesity*. (➤ predisposition は「(…になりやすい)体質, 素質」).

‖**肥満児** an overweight [obese] child.

びみ 美味な delicious ‖**美味な物** a delicacy.

ひみつ 秘密 a **secret** 一形 **秘密の secret, clandestine** /klændéstɪn/ (後者は堅い語で, 用心深さを強く暗示する); **confidential**(内密の, 機密の) ▶秘密を守る keep *a secret* ‖ 秘密を漏らす reveal [leak] *a secret* (➤ reveal は「意図的に漏らす」, leak は「こっそりと漏らす」) ‖ 秘密を打ち明ける confide *a secret* ‖ 強盗を企てるための秘密の集まり a *clandestine* meeting to plan a robbery ‖ これは二人だけの秘密だ This is *a secret* just between us. ／This is between you and me. (➤「これは二人だけの話だよ」の意) ‖ どこから秘密が漏れたのか緊急に調べる必要がある We must make an urgent investigation into who let that *secret* out [how that *secret* leaked out]. (➤ 前者は「だれが口外したか」, 後者は「どうやって漏れたか」) ‖ お互いに秘密はなしにしようね There'll be *no secrets* between us. OK?

▶ 対話「これ秘密よ」「だれにも言わないとも」"*This is* (*a*) *secret*." "I won't tell anybody." ‖ 医者は患者についての情報は秘密にしなければならない Doctors must *keep* all information concerning their patients *confidential*. ‖ 日本のたいていの城にはどこかに秘密の抜け穴がある Most Japanese castles have a *secret* [*hidden*] passage somewhere. ‖ あの二人が同せいしていることは公然の秘密だ It's *an open secret* that they are living together.

‖**秘密会議** a secret meeting ‖ **秘密警察** the secret police ‖ **秘密主義** secretiveness ‖ **秘密情報** secret [classified] information (➤ 後者は政府・軍関係の) ‖ **秘密文書** a secret [confidential] document ‖ **秘密漏えい** leakage of a secret ‖ **企業秘密** a trade secret.

びみょう 微妙な delicate /délɪkət/, **subtle** /sʌ́ṭl/ ▶微妙な問題 a *delicate* problem ‖ 彼はその2つの類義語の微妙な違いを説明することができなかった He could not explain the *delicate* [*subtle*] distinction between the two synonymous words. ‖ 二人の話は微妙に食い違っていた There was a *subtle* difference between the accounts of the two (people).

▶ 対話「このラーメンの味, どう？」「ビミョー」"How do you like this ramen?" "*It's hard to* [*I can't*] *say it's* (*either*) *good or bad.* ／*It's somewhere in between.*"

ひめ 姫 a **princess**(王女) ▶《慣用表現》寺沢さんのところは一姫二太郎だ Mr. and Mrs. Terasawa have two children—*an elder girl and a* (*younger*) *boy*.

‖**白雪姫** Snow White.

ひめい 悲鳴 a **shriek**, a **scream** (金切り声；前者がさらに甲高い); a **yell** (わめき) ▶ゆうべ10時ごろ悲鳴を聞きませんでしたか Did you hear *a shriek* [*a scream*] at around ten o'clock last night? ‖ 女の子は悲鳴をあげて助けを求めた The girl *cried out* [*screamed*] for help. (➤ cry out は「大声で叫ぶ」) ‖ 患者は痛くて悲鳴をあげた The patient *screamed* with pain.

▶《慣用表現》その製品の大量注文にメーカーはうれしい悲鳴をあげている The manufacturer *is swamped* [*is snowed under*] *with* orders for the product and *is loving* [*is enjoying*] *every minute of it*. (➤ be swamped with は「…で圧倒される」; love [enjoy] every minute of は「…を心から楽しむ」).

びめい 美名 ▶慈善という美名に隠れて多くの不正が行われた The many wrongful acts that were committed were hidden by the *euphemism* 'charity.'(➤ euphemism は「遠回しな言い方」).

ひめくり 日めくり a **daily calendar.**

ヒメマス《魚》a **kokanee salmon.**

ひめる 秘める keep ... to oneself (人に明かさない) ▶小百合は彼へのほのかな思いをひとり胸に秘めていた Sayuri *kept* her tender feelings for him *to herself*. ‖ さまざまな可能性を秘めた子供たちとともに学べ

るのは楽しい I'm enjoying learning with my students, who all *have* so much (*hidden*) *potential*.

ひめん 罷免する discharge +目; dismiss +目 (免職する) ▶首相は不穏当な発言をしたその大臣を罷免した The Prime Minister *dismissed* the Minister *from his post* for his improper remarks.

ひも 紐 (a) **string**(細い); (a) **cord** (string より太い); a **strap** (物を固定するための); a **lanyard** /lǽnjəʳd/ (笛・ストップウォッチなどを首からつるす); a **sash** (帯) ▶ひもを結ぶ[ほどく] tie [untie] a *string* ‖ ひもをかけたギフトボックス a gift box tied with *string*.
▶もっと太い[細い]ひも, ないの? Don't you have thicker [thinner] *string*? ‖ この小包にひもを掛けてくれ Please tie this package up with (*a piece of*) *string*.
▶《慣用表現》家では母が財布のひもを握っている In our family, my mother *holds the purse strings*.
‖ おんぶ[だっこ]ひも a baby strap [carrier] ‖ 洗濯ひも a clothesline.

ひ

ひもじい **hungry** ▶子供にはひもじい思いはさせたくない I don't want my children to ever go *hungry*.

ひもち 日持ち ▶日持ちのする食品 foods that *keep well* / 《主に英》*long-life* foods ‖ サバは日持ちがしない Mackerel *spoils* [*goes bad*] *easily*.

ひもつき 紐付き ▶ひも付きの融資ならお断りだ I don't need money *with strings* [*conditions*] *attached*. ‖ あのバーのオーナーはヤクザのひも付き(=と関係がある)らしい They say that the owner of that bar *has connections with* the yakuza.

ひもと 火元 **the origin of a fire**
▶警察で今火元を調査中だ The police are investigating *the origin of the fire*. ‖ 火元は台所と判明した It was proved that *the fire started* in the kitchen.

ひもとく 繙く ▶ときに古典をひもとくのも楽しいものだ It's enjoyable to *open and read* a classic from time to time.

ひもの 干物 (a) **dried fish**; (a) **stockfish** (塩引きをしない) ▶アジの干物 a *dried* horse mackerel.

ひやあせ 冷や汗 (a) **cold sweat** /swet/ ▶生徒に鋭い質問をされて冷や汗をかいた When I was asked a pointed question by a student, I broke out in *a cold sweat*.

ひやかす 冷やかす **tease** +目, 《インフォーマル》**josh** +目 (➤ 後者には悪意がこもらない) ▶友人たちは彼の奇妙な髪型のことでよく彼を冷やかす His friends often *tease* him about his strange hairstyle. ‖ ボーイフレンドのことで姉を冷やかしていたら姉は突然怒りだした I was *teasing* [*joshing*] my sister about her boyfriend, when suddenly she got angry. ‖ その少年は妹と二人乗り自転車に乗っていてみんなに冷やかされた (=からかわれた) The boy *was made fun of* by everybody when he was riding a tandem (bicycle) with his sister.
▶ぶらぶらと町を歩きながらお店を冷やかすのも楽しいでしょう I would enjoy *window shopping* while walking leisurely around town.

[1]**ひやく 飛躍** **1【大きな発展】**▶飛躍的な進歩を遂げる make *considerable* [*substantial*] progress ‖ スマートフォンの生産高は飛躍的に伸びている The production of smartphones is increasing *by leaps and bounds*.
✉ **(年賀状で) ことしこそ飛躍の年にしたいと思っております** I hope to make this the year when I (really) *spread my wings*. ➤ spread one's wings は「活動範囲を広げる」の意.
2【論理・話の】 a **jump**, a **leap** ▶あなたの論理には飛躍がある There's *a jump* [*a leap*] in your logic. ‖ 彼の話はときどき飛躍する He sometimes *jumps from one topic to another*.

[2]**ひやく 秘薬** a **secret medicine** [**remedy**].

びやく 媚薬 an **aphrodisiac** /æfrədíziæk/.

ひゃく 百

a [**one**] **hundred**; **the hundredth** (100番目)

語法 (1) one hundred は特に数字を強調する場合やインフォーマルで多く用いられる. (2) hundred は hundreds of ...(数百の…, 何百の…)のような連語のとき以外は単数形で用いる.

▶105人の子供 *a* [*one*] *hundred and five* children ‖ 300人の大学生 *three hundred* college students ‖ 480 *four hundred* (*and*) *eighty* (➤ and を入れるのは主に《英》) ‖ 311号室 Room No. *three eleven* (➤ 部屋番号やページは2けたずつ区切って読むこともある) ‖ 彼は数百冊の本を持っている He has *several hundred* books. (➤ 漠然と,「百を越えるたくさんの」の意味の「何百冊もの」ならば hundreds of books).
▶英語のテストで100点を取った I got (*a*) *hundred* [*a perfect score* / 《英》*full marks*] on the English test. ‖ ことし, わが校は創立百年目(の記念の年)を迎える Our school will celebrate *the hundredth anniversary* [*the centennial* / 《英》*the centenary*] of its founding this year. (➤ centennial, centenary /senténəri/ は「百年祭」) ‖ 成功率は100分の1だ The success rate is *one percent* [*one out of a hundred*].
▶《慣用表現》そんなことは百も承知だ I *know that one hundred percent*. / I'*m completely aware of* that. ‖ 自分がぐずだということは百も承知だ I'*m fully aware* that I'm a slowpoke.
‖ 百円ショップ a one-hundred-yen store (➤ アメリカには a dollar store (1ドル店)がある).

ひゃくがい 百害 ▶この種のサイトは百害あって一利なしだ This kind of website *does* (*you*) *no good and much harm*.

ひゃくしょう 百姓 →農民.

ひゃくとおばん 百十番 ▶110番する dial [call] *110* /wʌ́n wʌ́n óʊ/ / make *an emergency call* to the police 《参考》日本の110番と119番を統合した緊急電話番号はアメリカ・カナダでは911, イギリスでは999, オーストラリアでは000, ニュージーランドでは111が一般的に使われる.

ひゃくにちぜき 百日咳 **whooping cough** /kɔːf/ ▶百日ぜきにかかる catch [develop] *whooping cough*.

ひゃくにちそう 百日草 《植物》a **zinnia**.

ひゃくにんいっしゅ 百人一首 ***Hyakunin Isshu***; an anthology of 100 *well-known classical waka* poems (➤ 説明的な訳).

ひゃくねんさい 百年祭 a **centennial celebration**.

ひゃくはちじゅうど 百八十度 ▶政府は原子力政策を180度転換した The government changed its nuclear energy policy *180 degrees* [*completely*].

ひゃくぶん 百聞 ▶百聞は一見にしかずというからね. 自分の目で見なきゃ信じられないよ It is said *seeing is believing*. I'll believe it when I see it.

ひゃくぶんりつ 百分率 **percentage**.

ひゃくまん 百万 a [**one**] **million** ▶百万円 *a* [*one*] *million* yen ‖ 200万冊の本 *two million* books ‖ 数百万人 *several million* people ‖ 何百万匹ものバッタ

millions of locusts ‖ **100万分の1の地図** a map on a scale of *one to a million* ‖ 彼女たちのデビューCDは**200万枚売れた** *Two million copies* of their debut CDs were sold. ‖ 1999年5月, 仙台は日本で11番目の**100万都市になった** In May of 1999, Sendai became the 11th *city* in Japan *with a population of over one million*.
‖ **百万長者** a millionaire /mìljənéər/ (百万ドル以上の資産をもつ金持ち).

ひゃくめんそう 百面相 ▶おじいちゃんは**百面相をして**赤ん坊を笑わせた The grandfather made the baby laugh by *making all kinds of funny faces*.

びゃくや 白夜 **the night of the midnight sun** (➤ white night は「眠れぬ夜」の意) ▶**白夜の国** the land of *the midnight sun*.

ひゃくようばこ 百葉箱 an **instrument screen** [**shelter**].

ひやけ 日焼け (a) **(sun) tan**, (a) **sunburn** (➤ 前者は「ほどよい日焼け」, 後者は「過度の日焼け, 炎症」をいう)
一動 **日焼けする** **get suntanned** [**sunburned**], **get a suntan** ▶**日焼けした顔** a *suntanned* face ‖ 極度の**日焼け**は皮膚がんの原因になるといわれている It is said that too much *exposure to the sun* may cause skin cancer. (➤ exposure は「さらすこと」) ‖ **日焼けしたところがひりひりする** My *sunburn* smarts. ‖ 彼女はスキーで**日焼けした** She *got suntanned* from skiing. ‖ こんがり(小麦色に)**日焼けしたいな** I want to *have a nice tan*.
▶彼はひどく**日焼けしている** He is seriously [badly] *sunburned*.
‖ **日焼け止めクリーム** a sunscreen (lotion) ; a sunblock (lotion / cream) ‖ **日焼け用ローション [オイル]** suntan lotion [oil].

ひやしちゅうか 冷やし中華 Chinese noodles served cold with sliced ham, cucumber and other toppings (➤ 説明的な訳).

ヒヤシンス 《植物》a **hyacinth** /háɪəsɪnθ/.

ひやす 冷やす **cool** +目 (適度に) ; **chill** +目 (飲食物を) ▶熱があるのなら氷で**頭を冷やす**といいよ If you have a fever, the thing to do is *cool* your head with ice. ‖ スイカを冷蔵庫に入れて**冷やして**ちょうだい Put the watermelon in the fridge to *cool*, please. ‖ ワイン**冷やし**といたわよ I've *chilled* the wine. ‖ 飲み物を少し**冷やし**といてね Could you *ice* some drinks, please? (➤ ice は「氷で冷やす」) ‖ ねんざした足首を**冷やした**ほうがいいよ You'd better *put an ice pack on* your sprained ankle. ‖ 体を**冷やさない**ようにしてください *Keep* yourself *warm*. (➤ keep ... warm は「…を暖かく保つ」).
▶《慣用表現》**頭を冷やせよ** *Cool head*. (➤「冷静な頭(でいろ)」の意) / *Be calm*. / *Don't lose your cool*. ‖ 女の子が急に車の前に飛び出してきたので**肝を冷やした** I *almost jumped out of my skin* [*My heart jumped into my mouth*] when a girl ran out of nowhere right in front of my car. (➤「体が驚いてびくっと動く」,「心臓が口まで飛び出るほどびっくりした」の意).

ひゃっかじてん 百科事典 an **encyclopedia** /ɪnsàɪkləpíːdiə/.

ひゃっかてん 百貨店 a **department store**, 《英また》a **big store** ▶丸武**百貨店**に買い物に行く go shopping at Marutake *Department Store*.

ひゃっぱつひゃくちゅう 百発百中 ▶小野は試験のヤマかけがうまい. まさに**百発百中だ** Ono is great at guessing about what will be on the test. He *hits the mark ten times out of ten*. (➤ 射撃などの文字どおりの意味でも用いる).

ひやっと ▶**ひやっとする** *shiver* ‖ **背筋がひやっとした** *A chill ran down my spine*.

ひやとい 日雇い a **day laborer** (人) ▶当時私は**日雇い**で, まさにその日暮らしだった At that time I worked as *a day laborer* and barely scraped by from day to day.

ひやひや 冷や冷や ▶内心**ひやひやしていた**が気づかれずにすんだ Inside I *was on pins and needles*, but I made it through without their realizing it. ‖ 弟の無謀運転にはいつも**ひやひやさせられる** My (younger) brother's reckless driving always *has* me *on the edge of my seat* [*puts* me *on edge*]. (➤ どちらも「私をはらはらした状態にする」の意).

ひやむぎ 冷麦 ***hiyamugi*** ; chilled Japanese noodles served with a thick soy sauce-based dipping sauce (➤ 説明的な訳).

ひやめし 冷や飯 ▶あの部長のもとで私は5年間**冷や飯を食わされた** Under that manager I *was left out in the cold* for five years. (➤「無視された」の意).

ひややか 冷ややかな **cool**, **cold** (➤ 後者のほうが非友好性がより強く感じられる) ▶**冷ややかな応対** a *cool* [*cold*] reception ‖ 彼女は背中に同僚の**冷ややかな視線**を感じた She felt the *cold* stares of her coworkers on her back. ‖ 彼は私の提案に対して**冷ややかな態度**をとった He took a *cool* [*cold*] attitude toward my suggestion. ‖ 彼は**冷ややかな笑い**を浮かべて答えた He replied with *a sardonic grin*. (➤ sardonic は「冷笑的な」).

ひややっこ 冷や奴 ***hiyayakko*** ; a block of tofu served cold [chilled], topped with dried bonito flakes, grated ginger, and chopped green onions and soy sauce (➤ 説明的な訳).

ひやり ▶もう少しで対向車とぶつかりそうになり**ひやりとした** I almost collided with an oncoming car and *felt a rush of fear*.

ヒヤリング →ヒアリング.

ひゆ 比喩 a **figure of speech** (比喩的表現) ; a **metaphor** /méṭəfɔːr/ (隠喩) ; a **simile** /síməli/ (直喩).

ぴゅー ▶冷たい北風が**ピューと**吹き抜けた The cold north wind howled past (➤ howl /haʊl/ は「(風が)うなる」). / The cold north gale blasted. ‖ チューブを押したらケチャップが**ぴゅーと**飛び出した Some ketchup *spurted out* from the tube when I squeezed it.

ヒューズ a **fuse** /fjuːz/ ▶**ヒューズがとんでしまった** The *fuse* has blown [has gone]. ‖ 車の**ヒューズがとんだ** My car has blown *a fuse*. →ブレーカー.

ヒューストン **Houston** /hjúːstən/ (アメリカ, テキサス州の都市).

ビューティーサロン a **beauty salon**.

ビューティスト a **beautician** /bjuːtíʃən/ (「ビューティスト」は和製語).

ひゅーひゅー ▶外では木枯らしが**ヒューヒュー**吹いていた Outside the cold winter wind *was whistling*.

びゅーびゅー ▶強い風が**ビュービュー**吹いて飛ばされそうだった A strong wind *was howling*, and I felt like I was going to be blown away.

ピューマ 《動物》a **puma** /pjúːmə/.

ヒューマニスト a **humanitarian** (人道主義者) ; a **humanist** (人間主義者) (➤ 前者のほうが日本語に近い ; →ヒューマニズム).

ヒューマニズム **humanitarianism** /hju(ː)mænɪtéəriənìzəm/ (人道主義) ▶核実験は**ヒューマニズムの**

精神から見て許しがたい Nuclear tests cannot be condoned from a *humanitarian* point of view. ‖ 彼の作る映画はどれもヒューマニズムにあふれている There is great *humanity* in all the films he directs. (➤ humanity は「人間愛」).

危ないカタカナ語✹ ヒューマニズム

1 humanism ということばは, ルネサンス期に神のことばを研究する学者たちに対して, ギリシャ・ローマの先人たちの著作(古典)の研究を行う学者たちを,「人間のことばの研究者」の意味で *Humanistica* と呼んだことに由来する.

2 したがって, humanism は日本語の「人道主義」「博愛主義」を意味することばではなく, この意味では humanitarianism というのがふつう.

3「ヒューマニスト」(人道主義者)も humanist より humanitarian がよい.

ひ

ピューリタン a **Puritan.**

ピューレ **purée**

‖**トマトピューレ** tomato purée.

ヒュッテ a **mountain hut** [**cabin**] 《参考》「ヒュッテ」はドイツ語の *Hütte* から.

ビュッフェ a **buffet** /bəféɪ ‖ bʊ́feɪ/ (➤ フランス語から) ‖**ビュッフェ式朝食** (a) buffet breakfast, a breakfast buffet.

びゅんびゅん ▶彼は後ろにパトカーがいるのにびゅんびゅん飛ばした He *zoomed ahead at high speed* though he knew there was a police car behind him. ‖ 高速道路でびゅんびゅん飛ばしたいよ I want to get on the expressway and really *let her fly*. (➤ her は「車」の意).

ひょいと ▶電車をひょいと降りる *hop off* a train ‖ 車からひょいと降りる *hop out of* a car ‖ タクシーにひょいと乗る *hop in* a taxi ‖ 窓からひょいと顔を出す *pop* one's head out of a window ‖ 男は旅行かばんをひょいと(=楽々と)持ち上げた The man lifted his traveling bag *effortlessly*.

ひよう 費用 (an) **expense** (支出) ; **expenses** (支出金) ; a **cost** (代価) ; **costs** (経費) ▶新築の費用を見積もる estimate the *expense* [*cost*] of building a new house ‖ わずかの費用で家を増築する build an addition onto one's house *at* (*a*) *low cost* / build a *low-cost* addition onto one's house ‖ 今夜の宴会の費用は会社持ちだ We're having a banquet tonight at the company's *expense*. ‖ 対話「塀を直すのに費用はどれくらいかかった？」「30万円ほどだったよ」"How much did it *cost* you to get the wall fixed? / How much did they *charge* you for repairing the wall?" "It cost [They charged] me about three hundred thousand yen." ‖ 旅行の費用は各自持ちだった All of us *paid our own way* on the trip. (➤「旅行の費用」は travel(ing) expenses).

[1]**ひょう 表** a **list**(項目を羅列したもの) ; a **table** (縦横の区切りのある)

▶メンバー表 *a list* of members ‖ 調査の結果を表にする *set out* [*show*] the research results *in a table* ‖ 値段は表に載っているはずだ The price should be on the *list*. / The price should be listed. ‖ この地図帳の後ろには各地の年間降雨量が表になっている At the end of the atlas there is *a table* of annual rainfall for various places. ‖ 結果は下のような表にまとまりました The results are given in the following *table*.

‖**換算表** a conversion table ‖ **対数表** a logarithmic table ‖ **統計表** a statistical table.

[2]**ひょう 票** a **vote** ▶票集めをする canvass for *votes* ‖ その計画に賛成[反対]の票を投じる *cast a vote* for [against] the plan ‖ 票が割れるかもしれない The *votes* may be split. ‖ 私は上田氏に票を入れるつもりだ I will *vote for* [I will *give my vote to*] Mr. Ueda. ‖ あの候補者は大量の票を集めた The candidate got *a large number of votes*.

▶その法案は200票対50票で可決された The bill was passed by *a vote* of 200 to 50 [by 200 *votes* against 50].

‖**組織票** the organized vote ‖ **同情票** a sympathy vote ‖ **無効票** a spoiled vote.

☛ 白票, 浮動票 (→見出語)

[3]**ひょう 評** **reputation**(評判) ▶あの医者は仲間の評が芳しくない That doctor has an unsavory *reputation* among his fellow doctors. ‖ あの人は金に汚ないとの評がある He [She] *is notorious for* dirty money dealings.

[4]**ひょう 雹** **hail** /heɪl/ (➤ 1粒は a hailstone という) ▶こぶし大のひょう *hailstones* as big as fists ‖ ゆうべひょうが降り, 農作物に被害が出た *It hailed* last night and the crops were badly damaged.

[5]**ひょう 豹** 《動物》 a **leopard** /lépərd/ ; a **panther** (特に黒ヒョウ).

びよう 美容 ⚠「美容」にぴったり対応する英語はない. したがって, 文脈によって「美」「スタイルをよくすること」「健康を保つこと」などと考えて訳す. ▶自然食は健康と美容によい Natural foods are good for health and *beauty*. ‖ 姉は美容のためにダイエットをしている My (older) sister is dieting *to improve her figure* [*to keep herself slim*]. (➤ 前者は「スタイルをよくするために」の意).

▶妻と娘はここ4, 5か月美容体操をやっている My wife and daughter have been doing *calisthenics* [*exercises to improve their figures*] for the past several months. (➤ calisthenics は「(美容と健康のための)柔軟体操」).

‖**美容院** a beauty parlor [salon / 《米また》 shop] (➤美顔術なども行う) ; 《英》 a hairdresser's ‖ **美容学校** a beauty school ‖ **美容師** a hairdresser, a beautician ‖ **美容食** food for beauty, diet food ‖ **美容整形** cosmetic [plastic] surgery (➤ 顔のしわを取るのは face lift, 鼻[目, あご]の整形は nose [eye, chin] job, 胸の整形は breast augmentation [enhancement / enlargement] (surgery) という).

[1]**びょう 秒** a **second** ▶1秒は1分の60分の1だ *A second* is one-sixtieth of a minute. ‖ 5秒前, 4, 3, 2, 1, 始め! Five *seconds* (to go), four, three, two, one. Go! ‖ 滑降競技は100分の1秒を争う競技だ Downhill racing is an event in which even *a hundredth of a second* counts.

☛ 秒針, 秒読み (→見出語)

[2]**びょう 鋲** a **tack**(画びょう) ; a **rivet** (船舶・機械用の) ▶じゅうたんはびょうで留められてあった The carpet was fastened with *tacks*. ‖ 先生はその日本地図を壁にびょうで留めた The teacher *tacked* the map of Japan to [on] the wall.

[3]**びょう 廟** a **mausoleum** /mɔ̀ːsəlíːəm/, a **Confucian shrine**(孔子廟).

ひょういもじ 表意文字 an **ideogram.**

びょういん 病院

a **hospital** ; a **clinic** (診療所) ▶母は病院に入院しています

My mother *is in the hospital* [*is hospitalized*]. (➤《英》では the を省略する) ‖ 肺炎にかかった息子を**病院に入れた** I *sent* my son *to* (*the*) *hospital* [*put* my son *in the hospital*] because he got pneumonia.

▶彼女はリウマチの治療のために**週に1度病院へ通っている** She *goes to* (*the*) *hospital once a week* to be treated for rheumatism. ‖ 肝臓が悪いと思うのなら**病院へ行ったほうがいいんじゃない** If you think you have a liver problem, you had better *see a doctor* [*go to a doctor's office*]. (➤ go to the hospital はふつう「入院する」「見舞いで病院に行く」の意味で使われる) ‖ 急病人は救急車で**病院へ運ばれた** The emergency patient *was taken to* (*the*) *hospital* by [in an] ambulance.

‖**救急病院** an emergency hospital ‖ **精神病院** a mental [psychiatric] hospital ‖ **総合病院** a general hospital ‖ **大学病院** a university hospital ‖ **動物病院** an animal hospital, a veterinary hospital, 《インフォーマル》 a vet's.

「病院の診療科」のいろいろ **胃腸科** gastroenterology /**眼科** ophthalmology /**形成外科** plastic surgery /**外科** surgery /**産婦人科** obstetrics & gynecology /**耳鼻咽喉科** otolaryngology /**小児科** pediatrics /**神経科** neurology /**整形外科** orthopedic surgery /**精神科** psychiatry /**内科** internal medicine /**泌尿器科** urology /**皮膚科** dermatology /**美容整形外科** cosmetic surgery /**放射線科** radiology /**麻酔科** anesthesiology
注 病院内の部局を表すには, 例えば「外科」は the department of surgery のようにいう.

ひょうおんもじ 表音文字 a **phonetic sign** [**symbol**] ; a **phonogram**(表意文字に対して).

ひょうか 評価 **evaluation** ; a **valuation**(査定額) **一動 評価する evaluate** +目 (価値判断する) ; **value** +目 (値踏みする ; 価値を置く) ; **rate** +目 (段階をつける) ; **appraise** +目 (財産などを評価する)

▶学生のテストの点数で先生たちを**評価する** *evaluate* teachers based on student test scores ‖ 私は生徒を5段階に**評価する**方法には反対です I'm against the *evaluation* method of classifying students into five levels. ‖ その土地は駅に近いことから1億円に**評価された** The land *was valued* [*was appraised*] at one hundred million yen because it was located close to the train station. /*The value* of that land *was estimated* at one hundred million yen because it was near the train station.

▶日本製品はたいがい世界的に**評価が高い** Most Japanese products *are highly valued* world-wide. ‖ 黒澤明監督は日本よりも海外で**評価が高かった** Film director Kurosawa Akira *was* more *highly praised* abroad than at home. ‖ 私たちは彼の能力を**高く評価している** We *think highly of* [*have a high opinion of*] his abilities.

☛ **再評価** (→見出語)

ひょうが 氷河 a **glacier** /gléɪʃəʳ/ ▶北極圏の**氷河**が急速に溶けている The *glaciers* in the Arctic Circle are beginning to melt rapidly.

▶ここ数年**大卒者の就職氷河期**が続いている The past few years have been *a difficult period for college-graduate job seekers*.

‖**氷河期** the glacial period [epoch], the Ice Age.

ひょうかい 氷解 ▶教授の説明で疑問は**氷解した** My questions *melted away* when I heard the professor's explanation.

ひょうき 表記 ▶名前をローマ字で**表記する** *write* one's name in Roman letters.

✉ **このたび表記の場所に転居いたしました** We've recently moved to the place *indicated* on the front of the envelope [card]. ➤ envelope は封筒の場合, card ははがきの場合.

びょうき 病気

(a) **sickness**, (an) **illness** ; a **disease** (具体的な病名のある) **一形 病気で sick, ill 一動 病気になる get sick, become ill**

語法 (1)**sickness** と **illness** は「体調の悪い状態」をいい, **disease** は具体的な名前のついた病気を指す. (2)形容詞は《米》では **sick** がふつうで, **ill** はやや堅い語. 《英》では ill のほうがふつうで, sick は「吐き気がする」の意になることが多い. ただし, 次に名詞がくるときは《米》《英》とも sick を用いる.

▶**病気の**子 a *sick* child /a child who *is sick* [*ill*] (➤ (×)ill child とはしない) ‖ 現代医学がすべての**病気**を治せるわけではない Modern medicine cannot cure all *diseases*. ‖ 姉は**病気で寝ている**[亡くなった] My sister is *sick in bed* [died of *an illness*]. ‖ 林君は**病気で**欠席です Hayashi is absent *because of sickness* [*illness*].

▶私は**病気で**旅行に行けなかった I couldn't go on a trip *because I was sick* [*due to illness*]. /*Illness* prevented me from going on a trip. (➤ 堅い言い方) ‖ 前田さんから**病気**で休むと電話があった Maeda called in *sick*. (➤ call in sick は「電話をかけて病欠を告げる」) ‖ 彼の**病気は重い**[**軽い**] He is *seriously* [*slightly*] *sick*. ‖ 今までに**重い病気**にかかったことがありますか Have you ever suffered from *a serious disease*? ‖ 彼女の胃の**病気**は慢性のものだ Her stomach *trouble* is chronic. (➤ trouble は重大ではないが慢性的な病気を指すのがふつう) ‖ 対話「お父さんのご病気はいかがですか」「おかげさまでよくなってきました」"*How's* your (*sick*) father?" "He's getting better, thanks."

▶母は先月**病気になった** My mother *became* [*got*] *ill* last month. ‖ そんなに働くと**病気になる**よ You'll *get sick* if you work that hard. (➤ get sick はややインフォーマルな言い方) ‖ 私は子供のころ**病気がち**だった I was *sickly* [*frequently sick*] when I was a child. /I was a very *sickly* child. ‖ **病気がすっかり治った** I *am* quite *well* now. ‖ **病気が早く治る**といいね I hope you *get well* soon.

▶《比喩的》彼のカメラ好きもあそこまでいくと**ビョーキ**だね I know he's a camera addict, but to go that far is *too much* [*is weird*]. (➤ weird /wɪəʳd/ は「異様な」).

✉ **ご病気だそうですね. 早く元気になられるのを願っております** I'm sorry to hear you *are not well*. I look forward to seeing you up and about again soon. ➤ ill や sick の代わりに遠回しの表現を使うと感じがよい. up and about は「(病気で寝ていた人が)起きて歩き回って」の意.

ひょうぎいん 評議員 a **council(l)or**, a **member of a council**.

ひょうぎかい 評議会 a **council**.

ひょうきん 剽軽な **funny**, **comic(al)** (笑いたくなる, こっけいな) ▶彼はよくひょうきんなことを言う He often says *funny* things. ‖ 彼はクラス一のひょうきん者だ He is the greatest *joker* in my class. ／He is the greatest class *clown*.

びょうく 病苦 **pain from illness**（病気の苦しみ）; **illness, sickness**（病気）▶病苦と闘う fight [struggle against] *a disease* ‖ 病苦に打ち勝つ overcome the pain of an *illness*.

ひょうけいほうもん 表敬訪問 a **courtesy call** [**visit**].

1**ひょうけつ 票決** a **vote** 一動 **票決する vote** ▶この問題はクラスの票決で決めるべきだ The question should be put to a class *vote*. ／The class should *vote* on this question.

2**ひょうけつ 評決** a **verdict**（陪審員の）▶有罪[無罪]の評決を下す return *a verdict* of guilty [not guilty].

びょうけつ 病欠 **absence from school** [**work**] **because of sickness ; sick leave**（病気欠勤）
▶久米さんはきょうは病欠です Kume's *absent* today *because of sickness*. ／Kume's *out* [*off*] *sick* today.

ひ

1**ひょうげん 表現** (an) **expression** 一動 **表現する express** ＋目 ▶表現の自由 freedom of *expression* ／free *expression* ‖ 適切な[うまい]表現 a suitable [good] *expression* ‖ パントマイムでは(ことばを使わず)動きや顔の表情で気持ちを表現する In pantomime, actors *express* how they feel with actions and facial expressions. ‖ どう表現すればいいのか説明するのが難しい How should I *put* it? It's hard to explain. ‖ あのダンサーは表現力が豊かだ That dancer *has great power of expression*. ／That dancer *is highly expressive*.

2**ひょうげん 氷原** an **ice field**.

3**ひょうげん 評言** a **comment**.

びょうげん 病原 **the cause of a disease**
‖**病原体** a pathogen /pǽθədʒən/.

びょうげんきん 病原菌 **germs**.

ひょうご 標語 a **motto** /mɑ́ːt̬oʊ/（生活の指針などにする）; a **catchword**（うたい文句）; a **slogan**（政治運動・商品広告などのスローガン）▶わが社では自然保護のための標語を募集しています We are asking for [soliciting] good *slogans* for the conservation of nature.
‖**交通標語** traffic safety slogans.

びょうご 病後 ▶病後で弱っているんだから無理はするなよ Take it easy. You're still weak *after your illness* [*sickness*].

ひょうこう 標高 an **altitude** ▶この辺りは標高2000メートル以上の高山が連なっている There's a range of high mountains over 2,000 meters *above sea level* here.

ひょうさつ 表札 a **nameplate**, a **doorplate** 《参考》英米の家庭では表札は出さないのがふつうだが, メールボックスに house number（家屋番号）とともに自分の名前を書いている人も多い. (→番地).

ひょうざん 氷山 an **iceberg** ▶氷山の約86パーセントは水面下にある About 86 percent of *an iceberg* is underwater.
▶《慣用表現》今回のようなえん罪は氷山の一角にすぎない The present case of wrongful conviction is only [just] *the tip of the iceberg*.

1**ひょうし 拍子** **1**【音楽の】**time** ▶ドラムで拍子をとる *beat time* on the drums ‖ 彼女は足で拍子をとりながら歌った She sang a song, *beating* [*keeping*] *time* with her foot. ‖ ワルツは4分の3拍子だ Waltzes are in *three-four time*. 《参考》「4分の2拍子」は two-four time,「4分の4拍子」は four-four time という.
‖**拍子記号**《音楽》a time signature.
2【はずみ】▶くしゃみをした拍子に入れ歯が外れた My dentures came out *the moment* I sneezed. ／I sneezed *and* my dentures came out.
▶《慣用表現》彼女がパーティーに来られないと知って拍子抜けがした I *felt let down* to learn that she would not attend the party. (➤ let down は「失望した」の意).

2**ひょうし 表紙** a **cover** ▶赤い表紙の本 a book with a red *cover* ‖『タイム』の今週の表紙はオバマ大統領です President Obama is (featured) on the *cover* of "Time" this week. →カバー.

ひょうじ 表示 (an) **indication** 一動 **表示する indicate** /índɪkeɪt/ ＋目 ; **show** ＋目（見せる）▶製造年月日はラベルに表示してあります The manufacture date *is indicated* on the label. ‖ 原材料は箱の裏に表示されています The ingredients *are listed* [*are shown*] on the back of the box.
▶この計画について自分の意思表示をはっきりしなさい You should *express your opinion* about this plan clearly.

びょうし 病死 ▶彼女は昨年暮れに若くして病死した She *died* young *of sickness* [*of a disease*] at the end of last year.

ひょうしき 標識 a **sign**, a **mark** ; a **marker**（目印）▶(交通)標識を無視する[守る] ignore [follow ／observe] a (traffic) *sign* ‖ 標識に従って通路を進む walk (along the way) following the *markers*.
‖**標識灯** a beacon light ‖ **航空標識** an air beacon.

びょうしつ 病室 a **sickroom** ; a **hospital room**（病院の）; a **ward** /wɔːʳd/（病棟）.

ひょうしゃ 評者 a **reviewer**.

びょうしゃ 描写 (a) **description**（ことばによる）; (a) **portrayal** /pɔːʳtréɪəl/（絵や演技による）一動 **描写する describe** ＋目, **portray** ＋目 ▶この物語は戦争を生々しく描写している This story *gives a* vivid *description* of the war. ／The author vividly *describes* wartime scenes. ‖ その映画の中でヒロインは当時の強い女性として描写されていた In the movie, the heroine *was portrayed* as a strong woman for those days. ‖ その小説は人物の性格描写と心理描写においてすぐれている The novel is really good in terms of *character portrayal* and *psychological description*.

びょうじゃく 病弱な **sickly** ▶病弱な人 a person *in weak* [*poor*] *health* ／a *sickly* person ‖ 兄は病弱のため学業を諦めざるをえなかった My (older) brother was forced to give up his studies because of *poor health*.

ひょうじゅん 標準 a **standard** ; **the average** /ǽvərɪdʒ/（平均）一形 **標準の standard, average** ▶標準的な家庭 the *average* family ‖ 彼女の演奏は高校生としては標準以上だった Her performance was *above average* for a high-school student.
‖**標準語** the standard language ; standard Japanese（日本語の場合）‖ **標準時** standard time ; Japan Standard Time (JST)（日本の）; Universal Time Coordinated (UTC)（協定世界時）(➤従来の Greenwich Mean Time (GMT) という名称は公式には廃止) ‖ **標準体重** standard weight ‖ **標準**

偏差《統計学》a standard deviation ‖ **標準モデル** a standard model ‖ **業界標準** the industry standard.

ひょうしょう 表彰 commendation ━動 **表彰する** commend ＋目, honor /ɑ́:nə^r/ ＋目 ▶警察はその人の勇敢な行為を**表彰した** The police *commended* the man for his brave deed. ／The man *got* [*won*] official *commendation* from the police for his brave deed. (➤後者は「賞を受けた」の意) ‖ 彼女はベストドレッサーとして**表彰された**(＝ベストドレッサー賞を授けられた) She *was honored with* the Best Dressed *Award*. ／ She *received* the Best Dressed *Award*. ‖ 彼は最優秀選手として**表彰された** He *was honored* as the most valuable player (of the year).

‖ **表彰式** a commendation ceremony ; a prize-giving ceremony (運動競技などの) ‖ **表彰状** a certificate of commendation ; a testimonial (➤「感謝・表彰のしるし」ということで, 必ずしも紙に書かれたり印刷されていなくてもよい) ‖ **表彰台** an honor platform ; the winner's platform, a victory stand (運動競技などの).

ひょうじょう 表情 an expression ; a look (顔つき) ▶悲しそうな**表情** a sad *expression* ‖ その俳優は**表情**が豊かだ The actor has an *expressive* face. ‖ この仏像は穏やかな**表情**(＝顔つき)をしている This Buddhist statue has a calm *face*. (● 訳例は一般の仏像を念頭に置いたものだが, 釈迦の像であれば the statue of Buddha とする).

▶きみ, きょうは**表情**が明るい[硬い]ね You *look happy* [*stiff*] today. ‖ どんなときでも彼女は**表情**を変えない She never changes her *expression* under any circumstances. ／No matter what may happen, she always keeps a poker face. (➤ poker face は「無表情な顔」).

☞ 無表情 (→見出語)

びょうしょう 病床 a sickbed ▶**病床**に人を見舞う visit a person on his [her] *sickbed* ‖ 祖母はもう2年近く**病床にある** My grandmother *has been ill in bed* for nearly two years.

びょうじょう 病状 (a) condition (容体) ▶彼の**病状**はしだいに快方に向かっている His *condition* has improved.

[1]**びょうしん 病身** ▶**病身**をいたわる take good care of *oneself during sickness*.

[2]**びょうしん 秒針** the second hand (of a clock [a watch]).

[1]**ひょうする 表する** show ＋目 (示す, 見せる) ; express ＋目 (意見を言う, 感情を表す) ▶被災者に対する援助を惜しまれなかった皆さまに**謝意を表します** This is to *show our gratitude* to you for your assistance to the disaster victims.

▶私たちは国の民主化に尽力してきたその政治家に**敬意を表します** We hereby *express our respect* for [hereby *pay tribute* to] that statesperson who has worked so hard for the democratization of the country.

[2]**ひょうする 評する** ▶同僚は彼を**評して**「完全主義者」と呼ぶ His colleagues *call* him a 'perfectionist.'

ひょうせつ 剽窃 plagiarism /pléɪdʒərɪzəm/ ━動 **ひょうせつする** plagiarize /pléɪdʒəraɪz/ ＋目.

[1]**ひょうそう 表層** the outer layer ; the surface (表面).

‖ **表層なだれ** a surface avalanche.

[2]**ひょうそう 表装** mounting ▶書を**表装**してもらう *have* one's work of calligraphy *mounted*.

びょうそう 病巣 the focus of a disease.

びょうそく 秒速 speed per second

▶台風の接近で**秒速**30メートルに達する強風が吹き荒れている With the typhoon approaching, there are strong winds with *speeds* of up to 30 meters *per second*.

ひょうだい 表題・標題 a title ▶その本の**表題**は『すい星について』だ The *title* of the book is "About Comets." ‖ **標題音楽** program music.

ひょうたん 瓢箪 《植物》a gourd /gɔ:^rd/ ▶あの池は**ヒョウタン形**をしている That pond is *gourd-shaped*.

▶《慣用表現》その喫茶店でアルバイトをしていたら, **ひょうたんから駒**で, オーナーからそこをまかされた When I was working part-time at the coffee shop, *the most unexpected thing happened*. The owner left me in charge of the shop. (➤「予想もしなかったことが本当に起こった」の意).

ひょうちゃく 漂着する be washed up (波に打ち上げられる) ▶1543年にポルトガル船が種子島に**漂着した** In 1543, a Portuguese ship *was washed up* [*drifted ashore*] on Tanegashima Island.

びょうちゅうがい 病虫害 crop damage by disease and pests [harmful insects].

ひょうてい 評定 a rating, an evaluation.

ひょうてき 標的 a mark, a target (➤後者は比喩的な意味でも用いる)

▶彼は銃を構え**標的**をねらった He aimed the gun at the *target*. ‖ その空母を**標的**にしてミサイルを発射する launch a missile *targeted* [*aimed*] *at* the aircraft carrier.

びょうてき 病的な morbid ▶彼の描く絵はどこか**病的だ** His pictures have something *morbid* about them. ‖ その子は**病的**なまでに火をこわがる The child has an *abnormal* [a *morbid*] fear of fire.

‖ **病的虚言者** a pathological liar.

[1]**ひょうてん 氷点** the freezing point

▶**氷点下**の冬の夜 a *subfreezing* winter night ‖ けさは**氷点下**3度まで気温が下がった The temperature fell to three degrees *below freezing* [*below the freezing point*] this morning. ／It was three *below zero* this morning. (➤ zero の発音は /zíəroʊ/).

[2]**ひょうてん 評点** a grade (評価点) ; a mark (試験の点数) ▶英語の**評点**はBだった I got [was given] a B (*grade*) in English.

[1]**ひょうでん 評伝** a critical biography ▶フロイトの**評伝** *a critical biography* of Freud.

[2]**ひょうでん 票田** a voter base ▶大都市は伝統的に革新政党の**票田**だ Big cities are traditionally *voter bases* for reformist parties. ／Big cities traditionally *provide grass-roots support* for reformist parties.

ひょうど 表土 topsoil.

びょうとう 病棟 a ward /wɔ:^rd/

‖ **隔離病棟** an isolation ward ‖ **産科病棟** a maternity ward ‖ **小児病棟** a children's ward.

びょうどう 平等 equality /ɪkwɑ́:ləṭi/ ━形 **平等の** equal /í:kwəl/ ▶**平等**の権利 *equal* rights ‖ すべての人間は生まれながらにして**平等**であるとアメリカ合衆国の独立宣言書にうたわれている The U.S. Declaration of Independence proclaims that all men are created *equal*.

▶男女は性の差別なく**平等**に扱われるべきである Men and women should be treated *equally* without gender [sex(ual)] discrimination. ‖ 父は財産を

平等に分配するよう遺言書を書いた Our father made a will that stated that we should divide his fortune *evenly* [*equally*] among us. (➤ evenly は「均等に」).

☛ 悪平等, 不平等 (⇀見出語)

びょうにん 病人 a **sick person**; **the sick, the ill** (➤総称) ▶病人の世話をする take care of *a sick person*.

☛ 半病人 (⇀見出語)

ひょうのう 氷嚢 an **ice bag** [**pack**].

1**ひょうはく 漂白** **bleaching** ━動 **漂白する** **bleach** +目 ▶しみのついたワイシャツを漂白する *bleach* a stained shirt.

‖**漂白剤** bleach.

2**ひょうはく 漂泊** **wandering**(放浪); **drifting**(漂流) ━動 **漂泊する** **wander**; **drift**.

ひょうばん 評判 **1【世間の評価】** (a) **reputation**; **popularity** (人気) ▶渡辺さんは率直にものを言うと評判だ Mr. Watanabe has *a reputation* for being an outspoken man. ‖新潟の米は味がよいと評判だ Rice produced in Niigata *has a good reputation* because it tastes good. (➤ reputation は単に「世評」という意味なので,「よい評判」は good reputation とする) ‖あなた最近評判が悪いわよ You're getting a bad *reputation* these days.

▶その俳優の評判を著しく傷つけるおそれのある写真 an extremely *compromising* photo of that actor ‖目黒教授は学生の間で評判がいい[悪い] Professor Meguro *is popular* [*unpopular*] among the students.

▶市川先生は評判のいい歯科医だ Dr. Ichikawa is a *popular* dentist. ‖芸能人は世間の評判(＝人が何と言っているか)をとても気にする人たちだ People in show business care very much about *what people say* [*write*] *about them*. ‖贈賄事件であの代議士は評判を落とした The Dietman *lost popularity* [*got a bad name*] because of his involvement in the bribery case. ‖そのホテルはサービスがよいので評判です The hotel *is famous for* its good service. ‖彼女のご主人はすごいハンサムだという評判だ(＝みんながそう言っている) *Everybody says* her husband is very handsome.

2【うわさ】 ▶多田さんは今評判の漫画家だ Mr. Tada is today's most *talked-about* cartoonist. ‖角のパン屋のクロワッサンは, 今近所でちょっとした評判になっている The croissants from the bakery on the corner *are becoming popular* [*are causing* a little *sensation*] in the neighborhood.

ひょうひ 表皮 《解剖学》 **the epidermis**.

ひょうひょう 飄々 ▶ひょうひょうとした人物 a person *unconcerned about worldly matters* / a person *living aloof* [*apart*] *from the world*.

びょうぶ 屏風 a **byobu**

日本紹介 ✉ **屏風は木の枠に紙や布などをはった折り畳み式のついたてです. 仕切りや装飾品として使います** A *byobu* is a folding screen consisting of a wooden framework covered with paper or cloth. It is used as a room divider or an ornament.

びょうへき 病癖 a **bad habit**(悪い癖).

ひょうへん 豹変 ▶頼みを断ると彼の態度はひょう変した When I turned down his request, he *changed his tune abruptly*. (●「ことばづかい[態度, 意見]を急に変えた」と考えて訳す).

ひょうぼう 標榜する **advocate** +目 ▶自由主義を標榜する *advocate* liberalism.

ひょうほん 標本 a **specimen** /spésəmən/ (動植物の); a **sample**(統計・調査の) ▶ぼくは夏休みの宿題にカブトムシの標本を作った I prepared *specimens* of beetles for my summer vacation assignment.

‖**標本抽出** sampling.

ひょうめい 表明する **express** +目; **declare** +目 (宣言する); **announce** +目 (公表する) ▶野党指導者たちはその法案に反対の意向を表明した The opposition leaders *declared themselves* (to be) against the bill.

▶首相は辞意を表明した The Prime Minister *announced* his [her] intention to resign. ‖首相はその問題について所信を表明した The Prime Minister *expressed his* [*her*] *opinion* on the issue.

びょうめい 病名 **the name of a disease** ▶患者に病名を明かす tell a patient the *name of* his or her *disease*.

ひょうめん 表面 **1【外側の部分】** a **surface** /sə́ːrfɪs/ ▶地球の表面の4分の3は水である Three quarters of the earth's *surface* is water. ‖このテーブルは表面がぴかぴかに光っている This table has a shiny *surface*.

▶閣僚を巻き込んだ贈収賄疑惑が表面化した A suspicious case of bribery *has surfaced* that involves a Cabinet minister.

2【うわべ】 **the surface** ▶容疑者は表面上は冷静を装っていた The suspect pretended to be cool *on the surface*. ‖表面(＝外見)だけで人を判断すべきではない You should not judge people by their *appearances* only.

▶彼女は表面的には愛想がよい She is nice *on the surface*. / She is *superficially* nice.

‖**表面張力** 《物理学》 surface tension.

ひょうめんせき 表面積 **surface area** ▶この球の表面積を求めよ Calculate the *surface area* of this sphere.

びょうよみ 秒読み a **countdown** ▶ロケットの打ち上げは秒読みに入った The *countdown* has started for launching the rocket.

▶《慣用表現》2社の合併はいよいよ秒読みの段階に入った The merger of the two corporations is in *the countdown stage* [has entered *the final stage*].

ひょうりいったい 表裏一体 ▶医療費の増大と人口の高齢化は表裏一体の関係にある The increase in medical expenses and the aging of the population are *two sides of the same coin*. (➤「硬貨の裏表」の意).

びょうりがく 病理学 **pathology**.

ひょうりゅう 漂流 (a) **drift** ━動 **漂流する** **drift** ▶その船は航行不能になり1週間も漂流した The ship became incapable of sailing and *drifted* (for) as long as a week.

‖**漂流者** a castaway (島に漂着した).

びょうれき 病歴 one's **medical history** ▶彼女には大きな病歴はない She has no serious *medical history*. / She has had no serious *illness*(*es*).

ひょうろうぜめ 兵糧攻め ▶兵糧攻めにする *starve the enemy* (*into surrender*), *cut off the enemy's provisions*.

ひょうろん 評論 (a) **criticism** (批評); a **review** /rɪvjúː/ (新刊書・演劇などの批評); (a) **comment** (意見, 解説) ▶私はいつも映画評論を読んでから見る映画を決める I usually depend on the *reviews* to decide which movie(s) to see. ‖毎日曜日の朝彼はテレビで時事**評論**をしている He *comments* [*makes comments*] on current events on TV every Sunday morning.

‖**評論家** a critic (芸術関係の) ; an analyst (分析して解説する人) ; a commentator (スポーツ・時評などの) ; a reviewer(新刊書・演劇などの).

「評論家」のいろいろ **映画評論家** film critic ／**演劇評論家** drama critic ／**音楽評論家** music critic ／**教育評論家** education analyst ／**軍事評論家** military analyst ／**経済評論家** economic analyst ／**政治評論家** political commentator [analyst] ／**美術評論家** art critic ／**文芸評論家** literary critic ／**野球評論家** baseball commentator

ひよく 肥沃な **fertile** /fɜ́ːʳtl/, **rich** ▶この辺の土地は肥よくで米がよく取れる We have good rice crops around here because the soil is *fertile* [*rich*].

びよく 尾翼 a **tail**(➤ 後部機体も含む)

‖**垂直尾翼** a vertical tail ‖ **水平尾翼** a horizontal tail.

ひよけ 日除け a **sunshade** ; a **blind**(➤ しばしば複数形で),《米また》a (**window**) **shade** (窓の) ; an **awning** /ɔ́ːnɪŋ/ (店先の) ; a (**sun**)**visor** (車・帽子の)

▶よしずの**日除け** a reed *sunshade* ‖ **日除けを下ろす** pull down the *blinds* ／ lower the *shade* [*blinds*].

ひよこ a **chick**, a **chicken** ▶《比喩的》あいつはまだひよこ(＝青二才)だ He's still *a fledgling*. 《参考》英語の chicken は俗語で「憶病者」の意.

ひよこまめ ひよこ豆 a **chickpea**, a **garbanzo bean**.

ひょこひょこ ▶そのお年寄りはひょこひょこどこかに出かけて行って道に迷ってしまった The elderly man *toddled* off somewhere and got lost.

ぴょこん ▶小さな女の子は舞台に上がるとぴょこんとおじぎした When the little girl got up on the stage she gave a *quick* bow.

ひょっこり ▶長い間会わなかった友人にきのうひょっこり会った Yesterday I *ran into* a friend I hadn't seen for a long time.

▶なくしたとばかり思っていた財布がひょっこり出てきた The purse I thought I had lost *turned up* (*unexpectedly*).

ひょっとすると [したら] ▶ひょっとすると彼は世界記録を出すかもしれない He *may possibly* set a new world record. ‖ ひょっとしたらこの夏ハワイに行けるかもしれない I *just might* [*perhaps might*] go to Hawaii this summer. (➤ ともに実現性の薄い推測を表すが, just might には「普通なら思いもよらないことだが」と意外性のニュアンスがある).

ひょっとして ▶あの人はひょっとして森田君のお兄さんかもしれない He *might possibly* be Morita's brother. ‖ ひょっとして彼女の電話番号を知らない？Do you *happen to* know her telephone number ? ‖ ひょっとしてあなたは横井さんではありませんか Are you *by any chance* Mr. Yokoi ?

ひよどり 《鳥》a **brown-eared bulbul**.

ぴよぴよ ▶ヒヨコが箱の中でピヨピヨ鳴いている Chicks *are peeping* in the box.

ひより 日和 ▶いいおひよりですね What *a nice day* today ! ／It's *a lovely day*, isn't it ? ‖ きょうは絶好のピクニックびよりだ Today's *weather is ideal for* a picnic. ／It's *a perfect day for* a picnic.

ひよりみしゅぎ 日和見主義 **opportunism** /àːpəʳtjúːnɪzəm/ ▶彼は議論になると決まってひより見主義的態度をとる When it comes to an argument, he always *straddles* [*sits on*] *the fence*. (➤ straddle [sit on] the fence は「さくの上に座って[立って]成り行きを見る」が元の意味).

‖**ひより見主義者** an opportunist, 《インフォーマル》a fence-sitter.

ひょろながい ひょろ長い ▶今の高校生の中には足ばかりひょろ長くてひ弱そうなのもいる These days, some high school students have such *long* legs they look weak and *gangly*. (➤ gangly は「やせて背が高く手足の長い」) 《参考》「ひょろっとした背の高い人」を lanky person という.

ひょろひょろ ▶大沢さんは若い頃はひょろひょろだった Mr. Osawa used to be *lanky* [*weedy*] when he was young.

ひよわ ひ弱な **delicate** /délɪkət/ ; **weak** (弱い) ▶あの子は青白くてひ弱そうだ That child is pale and looks *delicate* (in health).

▶最近は甘やかされて**精神的にひ弱な**子が多い In recent years, many children are spoiled and *have weak characters*.

ぴょん ▶彼は塀の上から身軽にぴょんと飛び降りた He sprang *nimbly* down from the top of the fence. ‖ 彼女は水たまりをぴょんと跳び越えた She leaped [leapt] over the pool *lightly*.

ひょんな ▶彼女とはひょんなことから親しくなった I made friends with her *in a strange way* [*by chance*]. ‖ きのう旧友の１人とひょんな所で出会った I met an old friend of mine *where I* (*had*) *least expected to*. (➤「予想もしなかった所で」の意).

ぴょんぴょん ▶しのぶはうれしそうにぴょんぴょん跳んで帰った Shinobu went home *skipping* with joy. ‖ ウサギが庭でぴょんぴょんはね回っている A rabbit is *hopping around* the yard.

ピョンヤン 平壌 **Pyongyang** /pjʌ̀njáːŋ/ (朝鮮民主主義人民共和国の首都).

ひら 平 ▶入社して10年たっても私はまだ平だ I'm still *a member of the rank and file*, though I joined this company ten years ago. ‖ あいつはただの平だよ He's just *a peon*. (➤ peon /píːən/ は「単純労働者」ということで, 通例軽蔑的に, またはおどけて用いる) ‖ 彼はまだ**平社員**だ He is still *a rank-and-file* [*an ordinary*] *employee*.

びら a **flier**(広告・宣伝用のちらし) ; a **leaflet**(広告・宣伝・案内用の折り込み) ; a **poster**, 《主に英》a **bill**(はり紙) →ちらし ▶壁にびらをはる put up *a poster* on the wall.

ひらあやまり 平謝り ▶よその塀に車をぶつけたら, おっかないおやじが出てきたので**平謝りに謝った** When I drove my car into someone's fence, a tough-looking guy came out and *all I could do was* (*to*) *apologize profusely* [*repeatedly*].

ひらい 飛来 ▶ことしも出水にナベヅルが飛来した Hooded cranes *came flying* to Izumi again this year.

ひらいしん 避雷針 a **lightning rod** [《英》**conductor**].

ひらおよぎ 平泳ぎ **the breaststroke** ▶平泳ぎで泳ぐ do [swim] *the breaststroke* (➤「平泳ぎの泳者」は a breaststroker).

ひらがな 平仮名 ***hiragana*** ; a ***hiragana*** **letter** (１文字)

日本紹介 ✉ **ひらがなは漢字をくずしてできた表音文字です. 日本語は漢字と, ひらがな, カタカナ**

の２種類のかな文字を組み合わせて表記します *Hiragana* is a set of phonograms developed from cursive *kanji* (Chinese characters). Japanese is written using a combination of *hiragana* and *katakana* letters together with *kanji*.
▶私の名の「あかり」はひらがなで書きます My name 'Akari' is written in *hiragana*.

ピラカンサ 《植物》 a **pyracantha** /pàɪərəkǽnθə/, a **firethorn**.

ひらき 開き a **gap** (大きな隔り) ; (a) **difference** (差)
▶労使の見解には相当の**開き**がある There is a wide *gap* between the views of management and labor. ‖あの２人の投手は実力の**開き**はほとんどない There's very little *difference* in ability between those two pitchers.
‖**アジの開き** a horse mackerel cut open and dried.

ひらきど 開き戸 a **hinged door**.

ひらきなおる 開き直る ▶スランプに陥ったときは，いつまでも悩んでいないで**開き直る**と意外に早く脱出できるものだ Don't worry too much about it when you fall into a slump. If you *take a "so-what" attitude* instead, you'll snap out of it in no time. (➤ "so-what" attitude は「だから何だと言うんだという態度」).
▶電車の中で痴漢におしりをさわられたので抗議すると，その男は**開き直った** When I protested when a groper touched my bottom on the train, the man *turned defiant* [*assumed a defiant attitude*].

ひらく 開く

訳語メニュー
あける →open **1**, **3**
広げる →open **1**, **2**
始める →open **5**
催す →hold, have **6**

1【閉じていたものをあける】**open** +目 ; **unfold** +目 (たたんだものを広げる) →**あける** ▶新聞を**開く** *unfold* [*open*] a newspaper ‖ドアが**開**いた The door *opened*. ‖ドアを**開き**なさい *Open* the door. ‖ドアが**開**かない The door *won't open*. ‖ドアが**開**いたままになっている The door has *been left open*. ‖本の55ページを**開き**なさい *Open* your book to [《英》at] page 55. ‖まず足を少し**開**いて立ってください First, stand with your legs slightly *apart*.
▶ファイル[フォルダ]を**開く** *open* a file [folder] ‖作成したプログラムをインストールしていないのでファイルが**開**けない I can't *open* the file because I haven't installed the program it was created with.

2【全体に大きくする】**open** (+目) ▶つぼみがもうすぐ**開き**そうだ The buds are about to *open* [*unfold*]. (➤後者は「ほころぶ」に近い) ‖にわか雨でスタンドには傘の花が**開**いた When it suddenly began to rain, umbrellas *opened* on the stands like colorful flowers. ‖爆弾処理班は慎重にその小包を**開**いた The bomb disposal squad gingerly *opened* the parcel.

3【目・口・心を】**open** +目 ▶彼は口を**開**けば自慢話になる When he *opens* his mouth, it's only to boast. ‖閉じていた目を**開く**とそこには美しいお花畑が広がっていた When I *opened* my closed eyes, there was a beautiful field of flowers spread out before me.
▶《比喩的》彼女の意見に私は目を**開**かれた Her opinions *opened* my eyes.

4【自由に出入りできる】▶教会の扉は悩める人のためにいつでも**開**かれています Church doors are always *open* for those in need.

5【始める】**open** (+目) ▶店は午前９時に**開き**ます The store *opens* at 9 a.m. ‖今度駅前にブティックを**開き**ました We *opened* a boutique in front of the train station. ‖明海銀行に口座を**開く**つもりだ I'm going to *open* an account with Meikai Bank.

6【催す】**hold** +目, **have** +目, **give** +目 ▶会合を**開く** *hold* [*have*] a meeting ‖私たちは公会堂で音楽会を**開く**予定です We plan to *hold* [*give*] a concert at the town hall. (➤ hold は主催者・運営者が, give は演奏者・歌手などが用いる語) ‖次の土曜日にパーティーを**開き**ます We are going to *give* [*throw*] a party next Saturday. (「(改まらない)パーティーを催す」の意の場合は throw a party を，また改まったパーティーのニュアンスを出したいときには hold a party をそれぞれ用いるとよい).
▶この展覧会は東京でしか**開**かれない This exhibition will *open* only in Tokyo.

7【切り開く】▶北海道の開拓民は荒れ地を**開**いていった The settlers *opened up* the wasteland in Hokkaido. ‖千利休は茶道の流派を**開**いた Sen-no-Rikyu *started* [*created* / *founded*] a school of the tea ceremony. ‖釈迦は菩提樹(ぼだいじゅ)の下で悟りを**開**いた Sakyamuni *attained enlightenment* [*became enlightened*] under a linden tree.

8【離れる】▶先頭ランナーとあとの走者との差はどんどん**開**いた The distance between the front runner and the others *became wider and wider*. ‖西武とソフトバンクのゲーム差は５に**開**いた The Lions *widened* their lead over the Hawks to 5 games. ‖その試合は点差の**開**いた(＝一方的な)ゲームだった It was a *one-sided* game.
▶いちばん上の兄と私は年が**開**いている The age difference between my oldest brother and me is *large* [*wide*]. / My oldest brother and I are *far apart* in age.

ひらける 開ける **1**【展開する】**spread out** ▶すばらしい景色が眼下に**開**けた A panoramic view *spread out* below us. (➤ spread は無変化動詞) ‖南側の大木を切ったら急に視界が**開**けた When we cut down the big tree on the south side of the house, the view suddenly *expanded*.
2【開化する】**become civilized** ; **develop** (発展する) ▶その国には早くから文明が**開**けていた That country has *been civilized* since ancient times. ‖私たちの村も最近になって少しずつ**開**けてきた Our village *is* slowly *developing* these days.
3【運が】▶ことしになってから運が**開**けてきたようだ Since the beginning of the year, *my luck has changed for the better* [*fortune has begun to smile on me*].

ひらたい 平たい **flat** ▶平たいお皿 a *flat* plate.
▶平たく言えば語学を学ぶことは文化を学ぶことだ *In plain words* [*To put it plainly*], to study a language is to study culture.

ひらてうち 平手打ち a **slap** ▶彼女は痴漢を平手打ちにした She *slapped* the groper *in the face* [*on the cheek*].

ピラニア 《魚》 a **piranha** /pərɑ́ːnə/.

ひらひら ▶桜の花びらがどこからかひらひら飛んできた The cherry blossom petals *fluttered down* from somewhere or other.

ピラフ **pilaf(f)**
‖カレーピラフ pilaf with curry ‖エビピラフ shrimp pilaf.

ひらべったい 平べったい **flat** ▶平べったい魚 a *flat* fish (➤ flatfish と1語につづるとヒラメやカレイの類を指す) ‖平べったい顔 a *flat* face.

ピラミッド a **pyramid** /pírəmɪd/ ▶ピラミッド型の建物 a *pyramidal* building.

ひらめ 平目 《魚》a **flatfish**, a **flounder** (➤ ともに「カレイ」も指す) ; a **sole** (シタビラメ).

ひらめき 閃き a **spark**, a **flash** (➤ それぞれ「火花」「閃光」が原義) ▶彼はその詩で天才的なひらめきを見せた He showed *a spark* [*a flash*] of genius in that poem.

ひらめく 閃く **flash** ▶稲妻が夜空にひらめいた Lightning *flashed* across the night sky. ‖すばらしいアイディアがケンの頭にひらめいた A brilliant idea *flashed* into [through] Ken's mind.

ひらや 平屋 a **house of one story** ; a **one-storied** [**one-story**] **house** (➤ 《英》では storey, storeyed とつづる).

ひらり ▶彼はスポーツカーにひらりと飛び乗った He *sprang* [*lightly* jumped] into his sports car. (● lightly jumped ... は日本語的発想に基づく訳で, 英語では訳例のように動詞1語で表すのがふつう).

びり **the bottom, the last** ▶私は中学時代いつもクラスでびりだった When I was a junior high school student, I was always at *the bottom* [*foot*] of my class. ‖うちの息子は駆けっこでびり(から2番目)だった My son came in (*second to*) *last* in the race.

ピリオド 《米》a **period** /píəriəd/, 《英》a **full stop** ▶文の最後にはピリオドを打つのを忘れないように Don't forget to put [place] *a period* at the end of a sentence.
▶《比喩的》ついに事件の捜査にピリオドが打たれた At last the investigation of the case *came to an end*. →終止符.

ひりき 非力 ▶私は全くの非力ですから, お役には立てないと思います I'm completely *powerless*, so I don't think I'll be able to help you.

ひりつ 比率 (a) **ratio** /réɪʃou/, (a) **percentage** /pəˈséntɪdʒ/ ▶わが校は2対1の比率で女子が多い At our school, the *ratio* of girl students to boy students is 2 to 1. (● 日本語では「男子学生に対して女子学生が」と言わなくても意味は通じるが, 英語では必ず to boy students と言わなくてはならない) ‖昔は外で働く女性の比率はわずかなものだった In the past, only a small *percentage* of women had jobs outside the home.

ぴりっと ▶ぴりっと辛いカレー a (*spicy*) *hot* curry ‖ぴりっと肌を刺すように寒い There is a *cutting* [*keen*] chill in the air. ‖あの男はぴりっとしたところがない He has no *backbone*.

ひりひり ▶日に焼けたところがひりひりする My sunburn *stings* [*hurts*]. ‖切ったところがひりひりする The cut *smarts*. (➤ smart は切り傷などが「ずきずきする」) ‖喉がひりひりするよ. かぜをひいたのかなあ I have a *sore* throat. I might have caught a cold.

びりびり ▶一生懸命かいた絵を小さい弟にびりびりに破られた The picture I had so painstakingly drawn *was ripped to shreds* by my little brother.
▶電気の通っている柵にさわったらびりびりっときた I *got an electric shock* when I touched the electric fence.

ぴりぴり ▶トウガラシをもろにかんだので舌がぴりぴりする I bit down on a red pepper so my tongue *is burning*.
▶彼女は今ぴりぴりしているから近づかないほうがいいよ She *is* really *tense* [Her *nerves are on edge*] right now so you'd better not approach her.

ビリヤード **billiards** /bíljəʳdz/ ; **pool** (プールゲーム) ▶ビリヤードをする play *billiards*.
‖ビリヤード室[台] a billiard room [table].

びりゅうし 微粒子 a **minute** /maɪnjúːt/ **particle**.

ひりょう 肥料 (a) **fertilizer** ; **manure** /mənjóəʳ/ (肥やし) ; **compost** (たい肥) ▶農夫は土を耕してから肥料をまいた The farmhand *fertilized* [*spread manure*] over the soil after plowing.
‖化学肥料 (chemical) fertilizer ‖人工[合成]肥料 an artificial [a synthetic] fertilizer ‖有機肥料 an organic fertilizer.

びりょう 微量 a **very small amount** 《of》 ▶この薬には微量の睡眠薬が含まれています This medicine contains *a very small amount of* sleeping medication.

びりょく 微力 ▶まことに微力ながら最善を尽くす所存です *Though I fear my best efforts will accomplish little* [*will be of little avail*], I will do my best. (● 英語では I will do my best. とだけ言うほうがふつう).

[1]**ひる 昼** **1【昼間】the daytime, day** ▶昼が伸びて[短くなって]きた *The days* are getting longer [shorter]. ‖昼の間は眠り, 夜活動する動物も多い There are many animals that sleep *during the daytime* and become active after dark. ‖彼らは昼も夜も働いて金を貯めた They worked hard *day and night* and saved money. →昼間.
2【正午】noon, midday ▶昼時に at *noon* ; at *lunchtime* (昼食時) ‖昼日中から酔っ払う get drunk *in broad daylight* ‖今ちょうどお昼だ It's *twelve noon* now. (➤ noon には「ほぼ, だいたい」というニュアンスがあるので「ちょうど」と言いたいときには twelve をつける) ‖《アナウンサー》お昼のニュースの時間です It is time for the (*twelve*) *noon* news. ‖お昼になったから食事に行こう It's *noon*. Let's go for lunch. ‖昼までにはこの仕事を終えます I'll finish this work *by noon*. ‖昼から(＝午後に)出かけます I'm going out *in the afternoon*.
3【昼食】lunch ▶そろそろお昼にしようか How about having *lunch*? ／Isn't it about time for *lunch*?
☞ 昼休み (→見出語)

[2]**ひる 蛭** 《動物》a **leech**.

ビル a **building** ▶10階建てのビル a ten-story *building* ‖明治通りにはビルが立ち並んでいる Meiji Avenue is lined with *buildings*.
▶新宿には高層ビルがたくさんある There are many *high-rises* in Shinjuku.

> **危ないカタカナ語✹ビル**
> **1**「ビル」は「ビルディング」(building)の日本式略語. 日本では鉄筋コンクリート造りの建物に限って「ビル」ということばを使う傾向があるが, 英語の building は単に「建物」の意味.
> **2**「ボディービル」は body building の日本式短縮形だが, 「マネービル」はボディービルをもじって作った和製語で, moneymaking がこれに当たる.

‖ビル街 a street lined with large buildings.

ピル **the pill, the Pill** ▶ピルを飲む take *the pill* ‖彼女はピルを服用している She is *on the pill*.

ひ

ひるい 比類 ▶セリーヌ・ディオンの高音の美しさは**比類がない** The beauty of Celine Dion's high tones is *beyond compare*. ‖ **比類のない**壮麗な邸宅 a *one-of-a-kind* grand mansion.

ひるがえす 翻す **wave** +㊐(揺らす); **flutter** +㊐(布などをはためかせる); **overturn** +㊐(くつがえす)
▶旗を**ひるがえす** *wave* [*flutter*] a flag ‖ バットマンはマントを**ひるがえして**走り去った Batman ran off, *spreading* his cloak.
▶その科学者は自説を**ひるがえした** The scientist *overturned* his own theory. ‖ 証人は前言を**ひるがえした**(=正反対のことを言った) The witness *said the exact opposite of* what he had (first) testified. / The witness *contradicted* his original testimony.

ひるがえる 翻る **wave**(揺れる); **flutter** (はためく)
▶校旗が風に[ポールに]**翻っている** Our school flag *is waving* [*fluttering* / *flying*] in the wind [on the flagpole].
▶**翻って考えると** *upon reconsideration* / *on second thought*.

ヒルガオ 《植物》a **false bindweed.**

ひるさがり 昼下がり ▶夏の**昼下がり**, 聞こえるのはセミの鳴き声だけだ It is *early* on a summer *afternoon*, and nothing can be heard but the chirping of cicadas.

ひるね 昼寝 a **nap**, a **siesta** (➤ 後者はスペインなどで日中の暑い盛りにとる昼寝をいうが, 英語で「昼寝」をおどけて言う場合によく用いる) ▶祖父は午後は必ず**昼寝をする** My grandfather *takes* [*has*] *a nap* every afternoon.

ひるま 昼間 **the daytime, day** ▶**昼間**の暑さがうそのように涼しくなってきた The heat of *the daytime* has gone like magic and it has gotten very cool. ‖ ベビーシッターのおかげで彼女は**昼間**働ける Thanks to the babysitter, she can work *during the day*. ‖ 彼女は**昼間**は働いて夜は学校に通っている She works *by day* and goes to school by night. (➤ by は「…の間に」の意).

ひるむ 怯む **flinch** ▶銀行員は強盗のナイフを見ても**ひるま**なかった The bank teller didn't *flinch* at the sight of a knife in the robber's hand.

ひるめし 昼飯 (a) **lunch.** ⇀昼食 ▶**昼飯**食べた? Have you had *lunch* yet?

ひるやすみ 昼休み a **lunch break** [**hour**] ▶**昼休み**にバレーボールをしようよ Let's play volleyball during (*the*) *lunch hour*. ‖ 戸田は**昼休み**で(食事をしに)外へ出ております Toda is *out for lunch*.
✉ **昼休みは友だちとおしゃべりをして過ごします** I talk with my friends during (*the*) *lunch break* [*noon recess*]. ➤ lunch break は中学生以上の場合に用い, noon recess は小学生の場合に用いる.

ひれ 鰭 a **fin** ‖ **胸[背 / 尾]びれ** a pectoral [dorsal / caudal] fin.

ヒレ a **fillet** /fílɪt ‖ fɪléɪ/ (ヒレ肉) (➤《米》では filet ともつづる)
‖ **ヒレステーキ** (a) fillet steak.

ひれい 比例 **proportion** ▶トイレットペーパーの消費量は家族の人数に**比例する** The consumption of toilet paper *is in proportion to* the number of family members. ‖ XはYに**正[反]比例する** X *is directly* [*inversely*] *proportional to* Y.
‖ **比例式** a proportion ‖ **比例代表(選挙)** a proportional representative (election).

☛ 逆比例, 正比例, 反比例 (⇀見出語)

ひれつ 卑劣な **mean**; **dirty** (汚い); **contemptible** /kəntémptəbəl/ (軽蔑すべき); **despicable**(卑しむべき)
▶**卑劣な**手 a *dirty* trick ‖ 陰口を言うなんて**卑劣だ** It's *contemptible* to say bad things about people behind their backs [to backbite]. ‖ 試験でカンニングするのは**卑劣な**行為だ Cheating on exams is a *despicable* thing to do.

ひれふす ひれ伏す **prostrate** oneself ▶イスラム教徒はメッカの方角に**ひれ伏して**祈りをささげる When Muslims pray, they *prostrate themselves* in the direction of Mecca. ‖ 彼は祭壇の前に**ひれ伏した** He *lay prostrate* before the altar. (➤この prostrate は形容詞).

ひれん 悲恋 (a) **tragic love** ▶彼女の恋は**悲恋だった** Hers was *a tragic love*.

ひろい 広い **1【場所などが】large, big; wide, broad**

> **語法** (1)「面積が広い」というときは **large**, またはややインフォーマルな **big** を用いる. したがって,「広い部屋」は large room となる. ⇀**せまい**.
> (2)「幅が広い」というときは wide や broad を用いる. **wide** は端から端までの距離に, **broad** は表面の広がりに重点があるが, 区別なく用いられることも多い.

▶**広い**部屋[家] a *large* room [house] ‖ **広い**川 a *wide* [*broad*] river ‖ きみの大学のキャンパスは**広いなあ** The campus of your college is *large*. ‖ 海は**広い**な, 大きいな The ocean is so *wide* and so big. ‖ 長江は実に**広い** The Yangtze River is very *wide*. ‖ 彼は肩幅[額]が**広い** He is *broad*-shouldered [has a *broad* forehead].
▶門を**広く**開けなさい Open the gate *wide*. ‖ がらくたを片づけたら部屋がぐんと**広くなった** Once the junk was cleared away, the room looked quite *spacious* [*large*].

2【範囲が】wide, broad; extensive(広範囲の) ▶趣味の**広い**人 a person of *wide* interests ‖ 島田氏は政治的視野が**広い** Mr. Shimada has a *broad* outlook on politics. ‖ 彼は読書範囲が**広い** He reads *widely* on many subjects. ‖ 野村さんは野球について**広い**知識を持っている Mr. Nomura has an *extensive* [*a wide*] knowledge of baseball. / Mr. Nomura knows *a lot* about baseball. (➤ knows ... very well としないこと. ⇀**知る**) ‖ 黒澤明の名は**広く**世界に知られている The name of Kurosawa Akira is known *worldwide*. ‖ 彼女は各界の人と**広く付き合っている** She *knows a lot of people* in many different fields.

3【心が】 ▶心の**広い**人 a *broad-minded* [*large-hearted* / *generous*] person (➤ generous は「寛大な」).

ひろいあげる 拾い上げる **pick up.**

ヒロイズム **heroism.**

ひろいぬし 拾い主 **the finder** ▶**拾い主**が私の財布を警察に届けてくれた *The person who found* my wallet turned it in to the police.

ひろいもの 拾い物 a **found article**(拾得物) ▶帰宅の途中で**拾い物をした** I *found* [*picked up*] *something on the street* on my way home.
▶《比喩的》すってんてんにならなかっただけでも**拾い物だよ**(=運がよかったと思いなさい) You should *count yourself lucky* not to have gone broke. ‖ 広島は坂本のエラーで**拾い物**の2点を加えた The Carp added

two runs as *a windfall* on Sakamoto's error. (➤ windfall は「たなぼた」).

ひろいよみ 拾い読みする **browse** /braʊz/ 《through》 ▶新聞をあちこち拾い読みする *read at random* from the newspaper ／*read* the newspaper *at random* ‖ 辞書を拾い読みして楽しむ enjoy *browsing through* dictionaries.

ヒロイン a **heroine** /hérouɪn/ ▶彼女はまるで小説のヒロインにでもなったようなつもりでいる She thinks of herself as *a heroine* in a novel.

[1]**ひろう 疲労** **fatigue** /fətíːg/, **exhaustion** /ɪgzɔ́ːstʃən/ (➤ ともに極度に疲れることをいうが前者が上品な語)；**tiredness** (体力・忍耐力がなくなること) ▶精神的疲労 mental *fatigue* [*exhaustion*] ‖ 肉体的疲労 physical *fatigue* [*exhaustion*] ‖ 一晩ぐっすり眠ると疲労がとれる A good night's sleep will help you get over your *tiredness*.
▶兄は父の葬儀のあとも少しも疲労の色を見せなかったが，私は疲労困ぱいした My brother showed no *signs* [*traces*] *of fatigue* after my father's funeral, but I was *totally exhausted*.

[2]**ひろう 披露** **introduction** (紹介)；**announcement** (発表) **一動 披露する** **introduce** +目，**announce** +目 ▶小売業者に新製品を披露する *introduce* a new product to the retailers ‖ 婚約を披露する *announce* one's engagement ‖ はなはだせん越ですが国の民謡をご披露いたします Ladies and gentlemen, *please allow me to perform* a folk song from the area where I was born. ‖ それでは祝電の一部を披露させていただきます I will now *read* aloud some congratulatory telegrams. ‖ 《結婚式で》お式のあとに披露宴が行われます *A reception* will be held after the ceremony.
‖ **結婚披露宴** a wedding reception.

[3]**ひろう 拾う** **pick up** (拾い上げる)；**find** +目 (見つける) ▶ごみを拾う *pick up* trash ‖ 海岸で貝を拾う *pick up* [*gather*] shells on the seashore (➤ gather は「集める」) ‖ 少年は小石を拾い上げて池に投げた The boy *picked up* a pebble and threw it into the pond. ‖ 私は道端で千円札を拾った I *found* a thousand-yen bill on the roadside.
▶《比喩的》タクシーを拾う *take* [*get*] a taxi ‖ タクシーはどこで拾えますか Where can I *get* a taxi? ‖ 《車で》きみの家に寄って拾ってやるよ I'll come to your home and *pick* you *up*. (➤ 逆に「降ろす」は drop off) ‖ 相手投手の暴投で決勝点をあげ，ぼくらは勝ちを拾った Thanks to the pitcher's wild throw, we scored the deciding run and *won the game*. ‖ **対話**「その子猫どうしたの」「道で拾った」"What's with the kitten?" "I *found* it on the road."

ビロード **velvet** /vélvɪt/ ▶ビロードのジャケット a *velvet* jacket ‖ ビロードのような光沢 a *velvety* luster.

ひろがり 広がり an **expanse** ▶宇宙の広大な広がり the *vastness* [*vast expanse*] of the universe ‖ インフルエンザの広がりを食い止める check the *spread* of the flu.

ひろがる 広がる **1【周囲に伸びる】** **spread**；**widen** (幅が) ▶眼下には太平洋が広がっていた The Pacific Ocean *spread* (*out*) below us [below our eyes]. (➤ spread は無変化動詞) ‖ 川幅はその地点で広がっている The river *widens* at that point. ‖ 平原ははるか地平線にまで広がって(＝伸びて)いた The plains *extended* [*stretched*] as far as the horizon.
2【うわさなどが】 **spread** ▶世界に広がる反原発の動き the anti-nuclear power movement that *is spreading* worldwide ‖ その汚職のうわさは町中に広がった The rumor of the bribery scandal *spread* through the town.

ひろくする 広くする **widen** +目 (幅を)；**enlarge** +目 (面積を) ▶川[道]を広くする *widen* a river [a road] ‖ 店[庭]を広くする *enlarge* a store [a garden].

ひろげる 広げる **spread** +目；**open** +目 (開く)；**widen** +目，**broaden** +目 (幅を；後者は広々とした広がりを強調する)；**unfold** +目 (折ったりたたんだりしたものを)；**extend** +目 (範囲・長さなどを) ▶地図を広げる *open* [*spread* (*out*) ／*unfold*] a map ‖ 毛布を広げる *unfold* [*spread*] a blanket ‖ 公園の区域を海まで広げる *extend* the boundaries of a park to the sea ‖ 道幅を広げる *widen* a road ‖ ツルは翼を広げて飛び去った The crane *spread* its wings and flew away. (➤ spread は無変化動詞) ‖ 子供たちはおもちゃを部屋いっぱいに広げた The kids *scattered* toys all over the room.
▶彼女は包みを広げた(＝開けた) She *unwrapped* [*opened*] the package. ‖ 足を広げて! *Spread* your legs (*apart*)! ‖ 彼は両手を広げてその男の行く手をさえぎった He blocked the man's way by *extending* his arms.
▶父は去年から商売の手を広げている My father has been *expanding* [*growing*] his business since last year. ‖ 旅は人の心を広げるとよく言う They say that travel *broadens* the mind.

ひろさ 広さ (an) **area** /éəriə/ (面積)；**extent** (広がり)；(a) **width** (幅) ▶庭の広さは100平方メートルほどです The garden is about 100 square meters in *area*. ／The *area* of the garden is about 100 square meters. ‖ ぼくはその農場の広さに驚いた I was astonished at the *extent* [*size*] of the farm. ‖ この道路の広さはどのくらいですか How *wide* is this road? ‖ **対話**「このトウモロコシ畑の広さはどのくらいですか」「東京ドームの約 2 倍です」"*How large* is this cornfield?" "About twice the size of Tokyo Dome."

ピロシキ **pirozhki, piroshki** /pɪrɔ́ːʃki/.

ひろば 広場 a **square**, a **plaza** (都市の)；an **open space**, a **vacant lot** (空き地) ▶広場の噴水の前で 3 時ね We're going to meet at three in front of the fountain at the *square*, right?

ひろびろ 広々 ▶広々とした庭 a *spacious* garden ‖ 広々とした牧場に牛が群れているのが見える We (can) see herds of cows in the *open* meadow.

ひろま 広間 a **hall** ▶客たちを広間に通す usher guests into *a hall*.

ひろまる 広まる **spread**；**go around** (うわさが；主に進行形で)
▶彼女の名声は国中に広まった Her fame *spread* through the country. ‖ おかしなうわさが広まっている *There's a* strange *rumor going around*. ‖ 町長が辞職するといううわさが広まっている *There's a rumor* that the mayor is going to resign.
▶反原発運動が全国的に広まっている The movement against nuclear power *has been gaining ground* [*making headway*] throughout the nation. (➤ gain ground は「(運動・理論などが) 支持を得て広まる」, make headway は「前進する」の意).

ひろめる 広める **spread** +目 ▶そんなひどいうわさを広めたのは彼だ He is the one who *spread* [*put about*] that vicious rumor. (➤ put about はインフォーマル

な言い方) ‖ 法然はこの地方に仏教を広めた Honen *propagated* Buddhism in this district. (➤ propagate は「(思想などを)宣伝する」).

ピロリきん ピロリ菌《医学》**(Helicobacter) pylori** /paɪlóʊraɪ/.

ひろんりてき 非論理的な illogical ▶非論理的な考え an *illogical* idea.

ひわ 秘話 an **unknown episode** [**story**]
▶二人の結婚秘話 *an unknown episode* in their marriage.

1**びわ 枇杷**《植物》a **loquat** /lóʊkwɑːt/.

2**びわ 琵琶**《楽器》a ***biwa*** ; a **Japanese lute.**

ひわい 卑猥な obscene /əbsíːn/ (わいせつな) ; **dirty** (みだらな) ▶卑わいな写真[ことば] an *obscene* picture [expression] ‖ 子供の前で卑わいな話をするな Don't tell *dirty* stories in front of children.

ひわり 日割り ▶あなたの給料は日割り計算です Your pay is *calculated by the day*.

ひん 品 elegance (身につけた上品さ) ; **grace** (天性の優美さ) ; **dignity** (気高さ) ; **refinement** (洗練)
▶彼女はどことなく品がある There is something *elegant* [*refined*] about her. ‖ 雅子さんは実に品があるね Masako has real *class*. (➤ class は「気品」の意のインフォーマルな語) ／Masako's really *classy*, isn't she?
▶そんな品のないことばを使うもんじゃないわよ You shouldn't use such *vulgar* [*rude*] language. (➤ vulgar は「野卑な, 低俗な」, rude は「失礼な」).

1**びん 瓶** a (**glass**) **bottle** ; a **jar** (広口の) ▶しょうゆ[ビール]瓶 a soy-sauce [beer] *bottle* ‖ 瓶詰めのジャム *a jar of* jam ‖ 私は牛乳を1日1瓶[2瓶]飲む I drink *a bottle* [*two bottles*] of milk a day.

2**びん 便 1**【配達便】a **delivery van** [**truck**] (配送車) ▶ちょうどそちらへ行く便があるのでご注文の品をそれに載せます There happens to be *a delivery van* [*truck*] going out to your area. So we'll put your order on that truck.
2【交通】a **flight** (飛行機の) ; (a) **service** (バス・電車などの運行) ▶ **対話**「私がお出迎えにあがりましょう. 何便ですか」「JALの501便です」"I'll meet you at the airport. What's your *flight* number?" "JAL *flight* 501." ‖ その温泉へはバスの便があります *Bus service* is available to the hot spring.

3**びん 鬢 the hair at the temples.**

1**ピン** a **pin** ▶この写真を壁にピンで留めてください Could you *pin up* this photo on the wall? ‖ 告示はドアにピンで留めてあった The notice was fastened to the door with *a pin*. ／The notice was pinned up on the door.

2**ピン** ▶《慣用表現》医者にもピンからキリまである There are *doctors and* (there are) *doctors*. ／There are *all kinds of* doctors. (➤ 第1文は「良い医者もいれば良くない医者もいる」のニュアンスで, 第2文は「医者にもいろいろある」という意味の無色の表現).

ひんい 品位 dignity (気高さ, 尊厳) ; **class** (品の良さ)
▶そんなことをすると品位が下がるよ Such conduct will degrade your *dignity*. ‖ お客さまの前では品位を保ちなさい Behave (yourself) with *class and dignity* in the presence of our guests.

ひんかく 品格 dignity (気高さ・尊厳) ; **grace** (天性の優美さ) ▶会議で重役を罵倒するなんて, 社長としての品格も何もあったものではない Abusing one of the executives at a meeting put his [her] *dignity* as a company president in question. ‖ あの横綱の行動は品格に欠ける That yokozuna's behavior lacks *dignity*.

びんかん 敏感な sensitive ▶敏感な鼻[耳] a *sensitive* nose [ear] ‖ この植物は日光に敏感だ This plant is *sensitive* to sunlight. ‖ 彼女はにおいに対して異常なほど敏感だ She is *hypersensitive* to smell. (➤問題と考える場合) ／She is *extraordinarily sensitive* to smell. (➤ほめる場合) ‖ 若者は流行に敏感な傾向がある Young people tend to be *fashion-conscious*. (➤ -conscious は「…を意識した」. 名詞の前以外はハイフンを省くこともある) ‖ 娘は今, 敏感な年頃です My daughter is now at a *vulnerable* age. (➤ vulnerable /vʌ́lnərəbəl/ は「(人・感情などが)傷つきやすい」).

ひんきゃく 賓客 a **guest of honor.**

ひんく 貧苦 poverty.

ピンク pink ▶ピンクのブラウス a *pink* blouse ‖ ピンク色のほお *rosy* cheeks ‖ ピンクがかった色 a *pinkish* color
‖**ピンク映画** a porno movie, an adult [X-rated] film.

ひんけつ 貧血《医学》**anemia** /əníːmiə/ (貧血症) ━ 形 **貧血の anemic** /əníːmɪk/ ▶彼女は貧血のたちでよくめまいを起こす She often feels dizzy because she is *anemic*. ‖ きのう歯科医院で貧血を起こしてしまった (=気を失った) I *fainted* at the dentist's yesterday.

ビンゴ bingo /bíŋgoʊ/.

ひんこう 品行 conduct /kɑ́ːndʌkt/ (行い) ; **behavior** (行儀) ▶彼は品行が悪い[品行方正だ] He is a man of *loose morals* [*good conduct*].

ひんこん 貧困 poverty
▶世界には貧困にあえぐ大勢の人がいる There are a lot of people in the world living in *extreme poverty*. ‖ 石川啄木は貧困のうちに死んだ Ishikawa Takuboku died *in poverty*.
▶きみは発想が貧困だね You *don't come up with many creative ideas*, do you? ／You'*re lacking in* creative [original] ideas.
‖**貧困者** the poor (➤総称) ; a poor person (1人).

1**ひんし 瀕死の dying** (死にかかった)
▶ひん死の病人 a *dying* patient ‖ 少女はダンプカーにはねられてひん死の重傷を負った The little girl received *fatal* injuries [was *fatally* injured] when she was hit by a dump truck. (➤ fatal は「致命的な」の意. したがって, 英文は「結局死んだ」のニュアンス).

2**ひんし 品詞**《文法》a **part of speech**
▶英語の8品詞 the eight *parts of speech* in English.

ひんしつ 品質 quality /kwɑ́ːləṭi/
▶品質の良い[悪い]トイレットペーパー toilet paper of good [poor] *quality* ‖ 高い品質を維持する maintain *high quality*.
▶日本製品は品質の点で外国の製品よりすぐれたものも多い Many Japanese products are superior in *quality* to [are of better *quality* than] foreign-made ones. ‖《表示》品質保証 Quality Guaranteed /gæ̀rəntíːd/
‖**品質管理** quality control (略 QC).

ひんじゃく 貧弱な poor, meager (➤後者は堅い語で, 質・量などが一定の水準に達していないことを強調する) ▶貧弱な体格の人 a person of *poor* build ‖ 貧弱な胸 a *flat* chest (➤「あばら骨の見えるような胸」の意) ‖ そのパーティーで出た食事は実に貧弱だった The food served at that party was very *poor* [*meager*]. ‖ 彼の講義は中身が貧弱だ His lectures *don't have* *much real content.*

ひんしゅ 品種 a **breed**; a **variety** (変種); a **species** /spíːʃiːz/ (分類上の種) ▶コシヒカリは最も人気のある米の品種の１つだ Koshihikari is one of the most popular *breeds* of rice.

▶バラにはたくさんの品種がある There are many *varieties* [*species*] of roses. ‖ 農家の人たちは生産高を増やそうと品種改良の研究グループを作った The farmers formed a study group to research *selective breeding* for crop increases.

ひんしゅく 顰蹙 ▶彼の粗暴なふるまいはみんなのひんしゅくを買った His boorish behavior *drew frowns.* ／People *frowned at* his rude behavior. (➤ frown /fraʊn/ は「顔をしかめる」).

ひんしゅつ 頻出 ▶このイディオムは入試に頻出する This idiom *frequently appears* in entrance examinations.

びんしょう 敏捷な **quick** (すばやい); **agile** /ǽdʒəl/, **nimble** (身軽ですばしこい；ともに敏しょうなことをいうが，前者は身軽な中に優雅さが感じられるのに対して，後者は軽快さと機敏さを強調する) ▶彼は動作が敏しょうだ He is *quick* to act [in action]. ／He is *agile* [*nimble*]. ‖ 大型力士は概して敏しょう性に欠ける Large-sized sumo wrestlers generally lack *agility.*

びんじょう 便乗 **1【相乗り】**▶私は学校へ行く途中父の車に便乗させてもらった My father gave me *a ride* [*a lift*] on my way to school. ／I *got a ride* [*a lift*] in my father's car on my way to school.

2【利用】▶消費税アップに便乗して商品を値上げした店もある *Taking advantage of* the consumption tax hike, there were some stores which raised the prices of their products. (➤「便乗値上げ」は follow-up price increase [hike] という) ‖ わが社は健康食品ブームに便乗して業績を伸ばした Our company *jumped on the* health food *bandwagon* and succeeded in increasing profits [sales]. (➤ jump on the bandwagon は「勢いのあるほうに加わって時流に乗る」の意).

[1]**ひんする 瀕する** ▶ノグチゲラは絶滅の危機に瀕している The Okinawa woodpecker *is on the verge* [*brink*] *of extinction.* ‖ その国では王政は危機に瀕している In that country, the monarchy is now *in danger of being overthrown.*

[2]**ひんする 貧する** ▶貧すれば鈍する *Poverty dulls the mind.*

ひんせい 品性 **character** /kǽrəktəʳ/ ▶品性の立派な[下劣な]男性 a man of noble [low] *character* ‖ またそんな下劣な番組を見て．あなたの品性を疑うわ You're watching that vulgar [lowbrow] program again! I can't help wondering about your *character.*

ピンセット (a **pair of**) **tweezers** 《参考》「ピンセット」はフランス語の *pincette* から.

びんせん 便箋 **notepaper,** (a **sheet of**) **letter paper** [**writing paper**] (１枚)；a **letter** [**writing**] **pad** (１冊の)；**stationery** (ホテル名などの入った．封筒とのペアの場合もある) ▶彼は比呂美への思いを便せん10枚に書きつづった He wrote out his feelings for Hiromi on ten sheets of *letter paper.*

ひんそう 貧相な **poor** (貧弱な)；**miserable** (みじめな)；**shabby** (みすぼらしい)

▶やせて貧相な男 a thin and *unimpressive-looking* man ‖ 貧相な身なりをした男 a *poorly-dressed* [*shabbily-dressed*] man.

びんそく 敏速な **swift, prompt** (➤ 前者は文語的) ▶この件については敏速な対応が望まれる *Swift* action should be taken on this matter. ‖ 私の代理人は常に敏速に仕事をこなす My agent does everything *promptly.*

びんた ▶彼女は彼をびんたした She *slapped* him (on the cheek).

ピンチ a **pinch,** 《インフォーマル》a **fix,** a **jam** ▶力を合わせてこのピンチを切り抜けよう Let's combine our efforts and get over this *pinch*! ‖ うちのチームは今ピンチだ Our team *is in a jam* [*in a pinch*]. ‖ 彼はピンチに強い He is strong *in a fix* [*when the chips are down*]. (➤ when the chips are down は「せっぱ詰まったとき」の意) ‖ 今，懐がピンチだ(＝金がない) *I'm in a tight financial situation* now. ‖ 後ろは絶壁でホームズは絶体絶命のピンチに追い込まれた With a cliff at his back, Holmes found himself in *a desperate situation.*

▶《野球》満塁のピンチ a bases-loaded *jam* ／ *tough situation* with bases loaded ‖ 浅尾は打者２人を歩かせ，ピンチを招いた Asao found himself *in a jam* [*in trouble*] after he walked two.

> **危ないカタカナ語✹ ピンチ**
> **1** pinch には「危機，窮地」という意味があって，日本語の「ピンチ」と同義だが，日本語ほどは使われない．インフォーマルでは fix や jam がよく用いられる．ただし，野球の「ピンチヒッター」「ピンチランナー」は pinch hitter, pinch runner でよい．
> **2** tough situation (つらい状況) や critical time (危機) を使っても「ピンチ」の意を表せる．

ビンディング **binding** (スキーの).

ビンテージ ビンテージの **vintage** ▶ビンテージ物のジーンズ *vintage* jeans.

ヒント a **hint**; a **clue** (手がかり) ▶息子のおもちゃからヒントを得てこの装置を発明しました *A hint* from my son's toy helped me devise this gadget. ‖ 《クイズなどで》全然見当がつかないなあ．ヒントを出してよ I'll never guess the answer; give me *a clue*!

ひんど 頻度 **frequency** /fríːkwənsi/ ▶これらの俗語は学生の間で高い頻度で使われている These slang words are used with high [great] *frequency* among students.

ぴんと **1【強く張って】** **tight(ly), tautly** (➤ 張り方は後者が強い) ▶ロープをぴんと張ってくれ Stretch the rope *tight* [*taut*]. ‖ 試験場にはぴんと張りつめた空気があった The examination room was charged with *tension* [filled with a *tense* atmosphere]. ‖ 彼女は背筋をぴんと伸ばしていすに座った She sat on the chair, *spine erect.*

▶犬は耳をぴんと立てた The dog *cocked* [*pricked up*] its ears.

2【「ぴんとくる」の形で】▶彼の言おうとしていることはすぐにぴんときた What he was trying to say *clicked with* me immediately. ／I *sensed* at once [I immediately *got the point of*] what he was trying to say. (➤ 前者のほうが日本語の語感に近い言い方).

▶その少年２人が漫画本を盗んだのだとぴんときた I *felt* (*it*) *in my bones* that the two boys had stolen some comic books. (➤「直感的にわかった」の意) ‖ 彼のしゃれは私にはぴんとこなかった I *didn't* (*quite*) *get* the point of his joke. ／His joke *didn't click with* me. ‖ 今の若い歌手の歌はどうも私にはぴんとこない Popular songs by young singers today *don't*

appeal to me at all.
▶ 対話「野間君はどう？」「あんまりぴんとこないわね」“How do you like Noma？”“He'*s not my kind of guy* [*not my type*].”

ピント (a) **focus** ▶この写真はピントが甘い This picture is *a bit out of focus*.
▶《比喩的》彼の言うことはピントが狂っている(＝的はずれだ) His remark *misses the point*. ／His comment *is not to the point*.

危ないカタカナ語 ピント
1「ピント」はオランダ語の *brandpunt*(「点」の意)の前半を省略したもの. 英語では focus という.「ピントが合う」は in focus,「ピントが合わない(ピンぼけ)」は out of focus.
2「的が外れている」という意味で「ピントが合っていない」と言うことがあるが, その場合は off the point [mark], not to the point, beside the point などという.

ひ

ヒンドゥーきょう ヒンドゥー教 Hinduism
‖ヒンドゥー教徒 a Hindu.

ひんにょう 頻尿 frequent urination.

ひんのう 貧農 a **poor farmer.**

ひんぱつ 頻発 ▶この曲がり角では交通事故が頻発する Traffic accidents *happen frequently* at this corner. ／Traffic accidents *are frequent* at this corner. ／This corner is the scene of *frequent* accidents.

ピンはね ▶支配人が売り上げの30パーセントをピンはねしていたそうだ I hear the manager *took a kickback* of 30 percent on sales. (➤ kickback は「上前」) ‖社長は従業員たちの給料の一部をピンはねした The boss *raked off* part of the money his employees made. (➤ rake off は「上前をはねる」).

ひんぱん 頻繁な frequent /fríːkwənt/ **一副 頻繁に frequently** ▶最近強い地震が頻繁に起きている Severe earthquakes have been occurring *frequently* lately.
▶妻と娘は頻繁に買い物に出かける My wife and daughter go shopping *quite often*. ‖空港行きのバスは頻繁に出てますか Do the buses for the airport run *at frequent* [*short*] *intervals*？

ひんぴょうかい 品評会 a **show**；a **fair** (特に農・畜産物などの) ▶犬[家畜]の品評会 a dog [cattle] *show*.

ぴんぴん ▶祖父は82歳だが今も元気でぴんぴんしている My grandfather is 82 years old but he is still *alive and kicking*. ‖対話「お元気？」「ぴんぴんしてるよ」“How are you doing？”“*Couldn't feel* [*be*] *better*.” (➤「これ以上元気になりようがない」の意).

ひんぴんと 頻々と frequently ▶最近この空港では旅行客がひんぴんとスリにあっている Recently, tourists at this airport are *frequently* victims of pickpockets.

ひんぷ 貧富 wealth and poverty (➤ 英語では語順が逆になることに注意) ▶貧富の差は広がるばかりだ The gap between *the rich and the poor* is getting bigger and bigger. (➤ the rich は「富める人」) ‖貧富の別なく人を平等に扱うべきだ We should treat all people equally, whether they are *rich or poor*.

ピンポイント ▶位置をピンポイントで突き止める *pinpoint* a location ‖目標にピンポイントで当てる hit a target *with pinpoint accuracy*.

びんぼう 貧乏 poverty 一形 貧乏な poor
▶私は貧乏はもうこりごりだ I'm tired of *being poor*. ‖リンカーンは貧乏な家に生まれた Lincoln was born *in a poor family*. ‖あんまり貧乏たらしい格好しないでね Don't wear such *shabby* clothes. ／Don't dress *shabbily*.
▶貧乏暮らしには慣れていますよ I am accustomed to *living in poverty*. ‖彼は貧乏性だ He is *the type who is unable to enjoy* (*his*) *life*. ‖対話「忙しそうだね」「ああ, 貧乏暇なしでね」“You look busy.” “Yeah. *I've got to work day and night to make ends meet*.” (➤「やりくりするためには日夜働かないといけない」の意).
▶《慣用表現》彼は貧乏くじをひいた He *was left holding the bag*. ／He *got the short end of the stick*. ／He *drew the short straw*. ‖あなた, その貧乏ゆすりの癖を早く直しなさいよ You'd better get rid of that nervous habit of *shaking* [*tapping*] *your feet*. (➤ 片足をゆするのなら feet を foot に).

ピンポーン 1【ドアベルなどの音】ding-dong
▶玄関のチャイムがピンポーンと鳴った The chime at the door rang “*ding-dong*.”
2【正解であることを示して】Bingo！

ピンぼけ ▶彼女が撮ってくれた写真はみんなピンぼけだった The pictures she had taken were all *out of focus*. →ピント.

ピンポン ping-pong, table tennis (➤ 後者が正式名)
▶ピンポンをしませんか What do you say to a game of *ping-pong*？／How about playing *ping-pong*？
‖ピンポン玉 a ping-pong ball.

ひんみん 貧民 the poor, the needy.

ひんもく 品目 an **item.**

ひんやり ▶外のさわやかでひんやりした空気にあたったら気分が少しよくなった After getting some fresh, *cool* air, I felt a little better. ‖風がひんやりしてきて冬も近いようだ The wind feels *chilly*. It seems winter is approaching.

びんらん 便覧 a **handbook** (ハンドブック)；a **manual** (手引き)
‖学生便覧 a handbook for students ／a student manual, 《米また》a college catalog, 《英また》a (university) prospectus ‖法律便覧 a handbook of law.

びんわん 敏腕な shrewd (判断力に優れた, やり手の), **capable** (実際的・実務的能力を持った) ▶敏腕な刑事 a *shrewd* [(*highly*) *capable*] police detective ‖彼女は敏腕部長だ She's a *capable and efficient* general manager. ‖彼は事業の海外拡張に敏腕を振るった He *demonstrated his ability* in expanding his company's overseas business.
‖敏腕家 a capable person.

ふ・フ

[1]ふ 府 a **prefecture** /príːfektʃəʳ/ (➤「県」や「(北海)道」にも用いる; ⇀県) ━ 形 府の **prefectural** /prɪféktʃərəl/ ▶大阪府 Osaka *Prefecture* ‖ 京都府立植物園 Kyoto *Prefectural* Botanical Gardens
‖ 府議会 a prefectural assembly.

[2]ふ 負の 《数学》 **negative, minus** ▶正の数と負の数 positive and *negative numbers* ‖ 原発の負の遺産 the *negative legacy* of nuclear power ‖ 負の側面 *a negative aspect*.

[3]ふ 斑 a **speckle**, a **spot** ▶葉に斑の入ったゼラニューム a geranium with *speckled* [*variegated*, *spotted*] leaves.

[4]ふ 麩 *fu*; bread-like pieces of dried wheat gluten (➤説明的な訳).

[5]ふ 腑 ▶あの説明はふに落ちない That explanation *is not convincing*.

[1]ぶ 部 **1**【クラブ】a **club**; a **team** (➤運動部の中でチームを構成したり, 他校と試合をしたりすることが多いものは club でなく team と表現することが多い) ▶演劇部 a drama *club* ‖ 野球部 a baseball *team* [*club*] ‖ 部に入る join *a club* [*a team*] (➤「辞める」と言うときは quit や leave を使う) ‖ 私は放送部に入っている I'm a member of [I belong to／I'm in] the broadcasting *club*. (●「(体育会系の)部に入っている」は I'm a member of ... ／I belong to ... ／I'm on [《英》 in] ... を用いる) ‖ 何部に入っていますか What [Which] *club* are you in?／What [Which] *team* are you on [《英》 in]?
‖ 部活 (⇀見出語) ‖ 部室 (⇀見出語).

> 「部(クラブ)」のいろいろ 囲碁部 Go club／運動部 athletic club／英語部 English club (日本の学校, 特に大学では English Speaking Society のような名称を使うところもある. 略称 E.S.S.)／園芸部 gardening club／演劇部 drama club／華道部 ikebana [flower arranging] club／剣道部 kendo team／コーラス部 glee club, chorus club／コンピュータ部 computer club／サッカー部 soccer team／茶道部 tea ceremony club／山岳部 mountaineering club／自転車部 cycling team／自動車部 automobile team／写真部 photography club／柔道部 judo team／書道部 calligraphy club／新聞部 newspaper club／水泳部 swimming team／体操部 gymnastic team／卓球部 table tennis team／テニス部 tennis team／陶芸部 pottery club／バスケットボール部 basketball team／バドミントン部 badminton team／バレーボール部 volleyball team／美術部 art club／文化部 culture club (華道部・茶道部などを含む); academic club (ディベート部・英語部などを含む)／弁論部 debate team／漫画部 cartoon [comics] club／野球部 baseball team／ラグビー部 rugby team／陸上部 track(-and-field) team

2【部門】a **department**, a **division** (会社などの); a **school** (大学の学部; 校舎) ▶営業部 the sales *department* [*division*] ‖ 理学部 the *school* of science (⇀学部).

3【部分】a **part** ▶2部から成る公演 a performance in two *parts*.

4【冊】a **copy** ▶このパンフレットが2部欲しいのですが May I have two *copies* of this brochure?

[2]ぶ 分 ▶この試合は我々に分がない[ある] *The odds are against us* [*in our favor*] in this game.／*We are at a disadvantage* [*at an advantage*] in this game. ⇀勝ち目.

ファースト 《野球》 **first base** (一塁); **the first baseman** (一塁手)
‖ ファーストミット a first baseman's glove [mitt].

ファーストクラス **first class** ▶一度でいいからファーストクラスで旅行してみたいわ I'd like to travel *first-class* just once. (➤副詞用法).

ファーストフード **fast food**
‖ ファーストフード店 a fast-food restaurant.

ファーストレディー **the First Lady** (大統領夫人) (➤the first lady とも書く) ▶米国のファーストレディー the U.S. *First Lady*／the *First Lady* of the U.S.

ぶあい 歩合 **rate** (割合); **percentage** (百分率); a **commission** (手数料)
‖ 歩合制 a commission system ‖ 公定歩合 the official discount [bank] rate.

ぶあいそう 無愛想な **unsociable** (人が非社交的な); **unfriendly** (人が非友好的な); **blunt** (返事・態度などがぶっきらぼうな); **curt** (返事・態度などがそっけない); **ungracious** (友好的な相手に対して) ▶無愛想な男 an *unsociable* [*unfriendly*] man ‖ 彼女は美人だけど無愛想だ She is beautiful but *unfriendly*. ‖ 彼は私に無愛想な返事をした He gave me a *blunt* [*curt*] answer.／He answered me in an unfriendly way.

ファイト **fight, fighting spirit** (闘志) ▶あの男はファイトがある He has plenty of *fight*.／He is a *go-getter*. (➤go-getter は「やり手, がんばり屋」の意) ‖ 彼はあすの試合にファイトを燃やしている He is full of *fighting spirit* [is burning with *fight*] for tomorrow's match.
‖ ファイトマネー a guarantee /gæ̀rəntíː/.

> 危ないカタカナ語✹ ファイト
> **1**「闘志」の意味の「ファイト」には fight, fighting spirit が相当するが, 運動部の選手たちが走りながら叫ぶ「ファイト! ファイト!」を "Fight! Fight!" とするのは不可. "Let's go!" "Keep it up!" "Go, go, go!" などとする.
> **2** "Fight!" はボクシングの選手に向かってのかけ声ならば可. バスケットボールやフットボールなどのチームスポーツの場合には "Fight, team, fight!" や "Go, team, go!" などのようにいう.

ファイナル a **final**; **the finals** (決勝戦).

ファイバースコープ a **fiberscope**.

ファイル a **file** ━ 動 ファイルする **file** +目 ▶テキスト[画像／動画／音楽]ファイル a text [an image／a video／a music] *file* ‖ ファイルを開く[保存する] open [save] a *file* ‖ 新製品に関する記事はすべてファイル(に保存)してあります Articles about new products are all *kept on file*. ‖《コンピュータで》ファイルとして保存する save as *a file*.

ファインダー a **finder**(カメラ・望遠鏡の)(➤ カメラの場合は viewfinder ともいう) ▶ファインダーをのぞく look through *a finder*.

ファインプレー a **spectacular play** ▶ファインプレーをする make *a spectacular play* ／make a fine catch (➤ fine play はあまり一般的ではない).

ファウル 1【野球の】a **foul** /faʊl/ ▶ファウルフライ a *foul* fly ‖ファウルボール a *foul* (ball) ‖ 中村は2死満塁でライトのファウルフライに倒れた With the bases loaded after two outs, Nakamura *fouled out* to right. (➤ この foul は「ファウルを打つ」の意の動詞).

2【反則】a **foul** ▶ファウルを犯す commit *a foul*.

ファクシミリ (a) **facsimile** /fæksíməli/.

ファゴット a **bassoon** /bəsúːn/ 《参考》「ファゴット」はイタリア語の *fagotto* から. faggot はアメリカの俗語で「ホモ」の意なので注意.

ふ

ファジー **fuzzy**

‖ファジー・コンピュータ a fuzzy computer.

ファシズム **Fascism, fascism** /fǽʃìzəm/.

ファスナー a **zipper**, 《英また》a **zip (fastener)**(➤ fastener /fǽsənəʳ/ は留め金具の総称) ▶彼女はスカートのファスナーを上げた［下ろした］She *zipped* (*up*) ［*unzipped*］ her skirt.

ぶあつい 分厚い **thick** ▶分厚い胸 one's *thick* chest ‖ 分厚い百科事典 a *thick* ［*bulky*］ volume of an encyclopedia.

ファックス (a) **fax**; a **fax machine**(ファックス機) ▶彼にファックスを送る send him *a fax* ‖ 彼女に手紙をファックスで送る send a letter to her *by fax* ‖ 商品の注文をファックスで送ります I'll *fax* you my order for the products.

‖ファックス番号 a fax number ［code］.

ファッション (a) **fashion** ▶最近のファッションはますます多様化してきた Today's *fashions* are becoming more and more diverse. ‖ 彼女はいつも最新のファッションを追いかけている She always follows the latest ［newest］ *fashions*. ‖ Mデパートで春物のファッションショーをやっている They're having *a fashion show* of spring wear at M Department Store.

‖ファッション雑誌 a fashion magazine ‖ ファッションモデル a fashion model.

ファミコン a **video game** 《参考》「ファミコン」は任天堂が開発した家庭用テレビゲーム機の通称. 外国では Nintendo の名で親しまれている.

▶ファミコンで遊ぶ play *a video game*.

ファミリー a **family**

‖ファミリーレストラン a family restaurant.

ファラオ a **pharaoh** /féəroʊ/(古代エジプトの王).

ふあん 不安 **anxiety** /æŋzáɪəṭi/; **concern**(心配); **uneasiness**(落ち着かない気持ち) 一形 **不安な** **anxious** /ǽŋkʃəs/, **uneasy** →心配 ▶ルーキーたちは期待と不安の入りまじった顔をしていた The rookies seemed to be filled with (a mixture of) expectation and *anxiety*. ‖ 原子力発電所に対する不安が国民の間に高まっている *Concern* about nuclear power plants is growing among the people. ‖ 将来のことを考えると不安になった When I thought of my future, I *became uneasy*. ‖ 余震が続く中で我々は不安な一夜を過ごした We passed an *uneasy* ［*anxious*］ night as the aftershocks continued. ‖ 公演前はみんな不安だった We *were nervous* before the performance. (➤ nervous は「神経質な」) ‖ どの駅で降りればいいのかだんだん不安になってきた I *began to worry about* which station I should get off (the train) at.

ファン a **fan**, an **enthusiast** ▶サッカーファン a soccer *fan* ［*enthusiast*］ ‖ 映画ファン a movie *fan* ［*lover*］ ／a film *buff* ‖ 熱狂的なジャズファン an enthusiastic jazz *fan* ‖ 私は西武のファンだ I am *a* Lions *fan*. ‖ モーツァルトのファンは多い There are many *fans* ［*admirers*］ of Mozart's music. ‖ 久美子ちゃんは学校にたくさん男の子のファンがいるのよ Kumiko has got a lot of *admirers* among the boys at her school.

✉ **私は大のビートルズファンです** I am *a big fan* of the Beatles.

> **危ないカタカナ語✸ ファン**
> 多くの場合 fan が使えるが,「熱狂的なファン」は enthusiast /ɪnθjúːziæst/ を用いて (great) soccer enthusiast のように言うこともできる. ほかに lover(愛好者)や admirer(賛美者)を用いて上の用例のようにいうこともできる.

‖ファンクラブ a fan club.

☛ ファンレター (→見出語)

ファンクションキー 《コンピュータ》a **function key**.

ファンシー ‖ファンシーグッズ novelty goods ［items］, 《英》fancy goods ‖ ファンシーショップ a novelty (toy) shop.

ファンタジー **fantasy**.

ふあんてい 不安定な **unstable**(絶えず変化を続ける, 揺れ動く); **unsettled**(はっきり決まっていない, 未解決の); **unsteady**(安定性のない) ▶不安定な社会情勢 *unstable* social conditions ‖ 不安定なはしご an *unsteady* ladder ‖ この花瓶は上が重そうで少し不安定だ This vase looks a bit top-heavy and *unstable*. ‖ このところ天候が不安定だ The weather is *changeable* ［*unsettled*］ these days.

ファンデーション **(make-up) foundation** ▶ファンデーションを塗る［落とす］apply ［remove］ *foundation*.

ファンド a **fund**(基金)

‖投資ファンド an investment fund.

ふあんない 不案内 ▶私はこの辺は不案内です I *don't know* this area. ／I'm *new* to this area. (➤ ビジネス街では I'm a stranger (around) here. のように言うこともある) ‖ その町は私にとっては不案内の所だった The city was *strange* to me. ‖ 私は経済問題には全く不案内だ I *am* quite *unfamiliar with* economic issues. ／I *know nothing about* economic issues.

ファンファーレ a **fanfare** /fǽnfèəʳ/ ▶競技場にファンファーレが響きわたった The stadium resounded with *fanfares*. 《参考》「ファンファーレ」はフランス語の *Fanfare* から.

ファンブル a **fumble** ▶中村は稲葉のゴロをファンブルし, 三塁走者の生還を許した Nakamura *fumbled* Inaba's grounder, allowing the third runner to score.

ファンレター a **fan letter**; **fan mail** (➤ 総称) ▶AKB48にファンレターを出そうよ Let's write *fan letters* to AKB 48.

[1]**ふい 不意の** **unexpected**(予期しない); **sudden**(突然の) 一副 **不意に** **unexpectedly**; **suddenly**; **abruptly**(唐突に) ▶不意の来客［出来事］an *unexpected* visitor ［incident］ ‖ 前の車が不意にブレーキをかけたのであわてた I panicked because the car in front of me *suddenly* put on the brakes. ‖ 彼女は何も言わず不意に出て行った She *abruptly* left without a word.

‖警官たちは男の**不意をついて**その部屋に突入した The police officers *caught* the man *off guard* and rushed into the room. (→不意打ち).

²ふい ▶我々の努力は**ふいになった** Our efforts *were in vain.* ／Our efforts *came to nothing* [*went down the drain*]. ‖せっかくのチャンスを**ふいにした** I *missed* (*out on*) a great opportunity.

ぶい 部位 a **region**(体, 食肉の) ▶脳の各**部位** the *regions* of the brain.

ブイ a **buoy** /bú:i, bɔɪ/ ▶**ブイ**を越えたところで泳いではいけない Don't swim past the *buoys*.

フィアンセ one's **fiancé** (男); one's **fiancée** (女) (➤ 発音はともに /fi:ɑ:nséɪ/) ▶理恵には**フィアンセ**がいる Rie has *a fiancé*. ／Rie is engaged. (➤ 後者は「婚約している」の意).

フィート a **foot** [複 **feet**] ▶ 2 **フィート** 4 インチ two *feet* four (inches) ／2 *ft.* 4 in. ‖10**フィート**のさお a ten-*foot* pole ‖ジムは身長が 6 **フィート** 6 インチ(＝198センチ)ある Jim is 6 *feet* [*foot*] 6 (inches tall).

フィードバック **feedback** ▶利用者の声を**フィードバック**して製品改良に生かす *get feedback* from users and make use of it to improve a product.

フィーバー a **fad**, a **craze** (➤ fever は「熱病」の意.「熱狂」「一時的流行」の意では fad, craze を用いる).

フィーリング **feeling** (感情, 気分); (a) **taste** (好み) ▶彼とは**フィーリング**が合わないの I *don't get along with* him. ／He and I never did *hit it off*. (➤ ともに「仲よくやっていけない」の意).

フィールド a **field**
‖**フィールド競技** a field event.

フィールドアスレチック

> 《解説》フィールド(field)とアスレチック(athletic)を結合して作った日本フィールドアスレチック協会の登録商標で, 英語にぴったりの対応語はない. これに似た施設としては, obstacle course (アメリカ)や adventure playground (イギリス; 主に子供向け)がある.

ふいうち 不意打ち a **surprise attack** ▶**不意打ちの試験** a *surprise* exam ／《インフォーマル》a *pop* quiz ‖敵に**不意打ちを食わせる** make *a surprise attack* on the enemy ／*catch* the enemy *off guard*. (➤「不意打ちを食らう」は be caught [taken] off guard).

フィギュア **1**【スケート】**figure skating** (➤「フィギュアスケートの選手」は figure skater) ▶結弦は今**フィギュア**の演技をしている Yuzuru *is* now *figure skating* (on the ice).
2【人形】a **figurine** ▶彼はアニメの**フィギュア**をたくさん集めている He has a large collection of *anime figurines*.

フィクション **fiction** ▶この物語は全くの**フィクション**だ This story is pure *fiction*. ‖このドラマに登場する人物・出来事はすべて**フィクション**です All (the) characters and events in this drama are *fictitious*.

ふいご **bellows.**

ブイサイン Vサイン a **V sign**, a **sign of victory** ▶選手たちは観客に向かって**Vサイン**を出した The players *flashed V-signs* toward the spectators.

フィジー **Fiji** (南太平洋にある国)
‖**フィジー諸島** the Fiji Islands.

ふいちょう 吹聴する **broadcast** ＋㊐ ▶彼は息子が司法試験に合格したことを**ふいちょうして**回っている He *is broadcasting* his son's success in the bar examination. ‖自分の手柄をあまり**ふいちょうする**と仲間に嫌われるよ If you keep *bragging* about your achievements, you'll be disliked by your friends. (➤ brag は「(大げさに)自慢する」).

ふいっち 不一致 (a) **disagreement** ▶目撃者たちの話には**不一致な点が見られる** There are some *conflicts* [*discrepancies*] among the witnesses' accounts. ‖二人の離婚の原因は**性格の不一致**だ The cause of their divorce was *incompatibility*.

フィットネス **fitness** ▶彼は毎朝ジョギングして**フィットネス**に励んでいる He jogs every morning to *build up* [*increase*] *his fitness* (*level*).
‖**フィットネスクラブ** a fitness club.

ブイティーアール (a) **VTR** (➤ video tape recorder の略), (a) **VCR** (➤ videocassette recorder の略)《参考》英語では V C R のほうが一般的. なお, ハードディスクに録画するものは digital video recorder (デジタル録画機,《略》DVR)という.

ぷいと ▶彼女はすねて**ぷいと**横を向いてしまった She turned away *with a pout*. (➤ pout /paʊt/ は「ふくれっつら」).

フィナーレ **finale** /fɪnɑ́:li/《参考》*finale* はイタリア語から. ▶そのコンサートの**フィナーレ**では『ウィー・アー・ザ・ワールド』が歌われた The song "We Are the World" was sung as the *finale* of the concert.

ブイネック Vネック a **V neck** (➤ V-neck ともつづる) ▶ **V ネック**のセーター a *V-neck*(*ed*) sweater ／a sweater *with a V neck*.

ブイヤベース (a) **bouillabaisse** /bù:jəbéɪs/.

フィヨルド a **fiord**, a **fjord** /fiɔ́:ʳd ‖ fí:ɔ:d/.

ブイヨン (a) **bouillon** /bóljɑ:n ‖ bú:jɔn/ (スープ); a **bouillon cube** (固形の).

フィラデルフィア **Philadelphia** /fìlədélfiə/ (アメリカ, ペンシルベニア州の都市).

ふいり 不入り **poor attendance**;《インフォーマル》a **flop** ▶そのロードショーは**不入りだった** The (special) first-run showing of the film *was poorly attended* [*drew only a small audience*]. ‖その映画は**不入りだった** The film was *a flop*.

フィリピン **the Philippines** /fɪ́ləpi:nz/ 一形 **フィリピン(人)の** **Philippine**, **Filipino**
‖**フィリピン人** a Filipino /fɪ̀lɪpí:noʊ/.

フィルター a **filter**; a **filter tip** (たばこの) ▶**フィルター付きのたばこ** a *filter*(*-tipped*) cigarette (➤ フィルターの付いてないのは non-filter cigarette という).

フィルダーズチョイス 《野球》a **fielder's choice.**

> 《解説》野球用語の「野選」は fielder's choice の直訳である「野手の選択」の略. 日本では野手が送球判断を誤ってバッターとランナーの両方をセーフにした場合をいうが, アメリカではこのほか, 走者は二塁で封殺されたが, 一塁はセーフだった場合の, 打者の記録も fielder's choice と呼ぶ.

フィルハーモニー ▶ウィーン・**フィルハーモニー**管弦楽団 the Vienna *Philharmonic* Orchestra (➤ 固有名詞なので, 略すときも the Vienna Philharmonic がふつう).

フィルム (a) **film** ▶ 24枚撮りの**フィルム** a roll of 24-exposure *film* ‖このカメラ, **フィルム**が入っていますか Is there *film* in this camera? ／Is this camera loaded? (➤ load は「(フィルムを)装てんする」の意)
‖**フィルムライブラリー** a film library.

フィレンツェ **Florence** (イタリア中部の都市; Firenze はイタリア名).

フィン a **fin** (➤ 両足の場合は a pair of fins) ▶**フィン**

をつけてもぐる put on (*a pair of*) *fins* and dive.

ぶいん 部員 a **member** ▶彼は本校のテニス部員だ He's *a member of* [He's *on*] *the tennis team* at our school. ‖ 野球部の**新入部員**は全部で20名だ There are [We have] a total of 20 *new members* on our baseball team.

フィンランド Finland 一形 フィンランドの Finnish ‖**フィンランド語** Finnish ‖ **フィンランド人** a Finn.

1**ふう 封** a **seal** ▶手紙の**封をする** *seal* a letter ‖ **封のしてある封筒** a *sealed* envelope ‖ 彼は手紙の**封を切った** He *broke the seal* on the letter. / He *opened* the letter.

2**ふう 風** **1【格好, 様子】**▶ 対話「その泥棒はどんなふうな男でしたか？」「やくざふうでした」"*What sort of* person was the robber? / What did the robber *look like*?" "He *looked like* a yakuza (gangster)."

2【様式】 (a) **style** ▶韓国**風**のレストラン a Korean-*style* restaurant ‖ すき焼きには**関東風**と**関西風**がある There's *Kanto type* sukiyaki and *Kansai type*. ‖ カナダでは今, **日本風の**庭を造るのが流行している Building *Japanese-style* gardens is popular in Canada now. ‖ スティーブさんは**日本風に**(= 日本人のように)おじぎをした Steve bowed *like a Japanese man* [*in the Japanese style*].

3【方法, 具合】 a **way** ▶アップルパイはこんなふうにして作ります I make apple pie(s) *this way* [*like this*]. ‖ こんなふうにして彼は計画を実行した *This is how* he carried out his plan. ‖ 披露宴の司会はどんなふうにしたらいいか, どうか私に教えてください Please teach me *how* to emcee a wedding reception. ‖ 対話「お宅へは駅からどういうふうに行けばよろしいですか」「駅に着いたらお電話ください. 迎えに参りますから」"*How* can I get to your house from the train station?" "Please call me at home when you arrive at the train station. I'll go to meet you."

ふうあつ 風圧 wind pressure.

ふういん 封印 a **seal 一動 封印する seal** +目.

ブーイング booing(やじを飛ばすこと) ; a **boo**(やじ, やじる) ▶観衆はアンパイアの判定に**ブーイングした** The spectators *booed* the umpire's decision.

ふうう 風雨 wind and rain ; a **storm** (暴風雨) ▶夕方には**風雨が強まった** The *wind and rain* got worse in the evening. ‖ その廃墟は長い間**風雨にさらされている** The ruins *have been exposed to the weather* [*the elements*] for a long time.

ふううんじ 風雲児 a **hero in times of turmoil** [**in turbulent days**] ▶北条早雲は戦国時代の**風雲児**だった Hojo Soun was *a hero who rose to greatness* during the turbulent Sengoku period.

ふうか 風化 weathering 一動 風化する weather ▶風化と浸食で美しい富士山の姿がだいぶ損なわれている *Weathering* and erosion have done great damage to the beautiful outline of Mt. Fuji.

▶《比喩的》その痛ましい事故の記憶を**風化させては**ならない We must not *let* memories of the tragic accident *fade away*.

‖**風化作用** weathering.

ふうが 風雅 ▶**風雅な人** a person *with elegant, refined taste*.

フーガ《音楽》a **fugue** /fjuːg/.

ふうかく 風格 dignity(威厳) ▶ライオンには王者の**風格**がある The lion has the *dignity* of a monarch. ‖ 白鵬は大横綱の**風格**が出てきた Hakuho has begun to show the *dignity* of a great yokozuna champion.

ふうがわり 風変わりな strange(奇妙な) ; **odd** (常識をはずれている) ; **peculiar** (一風変わっている) ▶この島には**風変わりな**風習が伝わっている There is a *strange* custom handed down on this island. ‖ 彼はちょっと**風変わりな**男でね. 何を考えているかさっぱりわからないんだ He's an *odd* [*eccentric*] person, you see. You can never tell what he's thinking. (➤ 日本語の「エキセントリック」には批判的な響きがあるが, 英語圏では人と違っていることはむしろ個性として受け入れられやすいので, eccentric には必ずしも悪い意味はない).

ふうき 風紀 public morals (公共の道徳) ; **discipline** /dísəplɪn/ (規律) ▶**風紀**を乱す corrupt *public morals* ‖ 近頃世の中の**風紀**が乱れていると思いませんか Don't you think that *public morals* have gotten corrupt recently? ‖ うちの学校は**風紀**にやかましい Our school is very strict in *matters of discipline* [*morals*].

ふうきり 封切り (a) **release** ▶その映画は来週**封切り**になります That film will *be released* next week.

‖**封切り映画** a first-run [newly-released] movie ‖ **封切り館** a first-run theater.

ブーケ a **bouquet** /boʊkéɪ, bu-/.

ふうけい 風景 scenery /síːnəri/ (ある地域全体の ; 集合名詞で a はつかない) ; a **view** (見晴らし) ; a **scene** (情景) ▶松島の**風景**は美しい The *scenery* in Matsushima is beautiful. ‖ 男体山のてっぺんから見る**風景**はすばらしかった The *view* from the top of Mt. Nantai was terrific. ‖ 窓の外にはのどかな**農村風景**が広がっていた A peaceful *scene of a farming village* spread before us outside the window.

‖**風景画** a landscape (picture) ‖ **街頭風景** a street scene.

ブーゲンビリア《植物》a **bougainvillea** /bùːgən-víliə/.

ふうこうめいび 風光明媚 ▶十和田湖は**風光明媚**な所だ Lake Towada is *a place of scenic beauty*. / Lake Towada is *a scenic spot*.

ふうさ 封鎖 a **blockade** /blɑːkéɪd/ **一動 封鎖する block (up)** ▶空港へ通じるすべての道路が**封鎖された** All the roads to the airport *were blocked* (*up*).

‖**経済封鎖** an economic blockade.

ふうさい 風采 (an) **appearance** ▶**風采の立派な人** a person *of fine appearance* [*presence*] ‖ うちの亭主は**風采の上がらない**四十男よ My husband is an *unimpressive-looking* man in his 40s.

ふうさつ 封殺《野球》a **forced out.**

ふうし 風刺 (a) **satire** /sǽtaɪəʳ/ **一形 風刺の satirical** /sətírɪkəl/ **一動 風刺する satirize** +目 ▶**風刺**のきいたエッセー an essay full of *satire* ‖ ドーミエは当時の世相を痛烈に**風刺**した漫画を多く描いた Daumier drew many cartoons which were *a bitter satire* on the society of that time. (➤ cartoon は「風刺漫画」).

‖**風刺画** a caricature /kǽrɪkətʃʊəʳ/ ‖ **風刺画家** a caricaturist /kǽrɪkətʃʊərɪst/ ‖ **風刺作家** a satirist /sǽṭərɪst/ ‖ **風刺小説** a satirical novel.

ふうしゃ 風車 a **windmill**

‖**風車小屋** a windmill (shed).

ふうしゅう 風習 (manners and) customs ▶昔からの**風習** old *customs* ‖ 村には変わった**風習**が残っている The village retains some unique old *manners and customs*.

ふうしょ 封書 a **(sealed) letter.**

ふうじる 封じる ▶目撃者の口を封じる *shut up* the witness ‖ 警察はアジトに手入れして過激派の動きを封じた The police raided the radicals' hideout and *shut down* their activities.

ふうしん 風疹 **German measles** /míːzəlz/, **rubella** /ruːbélə/ 《参考》後者は本来は医学用語だが，前者が「ドイツ(人)」を連想させるため，最近では後者が好まれる.

ブース a **booth**

‖**展示ブース** an exhibit booth.

ふうすいがい 風水害 **storm and flood damage** ▶風水害に見舞われる meet with [encounter] *storm and flood damage*.

ブースター a **booster.**

ふうせつ 風雪 **wind and snow** ▶これらの松の木は300年もの間風雪に耐えてきた These pines have survived *wind and snow* for 300 years.

ふうせん 風船 a **balloon** ▶紙［ゴム］風船 a paper [rubber] *balloon* ‖「パン!」と風船が割れた Pop! The *balloon* broke [burst]. ‖ その女の子は風船ガムをふくらませた The girl blew *a bubble* with her gum [blew *a gum bubble*]. (➤ bubble は「泡」で，「風船ガム」そのものは bubble gum という).

ふうぜんのともしび 風前の灯火 ▶国王の運命も今や風前のともしびだ The king's life now *hangs by a thread* [*a hair*]. (➤「糸［髪の毛］1本でぶら下がっている」が原義) ‖ 後継者が絶えて地場産業も風前のともしびだ Local industry *is endangered* because no [few] people remain in (the) town to take over businesses. (➤「消滅の危険にさらされている」の意).

ふうそく 風速 **wind velocity** /vəlάːsəṭi/ [**speed**] ▶瞬間最大風速 the maximum instantaneous *wind velocity* ‖ 台風の影響で風速(秒速)15メートルの風が吹いている The typhoon is accompanied by [The typhoon has brought] *winds of up to 15 meters per second*.

‖**風速計** an anemometer /æ̀nɪmάːməṭəʳ/, a wind gauge /ɡeɪdʒ/.

ふうぞく 風俗 ▶どの国にもそれぞれ風俗習慣がある Each country has its own *manners and customs*. ‖**風俗営業** the entertainment and amusement business; the sex industry (セックス産業) ‖ **風俗犯罪** a vice.

ふうち 風致 **scenic beauty**

‖**風致地区** a nature preservation area.

ふうちょう 風潮 a **tendency** ▶最近ますます金がすべてという風潮が強まっている Today there is an increasing *tendency* (among people) to think that money is everything.

ブーツ (a **pair of**) **boots** ▶革のブーツ leather *boots* ‖ ブーツをはく［脱ぐ］ put on [take off] one's *boots*.

‖**厚底ブーツ** (super-)platform shoes.

ふうてい 風体 **appearance** ▶みすぼらしい風体の男 a *shabbily dressed* man.

ふうど 風土 (a) **climate** /kláɪmət/ ▶アジサイやサザンカは日本の風土によく合った植物だ Hydrangeas and sasanquas are well suited to *the Japanese climate*. ‖ 賢治の作品は花巻の風土を抜きには考えられない You can't think of Kenji's works without bringing to mind the *land and climate* of Hanamaki.

‖**風土病** an endemic (disease).

[1]**フード** 《食物》(a) **food** ▶キャット［ドッグ］フード cat [dog] *food*.

[2]**フード** 《ずきん》 a **hood** /hʊd/.

ふうとう 封筒 an **envelope** /énvəloʊp/ ▶切手をはった返信用の封筒 a stamped return *envelope* ‖ (書籍・小荷物用の)クッション入りの封筒 a padded bag, a Jiffy bag (➤ 後者は商品名だが多用される).

ふうどう 風洞 a **wind tunnel.**

フードコート a **food court.**

プードル 《動物》a **poodle.**

ふうび 風靡 ▶ビートルズの音楽は一世を風靡した The music of the Beatles *took the world by storm*. (➤ take ... by storm は「(聴衆などを)とりこにする」の意).

ブービーしょう ブービー賞 a **second-last prize** (日本の); a **booby prize** (英米の) 《参考》日本語の「ブービー賞」は「最下位から2番目の賞」をいうが，英語の booby prize は最下位賞を指すので，正確には訳語のようにする必要がある.

ふうひょう 風評 a **rumor**

‖**風評被害** damage caused by rumors, rumor-induced damage.

ふうふ 夫婦 **husband** [**man**] **and wife**, a (**married**) **couple** ▶あの二人は夫婦です They are *husband and wife*. (➤ a をつけないことに注意) ／They are married. ‖ 機内はどちらを向いても新婚夫婦ばかりだった In the plane, I found *newly married couples* [*newlyweds*] all around me. ‖ 田中さん夫婦はことし金婚式を迎えます *Mr. and Mrs. Tanaka* will celebrate their golden (wedding) anniversary this year. ‖ ゆうべは夫とつまらぬことから夫婦げんかをした Last night I *had a quarrel* [*row*] *with my husband* over a trivial matter. (➤ row /raʊ/ は「けんか」) ‖ 彼らは夫婦仲が良い They *are a happily married couple*.

☛ 夫婦別姓 (→見出語)

ふうふう ▶弟は宿題をため込んで，今ふうふう言いながらやっている My (younger) brother let his homework pile up and now he is *sweating his way through* it. (➤ sweat one's way は「汗水たらしてやる」) ‖ ふうふう言いながら富士山に登った *Huffing and puffing*, we climbed Mt. Fuji.

ぶうぶう ▶(車の)クラクションをブーブー鳴らす *honk* the (car) horn

▶彼は何かにつけてぶうぶう言って(＝こぼして)いる He's always *complaining* [*grousing*] about something.

ふうぶつ 風物 **things** (➤ この意味では形容詞はあとにくる) ▶日本の風物 *things Japanese* ‖ 外国の風物 *things foreign* ‖ う飼いは長良川の夏の風物詩だ Cormorant fishing is *a special attraction which gives poetic charm to summer* along the Nagara River. (➤「夏に詩情を与える特別な出し物」の意).

ふうふべっせい 夫婦別姓 ▶あなたは夫婦別姓をどう思いますか What do you think of *married women keeping their maiden names*? (➤ maiden name は「(女性の)結婚前の名」) ‖ うちは夫婦別姓です I *have kept my maiden name*. (➤ 妻が言う場合) ／My wife *has kept her maiden name*. (➤ 夫が言う場合).

ふうぼう 風貌 ▶彼は芸術家のような風貌をしている He *looks like* an artist. ／He *has the face and manner* of an artist.

ふうみ 風味 (a) **flavor** ▶ミント風味のガム mint-*flavored* chewing gum ‖ 新茶は風味がいい Freshly harvested green tea has a wonderful *flavor*. ‖ このマツタケは風味がない This *matsutake* has no *flavor*.

ブーム a **boom**; a **fad** (一時的な大流行); a **craze** (…

熱) ▶にわかブームに火をつける set off *a sudden boom* ‖ 今は海外旅行ブームだ An overseas travel *boom* [*craze*] is on. /Overseas travel is very popular at the moment. ‖ ゴルフブームは若い女性にまで及んでいる The golfing *boom* extends even to young women. ‖ ツイッターのブームがこれから何年も続くだろう The *popularity* of Twitter [The Twitter *boom*] will probably go on for many years. (➤ popularity は「人気」) ‖ 近年タンゴが一種のブームになった The tango has become something of *a fad* in recent years.

‖健康ブーム health awareness boom.

ブーメラン a **boomerang** /búːməræŋ/.

ふうらいぼう 風来坊 a **drifter**, a **wanderer** ▶あの男は風来坊で定職がない He is *a drifter* and has no stable [steady] job.

フーリガン a **hooligan**.

ふうりゅう 風流 ⚠「優雅な趣がある」の意では **elegant, exquisite, refined** などを用いることができるが,「詩歌や茶道などをたしなむ心」の意の「風流」にぴったり対応する英語はない. この意味では **poetic**(詩的な)などを用いて表す.

▶風流な庭 a garden arranged *in elegant taste* ‖ ダニエルズさんは風流な人だ Mr. Daniels *has exquisite taste*.

ふうりょく 風力 **the force of the wind, wind force**

‖風力計 an anemometer, a wind gauge ‖ 風力発電 wind power generation.

ふうりん 風鈴 a ***furin***; a hanging bell that tinkles in the wind(➤ 説明的な訳) ▶涼風に軒先の風鈴がチリンと鳴った The *wind-bell* under the eaves tinkled in the cool breeze.

[1]**プール** a **(swimming) pool**(➤ pool は「水たまり」の意が基本で, swimming をつけるのが正式だが, 文脈で明白なときは省略する) ▶25メートルプール a 25-meter *swimming pool* ‖ 屋内温水プール an indoor *heated pool* ‖ プールで泳ぐ swim in *a pool*.

‖プールサイド the poolside.

[2]**プール** **pool** +㊐ (ためる) ▶彼らはマンション改築の資金をプールした They *pooled* (their) money to remodel the condominium.

ふうん 不運 **bad luck**; (a) **misfortune**(不幸) 一㊜ **不運な** **unlucky, unfortunate**(➤ 後者のほうが堅い語) ▶人間には運・不運がある Some people have good luck, others *bad* (*luck*). ‖ その女性は不運な一生を送った The woman led an *unfortunate* life. /She was *unfortunate* all her life. ‖ 不運にも私の友人はその墜落した飛行機に乗り合わせていた *Unfortunately* [*Unluckily*], a friend of mine happened to be on board the plane that crashed. ‖ 不運な宿命を背負った航海 an *ill-fated* voyage (● 失敗するに決まっているという含みがある) ‖ ロミオとジュリエットは不運な宿命の恋人同士だった Romeo and Juliet were *ill-starred* lovers. (➤ ill-starred は「星回りの悪い」).

ぶーん ▶大きなハチがブーンと飛んで来て, 父の頭を刺した A huge bee came *buzzing* toward my father and stung him on the head.

ふえ 笛 a **whistle** /*h*wísəl/ (合図の); a **recorder** (縦笛); a **flute** (横笛) ▶笛を吹く play *the flute*(➤ 横笛の場合) ‖ 夜道であなたが人に襲われたらこの笛を吹きなさいね *Blow* this *whistle* if you're attacked on the road at night.

▶笛吹けど踊らず We played the pipe for you, but you didn't dance. (➤ 聖書のことば).

[1]**フェア** **1**【公明正大な】**fair** ▶フェアにやろう Let's play *fair*. ‖ きみはやり方がフェアじゃないよ I don't think you*'re playing fair*.

‖フェアプレー fair play.

2【野球】▶打球はフェアグラウンドに落ちた The ball fell in *fair territory*. (➤ fairground とすると「博覧会場」の意になる).

‖フェアボール a fair ball

[2]**フェア** (展示会) a **fair** ▶ブックフェア a book *fair*.

フェアウエイ (ゴルフ) a **fairway**.

ふえいせい 不衛生な **unsanitary** ▶不衛生な布巾 an *unsanitary* dishtowel.

フェイドアウト a **fade out** 一㊍ **フェイドアウトする fade out**.

フェイドイン a **fade in** 一㊍ **フェイドインする fade in**.

ふえいよう 富栄養化した **eutrophic** /jutróʊfɪk/ (➤「富栄養化」は eutrophication).

フェイント a **feint** ▶フェイントをかける make *a feint*.

フェーズ a **phase** ▶WHOは警戒レベルをフェーズ6とした The WHO set the alert level to *phase* 6.

フェーンげんしょう フェーン現象 (気象) a **foehn** /feɪn/ **phenomenon**.

フェザーきゅう フェザー級 **the featherweight division** [**class**] ▶フェザー級の選手 *a featherweight*.

フェスティバル a **festival**.

ふえて 不得手な **poor** (at), **weak** (in) ▶私は数学が不得手だ I *am poor* [*bad*] *at* math. /I *am weak in* math.

フェニックス a **phoenix** /fíːnɪks/.

ブエノスアイレス **Buenos Aires**(アルゼンチンの首都).

フェミニスト a **feminist** /fémənɪst/ (男女同権論者); a **gallant** (女性に優しい男性) ▶草野さんはフェミニストだ(=女性に優しい) Mr. Kusano *is always kind to women*.

> **危ないカタカナ語✸ フェミニスト**
> **1**「フェミニスト」は「女性に優しい男性」の意味で使われることも多いが, 英語の feminist は「男女同権主義者」のことで, 主に女性である.
> **2**「女性に優しい人」という意味なら gallant man や man who is kind to [considerate of] women などを用いる.

フェラチオ **fellatio** /fəléɪʃioʊ/.

フェリー a **ferry (boat)** ▶フェリーに乗る board *a ferry* ‖ 我々はフェリーで海峡を渡った We crossed the channel *by* [*on a*] *ferry*.

‖カーフェリー a car ferry(➤ 自動車のまま乗り込めるフェリーは drive-on ferry).

ふえる 増える **increase** /ɪnkríːs/ (数が; → 増やす); **gain** (体重が; 主語は人) ▶売り上げが先月より1割増えた Our sales *have increased* ten percent over last month. ‖ 海外で仕事をする日本人のビジネスマンが増えている *The number* of Japanese business people who work in foreign countries *is increasing*. ‖ 中国人観光客が著しく増えた Chinese tourists *have increased* significantly in number. ‖ 収入が増えれば支出も増す *The more you earn*, the more you spend. ‖ 交通量が増えるにつれて渋滞が激しくなっている As the traffic *becomes heavier*, the streets get more congested. ‖ 悪質な犯罪が増えている Vicious crimes *are on the rise*. ‖ 運動不足で体重が5キロ増えた I have *gained* [have *put on*] five kilos from lack

of exercise.
▶きみ, ずいぶん白髪が増えたね You'*ve got* a lot *more* gray in your hair, haven't you?／You'*ve gotten* a lot more white hair, haven't you? ‖この前お目にかかってから子供が1人増えました I *have had another* child since I saw you last.

フェルト **felt.**

フェルトペン a **felt(-tip) pen.**

プエルトリコ **Puerto Rico** /pwɜ̀:ˈtoʊ ríːkoʊ/ (西インド諸島にあるアメリカの自治領の島)
‖**プエルトリコ人** a Puerto Rican.

フェレット 《動物》a **ferret.**

フェローシップ a **fellowship**(研究奨学金).

フェロモン 《生化学》a **pheromone**
‖**ヒトフェロモン** a human pheromone.

ふえん 敷衍する **elaborate on, go into detail.**

フェンシング **fencing** ▶フェンシングの試合 a *fencing* match (➤「フェンシングをする」は fence,「フェンシングの選手」は fencer という).

フェンス a **fence** ▶レフトは背走また背走, フェンスに激突した The left fielder kept running backward and crashed into the *fence*.

フェンダー a **fender,** 《英》a **wing.**

ぶえんりょ 無遠慮な **rude**(ぶしつけな); **impolite**(礼儀作法を心得ていない) ▶無遠慮なふるまい *rude* behavior ‖そういう言い方は少し無遠慮だよ It's rather *impolite*［*rude*］to speak［put it］like that.

フォアグラ **foie gras** /fwɑ̀: grɑ́:/.

フォアボール 《野球》a **base on balls,** a **walk,** a **pass**
▶フォアボールで出塁する draw *a base on balls*／get *a walk* ‖ヒットとフォアボール2つでオリックスは満塁とした The Buffaloes loaded the bases on a single and two *walks*. ‖田中は次の打者をフォアボールで歩かせた Tanaka *walked* the next batter.

> **危ないカタカナ語✹ フォアボール**
> 「フォアボール」は和製語. 英語では「フォアボールによる出塁」を base on balls (略して BB) という. walk とか pass という言い方もある.「敬遠のフォアボール」は intentional walk［pass］である.

フォーカス a **focus**(焦点) ▶スポーツ選手のメンタル面にフォーカスをあてた特集 a feature article *focusing on* the players mental condition ‖その二人は深夜六本木で密会しているところをフォーカスされた The two *were photographed* during their late-night rendezvous in Roppongi.

フォーク a **fork** ▶ナイフとフォーク a knife and *fork* (➤1組とみる場合は fork に a をつけない. なおフォークの「歯」は tine という).
▶私はATMの前でフォーク並びをしていた I *was waiting in line for the next available* ATM. (➤銀行窓口ならば, ATM を counter や teller に変える;「フォーク並び」は英米で昔から行われていたものを日本で普及させるために名づけた呼称).

フォークソング a **folk** /foʊk/ **song**
‖**フォークソング歌手** a folk singer.

フォークダンス a **dance** 《参考》日本語の「フォークダンス」は学園祭やキャンプ場で踊るレクリエーション用のダンスを指すことが多いが, 英語の folk dance はあくまでも「民俗舞踊」の意である.

フォークボール 《野球》a **forkball.**

フォークリフト a **forklift (truck).**

フォークロア **folklore.**

フォースアウト 《野球》a **force-out** ▶新井のサードゴロで鳥谷は二塁フォースアウトとなった Toritani *was forced out* at second on Arai's grounder to third.

フォードア ▶フォードアの車 a *four-door* car.

フォーマット 《コンピュータ》a **format** ▶PDFフォーマットの文書 a document in PDF *format* ‖ディスクをフォーマットする *format* a disk.

フォーマル ‖**フォーマルウエア** a formal dress［suit］; formal wear(➤集合的).

フォーム (a) **form** ▶野茂投手のピッチングフォームはダイナミックだった Nomo had a dynamic *pitching form*. ‖彼女はすばらしいフォームで泳ぐ Her *form* in swimming is excellent.

フォーラム a **forum**(公開討論の場) ▶環境問題についての国際フォーラムが昨日開催された *An international forum* on environmental problems was held yesterday.

ぶおとこ 醜男 an **unattractive**［**ugly**］**man**(➤ ugly はしばしば性格の悪さを表す).

フォルダ 《コンピュータ》a **folder**(パソコンの) ▶フォルダを新規作成する create a new *folder*.

フォルテ 《音楽》**forte** /fɔ́:ˈteɪ/.

フォロー フォローする **follow up** 《on》(さらに補う, 徹底してやる) (➤ follow だけだと「…のあとをついて行く, を尾行する」の意) ▶大震災のその後をフォローしたテレビ番組 a *follow-up* TV program on the great earthquake ‖先生はいつも私たちの質問をきちんとフォローしてくれる Our teacher always *follows up on* our questions. (➤その場で答えられなくても, あとで調べて返事するの意) ‖私の説明不足を部長が上手にフォローしてくれた The (general) manager skillfully *clarified* some points that I had failed to explain fully. (➤ clarify は「きちんと説明して理解しやすくする」).
▶そのお客さんのクレームは私がフォローします I'll *take care of*［*handle*／*deal with*］the customer's complaint. ‖ショートがはじいた打球を二塁手がナイスフォローした The second baseman *nicely backed up* the shortstop to deal with the ball which he had missed.

フォワード 《球技》a **forward**(前衛)《略 FW》▶フォワードを務める play *forward*(➤守備位置の意味では a をつけない).

ふおん 不穏な **disturbing, alarming, disquieting, threatening** ▶不穏な情勢 a *disturbing* situation.

フォンデュ **fondue**(➤特に「チーズフォンデュ」というときは cheese fondue).

フォント 《印刷》a **font** ▶文書のフォントを平成明朝に変える change the document *font* to Heisei Mincho.

ふおんとう 不穏当な **improper** ▶不穏当なことば遣い use of *improper* language.

1**ふか 孵化する** **hatch**(+⾃) ▶このサケは人工ふ化したものだ These salmon *were hatched artificially*. (➤「人工ふ化」は artificial incubation) ‖ひなどりがふ化した The chickens *have hatched* (*out*).

2**ふか 不可** **unacceptable, unsatisfactory**; an **F**(学業成績) ▶辞書の使用は不可 The use of dictionaries *is not permitted* ‖地理が不可になる *get an F* in geography／*fail* geography (➤後者は「地理の試験に落ちる」).
▶《慣用表現》この作品は可もなく不可もなしだ There is *nothing outstandingly good or bad* about this work.／This work is *neither good nor bad*.／This work is so-so［mediocre］.

3**ふか 付加する** **add** +⾃ ‖**付加価値** added value ‖

付加価値税《英》a value-added tax《略 VAT》‖付加疑問 a tag question.

4ふか 鱶《魚》a **shark** ‖ フカひれ a shark fin ‖ フカひれスープ shark fin soup.

5ふか 負荷 a **burden**(マイナスの影響); a **load**(電気量) ▶環境負荷を極少にする minimize the *environmental burden* [*burden on the environment*] (➤ この表現では burden の代わりに, impact (影響)を使うことも多い).

ぶか 部下 one's **people**, one's **staff**(全員) ▶その部長は部下の面倒見がいい The manager takes good care of *his* [*her*] *people*. ‖部長は部下の一人一人に仕事を割り当てた The general manager assigned tasks to *everyone on his* [*her*] *staff*. ‖ 3年間あの人の部下として働いた I worked *for* [*under*] *him* for three years.

> **《解説》「部下」の言い方**
> (1)集合的には one's people, one's staff のようにいい, 1人の場合は例えば He [She] is one of my people [assistants /staff (members)]. のようにいうが, 一般的には He [She] works for [《英また》under] me. のような言い方が好まれる. ビジネス英語では He [She] reports to me. ともいう. one of my people は「仲間やメンバーの一人」の意味もある.
> (2) **subordinate** /səbɔ́ːrdənət/ は堅い語で, ときに軽蔑的に, または自虐的に用いられる.

1**ふかい 不快** **discomfort**(快適でないこと); **displeasure**(気に入らないこと) 一形 不快な **unpleasant**; **offensive**(ひどく不快な) ▶ごみ入れが不快なにおいを放っていた An *unpleasant* smell came from the garbage can. ‖不精ひげはまわりの人に不快感を与える Stubble *is unpleasant to look at* [*gives people a bad impression*]. ‖村長はその大臣の発言に不快感をあらわにした The village mayor expressed his [her] *displeasure* at the minister's remark. ‖彼女は家族のことを尋ねられると不快そうな顔をした She *looked displeased* [*offended*] when she was asked about her family.

‖不快指数 a discomfort index; a temperature-humidity index(温湿指数).

2ふかい 深い

> **訳語メニュー**
> 底や奥までの距離が長い →deep **1**
> 深遠な →profound **2**
> 関係が密接な →close **3**
> 霧などが濃い →dense, thick **4**

1【底・奥までの距離が】deep 一副 深く **deep**(➤ この意味では deeply はあまり使わない) ▶深い井戸 a *deep* well ‖ 深い穴 a *deep* hole ‖ 田沢湖は日本でいちばん深い湖です Lake Tazawa is *the deepest* in Japan. ‖この地方は冬の間は雪が深い In this area, the snow is *deep* in winter.

▶水中深く潜る dive *deep* in the water ‖ 雪が深く積もっている The snow lies *deep* [has piled up *deep*]. ‖この辺りは地面を深く掘ると温泉が出てくる If you dig *deep* (enough) around here, you can find hot-water springs.

2【程度が】deep; **profound** /prəfáʊnd/ (深遠な) 一副 深く **deeply** ▶彼女の両親は深い悲しみに沈んでいる Her parents are sunk in *deep* sorrow. ‖ 皇后陛下のスピーチは聴衆に深い感銘を与えた The empress's speech made a *deep* impression on the audience. ‖彼女は深いため息をついた She breathed a *deep* sigh. / She sighed *deeply*. ‖彼女は床につくとすぐ深い眠りに落ちた She fell into a *deep* [*sound*] sleep as soon as she got into bed. ‖このたとえ話には深い意味がある This allegory has a *profound* meaning.

▶我々は彼の勇気ある行動に深く感動した We were *deeply* moved by his brave deed. ‖あなたに悪いことをしたと深く反省しています I *deeply* regret having done a nasty thing to you.

3【関係が】close /kloʊs/ ▶この2つの事実の間には深い関係はない There is no *close* relation between these two facts. ‖二人は深い仲になった They became *intimately involved*. / They became *sexually intimate*.

4【生い茂った, 濃い】deep(深さ・奥行きなどが); **thick**(霧・樹木の生い茂り方などが); **dense**(気体の密度などが) ▶我々は深い森に迷い込んだ We wandered into [lost our way] in a *deep* [*thick*] forest. (➤ lost our way は道がわからなくなった場合) ‖エメラルドは深い緑色をしている Emeralds are *deep* green. ‖ 深い霧で我々の車は動けなかった Our car couldn't move because of the *dense* [*thick*] *fog*.

ぶかい 部会 a **club** [**team**] **meeting** ‖ 作業部会 a task force.

ぶがいしゃ 部外者 an **outsider**; a **person not concerned**(関係のない人) ▶《掲示》部外者立入禁止 Private.

ふがいない 腑甲斐ない ▶我々はふがいない(=屈辱的な)負け方をした We suffered a *humiliating* defeat. ‖なんてふがいない(=いくじのない)やつだ What a *spineless* guy!

ふかいり 深入り ▶こういうことにはあまり深入りしないほうがいい You'd be wise not to *get too deeply involved in* [*go too far into*] something like this.

ふかおい 深追い ▶女性を深追いする *pursue* a woman *(too) tenaciously*.

ふかかい 不可解な **mysterious**; **enigmatic**(謎めいた) ▶何とも不可解な事件だった The case was quite *mysterious*. ‖これは私には不可解だ This is *a mystery* to me. ‖彼の言動には不可解な点がある There is something *inscrutable* about what he says and does. ‖あの男は不可解な人物だ He is *a mystery* [*a mystery man*].

ふかぎもん 付加疑問《文法》a **tag question**.

ふかく 不覚 a **mistake**(誤り) ▶あの男を信用したのは私の一生の不覚だった It was the biggest *mistake* of my life to have trusted him. ‖不覚にも息子に碁で負けた *It was humiliating* [*embarrassing*] *to* have lost the Go match to my son. (➤ どちらも「不面目だ」の意) ‖ラストシーンで私は不覚にも涙を流した While watching the last scene, I shed tears *in spite of myself*. (➤ in spite of oneself は「思わず」).

ふかくじつ 不確実な **uncertain**; **unreliable**(信頼できない) ▶この情報は不確実だ This information is *uncertain* [*unreliable*]. ‖人生は不確実なことだらけだ Life is full of *uncertainties*. ‖不確実なことは言わないでください Don't tell me things you *are not sure of*.

ふかくてい 不確定な **uncertain**(はっきりしない) ▶その計画にはまだ不確定な要素がある Some elements of the plan are still *uncertain*.

ふかけつ 不可欠な indispensable《to, for》(欠かせない); essential《to, for》(あるものを成立させるために必須の) ▶外国語を勉強するには辞書は不可欠だ Dictionaries are *indispensable* when learning a foreign language.
▶きれいな水は半導体の生産上不可欠である Clean water is *indispensable for* the production of semiconductors. ‖ この計画を推進するためには彼は不可欠な人物だ He is *indispensable to* the project. ‖ 水と空気は生命に不可欠である Water and air are *essential to* life.

ふかこうりょく 不可抗力 ▶不可抗力の事故 an *unavoidable* accident ‖「地滑りは不可抗力だった」ではすまされない It's no excuse to say that the landslide was *a natural calamity* [*an act of God*]. 《参考》natural calamity は「天災」, act of God は法律用語で,「神の御業」の意なので英米人も日常的には使わない. 日本人も使用を避けたほうが賢明.

ふかさ 深さ depth ▶深さ最大1.2メートルの丸い穴 a round hole with a maximum *depth* of 1.2 meters ‖ この湖の深さはどのくらいありますか What is the *depth* of this lake? ／How deep is this lake?
▶この井戸は深さ約10メートルだ This well is about ten meters *deep*. ‖ その段ボールでは深さが足りない That cardboard box *isn't deep enough*.

ふかざけ 深酒 heavy [excessive] drinking ▶深酒しないようにね Take care not to *drink too much*.

ふかざら 深皿 a dish; a bowl(深鉢).

ふかさんめいし 不加算名詞《文法》an uncountable noun(➤ 本書では Ⓤ の記号で表している).

ふかしぎ 不可思議な mysterious; strange(奇妙な).

ふかしん 不可侵 ‖**不可侵条約** a nonaggression treaty.

[1]ふかす 蒸かす steam +ⓔ ▶ジャガイモをふかす *steam* potatoes.

[2]ふかす 吹かす **1【たばこを】** puff《at, on》▶父はうまそうにたばこをふかした My father *puffed on* a cigarette with evident enjoyment.
2【エンジンを】 rev (up) ▶うるさくエンジンをふかすな Don't *rev* (*up*) your engine so loudly.

ぶかつ 部活 club activities(クラブ活動); an extracurricular /èkstrəkəríkjələʳ/ activity(課外活動) ▶哲也は勉強より部活に熱心だ Tetsuya has more enthusiasm for his *club activities* than for his studies. ‖ 対話「部活は何をしていますか」「サッカーです」"What *club activities* do you take part in?" "I'm on the soccer team."
✉ **日本の中学では, 生徒に部活をすることを奨励しています** Japanese junior high schools encourage students to participate in *after-school activities* [*extracurricular activities*].
✉ **演劇部の部活のある日は帰りは8時ごろになります** On days *the drama club meets after school*, I get home (at) around eight. ➤ 個人のことについていうときには,「部活」と総称せず,「演劇(部)の練習があるとき」のように具体的にいうことが多い.

ぶかっこう 不格好な ill-shaped (形が悪い); unshapely(バランスが悪い); shapeless(見栄えがしない) ▶不格好な鼻 an *ill-shaped* nose ‖ 姉さんが編んでくれたセーターは少し不格好だけど大事にしている I treasure my (older) sister's hand-knitted sweater, though it is a little *shapeless* [*unshapely* ／ *ill-shaped*].

ふかっぱつ 不活発な inactive.

ふかづめ 深爪 ▶深爪をする *cut a fingernail* [*toenail*] *to the quick*(➤ to the quick は「生身のところまで」の意).

ふかのう 不可能な impossible ▶今さら日程を変更するなんて不可能だ It is *impossible* to change the schedule now. (● 不定詞に意味上の主語をつけるときには for us to change のようにする. (×)We are impossible のように人を主語にして言うことはできない) ‖ 19世紀には人間が月へ行くことなど不可能に思えた In the nineteenth century it seemed *impossible* that humankind could ever go to the moon. ‖ そんなの不可能に近いよ That's nearly [next to] *impossible*.
▶やる前から不可能だとあきらめてはだめだ Don't *give up* before you try. ‖ きみの要求は不可能だ You're asking for *the impossible*. ／Your request is *impossible*. ／Your demand is *out of the question*. ‖ 彼は決して「それは不可能だ」とは言わない He never says, "*It can't be done.*"

ふかひ 不可避の inevitable /ɪnévɪṭəbəl/, unavoidable (➤ 前者がより強意) ▶スト突入は不可避と思われる Going on strike seems *inevitable* [*unavoidable*]. ／It seems *impossible to avoid* a strike.

ふかふか ▶ふかふかのソファー a *soft and comfortable* sofa ‖ ふかふかのカステラ a *soft and light* sponge cake ‖ 布団を干したので今夜はふかふかの布団で寝られる I will be able to sleep on a *fluffy* futon tonight since I aired it today.

ふかぶか 深々と deeply ▶社長は遺族に深々と頭を下げた The president bowed his head *deeply* to the bereaved families. ‖ 彼はソファーに深々と座った He sat back *deep* in the sofa. (● 比喩的ではなく具体的な意味の場合は, deeply ではなく副詞の deep を用いることが多い).

ぶかぶか ▶弟はいつもぼくのお下がりのぶかぶかのズボンをはいている My brother always wears the *baggy* slacks that were passed down from me. ／My brother always wears the *baggy*, hand-me-down slacks from me. ‖ 福ちゃんはぶかぶかの帽子をかぶっている (Little) Fuku-chan is wearing a cap that is so big it *bobs around* on his head. (➤「大きすぎてかぶると動く」の意).

ぷかぷか ▶たばこをぷかぷか吸う *puff away at* a cigarette ‖ 川面をペットボトルがぷかぷか流れていた A plastic bottle was *bobbing up and down* on the river. (➤ bob は「ぴょこんと上下する」の意).

ふかぶん 不可分 ▶言語と文化の不可分性 *the inseparability* [*inseparableness*] of language and culture ‖ 生あるかぎり, 心と肉体は不可分だ Mind and body are *inseparable* as long as we're alive. 《参考》キリスト教徒だけでなく, イスラム教徒・ユダヤ教徒, いずれの人たちも, 心(や意識)は死の瞬間に肉体を離れ, the immortal soul (不滅の魂)となって別の生を生き続けると考える. これこそが the afterlife (来世)と呼ぶもので, 信仰の根本である.

ふかまる 深まる ▶彼らの愛は日増しに深まった Their love *deepened* [*grew deeper*] day by day. ‖ 彼女の個展を見て彼女の絵に対する理解が深まった Her solo exhibition gave me a *deeper* understanding of her paintings. ‖ 秋もだいぶ深まってきた Autumn has *deepened* considerably. ／We are well *into* autumn.

ふかみ 深み depth, profundity (➤ 後者は「深遠さ」に相当する堅い語) ▶芭蕉の芸術の深み the *profundity* of Basho's art ‖ 深みのあるブルー *deep* blue.

▶かけ事に夢中になって彼は深みにはまり込んだ He *got too involved in* gambling.

ふかみどり 深緑 deep green.

ふかめる 深める deepen ＋目 ▶私たちは休暇を一緒に過ごして友情を深めた Our vacation together *deepened* [*strengthened*] our friendship. (➤ strengthen は「強める」) ‖ 彼らは文通を通じて相互の理解を深めた They *deepened* their mutual understanding by exchanging letters.

ふかよみ 深読みする read too much《into》, overinterpret ＋目.

ぶかん 武官 a military officer ; a naval officer (海軍の).

1**ふかんしょう 不干渉** nonintervention, noninterference ‖内政不干渉 (a policy of) nonintervention in internal affairs.

2**ふかんしょう 不感症** ▶不感症の女性 a *frigid* woman.

▶《比喩的》我々はふつうの交通事故には不感症になっている We have *become immune to shock* from ordinary traffic accidents. (➤ immune /ɪmjúːn/ to は「…に免疫ができた」) ／We've *gotten used to* usual traffic accidents.

ふかんぜん 不完全な incomplete (必要なものがそろっていない) ; imperfect (完璧ではない) ▶曲はできたが, 詞のほうがまだ不完全だ I've made the melody of the song, but the lyrics are still *incomplete*. ‖ 人間はみな不完全なものだ Everyone is *imperfect*. ／We are all *imperfect*. (逆の表現だが, No one is perfect. (完璧な人などいない) という言い方がふつう) ‖ 製品には不完全なものが混じっていた There were some *defective* items among the products. (➤ defective は「欠陥のある」).

‖不完全燃焼 incomplete [poor] combustion.

1**ふき 蕗** 《植物》 a butterbur /bʌ́t̬ərbəːʳ/.

2**ふき 付記する** add ＋目 ▶「要再検討」と彼は付記した "It should be reviewed," he *added*.

ふぎ 不義 infidelity (不貞) ; adultery (姦通).

ぶき 武器 arms (➤ 戦闘用の武器の総称 ; 複数形で用いる) ; a weapon /wépən/ (➤ 個々の, 攻撃・防御用の道具) ▶武器を捨てる lay down one's *arms* [*weapons*] ‖ 農民たちは武器を取って政府軍と戦った The farmers and peasants took up *arms* and fought against the government forces. ‖ カニにとってははさみが最大の武器だ A crab's most powerful *weapon* is its claws.

▶《比喩的》ジャーナリストはペンを武器に世の不正に立ち向かう Journalists stand up against social injustice by using the pen as their *weapon*.

ふきあげる 吹き上げる・噴き上げる ▶木枯らしが落ち葉を吹き上げた The cold winter wind *made* the fallen leaves *whirl* (*in the air*). ‖ クジラが潮を吹き上げた A whale *spouted* (*water*). (➤ spout は「(液体などを)噴出する」の意) ‖ 浅間山は絶えず煙を噴き上げている Mt. Asama is *emitting* [*spouting*] *smoke* ceaselessly.

ふきあれる 吹き荒れる ▶風が一日中吹き荒れた It [The wind] *blew hard* all day.

ブギウギ 《音楽》 the boogie-woogie.

ふきかえ 吹き替え dubbing (音声の) ▶その映画は吹き替えですか, 日本語の字幕つきですか *Is* that movie *dubbed*, or does it have Japanese subtitles?

▶その俳優は危険な場面を吹き替え(＝代役)なしで演じた That actor did the dangerous stunts himself without *a stand-in*.

ふきかえす 吹き返す ▶人工呼吸のおかげで彼は息を吹き返した Artificial respiration *brought* him *back to life* [*revived* him].

▶《比喩的》その勝利でドラゴンズは息を吹き返した After the victory, the Dragons *have come back to life*. ／The victory *gave* the Dragons *a new lease on life*.

ふきかける 吹き掛ける blow《on》(息を) ▶少年は冷たい両手に息を吹きかけた The boy *blew* on his cold hands. ‖ 彼女はアイロンをかける前にシャツに霧を吹きかけた She *sprayed water* on the shirts before ironing them.

ふきけす 吹き消す blow out ▶彼女はバースデーケーキのろうそくを吹き消した She *blew out* the candles on her birthday cake.

ふきげん 不機嫌な bad-tempered (機嫌の悪い ; 一時的な状態は be in a bad mood で表す) ; cross (気に入らなくて怒った) ; sullen /sʌ́lən/ (気に入らなくて黙り込んだ, ぶすっとした) ; grouchy /ɡráʊtʃi/, grumpy (ぶつぶつ言う, 不平たらたらの ; 前者がよりインフォーマル) ▶たけしは家を出る前に姉とけんかしたので一日中不機嫌だった Takeshi was *in a bad mood* [*temper*] all day because he had quarreled with his sister before he left home. (temper は「かんしゃく」の意で使うことが多い) ‖ どうして彼はあんなに不機嫌なんだい? Why is he *in* such *a bad mood*? ／What makes him so *cross*?

▶母はなぜか朝から不機嫌だ I don't know why, but my mother has been *grumpy* since morning. ／My mother has been *out of sorts* since morning for some reason or other. ‖ 父はおなかがすくと不機嫌になる My father *gets grouchy* when he is hungry.

ふきこぼれる 吹きこぼれる boil over ▶気をつけないとスープが吹きこぼれるよ If you aren't careful, the soup will *boil over*.

ふきこむ 吹き込む **1【風や雨が】** blow into ▶戸の隙間から冷たい風が吹き込んでいた A cold draft *was blowing into* the room through the crack in the door. ‖ 高窓から雨が吹き込んだ Rain *came in* through the high window.

2【教え込む】 ▶子供に妙な考えを吹き込まないでくれ Don't *put* strange [weird] ideas *in* my child's head.

3【録音する】 record /rɪkɔ́ːʳd/ ＋目 ▶その男性アイドルグループが新曲を吹き込んだ The boy band *has recorded* a new song. ／The boy band *has cut* a new single.

ふきさらし 吹きさらし ▶このホームは吹きさらしだから冬は寒い Since the platform *is exposed* [*open*] *to the wind* [*is windswept*], it is freezing cold in winter.

ふきすさぶ 吹きすさぶ blow violently ; rage (荒れ狂う) ▶吹きすさぶ風 a *raging* wind.

ふきそ 不起訴 non-prosecution, non-indictment /nɑ̀ːnɪndáɪtmənt/ →起訴 ▶その総会屋は不起訴処分になった The corporate racketeer *was not prosecuted* [*indicted*]. (➤ prosecute, indict はともに「起訴する」の意) ／The *case* against the corporate racketeer *was dropped*.

ふきそうじ 拭き掃除 wiping ; mopping (モップを使っての).

ふきそく 不規則な irregular ▶不規則な生活 an *irregular* life ‖ 父はこの頃帰りが不規則だ My father comes home *at irregular times* these days. (➤ irregularly を用いると帰って来ないときもあると解釈される

恐れがある) ／My father hasn't been coming home at a set time recently.
▶この辺は道路が不規則に延びている In this area, the roads go *every which way* [are laid out *in no particular order*].

ふきたおす 吹き倒す blow down ▶嵐が公園の木をたくさん吹き倒した The storm *blew down* lots of trees in the park.

ふきだし 吹き出し a balloon,《英》a bubble.

ふきだす 吹き出す･噴き出す **1**【出る】gush [spurt] out(液体が勢いよく)；billow (out)(煙や炎が大きな塊となって)；break out(汗などが急に) ▶油井から石油が吹き出した Oil *gushed out* of the well. ‖ 爆発したガスタンクから煙が吹き出している Clouds of smoke *are billowing* from the exploded gas tank. ‖ 額から汗が吹き出した Sweat *broke out* on my forehead. ／My forehead *broke out* in (a) sweat. ‖ 燃えている車から炎が吹き出した Flames *leaped* from the burning car.
▶労働者の不満がいっせいに吹き出した The dissatisfaction of the workers *erupted* all at once. (➤ erupt は「爆発する」).
2【笑う】▶彼が変な間違いをしたのでクラスのみんなはふき出した All the class *burst out laughing* [*broke into laughter* ／*cracked up*], because he made a funny mistake. ‖ 息子が鼻の頭にケチャップをつけているのを見て母親はぷっとふき出した The mother *let out a giggle* when she saw her son had gotten some ketchup on the tip of his nose.

ふきだまり 吹きだまり a drift ▶道の片側は絶壁で,もう一方は雪の吹きだまりだ There's a cliff on one side of the road, and *a snowdrift* on the other. ‖ 落ち葉が校庭の片隅で吹きだまりになっていた Fallen leaves *had drifted into a pile* in a corner of the playground.

ふきつ 不吉な ominous /ɑ́ːmɪnəs/；unlucky(縁起の悪い) ▶不吉な前兆 an *ill* omen ‖ 西洋では13日の金曜日は不吉な日だといわれる In the West, Friday the 13th is said to be an *unlucky* day. ‖ 何か悪いことが起きるのではないかという不吉な予感がした I had an *ominous* feeling that something bad would occur.

ふきつける 吹き付ける spray +目 (吹きかける)；blow against(風がたたきつける) ▶父は外壁にペンキを吹きつけた My father *sprayed* paint on the outer wall.

ぶきっちょ ▶兄はぶきっちょだ My brother is *clumsy* [is *a klutz*]. (➤ klutz /klʌts/ は「下手くそ, 不器用な人」の意のアメリカ俗語). →不器用.

ふきでもの 吹き出物 a pimple(にきび)；a rash (発疹) ▶顔に吹き出物ができた I have *pimples* on my face. ／I have *a rash* on my face. ／*A rash* has broken out on my face.

ふきとばす 吹き飛ばす **1**【風が飛ばす】blow off [away] ▶ゆうべの嵐でうちの屋根が吹き飛ばされた The roof of my house *was blown off* in last night's storm. ‖ 彼は机の上のほこりを無造作に吹き飛ばした He casually *blew* the dust *off* the desk.
2【追い払う】▶ジョギングをして寒さを吹き飛ばそう Let's *shake off* the cold [Let's warm ourselves up] by jogging. ‖ 先生の励ましが彼の不安を吹き飛ばした His teacher's encouraging words *drove away* [*dispelled*] his anxieties.

ふきとぶ 吹き飛ぶ ▶突風で屋根がわらが吹き飛んだ The roof tiles *were blown off* [*away*] by the gust. ‖ 会社がつぶれて夢も希望も吹き飛んだ My hopes and dreams *vanished* when my company went under. (➤ vanish は「消えうせる」の意).

ふきとる 拭き取る wipe《off, away》▶皿の汚れをふき取る *wipe* a dish *clean* ‖ 汗をふき取る *wipe off* (the) sweat.

ふきながし 吹き流し a streamer.

ふきぬけ 吹き抜け a stairwell(階段の)；an atrium(ホテルなどの広い空間) ▶吹き抜けに置かれた巨大なクリスマスツリー a giant Christmas tree in *the atrium*.

ふきのとう 蕗の薹 《植物》a butterbur sprout.

ぶきみ 不気味な weird /wɪəʳd/ (不思議な, 気持ちの悪い)；eerie /íəri/ (恐怖と不安を呼び起こす) ▶時折水鳥が闇の中から不気味な声を出した Every now and then, some water birds gave off *eerie* cries from the darkness. ‖ 誰もいない家から不気味な音が聞こえてきた We heard an *eerie* sound from the empty house. ‖ 家は不気味なほど静まりかえっていた The house was so quiet that it *gave me the creeps*. (➤「ぞっとした」の意).

ふきや 吹き矢 a blowpipe, a blowgun.

ふきやむ 吹きやむ ▶北風が吹きやんだ The north wind *died down*.

¹ふきゅう 普及 the spread /spred/ **一動 普及する** spread (広まる)；become popular (人気が出てくる) ▶その童謡は小学校で歌われてから一般に普及した The children's song *spread* throughout the nation after being sung at elementary schools. ‖ フェイスブックはアメリカよりヨーロッパのほうが普及している Facebook is more *widespread* in Europe than in the U.S. ‖ 携帯電話の普及率は高い Cellphones *have become quite popular*. ／Cellphones *have come into widespread use*. ／Cellphones are here to stay. (➤ be here to stay は「定着している」).
‖普及版 a popular edition.

²ふきゅう 不朽の immortal, everlasting ▶ベートーベンの9つの交響曲は不朽の名作とされている Beethoven's nine symphonies are considered *immortal* masterpieces. ‖『風と共に去りぬ』でマーガレット･ミッチェルは不朽の名声を得た "Gone with the Wind" won Margaret Mitchell *immortal* [*everlasting*] fame.

¹ふきょう 不況 a recession (景気の後退)；(a) depression(GNPが10%以上減少するような極めて深刻で広範囲の)；stagnation(停滞) ▶日本経済の不況は深刻だ The economic *recession* [*slump*] in Japan is serious. ‖ 政府は不況を切り抜けるための政策を発表した The government announced its policies for pulling out of the *recession*.

²ふきょう 布教 missionary work(布教活動) **一動 布教する** spread +目 (➤「広める」の意の一般語)；propagate +目 (思想･主義などを広める) ▶キリスト教を布教するために多くの宣教師が日本にやって来た A large number of missionaries came to Japan to *spread* Christianity.

³ふきょう 不興 ▶彼は暴言を吐いて上司の不興を買ったようだ It seems he *has offended* the boss by shouting abusive language.

ぶきよう 不器用な clumsy/klʌ́mzi/, awkward/ɔ́ːkwəʳd/ (➤ 前者には軽蔑的なニュアンスがあることが多い) →ぶきっちょ ▶私は手先が不器用だ I'm *clumsy* with my fingers [hands]. ／I'm all thumbs. (➤ 後者は「5本とも親指である」が原義) ‖ 父は不器用な手つきでキャベツを刻んでいる My father is *awkwardly* cutting cabbage.

ふ

ふきょうわおん 不協和音 (a) **discord,** (a) **dissonance** (➤ともに比喩的な意味でも用いる) ▶《比喩的》最近, 社長と重役たちの間に**不協和音**が生じているらしい Lately, there are rumors of *discord* between the company president and the directors. ／The president is said to be on bad terms with the directors these days.

ぶきょく 舞曲 (a **piece of**) **dance music,** a **dance.**

ふぎり 不義理 **1**【忘恩】**ingratitude** ▶卒業以来, 恩師のところにはお礼にもうかがわず**不義理をしている** I *feel an uncomfortable debt* to my former teacher because I haven't gone to thank him properly since graduation.

2【借金があること】▶彼はあちこちに**不義理をしている** He *is in debt* to people all over.

ふきりつ 不規律 a **lack of discipline.**

ぶきりょう 不器量な **plain,**《主に米》**homely.**

[1]**ふきん 布巾** a **dishtowel**(食器用の)

‖**台ぶきん** a cloth used for wiping tables.

[2]**ふきん 付近** (a) **neighborhood** ▶**この付近にはいいレストランがたくさんある** We have a lot of good restaurants *in this neighborhood.* ‖**この付近に銀行はありますか** Is there a bank *near here*? ‖彼女はどこかこの付近に住んでいる She lives *somewhere around here.*

ふきんこう 不均衡 **imbalance** ━形 **不均衡な** **unbalanced** ▶貿易の不均衡を是正する必要がある We have to correct the trade *imbalance.* ‖男女の社会的地位はまだ**不均衡だ** The social positions of men and women *are* still *unbalanced.* →**アンバランス.**

ふきんしん 不謹慎な **indiscreet**(言動に思慮を欠く); **imprudent**(自分の言動のあと先を考えない; やや堅い語); **indecent**(品位を欠く) ▶**不謹慎な**発言をする make some *indiscreet* remarks ‖**不謹慎なふるまい** *imprudent* behavior ‖葬式のときに笑うのは**不謹慎だ** It's *indecent* to laugh at a funeral.

[1]**ふく 服** **clothes** /klouz/ (衣服); **clothing**(衣料品, 衣類; 集合的に指す語), a **suit** (スーツ); a **dress** (ドレス) →**衣服**

▶**夏服をしまう** put away one's *summer clothes* ‖**防護服を着る** wear *protective clothing* ‖**服を着なさい** Get dressed. ／Put on your *clothes.* ‖**服を脱ぎなさい** Take off your *clothes.* (➤「脱ぐ」は put off としない) ／Get undressed. ‖この**服**は小さくなった I've outgrown [grown out of] these *clothes.* (➤何着かある場合) ／I've outgrown this *suit* [*dress*]. (➤1着の場合は具体的にいう) ‖**服**は脱いだらきちんと畳みなさい Fold your *clothes* properly after taking them off. ‖あすのコンサートにどの**服**を着て行こうかな Which *dress* shall I wear to the concert tomorrow? ‖彼女は赤い**服を着ていた** She *was dressed in* red. ／She *was wearing* [*was in*] *a* red *dress.* ‖彼女は**服を着替える**のにずいぶん手間取った She took a long time to *change* (*her clothes*). ‖**紳士服** [**子供服**] **売り場**はどこですか Where's the *men's* [*children's*] *clothing department*?

[2]**ふく 福** (**good**) **luck, fortune** (➤前者はややインフォーマル) ▶西洋ではウサギの足は**福**をもたらすと信じられている In the West, a rabbit's foot is believed to bring *good luck.*

‖**福の神** the god of good fortune.

[3]**ふく 吹く・噴く** **1**【風が】**blow** ▶ゆうべは強い北風が夜通し**吹いていた** A strong north wind *blew* all night (long) yesterday. (➤ blew は blow の過去形) ‖風が強く**吹いている** *It* [*The wind*] *is blowing* hard. ／There is a strong wind. (インフォーマルでは It's windy. ということが多い) ‖さわやかな風が**吹いている** *There is* a refreshing breeze. ‖私たちは春風に**吹かれながら**土手を散歩した We took a walk along the bank *in* the spring breeze [*as* the spring breeze blew].

2【息をかける】**blow** 《on》 ▶**ろうそくを吹いて消す** *blow out* a candle ‖熱いお茶を**吹いて**冷ました I *blew on* the hot tea to cool it.

▶《慣用表現》うちの会社なんて**吹けば飛ぶような**零細企業ですよ Ours is such a small company that it can *be blown away* any time.

3【鳴らす】**blow** +目; **play** +目 (演奏する) ▶トランペットを**吹く**のは難しい It is difficult to *blow* a trumpet [*play* the trumpet]. ‖車掌が笛を**吹く**とドアが閉まった When the conductor *blew* the whistle, the doors closed.

4【勢いよく出る】▶**エンジンが火を噴いた** The engine *burst into flames.* ‖またまた阿蘇山が**火を噴いた**(＝噴火した) Mt. Aso *erupted* once again. ‖ほら, やかんのお湯が**噴いてる**よ Look! The kettle *is boiling over.* ‖ザトウクジラが**潮を吹いた** A humpback whale *spouted* [*blew*] water.

5【表面に出てくる】▶4月になるとシラカバがいっせいに**芽を吹く** In April, white birch trees *bud* all at once.

[4]**ふく 拭く** **wipe** (**away**)(ぬぐう); **clean** +目 (きれいにする); **dry** +目 (水気を取る) ▶**棚の上をふきなさい** *Wipe* [*Clean*] the shelves. ‖黒板を**ふいて**ください Can you please *clean* the blackboard? ‖母は食器を片づけ, テーブルを**ふいた** My mother cleared away the dishes and *wiped* the table. ‖私が食器を洗うから, あなたは布巾で**ふいて**ちょうだい I'll wash the dishes, so would you *dry* them with a dishtowel? ‖彼はハンカチで**涙をふいた** He *wiped his eyes* with a handkerchief. ／He *wiped his tears away* with a handkerchief.

ふく- 副-

> **解説**「副-」に相当する英語には vice-, deputy, sub- などがある. このうち vice- と deputy は官職・公職名の前につける. sub- は「次位の, 下位の」の意で用いる. assistant を使う場合もある.

▶我々は彼を**副議長**に選んだ We elected him *vice-chairman.* ‖新宿は東京の**副都心**である Shinjuku is *a subcenter* of Tokyo.

‖**副音声** a SAP channel (➤ SAP は secondary audio program の略) ‖**副会長** a vice-chairperson ‖**副教材** supplementary material ‖**副校長**《米》a vice-principal,《英》a deputy headteacher ‖**副社長** an executive [a senior] vice-president (of a company) ‖**副収入** (an) income from a side job ‖**副賞** an extra [a supplementary] prize ‖**副審** a sub-referee, a sub-umpire ‖**副操縦士** a copilot /kóupàilət/ ‖**副題** a subtitle ‖**副大臣** a senior vice-minister ‖**副大統領** a vice president (➤インフォーマルでは veep /viːp/ という) ‖**副知事** a vice-governor, a deputy governor ‖**副読本** a side [supplementary] reader.

-ふく -副 ▶申請書は**正副二通**を提出のこと The applications should be presented *in duplicate.*

‖**正副議長** the speaker and vice-speaker, the chairperson and vice-chairperson, the president and vice-president.

ふぐ《魚》a **globefish**, a **blowfish**, a **puffer**, a ***fugu***.

ふぐあい 不具合 a **defect**, a **fault**(欠陥); a **bug**(ソフトウエアの誤り) ▶システムにいくつかの**不具合**が見つかった Some *bugs* were discovered in the system.

ふくあん 腹案 ▶もし**腹案**がありましたら発表してください If you *have some plan in mind*, please explain it now.

ふくいくたる 馥郁たる **fragrant**(芳香のある); **aromatic**(コーヒーなど).

1**ふくいん 福音** **the Gospel**(キリスト教の); **good news**(吉報) ▶新しい治療法の発見は患者たちにはまさに**福音**となった The discovery of a new cure came as *good news* to the patients.
‖**福音書** the (four) Gospels.

2**ふくいん 復員** **demobilization** 一動 **復員する** **demobilize.**

ふぐう 不遇の **ill-fated**(不運な); **ill-starred**(星回りの悪い) ▶**不遇の**詩人 an *ill-starred* poet ‖その芸術家は才能があるにもかかわらず, 一生を**不遇のうちに**終えた Despite his talent, the artist ended his life *in obscurity*. (●「無名(状態)で」と考える) ‖モジリアニは**不遇のまま**死んだ Modigliani died *without getting his due recognition*. (●「正当に評価されることなく死んだ」と考える).

ふくえき 服役する **serve time** [**a sentence**] ▶刑務所に3年間**服役する** *serve* three years [a three-year sentence] in prison ‖彼女は詐欺罪で**服役中**だ She *is serving* [*doing*] *time* for fraud.

ふくえん 復縁 ▶彼は離婚した妻に**復縁**を迫った He urged his former wife [ex-wife] to *get back together with* him.

ふくがく 復学 ▶彼女は6か月後に**復学した** She *came back* [*returned*] *to school* after six months' absence.

ふくがん 複眼《生物学》**compound eyes.**

ふくぎょう 副業 a **job on the side**, a **sideline**, a **second job** ▶高田さんは**副業**として著述関係の仕事をしている Mr. Takada does some writing as *a sideline*. ‖公務員は**副業**を禁じられている Public servants are banned from *moonlighting*. →アルバイト.

ふくげん 復元 **restoration**(修復); **reconstruction**(再建) 一動 **復元する** **restore** +目; **reconstruct** +目(再建する) ▶登呂遺跡には弥生時代の住居が**復元されている** Several houses of the Yayoi era have *been reconstructed* at the Toro historic site. ‖ファイルを**復元する** *restore* a file.
‖**復元図** a diagram of a restored building.

ふくごう 複合 ‖**複合汚染** compound pollution ‖**複合企業** a conglomerate ‖**複合語** a compound word ‖(スキーの) **アルペン複合** Alpine Combined.

ふくさ 副査 ▶論文審査の**副査** *a* [*the*] *deputy chair* of a thesis evaluation committee (➤ the は副査が1人の場合).

ふくざつ 複雑な **complicated**, **complex**
語法 complicated は「各部分が入り組んでいて理解・分析などが困難な」という意味だが, しばしば「ごちゃごちゃした」というマイナスイメージが含まれる.complex は「(ごちゃごちゃしてはいないが)構造が込み入っていて専門的知識を必要としたり, 理解するまでには時間がかかる」の意.
▶**複雑な**機械 a *complicated* [*complex*] machine ‖**複雑な**法律問題 a *complicated* question of law ‖日本の年金制度は**複雑だ** The Japanese pension system is *complicated*. ‖人間の脳は**複雑な**器官である The human brain is a *complex* organ. ‖彼女の話を聞いて私は**複雑な気持ち**になった Hearing her story, I had *mixed feelings*.
▶彼の発言は問題をますます**複雑にした**だけだった His remark only *complicated* the matter further. / His comment only *made* the situation more *complicated*. ‖今や生活は**複雑化する**一方だ Nowadays, life *is becoming* more and more *complicated*.

ふくさよう 副作用 a **side effect**(➤しばしば複数形で用いる) ▶**副作用**のない薬はない No medicine is free from *side effects*. ‖この抗生物質は**副作用**の心配はありませんか Are there any fears of *side effects* with this antibiotic?

ふくさんぶつ 副産物 a **by-product**, a **spinoff** ▶軍事研究はさまざまな有用な**副産物**を生んだ Military research has spawned a wide variety of useful *by-products*.

1**ふくし 福祉** **welfare**, **well-being** (➤前者のほうが一般的) ▶もっと多くの税金が国民の**福祉**のために使われるべきだ More tax money should be used for the *welfare* [*well-being*] of the people. ‖彼女は一生を**公共福祉**にささげた She devoted herself to *public welfare*.
‖**福祉国家** a welfare state ‖**福祉サービス** welfare service ‖**福祉事業** welfare work ‖**福祉施設** welfare facilities ‖**福祉事務所** a (public) welfare office ‖**児童福祉** child welfare ‖**社会福祉** social welfare.

2**ふくし 副詞**《文法》an **adverb**
‖**副詞句** an adverbial phrase.

ふくじ 服地 **material for clothing.**

ふくしきこきゅう 腹式呼吸 **abdominal breathing** ▶**腹式呼吸をする** *breathe from the abdomen*.

1**ふくしゃ 複写** a **copy**, a **duplicate** /djúːplɪkət/ (複写されたもの) 一動 **複写する** **copy** +目, **duplicate** /djúːplɪkeɪt/ +目 (コピーする); **reproduce** +目 (絵画などの複製を作る) →コピー ▶これは古い写真から**複写した**ものだ This is a *duplicate* picture taken from an old photograph. / This is a photograph which has *been reproduced* from an old one. ‖この原稿を**複写してください** Please *copy* [*make a copy of* / *make a duplicate of*] this manuscript.
‖**複写機** a copy(ing) machine, a copier; a photocopier(写真複写機).

2**ふくしゃ 輻射** ‖《物理学》**輻射熱** radiant heat.

1**ふくしゅう 復讐** (a) **revenge** 一動 **復しゅうする** **take revenge on**(個人的なうらみを晴らす); **avenge** +目 (人のあだを討つ) →仕返し ▶彼は自分を裏切った男に**復しゅう**しようとした He tried to *take revenge on* the man who betrayed him. ‖身代わりになって監獄に送られた男は**復しゅう心**に燃えていた The man who had been sent to prison as a scapegoat was burning with *revenge*.

2**ふくしゅう 復習** 《米》(a) **review**, 《英》**revision** 一動 **復習する** 《米》**review**(+目), 《英》**revise**(+目) ▶私は英語の授業の**復習をした** I *reviewed* my English class [lessons]. / I *reviewed* my English textbook [my English class notes]. ‖すぐに**復習をしなさい** *Review* [*Go over*] your lesson(s) right now.
‖**復習問題** a review exercise.

ふくじゅう 服従 **obedience** /oʊbíːdiəns/ (命令に従うこと); **submission** (降伏) 一動 **服従する** **obey**(+目), **submit**(+目) ▶当時, 奴隷たちは主人への**服従**を拒めば

ひどい仕打ちを受けた In those days, if slaves refused *obedience* to [refused to *obey*] their master, they were punished harshly.

ふくじゅそう 福寿草《植物》an **adonis.**

ふくしょう 復唱する **repeat** +㊐ ▶復唱させていただきます Please let me *repeat* what you said.

1**ふくしょく 服飾** ▶彼女は服飾関係の仕事をしている She's in the *fashion industry* [*business*].
‖**服飾雑誌** a fashion magazine ‖**服飾デザイナー** a dress [fashion] designer ‖**服飾品** accessories /əksésəriz/.

2**ふくしょく 復職する** **return** [**come back** / **go back**] **to work** ; **be reinstated in** one's **office**(公職に) ▶彼女は育児休暇が終わって復職した She *returned to work* after her maternity leave finished.

3**ふくしょく 副食** →おかず, 主食.

ふくしん 腹心 ▶彼は私の腹心の部下だ He is one of my *most trusted people* [*men*]. / He is my *right-hand man*. (「最も信頼する男の一人」と考えて前者のように,「右腕である」と考えて後者のように訳す).

ふくじん 副腎《解剖学》an **adrenal gland.**

ふくじんづけ 福神漬け ***fukujinzuke*** ; sliced vegetables pickled in soy sauce and mirin (➤ 説明的な訳).

1**ふくすい 覆水** ▶ ことわざ **覆水盆に返らず** What's done is done [cannot be undone]. (➤ このことわざが日本語により近い) / It's no use crying over spilt milk.

2**ふくすい 腹水**《医学》**ascites** /əsáɪtiːz/.

ふくすう 複数の **plural** /plʊ́ərəl/ ▶"child" の複数形は何ですか What is the *plural* (*form*) of "child"?
▶複数の人がその事故を目撃した *More than one person* [*A number of people*] witnessed the accident.

ふくする 服する ▶彼は5年の懲役刑に服している He *is serving out* a sentence of five years' imprisonment. ‖彼女は夫の喪に服している She *is in* [*has gone into*] *mourning* for her husband.

ふくせい 複製 a **replica** /réplɪkə/ (きわめて忠実な) ; a **reproduction** (原物に似た絵画など) ; a **duplicate** /djúːplɪkət/ (本物と同時または同方式で作られた) 一動 **複製する** **reproduce** +㊐, **duplicate** /djúːplɪkeɪt/ +㊐ ▶今日残された古代ギリシャ彫刻の多くはローマ時代の複製である Most ancient Greek sculptures that remain today are *replicas* [*copies*] from the Roman period. ‖壁にはモネの複製画がかかっていた There was *a reproduction* of a Monet on the wall. / There hung a Monet *reproduction* on the wall.
▶この店は絵画の複製を専門に扱っている This store makes a specialty of *reproducing* [*duplicating*] paintings.

1**ふくせん 複線** a **double track**, a **two-track line** 《参考》「複々線」は a four-track line という.

2**ふくせん 伏線** **foreshadowing** ▶この小さな事件が後の大事件の伏線になっている This small incident *foreshadows* [*is the foreshadowing* of] a much bigger one.

ふくそう 服装

dress ; **clothes** /kloʊz/, **clothing** (➤ ともに「衣服」の意で, 後者は集合的) ; **costume** (ある民族・時代・職業などに特徴的な) ▶この高校は服装にうるさい This high school is strict about *dress*. ‖彼女はいつもきちんとした服装をしている She always *dresses neatly*. ‖彼は服装には全くむとんちゃくだ He pays no attention at all to *what he wears* [to *his clothing*]. ‖仮面舞踏会には凝った服装の人々が集まった People came in fancy *costumes* to the masquerade. ‖きょうは1日冷えますので, 暖かい服装でお出かけください It will be chilly all day today, so please go out wearing warm *clothing* [*clothes*].
▶セールスの仕事ですので服装には気をつかいます Since I'm a salesperson, I am careful about *what I wear*.
✉ **私たちの学校には厳しい服装規定があります** Our school has a strict *dress* code. ➤ code は「規則」の意.

ふくぞう 腹蔵 ▶腹蔵ないご意見を伺いたい I'd [We'd] like to hear your *candid* opinion(s).

ふぐたいてん 不倶戴天 ▶不倶戴天の敵 a *mortal* enemy.

ふくつ 不屈の **indomitable** (断固たる) ; **sturdy** (強固な) ; **invincible** /ɪnvínsəbəl/ (無敵の) ▶不屈の意志 an *indomitable* will ‖不屈の闘士 a *sturdy* fighter ‖彼は不屈の精神の持ち主だ He has an *invincible* spirit.

ふくつう 腹痛 (a) **stomachache** /stʌ́məkeɪk/ (胃痛) ; **abdominal** [**stomach**] **pain(s)** (腹部の痛み) ▶ひどい腹痛がする I've got a terrible *stomachache*. / I have terrible *abdominal* [*stomach*] *pain*(*s*). ‖真理子は腹痛のため学校を休んだ Mariko was absent from school because of (*a*) *stomachache*.

ふくどく 服毒 ▶男は服毒自殺を図った The man tried to *kill himself by taking* [*swallowing*] *poison*.

ふくびき 福引き a **lottery**, a **raffle** (➤ 後者は慈善目的が多い) ▶福引きを引く draw *a lottery* ‖福引きで韓国旅行 [1等賞] が当たった I won a trip to South Korea [(the) first prize] in *a lottery*.
‖**福引き券** a lottery [raffle] ticket.

ふくぶ 腹部 **the abdomen, the belly** 一形 **腹部の** **abdominal.**

ぶくぶく ▶お父さんはおなかのあたりがぶくぶく太っている Dad is getting a spare tire. (➤ spare tire は胴回りのぜい肉を「予備のタイヤ」とおどけて言ったもの) / Dad has a potbelly. (➤ potbelly は「太鼓腹」).
▶そのカニはぶくぶく泡を吹いた The crab blew bubbles—*pop! pop!*

ふくぶくしい 福々しい ▶彼の奥さんは福々しい顔をしている His wife has a *cheerfully round* face.

ふくぶくろ 福袋 a **grab bag of unknown contents.**

ふくぶん 複文《文法》a **complex sentence.**

ふくほん 複本 a **duplicate copy** (➤「(絵などの)複製」の意もある).

ふくまくえん 腹膜炎《医学》**peritonitis** /pèrətnáɪtɪs/.

ふくみ 含み an **implication** (言外の意味) ; a **connotation** (特に単語が持つ) ▶彼は彼のやる気を起こさせる唯一のものは金銭だという含みのことを言われて憤慨した He resented *the implication* that his only motivation was money. ‖ハトという語には平和という含みがあることが多い The word "dove" often has the *connotation* "peace." ‖首相は国会の解散について含みのある発言をした The Prime Minister made an *suggestive* [*equivocal*] remark about the dissolution of the Diet. (➤ suggestive は「ほのめかすような」, equivocal は「2つ(以上)の意味にとれる」) ‖**含み笑い**をしながら言ったので, 彼女の言っていることがうそだとわかった From her *suppressed laugh*, I could tell she was lying.

[1]**ふくむ 含む** **1【成分として持つ】contain** +目（成分として含有する）; **include** +目（全体の一部として含む）▶ルートビアはアルコールを含まない Root beer doesn't *contain* alcohol. ‖ コーヒーやお茶はカフェインを含んでいる Coffee and tea *contain* caffeine.（➤ 進行形にしない）‖ 豆類はビタミンBを多く含む Beans *have* a lot of vitamin B.

▶この料金にはサービス料は含まれておりません This price doesn't *include* the service charge. ‖ その飛行機事故で日本人乗客5人を含む130人が死亡した One hundred and thirty people, *including* five Japanese passengers, died in that airplane accident.

▶「やさしい」ということばは，いろいろな意味やニュアンスを含む The word *"yasashii" bears* [*carries*] many meanings and nuances.

2【口に入れておく】▶口に水を含む *hold* water in one's mouth.

3【心に留める】keep ... in mind ▶彼がまだ未成年であるということを含んでおいてください Please *keep* (it) *in mind* [*bear* (*it*) *in mind*] that he is still a minor.

[2]**ふくむ 服務** **service** ‖**服務規程** office regulations, employee work rules, service regulations.

ふくめる 含める **include** +目 ▶私も含めて全員に責任がある All the staff, *including* me [myself *included*], are to blame. ‖ その船には乗務員を含めて260名が乗っていた There were 260 people on board the ship, *including* the crew. ‖ 東京で暮らすには小遣いを含めなくても月10万円はかかる Living in Tokyo costs at least one hundred thousand yen a month, *excluding* [*not including*] pocket money.

ふくめん 覆面 a **mask** ▶強盗はストッキングで覆面をしていた The burglar *wore* a stocking *over his face*. ／The burglar *had covered his face* with a stocking.

‖**覆面強盗** a masked robber ‖ **覆面パトカー** an unmarked police car 《参考》(英)では an area car（俗称 "Z car"）ともいう.

ふくよう 服用する **take** +目 ▶薬を服用する *take* medicine ‖ この薬は食前に服用のこと This medicine should *be taken* before meals [eating].（➤ 注意書きには To be taken before meals. のように書いてあることも多い）.

‖**服用量** a dose（1回分の服用量）（➤ a dosage は1回分の投薬量）.

ふくよかな **buxom** /bʌ́ksəm/（肉づきのよい；女性に用い，豊満な胸をしているという含みがある）; **chubby** /tʃʌ́bi/（丸ぽちゃの）▶ふくよかな胸をした金髪女性 a *buxom* blonde ‖ 彼女はふくよかな胸をしている She *is full-breasted*.（➤「ふくよかな体型をしている」は She has an ample figure.）‖ この赤ん坊はふくよかな顔をしている This baby has a *chubby* [*round*] face.

ふくらしこ ふくらし粉 **baking powder.**

ふくらはぎ **the calf** /kæf/ [複 **calves**] ▶足がつってふくらはぎがこちこちになった I got a cramp in my leg and my *calf* became stiff.

ふくらます 膨らます **blow up**（吹いて）▶浮き輪を口でふくらます *blow up* a float (ring) by mouth.

▶彼女は先生になることが決まり，希望に胸をふくらませていた Having gotten a teaching position, she *was full of* [*was filled with*] *hope*.

ふくらみ 膨らみ a **swell**; a **bulge**（出っ張り）▶つぼみ[胸]のふくらみ the *swelling* of buds [breasts].

ふくらむ 膨らむ **expand**（膨張する）; **swell**（丸く）; **bulge**（出っ張る）▶気球がふくらんだ The balloon *expanded* [*swelled*]. ‖ 彼女の財布は小銭でふくらんでいた Her wallet *was bulging* with loose change. ‖ 暖かくなって桜のつぼみがふくらんできた It is getting warmer and the cherry buds *are ready to bloom*.（➤「咲きそうだ」の意）.

▶彼女の胸は期待にふくらんだ Her heart *swelled* with hope. ‖ 物価高の影響で旅行の費用が2割もふくらんだ（＝超過した）Because of a rise in prices, the final cost of our trip *exceeded* the original calculation(s) by a full 20 percent.

[1]**ふくり 福利** **welfare**

‖**福利厚生施設** welfare facilities.

[2]**ふくり 複利** 《金融》**compound interest.**

ふくりゅうえん 副流煙 **secondhand** [**sidestream**] **smoke.**

ふくれっつら 膨れっ面 a **sulky look**; a **pout** /paʊt/（口をとがらせること）▶父親に怒られて息子はふくれっ面をした Scolded by his father, the son *gave* him *a sulky look*. ‖ 何だ，そのふくれっ面は？ Hey！What are you *pouting* about？

ふくれる 膨れる **1【ふくらむ】swell** ▶もちは焼くとふくれる As the rice cakes are toasted, they *swell*. ‖ ご飯を3杯お代わりをしたらおなかがふくれた After having three helpings of rice, my stomach *was bloated*.

2【不機嫌になる】get sullen（むっつりする）; **sulk**（すねる）; **pout** /paʊt/（口をとがらせる）▶父親がおみやげを買ってくるのを忘れたのでその男の子はふくれていた The boy *was sullen* [*was sulky*] because his father had forgotten to buy a present for him. ‖ ふくれてないで何があったか言ってごらん Stop *pouting* and tell me what happened.

[1]**ふくろ 袋** a **bag**; a **sack**（布などの大きな）; a **pouch** /paʊtʃ/（小物入れ，ポーチ；腹の袋）; a **pack**, a **packet**（一包み）▶袋詰めにした駄菓子 cheap candies *packed in a bag*／*a packet of* cheap candies ‖ 袋一杯のジャガイモ *a bag of* potatoes ‖（店で）それ，袋に入れてくれますか Can you put that in *a bag*？‖ 女の子はビニール袋に入った金魚を持っていた The little girl had some goldfish in *a plastic bag*. ‖ カンガルーは子供をおなかの袋に入れている Kangaroos carry their young in *a pouch*.

bag

sack

pouch

▶《慣用表現》こそどろは袋のネズミ同然だった The sneak thief was just like *a cornered rat* [*a rat in a trap*]. ／There was no escape for the sneak thief.

‖**袋小路** a blind alley, a dead end, a cul-de-sac.

[2]**ふくろ 復路** **the way back**; a **return trip** [**journey**]（帰りの旅）.

ふくろう 梟 《鳥》an **owl** /aʊl/ ▶フクロウがホーホー鳴いている I hear *an owl* hooting.

ふくろだたき 袋叩き ▶ホームレスの男は少年たちに袋だたきにされた The homeless man *was beaten up* by some boys.

▶《比喩的》「たいていの主婦は気楽な生活をしている」と言ったら女性の聴衆から袋だたきにあった When I said that most housewives lead a carefree life, the women in the audience *jumped all over me*. (➤ jump all over は「(人を)激しく非難する，やり込める」の意のインフォーマルな言い方).

ふくわじゅつ 腹話術 ventriloquism /ventrílə-kwìzəm/ ▶彼は腹話術が使える He can use *ventriloquism*. ／He can throw his voice.
‖**腹話術師** a ventriloquist(➤ 腹話術師が持つ人形は dummy).

ふけ dandruff /dǽndrəf/ ▶きのうシャンプーしたばかりなのにもうふけが出ている I just shampooed (my hair) yesterday, but I already have *dandruff*. ‖ぼくはふけ性だ I *easily get dandruff*. ／I've got a *flaky scalp*. (➤ flaky scalp は「ふけの目立つ頭皮」).
‖**ふけ取りローション** anti-dandruff hair lotion.

ぶけ 武家 a samurai family.

¹**ふけい 父兄** one's parent(s) (親)；one's guardian (保護者). →父母会.

²**ふけい 不敬** disrespect.

³**ふけい 父系** on the father's side of one's family
‖**父系社会** a patrilineal society.

ぶげい 武芸 (Japanese) martial arts.

ふけいき 不景気 **1**【景気の悪いこと】a recession(景気の後退)；(a) depression(きわめて深刻な不況)；a slump(不振)；stagnation(停滞)；hard times(厳しい時勢) →不況 ▶こう不景気じゃ飯の食いあげだ I can't make ends meet in such *hard times*. ‖今出版業界は不景気だ The publishing industry *is in a recession* now. ‖その国は不景気で苦しんでいる That country is suffering from *a (business) recession*.
2【元気がないこと】▶おじは不景気な顔をしていた My uncle looked *cheerless* [*gloomy*].

ふけいざい 不経済な uneconomical ▶テレビを一日中つけっ放しにしておくのは不経済だ It is *uneconomical* to leave the TV (switched) on all day.

ふけこむ 老け込む age ▶彼は奥さんを亡くして急にふけ込んだ He *aged* quickly after his wife passed away [his wife died]. ‖まだふけ込む年じゃないだろう You're too young to *act so old*.

ふけつ 不潔な dirty, filthy (➤ 後者がより強意)；unsanitary(健康に悪い，非衛生的な) ▶そんな不潔な手で目をこすってはだめ Don't rub your eyes with such *dirty* [*filthy*] hands. ‖台所を不潔にしておくなよ Don't leave the kitchen *unclean* [*unsanitary*].
▶《比喩的》おとななんてみんなフケツよ！ All adults are *dirty*!

¹**ふける 耽る** give oneself up《to》, abandon oneself《to》(➤ 後者は主に文語)；be absorbed《in》(夢中になる) ▶ギャンブルにふける *give oneself up* [*abandon oneself*] *to* gambling ‖空想にふける *indulge in* excessive fantasizing [daydreaming] (➤ indulge (oneself) in で「(楽しみなどに)ふける」だが，インフォーマルでは「思う存分楽しむ」と肯定的に使う.「ふける」の語感は excessive や heavy を加えることで表す) ‖彼は以前よく飲酒にふけったものだ He used to *indulge in* heavy drinking often. ‖子供たちは夜遅くまでテレビゲームにふけった The children *were absorbed in* (playing) video games until late at night.
▶女の子はほおづえをつきながら物思いにふけっていた The girl *was lost in thought* with her chin propped up on her palm.

²**ふける 老ける** age, grow [become] old (➤ age には「比較的短期間に」という含みがある) ▶父はここ２，３年でめっきりふけた My father *has aged* terribly in the past few years. ‖彼女は年の割にはふけて見える She *looks old* for her age.
▶彼は私より５，６歳年下だが，私より10歳もふけて見える He is five or six years younger than I, but he *looks* a good ten years *older*. (➤ a good は「たっぷり，優に」の意).

³**ふける 更ける** ▶夜もふけてきた It's *getting late*. ／The night *is getting on*. ‖夜がふけるにつれて虫の音も絶えた As *the night went on* [*wore on*], the chirps of the insects died down. (➤ wear on は「時がゆっくり進む」).

ふげん 付言する make an additional remark.

ふけんこう 不健康な unhealthy ▶連日の夜更かしは不健康だ Staying up late every night *is bad for the health*. ‖一日中家にこもりっきりでは不健康だ It's *unhealthy* to stay cooped up in the house all day.
▶《比喩的》そういう考え方は不健康だ That type of thinking *is unhealthy* [*is not sound*].

ふけんしき ▶あの大臣は不見識な発言が目立つ That minister often makes *remarks that show that he lacks good sense*.

ふげんじっこう 不言実行 ▶私は不言実行の人になりたいと心がけている I try to be *a man of deeds rather than words*.

ふけんぜん 不健全な unwholesome (道徳的に有害な)；morbid(病的な) ▶きみの考え方は不健全だ Your way of thinking is *not healthy*. ／You have *morbid* ideas. ‖不健全な番組は長続きしない *Unwholesome* TV programs don't run long.

ふこう 不幸 unhappiness(幸せでないこと)；(a) misfortune (非常な不運) 一形 **不幸な** unhappy, unfortunate ▶不幸な生涯を送る lead an *unhappy* life ‖不幸な出来事 an *unhappy* [*unfortunate*] accident ‖不幸にも彼は交通事故で亡くなった *Unfortunately*, he was killed in a traffic accident. ／*It was unfortunate that* he was killed in a traffic accident.
▶《慣用表現》幸か不幸か彼女は生活のために働いたことがない *For better or for worse*, she has never worked to support herself. ‖その火事で１人も死者が出なかったのは不幸中の幸いだった *The only consolation* [*The one good thing*] is that nobody was killed in the fire. (➤ consolation は「慰め」).
▶彼女は親類の不幸できょうは休んでいます She is absent today due to the *death* of a relative.

¹**ふごう 符号** a symbol, a mark, a sign. →記号.

²**ふごう 富豪** a rich [wealthy] person；a millionaire /mìljənéə^r/(百万長者)；a billionaire /bìljənéə^r/, a multimillionaire(億万長者；大富豪). →金持ち.

³**ふごう 負号**《数学》a negative sign.

⁴**ふごう 符合** ▶今回の強盗事件の手口は10年前の同様の事件のそれと奇妙に符合する Curiously enough, the modus operandi of this burglary *corresponds with* that of a similar case ten years ago.

ふごうかく 不合格 failure (in an examination)(試験の) ▶彼女は大学入試で不合格になった She *failed* the entrance examination for the college. ‖私は面接で不合格になった I *was eliminated* after the interview. ／I *didn't pass* the interview. ‖そのミュージカルのオーディションを受けたが，不合格だった I auditioned for the musical but *didn't get in*. ‖このおもちゃは安全基準を満たせず不合格となった This toy *was rejected* because it failed to satisfy [meet] (the) safety criteria.

‖**不合格者** a failure ‖**不合格品** rejected goods, a reject /ríːdʒekt/.

ふこうへい 不公平 unfairness (同じ扱いでないこと); partiality /pàːrʃiǽləṭi/ (一方の肩をもつこと); favoritism (えこひいき) ━形 **不公平な** unfair, unjust; partial ▶双方の意見を聞かないのは不公平だ It is *unfair* not to hear the opinions of both parties. ‖その女性は職場で不公平な扱いを受けてきたと感じている The woman feels that she has received *unfair* treatment at the office.

▶子供は不公平には敏感だ Children are very sensitive to *partiality* [*favoritism*].

ふごうり 不合理な unreasonable (筋の通らない); irrational (理にかなわない) ▶古い法律にはときに不合理な面が見られる *Unreasonable* aspects are sometimes seen in old laws.

ふこく 布告 (a) declaration ━動 **布告する** declare +目 ▶その国に宣戦を布告する *declare* war on [against] the country.

ぶこつ 武骨な unrefined (洗練されていない) ▶熊さんも八っつぁんも武骨でそそっかしい Both Kumasan and Hattsuan are rash and *unrefined* [*rude*].

‖**武骨者** a boor, an unrefined fellow.

ふさ 房 a bunch (果物などの); a cluster (花・毛などの); a tassel (帽子・カーテンなどの房飾り) ▶バナナ[ブドウ]の房 *a bunch* of bananas [grapes] ‖フジの(花の)房が地面に届きそうだ The *clusters* of wisteria are almost touching the ground.

ブザー a buzzer /bʌ́zər/ ▶ブザーを鳴らす[押す] ring [press] *a buzzer* ‖開演のブザーが鳴った The *buzzer* sounded [rang] for the rise of the curtain.

¹**ふさい 夫妻** husband and wife ▶山本夫妻 *Mr. and Mrs.* Yamamoto / *The* Yamamotos (➤後者は「山本さん一家」の意にもなる) ‖中井さんはご夫妻でパーティーに出席される予定です Mr. Nakai is going to come to the party *with his wife*. (➤ Mrs. Nakai が主語なら with her husband となる).

²**ふさい 負債** (a) debt /det/; liabilities (債務) ▶彼は事業に失敗して多額の負債をかかえている He is heavily *in debt* [*has a* large *debt*] because he failed in business.

‖**負債者** a debtor /déṭər/.

ふざい 不在 absence ▶きのう家に寄ったとき, 彼は不在だった When I stopped by his house yesterday, he *was not at home*. ‖彼女の一家は北海道に行っていて不在だった Her family *was away* on a trip to Hokkaido. ‖火事は彼の不在中に起きた The fire broke out *during his absence*.

▶政治家たちは国民不在の政権抗争に明け暮れている The politicians are engaging in power struggles day and night, *paying little attention to the people's needs*.

‖**不在者投票** (an) absentee ballot.

ぶさいく 不細工な plain, 《米》homely (不器量な) ▶顔は多少不細工でも気立ての優しい女の子がいい I prefer a kindhearted girl, even if she is on the *plain* [*homely*] side. (➤ on the ... side は「…ぎみ」).

ふさがる 塞がる **1**【閉じる】close /klouz/; be blocked (詰まる) ▶傷口がしだいにふさがってきた The wound gradually *closed*. ‖枯れ葉で管がふさがってしまった The pipe *was blocked* by dead leaves.

2【使用中, いっぱい】be occupied (使用中である); be full (手いっぱい) ▶5つあるトイレ[駐車場]が全部ふさがっていた All of the five toilet stalls [All the parking spaces] *were occupied*. ‖私, 今手がふさがってるの My *hands are full* now. / I'*ve got my hands full* now. / I'*m tied up* at the moment. ‖**対話**「いつがご都合よろしいですか. あすの午後などは?」「そうですね. あすの午後はだめなんです. 完全にふさがっています」"When would be convenient (for you)? What about tomorrow afternoon?" "Mm. I'm afraid I can't manage tomorrow afternoon. My afternoon schedule *is full* [*I'm booked up* all afternoon]."

▶《プレーガイドで》あいにく3日はどの席もふさがっております(=予約されている) Unfortunately, all seats *are booked* on the third.

ふさぎこむ 塞ぎ込む get depressed ▶彼はどういうわけか最近ふさぎ込んでいる For some reason, he's *been depressed* [*gloomy*] recently. ‖恵美はたいていは快活だけれど, ときどき急にふさぎ込む Emi is generally cheerful, but every so often she *has sudden fits of the blues*. (➤ the blues は「憂鬱」) ‖そんなにふさぎ込むなよ Don't look so *glum*! (➤ glum は「暗く悲しそうな」) ‖何をふさぎ込んでるんだい? What're you *moping around* [*about*] for? (➤ mope around [about] は「暗い気持ちで過ごす」の意のややインフォーマルな言い方).

ふさく 不作 a poor crop [harvest] (農作物の) ▶去年は米が不作だった We had *a poor* [*bad*] *crop* of rice last year. / The rice crop failed last year. ‖ブドウはことしは不作だった The grapes *crop has been bad* this year. / This *has been a bad year* for grapes.

▶その年の芥川賞は不作だった There were *no good candidates* for the Akutagawa Literary Prize that year.

ふさぐ 塞ぐ **1**【閉じる】close (up); cover +目 (おおう); fill (in), plug (up) (物を詰めて) ▶傷口をふさぐ *close up* a wound ‖壁と柱の間をふさがないと隙間風が入る If you don't *close up* the area between the wall and the pillar, there's going to be a draft.

▶女の子は雷が鳴るたびに手で耳をふさいだ The little girl *covered* [*stopped up*] her ears with her hands every time it thundered. ‖その穴をふさいでくれる? Could you *fill in* that hole? / Could you *plug up* that hole?

2【邪魔になる, 邪魔をする】block (up), obstruct +目 (邪魔をする); occupy +目 (場所を占める) ▶大きなトラックが建物の入り口をふさいでいた A big truck *blocked* the entrance to the building. ‖雪崩が県道をふさいだ The avalanche *obstructed* the highway. ‖この食器戸棚が台所(のスペース)をずいぶんふさいでいる This cupboard *occupies* [*takes up*] a lot of space in the kitchen.

3【元気がない】get depressed. →ふさぎ込む.

ふざける **1**【おどける】fool around [about]; horse around [about] (ふざけてはね回る) ▶みんな, ふざけてないで席に戻りなさい Stop *fooling around* and go back to your seats, boys and girls. ‖子供たちはふざけているうちに花瓶を割ってしまった The children broke the vase while *horsing* [*fooling*] *around*.

2【不まじめな態度をとる】joke (冗談を言う); act up (子供が騒ぐ) ▶ふざけているのではない, まじめな話だ *I am not joking*. I am serious. ‖彼女はふざけてぼくにキスをした She kissed me *as a joke*. ‖子供たちは母親が出かけるといつもふざけた The children always *acted up* when their mother was out. ‖ ふざけるな！ *Don't be silly* [*ridiculous*]！／Stop that nonsense！‖ 1時間も遅れて来るなんて, ふざけた(＝失礼な)やつだ How *rude* [*inconsiderate*] of him to come an hour late！

ぶさた 無沙汰 →ご無沙汰.

ふさふさ ▶昔は私も髪がふさふさしていた My hair used to be *thick*. ‖ このえり巻きは毛がふさふさしている This muffler is *fluffy*.

ぶさほう 無作法 **bad manners**(行儀が悪いこと)；**rudeness**(無礼) 一形 **無作法な** **impolite, ill-[bad-]mannered, rude** ▶人の顔を見てくすくす笑うのは**無作法**だ It is *bad manners* [*impolite*／*rude*] to look at others and giggle. ‖ 彼が**無作法**なのにはあきれた His *rudeness* astonished us.

ぶざま 無様な ▶チャンピオンはぶざまな(＝屈辱的な)負け方をした The champion suffered a *humiliating* defeat. ‖ どぶからはい上がったときの彼は見るもぶざまなかっこうだった He was quite *a sight* when he crawled up from the muddy ditch. (➤ a sight は「ひどいありさま」の意のインフォーマルな語).

ふ

ふさわしい **suitable**《for》(人・目的・状況に)；**fit**《for》(ある目的にぴったりの)；**appropriate**《for》(特定の目的・用途に合う) ▶あなたにふさわしい仕事がある I've got a job *suitable for* you. ‖ 葬儀にふさわしい音楽というとおのずから限られてくる Only certain types of music are *appropriate for* a funeral. ‖ 友人の婚約をお祝いするのにふさわしい贈り物をさがしています I'm looking for an *appropriate* present to congratulate my friend on her [his] engagement. ‖ 彼はその場にふさわしいことばを選ぼうとした He tried to choose words *appropriate for* the occasion. ‖ あの人は首相としてふさわしい人物だろうか Is he the *right* person for (the) post of prime minister？‖ 大家の名にふさわしい(＝値する)みごとな作品だ This work *deserves* to be called a masterpiece. ‖ 彼は医者になるにはふさわしくない He is *not fit* to be a doctor. (➤ 単に「向いていない」というだけでなく, 資質・能力などに欠けるという強い意味).

✉ **《ラブレターで》達也, 私はきっとあなたにふさわしい奥さんになります** Tatsuya, I'm sure I'd be a *good* wife for you [I'd make you a *good* wife].

ふさんか 不参加 **nonparticipation.**

ふさんせい 不賛成 **disagreement**(不一致)；**disapproval**(不承知) ▶私は彼の意見には**不賛成**です I *don't agree with* him [his opinion]. ／I *disagree with* him. ‖ きみはこの計画に賛成ですか, **不賛成**ですか？Are you for or *against* this plan？‖ 両親は二人が若すぎるという理由で彼女の結婚に**不賛成だった** Her parents *did not approve of* her marriage because she and her boyfriend were too young. →**賛成.**

[1]**ふし 節** **1【結節】** a **knot** /nɑːt/ (木の)；a **joint** (竹の) ▶節の多い板 a board full of *knots* ‖ 竹をこの節のところで切ってください Cut the bamboo at this *joint*.

2【関節】 a **joint** ▶**指の節**をポキポキ鳴らす crack one's *finger joints* →**節々.**

3【旋律】 a **melody** (メロディー)；a **tune** (節回し) ▶この節, 知ってる？ Do you know this *melody* [*tune*]？‖ 覚えやすい**節**だね It's a catchy *tune*.

4【箇所】 ▶彼女の自殺には思い当たるふしは全くありません I can't think of *any reason* for her to have killed herself.

[2]**ふし 不死** **immortality** ▶**不死の神々** the *immortal* gods.

[3]**ふし 父子** **father and child**

‖**父子家庭** a single parent family (片親の家庭)；a motherless family (母親のいない家庭).

[1]**ふじ 藤**《植物》(a) **wisteria** /wɪstíəriə/

‖**ふじ色** light purple, lavender；mauve /moʊv/ (絵の具の) ‖ **フジ棚** a wisteria trellis ‖ **フジづる** a wisteria vine.

[2]**ふじ 不治** →ふち.

ぶし 武士 a **samurai** (➤ 英語化している)；a **warrior** (戦士) ▶**武士に二言はない** *A samurai* never takes back his words. ／As *a samurai*, I keep my word.

‖**武士道** *Bushido*, Japanese chivalry.

ぶじ 無事 **1【安全】** **safety** 一形 **無事な** **safe**；**trouble-free** (問題のない) 一副 **無事に** **safely** ▶**無事な**旅 a *safe* [*trouble-free*] journey ‖ **無事に**あちらに着いたら知らせてよ Let us know when you have (*safely*) arrived. (➤ 危険が予想される状況でなければ safely は不要) ‖ うれしいことに彼は**無事に**帰国した We're happy [glad] that he came back home *safe and sound*. (➤「安全に健康で」の意) ‖ 子供を**無事に**返してほしければ5000万円出せ If you want your child back *safe and alive*, pay us 50 million yen. (➤「安全に生きたままで」の意) ‖ 小包は**無事に**着きました The parcel reached us *in good condition*. ‖ 人質たちは**無事に**解放された The hostages were released *unharmed*. (➤ unharmed は「無傷で」).

▶**《旅立つ人に》どうぞご無事で(行ってらっしゃい)！** Have a nice trip！／Bon voyage！(➤ bon voyage /bɑ̀ːn vwaɪɑ́ːʒ/ はフランス語で「よい旅を」の意で, 今では古風な言い方) ‖ 両親は外国から帰った兄の**無事な**(＝元気な)顔を見てとても喜んだ My parents were very glad to see my (older) brother looking so *well* after returning from abroad.

✉ **無事にアテネ空港に到着しましたのでご安心ください** I arrived *safely* at Athens Airport. ➤「ご安心ください」は訳出不要.

2【平穏】 **peace** 一形 **無事な** **peaceful** 一副 **無事に** **peacefully** ▶紛争が**無事に**解決してよかった We are pleased that the dispute was settled *peacefully*. ‖ きょうも一日**無事に**終わった This has been another *peaceful* [*uneventful*] day.

ふしあな 節穴 a **knothole** /nɑ́ːthoʊl/ ▶**節穴からのぞく** peep through *a knothole*.

▶《比喩的》こんなミスに気がつかないなんて, おまえの目は節穴か？You failed to notice an error like this？Where on earth are your eyes？(➤「いったいどこに目がついているんだ」の意) ‖ 彼の目は**節穴同然**だ He sees but *doesn't grasp anything*. ／He looks but *sees nothing*.

ふしあわせ 不幸せ **unhappiness** 一形 **不幸せな** **unhappy** ▶不幸せな人生 *unhappy* life ‖ 母は**不幸せな**人を見るとじっとしていられなくなるらしい It seems that my mother can't sit still when she sees someone *unhappy* [*unfortunate*].

ふしぎ 不思議 (a) **wonder**(不思議なこと・物) 一形 **不思議な** **strange** (奇妙な)；**mysterious**(不可解な)；**wonderful** (驚くべき) ▶世の中には**不思議な**ことがいっぱいある The world is full of *wonders*. ‖ この寺では満月の夜に**不思議な**現象が起こるといわれている They say that *strange* things happen at this temple when the moon is full. ‖ この数週間, **不思議な**事件が連続して起きた A series of *mysteri-*

ous incidents have occurred in the past few weeks.

▶時計が机の上から消えたのは**不思議だ** *It's strange that* my watch should have disappeared from the desk. ‖ 彼が4打席とも三振するなんて**不思議だ**(＝信じられない) *It's hard to believe* he struck out (at bat) four times in a row. ‖ 毎日サラダしか食べないんじゃ, 貧血になるのも**不思議じゃない**よ If you're eating only salad every day, *it's no wonder that* you're anemic.

▶先生に診てもらったら**不思議と**痛みが消えた The pain went away *like magic* just after seeing the doctor. (➤ like magic は「またたく間に」) ‖ あの手相見の言うことは**不思議と**(＝驚くほど)よく当たる What that palm reader says is *amazingly* accurate. ‖ 子供たちは**不思議そうに**トランプの手品を見ていた The children were watching the card tricks *in amazement*.

▶**不思議なことに**その大歌手は日本では人気がない *Strange* (*to say*), that great singer isn't popular in Japan. (➤ インフォーマルでは to say を省略することが多い) ‖ 明夫は頭がいいのに, **不思議なことに**, 過去に自分の身に起きたことをあまり覚えていない Akio is a bright person, but *strangely enough*, he doesn't remember much of what happened to him in the past. (➤ strangely (enough) は一般の予想に反することを言うのに用いる) ‖ バビロンの空中庭園は古代の**世界七不思議**の1つだ The Hanging Gardens of Babylon are one of *the Seven Wonders of the* Ancient *World*.

ふしくれだつ 節くれだつ ▶**節くれだった**木 a *knotty* [*gnarled*] tree (➤ knotty /náṭi/, gnarled /nɑːˈld/ は「節[こぶ]だらけの」) ‖ 父の手は**節くれだっている** My father has *gnarled* hands.

ふしぜん 不自然な ▶若夫婦がセックスしないなんて**不自然**よ It *isn't natural* for a young married couple not to have sex. ‖ **不自然な**(＝いつもと違う)姿勢で寝ていたら腕がしびれた My arm went numb because I slept in an *unusual* position.

ふしだら ▶**ふしだらな**生活を送る lead a *loose* [*fast*] life (➤ loose /luːs/, fast はともに「性的にだらしない」の意).

ふじちゃく 不時着 an **emergency** [a **forced**] **landing**; a **crash landing** (不時着の結果破損した場合) ▶悪天候のためその旅客機は大島に**不時着した** Because of the bad weather, the passenger plane *made an emergency* [*a forced*] *landing* at Oshima.

ふしちょう 不死鳥 a **phoenix** /fíːnɪks/ ▶(大震災後)神戸は**不死鳥のごとく**よみがえった Kobe has risen from the ashes *like a* [*the*] *phoenix*.

ぶしつ 部室 a **clubroom** ▶新聞部のみなさんは放課後**部室**に集まってください Members of the newspaper club, please gather in the *clubroom* after school.

ぶしつけ 不躾な **impolite** ▶初対面で人の年齢を聞くのは**ぶしつけ**だ It is *impolite* [*bad manners*] to ask a person's age when you meet him or her for the first time. ‖ **ぶしつけな質問ですが**, お子さんはいらっしゃいますか *Excuse me for asking*, but do you have any children?

ふじつぼ 富士壺《動物》a **barnacle**.

ふしぶし 節々 ▶かぜをひいて体の**節々**が痛む I have a cold and my *joints* ache [hurt].

ふしまつ 不始末 **carelessness** (不注意); **misconduct** (不品行) ▶キャンプファイアの**不始末**から大火事になった *The careless handling* of a campfire was the cause of the huge destructive fire. ‖ 彼は仕事で**不始末**をしでかして首になった He was fired because of his *misconduct* in business.

ふじみ 不死身の **immortal** (不滅の) ▶そのスタントマンはまるで**不死身**のようだった That stunt man seemed to lead *a charmed life* [seemed *immortal*]. (➤ lead a charmed life は「魔法で守られたような生涯を送る」が原義).

1**ふしめ 伏し目** ▶私の質問に彼女は**伏し目**がちにうなずいた When I asked her a question, she nodded in assent *with eyes downcast* [*with downcast eyes*].

2**ふしめ 節目** ▶就職や結婚は人生の**節目**だ Getting a job and getting married are (two) *milestones* in life.

ふしゅ 浮腫《医学》**edema**,《英》**oedema** /ɪdíːmə/.

ふしゅう 腐臭 a **rotten smell**; a **putrid smell** (動植物の).

ふじゆう 不自由 **1**【不便】(an) **inconvenience** /ìnkənvíːniəns/ ━形 **不自由な** **inconvenient** ▶停電でずいぶん**不自由**をした The power failure caused us a lot of *inconveniences*. ‖ その島でのキャンプ生活はそれほど**不自由**ではなかった Camping on that island wasn't so *rough* (after all). (➤ 英語には, キャンプ生活などで不自由な暮らしをすることを表す rough it という表現がある).

▶彼はアメリカで5年間生活したので英語にはあまり**不自由しない** He *gets along quite well* in English since he lived in the U.S. for five years. (➤ get along は「何とかやれる」).

2【欠乏】**poverty** (貧乏) ▶**不自由な**(＝貧乏な)暮らしをする live in *poverty* [in *want*] ‖ 彼女は金に**不自由している** She is *short of money* (now). ‖ 彼は何**不自由なく**暮らしている He lives *in comfort*.

3【身体に障害がある】▶体の**不自由な人** a *physically disabled* [*challenged*] person ‖ 彼女は目が**不自由だ** She has *impaired vision* [*eyesight*]. (➤「目が見えない」の意の婉曲(えんきょく)表現) ‖ 彼は耳が**不自由だ** He is *hard of hearing*. ／He is *hearing-impaired*. (➤「耳が聞こえない」の意の婉曲表現).

ぶしゅうぎ 不祝儀 a **sorrowful occasion**; a **funeral** (葬儀) ‖**不祝儀袋** an envelope in which one puts a money gift for a bereaved family (➤ 説明的な訳).

ふじゅうぶん 不十分な **insufficient** /ìnsəfíʃənt/; **scanty** (乏しい) ▶**不十分な**燃料の供給 a *scanty* supply of fuel ‖ 彼は部長になるにはまだ実務経験が**不十分だ** His business experience is still *insufficient* for him to become a manager. ‖ 私の英語力はアメリカの大学で学ぶには**不十分だ** My English is *not good enough* to study at an American university. ‖ ポルトガルまで足を延ばすには**金が不十分だった** I *did not have enough money* to extend my trip as far as Portugal.

▶容疑者は**証拠不十分**で釈放になった The suspect was released *because of insufficient* [*for lack of*] *evidence*. ‖ 練習が**不十分**で思うように力が出せなかった Because I *didn't practice enough*, I wasn't able to give it all I had.

ふしゅび 不首尾 ▶**不首尾に終わる** end in *failure*.

1**ふじゅん 不順** ▶季節の変わり目は天候が**不順だ**(＝変わりやすい) The weather *is changeable* at the turn of the seasons. ‖ **天候不順**のため昨年は稲が不作だった Due to the *unfavorable* [*unseasonable*] *weather*, the rice crop was small last year. (➤ unfavorable は「好ましくない」, unseasonable は「季節外れの」の意) ‖ 彼女は**生理不順**に悩んでいる She is troubled by *menstrual irregularity*.

2**ふじゅん 不純な** **impure** ▶**不純な動機** an *impure* motive ‖ 純金も少量の**不純物**を含んでいる Even solid gold contains slight *impurities*.

1**ふじょ 婦女** a **woman** ▶その男は**婦女暴行**の罪で逮捕された The man was arrested for *rape*.

2**ふじょ 扶助** **aid**(援助；かなり大がかりな公的なものを指すことも多い)；**help**(助力)；**support**(扶養) ▶**相互扶助**の精神 the spirit of *mutual aid* [*help*].

ぶしょ 部署 one's **post** [**station**]；a **department**, a **division** (会社の) ▶新入社員はそれぞれの**部署に配属された** The newly hired staff members were assigned to various *departments of the company*.

1**ふしょう 負傷** an **injury** /índʒəri/；a **wound** /wuːnd/ **━動 負傷する be** [**get**] **injured** /índʒərd/, **get hurt** (事故などで)；**get wounded** (刃物などで攻撃されて) → けが ▶その列車事故で20人が**負傷した** Twenty people *were injured* in the train accident. ‖ 彼は交通事故で足を**負傷した** He *injured* his leg in a traffic accident. ／His leg *was hurt* in a traffic accident. ‖ その活動家は何者かに襲われて**負傷した** The activist was attacked by someone and *was wounded*. ‖ **負傷者**たちは救急車で近くの病院に運ばれた *The injured* [*The wounded*] were carried to the nearest hospital by ambulance.

2**ふしょう 不詳** ▶年齢**不詳**の女性 a woman of *no certain* [*uncertain*] age ／a woman whose age is *unknown* ‖ この小説は作者**不詳だ** This novel is of *unknown* authorship. (➤「作者不詳の小説」は anonymous /ənáːnɪməs/ novel).

1**ふじょう 浮上する rise** [**come** (**up**)] **to the surface, surface** ▶潜水艦が(海面に)**浮上した** The submarine *surfaced* [*came to the surface*]. ‖ 広島カープは中日ドラゴンズを５－０で退け，３位に**浮上した** The Carp beat the Dragons to *rise* [*go up*] to third place (in the Central League standings).

2**ふじょう 不浄な unclean** (汚れた)；**impure** (不純な) ▶イスラム教徒にとって豚肉は**不浄である** To Muslims, pork *is unclean*.

1**ぶしょう 不精** ▶彼は**不精者だ** He's *a lazy man* [*a lazybones*]. ／He's *lazy*. ‖ 彼は顔じゅう**不精ひげ**だらけだった His face was covered with (*beard*) *stubble*. (➤ 英語では He has three days' stubble [a three-day beard]. のように何日間伸びたかをいうのがふつう；また朝そって夕方には伸びてくるものを a five o'clock shadow という) ‖ 彼女はどちらかというと**出不精**のほうだ She is a bit of *a stay-at-home type*. ‖ 私は**筆不精**で，もらいもののお礼はいつも電話で済ませる I am *a poor* [*bad*] *letter writer*, so whenever I want to say thanks for a present, I prefer to call [phone].

2**ぶしょう 武将** a **feudal warlord**

‖**戦国武将** a warlord [samurai general] in the Sengoku period.

ふしょうか 不消化 indigestion.

ふしょうじ 不祥事 a **disgraceful affair**；a **scandal**(スキャンダル) ▶一連の**不祥事** a series of *disgraceful affairs*.

ふしょうじき 不正直な dishonest ▶彼があんな**不正直**な男とは思わなかった I never thought that he was such a *dishonest* man.

ふしょうち 不承知 disapproval.

ふしょうぶしょう 不承不承 reluctantly ▶**不承不承**ならやってくれなくて結構だ If you are so *reluctant* to do the job, you don't have to do it. ‖ メーカー側は**不承不承**商品の欠陥を認めた The manufacturer *reluctantly* admitted the product was defective.

ふしょうふずい 夫唱婦随 ▶あのうちは**夫唱婦随だ** In that family, *the woman does whatever her husband says*.

ふじょうり 不条理 absurdity, the absurd ━形 不条理な absurd.

ふしょく 腐食 corrosion /kəróʊʒən/ **━動 腐食する corrode** ▶トタン屋根が**腐食し始めた** The tin roof began to *corrode*.

ぶじょく 侮辱 (an) **insult** /ínsʌlt/ **━動 侮辱する insult** /ɪnsʌ́lt/ ＋目 ▶大臣の発言は芸術に対する**侮辱だ** The minister's remarks are *an insult* to art. ‖ 私は公衆の面前で彼に**侮辱された** I *was insulted* by him in public.

1**ふしん 不振** a **slump**(不調) ▶今シーズンの巨人は**不振**だ The Giants are in *a slump* this season. ‖ わが社は今期も**業績不振だ** Our company's performance has been *poor* again this fiscal year. ‖ 私は毎年夏になると**食欲不振**に陥る Every summer, I *lose my appetite* [my *appetite suffers*].

2**ふしん 不信** (a) **distrust** ▶政治に対して**不信の念**を抱いている人が多い Many people *have no trust in* [*have a distrust of*] politics. ‖ 彼女，恋人に裏切られてから**男性不信**に陥ってるのよ Since her boyfriend cheated on her, she *has been distrustful of* all men.

3**ふしん 不審な doubtful, suspicious** (➤ 後者は強い疑いを表す) ▶彼のアリバイには**不審な点**がある There are some *doubts* about his alibi. ‖ ご**不審**(＝疑問)の点があれば遠慮なくお尋ねください If you have any *questions*, please don't hesitate to ask me. ‖ 門の前に挙動の**不審な**男がいる There's a man in front of the gate who is *behaving suspiciously*. ‖ 成田空港に行く途中で警官に**不審尋問を受けた** I *was questioned* by a policeman on my way to Narita Airport. ‖ 近所で**不審火**が続いている There has been a series of *suspicious fires* in our neighborhood.

‖**不審者** a suspicious person.

4**ふしん 普請** ▶**普請中**の家 a house *under construction* ‖ **安普請**の家 a *jerrybuilt* house.

5**ふしん 腐心** ▶赤字対策に**腐心する** *struggle with measures to* reduce the deficit ／ *take great pains to* reduce the deficit.

1**ふじん 婦人** a **woman** [**複 women**]；a **lady** (目前の女性を指したり，elderly や old などの形容詞を前につけて) ▶親切な**婦人** a kind *woman* ‖ これは年配のご**婦人**たちのための特別講座です This is a special lecture for *elderly ladies*.

▶彼女は働く**婦人**の立場から意見を述べた She expressed her opinions from a *working woman*'s standpoint. ‖ これは**婦人向け**の雑誌です This is a magazine *for women* [*ladies*]. ／This is a *women's* magazine.

‖**婦人科** gynecology /gàɪnəkáːlədʒi/ ‖ **婦人科医** a gynecologist ‖ **婦人会** a women's club ‖ **婦人病** a women's disease ‖ **婦人服** women's [ladies'] clothing ‖ **婦人問題** a women's issue.

2**ふじん 夫人** a **wife**(妻) ▶アメリカの大統領が**夫人同伴**で来日した The U.S. president, *accompanied by the first lady*, paid a visit to Japan. ‖ 私はきのう

(ウィリアム・)ジョーンズ夫人に会った I met *Mrs.* (William) Jones yesterday.

ふしんじん 不信心な impious.

ふしんせつ 不親切な unkind ▶彼らは知らない人には不親切だ They are *unkind* to strangers. ‖あの店員は客に**不親切**だ That salesclerk is *not helpful* to customers. ‖このイラストマップは大ざっぱ過ぎて**不親切**だ This illustrated map is *too* simple *to be of any help*.

ふしんにん 不信任 nonconfidence ▶我々は議長の**不信任案**を提出した We moved *a vote of nonconfidence* in the chairman.

ふしんばん 不寝番 a night watch, a sleepless vigil.

ふず 付図 an appended figure.

ぶす a bag, an old bag(➤この bag は「袋をかぶせておきたくなるような不器量な女」が原義の俗語).

1**ふずい 付随** ▶英語学習に**付随する**問題点 problems that *accompany* [problems *incidental to*] the study of English (➤incidental to は「…に付きもの」).

‖**付随音楽** incidental music.

2**ふずい 不随** paralysis /pərǽləsɪs/ (まひ) ▶**半身**[**全身**]**不随**になる suffer *partial* [*complete*／*total*] *paralysis* ‖彼は落馬事故で全身[首から下が]**不随**になった He *was* completely *paralyzed* [*was paralyzed* from the neck down] after he fell off a horse.

ぶすい 無粋な・不粋な inelegant ; boorish (がさつな) ; insensitive (鈍感な) ▶ 対話「ゆうべ, あれから彼女とどこへ行ったんだい？」「**無粋**なことを聞くもんじゃないよ」"Where did you go with her last night after that?" "Don't ask such *boorish* [*insensitive*] questions."

ふすう 負数 《数学》a negative number.

ぶすう 部数 the number of copies (冊数) ; a circulation (新聞・雑誌の発行部数) ▶この月刊誌は**発行部数**が多い[少ない] This monthly magazine has a large [small] *circulation*.

ぶすっと ▶父は朝はいつもきげんが悪く**ぶすっと**している My father is moody in the morning and always *looks sullen* [*sulky*] then.

ふすま 襖 a *fusuma* ; a framed and papered sliding door (➤説明的な訳).

ぶすり ▶男はけんかして出刃包丁で**ぶすりとやられた** The man got in a fight and *was stabbed* with a kitchen knife.

1**ふせい 不正** (a) dishonesty (不正直 ; 不正行為) ; (an) injustice (不当な処置・行為) 一形 **不正な** wrong (反道徳的な) ; unfair, unjust (不公正な) ; unlawful, illegal (違法の) ; dishonest (ごまかしの, いんちきの) ; crooked (いんちきの ; インフォーマルな語) ▶**不正をあばく** expose *an injustice* ‖**不正を働く** commit *an injustice* [*a wrongful act*] ‖**不正な方法**で金をもうける make money by *dishonest* means ‖カンニングは**不正行為**だ Cheating *is dishonest*. ‖彼のやったことは**不正な行為**だ What he did was an *unlawful* [*illegal*] act.

▶その男は**不正乗車**でつかまった The man was caught *cheating on train fares*. ‖その会社の**不正取り引き**が発覚した The *unfair dealings* of that company were brought to light. ‖彼は多額の**不正利得**を得ている He has *made* a lot of *money by illegal means*.

2**ふせい 父性** paternity

‖**父性愛** paternal affection [love].

ふぜい 風情 ⚠ **その場の状況から感じられる, ことばでは説明しにくい風流な感じをいうが, これにぴったりの英語はない. したがって, 用例のように適宜言い換えて訳出するしかない.**

▶こけむした灯ろうが庭に**風情**(＝趣)を添えている A stone lantern covered with moss adds some *charm* to the garden. ‖雪をいただいた富士山には独特の**風情がある** A snow-capped Mt. Fuji has its own *charm*. ‖その城下町は今も**昔の風情を残している** The castle town still retains *some traces of its old days*.

ふせいかく 不正確な incorrect (正しくない ; 「間違っている」を遠回しに言った語) ; inaccurate /ɪnǽkjərət/ (精密でない, 正確ではない) ▶**不正確な情報** *incorrect* information ‖私の時計は**不正確**だ My watch is *not correct*. ／My watch does not keep good time. ‖彼女の話はときに**不正確**だ What she says is sometimes *inaccurate*.

ふせいこう 不成功 (a) failure ▶エンジントラブルでロケットの実験は**不成功**に終わった The rocket experiment *ended in failure* [turned out *unsuccessful*] because of engine trouble.

ふせいじつ 不誠実 insincerity ; dishonesty (不正直) 一形 **不誠実な** insincere, dishonest ▶あの男は**不誠実**だ He is *insincere* [*dishonest*]. ／He *lacks sincerity* [*honesty*]. ‖会社側の対応は**不誠実**だった The way the company handled the case was *insincere*.

ふせいしゅつ 不世出 ▶**不世出**の芸術家 an *unparalleled* artist (➤「比類なき芸術家」の意) ‖ベーブ・ルースは**不世出**のバッターだった Babe Ruth was a *one-in-a-million* batter. (➤「100万人に1人のバッター」の意).

ふせいせき 不成績 poor results ▶バレーボール部はことしは**不成績**で予選で姿を消した The volleyball team *did badly* this year and dropped out in the preliminaries.

ふせいみゃく 不整脈 a (cardiac) arrhythmia ; an irregular heartbeat ▶彼には**不整脈**がある He has *an irregular heartbeat*.

ふせいりつ 不成立 ▶予算案は**不成立**だった The budget *failed to pass*. ‖商談は**不成立に終わった** The business talk *ended in failure* [*fell through*]. (➤fall through は「だめになる」)／They *were unable to clinch the deal*. (➤clinch a deal は「取り引きをまとめる」の意).

ふせき 布石 ▶**布石を打つ** *make a strategic move*.

ふせぐ 防ぐ

1【食い止める】 protect ＋目 ; defend ＋目 (武器などで) ▶城の堀は敵の侵入を**防ぐ**目的で造られた The moats of castles were built to *protect* [*guard*] against enemy invasion.

▶彼らは敵を**防ぐ**ことができなかった They could not *defend themselves against* their enemy. ‖このテントでは雨を**防ぐ**ことはできないだろう This tent will *be no protection* [*defense*] *against* the rain. ‖このカーテンなら寒さを**防げる**はずだ This curtain should *keep out* the cold.

2【未然に防止する】 prevent 《A from B》(A が B しないようにする) ; check ＋目, stop ＋目 (阻止する) ▶感染症のまん延を**防ぐ** *prevent* [*stop*／*stem*] the spread of an infectious disease ‖もっと注意を払っていたら事故は未然に**防げた**かもしれないよ If you had been more careful, you might have *prevented* the accident. ‖患者の病状の悪化を**防ぐ**ために特別な治療が施された A special treatment was given to *prevent* the patient's condition *from* getting worse.

ふせじ 伏せ字 asterisks, x's, or other symbols used to hide names, passwords, obscene words, etc. ▶パスワードは伏せ字になっています The password *is hidden by asterisks*. (➤ 英米ではアステリスクを用いることが多い).

[1]**ふせつ 敷設する** lay +㊐ (レール・パイプなどを水平に敷く) ; construct +㊐ (大がかりなものを建設する) ▶2つの市の間に鉄道を敷設する *lay* train tracks [*lay* a railroad / *construct* a railroad] between the two cities.

[2]**ふせつ 付設** ▶X大学に日本研究センターを付設する *establish* a Japan research center *attached to* X University ⇀付属.

ふせっせい 不摂生 intemperance ▶日頃の不摂生がたたって佐藤さんは肝臓病になった Mr. Sato's chronic *neglect of his health* caused him to develop liver trouble. ‖ 不摂生な生活をしていると今にこたえるよ If you (continue to) lead an *unhealthy* lifestyle, you'll pay for it sooner or later.

ふせる 伏せる 1【下にする】 put ... face down ▶答案用紙は配り終わるまで机の上に伏せておいてください Please leave your answer sheets *face down* on the desk until I have handed them all out. ‖ 時間です. 答案を伏せ(＝裏返しにし)なさい Time's up. Please *turn* your answer sheets *over*. ‖ 爆発が起こったとたん我々は地面に身を伏せた The moment the bomb exploded, we *threw ourselves face down* on the ground.

▶ (床に)伏せろ! *Get down! / Drop!* ‖ ジュディーさん, おわんは伏せてテーブルに並べてね Judy, please set the bowls *upside down* on the table. (➤「上下逆に」の意).

2【隠す】 ▶このことはしばらく伏せておいてください Please *keep* this *to yourself* for a while.

3【床につく】 be sick in bed ▶彼は3年間病気でふせっている He *has been sick* [*ill*] *in bed* for three years.

ふせん 付箋 a slip ; a self-stick label (取りはがし自由の ; 商標のPost-it も用いる ; Post-it note ともいう) ; a tag (付け札) ▶私は試してみたいレシピのあるページに付せんをつける I put *stickers* on pages that have recipes I want to try.

ぶぜん 憮然 ▶父はぶ然とした表情で帰宅した My father came home looking *dejected* [*glum*].

ふせんしょう 不戦勝 an unearned win ; a bye (トーナメントでの) ▶1回戦で不戦勝になる draw a first-round *bye* ‖ 我々は1回戦は不戦勝だった We *got a bye* in the first round game. / We *won* the first game *by default*. (➤ by default は「欠場によって」).

ふせんめい 不鮮明な not sharp, not clear (不明瞭な) ; unclear (理解不十分な) ▶不鮮明な印刷 *illegible* print (➤ illegible /ɪlédʒəbəl/ は「読みにくい」) ‖ この写真は色が不鮮明だ The color of this photo *didn't come out well*. (➤「よく出ていない」の意) ‖ 首相の意図が不鮮明だ The Prime Minister's intention is *unclear*.

ぶそう 武装 armament **一動 武装する** arm oneself, be armed ▶核武装 nuclear *armament* ‖ ゲリラは銃で武装した The guerrillas *armed themselves* with guns. ‖ 完全武装の兵士たちが入り口を固めていた Several *fully-armed* soldiers guarded the gate.

‖**武装解除** disarmament.

☛ **非武装** (⇀見出語)

ふそうおう 不相応 ▶分不相応な暮らしをする live *above* [*beyond*] *one's means* (➤ means は「資力」) ‖ 彼は一般人には不相応な豪邸に住んでいる He lives in a mansion which is *beyond the means* of the average person.

[1]**ふそく 不足 1【足りないこと】** (a) shortage ; lack (欠乏) ; (an) insufficiency (必要なものが十分でないこと) ; deficiency (不可欠なものの) (➤ shortage は具体的なものや物質名詞に, lack は抽象名詞に用いることが多い) **一動 不足する** be short (不足している) ; be short of (➤ 主語は人. of のあとに不足しているものがくる) ▶その国は食糧の不足に苦しんでいる That country is suffering a terrible *shortage* of food. ‖ 戦時中は多くのものが不足していた During the war, many things *were in short supply* [*there were* many *shortages*].

▶今うちでは人手が不足している We'*re shorthanded* [*understaffed*] now. ‖ 日本では小児科医不足が深刻だ There's a severe *shortage* of pediatricians in Japan.

▶郵送料が50円不足です The postage *is short* by fifty yen. ‖ 1円玉が不足している We *are short of* one-yen coins. ‖ 資金が不足してきた We *are running short of* [*running out of*] money. (➤ be running short of は「…が残り少なくなっている [切れかかっている]」, run out of は「…を使い果たす」の意) ‖ 彼女は何不足なく育った She was raised *in comfortable circumstances*.

▶ビタミンB_1不足 a Vitamin B_1 *deficiency* ‖ 運動不足は肥満の原因となる *Lack of exercise* is a cause of obesity. ‖ きのう夜更かししたからきょうは睡眠不足だ I *didn't get enough sleep* because I stayed up late last night. ‖ 田舎は都会より住みやすいって? それはきみの認識不足だよ You say the country is easier to live (in) than the city? That shows *how little you know*.

▶水不足で稲が枯れかかっている The rice plants are dying for *lack of water* [due to *a lack of water*]. / Because of the *water shortage*, the rice plants are dying.

2【不平】 ▶T高校なら相手にとって不足はない T High School is a *worthy* opponent. (➤ worthy は「敬意を表すべきりっぱな」).

[2]**ふそく 不測の** unexpected ▶不測の災害に備える provide against an *unexpected* disaster ‖ 2人が到着していないところをみると不測の事態があったのかもしれない Judging from the fact that two people have not arrived yet, *something unexpected* might have happened.

[3]**ふそく 付則** a supplementary provision, an additional rule.

ふぞく 付属 ▶X大学付属病院 the X University Hospital ‖ 東京大学付属日光植物園 Tokyo University Botanical Gardens in Nikko (➤ 以上の2例では「付属」は訳には現れない) ‖ T高校はP大学の付属である T Senior High School *is affiliated with* [*to*] P University. (➤ affiliated は「提携した」; 「P大学付属T高等学校」なら T Senior High School affiliated with P University)

‖**付属品** an attachment ; accessories /əksésəriz/ (➤ 総称).

ぶぞく 部族 a tribe.

ふぞろい 不揃いの irregular ; uneven (表面が平らでない) ▶ここにあるティーカップは大きさがふぞろいだ These teacups are *not of the same size*. ‖ 私は歯並びがふ

ぞろいです I have *uneven* [*irregular*] teeth.

ふそん 不遜な **arrogant** ▶不そんな態度の人 an *arrogant* person.

ふた 蓋 a **lid**; a **cap**（キャップ）; a **top**（鍋・箱・瓶などの）; a **cover**（おおい） ▶箱にふたをする put the *lid* [*top*] on a box／shut a box ‖ 箱のふたを開ける take off the *lid* of a box／open a box ‖ 瓶のふたを(回して)取る unscrew the *top* [*cap*] of a bottle ‖ このふたがなかなか開かない This *cap* just won't come off.

▶《慣用表現》そのオペラ公演は前評判はすごかったが, いざふたを開けてみると観客はまばらだった The opera's advance publicity was terrific, but *when the opening came*, it drew only a small audience.

ふだ 札 a **sign**（看板）; a **label** /léɪbəl/（ラベル）; a **tag**（下げ札, タグ）; a **card**（トランプ）; a **talisman** /tǽlɪzmən/（お守り） ▶図書館の入り口のドアに「月曜休館」の札が下がっていた There was *a sign* on the front door of the library saying "Closed on Mondays." ‖ びんには「劇薬」という札がはってある The bottle *is labeled* "Poison."

▶自分の荷物には名前を書いた札をつけておくように Attach *tags* with your name written on them to your luggage. ‖ 彼女は巧みにトランプの札を切った She shuffled the *cards* skillfully. ‖ 私は成田山のお札を身につけている I keep *a talisman* from Narita-san Temple on me.

ぶた 豚 a **pig**, a **hog**, a **swine** /swaɪn/

> **《解説》** (1)最も一般的な語は **pig** だが, 《米》ではしばしば「子豚」を指し, 成長した豚には **hog** を用いる. また「雌豚」を特に **sow** ともいう. (2)**swine** は文語的な語で, 主に集合的に用いる. (3)鳴き声の「ブーブー」は oink /ɔɪŋk/, oink と表現する.

▶豚を飼育する raise *pigs* ‖ 豚がブーブー鳴いている Some *pigs* are grunting. ‖ そう豚みたいにがつがつ食うな Don't eat *like a pig*.

▶《慣用表現》あの子にそんな立派なネックレスを買ってやっても豚に真珠よ It is *like casting pearls before swine* to buy her such a fine necklace. (➤ cast pearls before swine は「豚の前に真珠を投げる」の意のことわざ).

‖豚小屋 a pigsty, a pig pen ‖ 豚肉 pork ‖ 焼き豚 roast pork.

ふたい 付帯的な **incident(al)**; **collateral**（付随的な）; **supplementary**（補足的な）

‖付帯事項 a supplementary item ‖ 付帯条件 a collateral [an incidental] condition.

ふだいだいみょう 譜代大名 a ***fudai daimyo***; a feudal lord who was a hereditary vassal of the Tokugawa family (➤ 説明的な訳).

1**ぶたい 舞台** **1【劇場の】** a **stage**; a **catwalk**（ファッションショーの長く突き出た） ▶舞台に立つ go [appear] on (the) *stage*. →初舞台.

2【活動の場】 ▶その物語は沖縄を舞台にしている The story *is set* in Okinawa. ‖ 彼女は国際舞台で活躍しているビジネスパーソンだ She is a businessperson (who is) active in the *international arena*. ‖ 舞台裏の取り引きがあったらしい There seem to have been *behind-the-scenes* dealings.

▶打って投げてきょうのゲームは斎藤の一人舞台だった Saito *played a key role*, both in hitting and pitching today.

‖舞台裏 backstage ‖ 舞台監督 a stage director ‖ 舞台げいこ a dress rehearsal ‖ 舞台芸術 the performing arts ‖ 舞台効果 stage effects ‖ 舞台照明 stage lighting ‖ 舞台装置 stage setting ‖ 舞台道具 setting（セット）; (stage) props（小道具）‖ 舞台俳優 a stage actor [actress].

☛ 清水の舞台（→見出語）

2**ぶたい 部隊** a **(military) unit** ▶戦闘部隊 a fighting *unit*.

ふたいてん 不退転 ▶不退転の決意 *indomitable* resolve.

ふたえ 二重 ▶紙を二重に折る fold a sheet of paper *in half* [*in two*] ‖ 由美は生まれつき二重まぶただ Yumi has natural *double eyelids*. **《参考》** 一重のまぶたはアジア人特有のもので, 英米では白人も黒人もラティーノ(ラテン系アメリカ人)の人たちも皆二重なので, 話題にならない. 初めてこの表現を聞く人は奇異に感じるだろう.

1**ふたく 付託する** **refer**《to》 ▶その法案は特別委員会に付託された The bill *was referred* to a special committee.

2**ふたく 負託** a **mandate** /mǽndeɪt/ ▶国民の負託にこたえる respond to the people's *mandate*.

ぶたくさ 豚草《植物》**ragweed.**

ふたご 双子 **twins**; a **twin**（双子の一方） ▶その双子の姉妹はうり二つなので互いによく間違えられる Those *twin sisters* closely resemble each other, so one is often taken for the other.

ふたござ 双子座 (a) **Gemini** /dʒémɪnaɪ/ ▶私は双子座です I'm *(a) Gemini*.／I'm *a Geminian*.

ふたことめには 二言目には ▶母は二言目には「お兄さんを見習いなさい」と言う *Every other thing* my mother says is "Be more like your (older) brother."

ふたしか 不確かな **uncertain** ▶不確かな情報 *uncertain* [*unreliable*] information ‖ その出来事については不確かな記憶しかない I have only an *uncertain* [a *vague*] memory of that incident.

ふたたび 再び **again**; **once more** [**again**]（もう一度） ▶二度と再び同じ間違いをするなよ Don't make the same mistake *ever again*.／Never repeat the same mistake. ‖ 再びこういうことがないように I don't want it to *ever* happen *again*. (➤ 叱るときによく使われる言い方).

▶エジンバラを訪れる機会が再び巡ってきた There came a chance for me to visit Edinburgh *a second time*.

ふたつ 二つ **two** ▶ 2つください Give me *two*, please. ‖ 《喫茶店で》コーヒー 2つ *Two* coffees, please. (➤ 正確には two cups of coffee だが, 注文では two coffees, two beers, two teas などと言う) ‖ 2つでいくらですか How much are *two*? ‖ 彼のほうが 2つ年上です He is *two years older* than I am [than me]. (➤ than me はインフォーマルな言い方) ‖ スイカを 2つに切った I cut the watermelon *into two*. ‖ それを 2つとも欲しい I want *both* of them. ‖ 2つとも気に入りません I don't like *either* of them. ／I like *neither* of them.

▶《慣用表現》こんな壮大な映画は二つとない *There couldn't be a more* spectacular movie *than* this. ‖ 二つとない命を粗末にするな Don't waste your life—it's *the only one* you've got. ‖ 彼は二つ返事でその仕事を引き受けてくれた He *promptly* accepted the job. ／He took the job *without a moment's hesitation*. ‖ イエスかノーか, 返事は二つに一つだ Yes or no. Answer *one or the other*.

ふだつき 札付きの **notorious** /noʊtɔ́ːriəs/, **infamous**

/ínfəməs/ ▶札付きの悪党 a *notorious* [an *infamous*] scoundrel ‖ あの子は近所で札付きの悪がきだ He *is known* as a brat all over the neighborhood.

ふたて 二手 ▶二手に分かれる divide [separate] *into two groups*.

ふたとおり 二通り ▶この問題の解き方は二通りある There are *two ways* of solving this problem. ／This problem can be solved in *two ways*.

ふたば 双葉 《植物》 **cotyledons** /kɑ̀:təlí:dnz/ (子葉).

ぶたばこ 豚箱 a **lockup** (留置場) ; **the clink** (刑務所). →刑務所.

ブダペスト Budapest (ハンガリーの首都).

ふたまた 二股 ▶この道は少し先で二またに分かれる This road *forks off* [*branches* (*off*)] a little way ahead. (➤「二またに分かれている所」は a fork [branch] in the road).

▶《慣用表現》公立大学と私立大学の二またかけて受験した I took exams for *both* private *and* public universities.

ふため 二目 ▶お岩はふた目と見られぬ顔になっていた Oiwa was *too ugly* [*frightening*] *to look at*.

ふたり 二人 1 【2人の人】 **two people** ▶バスには2人しか乗ってなかった There were only *two people* on the bus. ‖ うちには子供が2人います We have *two children*. ‖ このクラスには渡辺は2人います There are *two* Watanabes in this class. ‖ 彼らは2人とも警察官だ They are *both* police officers. ／*Both* of them are police officers. ‖ 2人ともたばこは吸わない *Neither of them* smokes. (➤ Both of them don't smoke. とするとどちらかは「吸う」の意となる).

▶きのう母と2人で(＝いっしょに)買い物に行った I went shopping *with my mother* yesterday. ‖ 自転車の二人乗りはするな Don't *ride double* on your bicycle.

2 【夫婦・恋人など】 ▶二人にはまだ子供がいない *They* [*The couple*] haven't had a child yet. ‖ 二人は恋人どうしだ *The two* are lovers. ‖ (新婚の)お二人の門出を祝って乾杯! Let's toast *the newlyweds*!

ふたん 負担 1 【重荷】 a **burden**, a **load** ▶負担の大きい仕事 *heavy* work ‖ 授業の進み方が速いので, 子供にはだいぶ負担になっているようだ The class is proceeding at such a fast rate that it seems to be a real *burden* for the children. ‖ 右足にけがをすると左足や腰によけいな負担がかかる If your right leg gets injured, an extra *load* [*burden*] is imposed on your left leg and back. ‖ 裁判員は精神的負担が大きいそうだ I hear that lay judges have to carry heavy *emotional burdens*.

2 【引き受けること】 ▶送料は当社で負担いたします We will *cover* postage. ／We will *pay* shipping charges. ／Free shipping. ‖ きみにも費用を負担してもらいたい We want you to *pay your share* of the expenses, too. (➤ share は「割り当て分」;「費用を負担する」は pay the expenses) ‖ 老人の医療費はかつては国庫負担であった Medical bills of the elderly *were* once *paid* out of the national treasury. ‖ (健康保険の)一部自己負担 a copayment, a copay.

1**ふだん 普段** **usually** (通常) ; **always** (常に) ▶税制についてはふだんから疑問に思っています I have *always* been skeptical about the tax system. ‖ ふだんの力が出せればいいのだが I hope I can do as well as I *usually* do. ‖ ふだんどおり5時半に帰宅した I got home at 5 : 30 *as usual*. ‖ 彼は試合の前日ふだんより早く寝た The night before the game, he went to bed earlier *than usual*.

‖ふだん着 everyday [casual] clothes, daily attire ; informal dress (略装).

2**ふだん 不断の** **ceaseless** (絶え間ない) ; **untiring** (たゆまぬ) ▶彼の成功は不断の努力によるものだ His success is due to his *ceaseless* [*untiring*] *efforts*.

1**ふち 縁** an **edge** (端) ; a **brink** (険しく切り立ったがけなどの) ; a **brim** (容器・河川・湖などの液体が入る側の) ; a **rim** (皿など円形物の外側の)

▶テーブルの縁を赤く塗ってください Paint the *edge* of the table red. ‖ 彼はがけの縁に立っていた He was standing on the *edge* [*brink*] of the cliff. ‖ 彼は広い縁(＝つば)のついた帽子をかぶっていた He had a broad-*brimmed* hat on. ‖ 彼は縁なしの眼鏡をかけている He wears *rimless* glasses. ‖ 彼女はプラチナ縁の眼鏡をかけている She wears platinum-*framed* glasses. (➤眼鏡の縁は frames がふつう) ‖ 私のコーヒーカップは縁が少し欠けている There's a chip on the *rim* [*edge*] of my coffee cup. ／The *rim* [*edge*] of my coffee cup is chipped. (➤コップの具体的な「縁」は rim または edge) ‖ 彼はコーヒーをカップの縁までいっぱいについだ He filled his cup *to the brim* with coffee. (➤液体が入る内側の最大限を想定する「縁」は brim).

▶アザミの葉は縁にとげがある There are thorns on the *tips* of the leaves of the thistle. (➤ tip は「先端」).

‖縁石(歩道の) a curb.

2**ふち 淵** a **deep place (in the water)** ▶川は曲がる辺りでふちになって(＝深くなって)いる The river *runs deep* at the bend.

▶《比喩的》マイスキーは絶望のふちからはい上がった音楽家だ The musician Maisky crawled out of *the depths of despair*.

3**ふち 不治の** **incurable** /ɪnkjʊ́ərəbəl/ ▶不治の病 an *incurable* disease.

ぶち 斑 ▶ぶちの猫 a *spotted* cat (はん点のある) ／a tabby (cat) (とら猫) ‖ 私は黒いぶちの犬を飼っている I have a dog *with black spots* [*spotted with black*].

プチー ▶プチ整形 *minor* cosmetic surgery ‖ ときにはプチぜいたくをして, フルコースのフランス料理を味わったりします From time to time I *indulge in small luxuries* such as enjoying a five-course French dinner.

‖プチブル(ジョア) a petit bourgeois /pèṭi bʊ́əʳʒwɑː/.

ぶちこむ ぶち込む 《米・インフォーマル》 **send up**, 《英・インフォーマル》 **send down** (刑務所に) ▶やつは最低でも10年は刑務所にぶち込まれるよ The guy'll *be sent up* for at least 10 years.

ぶちこわす 打ち壊す **destroy** +㊐ (破壊する) ; **ruin** +㊐ (台なしにする) ▶私たちの愛をぶちこわさないでよ Don't try to *destroy* our love. ‖ 彼女はあることないことを言って妹の縁談をぶちこわした She *ruined* her (younger) sister's marriage negotiations with (malicious) lies. (➤ malicious は「悪意のある」).

ふちどる 縁取る fringe +目 ▶レースで縁どったクッションカバー a cushion cover *fringed* [*edged*] with lace ‖ 隣の芝生はパンジーで縁どられている The next-door lawn *is bordered* [*is fringed*] with pansies. ／The next-door lawn has pansies around it.

ぶちぬく 打ち抜く 1【反対側まで穴をあける】▶弾丸が彼の脳天をぶち抜いた A bullet *went through* [*pierced*] his brain.

2【仕切りを取る】▶ 2 部屋ぶち抜けば100人は座れる At least one hundred people can be seated *if the partitions are removed* to make the two rooms into one.

ぶちまける vent +目, let out (感情を；後者はややインフォーマル)；dump +目 (ごみなどを) ▶私は日頃の不満を彼女にぶちまけた I *vented* [*let out* ／ *dumped*] all my complaints on her. ／I *hurled* all my complaints at her. (➤ 第 1 文は不満の原因はほかにあるが, 第 2 文は「彼女」が不満の対象).

▶トラックはその穴に生ごみをぶちまけた The truck *dumped* the garbage in the hole.

ふちゃく 付着する stick《to》▶いかりには無数のフジツボが付着していた There were innumerable barnacles *stuck to* the anchor. ‖ 彼のシャツには血痕(けっこん)が付着していた *There was a trace* of blood on his shirt.

ふちゅうい 不注意 carelessness 一形 不注意な careless；inadvertent (故意でなく, うっかり) ▶不注意な間違い a *careless* mistake ‖ 不注意からよく事故が起きる Accidents are often caused by *carelessness*. ‖ それに気づかなかったのは私の不注意だった It was due to my *carelessness* that I didn't notice that. ／I was *careless* not to notice that. ‖「進入禁止」の標識を見落とすなんて何て不注意なんだ It was really *careless* of you to have missed the "Don't Enter" sign !

1**ふちょう 不調** 1【状態や調子が悪いこと】a slump, bad form ▶その選手はこのところ不調だ The player *has been out of form* [*has been in a slump*] recently. ‖ 私は最近不調だ (＝体調が悪い) I *haven't been feeling well* recently. ‖ エンジンが不調だ *Something is wrong* with the engine. ／The engine *isn't working well*.

2【まとまらないこと】failure ▶商談は不調に終わった The business talks *ended in failure* [*broke down*].

2**ふちょう 符丁** a secret password；a secret price indication (値段札).

ぶちょう 部長 a general manager, a department head, a director (会社の)；the head (学校のクラブなどの) ⚠ (1) 会社組織が日･英･米で少しずつ異なるので,「部長」にぴったりの英語はない. (2) 英米では上司に対して部下がファーストネームで呼びかけることはごく普通であるが, 日本にはこの習慣はないので, 呼びかけるときは "Bucho !", "Manager !", "Boss !", または名前で "Mr. [Mrs. ／Miss ／Ms.] Sato !" などとする.

▶三田君は部員たちによって美術部の部長に選ばれた Mita has been elected *head* [*leader*] of the art club by the members. (➤ 1 名の役職の場合は Ⓤ 扱い).

‖部長代理 a deputy /dépjəṭi/ general manager, a deputy department head ‖ 営業部長 the sales manager [director] ‖ (大学の) 学生部長 (→学生).

ふちょうわ 不調和 disharmony.

ふちん 浮沈 sink or swim ▶景気の回復はわが国の浮沈にかかわる問題だ Putting [Getting] the economy back on track is *a matter of sink or swim* for our nation.

ぶつ 1【殴る】hit +目；slap +目, smack +目 (平手でぴしゃりと；後者はややインフォーマル)；spank +目 (おしおきにおしりを) ▶健二は私の頭をぶった Kenji *hit* me on the head.

2【しゃべる】▶おれが会議で一席ぶってやる I'll *give a talk* at the meeting.

1**ふつう 普通** 1【平均的】一形 ふつうの ordinary；common (ありふれた)；average /ǽvərɪdʒ/ (並の) ▶ふつうの女の子 an *ordinary* girl ‖ 彼の学校の成績はふつうだ His school record is *average*. (➤「ふつう以上 [以下]」は above [below] the average という).

2【正常】一形 ふつうの normal; usual (いつもの) ▶きょうの彼女はふつうじゃない She doesn't look her *usual* [*normal*] self today. ／She doesn't look herself today. ‖ 彼の態度はふつうではない His attitude is rather *unusual*.

3【通常】usually；generally (たいてい)；commonly (一般に)；normally (正常に) ▶私はふつう朝食前に新聞を読む I *usually* read the newspaper before breakfast. ‖ 対話「毎日何時ごろ家にお帰りになりますか」「ふつうは 8 時ごろです」"When do you come home every day ?" "*Usually* about eight." ‖ 夏は私はふつう半そでのシャツを着る In summer, I *generally* wear short-sleeve(d) shirts. ‖ フレンチフライはイギリスではふつう「チップス」という French fries are *commonly* called "chips" in Britain. ‖ ふつうならもうとっくに東京に着いていてもいい時間だ *Normally* [*Under normal conditions*], we should have already reached Tokyo. ‖ スズメやカラスは日本全国でふつうに見られる鳥の代表だ Sparrows and crows are *common* birds in Japan.

‖普通科 a day course (全日制の)；a general course (➤「商業科」などに対して) ‖ 普通教育 general education ‖ (文法) 普通名詞 a common noun ‖ 普通料金 the ordinary rate ‖ 普通列車 a local train.

2**ふつう 不通** ▶信越線は大雪のため不通だ (Train) service *has been interrupted* [*has been suspended*] on the Shin-Etsu Line due to (the) heavy snow. ／The Shin-Etsu Line *is not running* due to (the) heavy snow. ‖ 大地震で電話が不通になった Telephone service *was disrupted* [*interrupted*] by the big earthquake.

ふつか 二日 two days (2 日間)；(the) second (月の) ▶ 1 月 2 日 January *2* (➤ 2 は (the) second と読む) ‖ かぜで会社を 2 日間休んだ I stayed home from work *for two days* because of a cold.

ぶっか 物価 prices (➤ 通例複数形で) ▶日本では物価が0.4% 上がった *Prices* have gone up (by) 0.4 percent in Japan. (➤「下がる」は come down) ‖ 物価がこう上がったのではやりくりが大変だ With *prices* rising the way they are, it's getting hard to make ends meet. ‖ 東京の物価は高すぎる *Prices* in Tokyo are too high.

‖物価高 high commodity prices.

ふっかける 吹っ掛ける ▶酔っ払いがけんかを吹っ掛けてきた A drunk *picked a quarrel with* me. ‖ 彼らは私に無理難題を吹っ掛けてきた They *asked* me to do the impossible.

▶新宿のバーで法外な値段を吹っ掛けられた A bar in Shinjuku *stuck* me *with* a ridiculously high bill. (➤「請求書を突き付けた」の意)

ふっかつ 復活 (a) **revival** (再生) ; (a) **reinstatement** (制度・法律などの) **一動 復活する revive** ▶町議会は3年間中止していた祭りの復活を決めた The town council decided to *revive* the festival which had been suspended for three years. ‖ 徴兵制度の復活だなんて絶対反対です We are strongly opposed to *bringing back* the draft system.
▶キリストは死んで3日後に復活したと信じられている It is believed that Christ *was resurrected* three days after His death. (➤ その復活を the Resurrection /rèzərékʃən/ という).
‖**復活祭** Easter ‖ (予算の) **復活折衝** talks for budgetary restoration, negotiations to restore cuts in budget.

フッかぶつ フッ化物 《化学》 **fluoride.**

ふつかよい 二日酔い a **hangover, the morning after** (➤ 後者はよりインフォーマル) ▶けさはひどい二日酔いだ I *have* a terrible *hangover* this morning. ‖ きのうの夜はうんと飲んだの? 二日酔いって感じよ Did you drink much last night? You look a bit *hung over*.

ぶつかる

📖 **訳語メニュー**
衝突する →run into **1**
当たる →hit **1**
思いがけず直面する →meet with **2**
日時が重なる →fall on **3**

1【衝突する】run into ; **collide** /kəláɪd/ **with** (互いに) ; **bump into** (…にドシンと) ; **crash into** (激突する) ; **hit** +㊐ (当たる) →衝突 ▶レーシングカーがフェンスにぶつかった The racing car *ran into* the fence. ‖ 走っていて子供にぶつかった I *bumped into* a little child while I was running. ‖ 曲がり角でダンプがバスにぶつかった A dump truck *collided with* a bus at the corner. ‖ いや, 大した事故じゃないよ. ちょっとぶつかっただけだ No, it wasn't much of an accident, just *a fender bender*. (➤ fender bender はフェンダーをへこます程度の「小さな自動車事故」の意のインフォーマルな言い方) ‖ その飛行機は山にぶつかった(=墜落した)らしい It looks like the plane *crashed into* the mountain. ‖ オートバイが私の車の後ろにぶつかった A motorcycle *hit* the back of my car. ‖ ファウルボールが頭にぶつかった The foul ball *hit* my head [*hit* me on the head].

> **あなたの英語はどう響く?**
> 「彼は車にぶつかって死んだ」を直訳して, (×)He hit a car and died. とすることはできない. これでは車にパンチを加えたように響く. He *was hit* by a car and died. なら自然な英語となる.

2【直面する】meet with ▶この映画では主人公は多くの困難にぶつかり, それを一つ一つ乗り越えていく In this film the hero *meets with* a lot of difficulties and overcomes them one by one. ‖ 渋滞にぶつかって2時間も遅れてしまった We *were caught in* a traffic jam and arrived two hours late.

3【日時が重なる】fall on ▶残念! ことしはせっかくの開校記念日が日曜日にぶつかっている What a bummer! The anniversary of the foundation of our school *falls on* a Sunday this year! ‖ その時間だと別の会議とぶつかってしまう That time *clashes with* another meeting. (➤ clash with は「…とかち合う」).

4【対立する】▶私は結婚のことで母とぶつかってしまった I *clashed with* my mother about my marriage.

5【対戦する】▶ぼくたちは甲子園でK商業とぶつかる We are going to *play against* [*take on*] K Commercial High School team at Koshien. ‖ 彼は強敵にぶつかった He *was up against* [*was matched against*] a strong opponent.

ふっかん 復刊 a **reissue.**

ふっき 復帰 (a) **return**, a **comeback** (➤ 後者はややインフォーマルな語) **一動 復帰する return** 《to》
▶本間さんは3か月の闘病生活のあと, 職場に復帰した After fighting a disease for three months, Honma *returned to* work. ‖ 彼女は芸能界に復帰した She *came back* [*made a comeback*] *to* show business. ‖ 土井さんは今社会復帰を目指している Ms. Doi is now trying to *get back to normal life*.

ぶつぎ 物議 ▶大臣のその発言は物議をかもした The Minister's remark *has triggered a lot of criticism*.

ふっきゅう 復旧 restoration ▶道路はすぐに復旧した The road *was* soon *restored to normal*. ‖ 東北本線はまもなく復旧した The Tohoku Line soon *resumed normal service*. (➤ resume は「再開する」) ‖ 道路の復旧には数週間かかりそうだ It will take a few weeks to *reopen* the road. ‖ 彼らは直ちに堤防の復旧工事に取りかかった They set about *repair work* of the riverbank at once.

ぶっきょう 仏教 Buddhism /búːdɪzəm/ ▶仏教にはいくつもの宗派がある There are many sects in *Buddhism*. ‖ 仏教はキリスト教, イスラム教と並ぶ世界3大宗教の1つです Along with Christianity and Islam, *Buddhism* is one of the three major religions of the world.
‖**仏教国** a Buddhist /búːdɪst/ nation ‖ **仏教徒** a Buddhist ‖ **仏教美術** Buddhist art ‖ **小乗仏教** Theravada Buddhism ‖ **大乗仏教** Mahayana Buddhism ‖ **チベット仏教** Tibetan Buddhism.

ぶっきらぼう ぶっきら棒な blunt (相手の気持ちを考えない) ; **brusque** /brʌsk/ (無愛想で思いやりの感じられない) ; **surly** (むっつりしている) ; **gruff** (つっけんどんな) ; **curt** (そっけない) ▶ぶっきらぼうな人 a *blunt* [*brusque* / *surly*] person ‖ あの店員は口のきき方がぶっきらぼうだ That salesclerk speaks *curtly* [*bluntly* / *gruffly*]. / That salesclerk is *blunt* [*brusque*]. ‖ 彼は私の質問にぶっきらぼうに答えた He replied *bluntly* [*curtly*] to my question.

ぶつぎり ぶつ切り ▶鶏肉をぶつ切りにする *chop* chicken *into chunks*.

ふっきれる 吹っ切れる ▶その一言で迷いが吹っ切れた That one word helped *dispel* [*drive away*] my worries. ‖ 今回の判決は何か吹っ切れないものを残した The decision this time *has not cleared the air*.

ふっきん 腹筋 an **abdominal muscle** /mʌ́səl/ ▶起き上がり体操は腹筋をきたえるのに効果的だ Sit-ups are effective to strengthen [in strengthening] the *abdominal muscles*.

フック 《ボクシング》 a **hook** ; 《ゴルフ・テニス》 a **hook** ▶あごに右フックをくらわせる land [deliver] *a right hook* to the jaw.

ブックエンド bookends.

ブックカバー a **book** [**dust**] **jacket** (➤ book cover

は「本の表紙」).

ぶつくさ ▶何ぶつくさ言ってるの？ What *are* you *grumbling about*?

ブックマーク《コンピュータ》a **bookmark** ▶サイトにブックマークを付ける *bookmark* a site.

ふっくら ▶ほおのふっくらした娘 a young girl with *plump* cheeks ‖ パンがふっくらと焼きあがった The bread turned out *soft and fluffy*.

ブックレビュー a **book review**.

ぶつける **1【投げつける】throw**《at》; **fling**《at》(力を込めて) ▶男の子はほえる犬に石をぶつけた The boy *threw* [*flung*] stones *at* a barking dog (and *hit* it). (➤ hit は当たったことを明確にしたい場合).
▶《比喩的》彼女はもって行き場のない怒りを息子にぶつけた She *vented* [*verbally expressed*] her suppressed anger on her son. (➤ vent は「感情をはき出す」; take out one's anger on という表現もあるが, こちらは暴力を振るったり, 逆に, 冷酷に扱ったりを含む場合がある).
2【衝突させる】hit ＋目; **knock** /nɑ:k/ ＋目 (こつんと); **bump** ＋目 (どんと) ▶彼女は暗やみで頭をドアにぶつけた She *hit* [*knocked* / *struck*] her head *against* the door in the dark. (➤ strike は堅い語) ‖ 彼は石につまずいて塀に体をぶつけた He tripped on a rock and *bumped into* a wall.

ふっけん 復権 restoration of rights; **rehabilitation** (名誉回復); **reinstatement** (地位の回復).

ぶっけん 物件 (a **piece of**) **property** (➤ 具体的に an apartment, a house というのがふつう) ▶あの不動産屋は魅力的な物件をそろえている That real estate agency has many attractive *listings*. (➤「とりそろえた物件」は listing といい,「一戸建て物件リスト」は a list of houses (for sale) という).

ふっこう 復興 (a) **recovery** (失ったものなどを取り戻すこと); **reconstruction** (再建) 一動 **復興する recover, restore** (元に戻す) ▶その国の経済は近年めざましい復興を遂げた The economy of that country *has made a* remarkable *recovery* [*has recovered* remarkably] in recent years. ‖ その劇場街は火事で焼けたがすぐに復興した The theater district was burned down in a fire, but it was soon *restored to prosperity* [*rebuilt*].
‖ **復興庁** the Reconstruction Agency.

ふつごう 不都合 (an) **inconvenience** /ìnkənví:niəns/ 一形 **不都合な inconvenient** ▶もし不都合ならお知らせください If this is *inconvenient*, please let us know.

ふっこく 復刻する reproduce ＋目
‖ **復刻版** a reprinted edition.

ぶっさんてん 物産展 ▶このデパートでは今九州の物産展をやっている This department store is now having *a promotional display and sales for products* of Kyushu.

ぶっし 物資 goods (品物); **commodities** (商品; 経済用語); **supplies** (生活用品) ▶トラックで物資を輸送する transport *goods* by truck ‖ 遠征隊はカトマンズで物資を補給した The expedition party replenished *supplies* at Katmandu. ‖ 被災地に救援物資を運ぶ carry [transport] *relief supplies* to the stricken area.

ぶっしき 仏式 ▶仏式による葬儀 a *Buddhist* funeral ‖ 葬儀は仏式で行われた The funeral was held *according to Buddhist rites*.

ぶっしつ 物質 matter (精神に対して); a **substance** (物理的な意味での) 一形 **物質の material** /mətíəriəl/ ▶塩は人間の生命維持に不可欠な物質である Salt is *a substance* essential to the maintenance of human life. ‖ 石綿は発がん性の物質だ Asbestos is a *cancer-causing substance* [is *a carcinogen*].
▶物質的な援助 *material* help ‖ 日本は物質的には豊かになったのにより多くの社会問題に悩まされるようになったのはなぜだろう？ Why is it that Japan has been plagued by a lot more social problems despite the fact that it is better off *materially*?
‖ **物質文明** material civilization.

ぶっしゃり 仏舎利 a **bone of the Buddha**.

プッシュ プッシュする pitch ＋目 (…を売り込む); **put pressure**《on》(…に圧力をかける) ▶先方の態度がはっきりしないようだから, 再度プッシュしたほうがいい It looks like the other party hasn't made a clear decision. I think we'd better *put pressure on* them again. ‖ そのテレビ局はその新女性ニュースキャスターを猛プッシュしている The TV station is enthusiastically *promoting* [*pitching*] the new woman (news)anchor.

プッシュホン a **push-button (tele)phone**
《参考》「プッシュホン」は NTT の登録商標名であり, 和製語. 英語では push-button (tele)phone という. アメリカには同じく登録商標名に由来する touch-tone (tele)phone がある.《英》では keyphone ともいう.

ぶっしょう 物証 physical [**real**] **evidence** ▶容疑者をその犯罪と結びつける物証は何もない There's no *physical* [*real*] *evidence* linking the suspect to the crime.

ふっしょく 払拭する dispel ＋目 (不安や疑念などを) ▶政府は地元住民の原発に対する不安を払拭できなかった The government was unable to *dispel* [*eradicate*] the local people's anxiety over the nuclear power plants.

ぶっしょく 物色する look for ▶今, 借家を物色中です I *am* now *looking* [*shopping around*] *for* a house to rent. ‖ 何者かが室内を物色した形跡があった There were signs that someone *had ransacked* [*rummaged through* / *searched*] the room.

ぶっしん 物心 ▶東京ではおじが物心両面で支えてくれた My uncle supported me *both physically and mentally* in Tokyo.

ぶつぜん 仏前 ▶仏前に(＝位はいの前に)花を供える offer flowers *before the tablet of the deceased*.

フッそ フッ素《化学》**fluorine** /flɔ́əri:n/; **fluoride** (フッ化物; 歯科で用いるのはこちら) ▶フッ素で虫歯予防をする prevent tooth decay using *fluoride*.
‖ **フッ素樹脂** fluorocarbon polymers (➤「フッ素加工されたフライパン」は正式には a PTFE-coated fry pan であるが, 一般には商標名で a Teflon-coated fry pan と呼ぶ).

ぶっそう 物騒な dangerous (危険な); **unsafe** (安全ではない) ▶物騒な世の中だ It's a *dangerous* world. ‖ あの辺は暴力団の抗争があって物騒だ That part of (the) town *is dangerous* because the gangs are at each other's throats around there. ‖ 夜道のひとり歩きは物騒だ It *is unsafe* for you to go out alone at night.

ぶつぞう 仏像 a **statue** [an **image**] **of Buddha** /bú:də/, a **Buddhist** /bú:dɪst/ **statue** [**image**].

ぶっだ 仏陀 (**the**) **Buddha**.

ぶったい 物体 an **object** /ɑ́:bdʒekt/ (物); a **body** (物理学上の) ▶上空に変な物体を発見しました I saw a strange *object* up in the sky. ‖ 物体には固有の質量がある All *bodies* have a certain mass.

ぶつだん 仏壇 a **family Buddhist** /búːdɪst/ **altar**
日本紹介 ✉ **仏壇は, 位はいを納めて日々家族が礼拝するための箱型の祭壇です. 旧家では代々伝わる仏壇がありますが, 新しい家では家族が亡くなった場合にしばしば新たに購入します** A *butsudan* is a box-shaped altar that holds Buddhist memorial tablets of deceased family members for whom and to whom the family prays daily. In families with a long history, there are *butsudan* that have been passed down from generation to generation. In new families people often buy one when someone in the family has died.
▶仏壇に先祖の霊を祭る pay respect to one's ancestors at one's *family* (*Buddhist*) *altar*.

ぶっちぎり ▶彼はぶっちぎりでそのマラソンに優勝した He came in *way ahead of everyone else* in the marathon. (➤ way は「はるかに, ずっと」の意の副詞).

ぶっちゃけ **to be frank, to put things bluntly**(はっきり言って).

ぶっちょうづら 仏頂面 a **sullen face** ▶うちの部長はいつも仏頂面で, にこりともしない Our department head always *looks sullen* and you never see him smile.

ふつつか 不束 ▶ふつつか者ですが, よろしくお願いいたします Although *I'm inexperienced*, I'm excited and looking forward to working with you. (➤ 謙そんする言い方は英語ではことばどおり受け止められて, 必要以上に卑屈に響くので言わないのがふつう).

ぶっつけほんばん ぶっつけ本番 ▶ぶっつけ本番のスピーチ an *impromptu* [*off-the-cuff*] speech ‖ 彼女はぶっつけ本番で受けた試験で満点を取った She got a perfect score on the test she took *cold*. (➤ この cold は「準備なしで」の意のインフォーマルな副詞).

ぶっつづけ ぶっ続け →ぶっ通し.

ふっつり ▶あれほど好きだったマージャンを彼はふっつりとやめた He *completely* quit playing mah-jongg, which he used to love so much.

ぷっつり ▶風で糸がぷっつりと切れて, たこが空へ飛んでいってしまった The wind *snapped* the string and carried the kite away up in the sky.

プッツン ▶その歌手はすぐプッツンするので有名だ That singer is notorious for *losing it* [*losing his* [*her*] *temper*] *over nothing*.

ふってい 払底 ▶その機種の携帯電話は現在在庫が払底しています Cellphones of that model *are completely out of stock* at present.

ぶってき 物的 ‖**物的援助** material help [support] ‖ **物的資源** material resources ‖ **物的証拠** physical [real] evidence.

ふってわく 降って湧く ▶降ってわいたような大事件 a *totally unforeseen* major incident / an *out-of-the-blue* incident.

ふってん 沸点 **the boiling point.**

ぶってん 仏典 **the Buddhist scriptures.**

ふっと ▶ふっとため息を漏らす *breathe* [*heave*] *a sigh*.

ぷっと ▶彼の顔があんまりおかしかったのでついぷっとふき出してしまった His face was so funny that I *broke out into laughter*. ‖ ぼくが何か気にさわることを言ったのか, 彼女はぷっとふくれた I must have said something to offend her, because she *suddenly started pouting*.

ふっとう 沸騰 **boiling** 一動 **沸騰する boil** ▶水は摂氏100度で沸騰する Water *boils* at 100℃. ‖ ママ, お湯が沸騰してるわよ Mom, the water *is boiling*. ‖ みそ汁は沸騰させてはだめよ Don't *boil* your miso soup. / Don't *bring* your miso soup *to a boil*.
▶その運河を埋め立てる埋め立てないで議論が沸騰している The question of whether the canal should be filled in or not *has stirred up a heated controversy*. (➤「熱い論争を巻き起こす」の意).
‖**沸騰点** the boiling point.

ぶっとおし ぶっ通し ▶12時間ぶっ通しで働いた I worked (for) 12 hours *running* [*at a stretch*]. (➤ running は「連続する」の意の形容詞で, 複数名詞のあとに置く. at a stretch は「一気に, 休まずに」の意) ‖ 各テレビ局は何時間もぶっ通しで震災のニュースを伝えた Each TV station broadcast news about the great earthquake *for hours on end*. (➤ on end は具体的な数字がくるときは用いない).

フットサル **futsal ; five-a-side (football)** ▶私たちは土日によくフットサルをします We often *play futsal* on Saturdays and [or] Sundays.

ぶっとばす ぶっ飛ばす **beat up**(たたきのめす); **tear** /teəʳ/ +副 (猛烈な勢いで動く) ▶名神高速を120キロでぶっ飛ばした I *tore* down the Meishin Expressway at 120km per hour.

ふっとぶ 吹っ飛ぶ **blow away** [**off**] ▶突風で屋根が吹っ飛んだ A gust of wind *blew* the roof *off*.
▶子供づれで遊園地へ行ったらあっという間に1万円吹っ飛んだ When I went to the amusement park with my children, we *blew* 10,000 yen in no time at all. (➤ blow は「大金をぱっぱっと使い果たす, 見境なく使う」).

フットボール **football** 《参考》アメリカでは通例 American football を, イギリスや南米などでは soccer または rugby (football) を指す.
▶フットボールをする play *football* ‖ フットボールの選手 a footballer / a football player.

フットライト **footlights**(➤ 通例複数形で用いる) →脚光.

フットワーク **footwork** ▶あのボクサーは軽快なフットワークをしている That boxer has swift *footwork*.

ぶつのう 物納 ▶相続税を物納する *pay* an inheritance tax *in kind*.

ぶっぴん 物品 **goods**, an **article.**

ぶつぶつ **1**【粒状の突起物】a **rash** ▶彼は顔中にぶつぶつができている He has *a rash* all over his face.
2【状態・言動を示して】▶きりでボール紙にぶつぶつ穴をあけた I made *several holes* in the cardboard (*at random*) with a gimlet.
▶清水先生はいつも何かぶつぶつ言いながら教室に入って来る Mr. Shimizu, our teacher, always comes into the classroom *mumbling* [*muttering*] something to himself.
▶母は私の成績が悪いのでいつまでもぶつぶつ言った Mom *went on at* me about my poor grades. (➤ go on は「ずっと文句を言う」) ‖ ぶつぶつ文句ばかり言ってないで仕事をしろよ Now stop *grumbling* and get to work.

ぶつぶつこうかん 物々交換 **barter** 一動 **物々交換する barter** 《for》 ▶我々は食料を衣服と物々交換した We *bartered* [*exchanged*] food *for* clothes.

ふつぶん 仏文 **French literature**(文学); a **department of French literature**(仏文科).

ぶつめつ 仏滅 ***Butsumetsu***
日本紹介 ✉ **仏滅は大安の反対で, 6つある吉凶を元に名付けられた日の中で最も縁起の悪い日とされます. この日に結婚式などおめでたいことを**

行う人はほとんどいません In contrast to *Taian* (the luckiest type of day), *Butsumetsu* is considered the unluckiest of the six kinds of days based on good and bad luck. Few people hold happy events such as weddings on a day designated as *Butsumetsu*.

ぶつもん 仏門 ▶仏門に入る *become a Buddhist priest*.

ぶつよく 物欲 ▶物欲の強い人 a *materialistic* person ‖ 物欲にとらわれる become a slave to *materialistic desires*.

ぶつり 物理 **physics**(物理学) 一形 **物理の physical** ▶こんなに大量の仕事をあすまでにやるのは物理的に不可能だ It is *physically* impossible to get this much work done by tomorrow.

‖**物理学** physics (➤「物理学を学ぶ」は study physics) ‖ **物理学者** a physicist /fízɪsɪst/ ‖ **物理療法** physical therapy ‖ **応用物理学** applied physics ‖ **地球物理学** geophysics /dʒìːəfízɪks/ ‖ **理論物理学** theoretical physics.

ぷつり ▶バッグのひもがぷつりと切れて中身が床に散らばった The strap of the bag *snapped* and the things inside flew out all over the floor. (➤ snap は「(ひもなどが)ぷつりと切れる, (枝などが)ぽきっと折れる」の意).

ふつりあい 不釣り合いの **ill-matched** ▶不釣り合いのカップル an *ill-matched* couple ‖ 背広にげたは不釣り合いだ A business suit *does not match* [*go with*] wooden clogs.

ぶつりゅう 物流 **distribution**(配送) ; **logistics**(効率的管理)

‖**物流拠点** a logistics base ‖ **物流コスト** distribution costs ‖ **物流システム** a distribution system ‖ **物流センター** a distribution [shipping] center ‖ **物流倉庫** a distribution warehouse.

ぶつりょう 物量 an **amount of resources** [**materials**].

ぷつん ▶針金をぷつんと切る *snap* a wire.

ふで 筆 a **calligraphy brush**(毛筆) ; a **paintbrush** (絵筆) ▶祖父は年賀状を筆で書く My grandfather writes New Year's cards with *a calligraphy brush*. ‖ 筆に墨をつけなさい Dip your *brush* in sumi ink.

▶《慣用表現》彼女は筆が立つ She *writes well*. ／She *is a good writer*. ‖ 先生が私の原稿に筆を加え[入れ]てくださった The teacher *corrected* [*added corrections to*] my manuscript. ‖ その作家が筆を断ってから久しい It's been a long time since that writer *gave up* [*quit*] *writing*.

ことわざ **弘法にも筆の誤り** Even (the Great Priest) Kobo made a mistake with the brush. ／Even the best of us make mistakes. ／Even Homer sometimes nods. (➤第1文は日本語からの直訳, 第2文は意訳. 第3文は西洋のことわざで,「ホメロスのような偉い詩人でもときには不注意な誤りを犯す」の意. なお, 欧米人には Kobo より Kukai のほうが通りがいい).

ことわざ **弘法筆を選ばず** Kobo (the Great Priest) doesn't blame his brushes. (➤日本語からの直訳) ／A bad workman blames his tools. (➤「下手な職人は道具に文句を言う」の意).

‖**筆入れ** [**筆箱**] a pencil case [box] ‖ **筆立て** a pen [brush] stand.

☛ **筆不精, 筆まめ** (→見出語)

[1]**ふてい 不定の** **indefinite** /ɪndéfənət/ ▶その男は住所不定だ That man *has no fixed address*.

‖《文法》**不定冠詞** an indefinite article ‖《文法》**不定詞** an infinitive.

[2]**ふてい 不貞** (**marital**) **infidelity, adultery** ▶不貞を働く commit *adultery*.

ふていき 不定期の **irregular** ▶現地から不定期だが連絡はときどき来る We do get news from there from time to time, but *not on any regular basis*.

‖**不定期便** a nonscheduled flight (航空機の).

ブティック a **boutique** /buːtíːk/ ▶青山通りには高級なブティックが並んでいる Aoyama Dori is lined with exclusive *boutiques*.

ふてき 不敵な **fearless** ▶そのプロレスラーは不敵な面構えをしている That pro wrestler has a *fearless* look. ／That pro wrestler looks *fearless*. ‖ 死刑の判決に被告は不敵な笑いを浮かべた The accused grinned *defiantly* [*fearlessly*] when he was sentenced to capital punishment.

ふでき 不出来な **bad**(➤「悪い」の意の一般語) ; **poor** (不十分な, 出来がよくない ; 堅い語) ▶不出来な子 a *bad* child ‖ 不出来なケーキ a *poorly-made* cake ‖ ことしはクリが不出来だった The chestnut crop *has failed* [We have *had a poor crop* of chestnuts] this year.

▶その監督の最新作は彼にしては不出来だ The director's latest film *is not up to* his *usual standards*. (➤「いつもの水準に達していない」の意).

ふてきかく 不適格な **unqualified**(資格を持っていない ; ある基準に合っていない) ; **unfit**(目的・条件から見て) ; **ineligible**(…に選ばれる条件や資格をもたない) ; **incompetent**(あることを完ぺきに成し遂げることのできない).

ふてきせつ 不適切な **inappropriate**(目的・条件などにそぐわない) ; **unsuitable**(似つかわしくない) ▶《アナウンサー》ニュースの中で不適切な表現があったことをおわびいたします We apologize for having used an *inappropriate* expression in the news. ‖ 彼の気持ちはわかるが, 言い方が不適切だった I understand how he feels, but the way he expressed himself was *not appropriate*.

ふてきとう 不適当な **inappropriate** (適さない) ; **unsuitable** (合わない) ; **improper** (場所柄・しきたりなどから見て) ▶この雑誌は中学生には不適当だ This magazine is *inappropriate* for junior high students. ‖ 不適当な表現があったら指摘してください Please point out *unsuitable* [*unfitting*] expressions, if any.

ふてきにん 不適任な **unsuited**(…するのに人などが) ; **unfit**(目的・条件などに) ; **unqualified**(資格を持っていない) ▶彼は会計係には不適任だ He is *unsuited* to be an accountant. ／He is not the right person for accounting. ‖ 彼は暴力的な男性だから警官には不適任だ He is *unfit* to be a police officer because he is a violent man.

ふてぎわ 不手際 ▶不手際な処理 *untactful* [*inept*] handling ‖ 塁審の判定に不手際(＝ミス)があった The base umpire made *a mistake* in judgment. ‖ 事故をすぐに警察に知らせなかったのは不手際だったね It was *a mistake* not to have reported the accident to the police right away.

ふてくされる **sulk, get sulky** ▶母親が外に遊びに行かせてくれないのでその男の子はふてくされている That boy *is sulking* [*is sulky*] because his mother won't let him go out to play.

ふてってい 不徹底 ▶不徹底な処置 *halfway* measures ‖ あいつの仕事ぶりはいつも不徹底だ He *never does* his work *thoroughly*.

ふてね 不貞寝 ▶こら, 鉄矢, またふて寝してるな Hey, Tetsuya, I see you'*re sulking in bed* again.

ふでぶしょう 筆不精 ▶私は筆不精だ I'm *a poor letter writer* [*a poor correspondent*].

✉ **筆不精でごめんなさい** I'm sorry for *being so lazy about writing letters*.

ふてぶてしい **defiant**(ごう慢な, 挑戦的な) ; **forward**(あつかましい, 自信過剰の) ▶ふてぶてしい(=反抗的な)態度 a *defiant* attitude.

▶何てふてぶてしい(=ずぶとい)! What (*a*) *nerve* ! ‖ その選手は新人とは思えないふてぶてしさだった That player *was bolder* than you would expect of a rookie.

ふでまめ 筆まめ ▶兄は筆まめだ My (older) brother is *a great letter writer* [*a good correspondent*].

ふと **suddenly**(突然) ; **casually** (何げなく) ▶教会の前で彼はふと立ち止まった He stopped *suddenly* in front of the church. ‖ ふと手に取った雑誌に母校のことが出ていた A magazine I had picked up *casually* turned out to have an article about my alma mater.

▶ぼくはふと彼女がぼくの妻になるかもしれないと思った *It occurred to me that* she might become my wife. (➤ occur to は「(考えなどが)ふと…の心に浮かぶ」) ‖ 新聞の片隅の小さな記事がふと目に留まった A short article in a corner of the newspaper *caught my eye*.

☛ ふとした (→見出語)

ふとい 太い **1【周囲や幅が大きい】** **thick** ; **bold** (線や字が) ▶太い足 a *thick* leg ‖ ラグビーの選手は首が太い Rugby players have *thick* necks. ‖ 雪の重みで太い木の枝が折れた A *thick* bough broke under the weight of the snow. ‖ ジーンズには太いベルトが似合う A *thick* belt goes well with jeans.

▶太い線は国境を示す The *bold line* indicates the border. ‖ 指が太くなって指輪が簡単には抜けなくなった My finger's *gotten* so *fat* the ring doesn't come off as easily as it used to (do).

2【声が】 **deep** ▶弟は近頃声が太くなった Recently, my (younger) brother's voice has gotten *deep*.

3【ずうずうしい】 ▶人の自転車に黙って乗って行くとは太い野郎だ That guy *has got* (*some*) *nerve* taking my bicycle without permission.

[1]**ふとう 埠頭** a **wharf** /*h*wɔːʳf/ ; a **pier** (桟橋) ▶横浜港の山下埠頭 the Yamashita *Wharf* at Yokohama Port.

[2]**ふとう 不当な** **unreasonable**(不合理な, 法外な) ; **unfair**(不公平な) ; **unjust** (不公正な) ; **wrongful**(正当性を欠く) ▶彼らはそのジュエリーを不当な値段で彼女に売りつけた They forced the jewelry on her at an *unreasonable* price. ‖ その会社は脱税で不当な利益をあげた The company made *unfair* profits by tax evasion.

▶彼は解雇は不当だと主張した He claimed his dismissal was *wrongful*.

ふどう 不動の **unshakable** ▶不動の信念 *firm* [*unshakable*] belief ‖ 彼はイラストレーターとして不動の地位を築いている He has *unshakable* status as an illustrator. ‖ ガードマンたちは直立不動の姿勢をとった The guards *stood at attention*. ‖ 日本チームは全5試合を不動のメンバーで戦った The Japanese team played all the five games *with an unchanged lineup*.

ぶとう 舞踏 **dancing**(踊ること) ; a **dance** (1回の踊り) ▶舞踏会を催す give *a dance* [*a ball*] (➤ ball は正式で大きなものをいう).

‖**舞踏家** a dancer ; a ballet dancer(バレエの).

[1]**ぶどう 葡萄** a **grape**(1粒) ; a (**grape**)**vine** (木) ▶ブドウ1房 a bunch of *grapes* ‖ ブドウ狩りに行く go *grape-picking*.

‖**ブドウ園** [**畑**] a vineyard /vínjəʳd/ ‖ **ブドウ球菌** a staphylococcus [複 -cocci] ‖ **ブドウ酒** wine ‖ **ブドウ棚** a grape trellis [arbor] ‖ **ブドウ糖** glucose /glúːkoʊs/ ‖ **干しブドウ** a raisin /réɪzən/.

[2]**ぶどう 武道** **martial arts** ; **budo**(日本の) 《**参考**》日本の武道は budo として英語化しているが, martial arts と言えば中国, 韓国などのものも含める一般語.

▶武道に励む practice *martial arts*.

ふとういつ 不統一 **disunity** ; **inconsistency** /ìnkənsístənsi/ (一貫性に欠けること) ▶同じ本の中で用語の不統一があるのは望ましくない *Inconsistent* use of terms in a book is not desirable. ‖ エネルギー政策については閣内の意見に不統一がみられた The Cabinet ministers *were divided* on (the subject of) energy policy.

ふとうこう 不登校 **school refusal** ▶不登校の生徒が増え続けている The number of *students who refuse to go to school* is on the increase.

ふとうごう 不等号 《数学》 an **inequality sign, a sign of inequality.**

ふどうさん 不動産 **real estate** [**property**], **immovables** (➤ 後者は法律用語. なお家具・車・宝石などの「動産」は chattel と呼ぶ).

‖**不動産業** real estate business ‖ **不動産業者** a real estate agent [broker], 《米また》 a realtor /ríːəltəʳ/ 《**参考**》《英》では estate agent が好まれる. また, realtor は業者が好む語である.

ふどうとく 不道徳 **immorality** ━形 **不道徳な** **immoral** ▶妻子のある人を愛するのは不道徳でしょうか Do you think it's *immoral* to fall in love with someone who has a wife and children ?

ふどうひょう 浮動票 **swing votes, floating** [**undecided**] **votes** ▶その候補者は浮動票を多数獲得して当選した That candidate won the election by picking up a great number of *floating* [*undecided*] *votes*.

ふとうふくつ 不撓不屈の **unyielding, indomitable.**

ふとうめい 不透明な **opaque** /oʊpéɪk/ ▶不透明な氷 *opaque* ice.

▶《比喩的》日本の景気の見通しは不透明(=不確か)だ Japanese business prospects are *uncertain*.

ふとく 不徳 ▶今回の混乱は私の不徳の致すところです It is I who *am to blame* [who *am at fault*] for the current confusion. (➤「自分の行いや心がけが立派でなかったことに原因がある」という考えは英語にはないので,「それは自分の責任です」と考える).

ふとくい 不得意な **poor** ; **weak** (弱い) ▶私は暗算[パソコン]が不得意だ I'*m poor at* mental arithmetic [using a computer]. ‖ 彼は体育が不得意だ He *is poor at* [*weak in*] physical education. ‖ 私は泳ぎが不得意だ I am a *poor* swimmer. ‖ 不得意な科目は何ですか What subject *are* you *poor at* [*weak in*] ?

▶夏休み中にあなたの不得意科目をよく勉強しなさい Study all the *subjects you're not good at* during the summer vacation.

ふとくてい 不特定の **unspecified** ; **indefinite** /ɪndéfənət/ (不定の) ▶不特定の場所 an *unspecified* place ‖ 不特定の時 *indefinite* time ‖ 不特定多数の人々 (*many and*) *unspecified individuals* ‖ a や an は不特定の物を指すのに使われる 'a' or 'an' is used to indicate an *unspecified* object.

ふところ 懐 **1【胸部】** a **chest**, a **breast**; an **inside pocket**（内ポケット）▶彼女は子供を懐にしっかりと抱いた She clutched the child to her *chest*. ‖ 彼はメモしたものを大事そうに懐にしまった He carefully put the memo in his *inside pocket*.

2【所持金】▶きょう給料をもらったばかりだから，懐が暖かいんだ I got paid today, so I'*m rich* [*loaded*]. ‖ **対話**「帰りに一杯やらないか？」「いやあ，きょうは懐が寂しいんだ」"How about a drink on our way home?" "No, thanks. I'*m short of cash* today."

▶彼はいつも人の懐を当てにする He always wants *someone else to pay*.

ふとさ 太さ **thickness** ▶この丸太は太さが30センチある This log is 30 centimeters *thick* [*in diameter*]. / This log has *a thickness* [*a diameter*] of 30 centimeters.（➤ 形容詞 thick で表現するのが普通；diameter は「直径」）‖ シャープペンシルのしんの太さはふつう0.5ミリだ The lead of a mechanical pencil is commonly 0.5mm *in diameter* [0.5mm across].（➤ in diameter, across とも「直径で」の意）.

ふとじ 太字《印刷》**boldface** ▶太字で書かれた written *in boldface* [*bold letters*].

ふとした ▶今のガールフレンドとはふとしたことから知り合った I met my girlfriend *by* (*mere*) *chance*. ‖ ふとした(＝ささいな)ことからけんかになった A quarrel started over an *unimportant* matter.

ふとっちょ 太っちょ a **fatso**, a **fatty**.

ふとっぱら 太っ腹 ▶会長は太っ腹な人だ The chairman is a *big-hearted* [*generous*] man.

ふとどき 不届き ▶無断で人の本を持ち去るとはふとどきな(＝けしからん)やつだ I think it was *outrageous* of him to take my book without permission.

ぶどまり 歩留まり《ビジネス》**the yield**.

ふとめ 太め ▶私は太めの万年筆を持っている I have a fountain pen with a *broad* [*thick*] nib. ‖ やせた子よりちょっと太めの女の子のほうがいい I prefer girls *on the plump side* to slim ones.（➤ on the ... side は「…ぎみで」の意）.

ふともも 太腿 a **thigh** /θaɪ/

▶むっちりした太もも a fleshy [plump] *thigh*.

ふとる 太る

gain [**put on**] **weight**, **get** [**grow**] **fat** — 形 **太った** **fat**, **stout** /staʊt/, **plump**, **chubby**

> **語法**「太る」は gain [put on] weight（体重を増す）がいちばん無難な言い方. fat は直接的に響き，しばしば「でぶ」という軽蔑的なニュアンスを伴うので，代わりに chubby, stout, plump, a little overweight [on the heavy side] などが婉曲(えんきょく)表現として用いられる. 特に plump は女性や子供に対して使われることが多く，好ましいニュアンスがある.

▶彼は太っている He *is fat* [*overweight* / *stout* / *plump*]. ‖ そんなにアイスクリームばかり食べると太るよ You'll *get fat* if you eat so much ice cream. ‖ **対話**「ちょっと太ったんじゃない？」「うん．ことしになって5キロ太っちゃったよ」"It seems you'*ve put on* a little *weight*." "Yeah. I'*ve gained* [*I've put on*] five kilos this year."（➤ 英米ではこういう話題は避けるのがふつう）.

▶ **対話**「ポテトチップス，どう？」「ありがとう．でも，太るからやめとくわ」"How about some potato chips?" "No, thanks. They're *fattening*."（➤ No, thanks. I have to watch my weight.（体重に注意しなければならないので，やめておく）のほうが英語的）.

▶彼女の赤ん坊は丸々と太っている Her baby is *plump* [*chubby*].（➤ 後者は主に赤ん坊や子供に用いる）‖ 景子はこの頃太りぎみだ Keiko has gotten *a bit plump* recently. ‖ 彼女は3キロほど太り過ぎだ She is three kilograms *overweight*. ‖ 太り過ぎは健康によくない *Being overweight* is not good for the health.

ふとん 布団 a **futon**（➤ 英語化しているが，英米でいう futon は敷き布団のみを指す）; **bedding**（➤ 寝具の総称）; a **quilt**（掛け布団）;《米》a **comforter**,《英》a **duvet** /dúːveɪ/（羽毛掛け布団）

日本紹介 ✉ **布団は日本の伝統的な寝具です．寝るときは綿を詰めた敷き布団をマットレスのように下に敷き，寝た上から掛け布団をかけます．昼間は折り畳んで押し入れにしまっておきます** Futon refer to traditional Japanese bedding. When people go to bed, they spread a *shiki-buton* (a futon packed with cotton), lie down on it and put a *kake-buton* (comforter) over them. Futon are folded and stored in an *oshiire* closet in the daytime.

▶布団を敷く spread out (the) *futon*（➤ 欧米式には make [prepare] the bed）‖ 布団を上げる put away the *futon* ‖ 布団を畳む fold up the *futon* ‖ 布団を干す air out the *futon*.

▶ふかふかの布団［せんべい布団］に寝る sleep on *a soft and comfortable* [*a thin and uncomfortable*] *futon* ‖ 寒い朝はなかなか布団から出られない I find it hard [difficult] to get out of the *futon* on cold mornings.

☛ 掛け布団（→見出語）

ふな 鮒《魚》a **crucian** /krúːʃən/ (**carp**) ▶釣りはフナに始まりフナに終わるという People say that catching *crucian carp* is the A to Z of angling [angling begins and ends with *crucian carp*].

ふな- 船- ‖ **船遊び** boating, sailing ‖ **船会社** a shipping company ‖ **船大工** a ship carpenter, a shipwright [boatwright] ‖ **船積み** shipment（➤「船積みをする」は load a ship, make a shipment）‖ **船主** a ship [boat] owner.

ぶな 橅《植物》a **beech** (**tree**)
‖ **ブナ林** a beech forest.

ふなあし 船足 **the speed of a boat** [**ship**]（船の速さ）; **the draft of a ship**（喫水）.

ふなうた 舟歌 **a boat song**; a **barcarole**（ベニスの）.

ふなか 不仲 ▶富夫とアンナは不仲だそうだ I heard (that) Tomio *has fallen out with* [*has been estranged from*] Anna. ‖ 子供にとって親が不仲なことほど悲しいことはない Nothing makes children more unhappy than *discord* between their parents.

ふなたび 船旅 a **trip by sea**, a **voyage** /vɔ́ɪɪdʒ/; a **cruise** /kruːz/（遊覧航海）▶佐渡へは1時間半ほどの船旅です The *trip by sea* to Sado Island takes about an hour and a half. / It's about an hour and a half to Sado Island by boat. ‖ 一行は地中海一周の船旅に出かけた The party went on [for] *a cruise* around the Mediterranean.

ふなちん 船賃 a (**boat**) **fare**（乗客の）; a **sea freight charge** [**cost**]（貨物の）.

ふなつきば 船着き場 a **wharf** /hwɔːrf/.

ふなで 船出する **sail**《out》（船が）▶《比喩的》いよ

いよきょうはあなたがたが新たな人生に船出する日です This is a big day for you all as you *launch out into the sea of life* [*embark on a new life*].

ふなのり 船乗り a **sailor**; a **seaman** (特に「下級船員, 下士官」を指す) ▶船乗りになる become *a sailor* ／go to sea.

ふなびん 船便 **sea mail**; **surface mail** (➤ 航空便以外のもので, 船便のほかに陸上輸送郵便も含む) ▶これを船便でスペインへ送りたいのですが I would like to mail this to Spain *by sea* (*mail*).

ふなよい 船酔い **seasickness** ▶私は船酔いをしやすい[しない] I easily [never] *get seasick*.

ふなれ 不慣れな **unaccustomed** (慣れていない); **unfamiliar** (よく知らない) ▶不慣れな仕事でひどく疲れた I've gotten very tired because I'*m not used* [*accustomed*] *to* the job yet.

▶東京には不慣れなものだからよく道を間違えます Because I'm still *a stranger* in Tokyo [Because Tokyo is still *unfamiliar* to me], I often take the wrong street.

ぶなん 無難 **1【まずまずの】adequate** /ǽdɪkwət/ (まずまずの, 可もなく不可もない); **acceptable** (受け入れられる) ▶その新人女優は無難な演技を見せた That new actress gave an *adequate* performance. ／The new actress played her part adequately.

2【安全な】safer (より安全な) ▶この空模様では傘を持って行くほうが無難だろう Judging from the sky, it would be *safer* for you to carry an umbrella with you. ‖ 赤はどぎついよ. ベージュくらいが無難だよ Red is too flashy. Beige would be (*more*) *appropriate* [*a safer bet*], I guess. (➤ appropriate は「(場に)ふさわしい」; a safer bet は「よりうまくいきそうなもの [まちがいないもの]」).

ふにあい 不似合い ▶不似合いな夫婦 an *ill-matched* couple ‖ このドレスはきみには不似合いだ This dress *doesn't suit* [*look good on*] you. ‖ 彼女は顔に不似合いなきんきん声を出す She speaks in a shrill voice *unfitting* [*unbecoming*] *to* her (beautiful) face.

ふにおちない 腑に落ちない ▶きみの説明ではどうもふに落ちない I *am not quite satisfied with* your explanation. ／Your explanation does*n't sit well with* me.

ふにゃふにゃ ▶こんにゃくはふにゃふにゃしていてはしでつかみにくい *Konnyaku* is so *limp* [*floppy*] that it's not easy to hold it with chopsticks.

[1]**ふにん 赴任する** **leave for** one's **new post** ▶中村さんは札幌に赴任した Mr. Nakamura *went to* Sapporo *to take up a new post*.

☛ 単身赴任 (→単身)

[2]**ふにん 不妊** **infertility** 一形 **不妊の** **infertile, sterile** /stérəl/ ▶不妊症の女性 an *infertile* [a *sterile*] woman ‖ 彼は不妊手術(＝パイプカット)を受けた He had *a vasectomy*. (➤ 女性の場合は She had her tubes tied. (卵管をくくってもらった)という; 男女を合わせた総合的な呼称は sterilization (procedure)) ‖ 猫の不妊手術をしてもらった We *had* our cat *spayed*. (➤ spay は「(動物の)卵巣を除去する」. なお「(雄)を去勢する」は neuter).

‖**不妊症治療** infertility treatment ‖ **不妊治療** fertility treatment ‖ **不妊治療院** a fertility clinic.

ふにんき 不人気な **unpopular** ▶英夫はハンサムなのにクラスの女の子たちに不人気だ Although he is handsome, Hideo *is unpopular among* [*with*] the girls in his class.

ふにんじょう 不人情な **heartless** (無情な); **unkind** (不親切な); **cold-hearted** (冷たい心の) ▶不人情な人 a *heartless* [an *unkind* ／a *cold-hearted*] person ‖ 不人情な世の中になったものだ It's a *cold-hearted* world we live in.

ふぬけ 腑抜け a **coward** (いくじなし); an **idiot** (ばか) ▶このふぬけ野郎! What *an idiot* [*a jerk*]! (➤ 後者のほうがより侮辱的).

ふね 船 a **ship**, a **boat**, a **vessel** /vésəl/

> **《解説》** (1)**ship** は「船」を表す一般的な語だが, 主として大型船を指す. **boat** はインフォーマルでは ship と同義に用いるが, 一般的にはオールや小型エンジンなどで動く「小型の船」を指す. (2)**vessel** は「大型船」を指す堅い語.

▶2 隻の船が下田沖を航行している Two *ships* are sailing off Shimoda. ‖ 船から大勢の観光客が降りてきた A lot of tourists got off the *ship*. ‖ 私は船で下関をたちプサンへ向かった I left Shimonoseki for Pusan *by ship*. ／I took a ship at Shimonoseki for Pusan.

▶私たちは船で木曽川を下った We rode down the Kiso River *on a boat*. ‖ 私は船に乗るとすぐ酔ってしまう I get seasick easily when I *am on a boat* [*ship*]. ／I get motion sickness *on boats* [*ships*] easily. ‖ 彼は 3 日間船に乗っている He *has been on board* for three days. ‖ 船に乗ろう Let's *board* [*go on board*] *the ship*. ‖ 私は船に強い [弱い] I'm *a good* [*bad*] *sailor*.

▶《慣用表現》乗りかかった船だ. 最後まで付き合うとしよう Now that *I've committed myself to it*, I think I'll have to see it through. ‖ おばあちゃんがちゃぶ台に寄りかかって船をこいでいる Grandma *is nodding off* over the low dining table.

ふねっしん 不熱心な **unenthusiastic** (熱意がない); **half-hearted** (気乗りしない) ▶商売に不熱心な人 a person *unenthusiastic* about business ／ a person *with little interest* in business.

ふねん 不燃 ▶消防士の服は不燃性の素材でできている Firefighters' suits are made of *nonflammable* [*incombustible*] material.

‖**不燃建築** a fireproof [fire-resistant] building ‖ **不燃物** nonflammables.

ふのう 不能 ▶このテレビは修理不能だ This TV (set) is *beyond repair*. ‖ あの投手は再起不能らしい That pitcher seems *unable to make a comeback*.

▶彼は不能(＝インポ)になった He became *impotent*. (➤ impotent は社会的に受け入れられる表現ではなくなった. He suffered from erectile dysfunction. と表現するのがよい).

プノンペン **Phnom Penh** /pnɑ̀m pén/ (カンボジアの首都).

ふはい 腐敗 **1【腐ること】rot** (細菌やかびによる); **decay** (自然でゆっくりとした) 一動 **腐敗する** **rot, decay**; **spoil, go bad** (食べ物などが悪くなる) 一形 **腐敗した** **rotten** ▶落ち葉は腐敗して植物の養分となる Fallen leaves *rot* and become nourishment for plants. ‖ 梅雨時は食べ物が腐敗するのが早い Foods *spoil* [*go bad*] quickly in the rainy season.

2【堕落】corruption (特に汚職) 一形 **腐敗した** **corrupt** ▶我々は政治の腐敗を許してはならない *Corruption* in politics is something we must not allow. ‖

麻薬は精神を**腐敗させ**，そのうえ健康をもむしばむ Besides *corrupting* [*ruining*] our minds, drugs destroy our health.

ふばい 不買 ▶彼らは日本車の**不買運動**を始めた They launched *a boycott* of [started *boycotting*] Japanese-made cars. ／They started *a no-buy campaign* against Japanese-made cars.

‖**不買同盟** a boycott /bɔ́ɪkɑːt/.

ふはつ 不発 ▶何発かの爆弾は**不発だった** Several bombs *did not explode* [*go off*]. ‖彼らは**不発弾**を処理した They disposed of the *unexploded bombs*. (➤「不発弾」をインフォーマルでは dud という. また「不発弾処理部隊」は bomb disposal squad [unit] という).

▶柳田はきょうは**不発だった**(＝ホームランが出なかった) Yanagida *didn't hit a home run* today.

ふばらい 不払い **nonpayment** ▶団地の自治会は家賃の**不払い**を決めた The members of the residents' association at the housing complex have decided *not to pay* their rents.

ふび 不備 (an) **inadequacy** /ɪnǽdɪkwəsi/ (不十分) ; (a) **deficiency** (欠陥) ▶防火設備の**不備**が犠牲者の数を増やした The *inadequacy* of fire-prevention devices caused an increase in the number of casualties.

▶税制の**不備**がさまざまな立場から指摘された The *deficiencies* of the tax system were pointed out from various standpoints. ‖この書類には**不備なところがある** These documents *are incomplete* [*are not filled out properly*].

ぶひ 部費 **club dues** ▶今月末までに**部費**500円を払ってください Please pay 500 yen in *club dues* by the end of this month.

ふびじん 不美人 a **physically unattractive woman**, 《インフォーマル》 a **plain Jane**, 《米》 a **homely woman** (➤《英》ではプラスイメージの語).

ふひつよう 不必要な **unnecessary** ▶南紀に旅行したときは思ったよりも暖かかったので，持って行った衣服のほとんどが**不必要だった** Most of the clothes I took on the trip to Nanki *were unnecessary* since the weather was warmer than I expected. →不要.

1**ふひょう 不評** **unpopularity** (不人気) ; a **bad reputation** (悪評) ▶新しい制服は女子社員の間では**不評だ** The new uniform *is unpopular* among the female workers.

▶その映画は**不評だった** The movie *got poor reviews*. (➤ review は「批評, 評論」の意) ‖新空港は遠くて不便だと**不評を買っている** The new airport *is criticized* as being far (from downtown) and inconvenient.

2**ふひょう 付表** an **appended table**.

ふびょうどう 不平等 (an) **inequality** ▶待遇の**不平等**を是正する rectify the *inequalities* in treatment ‖3人の息子に**不平等にならないよう**，どう財産を分けるかで頭を痛めている I've been racking my brains about how to divide my property *equally* among my three sons.

▶彼と彼女は同じ仕事をしているのに給料に差があるのは**不平等だ**(＝不公平だ) *It's unfair that* there's a difference in pay for him and her, when both do the same work.

‖**不平等条約** an unequal treaty.

ふびん 不憫な **poor** (かわいそうな) ▶彼女は事故で両親を亡くした子供を**ふびんに思った** She *felt pity for* [*took pity on*] the child who had lost his [her] parents in the accident.

ぶひん 部品 a **part** ; a **component** (構成部分) ▶自動車[オーディオ]の**部品** auto [audio] *parts* ‖**部品**さえあればこの自転車，簡単に修理できるのになあ I could fix this bicycle easily if I had some *spare parts*.

ふひんこう 不品行 **loose morals** (身持ちの悪いこと) ; **immoral conduct** (不道徳な行為) ▶**不品行な人** a person *of loose morals*.

ふぶき 吹雪 a **snowstorm** ; a **blizzard** /blízəʳd/ (猛吹雪) ▶**吹雪**がやっとおさまった The *snowstorm* has finally let up [died down].

ふふく 不服 **dissatisfaction** (不満) ; (a) **complaint** (不平) ▶息子は1000円の小遣い増額では**不服らしい** My son seems to *be dissatisfied* [*be discontent*] *with* the 1,000 yen raise in his allowance. ‖彼女は**不服ばかり言っている** She *is* always *complaining* [*grumbling*].

ふぶく 吹雪く ▶**吹雪いてきた** *A blizzard* [*snowstorm*] has started [has arisen].

ふふん **Hah**! (➤ 驚きや疑念を表す) ; **Haha**! (➤ あざ笑いや愉快なことを表す) ▶ふふん! やつらに何ができるものか *Hah!* Let's see what they can do!

ぶぶん 部分 (a) **part** ▶ミロのビーナスは腕の**部分**が欠けている The arms of the Venus of Milo are missing. (●「腕が」と同意だから「部分」は訳出不要) ‖この協奏曲は3つの**部分**から成り立っている This concerto is composed of three *parts*. ‖興味ある**部分**には下線を引きなさい Underline the *parts* that interest you.

▶その報告書の**一部分**は作り話だ *Part* of the report is fictitious. (➤ part of ... のときは a をつけないことが多い) ‖彼の話は**部分的**には正しい His story is *partly* true.

‖(日食・月食の)**部分食** a partial eclipse /ɪklíps/ (➤「部分日食」は a partial solar eclipse,「部分月食」は a partial lunar eclipse).

☞ **一部分, 大部分** (→見出語)

ふぶんりつ 不文律 an **unwritten rule** [**code**] (➤ code は主に「行動規範」).

ふへい 不平 (a) **complaint** 一動 **不平を言う** **complain** ; **grumble** (ぶつぶつ言う) ▶あまり**不平を言うな** Don't *complain* [*grumble*] too much. ‖選手たちは合宿の食事のことで監督に**不平を言った** The players *complained to* the manager *about* the food at the training camp. ‖彼らは読書の時間がないと**不平を言う** They *complain that* they can't find time to read.

▶彼は**不平が多い** He makes a lot of *complaints*. ／He *complains* a lot. ‖息子は**不平も言わず**，よく農作業を手伝ってくれる My son often helps me with the farmwork *without* (*uttering*) *a word of complaint* [*without complaining*].

‖**不平家** a grumbler.

ぶべつ 侮蔑 →軽蔑.

1**ふへん 普遍** ▶ハトは平和の**普遍的な**シンボルだ The dove is a *universal* symbol of peace. ‖適者生存は**普遍的真理**だ The survival of the fittest is *a universal* [*universally acknowledged*] *truth*.

▶きわめて個性的な作品がかえって**普遍性**をもつ場合がある There are some cases in which a highly individualistic work can have greater *universality*.

2**ふへん 不変の** **unchanged** (変わらない) ▶**不変の真理** *eternal* truth ‖今回は失敗したけれど，我々の最終目標は**不変です** Although we failed this time, our ultimate goal remains *unchanged*.

ふべん 不便 **inconvenience** /ìnkənvíːniəns/ 一形 **不便な inconvenient** ▶ご不便をおかけして申しわけありません I'm sorry for the *inconvenience* (I've caused you). ‖ 多少の**不便**はがまんしなさい You should put up with a little *inconvenience*.

▶その学校は駅から遠いので**不便だ** The school *is inconvenient* because it is far [a long way] from the train station. ‖ このズボンはポケットがないので**不便だ** This pair of pants *is inconvenient* because it has no pockets.

▶そのノートパソコンは少しかさばって持ち歩きに**不便だ** That laptop is a bit bulky and *not handy* to carry around. ‖ 彼の店は**不便な**所にあるため, はやっていなかった Since his store *was inconveniently located*, business was poor.

▶携帯電話がないと**不便じゃありませんか** Isn't it *inconvenient* (for you) not to have a cellphone ? (● inconvenient は日本語の「不便な」と違い, 人を主語にしては用いないので, (×) Aren't you inconvenient ... ? のように訳さないこと) ‖ 車がないと**不便だ** Not having a car is *inconvenient*.

ふべんきょう 不勉強 ▶学生時代の**不勉強**を今になって後悔しています Now I regret that I *didn't study harder* while in college.

▶**不勉強**で御社のこの新製品のことは存じ上げませんでした Evidently I have*n't done my homework*. I don't know about this new product of your company. (➤ do one's homework は「(入念に)下調べをする」).

ふへんふとう 不偏不党 **neutrality** ▶当社の新聞はあくまで**不偏不党**を貫きます Our newspaper is committed to maintaining *neutrality*.

ふぼ 父母 one's **parents**

✉ **きのうは参観日だったので大勢の父母が私たちの学校に授業を見に来ました** Yesterday many *parents* came to watch classes at our school because it was school visitation day.

☛ **父母会** (→見出語)

[1]**ふほう 不法な** **illegal** /ilíːɡəl/ (違法の) ; **unlawful** (非合法的な) ▶**不法**行為 an *illegal* [*unlawful*] act ‖ その男はピストルを**不法**に所持していた The man possessed a handgun *illegally*. ‖ その男は日本に**不法入国**[を**不法出国**]した The man *entered* [*left*] Japan *illegally*. (➤「不法入国者」は illegal immigrant [alien], 「不法出国者」は a person who leaves one's country illegally).

‖ **不法就労者** an illegal worker ‖ **不法侵入** trespass (他人の土地などへの) ‖ **不法侵入者** a trespasser ‖ **不法占拠** squatting ‖ **不法占拠者** a squatter ‖ **不法滞在** an illegal stay ‖ **不法滞在者** an illegal alien [immigrant], a visa overstayer.

[2]**ふほう 訃報** ▶サンフランシスコで父の**訃報**に接した In San Francisco, I heard the *news of* my father's *death*.

‖ (新聞の)**訃報欄** an obituary.

ふぼかい 父母会 a **parents' association**, a **PTA** ▶来週の土曜日に**父母会**(の会合)がある There will be *a PTA meeting* on Saturday next week. (➤ PTA は Parent-Teacher Association の略).

ふほんい 不本意な **disappointing** (期待外れの) ; **unsatisfactory** (不満足な) ▶陸上競技会では私は**不本意な**成績に終わった My performance in the track meet was *disappointing* [*unsatisfactory*]. ‖ 私は**不本意**ながら彼の要求に従った I yielded to his demand *against my will* [*reluctantly* / *unwillingly*]. (➤ against one's will は「意志に反して」, reluctantly と unwillingly は「しぶしぶ」).

ふまえる 踏まえる ▶彼の意見は体験を**踏まえている**ので説得力がある His opinion is convincing because it *is based on* experience. ‖ これまでの経緯を**踏まえて**(＝考慮に入れて)議論していただきたい We'd like you to discuss this while *taking into consideration* the progress up to now.

ふまじめ 不真面目 ▶**不真面目**な生徒 a *bad* [*lazy*] student ‖ **不真面目**な答えをする give a *frivolous* reply (➤ frivolous は「真剣みのない」の意) ‖ 彼女は数学の授業になると**不真面目**な態度をとる She is *not serious* [*attentive*] in math classes.

ふまん 不満 **discontent, dissatisfaction** (➤ 後者のほうが不満度が高い) ; a **complaint** (不平) 一形 **不満な discontented, dissatisfied**

▶学生一人一人が**不満**の種を持っている Every student has some *source of discontent*. ‖ 彼らの**不満**の原因は何だろう What is the cause of their *dissatisfaction* ?

▶給料に**不満**を持っている人は多い Many people *are discontented* [*are dissatisfied* / *are not satisfied*] with their salaries. ‖ **対話**「日本の食事に何か**不満**はありますか」「全体的に味つけが薄いのが**不満**です」 "Do you have any *complaints* about Japanese food ?" "It generally tastes rather bland. That's my *complaint*." ‖ 彼女はいつも処遇についての**不満**を言っている She *is* always *complaining* about her treatment.

ふまんぞく 不満足な **unsatisfactory** ▶東京ではふつうの会社員は何らかの点で**不満足な**家かマンションしか持てない Ordinary office workers in Tokyo can only obtain a house or apartment that is in some way *unsatisfactory*.

ふみいし 踏み石 a **steppingstone** (➤ stepping stone ともつづる).

ふみいた 踏み板 a **step** ; a **tread**, a **footboard** (階段の).

ふみいれる 踏み入れる **step** 《into》 ▶この山には地元の人もほとんど足を**踏み入れた**ことがない Even the local people hardly ever *set foot on* this mountain.

ふみえ 踏み絵 a ***fumi-e*** ; an image of Christ or the Virgin Mary that suspected Christians were required to step on to reveal whether or not they were Christians (➤ 説明的な訳).

ふみかためる 踏み固める **stamp** [**tread**] **down** (➤「踏み固まった雪」は (hard) packed snow).

ふみきり 踏切 **1【鉄道の】** a **(railroad) crossing** ▶無人**踏切** an unattended [unmanned] *crossing* ‖ **踏切**を渡る go over *a railroad crossing* ‖ **踏切**で電車とトラックの衝突事故があった A collision took place between a train and a truck at the *crossing*.

‖ **踏切番** a crossing gateman.

2【体操・ジャンプ競技の】 a **takeoff**

‖ **踏切板** a springboard, a vaulting board.

ふみきる 踏み切る ▶ドコモは電話料金の値下げに**踏み切った** DOCOMO *decided* to reduce telephone charges.

▶由美子は真治との結婚に**踏み切れない**でいる Yumiko is still hesitant about *taking the plunge* (*into* marriage) with Shinji. (➤ take the plunge は

「思い切ってやる」).

ふみこむ 踏み込む 1【襲う】raid +目 ▶警察が犯人の隠れ家に踏み込んだ The police *raided* [*made a raid on*] the criminal's hideout.
2【本質に迫る】▶もう一歩踏み込んだ議論が欲しかった I wish your discussion (of the problem) had *gone into more depth*.

ふみしめる 踏みしめる step on ▶私たちは10年ぶりに横浜港に着き日本の土を踏みしめた We *stepped on* Japanese soil at Yokohama Port for the first time in ten years.
▶我々は険しい山道を一歩一歩踏みしめながら歩いた We walked the steep mountain path *taking each step slowly and firmly*.

ふみだい 踏み台 a stool; a stepladder (脚立); a stepstool (脚立式のスツール) ▶踏み台に乗る get on *a stool*.
▶《比喩的》彼は友人を踏み台にして出世した He achieved success by *walking all over* his friends.

ふみたおす 踏み倒す ▶借金を踏み倒す *welsh* [*welch*] *on* one's debt(● 「ウェールズ(人)の」の意の Welsh に由来するともいわれるくだけた言い方だが, 差別表現になりうるので, do not pay one's debt が無難) ‖ 勘定を踏み倒して逃げる skip out *without paying* one's bill(➤ タクシーの場合は jump a taxi fare とする).

ふみだす 踏み出す ▶行進のときは左足から踏み出すこと You should *step out* with your left leg when marching.
▶二人は夫婦として新たな人生に踏み出した They *embarked on* a new life as man and wife [a married couple].

ふみだん 踏み段 a step; a treadboard (エスカレーターや脚立などの).

ふみつける 踏みつける stamp 《on》; tread 《on》 (踏みつけて歩く) ▶男の子は空き缶を何回か踏みつけてぺしゃんこにした The boy *stamped on* the empty can several times until it was flat. ‖ 子供たちは花を踏みつけて歩いた The children *treaded on* the flowers. ‖ あれ, ガムを踏んづけちゃった Shoot! I *stepped on* some gum.

ふみつぶす 踏み潰す trample 《on》 ▶男の子は女の子の作った砂の城を踏みつぶした The boy *trampled on* the girl's sandcastle.

ふみとどまる 踏み止まる 1【残る】▶横綱は土俵際で踏みとどまった The yokozuna *stood firm* at the edge of the ring.
2【思いとどまる】▶彼女を抱き締めたい衝動に駆られたがあと一歩のところで踏みとどまった I felt an impulse to hold her in my arms, but I *held myself back* at the last moment.

ふみにじる 踏みにじる trample 《on》 ▶彼との友情を踏みにじるようなまねはできない I can't do something that is going to *trample on* my friendship with him. ‖ 報道の自由の名のもとにプライバシーが踏みにじられている Privacy *is being trampled* under the name of freedom of the press.

ふみば 踏み場 ▶部屋は足の踏み場もないほど散らかっていた The room was in such a mess that *there was no place to stand*.

ふみはずす 踏み外す miss one's step ▶足を踏み外して階段からころげ落ちた I *missed my step* [*took a false step*] and fell down the stairs. ／I *missed my footing* on the stairs.
▶若者たちが道を踏み外すのは悲しいことだ It is sad when young people *go wrong*. (➤ go wrong は日本語の「踏み外す」に似てやや古風).

ふみん 不眠 ▶不眠不休で働く work hard *night and day* ‖ 我々は不眠不休でその仕事を終えた We finished the work *without any sleep or rest*. ‖ この頃不眠症にかかっている I have [am suffering from] *insomnia* these days. ／I can't (get to) sleep these days.

ふむ 踏む 1【足で】step 《on》, tread 《on》 (➤ 後者は「踏みつける」の意味にもなる) ▶ブレーキ[アクセル]を踏む *step on* the brake [the accelerator] ‖ 落ち葉を踏むたびに乾いた音がした Each time I *stepped* [*trod*] *on* the fallen leaves, they made a dry, crackling sound. (➤ trod は tread の過去形).
▶満員電車の中で私はうっかり女性の足を踏んでしまった I carelessly *stepped on* a woman's foot in the crowded train. ‖ 私はバスの中で足を踏まれた I *had* [*got*] my foot *stepped on* in the bus. ‖ 彼女は軽やかなステップを踏んでワルツを踊った She danced a waltz *stepping* lightly.
▶《慣用表現》私はことし初めて外国の土を踏んだ This year I *set foot on* foreign *soil* for the first time in my life.
2【経験する】▶私は3歳のとき初舞台を踏んだ I *made my debut* (*on stage*) at the age of three. ‖ 骨とうの真贋(しんがん)を見抜くには場数を踏む必要がある You need to *acquire a lot of hands-on experience* to discern genuine from fake antiques.
3【手続きを経る】go through ▶正規の手続きを踏む *go through* the regular procedures.
☛ 踏んだりけったり (→見出語)

ふむき 不向きな unsuitable (条件・目的などにそぐわない) ▶きみはサラリーマンには不向きだね You are *unsuitable* to be an office worker. ／You are *not cut out for* office work. (➤ be cut out for は「(人が)生まれつき…に適している」の意で, 通例否定文で用いる) ‖ この映画は子供には不向きだ This movie is *not suitable* [*not suited*] *for* children.

ふめい 不明の unknown (わからない); unclear (はっきりしない) ▶この歌の作曲者は不明だ The composer of this song *is unknown* [*is unidentified*]. (➤ 後者は「確認できない」の意) ‖ その殺人の動機はまだ不明だ The motive for the murder *is* still *unclear*. ‖ 不明な点がございましたら, いつでもご連絡ください Please call us if you should ever need *additional* details. (● 英語では「不明な点」の「不明な」は unclear ではなく「追加の, さらなる」と考えて additional を用いるのがふつう) ‖ 酔っ払いが意味不明のことをわめきたてている The drunk is shouting things that *don't make sense*. ‖ 先月は原因不明の火事が相次いだ There was a series of fires *of unknown cause* last month.

ふめいよ 不名誉 disgrace ―形 不名誉な disgraceful ▶わが県は3年連続交通事故による死者数全国一という不名誉な記録を作った Our prefecture has set a *disgraceful* record of having the heaviest death toll in traffic accidents throughout the nation for three consecutive years.

ふめいりょう 不明瞭な not clear; obscure /əbskjúəʳ/ (意味内容が); inarticulate /ìnɑːʳ-tíkjələt/ (発音が) ▶電話の声は不明りょうで聞き取りにくかった The voice on the phone was *not clear* enough to catch. ‖ この記事には意味の不明りょうな箇所がいくつかある

There are some *obscure* points in this article.
▶彼はもぐもぐしたしゃべり方をするのでことばが不明りょうだ His words sound *unclear* because he talks in a mumble.

ふめいろう 不明朗 ▶バーの勘定は往々にして不明朗だ Bar tabs are often full of *questionable* charges.

ふめつ 不滅の immortal, undying ▶不滅の名声 *immortal* fame ‖『魔笛』は音楽史上不滅の作品である "The Magic Flute" is an *immortal* [a *monumental*] work in the history of music.
▶ダイヤは不滅の輝きで女性をとりこにする Diamonds fascinate women with their *undying* [*eternal*] splendor.

ふめん 譜面 music; sheet music (一枚刷りの); a score (総譜)
‖譜面台 a music stand.

ふもう 不毛の barren, sterile /stérəl/ (➤前者がより堅い語); waste (荒れた) ▶ここはかつては不毛の砂漠だった This place was formerly *barren* desert.
▶こんな議論はこれ以上続けても不毛(＝無駄)だ Continuing this kind of argument will *get us nowhere*. ／It *is fruitless* to keep on arguing like this.

ふもと 麓 the foot ▶雪がふもとの村にやってくるのももう間近だ It won't be long before it snows in the village *at the foot of the mountain*.

ふもん 不問 ▶経験不問 *Previous experience not required*. ‖若社長のミスは不問に付された The young president's mistake *was not made an issue* [*was overlooked* ／ *was passed over without mention*].

ぶもん 部門 a department, a division, a section (➤section が最も小規模); a category /kǽţəgɔ:ri/ (部類); a branch, a field (学問上の)
▶この映画はアカデミー賞の5部門にノミネートされている This movie has been nominated for Academy Awards in five *categories*.

ふやかす ▶豆を水につけてふやかします Soak the beans in water until they *become soft*.

ふやける ▶あんまり長く風呂に入っていたので指先がふやけてしまった Since I was in the bath too long, my fingertips got all *wrinkled*. (➤「しわになった」の意).

ふやじょう 不夜城 an all-night [a brightly lit up] entertainment district.

ふやす 増やす increase /ɪnkrí:s/ ＋㊐ ▶公園(の数)を増やす *increase the number of* parks (● increase parks とはしない. 数の場合は the number とはっきり言う).
▶(会社の)休みを増やしてほしい We want our company to *increase the number of* (our) days off. ／We want to have *more* days off. ‖これ以上人手を増やすわけにはいかない We can't *increase* our workforce any further. ‖新監督は我々の練習量を増やした Our new coach *increased the amount of* our practice. ／Our new coach made us practice *more*. (➤後者は「今まで以上に練習させた」の意).

ふゆ 冬 winter ▶ことしの冬は暖かい We are having a mild [warm] *winter*. ‖ことしの冬は雪が少なかった We have had little snow *this winter*. ‖冬の山に登るのは危険だ It is dangerous to climb *a mountain in* (*the*) *winter*. ‖冬らしくなってきた It is getting more *like winter*.
▶その地方の人々は11月になると冬じたくに忙しい Come November, people in the region are busy *preparing for winter*.
‖冬服 winter clothes [wear].

¹ふゆう 富裕な affluent ▶富裕な社会 an *affluent* society ‖この辺りには富裕層が住んでいる *Affluent* families live in this area.

²ふゆう 浮遊 floating; suspension(固体粒子の)
‖浮遊粒子 suspended particulates.

ぶゆうでん 武勇伝 a story of one's heroic acts [exploits] ▶社長の武勇伝は聞き飽きた I'm sick and tired of hearing the president talk about *his exploits*.

ふゆかい 不愉快な unpleasant; disagreeable (気に入らない) ▶彼は横柄で実に不愉快な男だ He is a very arrogant and *disagreeable* man. ‖妹は学校で何か不愉快なことがあったらしく, 難しい顔で帰って来た My (younger) sister came home with a frown (on her face) because she apparently had an *unpleasant* time at school. ‖彼のごう慢な態度に不愉快になった I *was annoyed* by his arrogant manner.

ふゆがれ 冬枯れ ▶冬枯れの那須を撮った写真 a picture of Nasu taken in *the bleak winter* (➤bleak は「荒涼たる」の意).

ふゆきとどき 不行き届き ▶監督不行き届きで部長まで訓戒を受けた Even the manager was admonished because of his *slack* [*lax*] *supervision*.

ふゆげしょう 冬化粧 ▶南アルプスの山々はもうすっかり冬化粧している The mountains in the Japanese Southern Alps *are* already *covered with snow* [*veiled deep in snow*].

ふゆごもり 冬籠り ▶まもなく雪国の人たちは長い冬ごもりに入る Soon the people in the snow country will *be snowbound for the long winter*.

ふゆしょうぐん 冬将軍 ▶いよいよ冬将軍の到来だ *Old Man Winter* [*Jack Frost*] is just around the corner. (➤ともに冬を擬人化した言い方).

ふゆぞら 冬空 the [a] winter sky ▶冬空の星を見上げる look up at the stars in *the winter sky*.

ふゆどり 冬鳥 a winter bird.

ふゆもの 冬物 winter clothing(衣料品) ▶冬物のコート a *winter* coat.

ふゆやすみ 冬休み the winter vacation [《英》holidays]; (a) winter break(学校の) ▶我々は冬休みに湯沢へスキーに行った We went skiing in Yuzawa during (*the*) *winter break*.
✉ **私たちの冬休みは12月21日に始まります** Our *winter vacation* starts on December 21.

ふゆやま 冬山 ▶冬山登山をする climb *a mountain in* (*the*) *winter* ‖冬山で遭難する人が毎年あとを絶たない Every winter, we hear about numerous climbers who die or go missing in the mountains.

¹ふよ 付与する grant ＋㊐, confer ＋㊐ ▶権利を付与する *grant* a right ‖特許を付与する *grant* a patent.

²ふよ 賦与 endowment ▶天から賦与された才能 *innate* talent.

ぶよ 蚋 《虫》a gnat /næt/ 《参考》《英》では gnat はふつう「蚊」も含む.

¹ふよう 不要の・不用の unnecessary(必要のない); discarded (捨てた); used /ju:zd/ (使用済みの) ▶自転車に乗るのに免許証は不要だ A driver's license *is not needed* to ride a bicycle. ‖台湾旅行にビザは不要だ Visas *are unnecessary* [*not required*] to travel to Taiwan. ‖不用になった(＝使用済みの)乾電池はこ

の箱にお入れください Please put *used* batteries in this box.
‖**不用品** an unneeded [a disused] item ‖**不用品セール** a used goods sale.

2**ふよう 扶養** support **一動 扶養する** support ▶彼は妻と3人の子供を扶養している He *has* a wife and three children *to support*. ‖彼には扶養家族が4人いる He has four *dependents*. ／He has *four mouths to feed*. (➤最後の文はくだけた言い方).
‖**扶養控除** an allowance [a tax exemption] for dependents ‖**扶養者** a supporter, a breadwinner ‖**扶養手当** a family allowance.

3**ふよう 芙蓉** 《植物》a **Confederate rose,** a **cotton rose-mallow.**

4**ふよう 浮揚** rise, come to the surface.

ぶよう 舞踊 dancing(踊ること); a **dance** (1回の踊り) ▶民俗舞踊 a folk *dance* ‖メアリーは日本舞踊を習っている Mary is taking lessons in *Japanese dancing*.
‖**舞踊家** a dancer.

ふようい 不用意な careless; thoughtless (思慮の足りない); inadvertent(うっかりした)
▶不用意な発言をする make a *careless* [*thoughtless*] remark ‖個人的なことは不用意に口にしないほうがいい You'd be wise not to talk about your personal matters *carelessly* [*thoughtlessly*].
▶私は不用意にも間違った人にメールを送ってしまった I *inadvertently* sent an email to the wrong person.

ふようじょう 不養生 ▶医者の不養生 *Doctors often neglect to take good care of themselves*.

ぶようじん 不用心な unsafe ▶そんな大金を持ち歩くのは不用心だ It is *unsafe* to carry such a large sum of money on you.

ふようど 腐葉土 leaf mold.

ぶよぶよ ▶彼女はおなかのあたりがぶよぶよだ She is *flabby* around the waist.

1**フライ** 《揚げ物》deep-fried food ▶私はヒラメのフライが好きだ I like *deep-fried flounder*. ‖母が夕食にエビのフライを揚げている My mother *is deep-frying* prawns for supper.
‖**フライ返し** a turner.

> **危ないカタカナ語✹ フライ**
> **1** 料理の「フライ」は fry とつづる. 名詞用法もあるが動詞用法が主で, fried rice (焼き飯), fried eggs (目玉焼き, 卵焼き)のように用いる.
> **2** 日本語の「フライ」がたっぷりの油の中で揚げることを指すのに対し, fry は「いためる」ことも含む. したがって,「揚げる」ことをはっきりさせるためには deep-fry という動詞を用いる必要がある.
> **3** 野球の「飛球」を指す「フライ」のつづりは fly である. 内野手への「小フライ」は pop fly または単に pop という.

2**フライ** 《飛球》a **fly (ball)** ▶中田はセンターに大きなフライを打ち上げた Nakata sent *a towering fly* to center. ‖阿部はセカンドへのフライに倒れた Abe *flied out* to second. (➤この fly は「フライを打つ」の意の動詞).

プライオリティ a **priority.**

フライきゅう フライ級 《ボクシング》 **the flyweight class** [**division**] ▶フライ級の選手 *a flyweight*.

ブライダル a **wedding** (➤ bridal は「花嫁の」の意で「結婚式」は表さない)
‖**ブライダルエステ** an esthetic treatment for brides ‖**ブライダル産業** the wedding industry ‖**ブライダルフェア** a bridal fair ‖**ブライダル用品** wedding supplies.

フライト a **flight**(飛行機の便) ▶本日のフライトはすべて欠航になっております All *flights* today are canceled.
‖**フライトレコーダー** a flight recorder, a black box.

プライド **pride** ▶あの男はプライドが高い He has too much *pride* in himself. ／He is overly proud (of himself). ‖頭を下げて援助を求めるなど彼女のプライドが許さなかった She *was too proud to* beg for help. (➤「プライドが高すぎてできなかった」の意) ‖大輔のことばに陽子はプライドを傷つけられた Daisuke's words hurt [wounded] Yoko's *pride*. ／Yoko's *pride* was hurt [was wounded] by Daisuke's words.
▶自分の仕事にプライドをもちなさい You should *take pride in* your work. (➤ take pride in は「…に誇りを持つ」で, プライドをもってそのプライドに恥じない良心的な仕事をしなさい, の意. be proud of は「…を誇りに思う」で, やり遂げたりっぱな仕事を誇りに思って[自慢して]いい, の意).

フライドチキン **fried chicken.**

フライドポテト **French fries.**

プライバシー **privacy** /práɪvəsi ‖ prívəsi/ ▶人のプライバシーを侵す violate [infringe on] others' *privacy* ‖人に細かい家族状況を聞くのはプライバシーの侵害だ Asking about people's families in too much detail is *an invasion of privacy*.
▶日本人はアメリカ人に比べプライバシーの意識が薄い Japanese people are *less privacy-conscious* than Americans.

フライパン a **frying** [**fry**] **pan,** 《米また》a **skillet** ▶タマネギのみじん切りをフライパンでいためた I *fried* [*stir-fried*] the chopped onion. (➤ stir-fry は中華料理の場合に多く用いられる).

フライフィッシング **fly fishing.**

プライベート **private** /práɪvət/ (私的な); **personal** (個人的な) ▶彼のプライベートなことはよく知らない I don't know much about his *private* affairs. ‖プライベートな質問をしないでください Please don't ask *personal* questions. ‖プライベート・レッスンを受ける take *private lessons*.

フライング **jumping** [**beating**] **the gun,** a **false start** ▶走者は1度でもフライングをすると失格になる If a runner *jumps the gun* [*makes a false start*] even once, he is disqualified.

ブラインド a **blind**(➤しばしば複数形で), 《米また》a **(window) shade**; a **Venetian** /vəníːʃən/ **blind** (板すだれ) ▶ブラインドを上げる draw up [raise] the *blinds* (➤「下ろす」は pull down).

ブラインドタッチ 《コンピュータ》**touch-typing.**

ブラウザ 《コンピュータ》a **browser**
‖**ウェブブラウザ** a Web browser.

ブラウス a **blouse** /blaʊs/ ▶彼女はスカートにブラウスというかっこうだった She had a skirt and *blouse* on. ／She wore a skirt and *blouse*.

ブラウンかん ブラウン管 a **(picture) tube,** a **cathode-ray** /kæθoʊdréɪ/ **tube** (略 CRT) 《参考》「ブラウン管」はこれを発明したドイツの物理学者 K. F. Braun の名にちなむが, Braun tube という語は日常的にはめったに用いられない.

プラカード a **placard** /plǽkɑːʳd/ (➤日常的には sign ということも多い) ▶彼らは「増税反対」のプラカードを掲げてデモをした They demonstrated holding up *placards* [*signs*] saying, "No Tax Increase."

ふ

ぶらく 部落 a **hamlet.**

プラグ a **plug** ▶プラグをコンセントに差し込む put *a plug* in the outlet／insert *a plug* into the outlet ‖プラグをコンセントから抜く pull *a plug* out of the outlet／unplug ‖ 彼女は電気がまのプラグを電源に差し込んだ She *plugged in* the electric rice cooker.

‖**プラグイン**《コンピュータ》a plug-in.

ぶらさがる ぶら下がる **hang** ▶鉄棒にぶら下がる *hang* from a horizontal bar ‖ 少年は父親の腕にぶら下がった The boy *hung on to* his father's arm.

ぶらさげる ぶら下げる **hang** +目 ▶軒に風鈴をぶら下げる *hang* a wind-bell from the eaves ‖ ガードマンは腰にかぎの束をぶら下げていた The security guard *carried* a bunch of keys *dangling* at his hip.

ブラシ a **brush** ▶たまにはスーツにブラシをかけなさいよ *Give* your suit *a brushing* sometimes. ／You should *brush off* your suit once in a while.

‖**歯ブラシ** a toothbrush ‖ **ヘアブラシ** a hair-brush ‖ **洋服ブラシ** a clothesbrush.

ブラジャー a **bra**, a **brassiere** /brəzíəʳ/（➤ 後者は堅い語で, 日常的にはあまり用いない）▶ブラジャーを着ける[外す] put on [take off] *a bra* ‖ フロント[後部]ホックのブラジャー a front-closing [back-closing] *bra* ／a front-fastening [back-fastening] *bra* ‖ Aカップのブラジャー an A-cup *bra*.

ブラジル **Brazil** /brəzíl/

‖**ブラジル人** a Brazilian.

ふらす 降らす ▶雨雲はあまり雨を降らさなかった The rain clouds did*n't bring* much *rain*.

プラス 1【加算】 **plus** 一動 **プラスする** **add**《to》▶ 3プラス4は7 Three *plus* four is [equals] seven.（➤ この場合の plus は前置詞扱い）／Three *and* four make seven.

▶私のボーナスは2か月分プラスアルファーだった My bonus was two months' salary *plus a little more*. ‖ あと1000円プラスしてくれませんか Could you *add* another 1,000 yen (*to* it)?

2【利益】 an **advantage** ▶黙っていても何のプラスにもならないよ Your silence won't be of any *advantage* to you. ／Keeping silent won't do you any *good* [won't *help* (you)]. ‖ この経験はきみにとって将来きっとプラスになると思うよ I think this experience will surely *give* you *an edge* in the future.（➤ edge は「人よりまさっていること」）／I think you will *gain something* from this experience *that will be valuable* in the future. ‖ プラスマイナスゼロだ *Plus minus zero*. ／There is *no gain* [*no profit*] for us. ／It adds up to nothing.

▶常に**プラス思考**で行こうよ Let's always practice *positive thinking*. ／ Let's always *think positively*.（➤ 後者は「常に前向きに考えましょう」に近い）.

> **危ないカタカナ語✸ プラス**
> **1** 数式を表す場合は plus が使えるが,「プラスする」という場合には add（追加する）という動詞を用いる必要がある. 英語の plus は前置詞および形容詞用法が主. →マイナス.
> **2** plus は「プラス（＝利益）になること」の意でも使われるが, ふつうは advantage や good などを使って表現する.

フラスコ a **flask** 《参考》「フラスコ」はポルトガル語の *frasco* から.

プラスチック (a) **plastic** /plǽstɪk/（➤ ビニールも含む）▶プラスチックのスプーン a *plastic* spoon ‖ プラスチックは成型が容易だ *Plastics* are easily cast in a mold.

‖**プラスチック製品** plastic goods, plastics.

フラストレーション **frustration** ▶思いどおりに行かないとフラストレーションがたまる When things don't go as smoothly as you expect, *frustration* builds up [mounts].

ブラスバンド a **brass band** ▶彼女はブラスバンドでトロンボーンを吹いている She plays the trombone in *a brass band*.

プラズマ《物理学》**plasma** ▶ 50インチのプラズマテレビ a 50-inch *plasma* television.

プラタナス《植物》a **plane (tree)**; a **buttonwood**, a **sycamore** /síkəmɔːʳ/（アメリカスズカケノキ）.

フラダンス **the hula** /húːlə/ ▶フラダンスをする dance *the hula*.

ふらち 不埒な **rude, outrageous.**

プラチナ **platinum** /plǽtnəm/ ▶プラチナのイヤリング *platinum* earrings.

ふらつく 1【ふらふらする】 ▶彼女は足がふらついている. ワインが回ったらしい She *is unsteady on her feet* [Her *steps are unsteady*]. The wine seems to have gone to her head. ‖ こんな遅くまでどこをふらついてたんだ Where have you been *hanging out* till this late at night?

2【定まらない】 ▶大学院へ進むか就職するかで私の気持ちはまだふらついている I *am* still *wavering* between going on to graduate school and getting a job.

ぶらつく **stroll**《about, around》（のんびりと歩く）; **loiter**《about, around》（立ち止まったりしながら徘徊(はいかい)する）▶彼は時間をつぶすためにデパートの中をぶらついた He *strolled about* in the department store to kill time.

▶男は公園をぶらついていて警官に職務質問された The man *loitering* [*hanging*] *around* the park was questioned by the police.（➤ hang around はインフォーマル）.

ブラック **black** ▶彼女はコーヒーはたいがいブラックで飲む She usually has [takes] her coffee *black*.

《参考》日本では砂糖およびミルクやクリームを入れないものを「ブラック（コーヒー）」と呼ぶが, 英語の black（coffee）はミルクやクリームを入れないものを指す語で, 砂糖の有無は問わない.

ブラックきぎょう ブラック企業 an **evil company.**

ブラックバス《魚》(a) **black bass.**

ブラックホール《天文学》a **black hole.**

ブラックリスト a **blacklist** ▶あの男は警察のブラックリストに載っている He is on the police *blacklist*. ／He has been *blacklisted* by the police.

フラッシュ a **flash (light)**; a **flashbulb**（電球）▶フラッシュをたく use *a flash* ／light *a flashbulb*.

ブラッシュアップ ブラッシュアップする **brush up**《on》（忘れかけていたものをやり直す）; **improve** +目（上達する）.

フラッシュバック a **flashback.**

ふらっと ▶起き上がろうとしたらふらっとした I *felt dizzy* [*My head swam*] when I got up.

▶ふらっと立ち寄った本屋でいい本を見つけた I *just wandered into* a bookstore and found a nice book.

フラット a **flat**（音楽の変記号）▶私の記録は50秒フラット（＝きっかり）だった My time was 50 seconds *flat*.

プラットホーム a **platform** ▶上り[下り]のプラットホーム an up [a down] *platform*.

フラップ a **flap.**

プラトニックラブ **Platonic love.**

プラネタリウム a **planetarium.**
プラハ **Prague** /prɑːg/ (チェコの首都).
フラフープ a **hula hoop.**
ふらふら ▶彼は足元がふらふらしている He's *unsteady* on his feet. ／He's *wobbly*. ‖校庭を10周したらもうふらふらだ I *feel ready to drop* after having run around the school yard 10 times. ‖ 3日間何も食べてないのでふらふらだ(＝気が遠くなりそうだ) I *am faint* with hunger because I haven't eaten anything for three days. ‖熱で頭がふらふらする I *feel dizzy* with a fever. ／My head *is swimming* with (a) fever.
▶病気になると体がふらふらすることがある Sickness can make you *feel weak*.
ぶらぶら ▶風にヒョウタンがぶらぶら揺れている The gourd is *swaying slowly* [*gently*] in the wind. ‖いすの上で足をぶらぶらさせるのはやめなさい Stop *swinging* your legs while sitting on the chair.
▶彼は会社を首になってぶらぶらしている After getting fired at the company, he *is* now *at loose ends* [《英》*at a loose end*]. (➤「身を持て余している」の意).
▶デパートの中をぶらぶらする *wander aimlessly* through a department store ‖あと30分あるからその辺をぶらぶらしてくるよ As I have half an hour to spare, I'll kill time *strolling around*.
ブラボー **Bravo!** ▶聴衆から思わずブラボーの声があがった The audience broke into spontaneous *bravos*.
フラミンゴ 《鳥》a **flamingo** /fləmíŋgoʊ/.
プラム 《植物》a **plum.**
フラメンコ (a) **flamenco** /fləméŋkoʊ/ (➤「フラメンコの曲[歌]」の意でも用いる) ▶フラメンコを踊る dance the *flamenco*.
プラモデル a **plastic model** ▶船のプラモデルを組み立てる build *a plastic model* of a ship.
ふらり ▶父はふらりと出かけて行った My father went out *without any definite purpose* [*aimlessly*]. ‖古くからの友人がふらりと訪ねてきた An old friend of mine *dropped in on me* [*dropped in at my house*].
ぶらり ▶木の枝から大きな蛇がぶらりと下がっていた A huge snake *was dangling* from a branch of the tree.
ふられる 振られる (● 英語では女が男を, または男が女を「振る」と表現するのがふつう) ▶俺, 彼女に振られちゃったよ She's *left* [*dumped*] me. (➤ dump は「(人を)見捨てる」).
▶私, 大輔さんに振られちゃった Daisuke has *turned* me *down* [*rejected* me]. ‖振られちゃったの？ かわいそう *Were you dropped?* Poor thing! (➤ drop は「(人と)絶交する」の意) ‖彼はいいやつなのに女に振られてばかりだ Though he is a nice guy, he always *gets the brush-off* from girls. (➤ get the brush-off は「ひじ鉄を食う」).
ふらん 腐乱する **decompose** ▶林の中で女性の腐乱死体が見つかった The *decomposed* body of a woman was found in the forest.
プラン a **plan** ▶プランを練る work out *a plan* ‖物事はプランどおりにはなかなかいかないものだ Things never go *according to plan*. ‖ハイキングのプランを立てよう Let's *make plans* for our hike.
ブランク a **blank** ▶次のブランク(＝空欄)を埋めなさい Fill in the following *blanks*.
▶その野球選手はけがで1年間のブランクがある That ball player *was sidelined* for one year because of injury. (➤ be sidelined は「試合に出場できない」の意).
プランクトン 《生物学》**plankton** ▶プランクトンの異常発生 the unusual growth of *plankton*.
フランクフルト **Frankfurt** /frǽŋkfəʳt/ (ドイツ中部の都市).
ぶらんこ a **swing**; a **swingboat** (向かい合って乗る舟形の大ぶらんこ; 箱形のものは box swing) ▶ぶらんこに乗ろうよ Let's get [sit] on the *swing*. ／Let's swing.
‖**空中ぶらんこ** a trapeze /træpíːz/.
フランス **France** 一形 **フランスの** **French** ▶彼女はフランス人です She is *French*. ／She is from France.
‖**フランス語** French ‖**フランス人** a Frenchman (男), a Frenchwoman (女) ‖**フランスパン** French bread ‖**フランス料理** French food [cuisine /kwɪzíːn/].
プランター a **planter** ▶プランターでハーブを育てる grow herbs in *a planter*.
ブランチ **brunch.**
フランチャイズ a **franchise**
‖**フランチャイズ店** a franchise, a franchised store.
ブランデー **brandy** ▶紅茶にブランデーをたらす spike [lace] tea with *brandy*.
‖**ブランデーグラス** a brandy glass.
プランテーション a **plantation.**
ブランド a **brand** ▶有名ブランド a name [famous] *brand* ‖ブランドもののネクタイ a *brand-name* tie ／a designer necktie ‖ミキはブランド志向だ Miki is *brand-conscious*. ／Miki has *a penchant for brand names*.
‖**ブランド商品** a brand-name item; brand-name goods (➤ 総称) ‖**自社ブランド** a house brand ‖**ノーブランド商品** an off-brand item.
プラント a **plant** (工場) ▶化学プラント a chemical *plant*.
‖**プラント輸出** plant export.
[1]**ふり 不利** (a) **disadvantage** /dìsədvǽnṭɪdʒ/ 一形 **不利な** **disadvantageous, unfavorable** (➤ 前者は堅い語) ▶相手が3人なのにこちらが2人では不利だ We're *at a disadvantage* because there are only two of us to [against] three of them. ‖この新しい契約はわが社に不利だ This new contract is *not to our advantage*. ／This new contract is *unfavorable* [*disadvantageous*] to our company. ‖証人は被告に対し不利な証言を行った The witness testified *against* the defendant. (➤「有利な」なら for) ‖試合はジャイアンツに不利な展開となった The game *went badly* for the Giants.
[2]**ふり 振り** **1【見せかけ】** 一動 **ふりをする** **pretend** (to do, that), **fake** ＋目 (➤ 後者はインフォーマルな語); **pose as ...** (…を装う, 自分を…に見せかける) ▶頭の痛いふりをする *fake* a headache

【文型】
…するふりをする
pretend to do
➤「…しないふりをする」は pretend not to do

▶彼女は母親が部屋を出て行くまで眠ったふりをしていた She *pretended to* be asleep [*faked* sleep ／*feigned* sleep] until her mother left the room. ‖電車の乗客は座席に寝そべっている酔っ払いを見て見ないふりをした The passengers on the train *pretended* not *to* see the drunk sprawled on the seat.
2【様子】▶ ことわざ 人のふり見てわがふり直せ Ob-

serve the behavior of others and correct your own.（➤日本語からの直訳）／Learn wisdom by observing the foolish behavior of others.（➤「他人の愚行から知恵を学べ」の意）.

3【振ること】 a **swing** ▶彼はバットの［クラブの］振りが鋭い His *bat* ［*club*］ *swing* is very sharp.

4【なじみでないこと】▶あのすし屋はふりの客でも歓迎する That sushi bar welcomes *casual customers* ［*first timers*］.

³ふり 降り ▶この降りではゲームは中止だろう The game will probably be called off due to this *downpour* （*of rain*）.

ぶり 鰤《魚》a **yellowtail.**

-ぶり 1【様子】 the way ... ▶口ぶりで彼女がうそをついていることがわかった I knew she was lying from *the way she spoke*.（→口ぶり）‖彼は飲みっぷりがいい *The way he drinks* is impressive. ‖彼女の熱心な勉強ぶりを見てください You should watch *how intensely she studies*.

2【時間の経過】

【文型】
～年ぶりに
for the first time in ～ years

《解説》(1)「何年かぶりに」のような言い方は，for the first time in years（何年かで初めて）で表すことが多い．また「最上級あるいは the first ... ＋ in ～ years」（何年かでいちばん「最初の…」）が当てはまることもある．
(2)「何日」「何週間」「何か月」の場合は years の代わりに，days, weeks, months を置けばよい．

▶彼女は40年ぶりに故郷の土を踏んだ She set foot in her homeland *for the first time in 40 years*. ‖ 3日ぶりの青空だ We've had a blue sky *for the first time in three days*. ‖当社の利益は昨年，5年ぶりの低水準に落ち込んだ Our company's profits last year fell to *the lowest level in five years*. ‖あなたにお会いするのは何年ぶりでしょうか *How many years ago was it that* I saw you last？‖ 対話「会うのは何年ぶりだろうね？」「3年は会ってないな」"*How long has it been since* we saw each other？" "It's been three years. ／I haven't seen you for three years." →久しぶり.

✉ **5か月ぶりのお手紙うれしく拝見しました** I was glad to read *the first letter I received from you in 5 months*.（➤英米では具体的に前回もらった月を示して I was glad to hear from you for the first time since June. などとすることが多い）.

ふりあげる 振り上げる ▶彼は怒ってぼくにげんこつを振り上げた He *raised* ［*shook*］ his fist at me in anger.

フリー free 一形 **フリーの freelance**（自由契約の）▶フリーのジャーナリスト［カメラマン］ a *freelance* journalist ［photographer］‖あの記者は現在はフリーだ［フリーランサーだ］ That man ［woman］ is now a *freelance* reporter. ／That reporter is now a *freelancer*. ‖彼は会社を辞めてフリーになった He quit the company to *become his own boss*.（➤「自分自身が指図する人になる」が原義）.

▶これはフリーサイズです This is *one-size-fits-all*.（➤「フリーサイズ」は和製語）.

‖**フリーエージェント** a free agent ‖**フリーキック** a free kick ‖**フリークライミング** free climbing ‖**フリースクール** a free school ‖**フリースタイル** freestyle ‖**フリースロー** a free throw ‖**フリーダイヤル**《米》a toll-free (phone) number,《英》a freephone ［freefone／freecall］ number ‖**フリードリンク** all-you-can-drink beverages ‖**フリーバッティング** batting practice ‖**フリーライター** a freelance writer（➤free writer とすると「ただで仕事をするライター」の意になる）.

> **危ないカタカナ語✹フリー**
> **1**「フリー」に free を当てはめただけでは通じない場合が多い．例えば「フリーダイヤル」や「フリーバッティング」は和製語で，別の言い方をする必要がある．また「フリーのジャーナリスト」のような場合も free journalist では日本語の意味を表さない．これは「組織に属さない」の意味の freelance という語を使う必要がある．
> **2**「フリーパス」も「無料の入場［乗車］券」の意味では free pass を使えるが，「…にフリーパスだ」というときは別の表現をする必要がある．→フリーパス．

フリーザー a **freezer.**

フリージア《植物》a **freesia.**

フリース fleece ▶フリースのジャケット a *fleece* jacket.

フリーズ《コンピュータ》a **freeze** 一動 **フリーズする freeze** ▶私のノートパソコンがまたフリーズした My laptop *froze* again.

フリーター a **(young) part-time worker** ▶とりあえず今はフリーターをやっています I *work part-time* for the time being.

フリーパス ▶私はあの動物園はフリーパスだ I *can get into* that zoo *free*. ‖外交官は税関がフリーパスだ Diplomats *can go through* customs *unchecked*.（→顔パス）.

フリーハンド freehand ▶フリーハンドで円を描く draw a circle *freehand*.

ブリーフ briefs.

ブリーフケース a **briefcase.**

フリーマーケット a **flea market**（ノミの市）（➤free market（自由市場）と混同しないこと）.

ふりえき 不利益 ▶自分の不利益になることは話さなくてよい You need not say anything *disadvantageous* to you.

ふりおとす 振り落とす ▶カウボーイは馬から振り落とされた The cowboy *was thrown off* ［*was shaken off*］ the horse.

ふりおろす 振り下ろす ▶棒［剣］を振り下ろす *swing* a stick ［sword］ *down* ‖おのを振り下ろす *bring* an axe *down*.

ふりかえ 振替 1【郵便振替】postal transfer ▶予約購読料を振替で送金する send one's subscription fee by *postal transfer*.

‖**自動口座振替** automatic bank payment.

2【交通機関の】▶山の手線で事故が発生し，乗客たちは地下鉄やバスで振り替え輸送された After the train accident on the Yamanote Line, the passengers *were given free transportation* by subway trains or buses.

‖**振り替え休日** a substitute holiday, a make-up holiday, a carry-over holiday《参考》説明的には a holiday making up for a public holiday that falls on a Sunday となる.

ぶりかえす ぶり返す ▶かぜがぶり返した My cold has *come back*. ‖せっかく治った腰痛がぶり返した I *had a relapse* of the backache I thought I had managed to get rid of. ‖この1週間，猛暑がぶり返している Sweltering hot weather *has returned* for this week.

ふりかえる 振り返る **1【振り向く】turn around ; look back**《at》(振り返って見る)
▶名前を呼ばれたので振り返って見たら山崎君だった Someone called my name from behind, so I *looked back* [*turned around to look*] and saw Mr. Yamazaki.
2【思い出す】look back《over, on》▶20世紀を振り返る *look back over* the 20th century ‖ 昨年を振り返ってみると実にいろいろなことがあった *Looking back over* the past year, I realize how much has happened!

ふりかかる 降り掛かる fall《on》▶松の枝を揺さぶったら細かい雪がさらさらと降りかかった When I shook a branch of the pine tree, snowflakes *fell on* me. ‖ 思わぬ災難が彼女の身に降りかかった An unforeseen misfortune *befell* her.

ふりかけ 振り掛け *furikake* ; dried seasoning that is sprinkled on top of rice (➤ 説明的な訳).

ふりかける 振り掛ける sprinkle +㊀ (一面にぱらぱらと) ; **shake** +㊀ (上下または左右に振り動かしながら) ▶イチゴに砂糖を振りかける *sprinkle* strawberries *with* sugar / *sprinkle* sugar *on* [*over*] strawberries ‖ 彼はラーメンにコショウを振りかけた He *shook* pepper *on* his ramen. (➤ shook は shake の過去形).

ふりかざす 振りかざす ▶刀を大上段に振りかざす *raise* a sword *over one's head*.
▶《比喩的》彼らは権力を振りかざしている They *are showing off* their authority.

ふりかた 振り方 ▶自分の身の振り方を考える think about how one will *get along* (*in the future*).

ふりがな 振り仮名 *furigana*
日本紹介 ✉ **ふりがなは,漢字の読み方を示すためにその上や横に添える小さなひらがな,またはカタカナのことです.つづり字に添える発音記号のようなものです** *Furigana* are small *hiragana* or *katakana* that are added above or along *kanji* to indicate how the *kanji* is pronounced. They are somewhat like phonetic symbols added after normal spelling to indicate the pronunciation.

ふりかぶる 振りかぶる ▶オーバースローのピッチャーはふつう振りかぶってから投げる An overhand pitcher usually *swings his arms over his head* before throwing the ball.

ブリキ tinplate, tin《参考》「ブリキ」はオランダ語の *blik* から ▶ブリキのおもちゃ a *tin* toy / a toy made of *tin*
‖ブリキ缶 a tin can.

ふりきる 振り切る shake off ▶男は追っ手を振り切った The man *shook off* the pursuers. ‖ 彼は母親が止めるのを振り切って嵐の中に飛び出した He ran out in the storm *ignoring* his mother's warnings. ‖ 彼女は両親が卒業まで待てというのを振り切って大学2年で結婚した She *brushed aside* her parents' suggestion that she (should) wait until graduation and got married when she was a college sophomore.

ふりきれる 振り切れる ▶地震計の針が振り切れた The needle of the seismograph *jumped off the paper* [*jumped erratically*].

プリクラ a ***purikura*** ; an instant photo machine to make tiny photo stickers (➤ 説明的な訳).

ふりこ 振り子 a **pendulum** /péndʒələm/ ▶ガリレオは振り子の原理を発見した Galileo discovered *the principle of the pendulum*.
‖振り子時計 a pendulum clock.

ふりこう 不履行 ▶契約の不履行 *breach* of contract (➤ breach は「(約束などの)違反」) ‖ 彼は契約不履行で訴えられた He was sued for *breach of promise*.

ふりこみ 振り込み ▶授業料を銀行振り込みで払う *pay* one's tuition fee *through the bank* ‖ 私の給料は銀行口座に自動振り込みにされる My salary *is paid* [*is transferred*] automatically *into* my bank account.

ふりこむ 振り込む transfer /trænsfə́ːʳ/ +㊀ ▶私は彼女の銀行口座に5万円を振り込んだ I *paid* 50,000 yen *into* her bank account. ‖ 父の給料は毎月25日に銀行に振り込まれる My father's salary *is paid into* his bank account on the 25th of every month.

ふりこめさぎ 振り込め詐欺 *furikome-sagi* ; telephone fraud in which someone, usually an elderly person, is talked into making a bank transfer (➤ 説明的な訳).

ふりこめる 降りこめる ▶新潟では一日中雪に降りこめられた We *were snowed in* all day in Niigata.

ブリザード a **blizzard.**

ふりしきる 降りしきる ▶きょうは雨が一日中降りしきっている *It has been raining hard* [*steadily*] all day today. ‖ 降りしきる雪の中を一行は山頂へ向かった The party headed for the top of the mountain in [through] the *heavy* snow.

ふりしぼる 振り絞る ▶その女性は声を振り絞って助けを求めた The woman cried for help *at the top of her lungs*.
▶彼女は高音域を出そうとのどを振り絞った She *strained* her voice by trying to reach the high notes. (➤ strain は「筋肉などを極度に使う」) ‖ 彼女は最後の力を振り絞ってゴールに倒れこんだ *Having put forth* [*exerted*] *her last ounce of strength*, she collapsed at the goal. (➤ ounce /aʊns/ は「微少,ごく少量」の意).

ふりすてる 振り捨てる throw off, cast off, abandon +㊀ ▶偏見を振り捨てる *throw off* [*abandon*] prejudice.

フリスビー a **Frisbee** /frízbi/ ▶フリスビーをする toss [play with] *a Frisbee*.

プリズム《光学》a **prism.**

ふりそそぐ 降り注ぐ ▶日の光が庭一面に降り注いでいた Sunlight *was streaming down* into the garden. / The garden was bathed in [was filled with] sunlight.

ふりそで 振り袖 a ***furisode***
日本紹介 ✉ **振りそでは長いそでのついた未婚の若い女性用の華やかな着物です.第一礼装として結婚式,成人式,卒業式など特別の機会に着ます** A *furisode* is a gorgeous kimono with long sleeves for young unmarried women. Since a *furisode* is considered the most formal wear, it is worn for special occasions such as wedding ceremonies, coming-of-age celebrations and graduation ceremonies.

ふりだし 振り出し square one(すごろくの) ▶振り出しに戻ってこの問題を考え直そう Let's think about this problem again *from the very beginning* [*from scratch*]. / Let's *go back to the drawing board*. ‖ 容疑者のアリバイが立証されれば,(捜査は)振り出しに戻らねばならない If the suspect's alibi is established, we'll have to *go back to* [*start again from*]

square one.
▶政府との交渉は振り出しに戻った The negotiations with the government *went back to where they started* [*went back to square one*].

[1]ふりだす 降り出す **begin to rain**(雨が；主語は it) ▶とうとう降りだしたね It's finally *begun to rain*. ‖ 夕刻には雪が降りだすでしょう It looks like it's *going to snow* this evening.

[2]ふりだす 振り出す ▶会社あてに手形を振り出す *draw* [*write*] *a bill* to a firm.

ふりちん ▶小さな男の子たちが何人か川でふりちんで泳いでいた Some small boys were swimming in the stream *stark naked* [*in their birthday suits*]. (➤ stark naked は「すっ裸で」, in one's birthday suit は「生まれたままの姿で」；英語では女子にも用いられる).

ふりつ 府立 →府.

ふりつけ 振り付け **choreography** /kɔ̀:riɑ́:grəfi/ ▶ミュージカルの振り付けをする *choreograph* a musical / *compose the dances* for a musical.
‖振り付け師 a choreographer.

ぶりっこ ぶりっ子 ▶わあ, 陽子って, すっごいぶりっ子! Oh, that Yoko's just *playing the cutie*. (➤ cutie は「かわい子ちゃん」の意のインフォーマルな語) / Oh, that Yoko *is acting innocent* [*helpless*]. (➤ innocent は「うぶな」, helpless は「自分では何もできない」).

ブリッジ **bridge**(トランプの)；a **bridge**(橋・歯・レスリングの) ▶《トランプで》ブリッジをする play *bridge*.

フリッター a **fritter** ▶小エビのフリッター a shrimp *fritter*.

ふりつづく 降り続く ▶北陸地方では昨夜から雪が降り続いております *It's been snowing* in the Hokuriku region since yesterday evening.

フリップ a **flip chart.**

ふりつもる 降り積もる ▶雪が降り積もった The snow *was piled up* [*was accumulated*].

ふりにげ 振り逃げ 《野球》 ▶内川選手は振り逃げで出塁した Batter Uchikawa got to first *because the catcher missed the pitch*. 《参考》「振り逃げ」に当たる英語はない.

ふりはらう 振り払う **shake off**(払いのける) ▶彼は消防士の制止を振り払って燃えさかる炎の中に飛び込んだ *Shaking off* the firefighter's restraining arm(s), he dashed into the roaring blaze.

ぷりぷり ▶ぼくがデブと言ったら, 彼女ぷりぷり怒って帰っちゃったよ When I said she was a fatso [a porker], she left *in a huff*.

プリペイドカード a **prepaid card.**

ふりほどく 振りほどく **shake oneself free** 《from》, **break free** 《from》 ▶彼女は彼の手を振りほどいた She *shook herself free from* his grasp.

ふりまく 振りまく ▶彼女はダンスパーティーで誰かれとなく愛きょうを振りまいた She *showered* smiles on everyone at the dance.

プリマドンナ a **prima donna.**

ふりまわす 振り回す **1**【振って回す】**swing around** ▶傘を振り回すのはやめろ Stop *swinging* your umbrella *around*. ‖ 彼は右腕を(ぐるぐる)振り回した He *waved* his right arm *about*.
2【かき回す】▶警察は誘拐犯人からの電話にすっかり振り回された The police *were led on a wild goose chase* by the kidnapper's phone calls. (➤ wild goose chase は「実体のないものを求めていつまでも続ける追跡」).
▶彼女の家族はわんぱく坊主にいつも振り回されている Her family *is ruled* by her rambunctious little boy. / Her mischievous little boy has her family *twisted around his little finger*. ‖ 彼はガールフレンドに振り回されている His girlfriend *leads* him *around by the nose*.

ふりみだす 振り乱す ▶美津子は髪を振り乱して踊った Mitsuko danced *with her hair flying loose* [*wild*]. ‖ 老婆は髪を振り乱しながら賊を追いかけた The old woman chased after the thief, her hair *flying in disarray*.

ふりむく 振り向く **turn around**(向きを変える)；**look back**(振り向いて見る)
▶振り向くと芳恵がそこに立っていた I *turned around* [*looked back*] to find Yoshie standing there. ‖ 理恵が通ると誰もが振り向いて彼女を見る When Rie passes by, everybody *turns around* to look at her.
▶秀美はぼくの方など振り向いてもくれない Hidemi *won't pay any attention* to me.

ブリュッセル **Brussels** /brʌ́səlz/ (ベルギーの首都).

ふりょ 不慮の **accidental**(偶然の)；**unforeseen**(予見できない) ▶私たちの教授は飛行機事故で不慮の死を遂げた Our professor met *an untimely* [*a sudden*] *death* in the plane crash.

[1]ふりょう 不良 **1**【非行者】a **delinquent** /dɪlíŋkwənt/ (未成年の非行者)；a **bad boy** [**girl**] (悪い少年[少女]) ▶うちの学校って, 不良が多いのよ There are lots of *delinquents* [*rowdy* students] in my school. (➤ 後者は「手に負えない乱暴な生徒」) ‖ 弟は悪い仲間と付き合ってとうとう不良になった My (younger) brother got mixed up with bad company and *went bad* in the end.
2【よくないこと】▶天候不良のため私たちは旅行を延期せざるをえなかった We had to put off our trip due to *bad weather*. ‖ 彼は成績不良で留年することになった He had to repeat the same year because his *grades were not good enough*. ‖ 私はピーナツを食べ過ぎて消化不良を起こした I got *indigestion* because I ate too many peanuts. ‖ 不良品はお取り替えいたします *Defective* [*Inferior*] *products* will be replaced.
‖不良債権 a bad [nonperforming] loan.

[2]ふりょう 不漁 ▶きょうは不漁だった We *had a poor catch of fish* [*had a poor haul*] today.

ふりょく 浮力 **buoyancy** /bɔ́iənsi/.

ぶりょく 武力 **force**；**military power** (軍事力) ▶武力に訴える resort to *force* ‖ 武力で紛争を解決する settle a conflict *by force*.
‖武力外交 power politics ‖ 武力干渉[介入] armed intervention ‖ 武力衝突 an armed conflict.

フリル a **frill** ▶フリルのついたスカート a skirt with *frills* / a frilly skirt.

ふりわける 振り分ける **divide** +㊐ ▶全校生徒が赤組と白組に振り分けられた All the students of the school *were divided* into two teams, Red and White.

ふりん 不倫 an **illicit** /ɪlísɪt/ [**extramarital**] **affair** (➤ illicit は「不義の」, extramarital は「婚外」の) ▶彼女, 奥さんのいる男性と不倫してるらしいわよ Somebody told me she's *having an affair with* [*running around with*] a married man. ‖ (騎士)ランスロットはアーサー王の王妃ギニビアと不倫の恋に落ちた Sir Lancelot *fell illicitly in love with* King Arthur's Queen Guinevere.

プリン (a) **caramel custard.**

危ないカタカナ語✹ **プリン**
1 日本語の「プリン」は英語の pudding の発音がなまったもので，卵・牛乳・砂糖・香料を混ぜて焼いたものを指すが，これは英語では custard pudding という．ふつうカラメルつきであるから，より正確には caramel custard または flan とする．
2 英語の pudding はデザートの一種であり，甘いものから甘くないものまで，多くの種類がある．

プリンス a **prince** ▶その若手代議士は「政界のプリンス」と呼ばれる That young Diet member is called "*the most promising young man* in the political world."

プリンセス a **princess.**

プリンター a **printer** ▶レーザー［インクジェット］プリンター a laser [an inkjet] *printer*.

プリント 1【印刷物】a **printed sheet,** a **copy**（写し）（➤集合的には printed material(s) という）; a **handout**（講演・会合・授業などで配る）▶先生は授業でよくプリントを配る Our teacher often passes out *printed sheets* [*printed material(s)*] in class.
2【染め付け】▶プリントの服 a *print* dress.
3【焼き付け】a **print** ▶このネガ，プリントしてみたら？ Why not *get* the negative *printed*?

プリントアウト (a) **printout** 一動 プリントアウトする **print out** ▶そのファイルは今プリントアウト中です The file is *being printed out* now.

1 **ふる 振る** 1【振り動かす】**shake** +目; **wave** +目（手・旗などを）; **swing** +目（丸く弧を描くように）; **wag** +目（尾などを）; **swish** +目（シュッ［ピュッピュッ］と勢いよく）▶旗を振る *wave* a flag ‖ バットを振る *swing* one's bat ‖（表示）よく振ってからご使用ください *Shake* well before use. ‖ 彼は信じられないと言うように首を振った He *shook his head* in disbelief.（● shake one's head は否定・疑い・失望などのため「首を横に振る」こと．「首を縦に振る」は nod）‖ 彼女は私たちにさよならと手を振った She *waved* good-bye to us.
▶その子犬はなでてやるとしっぽを振った The puppy *wagged* its tail when I patted it.
2【散らしてまく】**sprinkle** +目 ▶彼女はサラダに塩を振った She *sprinkled* salt on the salad.
3【捨てる】**dump** +目 ⇀振られる ▶あんな女，振っちゃえばいいのに You should *ditch* a woman [girl] like that.
4【わきに添える】▶係員は申込書に番号を振った The clerk in charge *assigned* a number to the application form.（➤ assign は「割り当てる」）.

2 **ふる 降る** **fall**（空から落ちる）; **rain**（特に雨が; 主語は it）; **snow**（特に雪が; 主語は it）▶雨が降っている It's raining.（➤ ふつう，The rain is falling. とは言わない．「雨が降り始めた」も It began to rain. がふつう）‖ きょうはよく降りますね It'*s raining* [*snowing*] *a lot* today.
▶あすは雨が降るだろうか Will *it rain* tomorrow? ／ Will *it be rainy* tomorrow? ‖ きょうは一日中降ったりやんだりでしょう It should *rain on and off* today. ‖ 外は今雨が降っていますか？ *Is it raining* outside now? ‖ 山では雪が降っているだろう I think *it is snowing* in the mountains. ‖ この20日間雨が降らない *It has not rained* for the past twenty days. ／We *have had no rain* for the past twenty days.
▶鹿児島市に大量の火山灰が降った A lot of volcanic ash *fell* on the city of Kagoshima. ‖ 降ろうと照ろうと行くよ I'll be there, *rain or shine*.
☛ 降ってわく（⇀見出語）

フル **full** ▶彼女は近くの図書館をフルに利用している She *makes full* [*makes the best*] *use of* the nearby library.
▶エアコンはフル回転していたが，それでも汗だらだらだった The air conditioner was *going full blast* [*going full force*] but I was still pouring sweat.

-ぶる ▶彼はときどきインテリぶる He sometimes *pretends* to be [*puts on the air of*] an intellectual. ‖ 小学校へ行くようになってから，直樹はいやにお兄ちゃんぶるわね Since he started school, Naoki has really begun to *act* [*behave*] *like* a big brother. ‖ 彼女があんなに学者ぶる［かわい子ぶる］人だとは思わなかったわ I didn't think she was the type to *act* so *pedantic* [*act like a cutie*].

1 **ふるい 篩** a **sieve** /sɪv/; a **sifter**（料理用の小型の）▶砂をふるいにかける sift sand in *a sieve*.
▶（比喩的）応募者全員が再度ふるいにかけられた All the applicants *were screened* again.

2 **ふるい 古い** 1【新しくない】**old**; **used** /juːzd/（使用済みの）; **ancient** /éɪnʃənt/（古代の）▶古い家 an *old* house ‖ 古い切手 an *old* [a *used*] stamp ‖ 古い都 an *old* capital ‖ 古き良きもの *oldies* but goodies（➤映画・音楽など）‖ 滝川氏は小学校時代からの古い友だちです Mr. Takigawa is an *old* friend (of mine) from elementary school. ‖ エジプトは古い文明で知られる Egypt is known for its *ancient* civilization. ‖ 私たちは古くからの友だちです We are *old* friends.
2【古くさい】**old-fashioned**（旧式な）; **outdated**（時代遅れの）▶社長は頭が古い The president has *old-fashioned* ideas.
▶男の子と付き合っちゃだめだなんて，お父さん古いわよ Dad, you're so *old-fashioned* (for) not letting me go out with boys. ‖ 古くなった情報は役にたたない *Outdated* data is useless. ‖ わが家は古くなってきた Our house *is getting old*. ‖ このハンドバッグはもう古くなった This handbag *is out of style* [*is old-fashioned*].
3【新鮮でない】**stale** ▶古い魚 *stale* fish ‖ そのソーセージ，ちょっと古いのよ That sausage's a bit *stale*.

ふるい 部類 a **class**（同じ条件のもとにあるものの集団）; a **category**（同じ特徴を持つものの集団）▶彼などはまだましな部類だ Oh, him—he's in the not-so-bad *category*.

ふるいおこす 奮い起こす ▶彼は勇気を奮い起こして飛行機からパラシュートで飛び降りた He *plucked up his courage* and parachuted from the airplane.

ふるいおとす ふるい落とす **screen out** ▶彼は面接でふるい落とされた He *was screened out* in the interview. ／He *was rejected* as a result of the interview.

ふるいたたせる 奮い立たせる ▶人を奮い立たせる本 an *inspiring* book ‖ 教師は生徒を奮い立たせることが必要だ Teachers should *inspire* their students. ‖ 彼の演説は人々の心を奮い立たせた His speech *stirred* [*inspired*] the people.

ふるいたつ 奮い立つ ▶サポーターたちの「ガンバ，頑張れ！」の声援に選手たちは奮い立った The players *were roused* by their supporters' shouting "Let's go, Gamba!"

ふるいつく 震いつく ▶かおるは震いつきたくなるような美人だ Kaoru is so beautiful you *can hardly resist* *hugging* her. ／Kaoru is *irresistibly* beautiful.

[1]**ふるう 振るう** **1【使う】**▶暴力を振るう *use* force／*resort to* violence.

2【存分に発揮する】▶存分に手腕を振るう *give full play to* one's ability ‖ 彼女はお客を招き，料理に腕を振るった She invited the guests to her home and *displayed*［*demonstrated*］her cooking ability.（➤「腕を見せびらかす」なら show off）.

▶総理は政治改革について熱弁を振るった The Prime Minister *spoke passionately* on the political reform.

3【勢いが盛んである】▶最近，商売が振るわない Business is *slow*［*slack*］these days. ‖ 彼女は試験の成績が振るわなかった She *didn't get a good grade*［*do well*］on the examination. ‖ きょうの試合でタイガースは全然振るわなかった The Tigers *made a very poor showing* in tonight's game.

☛ ふるった，ふるって（→見出語）

[2]**ふるう** ▶小麦粉をふるう *sift* the flour ‖ 志願者をふるう *sift through* the applicants.

ブルー **blue** ‖ **ブルーカラー** a blue-collar worker ‖ **ブルーフィルム** a blue film［movie］‖ **マリッジブルー** pre-nuptial blues.

ブルース **(the) blues** /bluːz/ ▶ブルースを歌う sing *(the) blues* ‖ ブルースの歌手 a *blues* singer.

フルーツ (a) **fruit** ▶娘はフルーツが好きだ My daughter likes *fruit*.（➤ 1つ1つの種類をいうとき以外は fruits としない）.

‖ **フルーツケーキ** (a) fruitcake ‖ **フルーツサラダ** (a) fruit salad ‖ **フルーツジュース** fruit juice ‖ **フルーツトマト** a campari tomato, a (Japanese) sweet tomato ‖ **フルーツパーラー** a coffee［tea］shop attached to a fruit store（➤ (×)fruits parlor とはしない）‖ **フルーツポンチ** fruit punch, a fruit cup.

フルーティー **fruity.**

フルート a **flute** ▶フルートを吹く play the *flute* ‖ 優子はドビュッシーの曲をフルートで演奏した Yuko played a Debussy piece on the *flute*.

‖ **フルート奏者** a flute player,《米また》a flutist,《英また》a flautist /flɔ́ːtɪst/.

ブルーベリー《植物》a **blueberry.**

プルーン《植物》a **prune.**

ふるえ 震え a **shake**; a **tremble**; a **shudder**; a **shiver**; a **quiver** →ふるえる ▶寒くて震えが止まらない I'm so cold I can't stop *shaking*［*trembling*／*shivering*］.

ふるえあがる 震え上がる **tremble**; **shiver** ▶あまりの恐ろしさに震えあがった I *trembled*［*shivered*］*all over* with terror.（➤ all over は「体中」）‖ 彼女は巨大なクモを見て震えあがった She *was terribly scared* when she saw a huge spider.

ふるえる 震える **shake**; **tremble**（寒さ・怒り・恐怖などで小刻みに）; **shiver**（寒さ・恐怖で瞬間的に）; **shudder**（恐怖などでがたがたと）; **quiver**（人・声・葉などが恐怖・喜びなどで小刻みに）

▶トラックが通ると窓ガラスが震えた The windowpane *shook* as a truck passed by.（➤ shook は shake の過去形）‖ 彼女は寒さで震えた She *shook*［*trembled*／*shivered*］with cold. ‖ 恐怖のあまりががたがた震えた I *shuddered* from terror. ‖ 緊張で彼の声は震えていた He was so nervous that his voice *was shaking*［*trembling*］.

▶新郎新婦は震える手でケーキにナイフを入れた The bride and groom cut the wedding cake with *trembling* hands.

プルオーバー a **pullover.**

フルカウント《野球》a **3－2 count**（➤ 英語ではボールの数をストライクより先に言う）.

ふるがお 古顔 an **old-timer** ▶斎藤さんは囲碁クラブの古顔だ Mr. Saito is *an old-timer*［*an old member*］in our 'Go' club.

ふるかぶ 古株 an **old (tree) stump**（木の）; an **old-timer**（古顔）.

ブルガリア **Bulgaria** /bʌlgéəriə/（ヨーロッパ南東部の国）‖ **ブルガリア人** a Bulgarian.

ふるぎ 古着 **old clothes** /kloʊz/, **used** /juːzd/［**second-hand**］**clothes**

‖ **古着屋** a secondhand-clothes store.

ふるきず 古傷 (an) **old injury,** (an) **old wound** /wuːnd/（➤ 後者は比喩的にも用いる；→傷）▶古傷に触れる (re)open *an old wound* ‖ ひざの古傷がときどき痛む My *old knee injury* sometimes hurts.

ふるくさい 古臭い **old-fashioned**; **outdated, out-of-date**（時代遅れの）▶古くさい考え方 an *old-fashioned*［*outdated*／*out-of-date*］way of thinking ‖ 古くさいしゃれ a *corny* joke ‖ 古くさい表現 a *hackneyed*［*corny*］expression.

フルコース ▶フルコース(の食事) a *full-course* dinner（➤ a five-course dinner のように品数をいうことが多い）.

プルコギ **bulgogi**; **Korean marinated barbecued beef.**

ふるさと 故郷 one's **home**; one's **hometown**（生まれた町や市）; one's **homeland**（故国）▶津軽は太宰治のふるさとだ Tsugaru was *the home* (*town*) of Dazai Osamu.（➤ 故人なので動詞は過去形にするのがふつう）‖ **対話**「ふるさとはどちらですか？」「広島県の三次です」"*Where are you from?*" "I'm from Miyoshi, Hiroshima Prefecture."／"*Where do you come from?*" "I come from Miyoshi, Hiroshima Prefecture." ‖ 北海道は私にとって第二のふるさとです Hokkaido is my *second home*.

ブルジョア a **bourgeois** /bɔ́əʳʒwɑː/; **the bourgeoisie** /bòəʳʒwɑːzíː/（➤ 総称）.

> **《解説》**(1)bourgeois は proletarian（無産階級者）に対する語で軽蔑的含みがある.
> (2)日本語では「金持ち」の意味で「ブルジョア」というが，英語の bourgeois は「労働者階級を搾取する資本家・有産者」のニュアンスが強い.

ふるしんぶん 古新聞 an **old newspaper.**

ふるす 古巣 one's **old place of work** ▶鈴木さんは古巣の経理部に戻った Suzuki returned to his *old position* in the accounting section.

フルスピード **full**［**top**］**speed** ▶赤いポルシェがフルスピードで走り去った A red Porsche drove off *at full*［*top*］*speed*.

ブルゾン a **blouson.**

フルタイム ▶彼女はフルタイムで働いている She works *full time*.／She is a *full-time* employee.（➤ 前者は副詞用法）.

プルダウンメニュー《コンピュータ》a **pull-down menu.**

プルタブ《米》a **pull-tab,**《英》a **ring-pull.**

ふるった ▶ふるったことを言う男だ He's a man who says *extraordinary* things.（➤ extraordinary /ɪkstrɔ́ːʳdnèri/ は「とっぴな」）‖ 最後に立った寺田さんのスピーチがふるっていた The speech by Mr. Terada, who was the last to speak, was *brilliant*.

ふるって 奮って ▶奮ってご参加ください You are cordially invited [are all welcome] to take part. ／Don't hesitate to join us.

ふるどうぐ 古道具 **used** /juːzd/ [**secondhand**] **goods**（中古品）; a **curio** /kjʊ́əriòʊ/（骨董品）; **old** [**used**] **furniture**（古家具）▶ノミの市で古道具を見て回る go around looking at the *curios* at a flea market.
‖古道具屋 a secondhand store, a junk shop（店）; a secondhand dealer, a junk dealer（人）.

ブルドーザー a **bulldozer** /bʊ́ldòʊzəʳ/.

ブルドッグ《動物》a **bulldog**.

プルトニウム《化学》**plutonium** /pluːtóʊniəm/.

ふるびる 古びる ▶その男は古びた上着を着ていた He wore an *old* jacket. ‖村外れに古びた神社がある There is an *old* Shinto shrine on the outskirts of the village.

ぶるぶる ▶寒くてぶるぶる震えた I *shivered* [*trembled*] from the cold. ‖おしっこをしたあと, 犬は体をぶるぶるっとさせた The dog *shook himself* after he had peed.

フルベース →満塁.

ブルペン《野球》a **bullpen**（➤この pen はもともとは「(家畜などの)囲い」の意）.

ふるぼけた 古ぼけた ▶古ぼけたかばん a *dilapidated* [*very old*] bag（➤dilapidated /dɪlǽpɪdèɪṭɪd/ は「ひどく傷んだ」）.

ふるほん 古本 a **secondhand** [**used** /juːzd/] **book** ▶この本は古本で買った I bought this book *secondhand*.
‖古本屋 a secondhand bookstore [bookshop], a used-book store [shop]（店）; a secondhand bookseller（人）.

ふるまい 振る舞い **behavior** ▶彼女の下品なふるまいに皆あきれた We were shocked at her coarse [vulgar] *behavior*.

ふるまう 振る舞う **1**【行動する】**behave, act** ▶別人のようにふるまう *behave* [*act*] like a different person.
2【もてなす】**entertain**（+目）▶彼女は夕食をふるまってくれた She *entertained* me at dinner.

ふるめかしい 古めかしい **old-fashioned**（旧式の）; **timeworn**（古臭い）; **hackneyed**（陳腐な）▶古めかしい考え an *old-fashioned* [*outdated*] idea ‖古めかしい表現 a *hackneyed* [*timeworn*] expression ‖教授の書斎にはマホガニーの古めかしい家具が置いてあった The professor's study was furnished with *old-fashioned* mahogany.

ふるわせる 震わせる **shake**; **tremble**（小刻みに）▶その少女は肩を震わせて泣いていた The girl's shoulders *were shaking* as she sobbed. ‖ジミーは恐ろしさに全身を震わせていた Jimmy *was trembling* all over with fear.

ぶれ a **motion blur**（被写体が動いてできる）; **camera shake**（カメラが動いてできる）▶画像のぶれ an image *blur* ‖カメラぶれを起こした写真 a *blurry* [*blurred*] photo *due to camera shake*.
☞ 手ぶれ（→見出語）

ふれあい 触れ合い **(human) contact**; a **close relationship**（親密な関係）▶家庭で大切なのは親子の触れ合いだ What is important in a family is to have *a close relationship* between parents and children. ／What is important in a family is *close* parent-child *communication*.

ふれあう 触れ合う **come into contact**《with》▶都会には自然と触れ合える場所が少ない There are few places in the city where you *can come into contact with* nature.

フレアスカート a **flared skirt**.

ぶれい 無礼な **impolite**; **rude**（粗野な）▶目上の人に向かってそういう言い方は無礼だよ It is *impolite* [*rude*] of you to talk like that to your superiors.

ブレイク an **overnight sensation**（突然の人気沸騰）; a **break**（突然のチャンス・幸運）▶あのお笑い芸人はことし大ブレイクした That comedian *had* [*got*] *an unexpected big break* this year.

ぶれいこう 無礼講 ▶今夜は無礼講でいこう *Let's let our hair down* tonight.（➤「今夜は髪を崩してやろう」の意）／Let's *party hearty*.（➤「(酒を飲んで)とことん騒ぐ」の意）／*Let's forget about work* and enjoy ourselves tonight.

プレー a **play** ▶珍プレー好プレー odd *plays* and nice *plays*.

プレーオフ a **playoff** ▶プレーオフを行う hold *a playoff*.

ブレーカー a **(circuit) breaker** ▶ブレーカーが落ちた The *breaker* has blown.

プレーガイド a **ticket agency**, a **ticket office** [**box**]（劇場内にある切符売り場）《参考》「プレーガイド」は Play Guide というアメリカの会社名に由来するとされる和製語. イギリスでは booking office ともいう.

ブレーキ **brakes**（➤しばしば複数形で）▶ブレーキをぐっと踏み込む slam [jam] on the *brakes*（➤「急ブレーキを踏む」にも相当）‖彼は坂の下でブレーキをかけた He *braked* [*put the brake on* ／ *hit the brakes* ／ *stepped on the brake*] at the foot of the slope. ‖ブレーキがきかなくて彼はあわてた He panicked when he found the *brakes* didn't work. ‖彼は子供をはねそうになって急ブレーキをかけた He *braked suddenly* [*slammed on the brakes*] to avoid hitting the child. ‖ドライバーはブレーキと間違えてアクセルを踏んだ The driver mistakenly pressed the accelerator instead of *the brakes*.
‖ブレーキオイル **brake fluid**（➤「ブレーキオイル」は和製英語）‖エアブレーキ an air brake ‖サイド[ハンド]ブレーキ《米》a parking brake,《英》a hand brake ‖フットブレーキ a foot brake.

ブレークスルー a **breakthrough** ▶半導体分野におけるブレークスルーの期待がかかる新材料 a new material which promises to be a *breakthrough* in the field of semiconductor technology.

ブレークポイント《テニス》a **break point**.

フレーズ a **phrase**（句）.

プレート《地質学》a **plate** ▶太平洋プレート the Pacific *Plate*.

フレーフレー ▶フレーフレー, ジャイアンツ *Come on*, Giants! ／*Go, Go*, Giants!

プレーボーイ a **playboy**; a **womanizer**（女たらし）; a **ladies' man**（女性を扱うのがうまい色男）.

> **危ないカタカナ語✹ プレーボーイ**
> **1** 英語の playboy は自由な時間のたっぷりある金持ちの男性で, 女性だけでなくさまざまな快楽を追求する人を指す. つまり, 日本語の「プレーボーイ」よりも意味の範囲が広い. したがって, 単なる「女好きの男」は playboy ではなく, womanizer（女たらし）とか woman chaser（女のしりを追い回す人）などというほうが適切.
> **2** 日本語の「プレーボーイ」の意で a Casanova ということもある. これは色事師として知られたイタリア人 G. J. Casanova に由来する言い方.

フレーム a **frame** ▶眼鏡のフレーム the *frames* of a

pair of glasses.

‖デジタル・フォトフレーム a digital photo frame.

フレームワーク a framework.

プレーヤー a player(選手, 演奏者); a (record／CD／DVD) player (レコードなどのプレーヤー)

▶彼女は一流のテニスプレーヤーだ She is one of the best [leading] *tennis players*.

ブレーン the brains(集団・組織の知的指導者); a brain trust (政府などから委嘱された専門顧問団); an adviser(助言者)

▶彼はこの会社のブレーンの1人だ He is a member of this company's *brain trust*. ‖ 大統領には有能なブレーンがついている The President has an able *brain trust*.

ブレーンストーミング brainstorm ▶次の会議では新商品の宣伝方法についてのブレーンストーミングを行います We're going to *brainstorm* (about) how to advertise our new products at the next meeting.

ふれこみ 触れ込み ▶その選手はホームラン打者というふれこみだった That player *was advertised as* a home run slugger.

ブレザー a blazer /bléɪzəʳ/ ▶紺色のブレザー a navy blue *blazer* (➤ (×)blazer coat としない).

プレス ▶プレスのきいたズボン *pressed* slacks ‖ このズボンをプレスしてください Please *press* this pair of trousers.

フレスコが フレスコ画 a fresco.

ブレスレット a bracelet /bréɪslət/; a bangle (留め金のない).

プレゼン(テーション) a presentation ▶我々は経営会議で新企画のプレゼンを行うことになっている We are supposed to give [make／do] *a presentation* on our new project at a management conference.

プレゼント a present, a gift (➤ 後者はより堅い語) ━ 動 プレゼントする give +目, present /prɪzént/ +目 (➤ 動詞の present は「贈呈する」に相当するかなり堅い語) ▶クリスマスプレゼント a Christmas *present* ‖ これはあなたへのプレゼントです This is *a present* for you. ／Here's something for you. ‖ 父親は息子の誕生日に自転車をプレゼントした The father *gave* his son a bicycle *as a* birthday *present*. ‖ それ, プレゼント用に包んでもらえますか? Could you please *gift-wrap* that?

✉ **すてきなプレゼントをお送りいただきありがとうございます** Thank you for the *wonderful present* you sent me.

✉ **ご結婚おめでとう! プレゼントとして日本の湯のみ一式を送ります** Best wishes on your marriage! I am sending you a set of Japanese teacups *as a wedding gift*.

フレックスタイム flextime, 《英また》 flexitime ▶フレックスタイムで働く work *flextime*.

▶うちの会社もやっとフレックスタイム制を採用した Our company has finally adopted *a flextime program*.

プレッシャー pressure ▶チャンピオンは初防衛戦でプレッシャーがかかっていた The champ felt considerable *pressure* since it was his first defending match. ‖ 彼にはだいぶプレッシャーがあるようだ He seems to *be under* a lot of *pressure*.

フレッシュ fresh ▶フレッシュな空気を吸う breathe *fresh* air ‖ フレッシュジュースを飲む drink *fresh juice*.

> **危ないカタカナ語✸ フレッシュ**
>
> **1** 英語の fresh の用法は日本語の「フレッシュ」とは異なる点が多い. 例えば「みずみずしい女の子」のつもりで fresh girl とすると「未熟な女の子」の意味にとられやすい. また男性についてこの語を用いれば「なれなれしい, 厚かましい」の意なので, Don't get fresh! は「なれなれしくしないでよ」.
>
> **2** また, 新入社員を「フレッシュマン」と呼ぶことがあるが, 英語の freshman は「(大学や高校の) 1 年生」を指すことばで, 社会人には使えない. new employee とか new worker という必要がある.

フレッシュマン a new employee.

プレハブ a prefabricated /prìːfǽbrɪkeɪtɪd/ house, 《インフォーマル》 a prefab /príːfæb/.

ふれまわる 触れ回る spread (about); broadcast +目 (広く人に知らせる) ▶彼は学校中にそのうわさをふれ回った He *spread* the rumor all over the school. ‖ 彼女は木村氏と尾崎さんが不倫の仲だということを社内のみんなにふれ回った She *broadcast* [*spread about*] the news to everyone in the office that Mr. Kimura and Ms. Ozaki were having an affair.

プレミアム a premium /príːmiəm/ ▶入場券はプレミアム付きで売られている The admission tickets are being sold *at a premium*.

プレリュード 《音楽》 a prelude.

ふれる 触れる **1【さわる】** touch (+目) ▶手を触れるな Don't *touch*! ／ (掲示) Hands off! ‖ 展示品には手を触れないでください Please do not *touch* the exhibit. (➤「見るだけにしてください」の意で Please touch with your eyes only. のように表記することもある) ‖ 電車の中でだれかの腕が私に触れた Somebody's arm *brushed against* me in the train. (➤ brush against は「(通りすがりなどに)軽くぶつかる」の意) ‖ 少年は道路に埋められた地雷に触れて片足を失った The boy lost one of his legs when he *hit* [*stepped on*] a landmine buried in the road.

▶《慣用表現》初めてオーストラリアに来たときは目に触れるものすべてが珍しかった When I first came to Australia, everything that *I saw* seemed unusual. ‖ アダルトサイトを子供の目に触れないようにすることが絶対に必要です It is absolutely necessary to *prevent* children *from viewing* adult (web) sites [to make sure that children do *not have access to* adult (web)sites].

2【言及する】 touch on, refer to ▶ここではその問題に触れないことにします I won't *touch on* the subject here. ‖ 作者はその説に全く触れていない The author does not *refer to* the theory at all. ‖ 後藤氏の発言は問題の核心に触れるものだった Mr. Goto's remark *got to the heart* of the matter.

3【抵触する】 ▶そういう行為は法律に触れる That kind of action *is against* the law.

▶そんな長い引用はたぶん版権に触れるだろう It will probably *be* a copyright *infringement* to use such a long quote. (➤ infringement は「(権利などの)侵害」).

ぶれる ▶ぶれた写真 a *blurred* photo ‖ この写真はぶれている This photograph is *out of focus* (because your hand wasn't steady).

▶ぶれない人 a *consistent* [*steady*] person ‖ 会社の経営方針がぶれて困る We're annoyed at our company's *frequent shifts* in management policy.

フレンチ **French**
‖**フレンチトースト** (a piece of) French toast ‖ **フレンチドレッシング** French dressing.

ブレンド a **blend** ▶ 対話「コーヒーは何になさいますか」「ブレンドをお願いします」"What kind of coffee would you like?" "I'll have the *house blend*, please." (➤ house blend は「店[自家製]のブレンド」の意).

フレンドリー **friendly.**

ふろ 風呂 a **bath** ▶**風呂にゆっくり入る** *have a* long *bath* ‖ **風呂に湯**[**水**]**を入れる** run the water for *a bath* ‖ **風呂を沸かす** *prepare* [*heat*] *the bath* (➤ boil は「沸騰させる」の意なので使えない) ‖ **彼はひどく汗をかいたので風呂に入った** He was terribly sweaty, so he *took* [*had*] *a bath*.
▶**お風呂が沸いてますよ** The *bath*'s ready. / Would you care for *a bath*? (➤ 後者は「お風呂に入りませんか」の意) ‖ **お風呂から上がったらよく体をふくのよ** Dry (yourself) well after you get out of the *bath*. ‖ **夫は毎日赤ん坊を風呂に入れてくれます** My husband *gives* the baby *a bath* [*bathes* the baby] every day. / 《英また》My husband *baths* the baby every day. (➤ bathe /beɪð/ [《英》bath /bɑːθ/] a baby で「赤ん坊を入浴させる」の意).
▶ 対話「**ジョージ君, お風呂の加減はどう?**」「**ちょっと熱いです**」"*How's the bath*, George?" "It's a little hot for me." (➤ 一般的に日本の風呂は外国人には熱く感じるといわれる. また「ぬるいです」なら It's not hot enough. という).
✉ **日本人はお風呂に入るのが大好きです** The Japanese people are very fond of [really enjoy] *taking baths*.
‖**風呂おけ** a bathtub ‖ **風呂場** a bathroom 《参考》(1)アメリカでは浴槽・トイレ・洗面所が1つの部屋に収められているのがふつうなので, 一般家庭で bathroom といえば「トイレ」の意にもなる. したがって「お風呂場はどちらですか」は Where is the bath? と言い, Where is the bathroom? とは言わないのがふつう. (2)イギリスではふろとトイレは別の場所であることも多い.

プロ a **professional**, 《インフォーマル》a **pro** /proʊ/ (プロの人) ▶**彼はプロ野球で通用するだろうか** Do you think he will make it as *a professional baseball player*? ‖ **そのスケート選手はプロに転向した** That skater has turned *professional* [turned *pro*]. ‖ **彼はプロ意識がある**[**ない**] He has [lacks] *professional pride*.
‖**プロ選手** a pro(fessional) player ‖ **プロ野球** pro(fessional) baseball.

ブロイラー a **broiler**(若鶏).

ふろうしゃ 浮浪者 a **tramp**, 《インフォーマル》a **bum**, 《米また》a **hobo** 《参考》法律・行政上は vagrant /véɪgrənt/ という. ⇀ホームレス.

ふろうしょとく 不労所得 (an) **unearned income** ▶**不労所得で暮らす** live on *unearned income*.

ふろうふし 不老不死 **eternal youth**(永遠の若さ); **immortality**(不滅).

ブロー a **blow-dry** 一動 **ブローする** **blow-dry** +目 ▶**毎朝私はシャワーを浴び, 髪を洗ってブローします** Every morning I take a shower, wash my hair and *blow-dry* my hair.

ブローカー a **broker.**

ブローチ a **brooch** /broʊtʃ/, a **pin** ▶**胸にブローチをつける** wear *a brooch* [*a pin*] on one's breast.

フローチャート a **flow chart.**

フロート a **float** ▶**コーラフロート** a cola *float*.

ブロードウェー **Broadway**(ニューヨーク市マンハッタン区の大通り; 劇場街, 娯楽街).

ブロードバンド 《通信》**broadband** ▶**インターネットのブロードバンド接続** a *broadband* Internet connection.

フローリング **flooring** ▶**木のフローリングを貼る** install wood *flooring*.

ふろく 付録 **something extra**, an **extra** (おまけ); a **supplement** /sʌ́plɪmənt/ (補遺); an **appendix** /əpéndɪks/ (巻末付録) ▶**この雑誌にはいつも付録がついている** You always get some *free extras* with this magazine. / This magazine usually comes with a number of *free supplements*. 《参考》英語には雑誌などにつく「別冊付録」にぴったりの対応語はない.

ブログ 《インターネット》a **blog** 《参考》ブログの公開運営者を blogger という ▶**このたびブログを開設しました** I've recently set up [started] *a blog*. ‖ **どうぞ私のブログを見に来てください** I invite you to visit my *blog*. ‖ **彼は毎日ブログに何か書き込む** He writes something on his *blog* every day.
▶**彼女は人気のブログを運営している** She's running a popular *blog*.

プログラマー a **(computer) programmer.**

プログラミング **programming**
‖**プログラミング言語** a programming language.

プログラム **1**【**予定表**】a **program** ▶**文化祭のプログラムができあがった** The *program* for the cultural festival is ready.
▶**次はプログラムの3番, 親子二人三脚です** Now comes the third event on the *program*: the parent-and-child three-legged race.
2【**コンピュータの**】a **program** ▶**プログラムを作る** write *a program* ‖ **コンピュータ用の新しいプログラムを開発する** develop a new computer *program*.
‖**プログラム学習** programmed instruction [learning] ‖ **プログラム学習課程** a programmed course.

プロジェクト a **project** ▶**巨大プロジェクト** a mammoth *project* ‖ **プロジェクトチームを組む** form [organize] *a project team*.

プロジェクター a **projector.**

ふろしき 風呂敷 a ***furoshiki***; a wrapping cloth, a cloth wrapper ▶**手みやげをふろしきに包む** wrap a present in *a furoshiki*.
‖**ふろしき包み** a parcel wrapped in a *furoshiki*.
日本紹介 ✉ **ふろしきは物を包んで持ち運ぶときに使う正方形の布です. 中央に包むものを置き対角線の端どうしを結びます. 使わないときは折り畳んでバッグに入れられます** A *furoshiki* is a square cloth used to wrap and carry things. You place an item or items [one or more items] in the center and tie the diagonally opposite ends. A *furoshiki* can be folded up and carried in a purse when it is not being used. 《参考》英米人の中にはふろしきをテーブルクロス, スカーフ, 壁掛けなどに使う人がいる.
☛ **大ぶろしき** (⇀見出語)

プロセス **process** ▶**それでは酒造りのプロセスを説明します** And now, I'll explain the *process* of sake-making [-brewing]. ‖ **結果よりプロセスが大切だ** The *process* is more important than the result.
‖**プロセスチーズ** processed cheese.

プロダクション a **talent agency**(人材を発掘したりプールしたりしておく); a **production company** (番組作成を手がける) ‖**芸能プロダクション** a talent agency.

ふ

ブロック **1**【建築資材】a **block**
‖ブロック塀 a concrete block wall ‖ **コンクリートブロック** a concrete block.
2【地区, 街区】a **block** ; a **bloc**（共通目的で提携した数か国・数団体から成る圏）▶そのデパートはここから３ブロック先にあります That department store is three *blocks* away [up] from here. ‖ ぼくたちのサッカーチームは四国ブロックで優勝した Our soccer team won the Shikoku *bloc* competition.
‖ブロック経済 bloc economy.
3【スポーツで】**blocking** 一動 **ブロックする** **block** ＋目 ▶シュートをブロックする *block* a shot ‖ そのキャッチャーはホームでランナーをブロックするのがうまい The catcher is good at *block*ing the plate.（日本語では「ランナーをブロックする」というが, 英語では「ホームプレートをブロックする」という）.
▶彼女は相手のスパイクをブロックした She *blocked* her opponent's spike.
‖ブロックサイン a block signal.
ブロッコリー **broccoli** /brɑ́:kəli/.
フロッピー a **floppy (disk)**, a **diskette.**
プロテイン **protein** /próʊti:n/（たんぱく質）.
プロテクター a **protector** ▶プロテクターを着ける wear *a protector*.
プロテスタント a **Protestant** /prɑ́:tɪstənt/（信者）; **Protestantism**（教義）▶プロテスタントの教会 a *Protestant* church.
プロデューサー a **producer** ▶映画のプロデューサー a movie *producer* ‖ ＡＢＣテレビのプロデューサー *a producer* at ABC Television.
プロバイダー《インターネット》a **provider**（➤ 正式には Internet service provider という）.
プロパガンダ **propaganda.**
プロパンガス《化学》**propane** /próʊpeɪn/ **(gas).**
プロフィール a **profile** /próʊfaɪl/ ▶入賞者のプロフィールを紹介します Here are the *profiles* of the prize winners.
プロフェッショナル **professional.**
プロペラ a **propeller** /prəpélər/
‖プロペラ機 a propeller plane.
プロポーション a **proportion** ▶彼女はプロポーションがいい[悪い] She has a *well-proportioned* [*a poorly-proportioned*] figure. ／She has an *attractive* [*unattractive*] figure.
プロポーズ a **proposal (of marriage)** 一動 **プロポーズする** **propose**《to》▶彼のプロポーズを受け入れる[断る] accept [refuse] his *proposal*（➤ refuse の代わりに turn down でもよい）.
▶良夫は久子にプロポーズした Yoshio *proposed to* Hisako. ／Yoshio *asked* Hisako *to marry* him.
《参考》プロポーズするときの言い方には May I have your hand in marriage?（古風）, Will you marry me?（ふつう）, Will you walk down the aisle with me?（しゃれた[きざな]表現 ; aisle は「教会の通路」）などいろいろな言い方がある.
ブロマイド a **picture (of a movie star)**（映画スターの）
《参考》歌手なら movie star を singer にして a picture of a singer とする.「ブロマイド」という語は bromide paper（ブロマイド印画紙）からきているが, この語に「スターの写真」という意味はない.
プロモーション (a) **promotion** ▶そのスターは自分の新作映画のプロモーションを行うために日本にやって来た The star visited Japan to *promote* his [her] new movie.
‖プロモーター a promoter（➤「ボクシングのプロモーター」は a boxing promoter）.
ふろや 風呂屋 a **public bath** ▶風呂屋に行く go to *a public bath*.
フロリダ **Florida**（アメリカ南東部の州 ; 略 FL, Fla.）.
プロレス **pro(fessional) wrestling** ▶父はテレビでプロレスを見るのが好きだ My father likes to watch *pro wrestling* on TV.
‖プロレスラー a pro(fessional) wrestler.
プロレタリア a **proletarian** /pròʊlətéəriən/（➤ 個人）; **the proletariat**（➤ 総称）
‖プロレタリア革命 a proletarian revolution.
プロローグ a **prologue** ▶その殺人事件がドラマのプロローグだった The murder case was the *prologue* to the drama.
フロンガス《化学》**chlorofluorocarbon** /klɔ̀:rəflɔ̀:roʊkɑ́:rbən/, **CFC (gases), CFCs**（➤「フロン」はその１種を指す Freon（商標名）から）
《参考》オゾン層を破壊しない代替フロン（ガス）を CFC substitute と呼ぶ.
ブロンズ **bronze** ▶ブロンズ像 a *bronze* statue.
フロンティア **the frontier**（アメリカの西部開拓時代の）
‖フロンティア・スピリット frontier spirit.
フロント **the front desk, the reception desk** ▶外出の際はお部屋のキーをフロントにお預けください Please leave your key at *the front desk* when you go out.

> **危ないカタカナ語✹ フロント**
> **1** ホテルの受付を「フロント」というが, これは英語の the front desk の日本式省略. 英語では必ず desk をつける. ただし, ホテル内にいるようなときは誤解のおそれはないので, 単に the desk でもよい.
> **2** プロ野球球団の経営首脳陣を指す「フロント」は front office の後半を略したものだが, 英語では略せない.
> **3** 自動車の前面のガラスを指す「フロントガラス」も和製語で, 英語では《米》windshield,《英》windscreen ということが多い.

ブロンド **blond(e) hair**（金髪）; a **blond(e)**（ブロンドの人）《参考》blond は男性, blonde は女性が原則だが, 今では区別なく blond を用いることが多い ▶彼女はブロンドだ She has *blond* hair. ／She is *a blond(e)*.
フロントガラス《米》a **windshield,**《英》a **windscreen.**
プロンプター a **prompter.**
ふわ 不和 **trouble**（もめごと）; **discord** /dískɔ:rd/（仲たがい）▶家庭の不和が原因で彼は非行に走った *Family trouble* [*discord*] drove him to delinquency.
ふわたり 不渡り **dishonor** ▶その手形は不渡りになった The bill *bounced* [*was dishonored*].（➤ bounce は「不渡りとして戻ってくる」, dishonor は「支払いを拒否する」）.
‖不渡り小切手 a dishonored check, a bad check,《インフォーマル》a rubber check.
ふわふわ ▶ふわふわのパン *soft* bread ‖ ふわふわのシフォンケーキ a *soft and fluffy* chiffon cake.
▶日に干したらふとんがふわふわにふくらんだ The futon became *soft and fluffy* after being aired in the sun.
ふわらいどう 付和雷同 ▶彼は付和雷同型だ He is the type who *follows the crowd*.
ふわり ▶猫はベランダから地上へふわりと降りた The cat jumped *lightly* from the balcony onto the ground. →ふんわり.
¹ふん 分 **1**【時間】a **minute** /mínɪt/ ▶５分の休憩をとる

take a five-*minute* break／rest for five *minutes*／《インフォーマル》take five(➤最後の例は「ちょっと休憩する」の意で用いられることも多い) ‖ あの時計は5分進んでいる［遅れている］That clock is five *minutes* fast [slow].

▶今3時15分です It is *fifteen minutes* [*a quarter*] *past three*. ／It's *three fifteen*. (➤後者のように数字をそのまま言うことが多い) ‖ 30分後にそちらへ行きます I'll come to see you in *thirty minutes* [in *half an hour*].

▶その店はここから歩いて10分です The store is *a ten-minute walk* from here. ‖ 対話「今何時でしょうか」「4時10分前です」"Do you have the time?" "*Ten* (*minutes*) *to* four."

2【角度·経緯度など】a **minute** ▶東京は北緯35度45分に位置している Tokyo is situated at 35 degrees 45 *minutes* north latitude. (➤35° 45′ N. Lat. と略記する).

▶この角度は厳密には20度30分だ This angle is 20 degrees 30 *minutes* to be exact.

2**ふん 糞** **droppings**(獣や鳥の)；**dung** (特に牛や馬の) ▶通りでは犬のふんは飼い主がきちんと始末すべきだ Dog owners should clean up their dogs' *droppings* [*poo*／*poop*] when on the street. ‖《掲示》犬［猫］のふんは飼い主がきちんと始末してください Clean up after your dog [cat], please. ⇀排泄.

‖ふん尿 feces /fíːsiːz/ and urine /jóərɪn/.

3**ふん** **Phooey!** /fúːi/ (➤嫌悪·不信などを表す)；**Hah!** (➤あざ笑いや喜びを表す) ▶ふん，そんなの信じないね *Phooey*, I don't believe it! ‖ ふん，俺にかけっこで勝てると思ってるのか. まあ見てろ *Hah!* So you think you can beat me in the race? We'll see. ‖ 父さんは私の話をふんふんうなずきながら聞いていた My father listened to what I had to say *with occasional nods* [*nodding occasionally*].

1**ぶん 文** a **sentence**(1つの) ⇀文章 ▶次の日本文を英語に直しなさい Put [Translate] the following Japanese *sentence*(*s*) into English. (● sentences はつながりのない複数の文の場合. まとまった文章の場合は passage とする. ⇀文章).

▶この文は何を言おうとしているのかさっぱりわからない I can't tell at all what this *sentence* is supposed to mean.

ことわざ 文は人なり An author's style reflects the author himself [herself].

2**ぶん 分** **1**【割り当て，分量】one's **share** ▶これがきみの分だ This is *your share*. ‖ 自分の分は自分で払います Let me pay *my share*. ‖ (お菓子など) 私の分も取っておいてよ Keep some *for me*, will you?

▶みんな自分の分だけ払った Everybody paid *their own bills*. (➤bill は「請求金額」) ‖ 《割り勘で》自分の分だけ払ってよ Just cover *yourself*. ‖ 私の分いくら? How much do I *owe*?

▶きょうは1人で2人分の仕事をこなした I did *the work of two people* today. ‖ 薬剤師が3日分の薬をくれた The pharmacist gave me medicine *for three days* [*three days' worth of* medicine]. ‖ 3月分の給料は予想よりも多かった My *pay for March* was more than I had expected.

2【身分】**means** (資力)；one's **place** (地位) ▶分不相応な暮らしをしているといつかそのつけが回ってくるぞ If you go on living *beyond your means*, you'll end up paying for it some day. ‖ きみは社長に口答えするのか. 分をわきまえろ Stop talking back to the president. *Remember your position* (in the company).

3【状態，程度】▶給料は少ないが1人で生活する分には十分だ Although my salary is not great, it is enough *to* support myself.

▶貸し出しはできませんが，図書館で読む分には差し支えありません You can read it in the library, but can't check it out. ‖ 足首を痛めたが，ゆっくり歩く分には(＝限りでは)差し支えない I've got a twisted ankle, but have no difficulty *as long as* I walk slowly. ⇀この分では.

4【分数】▶レポートは3分の2まで書き終えた I finished *two-thirds* of my term paper. ‖ 韓国では国民の4分の1以上がキリスト教徒だ More than *one fourth* of the South Korean population is [are] Christian. (➤名詞を使って are Christians でもよい) ⇀分数 ‖ この日本地図は縮尺1000万分の1だ This map of Japan is drawn to a scale of *one to ten million*.

ぶんあん 文案 a **draft** ▶講演の文案を作る make *a draft* of one's lecture／draft one's lecture.

ぶんい 文意 **the meaning of a sentence** [**passage**].

ふんいき 雰囲気 an **atmosphere** /ǽtməsfɪəʳ/；an **air** (独特の) ▶わが落語クラブには和やかな［家庭的な］雰囲気がある Our *rakugo* club has a friendly [family] *atmosphere*. ‖ 久美子にはおとなの雰囲気がある Kumiko has an adult [a grown-up] *atmosphere* about her.

▶あの女性には神秘的な雰囲気がある That woman has a mysterious *air* about her. ‖ 喫茶店内はやかましくて仕事の話ができる雰囲気ではなかった The coffee shop was noisy and didn't have *an atmosphere* conducive to talking about business. (➤conducive to ... は「…に資する」) ‖ おもしろいことを言ってその場の雰囲気をやわらげる *break the ice* by telling a humorous story.

ふんえん 噴煙 **smoke** (**of a volcano**) ▶阿蘇中岳から噴煙が上がっている *Smoke* is rising from the Nakadake crater on Mt. Aso. ／The Nakadake crater on Mt. Aso is letting off [emitting] *smoke*.

ぶんえん 分煙する **separate smoking and non-smoking areas.**

ふんか 噴火 (an) **eruption** 一動 噴火する **erupt** ▶五色沼は磐梯山の噴火でできた Goshikinuma was created after Mt. Bandai *erupted*.

‖噴火口 a crater.

1**ぶんか 文化** (a) **culture** 一形 文化の **cultural** ▶中国の文化 Chinese *culture* ‖ 文化程度の高い国 a country which has *a high level of culture* ‖ 日本文化の伝統を受け継ぐ inherit *the Japanese cultural tradition*.

▶外国の文化に接する come into contact with *foreign cultures* ‖ 異文化間コミュニケーションに関する講義 a lecture on *intercultural* [*cross-cultural*] communication.

▶どの国にも固有の文化がある Each country has its own unique *culture*. ‖ 木や竹は日本の文化に大きな影響を与えてきた Wood and bamboo have had a great influence on *Japanese culture*. ‖ ここでは古代ローマの文化遺産がよく保存されている The *cultural heritage* of ancient Rome has been well preserved here.

▶韓国との文化交流をいっそう促進する必要がある We need to further promote *cultural exchange* with South Korea.

‖文化勲章 an Order of Cultural Merit, a Cultural Medal ‖文化功労者 a person of Cultural Merit ‖文化国家 a nation with a high level of culture ‖文化祭（→見出語）‖文化財（→見出語）‖文化人 a man [woman] of culture（教養のある人）; a man [woman] in an academic [artistic] career（学問や芸術畑の人）‖文化人類学 cultural anthropology ‖文化庁 the Agency for Cultural Affairs ‖文化の日 Culture Day.

逆引き熟語 ○○文化
異文化 a different culture／外国文化 foreign culture／企業文化 corporate culture／現代文化 contemporary [modern] culture／情報文化 information culture, informatics and culture／食文化 food [culinary] culture（culinary は「料理の」）／大衆文化 mass [pop, popular] culture／多文化 multiculturalism, cultural diversity／使い捨て文化 a throwaway culture／伝統文化 traditional culture／比較文化 comparative culture／若者文化 youth culture

²ぶんか 文科 (the) humanities（人文科学）; (the) liberal arts（教養学科目）▶文科系の学生 a college student *studying the humanities* ‖きみは理科系よりも文科系のほうが向いているようだ It seems like (the) *humanities* would suit you better than (the) sciences.

³ぶんか 分化 differentiation ; specialization（特化）▶役割は明確に分化されている The roles *are* clearly *differentiated*.

ふんがい 憤慨 indignation /ìndɪgnéɪʃən/（不当な扱いや不正などに対する）; resentment（他人の言動や自分の置かれた状況などに対する）一動 憤慨する get indignant ▶ぼくは事務員のいいかげんな応対に憤慨した I *got indignant* with the clerk because of his lackadaisical attitude. ‖彼女は，女性は男性ほど頭がよくないという彼の性差別発言に憤慨した She *resented* his sexist remark about women not being as smart as men.
▶きみが憤慨するのも無理はない You have every reason to *be indignant* [*exasperated*].（➤ be exasperated は「激しいいらだちを感じる」の意）.

ぶんかい 分解する 1【物をばらばらに】take apart ; dismantle ＋目（機械・装置などを）▶テレビを分解する *take* a TV *apart* [*to pieces*] ‖故障の原因を調べるために車を分解する *dismantle* a car to find out what is wrong with it.
▶ヘリコプターが空中分解した The helicopter *fell apart* [*disintegrated*] *in midair*.
2【化学的に】resolve ▶水を酸素と水素に分解する *resolve* [*separate*] water into oxygen and hydrogen.

ぶんがく 文学 literature /lɪ́tərətʃəʳ/ 一形 文学の literary /lɪ́təreri/ ▶イギリス[アメリカ]文学 British [American] *literature*（➤ English literature とすると「イングランド文学」または「英語で書かれた文学」の意に解される）‖古典[現代／比較]文学 classical [modern／comparative] *literature* ‖文学を鑑賞する appreciate *literature* ‖文学を志す aspire to a *literary career*.
‖文学界 the literary world ‖文学作品 a literary work ‖文学史 a history of literature ‖文学者 a writer（作家）; a man [woman] of letters（著述家）; a literary man [woman]（文学研究家，作家）‖文学賞 a literary award [prize] ‖文学博士 a Doctor of Literature [Letters]《略 Litt. D.》‖文学部 the school [college] of literature ; the school [college] of the humanities（➤ 哲学科・心理学科・史学科などを含む）‖文学論 literary criticism.

ぶんかさい 文化祭 a cultural festival ; a school festival（学校の）
日本紹介 ✉ **文化祭は高校や大学で，年に1日～2日間行う催しで，文化サークルの研究発表，コンサート，演劇の上演，講演会などを行います．ふつう，学生たちが中心になって企画運営します** A *bunkasai* is an annual one or two day event held at senior high schools or colleges. It consists of presentations of research results by cultural societies, concerts, performances of drama, lectures and other activities. Usually the students plan and organize the entire event by themselves.
✉ **来週学校で文化祭があります．今その準備で大忙しです** We have *a school festival* next week. Now, we're very busy preparing for it.
✉ **文化祭では私たちのクラスはホットドッグの模擬店をやりました** During the *school festival*, our class ran a hot dog stand.

ぶんかざい 文化財 cultural assets
‖重要文化財 an important cultural asset ‖無形文化財 an intangible cultural asset（➤ intangible は「触れることができない」の意）.

ぶんかつ 分割 division 一動 分割する divide ＋目 ▶ドイツは大戦後2つに分割された Germany *was divided* into two parts after the war.

ぶんかつばらい 分割払い installment plan,《英また》hire-purchase (system) ▶冷蔵庫を10回の分割払いで買う buy a refrigerator on a 10-month *installment plan* ‖このコンピュータは分割払いで買えますか Can I buy this computer *on the installment plan* [*on easy payment*]?

ぶんかん 文官 a civil servant.

ふんき 奮起する rouse /raʊz/ oneself ▶今こそ奮起すべきときだ It is time for us to *rouse* [*stir*] *ourselves* (*to action*).
▶彼の話を聞いて奮起し，もっと努力する気になった His story *spurred* me on to greater effort.（➤ spur は「刺激する」）／His story *inspired* me to try harder.

ぶんきてん 分岐点 a fork（道路・川の）; a parting of the ways（道路の）; a crossroads（人生の岐路）▶きみは今人生の分岐点に立っている You're now (standing) at *a crossroads* in your life.
▶米原は東海道本線と北陸本線の分岐点にあたる The Hokuriku Trunk Line *branches off* from the Tokaido Trunk Line at Maibara.

ふんきゅう 紛糾 disorder（秩序などの乱れ）; (a) confusion（入り乱れていること）一動 紛糾する get complicated, confuse ▶その予算を通すかどうかで市議会は紛糾した The city assembly *fell into disorder* [*was thrown into confusion*] whether to pass the budget.
▶ここであなたが口出しすると事態はますます紛糾しますよ If you stick your nose into this business now, it's going to *get* more and more *confusing* [*complicated*].

ぶんきょう 文教 ▶八王子は大学がたくさんある文教地区だ Hachioji is *an education-oriented area* with

many universities.
‖文教予算 an education budget.
ぶんぎょう 分業 (a) division of labor ▶分業はしばしば製品を作る上で最も簡単で安上がりの方法だ *A division of labor* is often the easiest and cheapest way to make products.
ぶんきょくか 分極化 polarization.
ふんぎり 踏ん切り ▶転職すべきかどうか私はまだふんぎりがつかない I *have not* yet *made up my mind* whether to change my job or not. ／I *am* still *hesitating* [still *uncertain*] whether to change jobs or not.
ぶんけ 分家 a branch family 一動 分家する set up a branch family.
1ぶんけい 文系 the humanities [liberal arts] course → 文科.
2ぶんけい 文型 a sentence pattern.
ぶんげい 文芸 literature /lɪ́tərətʃəʳ/ (文学) ; art and literature (文学と芸術) 一形 文芸の literary /lɪ́təreri/ ▶私は文芸部員です I am *a member of the literature club*.
‖文芸作品 a literary work ‖ 文芸批評[評論] literary criticism ‖ 文芸復興 the Renaissance ‖ 文芸欄(新聞などの) a literary column [section／page].
1ぶんけん 文献 literature /lɪ́tərətʃəʳ/ ▶楼蘭に関する文献 *literature* on Loulan.
‖参考文献 reference books ; a bibliography /bìbliɑ́:grəfi/ (目録).
2ぶんけん 分権 decentralization (of authority) (地方分権).
ぶんこ 文庫 a library ▶学級文庫 a class *library* ‖ その作家の小説のほとんどは文庫本で読んだ I have read almost all the novels by that author *in pocket editions*. 《参考》英米とも本のサイズは規格化されておらず, 日本のような文庫本サイズは少ない.
ぶんご 文語 written language (書きことば) ; a literary word (雅語) ; classical(-style) language (古典様式の言語) ▶藤村の詩は文語(体)で書かれている Toson's poems are written *in classical-style Japanese*.
ぶんこう 分校 a branch school.
ぶんごう 文豪 a great writer, a literary giant ▶ロシアの文豪トルストイ Tolstoy, the Russian *literary giant* ‖ 森鷗外は文豪の名にふさわしい作家だ Mori Ogai deserves to be called *a great writer*.
ふんさい 粉砕する 1【細かく砕く】 shatter +目 ; pulverize +目 (粉末にする) ▶空き瓶を粉砕する *shatter* empty bottles ‖ 穀物を粉砕する機械 a machine that *pulverizes* grain ‖ ダイナマイトで岩石を粉砕する *break* rocks *into fragments* [*into small pieces*] with dynamite.
2【徹底的に打ち破る】 crush +目 ▶敵を粉砕する *crush* [*smash*] one's enemy ‖ 人員削減案断固粉砕! *Down with* the personnel reduction plan!
ぶんさい 文才 literary talent ▶谷崎は早くから文才をうたわれた Tanizaki was lauded for his *literary talent* from his early days.
ぶんさん 分散する scatter +目, disperse +目 ▶全国に分散している資料を1か所に集める collect reference material which *is* [materials which *are*] *scattered* throughout the country ‖ 我々はグループに分散してシカゴに向かった We *broke* [*split*] *up into groups* and headed for Chicago.
1ぶんし 分子 a molecule /mɑ́:ləkju:l/ (化学の) ; a numerator /njú:mərèɪtəʳ/ (分数の) ; elements (一部の者) ▶それは一部危険分子のしわざだ It was the work of *dangerous elements*.
‖分子式 a molecular formula ‖ 分子量 molecular weight.
2ぶんし 分詞 《文法》 a participle
‖分詞構文 a participial construction ‖ 過去[現在]分詞 a past [present] participle.
ふんしつ 紛失 loss 一動 紛失する lose +目 ▶どこかで定期券を紛失した I *lost* my commuter pass somewhere. ‖ 金庫の中のお金が紛失した The money in the safe *has gone missing*.
▶母は銀行にクレジットカードの紛失届けをした My mother *reported the loss* of her credit card to the bank.
‖紛失物 a lost [missing] article [item].
ぶんしつ 分室 a branch office.
ふんしゃ 噴射 ▶白い煙を噴射しながらロケットは空に吸い込まれていった A rocket disappeared into the sky *shooting out* white smoke.
ぶんしゃ 分社 ▶製造部門を分社化する *spin off* the production division *as a separate company*.
ぶんしゅう 文集 a collection of compositions ▶私たちは高校卒業記念に文集を作った We edited *a collection of our compositions* to commemorate our high school graduation.
‖卒業文集 a school yearbook.
ふんしゅつ 噴出する spout /spaʊt/ (+目), gush (out) (➤ gush は「多量にほとばしり出る」というニュアンス) ▶古い水道管が破裂して水が噴出した Water *spouted* [*gushed*] from a burst old pipe.
▶株主総会で株主から不満が噴出した *There was a barrage* [*torrent*] *of complaints* from stockholders at the general meeting. (➤ barrage は「集中砲火」, torrent は「嵐」).
ぶんしょ 文書 a document (公の, またはパソコンで作成した) ; papers (書類) ; writing (書き物) ▶極秘文書 a top-secret *document* ‖ 子供の出生は2週間以内に文書で届け出なければならない A child's birth must be reported *in written form* [*in writing*] within 14 days.
▶中身が何かはっきりわかっていない限り文書を開くな Do not open a *document* unless you are sure you know what it contains.
‖(会社などの)文書課 the legal section.
ぶんしょう 文章 writing (書いた物) ; a sentence (文) ; a composition (作文) ; a passage (1節) ▶自分の考えを文章にまとめる put one's ideas down in *writing* ‖ 作家にも読みやすい文章を書く人と難しい文章を書く人とがいる Some novelists write easy-to-read *sentences* and others hard ones. ‖ 次の文章を100語以内で要約せよ Summarize the following *passage* within 100 words. (● sentences としない. こうすると前後の脈絡のない複数の文章の意になる) ‖ 彼女の文章は難しい Her *writing style* is difficult. ‖ 彼は文章がうまい[下手だ] He *is a good* [*bad*] *writer*. ／He *writes well* [*poorly*].

直訳の落とし穴「文章がうまい」
文章＝sentence であることから,「彼女は文章がうまい」「彼女はいい文章を書く」などを (×) Her sentences are good., (×) She writes good sentences. などとしがち. 複数形の sentences は前後につながりのない個々の文になってしまう. どちらの英文も文法的には正しいが, 日本語でいっているのは個々の文章が悪文や誤文でないということではなく, 書くものに表現力があるということであるから, She writes well. または, Her writing is good. とする.「川端の文章は美しい」も Kawabata's writing is beautiful. となる.

[1]**ぶんじょう 分譲** subdivision /sʌ́bdɪvìʒən/ ▶土地を分譲する *sell* the land *by* [*in*] *lots* ‖ おじは最近郊外に分譲住宅を買った My uncle bought *a house in a subdivision* in the suburbs recently.

‖**分譲地** a subdivision, subdivided housing lots, land for sale in lots ‖ **分譲マンション** a condominium,《米・インフォーマル》a condo.

[2]**ぶんじょう 分乗** ▶我々は車3台に分乗した We *rode separately* in three cars.

ふんしょく 粉飾 embellishment, window dressing

‖**粉飾決算** accounting fraud.

ふんしん 分針 the minute hand (of a clock [watch]).

ふんじん 粉塵 dust ▶アスベスト[石炭]の粉塵 asbestos [coal] *dust*.

‖**粉塵公害** dust pollution.

ぶんしん 分身 an alter ego, an alternate self [identity].

ぶんじん 文人 a literary person, a man [woman] of letters (➤やや古風な言い方).

ふんすい 噴水 a fountain ▶噴水が出ていない The *fountain* isn't on. ‖ 噴水が勢いよく出ている The *fountain* is gushing vigorously.

ぶんすいれい 分水嶺 a watershed.

ぶんすう 分数《数学》a fraction ━形 **分数の** fractional

《解説》**分数の読み方**
(1)分数を読むときは分子を基数で先に, 分母を序数であとに読む. 例えば ⅓ は one third または a third と読む.
(2)分子が2以上の場合は, 分母は複数形になる. したがって, ⅔ は two thirds, ⅗ は three fifths と読む.
(3) $^{29}/_{33}$ のように複雑なものは over を用いて twenty-nine over thirty-three と表現するとよい.

‖**分数式** a fractional expression ‖ **仮分数** an improper fraction ‖ **帯分数** a mixed fraction.

ふんする 扮する ▶玉三郎は舞台で楊貴妃にふんした Tamasaburo *played the part* [*role*] *of* Yang Gui-fei on the stage.

[1]**ぶんせき 分析** (an) analysis [複 analyses] ━動 **分析する** analyze /ǽnəlaɪz/ +目 ▶分析の結果, そのジュースには毒が含まれていることがわかった *Analysis* showed that the juice contained poison. ‖ 調査団は事故の原因を分析した The panel *analyzed* the cause of the accident.

‖**化学分析** (a) chemical analysis ‖ **精神分析** psychoanalysis ‖ **データ分析** data analysis.

[2]**ぶんせき 文責** responsibility for the wording [content] of an article.

ふんせん 奮戦 ▶我々は奮戦及ばず1回戦で敗退した Though we put up *a hard* [*stiff*] *fight*, we lost the first match and were eliminated.

ふんぜん 憤然と ▶彼は憤然として席を立った He stood up from his seat *in a rage* [*indignantly*].

[1]**ふんそう 扮装** (a) make-up; (a) disguise /dɪsgáɪz/ (変装) ━動 **ふん装する** be made up《as》, be disguised《as》, disguise oneself《as》

▶校長先生は殿様のふん装をした The (school) principal *was made up as* a feudal lord. ‖ 彼は女性にふん装した He *was disguised* [He *disguised himself*] *as* a woman.

[2]**ふんそう 紛争** a dispute (争い); (a) conflict (矛盾対立して相いれないこと; 闘争) ▶国連はその国際紛争を平和的に解決した The United Nations settled the *international dispute* peacefully. ‖ 両国間で国境紛争が起こった *A border dispute* arose between the two countries.

‖**学園紛争** campus strife [dispute], a student riot ‖ **民族紛争** a racial dispute, an ethnic conflict.

ふんぞりかえる ふんぞり返る ▶社長は椅子にふんぞり返っていた Our boss *was sitting back proudly* in his chair.

▶《比喩的》彼は会社でふんぞり返っている (＝いばっている) He *behaves arrogantly* in the office.

ぶんたい 文体 (a) style ▶この小説は平易な文体で書かれている This novel is written *in* (*a*) *plain* [*simple*] *style*.

ふんだくる snatch +目 (ひったくる); rip off (ぼる) ▶スコッチウイスキー1本で1万円もふんだくられた I *got ripped off* ten thousand yen for one bottle of Scotch whisky.

ふんだりけったり 踏んだり蹴ったり ▶彼には振られるし, その彼ときたら私の親友と付き合い始めるし, 全く踏んだりけったりだわ My boyfriend just broke up with me. And *to add insult to injury*, he's now going out with one of my closest friends. (➤add insult to injury は「さらに追い打ちをかける」の意).

ふんだんに amply ▶地元の野菜をふんだんに使った料理 a dish cooked using *plenty of* local vegetables ‖ 草津では温泉がふんだんにわき出ている Hot water wells up *amply* at Kusatsu. ‖ これはカカオをふんだんに使ったまろやかなチョコレートです This is a mellow [mild] chocolate that contains *a generous amount of* cacao.

ぶんたん 分担 one's share ━動 **分担する** share +目 (仕事・費用などを); split +目 (費用・もうけなどを) ▶私は自分の仕事の分担は済ませた I did *my share* of the work. ‖ 我々は食費を分担し合った We *shared* [*split*] the food expenses.

▶各クラスで分担して校庭の掃除をした We *divided the work* among the classes and cleaned the schoolyard.

[1]**ぶんだん 文壇** the literary world, literary circles ▶その作家は文壇に新風を吹き込んだ That writer breathed new life into *the literary world* [into *literary circles*].

[2]**ぶんだん 分断する** divide into parts ▶朝鮮は南北2つに分断されている Korea *is divided* into two parts, North and South.

▶台風で鉄道が分断された Train service was *disrupted* [*cut off*] by the typhoon.

ぶんちょう 文鳥《鳥》a Java sparrow.

ぶんちん 文鎮 a paper weight.

ぶんつう 文通 correspondence ━動 **文通する** exchange letters《with》, correspond《with》

▶私はシンガポールの高校生と文通を始めた I began to *exchange letters* [*correspond*] *with* a high school student in Singapore.

✉ **私と文通していただけませんか** Can we start writing letters to each other?

✉ **宇宙探査に関心のある人, 英語で文通しませんか. 性別・年齢は問いません** I'm looking for a pen pal who is interested in space exploration and will correspond with me in English. Gender and age don't matter.

‖文通友だち a pen pal.

ふんとう 奮闘 a struggle **━動** **奮闘する** struggle ▶雄二はその幾何の問題を解こうと30分も奮闘した Yuji *struggled* [*worked hard*] for a whole 30 minutes trying to solve the geometry problem. ‖日本選手は奮闘したが皆予選落ちした Though they *fought hard*, the Japanese athletes were all eliminated in the preliminaries.

ぶんとう 文頭 the beginning of a sentence [document／passage] (➤カッコ内は「文章」の意).

ぶんどき 分度器 a protractor.

ふんどし 褌 a *fundoshi*; a (Japanese traditional) loincloth ▶ふんどしを締める wear *a fundoshi*.

▶《慣用表現》あいつは人のふんどしで相撲をとるのが得意だ He is good at *taking risks with other people's money*. (➤「他人の金で勝負する」の意).

ぶんどる 分捕る seize +目, grab +目 ▶次郎は子供たちのおやつを分捕った Jiro *grabbed* [*seized*／*snatched away*] the little boys' snacks.

ぶんなぐる ぶん殴る slug +目, wallop +目 ▶あのいじめっ子をぶん殴ってやりたい I'd like to *slug* the bully.

ふんにゅう 粉乳 powdered milk.

ふんにょう 糞尿 excreta /ɪkskríːṭə/ (排せつ物); human waste (人間の).

ぶんのう 分納 ▶授業料を分納する *pay* (one's) tuition *in installments*.

ぶんぱ 分派 a faction.

ぶんばい 分売する sell separately.

ぶんぱい 分配 division, (a) distribution **━動** **分配する** divide +目 (分ける); distribute /dɪstríbjuːt/ +目 (自分は取らずに人に分ける) ▶利益はみんなで分配しよう Let's *divide* the profits among us. ‖彼の父は財産を平等に3人の子供に分配した His father *distributed* [*divided*] his property equally among his three children.

ふんぱつ 奮発 ▶彼女はボーイにチップを奮発した She tipped the bellboy *generously*. (➤「気前よくチップを渡した」の意)／She gave the bellboy a *handsome* tip. (➤この handsome は「たっぷりの」の意) ‖奮発して3万円のセーター買っちゃった I *splurged on* a thirty-thousand-yen sweater. (➤ splurge は「ぜいたくをする」).

ふんばり 踏ん張り ▶もうひと踏ん張りだ We need to *make one last effort*!

ふんばる 踏ん張る stand firm ▶足を踏ん張る *stand firm* with one's legs wide apart ‖把瑠都は土俵際で踏ん張った Baruto *stood firm* so that he would not be pushed out of the ring.

▶《比喩的》踏ん張れ. もう一息だ One last effort [spurt]! ‖多くは脱落したが彼女は最後まで踏ん張った Many dropped out, but she *stuck with it* to the end. (➤ stuck は stick (しがみつく)の過去形).

[1]**ぶんぴ(つ) 分泌** 《生物学》secretion /sɪkríːʃən/ **━動** **分泌する** secrete +目 ▶胃は胃液を分泌する The stomach *secretes* gastric juices.

‖分泌腺 a secretory gland, a secretory ‖分泌物[液] a secretion.

[2]**ぶんぴつ 文筆** ▶彼は文筆で暮らしを立てている He writes for a living.

‖文筆家 a writer ‖文筆業 the literary profession.

ぶんぶ 文武 ▶わが校は伝統的に文武両道に秀でている Our (high) school has a tradition of excellence in *both learning* [*academic studies*] *and sports*.

ぶんぷ 分布 (a) distribution ▶人口の分布 the *distribution* of population ‖この種のチョウは日本に広く分布している This species of butterfly *is* widely *distributed* in Japan. ‖杉は北海道を除く日本各地に分布している Japanese cedars *grow* throughout Japan, excluding Hokkaido.

▶ビーバーはアメリカからカナダにかけて分布している Beavers *are found* in an area spanning from the U.S. to Canada.

‖分布図 a distribution map [chart].

ぶんぶつ 文物 the products of civilization ▶遣唐使は大陸の進んだ文物を日本に持ち帰った Envoys to China during the Tang Dynasty returned home with sophisticated *products* [*artworks*] *of* continental *civilization*.

ぶんぶん ▶ハエが(頭上で)ブンブン飛び回っている There are flies *buzzing around* (my head). ‖中村選手はバットをブンブン振り回す The player Nakamura *brandishes* his bat.

ぷんぷん ▶この辺りはガソリンのにおいがぷんぷんする There's a *strong* smell of gasoline around here. ‖エミはいつもニンニクのにおいをぷんぷんさせている Emi always *reeks of* garlic. (➤ reek of は「(強い臭いを)放つ」).

▶あの女の人ぷんぷん怒って帰って行ったけど, どうしたの? What happened to that lady? She left *in a huff*.

ふんべつ 分別 discretion /dɪskréʃən/ (自制する力, 思慮); good sense (良識)

▶分別のある人 a person of *discretion* [*good sense*]／a *sensible* person ‖彼は年の割には分別がある He *is sensible* for his age.

▶分別盛りのいいおとながなぜあんな事件を起こしたのかしら Why did an adult *old enough to know better* do such a thing? (➤ know better で「分別がある」) ‖うちの息子は17歳なのに分別臭いことをする Although he's only seventeen, my son acts *like a real know-it-all*. (➤「何でもわかっているという顔だ」の意).

ぶんべつ 分別 ▶我々はごみをきちんと分別すべきだ We should *sort* our trash properly.

‖分別ごみ sorted trash, divided garbage [rubbish].

ぶんべん 分娩 a delivery, childbirth **━動** **分娩する** give birth 《to》 ▶無痛分娩 a painless *delivery*.

‖分娩室 a delivery room ‖自然分娩 natural childbirth, a natural delivery.

ぶんぼ 分母 《数学》a denominator ▶分母をそろえる find the common *denominator* ‖分母を払いなさい Cancel the *denominator*.

ぶんぽう 文法 grammar **━形** **文法の** grammatical ▶日本語の文法 Japanese *grammar* ‖この表現は文法にかなっていない This expression is *ungrammatical* [is *not grammatical*]. ‖きみの作文は少数の文法上の誤りを除けば大変よろしい Your composition is very good except for a few *errors in grammar* [*grammatical errors*]. (● grammatical に「文法にかなった」の意があるため, grammatical error が「文法にかなった誤り」と解釈されかねないので前者のような言い方のほうがわかりやすい).

‖文法家[学者] a grammarian ‖文法書 a grammar (book).

ぶんぼうぐ 文房具 stationery, writing materials (➤ともに主に筆記に用いる鉛筆やペン, ノートや便せんなどを指す) ▶このボールペンは学校の近くの文房具店で買った I bought this ballpoint pen at *a stationery store* [*a stationer's*] near our school.

「文房具」のいろいろ 赤鉛筆 red pencil ／色鉛筆 colored pencil ／インク ink ／鉛筆削り pencil sharpener ／カッター (box) cutter ／紙 paper ／クリップ paper clip ／計算機 calculator ／消しゴム eraser ／コンパス compass ／サインペン felt-tip pen ／三角定規 triangle ／シャープペン mechanical pencil ／修正液 correction fluid ／定規 ruler ／セロテープ adhesive tape, Scotch tape ／ディバイダー dividers ／ノート notebook ／のり paste, glue ／バインダー ring binder ／はさみ scissors ／ 便せん notepaper, (a sheet of) letter paper [writing paper] ; a writing pad (１冊の) ／ファイル file ／封筒 envelope ／分度器 protractor ／ペン pen ／ボールペン ballpoint pen ／ホチキス stapler ／万年筆 fountain pen ／メモ帳 memo [scratch] pad ／ルーペ magnifying glass

ふんまつ 粉末 **powder** ; a **granule** /grǽnju:l/ (顆粒) ▶この薬には錠剤と粉末がある This medicine comes in pill or *powder form*.

ぶんまつ 文末 **the end of a sentence** [**document** ／ **passage**] (➤ カッコ内は「文章」の意).

ふんまん 憤懣 **indignation** ; (**righteous**) **anger** (義憤) ▶信頼していた男に裏切られてふんまんやるかたなしだ I'*m totally indignant* at him for betraying my trust. →やるかたない.

ぶんみゃく 文脈 (a) **context** /kά:ntekst/ ▶文脈からこの単語の意味を推測しなさい Guess the meaning of this word from its [the] *context*.

ぶんみん 文民 a **civilian**
‖**文民統制** civilian control.

ふんむき 噴霧器 a **spray**(**er**) ▶噴霧器を使って盆栽を消毒する use *a spray*(*er*) to fumigate the bonsai.

ぶんめい 文明 (a) **civilization** ▶西洋文明 *Western civilization* ‖古代メソポタミア文明 ancient Mesopotamian *civilization* ‖古代文明の発祥地 the birthplace of *ancient civilization* ‖文明の利器 *products of modern civilization* ／ *modern conveniences*.
▶文明の進歩に伴って我々はものぐさになっているようだ It seems that we are becoming lazy as *civilization* advances [with the advance of *civilization*]. ‖ユカタン半島には高度の文明が栄えた *A highly-developed civilization* flourished on the Yucatán Peninsula.
‖**文明国** a civilized country [nation] ‖**文明社会** a civilized society.

ぶんめん 文面 ▶手紙の文面からすると彼女は相当悩んでいるようだ Judging from her *letter*, she seems to be seriously worried.

ぶんや 分野 a **field**(領域) ; a **branch** (部門) ▶それは私の得意の分野です That's *a field* I'm good in [I'm knowledgeable about]. ／That *field* is my specialty.
▶科学といってもいろいろな分野がある There are many *branches* of science. ‖きみの研究分野は何ですか What is your *field of study* ? ‖彼は専門分野において多くの業績をあげている He has produced many works in *his own field*.
▶生物は私のいちばん苦手な分野（＝学科）だ Biology is my worst *subject*.

ぶんらく 文楽 **Bunraku**, a **Bunraku puppet show** [**theater**]
日本紹介 ✉ **文楽は日本の伝統的な操り人形芝居のことで, 太夫, 三味線弾き, 人形使いによって演じられます. 一体の人形は３人の人形使いが操ります** *Bunraku* is the traditional puppet theater. It is performed by a team made up of a ballad-reciting chanter, the *shamisen* accompanist, and the three operators required for each puppet.

ぶんり 分離 **separation** 一動 **分離する** **separate** /sépəreɪt/ 《from》 ▶油は水と分離する Oil *separates from* water. ‖ケベック州にはカナダからの分離独立を主張する人々がいる In Quebec, there are people who are demanding *separation and independence* from Canada.
▶彼らは党から分離した They *broke away from* the party.
‖**中央分離帯** 《米》 a median (strip), 《英》 a central reserve [reservation] ‖**歩車分離方式** a system of separate signals for traffic and pedestrians.

ぶんりつ 分立 **separation**
‖**三権分立** the separation of (executive, legislative and judicial) powers.

ぶんりゅう 分流 a **fork** (**of a river**).

ぶんりょう 分量 a **quantity** ▶そのケーキを作るのに小麦粉はどのくらいの分量が必要ですか *How much* flour do you need for that cake ? (➤ quantity を使うと堅い文になる) ‖砂糖と塩の分量を間違えないようにしましょう Let's not make a mistake in the *amount* of salt and sugar. ‖体調が悪いので仕事の分量を減らしてください Please *give me less work to do* because I don't feel well. ‖薬の分量 *the dosage* of a medicine.

ぶんるい 分類 (a) **classification** 一動 **分類する** **classify** +㊐ ; **group** +㊐ (大ざっぱに) ; **sort** +㊐ (えり分ける) ▶切手を発行年順に分類する *classify* stamps according to the year of issue ‖人間の血液型は基本的に４つに分類される Human blood *is classified* into four basic types.
▶先生は生徒たちにテーマ別に本を分類するように頼んだ The teacher asked his students to *classify* [*group*] the books by subject. (➤ classify はたとえば本を１冊１冊, 小説・歴史書・実用書など, どのカテゴリーに属するかを判断していくこと. group は同じカテゴリーの本を寄せ集めるということ) ‖どんな分類方法を用いたのですか？ What kind of *classification system* did you use ?
‖(動植物の) **分類法** [**学**] (a) taxonomy.

ぶんれつ 分裂 (a) **division** ; a **split** (仲間割れ) 一動 **分裂する** **divide, split** ▶ゾウリムシは22時間後に２つに分裂する The paramecium will *divide* into two after twenty-two hours.
▶その党は５派に分裂した The party (*was*) *split* into five factions.
‖**核分裂** nuclear fission ‖**細胞分裂** cell division.

ふんわり ▶ふんわりした生地 *light* [*fluffy*] material ‖ふんわりしたモヘアのセーター a *fluffy* mohair sweater ‖パラシュートがふんわり降りてくる様子は美しい It is wonderful to see a parachute *gently* float down.

へ・へ

へ 屁 a **fart** 一**動** **へをする fart, let out a fart** (➤ fart は露骨な語なのでふつうは pass gas またはその婉曲(えんきょく)表現の break wind を用いる) ▶《慣用表現》あいつが俺のことをどう思おうとへとも思わないね I *don't give a damn* [*a crap*] what he thinks about me. ‖ そんなのへのかっぱだよ It's *a piece of cake*. (➤「簡単だ, 朝めし前だ」の意). →おなら.

ーへ 1【動作の方向を示して】**to, toward, for**

> **語法** **to** は到着地点や目的の場所を示すときに, **toward** は単に運動の方向を示すときに, **for** は主に交通機関などの行き先を示すときに用いる.

▶この夏, 佐渡へ旅行に行く予定だ We're planning to take a trip *to* Sado this summer. ‖ 駅へはこの道でいいですか Is this the right way *to* the train station? ‖ 彼は玄関の方へ歩いて行った He walked *toward* the front door. (➤ 本当に玄関まで行ったかどうかは不明. to を使うとそこまで行ったことがはっきりする) ‖ たくさんの鳥が南へ飛んで行く A lot of birds are flying *south* [*toward the south*].

▶家へ帰る go *home* ‖ 外国へ行く go *overseas* [*abroad*] (➤ この2例では「へ」は home, overseas [abroad] という副詞の中に含まれている. 次の2例も同様) ‖ こっちへいらっしゃい Come *here*. ‖ 次の角で左へ曲がりなさい Turn *left* at the next corner.

▶これは千葉へ行く電車ですか Is this the train *for* Chiba? ‖ 彼女はきのうアメリカへたった She left *for* the U.S. yesterday.

▶母は日本橋へ[デパートへ]買い物に行った My mother went shopping *in* Nihonbashi [*at* a department store]. (➤ go shopping to Nihonbashi とは言わない).

▶彼らは鎌倉へ[郊外へ／新居へ]引っ越した They have moved *to* Kamakura [*into* the suburbs / *into* their new home]. ‖ 男はあっちの方へ行った The man went *in that direction*. ‖ こちらへお越しの節はぜひお立ち寄りください Please drop in when you happen to come *this way*.

▶彼は箱を棚の上へ上げた He put the box *on* the shelf. ‖ 猫は机の上へ飛び上がった The cat jumped *onto* the desk.

2【動作の対象を示して】**for, to** ▶これはあなたへのささやかな贈り物です This is a little gift *for* you. ‖《贈り物の上書き》隆君へ *To* Takashi.

3【「…ところへ」の形で】▶出掛けようとしているところへ電話がかかってきた *Just as* I was going out, the telephone rang. / I was *just* going out *when* the telephone rang.

ヘア hair(毛) ; **pubic hair** (陰毛)
‖ヘアクリーム hair cream ‖ ヘアスタイル a hairstyle ‖ ヘアスプレー hair spray ‖ ヘアダイ hair dye ‖ ヘアトニック a hair tonic ‖ ヘアドライヤー a hair dryer ‖ ヘアバンド a headband ‖ ヘアピース a hairpiece ‖ ヘアピン a hairpin (U字形のピン) ‖ ヘアブラシ a hairbrush ‖ ヘアローション hair lotion.

☞ ヘアマニキュア, ヘアリキッド (→見出語)

ベア →ベースアップ.

ペア a **pair** ▶友人たちはみんなペアになって歌った All of my friends sang together *in pairs*. ‖ 私はきのうテニスの試合で大学生とペアを組んだ I *was paired with* a college student in the tennis match yesterday. ‖ きみは誰とペアを組むの? Who are you going to *pair up with*? ‖ 彼は典子とペアを組んだ He *paired off with* Noriko.
‖ペアルック matching outfits [clothes], his-and-her outfits (➤ his-and-her outfits は広告用語)《参考》「ふたりはペアルックが好きだ」は The two like dressing alike. という.

ヘアピンカーブ a **hairpin curve** [**turn** / **bend**] ▶ヘアピンカーブを切り抜ける negotiate [swerve around] *hairpin curves*. →カーブ.

ヘアマニキュア demi-permanent hair coloring (色をつけること) ; a **demi-permanent hair color(ing) product** (製品) (➤ ヘアマニキュアは和製語 ; 「マニキュア」は手や指の手入れという意味であり, ヘアとは結びつかない ; demi- /démi/ は「半-」の意).

ヘアリキッド hair tonic (➤ ヘアリキッドは和製語で日本独自のもの).

1へい 塀 a **wall** (土・石・れんがなどの) ; a **fence** (囲い) ▶塀越しに見る look over *a wall* ‖ 猫がブロック[土/板]塀の上を歩いていた A cat was walking along on the *concrete block wall* [the *earthen wall* / the *board fence*]. ‖ 彼らは家の周囲に高い塀を巡らせた They built a high *wall* surrounding their house.

2へい 兵 an **army, troops** (➤ 前者は軍隊全部に, 後者は兵員に重点を置いた語. 1人1人の「兵士」は soldier) ▶兵を挙げる raise *an army* ‖ 兵を進める move *troops* ‖ 沖縄には2万以上のアメリカ兵が駐留している More than 20,000 *U.S. troops* are stationed in Okinawa. (➤ 1人1人の「アメリカ兵」は a U.S. soldier).
▶ナポレオンは60万の兵とともにロシアに攻め入った Napoleon marched into Russia with *an army* of six hundred thousand *men*.

へいあん 平安 peace ▶日々平安に暮らす live *peacefully* every day.
‖平安時代 the Heian period ‖ 平安京 Heian-kyo, the Heian Capital.

へいい 平易な easy (やさしい) ; **plain** (明白でわかりやすい) ; **simple** (簡単な) ▶平易な英語 *plain* English ‖ ウィリアム・ジェームズは平易な文章で哲学を説いた William James explained philosophy in *simple* prose.

へいえき 兵役 military service ▶彼は2年間兵役に服したことがある He *was* once *in the military* (*service*) for two years. / He once *served in the army* [*navy*] for two years. (➤ navy は海軍の場合) ‖ その国ではオリンピックのメダル受賞者は兵役を免除される Olympic medalists are exempt [exempted] from *military service* in that country.

へいおん 平穏な quiet (活動の少ない, 静かな) ; **tranquil** (穏やかで安らげる) ; **peaceful** (平安な) ; **uneventful**

(波乱のない) ▶被災された方々が一日も早く以前の**平穏**な日々[暮らし]に戻れますようにと心より願っております I sincerely hope that the disaster victims can go back as soon as possible to the *peaceful* days [*tranquil* life] they previously enjoyed. ‖ことしも**平穏無事**でありますように May we live *safely and peacefully* [*in peace and security*] this year, too!

へいか 陛下 **His Majesty** /mǽdʒəsti/ **(the Emperor)**(天皇); **Her Majesty (the Empress)**(皇后) (➤ 直接呼びかける場合は, 天皇・皇后ともに Your Majesty となる) ▶エリザベス女王**陛下** *Her Majesty* Queen Elizabeth ‖天皇皇后**両陛下** *Their Majesties* the Emperor and Empress.

べいか 米価 **the price of rice, (the) rice price**
‖**米価審議会** the Rice Price Council ‖**消費者[生産者]米価** (the) consumer [producer] rice price.

へいかい 閉会する **close (a meeting)** ▶会は校歌を歌って**閉会した** The meeting *was closed* after the singing of their school song. ‖会は5時に**閉会に**なった(=終わった) The meeting *ended* at five. ‖これで**閉会にいたします** This *concludes* [*wraps up*] *our meeting*.
‖**閉会式** a closing ceremony ‖**閉会の辞** a closing address

へいがい 弊害 a **bad effect**(悪い結果); a **harmful influence**(有害な影響) ▶飲み過ぎの**弊害**はいくら強調してもし過ぎることはない The *bad effects* of drinking too much (alcohol) cannot be emphasized enough.

へいかん 閉館 ▶《掲示》**閉館**(中) Closed ‖その図書館は午後7時に**閉館する** The library *closes* at 7 p.m.

へいがん 併願する **apply to more than one school for admission** (➤ school は college [university] (大学)などと置き換えられる) ▶第一志望は国立大学ですが, 私大も**併願します** My first choice is a national university, but I'm also going to *apply to* some private universities.

1**へいき 兵器** a **weapon** /wépən/, **arms**
‖**兵器庫** an arsenal /ɑ́ːʳsənl/ ‖**核兵器** nuclear weapons [arms] ‖**生物兵器** biological weapons ‖**通常兵器** conventional weapons.

2**へいき 平気** ▶彼女は人が何と言おうと**平気だ**(=気にしない) She *doesn't care* what other people say. ‖ 対話 「先生に怒られるぞ」「**平気, 平気**」"Your teacher'll get mad at you." "*I don't care*." (➤「全然気にしない」の意) ‖雪ぐらい**平気だよ**(=いやだと思わない) I *don't mind* the snow. ‖バス旅行は苦手だが飛行機なら**平気だ** I hate traveling by bus, but flying *is no problem* [I *don't mind* flying].
▶私は徹夜は**平気だ**(=苦にならない) Staying up all night *doesn't bother* me *in the least*. / I *think nothing of* staying up all night. ‖ 対話 「きみ, 半ズボンで寒くないの?」「**平気だよ**(=全然)」"Aren't you cold in your shorts?" "*Not at all*."
▶彼は**平気で**うそをつく He tells lies *shamelessly* [*nonchalantly* / *bold-facedly*]. (➤ それぞれ「恥ずかしげもなく」,「平然として」,「あつかましくも」の意) ‖彼女は**平気で**(=冷静に)カエルをつかんだ She held a frog *quite calmly*. ‖彼女は**平気で**脱税する She has *no scruples* [*qualms*] about cheating on her taxes. (➤ scruples, qualms /kwɑːmz/ はともに「やましさ」) ‖ぼくをすっぽかしておきながら次の日彼女は**平気な顔で**(=何事もなかったように)やって来た Although she stood me up, she appeared on the following day *as if nothing had happened*.

3**へいき 併記** ▶諮問文書には反対意見も**併記された** Opposing views were also *included in* the consultation document.

へいきん 平均 **1【ならすこと, 中間値】**(an) **average** /ǽvərɪdʒ/ 一形 **平均の average** ▶**平均を出す** calculate *an average* ‖2と6と10の**平均は**6だ The *average* of 2, 6, and 10 is 6. ‖この数字の**平均を出す**にはどうしたらいいですか What do you do to *find the average* of these figures? / How do you *average* these figures? (➤ この average は「(数を)平均する」の意の他動詞) ‖学校での彼の身長は**平均以上**[**以下**]だ His height is *above* [*below*] *the average* at his school. ‖きみの収入は**平均よりいい** Your income is better than [is above] *average*.
▶この組の生徒の**平均体重**は60キロだ The *average weight* of the students in this class is sixty kilograms. ‖ 対話 「月に何冊本を読みますか」「**平均して**2冊です」"How many books do you read a month?" "I read two (books), *on* (*the*) *average*. / I *average* two (books)." (➤ 後者は「平均すると…である」の意の動詞).
▶それが**平均的**日本人の考え方だ That's the opinion of *the average Japanese*. ‖1日**平均**500人の観光客がその寺を訪れる *An average* of 500 sightseers a day visit the temple.
▶全教科で**平均点**60点以上の者を合格とします I'll pass the students who get *an average score* of 60 or above in all subjects.
‖**平均寿命** the average life span [life expectancy] ‖**平均年齢** the average age ‖**平均余命** (the average) life expectancy.
2【つり合い】(a) **balance** ▶そのまま20秒間**平均を保っ**ていてください Keep your *balance* in that position for 20 seconds. / Stay balanced without moving for 20 seconds. ‖私は体の**平均を失って**倒れた I lost my *balance* and fell down.
‖**平均台** a balance beam.

へいけ 平家 **the Heike clan.**

へいけい 閉経 **menopause** ▶**閉経を迎える** reach *menopause* ‖**閉経を経験する** go through *menopause*.

へいげん 平原 a **plain**(平野); a **prairie** /préəri/ (特に北米ミシシッピー川流域の大草原) ▶目の前には見渡す限りの**平原**が広がっていた Before us the *plain* stretched as far as the eye could see.

べいご 米語 **American English.**

1**へいこう 平行の** **parallel** 《to》 ▶**平行する**2本の線は永久に交わることがない Two *parallel* lines never intersect each other. ‖これと**平行な**線を引きなさい Draw a line *parallel to* this one. ‖線路は川と**平行して**走っている The railroad runs *parallel to* [*with*] the river.
‖**平行四辺形** a parallelogram ‖**平行棒** parallel bars (➤「段違い平行棒」は uneven (parallel) bars という).
☞ **平行線** (→見出語)

2**へいこう 平衡** (a) **balance, equilibrium** /iːkwɪlíbriəm/ (➤ 後者はより堅い語) ▶**平衡を保つ**[**失う**] keep [lose] one's *balance*.
‖**平衡感覚** the [a] sense of balance [equili-

brium].

3へいこう 並行 ▶2人のランナーが並行して(＝並んで)走った Two runners ran *side by side*. ‖ 東京と京都で2つの会議が並行して(＝同時に)行われた The two conferences were held *simultaneously* in Tokyo and Kyoto. ‖ フィールドでは走り高跳びと三段跳びが並行して行われた The high jump was held *along with* the triple jump on the field.

4へいこう 閉口する **be annoyed**(悩まされる) ▶夜中に隣の犬がやかましくほえたてるのには閉口している *I'm annoyed by* the barking of the neighbor's dog in the middle of the night. ‖ こう暑くては閉口だ(＝この暑さには耐えられない) I *can't stand* [*bear*] this heat. ／This heat *is unbearable*. ‖ あの人のぐちには閉口するよ(＝うんざりだ) I'm *sick of* [*fed up with*] his grumbling.

▶その酔っ払いには閉口した I *didn't know how to handle* [*deal with*] the drunk. (➤「どう対処したらよいかわからなかった」の意).

へいごう 併合する **merge** ＋目 (会社などを対等な立場で合併する) ; **annex** /ənéks/ ＋目 (領土などを武力などで自国のものにする).

へいこうせん 平行線 **parallel lines** (2本) ▶この線に対する平行線を引きなさい Draw *a parallel* to the line.

▶《比喩的》議論は平行線のままだ(＝成果がない) They *are getting nowhere* in their argument. ‖ その点に関する彼らの話し合いは平行線をたどった(＝一致を見なかった) They *failed to reach agreement* on the points under discussion. (● 議論などがかみ合わないことを比喩的に「平行線をたどる」というが，この表現を parallel を使って訳すことはできない．英語の parallel は「同じ方向に進む」「類似の」の意味で，日本語の用法とは大きく異なるからである).

べいこく 米国 →アメリカ.

へいさ 閉鎖 **a closedown, a shutdown** (店・工場などの ; 前者は長期または永久の閉鎖，後者は一時的な閉鎖をいうのがふつう) 一動 閉鎖する **close** [**shut**] **down** ▶その会社は販売不振のため新潟支店を閉鎖した The company *closed down* the branch in Niigata because of its poor sales. ‖ 事故のため東名高速の上り線は閉鎖された The Tokyo-bound lanes of the Tomei Expressway *were closed* to traffic due to an accident. ‖ 山小屋は冬の間は閉鎖されます They *shut down* the mountain lodge during the winter.

▶閉鎖社会を形成する form *a closed society* ‖ 流感のため学校閉鎖になった *The school was closed* due to the flu. ‖ その島の人々は閉鎖的で外部の人間が移り住んでくるのを好まない The islanders are *exclusive* and dislike outsiders settling on the island.

べいさく 米作 **rice growing** (米の栽培) ; **a rice crop** (収穫) ▶砂地は米作に向かない Sandy soil is not suitable for *growing rice*. ‖ ことしの米作はほぼ平年並みだ This year's *rice crop* is about (the) average.

‖ 米作地帯 a rice-producing district.

へいさつ 併殺 →ダブルプレー.

へいざん 閉山 **a mine closing** (鉱山の).

へいし 兵士 **a soldier.**

へいじ 平時 **time of peace, peacetime** (平和な時) ; **normal** [**ordinary**] **times** (ふだん) ▶平時は *in times of peace* ／*normally*.

へいじつ 平日 **a weekday** ▶デパートは平日はわりあいすいている Department stores are less crowded *on weekdays*.

へいしゃ 兵舎 **a (military) barracks** (➤単複両扱い).

べいじゅ 米寿 **(a celebration on)** one's **88th birthday.**

へいじょう 平常 **normal** (いつもの状態) 一形 平常の **normal, usual** ▶新幹線の運行は正午前に平常に戻った Shinkansen service *returned to normal* before noon. ‖ 交通ストが行われてもあすは平常どおり授業があります We will have school *as usual* tomorrow, even if there is a transportation strike. ‖ こんなピンチにピッチャーに平常心でいろ[を保て]というのは無理だ It's too much to ask a pitcher to *stay calm* [*retain his presence of mind*] in a pinch like this. (➤「平常心を保つ」は堅い言い方では maintain (one's) equanimity とも言える) ‖ 我々は決勝戦には平常心で臨むことを確認した We made sure that we would *play* the final game *calmly*. ／We made sure that we would *keep our cool* [*maintain presence of mind*] in the final game. ‖ 成績には平常点を加味します Your *classwork will affect* your grade(s). (➤「授業での勉強ぶりが成績に影響する」の意).

べいしょく 米食 **a rice-based diet** ▶米食は健康によい *A rice-based diet* [*A diet based on rice*] is healthy.

へいじょぶん 平叙文 《文法》a **declarative sentence.**

へいしんていとう 平身低頭 ▶「スープにゴキブリが入ってるわ」と大声をあげたら，支配人が飛んで来て平身低頭して謝った When I cried out, "There's a cockroach in my soup !", the manager came running and *groveled* in apology. (➤ grovel は「ひれ伏す」).

1へいせい 平静 **composure** /kəmpóʊʒəʳ/, one's **presence of mind** 一形 平静な **calm** /kɑːm/, **quiet** ▶彼女はその知らせを聞いて平静を保つことができなかった She couldn't *keep her composure* when she heard the news.

▶地震がおさまると買い物客たちはすぐに平静を取り戻した The shoppers *recovered their composure* soon after the earthquake subsided. ‖ 彼は火事が起きたとき平静を失わなかった He *kept his presence of mind* [*didn't lose his head*] when the fire broke out.

2へいせい 平成 **Heisei** ▶平成16年に生まれた子 a child born in the 16th year of *Heisei* [in 2004] (● 日本独特の年号なので，日本の元号制度を知らない外国人には西暦を用いて言うほうがよい).

へいぜい 平生の **everyday** ▶平生の行い *everyday* conduct ‖ 入試でものをいうのは平生の努力だよ It is your *daily* effort that will make you successful in the entrance examination(s).

へいせつ 併設する ▶その大学には病院が併設されている A hospital *is attached to* the university.

へいぜん 平然と **calmly** /kɑ́ːmli/ ▶地震が来たとき父は平然としていた Dad remained *calm* [*cool* ／*unperturbed*] when the earthquake hit. ‖ その少年は平然とヘビをつかんだ The boy grabbed a snake *calmly*.

へいそ 平素 ▶彼女は平素から健康には注意している She is *always* careful about her health. ／She *always* takes good care of herself.

へいそく 閉塞 ▶長引く不況で日本は閉塞感に包まれている Due to the prolonged economic slump, Japan is enveloped in *a sense of stagnation*.

へいぞん 併存 **coexistence** 一動 併存する **coexist.**

へいたい 兵隊 **a soldier** (兵士) ; **troops** (軍隊) ▶兵

隊ごっこをする *play* (*at*) *soldiers*.

へいたん 平坦な flat (➤ 壁面のように水平でないものにも用いる); level (上下に傾いていない); even (むらのない) ▶日本は山がちで平たんな土地は少ない Japan is generally mountainous and has little *flat* [*level*] land. ‖飛行機が着陸するには平たんな地面が必要だ Airplanes need *level* ground to land on. ‖平たんな歩道はローラースケートにいい An *even* sidewalk is easy to skate on.

▶《比喩的》この事業で成功するまでの道は決して平たんではなかった The road to success in this business was not a *smooth* one.

へいち 平地 flatland (平らな土地); flatlands (平地地方); level land (水平な土地) ▶山を切り崩して平地にする level down a hill into *flatland* ‖平地では山よりも春の訪れが一月も早い Spring comes at least one month earlier in the *flatlands* than in the mountains.

へ

へいちゃら ▶彼が何と言おうとぼくはへいちゃらだ (=気にしない) I *don't care a bit* what he says. ‖昼飯くらい抜いてもへいちゃらだ Skipping lunch is *no problem* (*at all*) for me.

1へいてい 平定 ▶秀吉は戦乱の世を平定した Hideyoshi *subjugated* a war-torn society *to his rule*. (➤ subjugate は「征服する」).

2へいてい 閉廷 ▶これで閉廷とします *The court is adjourned*.

へいてん 閉店する close ▶きょうは何時に閉店ですか What time [When] do you *close* today? ‖この店は夜11時に閉店する This store *closes* at 11 p.m. ‖《掲示》本日は閉店しました We are closed for the day. / We're closed. / Closed. (➤ 第1例が最も日本語に近い. なお, 日本では店頭にしばしば Close と書いた札が下がっているのを見かけるが, これでは「閉めなさい」と命令している意味にしかとれない).

▶売り上げ不振で閉店(=廃業)せざるをえない We have to *close* (*down*) *our shop* because of poor business.

‖閉店時間 the closing hour [time].

へいねつ 平熱 normal temperature ▶患者は午前中は平熱だったが午後になって熱が出た The patient's *temperature was normal* in the morning but it went up in the afternoon.

▶妹の熱は平熱に戻った My sister's *temperature is back to normal*.

へいねん 平年 an average year (例年); a common year (うるう年に対して) ▶当地では平年だと11月には雪が降る We *usually* have snow in November. ‖ことしのミカンは平年作を30パーセント上回った This year's orange crop was 30% better than *in an average year*.

へいはつ 併発 ▶病人は(かぜから)肺炎を併発して亡くなった The patient died after *developing* pneumonia.

へいばんな 平板な flat ▶全体的に平板な印象の小説 a novel that gives an overall *flat* [*monotonous*] impression ‖平板な発音 *flat* pronunciation.

へいふく 平服 ordinary clothes (ふだん着)

✉ (招待状で) 平服でおいでください *Informal* dress. / Dress *informally*.

へいべい 平米 a square meter ▶このマンションの専有面積は約80平米だ Total living space in each of these condos comes to about 80 *square meters*.

ぺいぺい a nobody; small fry (ざこ).

1へいほう 平方 a square ▶3メートル平方の布 a piece of cloth three meters *square* ‖この家の面積は約180平方メートルです This house is about 180 *square meters* in area. 《参考》アメリカでは現在でも square feet (平方フィート), square mile (平方マイル)を用いるほうがふつう.

▶3の平方(=2乗)は9である The *square* of three is nine. ‖9の平方根は3である The *square root* of nine is three.

2へいほう 兵法 military tactics [strategy] (➤ 後者は「大局的な戦術」の意).

へいぼん 平凡な ordinary (ふつうの); average (平均的な); run-of-the-mill, trite /traɪt/ (陳腐な); mediocre /mìːdióʊkəʳ/ (ありきたりの; マイナスイメージの語) ▶父は平凡な会社員です My father is an *ordinary* [*average*] company employee. ‖そのテレビドラマはストーリーが平凡だった The plot of the TV drama was *run-of-the-mill* [*commonplace*]. (➤ commonplace は common より「平凡さ」を強調する) ‖彼女の今度の本は平凡だった Her latest book was *mediocre*.

▶平凡ですけど私は優しい男性が好きです *This may sound trite* [*This may not be at all original*], but I like men who are gentle. (➤ trite は表現法が「ありふれた」の意).

へいまく 閉幕 ▶昼の部の閉幕は午後4時だ The *closing time* for the matinee (performance) is 4 p.m. / The matinee (performance) *closes* at 4 p.m.

▶《比喩的》冬季オリンピックは無事閉幕した The Winter Olympic Games *came to an end* without any trouble.

へいめい 平明な plain (わかりやすい); clear (はっきりした); lucid /lúːsɪd/ (明快な, 明りょうな; 堅い語) ▶平明な英語 *plain* [*simple*] English ‖その小説は平明な文体で書かれている The novel is written in a *lucid* [*clear*] style.

へいめん 平面 a plane, a level ▶2つの三角形は同一平面上にある The two triangles are on the same *plane* [*level*]. ‖あなたの問題のとらえ方は平面的(=表面的)だ Your grasp of the problem is *superficial*.

‖平面鏡 a plane mirror ‖平面図 a ground [floor] plan (設計図の); a plane figure (図形としての).

へいや 平野 a plain ▶木曽川は濃尾平野を流れて伊勢湾に注ぐ The Kiso River flows through *the Nobi Plain* into Ise Bay.

へいよう 併用 ▶授業では教科書と新聞を併用している We *use* newspapers *together* [*along*] *with* the textbook in class. ‖バイアグラは心臓の薬と併用すると危険だ *Taking* Viagra *and* heart medicine *at the same time* can be dangerous.

へいりょく 兵力 military strength [power]; military force (軍事力) ▶両国とも兵力はほぼ互角だ The two countries are roughly equal in *military strength* [*power*]. ‖NATO軍はその戦闘に総勢3万の兵力を投入した The NATO army threw *a force 30,000* strong into that battle. (➤ strong は数詞のあとに置いて「総勢…人の」の意).

ベイルート Beirut (レバノンの首都).

へいれつ 並列 ▶乾電池を並列につなぐ connect dry cells *in parallel* ‖並列回路 a parallel circuit.

へいわ 平和 peace 一形 平和な peaceful 一副 平和に peacefully ▶恒久平和 lasting *peace* ‖平和を維持

する maintain *peace* ‖ 日本の**平和憲法** Japan's *pacifist* [*peace*] Constitution ‖ テロは**世界平和**に対する脅威だ Terrorism is a threat to *world peace* [*the peace of the world*]. ‖ 原子力は**平和目的**に利用するよう努めるべきだ We should endeavor to utilize nuclear energy for *peaceful purposes*. ‖ 津波で漁村の**平和な暮らし**はくずれさった The tsunami completely disrupted the *peaceful* lives in the fishing village.
▶私たちは**平和な世の中に暮らしている**が，今も世界のどこかで戦争をしているのだ Although we *live in peace*, there are wars going on around the world at this very moment. ‖ **家庭の平和**を乱さないでください Don't disturb *the peace of our home*. ‖ 両国は紛争の**平和的**解決に努めるべきだ The two countries should try to find a *peaceful* solution to the conflict.
‖**平和維持活動**（国連の）peacekeeping operations《略 PKO》‖ **平和運動** a peace movement ‖ **平和主義** pacifism ‖ **平和主義者** a pacifist.

へえ **Well**!, **So** [**Hmm**]!; **What**!（何だって）; **Indeed**!, **Oh**!, **Really**!（本当？）▶へえ，何だって *Well!* What did you say? ‖ へえ，で，彼は何と言ったの？ *So* [*Hmm*], what did he say then? ‖ へえ，驚いたわ *Wow!* That's amazing!
▶ 対話「おやじにバイク買ってもらったんだ」「へえ，ほんと」"My dad bought me a motorcycle." "*Oh, really?*"（➤ really の語尾を上げると疑問文になるが，平板に発音すると納得を表す）．

ベーカリー a **bakery**.

ベーキングパウダー **baking powder**.

ベーコン **bacon** ▶ベーコン１切れ a slice of *bacon*.
‖**ベーコンエッグ** bacon and eggs.

ページ a **page** ▶ページをめくる turn *a page* ‖ この本は本文が150ページ，注釈が25ページついている This book contains 150 *pages* of text and 25 *pages* of explanatory notes. ‖ 20ページを開けなさい Open your book(s) to [《英》at] *page* 20. ／Turn to *page* 20. ‖ 25ページから始めましょう Let's begin at [from] *page* 25. ‖ 30ページ[反対ページ]の地図を見てください Look at the map *on page 30* [*on the facing page*]. ‖ 詳しくはその本の51ページから56ページを参照のこと For further information [For (more) details], see *pages* 51 *to* 56 of the book.（➤ pages の略号は pp. で，pp. 51-56 のように書く）‖ 彼は雑誌のページをぱらぱらとめくった He *leafed through* a magazine.
▶《比喩的》土星探査は宇宙開発の歴史に**新しいページを加えた** The exploration of Saturn *has added a new page to* the history of space development.

ベージュ **beige** /beɪʒ/ ▶ベージュのズボン a pair of *beige* trousers.

1**ベース** **1**【基準】a **basis**; a **base**（土台）▶わが社は賃金ベースが低い Our *base salary* is low.
2【野球】a **base** ▶村田の当たりは三塁ベースに当たって二塁打になった Murata's grounder bounced off (the) third *base* for a double.

2**ベース**《音楽》**bass** /beɪs/（バス）
‖**ベースギター** a bass guitar ‖ **ダブルベース** a (double) bass.

ペース (a) **pace** ▶ペースを速める[遅くする] quicken [slacken] one's *pace* ‖ 1時間6キロのペースで歩く walk *at a speed* [*a pace*] *of* six kilometers per hour ‖ レースで同じペースを保つ maintain [keep (up)] the same *pace* in a race ‖ **きみは自分のペースで勉強すべきだ** You should study *at your own pace*.
▶彼のペースにはついて行けない I can't *keep pace with* him [can't *keep up with* him]. ‖ 30キロを過ぎると藤原のペースは急に落ちた After 30 kilometers, Fujiwara's *pace* suddenly fell off.

ベースアップ ▶労働組合は5パーセントのベースアップを要求した The labor union demanded a 5-percent *increase in base pay*.

> **危ないカタカナ語✹ ベースアップ**
> 給与体系を物価指数などとの関連で一定の率で上げることを「ベースアップ」といっているが，これにぴったりの英語はない．pay raise [《英》rise], wage raise [hike], あるいは単に raise [《英》rise] などの言い方はあるが，これらは「昇給」に当たることばである．したがって，「ベースアップ」は increase in base pay のようにいうしかない．

ベースキャンプ a **base camp**.

ペースト (a) **paste**
‖**レバーペースト** liver paste.

ペースメーカー a **pacemaker**.

ベータ **beta** ▶そのソフトウェアのベータ版 the *beta version* of the software.
‖**ベータカロテン**《生化学》beta carotene ‖ **ベータテスト** a beta test.

ペーハー《化学》(a) **pH** /piːéɪtʃ/（➤「ペーハー」はドイツ語読み）▶海水のペーハーは8前後だ The water of the ocean has *a pH* of around 8.

ペーパー **paper**（紙）
‖**ペーパータオル** a paper towel ‖ **ペーパーナイフ** a paper knife, 《米また》a letter opener ‖ **ペーパーバック** a paperback.

> **危ないカタカナ語✹ ペーパー**
> 頭に「ペーパー」のつくことばには和製語が多いので注意が必要である．
> **ペーパーカンパニー** 税金対策のために作った書類上だけの会社をこういうが，和製語．paper company では「製紙会社」の意味になってしまう．英語では bogus company（いんちき会社），company on paper（紙の上での会社），nominal company（名目上の会社）などという．
> **ペーパーテスト** 英語では written test という．paper test では「紙質検査」の意味にしかならない．
> **ペーパードライバー** 免許証は持っているが実際に運転をしていない人のことをこういうが，相当する英語はない．I have a driver's license but do not drive. とか I am a driver on paper only. のように説明的にいうしかない．

ベール a **veil** ▶アラブの女性は人前ではベールをかぶることになっている Arab women are expected to wear *veils* in public.
▶《比喩的》その殺人事件の真相は(なぞの)**ベールに包まれている** The real facts of the murder case *are under a veil of mystery*.

-べからず **No ...**, **Don't ...** ▶壁に落書きをするべからず *No* graffiti [scribbling] on the wall. ‖ ごみを散らかすべからず *No* littering. ‖ 動物に食べ物を与えるべからず *Don't* feed the animals.
▶**手を触れるべからず** *Hands off*. ‖ **芝生に入るべからず** *Keep off* the grass. ‖ **エチケットべからず集** a list of *don'ts* of etiquette.

-べき must, should（➤ must は選択の余地のない義務や必要を, should は「…するほうがいい」という勧めを表す).

【文型】
…すべきだ
must do／have to do
should do
ought to do
《解説》must や have to が「…しなければならない」という, 必ず行うべき義務を表すのに対し, should や ought to は良識や良心に照らして「…すべきだ」や忠告としての「…すべきだ, …するのがよい」を表す. →-ならない.

▶市長は公約を実行すべきだ The mayor *must* [*has to*] carry out his campaign pledge(s). ‖彼女は仕事を辞めるべきかどうか迷っている She can't decide if she *should* quit her job or not. ‖あなたにはもっと早くすべてを打ち明けるべきだった I *should* [*ought to*] *have* told you everything earlier. ‖きみは高校を中退すべきでない You *shouldn't* quit high school. ‖高校生は喫煙すべきでない High school students *shouldn't* [*mustn't*] smoke. (➤後者のほうが意味が強い；don't have to とすると「…する必要はない」の意になる).
▶試験中カンニングすべきではない There *must be no* cheating in [during] the exam.
▶私にはまだやるべき仕事がたくさん残っている I still have a lot of work *to* do.

へきえき 辟易 ▶部長の長話にはへきえきした We *were annoyed by* [*grew weary of*] the general manager's endless talking. ‖トムの常習的な遅刻に教師たちはへきえきしている The teachers *are fed up with* Tom's habitual tardiness. (● be fed up with はこの例のように常習的な事に言及する句であるため, 第1例の場合に用いるのは不適当).

へきが 壁画 a mural /mjóərəl/, a wall painting；a fresco（フレスコ画法のもの).

へきち 僻地 a remote place [area], an out-of-the-way place [area].

ペキン 北京 Beijing /bèɪdʒíŋ/, Peking /pìːkíŋ/（➤英語では前者が多い）‖北京原人 Peking man.

ヘクタール a hectare /héktеəʳ/《略 ha.》.

ヘクトパスカル《気象学》hectopascal《略 hPa.》（➤気圧の単位).

ベクトル《数学》a vector.

ベクレル《物理学》a becquerel /békərəl, bekərél/（放射能の単位, 略号 Bq）▶キロ当たりセシウム137が5000ベクレル以上の土に米を植え付けることを禁じる ban the planting of rice in soil that has more than 5,000 *becquerels* of cesium-137 per kilogram of soil.

ペケ no good（だめ）；a cross（×印). →ばつ.

へこたれる get discouraged /dɪskə́ːrɪdʒd/（がっかりする）；lose heart（元気をなくす）▶1回試合に負けたくらいでへこたれるな Don't *get discouraged* [*lose heart*] at losing just one game.
▶このくらいの失敗ではへこたれないぞ I won't let such a (minor) failure *get* me *down*. (➤「こんな失敗に私をくじけさせない」が原義).

ベゴニア《植物》a begonia /bɪgóʊnjə/.

ぺこぺこ ▶おなかがぺこぺこだ. けさから何も食べてないんだから I'*m starved* [*starving*] because I haven't eaten anything since this morning.
▶父が人にぺこぺこ頭を下げるのは見ていて気分が悪い It makes me sick to see my father *groveling* [*kowtowing*] *to* others. ‖人にぺこぺこするのはやめろ Don't *bow and scrape* [*suck up*] *to* others. (➤後者はアメリカの俗語表現).

へこます 凹ます dent ＋目 ▶車を壁にぶつけてバンパーをへこませてしまった I ran the car into the wall and *dented* [*got a dent on*] the bumper.
▶何とかしてあいつをへこましてやりたい I'd like to find some way to *take* him *down a peg* (*or two*). (➤ take ... down a peg (or two) は「…をやり込める」の意のインフォーマルな表現).

へこみ 凹み a hollow；a dent（外からの強い力によってできた）▶麦わら帽子のへこみ the *hollow* in a straw hat ‖鈴木先生の車のドアには大きなへこみがある Mr. Suzuki's car has a big *dent* on the door.

へこむ 凹む ▶きみの車の屋根はひどくへこんでいるね Your car roof *is* badly *dented*, isn't it？‖この空き缶はぎゅっと押すと簡単にへこむ This empty can easily *yields to pressure*. (➤「圧力に屈する」の意).
▶そんなことでへこむなよ Don't *let* it *get* you *down*. (➤ get ... down は「(人)をがっかりさせる」の意のインフォーマルな言い方).

ぺこり ▶ケンとマイクは私にぺこりと頭を下げた Ken and Mike *nodded* (*their heads*) when they saw me.

へさき 舳先 a bow /baʊ/（➤しばしば複数形で用いる).

へしおる へし折る break（折る）；break off（折り取る）▶木の枝をへし折って薪を作った We *broke* branches and made firewood.
▶《慣用表現》彼女の鼻っ柱をへし折ってやりたい I'd like to *take* her *down a peg* (*or two*). (➤ take ... down a peg (or two) は「…をやり込める」の意のインフォーマルな表現).

ベジタリアン a vegetarian（菜食主義者). →菜食.

ペシミスト a pessimist.

ペシミズム pessimism.

ぺしゃんこ →ぺちゃんこ.

[1]**ベスト**《最善》(the) best ▶ベストを尽くせ Do your *best*.／Do *the best* you can. (➤下のコラムを参照) ‖先生のおっしゃるようにするのがベストだと思うよ I think it *best* to do as our teacher told us. ‖私たちはベストコンディションでその試合を戦った We played the game *in top form*.
✉ **英語スピーチコンテストではベストを尽くしましたが, 4位でした** I *did my best* in the English speech contest, but I came in fourth.
‖ベストドレッサー the best-dressed person, a best dresser (➤ dresser には「化粧台,《英》食器戸棚」の意もあって誤解を招きやすいので前者の言い方がよい).

> **あなたの英語はどう響く?**
> 日本人は「ベストを尽くします」の意味で I'll do my best. や I'll do the best I can. のように言うことが多いが, この英語には「やれるだけはやってみます（ただし, 成果が出るかどうかは保証できませんが)」という含みを持つことがある. I'll give it my all., I'll give it all I've got., I'll give it my best shot. などにすれば積極性がより明確に伝わる.

[2]**ベスト**《チョッキ》《米》a vest,《英》a waistcoat /wéskət, wéɪstkoʊt/《参考》《英》の vest は「肌着」の意 ▶上着の下にベストを着る wear *a vest* under a jacket.

ペスト the plague /pleɪg/
‖ペスト菌 a plague bacillus /bəsɪləs/《参考》「ペ

スト」はオランダ語の *pest* から.

ベストセラー a **bestseller** ▶村上春樹の新しい小説がベストセラーになった Murakami Haruki's new novel has become *a bestseller*. ‖ベストセラー小説 a *best-selling* novel.

ベストテン **the top ten, the ten best** ▶《ヒット曲など》今週のベストテン this week's *top 10* / *the ten best songs* of this week ‖川端がとうとう打撃ベストテンに顔を出した Kawabata finally made the list of *the 10 best hitters*.

危ないカタカナ語✹ ベストテン
1「ベストテン」を the best ten の語順にするのは日本式. 英語では the ten best とする. したがって,「ベストテンに入っている打者」は the ten best hitters となる.
2 トーナメントなどの準決勝, 準々決勝の出場者を「ベストフォー」「ベストエイト」というが, これらの場合英語では best は用いず, それぞれ semifinalists, quarter-finalists という.

へそ 臍 a **navel** /néɪvəl/, 《インフォーマル》 a **bellybutton** (➤ 後者はやや子供っぽいが大人も普通に用いる) ▶かわいいおへそ a cute *bellybutton* ‖哺乳動物にはへそがある Mammals have *a navel*. ‖富良野は「北海道のへそ」と呼ばれている Furano is called '*the navel* of Hokkaido' (because it's located at the very center of Hokkaido).
▶《慣用表現》その男の子はお兄ちゃんがおもちゃで遊ばせてくれなかったのでへそを曲げていた The little boy *was sulking* [*was cranky*] because his brother wouldn't let him play with his toys. (➤ sulk /sʌlk/ は「すねる」, cranky は「つむじが曲がった」).
‖へその緒 the umbilical cord, the navel cord.
☞ へそ曲がり (→見出語), 出べそ (→見出語)

べそ 一動 べそをかく **sob** (しくしく[くすんくすん]泣く) ; **sniffle** (泣きながら鼻声で言う) ; **whimper** (めそめそ泣く) ▶少年は母親にしかられて今にもべそをかきそうだった The little boy was scolded by his mother and was *on the point of tears*. ‖女の子はべそをかきながら家に帰った The girl went home *sobbing* [*in tears*]. ‖「ママがいないよ」とその男の子はべそをかきながら言った "I lost my Mommy," the little boy *sniffled*. ‖男の子はころんでべそをかいた The boy fell down and *whimpered*.
▶《比喩的》偉そうなことを言ってあとでべそをかく(=後悔する)なよ Stop talking big, or you'll *be sorry later*.

へそくり **secret savings** ; a **nest egg** (何かを買うためにためている金) 《参考》西洋ではよく砂糖つぼやコーヒーの缶などが典型的な隠し場所といわれ, sugar bowl savings とか, coffee can savings のような言い方がある ▶お母さんはへそくりをしているらしいが, どこにあるかは知らない My mother seems to *have* some *money stashed away* (somewhere), but I don't know where she has hidden it. (➤ stash away は「のちのちのために, こっそり隠す」)

へそくる ▶母は家計費から少しへそくっている My mother has been *saving* some *money secretly* out of the family budget.

へそまがり 臍曲がりの **contrary** (意識的に人に逆らう) ; **perverse** (ひねくれた ; 堅い語) ▶へそ曲がりの少年 a *contrary* [*perverse*] boy ‖あいつはへそ曲がりでいつも人と反対のことをする He is so *perverse* that he always does just the opposite of what other people do.

[1]**へた 下手 一形 へたな** **poor, bad** (➤ 後者が意味が強い) ▶料理のへたな人 a *poor* cook ‖へたな歌を歌う sing (a song) *poorly*.

【文型】
物事(A)がへたである
be not very good at A
be bad at A
be poor at A
➤ A は名詞・動名詞
《解説》(1)「…がへた」は **be not very good at** (あまり上手ではない)と表現するのがふつう. **be poor at** は「不得手」で, **be bad at** はより強意の「へたくそ」の意. poor よりは bad を使うことが多い.
(2)「…するのがへた」は A に doing を入れて表す.
(3) not very good, bad, poor を「…する人」を表す名詞につけて表現することも多い.

▶弟は野球がへただ My brother *is not very good* [*bad* / *poor*] *at* (playing) baseball. ‖彼は絵がへただ He *isn't good* [*skillful*] *at* painting. / He's an *unskillful* painter. (➤「へたな絵」は a badly [poorly]-painted picture).
▶父は字がへただ My father has *poor* handwriting. / My father's handwriting is *poor*. ‖彼は英語を話すのはへただけど英米人の友だちが多い Though he speaks *poor* [*broken*] English, he has lots of British and American friends. ‖はしを使うのがへたな若者が多い Many young people use chopsticks *awkwardly*. (➤ awkwardly は「ぎこちなく, 不器用に」) ‖あなたはうそがへたね You're a *bad* [*lousy*] liar. (➤「ひどいうそつき」という意味もあるが, ふつうは「うそがへた」という意味で使われる).
ことわざ へたな鉄砲も数撃ちゃ当たる Even a bad shooter will eventually hit the mark, if he shoots often enough [keeps on trying].
ことわざ へたな考え休むに似たり If you can't come up with a good idea, you might as well be asleep. (➤ 直訳) / It's a waste of time to think about the matter if you cannot come up with a good idea.
▶《慣用表現》あのイギリス人タレントはへたな日本人より日本語がうまい That British TV personality speaks *better* Japanese *than most Japanese* (*do*). ‖あいつが仕事に熱中しているときはへたに口出ししないほうがいい It's better not to *butt in with needless suggestions* when he's concentrating on his work. ‖へたをすると日本の体操チームは金メダルを1つも取れないかもしれない *If we put a foot wrong*, our (Japanese) gymnastic team will fail to get a single gold medal. ‖ 対話 「ゴルフはなさいますか?」「ええ, へたの横好きで」"Do you play golf?" "Yes, I enjoy (playing) it, although I'*m not very good at* it."

[2]**へた** 《植物学》 a **calyx** /keɪlɪks/ (がく) ▶なすのへた *the calyx* of an eggplant.

へたくそ 下手糞な **lousy** /láʊzi/ (お粗末な) ; **terrible** (ひどい) ▶彼は字がへたくそだ His handwriting is *lousy* [*sloppy*]. ‖私は英語を話すのがへたくそです I am a *terrible* speaker of English. ‖へたくそ! もういいよ *What a klutz!* / You *klutz*! Just forget about it. (I'll do it myself.) (➤ klutz は「不器用な人, どじ」の意のアメリカ俗語).

へだたり 隔たり (a) **distance** (時間・空間の) ; a **gap**

（ずれ）; a **difference**（違い） ▶太陽から地球までの隔たり the *distance* from the sun to the earth.
▶両者の主張には大きな隔たりがある There is a wide *gap* [a great *difference*] in the claims of those two.
▶私と結婚してくれる人がいるなら年齢の隔たりなんか気にしない If there was someone who was willing to marry me, *a difference* in (our) ages wouldn't matter at all.

へだたる 隔たる ▶京都は東京から約500キロ隔たっている Kyoto *is* about 500 kilometers *distant* [*away*] *from* Tokyo. ‖ 現実は我々の理想とは遠く隔たっていた The reality *was light-years away from* our ideal. (➤ light-years は文字どおりには「何光年も」).

べたつく **be sticky, be gooey**(➤ 後者はインフォーマル) ▶手が油でべたついている My hands *are sticky* [*gooey*] with oil.
▶《比喩的》雄太はいつもしのぶとべたついている Yuta *is* always *carrying on with* Shinobu.

べたっと ▶値段を書いたシールが茶わんにべたっとくっついていて取れない The price sticker is glued so *firmly* to the cup that it won't come off.

へだて 隔て ▶私はどの生徒とも一様に隔てなく（＝等しく）接するようにしている I try to treat every student *equally*.

へだてる 隔てる **separate** /sépəreɪt/ ▶職員室と講師室はついたてで隔てられている The teachers' room and the part-time lecturers' room *are separated* by [*are partitioned off* with] a wooden screen. (➤ partition off は「…を仕切る」の意) ‖ その町から30キロ隔てて原子力発電所がある There is a nuclear power plant *at a distance of* thirty kilometers from the town.
▶通りを隔てた向こう側に小さなパン屋さんがある There is a small bakery *across* [*on the other side of*] the street. ‖ 伊藤教授の研究室は一部屋隔てた向こうです Professor Ito's office is *two doors down* the hall.
▶あのビルに隔てられて（＝さえぎられて）ここから富士山は見えない We can't see Mt. Fuji from here with that building *blocking the view*.
▶彼女がアメリカ留学をしたために，ぼくらの仲は隔てられてしまった Because she went to study abroad in the United States, we began to *go* our *separate ways*. (➤ go one's separate ways は「別々の道を行く」).

へたばる **get tired out** ▶テニスを６ゲームしてへたばった I *was tired out* [*was done in* ／ *was completely exhausted*] after playing six games of tennis. (➤ 最後の言い方はやや堅い).

べたべた **1【粘つく】**▶手がべたべたする My hands *are sticky* [*gooey*]. →べたつく ‖ 汗で体中がべたべたした I *was sticky* [*clammy*] all over with sweat.
2【一面につける】▶壁一面に抗議のビラがべたべたと貼ってあった The wall *was plastered* [*covered all over*] with protest fliers. ‖ その歌舞伎役者は顔におしろいをべたべた塗っていた The Kabuki actor's face was *thickly* powdered.
3【離れない】▶彼はいつも恋人とべたべたしている He and his girlfriend are always *clinging to* each other.

ぺたぺた ▶女の子がはだしでペタペタ歩いて来る Here comes a little girl *pattering* barefoot. ‖ 弟はノートにシールをぺたぺたはっている My (younger) brother *put* stickers *all over* his notebooks.

べたぼめ べた褒め ▶すべての批評家が彼の音楽の技量をべたぼめしている Every critic *praises* him *very highly* for [*raves about*] his musical skill. ‖ あそこの社長はきみをべたぼめしていたよ That (company) president *spoke very highly of* [*raved about*] you. ／That (company) president *praised* you *highly*.

べたぼれ ▶彼は奥さんにべたぼれだ He's *madly* [*totally*] *in love with* his wife.

へたりこむ へたり込む ▶優勝したマラソンランナーはテープを切ったあとその場にへたり込んでしまった After breaking the tape, the winner of the marathon *fell to her knees*.

ペダル a **pedal** ▶彼はゆっくりと自転車のペダルをこいだ He *pedaled* his bicycle slowly.

ぺたん ▶おばあさんは畳の上にぺたんと座り込んだ The elderly woman sat down *with a flop* on the tatami mat.

へちま 糸瓜《植物》a **sponge gourd** /spʌ́ndʒ gɔːrd/, a **loofah** /lúːfə/ (➤ 入浴時にスポンジの代わりに用いるものには後者をあてる) ▶《慣用表現》嫌いなものは嫌いだ. わけもへちまもない I don't like it because I don't like it, and I *do not have any particular reason* [*there's no rhyme or reason why* (I don't)]. (➤「それ以上言うことはない」の意味で and that's that. としてもよい).

ぺちゃくちゃ ▶ぺちゃくちゃしゃべる chatter *noisily* ‖ 友達から電話があると妹はいつまでもぺちゃくちゃしゃべっている When a friend calls her up, my sister *rattles on* [*chews the fat*] forever. ‖ 生徒たちは部屋の中でぺちゃくちゃしゃべっていた The students were *chatting away* in the classroom.

ぺちゃっと ▶チンの鼻はぺちゃっとしている Japanese spaniels have *flat* noses.

ぺちゃぱい ▶ぺちゃぱいの女の子 a *flat-chested* girl.

ぺちゃぺちゃ ▶子犬がミルクをペチャペチャ飲んでいる The puppy *is slurping* the milk.

ぺちゃんこ **flat**（鼻などが平べったい）; **flat-chested**（胸が） ▶ぺちゃんこになった自動車 a *crushed* car ‖ ぺちゃんこのざぶとん a *flattened* seat cushion ‖ 台風で物置小屋がぺちゃんこになってしまった The typhoon *leveled* the shed.

ペチュニア《植物》a **petunia** /pɪtjúːnjə/.

べつ 別

訳語メニュー
ほかの →other **1**
もう１つの →another **1**
区分けした →separate **2**
余分の →extra **3**
…を除いて →except for **4**

1【ほかの】 **other**; **another**（もう１つの）; **different**（違った） ▶それはまた別の機会に話そう Let's talk about it some *other* time. ‖ 別のパソコンを見せてください Could you show me *another* (personal) computer? ‖ 父とは別の研究分野に進みたい I'd like to major in something *different* from my father's field of study.
▶みんなビーフシチューにするの？ じゃあ，私は別なのを頼むわ Is everyone going to order beef stew? Then I'll have *something else*. ‖ どうしてこの写真だけ別にしてあるんだろう Why has this picture *been put aside from the others*? (➤ put aside は「わきへ取

りのけておく」).

▶スキーは得意だが，教えるとなると全く別だ I'm good at skiing, but when it comes to teaching it, that's a completely *different matter*. ‖ 英語を読むことと話すことは別だ Reading English *is one thing*, and speaking it *is another*.

2【区分けした】separate /séprət/ ▶車を買う金は別の口座に貯金しているんだ I have been saving money to buy a car in a *separate* account. ‖ 彼はいいことと悪いことの別がわかっていないようだ He doesn't seem to *know* right *from* wrong. ‖ このハンカチを1枚ずつ別に包んでもらえますか Please wrap these handkerchiefs *one by one* [*separately*].

▶都道府県別の(＝各県の)人口が知りたい I want to know the population of Japan *by* prefecture. ‖ この旅行は年齢[男女]の別なく(＝関係なく)参加できます Anybody can join this tour, *regardless of* their age [sex]. ‖ この棚の本はテーマ別に分けてあります The books on the shelf are categorized *according to topics*. ‖ 昨年度の月別販売額 last year's *monthly* sales figures ／last year's sales figures *listed by month* ‖ 本年度の月別販売目標額 the *monthly* sales targets for the current fiscal year.

3【余分の】extra ▶夜勤をすると別に手当がもらえる You'll get *extra* pay if you work (the) night shift. ‖ 父は給料とは別に(＝に加えて)印税をもらっている My father gets royalties *in addition to* his salary.

4【除いて】except for ▶彼は別として，チームの他のメンバーとはうまくいってる *Except for* [*Apart from*] him, I'm getting along well with the members of the team. ‖ テストが難し過ぎる点を別にすれば竹田先生はいい先生です Miss Takeda is a good teacher, *except that* her tests are too hard.

▶冗談は別にして，誠さんはいつまでもひとりでいるつもり？ *Joking aside*, are you going to stay single (forever), Makoto?

5【特別には】particularly ▶きょうは別に予定はありません I have nothing (*particular*) (I have) to do today. ‖ 対話「今，お忙しいですか」「いや別に」"Are you busy now?" "No, not *particularly*." ‖ 対話「どうかしたの？」「別に」"Is something bothering you?" "*No, nothing* (*in particular*)." ‖ 対話「彼の学説はいかがですか」「別に目新しいものでもないね」"What do you think of his theory?" "It's not *particularly* original."

▶隣でたばこを吸っていても私は別に気にならない It doesn't *especially* bother me if someone smokes next to me. ‖ あの日，彼女には別に変わったところはなかったようだったけど There was nothing unusual about her that day. (➤この場合，「別に」は訳文には現れない).

べつうり 別売り ▶プリンターは別売りです Printer *not included*.

べっかく 別格 ▶そのルーキーは別格の扱いを受けてきた The rookie has been given *special* [*exceptional*] treatment. ‖ ポップのシンガーグループとしてビートルズは別格だった(＝格が違った) As a pop singers' group, the Beatles *were in a class of their own* [*were something else*].

べっかん 別館 an **annex** /ǽneks/ ▶私たちのクラスはそのホテルの3階建て別館に泊まった Our class stayed at the three-story *annex* to the hotel. (➤前置詞 to に注意).

べっきょ 別居 **separation** ▶あの夫婦は現在別居中だ The couple *are* now *living separately*. ‖ 息子は別居して大阪にいます My son is *living apart from* us in Osaka.

‖別居(結)婚 a commuter marriage.

べっけん 別件 **another matter**(別のこと) ▶別件逮捕する *arrest* someone *on a separate charge*.

べっこ 別個に **separately** /sépərətli/ ▶プロの選手とアマの選手は別個に扱われるべきだ Professionals and amateurs should be considered *separately*. ‖ 冷蔵庫の飲み物代は(宿泊費とは)別個にフロントでお支払いください Please pay for drinks from the fridge *separately* at the front desk.

べっこう 鼈甲 **tortoiseshell** /tɔ́ːrṭəsʃel/ ▶べっ甲縁の眼鏡 *horn-rimmed* glasses (➤horn-rimmed は「眼鏡のフレームが角製(またはそれに似たもの)の」の意).

‖べっ甲細工 tortoiseshell work.

べっさつ 別冊 a **supplement**, an **extra**(雑誌・全集などの付録本); an **extra number** [**issue**](雑誌の増刊号) ▶雑誌『カントリー』の正月号別冊付録 *a supplement* [*an extra*] to the New Year issue of "Country" (magazine).

¹べっし 別紙 ▶詳細は別紙のとおりです The details are given on the *attached sheet*.

²べっし 蔑視 ▶(周囲の)蔑視に耐える endure *scornful* [*contemptuous*] *stares* ‖ この国には女性蔑視の風潮がいまだに残っている In this country, it is still the tendency to *look down on* women.

べっしつ 別室 **another room** ▶客人を別室に案内する show a guest into *another room*.

べつじょう 別条 ▶さしあたり生命には別条ありません His life *is not in imminent danger*. ／He *is in no immediate danger* of losing his life.

べつじん 別人 a **different person** ▶大木君かと思ったが別人だった I thought it was Oki, but it was *someone else*. ‖ 彼は貫録が出てきて昔の彼とは別人のようだ He has become a man of dignity. He *looks quite different* [*like another person* ／*like a different person*] from what he used to be. ‖ 彼女は絵を描いているときは別人だ She's *like a different person* when she is painting.

べっせい 別姓 →夫婦別姓.

べっせかい 別世界 ▶別世界からやって来た生物 a creature from *outer space*.

▶夏の高原は蒸し暑い都会とは別世界だ In summer, the highlands are *a different world* from the hot, humid cities.

べっそう 別荘 a **cottage** /kɑ́ːṭɪdʒ/ (小規模な); a **summer house** (夏用の); a **vacation house** (休暇に利用する); a **villa** (海辺などにある大邸宅) ▶我々はその夏を海の近くの小ぢんまりした別荘で過ごした We spent the summer at a cozy *cottage* near the sea.

へったくれ ▶自転車に乗る人には規則もへったくれもないようだ. 赤信号は無視するし，夜は無灯で走るし Many bicycle riders *don't care about* rules *a bit*. They run red lights and ride without a light at night.

べったり ▶ガムが床にべったりくっついてなかなか取れない The gum *is stuck* so *tight*(*ly*) [*firmly* ／*fast*] to the floor that I can't get it off. ‖ 彼の背中にはべったり(＝一面に)ペンキがついていた His back was covered *all over* with paint.

▶あの二人はいつもべったりだね Those two are always *lovey-dovey*. (➤「アツアツで」の意) ‖ その少女は母親にべったりとくっついていた The little girl *clung* [*stuck*] *to* her mother. (➤clung は cling (まといつく)の過

去形).

べつだん 別段 ▶彼は別段理由もないのによく授業をサボる He often cuts classes for no *special* [*particular*] reason.

へっちゃら →平気.

べってんち 別天地 ▶美しいマウイ島は別天地のようだ The beautiful island of Maui is like *a paradise*.

べっと 別途 ▶交通費は別途に支払います Transportation expenses will be paid *separately*. (➤ separately /séprətli/ は「別に」) ‖ 旅行の日程については別途(＝追って)ご連絡いたします We will inform you about the itinerary *later*.

ベッド a **bed** ; a **berth**(列車など乗り物の) ; a **canopy bed**(天蓋付きの) ▶ベッドで寝る sleep in *a bed* ‖ ベッドから飛び起きたら8時だった I jumped out of *bed* to find it was eight o'clock. ‖ マリちゃんはけさ自分ひとりでベッドを整えたのよ Mari *made her bed* this morning all by herself.

▶彼女は子供をベッドに入れてふとんをかけた She *tucked* her child *into bed*.

‖**ベッドカバー** a bedcover, a bedspread ‖ **ベッドシーン** a bedroom scene ‖ **ベッドタウン** a bedroom community [suburb], 《おもに英》 dormitory town (➤ bedroom town, commuter town ということもある).

逆引き熟語 ○○ベッド
折り畳み式ベッド a camp bed, a turndown bed, a collapsible bed ／**簡易ベッド** a cot ／(病院などの)**差額ベッド** an amenity bed, a pay bed ／**シングル[ダブル, ツイン]ベッド** a single [double, twin] bed ／**ソファーベッド** a sofa bed, a convertible bed, a daybed ／ **2段ベッド** bunk beds ／**ベビーベッド** a crib, 《英》 cot

ペット a **pet** 《参考》 (1) pet を避けて companion animal という言い方を好む人もいる. (2) 飼い主の留守中, ペットの世話をすることを petsit という(pet と babysit の sit による合成語) ▶弟はペットとしてイグアナを飼いたがっている My (younger) brother wants (to have) an iguana as *a pet*. ‖ 《掲示》ペットの同伴お断り No *Pets* Allowed. ‖ ペットの飼い主 a *pet* owner.

✉ **ペットは何を飼っていらっしゃいますか. うちでは犬を2匹飼っています** What kind of *pet* do you have? We have two dogs.

‖**ペット預り所** a kennel ‖ **ペットショップ** a pet store [shop] ‖ **ペット動物園** a petting zoo ‖ **ペットフード** pet food ‖ **ペットロス** pet loss, loss of a pet.

ヘッドスライディング 《野球》 a **headfirst slide, headfirst sliding** (➤ (×)head sliding とはしない) ▶ヘッドスライディングをする *slide headfirst*.

ヘッドハンター a **headhunter** 一動 **ヘッドハントする headhunt** +目 ▶ヘッドハントされる *be headhunted*.

ペットボトル a **PET bottle**, a **plastic bottle** (➤ 日常的には前者は用いない. PET は polyethylene terephthalate(ポリエチレンテレフタレート)の略).

ヘッドホン a **pair** [**set**] **of headphones**, a **headset** ▶彼はヘッドホンで CD を聴いている He's listening to a CD on his *headphones*.

ヘッドライト a **headlight**, a **headlamp**.

べっとり ▶どうしたの? そでに絵の具がべっとりついているよ What happened? Your sleeve *is smeared with* paint. ‖ 指にべっとり油がついた My fingers *were covered with* oil.

べつに 別に →別.

べつばら 別腹 ▶チーズケーキは別腹だ I *always have room* for cheesecake. (➤「〜のためには常に余裕[空間]がある」) ／I *have a separate stomach* for cheesecake.

べっぴょう 別表 an **attached table** [**chart**].

へっぴりごし 屁っぴり腰 ▶そんなへっぴり腰ではボールは打てないよ You can't hit the ball *with your rear end stuck out* like that. (➤「おしりを突き出して」の意).

べつびん 別便

✉ **祝いの品を別便で送ります** I am sending a congratulatory gift *separately*. ／I'll send a congratulatory gift *under separate cover* [*by separate mail* ／《英また》 *by separate post*].

べっぴん a **good-looker** (➤「イケ面」もさす).

べっぷう 別封する send separately, send in a separate envelope [**package**], **send under separate cover.**

べつべつ 別々の separate /séprət/ ▶うちは祖父母とは別々の家に住んでいる We live in a *separate* house [live separately] from our grandparents. ‖ 姉妹は別々の学校へ行っている The sisters go to *different* schools.

▶《レストランなどで》勘定は別々にしてくれませんか Could we have *separate* checks, please? ／*Separate* checks, please. ‖ これ[それ]は別々に包んでください Could you wrap these [them] *separately*, please?

べつめい 別名 another name ; an **alias** /éiliəs/ (➤ 通例犯罪人などの偽名として) ▶琵琶湖には「鳰(にお)の海」の別名がある Lake Biwa has *another name*, 'Niono-umi.' ／Lake Biwa is *also known as* 'Niono-umi.'

▶山口という別名を使っている go by *the alias* of Yamaguchi.

べつもの 別物 ▶恋愛と結婚は別物よ, ごっちゃにしないで Love and marriage are *two different things*. Don't mix them up.

べつもんだい 別問題 ▶彼女がいくらピアノが上手に弾けると言っても本当に才能があるかどうかは別問題だ Even though she plays the piano skillfully, whether or not she has real talent is *another matter*. (➤ 後半は that doesn't mean she has real talent のように言ってもよい).

へつらい flattery, obsequiousness, brown nosing.

へつらう play [**butter**] **up to** ; **flatter** +目 (大げさな・心にもないことを言う) ▶彼は部長にへつらってばかりいる He is always *playing up to* the general manager.

べつり 別離 parting, separation ▶別離は悲しいがいつの日か必ず訪れる Though (it may be) sad, the day (when) *we have to say "goodbye"* (*to each other*) will surely come.

ペディキュア (a) **pedicure**(足の指や爪の手入れ. 足の爪をきれいに飾ることは (toe)nail polishing で, おしゃれに飾るのは (toe)nail art という).

ヘディング 《サッカー》 **heading**(行為) ; a **header**(ヘディングされた球, およびヘディングによるシュート[パス]) 一動 **ヘディングする head** +目 ▶ヘディングで得点する score on *a header* ‖ ヘディングでゴールを決める *head* the ball into the net.

ベテラン a **veteran** /vétərən/ (老練な人) ; an **expert** /ékspəːrt/ (熟達者) ▶ベテラン教師 an *experienced* teacher ‖ ベテラン選手 a *veteran* player ‖ ベテランドライバー an *expert* driver.

▶彼はベテランの医者[操縦士]だ He is a *veteran*

doctor [pilot].

危ないカタカナ語✹ ベテラン
英語の veteran は《米》では「退役軍人」,《英》では「古参兵」の意味で用いられることが多いが, 日本語の「ベテラン」と同じ用法もある. ただし,「経験豊富な」の意では experienced を,「熟達した」の意では expert を用いるほうがよい.

ぺてん a trick ; a swindle(詐欺) ▶彼は友人たちをぺてんにかけた He played *a trick* on his friends. ‖ その男は私をぺてんにかけて金を取った The man *swindled* [*conned*] me out of my money.
‖**ぺてん師** a con man [artist] (➤ 後者は女性にも用いる) ; a swindler(詐欺師).

へど 反吐 vomit,《インフォーマル》puke (➤ 後者は品の悪い語) **一動 へどを吐く** vomit,《インフォーマル》throw up ▶彼は酔っぱらって道路にへどを吐いた He got drunk and *threw up* [*puked*] on the street.
▶《慣用表現》あいつのおべっかにはへどが出る I *am disgusted* by [with] his flattery. / His flattery *makes* me *sick*. ‖ あいつの顔を見ただけでへどが出そうだ The very sight of him *disgusts* me [*is revolting*].

べとつく be sticky ▶車にワックスをかけたので手がべとつく My hands *are* all *gooey* [*sticky*] from waxing my car.

ベトナム Vietnam /vì:etnɑ́:m/ **一形 ベトナムの** Vietnamese /vìetnəmí:z/
‖**ベトナム語** Vietnamese ‖ **ベトナム人** a Vietnamese (person) ‖ **ベトナム戦争** the Vietnam War.

へとへと ▶朝から赤ん坊のお守りでへとへとだ I *am dead tired* [*am dog-tired*] *from* taking care of the baby all day.

べとべと ▶暑い中で仕事をしたので汗で体中がべとべとだ Since I've been working in the heat, my whole body is *sticky with sweat*.

へどろ ooze /u:z/ (海底・湖底・川底などの) ; sludge (排水処理タンク・ボイラーなどの底にたまる) ; slime (ナメクジなどのぬめりを連想させるべとついた泥土) ▶湾内の海底は厚いへどろでおおわれている The bottom of the bay is covered with (a) thick *ooze*. ‖ 水槽の底のへどろを掃除する clean the *sludge* from the bottom of a water tank.

へなちょこ a wimp, a pipsqueak ▶あんなへなちょこ野郎に負けるもんか I won't be beaten by such a *wimp*.

へなへな ▶そんなへなへなした男とは付き合うな Don't go out with *a weak-kneed* [*spineless*] *guy* like him. ‖ このドアは薄いベニヤ板で作られているからへなへなだ This door is *flimsy* because it is made of thin plywood.
▶自分の家が焼け落ちるのを見て彼はへなへなと座り込んでしまった When he saw his own house burned to the ground, he *sank down* [*collapsed*] *to his knees*.

ペナルティー a penalty /pénəlti/ ▶違反者にペナルティー(＝罰金)を科す impose *a penalty* on an offender.
‖**ペナルティーエリア** a penalty area ‖ **ペナルティーキック** a penalty kick ‖ **ペナルティーキック合戦** a penalty shoot out.

ペナント a pennant ▶ベイスターズがペナントを握るのは(いったい)いつのことだろう When will the BayStars (ever) win the *pennant* [*championship*] ?
‖**ペナントレース** a pennant race.

べに 紅 crimson(深紅色) ▶薄紅色の花びら a *reddish* (flower) petal.

ペニー a penny [複 pence]《略 p》(➤ イギリスの貨幣単位で100分の1ポンド ; アメリカでは penny は1セント玉をさすが, 金額をいうときには使わない. その複数形は pennies) ▶1ペニー a [one] *penny* / one [1] *p* (➤ one pence ということもある).

べにざけ 紅鮭《魚》a sockeye salmon.

べにしょうが 紅生姜 red pickled ginger.

ペニシリン《薬学》penicillin /pènəsílɪn/
‖**ペニシリン軟こう** a penicillin ointment.

ベニス Venice(イタリア北東部の都市の英語名).

ペニス the penis /pí:nɪs/. →おちんちん.

べにばな 紅花《植物》safflower /sǽflaʊəʳ/
‖**紅花油** safflower oil.

ベニヤいた ベニヤ板 (a sheet of) plywood /pláɪwʊd/.

危ないカタカナ語✹ ベニヤ
「ベニヤ」は veneer とつづるが, この語は日本でいうベニヤ板の表面に張った上質の薄い板のことである. いわゆる「ベニヤ板」はその veneer を張った合板のことで, 英語では plywood という別の語を用いる.

ベネズエラ Venezuela /vènəzwéɪlə/ (南米北部の国).

ベネチア →ベニス.

へのへのもへじ *henohenomoheji* ; a face drawn by using Japanese hiragana characters, namely two he(へ) for eyebrows, two no(の) for eyes, mo(も) for the nose, he(へ) for the mouth and ji(じ) for the outline of the face (➤ 説明的な訳).

ペパーミント peppermint
‖**ペパーミントキャンディー** peppermint candy.

へばりつく cling《to》▶風にあおられないようにクライマーは岩にへばりついた The climbers *clung to* the rock so that they would not be blown off by the wind. (➤ clung は cling の過去形).

へばる get tired out ▶彼女はちょっと運動するとすぐにへばってしまう She *gets tired out* [*gets exhausted*] after the slightest exercise.
▶この暑さにへばっている This hot weather *has taken a lot out of* me. (➤ take a lot out of は「…を大いに疲れさせる」の意).

へび 蛇 a snake, a serpent (➤ 前者が一般語. 後者は文学的な語で特に大きなものを指す. また, エデンの園でイブを誘惑したのが蛇(serpent)に変装した悪魔であることから, 悪魔を連想することも多い) ▶蛇がするすると草むらを逃げて行った *A snake* slithered away through the grass.
‖**蛇使い** a snake charmer.

ヘビー heavy ▶ヘビー級 the heavyweight division [class] ‖ ヘビー級の選手 a heavyweight.
‖**ヘビースモーカー** a heavy smoker, a chain smoker ‖ **ヘビードリンカー** a heavy drinker ‖ **ヘビーユーザー** a heavy user.

ベビー a baby
‖**ベビーブーマー** a baby boomer ‖ **ベビーブーム** the baby boom ‖ **ベビー服** baby wear [clothes] ‖ **ベビー用品** baby goods [articles].

危ないカタカナ語✹ ベビー
「ベビー」のつくカタカナ語で注意すべきものに次のようなものがある.
ベビーカー 4輪で箱型のものは《米》baby buggy また

は baby carriage, 《英》pram といい, 腰かけ型のものは《おもに米》stroller, 《おもに英》pushchair という. baby car とすると「子供用のおもちゃの自動車」の意になる. (→うば車).
ベビーサークル これは和製語で, 英語では playpen という. pen は「囲い」.
ベビーベッド 《米》では crib, 《英》では cot ということが多い. baby bed とはしない.
ベビーホテル 乳幼児を一時的に預かる施設をこう呼ぶことがあるが, 和製語. child care center というのがよい.

ベビーシッター a **babysitter** ▶来週の金曜日の夜, ベビーシッターをお願いできますか Can you *babysit for* us next Friday night? ‖ 私はよく隣の子供たちのベビーシッターをする I often *babysit* (*for*) my neighbor's children.

ヘビメタ 《音楽》**heavy metal**(ロック音楽)
‖ヘビメタバンド a heavy metal band.

ヘブライご ヘブライ語 **Hebrew**(イスラエルの公用語).

へべれけ ▶へべれけに酔って *be blind drunk.*

へぼ ▶あんなへぼ将棋なんか見てもしかたがないよ It is not worth your time to watch such a *poor* [*sloppy*] game of shogi.
‖へぼ医者 a quack (doctor).

へま a **blooper**; a **blunder** (大失敗) ▶今度こそへまをするなよ Don't *make* [*pull*] *a blooper* this time around. / Now, this time be sure not to *make any mistakes.* ‖ やつはへまをやった He *put his foot in it.* (➤ put one's foot in it は「うっかり犬のふんに足を突っ込む」が原義のインフォーマルな表現; 次例のような類似の言い方もある) ‖ 彼は口を開くとへまなことを言う Whenever he opens his mouth, he *puts his foot in it.* (➤ put one's foot in it [in one's mouth] で「へまなことを言う」) ‖ きょうの試験, ほんとへまやっちゃったよ I really *goofed up* on the exam today. (➤ goof up は「ばかなこと[まね]をする」の意のインフォーマルな言い方).

へや 部屋 **1**【一室・ひと間】a **room** ▶広い[狭い]部屋 a large [small] *room* ‖ 6 畳の部屋 a six-mat *room* ‖ 部屋を片づける tidy up one's *room* ‖ ホテルに部屋を予約する reserve [《英また》book] *a room* at a hotel ‖ 私の家は 5 部屋ある My house has five *rooms.* ‖ 対話 (ホテルで)「今晩部屋は空いてますか」「あいにく満室です」"Do you have any *rooms* for tonight?" "I'm sorry but we have no vacancies."
▶梅雨時は洗濯物をどうしても部屋干しすることが多い I often have to hang my laundry *inside to dry* during the rainy season.
✉ (ホームステイに来る人に) 私と一緒の部屋でもかまわないですよね I hope you don't mind *sharing the room* with me. ➤「部屋を共用する」の意.
2【アパート・マンション】an **apartment** ▶もっと広い部屋をさがしています I'm looking for a larger *apartment.*
‖部屋着 loungewear(➤「ルームウェア」は和製語); a housedress (女性用の簡素な服); a dressing gown (ガウン) ‖ 部屋代 room rent (アパートなどの); room charge(ホテルの).

へら 箆 a **spatula** /spǽtʃələ/.

へらす 減らす **reduce** +⑬; **cut down** 《on》(切り詰める) ▶費用を 2 割減らしなさい *Reduce* [*Cut down*] expenses by 20 percent. ‖ 塩の摂取量を減らすよう医者に言われた The doctor advised me to *cut down on* (my intake of) salt. ‖ 体重を減らすいちばん手っとり早い方法は食事を減らすことだ The quickest way to *lose weight* is to *eat less.* ‖ 仕事の量を減らしなさい *Cut back on* work. / Work *less.* ‖ 従業員の数は30名に減らされた The number of employees *was decreased* [*was reduced*] to 30. ‖ 健康を保つためにはたばこの本数を減らしビールの量を減らさなければいけないよ You ought to smoke *fewer* cigarettes and drink *less* beer in order to keep yourself in good health.

へらずぐち 減らず口 ▶減らず口をたたくな Don't talk back! / None of your back talk! (➤ともに「口答えするな」の意) / None of your lip! (➤「生意気言うな」の意).

ヘラブナ 《魚》a **deepbodied crucian carp.**

へらへら ▶彼はいつもへらへら笑ってばかりいる He's always *laughing like an idiot* [*for no good reason*].

べらべら ▶秘密だとあれほど言ったのにあいつったら全部べらべらしゃべっちまった Even though I made it clear to him that it was a secret, he *went and blabbed* everything [*spilled the beans*]. (➤ blab は「(秘密を)べらべらしゃべる」, go and do は「…するようなばかなことをする」, spill the beans は「うっかり秘密をもらす」の意).

ぺらぺら ▶ぺらぺらの紙 *thin* paper.
▶彼女は英語とフランス語がぺらぺらだ She is *fluent* in both English and French.

べらぼう ▶このところべらぼうに忙しい I have been *awfully* [*terribly*] busy recently. ‖ その車はべらぼうに高いので手が出ない I cannot afford (to buy) the car because it is *way too* expensive. (➤ この way は「とても」の意のインフォーマルな副詞).

ベランダ a **veranda**(**h**) /vərǽndə/, 《米また》a **porch** (屋根付きで張り出した)

危ないカタカナ語 ✹ ベランダ
(1) 日本語では「ベランダ」と「バルコニー」が混乱して使われているようだが, 厳密にいえば veranda(h) は一階部分の外に屋根をつけた一種の外廊下, balcony /bǽlkəni/ は地面から離れた部分に張り出した屋根のない台をいう.
(2) ただし最近ではマンションのベランダをさして (covered) balcony ということも多い.

へり 縁 an **edge**; a **hem** (衣服の); a **border** (畳・ござなどの).

ベリーダンス **belly dancing.**

ヘリウム 《化学》**helium** /híːliəm/.

ペリカン 《鳥》a **pelican.**

へりくだる **humble** one**self** ▶あんまりへりくだるのもどうかと思う I don't think you need to *humble yourself* [*put yourself down*] too much. (➤ put oneself down は「自分を悪く言う」の意のインフォーマルな表現) ‖ 彼女はいつもへりくだったものの言い方をする She always *speaks humbly* [*in a modest way*].

へりくつ 屁理屈 a **quibble** /kwíbəl/ ▶そんなのへ理屈だよ That's nothing but *quibbling.* ‖ 彼はつまらないことによくへ理屈をつける He often *quibbles* over trivial matters.

ヘリコプター a **helicopter** /hélәkɑːptəʳ/ 《参考》(1) 日本語ではしばしば「ヘリ」と略すが英語では copter と前半を略す. (2) インフォーマルでは chopper ともいう. ▶ヘリコプターは頭上でブンブン旋回した The *helicopter* whirred directly overhead.

ヘリポート a **heliport.**

1**へる** **減る** **1**【**減少する**】**decrease** /dìːkríːs/ ; **lose** (体重が) ▶T 大志願者の数が減った The number of applicants for admission to T University *has decreased*. ／Applicants to T University *have decreased in number*. (➤ 人数の場合は in number を省略しないのがふつう) ‖ ことしは交通事故が目立って減った Traffic accidents *have decreased* (*in number*) markedly this year. ／This year has seen a marked *decline* in (the number of) traffic accidents.

▶夏の間に体重が 2 キロ減った I *lost* two kilograms during the summer. ‖ お母さん, 砂糖が減ってきてるよ We're *running short of* [*on*] sugar, Mom! /We're *running low on* sugar, Mom! ‖ 今月は売り上げが減った Sales *have fallen off* [*have gone down*] this month.

2【**磨滅する**】**wear out** ▶靴のかかとが減ってしまった The heels of my shoes *are worn out*.

▶口の減らないやつだな You've *got a rejoinder for everything* (I say). (➤ rejoinder は「言い返し」「反論」).

3【**腹がすく**】▶おなかが減ってきた I began to feel *hungry*. ／I'm getting *hungry*. →腹ぺこ ; ぺこぺこ.

2**へる** **経る** **1**【**経過する**】**pass, go by** ▶日を経るにしたがって彼の病は重くなった His condition grew worse as the days *went by*. ‖ 法案は紆余(うよ)曲折を経てようやく可決された The bill was finally passed *after* many twists and turns.

2【**経由する**】▶彼女はパリを経てローマへ行った She went to Rome *by way of* [*via*] Paris.

3【**経験する**】**go through** ▶初心者コースを経てから中級コースに入るのがいいでしょう You'd better *go through* the introductory course before trying the intermediate class.

ベル a **bell** ▶ベルを押す push *a bell button* ‖ ベルを鳴らす ring *a bell* ‖ 発車のベルが鳴った The *bell* sounded to indicate the departure of the train. ‖ 伊藤先生はベルとともに教室に入って来る Mr. Ito enters the classroom *at the sound of the* (*school*) *chime*. ‖ 風呂に入っていたら玄関のベルが鳴った When I was taking a bath, the *doorbell* rang.

‖**ベルボーイ** a bellhop, a hotel porter (➤ a bellboy, a bellman ともいうが, 性差の観点から使用を避けたほうがよい).

ペルー **Peru** /pərúː/ (南米の太平洋岸の国)

‖**ペルー人** a Peruvian.

ベルギー **Belgium** /béldʒəm/ (ヨーロッパ中西部の国)

‖**ベルギー人** a Belgian.

ベルサイユ **Versailles** /vəʳsáɪ/ (パリの南西にある都市)

‖**ベルサイユ宮殿** the Palace of Versailles.

ヘルシー **healthy** ▶ヘルシーなメニュー a *healthy* menu item (メニューの中の 1 品 ; 全品がヘルシーなものならば a healthy menu).

ペルシャ **Persia** /pə́ːʳʒə/ (イランの旧称) 一形 **ペルシャの** **Persian** ‖**ペルシャ猫** a Persian cat ‖ **ペルシャ湾** the Persian Gulf.

ヘルシンキ **Helsinki** (フィンランドの首都).

ヘルス **health** (健康)

‖**ヘルスクラブ** a health club ‖ **ヘルスセンター** a relaxation spa ‖ **ヘルスメーター** bathroom [bath] scale(s).

ヘルツ 《物理学》 **hertz** /həːʳts/ 《略 Hz》 (➤ 単複同形) ▶ラジオ日本は 1422 キロヘルツで放送している Radio Nippon broadcasts on 1,422 *kilohertz* [*kHz*].

‖**メガヘルツ** megahertz 《略 MHz》.

ベルト a **belt** ▶安全ベルト a safety *belt* ‖ ベルトを締める fasten [buckle] one's *belt* ‖ ベルトをゆるめる loosen one's *belt* ‖ ベルトにおつかまりください Hold onto the *belt*.

‖**ベルトコンベヤー** a conveyor belt (➤ 語順に注意. 単に conveyor ともいう) ‖ **ベルト通し** a belt loop.

ヘルニア 《医学》 (a) **hernia** /hə́ːʳniə/, a **rupture**

‖**椎間板ヘルニア** a slipped disk [disc].

ヘルパー a **caregiver**, a **home helper** (家事と合わせて介護も行う人) ; a **home health aide**, a **home care worker**, 《英》 a **home help** (正式な資格を持った「ホームヘルパー(訪問介護員)」に相当) ; a **domestic** [**household**] **helper**, a **help** (家事を手伝う人) ▶85歳の父にはヘルパーが必要だ My 85-year-old father needs *a caregiver* [*a home care worker*].

ベルファスト **Belfast** /bélfæst ‖ bèlfáːst/ (北アイルランドの都市).

ヘルペス 《医学》 **herpes** /hə́ːʳpiːz/ ; a **cold sore** (口辺ヘルペス) ▶口の隅にヘルペスができている I have *a cold sore* on the corner of my mouth.

ヘルメット a **helmet** ; a **crash helmet** (特にレーサーなどがかぶるがんじょうなもの) ; a **hard hat** (作業現場でかぶるもの) ▶バイクに乗るときにはヘルメットをかぶりましょう Be sure to wear *a* (*safety*) *helmet* when you ride a motorcycle.

ベルモット **vermouth** /vəːʳmúːθ ‖ vɜ́ːməθ/.

ベルリン **Berlin** /bəːʳlín/ (ドイツの首都).

ベレー a **beret** /bəréɪ/.

べろ a **tongue** (舌).

ヘロイン **heroin** /héroʊɪn/.

べろべろ ▶最初のデートだってのに彼ったらべろべろに酔って来たのよ Believe it or not, my boyfriend *was smashed* [*plastered*] when he came to our first date.

ぺろぺろ ▶猫が自分の足をぺろぺろなめている A cat *is licking* its paws. ‖ 猫がぺろぺろとミルクをなめている A cat *is lapping* [*slurping*] *up* the milk. (➤ lap は「液体をなめて飲む」, slurp は「ペチャペチャ音を立てて飲む」の意).

ぺろり ▶男はご飯をどんぶりで 5 杯ぺろりと平らげた The man *gobbled up* five big bowls of rice *in a flash*. ／The man *devoured* five huge bowls of rice *in no time*. (➤ devour /dɪváʊəʳ/ は「むさぼり食う」の意の堅い語で, ややおどけた感じがする) ‖ その競技参加者はホットドッグ20個をぺろりと平らげた The contestant ate twenty hot dogs, *just like that*. (➤ just like that は「あっさりと, やすやすと」の意のインフォーマルな言い方).

▶犬が私の手をぺろりとなめた The dog *gave* my hand *a lick*. ‖ 彼は私に向かってぺろりと舌を出した He *stuck out his tongue* at me.

べろんべろん ▶彼はべろんべろんに酔っぱらって立ち上がることもできなかった He was so *plastered* [*drunk*] (that) he couldn't get to his feet.

1**へん** **辺** **1**【**あたり**】a **part** ; a **region**, a **district** (地域 ; 後者のほうが狭い) ▶町もこの辺は人通りが少ない This is a fairly quiet *part* of town. ‖ この辺はお茶の産地だ Tea is produced in this *region* [*district*]. ‖ 彼はどこかその辺に住んでいる He lives somewhere *around there* [*in that neighborhood*]. ‖ (背中の)

どの辺がかゆいの？この辺？それともこの辺？ *What part* (of your back) itches [*Where* does your back itch]? *Here?* Or *here?*

2【程度】▶その辺で休憩にしたらどうだい？How about taking a break *now*? ‖きょうはこの辺にしておこう *That's all* for today.（➤ 授業を終えるとき）／Let's *call it a day*.（➤ 仕事を切り上げるとき）.

3【図形の】a **side** ▶正三角形の３つの辺の長さは等しい The three *sides* of a regular triangle are equal in length.

²**へん 変** **1【おかしい】strange**（奇妙な）；**odd**（普通でない，見慣れない）；**unusual**（普通のものとは違っている）；**queer**（ふだん見かけるものと違う）；**weird** /wɪəʳd/（異様な）；**suspicious**（怪しい）；《インフォーマル》**funny**（変てこな）

▶庭の方で変な音がしたよ I heard a *strange* sound in the garden. ‖田中さんのことで変なうわさが広まっている There is a *strange* rumor about Tanaka going around.

▶そんな変な話は聞いたこともない I've never heard such a *strange* story. ‖祐美子は変な服を着て卒業式に来た Yumiko wore *strange* clothes to the graduation ceremony. ‖変な男が近寄ってきて，「どこへ行くの？」と聞いた A *strange-looking* [*-acting*] man came up to me and asked, "Where are you going?"（➤ strange man だと「見知らぬ男」の意にもなる）.

▶５時到着予定の飛行機がまだ着かないのは変だ *It's strange that* the flight scheduled to arrive at five o'clock hasn't arrived yet. ‖きょうのあなた，変よ You *are acting strange* today. ‖変な話だが，夢に出てきたのと同じ事が起こったんだ It may sound *strange*, but the things I saw in my dreams really happened.

▶ロック歌手には変な髪型の人が多い Many rock singers have *unusual* hairstyles. ‖あの博物館，変なものばかりだったよ I saw only *weird* things with that museum. ‖網棚に変な包みが置き放しになっている A *suspicious* package has been left on the rack.

▶この頃どうも体調が変だ（＝どこか悪いところがある）Something seems to be *wrong* with me these days. ‖彼は箸の使い方が変だ He is *awkward* at handling chopsticks.（➤ awkward は「ぎこちない」；→おかしい）.

▶こんなにやかましいんじゃ，頭が変になっちゃうよ All this noise is *driving me crazy* [*out of my mind* ／ *up the wall*].

2【異変】an **incident**（事件）▶本能寺の変 the *incident* at the Honnoji Temple ‖井伊直弼は1860年，桜田門外の変で暗殺された Ii Naosuke was assassinated in the Sakurada Gate *Incident* of 1860.

3【音楽】▶変ホ長調 E *flat* major.

³**へん 編** **1【作品の】**▶全３編から成る書物 a three-*part* [*-volume*] book.

2【編集】▶山田太郎編の辞典 a dictionary *edited* [*compiled*] *by* Yamada Taro.

¹**べん 弁** **1【バルブ】**a **valve** ▶安全弁を閉じる close a safety *valve*.

2【方言】a **dialect** /dáɪəlekt/；an **accent**（話すときのなまり）▶東北弁の研究 a study on Tohoku *dialects* ‖彼女は京都弁で話す She speaks with a Kyoto *accent*.

3【話すこと】(a) **speech** ▶土井さんは弁がたつ Mr. Doi *is an eloquent speaker*.

²**べん 便** **1【便宜】convenience**；(a) **service**（交通の）

▶駅から学校までバスの便がある There is *bus service* [*Bus service* is available] from the train station to the school.

▶ここは電車の便がとてもいい *The train station is conveniently located* near here. ‖私の住んでいる所は交通の便が悪い The place where I live *doesn't have good transportation* [*isn't convenient to transportation* ／ *isn't conveniently located to transportation*].

2【大便】stools, feces /fíːsiːz/（➤ 後者は専門用語）▶硬い[やわらかい／異常な]便 hard [loose ／ abnormal] *stools* ‖便を検査してもらった I had my *stools* examined.（➤ 検便用の便を stool specimen という）‖きょうはまだ便が出ない（＝便通がない）I *haven't had a bowel movement* yet today.

ペン a **pen**（➤ 英語の pen はボールペンも含む）▶このペンはとても書きやすい This *pen* is very easy to write with. ／This *pen* writes very well. ‖ここにペンでサインしてください Please sign here *with a pen*. ‖手紙はペンで書かれていた The letter was written *in ink*.（➤ with a pen は「ペンという道具を使って」，in ink は「（鉛筆でなく）インクで」の意）.

ことわざ ペンは剣よりも強し The pen is mightier than the sword.

‖**ペン画** a pen(-and-ink) sketch [picture] ‖**ペン先** a penpoint；a nib（万年筆の）‖**ペン習字** penmanship ‖**ペンフレンド**《米》a pen pal,《英》a penfriend →ペンパル ‖**ペンライト** a penlight（➤ penlite ともつづる）.

☛ **ペンネーム**（→見出語）

へんあい 偏愛 **partiality**（意識的・無意識的な）；**favoritism**（意識的な）.

へんあつき 変圧器 a **transformer.**

へんい 変異《生物学》(a) **variation**；a **mutation**（突然変異）

‖**遺伝子変異** a genetic [gene] mutation.

べんい 便意 ▶冷たい牛乳を飲んだら急に便意を催した After I drank a glass of cold milk, I suddenly *had an urge to use* [*go to*] *the bathroom*.（➤《英》では toilet でよい）.

へんおんどうぶつ 変温動物《動物学》a **poikilotherm** /pɔɪkíləθəːʳm/, a **poikilothermic animal**（➤ ともに専門用語で，日常的には a cold-blooded animal と呼ばれる）.

へんか 変化 **1【変わること】**(a) **change** ━動 **変化する change**

▶小さな生き物たちは季節の変化を敏感に感じ取る Small creatures are sensitive to the *change* of seasons. ‖あなたは息子さんの行動の変化に気づくべきだったのです You should have noticed *a change* in your son's behavior.

▶山間部は平地に比べて気温の変化が激しい Temperature *changes* are more extreme in mountain areas than in flatlands. ‖体積は温度によって変化する The volume *changes* with the temperature. ‖過去数十年間に日本は大きく変化した Japan *has* greatly *changed* [*has undergone* great *changes*] in the past few decades. ‖ここ数年世界各地で政治的に大きな変化が起こりつつある The world has undergone many political *changes* over the past few years.

‖**変化球**《野球》a breaking ball [pitch].

2【多様な趣】variety /vəráɪət̬i/ ▶この辺の景色は変化に富んでいる The scenery around here *is varied*. ‖私の学園生活は変化に乏しかった My college days *were* rather *dull.* ／My college days *lacked variety* [*were monotonous*].

べんかい 弁解 (an) **excuse** /ɪkskjúːs/ (言い訳) ; (an) **explanation** (説明, 弁明) ; **justification** (正当化) ; a **defense** (弁護) **一動 弁解する excuse** /ɪkskjúːz/ 《oneself》, **make** [**give**] **an excuse** ▶彼は遅れて来たことをいろいろ**弁解した** He *made* a lot of *excuses* for coming late. ‖ 彼女は先に帰ったことを**弁解した** She *explained* [*justified*] why she had gone home early. ‖ 知らなかったでは**弁解**にならない Ignorance is no *excuse.* ／The fact that you didn't know is no *excuse.* ‖ **弁解**など聞きたくもない I don't want to listen to your *excuses.* ‖ **弁解無用** *Don't make excuses.*
▶おまえの遅刻は**弁解の余地がない**よ You *have no excuse* for arriving late. ‖ あいつは**弁解がましいことばか**り言って自分の誤りを認めようとしない He always *makes* (*up*) *excuses* and won't admit his own mistakes.

へんかく 変革 (a) **reform** (改善) ; (a) **change** (変化) ; (a) **revolution** (革命) ▶教育制度の根本的な**変革** fundamental *reforms* in the education system.

べんがく 勉学 study (勉強) ; one's **studies** (個人の学業) ▶彼女は日夜**勉学**にいそしんでいる She is occupied with her *studies* [in *studying*] day and night.

1**へんかん 変換 conversion 一動** …を(…に)**変換する convert** /kənvə́ːʳt/ 《to》 ▶ひらがなを漢字に**変換する**ときはこのキーを押してください When you want to *convert* hiragana *to* kanji, press this key.

2**へんかん 返還** (a) **return** ; (a) **reversion** (復帰) **一動 返還する return** +⽬ ▶基地の**返還**を求める demand the *return* of the base ‖ 1997年の中国へのホンコン**返還** the *reversion* of Hong Kong to China in 1997.

べんき 便器 a **toilet** ; a **urinal** /jʊ́rənəl/ (壁につけた男子用の) ; a **bedpan** (病人用 ; ベッドの中で使用する).

べんぎ 便宜 convenience ▶**便宜的**措置をとる adopt *temporary* [*stopgap*] measures (➤ それぞれ「一時的な」「間に合わせの」の意) ‖ できるだけ**便宜**をお計らいしましょう We'll *do everything possible* [*everything we can*] *to help* you. ‖ 100キロ以上の運賃は**便宜上**東京駅を起点に計算される In calculating fares for rides of 100km or more, Tokyo Station is used as the starting point *for the sake of convenience.*

ペンキ paint ▶ペンキがはげてしまった The *paint* has come off. ‖ 家のひさしをペンキで白く塗ってもらった I *had* the eaves of my house *painted* white. ‖ 《掲示》ペンキ塗りたて Wet [《米また》 Fresh] Paint.
‖**ペンキ屋** a painter (人).

へんきごう 変記号 《音楽》 a **flat.**

へんきゃく 返却 (a) **return 一動 返却する return** +⽬
▶本は必ず期限内に**返却してください** Please remember to *return* the book by the due date. ‖ 読み終わった本は元の場所に**返却してください** Please *put* the book *back* when you're finished with it.

へんきゅう 返球 ▶外野から(二塁へ)の**返球**がそれて一塁ランナーが一挙に生還した The ball *thrown back* from the outfielder went wide (of the second baseman), allowing the runner to score all the way from first.

1**へんきょう 辺境** a **frontier** /frʌntíəʳ/ ; a **remote region** (人里離れた地) ; a **borderland** (国境地帯) ▶**辺境**の村 a village on the *frontier.*

2**へんきょう 偏狭** ▶**偏狭な**ナショナリズムは危険だ *Narrow-minded* nationalism is dangerous.

べんきょう 勉強

1【勉学】 **study** ; one's **studies** (個人の学業) **一動 勉強する study, work** (➤ 後者は意味が広く, 仕事[作業]をする場合にも用いる) ▶**勉強**をなおざりにしたことを後悔しています I regret having neglected my *studies.* ‖ 大学では宇宙科学を**勉強する**つもりです I'm going to *study* space science in college. ‖ 日本では高校時代によく**勉強して**大学では怠ける傾向にある Though they *study* [*work*] hard in high school, Japanese students tend to be lazy in college. ‖ 彼は頭はいいが**勉強**が嫌いだ He is smart, but doesn't like *studying* [*to study*].
▶クラスでいちばん**勉強ができる**のは北川さんだ Kitagawa always *gets better grades* than any other student in our class. (➤「いい成績をとる」の意) ‖ 弟は**勉強ができる** My (younger) brother *does well at school* [*in his studies*]. ‖ 山本さんは**勉強家**だ Yamamoto is *a really diligent student* [*a* (*real*) *hard worker*].
▶彼女は教科書と悪戦苦闘しながら**勉強した** She *plowed her way* through her textbook. (➤ plow through は「かきわけて進む」の意) ‖ 彼らは毎週土曜日, 司法試験のため**勉強会**を開いている Every Saturday they hold *study sessions* to prepare for the judicial examinations.
‖**勉強部屋** a study (おとな用の書斎) 《参考》子供の勉強部屋はふつう one's (bed)room という.

2【経験, 教訓】▶今回のキャンプは息子にはいい**勉強**になったと思う I think my son *learned a lot* from this camp. ‖ 今回の失敗はいい**勉強**になりました I *learned a* (*good*) *lesson* from this mistake. (➤ lesson は「教訓」)

3【安く売ること】▶少し**勉強して**くれない? How about (*giving* me) *a* little *discount*? ／Can't you *give* me *a* small *discount*? (➤ give a discount は「値引きをする」) ‖ せいぜい**勉強して**おきます I'll *give* you as big *a discount* as possible. ／I'll *discount* it as much as possible.
☛ 不勉強 (→見出語)

へんきょく 編曲 (an) **arrangement** (➤ 曲そのものを指すときは an をつける) **一動 編曲する arrange** +⽬ ▶バッハの組曲をギター曲に**編曲する** *arrange* a Bach suite for the guitar ‖『展覧会の絵』はラベルのオーケストラ**編曲**版で有名だ "Pictures at an Exhibition" is well known for the orchestral version *arranged* by Ravel.
‖**編曲者** an arranger.

へんきん 返金 (a) **repayment,** (a) **refund** /ríːfʌnd/ **一動 返金する pay back, repay** +⽬, **refund** /rɪfʌ́nd/ +⽬ ▶一度納めた入学金はいかなる場合でも**返金**いたしません Once the admission fee has been paid, it will not *be refunded* under any circumstances.

ペンギン 《鳥》 a **penguin** /péŋgwɪn/
‖**イワトビペンギン** a rockhopper penguin ‖ **コウテイペンギン** an emperor penguin.

へんくつ 偏屈な perverse /pəʳvə́ːʳs/ (ひねくれた) ; **stubborn** (性格的に強情な) ; **obstinate** (がんこで意見を変えない) ; **eccentric** /ɪkséntrɪk/ (変わり者の) ▶**偏屈**じいさん a *stubborn* old man ／a codger (➤ 後者はインフォーマルな語).

へんけい 変形 (a) **transformation** (形を変えること) ; (a) **deformation** (形を崩すこと) **一動 変形する be de-**

formed ▶熱湯をかけたらプラスチックの容器はすっかり変形してしまった The plastic container *was* completely *deformed* when I poured hot water on it.

‖変形文法 transformational grammar.

べんけい 弁慶 ‖**弁慶の泣き所** Benkei's weak point, a chink in one's armor ; one's Achilles' heel.

へんけん 偏見 (a) **prejudice**(不合理な毛嫌い) ; (a) **bias** /báiəs/ (偏った好悪) ▶両親はヒップホップに対して偏見を持っている My parents have *a prejudice* [*a bias*] against hip-hop music. (➤ against を in favor of や for に変えると「えこひいきしている」の意になる) ／My parents are prejudiced against hip-hop music.

▶偏見のある見方 a *prejudiced* [*biased*] view ‖人種的偏見を克服するよう努めなければならない We must try to break down *racial prejudice* [overcome *racial bias*].

べんご 弁護 **defense** 一動 **弁護する** **defend** +目 ▶その大臣は自分の秘書を弁護するために若い有能な弁護士を雇った The Minister hired a young and capable *lawyer* to *defend* his secretary. ‖彼女はいつも自己弁護しようとする She always tries to *defend herself* [to *say she is right*].

‖**弁護団** the (defense) counsel ‖**弁護人** a counsel.

☛ 弁護士 (→見出語)

[1]**へんこう 変更** (a) **change** ; (an) **alteration** /ɔ̀:ltəréiʃən/ (部分的な) 一動 **変更する** **change** +目, **alter** /ɔ́:ltəʳ/ +目 ▶計画に変更がある場合は追ってお知らせします We will inform you later if there is any *change* [*alteration*] in the plan. ‖場合によりプログラムの一部を変更することがあります *There will be a change* in the program [The program *will be changed*] due to unforeseen circumstances. ‖集合時間が7時半から7時に変更された The meeting time *has been changed* from 7 : 30 to 7 : 00.

[2]**へんこう 偏向** (a) **bias** /báiəs/ ▶偏向した報道 a *slanted* [*biased*] report.

‖**偏向教育** a politically [an ideologically] biased education.

[3]**へんこう 偏光** 《光学》**polarization**

‖**偏光レンズ** a polarized lens ‖**偏光フィルター** a polarizing filter.

べんごし 弁護士 a **lawyer**, 《米また》a **counselor**, 《米また》an **attorney (at law)** (➤ 最後の語が前の2語よりさらに上品な響きを持つ) ▶弁護士を頼む hire [engage] *a lawyer* ‖弁護士に相談する see [consult ／confer with] *a lawyer* ‖兄は大阪で弁護士を開業している My (older) brother *practices law* in Osaka.

べんざ 便座 a **toilet seat**

‖**便座カバー** a toilet seat cover ‖**温水洗浄便座** a toilet seat with a hot-water bidet-like spray (➤ 説明的な訳).

へんさい 返済 (a) **payment**(支払い) ; (a) **repayment** (払い戻し) 一動 **返済する** **pay (back), repay** +目 ▶私はまだ借金を返済していない I haven't *paid back* [haven't *repaid*] my debt yet. ‖彼はすぐにその金を返済せよと迫った He demanded prompt *payment* of the money. ‖このローンを返済し終えるのに20年かかる It will take me twenty years to *pay off* the loan. (➤ pay off は「(借金などを)全部払う」) ‖返済期限は3月末日です The *repayment is due* on March 31.

‖**返済期日** a repayment due date.

[1]**へんざい 偏在** **uneven distribution** ▶偏在する *be unevenly distributed*.

[2]**へんざい 遍在** **omnipresence** 一形 **遍在する** **omnipresent**.

へんさち 偏差値 ***hensachi***, a **standard score** (whose distribution has a mean of 50 and a standard deviation of 10) (➤ カッコ以下は説明的 ; 統計学では T-score と呼び, これの使用も可)

‖**偏差値教育** education which places too much importance on test results [on the T-score].

へんさん 編纂 **compilation**(資料を集めてまとめること) ; **editing** (編集) 一動 **編さんする** **compile** /kəmpáil/ +目, **edit** +目 ▶辞書を編さんする *compile* a dictionary.

‖**編さん者** a compiler.

へんし 変死 an **unnatural death**(不自然な死) ; a **mysterious** [**suspicious**] **death** (不可解な死) ▶警察は川で発見された変死体の身元確認に全力を尽くしている The police have been doing their utmost to identify the (*dead*) *body* found in the river.

へんじ 返事 an **answer**, a **reply**(➤ 後者は前者より堅い語) 一動 **返事する** **answer** (+目), **reply** 《to》 ▶呼ばれたら返事をしなさい *Answer* (me) when you are called. ‖《声をかけたのに黙っている相手に》返事ぐらいしろよ! *Talk to me!* ／*I'm talking to you!* ‖チャイムを鳴らしても返事がなかった I rang the bell, but nobody *answered*.

▶できるだけ早くご返事をください Please give me your *answer* as soon as you can. ／Please *answer* [*respond* ／*reply*] as soon as possible.

✉ **ご返事が遅れてすみません** I am sorry I didn't *answer* [*reply to*] you sooner. ／I'm sorry for not having *written* you sooner.

✉ **お返事を待っています** I am looking forward to *hearing from you* [*your reply*].

✉ **5月10日までにお返事ください** *R.S.V.P.* by May 10. ➤「どうぞ返事してください」の意のフランス語 Répondez s'il vous plaît. の頭文字 ; 招待状などによく使う.

べんし 弁士 an **orator**.

へんしつ 変質 ▶湿気はこの粉を変質させる Moisture will *cause* this powder *to deteriorate*. (➤ deteriorate は「品質が低下する」) ‖この牛乳は封を切らなければ90日は変質しない This carton of milk will *keep* [will *not spoil*] for 90 days unless it is opened.

‖**変質者** a pervert /pə́:ʳvə:ʳt/ (性倒錯者) ; a psychopath /sáikəpæθ/ (精神病質者).

へんじゃ 編者 an **editor**, a **compiler**.

へんしゅ 変種 《生物学》a **mutation**, a **variety**.

へんしゅう 編集 **editing** ; **compilation** (編さん) 一動 **編集する** **edit** +目, **compile** /kəmpáil/ +目 ▶新しい雑誌を編集する *edit* a new magazine ‖このビデオカメラは編集が容易だ It's easy to *edit* using this camcorder. ‖彼は編集部の一員だ He is *on the editorial staff*.

‖**編集会議** an editorial [an editors'] meeting ‖**編集後記** an editor's postscript [note(s)] ‖**編集者** an editor(責任者) ; a member of the editorial staff (編集部員) ; a compiler (辞典・選集などの) ; a (film) cutter (映画の) ‖**編集主幹** the editor in chief, the executive editor ‖**編集長** the chief editor, the editor in chief ‖**編集部** an editorial department.

べんじょ 便所 a **bathroom**,《英また》a **toilet**(家の); a **restroom**, a **lavatory**(公共の場所の). →トイレ.
‖**公衆便所** a (public) restroom ‖(野営地・キャンプ場などで, 土を掘って作った)**簡易便所** a latrine /lətríːn/.

へんじょう 返上する **give up** ▶彼女はミスでないことがばれてミス東京の名を返上した When it came out that she was married, she *gave up* the title of Miss Tokyo.
▶我々は夏休みを返上して学園祭の準備をした We *gave up* (most of) our summer vacation to make preparations for our school festival.

べんしょう 弁償 **compensation** 一動 (…を)**弁償する** **compensate**《for》; **pay**《for》(支払う) ▶弁償してよ You have to *pay for* it. ／You have to *pay* (me) *compensation* (*for* it). ‖彼らは損害の弁償を要求している They are demanding *compensation* for their loss. ／They are claiming damages for their loss.

【文型】
人(A)に損害(B)を弁償する
compensate A **for** B

▶そちらが悪いのだから自転車の修理代を弁償してほしい I want you to *compensate* [*pay*] me *for* the repairs to my bicycle because you're the one who broke it.
▶ 50万円の損害は保険で弁償された Five hundred thousand yen in damages *was covered* by insurance.

べんしょうほう 弁証法《哲学》**dialectic**.

1**へんしょく 変色** **discoloration** 一動 **変色する** **discolor**(色が変わる); **fade**(色があせる); **tarnish**(光沢・つやのある物をくもらせる) ▶このカラー写真は100年間変色しません These color prints will not *fade* for one hundred years.

2**へんしょく 偏食** an **unbalanced diet**(バランスのよくない食事);《インフォーマル》**picky eating**(えり好みをして食べること) ▶偏食は体に悪い *Eating only what you like* [*your favorite foods*] is bad for your health.

ペンション a **lodge**, a **resort inn** ▶今度のゴールデンウイークに清里のペンションに泊まりに行きます We are going to stay at *a resort inn* at Kiyosato this coming Golden Week.

危ないカタカナ語✹ ペンション
1 民宿風の小ホテルを指す「ペンション」はフランス語の *pension*(下宿屋)からきているが, 英語としては通じない. 英語の pension は「年金」の意味である.
2 日本でいう「ペンション」を表すには lodge(山小屋), resort inn(保養地の旅館), small hotel(小ホテル)などを用いる.

ペンシルベニア **Pennsylvania** /pènsəlvéɪnjə/ (アメリカ東部の州; 略 PA, Pa., Penn.).

1**へんしん 返信** an **answer**, a **reply**(➤ 後者は前者より堅い語) ▶切手をはった返信用封筒を同封のこと Please enclose *a self-addressed, stamped envelope*. 《参考》しばしば SASE と省略される. また stamped, self-addressed envelope の語順になることもある.

2**へんしん 変身** (a) **transformation** 一動 **変身する** **be transformed**《into》, **transform**《into》 ▶けものはハンサムな王子に変身した The beast *was transformed into* a handsome prince. ‖おとぎ話では動物が人に変身することが多い In fairy tales, animals often *change* [*transform*] *into* people.

3**へんしん 変心** a **change of heart**, a **change of mind**. →心変わり.

へんじん 変人 an **odd** [**eccentric**] **person**(➤ eccentric は好意的に見られる場合もある); a **crank**(変わり者); a **crackpot**(頭がいかれたやつ); a **weird person**, a **weirdo**(奇妙な人) ▶ぼくを変人扱いするな Don't treat me like *a crank*!

ベンジン《化学》**benzine** /bénziːn/.

ペンス **pence**《略 p》(➤ ペニー (penny) の複数形). →ペニー.

へんすう 変数《数学》a **variable**.

へんずつう 偏頭痛 a **migraine (headache)**
▶私はときどき偏頭痛がある I sometimes *have* [*get*] *migraines*.

へんせい 編成 **organization** 一動 **編成する** **organize** +Ⓞ(組織する) ▶彼らは新しい歌のグループを編成した They *have organized* a new singing group. ‖ 1年生は5クラスに編成された(＝分けられた) The first-year students *were divided into* five homeroom classes.
▶このローカル線では2両編成の列車が走っている Trains on this local line *are made up* [*are composed*] *of* only two cars. ／Trains on this local line have only two cars each. ‖彼らは特別番組の編成に追われていた They were busy *making* [*planning*] a special program. ‖政府は来年度の予算編成に取り組んでいる The government is now busy *making up* [*drawing up*] the budget for the next year.
☛ 再編成 (→見出語)

へんせいき 変声期 ▶息子は今変声期です My son is going through *a change-of-voice* (*stage*). ／My son's voice is changing now.

へんせいふう 偏西風 **the westerlies, prevailing westerlies.**

べんぜつ 弁舌 ▶PTA会長はいつも弁舌さわやかだ The president of the PTA always *speaks eloquently* [*fluently*].

へんせん 変遷 (a) **change**(変化); (a) **transition**(移行, 推移) ▶社会的変遷 (a) social *transition* ‖時代は変遷する Times *change*. ‖首相官邸は幾多の歴史的変遷を見てきた建物だ The prime minister's official residence has seen many historical *changes*.

ベンゼン《化学》**benzene** /bénziːn/.

1**へんそう 返送する** **return** +Ⓞ, **send back**(➤ 後者は「送り返す」という日本語に近い) ▶その荷物はあて先が間違っていたので返送されてきた The parcel *was sent back* [*was returned*] to me because it was wrongly addressed.
✉《通信販売》注文書にご記入のうえご返送ください Please fill in [out] the order form and *send* it *to us*.

2**へんそう 変装** (a) **disguise** /dɪsgáɪz/ 一動 **変装する** **disguise** oneself《as》 ▶彼は変装のためかつらとつけひげをつけた He put on a wig and a false mustache for *disguise*. ‖犯人たちは警備員に変装して, 美術館に侵入した The perpetrators *disguised themselves as* security guards and broke into the museum.

へんぞう 変造 ▶変造紙幣 an *illegally altered* bill.

へんそうきょく 変奏曲《音楽》a **musical variation** ▶バッハのゴルトベルク変奏曲 Bach's Goldberg *Var-*

iations.

[1]へんそく **変則の** **irregular** ▶期末テスト後は時間割は変則になる We will have a *special* [an *irregular*] class schedule after the term exams. ‖彼のピッチングフォームは変則的だ His pitching form is *unorthodox*.

[2]へんそく **変速** ▶ギアをローに変速する *shift* [*change*] *into* low [bottom／first] gear ‖この自転車は10段変速です This is a *ten-speed* bike.
‖**変速レバー** a gearshift, a shifter.

[1]へんたい **変態** 1【昆虫などの】(a) **metamorphosis** /mèṭəmɔ́ːʳfəsɪs/ [複 **metamorphoses**] ▶昆虫は数回変態する Insects go through several *metamorphoses*.
▶この絵は幼虫がチョウに変態する過程を示したものです These pictures show how a caterpillar *changes into* a butterfly.
2【性的な】**abnormality**（異常）; **perversion** /pəʳvə́ːʳʒən/（性的倒錯）; a **pervert** /pə́ːʳvəːʳt/（人）▶あいつは少し変態だ He's a little *abnormal*. ／He's a bit of *a pervert*. ‖変な所を触らないでよ, ヘンタイ! *You pervert!* Get your hands off me!（➤ pervert は非難のニュアンスが強い）.

[2]へんたい **編隊** (a) **formation** ▶ほら, 戦闘機が編隊を組んで飛んでいる Look! Some jet fighters are flying *in formation*.
‖**編隊飛行** a formation flight.

へんたいがな 変体仮名 a **variant form of a kana letter**.

ペンタゴン **the Pentagon**（アメリカ国防総省の通称）.

べんたつ 鞭撻 **encouragement**
✉ **今後ともいっそうご指導ご鞭撻くださいますようお願い申し上げます** We hope to benefit from your continued guidance and *encouragement*. ➤ 日本語の直訳であり, 英語では卑屈に響いたり, 自主性に欠けるように思われたりするおそれがある. 英語的には, 例えば It is our [my] earnest hope that our business relations may long continue.（仕事の関係が今後長く続くことを切望します）のように表現するほうがよい.

ペンダント a **pendant** ▶ペンダントをつけている wear *a pendant*.

ベンチ 1【長いす】a **bench**; a **pew** /pjuː/（教会内の会衆用の）▶ベンチに座る sit on *a bench*.
2【野球場の】**the bench**; a **dugout**（ダッグアウト）▶代打要員が2人ベンチに控えている Two pinch hitters are warming *the bench* [are waiting on *the bench*].
▶その選手はエラーをしてベンチに下げられた The player *was benched* after committing an error.

ペンチ (a **pair of**) **pliers** 《参考》pliers は「やっとこ」「くぎ抜き」などの工具の総称でもある. また,「ペンチ」の語源とされる pincers や pinchers も pliers の一種.

ベンチャー a **venture**（事業）
‖**ベンチャー企業** a venture company ‖**ベンチャー資本家** a venture capitalist.

[1]へんちょう **偏重** ▶日本の社会は学歴偏重だ Japanese society *puts too much stress on* (*a person's*) *academic background*. ／Japanese society *is extremely diploma-oriented*.（➤ diploma-oriented は「卒業証書重視の」の意）‖知育をあまり偏重すべきでない We should not *attach too much importance to* intellectual training. ／We shouldn't *put too much weight* [*emphasis*] *on* academic skill.

[2]へんちょう **変調** ▶彼女はこの2, 3日体に変調をきたしている She has *been in poor health* [*hasn't been up to par*] for the last few days.

べんつう 便通 **bowel** /báʊəl/ **movements**（➤ インフォーマルな会話では頭文字の BM をよく使う）→通じ ▶野菜は便通を助ける Eating vegetables will help you have regular *bowel movements*.

ペンディング ▶その件はペンディングになったままだ That matter is still *pending*.

へんてこ 変てこな **queer, odd**（➤ 前者のほうが変わっている度合いが強く, 日本語の場合と同様やや古風）; **weird** /wɪəʳd/, **funny**（➤ 前者は人に用いると「うす気味悪い」という変質者的イメージを生む）
▶変てこな服着るなよ Don't wear *weird* [*funny*] clothes.

へんてつ 変哲 ▶《手品師のことば》皆さん, これは何の変てつもない帽子です Boys and girls! This is just an ordinary hat, *nothing strange* [*unusual*] about it.

へんでんしょ 変電所 a (**transformer**) **substation**.

へんとう 返答 an **answer**, a **reply**（➤ 後者は前者より堅い語）▶生徒たちに,「なぜ長髪はいけないのですか」と聞かれて返答に窮した When my students asked me, "what's wrong with long hair?" I did *not know how to answer* them.

へんどう 変動 (a) **change**（変化）; (a) **fluctuation**（物価・株価などの）一動 **変動する** **change, fluctuate** ▶変動する世の中 a *changing* world ‖このところ株価が激しく変動している Stock prices have been *fluctuating* a lot recently.
‖**変動為替相場制** a floating exchange rate system ‖**変動期** uncertain times, an age of transition.

べんとう 弁当 a ***bento***（➤ 英語化している）; a **box lunch**, a **box meal**（箱に詰めた）▶弁当を食べる eat one's *bento* ‖弁当を広げる open one's *box lunch* ‖きょうは弁当を持って来た I brought *a lunch* [*bento*] with me today. ‖母が毎朝弁当を作ってくれる My mother makes *a bento* for me every morning.
‖**弁当箱** a bento [lunch] box ‖**愛妻弁当** a lunch one's (loving) wife has made 《参考》「愛妻弁当」にぴったりの対応語はない. アメリカの勤め人の中にはサンドイッチ, ハンバーガーなどの自家製の弁当を brown bag と呼ばれる褐色の紙袋に入れて勤め先に持って行く人も多く, そういう人を brown-bagger という.

へんとうせん 扁桃腺《解剖学》**tonsils** /tɑ́ːnsəlz/（➤ 通例複数形で）
▶へんとうせんがはれています You have swollen *tonsils*. ／Your *tonsils* are swollen.
‖**へんとうせん炎** tonsillitis.

へんにゅう 編入 **admission**（学校への）; **incorporation**（町などの合併）一動 **編入する** **admit** +目（入学を許可する）; **incorporate** +目 ▶彼は2年の編入試験を受けた He took *an examination for admission* into the sophomore class.
▶私はX大の3年に編入を希望している I want to *transfer to* [*be admitted* (*to*)] X University as a third-year student. ‖その村は昨年この市に編入された The village *was incorporated* into this city last year.

ペンネーム a **pen name**, a **pseudonym** /sjúːdənɪm/, a **nom de plume** /nɑ̀ːm də plúːm/（➤ 最後の言い方はフランス語で, name of pen の意）▶夏目金之助は夏目漱石というペンネームを使った Natsume Kinnosuke used the *pen name* of Natsume Soseki. ／Natsume Soseki is the *pseudonym* used by Natsume Kinnosuke.

へんぱい 返杯する **offer a cup of sake in return.**

ペンパル 《米》a **pen pal,** 《英》a **penfriend.**

✉ **私のよいペンパルになってくださることを願ってます** I hope you will be a good *pen pal* [*penfriend*] of mine.

✉ **アメリカ人のペンパルを１人紹介してください** Could you introduce me to an American *pen pal* [*penfriend*]?

へんぴ 辺鄙な **remote** ▶その詩人は都会から遠く離れたへんぴな村に住んでいる The poet lives in a *remote* [*out-of-the-way*] village far from any city.

べんぴ 便秘 **constipation** /kɑ̀ːnstɪpéɪʃən/ **―動 便秘する** **be constipated** /kάːnstɪpèɪt̬ɪd/ ▶私は便秘ぎみです I'*m a little constipated*.
▶私はしつこい便秘に苦しんでいます I'm suffering from a bad case of *constipation*. 《参考》英語圏では「便秘」や「下痢」に関しては口にするのも恥ずかしいと考える人が多い.
‖**便秘薬** a laxative /lǽksət̬ɪv/ (下剤).

へんぴん 返品 **returned goods** [**articles**] ▶返品の山 a heap of *returned goods* ‖《掲示》特売品の返品はご容赦願います Sale items cannot *be returned* [*taken back*].

✉ **《通信販売で》送られてきたジーンズはサイズが違っていましたので返品いたします** Since the jeans you sent are the wrong size, *I am returning them*. ➤ このあとに Please send me in exchange another pair in size S. (サイズＳのと取り替えてください)などと続ける.

へんぺいそく 扁平足 a **flatfoot.**

へんぼう 変貌 a **transformation** ▶シンガポールは著しい変ぼうを遂げている Singapore *has undergone a dramatic transformation*.

べんぽう 便法 an **expedient** /ɪkspíːdiənt/ **measure** (便宜的手段); an **expedient policy** (ご都合主義) ▶プライムレートの引き下げは景気押し上げのための便法だ Lowering the prime rate is *an expedient measure* [*a temporary measure*] to boost the economy.

べんむかん 弁務官 a **commissioner**
‖**国連難民高等弁務官** a United Nations high commissioner for refugees.

へんめい 変名 an **assumed name**; a **false name** (事実に反する不正確な名) ▶変名を用いる assume *a false name*.

べんめい 弁明 (an) **excuse** (自分の言動に対する言い分) ⇀弁解 ▶自分の行為に対して弁明する *make an excuse* for one's behavior ‖きみの失敗は弁明の余地のないものだ *There is no excuse* for your mistake. ／Your mistake is *inexcusable*. ‖その男は万引きの現行犯で捕まったのだから弁明のしようがない Since the man was caught in the act of shoplifting, he doesn't have any *defense*.

へんよう 変容 (a) **metamorphosis** /mèt̬əmɔ́ːʳfəsɪs/ (不可思議な力による一大変化); (a) **transformation** (大変身) **―動 変容する** **metamorphose** /mèt̬əmɔ́ːʳfouz/, **be transformed.**

べんり 便利 **convenience** **―形 便利な** **convenient**; **handy** (扱いやすい); **useful** (役に立つ) ▶便利な道具 a *useful* [*handy*] tool ‖車があると便利だ It is *convenient* to have a car. ‖車はとても便利なものだが公害の元凶でもある Although a car is *a* great *convenience*, it is also a source of environmental pollution. ‖電話のそばに鉛筆とメモ帳を置いておくと伝言を書くのに便利だ Having a pencil and a memo pad near the telephone *is convenient* for taking messages. ‖私の家は地下鉄の駅へ出るのに便利なところだ My house is *convenient* for the subway station.
▶ふろしきは必要がなければ畳んでポケットに入るので便利だ A furoshiki is *handy* because it can be folded and kept in your pocket when not needed. ‖私たちの学校は便利な場所にある Our school is *conveniently* located.
▶彼は何かと便利な男だ He is a *handy* person to have around. ‖私は都会の便利さより田舎の新鮮な空気のほうが大切だと思う I prefer the fresh air in the country to urban *conveniences*. ‖この台所は便利に(＝働きやすく)できている This kitchen is *easy to work* in.

べんりし 弁理士 a **patent attorney** (弁護士); a **patent agent** (代理人).

へんりん 片鱗 ▶こういう土器から我々は古代の人々の生活の片りんをうかがうことができる These earthenware pots give us *a glimpse* of the way people lived in ancient times.
▶新人投手はその試合で大物の片りんを見せた In that game, the rookie pitcher showed *signs* of becoming a great pitcher.

へんれい 返礼 ▶頂き物には返礼の必要がある場合がある There are some cases in which you need to *give* something *in return* for a gift you have received.

へんれき 遍歴 **1**【巡り歩くこと】**wandering** ▶その画家は若い頃ヨーロッパの国々を遍歴した The artist *wandered about* in Europe [*visited one* European country *after another*] when he was a young man.
2【さまざまな経験】▶そのロック歌手は多くの女性遍歴がある That rock singer *has been* (*sexually* ／ *romantically*) *involved with many women*.

へんろ 遍路 (a) **pilgrimage** (巡礼); (a) **pilgrim** (巡礼者) ▶四国遍路に出かける go on *a Shikoku pilgrimage*.

べんろん 弁論 **public speaking** (演説); (a) **debate** (討論); an (**oral**) **argument** (裁判での) ▶彼は英語の弁論大会で２等になった He won second prize in the English *speech* [*oratorical*] *contest*. (➤ 後者は堅い語).

✉ **10月に英語の弁論大会があります** There will be *an* English *speech contest* in October.
‖**弁論部** a public speaking club; a debate team (ディベートを目的とする) ‖**最終弁論** a closing argument ‖**冒頭弁論** an opening argument.

ほ・ホ

[1]ほ **帆** a **sail** ▶帆を下ろす[上げる] lower [hoist] *a sail* ‖その船は帆をいっぱいに張って走った The yacht sailed (*in*) *full sail* [*with all the sails set*].

[2]ほ **穂** an **ear** ▶穂の出た稲 rice plants *in* (*the*) *ear* ‖トウモロコシの穂 *an ear* of corn ‖小麦の穂が出てきた The wheat has *come into ear*.

[3]ほ **歩** a **step**; a **pace** (歩行の際の歩幅に基づく1歩) ▶2, 3歩前へ出[後ろへ下がり]なさい Take *a few steps* forward [backward]. ‖彼らは一歩一歩進んでいった They advanced *step by step*. ‖疲れてもう一歩も歩けません I'm so tired I can't walk *another step*.

ほあんかん 保安官 a **sheriff**
‖保安官代理 a deputy sheriff.

ほい 補遺 a **supplement**; an **appendix** (巻末付録) ▶『ブリタニカ百科事典』の補遺 the *supplement* to the Encyclopedia Britannica.

ぽい ▶彼はごみ箱にぽいと空き缶を捨てた He *chucked* [*tossed*] an empty can into the trash can.

-ぽい -ish ▶赤っぽい車 a *reddish* car ‖素人っぽい絵 an *amateurish* painting ‖ほこりっぽい道 a *dusty* road ‖ささいなことで感情的になるなんて彼も子供っぽいね It is *childish* of him to get upset over such a small matter. (➤よい意味の「子供らしい」は child-like) ‖このビールは水っぽい This beer *tastes watery* [*tastes like water*]. ‖彼の話はうそっぽい His story *sounds false*. /His story *doesn't ring true*. (➤sound, ring とも「…のように聞こえる」の意).

ホイール a **wheel**
‖ホイールキャップ a hubcap.

ほいく 保育 child care ▶この保育所[保育園]は3年保育だ They *take care of children for three years* up to school age at this *day care center* [*day nursery*]. (➤child(-)care center ともいう).
‖保育器 an incubator /íŋkjəbèɪṭəʳ/ (未熟児用の) ‖保育士 a nurse (女性の); a male nurse (男性の)《参考》幼稚園教諭は kindergarten teacher.

ボイコット a **boycott** 一動 **ボイコットする boycott** +目 ▶彼らは日本製品のボイコットを始めた They launched *a boycott* of [against] Japanese products. ‖私たちは石井先生の授業をボイコットするつもりだ We are planning to *boycott* Mr. Ishii's classes.

ぽいすて ぽい捨てする toss +目, **throw away**; **litter** ▶《掲示》ぽい捨て禁止 No Littering. /Littering Forbidden.

ボイスレコーダー a **voice recorder**.

ホイッスル a **whistle** /hwísəl/ ▶ホイッスルが鳴った *A whistle* was sounded. /The *whistle* blew.

ホイップ ホイップする whip (up) ▶ホイップ(した)クリーム *whipped* cream.

ほいほい ▶子供の言うことをほいほい聞いてやっていると子供はだめになる You'll spoil your child if you *rush to do everything* he [she] wants (you to do).

ボイラー a **boiler** ‖ボイラー室 a boiler room ‖ボイラーマン a boilerman.

ホイル foil ▶魚をホイルに包む wrap a fish in *foil*.
‖アルミホイル aluminum foil, tinfoil.

[1]**ぼいん 母音** 《音声学》a **vowel** /váʊəl/ **(sound)**
‖短[長]母音 a short [long] vowel ‖二重母音 a diphthong /dífθɔːŋ/ (➤/aʊ/, /eɪ/ など) ‖半母音 a semivowel (➤/w/, /j/ など).

[2]**ぼいん 拇印** a **thumbprint** /θʌ́mprɪnt/ ▶書類に拇印を押す put one's *thumbprint* on a document. 《参考》英米では, 一般に書類に拇印を押す習慣はないが, ほかに身分を証明するものがないときや, 文字が書けない人がサインの代わりに押すことはある.

ボイン ▶彼女はボインだ(=胸が大きい) She is *stacked* [*busty* /*buxom* /*chesty*]. /She has *big boobs*.

ポインセチア 《植物》a **poinsettia** /pɔɪnséṭiə/.

ポインター 《動物》a **pointer**.

ポイント 1【要点】the point ▶お話のポイントがわかりません I don't understand *the point* you're trying to make. ‖きみの質問はポイントをついていない Your question is *off the point*. ‖彼は取りとめもないことばかり言って, ポイントをつくことを言わなかった He rambled on and on without *coming to the point*. ‖きょうは実戦的なプレーにポイント(=力点)を置いて練習しよう During today's practice, I want to put *emphasis* on actual playing strategies.

2【「…ポイント」の形で】 ▶チェックポイント *points to check* (⇀チェック) ‖この事件を解決するキーポイント the *key* to solving this case ‖彼女はえくぼがいちばんのチャームポイントだ Her dimples are her most *attractive* [*charming*] *feature*.

3【得点・点数】 a **point** ▶我々は速攻でポイントを稼いだ We gained [picked up] *points* with a quick offensive. ‖彼女はチームのポイントゲッターだ She is the *point getter* [*high scorer*] of our team.
▶その新入社員はパソコンにたけているところを見せてポイントを稼いだ That new employee *got* [*earned*] *brownie points* by showing how proficient he [she] was at using computers. (➤brownie points は先生や上司の「評価点」「覚え」).
‖ポイントカード a (customer) loyalty card, a reward(s) card ‖マッチポイント a match point.

4【鉄道の】《米》a **switch**, 《英》**points**.

☛ ウイークポイント, セールスポイント (⇀見出語)

[1]**ほう 法 1【法律】(the) law** (➤総称); an **act** (議会などが制定した個々の) 一形 **法の legal** ▶法を守る obey [observe] *the law* ‖法を破る break *the law* ‖法を廃止する repeal *an act*.
▶人は皆法の下では平等だ People are all equal *before* [*under*] *the law*. ‖その町では法と秩序(=治安)が維持されている *Law and order* is maintained in the town.

2【方法】 a **method**, a **way** ▶わが国の英語教授法はずいぶん改善された *Methods of English teaching* in our country have been greatly improved. ‖早寝早起きが私の健康法(=健康の秘けつ)だ My *secret for staying healthy* is going to bed and getting up early.

[2]**ほう 報 news** (知らせ); a **report** (報告) ▶飛行機墜落の報に接したのは外出しようとしていたときだった I was just about to go out when I heard the *news* [*re-*

port] of the plane crash.
✉ **お父上ご逝去の報に接し，悲しみに堪えません** I was terribly sad to *hear of* your father's passing away.

[3]**ほう 方** ⚠ **日本語の「方」「ほう」は省略しても意味の通じる場合が多い．例えば「後ろの方から」「あちらの方に」「お体のほうは」はそれぞれ「後ろから」「あちらに」「お体は」としても意味はほぼ同じである．したがって，これらの「ほう」は訳文に現れないことが多い．**

1【方向】▶弾は後ろの方から飛んで来た The bullet came *from behind.* ‖ そのレストランなら左の方へ曲がるとすぐです Turn *to* the left, and you'll soon find the restaurant. ‖ 大勢の人が国会議事堂の方へ歩いていった A great crowd of people walked *toward* the Diet Building. ‖ 対話「お兄さんは今どちらですか」「関西の方に居ます」"Where is your brother these days?" "*In* the Kansai area." ‖ 対話「その飛行機はどちらの方へ飛んでいきましたか」「北の方[あちらの方]です」"*Which direction* [*way*] did the airplane fly?" "It flew *north* [*in that direction* / *that way*]."

2【方面，分野】▶その計画には経理部のほうから強硬な反対意見が出た The plan met with strong opposition *from* the accounting division. ‖ 走るほうでは(＝ことにかけては)私はクラスの誰にも負けない *When it comes to* running, I'm second to none in my class. ‖ お体のほうはその後いかがですか How are you feeling these days?

3【対比，比較】▶あなたのほうが私より背が高い *You* are taller than I am. ‖ こちらのほうがあちらより少しお安くなります *This one* is less expensive than that one. ‖ 大きいほうをちょうだい Give me *the larger one.*

▶2個のリンゴの大きいほうはもう一方の2倍の重さがある *The bigger* of the two apples is twice as heavy as *the other one.* ‖《面会の取り決めで》午後のほうが(都合が)いいのですが The afternoon would be *better.*

▶私は秋より春のほうが好きだ I *like* spring *better than* fall. / I *prefer* spring *to* fall. (→好き) ‖ 私は家に居るほうがいい I *prefer to* stay home. ‖ 多くの人がネットでショッピングをするほうを好む Many people *prefer to* shop [shopping] online. ‖ 対話「卓球やらない？」「ぼくは座って見てるほうがいいよ」"How about playing ping-pong?" "I'*d rather* sit and watch." (● I'd rather do ... は可能性のあるもののうち，好ましいほうを言う).

▶母はぽっちゃりしているほうだ My mother is *on the* plump *side.* (➤ on the ... side で「やや…で」の意で，…の部分には高低・大小・軽重を表す形容詞がくる).

4【「…したほうがいい」の形で】 should

> **《解説》should と had better**
> (1) 自分の意見として相手の人に「…したほうがいい(ですよ)」と言う場合は **should** や **ought to** を用いるのが最も一般的.
> (2) **had better** は「…しないと困ったことになる[あなたのためにならない]」という響きを持つので，年長者やあまり親しくない人などには用いないほうがよい.

▶そろそろ試合の練習を始めたほうがいい You *should* [*ought to*] go into training for the match now. ‖ あの子とはもう付き合わないほうがいいわよ You'*d better* stop seeing him [her]. / You'*d better not* go out with him [her] any more. (➤'d better は had better の省略形) ‖ いずれ本当のことがわかってしまうのだから，今白状したほうがいい We'll find out the truth sooner or later, so you *might as well* confess now. (● might as well は「…したらどうですか」に近い控えめな言い方).

[4]**ほう**《感心して》▶ほう，それはすばらしい *Oh* [*Why*], that's fantastic! ‖ ほう，きみにピアノが弾けるとは知らなかった *Well,* I didn't know that you could play the piano.

ほう- 訪- ▶訪欧 *a visit to Europe* (➤「訪欧する」は visit Europe) ‖ 訪米中の野田氏 Mr. Noda, who is *on a visit to the United States.*

ぼう 棒 1【細長い物】 a **stick** (木切れ); a **pole** (さお); a **bar** (棒状の物) ▶鉄の棒 a steel [an iron] *bar* ‖ 彼はぼくを棒で打った He hit me with *a stick.* ‖ 手が届かなければ棒を使って取ればいい If it's out of your reach, why not use *a pole* to get it?

2【慣用表現】▶彼は足を棒にしていなくなった猫を捜した He searched for the lost cat *till his legs felt like they had turned to lead.* (➤ lead /led/ は「鉛」) ‖ 彼はその汚職事件に巻き込まれて一生を棒に振った He *ruined his life* [*made his life a mess*] by getting involved in that scandal. ‖ そのスキャンダルで彼は社会的地位を棒に振った The scandal *cost* him his social position. ‖ (歴史の)年号をただ棒暗記しても無駄だ There is no point in just *learning* the dates *by rote.* (➤ learn by rote は「機械的に覚える」).

‖**棒グラフ** a bar graph.

ぼう- 某- a **certain ...** ▶某氏 *a certain* person / Mr. *So-and-so* ‖ 私は中川氏に某所で会った I met Mr. Nakagawa at *a certain* place. ‖ 彼は去年の某月某日に某国に向け出国した He left for *a certain* country on *a certain* date last year.

ほうあん 法案 a **bill** ▶武器の輸出を禁止する法案 *a bill* banning the export of weapons ‖ 法案を提出する introduce [propose] *a bill* ‖ 減税法案が成立した The tax reduction *bill* passed the Diet. 《参考》アメリカでは法案が議会を通過したあと，大統領や州知事などの首長が署名して初めて法律となる．したがって The tax reduction bill passed Congress and was signed into law. などと表現される．当然，拒否権もあり，その場合は veto the bill という.

[1]**ほうい 方位** (a) **direction**(方角); a **bearing** (方位計による方向) ▶磁石で方位を確かめる *take* one's *bearings* with a compass.

[2]**ほうい 包囲** (a) **siege** /siːdʒ/ ━動 **包囲する surround** ＋目 (敵などを); **siege** ＋目, **besiege** ＋目 (占領目的で) ▶その町は敵に包囲された The town *was besieged* by the enemy. / The enemy *laid siege to* the town.

ほういがく 法医学 forensic medicine, forensics ▶(血液・毛髪などの)法医学根拠 *forensic* evidence.

ぼういん 暴飲 excessive drinking ▶暴飲暴食をしていると体を壊すよ *Eating and drinking too much* [*Overindulging*] will ruin your health. (● 日本語とは逆に通例 eat が先にくる).

ほうえい 放映する televise ＋目, **broadcast ... on television** ▶ゴールを決めたシーンは何度も放映された The goal-scoring play *was televised* [*was telecast*] repeatedly. ‖『駅馬車』はテレビで放映されたのを見た I saw "Stagecoach" *on* TV.

ぼうえい 防衛《米》**defense,**《英》**defence** ━動 **防衛する defend** ＋目 ▶国家の防衛 national *defense* ‖ 正当防衛 legitimate self-*defense* ‖ そのボクサーはタイ

トルを防衛することができなかった The boxer could not *defend* his title.
▶空手は自己防衛の手段として始まった Karate started as a means of *self-defense*. ‖ ふつうの日本人は国家防衛意識が希薄だ Ordinary Japanese don't have a strong awareness of (the need for) *national defense*.
‖防衛省 the Ministry of Defense (➤ the Defense Ministry ともいう) ‖ 防衛大学校 National Defense Academy of Japan ‖ 防衛大臣 the Minister of Defense, the Defense Minister ‖ 防衛費 the defense budget ‖ 防衛力 defense capacity, defensive strength.

1**ぼうえき 貿易** **trade ; commerce**(国際間の通商) **一動** (…と)貿易する **trade**《with》▶外国貿易 foreign *trade* ‖ 日中貿易 the Japan-China *trade* ‖ オランダは東洋と香辛料の貿易を行っていた The Netherlands carried out *trade* in spices with the East. ‖ その商社はメキシコと貿易している The firm *trades with* Mexico.
▶アメリカは日本に対する貿易不均衡を憂慮していた The United States was worried about its *trade imbalance* with Japan.
‖貿易赤字 [黒字] a trade deficit [surplus] ‖ 貿易会社 a trading company ‖ 貿易協定 a trading agreement ‖ 貿易交渉 trade talks ‖ 貿易自由化 trade liberalization ‖ 貿易風 trade winds ‖ 貿易摩擦 trade friction, trade conflict.

2**ぼうえき 防疫** ▶防疫対策を行う take *preventive measures against an epidemic*.

ぼうえん 望遠 ‖望遠レンズ a telephoto lens.

ぼうえんきょう 望遠鏡 a **telescope** ▶土星の輪は望遠鏡ではっきり見える Saturn's rings are clearly visible *through a telescope*.
‖天体望遠鏡 an astronomical telescope ‖ 反射[電波]望遠鏡 a reflecting [radio] telescope.

1**ほうおう 法王** a **pope**
‖ローマ法王 the Pope, the Holy Father (➤ 後者は主にカトリック信者が使う言い方).

2**ほうおう 法皇** ▶後白河法皇 *the cloistered* [*retired*] *Emperor* Go-Shirakawa.

3**ほうおう 鳳凰** a ***Ho-o*** ; a phoenix-like auspicious bird in Chinese mythology (➤ 説明的な訳).

1**ぼうおん 防音** **soundproofing** ▶窓を二重にするだけでかなりの防音効果がある Putting in double-paned glass will do a lot to *cut down on sound*. ‖ この部屋は防音装置がしてある This room is *soundproof*.

2**ぼうおん 忘恩** **ingratitude.**

1**ほうか 放火** **arson,** 《英また》**fire-raising** **一動** 放火する **set fire**《to》, **set ... on fire** ▶ゆうべの火事は放火によるものだった The fire last night was a case of *arson*. ‖ 彼は保険金欲しさに自分の家に放火した He *set fire to* his own house [*set* his own house *on fire*] in order to collect the insurance.
‖放火犯人 an arsonist, 《英また》a fire-raiser ‖ 放火魔 a habitual arsonist, 《インフォーマル》a firebug.

2**ほうか 砲火** **(artillery) fire** ▶敵の砲火を浴びる be under heavy enemy *fire*.

3**ほうか 法科** **the law department [faculty], the department [faculty] of law ; the law school** (大学院クラス) ▶法科の学生 a student *in the department* [*faculty*] *of law* / a *law* student.
‖法科大学院 a graduate law school.

1**ほうが 邦画** a **Japanese film [movie].**

2**ほうが 萌芽** **budding ; the germ**(比喩的に)
‖ほう芽研究 exploratory [germinating] research.

ぼうか 防火 **fire prevention ; fireproofing**(耐火) ▶そのホテル火災では防火設備が働かなかった In that hotel fire, the *fire prevention system* failed to work. ‖ 私たちの学校は防火構造だ Our school buildings are *fireproof*.
‖防火訓練 a fire drill ‖ 防火シャッター a fireproof shutter ‖ 防火週間 Fire Prevention Week ‖ 防火扉 a fire door ‖ 防火壁 a firewall ‖ 防火用水 water for putting out fires.

ほうかい 崩壊 **collapse, a fall** (➤ 日常語としては後者がふつう) ; **a washout** (水による堤防・道路などの) ; **(a) disintegration** (国家などの) **一動** 崩壊する **collapse, fall [break] down ; be pulled down** (取り壊される)
▶学級崩壊 the *collapse* [*breakdown*] of order in classrooms (➤「学級崩壊」はほかに, classroom chaos, classroom dysfunction などとも表現される) ‖ ソ連邦の崩壊 the *collapse* [*disintegration*] of the USSR ‖ 独裁政権の崩壊を人々は歓迎した People welcomed the *fall* of the dictatorial regime. ‖ その地震でいくつかの高層アパートが崩壊した Some high-rise apartment houses *collapsed* [*fell down*] in the earthquake. ‖ 夫婦の不和がその家庭の崩壊を招いた Discord between the husband and wife *broke up* the family. ‖ 1989年, ベルリンの壁が崩壊した In 1989, the Berlin Wall *was torn* [*pulled*] *down*.
‖深層[表層]崩壊 a deep-seated [a shallow] landslide.

ほうがい 法外な **exorbitant** /ɪɡzɔ́ːˈbətənt/ ; **unreasonable** (不合理な) ▶法外な値段 an *exorbitant* price ‖ そのブランドもののバッグは法外に高い That brand-name bag is *unreasonably* expensive [is *a real rip-off*]. (➤ rip-off は「べらぼうに高い品」に相当するインフォーマルな語).

1**ぼうがい 妨害** **disturbance**(騒いで邪魔をすること) ; **obstruction**(遮ること) ; **interference**(手出しをして邪魔すること) **一動** 妨害する **disturb** +Ⓐ, **obstruct** +Ⓐ, **interfere**《with》▶治安の妨害 *a disturbance* of the (public) peace ‖ 安眠を妨害しないでくれ Don't *disturb* my sleep. ‖ 違法駐車の列が交通を妨害した A row of illegally parked cars *obstructed* (the) traffic. ‖ デモ参加者たちが市長の演説を妨害した Demonstrators *interrupted* the mayor's speech. ‖ ランナーは守備妨害でアウトになった The runner was called out for *interfering with fielding*.
‖電波妨害 jamming.

2**ぼうがい 望外** ▶亡き父の蔵書が皆さまのお役に立てば望外の幸せです It will be *an unexpected pleasure* if my late father's books are of some help to you.

-ほうがいい →ほう.

1**ほうがく 法学** **law** →法科 ▶法学を学ぶ study *law*.
‖法学者 a jurist ‖ 法学博士 a doctor of laws (➤ 学位は Doctor of Laws で LL. D. と略す).

2**ほうがく 方角** a **direction,** a **way** (➤ 後者はややインフォーマルな語) ▶山ではよく方角がわからなくなる In the mountains, people often lose their sense of *direction*. ‖ 対話「伊吹山はどの方角ですか？」「あっちです」"Which *direction* [*way*] is Mt. Ibuki?" "It's that way." (伊吹山が見える場合は It's over there. でよい).

「方角」のいろいろ 北 north (N)／北北東 north-northeast (NNE)／北東 northeast (NE)／東北東 east-northeast (ENE)／東 east (E)／東南東 east-southeast (ESE)／南東 southeast (SE)／南南東 south-southeast (SSE)／南 south (S)／南南西 south-southwest (SSW)／南西 southwest (SW)／西南西 west-southwest (WSW)／西 west (W)／西北西 west-northwest (WNW)／北西 northwest (NW)／北北西 north-northwest (NNW) 注 ( )内は略号.

3**ほうがく 邦楽** Japanese music ; Japanese traditional music(伝統音楽).

ほうかご 放課後 after school ▶放課後プールで泳いだ We swam in the pool *after school* (*was over*). ‖放課後, 残りなさいよ. いい? Stay (behind) *after school*. Got it? ‖放課後まで彼女に会えなかった I couldn't see her *until school was over* [*out*].

ほうかつ 包括 ▶会議の包括的な報告書を作成する make a *comprehensive* report of a conference ‖彼の報告はその事故に関するすべてを包括している His report *includes* [*covers*] everything related to the accident.

1**ぼうかん 暴漢** a thug ▶その政治家は演説中に暴漢に襲われた The politician was assaulted by *a thug* while giving a speech.

2**ぼうかん 傍観する** look on ▶彼は傍観するだけで何もしなかった He merely *looked on* and did nothing. ／He *just stood watching*.

‖傍観者 an onlooker, a bystander.

ほうがんし 方眼紙 graph [section／squared] paper.

ほうがんなげ 砲丸投げ the shot put ▶砲丸投げをする put the shot.

‖砲丸投げ選手 a shot-putter.

ほうがんびいき 判官贔屓 ▶日本人は大概判官びいきだ Most Japanese *root for the underdog*. (➤「弱いほうを応援する」の意).

ぼうかんふく 防寒服 clothes [gear] for cold weather ▶ダウンのコートは防寒性に優れている Down jackets *are effective in keeping out the cold*.

1**ほうき 箒** a broom ▶教室をほうきで掃く *sweep* the classroom *with a broom*.

‖ほうき星 a comet.

2**ほうき 法規** (laws and) regulations ▶交通法規を守る[破る] obey [violate] *traffic regulations*.

3**ほうき 放棄** renunciation (権利などの) ; abandonment (計画などの) 一動 放棄する renounce +目, abandon +目 ; give up (諦める) ▶権利を放棄する *waive* [*give up*] one's right ‖彼は足首を捻挫したために試合を途中で放棄しなければならなかった He had to *give up* partway through the game because he sprained his ankle. ‖日本国憲法には戦争の永久放棄がうたわれている The Constitution of Japan proclaims that the Japanese people forever *renounce* war.

4**ほうき 蜂起** revolt 一動 蜂起する rise (up) in revolt [rebellion] (➤rise (up) against でも「…に対して蜂起する」の意になる) ▶学生たちは新政府に反対して各地で蜂起した Students in various parts of the country *rose* (*up*) *in revolt* against the new government.

ぼうきゃく 忘却 oblivion ▶人間は皆死ぬと忘却されていくものだ All people *pass into oblivion* when they die.

ぼうぎゃく 暴虐 atrocities ▶暴虐の限りを尽くす commit all kinds of *atrocities*.

ぼうきょ 暴挙 a reckless attempt (無謀な企て) ; an outrage (不法行為) ▶公海上での爆撃は国際法を踏みにじる暴挙だ Bombing ships in international waters is *an outrage* against international law.

ぼうぎょ 防御 《米》defense, 《英》defence 一動 防御する defend +目 ▶攻撃は最大の防御なり A good offense is the best *defense*. (➤英語のことわざ ; アメリカでは The best *defense* is a good offense. ということが多い). ‖防御率 《野球》 an earned run average 《略 ERA》.

ほうきょう 豊胸 large [well-developed] breasts. →美容.

ぼうきょう 望郷 homesickness ▶メキシコに来て20年, 望郷の念はますます強くなっています I've been here in Mexico for twenty years, and my *feelings of homesickness* have grown (more and more) intense.

ぼうきれ 棒切れ a stick.

ぼうぐ 防具 protective gear.

ぼうくう 防空 air defense

‖防空ごう an air-raid shelter, a bomb shelter ‖防空頭巾 an air-raid hood.

ぼうくん 暴君 a tyrant /táɪərənt/ (圧制者) ; a despot (専制君主) ▶うちの旦那, ああ見えて家では意外に暴君なのよ My husband may look mild, but he's a real *tyrant* at home.

ほうけい 包茎 《医学》 (a) phimosis /faɪmóʊsəs/

‖仮性包茎 an uncircumcised penis (➤circumcise は「包皮を切除する」).

ほうげき 砲撃 fire, bombardment (➤後者が大規模) 一動 砲撃する bombard +目, fire +目 ▶砲撃を開始する[やめる] open [cease] *fire*.

ほうけん 封建 一形 封建的な feudalistic ; feudal (封建制の) ▶彼女の父親はとても封建的だ Her father is very *old-fashioned*. (➤「古めかしい考え方をする」の意. feudalistic を使うと少し滑稽に響く).

‖封建時代 the feudal age [times] ‖封建社会 a feudal society ‖封建主義 feudalism ‖封建制度 feudalism, the feudal system.

1**ほうげん 方言** a dialect /dáɪəlekt/ ; (an) accent (なまり) ▶この劇は出雲地方の方言で話されます The actors and actresses speak in (the) Izumo *dialect* in this play.

✉ 日本には方言がたくさんあります We have many *dialects* in Japan.

2**ほうげん 放言** irresponsible remarks (無責任な発言) ; careless talk (不注意な談話) ; a slip of the tongue (失言).

ぼうけん 冒険 an adventure ; a risk (自分から冒す危険) ▶ぼくたちはその島で多くの冒険をした We had a lot of *adventures* on the island. ‖少年は一般に冒険心に富んでいる Boys are generally full of *adventurous spirit*. ／Boys are generally *adventurous*.

▶その投資は冒険だよ I am afraid that investment is rather *risky*. ‖何も今冒険することはないよ You have no reason to *run a risk* now.

‖冒険家 an adventurer ‖冒険談 an adventure story.

ぼうげん 暴言 abusive [violent] language (➤abusive は「口汚い」, violent は「乱暴な」) ; an unreasonable statement (筋違いの発言) ▶父親に暴言を吐く *use abusive language* against one's father.

ほうこ 宝庫 a treasury, a treasure house ; a repository

（置き場）▶書物は知識の**宝庫**だ Books are *a treasury* [*a treasure house*] of knowledge. ‖ 海は資源の**宝庫**だ The sea is *a rich repository* of natural resources. ‖ オーストラリアは珍獣の**宝庫**だ Australia *abounds in* [*with*] rare animals. (➤ abound in [with] は「…が豊富である」の意).

ぼうご 防護する protect +⑪ 一形 **防護の** protective ‖**防護服** a protective suit, protective gear [clothing] ‖ **防護壁** a protective barrier.

1**ほうこう** 方向 **1**【方角】a **direction**, a **way** (➤後者はややインフォーマル) ▶船は正しい[反対の]**方向**に進んでいる The ship is moving in the right [opposite] *direction*. (➤前置詞は to でなく in) ‖ **方向**を間違えたようだ We seem to have come in the wrong *direction*.

▶私は声のする**方向**を見た I looked in the *direction* of the voice. ‖ 私も同じ**方向**に行くところです I am going the same *way* myself. ‖ 登山者たちは霧の中で**方向を失った** The climbers *lost their bearings* in the fog. (➤ lose one's bearings で「方角がわからなくなる」).

▶彼は**方向感覚**がない(＝方向音痴だ) He has no *sense of direction*. ‖ 銀座はこっちの**方向**よ. あなたも相当な**方向音痴**ね Ginza is *this way*. You sure have *a terrible* [*lousy*] *sense of direction*. ‖ 彼らは学校のとるべき**方向性**を話し合った They discussed the *direction* the school should take. ‖ 通りを横断するときは**両方向**を見なさい *Look both ways* before you cross the street.

‖**方向指示器** a turn signal, 《米・インフォーマル》 a blinker, 《英・インフォーマル》 a winker ‖ **方向舵**(だ) a rudder ‖ **双方向テレビ** interactive television.

2【進路, 方針】a **course** ▶将来の**方向**を決めるべき時が来た The time has come for you to decide (on) your *future course*. ‖ この小さな経験が私の人生の**方向**を決定した[変えた] This small experience determined [changed] the *course* of my life. ‖ 労使の交渉は 3 % 賃上げの**方向**で妥協が成立した The labor-management negotiations have reached a compromise *aiming at* a 3 percent salary increase.

2**ほうこう 芳香** fragrance /fréɪgrəns/, **perfume** ▶クチナシは**芳香**を放つ Gardenias give off [emit] a (sweet) *fragrance*.

‖**芳香剤** an aromatic /ærəmæṭɪk/.

3**ほうこう 放校** ▶彼女は非行のため**放校処分**になった She *was expelled from school* for delinquency.

4**ほうこう 奉公** service ; **apprenticeship** (弟子入りしての) ▶家具職人に 4 年間の**弟子入り奉公**をする serve a four-year *apprenticeship* with a cabinetmaker.

1**ぼうこう 膀胱** 《解剖学》 **the bladder** ‖**ぼうこう炎** cystitis /sɪstáɪṭɪs/, bladder infection.

2**ぼうこう 暴行** violence (暴力行為) ; (a) **rape** (強姦(ごうかん)) 《参考》 assault, attack, outrage, violate (いずれも「暴行する」の意)などを婉曲(えんきょく)語として用いることもあるが, 英語では rape は rape と明確にいうのがふつう.

▶彼はその女性に**暴行を加えた** He *used violence* against the woman. ／He *assaulted* the woman (*sexually*). (➤ sexually をつけると強姦であることがより明確になる) ‖ 男は**婦女暴行**の罪で逮捕された The man was arrested on a charge of *rape*.

ほうこく 報告 a **report** 一動 **報告する report** (on), **make a report** ▶主将が全校生徒を前に大会での成績を**報告した** Our captain *made* [*gave*] *a report on* the outcome of the tournament to the entire student body. ‖ クラス委員はクラス会の結果を先生に**報告した** The class representative *reported* to the teacher *on* the results of the class meeting. ‖ 彼は実験が成功したことを**報告した** He *reported* that the experiment had been successful. ‖ もし何かあったら逐一**報告**してくれ Please *keep* me *informed* [*posted*] if something happens. (➤ keep A informed [posted] は「A (人)に連絡を取り続ける」).

‖**報告書** a (written) report ‖ **中間報告** an interim report.

ぼうさい 防災 prevention of disasters, disaster prevention ▶ホテルの支配人たちはもっと**防災**に気をつけるべきだ Hotel managers should be more concerned about the *prevention of disasters*. ‖ 都市部の**防災対策**はまだ不十分だ *Disaster prevention measures* in urban areas are still inadequate.

‖**防災グッズセット** a disaster kit ; emergency supplies (非常時用の備蓄物) ‖ **防災訓練** a disaster [fire] drill ‖ **防災計画** a disaster plan (災害対応策) ‖ **防災センター** a center for disaster preparedness (災害に備える知識などを広めるための) ; an emergency center (非常時に使う施設) ‖ **防災の日** Disaster Drill Day ‖ **防災パック** a survival kit ‖ **防災マップ** a disaster preparedness map, a map for disaster preparedness.

1**ほうさく 豊作** a **good** [**rich**] **harvest** ; a **bumper crop** (大豊作) ▶去年は**豊作**だった We had *a rich harvest* last year. ‖ ことしは米は**豊作**の見込みだ We are expecting *a good harvest* of rice [*a big* rice *crop*] this year. ／The rice *harvest* [*crop*] *looks good* this year.

2**ほうさく 方策** measures (➤通例複数形で) ▶適当な**方策**が思い浮かばない I have yet to come up with suitable *measures*.

1**ぼうさつ 忙殺** ▶私は仕事に**忙殺**されています I *am swamped* [*am inundated*] *with* work. (➤ be inundated /ínʌndeɪtɪd/ with ... は「…であふれる」の意).

2**ぼうさつ 謀殺** premeditated murder.

ほうさん ホウ酸 《化学》 **boric acid.**

1**ほうし 奉仕** service ; **volunteer** [《英》 **voluntary**] **work** (ボランティア活動) 一動 **奉仕する serve** +⑪ ▶みんなが何らかの形で社会に**奉仕**すべきだ Every one should *serve* the community [*contribute to* society] in one way or another. ‖ 彼は老人ホームで**奉仕活動**をしている He is doing *volunteer work* at a nursing home for elderly people.

‖**奉仕価格** a bargain price ‖ **奉仕品** a bargain (→サービス).

2**ほうし 胞子** 《生物学》 a **spore** ▶炭疽(たんそ)菌の**胞子** anthrax *spores*.

ほうじ 法事 a (**Buddhist**) **memorial service** (追悼会) ▶両親は親戚の**法事**に出かけています My parents are away to attend *a memorial service* for one of my relatives. →回忌.

1**ぼうし** 帽子 a **cap** (ひさしのある) ; a **hat** (縁のある) ▶**帽子**をかぶる put on *a hat* [*a cap*] ‖ 挨拶するときには**帽子**を取りなさい Take off your *hat* when you greet people. ‖ つばの広い**帽子**をかぶっているあの女性は誰ですか Who is that woman wearing a broad-brimmed *hat*?

‖**帽子掛け** a hatrack, a hatstand ‖ **帽子屋** a hat shop (店) ; a hatter (人).

2ぼうし 防止 **prevention** 一動 防止する **prevent** +目; **check** +目 (食い止める) ▶犯罪［交通事故］の防止 the *prevention* of crime [traffic accidents] ‖ 災害を未然に防止する *prevent* disasters *from* happening ‖ B型肝炎がこれ以上広がるのを防止しなければいけない We have to *prevent* Hepatitis B *from* spreading further. ／We have to *stop* [*check*] the further spread of Hepatitis B.

ほうしき 方式 a **form** (形式); a **method** (方法); a **type** (型) ▶所定の方式に従って申込書を書く make an application following the standard *form* ‖ あの学校は新しい方式で英語を教えている They use a new *method* of teaching English at that school.

ほうじちゃ 焙じ茶 **roasted** [**toasted**] **tea**.

ぼうじゃくぶじん 傍若無人 ▶傍若無人な人 a person *with little concern* [*respect*] *for others* ‖ 彼女は職場で傍若無人にふるまっている She just does what she likes, *with no regard for others* at her workplace.

ほうしゃじょう 放射状の **radial** ▶その駅を中心に道路が放射状に伸びている Streets spread out *radially* from that station.

ほうしゃせい 放射性の **radioactive** ▶放射性物質の大規模な放出 a large-scale release of *radioactive material(s)* ‖ この石には放射性反応がある This rock *is radioactive*.

‖放射性元素 a radioactive element ‖ 放射性降下物 (radioactive) fallout ‖ 放射性廃棄物 radioactive waste ‖ 放射性ヨウ素 radioactive iodine /áɪədaɪn ‖ -diːn/.

ほうしゃせん 放射線 **radiation** ▶線量計で放射線量を測定する measure the *radiation level* with a dosimeter ‖ 安全な被ばく放射線量 a safe *radiation dose* ‖ 放射線を浴びる be exposed to *radiation*.

‖放射線技師 a radiologist ‖ 放射線治療 radiation treatment ‖ 放射線治療法 radiotherapy, radiation therapy ‖ 放射線被ばく exposure to radiation.

ほうしゃのう 放射能 **radioactivity** ▶原発のメルトダウン後に通常の2倍の放射能が検出された *Radioactivity* twice the normal level was detected after the nuclear power plant meltdown. ‖ この野菜は放射能に汚染されている These vegetables are contaminated by *radioactivity*.

‖放射能汚染 radioactive contamination ‖ 放射能汚染水 radioactive water.

ほうしゃれいきゃく 放射冷却 **radiative cooling**.

ぼうじゅ 傍受する **monitor** +目, **intercept** +目 (➤後者には「通信文を盗み見る」の意もある) ▶北朝鮮のラジオニュースを傍受する *monitor* [*intercept*] North Korean radio news (🔘単に海外の短波放送などを受信する場合は receive や pick up でよい).

ほうしゅう 報酬 (a) **reward** (褒美); a **return** (返礼); 《米》 **compensation** (役員の); **pay** (金の支払い) ▶親切にしてあげたからといって報酬を期待してはいけない You should not expect any *reward* [anything *in return*] for your kindness. ‖ 仕事をして報酬を得るのは当たり前だ You should *be paid* [*get some pay*] for the work you have done.

☞ 無報酬 (→見出語)

ぼうしゅうざい 防臭剤 an **air freshener**; (a) **deodorizer** (トイレ用などの).

ほうしゅつ 放出 **1**【物資などの】**release** 一動 放出する **release** +目 ▶政府は緊急用食糧を放出した The government *released* emergency food supplies.

2【ガス・熱などの】**emission** 一動 放出する **emit** +目 ▶車からの排気ガスの放出 the *emission* of exhaust gas from cars ‖ 大気中に温室効果ガスを放出する *emit* greenhouse gases into the atmosphere.

ほうじゅん 芳醇な **mellow** ▶芳じゅんなチリワイン (a) *mellow* Chile wine.

ほうじょ 幇助 **assist** ▶自殺をほう助する *help* someone commit suicide ‖ テロをほう助する *provide aid* to a terrorist group.

ほうしょう 褒章 a **medal of honor**

‖紫綬(じゅ)褒章 a Medal with a Purple Ribbon.

1ほうじょう 豊穣 a **prolific growth of a grain crop**

‖五穀豊穣 an abundant crop, a huge harvest.

2ほうじょう 豊饒 **fertility** (肥沃); **productiveness** (多産) ▶豊饒な土地 *fertile* [*productive*] land ／*rich* soil.

ほうしょうきん 報奨金 a **reward** (報酬); a **bonus** (特別手当).

ほうしょく 飽食 **satiation** ▶飽食の時代 an age of *excessive eating* ／ an age *when you can eat more than you need*.

ほうしょく(ひん) 宝飾(品) **jewelry**

‖宝飾店 a jewelry store.

ほうじる 報じる **report** (+目) (報道する); **say** (+目) (言う) ▶新聞の報じるところによると東北地方の農作物は大雨のため大きな被害を受けた The newspaper *says* [*reports*] that a heavy rain badly damaged crops in the Tohoku district. ／*According to* the newspaper, crops in the Tohoku district were badly damaged by (a) heavy rain.

1ほうしん 方針 a **policy** (会社・政党などの政策); a **principle** (主義) ▶体罰は本校の教育方針に反する Corporal punishment is against this school's educational *policy*. (➤ education policy は「教育政策」).

▶高品質の物だけを売るのが当店の方針です It is our store's *policy* to sell only high-quality goods. (➤「社の方針」は company policy).

‖営業方針 a business policy ‖ 外交方針 a foreign policy.

2ほうしん 放心する **be stunned** (ぼう然自失する) ▶炎に包まれたわが家を見て彼女は放心したように立ち尽くした She stood *stunned* [*thunderstruck*] when she saw her house in flames.

1ほうじん 法人 a **legal** [**juridical**] **person**; a **corporation** (会社) ▶小さな会社を法人(組織)にする *incorporate* a small company.

‖法人税 a corporation tax ‖ 学校法人 an educational foundation ‖ 公益法人 a public-interest corporation ‖ 宗教法人 a religious corporation ‖ 特殊法人 a special public corporation ‖ 独立行政法人 an independent administrative institution [agency] ‖ 認可法人 a government-authorized corporation.

2ほうじん 邦人 a **Japanese national** (国外に住む日本人); a **Japanese**, a **Japanese citizen** [**person**] (日本人) ▶ブラジル在留邦人 a *Japanese national* in Brazil ／*a Japanese* who is living in Brazil.

ぼうじん 防塵 ‖防塵マスク a dust mask.

ぼうず 坊主 a **Buddhist priest**; a **Buddhist monk** (修行僧) ▶彼は頭を坊主刈りにした He *had his hair close-cropped*. (🔘毛をそってしまったのなら had his head

shaved となる).
☛ 丸坊主 (→見出語)

ほうすい 放水 ▶消防士たちは炎上中の建物に放水した The fire fighters *sprayed water* [*played water hoses*] on the burning building. ‖ 機動隊は群衆に向けて放水した The riot police *turned the water cannon* on the crowd.
‖**放水車** a truck with a water cannon ‖ **放水路** a drainage canal ; a sluice (ダムの).

ぼうすい 防水の waterproof
‖**防水シート** a waterproof canvas, a tarpaulin ‖ **防水時計** a waterproof watch ‖ **生活防水** home waterproofing.

1**ほうせい 縫製** sewing (by machine) ▶縫製がしっかりした *well sewn* / *well made* ‖ 縫製が甘い *poorly-sewn* / *poorly made*.

2**ほうせい 砲声** the roar [rumble] of artillery.

ほうせき 宝石 a gem (カットして磨いた石) ; a jewel (装身具用の石) ▶その小箱には宝石がちりばめられている The small box is studded [is set] with *gems*. (➤「宝石をちりばめた時計」は a jewel [gem]-encrusted watch) ‖ その女優はたくさんの高価な宝石を持っている The actress has lots of [many pieces of] expensive *jewelry*. (➤ 指輪, イヤリング, ネックレスなど身に着けられるものは jewelry で, 石そのものは gem または stone).
‖**宝石商** (米) a jeweler, (英) a jeweller ‖ **宝石店** (米) a jewelry store [shop], (英) a jewellry shop [store] ‖ **宝石泥棒** a jewel thief ‖ **宝石箱** a jewel [jewelry] box.

「宝石」のいろいろ アメジスト amethyst / エメラルド emerald / オニックス onyx / オパール opal / ガーネット garnet / 血石 bloodstone / サードニクス sardonyx / サファイア sapphire / ジルコン zircon / 真珠 pearl / ダイヤモンド diamond / トパーズ topaz / トルコ石 turquoise / 猫目石 cat's-eye / ひすい jade / めのう agate / ルビー ruby

ぼうせき 紡績 spinning
‖**紡績工場** a spinning mill.

1**ぼうせん 傍線** ▶傍線の語に注意しなさい Pay attention to the words with *a line drawn beside them*. (➤ 英語の場合は横書きなので beside them を under them にして「下線」の意味にする, もしくは underlined words で「下線が引かれた語」として理解してもらう).

2**ぼうせん 防戦する** defend oneself (against).

ぼうぜん 茫然 ▶死刑の判決に被告はぼう然となった The accused *was stunned* when he was sentenced to death. ‖ 彼女の自殺の知らせを聞いてぼう然となった I *was struck dumb* [*speechless*] at the news of her suicide. (➤ どちらも「ショックでことばにならない」の意) ‖ 彼は火事で全焼したわが家を前にぼう然と立ち尽くした He *kept standing stupefied* [*thunderstruck*] in front of his burnt-down house.

ほうせんか 鳳仙花 《植物》 a (garden) balsam /bɔ́ːlsəm/, a touch-me-not.

ほうそ ホウ素 《化学》 boron.

1**ほうそう 放送** broadcasting (放送すること) ; a broadcast (1回の放送) ; an announcement (駅などの) 一動 **放送する** broadcast (+目) ; 《インフォーマル》 air +目 ; televise +目 (テレビで) ▶テレビ放送 television *broadcasting* (放送を行うこと) ; a television *broadcast* (1回1回の) ‖ その公開討論会はテレビで [ラジオで] 放送された The open forum *was broadcast* on TV [on the radio]. (➤ この broadcast は過去分詞) ‖ その記録映画は今夜テレビ放送される The documentary film will *be televised* tonight. ‖ (ゴルフの) マスターズの模様はジョージア州から生中継で放送された The Masters Tournament *was broadcast* [*was aired*] *live* from Georgia. (➤ live /laɪv/ は「生で」) ‖ そのドラマは毎週日曜日に放送されている The drama *is broadcast* (*ed*) [*aired*] every Sunday. ‖ NHKは甲子園の全国高校野球の全試合を全国ネットで放送している NHK *broadcasts* all the games of the National High School Baseball Tournament at Koshien *over a nationwide network*. ‖ 《掲示》 放送中 On (the) Air.
▶私は学校の運動会で放送を担当した I *did the announcing* [I *served as announcer*] for the school athletic meet.
‖**放送衛星** a broadcasting satellite ‖ **放送局** a broadcast station ‖ **放送劇** a radio drama ‖ **放送時間** air time, on-the-air hours ‖ **放送室** a broadcasting studio ‖ **放送大学** the University of the Air, 《英》 the Open University ‖ **放送番組** a broadcast program.
☛ 再放送 (→見出語)

逆引き熟語 ○○放送
ウェブ放送 webcasting / 衛星放送 a satellite broadcast / 海外放送 an overseas broadcast / 校内 [社内] 放送 an announcement over the school [in-house] PA system (➤ PA system は public-address system の意で「校内 [館内] 放送」のこと) / 国営放送 a government-operated [-run] broadcast / 実況放送 an on-the-spot [a play-by-play] broadcast / 深夜放送 a late-night [midnight] broadcast / 政見放送 a campaign [an election] broadcast / 全国放送 a nationwide broadcast / 中継放送 a relay broadcast / デジタル放送 a digital broadcast / 生放送 a live broadcast / 2か国語放送 a bilingual broadcast / 有線放送 a cable [wire] broadcast, closed-circuit broadcast / ローカル放送 a local broadcast

2**ほうそう 包装** wrapping ; packing (こん包) ; packaging (包装材料およびそれを使っての包装) 一動 **包装する** wrap +目, pack +目 ▶店員はその品をきれいに包装した The salesclerk *wrapped* the article neatly. ‖ この本を贈り物用に包装してください Could you *giftwrap* this book [*wrap* this book *as a gift*], please ?
‖**包装紙** wrapping paper ‖ **食品包装** food packaging.

ぼうそう 暴走 ▶トラックが暴走して人家に突っ込んだ The truck *went out of control* and crashed into a house.
▶《野球》 鳥谷は暴走して三塁で刺された Toritani tried to get an extra base, but was tagged out at third. (「暴走」に当たる英語はないので「余分のベースを取ろうとした」と考える).
‖**暴走族** a motorcycle gang (オートバイに乗った) ; 《インフォーマル》 (a group of) hot-rodders (改造車に乗った).

ほうそうかい 法曹界 legal circles, the judicial world.

ほうそく 法則 a law, a rule ▶物理学の法則 a *law* of physics ‖ メンデルの法則 Mendel's *laws* ‖ 需要と供給の法則 the *law* of supply and demand ‖ 新しいものが古いものに取って代わるのは自然の法則だ It is *a*

law of nature that the old gives way to the new.

ほうたい 包帯 a **bandage** /bǽndɪdʒ/ ▶彼は腕に包帯をしていた He had *a bandage* around his arm. ／His arm was bandaged (up).

ほうだい 砲台 a **battery**.

-ほうだい -放題 ▶食べ放題のレストラン(＝バイキング) an *all-you-can-eat* restaurant／a *buffet* [*smorgasbord*] restaurant. ‖プラス1500円で, 90分飲み放題です For another 1,500 yen, you *can drink as much as you like* for 90 minutes. ‖彼はわがままのし放題だ He is *shamelessly selfish*. (➤ shamelessly は「厚かましいほど」) ‖住む人がいなくなって, その家は荒れ放題になっている The house has *gone to total ruin* with no one living in it.

ぼうだい 膨大な **huge, enormous** (➤後者はやや堅い語) ▶そのダムの建設には膨大な資金がつぎ込まれた A *huge* [An *enormous*] amount of money was poured into the construction of that dam. ‖コンピュータは膨大な量の情報を処理することができる A computer has the capacity to process an *enormous* [a *vast*] amount of data.

ぼうたかとび 棒高跳び **the pole vault** ▶彼は棒高跳びで6メートルを跳んだ He *vaulted* [*pole-vaulted*] 6 meters.

‖棒高跳び選手 a pole vaulter.

ぼうだち 棒立ち ▶彼はエレベーターの中でいきなりピストルを胸に突きつけられ, 棒立ちになった He *stood petrified* after he was suddenly stuck in the ribs with a gun in the elevator. (➤ petrify は恐怖などのショックで「石のように身を硬くさせる」の意).

ほうだん 砲弾 a **shell** ▶敵に砲弾を浴びせる fire *shells* over the enemy.

ぼうだん 防弾の **bulletproof** ▶その車は防弾車だ The car is *bulletproof*.

‖防弾ガラス bulletproof glass ‖防弾チョッキ a bulletproof vest [jacket], a flak jacket.

1**ほうち 放置する** **leave** +⦅目⦆ ▶少年は新しい自転車を雨の中に放置した The boy *left* his new bicycle in the rain.

2**ほうち 法治** ▶法治国家 a country *governed by law* [*under the rule of law*]／a *law-governed* state／a *law-abiding* nation.

ほうちき 報知機 an **alarm**(警報)

‖火災報知機 a fire alarm.

ぼうちゅうざい 防虫剤 (an) **insect** [(a) **bug**] **repellent**; a **mothball**(衣類の; 通例複数形で).

ほうちょう 包丁 a **kitchen knife**.

1**ぼうちょう 膨張** (an) **expansion** 一⦅動⦆ **膨張する** **expand**; **swell**(膨らむ) ▶木材の自然な膨張と収縮 the natural *expansion* and contraction of wood ‖熱は金属を膨張させる Heat *expands* metals. ‖木材は水分を吸収すると膨張する Wood *swells* when it absorbs water. ‖この町の人口は過去10年間で2倍に膨張した The population of this town *has expanded* to twice its original size in the past ten years.

‖膨張率 the expansion rate ‖熱膨張 thermal expansion.

2**ぼうちょう 傍聴** **listening, hearing** 一⦅動⦆ **傍聴する** **listen** ⦅to⦆, **hear** ▶私はその裁判を傍聴するため裁判所に行った I went to the court to *hear* the trial. ‖傍聴券 a public observer ticket; an admission ticket (入場券) ‖傍聴席 the (public) gallery.

3**ぼうちょう 防潮** ‖防潮水門 a tide gate ‖防潮堤 a storm surge barrier, a coastal levee.

ほうっておく 放っておく **leave** +⦅目⦆ →ほっとく ▶事態をこのまま放っておくわけにはいかない We can't *leave* things *as they are*. ‖この傷は放っておいてはいけない You shouldn't *leave* that cut *untreated*. ‖少し放っておいてよ *Give* me *a break*. ／Please *let* me *alone*. ‖**対話**「彼女, 泣いてるぜ」「放っておけよ」"She's crying." "*Leave* her *alone*."

ぼうっと →ぼーっと ▶ぼうっとしていて肝心なところを聞き漏らした I *was daydreaming* [*I wasn't paying attention*／My *mind was somewhere else*] and missed the main points (of the lecture). (➤ daydream は「夢想する」と訳されることが多いが, 単に目の前のことに集中しないで別のことを考えることで, 「ぼんやりする」に当たる. 長時間のこともあれば, 数秒間のこともある) ‖富士山が春がすみにぼうっとかすんでいる I (can) see a blurred Mt. Fuji in a spring haze. ‖毎日をぼうっと過ごしているうちに夏休みも終わりに近づいた The summer vacation during which I have spent every day *idly* is almost over.

1**ほうてい 法廷** a (**law**) **court**; a **court of justice** (裁判所; 正式な言い方) ▶彼は法廷で真実を述べた He stated the truth *in court*. ‖我々はその会社と法廷で争った We *took* the company *to court*.

2**ほうてい 法定の** **legal** /líːɡəl/

‖法定金利 the legal interest (rate) ‖法定相続人 a legal heir /eəʳ/ ‖法定代理人 a legal representative.

ほうていしき 方程式 an **equation**(数学の); a **formula**(結果につながるやり方) ▶次の方程式を解きなさい Solve the following *equations*. ‖勝利の方程式 a winning *formula*.

‖一[二／三]次方程式 a simple [quadratic／cubic] equation.

ほうてき 法的な **legal** /líːɡəl/ 一⦅副⦆ **法的に** **legally** ▶我々の主張には法的な根拠がある Our claim has a *legal* basis [has *legal* grounds]. ‖我々は法的措置を取るつもりだ We intend to take *legal* action. ‖安楽死は法的に認められていない Mercy killing [(Active) euthanasia] is not *legally* permitted.

ほうてん 法典 a **code** (**of laws**)

‖ハムラビ法典 the Code of Hammurabi ‖ナポレオン法典 the Napoleonic Code.

ほうでん 放電 (an) (**electric**) **discharge** 一⦅動⦆ **放電する** **discharge electricity** ▶空中[真空]放電 an atmospheric [a vacuum] *discharge*.

ぼうと 暴徒 a **mob**(➤集合的に) ▶警察は暴徒を鎮圧した The police suppressed the *mob* [*rioters*]. ‖デモ隊の一部が暴徒化して商店を略奪した Some protesters *formed a mob* and looted stores.

ほうとう 放蕩 **dissipation** (金銭・精力などの); **debauchery** /dɪbɔ́ːtʃəri/ (酒・女遊びなどの) ▶放とう三昧の日々を送る lead *a life of dissipation* [*debauchery*].

‖放とう息子 a dissipated son; the prodigal son (聖書に出てくる).

ほうどう 報道

ほうどう 報道 a **report**; **news** /njuːz/ (ニュース) 一⦅動⦆ **報道する** **report** (+⦅目⦆); **cover** +⦅目⦆ (記者が取材して) ▶新聞は日々の出来事を報道する The newspaper *reports* daily events. ‖景気は上向き始めたと報道されている *On the news they're saying* that business has started to pick up. ‖彼は大統領選挙を報道するためにアメリカへ渡った He went to the U.S. to *cover* the presidential election.

▶彼の死は世界中の新聞に大きく報道された His death *hit* [*made*] *the headlines* all over the world. (➤ hit [make] the headlines は「大見出しで報じられる」の意の熟語).

▶この事件に関するテレビの報道は間違っていた The television *news reports* on this incident turned out (to be) false. ‖新聞の報道によれば出生率は幾分回復しつつある *According to the newspapers* [*newspaper reports*], the birth rate has been increasing slightly.

▶王子のきたるべき結婚式を巡ってマスコミ報道が過熱気味だ There's been too much *media reporting* on the prince's coming wedding. ‖事故の現場は報道陣でごった返していた The site of the accident was swarming with *reporters* [*members of the press*]. ‖報道の自由は守られなければならない Freedom of the press must be protected. (➤ the press は「新聞・雑誌などの出版物」).

✉ **あなたの国を襲ったハリケーンは日本でも報道されました** The hurricane which hit your country *was reported* [*was on the news*] in Japan, too.

‖**報道機関** the press, the news media /míːdiə/ ‖**報道写真** a news photo(graph) ‖**報道写真家** a photojournalist ‖**報道番組** a news program.

1ぼうとう 冒頭 **the beginning, the opening** ▶冒頭の数行を読めば大概おもしろい小説かどうかがわかる You can generally tell if a novel is interesting or not by reading a few *opening* lines. ‖会議は冒頭から激しい口論になった The meeting *opened* [*began*] *with* a sharp exchange of words.

2ぼうとう 暴騰 a **sudden** [**sharp**] **rise** 一動 **暴騰する** **rise suddenly** [**sharply**]; 《インフォーマル》 **skyrocket** ▶地価が暴騰した There was *a sudden rise* in land prices. ／Land prices *shot up*. ‖中国では株価の暴騰はまだ続いている Stock prices are still *soaring* in China.

3ぼうとう 暴投 《野球》 a **wild pitch**.

ぼうどう 暴動 a **riot** /ráiət/ ▶暴動が起こったがすぐに鎮圧された *A riot* broke out, but it was soon suppressed. ‖新政権に反対し, 市民が暴動を起こした The citizens *started a riot* protesting the new government.

ぼうとく 冒瀆 **blasphemy** /blǽsfəmi/; **profanity** (神聖を汚すこと); **disrespect**(尊敬を示さないこと) ▶神を冒とくする *blaspheme* against God ‖それは戦没者に対する冒とくだ That shows *disrespect* for the war dead.

ぼうどくマスク 防毒マスク a **gas mask** ▶防毒マスクをかぶる put on *a gas mask*.

ほうにち 訪日 a **visit to Japan** ▶フランスの大統領が来月訪日する予定です The President of France is planning an official *visit to Japan* next month.

ほうにょう 放尿 **urination** 一動 **放尿する** **urinate**.

ほうにん 放任 ▶子供を放任する親が多い Many parents are *too permissive* [*leave* their children *to do as they like*]. ‖放任主義は子供の成長を妨げる (*Parental*) *permissiveness* prevents children's growth.

ほうねつ 放熱する **radiate heat**

‖**放熱器** a radiator /réidieiṭəʳ/.

ほうねん 豊年 ▶ことしは豊年満作間違いなしだ This year we'll have *a good harvest* [*a bumper crop*] for sure.

ぼうねんかい 忘年会 a **year-end party**, a **forget-the-year party** 《参考》 英米には無い習慣なので, a *bonenkai* party とするのも可.

日本紹介 ✉ **忘年会は「その年を忘れるための会」という意味で, ふつう12月に仕事仲間または親しい友人たちが1年の締めくくりとして催す打ち解けたパーティーです** *Bonenkai* are parties for "forgetting the year." They are informal parties with co-workers or close friends, usually held in December, that provide a sense of closure at the end of the year.

ほうのう 奉納 (a) **dedication** 一動 **奉納する** **dedicate** +目 ▶神楽を奉納する *dedicate* kagura music to the god of a Shinto shrine.

‖**奉納相撲** sumo performed in the precincts of a shrine or temple.

ぼうはつ 暴発 ▶ライフルは子供がいじっている最中に暴発した The rifle *went off* [*was discharged*] *accidentally* while the child was playing with it.

ぼうはてい 防波堤 a **waterbreaker**, a **surfbreaker**(波浪から港湾・海岸を守る); a **groyne** /grɔin/ (海岸の浸食を防ぐ).

ぼうはん 防犯 **crime prevention, prevention of crime(s)** ▶防犯は全市民の願いだ *Prevention of crime* is the wish of every citizen. ‖あなたの勇気が防犯に役立ちます Your courage will help (to) *prevent crime*. ‖万引きの犯人がスーパーの防犯カメラに写っていた A shoplifter showed (up) on the *security camera* in the supermarket.

‖**防犯ベル** a burglar alarm; a crime prevention buzzer /bʌ́zəʳ/ (ハンドバッグなどに入れておく).

1ほうひ 包皮 one's **foreskin, prepuce** /príːpjuːs/ (ペニスの; 後者は医学用語).

2ほうひ 放屁する **pass gas, break wind, fart.**

ほうび 褒美 a **reward**(功労・善行・努力などに対する報酬); a **prize**(賞品, 賞金) ▶満点を取ったご褒美に両親に東京ディズニーランドへ連れていってもらった As *a reward* for getting a perfect score, my parents took me to Tokyo Disneyland.

ぼうび 防備 (a) **defense** [《英》**defence**] 一動 **防備する** **defend** +目; **guard** +目 (警戒する) ▶我々は敵の侵入に対して防備を固めた We strengthened our *defenses* against the enemy invasion.

ぼうびき 棒引き ▶借金を棒引き(＝帳消し)にしてもらった I had my debts *written off* [*canceled*].

1ほうふ 抱負 one's **plan**(計画); one's **resolution** (決心); one's **hopes** (大志) ▶総理は新年の抱負を語った The Prime Minister told us about his *plans* for the new year. ‖これから1年, 英語で日記をつけるというのがことしの私の抱負です My New Year's *resolution* is to keep a diary in English for a year. ‖あなたは歌手としてデビューされたわけですが, これからの抱負を聞かせてください Now that you have made your debut as a singer, tell us *what you would like to do* from now on.

2ほうふ 豊富な **rich** 《in》 ▶彼は話題が豊富だ He *has a wide repertoire of* topics he can discuss. ／He can talk on *a variety* [*range*] *of* topics. ‖その店は品数が豊富だ The store carries *a wide variety of* goods. ‖あのアイスクリーム店は種類が豊富だ That ice cream parlor serves *a lot of* flavors.

> **〖文型〗**
> **資源など(A)が豊富だ**
> **have abundant** A
> **be rich in** A

▶古田先生は教職経験が豊富だ Mr. Furuta *has abundant* teaching experience. ‖ 部長はその方面では経験が豊富だ Our manager *has a great deal of* experience along that line. ‖ インドネシアは天然資源が豊富だ Indonesia *is rich in* natural resources. ‖ ブロッコリーはビタミンCが豊富だ Broccoli *is rich in* vitamin C. ‖ 琵琶湖は魚が豊富だ Lake Biwa *abounds in* [*with*] fish. (➤ abound in [with] は「(場所などが)…に富む」の意の改まった言い方) ／ Fish *abound* in Lake Biwa. (➤ この abound は「(生物・資源などが)…に多い」の意) ‖ 四万十川は豊富な水量をたたえている The Shimanto River has *a great amount of* water.
▶英文をたくさん読めば英語の語彙は豊富になる If you read a lot in English, you'll *enlarge* [*enrich*] your English vocabulary.

ぼうふ 防腐 prevention against decay
‖**防腐剤** a preservative.

ぼうふう 暴風 a **windstorm**, a **storm** ▶暴風が一晩中吹き荒れた The *windstorm* raged all through the night. ‖ 私たちの船は暴風に遭った Our ship was caught in *a storm*.
‖**暴風雨** a rainstorm (➤ 暴風も暴風雨も区別しないで単に storm と呼ぶことが多い) ‖ **暴風警報** a storm warning ‖ **暴風雪** a blizzard, a snowstorm.

ぼうふうりん 防風林 a **windbreak (forest)**.

ほうふく 報復 **revenge**(自分の恨みを晴らすこと); **retaliation**(対抗手段での仕返し) 一動 **報復する** **avenge** +⑪, **revenge oneself on, take revenge on, retaliate against**
▶彼らは旅客機を乗っ取ることでアメリカに報復した They *retaliated against* the U.S. by hijacking an airliner. ‖ この不当な扱いの報復は必ずしてやる I will *avenge* this injustice at any cost.
‖**報復攻撃** a revenge [retaliatory] attack.

ほうふくぜっとう 抱腹絶倒 ▶抱腹絶倒のコメディー a *hilarious* [*sidesplitting*] comedy ‖ そのコントに聴衆は抱腹絶倒した The audience *burst* [*split*] *their sides with laughter* at the comic skit. ／The audience *laughed their heads off* at the comic skit. (➤ いずれも「腹を抱えて笑う」の意の熟語).

ぼうふざい 防腐剤 an **antiseptic** /æ̀ntəséptɪk/ (殺菌用の); a **preservative**(保存可能にする).

ほうふつ 彷彿 ▶彼女は亡くなった彼女の父親をほうふつさせる Seeing her *brings to mind* the image of her late father. ‖ その天井の高い建物は古き良き時代をほうふつさせる The high-ceilinged building *reminds* you *of* the good old days.

ほうぶつせん 放物線 《数学》a **parabola** ▶白球は放物線を描いてレフトスタンドに飛び込んだ The white ball described *a parabola* as it flew into the left field stands.

ぼうふら 《虫》a **mosquito larva**(➤ larva の複数形は larvae), a **wriggler**.

ほうへい 砲兵 an **artillerist**; an **artilleryman** (男の)
‖**砲兵隊** the artillery (➤ 集合的).

ほうほう 方法 a **way**; a **method**(体系だった) ▶英語を習得する最良の方法は何ですか What is *the best way* to learn English [*method* of learning English]? (➤ method の場合は method of [for] doing が多いが, method to do も使われる) ‖ このピンチを切り抜ける方法はないだろうか Isn't there *a way* to get out of this difficult situation? ‖ 彼女を説得するにはあの人に頼むしか方法はない There is no (other) *way* to persuade her but to ask him.
▶この方法で勉強すればフランス語は半年で話せるようになる If you study French *using this method* [(*in*) *this way*], you'll be able to speak it in six months. (➤ way に this, that がつくときは in は省略されることが多い) ‖ この方法でだめなら別の方法を試してみよう If this *method* doesn't work well, let's try another one. ‖ 万里の長城がどんな方法で築かれたのか知りたいものだ I would like to know *how* they built the Great Wall of China.

ほうぼう 方々 **many different places**(いろいろな場所); **everywhere**(あらゆる所) ▶ほうぼう旅をしたがやっぱり奈良がいちばんいい I have visited *many different places*, but in the end I think Nara is best. ‖ 妹がいないか近所をほうぼう捜し回った I looked for my sister *everywhere* in the neighborhood. ‖ 暴走族がほうぼうから広場に集まって来た Hot-rodders gathered at the square *from all directions*.

ぼうぼう ▶火がぼうぼう燃えている The fire is burning *furiously* [*vigorously*]. ‖ 気がつくと辺り一面火がぼうぼうだった I found myself surrounded by a *blazing* fire.
▶ひげぼうぼうの男 a man with *a bushy beard* ‖ その庭は草ぼうぼうだった The garden *was overgrown* (*thickly*) *with weeds*. ／Weeds were growing all over the garden.

ほうほうのてい 這う這うの体 ▶大きな番犬に追い立てられて泥棒はほうほうの体で逃げ去った The burglar who was chased by a big watchdog ran *for all he was worth* [ran away *for dear life*].

ほうぼく 放牧 **grazing**(家畜に草を食わせること); **pasturing**(家畜を牧草地に放すこと;「家畜が草を食うこと」の意もある) 一動 **放牧する** **graze** +⑪, **pasture** +⑪ ▶この山の牧場では羊を放牧している They *graze* sheep in this mountain pasture.
‖**放牧地** a pasture 《参考》《米》では大規模な放牧場を ranch, 囲いのないものを the (open) range ということがある.

1**ほうまん 放漫な** **loose** /luːs/ (ルーズな); **sloppy** (ずさんな); **lax** (放縦な; 堅い語) ▶その会社は放漫経営により倒産した The company went bankrupt because of its *irresponsible* [*careless* ／ *loose*] *management*.

2**ほうまん 豊満な** **voluptuous** ▶豊満な肉体 a *voluptuous* body ‖ 豊満な胸の女性 a woman with *ample breasts*.

ほうむ 法務 ‖**法務省** the Ministry of Justice ‖ **法務大臣** the Minister of Justice.

ほうむる 葬る **bury** /béri/ +⑪ ▶彼は一家の墓地に葬られた He *was buried* in the family graveyard.
▶《比喩的》その事件は闇に葬られた The case *was hushed up*. (➤ hush up は「もみ消す」) ‖ 彼はそのスキャンダル以来社会から葬られた After that scandal he *was ostracized* [*was shut out from society*].

ぼうめい 亡命 **defection**(自分の国を捨てること;「国家機密などを握っての亡命」という含みをもつことが多い) 一動 **亡命する** **seek (political) asylum**(大使館などに(政治的)保護を求める); **defect** 《to》(国を捨てる) ▶そのバレエダンサーはアメリカに亡命した The ballet dancer *sought asylum* in the U.S. (➤ sought は seek の過去形) (● 亡命に成功したことを明確にしたい場合は find asylum を用いる. この場合はその過去形 found にすればよい).
‖**亡命者** a refugee /rèfjudʒíː/, a defector.

1**ほうめん 方面** 1【地域】a **direction**(方向); an **area**,

a **district**（地域；後者のほうが小さい地域を指す）▶容疑者は金沢**方面**へ逃走中です The suspect is fleeing *in the direction of* Kanazawa. ‖関東**方面**には大雨・洪水注意報が出ている A heavy rain and flood warning has been issued in the Kanto *area* [*district*].

2【分野】a **field** ▶彼はその**方面**に詳しい He is well versed in that *field* [*line*].

[2]**ほうめん 放免** ▶被告は無罪**放免**になった The defendant *was acquitted* (*of the criminal accusation*).

ほうもつ 宝物 (a) **treasure**

‖**宝物館**[**殿**] a treasure repository [house].

ほうもん 訪問 a **visit**, a **call** 一動 **訪問する visit** +目, **call on** [**at**] →訪ねる ▶きのう野口先生のお宅を**訪問した** Yesterday I *visited* [*called on*] Mr. Noguchi. (➤「人」を訪問するときは call on) ／Yesterday I *called at* Mr. Noguchi's house. (➤「家」を訪問するときは call at) ‖きょうは**訪問客**が多かった I had many *visitors* today. ‖兄は連日**会社訪問**をしている My brother is *visiting one company* after another (*to find a job*). ‖来週黒川先生の**家庭訪問**があります Mr. Kurokawa, my teacher, will be *visiting* [*calling at*] *my house* next week.

‖**訪問介護** home help service (➤ 世話をする人は home helper) ‖**訪問看護** home-visit nursing (care) ‖**訪問看護師** a visiting nurse, a home-visit [visiting] nurse ‖**訪問着** a semi-formal kimono ‖**訪問販売** door-to-door sales ‖**訪問販売員** a door-to-door [visiting] salesperson ‖**表敬訪問** a courtesy call.

ぼうや 坊や a **boy**; a **son**（息子）(➤ 呼びかけのときは boy, son, sonny などを使う) ▶**坊や**, いい子だね That's [There's] a good *boy*. ‖**坊や**, こんな所で遊んじゃだめだよ You shouldn't play [be playing] here, *young man*.

ほうやく 邦訳 (a) **Japanese translation**, (a) **translation into Japanese** ▶この本の**邦訳**は出ていますか Is *a Japanese translation* of this book available?

[1]**ほうよう 法要** a (**Buddhist**) **memorial service** ▶祖母の七回忌の**法要**を営んだ We held *a memorial service* on the sixth anniversary of our grandmother's death. →回忌.

[2]**ほうよう 抱擁** an **embrace**, a **hug** (➤ 前者が日本語に近い堅い語で濃密なもの；後者は挨拶代わりの短時間のもの) 一動 **抱擁する embrace** +目, **hug** +目 ▶熱烈な**抱擁** a passionate *embrace* ‖母親はわが子を**抱擁した** The mother *embraced* [*hugged*] her child. ／The mother *gave* her child *a hug*.

ほうようりょく 包容力 ▶中江先生は**包容力がある** Miss Nakae *is broad-minded* [*is understanding*].

ぼうよみ 棒読み ▶その政治家はスピーチ原稿を**棒読みした** That politician *read* his speech *in a monotone*. ‖卒業式では市長の代理が祝辞を**棒読みした** At the graduation ceremony, the mayor's deputy *read* his congratulatory speech *in a monotone* [*singsong*] *voice*. (➤ singsong は「一本調子の」).

ほうらく 崩落 a **collapse** ▶つり橋の**崩落** *the collapse* of a suspension bridge.

ぼうらく 暴落 a **sudden** [**sharp**] **fall**,《インフォーマル》a **nose dive**; a **slump**, a **crash**（相場などの）▶石油価格の**暴落**は石油輸出国に打撃を与えた The *sudden fall* in oil prices hit the oil exporting countries. ‖株価が**暴落した** Stock prices *have slumped* [*have plummeted* ／ *have fallen sharply*].

ぼうり 暴利 **excessive profits** ▶彼は不当な土地の売買で**暴利をむさぼった** He *made excessive* [*enormous*] *profits* from unfair land sales.

ほうりあげる 放り上げる **throw** [**toss**] **up** ▶2階の窓の所に居る兄さんにラグビーボールを**放り上げた** I *tossed up* a rugby ball to my brother at the upstairs window. ‖雄牛はその闘牛士を角で**放り上げた** The bull *tossed* the matador.

ほうりこむ 放り込む **throw in** [**into**] ▶ぼくは彼女の部屋の窓にラブレターを**放り込んだ** I *threw* my love letter *into* her room through the window. ‖その男は刑務所に**放り込まれた** The man *was thrown into* prison. ‖稲葉は右翼上段に特大のホームランを**放り込んだ** Inaba *slammed* an extra-big homer high [deep] *into* the right field seats.

ほうりだす 放り出す **throw out** ▶彼は猫を通りに**放り出した** He *threw* the cat *out* into the street.

▶勉強を**放り出して**映画に行った I *dropped* my work and went to see a film. ‖子供を**放り出して**こんな遅くまでどこへ行っていたんだ？ Where have you been until this late, *neglecting* your child?

ほうりつ 法律 a **law**（個々の）; (**the**) **law**（➤ 総称）一形 **法律の legal** ▶**法律**を勉強する study *law* ‖**法律**は守らなければならない We must obey *the law*. ‖未成年の喫煙は**法律で禁じられている** Minors are prohibited *by law* from smoking. ／*The law* forbids minors to smoke [from smoking]. ‖日本では（選挙での）戸別訪問は**法律違反**だった In Japan, door-to-door canvassing was *against the law*.

‖**法律家** a lawyer ‖**法律事務所** a law office ‖**法律用語** a legal term;《インフォーマル》legalese /lìːgəlíːz/（小難しい）.

ほうりなげる 放り投げる **throw** +目; **toss** +目（軽くぽいと）▶彼は上着を椅子の上に**放り投げた** He *threw* his jacket *over* the chair. ‖車の窓から空き缶を**放り投げる**人がいる There are some people who *toss* empty (beverage) cans from their car windows.

ぼうりゃく 謀略 a **plot**; a **conspiracy**（徒党を組んでの）▶それは私を陥れるための**謀略**だ！ That's *a plot* to trap me!

ほうりゅう 放流する **discharge** +目（水を）; **stock** +目（魚を）▶ダムの水を**放流する** *discharge* water from a dam.

▶多摩川にサケの稚魚が**放流された** The Tama River *was stocked* with salmon fry.

ほうりょう 豊漁 a **good** [**big** ／ **large**] **catch**, a **good haul** ▶ことしはサバが**豊漁**だ We had *a big catch* [*a good haul*] of mackerel this year.

ぼうりょく 暴力 **violence**; **force**（実力行使）; an **act of violence**（暴力行為）; **organized crime**（組織犯罪）▶**暴力**はやめろ！ Don't use *violence*! ‖彼はクラスメートに**暴力を振るう** He *is violent* with his classmates. ‖**暴力追放運動** a campaign against *organized crime*.

‖**暴力団** a criminal [gangster] organization (➤ 暴力団員は a gangster) ‖**家庭内暴力** domestic [family] violence ‖**校内暴力** school violence, violence in schools.

ボウリング **bowling** 一動 **ボウリングをする bowl**; **go bowling**（ボウリングをしに行く）▶**ボウリング**をしに行こう Let's *go bowling*. (➤ play は用いない).

‖**ボウリング場** a bowling alley.

ほうる 放る throw +㊀; toss +㊀ (軽く投げる) ▶バスの窓から空き缶を放るな Don't *throw* empty cans from the windows of buses. ‖ 消しゴムを彼に放ってやった I *threw* [*tossed*] an eraser to him. (➤ at him とすると「怒って投げつけた」の意).

ボウル 《容器》 a **bowl** /boʊl/ ▶サラダボウル a salad *bowl* ‖ 材料をボウルでよく混ぜ合わせます Mix the ingredients well in a *bowl*.

ほうれい 法令 a **law**; a **statute (law)** (成文法); an **ordinance** (条例)

‖法令集 a statute book, a book of statutes.

ぼうれい 亡霊 **the soul of a dead person**; a **ghost** (死霊); a **spirit** (霊).

ほうれんそう 《植物》 **spinach** /spínɪtʃ ‖ -nɪdʒ/ ▶ホウレンソウ1束 a bunch [a bundle] of *spinach*.

1**ほうろう 放浪** **wandering** 一動 **放浪する** **wander** [**roam**] (**around**) ▶画家は放浪の旅に出た The artist started on *a wandering journey*. ‖ 彼には放浪癖がある He has *the habit of bumming around*. ／He has *wanderlust*. (➤ 前者は否定的, 後者は肯定的な意味合い).

‖放浪者 a wanderer.

2**ほうろう 琺瑯** **enamel** /ɪnǽməl/ ▶ (浅い) ほうろう鍋 an *enamel* pan.

ぼうろん 暴論 ▶暴論を吐く make *an absurd remark* ‖「入試を全廃せよ」というのは暴論だ To call for abolishing all entrance exams *is absurd* [*irresponsible* ／*ridiculous*].

ほうわ 飽和 **saturation** ▶食塩の飽和溶液 *a saturated solution* of salt ‖ 今夜の東京ドームはすでに飽和状態です Tokyo Dome has already *reached full capacity* tonight.

ほえごえ 吠え声 a **bark**; a **howl** (犬やオオカミの遠ぼえ); a **roar** (猛獣の) ▶近所の犬のほえ声がやかましい The *barking* of neighborhood dogs is very noisy. 《参考》 犬のほえ声は bow-wow, 子犬の場合は yelp, yap という.

ほえづら 吠え面 ▶偉そうなこと言ってあとでほえ面かくなよ Don't talk so big. You*'re sure to* (*cry and*) *be sorry* later.

ほえる 吠える **bark** (犬が); **yelp** (犬がキャンキャンと); **roar** (猛獣が); **howl** (遠ぼえする) ▶スヌーピーは誰にもほえたことがない Snoopy has never *barked* at anybody. ‖ ほえる犬はめったにかまない *Barking* dogs seldom bite. (➤ 英語のことわざ).

1**ほお 頬** a **cheek** ▶彼女は頬が落ちくぼんでいる Her *cheeks* are sunken. ／She is hollow-cheeked. ‖ 涙が彼女の頬を伝って流れた Tears ran down her *cheek*(*s*).

▶《慣用表現》 大輔は美少女の前で頬を赤らめた Daisuke *blushed* [*flushed*] before the pretty girl. ‖ 彼女は気に入らないことがあるとすぐ頬を膨らます She *pouts* [*puffs out her cheeks*] when she is not pleased with something. (➤ pout /paʊt/ は「すねて口をとがらす」の意).

▶そのメロンは甘くて頬が落ちそうだった The melon was sweet and *melted in my mouth*. (➤「口の中で溶けた」の意).

‖頬ひげ whiskers (➤ 通例複数形) ‖ 頬紅 (a) blusher ‖ 頬骨 a cheekbone.

☞ 頬ずり, 頬づえ (→見出語)

2**ほお 朴 (の木)** 《植物》 a **Japanese big-leaf magnolia**.

ボーイ a **waiter**, a **server** (レストランの接客係; 後者は性差のない語); a **bellhop** (ホテルの); a **steward** /stjúːəʳd/ (客船・列車などの) ▶ボーイさん, 勘定をお願いします Excuse me, Tom. May I have the check [bill], please? (● 呼びかけるときは Waiter! などと言わないで名前を呼ぶのがふつう. 向こうから自己紹介するか, 大きな名札をつけている).

> **危ないカタカナ語✸ ボーイ**
> **1** レストランの「ボーイ」は waiter, ホテルの「ボーイ」は bellhop という.
> **2** レストランで客が食べたあと食器を皿洗いの所へ運ぶ人は waiter ではなく busperson と呼ばれる.

‖ボーイソプラノ a boy soprano.

ボーイスカウト **the Boy Scouts** (➤ その一員は a boy scout) ▶ぼくは子供の頃ボーイスカウトに入っていた I was *a boy scout* [I belonged to *the Boy Scouts*] when I was a boy.

ボーイッシュ **boyish** ▶女の子のボーイッシュなヘアスタイル a girl's *boyish* hairstyle ‖ 妹は髪を短く切ってボーイッシュに見える Since my sister had her hair cut short, she *looks like a boy*.

ボーイフレンド a **boyfriend**

> **危ないカタカナ語✸ ボーイフレンド**
> 英語の boyfriend は「恋愛関係にある特定の男性, 恋人, 彼(氏)」の意. 日本語でいう「男友だち」の意味は friend (of mine) だけで十分. 特に性別を示したいときは male friend とか, 年配者なら gentleman [man] friend とする.

▶杉野君は私のボーイフレンドのひとりですが, 恋人ではありません Sugino is *a friend* of mine, but not my boyfriend.

ポーカー **poker** (トランプのゲーム) ▶ポーカーをする play *poker* ‖ ポーカーフェースを装う[装っている] put on [keep ／wear ／have] *a poker face*.

ほおかぶり 頬被りする **1【手拭いで覆う】** **cover one's head and cheeks with a towel**.

2【知らないふりをする】 **pretend not to know**; **shut one's eyes to** (…に目をつぶる) ▶首相はその疑惑に頬かぶりを決め込むつもりだ The prime minister intends to *feign ignorance* of [*pretend to be unaware of*] the allegations.

ボーカル a **vocal** (➤ しばしば複数形で) ▶男性[女性]ボーカル male [female] *vocals* ‖ ひろしはロックバンドでボーカルを担当している Hiroshi is *a vocalist* in a rock band.

‖リードボーカル a lead vocal [singer].

ボーク 《野球》 a **balk** /bɔːk/ ▶ボークを犯す commit *a balk* ‖ 主審がボークを宣した The umpire called *a balk*.

ポーク **pork**

‖ポークカツ a breaded deep-fried pork cutlet ‖ ポークソテー a pork sauté, sautéed pork.

ボージョレヌーボー **Beaujolais nouveau** (新酒).

ホオジロ 《鳥》 a **meadow bunting**.

ホース a **hose** /hoʊz/ (➤ 発音に注意) ▶ゴムホース a rubber *hose* ‖ ホースで水を掛けて車を洗う rinse the car off using *a hose* ／*hose down* the car (➤ この hose は動詞) ‖ 父は毎日庭にホースで水をまく My father waters the garden *with a hose* every day.

1**ポーズ** 《姿勢》 a **pose** /poʊz/ ▶彼女はカメラの前でポーズをとった She *posed* for a picture. ／She *struck a pose* in front of the camera. ‖ はい, ポーズ! Hold that *pose*!

▶彼は同情してくれているようだが単なる**ポーズ**だ He seems sympathetic, but it's just *a pose* [*an act*].

[2]**ポーズ**《休止》a **pause** /pɔːz/ ▶校長先生はちょっと**ポーズ**をおいてせき払いをし, 式辞を続けた The principal *made a* brief *pause* [*paused* briefly], cleared his throat, and continued his speech.

ほおずき《植物》a **ground-cherry**, a **Chinese lantern plant**
‖**ホオズキ市** a "hozuki" market.

ほおずり 頬擦り ▶おじいさんは孫に**頬ずり**をした The grandfather *pressed his cheek against* his grandson's.

ポーター a **porter**.

ボーダーライン a **borderline** ▶多くの受験生が合否の**ボーダーライン**にいる Many examinees are on the *borderline* between passing and failing (the exam).

ポータブル portable ▶**ポータブル音楽プレーヤー** a *portable* music player ‖**ポータブルトイレ** a *portable* toilet.

ポータルサイト《コンピュータ》a **portal site** [**website**].

ボーダレスな borderless.

[1]**ポーチ** a **porch** ▶**ポーチ**で夕涼みをする enjoy the evening cool *on a porch*.

[2]**ポーチ** a **pouch** /pautʃ/ (小物入れ).

ホーチミンし ホーチミン市 Ho Chi Minh City(ベトナム南部の都市; 旧称 Saigon).

ほおづえ 頬杖 ▶彼女は**頬づえ**をついて何か考え込んでいる She is *resting her cheek on one hand*, absorbed in thought.

ぼーっと ▶霧のため景色が**ぼーっと**している The scenery *is blurred* because of the fog.
▶**ぼーっと**してないで手伝ってちょうだい Don't *just stand* there *in a daze*; give me a hand. ‖**ぼーっと**していて名前を呼ばれたのに聞こえなかった I *was daydreaming* and I didn't hear my name (being) called. ‖彼女は最近**ぼーっと**していることが多い She's often *out of it* [*out to lunch*] these days. (➤インフォーマルな言い方) ‖あまりの暑さに頭が**ぼーっと**なった My mind *went blank* because of the heat.
▶**ぼーっと**してんじゃないよ! *Keep your eyes* [*ears*] *open*! / *Wake up*! ‖ごめん. **ぼーっと**してた Sorry. I *was somewhere else*.

ぽーっと ▶おまえさんは美人を見るとすぐ**ぽーっと**なるんだねえ You *lose your head* at the sight of a pretty girl. / You*'re swept off your feet* by pretty girls. (➤ sweep A off A's feet は「たちまちA(人)の心を奪う」).

ボート a **rowboat**,《英また》a **rowing boat**(手こぎボート); a **boat**(大型の船·汽船を含む) ▶貸し**ボート** *a rowboat* for hire ‖ゴム**ボート** a rubber *raft* [*dinghy*] ‖我々は交代で**ボート**をこいだ We rowed the *boat* by turns. / We took turns rowing the *boat*. ‖**ボート**乗りに行こう Let's *go boating*. ‖ことしの大学対抗**ボートレース**ではオックスフォード大学が優勝した The Oxford University crew won the championship in the intercollegiate *boat race* this year.

ボードセーリング boardsailing. →ウインドサーフィン.

ポートレート a **portrait** ▶人気女優の**ポートレート**を満載した週刊誌 a weekly magazine full of (*photo*) *portraits* of popular actresses.

ボーナス a **bonus** /bóunəs/

> **《解説》** 欧米では日本のようにまとまった額のボーナスが定期的に支払われるのは一般的ではない. 英語の bonus は「特別手当」「配当」の意味で, 好成績をあげたセールスマンに対してや, 会社が大きな利益を得たときなどに支払われる.

▶多くの会社では**ボーナス**は6月と12月に出る In many companies, *bonuses* are given [are paid] in June and December. ‖**ボーナス**出た? Did you get your *bonus*?

ほおばる 頬張る ▶彼はすしを一度に2個も**頬張った** He *crammed* [*stuffed*] two pieces of sushi *into his mouth* at one time. ‖食べ物を**頬張った**まま話すな Don't speak *with your mouth full*.

ホープ a **hopeful** (**person**); a **hope** (頼みの綱) ▶彼女はわがバレーボールチーム最大の**ホープ**だ She is the most *promising* [*hopeful*] player on our volleyball team. (➤「将来を期待されている人」の意) / She is the greatest *hope* of our volleyball team.

ホーマー《野球》a **homer**, a **home run** →ホームラン ▶阿部選手が30号**ホーマー**を放った Abe slammed his 30th *home run* (of the season).
‖**ソロホーマー** a solo homer ‖**満塁ホーマー** a grand slam, a bases-loaded home run ‖**ランニングホーマー** an inside-the-park homer.

[1]**ホーム**《駅の》a **platform**,《米また》a **track** ▶我々は**ホーム**で新婚カップルを見送った We saw the newly-wed couple off on the *platform*. ‖日光行きの電車は1番**ホーム**から出ます Trains for Nikko leave from *Track* No. 1 [*Platform* No. 1].
‖**ホームドア** a platform door.

[2]**ホーム** **1【家庭】**(a) **home**
‖**ホームショッピング** telephone [catalog] shopping ‖**ホームセンター** a home improvement store [center] ‖**ホームドラマ** a family drama, a soap opera (➤後者には「お涙頂戴の, 安っぽい」という軽蔑的な含みがあることが多い) ‖**ホームパーティー** a (house) party ‖**ホームビデオ** a home video.
2【施設】 a **home** ▶両親を老人**ホーム**に入れる send one's parents to *a home for elderly people*.
3【野球の】home plate, home base, home, the plate ▶ランナーはレフトからの好返球で**ホーム**でタッチアウトになった The runner was tagged out at *the plate* on a good throw from the left fielder.

> **危ないカタカナ語✸ホーム**
> **1**「家庭」の意味の「ホーム」のついた語には和製語が多い. 掛かりつけの医者を指す「ホームドクター」は英語では family doctor という. また「ホームドラマ」は family drama か soap opera である.
> **2** 野球用語の「ホームイン」「ホームスチール」も和製語. 英語ではそれぞれ reach home, steal home のように動詞表現をとるのがふつう.
> **3** プラットホーム (platform) を略して「ホーム」というが, 英語では form とは略せない. また, platform は乗客の乗降のために軌道よりも高くした場所のことで, 軌道と同じ(くらいの)高さの場合には track と呼ぶ.

ホームイン《野球》▶高橋君の二塁打でランナー2人が**ホームイン**した Two runners *reached home* on Takahashi's double.

ホームグラウンド《野球》one's **home ballpark**, one's **home** (**grounds**) ▶中日は**ホームグラウンド**では勝率が高い The Dragons have a high winning percentage at their *home ballpark*. 《参考》「ホームグラウンドでの試合」を a home game という. 反対は an away [a road] game.

ホームシック **homesickness** ▶ロンドンに着いて2か月もするとホームシックになった I *got homesick* two months after I arrived in London.

ホームスチール 《野球》a **steal of home** [**home base**] ▶松田がホームスチールに成功した Matsuda *stole home*.

ホームステイ a **homestay** 一動 ホームステイする **homestay** 《with, at》 ▶カナダにホームステイに行く[行っている] go [be] on *a homestay visit* to Canada ‖ この夏アメリカにホームステイしに行きます I'm going to *stay with* an American *family* in the U.S. for the summer. ／I'm going to *homestay* in America this summer. ‖ 去年の夏休みはロンドンの家庭にホームステイした Last summer I *stayed* [*had a homestay*] with a family in London.

ホームストレッチ **the homestretch**.

ホームページ 《インターネット》a **web page**(通例, ウェブサイト上の1ページを指す) ; a **website**(複数のページからなる全体. web [Web] site ともつづる) ▶Amazon のホームページにアクセスする access Amazon's *website* ‖ ホームページを作成する make *a website* ／create *a web page*.

✉ **3月1日よりホームページを開きます. どんどんご利用ください** I'm going to *launch my website* on March 1st. I hope you check it out often!

ホームヘルパー a **home health aide**, a **home care worker**, 《英》a **home help**（正式な資格を持った）; a **caregiver**, a **home helper**（お年寄り・病人などの世話をする人）; a **domestic helper** [**worker**]（家事手伝い）; a **maid**（住み込みのメイド）.

ホームラン 《野球》a **home run** ; a **homer**, a **round-tripper**（➤ 後者2つはよりインフォーマル）▶大きなホームラン a long *home run* ‖ ホームランをかっ飛ばす hit [belt ／slam ／slug] *a home run* ‖ ホームランを許す give up *a home run* ‖ 同点［さよなら／決勝］ホームラン a game-tying [-ending ／winning] *home run*. ‖ **ホームラン王** a home run king [leader] ‖ **ホームランダービー** a home run derby ‖ **ホームランバッター** a home run hitter.

ホームルーム 《米》(a) **homeroom**, 《英》(a) **form room**

> **解説** **英米のホームルーム**
> アメリカの高校やイギリスの中等学校では日本と違い同一クラス内でも専攻により各生徒の時間割が異なり, 教科ごとに教室を移動する. したがって, 朝クラスの全員が集まり, 担任の先生とクラスの問題や連絡事項などを話し合う教室のことを a homeroom [form room] と呼び, その時間を homeroom [form room] または a homeroom [form room] hour と呼ぶ.

▶ホームルームで今度の運動会について話し合った We discussed the coming field day in *homeroom* (*hour*).

ホームレス a **homeless** [**street**] **person** ▶ホームレスの人々の手助けをする help *homeless people* [*the homeless*].

ポーランド **Poland** 一形 ポーランドの **Polish** ‖ **ポーランド語** Polish ‖ **ポーランド人** a Pole.

[1]**ボーリング** 《スポーツ》→ボウリング.

[2]**ボーリング** **boring**(掘削).

[1]**ホール** 《広間》a **hall** ; an **auditorium**（音楽会・演劇などのための）‖ **コンサートホール** a concert hall ‖ **展示ホール** an exhibition hall.

[2]**ホール** 《穴》a **hole** /hoʊl/ ▶《ゴルフ》ホールインワンをする get *a hole-in-one* [《米また》*an ace*].

[1]**ボール** **1**【球】a **ball** ▶サッカー[テニス]ボール a soccer [tennis] *ball*.

2【野球】a **ball** ▶ボール球を打つ hit *a bad pitch*（➤ pitch は「投球」）‖ ボール！ *Ball!*

[2]**ボール** 《容器》a **bowl** /boʊl/. →ボウル.

ボールがみ ボール紙 **cardboard**, **pasteboard** ▶私たちは学校祭で引く山車をボール紙で作った We made a float out of *cardboard* for our school festival.

ボールドたい ボールド体の 《印刷》**bold**, **boldface**(**d**) ▶ボールド体の文字で in *bold* letters ／in *bold type*.

ボールペン a **ballpoint** (**pen**) ▶用紙にはボールペンで記入してください Please use *a ballpoint pen* to fill out the form. 《参考》イギリスではふつう biro /báɪəroʊ/ という.

ほおん 保温する **keep ... warm** ▶アクリル繊維は軽くて保温性に優れている Acrylic fiber is light and *retains heat well*.

ホーン a **horn**(警笛) ▶車のホーンを鳴らす honk one's *horn*.

ボーンヘッド 《野球》▶ライトのボーンヘッドでベイスターズは労せずして1点をあげた The right fielder's *bonehead play* gave the BayStars an easy run. (➤ bonehead は主に人を指す).

ほか 外・他 **1**【別の物・人】一形 ほかの **other** ; **another**（もう1つの）; **else**（➤ 疑問詞や, something, anything, someone などのあとに置く）▶ほかに何か意見はありませんか Are there any *other* opinions?（➤ 会議などで）／Do you have any *other* opinions?（➤ 個人に対して）‖ トマトばかりでなくほかの野菜も食べなさい You should eat not only tomatoes but *other* vegetables as well. ‖ **対話** 「ほかの大学も受験してみたらどうなの？」「うん, そうするよ」 "Why don't you try *other* universities, too?" "OK. I will." ‖ ほかの人の助けを当てにするな Don't expect help from *other* people. ‖ またほかの日に来てください Please come *another* [*some other*] day. ‖ このネクタイは気に入らないな. ほかのを見せてください I don't care for this tie. Could you please show me *another one* [*some others*]?（➤ another one は「別の1本」, some others は「別のものを何本か」）‖ 大臣ほか12名の一行は今夜成田をたちました The Minister *and* twelve *others* departed from Narita this evening.

▶ほかに欲しいものは？ Do you want anything *else*? ‖ おっと, 誰かほかの人の傘を持って来てしまった Oh! I've taken *someone else's* umbrella with me! ‖ 子供は公園に居ない. ほか(の所)を当たってみよう I couldn't find the child in the park. Let's search *elsewhere*.

2【…以外】**except for**, **except** ; **but**（➤ no や nothing との相関で用いることが多い）

> **語法** (1)「…を除いては, …という点以外は」の意の場合は **except for** または **except** を用いる. except for は文全体に対するただし書きのようなもので, except はその前にくる語・句・節と同等のもの, すなわち文の一部を除外する場合に用いる.
> (2)「AだけでなくBも(また)」の意の場合は **not only A but** (**also**) B, あるいは B **as well as** A を用いる. また「…に加えて, …の上に」の意の場合は前置詞の **besides** を用いる. →**3**.

▶声が少し小さかったほかは，きみの歌なかなかよかったよ You sang very well, *except that* your voice was a bit weak. ‖ 足に数か所打ち身があるほかはけがはなかった I wasn't hurt *except for* a few bruises on my legs. ‖ 父は日曜日のほかは毎日会社に行く My father goes to work every day *except* Sunday. ‖ 期末では数学のほかはまあまあだった I did fairly well on the finals, *except for* math.

▶きみのほかにこの仕事のできる人間はいない *No* one *but* you could do this job. ‖ 芳夫は彼女のことを諦めるほかはなかった Yoshio had *no* (*other*) *choice but* to forget about her. ／*There was nothing* Yoshio could do *but* forget about her. ‖ テレビを見る以外，ほかにすることはないの？ Don't you have anything to do *besides* watch TV？（➤否定文・疑問文での besides は except と同義）‖《店員が客に物をすすめて》こんなの，ほかにありませんよ It's *one of a kind*.（➤ one of a kind は「ひとつだけでほかに類のないもの」の意）.

3【「AのほかにBも」の形で】not only A **but** (**also**) B ; B **as well as** A（➤ not only A but (also) B の場合と異なり，強調する語が as well as の前にくるのがふつう）▶山川さんは中国語のほかに韓国語も話せるんだよ Ms. Yamakawa speaks *not only* Chinese *but* (*also*) Korean.（● also はインフォーマルでは省くのがふつう）.

▶私たちは仙丈ヶ岳のほかに駒ヶ岳にも登った We climbed Mt. Koma *as well as* Mt. Senjo. ‖ ビンディーさんはインド料理店のほかに喫茶店も経営している *Besides* an Indian restaurant, Bindi runs a coffee shop. ‖ 私たちは定期試験を受けるほかに長いレポートを提出しないといけない *In addition to* taking regular tests, we have to hand in a long paper.（➤ in addition to は「…に加えて」の意）.

☛ ほかならない（→見出語）

ぽか a **blunder**（ばかな間違い）▶やつはまたポカをやったぜ He has *made a blunder* again. ／He *goofed* [*screwed up*] again.

ほかく 捕獲する catch +目，**capture** +目（➤後者は生け捕りを強調する）▶資源調査のため鯨を捕獲する *catch* whales for the purpose of resources research.

‖捕獲高 a catch.

ぼかし blurring ; **pixelization**（画像のピクセル化）; **gradation**（色調の）. →モザイク.

ぼかす blur +目 ; **pixelate** /píksəleɪt/（モザイク処理する）; **gradate** +目，**obscure** +目（曖昧にする）▶画像をぼかす *blur* [*pixelate*] an image ‖ 色をぼかす *gradate* a color ‖ 背景をぼかせばもっといい写真になるよ If you *blur* the background, it will be a better picture.

▶《比喩的》肝心なところをぼかさないでくれ Don't *obscure* the point.

ほかならない 他ならない ▶彼のした行為は性犯罪にほかならない What he did was *nothing short of* [*nothing less than*] a sex crime.

ほかならぬ 他ならぬ ▶その指輪はほかならぬ盗まれた彼女自身のものだった The ring was *none other than* the one that had been stolen from her. ‖ ほかならぬきみの頼みだから金を貸してあげよう Since you are the one [Only because it's you] who is asking, I will lend you the money.（➤前半の部分はともに「頼んでいるのがきみだから」の意）.

ほかほか ▶ほかほかのお芋 a *piping* [*steaming*] *hot* sweet potato ‖ パンは焼きたてでほかほかしたのが好きだ I like bread *fresh from the oven* [*freshly baked* bread].

ぽかぽか ▶春の日ざしはぽかぽかと気持ちがいい The spring sun makes you feel *nice and warm*. ‖ この手袋はぽかぽかして温かい These gloves keep my fingers *nice and warm*.

▶少年たちは彼の頭をぽかぽか殴った The boys *showered* his head *with blows*.

ほがらか 朗らかな cheerful, **sunny**（➤ともに性格的に）; **merry**（浮き浮きした）▶朗らかな女の子 a *cheerful* [*sunny*] girl ‖ 彼は朗らかな性格だ He has a *cheerful* disposition. ‖ 少女たちが朗らかに笑いながら歩いていく A bunch of girls are walking by, laughing *cheerfully*.

¹ほかん 保管する keep +目 ▶原稿は私が大事に保管しておきます I'll *keep* the manuscript with care. ／I'll *take* good *care of* the manuscript. ‖ 大事な物は貸し金庫に保管してある（＝預けた）I *have deposited* my valuables in a safety-deposit box.

²ほかん 補完する supplement +目 ▶本編を補完する別冊が出版された An additional volume that *supplements* the main volumes was published.

ぽかん ▶弟は口をぽかんと開けて眠っていた My brother was sleeping *with his mouth wide open*. ‖ 子供たちは口をぽかんと開けてその相撲取りに見とれた *The children gaped at* the sumo wrestler. ‖ そんな所にぽかんと突っ立ってないで座ったらどう？ Why not sit down instead of standing there *absent-mindedly* [*in a daze* ／*vacantly*]？

ぼき 簿記 bookkeeping ▶簿記をつける keep *books* [*accounts*].

‖簿記係 a bookkeeper ‖ 商業簿記 commercial bookkeeping.

ボギー《ゴルフ》a **bogey** /bóugi/ ▶8番でボギーをたたく make (*a*) *bogey* on [at] the 8th.

ぼきっ ▶倒れた拍子にそのおばあさんの腕の骨がボキッと折れた The moment the elderly lady fell to the ground, her arm broke *with a snap*.

ぽきぽき ▶子供たちははしゃいで枯れ枝をポキポキと折った The children were amusing themselves by *snapping* the dead twigs in two. ‖ 指をポキポキ鳴らすのはやめなさい Stop *cracking* your knuckles.

ボキャブラリー (a) **vocabulary** ▶彼はボキャブラリーが豊富［貧弱］だ He has a rich [limited] *vocabulary*.（➤個人の「語彙」全体が vocabulary で（×）vocabularies としない.「多くのボキャブラリー」は many words）.

ほきゅう 補給 (a) **supply**, **replenishment**（➤後者は堅い語）**一動 補給する supply** +目，**replenish** +目 ▶戸棚に食料品を補給する *replenish* the cupboard with food ‖ 台風のため食料の補給が遅れた［途絶えた］Because of the typhoon, the food *supply* was delayed [was cut off]. ‖ 被災地に食糧を補給した They *supplied* the disaster areas with food. ‖ 飛行機は燃料補給のため着陸した The plane landed to *refuel*.

▶その漁船は燃料と水を補給するために寄港した The fishing boat stopped at the harbor to *be supplied* with [to *take on*] fuel and water.

ほきょう 補強 reinforcement 一動 補強する reinforce +目 ▶台風に備えて塀を補強しておこう Let's *reinforce* the wall against the coming typhoon. ‖（球団は）チームの補強のために外国人選手を雇った They hired foreign players to *reinforce* [to *beef up*] their team.（➤ beef up はインフォーマル）.

‖補強工事 reinforcement work.

ぼきん 募金 fund-raising **一動 募金する** raise funds ▶学校は体育館を建て直すため**募金**を行っている The school *is raising funds* [*is collecting contributions*] to rebuild the gym. ‖交通遺児の**募金運動**に参加した I joined *a fund-raising campaign* for the children of traffic accident victims.
‖**募金箱** a donation box ‖**共同募金** the community chest. →**赤い羽根**.

ぼきん ▶小枝が雪の重みでポキンと折れた The twig broke *with a snap* under the weight of the snow.

ほきんしゃ 保菌者 a carrier ▶コレラの**保菌者** a cholera *carrier* ‖この病気の**保菌者**が発病するとは限りません *Carriers* of this disease don't always become sick.

ぼく 僕 I →**私** ▶ぼくは優作です *I* am [*I'm*] Yusaku. ／My name is [My name's] Yusaku. ‖**ぼくの番だ** It's *my* turn. ‖**きみはぼくのものだ** You are *mine.* ‖(よその子に声を掛けて)**ぼく，ここら辺りで三木さんっていううち知ってる？** Do you (happen to) know a Mr. Miki around here(, *little boy*)? ‖**ぼくたちはきのうそこに行った** *We* went there yesterday. ‖**きみのものはぼくのもの．ぼくのものはぼくのもの** What's yours is *mine* and *what's mine* is *mine.* ‖ **対話** (ノックに対して)「だあれ？」「ぼくだよ」"Who is it?" "It's *me.*" (● It's I. は，まれ；It's Bill.（ビルです）のように名乗るのがふつう).

ほくい 北緯 the north latitude ▶京都は**北緯35度**にある Kyoto is situated in [at] *lat. 35° N.* (➤ latitude thirty-five degrees north と読む；latitude は l. とも略す).

ほくおうしょこく 北欧諸国 the Nordic countries (デンマーク・スウェーデン・ノルウェー・フィンランド・アイスランドなど)；Northern European countries (ドイツやイギリスを含む場合もあり，曖昧)；Scandinavia (スカンジナビア).
‖**北欧人** a Northern European, a Scandinavian ‖**北欧神話** Norse mythology.

ほくげん 北限 ▶ブドウ栽培の**北限** *the northern limit* of grape cultivation [growing] ‖**北限の猿** *a Japanese macaque, Nihonzaru* (➤ snow monkey ともいう).

ボクサー a boxer (➤ ボクサー犬にもいう)；a prizefighter (プロボクサー).

ぼくし 牧師 **《解説》** (1)プロテスタントの牧師は一般に pastor, minister, clergyman／clergywoman といい，教区(主任)牧師は英国国教会では parson，それ以外では pastor，米国聖公会では rector という．(2)「…師」に相当する敬称は Reverend. →**神父** ▶メソジスト教会の**牧師** *a minister* of the Methodist Church ‖キング**牧師** the *Reverend* King／the *Reverend* Mr. King (● 後者はより改まった書き方；直接呼びかけるときは Reverend King).

ぼくじゅう 墨汁 sumi ink, India ink.

ほくじょう 北上する go north [northward] ▶桜前線が**北上**中である The 'cherry blossom front' is *moving north.*

ぼくじょう 牧場 a stock farm, 《米》 a ranch；(a) pasture (放牧場)；a meadow (干し草を作るための) **《参考》** アメリカ西部の観光用牧場は dude ranch といい，多くは宿泊施設を持つ ▶この夏は北海道の**牧場**で働くつもりだ I'm going to work on *a stock farm* in Hokkaido this summer.
‖**牧場主** a stock farmer, a rancher

ボクシング boxing ▶プロボクシングの**試合** a professional *boxing match.*

ほぐす 1【解く】 disentangle ＋目 ▶もつれた毛糸をほぐす *disentangle* [*unravel*] the twisted yarn ‖魚の身をほぐす *flake* the fish (away from the bone).
2【和らげる】 ease ＋目 ▶温泉につかって肩凝りをほぐした I *eased* my stiff shoulders by soaking in the hot spring. ‖父の肩の凝りをほぐした I *massaged* the stiffness out of Dad's neck and shoulders. ‖彼のジョークがその場の緊張をほぐした His joke *eased* the tense atmosphere [*broke the ice*]. (➤ break the ice は「緊張[堅苦しさ]をほぐす」の意のインフォーマルな言い方).
▶彼女には人の気持ちをほぐす才能がある She has the ability to *make* people *feel at ease.*

ほくせい 北西 the northwest (略 NW) ▶**北西**の風が吹いている A *northwest(erly)* wind is blowing.／The wind is blowing *from the northwest.* ‖船は**北西**に進んでいる The ship is sailing (*toward the*) *northwest.*
‖**北北西** NNW, north-northwest.

ぼくそう 牧草 grass ▶牛が**牧草**を食べている The cows are feeding on *grass.* ／The cows are grazing.
‖**牧草地** a meadow, (a) pasture.

ほくそえむ ほくそ笑む gloat (over) ▶他人の不幸を見て**ほくそ笑む** *gloat over* other people's misfortunes ‖強盗は自分の銀行強盗のニュースを見て**ほくそ笑んだ** The robber *chuckled to himself* as he watched the news of his bank robbery. (➤「ひとりでクックッと笑った」の意).

ほくたん 北端 the northernmost part [point], the northern end [tip] ▶その岬の**北端**に灯台があった There was a lighthouse at *the northern end* [*tip*] of the cape.

ぼくちく 牧畜 cattle raising [breeding], live-stock [stock] farming ▶この地方では**牧畜**が盛んだ *Cattle breeding* is widely practiced in this area.
‖**牧畜業者** a stock breeder.

ほくとう 北東 the northeast (略 NE) ▶**北東**の風が吹いている *A northeast(erly)* wind is blowing.／The wind is blowing *from the northeast.* ‖台風は**北東**に進んでいる The typhoon is moving (*to the*) *northeast.*
‖**北北東** NNE, north-northeast.

ぼくとう 木刀 a wooden sword.

ほくとしちせい 北斗七星 《米》 the Big Dipper, 《英》 the Plough /plaʊ/.

ぼくとつ 朴訥 ▶**朴とつ**な性格 *simple, unaffected* character ‖私は**朴とつ**な人が好きだ I like *quiet, unsophisticated* (types of) people. (➤ unsophisticated は「すれていない」).

ほくぶ 北部 the north, the northern part ▶私の田舎は新潟県の**北部**にあります My hometown is in *the north* [*the northern part*] of Niigata Prefecture.

ほくべい 北米 North America
‖**北米大陸** the North American continent.

ほくほく ▶事業が大成功だったので彼は**ほくほく顔**だ He *looks quite pleased* with his big success in business.
▶この焼き芋は**ほくほく**しておいしい This roasted sweet potato is *light and dry.* It tastes good.

ぼくめつ 撲滅 eradication **一動 撲滅する** eradicate ＋目；stamp out (踏み潰す)；wipe out (一掃する) ▶がん**撲滅運動** a *campaign against* cancer ‖性病の**撲滅**はまだ成功していない We still have not succeeded in *eradicating* sexually transmitted diseases. ‖ 人類はついに天然痘を地球上から撲滅した Human beings have finally *wiped* [*stamped*] *out* smallpox from the face of the earth.

ほくよう 北洋 **the north seas**
‖**北洋漁業** north-sea fisheries.

ほぐれる 1【解ける】 **come loose** ▶このもつれた糸はなかなかほぐれない This knotted thread just won't *come loose*.
2【和らぐ】 ▶彼女のマッサージで肩の凝りがほぐれた Her massage helped *lessen* [*relieve*] the stiffness in my shoulders. ‖ パーティーが進むにしたがってみんなの気分がほぐれてきた They all *relaxed* [*loosened up*] as the party went on.

ほくろ 黒子 a **mole** ▶はるみは右目の上にほくろがある Harumi has *a mole* over her right eye.
‖**泣きぼくろ** a mole under the eye.

1**ぼけ 惚け** **senility** /sənɪ́ləṭi/ (老人ぼけ; 婉曲(えんきょく)に a [one's] second childhood ともいう) ▶ぼけが始まる begin to *get senile* ‖ 祖母には少しぼけの症状が見られる My grandmother shows slight signs of *senility*. ‖ まだ連休ぼけだ *My head is still on vacation.* 《参考》休日明けに感じる休みぼけのことを social jet lag と呼ぶことがある.
‖**ぼけ老人** a senile person.

2**ぼけ 木瓜** 《植物》 a **Japanese (flowering) quince.**

ほげい 捕鯨 **whaling** ▶日本はかつて世界有数の捕鯨国だった Japan was once one of the leading *whaling countries* in the world.
‖**捕鯨船** a whaling ship, a whaler.

ぼけい 母系 **on the mother's side of** one's **family**
‖**母系社会** a matrilineal society.

ほけつ 補欠 a **substitute** /sʌ́bstɪṭjuːt/ (交代要員); a **reserve** (控え選手) ▶彼は野球部の補欠だ He is *a substitute player* [*a bench warmer*] on the baseball team. ‖ 兄は大学に補欠で入学した My brother was admitted to the university *to fill a vacancy*. (➤「空きを埋めるために」の意).
‖**補欠選挙** an election to fill a vacancy, 《英また》 a by-election.

ぼけつ 墓穴 a **grave** ▶《慣用表現》うそをついてばかりいるといずれ墓穴を掘ることになるよ If you keep telling lies, you're *digging your own grave*.

ぼけっと ▶祖父はこの頃何ひとつしないでぼけっと過ごしている These days, my grandfather *just watches the world go by*.

ポケット a **pocket** ▶上着[ズボン]のポケット a coat [pants] *pocket* ‖ 内ポケット an inside [inner] *pocket* ‖ 後ろのポケット a back *pocket* / 《英また》 a hip *pocket* ‖ 胸のポケット a breast *pocket* ‖ ポケット版の辞典 a *pocket-size*(*d*) dictionary.
▶彼は釣り銭をポケットにしまった He put the change in [into] his *pocket*. ‖ 警官はポケットから手帳を取り出した The police officer took a notebook out of his *pocket*. ‖ 少年はポケットに両手を突っ込んで立っていた The boy was standing *with his hands in his pockets*. ‖ 彼は手土産をポケットマネーで買った He paid for the present *out of his own pocket*. (➤ 経費などではなく「自腹で」の意. pocket money は「小遣い銭」).
‖**ポケットカメラ** a pocket camera.

ポケベル a **pager**; 《米また》 a **beeper**, 《英また》 a **bleep(er)** (➤ (×)pocket bell とはしない).

ぼける 惚ける **1【もうろくする】** **become** [**get** / **go**] **senile** /síːnaɪl/ ▶頭を使わないとぼけますよ You'll *become* [*get*] *senile* if you don't keep your mind active. ‖ ひいおじいちゃんは90歳になるけど全然ぼけていない My great-grandpa, though 90 now, *is* not the least bit *senile*.
2【ぼやける】 **be blurred** [**blurry**] ▶この写真はぼけている This picture is *blurred* [*out of focus*]. (➤ out of focus は「ピンぼけの」) ‖ ぬれた窓ガラスを通して見るとすべてがぼけて見えた Everything looked *blurred* through the wet window. ‖ このテレビは映像がぼけている We get a *fuzzy* picture on this TV.

1**ほけん 保険** **insurance** /ɪnʃʊ́ərəns/ ▶保険に入る buy [take out] *insurance* / take out an *insurance* policy ‖ 保険の契約をする make [sign] an *insurance* contract ‖ 車の保険を払う pay the *insurance* on a car (➤「自動車保険」は car [motor] insurance という) ‖ 《病院で》保険は利きますか Will my *insurance* cover this? ‖ 美容整形は大概保険が利かない Cosmetic surgery *is* typically *not covered by insurance*.
▶修理費は保険から支払われます Repairs will be paid for by the *insurance*. ‖ 私は2000万円の生命保険に入っています I have a 20-million-yen *life insurance policy*. / I carry twenty million yen of *life insurance*. (➤ この policy は「保険証書」) ‖ 私の家には(1000万円の)火災保険が掛けてある My house *is insured against fire* (for ten million yen). (➤「家に火災保険を掛ける」は, insure a house against fire のようにいう) ‖ 今度太陽生命の保険に入った I have *taken out a life insurance policy* [I have *insured myself*] with the Taiyo Life Insurance Company.
‖**保険外交員** an insurance salesperson ‖ **保険会社** an insurance company ‖ **保険金** insurance (money); benefits (給付金) 《参考》「保険金殺人」は a murder for insurance,「保険金詐欺(事件)」は life insurance fraud (case) という ‖ **保険金受取人** a beneficiary ‖ **保険契約者** a policyholder ‖ **保険証書** an insurance policy ‖ **保険代理店** an insurance agency ‖ **保険料** an insurance premium ‖ **健康保険証** a health insurance card.

「保険」のいろいろ **医療保険** medical insurance / **海外旅行保険** overseas travel accident insurance / **介護保険** nursing care insurance / **海上保険** marine insurance / **火災保険** fire insurance / **簡易保険** postal life insurance / **がん保険** cancer insurance / **グループ保険** group insurance / **健康保険** health insurance / **国民保険** national insurance / **雇用[失業]保険** unemployment insurance / **地震保険** earthquake insurance / **自動車保険** 《米》 auto (mobile) insurance, 《英》 motor insurance / **社会保険** social insurance / **終身保険** whole-life insurance / **障害保険** personal accident insurance / **生命保険** life insurance / **損害保険** damage insurance / **労災保険** workers' (accident) compensation insurance

2**ほけん 保健** **(preservation of) health** ▶彼女はこの地域の保健衛生のため頑張っている She is working hard to promote public *health* (*and hygiene*) in this area. (➤ hygiene /háɪdʒiːn/ は「衛生」).
‖**保健師** a public health nurse (➤ 学校の保健師(保健室の先生)は school nurse という) ‖ **保健室** the nurse's room [infirmary], 《英》 the dispen-

sary(→医務室)‖**保健所** a (public) health center ‖(学科の)**保健体育** health and physical education.

[1]**ほご 保護** **protection**(守ること); **conservation**(維持すること); **preservation** (安全確保) ━動 **保護する** **protect** ＋目, **conserve** ＋目, **preserve** ＋目 ▶環境を保護する *protect* [*preserve*] the environment ‖椅子の保護カバー a *protective* cover for a chair ‖夏は強烈な太陽光線から肌を保護する必要がある In (the) summer, it is necessary to *protect* your skin from the glaring sunlight. ‖自然を保護しよう Let's *protect* nature. ‖道路建設案は自然保護の立場から取りやめになった The road construction plan was canceled in the interest of *nature conservation* [*protection*].
▶その迷子の女の子は警察に保護された The lost little girl *was taken into protective custody by the police*.
‖**保護者** a protector (保護する人); a guardian (未成年者の後見人); a patron (芸術家などの); a parent (親) ‖**保護者会** a parent association(➤ a PTA meeting は保護者だけでなく教員なども含まれる) ‖**保護主義** protectionism ‖**保護色** a protective color ‖**保護鳥** a protected bird ‖**保護貿易** protective trade.

[2]**ほご 補語** 《文法》a **complement**
‖**主格**[**目的格**]**補語** a subjective [an objective] complement.

[3]**ほご 反故** ▶約束[契約]をほごにする *renege on* one's promise [contract] (➤ renege の発音は /rɪníg ‖ -níːg/).

ぼご 母語 one's **mother tongue** /tʌŋ/

《解説》母語と母国語
(1)「母語」とは, ある人が幼児期に最初に習得する言語のことで, 英語では one's mother tongue とか one's native language [tongue]という. これに対して, 「母国語」とは「母国[祖国]の言語」「国語」の意.
(2)「母語」と「母国語」が同一である場合もあれば, そうでない場合もある. 例えば, イギリス西部でウェールズ語を聞いて育った人が, ウェールズ語以外に, イギリスの国家語 (national language)としての英語を話すようになった場合, この人にとって母語はウェールズ語で, 母国語は英語である. →**母国語**.

[1]**ほこう 歩行** **walking** ▶彼は右半身がまひしていて歩行が困難だ The right half of his body is paralyzed, and he has difficulty (in) *walking*.
‖**歩行器** a walker (➤ 幼児用・病人用) ‖**歩行喫煙** smoking (a cigarette) while walking (along) ‖**歩行者** a walker, a pedestrian (➤ 後者はやや改まった語だが Yield to Pedestrians(歩行者優先) のように交通用語としてはよく用いられる); a passer-by(道行く人; 複数形は passers-by) ‖**歩行者専用道路** a pedestrians-only street ‖**歩行者天国** a vehicle-free mall [street], a Pedestrians-Only Area.

[2]**ほこう 補講** a **make-up class** ▶ 12月の第3週に補講をします There will be *a make-up class* in the third week of December.

[1]**ぼこう 母校** one's **old school**, one's **alma mater** /ælmə máːtəʳ/ (➤ 後者は改まった語で, 厳密には高校・大学の母校を指す) ▶私の母校は横浜高校です I graduated from Yokohama High School. ‖小山先生は今, 母校で教えている Mr. Koyama is teaching at *his alma mater* now.

[2]**ぼこう 母港** a **home port**.

ほごかんさつ 保護観察 **probation** ▶少年は保護観察処分となった The boy *was placed on probation*.

ぼこく 母国 one's **home** [**mother**] **country** ▶母国を離れて6年になる It has been six years since I left *my home country*.

ぼこくご 母国語 one's **national language** (自分たちが帰属する国家の共通語; 国家語); one's **mother tongue**, one's **native tongue** [**language**](母語). →母語.

ほこさき 矛先 ▶野党議員の質問の矛先は財務大臣に向けられた The Opposition member's questions *took aim at* [*zeroed in on*] the finance minister. (➤ zero in on は「…に照準を合わせる」の意).

ぼこぼこ ▶ぼこぼこ穴のあいた道 a road *full of potholes* (➤ pothole は「(道路の)穴ぼこ」) ‖お湯がぼこぼこ煮立ってきたらタコを入れてください Put the octopus in when the water *reaches a rolling boil*.
▶あのすりめ, 今度会ったらボコボコにしてやる I'll *beat up* that damn pickpocket the next time I see him.

ほこら 祠 a ***hokora***; a **miniature Shinto shrine**.

ほこらしい 誇らしい **proud** ━副 **誇らしげに** **proudly** ▶私は自分の国が誇らしい I *am proud of* my country. ‖彼は自分の勝利を誇らしげに語った He talked about his victory *proudly*.

[1]**ほこり 埃** **dust** ▶古い家具が地下室でほこりをかぶっていた The old furniture in the basement was covered with *dust*. ‖ダンプカーはもうもうとほこりを立てて通り過ぎた The dump truck raised a cloud of *dust* as it passed by. (➤ a cloud of dust は「立ち上る砂ぼこり」) ‖こんなほこりだらけの本は読みたくないわ. ちゃんとほこりを払ってよ I don't want to read such a *dusty* book. *Dust* [*Wipe*] it *off* properly. (➤ wipe off は「拭いてほこりを落とす」の意).
☛ **ほこりっぽい** (→見出語)

[2]**ほこり 誇り** **pride**; **self-respect**(自尊心) ▶彼女は郷土の誇りだ She is *the pride of our hometown*. ‖彼女は夫の誇りを傷つけてしまった She *hurt* her husband's *pride* [*self-respect*]. ‖祖母は誇り高き女性だった My grandmother was a *proud* woman.

【文型】
人・物(A)を誇りに思う
be proud of A
➤ Aは名詞・動名詞
人・物(A)に誇りをもっている
take pride in A
➤ Aは名詞・動名詞

▶あなたが学校の代表選手になってお母さまはあなたを誇りに思っているに違いないわ Your mother must *be proud of* you for being selected as one of the athletes to represent your school. ‖私たちは世界チャンピオンになったことをとても誇りに思います We *are very proud of* becoming the world champions. (➤ be proud of はやり遂げたことを「誇りに思う」) ‖彼は自分の仕事に大いに誇りをもっている He *takes* great *pride in his work*. (● take pride in は「…に誇りをもっている」で, 単に心情を表すのでなく, 「誇りに恥じない入念な[いい]仕事をしている」の意. また, この work は仕事ぶりだけでなく, 出来上がった作品全般も指すことがある).
▶私たちの町には誇りになるような立派なコンサートホールがある Our town *boasts* a fine concert hall. (➤ boast は「(誇りになるものを)持っている」の意).

ほ

ほこりっぽい 埃っぽい dusty ▶ほこりっぽい道 a *dusty* road ‖ きょうは風が強くてほこりっぽい Today it's windy and *dust is flying around*.

ほこる 誇る be proud ((of)), **take pride** ((in)) (…に誇りをもつ) ; **pride oneself** ((on)) (…を特に誇る ; 得意がる) ▶彼女は家柄を**誇っている** She *is proud of* her lineage. ‖ 職人の父は自分の技術を**誇っている** My father *takes pride in* his craftsmanship. ／My father *prides himself on* his craftsmanship. ‖ これはわが社の誇る製品の1つです This is one of the products that *we are proud of*.

ほころび 綻び a **split** [an **open**] **seam** ; a **rip**, a **rent** (裂け目) ▶綻びを縫い直す sew up *a split seam*.

ほころびる 綻びる **1**【衣類が】**come apart** [**loose**] ; **be torn** (破れる) ▶袖の縫い目が綻びた The seam of my sleeve *has come apart* [*loose*]. ‖ ズボンのお尻が綻びた (＝裂けた) The seat of my pants *ripped open*.

2【花が咲く】**begin to bloom** [**come out**] ▶庭の梅がちらほらほころび始めている The *ume* blossoms in my garden are beginning to *unfold* [*come out*] here and there.

ほさ 補佐 an **assistant**, an **aide** /eɪd/ (➤ 後者は特に高官を補佐する人をいう) **一動 補佐する assist, help** ▶誰かが彼女を**補佐しなければならない** Somebody must *help* [*assist*] her. ／She needs an assistant. ‖ 彼は課長補佐になった He became *an assistant section chief*.

‖ (アメリカ大統領の)**補佐官** a presidential aide (➤「首席補佐官」は chief of staff).

ほざく ▶ほざくな, 小僧! *Shut up* [*Shut your trap*], you little squirt! (➤ trap は「口」の意の俗語) ‖ よくもほざいたな! You've said enough!

ぼさつ 菩薩 a **Bodhisattva** /bòʊdəsʌ́tvə/.

ぼさっと ▶そんな所にぼさっと立っていると掃除の邪魔よ I can't get the cleaning done with you *standing* (*around*) in the way.

ぼさぼさ ▶M教授はいつも髪をぼさぼさにしている Professor M's hair is always *messy* [*uncombed*]. (➤ 後者は「くしが入っていない」).

ぼさん 墓参 ▶久しぶりにおじの**墓参をした** I *visited* my uncle's *grave* for the first time in a long while.

ほし 星

1【空の】**a star** (恒星) ; **a planet** (惑星) ▶星が出ている The *stars* are out. ‖ 空には無数の星が瞬いている Millions of *stars* are twinkling in the sky. ‖ その夜は1つも星が見えなかった We couldn't see any *stars* that night. ‖ 今夜は星が多い The sky is *starry* tonight.

《参考》日本語では「青い星, 地球」などというが, 地球は惑星なので planet であり, star と呼ぶことはない. the planet や this [our] planet が地球を表すごくふつうの言い方で Planet Earth と呼ぶこともある.

▶《比喩的》ダルビッシュはプロ野球界の星だ Darvish is the *star* [*hope*] of professional baseball.

2【運勢】▶彼は幸運な[悪い]星の下に生まれた He was born *under a lucky* [*an unlucky*] *star*.

3【星形】**a star** ; **an asterisk** (＊印) ▶アメリカの国旗には50の星がある The U.S. national flag has 50 *stars* on it.

4【犯人】▶ホシはまだ挙がっていない The *perp* has not yet been caught. (➤ perp はもとアメリカの警察俗語で perpetrator (犯人) の略だが, 日本語の「ホシ」ほどには一般的ではないので次例の言い方がよい) ／The *culprit* is still at large. (➤ at large は「(犯人などが)逃走中で」の意).

5【「…星」の形で】▶東京の2つ[3つ]**星レストラン** a two- [three-] *star* restaurant in Tokyo ‖ 期待の星 a rising *star*.

☞ **勝ち星, 星占い, 星回り** (→見出語)

ほし- 干し- dried ▶干し柿 a *dried* persimmon ‖ 干しあわび *dried* abalone ‖ 干し芋 *dried* sweet potato.

ほじ 保持 maintenance /méɪntənəns/ **一動 保持する maintain** +目, **hold** +目 (➤ 前者は堅い語) ▶選手権**保持者** a title*holder* ‖ 日本[世界]記録**保持者** a Japan [world] record *holder* ‖ 彼は陸上10,000メートルの世界記録**保持者だ** He *holds* the world record for the 10,000-meter race.

ぼし 母子 mother and child (母と子) ▶**母子ともに健康です** *Both the mother and her baby* are doing well. ‖ 彼女の家は**母子家庭**だ (＝父親がいない) She is from *a fatherless family*. ／She doesn't have a father. (💰 第1例を She is from a single parent family. と訳すこともできるが, single parent family は親の性別を問題としない言い方なので「父子家庭」の訳語としても使える).

‖ **母子手帳** a maternity health record book.

ポジ a **positive** ‖ **ポジフィルム** a positive film.

ほしあかり 星明かり starlight ▶**星明かりの道** a *starlit* road.

ほしい 欲しい

1【手に入れたい】**want** +目, **would like** +目 (➤ 後者は前者の丁寧な言い方で,「頂きたい」に近い) ▶どうしてもこれが欲しい I really *want* this (one). ‖ 対話「何か欲しい物はない?」「デジタル音楽プレーヤーが欲しい」"Is there anything you *want*?" "I *want* a digital music player." ‖ 何か飲み物が欲しいな I'*d like* (to have) something to drink. (➤ I'd like は I would like の短縮形) ‖ お茶が1杯欲しいわね I'*m dying for* [I *could* (really) *use*] a cup of green tea. (➤ be dying for も could use も「…が欲しくてたまらない」の意) ／I'*d love* a cup of green tea. (➤ I'd love は I'd like と同義で女性に多い言い方) ‖ 早く一雨欲しい I sincerely *hope* we'll have rain soon. ‖ 今はとにかく時間が欲しい I'm desperately *in need of* time now. (➤ in need of は「…を差し迫って必要として」) ‖ 長年欲しかったオートバイをやっと手に入れた I finally got the motorcycle that I *had been wanting* [I *had wanted*] for many years.

✉ **ロックの歴史の本ありがとう. これこそ私の欲しかった物です** Thank you for the book on the history of rock music. It is exactly what I *wanted*.

2【「…してほしい」の形で】**want ... to do** (➤ …には「人」がくる ; 指図・軽い命令を表す)

> **【文型】**
> **人(A)に…してほしい**
> **would like A to do**
> **want A to do**
>
> **《解説》**(1)**would** (＝'**d**) **like** A **to** do は「(できたら)…してほしい」という, 丁寧な願望表現である. しかし, いかに丁寧でも言い切りの形なので A が you の場合には聞き手にプレッシャーがかかり, 命令されているように響くことも少なくない. したがって, 目上の人や年長者には使わない. **want** A **to** do はよりストレートな欲求を表し, 命令に近くなる. どちらも頼み事には使わないほうがよい. 次のページの囲みを参照.
> (2)to do の主語(A)はその前に置く. 代名詞は目的格にする.

▶きみにはバントでランナーを送ってほしい *I want you to* advance the runner on a bunt. ‖ これから言うことを注意して聞いてほしい *I want* [*ask*] *you to* listen to me carefully. ‖ きみにはもう少し情熱というものをもってほしい *I'd like you to* show a little more enthusiasm. ‖ おまえには銀行員になってほしい *I'd like you to* become a bank clerk. ‖ 横から口を出してほしくないね *I don't want you* butting in. (➤ 否定文では to do の代わりに doing の形を用いることがある. また, ストレートに命令形で Don't butt in (when I'm talking). と言うことも多い).

▶春が早く来てほしいな *I hope* spring comes soon. (●「早く来るといいな」の意 ; I wish spring would come soon. は春がなかなか来ないことへの不満を表す. →-のに) ‖ 田中には満塁のピンチを切り抜けてほしかった *I wish* Tanaka had pitched himself out of the bases-loaded jam. (➤ I wish (that) ~ had done は「～が…すればよかったんだが」の意で過去の実現しなかった願望を表す).

▶ **対話**「大阪を案内してほしいんですが」「どの辺へ行きたいですか」"*I'd* (*really*) *like it if* you could show me around Osaka." "Where would you like to go ?" ‖ ほしい物リスト a *wish* list.

✉ **何か日本から送ってほしい物があったら, おっしゃってくださいね** If you *want me to send anything* from Japan, please let me know.

直訳の落とし穴「…してほしいんですが」

I'd like you to do が丁寧な依頼を表すと考えて,「英語の作文をチェックしてほしいんですが」のつもりで, I'd like you to check my English composition. と言う人がいるが, 部下への指示ならともかく, 先生や目上の人への頼みであればふさわしくない. 頼み事は相手が Yes または No の選択の余地のある疑問文を使うのが礼儀である. したがって,「…していただけませんか」に当たる Could you please ...? を用いる. 多少頼みにくいときにはより間接的な表現で I was wondering if you could check my English composition. または, I'd appreciate it if you could check my English composition. とすることもできる. 学習者が使いがちな I wish you would ... は頼み事でなく, 現状への不満を表す言い方で,「…してくれてもいいものを」の意になるので注意が必要である. →いただく.

ほしいまま ▶彼は権力をほしいままにした He *abused* his authority. (➤ abuse /əbjúːz/ は「乱用する」) ‖『ハリー・ポッター』で作者は想像をほしいままにして魅力ある登場人物を創造した In Harry Potter, the author *put her imagination to full play* to create fascinating characters.

ほしうらない 星占い astrology /əstrɑ́ːlədʒi/ (占星術) ; a **horoscope** (占ったもの) ▶星占いをする cast *a horoscope* ‖ 私は雑誌で自分の星占いをよく見ます I often read my *horoscope* in the magazine. ‖ 彼女の星占いはよく当たる Her *horoscopes* often prove right.

ポシェット a **pochette.**

ほしがる 欲しがる **want** +Ⓞ ▶息子はクリスマスプレゼントにノートパソコンを欲しがっている My son *wants* a laptop for Christmas. ‖ 見る物見る物, 欲しがるんじゃありません Don't *ask me to buy* you every little thing you see. ‖ 赤ん坊はミルクを欲しがって泣いた The baby *cried for* milk.

ほしくさ 干し草 **hay.**

ほじくりかえす ほじくり返す ▶過去をほじくり返すのはよくない It's not good to *dredge up* the past.

ほじくる **pick** ▶人前で鼻[歯]をほじくるのは不作法だ It is bad manners to *pick* your nose [teeth] in public.

-ほしさ -欲しさ ▶相手欲しさ *a desire* to be with someone.

ポジション a **position** ▶ **対話**《野球で》「きみのポジションはどこですか」「ショートです」"What's your *position* ?" "(I'm a) shortstop."

ほしぞら 星空 a **starlit** [**starry**] **sky,** (**the**) **starry skies** (➤ 後者は空の広がりを強調した言い方) ▶二人は黙って星空を眺めていた The couple looked up into the *starlit sky* in silence.

ほしつ 保湿 ‖**保湿クリーム** (a) moisturizing cream, (a) moisturizer.

ポジティブな **positive** ▶ポジティブな態度 a *positive* attitude.

ほしぶどう 干し葡萄 a **raisin** /réɪzən/.

ほしまわり 星回り ▶星回りが悪い人 an *unlucky* [an *ill-starred*] person (➤ 後者は文語的 ;「星回りのよい人」は lucky person).

ほしもの 干し物 **the washing** (洗濯物) ▶干し物を干す hang *the washing* out to dry ‖ 夕方になったら干し物を取り込んでね Please bring [take] in *the washing* before dark.

ほしゃく 保釈 **bail** /beɪl/ (➤「保釈金」の意味にもなる) **一動 保釈する** **release ... on bail** ▶その容疑者は(保釈金を払って)保釈された The suspect *was released on bail.* / The suspect *was bailed out.* ‖ 彼は200万円の保釈金を払った He paid [put up / posted] two million yen in [for] *bail.*

ぽしゃる ▶参加者が少なくて, 探鳥会の計画はポシャった The bird watching plan *fell through* [*fell flat*] because there were too few participants. (➤ fall through, fall flat はともに計画が「だめになる」).

¹**ほしゅ 保守** **1【制度・考え方を変えないこと】一形 保守的な** **conservative** ▶保守的な意見[社会] a *conservative* opinion [society] ‖ うちの父は考え方が保守的だ My father is *conservative* in his views. ‖ 日本の医学界には臓器移植に対して保守的な人も多い In Japanese medical circles, many people still have a *conservative* attitude toward organ transplants. ‖ 若者の保守化が進んでいる The young generation is *getting* (*more*) *conservative.*

‖**保守主義** conservatism ‖ **保守主義者** a conservative ‖ **保守党** a conservative party ; the Conservative Party (イギリス・カナダの).

2【設備などを正常な状態に保つこと】 **maintenance** ▶道路の保守 road *maintenance* ‖ コピー機を定期的に保守点検する *do* [*perform* / *conduct*] *maintenance on* a copying machine regularly.

²**ほしゅ 捕手** a **catcher** ▶捕手を務める *play catcher.*

¹**ほしゅう 補習** a **supplementary lesson** ▶ 3 時から英語の補習(授業)を受けなくてはならない I have to attend [take] *a supplementary lesson* in English at three.

²**ほしゅう 補修** **repair** **一動 補修する** **repair** +Ⓞ, **mend** +Ⓞ, **fix** +Ⓞ ▶この外壁は補修の必要がある This outer wall needs *repairing.*

‖**補修作業** repair work. →修理.

ほじゅう 補充する **replenish** +Ⓞ ; **fill up** (いっぱいにする) ▶冷蔵庫(の中身)を補充する *replenish* the refrigerator ‖ チームの欠員を補充する *fill* (*up*) *the va-*

ほ

cancies in the team ‖ タンクに水を補充しなさい *Fill up* the tank with water.

ぼしゅう 募集 recruitment（新人の）**一動 募集する** recruit ＋目; accept applications（申し込みを受け付ける）; invite ＋目（質問や提案を求める）▶新入社員を募集する *recruit* new employees ‖ 当社では事務員を１人募集して（＝募集広告を出して）います Our company is *advertising for* a clerk. ／Our company *has put out a job ad for* a clerk. ‖ 製品改良の提案を募集中です Suggestions for improving our products *are invited*. ‖ 新しい乗用車の愛称を募集しています Nicknames for the new passenger car are now *being solicited*. ／We *are now soliciting* [*inviting suggestions for*] nicknames for the new passenger car. (➤ solicit は「募金や援助を求める」の意の堅い語).

▶その料理学校は目下生徒を募集中だ The cooking school *is now accepting enrollment applications*. (➤ 貼り紙の「生徒募集中」は New Students Invited) ‖ 英語学科の募集人員は100名だ The number of students to *be admitted to* the English Language Department is 100. ‖《貼り紙》アルバイト募集中 Part-timers *Wanted* ／Part-time Help *Wanted*.

‖募集広告 a want ad ‖ 募集要項 an application booklet.

ほじょ 補助 assistance, aid /eɪd/, help (➤ aid は堅い語) **一動 補助する** aid ＋目, help ＋目 ▶生活困窮者は政府の補助を受けられる Needy persons can receive *assistance* [*aid*] from the government. ‖ わが国の私立大学は国庫の補助を受けている Private universities in our country *are subsidized* by the government. (➤ subsidize は「補助金を出す」).

▶おじが私の学費を補助してくれています My uncle *helps* me *with* my school expenses.

‖補助椅子 a spare chair; a jump seat（バスなどの）‖ 補助教材 supplementary teaching materials ‖ 補助金 a subsidy /sʌ́bsədi/ ‖（自転車の）補助輪 stabilizers ‖ 栄養補助食品 nutritional supplements.

[1]**ほしょう 保証** a guarantee /gæ̀rəntíː/, a warranty (➤ ともに「メーカーや店が消費者にする約束」の意) **一動 保証する** guarantee ＋目, warrant ＋目; assure ＋目（請け合う）▶この時計は２年間の保証付きです This watch has a two-year *guarantee* [*warranty*]. ／This watch *is guaranteed* [*is warranted*] for two years.

▶この車の保証期間はどれだけですか How long is the *guarantee* [*warranty*] on this car? ‖ この冷蔵庫にはまだ保証がついている This refrigerator *is* still *under warranty*.

▶彼が正直であることは私が保証します I *assure* you of his honesty. ／I can *vouch for* his honesty. (➤ vouch /vautʃ/ for は「…の保証人になる」の意で, 推薦状などで用いる) ‖ そのことは私が保証するよ You *have my word* on it. ‖ うまくいくかどうかは保証の限りではない I *can't promise* you that all will go well.

‖保証期間 the term of guarantee ‖ 保証金 security money; a deposit（手付け金）‖ 保証書 a warranty, a written guarantee.

☛ 保証人（→見出語）

[2]**ほしょう 保障** security（安全の）; guarantee（権利の）**一動 保障する** guarantee ＋目 ▶社会保障 social *security* ‖ 言論の自由を保障する *guarantee* freedom of speech ‖ 私には老後の保障は何もない I have no *guaranteed* [*assured*] *source of income for my old age*. ‖ 日米安全保障条約 the Japan-U.S. *Security* Treaty.

[3]**ほしょう 補償** compensation, recompense **一動**（…を）**補償する** compensate《for》, recompense《for》▶彼は運転手に事故の補償（金）を要求した He demanded *compensation* from the driver for the accident. ‖ 政府がこの風評被害を補償すべきだ The government should *compensate* us *for* the damage caused by this rumor.

‖補償金 compensation (money).

ぼじょう 慕情 a longing, a yearning《for》.

ほしょうにん 保証人 a guarantor /gæ̀rəntɔ́ːʳ/, a surety /ʃʊ́ərəṭi ‖ ʃɔ́ːrəti/（借金・約束などの; 前者は堅い語で法律用語として用いることが多い）; a voucher /váʊtʃəʳ/（物事・人の）; a cosigner /kòʊsáɪnəʳ/（連帯保証人）▶私が彼の保証人になります I will *stand surety* for him. ‖ 銀行ローンの保証人になっていただきたいのですが I would appreciate it if you would *cosign on* this bank loan for me [《英》if you would be my *guarantor* for a bank loan]. ‖ 私は彼の人物を保証します I can *vouch for* his character.

ほしょく 補色《美術》a complementary color.

ほじる pick ＋目（鼻や歯を）. →ほじくる.

ほす 干す dry ＋目（ぬれた物を）; air ＋目（空気に当てる）▶ぬれた服を日［火］に干す *dry* one's wet clothes in the sun [by the fire] ‖ 洗濯物を外に干した I *hung out* the wash *to dry*. ‖ 布団はたびたび干したほうがいい Futon(s) should *be aired* frequently.

▶最近彼は会社で干されている Recently he *has been left out in the cold* in his company. (➤ (out) in the cold で「無視されて」の意のインフォーマルな言い方).

ボス a boss; a head, a gang leader（ギャングの）; a ringleader（不良グループなどの）▶政界のボス a political *boss* ／a kingmaker ‖ 警察は不良グループのボスを逮捕した The police arrested the *ringleader* of the gang.

ほすうけい 歩数計 a pedometer.

ポスター a poster ▶宣伝ポスター a publicity *poster* ‖ 壁にポスターを貼る put up *a poster* on the wall.

‖ポスターカラー poster paint.

ホステス a hostess

> **危ないカタカナ語✹ ホステス**
> **1** hostess は「（家庭でのパーティーで来客をもてなす）接待役の女性」が第一義で, host（接待役の男性）に対する語.「（社交クラブなどで客の踊りの相手をしたり, 話し相手になったりする）コンパニオン」の意もあるが, 日本の「バーのホステス」のイメージとはかなりずれる.
> **2**「バーのホステス」は bar hostess とする. なお, barmaid は「女性のバーテン」の意.

ホスト a host（パーティーなどで客をもてなす主人役）

‖ホストクラブ a "host" club; a drinking establishment where male attendants entertain women patrons ‖ ホストコンピュータ a host computer.

[1]**ポスト**《郵便ポスト》《米》a mailbox;《英》a pillar box, a postbox ▶手紙をポストに入れた I *mailed* [《英また》*posted*] the letter. ／I *put* the letter *in the mailbox*.

[2]**ポスト**《地位》a post, a position ▶父は会社で重要なポストを与えられた My father was given an important *post* [*position*] in his company.

ホストファミリー a host family
✉うちでホストファミリーをやってみたいと思っています We're interested in being [in serving as] *a host family*.
✉皆さまは最高のホストファミリーでした. ありがとうございました You were the greatest *host family*. Thank you (for everything).

ボストンバッグ a Boston bag.

ホスピス a hospice ▶末期患者用のホスピス *a hospice* for terminal patients.
‖在宅ホスピス home hospice care.

ほせい 補正 (a) revision ━動 補正する revise +目
‖補正予算 a revised [supplementary] budget (➤前者は修正した, 後者は補足した予算).

ぼせい 母性 motherhood, maternity /mətə́ːrnəti/ ━形 母性の maternal ▶母性的な女性 a *motherly* woman ‖子供には母性愛が必要だ Every child requires *a mother's love* [*maternal affection*]. ‖彼みたいにだらしない男性のほうが母性本能をくすぐるわ A scruffy man like him really appeals to my *maternal instincts*.

ぼせき 墓石 a gravestone, a tombstone.

ほせん 保線 rail(road) maintenance.

ほぜん 保全 conservation (損なわれないように守ること); maintenance (維持) ━動 保全する conserve +目, maintain +目 ▶高速道路の保全 *maintenance* of expressways.
‖環境保全 environmental conservation.

ぼせん 母船 a mother ship.

ほそい 細い

thin (➤人体に用いた場合, しばしば「不健康に痩せた」の意になる); fine (ごく細かい); narrow (幅が狭い) ▶細い針金[首] a *thin* wire [neck] ‖彼女は細い指をしている She has *thin* [*slender*] fingers. (➤slender は「ほっそりして魅力的な」) ‖その少女は手足が細い The girl has *slender* limbs. ‖細い線は町の境界を示す The *fine* lines (on the map) designate city limits.
▶我々は峠に通じる細い道をたどった We hiked along a *narrow* trail leading to the pass. ‖「ごめんなさい」と彼女は蚊の鳴くような細い声で謝った "I'm sorry," she apologized *in a thin voice* like a mosquito's whine.
▶ガスの火を細くしてちょうだい *Turn down* the gas, please. ‖娘は食が細い My daughter *is a light eater*. / My daughter *doesn't eat much*.

ほそう 舗装する pave +目 ▶舗装していない道 an *unpaved* road ‖その道路はアスファルトで舗装してある The street *is paved* [*is surfaced*] with asphalt. ‖その通りは舗装工事中だ They *are paving* the street.
‖舗装道路 a paved [a surfaced] road, a pavement.

ほそうで 細腕 ⚠英語には「細腕」(a thin arm) を比喩的に用いることはないのでぴったりの対応語はない. したがって用例のように適宜内容の意味をくんで言いかえる必要がある.
▶彼女は女の細腕一つで7人の子供を育て上げた She brought up seven children *on her meager earnings* [*all by herself*]. (➤meager earnings は「少ない稼ぎ」; all by herself は「自分で」).

ほそおもて 細面 ▶彼女は細面の純日本風の美人だ She's a classic Japanese beauty with *a slender face*.

ほそく 補足の supplementary (不完全さを補う); complementary (補完的な) ━動 補足する supplement +目 ▶補足説明 a *supplementary* explanation ‖彼の説明不十分のところを私が補足いたします I will *fill in* the parts that weren't (sufficiently) covered in his explanation.

ぼそっと ▶「俺結婚したよ」と彼はぼそっと言った "I got married," he said *in a low and indistinct voice*. (➤「低くはっきりしない声で」の意).

ほそながい 細長い ▶細長い紙 a *long, narrow* piece of paper ‖あの細長い建物が本社です That *tall, slender* building is our head office.

ほそぼそ 細々 ▶私の年老いた両親は信州で細々と暮らしています My aged parents are making a *meager* living in Shinshu. (➤meager は「貧弱な」) ‖祖父は田舎で細々と店をやっている My grandfather runs a shop in the country(side) *which brings in very little money*.

ぼそぼそ ▶ぼそぼそした話し方をする talk *in a low and inarticulate voice* (➤「低く不明瞭な声で」の意).
▶ぼそぼそしたクッキー *dry and crumbly* cookies.

ほそみち 細道 a narrow road; a lane (小道)
‖『おくのほそ道』"The Narrow Road to the Far North."

ほそみの 細身の slender, slim ▶細身の女性 a *slender* woman.

ほそめ 細め ▶彼女はどちらかというと細めだ She is a bit *on the slender side*. ‖彼は細めの(=ぴったりした)ズボンが好きだ He likes *rather tight* pants.

ほそめる 細める ▶その老人は孫が歩くのを目を細めて眺めていた The old man *fondly* watched his grandson walk. (➤fondly は「愛情を込めて」; →かこみ記事).

> **あなたの英語はどう響く?**
> 日本語で「父親は幼い息子が歌を歌うのを目を細めて見た」と言うと, ほほえましさを連想させるが, これを (×) The father *narrowed his eyes* as he saw his little son singing. としたり, (×) The father looked *with his narrowed eyes* at his little son singing. としたりすることはできない. 英語では斜体字部分は「疑惑の目で(見た)」という意味になるからである. 日本文に当たる英語は The father *beamed with delight* [The father *grinned*] as he watched his little son singing. である.

ほそる 細る ▶彼女は身の細る思いできみに焦がれているそうだ She *has lost her appetite* pining for you. (➤「食欲を無くしてしまった」の意).

ほぞん 保存 preservation ━動 保存する preserve +目; keep +目 (しまっておく); save +目 (データを残す) ▶市の歴史保存地域 the city's *historic preservation district* ‖私たちはこの町の歴史的建物の保存に努めています We're making an effort to *preserve* the historical buildings in this city. ‖古代エジプト人はファラオをミイラにして保存した The ancient Egyptians *preserved* their pharaohs as mummies.
▶この薬は冷暗所に保存してください *Keep* this medicine in a cool place away from direct sunlight. ‖こまめにデータを保存することをお勧めします I advise you to *save* your data frequently.
‖保存食 preserved food ‖保存料 a preservative.

ポタージュ potage /poutáːʒ/, thick soup (➤英語では後者がふつう).

¹ぼたい 母体 ▶母体の安全のために中絶が必要かもしれない We may have to perform an abortion to

save the *mother*.
▶労働組合がその組織の母体(＝核)だ The labor union forms the *nucleus* of the organization.
‖支持母体 a power base.

[2]**ぼたい 母胎** one's **mother's womb.**

ぼだいじ 菩提寺 a **Buddhist temple that takes care of a family's deceased members.**

ぼだいじゅ 菩提樹《植物》a **linden, a lime (tree)** (セイヨウボダイジュ); a **bodhi-tree**(インドボダイジュ).

ほだされる ▶あいつは情にほだされやすいやつなんだ He *is* easily *moved* by compassion.

ほたてがい 帆立て貝 a **scallop.**

ぼたぼた ▶油がタンクからぼたぼた落ちていた Oil *was dribbling down* from the tank. →ぽとぽと.

ぽたぽた ▶葉から雨の滴がぽたぽた落ちていた The rain was *dripping* from the leaves. ‖引っ越し屋さんは額から汗をぽたぽたたらしながら家具を運び入れた Sweat *was dripping* [*trickling*] *down* the movers' faces as they carried the furniture into the house. ‖水がしたたるぽたぽたぽたという音 the *drip, drip, drip* of a leak.

ぼたもち ぼた餅 ***botamochi***
日本紹介 ✉ **ぼた餅は, 餅米とうるち米を混ぜて炊いて作った餅を丸めて, あん, きな粉などをまぶしたものです. おはぎとも呼びます. お彼岸に食べます** *Botamochi* are round rice cakes made from glutinous rice mixed with non-glutinous rice that is boiled, rounded into cakes and covered with *an* (sweet azuki bean paste) or soybean flour. They are also called *'ohagi.'* People eat them during *ohigan* (a seven-day period with the spring or autumnal equinox falling on the middle day).
▶《慣用表現》1位と2位の選手が失格になったので3位の選手が棚からぼた餅で金メダルを手にした Because the first- and second-prize winners were disqualified, the person who came in third got the gold medal as *a windfall*. (➤ windfall は「風で落ちた木の実」. 転じて,「意外な授かり物」; →たなぼた).

ほたる 蛍 a **firefly,** a **lightning bug**(➤ イギリスにはいない) ‖**蛍狩り** firefly catching.

ホタルイカ《動物》a **firefly squid.**

ぼたん 牡丹《植物》a **(tree) peony** /píːəni/.

ボタン 1【洋服の】 a **button** /bʌ́tn/ ▶ボタンを掛ける[外す] do [undo] *buttons* ‖このボタンは取れそうだ This *button* is loose. ／This button *is coming* [*falling*] *off*.
▶(ワイシャツの)ボタンが1つ取れた *A button* has come off (my shirt). ‖いちばん上のボタンが外れてますよ Your top *button* is undone. ‖コートのボタンを掛けなさい *Button* (*up*) your coat.
2【押しボタン】 a **button** ▶エレベーターのボタンを押す push [press] an elevator *button* ‖ご用の方はボタンを押してください Please press [push] this *button* if you need us. (➤ ファミレスなどの場合, if 以下を for service に言い換えて使うことができる).

ぼたんゆき 牡丹雪 **large flakes of snow** ▶ぼたん雪が降っている *Snow is falling in large flakes*.

ぼち 墓地 a **cemetery**(共同墓地); a **churchyard**(教会付属の); a **graveyard** (➤ cemetery と同義に用いるが, 今は婉曲(えんきょく)的に memorial park で代用することが多い).

ホチキス a **stapler** ▶レポートはホチキスで留めること Be sure to *staple* your report.
《参考》(1)「ホチキス」はこれを売り出したアメリカの会社 Hotchkiss and Company の社名から. (2)ホチキスの針1本は a staple, つながったものは a strip of staples という.

ぼちぼち ▶ぼちぼち仕事に取りかかろうか Well, let's get down to work *now*.
▶ 対話「調子はどうだい?」「まあ, ぼちぼちだねえ」"How's everything?" "Not bad. ／We're *getting there*."

ぽちゃぽちゃ ▶ぽちゃぽちゃっとした顔の女の子 a *plump*-faced girl ‖赤ん坊の手足はぽちゃぽちゃしている Babies have *chubby* arms and legs.

ぽちゃん ▶ゴルフボールがポチャンと池に落ちた A golf ball fell into the pond *with a splash*.

ほちゅう 補注 a **supplementary note.**

ほちゅうあみ 捕虫網 an **insect net.**

ほちょう 歩調 a **step**; a **pace** (歩く速さ) ▶彼は突然歩調を速めた[緩めた] He suddenly quickened [slowed down] his *pace*.
▶兵士たちは歩調をそろえて行進した The soldiers marched *in step*. ‖ほかの人と歩調を合わせなさい *Keep step* [*pace*] with others. ‖歩調を乱すな! Don't *break step*!
▶《比喩的》彼はその企画では同僚たちと歩調を合わせることができなかった He could not (*bring himself to*) *fall in line with* his co-workers on that plan.

ほちょうき 補聴器 a **hearing aid.**

ぼつ 没 ▶1995年没 *Died* in 1995. (➤ 事典などでは d.1995 と略す) ‖彼の原稿は没になった His manuscript *was rejected*.

ほっかい 北海 **the North Sea.**

ぼっかてき 牧歌的な **pastoral** ▶突然目の前に牧歌的な風景が開けた All of a sudden, a *pastoral* panorama unfolded before me.

ぽっかり ⚠「ぽっかり」に相当する英語はないので, 強いて訳す必要はない.
▶大地震で道路にぽっかり大穴があいた The big earthquake opened a huge hole in the street.
▶山の上にぽっかり満月が出た A full moon emerged [came out] above the mountain.

ぼっき 勃起 an **erection,**《インフォーマル》a **hard-on** ▶勃起する get *an erection* ‖勃起したペニス an *erect* penis.
‖勃起不全 erectile dysfunction (➤ ED と略す).

ほっきにん 発起人 an **initiator**(組織・企画などの首唱者); a **promoter** (会社設立などの推進役); a **proposer** (計画などの提案者); an **organizer** (会などの世話役)
▶私は学校創立100周年記念募金の発起人になった I became one of *those who took the initiative* to raise [in raising] funds for the 100th anniversary of our school. (➤ take the initiative は「率先して…する」).

ほっきょく 北極 **the North Pole**(極点); **the Arctic** (北極地方) 一形 **北極の arctic**
‖**北極海** the Arctic Ocean ‖**北極グマ** a polar bear ‖**北極圏** the Arctic Circle ‖**北極星** the polestar, the North Star ‖**北極探検** an Arctic [a polar] expedition.

ぽっきり ▶あんな大木があの強風でぽっきり2つに折れてしまうとは It's amazing that such a huge tree *snapped in half* in the strong wind.
▶よし, まけてやろう. 1000円ぽっきりでどうだ OK. This is a big bargain. *Just* [*Only*] 1,000 yen.

ホック a **snap fastener,**《英》a **press stud**; a **hook** /hʊk/ (かぎホック) (➤ 留めるところと一体のものは hook and eye という) ▶フロントホックのブラジャー a *front-closing* [*-fastening*] bra ‖このホックを留めて[外して]くれない? Will you *hook* [*unhook*] this for me?

ボックス ‖**キャッチャーボックス** the catcher's box ‖**検索ボックス** a search box ‖**電話ボックス** a telephone booth ‖**バッターボックス** the batter's box ‖**ペナルティーボックス** the penalty box ‖**ロイヤルボックス** the royal box.

ぽっくり ▶山田君のところのおじいさん, きのうの晩, ぽっくりいったんだってね Did you hear that Yamada's grandfather *dropped dead* [*popped off* / *kicked the bucket*] last night? (➤ pop off は主に《英》で「あっけなく死ぬ」の意; kick the bucket は「死ぬ」の意のおどけた言い方).

‖**ぽっくり病** (a) sudden death.

ほっけ 鯱 《魚》an **Arabesque greenling.**

ホッケー **hockey** ▶ホッケーをする play *hockey* 《参考》アメリカでは単に hockey といえばアイスホッケー(ice hockey)を指し, 陸上ホッケーは field hockey という.

ぼつご 没後 ▶作家の没後50年を記念して全集が刊行された The complete works of the author were published to commemorate the fiftieth anniversary of his [her] *death*. ‖その小説は彼女の没後出版された The novel was published *after her death* [*posthumously*].

ぼっこう 勃興 (a) **rise** ▶明(みん)王朝の勃興 the *rise* (*to power*) of the Ming dynasty ‖新勢力が勃興した A new power *has risen*.

ぼっこうしょう 没交渉 ▶私は同窓生とは没交渉だ I *have no contact* [do *not socialize*] *with* my former classmates. ‖彼は職場で同僚と没交渉だ(=孤立している) He *is isolated* in his workplace.

ほっさ 発作 a **fit**, an **attack** (➤ 後者は主に重大な病気について用いる) ▶せきの発作に襲われた I had *a fit* of coughing. ‖彼は(心臓)発作を起こした He had *a heart attack*. ‖少女は発作的に橋から身を投げた The girl jumped off the bridge into the river *on a sudden impulse*.

ぼっしゅう 没収 **confiscation** 一動 **没収する** **confiscate** /kɑ́ːnfɪskeɪt/ +⊞ ▶新政府は前大統領の財産を没収した The new government *confiscated* the former president's property. ‖カンニングペーパーを学校に持って来た場合は没収するぞ If you bring cheat sheets to school, they will *be confiscated*.

ほっしん 発疹 a **rash** →はっしん.

ほっする 欲する **desire** +⊞ (強く望む); **long for** (手に入りにくいもの, 実現しそうもないことを) ▶人は皆平和を欲する All people *desire* peace. ‖彼女は富と名誉を欲していた She *longed for* fame and fortune. ‖己の欲するところを人になせ Do unto others as you *would have* them *do* unto you. / Always treat others as you *would like* them to treat you. (➤ ともに聖書のことばで「黄金律」(the Golden Rule)と呼ばれている. 前者は広く知られている言い方, 後者は現代語訳聖書から).

ぼっする 没する **sink**, **set**(日が); **die**, **pass away**(人が; 後者は「亡くなる」に相当) ▶やがて日は西の空に没した Soon the sun *set* [*sank*] in the west.

ほっそく 発足する **be established**(設立される); **be organized**(組織される) ▶宇宙開発委員会を発足させる *launch* a space exploration committee ‖わが社でもようやく労働組合が発足した A labor union *was* finally *organized* in our company.

ほっそり ▶ほっそりした女の子 a *slender* [*slim*] girl ‖彼女はウエストがほっそりしている She is *slim*-waisted. / She has a *slim* [*slender*] waist.

ぼったくり a **rip-off.**

ほったてごや 掘っ立て小屋 a **hut**, a **shanty**; a **shack**(あばら家).

ほったらかす **leave ... undone**; **neglect** +⊞ (なおざりにする) ▶宿題をほったらかしてテレビを見てしまった I watched television *leaving* my homework *undone* [*unfinished*]. ‖彼女はよく子供をほったらかしにする She often *neglects* her children. / She often *leaves* her children *to themselves*. ‖私が留守している間, 主人は庭を1か月もほったらかしていたので, ジャングルみたいになってしまった While I was gone, my husband *neglected* the garden [*let* the garden *go untended*] for a month, and it turned into a jungle.

ほったん 発端 **the beginning** ▶彼女の失踪が事件の発端だった Her disappearance marked *the beginning* of the case. / The case began [started] with her disappearance.

ぼっち →ひとりぼっち ▶彼は昼によく学食でぼっち飯している He often *eats* lunch (*all*) *alone* at the school cafeteria. (➤ alone だけでは単に客観表現で「ひとりで」だが, all alone は「(付き合う人もなく)寂しく」のニュアンスがある).

ホッチキス a **stapler.** →ホチキス.

ぽっちゃり ▶彼女は小柄でぽっちゃりしている She is small and *plump* [*chubby* / *well-rounded*].

ぼっちゃん 坊ちゃん one's **son** (息子); a **boy** (男の子) ▶ 対話「坊ちゃんは(小学校の)何年生ですか?」「2年生です」"What grade is *your son* in?" "He is in the second grade."

☛ **お坊ちゃん** (→見出語)

ほっつきあるく ほっつき歩く ▶彼は当てもなく町をほっつき歩いた He *walked about* the town aimlessly.

▶こんな遅くまでどこをほっつき歩いてたんだ? Where have you been *wandering* [*gallivanting*] *about* until this late? (➤ gallivant about は「(仕事をしないで)遊び歩く」).

ぼってり ▶彼女のぼってりした唇 her *plump* [*full*] lips.

ほっと 一動 **ほっとする** **be** [**feel**] **relieved**

> 【文型】
> **…してほっとする**
> **be relieved to** do
> **It is a relief to** do.

▶彼のけがが大したことがなくてほっとしたよ I *was relieved* [*It was a great relief*] *to* hear that his injury wasn't so serious.

▶ああ, ほっとした *What a relief!* ‖彼女はほっとため息をついた She *breathed* [*gave*] *a sigh of relief*.

ホット **hot** ▶《喫茶店で》ホットを1つください I'd like *a* (*hot*) *coffee*. (➤ hot は略せるが coffee は略せない) ‖このDJはいつもホットな話題を取り上げる This deejay always brings up *hot* [*trendy*] topics.

‖**ホットカーペット** an electric carpet ‖**ホットスポット** a hot spot ‖**ホットニュース** hot news ‖**ホットプレート** a hotplate ‖**ホットライン** a hotline.

ぽっと ▶彼女はぽっと頬を赤らめた Her cheeks blushed *bright red*.

ポット a **thermos** /θɔ́ːʳməs/ (**bottle**)(魔法瓶); a **teapot**(紅茶用の); a **coffee pot**(コーヒー用の) ▶お湯はポットに入っています There is hot water in the *thermos*.

危ないカタカナ語✷ ポット
1「コーヒーポット」「ティーポット」という場合の「ポット」は pot でよい. pot は「つぼ」「かめ」「深鍋」など丸くて深い容器を指すことば. →**鍋**.
2 日本語では魔法瓶のことを「ポット」というが, これは日本だけの用法. 英語では thermos (bottle) という. Thermos という商標名からきている.

ぼっとう 没頭する **be absorbed** 《in》(夢中になる) ; **be immersed** 《in》(ふける) ; **be devoted** 《to》(献身する) ▶彼は日夜小説を書くことに没頭している He *is absorbed* [*is immersed*] *in* writing a novel day and night. ‖ 彼女は今子育てに没頭している She *is devoting herself* [*is devoted*] *to* raising her children now. ‖ 何か没頭できるものがあればなあ I wish I had something to *throw myself into* [to *get into*]. ‖ 彼は死んだ妻と子供のことを忘れようと仕事に没頭した He *buried himself in* his work so that he could forget about his deceased wife and children.

ほっとく **leave ... alone** ▶ほっといてよ! *Leave me alone!* / *Don't bother* [*bug*] *me*. ‖ ほっとけよ! *Leave* her [him / them] *alone*. / *Leave* it *as it is*. (➤ 前者は人, 後者は物の場合) ‖ きみには関係ないんだからほっときなよ Just *lay off* [*back off*]. It's none of your business. (➤ lay off は「…をそっとしておく」). →**放っておく**.

ホットケーキ a **pancake** 《参考》griddle cake, flapjack など多くの異称がある. hot cake という語はあまり用いられない.

ぽっとで ぽっと出 ▶ (田舎から)ぽっと出の少女 a girl *fresh from the country*.

ホットドッグ a **hot dog** ▶ホットドッグを2本ください. マスタードをたっぷりつけて Two *hot dogs*, please. With extra mustard. 《参考》ホットドッグを売る屋台を hot dog stand という.

ぽつねん ▶待合室でおばあちゃんはぽつねんと座っていた Grandma was sitting *all alone* in the waiting room.

ぼっぱつ 勃発 an **outbreak** 一動 **勃発する** **break out** ▶暴動勃発のニュースは市民を不安に陥れた The news of *an outbreak* of riots made the citizens nervous.

ホップ 《植物》a **hop** ▶ホップの心地よい苦味のあるビール beer with a pleasing bitterness from *hops*.

ポップ **pop**
‖**ポップアート** pop art ‖ **ポップコンサート** a pop(s) concert ‖ **ポップシンガー** a pop singer ‖ 《野球》**ポップフライ** a pop fly.

ポップコーン **popcorn**.

ポップス **pop (music)** (音楽) ; a **pop song** (歌).

ほっぺた a **cheek** ▶この桃はみずみずしくてほっぺたが落ちそうだ(=とてもおいしい) This peach is juicy and so *delicious* (that *it melts in your mouth*).

ほっぽう 北方 **the north** ▶北海道は本州の北方にある Hokkaido lies (*to the*) *north of* Honshu.
‖**北方領土** the Northern Territories.

ぼつぼつ ▶ぼつぼつ始めましょうか Shall we get started? / Let's get started, shall we? →**そろそろ**.
✉ **こちらでは桜の花がぼつぼつ咲き始めました** The cherry trees are beginning to blossom *little by little* here.

ぽつぽつ ▶そのボール紙にはぽつぽつ小さな穴があいていた There were *tiny* holes punched in the cardboard. ‖ 妹の顔にはにきびがぽつぽつある My sister has *a few* pimples on her face.
▶雨がぽつぽつと降ってきた It has begun to rain *slightly* [*in small drops*].

ほっぽる ▶帽子をほっぽる *toss* one's hat [cap] ‖ 部長は仕事をほっぽってテレビでサッカー観戦している The department head *is ignoring* his work and watching a soccer game on TV.

ぼつらく 没落 (a) **fall**, (a) **downfall** (落ちぶれること) ; **ruin** (破滅) ▶彼女の家は父親の死後すっかり没落した Her family *suffered a* great *fall* [*downfall*] after her father's death. ‖ 明治維新で武士階級は没落した The Meiji Restoration caused [brought about] the *ruin* [*downfall*] of the samurai class.

ぽつり ▶雨がぽつりと落ちてきた *A drop* of rain [A raindrop] fell.
▶「だめだった」と彼はぽつりと言った "I failed," he said *in a low whispering voice*. (●「思いがけなく」の意なら,「ぽつりと」に unexpectedly を当てることもできる).

ほつれる **become frayed** (衣服が) ; **come loose** /luːs/ (髪などが) ▶彼女のスカートは裾がほつれていた Her skirt *was frayed* at the hem. ‖ 母はほつれた髪をかき上げた My mother combed up her *loose* [*stray*] hairs.

ぽつん ▶広々とした荒野に家が一軒ぽつんと立っている In the vast wilderness stands a *lone* house.

ボディーガード a **bodyguard**
▶大統領はいかついボディーガードに守られて出てきた The President came out guarded by sturdy *bodyguards*.

ボディーチェック a **body search**, 《インフォーマル》a **frisk** ; a **pat-down** (身体に触れて調べる) ▶乗客は搭乗口で再びボディーチェックされた The passengers *were frisked* again at the boarding gate. / The passengers had to *go through security* [*a body search*] again at the boarding gate.

危ないカタカナ語✷ ボディーチェック
1 空港などで行う「ボディーチェック」は security check というが, この語は単に身体検査だけでなく荷物などを調べることも含む.「身体検査」の意味では body search, frisk, pat-down などという.
2 body check はアイスホッケーの用語で, 相手の動きを体当たりで阻止することをいう.

ボディービル **body building**.

ボディーランゲージ **body language**.

ボディコン ▶ボディコンのドレス a *figure-fitting* dress.

ポテトチップ(ス) 《米》**potato chips**, 《英》**(potato) crisps** 《参考》イギリスで potato chips といえば「(拍子木に切った細長い)フライドポテト」(French fries)を指す.

(米) **potato chips**
(英) **(potato) crisps**

(米) **French fries**
(英) **potato chips**

ポテトフライ **French fries** (➤ 単に fries ともいう).

ぼてぼて ▶彼はぼてぼてのゴロをショートに打った He hit *a slow grounder* to shortstop.

ほてり 火照り a **blush**, a **flush**.

ほてる 火照る **feel hot**, **burn** ; **flush** (紅潮する) ▶たき

火に当たっていたら顔がほてってきた My face *felt hot* in front of the fire. ‖ 熱があるのか, 体がほてる I *feel hot*. Maybe I have a fever. ‖ 彼女の顔は恥ずかしさでほてった Her face *burned* with embarrassment. ／ She *flushed* in embarrassment. ‖ 彼はグラス1杯のビールで顔をほてらせた After one glass of beer, his face *became flushed*. ／One glass of beer made his face *flushed*.

ホテル a **hotel** /houtél/ ; an **inn** (古風な) ▶三つ星ホテル a three-star *hotel* ‖ ホテルにチェックインする check in at [check into] *a hotel* (➤「チェックアウトする」は check out of a hotel) ‖ ホテルに部屋を予約する reserve a room at *a hotel* ／make a *hotel* reservation (●ホテル全体を借り切るのでない限り, reserve a hotel とはしない) ‖ 我々は明治時代からの格式あるホテルに泊まった We stayed at a prestigious *hotel* dating from the Meiji era.

‖ホテル客 a guest ‖ ホテル代 hotel charges [rates].

ほてん 補塡をする **compensate for** ; **offset** ＋⊞ (埋め合わせる) ▶損失を補塡する *compensate for* the loss (es) ‖ 多くの会社が住宅費を一部補塡するために手当を支給している Many companies provide benefits to employees to partly *offset* housing costs.

ポテンシャル **potential** ▶中国の経済成長のポテンシャルは高い *The potential* for China's economic growth is high. (➤「低い」なら low).

ぽてんヒット 《野球》a **Texas leaguer**, a **blooper** (➤後者のほうが多用される).

ほど 程 **1【およそ】about**, **around** (➤後者はややインフォーマル) ; **or so** (…かそこら) ; **approximately** /əprɑ́:ksɪmətli/ (およそ) ; **some** (約, およそ… ; 切りのよい数字があとにくる) →約

▶新入社員を500名ほど採用します We are going to hire *about* 500 new employees. ‖ 父は1週間ほどで戻ります My father will be back in *about* a week. ／My father will be back in a week *or so*. ‖ この車は500万円ほどします This car costs *around* five million yen. ‖ 日本の人口はイギリスの2倍ほどだ The population of Japan is *approximately* double that of the UK. ‖ 400人ほどの人がパレードを行った *Some* 400 people marched in the parade.

2【程度】▶きのうは声がかれるほど千葉ロッテの応援をした I cheered for the Marines *so* hard yesterday *that* my voice became hoarse. (➤「懸命に応援したので声がかれてきた」の意) ‖ その暴動は機動隊が出動するほどのものではなかった The riot wasn't *so* violent *that* riot police needed to be mobilized. ‖ 父は早朝の散歩に出かけられるほど体力を回復した My father has recovered *enough* of his strength *to* take his early morning walks. ‖ 写真を撮れるほどの明るさがない There isn't *enough* light *to* take a picture.

▶彼はそんな手に乗るほどの愚か者ではない He is not *such* a fool *as to* be taken in by such a trick. ‖ 彼は私がショックを受けるほどに変わっていた He had changed *to a shocking extent*. ／ He had changed *so much* it shocked me. (➤後者はややインフォーマルな言い方).

▶死ぬほど怖かった I was scared [frightened] *to death*. ‖ 冗談だよ. 腹を立てるほどのことじゃないじゃないか It's only a joke. *It isn't worth* getting angry about it, is it ?

3【比較】▶日本ほど良い水に恵まれた国はない *No other* country is more blessed with good water *than* Japan. ‖ 真夏には冷えたスイカほどおいしいものはない *There is nothing like* (a) cold watermelon in midsummer. ／*Nothing can beat* (a) cold watermelon in midsummer. ‖ イチローほどのプレーヤーはもう出ないだろう A baseball player *like* Ichiro will probably never appear again.

> **【文型】**
> A ほど〜ではない
> **not as [so] 〜 as** A
> ➤〜は形容詞・副詞
> **《解説》** not のないときと同様, as 〜 as がふつうの言い方で, **not so 〜 as** は少し改まっていて, 《米》ではあまり使わない.

▶ことしの冬は去年ほどは雪が降らなかった We did*n't* have *as much* snow this winter *as* we did last winter. ‖ 東京はボストンほど寒くはない Tokyo is *not as* [*so*] cold *as* Boston. ‖ 彼の病気はきみが思っているほど深刻なものではない His sickness is *not as* serious *as* you think. ‖ **対話**「あなたの料理はどれも本当においしいわね」「ありがとう. でも, あなたほど上手じゃないわ」 "Everything you cook is really delicious." "Thanks, but I don't think I'm *as* good a cook *as* you."

▶この本はその本ほど高価ではない This book is *less* expensive *than* that one. ‖ 以前ほど疲れなくなった I feel *less* tired *than* before.

> **【文型】**
> A であればあるほど B だ
> **The more** A, **the more** B.
> **The ＋比較級** A, **the ＋比較級** B.

▶パンダって見れば見るほどかわいいわね *The more* you look at pandas, *the cuter* they look.

✉ **パーティーにはなるべく多くのお友だちをお連れください. 多ければ多いほど楽しいですから** Bring as many of your friends as possible to the party. *The more, the merrier*.

4【限度】a **limit** ▶何事にも程がある There is *a limit* to everything. ‖ 冗談にも程があるぞ You're carrying the joke too far. ‖ ずうずうしいにも程がある You have no shame ! ／You should be ashamed of yourself.

5【様子】▶その情報については真偽の程を確かめる必要がある We need to make sure *whether* the information is true *or not*.

¹ほどう 歩道 《米》a **sidewalk**, 《英》a **pavement** ▶動く歩道 a moving *walkway*.

‖歩道橋 a pedestrian bridge [overpass], a (public) footbridge.

²ほどう 補導 ▶彼はシンナー遊びをして警察に補導された He *was put under police guidance* for sniffing paint thinner.

ほどく 解く **undo** ＋⊞ ; **untie** ＋⊞ (結び目を) ▶ひもの結び目をほどく *undo* [*untie*] a knot in a cord ‖ スニーカーのひもをほどく *unlace* one's sneakers (➤ unlace は「靴ひもをほどく」の意) ‖ この包みをほどいてください Can you *undo* [*unwrap* ／ *unpack*] this package ?

ほとけ 仏 **the Buddha** /bú:də/ (お釈迦(しゃか)さま) ; a **Buddha** (悟りを得た人) ▶仏の道に従って悟りを得る follow *the Buddha's Noble Path* to enlightenment ‖ 毎朝仏さまを拝む worship (Amida) *Buddha* eve-

ry morning (➤「仏陀(ぶっだ)を拝む」の意) ／offer prayers to (and for) *one's departed ancestors* every morning (➤「亡き先祖を供養する」の意. for は「先祖の冥福を祈って」) ‖ おじは仏さまのような人だ My uncle is a *saint* of a man. (➤「聖人のような人だ」の意) ／My uncle is a *merciful* person. (➤「慈悲深い人だ」の意) ‖ **仏の道に入る**(＝僧侶になる) become a Buddhist priest ‖ **仏の顔も三度** Even (the) Buddha gets angry the third time you misbehave. ／There's a limit to anyone's patience. (➤ 後者は「忍耐には限度がある」) ‖ **仏作って魂入れず** You can make a Buddhist image but fail to put a soul into it. ／You neglect to put the finishing touches to your work. (➤ 後者は「最後の仕上げを怠る, 画竜点睛(がりょうてんせい)を欠く」).
▶**ホトケ**(＝遺体)の身元は割れたかい？ Did you identify the *body* (of the deceased person)？ ‖ きのうの夜, また川から**ホトケさん**を引き上げた They pulled another *stiff* out of the river last night. (➤ stiff は死体をおどけていうくだけた語).
▶ 対話「どうしてなのか教えてよ」「気にしないほうがいいよ. 知らぬが仏って言うから」"Tell me why？" "Never mind. *What you don't know won't hurt you.*" (➤「知らなければ傷つくことはない」の意；「知らぬが仏」に相当する英語のことわざは Ignorance is bliss. だが, 日本語のことわざと異なり「気づいていないのは当人だけだ」というあざ笑う気持ちは含まれない).

ほどける 解ける get untied ; come loose /luːs/ (緩む) ▶靴のひもがほどけていますよ Your shoelace has *got untied*. ‖ すぐにほどけないようにロープをしっかり結わえなさい Tie the rope tightly so it won't *come loose* easily.

ほどこしもの 施し物 charity, alms /ɑːmz/ (➤ 後者は古風な語) ▶人からの施し物は受けない I don't beg for [seek] *alms*. ／I don't accept charity from others.

ほどこす 施す ▶古い壁画に**修理を施す** *carry out repairs* to the old mural painting ‖ その土器には**装飾が施されていた** Ornamental designs had been *applied to* the earthenware. ‖ その患者は**手の施しようがなかった** *There was no cure* for that patient's disease. ／*Nothing could be done to cure* the patient.

ほどとおい 程遠い

> 【文型】
> A **は** B **には** [**…するには**] **程遠い**(＝先のことだ)
> A **has a long way to go before** S ＋ V [**to** do].
> A **は** B **とは程遠い**(＝全く違う)
> A **is far from** B.
> A **is a far cry from** B.
>
> 《解説》**be far from** は「かけ離れている」の意で, あとには名詞・動名詞・形容詞がくる. **a far cry** は「かけ離れたもの, 遠く及ばないもの」の意で, B は名詞・動名詞. ほかに fall well short of (…にまるで及ばない)も使える.

▶この研究は完成にはまだ**程遠い** I still *have a long way to go before* I finish [complete] this research (project). ‖ その地域は原発事故からの完全復興には**程遠い** That district *has a long way to go to* completely recover from the nuclear disaster. ‖ デートの相手は夢に描いていた人とは**程遠かった** My date *was far* [*a far cry*] *from* what I had been dreaming of.

ほととぎす 《鳥》a **lesser cuckoo** (➤ アジアにしかいない)；《植物》a **toad lily.**

ほどなく 程なく shortly(じきに)；soon, before long (まもなく) ▶社長は程なく参ります Our president will come *shortly* [*soon* ／*before long*].

ほとばしる 迸る ▶レスラーの顔から鮮血がほとばしった Blood *gushed* from the wrestler's face.

ほとほと ▶勉強嫌いの息子にほとほと手を焼いています I am *quite* [*totally*] at a loss (as to) how to deal with my son who doesn't like to study. ‖ 派閥争いがほとほと嫌になった I'*m completely* [*really*] *fed up with* factional strife.

ほどほど 程々 ▶悪ふざけするのもほどほどにしなさい *Don't carry* your practical jokes *too far*. (➤ carry … too far は「…をやり過ぎる」) ‖ 私は酒はほどほどに飲みます I'm a *moderate* drinker. ‖ ほどほどの酒は体にいい *Moderate* drinking is good for your health.

ぽとぽと ▶洗濯物から水がぽとぽと落ちている The laundry is *dripping*.

ほとぼり 熱 ▶事件のほとぼりが冷めた頃, 彼は町にふらっと戻って来た He slipped back into town after people's *interest* in the incident had died down.

ボトムアップ ▶日本の経営はボトムアップで, アメリカはトップダウンと言われる It is said that Japanese management is *bottom-up* while American management is top-down.

ほどよい 程好い moderate /mɑ́ːdərət/ (適度の)；proper (適切な) ▶程よい湯加減です The bath (temperature) is *just right*. ‖ このチーズケーキは程よい酸味があっておいしい This cheesecake has *a moderate amount of* tartness and tastes good. ／This cheesecake is *pleasantly* tart and tastes good.

ほとり 辺 ▶ロンドンはテムズ川のほとりにある London is (situated) *on* the Thames. ‖ 湖のほとりに教会がある There is a church *on* [*by* ／*near*] the lake. (➤ 接触を表す on が最も湖に近い).

ぽとり ▶柿の実がぽとりと池に落ちた A persimmon fell *plop* into the pond. (➤ plop は「ポチャン」と水に落ちた様子を表す).

ボトル a **bottle**
‖ステンレスボトル a stainless thermos bottle.

ほとんど

1【大部分, 大体】**almost, nearly**
━形 **ほとんどの most, almost all**

> 語法 (1)almost, nearly は時間・空間など計測可能なものについていう場合はほぼ同義だが, 前者が接近の度合いが強く, 意味も強い.
> (2)計測不可能なものについては nearly は使えない.
> (3)形容詞の most は全体の50〜70％程度, almost all は全体の90％程度の事柄に言及する場合に用いる.

▶世界のほとんどの国は国連に加盟している *Almost all* countries in the world are members of the United Nations. (➤ (×)almost countries としないこと) ‖ その模試にはうちの学生のほとんどが参加した *Most* of the students [*Almost all* the students] in our school took the trial exam. ‖ 病気はもうほとんど(完全に)治りました I'm *almost completely* well. ‖ ほとんど毎日どこかで交通事故が起きる *Almost* every day there is a traffic accident somewhere. ‖ 父はほとんどいつも車で出勤する My father *nearly always* drives to work. ‖ 彼らのスーツは色を別にすればデザインはほとんど同じだ Their suits are *almost the same* in design though the colors are different. ‖ 仕事はほとんど終わった I've *just about* [*almost*] finished my work. (➤ just about はくだけた言い方).

2【「ほとんど…ない」の形で】hardly（ほとんど…ない）; **seldom**（めったに…ない）; **only a few** [**little**]（少ししかない）▶その英国人学者の講演は私にはほとんど聞き取れなかった I could *hardly* understand the lecture by the English scholar. ／I understood *little* of the lecture by the English scholar. ‖ 私はテレビはほとんど見ない I *hardly ever* [*almost never*] watch TV. ／I watch (*very*) *little* TV. ‖ 彼女は学校に遅れたことはほとんどない She is *rarely* [*seldom*] late for school. ‖ スミスさんは刺身はほとんど食べない Mr. Smith *seldom* [*rarely*] eats sashimi. ‖ 彼には友だちがほとんどいない He has *few* [*only a few*] friends. ‖ ボトルにはウイスキーはほとんど残っていない *Little* [*Only a little*] whisky is left in the bottle. ／There is *hardly any* whisky left in the bottle. ‖ 私の友だちの多くは相撲にほとんど何の興味も示さない Many of my friends show *almost no* interest in sumo. ‖ 私は朝食を抜くことはほとんどない I *almost never* skip breakfast.

▶両国の停戦の可能性はほとんどない There is *virtually no* possibility of a cease-fire between the two nations. (➤ virtually は「事実上」) ‖ 1か月でこの問題集を終えるなんてほとんど不可能だ It is *almost* [*nearly*] impossible to finish this workbook in a month. ／I can *hardly* finish this workbook in a month. (➤ 後者のほうがややインフォーマル).

3【もう少しで】almost ▶きのうの集中豪雨で川の水がほとんどあふれそうになっている The river is *almost* overflowing from yesterday's heavy rain. ‖ 女の子はほとんど泣き出しそうだった The girl came *near to tears*. ／The girl was *close to* [*on the verge of*] *tears*.

ポニーテール a **ponytail** ▶彼女は髪をポニーテールにしている She wears her hair in *a ponytail*.

ほにゅう 哺乳 ‖**哺乳動物** a mammal /mǽməl/ ‖ **哺乳瓶** a (baby's) bottle, a (formula) bottle ‖ **哺乳類** the mammals.

ぼにゅう 母乳 **mother's milk** ▶母乳による育児 breast-feeding (➤「粉ミルクによる育児」は bottle-feeding) ‖ 母は私を母乳で育てた My mother fed me *on her milk*.

ほね 骨

訳語メニュー
人・動物の骨 →bone **1**
障子の骨 →frame **2**
傘の骨 →rib **2**
気骨 →fortitude, backbone **4**

1【人・動物の】 a **bone** ▶年配の女性の骨はもろい The *bones* of elderly women break easily [are fragile]. ‖ 魚の骨が喉に引っかかった A fish *bone* got stuck in my throat. ‖ この魚は骨が多い This fish is *full of bones*. (➤ This fish is bony. とすると「身がほとんどなく骨ばかり」のニュアンス) ‖ こちらの魚は骨ごと食べられます You can eat these fish, *bones and all*. ‖ サッカーをして足の骨を折った I *broke my leg* while playing soccer. (●「足の骨」は the bone of my leg であるが, この場合は my leg でよい) ‖ 彼女, 女性にしては骨太だね She has *large bones* for a woman.

▶《慣用表現》彼女はダイエットのし過ぎで骨と皮ばかりだ Her extreme dieting has made her (all) *skin and bones*. ‖ あいつは骨の髄まで腐っている He's rotten *to the core*. ‖ 彼らはカナダに骨をうずめる覚悟で移住を決意した They decided to move to Canada to *live for the rest of their lives*. (➤「一生暮らす決心をした」の意).

‖**骨接ぎ** a bonesetter（人；通例無資格；→接骨（医））.

2【器物の】 a **frame**（骨組み）; a **rib**（骨の1本）▶この障子の骨(＝桟)は木でできている The *frames* in this shoji (screen) are made of wood. ‖ 傘の骨が折れちゃったんですけど直りますか *A rib* of this umbrella is broken. Can you repair it?

3【困難, 面倒】 →骨折り, 骨折る ▶骨の折れる仕事 *hard* work ‖ 今夜中にこれだけの書類を読み終えるのはかなり骨だ(＝大変だ) It will *be* rather *hard* to read all these papers before the night is out. ‖ きみのご両親を説得するのは骨が折れそうだ It looks like it will *be difficult* to persuade your parents. ‖ 指導教授が勤め口を見つけるのに大いに骨を折ってくれた My advisor *took* great *pains* to find a job for me.

4【気骨】 **fortitude**（耐える力）; **backbone**（精神的強さ）▶彼は絶対に泣き言を言わない. なかなか骨のあるやつだ He never complains. He's *a man with* real *fortitude*.

逆引き熟語 ○○骨
肩甲骨 a shoulder blade, a scapula ／**鎖骨** a collarbone, a clavicle ／**座骨** a hipbone ／**頭蓋骨** a skull, a cranium ／**背骨** the backbone ／**大腿**(だいたい)**骨** a thighbone ／**軟骨** cartilage ／**鼻骨** a nasal bone ／**頬骨** a cheekbone ／**肋**(ろっ)**骨** a rib

ほねおしみ 骨惜しみ ▶あの旅館のおかみさんは少しも骨惜しみせずに働く The Okami-san of that inn works hard *without sparing herself* in the least.

ほねおり 骨折り **pains**; **trouble**（苦労）; **effort(s)**（努力）▶骨折りがいがあった My *pains* [*efforts*] have been amply rewarded. (➤「苦労は十分に報われた」の意).

✉ **いろいろお骨折りいただきありがとうございます** I sincerely thank you for all the *trouble* you have taken for me. ／Thank you very much for all [everything] you have done for me.

[ことわざ] **骨折り損のくたびれもうけ** I went to a lot of trouble, but it was all for nothing. ／Great pains but all in vain. (➤ 後者は英語のことわざ).

ほねおる 骨折る **take pains, go to great pains** ▶池沢さんは娘の就職のためにいろいろ骨折ってくれた Mr. Ikezawa *took great pains* [*put a lot of effort*] to help find a job for my daughter. ／Mr. Ikezawa *went to a lot of trouble* to help my daughter find employment.

ほねぐみ 骨組み **1【構造】** a **framework**（基本的な仕組み）; a **skeleton**（あらましの枠組み）▶この家の骨組みは地震に耐えるように丈夫に作られている The *frame* [*shell*] of this house is built strongly so as to withstand earthquakes.

2【骨格】 a **frame**, a **build** ▶あのフットボール選手はがっしりした骨組みをしている The football player has a strong *build* [*physique*]. ／The football player is well built. (➤ well built は「体格のよい」).

▶その計画の骨組み(＝概要)を述べる give *an outline* [*a general idea*] of the plan.

ほねっぽい 骨っぽい ▶骨っぽい魚はどうも苦手です I

ほ

just don't like fish *with a lot of small bones.* ▶あの娘はスティーブ・ジョブズのような骨っぽい(＝気骨のある)男に憧れている She admires men *with backbone* like Steve Jobs.

ほねぬき 骨抜きの **boned**(骨を取った)；**watered-down**(➤比喩的に「弱められた」) ▶骨抜きの法律 a *toothless* law(➤toothless は「効力のない」).

ほねばった 骨張った **angular, bony** ▶骨張った手 *bony* hands ‖ 兄は骨張った顔をしている My brother has an *angular* [*bony*] face.

ほねぶと 骨太の **thick boned**；**sturdily built**(骨格ががっしりした) ▶骨太の足 *thick-boned* legs ‖ 骨太の男 a *sturdily-built* man.
▶骨太の改革案 a *muscular* [*basic*] reform proposal ‖ 骨太のドラマ a *dynamic* [*muscular*] drama.

ほねみ 骨身 ▶母は骨身を惜しまず働いた My mother worked *without sparing herself.* ‖ おじは骨身を惜しまず助力してくれる My uncle *bends over backward* to help me. (➤bend over backward は「(人のために)一生懸命努力する」の意のインフォーマルな言い方) ‖ 太田先生のお説教は骨身にこたえた Mr. Ota's admonition (really) *hit* [*struck*] *home.* (➤home は「深く, ぐさりと」の意の副詞).

ほねやすめ 骨休め **rest** ▶きみは働き過ぎだ. 温泉にでも行って骨休めして来いよ You're working too hard. Go to a hot spring to *get some rest.* (●「でも」は訳出不要).

ほのお 炎 a **flame**；a **blaze**(勢いよく燃え上がる大きな炎) ▶ろうそくの炎 a candle *flame* ‖ 瞬く間に炎は家をなめ尽くした The *flames* swallowed up the house in no time. ‖ その建物は炎に包まれた The building went up *in flames.* ／The building was *ablaze.* ‖ その家は真っ赤な炎を上げて燃えていた The house was burning in *a blazing fire.*
▶《比喩的》彼はその事件に対して怒りの炎に燃えていた He *was burning with anger* about the incident. ‖ 彼女に対する恋の炎は燃え上がるばかりだった *The flame of my passionate love* toward her burned ever brighter.

ほのか 仄かな **slight**(僅かな)；**faint**(かすかな)；**dim**(明かりが) ▶遠くにほのかな明かりが見えた I saw a *dim* light in the distance. ‖ そよ風に若葉がほのかに香った The breeze wafted *a hint of* fresh greenery to me. (➤hint は「気配」).

ほのぐらい 仄暗い **dim** ▶ほの暗いバーで愛のことばを交わす exchange words of love in a *dim* [*dimly lit*] bar (➤lit は light の過去分詞で「電灯に照らされた」の意) ‖ 成田空港をたったときはまだほの暗かった It was still *a little dark* when I left (from) Narita Airport.

ほのじ ほの字 ▶兄はあの娘にほの字だ My brother *is attracted to* [*is in love with*] that young woman.

ほのぼの ▶その画家のほのぼのしたイラスト the artist's *heartwarming* illustrations.
▶やっと仕事が終わったときにはほのぼのと夜が明け始めていた Day [Morning] was beginning to break when I finally finished the work. (➤「ほのぼの」は訳文に現れない).

ほのめかす 仄めかす **hint** 《that》(それとなく言う)；**suggest** 《that》(連想・暗示によってわからせる) ▶吉田君は退学の決意を私にほのめかした Yoshida *hinted* to me that he intended to quit school. ‖ 新しい研究員は処遇に対しての不満をほのめかした The new researcher *suggested* that he was dissatisfied with the way he was treated.

ホノルル **Honolulu** /hɑ̀ːnəlúːluː/ (アメリカ, ハワイ州の州都).

ホバークラフト a **Hovercraft**, a **hovercraft** (➤もと商標名).

ほばしら 帆柱 a **mast.**

ほはば 歩幅 a **step**；a **stride** (大股の1歩) ▶あいつは足が長い分歩幅が広い Because he's got long legs, he walks with long *steps* [*strides*].

ぼひ 墓碑 a **gravestone**, a **tombstone** (→墓石)；a **grave marker**, a **headstone.**

ぼひめい 墓碑銘 an **epitaph**；an **inscription on a gravestone** [**tombstone** ／**grave marker**].

ポピー 《植物》a **poppy.**

ポピュラー **popular**(人気がある, 多くの人に評判がよい)；**common** (ありふれた) ▶『坊ちゃん』は漱石の最もポピュラーな作品だ "Botchan" is one of the most *popular* works by Soseki. ‖ 日本では鈴木はポピュラーな名字です In Japan, Suzuki is a *common* family name.
‖ポピュラー音楽 popular [pop] music(➤歌なら popular song) ‖ ポピュラー歌手 a popular [pop] singer.

ぼひょう 墓標 a **grave marker** ▶墓標のない墓 an *unmarked* grave.

ほふ 保父 →保育(士).

ボブスレー a **bobsled**, 《英》a **bobsleigh** /bɑ́ːbsleɪ/ (そり)；**bobsledding**(競技).

ポプラ 《植物》a **poplar** ▶ポプラ並木の道 a road lined with *poplars.*

ポプリ a **potpourri** /pòʊpʊríː ‖ -póri/.

ほへい 歩兵 a **foot soldier**；an **infantryman** (➤集合的には infantry という).

[1]**ほぼ 保母** →保育(士).

[2]**ほぼ** **almost, nearly**(ほとんど)；**about**(およそ) ▶トンネル工事はほぼ完成した Work on the tunnel is *nearly* [*almost*] completed. ／The tunnel is *near* completion.
▶彼の身長はほぼ2メートルある He is *about* two meters tall. ‖ 大雪山は北海道のほぼ中央にある Mt. Daisetsu is located in the *approximate* center of Hokkaido. (➤approximate は「極めて近い」の意) ‖ その城はほぼ元どおりに復元された The castle was restored to *practically* its original state. (➤practically は「事実上」).

ほほえましい 微笑ましい **heartwarming**(心温まる)；**amusing** (人を楽しくさせる)；**pleasant** (心地よい) ▶小さな少年が弟の面倒を見ている姿はほほえましかった *It was heartwarming* to see the little boy looking after his little brother. ‖ その幼児が歩こうとして突然転んだのがほほえましかった *It was amusing* to see the toddler tumble (about) as he tried to walk. ‖ それはほほえましい光景だった It was a *pleasant* sight.

ほほえみ 微笑み a **smile** ▶常にほほえみを忘れないように Never forget to have *a smile* on your face at all times. ‖ タイはほほえみの国と呼ばれている Thailand is called '*the Land of Smiles.*'

ほほえむ 微笑む **smile** 《at》 ▶ついに勝利の女神が我々にほほえんだ Finally Victory *smiled upon* us. ‖ 多くのアメリカ人は知らない人にもほほえみかける Many Americans *smile* even *at* strangers. ‖ 彼女はほほえみながら「ありがとう」と言った She said "thank you" *with a smile.*

ポマード **pomade.**

ほまれ 誉れ (an) **honor** /ɑ́:nəʳ/ (名誉) ; a **credit**(名誉になるもの) ▶松坂君, きみはわが校の誉れだ Matsuzaka, you are *an honor* [*a credit*] to our school. ‖ ヤッシャ・ハイフェッツは名手の誉れ高いバイオリニストだった Jascha Heifetz was a violinist of *acclaimed* virtuosity.

ほめごろし 褒め殺し a **backhanded compliment** 一動 褒め殺しにする **give** someone **a backhanded compliment.**

ほめそやす 褒めそやす acclaim +目 ▶批評家たちは彼の新しい芝居を褒めそやした Critics *acclaimed* his new play.

ほめたたえる 褒め称える praise +目 ; **acclaim** +目 (褒めそやす) ▶彼の勇気を褒めたたえる *praise* him for his courage.

ほめちぎる 褒めちぎる praise ... to the skies ; **rave about**(絶賛する).

ポメラニアン《犬》a **Pomeranian.**

ほめる 褒める praise +目 (公に賞賛する), **compliment** +目 (褒めことばを言う) ; **admire** +目 (感心する) ; **speak well** [**highly**] **of** (よく言う) ▶誰もがさゆりを褒める Everybody *praises* [*speaks well of*] Sayuri. ‖ 先生は私の作文を褒めてくれた The teacher said my composition was very good. / The teacher *praised* my composition.

> 【文型】
> 人(A)の物(B)を褒める
> **praise** A **for** B
> **compliment** A **on** B

▶皆が彼の勇気を褒めた Everybody *praised* [*admired*] his courage. / Everybody *praised* [*admired*] him *for* his courage. ‖ 彼は妻の新しいスカーフを褒めた He *complimented* his wife *on* her new scarf.

▶子供が満点を取ったので褒めてやった I *gave* my son *credit* [*a pat on the back*] because he got a perfect score. (➤ give ... credit で「…を評価する」の意 ; a pat on the back は「褒めことば」の意でインフォーマル).

▶それは褒め過ぎだ That is *undue* [*excessive*] *praise*. ‖ お褒めにあずかって恐縮です Thank you for the *compliment*. ‖ 喫煙を先生に見つかって停学になるなんて決して褒められたことじゃないぞ Being suspended from school for smoking is *nothing to be proud of*. (➤「自慢することではない」の意).

ホモセクシュアル a **homosexual**, a **gay (man)** ▶彼はホモセクシュアルだ He's (*a*) *homosexual* [*gay*]. (➤ 当事者が自身を肯定的にとらえる語として queer を使うこともあるが, fag, faggot, homo と同様, 差別的・軽蔑的なニュアンスがあるので普通は使用しない).

ほや 海鞘《動物》a **sea squirt.**

ぼや 小火 a **small fire** ▶ゆうべこの近くでぼやがあったそうだ I hear that *a small fire* broke out near here last night.

ぼやく complain《about, of, that》(不平を言う) ; **grumble**《about, that》(ぶつぶつ言う) ▶彼女は口うるさい上司のことをいつもぼやいている She always *complains about* [*of*] her nagging boss. / She always *complains* that her boss nags (at) her. ‖ まあ, そうぼやくなよ Don't *grumble* [Stop *grumbling*] all the time!

ぼやける get blurred, become fuzzy (➤ 後者はややインフォーマル) ▶昔の記憶は時がたつにつれてぼやけてきた My memories of the old days have *blurred* [*have become fuzzy*] with (the passing of) time. ‖ この頃小さな字がぼやけて見えます These days when I read fine print it looks *blurred*. ‖ この写真はちょっとぼやけている This photograph is a bit *blurry* [*out of focus*]. (➤ out of focus は「焦点が合っていない」).

ほやほや ▶このサツマイモは焼きたてのほやほやだよ This sweet potato is *hot from the oven*. ‖ こちら志村君, まだ新婚ほやほやだ This is Mr. Shimura, who *has just got married*.

ぼやぼや ▶ぼやぼやしてちゃだめよ! 車が多いんだから *Watch out* [*Pay attention*]! There are a lot of cars on the street. ‖ ぼやぼやしてるから電車に乗り遅れるんだよ The reason you missed the train is that *you're so absent-minded*.

ほゆう 保有 possession /pəzéʃən/ 一動 **保有する possess** +目, **hold** +目 ▶日本は現在核兵器を保有していないし, これからも保有しないことを祈る Japan doesn't *possess* nuclear weapons at present and I hope it never will (*possess* them).
‖ **核保有国** a nuclear power [state].

ほよう 保養 relaxation(骨休め) ; (a) **rest** (休息) ; **recuperation**(病後の) 一動 **保養する relax, recuperate, rest** ▶温泉へ保養に行く go to a hot spring to *relax* [*recuperate* / *rest*] ‖ おばは箱根で病後の保養をしている My aunt *is recuperating* in Hakone after her illness.
▶《慣用表現》水着姿の美女を見て目の保養をした We *feasted our eyes* on the beauties in bathing suits [on the bathing beauties].
‖ **保養所** a resort house ‖ **保養地** a health resort.

[1]**ほら 法螺 big talk, boasting, bragging** ▶ほら吹くなよ Don't *talk big*! (➤「偉そうな口を利く」の意にもなる) ‖ 彼は自分のうちのことでほらばかり吹いている He is always *bragging* [*boasting*] about his family.
‖ **ほら吹き** a big talker, a blowhard (➤ 後者は《米・インフォーマル》).

[2]**ほら** ▶ほら(=見てごらん)! チョウチョが飛んでるよ *Look!* A butterfly is flying. ‖ ほら(=聞いてごらん)! この辺でコオロギが鳴いている *Listen!* A cricket is chirping somewhere around here. ‖ ほらね, 私の言ったとおりでしょう *See*, I told you so. ‖ ほら, ほら, もう泣かないで *There, there*, don't cry.
▶ほら, バスが来たよ *Here* comes the bus. ‖ ほら, 湯川先生よ *There* goes Mr. Yukawa. / *Here* comes Mr. Yukawa. (➤ 前者は「あそこに…が行く」, 後者は「こちらに…が来る」の意) ‖ (小言や自慢話などが)ほら, また始まった *There* he [she] goes again. (➤ 動作主によって人称を変える).

ぼら 鯔・鰡《魚》a **mullet** /mʌ́lɪt/.

ホラー horror ‖ **ホラー映画** a horror movie [film].

ほらあな 洞穴 a **cave** ; a **cavern** /kǽvəʳn/ (大きな).

ほらがい 法螺貝 a **Triton's trumpet**(貝) ; a **horagai**, a **conch** [**trumpet**] **shell**(楽器).

ぼられる →ぼる.

ポラロイド a **Polaroid** /póʊlərɔɪd/ (カメラ, およびそれで撮った写真).

ボランティア a **volunteer** /vɑ̀:ləntíəʳ/ (人) ▶将来ボランティア活動をして困っている人を助けたい I'd like to *work as a volunteer* and help needy people someday. ‖ 母はボランティアで外国の人に日本語を教えている My mother teaches foreigners Japanese *as a volunteer*. ‖ 彼女は病院でボランティアの仕事をしている She does *volunteer* [*voluntary*] *work* at the hospital.

✉ **あなたは何かボランティア活動をしていますか** Are you doing any *volunteer work*?

[1]**ほり 堀** a **moat**(城の); a **canal** /kənǽl/ (水路) ▶その城の周りには**堀**が巡らしてある There is *a moat* around the castle. / The castle is surrounded by *a moat*.

[2]**ほり 彫り** ▶彼女は日本人にしては**彫りの深い顔をしている** She has *sharp* [*finely-chiseled*] features for a Japanese person.

ほりあてる 掘り当てる ▶石油を**掘り当てる** *strike* [*hit*] oil.

ポリープ 《医学》 a **polyp** /pá:lɪp/ (➤ 専門用語), a **small tumor** ▶良性[悪性]の**ポリープ** a benign [malignant] *polyp* ‖ 胃に**ポリープ**ができているらしい It seems I have *a small tumor* in my stomach.

ポリウレタン 《化学》 **polyurethane** /pà:lijóərəθeɪn/.

ポリエステル 《化学》 **polyester** ▶**ポリエステル**100%のシャツ a 100% *polyester* shirt.

ポリエチレン 《化学》 **polythene** /pá:lɪθi:n/, 《米また》 **polyethylene** /pɑ:liéθəli:n/.

ポリオ 《医学》 **polio** (➤ poliomyelitis の略) ▶**ポリオ**にかかる contract [develop] *polio* (➤ develop は「発症する」に相当).

‖**ポリオワクチン** polio vaccine.

ほりおこす 掘り起こす **dig up** ▶道路を**掘り起こす** *dig up* a road ‖ 事件の真相を**掘り起こす** *dig up* [*out*] the truth of the case ‖ 埋もれた人材を**掘り起こす**(＝発見する) *discover* [*find*] people with hidden talent.

ほりかえす 掘り返す **dig up** ▶発掘調査のため畑を**掘り返している** They *are digging up* the field for an excavation. ‖ この道は年中**掘り返されている** This road is *being dug up* all year round.

ポリグラフ a **polygraph**; a **lie detector**(うそ発見器).

ほりごたつ 掘り炬燵 a ***horigotatsu***; a *kotatsu* placed over a recessed floor (➤ 説明的な訳).

ほりさげる 掘り下げる **delve into** ▶この問題をもっと**掘り下げて**(＝探究して)いくべきだ We should *delve* further *into* this issue. / We should *explore* this matter *further*.

ポリシー a **policy**; a **principle**(信念・主義) ▶**ポリシー**を持つ have one's *principle* (➤ have a policy だと「保険に入っている」) ‖ 人の陰口を言わないのが私の**ポリシー**だ It is my *policy* not to talk behind people's backs.

ほりだしもの 掘り出し物 a **find**(めっけ物); a **buy**, a **bargain**(格安品) ▶その骨とう屋ですばらしい**掘り出し物**を見つけた I *made a* great *find* in the antique shop. ‖ 奥さん, これは**掘り出し物**だよ Ma'am, this is *an excellent buy*.

ほりだす 掘り出す **dig out** [**up**] ▶ポチが裏庭からつぼを**掘り出してきた** Pochi *dug up* a vase from the backyard. (➤ dug は dig の過去形).

ポリタンク a **plastic canteen**.

ポリネシア **Polynesia** /pà:ləní:ʒə, -ʃə/ (太平洋の東部, ハワイ諸島・ニュージーランドを含む地域)

‖**ポリネシア人** a Polynesian.

ポリバケツ a **plastic bucket**.

ボリビア **Bolivia**(南米中西部の国).

ポリぶくろ ポリ袋 a **plastic bag**.

ぼりぼり ▶人前で頭を**ぼりぼり**かくのはやめたほうがいい You should stop [refrain from] *scratching* your head in public.

ポリマー 《化学》 a **polymer**.

ほりもの 彫り物 (a piece of) **carving**; a **tattoo**(入れ墨).

ほりゅう 保留する **suspend** +目 (決定・承諾などを); **reserve** +目 (判断を); **defer** +目 (延期する) ▶彼は判断を**保留した** He *suspended* judgment. ‖ その提案については最終判断を**保留します** I *reserve* final judgment on the proposal. ‖ 支店への転勤を打診されたが, まだ返答を**保留している** Although I was asked if I would be interested in a transfer to a branch office, I *haven't decided* how I will answer [I *have deferred* my reply]. ‖ その計画はしばらく**保留**しよう Let's *put* the project *on hold* [*on ice*] for a while. (➤ 後者は「凍結する」の意).

ボリューム **1【音量】** **volume** ▶**ボリュームのある**声 a voice *of great volume* ‖ テレビの**ボリューム**を下げ[上げ]ましょう I'll turn down [up] (the *volume* on) the TV.

2【分量】 ▶**ボリュームのある**食事 a *big* [*hearty* / *substantial*] meal ‖ あの店のカレーライスは**ボリュームがある** The curry and rice at that restaurant *is very filling*. (➤ filling は「(腹を)満たす」) ‖ (美容師が客に) パーマをかけると**ボリューム**が出ますよ A perm would give your hair *volume*.

ほりょ 捕虜 a **prisoner**; a **prisoner of war**(戦争の; POW と略す) ▶**捕虜になる** *be taken prisoner* ‖ 祖父は2年間**捕虜**としてその**捕虜収容所**に入れられていた My grandfather was held in the *prison camp* for two years as *a prisoner of war* [*a POW*].

ほりわり 掘り割り a **canal** /kənǽl/ (船舶用・かんがい用の運河); a **ditch**(細長い水路・溝).

[1]**ほる 掘る** **dig** +目; **mine** +目 (採掘する) ▶土を**掘る** *dig* dirt ‖ トンネルを**掘る** *dig* [*bore*] a tunnel (➤ bore は「ドリルで穴をあける」) ‖ 石炭を**掘る** *dig* [*mine*] coal ‖ 温泉を**掘る** *dig* a hot spring.

▶彼らは地面に深さ2メートルの穴を**掘った** They *dug* a hole [the ground] two meters deep. (「地面に穴を掘る」は dig a hole でも dig (in) the ground でもよい) ‖ 子供たちは皆畑へ出てジャガイモを**掘っていた** All the children were out in the field *digging* potatoes.

[2]**ほる 彫る** **carve** +目 (彫刻する); **engrave** +目 (文字などを) ▶上野の西郷隆盛の像は高村光雲が**彫った** Takamura Koun *carved* [*sculpted*] the statue of Saigo Takamori at Ueno Park. ‖ 私は指輪に自分の名前を**彫ってもらった** I had my name *engraved* on the ring.

ぼる **rip ... off** ▶あのバーは**ぼる** They really *rip* you *off* at that bar. ‖ タクシーの運転手に**ぼられた** The taxi driver *ripped* me *off* [*overcharged* me].

ポルカ 《音楽》 a **polka**.

ホルスタイン a **Holstein**.

ポルターガイスト a **poltergeist** ‖**ポルターガイスト現象** a poltergeist phenomenon.

ボルダリング **bouldering**.

[1]**ボルト** 《ねじ》 a **bolt** ▶**ボルト**を締める tighten *a bolt* ‖ **ボルト**で本棚を壁に固定した I *bolted* the bookcase to the wall.

[2]**ボルト** 《電圧》 a **volt** 《略 V, v》 ▶その電線には3000**ボルト**の電流が流れている The wire is charged with a 3,000-*volt* current.

ボルドー **Bordeaux** /bɔ:ʳdóʊ/ (フランス南西部の河港; ワインの名産地).

ポルトガル **Portugal** /pɔ́:ʳtʃəgəl/ 一形 **ポルトガルの** **Portuguese** /pɔ̀:ʳtʃəgí:z/

‖**ポルトガル語** Portuguese ‖ **ポルトガル人** a Portuguese person.

ボルネオとう ボルネオ島 Borneo（東南アジアの大きな島；マレーシア領・ブルネイ・インドネシア領に分かれる）.

ポルノ pornography /pɔːˈnáːɡrəfi/,《インフォーマル》porn(o) **一形 ポルノの** pornographic,《インフォーマル》porn(o)（➤ porn がふつう）

‖**ポルノ映画** a porn(o)［pornographic］film（➤ 俗語で skin flick ともいう）‖**ポルノ作家** a pornographer ‖**ポルノショップ** a porn(o)［sex］shop ‖**ポルノ女優** a porn(o) queen［star］‖**ポルノビデオ** a porn(o) video ‖**児童ポルノ** child pornography.

ホルマリン《化学》formalin /fɔ́ːˈməlɪn/.

ホルモン (a) hormone /hɔ́ːˈmoʊn/ **一形 ホルモンの** hormonal ▶ヒト成長**ホルモン** (a) human growth *hormone* ‖ひげが生えるのは**男性ホルモン**の働きによる The growth of facial hair on men is caused by *male sex hormones*.（➤「女性ホルモン」は female sex hormones）. ‖**ホルモン焼き** *horumon-yaki*; grilled beef or pork offal（➤ offal /ɔːfəl/ は「(食用の)臓物，もつ」）.

ホルン a French horn ▶**ホルン**を吹く play the French *horn* ‖**ホルン奏者** a French horn player, a hornist ‖**イングリッシュ・ホルン** an English horn, a cor anglais.

ボレー a volley.

ほれこむ 惚れ込む ▶彼女に**ほれ込んだ**いきさつを話してくれよ Could you tell me what has made you *fall for* her? ‖あいつはあの女優にぞっこん**ほれ込んでいる** He *is crazy*［*head over heels*］*about* the actress. ‖ぼくはこの写真集に**ほれ込んでいる**んだ I'*m in love with* this photograph collection.

ほれっぽい 惚れっぽい ▶あいつは**ほれっぽい**男だ He'*s always falling in love*.

ほれぼれ 惚れ惚れ ▶レオタード姿のパメラには**ほれぼれ**してしまった I *was charmed*［*was attracted*］by the sight of Pamela in a leotard. ‖スカーレット・ヨハンソンは**ほれぼれ**するようないい女だ Scarlett Johansson is *really a charming*［*fascinating*］*woman*.

ほれる 惚れる 1【好きになる】 fall in love《with》; love ＋目（ほれている）▶おまえに**ほれてる**んだよ I *love* you. ／I'*m in love with* you. ‖二人は**ほれ合った**仲だ They *love each other*.

2【引かれる】 be impressed（感心する），be attracted（心を引かれる）▶私は彼の心意気に**ほれた** I *was impressed*［*was attracted*］*by* his spirit.

ボレロ《音楽》a bolero /bəléəroʊ/.

ほろ 幌 a hood, a top ▶ベビーカーの**幌** the *hood* of a baby stroller.

ぼろ 1【布】 a rag, old cloth（ぼろ切れ）▶**ぼろ**を着たこじき a beggar *in rags*［*tatters*］‖**ぼろ切れ**で機械の汚れを取る clean a machine with *a rag*.

‖**ぼろ靴** worn-out shoes ‖**ぼろ家** a shack.

2【欠点】 ▶**ぼろ**を出し（＝無知をさらし）たくなかったので難しい話は避けた I avoided difficult topics because I didn't want to *expose my ignorance*. ‖彼女はいつも**ぼろ**を出さないようにしている She always tries to *keep up appearances*.（➤ keep up appearances は「体面を維持する」）.

ぼろい 1【古い】 worn-out（使い古した）; poor, bad（粗悪な）▶**ぼろい**靴 *worn-out* shoes ‖何だ，おまえの車ずいぶん**ぼろい**な Your car is *a real clunker*, isn't it?（➤ clunker は「おんぼろ車」の意のインフォーマルな語）.

2【もうけが大きい】 ▶**ぼろい**仕事 a *soft* job（➤「楽でもうかる仕事」の意）‖あいつ近頃**ぼろい**商売をやってるらしい I hear he *is making easy money*［*is on the gravy train*］these days.

ぼろがちする ぼろ勝ちする《米・インフォーマル》cream ＋目; defeat overwhelmingly.

ぼろくそ ▶上司に**ぼろくそ**に言われてしまった My boss sure said *nasty things* to me. ‖その評論家は彼女の新作を**ぼろくそ**にけなした The critic *picked* her new work *to pieces*.

ホログラフィー holography.

ホログラム a hologram.

ポロシャツ a polo shirt.

ぽろっと ▶彼女はその劇のオーディションを受けていたことを**ぽろっと**漏らしてしまった She *let* it *slip out* that she had had an audition for the play.

ほろにがい ほろ苦い slightly bitter（少し苦い）; bittersweet（甘いような苦いような）▶フキノトウは**ほろ苦い**味がする A butterbur sprout tastes *slightly bitter*. ‖初恋(の思い出)は誰にとっても**ほろ苦い** First love is a *bittersweet* experience for everyone.

ポロネーズ《音楽》a polonaise.

ほろばしゃ 幌馬車 a covered wagon; a prairie schooner /skúːnəˈ/（アメリカ西部開拓時代に使われた大型の馬車）.

ほろびる 滅びる die out, perish（➤ 後者は文語）; become extinct（絶滅する）; be destroyed（攻撃に跡形もなく）; be wiped out（全滅させられる）▶将来の戦争で核兵器が使われるようなことにでもなれば人類は結局は**滅びて**しまうかもしれない If nuclear weapons are ever used in future wars, the human race could end up *perishing*［*being wiped out*］. ‖マンモスは先史時代に**滅びた** Mammoths *died out*［*became extinct*／*were wiped out*］in prehistoric times. ‖アステカ文明はスペイン人の侵入によって**滅びた** The Aztec civilization *was destroyed* by the invasion of the Spaniards. ‖古い習慣はなかなか**滅びない** Old customs *die hard*.

ほろぼす 滅ぼす destroy ＋目（死滅させる）; ruin ＋目（破滅させる）▶徳川は豊臣を**滅ぼした** The Tokugawas *destroyed* the Toyotomis. ‖彼は酒で**身を滅ぼした** He *ruined himself* by drinking too much. ／Too much drinking was his ruin.（➤ 後者の ruin は「身を滅ぼす原因」の意）.

ぼろぼろ 一形 ぼろぼろの worn-out（擦り切れた）; ragged, tattered（ぼろ切れのようになった）▶この**ぼろぼろ**になった辞書が私の宝だ This *worn-out* dictionary is my treasure. ‖男は**ぼろぼろ**のコートを着ていた The man was wearing a *ragged*［*tattered*］coat. ‖この壁は手を触れると**ぼろぼろ崩れる** This wall *crumbles easily* when you touch it.

ぽろぽろ ▶男の人が話しかけると迷子の少年は涙を**ぽろぽろ**流した When a man spoke to the lost boy, tears ran down his cheeks (*in large drops*). ‖食事のときご飯を**ぽろぽろ**こぼさないようにしなさい Please don't *scatter*［*spill*］(grains of) rice *all over* when you eat.

ほろほろちょう ほろほろ鳥《鳥》a guinea /gíni/ fowl［hen］（➤ 後者は雌）.

ぼろまけする ぼろ負けする《米・インフォーマル》be creamed; be defeated overwhelmingly.

ぼろもうけ ぼろ儲け ▶あの人は株で**ぼろもうけ**をしたらしい I've heard he *hit it big*［*made a killing*］in the stock market.

ほろよい ほろ酔い ▶**ほろ酔い**のおじいさん a *tipsy* old man ‖お父さんが**ほろ酔い**機嫌で帰って来た Dad came home *in a happy mood after a few drinks*.

ほろり ▶彼の目から涙がひと滴**ほろり**とこぼれた A teardrop fell from his eye(s). ‖ 少年の苦労話に私はほろりとさせられた I *was moved to tears* by the boy's hard-luck story. (➤「ほろりとさせる話」は touching [moving] story).

ぽろり ▶その役者がおじぎをしたとたん, かつらがぽろりと落ちた The moment the actor bowed, his wig *fell off*.

ホワイトカラー a **white-collar worker**.

ホワイトデー "**White Day**" ▶ホワイトデーは和製語で, 男性が女性にバレンタインデーのお返しのプレゼントをする日です "*White Day*" is a Japanese coinage that refers to the day when men give gifts to women in return for the women's Valentine gifts.

ホワイトニング **whitening** ▶歯のホワイトニングをする *do* a teeth *whitening* / *whiten* one's teeth.

ホワイトハウス **the White House** /*h*wáɪt hàʊs/.

ホワイトボード a **whiteboard**.

ほん 本 a **book**(単行本); a **magazine** (雑誌) ▶漫画の本 a comic *book* ‖ 私の趣味は歴史の本を読むことです I'm interested in reading *history books*. ‖ インドの踊りについて書いた本はありませんか Do you have *books* about Indian dances? ‖ 彼は長い間に書きためた論文をまとめて一冊の本として出版した He collected all the papers he had written over the years and had them published *in a single volume* [*in book form*]. ‖ 1枚の古い写真が父の本の間に(=ページの間に)挟んであった I found an old picture *between the leaves of* my father's *book*. ‖ 彼女は本の虫だ She is *a bookworm*. ‖ この本は40冊まとめて出版社に注文しておきました I ordered *forty copies of this book* from the publisher. (⚠ (×)forty books としないこと. これでは別々の40種類の本という意味になる →-冊).

ほん- 本- **1【真の】** **real** (本当の); **genuine** (本物の) ▶本名 one's *real* name ‖ 本真珠 a *genuine* pearl ‖ きのうから(舞台の)本稽古に入った Since yesterday we've been having *full-dress rehearsals*.

2【主な】 **main** ▶本館 the *main* building ‖ 本通り the *main* street ‖ 本会議 a plenary [full] session.

3【この】 **this** ▶本年 *this* year / the *current* year ‖ 本件は継続審議とします We will take up *this* subject [issue] in the next session.

-ほん -本 【解説】日本語では物によって「…本」「…冊」のように使い分けるが, 英語では数えられる名詞の場合は複数形の前に数詞をつけるだけでよい.
▶5本の鉛筆 *five* pencils ‖ たばこ1本 *a* cigarette ‖ チョーク3本 three *pieces* of chalk ‖ ビール2本 two *bottles* of beer.

1ぼん 盆 《器》a **tray** /treɪ/ ▶お茶をお盆に載せて運ぶ take a cup of tea on *a tray*.
ことわざ 覆水盆に返らず (→覆水).

2ぼん 盆 《行事》***Bon*, the *Bon* festival**
日本紹介 ✉ **盆またはお盆は先祖の霊を供養する仏教徒の行事で, 多くの地方では8月13日から15日に行います. この期間だけ先祖の霊がこの世に戻って来ると考えられています. 盆踊りも全国各地で行われます** *Bon*, or *obon*, is the Buddhist festival for paying respect to the spirits of ancestors. In most districts, it is held from August 13 through 15. It is believed that the spirits of the ancestors return to this world only during this period. *Bon* dances are also held in many places throughout Japan.
▶盆と正月が一緒に来たようだ I'm as happy as can be. It's like *the Bon festival and New Year's have come all at once*. (➤ 後半は直訳. 英米人はうれしいことが重なったときに I feel so happy. It's like Christmas and my birthday all at once. と表現することはある).
‖ **盆踊り** the *Bon* (festival) dance.

ボン **Bonn**(旧西ドイツの首都).

ぽん ▶誰かがポンと背中をたたいた Someone *gave* me *a pat* [*tapped* me] on the back. ‖ ワインの栓を引っ張るとポンと抜けた The cork of the wine bottle *popped* when I pulled on it. ‖ 弟は辞書をぽんと投げてよこした My brother *tossed* me the dictionary. ‖ おじさんは海外旅行の費用をぽんと50万円出してくれた My uncle *willingly plunked down* a half million yen to pay for my overseas trip. (➤ plunk down は「ドスンと置く」の意).

ほんあん 翻案 an **adaptation** ▶黒澤明の『乱』はシェークスピアの『マクベス』の翻案だ Kurosawa Akira's "Ran" is *an adaptation* of Shakespeare's "Macbeth."

1ほんい 本意 one's (**true** / **real**) **intention** ▶それが彼の本意だったとは思えない I don't think that was his (*true* / *real*) *intention*.

2ほんい 本位 ▶学習者本位の教育 *learner-centered* education ‖ 彼は自分本位の人間だ He is a *self-centered* person. ‖ 当店ではサービス本位です We *give service top priority* at this store. (➤「サービスを最優先にしている」の意) ‖ 彼女は品質本位で物を買う She buys things *for their quality*.

ほんかい 本懐 ▶本懐を遂げる *achieve* [*fulfill*] one's *long-cherished ambition*.

ほんかくてき 本格的な **real**(本物の); **full-scale** (全面的な); **authentic**(真正の); **serious**(真剣な); **full-fledged** (一人前の); 《インフォーマル》 **honest-to-goodness**(正真正銘の) ▶本格的な調査 a *full-scale* investigation ‖ 本格的な中国料理 *authentic* Chinese cuisine ‖ 本格的な海浜リゾート an *honest-to-goodness* beach resort ‖ 本格的な発掘調査が始まった *Full(-scale)* excavation has begun. ‖ あと2週間もすれば本格的な夏が来る Summer will be *in full swing* in two weeks. (➤ in full swing は「真っ盛りで」の意) ‖ 雨が本格的に降ってきた It's *really* pouring [coming down]. / It's raining *in earnest*. ‖ あなたのフランス料理は本格的(=プロ並み)ね You cook French food *as well as a professional* [*like a pro*].

ポンがし ポン菓子 **puffed rice**.

ほんかん 本管 a **main**
‖ **ガス本管** a gas main ‖ **水道本管** a water main.

ほんがん 本願 **the original vow of Amida Buddha**(阿弥陀の); a **long-cherished wish**(比喩的に)
‖ **自力本願** salvation by one's own efforts; self-reliance (比喩的に) ‖ **他力本願** salvation through the benevolence of Amida Buddha; reliance on other people (for help) (比喩的に).

ほんき 本気の **serious**(真剣な); **earnest** (ひたむきな)
一副 **本気で** **seriously, in earnest** ▶私, 本気であなたが好きよ I'm *serious* about you. ‖ ちょっとからかったら弟は本気で怒った I played a practical joke on my (younger) brother and he got mad *for real*. (➤ for real はインフォーマル) ‖ あいつの言うことなど本気にするな Don't *take* him *seriously*. ‖ きみの話を誰が本気にするだろうか Who would *believe* your story? ‖ 彼は本気になって勉強し始めた He began to study *in earnest* [*seriously*]. ‖ 対話「きみは本気でそう言う

のか」「本気だとも」"Are you *serious*?" "Sure (I am)." ／"Do you (*really*) *mean it*?" "Sure (I do)." ‖きみが本気になればできるさ You can accomplish it if you *put your mind to it* [if you *put your heart into it*]. ‖刃向かうな. やつは本気だ Don't go against him—he *means business*. (➤ mean business は「(遊びでなく)真剣だ」の意).

ほんぎ 本義 the original meaning(元の意味); the true meaning(本当の意味).

ほんぎまり 本決まり ▶本決まりになるまではこのことは伏せておいてください Please keep this secret until *the final decision is made* [*it is decided formally*].

ほんきょ 本拠 a base; headquarters(本部) ▶名古屋に本拠を置く予備校グループ a Nagoya-*based* chain of (college entrance exam) prep schools ‖我々はその村に演劇活動の本拠を置いた We set up the *base* [*headquarters*] for our theatrical activities in the village.

ほんぎょう 本業 one's main occupation, 《インフォーマル》one's day job; core business(企業の中核業務) ▶この辺りではもはや農業を本業にする人はいない There are no longer any people around here who *make their living* (*chiefly*) *by* farming.

ほんぐもり 本曇り ▶午前中は雲が少し出ている程度だったが, 午後から本曇りになった It was partly cloudy in the morning, but *became completely overcast* in the afternoon.

ぼんくら a blockhead.

ぼんくれ 盆暮れ ▶指導教授には盆暮れの付け届けをしている I never fail to send my academic adviser *midyear* [*Bon*] *and year-end gifts*. 《参考》英米にはこの習慣がないので, 賄賂を贈っていると受け取られるおそれがある.

ほんけ 本家 the head [main] family (分家に対して); the originator (創始者) ▶野球はアメリカが本家(＝元祖)だ The U.S. is *the birthplace* of baseball. ／Baseball originated in the U.S.

ぼんご 梵語 Sanskrit.

ほんこう 本校 **1**【当校】this school, our school ▶本校は来年で創立100年です *This school* will celebrate the 100th anniversary of its founding next year.
2【分校に対して】the main campus, the main [head] school.

ほんごく 本国 one's (own) country, one's home [native] country ▶その外交官は本国に強制送還された The diplomat was forcibly repatriated to *his own country* [*his home country*].

ほんごし 本腰 ▶あいつもようやく本腰を入れる気になったな It looks like he finally decided to *be serious* about it, doesn't it? ‖年が明けたら卒論に本腰を入れるつもりだ I am going to *get* [*settle*] *down to* working (*in earnest*) on my graduation thesis once we get into the new year.

ぽんこつ junk(廃品, くず)
‖ぽんこつ車 a junk car.

ホンコン 香港 Hong Kong /hɑ̀ːŋ kɑ́ːŋ/ (中国南東部の都市; 元イギリス植民地).

[1]**ぼんさい 盆栽** (a) bonsai(➤ 英語化している)
日本紹介 ✉ **盆栽は小さな植木鉢にごく小型の木, 石, コケなどを配して自然の美を表現したものです** A bonsai is a dwarf tree with stones (or pebbles) and /or moss in a small earthen pot. Bonsai are arranged in such a way as to express the beauty of nature.

[2]**ぼんさい 凡才** a person with average ability, a mediocre person.

ほんしき 本式の formal (正式の); regular (正規の) ▶本式に英会話を習う take *formal* [*regular*] lessons in conversational English ／learn conversational English *formally* ‖お茶を入れるときは, 急須を温め, 1人につき茶さじ1杯の茶葉を入れるのが本式だ *The proper way of* brewing green tea is to heat the teapot (*kyusu*) and put in one scoop of tea leaves per person.

ほんしつ 本質 essential [true] nature; essence (問題の根本要素, 核心); substance(実体, 実質) ▶彼には問題の本質がわかっていないようだ Apparently, he fails to grasp the *true nature* of the problem. ‖自由の本質は責任だ The *essence* of freedom is responsibility. ‖水と氷は状態は異なっているが本質は同じだ Though they are in different states, water and ice are the same *substance*. ‖その両者には本質的な(＝根本的な)差がある The two are *fundamentally* different. ‖彼女は本質的に(＝本来)自分勝手な人だ She is *essentially* a selfish person.

ほんじつ 本日 today; this day(➤ 正式のスピーチなどで用いる) ▶《掲示》本日休業 Closed Today ‖本日はお忙しい中をお集まりいただきましてありがとうございます We thank (all of) you very much for taking time off to attend the party *today*. (● 英語では「本日はこのパーティーに出席するための時間を取ってくださり感謝します」と発想する) ‖本日は当校の創立25周年でございます *This day* marks the 25th anniversary of our school's founding.

ほんしゃ 本社 the head [home] office ▶トヨタ自動車東京本社 Toyota Motor's Tokyo *head office* ‖本社と支社の連絡をきちんとする必要がある We must make sure that there is smooth communication between *the home office* and branch offices.

ほんしゅう 本州 Honshu

> 《解説》「本州」の訳語に mainland を当てることがあるが, これは「大陸または大陸の主要部分」の意で用いられることが多い.「本州」は固有名詞と考えて Honshu とするのがよい.

▶本州と北海道は青函トンネルで結ばれている *Honshu* and Hokkaido are linked (to each other) by the Seikan Tunnel.

ほんしょ 本署 the headquarters; this office, this (police) station(➤「この [当] 警察署」の意).

ほんしょう 本性 one's true nature [colors ／character] ▶あいつもとうとう本性を現したな So he's finally revealed his *true nature*. ／So he finally showed his *true colors*!

ほんしょく 本職 one's main occupation ▶本職の歌手 a *professional* singer ‖あのテレビタレントの本職は大学教授だ That television personality's *main occupation* is teaching at a university. ‖藤本さんの本職は作家だ Mr. Fujimoto is a writer *by profession*.

ほんしん 本心 one's real [true] intention ▶彼の本心がわからない I don't understand his *real intention* [*what he really means* ／*what he intends* (*to do*)]. ‖あなたの本心を話してよ Tell me *what you really think*. ‖彼女はああ言っているが本心ではどう考えているかわからない Although she's talking like that, you can't tell what she's thinking *deep down*. (➤ deep down は「腹の底で」の意のインフォーマルな言い方) ‖ 彼が本心からそう言っているとは思えない I don't think he *really means what he is saying*.

ぼんじん 凡人 an **ordinary person** ▶所詮我々凡人にはまねのできないことだ After all, it just isn't something we *ordinary people* can do.

ポンず ポン酢 ***ponzu*** ; **citrus juice with added soy sauce.**

ほんすじ 本筋 the (main) subject (話題の) ▶あの教授の講義はすぐ本筋からそれるので有名だ Everyone knows that professor always *strays from his main subject* [*goes off on a tangent*] during his lectures.
▶まず上司に挨拶するのが本筋(＝適切)でしょう It would be *proper* to greet your supervisor first.

ほんせき 本籍

【解説】英米では日本のような戸籍制度を採用していないので,「本籍(地)」に当たる単語はない. 日本の「本籍(地)」は one's permanent official address, one's permanent legal address, one's legally recognized permanent address などと表現するのがよい.

▶私の本籍は千葉だ My *permanent official* [*legal*] *address* is in Chiba. ‖ 本籍を父の田舎から東京に移した I transferred my *permanent official* [*legal*] *address* from my father's hometown to Tokyo.

ほんせん 本線 the main [**trunk**] **line** ▶東海道本線 the Tokaido *Main* [*Trunk*] *Line*.

ほんそう 奔走する make every effort (to do) ▶彼は資金集めに奔走している He *is busy* raising funds. ／He *is making every effort* to raise money. ‖ おじが奔走して(＝世話をして)くれたので就職できた I got a job *through the influence of* [*with the help of*] my uncle. (➤ with the help of は「…が援助してくれて」の意).

ほんぞん 本尊 a ***gohonzon*** ; an object of devotion in Buddhism (➤「仏教で信仰の対象物」の意の説明的な訳).

ぼんだ 凡打《野球》▶井口は3打席凡打のあと満塁ホームランを打った After *going hitless* in his first three trips to the plate, Iguchi clouted a bases-loaded home run.

ほんたい 本体 the (main) body ▶あとはこの部品を本体に取り付けるだけだ All I have left to do is attach this part to *the body*. ‖ 遺伝子の本体はDNAである *The main part* of a gene consists of DNA.

ほんだい 本題 the main point ▶日本人は交渉の際すぐには本題に入ろうとしない Japanese tend to take time before they *get to the main point* [*get down to business*] when negotiating.

ぼんたい 凡退《野球》▶広島は5回以降3者凡退を続けた From the fifth inning on, the Carp batters *were* all *retired* in order.

ほんたて 本立て bookends.

ほんだな 本棚 a **bookshelf** (本箱の棚の1枚) ; a **bookcase** (本箱) ▶本棚に本を並べる arrange books on *bookshelves*.

ぼんち 盆地 a **basin** /béɪsən/ ▶福知山盆地 the Fukuchiyama *Basin* ‖ 盆地は夏は暑く, 冬は寒い In *basins* it is hot in summer and cold in winter.

ほんちょうし 本調子 ▶今シーズンのライオンズはまだ本調子ではない The Lions are not yet *in full swing* this season. ‖ きょうはどうも本調子じゃない(＝気分がすぐれない) I'm *feeling* a little *under par* today.

ほんてん 本店 the head [**main**] **office** ▶みずほ銀行の本店 *the head office* of Mizuho Bank ‖ 三越本店 *the main store* of Mitsukoshi ‖ 本店のほうに在庫があるか問い合わせてみます I'll call *the main store* and ask if they have any in stock.

ほんでん 本殿 the main shrine.

ほんど 本土 the mainland ▶日本本土 Japan *proper* ‖ アメリカ本土 *the mainland* of the U.S. ‖ 台風は明朝, 本土に上陸するでしょう The typhoon will hit *the main islands* (of Japan) tomorrow morning.

ボンド (a) **glue** /gluː/ (接着剤).

ポンド 1【重量の単位】 a **pound** /paʊnd/ (➤ 略号は lb.) ▶3ポンドのバター three *pounds* of butter.
2【貨幣の単位】 a **pound** /paʊnd/ (➤ 略号は£) ; **the pound sterling** (英貨ポンド) 《参考》《英・インフォーマル》では pound を quid (単複同形) ということも多い.
▶その本は1冊6ポンドです That book costs *six pounds* [*£6.00*／*six quid*] a copy. ‖ ポンドが値下がりした The value of *the sterling* [*the British pound*] has fallen.

¹ほんとう 本島 the main island ▶沖縄本島のかなりの部分が現在でも米軍基地として使われている A large part of *the main island* of Okinawa is still used for U.S. military bases.

²ほんとう 本当 1【現実, 真実】reality (現実) ; **truth** (真実) ; **actuality** (実在) ━ 形 本当の **real, true, actual** ━ 副 本当に **really, truly, actually** ▶あの人, 強がりを言ってるだけで, 本当は気が小さいんだ He may talk tough, but *in reality* he's a wimp. ‖ きみは本当にカナダへ移住する気かい Do you *really* plan to emigrate to Canada?
▶あの子, 幽霊の話を本当にしてすっかりおびえてるよ She is (so) scared because she *believed* the ghost story. ‖ 夢は本当の体験ではない Your dreams are not *actual* experiences. ‖ 本当のことを言ってよ Give me *the truth*. ‖ 本当のことを言うとこの指輪はイミテーションなの *To tell* (you) *the truth*, this ring is an imitation.
▶ 対話「あの子が婚約したって本当?」「ほんとだとも」"Is it *true* that she got engaged?" "Yes, it is. [*That's right*.]" (➤ is を強く発音する) ‖ 対話「俺, ノートパソコン買ったよ」「本当?」"I bought a laptop computer." "*Oh, did you* [*really*]?" (➤ 驚きや疑いの気持ちを表す言い方. 英語ではここで止めないで, Where did you buy it? など関連質問をして会話を続けるのが普通) ‖ 対話「きみは本当にインスタント食品が好きだね」「ほんとはそうでもないんだけど, 手軽だからね」"You *really* like convenience food(s), don't you?" "*Actually*, I don't like them so much. But they're convenient."
2【本物】 ━ 形 本当の **real** (本物の) ; **genuine** /dʒénjuɪn/ (真の, まがい物でない) ; **absolute** (完全な, 全くの) ▶これこそ本当の大リーグ野球だ This is what I call *real* major league baseball. ‖ 私はまだ本当のモロッコ料理を食べたことがない I have never eaten *genuine* Moroccan cuisine. ‖ 本当の(＝正式の)紅茶の入れ方を教えてやろう Let me show you how to make tea *properly*. ‖ 父はきのうようやく退院したが, 体はまだ本当ではない My father was at last discharged from the hospital yesterday, but he *hasn't fully recovered* yet.
3【非常に】 ▶本当にありがとう Thank you *very much*. ‖ 本当にごめんなさい I'm *really* [*awfully*／

terribly] sorry. (➤ カッコ内の2語はインフォーマル) ‖ 富士山って本当にきれいだね Mt. Fuji *sure* is beautiful, isn't it?

ほんどう 本堂 the main building of a Buddhist temple.

ほんにん 本人 the person himself [herself] ▶ぜひご本人に会ってお話をしたい I really want to see and talk to *him* [*her*] *in person*. (➤ in person は「代理でなく当人の」) ‖ 申し込みには本人が来ること Applications must be submitted *in person*. ‖ 本人の口から真実を聞きたい I'd like to hear the true story from *the person in question*. (➤ the person in question は「問題の当人」).

ほんね 本音 ***honne***, one's **real** [**true**] **intention(s)** ➡建て前 ▶建て前ではなく社長の本音が知りたい I want to know the president's *honne* [*true intentions*], not his *tatemae* [public stance]. ‖ 本音を言うと, K大よりP高専に行きたいんだ *To tell* (you) *the truth*, *what I really want* is not to go to K University but to P Technical School. ‖ 彼女の言ったことのどこまでが本音なのかわからない I don't know how much of what she said reflected her *true opinion* [*feelings*]. ‖ 思わず彼の本音が出た He inadvertently *gave himself away*. (➤ give oneself away は「思わず正体を現す」).

ボンネット 《米》 a **hood** /hʊd/, 《英》 a **bonnet**.

> **危ないカタカナ語✸ ボンネット**
> 自動車の「ボンネット」は《英》の bonnet からきていて, 《米》では hood という. ただし, 帽子の「ボンネット」は英米ともに bonnet である.

ほんの only, just (ただ…だけ); **mere** (単なる) ▶本気になるなよ. 相手はまだほんの子供だ Don't take it seriously. She is a *mere* child [*only* a child]. (➤ mere, only の位置に注意) ‖ 地下鉄の駅まではほんの数歩です The subway station is *only* [*just*] a few steps away. ‖ ビールをほんの少し飲んだだけなのに顔が赤くなった I drank *only* a little beer but my face turned red. ‖ この肉は1キログラムにほんの僅かだけ足りない This piece of meat weighs *a bit* less than one kilogram. (➤ 副詞的に用いて「ごく僅かに」の意) ‖ ほんの2, 3分待ってください Would you wait *just* a few minutes?

ほんのう 本能 (an) **instinct** /ínstɪŋkt/ ▶動物本能 animal *instincts* ‖ 母性本能 maternal *instinct(s)* ‖ 本能のままに行動する act *on instinct alone* ‖ 人間は本能的に暗闇を恐れる Humans have an *instinctive* fear of darkness. / Humans fear darkness *by instinct*. ‖ すべての動物には危険に対する自己防衛本能が備わっている Every animal has *the instinct to protect itself* against danger [*the instinct of self-preservation*]. (➤ 後者は「自己保存の本能」).

ぼんのう 煩悩 worldly desires [**passions**] ▶煩悩を断ち切る cut off one's *worldly desires* ‖ 人は死ぬまで煩悩に翻弄される People are at the mercy of *worldly desires* until they die.

ほんのり ▶リンゴがほんのり色づき始めた The apples began to color *faintly*. ‖ ワインのせいで彼女の頬がほんのりピンクに染まった Her cheeks were *slightly* flushed with wine.

ほんば 本場 a **home** (産地); a **center (of production)** (生産の中心地) ▶志摩は真珠の本場だ Shima is the *home* [*center*] of Japanese pearl production. ‖ イングランドはサッカーの本場(=発祥地)だ England is the *birthplace* of soccer. ‖ あのレストランは本場の(=本物の)イタリア料理を出す They serve *genuine* [*authentic*] Italian dishes at that restaurant. ‖ メキシコへ行って本場の(=実際に使われている)スペイン語を勉強したい I'd like to go to Mexico to study *real-life* Spanish. / I'd like to go to Mexico to study *real Spanish as it is spoken in everyday life*.

ほんばこ 本箱 a **bookcase**.

ほんばしょ 本場所 a **regular** [**seasonal**] **sumo tournament** (相撲の) ▶相撲の本場所は1年に6回行われる Six *regular sumo tournaments* are held (in) a year.

ほんばん 本番 ▶彼は本番(の試験)で力を発揮できなかった When it got to the *real* [*actual*] exam, he was unable to demonstrate his ability. ‖ 彼女は本番(の演技)で本当に泣いてしまった She actually wept during the *performance*.
☛ ぶっつけ本番 (➡見出語)

ポンびき ポン引き a **pimp**; a **toot** (客引き).

ほんぶ 本部 the head office; **the headquarters** (警察・軍隊などの) ▶この会の本部は京都にある The *head office* of this association is in Kyoto. ‖ 警察はその殺人事件の捜査本部を設置した The police set up *an investigation headquarters* to investigate the murder case.

ポンプ a **pump** /pʌmp/ ▶ここでは田んぼへポンプで水をくみ上げています We use *a pump* to draw water into the paddy. ‖ ポンプでタイヤに空気を入れた I *pumped* air into the tires. / I *pumped up* the tires.
‖ 排水ポンプ a drainage pump.

ほんぶり 本降り ▶本降りになる前に家に帰ろう Let's get home before *it really starts to pour*.

1ほんぶん 本文 text; **the body** (手紙などの) ▶詳しくは本文参照のこと Please refer to the *text* for further details.

2ほんぶん 本分 one's **duty** ▶学生としての本分を尽くしなさい You should fulfill [do] your *duty* as a student.

ボンベ a **cylinder**; an **air tank** (ダイビング用の) ▶酸素ボンベ an oxygen *cylinder* 《参考》「ボンベ」はドイツ語の *Bombe* (爆弾)から.

1ほんぽう 奔放な uninhibited (自制しない, のびのびした); **free** (自由な) ▶奔放な生活を送る lead an *uninhibited* [*a free*] life ‖ 彼女は自由奔放に生きたいと思っている She wants to live *freely without inhibitions*.

2ほんぽう 本俸 basic pay.

3ほんぽう 本邦 this [**our**] **country** ▶このフェルメールの名画は本邦(=日本)初公開です This famous painting of Vermeer's will *be shown to the public for the first time in Japan*.

ボンボン a **bonbon** (糖菓).

1ぽんぽん ▶お父さんは自分のおなかをポンポンたたいた Dad *thumped* his belly.
▶日本女性としては真紀子はぽんぽん言う(=物をはっきり言う)ほうですね Makiko is quite *outspoken* for a Japanese woman.

2ぽんぽん 《小児語》 one's **tummy**, one's **tum-tum**.

ポンポン a **pompom**, a **pompon** ▶チアガールたちはポンポンを振りながら声援した The cheerleaders rooted (for their team) shaking their *pompoms*.

ほんまつてんとう 本末転倒 ▶塾の勉強が忙しくて学校の宿題に手が回らないなんて本末転倒だ When you say you don't have enough time to do your school homework because you are too busy with study at the cram school, you are *putting the cart before the horse* [you are *getting your priorities mixed up*]. (➤ put the cart before the horse は「馬の前に荷車をつなぐ」の意で, 英語のことわざ).

ほんみょう 本名 one's **real name.**

ほんめい 本命 the favorite ; the target(目標) ▶本命(の馬, または選手)が予想どおり勝った *The favorite* won the race as expected. ‖ 田川氏が次期社長の本命だ Mr. Tagawa is *the most likely* (*candidate*) to be the next president. ‖ ことしのセ・リーグのペナントレースは中日が本命だ The Chunichi Dragons are *the leading* [*top*] *contenders* for the Central League pennant this season. (➤「最有力チーム」の意).

ほんもう 本望 ▶ここまでやれれば本望です It *is more than enough* for me to have come this far. ‖ 好きな山で死ねれば本望だ I would *be happy* [*be satisfied*] to die in the mountains I love.

ほ

ほんもの 本物 a **real** [**genuine**] **thing,** the **real McCoy** (➤後者はインフォーマル) 一形 **本物の real ; genuine** (まがい物でない) ▶本物のダイヤ a *real* [*genuine* / *natural*] diamond (➤ natural は「天然の」) ‖ この 2 枚のお札, どちらが本物でどちらが偽物かわかりますか Can you tell which of these two bills is *genuine* and which is (a) counterfeit? ‖ 版画を買ったとき, 画商は間違いなく本物だと太鼓判を押した When I bought the woodblock print, the dealer assured me it was *authentic*. (➤ authentic は美術品などについていうことば).
▶彼女の英語は本物だ Her English is *the real thing*.

ほんもん 本文 →ほんぶん.

ほんや 本屋 《米》 a **bookstore,** 《英》 a **bookshop** (店) ; a **bookseller**(人).

ほんやく 翻訳 (a) **translation** 一動 **翻訳する translate** +目 ▶アメリカ人の友人は安部公房の小説を翻訳で楽しんでいる One of my American friends enjoys reading Abe Kobo's novels *in translation*. ‖ 詩の翻訳では多くのものが失われてしまう Much is lost in *translation* of poetry. ‖ 私は日本の民話を英語に翻訳中です I have *been translating* some Japanese folktales into English. ‖ この歌詞を日本語に翻訳してもらえますか Could you please *translate* [*put*] the words of this song *into* Japanese?
‖**翻訳者** [**家**] a translator ‖ **翻訳書** a translation.

ぼんやり

訳語メニュー
不明瞭な →vague **1**
ぼやけた →dim **1**
うわの空の →absent-minded **2**

1【不明瞭な】vague /veɪg/, **dim** ▶祖父のことはぼんやり覚えているだけです I remember my grandfather only *vaguely*. ‖ 前方の車のテールランプがぼんやり見えた I saw the *dim* taillights of the car ahead. ‖ 私は睡眠が十分でないと頭がぼんやりする My head *gets foggy* if I don't get enough sleep. ‖ その船はぼんやりとしか見えなかった I saw the ship only *faintly* [*indistinctly*].

2【不注意な, ぼう然とした】absent-minded (うわの空の) ▶ぼんやりしていて有楽町で降りるのを忘れてしまった I was so *absent-minded* [*preoccupied*] that I forgot to get off at Yurakucho. (➤ preoccupied は「何かに気をとられて」) ‖ ぼんやりしているとファウルボールが当たるぞ If *you don't pay attention*, a foul (ball) will hit you. ‖ ぼんやりしてないで仕事をしろ Stop *daydreaming* [*gazing into space*] and get to work. (➤ gaze into space は「空(くう)をじっと見つめる」) ‖ 何をぼんやり考えてるの? What *are* you *dreaming about*?

3【何もしない様子】▶忙しいんだからそんな所にぼんやり突っ立ってないでくれ There's a lot to be done. Don't stand there *idly* [*doing nothing*]. ‖ ぼんやりしていると 1 年はあっという間に過ぎてしまう A year passes before you know it if you *idle the time away*.

ぼんよう 凡庸 mediocrity /mìːdiɑ́ːkrəṭi/ (そこそこであること) 一形 **凡庸な mediocre** /mìːdióʊkəʳ/ ; **ordinary** (平凡な) ▶この小説は凡庸だ This novel is *mediocre*. ‖ 私は凡庸な人間です I'm an *ordinary* person.

ほんらい 本来 1【もともと】originally (最初は) ; **essentially** (本質的に) ; **by nature** (生まれつき) ▶この学校は本来男子校だった This school was *originally* for only boys. ‖ 子供は本来活動的だ Children are active *by nature*. ‖ 本来良い物でも用い方によっては悪くもなる A thing that is good *in itself* may become harmful depending on the way it is used. (➤ in itself は「それ自体では」).

2【正式】▶本来ならここで社長がひと言ご挨拶すべきなのですが *The proper thing would be* for our president to make a little speech here.

[1]ほんりゅう 本流 the mainstream ▶この川は 3 キロ先でアマゾン本流と合流する This river merges with *the Amazon* three kilometers ahead.
▶《比喩的》彼は保守の本流に身を置いている He belongs to the conservative *mainstream*.

[2]ほんりゅう 奔流 a **torrent,** a **strong current,** a **rapid** [**rushing**] **stream** (急流) ▶雪解けの奔流 *a torrent* of water from melting snow ‖ 釣り人が奔流にのまれた A fisherman was swallowed up in the *torrent* [*rapid stream*].

ほんりょう 本領 ▶彼女はやっと本領を発揮できる仕事を見つけた She has finally found a job which *maximizes her talents* [in which she *can show real ability*]. (動詞の show の代わりに demonstrate や exhibit を使うこともできる) ‖ 企画部門に配属になれば彼は本領を発揮するだろう He will *be in his element* when assigned to the planning division. (➤ in one's element は「水を得た魚のよう」の意).

ほんるい 本塁 《野球》 **home plate, the plate**
‖**本塁打** a home run, a homer.

ほんろう 翻弄 ▶嵐の中で小船は波に翻弄された The small boat *was tossed about by* [*was at the mercy of*] the waves in the storm. (➤ at the mercy of は「…のなすがままになって」).

ほんろん 本論 the main subject [**issue**] ▶それでは本論に入りましょう Now let's take up *the main issue*.

ほんわか ▶このイラストレーターはほんわかした優しい気持ちになる絵を描く This illustrator draws *heartwarming and soothing* pictures. ‖ そのテレビドラマはほんわか暖かいものが残るいい作品だった That TV drama was excellent and left (me with) a *nice, heartwarming* afterglow.
▶お酒が回ってほんわかしてきた I'm a little tipsy and *feeling good* [*mellow*]. / I'm *feeling a nice buzz*. (➤ この buzz は「ほろ酔い気分」).

ま・マ

1ま 魔 ▶魔の(＝危険な)踏切 a *fatal* [*dangerous*] railroad crossing.
▶《慣用表現》明子が万引きをするなんて魔がさしたとしか思えない *Something must have come over* [*must have got into*] Akiko to make her shoplift. (➤「何かが明子を襲った[明子の頭にとりついた]に違いない」の意).
‖電話魔 a telephone addict, a phone freak(➤ addict, freak はともに「…マニア」の意) ‖通り魔(→見出語).

2ま 間 1【時間】time ▶飛行機が出るまでにまだ間がある We still *have some time* before the airplane leaves. ‖この会社で働くようになってまだ間がない I *haven't been working* for this company *for very long*. (➤後者のほうがややインフォーマル) ‖おじさんが亡くなったことは少し間を置いてから彼に話そう I'll *wait a little while before* I talk to him about his uncle's death. (➤「話す前に少し待とう」の意) ‖彼女は毎日帰宅すると休む間もなく夕食のしたくにかかる *The moment* she gets home from work (every day), she begins to prepare supper.
▶せりふを言うときは間のとり方(＝タイミング)に気をつけなさい Pay attention to the *timing* when you say your lines. ‖日本の舞台芸術では間の取り方が極めて重要だ *The skillful use of silence*(*s*) [*pauses*] is considered all important in Japanese performing arts.
2【空間】▶私は姉の隣に間を空けて座った I sat *a little away from* my (older) sister.
3【部屋】a room ▶六畳間 *a six-mat room* ‖私は洋間よりも日本間が好きだ I prefer *Japanese-style rooms* to *Western-style rooms*. ‖彼女のアパートは2間しかない Her apartment has only two *rooms*.
4【慣用表現】▶社長と1時間一緒だったが，間がもてなくて苦労した When I had to spend an hour with the president, I found it difficult to *keep the conversation going*. (➤「話を途切れないようにするのが難しかった」の意).
▶デートの日にちを間違えるなんて，あいつも間が抜けてるよ *How stupid* of him to have mistaken the day of his date with her! ‖ぼくはまわりが女性ばかりで間の悪い思いをした I *felt awkward* when I found myself surrounded by women.

> **逆引き熟語 ○○間**
> 居間 a living [sitting] room, a family room ／応接間 a drawing room ／茶の間 a living room, a family room ／日本間 a Japanese-style room ／広間 a hall ／仏間 a (family) Buddhist altar room ／洋間 a Western-style room ／六畳間 a six-mat room

まー 真ー ▶その湖はB市の真東[北]にある The lake lies *due* east [north] from B City. (➤ due は「(方位が)まさしく」の意).

まあ 1【自分の気持ちや判断をぼかして】well《参考》日本人の多くがこの用法を好むが，例えば人からお茶や食事に誘われたような場合に不用意に Well, … と言うと，いかにも気乗りがしていないように解釈されるおそれがあるので注意.
▶まあ，そうですねえ *Well*, let me see. ‖ 対話「先生，ここの who は that じゃだめですか？」「まあ，that でもいいでしょう」"I can replace this *who* with *that*, can't I?" "*Well*, yes." ‖ 対話「この絵はどのくらいの価値があるでしょうか」「まあ，そうですねえ」"About how much do you think this painting is worth?" "*Well*, let me see."
▶ 対話「英語のテスト，満点だったんだって？」「まあ，ついていたんだろうね」"Somebody told me you got a perfect score in English." "*Yeah* [*Well*], I must have been lucky." (➤ Well だと満点だったことをあたかも本人が知らないように響くので，英米人ならば上昇調で "Yeah, …" と言って，そうであることを認めるような表現のほうが自然であると思われる) ‖ 対話「きみは彼女のこと好きだろ？」「うん，まあね」"You like her, don't you?" "*Yeah, you could say that.* ／*Well, kind of* [*sort of*]." (➤ *kind of* [*sort of*] は「ちょっと」の意のインフォーマルな言い方で，日本人的な応じ方であるが，英米人ならば "*Yeah, you could say that.*" とより積極的に肯定すると思われる) ‖この本ならまあ(＝少なくとも) 1万部は売れるでしょう We can sell *at least* 10,000 copies of this book.
2【相手の感情をなだめたり，軽くたしなめたりして】▶まあやってごらんよ *Just* try it. ／*Just* give it a try. ‖突っ立ってないで，まあ入りなさいよ Don't keep standing there. *Why don't you just* come on in? ‖ 対話「最近の政治家はいったい何をやってるんだ」「まあ，そうかっかしなさんな」"What on earth are politicians doing these days?" "*Hey* (*now*), don't get all hot and bothered."
3【驚きを示して】oh, how ▶まあ，驚いた *Oh*, my goodness! (➤女性の言い方) ‖《写真などを見て》まあ，きれい *How* beautiful! ／*Wow*, it's (really) beautiful.
▶まあ，すてき *Oh*, how lovely!

マーカー a marker, a marking pen ; a highlighter (pen) (蛍光ペン).

マーガリン margarine /mάːʳdʒərɪn/, 《英・インフォーマル》marge ▶パンにマーガリンを塗る spread *margarine* on bread.

マーガレット《植物》a marguerite /mὰːʳɡəríːt/.

マーク 1【印】a mark(記号) ; a sign(標識) ; a trademark(商標) ▶わからない文章の箇所にはマークをつけておきなさい *Mark* the passages you don't understand. ‖地図の赤い十字のマークは病院を表します A red cross (*mark* ／*symbol*) on the map indicates a hospital.
2【見張ること】一動 マークする mark ＋目 ; cover ＋目 (スポーツで相手をチェックする) ▶彼は麻薬密売人として警察からマークされている He *is marked* by the police as a drug dealer. ／ The police *are keeping an eye on* him because they suspect that he is a drug dealer.
▶8番の選手をしっかりマークしろ *Cover* [《英》*Mark*] the No. 8 player tight.
3【達成すること】▶国内最高記録をマークする *make* [*set*] a national record.

逆引き熟語 ○○マーク
アットマーク an at sign, an at-mark (@) ／**ウールマーク** Woolmark ／**エコマーク** an eco-mark [-label] ／**キスマーク** a hickey, a love bite ／**シンボルマーク** an emblem ／**チェックマーク** a check, a tick ／**トレードマーク** a trademark ／**ビックリマーク** an exclamation mark [point] ／**ロゴマーク** a logo ／**初心者マーク** a newly-licensed driver's sticker (➤ これは日本独自だが, イギリスなどでは仮免講習中の車につける標示板として L-plate がある) ／**高齢者マーク** a senior driver sticker

危ないカタカナ語✹ マーク
「目印」とか「記号」の意味の「マーク」は mark でよいが, 他の語を用いたほうがよい場合もある. 例えばトイレや非常口などを示す「標識」の意味では sign を用いる. また, 商品のマーク(商標)には trademark が, 会社などの組織のマークには logo が相当する.

マークシート an **OMR (answer) sheet**, a **bubble sheet**.

マーケット a **market** ▶母は週 2 回マーケットに買い物に行く My mother goes shopping at the *market* twice a week.
▶南米にマーケット(＝市場)を広げるために, まずマーケットリサーチをした We initially conducted *market* [*marketing*] *research* to determine the feasibility of opening up a new *market* in South America.

マーケティング **marketing**.

マージャン **mah-jongg** /mɑ̀ːdʒɑ́ːŋ/ (➤ (英) では mah-jong ともつづる) ▶マージャンのパイ a (*mah-jongg*) tile ‖マージャンをやろうよ Let's play *mah-jongg*. ／How about a game of *mah-jongg*?
‖**マージャン店** a mah-jongg parlor [saloon].

マージン a **(profit) margin**, a **margin of profit** (利ざや) ; a **margin** (余白) ▶このビジネスはマージンが多い[少ない] This business has a wide [narrow] *profit margin*.
▶ページの左右のマージン left and right *margins* (on a page).

まあたらしい 真新しい **brand-new** ▶ケンとメアリーは真新しいベンツを乗り回していた Ken and Mary were driving around in a *brand-new* Mercedes. (➤ 英語では「ベンツ」を Benz とはいわない).

マーチ a **march** (行進曲)
‖**ウエディングマーチ** a wedding march.

マーボーどうふ 麻婆豆腐 **mabo dofu, mapo doufu** (➤ 後者は中国語の発音).

まあまあ 1【まずまず】▶彼女の学業成績はまあまあでした Her grades were *just average* [*so-so*]. ／Her grades were *passable*. ‖ 対話「その映画はどうでしたか」「まあまあだね」"How did you like the movie?" "It was *OK* [*so-so*]." (➤ この OK は「けっこう」や「いい」ではなく「可もなく不可もなく」に近い) ‖ 対話「試験の成績どうだった？」「まあまあだったよ」"How did you do on your exam(s)?" "I did *OK* [*all right* ／ *fairly well*], *I think*." (➤ all right は下降調で発音すれば「まあまあ」の意味になり, right を強めれば「最高」の意味になる).
2【なだめて】▶まあまあ, 落ち着いて *Now, now*, calm down.

マーマレード **marmalade** /mɑ́ːrməleɪd/.

まい- 毎- **every** (…ごとに) ; **each** (各…) ▶毎朝[晩]テレビで 7 時のニュースを見ます I watch the seven o'clock news on television *every morning* [*evening*]. ‖私たちは毎日曜日テニスをします We play tennis *every Sunday* [*on Sundays*].
☞ **毎回, 毎時, 毎週, 毎月, 毎度, 毎年, 毎日** (→見出語)

マイ- **my** (自分の) ; one's **own** (自分自身の) ▶マイバッグ one's *own* shopping bag ‖マイボトル one's *own bottle* ‖マイカップ one's *own* (coffee) cup [mug ／tumbler].
☞ **マイカー, マイホーム** (→見出し語)

1**-まい -枚** ... **sheet** 《of》, ... **slice** 《of》 (➤ of のあとに数えられない名詞がくる) ▶画用紙を10枚買った I bought *ten sheets* of drawing paper. ‖朝食にトーストを 2 枚食べた I had *two slices* of toast for breakfast. (➤ slice は「(パン・肉などの) 薄切り 1 枚」) ‖84円切手 2 枚とはがきを10枚ください *Two* 84-yen *stamps* and *ten postcards*, please. (➤ 数えられる名詞の場合はこのように数詞をつけて複数形にすればよい).
▶大阪行きの切符を 2 枚ください *Two tickets* to Osaka, please. ‖もう 1 枚お皿を取ってちょうだい Can you get me *one* more *plate*? ‖あらしで窓ガラスが 4 枚割れた *Four panes* [*sheets*] of glass were broken in the storm.

2**-まい** 1【推量の打ち消し】▶ 対話「近い将来, 富士山は噴火するでしょうか」「いや噴火はすまい」"Will Mount Fuji erupt in the near future?" "I *don't think* so [I *don't think it's likely*]."
▶ファストフードを食べようと食べまいと俺のかってだ It's none of your business *whether or not* I eat fast food.
2【意志の打ち消し】**will not, won't** ▶あの人にはもう会うまい I *won't* see him any more. ‖江美子との別れはつらかった. もう二度と恋はすまい It was hard when I broke up with Emiko. *I'll never* fall in love again.
3【理由の打ち消し】▶子供じゃあるまいし, 一人で行けるでしょう You should be able to go (there) by yourself *since you're not a child* any more. (➤「もう子供じゃないのだから」の意).

まいあがる 舞い上がる **soar (high)** (鳥などが) ; **be raised** (ほこりが) ▶ダンプが走り去るとほこりがもうもうと舞い上がった A heavy cloud of dust *was raised* when the dump truck sped away. ‖ヒバリが 1 羽空高く舞い上がった A lark *soared* high into the sky.
▶枯れ葉が風に舞い上がった Dead leaves *were stirred up* by the wind. ‖桜の花びらが風に舞い上がった The cherry blossom petals *swirled* [*whirled*] in the wind. (➤ swirl は「渦まく」).
▶彼におだてられて私はすっかり舞い上がってしまった I *was beside myself* [*walked on air* ／ *was on cloud nine*] when he complimented me. ／I *was overjoyed* when he flattered me. (➤ いずれも「有頂天になった」の意).

まいあさ 毎朝 →毎-.

マイアミ **Miami** /maɪǽmi/ (アメリカ, フロリダ州の都市).

まいおりる 舞い降りる **flutter down** ▶見た事もない鳥が舞い降りてきてマストに止まった A bird we had never seen *fluttered down* and landed on the mast. ‖タカは野ウサギ目がけてさっと舞い降りた The hawk *swooped down on* the hare.

マイカー one's **own car** (➤ 自分のものである車) ; a **car**

of one's own(しばしば，願い事の対象としての自分の車) ▶やっとマイカーが手に入った I've finally bought *a car* (*of my own*). (「自分の所有する車を自分が買う」というのは論理が成り立たないので，my car としない) ‖ 秋になると多くのマイカー族が河口湖にやって来る A lot of *motorists* come to Lake Kawaguchi in the fall. →自家用車.

まいかい 毎回 every [each] time ▶あなたに会うと毎回(＝会うたびごとに)同じ話を聞かされるね *Every time* I see you, I have to listen to that same old story. ‖ 母はそのドラマを毎回楽しみにしている My mother looks forward to *each episode* [*installment*] of that drama. (➤ episode, installment はともに「(連続物の) 1回分」) ‖ 毎回同じことを言わせないでちょうだい *How many times* do I have to tell you the same thing? (➤「何回言ったらわかってもらえるの？」の意).

まいきょ 枚挙 ▶古賀政男のヒット曲は枚挙にいとまがない Koga Masao has so many hit songs that I *can't remember* [*enumerate*] them *all*. (➤ enumerate は「数え上げる」の意の堅い語).

マイク a mike ▶次に生徒会長がマイクの前に立った Next, the president of the student council stepped up to the *mike*. ‖ マイクが入ってませんよ The *mike* is not on [is dead]. 《参考》マイクの調子をテストするとき日本では「本日は晴天なり」「ただ今マイクのテスト中」などと言うが，英語では "Testing, testing, one, two, three." などと言う.

マイクロシーベルト 《物理学》microsievert(人体への放射線被曝線量の単位；1シーベルトの100万分の1).

マイクロバス a minibus, a microbus.

マイクロホン a microphone. →マイク.

まいこ 舞子 a dancing girl; a young apprentice geisha (➤説明的な訳).

まいご 迷子 a lost child 一動 迷子になる get lost, lose one's way (➤ 後者は「道順がわからなくなる」. 前者のほうが深刻な状況を暗示する); stray(帰り道がわからなくなるほど遠くへ行く)

▶うちの息子はきのうデパートで迷子になった My son *got lost* at a department store yesterday. ‖ 私は山の中で迷子になった I *got lost* [*lost my way*] in the mountains. ‖ 小さな子はよく家から離れて迷子になる Little children often *stray* from their homes.

まいこむ 舞い込む ▶戸の隙間から雪が舞い込んだ Snow *came in* through a crack in the door. ‖ 妙な手紙が舞い込んだ I *received* a strange letter.

マイコン a microprocessor (➤「マイコン」は本来 microcomputer の略だが，現在では電気製品などに組み込まれたコンピュータ・チップを指すことが多い).

まいじ 毎時 every hour ▶毎時100キロのスピードで走る go at (a speed of) 100 kilometers *per* [*an*] *hour* (➤ at 100 kph と略す場合が多い；kph は kilometers per hour と読む) ‖ バスは毎時15分にここを発車する Buses leave here *every hour on the quarter hour*. (➤「毎時 0 分」つまり「毎正時」は every hour on the hour).

まいしゅう 毎週 every week ▶毎週英語の小テストがある We have an English quiz *every week*. ‖ 毎週月曜日の朝に打ち合わせがある We have a meeting *every Monday morning*.

✉ **私は毎週 2 回ピアノを習っています** I take piano lessons *twice a week*.

まいしん 邁進 ▶市長に当選したからには公約実現にまい進いたします Now that I have been elected mayor, I will *proceed boldly* [*single-mindedly*] to fulfill my campaign promises.

まいすう 枚数 the number of sheets ▶答案用紙の枚数を確認してください Check *the number of* answer *sheets*. ／Please check how many exam papers there are.

まいせつ 埋設する lay under the ground, bury +(目) ▶電線を埋設する *lay* power lines *underground*.

‖ **埋設ケーブル** a buried cable.

まいそう 埋葬 (a) burial /bériəl/ 一動 埋葬する bury /béri/ +(目) ▶モーツァルトは共同墓地に埋葬された Mozart *was buried* in a public cemetery.

‖ **埋葬許可書** a burial permit.

まいぞう 埋蔵 ▶北海の石油埋蔵量はかなりのものだ There are rich *deposits* [*reserves*] of oil in the North Sea. ／The North Sea is rich in oil *deposits* [*reserves*]. (➤ 前者は地中にある量，後者は採掘可能な量) ‖ 霞ヶ関に眠っている埋蔵金 (*government) slush funds* buried in Kasumigaseki ‖ 彼は江戸時代の埋蔵金を掘り当てた He dug out *a cache of coins buried* (*underground*) in the Edo period. (➤ cache /kæʃ/ は「(盗品などの) 隠した物」).

まいちもんじ 真一文字 ▶武蔵は口を真一文字に結んだ Musashi closed his lips *in a straight line* [closed his lips *tight*].

まいつき 毎月 every month 一形 毎月の monthly (➤名詞の前で用いる) ▶この雑誌は毎月発行される This magazine is published *every month*. (➤「毎月 5 日に」なら on the 5th of each month) ／This is a *monthly* magazine.

まいった 参った →参る.

まいど 毎度 every time (毎回); always (いつも); as usual (いつものごとく) ▶おじいちゃんの話は毎度同じさ My grandfather tells (me) the same story *every time* I see him. ／My grandfather repeats the same old story *all the time*. ‖ 彼の遅刻は毎度のことさ He is *always* late. ‖ 毎度(＝たびたび)お騒がせいたします We apologize for the *frequent* announcements. ‖ 毎度ありがとうございます Thank you *again*. (➤ これに It's always a pleasure to serve you. をつけ加えてもよい. 掲示などの表記としては We appreciate [We thank you for] your patronage. のような言い方がよい).

まいとし 毎年 every year ▶村野教授は毎年本を 1 冊出版する Professor Murano publishes a book *every year*. ‖ 毎年夏に家族と一緒に北海道へ行きます I go to Hokkaido with my family *every summer*. ‖ 毎年恒例の平和会議が 8 月にハワイで開かれます The *annual* peace conference will be held in Hawaii in August. (➤ annual は「年 1 回の」) ‖ 毎年今頃は雨が多い It rains a lot *around this time of* (*the*) *year*.

マイナー minor ▶彼は詩人としては偉大だが，小説家としてはマイナーだ He's a major poet but a *minor* novelist.

マイナス 1 【数】 minus ▶ 10マイナス 6 は 4 である Ten *minus* six equals four. ‖ 6 引く10はマイナス 4 である Six minus ten is *minus* four. ‖ 気温はマイナス(＝零下)15度に下がった The temperature dropped to fifteen (degrees) *below zero* [*below freezing*]. ‖ わが家の先月の家計は 2 万円のマイナス(＝赤字)だった Our family budget last month went twenty thousand yen *into the red*.

‖ **マイナスイオン** a negative (air) ion, an aeroanion (➤「マイナスイオン」は定義も実態も不明確な和製語）‖**マイナス記号** a minus [negative] sign（➤ negative は専門用語）‖（経済の）**マイナス成長** negative economic growth.

2【欠点，不利】▶わがままなところが彼女の性格のマイナス面だ Her *biggest fault* is (her) selfishness. ‖今彼を叱るのはかえってマイナスだろう Scolding him now would have *the opposite* [*an adverse*] *effect* of what you intended.（➤ 前者は「逆効果」, 後者は「よくない影響」）.

> **危ないカタカナ語✹ マイナス**
> **1**「マイナス」は数学の引き算の記号や負数を表すのに用いられるが，これらの場合は minus がそのまま使える．→プラス．
> **2** 日本語では「欠点」とか「不利」の意味で「マイナス」というが，この用法は英語の minus にはない．また「赤字」の意味では，個人の場合は the red を，企業や国の場合は deficit を用いる．商売上の「マイナス」は loss がよい．

まいにち 毎日 every day ━形 **毎日の** everyday, daily ▶毎日の生活 *everyday* life ‖辞書の校正が**毎日の**仕事です Proofreading dictionaries is my *daily* work. ‖健康な体を維持するには**毎日**適度な運動が必要だ You need moderate exercise *every day* to stay healthy. ‖ 9 月に入って**毎日のように**雨が降っている It has been raining *almost every day* since the beginning of September. ‖**毎日毎日**見えるものは砂漠だけだった I could see nothing but desert *day after day*.（➤ day after day は「来る日も来る日も」）.

まいねん 毎年 →まいとし.

マイノリティー a minority（少数派）.

まいばん 毎晩 →毎-.

マイブーム one's personal obsession ▶ホラー映画を見るのが今私のマイブームです I'*m really into* horror movies now.

マイペース ▶人のことは気にしないで，マイペースで勉強しようと思う I am going to study *at my own pace* without worrying about what other people [students] do.

> **危ないカタカナ語✹ マイペース**
> 英語の pace はスピードを表す語で，at one's own pace は「自分に合ったスピードで」の意味である．「自分流のやり方で」の「マイペース」ならば do something (in) one's way，他人におかまいなしにわが道を行く「マイペース」には go one's own way という表現が当てはまる．

マイホーム one's own house [home], a house [home] of one's own ▶私たち，やっとマイホームを買うことができました We have finally managed to buy *our own house*.（●「自分の所有物である家を自分が買う」というのは筋が通らないので，my home としないことに注意）.

▶最近は**マイホーム主義の人**が増えている There has been an increase in the number of *people who value family* (*time*) *above work* [*who put their family first*].（➤「仕事より家庭を重視する人」の意；「マイホーム主義の男性」を family man ともいう）‖国民の 7，8 割が郊外の庭付き一戸建てを理想の**マイホーム**と考えている Surveys show that 70–80% of the population believe that the ideal *home* is a house with a garden in the suburbs.

まいぼつ 埋没する be buried /bérid/ ▶山崩れで多くの家が埋没した Many houses *were buried* under the landslide.

まいもどる 舞い戻る ▶犯人は故郷に**舞い戻った**ところを逮捕された The culprit was arrested when he *returned* [*came back*] *to* his hometown.

まいる 参る 1【行く，来る】 go, come ▶さあ，参りましょうか Shall we *go* now? ‖すぐに参ります I'*m coming* now.（➤ come は相手の所へ行く場合）.

2【参拝する】▶伊勢神宮に参る *visit* [*worship at*] (the) Ise Shrine.

3【降参する，閉口する】 give up（降参する）；can't stand（耐えられない）▶彼女の短気には参るよ I *can't stand* [*can't put up with* / *can't tolerate*] her short temper. ‖この猛暑には**参った** This intense heat *has* really *gotten to* me.（➤ get to は「…にこたえる，…を苦しめる」の意）/ I *can't stand* this intense heat. ‖そんなに働きづめでは体が**参っちゃう**よ You'll *burn* (*yourself*) *out* if you keep working that hard.（➤ burn (oneself) out は「燃え尽きる」）/ Working that hard will *do* you *in*.（➤ do ... in は「へとへとに疲れさせる」の意のインフォーマルな言い方）‖彼のがんこなのには**参る**よ I'*m at a total loss* as to how to deal with his stubbornness. ‖彼女は**精神的に参っている**ようだ She seems to *be emotionally exhausted*. ‖ 対話「どうだ，参ったか」「参った，降参だ」"Well, do you *give up*? / Now cry [say] uncle!" "You win. I give up."（➤ cry [say] uncle は《米・インフォーマル》で「参ったと言う」の意）‖ 対話「東海道線は事故のため現在運転を見合わせております」「**参ったなあ！**」"Service on the Tokaido Line has been suspended due to an accident." "*Oh, shoot!*"

4【好きになる】▶光一のやつ，すっかり雅子に**参っちゃったらしい** It looks like Koichi *is smitten with* Masako.

マイル a mile（➤ 1 マイルは約1,609メートル）▶アメリカでは日常的にはキロよりマイルが多く使われる In the U.S., people usually measure distance in *miles*, not (in) kilometers.

マイルド mild ▶マイルドなチーズ *mild* cheese ‖**マイルドな風味** a *mild* flavor.

マイレージ mileage ‖**マイレージプログラム [サービス]** a mileage program.

マインドコントロール mind control ▶あのカルト教団の信者はマインドコントロールされている The members of that cult *are mind controlled*.

まう 舞う dance（踊る）；whirl /hwəːrl/（ぐるぐる動く）；circle（旋回する）▶枯れ葉が風に**舞って**いる Dead leaves are *whirling* [*dancing*] in the wind. ‖トンビが上空を**舞っている** A kite is *circling* high up in the sky. ‖空中にほこりが**舞っていた** Dust *was hanging* in the air.

まうえ 真上に right over ..., just above ... ▶頭の**真上**をハトが数羽飛んで行った Several pigeons flew *right over* our heads. ‖おじさんはこの（階の）**真上**に住んでいる My uncle lives *just above* us. →上.

まうしろ 真後ろに right [just] behind ... ▶私はそっと彼女の**真後ろ**に立った I stood *right* [*just*] *behind* her without her noticing (me). ‖ 2 位の選手が先頭ランナーの**真後ろ**に迫った The second place runner *came close on the* front-runner's *heels*.

マウス a mouse（ネズミ，またパソコンの）（➤ 複数形は mice；「パソコンのマウス」の意味では mouses とするのがふつう）▶マウス（ボタン）をクリックする click *a mouse* (*button*) ‖ マウスでコンピュータを操作する operate a computer with *a mouse* ‖ コンピュータを使えばいろいろなものがマウスを数回クリックするだけで買える You can buy all kinds of things with *a few mouse clicks* on your computer.

‖ マウスパッド a mouse pad.

マウスピース a **mouthpiece**.

マウンテンバイク a **mountain bike**.

マウント マウントを取る **try to assert dominance over, try to one-up** +⊞ ▶彼はいつも私に向かってマウントを取ってくる He always *tries to one-up* me. ／He always *tries to assert dominance over* me.

マウンド 《野球》 **the mound** ▶中日は浅尾投手がマウンドに上がった Asao *took the mound* [*pitched*] for the Dragons.

まえ 前

1【位置, 方向】the front /frʌnt/ (前部)

語法 (1)場所的に「…のすぐ前に」の意の場合は **in front of** または **before** を用いるが, before は堅い語. (2)進行方向の「前方に」の意の「前に」には **ahead of** を用いる.

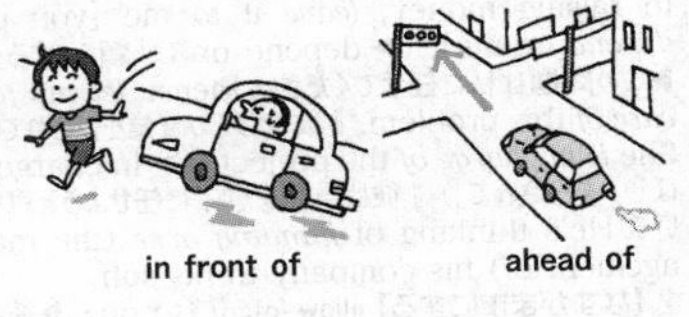

▶郵便ポストならあのビルの前にありますよ There's a mailbox *in front of* that building. ‖ 私の前に３人並んでいる Three people are lined up *in front of* [*ahead of*] me. ‖ 人の前で話をするのは苦手です I'm not good at speaking *in front of* [*before*] people. ‖ 私のすぐ目の前で交通事故が起きた A traffic accident occurred *right before my eyes*. ‖ 彼の家は(道路を挟んで)私の家の前にある His house is *across* (*the street*) *from* mine. ／His house is *opposite* mine. ‖ 竜夫の前では「落ちる」なんてことば使わないでよ Don't use the word "fail" *around* Tatsuo. (➤ around は「…のいる所で」).

▶前へ出なさい Please come to *the front*. ‖ 私たちは前から３列目(の席)に座った We sat in the third row from *the front*. ‖ 全体, 前へ進め *Forward march!* (➤ 号令) ‖ 彼女は私たちの前(＝前方)を歩いていた She was walking *ahead of* us. ‖ 山田君, ちゃんと前を向きなさい Yamada, *look forward* [*face the front*].

2【今より以前】before ; ago ▶(医者が患者に)前にもこんなことがありましたか Have you had this (problem) *before*? ／Has this been a problem *before*? ‖ 太田君は前よりずっと堂々として見える Ota looks a lot more confident than *before*. ‖ 吉田さんには前に一度会ったことがある I have met Yoshida once *before*.

▶野田さん一家は(今から)３年ほど前に青森へ引っ越していった The Nodas moved to Aomori three years *ago*. ‖ そのバス路線はずっと前に廃止になった The bus service on that route was discontinued *long ago*. ‖ こちらが前に(＝先日)お話しした井上さんです This is Mr. Inoue, who(m) I told you about *the other day*.

語法 before と ago
(1)時間的に「今より前」を表すとき, **before** は漠然と「以前に」の意で用いる. **ago** は「今から…(年)前に」と時間を表す語句を伴い, 過去の文で用いる.
(2)before はまた **3** の例のようにある時点を基準にして「その時より以前に」の意でも用いる.

▶このマウンテンバイクは前から(＝長い間)欲しいと思ってたんだ I've been wanting this mountain bike *for a long time* [*for ages*]. ‖ ぼくは数年前からピラニアを２匹飼っている I have had two piranhas *for the past few years*. ‖ うちのチームは前はとても強かった Our team *used to* be very strong. (➤ used to do は現在と対比して過去の状態や事実を述べる) ‖ この辺りは前とすっかり変わってしまった This neighborhood looks quite different than (it did) *before*.

3【ある時より以前】before ▶試合の前, 選手たちはひどく緊張していた The players were very nervous *before* the game. ‖ 彼女は３時ちょっと前に姿を現した She showed up shortly *before* three. ‖ 鈴木さんは女優になる前はモデルをしていた Ms. Suzuki was a model *before* she became an actress. ‖ テレビを見る前に宿題を済ませてしまいなさい Finish your homework *before* watching TV. ‖ 試験開始の10分前には入室してください Please be in the room at least ten minutes *before* the exam starts. ‖ 数日前に現地に行っているつもりです I'll be there a few days *before*. ‖ 彼女を紹介されたとき, 私は前に会ったことがあると思った When she was introduced (to me), I realized we had met *before*. ‖ 彼女は２, ３日前に私のおばに会ったと言った She told me that she had met my aunt a few days *earlier*.

▶約束の時間より30分も前に着いてしまった I arrived 30 minutes *before* my appointment. ‖ 船は定刻より(５分)前に出港した The ship left (five minutes) *ahead of time*. ‖ 今ちょうど６時15分前だ It's exactly fifteen minutes *to* six. ／It's five forty-five sharp [on the dot].

4【順序が先】▶前の社長は美術品を集めるのが趣味だった Our *former* president collected works of art as a hobby. ‖ 前の車は小さかったので大きなのに買い替えた Because the *last* car we had was too small, we bought a bigger one this time. (➤ last は「すぐ前の」) ‖ 前のページをもう一度見なさい Take another look at the *preceding* page. ‖ 野田さんの前の首相は誰でしたっけ Who was the Prime Minister *prior to* Mr. Noda? ‖ 彼はその前の日に電話をくれた He phoned me on *the previous day*. ／He phoned me *the day before* (*that*). ‖ 祖父は日米開戦の前の年に生まれた My grandfather was born *in the year before* the war broke out between Japan and the U.S.

5【…人分】▶ラーメン５人前お願いします Five *bowls* of ramen, please. ‖ 弟は２人前の牛どんをぺろりと平らげた My brother ate up two *bowls* of rice with beef.

まえあし 前足・前脚 a **forefoot**(前足) ; a **foreleg**(前脚) ▶この犬, 前足にとげがささってるみたい This dog seems to have a splinter in his (*front*) *paw* [*forepaw*].

まえうり 前売り (an) **advance sale** ▶前売り券発売中 *Advance tickets* on sale now. ／*Advance tickets* available. ‖ ９月20日の巨人対広島戦の前売り券を買った I got *an advance ticket* for the Giants-

Carp game on the 20th of September.

まえおき 前置き ▶彼の演説は前置きが長過ぎた In his speech, he spent too much time on the *opening statement*. ‖ 前置きはこのくらいにして, 早速ショーをご覧にいれます *Without any more preliminaries* [*Without further ado*], please enjoy the show. (➤ without further ado は「遅れたりせずに, さっさと」の意).

まえかがみ 前屈み a **slouch** /slaʊtʃ/ (姿勢の悪さによる) ; a **stoop** (加齢による腰の曲がり) ▶彼は前かがみになって歩く He walks *with a slouch* [*with a stoop*]. ／He has a *slouchy* way of walking. ／He *leans forward* when he walks.

まえがき 前書き a **preface** /préfəs/ ; a **foreword** (特に著者以外による略式のもの).

まえかけ 前掛け an **apron** /éɪprən/.

まえがみ 前髪 **bangs** (切り下げた) ▶きみは前髪を垂らしたほうが似合うよ You look better with *bangs* [《英》 with *a fringe*].

まえがり 前借り ▶私は給料から3万円前借りした I *got a* 30,000-yen *advance* on my salary. ‖ 彼は退職金を前借りして(＝前払いしてもらって)家を新築した He *had* his retirement money *paid in advance* and built a (new) house.

まえきん 前金 (an) **advance (payment)** ▶1万円を前金でお支払い願います We ask for *an advance payment* of 10,000 yen. ／We request you to pay ten thousand yen in advance.

まえだおし 前倒し ▶予定を前倒しする *advance* [*move up*] a schedule.

まえのめり 前のめり ▶タクシーが急ブレーキをかけたので我々は反動で前のめりになった When the taxi stopped abruptly, we *lurched forward* in reaction.

まえば 前歯 a **front tooth**.

まえばらい 前払い (an) **advance (payment)** ▶給料の前払いを頼んだ I asked for a month's *pay in advance*. ‖ 料金は前払いでお願いします Please *pay in advance*.

まえひょうばん 前評判 ▶その映画は前評判がいい That movie *has received good advance reviews*. ‖ その映画は前評判ほどではなかった That movie *wasn't all it was cracked up to be*.

まえぶれ 前触れ a **sign**, a **herald**, a **harbinger** (➤ 後の2つは文語) ; a **precursor** (先ぶれ) ; an **omen** (吉凶などの) ; **notice** (予告) ▶人々はその群発地震が噴火の前触れではないかと恐れた People feared that the frequent earthquakes were the *sign* of an impending (volcanic) eruption. ‖ コマドリは春の前触れだ The robin is *a harbinger* [*a herald*] of spring. ‖ おやじが前触れもなくアパートを訪ねて来た My dad *made* [*paid*] *a surprise visit* to my apartment.

まえまえ 前々 ▶前々から一度お会いしたいと思っていました I've been wanting to meet you *for a long time*.

まえむき 前向きの **positive** (積極的な) ▶若者は将来に対して前向きであってほしい I want young people to *be positive* about their futures. ‖ 前向きに生きて行こう Let's all take a more *positive attitude* [*forward-looking approach*] toward life.

まえもって 前以って **beforehand**
✉ 前もって成田に到着する時間をお知らせください Please let me know *beforehand* [*in advance* ／ *ahead of time*] when you will arrive at Narita. ➤ ahead of time は《米》に多い言い方.

まおう 魔王 **the Devil, Satan** /séɪtn/.

まがいもの 紛い物 an **imitation** ▶宝石商にまがい物のダイヤをつかまされた The jeweler palmed off *an imitation* [*a fake*] diamond on me.

まがお 真顔 ▶彼女の名前が出たら彼は急に真顔になった He suddenly *got a serious look on his face* when someone mentioned her name. ‖ あの人はよく真顔で冗談を言う He often tells jokes *with a straight face*.

まかす 負かす **defeat** ＋目, **beat** ＋目 (➤ 後者は前者よりややくだけた語) ▶わが校は野球でS高校を負かした Our school *defeated* [*beat*] S High School at baseball.

まかせる 任せる **1【ゆだねる】** **leave** ＋目 ; **entrust** ＋目 (信頼して)

> **【文型】**
> 人(A)に物事(B)を任せる
> **leave** B **to** A

▶決定はあなたに任せます I *leave* the decision *to* you. ‖ 金の工面ならおれに任せておけ When it comes to raising money, *leave* it *to* me [you can *depend on* me]. (➤ depend on は「頼りにする」) ▶この問題は私に任せてください Please *let me take care of* this problem. ‖ 彼女はその事業を任されている She *is in charge of* the project. (➤ in charge of は「…を託されて」) ‖ 彼は会社を息子に任せようと思っている He's thinking of *handing over* (the management of) his company to his son.

2【なすがままにする】 **allow** /əláʊ/ 《to do》 ▶彼はうずくまったまま, 相手の殴るに任せた He kept on squatting, which *allowed* his opponent *to* beat him easily. ‖ この頃は思うに任せぬことばかりだ I have met with too many *setbacks* recently.

3【放置する】 **leave** ▶父親が入院して以来, 庭は荒れるに任されている The garden *has been left* uncared-for [untended] since my father was hospitalized. ‖ 二人のことは成り行きに任せるしかないと思うね The only thing we can do in their case is to *let things take their natural course*.

まがった 曲がった **bent** ; **curved** (湾曲した) ; **winding** /wáɪndɪŋ/ (曲がりくねった) ▶曲がった線 a *curved* line ‖ くねくねと曲がった道 a *winding* [*snaked*] road ‖ 腰の曲がった老婆 an old woman with a *bent* [*crooked*] back.
▶《比喩的》私は曲がったこと(＝不正)が大嫌いだ I hate *dishonesty* [*unfairness*].

まかない 賄い **board** ▶私は賄い付きの下宿で月10万円払っています I pay 100,000 yen a month *for room and board*.
‖賄い付き下宿 a boardinghouse.

まかなう 賄う **manage** (やりくりする) ; **cater** (業者が出向いてパーティーなどの料理を) ▶パーティーの料理を賄う *cater* (*for*) a party (➤ for を省略するのは主に《米》) ‖ 50人分の料理を賄う *cater for* fifty people (➤ この場合の for は省略不可) ‖ 私は毎月15万円で家計を賄わ(＝切り盛りし)なければならない I have to *manage the household* on 150,000 yen a month.

マガモ 《鳥》 a **mallard** /mǽləʳd ‖ -lɑːd/.

まがり 間借りする 《米》 **room**, 《英》 **lodge** ▶私は伊藤さんの家に間借りしている I'*m rooming at* Mr. Ito's.
‖間借り人 《米》 a boarder, 《英》 a lodger.

まがりかど 曲がり角 a **turn in a road** ; a **street corner** (街角) ▶あの曲がり角を左に曲がると右手に薬局がありま

す Turn left at that *corner*, and you will find a drugstore on your right. ‖ 曲がり角ではスピードを落としなさい Slow down *when driving around a corner*.

▶《比喩的》日本経済は今曲がり角(＝転換期)に来ている The Japanese economy is now at *a turning point*. ‖ 25歳はお肌の曲がり角と言われる At twenty-five *your skin starts to show signs of aging*.

まがりくねる 曲がりくねる wind /waɪnd/ ; meander /miǽndəʳ/ (特に川が) ▶長くて曲がりくねった道 a long and *winding* road ‖ 曲がりくねった木 a *crooked* tree ‖ 道路は曲がりくねって丘を上っている The road *winds* up the hill. ‖ 千曲川は長野県を曲がりくねって流れている The Chikuma River *winds* [*meanders*] *through* Nagano Prefecture.

まかりとおる まかり通る ▶警察は暴力団の違法行為がまかり通るのを許してはならない The police should not allow the illegal activities of criminal organizations to *go unchecked*. ‖ 当時は権力者の極悪非道がまかり通っていた In those days atrocities were committed *rampantly* by those in power. (➤ rampantly は「どうしようもなく頻繁に」の意) ／At the time, those in power committed atrocities *with impunity*. (➤ with impunity は「罰せられることなく」).

まがりなりにも 曲がりなりにも ▶弟は曲がりなりにも(＝どうにかこうにか)夏休みの自由研究を一人でやりとげた *Somehow or other* my brother managed to finish his summer project by himself. ‖ 夫は曲がりなりにも大学を出ている My husband is a college graduate, *even though he wasn't a great student*. (➤「すばらしい学生ではなかったが, 学卒である」) ／My husband managed to graduate from college, *though he didn't get the best grades*. (➤「最高の成績ではなかったが, なんとか卒業した」) ‖ 曲がりなりにも(＝完璧とは言えないが) 彼は使命を果たした He accomplished his mission, *though not perfectly*.

まかりまちがう まかり間違う ▶バンジージャンプだなんて, まかりまちがえば(＝失敗すると)命にかかわるよ Bungee jumping? But if you *make one false move* doing that, it may mean your life. ‖ まかりまちがっても麻薬には手を出すな Never touch drugs *no matter how much you want to try them*! (➤「どんなに試してみたい気持ちになっても」の意).

まがる 曲がる 1【物がまっすぐでなくなる】 bend ; be crooked /krʊ́kɪd/ (背中などが) ; tilt (傾く) ▶竹は弾力性に富み, たやすく曲がる Bamboo is very flexible and *bends* easily. ‖ 大雪で鉄塔がくの字に曲がってしまった The pylon *was badly bent* by the heavy snow. (➤ bent は bend (曲げる)の過去分詞形).

▶その行商人は年を取って腰が曲がっている The peddler *is bent* with age. ‖ ヒロシちゃん, 背中が曲がっているわよ. まっすぐに座りなさい You'*re slouching*, Hiroshi. Sit up straight. (➤ slouch は「前かがみになっている」).

▶ネクタイが曲がってるわよ. 直してあげる Your tie *is (on) crooked*. Let me straighten it for you. ‖ あの額少し曲がってない? *Isn't* that picture *tilted* a little?

2【方向を変える】 turn ; curve (道が湾曲する) ; wind /waɪnd/ (曲がりくねる) ▶次の交差点を右[左]に曲がってください *Turn* (to the) right [left] at the next intersection. (➤ to the は省略するほうがふつう) ‖ どうも曲がる所を間違えたようだ It seems that we may *have taken the wrong turn*. ‖ うちはその角を曲がったところです My house is just *around the corner*.

▶道は教会の前で大きく右に曲がっている The road *curves* sharply to the right in front of the church.

3【心がゆがんだ】 ▶あの少年は根性が曲がっている That boy is *crooked to the core*. (➤ to the core は「芯まで」「とことん」).

☛ 曲がった (→見出語)

マカロニ macaroni ▶マカロニグラタン *macaroni* au gratin ‖ マカロニサラダ *macaroni* salad.

‖ マカロニウエスタン a Spaghetti Western.

まき 薪 firewood, wood.

まきあげる 巻き上げる roll up (巻いて上げる) ;《インフォーマル》 fleece ＋目, skin ＋目 (金や物をだまし取る ; 前者には「大金を」という含みがある) ▶すだれを巻き上げる *roll up* a bamboo blind.

▶車がほこりをもうもうと巻き上げた(＝立ち上らせた) The car *raised* a cloud of dust.

▶詐欺師はおばあさんから金を巻き上げた Tha con man *fleeced* [*skinned*] the elderly woman. ‖ 彼はうまいことを言って母親から 1 万円を巻き上げた He *wheedled* 10,000 yen *out of* his mother. (➤ wheedle A out of B で「うまいことを言って B (人)から A (物)を巻き上げる」).

1**まきえ 蒔絵** *makie* ; a Japanese lacquerware technique in which the lacquered object is dusted with gold or silver while the lacquer is still wet (➤ 説明的な訳).

2**まきえ まき餌** 《主に米》 chum, 《主に英》 ground bait ▶まき餌で魚を寄せる attract fish with *chum* [*ground bait*].

まきおこす 巻き起こす ▶その遺跡の発見は考古学者たちの間にセンセーションを巻き起こした The discovery of those ruins *created* [*produced*] a big sensation among archaeologists.

まきがい 巻き貝 《動物》 a conch /kɑːŋk/.

まきかえし 巻き返し a comeback ▶自民党は今回の選挙で巻き返しを図っている The Liberal Democratic Party is trying to make [stage] *a comeback* in the upcoming election. ‖ ペナントレースの終盤近くになって巨人は巻き返しに出た Toward the end of the pennant race, the Giants began to *rally*. (➤ rally は「盛り返す」の意).

まきかえす 巻き返す ▶《ボクシング》このラウンドでは挑戦者が巻き返した In this round, the challenger *regained lost ground* [*his strength*].

まきげ 巻き毛 curly hair, (a) curl 一形 巻き毛の curly-haired.

まきこむ 巻き込む ▶船は渦に巻き込まれた The boat *was caught* [*was engulfed*] *in* a whirlpool. ‖ その作業員は腕を機械に巻き込まれた The worker *got* his arm *caught in* a machine.

▶きみたちのもめごとに私を巻き込まないでくれ Don't *involve* me in your dispute. (➤ involve A in B で「A (人)を B (事件)に巻き込む」) ‖ 彼は殺人事件に巻き込まれた He *got involved* in a murder. ‖ こんなごたごたに巻き込んでしまって申しわけありません I'm sorry to *have gotten* you *involved in* this mess.

まきじた 巻き舌 ▶巻き舌で話す *roll* [*trill*] one's *r's*.

まきじゃく 巻尺 a tape measure.

まきずし 巻き寿司 a sushi roll.

まきぞえ 巻き添え ▶彼はけんかの巻き添えを食ってけが

をした He *was involved* [*was mixed up*] *in* a fight and got injured.

まきちらす まき散らす scatter +⑩ ▶道路に砂利をまき散らす *scatter* gravel on the road.

まきつく 巻き付く coil [wind /waɪnd/] around ▶アサガオのつるが支柱にくるくる巻きついている The morning glory vines are *coiling* [*winding*] *around* the pole. (➤ coil [wind] itself around の形で用いることもある).

まきつける 巻き付ける coil ... [wind /waɪnd/] around ▶蛇が木の枝に体を巻きつけていた A snake *coiled itself around* the branch. ‖ 彼はマフラーを巻きつけて出て行った He *wound* his scarf *around* his neck and went out. (➤ wound /waʊnd/ は wind の過去形).

まきとる 巻き取る wind /waɪnd/ +⑩ ▶漁網を巻き取る *wind up* a fishing net ‖ フィルムを巻き取る(＝元の状態に巻いて戻す) *rewind* film (➤「フィルムを別のリールに巻き取る」なら wind film onto another reel).

まきば 牧場 a stock farm(牧畜場); a pasture(牧草地) →牧場(ぼくじょう).

まきもどし 巻き戻し →巻き戻す.

まきもどす 巻き戻す rewind /riːwáɪnd/ +⑩ ▶ビデオテープを巻き戻す *rewind* a videotape
‖巻き戻しボタン a rewind button, a review button.

まきもの 巻物 **1**【軸に巻いた紙・布地】a scroll(軸物); a roll of cloth (巻いた反物).
2【巻き鮨】*makizushi*, rolled sushi.

まぎらす 紛らす ▶悲しみを酒に紛らす *drown* one's sorrows in liquor [alcohol].

まぎらわしい 紛らわしい confusing; misleading (誤解を与えやすい) ▶紛らわしい説明 a *misleading* explanation ‖ うちの親類には恵美子が何人かいて紛らわしい We have several relatives named Emiko. It is *very confusing*.

まぎれこむ 紛れ込む ▶どういうわけか, きみの鉛筆がぼくの筆箱に紛れ込んでいたよ Your pencil somehow *got into* my pencil case. ‖ すりは雑踏の中に紛れ込んでしまった The pickpocket *managed to hide* [*conceal*] *himself in* the crowd.

-まぎれに -紛れに ▶彼女は腹立ちまぎれに皿を数枚割った She broke several dishes *in a fit of anger*. (➤ fit は「一時的興奮」) ‖ 火事場のどさくさまぎれに(＝混乱のさなかで)金を盗まれた I had my money stolen *in the confusion* caused by the fire.

まぎれもない 紛れもない ▶その事故で日本の原子力政策が多大な影響を受けたのは紛れもない事実だ It's *definitely* true that the accident had a major impact on Japan's nuclear policy. ‖ それは紛れもなく彼女のスカーフです It's *unmistakably* her scarf. ／*Without* (*a*) *doubt* it's her scarf.

まぎれる 紛れる **1**【入りまじる】get mixed up ▶あなたの手紙がほかのものと紛れてしまって見つからない Your letter *got mixed up* among others and I can't find it. ‖ その子供は人込みに紛れてしまった I *lost sight of* the child in the crowd. ‖ どろぼうは暗やみに紛れて逃げた The thief ran away *under* (*the*) *cover of night* [*darkness*].
2【気を奪われる】▶散歩をしたら気が紛れた Taking a walk *took my mind off things* [*diverted* me]. (➤後者は文語的表現) ‖ 友だちと電話でしゃべったらいくらか気が紛れた I *felt* somewhat *better* after I talked to a friend (of mine) over the phone.
✉ **このところの忙しさに紛れてお手紙のご返事が遅くなってしまいました. お許しください** I'm sorry for not replying (to your letter) sooner, but I've been very busy [things have been really hectic] recently.

まぎわ 間際 ▶ゲーテは死ぬ間際に「もっと光を」と言った *Just before* his death, Goethe said, "More light." ‖ 発車間際にプラットホームに着いた I made it to the platform *just before* the train left. ‖ 彼女は間際(＝土壇場)になって気が変わった She changed her mind *at the last moment*.

[1]まく 幕 **1**【舞台などの】a curtain ▶芝居の幕が上がった[下りた] The *curtain* has risen [has fallen] on the drama. (➤ 横開きの幕の場合は pull や draw を用いる).
▶《慣用表現》選挙戦の幕が切って落とされた The candidates *kicked off* their election campaigns. (➤ kick off は「始める」) ‖ ペナントレースは坂本の2発のホームランで幕を明けた The pennant race *was kicked off* by Sakamoto's two homers.
2【劇の区切り】an act ▶2幕8場の芝居 a play with [in] two *acts* and eight scenes.
▶《比喩的》きみの出る幕じゃない(＝きみには関係の無いことだ) It's none of your business. ／This is no time for you to butt in.

[2]まく 膜 a film, a membrane (➤ 後者は生物・化学用語) ▶温めた牛乳の表面に薄い膜ができた A thin *film* formed on the surface of the warmed milk.
‖鼓膜 a tympanic membrane ‖ 細胞膜 a cell membrane ‖ 粘膜 a mucous membrane ‖ 油膜 a film of oil.

[3]まく 巻く **1**【うずまき状にする】coil ▶うちの犬のしっぽは右に巻いている Our dog's tail *is coiled* clockwise.
2【物をねじって回す】wind /waɪnd/ +⑩ (➤ 過去・過去分詞は wound /waʊnd/); roll +⑩ (丸める) ▶柱時計のねじを巻く *wind* (*up*) a wall clock ‖ セーターをほどいて毛糸を玉に巻く undo [unravel] a sweater and *wind* its wool into a ball ‖ 証書を巻いて紙筒に入れた I *rolled up* my certificate and put it into a paper cylinder.
3【包む】bind +⑩ (巻きつける); wrap +⑩ (包む) ▶おにぎりをのりで巻く *wrap* an *onigiri* with laver ‖ 看護師はねんざした足首に包帯を巻いてくれた The nurse *bandaged* my sprained ankle. ／The nurse *bound up* my sprained ankle *with a bandage*. (➤ bound は bind の過去形) ‖ その女の子は首に赤いスカーフを巻いていた That girl *had* a red scarf *around* her neck.
▶3人が煙にまかれて火事の犠牲になった Three people *suffocated* to death (from smoke inhalation) in the fire. (➤ suffocate は「(煙などで)息が詰まる」の意).
▶誰かあとをつけてくるぞ. まこう(＝くらましてやろう) Someone's tailing us. Let's *give him the slip*.

[4]まく 撒く water +⑩ (水をかける); sprinkle +⑩ (振りかける); scatter +⑩ (ぱらぱらとまき散らす); dust +⑩ (殺虫剤などの粉末を散布する); spray (液体の殺虫剤の場合) ▶庭に水をまく *water* the garden ‖ 道路に砂をまく *sprinkle* sand on the street ‖ 街頭でビラをまく *distribute* fliers on the street ‖ バラの木に殺虫剤をまく *dust* an insecticide on rosebushes ／*dust* rosebushes with an insecticide (➤ 液体の殺虫剤の場合は spray という).
▶両力士は土俵を清めるためにひとつかみの塩をまいた The two sumo wrestlers *scattered* handfuls of salt to purify the ring.

5**まく 蒔く** sow +⊞ (種を) ; plant +⊞ (植え込む)
▶花壇にコスモスの種をまく *sow* cosmos seeds in a flowerbed ‖ 庭にヒマワリの種をまいた I *planted* sunflower seeds in the garden.

まくあい 幕間 《米》 an intermission, 《英》 an interval
▶幕あいにアイスクリームでも食べよう Let's get some ice cream *during the intermission* [*interval*].

まくあけ 幕明け ▶4月に入るといよいよプロ野球の幕明けだ In April, the professional baseball *season opens*.

マグカップ a (coffee) mug (➤ (×) mug cup とはいわない).

まくぎれ 幕切れ an ending (物語・映画などの) ; an end (終わり) ▶『賢者の贈り物』は思いがけない幕切れだ "The Gift of the Magi" has an unexpected *ending*. ‖ ゲームはあっけない幕切れだった The game came to an abrupt *end*. / The game ended abruptly.

まぐさ fodder (かいば) ; hay (干し草).

まくしたてる ▶候補者は自分の見解をとうとうとまくしたてた The candidate *spouted* his opinions. (➤ spout /spaʊt/ は「えんえんとしゃべり続ける」の意のインフォーマルな語) / The candidate *went on and on* giving his opinions.

まぐち 間口 ▶うちは間口は10メートルほどあるが奥行がない My house is about ten meters *wide* (*at the front*) but doesn't go back very far.

マグニチュード a magnitude ▶マグニチュード5.1の地震 an earthquake with *a magnitude* of 5.1 / a 5.1-*magnitude* earthquake ‖ けさの地震はマグニチュード5.2だった This morning's earthquake measured 5.2 *on the Richter scale*. (➤ 英米ではマグニチュードはリヒタースケールで表す. 数値は同じ, Richter の発音は /rɪktəʳ/).

マグネシウム 《化学》 magnesium /mæɡníːziəm/.

マグネット a magnet.

まくのうちべんとう 幕の内弁当 a Japanese box lunch, which consists of fish, meat and vegetables with cooked rice (➤ 説明的な訳).

まくひき 幕引きする close the curtain
▶《比喩的》ソビエト連邦の幕引き *the demise* of the Soviet Union.

マグマ 《地質学》 magma.

まくら 枕 a pillow ▶まくらが低いと眠れない I can't sleep on a flat *pillow*. ‖ 宏は授業中腕をまくらにして眠っていた Hiroshi was sleeping *with his head on his arm* during class.
▶連続放火魔が捕まったので, 住民たちはようやく枕を高くして (= 安心して) 寝られる Now that the serial arsonist has been arrested, the residents can *sleep easy* (at night). (● sleep easy を sleep in peace とすると, 今まで暴走族などに睡眠を妨げられていたように響く).
‖まくらカバー a pillowcase ‖ まくら木 《米》 a (railroad) tie, a (cross) tie, 《英》 a (railway) sleeper ‖ 抱きまくら a body [huggable / hug] pillow.

まくらもと 枕元 bedside ▶子供たちが病気の母のまくら元に呼ばれた The children were called to the *bedside* of their sick mother. ‖ 彼女はきちんと洋服を畳んでまくら元に置いた She folded her clothes neatly and put them *by* [*at*] *her bedside*. (➤ next to her bed としてもよい).

まくる 捲る roll up, tuck up (➤ 後者には「まくり上げてたたむ」という含みが強い)
▶そでをまくる *roll* [*tuck*] *up* one's sleeves ‖ そでをまくらないとぬれるよ *Roll* your sleeves *up* if you don't want them to get wet. ‖ 私たちはズボンのすそをまくり上げて海岸を散歩した We strolled along the seashore with our trousers *rolled up*. ‖ いたずら坊主が女の子のスカートをまくった The mischievous boy *flipped* the girl's skirt to get a peek. (➤ flip は「さっと裏返す」, peek は「のぞき見」).

-まくる ▶買いまくる *go on a buying spree* [*binge*] (➤ binge /bɪndʒ/ には「歯止めがかからない」という含みがある) ‖ 彼女は寂しくなると友人に電話をかけまくる Whenever she feels lonely, she calls *one* friend *after another*. ‖ 雅治は新しいオートバイのことをしゃべりまくった Masaharu *went on and on* about his new motorcycle. ‖ きのうの夜はパチンコでつきまくった I *had a run of luck* at pachinko last night. (➤ a run of luck は「運がついている時間[期間]」の意).

まぐれ a fluke /fluːk/ ▶ど真中に当たったのはまぐれだよ Your (hitting the) bull's eye was *a fluke*. ‖ あんなのまぐれですよ (= 運がよかっただけです) I was just *lucky*. ‖ まぐれで賞を取った I won the prize *by chance*. / I got the award through *dumb luck*. (➤ dumb luck は「まぐれ」に相当するインフォーマルな言い方) ‖ 対話「初めてにしては上出来だ」「まぐれよ」 "Considering this is your first time, you're doing pretty well." "*Beginner's luck*, I guess." (➤ beginner's luck は「初心者のまぐれ当たり」の意).

まくれる 捲れる ▶スカートのすそがまくれてますよ The hem of your skirt *is turned up* [*is rolled up*].

まぐろ 鮪 《魚》 a tuna ▶マグロの刺し身 slices of raw *tuna*
‖キハダマグロ a yellowfin tuna ‖ クロマグロ a bluefin tuna.

まけ 負け a loss (試合などの) ; (a) defeat (➤「敗北」の意の一般語) ▶この勝負はきみの負けだ You're going to *lose* this game. ‖ 裁判は彼の負けだった He *lost* the case. / The judgment went *against* him. ‖ 1点差でも負けは負けだ *A loss* is *a loss* even if the margin is just one point. ‖ 最初に笑った者が負けだよ The one who laughs first is *the loser*. ‖ 最初から負けいくさだとわかっていた We knew we were fighting *a losing battle* from the start.
‖負け犬 a loser (敗者, 不成功に終わった人) ; an underdog (勝ち目のない側) ‖ 負け投手 the losing pitcher, the loser.

まげ a topknot /tάːpnɑːt ‖ tɔ́pnɔt/ ▶相撲取りはまげを結う Sumo wrestlers wear their hair in *a topknot*.

まけおしみ 負け惜しみ ▶かぜ気味で力が出せなかっただなんて, あいつの負け惜しみだよ He said he was unable to do his best because he was coming down with a cold, but I think he's just *a poor loser* [it's just *sour grapes*]. (➤ poor loser は「負け惜しみを言う人」. また, sour grapes はイソップ物語から出た表現. 「酸っぱいブドウ」が原義で「負け惜しみ」の意で用いる). ‖ 彼は負け惜しみが強い He is *a bad loser*.

まけこす 負け越す ▶その力士は今場所, 7勝8敗で負け越した That sumo wrestler *ended with an overall losing record* of 7 wins and 8 losses.

まけじだましい 負けじ魂 an unyielding spirit.

まけずおとらず 負けず劣らず ▶その三姉妹は負けず劣らずの (= 等しく) 美人だ The three sisters are *equally* beautiful. ‖ 秋夫は春夫に負けず劣らず (= 同

じように)頭がいい Akio is *just as* smart *as* Haruo.

まけずぎらい 負けず嫌い ▶負けず嫌いの人 a person who *hates to lose* ‖ピッチャーは負けず嫌いでなくては務まらない To be a pitcher, one must have *a competitive spirit* [one has to be *unyielding*]. (➤ a competitive spirit は「競争心」, unyielding は「妥協しない」の意).

まけっぷり ▶負けっぷりが良い[悪い]人 a good [poor /bad] loser. (➤ good loser は「負けても悪びれない人」のこと).

まける 負ける

1【競技などで】lose /luːz/ (+㊐), **be beaten**

> **語法** lose は「試合を落とす」の意で, lose a game [a match] の形で用いる. 人や相手チームに負けるときは lose to ... または be beaten by ... とする.

▶阪神タイガースが試合に負けると父は不機嫌になる My father gets grumpy whenever the Hanshin Tigers *are beaten* [*lose a game*]. ‖渡辺選手はボクシングの試合で判定で負けた Watanabe *lost* the boxing match by decision.

ま

【文型】
相手(A)に負ける
lose to A

▶うちの野球チームは相手チームに 2 対 1 で負けた Our baseball team *lost to* [*was beaten by*] the opposing team by a score of 2-1. (➤ 2-1 は two-to-one と読む).

▶彼は将棋では誰にも負けない Nobody can *beat* him at *shogi*. (➤「彼には誰も勝てない」の意) ‖《サッカーで》マリノスは前半 2 点負けていたが後半盛り返した The Marinos *were* two goals *behind* in the first half, but came roaring back in the second half. ‖生産性という点では日本はほかのどの国にも負けない Japan *is second to none* in productivity.

ことわざ 負けるが勝ち Sometimes you gain more by losing (than by winning).

2【屈する】give in《to》▶暴力の脅しには決して負けないぞ I'll never *give in to* threats of violence. ‖口げんかになると妹のほうも負けてはいない When it comes to an argument, my (younger) sister *gives as good as she gets*. (➤「負けずにやり返す」の意のインフォーマルな表現) ‖寒さに負けない丈夫な体を作りなさい Build up your strength so you can *beat* [*cope with*] the cold. ‖きみには負けたよ! *I give up. You win!*

3【かぶれる】▶かみそりにまけるたちなので必ずローションをつけます My skin is *sensitive to* [*is irritated by*] razors, so I always apply lotion.

4【値引きする】give ... a discount,《インフォーマル》**knock ... off** ▶少しまけてください Please *give* me a little *discount*. (➤「少しまけてくれませんか」なら Can you take [knock] a bit off (the price)? と言う) ‖この車, 20万円まけますよ I'll *give* you *a discount* of 200,000 yen on this car. ‖あの八百屋さんはいつもよくまけてくれる That vegetable store always *gives* good *bargains*. ‖果物屋でりんごを 5 つ買ったら, 1 つまけてくれた When I bought five apples at that fruit store, the storekeeper *gave me an extra one* [*threw in one more for free*]. (➤ throw in は「おまけに付ける」).

まげる 曲げる **1【まっすぐでなくする】bend** +㊐; **twist** +㊐ (ねじる) ▶もう少しひざを曲げなさい *Bend* your knees a little more. ‖スーパーマンは鉄の棒を苦もなく曲げた Superman easily *bent* the iron bar. ‖彼女は針金を曲げてハンガーを作った She made a hanger by *twisting* the wire. ‖彼は腕を曲げて力こぶを作って見せた He *flexed* his arm and made his biceps bulge. (➤ flex は「(手・足を)曲げる」の意).

2【途中で変える】▶何があっても私は信念を曲げない(=固執する)つもりだ I am going to *stick to* my beliefs no matter what. ‖山岡教授は自説を曲げなかった Professor Yamaoka *stuck to* his own views. ‖そこを何とか曲げてお願いします Please *be more flexible*.

3【正しくなくする】distort +㊐ (ゆがめて伝える); **twist** +㊐ (曲解する) ▶マスコミは事実を曲げてはならない The media should not *distort* the facts. ‖私のことばを曲げて取らないでほしい Please don't *twist* my words.

まけんき 負けん気 ▶彼は負けん気が強くて決して降参しない He *doesn't like to be beaten* and never gives up easily.

まご 孫 a **grandchild** [複 **grandchildren**]; a **grandson** (男), a **granddaughter**(女) ▶今度初孫が生まれる I'm soon going to be *a grandmother* [*grandfather*] (*for the first time*). ‖私には孫が 5 人いる I have five *grandchildren*.

‖**孫の手** a back scratcher.

まごころ 真心 sincerity /sɪnsérəṭi/ (誠意) ▶佐和子は真心をこめて彼氏のためにセーターを編んだ Sawako *put her whole heart into* knitting the sweater for her boyfriend. ‖私は彼女から真心のこもった贈り物をもらった She sent me a *thoughtful* gift.

まごつく get confused ▶シカゴではどのバスに乗っていいかまごついた In Chicago I *got confused* as to which bus to take. /In Chicago I *had a hard time* figuring out which bus to take. ‖彼女は思いがけない質問にまごついたようだった She seemed to *be embarrassed at* [*be rattled by*] the unexpected question.

まこと 誠 truth ▶ ことわざ うそから出たまこと Out of falsehood comes truth. /What started as a falsehood has become the truth.

まことしやかな plausible /plɔ́ːzəbəl/ (もっともらしい) ▶彼はまことしやかなうそをつく His lies always sound so *plausible* [*believable*]. ‖彼がまことしやかにその話をしたので多くの人が信じてしまった He told us the story *as if it were true*, so many of us believed it.

まことに 誠に very(たいへん); **truly**(ほんとうに); **quite** (全く) ▶お邪魔をしてまことに申しわけありません I'm *very* sorry to disturb you like this. ‖あなたのおっしゃることはまことにもっともです What you say *is quite right*.

✉ **ご返事が遅くなりまことに申しわけございませんでした** I am *very* sorry that I could not answer you sooner. /I am *very* sorry for not replying (to your letter) sooner.

まごびき 孫引き requotation (行為); a **requotation** (再引用の語句) **一動 孫引きする requote** +㊐ ▶その参考書はほかの本からの孫引きばかりだよ That reference book has too many passages *requoted* from other books.

まごまご ▶駅前がすっかり変わってしまっていたのでまごまごしちゃった I *was at a loss as to where to go* [*I got confused*] because the area in front of the station had completely changed. ‖まごまごしているとあっという間にひと月がたってしまう When you'*re* *dilly-dallying*, one month passes without your knowing it. →まごつく.

まさか ▶ 対話「おれ, 通知表, オール5だったよ」「まさか」"I got straight 5's on my report card." "*You don't say!*／*No kidding.*／*Don't pull my leg.*" ‖「高見さん夫婦が離婚した」「まさか!」"The Takamis have divorced." "*You must be kidding.*／*I can't believe it.*"

▶ 対話「会社をやめて自分で商売を始めたいよ」「まさか本気じゃないでしょうね」"I want to quit my job and start my own business." "*Are you serious?*" (➤ より信じがたい気持ちで言うときは You can't be serious. という).

▶まさか彼女があんないいモデルになるとは思わなかったよ I *never dreamed* she would make such a good model. ‖ まさかあそこにいるのはうちのお父さんじゃないでしょうね That *can't be* Dad over there. ‖ まさかとお思いでしょうが, 一目で彼が好きになりました *Believe it or not*, I fell in love with him at first sight. (➤「こんなこと言っても信じられないだろうが」の意).

▶まさかの時にはこれを売りなさい *If you get in a pinch*, you can sell this. ‖ ブラジルチームが日本チームにまさかの負けを喫した The Brazilian team suffered *an upset loss* to the Japanese team.

まさかり a **broad ax(e).**

まさぐる finger +㊐, **toy with.**

マザコン ▶私の彼氏, どうしようもないマザコンなの My boyfriend is a hopeless *mama's boy*.

> **危ないカタカナ語✸ マザコン**
> 「マザコン」は「マザーコンプレックス」を略したものだが, mother complex という英語はない. なお,「彼はマザコンだ」をインフォーマルで He's a mama's boy. とか He's still tied to his mother's apron strings. などのようにいう.

まさしく 正しく certainly, surely (➤ 前者は客観的な証拠や事実があって, 後者は主観的に確信してという含みがある); **undoubtedly** (疑問の余地もなく) ▶これはまさしく本物の小判だ This is *surely* [*undoubtedly*] a genuine koban [old Japanese oval gold coin].

マサチューセッツ Massachusetts (アメリカ北東部の州; 略 MA, Mass.).

まさつ 摩擦 friction; **rubbing** (こすること) 一動 **摩擦する rub** ▶両国間に貿易摩擦が生じた *Trade friction* has arisen between the two countries ‖ ぼくは毎朝冷水摩擦をする I *rub myself down with a cold wet towel* every morning.

‖**摩擦熱** frictional heat.

まさに 正に 1【全く, 確かに】**really, truly** ▶彼はまさに自由奔放な生活をした人だった He led a *really* [*truly*] Bohemian life. ‖ 宮本武蔵はまさに剣豪であった Miyamoto Musashi was a *splendid* swordsman. ‖ 対話「教科に興味をもてば生徒はよく勉強する」「まさにそのとおりだ」"Students study hard when they're interested in a subject." "*That's right.*／*Exactly.*／*You can say that again.*"

2【ちょうど】**the very** (➤ あとに名詞がくる); **just about to** do (…しようとしていた) ▶彼女はまさに私がさがしていた女性だった She was *the very* woman [*just the* woman] I had been looking for. ‖ 電車はまさに駅を出ようとしていた The train was *just about* [*ready*] *to* leave the station.

まざまざと clearly (はっきりと); **vividly** (鮮やかに) ▶この映画は人間の愚かしさをまざまざと教えてくれる This film *vividly* portrays human folly. ‖ その交通事故の状況は今でもまざまざと思い出すことができる I can *clearly* remember the scene of the traffic accident. ／The scene of the traffic accident comes *vividly* to mind (whenever I remember it).

まさゆめ 正夢 ▶彼女とデートする夢を見たけどそれが正夢になった I dreamed I had a date with her, and then the *dream came true*.

まさる 勝る be superior to (…より優れている); **surpass** /sərpǽs/ +㊐ (…をしのぐ); **be better than** (…よりもよい) ▶耐久性では石の家は木の家よりも勝っている Stone houses *are superior to* wooden ones in terms of durability. ‖ 料理にかけては恵美は久美よりも勝っている Emi *surpasses* Kumi in cooking. ／Emi is a *better* cook *than* Kumi. ‖ 彼女は歌唱力において他の歌手よりも勝っている She has *more* singing *ability than* other singers. ／She can sing *better than* other singers.

▶健康は何ものにも勝る Health *is more important than* anything else. ／Health is the most important thing. ‖ わが家に勝る所はない *There is no* place *like* home.

▶《慣用表現》彼はお兄さんに勝るとも劣らず勤勉だ He is *no less* hardworking *than* his (older) brother.

まざる 混ざる・交ざる →まじる.

まし ▶思ったよりもましな映画だった The movie was *better than* I expected. ‖ もっとましなことが言えないのかい Can't you say anything *better than* that? ‖ あの人と一緒にやっていくくらいなら死んだほうがましよ I *would rather* die *than* live with him. (➤ would rather A than B で「BするくらいならむしろAしたい」の意) ‖ いくらかでもあるほうがないよりはましだ Something *is better than* nothing. (➤ 英語のことわざ) ‖ 遅くともしないよりはまし *Better* late *than* never. (➤ 英語のことわざ) ‖ 対話「オンボロ車だね!」「歩くよりはましだよ」"What a clunker!" "It *beats* walking." (➤この beat は「…にまさる, 打ち負かす」の意のインフォーマルな語).

-まし -増し ▶午後10時以降はタクシーは2割増しの料金になる After 10:00 p.m. taxis charge an *extra* 20 percent. ／Taxi fares *increase* 20% after 10 p.m. ‖ ことしの稲の収穫は去年の5パーセント増しだった The rice crop this year *increased* by 5 percent over last year.

まじ ▶それ, マジ? *Are you serious?* ／*You really mean it?* ／*Is it* (*really*) *true?* (➤ 最初の表現が最も強意) ‖ あいつ, 目がマジだぜ He has *a serious look* in his eyes. ‖ 冗談で言ったんだ, マジにとるなよ It was only a joke; don't *take it seriously*. ‖ 対話「来月ニューヨークへ行こう」「え, マジ?」"What do you say to going to New York next month?" "*Are you serious?*／*Seriously?*"

まじえる 交える ▶裁判官は判断に私情を交えてはならない Judges should not *bring* personal feelings *into* [*let* personal feelings *influence*] their decisions.

▶先生は生徒とひざを交えて(=腹を割って)話をした The teacher had a *heart-to-heart* talk with his students.

まじかく 真四角 a (**perfect**) **square** 一形 **真四角の square.**

まじきり 間仕切り a **partition** 一動 **間仕切りする partition off.**

ました 真下に just [right] under ... ▶地下鉄の駅はこの交差点の真下にある The subway station lies *just* [*right*] *under* this intersection.

マジック magic(魔法, 奇術) ; a magic trick(手品) ▶マジックを行う do [perform] *magic* (*tricks*).

> **危ないカタカナ語✸ マジック**
> 「マジック」のつくことばには和製語が多いので注意が必要.
> **マジック(インキ)** 日本での商標名で, 英語では太いものは marker とか marking pen, 細めのものは felt-tip (pen) という. アメリカの商標名の Magic Marker を用いることもある.
> **マジックテープ** a hook-and-loop fastener, 《商標》Velcro.
> **マジックナンバー** プロ野球のシーズンの終わり近くに出る「マジック(ナンバー)」は, 英語でも magic number でよい.
> **マジックミラー** 片面が鏡になり, 片面がガラスのように素通しに見える「マジックミラー」も和製語で, 英語では one-way mirror という.

まして let alone, much less(➤どちらも「まして…ない」の意で, 通例否定文のあとに用いる) ▶私はフランス語は読めません. まして話すことなどできません I can't read French, *let alone* [*much less*] speak it. ‖ 車も買えないのに, まして家を買う余裕などはない I can't afford to buy a car, *let alone* [*not to mention* ／*to say nothing of*] a house. (➤言い換え 2 つは「…は言うまでもなく」の意) ‖ おとなだってこのテレビは持ち上げられないのだから, まして子供にできるはずがないよ Since an adult can't lift this TV set, *of course* a child *couldn't* do it either. (➤この could は仮定法).

まじない 呪い a spell (魔力をもつと信じられていることば) ; a charm (幸運をもたらすと信じられていることばや物) ▶魔法使いのおばあさんは少女にまじないをかけた The old witch put [cast] *a spell* on the girl. ／The old witch bound the girl with *a spell*. ‖ 小指に巻いた赤い糸は物忘れしないためのおまじないです (Tying) a red thread around the little finger is *a charm* against forgetfulness.

まじまじ ▶子供たちはまじまじと私の顔を見た The children *stared* me in the face.

まじめ 真面目 一形 **まじめな** serious (真剣な) ; honest (正直な) ; earnest (熱心な) 一副 **まじめに** seriously ▶彼はまじめな男だ He is a man of *honesty*. ／He is *honest*. ‖ 対話「真奈美さんはどんな生徒でしたか」「まじめな生徒でしたよ」"What kind of student was Manami ?" "She was an *earnest* [*a hardworking*] student." ‖ 彼女はまじめそうだけどよく冗談を言う She looks *serious*, but she often cracks jokes. ‖ 小林はまじめな仕事についたことがない Kobayashi has never had a *respectable* [*decent*] job. (➤respectable は「まともな, 堅気の」, decent は「きちんとした」の意).
▶最近彼はまじめに(＝しっかり)働いている He is working *earnestly* [*hard*] these days. ‖ 将来のことをもっとまじめに考えなくちゃだめだ You should take your future more *seriously*. ‖ まじめに話しているときにからかわないでよ Don't make fun of me when I'm talking *seriously*. ‖ 私が書いたことをあまりまじめにとらないでよ Don't take what I just wrote too *seriously*. ‖ 私はまじめに(＝本気で)言っているのよ I'm very *serious*. ／I really mean it. ‖ もっとまじめにやれ *Be* more *serious*. ‖《先生が生徒に》先生の言うことをまじめに聞きなさい *Take* what I'm telling you *seriously*.
☛ 不まじめ (→見出語)

まじめくさる 真面目くさる ▶私たちの担任の先生はよくまじめくさった顔で冗談を言う Our homeroom teacher often tells jokes with *a straight face*.

まじゅつ 魔術 magic ▶我々は彼のすばらしい魔術に魅了された The magician thrilled us with his *magic tricks* [feats of *magic*].
‖魔術師 a magician.

マシュマロ a marshmallow.

まじょ 魔女 a witch, an enchantress(➤後者にはプラスイメージがある) ▶魔女狩り a *witch*-hunt.

ましょう 魔性の devilish, diabolical(悪魔のような).
‖魔性の女 a femme fatale (男を破滅させる妖婦) ; a seductive woman (男を惑わす女性).

ましょうめん 真正面 ▶打球は真正面で捕れ Try to catch the ball *just in front of you*. ‖ 真正面の建物が本社です The building *right ahead of us* is our home office. ‖ この問題は真正面から取り組むべきだ You should tackle this problem *head-on*.

まじりけ 混じり気 ▶混じりけのないコシヒカリ *100%* Koshihikari rice.

まじる 交じる・混じる **1**【2つ以上のものが混合する】mix《with》; blend(境界がわからないくらいに) ▶水と油は混じらない Water and oil *do not mix*. ／Oil *does not mix* [*blend*] *with* water. ‖ このごはん, 小石が混じってるよ *There are* some pebbles *mixed in* with this rice. ‖ この布地は30パーセントのポリエステルが混じって(＝入って)いる This cloth *contains* thirty percent polyester.
▶英語が交じったたどたどしい日本語 broken Japanese *mixed* with English words ‖ 彼の髪には少し白いものが交じっている His hair *is* lightly *streaked with* gray. (➤「白くしまになっている」の意).
2【仲間に加わる】join ＋目 ▶私は群衆に交じってパレードを見た I *joined* the crowd and watched the parade. ‖ 妹は男の子たちに交じって(＝と一緒に)野球をした My sister played baseball *with* the boys. ／My sister *joined* the boys who were playing baseball.

まじわり 交わり →交際.

まじわる 交わる cross (＋目), intersect (＋目) (➤後者は前者より堅い語) ▶ブロードウェーと 7 番街が交わる所がタイムズスクエアだ Times Square lies where Broadway and Seventh Avenue *intersect* [*cross each other*].
▶悪い友だちと交わる(＝交際する)な Don't *keep* bad *company*.

マシンガン a machine gun(機関銃).

¹ます 鱒《魚》a trout /traʊt/ ▶マス釣りに行く go *trout-fishing*.
‖ニジマス a rainbow trout ‖ ヒメマス a kokanee /koʊkǽni/.

²ます 升・枡 **1**【計量器】a wooden box used to measure grain or liquid ; a measure (box) ▶一合ます a one-*go measure*.
2【ます形】▶原稿用紙のますを埋める fill out the *squares* on Japanese manuscript paper.
‖ます席 a box (seat) ‖ ます目 a (square) grid.

³ます 増す increase /ɪnkríːs/ (数量・程度などが[を]) ; gain (速力・高度・力などが[を]) ; multiply ＋目 (数量・問題・危険などが[を]) ▶集中力を増す *increase* (one's) power of concentration ‖ ジェット・コースターはしだいに速さを増した The roller coaster *gathered*

[*picked up*] speed. ‖ 飛行機は**高度を増した** The plane *gained altitude*. ‖ あの歌手は人気が**増してきた** That singer *has been gaining* [*growing*] in popularity.
▶麻薬を常用するようになると問題が**増す**だけだ Taking drugs will *multiply* your problems. ‖ その詩で彼の名声はさらに**増した** The poem further *enhanced* his reputation. (➤ enhance は「価値や魅力を高める」) ‖ 雨で川の**水かさが増した** The river *has risen* after the rain. ‖ 共通の趣味をもっとわかって彼女への**親しみが増した** After I found that she and I had the same interest(s), I *felt closer to* her.
▶3分**増す**ごとに10円払わなければならない We have to pay 10 yen for each *additional* three minutes. (➤ additional は「追加の」).

まず **1**【最初に】**first, first of all** ▶まず，一人ずつ自己紹介をしましょう *First of all* [*For starters*], let's introduce ourselves. (➤ for starters はインフォーマルな言い方) ‖ まず本田君の意見を聞こう Let's hear your opinion *first*, Honda. ‖ 博多駅に着いたらまず電話をちょうだい Please call me (*the*) *first thing* when [after] you arrive at Hakata Station. (➤ 副詞的用法で the をつけないのがふつう).
2【だいたいのところ】**probably**(たぶん)；**almost**(ほとんど) ▶きょういっぱいまず雨は降らないだろう We *probably* won't have rain (all day) today. ‖ 彼が回復することはまずあるまい The *possibility* of his recovery *is very slim*. ‖ 私の勘にまず間違いはありません I'm *almost* [*pretty*] sure my hunch is right.

ますい 麻酔 **anesthesia** /ænəsθíːʒə/ ▶人に**麻酔をかける** put a person under *anesthesia* ／anesthetize a person ‖ **麻酔**は1時間で切れた The *anesthesia* wore off in an hour. ‖ **全身麻酔**をかけられて腹膜炎の手術を受けた I had an operation for peritonitis under *general anesthesia*. (➤「局部麻酔」は local anesthesia).
‖**麻酔医** an anesthetist /ənésθətəst/ ‖ **麻酔薬** an anesthetic.

まずい **1**【おいしくない】**bad, not good；unappetizing**(食欲をそそらない) ▶このコーヒーはまずい This coffee *doesn't taste good* [*tastes bad*]. (➤「まずい！」と言うときのインフォーマルな語に Yuck(y)！がある) ‖ 社長の退屈なスピーチで**食事がまずくなった** The president's boring speech *has spoiled* our dinner. (➤ spoil は「台なしにする」).
2【へたな】**poor；sloppy**(いい加減な，ぞんざいな) ▶彼はまずい字を書く He has *poor* [*sloppy*] handwriting. ／His handwriting is *poor*. ‖ まずい言い訳だね What a *poor* [*lame*] excuse!
3【不都合な，不適切な】**wrong；awkward**(問題などがやっかいな) ▶まずい時に帰って来たね．お父さんが怒っているよ You've come home at the *wrong* time. Dad's angry with you. (➤「ちょうどいい時に」は at the right time).
▶ぼく，まずいこと(＝よくないこと)言ったみたいだね I seem to have said *the wrong thing*. ‖ この事件が表沙汰になってはまずい It would *be awkward* if this matter were known to the public. ／We'll *be in a* (*tight*) *spot* if news of this incident leaks out. (➤ in a (tight) spot で「ひどく困って」の意のインフォーマルな言い方).
▶まずいこと(＝軽率なこと)言っちゃった．ごめんね．I spoke *out of turn*, and I am sorry. ‖ 彼が暴力に訴えたのはまずかった It *was unwise* [*stupid*] of him to have resorted to violence. ‖ きみと一緒のところを誰かに見られたらまずいよ *It would be awkward* [*It wouldn't be a good idea*] *to* be seen with you. ‖
対話「あした遊びに来いよ」「あしたはちょっとまずいんだ」"Why don't you come and see me tomorrow?" "Sorry, I *can't make it* tomorrow [tomorrow's *not good* for me]."

マスカット a **muscat** /mʌ́skət/.

マスカラ **mascara** /mæskǽrə/ ▶マスカラをつける apply [put on] *mascara* (to one's eyelashes).

マスク a **mask** ▶酸素マスク an oxygen *mask* ‖ 白い外科用マスクをした医師 a doctor *in a* white surgical *mask* ‖ 杉山先生は花粉症なので春先はいつもマスクをしている Mr. Sugiyama always wears *a mask* in early spring because of his pollen allergy.
▶その俳優は甘いマスク(＝顔)をしている The actor is *good looking* [has *good looks*].

マスクメロン a **muskmelon**.

マスゲーム **mass gymnastic exercises**(➤ しばしば複数形で用いる；「マスゲーム」は和製語).

マスコット a **mascot** /mǽskɑːt/ ▶この人形はうちのチームのマスコットだ This doll is our team's *mascot*.

マスコミ **mass communications；the (mass) media**(報道機関；→マスメディア) ▶息子は将来マスコミで働きたがっている My son wants to work in (the field of) *mass communications* in the future. ‖ 彼女の自殺はマスコミを大いに騒がせた Her suicide attracted considerable attention from *the* (*mass*) *media*.

> **危ないカタカナ語✹ マスコミ**
> 「マスコミ」は「マスコミュニケーション」の省略．日本語では「マスコミの暴力」のような使い方をするが，この場合の「マスコミ」はラジオ，テレビ，新聞などの報道機関を指しているので the (mass) media を用いるべきである．mass communications は「(大衆への)情報伝達」という概念を表すことば．→ロコミ．

まずしい 貧しい **poor** ▶**貧しい**国 a *poor* country ‖ **貧しい**人 a *poor* person ‖ **貧しい人々** *the poor* ／*needy people* ‖ 彼は**貧しい家に生まれた**のでよい教育が受けられなかった He *was born poor* [*was born into a poor family*], so he was unable to get a good education. ‖ 島民は**貧しい暮らしをしている** The islanders *live in poverty*. ‖ 昔の芸術家の多くは**貧しい生活に耐えなければならなかった** In the past, most artists had to endure *a life of poverty*.
▶私の中国語の語いはきわめて**貧しい** My vocabulary in Chinese is quite *poor* [*meager*].

マスター **1**【バーなどの】a **manager** (経営者)；an **owner**, a **proprietor** /prəpráɪəṭəʳ/ (所有者) ▶正木さんはあのバーのマスターです Mr. Masaki is the *manager* [*owner* ／*owner and manager*] of that bar. (➤ 最後は経営者であり，オーナーでもある場合).

> **危ないカタカナ語✹ マスター**
> **1**「(バー・喫茶店などの)マスター」に相当するのは manager, owner, proprietor などであるが，あとの2語が所有者自身を指すのに対して，manager は他人に雇われているマスターにも用いる．英語の master は「(動物，特に犬の)飼い主」「(奴隷の)主人」「修士」などの意．
> **2** 客が「マスター」と呼びかける場合は，Excuse me, sir [Mr. ...]！のように言うか，親しい間柄であればファーストネームを用いる．

2【熟達する】**一動** **マスターする** **master** ＋目 (完全

に身につける）; **learn** +⽬（習得する）▶ゲームのルールをマスターする *master* the rules of a game ‖ 私は英語をマスターしたい I want to *become fluent* [*proficient*] in English. ／I want to become a good English speaker.

直訳の落とし穴「英語をマスターする」
「英語をマスターする」は日常生活で困らない程度に英語を身につけることにもいうが，英語の master は何不自由なく完全に使いこなせるレベルの知識・技術の習熟を指す．したがって，「ニュージーランドに滞在している間に英語をマスターしたい」は（×）I want to master ... ではなく，I want to improve [brush up] my English during my stay in New Zealand. など「上達する」（improve）や「やり直して磨きをかける」（brush up）が適当．単に，「勉強して習得する」という意味ならば learn English である．

3【修士】Master ▶彼は電子工学のマスターコースを終了した He completed his *Master's degree* in electronics.

‖**マスターキー** a master key ‖ **マスタークラス** a master class ‖ **マスターテープ** a master tape ‖ **マスタープラン** a master plan.

マスタード **mustard.**

マスターベーション **masturbation** 一動 **マスターベーションする** **masturbate** ／**do masturbation.**

マスト a **mast** ▶ 3本マストの帆船 a sailing ship with three *masts* ／a three-*masted* sailing ship.

マスプロ **mass production**（大量生産）

‖**マスプロ教育** conveyor-belt [assembly-line] education ‖ **マスプロ大学** a mass-production university, a university that churns out graduates（➤ churn out は「…を粗製乱造する」）.

ますます 益々

《解説》（1）「だんだん，しだいに」の意は「比較級 + and ＋比較級」で表す．
（2）「これまで以上に，さらに」の意は，「比較級＋ than ever」で表す．
（3）「…であればあるほどますます」は「the ＋比較級，the ＋比較級」で表す．
（4）「それだけますます」は「all the ＋比較級」で表す．all は強めるための語．

▶ますます暗くなってきた It is getting *darker and darker*. ‖ 事態はますます悪化している Things are getting *worse and worse*. ／Things are *going from bad to worse*. ‖ アリサは最近ますますきれいになった Arisa has become *even more beautiful* recently.（➤ この even は「さらに」の意で比較級を強める；下の文型を使って，Arisa is more beautiful than ever these days. とすることもできる．これを more beautiful than before と before にすると，以前との対比を表すので，以前はきれいとは言えなかった，というニュアンスになってしまう）.

【文型】
前よりますます…だ
比較級＋ than ever
increasingly ＋原級
《解説》 ever は「これまで」の意なので，「**比較級＋ than ever**」は「これまで以上に，ますます」に当たる．

▶サッカーは（前以上に）ますます人気だ Soccer is *more popular than ever*. ／ Soccer is *increasingly* popular. ‖ 花粉症はますますありふれたものになってきている Pollen allergy is becoming *increasingly* common. ‖ 日中関係はますます重要になってきている Japan-China relations have become *more* important *than ever* [*increasingly* important].

▶実情を聞けば聞くほどますます心配になった *The more* I hear about the actual state of affairs, *the more* worried I become. ‖ 山の上の方に登れば登るほどますます寒くなる *The higher* you go up a mountain, *the colder* it gets. ‖ 健康的な日焼けで彼女はますます魅力的になった Her healthy tan makes her *all the more* attractive.

✉ **貴社のますますのご発展とご繁栄をお祈りします** My best wishes for your company's *future growth and prosperity*.

まずまず ▶まずまずの値段 a *reasonable* price ‖ 当日の天気はまずまずだった The weather was *not bad* [was *fairly good*] that day. ‖ **対話**「景気はどうですか」「まずまずです」"How's business going?" "*Can't complain.* ／*Pretty good.* ／*OK.* ／*Not bad.*"（➤ Can't complain. は文頭に I が省略されており，「不平は言えない」が原義．この場合 So-so. と言うとあまりよくないというニュアンスになる）.

マスメディア **the mass media** ▶マスメディアを通じて大宣伝する advertise extensively through *the mass media*.

マズルカ《音楽》a **mazurka.**

まぜあわせる 混ぜ合わせる **mix** ▶小麦粉と卵をボウルに入れ，よく混ぜ合わせてください Put the flour and eggs into a bowl and *mix* well.

まぜかえす 混ぜ返す →混ぜっ返す.

まぜこぜ a **jumble**（ごちゃ混ぜ）▶おもちゃ箱にはいろいろなおもちゃがまぜこぜになっていた Many different toys were *all jumbled up* in the toy box.

まぜごはん 混ぜご飯 cooked rice mixed with vegetables and fish or meat（➤ 説明的な訳）.

まぜっかえす 混ぜっ返す ▶彼は人の話を混ぜっ返す癖がある He often *confuses* people when they are talking. ／He often *makes people lose their train of thought* (when they are talking) *by joking too much*.

まぜもの 混ぜ物 a **mixture**（混合物）; an **adulterant** /ədʌ́ltərənt/（不純物）; an **additive**（添加物）.

ませる 一形 **ませた** **precocious** /prɪkóʊʃəs/ ▶あの子は年の割にませている That child *is precocious*. ‖ あの女の子はませた（＝おとなのような）口のきき方をする That girl talks *like a grown-up*.

まぜる 交ぜる・混ぜる **mix** +⽬; **combine** +⽬（結合させる）; **blend** +⽬（混ぜて新しい色・味を出す）; **stir** +⽬（かき混ぜる）▶ボウルにバターと砂糖と卵を入れてよく混ぜなさい Put butter, sugar, and eggs in a bowl and *mix* well. ‖ 赤と青を混ぜると紫が作れる If you *combine* [*blend*] red and blue, you'll get purple. ／Purple is made by *combining* [*blending*] red and blue. ‖ このコーヒーは何種類の豆を混ぜて作るのですか How many kinds of beans do you *blend* to make this coffee?

▶トランプを交ぜる *mix up* [*shuffle*] cards ‖ 麻を交ぜた絹 silk *interwoven* with linen.

▶卵をよく混ぜる *beat* an egg thoroughly ‖ シチューは弱火にかけてときどき混ぜます Put the stew on a low flame and *stir* it from time to time.

-ませんか **1【疑問】**▶ボールペンか何かお持ちではありませんか *Do you* (happen to) have a ball-point pen or something to write with？（➤ happen to を用いるほうがより丁寧になる）‖ おけがはありませんか *Did you* get hurt？

あなたの英語はどう響く？
「彼女の住所を知りませんか」を *Don't you* know her address？とすると，「あなた，知らないんですか」「知ってなきゃ困るでしょ」といった響きをもつのがふつう．この場合は Do you …？がよい．これは日本語では「…を知ってますか」とも「…を知りませんか」とも言うところから生じる食い違いである．

2【勧誘】**How about … ?** ▶ 対話「今夜映画を見に行きませんか」「悪くないね」"*How about* going to the movies tonight？" "Not a bad idea." ‖ 対話「私たちの学園祭に来ませんか」「ぜひ行きたいです」"*Would you like to* come to our school festival？" "I'd love to."

マゾ ‖ **マゾヒズム** masochism /mǽsəkizəm/ ‖ **マゾヒスト** a masochist /mǽsəkist/.

[1]**また 股** a **crotch** ▶このズボンはまたのところが少しきつい These pants are a little tight in *the crotch.* ▶《慣用表現》森田さんは**世界をまたにかけて**活躍している Ms. Morita is active *all over the world.*

[2]**また 又** **1**【複数回繰り返して】**again**（再び）；**another**（もう１つの）▶またかぜをひいてしまった I've caught cold *again.* ／I have caught *another* cold. ‖ あの交差点でまた事故があった There has been *another* accident at that intersection. ‖ どうぞまたいらしてください Please come *again.* ‖ いずれまたお伺いします I'd like to visit [call on] you *again* some other time [day]. ‖《店で》また（今度）にします I'll come *another day.* ‖ **またのお越し**をお待ちしております Please *come again.* ‖ **またのご来店**をお待ちしております We are looking forward to serving you *again in the future.* ‖ **また会いましたね** So we meet *again.* ‖ きょうはお忙しいようなので，**また後日**伺います You look busy today. I'll come back *again some other day.* → **またまた**.

直訳の落とし穴「じゃ，また」
(1)「また」＝again なので，別れ際の「じゃ，また」を See you again. だと思って使う人がいる．これは日本語の「また会いましょう」に似て，すぐにはまた会えそうもない人，会えたらいいなと思っている人に向かって言う．同じニュアンスでは See you around. ともいう．会いたい気持ちをもう少し積極的に出すには See you soon. という．いっぽう，ふだん付き合っている友人に対して，あとで，または後日，また会うことがわかっているときの言い方は I'll see you !, (I'll) be seeing you !, See you (later) ! などである．会える日時がはっきりしているときは，See you tonight [on Monday].（じゃあ今夜［月曜日に］）のように具体的に言う．
(2) また，「じゃ，またあす」のつもりで「あす会いましょう」を（×）Let's see tomorrow. などという人がいる．「人に会う」という意味の see には「人に」に当たる語が必要．See you tomorrow. または Let's meet tomorrow. とする．「我々はよく日曜日に会う」も（×）We often see on Sundays. は不可で，We often see each other on Sundays. とする．

2【同様に】**too, also**（➤ 後者はやや堅い語）▶これもまた珍しい切手ですね This is a rare stamp, *too.* ‖ 確かに彼の言うことにもまた一理ある I have no doubt he *also* has a good point.

3【別の事がらを列挙して】▶斎藤茂吉は歌人であり，また医者でもあった Saito Mokichi was *both* a poet *and* a doctor. ‖ 彼女は昼間は会社で働き，夜はまた大学に通っている She studies at a college in the evenings *besides* [*in addition to*] working in an office during the day.
▶私はきみの言い訳なんか聞きたくないし，また聞く暇もないね I don't want to hear your excuses, *nor* do I have time to do so.

4【重なることを示して】▶一人また一人とその村から若者がいなくなる *One* young person *after another* is leaving the village. ‖ 行く手には山また山が続いている We have to go over *one* mountain *after another.*

5【感情を強調して】▶何でまたあんなへんぴな所に土地を買ったんだい？ *Why on earth* [*in the world*] did you buy land in such a remote place？

まだ **1**【予定の段階・状態に至っていない】**not … yet**（まだ…でない）；**never**（一度も…ない）▶彼女からの返事の手紙がまだ来ない Her letter of reply *hasn't* arrived *yet.* ／Her letter of reply *still hasn't* arrived.（➤ 否定文では still は not よりも前にくる．not … yet よりも強意でしばしばいらだちや驚きを表す．実際に来るかどうかもわからない，という含みがある）‖ 対話「昼飯は食べたの？」「いや，まだです」"Have you had lunch？" "(No,) *not yet.*" ‖ 対話「もういいかい」「まあだだよ」"Are you ready？" "(No,) *not yet.*"
▶私はまだ（＝一度も）雪を見たことがない I have *never* seen snow. ‖ 私はまだ17歳です I'm *only* [*just*] seventeen.

2【ある状態がずっと続いている】**still** ▶彼はまだ寝ている He is *still* in bed. ‖ きみ，まだいたの？ Are you *still* here？ ‖ ヤクルトスワローズがまだリードしているよ The Swallows are *still* in the lead. ‖ 新製品に関して今の所まだ苦情はない I haven't received any complaints about the new product *so far* [*to date* ／*as yet*].（➤ as yet は主に否定文で使う）.

3【ある状態に至るには余地がある】**still**；**only**（やっと）▶映画が始まるまでにまだ30分ある We *still* have 30 minutes before the movie starts. ‖ おやつはまだいくらか残っている There are *still* some snacks left. ‖ チャンスはまだあるさ You'll have *another* chance.（➤ another は「もう１つの」）‖ まだ９時になったばかりだ It's *only* nine o'clock. ‖ 対話「疲れちゃったよ」「あら，だってまだ20分しか歩いてないじゃないの」"I'm beat." "Really？ We've been walking (for) *only* twenty minutes."

4【さらに付け加える】▶事故の原因はまだほかにもある There are some *other* causes of the accident.

5【比較して少しは良い】▶負けるより引き分けのほうがまだましだ A draw is *better* than a loss. ‖ 英語の点数は数学よりまだましだった I did poorly in math, and only *a little better* in English.

まだい 真鯛《魚》a **red sea bream.**

またいとこ a **second cousin.**

またがし 又貸し a **sublease**（土地・部屋などの）一動 **また貸しする sublet** ＋目，**sublease** ＋目 ▶去年の夏休み，友人にアパートをまた貸しした I *sublet* [*subleased*] my apartment to a friend of mine during the last summer vacation.

またがり 又借りする **sublease** ＋目，**borrow … secondhand.**

またがる 跨がる **1**【乗る】**straddle** ＋目，**sit astride** ▶塀にまたがって座る sit *straddling* a fence ‖ 馬にまた

がる *straddle* a horse ／ *sit astride* a horse.

2【広がる】stretch, extend ▶関東平野は１都６県にまたがっている The Kanto Plain *stretches* [*extends*] *over* Tokyo and much of the six adjoining prefectures.

またぎき 又聞き secondhand information（間接情報）▶この話はまた聞きだから，本当かどうかはわからない I *heard* this *secondhand* [This is *secondhand information*], so I'm not sure whether it's true or not.

またぐ 跨ぐ step over [**across**]；**stride over** [**across**]（大またで）▶ぼくのプラモデルをまたぐな Don't *step over* my plastic model.

▶《慣用表現》二度とこの家の敷居をまたがせないからな I'll *never let* you *set foot on my property* [*in my house*] again. ／I'll see to it that you *never darken my door* again.（➤ darken one's door は「玄関口に立って暗くする」が原義）.

またした 股下《主に米》an **inseam**,《主に英》an **inside leg** ▶股下75 cm のジーンズ a pair of jeans with a 75 cm *inseam* [*inside leg*].

ま

またしても 又しても yet again ▶巨人はまたしてもヤクルトに負けた The Giants were beaten by the Swallows *yet again*.

まだしも ▶父さんたら，傘だけならまだしもかばんまで電車の中に忘れてきた *As if* forgetting his umbrella *wasn't enough*, Dad had to go and leave his briefcase on the train as well.（➤「まるで…するのが十分でないかのように」の意）.

またせる 待たせる keep ... waiting ▶長い間お待たせしてすみません I'm sorry to *have kept* [*to keep*] you *waiting* so long. ‖タクシーを待たせてありますからすぐ失礼します Since I *have* a taxi *waiting* for me, I have to leave right away.

またぞろ ▶与党内ではまたぞろ内輪もめをしている They're having *yet another* squabble within the ruling party.（➤ yet another は「さらにもう１つ別の」）.

またたく 瞬く flicker, blink（光が）；**twinkle**（星が）▶遠くで明かりがまたたいていた A light *was flickering* [*blinking*] in the distance. ‖シリウスが東の空にまたたいている Sirius *is twinkling* in the eastern sky.

またたくまに 瞬く間に in an instant ▶火はまたたく間にホテル全館に広がった The fire spread through the entire hotel *in an instant* [*in the twinkling of an eye*]. ‖携帯電話は多くの人にとってまたたく間に必需品となった The cellphone became a must-have for many people *in no time*.（➤ in no time は「時を置かずに，すぐに」の意）.

またとない 又とない ▶これはまたとないチャンスだ It's *the chance of a lifetime*. ／It's *a golden opportunity*. ‖この絵の静かな美しさはまたとない（＝匹敵するものがない）ものだ The tranquil beauty of this painting is *unparalleled* [*unequaled* ／*unmatched*].

マタニティ maternity（妊婦のための）（➤「妊婦」という意味はない）.

‖マタニティドレス maternity clothes, a maternity dress.

またのな 又の名 ▶中村次郎吉またの名をねずみ小僧次郎吉 Nakamura Jirokichi, *also known as* Nezumikozo Jirokichi（➤ also known as は a.k.a., aka と略記されることも多い）.

または 又は (either) A or B（➤ either を入れたほうが強意）▶コンサートのお申し込みはインターネットまたはお電話でどうぞ Order your concert ticket online *or* by phone. ‖息子または私が間違いなくお支払いいたします *Either* my son *or* I will pay for it, I assure you.（➤ either A or B が主語になった場合，動詞は B に一致させるのが原則）.

またまた ▶打ち合わせがまたまた延期になった The meeting was postponed *yet again*. ‖またまたお会いしましたね Our paths seem to cross *often*, don't they？

まだまだ still ▶あいつはまだまだひよっこだ He's (*still*) wet behind the ears.（➤ wet behind the ears は「(まだ)青二才だ」の意）‖おみやげひとつでだまされるなんて，あの子まだまだ子供だね Being taken in by a single gift shows he's *still* a child. ‖まだまだ夜はこれからだ The night's *only just* begun. ／The night's *still* young. ‖**対話**「降参か？」「まだまだ」"Are you ready to give up [cry uncle]？" "*I'm not even close* (to giving up)." ‖**対話**「きみ，ずいぶん英語が伸びたね」「ありがとうございます．でも，まだまだです」"You've made a lot of progress in English so far." "Thank you, but I (*still*) *have a long way to go*."

マダム madam（➤ Ⓤ 扱いで女性への呼びかけに用いる）‖有閑マダム a rich [wealthy] woman of leisure.

またもや 又もや again ▶またもや山本氏が当選した Mr. Yamamoto won the election *again*. ‖妹はまたもや事故を起こしてしまった．免許を取って以来３度目だ My (younger) sister had *yet another* car accident. That's her third since she got her driver's license.

まだら 斑 a **spot**；a **speckle**（皮膚のはん点）▶まだらのシカ a *speckled* deer ‖白黒まだらの犬を飼っている I have a *black and white* dog.

まだるっこい slow（のろい）；**roundabout**（まわりくどい）▶祖母の話し方はまだるっこい My grandmother is *slow* of speech. ‖まだるっこい言い方はやめてずばり要点を言ってくれ Stop talking in such a *roundabout* way [Don't beat around the bush] and get to the point.（➤ beat around the bush は「遠回しに言う」）‖**対話**「つまり，ええと，何と言うか」「まだるっこいなあ！」"In other words ..., well, what can I say ..." "*Get to the point!*"（➤「要点を言え」の意）.

まち 町・街 a **town**（町）；a **city**（市）；a **street**（通り）

> **《解説》**(1)**town** は village より大きく，**city** より小さい自治体を指すが，会話では town と city に厳密な区別は見られない．また town は繁華街（downtown）の意味でも用いられる．
> (2)**street** は「にぎやかな通り」の意味で用いる．
> (3)手紙などのあて名の「－町」は「－市」と同じように -machi でよい．

▶両親は東京の近くの小さな町に住んでいます My parents live in a small *town* [*city*] near Tokyo. ‖町中の人が彼のことを知っている *The whole town* has heard of him. ‖街へ行って楽しくやろう Let's *go to town* [*go downtown*] and enjoy ourselves.（➤ town は話し手の住んでいる町やその付近の特定の町を指す場合は Ⓤ 扱い）.

▶八王子は今や学生の街になった Hachioji has become *a student town* now. ‖池袋は大衆的なショッピングと歓楽の街だ Ikebukuro is a popular shopping and entertainment *district*.（➤ この district は「(小)地域」の意）.

▶きのう街で恩師に会った I met a former teacher of mine *on the street* yesterday. ‖ ウインドーショッピングをしながら三宮の街を歩いた I walked along *the streets* in [of] Sannomiya window-shopping.
‖**町医者** a general practitioner《略 G.P.》‖**町役場** a town [city] office ; a town [city] hall（建物）.

-まち -待ち ▶キャンセル待ち *waiting* for a cancellation ‖ 空き席待ち *waiting* for an available table ‖ 三か月待ち a three-month *wait*.

まちあいしつ 待合室 a **waiting room** ▶待合室でお待ちください Please have a seat in the *waiting room*.

まちあぐむ 待ち倦む ▶原宿駅で彼女を待ちあぐみ（＝待ち切れずに），私は家に帰った I could*n't stand waiting* for her any longer at Harajuku Station, so I came home.

まちあわせる 待ち合わせる meet ＋目（会う）; **wait for**（待つ）▶私たちは８時に新宿駅西口で待ち合わせている We are to *meet* at the west entrance of Shinjuku Station at eight. ‖ 彼女はだれかと待ち合わせているらしい She seems to *be waiting for* somebody.

まちうける 待ち受ける ▶過酷な運命が主人公を待ち受けていた A cruel fate *awaited* the hero.（➤ await は wait for の堅い言い方）‖**待ち受け画面** an idle screen, a standby screen.

まぢか 間近に **1【時間的に】near** ▶期末試験が間近だ The final exams *are approaching* [*are around the corner*]. ‖ 息子の結婚式の日が間近に迫った The day of our son's wedding *is coming up* (*soon*).（➤ be coming up (soon) は大事な行事やめでたい行事に関して用いる）.

2【距離的に】close /kloʊs/《to, by》▶本物のシャチをこんなに間近で見るのは初めてだ This is the first time for me to see real killer whales *close-up* [*at close range*] like this. ‖ 彼は学校の間近に住んでいる He lives *close to* [*by*] the school.

まちがい 間違い

1【誤り】 a **mistake**, an **error** /érəʳ/

> **《解説》mistake** は不注意や思い違いなどに起因する間違いをいうことが多く，非難のニュアンスは少ない．それは，We all make mistakes. または Everybody makes mistakes.（間違いは誰にでもある）という表現にも表れている．これに対して，**error** は正解・基準・道徳などからはずれた誤りや判断の誤りをいうことが多く，非難のニュアンスがある．

▶試験で大きな間違いをした I made a big *mistake* [*error*] on an examination. ‖ つづりの間違いをする *make a* spelling *mistake* [*error*] ‖ 先生は私の英語の手紙の間違いを直してくださった My teacher corrected the *mistakes* in my English letter. ‖ きみの計算には間違いがたくさんあったよ I found a lot of *errors* in your calculations. ‖ 私の記憶に間違いがなければ（＝記憶が正確ならば），彼は平泳ぎの日本記録を持っていた人だ *If I remember correctly* [*right*], he held the Japan record for the breaststroke.
▶**対話**「だれから？」「間違い電話よ」"Who was that?" "It was *a wrong number*."

2【失敗，勘違い】 a **mistake** ▶間違いから多くのことを学んだ I've learned a lot from my *mistakes*. ‖ この学部を選んだのは大間違いだった．向いてないんだ Choosing this school was *a big mistake*. I don't belong here [I don't fit in here]. ‖ 私の援助を当てにしているのなら大きな間違いだよ If you're relying on me to help you out, you'*re making a big mistake*. ‖ あの監督が誘拐犯だなんて，何かの間違いでしょう That coach is a kidnapper? It must be *some kind of mistake*.
▶あいつを信用したのが間違い（の元）だった It was *a mistake* to have trusted him.

3【事故，事件】 ▶由里子がまだ帰らない．間違いでもなければいいが Yuriko has not come home yet. I hope nothing has happened.

4【「間違いなく」「間違いない」の形で】 ▶彼が来るのはほぼ間違いない *It is* almost *certain that* he will come. ／He will almost *certainly* come. ‖ 田中投手が今シーズンも活躍することは間違いない *I'm sure* the pitcher Tanaka will perform well again this season.（➤「確信している」の意）‖ 彼はもうじき横綱になるよ．間違いないよ He'll be yokozuna before long, *make no mistake about it* [*that's for sure*].（➤ 前者のほうが強意）‖ あの弁護士さんなら間違いない（＝信頼できる）You can't go wrong with that lawyer. ／That lawyer is really a *reliable* person. ‖ 間違いなくこのお金を持ち主に返してくださいね Please *be sure to* return this money to the rightful owner.

5【「…間違い」の形で】 ▶書き [言い] 間違い *a slip of the pen* [*the tongue*] ／*a mistake in writing* [*speaking*] ‖ きみの答案には計算間違いが多過ぎるね Your answer sheet is full of *miscalculations*. ‖
対話「きみのお父さんはたしかお医者さんだったよね」「あら，弁護士よ」「じゃ，ぼくの聞き間違いだ」"Your father is a doctor, isn't he?" "No, he is an attorney." "Oh, I guess I *misheard* (you)."
☛ **大間違い**（→見出語）

まちがう 間違う make a mistake [**an error**] ; **be wrong**（まちがっている）▶間違った答えを出す give an *incorrect* [*a wrong*] answer ‖ 名医でも診断を間違うことがある Even an experienced doctor sometimes *makes a mistake* in diagnosis [makes an incorrect diagnosis]. ‖ きみの考えは間違っている You'*re wrong* to think like that. ／Your thinking (about that) *is wrong*. ‖ 彼女を責めるのは間違っている You *are wrong* [*It is wrong* of you] to blame her.
✉ **（通信販売で）デニムのジャケットを注文しましたが，間違った商品が送られてきました** I ordered a denim jacket, but you sent me the *wrong item*.
☛ **間違っても**（→見出語）

まちがえやすい 間違え易い ▶この問題は間違えやすい This question *is easy to get wrong*. ‖ 浦和じゃなくて南浦和で降りるのよ．わかった？ 間違えやすいから気をつけて Get off at Minami-Urawa, not Urawa, OK? They'*re easy to confuse* (*with each other*), so be careful.

まちがえる 間違える

1【誤りを犯す】make a mistake, err /əːʳ/（➤ err は堅い語）▶英語の試験で２か所間違えた I *made* two *mistakes* on the English exam. ／I *got* two questions *wrong* on the English exam. ‖ 漢字を間違えて書いてしまった I *made a mistake* writing the kanji. ／I wrote the kanji *incorrectly*. ‖ その店員はつり銭を間違えた The clerk gave me the *wrong* change. ‖ 道を間違えて約束に遅れてしまった I took the *wrong* street and was late for my appointment.

ま

▶《電話で》すみません，間違えました I'm sorry. I must have the *wrong* number.（➤くだけた言い方で Sorry, wrong number. とだけ言うこともある）‖間違えるのが人間だ It is natural for people to *make mistakes*. ／To *err* is human.（➤後者は「過つは人の常」に相当する堅い言い方）.

2【取り違える】

【文型】
AをBと間違える
mistake A **for** B
take A **for** B
➤ 前者は完全な間違い，後者はしばしば「AをBと受け止める」

▶車を運転していた人はアクセルとブレーキを間違えたらしい It looks as if the motorist *mistook* the gas pedal *for* the brake. ‖ベトナムに住んでいたとき，兄はよくベトナム人に間違えられた My brother *was* often *mistaken for* a Vietnamese person while he was living in Vietnam. ‖彼女のきみへの優しさを愛情と間違えてはいけない You shouldn't *mistake* [*take*] her kindness toward you *for* love.
▶間違えて店員に別の店のポイントカードを渡してしまった I *mistakenly* handed the clerk another store's loyalty card. ／I handed the clerk the *wrong* loyalty card. ‖先生はよくその双子のきょうだいを間違える The teacher often *gets* the twins *confused*.

まちがっても 間違っても ▶間違ってもおじさんの前でがんだなんて言ってはいけないよ *Whatever you do*, don't mention the word cancer around your uncle.

まちかど 街角 a **street corner**（曲がり角）▶街角の広告塔 a billboard at *a street corner* ‖街角（＝通り）で知らない人に呼び止められた A stranger spoke to me *on the street*.

まちかねる 待ち兼ねる ▶彼女は久しぶりに両親に会えるのを待ちかねていた She *could hardly wait* to meet her parents for the first time in a long while. ‖かわいいお嬢さんが先ほどからあちらでお待ちかねよ There's a cute young woman (who'*s been*) *waiting for* you for some time. ‖生徒たちはバスが出るのを待ちかねていた The students were *impatient* for the bus to leave.

まちかまえる 待ち構える **wait** ▶カメラマンたちは映画スターが到着ロビーに現れるのを待ち構えていた The photographers *were waiting impatiently* for the movie star to appear in the arrival lobby.

まちくたびれる 待ちくたびれる ▶子供は母親の帰りを待ちくたびれて眠ってしまった The child *got tired of waiting for* her mother (to return home) and fell asleep.

まちこうば 町工場 a **small factory (in town)** ▶下請けの町工場 *a small factory in town* doing subcontract work ／a small, subcontract factory.

まちこがれる 待ち焦がれる ▶子供たちは新しい先生に会える日を待ち焦がれていた The children *were looking forward to* the day when they would meet their new teacher.
✉ **あなたからのお手紙を待ち焦がれています** I *am dying to* hear from you. ➤「…したくてたまらない」という強い願望を表すインフォーマルな言い方.

まちじかん 待ち時間 a **wait** ▶待ち時間はどのくらいですか *How long do I need to wait?* ／*How long is the wait?* ‖この病院での平均的待ち時間は2時間だ The average *wait* at this hospital is two hours.

まちどおしい 待ち遠しい **look forward to**（➤あとに名詞または動名詞がくる）; **just can't wait**《for, to do》（待ち切れない）▶クリスマス［夏休み］が待ち遠しい I *am looking forward to* Christmas [the summer vacation]. ‖注文したパソコンが届くのが待ち遠しくてたまらない I *can hardly wait to* get the personal computer I ordered.
✉ **夏休みに家族と海に泳ぎに行くことにしていますが，待ち遠しいです** My family and I plan to go swimming in the ocean during the summer vacation. And *I* (*just*) *can't wait*.

まちなか 町中 **downtown**（繁華街）▶町中にあるコンビニ a convenience store *downtown* ／a *downtown* convenience store（➤後者は形容詞用法）.

まちなみ 町並み ▶この辺は古い町並みが残っている There still remain *some old houses* [*buildings*] around here.

まちにまった 待ちに待った ▶待ちに待った合格通知がけさ届いた This morning, I finally got the admission notice I'*d been anxiously* [*eagerly*] *waiting for*. ‖あすから待ちに待った夏休みだ The *long-awaited* summer vacation will start tomorrow.

マチネー a **matinee** /mæ̀tənéɪ ‖ mǽtɪneɪ/.

まちのぞむ（…を）**待ち望む** **wait**《for》（待つ）▶家族全員があなたの帰国の日を待ち望んでいます We all are *waiting for* you to come back [*looking forward to* your return].

まちはずれ 町外れ **the outskirts of town** ▶歴史博物館は町外れにある The history museum is *on the outskirts of town* [*at the edge of town*].

まちびと 待ち人 ▶待ち人来たらず *The person I'm waiting for hasn't come yet*.（➤「まだ来ない」）／*The person I waited for didn't come*.（➤「来なかった」）.

まちぶせ 待ち伏せ (an) **ambush** ▶明智光秀は農民の待ち伏せにあった Akechi Mitsuhide fell into the peasants' *ambush*. ‖待ち伏せするとはひきょうだぞ It was cowardly of you to *wait* [*lie*] *in ambush* for me.

まちぼうけ 待ち惚け ▶アキ子はまた私に待ちぼうけを食わせた Akiko *stood* me *up* again.（➤ stand ... up は「（デートの相手に）待ちぼうけを食わせる」の意のインフォーマルな表現）.

まちまち ▶いつから英語教育をしたらよいかについて学者の間でも意見はまちまちだ Opinions *vary* greatly among experts [Experts have *various* opinions] as to when to start English education.

まちわびる 待ち侘びる ▶彼女は息子からの便りを待ちわびていた She *eagerly waited* to hear from her son.

¹まつ 松 a **pine (tree)**
‖松かさ a pine cone ‖松飾り a New Year's pine decoration（→門松）‖松の実 pine nuts ‖松葉 pine needles ‖松林 a pine grove [forest／wood] ‖松やに pine resin, rosin.

²まつ 待つ **1【待ち受ける】** **wait**《for》

【文型】
人・物事(A)を待つ
wait for A
人(A)が…するのを待つ
wait for A **to** do

▶私は姉（が着くの）を待っているのです I'*m waiting for* my sister (*to* arrive). ‖人々は梅雨が終わるのを待っている Everyone *is waiting for* the rainy season

to end [*for* the end of the rainy season].
▶もう少し待ってください Please *wait* a little longer. ‖電話を待っているんです I'*m expecting* a phone call. (➤ be expecting は「(電話がある予定なので)待ち受けている」の意).

あなたの英語はどう響く?
(1)来客を迎えて「お待ちしていました」というとき，そのまま過去進行形で，(×)We were waiting for you. などというと客はびっくりする．英語の過去形はすでに終わったことを表すので，それはいつのこと？きのうの話？などと反応してしまう．現在までずっと待っていたのであるから，現在完了形で We've been waiting for you. とするのが正しい．ただし，この言い方は相手が予定より遅れているので待っていました，というニュアンスもあり，「楽しみに待っていました」には We've been expecting you. または，We've been looking forward to seeing you. (初対面ならば to meeting you；→楽しみ)とするのがよい．
(2)仕事上の得意先である外国人に「１時に(下の)ロビーでお待ちしております」のつもりで I'll *wait for* you at 1 o'clock (down) in the lobby. と言う人が少なくないが，これは「待ってますよ」という感じで，なれなれしく響く．客に対して丁寧に言うのであれば，未来進行形にするか see を用いて I'll *be waiting for* [I'll *see*] you at 1 o'clock (down) in the lobby. とすると「(そちらで)お待ちしていますので」という感じになり，やわらかく響く．

▶ちょっと待ってください *Wait a minute*, please. ／*Just a moment*, please. ／*Hold on* (*a moment*), please. (➤ 最後の文は電話の場合) ‖じゃあ，あした待ってるよ OK. I'll *see you* tomorrow. (➤「あした会おう」の意) ‖母は父が帰るのを毎晩寝ないで待っています My mother *waits up for* my father every night. ‖私が遅れたら待たずに行ってください In case I'm late, go on [ahead] *without me*.
▶ロシア側の出方を待ってわが国の対策を決めよう We'll *wait* to see what Russia does before deciding anything.
✉ **お便り[メール]を待っています** I'*ll be waiting for* your letter [e-mail]. ／I'*m looking forward to* hearing from you.
✉ **手紙を書いてね，待ってるわ** Please write; *I'd love to hear from you.*
2【相手の行動を中止させる】Wait! ▶こら，逃げるな．待て！ Hey, don't run away. *Wait!*
☛ 待ちに待った，待った，待てど暮らせど(→見出語)

まつえい 末えい a **descendant**.

まっか 真っ赤な (**deep**) **red**; **crimson** (深紅色の); **scarlet**(朱色を帯びた深紅色の) ▶真っ赤なドレス a *vivid* [*bright*] *red* dress ‖カエデの葉が真っ赤になった The leaves of the maple trees have turned *deep red* [*crimson*].
▶木村さんは怒って真っ赤になった Mr. Kimura *turned* [*flushed*] *red* with anger. ‖彼女は恥ずかしさのあまり真っ赤になった She *blushed scarlet* [*Her face turned as red as a beet*] with embarrassment. (➤ beet は「赤大根」) ‖彼の目は睡眠不足で真っ赤だった(＝充血していた) His eyes were *bloodshot* from lack of sleep.
▶彼は真っ赤なうそをついた He told *a downright* [*barefaced*] *lie*. ／He lied through his teeth.

まっき 末期 the end of a period; the last stage(最後の段階) 一形 (病気が)**末期の terminal** ▶江戸時代の末期に黒船が日本に来た The Black Ships came to Japan at *the end* of the Edo period.
▶末期の病気 (a) *terminal* illness ‖この患者はもうがんの末期だ This patient is in *the last* [*final*] *stage* (*s*) of cancer. (➤「末期がん」は terminal cancer, 「末期がん患者」は a person with terminal cancer とか a patient terminally ill with cancer という).
▶《比喩的》O 政権は末期症状を呈していた(＝崩壊寸前だった) The O Administration was *on the verge of collapse*.

マッキンリー マッキンリー山 Mount McKinley (アラスカにある北米大陸の最高峰．正式名称は Denali(デナリ)).

まっくら 真っ暗な pitch-dark [**-black**] ▶起きたとき，外はまだ真っ暗だった It was still *pitch-dark* outside when I woke up.
▶《慣用表現》この研究プロジェクトの見通しはお先真っ暗だ *Prospects* for this research project *are quite bleak*. ‖退職金が出ないと聞いて目の前が真っ暗になった When I heard that I would not get my retirement money, I *was stunned* [I *plunged into despair*]. (➤ 前者は「ぼう然となった」，後者は「絶望的な気持ちになった」の意. I fell into despair. としてもよい).

まっくらやみ 真っ暗やみ ▶突然の停電で一帯は真っ暗やみになった Due to a sudden power failure, the neighborhood was plunged in *total* [*complete*／*pitch*] *darkness*.

まっくろ 真っ黒な pitch-black, jet-black (漆黒の) ▶彼女の髪は真っ黒だ Her hair is *black as a raven*. (➤ raven は「ワタリガラス」で，黒くてつやのある髪の形容に用いられる) ／She has *jet-black* hair. ‖ステーキを真っ黒に焦がしてしまった I burned the steak *black*. ‖子供たちは真っ黒に日焼けして海から戻ってきた The children returned home from the beach *tanned all over* [*with dark tans*].

まつげ 睫毛 eyelashes ▶長いまつ毛の女の子 a girl with long *eyelashes*.
‖付けまつ毛 false eyelashes.

まつご 末期 one's **dying moments** ▶祖父の末期を看取った I was with my grandfather *when he died* [*at his deathbed*].

まっこうから 真っ向から ▶両親は私の冒険計画に真っ向から反対した My parents were *dead set* against my adventure plan. (➤ be dead set against で「…に絶対反対する」) ‖ランナーたちは真っ向から(＝まともに)風を受けて走らねばならなかった The runners had to run *directly* into the wind.

マッサージ (a) **massage** /məsɑ́ːʒ ‖ mǽsɑːʒ/
‖マッサージ医院 a massage clinic ‖マッサージ師 a massage therapist; a masseur /mæsə́ːʳ/ (➤ 女性は masseuse /mæsúːz/. 後者は性的サービスの連想もあるので前者を使うのが無難).

まっさいちゅう 真っ最中 ▶楽しい夢の真っ最中に雷鳴で目が覚めた *In the middle of* a pleasant dream, I was awakened by the sound of thunder. ‖ナゴヤドームに着いたときにはゲームの真っ最中だった When we arrived at Nagoya Dome, the game was *in full swing*.

まっさお 真っ青な deep blue; deathly pale (顔が死者のように青白い) ▶真っ青な空 a *deep blue* sky.
▶顔が真っ青だよ．どうしたの？ You look *very* [*deathly*] *pale*. What's the matter? ‖その知らせを聞いて彼女は真っ青になった She turned *white as a sheet* when she heard the news.

まっさかさま 真っ逆様に headfirst ▶その若い大工ははしごから真っさかさまに落ちた The young carpenter fell *headfirst* [*headlong* ／ *head over heels*] from the ladder.

まっさかり 真っ盛り ▶わが家の庭の梅は今が真っ盛りだ The *ume* blossoms in our garden are now *in full bloom* [*at their best*].
▶ここ数日まさに夏の真っ盛りだ We've been *in the height of summer* (for) the past few days.

まっさき 真っ先に ▶山本君はいつも真っ先に下校する Yamamoto is always *the first* to leave school. ‖ 父は帰宅するといつも真っ先に風呂に入る My father always takes a bath *first thing* upon arriving home.

まっさつ 抹殺する erase ＋目(消す); annihilate /ənáɪəleɪt/ ＋目(全滅させる) ▶ヒットラーはユダヤ人を地球上から抹殺しようとした Hitler tried to *annihilate* [*wipe out*] the Jews from the face of the earth. (➤ wipe out は「消す(＝殺す)」に相当するインフォーマルな表現).

まっさら 真っ新 ▶まっさらなゆかた a *brand-new* yukata.

まっしぐら ▶そのフットボール選手はボールを抱え，ゴールライン目指してまっしぐらに走った The football player rushed *straight* [*headlong*] toward the goal line with the ball.

マッシュポテト mashed potatoes.

マッシュルーム a mushroom.

[1]まっしょう 末梢 ▶そんな末梢的な事にこだわるな Don't fuss over such *trivial* things.
‖末梢神経 a peripheral nerve.

[2]まっしょう 抹消する delete ＋目 ▶会員名簿から彼の名を抹消する *delete* his name from [*cross* his name *off*] the membership list ／ *strike* his name from the membership list.

まっしょうじき 真っ正直な very honest ▶真っ正直に生きる *lead an honest life*.

まっしろ 真っ白な snow-white, pure white ▶その老人のひげは真っ白だった The old man's beard was (*as*) *white as snow*.
▶彼女の答案用紙は(何も書かず)真っ白だった Her answer sheet was *all* [*completely*] *blank*. (➤ blank は「白紙の」) ‖ 不二夫が江梨とデートしたと聞いて，ぼくは頭の中が真っ白になった When I heard Fujio had gone on a date with Eri, my *mind went blank*.

まっすぐ 真っすぐ 1【曲がっていない】straight /streɪt/ ▶まっすぐな線を引く draw a *straight* line ‖ 道はどこまでもまっすぐに伸びていた The road stretched out *straight* as far as the eye could reach. ‖ この通りをまっすぐに行くと二条城があります Go *straight* along this street, and you'll see Nijo Castle.
▶この道をまっすぐに行けばいいんですか Is it *down* this road? ‖ あの額をまっすぐに直してください Can you put that picture *straight* [*right*]? ／ Can you *straighten* that picture? ‖ 背筋をまっすぐに伸ばしなさい *Sit up* [*Stand up*] *straight*. ／Don't slouch. (➤ slouch /slautʃ/ は「前かがみになって(だらしなく)座る[立つ]」の意).
2【寄り道しないで】straight, direct(ly) ▶会議が終わったらまっすぐ空港へ向かうつもりだ I'm going *straight* [*directly*] to the airport after the meeting. ‖ 学校が終わるとまっすぐ家に帰った I went *straight* home after school.
3【正直な，自然な】straightforward(正直な，率直な); upright(高潔な) ▶彼はまっすぐな(＝正直な)人だ He is an *honest* person. ／He is an *upright* guy. ‖ この子がまっすぐに才能を伸ばしてくれるよう願っています I hope my son will develop his talent *naturally*.

まっせき 末席 ▶新人は末席に座るのが習わしだ It is customary for people with the least seniority to take *the seats furthest from that of the main guest* [to sit in *the* (*lowest status*) *seats by the door*]. (➤ 後者は「出入口のそばの(いちばん地位の低い)席」).

まった 待った ▶ちょっと待った(＝待て). きみ，今何て言った? *Wait* [*Just*] *a moment*. What did you say just now? (➤ 後半は What did you just say? と言ってもよい) ‖ 新ダムの建設計画に待ったがかかった The construction plan for the new dam *was put on hold*. (➤ put ... on hold で「…を一時的に保留する」の意).
▶日本の財政再建は待ったなしの状態だ Japan must rebuild its finances *as quickly as possible*. *There's no time to lose*.

マッターホルン the Matterhorn /mǽt̬ərhɔːrn/ (アルプスの高峰).

まつだい 末代 ▶こんな醜聞(しゅうぶん)はわが家の末代までの恥だ This scandal is an *eternal* disgrace to our family.

まったく 全く 1【完全に，全然】completely; absolutely (絶対に); not [no] ... at all(全く…でない) ▶全くおっしゃるとおりです You are *completely* correct. ／I agree with you *completely*. ‖ そんな計画は全く不可能だ The project is *absolutely* unfeasible. ‖ 彼の言ったことは全くの間違いだった What he said was *completely* [*entirely* ／ *totally*] wrong. ‖ 彼女は全くのうそつきだ She is *an out-and-out liar*. (➤「全くのうそ」は out-and-out lie) ‖ 対話「消費税を上げるべきだと思います」「全く同感です」"I think the consumption tax should be raised." "I *couldn't agree more*. ／ I *agree 100%*." ‖ 食欲が全くないんです I have *no* appetite *at all*.
▶彼女は全く問題なく英語が話せる She can speak English *without any problem* [*difficulty*] *at all*. ‖ そんなうわさのことは全く知りませんでした I did*n't* know *anything* about the rumor. ‖ 彼は全くのお調子者だ He's a *real* featherbrain.
2【ほんとうに】really ▶彼の無作法には全く困ったものだ I was *really* embarrassed by his rude behavior. ‖ 対話「きょうはすごい暑さですね」「全く」"It's really hot today." "*It sure is*."
3【怒りを示して】▶またスピード違反で捕まったのか. 全くしょうがないやつだな You were caught speeding again? You're (*completely*) impossible.

まつたけ 松茸 a *matsutake* mushroom.

まっただなか 真っ只中 ▶船はあらしの真っただ中を航行した The ship sailed *in the middle of* the storm. ‖ 私はその頃青春の真っただ中で，将来の不安など何も無かった I was then *right in the prime of my youth* and had no anxiety about the future.

まったり 1【味わいなどが】rich(豊かな); full-bodied(こくのある); mellow(まろやかな) ▶まったりしたバニラアイスクリーム *rich* vanilla ice cream ‖ まったりしたワイン a *full-bodied* wine.
2【人が】relaxed(くつろいだ); laid-back(のんびりした); mellow(角のとれた) ▶まったりした人 a person *of mellow disposition* ‖ まったりした気分でいる I am in a

relaxed mood. ‖まったりできる音楽 *relaxing* music.

まったん 末端 the end ▶幹部の意向が末端にまで伝わらなかったようだ It seems the leaders' intentions were not conveyed *all the way down the line.* ‖末端価格 1億円のヘロイン heroin with *a street price* [*value*] of one hundred million yen.

‖**末端消費者価格** an end-user [end-consumer] price, a street price [value].

1**マッチ**《火をつける道具》a **match** ▶マッチ1箱 a pack [box] of *matches* ‖マッチをする light [strike] *a match* ‖彼女はマッチでろうそくに火をつけた She lit a candle with *a match*.

‖**マッチ箱** a matchbox ‖**マッチ棒** a matchstick.

2**マッチ**《試合》a **match** ▶挑戦者はタイトルマッチに備えて猛練習をしている The challenger is practicing hard for the *title match*.

‖**マッチポイント** a match point.

3**マッチ**《調和》一動 **マッチする** **match** +目, **go well with** ▶洋服と靴をマッチさせる *match* one's shoes *with* one's dress ‖そのネクタイはあなたのスーツによくマッチしている The tie *goes well with* your suit [*matches* your suit *well*]. ‖あの茶室は庭によくマッチしている That tea-ceremony cottage *blends* [*harmonizes*] *well with* the garden.

まっちゃ 抹茶 ***matcha*** **(tea)**; **powdered green tea.**

マッチョ マッチョな **very muscular**(筋肉質の)(➤英語の macho は必要以上に男らしさを誇示する, 優しさ・繊細さに欠けるというようなマイナスイメージが強い).

マット a **mat** ▶マットで泥をよく落としなさい Scrape off the mud on the (*door*)*mat* carefully.

‖**バスマット** a bath(tub) mat.

まっとう 真っ当な **decent**(ちゃんとした); **respectable**(社会的にまともな); **honest**(正直な) ▶建築業者がまっとうであることを調べたほうがいいよ You should make sure that your builder *is on the level*.

まっとうする 全うする ▶彼は任務を全うするために全力を尽くした He did his utmost to *fulfill* his mission. ‖祖父は天寿を全うした My grandfather *lived a long life* [*died at an old age*／*died at an advanced age*].

マットレス a **mattress** ▶床にマットレスを敷く spread *a mattress* on the floor.

まつのうち 松の内 **the New Year's Week** ▶年賀のあいさつ回りは松の内にすませなさい Get your New Year's courtesy calls done *before the first seven days of the New Year are over*.

マッハ **Mach** /mɑːk/ (速度の単位) ▶マッハ2で飛行する fly at (the speed of) *Mach* 2.

まっぱだか 真っ裸の **stark naked.**

まつばづえ 松葉杖 (a **pair of**) **crutches** (➤1本は a crutch) ▶右足を骨折して, 今松葉づえで歩いてるんだ I broke my right leg and am walking *on crutches* [*on a crutch*] now.

まつび 末尾 **the end**(端, 最後); **the close** /klous/ (結末) ▶報告書の末尾に署名する put one's signature at *the end* [*close*] of a report ‖7等は宝くじ券末尾の数字が5の方です The seventh level prize winners are those whose lottery tickets *end with the number* 5.

まっぴつ 末筆

✉ **末筆ながらご両親様にくれぐれもよろしくお伝えください** *Lastly*, please give my best regards to your parents.

まっぴら 真っ平 ▶うそをつくのはまっぴらだ I *wouldn't tell a lie for anything*. ‖あんな人のお嫁さんになるなんて, まっぴらよ *There's no way* I'm marrying a man like that!

まっぴるま 真っ昼間に **in broad daylight**(白昼) ▶その銀行は真っ昼間に強盗に襲われた The bank was robbed *in broad daylight*. ‖あの野郎, 真っ昼間から酔っ払ってるよ That guy is drunk *in broad daylight*.

まっぷたつ 真っ二つ ▶その事故で機体は真っ二つに折れた The plane broke *in half* in the accident. ‖その問題をめぐってクラスの意見は真っ二つに割れた The class *split in two* over that question.

まつり 祭り a **festival**; a **fair** (➤アメリカなどで農産物・家畜などを対象とする品評会) ▶村の祭り a village *festival* ‖八幡神社のお祭りに行こうか How about going to the *festival* at the Hachiman Shrine? ‖札幌の雪祭りは2月に催される The *snow festival* in Sapporo is held in February.

✉ **ねぶたは東北地方の伝統的な夏祭りです** Nebuta is a traditional *summer festival* in the Tohoku district.

✉ **あなたの町には何か特別なお祭りはありますか** Does your town have any special *festivals*?

☛ **あとの祭り, お祭り気分, お祭り騒ぎ** (→見出語)

まつりあげる 祭り上げる ▶みんなで木村君を生徒会長に祭り上げた We *set* Kimura *up as* chairman of the student council.

まつる 祭る ▶祖先の霊を祭る *hold services for* the repose of one's ancestors' souls ‖東照宮には徳川家康が祭ってある The Toshogu Shrine *enshrines* [*is dedicated to*] Tokugawa Ieyasu.

まつろ 末路 ▶かつてのチャンピオンも末路は哀れだった The former champ's *last days* were miserable. ／The former champ died in misery. (➤後者は「困窮して死んだ」の意).

まつわりつく **follow about**(つきまとう) ▶あの子は一日中母親にまつわりついて離れない The little girl *follows* her mother *about* [*clings to* her mother] all day long. (➤cling to は「ぴったりとつく」).

まつわる 纏わる ▶この池にまつわる悲しい伝説があります There is a sad legend *about* [*associated with*] this pond.

▶マネージャーは彼女の自殺にまつわる秘密を知っているに違いない I bet her manager knows some secret *related* [*connected*] *to* her suicide.

-まで **1【時間の期限を示して】until, till**; **by** (…までには); **to**(➤from と呼応することが多い)

> **語法** (1)**until, till** は「…までずっと」の意.《米》では日常語としては until が好まれ, till ははるかに頻度が低い.《英》では till が好まれる.
> (2)「(遅くとも)…までには」という場合は **by, by the time, before** などを用いる.

▶私たちは8月の終わりまでカナダにいます We will be staying in Canada *until* the end of August. ‖彼女が来るまでもう少し待っていよう Let's wait *until* she turns up. (➤until に続く節中では未来のことでも現在形で表し, 未来形は使わない) ‖**対話**「こんなに遅くまでどこにいたの?」「映画を見てたんだ」"Where have you been *till this late*?" "I was at the movies."

▶あの書店なら朝9時から夜11時まで開いているよ That bookstore is open *from* 9 a.m. *to* 11 p.m. ‖**対話**「お店, 土曜日は何時まで開いてますか」「7時半までです」"*How late* are you open on Saturdays ?" "We're open *until* 7 : 30." ‖展覧会はあすから15日まで開かれる The exhibition will be held *from* tomorrow *through* the 15th [*from* tomorrow *until* the 15th *inclusive*]. ‖最後まで勝負をあきらめてはだめだ Don't give up your hope of winning *until the very end*.

▶《期限を示して》11時までに家に帰らないと父にしかられる My father will scold me if I don't get home *by* 11 o'clock. ‖名古屋に着くころまでには雨はやむだろう It will probably stop raining *by the time* we arrive in Nagoya. ‖夕ごはんまでには帰ります I'll be back *before* dinner. ‖現在までに30人ががれきの下から救出されています *To date* [*Up to now*] thirty people have been rescued from under the debris. (➤ 前者は「きょうまでに」, 後者は「今の瞬間までに」) ‖5年前までは私は香港駐在でした I was stationed in Hong Kong *up until* five years ago. (➤ up は強調).

✉ **3月10日までに到着の時間を知らせてください** Please let me know your arrival time [when you'll arrive] *by* March 10.

2【場所の限度を示して】to, as far as (➤ 後者には「…くらい遠くまで」と距離を強調する響きがある) ▶水戸駅まで車でお送りしましょう I'll drive you *to* Mito Station. ‖博多まで往復でください A round trip ticket *to* Hakata, please. ‖富士山は5合目までは車で行けるがそこから先は歩きだ You can drive *to* the fifth station of Mt. Fuji, but from there (up) you have to walk. ‖私たちは京都まで自転車旅行をした We rode our bicycles *to* [*as far as*] Kyoto. (➤ (×)until Kyoto としないこと. until は時間や期間の限度に用いる).

3【範囲や程度の限界を示して】(up) to ▶試験の範囲は教科書の52ページまでだ The test will cover *up to* page 52 of the textbook. ‖駐車料金は1時間までは500円です The parking fee is 500 yen for *up to* one hour. ‖きょうの授業はここまで *That's all* for today. (➤ 先生のことば) ‖ジャガイモをやわらかくなるまでゆでなさい Boil the potatoes *until* they become tender. ‖あの人の言うことはどこまでが本当だかわからない I don't know *to what extent* [*how far*] we can believe what he says. ／I can't tell *how much* of what he says is true.

▶あそこまで言うことはなかったね You shouldn't have said *that* [told them *that*]. ／You said *more than you should have* (*said*). ‖彼は私のことを卑きょう者とまで呼んだ He even *went so far as to* call me a coward.

4【強調を示して】even (…でさえ) ▶近頃は高校生までが髪を染めている *Even* some high school students have their hair dyed these days. ‖リリーフ投手まで打ち込まれてしまった *Even* the relief pitcher was knocked out.

5【その他】▶この計画については皆さんご存じですから説明するまでもないでしょう Since you are all familiar with this project, I *won't have to* explain it to you. ‖言うまでもないが反則行為をした者は退場してもらう *It goes without saying that* if you commit a foul, you will be kicked out of the game.

まてどくらせど 待てど暮らせど ▶待てど暮らせど約束の電話はかかってこなかった I *waited and waited*, but the promised call never came.

まてんろう 摩天楼 a **skyscraper**.

まと 的 1【射撃の標的】a target, a mark ▶弾丸は的に当たった[を外れた] The bullet hit [missed] the *target*.

▶《比喩的》あなたの質問は的を射ている[外れている] Your question *is to the point* [*misses the point*].

2【対象】an object ; (a) **focus** (焦点) ▶小泉さんは私たちのあこがれの的です Ms. Koizumi is the *object* of our admiration. ‖彼女はみんなの注目の的だ She's *the center of attention*. ‖大統領夫人のファッションはいつも注目の的だ The First Lady's fashions always *draw attention*. ‖赤ん坊を救出した犬は人々の賞賛の的になっている After rescuing the baby, the dog *drew* [was *the object of*] *great admiration*.

▶ **対話**「自然科学を専攻したいんです」「もう少し的を絞ったら？」"I'd like to major in natural sciences." "I suggest that you (should) *narrow* your focus (a bit)."

まど 窓 a **window** ▶開き[上げ下げ]窓 a casement [sash] *window* ‖窓を開けて[閉めて]ください Please open [shut ／ close] the *window*. ／Please raise [lower] the *window*. (➤ 後者は上下させる窓の場合) ‖バスの窓から顔や手を出してはいけません Do not stick your head or hands out (of) the *bus window*. 《参考》車内の注意書なら Caution : Keep head and hands inside the window while the bus is in motion. とか Keep your head and hands inside the bus. のように書けばよい.

▶彼女は電車の窓から手を振った She waved her hand from [through] the *train window*.

▶《慣用表現》課長, 社会の窓が開いてますよ Excuse me, Chief, but your *fly*'s open.

‖窓ガラス a windowpane ‖窓枠 a window frame [sash].

まとう 纏う wear +⑥ ; **put on** ▶彼女の結婚披露宴には華やかなドレスをまとった有名人が集まった Beautifully-*dressed* [*-clad*] celebrities gathered at her wedding reception. ‖私たちはバスローブをまとってサウナに入った We took a sauna, while *wrapped in* our bathrobes.

まどう 惑う ▶四十にして惑わず At forty, I'*m no longer unsure where I stand*. ／I will *hesitate no more*, now that I have turned forty.

まどぎわ 窓際 ▶彼女は窓際に座って本を読んでいた She sat reading a book *by the window*. ‖私は窓際の席に座った I took a seat *by* [*near*] *the window*. ／I took a *window* seat. (➤ 後者は an aisle seat(通路側の席)に対する言い方).

‖窓際族 an employee with a nominal position and little responsibility who is seated near a window (➤ 説明的な訳) ; a marginalized employee.

まどぐち 窓口 the window, a **wicket** (切符売り場や銀行などの) ▶住民票は5番の窓口です Residency certificates are *Window* No. 5.

まとはずれ 的外れ ▶あの議員の質問は的はずれだ That Diet member's question is *beside the point*. ‖彼の主張はしばしば的はずれだ His arguments are often *irrelevant*.

まどべ 窓辺 ▶窓辺のアジアンタムの鉢 an adiantum pot *by* [*near*] *the window*.

まとまり 纏まり unity (統一) ; **coherence** (首尾一貫していること) ▶私たちのチームはまとまりがある There is *unity* in our team. ‖彼女の話はほとんどまとまりがない Most of what she says *lacks coherence* [*is poorly organized*].

まとまる 纏まる 1【集まる】**be collected, be put together** ▶彼女が新聞に寄稿していた随筆が本にまとまった The essays she had written for the newspaper *were collected* [*were put together*] into a book. ‖家を建て替えるにはまとまった金がいる You need *a large amount of money* to rebuild your house.
2【整理される】▶考えがまとまった My ideas *took shape* [*came together*]. ‖あなたの期末レポートはよくまとまっています Your term paper *is well organized*.
3【解決がつく】**be settled** ▶話し合いはまとまった The discussion *has been concluded* [*has been settled*]. ／We *have come to an agreement*. ／The negotiations *were completed*.

まとめ 纏め a **summary**（要約）; a **conclusion**（結論）▶討議のまとめを発表する read *a summary* [*the conclusions*] of the discussion.
‖**まとめ役** a facilitator, a coordinator（調整役）; an organizer（世話役）; a mediator（調停者）.

まとめる 纏める 1【集める】**gather** +目, **gather ... up, put ... together; collect** +目 ▶彼は自作の詩を1冊にまとめた He *gathered* (*together*) [*collected*] his own poems into one volume. ／He *put* his own poems *together* in one volume. ‖自分の持ち物をまとめておきなさい *Keep* [*Get*] your things *together*. ／*Gather up* your things. ‖食料品を1週間分まとめて買った I have bought enough groceries for the whole week.
2【整理する】▶卒論をまとめる(＝完成させる) *complete* one's graduation thesis ‖今読んだ物語の内容を簡単にまとめ(＝要約し)なさい *Summarize* the story you have just read. ‖考えをまとめる時間をいただけますか Can you give me (some) time to *gather* [*collect*] my thoughts?
3【解決する】**settle** +目 ▶けんかをまとめる *settle* [*patch up*] a quarrel ‖商談をまとめる *wrap up* a deal ／make a bargain ‖おばは縁談をまとめるのが上手だ My aunt is good at *arranging* marriages.

まとも 1【正面から】**head-on** /hèdɑ́:n/（正面から）; **straight**（まっすぐ, もろに）▶まともに攻めたのでは, 誰もその横綱には勝てない Nobody can beat the yokozuna by fighting him *head-on*. ‖息子は父親の顔をまともに見ることができなかった The son could not look his father *straight* in the face.
2【ちゃんとした】**respectable**（世間に認められるような）; **decent** /dí:sənt/（きちんとした）; **honest**（正直な）; **proper**（正式の）; **sane**（正気の）.
▶もっとまともな仕事に就いたらどうだい Why don't you find a more *respectable* job? ‖葬式のときくらいまともな格好をしろよ Dress *properly* [*decently*] at least when you attend a funeral. ‖兄貴に比べれば弟はよほどまともだ My younger brother is a lot more *serious* (*about life*) than my older brother.
▶朝からまともな物を食べていない I haven't had anything *decent* to eat since morning. ‖まともな人間ならそんなことはしないだろう No *sane* person would do a thing like that.

まどり 間取り **the plan** [**layout**] (**of a house**) ▶この家は間取りがいい[悪い] This house *has a good* [*bad*] *layout*. ／This house *is laid out well* [*badly*]. ‖この間取りだと台所が狭過ぎる The kitchen is too small in this *floor plan*.

マドリード **Madrid** /mədríd/（スペインの首都）.

マドレーヌ a **madeleine** /mǽdlɪn/（菓子. もともとフランス語）.

まどろっこしい →まだるっこい.

まどろむ **doze** (**off**).

まどわす 惑わす **seduce** /sɪdjú:s/ +目（甘いことばで異性などに言い寄る）; **tempt** +目（…する気を起こさせる）; **mislead** +目（あざむく）▶少女は男の甘いことばに惑わされた The girl *was seduced* by his honeyed words [his sweet talk]. ‖宣伝文句に惑わされて高い腕時計を買ってしまった The advertising *tempted* me into buying the expensive watch. ‖一人暮らしのお年寄りはでたらめな宣伝に惑わされやすい Elderly people living alone *are* easily *misled* by false advertisements.

まとわりつく **cling to**（体にくっつく）; **follow around**（つきまとう）.

マトン **mutton**（羊肉）.

マドンナ **the Madonna**（聖母）▶小百合はわが校のマドンナだ Sayuri is *the idol of the boys* at our school.
‖**マドンナ候補** a female candidate.

マナー **manners**（➤常に複数形で用いる）▶あの新人歌手はマナーがいい That new singer has good *manners*. ‖全くマナーの悪いやつらだ They *have no manners* at all.
‖**テーブルマナー** table manners.

マナーモード (a) **silent** [**vibrating**] **mode**（➤(×) manner mode とはいわない. そもそも「マナー」は英語では manners である）▶優先席の近くでは携帯電話は電源をお切りになるか, マナーモードにしてください When (you are) near the priority seats, please switch your cellphone to *silent mode* or turn it off.

まないた 俎 a **chopping** [**cutting**] **board** ▶まないたの上で on *a chopping board*.

まなこ 眼 an **eyeball**（眼球）; an **eye**（目）▶彼はねぼけまなこで玄関に出て来た He *looked sleepy* when he came to the door.

まなざし 眼差し a **look** ▶彼女は愛情のこもったまなざしで夫を見た She gave her husband a loving *look*. ／She looked [gazed] at her husband with deep affection in her eyes.

まなつ 真夏 **the height of summer; midsummer**（➤イギリスでは夏至の頃の快適な時期を指す）▶ぎらぎらした真夏の太陽 the glaring *midsummer* sun ‖この辺は真夏でも気温は20℃以上にはならない The temperature doesn't rise above 20℃ here, *even at the height of summer*.
‖**真夏日** a ***manatsubi***; a day with a high of 30℃ or above（➤説明的な訳）.

マナヅル《鳥》a **white-necked crane**.

まなでし 愛弟子 one's **favorite pupil** ▶アリストテレスはプラトンのまな弟子だった Aristotle was Plato's *favorite pupil*.

まなぶ 学ぶ **learn** +目（学んで身につける）; **study** +目（勉強・研究する）▶短歌の作り方を学ぶ *learn* how to write a *tanka* ‖歴史から多くのことを学ぶことができる We can *learn* a lot from history.（➤この場合の learn は「(見て・聞いて)知る」の意）.
▶彼は西沢教授のもとで物理を学んだ He *studied* physics under Professor Nishizawa. ‖息子は鈴木先生からバイオリンを学んで(＝レッスンを受けて)います My son has been *taking* violin *lessons* from Mr. Suzuki.
ことわざ よく学びよく遊べ Study a lot and play a lot.（➤日本語からの直訳）／All work and no play makes Jack a dull boy.（➤「勉強ばかりで遊ばないと子供はばかになる」の意の英語のことわざ）.

ま

まなむすめ まな娘 one's **beloved daughter.**

マニア a **maniac** /méıniæk/, an **enthusiast**（熱狂者），《インフォーマル》a **buff** ▶彼は記念切手マニアだ He is a commemorative stamp *buff*. ／He is *an avid collector* of commemorative stamps.

> **危ないカタカナ語✹ マニア**
>
> **1** 英語の mania /méıniə/ が語源だが，これは「病的な執着心」を指す語で，日本語と異なり，人は指さない．人の場合は maniac といい，a fishing maniac（釣りマニア）などのように用いる．ただし，maniac は「病的」のイメージが強く，他人に面と向かってこの語を用いるのは不適当．
>
> **2** 日常的には，「…狂」に相当する buff, bum, nut などを用いて a car buff（カーマニア）とか a railroad bum（鉄道マニア）などのようにいい，丁寧に My uncle is an enthusiastic golfer.（おじはゴルフマニアだ）のようにいう．

まにあう 間に合う **1【時間に遅れない】be in time**

> **【文型】**
> A に間に合う
> **be in time for** A
> ➤ Aは名詞

▶今出れば11時の電車に間に合う If you leave now, you'll *be in time for* [you *can catch*] the eleven-o'clock train.（➤ カッコ内の言い方のほうがよりふつう）‖授業に間に合った I *was in time for* (the) class.

▶タクシーで行けば今からでもきっと間に合うよ If we take a taxi now, I'm sure we'll *make it* [*get there on time*].（➤ make it は「間に合うように着く」の意のインフォーマルな言い方．on time は「時間ぴったりに」）‖全日空の11便には間に合わなかった（＝乗りそこねた）I *missed* ANA flight No. 11.

2【足りる】be enough ▶1600ccの車を買うなら200万円あれば間に合う（＝十分だ）Two million yen *is enough* to buy a 1600cc car. ‖ **対話**「金はいくら欲しいんだ」「5万円あれば間に合うよ」"How much money do you want?" "Fifty thousand yen *should do it*." ‖ **対話**「野菜はいかがですか」「きょうは間に合ってます」"Do you need any vegetables?" "No, we *have enough* for today [we don't need any today]."

▶小さいけど，この案内書で結構間に合った（＝役だった）Though small in size, this guidebook proved to *be useful*. ‖この古い車で結構間に合っている This old car *serves* me *well enough*.

まにあわせ 間に合わせの **makeshift** ▶私は本箱の間に合わせに空き箱を使った I used an empty box as a *makeshift* bookcase.

まにあわせる 間に合わせる **1【遅れないようにする】get ... ready**（用意する）; **get ... done**（済ませる）▶その資料は月曜日の会議に間に合わせてくれ Please make sure the materials *are ready* for the meeting on Monday. ‖この仕事はあすの朝までに間に合わせるつもりだ I'll *get* this job *done* by tomorrow morning.（➤「やってしまう」の意）．

2【代用する】make do with（…で済ませる）▶成人式に着る服が無かったので兄ので間に合わせた I didn't have a suit for the coming-of-age ceremony, so I *made do with* my brother's. ‖レモンジュースが無いのなら酢で間に合わせなさい If you're out of lemon juice, *use* vinegar *instead* [*as a substitute*].

まにうける 真に受ける **take ... seriously**（本気にする）▶やつはからかっているんだから真に受けるな He's just kidding you. Don't *take* it *seriously*. ‖あんなプレイボーイのことばを真に受けると，あとで泣くよ You'll regret it later if you *take* that playboy *seriously*.

マニキュア (a) **manicure** /mǽnıkjʊəʳ/（手のつめを手入れすること；足の場合は **pedicure**）; **nail polish** [**enamel** ／《英また》**varnish**]（マニキュア液）▶（つめに）マニキュアをする *polish* [*do*] *one's nails* ‖マニキュアを落とす remove the *polish* from one's nails ‖姉はピンクのマニキュアをしている My sister has pink *nail enamel* on.

‖マニキュア除光液 (a) nail-polish remover.

マニフェスト a **manifesto.**

マニュアル a **manual**, an **instruction manual**; a **script**（前もって用意された原稿・台本）▶コンピュータ[プリンター]のマニュアル a computer [printer] *manual* ‖コンビニの店員はマニュアルどおりの事しか言わない Clerks at convenience stores only speak *according to the manual*. ‖マニュアルどおり行かないことが多い Things don't always go *according to* (*the*) *script*.

‖マニュアル人間 a person who goes by the manual.

マニラ **Manila** /mənílə/（フィリピンの首都）．

まにんげん 真人間 ▶罪を悔いて真人間になる express remorse for one's crime and *get back on the straight and narrow*.

まぬがれる 免れる **1【逃れる】escape** ＋目; **be spared**（(命を)助けられる）▶私はその列車に乗り遅れたために運よく事故を免れた I was lucky enough to *escape* the accident because I missed the train.

▶彼は危うく死を免れた He *had a narrow escape from* death. ‖あやうくおぼれるところだったが，イルカに岸に運んでもらって死を免れた I almost drowned but *my life was spared* by a dolphin who carried me to shore.

2【回避する】avoid ＋目 ▶責任を免れようったってだめだよ You can't *avoid* [*get away from*] your responsibility.

まぬけ 間抜け a **fool**, an **idiot**, a **goof**（人）（➤ 後の2語はよりくだけた語で，a goof は《米》に多い）▶また同じ間違いをするとはおまえは何とまぬけなんだ What *a fool* [*an idiot*] you are to make the same mistake twice [again]!

まね 真似 **imitation**（模倣）; **mimicry**（特に人のしゃべり方などの）**一動** **まねをする** **imitate** ＋目, **copy** ＋目（➤後者には「そっくりそのまま」という含みがある）; **mimic** ＋目 →まねる

▶彼女は映画スターのまねをして髪型を変えた She changed her hairstyle *in imitation of* a movie star. ‖松田君は井上先生のまねをするのがうまい Matsuda can *imitate* [*mimic*] Mr. Inoue very well. ／Matsuda *does a* great *impression* of Mr. Inoue. ‖《テレビで視聴者に注意をうながして》まねをしないでください *Don't try this at home.* ‖少年たちは海賊のまねごとをして（＝海賊ごっこをして）遊んでいる The boys *are playing* (*at*) pirates.

▶ばかなまねはやめろ Stop *acting stupid* [*like a fool*]. ／Don't be foolish. ‖汚いまねはやめろよ Stop *acting like a dirty rat*.（➤「汚いネズミのようなまねをするな」の意）．

マネー money
‖**マネーゲーム** a money game ‖ **ウェブマネー** WebMoney (➤ 商標；一般語としても使われる) ‖ **電子マネー** electronic money, e-money, e-cash.

マネージャー a **manager** /mǽnɪdʒəʳ/ (店の支配人；スポーツチームの監督)；a **caretaker**(学校の運動部などの世話役)
▶レストランのマネージャー the *manager* of a restaurant ‖ ラグビー部のマネージャー the *caretaker* of a rugby club.

まねき 招き an **invitation** ▶招きに応じる［を断る］accept［decline］*an invitation* ‖ その国の皇太子が政府の招きで来日した The prince of that country came to Japan at the *invitation* of the government.
✉ **パーティーへお招きにあずかりありがとうございます. 喜んで出席させていただきます** Thank you for your kind *invitation* to the party. I will be very glad to attend (it).

マネキン a **mannequin** /mǽnɪkɪn/ (人形；manikin ともつづる)；a **model**(ファッションモデル；デパートのマネキンガールをいうこともある).

まねく 招く **1【招待する】invite** +㊐；**ask** +㊐ (呼ぶ)

【文型】
人(A)を会(B)に招く
invite A **to** B
ask A **to** B

▶私は彼女をパーティーに招いた I *invited*［*asked*］her *to* the party. ‖ きのうは数人の友人を夕食に招いた We *invited*［*had*］several friends *over* for dinner yesterday. (➤ have ... over は「(人を)食事などに招く」の意のインフォーマルな言い方) ‖ 披露宴にお招きいただきありがとうございます Thank you for *inviting* me *to* your wedding reception.
2【頼んで来てもらう】invite +㊐ ▶木村さんを(講演の)講師に招こう Let's *invite* Mr. Kimura as a speaker.
3【引き起こす】invite +㊐；**cause** +㊐ (原因となる)；**bring about** (…の結果をもたらす) ▶ドライバーの不注意がその事故を招いた The driver's carelessness *invited*［*caused*／*brought about*］the accident. ‖ 彼は正直過ぎるのでしばしば他人の誤解を招く He *is* often *misunderstood* because he is too straightforward.

まねごと 真似事 ▶書道の真似事をする *dabble in* calligraphy(➤ dabble in は「遊び半分で手を出す」) ‖ その裁判は真似事にすぎなかった That trial was *a mockery*［*travesty*］*of justice*. (➤ ともに「茶番」)／That trial was *a charade*. (➤ charade は「見え透いたお芝居」) ‖ **対話**「山本さん, 油絵やるんだって？」「いや, ほんの真似事です」"You do oil paintings, don't you, Yamamoto?" "Well, *sort of*." (➤ sort of は「多少」の意のインフォーマルな表現で「まあね」くらいに当たる).

まねる 真似る **imitate** +㊐, **copy** +㊐ (➤ 後者には「できるだけ正確に」という含みがある)；**mimic**(ことば・身ぶりなどをふざけて) ▶他人をまねる必要はない You don't need to *imitate* others. ‖ あのコメディアンは有名歌手の声をまねるのがうまい That comedian is good at *copying*［*mimicking*］the voices of famous singers. (➤ -ic で終わる動詞は ing をつける際に k が付加される) ‖ 木村君は先生をまねては皆を笑わせる Kimura often makes us laugh by *doing a takeoff* of our teacher. (➤ takeoff は「物まね」の意のインフォーマルな語).
▶私がスマホに替えたら, 美恵子もまねた I changed to a smartphone and Mieko *followed suit*. (➤ follow suit は「人まねをする」).

まのあたり 目の当たり ▶大惨事をまの当たりにして, 女の子はわなわなと身を震わせた The girl trembled like a leaf as a big disaster occurred *right before her eyes*.

まのび 間延び ▶間延びした顔のサル a *stupid-looking* monkey ‖ 彼女の動作はどこか間延びしている She is somewhat *slow* (in her behavior).

まばたき 瞬き a **blink**, a **wink**(➤ 前者は無意識の, 後者は意識しての) **━動 まばたきする blink, wink** ▶彼はまばたきひとつせずにフロアショーを見つめていた He (intently) watched the floor show without so much as *a blink*.

まばゆい →まぶしい.

まばら 疎らな **sparse** ▶彼の髪の毛はまばらだ His hair is *thin*［*sparse*］. ‖ 不評のためにその映画は観客がまばらだった The movie *was sparsely attended* because of its poor reviews. ‖ 雨の日で公園は人影がまばらだった(＝人がほとんどいなかった) I saw *very few people* in the park on that rainy day.／It was a rainy day, and the park *was almost deserted*. ‖ その新興住宅地は人家がまばらだった *There were only a few houses scattered* through the new residential tract.

まひ 麻痺 **paralysis** /pərǽləsɪs/ **━動 まひする get paralyzed** /pǽrəlaɪzd/ ▶彼は脳血栓のために右半身がまひしている He *is paralyzed*［He *developed paralysis*］on his right side due to cerebral thrombosis. ‖ 彼女は腰から下がまひしている She *is paralyzed* from the waist down.
▶しばらく氷を持っていたら指の感覚がまひした My fingers *got numb* after holding an ice cube for a while. (➤ numb /nʌm/ は「感覚が(一時的に)なくなって」).
▶《比喩的》事故のために東名高速は交通がまひしている Traffic *is tied up* on the Tomei Expressway［The Tomei Expressway *is paralyzed*］because of a car accident. (➤ tie up は「(鉄道などを)不通にする」) ‖ 多額の金をやりとりしているうちにその証券マンは金銭感覚がまひしてしまった In the course of dealing with such large sums of money, the stockbroker *became insensitive*［*habituated*］*to* money.

まびきうんてん 間引き運転 ▶この鉄道は昼間は間引き運転になる *The number of trains* running on this track during the day will *be cut*［*reduced*］.

まびく 間引く **thin (out)** ▶ダイコンの芽を間引く *thin out* daikon seedlings.

まひる 真昼 **midday**(正午) ▶真昼の太陽が照りつける中, 試合は続行された The game went on in the *midday sun*. →まっぴるま.

マフィア **the Mafia** /mɑ́:fiə, mǽfiə/.

マフィン a **muffin**.

まぶか 目深 ▶あの男, 帽子を目深にかぶって, どうも怪しい That man looks quite suspicious with his hat *pulled down over his eyes*. ‖ 少年は野球帽をぐいと引っ張って目深にかぶった The boy *jerked* his baseball cap *down*.

まぶしい 眩しい **dazzling**(まばゆい；比喩的に用いるときはプラスイメージ)；**glaring**(ぎらぎらする；比喩的に用いるときはマイナスイメージ) ▶浜辺では太陽がまぶしかった The

sunshine was *glaring* [*painfully bright*] on the beach. ‖ 雲一つない空から太陽がまぶしく照りつけた The sun *glared down* from a cloudless sky.
▶《比喩的》きょうのきみはとてもまぶしいよ You look *dazzlingly beautiful* [look *gorgeous*] today.

まぶす **coat** +目, **dredge** +目 (➤ 後者のほうが「軽く」というニュアンスを伴う) ▶肉に小麦粉をまぶして焼きなさい *Coat* [*Dredge*] the meat *with* flour before frying it.

まぶた 瞼 **an eyelid** ▶彼は一重[二重]まぶただ He has single [double] *eyelids*.
▶《慣用表現》ときどき故郷の村がまぶたに浮かぶ Sometimes I can *see* my home village *when I close my eyes*. ／ Sometimes I *vividly recall* my home village.

まふゆ 真冬 **midwinter** ▶彼は真冬でも冷水浴を欠かさない He regularly takes a cold bath, even in *midwinter* [*the middle of winter*].
‖**真冬日** a ***mafuyubi*** ; a day with a high of 0℃ or below (➤ 説明的な訳).

マフラー **1【えり巻き】a scarf** ▶外は寒いからマフラーをしたら？ It's cold outside, so how about wearing *a scarf*?
2【消音器】《米》a **muffler**, 《英》a **silencer**.

> **危ないカタカナ語✹マフラー**
> **1**「えり巻き」の意の「マフラー」は英語の muffler からきているが，最近ではこの英語は古風になっており，代わりに scarf が「マフラー」の意でも用いられることが多い．
> **2**「(自動車などの)消音器」の意では muffler が用いられるが主に《米》.《英》では silencer が一般的.

まほう 魔法 **magic** ▶魔法を使う use *magic* ‖ 魔法のじゅうたん[ランプ／つえ] a *magic* carpet [lamp／wand] ‖ アラジンが魔法の呪文を唱えるとドアが開いた The door opened when Aladdin said [chanted] the *magic* words.
‖**魔方陣** a magic square ‖ **魔法使い** a wizard(男の) ; a witch ; an enchantress (魔女；後者にはプラスのイメージがある) ‖ **魔法びん** a thermos (bottle) (➤ pot とはいわない；→ポット)；《英また》a thermos flask.

マホガニー (a) **mahogany** ▶マホガニーの机 a *mahogany* desk.

まぼろし 幻 **a phantom** /fǽnṭəm/, **a vision** ▶船員たちは幻の船を見た The sailors saw a *phantom* [*ghost*] ship.
▶イトウは幻の魚と呼ばれている The *ito* is now so rare people call it a "*phantom* fish." ‖ 人の世は夢幻の如くなり Human life is *like a dream or* (*an*) *illusion*.

[1]**まま** **1【そのまま】**

> **【文型】**
> **もの(A)をある状態(C)のままにして**
> **with** A C
> ➤ Cは形容詞・副詞(句)・分詞など

▶彼は口を開けたまま寝ていた He was sleeping *with his mouth open*. ‖ ヘンリーさんは靴をはいたまま[オーバーを着たまま]客間に入って来た Henry came into the living room *with his shoes* [*overcoat*] *on*. (➤ on は「(衣服などを)身につけて」) ‖ 男は腕組みをしたまま座っていた The man sat *with his arms crossed* (*over his chest*).

> **【文型】**
> **人・物(A)があるまま**
> **as** A **is** ／**the way** A **is**

▶今のままがいい I like things *as* [*the way*] *they are*. (➤ things は漠然と「状況」や「状態」全般を表し, as [the way] they (＝things) are は「現在の状態のまま，現状のままに」の意.「今のままのきみがいい」なら I like [love] you the way you are. とする) ‖ 私たちは今のままでしあわせです We're happy *the way things are*.

> **【文型】**
> **ある状態(A)のままでいる**
> **stay** A ／**keep** A
> **remain** A
> ➤ Aは形容詞・-ing 形・名詞など

▶毎年，年は取るが気持ちは若いままだ Though I'm getting older every year, I *stay* [*remain*] *young* at heart. ‖ 父は一日中黙ったままだった My father *remained* [*kept*] *silent* all day long. (➤ keep のほうが意識的).

> **【文型】**
> **A を B のままにしておく**
> **leave** A B
> **keep** A B
> ➤ Bは形容詞・副詞句・-ing 形など
>
> **《解説》leave** は「…のままにほうっておく」の意. **keep** は「努めてその状態を保つ，その状態を続ける」なので，日本語では「－にしている」になることが多い.

▶ドアは開けたままにしておいてください Please *leave* [*keep*] the door *open*. ‖ 机の上(の物)をこのままにしておいてくれますか Will you *leave* the things on my desk *as they are*? ／Will you *leave* my desktop *as* (*it*) *is*? ‖ あの障子はあちこち破れたままになっている That shoji has *been left with* (*numerous*) *tears* here and there.
▶母は買い物に出かけたままです My mother *is* (*still*) *out* shopping.
2【…に従って】▶彼のしたいままにさせてやれ *Let* him *have his own way*. ／*Let* him *do whatever he likes*. ‖ 彼は上司に命ぜられるままに書類を改ざんした He doctored the documents *just as* his boss told him to (do).
▶彼女は自分の見たままを正直に述べた She *truthfully* described what she had seen.

[2]**まま 間々** **from time to time**(ときに) ; **sometimes**(ときどき). →ときどき.

ママ a **mother**(母親) ; **Mom, Mommy**(呼びかけで) ▶ママさんバレーのチーム a *mothers'* volleyball team.
‖**教育ママ** an education-conscious [education-minded] mother ／a mother overly concerned with her child's education (➤ 後者は批判的な言い方) ‖ **ママ友** mothers who are friends.

> **危ないカタカナ語✹ママ**
> **1** mama, mamma は英語では古風な語で，日常語としては，今は《米》では mom, mommy が，《英》では mum, mummy が用いられる. mommy, mummy は小児語.
> **2** 日本語では飲み屋やスナックの女性経営者を「ママ」というが，英語の mama にはその意味はないので，(female) owner あるいは proprietress というほうがよ

い. ただし,「ママさん」と言ったり呼び掛けたりする場合は Mama-san でよい. なお,「雇われママ」は the (female) manager, the head hostess などで表せる.
3 日本語では夫が(子供の面前であるとないとにかかわらず)妻に「ママ」と呼びかけることはふつうであるが, 英語では子供の面前を除いては夫が妻に Mom, Mommy と呼びかけることはふつうではない.

ままこ 継子 a **stepchild**(男女とも); a **stepson**(男), a **stepdaughter**(女).

ままごと ▶ままごとしようよ. ぼくがお父さん, きみがお母さん Let's *play house*. I'll be the daddy, and you can be the mommy.

ままちち 継父 a **stepfather**.

ままならぬ ▶年金だけでは老後の生活はままならない My pension *is not enough to cover my living expenses* in my old age. ‖ とかくこの世はままならぬ In this world, *things do not* (*always*) *turn out as you wish*.

ままはは 継母 a **stepmother** ▶シンデレラはまま母にいじめられた Cinderella was ill-treated by her *stepmother*.

まみず 真水 **fresh water**.

-まみれ ▶彼の靴は泥まみれだった His shoes *were covered with mud*. ‖ 殺人犯は血まみれの上着を着ていた The murderer wore a *blood-stained* jacket.

まみれる ▶作業員の上着は油[泥]にまみれていた The worker's clothes were *smeared with* grease [were *covered with* mud].

まむかい 真向かいに **right in front of ...** (…の真ん前に) ▶駅の真向かいに本屋がある There is a bookstore *right in front of* the train station. ‖ 彼はテーブルで彼女の真向かいに座った He sat *just* [*right*] *across* the table from her.

まむし 蝮《動物》a ***mamushi***, a **pit viper**.

1**まめ 豆** a **bean**; a **soybean**(大豆); a **pea**(エンドウ豆) ▶ハトに豆をやる feed *beans* to pigeons ‖ ゆでる前に豆を一晩水につけておきなさい Soak the *beans* in water overnight before boiling them. ‖ コーヒー豆をひいてください Could you (please) grind the (*coffee*) *beans*?
‖豆台風 a small typhoon ‖ 豆電球 a miniature bulb.

2**まめ** a **blister**(水ぶくれ); a **corn**(たこ, うおのめ) ▶足にまめができた I've got *a blister* on my foot. ‖ 足の裏のまめがつぶれた The *blister* on the sole (of my foot) popped.
‖血まめ a blood blister.

3**まめ** ▶夫は本当にまめな人です My husband is *a* really *diligent*, *hard-working man*. / My husband doesn't *have a lazy bone in his body*. (➤後者は「怠け癖がこれっぽっちもない」のおどけた言い方) ‖ そのお手伝いさんはまめによく働く The housekeeper *is a hard worker* [*works hard*].
▶彼はまめに手紙を書く He *is a good* [*regular*] *correspondent*. ‖ 辞書をまめに引く *make frequent use* of one's dictionary.
▶故郷の両親はまめに暮らしています My parents back home are *living happily and healthily*.

まめつ 摩滅する **wear out** ▶摩滅した古タイヤ a *worn-out* old tire ‖ CD はレコードと違って摩滅することがない Unlike records, CDs never *wear out*.

まめつぶ 豆粒 ▶展望台から見下ろすと, 人間が豆粒のように見えた When I looked down from the observation deck, the people on the ground looked *just like ants*. (➤「アリのように」の意).

まめまき 豆まき a **bean-scattering ceremony** ▶節分に豆まきをする scatter roasted beans to drive out evil spirits [influences] on *Setsubun* (➤日本独特の行事なので「悪霊を追い払うために」などと説明する必要がある; →節分).

まめまめしい ▶まめまめしく働く work *like a beaver* (➤「(働き者の)ビーバーのようによく働く」の意) ‖ 母が寝込んだので父がまめまめしく家事をしている With my mother ill in bed, my father is doing the household chores *conscientiously*. (➤ conscientiously は「誠実に」の意).

まもう 摩耗 **wear, abrasion**.

まもなく 間もなく **soon, before long**(➤後者はやや堅い言い方) ▶バスはまもなく来ますよ The bus will come *soon* [*shortly* / *before long*]. ‖ (その後)まもなくして雨が降り出した *It was not long before* the rain started. / The rain started *a little later*. ‖ まもなく夏がやって来る Summer *is just around the corner*. / Summer *is not far away*. (➤ともに「すぐ近くまで来ている」の意) ‖ まもなく7時です *It is going* (*on*) seven o'clock. ‖ 生まれてまもなく赤ちゃんパンダは死んだ The baby panda died *soon* [*shortly*] after it was born.

まもの 魔物 an **evil spirit**(悪霊); a **devil**, a **demon** (➤前者はキリスト教, 後者はギリシャ神話でいう「悪魔」) ▶金は魔物だ The love of money is the root of all evil. (➤「金銭愛は諸悪の根源だ」の意).

まもり 守り **defense** ▶国の守り national *defense* ‖ ライオンズの内野の守り(=守備)は堅い The Lions *have a tight infield*. ‖ 私たちのチームは守りについた[守りを固めた] Our team *took to the field* [*solidified our defense*].
‖守り神 a guardian deity.

まもる 守る **1【防護する】** **defend** +目 (攻撃や危険を積極的に防ぐ); **protect** +目, **shield** +目 (保護する); **guard** +目 (見張る) ▶祖国を守る *defend* one's own country / *protect* one's homeland ‖ 自然を守る *protect* [*preserve*] nature ‖ その盲導犬は主人を危険から守った The guide [seeing-eye] dog *defended* [*protected*] his master from danger. ‖ マイケルは両わきをボディーガードに守られてホテルに入った Michael entered the hotel *guarded* by bodyguards on either side. ‖ 平和を守る(=維持する)のは我々の義務である It is our duty to *maintain* peace.
▶あの選手は一塁も三塁も守れる That player *can play* both first and third.
2【約束・法律などを】 **keep** +目; **obey** +目 (従う); **observe** +目 (規則を); **live up to** (主義・信念などを) ▶彼女はいつも約束を守る She always *keeps her promises*. / She *is as good as her word*. / She *is a woman of her word*. ‖ 秘密を守ってね Be sure to *keep* the secret. ‖ 守る気のない約束をしてはいけない Don't make promises (that) you *don't intend to keep*.
▶皆が規則を守らなければならない Everybody should *obey* [*observe*] the rule(s). ‖ 校長先生は時計のように時間をきちんと守る Our principal *is as punctual* as a clock. ‖ たかしは言いつけをよく守る子だ Takashi is an *obedient* boy.
▶私はできるだけ車線を守るようにしている I try to *keep in the same lane* as much as possible.

まやかし まやかしの **false** (人を迷わせる); **phon(e)y** (いんちきの) ▶そんなまやかしの宗教を信じるな Don't believe in such a *false* [*phony*] religion. (➤ false religion は「邪教」に近い) ‖ 彼の微笑はまやかしの微笑だ His is a *false* [*fake* ／*phony*] smile.

まやく 麻薬 a **drug**(➤ 通例, 複数形で用いる) ; a **narcotic** (鎮痛などを目的とした麻酔薬) ▶麻薬をやる take *drugs* ‖ 彼らは麻薬をやっている(＝常用している) They *do drugs*. ‖ 彼には麻薬の常習癖がある He has a *drug* habit. ／He's a *drug* addict.

‖麻薬常用者[中毒患者] a drug user [addict] ‖ 麻薬中毒 drug addiction ‖ 麻薬密売人 a narcotic [drug] dealer ‖ 麻薬乱用 drug abuse.

[1]**まゆ 繭** a **cocoon** /kəkúːn/.

[2]**まゆ 眉** an **eyebrow** /áɪbraʊ/, a **brow** (➤ 後者は下記の用例のように熟語的に用いられるのでなければ古風な語) ▶ 《化粧で》まゆを描く pencil one's *eyebrows* ‖ 彼はまゆが濃い He has thick *eyebrows*.

▶父は私の試験の結果を聞いてまゆをひそめた My father *frowned* [*knitted his brows*] when he heard the results of my exams. ／My father listened to the results of my exams *with a frown* [*with knitted brows*].

まゆげ 眉毛 an **eyebrow** /áɪbraʊ/ ▶濃い[薄い]まゆ毛 thick [thin] *eyebrows* ‖ もじゃもじゃのまゆ毛 shaggy [bushy] *eyebrows*.

まゆつば 眉唾 ▶あいつはおぼれた子を助けたと言っているがまゆつばものだ(＝信じがたい, 疑わしい) He said that he rescued a drowning child, but that'*s hard to believe* [*dubious*]. ‖ そんなうまい話はまゆつばだよ The story sounds too good (to be true). *You should take it with a grain of salt*. (➤「割り引いて考えるべきだ」の意).

まよい 迷い **hesitation**(ためらい) ▶この車を手離すことにはまだいくらか迷いがある I still have some *hesitation* about letting this car go. ‖ 大学に進学すべきかどうか気持ちの上で迷いがある(＝決められない) I'*m* still *wavering about* [I'*m* still *of two minds* (*about*)] whether to go to college or not.

まよう 迷う

1【道に】 **lose** one's **way**, **get lost**(➤ 後者のほうがしばしばより深刻) ; **stray** (仲間にはぐれる) ▶我々のパーティーは下山の途中で道に迷った Our party *lost its way* [*got lost*] while coming down the mountain. ‖ この猫はこの間わが家に迷い込んで来た This cat *strayed into* our house the other day.

2【決められない】 **can't decide**, **can't make up** one's **mind** ; **be at a loss**(途方に暮れる) ▶彼の申し出を受けるべきか迷っています I *can't decide* [*can't make up my mind*] whether to accept his offer. ／I'*m of two minds as to* whether I should accept his offer. ‖ ぼくは彼女の部屋に入るべきかどうか迷った I *was at a loss* (as to) whether I should enter her room.

▶このバッグにしようかあのバッグにしようか迷っているんです I *don't know* which purse to buy, this one or that one. ‖ 彼は美樹に婚約指輪を渡すべきか迷い始めた He was *having second thoughts* about giving Miki the engagement ring. (➤ have second thoughts は「(よい判断か)疑問を持ち始める」).

✉ **大学に進学しようかどうかまだ迷っています** I'*m* still *wondering* whether I should go on to college or not.

3【惑う】 ▶彼女の色香に迷って道を踏み外した男は少なくない Quite a few men strayed from the path of virtue after becoming *fascinated* [*captivated*] *with* her beauty.

まよえる 迷える **stray** ▶迷える羊 a *stray* sheep.

まよけ 魔除け a **charm** (**against evils**), an **amulet** /ǽmjələt/.

まよこ 真横 ▶すごい美人がぼくの真横に来て座った A real beauty came and sat *right beside* [*right next to*] me. ‖ あの枝だけ真横に(＝水平に)伸びている Only that (one) branch sticks out *horizontally*.

まよなか 真夜中 **the middle of the night**(夜中) ; **midnight**(夜の12時)

> **解説** 日本語の「真夜中」は漠然と12時頃から2時頃を指すので the middle of the night がよい. midnight は午前0時ちょうどである.

▶火事は真夜中に起きた The fire broke out *in the middle of the night* [*at midnight*]. ‖ 父は真夜中過ぎに帰宅した My father returned home *after midnight*. ‖ 私は真夜中まで一生懸命勉強した I worked hard *far into the night*.

マヨネーズ **mayonnaise** /méɪəneɪz/ ▶サラダにマヨネーズをかける put *mayonnaise* on the salad.

まよわす 迷わす **puzzle** ＋㊐ (当惑させる) ; **mislead** ＋㊐ (判断を誤らせる) ▶彼の説は初学者を迷わすかもしれない His theory might *puzzle* [*perplex*] beginners.

▶いい加減なうわさに迷わされないように用心しなさい Take care not to *be misled* by idle rumors. (➤ misled は mislead の過去分詞形).

マラソン a **marathon** (**race**) (競技) ; **jogging**, **running** (運動のための) ▶マラソン大会に出る run (in) *a marathon* ／take part in *a marathon* (➤「大会」は訳出しなくてよい).

▶私は初マラソンを完走した I completed [finished] *my first marathon*. ‖ 人生は私にとっては短距離走ではなくマラソンなのです To me life isn't a sprint but *a marathon*.

‖マラソン完走者 a marathon finisher ‖ マラソンランナー a marathon runner, a marathoner ‖ ハーフマラソン a half marathon.

> **危ないカタカナ語✸ マラソン**
> **1** 英語の marathon は競技としての「マラソン」にしか使わない. 健康を維持するためのマラソンは jogging (ジョギング)である.
> **2** 公園などにある「マラソンコース」は jogging track という. また「マラソンシューズ」は running shoes(競走用), jogging shoes(ジョギング用)という.

マラリア 《医学》**malaria** /məléəriə/.

まり 毬 a **ball** ▶まりを投げる[つく] throw [bounce] *a ball*.

マリア ‖聖母マリア the Blessed /blésɪd/ Virgin, the Virgin Mary, Our Lady(➤ 最後は主にカトリック教徒が用いる言い方).

マリネ a **marinade** ▶いわしのマリネ *marinated* sardine.

マリファナ **marijuana** /mæ̀rɪhwáːnə/, 《インフォーマル》**weed** ; 《俗》**grass**, **pot** ▶マリファナを吸う smoke *marijuana* [*weed*].

マリモ 《植物》a **marimo**.

まりょく 魔力 **magic power** ; (a) **charm** (魅力)

▶ダイヤは女性にとって不思議な魔力があるようだ Diamonds seem to hold a mysterious *charm* [*fascination*] for women.

マリン **marine**

‖マリンスポーツ marine [ocean] sports.

「マリン・スポーツ」のいろいろ ウインドサーフィン windsurfing／海釣り ocean fishing／カヌー canoeing／カヤック kayaking／サーフィン surfing／サーフボード surfboarding／ジェットスキー jet-skiing／シュノーケル snorkeling／スキューバダイビング scuba diving／スポーツフィッシング sport-fishing／ヨット sailing

マリンバ a **marimba** ▶マリンバを演奏する play the *marimba*.

まる 丸 a **circle** ▶黒板に丸を描く draw *a circle* on the blackboard ‖ 該当する項目の番号を丸で囲みなさい *Circle* each applicable item.

まる- 丸- **full**（正味…）; **whole**（全…）▶私は彼にまる1時間待たされた He kept me waiting (for) a *full* [*whole*] hour. ‖ 私たちが結婚してからまる1年になります It has been a *full* [*whole*] year since we got married. ‖ 私はまる2日間眠っていない I haven't slept for *two full* [*a full two*] *days*.
▶着物を丸洗いする *wash* a kimono *without taking it apart* ‖ りんごを丸かじりする *eat* an apple *skin and all* ‖ 豚の丸焼き *roast pig*.

まるあんき 丸暗記 **rote-learning** 一動 まる暗記する **learn ... by rote** [**by heart**] ▶数学の公式をまる暗記する *learn* mathematical formulas *by rote*.

まるい 丸い **round**; **circular**（円形の）; **spherical** /sférɪkəl/（球形の）▶丸いテーブル a *round* table ‖ 地球は丸い The earth is *round* [*spherical*]. ‖ その劇場は中央に丸い舞台がある The theater has a *circular* stage at the center. ‖ 鉛筆のしんが丸くなった The pencil has gotten *blunt*. (➤ blunt は「(ナイフなどが)鈍い」).
▶全選手が丸くなって座った All the players sat *in a circle*. ‖ 猫がこたつの上で丸くなっている The cat *is curled up* on the kotatsu.
▶《比喩的》事態は何とか丸く収まるだろう Somehow things will *work out*. (➤「自然に解決する」の意) ‖ あの角のあった父も50を越えてすっかり丸くなった My father, who used to be so abrasive, *has* completely *mellowed* since he turned fifty.

まるうつし 丸写し ▶彼は私の練習問題の答えをノートに丸写しした He *copied all* of my answers to the exercises into his notebook.

まるがお 丸顔 a **round face** ▶丸顔の男の子 a *round-faced* boy／a *chubby* boy (➤ 後者は「太った」の意にもなる) ‖ 妹は丸顔でぽっちゃりしている My (younger) sister is plump with *a round face*.

まるがかえ ▶その国会議員たちは某企業の丸抱えで中国旅行をした The Diet members took a trip to China, in which *all the expenses were paid* by a certain corporation.

まるがり 丸刈り **close-cropped hair**; a **buzz cut**（スポーツ刈り）▶野球部に入ったら丸刈りにするように言われた When I joined the baseball club, I was told to get *a close haircut* [to have my hair cropped closely]. →丸坊主.

まるきぶね 丸木舟 a **dugout (canoe)** ▶丸木舟で川を下る go down a river by *dugout* [*in a dugout*].

まるくび 丸首 ▶丸首のセーター a *round-neck* [*crew-neck*] sweater.

まるごし ▶警備員は丸腰で刃物を振り回す強盗に立ち向かった An *unarmed* security guard confronted the knife-wielding burglar.

まるごと 丸ごと ▶文章を丸ごと暗記する learn the *whole* passage by heart ‖ 私はリンゴを丸ごと(＝皮ごと)かじった I ate the apple, *peel and all*. ‖ その猫はイワシを丸ごと(＝骨ごと)食べた The cat ate the sardine, *bones and all*.

マルセーユ **Marseille(s)** /mɑːˈséɪ/（フランス南部の地中海岸の都市; 原語に最後の s はないが, 英語ではつけることがある).

まるぞん 丸損する **suffer a total** [**complete**] **loss** ▶妻は株の暴落で丸損した My wife *lost all she had invested* [*suffered a total loss of all she had invested*] in the stock market crash.

まるた 丸太 a **log** ▶丸太の橋 a *log* bridge.
‖丸太小屋 a log cabin ‖ 丸太置き場 a log dump.

まるだし 丸出し ▶その赤ちゃんはおしりを丸出しにしていた The baby's bottom was *completely exposed*.／The baby's buttocks were *in full view*. ‖ 彼女はお国なまり丸出しでしゃべった She talked *with a strong provincial accent*. ‖ 対話「眼鏡をかけたまま, 顔洗っちゃったよ」「ばか丸出し!」"I washed my face with my glasses on." "*Shows how stupid you are*." (➤ 文頭に That が省略されている).

マルチ **multi-** ▶マルチタレント a *versatile* actor [personality].
‖マルチ商法(ネットワークビジネス) a pyramid (sales) scheme [system]; a Ponzi scheme (ねずみ講) ‖ マルチリンガル multilingual.

マルチメディア **multimedia**.

まるっきり 丸っきり **absolutely**（絶対に）; **completely**（完全に）; **not** [**no**] **... at all**（全く…でない）▶彼の言ったことはまるっきりうそだった What he said was an *absolute* [*a complete*] lie. ‖ 私はラップにはまるっきり興味がない I'm *not* interested [I have *no* interest] in rap music *at all*.／Rap music does*n't* interest me *at all*.
▶あいつのかっこう見ろよ. まるっきりクマだぜ Look at him! He looks *just* like a bear!

まるっこい 丸っこい ▶背が低くて丸っこい感じの男の人 a short, *round* [*plump*] man ‖ 彼女は丸っこい字を書く She writes *roundish* characters.

まるつぶれ 丸潰れ ▶落第点でも取れば彼女に対してメンツ丸つぶれだ I will *utterly lose face* with her if I flunk the exam. (➤ lose face は「面目を失う」).

まるで **1【全く】** **absolutely**（絶対に, 全然）; **completely**（完全に）; **not ... at all**（全然…でない）▶このガイドブックはまるで役にたたない This guidebook is *absolutely* useless. ‖ 母はまるで泳げない My mother can*not* swim *at all*. ‖ 彼はカラオケにまるで興味がない He is *completely* [*totally*] uninterested in karaoke. (➤ totally は completely よりややくだけた語)／He is *not* interested in karaoke *at all*. ‖ 私は政治のことはまるで(＝何も)わからない I know *nothing* about politics. ／I'm *completely* ignorant about politics. ‖ その選手がこんなに早く引退するなんて, まるで考えていなかった I never had the *slightest* idea that the player would retire so early. ‖ きみはぼくをまるで信用してないみたいだね You don't seem to trust me *at all*.

2【あたかも】 **just like**; **as if ...**（➤ あとには仮定法の文がくる）

【文型】
まるで A のように
(just) like A ➤ Aは名詞
as if [as though] S + V

《解説》(1)「まるで」はしばしば現実とは違うことを表すが, as if でその意味を表すには動詞に仮定法過去形を用いる. be 動詞は主語に関係なく were が正式だが, 口語では単数の主語の後に was を用いることもある. →もし, -よう.
(2)as if は look, smell, sound, feel その他の動詞の後に続けて用いる. 単に現在の様態を述べる場合は, as if の文の動詞に現在形がくることもある. また, look や sound の後では口語では as if の代わりにしばしば like を用い, S + V を続ける.

▶この試合に勝てたなんてまるで夢のようです Winning this game is *just like* a dream. ‖ 彼はまるで大きなだだっ子のようだ He is *just like* a big spoiled child. ‖ 妻との初デートをまるできのうのことのように覚えている I remember the first date with my wife *as if* it were [was] yesterday.
▶まるで今にも降り出しそうな空模様だ It looks *as if* [looks *like*] it might begin to rain at any moment. (➤ like のあとに文を続けるのはインフォーマルな会話に多い) ‖ 二人はお互いにまるで何事もなかったようなそぶりだった The two acted *as if* [*as though*] nothing had happened between them.

まるてんじょう 丸天井 a **circular ceiling**(円天井); a **vaulted ceiling**(アーチ型天井).

まるなげ 丸投げする leave everything up to ... ▶仕事を丸投げする(=外注に出す) *farm out* all the work ‖ 受験勉強を塾に丸投げする *let* cram schools *decide everything* about studying for (entrance) exams.

まるのみ 丸呑み ▶その蛇は獲物を丸のみにした That snake *swallowed* its prey *whole*.
▶専門家の予想を丸のみする(=頭から信じる)のは危険だ It is dangerous to *swallow* (even) experts' predictions *whole*.

まるはだか 丸裸の stark naked ▶子供たちは丸裸になって水に飛び込んだ The children *stripped off* [*took off all their clothes*] and jumped into the water.
▶《比喩的》彼は火事で[ばくちで]丸裸になった(=全財産を失った)そうだ They say he *lost his entire fortune* in the fire [*gambled away all his money*].

まるばつしき ○×式 ‖○×式テスト a **true-false test**(➤ ふつうTまたはFで答える); a **multiple-choice test**(選択肢の多いテスト).

マルひ マル秘 ▶その書類にはマル秘の判が押してあった The document was stamped "*Confidential*."
《参考》(1)英語国では「部外秘」に internal use only や restricted,「マル秘」に confidential,「極秘」に secret,「最高機密」に top secret などを用いる. (2)日本では「秘」「極秘」「機密」のように分ける.

まるぼうず 丸坊主 ▶丸坊主の頭 a *close-cropped* head / a *close-shaved* head(➤ 後者は「そって丸坊主の」).
▶彼は交通事故を起こしたことを反省して丸坊主になった Feeling remorse for having caused a traffic accident, he *cut off his hair*. **《参考》**英語国には反省の気持ちを表すために頭を丸める習慣はない.

まるぽちゃ 丸ぽちゃの plump (➤ 主に女性・子供が); **chubby** (➤ 主に赤ん坊・子供が) ▶丸ぽちゃの女の子 a *plump* [*chubby*] girl.

まるまっちい 丸まっちい round ▶丸まっちい字 *round* (, small) letters.

まるまど 丸窓 a **round window**.

[1]**まるまる 丸まる curl (up)** ▶彼女はベッドに丸まって寝ていた She was *curled up* in bed asleep. ‖ アルマジロは攻撃されるとボールのように丸まる An armadillo *curls* [*rolls*] *into* a ball when (it is) attacked.

[2]**まるまる 丸々 1【太っている様子】**▶丸々と太った子供 a *chubby* kid(➤ fat は「デブ」という悪いイメージがあるので, ここでは不適当).
2【皆, 全部】▶まるまる一日の旅行 a *good* day's journey ‖ 私はまるまる1か月両親と口をきいていない I haven't talked to my parents *for a whole* [*entire*] *month*. ‖ まるまる3時間待った I waited three *solid* hours [three hours *solid*]. (➤ solid はインフォーマルな語).

まるみ 丸み roundness ▶思春期になると女の子は体に丸みが出てくる Girls' figures *round out* [*develop curves*] at puberty.
▶《比喩的》2, 3年すれば彼にも丸み(=円熟さ)が出てくるだろう He will become more *mature* [*mellow*] in a few years.

まるみえ 丸見え ▶カーテンをしないと部屋の中が丸見えだよ People can *see everything* in [People can *get a full view* of] the room without a curtain.

まるめこむ 丸め込む wheedle +㊐, **coax** /kouks/ +㊐ ▶少年は母親を丸め込んでオートバイを買わせた The teenage boy *wheedled* [*coaxed*] his mother into buying a motorcycle. (➤ wheedle [coax] A into doing で「A(人)に甘えて[心にもないことを言って]…させる」の意).

まるめる 丸める roll (up) ▶女の子は泥を丸めてお団子を作った The little girl *rolled* some mud *up* into balls. ‖ この子はいつも体を丸めて寝る This boy always *curls up* when he sleeps.

まるもうけ 丸儲け ▶その商売で30万円, 丸もうけした I *made a clear profit of* 300,000 yen on the sale. / I *cleared* 300,000 yen on the sale. (➤ 後者の clear は「純益をあげる」).

まるやけ 丸焼け ▶火事で風下の家は丸焼けになった The houses downwind of the fire *were burned down* [*were burned to the ground*].

まれ 稀な rare; **unusual** (いつもとは違う, 珍しい); **uncommon**(一般的ではない) **一副 まれに rarely, seldom** (まれにしか…しない) ▶まれな出来事 an *uncommon* [a *rare*] occurrence ‖ 彼が冗談を言うのはまれだ He *rarely* tells jokes. (➤ 習性をさす. 今実際に冗談を言ったことに対するコメントなら It's rare [unusual] for him to make a joke. という) ‖ 20歳まで生きる犬はごくまれだ(=ほとんどいない) *Very few* dogs live to be twenty years old.
▶《慣用表現》アインシュタインはまれに見る天才だった Einstein was a *one-in-a million* genius. (➤ 文字どおりには「百万人に1人の」).

マレーシア Malaysia /məléɪʒə, -ʃə/ (東南アジアの国) **一形 マレーシアの Malaysian**
‖マレーシア人 a Malaysian.

マレーはんとう マレー半島 the Malay Peninsula(アジア南東部の半島).

マロニエ《植物》a **horse chestnut (tree)** (セイヨウトチノキ).

まろやか 円やかな mellow(こくのある); **mild** (口あたりのよい) ▶このワインはとてもまろやかだ This wine tastes quite *mellow*.

マロングラッセ (フランス語から) a **marron glacé** [複 **marrons glacés**], a **candied** [**glazed**] **chestnut**.

まわし 回し a ***mawashi***, a **belt**(相撲の).

まわしのみ 回し飲みする ▶ウイスキーを回し飲みする *pass around* a bottle of whiskey.

まわしもの 回し者 a **spy** ▶敵の回し者 an enemy

spy.

まわす 回す **1【回転させる】turn** +㊀；**spin** +㊀（くるくると）▶ドアの取っ手を回したらドアが開いた The door opened when I *turned* the doorknob. ‖ 男がダイヤルを回すと金庫はガチャリと開いた The safe opened with a clink when the man *turned* the dial. ‖ あの奇術師は頭の上でこまを回せる That juggler *can spin* a top on his head.

2【順に送る】pass +㊀ ▶答案用紙を１枚ずつ取って後ろの人へ回してください Please take one answer sheet for yourself and *pass* the rest *on* (*to* those in the) back rows. ‖ これから中田さんの手紙を回します（＝回覧します）から読んでください I'll *pass* Mr. Nakata's letter *around*, so please read it. ‖ すみません, こしょうを回してください Excuse me. Could you please *pass* the pepper?

▶難しい問題は後に回しなさい（＝後に残しなさい）*Leave* the hard questions *till later*.

3【別の所に移す】▶贈り物をよそへ回す *recycle* a gift by sending it to another person ‖ 車を西門に回してください Please *bring* the car *around to* the west gate. ‖ この電話を山田さんに回してください Please *transfer* this call to Mr. Yamada.

▶私は食費を削って遊ぶ金に回している I'm cutting down on food expenses so that I'll have more money to spend on having fun (with my friends). ‖ 私は練習の調子がいまひとつだったので, 補欠に回された I was told to warm the bench because I wasn't in the best condition during the practice.

4【相手とする】▶挑戦者は世界チャンピオンを向こうに回して善戦した The challenger put up a good fight *against* the world champion. ‖ 安岡君は頼もしいやつだが, 敵に回せばこわい男だ Yasuoka is a good friend *but a bad enemy*.

まわた 真綿 **floss silk**.

[1]**まわり 周り** **1【周　囲】circumference** /səʳkʌ́mfrəns/（円周）→**周囲**

▶河口湖のまわりは16キロある The *circumference* of [The distance *around*] Lake Kawaguchi is sixteen kilometers. ‖ カリフォルニアにあるセコイアの巨木はまわりが10メートル以上もある There's a giant sequoia tree in California that is more than ten meters *in circumference*. ‖ 学生たちは飯島教授のまわりに座って討論をした The students sat *around* Professor Iijima and carried on a discussion. ‖ 対話「この湖はまわりがどのくらいありますか」「20キロです」"*How far is it around* this lake?／*What is the circumference of* this lake?" "It's twenty kilometers around."

2【周辺に】around ▶私の大学のまわりには喫茶店が多い There are a lot of coffee shops *around* our college. ‖ 怪しげな男が郵便局のまわりをうろついていた There was a strange man *hanging around* the post office. ‖ 姉は毎晩家のまわりをジョギングしている My sister jogs (*around*) *the neighborhood* every evening.

▶まわりの者の言うことを気にするな Don't worry about what *people* say.（➤ people around you とする必要はない）‖ まわりの人に聞いてください Ask *around*.

[2]**まわり 回り** ▶そのホテルでは火の回りが早くて５人が焼死した The *fire spread quickly* through the hotel, and five people were killed. ‖ 私たちは東大阪市を車で一回りした We *drove around* Higashi-Osaka. ‖ 仙台から酒田回りで（＝を経由して）秋田へ行った I went from Sendai to Akita *by way of* [*via*] Sakata.

▶（電話）沼田はただ今お得意様回りに出ております Mr. Numata is out *calling on* [*visiting*] his clients now.（➤ 英語では敬称をつけるのがふつう）.

‖**回り舞台** a revolving stage.

まわりくどい 回りくどい **roundabout** ▶彼はいつも回りくどい言い方をする He always speaks in a *roundabout* way. ‖ わたしは回りくどいのは嫌いだ. 要点を言ってくれ Stop *beating around the bush*. Get to the point.（➤ beat around the bush は「遠回しに言う」の意の熟語）.

まわりこませる 回り込ませる ▶左足の外側にボールを回り込ませる *circle* a ball *around* the outside of one's left leg ‖ テキスト（文章）を画像に回り込ませる *get* text *to wrap around* an image.

まわりこむ 回り込む ▶（相撲で）相手の背後に回り込む *circle* (*around*) *behind* the opponent ‖ 土俵際を右に回り込む *move* along the inner edge of the (sumo) ring *to the right*.

▶建物の裏手に回り込む *go around to the back* of a building.

まわりまわって 回り回って **eventually**（最終的に）；**finally**（最後に）.

まわりみち 回り道 a **roundabout route** [**course**／**way**]；a **detour** /díːtʊəʳ/（う回路）▶きょうは回り道をして帰宅した I came home by *a roundabout route*.／I took *a roundabout way* home. ‖ 回り道をして彼女を家まで送った I *made a detour* to take her home.

まわりもち 回り持ち →**持ち回り**.

まわる 回る **1【回転する】turn**；**spin**（くるくると）；**rotate**（軸を中心に）▶風が強いので風力計が猛烈な速さで回っている The anemometer *is turning* [*spinning*] very fast in the strong wind. ‖ フィギュアスケートの選手はあんなにくるくる回って, 目が回らないんだろうか It's a wonder figure skaters don't *get dizzy* from *spinning* so much. ‖ 自動車の車輪は車軸を中心に回る The wheels of an automobile *rotate* on their axles.

2【ほかのものの回りを動く】go around；**circle**（円を描いて）；**revolve**（軌道を描いて）；**orbit**（人工衛星などが軌道に乗って飛ぶ）

▶スピードスケートの選手はみごとにコーナーを回る Speed skaters *go around* the turns beautifully. ‖ 坂本は二塁を回って三塁へ向かっています［ダイヤモンドを回っています］Sakamoto *has rounded* second and is heading for third [*is running around* the diamond].（➤ この round は「（角などを）曲がる」）‖ 幼稚園児たちは手をつないで先生のまわりを回った The kindergarten children joined hands and *circled* their teacher. ‖ 気象衛星「ひまわり」は地球のまわりを回っている Himawari weather satellites *are orbiting* the earth.

3【いろいろな所に順々に行く】▶外務大臣一行は南米５か国を回って（＝訪れて）帰国した The Foreign Minister and his aides *visited* five South American countries before returning home. ‖ 一度四国を回ってみたい（＝旅して回りたい）Just once I'd like to *take a trip* [*to travel*] around Shikoku. ‖ きょうの午後は得意先を回らないといけない I must *call on* [*visit*] my customers this afternoon. ／I must *make* some business *calls* this afternoon. ‖ さあ, 館内を回ってくる時間だ Well, it's time to *make my rounds*.（➤ make one's rounds は

「(医者や警官が)巡回する」) ‖ 引っ越してきたのだから挨拶にご近所を回らなくちゃ Since we are new to the neighborhood, we have to *go around* to meet our neighbors.

4【寄る】drop by ▶クリーニング屋さんに回ってコートを取って来てくれませんか Could you *drop by* the cleaners to pick up my overcoat? ‖ 裏口に回ってください Please *come around to* the back door.

5【順番が来る】▶やっと私に打順が回ってきた At last it was *my turn* at bat. ／Finally my batting turn *came*. ‖ 町会の回覧板が回ってきた The neighborhood notice board *came around* to our house.

6【全体に行き届く】▶彼はなかなか知恵の回る男だよ He is pretty *intelligent*. ‖ 酒が回ってきた I'*m beginning to feel* the sake. ‖ その男はコブラの毒が全身に回って死んだ The man died when the cobra venom *spread* throughout his body. ‖ 彼女は酒［酔い］が回ると歌を歌いたがる When she *gets tipsy*, she likes to sing. ‖ 忙しかったのでそこまで気が回らなかった I was so busy that I didn't even *think of* (doing) that.

7【慣用表現】▶あの司会者はよく口が回る That M.C. sure *has the gift of the gab*. ‖ 長年の友人が意外にも敵に回った A long-time friend of mine has unexpectedly *gone over to the enemy*.

まわれみぎ 回れ右 ▶《軍隊の号令》回れ右!《米》*About face!* ／《英》*About turn!* (➤「回れ右をする」は do an about-face [about-turn]) ‖ ぼくの顔を見るとその子は回れ右して逃げ出した When he saw me, the boy *turned* and fled.

¹まん 万 ten thousand (➤ thousands と複数形にしない)
⚠ **英語には「万」に相当する語はないので,「1000の10倍」と考え ten thousand という.「2万」は twenty thousand である.** →億.
▶5万人の観客 *fifty thousand* spectators ‖ そのバッグに1万5千円を支払う pay *fifteen thousand yen* for that bag ‖ その図書館の50万冊の本 *five hundred thousand* [*a half million*] books at that library.
▶このスタジアムは1万人を収容できる This stadium seats *ten thousand* people. ‖ この市の人口は10万人になろうとしている The population of this city will soon reach *a* [*one*] *hundred thousand*. ‖ 何万という人がアフリカで餓死した *Tens of thousands* [*Many thousands*] *of* people died of hunger in Africa. (➤ この場合は複数形を使う).
▶宝くじの一等が当たることなど万に1つもない The chance of winning the first prize in the lottery ticket is *none in a million*. ‖ あのチームには万に1つの勝ち目もない *Never in a million years could we beat* that team.

²まん 満 ▶私が東京に来てから満3年になる It's been a *full* three years [three *full* years] since I came to Tokyo. ‖ 私は満18歳です I am eighteen (years old). (英米では常に満年齢で数えるので特に訳出しない).
▶チャンピオンは満を持してその試合に臨んだ The champion *was very well prepared* for the match.

まんいち 万一 if ... (should), (just) in case (万一…ならば;後者はややインフォーマル) ▶万一試験に落ちたらどうしよう What shall I do *if by some chance* I (*should*) fail the examination? (➤ by some chance は「何かのはずみで, 何かの拍子で」の意) ‖ 万一の場合(＝緊急時)はこのかばんを持ち出そう *In case of emergency* [*In an emergency*], I'll take this bag with me. ‖ 万一のためにホテルの電話番号を教えといて Can you tell me your hotel's phone number, *just in case*?

まんいん 満員の full; crowded, (jam-) packed (➤ (jam-)packed には「気持ちが悪いくらい満員の」という含みがある)
▶夕食時でレストランは満員だった The restaurant *was full* at dinner hour. ‖ 電車は満員だった The train *was crowded* [(*jam-*)*packed*] *with passengers*. (➤「満員電車」は a crowded [(jam-) packed] train).
▶コンサート会場は大入り満員だった The concert hall *was filled to capacity*. (➤ capacity は「最大収容人員」) ／The concert hall *had a capacity crowd* [*audience*]. ‖ 少女は満員の聴衆を前にコンチェルトを弾いた The girl played a concerto before *a capacity audience*.
▶《掲示》満員 *Full House* (➤ レストラン・劇場などで;→満席).

まんえつ 満悦 ▶私のプレゼントに妻はご満悦のようだった My wife looked *delighted* with my gift.

まんえん 蔓延 spread(広がること); **prevalence**(広く生じている状態) **一動 まん延する spread, prevail; pervade**(～じゅうに広がる)
▶適切な対策を講じれば赤痢のまん延は食い止められる The *spread* of dysentery can be stopped if proper measures are taken. ‖ 最近東京ではインフルエンザがまん延している The flu *is spreading* in Tokyo these days. ‖ 当時ヨーロッパではコレラがまん延していた Cholera *was widespread* [*prevalent*] in Europe in those days. ‖ いじめが多くの公立校にまん延していた Bullying *pervaded* in many public schools.

まんが 漫画 manga(➤ 英語化しており, 単複同形); **a comic strip**(4コマ前後の); **comics**(4コマ以上の); **a cartoon**(アニメ漫画・政治漫画); **a caricature**(風刺漫画) ▶漫画を描く draw *manga* [*a comic strip*] ‖ 日本語の「漫画」は多くの国で通用する語になっている The Japanese word '*manga*' has become a word that can be understood in many countries.
✉ **漫画は日本の若者にすごく人気があって, 多くが英訳されています** *Manga* [*Comic books*] are extremely popular among young people in Japan, and many have been translated into English.
‖**漫画映画** a manga film, an animated cartoon (film), a cartoon (film) ‖ **漫画家** a mangaka(➤ 英語化している), a manga artist, a cartoonist, a comic artist ‖ **漫画雑誌[本]** a manga magazine [book], a comic magazine [book].
ディベートルーム 「漫画は子供に悪影響を与えている」

まんかい 満開で in full bloom, at one's best (➤ 後者は「見ごろで」の意) ▶梅の花は今満開だ The *ume* trees are *in full bloom* now. ／The *ume* blossoms are *at their best* now.
▶桜は今月末に満開になるだろう The cherry blossoms will *come into full bloom* [*open fully*] at the end of this month.

マンガン《化学》**manganese** /mǽŋgəniːz/.

まんき 満期 ▶この定期預金は今月の10日で満期になる[5年満期だ] This time deposit *matures* on the 10th of this month [*matures* in five years]. ‖ 私の保険はまもなく満期をむかえる My insurance policy is near its *term*. (➤ term は「決められた期間，期限」). ‖満期日 the day of maturity, the due date.

まんきつ 満喫 ▶姉はハワイで学園生活を満喫している My sister is *enjoying* campus life in Hawaii *to the full*.

マングース 《動物》a **mongoose**.

マングローブ 《植物》a **mangrove**.

まんげきょう 万華鏡 a **kaleidoscope** /kəláɪdəskòʊp/.

まんげつ 満月 a **full moon** ▶今夜はちょうど満月だ *The moon is full* tonight.

マンゴー 《植物》a **mango**.

まんさい 満載 a **full load** [**cargo**]（いっぱいの積み荷）(➤ cargo は主に船や飛行機の積み荷) ▶ダンプカーは産業廃棄物を満載していた The dump truck *was carrying a full load of* industrial waste. ／The dump truck *was fully loaded* with industrial waste. ‖そのタブロイド版の新聞は地域の情報を満載している That tabloid (newspaper) *is full of* local information.

まんざい 漫才 ***manzai***; a rapid-fire comic dialogue by a comic duo (➤ 説明的な訳).
‖漫才師 a *manzai* comedian.

まんざら ▶彼女はまんざら料理がへたというわけではないようだ It seems she is *not* (*all*) *that* bad a cook. (➤ この that は「そんなに，それほど」の意のインフォーマルな副詞) ‖私たちはまんざら知らない仲ではない We are *not complete* strangers to each other. (➤ complete は「全くの」) ／We know each other to some extent.
▶彼の言うこともまんざらうそではない What he says is *not all* untrue. ‖父は仲人を頼まれて，まんざらでもなさそうだった My father *didn't look completely* [*altogether*] *unwilling* when asked to act as a matchmaker.

まんじ 卍 a **swastika** /swɑ́:stɪkə/.

まんしつ 満室 ▶奈良のホテルは現在どこも満室だ All of the hotels in Nara *are full* [*are fully booked*] now.
▶《掲示》満室 No Vacancy. ‖《ホテルのフロント係が客に》ただ今満室でございます *All the rooms are taken* [*full* ／ *booked* (*up*)] now.

まんしゃ 満車 ▶この辺の駐車場は全部満車になっている All the parking lots near here are *full*. ‖《掲示》満車 No Vacancy.

まんしゅう 満州 Manchuria /mæntʃʊ́əriə/.

まんじゅう 饅頭 a ***manju***
日本紹介 ✉ **まんじゅうは伝統的な和菓子で，小麦粉で作った皮にあんを詰めて蒸して作ります．おめでたい行事には紅白のまんじゅうが，葬式には模様や図案の焼き目を入れた葬式まんじゅうが配られます** A *manju* is a traditional Japanese confection, made by steaming buns of sweet dough stuffed with *an* (sweet azuki bean paste). *Manju* in red and white pairs are often given to guests on auspicious occasions. *Manju* that have been singed on the top to create various patterns or designs are distributed at funerals.

まんじょう 満場 ▶その小説家の講演は満場の聴衆に深い感銘を与えた The novelist's lecture deeply impressed *the full-house* [*capacity*] *audience*. ‖満場一致でその法案は可決された The bill passed *unanimously*.

マンション an **apartment** (**house**)（賃貸式）; a **condominium** /kɑ̀:ndəmíniəm/,《インフォーマル》a **condo**（分譲式）▶私たちはマンションに住んでいる We live in *a condominium* [*an apartment*].

> **危ないカタカナ語✹ マンション**
> **1** 日本語の「マンション」はふつう高層の集合住宅を指すが，英語の mansion は部屋数が何十もあるような豪壮な大邸宅を指す語で，全く意味が異なる．ただし，《英》では豪華マンションの名称として，例えば Diamond Mansions（ダイヤモンドマンション）のように複数形の mansions を用いることは多い．
> **2** 日本語の「マンション」は賃貸式のものは apartment house，分譲式のものは condominium という．→アパート．
> **3**「ワンルームマンション」は《米》では studio (apartment)，《英》では bed-sitting room または bed-sitter という．

まんじり ▶試験の結果が心配でまんじりともできなかった I *spent a sleepless night* worrying about how I had done on the exam. ／I was so worried about the results of the exam that I *couldn't sleep a wink* [*get a wink of sleep*]. (➤ 後者の文のほうがインフォーマル).

¹まんしん 満身 ▶岡選手は満身の力を込めてバーベルを持ち上げた Oka *exerted all his strength* to lift the barbell.

²まんしん 慢心する get conceited ▶一度ぐらい勝ったからといって慢心するんじゃない Don't *get conceited* [*bigheaded*] just because you won one game!

まんすい 満水 ▶貯水池は満水になっている The reservoir *is filled to capacity*.

まんせい 慢性の chronic /krɑ́:nɪk/ ▶慢性的な人手不足 a *chronic* labor shortage ‖父は慢性胃炎にかかっている My father suffers from *chronic* gastritis. ‖その国ではインフレが慢性化している Inflation is *becoming chronic* in that country.
‖慢性病 a chronic disease.

まんせき 満席 ▶ただ今満席です We are *full* right now. ／We are completely *full* now. (➤ 後者がより強意) ‖この映画館は満席だ This movie theater *is full*. ／*All the seats are filled* (*to capacity*) in this movie theater. 《参考》掲示は "House Full", "Full House", "Standing Room Only"（立見席のみ）となる.

まんぜん 漫然 ▶漫然と夏休みを過ごしてしまった I spent the summer vacation *aimlessly* [*idly*]. (➤ 前者は「目的もなく」，後者は「怠惰に」) ／I idled the summer vacation away. ‖あの子は漫然と机に向かっているだけだ She just sits *idly* at her desk.

まんぞく 満足

1【満ち足りること】**satisfaction** 一動（…に）満足する **be satisfied**《with》, **be happy** [**content(ed)**]《with》▶満足した表情 a *satisfied* [*contented*] look (➤ この場合の contented の代わりに content は不可．content は名詞の前では用いない) ‖彼は彼女を精神的に満足させられなかった He could not *satisfy* her emotionally. ‖富は必ずしも人に満足を与えない Wealth does not always *satisfy* people [*make* people *happy*]. ／Wealth doesn't always *bring* (people) *satisfaction* [*happiness*].

> 【文型】
> A に満足している
> **be (very ／ quite) satisfied with** A
> **be content with** A

《解説》be satisfied は，希望や欲するものが最低限満たされている，という意味合いで「可ではあるが，格別良くもない」というニュアンス．ふつう日本語でいう「満足している」はかなり高い評価を表すので，very や quite などをつける必要がある．くだけた日常語では **be happy** という．**be content** はふつう肯定的な「現状で十分でそれ以上望まない」という穏やかな知足の状態．

▶あなたは大学生活に**満足していますか** *Are you satisfied with* your college life？‖私は今の仕事に一応**満足しています** I*'m* mostly *content with* my present job.

直訳の落とし穴「仕事ぶりに満足だ」
「…に満足です」は be satisfied with であるが，上司が言う「きみのすばらしい仕事ぶりには満足だ」をそのまま（×）I'm satisfied with your excellent job performance. などとするのは不自然．日本語の「満足」はそれだけで十分な評価を表すが，be satisfied with は期待の大きさに合わせて満足も相対的であるが，しばしば「何とか満足できる」というニュアンスで大きなプラスの評価にならない．excellent と言いながら単に satisfied では合わないのだ．「大いに評価できる」というには satisfied に very, quite, completely（文句のつけようがなく），fully（十分に），more than（大いに）などをつけて強める必要がある．また，「そのコンサートを聞いて満足しました」のつもりで，I was satisfied to hear the concert. というような不定詞の使い方も不自然．I really enjoyed the concert. などとする．

▶現状［現在の地位］に**満足している**ようじゃ向上は望めないぞ You can't hope to improve yourself as long as you *are complacent with* your present situation［*in* your present post］.（➤ complacent は「自己満足の」）‖ジャイアンツを破って小川監督は**満足そうだった** Manager Ogawa *looked satisfied*［*looked pleased*］when his team beat the Giants.
▶あなたといっしょにいられるだけで**満足よ** I*'m happy* just to be with you.‖この前のテストでは**満足のいく**成績は取れなかった I was unable to get a *decent* score on the last test.（➤ decent は優秀ではないが，「それなりにいい，（体裁の悪くない）まずまずの」で，5段階評価では平均より少し上の3.5くらいに相当する）‖その件は**満足のいく**解決をみた The matter was *satisfactorily* resolved.／The matter was resolved *to everyone's satisfaction*.‖《広告などで》万一ご**満足いただけない**場合は代金はお返しいたします *Satisfaction* or your money back.‖**対話**「イタリア旅行はご**満足いただけた**でしょうか（＝楽しめましたか）」「ええ．とってもよかったです」"Did you *enjoy* the trip to Italy？" "I sure did. It was superb."‖彼はやるだけのことはすべてやったという**満足感**を味わっていた He was experiencing *a feeling of satisfaction* from having done all he could do.
2【十分，完全】**一形 満足な** **satisfactory**（特定の目的・用途などに十分な，まずまずの）；**satisfying**（満足感を与える）**一副 満足に** **satisfactorily**；**properly**（きちんと）
▶賃上げ要求に対して，経営側からは**満足のいく**解答は得られなかった We didn't receive a *satisfactory* answer to our demand for a pay raise from the management.
▶その金額では**満足な**パソコンは買えないよ That is not enough money to buy a (personal) computer that you'll *be satisfied with*.
▶今シーズンはイチローにとって，たぶん最も**満足のいく**シーズンだったろう This has been perhaps Ichiro's most *satisfying* season.‖ここ2，3日忙しくて食事も**満足**にしていない I've been so busy for the past few days I haven't had time for a *decent* meal.（➤ decent は「ちゃんとした」）‖何だ，あの男はあいさつも**満足**にできないじゃないか He doesn't know how to greet people *properly*.
☛ 不満足（→見出語）

まんだら 曼荼羅 a **mandala.**

まんタン 満タン ▶**満タン**にしてください *Fill it up*, please.（➤ 男性は it の代わりに her と言うこともある）‖**満タン**になってますよ The tank is *full*.

まんだん 漫談 a **stand-up comedy**；a **humorous story**［**conversation**］（愉快な話）；a **rambling story**（とりとめのない話）
‖**漫談家** a comic storyteller.

まんちょう 満潮 (a) **high**［**full**］**tide** ▶**満潮**は午後4時です．*High tide* is［The tide will be high］at 4 p.m.

マンツーマン ▶**マンツーマン**の特訓 *one-to-one* special training／*one-on-one* training‖彼に**マンツーマン**で水泳を教える give him a *private* swimming lesson（個人教授する）.
‖**マンツーマンディフェンス** (a) man-to-man defense, (a) one-on-one defense.

¹まんてん 満点 **1**【規定の最高点】a **perfect score**,（英）**full marks** ▶数学の試験で**満点**を取った I got *a perfect score*［*full marks*／*100 percent*］on the math test.‖**100点満点**のうち80点を取ったら合格です If you get eighty points *out of a hundred*, you'll pass the exam.／The passing score is 80 *out of 100 points*.
2【欠点のないこと】▶彼女の着こなしはいつも**満点**だ She's always dressed *perfectly*［*impeccably*］.‖あのホテルはサービス**満点**だ They provide *excellent service* at that hotel.
▶牛乳は栄養**満点**だ Milk *is very nutritious*.（➤「栄養分に富む」の意）.

²まんてん 満天 ▶**満天の星** *a stadium of stars*／*a sky full of stars*‖**満天の星**の下で under *a star-filled*［*starry*］*sky*.

マント a **cloak**；a **cape**（肩からかける短いもの）《参考》「マント」はフランス語の *manteau* から．なお，英語の mantle も「マント」だが，今では古風な語で，主に婦人用のものをいう．

マンドリン a **mandolin** /mæ̀ndəlín/（➤ mandoline ともつづる）▶**マンドリン**を弾く play the *mandolin*.
‖**マンドリン奏者** a mandolinist.

マントル《地質学》a **mantle.**

まんなか 真ん中 **the center**；**the middle**（➤ 通例前者は「厳密に測定した中心点」，後者は「ほぼ中心点」を指す）▶湖の**真ん中**に小さな島がある There is a small island *in the center of* the lake.‖座礁して船体は**真ん中**で2つに折れた After the ship went aground, the hull split into two *right down the middle*.‖彼は髪を**真ん中**で分けている He parts his hair *in the middle*.‖仙台は東京と青森の**真ん中**にある Sendai lies *halfway*［*midway*］between Tokyo and Aomori.
☛ ど真ん中（→見出語）

マンネリ ▶**マンネリ化**した（＝型にはまった）テレビドラマ a *stereotyped* TV drama‖学園祭の趣向も**マンネリ化**して新鮮味に乏しい Ideas for the school festival *have become routine*［*boring*］and uninspiring.

危ないカタカナ語✹ マンネリ
「マンネリ」の語源は英語の mannerism だが, この語は芸術様式や言動の癖をいう語で, ふつうはあまり使われない. 行動・考え方・生活などが「マンネリ化する」は get into a rut, 場所や活動が「マンネリでおもしろくなくなる」は become stale (新鮮さを失う), become routine [stereotyped] (やり方が固定的なものになる), become boring (人を退屈させるようになる) などのようにいう.

まんねんどこ 万年床 ▶彼の部屋は万年床だ He never puts away his futon. (➤「万年床」に当たる英語はないので「ふとんを上げることをしない」と考える; futon は /fúːtɑːn/ と発音).

まんねんひつ 万年筆 a (fountain) pen ▶万年筆で書く write with *a (fountain) pen*.

まんねんゆき 万年雪 perpetual snow ▶万年雪を頂くキリマンジャロ Mt. Kilimanjaro (which is) crowned with *perpetual snow*.

まんぱい 満杯 ▶冷蔵庫は肉や果物や野菜で満杯だ The refrigerator *is full of* [*is filled with*] meat, fruit, and vegetables. ‖ 駐車場は満杯だった The parking lot *was filled to capacity* [*was packed*].

マンハッタン Manhattan (ニューヨーク市の中心を成す島).

マンパワー manpower.

まんびき 万引き shoplifting (行為); a shoplifter (人) 一動 **万引きする** shoplift (+目) ▶万引きは犯罪です *Shoplifting* is a crime. ‖ 男の子がガムを万引きした A boy *shoplifted* some chewing gum. ‖ 彼は本を万引きするところを店員に見つかった The clerk caught him *shoplifting* a book.

まんびょう 万病 ▶かぜは万病のもと Colds are the root of *all sickness* [*illness*]. ‖ アロエは万病に効くという人もいる There are some people who say that aloe is *a panacea for everything*. (➤ panacea /pænəsíːə/ は「万能薬」).

まんぷく 満腹 ▶私たちは満腹するまで食べることができた We could *eat our fill* [*eat to our heart's content*].
▶ 対話「お代わりいかが?」「もう満腹です」"How about another helping?" "No, thanks. *I'm full*." (➤「十分いただきました」なら I've had enough. と答える). →十分.

まんべんなく ▶どの学科もまんべんなく勉強するのは大変だ It is no easy matter to study every subject *equally well*.
▶エビにかたくり粉をまんべんなくまぶして揚げた I deep-fried the shrimp after covering them *completely* in katakuri starch.

マンボ (a) mambo (音楽, 踊り).

マンボウ 《魚》an ocean sunfish, a sunfish.

マンホール a manhole, a sewer /sjúːəʳ/ hole, a utility access hole (➤ あとの2語は無性差語).

まんぽけい 万歩計 a pedometer /pɪdɑ́ːmət̬əʳ/ ▶祖父は万歩計をつけて歩く My grandfather walks with *a pedometer*.

まんまえ 真ん前に right in front of ... ▶門の真ん前に車を止めたのはだれだ Who parked their car *right* [*just*] *in front of* the gate? ‖ わが家の真ん前に新しいビルが建った A new building was built *just across from* [*just opposite to*] my house. (➤ across from は「通りをはさんで向こう側に」, just opposite to は「真向かいに」) ‖ 真ん前を走っていた車が急に止まった The car *directly ahead of* mine stopped suddenly.

まんまと ▶多くのお年寄りがその口のうまい販売員にまんまとだまされた Many elderly people were *completely* taken in by that smooth-talking salesperson. ‖ 母からまたまんまとこづかいをせしめた I *successfully* wheedled some spending money out of my mom again.

まんまる 真ん丸 ▶今夜は真ん丸な十五夜の月だ The moon is *perfectly round* tonight. / There's a beautiful harvest moon tonight. (➤ harvest moon は「中秋の名月」).

まんまん 満々 ▶バイカル湖は満々と水をたたえていた Lake Baikal was *brimming over with water*. ‖ 自信満々で入試に臨んだが, 見事に失敗した I *was full of confidence* as I took the entrance examination, but I failed it completely. ‖ その新入社員はやる気満々だった That new employee *was highly motivated* [*had lots of drive*].

まんまんなか まんまん中 the exact [dead] center.

まんめん 満面 ▶彼は満面に笑みを浮かべた He smiled *all over* [*broadly*]. / He *was all smiles*. / He beamed with joy. ‖ 彼女は得意満面でイタリア旅行の話をした When she talked about her trip to Italy, *her face* was *full of smiles* [*full of self-satisfied smiles*].

マンモス a mammoth /mǽməθ/ ▶日本にもかつてマンモスが生息していた Once *mammoths* lived in Japan, too.
‖**マンモス大学** a huge university ‖**マンモスタンカー** a gigantic /dʒaɪgǽnt̬ɪk/ tanker, a megatanker.

危ないカタカナ語✹ マンモス
「巨大な」の意味で「マンモス…」というが, 英語でも mammoth を形容詞として用いることができる. ただし, 用法の違いはある. 例えば「マンモスビル」は megastructure がふつうであるし,「マンモス都市」は megalopolis という.「マンモス企業」は mammoth enterprise といってもよいが, huge corporation のほうが英語としてはより自然である.

まんゆう 漫遊 ▶ドン・キホーテは諸国を漫遊した Don Quixote *rambled over* many lands (in his travels).

まんりき 万力 《米》a vise, 《英》a vice.

1**まんりょう 満了** expiration, expiry (➤《米》では前者が,《英》では後者がふつう) 一動 **満了する** expire, end ▶学長は任期満了で退職した The university president retired *when his term ended*.
‖**任期[刑期]満了** the expiration of one's term of office [one's prison term].

2**まんりょう 万両** 《植物》a coral bush.

まんるい 満塁 ▶二死満塁で with *the bases loaded* and two out(s) ‖ 鈴木は四球を選び満塁とした Suzuki got a walk to *load the bases*. 《参考》満塁のことを日本語では「フルベース」ともいうが, これは和製語.
‖**満塁ホームラン** a grand slam, a bases-loaded home run.

み・ミ

[1]**み 身** **1【体】** a **body** ▶身をかがめる bend one's *body* ‖身につけるもの(＝衣類)は清潔にしておきなさい Keep your *clothes* clean. ‖彼は身が軽い(＝機敏だ) He's *agile* [*nimble*]. (➤ 前者は身軽な中に優雅さが感じられる場合, 後者は軽快さと機敏さを強調する場合) ‖彼女, バレエを習っているだけあって身のこなしがきれいだね She *moves* very elegantly, because she takes ballet (lessons).
▶日本語の発音を直されたとき, トムは身の縮む思いがした Tom *felt embarrassed* when his Japanese pronunciation was corrected. ‖アラスカの風は身を切るように冷たかった The wind in Alaska *was piercing cold*. ‖彼女は橋の上から身を投げた She *threw herself off* a bridge.
2【立場, 身分】 one's **place** ▶私の身にもなってくれよ Just *put yourself in my place* [*in my shoes*]. (➤ 後者はよりくだけた言い方).
3【魚などの肉】meat, flesh (➤ 後者は堅い語) ▶カニの身 crab *meat* ‖このサケはよく身が締まっている The *flesh* of this salmon is firm.
‖赤身 lean meat ‖脂身 fatty meat.
4【慣用表現】
身が入る ▶この頃, 秀夫も勉強に身が入ってきたようじゃないか Hideo seems to *be serious about* his studies these days. ‖この仕事にはどうも身が入らない I just can't *get interested in* this job. **身がもたない** ▶いくら若くても連日徹夜で仕事じゃ身がもたないよ Although I am still young, I'll *ruin my health* if I keep on working all night every night. **身から出たさび** →さび **身に余る** ▶まことに身に余る光栄です This is a *greater* honor *than I deserve*.
身に覚えがない ▶容疑者は放火については身に覚えがない(＝関係がない)と主張した The suspect claimed that he [she] did *not* have *anything to do with* the arson. ‖彼は身に覚えのない高額の請求を受けた He was charged a lot of money for something *he didn't remember buying*. **身にしみる** ▶寒さが身にしみる The cold *cuts to the bone*. ‖一人暮らしをするようになってから親の愛情が身にしみてわかるようになった Since I began living by myself, I have come to *appreciate* my parents' love. **身につく** ▶外国語は失敗して身につくものだ A foreign language *is learned* by making mistakes. **身につける** ▶父は再就職するために何か技術を身につけたいと言っている My father says he wants to *learn* a skill before he reenters the job market. **身につまされる** ▶彼女の苦労話を聞いて身につまされた I *became sympathetic* to her when I heard her hard luck story. ‖《他人事ではない話を聞いて》身につまされるなあ That *hits close to home*.
身のため ▶おとなしく白状したほうが身のためだぞ *If you know what's good for you*, you'd better confess. ‖あまりうまい話には安易に乗らないほうが身のためだ *It would be wise* (*for you*) not to jump too quickly at that kind of too-good-to-be-true offer. **身の振り方** ▶退職後の身の振り方(＝何をするか)はまだ決まっていません I haven't decided yet *what to do* after I retire. **身の程** →見出語 **身もふたもない** ▶そういう言い方をしては身もふたもない That's *too direct* a way of saying it.
身を入れる ▶もう少し身を入れて勉強したらどうだ How about *putting* more *effort into* your studies ? **身を固める** ▶結婚して身を固める marry and *settle down* ‖きみもそろそろ身を固めた(＝結婚して家庭を作る)ほうがいい It's about time you *married and started a family of your own*. (➤ It's about time のあとの節中の動詞は過去形). **身を粉**(こ)**にする** ▶彼は借金を払うために身を粉にして働いた He *worked his fingers to the bone* to pay back the loan. (➤ work one's fingers to the bone は「指がすりむけて骨になるまで働く」が原義).
身を立てる ▶おじは日本画家として身を立てた My uncle *established himself* as a Japanese-style painter. (➤ establish oneself as は「(職業人として)地位を確立する」) / My uncle *made* Japanese-style painting *his career*. **身を投じる** ▶彼は民主化運動に身を投じた He *threw himself into* the democracy movement. **身を引く** ▶私は70歳になったらすべての公職から身を引くつもりだ I'm going to *step down from* [*to leave*] all public posts when I turn seventy. **身をもって** →見出語.

[2]**み 実** **1【果実, 木の実】** (a) **fruit** (果物の) ; a **nut** (木の実) ; a **berry** (イチゴなどの) ▶この柿(かき)の木には秋にたくさんの実がなる This persimmon tree *bears* a lot of *fruit* in the fall. ‖子供たちは木の実を拾いに森へ出かけた The children went gathering *nuts* in the woods. ‖うちの桜の木は今年は実がいっぱいなった Our cherry tree was loaded with *cherries* this year. (➤ cherry は「さくらんぼ」).
2【慣用表現】 ▶彼の研究 [努力] はいつか実を結ぶだろう His study [efforts] will *bear fruit* some day. ‖先方と実のある話し合いができた We had a *fruitful* talk with the other party.

[3]**み 巳** **the snake, the sixth of the signs of the Chinese Zodiac**(十二支の6番目).

-み -味 ▶赤みがかった茶色の服 a *reddish* brown suit ‖このリンゴは甘みが強い This apple tastes very *sweet*.

みあい 見合い ***miai***
日本紹介 ✉ **見合いは, ていねいにはお見合いといい, 結婚相手を求める男女が第三者を仲立ちとして初めて会うことをいいます. お互いが気に入って結婚に進む場合が見合い結婚です** *Miai*, or a little more politely *omiai*, is the first formal meeting of a man and a woman who are seeking a marriage partner. A *miai* is arranged by a third person. If the two are attracted to each other and decide to marry, the resulting marriage is called a '*miai kekkon*,' or arranged marriage. **《参考》**最近では *miai* marriage と言っている英米人も少なくない.
‖**集団見合い** a singles' party for people seeking a marriage partner.

みあう 見合う ▶収入に見合った生活をする live *within one's means* ‖我々は仕事に見合う賃金を会社に要求する We demand that the company pay us what our work *is worth*.

みあきる 見飽きる ▶深夜番組は**見飽きた** I'*m tired of watching* late night TV programs. ‖ ゴッホの『ひまわり』は何度見ても**見飽きない** One can *never tire of looking at* van Gogh's "Sunflowers."

みあげる 見上げる **1**【上を見る】**look up**《at》▶夜空を**見上げる** *look up at* the night sky ‖ 子供は恨めしそうに母親を**見上げた** The child *looked up at* [*turned his face up toward*] his mother reproachfully. ‖ そのバレーボール選手は**見上げるような大男**だった The volleyball player was *a man of towering height*.

2【感心する】**admire** +㊐ ▶あの消防士の勇敢さは**見上げたものだ** I *admire* that fire fighter for his bravery. ‖ あんな若者が店一軒持つとは**見上げたものだ** It is *wonderful* [*admirable* / *praiseworthy*] for such a young man to run his own shop. (➤ それぞれ「すばらしい」「実にりっぱな」「賞賛に値する」の意).

みあたらない 見当たらない ▶お母さん, 私の時計が**見当たらないんだけど** Mom, I *can't find* my watch. ‖ きみの論文にはこれといった欠点は**見当たらない**が, 新味に欠けるね *There aren't* any particular problems with your paper, but it lacks originality.

みあやまる 見誤る ▶数字[信号]を**見誤る** *misread* a figure [a signal] ‖ 私はその男性を友人と**見誤った** I *mistook* [*took*] that man *for* one of my friends. / When I saw that man, I thought he was a friend of mine. (➤ 前者はやや堅い言い方).

みあわせる 見合わせる **1**【たがいに見る】▶佳子と裕司は**顔を見合わせて**ぷっとふき出した Yoshiko and Yuji *glanced at each other* and burst into laughter.

2【やめる】▶天気が崩れそうなので, ピクニックは**見合わせ**(＝中止し)ましょう Let's *cancel* [*call off*] our picnic because the weather is likely to change for the worse.
▶強風のため, 電車の運行は**見合わせております** Train services have *been suspended* due to the strong wind. ‖ 彼が急病になったので我々は出発を**見合わせた**(＝延期した) We *put off* [*postponed*] our departure because of his sudden sickness.

みいだす 見出す **discover** +㊐, **find** +㊐ →見つける ▶高木先生は彼女の隠れた才能を**見いだした** Mr. Takagi *discovered* her hidden talents. ‖ 問題解決の糸口が**見いだせない** We cannot *find* any clues to the solution of the problem.

ミーティング a **meeting** ▶毎朝**ミーティングがあります** We *have a meeting* [We *meet*] every morning.

[1]**ミート**《野球》▶イチロー選手は**ミートがうまい** Ichiro is good at *connecting with* the ball. / Ichiro *meets* the ball well.

[2]**ミート**《肉》**meat**
‖**ミートソース** meat sauce ‖ **ミートパイ** a meat pie ‖ **ミートボール** a meatball ‖ **ミートローフ** a meat loaf.

ミーハー a **lowbrow** /lóʊbraʊ/ (知性の低い人) ; a **teenybopper**(最新の音楽や流行に夢中になる10代の女の子 ; 古風な語) ▶妹はちょっと**ミーハーっぽい** My little sister is a bit of *a teenybopper*.

ミイラ a **mummy** /mʌ́mi/ ▶古代エジプト人は死体を**ミイラにして保存した** Ancient Egyptians preserved dead bodies as *mummies*.

みいられる 魅入られる ▶彼女は悪魔に**魅入られている**ようだ She seems to *be possessed by* an evil spirit.

みいり 実入り ▶**実入りのいい仕事** a *profitable* [*lucrative*] job (➤ 後者は堅い語) ‖ 税金が高いから我々の**実入り**(＝実収入)は少ない Because taxes are high, our *net income* is small.

みいる 見入る ▶飛行機の窓から見えた大阪の夜景がすばらしく, 思わず**見入ってしまった** I *was spellbound* [*mesmerized*] by the magnificent night view of Osaka seen from the plane window. / The night view of Osaka seen from the plane window was so magnificent that I *couldn't take my eyes off* it.

みうける 見受ける **seem, look**(思える) ; **see**(見る) ▶彼はわがままな人のように**見受けました** He *seemed* to be a selfish person.

みうごき 身動き ▶聴衆は**身動きひとつしないで**彼の話に聞き入っていた The audience was listening *motionless* to his lecture. ‖ 朝の電車は込んでいて**身動きもできない** The trains are so jam-packed in the morning that you *can't move even an inch*. ‖ 彼の車はぬかるみにはまって**身動きがとれなくなった** His car *got bogged down* in the mud.
▶《比喩的》彼は借金で**身動きできない** He *is deeply in debt*.

みうしなう 見失う **lose sight of** ▶遊園地の人込みで友人を**見失った** I *lost sight of* my friend in the crowd at the amusement park. ‖ 刑事は神戸駅で容疑者を**見失った** The detective *lost track of* the suspect at Kobe Station. (➤ lose track of は「(犯人などの行方を)見失う」の意).

みうち 身内 a **relative**(親せき) ▶新社長は会長の**身内**から選ばれた A new president was picked from among the chairman's *relatives*. ‖ 野田君は私の**身内同然**だ Noda is like *a member of my family*.

みうり 身売り ▶(会社を)**身売りする** *sell out* (one's company).

[1]**みえ 見栄** **show**(見せびらかし) ; **vanity**(虚栄心) ▶彼は**見えを張って**外車を買った He bought a foreign car *to show off* [*only for show*]. (➤ show off は「見せびらかす」) ‖ **見えを張るな** Don't *try to make yourself look good* [*look better than you are*]. ‖ 彼女は**見えで**息子を無理に大学へ行かせようとしている She is pushing her son to go to college *just to satisfy her own ego*. (●「単に自尊心を満足させるために」と考えて訳すとよい).

[2]**みえ 見得** a **pose**(意識的なポーズ) ; a **posture**(立っている[座っている]ときの体の構え・格好) ▶**見得を切る** *pose* ; *assume a posture*.

みえがくれ 見え隠れ ▶高い木々の間から月が**見え隠れしていた** The moon could *be seen intermittently* [*on and off*] through the branches of the tall trees.

みえすいた 見え透いた **transparent** /trænspǽrənt/, **blatant** /bléɪtnt/ (➤ 後者はやや堅い語) ; **obvious**(明白な) ▶**見え透いたうそ**を言うな! Don't tell me such a *transparent* [*a blatant* / an *obvious*] lie ! ‖ 彼はいつも**見え透いたお世辞**を言う He always uses *obvious* flattery. ‖ 彼はいつも**見え透いた言い訳**ばかりしている He always makes *transparent* [*flimsy*] excuses. (➤ flimsy は「(言い訳などが)見え透いた」).

みえっぱり 見栄っ張り a **vain person**(人) ; **vanity**(虚栄心) ▶**見えっ張り**なところが明美のいちばん悪いところだ *Vanity* [*Being fond of show*] is Akemi's chief fault. (➤ show は「見せびらかし」) ‖ 彼女にダイヤの指輪を買ってやるなんてあいつも**見えっ張り**だね Don't you think he is *showing off* by buying her a diamond ring？(➤ show off は「いいところを見せようとする」).

みえみえ 見え見え ▶彼は小学校に大口の寄付をしたが，町長選挙での人気とりが**見え見え**だ He made a large monetary donation to the elementary school, but it was *obviously* done (just) to collect votes in the mayoral election.

みえる 見える **1【目に映る，見る能力がある】see** (➤ 主語は「見る人」)；**show** (➤ 主語は「物」) ▶私は眼鏡をかけなくても(物が)とてもよく**見える** I *see* very well without glasses. ‖ このマンションの屋上からは大島が**見える** You *can see* Oshima [Oshima *can be seen*] from the roof of this apartment building. ‖ きみの家から富士山は**見えますか** *Can you see* Mt. Fuji from your house？‖ 暗くて部屋の中は何も**見えない** I *can't see* anything in this room. It's too dark. ‖ 彼は物がかすんで[**二重に**]**見える** He *has blurred* [*double*] *vision*. ‖ 彼は右目がほとんど**見えない** He *can hardly see* with his right eye. ／He *is almost blind* in his right eye. (➤ 後者のほうがインフォーマル).

▶きみ，下着が**見えてるよ** Your underwear *is showing*. ‖ 遠くに船が**見えてきた** A ship *came in sight* far away. ‖ ペルセウス座流星群は肉眼でも**見えた** The Perseid meteor shower *was visible* to the naked eye. ‖ 中性子爆弾は目に**見えない**光線で人を殺す A neutron bomb can kill people with its *invisible* rays. ‖ 彼女の姿が**見えなくなる**まで見送った I watched her until I *lost sight of* her [until she *went out of sight*].

2【…のように見える】look, seem, appear

【文型】
A [B] であるように見える
look A ➤ A は形容詞
seem (**to be**) B
appear (**to be**) B
➤ B は主に形容詞・名詞

【解説】(1) **look** は顔つきや様子から「(実際)…のように見える」，**seem** は話し手の主観的判断で「…と思われる」の意．**appear** は少なくとも「外見はそう見える」の意で，しばしば実際はどうかわからない，そうでないかもしれない，という含みをもつ．
(2) A に名詞がくると，**look like** A とする．(→-よう) また，しばしば seem like ともなるが，appear like とはいわない．
(3) **It seems** [**appears**] **that** S + V. や **It looks as if** [**like**] S + V. の言い方もよく使われる．

▶彼は60歳くらいに**見える** He *looks* about sixty. ／He *looks* sixtyish. (➤ -ish は数詞につけて「だいたい［およそ，約］」の意を表す) ‖ きみは二十歳には**見えない** You do*n't look* twenty. ‖ 彼女は病人のように**見える** She *looks* sickly. ／It *looks like* she's sick. ‖ あの男の子は賢そうに**見える** He *looks like* a smart boy. ‖ 彼女は**年齢相応に見えた** She *looked her age*. (➤ look one's age や look one's best (一番かっこよく見える)は例外的な決まった言い方) ‖ ヤクルトは今好調に**見える** The Swallows *seem to be* in good shape. ‖ 心配事があるように**見える**けど，どうしたの？You *seem* (*to be*) worried—what's the matter？‖ 彼女はいい人のように**見える** She *seems to be* a good person. ／She *seems like* a good person. (➤ 第1文のように seem は名詞が後続する場合は to be を省かない；インフォーマルな言い方では第2文が好まれる) ‖ 彼はインテリに**見える**が頭はあまりよくない He *appears* (*to be*) intelligent, but he is not very smart.

▶ああ**見えて**彼女はなかなか頼りになる人だ She *may not look it*, but she is a quite reliable person.

3【実態を理解できる】▶彼女の今度の作品には大幅な進歩の跡が**見える** This work of hers *shows* great improvement in her artistic skills. ‖ 彼の態度には少しも反省の**色が見えない** The way he behaves *doesn't give the slightest impression* that he really feels sorry. ‖ 自分の欠点は**見えない**ものだ People *are blind to* their own shortcomings.

4【「来る」の尊敬語】▶パパ，池田さんが**お見えになりました** Dad, Mr. Ikeda *has arrived*. ‖ きょうは5人のお客様が**お見えになる** We *are expecting* five guests today. (➤「来ることを予期している」の意).

みおくり 見送り **1【人を送ること】a send-off** ▶ジュリーを**見送りに**成田空港へ行った I went to Narita Airport *to see* Julie *off*.

✉ **空港まで見送りに来てくださってどうもありがとう** Thank you very much for coming to the airport *to see* me *off*.

2【そのままにすること】▶減税法案は国会において**見送りとなった** The tax-cut bill *was shelved* [《米また》*was tabled*] in the Diet. ‖ 石川は**見送りの三振に**倒れた Ishikawa struck out *without swinging*. ／Ishikawa watched the third strike.

みおくる 見送る **1【人を送る】see ... off** ▶羽田空港でおじを**見送った** I *saw* my uncle *off* at Haneda Airport. ‖ 彼らは駅のホームで新婚カップルを盛大に**見送った** They *gave* the newlyweds *a* grand *send-off* on the station platform. →見送り.

2【やり過ごす】▶練習不足で，彼女は今回のピアノコンクール出場を**見送った** She *gave up* (the idea of) participating [*decided not to* participate] in the piano competition this time (around) because she hadn't practiced enough.

みおさめ 見納め ▶それが祖父の**見納め**になった It was *the last time for me to see* my grandfather.

みおとし 見落とし (an) **oversight** ▶**見落とし**のないようにもう一度チェックしなさい Check again to make sure there are no *oversights*.

みおとす 見落とす **overlook** +㊐ (見ていながら気がつかない)；**miss** +㊐ (見損なう) ▶その事故は運転士が停止信号を**見落とした**のが原因だった The accident resulted from the train driver's *overlooking* [*missing*] a stop signal. ‖ 我々はリストにある倉田君の名を**見落とした** We *failed to notice* Kurata's name on the list.

みおとり 見劣り ▶この半導体は日本製のものと比べて**見劣りがする** The quality of this semiconductor *is visibly inferior* [*pales in comparison*] *to* that of Japanese ones.

▶複製は当然のことながら原画に比べて**見劣りする** Reproductions naturally *pale in comparison to* their originals. ‖ ドラゴンズの戦力はジャイアンツに比べても**見劣りしない** (＝同等だ) The Dragons are *just as* strong *as* the Giants.

みおぼえ 見覚え ▶あの記者には**見覚えがある** I *recognize* that reporter. ／That reporter *looks familiar to* me. (➤ I remember that reporter's face. はふつうではない).

みおも 身重 ▶**身重**の女性 a woman who *is expecting* (*a baby*).

みおろす 見下ろす **look down** 《on》(下を眺める)；**overlook** +㊐；**look over** (見渡す) ▶海を**見下ろす**丘 a hill *overlooking* the sea ‖ 展望台から下を見下ろしたら目が回った I felt dizzy when I *looked down* from the observation deck.

みかい 未開の **uncivilized**（文明化していない）; **undeveloped**（未開発の）; **primitive**（原始的な）▶未開の国 an *uncivilized* [a *primitive*] country ‖ その国の北部は長い間未開のままであった The northern part of the country has been *undeveloped* for a long time.

みかいけつ 未解決の **unsolved**; **pending**（未処理の）▶その誘拐事件は未解決だ That kidnapping (case) *remains unsolved.* ‖ 大臣は多くの未解決の問題を残したまま辞任した The minister resigned leaving a lot of problems *unsolved.* ‖ それは未解決の問題だ That's a *pending* question. ／That question is *unresolved.*

みかいたく 未開拓 ▶19世紀の中頃, アメリカ西部はまだ未開拓だった The West was still *undeveloped* in the middle of the nineteenth century.
▶《比喩的》この地域はファーストフード産業の未開拓市場だ This area is an *untapped* [a *potential*] *market* for the fast-food industry. (➤ potential は「潜在的な, 可能性のある」).

みかいはつ 未開発 ▶未開発（＝未開拓）の分野 an *unexplored* field (of study) ‖ その島は未開発の天然資源が豊富だ That island has an abundance of *untapped* [*unexploited*] natural resources.

みかえし 見返し **endpapers**（本の最初と最後で表紙とつながっているページ）.

みかえす 見返す **1**【見直す】▶もう一度論文を見返しなさい *Look over* your paper again.
2【かつてのあなどりに報いる】▶いつかあのいやな監督を見返してやる Someday I'll *get even with* that nasty manager. ‖ いつかあの人たちを見返してやりたい I want them to *recognize my worth* someday. (●こういう場合, 英語では「自分の値打ちを認めさせたい」と考える).

みかえり 見返り ▶その課長は便宜を図る見返りにその建設業者に100万円を要求した The section chief demanded one million yen from the construction firm *in exchange for* accommodating them [their wishes].

みがき 磨き ▶ワックスを塗って床に磨きをかける *shine* the floor after applying wax to it.
▶《比喩的》きみのタイ語に磨きをかけるにはタイに行くに限るよ The best way to *brush up* (*on*) [*polish* (*up*)] your Thai is to go to Thailand. (➤ brush up には「忘れかけたことをやり直して磨きをかける」の含みがあるが, polish up にはそれがないのがふつう).

みかぎる 見限る **give up**《on》▶彼は発展性のない会社を見限って独立した He has started his own business after *giving up on* working for a company with no future.
▶しっかりしないと彼女に見限られるよ Your girlfriend will *leave* you if you don't shape up! (➤ leave は「人のもとを去る」).

みかく 味覚 **the (sense of) taste, the palate** /pǽlət/ ▶料理人は鋭い味覚をもっていなければならない A cook must have a keen *sense of taste* [a delicate *palate*].

みがく 磨く **1**【こすってきれいにする】**brush** +目（ブラシで）; **shine** +目, **polish** +目（つやを出す）▶歯をよくみがきなさい *Brush* your teeth well. ‖ お父さん, 靴をみがいておいたからね Dad, I've *shined* [*polished*] your shoes. ‖ 床をみがかなくっちゃ I've got to *clean* [*wax*] the floor. ‖ クレンザーで流しをみがいてくださらない？ Could you *scrub* the sink with cleanser? (➤ scrub は「ごしごしこする」).
▶《慣用表現》彼はみがけば光る逸材だ He's *a diamond in the rough.* (➤「未加工のダイヤモンド」が原義).
2【向上させる】**polish (up), brush up; enhance**（…を高める）→磨き ▶彼女はパリでデザイナーとしての腕をみがいた She *polished up* [*honed*] her designing skills in Paris. (➤ hone は「といしで研ぐ」が原義) ‖ きみは英語をさらにみがく必要がある You need to *polish* (*up*) [*brush up* (*on*)] your English. ‖ 自分をみがく *develop* [*train*] one's mind ‖ 女子力をみがく *enhance* one's feminine charm.

みかくにん 未確認の **unconfirmed**; **unidentified**（正体不明の）▶その情報は未確認です That information has *not* yet *been confirmed.* ／That information is still *unconfirmed.* ‖ 未確認飛行物体 a UFO (＝unidentified flying object).

みかけ 見掛け an **appearance**, a **look**（➤ともにしばしば複数形で用いる）▶人を見かけだけで判断してはいけない Don't judge a person only by his or her *appearance* [*looks*]. ‖ 彼は見かけは武骨だが, 実は繊細な神経をしている He *looks* uncouth, but in reality he's quite sensitive. ‖ 母は見かけより丈夫だ My mother is healthier *than she looks.*
▶それは見かけだけさ It's *just a façade.* (➤ façade /fəsɑ́:d/ は「(建物の通りに面した)正面」の意から「(偽りの)外見」) ‖ あんな大男がころりと負けるなんて, 見かけ倒しだね He *can't have been as* strong *as he looked,* or he wouldn't have been beaten so easily. (➤「見た目ほど強くはなかった」の意) ‖ このオートバイは見かけによらずスピードが出る This motorcycle goes fast, *despite its appearance.* ／This motorcycle goes faster *than it looks.* (➤「見かけ以上に」) ‖ あのけちな社長が福祉団体に属していたなんて, 人は見かけによらないね Our stingy president is a member of a charitable organization; *you can't judge people by their looks,* can you?

みかける 見掛ける **see** +目 ▶今しがた彼女が買い物に出かけるところを見かけた I *saw* her leave to go shopping just now. ‖ あの人はこの辺でよく見かける人だ That man *is often seen* around here. ‖ 閉店してシャッターを閉めた店舗は商店街でよく見かける光景だ Shuttered stores are *a familiar sight* in many shopping streets.

¹みかた 見方 a **point of view**, a **viewpoint**（視点）; an **angle**（物事を見る角度）▶あなたと私とでは物の見かたが違う My *point of view* is different from yours. ／We see things differently. ‖ 歴史家と文学者とでは歴史に対する見かたが違う Historians and novelists *look at* history *from different angles.*
▶この表の見かた（＝読み方）がわからない I can't understand *how to read* this table.

²みかた 味方 a **friend** 一動 **味方する** **stand by; take ~'s side, take sides with, side with**（…の側につく）▶撃つな！我々は味方だ Don't shoot! We're *friends*! ‖ スーパーマンはいつも弱い者の味方だ Superman is always *a friend* of the weak [*on the side of* the weak]. ‖ どんなことがあってもきみの味方だよ I'll *stand by* you, no matter what. ‖ 対話「お父さんとお母さんがけんかしたときはどっちの味方をするの？」「どっちの味方もしないさ」"*Whose side* do you *take* when your dad and mom quarrel?" "I *take neither side.*" ‖ 私が反対したとき, 誰も味方をしてくれなかった When I objected, nobody *sided with* me. ‖ 私が味方についているから安心しなさい I'll always *be on your side*, so don't worry. (➤ be on ~'s side で「~の味方をしている」).

みかづき 三日月 a **crescent (moon)** ; a [**the**] **new moon**(ごく細い月) ▶三日月が空にかかっている *A crescent moon* is hanging in the sky.

みがって 身勝手な selfish ▶子供たちはときに身勝手な行動をする Children sometimes act *selfishly*. ‖ きみたちの身勝手なふるまいは許さない(=好きなようにはさせない) I won't let you have your own way.

みかねる 見かねる ▶私は高校生たちがたばこを吸っているのを見るに見かねてやめろと言った I *couldn't stand* [*bear*] *to see* the high school students smoking, so I told them to stop (it). (➤ この stand は「がまんする」).

みがまえる 身構える ▶彼は自分を守ろうと身構えた He *took a* defensive *stance*. (➤「防御の姿勢をとった」の意) ‖ 私は外国人に話しかけられると何となく身構えてしまう I *become* somewhat *nervous* when a foreigner speaks to me.

みがら 身柄 ▶先生は問題の生徒の身柄を引き取りに警察に行った The teacher went to the police *to take* the delinquent student *under his charge*. (➤「自分の監督下に置くために」の意) ‖ 警察は容疑者の身柄を確保した The police *captured* the suspect.

みがる 身軽 ▶彼は身軽に小川を飛び越えた He *nimbly* jumped across the brook.
▶旅行は身軽(=軽装)がいい Travel *light*. (➤ 決まった言い方) ‖ 彼は身軽な服装をしていた He *was lightly dressed*.
✉ **子供が小学校へ行き始めたので昼間は身軽になりました** I'm now *free* in the daytime because my son [daughter] started going to elementary school.

みがわり 身代わり a **scapegoat**(代わりに罪を負う人) ▶牧師が人質の身代わりになった The minister *took the place of* the hostages.

¹みかん 蜜柑 a ***mikan*** ; a **satsuma**

> **《解説》** 日本の「温州(うんしゅう)ミカン」は日本語から英語化した *mikan* や satsuma (orange) を用いるのがよい (satsuma は「薩摩」から). ほかに日本のミカンに近いものに tangerine や mandarin orange, clementine があり, ともに日本のミカンを指すのに用いられることがある.

²みかん 未完の unfinished(終わってはいない) ; **incomplete**(完全ではない) ▶作家の死で小説は未完のまま残された The author died leaving the novel *unfinished* [*incomplete*].
▶《慣用表現》その投手は未完の大器だ He is a *great* pitcher *in the making*. (➤ in the making は「完成への道を歩んでいる, 修業中の」の意).

みかんせい 未完成の unfinished(完成してはいない) ; **incomplete**(完全ではない) ▶モーツァルトは『レクイエム』を未完成のまま死んだ Mozart died with his "Requiem" *unfinished* [*incomplete*]. / Mozart died *before* he *had completed* composing his "Requiem."

みき 幹 a **trunk** ▶この杉は幹の太さが8メートルある The *trunk* of this Japanese cedar is eight meters thick. ‖ セミが1匹木の幹に止まった A cicada alighted on *a tree trunk*.

みぎ 右 **1【右側】the right** 一形 **右の right** ▶次の角を右に曲がりなさい Turn (*to the*) *right* at the next corner. (➤ カッコ内は言わないほうがふつう) ‖ 右側に海が見えてきた The sea came into view *on the* [*my*] *right*. ‖ アメリカでは車は右側通行だ Cars and trucks are supposed to *keep to the right* in the United States. ‖ 右回りに自己紹介してください Please introduce yourselves *in clockwise order*. (➤ clockwise は「時計回りの」の意) ‖ 右へならえ! *Dress right!*
▶右向け右! *Right face!* ‖ **対話** 《写真を見せて》「私は右から3番目」「その右の人は誰?」"I am the third *from the right*." "And who is *on your right*?" ‖ 彼は右上がりで字を書く His handwriting *slants upward*.
✉ **家族の動画を送ります. 私の右でギターを弾いている人が兄の圭介です** I'm sending video taken of my family. Here *on my right*, playing the guitar, is my older brother Keisuke.
▶《慣用表現》暗算にかけては彼女の右に出る者はいない She *is second to none* in mental arithmetic. (➤「誰にも負けない」の意) ‖ 友だちが焼きそばを注文したので, 私も右へならえした My friends ordered fried noodles, and I *followed suit* [*followed their example*].
‖ 右上 upper right ‖ 右下 lower right.
2【右翼】the right wing(政党などの) ▶あの大臣は右寄りだ That Minister is *a rightist*. (➤ rightist は「右派の人」).

みぎうで 右腕 the right arm(右の腕) ; a **right hand**(頼りにする人) ▶彼は長年, 社長の右腕として働いてきた He has been the president's *right-hand man* for many years.

みぎかた 右肩 one's **right shoulder** ▶右肩上がりの売り上げ *ever increasing* [*steadily growing*] sales.

みきき 見聞き ▶私は中国旅行中に見聞きしたことを彼女に話した I told her what I *saw* (*and heard*) during my trip to China.

みぎきき 右利き a **right-handed person**, a **right-hander** ▶私は右利きだ I am *right-handed*.

ミキサー a **blender**, 《英また》a **liquidizer** /líkwɪdaɪzəʳ/ (台所用の) ; a **concrete mixer** (コンクリートミキサー) ; a **mixer** (音声調節者) ▶ミキサーでトマトジュースを作る make tomato juice with [in] *a blender*.

> **危ないカタカナ語✹ミキサー**
> **1** 日本では果物や野菜をくだいてジュースを作る機械を「ミキサー」と呼んでいるが, 英語では blender, 《英また》liquidizer という.
> **2** 英語の mixer は混合する機械や人を指す. food mixer や concrete mixer のほか, 放送局などで音声や画面を調整する装置, およびその係の人も mixer である.

みぎて 右手 the right hand(右の手) ; **the right**(右の方向) ▶大半の人は右手で書く Most people write with *their right hand*.
▶まもなく右手に東京都庁舎が見えます You will soon see the Tokyo Metropolitan Government Office *on* [*to*] *the right*.

みぎひだり 右左 right and left ▶通りを渡るときは右左をよく確かめて Look (to *the*) *right and left* [*both ways*] before you cross the street. (➤ 後者の言い方がふつう).

みきり 見切り ▶その計画は見切りをつけなさいよ *Give*

up on [*Forget* (*all*) *about*] that plan.
‖**見切り発車** starting a train [bus] before all passengers are on board, rushing to act(➤ 比喩的) ‖**見切り品** a bargain.

みぎれい 身奇麗 ▶あの老婦人はいつもみぎれいにしている That elderly lady always *keeps herself clean and tidy*.

みきわめる 見極める ▶情勢を見極めたうえで対応を決める *carefully assess* [*investigate*] the situation and then decide how to respond ‖論文を書くときはまず問題が何であるかを見極める(＝はっきりさせる)ことが大切だ When writing a paper, it is essential to first *ascertain* the issues to be dealt with.

みくだす 見下す **look down on** ▶日本人の中には東南アジアの人を見下す人がいる Some Japanese *look down on* Southeast Asians. ‖あいつの人を見下したような(＝横柄な)口のきき方が気に食わない I don't like his *arrogant* way of speaking.

みくだりはん 三行半 a short letter of divorce (given by a husband to his wife during the Edo period) (➤ 説明的な訳).

みくびる 見くびる **underestimate** +目 (過小評価する); **make light of, sell ... short** (軽んじる; 後者の言い方が「見くびる」に近い) ▶年下だからといってあいつを見くびるとやられるぞ If you *underestimate* him just because he's younger, you'll lose. ‖俺を見くびるなよ Don't *underestimate* me. / Don't *sell* me *short*.

みくらべる 見比べる **compare** 《with》 ▶私は自分の英語の点数を彼のと見比べてみた I *compared* my score on the English test *with* his. ‖どっちの絵がいいか, 2つをじっくり見比べてみよう *Compare* the two pictures carefully to see which is better.

みぐるしい 見苦しい **ugly** (醜い); **shameful** (恥ずべき) ▶丘の上のあの塔は全く見苦しい That tower on the hill is really *ugly*. ‖酔っ払った男たちのふるまいは見苦しかった The behavior of the drunk men was *shameful* [*disgraceful*]. ‖あの汚れたカーテンは見苦しい Those dirty curtains are *an eyesore*. (➤ eyesore は「目ざわりなもの」の意) ‖お見苦しいところをお目にかけました I'm sorry you had to witness such a *disgraceful* display.

みぐるみ 身ぐるみ ▶私はニューヨークの路上で身ぐるみはがれた I was robbed of *everything I had* on the street in New York.

ミクロ **micro** /máɪkroʊ/ ▶ミクロの世界 the *microscopic* world / the world *of microorganisms* (➤ それぞれ「顕微鏡的な世界」「微生物の世界」が原義).
‖**ミクロ経済学** microeconomics ‖**ミクロコスモス** a microcosm.

ミクロネシア **Micronesia** /màɪkrəníːʒə/ (フィリピンの東方, 日付変更線に至る島々)
‖**ミクロネシア人** a Micronesian.

ミクロン a **micron** /máɪkrɑːn/ (100万分の1メートル).

みけいけん 未経験の **inexperienced** ▶私はキャッチャーは未経験だからやりたくない I don't want to play catcher because I'm *inexperienced* in that position.
▶私たちはみんな乗馬は未経験だった *None* of us *had any previous experience* in horse riding. ‖**未経験者** an inexperienced person.

みけつ 未決の **pending** (未解決の); **undecided** (未決定の) ▶その問題は未決である That matter is still *pending* [*undecided*].
‖**未決囚** an unconvicted prisoner ‖**未決書類** pending documents.

みけねこ 三毛猫 a **tortoiseshell** /tɔ́ːrṭəsʃel/ (**cat**).

みけん 眉間 **the space between the eyebrows** /áɪbraʊz/ ▶彼はみけんにしわを寄せた(＝まゆをひそめた) He *knitted his brows*.

みこ 巫女 a ***miko***, a **shrine maiden**; a **girl in the service of a Shinto shrine** (神社に仕える少女); a **shaman** (まじない師).

みこうにん 未公認の **unofficial** ▶未公認記録 an *unofficial* record.

みこし 神輿 a ***mikoshi***
日本紹介 ✉ **みこしは, おみこしともいい, 神道のご神体を乗せる輿(こし)です. 祭礼のときに地元の人々が肩にかついで通りを練り歩きます** A *mikoshi*, or *omikoshi*, is a portable Shinto shrine that holds a sacred object of worship. During festivals, local people parade through the streets carrying *mikoshi* on their shoulders.
▶《慣用表現》政府は財政再建にようやくみこしを上げた(＝取りかかった) The government has finally *started taking action* to put its finances in order.

みこす 見越す **expect** +目 ▶私たちは地価の騰貴を見越して土地を買った We bought land because we *expected* [*anticipated*] that land prices would skyrocket. ‖インフレを見越して金(きん)を買う人がいる Some people buy gold *in anticipation of* inflation.

みごたえ 見応え ▶そのプロレスの試合は本当に見ごたえがあった The professional wrestling match *was* really *worth watching*. (●「見る価値があった」と考えて訳す) ‖この頃は見ごたえのある映画が少ない Nowadays, there are very few movies (really) *worth seeing*. (➤ see は「何かが目に入る」の意で, 映画の場合はこの動詞がふつう).

みごと 見事

一形 みごとな **fine** (りっぱな); **wonderful** (すばらしい); **excellent** (すぐれた); **beautiful** (美しい); **superb** (とびきりりっぱな, 最高の); **amazing** (驚異的な) **一副 みごとに** **beautifully** (美しく); **successfully** (首尾よく)
▶ほら, みごとな夕焼けだよ Look at the *beautiful* [*wonderful*] sunset! ‖社長室にはみごとなびょうぶが飾ってある A *superb* [*fine*] folding screen is displayed in the president's office. ‖コックはみごとな包丁さばきを見せた The cook demonstrated *amazing* knife-cutting skills. ‖おみごと! *Well done!* (➤ よくできたね の意) / *Beautiful!* / *Wonderful!*
▶ことしもバラがみごとに咲いた The roses bloomed *beautifully* again this year. ‖三田氏は初挑戦でみごとに当選した Mr. Mita was *successfully* elected on his first time in the election. ‖娘は入試で苦戦するかと思ったが, みごとに合格した We thought our daughter might have difficulty with the entrance examinations, but she came through *with flying colors*. (➤ with flying colors は「大成功を収めて」の意のインフォーマルな表現).
▶《反語的》ロケットの打ち上げはみごとに失敗した They failed *completely* [*miserably*] in the attempt to launch the rocket. ‖あの詐欺師にはみごとにだまされた I was *completely* taken in by that con man.

みこみ 見込み **1** 【予想】(an) **expectation** ▶新幹線は午後運転再開の見込みです Shinkansen service *is expected* to resume in the afternoon. ‖彼の仕事ぶりはだいぶ見込み外れだった His work fell far short of our *expectations*. ‖それは私の見込み違いだった It was my *miscalculation.* (➤ miscalculation は「誤算」).

2【可能性】 (a) **chance**; **possibility** (状況判断によった); **hope** (望み) ▶この病人の回復の**見込みは十分ある** This patient has a good *chance* of recovery. ‖ この患者の回復の**見込みはほとんどない** There is little *hope* [*possibility*] of this patient's recovery. ‖ 今度のダービーであの馬が入賞する**見込みは少ない** That horse *doesn't stand a chance of* placing in the next Derby. (➤ stand a chance of で「…する見込みがある」の意; 否定文で用いることが多い) ‖ ぼくたちが試合に勝つ**見込みがないではない** We *do have a slim chance of* winning the game. (➤ 強調の do で,「わずかながら見込みがある」となり, do がないと「望み薄」になってしまう) ‖ 石原氏がうちの会社の社長になる**見込み**はどうですか How good are Mr. Ishihara's *chances* of becoming our company's president?

3【将来性】 ▶この若い芸術家は**見込みがある**(=有望だ) This young artist *is very promising.* ‖ きみはコックとして**見込みがない** You *have no future* as a cook.

みこむ 見込む **1【可能性があると頼りにする】** ▶きみを**見込んで**(=頼りがいのある人物と思って)頼みがある I think you're *a reliable person*, so I'd like to ask you a favor. ‖ 正夫は社長に**見込まれて**その社長の娘と結婚した *Winning the confidence of* [*Winning favor with*] the company president, Masao married his daughter.

2【予想する】 **expect** +㊐ (期待する); **anticipate** +㊐ (見越す) ▶昇給を**見込んで**背広を新調した I had a new suit made *in anticipation* [*expectation*] *of* a pay raise. ‖ 今回その水泳選手の入賞は**見込めそうもない** This time *there is little hope* for that swimmer to win any prizes. ‖ 初もうでの人出は500万人を超すものと**見込まれている** The turnout at shrines and temples during the New Year holidays *is expected* to top the five million mark.

みごもる 身籠る **get** [**become**] **pregnant** ▶彼女は有名な俳優の子を**身ごもった** She *got pregnant* by a famous actor.

みごろ 見頃で **at** one's **best**; **in full bloom** (花が) ▶上野公園の桜は今が**見頃です** The cherry blossoms in Ueno Park are now *at their best* [*in full bloom*]. ‖ 箱根の紅葉はいつが**見頃**ですか When are the autumn leaves in Hakone *at their peak* [*at their best*]?

みごろし 見殺し ▶きみはどうして彼が3人の男に袋だたきにされているのを**見殺しにした**のだ Why did you *stand by and watch* him being beaten by three men? (➤「傍観する」の意) ‖ 囚人2人は仲間1人を**見殺しにして**逃げた The two inmates ran away *leaving* their buddy *in the lurch.* (➤ leave ... in the lurch は「困っている…を見捨てる」).

みこん 未婚の **unmarried, unwed** (➤ 前者がふつう) ▶**未婚の**母 an *unmarried* [*unwed*] mother (➤ 最近では a single mother という言い方が好まれるが, この語は「離婚して一人の」の意にもなる) ‖ この学校には**未婚の**先生が多い There are many *unmarried* [*single*] teachers in this school.

ミサ (a) **Mass** /mæs/ (カトリックの) ▶**ミサ**に参列する attend [go to] *Mass* ‖ 世界平和のために**ミサ**がささげられた *Masses* were offered for world peace.

‖**ミサ曲** (a) mass.

ミサイル a **missile** /mísəl/ ▶**ミサイル**を発射する fire [launch] *a missile* ‖**ミサイル基地** a missile site [base] ‖ **巡航ミサイル** a cruise missile ‖ **弾道ミサイル** a ballistic missile.

みさお 操 **chastity** (貞操); **fidelity** (節操).

みさかい 見境 ▶彼は前後の**見境なく**上司を殴ってしまった He punched his boss *without thinking what might happen* to him *afterward.* ‖ ゲリラは**見境なく**(=無差別に)発砲した The guerrillas fired *indiscriminately.* ‖ 彼は酒を飲むと**見境がなくなる**(=手がつけられなくなる) He *loses all self-control* when he drinks.

みさき 岬 a **cape**; a **point** (突端) ▶足摺岬 *Cape* Ashizuri ‖ 室戸岬 Muroto *Point.*

みさげはてた 見下げ果てた **despicable** (卑しむべき); **contemptible** (軽べつに値する); **mean** (卑劣な); **miserable** (ひどく不快感をもよおす) ▶**見下げ果てた**うそつき a *miserable* liar ‖ 彼は友人たちを裏切るという**見下げ果てた**ことをした It was *despicable* of him to betray his friends.

みさげる 見下げる **look down on** [**upon**] ▶人を**見下げる** *look down on* [*upon*] a person.

みさだめる 見定める ▶転職するなら状況を**見定めて**から上司に伝えなさい If you (plan to) change jobs, *make sure where* [*how*] *things stand* before you tell your current boss (about it).

みざる 見猿 ▶**見猿, 聞か猿, 言わ猿** See no evil, hear no evil, speak no evil.

みじかい 短い

short; **brief** (簡潔な) **━動 短くする** **shorten** +㊐ ▶父さんは胴が長く, 足が**短い** My father has a long torso and *short* legs. ‖ このゆかた, ぼくには少し**短過ぎる** This yukata is a little (too) *short* for me. ‖ **短くて**しかも印象に残る話をするのはそう簡単ではない It is not all that easy to make a *brief* yet impressive speech.

▶休暇を3日間**短くした** I *shortened* my vacation by three days. ‖ 日がだいぶ**短くなってきた** The days have gotten much *shorter.* ‖ この鉛筆はだいぶ**短くなってきた** This pencil has become very *short.* / This pencil has worn down. (➤ wear down は「すり減る」) ‖ **短い**間ですがロンドンで生活したことがあります I once lived in London for a *short* (period of) time.

▶髪を**短くしてもらった** I had my hair *trimmed* [*cut short*]. ‖ 報告はできるだけ**短くしてくれますか** Could you make your report as *brief* as possible? ‖ 彼女の姓は山田だが, 私たちは**短く**「山」と呼んでいる Her family name is Yamada, but we call her "Yama" *for short.* ‖ この原稿, 少し**短くしてください** Please *shorten* the manuscript a little.

▶兄は**気が短い** My older brother is *impatient* [*short-tempered*]. ‖ あの患者は末期癌(がん)でもう**先が短い** That patient *doesn't have long to live* [That patient's *days are numbered*] since he has terminal cancer.

ミシガン **Michigan** (アメリカ中北部の州; 略 MI, Mich.).

ミシシッピー **Mississippi** (アメリカ南部の州; 略 MS, Miss.) ‖**ミシシッピー川** the Mississippi.

みじたく 身支度する **dress oneself, get dressed** ▶姉はいつも**身じたく**に時間がかかる My (older) sister always takes a lot of time *to get dressed.* ‖ 運動のできる**身じたくをして**校庭に集まりなさい Come to the playground *dressed* for exercise.

みしみし ▶わが家は小さな地震でも**みしみしする** Our

house *creaks* even in a slight earth tremor.

みじめ 惨めな **miserable**, **wretched** /rétʃɪd/ (➤ 後者がより強意); **sorry** (悲しい, おそまつな) ▶みじめな敗北 a *miserable* [*wretched*] defeat ‖ 金をためておかないと老後みじめな思いをするぞ If you don't save money, you'll be *miserable* when you're old. ／Save money, or you'll *regret* it when you're old. ‖ 彼らの大計画はみじめな結果に終わった Their ambitious plan *came to a sorry end*. ‖ 対話「今月, 小遣いあと500円しかないんだ」「みじめー!」 "There's only 500 yen of my spending money left this month." "*Poor you!*" (➤ この poor は「かわいそうな」の意).

みじゅく 未熟な **immature** /ìmətjóəʳ/ (未完成の); **poor** (へたな); **unskilled** (熟練していない) ▶未熟な女優 an *immature* actress ‖ 未熟な運転 *unskilled* driving ‖ 彼女の運転はまだ未熟だ She's still a *poor* driver. ‖ 教師としては未熟です I *don't have much* [*a lot of*] *experience* as a teacher.
▶おまえのような未熟者が何を言うか That's a fine thing for *a greenhorn* [*a novice*／*a newcomer*] like you to say. (➤ novice は「新米」, newcomer は「新入り」) ‖ 未熟者ですが, よろしくお願いします I'*m new at this*, but I promise I'll give it my best. (🏺「慣れていませんけれどがんばります」と積極性を示すのが英語的).
‖未熟児 a premature baby, 《米・インフォーマル》 a preemie /príːmi/.

[1]**みしょう 未詳の** **unknown**; **unidentified**.

[2]**みしょう 実生** a **seedling**(苗木).

みしらぬ 見知らぬ **unknown**(知られていない); **unfamiliar** (なじみのない); **strange** (見たことも聞いたこともない) ▶見知らぬ国 an *unknown* [an *unfamiliar*] country ‖ 見知らぬ人 *a stranger* ‖ そのパーティーに行ってみたが見知らぬ顔ばかりだった I went to the party, but there was no one I knew there [but all the people there were *new to me*].

みじろぎ 身じろぎ ▶彼女は外の雨を見つめたまま身じろぎもせず立っていた She was standing *motionless* looking at the falling rain outside. ‖ うちの子供たちはドラえもんのテレビ番組をいつも身じろぎもせずに見ている Our children *are* always *glued to* the TV when the Doraemon show comes on. (➤「くぎづけになっている」の意).

ミシン a **sewing** /sóʊɪŋ/ **machine** ▶彼女はミシンでスカートを縫っている She is sewing a skirt on the *sewing machine* [by *machine*]. ‖ この着物はミシン縫いですか, 手縫いですか Is this kimono *machine-sewn* or hand-sewn?

みじん 微塵 **1【細かいもの】** a **particle** (微粒子); a **piece** (小片, 断片) ▶フロントガラスが粉みじんに壊れた The windshield was smashed *into little pieces* [*smithereens*]. ‖ タマネギをみじん切りにしてください *Chop* the onions *finely*. ／*Mince* the onions.
2【わずか】 ▶傭兵たちには大統領に対する忠誠心はみじんもなかった The mercenary soldiers didn't have *a speck of* loyalty to the president.

[1]**ミス** 《間違い》 a **mistake**, an **error** 一動 ミスする **make a mistake**, **err** /əːʳ/ (→かこみ記事, 間違い) ▶つづり [スペリング] のミス a spelling *mistake* ‖ 同じミスを繰り返すな Don't repeat the same *mistake(s)* [*error(s)*]! ‖ ミスは誰にでもある *Everybody makes mistakes*. ‖ 1つミスすると最初からやり直しだ If I *make one mistake*, I have to start all over. ‖ あいつ, またミスったぞ He *goofed* again! (➤ goof は「へまをする」の意のインフォーマルな語).
‖ミスプリント a misprint.

[2]**ミス** 《未婚の女性》 **Miss** (➤ 敬称として); an **unmarried woman**, a **single woman** (➤ 最近では後者が好まれる) ▶ミスアメリカがミスユニバースに選ばれた *Miss* USA won the *Miss* Universe title. ／*Miss* USA was chosen *Miss* Universe.

> **危ないカタカナ語✹ ミス**
> **1**「失敗」の意の「ミス」は miss よりも mistake や error が近い. miss は「(的などへの)当て損ない」の意味で用いることが多く, 動詞の miss も「当て損なう」「捕まえ損なう」「見逃す」などの意味. 日本語の「ミスをする」に当たるのは make a mistake である. →間違い.
> **2** 日本では未婚の女性を指して「ミス」というが, この用法は英語にはない. unmarried woman とか single woman のようにいう. 英語の Miss は未婚女性の姓または姓名の前につける敬称である. なお, 未婚・既婚の別を明示したくない場合は Ms. /mɪz/ を用いる. →ミズ, ミセス.

みず 水 **1【飲料水など】** **water**, **cold water** →湯 ▶蛇口から水が漏れている *Water* is dripping from the faucet. ‖ 水を1杯頂けますか? May I have a glass of *water*, please? ‖ 東京では今水が不足している Tokyo *is suffering from a water shortage* [*a shortage of water*]. ‖ この川の水は飲めるのかな Is the *water* from this stream safe to drink [drinkable]?
▶砂糖は水よりお湯のほうがよく溶ける Sugar dissolves more (easily) in hot water than in *cold water*. (➤ この場合は hot water との対比になっているので cold は省けない) ‖ 水を節約しましょう Save [Conserve] *water*. ‖ 彼は水を出して足を洗った He *turned on the water* [*ran water*] to wash his feet. (➤ ともに「水道の水を出す」の意.「止める」は turn off) ‖ 陽子, 花壇に水をやってくれない? Yoko, will you *water* the flowerbed? (➤ この water は「水をやる」の意の動詞).
‖水あか (water) scale ‖ 水薬 a liquid medicine ‖ 水栽培 water culture.
2【洪水】 a **flood** /flʌd/ ▶豪雨で水が出た(=川がはんらんした) Due to the heavy rain, *the river overflowed* (its banks). ‖ 神田川周辺の30世帯が水につかった Thirty houses near the Kanda River *were flooded*. ‖ 水は午後になって引き始めた *The water* [*flood*] began to recede in the afternoon.
3【慣用表現】
水と油 ▶久美と理恵はまるで水と油だ(=仲が悪い) Kumi does*n't get along with* Rie. ／Kumi and Rie *are oil and water*: they just don't mix. (➤ 語順の違いに注意). **水に流す** ▶俊夫と京子は昔のことを水に流して(=忘れて)仲直りすることにした Toshio and Kyoko decided to *forget* (*about*) the past and make up. ‖ 過ぎたことは水に流せ Let's forgive and forget. ／Let bygones be bygones. (➤ ともに決まった言い方). **水の泡** →見出語 **水も滴る** ▶水も滴るいい男 a *strikingly handsome* man ‖ 水も滴るいい女 a *stunning*(*ly beautiful*) [*ravishing*] woman.
水をあける ▶1位の泳者は2位の選手に大きく水をあけた(=リードを広げた) The first swimmer *widened his* [*her*] *lead* greatly over the closest competitor. **水を打ったよう** ▶聴衆は水を打ったように静かだった The audience was so quiet that you could

have heard a pin drop. (➤「とても静かだったのでピンが1本落ちても聞こえただろう」の意). **水を得た魚** ▶彼女は勉強しなければならないときはあまり楽しそうではないが, テニスをするときはまるで水を得た魚のようだ She doesn't look so happy when she has to study, but she is *like a fish back in water* [is *in her element*] when she plays tennis. (➤ in one's element は「本領を発揮して」の意).
水をさす ▶せっかくのお祝いのパーティーに水をさすようなことを言うな Don't *throw a wet blanket* over the celebration. ／Don't *be a wet blanket* at the celebration. ‖ぼくたちの関係に水をささないでよ Don't try to *ruin* [*destroy*] our relationship. **水を向ける** ▶「好きな人はいないの？」と水を向けたら, 彼女は恋人のことをいろいろと話し出した When I tried to *draw* her *out* by asking if she had someone she was in love with, she began to talk a lot about her boyfriend.

逆引き熟語 ○○水
雨水 rainwater／**飲料水** drinking water／**温水** heated water／**海水** seawater／**下水** sewage, wastewater／**工業用水** industrial water／**工場廃水** industrial wastewater／**上水** a water supply, clean water／**蒸留水** distilled water／**生活排水** household wastewater／**精製水** purified water／**ソーダ水** soda (water), (soda) pop／**炭酸水** carbonated water, soda (water)／**淡水** fresh water／**地下水** ground water／**天然水** natural water／**冷却水** (a) coolant／**冷水** cold [chilled] water

ミズ **Ms., Ms** /mɪz/《参考》ウーマンリブ運動の結果生まれた呼称で, 未婚・既婚を問わず女性の姓または姓名の前につける. 仕事ではMs. を用い, 社交ではMrs. を用いるというように使い分けている女性も多い.

みずあげ 水揚げ **1**【陸揚げ】**unloading** ▶船荷を水揚げする *unload* a ship.
2【漁獲高】a **catch (of fish)**, a **haul (of fish)** ▶ことしはサバの水揚げ高が少ない We've had a poor *catch* [*haul*] of mackerel this year.
3【売上高】**takings**; **profits** (利益) ▶きょうそのタクシーの水揚げは少なかった Today, the taxi *did not make much money* [*profit*].

みずあそび 水遊び ▶幼い頃よく妹と水遊びをしたものです When we were children, my (younger) sister and I often used to *play in the water* [*have water fights*]. (➤ 後者は「水のかけっこ」など).

みずあび 水浴びする **take a bath,**《英》**have a bathe** /beɪð/ ▶スズメが水たまりで水浴びをしている A sparrow is *taking a bath* in the puddle.

みずあめ 水あめ **starch syrup.**

みずあらい 水洗いする **rinse** +㊀ ▶ホウレンソウをよく水洗いする *rinse* the spinach well.

みすい 未遂の **attempted**; **abortive** (失敗の) ▶その男は自殺を企てたが未遂に終わった(＝失敗した) He attempted suicide but *failed*. (➤ attempt には「不成功」のニュアンスがある) ‖彼らのクーデターは未遂に終わった Their coup *was aborted*. ‖先週3件の殺人未遂事件があった There were three cases of *attempted murder* last week.

みずいぼ 水いぼ《医学》**molluscum contagiosum** /məlʌ̀skəm kənteɪdʒióʊsəm/ (伝染性軟属腫).

みずいらず 水入らず ▶元旦(がんたん)は必ず自宅で家族水入らずで過ごします Our family always spends New Year's Day at home *by ourselves*. (➤「自分たちだけで」と考える). ／We always spend New Year's Day at home *as a family*.

みずいろ 水色 **light blue.**

みずうみ 湖 a **lake** ▶琵琶湖は日本でいちばん大きな湖だ Lake Biwa is the largest (*lake*) in Japan. ‖私たちは湖でボート遊びを楽しんだ We enjoyed boating on the *lake*.

ミズーリ **Missouri** (アメリカ中部の州; 略 MO, Mo.).

みすえる 見据える ▶政府は10年先を見すえた財政政策を作るべきだ The government should always *look* ten years *ahead* when making economic policy.

みずかき 水搔き a **web** (水鳥などの); a **flipper** (イルカやアザラシのひれ足).

みずかけろん 水掛け論 an **unsuccessful** [a **useless**] **argument** (むなしい議論) ▶どちらにおちどがあるかの話し合いは水掛け論に終わった The discussion between the two parties as to which was to blame *was unsuccessful* [*was useless*／*got* them *nowhere*].

みずかさ 水嵩 ▶水かさの増した[減った]川 a *swollen* [*fallen*] river ‖長良川は今の時期にしては水かさが多い The Nagara (River) is *higher than usual* at [for] this time of (the) year.

みすかす 見透かす **see through** ▶老人の鋭い目にこちらの意図が見透かされているように感じた It felt as if the old man had *seen through* my intentions with his sharp intuition. ‖彼は交渉を始める前にすでに相手の腹を見透かしていた He had *read* [*seen through*] the other person's intentions even before beginning negotiations.

みずがめざ 水瓶座 (an) **Aquarius.**

みずから 自ら **oneself** (自分自身で); **personally** (自分で直接) ▶社長はみずから大臣に会いに行った The president went to talk to the Minister *personally*.
▶きみがみずから行くこともないよ I don't think you have to go *yourself* [*in person*]. ‖グレン氏はみずから進んで宇宙飛行士になった Mr. Glenn became an astronaut *of his own accord*.

みずがれ 水涸れ (a) **drought** /draʊt/ (干ばつ); (a) **water shortage** (水不足).

みずぎ 水着 a **bathing** /béɪðɪŋ/ **suit**, a **swimsuit** (➤《英》では後者は女性用であることが多い); **swimming trunks** (男性用の水泳パンツ).

ミスキャスト **miscasting** ▶彼女の芸者役はミスキャストだと言われている People say that she *was miscast* as a geisha.

みずきり 水切り ▶水切り遊びをする play *ducks and drakes* ‖**水切り台**《米》a drainboard,《英》a draining board ‖**水切りボール** a colander.

みずぎわ 水際 **the water's edge** ▶水際からカワセミが飛び立った A kingfisher took to flight at *the edge of the water*.
▶水際だった手腕を発揮する show one's *outstanding* [*splendid*／*superb*] ability (➤ いずれも「際だってすぐれた, すばらしい」の意).
‖**水際作戦** shoreline operations.

みずくさ 水草 a **waterweed**, a **water plant.**

みずくさい 水臭い ▶ 対話「この写真おいくら？」「水臭いわね, あげるわよ」"How much do I owe you for this photo?" "*We're friends, aren't we?* Just take it." (●「友だちじゃないの」と考えて訳す).

みずけ 水気 **water** (水分); **juice** (汁) ▶野菜の水気を切る (wash and) *drain* vegetables ／(wash and) *drain the water off* the vegetables (➤「(タオルなどで)水気を拭き取る」ならば dry (off) vegetables (with a cloth)) ‖ 水気の多いナシ a *juicy* pear ‖ このリンゴは水気が多い[少ない] This apple is *juicy* [*dry*]. (➤ watery にすると飲み物などが「水っぽい」の意になる).

みずけむり 水煙 a **cloud of spray** ▶モーターボートが水煙をあげて走り去った A motorboat spun away sending up *a cloud of spray*.

ミズゴケ 《植物》**sphagnum** /sfǽgnəm/, **bog moss.**

みすごす 見過ごす **overlook** +㊐ (見落とす; 大目に見る) ▶彼が本当にそう書いたのなら見過ごすことはできない If he actually wrote that, then we cannot *overlook* it.
▶原発の危険性は専門家たちからもほとんど見過ごされてきた The dangers posed by nuclear power plants have *been* largely *overlooked* even by specialists.

みずさいばい 水栽培 **hydroponics, hydroponic cultivation** ▶水栽培のトマト a *hydroponic* tomato ‖ ヒヤシンスを水栽培で育てる grow hyacinths by *hydroponics*.

みずさかずき 水杯 ▶(別れの)水杯を交わす exchange *a farewell cup of water*.

みずさきあんない 水先案内 a **pilot**(人).

みずさし 水差し 《米》a **pitcher,** 《英》a **jug.**

みずしごと 水仕事 **scrubbing and washing** (掃除洗濯); **kitchen work** (台所仕事).

みずしぶき 水しぶき a **splash** (はねた水); (a) **spray** (水煙) ▶(リレーの)第一泳者たちは水しぶきをあげてプールに飛び込んだ The first swimmers (in the relay) jumped into the pool *with a splash*. ‖ 船のデッキに出ていて水しぶきでぬれてしまった I got wet with *spray* on the deck of the ship.

みずしょうばい 水商売 **the restaurant and bar business**(飲食業); **the entertainment business** (芸能関係の仕事); a **chancy business** [**trade**] (不安定な仕事) ▶彼女の母親は水商売をしている Her mother *works in a bar* [*a nightclub* / *a cabaret*].

みずしらず 見ず知らずの **strange** ▶私はパチンコ店の前で見ず知らずの人に話しかけられた *A total* [*complete*] *stranger* accosted me in front of the pachinko parlor.

みずすまし 水澄まし 《虫》a **whirligig beetle.**

ミスター **Mr.** (➤男性の姓または姓名の前につける敬称).

みずたき 水炊き ***mizutaki*** ▶鶏の水炊き a chicken *hotpot*.

みずたまもよう 水玉模様 **polka dots** ▶水玉模様のブラウスを着た女の子 a girl in a *polka-dot* blouse.

みずたまり 水溜まり a **pool**; a **puddle** (小さな) ▶ゆうべの豪雨で庭に大きな水たまりができた Last night's heavy rain formed [made] a large *pool* in the garden.

みずっぽい 水っぽい **watery**(水気の多い); **thin, weak** (薄い) ▶水っぽいスープ (a) *watery* [*thin* / *weak*] soup.

みずでっぽう 水鉄砲 a **water pistol,** a **squirt (gun).**

ミステリー (a) **mystery** ▶彼がどのようにして試験に合格したかは我々にはいまだにミステリー(=なぞ)だ How he passed the exam is still *a mystery* to us.
‖ミステリー小説[映画] a mystery.

みすてる 見捨てる **abandon** +㊐ (➤「見捨てる」の一般語で堅い語); **desert** /dɪzə́ːrt/ +㊐ (法律上・道義上見捨ててはいけないものを); **leave** +㊐ (置いて行ってしまう) ▶わが子を見捨てる *abandon* [*leave* / *desert* / *forsake*] one's own child ‖ 彼に限って私を見捨てるはずがない He would be the last person to *leave* me *in the lurch*. (➤ leave ... in the lurch は「(窮地に立っている人を)見殺しにする」の意のインフォーマルな言い方).

みずとり 水鳥 a **water bird**; **waterfowl** (➤集合的).

みずのあわ 水の泡 ▶体育大会は雨で中止になり，我々の努力はすべて水の泡となった All our efforts *went down the drain* [*were wasted*] because the athletic meet was rained out. (➤前者は「下水に流れた」が原義).

みずのみば 水飲み場 a **place for drinking water**; a **drinking fountain** (駅・公園などの噴水式の水飲み器); a **watering place** (動物の).

みずはけ 水捌け **drainage** /dréɪnɪdʒ/ ▶本校のグラウンドは水はけがよい[悪い] Our school sports field *is well* [*badly*] *drained*. / Our school sports field *drains well* [*badly*].

みずびたし 水浸し ▶水浸しのカーペット a *soggy* carpet ‖ 洪水で市全体が水浸しになった The whole city *was flooded* [*was inundated*].

みずぶくれ 水脹れ a **(water) blister** ▶足の指に水ぶくれができた I got *a blister* on my foe. ‖ やけどが水ぶくれになった The burn *blistered*.

みずぶそく 水不足 (a) **water shortage.**

ミスプリ(ント) →誤植.

みずべ 水辺 **the waterside** ▶水辺の散歩道 a *waterside* promenade ‖ 水辺の植物 *waterside* plants.

みずぼうそう 水ぼうそう 《医学》**chickenpox.**

みすぼらしい 見すぼらしい **shabby,** 《インフォーマル》**seedy** ▶みすぼらしい家 a *shabby* [*seedy*] house ‖ 彼はみすぼらしい身なりをしていた He was *shabbily* [*poorly*] dressed.

みずまき 水撒き **watering, water sprinkling.**

みずまし 水増し ▶旅費の水増し請求は厳禁です Don't *claim more money* for your travel expenses *than you* (*actually*) *spent*. ‖ 私は決して水増し請求はしてません I never *padded* the bills. (➤ pad は「(勘定などを)不正に水増しする」の意) ‖ あの大学は水増し入学を行っている That college *admits more students than it is supposed to*.

ミスマッチ a **mismatch.**

みずまわり 水回り ▶家を買うときは水回りをしっかりチェックしたほうがよい When you buy a house, you should check the *plumbing*. (➤ plumbing は「(上下水道)配管」).

みすみす ▶私たちのチームは拙攻でみすみす得点のチャンスを逃した Our team *let* the chance to score *slip by* because of our poor offensive.

みずみずしい 瑞々しい **fresh**(新鮮な); **juicy** (汁・水分が多い); **succulent** /sʌ́kjələnt/ (水気があっておいしい) ▶みずみずしい桃 a *juicy* [*succulent*] peach ‖ このブドウはとてもみずみずしい These grapes are very *fresh and juicy*. ‖ 麻衣子は肌がみずみずしい Maiko has *fresh and youthful* [*smooth and beautiful*] skin.

みずむし 水虫 **athlete's foot** ▶水虫に悩まされる be afflicted with *athlete's foot*.

みずもれ 水漏れ a **water leak** 一動 **水漏れする** **leak** ▶天井から水漏れがしている *Water is leaking* through the ceiling. / The ceiling *is leaking*. ‖ このやかんは水漏れする This kettle *leaks*.

みずわり 水割り ▶ウイスキーの水割り (a) whiskey *and water*.

みせ 店

《米》a **store,** 《英》a **shop**; a **restaurant**(レストラン)

《解説》store と shop
(1)《米》では一般に, 商品を売る店は bookstore, drugstore のように **store** を用い, 専門店やサービスを売る店は barbershop, coffee shop のように **shop** を用いる. しかし flower shop, pet shop など, 慣用的に shop を使う場合もある.
(2)《英》では **store** は大規模な百貨店や, 倉庫などを指す.

▶店を開ける[閉める] open [close] *a store* ‖ 店を手伝う help out in *a store* ‖ あの店は品数が多くて安い That *store* has a wide selection, and it is cheap. ‖ あの店は何でも高過ぎる Everything at that *store* [*shop*] is too expensive. ‖ おいしい店 a good *restaurant* / *a restaurant* that serves delicious food ‖ 店を出す *open a store* / *set up shop* ‖ 彼女は六本木に店を2軒持っている She runs two *shops* [*bars*] in Roppongi. ‖ 売れ行き不振で店を畳んだ We *closed our business* because of poor sales.

「店」のいろいろ 衣料品店 clothing store / おもちゃ屋 toy store / 家具店 furniture store / 金物店 hardware shop [store] / 喫茶店 coffee shop / 果物店 fruit store / 靴店 shoe store / 靴の修理店 a shoe-repair shop / クリーニング店 cleaner's, laundry / コンビニ convenience store / 酒店 liquor store / 自転車店 a bicycle shop / 食料品店 grocery store / 書店 bookstore / スーパーマーケット supermarket / 生花店 flower shop / 青果店 greengrocer's, vegetable shop / 精肉店 a butcher (store / shop) / 鮮魚店《米》fish store,《英》fishmonger's / たばこ店 tobacco shop / デリカテッセン delicatessen / 電気(器具)店 electrical appliance store / パン店 bakery / 美容院 beauty parlor / ブティック boutique / 文房具店 stationery store / ペットショップ pet shop / 宝石店 jewelry store / みやげ物店 souvenir shop / 眼鏡店 optician's / 薬局 pharmacy, drugstore / 理髪店 barbershop / レストラン restaurant

逆引き熟語 ○○店
◆アウトレット店 an outlet store / 飲食店 a restaurant / 小売店 a retail store [shop] / チェーン店 a chain store / 直販店 a direct sales store, an outlet store / 日曜大工店 a home improvement store / パチンコ店 a pachinko parlor / 百貨店 a department store / ファーストフード店 a fast-food shop [restaurant] / 風俗店 a sex trade shop / 免税店 a duty-free shop / レンタルビデオ店 a video rental store
◆支店 a branch / 売店 a stand / 本店 the head [main] office (本社), the main store (店) / 輸入代理店 an import agent / 露店 an open-air stall, a street stall, a roadside stand

みせいねん 未成年 a **minor** (未成年者; 法律用語) ▶きみ, 未成年者はたばこを吸ってはいけないことを知らないのか Don't you know that *minors* are prohibited from smoking? ‖ この映画は未成年者お断りです This movie is *NC-17*. (➤ NC-17は No children 17 and under admitted を表し,「17歳以下入場禁止」「成人向」を表す) ‖《掲示》未成年者はお断り No Minors.

みせかけ 見せかけ (a) **pretense**, a **show** (➤ 後者はややインフォーマルな語); a **pose** (ポーズ) ▶彼の勇敢さは見せかけだけさ His bravery is only *a show*.

みせかける 見せかける **pretend** 《to do, that》; **pose as** ... (自分を…に) ▶彼は私に誠実だと見せかけた He *pretended* to be loyal to me. ‖ 彼はいかにも金持ちらしく見せかけた He *posed as* a rich man. ‖ そのスニーカーはアメリカ製のように見せかけているが, 実はベトナム製だ Those sneakers *are made to look as though* they were manufactured in the U.S., but actually they were made in Vietnam. ‖ 店主は店が押し込み強盗に入られたように見せかけた The storekeeper *made* his store *appear as if* it had been broken into.

みせさき 店先 a **storefront** ▶店先に自転車を置かないでください Don't leave bicycles *in front of the store*. ‖ 店先で新製品の宣伝をしている The new product is being advertised [demonstrated] *at the entrance of the store*.

みせじまい 店仕舞いする **close** (終了する); **close (down)** (廃業する) ▶その本屋は毎日午後10時に店じまい(=閉店)する The bookstore *closes* at 10 p.m. every day.
‖店じまいセール a closing down sale, a going-out-of-business sale; a closeout sale (➤「在庫一掃セール」, あるいは「売り尽くしセール」の意でも用いる).

みせしめ 見せしめ a **warning** (警告); an **example** (戒め); a **lesson** (思い知るべきこと) ▶謀反人は見せしめにさらし首にされた The traitors had their heads severed and gibbeted *as a lesson* (*to others*). ‖ 大尉は捕虜の1人を(他の捕虜への)見せしめに一発殴った The captain hit one of the prisoners *as an example to the rest*.

ミセス a **married woman** (既婚の女性); a **housewife** (主婦) ▶このサークルはヤングミセスを対象にしています This circle is intended for *young married women* [*housewives*].

危ないカタカナ語✹ ミセス
「ミセス」は Mrs. /mísiz/ からきているが, Mrs. は既婚女性の夫の姓(正式には姓名)の前につける敬称である. 日本では結婚している女性を指して「ミセス」ということがあるが, これは日本的用法. 英語では married woman という.

みせつける 見せつける ▶洋平と今日子は熱々ぶりをみんなに見せつけた Yohei and Kyoko *made a show* [*made a display*] of how deeply in love they were. →見せびらかす.

みせどころ 見せ所 ▶さあ満塁. きみの腕の見せどころだ OK, the bases are loaded. Now you *can show* your batting power [*can show* your stuff]. ‖ ここが首相の指導力の見せどころだ This is where the Prime Minister *must demonstrate* [*show*] his leadership skills.

みぜに 身銭 one's **own money** ▶私たちの上司はけちで我々のために決して身銭を切ろうとしない Our boss is stingy and will never *spend his own money* on us.
▶これらの資料は身銭を切って集めたものだ I paid for all these materials *out of my own pocket*.

みせば 見せ場 a **high point**, a **highlight** ▶ゆうべの中日対巨人戦は見せ場が多かった The Dragons-Giants game last night had a lot of *high points*.

みせばん 店番 ▶留守の間, 店番(＝店の番)を頼みます Could you please *tend* [*mind*] *the store* while I am away?

みせびらかす 見せびらかす **show off** ▶彼はスイス製の高級腕時計を見せびらかしている He's *showing off* his expensive Swiss watch. ‖ そんなにお金を見せびらかすもんじゃない. すりに「どうぞ, すってください」と言ってるようなものだ Don't *flash* your money *around* like that. It's an open invitation to pickpockets to take it.

みせびらき 店開きする **open** ▶この付近に喫茶店が店開きするそうだ I hear that a (new) coffee shop will *open* (*for business*) near here. ‖ 店開きの日に行くと景品をもらえるよ If you go to that store [restaurant] *on their opening day*, you'll get a free (promotional) gift.

みせもの 見せ物 a **show**, an **exhibition** /èksɪbíʃən/ ▶ほら, 行った行った, これは見世物じゃない Go away! This *isn't a show*.
‖見せ物小屋 a show tent.

みせられる 魅せられる ▶冬山に魅せられる *be fascinated* [*be enchanted*] by winter mountains ‖ 彼はコアラのかわいらしいしぐさに魅せられてしまった He *was fascinated* by the koala's endearing poses.

みせる 見せる **1【人が見るようにする】show** +㊐, **let ... see** (➤…には見る人がくる)

【文型】
人(A)に物(B)を見せる
show A B
show B **to** A

▶運転免許証を見せてください Please *show* me your driver's license. ‖ あなたに見せたいものがある I have something to *show* you. ‖ 私にも見せて Show me, too! ‖ 彼女はその写真を社内の誰かれなく見せたがる She wants to *show* the photo *to almost everyone* she meets at the office.

▶それ, 見せてくれる? Can I *see* that? ‖ 読み終わったらその新聞を見せてください Could you *let me see* the newspaper when you are through with it? ‖ それ, 何? 隠さないで見せてよ What's that? Don't hide it, *let me have a look at* it.

▶私たちは工場内を見せて(＝案内して)もらった We *were shown around* the inside of the factory. ‖ 消防士たちは日頃鍛えた腕まえを見せた The firefighters *displayed* [*demonstrated*] the skills they had acquired through years of training. ‖ 彼女のビキニ姿をきみにも見せたかったよ You *should've seen* her in a bikini. (➤「見られないで惜しいことをした」のニュアンス) ‖ たまには顔を見せろよ Why don't you *come* (*and*) *see* us sometimes?

2【意図して人にそう思わせる】▶あの司会者は自分を若く見せようと努力をしている That emcee tries to *make* herself *look* young. ‖ 彼はいつも人前で格好よく見せようとする He always *shows off* in front of other people. (➤ show off は「気取る」).

3【診察してもらう】▶次郎がひどい熱よ. 医者に見せましょう Jiro has a high fever. Let's *take* him *to a doctor*. ‖ すぐに医者に見せたほうがいい You should *see a doctor* immediately.

4【「…してみせる」の形で】▶太郎は新入部員たちにトランペットを吹いてみせた Taro *showed* the new club members *how to* play the trumpet. (➤「吹き方を実演した」の意) / Taro *showed* the new club members *how well* he *could* play the trumpet. (➤「腕まえのほどを見せた」の意) ‖ 彼女は無理にほほえんでみせた She *forced* a smile.
▶今度こそあいつをぎゃふんと言わせてみせる *I'll make* him *cry uncle* for sure this time; *wait and see*. (➤ cry uncle は「参ったと言う」) / *I'll show* him this time or never.

みぜん 未然 ▶交通事故を未然に防ぐために努力する work hard to *prevent* traffic accidents (➤ prevent だけで「未然に防ぐ」の意味になる) ‖ 大統領はクーデターを未然に防ぐ手段を講じた The president took *preventive measures* against a coup. ‖ その陰謀は未然に防がれた The conspiracy *was nipped in the bud*. (➤ nip ... in the bud は「…をつぼみのうちに摘み取る」が原義).

みそ 味噌 **1【食品】miso,** (**fermented**) **soybean paste** ▶《慣用表現》首相は大臣の人選を誤りすっかりみそをつけた The Prime Minister chose the wrong man as minister and *got mud on his face* [*lost face*].
‖みそ汁(→見出語) ‖ みそ漬け vegetables [fish] preserved in miso ‖ みそっ歯 a decayed baby tooth.

2【利点】▶初心者でも失敗なくできるところがみそだ *The great thing* is that even a beginner can be successful.

みぞ 溝 **1【水路】**a **ditch** (掘割); a **gutter** (道路の排水溝); a **drain** (下水溝); a **groove** (敷居などの) ▶溝を掘る dig *a ditch* ‖ この溝は詰まっている This *drain* is clogged up.

2【隔たり】a **gap**; a **gulf** (越えがたい障壁) ▶新旧の世代間の溝は大きい The *generation gap* between young and old people is large. ‖ 彼と彼の妻との間には心の溝がある There is *a rift* between him and his wife. (➤ rift は「不和」).

みぞう 未曾有 ▶未曾有の豪雨 an *unprecedented* heavy rainfall / the heaviest rainfall we've ever experienced (➤ unprecedented は「先例のない, 空前の」の意).

みぞおち **the pit of the stomach,** 《インフォーマル》 **the solar plexus** /pléksəs/.

みそぎ 禊 a **purification ceremony** (**performed with water**); **ablutions** ▶みそぎをする *perform* [*make*] one's *ablutions* / *wipe the slate clean*(➤ 比喩的に「(過失など)過去のことを忘れて新しく出直す」).

みそこなう 見損なう **1【見ないでしまう】miss** +㊐ ▶ゆうべはそのテレビドラマの最終回を見損なってしまった I *missed* the last episode of the TV drama last night.

2【評価を誤る】misjudge +㊐ ▶人を見損なう *misjudge* a person (➤ 英語では自分が下した評価よりも相手がよかった場合にも「見誤る」の意で用いる) ‖ ティム君を見損なった(＝には失望した). 彼は工科大を出てるのにパソコンも満足に扱えないんだ I am *disappointed in* Tim. Although he graduated from a technical college, he can't use a computer properly. ‖ おれを見損なわないでくれ Don't *sell* me *short*. (➤ sell ... short で「…を見くびる」の意).

ミソサザイ 《鳥》 a **wren** /ren/.

みそしる 味噌汁 **miso soup** 《参考》すでに英語に入った言い方だが, この語から英語国の多くの人々はみそ汁をスープの一種だとみなし, 塩辛さの程度も野菜スープやコンソメスープ並みだと思いがちである. したがって, 適宜 'miso-shiru' を用いるのもよい ▶大根のみそ汁 *miso soup* with daikon ‖ みそ汁を飲む drink *miso soup*.

みそめる 見初める **fall in love at first sight**(一目ぼれす

る）▶彼はスキー場で見初めた子と結婚した He married a girl he met at a ski resort and *fell in love with at first sight*.

みぞれ **sleet** ▶みぞれが降っている It is sleeting. ／*Sleet* is falling. ‖ この雨はみぞれに変わります The rain will turn to *sleet*.
▶みぞれ模様の天気が続きます *Sleety* weather will continue.

-みたい **1【他に類似していることを示して】**▶あの人形はまるで生きているみたいだ That doll *looks as if* it were alive.（➤ as if 以下はしばしば仮定法になる）‖ ヨーロッパへ行けるなんて夢みたい Me, going to Europe! *It seems too good to be true*.
2【具体例を示して】▶あなたみたいなわからず屋は初めてよ I've never met a man *as* stubborn *as* you.
3【不確かさを示して】 **look**, **look like**（…のように見える）; **seem**（…のように思える）▶あなた，熱があるみたいよ You *look like* you have a fever.
▶みんな帰ったみたい It *looks like* everybody went home. ‖ 少女は何かにおびえているみたいだった The girl *seemed*［*appeared*］to be frightened by［of］something.

み

みだし 見出し a **headline**（新聞の）; a **banner**（トップ抜き特大見出し）; **contents**（目次）; an **entry** (**word**), a **headword**（辞書の見出語）▶保険金詐欺事件が大きな見出しで出ている The insurance fraud case *is in the headlines*.

みだしなみ 身嗜み **appearance(s)** ▶俳優たちはいつも身だしなみに気をつけている Actors and actresses are always careful about their *appearances*. ／Actors and actresses always pay attention to *what they wear*. ‖ かおりはいつも身だしなみがいい Kaori *is* always *dressed neatly*.

みたす 満たす **fill** +目（いっぱいにする）; **satisfy** +目（満足させる）

> **【文型】**
> **場所(A)を(B)物で満たす**
> **fill** A **with** B

▶豪雨が貯水池を満たした Heavy rains *filled* the reservoir. ‖ バラが庭園を甘い香りで満たしていた The roses *filled* the garden *with* a sweet fragrance.
▶空腹を満たす *satisfy* one's hunger ‖ 国はすべての人の要求を満たすことはできない The government can't *satisfy* everybody's demands.
▶満たされた心 a *contented* mind ‖ 満たされた生活 a (*fully*) *satisfying* life ‖ 満たされた日々 *fulfilling* days.

みだす 乱す **disturb** +目（人を不安に陥れる，不愉快にする）; **trouble** +目（人を悩ます）; **confuse** +目（人を当惑させる）▶人の心を乱す *disturb*［*trouble*／*confuse*］a person ‖ 頻発するテロが世界の平和を乱している Frequent terrorist activities *disturb* world peace.
▶こら，列［歩調］を乱すな！ Hey, don't *get out of line*［*step*］!

みたて 見立て a **diagnosis** /dàɪəgnóʊsɪs/（医師の診断）; **choice**（選択）▶このスーツは妻の見たてです This suit was my wife's *choice*.

みたてる 見立てる **pick** +目（➤「いくつかの中から気に入ったものを選ぶ」の意だが，ややくだけた語）; **choose** +目（➤「選ぶ」の意の一般語だが，しばしば 2 つの中から選ぶ場合に用いる）▶ネクタイを買うときは彼女が見たててくれる When I buy ties, my girlfriend *picks*［*chooses*］them for me.

みたま 御霊 a **soul** ▶死者の御霊 the *soul* of a deceased person ‖ 御霊よ安らかなれ *May he*［*she*／*they*］*rest in peace*. ／*May his*［*her*］*soul rest in peace*. ／*May their souls rest in peace*.

みため 見た目 ▶この服，見た目はいいけどすぐ飽きそうだな It is a *nice-looking* suit, but I'm afraid I'll get tired of it soon. ‖ そのレストランの料理は見た目はきれいだが味はひどい The food in the restaurant *looks beautiful*, but tastes awful. ‖ 彼は見た目ほどだらしなくはない He is not as slovenly *as he looks*. ‖ 見た目にはわからないだろうが，彼女はすごい飲んべえだ *You can't tell by looking at* her, but she drinks like a fish. ‖ ときには見た目が大事なこともある Sometimes *appearances* (do) matter. ‖ 見た目は華やかだがスターたちの中には結構きつい生活を送っている者もいる In spite of their *glamorous appearance*, some stars lead quite a strenuous life.

みだら 淫らな **obscene** /əbsíːn/, **dirty**（わいせつな）; **indecent** /ɪndíːsənt/（下品な）▶みだらな話 a *dirty* story ‖ みだらな行為を行う commit an *indecent* act ‖ アダルト映画はみだらだ Adult movies are *obscene*［*pornographic*］. ‖ そのコーチは女子学生にみだらなことをした The coach (*sexually*) *molested* a female student.（➤ molest は「性的ないたずらをする」の意）.

みだりに ▶女子の部屋へみだりに（＝ちゃんとした理由もなく）行ってはいけない You mustn't go into a girl's room *without a proper reason*.

みだれ 乱れ ▶服装の乱れを直しなさい *Tidy* your clothes. ‖ 彼女は髪の乱れを直した She smoothed her *ruffled hair*. ‖ ダイヤの乱れはしばらく続くだろう The train schedule will remain *disrupted* for some time.

みだれる 乱れる **⚠どの場合にも使える言い方はない．何が乱れるかによって訳し方を工夫する．**
▶髪が風で乱れた My hair *was disheveled* by the wind. ／The wind *messed up* my hair. ‖ 病人の脈は乱れていた The patient's pulse *was irregular*. ‖ 地震のため電車のダイヤが乱れています The train schedule *is* now *in disorder*［*has been disrupted*］due to the earthquake. ‖ その老国語学者は日本語が乱れていると嘆いている The old scholar of Japanese is lamenting over how *corrupted* the language *has become*. ‖ ローマ帝国も末期には風紀が乱れた Morals *decayed*［Discipline *was lost*］in the last days of the Roman Empire. ‖ 若者たちは乱れた生活をしていた The young people were leading *dissolute*［*loose*］lives.

[1]みち 道

> **訳語メニュー**
> 道路 →road **1**
> 街路 →street **1**
> 細い道 →path **1**
> 通路，道のり →way **1, 2**
> 手段 →way, means **3**
> 領域 →field **4**

1【道路】 a **road**（都市・府県を結ぶ道路・車道）; a **street**（市街地を走る道路）; a **path**（細道，小道）; a **way**（ある場所へ行くための道順）▶この道は長野県に通じています This *road* goes to Nagano Prefecture. ‖ この道をまっすぐ行ったところが金閣寺です Go straight along this *street*, and you'll come to Kinkakuji Temple. ‖ 山道［でこぼこ道］でころんだ I fell on the *mountain path*［*bumpy path*］. ‖ 四谷駅へ行く道を

教えてください Could you tell me *the way to* Yotsuya Station? ‖ 彼女は西川さん宅への道を聞いた She asked *the way* [She asked for *directions*] *to* the Nishikawas' (house). (➤ directions は「道順の指示」) ‖《タクシーの運転手が客に》どの道を行きますか Which *way* do you want me to go?

直訳の落とし穴「道を教える」
「教える」＝teach であるが,「図書館に行く道を教えてください」というときの「教える」に teach は用いない. teach は教科や技能を伝えて身につけさせることである.「道を教える」には tell (指示して言う)や show (図に描いて示す, 同行して教える)を用いる. したがって, Could you tell [show] me the way to the library? となる.

▶道をまちがえて, パーティーに10分遅れた I was ten minutes late for the party because I *took the wrong way*. ‖ 道に迷ってしまったみたい We seem to have *lost our way*. ‖ 救急車が通ります. 道を空けてください *Clear the road*; an ambulance is coming. / Please *make way for* the ambulance. ‖ 探検隊は道なき道を進んだ The expedition proceeded through *the wilderness*. (➤ wilderness /wíldərnəs/ は「原始的な密林地帯」).

逆引き熟語 ○○道
石畳の道 a stone-paved street / 田舎道 a country [rural] road / 裏道 a back street, an alley / 帰り道 one's way home / 小道 an alley, a path, a lane / 坂道 an uphill [downhill] road [path], a sloping road / 砂利道 a gravel road / でこぼこ道 a bumpy road / 近道 a shortcut / 曲がりくねった道 a winding road [path] / まわり道 a roundabout route, a detour / 山道 a mountain road [path] / 雪道 a snowy road

2【距離, 道のり】 a **way** ▶疲れたのか. まだ道は遠いぞ Are you tired? *It's a long way* ahead. ‖ 両国の和平への道は険しかった The *road to peace* between the two countries has been rough.

3【手段, 方法】 a **way**, a **means** ▶定年(退職)後の生活の道は考えていますか Have you thought of *a way* [*of how*] to support yourself after retiring (from your company)? ‖ 会社が現在の苦境から脱出する道が何かあるはずだ There must be *a way* [*a means*] for our company to get out of the current difficulties.

4【領域】 a **field**; a **subject**(事がら); a **career**(ずっと続ける職業) ▶その道の大家 an authority on that *subject* [in that *field*] ‖ 彼はその道ではかなり有名だ He is quite famous *in his own field*. ‖ その道をきわめた人のことばは重い The words of *a person who has perfected his or her art* carry weight. ‖ ｉＰＳ細胞の実用化は再生医療の道を拓くものと期待されている If iPS cells are put to practical use, they are expected to *clear the way* for regenerative medicine.

▶教師の[学者の] 道を選んだことに後悔はない I never regret that I chose *a teaching career* [*an academic career*].

▶ 対話「将来はどんな道に進むつもり?」「酪農をやりたいと思っています」"*What career do you want to pursue* [*go into*] in the future? / *What kind of work* [*job*] *do you want to do* in the future?" "I'm going to be a dairy farmer."

5【道徳】 ▶人々に道を説く teach people the *moral principles* ‖ 生徒が先生に暴力を振るうなんて全く道に外れている(＝全くの非行だ) It is totally *out of line* [It's definitely *misconduct*] for students to hit their teacher. ‖ 人の道に外れたことだけはするな Just be careful not to do *anything morally wrong*.

²みち 未知の **unknown** ▶未知の世界 the *unknown* world ‖ 未知の領域 an *uncharted* territory ‖ 地球上に未知の島は無くなった There are no *unknown* islands left on earth. ‖ それまではブータンは私にとって未知の国でした Before that, I *didn't know* [*hadn't learned*] *anything* about Bhutan.

みちあんない 道案内 a **guide**(人) ▶私はその学生に駅までの道案内を頼んだ I *asked* the student *to show* me *the way* [*to lead the way* / *to guide* me] *to* the railway station. ‖ 彼が運転するというので私が道案内した He said he would drive, so I *navigated*. (➤ navigate は「(車の同乗者が)導く」の意).

みぢか 身近 ▶私の身近な人たち people *close to* me ‖ その男性の顔は妙に身近に感じられた The man's face was oddly *familiar*. ‖ 彼の失敗談を聞いたら, 急に彼を身近に感じた After I heard about his blunder, I suddenly began to *feel friendly toward* him. (➤ 家族のようなごく身近な感じは feel close to で表す) ‖ 私は和英辞典をいつも身近に置いている I always *keep* a Japanese-English dictionary *by my side*. (➤ 斜体部分を have ... at hand としてもよい).

みちがえる 見違える ▶比呂はとても背が高くなったので見違えてしまった Hiro had become so tall that I *could hardly recognize* him. (➤ recognize は「誰であるかがわかる」の意) ‖ 壁紙を替えれば部屋は見違えるようになりますよ Repapering the walls will *make a big difference* to the room.

みちかけ 満ち欠け ▶月は満ち欠けする The moon *waxes and wanes*.

みちくさ 道草 ▶高校生の中にはゲームセンターに立ち寄って道草を食う者がいる Some high school students *hang out* [*around*] in video arcades after school (before going home). (➤ hang out [around] は「うろつく」) ‖ どこで道草を食っていたの? Where have you been *wasting your time* [*goofing off*] *along the way*? (➤ goof off は「怠ける」) / Did you take a nap on the way or something? (➤ take a nap の部分は, 時間がかかるような他のことにも置き換え可能).

みちしお 満ち潮 a **flood** [**rising**] **tide** ▶今は満ち潮だ *The tide is coming in* [*is rising* / *has begun to flow*].

みちじゅん (…への)**道順** **the way**《to》 ▶ヒルトンホテルへの道順を教えてくれませんか Can you tell me *the way to* the Hilton Hotel? / Could you give me *directions to* the Hilton Hotel? ‖ 会場への道順を間違えて15分遅れてしまった I *took the wrong way to* the meeting place and was 15 minutes late.

みちしるべ 道標 a **guidepost**, a **signpost** ▶道しるべに従えば山頂に着けます You can reach the top of the mountain if you follow the *guideposts* [*signposts*].

みちすう 未知数 an **unknown quantity**(➤ 数学用語だが, 比喩的にも使われる) ▶彼はかつて大リーグにいたことがあるが, 日本では全く未知数だ He was once a major leaguer, but he is still entirely *an unknown quantity* in Japan.

み

みちすがら 道すがら ▶大学への道すがら市立図書館に立ち寄った I dropped in at the municipal library *on my way to* college.

みちすじ 道筋 a **route** ; a **course**（進路）; a **road map**（《比喩的に》行程表）▶一行は公会堂に至る道筋で熱烈な歓迎を受けた The party received an enthusiastic welcome *en route* to the hall.（➤ en route /ὰ:n rú:t/ はフランス語起源の言い方で「(…への)途中で」の意）‖その本屋は駅に行く道筋にある That bookstore is located *on the way to* the train station.

▶財政再建の道筋をつけるのが現内閣の主要課題の１つだ It's one of the major tasks the current Cabinet should tackle to *pave the way* [*set a practical course*] *for* fiscal reconstruction.

みちたりる 満ち足りた **satisfying** ▶妻のおかげで私はきわめて満ち足りた結婚生活を送っている Thanks to my wife, I've had a most *satisfying* marriage. ‖退職した叔父夫婦はシンガポールに移り住んで満ち足りた(＝充実した)日々を過ごしている My uncle and his wife, who retired and moved to Singapore, are leading a *fulfilling* [*contented*] life there.

みちづれ 道連れ a **traveling companion**, a **fellow traveler** ▶ボストンからニューヨークへ行く途中おもしろい人と道連れになった I *had an* interesting *traveling companion* on my way from Boston to New York.

▶彼女は２人の幼児を道連れに自殺した She committed suicide *taking* her two young children *with her*.

みちなり 道なり ▶道なりに行けば神社に出ます *Follow the road*, and you'll come to the Shinto shrine.

みちのり 道のり a **distance** ▶空港まではバスで［車で／歩いて］20分の道のりです It's *a 20-minute bus ride* [*drive* ／ *walk*] to the airport. ‖ダブリンまでは長い道のりです Dublin is *a long way off*.

対話「大分から別府までの道のりはどのくらいですか」「10キロです」"What's the *distance* between Oita and Beppu ?" "Ten kilometers."

▶《比喩的》田部氏が社長になるまでの道のりは厳しかった Mr. Tabe had a hard time on his *way* to becoming president. ‖彼が一人前の漫画家になるまでにはまだまだ道のりがある He *has a long way to go* to become a manga artist in his own right.（➤「まだ力不足だ」の意）.

みちばた 道端 a **roadside**, a **wayside**（➤ 後者は古風な語で「路傍」に近い）▶道端に三輪車が１台置き忘れてある A tricycle has been left *by the roadside* [*wayside*].

みちはば 道幅 **the width of a road** [**street**] ▶この道路は道幅が広い［狭い］This street *is wide* [*narrow*].

みちひ 満ち干 **the ebb and flow** ▶潮の満ち干 *the ebb and flow* of the tide [sea] ‖その入り江は潮の満ち干が大きい *The range of the tides* is great in the inlet. ／*The tide* varies greatly in the inlet.

みちびく 導く **lead** ＋目（先導する）; **guide** ＋目（案内する）▶ガイドは旅行者たちを陽明門へ導いた The guide *led* [*guided*] the tourists to the Yomeimon Gate.（➤ led は lead の過去形）‖2018年，辻監督は西武ライオンズを10年ぶりの優勝へ導いた Manager Tsuji *led* the Lions to their first championship in 10 years in 2018.

みちる 満ちる **be filled**《with》; **be full**《of》（満ちている）▶スリルと冒険に満ちた物語 a story *full of* thrills and adventures ‖横綱は自信に満ちあふれていた The yokozuna *was overflowing with* confidence.

▶年の瀬になり商店街は買い物客で活気に満ちていた As the year drew to an end, the shopping district *was alive with* shoppers. ‖潮が満ちてきた The tide is *coming in* [began to *rise*].

[1]**みつ 蜜** **honey**（はちみつ）; **nectar**（花のみつ）; **syrup**（糖みつ）▶ハチは花から花へ飛んでみつを集める Bees fly from flower to flower to get [gather] *honey*. ‖ハチドリは花のみつを吸う Hummingbirds suck *nectar* from flowers.

▶パンケーキにみつをかけて食べる put *syrup* on pancakes and eat them.

[2]**みつ 密** ▶私たちはもっと連絡を密にすることを約束した We promised to *keep in closer contact* [*touch*] *with each other*.

みつあみ 三つ編み《米》**braids** /breɪdz/,《英》**plaits** ▶あの子はいつも三つ編みにしている That girl always wears her hair *in braids*.

みっか 三日 **three days**（３日間）; **the third**（各月の）▶三日にあげず *almost every other day* ／ *very frequently* ‖３日間休みを取りたいのですが I'd like to take *three days* off. ‖３日目ごとに［３日おきに］娘から電話がある My daughter calls me up *every three days* [*every four days*]. ‖11月３日は文化の日です *The third* of November [November (*the*) *third*] is Culture Day.

みっかい 密会 a **secret meeting** ; a **secret rendezvous** /rɑ́:ndeɪvu:/（ランデブー）.

みっかぼうず 三日坊主 a **quitter**（やりとげないで途中でやめてしまう人）▶どうせあの子はまた三日坊主よ He *can't stick to anything for long*. ／I bet he'll give up soon.（●「何事もやり通すことができない」と考えて前者のように，「きっとすぐに投げ出すだろう」と考えて後者のように訳すことができる）.

みつかる 見つかる **1【さがしていたものが】be found**（紛失物などが）; **be discovered**（知られていなかったものが）▶眼鏡が見つからないよ I *can't find* my glasses. ‖父の財布はまだ見つかっていない My father's wallet *hasn't been found yet*. ／My father's wallet *is still missing*.（➤ 後者は「紛失中だ」の意）‖いい仕事が見つかるといいね I hope you *find* a good job. ‖中国で恐竜の骨がたくさん見つかった Many dinosaur bones *were discovered* in China.

2【人に見つけられる】be caught doing（悪いことをしているところを）; **be found out**（発覚する）▶誰にも見つからず庭に忍び込んだ I sneaked into the garden *without being seen* by anybody.

▶彼は万引き［カンニング］している所を見つかった He *was caught* shoplift*ing* [cheat*ing*]. ‖彼らの悪だくみはすぐに見つかった Their evil scheme *was* soon *found out*.

みつぎもの 貢ぎ物 a **tribute**.

みっきょう 密教 **Esoteric Buddhism**（➤ esoteric は「秘教的な」）.

みつぐ 貢ぐ ▶５億円を横領した女性銀行員はその金をすべて愛人に貢いだ The female bank teller who embezzled half a billion yen *used* it all *as a gift* to her lover.

ミックス 一動 ミックスする **mix** ＋目 ▶卵と牛乳をミックスしたもの *a mixture* of eggs and milk ‖小麦粉と牛乳をよくミックスしなさい *Mix* the flour and milk well.

‖ミックスジュース mixed fruit juice ‖ミックスダブルス（テニスなどの）mixed doubles.

危ないカタカナ語✸ ミックス
「AとBをミックスする」という言い方のほか,「ミックス…」の形でよく使われる. 前者は mix でよいが, 後者は和製語の場合が多い.
ミックスサンド ハム, 卵などさまざまの種類のサンドイッチのとり合わせだが, これは日本独特のもの. あえて言えば《米》の club sandwich(3枚重ねのサンドイッチ) や submarine (sandwich)(大型ロールパンにいろいろはさんだもの)がやや近い.
ミックスジュース mix juice でなく, mixed (fruit) juice のようにいう.

みづくろい 身繕いする dress oneself ▶洗面所で身繕いする *fix one's clothes* (*and make-up*) in the restroom.

みつくろう 見繕う ▶《飲食店で》すみません, お刺し身を適当に見繕ってください (Excuse me.) We'd like sashimi, please. We'll *leave the choice to you*. (➤「あなたに任せます」の意) ‖ 女店員に花束を見繕って作ってもらった I had a salesgirl *choose* flowers and make a bouquet. / I had a salesgirl *put together* a bouquet (for us).

みつけだす 見つけ出す find +目, find out (➤前者が単に「物や人を見つけ出す」の意であるのに対して, 後者は「知らなかった[隠されていた]事実を思考力や推理力を用いて知るようになる」の意) ▶母は父のへそくりを見つけ出した My mother *found* the money my father had stashed away. / My mother *found out* where my father had stashed his money away.

みつげつ 蜜月 a honeymoon →ハネムーン ▶マスコミとの蜜月は終わった The *honeymoon* with the media is over. ‖ A社とB社は昨年まで蜜月関係にあった Company A had *a honeymoon relationship* with company B until last year.

みつける 見つける
find +目, find out ; discover +目, detect +目, locate +目, spot +目, catch +目

語法 **find** は「偶然に, またはさがして見つける ; 今まで知らなかったことを知るようになる」の意. **find out** は「思考力・推理力を働かせたり, 調査の結果見つけ出す」の意. **discover** は「前からあったのだが, 誰も知らなかったようなものを発見する」の意. **detect** は「欠点・欠陥などを見つけたり, 注意深くさがして隠されていたものを見つけ出したりする」の意. **locate** は「何かの場所や位置を見つけ出す」の意. **spot** は「見つけにくいものを見つけ出す」の意. **catch** は「よくないことをしている人を見つける」の意.

▶父の本の間から1万円札を見つけた I *found* a ten-thousand-yen bill among the pages of my father's book. ‖ 姉は新しい仕事を見つけて意気ごんでいる My big sister is feeling enthusiastic because she *got* [*found*] a new job. ‖《隠れんぼなどで》太郎ちゃん, 見いつけた! *I found you*, Taro-chan! ‖ 彼はついに英単語が覚えられるいい方法を見つけた At last he *found out* a good way [*devised* a good method] to memorize English words. ▶帯広ですてきな喫茶店を見つけた I *discovered* [*came across*] a nice coffee shop in Obihiro. (➤ come across は「偶然出くわす」の意のややインフォーマルな言い方) ‖ 中島君が遠くから私を見つけて手を振った Nakajima *spotted* me from afar and waved at me. ▶生きがいを見つけられない高齢者が多い There are many elderly people who can't *find* something to live for.

【文型】
人(A)が…しているのを見つける
find A doing
catch A doing

《解説》 **catch** は「現場をつかまえる」が元の意味で, 相手がしてはいけないことをしている所を, または見つかると当惑するようなことをしている所を, の含みがある.

▶警備員は社長が執務室で倒れている所を見つけた A guard *found* the president ly*ing* on his [her] office floor. ‖ 先生は吾郎が教室をこっそり抜け出そうとしている所を見つけた The teacher *caught* Goro try*ing* to sneak out of the classroom.

みつご 三つ子 triplets (➤その中の1人は a triplet) ▶妻は排卵誘発剤を使用したため三つ子を生んだ My wife gave birth to *triplets* after using a fertility drug.
ことわざ 三つ子の魂百まで A person's character is fixed by the age of three. / A leopard never changes its spots. (➤「ヒョウは自分の斑点を変えない」の意) / The child is father of the man. (➤「子供はおとなの父だ」の意の英語のことわざ).

みっこう 密航する stow away (船や飛行機などに隠れて無賃旅行する).
‖密航者 a stowaway.

みっこく 密告する inform 《against, on》, 《インフォーマル》 tip off ▶彼はテストでカンニングをした他の生徒のことを密告した He *informed on* [*against*] other students who cheated on the test. ‖ 誰かが税務署に会社の不当利益を密告した Somebody *tipped off* the tax office about the firm's illegal windfall.
‖密告者 a whistle-blower, an informer, a tipster ; a stool pigeon (警察のスパイ).

みっしつ 密室 a locked [sealed] room ; a secret room (秘密の部屋) ▶密室殺人事件 a case of murder in *a locked* [*sealed*] *room*.
‖密室会議 a closed-door session.

みっしゅう 密集した dense (密度の濃い) ; thick (密生した) ▶東京は家が密集し過ぎている Houses in Tokyo are built much too *close together*. ‖ メキシコシティーは人口密集地である Mexico City is *densely populated*. ‖ バラが密集して茂っていた The roses grew *thick*(*ly*).

ミッション a mission (任務) ▶ミッション完了 *Mission* accomplished [completed].

ミッションスクール a Christian school, a church-supported school

危ないカタカナ語✸ ミッションスクール
1 英語の mission は「布教, 伝道」の意で, mission school は本来「(宗教の)布教のための学校」を指す. したがってこれは「文化的に後進地域にある」というイメージを伴うことばでもある.
2 日本語の「ミッションスクール」を説明するときは Christian school (キリスト教の学校)や Catholic school (カトリックの学校)というほうが適切である.

みっせい 密生 ▶斜面にはササが密生している Bamboo grass *grows thick*(*ly*) on the slope. / The slope *is thick* [*is densely covered*] with bamboo grass.

みっせつ 密接な close /kloʊs/ 一副 密接に closely

▶栄養と成長の間には密接な関係がある There is a *close* relation between nutrition and growth. ‖ 政治と経済は密接に関連している Politics and the economy are *closely* connected. ‖ A党とB党はより密接になった A Party and B Party *have become closer*.

みっそう 密葬 a **private funeral** ▶ご遺族の希望により葬儀は密葬にて執り行いました According to the (bereaved) family's wishes, the funeral was held *privately*.

みつぞう 密造する **manufacture** [**produce**] **illegally**; **brew** [**distill**] **illegally**(酒を) ‖ **密造酒** an illicit liquor; 《インフォーマル》 moonshine (➤ もともとアメリカ南部の密造バーボンウイスキーを指した語).

みつぞろい 三つ揃い a **three-piece suit**.

みつだん 密談 a **confidential meeting** ▶両党の指導者が料亭で密談した The leaders of the two parties *had a confidential meeting* [*talked secretly*] at a restaurant.

みっちゃく 密着 ▶ウエットスーツは肌に密着する A wet-suit *fits skin-tight*. ‖ どうしてあんなに大勢の記者が俳優のハネムーンの密着取材をするのだろう Why are so many reporters *covering* the actor's honeymoon *so closely*?

みっちり ▶おまえが本気で柔道をやる気なら, みっちり仕込んでやる If you sincerely want to learn judo, then I'll give you a *real* workout. ‖ いたずらをして, おやじにみっちりしぼられた My old man gave me a *good* scolding for my misbehavior.

みっつ 三つ **three** ▶グレープフルーツを3つください *Three* grapefruits, please.

みってい 密偵 a **secret agent**, a **spy**.

ミット a **mitt** ▶ミットをはめる put on *a mitt*. ‖ **キャッチャーミット** a catcher's mitt.

みつど 密度 **density** ▶空気は寒いときのほうが密度が高い The *density* of air is higher when it is cold. / Air is denser when it is cold. ‖ 日本の人口密度は1平方キロ当たり337.4人だ Japan's *population density* is 337.4 per square kilometer. ‖ シンガポールは人口密度が高い Singapore *is densely populated*. ‖ カナダは人口密度が低い Canada *is sparsely populated*. ‖ **骨密度** bone density.

みつどもえ 三つ巴 ▶今度のマラソンは伊藤・加藤・江藤による三つどもえの争いになるだろう The coming marathon will shape up into *a three-way* [*triangular*] *struggle* among Ito, Kato and Eto.

みっともない **shameful**(恥ずかしい)

> **解説** 「みっともない」は「(世間に対して)体裁が悪い, 人に見せられない」の意味であるが, これにぴったりの英語はない. やや近い語に shameful があるが, これは「(恥ずべきことをしたので)恥ずかしい」の意であって, 「みっともない」のように他人を意識した語ではない. あくまで自分の良心に照らして「恥ずかしい」のである. →**恥, 恥ずかしい**.

▶みっともない行為 a *shameful* act ‖ 同じチームに3連敗するなんてみっともないぞ! *How shameful* [*disgraceful*] that you lost three games in a row to the same team! ‖ 別れた女房に借金を申し入れるなんてみっともないことができるか! *How can you do such a shameless thing* as to ask your ex-wife for a loan! (➤ shameless は「恥知らずな」) ‖ こんなみっともない服, 着るのいやだ I'd hate to wear an *ugly* [*unshapely*] dress like this. ‖ 道を歩きながら物を食べるのはみっともない(=無作法)ですよ It's *bad manners* to eat while you're walking along the street.

みつにゅうこく 密入国 **smuggling** 一動 **密入国する** **smuggle** oneself [**sneak**] **into a country** ▶国境警備隊は密入国者(=不法入国者)に目を光らせている The border patrol is keeping an eye out for *illegal entrants*.

みつば 三つ葉 《植物》 a **Japanese honewort**.

みつばい 密売 an **illicit sale**; **trafficking**(違法な売買) 一動 (…を)**密売する** **sell illegally** [**secretly**], **traffic** 《in》 ▶麻薬の密売 the *illicit sale* of drugs / drug *trafficking*. ‖ **密売人** an illicit dealer [merchant].

みつばち 蜜蜂 a **honeybee**, a **bee** ▶ミツバチを飼う keep *bees* ‖ **ミツバチの巣** a honeycomb /hʌ́nikoʊm/; a beehive (巣箱).

みっぷう 密封する **seal** (**up**) ▶瓶を密封する *seal* a jar (*up*) ‖ 申告書は密封の上, 社長あて送付のこと Send the report to the president after *sealing* it.

みっぺい 密閉する **make … airtight** (気密にする); **seal up** (密封する) ▶のりは容器に入れて密閉しておかないとすぐにしける Nori [Dried laver] soon gets soft if you don't *keep* it *in an airtight container*.

みつぼうえき 密貿易 **smuggling** ▶兵器の密貿易 arms *smuggling* ‖ 覚せい剤を日本に[から]密貿易する *smuggle* (illegal) stimulants into [out of] Japan.

みつぼし 三ツ星の **three-star** ▶三ツ星ホテル[レストラン] a *three-star* hotel [restaurant].

みつまた 三つ股 ▶三つまたのコンセント[ソケット] a *three-way* outlet [socket] ‖ 三つまたの道路 a *three-forked* road.

みつまめ 蜜豆 ***mitsumame***; a dessert made with boiled red beans, agar-agar cubes, syrup, and fruit (➤ 説明的な訳).

みつめる 見つめる **gaze** 《at》, **stare** 《at》, **look hard** 《at》

> **語法** **gaze** は「何かを長い間じっと見る」の意で, プラスイメージの語. これに対して, **stare** は「(驚き・驚嘆・恐怖などのために)まばたきもしないで見る; じろじろ見る」の意で, しばしばマイナスイメージを伴う. **look hard** は「何かを意識してしっかりと見る」の意.

▶漁師が海を見つめて立っていた A fisherman stood *gazing at* the sea. ‖ そんなに私を見つめないで Don't *stare at* me [*stare* me *in the face*] like that! ‖ 彼はしばらく私の顔をじっと見つめた He *stared at* me [*studied* my face] for a moment. (➤ study は「探るように見る」) ‖ 赤ん坊は母親の目を一心に見つめていた The baby was *looking hard at* her mother's eyes. / The baby was *watching* her mother's eyes *intently*.

▶今世界で何が起きているかをしっかり見つめてほしい I want you to *keep a careful eye on* what's happening in the world.

みつもり 見積もり an **estimate** /éstɪmət/ (コストなどの); a **quotation**, 《インフォーマル》 a **quote**(請負仕事などの) ▶修理費の見積もり *an estimate* of repair costs ‖ あすお電話をくだされば見積もりをしておきます If you call me tomorrow, I can give you *an estimate*. ‖ 披露宴の費用の見積もりをしてください Please submit *a quotation* for what you would

charge to cater the reception.
‖見積書 a written estimate.

みつもる 見積もる estimate /éstimeɪt/ +目, make an estimate《of》▶我々は旅行の費用を60万円と見積もっている We *estimate* the cost of our trip at six hundred thousand yen. ‖店のおよその改装費を見積もってくれますか Could you *make a* rough *estimate of* the expenses for remodeling the store？‖葬式は控えめに見積もっても70万円はかかりそうだ The funeral will cost 700,000 yen *at a conservative* [*moderate*] *estimate*.

みつやく 密約 a secret promise ; a secret agreement (秘密の協約) ▶両国首脳の間には密約が取り交わされていた There was *a secret agreement* between the two nations' leaders.

みつゆ 密輸 smuggling 一動 (…に, …から)密輸する smuggle《into, out of》▶大量のフィリピン製ピストルが日本に密輸された Many Philippine-made pistols *were smuggled into* Japan.
‖密輸業者 a smuggler ‖密輸団 a smuggling ring ‖密輸品 smuggled goods.

¹みつりょう 密猟 poaching 一動 密猟する poach +目 ▶角を得るためにサイを密猟する *poach* rhinos for their horns.
‖密猟者 a poacher.

²みつりょう 密漁 poaching of fish 一動 密漁する poach +目.

みつりん 密林 a dense forest, a jungle ▶熱帯の密林に住む動物たち animals inhabiting *dense tropical forests*.

みてい 未定の undecided (未決定の) ; not fixed (日取り・値段などが確定していない) ▶開所式の日取りは未定です The date of the opening ceremony *hasn't been set* [*decided* / *fixed*] *yet*. / The date of the opening ceremony *is still undecided*. ‖ 対話 「卒業後のご計画は？」「未定です」"What are you going to do after graduation?" "*I haven't decided yet*."

ミディ 《コンピュータ》MIDI /mídi/ (➤ musical instrument digital interface の頭字語)
‖ミディファイル a MIDI file.

ミディアム medium.

みてくれ 見てくれ (an) appearance (体裁) ▶見てくれで人を判断してはならない Never judge people by *appearances*. ‖大切なのは見てくれではなく, きみたちの生き方だ What counts is not *how you look* but how you live. ‖見てくれはりっぱだが, この家は欠陥住宅だ Although it *looks nice* [*great*], this house is in fact full of problems.

みてとる 見て取る ▶夫婦のぴりぴりした関係が見て取れた(＝を感じた) I *sensed* the couple's tense relationship.

みてまわる 見て回る look around, go around ; surf (ウェブサイトを漠然と) ▶デパートを見て回る *look around* (in) a department store (➤ 1店を見て回る場合) / *make the rounds of* department stores (➤ 何店も見て回る場合) ‖博覧会場を見て回る *tour* [*go around*] the exhibition grounds ‖インターネット上を見て回る *surf* [*troll*] the Net (➤ 後者は何かをさがす目的で) ‖ネットオークションサイトを見て回る *troll through* online auction sites ‖館内の展示物を見て回る *look at* all the exhibits in the hall ‖どのパソコンにするか決める前に少し見て回ろうと思う I think I'll *look around* [*shop around*] a bit before deciding which personal computer to buy.

みてみぬふり 見て見ぬふり ▶大部分の乗客は酔っぱらいの乱暴を見て見ぬふりをした Most passengers *turned a blind eye* [*shut their eyes*] *to* the drunk's violent behavior. (➤ shut の代わりに closed でもよい).

みてもらう 診てもらう see +目 (会って相談する) ▶痛みがあるのなら医者に診てもらいなさい If you're in pain, *see* a doctor. ‖おでこのできものを医者に診て(＝診察して)もらった I asked my physician to *examine* a boil on my forehead.

みとう 未踏 ▶人跡未踏の極地 the *untrodden* polar region ‖1969年7月20日ニール・アームストロングは人跡未踏の月に降り立った On July 20, 1969, Neil Armstrong stepped down onto the moon, which had *never been trodden by human feet* [hitherto *known no human footprint*].

みとおし 見通し **1**【視界】visibility ▶東京湾は霧できょうは見通しが悪い *Visibility* is quite bad [poor] today in Tokyo Bay due to the fog. ‖吹雪ではとんど見通しがきかなかった *Visibility was* almost *nil* in the snowstorm. ‖見通しのきかない曲がり角では必ずスピードを落としなさい Be sure to slow down at *blind corners*.

2【予測】prospects, an outlook (➤ 後者のほうがより客観的な見通しを表す) ▶我々の事業の見通しは明るい[暗い] The *prospects* for our business are bright [gloomy]. / Our business *outlook* is bright [gloomy]. ‖政府の景気対策は見通しが甘い The government's *predictions* for the economy are overly optimistic.
▶中央線は午後には復旧の見通しです[復旧の見通しが立っておりません] The Chuo Line *is expected to* resume its service in the afternoon [*isn't expected to* resume service *any time soon*].
▶そんなことは先刻お見通しだよ *I've already foreseen that*.

みとおす 見通す ▶ここから遠くまで見通せる You *can see far* (*into the distance*) from here. ‖10年先を見通す(＝予測する)のは難しい It is difficult to *foresee* [*predict*] how things will be ten years from now.

みどく 味読 ▶これは多くの人に味読してほしい文学作品です This is a literary work that I hope many people will *read and appreciate*.

みどころ 見所 **1**【見せ場】a highlight ▶その映画の見どころは最後の場面だ The *highlight* of the film is the last scene. →山場.

2【見込み】promise ▶彼は見どころのある学生だ He is a *promising* student.

みとどける 見届ける ▶きみはセンターがボールを捕ったことを見届けて(＝確かめて)から三塁を離れるべきだった You should have *made sure that* the center fielder (had) caught the ball before you left third base. ‖生きている間にふるさとが復興した姿を見届けたい I'd like to *see* my hometown restored *with my own eyes* before I die.

みとめいん 認め印 an informal *hanko*, an approval seal [*hanko*].

みとめる 認める

📖 **訳語メニュー**
受け入れる, 承認する →accept, admit **1**
許可する →allow, permit **2**
評価する →recognize **3**

1【承認する】admit 《to》（好ましくないことを，しばしば圧力に屈してしぶしぶ）; **accept** +目（適切であるとみなして受け入れる）; **acknowledge** +目（隠していた事実を，また真価を）; **concede** +目（しぶしぶ，不本意ながら）▶挑戦者は負けを認めようとしなかった The challenger would not *admit* [*concede*] defeat. ‖ 容疑者は犯行を認めた The suspect *admitted* (to) his crime. ‖ 先生は私が遅刻した理由を認めようとしなかった My teacher wouldn't *accept* my reason for being late for school. ‖ メーカーはエンジンに欠陥があることを認めた The manufacturer *acknowledged* that the engine had a defect.

【文型】
～であると認める
admit (that) S + V
admit (to) being ～

▶その選手は禁止薬物を使用したことを認めた The athlete *admitted that* he [she] had used banned substances. ／The athlete *admitted to* having used banned substances. ‖ 認めようが認めまいが，我々はみな偏見を持っている *Admit it or not*, we all have prejudices.

2【許可する】allow /əláʊ/ +目（止めないでやらせる）; **permit** +目（正式に許可する）; **approve** 《of》（賛成する）▶うちの学校ではバイク通学は認められていない Our school doesn't *allow* [*permit*] us to use motorcycles to get to school. ‖ 両親はぼくが彼女と付き合うのを認めている My parents *approve of* my going out with her.

3【正当に評価する】recognize +目 ▶高山氏はすぐれた画家として広く認められている Mr. Takayama *is* widely *recognized* as an outstanding artist.

4【発見する】▶船長ははるかかなたに島影を認めた The captain *saw* an island far off in the distance. ‖ 検査の結果，異常は認められませんでした The results of the checkup *show there is nothing* wrong with you.

みどり 緑 green（色）; **greenery**（緑の草木）▶緑のひすい *green* jade ‖ 別荘は高原の豊かな緑に囲まれている The summer house is surrounded by the lush *greenery* of the highlands. ‖ 昔は東京も緑が多かった Years ago, Tokyo had a great deal of *greenery*. ‖ このキャンパスには緑がたくさんある This campus has a lot of *trees and plants*.

‖みどりの日 Greenery Day (➤ 日本だけの祝日).

みとりず 見取り図 a (rough) sketch（スケッチ）; **a plan**（設計図）▶店の見取り図をかく make *a sketch* of a store ‖ 新しい家の見取り図 *a plan* for [of] a new house.

みとる 看取る ▶老人は妻にみとられてこの世を去った The elderly man passed away *with* his wife *at his bedside*.

ミドルきゅう ミドル級 the middleweight class [division] ▶ミドル級の選手 *a middleweight*.

みとれる 見とれる be lost in admiration ▶観光客たちはフィヨルドの壮大な眺めに見とれていた The tourists *were lost in admiration* of the spectacular view of the fjord. ‖ 私は美人に見とれていて駅を乗り過ごしてしまった I *was* so *fascinated* by the beautiful woman I forgot to get off at my station. (➤ be fascinated は「うっとりする」).

ミトン a mitten.

みな 皆 1【すべての人】everybody, everyone (➤ 後者はやや堅い語) ▶会社の人は皆いい人ばかりです *Everybody* at the office is kind. ‖ うちの家族は皆阪神ファンだ *All* my family members are fans of the Tigers (baseball team). ‖ 人間は皆平等だ *All* people are equal. →みんな.

2【全部】all ▶広告の品は皆売り切れです The advertised product is *all* sold out. ‖ 持って行く物は皆かばんに詰めた I packed *all the things* [*everything*] to take with me. ‖ こんなことになったのは皆私のせいだ This is *all* my fault.

☛ みなさん (→見出語)

みなおし 見直し ▶選挙制度の早急な見直しが必要だ The election system needs to *be reviewed* as soon as possible.

みなおす 見直す 1【再度見る】look over (again); **double-check**（もう一度チェックする）▶答案は提出する前に必ず見直しましょう Be sure to *look over* [*double-check*] your answers before you hand in your exam paper. ‖ 看護師が比呂子にそっくりだったので，驚いて見直した I *did a double take* because the nurse looked very much like Hiroko. (➤ do a double take は「(最初は気がつかず)あとではっと驚いて見直す」の意のインフォーマルな言い方).

2【再検討する】review +目, **reconsider** +目; **reexamine** +目（再びよく調べる）▶その開発計画は見直す必要があると思う I think the development plan needs to *be reviewed* [*be reconsidered*／*be reexamined*].

3【再評価する】revalue +目, **have a better opinion** 《of》▶監督としての彼を見直す *have a better opinion* of him as manager／*recognize again his worth* as manager ‖ 漢方薬の穏やかな効きめが見直されている Chinese herbal medicine has *undergone a revaluation* in view of its more natural effects. ‖ まあ，安夫君ってピアノが上手ね. 見直しちゃったわ Why, Yasuo, you can play the piano very well. I'll have to *revise my opinion of* you. (「あなたに対する評価を修正しなければならない」と考えて訳す).

みなぎる be full 《of》, **be filled** 《with》▶平和部隊の隊員たちには誇りがみなぎっていた The members of the Peace Corps *were full of* pride. ‖ 新人選手たちは闘志がみなぎっていた The rookies *were filled with* fighting spirit. ‖ 街には活気がみなぎっていた The streets *were alive with* activity.

みなげ 身投げ ▶若い女性が橋の上から身投げした A young woman *threw herself* (*to death*) from the bridge. (➤ to death は死亡したことをはっきりさせるとき).

みなごろし 皆殺し genocide /dʒénəsaɪd/（大量虐殺）▶その男は機関銃で敵を皆殺しにした The man *killed* [*murdered*] *all* his enemies with a machine gun.

みなさん 皆さん everybody, everyone (➤ 後者はやや堅い語) ▶みなさん，こんにちは Hi, *everyone*. ‖ みなさん，きょうは「日本の将来」についてお話ししたいと思います *Ladies and gentlemen*, today I'd like to talk about Japan's future.

▶私はみなさんの誰より速く走ることができます I can run faster than *any of you*. ‖ みなさんに心から感謝いたしたいと思います I'd like to express my sincere thanks to *you all*.

✉ **ご家族のみなさんはいかがお過ごしですか** How's *everybody* in your family?

✉ **ご家族のみなさんによろしく** My best wishes to *you all*.

みなしご 孤児 an **orphan** 《参考》orphan は片親だけを失った子供にも用いることがある.

みなす 見做す **consider** 《to be》, **regard** 《as》 (➤ regard のほうが主観的な判断という含みがある)

【文型】
A を B **とみなす**
consider A (**to be**) B
regard [**view**] A **as** B ➤ B は名詞・形容詞

《解説》**consider** が最もふつうの語で,「…と思う, …と考える」に当たることも多い. また, consider が熟慮のうえの結論というニュアンスがあるのに対し, **regard** は元の「見る」の意を残して, しばしば外見上の判断や個人的な見方を表すことがある.

▶欠席者は棄権 [失格] **とみなします** Absentees will *be considered* (*to be*) disqualified. ‖ スティーブ・ジョブズはパソコンの生みの親の一人**とみなされている** Steve Jobs *is considered* [*is regarded as*] one of the fathers of the personal computer. ‖ 反対意見がなければ承認されたもの**とみなします** If you give no opposing opinions, we will *consider* that you have given your approval. (➤ ちなみに, Silence gives [is] consent. (沈黙は同意と同じこと) ということばがある).

みなと 港 a **harbor** (外海から守られた) ; a **port** (商港 ; しばしば「港町」の意で用いる) ▶**港**に韓国船が着いた A South Korean ship arrived in the *harbor*. ‖ **港**にクイーンエリザベス 2 号が停泊している The QE 2 is in *port*. (➤ in port は「入港中で」) ‖ **港**を出て行く船を大勢の人が見送った A great many people saw the ship out of *port*.
‖**港町** a port town [city].

みなみ 南 **the south** 一形 **南の** **south, southern** /sʌ́ðəʳn/ ▶奈良は京都の**南**にある Nara is (to *the*) *south* of Kyoto. (➤ カッコ内は言わないほうがふつう) ‖ 鹿児島は**南九州**にある Kagoshima Prefecture is in *southern Kyushu*. ‖ 船は**南**に向かって航海していた The ship was sailing *to the south* [sailing *southward*].
▶**南**の空を見上げてごらん Look up at the *southern* sky. ‖ 新宿駅の**南口**で会おう I'll see you at the *south exit* of Shinjuku Station. ‖ うちの子供部屋は**南向き**です My child's room *faces south*. (➤ この south は副詞).
‖**南アフリカ** South Africa ‖ **南アメリカ** South America ‖ **南回帰線** the Tropic of Capricorn ‖ **南風** a south wind ‖ **南十字星** the Southern Cross ‖ **南太平洋** the South Pacific ‖ **南半球** the Southern Hemisphere.

みなも 水面 **the surface of the water** ▶月影が湖の**みなも**に揺れていた The moonlight was shimmering on *the surface* of the lake.

みなもと 源 **the source** (何かが始まる所) ; **the origin** (あるものの起源) ▶相模川の**源**は山中湖である The Sagami River has its *source* in [rises in] Lake Yamanaka. (➤ この rise は「源を発する」).
▶仏教の**源**は古代インドにさかのぼる Buddhism originated in ancient India. ／*The origins* of Buddhism lie in ancient India.

みならい 見習い a **trainee** /trèɪníː/ (実習生) ; an **apprentice** (徒弟) ▶この店員たちは**見習い中です** These salesclerks *are trainees*. ‖ ぼくは大工**見習い**だ I'm a carpenter's *apprentice*. ‖ **見習い期間**は半年間です The *probationary period* is six months.

みならう 見習う **follow the example** 《of》 ▶野球選手はイチローを**見習う**べきです Baseball players should *follow* Ichiro's *example*. ‖ 良夫君を**見習い**なさい. ほんとうによく勉強するから *Be more like* Yoshio ; he works so hard.

みなり 身なり one's (**personal**) **appearance** ▶私たちの教授は**身なり**に全く無頓着だ Our professor is quite careless about *his* (*personal*) *appearance* [*what he wears*]. ‖ 入社試験の面接に行くときは**身なりをきちんとする**ことが大切だ It is important to *dress properly* [*to be neatly dressed*] when you go for a job interview. ‖ 彼はいつも**りっぱな** [**質素な**] **身なりをしている** He *is* always *nicely* [*simply*] *dressed*. ‖ 面接の前に**身なりを整え**たほうがいいよ You'd better *tidy* (*yourself*) *up* [*make yourself presentable*] before the interview.

みなれる 見慣れる 一形 (…には) **見慣れた** **familiar** 《to》 ▶**見慣れた** [**見慣れない**] 顔 a *familiar* [*an unfamiliar*] face ‖ 長い入院生活のあとでは**見慣れた光景** [**景色**] も新鮮に映る Even *a familiar sight* [*view*] looks fresh after a long stay in the hospital. ‖ 私は警察官なので交通事故は**見慣れている** I'*m used* [*accustomed*] *to seeing* car accidents since I'm a policeman. (➤ to のあとは名詞または動名詞) ‖ **見慣れぬ人**が戸口に立っている There's *a stranger* at the door.

ミニ ‖**ミニコンポ** a miniature stereo system (with components) ‖ **ミニスカート** a miniskirt, 《インフォーマル》a mini ‖ **ミニバン** a minivan.

ミニカー a **minicar**

> **危ないカタカナ語✹ ミニカー**
> **1** 日本語では「小型自動車」「模型自動車」の両方の意味に使われるが, 英語の minicar はもっぱら前者を指す. またイギリスには客からの電話呼び出しにだけ応じるタクシーがあって, それを minicab と呼んでいる.
> **2**「模型自動車」の意味の「ミニカー」は model car とか miniature /míniətʃəʳ/ of a car という.

¹みにくい 醜い **ugly** ; **shameful, disgraceful** (恥ずべき ; 後者は強い調子の語) ▶**醜い**アヒルの子 an *ugly* duckling ‖ 遺産相続をめぐって**醜い**争いになった An *ugly* struggle developed over the inheritance. ‖ 選挙での票の買収ほど**醜い**ものはない Nothing is more *shameful* [*disgraceful*] than to buy votes in an election.

²みにくい 見難い ▶雨が強くなって, 前方が**見にくくなった** It started to rain harder and it was getting *harder to see* in front of me. ‖ コピーが小さくて**見にくい** It's *hard to read* this photocopy because the print is too small. (➤ この場合は文字などが読みにくいことなので, read を用いる).

ミニコミ ‖**ミニコミ誌** a magazine circulated among a limited number of readers.

ミニチュア a **miniature** /míniətʃəʳ/ ▶**ミニチュアカー** a model car ／*a miniature* of a car.

みにつける 身につける **learn** +目. →**身**.

みぬく 見抜く **see through** ; **read** +目 (人の心を読む) ; **pierce** +目 (変装などを) ▶ 1941年, アメリカの指導者は日本軍戦術家の意図を**見抜いていた** In 1941, American leaders *saw through* the intentions of Japanese military strategists. ‖ 田中先生は人の心をよく**見抜く** Mr. Tanaka is a good *mind reader*. ‖ 彼女には人を**見抜く**力がある She has good *insight* into people's character. (➤ insight は「洞

察力」）‖彼女の変装［なぞの真相］を見抜く *pierce* her disguise [a mystery].

みね 峰 a **peak**; a **summit, the top**（山頂）; a **ridge**（尾根）▶雲海の上にいくつかの峰々がそびえ立っている Several *peaks* rise above the sea of clouds.

ミネソタ **Minnesota**（アメリカ中北部の州；略 MN, Minn.）.

ミネラル a **mineral** ▶海草はミネラル分が豊富だ Seaweed is rich in *minerals*.

‖ミネラルウォーター mineral water.

みのう 未納 ▶あなたは家賃が未納です You *are behind* with [in] your rent. ／Your rent *is past due*.

▶未納額は10万円です The *balance owed* (*due immediately*) is 100,000 yen.

みのうえ 身の上 **circumstances**（境遇，暮らし向き）; one's **situation**（立場）▶私は彼女の気の毒な身の上に同情した I felt pity for her unfortunate *circumstances*. ‖あのおばあさんは誰にでも身の上話をする That elderly woman tells *the story of her life* to anybody (who will listen). ‖ご両親はあなたの身の上を案じているに違いない Your parents must be concerned for *your well-being* [about *how you are getting along*].（➤ well-being は健康で経済的にも困らない「幸福な状態」）.

‖身の上相談欄 a personal advice column,《英・インフォーマル》an agony column.

みのがし 見逃し ▶《野球》（打者が）見逃しの三振をする *strike out looking*／*take a called third strike* ‖見逃しの三振に倒れる *be called out on strikes*.

みのがす 見逃す **1【見落とす】overlook** +目（見ていながら気がつかない）; **miss** +目（見損なう）▶誤りを見逃す *overlook* a mistake（➤「大目に見る」の意にもなる）‖ああ残念！『レ・ミゼラブル』を見逃した What a shame! I *missed* (*seeing*) "Les Misérables." ‖あすの新聞にくじの当選番号が出るから見逃さないように Don't *forget to check* the winning numbers of the lottery in the newspaper tomorrow.

2【大目に見る】overlook +目 ▶きみの過ちを今回だけは見逃してやる I'll *overlook* your mistake this once.（➤「今回は見逃してやる」なら I'll let you go this time.）‖子供のいたずらを見逃してやった I *let* the child's misbehavior *go by*.

3【やり過ごす】▶阿部選手は絶好球を見逃した Abe *let* a perfect pitch *go by*.

みのけ 身の毛 ▶身の毛のよだつような話 a *hair-raising* [*gruesome*] story ／a spine-chiller（➤ hair-raising が日本語に近く，gruesome は「ぞっとするような」の意で，死・幽霊などを連想させる．また spine-chiller は「背筋を冷やすもの」が原義．映画・小説などにも使える）‖事故の様子を見て身の毛がよだった The sight of the accident *made my hair stand on end*. ／I *was horrified* at the sight of the accident.

みのしろきん 身代金 a **ransom** ▶誘拐犯人は1億円の身代金を要求した The kidnapper demanded *a ransom* of 100 million yen [*a* hundred-million-yen *ransom*]. ‖犯人は身代金目当てに子供を監禁した The criminal held the child *for* [*to*] *ransom*.

みのたけ 身の丈 one's **height**（身長）▶身の丈に合った生き方をする live *within one's means*.

みのほど 身の程 ▶T大を受けようなんて，おまえも身の程知らずだな You're planning to try and get into T University? You do*n't know your* (*own*) *limitations*, do you? ‖あの男は身の程を知らない That man does*n't know his place*.

みのまわり 身の回り ▶彼はいつも身の回りをきれいにしている He always *keeps himself neat and clean*. ‖すりがいますので身の回り品にご注意ください Watch *your personal belongings* and be on guard against pickpockets. ‖姉はお年寄りたちの身の回りの世話をしています My sister *looks after* [*takes care of*] elderly people.

みのむし 蓑虫《虫》a **bagworm**.

みのり 実り a **harvest**, a **crop**（➤ 後者はややインフォーマルな語）▶ことしはブドウの実りがよかった We've had a great grape *harvest* this year. ‖いよいよ実りの秋だ It's finally *fall, the harvest season*.

▶《比喩的》研究会は実り多いものだった The workshop turned out to be *fruitful*.

みのる 実る **bear fruit**（果樹が）; **ripen, become ripe**（果実・穀物が）▶柿（かき）は秋に実る Persimmon trees *bear fruit* in the fall. ‖ことしは稲がよく実るだろう The rice will *ripen well* this year. ／We'll *have a good crop* of rice this year.（➤「よい収穫がある」の意）.

▶《比喩的》きみの努力はいつか実ると信じています I believe your hard work will *bear fruit* [*pay off*] some day.

みばえ 見栄え ▶見栄えのしないネクタイ a *dull* [*boring*] tie ‖友恵はウエディングドレスを着たら見栄えがした Tomoe *looked lovely* [*attractive*] in her wedding dress.（➤ lovely は「愛らしい」, attractive は「魅力的な」）.

▶ちゃんとした額に入れたら絵はぐっと見栄えがよくなった The picture *looked all the better* after it had been set in a proper frame.

みはからう 見計らう ▶ぼくが時機を見計らって慶子にとりなしてやるよ *When* I *get a chance*, I'll talk to Keiko for you.

みはったつ 未発達の **undeveloped**; **underdeveloped**（発達不十分の）▶彼女は精神面で未発達なようだ She seems emotionally *underdeveloped*.

みはっぴょう 未発表の **unpublished** ▶応募作品は未発表のものに限ります Entries must be [are limited to] *unpublished* works.

みはてぬ 見果てぬ ▶世界平和の達成は見果てぬ夢に思われる Achieving world peace seems like *an impossible dream*.

みはなす 見放す **give up**《on》, **abandon** +目（➤ 後者は堅い語）▶医師はその患者を見放してしまった The doctor has *given up on* the patient. ‖岡田さんは非行の息子を見放すことはしなかった Mr. Okada never *abandoned* his delinquent son.

みはらい 未払い ▶未払いの給料 *unpaid* salary ／*back* pay ‖500万円の未払い金 five million yen *in arrears* ‖その仕事の報酬は未払いだ（＝まだもらっていない）We *haven't been paid* for the job yet.

みはらし 見晴らし a **view** ▶見晴らしのいい丘 a hill *with a fine view* ‖サンフランシスコのテレグラフヒルはとても見晴らしがいい Telegraph Hill in San Francisco *has a great view*. ／You *can get* [*enjoy*] *a beautiful view* from Telegraph Hill in San Francisco.

みはらす 見晴らす ▶このマンションの屋上から東京ディズニーランドが見晴らせる You *can see* [*get a view of*] Tokyo Disneyland from the rooftop of this apartment house.

みはり 見張り a **guard** ▶とばく師たちは戸口に見張りを置いた The gamblers placed *a guard* at the door.

みはる 見張る 1【監視する】**watch** +目, **guard** +目; **stake out**（張り込む；インフォーマルな言い方）▶容疑者のアジトを見張る *stake out* the suspect's hideout ‖ 刑事たちが先週から彼の行動を見張っている The detectives *have been watching* his movements since last week. ‖ 数名の警備員が展示中の王冠を常時見張っていた Several security guards *were keeping watch on* [*were guarding*] the crown on display the whole time.

2【目をみはる】▶我々は聖ソフィア大聖堂の壮麗さに目をみはった *Our eyes opened wide* at the splendor of St. Sophia.

みびいき 身贔屓 **favoritism**（えこひいき）; **nepotism**（縁者びいき）▶身びいきする *practice favoritism* ‖ 隣の奥さんは身びいきな人だ The woman next door *is overly partial to her family*.（➤「自分の家族を過度にえこひいきする」の意；英語圏ではそういう態度を他人が非難することは一般的ではない）.

みひらき 見開きの **two-page** ▶見開き全面広告を載せる run a *two-page* ad（➤ two- [double-] page spread ともいう. これは記事を指すこともある）.

みぶり 身振り a **gesture**（しぐさ）▶あの候補者は大げさな身ぶりで話す That candidate talks with exaggerated *gestures*. ‖ その外国人は困ったという身ぶりをした The foreigner *made a gesture* of puzzlement.

▶彼は身ぶりで逃げろと合図した He *motioned* [*signaled*] me *to* run away. ‖ 身ぶり手ぶりで何とか意思が通じた I somehow managed to make myself understood *with a lot of gestures*.

みぶるい 身震いする **shudder**（恐怖・寒さなどで激しく震える）; **tremble**（恐怖・寒さなどで小刻みに）▶興奮で身震いする *tremble* with excitement ‖ 毛虫って, 身震いするほど嫌い！I hate caterpillars so much that I *shudder* at the mere sight of them.

みぶん 身分 a (**social**) **position,** (**social**) **status** [**standing**]（➤ いずれの言い方も「社会的地位」を指す）; **identity**（身元）▶身分の低い男 a man of *low social status* ‖ 昔は身分の違いによってさまざまな制約があった A lot of restrictions used to be placed on people according to their *social positions* [*standing*]. ‖ あなたの身分を証明するものを提示してください Please show me some form of *ID*. ‖ 身分相応の暮らしをしなさい Try to live *within your means*.（➤ means は「収入」）‖ 平日に休みを取れるような身分ではない I *can't afford to* take a weekday off (from work).（➤「ゆとりがない」の意）.

‖ 身分証明書 an identification [ID] card.

みぼうじん 未亡人 a **widow** ▶Tさんの未亡人 Mr. T's *widow* / the wife of the late Mr. T（➤ 後者は「故T氏の妻」の意）‖ おばは40歳で未亡人になった My aunt became [was left] *a widow* at the age of forty.

みほん 見本 1【サンプル】a **sample**（同類のものの代表例）; a **specimen**（科学[技術]研究の目的のための）▶無料見本進呈 A free *sample* is available. ‖ 実物は見本とだいぶ違う The real thing differs greatly from the *sample*.

▶宇宙飛行士たちは月の岩石の見本を持ち帰った The astronauts brought back *specimens* of moon rocks.

‖ 見本市 a trade fair（➤「国際見本市」は international trade fair）‖（採用）審査見本 an examination copy ‖ 製品見本 a product sample.

2【手本】an **example**; a **model**（模範）▶すぐれた文章の見本 *a model* of good writing ‖ 彼女は成功したミュージシャンの見本だ She is *an example* of a successful musician.

▶オーバーヘッドキックの見本を見せてあげよう Let me *demonstrate* an overhead kick.（➤ demonstrate は「目の前で実演する」）.

みまい 見舞い an **inquiry** /ɪnkwáɪəri/（人の容体を尋ねること）; a **visit**（訪問）▶体育の先生のお見舞いにきのう病院へ行った We *visited* our P.E. teacher in (the) hospital yesterday.（➤《英》では the を省く）‖ お見舞いの手紙がたくさん届いてますよ There are a lot of *get-well letters* for you. ‖ さっそくのお見舞いをありがとうございました Thank you for *coming to see me* so soon.

▶あの野郎に一発（パンチを）お見舞いしてやったよ I *gave* that guy *a blow*.

✉ **ご病気とのこと, お見舞い申し上げます** Sorry to hear of your illness. *I hope you will be feeling better soon.* ➤ 親しい人へのくだけたお見舞いで「早い回復を祈っています」の意. Get well soon.（早くよくなってね）とだけ書いてもよい.

✉ **お父さまが癌（がん）とうかがい, 心からお見舞い申し上げます** I am shocked to hear that your father has cancer. *I am sending you my heartfelt wishes for his* (*complete*) *recovery*. ➤ 少し改まったお見舞い.

✉ **ハリケーンとはとんだ災難でしたね. 心からお見舞いを申し上げます** What a terrible thing for you to have been hit by a hurricane. *Allow me to express my sincere sympathy* [*I wish to offer my sympathy*].

‖ 見舞い客 a visitor (to a sick person); a well-wisher（回復を願う人）‖ 見舞い金 a gift of money (in token of one's sympathy) ‖ 見舞いの品 a gift [a present] for a convalescent.

みまう 見舞う 1【病人を】**visit** +目（訪問する）; **inquire**《after》（容体を聞く）▶花を持って病院に友人を見舞った I *visited* [*went to see*] a friend of mine in the hospital with some flowers. ‖ 病気のいとこを見舞う手紙を書いた I wrote a *get-well* letter to my cousin who is sick. / I wrote a letter to *inquire after* my cousin who is sick.（➤ inquire after は医師・看護師など, 第三者に患者の病状を尋ねる場合）.

2【襲う】**hit** +目, **strike** +目 ▶沖縄地方はたびたび台風に見舞われる The Okinawa district *is* often *hit* [*struck*] by typhoons.

みまがう 見まがう ▶雪が積もったかと見まがうばかりの月明かりの道 a road brightly lit by the moon *that could be mistaken for* a snow-covered one.

みまちがえる 見間違える **mistake ... for** ▶この2枚の切符は似ているから見間違えないように These two tickets look similar, so don't *mistake* one *for* the other [don't *get* them *mixed up*].

みまもる 見守る **watch** +目 ▶水泳監視員たちは常にプールの中の子供たちを見守っている The lifeguards continually *watch* [*keep their eye*(*s*) *on*] the children in the swimming pool.

みまわす 見回す **look around** ▶子供たちはもの珍しそうに国会議事堂の中を見回した The children *looked around* the Diet building with curious eyes.

みまわり 見回り **patrol** /pətróʊl/（巡視）▶警官がその地区を見回りしている Police officers *are patrolling* the area.

▶先生方は放課後に校舎の**見回りをする**ことになった The teachers were required to *go around and inspect* the school building after school. (➤ inspect は「点検する」).

みまわる 見回る **patrol** +目 (特定の地域を異状はないかと) ; **make** [**do** ／**go**] one's **rounds** 《**of**》 (受け持ち区域を職務として) ; **inspect** +目 (視察する) ▶夜警が構内を１時間おきに**見回る** A night watchman *patrols* [*makes the rounds of*] the premises every hour.

みまん 未満 **under …** (➤ under はその数を含まない) ▶《掲示》18歳**未満**入場お断り No One *Under* Eighteen Admitted. ‖ 銀行は１円**未満**の利子は切り捨てる When paying interest, the bank drops fractions of *less than* one yen. (➤ less than は「…より少ない」の意) ‖ 遼君は「友だち以上, **恋人未満**」というところよ Ryo is more than a friend, but *not quite my boyfriend*.

みみ 耳

📖 **訳語メニュー**
耳 →ear **1**
聴力 →hearing **2**

1【**器官**】an **ear** ▶ウサギの**耳**を持ってぶら下げる hold a rabbit by the *ears* ‖ 風船が今にも割れそうだったので私は手で**耳**をふさいだ I covered my *ears* with my hands when the balloon was about to break. ‖ ママ, **耳**のあかを取ってよ Mom, could you clean my *ears*?

▶妙な音がしたので犬は**耳をぴんと立てた** The dog *pricked* [*perked*] *up its ears* at the strange noise. ‖ 彼は私の**耳もと**で「好きだよ」とささやいた He whispered *into my ear*, "I love you."

‖**耳あか** earwax, wax in the ears ‖ **耳かき** an earpick ‖ **耳栓** an earplug.

2【**聞く能力**】**hearing** ▶祖父は**耳がいい**[**遠い**] My grandfather *has good ears* [*is hard of hearing*]. ‖ エジソンは若い頃から**耳が遠かった** Edison *had poor hearing* since childhood. ‖ ものすごい爆発音がして一瞬**耳が聞こえなくなった** I *couldn't hear anything* for a minute because of the earsplitting noise of the explosion.

3【**物の耳**】▶パンの**耳**を捨てないで Please don't throw away *the crusts* [*ends*] of the bread.

4【**慣用表現**】

耳が痛い ▶それを言われると耳が痛いね That's *a sore spot* (for me). ‖ **対話**「お隣のご主人は食事のあとの洗い物をしてくれるそうよ」「耳が痛いな」"I hear that the husband next door washes the dishes after meals." "*Ouch! That hurts.*" (➤ 決まった言い方). **耳が早い** ▶もう知ってるの？ 耳が早いなあ You know it? You *have quick ears* [You*'ve* sure *got your ear to the ground*]. (➤ have sharp ears ともいう). **耳に入れる** ▶きみの耳に入れておきたいことがあって電話したんだ I called you up because there's something I think you *should know*. **耳にする** ▶宮本さんが国会議員に立候補するという話を耳にした I *heard* [*happened to hear*] that Mr. Miyamoto will run for the Diet. **耳にたこができる** ▶監督の説教は耳にたこができるほど聞いた (＝聞き過ぎてうんざりだ) I've heard the same old lecture from the manager so often; I'*m sick and tired of* it. **耳につく** ▶雨の音が耳について (＝邪魔になって) 寝つけなかった I couldn't get to sleep because I was *disturbed by* the sound of rain. **耳に残る** ▶あのときの彼の笑い声が今でも耳に残っている The sound of his laughter still *rings in my ears*. **耳に入る** ▶いやなうわさが耳に入った Some unpleasant gossip *reached my ears*.

耳を疑う ▶うちの社長が贈賄で捕まったことを聞いたときは耳を疑った (＝信じられなかった) I *couldn't believe my ears* when I heard that our president got caught for bribery. **耳を貸す** ▶ちょっと耳を貸してよ I have something to tell you that I'd like you to keep (a) secret. ／This is just between you and me [the two of us]. (➤ ともにないしょ話をする場合. Could you lend me an ear? は「私の悩みごとを聞いて」という場合に用いる) ‖ あの国会議員は我々の訴えに耳を貸そうとしなかった That Dietman *shut his ears* [*turned a deaf ear*] *to* our complaint. **耳を傾ける** ▶人の話に少しは耳を傾けたらどうだい Why don't you try to *listen to* other people? ／Why don't you try *paying* a little *attention to* what other people (have to) say?

耳を澄ます ▶耳を澄まして (＝注意して聞いて) ごらん, ウグイスが鳴いている *Listen* (*attentively*). A bush warbler is singing. **耳をそばだてる** ▶prick (up) one's ears; listen attentively [carefully] (注意深く聞く). →**そばだてる** **耳をそろえる** ▶貸した金はあした耳をそろえて返してもらうよ I want you to pay back *every single one* of your debts tomorrow.

耳をつんざく ▶ライブハウスから耳をつんざくような音楽が聞こえてきた I heard *earsplitting* [*deafening*] sounds from the bar with live music.

みみあたらしい 耳新しい **new**, **fresh** ▶**耳新しい**情報 *new* information.

みみうち 耳打ち ▶王妃は国王に何か**耳打ちした** The queen *whispered* something to the king [in the king's ear].

みみがくもん 耳学問 ▶祖父は**耳学問**で多くのことを知っている My grandfather is full of *knowledge* that he's *picked up* here and there. ／My grandfather has *picked up* many things (by listening to others). (➤ pick up は「聞き覚える」).

みみかざり 耳飾り an **earring** ▶**耳飾り**をつける [つけている] put on [wear] *earrings*. ‖「真珠の**耳飾り**の少女」Girl with a Pearl *Earring* (➤ フェルメールの肖像画の題名).

みみざわり 耳障り ▶この自転車のキーキーいう音は**耳ざわりだ** The way this bicycle squeaks *grates on my ears* [*on my nerves*]. ‖ 私の古いパソコンのプリンターの音は全く**耳ざわりだ** The noise from my old (PC) printer *is* really *irritating*. (➤「いらいらさせる」の意).

みみず《動物》an **earthworm** ▶釣り針に**ミミズ**をつける put *an earthworm* on a hook.

▶《慣用表現》**ミミズがはったような字** handwriting *like chicken scratches* (🔴 英語では「ニワトリが引っかいたような字」と考えて用例のようにいう).

みみずく《鳥》a **horned owl** /aʊl/.

みみずばれ みみず腫れ a **welt**, a **wale** ▶彼女は私の腕を引っかいて**みみずばれ**にした She scratched me and left *a welt* [*wale*] on my arm [*waled* my arm].

みみたぶ 耳朶 an **earlobe**.

みみっちい **stingy** (けちな) ▶これっぽっちしかくれないの？ **みみっちい**なあ This is all you're giving me? How *stingy* of you! ‖ **みみっちい**ことをするな Don't be *petty-minded*!

みみなり 耳鳴り **ringing in the ear(s)** (➤ 両耳の場合

は ears)；**tinnitus**（➤医学用語）▶耳鳴りがする My ears are [My ear is] ringing. ／I have *ringing in my ear*(*s*).

みみなれない 耳慣れない **unfamiliar** ▶彼女は耳慣れない外来語ばかり使いたがる She tends to use *unfamiliar* loanwords too much.

みみより 耳寄り ▶耳寄りな情報 *a tidbit* ‖ 耳寄りな話があるのよ. 今, ブランドもののバッグが半額で手に入るって *Good news!* I hear you can get designer bags at half prices now.

みむき 見向き ▶パーティーで純子はぼくの方を見向きもしなかった At the party, Junko *ignored* me [*didn't even look at* me].

▶彼はギャンブルなど見向きもしない(＝興味がない) He *has no interest in* gambling.

みめい 未明 ▶我々は10日の未明にベースキャンプを出発する予定だ We plan to leave the base camp *before dawn* [*daybreak*] on the 10th. (➤ dawn は「夜明け」) ‖ けさ未明の火事で3軒が焼けた The fire *at early dawn* this morning destroyed three houses.

ミモザ 《植物》a **mimosa** /mɪmóʊsə ‖ -zə/.

みもだえ 身悶え ▶耐え難い痛さに身もだえする *writhe* in unbearable pain.

みもち 身持ち **morals**(品行) ▶身持ちの悪い女とは付き合うな Avoid women *of loose morals*. ‖ 気をつけろ, あの男は身持ちがよくないぞ Be careful. He lives a *dissipated* life.

みもと 身元 one's **identity**（どこの誰であるか)；one's **background**（生い立ち）▶ひき逃げ事故の被害者の身元はまだわかっていない The *identity* of the hit-and-run accident victim has not yet been established. ／The victim in the hit-and-run accident has yet to be identified. ‖ 警察は被害者の身元を調査している The police are making inquiries into the victim's *background*.

▶おじは快く私の身元を引き受けて(＝保証人になって)くれた My uncle agreed to *be my guarantor*. ／My uncle *stood surety* [*stood guarantor*] *for* me.

‖ **身元引受人** a surety, a guarantor（➤両語とも「負債に対する保証人」の意にも用いる).

みもの 見物 ▶巨人対西武の日本シリーズは見物だ The Japan Series between the Giants and the Lions will be *exciting* [*worth watching*]. ‖ 誰が次の首相になるか見物だね *I'm curious to see* who will be the next prime minister.

みや 宮 a **Shinto shrine** ▶宮参りをする *visit a Shinto shrine*.

‖ **宮大工** a carpenter who specializes in building shrines or temples.

みゃく 脈 **1**【脈拍】a **pulse** /pʌls/ ▶私の脈は平常で70くらいだ My *pulse* is around 70 normally. ‖ 彼の胸に耳を当てたら, 脈が驚くほど速かった When I put my ear against his chest, I found his *pulse* was extremely fast.

▶看護師が私の脈をとった The nurse *took* [*felt*] *my pulse*.

▶わが校には建学の精神が今なお脈打っている Our school's [college's] founding spirit *still lives* (*on*).

2【望み】**hope** ▶脈がなさそうなら早く彼女のことは忘れたほうがいい Forget about her if *there is no hope* [she *is not interested in* you].

‖ **金脈** a vein of gold (金鉱脈)；a source of funds [financial backing]（➤「不正金脈」は shady financial dealings) ‖ **水脈** a (ground) water vein.

みゃくはく 脈拍 a **pulse** ▶脈拍を計る take one's *pulse*.

‖ **脈拍数** a pulse rate, (a) pulse frequency.

みゃくみゃく 脈々 ▶開拓者魂は脈々とアメリカ人の中に生きている The Pioneer [Frontier] Spirit *has been in the blood* of Americans throughout their history.

みゃくらく 脈絡 **coherence** /koʊhíərəns/（首尾一貫性)；**connection**（関係）▶その作家はふいに前の話と全く脈絡のないことをしゃべり出した The writer abruptly began to talk on a topic that had no *connection* with the previous one.

みやげ 土産 a **present**, a **gift**（贈り物)；a **souvenir** /sùːvəníəʳ/（記念の品）

> **《解説》** (1)「みやげ」にぴったりの語はないので, present（プレゼント), gift（贈り物), souvenir（記念の品)を適宜用いる. present と gift では後者が堅い語.
> (2) souvenir が日本語の「みやげ」の相当語として用いられることが多いが, これは「思い出のための品, 記念の品」の意で, 自分のために買い求めた品を含む.

▶多くの外国人は日本人は旅行でなぜあんなにたくさんのみやげを買うのだろうかと思っている Many foreigners wonder why Japanese buy so many *gifts* when traveling. ‖ ほら, 沖縄に行ったおみやげよ Here's *a present I brought back* for you from Okinawa. ‖ インド旅行のみやげにこのサリーを買った I bought this sari as *a souvenir* of my trip to India. ‖ トルコ, どうだった？ みやげ話を聞かせてよ How was your trip to Turkey? Let me hear *all about your trip* [*stories from your trip*].

✉ **こけし人形は東北地方の人気のあるおみやげです** A kokeshi (wooden) doll is *a* popular *souvenir* of the Tohoku region.

‖ **みやげ物店** a souvenir [gift] shop.

☛ **置きみやげ**（→見出語)

みやこ 都 a **city**(都市)；**the capital**（首都）▶ウィーンは音楽の都といわれる Vienna is known as *the city* [*capital*] *of music*.

ことわざ 住めば都 Wherever you live will be the best place for you. ／Any place can be home once you get used to it.

みやすい 見易い ▶彼の字は見やすい His writing is *easy to read*. ‖ 黒板の字は見やすいように書いてください Please write *clearly* on the blackboard.

みやび 雅 **elegance** ▶平安時代の女官たちの雅な世界 the *elegant* world of court ladies in the Heian period.

みやぶる 見破る **detect** ＋目 ▶バッテリーは相手のスクイズのサインを見破った The battery *detected* their opponents' signal to stage a squeeze play. ‖ カウンセラーはすばやくぼくの心を見破った The counselor quickly *read my mind*.

ミャンマー **Myanmar** /mjáːnmɑːʳ/（東南アジアの国；旧称は「ビルマ」(Burma))

‖ **ミャンマー人** a Myanmarese（➤英米とも旧称の「ビルマ人」(Burmese) を用いる人は少なくない).

ミュージカル a **musical** ▶ブロードウェー・ミュージカルを見る see a Broadway *musical*.

ミュージシャン a **musician** /mjuːzíʃən/.

ミュンヘン **Munich** /mjúːnɪk/（ドイツ南部の都市).

みょう 妙な **strange**（見慣れない, 聞き慣れない)；**funny**

(おかしな)；odd(奇妙な) ▶地下室から妙な音がする I hear a *strange* sound coming from the basement. ‖この子は妙なはしの持ち方をする He [She] holds chopsticks in a *funny* [*strange*] way. (➤「この子」は文字通りには this child だが, 英語ではその性別によって he か she でよい).

▶妙なことにそのルームメートは事件以来姿を消した *Strange to say* [*Strange* (*ly*) *enough* ／ *Oddly enough*], the roommate disappeared after the incident. ‖秋の夕暮れは妙に(＝どういうわけか)もの悲しくなる *I don't know why*, but I feel a little sad on autumn evenings.

みょうあん 妙案 a **great** [an **excellent** ／ a **wonderful**] **idea** ▶妙案が浮かんだ I got *a great idea*. ‖それは妙案だ It's *an excellent* [*a wonderful*] *idea*.

みょうが 《植物》(a) *myoga*.

みょうぎ 妙技 **marvelous skill**(すばらしい技術)；a **skillful performance**(みごとな演技)；a **feat**(曲芸)；**virtuosity**(芸術, 特に楽器演奏などの) ▶中国の体操選手たちは競技会ですばらしい妙技を見せた The Chinese gymnasts displayed *marvelous skill* in the competition.

みょうごにち 明後日 **the day after tomorrow** ▶明後日また伺います I'll call on you again *the day after tomorrow*. ‖明後日の夕方お会いしたいのですが I'd like to see you *the evening after next*.

みょうじ 名字 a **family name**, a **surname** ▶きみの名字は何というのですか What is your *family name*? ／ Your *family name*, please? (➤欧米人の場合は last name ともいえるが, 日本人の場合には不適当) ‖彼女の結婚前の名字は冬岡です Her *maiden name* is Fuyuoka.

みょうじょう 明星 **Venus** /víːnəs/ (金星) ▶明け[宵]の明星が出ている *The morning* [*evening*] *star* has appeared.

みょうちきりん 妙ちきりんな **peculiar** ▶彼は妙ちきりんな服装でパーティーにやって来た He came to the party in *peculiar* clothes.

▶その妙ちきりんな形の飾りは何だい? What is that *odd-shaped* ornament?

みょうちょう 明朝 **tomorrow morning** ▶明朝8時までにいらっしゃい Come to my house by eight *tomorrow morning*.

みょうに 妙に →妙.

みょうにち 明日 **tomorrow**. →あす.

[1]みょうばん 明晩 **tomorrow evening** [**night**].

[2]みょうばん 《化学》**alum** /ǽləm/.

みょうみ 妙味 ▶ルアーフィッシングの妙味 the *fascination* of lure fishing.

みようみまね 見様見真似 ▶昔は見よう見まねで大工仕事を覚えたものだ People used to learn carpentry *by imitating* [*following the example of*] *older carpenters*.

みょうやく 妙薬 a **specific medicine**(特効薬) ▶これは水虫に効く妙薬です This is *a specific medicine* for athlete's foot.

▶《比喩的》うちの息子を勉強する気にさせる妙薬はないかね Is there any *miracle medicine* for getting my son to study hard? (➤ほかに a wonder [miracle] drug, a magic [silver] bullet なども用いる).

みょうり 冥利 ▶こんな優秀な学生を教えることができて教師みょうりに尽きます With such excellent students, I feel (that I'*m*) *blessed to be a teacher* [*I'm really enjoying my job as a teacher*]. ／With such excellent students, I'*m enjoying teaching* [*being a teacher*] *to the fullest*.

みより 身寄り a **relative** ▶そのお年寄りには身寄りがない The elderly man has no *relatives*. ／The elderly man has nobody to depend on.

ミラーボール a **mirror ball**.

みらい 未来 **the future** 一形 **未来の future** ▶過去, 現在, 未来 the past, the present and *the future* ‖未来のある青年 a young man with *a future* (before him) (➤「将来性」の意味では a future となる) ‖100年後の未来を予測することは困難だ It is difficult to predict what *the future* will be like one hundred years from now. ‖子供たちは未来都市や未来の夢の車を絵にかいた The children drew pictures of *futuristic cities* and dream cars *of the future*.

▶こちらがぼくの未来の妻です This is my *future* wife [my wife-*to-be* ／ my *fiancée*]. (➤ fiancée /fìːɑːnséɪ/ は「(男性から見た)婚約者」; 女性から見た男性の婚約者は fiancé で発音は同じ).

‖**未来学** futuristics, futurology ‖《文法》**未来時制** the future tense ‖**未来図** a vision of the future ‖**近未来** the near future.

ミラクル a **miracle**.

ミラノ **Milan** /mɪlǽn/ (イタリア北部の都市).

ミリ **milli-** ▶直径5ミリ(＝ミリメートル)の丸をかきなさい Draw a circle with a diameter of 5 *millimeters*. ‖この薬の重さは10ミリグラムだ This medicine weighs 10 *milligrams*.

‖**ミリシーベルト** a millisievert《略 mSv》‖**ミリバール** a millibar《略 mb》‖**ミリリットル** a milliliter《略 ml》.

ミリオンセラー a **million seller**.

ミリタリー **military** ▶ミリタリー系ファッション *military* fashion.

みりょう 魅了する **fascinate** /fǽsɪneɪt/ ＋目 ▶聴衆は真由子の演奏に魅了された The audience *was fascinated* [*was captivated*] by Mayuko's performance. (➤後者は前者より堅い言い方).

みりょく 魅力 an **attraction**(人の心を引きつけたり楽しくさせたりする)；a **fascination**(人の心を奪うほどの)；**appeal**(人の心に訴える)；(a) **charm**(言動が優美で人をうっとりさせる) 一形 **魅力的な attractive, charming, fascinating** →チャーミング ▶女性的[男性的]魅力 feminine [masculine] *charms* ‖パリは芸術家にとって今日でもとても魅力がある Paris holds a great *fascination* for artists even today. ‖ミッキーマウスは誰からも愛される魅力がある Mickey Mouse has universal *appeal*.

▶彼に[彼の人柄に]魅力を感じます I'*m attracted* to him [by his personality]. ‖彼女のお母さんは思ったとおりの魅力的な女性だった Her mother was an *attractive* [a *fascinating* ／ a *charming*] woman, just as I had imagined. ‖グアム島旅行は安さが魅力だ The most *appealing thing* about going to Guam is its inexpensiveness.

みりん 味醂 ***mirin***; sweet rice wine for seasoning [cooking] (➤説明的な訳).

みる 見る・診る **1【目で】see** (＋目), **look** 《at》, **watch** (＋目) →見つめる

【文型】
人・物(A)を見る
look at A
see A ／**watch** A

◀解説▶ **look** 《at》は「意識的に視線を向ける, 気をつけて見る」の意. **see** は「自然に, または偶然に目に入る, 見える, 見かける」の意で, ふつう進行形にしない. **watch** は「動きや変化のあるものをしばらくじっと見守る」の意.

▶**私(の顔)を見なさい** *Look at* me. (➤「私のすることを注意して見なさい」は Watch me carefully.) ‖ **この本をちょっと見てもいいですか** May I *have a look at* this book? ‖ **きのう動物園で初めてコアラを見た** I *saw* koalas for the first time at a zoo yesterday. ‖ **私たちはその歌手を近くでよく見ようと近づいた** In order to *see* the singer well from close up, we approached him [her]. ‖ **私のバッグ, 見なかった?** Have you *seen* my bag? ‖ **テレビ[映画／ビデオ／試合]を見る** *watch* television [a movie／a video／a game] ‖ **その動画はこれまで100万回以上見られている** The video *has been viewed* more than a million times. (➤ view は「画面で見る」).

【文型】
人(A)が…するのを見る
see A do
人(A)が…しているのを見る
see A doing

◀解説▶ (1)**see A do** は「…するのを一部始終見る」の意. **see A doing** はその行為中の「一部分…しているところを目にする」の意.
(2)「じっと見守る」のときは watch を使う. look at もこの文型をとることがあるが, see や watch ほどには使われない.

▶**日本チームがもうひと試合勝つのを見たいものだ** I'd like to *see* the Japanese team *win* another game. ‖ **孫の成長を見るのが楽しみです** It's a pleasure to *see* [*watch*] my grandson *grow up*. ‖ **きみのところの犬が猫を追いかけているのを見たよ** I *saw* your dog *running after* a cat. ‖ **私はそこに座って人々が通り過ぎるのを見ていた** I sat there *watching* the people *pass* [*passing by*].

▶**彼は彼女の顔[空の星]をじっと見た** He *gazed into* her face [*at* the stars in the sky]. ‖ **彼女は私の指輪をちらりと[じろじろ]見た** She *glanced* [*stared*] *at* my ring. ‖ **見て, あの人たち, ビルの屋上で踊ってるわ** *Look*! Those people are dancing on the roof of the building. ‖ **おい, あの車, 見てみろよ!** Hey, *check out* that car! (➤ check out は「よく見る」の意のインフォーマルな言い方) ‖ **運転するときは前をしっかり見なさい** *Keep your eyes on* the road ahead when you are driving. ‖ **あの人は顔を見るのもいやだ** I *can't stand the sight of* him.

▶**彼ほどの才能のあるバスケットボールの選手はまだ見たことがない** I'*ve never seen* a more gifted basketball player than him. ‖ **きょうはきみの意外な一面を見た(＝見つけた)ような気がするよ** I think I have *found* a surprising side of your character today. ‖ **このろう人形, 見れば見るほどオバマ大統領に似ているね** *The more I look at* this wax figure, the more it looks like President Obama.

2【見物する, 観察する】 **see**(+目) ; **observe** +目 (注意深く) ▶**富士五湖の辺りには見る所がたくさんある** There are a lot of places to *see* around Fuji Five Lakes. ‖ **私たちは一日中ロンドン市内を見て歩いた** We spent the whole day *looking* [*sightseeing*] *around* London. ‖ **野球[映画]を見に行こう** Let's go to *see* a ball game [go to the movies]. ‖ **私はまだ能を見たことがない** I have never *seen* a Noh play.

▶**向こうの反応を見てこちらの態度を決めよう** Let's decide our stance after *observing* how they react. ‖ **もうしばらくこの薬を続けて様子を見てみましょう** Keep taking this medicine for a little longer and (we'll) *see* how it is working [affecting you]. ‖ **最近の為替相場は顕著な円高の傾向が見られる** In the recent currency exchange market, a clear tendency of the yen to appreciate can *be observed*. ‖ **来年の運勢を見て(＝占って)もらった** I *had* my fortune for the coming year *told*.

▶**今に見てろ. この借りは返してやるからな!** *Just wait* (*and see*). I'll get even with you!

3【診察する】 **see** +目 ; **examine** +目 (徹底的に) ▶**あの先生は1日に何十人もの患者を診る** That doctor *sees* dozens of patients a day. ‖ **斉藤先生に診ていただきたいのですが** I'd like Dr. Saito to *examine* me. ‖ **胸が痛いんですが, 診ていただけますか** I have a pain in my chest. Will you *examine* [*take a look at*] it?

4【調べる, 読む】 **check** +目 ; **look over** (目を通す) ▶**窓が閉まっているか見てくれますか** Could you *check* the windows?／Could you *check to see* if the windows are closed? ‖ **私の論文, 見ていただけましたか** Did you *look over* my paper? ‖ **みんなの答案は今見て(＝採点して)いるところだ** I'*m grading* your exam papers. ‖ **このスープの味を見てくれない?** Will you *taste* [*have a taste* of] this soup?

5【判断する, 推測する】 **judge** (+目) ; **regard** +目 (みなす) ▶**話し方から見ると佐々木さんは栃木の出身だろう** *Judging from* the way he talks, Mr. Sasaki is from Tochigi.

▶**私の見るところではここ当分景気は回復しそうにない** *In my opinion*, the economy isn't going to pick up in the immediate future. ‖ **どう見てもあの子は中学生だ** *To all appearances*, the girl is a junior high school student.

▶**警察ではこの一件はその男の犯行と見ています** The police *regard* that man *as* the offender in this case. (➤ regard A as B で「AをBとみなす」) ‖ **一行はアルプス山中で道に迷ったものと見られます(＝推測される)** *It is presumed that* the group got lost in the Alps.

6【世話をする】 **look after** ▶**買い物をして来ますから子供を見ていてください** Could you *look after* [*watch*] the children while I'm out shopping? ‖ **しばらくかばんを見てて(＝見守っていて)くれませんか** Could you *keep an eye on* my bag for a while? ‖ **田舎の両親は兄夫婦がめんどうを見ています** My (older) brother and his wife *are taking care of* our parents in our hometown. ‖ **うちの息子の英語を見てもらえませんか(＝教えてください)** Please *give* my son *private lessons* [*tutor* my son] in English. ‖ **宿題を見てあげるから持って来なさい** I'll *take a look at* your homework, so bring it here.

7【経験する】 ▶**あんな寒い所で待っていてばかを見ちゃった** I *shouldn't have* waited in such a cold place. (➤「…するべきではなかった」の意)／*It was stupid of me* to wait (around) in such a cold place. ‖ **それ見たことか** I told you that would happen. (→**それ見たことか**).

8【…してみる】 **try**(+目) ▶**きみ, 京都大学を受けてみなさい** *Try for* Kyoto University. ‖ **この服を着てみたら?** *Why don't you try* this suit (*on*)? ‖ **考えてみ**

み

ると，世の中何もかもそう自分の思いどおりにいくはずがない (But) *thinking it over*, you can see that you can't always have your own way.

☛ 見て見ぬふり，見るからに，見るべき，見る見る (→見出語)

みるかげもない 見る影もない ▶あの大女優も今や年老いて見る影もない That great actress has gotten old and is now *a mere shadow of her former self*.

みるからに 見るからに ▶見るからに彼はプロレスラーだ (*Judging*) *from the way he looks*, he must be a pro wrestler. ‖ 島田さんは見るからに弁護士らしい Mr. Shimada is a lawyer *from head to toe*. (この日本語の場合，英語では用例のように「頭のてっぺんからつま先まで」の意の成句を用いる) ‖ 見るからに意地悪そうなおばあさんだな *At a glance, you can tell* she's a mean old woman.

ミルク milk ▶彼女は(母乳でなく)ミルクで育った She *was bottle-fed*. ／She *was brought up on the bottle*. (➤ bottle は「哺乳びん」;「母乳」に対して赤ちゃん用に調合したミルクは《米》baby formula,《英》baby milk という).

▶コーヒーにミルクを入れますか Would you like *cream* in your coffee? (➤ コーヒー用の「(濃い)ミルク」は cream というのがふつう).

‖ミルクセーキ a milk shake ‖ ミルクティー tea with milk ‖ 粉ミルク dried [powdered] milk, milk powder ‖ スキムミルク skim [skimmed] milk.

みるにみかねて 見るに見かねて ▶息子が危なっかしい手つきでまきを割るのを見るに見かねて私が代わってやった *Because I couldn't bear to watch* my son chop firewood awkwardly *any longer*, I took his place.

みるべき 見るべき ▶その博物館には見るべき物はほとんどなかった There were few exhibits *worth seeing* in the museum. ‖ 彼のその試合での活躍には見るべき(＝めざましい)ものがあった He played a *conspicuous* part in the game.

みるまに 見る間に in an instant ▶巨大なビルが地震で見る間に倒壊した A huge building collapsed *in an instant* [*right before our eyes*] when the earthquake hit.

みるみる 見る見る ▶噴煙が見る見る火口から空へかけ昇った *Even as we watched*, huge clouds of smoke climbed into the sky from the volcano's smoking crater. ‖ 私の友人は20歳を過ぎて見る見る太った A friend of mine grew fat *very fast* after turning twenty. ‖ 娘のピアノは見る見る上達してきた My daughter has *quickly* improved at playing the piano.

みるめ 見る目 ▶黒沢さんは骨とう品を見る目がある Kurosawa *has an eye for* antiques. ‖ あんな男を信用するとは私も人を見る目がなかったなあ I must be *a poor judge of character* to have trusted that man.

ミレニアム a **millennium** [複 **millennia** または ~ **s**].

みれん 未練 an **attachment**(愛着); **regrets** (なごり惜しい気持ち) ▶この家には未練があって手放せない I can't sell this house because I *feel attached to* it. ‖ もうこの世に未練はない I feel no *regrets* about leaving this world. ／I don't have any reason to live any longer. ‖ 雅子にはまだ未練がある I still *have lingering love* for Masako. ‖ 未練がましいことは言いっこなしだよ Let's not talk about *might-have-beens*. (➤ might-have-beens は「もしかしたらそうなったかもしれないこと」の意).

みわく 魅惑 fascination 一動 **魅惑する fascinate** /fǽsəneɪt/ +目, **captivate** +目 (➤ 後者は堅い語) ▶ダイヤモンドの永遠の輝きが女性を常に魅惑してきた The eternal brilliance of diamonds *has* always *fascinated* [*captivated*] women.

みわけ 見分け distinction(区別) ▶あの双子は全くよく似ているので見分けがつかない The twins look so much alike I *can't tell which is which*. ‖ その子はまだほんの子供なので良いことと悪いことの見分けがつかない Being a mere child, he *doesn't know* right *from* wrong.

みわける 見分ける tell 《A from B》; **distinguish** 《A from B》(特徴によって；堅い語)

> 【文型】
> A と B を見分ける
> (can) tell A from B
> distinguish A from B

▶ひよこの雄雌を見分けられますか Can you *tell* a male chick *from* a female one? ‖ 私のようなしろうとでもダイヤモンドとガラス玉くらい見分けられる Even a layman like me can *distinguish* a diamond *from* glass [*tell the difference between* a diamond *and* glass].

みわたす 見渡す look out 《over》; **overlook** +目 (場所・建物などが) ▶講師は聴衆をさっと見渡した The lecturer *looked out* [*ran his eyes*] *over* the audience briefly. ‖ 居間の窓から公園が見渡せる The living room window *overlooks* the park. ／You *can see the whole* park from the living room window.

▶青葉山の上からは仙台市内を見渡せる You can *get a view of* the city of Sendai from the top of Mt. Aoba. ‖ 目の前は見渡す限りの大草原だった A vast grassy plain stretched before us *as far as we* [*the eye*] *could see*.

みをもって 身を以て ▶父は人生とは何かを身をもって示してくれた My father showed me what life is (all about) *through his own example*. ‖ ジャーナリストはその内戦の悲惨さを身をもって体験した The journalist *personally* experienced the misery of the civil war.

みんい 民意 the will of the people; public opinion (世論) ▶民意を反映する reflect *the will of the people* ／reflect *public opinion* ‖ 民意を問う elicit *public opinion*.

みんえい 民営 private ownership 一動 **民営化する privatize** /práɪvətaɪz/ +目 (➤「民営化」は privatization) ▶近年国営企業が次々に民営化されている In recent years, government-owned enterprises have *been privatized* [have *been sold to private owners*] one after another.

みんか 民家 a (**private**) **house** 《参考》英語では特に「民家」といわず house で通用するが，公共施設と区別する場合の掲示は PRIVATE とする ▶戦闘機が民家に突っ込んだ A fighter plane crashed into *a* (*private*) *house*.

みんかん 民間 1【公の機関に属さないこと】一形 **民間の private** (私営の); **civilian** (軍に対して)

‖民間企業 a private enterprise [company] ‖ 民間航空機 a commercial [civilian] aircraft (➤ private aircraft は「自家用機」) ‖ 民間人 a civilian (軍人・警察官などに対して；「民間人の犠牲者」は

civilian casualties) ; a private citizen(公人に対して) ‖ **民間部門** the public sector ‖ **民間貿易** private foreign trade.

2【世間】▶民間に広く知られた話 a story well-known *to most people*.

‖**民間信仰** (a) folk belief ‖ **民間伝承** folklore ‖ **民間療法** a folk [home] remedy.

みんぎょう 民業 a **private-sector business.**

ミンク a **mink**(動物) ; **mink** (毛皮) ▶ミンクのコート a *mink* coat. ‖**ミンク鯨**《動物》a mink whale.

みんぐ 民具 everyday tools [implements] regarded as folk art.

みんげい 民芸 folk art ▶民芸調の柄 *folk* print design ‖**民芸館** a folkcraft museum ‖ **民芸品** a folkcraft, a folk handicraft ‖ **民芸品店** a folkcraft shop.

みんじ 民事 civil affairs ▶民事訴訟を起こす bring *a civil action* [*suit*] ‖**民事再生法** the Civil Rehabilitation Act ‖ **民事裁判** a civil trial ‖ **民事訴訟法** the Code of Civil Procedure.

みんしゅ 民主 一形 **民主的な democratic** ▶民主的な政府 a *democratic* government ‖ 民主的な解決方法 a *democratic* way of solving a problem ‖ 校長が独断でこの問題に結論を出したのは全く民主的でない It was not at all *democratic* for the principal to make the final decision concerning this matter by himself.

▶民主政治が彼らの願いだ *Democratic government* is what they want. ‖ その国では民主化が進んでいる [遅れている] *Democratization* is well under way [lags] in that country. ‖ アメリカには民主党と共和党がある In America there are [America has] two major parties : *the Democratic Party* and the Republican Party.

‖**民主国家** a democratic nation [country], a democracy /dɪmɑ́:krəsi/ (➤「日本は民主国家だ」は Japan is a democratic country.) ‖ **民主主義** democracy ‖ **民主党員** a Democrat /déməkræt/.

みんしゅう 民衆 the people ▶その独裁者は民衆によって追放された The dictator was driven out by *the people*. ‖ デモ隊は一般民衆を巻き込んで暴徒化した The demonstrators, with members of *the general public* [*the citizens*] caught up among them, became violent.

みんしゅく 民宿 a **tourist home,** (a) **bed and breakfast**《略 B & B》,《英また》a **guesthouse** ▶私たちは海辺の民宿に泊まった We stayed at *a tourist home* by the sea.

みんせい 民政 civil [civilian] government.

みんせいいいん 民生委員 a **welfare volunteer.**

1**みんぞく 民族** a **people,** a **nation,** an **ethnic group** 一形 **民族の national, ethnic**

《解説》(1)**people** と **nation** は「(ある国の)国民」の意で用いられ, 前者は社会的・文化的特徴から, 後者は政治的統一体として見た場合に用いることが多い. (2)**ethnic group** は特に言語・文化・出身国・宗教などが同じであることを強調する語. (3)**race** はふつう the white race (白人種), colored races (有色人種)のように, 皮膚の色による民族分けの際に用いられるもので, 最近では使用を避けるべき語の1つとされている.

▶日本民族 the Japanese *people* ‖ アジア民族 *the peoples* of Asia / Asian *peoples* (➤ people は「国民, 民族」の意では数えられる名詞) ‖ ゲルマン民族 the Germanic *peoples* ‖ アメリカ合衆国は多民族国家だ The United States (of America) is *a nation of diverse ethnic groups* [is *a multiethnic country*]. (➤ nation of diverse /dəvə́:ʳs/ ethnic groups は「多様な民族集団から成り立っている国家」の意で, カッコ内の multiethnic を使った言い方より好ましい ; 「単一民族国家」は (ethnically) homogeneous nation).

▶どの国も何らかの形で少数民族の問題を抱えている Every nation has (*ethnic*) *minority* problems in one form or another.

‖**民族意識** nationalism, ethnicity consciousness ‖ **民族衣装** (a) folk costume ‖ **民族音楽** ethnic music ‖ **民族学** ethnology ‖ **民族自決** self-determination of a people, ethnic self-determination ‖ **民族主義** (ethnic) nationalism ‖ **民族性** national traits, ethnicity ‖ **民族紛争** an ethnic conflict.

2**みんぞく 民俗 folk customs**

‖**民俗学** folklore (studies) ‖ **民俗学者** a folklorist ‖ **民俗楽器** a folk instrument ‖ **民俗芸能** folk entertainment ‖ **民俗舞踊** a folk dance.

ミンチ →メンチ.

ミント《植物》**mint.**

みんど 民度 living and cultural standards of a people.

みんな 皆 1【すべての人】**everybody, everyone** (➤後者はやや堅い語) ; **all** (全部) ▶みんながそろったら乾杯しよう Once *everybody* is here, let's drink a toast. (➤ everybody は単数扱い) ‖ この辺りではみんなお互いに知っている *Everybody* knows everybody else around here. ‖ 私が家に着いたときには家族はみんな寝てしまっていた When I got home, my family had *all* gone to bed. ‖ 対話「友だちはみんなスマホ持ってるんだ」「みんながみんなってわけじゃないでしょう?」"*All* my friends have smartphones." "Surely not *all of them*?"

▶みんな(＝誰も)その問題が解けなかった *None of us* could solve the problem. (➤ All of us couldn't solve ... では「みんなが解けたわけではない」).

2【全部】**everything, all** ▶知ってることをみんな話してくれ Tell me *everything* you know. ‖ テーブルに出てたもの, きみたちでみんな食べてしまったの? Did you eat up *all* the food on the table? ‖ みんなでいくら? How much is it *altogether*?

みんぺい 民兵 a **militant,** a **militiaman** [**militiawoman**] ; a **militia**(民兵組織).

1**みんぽう 民放 commercial broadcasting**

‖**民放局** a commercial broadcasting station ‖ **民放テレビ番組** a commercial TV program.

2**みんぽう 民法 civil law** ; **the civil code** (法典).

ミンミンゼミ《虫》a ***minminzemi*** **(a kind of cicada).**

みんよう 民謡 a **folk song**(歌) (➤日本のものは Japanese folk song または文脈によっては *min-yo* としてもよい) ; **folk music** (曲) ; a **ballad** (伝承的な物語を含む) ▶アイルランド民謡 an Irish *folk song* / an Irish *traditional song*.

‖**民謡歌手** a folk singer ; a *min-yo* singer(日本の) ‖ **民謡大会** a Japanese folk song competition [festival].

みんわ 民話 a **folk tale,** a **folk story** (民間に伝わる説話) ; **folklore** (民間伝承) ▶東北地方は民話の宝庫である The Tohoku district is rich in *folk tales* [*folklore*].

む・ム

む 無 nothing ; zero (零) ▶無から有は生じない Nothing will come of *nothing*. (➤ 英語のことわざ) ／You can't get something from *nothing*. ‖ 唯物論者は人は死ねば無であると考えている Materialists believe that humans *do not exist* after death. ‖ 我々の努力が無になった Our efforts *have come to nothing*.
▶人の好意を無にしてはいけない You should not *let* other people's kindness *come to naught*. (➤ naught は nothing の文語) ‖ その飛行機は無給油・無着陸で地球を一周した The plane circled the globe *without* landing or being refueled.

むい 無為 ▶無為に時を過ごしている人は多い There are many people who *lead idle lives*. ‖ どうか大学生活を無為に送らないでください Please don't *idle away* your college days. →無策.

むいしき 無意識 unconsciousness (無意識の状態) ━ 形 無意識の unconscious ▶彼は無意識に頭をかいた He scratched (at) his head *unconsciously*.

むいそん 無医村 a doctorless village, a village without a doctor.

むいちもつ 無一物 ▶私はこの間の大火で無一物になった I *lost everything* in the recent big fire. ‖ その俳人は無一物で全国を放浪した The haiku poet wandered all over the country *with few worldly goods*. (➤「俗人の持つものはほとんど何も持たずに」の意).

むいちもん 無一文 ▶私は無一文だ I'*m penniless*. ／I'*m broke*.

むいみ 無意味な meaningless ▶無意味な戦い a *meaningless* battle ‖ これ以上彼と議論しても無意味だ It would be *fruitless* [*useless*] to argue with him any further. (➤ ともに「無駄だ」の意) ‖ そんなことをしても無意味だ You will only *waste your time* doing that. (➤「時間の浪費だ」の意).

ムース (a) mousse /muːs/.

ムード (an) atmosphere /ǽtməsfɪəʳ/ (雰囲気) ; a mood (気分) ; an air (人が持つ) ▶ムードのある喫茶店 a coffee shop with *atmosphere* ‖ このクラスのムードはなかなかいいね This class has *a* nice *atmosphere*. (➤ 前に形容詞がくるときは a や the を伴う) ‖ あのときはそんなお涙ちょうだいの映画を見るようなムードではなかった At that time, I was not *in the mood* to see such a tearjerker. ‖ その俳優はどことなくムードがある The actor has a certain *air* [*aura*] about him. ‖ もっとムードのある音楽が聴きたい I'd like to listen to some more *romantic* music [music *with* more *atmosphere*].

> **危ないカタカナ語✸ ムード**
> **1** 英語の mood は「機嫌, 気分」の意で, 楽しい気分のほか, 不快な気分も指す. これに対して日本語でいう「ムード」は「いい雰囲気」に近く, atmosphere で表すほうが適切. ただし, 人についていう場合は air を用いる.
> **2**「ムードがある」に moody を使うことはできない. moody は「気難しい」とか「不機嫌な」の意味である. したがって「ムードのある音楽」は romantic music,
> 「(バックグラウンドに流れる)ムード音楽」は background music のようにいう. ただし, 最近ではオーケストラによるポップスのイージーリスニング(タイプの)音楽のことを mood music ということもある.

ムールがい ムール貝 a blue [common] mussel /mʌ́sl/.

むえき 無益な useless ▶無益な論争には巻き込まれたくない I don't want to get involved in a *useless* [*profitless*] argument.
▶子供の宿題を手伝ってやるのは有害無益だ Helping children with their homework *does more harm than good*.

むえん 無縁 ▶この問題は科学とは無縁だ This question *has no relation to* science. ‖ 彼を一目見れば金とは無縁の男だということがすぐわかる A glance at him will show that he *has nothing to do with* money.
‖ **無縁墓地** a cemetery for those who have no surviving relatives.

むが 無我 selflessness ▶ヨガは無我の境地になることを目指す一種の行であるYoga is a (physical) discipline which aims at the attainment of *a spiritual state of selflessness*.
☛ 無我夢中 (→見出語)

むかい 向かい ▶小林さん宅は(通りを挟んで)お向かいです Mr. Kobayashi's house is *across the street* (*from us*). ‖ 彼はテーブルを挟んで私の向かいに座った He sat *across* the table *from* me. ／He sat *opposite* me *across* the table. ‖ インド人家族が(うちの)向かいに引っ越して来た An Indian family moved into the house *opposite* ours.

1むがい 無害な harmless ▶このせっけんは万一のみ込んでも無害です This soap *is harmless* even if you happen to swallow a piece of it.

2むがい 無蓋 open
‖ **無蓋貨車** an open freight car.

むかいあう 向かい合う face ＋目 ▶私たちの会社は大きなホテルと向かい合っている Our office *faces* [*is opposite*] a big hotel. ‖ 試験官と私は向かい合って座った The examiner and I sat *facing each other* [*face to face*].

むかいあわせ 向かい合わせ ▶新幹線で私たちは向かい合わせの席を取った We sat on seats *facing each other* on the Shinkansen train. ‖ きょう電車ですごい美人と向かい合わせに座った I was sitting *face to face with* [*opposite*] a stunningly beautiful woman on the train today.

むかいかぜ 向かい風 a head [an adverse ／an unfavorable] wind ▶強い向かい風を受けて走る run against a strong *head wind* (➤ ヨットの場合なら動詞は sail か go) ‖ 向かい風が強かったので力いっぱいペダルをこがなければならなかった The *head wind* was so strong I had to pedal with all my might.

むかう 向かう **1【目指す】** head《for》▶探査機は一路火星に向かっている The probe *is heading* straight *for* Mars. ‖ 一行は丸山古墳へ遺跡調査に向かった The group *headed for*

the Maruyama Tumulus Mounds to investigate the ruins. ‖ あす成田をたってハワイに向かいます I'*m leaving* Narita *for* Hawaii tomorrow. (➤ leave A for B で「Bに向かってAをたつ」) ‖ 鳥は北に向かって飛んでいる The birds are flying (*toward* the) north.
▶彼は得意先に向かう途中で交通事故に巻き込まれた He got (involved) in a traffic accident *on the way to* his customer's office.
✉ **だんだん寒さに向かいますので, かぜなどひかぬようご注意ください** *The weather is getting cooler*, so please be careful not to catch a cold.
2【面する】face ＋目 ▶寮生たちは毎晩消灯時間まで机に向かっている Every night, the dorm students *sit at their desks* till lights-out. ‖ 駅を出ると向かって左側に(＝あなたの左側に)大きなデパートがあります You'll see a big department store *on your left* when you come out of the station. ‖ 舞台に向かって右側を「上手」という The right side of the stage *as you face it* is called the 'kamite.'
3【対立する, 攻撃する】▶彼に面と向かってそんなこと言えないよ I could never say that *to his face*. ‖ 親に向かってそんな口の利き方があるか Is that the way you talk *to* your parents? (➤ that に強勢を置く) ‖ 強い風に向かって歩くのはきつい It's tough to walk *against* a strong wind. (➤ against は「…に逆らって」).
▶少年は棒を持って向かって来た The boy *struck at* [*rushed at*] me with a stick. ／The boy *attacked* me with a stick. (➤ 後者は実際にぶたれたことを意味する).

むかえうつ 迎え撃つ ▶敵を迎え撃つ *mount an attack against* the enemy ‖《ボクシングで》挑戦者を迎え撃つ *take on* the challenger.

むかえび 迎え火 a ***mukaebi***; a small ritual fire to welcome back the spirits of one's ancestors [one's departed family members](➤説明的な訳).

むかえる 迎える **1【会う】meet** ＋目; **welcome** ＋目(歓迎する); **receive** ＋目(迎え入れる); **greet** ＋目(挨拶する); **pick up** (車で迎えに行く) ▶駅まで迎えに来てください Please (*come to*) *meet* me at the station. ／Please *come and pick* me *up* [*get* me] at the station. ‖ ホストファミリーが私を笑顔で迎えてくれた My host family *welcomed* me with a smile. ‖ スミス家の人たちは私を気さくに迎えてくれた I *received a* friendly *welcome from* the Smiths. (➤「歓迎を受けた」の意) ‖ 道子, 玄関へ行っておじいちゃんたちをお迎えしてちょうだい Michiko, will you go and *greet* your grandparents at the door? ‖ ホテルまで車で迎えに行くよ I'll *pick* you *up* at the hotel.
✉ **セントラルパーク駅には7時30分に到着の予定です. 迎えに来ていただけるとありがたいのですが** I'm due in Central Park Station at 7 : 30. I'd really appreciate it if you would *come to meet* me.
2【招く】invite ▶林氏はABC社に重役として迎えられた Mr.Hayashi *was invited to join* ABC Company as a member of the board of directors. ‖ 太郎は良子を妻に迎えた Taro *has taken* Yoshiko for his wife.
3【時になる】▶オーストラリアでは夏にクリスマスを迎えます Christmas *comes* in summer in Australia. ‖ 正月は立山山頂で迎える予定です I plan to *greet* the New Year on the summit of Mt. Tateyama. ‖ あとひと月で卒業の日を迎える We have one month to go before the day of our graduation. (➤ to go は数詞のあとに置いて「残された, 残りの」の意を表す) ‖ おじいちゃんはあした70歳の誕生日を迎える(＝祝う) My grandpa will *celebrate* his seventieth birthday tomorrow.
✉ **どうぞよいお年をお迎えください** I hope you'll *have* a happy New Year. ／I wish you a Happy New Year. 《参考》後者は「新年おめでとう」の意で元日にも言うが,「よいお年を!」の意で年内にも言う. なお happy の h は大文字でも小文字でもよい.

むがく 無学の uneducated /ʌnédʒəkeɪtɪd/ ▶無学の人 an *uneducated* person ／a person *without an education*.

むかし 昔 the old days; ancient times (古代); the past (過去) ━形 **昔の old**; **ancient** (大昔の); **former** (以前の)
▶昔々 *once upon a time* ／*long, long ago* (➤ ともに昔話の書き出し) ‖ 昔の人がいみじくも言ったように「去る者は日々に疎し」だ As *people in the old days* aptly put it, "Out of sight, out of mind." ‖ 年とともに昔が懐かしくなる As I grow older, I miss *the good old days*. (➤ the good old days は「古き良き時代, 懐かしい昔」).
▶昔, この辺は海の底だった *In ancient times*, this area was at the bottom of the sea. ‖ 昔, 仕事でロンドンを訪れたことがある *Years ago*, I visited London on business. ‖ 昔はほとんどの日本人が農業を営んでいた *In the past*, most Japanese people were engaged in farming. ／Most Japanese people *used to* be engaged in farming. (➤ used to do は「昔は…だった」の意で, しばしば現在はそうでないという含みをもつ) ‖ 昔, ここに大きな映画館があった There *used to* be a big movie theater here.
▶昔からの伝統 an *old* tradition ‖ 中村さんは昔から(＝昔も今も)頭が良かった Mr. Nakamura *was and is* still very smart. ‖ 池田君は昔からの友だちです Ikeda is an *old* friend of mine. ／Ikeda and I have been friends for a long time. ‖ 私は昔の私ではない I am not *what I was*. ‖ あの女優には昔の面影がない That actress *doesn't look the way* she *used to*.
▶《慣用表現》昔とった杵柄(きねづか)でおじいちゃんは多少の中国語なら話せる My grandpa can speak a little Chinese *based on his experience using it when he was younger*.
✉ **私たちの町ではお盆に灯籠流しをするのが昔からの習わしです** In our town, it is a *traditional* [*an old*] custom to float paper lanterns out to sea during the *Bon* festival. (➤ 川に流す場合は out to sea の代わりに down the river とする).
☛ **大昔** (→見出語)

むかしかたぎ 昔気質 ▶昔かたぎの大工は今や少ない Nowadays, very few carpenters *stick to the old* [*traditional*] *ways*.

むかしながら 昔ながら ▶飛騨の白川郷には昔ながらの家々が保存されている *Old-style* houses have been preserved in Shirakawa Village in the Hida district (of Honshu). ‖ 妻籠には昔ながらの町並みが続いている The streets and houses in Tsumago have remained *unchanged since olden times*. ‖ そのみそは昔ながらの方法で作られている That (brand of) miso is produced using a *traditional* method.

むかしなじみ 昔馴染み an **old friend** ▶同窓会で多く

む

の昔なじみに会った I met a lot of *old friends* at the class reunion.

むかしばなし 昔話 an **old story** [**tale**] (古い話) ; a **story of** one's **youth** (昔の思い出) →民話 ▶同窓会では昔話に花が咲いた We *talked about the good old days* at the class reunion. (➤「懐かしい昔の話をした」の意).

むかつく **feel sick** (**to** one's **stomach**) (気分が悪くなる) ▶船に乗ったとたんに胸がむかついてきた Right after I boarded the ship, I started to *feel sick to my stomach* [*felt like throwing up*]. (➤ throw up は「吐く」).
▶《比喩的》あいつの顔を見るだけでむかつく The mere sight of him *makes* me *sick*. ‖ 車内で足を投げ出して漫画本を読んでいるやつを見ると全くむかつく It *makes* me *angry* when I see guys reading comic books on the train with their legs sprawled out. ‖ あいつはむかつくやつだなぁ He *gets on my nerves*. ／He's *disgusting*.

むかって 向かって →向かう.

むかっぱら むかっ腹 ▶むかっ腹を立てる *get angry* ／*lose one's temper*.

むかで 百足 《虫》 a **centipede** /séntəpi:d/ ▶ムカデが床をはっている *A centipede* is crawling on the floor.

むかむか ▶胸がむかむかする (＝気持ちが悪い) I *feel sick* (*to my stomach*). ／I *feel nauseous*. (➤ nauseous の発音は /nɔ́:ʃəs/) ‖ 兄貴のことばにむかむかっときて, 机を蹴飛ばした What my brother said *made me* so *mad* that I kicked (at) the desk.

むがむちゅう 無我夢中 ▶あのときは彼女に会いたい一心で無我夢中だった At that time I *was overtaken by* a longing [*I could think of nothing but my desire*] to see her. (➤ be overtaken by は「ある感情や事態に突然襲われる」) ‖ イノシシに追いかけられて無我夢中で逃げたよ A wild boar came after me and I *ran for my life*. (➤ for one's life は「命からがら」).

むかん 無冠の **uncrowned** ▶無冠の王 [女王] an *uncrowned* king [queen].

むかんかく 無感覚な **insensitive** ; **numb** /nʌm/ (寒さなどでまひした) ▶寒さで手の指が無感覚になった My fingers *became numb* from the cold. ／The cold *numbed* my fingers. ‖ 官僚たちは汚職に対して無感覚 (＝慣れっこ) になっているようだ Government officials seem *insensitive* to (the evil of) corruption.

むかんけい 無関係な **irrelevant** /ɪréləvənt/ ▶彼の質問はこのテーマとは無関係だ His question *is irrelevant to* this topic. (➤やや堅い言い方) ／His question *has nothing to do with* this topic. ‖ 私も夏目ですが, 漱石とは全く無関係です I'm also a Natsume, but *not related to* Soseki in any way. ‖ 私はこの事件には無関係だ I *am not involved in* this case.

むかんしん 無関心 **indifference** 一形 (…に) 無関心な **indifferent** 《to》 (➤「冷淡」の含みが強い) ; **uninterested** 《in》 (興味がない) ; **nonchalant** /nɑ̀:nʃəlɑ́:nt ‖ nɔ́nʃələnt/ (平気な ; 堅い語) ▶彼は女の子に無関心だ He *is indifferent to* girls. (➤ やや堅い言い方) ／He *doesn't care about* girls.
▶母は野球には全く無関心だ My mother *is* quite *uninterested in* baseball. ‖ 父はPTAの活動には無関心だ My father *is not concerned with* PTA activities. ／My father *doesn't take* [*show*] *any interest in* PTA activities. (➤ 後者は「関心をもつべきなのに無関心だ」のニュアンス) ‖ 無関心を装う assume *a nonchalant air*.

むかんどう 無感動 **apathy** ▶無感動な若者たち *apathetic* youth.

[1]**むき 向き** **1【方向】** a **direction** ▶バックミラーの向きを変える change [adjust] the *direction* of a rearview mirror ‖ 風の向きが変わった The *direction* of the wind has changed. ／The wind has shifted. ‖ 机の向きを窓の方へ変えなさい *Turn* the desk *toward* the window.
▶この窓はどちら向きですか *Which direction* does this window *face*? ‖ この部屋は東向きです This room *faces east*.
2【合っていること, 適性】 ▶子供向きのアニメ映画 a [an animated] cartoon *for* children ‖ この車のデザインは若者向きだ This car is designed *for* young people. ‖ 人には向き不向きがある Each person *is suited for* [*good at*] *some things and not others*. ／Everyone has their own forte.

[2]**むき** ▶彼はすぐにむきになる He *gets upset* easily. ‖ そんなにむきになるなよ (＝気を落ち着けて) Take it easy. ／Don't *get* so *worked up*. ‖ 子供相手の腕相撲でそんなにむき (＝本気) になるなよ Don't *get* so *serious* when you're arm-wrestling with a little child. ‖ 彼は怜子との交際をむきになって (＝強く) 否定した He *strongly* [*emphatically*] denied that he had been seeing Reiko.

[3]**むき 無期の** **indefinite** /ɪndéfənət/ (無期限の) ▶会合は無期延期となった The meeting *was postponed indefinitely*. ‖ その男は無期懲役 (＝終身刑) に処せられた The man *was sentenced to life imprisonment*.

[4]**むき 無機** ▶コンクリートむき出しの無機的な建物 an *inorganic* building of bare concrete.
‖ **無機化学** inorganic chemistry ‖ **無機化合物** an inorganic compound ‖ **無機質** mineral matter ‖ **無機肥料** inorganic fertilizer ‖ **無機物** (→見出語).

むぎ 麦 **barley** (大麦) ; **wheat**, 《英また》 **corn** (小麦)
‖ **麦茶** barley tea ‖ **麦畑** a wheat [barley] field, 《英また》 a cornfield ‖ **麦飯** rice cooked with barley.

むきあう 向き合う **face each other**. →向かい合う.

むきげん 無期限の **indefinite** ▶無期限ストに突入する go on strike *for an indefinite period* ／go on an *indefinite* [*a no-time-limit*] strike.

むきず 無傷の **unhurt** ; **uninjured** (けがのない) ▶交通事故に遭いましたが幸い無傷でした I got (involved) in a traffic accident, but luckily was *unhurt*. ‖ 盗まれた絵は無傷で持ち主に返された The stolen painting was returned to the owner *in perfect condition*.
▶《比喩的》そのボクサーはいまだ無傷で連勝記録を伸ばしている That boxer is still enjoying his *perfect* winning streak. (➤ streak は「連続」).

むきだし 剝き出し ▶むき出しの背中 one's *bare* back ‖ 敵意をむき出しにする *show* one's hostile feelings *openly*.
▶お金を贈るのにむき出しのまま渡すのは失礼だ It is rude to give other people a gift of money *without putting it in an envelope*.

むきどう 無軌道な **wild** (手に負えない) ; **unruly** (抑えの利かない) ▶無軌道な息子 my *wild* [*unruly*] son ‖ いいかげんに無軌道な生活はやめなさい It is high time you quit leading such an *undisciplined* [such a *dissipated*] life. (➤ dissipated /dísɪpèɪṭɪd/ は「放とうの」).

むきなおる 向き直る turn around ▶彼女は向き直るともう一度私に手を振って別れの挨拶をした She *turned around* and waved good-bye to me once again.

むきぶつ 無機物 inorganic matter, inorganic substance.

むきめい 無記名の unsigned ▶無記名投票によって代表が選出された The representative was elected by *secret ballot* [*vote*]. ‖ 無記名の提案は採用しません *Unsigned* suggestions will be disregarded.

1**むきゅう 無休** ▶昔は労働者は無休で働いた In the old days, workers *had no days off* [worked *without days off*].
▶《掲示》年中無休 *Open year-round* / *Always Open* / *Open 24/7*(➤24/7は twenty-four seven と読む).

2**むきゅう 無給の** unpaid ▶無給で働く work *without pay* ‖ イギリスでは一部の治安判事は無給である In Britain, some magistrates are *unpaid*.

むきょういく 無教育な uneducated; uncultured (教養のない).

むきょうよう 無教養な uncultured.

むきりょく 無気力 ▶無気力な若者たち *lethargic* [*apathetic*] young people ‖ 奥さんを亡くしたあと彼は長いこと無気力に見えた He seemed to *have no energy* for some time after his wife's death.

むぎわら 麦藁 straw
‖麦わら帽子 a straw hat.

むきん 無菌の germ-free, sterile (殺菌した); aseptic /eɪséptɪk/ (傷・器材などが消毒済みの) ▶手術は無菌状態で行わなければならない Surgery must be performed *under sterile conditions* [*in a sterile environment*].
‖無菌室 a germ-free [sterilized] room.

1むく 向く

📖 訳語メニュー
…の方を向く →look **1**
面する →face **1**
合う →be suitable **2**
気が向く →feel like **3**

1【顔などを向ける】 look(見る); turn(向きを変える); face(面する) ▶上[下]を向く *look* up [down] ‖ こっちを向きなさい *Look* this way. / *Look at* me. ‖ 後ろを向くな Don't *look behind* you. / Don't *look back*. (➤「過去を振り返るな」という意味にもなる) / Don't *turn around*. (➤ turn around は「ぐるりと向きを変える」) ‖ 横を向きなさい *Turn* sideways.
▶父の書斎は庭に向いている My father's study *faces* [*looks out on*] the garden.
▶運が向いてきた Luck *has turned in my favor*. / (Lady) Luck is smiling on me.
▶《慣用表現》足の向くまま旅に出たい I would like to travel around *wherever my legs lead* [*take*] me.

2【合っている】 be suitable [suited] 《for, to》

【文型】
人(A)が仕事(B)に向いている
A is suited to [for] B.
➤ to do や to doing の形もある
物(C)が人(D)に向いている
C is suitable for D.

【解説】 be suited は人が「資質を備えていて適任だ」の意. be suitable は「ふさわしい, 適している」の意. ほかに, be cut out for も「生まれつき・性格的にぴったり合っている」の意だが, しばしば否定形で使う.

▶どの候補者がいちばん首相に向いているだろうか I wonder which candidate *is* most *suited to* be [most *suited for*] prime minister. ‖ このアパートは子供のいる家族[独身者]に向いている These apartments *are suitable for* [*are suited to*] families with children [singles]. ‖ 当地の冷涼な気候はリンゴの栽培に向いている The cool climate here *is suitable for* [*is suited to*] growing apples. ‖ 私はこの仕事には向いていないと思う I don't think *I'm suited to* [*for*] this job. (➤ to がふつう) / This job *is* not *suitable for* me. (➤ I'm not suitable for this job. は相性でなく,「自分は (能力的に) ふさわしくない」) / I don't think I *am cut out for* [*am cut out to* do] this job. / I don't think I am *the right person for* this job. ‖ 彼はその仕事に向かない He *is ill suited to* [*for*] the job.
▶学生さんに向いたアルバイトがあるよ I have a part-time job that is (*suitable*) *for* students. ‖ 介護の仕事は私に向いている Working as a caregiver *suits* me.

3【気持ちになる】 ▶日曜日に仕事というのはどうも気が向かない I (just) *don't feel like* working on Sundays. ‖ 気が向くと彼女はお茶を入れてくれる She serves us tea when she *is in the mood*.

2**むく 剝く** peel +㊐ (皮を手や刃物で); pare +㊐ (皮を刃物で); shell +㊐ (エビ・貝などを) ▶バナナ[リンゴ]の皮をむく *peel* a banana [an apple] ‖ ジャガイモの皮をむく *pare* a potato ‖ 木の皮をむく *bark* a tree ‖ エビの殻をむく *shell* prawns [shrimp].

3**むく 無垢な** innocent; pure (純真な) ▶子供たちの無垢な心 the *pure* hearts of children.

むくい 報い a reward(報酬); punishment(罰) ▶親は子供を育てたからといって報いを求めたりはしないものだ Parents do not expect *a reward* for raising their children. ‖ さんざんだらしのない生活をした報いが今きたというわけか This may be the *punishment* for the loose life I have led so far.

むくいぬ 尨犬 a shaggy dog.

むくいる 報いる reward +㊐ (善行・功労などに対して); repay +㊐ (恩・親切などに対して) ▶社長は多額のボーナスを出してその社員の多年の労に報いた The company president *gave* the employee a big bonus *to reward* him [*as a reward*] for his long years of service. ‖ 彼の親切にはどう報いてよいかわかりません I don't know how to *repay* him *for* his kindness.

むくげ 木槿 《植物》a rose of Sharon, an althea.

むくち 無口な silent; quiet (もの静かな) ▶彼は無口な人だ He is *a man of few words*. / He's the *silent* [*quiet*] *type*. / He doesn't talk much. ‖ 西郷隆盛は無口で有名だった Saigo Takamori was known for his *taciturnity* [*reticence*]. (➤ reticence /rétəsəns/ は「押し黙っていること」の意の堅い語).

むくどり 椋鳥 《鳥》a starling.

むくのき 椋の木 《植物》a Muku tree.

むくみ swelling, edema /ɪdíːmə/ (➤後者は医学用語).

むくむ swell, become swollen ▶どうしました？ 顔がむくんでますよ What's the matter? Your face looks *swollen* [You have a *bloated* face]. ‖ 薬の副作用で足がむくんだ My legs *have become swollen* as a side effect of the medicine I'm taking.

むくむく ▶りょう線に入道雲がむくむくと湧いてきた A huge mass of thunderheads was rising over the ridge.

▶好機到来でマクベスの野望がむくむくと頭をもたげ始めた When his golden chance came, Macbeth began to *swell* with ambition [Macbeth's ambition began to *swell* within him].

むくれる ▶彼は思いどおりにならないとすぐむくれる He *gets miffed* easily when he can't have his way. ‖うっかり結婚記念日を忘れたら女房のやつ, すっかりむくれてしまった I completely forgot our wedding anniversary, and now my wife is *in a bad mood* [*temper*].

むくわれる 報われる **be rewarded** ▶きみの努力は必ず報われるよ Your effort will definitely *be rewarded*. ／Your effort will surely *bear fruit* [*pay off*]. (➤ bear fruit は「実を結ぶ」; pay off は「うまくいく」の意のインフォーマルな言い方) ‖PTAの役員は報われることの少ない仕事だ Serving on the board of the PTA is very often a *thankless* [*an unrewarded*] task.

‐むけ ‐向け ▶これは南米向けの陶器です This chinaware is made *for* South America. ‖いいかい坊や, これは大人向けの番組なんだから見ちゃだめだよ Listen, son! This program is *for* grown-ups, so you can't watch it. ‖主婦向けの番組 a program *aimed at* [*geared to* ／*targeted at*] housewives.

むけい 無形 ▶きみに対して有形無形の援助を惜しみません I'm ready and willing to provide *tangible and emotional* support.

‖無形文化財 an intangible cultural asset /æset/; a living national treasure (人間国宝).

むけいかく 無計画な **unplanned** ▶無計画な土地開発 *unplanned* land development ‖私は無計画でよく旅に出る I often take trips [go on a trip] *with no plan at all* [*without making any plans in advance*].

むけつ 無血の **bloodless**

‖無血革命 a bloodless revolution.

むけっきん 無欠勤 ▶父はこの20年間無欠勤だ My father *has never missed a day of work* for the past twenty years.

むけっせき 無欠席 **perfect attendance.**

むげに 無下に **flatly** ▶親友の頼みなのでむげに断るわけにもいかない Because it's my best friend's request, I can't refuse it *out of hand* [*bluntly*]. (➤ この out of hand は「(検討もせずに) 即座に」, bluntly は「そっけなく, 単刀直入に」; 日常的には I can't just refuse it. で表すことが多い).

▶私たちの提案をそうむげに却下しないでください Don't reject our proposals so *flatly* [*flat out*]. (➤ 後者のほうがくだけた言い方).

[1]**むける 向ける** **turn** +㊀ (向きを変える); **direct** +㊀, **point** +㊀, **aim** +㊀ (狙う) ▶すねてないで, こっちに顔を向けてよ Stop sulking and *turn* your face toward me [*let* me *see* your face]. ‖インタビュアーは受賞者にマイクを向けた The interviewer *directed* [*pointed*] his mike at the winner. ‖候補者は有権者に向けてテレビで政見放送を行った The candidates made televised campaign speeches *aimed* [*targeted*] *at* the voters. ‖一行はアメリカに向けて出発した The party left *for* the United States.

▶次のオリンピックに向けて準備はすでに着々と進んでいる Preparations are already well under way *for* the next Olympic Games.

[2]**むける 剝ける** **peel** 《off》 ▶日焼けして顔の皮がむけた I got sunburnt, and my face *is peeling*.

むげん 無限の **infinite** /ínfɪnət/; **unlimited** (際限のない) ▶宇宙は無限の空間に向かって広がっていると言われる The universe is said to be expanding into *infinite* [*boundless*] space. ‖きみたちには無限の可能性がある You have *unlimited* potential.

‖無限大 infinity /ɪnfínəṭi/.

むこ 婿 a **son-in-law** (娘の夫); a **bridegroom** (花婿) ▶こちらが私の娘婿です This is my *son-in-law*. ‖西田氏は娘さんの婿探しをしている Mr. Nishida is searching for a future *husband* for his daughter. ‖彼は岸家の婿養子になった He *married into* the Kishi *family*. ／He *married* the Kishis' daughter and *was adopted* by her family.

むごい 酷い **horrible** (恐ろしい); **tragic** (悲惨な); **brutal** (残忍な); **cruel** (残酷な) ▶むごい犯罪 a *horrible* [*brutal*] crime.

▶むごい仕打ち *brutal* [*cruel*] treatment ‖あんな小さな子を殺すなんて何てむごいことを! What a *brutal* [*heinous* ／*cruel*] thing to have killed such a little child!

[1]むこう 向こう

📖 **訳語メニュー**
- 反対側 →the other side **1**
- あちら →there **1**
- 相手側 →they **2**

1【反対側, 遠方】 **the other side** (向こう側) 一副 **向こうに** **over there** ▶湖の向こう側にはホテルがある There are hotels *on the other side* of the lake. ‖通りの向こう側に警官が立っている A police officer is standing *on the other side of* [is standing *across*] the street. ‖向こう三軒両隣 *three houses opposite yours and two next-door neighbors* (*on both sides*).

▶あの山並みの向こうは長野県になる *Beyond* [*The other side of*] those mountains lies Nagano Prefecture. ‖向こうに見えるのが劔岳だ What you see *over there in the distance* is Mt. Tsurugi. ‖向こうに白いきれいなホテルが見える You can see a beautiful, white hotel *over there*.

▶ずっと向こうに灯台が見えた A lighthouse came into view *far ahead* [*way ahead*]. ‖着替えるから向こうを向いてて I'm changing, so face *the other way*, please.

▶向こう(＝あちら)へ着いたらすぐに電話をよこしなさい Call us as soon as you get *there*. ‖向こうはもう雪が降り始める頃だ It's about time it starts snowing *there* now.

2【相手側】 **they** ▶先に手を出したのは向こうのほうです *They* are the ones who started the fight. ‖まあ, 向こうの言い分も聞こうじゃないか Let's give *them* a chance to talk [to have *their* say]. ／Well, but let's hear *the other side's* view.

3【今後】 ▶きょうから向こう1か月間, 図書館は閉館になる The library is closed for a month from [starting] today.

▶きょう, 向こう3か月間の天気予報が発表された The weather forecast for the *next* three months was announced today.

4【対抗】 ▶マクドナルドの向こうを張って(＝に負けじと)ロ

ッテリアでも新メニューを出した *Not to be outdone by* McDonald's, Lotteria has come up with new menu items.

²**むこう 無効の** invalid /ɪnvǽlɪd/ ▶販売店の押印のない保証書は**無効**です Warranties without the stamp of the store where you made your purchase are *invalid*. ‖ この入場券は4月1日以降は**無効**です This admission ticket is good only through the end of March.
▶切り離し**無効** *Void* if detached. (➤ void は法律用語) ‖ 二社間の契約は**無効となった** The contract between the two companies *was nullified* [*was annulled*]. (➤ nullify, annul はともに「無効にする」の意の法律用語).
‖**無効票** an invalid vote.

むこういき 向こう意気 ▶徹は**向こう意気の強い**子だ Toru doesn't give in easily. (➤ give in は「降参する」) ／Toru is a *scrappy* boy. (➤ scrappy は「引き下がらずに人と張り合う」の意) ‖ この仕事には**向こう意気の強い**男が必要だ This job requires *aggressive* men.

むこうぎし 向こう岸 the opposite bank, the other side of the river ▶川の**向こう岸に**釣り人が大勢いる There are many anglers *on the opposite bank* of the river. ‖ **向こう岸まで**泳いで渡ろうか Shall we swim *across the river*? ／Shall we swim *to the other side of the river*?

むこうずね 向こう脛 a shin ▶机に**向こうずね**をぶつけて思わずギャッと叫んだ I yelled with pain when I banged my *shin* against the desk.

むこうみず 向こう見ずな reckless ▶**向こう見ずな**勇気 *reckless* courage ‖ あいつは**向こう見ずだ** He's *a daredevil*. (➤「人をあっと言わせようとあえて危険な行為を行う人」の意).

むこくせき 無国籍 ▶不法滞在の外国人から生まれる子供は**無国籍**になることがある Children who are born of [to] illegal immigrants are sometimes *stateless*.
‖**無国籍料理** fusion food.

むごたらしい 酷たらしい cruel (残酷な); brutal (残虐な); merciless (無慈悲な) ▶捕虜に対する**むごたらしい**扱い *brutal* treatment of prisoners.

むごん 無言の silent ▶彼らは死者の冥福を祈って**無言**の祈りをささげた They offered a *silent* prayer for the peaceful repose of the dead. ‖ 母は**無言で**私に金をくれた My mother gave me some money *without saying anything* [*without a word*]. ‖ 彼らの間にはその件には触れないという**無言の**(＝暗黙の)約束があった There was *a tacit agreement* between them that they would not mention the matter.
‖ 最近わが家に頻繁に**無言電話**が掛かってくる We've been getting frequent *silent* [*prank*] *phone calls* recently. (➤ prank call は「いたずら電話」).

むざい 無罪 innocence (潔白) 一形 **無罪の** innocent (潔白な), not guilty (有罪でない; 主に, 英米の裁判中に使われる言い方) ▶弁護士は被告の**無罪**を主張した The attorney insisted that the accused was *not guilty*. ／The attorney insisted on the accused's *innocence*. ‖ 裁判官は被告人を**無罪とした** The judge *ruled* the accused *not guilty*. 《参考》陪審制度のあるアメリカではまず陪審が評決を出すが, そのときの表現は We, the jury, find the accused not guilty. または The accused is found not guilty. という. ‖ 彼はすべての容疑で**無罪となった** He *was acquitted of* all charges.

> **解説** innocent が「罪を犯していない」こと, すなわち「潔白である」ことを指すのに対して, not guilty は「有罪でない」の意. 英米の裁判においては, 提出された証拠によって, "guilty (有罪)" か "not guilty (有罪でない)" かを判断するので, 評決・判決では innocent (潔白)という語ではなく, "guilty" または "not guilty" が用いられる. 疑わしいが罪を十分に立証できない場合(俗にいう「グレーな」場合)は日本では「無罪」だが, 英米ではことばどおり, not guilty (有罪でない)である.

むさく 無策 ▶学校当局はいじめ問題に対して**無為無策**だった The school authorities *had no policy and took no measures* against bullying.

むさくい 無作為の random ▶世論調査の回答者は**無作為に**選ばれなければならない Respondents to a public opinion poll must be chosen *randomly*. ‖ 被験者は応募者の中から**無作為に**選ばれた Examinees were chosen *randomly* from among the applicants.

むさくるしい むさ苦しい messy (乱雑な); untidy (だらしない); dingy /díndʒi/ (薄汚れた); cramped (狭苦しい) ▶そんな**むさ苦しい**頭で人の家へ行ってはいけないよ You shouldn't visit people with your hair in such *a mess* [with such *disheveled* hair]. (➤ disheveled は髪が「ぼさぼさの」).
✉ **むさ苦しい家ですがいつでもおいでください** I'm almost ashamed to invite you over to such a *messy* house, but do feel welcome to come anytime. ➤ こういう卑下する表現を英米人はふつう用いないので, 真意が伝わらないおそれがある.

むささび 鼯鼠 《動物》a flying squirrel.

むさべつ 無差別な indiscriminate /ìndɪskrímɪnət/ ▶その町に対する**無差別攻撃**で多数の小さな子供たちが殺された In the *indiscriminate* [*all-out*] *attack* on the city, numerous small children were killed.
‖ (柔道の)**無差別級** the open-weight division.

むさぼる 貪る devour /dɪváʊəʳ/ ＋自 (➤ 読むことにも食べることにも用いる) ▶待ちに待った手紙が来て, みゆきはそれを郵便受けのそばで開けて**貪るように読んだ** When the long-awaited letter arrived, Miyuki tore it open and *devoured* it right at the mailbox. ‖ 練習のあと彼らはスナック菓子を**貪り食った** They *devoured* [*wolfed down*] snack foods after their practice. ‖ 彼はその漫画を**貪るように**読んだ[貪り読んだ] He *voraciously* read the comic book. ‖ **暴利を貪る**企業はメディアにたたかれる Enterprises that *make excessive profits* [*Profiteering* enterprises] are hounded by the media.

むざむざ ▶あんな数段格下のチームに**むざむざ**負けて悔しくないのか Don't you feel like kicking yourselves after being beaten *so easily* by a team several notches below yours? ‖ 長年集めた切手のコレクションを**むざむざ**手放してなるものか I (*just*) *can't bring myself to* part with my stamp collection that I have built up [put together] over so many years. (➤「とてもその気にならない」の意).

むざん 無残な horrible (恐ろしい); tragic (悲劇的な); cruel (残酷な); distressing (悲惨な; 堅い語) ▶**無残**な光景 a *horrible* [*cruel*] sight ‖ **無残な事件** a *tragic* incident ‖ **無残な結果** *distressing* results ‖ 津波に襲われて残った家々は見るも**無残な**姿をさらしていた After the tsunami hit, the remaining houses presented a *miserable* [*pitiful*] sight. ‖ 開発の結

む

果，美しい森が無残にも荒れ地と化した It's *distressing* how development has turned the beautiful forest into a wasteland.

[1]**むし 虫** **1【動物の】** an **insect**, a **bug**（昆虫）; a **worm** /wəːrm/（ミミズ・毛虫・寄生虫などのはう虫）; a **moth**（衣類につく虫）

▶庭で虫が鳴いている Some *insects* are chirping in the garden. ‖ おでこを虫に刺された I was bitten on the forehead by *a bug* [*an insect*]. ‖ このオレンジ，虫がついている This orange has *a worm* in it. ‖ 大事なコートが虫に食われてしまった My treasured coat is *moth-eaten*.

ことわざ 一寸の虫にも五分の魂 Even a worm will turn.（➤「虫けらでも（攻撃されれば）反撃に転じる」の意）.

‖ 虫かご an insect cage ‖ 虫よけ（→見出語）.

2【熱中する人】▶内田君は本の虫だ Uchida is *a bookworm*. ‖ 大久保さんは仕事の虫だ Mr. Okubo *lives for work*.

3【慣用表現】

虫がいい ▶練習はサボって試合には出たいなんて，虫がよ過ぎるよ To say you want to skip practice but still play in the game *is asking too much*. **虫が知らせる** ▶虫が知らせたので（＝事故の起きそうな予感がしたので）あの飛行機の予約は取り消したんだ I *had a premonition* [*presentiment*] about the accident, so I canceled my reservation for the flight.（➤ presentiment のほうが堅い語）‖ 対話「ちょうど今そっちに行こうと思ってたとこなの．どうしてわかった？」「虫の知らせでね」"How did you know I was thinking about going to your place ?" "*I* (*just*) *had a hunch*."（➤ hunch は「予感」の意のインフォーマルな語） **虫が好かない** ▶虫の好かないやつ a *disagreeable* [*disgusting*] guy **虫がつく** ▶娘に悪い虫がつきはしないかと心配です I'm worried that my daughter may *get a bad boyfriend*.

虫の息 ▶拾って来たときは虫の息だった子猫もだいぶ元気になった The kitten was *half alive* when we found it, but it has gotten much better now. ／ Although the kitten *was at death's door* when found, it has recovered considerably. **虫の居所** ▶マネージャーはきょうは虫の居所が悪い The manager *must have gotten out of the wrong side of* (*the*) *bed* today.（➤「（就寝時にベッドに入ったのと）逆の側から起きる」が原義の不吉な迷信に由来する言い方で，「朝から機嫌が悪い」の意）. **虫も殺さない** ▶彼女は虫も殺さないような顔をしているけど，本当はすごい意地悪なんだ She *looks as though she wouldn't hurt* [*harm*] *a fly*, but actually she is quite mean.（➤ 日本語に似た表現）.

[2]**むし 無視する** **ignore** +㊐（わざと）; **disregard** +㊐（軽く見る）; **neglect** +㊐（おろそかにする）; **defy** +㊐（ものともしない）▶警告を無視する *ignore* a warning ‖ 法律を無視する *defy* the law ‖ あのトラックは赤信号を無視した That truck *ignored* the red light. ／That truck *ran the light*. ‖ ハイカーたちはガイドの忠告を無視して山に入った The hikers went into the mountains, *ignoring* [*disregarding*] the guide's advice. ‖ 私の分のおやつがなくて無視されたような気がした They had left no snacks for me, so I felt *neglected*. ‖ 誤差は無視できる程度だ The margin of error *is negligible*. ‖ そんないいかげんなうわさは無視しなさい（＝注意を払うな）*Don't pay any attention to* such a silly rumor.

[3]**むし 無私の** **selfless**（利己的でない）; **impartial**（えこひいきしない）▶わが子に対する彼女の無私の愛情 her *selfless* love for her children ‖ 先生というものは生徒に対して公平無私でなければならない A teacher should be *fair and impartial* to all the students. ‖ 私たちは裁判官が公平無私の判断を下すものと期待している We expect a fair and *disinterested* ruling from the judge.

[4]**むし 無死**《野球》▶無死満塁 The bases are loaded [full] *with no outs*.

むじ 無地の **plain** ▶無地の布 (a) *plain* cloth ‖ 黒い無地のネクタイ a tie of *solid* [*plain*] black（➤ solid は「一色の」）.

むしあつい 蒸し暑い **hot and humid, muggy, sultry** 《参考》sultry には「セクシーな」の意味もあるので，《米》では muggy のほうが好まれる. ▶蒸し暑い日 a *muggy* day ‖ ただ暑いのは我慢できるが蒸し暑いのはたまらない I can bear it when it's just hot, but I can't stand *humid heat* [*muggy weather*].

むしかえす 蒸し返す **repeat** +㊐（繰り返す）▶その議論を蒸し返してみても何にもならない It is no use *repeating* [*rehashing*] the argument *again*. ‖ 同じ問題を何度も蒸し返すのはやめようよ Let's not *bring up* that old issue (*yet*) *again*.（➤ yet again は「またしても」）／Let's not *go there* again.（➤ go there は「その話を持ち出す」で否定形で用いる）.

むしかく 無資格の **unqualified**（資格のない）; **unlicensed**（免許を持たない）▶無資格の医師 an *unlicensed* 'doctor'（➤ 引用符は「自称」の含みを表す）‖ その男は無資格診療を行い逮捕された He was arrested for practicing medicine *without a license*.

むしき 蒸し器 a **steamer**.

むしくい 虫食い ▶虫食いの着物 a *moth-eaten* kimono（➤ この場合の moth は衣類を食い荒らす「イガ (clothes moth)」の幼虫のこと．一般的な意味での「虫に食われた着物」なら a worm-eaten kimono でもよい）‖ 虫食いの穴のある机 a desk with *a wormhole* ‖ このリンゴは虫食いだ This apple *is worm-eaten*.（➤「虫食いリンゴ」は a worm-eaten apple, a wormy apple などとなる）.

むしけん 無試験 ▶彼は無試験で大学に入学を許可された He was admitted into college *without* (*having to take*) *an examination*. ‖ 彼女は無試験でその会社に採用された The company hired her *without giving her an employment test*.

むじこ 無事故 ▶この飛行機は5年間無事故です This aircraft has been *free from accidents* [*accident-free*] for five years.（➤ free from は「（通例好ましくないものが）ない」の意）.

▶私は10年間無事故無違反だ I've driven *without an accident* or offense for ten years. ／My driving record has been clean for ten years. ‖《標語》無事故週間 Safety Week.

むしさされ 虫刺され an **insect bite** 《参考》ハチの場合は a sting ▶この薬は虫刺されに効く This medicine [ointment] works on *insect bites*. ‖ 虫刺されの痕が腫れ上がっている This *insect bite* [*bugbite*] is swollen.

むしず 虫酸 ▶あの大臣の顔を見ると虫ずが走る The sight of that minister's face *disgusts* me. ／The mere sight of that minister's face *makes* me *sick*.
▶あの男の気取ったおしゃべりを聞くと虫ずが走る His affected speech *is just disgusting*.

むじつ 無実 **innocence** 一形 **無実の** **innocent** ▶無実を証明するのは必ずしも容易ではない Proving your *innocence* is not always easy. ‖彼が無実だったとは意外だ It is a surprise that he *was found not guilty*. (➤日本の裁判では「無罪」「無実」であるが, 英語は not guilty ; →無罪) ‖彼は自分が無実であると主張した He insisted on his *innocence*. ／He pleaded *not guilty*. ‖彼は無実の罪を晴らした He has cleared himself of *a false accusation*.

むしば 虫歯 **tooth decay** ; a **decayed** [**bad**] **tooth** (虫歯の1本) ; a **cavity** (虫歯でできた空洞 ; 日常的にはこの語を「虫歯」の意味で使う) ▶下の奥歯が虫歯になった I've got *a cavity* in a lower back tooth. ‖私は虫歯が3本ある I have *three bad teeth*. ／I have *three teeth with cavities*. ‖虫歯を予防するには甘い物を食べないことです To *prevent your teeth from decaying* [To *prevent cavities*], don't eat sweets.

むしばむ 蝕む **eat away** 《at》 ▶彼の肉体は原因不明の病気にむしばまれていった His flesh *was being* gradually *eaten away* by a mysterious disease. ‖最も心をむしばむものは怠惰である What *eats away at* our heart most is laziness.

むじひ 無慈悲な **merciless** ▶そんな無慈悲なことばをきみの口から聞こうとは思わなかったよ I hardly dreamed that I would ever hear such *merciless* [*cruel*] words from you.

むしぶろ 蒸し風呂 a **steam bath** ▶会場は蒸し風呂のような暑さだった The assembly hall was as hot and sticky as *a steam bath*.

むしぼし 虫干し (an) **airing** 一動 **虫干しする** **air** +目 ▶衣類を虫干しする *air* clothes ／*give* clothes *an airing* ‖その洋服はたんすにしまう前に虫干ししなさい *Air* that suit (*out*) before you put it into the wardrobe.

むしむし ▶きょうはやけにむしむしするね It *is* unbearably *muggy* today, isn't it? ／It'*s* very *hot and humid* today, isn't it?

むしめがね 虫眼鏡 a **magnifying glass** ▶虫眼鏡で新聞を読む read a paper using [with] *a magnifying glass*.

むしゃ 武者 a **warrior** ; a **samurai** ▶挑戦者はリングに上がる前にひとつ大きく武者震いした The challenger *shook with visible excitement* before climbing into the ring.
‖**武者修業** travel around the country to acquire greater swordsmanship skills (「料理の武者修業」なら swordsmanship を cooking に換えればよい).

むしやき 蒸し焼き ▶サツマイモをアルミホイルに包んで蒸し焼きにする *bake* a sweet potato *wrapped in aluminum foil*.

むじゃき 無邪気 **innocence** 一形 **無邪気な** **innocent** ▶無邪気な子供たち *innocent* children ‖私のおばあちゃんはとっても無邪気なんだよ My grandmother is quite *childlike*. (➤ childish とすると「子供じみた」という好ましくない意味になる).

むしゃくしゃ ▶おふくろとけんかしたからきょうは朝から気分がむしゃくしゃしてるんだ I *have been in a foul mood* since this morning because I had an argument with my mother.

むしゃぶりつく ▶腹の減ったライオンはその肉にむしゃぶりついた The hungry lion *devoured* the meat.

むしゃむしゃ ▶彼女はテレビを見ながらドーナツをむしゃむしゃ食べ続けた She went on *munching* doughnuts while watching TV.

むしゅう 無臭の **odorless, unscented** ▶無色無臭の気体 a colorless, *odorless* gas ‖無臭のヘアスプレー *unscented* [*odorless*] hair spray.

むしゅうきょう 無宗教 ▶日本人はよく「私は無宗教です」と言う Japanese often say, "I do*n't believe in any* (*particular*) religion." →宗教.

むじゅうりょく 無重力 **zero gravity, weightlessness** ▶宇宙飛行士たちは無重力状態に慣れる訓練をした The astronauts practiced acclimatizing themselves to *zero gravity*.
‖**無重力飛行** a weightless flight.

むしゅみ 無趣味 ▶彼は無趣味でつまらない男だ He is quite a dull person with *no interests*. →趣味.

むじゅん 矛盾 (an) **inconsistency** (不一致) ; (a) **contradiction** (両立しないこと) 一動 **矛盾する** **be inconsistent with, contradict** /kɑ̀ːntrədíkt/ +目 ▶社会にはいろいろな矛盾や不合理がある There are a lot of *inconsistencies* and unreasonable things in society. ‖今のおことばはあなたがさっきおっしゃったことと矛盾しています What you just said *is inconsistent with* what you said just a while ago. ／You *are contradicting* yourself. ‖容疑者の自供は目撃者の証言と矛盾している The suspect's confession *conflicts* [*is in conflict*] *with* the testimony of the witness.

むしょう 無償 ▶無償奉仕 *voluntary* service ‖義務教育の教科書は無償で配布される Compulsory education textbooks are distributed to students *free* (*of charge*).
▶子に対する親の愛は無償の愛である The love of parents for their children is *a love that demands nothing in return*.

[1]**むじょう 無情な** **heartless** (心ない) ; **inhuman** (人間味に欠ける) ; **merciless** (慈悲の心に欠ける) ▶1つミスしたからといって給料を半分にするとは無情な仕打ちだ Just because I made one mistake, they slashed my pay in half—*that's heartless* [*inhuman*].

[2]**むじょう 無上** ▶このすばらしい祝典にご招待いただき無上の光栄に存じます I appreciate the *great* honor of being invited to this wonderful celebration. ‖初孫の誕生は彼にとって無上の喜びであった The birth of his first grandchild gave him the *greatest* joy.

[3]**むじょう 無常** **impermanence** (はかなさ) ; **transitoriness** (移ろいやすさ) ; **uncertainty** (不確かさ) ; **transience** [**-cy**] (一時的であること) 《参考》以上の語が仏教用語としての「無常」を英訳する場合に用いられているが, 一般に「人生のはかなさ」をいう場合に用いることもできる.
▶この世に存在するものすべてが無常である All things (that exist) in this world are *impermanent* [*transitory* ／*uncertain* ／*transient*]. ‖『平家物語』を貫く主題は無常観である The leitmotif that permeates "The Tale of Heike" is *a sense of transience*.

むじょうけん 無条件の **unconditional** ▶無条件降伏 *unconditional* surrender ‖無条件でこの車をおまえにやるわけにはいかないよ I can't (agree to) give you this car *without any conditions*.

む

むしょうに 無性に ▶彼女はその男に無性に腹が立った She felt *unbridled* anger toward that man. ‖ 海を見ていたら無性に旅に出たくなった As I looked at the sea, I had *a craving* [*a longing*] to travel. (➤ともに「切望」の意) ‖ 無性にマンゴーが食べたくなった I'*m dying for* [I *have a* (*strong*) *craving for*] a mango.

[1]**むしょく 無色の** colorless ▶アルコールは無色透明の液体だ Alcohol is a *colorless*, transparent liquid.

[2]**むしょく 無職の** unemployed (失業中の；就業先を持たない)；retired (退職した) ▶私は現在無職です I'm *unemployed* [*jobless*] now. ／I'm now *out of a job* [*between jobs*]. (➤ともに「失業中です」の意) ‖ 無職の人はアパートを借りるとき困ることが多い People *without a job* often have difficulty renting apartments.

むしよけ 虫除け an insect [《米また》a bug] repellent；a moth repellent (衣類用の)；a mothball (ボール状の).

むしょぞく 無所属の independent (独立した)；unaffiliated (提携・加盟していない)；unattached (組織などの一員でない) ▶この前の市長選に彼は無所属で立候補した He ran as an *independent* [*unaffiliated*] candidate in the last mayoral election.

むしる 毟る pull +目 (引っ張る)；weed +目 (草取りをする)；pluck +目 (鳥の羽を) ▶俺の胸毛をむしるなよ Don't *pull* the hair on my chest. ‖ 彼は裏の庭で草をむしっているよ He is *weeding* (in) the back garden. ‖ 鶏の羽をむしる *pluck feathers* from a chicken ／*pluck* a chicken ‖ 魚の身をむしる *pick off* the flesh of a fish from the bone (s) (with one's chopsticks).

[1]**むしろ 蓆** a (straw) mat. →ござ.

[2]**むしろ** more《than》；rather《than》

> 【文型】
> A であるよりむしろ B
> more B than A
> ➤ A, B は形容詞
> B rather than A
> ➤ A, B は名詞・形容詞・動詞
>
> 《解説》(1)「A ではあるが, むしろ B」というには **more** B **than** A (A よりもっと B) を使う. B が名詞の場合は **more** of B **than** A という. 少し改まった言い方では not so much A as B という言い方も使う.
> (2)「A でなくてむしろ B」と A を否定する感じでは B **rather than** A という.

▶彼女は美人というよりむしろかわいい感じだ She's *more* cute *than* beautiful. (➤「美人でないとは言わないが, むしろかわいい感じだ」の意) ／She is cute *rather than* beautiful. (➤「かわいいが美人とは言えない」の意) ‖ 彼女は歌手というよりもむしろ女優だ She is *more of* an actress *than* a singer. ／She is *not so much* a singer *as* an actress. (🏺どちらも「歌手でもあるが, むしろ女優だ」の意. She is an actress rather than a singer. とすると「歌手と思い違いされているかもしれないが, そうではなくて実際は女優だ」の意になる).

> 【文型】
> むしろ…したい
> would rather do
> would prefer to do [doing]
> A するよりむしろ B するほうがいい
> would rather B than A
> ➤ A, B とも動詞の原形
>
> 《解説》(1) would は主語が代名詞のときはしばしば 'd を使い, I'd のようになる.
> (2) would は仮定の話としての好みを表している (例えば, 選べるとしたらそうする) だけなので, 実際にそうするかどうかはわからない.
> (3) would なしの prefer to do [doing] は「実際にそのほうが好きでそうしている」を表す.
> (4)「A するより B したい」は **would prefer** B (**rather**) **than** A でも表せる. A, B は to do でも doing でもよい.

▶きょうは疲れているので (外出するより) むしろ家に居たい Since I'm tired, I'*d rather* stay at home (*than* go out) today. (➤'d rather do は「どちらかと言えば…したい」という仮定的な言い方) ‖ 私は都会よりもむしろ田舎に住むほうがいい I'*d prefer to* live in the country *rather than* in a city. ／I'*d like to* live in the country *better than* [*more than*] in a city. (🏺'd を使った場合はどちらも現在都会に住んでいる人が選べると仮定しての文. I prefer … や I like … では現在田舎に住んでいるか, その経験のある人が自分の体験から行う発言となる) ‖ 修理してもらうよりむしろ新しいのを買ったほうが賢明だと思うよ I think you'd be wiser to buy a new one (*rather*) *than* to have it fixed. ‖ 私はむしろ何も知らないほうがいい I'*d rather not* know (anything).

むしん 無心 innocence ▶無心に遊ぶ子供の姿は天使のようだ Children playing *innocently* look like angels.

[1]**むじん 無人** ▶無人の家 a *vacant* [an *empty*] house ‖ 無人ロケットがきょう打ち上げられた An *unmanned* rocket was launched today.
‖無人駅 an unstaffed [unmanned] railroad station ‖ 無人島 an uninhabited island；a desert island (熱帯の).

[2]**むじん 無尽** a mutual financing association.

むしんけい 無神経な insensitive (他人の感情に対して), thick-skinned (批判・侮辱に対して鈍感な) ▶クラスの生徒たちの前で太郎を叱るとはあの人も無神経だ How *insensitive* of him [her] to have scolded Taro in front of the class! ‖ 彼は無神経で人の言うことを気にしない He is *thick-skinned* and doesn't care what other people say.

むじんぞう 無尽蔵の inexhaustible /ìnɪgzɔ́:stəbəl/ ▶私たちは天然資源が無尽蔵だと思いがちだ We tend to think that natural resources are *unlimited* [*inexhaustible*].

むしんろん 無神論 atheism /éɪθiìzəm/
‖無神論者 an atheist.

むす 蒸す 1【ふかす】 steam +目 ▶サツマイモを蒸す *steam* sweet potatoes ‖ 蒸したタオル a *steamed* towel.
2【蒸し暑い】 be muggy ▶ここは蒸すねえ. エアコンをつけてよ It *is* quite *muggy* in here, isn't it? Why don't you turn on the air conditioner?

むすう 無数の countless, innumerable /ɪnjú:mərəbəl/ (➤後者は堅い語) ▶空にきらめく無数の星 *countless* [*innumerable* ／*myriads of*] stars twinkling in the sky (➤myriads of は文語的な言い方) ‖ 人知の及ばぬことは無数にある There are *countless* things that are beyond our knowledge.

むずかしい 難しい

1【難解な】 hard, difficult ▶あの先生はいつも難しい問題を出す That teacher always asks us *hard* [*difficult*] questions. ‖ 手続きが難しいので申請は諦めた I gave up on applying because the procedure was too *complicated*. (➤ complicated は「複雑な」).

2【困難な】difficult ▶部下の離反で課長は難しい立場に立たされた Losing the support of his staff (members) put the section chief in a *difficult* spot [situation].

【文型】
人(A)が…するのが難しい
It is difficult [**hard**] **for** A **to** do.

【解説】(1) difficult は困難を克服するのに技術・工夫・能力・知識などが必要な難しさを指し, hard は肉体的に大変な, あるいは精神的にきつい, を表す. difficult のほうが深刻で少し改まった響きがあるのに対し, hard はより口語的だが多義のため漠然としている.
(2) くだけた言い方では tough も使われる.

▶一度失った信頼を取り戻す**のは難しい** *It's difficult* [*hard*] *to* restore confidence once it has been lost. ‖ 日本選手がオリンピックの100メートルでメダルを取る**のは難しい** *It's difficult for* a Japanese athlete *to* win a medal in the 100 meters at the Olympics.

✉ **英語で自分の思っていることをわかってもらうのは難しいですね** I realized that making myself understood in English was *difficult*.

3【気難しい】difficult ▶うちの娘は今**難しい**年頃だ My daughter is now at a *difficult* [*delicate*] age. (➤ 後者は「傷つきやすい」) ‖ 今野さんは**難しい**人だからみんなが避けようとする Everybody tries to avoid Mr. Konno because he is a very *difficult* person. ‖ **難しい**こと言わないで, やってくれよ Please don't be *difficult*; just do it. ‖ 監督はきょうは**難しい**顔をしている The manager looks *grumpy* today. (➤ grumpy は「むっつりと不機嫌な」) ‖ 目が肥えているから, あの奥さんは着物の注文が**難しい**(＝なかなか満足しない) That lady is a *difficult* customer *to please* because she has an eye for good kimonos.

4【見込みが少ない】 ▶このしけでは漁師たちの生還は**難しい** *It is doubtful* [*unlikely*] *that* the fishermen can return safely in this stormy weather. (➤ be unlikely は「ありそうもない」).

むずがゆい むず痒い itchy ▶足の裏が**むず痒い** The sole of my foot *feels itchy*.

むずかる fret ▶弟はおなかがすいて**むずかっていた** My little brother got *fretful* because he was hungry.

むすこ 息子 a **son** ▶一人**息子**はとかく甘やかされがちだ *An only son* tends to be spoiled [pampered].

むすっと ▶何, **むすっと**しているんだ？ Why *are* you *sulking*?

むすばれる 結ばれる ▶太一と美恵はお互いの両親の反対にもかかわらずついに**結ばれた**(＝結婚した) Taichi and Mie finally *got married* despite their parents' disapproval.

むすび 結び an **end**(終わり); a **conclusion** (結論) ▶**結び**のことばを述べる make *closing* [*concluding*] *remarks* ‖ きょうの**結び**の一番は横綱どうしの対戦だ The *closing bout* in today's sumo will be a match between the two yokozuna (grand champions).

むすびつき 結び付き (a) **connection**; **relation(s)** (関係); **ties** (きずな).

むすびつく 結び付く connect《to》 ▶彼の話とこの事件がどう**結び付く**のか私にはわからない I don't know how his account *is connected* [*is related*] *to* this case. ‖ 合格に**結び付く**勉強のしかたを工夫しなければならない You must figure out a way of studying which will bring success in the exam.

むすびつける 結び付ける fasten /fǽsən/ ＋目, **tie** ＋目 (ひもなどで); **link** ＋目 (関係づける) ▶ザイルを腰に**結び付け**, 岩をよじ登った I climbed up the rock *with* a rope *fastened* to my belt. ‖ その2つの事件を**結び付ける**証拠は何もない There's no evidence that *links* those two cases.

むすびめ 結び目 a **knot** /nɑːt/ ▶**結び目**をほどく untie [undo] *a knot* ‖ **結び目**が緩んだ[きつくなった] The *knot* has loosened [tightened].

むすぶ 結ぶ

📖 **訳語メニュー**
ひもなどを結ぶ →tie **1**
結び付ける →link, connect **2**
協定などを →conclude **3**
締めくくる →close **4**

1【結わえる】tie /taɪ/ ＋目 ▶三塁手が靴のひもを**結ぶ**間, タイムがかけられた A time-out was called while the third baseman *tied* his shoelaces. ‖ 父がネクタイの**結び**方を教えてくれた My father taught me how to *tie* my tie. ‖ 髪にこのリボン**結んで**くれない？ Please *tie* my hair *up* with this ribbon. ‖ 母に帯を**結んで**もらった I *had* my mother *tie* my obi.

2【つなぐ】connect ＋目, **link** ＋目 (➤ 意味に大差はなく, 前者のほうがふつう)

【文型】
場所(A)と場所(B)を結ぶ
connect A **and** B ／**connect** A **to** [**with**] B
link A **and** B ／**link** A **to** [**with**] B

▶レインボーブリッジは芝浦とお台場を**結んでいる** The Rainbow Bridge *connects* [*links*] Shibaura *and* Odaiba. ／ The Rainbow Bridge *connects* [*links*] Shibaura *to* Odaiba. (➤ 後者は with Odaiba も可) ‖ 東京と博多は新幹線で5時間半で**結ばれている** Tokyo *and* Hakata *are linked* by a five-and-a-half-hour Shinkansen train ride. ‖ 本社と全支社は高速のコンピュータ・ネットワークで**結ばれている** The head office *and* all the branches *are connected* [*linked*] by a high-speed computer network. ‖ 点A, Bを直線で**結びなさい** *Connect* points A *with* B with a line. ／Draw a line *connecting* A *to* B. 《参考》点と点を順に結んでいくと絵が出来上がる子供の遊びは connect [《英》join] the dots といい, これは「点を結ぶ」のほか, 比喩的に「いくつかの事実を結び合わせて全容を明らかにする, 結論を引き出す」あるいは「点を結んで全体像を作り上げる」という意味にもなる.

3【取り決める】conclude ＋目 ▶大手石油会社はガソリン価格値下げの協定を**結んだ** The big oil companies *concluded* an agreement to lower the price of gas. ‖ その選手は年俸6000万円で中日と契約を**結んだ** The player *concluded* [*signed*] a sixty million yen annual contract with the Dragons.

4【締めくくる】close /kloʊz/ ＋目 ▶彼女は両親への感謝のことばでスピーチを**結んだ** She *closed* [*concluded*] her speech by expressing her thanks to her parents.

5【固く閉じる】shut ＋目 ▶その男の子は口を真一文字に**結んで**ひと言もしゃべらなかった The boy *shut* his lips *tight* [*clamped* his lips *shut*] and didn't say a word.

むずむず ▶背中がむずむずする *It feels like* [*I feel like*] *something is crawling* on my back. (➤「何かが背中をはっているような感じがする」の意) ‖ 鼻がむずむずする My nose *tickles*.
▶息子は隣の子がプレゼントに何をもらったか知りたくてむずむずしている My son *is itching to* find out what the boy (sitting) next to him has gotten as a present. ‖ 早く打順が回ってこないかなあ. 腕がむずむずするよ I *can hardly wait* for my turn at bat.

むすめ 娘 **1**【女の子供】a **daughter** ▶上の[下の]娘 one's older [younger] *daughter* (➤「いちばん上の」は oldest または eldest,「いちばん下の」は youngest) ‖ 私には娘が2人いる I have two *daughters*. ‖ 娘たちはどこ? Where are *the girls*? (➤ 父親が母親に, または母親が父親に向かって言うような場合).
‖娘婿(むこ) a son-in-law.
2【若い女性】a **young woman**, a **(young) girl** ▶こんにちは, 娘さん Good afternoon, *young lady*. (➤ 呼びかけるときはこのように lady を使うのがふつう) ‖ 私だって, 娘の頃には燃えるような恋を夢見たものよ I, too, used to dream of passionate love *when I was a young girl*.

むせい 夢精 a **wet dream**, (a) **nocturnal emission** (➤ 後者は医学用語) ▶夢精をする have *a wet dream*.

むぜい 無税の **tax-free** (税金なしの) ; **duty-free** (関税なしの) ▶少額の遺産は無税です Small inheritances *are not taxed*.

むせいえいが 無声映画 a **silent movie** [**film**].

むせいげん 無制限の **unlimited** ▶無制限に石油を消費すると人類は苦境に立つことになるだろう *Unlimited* consumption of oil will eventually get us into trouble.

むせいふ 無政府 ▶その国は内乱で無政府状態になっている That country has been in *a state of anarchy* because of civil war.
‖無政府主義 anarchism /ǽnəʳkìzəm/ ‖ 無政府主義者 an anarchist /ǽnəʳkɪst/.

むせいぶつ 無生物 an **inanimate object**.

むせきついどうぶつ 無脊椎動物 (動物学) an **invertebrate (animal)**.

むせきにん 無責任 **irresponsibility** 一形 **無責任な** **irresponsible** /ìrɪspáːnsəbəl/ ▶あいつは無責任なやつだ He is an *irresponsible* guy. ‖ 自分がよく知りもしない男を彼女に紹介するなんて無責任だよ It *is irresponsible* of you to introduce to her a man you don't know well.

むせっそう 無節操 ▶無節操な政治家 an *unethical* [*unprincipled*] politician.

むせぶ ▶涙にむせびながら, 彼女はその不幸な結婚のことを話した *Choked with tears*, she told the story of her unhappy marriage. / She *sobbed out* the story of her unhappy marriage. (➤ sob out は「むせび泣きながら語る」).

むせる ▶煙にむせて盛んにせき込む *be choked with smoke* and have a coughing fit ‖ 一気にお握りにかぶりついたらむせてしまった When I took a big bite of a rice ball, I *nearly choked on it and coughed violently*.

¹むせん 無線 **radio**, **wireless** ▶無線操縦の飛行機 a *radio-controlled* airplane / a drone ‖ 無線で救助を求める ask for rescue *by radio*.
‖無線送信機 a radio transmitter ‖ 無線装置 a wireless telegraphic apparatus ‖ 無線電信 wireless telegraph, radiotelegraph.

²むせん 無銭 ▶無銭旅行をする travel *without money* ‖ 彼のような金持ちがどうして無銭飲食なんかしたんだろうか? What on earth made a rich man like him *walk* [*skip*] *out of the restaurant without paying his bill*?

むせんまい 無洗米 **pre-washed rice, rinse-free rice.**

むそう 夢想する **dream** 《of, that》▶彼がこんな大作家になろうとは誰も夢想だにしなかった *Nobody dreamed* [*imagined*] that he would become such a great novelist.
‖夢想家 a dreamer.

むぞうさ 無造作に **casually** (さりげなく) ; **carelessly** (無頓着に) ▶彼女は髪を無造作に束ねていた Her hair was tied up *casually*. ‖ 彼は100万円の札束を無造作に机の上に置いていた He had *carelessly* put a wad of bills totaling one million yen on the desk.

むだ 無駄

1【浪費】(a) **waste** ▶そんな本を読むのは時間の無駄だ Reading that kind of book is *a waste of time*. ‖ 時間[金]を無駄にするな Don't *waste* your time [money]. ‖ 無駄を省いて効率的に働こう Let's cut down on *waste* and work efficiently.
2【無益】一形 **無駄な** **useless** ; **idle** (無益な, たわいのない)

> 【文型】
> …しても無駄だ
> **It is no use** [**useless**] **doing** [**to do**].
> **There is no point in doing.**

▶ケーキを捜しても無駄だよ, 食べちゃったんだから *It is useless to* look for the cake ; I already ate it. ‖ 誰の言うことも聞かないんだから, この子には何を言っても無駄だ He won't listen to anybody, so *it's no use* [*no good*] tell*ing* him anything. ‖ 同じことの繰り返しなのだから, これ以上議論しても無駄だ *There's no point in* continu*ing* the discussion because we're repeating the same thing. (➤ There is no point in doing は「…しても無意味だ」の意. 会話では in を省略することがある).
▶我々の努力は無駄だったようだ Our efforts seem to *have been in vain* [*to have gone down the drain*].

むだあし 無駄足 ▶あの人は不在のことが多いから, 無駄足を踏まないよう前もって約束してから事務所を訪ねなさい Since he is often out of the office, be sure to make an appointment before visiting him, unless you want to *waste your time* [*make a fruitless visit*].

むだがね 無駄金 ▶無駄金を使う *waste money*.

むだぐち 無駄口 ▶無駄口を利くな Don't *talk nonsense* [*rubbish*]! ‖ 無駄口ばかり利いていないでせっせと仕事をしなさいよ Just do your work and don't *talk so much*. / Stop *shooting the breeze* [*goofing around*] and get down to work. (➤ shoot the breeze は「ばか話をする」, goof around は「無駄に時間を過ごす」の意のインフォーマルな言い方).

むだげ 無駄毛 ▶無駄毛をそる shave off (women's) *facial or other unwanted hair*.

むだじに 無駄死に ▶無駄死にする *die in vain* / *die for nothing*.

むだづかい 無駄遣い (a) **waste** 一動 **無駄遣いする** **waste** ▶無駄遣いをやめれば月に3万円は貯金できる If you stop *wasting money*, you'll be able to save up to 30,000 yen a month.

むだばなし 無駄話 idle talk [chatter] ▶無駄話をする *shoot the breeze* / *chew the fat*(➤どちらもくだけた表現).

むだぼね 無駄骨 (a) waste of labor ▶このぽんこつテレビを直そうとしても無駄骨を折るだけだ It would be just (a) *waste of labor* to try to repair this old junk TV set.

むだん 無断で without permission(許可なく) ▶裕子は親に無断で外泊した Yuko spent the night away from home *without* (*getting*) *her parents' permission.* ‖伸宏は無断で学校を休んだ Nobuhiro was absent from school *without notice.* (➤notice は「(前もって)知らせること」) ‖無断欠勤[欠席]する *play truant* ‖無断借用禁止 *Unauthorized* borrowing is prohibited. / Borrowing *without* (*the owner's*) *permission* is prohibited. ‖画像の無断使用は禁止です *Unauthorized use* of images is prohibited.

むたんぽ 無担保の unsecured
‖無担保ローン an unsecured loan.

1**むち 鞭** a whip; a rod (棒状の); a lash (むち打ち) ▶教育にむちは要らない The *whip* [*rod*] has no place in education. ‖ピシリとむちを当てたとたん彼は馬から振り落とされた No sooner had he *laid whip to* the horse than it threw him. ‖囚人はむち打ち20回の刑に処せられた The prisoner received (a sentence of) 20 *lashes*.
▶《慣用表現》それはきみに対するお父さんの愛のむちだよ That is your father showing his belief "*Spare the rod and spoil the child.*" (➤引用符の中は「むちを惜しめば子供はだめになる」という英語のことわざ) / That is your father's *strict but loving discipline* toward you.

2**むち 無知** ignorance 一形 無知な ignorant ▶無知な人々 *ignorant* people ‖無知であることは恥ではない You should not be ashamed of your *ignorance*. / *Ignorance* is nothing to be ashamed of. ‖私は法律関係は全く無知だ I'm totally *ignorant* of [about] legal matters.

むちうちしょう 鞭打ち症 whiplash, a whiplash injury ▶車がダンプカーと衝突し, 彼はむち打ち症で病院へ送られた His car collided with a dump truck, and he was sent to the hospital with *whiplash*.

むちうつ 鞭打つ whip +目, lash +目 ▶騎手が馬にむち打つと馬は狂ったように走り出した The horse started running frantically when the jockey *whipped* it.
▶《慣用表現》山田氏は老骨にむち打って(=老齢にもかかわらず)会社再建に取り組んだ Mr. Yamada, *in spite of his advanced age*, tackled the rebuilding of his corporation (aggressively).

むちつじょ 無秩序 disorder; chaos /kéɪɑːs/ (混とん状態) ▶その国は左翼のクーデターで無秩序の状態に陥った The country was thrown into *disorder* following the leftist coup d'état.

むちむち ▶むちむちに太った赤ちゃん a *chubby* baby ‖彼女のむちむちした太もも her *plump* thigh(s) ‖むちむちボディーのギャル a *curvaceous* girl (➤curvaceous /kəːˈvéɪʃəs/ は「肉体美の」の意で, おどけた響きがある).

むちゃ 無茶な unreasonable (理不尽な); reckless (無鉄砲な); ridiculous (ばかげた); foolhardy (無謀な) ▶きみの言うことは無茶だ What you have said is *unreasonable*. ‖息子が無茶なことをしないかと心配です I'm afraid my son may do something *reckless* [*desperate*]. (➤後者は「自暴自棄の」) ‖母は時々無茶な運転をする My mother sometimes drives *recklessly*.
▶この天気に頂上アタックなんてあの人たちは無茶だ It's *foolhardy* for [of] them to set out to scale the peak in this weather. ‖3日連続徹夜で勉強だなんて無茶だよ(=やり過ぎだ) You'*re pushing yourself too hard* by staying up all night studying three nights in a row.

むちゃくちゃ 無茶苦茶 ▶むちゃくちゃに泳いで気がつくと湖の真ん中だった I swam *desperately* and found myself in the midst of the lake. ‖この問題はむちゃくちゃに難しい This quiz is *terribly* difficult. ‖徹夜で仕上げろだなんてむちゃくちゃだよ It's *outrageous* [*ridiculous*] to ask me to work all night to finish this job. (➤outrageous は「あまりにもひどい, とんでもない」, ridiculous は「とんでもない, ばかげている」).

むちゃくりく 無着陸 ▶無着陸飛行をする make *a nonstop flight* / fly nonstop.

むちゅう 夢中

> **【文型】**
> 物事(A)に夢中になっている
> be absorbed in A
> be crazy about A
>
> **《解説》be absorbed in** は「現に今ある活動に注意を集中し, 没頭している」の意. 同じような意味の少し改まった言い方に be engrossed in がある. **be crazy about** は「夢中になるほど大好き」の意のくだけた言い方.

▶その少年は漫画に夢中だ The boy *is absorbed* [*is engrossed*] *in* (reading) comic books. ‖電車内でスマートフォンに夢中になっている通勤客が多い Many commuters on the train *are absorbed in* their smartphones. ‖私はディカプリオに夢中です. 彼の出た映画は全部見ました I'*m crazy about* DiCaprio. I have seen all of his films.
▶最近私はブログに夢中です I'*m hooked on* blogging these days. (➤be hooked on は「…にはまっている」の意のインフォーマルな言い方) ‖買い物に夢中だったので家に電話するのをすっかり忘れていた I *was so busy* shopping that I completely forgot to call home. ‖話に夢中で時のたつのを忘れた We *were so deep* [*lost*] *in* conversation that we forgot the time.
▶我々は夢中でグランパスを声援した We rooted for Grampus *like mad* [*like crazy*]. ‖逃亡者は闇の中を夢中で(=必死で)逃げた The fugitive *ran for his* (*dear*) *life* in the dark.
☛ 無我夢中 (→見出語)

むちんじょうしゃ 無賃乗車 a free ride 一動 無賃乗車する steal a ride (on a train or bus).

むつう 無痛の painless ‖無痛分べん painless childbirth, a painless delivery.

むつかしい →難しい.

ムック a magazine-like book.

むっくり ▶ライオンはむっくりと起き上がった The lion got up *heavily*.

むつごろう 鯥五郎 《魚》 a bluespotted mud hopper.

むっちり ▶チアリーダーたちがジャンプすると, むっちりした太ももが見えた As the cheerleaders jumped in the air, I caught sight of their *plump* [*well-rounded*] thighs.

む

むっつり ▶お母さんはけさはなぜむっつりしているんだろう What's making Mom *look* so *sullen* [*moody*] this morning, I wonder? ‖ ああいうのを「むっつりすけべ」って言うのよ. 気をつけて Be wary of that type. He *doesn't say much, but he's a real lech.*

むっと ▶リポーターのぶしつけな質問にその歌手はむっとなった The singer *went into a huff* [*looked offended*] when asked a rude question by a reporter. ▶部屋はむっとするほど暑かった The room was very hot and *stuffy*.

むつまじい 睦まじい **harmonious** ▶むつまじい老夫婦 a *harmonious* elderly couple.

むていけん 無定見 ▶政治家の中には無定見な人もいる Some politicians *have no fixed* (political) *principles*.

むていこう 無抵抗 **nonresistance** 一形 無抵抗の **nonresistant** ▶ガンジーの無抵抗主義はよく知られている Gandhi's principle of *nonresistance* is widely known. ‖ その少年はひどく殴られても無抵抗だった Even when hit severely, the boy *put up no resistance at all*.

1**むてき 無敵の** **invincible** ▶無敵のチーム an *invincible* team ‖ 腕力だけで言えば彼は無敵だ For sheer strength, he *has no rivals* [*there is no one to rival* him].

2**むてき 霧笛** a **foghorn** ▶霧笛を鳴らす sound *a foghorn*.

むてっぽう 無鉄砲な **reckless** ▶無鉄砲な男 a *reckless* man ‖ あの体でマラソンに参加するなんて無鉄砲というものだ He is *reckless* to take part in the marathon in spite of his poor health.

むでん 無電 **radio, wireless** ▶この船は無電で港と連絡しています This ship keeps in touch with the port *by radio* [*wireless*]. ‖ 私たちは遭難船からの無電を傍受した We picked up *a radio* [*wireless*] *message* from a ship in distress.

むてんか 無添加の **additive-free** (添加物を使っていない) ▶このパンは無添加だ This bread is *additive-free*.
‖無添加食品 an additive-free food.

むとう 無灯 ▶無灯の自転車が多い Many people ride their bikes *without a light on*.

むとうはそう 無党派層 **independent voters.**

むとうひょう 無投票 ▶村長は無投票で再選された The village mayor was re-elected *by default*. (➤ by default は「対抗馬がなく」).

むとくてん 無得点の **scoreless** ▶そのサッカー試合は両チーム無得点に終わった The soccer game ended *scoreless*. ／Neither team could obtain any points in the soccer game. ‖ 《野球で》両チーム無得点のまま 9 回を迎えた They have come to the ninth inning, with both teams *scoring no runs* so far.

むとどけ 無届け ▶警察に無届けでデモをするとやっかいなことになるよ If you start a demonstration *without prior notice* to the police, you will get in trouble.

むとんちゃく 無頓着な **unconcerned**, **indifferent** (無関心な；後者が強意)；**careless** (気にかけない；やや文語的な言い方) ▶彼は服装には無頓着だが, 食べ物にはうるさい He *is indifferent to* [*is unconcerned about*] clothes, but is particular about food.

むないた 胸板 a **chest** ▶彼は胸板が厚い He has a (well-)defined *chest* [a thick *chest*].

むなくそ 胸糞 ▶あの政治家の声を聞くと胸くそが悪くなる The way that politician talks *is disgusting*. ／That politician's voice *makes* me *sick*.

むなぐら 胸倉 ▶アンパイアの判定に怒ったM監督は彼の胸倉をつかんで抗議した Upset about the umpire's decision, team manager M *grabbed* him *by the shirt* and yelled at him. (➤ 英語では「シャツをつかむ」という).

むなぐるしい 胸苦しい ▶深夜胸苦しくなって私は目が覚めた I woke up in the middle of the night *feeling tight* [*feeling oppressed*] *in the chest*.

むなげ 胸毛 **chest hair** ▶私は胸毛のある男に魅力を感じる I am attracted to men *with hairy chests*.

むなさわぎ 胸騒ぎ ▶何となく胸騒ぎがして彼女は一睡もできなかった For some reason, she *felt* so *uneasy* that she couldn't sleep a wink. ‖ 彼女の身に何かが起きるのではと彼は胸騒ぎがした He *had a feeling* [*had a premonition*] that something bad was about to happen to her. (➤ premonition は「予感, 前兆」).

むなざんよう 胸算用 ▶このつぼを売ればいくらもうかるか胸算用してみた I *mentally calculated* how much I would get if I sold this pot.

むなしい 空しい・虚しい **empty** (空虚な)；**fruitless** (実りのない)；**futile** /fjúːtl/ (無駄な) ▶生きがいのない人生なんてむなしい A life without (a) purpose is *empty*. ‖ ことしもむなしく終わってしまった This year, too, ended *in meaninglessness*. ／This has been another *meaningless* year for me. ‖ 母親は娘と連絡を取ろうと何度もむなしく試みた The mother repeatedly made *fruitless* [*futile*] efforts to get in touch with her daughter. ‖ 会社を倒産させまいとする我々の努力はむなしかった Our efforts to save the company from bankruptcy *were in vain* [*were fruitless*]. ‖ わがチームは善戦むなしく(＝よく戦ったが)敗れた Our team was beaten, *though we put up a good fight*.

むなしさ 空しさ・虚しさ **emptiness.**

むなもと 胸元 a **chest**, a **breast** →胸 ▶メアリーは胸元に十字架のペンダントをしていた Mary wore a cross pendant (on her *chest*). ‖ この服は胸元があき過ぎている This dress is too big *around the chest*. ／This dress is too low-cut. (➤ 後者は「襟ぐりが深すぎる」の意) ‖ 強盗は社長の胸元にナイフを突きつけた The burglar put a knife to the president's *chest*.

むに 無二 ▶父は無二の親友に死なれてがっくりしている My father is upset because his *best friend* has just died. ‖ 中村君は無二の親友です Nakamura is my *best* [*closest*] *friend*.

ムニエル **meunière** /mʌnjéəʳ/ (➤ フランス語から) ▶シタビラメのムニエル sole *meunière*.

むにゃむにゃ ▶あなた寝言で何かむにゃむにゃ言ってたわよ You were *mumbling* something in your sleep.

1**むね 胸** **1**【胸部】a **chest**; a **breast** (特に女性の乳房)；a **bust** (バスト；特に女性の胸回りの寸法) ▶胸のポケット a *breast* pocket ‖ 胸に校章をつける wear the school badge *on one's jacket* (➤ on one's chest とすると裸の胸に直接つけるようにもとれる) ‖ 胸が痛いんです I have pain in my *chest*. ‖ 彼は胸が厚い[広い] He has a broad *chest*. ／He's broad-chested. ‖ 彼女は胸が小さい[大きい] She has small [big] *breasts*. ／She has a small [big] *bust*. ‖ 医者は胸に聴診器を当てた The doctor put the stethoscope to my *chest*. ‖ 《医師のことば》胸を出してください(＝下着を取ってください) Take off your underwear, please. ‖ 胸を張って Sit up. ／Hold your head high. ‖ 彼女は胸に子供を抱き締めた She *held* her child *to her bosom*. (➤ bosom は文語的な語).

2【胃, 心臓】 a **heart** ▶焼き芋を食べると胸が焼ける I *get heartburn* when I eat baked sweet potatoes. ‖ そのサイトで知り合った葉子と実際に初めて会うときは胸がどきどきした *My heart beat fast* [*skipped a beat*] when I met Yoko, who(m) I had gotten to know through the website, for the first time in real life.

3【慣用表現】

胸が痛む ▶今なお原爆(後遺)症に苦しんでいる人を見ると胸が痛む(＝悲しい気持ちになる) *It is painful* [*heart-rending*] to see those people who are still suffering from A-bomb disease. **胸がいっぱい** ▶電話で田舎の父の声を聞いたら胸がいっぱいになった I *got all choked up* [*felt a lump in my throat*] when my father called me from home, and I heard his voice. ‖ 新人王に選ばれたときは胸がいっぱいになった(＝非常にうれしかった) I *was extremely happy* [*My heart was filled with joy*] when I was elected "rookie of the year". **胸がすっとする** ▶彼をどなりつけてやったら胸がすっとした I *felt better* [*relieved*] after I yelled at him. **胸が張り裂ける** ▶故郷の惨状を目の当たりにして胸が張り裂けそうだった It was *heart-rending* to see my hometown after the disaster wreaked havoc on it.

胸に描く ▶彼はニューヨークでの生活を胸に描いた He *pictured himself* living in New York. **胸にこたえる** ▶彼女の私の作品への率直な批評は本当に胸にこたえた Her frank criticism of my work really *hit me hard* [*hit home*]. **胸にしまう** ▶物事を胸にしまっておいちゃだめよ Don't *keep* things *to yourself*. **胸に迫る** ▶その難民の写真には見る人の胸に迫るものがあった The picture of the refugees was *deeply moving*. **胸に手を当てて** ▶おまえにも悪いところはある. 胸に手を当てて考えてみろ You too are to blame. *Search* [*Examine*] *your own heart*.

胸を打つ ▶胸を打つ話 a *moving* story ‖ 私はマザー・テレサの生き方に深く胸を打たれた I *was* deeply *moved by* Mother Teresa's way of life. **胸をなで下ろす** ▶国体が無事に済み, 主催者側はほっと胸をなで下ろした The organizers *were relieved* when the National Athletic Meet ended in success. **胸を張る** ▶私たちはよく戦ったじゃないか. さあ, 胸を張って帰ろう We played a good game. Let's go home *with our heads high*. **胸を膨らませる** ▶彼は4月からの大学生活を思い描いて, 期待に胸を膨らませている *His heart is filled with hope* as he pictures his life at college which will start in April.

²むね 棟 **the ridge (of a roof)** ; a **house** (家屋) ▶崖崩れで5棟が全壊した Five *houses* were completely destroyed by a landslide.

‖**棟上げ式** a framework-raising ceremony, the ceremony of the completion of the framework of a house (➤ 英語圏にはない).

³むね 旨 ▶彼女からプロポーズはお受けできませんという旨(＝意向)の手紙が届いた I received a letter from her *to the effect that* she couldn't accept my marriage proposal.

▶彼は誠実を旨(＝信条)として生きてきた He has made honesty his *creed* [*motto*] in life.

むねやけ 胸焼け **heartburn** ▶胸焼けを鎮める alleviate (one's) *heartburn* ‖ 胸焼けがするのなら, この胃薬をのんでみたら? If you have *heartburn*, why don't you take this stomach medicine?

むねん 無念 **regret**(後悔) ▶無念にも彼を説得できなかった *To my regret* [*Regrettably*], I couldn't persuade him.

▶無念無想の境地に達することは難しい It is hard to *remove all distracting thoughts from your mind*.

むのう 無能な **incapable**(本来的に能力が備わっていない) ; **incompetent** (ある特定の仕事に対して不適格な) ▶無能な経営陣 *incapable* management ‖ 無能な総理大臣 an *incompetent* prime minister.

むひ 無比 ▶彼女の計算は正確無比だ Her (mathematical) calculations *are more accurate than anyone else's*. ‖ あの歌舞伎俳優の芸は当代無比である *No one today can match* that kabuki actor in performance.

むひはん 無批判 ▶これらの説を無批判に受け入れるのは危険です It is dangerous to adopt these theories *uncritically*.

むひょう 霧氷 **rime**.

むひょうじょう 無表情な **expressionless** ; **detached** (超然とした) ▶無表情な顔 an *expressionless* face ‖「勝手にしろよ」と彼は無表情で言った "Do as you like," he said *with an expressionless face* [*with an emotionless expression*].

むびょうそくさい 無病息災 ▶神社に詣でて無病息災を祈願する visit a Shinto shrine to *pray for good health* (*and protection from sickness*).

むふう 無風の **windless** ; **calm** (穏やかな) ▶無風状態で旗がだらりと垂れている The flag is hanging limp *in the calm air*. ‖ その日, 太平洋は無風状態だった On that day, there was *a dead calm* on the Pacific.

むふんべつ 無分別な **thoughtless**(考えなしの) ; **indiscreet** (事を行うのに必要な思慮分別を欠いた) ▶無分別な行動をする behave *thoughtlessly*.

むほう 無法な **lawless** ▶全市が一時無法地帯と化した The entire city turned into a *lawless* zone for a while. ‖ ビリー・ザ・キッドは名だたる無法者だった Billy the Kid was a notorious *outlaw*.

むぼう 無謀な **thoughtless**(考えなしの) ; **reckless**(むちゃな) ▶無謀な企て a *thoughtless* attempt ‖ 無謀な運転は事故のもとだ *Reckless* driving causes accidents.

むほうしゅう 無報酬 ▶無報酬の仕事 *unpaid* work / *volunteer* work (➤「ボランティアの仕事」の意) ‖ 無報酬で働く work *without pay* [*on a volunteer basis*] ‖ この仕事は無報酬ですが, よろしいでしょうか *There's no pay* for this work. Can you accept that (condition)?

むぼうび 無防備な **defenseless** ; **unfortified** (防御工事が施されていない) ; **unarmed** (非武装の) ; **vulnerable** (攻撃されやすい) ▶無防備の兵士 an *unarmed* soldier ‖ 彼らは敵の攻撃に対して全く無防備だった They were completely *defenseless* against the enemy attack.

むほん 謀反 a **rebellion** /rɪbéljən/ (反乱) ; **treason**(反逆) ▶明智光秀は織田信長に対して謀反を起こした Akechi Mitsuhide *started a rebellion* against Oda Nobunaga.

むみ 無味の **tasteless, odorless** ▶無味無臭の液体 a *tasteless* and odorless liquid ‖ こんにゃくは無味だ Konnyaku is *tasteless* [has *no taste*].

むみかんそう 無味乾燥な **dull** (退屈な) ; **uninteresting**(おもしろみのない) ▶国際会議での日本代表の演説はよく無味乾燥だと言われる The speeches of Japanese delegates at international conferences

む

have a reputation for being *dull and uninteresting.*

むめい 無名の unknown(知られていない); nameless(名もない); obscure(隠れた); anonymous /ənɑ́:nɪməs/(匿名の) ▶無名の画家 an *unknown* [*nameless* / *obscure*] painter ‖ 無名の新人がドラマの主役に選ばれた An *unknown*, new actor was chosen for the leading role in the drama.

‖無名戦士 the Unknown Soldier [《英》Warrior].

むめんきょ 無免許 ▶彼は車を無免許で運転していて捕まった He was caught driving a car *without a driver's license*. ‖ 無免許では開業医にはなれない You cannot become a practicing physician *without a license*.

むやみ 無闇に thoughtlessly(よく考えもしないで); indiscriminately(無差別に) ▶むやみに人の悪口を言うものではない Don't criticize others *thoughtlessly*. ‖ むやみに生き物を殺してはいけない Don't kill creatures *indiscriminately*. ‖ おじはむやみやたらと酒を飲む My uncle drinks *excessively* [*too much*]. (➤ excessively は「過度に」の意).

むゆうびょう 夢遊病 sleepwalking; somnambulism /sɑːmnǽmbjəlɪzəm/(睡眠時遊行症) (➤ 後者は専門用語)

‖夢遊病者 a sleepwalker, a somnambulist.

むよう 無用 ▶お金のことなら心配無用だ *There's no need* to worry about money. / Don't worry about (the) money. ‖ 弁解は無用だ Excuses (trying to explain your way out of it) *won't do you any good*. (➤「弁解しても何の役にも立ちませんよ」の意).

▶大部の百科事典は無用の長物となった Multivolume encyclopedias have become a kind of *white elephant*. (➤ white elephant は「(贈られてありがた迷惑の珍しい)白い象」が原義) ‖ (掲示) 無用の者, 立ち入るべからず No trespassing.

むよく 無欲 ▶きょうのゲームはいわば無欲の勝利と言えよう Today we gained an *unsolicited* victory, so to speak. (➤ unsolicited は「求めないのに与えられた」の意) ‖ あの人は実に無欲な人だね He is truly *indifferent to worldly gains*, isn't he?

¹むら 村 a village

‖村人 a villager ‖ 村役場 a village office.

> 《解説》(1)イギリスでは village と town(町)を区別するのに対して, アメリカでは town より小さいものを village と呼び, an Indian [Eskimo] village のように使ったりする. また, 店の名前の一部に使うこともある.
> (2)日本の「村」は village でよいが, 郵便の宛名などでは -mura のようにするほうがよい.

²むら ▶この芝の植え方にはむらがある. 素人の仕事に違いない The lawn is planted *unevenly*. It must be the work of an amateur. ‖ きみの仕事にはどうもむらがあるね Your work *lacks consistency*. (➤「一貫性に欠ける」の意) / You're *erratic* in your work. (➤ erratic は「出来不出来がある」) ‖ 彼の投球にはむらがあった He pitched *erratically*.

むらおこし 村興し ▶私たちは村興しのためにコンピュータ工場を誘致することにした We decided to try to get a computer factory to come to our village, *so as to revitalize the village economy*. (➤ revitalize は「(組織など)を再活性化する」の意).

むらがる 群がる gather(集まる); cluster(群れを成して集まる); crowd(人・動物などが一か所にあふれるほど); swarm(虫などが) ▶交番の前に人が群がっていた A large crowd *had gathered* [People (*were*) *clustered*] in front of the police box. ‖ 馬のふんにハエが群がっていた Flies *swarmed* on the horse dung.

むらさき 紫 purple(赤紫色); violet(スミレ色) ▶紫は昔は高貴な色とされた *Purple* was considered a noble color in olden times. 《参考》紫は violet が近いが,「高貴」の連想は purple にある.

むらはちぶ 村八分 (social) ostracism /ɑ́:strəsɪzəm/ ▶人を村八分にする *ostracize* a person.

むらむら ▶デブと言われて怒りがむらむらと湧いてきた Anger *surged within me* when someone called me a fatso. ‖ (性的興奮を覚えて)むらむらとなる *become sexually aroused* / *get hot and bothered* (➤ 後者はインフォーマル).

むり 無理

1【不合理な, 不自然な】 unreasonable, unnatural ▶無理な要求 an *unreasonable* demand ‖ 彼の議論にはやや無理がある His argument *is* a bit *unreasonable*. ‖ 無理を言われても困る Don't be *unreasonable*. ‖ 大谷の投球フォームには無理がない Ohtani's pitching form *is very smooth*. ‖ 無理が通れば道理が引っ込む When unreason prevails, reason gives way. / Where might is master, justice is servant.

> 【文型】
> ～であるのも無理はない
> (It is) no wonder S + V.
> It is natural that S + V.
> 人(A)が…するのも無理はない
> It is natural for A to do.
>
> 《解説》(1)**no wonder** は「不思議でない, 驚くに当たらない」の意. **be natural** は「自然なことだ, 当然だ」の意.
> (2)**It is natural** に続く文では, 事実を述べるにはふうに現在形や過去形を使うが, 仮定法で一般論化して would や should を使うことがある.

▶あの子, いい子だもの. 母親が自慢に思うのも無理ないよ He's such a good boy. *No wonder* his mother is proud of him. ‖ 無断欠勤があぁ多くては, 彼女が会社を辞めさせられたのも無理はない *It was only natural that* she got fired [should get fired] after being absent from work so many days. / Because she was absent from work so many days, she was fired *as a matter of course*. (➤ as a matter of course は「当然のこととして」) ‖ あんなだらしない試合をしては監督が怒るのも無理はない Since you played such a sloppy game, *I can* (*easily*) *understand* why the manager got mad [would get mad]. (● 後半を I don't blame the manager for getting angry. / it is only natural for the manager to get angry. としてもよい. 最後の it is ... for の構文は客観的で堅い言い方).

‖無理難題 an unreasonable demand, a tall order.

2【不可能な】 impossible ▶ニューヨークを1日で見物しようなんて無理だよ *It's impossible* to see the sights of New York in a day. ‖ 今すぐ車を買ってくれと言われてもそれは無理だよ You're *asking the impossible* if you expect me to buy you a car right away. ‖ 子供に服を汚すなと言っても無理だ *It is too much to expect* children to keep their clothes clean.

3【過度】 ▶私は無理(＝働き過ぎ)がたたって体を悪くし

た I got sick due to *overwork*. ‖ 疲れたら**無理をせず**に休みなさい *Don't overdo yourself*, but take a rest when you get tired. ‖ あまり**無理をするな**(＝のんびりやれ) Take it easy. ‖ **無理が利くのは**30代までだ It is only until your thirties that you *can push yourself too hard*. ‖ 対話「あすは社員旅行だけど, かぜで熱があるんだ」「**無理しないほうがいいね**」"There's a company trip tomorrow, but I have a fever from a cold." "*You shouldn't force yourself* (to go)." ‖ 後ろから**無理に押さないでください** Don't push *too hard* from the back.

4【強制】→させる

【文型】
人(A)に無理に…させる
force A **to** do
make A do
【解説】force は嫌がる者を「力ずくで無理やりさせる」の意. **make** は「させる」に重点があるが, やらないでよいという選択の余地はない. →させる.

▶彼女は3歳の息子に**無理にピアノを習わせた** She *forced* her three-year-old son *to take* piano *lessons*. ／ She *made* her three-year-old son *learn* to play the piano (against his will). (●「無理に」の語感を出すには make A do のあとに against ～'s will を足すとよい) ‖ 彼女は体調はよくなかったが, 職場では**無理に笑顔を作った** Although she was not feeling well, she *forced herself to smile* at the office.

▶お子さんに**無理に勉強させても**, あまり身につきません If you *force* your child *to study* [*make* your child *study*], he [she] won't be able to learn much. ‖ 食欲が無いのなら, **無理に[無理して]食べることはありません** If you don't have an appetite, you shouldn't *force yourself to eat*.

▶自分の提案を**無理押しするな** Don't *push* your own proposal *too hard*. ‖ 彼は妻と**無理心中した** He killed his wife and *committed suicide*. (➤「妻を殺して自殺した」と表すしかない).

‖**無理数**《数学》an irrational number.

むりかい 無理解 ▶大衆のうつ病に対する**無理解**を改める必要がある It is necessary to correct the public's *lack of understanding* about depression. ‖ 彼女は妻の立場に全く**無理解な**夫にうんざりしてしまった She was disgusted with her husband's *lack of sympathy* for her situation.

むりし 無利子 no interest ▶10万円まで1週間**無利子**でお貸しします We offer a loan of up to a hundred thousand yen and charge *no interest* for a week.

むりじい 無理強い compulsion 一動 **無理強いする force**《to do》▶彼女は嫌がる子供を**無理強いして**学校へ行かせた She *forced* her reluctant child *to* go to school. ‖ **無理強いしても**だめだよ. 彼女は絶対にお酒は飲まないから It is no use *forcing* her (*to* drink). She simply does not drink.

むりやり 無理矢理に against one's **will**(意思に反して) ▶嫌がる子供を**無理やり**勉強させてもだめだ It's no use *forcing* children *to* study *against their will*. ‖ 彼女は好きでもない男と**無理やり結婚させられた** She *was forced into* marrying a man she did not (really) love. ‖ 姉貴はきついジーパンを**無理やりはいて**苦しがっている My (older) sister *squeezed herself* into a tight pair of jeans and is complaining that it pinches.

むりょう 無料の free 一副 **無料で free, for nothing,**《インフォーマル》**for free** ▶**無料の**コンサート a *free* concert ‖ 参加者にはオレンジジュースが**無料で**サービスされた Orange juice was served *free* [*for nothing* ／ *for free*] to the participants. ‖ このパンフレットは**無料**です. ご自由にお持ちください These brochures are *free*. (Please) take one. ‖ 30分以内にお届けできない場合, (ご注文の)ピザは**無料**になります If the pizza you ordered doesn't come within 30 minutes, you can get it *free* (*of charge*).

‖《掲示》**入場無料** Admission Free.

むりょく 無力な powerless(力がない); **helpless**(自分の力では何もできない) ▶相手チームの速攻にわがチームは全く**無力**だった We were utterly *helpless* [*powerless*] in the face of the lightning offense of the rival team. ‖ **無力で**その仕事のお役に立てません I am *powerless* [*unable*] to help you with the project.

むるい 無類の unequalled(匹敵するものがない); **matchless**(無比の); **unparalleled**(並ぶもののない); **unique**(独特の) ▶スティーブ・ジョブズは先見の明のある人として**無類**であった Steve Jobs was an *unparalleled* [*unequalled* ／ *matchless*] visionary. ／ Steve Jobs was a *one-of-a-kind* visionary. (➤ one-of-a-kind は「それだけで一種を成す, ユニークな」の意) ‖ ここに集まったのは**無類の**野球好きばかりだ The people assembled [gathered] here are all *dyed-in-the-wool* baseball fanatics. (➤ dyed-in-the-wool は「筋金入りの」).

むれ 群れ a **group**(集団); a **crowd**(人の) ▶若者の**群れ** *a group* of young people ‖ **群れをつくる**習性 the herd instinct ‖ イルカは**群れをつくって**海中にすむ Dolphins live *in schools* (in the ocean).

「**群れ」のいろいろ** **イナゴ[ハチ, アリ]の群れ** a *swarm* of locusts [bees, ants] ／**牛[象, アザラシ]の群れ** a *herd* of cattle [elephants, seals] ／**オオカミ[猟犬, 犬]の群れ** a *pack* of wolves [hounds, dogs] ／**魚[サメ, 鯨]の群れ** a *school* of fish [sharks, whales] ／**猿[シカ]の群れ** a *troop* of monkeys [deer] ／**鳥[ハト, 白鳥]の群れ** a *flock* of birds [pigeons, swans] ／**羊[ヤギ]の群れ** a *flock* of sheep [goats] ／**ライオンの群れ** a *pride* of lions

1むれる 蒸れる be steamed(蒸される); **get sweaty**(汗じみる) ▶もうご飯が十分**蒸れている**頃だ The rice should *be* well *steamed* by now.

▶一日中靴を履いていると足が**蒸れる** If you wear shoes all day, your feet will *get sweaty*.

2むれる 群れる throng ▶湖に白鳥が**群れている** Swans *are thronging* (*together*) on the lake.

むろん 無論 of course ▶**無論**彼女のことは覚えています *Of course* I remember her. ‖ きみは**無論**ぼくの考えに賛成だね *I am sure* you will agree to my idea. ‖ 運転手は**無論**(＝言うまでもなく), 乗客たちも大けがをした The passengers were badly injured, *to say nothing of* the driver [*not to mention* the driver]. →もちろん.

むんむん ▶窓を開けよう. 部屋が**むんむんしている** Let's open the windows ; it's *stifling* [*stuffy*] in here. (➤ stifling は「息が詰まる」, stuffy は「風通しが悪くてむっとする」) ‖ 会場は若者たちの熱気で**むんむんしていた** The hall was *pulsating* with the excitement of the young people.

む

め・メ

[1]め 目

📖 訳語メニュー
目 →eye 1
視力 →(eye)sight 2
視線 →eyes 3
目つき →look 4
経験 →experience 5
見方 →point of view 6

1【器官としての】 an **eye** ▶彼女は目が大きい She has big *eyes*. ‖ 目が痛い［かゆい］ My *eye* hurts [feels itchy]. ‖ 目がごろごろする I've got something gritty in my *eye*. (➤ gritty は「砂が入ったような」) ‖ どうしたの. 目が赤いよ What's the matter? Your *eyes* are bloodshot. ‖ 目に何か入った Something is in my *eye*. ‖ せっけんが目に入ってとてもしみる I got soap in my *eyes* [Soap got into my *eyes*], and it really stings. ‖ 彼女の目には涙が浮かんでいた I saw tears in her *eyes*. ‖ エミリーは緑色の目をしている Emily has green *eyes*. (➤日本人の「黒い目」は brown eyes または dark eyes という; black eye は殴られてできた「目の回りのあざ」) ‖ 目を開けて［閉じて］ごらん Open [Close] your *eyes*. ‖ 人と話すときは目を伏せずに相手の目を見なさい When you talk to someone, you should meet his [her] *eyes* without *looking down* [you should maintain eye contact]. ‖ 彼は目をしょぼつかせながら部屋から出て来た He came *blearily* out of his room. ‖ 自分の目で確かめたらどうですか How about checking it *with your own eyes*?

2【視力】 (eye)sight, vision →視力 ▶私は目がいい［悪い］ I have good [poor／bad] *eyesight*. ‖ 50歳を過ぎると目が弱る［悪くなる］ After fifty, your *eyesight* declines [worsens]. ‖ 最近目が悪くなったみたい. 黒板の字が見にくいの Recently, my *eyes* seem to have gotten worse. I have trouble making out the characters on the blackboard with ease. (➤ make out は見たり聞いたりしたものが「何であるかをなんとか理解できる」で, しばしば否定語とともに用いる) ‖ 私の目は(視力表の)1.0まで見える My *vision* is 1.0, which means I have twenty-twenty vision. 《参考》 have twenty-twenty vision はアメリカ式表現で,「20フィートの距離から検査表が右目, 左目とも読める」の意で, 正常視力をいう.
▶目の不自由な人 a *visually-impaired* person ‖ 目の見えない人 a *blind* person ‖ 彼は15歳のとき目が見えなくなった He *went blind* [*lost his eyesight*] when he was fifteen. (➤ lose one's eyesight は「失明する」に相当する) ‖ 伯父は(右の)目が見えない My uncle is *blind* (in his right eye).

3【視線】 eyes ▶試験中, 顔を上げたら先生と目が合ってしまった When I looked up during the test, *my eyes* met the teacher's. ‖ 先生のお宅にうかがったらすててこ姿で出てくるんだもの, 目のやり場に困ったわよ When we went to our teacher's home, he came out in *suteteko* [summer long johns]. We *were so embarrassed* we *didn't know where to look*. ‖ 彼ったら私と会ったとき目をそらしたのよ He *turned his eyes away* when he met me.

4【目つき】 a **look** ▶あらぬ疑いをかけられて同僚たちから白い目［不信の目］で見られた My colleagues were mistakenly suspicious of me and gave me *cold* [*distrustful*] *looks*. ‖ その男は私をおどすような［きつい］目でにらんだ The man gave me *a threatening* [*sharp*] *look*. ‖ 彼女は私に部屋から出て行くよう目で合図した She *winked at* me to leave the room. ‖ きみの目を見ればもうぼくを好きでないことがわかる Your *eyes tell* me that you don't love me any more. ことわざ 目は口ほどに物を言う The eyes are as eloquent as the tongue. (➤ The eyes speak volumes. (目は雄弁である) という言い方もある).

5【経験】 an **experience** /ɪkspíəriəns/ ▶パリではさんざんな目にあった I *had a terrible experience* in Paris. ‖ きょう会社でひどい目にあった I *had a tough time* at the office today. ‖ ニューヨーク市は危ないとよく言われるが, 私はこわい目にあったことがない They often say New York City is dangerous, but I *have* never *had anything scary happen* to me (there). ‖ どうして私がこんな目にあわなきゃいけないの What did I do to deserve this? (➤「こんな報いを受けるようなどんなことをしたのか」の意).

6【見方, 意見】 a **point of view** ▶事故の原因について専門家の目から見てどう思われますか What do you think about the cause of the accident from an expert's *point of view*? ‖ 親の目から見ると自分の子はちっとも成長していないように見える *In the eyes of* most parents, children never seem to grow up. ▶《慣用表現》新人は長い目で見て育ててやってほしい I would like you to *take a long-term view* in training the new employees.

7【会うこと, 見ること】 ▶お目にかかれて光栄です I'm glad to *meet* you. (➤ meet は紹介されて初めて会ったとき) ‖ またお目にかかりましたね It's good [nice] to *see* you again. ‖ どこかでお目にかかりましたか Don't I know you from somewhere? ‖ では, 広重の絵をお目にかけましょう I'll *show* you a Hiroshige picture. ／Let me *show* you a Hiroshige.

8【物の目】 ▶台風の目は硫黄島付近にあります The *eye* of the typhoon is over Iwo Jima. ‖ 《さいころ遊びで》いい目が出ますように I hope I can get *a lucky roll* [*spot*]. ▶この生地は目がつんでいる［粗い］ This fabric has a fine [loose] *texture*. ‖ 目の大きい［細かい］方眼紙を使いなさい Use graph paper with big [small] *squares*.

9【慣用表現】
目がきく ▶彼女は骨董品にかけては目がきく She *has an eye for* antiques. ／She *is expert in* appraising antiques. **目がくらむ** ▶自動車のヘッドライトに目がくらんだ I *was blinded* by the headlights of a car. ‖ 私は高い所に立つと目がくらむ(＝めまいがする) I *feel dizzy* in high places. ‖ 彼は欲に目がくらんで賄賂を受け取ったようだ It seems that he *was blinded* by greed and accepted the bribe. **目が肥えている** ▶このごろの若い人は着る物には目が肥えている Young people these days *can easily tell* good

clothes *from* bad. (➤「良し悪しをすぐ見分ける」の意). **目がさえる** ▶きのうは妙に目がさえて4時ごろまで眠れなかった I *was wide awake* and couldn't get to sleep till around 4 this morning. **目が覚める** ▶きょうは5時に目が覚めた I *woke* at five this morning. ‖ 彼女は目の覚めるようなピンクのドレスで現れた She appeared in a *shocking*-pink dress. **目が据わる** ▶あいつにはもう飲ませるな. 目が据わっている Don't give him anything more to drink. His *eyes look glassy* [*glazed*].

目が高い ▶このネクタイをお選びになるとはさすがにお目が高い You must be *a good judge of quality* to pick this tie. ／Picking this tie shows that you *have good taste*. (➤後者は「センスがいい」の意). **目が届く** ▶1クラス50人では担任の目が全員に届くはずがない(＝監督できない) If there are fifty students in a class, there's no way the teacher in charge can *take care of* all of them. **目がない** ▶私, 甘い物には目がないんです I have a sweet tooth. ／I'*m fond of* sweets. (➤後者は女性の好む言い方) ‖ 父はキャビアに目がない My father *has a weakness for* caviar. **目が離せない** ▶このくらいの年頃の子は目が離せない You *can't take your eyes off* children this age. **目が回る** ▶展望台から下を見下ろしたら目が回った(＝めまいがした) My *head swam* [*reeled*] when I looked down from the observation deck. (➤I felt dizzy when ... としてもよい) ‖ 昼休みの学生食堂は目が回るような忙しさだ It is *hectic* in the school cafeteria during lunch time. (➤hectic は「大忙しの」の意).

目から火が出る ▶ラグビーの試合でタックルされたときは目から火が出た I *saw stars* when I was tackled in the rugby game. **目じゃない** ▶部長なんて目じゃない. 目ざすは社長だ Becoming a general manager is *no big deal* to me. What I'm aiming at is becoming president. **目と鼻の先** ▶国会図書館なら議事堂のつい目と鼻の先です The National Diet Library is *just a stone's throw from* [is *within easy walking distance of*] the Diet Building.

目に余る ▶若者たちの無謀運転は目に余る I *can't stand* young people's reckless driving. ／The reckless way young people drive is *simply outrageous*. (➤前者は「がまんできない」, 後者は「あきれるほどだ」の意). **目に入れても痛くない** ▶孫は目に入れても痛くないほどかわいい I *love* my grandchild *more than anything else*. ／My grandchild is *the apple of my eye*. (➤the apple of one's eye は「非常に大切にしているもの」の意). **目に浮かぶ** ▶箱を開けたときの彼の驚いた顔が目に浮かぶ I *can imagine* [*picture*] his surprised face when he opens the box. (➤この picture は「心に描く」の意の動詞). **目に狂いはない** ▶あの選手をスカウトした私の目に狂いはなかった *My judgment was right* when I recruited that player.

目につく ▶岡山さんは背が高いから人込みでも目につく Mr. Okayama is tall and he *stands out* in a crowd. ‖ その理髪店は目につく[つきにくい]場所にある The barbershop *can be easily spotted* [*is hard to find*]. **目に留まる** ▶彼はテレビのディレクターの目に留まり, 俳優になった He *caught a* TV director's *eye* [*attention*] and landed an acting job. **目に入る** ▶長い入院生活のあと, 外界の目に入るものすべてが新鮮だった After a long stay in the hospital, everything I *saw* in the outside world looked fresh. ‖ 理恵は太郎にべたぼれで, 他の男性は目に入らないようだ Rie is madly in love with Taro and does*n't pay any attention to* other men. (➤後半を and doesn't give other men a (second) glance. (他の男性の方は(もう一度) ちらっと見ようともしない) としてもよい).

目には目, 歯には歯 An eye for an eye, a tooth for a tooth. **目に見える** ▶病気だった父は目に見えて回復してきている My father is *rapidly* recovering from sickness. ／My father is getting *noticeably* better. ‖ 彼のピッチングは目に見えて上達した He has made *remarkable* progress in his pitching. ‖ 彼が試験に落ちることは目に見えていた *Anyone could see* [*It was obvious*] that he would flunk the examination. **目にも留まらぬ** ▶リニアモーターカーは目にも留まらぬ速さで走って行った A maglev train sped away *faster than the eye could follow*. (➤「目で追えないほど速く」の意). **目に物見せる** ▶今度こそいじめっ子に目に物見せてやる I'll *teach* the bully *a lesson* [*give* the bully *a hard time*] this time.

目の色が変わる ▶美佐子は猫の話になると目の色が変わる When the conversation turns to (the subject of) cats, Misako *gets really engrossed* [*absorbed*]. **目の色を変える** ▶学校を辞めたいと言うと父は目の色を変えて怒った When I told my father that I wanted to quit school, he *blew his top*. (➤blow one's top は「激怒する」の意のインフォーマルな言い方). **目のかたき** →見出語 **目の黒いうち** ▶私の目の黒いうちは勝手は許しませんよ You'll have [get] your own way *over my dead body*. (➤文字通りには「私の死体を飛び越えて…しろ」から「絶対に…させないぞ」の意). **目のつけどころ** ▶きみの論文は目のつけ所がいいね Your *approach* to the subject in the paper is very good.

目の毒 ▶そのテレビショッピング番組は明子にとって目の毒だ. 見る物見る物が欲しくなる That TV shopping program is *tempting* to [*a temptation* for] Akiko. She wants to get everything she sees (on it). **目の前が暗くなる** ▶S商事の破産を聞いたときは目の前が真っ暗になった I *was stunned* when I heard that S Trading Company had gone bankrupt. (➤「ぼう然となった」の意).

目も当てられない ▶模擬試験の結果は目も当てられなかった I *couldn't bear to look at* the (awful) results of the trial examination. **目もくれない** ▶少年はおやつには目もくれず, バットを持って飛び出して行った The boy did*n't even glance at* his afternoon snack before rushing out with a bat in his hand.

目を疑う ▶(新聞の)その大見出しを見たときは目を疑った I *couldn't believe my eyes* when I saw the banner headline. **目を奪う** ▶ロビーにいた人たちは皆その有名な女優に目を奪われた All the people in the lobby *had their eyes glued to* that famous actress. (➤「目がくぎづけになった」の意). **目をおおう** ▶ガス爆発の事故現場の惨状は目をおおうばかりだった The horror at the site of the gas explosion was so bad that I *could not bear to look at* it. **目をかける** ▶監督はそのルーキーに目をかけている The manager *favors* the rookie. ‖ 課長にはずいぶん目をかけて(＝親切にして)もらった The section chief *was particularly kind to* me. **目をかすめる** ▶囚人たちは看守の目をかすめて壁に穴を掘った The convicts dug a hole through the wall when the prison guards were not looking. **目をくらます** ▶犯人は警察の目をくらますため, 逃走に別のライトバンを使った

The criminals used a different station wagon for their getaway to *deceive the eyes* of the police. **目を凝らす** ▶目を凝らして見たが, 洞くつの中は真っ暗で何があるのかわからなかった The cave was so dark (that) I couldn't make out what was in it, no matter how hard I *strained my eyes*. **目を覚ます** ▶目を覚まして現実を見ろよ! *Wake up* to reality! / *Wake up* and smell the coffee. ‖ あいつは詐欺師だ, わかってるだろ. いい加減に目を覚ませよ You know he's a con man. It's about time you *came to your senses*. **目を皿のようにする** ▶子供たちは卵からひながかえる様子を目を皿のようにして見た The children watched the egg hatch *with rapt attention* [*very attentively*]. / The children *were all eyes* when the egg hatched. **目を白黒させる** ▶男はステーキがのどに詰まって目を白黒させていた The man's *eyes were rolling* in agony when the piece of steak got stuck in his throat. **目をつける** ▶おれもあの子には前から目をつけてたんだ I, too, *have had an eye on* that girl. ‖ あの病院は脱税の疑いで税務署に目をつけられている That hospital *is under surveillance* [*is being watched*] by the tax office on suspicion of tax evasion. **目をつぶる** ▶目をつぶってごらん *Close your eyes*. ‖ ホームランを打ったからさっきのエラーには目をつぶってやろう I'll *overlook* your error now that you have hit a home run. **目を通す** ▶朝食を食べながらさっと新聞の見出しに目を通した I *scanned* [*browsed* (*through*)] the newspaper headlines while eating breakfast. (➤ scan は興味を引くものや目的のものがないか「さっと目を通す」) ‖ きみの報告書に目を通しておいたよ I *skimmed through* your report. (➤ skim は内容をつかむために「全体をさっと読む」) ‖ 誤りがないかこの作文に目を通していただけますか Could you please *look over* [*through*] this essay and check if there are any mistakes? **目を留める** ▶首相のボディーガードは群衆の中の不審な男に目を留めた The bodyguard of the Prime Minister *detected* [*noticed*] a suspicious-looking man in the crowd. **目を盗む** ▶数人の生徒たちが先生の目を盗んで学校で酒を飲んでいた Several students were drinking (alcoholic beverages) at school *behind* the teacher's *back*. **目を離す** ▶荷物から目を離さないように *Keep an eye on* your baggage. ‖ ちょっと目を離したすきにかばんがなくなった My bag disappeared when I *looked away* for a moment. **目を光らせる** ▶税関では麻薬の密輸に特に目を光らせている Customs *keeps an* especially *sharp eye out for* drug smuggling. (➤ keep an eye out for で「…を油断なく見張る」). **目を引く** ▶近頃, 女性作家の活躍が目を引く Recently, the achievements of women writers have *attracted attention*. / Lately, women writers have *been moving into the limelight*. (➤「脚光を浴びている」の意) ‖ はでなドレスを着た女性たちの中で, 品のよい着物姿の香織が目を引いた(=目だった) Among the women wearing brightly colored dresses, Kaori *stood out* in her elegant kimono. **目を細める** ▶孫娘のピアノ演奏を彼は目を細めて見ていた He *fondly* watched his granddaughter playing the piano. (➤「愛情を込めて」の意; 直訳して narrow one's eyes とすると人を疑うときの目つきになるので注意). **目を丸くする** ▶子供たちはスクリーンの怪獣に目を丸くした(=驚いて見た) The children *looked* at the monster on the screen *in amazement*. **目を回す** ▶彼は殴られて目を回した He *was knocked out* (*unconscious*). **目を見張る** ▶その選手は1年間で目を見張るほど上達した That player has improved *amazingly* over the past one year. **目をむく** ▶そう目をむいて怒るほどのことでもないだろう Don't *glare at* me like that over such a small thing!

☛ **お目にかかる, 見る目** (→見出語)

²め 芽 a **sprout** /spraʊt/, a **shoot** (将来枝になる芽); a **bud** (葉の芽, つぼみ); a **seedling** (種から出た芽) ▶この暖かい陽気で柳の**芽が出**始めた The willows are beginning to *bud* [*put forth bud* / *come into bud*] in this warm weather. ‖ 種から**芽が出た** The seeds *have sprouted*.

▶《比喩的》ようやく彼の商売も**芽が出た** At long last, his business *has begun to take off*. ‖ その力士は15年間角界にいたが, 結局**芽が出なかった** That sumo wrestler was active for fifteen years but *never got anywhere* [*never achieved much success*]. ‖ 悪は**芽のうちに摘まなければならない** Crime [Evil] must *be nipped in the bud*.

-め -目 **1【順序, 回数】**▶右から**3番目の**男の子が青木君です *The third* boy from the right is Aoki. ‖ あれが世界で**2番目に高い**山です That is *the second highest* mountain in the world. ‖ 対話「宇治駅はいくつ目ですか」「6つ目です」"*How many stops* is it to Uji?" "It's six stops from here." ‖ 何度同じことを言うの? 今度で**5度目よ** How many times are you going to repeat that? This is *the fifth*! ‖ 結婚**10年目**に私たちに子供が生まれた *In the tenth year* of our marriage, we had a baby.

2【程度】▶きみは**早め**に出発したほうがいいよ You'd better get an *early* start. ‖ ぼくは**太めの**女の子のほうが好きだ I prefer girls *on the plump side*. (➤ on the ... side は「…ぎみで」) ‖ お茶は濃いめにしてください Please make the tea strong.

めあたらしい 目新しい **novel**; **new** (新しい); **original** (独創的な) ▶**目新しい**デザイン *novel* [*eye-catching*] design (➤ eye-catching は「人目を引く」) ‖ ネパールでは見るものすべてが**目新しかった** Everything I saw in Nepal was *new* to me. ‖ きみの案には何も**目新しいもの**はないね There is nothing *new* [*original*] in your proposal.

めあて 目当て **1【目印】** a **guide**; a **landmark** (遠方からでもひときわ目立つ建築物) ▶我々は消防署の塔を**目当て**にしながらホテルに着いた We reached the hotel with the fire station tower as *a guide* [*landmark*].

2【目的】 a **purpose** ▶きみは何が**目当て**でぼくに取り入ろうとするんだ? For what *purpose* are you trying to play up to me? ‖ 私はお礼**目当てに**(=お礼を期待して)猫を捜してやったんじゃない I didn't look for the cat *expecting* a reward [*in expectation of* a reward]. ‖ 伊藤は近頃よく遊びに来るが, **お目当て**は実は妹らしい Ito has been coming to see me a lot recently, but in fact he seems to *be after* my (younger) sister. (➤ after は「…を求めて」) ‖ あの女は財産**目当て**に老実業家と結婚した That woman married the (rich) old businessman *for* money.

¹めい 姪 a **niece** /niːs/ ▶《紹介して》めいの久子です Let me introduce my *niece* Hisako.

²めい 銘 ▶この刀には村正の**銘**が入っている This sword has the *inscription* "Muramasa" on it.

めい- 名- **great** (偉大な); **famous** (有名な) ▶**名君** a

great monarch [lord] (➤ monarch は王や女王, lord は領主) ‖ 名犬 a dog that is famous for its intelligence, loyalty etc ‖ 名車 a *well-known* car ‖ 名将 a *great* general ‖ 名城 a *famous* castle ‖ 名水 *famous* spring water ‖ 名湯 a *famous* hot spring ‖ 名ピアニスト a *great* [*master*] pianist ‖ 名選手 a *great* [*famous*] player.

☛ 名演, 名画, 名器, 名曲, 名月, 名作, 名産, 名著, 名盤, 名訳 ほか(→見出語)

1めいあん 名案 a **good idea**, a **wonderful idea** ▶突然私に名案が浮かんだ *A good* [*wonderful*] *idea* came to me suddenly. /I hit on *a good idea* suddenly. ‖ そいつは名案だ That's *a good idea*.

2めいあん 明暗 **light and shade**(光と陰) ▶人生には明暗がある Life has (both) *bright and dark sides*. ‖ その1球が試合の明暗を分けた That pitch *decided* the game.

めいい 名医 a **skilled physician** [**doctor**](腕のいい医者); a **doctor with an established reputation**(定評のある医者).

めいうん 命運 ▶このプロジェクトには会社の命運がかかっている The *fate* of the company depends on this project.

めいえん 名演 an **excellent performance** ▶三郎の名演に観客は盛大な拍手を送った The audience applauded Saburo's *excellent* [*superb* / *impressive*] *performance*.

めいおうせい 冥王星《天文学》**Pluto**.

めいか 名家 a **prominent** [**well-known**] **family**.

めいが 名画 a **famous picture**(絵画); a **noted** [**an excellent**] **film**(映画) ▶きのう日本画の名画展を見に行った I visited an exhibition of *famous* Japanese *paintings* yesterday.

▶あの映画館で古い名画をやっている A *famous* old *film* is now showing at that movie theater.

めいかい 明快な **clear**; **understandable**(わかりやすい) ▶明快な説明 a *clear* explanation ‖ この辞書は定義が明快だ The definitions in this dictionary *are clear*. /This dictionary gives *clear* definitions. ‖ Y教授の講義はおもしろくて明快だ Professor Y's lectures are interesting and *easy to understand* [*follow*].

めいかく 明確な **definite** /défənət/, **clear** ▶政治家は明確な回答を避ける傾向がある Politicians tend to avoid making a *definite* answer. ‖ 三重方言と和歌山方言を明確に区別するのは私には難しい It's difficult for me to make a *clear* distinction [to *clearly* distinguish] between Mie and Wakayama dialects.

めいがら 銘柄 a **brand** ▶ウイスキーは銘柄によって価格に大きな差がある Whiskey prices differ greatly according to *brand*.

めいかん 名鑑 a **directory** ▶美術家名鑑 *a directory* of (noted) artists.

1めいき 名器 ▶このバイオリンは名器だ This violin is *famous* [*noted*] *for its excellence*.

2めいき 明記する **write clearly** ▶校則の中に生徒の禁煙を明記すべきだ It should *be clearly written* [*made clear*] in the school regulations that students are prohibited from smoking. ‖ 戦争の放棄は憲法第9条に明記されている The renunciation of war *is clearly stipulated* in Article 9 of the Constitution. (➤ stipulate は「規定する」).

3めいき 銘記 ▶「生者必滅」ということを心に銘記せよ "All living things must perish" are words you must *always bear firmly in mind* [are words you should *engrave in your memory*].

めいぎ 名義 a **name** ▶この土地は父の名義になっている This piece of land is in [under] my father's *name*. ‖ 私は不動産の一部を息子の名義に書き換えた I *transferred* part of my real estate to my son. (➤「譲渡した」の意).

‖名義貸し name-lending, a nominal transfer ‖ 名義変更 (a) change of ownership.

めいきゅういり 迷宮入り ▶その殺人事件は迷宮入りとなった The murder case *remains a mystery* [*remains unsolved*].

めいきょく 名曲 a **musical masterpiece**(傑作); a **famous** [**great**] **piece of music**(有名な[すぐれた]曲) ▶趣味はクラシックの名曲鑑賞です My favorite pastime is listening to classical music *masterpieces*. ‖『枯葉』は名曲中の名曲だ "Autumn Leaves" is *a masterpiece among masterpieces*.

メイク →メーキャップ.

めいげつ 名月 a **bright moon**; a **full moon**(満月)

‖中秋の名月 the harvest moon.

1めいげん 名言 a **wise** [**good**] **saying**, a **witty remark** ▶芥川は随筆でたくさんの名言を残した Akutagawa left a lot of *witty remarks* in his essays. ‖「時は金なり」というのは名言だ It *is aptly said* that time is money. (➤ aptly は「適切に, うまく」).

2めいげん 明言 a **definite statement** 一動 明言する **state** [**say**] **definitely**《that》; **declare**《that》(宣言する) ▶社長はことしは賃金カットはしない, と明言した The president *clearly stated* that there will be no pay cut this year.

1めいさい 明細 **details** ▶支出の明細が知りたいのです I would like to have *detailed information* on [about] the expenses. ‖明細書 a (detailed) statement(計算書); specifications(仕様書).

2めいさい 迷彩 ▶迷彩を施した装甲車 an armored car painted with *camouflage*.

‖迷彩服 camouflage fatigues [clothes].

めいさく 名作 a **masterpiece**(傑作); a **great work**(すぐれた作品) ▶『こころ』は漱石の名作の1つだ "Kokoro" is one of Soseki's *masterpieces* [*great*(*est*) *novels*]. ‖ この絵はダリの名作の1つだ This painting is one of Dali's *finest works*.

めいさん 名産 a **special product**; a **specialty** /spéʃəlti/(特産品) ▶三重県の名産は真珠だ Pearls are *a special product* of Mie Prefecture. /Mie is noted for its excellent pearls.

1めいし 名士 a **person of distinction**, a **noted person**; a **celebrity** /səlébrəṭi/ ((芸能・スポーツ関係の)有名人) ▶文壇の名士たち *prominent figures* in literary circles ‖ 多数の名士が一堂に会した Many *celebrities* met together in the hall.

2めいし 名刺 a **business card**, a **name card**

> **解説** **名刺について**
> (1) 業務用の名刺を指す一般的な語は business card であるが, 日本人が業務以外で自己紹介用に使う名刺は name card でよい.
> (2) 英米では名刺交換は一般的ではなく, 商取り引きに従事する人々は business card を使用するが, 一般人は名刺を持ち歩かない. ただし,《米》calling card,《英》visiting card と呼ばれる個人用名刺(通例, 氏名と住所のみ印刷)を他家などを訪問する際に使用する人はいる.

め

[3]めいし 名詞《文法》a **noun**
‖**可算名詞** a countable [count] noun ‖**固有名詞** a proper noun ‖**集合名詞** a collective noun ‖**抽象名詞** an abstract noun ‖**不可算名詞** an uncountable noun ‖**普通名詞** a common noun ‖**物質名詞** a material noun.

[1]めいじ 明示する **indicate clearly**; **specify** +目 (明細に述べる) ▶手紙には会合の場所が明示されていない The place of the meeting *is not clearly indicated* [*is not specified*] in the letter.

[2]めいじ 明治 ***Meiji*** ▶宮沢賢治は明治29年生まれだ Miyazawa Kenji was born in the 29th year of *Meiji*.
‖**明治維新** the Meiji Restoration ‖**明治時代** the Meiji era /fɪ́ərə/ ‖**明治天皇** the Emperor Meiji.

めいじつともに 名実ともに ▶ルービンシュタインは名実ともに一流のピアニストだった Rubinstein was one of the world's greatest pianists, *both in name and reality*.

めいしゃ 目医者 an **eye doctor**, an **ophthalmologist** /ɑ̀ːfθælmɑ́ːlədʒɪst/ (➤後者は「眼科医」に当たる堅い言い方).

めいしゅ 名手 ▶辻は守備の名手だった Tsuji was *an excellent fielder*. ‖舞の名手 *a notably accomplished dancer*.

めいしょ 名所 **the sights** (観光名所); a **famous** [**noted**] **place** (有名な場所); a **place of interest** (興味・関心を引く場所) ▶名所を見物する *see* [*do*] *the sights* (➤ do はやや古風) ‖私たちはローマの名所をたくさん見た We saw a lot of *famous places* in Rome. / We saw a lot of *places of* (*historical*) *interest* in Rome. ‖吉野は桜の名所だ Yoshino *is famous for its cherry blossoms*. (➤「桜で有名だ」の意).
‖**名所旧跡** famous places of scenic beauty and historical interest.
✉ **私の故郷は紅葉の名所です** The autumn [fall] foliage *is particularly beautiful* in my hometown.

[1]めいしょう 名称 a **name** ▶中国の正式名称は何といいますか What is the *official name* of China?

[2]めいしょう 名勝 a **place of scenic beauty** ▶東北の名勝の地を訪ねる visit *places of scenic beauty* in the Tohoku district.

めいしょく 明色 a **bright color**.

めいじる 命じる **1**【命令する】**order** +目; **command** +目 (指揮官などが; 堅い語); **tell** +目 (用を言いつける) ▶警察はデモ隊に解散を命じた The police *ordered* the demonstrators to disperse. ‖裁判所は会社に100万円の賠償を行うように命じた The court *ordered* the company *to* pay one million yen in damages. / The court *ordered that* the company (should) pay one million yen in damages. (→命令) ‖指揮官は兵士たちに「撃ちかたやめ」を命じた The officer *commanded* the soldiers to cease fire. ‖社長は秘書に書類のコピーを命じた The president *told* his secretary to make a copy of the paper.
2【任命する】**appoint** +目, **assign** /əsáɪn/ +目 (➤前者がより堅い語) ▶4月1日付けをもって販売課長を命ず *Appointed* (to the post of) section chief in the sales department as of April 1. (➤文頭に昇格者の氏名を書く).

めいしん 迷信 (a) **superstition** ▶鏡を割ると7年間不運だという迷信がアメリカにある There is *a superstition* in America that if a person breaks a mirror, he or she will have bad luck for seven years. ‖私は迷信を信じない I'm *not superstitious*.
✉ **日本にも迷信があります. 例えば夜に口笛を吹くと蛇が来るというんですよ** We also have some *superstitions* in Japan. For example, we say that if you whistle in the evening, a snake will come.
‖**迷信家** a superstitious person.

めいじん 名人 **1**【上手な人】an **expert** (熟練者, 専門家); a **master** (大家, 達人) ▶きみは金もうけの名人だね You are *an expert* at making money. / You've got the Midas touch. (➤ Midas は手に触れる物をすべて黄金に変える力を与えられたギリシャ神話の王の名; この故事から the Midas touch は「金もうけの才能」の意を表す) ‖川口さんは陶芸の名人だ Mr. Kawaguchi is *a master* at making pottery [*a master* potter]. ‖川野さんはアユ釣りの名人だ Mr. Kawano is a *skillful* ayu fisherman.
‖**名人芸** a masterly performance.
2【最高位の人】▶碁[将棋]の名人 *a* (*grand*) *champion* Go [shogi] player.

めいせい 名声 **fame**, **renown** (➤後者のほうが意味が強い) ▶世界的名声のある指揮者 a *world-famous* conductor ‖名声にあこがれる人は多い Many people *long for fame* [*to be famous*]. ‖吉本ばななは『キッチン』で名声を得た Yoshimoto Banana *gained fame* with her novel "Kitchen."

めいせき 明晰な **clear** ▶彼は頭脳明せきだ He *is a clear thinker*. / He *has a sharp mind* [*a clear intellect*]. ‖明せきな文章は明せきな思考から生まれるものだ *Clear* writing comes from *clear* thinking.

[1]めいそう 瞑想 **meditation** 一動 **めい想する** **meditate** /médɪteɪt/ ▶私はときどきめい想をしてストレスを解消する I practice *meditation* from time to time to get rid of stress. ‖あの高僧はめい想にふけっている That high priest *is lost in deep meditation*.
‖**めい想録** meditations.

[2]めいそう 迷走する **stray** (コースをそれる); **wander** (さまよう)
‖**迷走台風** a stray typhoon, a typhoon that takes an irregular course.

めいだい 命題《論理学》a **proposition**, a **thesis**.

めいちゅう 命中する **hit** +目 ▶ミサイルは的に命中した[しなかった] The missile *hit* [*missed*] the target.

めいちょ 名著 a **famous** [**notable**] **book** (有名な書物); a **great book** [**work**] (すぐれた書物); a **masterpiece** (傑作).

めいっぱい 目一杯 ▶ラジオのボリュームを目いっぱいあげてください Please turn up the radio *as far as it will go* [*as loud as possible*]. ‖短い休暇だったが私たちは目いっぱい楽しんだ It was a short vacation, but we enjoyed it *to the full*. (➤ to the full は「心ゆくまで」の意).

めいてい 酩酊 **intoxication** 一動 **酩酊する** **be intoxicated**.

めいてんがい 名店街 a **street of well-known stores** (通り); an **arcade** /ɑːrkéɪd/ **of noted stores** (デパートなどの) ▶母はあのビルの地下名店街でよく買い物をする My mother often shops at the underground *shopping mall* in that building.

[1]めいど 冥土 **the land of the dead**; **the other world** (あの世) ▶めい土に旅だつ go to *the other world* ‖めい土のみやげにオーロラを見たい I want to see the aurora borealis [the Northern Lights] *once in my life*. / I want to see the aurora borealis [the Northern Lights] (*once*) *before I die*.

2めいど 明度 brightness.

メイド a maid(➤ houseworker, household worker, housekeeper などの表現のほうが好まれる)

‖(ホテルの)ルームメイド a (room) maid, 《英また》a chambermaid.

1めいとう 名答 the right [correct] answer(正しい答え) ▶ご名答! You've guessed right! / You're right on the button! / An excellent answer!

2めいとう 迷答 an off-the-wall [interesting but wrong] answer ▶第3問には迷答がいくつもあったぞ There were several *off-the-wall answers* to Question 3.

めいにち 命日 ▶彼は祖父の命日に墓参りをした He visited the grave on *the anniversary of* his grandfather's *death*.

めいはく 明白な clear(はっきりしている); obvious(すぐに判断できる); evident(証拠がある); apparent /əpǽrənt/ (見た目に明らかな) ▶事故の原因は明白だ The cause of the accident is *clear* [*obvious*]. ‖少年がうそをついているのは明白だ It is *obvious* [*evident*] that the boy is lying.

めいばん 名盤 a great (phonograph) record.

めいびん 明敏な sharp(鋭敏な); bright(利発な); quick-witted(頭の回転の早い) ▶彼は明敏な頭脳の持ち主だ He is *sharp* [*bright*].

めいふく 冥福 ▶私はその事故の犠牲者の冥福を祈った I prayed for *the peaceful repose* of (the souls of) the victims of the accident. (➤ the peaceful repose of ... は「…の安らかな休息」の意).

✉ お母さまのご冥福をお祈りいたします I pray your mother's soul *may rest in peace*. / *May* your mother *rest in peace*. ➤「安らかに休息できますように」の意. →眠り.

めいぶつ 名物 **1**【名産】a special product, a specialty /spéʃəlti/ ▶ピーナツは千葉県の名物です Peanuts are *a regional specialty* of Chiba Prefecture. ‖ ことわざ 名物にうまい物なし Famous specialties often fail to live up to their reputations. (➤「評判ほどではない」の意).

2【評判のもの】an attraction ▶朝倉さんはこの大学の名物教授だ Mr. Asakura is *a popular professor* [*an institution*] at this university. (➤ institution は「(長い間そこにいて)名物的になった人」の意; 少しおどけた言い方).

✉ ラクダ乗りは鳥取砂丘の観光名物です Camel rides are a famous tourist attraction of the Tottori Sand Dunes.

めいぶん 名文 a beautiful passage(すぐれた文章); a literary gem(文学上の逸品) ▶石川淳ほどの名文家はもう出ないだろう There'll never be another *writer who writes prose as great as* Ishikawa Jun.

めいぼ 名簿 a list (of names); a directory /dəréktəri/ (住所が併記してあるもの); a roster /rɑ́:stəʳ/ (大学などの履修登録者名簿; 当直者名簿) ▶きみの名前が名簿に載っている[からもれている] Your name is on [is not on] the *list*. ‖この学生は私の名簿には登録されていないのに授業に出ている This student is attending my class, although he isn't listed on the (class) *roster*.

‖会員名簿 a membership directory [list] ‖顧客名簿 a customer list ‖乗客名簿 a passenger [boarding] list ‖選挙人名簿 a pollbook ‖同窓会[職員]名簿 an alumni /əlʌ́mnaɪ/ [a staff] directory.

めいみゃく 命脈 life ▶わが応援団の輝かしい伝統は今やかろうじて命脈を保っている The brilliant tradition of our cheerleading squad *barely survives*.

1めいめい 命名する name +目 ▶彼は赤ん坊を宏奈と命名した He *named* the baby Hirona. ‖インディアナ州のイエドは日本の江戸にちなんで命名された Yeddo, Indiana, *was named for* [*after*] Edo of Japan.

2めいめい 銘々 each ▶従業員にはめいめいロッカーがある *Each* employee has a locker. ‖生徒はめいめい弁当持参のこと All students are to bring their own lunches. (➤ Each student should bring his or her own lunch. とも書けるが, ぎこちない文になる) ‖願書はめいめいで出してください Would *each* of you please send in an application? ‖先生はクラスのめいめいに資料を配った The teacher passed materials out to *everyone* in the class.

‖銘々皿 a small individual plate.

めいもく 名目 (a) name 一形 名目上の nominal ▶彼は名目だけの理事だ He is a *nominal* director. / He is a director *in name only*. ‖その金は募金の名目で集められたが実際は半強制的なものだった The money was *ostensibly* a contribution but in fact was largely compulsory. (➤ ostensibly は「表向きは」) ‖ 対話「あいつら, 研修で伊豆へ出張だそうだ」「なあに, どうせ研修なんて名目だけさ」"I hear they are on a trip to Izu to attend a training camp." "That's *only an excuse* for partying." (➤「遊ぶための口実にすぎない」の意).

めいもん 名門 a distinguished [noted] family(名家) ▶その女性は名門の出だ That lady comes from *a distinguished family*. ‖東福岡高校はサッカーの名門だ Higashi-Fukuoka High School *is famous for its brilliant record* [*history*] in senior high school soccer tournaments.

‖名門校 a prestigious [prestige] school.

めいやく 名訳 an excellent [a fine] translation.

めいゆう 名優 a great actor [actress](すぐれた俳優) ▶オーソン・ウェルズは若くして名優と呼ばれるようになった Orson Welles established his name as *a distinguished actor* at an early age.

めいよ 名誉 (an) honor /ɑ́:nəʳ/ (誇りに思うこと); a privilege /prívəlɪdʒ/ (望外の喜び) 一形 名誉ある honorable ▶このような名のある劇場で公演できることは我々にとって大変な名誉です It is a great *honor* [*privilege*] for us to give a performance at a prestigious theater like this. ‖母校の名誉(=名前)を傷つけることのないよう全力を尽くします We'll do our best *not to disgrace the name* of our school. 《参考》これは日本的な考え方. 英語では to bring honor to our school (母校に名誉をもたらすために)のように前向きに考えるのがふつう ‖名誉にかけて(=誓って)うそはついていない *On my honor*, I (swear that I) didn't tell a lie. ‖彼は名誉毀(き)損で訴えられた He was sued for *libel*. (➤ libel /láɪbəl/ は「文書による名誉毀損」; 「発言による名誉毀損」は slander).

‖名誉会員 an honorary /ɑ́:nərəri/ member ‖名誉教授 a professor emeritus /ɪmérɪṭəs/ ‖名誉市民 an honorary citizen.

めいりょう 明瞭な clear(まちがいなく知覚・理解できる); distinct(相違が明らかな); articulate /ɑ:ʳ-tíkjələt/ (発音・言語がわかりやすい) ▶彼の発音は明りょうだ His pronunciation *is clear*. ‖明りょうな話し方はアナウンサーにとって不可欠のものだ *Articulate* speech is essential for an announcer. ‖彼女がデートを断った理由は簡単明りょう, きみが嫌いなのさ It is *simple and clear* why she turned down a date ; she simply doesn't like you. ‖ 政治家の発言はしばしば**明りょうさを欠く** Politicians' remarks *are* often *unclear* [*vague* / *ambiguous*].

☛ **不明りょう** (→見出語)

めいる 滅入る get depressed ▶ぼくはガールフレンドに振られて**気がめいっている** I'*m depressed* because I was dumped by my girlfriend. / I'*m feeling blue* because my girlfriend left me. ‖ こう天気が悪いと**気がめいってしまう** This bad weather *makes* me *feel blue* [*low*]. / This bad weather really *gets* me *down*.

めいれい 命令 an **order** ; a **command** (特に軍隊などでの絶対的な) 一動 **命令する order** +目, **command** +目 ; **tell** +目 (用を言いつける)

▶**命令**に従う obey *an order* ‖ **命令**を出す issue [give] *an order* ‖ 田宮君は上司の**命令**に背いたので, 支店に飛ばされてしまった Tamiya has been packed off to a branch office because he disobeyed his boss's *orders*. ‖ **命令は命令だ** *Orders are orders*. ‖ 中尉の**命令**で小隊は敵陣に突撃した The platoon rushed the enemy at the lieutenant's *command*. / At the lieutenant's *order*, the platoon charged the enemy. ‖ そういう**命令するような言い方**はやめてちょうだい Please don't *order* me *around* like that. (➤ order around は「(人に)あれこれ言いつける」).

【文型】
人(A)に…するよう命令する
order A **to** do
➤ A に向かって直接出す命令を意味する
order that A (**should**) do
➤ 間接的な場合もあり. しばしば, A (should) be done のように受け身形で用いる

▶コーチは選手たちに20回の腕立て伏せを**命令した** The coach *ordered* the players *to* do 20 push-ups. ‖ 部長はスタッフに計画を練り直せと**命令した** The manager *ordered* [*directed*] his staff *to* revise the plans. (➤ direct は「指示する」) ‖ 大統領は捕虜全員の即時解放を**命令した** The president *ordered that* all prisoners (*should*) be released immediately.

‖**命令形**《文法》the imperative form ‖ **命令文**《文法》an imperative sentence.

めいろ 迷路 a **maze** /meɪz/, a **labyrinth** /lǽbərɪnθ/ (➤ 後者はやや文語的) ▶**迷路**のような狭い曲がりくねった通り a *maze* [*labyrinth*] of narrow winding streets ‖ この**迷路**は1時間以内に抜けられなければ失格です You'll be disqualified if you fail to get through this *maze* within one hour.

めいろう 明朗な 1【明るい】cheerful ▶俊彦は**明朗快活な**青年だ Toshihiko is a (*bright and*) *cheerful* young man.

2【うそのない】clean (公正な) ; **clear** (明確な) ; **honest** (偽りのない) ▶**明朗な政治** *clean* [*honest*] politics ‖ 会計を**明朗化する** *make* the accounting *transparent* [*clear*].

めいわく 迷惑 trouble (煩わしいこと) ; (an) **annoyance** (いらいらさせる事・物) ; a **nuisance** /njúːsəns/, a **bother** (不愉快な行為・人) 一形 **迷惑な annoying** ; **inconvenient** (不都合な)

▶彼女にはたいへん**迷惑をかけた** I *gave* her a lot of *trouble*. ‖ いろいろご**迷惑をおかけして**申しわけありません I'm sorry to *have put* you *to* so much *trouble*. (➤ これから迷惑をかけそうな場合は I'm sorry to trouble [bother] you. のように言う) ‖ 人の**迷惑にならない**ようにしなさい Don't make *a nuisance* of yourself. / Don't be *a nuisance* [*a bother*] to others. ‖ 工事の騒音で我々は大変**迷惑している** We *are* very *disturbed* by the construction noise. ‖ ご**迷惑でなければ**途中までご一緒させてください If it isn't any *bother* [*trouble*], let me go with you part of the way. ‖ 車内での携帯電話の使用はほかのお客さまのご**迷惑**になりますのでご遠慮ください In consideration of the other passengers, please refrain from using cellphones on the train. (➤ consideration は「思いやり」).

☛ **ありがた迷惑** (→見出語)

¹メイン main ▶清水さんが**メイン**になってこの学会を作った Mr. Shimizu *played a key role* [*took the lead*] in organizing this academic society. ‖ 本日の**メインイベント**はイノキ対ウノキのタイトルマッチだ Today's *main event* is the title match between Inoki and Unoki. ‖ きょうの**メインディッシュ**はローストポークです Today's *main course* is roast pork.

‖**メインスタンド** the grandstand ‖ **メインストリート** the main street ‖ **メインテーブル** the main table.

²メイン Maine (アメリカ北東端の州 ; 略 ME, Me.).

めうえ 目上 one's **elder**, one's **senior** (年上の人) ; one's **superior** (上司) ▶**目上の人**をうやまいなさい Respect your *elders* [*superiors*].

めうつり 目移り ▶ごちそうがあり過ぎて**目移りがする** There are so many delicious dishes that I *can't decide which to choose*. (➤「どれを選んだらいいか決められない」の意).

メーカー a **manufacturer** /mæ̀njəfǽktʃərəʳ/, a **maker** ▶電器**メーカー** an electrical appliance *manufacturer* [*maker*] ‖ 医薬品**メーカー** a drug *maker* ‖ 日本の自動車**メーカー**数社がアメリカに工場を持っている Several Japanese *automakers* [*car manufacturers*] have factories in the USA.

‖**メーカー希望小売価格** the manufacturer's suggested retail price ‖ **メーカー品** a brand-name product.

> **危ないカタカナ語✸ メーカー**
> 「製造業者」の意味の「メーカー」は manufacturer または maker という. maker は automaker, dressmaker, watchmaker のように複合語として使われることが多い.

メーキャップ makeup, make-up /méɪkʌp/ 一動 **メーキャップする make up, put on** (one's) **makeup** ▶彼女は**メーキャップ**をしていない She has no *makeup* on. / She isn't wearing *makeup*.

メーク →メーキャップ.

メーター a **meter** /míːt̬əʳ/ ▶毎月検査員が来てガスの**メーター**を調べていく The inspector comes and reads the *gas meter* once a month.

‖(タクシーの)**料金メーター** a taximeter.

メーデー May Day ▶**メーデー**の集会に参加する take part in *a May Day rally*.

メートル a **meter** /míːt̬əʳ/ ▶それは長さ[深さ]が3**メートル**ある It is three *meters* long [deep]. ‖ 日本では**メートル法**を採用している We use [are on] *the metric system* in Japan.

メール mail (郵便物) ; (an) **email**, (an) **e-mail** (電子メール), a **text message** (携帯メール)

《解説》(1) 日本語でいう「メール」は電子メールや携帯メールを指すことが多いが, 英語ではそれぞれ, email [e-mail], text message という. mail は発送または配達される「郵便物」を指すのがふつう. mail は Ⓤ 扱いなので, email も本来は Ⓤ 扱いだが, message が省略されたものと感じて, Ⓒ 扱いすることも多い. 具体的には数字や many, a few など数に結びつく語がつくと Ⓒ に, much, little など量に結びつく語がつくと Ⓤ になる. a lot では Ⓒ も Ⓤ もある.
(2) 携帯電話でメールすることは text messaging または texting という.

▶メールを送っといたけど読んでくれた？ I sent *an email* (*message*). Have you read it？ ‖ ご質問はメールでお寄せください Questions may be sent *by email* [*by text* (*message*)].
▶日程が決まったらメールして Please *email* [*text*] *me* when the date is fixed. (➤この email [text] は動詞) ‖ 私は友におわびのメールをしておいた I *emailed* [*texted*] my friend *an apology*. ‖ 姉は携帯電話を友だちへの通話よりメールに使うことのほうが多い My sister uses her cellphone to *text* her friends more often than to call them.
‖チェーンメール chain mail ‖ 迷惑［スパム］メール spam (email)；junk (e)mail (➤ junk mail はダイレクトメールも含む).

メカ ▶私はメカ(＝機械)に弱い I'*m not mechanical*. ／I'*m not mechanically-minded*. ‖ 父はメカに強く, 電気製品や車など何でも直せます My father *knows quite a bit about machinery*. He can repair electrical appliances, cars, and lots of other things.

メガ 《コンピュータ》 **mega-** (➤ 100万または2の20乗を表す) ▶メガバイト a *mega*byte. ⇀メガバイト, メガヘルツ.

めかくし 目隠し a **blindfold** (目をおおうもの) 一動 目隠しをする **blindfold** ＋㊐ ▶スイカ割り遊びをするとき, 棒を持った人は目隠しをする In the game of "split-the-watermelon," we *put a blindfold over the eyes* of the person with the stick.
▶目隠し(＝おおい)のため窓際に木を植えた We planted trees by the window to *screen* the inside of the house *from view*.

めかけ 妾 a **mistress**；a **kept woman** (囲い者).

めがけて 目がけて ▶ライオンは獲物目がけて飛びかかった The lion jumped *at* its prey. ‖ 走者はゴール目がけてまっしぐらに走った The runners ran like mad *toward* the goal.

めがしら 目頭 ▶戦争孤児が母親と再会した光景をテレビで見て目頭が熱くなった(＝感動した) I *was moved to tears* when I saw a war orphan being reunited with his [her] mother on TV. ‖ 母は息子の雄姿を見てそっと目頭を押さえた When she saw her son's proud appearance, the mother *wiped* (*away*) *her tears* [*dabbed at her eyes*].

めかす **dress up** (盛装する)；**primp** (鏡を見て, 服や髪を直す) ▶まりちゃん, やけにめかしこんでるじゃない？ You'*re* quite *dressed up* [*primped*], aren't you, Mari？ (➤ be spruced up, be dressed to kill, be dolled up などともいう).

めかた 目方 **weight** ▶目方で売る sell by *weight* ‖ その力士は最近目方が増えた［減った］ The sumo wrestler *has gained* [*has lost*] *weight* recently. ‖ この小包の目方を量ってください Can you please *weigh* this parcel？ ⇀体重.

メカニズム a **mechanism** /mékənìzəm/ ▶コンピュータのメカニズム the *mechanisms* of a computer ‖ 記憶のメカニズムはまだよくわかっていない The *mechanism* of memory still remains a mystery.

めがね 眼鏡 (a **pair of**) **glasses**, (a **pair of**) **spectacles** (➤ 前者がふつう)；**goggles** (水泳・スキーなどの) ▶縁なしの眼鏡 rimless *glasses* ‖ 眼鏡を掛ける［外す］ put on [take off] one's *glasses* ‖ ずいぶん度の強い眼鏡を掛けているね You are wearing very strong [thick] *glasses*, aren't you？ (➤ thick は「(レンズが)厚い」) ‖ 新しい眼鏡を買った I got new *glasses* [a new pair of *glasses*].
▶《慣用表現》姉には, 母のめがねにかなうような男性は見つかりそうにない It's not likely that my (older) sister will be able to find a man who *can measure up to my mother's expectations* [*can win my mother's favor*]. (➤ 前者は「期待に添える」, 後者は「気に入られる」の意. measure up の代わりに come up ともいう).
‖眼鏡店 an optician's (店)；an optician (人) 《参考》検眼をし, 処方せんを書く資格のある人を ophthalmic /ɑːfθǽlmɪk/ optician (検眼眼鏡士), その処方せんによって眼鏡を作って売る人を dispensing optician (処方眼鏡士) という. 《米》では前者を optometrist /ɑːptɑ́ːmətrɪst/ といい, optician といえば後者を指す.

メガバイト 《コンピュータ》 a **megabyte** 《略 MB》.

メガヘルツ **megahertz** 《略 MHz》(➤単複同形；周波数の単位). ⇀ヘルツ.

メガホン a **megaphone** ▶メガホンを使って話す speak through *a megaphone*.

めがみ 女神 a **goddess** ▶幸運の女神 *Lady Luck* (➤運・不運を司る女神) ‖ 勝利の女神が我々にほほ笑んだ *Victory* smiled on us.

めきき 目利き a **good judge**；a **connoisseur** /kɑ̀ːnəsə́ːʳ/ (鑑定家) ▶彼は書画にかけてはひとかどの目利きだ He is *a good judge* [*a connoisseur*] of paintings and calligraphic works.

メキシコ **Mexico** 一形 メキシコの **Mexican**
‖メキシコ人 a Mexican.

めきめき **remarkably** (めざましく) ▶彼は英語がめきめき上達した He has made *remarkable* progress in English.

めキャベツ 芽キャベツ (**Brussels** /brʌ́səlz/) **sprouts** (➤ 通例複数形で用いる).

-めく ▶すっかり春めいてきた It's getting quite *spring-like* [*like spring*]. ‖ 和夫のことばは皮肉めいて聞こえる There is *a touch of irony* in what Kazuo says. (➤ touch は「気味」) ／What Kazuo says sounds *somewhat sarcastic*.

めくじら 目くじら ▶ささいなことに目くじらを立てるな Don't *carp* (at me) *about* such trivial things.

めぐすり 目薬 **eye drops**；(an) **eyewash**, (an) **eye lotion** (洗眼液) ▶目薬をさす put some *eye drops* in one's eyes.

めくばせ 目配せ a **wink** 一動 目くばせする **wink** 《at》 ▶彼らは互いに目くばせした They *exchanged glances*. ‖ 彼は私に意味ありげに目くばせした He *gave* me *a* meaningful *wink* [*winked at* me meaningfully]. ‖ 彼はすぐ出発するように私たちに目くばせした He *indicated with his eyes* that we should leave at once.

めくばり 目配り ▶新人に対してはしばらくの間いろいろと目配りしてやらねばならない We have to *look after* the newcomers for the time being. ‖ プールの監視人

は子供たちに絶えず目配りをしていた The lifeguard at the swimming pool *kept a constant watch on* the children.

めぐまれる 恵まれた **gifted**(才能など生まれつきのものに); **lucky**(幸運な) ▶才能に恵まれたピアニスト a *gifted* pianist ‖ 彼女は絵の才能に恵まれている She *is gifted with* artistic talent. ‖ こんな良い環境で育つきみたちは恵まれている You *are lucky* to grow up in such a good environment. ‖ 彼女は恵まれた生活を送っている She's leading *a comfortable life*. ‖ 彼はいろいろなものに恵まれている He *has a lot going for* him. (➤「能力, 財産, 美貌など, 幸運な人生を送るために有利なものがそろっている」の意).

▶世の中には恵まれない人が大勢いる There are many *underprivileged people* in the world. (➤ underprivileged は poor のえん曲語).

〘文型〙
好ましいもの(A)に恵まれている
be blessed with A

▶その俳優は美貌[美声]に恵まれている The actor *is blessed with* good looks [a sweet voice]. ‖ 南アフリカは豊かな鉱物資源に恵まれている South Africa *is blessed with* abundant mineral resources. ‖ 運動会は好天に恵まれた Our athletic meet *was blessed* [*was favored*] *with* fine weather.

めぐみ 恵み a **blessing**(恩恵); **charity**(施し) ▶農作物は自然の恵みである Agricultural products are *a blessing from nature*. ‖ 中日ドラゴンズにとって, それは恵みの雨だった It turned out to be *a welcome rain* for the Dragons.

めぐむ 恵む **give** +⑩ ▶100円恵んでよ Will you please *give me* 100 yen?

めぐらす 巡らす 1【囲む】**surround** +⑩ (取り囲む); **enclose** +⑩ (四方八方を囲む) ▶農夫は果樹園にさくを巡らした The farmer *surrounded* [*enclosed*] the orchard with a fence.

2【考える】▶子供たちはいじめっ子をわなにはめようと計略を巡らした The children *cooked up* a scheme to trap the bully.

-めぐり -巡り ▶お寺巡りをする make *a tour* of [*a pilgrimage* to] Buddhist temples(➤ pilgrimage は「巡礼の旅」) ‖ 我々は奈良の名所巡りを楽しんだ We enjoyed *sightseeing* in Nara. ‖ 島巡りをするにはどの船に乗ってもかまいません It doesn't matter which boat you take to *go around the islands*.

めぐりあう 巡り会う **meet (by chance)** ▶宏美は10年ぶりにかつての恋人に巡り会った Hiromi *met* her ex-boyfriend *by chance* for the first time in ten years. / Hiromi *happened to meet* her ex-boyfriend after a separation of ten years.

めぐりあわせ 巡り合わせ ▶不思議な巡り合わせでぼくは昔の恋人と隣どうしで住むようになった *By a curious* [*strange*] *chance of fortune*, I ended up living next door to my ex-girlfriend. ‖ きみは彼女とは結婚できない巡り合わせなのだ I'm afraid you'*re* not *fated to* marry her.

めくる 捲る 1【裏返す】**turn (over)** ▶本をぱらぱらめくる *leaf through* a book ‖ ページをめくりなさい *Turn* the page. ‖ 猫が寒そうにしていたので, 布団をめくってやったらもぐりこんできた Because the cat seemed to be cold, I *lifted* the comforter and let her sneak in.

2【はぎ取る】**tear** /teəʳ/ **off** ▶カレンダーを1枚めくり取る *tear off* a leaf from the calendar.

めぐる 巡る 1【移る】**come around**(回って来る) ▶雪国に春が巡って来た Spring *has come* [*has rolled*] *around* to the snow country. ‖ 養蜂家たちは花を求めて日本中を村から村へと巡り歩く Beekeepers *travel* [*move*] all over Japan from one village to another in search of flowers and blossoms.

2【中心にする】▶兄弟たちは遺産をめぐって争っている The brothers are at odds with each other *over* the inheritance.

めくれる 捲れる ▶風で机の上の本のページがめくれた The wind *turned over* some pages of the book on the desk.

めげる **feel discouraged**(気がくじける) ▶全くめげちゃうよ I *feel* really *down*. ‖ 彼女は簡単にめげたりしない Nothing *gets* her *down*. (➤ get ... down は「…の元気をくじく」の意のインフォーマルな言い方) / She isn't the type to get down in the dumps over nothing. (➤ get down in the dumps は「ふさぎ込む」の意のインフォーマルな言い方) ‖ 幾多の困難にもめげず, 彼はエベレストの登頂に成功した *Undaunted* by hardships [*Not discouraged* by difficulties], he conquered Mt. Everest.

めさき 目先 1【当座】▶目先の利益を追う try to gain an *immediate* profit ‖ 目先のことばかり考えるな Don't think only of *the present*. / Don't *be shortsighted*.

2【先の見通し】▶あの男は目先がきく[きかない] He *has foresight* [*is lacking in foresight*]. (➤ foresight は「先見の明」).

めざし 目刺し (a **string of**) **salted and dried sardines** /sɑːʳdíːnz/ (イワシの).

めざす 目指す **aim** ((at, for, to do)) ▶相撲取りになるのなら横綱を目指すべきだ If you enter the sumo world, you should *aim to* become a yokozuna. ‖ 全部員が優勝を目指して練習に励んでいる All the club members are practicing all out *aiming at* the championship. (➤ all out は「全力をあげて」) ‖ 観測船は南極大陸を目指して(=に向けて)出航した The observation ship set out *for* Antarctica.

✉ **あなたはどこの大学を目指していますか. 私は東大です** Which college are you *aiming at*? For me, it's the University of Tokyo.

めざとい 目ざとい **keen-** [**sharp-**] **eyed** ▶優秀な校正者は小さなミスプリントも目ざとく見つける An excellent proofreader has a *keen* [*sharp*] eye for the slightest misprint. ‖ 彼女は人込みの中に目ざとく私を見つけて手を振った She *quickly* spotted me in the crowd and waved to me.

めざまし 目覚まし 1【時計】an **alarm clock** ▶目覚ましを5時にセットした I set the *alarm clock* for [to ring at] five. ‖ 6時に目覚ましが鳴った My *alarm* rang [went off] at six. (➤ go off は「急にやかましく鳴る」).

2【眠け覚まし】an **eye-opener** ▶私は目覚ましにコーヒーを1杯飲んだ I drank a cup of coffee for *an eye-opener*.

めざましい 目覚ましい **remarkable**(著しい); **marvelous** [((英)) **marvellous**](感嘆する[驚く]ほど) ▶最近の彼女の英語の上達ぶりにはめざましいものがある Her English has made *remarkable* progress recently. ‖ その投手はことしの日本シリーズでめざましい活躍をした The pitcher performed *outstandingly well* in this year's Japan Series.

めざめる 目覚める 1【目が覚める】**wake up, awake**

(➤ 前者がふつう) ▶けさは5時に目覚めた I *woke up* at five this morning. ‖ 春になると冬眠していた動物たちは長い眠りから目覚める When spring comes, animals that have been hibernating *wake up* from their long sleep.

2【自覚する】▶息子は性に目覚めたようだ My son seems to *have become sexually aware* [*have awakened sexually*]. ‖ きみは現実[変わりゆく世界]に目覚めなくてはならない You should *open your eyes to* reality [the changing world].

めざわり 目障り an **eyesore**(目ざわりな物) ▶古都に高い建物は目ざわりだ A tall building in a historic city *is an eyesore* [*spoils the view*]. (➤ 後者は「眺めを損なう」の意).

めし 飯 **(boiled) rice**(ごはん) ; a **meal**(食事) ▶飯を炊く cook [boil] *rice* ‖ 飯にしようよ Let's have [take] *a meal*. (➤ ふつうは have lunch, have dinner と具体的にいう) ‖《慣用表現》父は三度の飯より釣りが好きだ My father likes fishing *better than anything else*. ‖ このまま不景気が続けば飯の食い上げだ We'll *starve* if this recession continues. (➤ starve は「餓死する」) ‖ 彼は雑誌のコラムの執筆で飯を食っている He *makes* [*earns*] *his living* by writing columns for magazines.

めしあがる 召し上がる ⚠これは「飲む」「食べる」の尊敬語であるが, 英語にはこれの対応語がないので, 例文のように would like to have [drink] や help oneself to の形を使ってていねいさを表すしかない. ▶何を召し上がりますか What *would you like to have*? ‖ 何か飲み物を召し上がりますか *Would you like* something to drink? ‖ どうぞフライドチキンを召し上がってください Please *help yourself to* the fried chicken.

めした 目下 one's **junior**(年下の人) ; one's **subordinate** /səbɔ́ːrdənət/ (自分より地位の低い人) ▶彼は目上の人にも目下の者にも礼儀正しい He is polite to both his *juniors* as well as (to) his seniors.

めしつかい 召使い a **(domestic) servant**.

めしべ 雌蕊《植物学》a **pistil**.

[1]メジャー《巻き尺》a **tape measure**
‖メジャーカップ a measuring cup.

[2]メジャー《主要な》**major** /méɪdʒər/ ▶彼はメジャー(リーグ)で通用するだろうか I wonder if he has the ability to succeed in *major league baseball*. **‖メジャーリーグ** the Major Leagues, the Majors.

めじり 目尻 ▶彼女は目じりがつり上がっている She has *upward slanting eyes*. ‖ 年を取ると目じりにしわがよる When you get old, you get crow's-feet. (➤ crow's-feet は「目じりのしわ」, いわゆる「カラスのあしあと」). ▶祖父は孫たちに囲まれて目じりが下がりっぱなしだ Surrounded by his grandchildren, the grandfather *is all smiles*. (➤ be all smiles は「満面に笑みを浮かべている」の意).

めじるし 目印 a **mark**(しるし) ; a **landmark**(目標となるもの) ▶地図に目印をつける put *a mark* on a map ‖ 目印にページの端を折る fold down a corner of a page *to mark* the place / make a dog-ear ‖ きみの家に行くとき, 何か目印はあるかい? Are there any *landmarks* to help me find your home?
✉ **空港まで出迎えをお願いします. 私は目印に赤い野球帽をかぶっています** Can you please come to the airport to meet me? I'll be wearing a red baseball cap *so that you can recognize me* [*find me easily*]. ➤ 前者は「あなたが私だとわかるように」の意.

めじろ 目白《鳥》a **(Japanese) white-eye**.

めじろおし 目白押し ▶1月のテレビはスポーツ番組が目白押しだ The January TV schedule *is crowded with* sports programs.

めす 雌 a **female** /fíːmeɪl/,《インフォーマル》a **she**
—形 雌の female, she- ▶これは雌犬です This is *a female dog* [*a bitch*]. (➤ bitch はインフォーマルでは「あばずれ, あま」の意の軽べつ的な語として用いることが多いので, 前者を用いるのがよい) ‖ この猫は雄ですか, 雌ですか Is this cat a he or *a she* [a male or *a female*]?

メス a **scalpel**, a **surgical knife** ▶外科医が患部にメスを入れた The surgeon inserted his *scalpel* into the affected part. ‖《比喩的》警察がその事件にメスを入れ始めた The police began to *investigate* [*probe into*] the case. (➤ probe into は「探る」).

> **危ないカタカナ語✹ メス**
> **1** 外科医が手術のときに用いる「メス」はオランダ語の *mes* からきている. 英語では scalpel または surgical knife という.
> **2** 比喩的に「(事件などに)メスを入れる」という場合, 英語ではこれらの語を使わず, 「探る」の意味ならば investigate や probe into を, 「根本的な処置をする」の意味ならば take drastic measures [steps] などを用いる.

めずらしい 珍しい **rare**(まれな) ; **unusual**(ふつうでない) ; **unique**(独特の) ; **uncommon**(一般には見られない) ▶珍しい鳥 a *rare* (kind of) bird ‖ 4月に雪とは珍しい It's *rare* [*unusual*] to have snow in April. ‖ きみに食欲がないなんて珍しいね It's *unusual* for you to have no appetite, isn't it? ‖ おまえが英語で100点取ったって? 珍しいことがあるもんだ You got a perfect score in English? *That's certainly unusual* for you. ‖ 佐渡島には珍しい風習が残っている Sado Island retains some *unique* [*uncommon*] customs. ‖ メキシコでは見るものすべてが珍しかった The things I saw in Mexico *were* all *new to me*. ‖ 父さんがケーキを買ってくるなんて珍しい. 雪でも降るんじゃないかしら It is quite *out of the ordinary* for my dad to bring home a cake. I wonder what will happen next. (➤ 英語では珍しいことの強調に,The next thing you know it'll start snowing. という言い方がある. 珍しい出来事なら何でも使える. この場合 It is quite out of the ordinary for my dad to bring home a cake. The next thing you know it'll start snowing. のようにいう) ‖ 最近ではキリスト教国でも死者を火葬に付すことは珍しくない Nowadays, cremation (of the dead) *is not uncommon* even in Christian countries.

> **あなたの英語はどう響く?**
> 「あなたの名前は珍しいですね」のつもりで Your name is *strange*. などとしてはいけない. 「へんてこな名前ですね」というニュアンスになるからである. この場合は unusual や uncommon を使うのが正しく, 「非常に珍しい」ならば rare でもよい. しかし, 相手の名前が珍しいからといって, それを話題にするのは避けるほうがよい.

▶父は私がタヒチから持ち帰った貝殻を珍しがった My father *marveled* over the seashells I brought back from Tahiti. ‖ そのアメリカ人の少年はタヌキを珍しそうに見つめた The American boy gazed at the tanuki raccoon *amazedly* [*interestedly* / *with curiosity*]. ‖ この夏は珍しく涼しかった This summer has been *exceptionally* [*unusually*] cool. ‖ いやあ, これはこれは珍しい所で会いましたね What a surprise to meet you here!／*Fancy* meeting you *here*. (➤ Fancy doing は「…するなんて驚いた」の意で,《英》に多い言い方)／Well, well. This is *the last place* I expected to see you! ‖ 彼の机(の上)は珍しく片付いている His desk is tidy *for a change*. (➤ for a change は「ふだんと違って」).

めせん 目線 ▶あの子はばっちりカメラ目線を決めていた She *looked straight at* [*into*] *the camera*. (➤「まともにカメラを見て」の意) ‖ 消費者の目線で商品を開発する必要がある We need to develop products *from a consumer('s) perspective* [*standpoint*]. ‖ 彼はよく上から目線でものを言うから好きでない I don't like him because he tends to speak *in a patronizing way* [*as if he thinks he's more important*]. (➤ 前者は「相手を一人前扱いしないで見下すようにして」, 後者は「自分は人より偉いと考えているかのように」の意).

メゾソプラノ《音楽》(a) **mezzo-soprano**.

めそめそ ▶令子はおセンチで, すぐめそめそする(＝涙ぐむ) Reiko is such a softie and easily *gets tearful*.

めだか《魚》a ***medaka***, a **killifish** ▶メダカの群れ a school of *killifish*.

めだつ 目立つ **stand out**(際立っている); **show up**(はっきり見える); **be conspicuous** /kənspíkjuəs/ (人目を引く) 一形 **目だった** **remarkable, striking** ▶かおるははでな服を着ていたので目だった Kaoru *stood out* [*was conspicuous*] among the others because of her showy dress. ‖ この黄色のジャケットはオートバイに乗るときに暗い場所で目だつ This yellow jacket *shows up* in the dark when I ride my motorcycle. ‖ その会社はことし目だった実績をあげた The company has performed *remarkably* well this year. ‖ 働く高齢者の数が目だって増えてきた The number of elderly people who still work has increased *remarkably* [*noticeably*]. (➤ noticeably は「はっきりわかるほど」).
▶目だたない人 an *inconspicuous* person ‖ こんな装丁では書店で目だたない This book jacket *won't draw (people's) attention* in bookstores. (➤「注目を引かない」の意) ‖ 日本の労働者の多くは職場で目だたないようにしている Many Japanese workers try to *keep a low profile* at the office. (➤ keep a low profile /próofaıl/ は「低姿勢をとる」).
▶美恵子は目だちたがり屋だ Mieko *likes to draw* [*get*] *attention*.／Mieko is *a show-off*.

メタノール《化学》**methanol** /méθənɔ:l/.

メタボ ▶メタボ体型の人 a person *with a midriff bulge* (➤「おなかの出っ張った」の意).
‖ **メタボリック症候群** metabolic syndrome.

めだま 目玉 an **eyeball** →目の玉 ▶目玉をぎょろつかせる roll [goggle] one's *eyes* ‖ その外車には目玉が飛び出るような値がついていた That imported car had an *eye-popping* price (tag). ‖ **目玉商品** a (loss) leader ‖ **目玉番組** a special-feature program.
☛ 大目玉, お目玉 (→見出語)

めだまやき 目玉焼き a **sunny-side up egg** ▶卵は目玉焼きにしてください I'd like my egg(s) (*fried*) *sunny-side up*.

メダリスト a **medalist** ▶彼女は柔道の金メダリストだ She is *a gold medalist* in judo.

メタル (a) **metal** ▶メタルフレームの眼鏡 *metal-rimmed* glasses.

メダル a **medal** ▶彼はスピーチコンテストで金[銀／銅]メダルを授与された He was awarded a gold [silver／bronze] *medal* in the speech contest.

メタンガス《化学》**methane** /méθeın/ **gas**.

めちゃくちゃ 滅茶苦茶な **messy** (乱雑な); **unreasonable** (話にならない); **outrageous** (けしからぬ) ▶机の上がめちゃくちゃだ My desk is *a mess*.／Everything is *in disorder* on my desk. ‖ テストの点が悪かったから来月の小遣いは半分にするなんてめちゃくちゃだ It's *unreasonable* [*outrageous*] to cut my allowance in half next month just because I got a low score on the test. ‖ 今週はめちゃくちゃに忙しかった I've been *insanely* [*super*] busy this week. ‖ あのぐうたら亭主は彼女の人生をめちゃくちゃ(＝台なし)にした Her lazy husband *ruined* her life.

めちゃめちゃ 滅茶滅茶 ▶隣の犬が入って来てうちの庭をめちゃめちゃにした The neighbor's dog *made a total mess of* our garden. (➤ mess は「混乱した[乱雑な]状態」の意) ‖ スポーツカーが塀に激突してめちゃめちゃになった A sports car crashed into the wall and *was totaled*. ‖ 地震で棚から花びんが落ちてめちゃめちゃに(＝粉々に)こわれた During the earthquake, a vase fell from the shelf and broke *into smithereens*.

メチルアルコール《化学》**methyl** /mèθəl/ **alcohol, methanol**.

メッカ a **mecca** (あこがれの土地) ▶バリ島のクタビーチはサーファーたちのメッカだ Bali's Kuta Beach is *a mecca* for surfers.

めつき 目つき a **look** ▶鋭い目つき a sharp *look* ‖ あの男は目つきが悪い He has a menacing [nasty] *look*. (➤ menacing は「威嚇的な」, nasty は「いじわるそうな」) ‖ 彼女は怒ったような目つきで私を見た She gave me an angry *look*.

めっき **plating** (金属の); **gilding** (金の) ▶金めっきのスプーン a *gold-plated* [*a gilded*] spoon ‖ この皿はめっきがはげてきた The *gilt has come off* from this dish.
▶《比喩的》彼女は英語がわかると言っていたが, 面接でめっきがはげてしまった She had pretended to know English, but *the truth came out* [*she betrayed herself*] during the interview.

めっきり **noticeably** (はっきりわかるほど) ▶父は最近めっきり白髪が増えた My father's hair has gotten *quite a bit* [*noticeably*] whiter lately. ‖ 10月に入ってめっきり涼しくなった It's gotten *noticeably* [*appreciably*] cooler since the beginning of October.

めっけもの 目っけ物 a **find** (➤ 人についても用いることができる) ▶この古本は本当にめっけ物だ This second-hand book is a real *find*.

メッシュ (a) **mesh** ▶メッシュの靴 *mesh* [*netted*] shoes.

メッセージ a **message** /mésıdʒ/ ▶何か彼にメッセージはありますか Do you have *a message* for him?／May I take *a message* for him? ‖ ピーと鳴ったらメッセージを入れてください Please leave *a message* at the sound of the beep. ‖ めいにお祝いのメッセージを送りたいのですが I'd like to send *a message of congratulations* to my niece.

めった ▶めったなことは言うものではありません You shouldn't say such *outrageous things*.

めったうち めった打ち ▶彼らはその犬をめった打ちにした They *beat up* the dog (*mercilessly*).
▶《野球》広島カープのバッターはその投手をめった打ちにし, 降板させた The Carp batters *showered hits on* the pitcher until he was taken off the mound.

めったに **rarely, seldom** (めったに…しない; 後者はやや堅い語）; **hardly ever**（ゼロに近い）; **not ... very often**（あまり多くない）▶めったにないチャンス *a* chance *in a million*（➤ 文字通りには「100万回に１回」の意）‖ 私はめったにタクシーには乗りません I *rarely* [*seldom*] take a taxi.（➤ ネイティブ・スピーカーはやや堅い seldom よりも rarely のほうを好むが, 日本人学習者には発音が難しく通じない可能性があるので, 会話では seldom を使うほうが無難）／I *hardly ever* take a taxi.（➤ hardly ever はほとんどゼロの場合）‖ こんなことはめったにありません This does*n't* happen *very often*.／This *rarely* [*seldom*] happens. ‖ 智恵子とはめったに会わない I do*n't* see Chieko *very often*.／I *hardly ever* [*scarcely ever*] see Chieko.（➤ たとえば前者は月に１～２度, 後者は数年に１度というような頻度を表す）.

めったやたらに ▶フルートはめったやたらに吹いてもいい音は出ません You won't get a good sound from a flute by blowing into it *with all your might* (like that).

めつぼう 滅亡 **ruin**（復旧不可能なまでの）; a **fall**（破壊）**一動 滅亡する** **end**（終わる）; **collapse**（崩壊する）; **perish**（滅びる）▶国の滅亡 the *fall* [*collapse*] of a nation ‖ 帝国の滅亡 the *fall* of an empire ‖ インカ帝国は1533年に滅亡した The Inca Empire *ended* [*collapsed*] in 1533. ‖ 全面的な核戦争が起これば人類は滅亡するだろう An all-out nuclear war would *exterminate* the human race.（➤ exterminate は「絶滅させる」）.

めっぽう **really**（実に）; **awfully**（ものすごく）; **terrifically**, **terribly**（ひどく; 前者は後者よりくだけた語）
▶その小説はめっぽうおもしろかった The novel was *really* interesting. ‖ ビルは腕ずもうがめっぽう強い Bill is *terrifically* good at arm wrestling.

めづまり 目詰まり **clogging** ▶フィルターが目詰まりした The filter *is clogged*.

メディア **the media**（マスコミ）（➤ 本来 medium の複数形. 「記憶媒体」(storage medium) など「媒体」の意の単数形は medium）▶マスメディア *the mass media*／*the media* ‖ 我々はテレビや新聞などのメディアを通じて世の中の出来事を知る We know what is going on in the world through TV, newspapers and other *media*. →マスメディア.

めでたい **happy** ▶わが校が創立100周年を迎えたことはたいへんめでたいことだ Our school's celebration of the 100th anniversary of its founding was a very *joyous* [*happy*] event. ‖ 新しい橋はめでたく完成した The new bridge was *successfully* completed. ‖ 二人はめでたく結ばれた *To everyone's joy*, the couple got married. ‖ 日本ではおとぎ話の多くはめでたしめでたしで終わる Most Japanese nursery tales *have happy endings*.
✉ **日本人はめでたいことがあると赤飯を炊きます** Japanese make *sekihan* (rice with red beans) when there is a *joyous* [*happy*] event.
☛ **おめでたい**（→見出語）

めでる 愛でる ▶月を愛でる *admire* the moon／*enjoy viewing* the moon.

めど 目処 ▶東海道線は復旧のめどが立っていない *There is no telling* [*It's uncertain*] when service will be restored on the Tokaido Line.（➤「いつ復旧するかわからない」の意）‖ ようやく仕事の完成のめどがついた The completion of the job *is in sight*.（➤「見えるところまで来た, 間近だ」の意）‖ 今年末をめどにその計画の概略を決めることにしている We have to have an outline of the plan prepared *by* the end of the year at the latest.（➤「遅くとも年末までに」の意）.

メドレー a **medley** /médli/ ▶400メートル・メドレー・リレー the 400(-meter) *medley relay* ‖ 彼は個人メドレーに優勝した He won the individual *medley*. ‖ 小学唱歌のメドレーを楽しく聞いた We enjoyed listening to *a medley* of school songs.

メトロ **the metro**（パリなどの地下鉄）.

メトロノーム《音楽》a **metronome**.

メトロポリス a **metropolis** /mətrɑ́:pəlɪs/.

メニュー a **menu** ▶メニューを見て注文する order off *a menu* ‖ メニューを見せてください Could you show me [May I see] the *menu*, please? ‖ きょうのメニューは何ですか What's on the *menu* today?／What are you serving today? ‖ あのレストランでは新しいメニューが増えた That restaurant *has added several new items* to its *menu*.（➤ several new menus としない. menu は「献立表」で, 個々の料理ではない）.
▶トレーニングメニューをこなす go through one's *workout menu*.
▶《コンピュータ》ファイル・メニューから「保存」を選びます Select "Save" from *the File menu*（➤「編集メニュー」は Edit menu,「ツールメニュー」は Tools menu）‖《表示》メイン・メニューに戻る Back to *Main menu*.
‖**プルダウン・メニュー** a pull-down menu ‖**ポップアップ・メニュー** a pop-up menu.

メヌエット《音楽》a **minuet** /mɪ̀njuét/.

めぬきどおり 目抜き通り a **main street** ▶彼の店は銀座の目抜き通りにある He has a store on *the main street* [in *the busiest section*] in Ginza.

めのう 瑪瑙《鉱物》(an) **agate** /ǽgət/.

めのかたき 目の敵 ▶彼女は私を目のかたきにしているようだ She seems to *have it in for* me.（➤「ひどく恨んでいる」の意）‖ 彼はぼくを目のかたきにしていて, 町で出会っても知らん顔をする He *has a grudge against* me and pretends not to know me when we encounter each other in public.

めのたま 目の玉 an **eyeball** ▶目の玉が飛び出るような値段 an *eye-popping* price ‖ おれの目の玉の黒いうちは(＝生きてる限り)絶対にそんな事はさせないぞ I won't let you do it *as long as I live*.

めのまえ 目の前で **before** one's **eyes** ▶私の目の前で高校生がたばこを吸った Some high school students smoked *right in front of me* [*before my eyes*].
▶《比喩的》春はすぐ目の前だ Spring *is* (*near*) *at hand*.／Spring *is just around the corner*. ‖ 受験した大学のすべてに落ちたことがわかったときには一瞬目の前が真っ暗になった When I learned that I had failed every college entrance exam (that) I took, I momentarily *lost all hope* [*was plunged into despair*].

めばえ 芽生え **sprouting**.

めばえる 芽生える **bud**（芽が出る）▶二人の間に愛が芽生えた Tender feelings *awoke* [*were awakened*] in the hearts of the two.

めはな 目鼻 ▶その計画もやっと目鼻がついた The plan *has* finally *taken shape*.

めばな 雌花 a **female flower**.

めはなだち 目鼻立ち **features** ▶久美は目鼻立ちが整っている Kumi *has fine* [*has finely chiseled*] *features*.

めばり 目張り ▶窓をガムテープで目張りする *seal up* the windows with packing tape（➤「ガムテープ」を gummed tape とはあまり言わない）.

めぶく 芽吹く **bud, come into bud** ▶春になると草木が芽吹き始める Plants begin to *bud* [*come into bud*] when spring comes.

めぶんりょう 目分量 ▶砂糖を目分量で計る measure sugar *by eye*.

めべり 目減り ▶最近は貯蓄の目減り(＝価値の低下)が激しい Recently, savings *have* greatly *diminished in value*.

めぼし 目星 ▶刑事たちはその女性がスパイではないかと最初から目星をつけていた From the beginning, the detectives had *marked* the woman as a spy.

めぼしい main(主な)；valuable(価値のある) ▶アガサ・クリスティのめぼしい作品はほとんど読んだ I've read most of Agatha Christie's *main* [*important*] works. ‖ めぼしい骨董品はすべて売り払った I sold all my *valuable* antiques. ‖ めぼしい(＝傑出した)高校球児のほとんどがプロ球団にスカウトされた Most of the *outstanding* high school baseball players were recruited by pro teams.

めまい dizziness,《医学》vertigo /vɔ́ːrṭɪgoʊ/ ▶めまいのするような高所 a *dizzying* height ‖ 急にめまいがして倒れそうになった Suddenly I *felt dizzy* [*giddy*] and nearly fell down. ／Suddenly *my head started swimming*, and I nearly fainted.

め

めまぐるしい 目まぐるしい quick, rapid (➤後者が堅い) ▶世の中のめまぐるしい動き the *quick* [*rapid*] developments of the world ‖ めまぐるしい時代の変化に応じる respond to the *quick* [*rapid*] changes of the times ‖ きょうは天気がめまぐるしく変化した Today the weather changed *rapidly*. ‖ 監督はめまぐるしく投手を替えた The manager changed pitchers *frequently* in the game.

めめしい 女々しい sissy；unmanly(男らしくない) ▶あいつはめめしい男だ He is such *a wimp* [*sissy*]. ‖ ぐちをこぼすのはめめしいぞ How *unmanly* of you to complain so much !

メモ a memo, a note 一動 メモする write down, make [take] a note《of》▶本の余白にメモをする *make a note* in the margin of a book ‖ 授業中, 和美は伸夫にそっとメモを渡した Kazumi slipped *a memo* [*a note*] to Nobuo during class. ‖ 私は彼女の電話番号を紙切れにメモした I *jotted down* her phone number on a piece of paper. ‖ この花の名をメモっておこう I think I'll *write down* the names of these flowers. ‖メモ帳 a memo pad,《米また》a scratch pad ‖メモ用紙 memo paper,《米また》scratch paper,《英また》scrap paper.

> **危ないカタカナ語✹ メモ**
> **1**「メモ」は英語の memorandum (短縮形が memo)に由来するが, 英語では主として「非公式の記録または連絡事項」「記憶するために書き記すもの, また注意すべきことを書いて他人に渡すもの」の意で用いる.
> **2** 日本語でいう「メモ」は note に当たり,「メモをする」は make [take] a note という.

めもと 目元 ▶目もとの涼しい[かわいい]女の子 a girl with clear [lovely] *eyes*(➤ eyes の前には beautiful, liquid, bright なども くるが,「涼しい」は日本語特有の表現と思われる) ‖ 彼女は特に目もとが母親に似ている She looks like her mother, especially *around the eyes*.

めもり 目盛り a scale, a graduation (➤後者は堅い語) ▶瓶に目盛りをつける mark *a scale* on a bottle ‖ この計量カップは1目盛りが50cc です This measuring cup indicates 50 cc *per graduation*.

メモリー (a) memory(記憶, 思い出；記憶容量) ▶パソコンのメモリーを4ギガから8ギガに増設する increase a PC's *memory* from 4 to 8 gigabytes. ‖メモリーカード a memory card.

めやす 目安 **1**【見当】a rough estimate(おおよその) ▶1日に何ページ読めるかおおよその目安を立ててごらん Try to get *a rough idea* of how many pages you can read a day.
2【基準】a standard ▶あなたは会社を選ぶとき何を目安にしますか？知名度, 安定性, それとも給料？ By what *standard* (*s*) [*criteria*] do you select a company to work for ? Name recognition ? Stability ? Or salary ? ‖ 試験の合否の目安は60点である The *passing mark* is 60. (➤ passing mark は「合格点」).

めやに 目脂 eye mucus /mjúːkəs/,《インフォーマル》sleep ▶目やにがこびりついて目が開かない My eyes are gummed shut. ‖ 目やにがついてるよ You've got *sleep* in your eyes.

メラニン 《生化学》melanin
‖メラニン色素 melanin pigment.

めらめら ▶火が障子に移ってめらめらと燃え上がった The shoji screen caught fire and *blazed* [*flamed*] *up*.

メランコリー melancholy.

メリーゴーラウンド a merry-go-round,《米また》a carousel /kærəsél/,《英また》a roundabout ▶メリーゴーラウンドに乗る ride (on) *a carousel*.

メリーランド Maryland(アメリカ東部の州；略 MD, Md.).

メリケンこ メリケン粉 flour /fláʊəʳ/ (小麦粉).

めりこむ めり込む get stuck《in》▶月面車は砂の中にめり込まないよう設計されている The lunar module is designed so as not to *get stuck in* the sand.

メリット (a) merit；an advantage(利点) ▶私たちは共学のメリットとデメリットについて論じた We discussed the *advantages* and disadvantages of coeducation. ‖ 英語ができるのは大きなメリットだ Knowing English is a great *advantage*. ‖ 我々が別会社として独立しても何のメリットもない *There is no merit* (for us) *in* becoming independent and forming a new company. ‖ そんなことをして何のメリットがあるのか *What will you gain* if you do that ?

> **危ないカタカナ語✹ メリット**
> **1** 英語の merit は「(賞賛に値する)美点・長所」の意で, his merit(彼の美点)のように人についても用いられる. 日本語では「メリット」は「有利な点, 強み」の意味で用いられることが多いが, その場合は advantage のほうが近い.
> **2** 反対の「デメリット」についても同様で, disadvantage のほうが日本語に近い. demerit は堅い語で, 日常的にはあまり用いられない.

めりはり ▶めりはりの効いた声 a *well-modulated* voice ‖ めりはりの効いた文章 *resonantly-phrased* writing.

めりめり ▶落雷で大木がめりめりっと裂けた Lightning struck and split the big tree *with a crack*.

メリヤス knit(ted) goods；knitwear(メリヤス製品) ▶メリヤスのシャツ a *knit*(*ted*) undershirt.

メルとも メル友 an e-mail friend；a cyber friend(ネット上の).

メルヘン a fairy tale(おとぎ話) (➤「メルヘン」はドイツ語の *Märchen* から) ▶彼の描く童画はさながらメルヘンの世界だ His paintings for children create [portray] *a fairy-tale world.*

メロディー a **melody**(旋律); a **tune**(節) ▶美しいメロディー a sweet *melody* ‖私はこの曲のメロディーが好きだ I like this *tune* [*melody*]. →なつメロ, 着メロ.

メロドラマ a **melodrama** /mélədrɑ̀:mə/; 《インフォーマル》 a **soap opera**(主婦向けの連続ドラマ) ▶彼女はまるでメロドラマの主人公になった気でいる She fancies herself the heroine of *a melodrama*.

めろめろ ▶おじいちゃんは孫の顔を見るとめろめろになる Grandpa *gets* (*all*) *sentimental* [*melts with love*] when he meets his grandchildren.

メロン a **melon** ▶デザートにメロンが出た A slice of *melon* was served for dessert. 《参考》日本ではメロンは高価な果物とみなされることが多いが, アメリカではむしろ安価なものというイメージがある. なお, レストランなどでメロンを注文するときは cantaloup(e)(果肉はオレンジ色), honeydew melon(果肉は緑)などのように種類を言うのがふつう. ‖マスクメロン a muskmelon.

1**めん 面** **1**【顔につけるもの】a **mask**(仮面); a **face guard** [**protector**/**mask**](顔面・頭部用防具) ▶その男はオオカミの面をかぶって彼女の部屋に侵入した The man broke into her room wearing a wolf's *mask*.

2【表面】a **surface** /sə́:ʳfɪs/; a **side**(側面); a **plane**(平面); a **face**(特に多面体の) ▶ざらざらした[平らな]面 a rough [plane] *surface* ‖立方体には6つの面がある A cube has six *surfaces* [*faces*].

3【局面】a **side**(対立するものの1つの側); a **respect**(点) ▶人生の明るい[暗い]面 the bright [dark] *side* of life ‖彼女にはひょうきんな面がある She has a humorous *side*. ‖おまえはあらゆる面でまだ未熟だ You're still immature in every *respect*.

4【新聞の】a **page** ▶第一面 the front *page* ‖社会面 the city news *page*.

5【慣用表現】▶この男の子たちは面と向かって私をばかにした These boys made fun of me *to my face*.

2**めん 綿** **cotton** ▶このシャツは綿でできている This shirt is (made of) *cotton*. ‖綿織物 cotton fabric ‖綿製品 cotton goods.

3**めん 麺** **noodles**(➤通例複数形); **vermicelli** /vɜ̀:ʳmɪtʃéli/(細いもの) ▶私はめん類が大好物だ I love *noodles*.

めんえき 免疫 《医学》**immunity** /ɪmjú:nəṭi/ 一形 免疫の **immune** /ɪmjú:n/ 《to》 ▶私ははしかには免疫がある I *am immune to* measles. ‖エイズは人間の免疫機能を破壊する AIDS destroys people's *immune system*. ‖《比喩的》私たちは上司のぐちにはもう免疫ができている We *are immune to* our boss's complaints.

めんか 綿花 (**raw**) **cotton** ▶綿花を栽培する[摘む] grow [pick] *cotton* ‖綿花畑 a cotton field.

めんかい 面会 a **meeting**; an **interview**(取材の面談) 一動 面会する **see** +目(会う); **meet** +目(初めて会う, 対面する); **have an interview** 《with》(面談する) ▶ご面会の方がいらっしゃってます *Someone* wants to see you. ‖きょうは誰とも面会したくない I don't want to *see* any visitors today. ‖彼は社長に面会を申し込んだ He requested *a meeting* with the president of the company. ‖この患者は面会謝絶だ This patient *is not allowed* (*to have*) *any visitors*. ‖《掲示》面会謝絶 No Visitors. ‖面会時間 visiting hours ‖面会人 a visitor ‖面会日 a visiting day.

めんきょ 免許 《米》a **license**, 《英》a **licence**; a **certificate** /səʳtífɪkət/(免状, 証明書) ▶免許を更新する renew *a license* ‖医師の免許を取る obtain a medical [doctor's] *license* ‖母は運転免許を持っている My mother has *a driver's license* [《英》*a driving licence*]. ‖彼は飲酒運転で免許停止[取り上げ]になった He had his *driver's license* suspended [canceled] for drunk driving. (→免停)

‖営業免許 a business license ‖仮免許 a temporary permit ‖教員免許(状) teaching certificate [license] ‖狩猟免許 a hunting license.

☛ 無免許 (→見出語)

めんくい 面食い ▶彼は面食いだ He *only likes good-looking girls*. / He *picks his women for their looks* (*only*). ‖私って面食いなの I'*m only interested in handsome* [*good-looking*] *men*.

めんくらう 面食らう **be taken unawares**(不意打ちを食らう); **get flustered**(あわてふためく) ▶山田先生に突然質問されてめんくらってしまった I *was taken unawares* [*got flustered*] when Mr. Yamada called on me suddenly. / Mr. Yamada's unexpected question *threw* me *for a loop*. (➤ throw A for a loop は「不意打ちを食らって混乱する」).

めんこ ***menko***; a children's card game in which a thick card with a picture on it is slapped on the floor. If (one of) his opponents cards is flipped, he keeps both cards (➤ 説明的な訳).

めんしき 面識 **acquaintance** ▶父はその社長と面識がある My father *is acquainted with* the president. / My father *knows* the president *personally*. ‖私は彼とは一面識もない He *is a total stranger to* me.

めんじょ 免除 (an) **exemption** 一動 免除する **exempt** [**excuse**] 《A from B》 ▶災害にあった人々は税金が免除される Disaster victims *are exempt from* taxes. (➤ この exempt は形容詞) ‖ジョンは目が悪いため兵役を免除された John *was exempted* [*was excused*] *from* military service because of bad eyesight.

めんじょう 免状 a **diploma** /dɪplóʊmə/(卒業証書); a **license**(運転免許証・教員免許状など公的機関発行の); a **certificate** /səʳtífɪkət/(免許状, 修了証書) ▶花子さんは茶道の先生になる免状を取った Hanako obtained [got] *a certificate* to be a teacher of the tea ceremony.

めんしょく 免職 (a) **dismissal** /dɪsmísəl/ 一動 免職する **dismiss** +目, **discharge** +目 ▶その警官は収賄をして免職になった The police officer *was dismissed* [*discharged*] for taking a bribe.

めんじる 免じる ▶ソーシャルワーカーとしての熱心な活動に免じて(=を考慮して)裁判官は彼に執行猶予つきの判決を下した He was given a stay of execution *in consideration of* his devoted activities as a social worker.

めんしん 免震 ‖免震構造 (a) seismically isolated structure.

メンス 《医学》(a) **menstruation**, **the menses** /ménsi:z/, a **period** →生理.

めんする 面する **face** +目 ▶彼女は海に面した別荘で週末を過ごす She spends the weekends at her cottage, which *faces* [*looks* (*out*) *onto*] the sea. (➤ look (out) onto は「…に向いている」) / She spends the weekends at her seaside cottage.

めんぜい 免税の **duty-free** ▶私は飛行機の中でウオツカを1本免税で買った I bought a bottle of vodka *duty-free* on the plane. ‖免税店 a duty-free shop ‖免税品 duty-free [tax-free] goods.

1**めんせき 面積** (an) **area** /éəriə/ ▶日本の面積は約37万8000平方キロメートルです Japan is about 378,000 square kilometers in *area*. / Japan has [cov-

め

ers] *an area* of about 378,000 square kilometers. ‖この三角形の面積を求めなさい Find the *area* of this triangle.

²**めんせき 免責** (an) **exemption from responsibility** ‖**免責事項** a disclaimer ‖**免責条項** an escape [exemption] clause.

めんせつ 面接 an **interview**; an **oral examination**(口頭試問) **━動 面接する interview** +目, **examine orally** ▶我々は就職希望者20人の面接を行った We *interviewed* twenty applicants for the job. ‖私はあす就職の面接試験を受けなければならない I have *a job interview* tomorrow. /I'm going to *be interviewed for a job* tomorrow.

めんぜん 面前で in one's **presence**(いるところで) ▶彼はぼくの面前でぼくのガールフレンドの悪口を言った He said bad things about my girlfriend *in my presence* [*in front of me*]. ‖日本人は公衆の面前で恥をかかされることを恐れる Japanese are generally afraid of being humiliated *in public*.

めんたいこ 明太子 ***mentaiko***; Alaska pollack roe marinated with red pepper(辛子明太子) (➤ 説明的な訳).

メンタル mental ▶あのテニス選手はメンタルが強いことで知られている That tennis player is known for his *mental strength* [*toughness*]. (➤「弱い」は mental weakness) ‖**メンタルトレーニング** mental training ‖**メンタルヘルス** mental health.

めんだん 面談 an **interview ━動 面談する have an interview** 《with》 ▶《広告》委細面談 Apply personally [in person] for particulars. /Particulars [Details] to be arranged in person [personally].

メンチ ‖**メンチカツ** a deep-fried patty of breaded, ground [minced] meat (with finely-chopped pieces of onion in it) (➤ 説明的な訳) ‖**メンチボール** a fried meatball.

メンツ 面子 face; **honor**(名誉) (➤「メンツ」は中国語から) ▶メンツを保つ save (*one's*) *face* ‖それはメンツにかかわる問題だ It's a matter of losing *face* or not. ‖浅野長矩はメンツを丸つぶれにされた Asano Naganori completely lost *face*. ‖彼はひどくメンツにこだわる He is too concerned about his own personal *honor*.

めんてい 免停 suspension of a license ▶彼女はスピード違反で1か月の免停をくらった She *had her* (*driver's*) *license suspended* for one month for speeding.

メンテナンス maintenance /méɪntənəns/ ▶サウナを作ったがメンテナンスが大変だ We have built a sauna, but *maintaining* it is a lot of trouble.

めんどう 面倒 **1【煩わしいこと】trouble**; a **bother**(やっかいなこと) **━形 面倒な troublesome, bothersome**; **difficult**(難しい) ▶面倒な仕事 a *troublesome* job ‖パジャマに着替えるのが面倒だったので, セーターを着たまま寝た Since it seemed *too much trouble* to change into pajamas, I went to bed with my sweater on. ‖対話「水野さん, この雑誌, いるのといらないのに分けてよ」「面倒だなあ」"Mr. Mizuno, can you sort these magazines into those you need and those you don't?" "*How troublesome*! /*What a bother*!" ‖**ご面倒ですが**, ここにお名前をお書きください *I'm sorry to trouble you*, but will you please write your name here? ‖**ご面倒をおかけしました** I'm sorry I *put* you *to* so much *trouble* [*caused* you so much *trouble*]. (➤ 相手に感謝するつもりなら Thank you very much for your trouble. などという) ‖もう面倒は起こさないでくれ Don't cause [start] any more *trouble*. ‖面倒な(=込み入った)事になりだした Things are getting *complicated*.

2【世話】care ▶私が働いている間, しゅうとめが赤ん坊の面倒を見てくれる While I work, my mother-in-law *takes care of* [*looks after*] my baby. ‖彼は部下の面倒見がいい He *takes good care of* the people who work for him.

めんどうくさい 面倒臭い ▶毎朝出勤前にひげをそるのは面倒くさい *It's a bother* [*a hassle*] to (have to) shave every morning before going to work. ‖パイナップルは好きだが切るのが面倒くさい I like pineapples, but they *are a bother* to cut. ‖こんな宿題, 面倒くさいなあ This assignment is *bothersome* [*troublesome*].

めんとおし 面通し ▶面通しですりを特定する identify a pickpocket *in a* (*police*) *lineup*.

めんとり 面取りをする chamfer +目(木材の); **round off the corners**(角を丸める).

めんどり 雌鳥 a **hen**(鶏); a **female bird**(鳥一般) ▶うちのめん鳥はよく卵を産む Our *hen* lays a lot of eggs. /Our *hen* is a good egg-layer.

メンバー a **member** ▶クラブのメンバー a club *member* ‖彼は委員会のメンバーだ He *is a member* of the committee. /He *is on* the committee. ‖彼女はテニスクラブのメンバーだ She is *a member* of the tennis club. /She *is in* the tennis club.

語法 日常的には member を用いずに be on [in] ... の形で表現することが多い.

▶阪神はベストメンバーで試合に臨んだ The Tigers started the game with its *best players*. ‖マージャンをするにはメンバーが1人足りない We have to get one more *person* for mah-jongg. (➤ グループが組織される前は member とは言えない. person や people を用いる) ‖会社のメンバー4人と三浦に釣りに行った I went fishing at Miura with four *people* [*friends* / *co-workers*] from my company.

めんぼう 綿棒 a **(cotton) swab**, a **Q-tip**, 《英》a **cotton bud**.

めんぼく 面目 face(メンツ); **honor** /ɑ́:nəʳ/ (名誉) ▶二度も犯人逮捕のチャンスを逃して, 警察の面目は丸つぶれだ The police *lost face* by missing two chances to arrest the culprit. ‖その横綱は10勝して何とか面目を保った The yokozuna managed to *save face* by winning 10 bouts. ‖あんな名もないチームに負けて面目ない(=恥ずかしい) We *are ashamed of ourselves* for having lost to such a minor team.

めんみつ 綿密な elaborate /ɪlǽbərət/ (入念な); **close** /kloʊs/ (精密な); **thorough** /θə́:roʊ ‖ θʌ́rə/ (徹底した) ▶綿密な計画を立てる make an *elaborate* plan ‖予定を綿密に打ち合わせる go over the schedule *carefully* ‖地震学者たちは火口を綿密に調査した The seismologists made a *close* [*thorough*] investigation of the crater. ‖ヨット乗りは航海の綿密な記録をつけていた The yachtsman kept a *detailed* [*minute*] record of the voyage. (➤ detailed, minute /maɪnjú:t/ はともに「詳細な」).

めんめん 面々 ▶チームの面々を紹介する introduce *everyone* on the team.

めんめんと 綿々と ▶おじは父に借金を申し込みに来たとき苦境を綿々と訴えた When my uncle came to ask for a loan, he *went on and on* telling my father about his (financial) difficulties.

も・モ

[1]も 藻 algae /ǽldʒiː/ ; seaweed (海草) ; waterweed (水草).

[2]も 喪 mourning ▶彼は妹の喪に服している He is *in mourning* for his younger sister. ‖ 来年, 母の喪が明ける The *period of mourning* for my mother ends next year.

ーも **1【同様であることを示して】too, also, as well ; either**(➤ 否定文で用いる)

> 【文型】
> **…もまた～である [～する]**
> S + V(,) **too.**
> **So** V + S.
>
> 【解説】(1)「…もまた」は肯定文では **too** や **as well** を文尾につけて表す. **too** がふつうで, 直前にコンマを置くこともある. 意味が紛らわしい場合は **too** は修飾する語の後ろに置く. 書きことばでは also を動詞の前 (be 動詞の場合はその後) に置いて表すこともできる.
> (2)前の文全体を受けるときは so も使える. **so** の後では「(助)動詞＋主語」の語順にする. この場合の動詞は代動詞 do, does, did や助動詞・be 動詞に限られる.

▶あすもたぶん晴れるだろう Probably tomorrow will be a fine day, *too.* ／We'll probably have *another* fine day tomorrow. ‖ 私もジョンソンさんを知っている I know Mr. Johnson, *too.* ／I *also* know Mr. Johnson. (● 後者は文脈によっては「私はジョンソンさんも知っている」の意になる. also を文尾に置けば「私はジョンソンさんも」の意のみ) ‖ 彼女は男に食べ物を与え, なにがしかの金も与えた She gave the man food and some money *as well.*

▶ 対話「私は神戸が大好きです」「私も」"I love Kobe." "*I do, too.* ／*Me, too.* ／*So do I.*" (● Me, too. は仲間どうしや家庭内でごくふつうに使うくだけた言い方で, So do I. はやや改まった言い方) ‖ 対話「疲れました」「私もです」"I'm tired." "*I am, too.* ／*So am I.*" (➤ (×)I am so. とはしない. くだけた言い方では Me, too.).

▶これも一緒に包んでください Could you (please) wrap this *together* with the other items ? ‖ ことしも優勝するぞ We're going to win the pennant *again this year* !

> 【文型】
> **…もまた～でない [～しない]**
> S + **not** V(,) **either.**
> **Neither** [**Nor**] V + S.
>
> 【解説】否定文の「…もまた～ない」は **not … either** で表す. either の前にコンマを置くこともある. 前の文全体を受けるときは neither または nor も使えるが, その後は「(助)動詞＋主語」の語順にする.

▶明はギターが弾けないし, 私も弾けない Akira can't play the guitar, and *neither can I* [and *I can't either* ／*nor can I*]. ‖ 対話「株のことは何もわかんないよ」「俺もさ」"I don't know anything about the stock market." "*I don't, either.* ／*Me, neither.*" (➤ Neither do I. と答えてもよいが, やや堅い言い方になる).

▶わが校の野球チームは今回も甲子園出場はならなかった Our school's baseball team could*n't* make it to the Koshien tournament *this time either* [*again*]. (➤ again には「また(しても)」という感情的なニュアンスがこもることもある).

2【複数のものを列挙して】both A **and** B ; **neither** A **nor** B(➤ 前者の否定形)

> 【文型】
> **A も B も**
> **both** A **and** B
> **not only** A **but also** B (＝Aばかりでなく B も)
> A **as well as** B (＝B はもちろん A も)
> **A も B も…(どちらも)ない**
> **neither** A **nor** B ／**not … (either)** A **or** B
>
> 【解説】(1)**not … both** A **and** B とすると「A も B も…というわけではない」と片方だけを否定する言い方(「部分否定」)になる.
> (2)「どちらも(…ない)」を強調して **either** をつけることがある.

▶彼も私も旅行が好きです *Both* he *and* I like traveling. ‖ 彼とは行きも帰りも一緒の列車だった He and I were on the same train (*both*) *going and coming* (*back*). ‖ 私はロンドンにもパリにも(どちらにも)行ったことがある I've been to *both* London *and* Paris. ‖ 雲仙にも長崎にも行きました I visited *not only* Unzen *but* (*also*) Nagasaki. ／I visited Nagasaki *as well as* Unzen. ‖ 八丈島へは飛行機でも船でも行ける You can go to Hachijo Island *either* by plane *or* by ship.

▶彼は酒もたばこもやらない He *neither* drinks *nor* smokes. (➤「どちらも(やらない)」を強調) ／He does*n't* drink *or* smoke. (➤ 単に「酒は飲まない, また, たばこは吸わない」を表す) ‖ 議員は疑惑を肯定も否定もしなかった The Diet member *neither* admitted *nor* denied the allegations. ／The Diet member did*n't* admit *or* deny the allegations. ‖ 私はフランス語もドイツ語もどちらも話せない I ca*n't* speak *either* French *or* German. ‖ その俳優は好きでも嫌いでもない I *neither like nor dislike* the actor. ‖ 私はロンドンにもパリにも(どちらにも)行ったことがない I have *never* been to *either* London *or* Paris. ‖ 彼女も私も何も言わなかった *Neither* she *nor* I said anything. ／*Neither of* us said anything. (➤ 後者がふつうの言い方).

> **直訳の落とし穴「どちらも来なかった」**
> (1)「A も B もどちらも」は both A and B,「彼らはどちらも」は both of them であることはだれでも知っている. また,「A も B もどちらも…でない」は neither A nor B であることを知っている人も多い. しかし,「彼らはどちらも来なかった」のつもりで, Both of them didn't come. と言ってしまう人が多い. 日本語は否定語を最後にもってくる特性があることが影響しているのかもしれないが, 英語では否定語は動詞より前が原則である. この英語は「二人が来たわけではない」つまり,「一人は来な

かった」ということであり，英文法でいう部分否定になる．二人が来なかったは Neither of them came. である．
(2)同様に，「彼らはみな来た」は All of them came. であるが，「みな来なかった」を All of them didn't come. あるいは，Not all of them came. とするのはあやまり．これは「全員が来たわけではない」つまり，「来なかった人がいた」ということである．「全員が来なかった」は None of them came. である．(1)の neither とこの none は日本人学習者の苦手とする語で，なかなかきちんと使えない．
(3)I like natto.（私は納豆が好き）に対して，「私も」はくだけた表現では，Me, too. でよいが，I don't like natto.（私は納豆が好きでない）に対して「私も(好きでない)」はもちろん（×）Me, too. でなく，Me, neither. である．これをアメリカ人でも（△）Me, either. と言ってしまう人がいるようであるが，正しい言い方とはされていない．

3【否定の意味を強めて】even ▶会社じゃ忙しくてコーヒーを飲む時間もない We are so busy at the office that we have no time *even* to drink coffee. ‖ 声を掛けたのに彼は振り向いてもくれなかった I spoke to him, but he didn't *even* turn around. ‖ スイスへは一度も行ったことがない I have *never* been to Switzerland.

4【数･量などが多いことを強調して】as … as ▶父は3000冊も本を持っている My father has *as many as* 3,000 books. ‖ きのう私は８時間も勉強した Yesterday I studied (for) *as long as* eight hours [for eight *long* hours]. ‖ 彼はゲームソフトに３万円も使った He spent *as much as* 30,000 yen on game software.

▶きょうで１週間も雨が続いている As of today, it *has been raining* for a whole week. ‖ 遅かったわね．1時間も待ったのよ！You're (so) late. I*'ve been waiting* for an hour！(➤ この２つの用例では，「も」は口調と現在完了進行形で表す)．

5【おおよそを表して】▶この仕事は１週間もあれば終わるだろう A week will be *enough* to finish this job. ‖ 電気自動車は200万もしないで買える You can get an electric car *for less than* [*for under*] two million yen.

6【その他】▶ヒロシもヒロシだが，おまえもおまえだ (I know) Hiroshi is *a problem*, but *so* are you.

もう **1【すでに】already**（平叙文で）；**yet**（疑問文で）▶あれ，もう午前２時だよ Gee, it's *already* 2 a.m. ‖ 沖縄ではもう桜の花が満開です Cherry blossoms are *already* in full bloom in Okinawa.

【文型】
もう…しましたか
Have you done **yet ?**
➤ 主に現在完了形の疑問文で用いる
もう…ですか
Are you … yet ?

▶もうお昼は食べましたか *Have you* had lunch *yet ?* ‖ **対話**「もう宿題は終わった？」「まだだよ」"*Have you* finished [done] your homework *yet ?*" "No, not yet." ‖（食事などが）もう終わりましたか *Have* [*Are*] *you* finished (with your breakfast [lunch／dinner]) *yet ?* (➤「お済みですか」の意．単に，Have [Are] you finished？がふつう) ‖ おたくはもう利益を上げていますか *Are you* profitable *yet ?*

▶あなたたちもう別れたの？ 半年前に結婚したばかりなのに *Have you* split up *already ?* You just got married a half year ago. (● already を疑問文で用いると「もう…したのか」という驚きを表す) ‖ もう帰るの？ *Are you* leaving *already* [*so soon*／*so early*] *?* (➤ so soon は「来てまもないのにもう」，so early は「まだ早い時刻なのに」)．

▶もう(＝今や)彼女は何でも食べられるのだから特別の食事は不要だ *Now that* she can eat anything, she doesn't need a special diet. ‖《遊びで》もういいかい？ *Are you ready ?*／*Ready or not, here I come.* (➤ 隠れんぼのときの決まり文句)．

2【限度を超えて】anymore（これ以上；内容によって「any ＋ほかの形容詞・副詞の比較級」を用いる）▶もうそのことは考えるのをよそう Let's *not* think about it *anymore*. ‖ もう彼の言うことなど信じない I do*n't* believe him *anymore*. ‖ 彼女のわがままにはもう(＝これ以上長くは)我慢できない I can't put up with her selfishness *any longer*. ‖ 疲れてもう(＝これ以上遠くへは)歩けない I'm so tired that I can't walk *any farther*.

▶今からではもう遅過ぎる It's *too late now*. ‖ 言い訳はもうたくさんよ I*'ve had enough of* your excuses.／I*'m fed up with* your excuses.

3【まもなく】soon ▶彼ももう来るころだ He should be here *any moment*. ‖ もうそろそろ夕飯のしたくを始めなくては *It is about time to* begin fixing supper. ‖ もう失礼しなくちゃ I'd better be going *now*. ‖ 彼女はもう(＝今頃は)家に着いてるわよ She should be home *by now*.

4【さらに付け加えて】more（さらに…だけ多くの）；**another**（もう１つ［１人］の…）▶写真をもう１枚撮りましょう Let me take *one more* picture. ‖ もう２週間待ってください Please wait two *more* weeks. ‖ 水をもう１杯ください Could I have *another* glass of water, please？‖ もう１週間入院していなくてはいけません You'll have to stay in the hospital *another* [*one more*] week.

5【感情的になって】▶ひどいなあ，もう *Oh*, this is too much！‖ 次から次へと買い物して，全くもう！You buy one thing after another. *I'm fed up with* your constant shopping. ‖ 全くもう，少しは静かにできないの？ *For heaven's sake*, can't you keep quiet for even a minute？

☛ **もう一度，もうすぐ，もう少し，もう一つ** (→見出語)

もう- 猛- ▶猛練習 *hard* [*intensive*] practice ‖ 山本さんは娘さんがそのドイツ人と結婚することに**猛反対した** Mr. Yamamoto was *dead set against* his daughter marrying that German. (➤ dead set は「断固」の意)．→**猛勉強**．

もうい 猛威 rage ▶そのころ，パリの街ではペストが**猛威をふるっていた** The plague *was raging* in Paris at that time. ‖ 台風12号が西日本に**猛威をふるった** Typhoon No. 12 *caused a lot of damage* [*wreaked havoc*] in western Japan.

もういちど もう一度 again ▶もう一度やってごらん Try *again*. ‖ もう一度言ってみろ *If you say that again* [*once more*]！‖ その質問をもう一度言っていただけませんか Would you please *repeat* the question？

もういっぽう もう一方の the other ▶私がロープの一方の端を持ち，父がもう一方の端を持った I held one end of the rope and my father *the other*.

もうか 猛火 ▶地震のあと，神戸の家々は多くが**猛火**に包まれた After the earthquake, many houses in Kobe were engulfed in *raging* [*uncontrollable*] *flames*.

もうがっこう 盲学校 a school for the blind.

もうかる 儲かる ▶もうかる商売 a *profitable* [*lucrative*] business ‖この商売はあまりもうからない This business *isn't very profitable*. / *There's not much profit* in this business. ‖友だちにチケットを10枚売ったら3000円もうかった I *made a profit of* [*gained*] three thousand yen when I sold ten tickets to my friends.

▶ 対話「もうかりまっか？」「ぼちぼちでんな」"So, *how's business*?" "Hey, can't complain." (● can't complain は I can't complain. (まあまあです)の I が省略されたもの).

もうかんげんしょう 毛管現象 《物理学》a capillary phenomenon. → 毛細(管現象).

もうきん 猛禽 a bird of prey, a raptor.

もうけ 儲け (a) profit (経費を差し引いたあとの利潤)；gains (利益金，利得) ▶卸売り業はもうけが多い[少ない] The wholesale business yields large [small] *profits*.

▶古い背広のポケットから1万円札が出てきて，もうけもの(＝拾い物)をした気になった It was *a stroke of good luck* [*a windfall*] when I found a ten-thousand-yen bill in the pocket of an old suit.

☞ 大もうけ，ひともうけ (→見出語)

[1]**もうける 儲ける 1**【金を】make money, make a profit ▶投資で300万円もうける *make* 3,000,000 yen from [on] an investment ‖あの男は株で大金をもうけた That man *has made* a great deal of *money* on stocks. / That guy *made a fortune* in the stock market. ‖たんまりもうけたらこの仕事から足を洗うつもりだ I'm going to quit this business after *making* a large *profit* [a lot of *money*]. ‖あの不動産屋さんは土地の急騰でもうけた That realtor *cashed in on* soaring land prices. (➤ cash in on は「…に便乗してもうける」の意のインフォーマルな表現).

2【得をする】▶きょうは先生に指されないでもうけた(＝幸運だった) I *was lucky* enough today not to be called on by the teacher. ‖《締切が延びて》よし，1日もうけたぞ I'm in luck! *I've got* one extra day. ‖《ただで何かを手に入れて》何だかもうけたような気がするな I feel like I *got something for nothing*.

[2]**もうける 設ける 1**【設置する】set up ▶委員会を設ける *set up* a committee ‖当校には優秀な生徒のための特別クラスが設けてある A special class for gifted students *has been established* [*been set up*] in our school. ‖電車やバスにはお年寄りや体の不自由な人のために優先席が設けてある Priority seating for elderly and disabled persons *is provided* on trains and buses.

2【用意する】▶彼は適当な口実をもうけて忘年会を欠席した He didn't attend the year-end party *on some pretext* or other [*on some pretext*].

3【子供を作る】have ▶彼は結婚して一子をもうけた He got married and *had* a child.

もうけん 猛犬 a fierce dog ▶《掲示》猛犬注意 Beware of (the) dog.

もうこう 猛攻 ▶(…の)猛攻にあう meet with a *fierce* [*violent*] *attack* (by …).

もうこはん 蒙古斑 《医学》a Mongolian (blue) spot.

もうさい 毛細 ‖毛細管《解剖学》a capillary ‖毛細管現象《物理学》capillary phenomenon ‖毛細管作用 capillary action.

もうしあげる 申し上げる ▶この件に関し特に申し上げることはございません I don't have any special comments to *offer* on this matter. ‖《場内放送など》皆さまに申し上げます May I have your attention, please? / Attention, please!

もうしあわせ 申し合わせ (an) agreement ▶市当局との申し合わせによりごみの収集は週2回になりました In accordance with *an agreement* with the city authorities, garbage pickups have been changed to twice a week.

もうしあわせる 申し合わせる agree ▶住民たちは産業廃棄物処理施設の建設に反対することを申し合わせた The residents *agreed* that they would oppose the construction of an industrial waste treatment facility.

▶学生たちは申し合わせたように就職試験には紺のスーツを着ていく Students all go to take employment exams in dark blue suits, *as if by some tacit* [*previous*] *agreement*. (➤ tacit は「暗黙の」，previous は「事前の」).

もうしいれ 申し入れ an offer /ɔ́ːfəʳ/, a proposal (提案)；a request (要請) ▶彼らは私の申し入れを断った They declined my *offer* [*proposal*].

もうしいれる 申し入れる request 《that》(要請する)；propose 《that》(提案する)；ask for (➤ ask for はややくだけた言い方) ▶市民たちは競馬場の建設を撤回するよう市当局に申し入れた The citizens *requested* that the city government drop its plan to construct a horse track. (● that 以下の節は仮定法現在なので動詞は原形) ‖労働組合は会社側に一律5パーセントの賃金引き上げを申し入れた The labor union *made a request* to the company for a five percent pay hike across the board. ‖米農家の代表たちは大臣に会見を申し入れた Representatives of rice farmers *asked for* an interview with the Minister.

もうしおくる 申し送る send word (to someone) 《about》.

もうしおくれる 申し遅れる ▶申し遅れましたが，本日司会を務めさせて頂く田中でございます I *should have introduced myself earlier*. My name is Tanaka, and I will be your emcee today.

もうしこみ 申し込み an application (応募)；a reservation (予約)；an order (注文) ▶コンサート・チケットの申し込みをインターネットで行う *order* one's concert ticket online ‖その分譲地に申し込みが殺到した *Applications* poured in for the subdivided residential lots. ‖申込期限はいつですか When is the *application deadline*? (➤ a time limit [a deadline] for application も可) ‖商品のお申し込みからお届けまでは1週間ほどかかります Products will be delivered about a week after we receive your *order*.

▶《掲示》ただ今，お申し込み受付中 *Applications* [*Reservations*] Now Being Accepted.

‖申込金 an application fee ‖申込者 an applicant /ǽplɪkənt/ ‖申込用紙 an application form.

もうしこむ 申し込む apply 《to, for》(手続きをする)；order ＋目 (注文する)；sign up 《for》(履修届などを出す；クレジットカード・保険などの契約をする)；propose 《to》(結婚を)

> **【文型】**
> 人(A)に物(B)を申し込む
> apply to A for B

▶入会を申し込むにあたって入会金は不要です No application fee is required when *applying for* membership. ‖ 彼はM銀行に500万円の融資を申し込んだ He *applied to* M Bank *for* a five million yen loan.

▶インターネットで切符を申し込む *order* a ticket online ‖ 私は山野井教授のゼミに履修を申し込んだ I *signed up for* Professor Yamanoi's seminar. ‖ きみは彼女に何と言って結婚を申し込んだの？ What did you say when you *proposed to* her?

▶プレゼントご希望の方はこちらのあて先にお申し込みください To receive your free present, please *write to* the address shown here. (➤「手紙を書く」の意) ‖ 私たちは大学生チームにサッカーの試合を申し込んだ We *challenged* the college team to a soccer game. ／We *invited* [*asked*] the college team to play soccer with us.

もうしたて 申し立て a **statement** ▶どうしてきみは虚偽の申し立てをしたのか Why did you *make a false statement* [*accusation* ／ *allegation*]? ／ Why did you *perjure yourself*? ‖ 被告は正当防衛の申し立てをした The defendant *pleaded self-defense.* ‖ (裁判官が)意義申し立てを却下する dismiss *an objection.*

もうしたてる 申し立てる **state**; **appeal** 《against》(上訴する) ▶町役場に苦情を申し立てる *file* a complaint at the town office ‖ 証人はその男性を目撃したと申し立てた The witness *stated* that he had seen the man with his own eyes. ‖ 被告人は判決に対して不服を申し立てた The accused *appealed* (*against*) the court decision.

もうしで 申し出 an **offer** /ɔ́:fəʳ/; a **request** (要請) ▶皆さまのお申し出の件につきましては慎重に考慮いたしました We have given your *request* careful consideration.

✉ **せっかくですが, 献花のお申し出はお断りさせて頂きます** We appreciate your consideration, but we must decline your *offer* to send a floral tribute. ➤ 英米ではこの場合断ることは通例しない.

もうしでる 申し出る **offer** +㊀ (「…を差し上げましょう[いたしましょう]」と言う); **volunteer** /vɑ̀:ləntíəʳ/ +㊀ (援助を申し出る)

【文型】
人(A)に物事(B)を申し出る
offer A B ／ **offer** B **to** A
…しようと申し出る
offer to do

▶困っている人に援助を申し出る *offer* help *to* a person in trouble ‖ S氏は100億円の寄付を申し出た Mr. S *offered to* make a ten billion yen donation.

▶何人かの市民が誘拐犯人の捜査への協力を申し出た Some citizens *volunteered* to help look for the kidnapper. ‖ この日に都合が悪い人は申し出てください Those who can't make it this day, please *let* me *know* [*tell* me].

もうしひらき 申し開き **self-defense** (自己弁護); **self-justification** (自己正当化); (an) **excuse** (言い訳) 一動 **申し開きをする** **defend** [**justify**] (oneself); **excuse.**

もうしぶん(の)ない 申し分(の)ない **perfect** (完璧な); **ideal** (理想的な) ▶申し分のない天気 *perfect* [*ideal*] weather ‖ ミラノはファッションデザインの勉強には申し分のない所だ Milan is an *ideal* place to study fashion design. ‖ 兄は申し分のない成績で大学を卒業した My (older) brother graduated from college with *excellent* grades. ‖ 彼は申し分のない父親だ He is a *perfect* father. ／He *leaves nothing to be desired* as a father.

▶あのホテルのサービスは申し分なかった The service *was impeccable* at that hotel. (➤「非の打ちどころのない」の意).

もうじゃ 亡者 ▶権力の亡者たち *insatiable power-seekers* (➤ insatiable は「飽くことのない」の意) ‖ あの老人は金の亡者だ That old man *is obsessed with money* [*is money mad*].

[1]**もうじゅう 猛獣** a **fierce animal**; a **beast of prey** (肉食獣) ‖猛獣使い a wild animal trainer [tamer].

[2]**もうじゅう 盲従** **blind obedience** 一動 **盲従する** **obey blindly** ▶権威に盲従するな Don't *obey* authority *blindly.* ‖ 多くの日本人は戦争中軍部に盲従した Many Japanese *followed* the military leaders *blindly* during the war.

もうしょ 猛暑 **intense** [**severe**] **heat**

✉ **こちらは連日の猛暑でうだっています. そちらはどうですか** I'm sweltering in the *terrible heat spell* here. How is the weather where you are? ➤ spell は「(天候の)ひと続き」.

もうしわけ 申し訳 **1**【言い訳】an **excuse** /ɪkskjú:s/ (弁明) ▶本当に申し訳ありません *I'm* very [so ／ terribly ／ awfully] *sorry.* ‖ 遅れて申し訳ない *I'm sorry* I'm late. ／*I'm really sorry* to be late [for being late]. ‖ 何のお役にも立てず申し訳ありません *I'm terribly sorry* that I couldn't be of any help to you. ／*I'm very sorry* for not having been able to help you.

▶あなたをこんなごたごたに巻き込んでしまって申し訳ありません *I'm sorry* to have gotten you into this trouble. ‖ 申し訳ありませんが, もう帰らなければなりません *I'm sorry, but* I have to leave now.

✉ **お借りした本を汚してしまい申し訳ありません** *I have to apologize* to you for having soiled the book I borrowed from you.

✉ **長い間ご無沙汰いたしておりまして申し訳ございません** *Please forgive me* for not writing to you for so long. ／*I'm sorry* I haven't written (to you) for a long time.

2【形ばかり】▶申し訳程度の水着 *a poor excuse for* a bathing suit (➤この excuse は「申し訳程度のもの」の意のおどけた言い方) ‖ こんな申し訳程度の(＝わずかばかりの)昇給では満足できない We won't be satisfied with these *small* wage increases.

もうしん 盲信 **blind faith** 一動 **盲信する** **believe** [**trust**] **blindly** 《in》 ▶薬の効果を盲信する人が多い Many people *have blind faith in* the power of medicine. ‖ 自分の実力を盲信するのはよくない It's not good to *trust blindly in* your (own) ability.

もうじん 盲人 a **blind person** (➤最近では a visually impaired person (目の不自由な人)という表現が好まれる); **the blind** (盲人たち) ▶盲人になる become *blind* ‖ 彼はその盲人が通りを渡るのを助けた He helped the *blind person* cross the street.

もうす 申す ▶父はどなたにもお会いしたくないと申しております My father *says* he doesn't want to see anybody. ‖ わたくしは伊集院と申す者でございます My name is Ijuin. (➤ I'm Ijuin. はややくだけた言い方になる).

もうすぐ **soon, in no time** (➤後者はややくだけた言い方)

▶彼はもうすぐ来る He'll *soon* be here. ／He'll be here *shortly*. ‖梅雨はもうすぐ終わる The rainy season will *soon* be over. ‖もうすぐ終わります I'll be finished *in no time*.
▶もうすぐ夏だ Summer is *just around the corner*. (➤ just around the corner は「すぐそこに」の意のインフォーマルな表現).

もうすこし もう少し **a little more**(量・程度が); **a few more**(数が) ▶もう少し席を詰めてください Move over *a little*, please. ／Please move over *a little*. (後者のように please を文頭に置くほうがより丁寧な言い方) ‖もう少しゆっくり話してくれませんか Could you speak *a little more* slowly? ‖もう少しゆっくりしていってください Won't you stay *a little longer*? ‖お茶をもう少し(たくさん)頂けますか Could I have *some more* tea? ‖もう少し待ってくれますか Can you wait *a few more minutes* [*days*]?
▶もう少しで終わります I'm *almost* finished. ／I'll be finished *shortly*. ‖私はもう少しで溺れそうになった I *nearly* [*almost*] drowned.

もうせい 猛省 ▶今回の事件について, きみの猛省を促したい I urge you to *reflect very seriously* on your conduct in this incident.

もうぜん 猛然と **fiercely** /fíəˊsli/ (猛烈に); **strongly** (強く) ▶島民は空港の建設に猛然と反対した The islanders *strongly* [*fiercely*／*vehemently*] opposed the construction of the airport.

もうそう 妄想 a **delusion**; a **wild fancy**(たわいもない; 文語的な言い方) ▶彼女は妄想にふけっているようだ She appears to *be delusional* [*be lost in wild fancies*]. ‖彼は警察に追われているという妄想に取りつかれている He suffers from the *delusion* that he is wanted by the police. ‖あいつは自分が天才であるかのような妄想を抱いている He *regards* [*fancies*] *himself as* a genius. ‖彼は被害妄想に駆られている He *is paranoid*.

もうだ 猛打 ▶オリックスはソフトバンクの4人の投手に16安打の猛打を浴びせた The Buffaloes collected [racked up] *16 hits* off four Hawks hurlers.

もうちょう 盲腸 《解剖学》 an **appendix** /əpéndɪks/ (虫垂); **appendicitis** /əpèndəsáɪtɪs/ (虫垂炎); **the cecum** /síːkəm/ (盲嚢(のう); その末端が appendix) ▶彼は盲腸炎で入院した He was hospitalized with *appendicitis*. ‖私は2年前に盲腸の手術をした I had *an appendectomy* two years ago.
‖急性盲腸炎 acute appendicitis.

もうでる 詣でる **go to pray** [**worship**] 《at》 ▶神社に詣でる *go to pray at* a Shinto shrine.

もうてん 盲点 a **blind spot**(➤ 網膜上の盲点のほかに比喩的にも用いる); a **loophole**(抜け穴) ▶税法の盲点を突いて荒稼ぎする人が多い Many people take advantage of *loopholes* in the tax law to make a lot of money.

もうとう 毛頭 ▶あなたを非難する気は毛頭ないわ I *don't have the slightest* [*least*] intention of criticizing you.

もうどうけん 盲導犬 a **guide dog**, a **Seeing Eye dog** (➤ 後者はアメリカの盲導犬訓練団体の名前から).

もうどく 猛毒 **deadly poison**.

もうはつ 毛髪 **hair**. →髪.

もうひつ 毛筆 a (**writing**) **brush**, a **calligraphy** /kəlígrəfi/ **brush**.

もうひとつ もう一つの **another**; **one more**(さらに1つ) ▶もう1つケーキを食べていいですか May I have *another* [*one more*] piece of cake? (another は2切れ目, one more はそれ以上を暗示する) ‖もう1つキャンデーがあれば均等に分けられるのに I could divide the candy equally between us if I had *one more*. (➤ この one more は名詞用法).
▶きょうはもうひとつ調子が出ない Today isn't my day. ／For some reason [Somehow] I can't do anything right today. ‖対話「私の絵, どうでしょうか」「うーん, もうひとつだね」"How is my drawing?" "Hmm ... It *needs a little something* (*more*). ／Well, *it's not quite there yet*." (➤ 後者は「あと一歩, 目標に届いていない」).

もうふ 毛布 a **blanket**; 《米また》 a **throw** (薄手の) ▶純毛の毛布 an all-wool *blanket* ‖私は冬は毛布を2枚掛けます I sleep under two *blankets* in the winter. (英語では「2枚の毛布の下で眠る」とする) ‖《機内で》毛布をください May I have *a blanket*? (Give me ... とは言わない).

もうべんきょう 猛勉強する **grind away** 《at》, 《英また》 **swot** ▶兄は司法試験目指して猛勉強している[猛勉中だ] My (older) brother *is grinding away* [*is swotting*] for the bar exam.
‖猛勉強家 《米》 a grind, 《英》 a swot.

もうまく 網膜 《解剖学》 **the retina** /rétnə/
‖網膜はく離 detachment of the retina.

もうもう ▶もうもうたる砂ぼこりをあげて1台の車がサハラ砂漠を走っていった A car raised *thick clouds of* dust as it sped across the Sahara. ‖工場の煙突はもうもうと黒煙を吐いていた The factory smokestacks were belching *columns of* black smoke.

もうもく 盲目 **blindness** 一形 **盲目の** **blind**(➤ 最近では visually impaired (目の不自由な)という表現が好まれる) ▶盲目のギタリスト a *blind* guitarist.
▶民衆は盲目的に政治家に従ってはならない People should not *blindly* [*unquestioningly*] follow the lead of politicians.

もうら 網羅する **cover** +目 (扱うべき範囲を); **include** +目 (含む) ▶網羅的なリスト an *exhaustive* list ‖この白書は重要問題を網羅している This white paper *covers all* the important problems. ‖その辞書はアメリカの方言を網羅している That dictionary *includes all* dialectal variations of American English.

もうれつ 猛烈な **awful**(すごい); **violent**(激しく破壊的な); **fierce**(残酷なまでの); **terrible**(苦痛に感じるほど不愉快な) 一副 **猛烈に** **terribly, awfully**; **like mad** (がむしゃらに) ▶船は猛烈な嵐に襲われた The ship was caught in a *violent* [*fierce*] storm. ‖この夏は猛烈な暑さだった It was *terribly* [*awfully*] hot this past summer.
▶私の提案は猛烈な反対にあった My proposal met with *strong* [*fierce*] opposition. ‖高校のときは猛烈に勉強した I studied *like mad* while in high school. ‖あの店のカレーは猛烈に辛い The restaurant serves *intensely* [*fiercely*] hot curry. ‖猛烈に暑い日 a *sweltering* day.

もうれんしゅう 猛練習 **hard** [**intense**] **training** ▶そのボクサーはリターンマッチに向けて猛練習した The boxer *underwent hard* [*intense*] *training* for the return match. ／The boxer *trained hard* for the return match. ‖私たちは今, 秋のリーグ戦に向けて猛練習をしています We are now *training intensely* for the fall league game.

もうろう 朦朧 ▶その患者は意識がもうろうとしている The patient is *only half conscious*. ‖ボクサーはノックアウトされる寸前でもうろうとしていた The boxer *was dazed* [*was stunned*] when he was almost

も

knocked out.
▶おじに関する記憶はもうろうとしている I have only a *dim* [*vague*] memory of my uncle.

もうろく 耄碌 **dotage** /dóʊṭɪdʒ/ (➤ 日本語と同じくユーモラスな感じのある語) ; **senility** /sənílәṭi/ (老化によるぼけ) **一動** **もうろくする** **fall into dotage, get** [**become**／**go**] **senile** /sí:naɪl/ ▶年を取ってももうろくしたくないものだ I don't want to *get* [*go*] *senile* when I get old. ‖ 祖母はもうろくしている My grandmother *is in her dotage* [*is senile*].

もえ 萌え ***moe*** ; **geek affection.**

もえあがる 燃え上がる ▶墜落した飛行機はあっという間に燃え上がった The crashed plane *burst into flame(s)* [*went up in flames*] in an instant.

もえうつる 燃え移る **spread** 《to》(広がる) ▶火はぼくの家に燃え移った The fire *spread to* my house. ‖ たき火にあたっているうちに服に火が燃え移った My clothes *caught fire* while I was warming myself by an open-air fire.

もえがら 燃え殻 **cinders** (石炭・木材などの) (➤ 通例複数形で) ; **ashes** (灰).

もえさし 燃えさし an **ember** (石炭・木材などの) ; a **stub** (たばこ・ろうそくなどの).

もえつきる 燃え尽きる **burn up** [**out**] ▶スパイ衛星は大気圏に再突入して燃え尽きた The spy satellite re-entered the earth's atmosphere and *burned* [《英》 *burnt*] *up*.
▶《比喩的》敗れたチャンピオンは「もう燃え尽きた」と語った The defeated champion said, "I'm *burned out*." **‖燃え尽き症候群** burnout syndrome.

もえひろがる 燃え広がる **spread** ▶火事はまもなく町全域に燃え広がった The fire soon *spread* through the whole town.

[1]**もえる 燃える** **1【火が】** **burn** ; **blaze** (炎をあげて) ▶このまきはよく燃える This wood *burns* well. ‖ こげ臭い. 何か燃えてるんじゃないかい? I smell something *burning*. ‖ 救助隊は燃えさかるビルに飛び込んで行った The rescue team rushed into the *blazing* building.
▶木造家屋は簡単に燃える (= 火がつく) Wooden houses *catch fire* easily. ‖ 旅館が燃えていた An inn *was on fire*.
▶燃えるごみと燃えないごみを分別して出してください Separate (your) trash into *burnable and unburnable items* before putting it out for collection. ‖ ストーブの近くに燃えやすい物を置くな Don't leave *(in)flammable* objects close to the heater.
2【燃えたような状態になる】 **blaze** ▶夕日が(真っ赤に)燃えている The setting sun *is blazing* scarlet. ‖ メアリーの髪は燃えるような赤毛だ Mary's hair is *blazing* red [scarlet].
3【気持ちが】 ▶ゲリラたちは復しゅうの念に燃えている The guerrillas *are burning furiously* with a desire for revenge.
▶我々はこの企画を成功させようと燃えています We *are burning with enthusiasm* for the success of this project. (➤ enthusiasm /mθjú:ziæzәm/ は「熱意」).

[2]**もえる 萌える** **bud** (芽ぐむ) ; **sprout** (葉や芽が) ▶草木の萌える春 spring when *grass grows abundantly and trees bud* ‖ 木々の葉が新しく萌え始めている New leaves are beginning to *sprout* from the trees. ‖ 古木から若葉が萌え出た The old tree *has sprouted* new leaves.

モーグル(スキー) **mogul** /móʊgәl/ **skiing.**

モーション a **motion** ▶ピッチャーは投球モーションに入りました The pitcher is going into his *windup*.
▶多くの男がみゆきにモーションをかけた (= 言い寄った) が, 皆だめだった Many men *made passes at* Miyuki, but all without success.

> **危ないカタカナ語✹ モーション**
> **1** 野球では投手の投球動作全体を motion という. 日本では「ワインドアップ」(ふりかぶる動作)のことを「モーション」ということが多いので, その場合は windup /wáɪndʌp/ を用いる.
> **2**「(女性に)モーションをかける」というが, これは和製用法.「言い寄る」の意味だから, make a pass at や make advances to などを用いる.

モーター a **motor** ; an **engine** (エンジン) ▶モーターを動かす[止める] start [stop／turn off] *a motor* ‖ モーターが回っている The *motor* [*engine*] is running.
‖モーターバイク a motorbike **‖モーターボート** a speedboat (➤ motorboat は「エンジン[モーター]で動く船」の意で, speedboat はその1つ).

モーテル a **motel** /moʊtél/, a **motor inn**, a **motor lodge** ▶モーテルで1泊する stay overnight at *a motel*
《参考》英語の motel は自動車旅行者のための簡易宿泊所を指し, 日本でいう「モーテル」とはかなり異なる.

モード **1【方式・態勢・気分】** **mode** ▶二学期になったけど私はまだ夏休みモードなの The second term has begun, but my mind is still in (summer) vacation *mode* [my mind still hasn't switched to study *mode*].
2【流行】 **fashion** ▶最新モード the latest *fashion*.
‖モード雑誌 a fashion magazine.
☛ マナーモード (→見出語)

モーニング **1【朝】** **morning.**
‖モーニングカップ a mug [cup] for morning coffee **‖モーニングコーヒー** morning coffee **‖モーニングコール** a wake-up call **‖モーニングサービス** a cut-price breakfast set (during the morning hours) **‖モーニングショー** a morning show.
2【礼服】 (a) **morning dress** (上着とズボン) ; a **morning coat**, a **cutaway** (上着).

> **危ないカタカナ語✹ モーニング**
> **1**「モーニング」は英語の morning (朝, 午前中) からきているが, 注意すべきは日本の喫茶店などでいう「モーニングサービス」で, morning service とすると「朝の礼拝」の意味になる. したがって a cut-price breakfast set (during the morning hours) のように説明する必要がある.
> **2** 電話で起こすことを「モーニングコール」というが, 英語では wake-up call がふつう.
> **3** 礼服の「モーニング」は morning dress という. morning coat とすると上着だけしか指さないので注意.

モーモー ▶牛がモーモーと鳴いていた The cow was *mooing*. (➤ moo の発音は /mu:/).

モーリシャス **Mauritius** (インド洋南西部, マダガスカル島東方にある島国).

モール **1【商店街】** a **mall.**
2【織物】 **braid.**
‖金モール gold braid.

モールス **‖モールス信号** the Morse /mɔ:ʳs/ code.

もがく **struggle** (何かに抵抗して) ; **writhe** /raɪð/ (苦痛な

どで)；squirm (体をよじる, もぞもぞする) ▶幼児は母親の手を離れようとしてもがいた The little boy *struggled* to get free from his mother's arms. ‖ 病人は苦しさのあまり床の中でもがいた The sick man *writhed* in the bed with pain.

もぎ 模擬の mock；trial (試しの) ▶あす模擬試験がある We are going to have *a mock* [*trial*／*practice*] *examination* tomorrow. (➤ mock examination は単に mock ということもある) ‖ 学園祭のときは模擬店が 10 くらい出る During the school festival, there will be about ten *refreshment stands*. ‖ 面接の一環としての模擬授業 *a trial lesson* as part of the interview process.
▶面接官たちの前で [教授たちに対して] 模擬授業を行う give *a teaching demonstration* before the interview committee [for an audience of faculty members].
‖模擬裁判 [法廷] a moot court (法学生の) ‖ 模擬実験 (a) simulation.

もぎたて ▶もぎたてのリンゴ a *freshly-picked* apple.

もぎとる もぎ取る pick ＋㊐ (果実などを)；wrench ＋㊐, wrest ＋㊐ (力ずくで；後者は堅い語または文語で, 武器や比喩的に人の地位などを無理に奪い取ることをいう) ▶行楽客たちはリンゴを木からもぎ取って食べた The vacationers *picked* apples and ate them. ‖ 警官はその暴漢からナイフをもぎ取った The policeman *wrenched* [*wrested*] a knife from the hoodlum.

もく 目 《生物学》an order (分類上の単位).

もぐ pick ＋㊐ ▶父は今, 裏庭でナシをもいでいます My father *is picking* pears in the backyard now.

もくぎょ 木魚 a *mokugyo*, a wooden fish.

もくげき 目撃する witness ＋㊐ ▶多くの人がその事件を目撃した A lot of people *witnessed* the incident. ‖ 彼は逃げて行くところを近所のみんなに目撃された (＝見られた) He *was seen* running away by everyone in the neighborhood.
‖目撃者 a witness, an eyewitness.

もぐさ moxa /máːksə/. →おきゅう.

もくざい 木材 wood (材木)；《米》lumber, 《英》timber (製材した).

もくさつ 黙殺する ignore ＋㊐ (completely) ▶彼らは私の意見を黙殺した They *ignored* [*took no notice of*] my opinion. ‖ 日本側代表団はそれを黙殺した The Japanese delegation *refused* to even comment on it. (➤「論評することさえ拒んだ」の意).

もくさん 目算 **1**【見当】a rough estimate ▶目算を立てる make *a rough estimate*.
2【見込み】expectations ▶月々の小遣いを増やしてもらえず目算が外れた My *expectations* were crushed when I was refused a raise in my monthly allowance.

もくし 黙視する observe silently；overlook (大目に見る)；close one's eyes to (…に目をつぶる).

もくじ 目次 (a table of) contents 《参考》目次の見出しには通例 Contents と書く.

もくじゅう 黙従 blind obedience.

もくしろく 黙示録 the Book of Revelation, the Apocalypse /əpáːkəlɪps/ (聖書の).

[1]**もくせい 木星** 《天文学》Jupiter ▶木星は太陽系の惑星のうちで最も大きい *Jupiter* is the largest planet in the solar system.

[2]**もくせい 木犀** 《植物》a fragrant [sweet] olive.

[3]**もくせい 木製の** wooden ▶木製の机 a *wooden* desk／a desk *made of wood*.

もくぜん 目前 ▶入学試験は目前に迫っている The entrance examinations *are drawing near* [*are just around the corner*]. ‖ 田中は勝利を目前にして一発に泣いた Tanaka lost the game by giving up a home run just when (we thought) victory was *within his reach*.
▶2 台の車が私の目前で衝突した Two cars collided *right before my eyes* [*right in front of me*].

もくぞう 木造の wooden ▶木造の家 a *wooden* house ‖ その旅館は木造だ The inn is *made* [is *built*] *of wood*. (● wooden は名詞の前で用いる形容詞なので, (×)The inn is wooden. とはしない).

もくそく 目測 ▶適当な計器を持っていなかったので距離を目測した We *measured* the distance *by eye*, since we had no proper instruments.
▶彼は岩棚へ飛び移ろうとして目測を誤り, 谷底へ転落した When he tried to jump to the ledge, he *misjudged* the distance and fell to the bottom of the gorge.

もくたん 木炭 charcoal /tʃáːʳkoʊl/ ▶木炭で絵を描く draw with a piece of *charcoal*.

もくてき 目的

a purpose /páːʳpəs/；an aim /eɪm/ (ねらい)；an intention (意図)；an objective (目標)；a goal (最終的な目標) ▶首相の今回のアメリカ訪問の目的は何ですか What is the *purpose* of the Prime Minister's current visit to the U.S.? ‖ 英語を身につける目的で英字新聞を取っています I take an English language newspaper *for the purpose of* learning English [*in order to* learn English]. (● I take an English language newspaper to learn English. が最も簡単な言い方).
▶何のために大学に行くのか目的をはっきりさせたほうがよいと思う I think you should make your *aim* in going to college clear. ‖ 彼女は金を借りる目的でおじを訪ねた She visited her uncle *with the intention of* asking for a loan. ‖ 探検隊は目的を果たせず途中で引き返した The expedition was unable to fulfill its *objective* [*goal*] and turned back partway. ‖ 何の目的で (＝なぜ) あんなくだらない番組を放送するんだろう *Why* are they broadcasting such a worthless program? ‖ 目的地に近づいたぞ We'll soon be arriving at our *destination*.

> **あなたの英語はどう響く?**
> 「日本へいらっしゃった目的は何ですか」といった質問を日本人はしがちだが, What is your purpose in coming to Japan? や Why did you come to Japan? では警察官などが「何の目的で日本へ来たんだ?」と問い詰めるときの質問になってしまう. Is this a sightseeing trip? (観光旅行ですか), Are you here on business? (こちらにはお仕事で来られたのですか) のように言ったほうがよい.

‖《文法》目的格 the objective case ‖ 目的語 an object.

もくとう 黙祷 a silent prayer /preəʳ/ ▶私たちは震災の犠牲者の霊に 1 分間の黙とうをささげた We offered a one-minute *silent prayer* for the souls of the (departed) earthquake victims.

もくどく 黙読 silent reading 一動 黙読する read to oneself ▶英語の勉強には黙読より音読のほうが効果がある In studying English, reading out loud is more effective than *reading silently* [*to yourself*].

もくにん 黙認 silent approval 一動 黙認する overlook

+㊐ (大目に見る) ; **condone** +㊐ (非合法行為などを) ▶上司は私の失敗を黙認してくれた My boss *overlooked* my mistake. ‖ 親は子供の喫煙を黙認すべきではない Parents mustn't *give their silent approval to* their children's smoking. ‖ 警察は右翼の暴力行為を黙認すべきでない Police should not *turn a blind eye to* the violent activities of right-wingers. (➤「見て見ぬふりをする」の意).

もくば 木馬 a **wooden horse** (木製の馬) ; a **rocking horse** (揺り木馬).

もくはん 木版 a **woodblock** (版木) ; **woodblock printing** (技法)
‖**木版画** a woodblock print, a woodcut.

もくひ 黙秘する **refuse to answer, stand mute** (➤後者は法律用語) ▶容疑者は黙秘権を行使した The suspect *exercised his right to remain silent* [《米また》*took the Fifth* (*Amendment*)]. 《参考》後者の take the Fifth [Amendment] は黙秘権に言及した合衆国憲法修正第5条に由来する表現.
‖**黙秘権** one's right to remain [keep] silent.

もくひょう 目標 **1**【目印】a **landmark** ; a **target** (攻撃の的) ▶教会を目標においでください Use the church as *a landmark* when coming here. ‖ 軍事目標を攻撃する attack *a military target*.
2【目的】an **aim** /eɪm/ (ねらい) ; an **objective** /əbdʒéktɪv/ (目的) ; a **goal** (最終目標) ▶当面の目標は茶道の基本を学ぶことだ My present *aim* is to learn the basics of (the) tea ceremony. ‖ 市長の目標は犯罪を減らすことであった The mayor's *objective* was to reduce crime.
▶募金はとうとう目標の金額に達した We have finally reached our *goal* [*target*] in fund-raising. ‖ 私にはもう生きていく目標がない I don't have anything to live *for* anymore [any longer]. (➤ for は「…のために」で目標を表す).
‖**目標額** a target (figure).

もくへん 木片 a **block of wood** ; a **chip** [**small piece**] **of wood**, a **wood chip** (小さな).

もくめ 木目 (**wood**) **grain** ▶木目調のテーブル a *wood-grain* table.

¹**もくもく** ▶入道雲がもくもくとわき上がった Thunderheads have risen *massively* in the sky. ‖ 工場の煙突がもくもくと煙を吐いている The factory smokestacks *are sending up billows of smoke*. ／*Billows of smoke are pouring* from the factory smokestacks.

²**もくもく 黙々と** **silently** ▶福井氏は朝から晩まで黙々と(＝黙って一生懸命)働く Mr. Fukui works *hard silently* (*and steadily*) from morning till night. ‖ 彼女は黙々と仕事をしている She'*s absorbed in* her work. ／She *is* completely *wrapped up in* her work. (➤ともに「没頭している」の意).

もぐもぐ ▶老婆は一言二言何やらもぐもぐ言った The old woman *mumbled* a few words.

もくよう(び) 木曜(日) **Thursday** /θə́ːrzdeɪ, -di/ 《略 Th., Thur., Thurs.》▶先週の木曜日に学校で火災避難訓練があった We had a fire drill at school last *Thursday*. →曜日.

もくよく 沐浴する **wash** oneself (体を洗う) ; **take a ritual bath, perform** one's **ablutions** (宗教的な清めを行う).

もぐら 《動物》a **mole**.

もぐり 潜り **1**【潜水】**diving** ▶彼は潜りが得意だ He's good at *swimming underwater*.
2【無免許】▶もぐりの医者 a *phony* doctor (➤「無免許の医者」は an unlicensed doctor) ‖ あの男はもぐりでレストランを経営している He runs a restaurant *without a license*.
3【偽者】a **phony**.

もぐりこむ 潜り込む **crawl into** ; **get into** (入り込む) ▶ベッドにもぐり込む *crawl* [*get*] *into* bed ‖ 蛇がテントにもぐり込んだ A snake *slithered into* the tent.
▶《比喩的》暴力団員がこの会場にもぐり込んでいるらしい Gangsters seem to have *slipped into* the hall. ‖ 彼はS大に何とかもぐり込んだ He *managed to get into* S University.

もぐる 潜る **1**【水中に】**dive** ▶漁師たちはアワビを採りに海に潜った The fishers *dived into* the sea for abalone. ‖ プロの潜水夫は素潜りでどのくらい潜っていられますか How long can a professional diver *stay underwater* without oxygen?
2【物の下に】**crawl** 《under》▶修理工は何か調べるために車体の下に潜った The mechanic *crawled under* the chassis to check something. ‖ 休みの日は昼近くまでふとんに潜っています I *stay in bed* until around noon on my days off.
3【目立たない所に】▶戦前の共産党員は地下に潜って執ように活動を続けた The prewar communists *went underground* [*went into hiding*] while persisting with their activities.

¹**もくれい 目礼する** **greet with** one's **eyes** ▶きれいな女の子が通りすがりに私に目礼した A pretty girl *greeted* me *with her eyes* as she passed.

²**もくれい 黙礼** a **bow** /baʊ/ ―動 **黙礼する** **bow** 《to》▶母は校長先生に黙礼した My mother *bowed* [*made a bow*] *to* the principal.

もくれん 木蓮 《植物》a **magnolia** /mæɡnóʊliə/ (➤《米》ではふつうタイサンボクを指す).

もくろく 目録 a **catalog**(**ue**) (カタログ) ; a **list** (一覧表) ; an **inventory** (商品の在庫目録) ▶コレクションの目録を作る make *a catalog* [*list*] of one's collection ‖ その本はもう目録にありません The book is no longer on the *list* now.
‖**オンライン目録** an online catalog ‖ **図書目録** a book catalog [list].

もくろみ 目論見 a **plan** (計画) ; an **attempt** (企て) ▶株でひともうけしようという彼のもくろみは外れた His *scheme* [*plan*] to make a killing on the stock market failed.

もくろむ 目論む **plot** +㊐ ▶1936年青年将校たちはクーデターをもくろんだ In 1936, young officers *plotted* a coup d'état. ‖ 彼らはいったい何をもくろんでいるんだろう Just what do they *have in mind*? ／What on earth *are* they *up to*? (➤後者がよりインフォーマル).

もけい 模型 a **model** ; a **miniature** /míniətʃəʳ/ (特に小型の) ▶実物大[10分の1]の模型 a life-size [one-tenth scale] *model* ‖ 息子は帆船の模型を作った My son made *a model* [*a miniature*] of a sailing ship.
‖**模型飛行機** a model (air)plane.

もげる **come off** (取れる) ; **drop off** (落ちる) ▶スーツケースがあまりに重くて手がもげそうだった The suitcase was so heavy I felt as if my arms would *drop off*.

もこもこ ▶もこもこしたダウンジャケット a *plump* down jacket.

もごもご ▶口の中でもごもご言ってないで, はっきり言いなさい Don't *mumble*. Speak clearly.

もさ 猛者 a **strong man**, a **tough guy**.

モザイク (a) **mosaic** /moʊzéɪɪk/ ▶モザイク模様の歩道 a *mosaic* sidewalk ‖ モザイクタイルの床 a *mosaic tile* floor.

▶モザイクのかかった画像 a *pixelated* [*pixelized*] image (➤ pixelate, pixelize はコンピュータ用語で「画素数を減らしてぼかす」) ‖ 容疑者の顔はモザイクがかけられていた The suspect's face *was pixelated*.

もさく 模索する struggle(…しようと努力する) ; grope 《for》(さがし求める) ▶政府は金融問題解決の道を模索中だ The government *is struggling to find* ways [*is groping for* measures] to resolve the financial problems.

もさっと ▶もさっとした少年 a *sluggish* [*clumsy*] boy.

1**もし 模試** a mock [trial／practice] exam ▶模試を受ける take *a mock* [*practice*] *exam*.

2もし

《解説》日本語の「もし…ならば」はそれがありうる条件か, 全くの仮想の話かはあまり意識されないが, 英語では明確に区別されるので, 英文にする際にははっきり意識する必要がある.「もし…ならば」に英語では if を用いるが, 大きく異なる 2 つの使い方がある. ふつうに「もしあす雨なら」(If it rains tomorrow)というのは単にありうる条件を示している(これも日本語では「仮定」に入るが, ここでは後述のものとの区別上,「ありうる条件」とする)だけであり, この場合, if は when や though などほかの接続詞と同じように使えばよい(→**1**). いっぽう,「もし私が鳥であったなら」(If I were a bird)とか「もし私がきみなら」(If I were you), あるいは「もし宝くじで1000万円当たったら」(If I won ten million yen in a lottery)というのは現実にはありえないことや可能性のきわめて低いことを純粋に「仮定」の上で発話しているので, 英文法でいう「仮定法」を用いる(→**2**).

1【条件を示して】 if ; in case(…の場合は, …かもしれないので).

【文型】
もし A ならば B だ
If S + V(現在形), S + V(現在形・未来形).

《解説》(1)現在あるいは未来に関して,「もし」とありうる条件を示すには **if** を使う. この場合の **if** は when, though, after などの他の接続詞と基本的に使い方は同じで, if の文 A では動詞は現在形, その後の文 B では内容に応じて, 現在形または未来形にする.
(2)A の動詞は未来を表すときも主に現在形を使う. また, **if** の文 A が文章の後半にくることもある.

▶もしきみが遅れたら, きみを置いて先に行くよ *If* you're late, I'll go ahead without you. (● if you'll be late とはしない) ‖ もしあした雨が降ったらバーベキューはできないね We won't be able to have a barbecue *if* it rains tomorrow.

▶もしパスワードをお忘れの場合はこちらをクリックしてください *If* you (*should*) forget [*In case* you forget] your password, please click here. (➤ if を用いるのがふつう. should は「万が一」のニュアンス) ‖ もしお昼がお済みでなかったら, ご一緒にいかがですか *If* you haven't had lunch yet, how about going out (for lunch) with me?

▶もしご宿泊を延長される場合は午前 9 時までにフロントにご連絡ください *Should* you wish to extend your stay, please contact the front desk before 9 a.m. (➤ Should … は「万一…ならば」の意の堅い言い方).

2【現実とは違う状況を仮定して】 if ; suppose (➤ Suppose … (…と仮定して) の形で用いることが多い).

【文型】
もし A ならば B なのに
《現在・未来のことは》
If S + V (過去形), S + would +原形.
《過去のことは》
If S + V (過去完了形),
S + would have +過去分詞.

《解説》「もし」は現実にはありえない, あるいは事実に反する仮想の条件, 実現が難しいと考えている条件などでも使われる.
(1)現在の事実に反する仮想の文では if の文 A の動詞は過去形にして, 後の文 B の動詞は「**would** +原形」にする. if の文 A の be 動詞は主語が単数でも were が正式だが,《インフォーマル》では was にすることもある. また, B には would の代わりに意味に応じて, could (…できるのに), might (…かもしれないのに)などもくる.
(2)過去の事実に反する仮想の文では, if の文 A の動詞は「**had** +過去分詞」の過去完了形を, B の文は「**would have** +過去分詞」を用いる.

▶もし私があなたなら, そんなことはしないと思います *If* I were you, I *would*n't do that. (➤ この文と次の文は仮定法過去) ‖ もしお金があればこのカメラを買うのだが *If* I had money, I *would* buy this camera. ‖ もし(あのとき)知っていたら教えてやったさ *If* I had known about it, I *would have* told you. (➤ 仮定法過去完了).

▶もし宝くじで1000万円当たったらどうしますか *Suppose* you won ten million yen in the lottery, what would you do with it? ‖ 彼の主張には「もし…だったら」という仮定が多すぎる There are too many *ifs* in his argument.

✉《ラブレターで》**もし私が鳥だったらすぐにでもあなたのもとへ飛んでいくのに** *If* I were a bird, I would fly to you right now.

3【提案・勧誘して】 ▶もし(都合が)よかったら, 今度の日曜日にうちに来てください *If it is convenient* (*for you*), I'd like to invite you to my house next Sunday. (➤ if your schedule permits, あるいは if you have no other plans, といういい方もよく使われる).

もじ 文字 a letter(英字などの表音文字) ; a character /kǽrəktəʳ/ (漢字などの表意文字) ▶大 [小] 文字で書く write in *capital* [*small*] *letters* ‖ その部族は文字を持たないといわれている That tribe is said to have no *writing system*.

‖ (放送・講演などの)**文字起こし** a transcript ‖ **文字化け** garbled letters [characters／text] (文字) ; text garbling (化けること) 《参考》英数字は 1 バイトで表せるので, 全角の日本語文字のように, 文字化けが起こることは少ない ‖ (時計などの)**文字盤** a dial, a face.

逆引き熟語 ○○文字
上付き文字 a superscript／**絵文字** a pictorial symbol, a pictogram／**大文字** a capital letter／**顔文字** a smiley, an emoticon／**頭文字** an initial (letter)／**ギリシャ文字** a Greek letter／**くさび形文字** a cuneiform (character)／**小文字** a small letter／**象形文字** a hieroglyph／**表意文字** an ideograph／**表音文字** a phonogram

もしかしたら possibly ; maybe, perhaps（➤ あとの２つのほうが可能性が高い；→たぶん）▶もしかしたら彼女はうそをついたのかもしれない *Possibly* she lied to me. ／*It could be that* she lied to me. ‖ もしかしたらあいつは遅れて来るかもしれない *Maybe* [*Perhaps*] he will be around later. ‖ もしかしたら大当たりするかもしれないと思って宝くじを買った I bought lottery tickets *on the chance of* hitting [*thinking I just might* hit] the jackpot.

もしかして ▶もしかして馬場さんの住まいをご存じかと思って I thought you *might happen to* [*might possibly*] know where Ms. Baba lives. ‖ もしかして小室さんではありませんか Are you Mr. Komuro *by any chance*?／ You wouldn't be Mr. Komuro, would you?《参考》Google 検索の際の間違った語や綴り字に対して示される「もしかして」は英語では Did you mean : …? のようになる.

もしくは (either) … or ▶お申し込みはお電話もしくはファックスでどうぞ Please apply by phone *or* by fax. ‖ 両親もしくは兄が試合を見に行きます *Either* my parents *or* my (older) brother is coming to see the game. (● 動詞は or のあとの(代)名詞に合わせる).

もじどおり 文字通り literally ▶あきらはその英文を文字どおりに訳した Akira translated the English sentence *literally* [*word for word*].
▶ (映画の)黒澤明監督は文字どおりの巨匠だった Director Kurosawa Akira was *literally* one of the greatest masters of film ever.

もしも if ▶もしも私がきみの立場だったとしたら, そんな大金は貸さないね *If* I were you, I would never lend (anyone) such a large sum of money. →もし.
▶もしものことがあったらこの番号に電話をしなさい Call this number *in case of emergency* [*if anything should happen*]. ‖ 妊娠してるのにスキーに行こうなんて, もしものことがあったらどうするんだ You're going skiing when you're pregnant ! What *if something (unexpected) should happen*? ‖ もしものときのためにお金を蓄えておきなさい Save money (*just*) *in case* [*for a rainy day*].

もしもし excuse me（人に注意を促して）; hello（電話で）▶もしもしお嬢さん, 傘を忘れてますよ *Excuse me, miss*… you've forgotten your umbrella. ‖ もしもし, ちょっとお尋ねします *Excuse me*. May I ask you something?
▶ 対話《電話で》「もしもし, 吾郎君？」「いえ, 今代わります」"*Hello*. Is this [《英》that] Goro?" "No, just a sec. I'll put him on."

もじもじ ▶女の子は母親の陰でもじもじして, ぼくに「こんにちは」も言わなかった The little girl was hiding *hesitantly* [*bashfully*] behind her mother and didn't even say hello to me. (➤ hesitantly は「ちゅうちょして」, bashfully は「はにかんで」) ‖ ぼくは美人の横に座るとついもじもじしてしまう I can't help *getting jittery* [*nervous*] when I sit next to a beautiful woman.

もしや ▶もしや彼の住所をご記憶ではありませんか Do you *happen to* remember his address? (➤ happen to は「たまたま…する」).

もしゃ 模写 a copy 一動 模写する copy ＋目 ▶歌麿を模写する *copy* an Utamaro ‖ この絵はラファエロの模写だ This picture is *a copy* of a Raphael.

もじゃもじゃ ▶もじゃもじゃのひげ a *scraggly* beard (➤ scraggly は「手入れもしていない」) ‖ その女の子のもじゃもじゃの毛 the girl's *scraggly* hair ‖ 人前でそのもじゃもじゃ頭をかかないでよ It's rude to scratch your *shaggy hair* in front of people.

もしゅ 喪主 the chief mourner ▶喪主を務める act as *the chief mourner* ‖ 喪主はどなたですか Who is (to be) *the chief mourner*? (➤ to be はこれから喪主を務める場合).

もしょう 喪章 a mourning band（上着の袖に巻く）; a mourning ribbon（胸の）.

もじり a parody.

もじる parody ＋目 ▶これはミルトンの詩をもじったものだ This is *a parody* of one of Milton's poems.

もす 燃す →燃やす.

もず（鳥）a shrike ▶モズの鳴き声は鋭い *A shrike* cries shrilly.

モスク a mosque（イスラム教寺院）.

もずく *mozuku* ; a type of edible seaweed usually served in vinegar (➤ 説明的な訳).

モスグリーン moss green.

モスクワ Moscow（ロシア連邦の首都）
‖ モスクワ市民 a Muscovite /mʌ́skəvaɪt/.

もぞう 模造 imitation ▶模造ダイヤ an *imitation* [*artificial*] diamond (➤ 後者は「人工の」の意) ‖ この真珠は模造品だ This pearl is *an imitation* [*a fake*]. (➤ fake は「偽物, いんちき」といった悪い意味で用いる).
▶ヒット商品が出ると必ず模造品が作られる If there is a hit product, *fakes* [*counterfeits*] of it will surely be made. →イミテーション.

もそもそ ▶おまえ, 何もそもそ言ってるんだい？ What're you *mumbling* (*about*)?

もぞもぞ ▶背中がもぞもぞする. シャツの中に何か入ったらしい I *feel something creeping* [*crawling*] on my back. Something must be in my shirt. ‖ 何, もぞもぞやってんの？ What are you *fidgeting* for?

もだえる 悶える writhe /raɪð/ ▶患者は苦痛にもだえている The patient is *in agony* [is *writhing in pain*].

もたげる ▶蛇は頭をもたげて私を見た The snake *raised* [*reared*] its head and looked at me. ‖ その国では再び独裁政権が頭をもたげてきた In that country, dictatorship has once again *reared* its head.

もたせかける rest《on, against》▶彼女は頭を椅子の肘かけにもたせかけて居眠りを始めた *Resting* her head *on* the arm of the chair, she began to doze off.

もたせる 持たせる **1**【運ばせる】have … carry (➤ …にくるのは持つ人) ▶彼女はよく夫に買い物袋を持たせる She often *has* her husband *carry* her (shopping) bags (for her). (● gets her husband to carry ともいえる) ‖ 代金は息子に持たせます I'll *send* my son along with the money.
2【支払わせる】▶これは私にもたせてください *Let* me *pay* [*foot the bill*] for this.
3【もちこたえさせる】▶この冬いっぱいはなんとかこのおんぼろストーブをもたせなくっちゃ Somehow (or other) I have to *make* this old heater *last* till the end of winter.

もたつく ▶お年寄りが小銭を探してもたついていたので, バスの運転手はいらいらした The bus driver was irritated because the elderly man *was* so *slow* in finding change for the fare. ‖ 交渉はもたついた The negotiations *hit a snag*. (➤ snag は「障害」).

もたもたする dawdle /dɔ́:dl/ ▶何もたもたしてるんだ What are you *dawdling* for? ‖ もたもたするな *Be* *quick about it.* ／*Make it snappy.* ／*Get a move on.* ／*Stop dawdling*！‖もたもたしてるうちにほかのお客さんがそのブーツ買ってっちゃうよ Some other customer will snatch up these boots while you*'re dillydallying*. (➤ dillydally /dílidæ̀li/ は「決心がつかずぐずぐずする」).

もたらす **bring about**(変化などを引き起こす)；**introduce** +目 (紹介する) ▶コンピュータは私たちの生活に多くの変化をもたらした Computers have *brought about* many changes in our life [have changed our lives in many ways]. ‖豪雨が九州に大きな被害をもたらした The heavy rain *caused* serious damage in Kyushu.
▶西洋医学は最初にオランダ人によって日本にもたらされた Western medicine *was introduced* into Japan by the Dutch.

もたれかかる **lean**《against》▶その通勤者は電車のドアにもたれかかって小説を読みふけっていた The commuter *was leaning against* the train door, absorbed in a novel.

もたれる **1**【寄りかかる】**lean**《against, on》▶彼氏にもたれる *lean against* [*on*] one's boyfriend ‖椅子の背にもたれる *lean against* the back of a chair ‖壁にもたれて座ってはいけない Don't sit *with your back against* the wall.
2【胃に重く感じる】▶このピザは胃にもたれる This pizza *is heavy on* the stomach.

モダン **modern** ▶この付近はモダンな建物が多い There are many *modern* buildings around here. ‖高齢にもかかわらずあの人の考えはなかなかモダンだ His ideas are quite *up-to-date*, in spite of his advanced age.
‖モダンジャズ modern jazz ‖モダンダンス modern dance.

[1]**もち 餅** ***mochi***；a **rice cake**
日本紹介 ✉ **もちはもち米を蒸して臼(うす)と杵(きね)でついて作った食品です. 正月を代表する食べ物ですが, 最近では一年中スーパーなどで売っています** *Mochi* is a food made from glutinous rice that is steamed and then pounded using a mortar and a mallet. It is one of the typical foods eaten during the Japanese New Year holidays. Nowadays, *mochi* is available at supermarkets all year round.
▶もちを焼く grill [toast] a cake of *mochi* ‖幼稚園でもちつき大会が開かれた The kindergarten class had a party *making and eating sticky mochi rice cakes*.
ことわざ もちはもち屋 Leave *mochi*-making to the *mochi*-maker. (➤ 日本語からの直訳) ／(Better) leave it to an expert.

[2]**もち 持ち** **1**【物の寿命】▶もちのいい商品 a *durable* product ‖もちのよい布 *serviceable* cloth (➤ serviceable は通例服の生地に使う) ‖この靴はもちがいい[悪い] These shoes *wear well* [*badly*]. →日持ち.
2【負担】▶旅費は各自もちです Everyone *must pay* his [her] own traveling expenses. ‖今夜の宴会は会社もちですから心ゆくまで飲んでください Please drink as much as you want tonight because our company is *footing the bill*. (➤ foot は「(勘定を)払う」の意のインフォーマルな語) ／Please drink to your heart's content tonight because *our company is taking care of all the expenses*. (➤ 改まった文).

もちあがる 持ち上がる **1**【上へ上がる】▶このハンマーは重くて私には持ち上がらない This hammer is too heavy for me to *lift*. ‖飛行機が離陸するとき, 体が持ち上がるような気がした It felt like I was *being lifted up* as our plane took off.
2【事が起こる】**come up** ▶また別の問題が持ち上がった Another problem *has come up*.
3【クラス担任が】▶本田先生は持ち上がる予定だ Mr. Honda will *remain in charge of the same class he had last year*.

もちあげる 持ち上げる **1**【上へ上げる】**lift** +目, **raise** /reɪz/ +目 (➤ 前者は意識[努力]して上げるというニュアンス) ▶その選手は150キロのバーベルを頭上に持ち上げた The weight lifter *lifted* a 150 kilogram barbell above his head. ‖頭を持ち上げろ *Raise* your head.
2【おだてる】**flatter** +目 ▶部員たちは盛んに課長を持ち上げた The staffers *flattered* the section chief enthusiastically.

もちあじ 持ち味 ▶そのデザインは絹の持ち味を十分生かしている That design uses the *special qualities* of silk to full advantage. ‖ひょうひょうとしたところがあの役者の持ち味だ (Noble) aloofness is that actor's *trademark* [*characteristic style*].

もちあるく 持ち歩く **carry** +目 ▶外国旅行をするときに現金を(ポケットに入れて)持ち歩くのは危険だ It is not safe to *carry* cash *with you* (in your pocket) when you travel abroad.

もちあわせ 持ち合わせ ▶すてきなブラウスを見つけたので買いたかったが, お金の持ち合わせがなかった I found a nice blouse and wanted to buy it, but I *didn't have enough money* (*with me*).

もちあわせる 持ち合わせる **have ... with** [**on**] one (➤ one は目的格の人称代名詞) ▶たまたまそのとき私は保険証を持ち合わせていた By chance, I *had* my health insurance card *with me* at the time. ‖手元には１円も持ち合わせていない I *have*n't *got* a penny *on me*. ／I don't *have* a dime *on me*. (➤ dime は「(アメリカ・カナダの)10セント硬貨」の意).

もちいえ 持ち家 one's **own house**(➤ 自分のものである家)；a **house of** one's **own**(しばしば, 夢の実現としての自分の家) ▶たいていの人が自分の持ち家を欲しがっている Most people would like to have *their own house*. ／Most people would like (to have) *a house of their own*. ‖このマンションは私の持ち家だ I *own* this condominium.

モチーフ a **motif** /moʊtíːf/ ▶シャガールは動物をモチーフにした絵を数多く描いている Chagall painted many pictures with animal *motifs*.

もちいる 用いる **use** /juːz/ +目；**utilize** +目 (利用する) ▶消毒にアルコールを用いる *use* alcohol for disinfection ‖その問題を解くにはピタゴラスの定理を用いよ *Utilize* the Pythagorean theorem to solve the problem.

もちうた 持ち歌 one's **repertory** [**repertoire** /répəʳtwɑːʳ/] (**of songs**)《参考》歌を聞けば歌っている有名歌手とすぐ結びつく代表的な持ち歌を signature song という.

もちかえり 持ち帰り 《参考》持ち帰り用の料理などのことを (a) takeout,《英また》(a) takeaway という.
▶ホットドッグを４つ持ち帰り用にしてください Four hot dogs *to go* [*to take out* ／《英また》*to take away*], please.
▶ 対話「お持ち帰りですか, それともここで召し上がりますか」「持ち帰りにしてください」"Is this to eat [drink] here or *to go*? ／(For) here or *to go*?" "*To go*,

も

please. ／I'd like that *to go.*"(➤「ここで食べます［飲みます］」は "(For) here, please. ／I'll eat here. ／It's for here." などと言えばよい).

[1]**もちかえる 持ち帰る** bring back ; take home（家へ）▶機密書類を自宅に持ち帰ることはできない You must not *take* classified documents *home.*

[2]**もちかえる 持ち替える** ▶彼女はバッグを右手から左手に持ち替えた She *shifted* her bag from her right arm to her left.

もちかける 持ちかける ▶うまい話を持ちかけてくる人には気をつけなさい Be careful when people *approach* you *with* offers［deals］(that seem almost) too good to be true.

もちかぶ 持ち株 ‖持ち株会社 a holding company.

もちきり 持ち切り ▶翌日, 教室は先生の秘密デートの話でもちきりだった The next day the entire class *was buzzing* with the story of the teacher's clandestine date. (➤ buzz は「ざわざわする, わきたつ」) ‖ 学校中が新しい転校生のうわさでもちきりだ The new transfer student is now *the talk of* the whole school. (➤ the talk of は「…のうわさの種」).

もちぐされ 持ち腐れ ▶この高価なギターは私には宝の持ち腐れだ It's *a waste* (*of a good thing*) for me to own this expensive guitar.

もちくずす 持ち崩す ruin oneself ▶彼の息子は10代で身を持ち崩した His son *ruined himself* in his teenage years.

もちこす 持ち越す ▶結論は次回に持ち越された(＝延期された) Making a decision *was put off* until the next meeting. ‖ この仕事は先月から持ち越されたものだ This work *is left over* from last month. ‖ ライオンズはきょう負けたため優勝は来週に持ち越された The Lions lost the game today, so they *have to wait until* next week to clinch the pennant.

もちこたえる 持ちこたえる bear ＋目（重さなどに）; pull through（切り抜ける）▶この橋はトラックの重みには持ちこたえられないだろう This bridge won't *bear*［*support*／*hold*］the weight of a truck. ‖ 患者は5日間重体だったが, どうやら持ちこたえた The patient was in serious condition for five days, but somehow he *pulled through.*

もちこみ 持ち込み ▶バスの中へのスキーの持ち込みはお断りします Please don't *bring* skis *into* the bus. ／《掲示》No Skis on Bus ‖《掲示》危険物の持ち込み禁止 Dangerous Articles Prohibited ‖ 教科書持ち込み可［不可］の試験 an *open*［a *closed*］*book* examination.

▶持ち込み手荷物はいくつ大丈夫ですか How many items of *carry-on luggage* are permitted［am I allowed］? ／How much *carry-on luggage* is permitted［am I allowed］?

もちこむ 持ち込む **1【運び入れる】**bring in ▶危険物を持ち込む *bring*［*carry*］*in* dangerous things ‖ 東京ディズニーランドには飲食物を持ち込むことはできない You are not allowed to *take* food or drinks *into* Tokyo Disneyland. ‖ このスーツケースは機内に持ち込めますか Can I *take* this suitcase on the plane?

2【用件などを持ってくる】▶区役所に苦情を持ち込む *complain to* the ward office ／*file a complaint with* the ward office ‖ あの男はしょっちゅう難題を持ち込んでくる He always *turns up with* some sort of problem. ‖ その問題は裁判に持ち込まれた The problem *was taken to* court.

3【ある状態に持っていく】▶試合を延長戦に持ち込む *send* the game *into* extra innings［*into* overtime］.

もちごめ 糯米 glutinous /glúːtənəs/ rice.

もちさる 持ち去る make［walk］off with ▶今夜の客の誰かがここにあった灰皿を持ち去った One of our guests tonight *made*［*walked*］*off with* the ashtray that was here.

もちじかん 持ち時間 ▶スピーチの持ち時間は3分です You *have*［*are allowed*］*three minutes* for your speech.

もちだし 持ち出し **1【外へ持って出ること】**▶図書館から辞書類は持ち出し禁止ですよ Dictionaries *may not be taken out of* the library.

2【自分で超過分を負担すること】▶私は学生のパーティーに招待されるといつも持ち出しになる(＝いくらかお金を負担しなければならない) Whenever I'm invited to a student party, I always *end up having to foot part of the bill*［*to pay part of the cost of the party*］. (➤ foot は「支払う, 負担する」の意のインフォーマルな語).

もちだす 持ち出す **1【持って出る】**take［carry］out ▶火の回りが早くて(家から)何も持ち出せなかった The fire spread so quickly we couldn't *take*［*carry*］anything *out* (of the house).

2【問題などを取り上げる】bring up ; pose ＋目（提起する）; drag up《インフォーマル》（相手にとって嫌な話題をわざと）▶決まったことなのだから, もうその話は持ち出さないでくれよ Don't *bring up* the issue any more now that it has been decided. ‖ 学生に難問を持ち出す *pose* a difficult question to students ‖ 古い話を持ち出す *drag up* old stories.

もちつもたれつ 持ちつ持たれつ ▶二人の姉妹は持ちつ持たれつの関係だ The two sisters have *a give-and-take relationship.* ／The two sisters are *interdependent.* ‖ 世の中は持ちつ持たれつ Give and take is what life is all about.

もちなおす 持ち直す **1【持ち替える】**▶荷物を右手に持ち直す *shift* a package *to* one's right hand.

2【状態が良くなる】improve（良くなる）; rally（回復する）▶天気は持ち直してきた The weather *is improving*［*is getting better*］. ‖ 母の病気は持ち直した My mother's illness *took a turn*［*changed*］*for the better.* ‖ その特効薬を使ってから父の病状は持ち直した My father's condition *has improved* since he began to be treated with that miracle drug. ‖ 景気は最近だいぶ持ち直してきた Business *has recovered*［*picked up*］considerably lately.

もちにげ 持ち逃げする go［run］away《with》, make［run］off《with》▶ちょっと目を離したすきにスーツケースを持ち逃げされた Someone *went away*［*made off*］*with* my suitcase during the one moment I took my eyes off of it.

もちぬし 持ち主 an owner ▶この車の持ち主は誰かしら I wonder who the *owner* of this car is. ／I wonder whose car this is. ‖ このパチンコ屋は何度か持ち主が変わった This pachinko parlor *has changed hands* several times.

もちば 持ち場 one's post ▶5時までは持ち場を離れないでください Please do not leave your *post* until 5 : 00 p.m.

もちはこび 持ち運び ▶このコピー機は持ち運びができる This copier *is portable.* ／This is a *portable* copier. ‖ このノートパソコンは持ち運びが便利だ This laptop *is easy to carry.*

もちはだ もち肌 supple［soft／smooth］skin.

モチベーション motivation ▶モチベーションを上げる increase [raise] one's *motivation* ‖ 私のモチベーションが下がった My *motivation* has decreased [gone down]. ‖ モチベーションを常に高く保つようにしています I always try to *keep my motivation high*. ／I always try to *stay highly motivated*.

もちまえ 持ち前 ▶彼女は持ちまえの頑張り精神で困難を乗り越えた She got over the difficulty with her *characteristic* [*usual*] tenacity.

もちまわり 持ち回り ▶私たちの研究会の会計係は会員の持ち回りになっている The post of treasurer of our study group *rotates among the members*.

もちもの 持ち物 one's belongings, 《インフォーマル》one's things ▶自分の持ち物にはすべて名前をつけなさい Put your name on all your *belongings* [*things*]. ‖ そのハンカチは久美子さんの持ち物です The handkerchief *belongs to* Kumiko.

もちゅう 喪中 be in mourning
✉ 喪中につき新年のご挨拶を失礼させていただきます We are *in mourning* and will therefore not be sending New Year's cards. ➤ 英語圏ではこのような挨拶状は出さない.

もちよる 持ち寄る ▶各人が月曜日の朝, プランを持ち寄ることにした It was decided that each member would *bring* a plan of his or her own *to the table* on Monday morning. (➤ この the table は議論や討論の「場」)
✉ 5月30日の土曜日わが家で持ち寄りパーティーをしませんか Why don't we have *a potluck party* [*potluck dinner*] at my place on Saturday, May 30？ ➤ potluck party は「あり合わせの食べ物でするパーティー」.

もちろん 勿論 of course, sure (いいとも)；go ahead (遠慮なくどうぞ)；you bet (間違いなく)

> 語法 (1)「もちろん(いいですとも)」に相当する一般的な表現は of course で, これよりもくだけた言い方が sure や go ahead.
> (2)you bet はさらにくだけた表現であるが, これは相手が言ったことに受け答えして間投詞的に用いることが多い.

▶ 対話「質問していいですか」「もちろん」"Can I ask you something？" "*Of course*." ‖ 対話「本当に私のこと, 愛してる？」「もちろん(愛してる)さ」"Do you really love me？" "*Of course* (I do)." ‖ 対話「お父さんは私が弘君と付き合うのをやめてほしいのかな」「もちろん, そんなことないよ」"Does Dad want me to stop seeing Hiroshi？" "*Of course not*." (● 否定の内容で答えるときはこのように Of course not. となる. Certainly not. と答えてもよい) ‖ 対話「パパ, 日曜日の試合に来てくれる？」「もちろん行くとも」"Dad, are you coming to our game on Sunday？" "*You bet*." ‖ 対話「チキンもう1つもらっていい？」「もちろん」"Can I have another piece of chicken？" "*Sure*. ／ *Go ahead*."

> **あなたの英語はどう響く？**
> 外国人から Can I borrow your calculator？(計算器をお借りしていいですか)と聞かれたような場合に, Yes, of course. (ええ, もちろん) と答えると, 相手には尊大な答え方をしているように響くことが多い. Sure, go ahead. (ええ, どうぞ) のような答え方が無難.

▶もちろん, 今月中にはそれを終えられるよう, できるだけのことはやります *Naturally*, I will do everything I can to get it done before the end of the month. (➤ naturally は「当然」の意で, 文全体を修飾することが多い) ‖ もちろん, きみも賛成だよね *I'm sure* you agree with me, too. (● of course で始めると断定的で失礼なので, I'm sure(きっと…と思う)を用いる).
▶あの経済学者は国内はもちろん(＝国内だけでなく)世界中に名が通っている That economist is well known *not only* in this country, *but* (*also*) around the world [internationally *as well as* domestically]. ‖ 父は酒はもちろん, コーヒーも飲まない My father never drinks coffee, *not to mention* alcohol.

もつ 持つ

> 📖 訳語メニュー
> 持つ →have **1**
> 所有する →have, own **2**
> 心に抱く →have **3**
> 金を負担する →pay **4**
> 担当する →take charge of **5**
> 持ちこたえる →last, keep **6**

1【手に持つ】have ＋Ⓞ；hold ＋Ⓞ (しっかり持つ)；carry ＋Ⓞ (持ち運ぶ) ▶右手に何持ってるの？ What do you *have* in your right hand？ ‖ ナイフは右手で, フォークは左手で持ちなさい *Hold* the knife in your right hand and the fork in your left (hand). ‖ ちょっとはしごを持ってて(＝押さえてて)ちょうだい Could you *hold* the ladder a minute, please？ ‖ 卒業する生徒たちは皆手に花束を持っていた All the graduating students *held* bouquets in their hands. (➤ held は hold の過去形) ‖ 入場券は各自でお持ちください Everyone is requested to *have* his or her admission ticket in hand. ‖ かばんをお持ちしましょう *Let* me *hold* [*carry*] your bag.

2【所有する】have ＋Ⓞ, own ＋Ⓞ；run ＋Ⓞ (経営する) ▶私は自転車も車も持っていない I *have* neither a bicycle nor a car. ‖ 奥野君, 今お金いくら持ってる？ How much money do you *have* on you now, Okuno？ ‖ この辺では車を2台持っている家も珍しくない It is not uncommon for families around here to *own* two cars. ‖ 鬼頭さんは横浜に法律事務所を持っている Mr. Kito *runs* a law firm in Yokohama.
▶持つべきものは友だね What you (really) need is a good friend [are a few good friends]. ‖ 持てば持つほど欲しくなる *The more you get*, the more you want. ‖ 彼女は驚くべき記憶力を持っている(＝に恵まれている) She *is gifted with* a fantastic memory.

3【心に抱く】have ＋Ⓞ ▶彼女は将来, 自分の会社を作る夢をもっている She *has* a dream of establishing a company of her own in the future. ‖ もっと自分に自信をもちなさい You should *have* more confidence in yourself. ‖ 私も彼女と同じ悩みをもっている I *have* the same trouble as she does. ‖ 犯人は被害者に恨みをもっていた The culprit *had* [*bore*] a grudge against the victim. (➤ bore は bear の過去形).

4【金を負担する】pay (＋Ⓞ) ▶ここの勘定は私がもつよ Let me *pay* the bill. ／This is on me. (➤ 後者は「私がおごるよ」の意のインフォーマルな言い方；もっと丁寧に言うときは Let me treat you (this time).) ‖ 旅費は会社がもってくれる Our company will *pay* trav-

も

eling expenses.
5【担当する】take charge of ▶私は高校2年生のクラスを持っている I *am in charge of* a class of second year high school students. ／I teach eleventh graders at a high school.
6【持ちこたえる】last（病人・天気などが）; **keep**（食物が腐らないで）▶病人は秋までもつまい The patient may not *last*［*live*］until fall. ‖ 祖父は**長くはもたない**だろう My grandfather *doesn't have long to live*. ‖ この好天は週末までもつだろうか I wonder if this fine weather *last* till the weekend. ‖ 毎日4，5時間の睡眠でよく**体がもつ**なあ How can you *get by*［*stay healthy*］with only four or five hours of sleep every day, I wonder? ‖ この菓子は冷蔵庫に入れておけば1か月はもちます These sweets will *keep*［*stay good*］for a month in the refrigerator. ‖ このコートは10年はもちます This coat will *last* you (at least) 10 years.
7【その他】▶新しいダム計画に関して地元住民への**説明会をもつ**予定です We're planning to *have*［*hold*］*an explanatory meeting* for the residents concerning the new dam project.
▶楽天は田中（の人気）でもっている The Eagles *depend solely on* the popularity of Tanaka.

もっか 目下 at present, currently, presently（➤ presently は《米》で好まれる）; **now**（➤「今」の意の一般語）▶地盤沈下の原因は目下調査中です The cause of the subsidence is *now*［*currently* ／*presently*］under investigation. ‖ パ・リーグでは目下オリックスが首位を走っている *At present*, the Buffaloes are the front-runners in the Pacific League pennant race.

もっかん 木管 ‖木管楽器 a woodwind instrument.

もっきん 木琴 a **xylophone** /záɪləfòʊn/（➤発音に注意）▶木琴を弾く play the *xylophone*.
‖木琴奏者 a xylophonist.

もっけのさいわい もっけの幸い a **stroke of (good) luck**（思いがけない幸運）▶2時限めが自習になったのをもっけの幸い，数学の宿題をやった *Luckily*, the second period was changed into a self-study［study hall］hour, so I did my math assignment. ‖ そのとき玄関のチャイムが鳴ったのを**もっけの幸いと**席を立った Just then the doorbell rang, and I *jumped at the chance* to get out of my chair.（➤「それをいい機会にして」の意）.

もっこう 木工 woodworking,《主に英》**woodwork**
▶木工をする do *woodwork*.
‖木工所 a woodworking plant ‖ **木工職人** a woodworker ‖ **木工品** (a piece of) woodwork.

もっさり ▶彼って，もっさりしてあか抜けない感じだね He looks *dull*［*clumsy*］and unsophisticated.

もったい ▶彼女の写真，見せろよ．そんなもったいつけるなよ Come on and show me a photo of your girlfriend. Don't *make such a big deal of*［*about*］*it*.（➤ make a big deal of［about］は「…をおおごとに考える」の意のインフォーマルな言い方; It's no big deal, is it? としてもよい）. →もったいぶる.

もったいない ⚠**この日本語にぴったりの英語はない．「無駄である」の意味では be wasteful を，「(…には)良過ぎる」の意味では be too good (for ...) などを使って表現する．** ▶誰もいない部屋に電気をつけっ放しにしておくのはもったいない It *is wasteful* to leave the lights on in a room when no one is around. ‖ 食べ残してはもったいないよ It's *a waste* to leave so much food.
▶ああ，もったいない．きっとこの洗濯機まだ使えるよ *What a waste*［*a shame*］! I bet this washing machine is still usable.（➤この shame は「残念なこと」の意のインフォーマルな語）‖ **まだ捨てるのはもったいない** It's still *usable*. ‖ あんな会議に出るなんて**時間がもったいない**よ It's *a waste of time* to go to a meeting like that. ‖ 彼女はきみにはもったいない She *is too good for* you. ‖ **もったいないような話だ** That's *too good to believe*.

もったいぶる ▶住職はもったいぶって（＝大事そうに）その小箱を開けた The head priest opened the small box *with an air of great importance*. ‖ 彼はもったいぶって（＝気取って）自作の詩を読んだ He read his own poem *pompously*［*with an air of self-importance*］. ‖ **もったいぶらないで教えて** *Stop acting like it's* (*such*) *a big deal*, just tell me about it. ‖ もったいぶらないで（＝じらさないで）早くビデオを見せてよ Don't *keep* us *in suspense*; hurry up and show us the video.

もって 以って ▶**書面をもって返事をする** reply *in writing*.

もっていく 持って行く take +目; **carry** +目（運ぶ）

> **【文型】**
> **人(A)に物(B)を持っていく**
> **take** B **to** A ／**take** A B
>
> **【解説】**(1)**take** は「(話し手・聞き手から離れた別の人のもと［場所］へ)持っていく」を表す．
> (2)「自分で持っていく，携帯していく」を明確に表すために with me［you, ...］をつけることがある．

▶外国へ行くときはクレジットカードを**持っていく**のを忘れないように Be sure to *take* your credit cards (*with you*) when you go abroad. ‖ 彼女はふだん会社に弁当を持っていく She usually *takes* her box lunch *to* the office.
▶ **対話**「このスーツケースを2階に持っていってくれますか」「いいですよ」"Can you *carry* this suitcase upstairs?" "Sure."
▶土曜日の忘年会には酒を1本**持っていく**よ I'll *bring* a bottle of sake to the year-end party on Saturday.（● bring は基本的には「(話し手の方に)…を持ってくる」の意だが，「(聞き手の方に)…を持っていく」の意にも使い，ここではその例）.
▶給料の5分の1以上が税金で**持っていかれてしまう** Over a fifth of my pay *is taken away* for taxes. ‖ 誰かがぼくの教科書を持っていった（＝盗んだ）Someone *stole*［*ripped off*］my textbook.（➤ rip off は「かっぱらう」の意の俗語）.

もってうまれた 持って生まれた innate /ìnéɪt/, **inborn** ▶彼には持って生まれた音楽の才能があった He had an *innate* talent for music. ‖ 私が短気なのは**持って生まれた性質だ** I *was born with* a short temper.

もってくる 持って来る bring +目

> **【文型】**
> **人(A)に物(B)を持ってくる**
> **bring** A B
> **bring** B **to**［**for**］A
>
> **【解説】**(1)**bring** は「(話し手・聞き手のいる所に)持ってくる」を表す．**to** は「…のもとに」，**for** は「…のために」を表す．
> (2)「行って持ってくる，取ってくる」は明確には go (and) get という．

▶水を1杯持ってきてくれ Could you *bring* [*go* (*and*) *get* ／*get*] me a glass of water, please？(➤ get はインフォーマル) ‖ ゲーム機を学校に持ってきてはいけません Don't *bring* your game devices *to* school.

▶私の机の上から免許証を持ってきてちょうだい Will you *bring* [*get*] me my driver's license？It's on the desk. ‖ 今にも雨が降りそうだ. 傘を持ってくるんだった It looks like rain. I should *have brought* an umbrella.

もってこい 持って来いの **ideal** /aɪdíːəl/ (理想的な)；**perfect** (完璧な) ▶谷田はキャッチャーにはもってこいだ Tanida is the *ideal* person to be a catcher. ‖ きょうは運動会にもってこいの天気だ This is *ideal* weather for a field day. ‖ その地域は大学を建てるのにもってこいの場所だ That area is *perfect* for building a college.

もってのほか ▶高校生が酒を飲むなんてもってのほかだ It is *out of the question* for high school students to be drinking liquor. (➤ out of the question は「問題外だ, 絶対にしてはいけない」の意).

もってまわった 持って回った **roundabout** (回りくどい) ▶彼は持って回った言い方で彼女と離婚したいと言った He said *in a roundabout way* that he wanted to divorce her. ‖ 持って回った言い方はやめて欲しい物を言いなさい Stop *beating around* [*about*] *the bush* and tell me what you want. (➤ beat around [about] the bush は「茂みの周りをたたいて獲物の鳥を追い出す」が原義).

もっと **more** (より多くの)；**better** (よりよい) ➤形容詞・副詞の比較級で表す ▶もっとお小遣いが欲しい I want *more* pocket money [a *bigger* allowance]. ‖《食事中に飲食物に言及して》これ, もっとある？Is there any *more* of this？‖ 世界のことをもっとたくさん知りたい I want to learn *more* about the world. ‖ 耳かきがない？箱の中をもっとよく捜してごらんなさい You can't find the ear pick？Look in the box again, this time *more carefully*. ‖ 勉強のほう, もっと頑張ってほしいな I'd like you to put *more* effort into your studies. ‖ もっといいものを見せてやるよ I'll show you a *better* one. (➤「もっとましな」の意にもなる).

▶もっと安いのはありませんか Do you have a *less expensive* one？(➤「より高くない」の意) ‖ ロープをもっと強く引いて Pull the rope *harder*. ‖ どうしてもっと早く言ってくれなかったの？How come you didn't tell me about that *earlier*？

モットー a **motto**；a **watchword** (標語) ▶「良い品を安く, 早く」が当店のモットーです "Good quality, low prices and quick service" is our *motto* [*policy*] (at this store). ‖ 我々のモットーは「効率」である Our *watchword* is "efficiency."

[1]**もっとも 最も** →いちばん ▶鯨は地球上で最も大きな哺乳類だ Whales are *the biggest* mammals on earth. ‖ ロッククライミングは最も危険なスポーツの1つだ Rock climbing is one of *the most dangerous* sports of all. ／Rock climbing is *more dangerous than* (*almost*) *any other* sport. ‖ 最も苦心したところはどこですか What part gave you *the greatest* difficulty？‖ カーペットをきれいにする最もよい方法は何ですか What is *the best* way to clean a carpet？‖ 最も好きな歌手は誰ですか What singer do you like *best*？／Who is your favorite singer？(☞ favorite は「いちばん気に入りの」の意なので most は不要) ‖ 恵子が女の子では最も英語を読むのがうまい Keiko reads English (*the*) *best* of all the girls. (➤この例のように特定の人たちの中で最もよくという意味の場合, 副詞の best に the をつけることがある).

[2]**もっとも** **1**【正しい】**natural** (当然の) ▶文法ばかり教える先生に生徒が不満をもつのはもっともだ *It is only natural that* students are dissatisfied with teachers who teach only grammar. ‖ きみが怒るのはもっともだ You *have good reason* to be angry.／Your anger *is justified*. ‖ おっしゃることはもっともです What you say *is perfectly reasonable* [*makes perfect sense*].／You're quite *right* to say so. (➤後者は「おっしゃるとおりだ」) ‖ 勇樹が働かないのにはもっともな理由があった Yuki had a *good* reason for not working.

2【ただし】**though** (…だけれども)；**but** (しかし) ▶カナダは大きい. もっとも人の住めない土地も多いがね Canada is large, *though* much of it is uninhabitable.

☛ごもっとも (→見出語)

もっともらしい **1**【理屈に合っているような】**plausible** /plɔ́ːzəbəl/ ▶もっともらしい言い訳をする make a *plausible* excuse.

2【まじめくさった】▶敬三はもっともらしい顔つきで冗談を言った Keizo made jokes *with a straight face*.／Keizo joked *deadpan*. (➤ deadpan は「無表情で」の意のインフォーマルな語).

もっぱら 専ら ▶彼女は最近はもっぱら絵を描いている She is devoting herself *wholly* [*entirely*] to painting (pictures) these days.／She spends most of her time painting (pictures) these days. (➤後者は「時間のほとんどを絵を描くのに費やしている」の意) ‖ 祖父母はもっぱら庭いじりをして時間を過ごしている My grandparents *occupy themselves with* gardening. (➤ occupy oneself with で「…で忙しい」) ‖ その歌手は近く引退するというもっぱらのうわさだ It *is widely rumored* that the singer will retire soon.

モップ a **mop** ▶母は台所の床をモップでふいた My mother *mopped* the kitchen floor.

もつれ 縺れ a **tangle** ▶髪のもつれをくしでとかす comb *a tangle* out of one's hair ‖ 糸のもつれをほぐす *untangle* thread ‖ 二人の間に感情のもつれが生じた The two ran into (*emotional*) *difficulties* in their relationship.

もつれる **get tangled** (からみあう) ▶糸がもつれた The thread *got tangled*. ‖ 足がもつれてよろけた I *tripped* (*over my own feet*) and stumbled. (➤ trip は「つまずく」) ‖ 父は舌がちょっともつれる My father's speech *is* slightly *slurred*. ‖ 日米交渉は話がもつれてきた The Japan-U.S. talks *have become complicated*.

もてあそぶ 弄ぶ **play** [**toy**] **with** ▶けん銃をもてあそぶ *toy* [*play*] *with* a gun ‖ 弟は年上の女性にもてあそばれているようだ It seems that my (younger) brother *is being toyed with* by an older woman.

もてあます 持て余す ▶私は息子を持て余している (＝手に負えない) I *don't know how to deal with* my son.／My son *has gotten out of hand*. ‖ きのうは出かける予定が急に取りやめになって体[時間]を持て余した Yesterday I *was at loose ends* [*I was left with time on my hands*] because our plans for an outing were suddenly canceled. (➤ at loose ends は「手持ちぶさたで」).

▶父は退職したので体を持て余している Now that my father is retired, he *doesn't know what to do with himself*. (「どう身を処したらよいかがわからない」と考える).

もてなし **hospitality** /hɑ̀:spətǽləṭi/ (歓待); a **welcome** (歓迎) ▶今夜はおもてなしありがとうございました. すてきなお食事でした Thank you for your (kind) *hospitality* tonight. I enjoyed the dinner very much.

▶親善団はカナダで温かいもてなしを受けた The goodwill mission received a warm [hearty] *welcome* in Canada. ‖ 私はそのお寺でお茶のもてなしを受けた I *was served* tea at the temple.

▶《客を送り出すとき》何のおもてなしもできませんで I'm glad you could come. ／I hope you have enjoyed yourself. 《参考》「何のおもてなしもできませんで」は極めて日本的な発想. 英語では I'm afraid I have not been much of a host [hostess] to you. (大した主人役ができなくてすみません) のように言うか, よりふつうには訳例のように言う.

✉ **あなたの温かいおもてなしのおかげでとても思い出深い旅になりました** Your warm *hospitality* has made my trip very memorable.

もてなす **entertain** +目 (接待する) ; **treat** +目 (ごちそうする) ▶客をもてなす *entertain* a guest ‖ 日本人はもっと外国人 [客] を家庭料理でもてなすべきだ Japanese should *treat* foreigners to [*entertain* guests *with*] home cooking more often. ‖ アメリカ南部の人々は客を手厚くもてなす (U.S.) Southerners *are very hospitable*.

もてはやす ▶彼はコピーライターとしてもてはやされている He *is very highly regarded* as a copywriter. ‖ その漫画は若者たちの間でもてはやされている That comic book *is very popular with* young people.

モデム 《コンピュータ》 a **modem** /móʊdem/.

もてもて ▶あのＫポップ歌手は少女たちにもてもてだ That K-pop singer *is very popular with* [*is adored by*] young girls.

モデラート 《音楽》 **moderato** /mɑ̀:dərɑ́:ṭoʊ/.

もてる **1【人気がある】be popular** 《with》 ▶ボブはどこへ行っても女の子にもてる Wherever Bob goes, he *is popular with* girls.

2【富のある】▶どの社会にも持てる者と持たざる者とがいる There are (*the*) *haves* and (the) have-nots in every society.

モデル **1【絵や小説などの】**a **model** ▶画家のモデルになる serve [sit] as *a model* for an artist ／pose [model] for an artist.

▶彼女は世界中で引っ張りだこのファッションモデルだ She is one of the most sought-after *models* in the world.

> **危ないカタカナ語✸ モデル**
> 「ヌードモデル」「ファッションモデル」はそれぞれ nude model, fashion model でよいが, 英語ではどちらも単に model というほうがよりふつう. なお, 画家などのモデルは artist's model ともいうが, ヌードとは限らない.

2【型, 見本】a **model** ▶その車はことしの春全面的なモデルチェンジをした The car underwent a full *model change* this spring. ‖ 名古屋のテレビ塔はパリのエッフェル塔をモデルにして作られた Nagoya's TV Tower *was modeled on* the Eiffel Tower in Paris.

‖**モデルカー** a model car ‖ **モデルガン** a model gun ‖ **モデルケース** a model case ‖ **モデルハウス** a model house [home] ‖ **モデルルーム** a model room.

モデレーター a **moderator** (仲裁者).

もと 元·本·基·下

> 📖 **訳語メニュー**
> 起源 →origin **1**
> 出所 →source **1**
> 根本 →base **1**
> 原因 →cause **2**
> 資金 →capital **4**

1【根元, 根源, 根本】the origin (起源) ; **the source** (出所) ; a **base** (根本) ▶この木は元から枯れてしまった This tree is dead *from the root*. ‖ 日本人の考え方の元には儒教と仏教がある Confucianism and Buddhism lie at the *base* of the Japanese mentality. ／The mentality of the Japanese *is rooted* in Confucianism and Buddhism. ‖ そのうわさの元を確かめなくちゃ I have to check *the source* of that rumor.

▶「カクテル」ということばの元ははっきりとはわかっていない *The origin* of the word "cocktail" is not known for sure. ‖ この事業はもとの計画からだいぶ変わった This project has changed considerably from the *original* plan. ‖ この小説は作者が少年院に入っていたときの体験がもとになっている This novel *is based on* the writer's own experiences of life at reform school.

▶元をただせばここの人たちはみんな外国からの移民だったのです *Originally*, all settlers here were immigrants from other countries.

2【原因】a **cause** ▶口論の元 the *cause* of an argument ‖ 日焼けのしすぎはしみの元になる Too much suntanning *can cause* skin blemishes. ‖ 内野手のエラーが元で負けてしまった We lost the game *because of* an error by an infielder.

▶その男の人は刺された傷が元で亡くなりました The man died *from* a stab wound. ／The stab wound *led to* his death. (➤ lead to は「(ある状態に)つながる」).

3【原材料】▶この薬はカニの甲羅を元にしたものです (＝から作られている) This medicine *is made from* the shells of crabs. ‖ このラーメンのスープの元は秘密です We use a special secret *soup stock* in this ramen.

4【元手】(a) **capital** (資本金) ▶このレストランを始めるには大変な元がかかった We invested a huge amount of *capital* [a lot of *money*] into opening this restaurant. ‖ 土地を売った金を元にマンションを建てた I sold some land and built a block of condos with the *proceeds*. (➤ proceeds は「収益」).

▶喫茶店を始めて３年で元を取り返した We recovered [recouped] our *original investment* in the coffee shop after three years. (➤ investment は「出資金」) ‖ この値段では元が取れない We can't *break even* at this price.

▶《慣用表現》ここで諦めると元も子もなくなるよ If you give up now, you'll *lose everything*. (➤「すべてを失う」の意).

5【時間的に以前】▶元首相 a *former* prime minister ‖ 元カレ [カノ] an *ex*-boyfriend [*ex*-girlfriend] ‖ 安部さんは元新聞記者だった Mr. Abe *used to be* a reporter. (➤ used to do は過去の状態·事実を表す) ‖ 今の郵便局の場所に元は教会があった *There used to be* a church where the post office now. ‖アキレス腱(ケン)を切ったら，もう元のように速くは走れないよ If you break your Achilles' tendon, you will never be able to run *as fast as before* again. ‖ぼくはりえ子と元から仲がよかったんだ I have gotten along well with Rieko *from the beginning* [*start*]. ‖もと住んでた家はもう人手に渡っている The house where we lived *before* [Our *former* house] has already passed into other hands.

▶読んだ本は元の場所にお返しください Please put the books back (*where they were*) after you finish reading them.

▶関係がここまでこじれたらもう簡単には元へ戻れない Once a relationship has gone sour to this extent, it can't *be* easily *restored*. (●「関係が修復される」と考える).

6【「…のもとに」の形で】▶民衆は自由と平等と博愛の旗のもとに蜂起した The people rose in revolt *under* the flag [banner] of liberty, equality and brotherhood. ‖平和維持の名のもとに自衛隊が派遣された Self-Defense Force was dispatched *in* the name [*under* the pretext] of peacekeeping.

もどかしい **feel frustrated**(思うようにいかずにストレスがたまる)；**feel impatient**(じれったい) ▶英語で思うように話せないのがもどかしい I *am* [*feel*] *frustrated* because I cannot express myself well in English. ‖救急車がなかなか来ないので，もどかしかった It took a longer time than I had thought for the ambulance to arrive, so I began to *feel impatient*.

▶先生はもどかしそうに口をはさんだ The teacher *impatiently* broke in. (➤「待ち切れないという感じで」の意).

モトクロス **motocross** /móʊṭoʊkrɔːs/.

もとじめ 元締め a **manager**(監督する人)；a **controller**(仕切る人)；a **boss**(親分，長)

‖**総元締め** a general manager (総支配人)；a chief controller (総括管理者).

もどす 戻す 1【もとの場所・状態に返す】put [**bring**] **back**；**return** +㊐ (返却する)；**reconstitute** +㊐ (水・湯で乾燥食品などを) ▶使用後は用具は必ず元あった場所に戻すこと Be sure to *put* the tools *back* (to where they were) when you are through with them.

▶画面表示を最初の大きさに戻すにはどうすればよいのですか Can you show me how to *bring* the display on the screen *back* to the initial size? ‖話を本題に戻しましょう Let's *bring* the story *back* [Let's go back] to the main subject. ‖乾燥豆腐をぬるま湯に浸して元に戻す *reconstitute* dried tofu by soaking it in lukewarm water.

▶時計の針を30分戻した I *set* the clock *back* (by) thirty minutes.

2【吐く】vomit(+㊐), **throw up** (➤後者はインフォーマル) ▶赤ん坊はミルクをもどした The baby *threw up* [*vomited*] milk.

▶バスに乗っていて，もどしそうになった(＝むかむかした) I *felt sick to my stomach* [*felt nauseous*] on the bus.

もとせん 元栓 **the main (stop) cock** ▶ガスを使ったら必ず元栓を閉めてください Be sure to turn off the gas at *the main* when you are finished using it.

もとづく 基づく **be based**《on》▶この話は事実に基づいている This story *is based on* facts [*is factual*]. ‖政治家は信念に基づいて行動すべきだ Politicians should act *on* (*the basis of*) their convictions. ／Politicians should act *according to* what they believe.

もとで 元手 **capital**(資本)；**seed money**(事業資金) ▶彼は500万円の元手で商売を始めた He started business with *capital* of five million yen. ‖この商売にはかなりの元手がいる A fairly large sum of *money* [*capital*] is necessary to start this kind of business.

もとどおり 元通り ▶心配しなくてもこの機関車はすぐ元どおりに直してあげるよ Don't worry. I'll *restore* this locomotive *to its original condition* in no time. ‖椅子を元どおりにしておきなさい *Put* the chairs *back* (*to where they were*).

もとね 元値 **cost**, a **cost price** ▶元値で［を切って］売る sell *at* [*below*] *cost* (*price*).

もとのもくあみ 元の木阿弥 ▶この前のテストでいい点を取って先生の受けがよかったのに，今回がこんな低い点数では元の木阿弥だ Although my high grades on the last exam put me in my teacher's good books, my low grades this time will *bring* me *back to square one*. (➤ back to square one は「振り出しに戻って」の意).

もとめ 求め (a) **request**(依頼)；a **demand** (要求) ▶出版社の求めに応じて私は本を書いた I wrote a book *at the request of* a publisher.

もとめる 求める

1【手に入れようとする】seek +㊐ ▶幸福を求める権利は誰にもある Everybody has the right to *seek* happiness. ‖コンピュータ業界は多くの若いプログラマーを求めている(＝必要としている) The computer industry *needs* a lot of young programmers. ‖上野公園には職を求める多くの外国人労働者がたむろしていた Many foreign laborers *seeking* [*looking for*] jobs used to gather in Ueno Park. ‖彼は2回目のデートで私の体を求めてきた He *tried to get physical* on our second date.

2【頼む】ask《for》；**request** +㊐ (要請する)；**require** +㊐ (要求する；堅い語)；**urge**《to do》(…することを強く求める) ▶教え子がアドバイスを求めてきた My former student *asked* me *for* some advice. ‖求めよ，さらば与えられん *Ask, and it shall be given you.* (➤聖書のことば).

【文型】
人(A)に…するよう求める
request A **to** do
call on A **to** do

▶政府は国民に対して可能なかぎり節電に努めるように求めた The government *requested* [*called on* ／*appealed to* ／*urged*] the citizens *to* save as much electricity as possible. (➤ call on は「呼び掛ける」, appeal to は「訴えるように真剣に求める」. この2つは主に対象を個人でなく，グループとして捉えている場合) ‖野党側は政府に大幅な減税を求めた The opposition parties *called on* the government *for* a big tax reduction.

▶屋根の上で男が助けを求めていた A man *was crying* [*calling*] *for help* on the roof. ‖WWFは絶滅のおそれがある動植物を保護するように，各国政府に強く求めた The WWF *strongly urged* the government of each country *to* protect endangered plants and animals. ／The WWF *demanded that* the government of each country (*should*) protect endangered plants and animals. (➤ urge と

demand の構文の違いに注意；demand は request より強意で「要求する」）‖会社への忠誠心は私に何を求めているのか What does company loyalty *require of* me？

3【さがす】search for, look for ▶ヘリコプターは行方不明のパーティーの手がかりを求めて飛びたった The helicopter took off *in search of* some clues to finding the missing party. ‖（掲示）パートタイマー求む Part-timers *Wanted*.

4【答えを出す】find ＋㊐ ▶次の数の平方根を求めよ *Find* the square roots of the following numbers.

5【買う】buy ＋㊐, **purchase** /pə́ːʳtʃəs/ ＋㊐（➤後者は堅い語）▶当社の製品をお求めくださいましてありがとうございます Thank you very much for *purchasing* our product.

もともと 元々 **1【元から】from the beginning**［**the first**］（最初から）; **originally**（本来）; **by nature**（生まれつき）▶だから私はもともと娘の結婚には反対だったんだ That's why I was against my daughter's marriage *from the beginning*［*the first*］. ‖もともと横浜はほんの小さな漁村にすぎなかった *Originally*, Yokohama was just a small fishing village. ‖息子はもともと口数が少ない My son is quiet *by nature*. ‖私にはもともと絵の才能はないんだ I don't have any talent for painting *in the first place*.

2【プラスマイナスゼロ】▶だめでもともとだ I *have nothing to lose* if I fail.（➤「失うものは何もない」の意）.

もとより ▶そのことはもとより（＝最初から）気がついていました I was aware of it *from the beginning*［*the first*］. ‖この映画は子供はもとより, 大人も楽しめる This is an enjoyable film for grown-ups *as well as* for children.

もとる 悖る ▶法の精神にもとる *be against*［*contrary to*］the spirit of the law ‖人道にもとる行為 an act that *goes against humanitarian principles* ／an *inhuman* act／an outrage *against humanity*.

もどる 戻る **1【返る, 帰る】go**［**come**］**back**《to》, **return**《to》（➤return はやや堅い語. go back と come back の違いについては「行く」の語法を参照）

▶すぐ戻るよ I'll *be back* soon.（➤be back は「戻っている」という状態を表す）‖席に戻ってよろしい You may *go back to* your seat. ‖（犬に向かって）シロ, 戻って来い *Come back*, Shiro！‖サケが川に戻って来た The salmon *came back to* the river (they were born in). ‖家に戻ったら誰もいなかった No one was home when I *got back*. ‖ブーメランは投げた人の所に戻って来る A boomerang *comes back*［*returns*］*to* the thrower.

▶急いで会社に戻った I *hurried back to* the office. ‖ここまで来たらもうあとへは戻れない We *can't turn back* now that we've come this far. ／We're already beyond the point of no return.

2【元の状態になる】get back《to》▶あの話に戻るけど, どう思う？ *Getting back to* that subject, what do you think？‖彼女にいつもの笑顔が戻った She *got back* her usual smile. ‖けさは体温が平熱に戻った My temperature *was back to* normal this morning.

▶一度破壊された自然は元には戻らない（＝回復できない）Nature *cannot be restored to* its original state once it has been destroyed.

もなか 最中 a *monaka*; a sweet made of sweetened azuki bean jam sandwiched between two crisp wafers made from mochi（➤説明的な訳）.

モニター a **test viewer**（テレビの）; a **test listener**（ラジオの）; a **test user**（商品などの）; a **monitor**（テレビ・コンピュータなどの画像表示装置）▶NHKではただ今, 番組の感想をお寄せくださるモニターを募集しております NHK is looking for *test viewers* to give opinions on its programs.

> **危ないカタカナ語✸モニター**
> monitor から出た語だが, 一般に用いられている「依頼されて放送・商品などの状態を調べて感想を述べる人」の意は英語の monitor にはない. この意味を英語で表すには test viewer（テレビの）, test listener（ラジオの）, test user, consumer (reception) tester（ともに商品の）などとする.

‖**モニターテレビ** a monitor screen.

モニュメント a **monument**.

もぬけのから もぬけの殻 ▶警察が踏み込んだときにはアジトはもぬけの殻だった When the police raided the hideout, it had *been left completely empty*.

[1]**もの 物** **1【品物, 物体】a thing**; **something**（何か）▶物を大切にしなさい Don't waste *things*. ‖子供は甘い物が好きだ Children like *sweet things*. ‖肩に何か白い物がついてますよ I see *something white* on your shoulder. ‖何かおいしい物を食べようよ Let's eat *something tasty*［*delicious*］. ‖何か食べる物ない？Is there *anything to eat*？（◆疑問文や否定文では anything となる）.

2【所有物】one's **things**; one's (**personal**) **belongings**（身の回りの品）▶この CD は姉の物です This CD *belongs to* my sister. ／This CD is my sister's.（➤後者のほうがインフォーマル）‖自分の物は各自で気をつけてください You should all take care of *your own belongings*.

▶俺の物を黙って使うな Don't use my *things*［*stuff*］without asking (me).（➤stuff は「持ち物」の意のインフォーマルな語）‖20年たってローンが終わればこの家は自分の物になる Twenty years from now we will have paid off the loan, and this house will be *our own*. ‖それは私の物ではありません That's not *mine*.

3【品質】▶ 対話「これは高いな」「そこいらの品とは物が違いますから」"This is expensive." "(Because) it's *in a different class*."

4【不特定の事物】▶ものには限度がある *Everything* has its limit. ／There is a limit to *everything*. ‖嫌いなものは宿題, 試験, 月曜日 *What* I don't like are homework assignments, exams and Mondays.

▶ものは考えようだよ It all depends on how you look at *it*. ‖彼はものにつかれたように研究に没頭している He is absorbed in his research *as if* he *were possessed by something*. ／He is obsessed with his research.

▶近頃ものを忘れやすくなってね I've *been* very *forgetful* recently. ‖あの子はものを覚えるのが早い He［She］*learns* quickly. ／She［He］is a quick *learner*. ‖あの人は実によくものを知っている He［She］*is* very *knowledgeable*. ／He［She］*knows a lot about many things*.

▶本当に大事なものは目には見えないんだ *What is essential* is invisible to the eye.（➤『星の王子さま』の中

のことば).
［ことわざ］**物も言いようで角が立つ** Oftentimes, it's not what you say, but how you say it that causes trouble.
5【道理】▶ものの**わかった人** a *sensible* [*perceptive*] person ‖ものの**わからない人** an *unreasonable* person. →物分かり.
6【慣用表現】
ものにする ▶巨人は3連戦の初戦をものにした The Giants *won* [*captured*] the first of the three consecutive games. ‖外国語をものにするには努力と根気がいる It takes effort and patience to *learn* [*master*] a foreign language. (➤ learn は「身につける」, master は自在に使えるくらい「熟達する」). **ものになる** ▶あの投手はプロに入ってものになるだろうか I wonder if that pitcher will *be a success* in professional baseball. (➤ a success は「成功した人」). **ものの数に入らない** ▶あの人の撮る写真に比べたら私のなどものの数にも入りませんよ Compared with his photographs, mine *are nothing* [*are insignificant* / *don't count*]. **ものは試し** ▶ものは試しだ(＝やってみなければわからない) You'll never know unless you try. **ものを言う** ▶こういうピンチには彼の経験がものを言う At tough times like this, his experience is *what counts* [is *what makes the difference*]. (➤ この count は「役に立つ」の意). **ものを言わせる** ▶そのチームは金にものを言わせて有力選手を次々と入団させた That team *made money talk* and persuaded one promising player after another to join them.
☛ものともせず[しない], もののみごとに(→見出語)

[2]もの 者 a **person**(人); **people**(人々) ▶あわて者 a hasty *person* ‖彼の悪口を言う者もいるし, 褒める者もいる Some *people* say bad things about him, while others praise him. ‖きみたちのような若い者には, わしの気持ちはわかるまい Young *people* like you could hardly understand how I feel. ‖この落書きをした者は前に出なさい Will the *person* who wrote this graffiti step forward! ‖誰かこの問題に答えられる者はいるかな? Can *anybody* answer this question?
▶私は宇野という者です I'*m* Uno. ‖ガス会社の者ですが I'*m from* the gas company. (➤「ガス会社から来ました」の意).

-もの **1**【傾向を示して】▶いくら注意しても事故は起こるものだ No matter how careful you are, accidents *will* (still) occur. (➤ この will は「習性, 習慣」を表す) ‖人生はそんなものさ *Such is life.* / *That's life* (*for you*). / *That's the way the cookie crumbles.* (➤「クッキーはそのようにこわれるもの」の意) / *That's the way the ball bounces.* (➤「ボールはそのようにはずむもの」の意).
2【過去の習慣を示して】

【文型】
よく…したものだ
used to do
would do

【解説】(1)「よく…したものだ」という過去の習慣は **used to** do または **would** do で表す. **used to** は /júːstə/ と発音する. **used to** は「…であったものだ」という状態や状況も表すことができる.
(2) **used to** はしばしば, 以前はそうであったが現在はそうでないというニュアンスで使われる. **would** にはその含みはない.
(3)ともに「子供［中学生］のとき」「しばしば」など少し漠然とした語句とともに使う. 具体的な「…年前」「…回」などが示されるとこれらは使わず単に過去形を使う.
(4) would は be, like, have などの状態動詞とともには用いない.

▶若い頃はよく旅行をしたものだ I *used to* travel a lot when I was young. ‖あの頃は週末によく映画を見たものだ In those days I *would often go to the movies* on weekends. 《参考》would を用いるときは used to より多少とも多くの説明句が必要で, 第1例に would を用いるのは不自然. 第2例でも on weekends あるいは with my girlfriend などがないとネイティブには自然に響かないようだ.
3【願望を示して】▶いつの日か自分の会社の社長になってみたいものだ Some day I'*d like to* be the president of my own company. (➤ 'd like は would like の短縮形).
▶億万長者になってみたいものだ *I wish I were* [*was*] a millionaire. (➤ 実現の望みが薄いときの言い方; インフォーマルでは was がふつう).
4【理由を示して】▶ 対話「なぜ弟に少し分けてあげないの」「だって少ししかないんだもの」"Why don't you give some to your brother?" "*Because* ['*Cause*] I have only a little." (➤ 'cause は because を省略した形でインフォーマル).
5【判断を示して】▶《反抗している子供に》親の言うことは聞くものだよ You *should* always obey your parents. ‖あいつの言うことなど怪しいものだ(＝信じられない) I can never believe what he says.
6【感心していることを示して】▶ふるさとに帰るのはいいものだ It *always* feels great to be back home. ‖言って［頼んで］みるものだね *I'm glad* (*that*) I said that [(that) I asked]. (➤「言って［頼んで］よかった」の意).
7【「…というもの」の形で】(● 英訳の際には訳出しないでよい) ▶日本に来て初めて地震というものを知りました I experienced *an earthquake* for the first time when I came to Japan. (●「日本に来て初めて地震を知った」と考える).
▶祖父はよく, 今の若者は苦労というものを知らないという My grandfather often says that young people today don't know *the hardships of life*. (●「…苦労を知らない」と考える).
8【多さを強調して】**as ... as** →-も **4** ▶沿道には30万人もの人が集まってメダリストたちを歓迎した *As many as* three hundred thousand people gathered along the street(s) and welcomed the medalists.

ものいい 物言い an **objection** ▶行司の判定に対し勝負審判から物言いがついた A member of the (sumo) judge panel entered *an objection* to the referee's decision on who had won.

ものいり 物入り ▶年末は何かと物入りだ(＝出費が多い) We *have many expenses* for one thing or another at the end of the year.

ものいれ 物入れ a **container**(容器); a **storeroom**, a **storage room**(収納室, 物置).

ものうい 物憂い **melancholy** /mélənkɑ̀ːli/ (憂鬱な) ▶彼女には何となくもの憂い様子がうかがわれた There was something *melancholic* [*gloomy*] about her.

ものうり 物売り 《米》a **peddler**, 《英》a **pedlar**(行商人); a **street vendor**(街頭の).

ものおき 物置 a **storeroom**, a **storage room**(建物の中

の)；a **barn**, a **shed**（物置小屋）.

ものおじ 物怖じ ▶あの子は何をするにも決して物おじしない The boy is never *timid* [*shy*] about anything.

ものおしみ 物惜しみ ▶たくさん持っている人に限って物惜しみする People who have a lot *are* generally *stingy*.

ものおと 物音 a **sound**；a **noise**（雑音）▶変な物音で私は目を覚ました I was awakened by a strange *sound*. ‖ 裏口で物音がしたので行ってみたら猫だった I heard *a sound* at the backdoor and rushed to look, but it was only a cat.

ものおぼえ 物覚え ▶妹は物覚えがいい My little sister *learns* (*things*) *fast* [*quickly*]. ／My little sister *is quick to learn*. (➤ 2 文とも「のみ込みが早い」の意）／My little sister *has a good memory*. (➤「記憶力がいい」の意）／My little sister *is a quick study*. (➤ a quick study はもともとせりふを覚えるのが早い俳優を指した言い方).

ものおもい 物思い ▶彼女は何時間もひとり物思いにふけっている She *has been lost in thought* by herself for hours. ‖ 秋は読書と物思いによい季節だ Fall is a good season for reading and *thinking*.

-ものか ▶もうあんなやつと口をきくものか I'll *never* speak to him again. ／I'll *be damned if* I (will) speak to him again. (➤ 後者は「絶対に…しないぞ」の意のインフォーマルな表現) ‖ そんなことがあるものか That *can't be* true！(➤ can't be で「…のはずがない」)／That's impossible！‖ あいつが学者だって？へん，何が学者なものか Are you saying he is a scholar？No way！He is *far from it*.

ものかき 物書き a **writer**.

ものかげ 物陰 ▶物陰から何かがいきなり飛び出したのでぎょっとした I was frightened when something suddenly dashed *out of nowhere*. (➤「どこからともなく」の意).

▶こっそり自分をつけてくる足音がしたので，彼は物陰に隠れた When he heard the sound of footsteps following him secretly, he *hid himself*.

ものがたり 物語 a **story**, a **tale**（お話）；a **fable**（ぐう話）；a **romance**（伝奇・空想物語）▶源氏物語 The *Tale* of Genji ‖ イソップ物語 Aesop's *Fables* ‖ その村には昔から悲しい物語が伝わっている A sad *story* has been handed down in the village since ancient times.

▶聞きたいですか？話せば長い物語ですよ Would you like to hear it？It's a long *story*.

‖ **物語作家** a storywriter.

ものがたる 物語る **tell**《of》▶その男の顔の傷は彼の長いプロレス生活を物語る The scars on that man's face *testify to* [*tell of*] his long career as a pro wrestler.

ものがなしい 物悲しい **sad**；**plaintive**（哀れを誘う）▶もの悲しい古い歌 a *sad* [*woeful*] old song ‖ 風がもの悲しげに吹いていた The wind was blowing *plaintively*.

ものぐさ 物臭 a **lazybones**(人) 一形 **ものぐさな lazy** ▶彼は大変ものぐさな男だ He is such a *lazy person*. ／He is a great *slacker* [*slouch* ／*lazybones*].

モノクロ monochrome, black and white ▶私はカラー映画よりもモノクロ映画のほうが好きだ I prefer *movies in monochrome* [*in black and white*] to ones in color.

ものごい 物乞い **begging**(行為)；a **beggar**(人) ▶数人の路上生活の子供たちが観光客に物乞いした Several street children *begged* (money) from passing tourists.

ものごころ 物心 ▶物心がついて以来，和歌山県から外へ出たことはありません *For as long as I can remember*, I've never left Wakayama. ／*Ever since I can remember*, I've always stayed in Wakayama. ‖ 物心がついた頃には父は亡くなっていました *By the time I was old enough to understand what was happening around me*, my father had already passed away. (➤「周囲の事情が理解できる年になったときには」の意)《参考》英語にはこの日本語に対応する言い方はなく，ふつうは I have no recollection of my father. I was too young when he died.（父の記憶はありません. 父が死んだときはまだごく小さかったので）などと言う.

ものごし 物腰 **bearing, manner**(➤ 前者は堅い語) ▶物腰のやわらかい人 a *gentle-mannered* person ‖ 彼女の母親は上品な物腰の人です Her mother *carries herself* gracefully. (➤ carry oneself ... で「立ち居ふるまいが…だ」).

ものごと 物事 **things** ▶物事はいつもきみの思いどおりにいくとは限らないよ *Things* don't always go as you would like them to. ‖ 物事をあるがままに受け止めることを学ばねばならない You should learn to accept [take] *things* as they are.

▶物事には順序というものがある There is a proper order to *everything*.

ものさし 物差し **1**【道具】a **ruler**, a **rule**（定規）；a **measure**(巻尺など) ▶私はその布をものさしで測った I measured the cloth with *a ruler*.

2【判断の基準】a **yardstick** ▶あの人は自分のものさしでしかものを見ない He always measures things using his own *yardstick*. (➤ yardstick は「1ヤードのものさし」が原義で，ここはその比喩的用法）／He judges things only from his own *point of view*.

ものさびしい 物寂しい **forlorn** /fəˈlɔ́ːn/ ▶冬の海辺は何となくもの寂しい I *feel rather forlorn* at the seaside in winter.

ものしずか 物静かな **quiet** ▶前の校長先生はもの静かな方でした The former principal was a *quiet* man. ‖ その中年の女性はとてももの静かに話した The middle-aged lady spoke in a very *calm and gentle* manner.

ものしり 物知り a **knowledgeable person** ▶父は物知りです My father is a *knowledgeable* person. (🔴「教育があり知識が広い」といったニュアンス；My father knows everything. とすると，「雑多なことを知っている」というニュアンスになる).

▶物知り顔で話す人は多い Many people talk *as if they know everything*.

ものずき 物好きな **curious** ▶物好きな人 a *curious* person ‖ 売れない作家の小説ばかり読むなんて，きみも物好きだね You *must be a real bookworm* [*must be really full of curiosity* (about books) ／*must have a passion for novelty*] to read stories that unpopular novelists wrote.

ものすごい **1**【こわい】**terrible**（恐ろしい）；**horrible**（身の毛のよだつような）▶崖はものすごい音を立てて崩れた The cliff collapsed with a *terrible* rumble. ‖ ものすごい衝突事故だった It was a *horrible* collision. ‖ それはものすごい(＝ぞっとするような)光景だった It was a *ghastly* [*horrible* ／*dreadful*] sight.

2【非常な】**awful, terrific** /tərífɪk/ 一副 **ものすごく awfully** ▶フェラーリがものすごいスピードで走り去った A Ferrari zipped past at a *terrific* speed. ‖ 課長はものすごく忙しそうだった The section chief seemed to be *awfully* busy. ‖あの歌手はものすごく稼いでいる That singer is making money *hand over fist* [*like mad*]. (➤ hand over fist は「がっぽがっぽ」, like mad は「猛烈に」の意のインフォーマルな表現) ‖ ものすごく怖かった I was scared *to death* [scared *stiff*].

ものたりない 物足りない ▶彼の説明は少しもの足りなかった His explanation *was not* completely *satisfactory*. ‖給料がよいだけではもの足りない A well-paying job *isn't enough* for me. /I *want something more than* just good pay.
▶マチス展は少々もの足りなかった The Matisse Exhibition *left something to be desired*. (➤「こうあってほしいというようなものを残した」の意) ‖あの俳優, ハンサムなだけでどこかもの足りないわね I agree that the actor is handsome, but he *lacks something*, wouldn't you say ?

モノトーン ▶冬のわびしいモノトーンの風景 a dreary, *colorless* [*black-and-white*] winter landscape.

危ないカタカナ語✹ モノトーン
モノトーンは英語では monotone で,「一本調子」の意から主に音声を形容するのに用いる. 明確な抑揚を生命とする英語では monotone は聞く者をいらだたせ,「退屈な」「単調な」(monotonous) に結びつく. 日本語では「モノトーンのシックなセーター [内装]」などとプラスイメージに用いることがあるが, 英語にはその使い方はない. a chic black-and-white sweater [decor] とする. monotone =「白黒」あるいは「単色」という連想もない.

ものともせず [しない] 物ともせず [しない] ▶法律をものともしない *defy* the law ‖彼は100キロぐらいの重さはものともせず持ち上げる He *thinks nothing of* lifting objects weighing as much as 100 kilograms. (➤ think nothing of は「…を何とも思わない」) ‖彼らは嵐をものともせず山頂を目指して出発した They started for the mountaintop, *braving* [*undaunted by*] the raging storm. (➤ brave は「勇敢に立ち向かう」, undaunted は「ひるむことなく」) ‖彼女は危険をものともしなかった She was *careless of* danger.

-ものなら ▶ホームランを打てるものなら打ってみろ *If you think* you can hit a home run, go ahead and try it. ‖遅刻を繰り返そうものなら首になってしまう I'll be fired *if* I'm late too often.

ものの only(ほんの) ▶その問題を解くにはものの1分もあればいい It will take me *only* [*no more than*] one minute to solve the problem.

-ものの though, although (➤ 後者は前者よりやや堅い語) ▶そのレスラーはやっと立ち上がったものの歩けなかった *Though* he managed to stand up, the wrestler could not walk. ‖同意したものの私はちょっと心配だ I agreed to it, *yet* I cannot help (feeling) some uneasiness.

もののあわれ 物の哀れ the pathos of things(万物の哀れ); the pathos of transience [evanescence](はかなさ) ▶日本人は落花に物の哀れを感じる Japanese feel *the evanescence* [*transience*] *of life* at the sight of falling cherry blossoms. (➤「生のはかなさ [移ろいやすさ]」の意) /Falling cherry blossoms remind Japanese people of *the transience* [*evanescence*] *of life* (*and beauty*).

もののけ 物の怪 an evil spirit(悪霊).

もののみごとに 物の見事に ▶彼は危ない綱渡りをもの見事にやってのけた He performed the dangerous ropewalking trick *masterfully*. ‖実験はものの見事に失敗した The experiment failed *spectacularly* [*miserably*].

ものほし 物干し a clothesline /klóʊzlaɪn/,《英また》a washing line(物干し綱); a clotheshorse(室内の物干し掛け)
‖物干しざお a pole for hanging out the washing, a clothes-drying bar ‖物干し台 a balcony for drying the washing (➤ ともに英米にはない).

ものほしげ 物欲しげ ▶おなかをすかした子猫はもの欲しげに私の顔を見た The hungry kitten looked at me *wistfully*.

ものまね 物真似 mimicry /mímɪkri/ 一動 物まねをする mimic +目 ▶青木隆治は物まねがうまい Aoki Ryuji is a good *mimic*. (➤ mimic は「物まねする人」).
▶そのコメディアンはマイケル・ジャクソンの物まねをした The comedian *mimicked* [*imitated*] Michael Jackson's voice and gestures. /The comedian *did a takeoff of* [*on*] Michael Jackson. (➤ takeoff は「おもしろおかしくまねること」).

ものみだかい 物見高い curious ▶火事現場は物見高い見物人でいっぱいだった The scene of the fire was crowded with *curious* onlookers [rubberneckers]. (➤ rubbernecker は「好奇心丸出しの人」をあざけっていう語).

ものめずらしい 物珍しい ▶もの珍しい光景 an *unusual* [*a curious*] sight ‖生徒たちはもの珍しそうにそのロボットを見つめた The students watched the robot *with curious eyes*.

ものもち 物持ち ▶私の父は物持ちがいい My father *takes good care of his things, so they last long* [*for a long time*].

ものものしい 物々しい ▶空港はものものしい警戒ぶりだった The airport was *heavily* [*tightly*] guarded by the police. /The airport was under *heavy* security.

ものもらい 1【まぶたの炎症】 a sty(e) /staɪ/ ▶目にものもらいができる have *a sty*(*e*) on one's eyelid.
2【物乞い】 a beggar(人); begging(行為).

ものやわらか 物柔らかな gentle ▶私たちの教授は物腰がものやわらかだ Our professor is *gentle-mannered*.
▶先生は彼に二度とそんなことをしないようにとものやわらかに諭した Our teacher *gently* admonished him not to do such a thing again.

モノラル monophonic, monaural,《インフォーマル》mono ▶この歌はモノラル盤である This song is recorded in *mono*. (➤ mono は「モノラル(方式)」の意).
‖モノラル録音 mono recording.

モノレール a monorail /má:nəreɪl/ ▶浜松町駅から羽田空港までモノレールに乗った I took the *monorail* from Hamamatsucho to Haneda Airport.

モノローグ a monologue,《米また》a monolog.

ものわかり 物分かり ▶私の父は物分かりがいい My father *is understanding*. ‖市長は物分かりがいい(=理解が早い) The mayor *catches on quickly*. ‖きみはもっと物分かりがいい(=分別がある)と思っていたんだが… I thought you'd *be* more *sensible*.

ものわかれ 物別れ ▶労使間の話し合いは物別れに終わった The management-labor talks *broke down*. /Management and labor *failed to come to an agreement* in their talks.

ものわすれ 物忘れ ▶最近私は物忘れがひどい I *am*

very forgetful these days.

ものわらい 物笑い ▶日本人の中には間違いを犯して物笑いになりたくないという理由で英語を話そうとしない人がいる Some Japanese don't try to speak English because they are afraid of *being laughed at* when they make mistakes.

▶他人を物笑いの種にしてはいけません Don't make someone *a laughingstock*. ／Don't *ridicule* other people.

モバイル **mobile** /móʊbəl ‖ -baɪl/ ▶モバイル機器 a *mobile* device.

‖モバイル・コンピューティング mobile computing ‖モバイル通信 mobile communications.

もはや 最早 ▶あの国ではもはや(＝すでに)秩序が失われている Law and order have *already* broken down in that country. ‖もはや(＝もう)彼女の言うことなど信用できない I can*not* believe her *any longer*. ／I can *no longer* believe her. (➤ 後者はやや堅い言い方) ‖もはやこれまで *The game is up* [*over*]. (➤「万事休す」の意).

もはん 模範 a **model**(手本)；an **example** (実例) ▶自分の子供たちに模範を示す set *a good example* for one's children ‖彼は俳優から政治家になった人たちの模範です He is *a role model* for actors who have become politicians. (➤ role model は「理想像」) ‖私はトマス・エジソンの生き方を模範にしたい I'd like to follow the *example* of Thomas Edison's way of life. ‖彼女は模範的な学生[奥さん]だ She's a *model* student [wife]. ‖純子はフィギュアの模範演技を行った Junko put on a figure-skating *exhibition*.

‖模範解答 a model answer ‖模範試合 an exhibition game [match].

モビール a **mobile** /móʊbiːl ‖ móʊbaɪl/ (動く作品).

もふく 喪服 a **mourning dress, mourning** ▶夫の死後彼女はしばらく喪服を着ていた After her husband's death she *wore mourning* [*black*] for some time.

もほう 模倣 (an) **imitation**, a **copy** (➤ 後者には「そっくりの模倣」という含みがある) **━動 模倣する imitate** +㊐, **copy** +㊐；**model** A《on B》(Bにならって Aを作る) ▶これはわが社のロゴマークの模倣だ This is *a copy* [*an imitation*] of our company logo. ‖日本の医療制度はドイツの模倣であった The Japanese medical system *was modeled on* [*after*] that of Germany.

もまれる 揉まれる ▶世間の荒波にもまれる *experience the hardships of life* ‖彼も会社でもまれればりっぱなビジネスマンになるだろう He'll probably become a fine businessman once he has *experienced the trials of corporate life*.

[1]もみ 樅 《植物》 a **fir (tree)** ▶私たちはモミの木をクリスマスの飾りつけで飾った We decked the *fir* (*tree*) with Christmas ornaments.

[2]もみ 籾 **unhulled rice, paddy** (もみ米)；**chaff** (もみ殻).

もみあう 揉み合う **jostle** /dʒɑ́ːsəl/ ▶デモ隊は機動隊ともみ合った The demonstrators *jostled against* the riot squad.

もみあげ 《米》 **sideburns**, 《英》 **sideboards**.

もみくちゃ ▶紙をもみくちゃにする *crumple up* a piece of paper ‖その映画スターは会場を出ようとしてティーンエージャーたちにもみくちゃにされた The movie star *was pushed and shoved* by teenagers as he tried to get out of the hall.

もみけす 揉み消す **stub out**(押しつけて消す)；**cover up** (隠す)；**hush up**(スキャンダル・秘密などを) ▶父はたばこを灰皿でもみ消した My father *stubbed out* his cigarette in the ashtray.

▶《比喩的》その政治家はスキャンダルをもみ消そうとした The politician tried to *cover up* [*hush up*] the scandal.

もみじ 紅葉 a **maple**(カエデ)；**autumn leaves** [**foliage** /fóʊliɪdʒ/](紅葉) ▶もみじ狩りに行く go to *view autumn leaves* ‖日光はもみじの名所だ Nikko is noted for the glorious colors of its *autumn leaves*.

もみで 揉み手 ▶土産物店の主人は通りがかりの観光客をもみ手をして迎えた The keeper of the souvenir shop *rubbed his hands eagerly as he welcomed* the tourists.

もむ 揉む ⚠「もむ」は手でつかんで力を加える行為だが，英語にはこれに対応する語がないので，**massage**(マッサージする)や **rub**(さする)で代用する.

▶息子が肩をもんでくれた My son *gave* me *a* shoulder *massage*. ‖《料理番組などで》薄切りにしたキュウリを塩で軽くもみます *Rub* the sliced cucumbers lightly with salt.

▶ひとつもんで(＝鍛えて)やろう I'll *give* you *a good workout*. ‖祖母は私の縁談がうまくいくかどうか気をもんでいる My grandmother *is concerned about* whether the marriage offer I received will result in my getting married. (➤ be worried を用いると深刻さが増すので，縁談に反対のニュアンスになってしまう；→心配)

もめごと 揉め事 (a) **trouble** ▶家庭内のもめ事 family [domestic] *trouble*(*s*) ‖チーム内でもめ事があるらしい There seems to be *discord* within the team. (➤ discord /dískɔːʳd/ は「うちわもめ」) 《参考》「もめ事を起こす人」を troublemaker という.

もめる 揉める ▶彼らは賃上げをめぐって会議でもめている They *are having a* (*heated*) *dispute* in the meeting over the pay hike. ‖二人はその金のことでもめた The two *quarreled* over the money. ‖姉夫婦のところがもめているようだ My (older) sister and her husband seem to *be having some* (*domestic*) *problems*.

▶母親は娘の帰りが遅いので気がもめた The mother *felt anxious* [*uneasy*] because her daughter was late coming home.

もめん 木綿 **cotton (cloth)** ▶木綿の下着 *cotton* underwear.

[1]もも 桃 a **peach** ▶桃の花 *peach* blossoms.

‖桃色 pink.

[2]もも 腿 a **thigh** /θaɪ/ ▶久しぶりに山登りをしたのでももの筋肉が痛い My *thighs* ache because I went climbing for the first time in a long while.

‖もも引き long johns.

もや 靄 (a) **haze**, (a) **mist** (➤ 後者のほうが濃い) ▶川にはもやが立ちこめていた *A mist* hung over the river.

もやし **bean sprouts** /spraʊts/

‖もやしっ子 a (pale) weedy kid (➤ weedy は「ひょろひょろした」の意).

もやす 燃やす **burn** +㊐ ▶神社の境内で落ち葉を燃やしている They *are burning* fallen leaves in the grounds of the shrine. ‖暖炉に火を燃やした We *made* [*built*] *a fire* in the fireplace. (➤「火をおこした」の意).

▶《比喩的》父は新しい仕事に情熱を燃やしている My father *is fired up with enthusiasm* for his new job.

▶《比喩的》選手たちは決勝戦を控えて**闘志を燃やしている** With the finals coming soon, the players *are full of fighting spirit* [*are fired up*].

もやもや ▶寝不足のせいか頭が**もやもやする** My head *feels dull*, maybe because of lack of sleep.

もよう 模様 **1**【柄】a pattern /pǽṭərn/（図柄）; a design（図案，デザイン）▶水玉**模様** a polka-dot *pattern* ／polka dots ‖ 幾何学**模様** geometrical *patterns* ‖ 杉あや**模様** herringbone *patterns* ‖ しま**模様**のネクタイ a *striped* tie ‖ 唐草**模様**のふろしき a Japanese wrapping cloth with arabesque *patterns* [*designs*] ‖ ペーズリー**模様**のショール a *paisley* shawl.

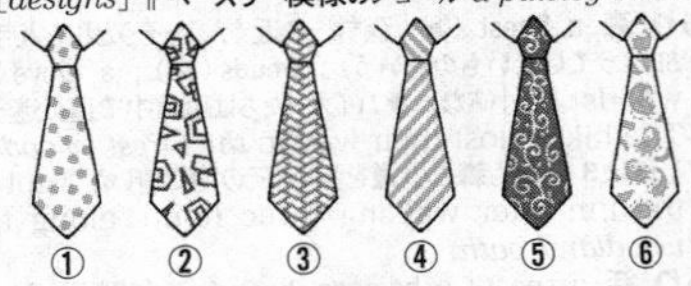

① polka-dot ② geometrical ③ herringbone
④ striped ⑤ arabesque ⑥ paisley

2【状態，様子】a look ▶空**模様**はどうですか What does the weather *look like*? ‖ スポーツニュースで試合の**模様**（＝経過）が放送された The sports news program broadcast the *game in progress*. ‖ 事故の**模様**を聞かせてください Please tell us *how* the accident *happened*.

▶救助された少年は一命を取り留めた**模様**です *It seems* that the boy who was rescued is now in stable condition.

もようがえ 模様替え (a) rearrangement（家具などの配置替え）; a face lift, (a) redecoration（改装）; remodeling（大改造）**一動** 模様替えをする rearrange ＋目, redecorate ＋目, remodel ＋目 ▶気分転換に部屋の**模様替え**をしようとしてたところなの I was just about to *rearrange* [*redecorate*] my room for a change.

もよおし(もの) 催し(物) a meeting（会合）; a party（パーティー）; an event（行事）.

もよおす 催す **1**【開催する】hold ＋目, give ＋目（➤ 前者は後者より堅い語）▶来月，クラス会を**催します** We are going to *hold* a class reunion next month.
2【感じる】feel ▶退屈な講義を聞いているうちに**眠気を催した** I *became* [*felt*] *sleepy* while listening to the dull lecture. ‖ 私はにわかに**便意を催した** I *had a* sudden *urge to go to the bathroom*. ／Suddenly *nature called*.

もより 最寄りの the nearest（いちばん近い）; nearby（近くの）▶**最寄りの**駅 *the nearest* [*a nearby*] train station.
▶詳細は**最寄りの**当社支店にお問い合わせください For more information, please contact *the* [our] *nearest* branch office.

もらいて 貰い手 ▶子猫の**もらい手**がいない There is *nobody who wants* [*will take*] our kitten.

もらいなき 貰い泣き ▶テレビで涙の再会シーンを見て**もらい泣き**した When I saw the tearful reunion on TV, I *shed tears* [*cried*] *along with the people* who were reunited.

もらいび 貰い火 ▶**もらい火**でマンションが全焼した The apartment building was burned down by *a fire that started in the neighboring house*.

もらいもの 貰い物 a gift, a present（➤ 前者は後者より堅い語）▶このクッキーは**もらい物**ですけど，どうぞ召し上がってください These cookies were *a gift from a friend*. Would you like some?

もらう 貰う **1**【受ける】be given（与えられる）; take ＋目（差し出されたものを）; receive ＋目, have ＋目, get ＋目（受け取る）; be awarded（賞を）; be granted（許可・権利などを）
▶ぼくはバレンタインデーにチョコレートをたくさん**もらった** I *was given* a lot of chocolates on St. Valentine's Day. ‖ 高野君からラブレターを**もらった** I *had* [*got* ／ *received*] a love letter from Takano.
▶石川遼選手にサインを**もらった** I *got* Ishikawa Ryo's autograph. ‖ その選手は新人賞を**もらった** The player *won* [*was awarded*] the Rookie-of-the-Year prize. (➤ win は「勝ち取る」) ‖ この仕事をしたらいくら**もらえる**んですか How much will I *get* for this job?
▶このパンフレットを**もらって**いいですか？ May I *have* [*take*] this brochure? ‖ この子犬を**もらって**ください Won't you please *take* this puppy *home* with you? ‖ 早く嫁さんを**もらい**なさい Hurry up and *find* yourself a wife. ‖《店で》このハンカチ**もらい**（＝買い）ます I'*ll take* this handkerchief. (● buy としないことに注意) ‖ 金を持ってこないと子供の命を**もらう**ぞ（＝殺すぞ）Bring money. Otherwise, I'*ll kill* your son.

2【…してもらう】

> 【文型】
> 人(A)に頼んで…してもらう
> have A do
> 人(A)を説得して…してもらう
> get A to do
>
> 【解説】(1) **have** A do はしばしば，そうするのがその人の職務，当然の務めであるので，というニュアンスがある.
> (2) ほかに，for（…のために）を使ったり，動詞自体に「（人の）ために」の意があって，それで表せたりすることもある.
> (3) **have** A do は間接的に頼む場合にも用い，ふつう結果に重点がある.「（自ら）依頼する」では ask A to do も用いる.

▶自転車屋さんにパンクを直して**もらった** I *had* a bicycle mechanic fix my flat tire. ‖ 友だちに講義のノートを貸して**もらった** I *got* a friend of mine *to* lend me his lecture [class] notes. (➤ asked では貸してもらえたのかは不明).
▶父に新しい自転車を買って**もらった** I *got* my father *to* buy me a new bicycle. ‖ 彼にビデオカメラを持って来て**もらおう** I'll *get* him *to* bring his camcorder. ／I'll *have* him bring his camcorder. ‖ 友だちに校門のところで待って**もらっている**の I *have* my friends waiting for me at the school gate.

> 【文型】
> 物(B)を…してもらう
> have B done
> get B done
>
> 【解説】(1) **have** B done が主に「他人」に頼むことを表すのに対し，**get** B done は「自分でやります」ときにも使われる.
> (2)「…してもらう」の意の get には「骨折って」や「難しさ」のニュアンスが加わることがある.
> (3) ふつう「人（A）に」を言う必要がないときに用いるが，加えるときは後に **by** A をつける.

▶彼女は携帯をデコって**もらった** She *had* [*got*] her cellphone decorated. ‖ この扇風機は配達して**もらえ**ますか Could I *have* this fan delivered? ／Could

I *have* you deliver this fan？‖髪をカットしてもらいなさい *Get* your hair cut. ／*Get* a haircut.（● ともに文頭に You should を補うと，やわらかい口調になる）‖部屋の壁紙を張り替えてもらった We *had*［*got*］the walls repapered.

【文型】
人(A)に…してもらいたい
want A to do ／would like A to do
人(A)に…してもらいたいのですが
Could［Can］I ask you to do？／Would you mind doing？

◆解説◆ (1) **want** は「(強い希望として)…してほしい」に対し，**would like** は「…してほしいんだが」というわずかに丁寧な言い方．どちらも命令と受け止められる．
(2) would は I'd, We'd のように代名詞と続けて短縮形で用いるのがふつう．
(3) 人への頼みごとは **Could［Can］I ask you to** do？や **Could［Can］you please** do？など疑問文を用いる．→ほしい，くれる．

▶次回はもっと気をつけてもらいたい I *want* you *to* be more careful next time. ‖駅まで車で送ってもらいたいんだけど *Could I ask you to* drive me to the train station？（➤ I'd like you to … では目上の人からの命令のように響く）‖おまえには弁護士になってもらいたい *I'd like* you *to* become a lawyer. ‖《近くにいる人に》写真を撮ってもらえますか？ *Could you* take my picture？／*May*［*Could*］*I ask you to* take a picture of me？／*Would you mind* taking my picture？（➤ あとの2つは丁寧なお願い；写真屋で頼む場合は I'd like to have my picture taken, please. など）‖ここでは靴を脱いでもらえますか *Could I ask you to* take off your shoes here？／*Would you mind* taking off your shoes here？（➤ この場合はかなりきつく響く指示）‖《バスで運転手が》もう少し奥へ詰めてもらえますか *Would you mind* moving further back？

▶きょうは松井君に昼ご飯をおごってもらった Matsui *bought* me lunch［*treated* me *to* lunch］today.

もらす 漏らす **1【小便などを】**▶つとむはときどきおしっこを漏らす Tsutomu sometimes *wets his pants*.（→おもらし）.

2【秘密などを】 **leak** +目, **let out**（➤ 前者は「液体・気体を漏らす」の比喩的用法）; **reveal** +目（明るみに出す）▶うっかり秘密を漏らす *spill the beans* ‖敵に秘密を漏らす *leak* a secret to the enemy ‖秘密を漏らすなよ Don't *let the secret out*. ／Don't *let the cat out of the bag*.（➤ 後者は「うっかり秘密を漏らす」の意の熟語）.

▶秘密を漏らしてしまう人がいる Some people *reveal* secrets. ‖彼女は亭主の給料が少ないと不満を漏らした She *complained about* her husband's small salary.

3【…し損なう】 **fail to** do; **miss** +目（見逃す，聞き損なう）▶私は先生が言ったことを書き漏らした I *failed to take notes of* what the teacher said. ‖大事な点を聞き漏らした I *missed* the important point.

モラトリアム a **moratorium**（一時的停止）.

モラル **morals, morality** ▶公衆のモラル public *morals*［*morality*］‖モラルのない女性 a woman *of loose morals* ‖そのレポーターにはモラルがあるのかとときどき疑ってしまう I sometimes wonder if that reporter has *any sense of morality*［*decency*］. ‖そんな古くさいモラルは今の若者には通用しないよ That kind of out-of-date *morality* doesn't wash with young people today.（➤ not wash with で「(人)に受け入れられない」）.

危ないカタカナ語✱モラル
1 日本語では「道徳」の意味で「モラル」というが，英語ではこの意味では morals と複数形にするか，morality という語を用いる．単数形の moral は「教訓」の意．
2 似た語に morale があるが，これは「士気」の意で，発音は /mərǽl/.

[1]もり 森 a **forest**（➤「森林」に近く，うっそうとして人手の加わっていないものをいう）; **woods**（林）; a **grove**（➤ woods より小さな）▶ハイカーたちは森の中で道に迷った The hikers lost their way in *the forest*［*woods*］. ‖私は3時間も森の小道を歩いてその宿に着いた I got to the inn after walking three hours along the *woodland path*.

[2]もり 銛 a **spear**; a **harpoon** /hɑːˈpúːn/（捕鯨用の）▶魚をもりで突く *spear* fish.

もりあがり 盛り上がり ▶この芝居は盛り上がりに欠けている This play is lacking in *dramatic tension*. ‖夏の甲子園大会は毎年大変な盛り上がりを見せる The high school baseball tournament at Koshien generates great *excitement* every summer.

もりあがる 盛り上がる **1【隆起する】** **rise** ▶地震の際に地面が盛り上がった The ground *rose* during the earthquake. ‖兄貴の両腕は筋肉が盛り上がっている My brother has *bulging* arm muscles.

2【高まる】 **arise** ▶増税反対運動が民衆の間に盛り上がった A tax hike opposition movement *arose* among the general public. ‖カラオケが始まり宴会は盛り上がってきた Once the karaoke started, the party began to *swing*［*to go with a swing*］.（➤ swing［go with a swing］は「盛況である」）‖討論会は終わり近くになって盛り上がり始めた The debate began to *heat up* near the end.（➤ heat up は「(討論・議論などが)熱を帯びる」の意）.

もりあげる 盛り上げる ▶みんな，このコンサートを盛り上げてくれてありがとう Thank you, everybody, for *making* this concert *a success*. ‖みんなで協力してこの会を大いに盛り上げよう Let's all pull together to *make* this meeting *a great success*. ‖彼はパーティーを盛り上げようとおもしろおかしい話をした He told some jokes to *liven up* the party.

もりあわせ 盛り合わせ ▶刺し身の盛り合わせ（*a plate of*）*assorted* sashimi（➤ assorted は「各種を取り合わせた」の意）.

もりかえす 盛り返す ▶ヤクルトは負けていたが後半に盛り返した The Swallows were losing, but *made a comeback*［*rallied*（*back*）］in the latter half of the game.

もりこむ 盛り込む **incorporate** +目（組み込む）; **include**《in》（含める）▶彼らはその少年の新しいアイデアを計画に盛り込んだ They *incorporated* the boy's new idea into their plan.

もりそば 盛りそば ***morisoba***; buckwheat noodles boiled and served cold on a bamboo colander（➤ 説明的な訳; colander は「水切りざる」）.

もりだくさん 盛り沢山 ▶今夜のコンサートの曲目は盛りだくさんだった［あまりに盛りだくさんだったので疲れた］The concert program this evening was *rich and varied*［was so *jam-packed* that I got tired (of listening)]. ‖ 盛りだくさんの料理を出す serve *a host* [*variety*] *of* dishes. (➤ a host of は「たくさんの」).

もりたてる 守り立てる back (up)(後援する); support +目(援助する); shore up(てこ入れする) ▶会社のブレーンが若い社長をもり立てた The people who were the brains of the company *backed* [*supported*] the young company president. ‖ この運動をもり立ててきたのは若い主婦たちだった It was young housewives who *shored up* [*backed*／*supported*] this political movement.

もりつける 盛り付ける arrange +目(配置する); garnish +目(添える) ▶刺し身を皿に盛り付ける *arrange* sashimi on a plate.

もりつち 盛り土 ▶盛り土をする raise the ground level (of a building site).

もりもり ▶もりもり食べて早く大きくなれよ Eat *a lot* and grow up fast. ‖ お前たちみんなのためにもりもり働くぞ I'm going to work *hard* for each and every one of you.

▶彼はいつも元気もりもりだ He is always *full of* energy. ‖ 彼は腕の筋肉がもりもりしている He has *bulging* biceps. (➤ bulging は「盛り上がった」, biceps /báɪseps/ は「二頭筋」の意).

¹**もる 盛る** **1**【積み上げる】heap [pile]《up》▶土を盛る *heap* [*pile*] *up* earth ‖ ミカンを山と盛った盆 a tray with *a heap* [*pile*] *of* mikans on it.

2【器に入れる】▶皿に盛って出す *serve* on a plate [a dish] ‖ 私は自分で茶わんにご飯を盛った I *filled* my bowl with rice. (●「山盛りに盛った」ならば filled を heaped にするか, I heaped rice into my bowl. とする).

3【毒をまぜる】poison +目 ▶殿様の膳には毒が盛られていた The dishes for the lord *were poisoned*.

4【大げさに言う】exaggerate, stretch the truth ▶若者の多くは SNS で話を盛っている Many young people *exaggerate* in their SNS posts.

²**もる 漏る** leak ▶このバケツは水が漏る This bucket *leaks*. ‖ 屋根が漏るので修理した The roof (of my house) *leaked*, so I had it repaired. ‖ 雨があちこちから漏り始めた The rain began to *come through* here and there.

モルタル mortar /mɔ́ːʳt̬əʳ/ ▶木造モルタル塗りの家 a *stucco(ed)* wooden house (➤ stucco /stʌ́koʊ/ は「化粧しっくいで塗る」).

モルディブ the Maldives /mɔ́ːldɪvz/ (スリランカ西方のさんご礁から成る島国).

モルト malt(麦芽)
‖モルトウイスキー malt whisk(e)y.

モルヒネ morphine /mɔ́ːʳfiːn/
‖モルヒネ中毒 morphine addiction ‖ モルヒネ中毒患者 a morphine addict.

モルモット a guinea pig /gíni pɪg/ ▶モルモットは実験にどうしても欠かせない *Guinea pigs* are indispensable for scientific experiments.

危ないカタカナ語✹ モルモット
1「モルモット」はオランダ語の *marmotje* が語源. 英語にも marmot という語はあるが, これは「マーモット」というアルプスやピレネーに生息するリスに似た動物のこと. 実験などに使ういわゆる「モルモット」は guinea pig または cavy /kéɪvi/ といい, 和名はテンジクネズミである.
2 比喩的な意味で「モルモット」ということがあるが, この場合も guinea pig を使う.

もれ 漏れ a leak(ガス・水などの); (an) omission(脱落) ▶会員リストに漏れがあったことをおわびいたします We are sorry that the list of members contains some *omissions*.
▶そのレースの参加者全員にもれなく参加賞を差し上げます All the entrants for the race will receive an entry prize (*without exception*).

もれきく 漏れ聞く overhear +目(ふと耳にする); hear secondhand(人づてに聞く) ▶漏れ聞くところによればあの先生の父親は大会社の社長さんだそうだ *I hear* (*that*) that teacher's father is the president of a large company.

もれる 漏れる **1**【水·ガスなどが】leak, escape (➤前者には「故障などで」という含みがある) ▶ガスが漏れている The gas *is leaking*. ‖ 漏れた場合すぐ気づくように天然ガスには臭いがつけてある An odor is added to natural gas so that it can be detected quickly if *there is a leak*. ‖ 木々の間から朝日が漏れている The morning sunshine *is streaming* [*coming*／*shining*] through the trees. ‖ 彼の口から思わずため息が漏れた A sigh *escaped* him [his lips].
▶(おしっこが)漏れちゃうよ I *can't keep it in* any longer. (➤「もう我慢できない」の意)／I'*m about to wet myself*. (➤後者が日本語に近い) ‖ あの若者のヘッドホンからはけっこう音が漏れている A lot of sound *is leaking* [*escaping*] from that young man's headphones.

2【秘密などが】leak《out》▶機密情報が社外に漏れた Some confidential information *has leaked out* of the company. ‖ 入試問題が事前に漏れてしまった Some of the entrance examination problems *have leaked out*.

3【抜け落ちる】▶私の名が名簿から漏れていた My name *was left out of* [*was left off*／*was omitted from*] the list. ‖ 彼女の絵は今回も選に漏れた Her painting *was not accepted* [*chosen*] this time either.

もろい 脆い **1**【壊れやすい】fragile /frǽdʒəl/ (慎重に扱わないとすぐに壊れる); brittle(柔軟性に欠け, 折れやすい); delicate(非常に壊れやすい) ▶ガラス製品はもろい Glassware *is easily broken* [*is fragile*]. ‖ 薄手のガラス製品はもろいので取り扱いに注意が必要だ Thin crystal is *delicate* and must be treated with care. ‖ 年を取るにつれて我々の骨はもろくなる As we age, our bones become *brittle*. ‖ 近年子供の骨はもろくなった In recent years, children's bones have become *weak*.

2【心を動かされやすい】▶情にもろい日本人が多い Many Japanese *are sentimental* [*are easily moved*].

もろくも ▶横綱はもろくも敗れた The yokozuna was defeated *too easily*.

モロッコ Morocco(アフリカ北西部の国).

もろて 諸手 ▶会社のリストラにもろ手を上げて賛成した人もいた Some people were *absolutely in favor of* the restructuring of my company. ‖ その案にもろ手を上げて賛成します I'*m all for* the plan.

もろとも ▶多くの財宝がタイタニック号もろとも沈んだ Many treasures sank (*along*) *with* the Titanic. ‖ ドライバーは車もろとも谷底に転落した The driver tumbled to the bottom of the gorge *together with* his [her] car. (➤ふつうは in his [her] car).

もろに smack; straight (じかに) ▶オートバイはもろにガードレールにぶつかった The motorcycle ran *smack* into the guardrail.

も

▶わが社は円高のあおりをもろに受けた Our company was hit *hard* [was *hard* hit] by the appreciation of the yen. (➤ be hit hard, be hard hit はともに「経済的に打撃を受ける」の意).

もろは もろ刃の double-edged, two-edged ‖**もろ刃の剣** a double- [two-] edged sword (➤ 前者がふつう).

もろもろ 諸々の various ▶もろもろの事情で計画は中止になった The plan was dropped due to *various* circumstances.

1**もん 門 1【入り口の】a gate** ▶門を開く[閉める] open [close／shut] *a gate*.

▶《比喩的》G大は狭き門だ It's *hard to get into* G University. ‖ 彼は小遊佐の門をたたいた He *asked* Koyuza *to accept him as a student*.

2【分類上の】《動物学》a **phylum** /fáɪləm/;《植物学》a **division.**

2**もん 紋** a **crest** 《解説》crest は西欧の盾形の紋章(coat of arms, heraldry)のいちばん上の部分にある家紋を指す語で family crest ともいう. 日本の紋 [紋所] はこの語で表してよい.

▶徳川家の紋は三葉葵(みつばあおい)だった The *crest* of the Tokugawa family was three asarum leaves.

‖**紋付き** a kimono with family crests (worn on formal occasions).

3**もん 問** a **question** ▶テストは全部で25問です There are 25 *questions* on the test [exam]. ⇀問題.

もんえい 門衛 a **gatekeeper,**《英また》a **porter.**

もんか 門下 ▶斎藤秀雄の門下からは多くの優れた音楽家が出た Saito Hideo produced many distinguished musicians from *among his former pupils* [*students*].

‖**門下生** a pupil (生徒); a disciple /dɪsáɪpl/ (信奉者).

もんがいかん 門外漢 a **layperson**(しろうと; 男女を明確にする場合は a layman, a laywoman で, 複数はすべて laypeople) ▶釣りについては私は全くの門外漢でほとんど何も知らない When it comes to fishing, I am only *a layman* and know next to nothing.

もんがいふしゅつ 門外不出 ▶この刀は門外不出の名刀だ This is a famous old sword and is *strictly not to be taken off the premises*. (➤ premises は「屋敷」).

もんかしょう 文科省 the Education Ministry, the Ministry of Education. ⇀文部科学省.

もんがまえ 門構え ▶りっぱな門構えの家 a house with an imposing *gate*.

もんきりがた 紋切り型の stereotyped(型にはまった); **conventional**(月並みな); **hackneyed**(陳腐な); **scripted**(台本[マニュアル]通りの) ▶紋切り型の挨拶 a *conventional* [*stereotyped*／*scripted*] greeting ‖ 紋切り型のスピーチ a speech *full of clichés* [*hackneyed expressions*].

もんく 文句

1【ことば】a phrase (語句); an **expression** (表現); **words, lyrics** (歌詞; 前者には「せりふ」の意もある) ▶決まり文句 a set *phrase* ‖ 名文句 a famous *expression* (➤「有名な」)／a well-turned *phrase* (➤「言い回しの見事な」) ‖ この歌の文句にはきっとぐっとくると思うよ I think the *words* [*lyrics*] of this song will really grab you.

2【不平】a complaint; a grumble (ぐち); an **objection** (異議) 一動 **文句を言う complain, make a complaint; get at**(がみがみ言う; 通例進行形で用いる) ▶今さら文句を言っても始まらない It's no use *complaining* [*making a complaint*] now. ‖ 文句を言わずにもっと働けよ *Stop complaining* [*grumbling*] and work harder.

▶文句(＝反対意見)のあるやつは前へ出ろ Step forward if you have any *objections*. ‖ 彼はいつも食べ物に文句ばかり言っている He *is always complaining* about the food.

▶上司は私のすることにいちいち文句をつける My boss *finds fault with* everything I do. (➤ find fault with は「…のあらを捜す」).

▶ここのラーメンは文句なしにうまい This ramen tastes *just perfect* [is *absolutely* delicious]. ‖ 彼女のピアノは文句のつけようのない演奏だった She played the piano *perfectly*. ‖ あなたの仕事ぶりは文句のつけようがない I *have nothing to complain about* in your work. ／Your work *is completely satisfactory* [*above reproach*].

もんげん 門限 (the) curfew /kə́ːʳfjuː/ ▶急がないと門限に間に合わないぞ Hurry up, or you won't get back before *curfew*. ‖ 寮の門限は何時? What time is your dorm door locked? (➤「寮のドアは何時に閉まるのか」の意)／When is your dorm *curfew*?

もんこ 門戸 the door(戸口); **the gate**(門); **the portal**(堂々とした表玄関) ▶外国人に大きく門戸を開く open *the door* wide to foreigners ‖ アメリカは世界中の難民に門戸を開放している The U.S. *has kept its doors open* to the refugees from around the world.

モンゴル Mongolia(ロシアと中国に挟まれた国)

‖**モンゴル語** Mongolian ‖ **モンゴル人** a Mongolian.

もんし 門歯《解剖学》an **incisor** /ɪnsáɪzəʳ/.

もんしょう 紋章 a **coat of arms**, a **crest** ▶その墓石には詩人の氏名と紋章が刻まれていた The tombstone was inscribed with the poet's full name and his *coat of arms*.

もんしろちょう 紋白蝶《虫》a **cabbage butterfly.**

もんしん 問診 ‖**問診票** a medical questionnaire.

モンスーン the monsoon.

モンスター a **monster**

‖**モンスターペアレント** a problem parent ‖ **モンスターペイシェント** a problem patient (➤ いずれの場合も monster とはいわない).

もんせき 問責 censure ▶(…に対する)問責決議を提出する introduce *a censure motion* (against).

もんぜんばらい 門前払い ▶その作家に会いたくて自宅を訪ねたが, 門前払いを食わされた I visited the writer's home wishing to meet him, but he *shut the door on me* [*I was turned away at the door*].

もんぜんまち 門前町 a ***monzenmachi***; a town that has developed in front of the gateway to a major Buddhist temple or a Shinto shrine (➤ 説明的な訳).

モンタージュ (a) **montage** /mɑːntáːʒ/; a **composite photo(graph)**(合成写真) ▶警察は容疑者のモンタージュ写真を公表した The police made public *a composite photo* of the suspect.

もんだい 問題

訳語メニュー
- 試験問題 ⇀question, problem **1**
- 疑問 ⇀question **2**
- 面倒な事 ⇀trouble **6**

1【設問】 a **question**(問いに「答える」); a **problem** (主に理数系の解く) ▶**問題**を解く answer *a question* / solve *a problem* ‖ 木村先生は試験でいつも難しい**問題**を出す Mr. Kimura always gives us difficult *questions* on the exams. ‖ 出そうな**問題**の勉強を忘れないように Don't forget to study *questions* likely to come up (on the test).
▶この数学の**問題**を解くのに半日かかった It took me a half day to solve this math *problem*. ‖ この**問題**は絶対テストに出るぞ This *question* will be on the test for sure.
‖**問題集** a drill book ‖ **問題用紙** a question sheet.
2【疑問】 a **question** ▶**問題**は誰が猫に鈴をつけるかだ The *question* is who dares to bell the cat. ‖ この仕事を全面的に彼に任せるというのは**問題**だ It's *questionable* to leave everything in his hands.
3【検討・解決すべきこと】 a **question**; a **problem** (難問); an **issue** (争点) ▶政治**問題** a political *issue* ‖ 10代の飲酒が社会**問題**になってきた Teenage drinking has become *a social problem*. ‖ 不公平税制が国会で**問題になった** Inequity in taxation *was pointed out* [*was taken up as a problem* / *was criticized*] in Diet deliberations.
▶これは説明するのがとても困難な**問題**だ This is *a problem* [*an issue*] that is very difficult to explain. ‖ 年功序列の給与制度にはいくつかの**問題点**があると私は思う I think there are some *problems* with the corporate system of compensation based on seniority.
▶彼の昔の失敗を今**問題**にしなくてもいいだろう Don't *rehash* his old mistakes. (➤ rehash は「蒸し返す」) / There's no need to *bring up* his past mistakes. ‖ この程度の誤差はほとんど**問題にならない** An error of this degree should *not make a difference*. ‖ 誰がそう言ったかは**問題ではない** It *does not matter* who said so. / It *is not important* who said it.
▶戦争放棄の憲法がある以上, 核兵器を持つなど**問題外**だ Because we have a war-renouncing constitution, it is *out of the question* for us to have nuclear weapons.
4【事情, 事柄】 **affairs** (情勢・事情); a **problem**, a **question** (個々の問題); a **matter** (…にかかわりのあること) ▶鈴木さんは中東**問題**に通じている Mr. Suzuki is well versed in Middle East *affairs*. ‖ 円高は中小企業にとって深刻な**問題**だ The strong yen is a serious *problem* to medium-and-small-sized businesses.
▶私はこの夏にオーストラリアには行くことはできません. **お金の問題**ではなく**時間の問題**があるのです I can't go to Australia this summer. It's not *a question of money*. It's *a question of time*. ‖ それは**好みの問題**です It is *a matter of preference*.
5【話題・議題】 a **subject**, a **topic** (➤ 後者のほうがカバーする範囲が広く, 小さなものから大きなものまで含む) ▶彼の話は**問題**からそれた He strayed from *the subject* [*topic*].
▶きみの言っていることはこの**問題**と無関係だ What you're saying has nothing to do with this *subject* [*topic*].
6【面倒な事】 **trouble** ▶うちの息子がまた学校で何か**問題を起こしたらしい** My son seems to have caused some *trouble* at school again. ‖ どこの学校にも**問題を起こす生徒**(=問題児)はいるものだ *Problem children* are found at any school.
7【関心事】 ▶これは彼が愛人と一緒に写っている**問題の写真だ** This is the picture *in question* showing him with his lover.

逆引き熟語 ○○問題
◆**試験問題** a test question / **ひっかけ[ひねった]問題** a trick question / **マークシート式問題** a multiple-choice question / **○×問題** a true-false question
◆**ありがちな[よくある]問題** a common problem / **金の問題** a question [matter] of money / **好みの問題** a matter of choice [preference] / **時間の問題** a question [matter] of time / **社会問題** a social problem / **重大な問題** a crucial problem [issue] / **深刻な問題** a serious problem / **政治問題** a political issue

もんだいし 問題視 ▶それを問題視する *regard* [*see*] it *as a problem*.
モンタナ **Montana** (アメリカ北西部の州; 略 MT, Mont.).
もんちゃく 悶着 ▶きのう谷山さんが課長とひと悶着起こしてね Yesterday, Mr. Taniyama *had a run-in with* the manager. / Yesterday, Mr. Taniyama *locked horns with* the manager. (➤ lock horns は「(人と)意見が衝突する」).
もんちゅう 門柱 a **gatepost**.
もんつき 紋付き a ***montsuki***; a Japanese formal kimono with a family crest (➤ 説明的な訳).
もんと 門徒 a **follower**; a **believer** (信者).
もんとう 門灯 a **gate light** [**lamp**].
もんどう 問答 **questions and answers** ▶**問答無用** There's no use (in) talking! / No more discussion! ‖ 禅僧は弟子たちと(禅)**問答した** The Zen priest *had a dialog* with his pupils (in which he asked them to explain the meanings of koans).
モントリオール **Montreal** (カナダ南東部の都市).
もんなし 文無しの **penniless** ▶20年前に東京に出て来たとき私は全くの文無しだった When I came to Tokyo twenty years ago, I was absolutely *penniless* [*flat broke*].
もんばん 門番 a **gatekeeper**; a **doorkeeper** (ビルなどの正面玄関の).
もんぶかがくしょう 文部科学省 **Ministry of Education, Culture, Sports, Science and Technology** (➤「文科省」と略称するように the Ministry of Education と省略することが多い).
モンブラン **Mont Blanc** /mɔ̃:nblɑ́:ŋ/ (フランスとイタリア国境にあるアルプスの最高峰).
もんぴ 門扉 the **door(s) of a gate**
もんぺ a ***mompe***; a women's loose work pants (tucked at the hem) (➤ 説明的な訳).
もんもう 文盲 →**非識字**.
もんもん 悶々 ▶彼女は自分はがんなのではないかと悶々として数日を過ごした She spent a few days *brooding over* the possibility of having cancer. (➤ brood over は「…をくよくよ気に病む」の意).
もんよう 文様 a **pattern** ▶波の文様 a wave *pattern*.

も

や・ヤ

や 矢 an **arrow**(弓で引く矢) ; a **dart**(投げ矢) ▶的に向かって矢を放つ shoot *an arrow* at a target.
ことわざ 光陰矢のごとし Time flies. (➤ 英語のことわざ ; like an arrow をつけるのは日本語からの直訳).

-や **and**(そして) ; **or**(または) ▶旅館ではウニや, アワビや, ホヤなどのごちそうが出ました They served us such delicacies as sea urchins, abalones(,) *and* sea squirts. (➤ 3つ以上列挙するときは A, B, C(,) and … の形になる).
▶ほとんどの生徒はバスや電車で登校して来る Most of the students come to school by bus *or* by train. ‖ こちらには友だちや親戚はあまり居ない I don't have many friends *or* relatives here. (➤ 否定語のあとでは or を用いる).

やあ **Hi**!, **Hey**! ▶やあ, かわい子ちゃん *Hey*, good-looking!／*Hey*, baby! ‖ 対話「やあ, 久しぶり」「やあ, どうしてた?」"*Hi!* It's been a while." "*Hi!* How have you been?"

ヤード a **yard**(➤ 1ヤードは 91.44センチメートル).

やい **Hey**! ▶やい, この野郎 *Hey*, you (idiot)! ‖ やい, こっちを向け *You!* Look here! ‖ やい, やめろってんだ *Come now*, stop it!／Come off it!

-やいなや や否や →-いなや.

やいのやいの ▶いくらきみがやいのやいの言っても, 返す金が無いんだ. 無い袖は振れないよ *No matter how hard* you *press me*, I don't have money to pay you back. You can't get blood out of a turnip [get water out of a stone], you know. (➤「カブから血[石から水]は取れない」が文字どおりの意).

やえ 八重 ▶八重咲きの花[チューリップ] a *double* flower [tulip].
‖八重桜 double cherry blossoms(花) ; a double(-flowering) cherry tree(木).

やえい 野営 **camping**(キャンプ) 一動 **野営する** **camp (out)** ▶彼らは湖のそばで野営した They *camped* [*pitched camp*] by the lakeside.
‖野営地 a camp.

やえば 八重歯 an **overlapping canine (tooth)**, a **double tooth**, a **redundant tooth** (➤ canine (tooth)は「犬歯」. おどけて a vampire tooth ともいう) ▶あの子は八重歯がかわいい That girl looks cute with her *double tooth*. 《参考》欧米人は一般に八重歯を気味悪く感じ, 早期に治療するのがふつう. 歯並びの悪い人は貧しくて歯医者に行くゆとりのない人と見られる傾向もある.

やおちょう 八百長 a **fix** ; a **rigging**(不正) ; a **fixed** [**rigged**] **game**(八百長試合) ▶八百長をする play *a fixed game*／rig [fix] a game ‖ あの試合, きっと八百長だぜ That game must have *been fixed* [*been rigged*／*been put up*／*been a put-up job*].

やおもて 矢面 ▶財務大臣はマスコミの非難の矢面に立たされている The Finance Minister *is bearing* [*taking*／*carrying*] *the brunt* of the media's criticism. (➤ brunt は「(攻撃の)矛先」の意).

やおや 八百屋 a **vegetable store**, 《英》a **greengrocer's (shop)**(店) ; a **greengrocer**(人) 《参考》アメリカではこのほかに農産物一般を扱う大規模な店を farmer's market とか produce market と呼ぶ.

やおよろず 八百万 ▶やおよろずの神 a *myriad of kami* [*gods*].

やおら **slowly**(ゆっくりと) ; **suddenly**(突然 ; この意味での日本語は本来は誤用) ▶やおら立ち上がる rise *slowly* [*suddenly*] to one's feet.

やかい 夜会 an **evening party**, a **soiree** /swɑːréi/
‖夜会服 (formal) evening wear [attire] ; an evening dress(女性の).

やがい 野外の **outdoor**, **open-air** 一副 **野外で** **outdoors** ▶野外スポーツ *outdoor* sports ‖ 私たちは湖畔で野外コンサートを楽しんだ We enjoyed *an open-air concert* by the lake. ‖ 私たちは野外でバーベキューパーティーをした We had a barbecue *outdoors* [an *outdoor* barbecue].
‖野外劇場 an open-air theater.

やがく 夜学 an **evening** [a **night**] **school**.

やかた 館 a **mansion** ; a **castle**(城).

やかたぶね 屋形船 a ***yakatabune*** ; a Japanese party boat with a roof(➤ 説明的な訳).

やがて **1【まもなく】before long**(遠からず) ; **soon**(すぐに) ; **by and by**(そのうちに ; 文語) ▶やがて夏休みも終わる The summer vacation will be over *before long*.
▶その食べ物は最初は変な味と思ったがやがて慣れてしまった I found that food (to be) strange-tasting at first, but I *soon* got used to it. ‖ 真実はやがて明らかになるだろう The truth will come to light *by and by* [*in the course of time*].
2【いつかは】▶地道に努力していればやがていいことがあるよ Constant, steady effort will pay off *in the end*. ‖ 父もやがては折れるだろう My father will give in *eventually* [*sooner or later*]. (➤ 前者は「結局は」, 後者は「いずれは」).
3【かれこれ】nearly, **almost** ▶教師になってやがて10年になる It has been *nearly* [*almost*] ten years since I became a teacher.

やかましい 喧しい

訳語メニュー
騒がしい →noisy 1
人が厳しい →strict 2
気難しい →particular 3

1【騒がしい】noisy ; **loud**(音が大きい) ▶やかましいぞ! (*Be*) *quiet!*／*Pipe down!*／*Tone it down!* (➤ 後者2つは俗語的) ‖ 隣の部屋がやかましい It's *noisy* in the next room. ‖ 隣の家のステレオがやかましくて迷惑だ The next-door neighbor's *loud* stereo bothers us.
2【厳しい】strict ▶監督は選手の私生活に対してやかましい Our manager *is strict* with the players about their personal conduct.
▶彼は時間[しつけ]にやかましい He'*s a stickler for* punctuality [discipline]. (➤ a stickler for A は「A にやかましい人」).
3【細かい】particular(こだわりがある) (➤「えり好みする, 気難しい」の意では fussy や picky を用いる) ▶父は食べる物にやかましい My father *is particular about* food.

▶夫は家のことをいつもやかましく言う My husband always *nags at* me about household matters. (➤ nag は「がみがみ小言を言う」).

やから 輩 ▶あんなやからと一緒に仕事をしたくない I don't want to work with that *bunch*.

1**やかん 薬缶** a **kettle**, a **teakettle** ▶やかんを火に掛ける put *a kettle* on the stove.

2**やかん 夜間** **night** ━副 **夜間に at night**(夜に); **in** [**during**] **the night**(夜のうちに) ▶彼女はふだん夜間は外出しない She usually doesn't go out *at night*. ‖ 午後 7 時以降は夜間割引があります There is *a night-time discount* after 7 p.m. ‖ 父は学校の夜間部に通った My father attended *night school* [*evening classes*].

‖**夜間外出禁止令** a nighttime curfew ‖ **夜間金庫** a night safe [depository] ‖ **夜間勤務** (→夜勤) ‖ **夜間飛行** a night flight.

やき 焼き **1【焼きかげん】**▶この魚は焼きが足りない This fish isn't *cooked* enough. ／ This fish needs to be *cooked* longer.

2【慣用表現】▶ちょっとたるんでいるから，きょうは部員に焼きを入れて(＝鍛えて)やろう Since the boys and girls have been a little slack lately, I'll *give* them *a hard workout* today. (➤ workout は「練習」).

▶こんな簡単なミスを見逃すようじゃあ，うちのおやじも焼きが回ったな I'm surprised my father missed this kind of easy mistake. I must say he *is not as sharp as* he used to be.

> **逆引き熟語 〇〇焼き**
> あぶり焼き broil ／うなぎのかば焼き grilled eel ／ステーキの炭火焼き charbroiled steak ／卵焼き an omelet ／照り焼き teriyaki ／豚のしょうが焼き grilled ginger pork ／目玉焼き(片面焼き) a fried egg sunny-side up ／目玉焼き(両面半熟焼き) a fried egg over-easy ／目玉焼き(両面焼き) a fried egg over-hard

やぎ 山羊 《動物》 a **goat**; a **kid**(子ヤギ) 《参考》ヤギの鳴き声を表す動詞は bleat や baa

‖**やぎひげ** a goatee /goʊtíː/.

やきあみ 焼き網 a **grill**, a **gridiron** /grídàɪərn/.

やきいも 焼き芋 *yakiimo*; a baked [roast] sweet potato (➤ 説明的な訳)

‖**焼き芋屋** a *yakiimo* seller [vendor] ‖ **石焼き芋** a sweet potato baked among hot pebbles.

やきいろ 焼き色 ▶鶏肉に焼き色をつける *brown* the chicken.

やきいん 焼き印 a **brand** ▶牛に焼き印を入れる *brand* a cow.

やぎざ 山羊座 (a) **Capricorn**.

やきざかな 焼き魚 a **broiled** [**grilled**] **fish**.

やきすてる 焼き捨てる ▶私が差し上げた手紙は全部焼き捨ててください Please *burn* all the letters I sent you.

やきそば 焼きそば **chow mein** /tʃàʊméɪn/, **fried noodles**.

やきたて 焼き立て ▶焼きたてのミートパイをどうぞ Please help yourself to the meat pies. They're *hot* [*fresh*] *from the oven*. (●「オーブンから出したばかりの」と考えて訳す).

やきつく 焼き付く **be burned** 《into》; **be engrave** [**imprinted**] 《on》 ▶凄まじい破壊力を持った津波が多くの日本人の記憶に焼き付いている The devastating tsunami *is burned into* [*is imprinted on* ／ *is engraved on*] the memories of most Japanese people.

やきつくす 焼き尽くす **burn down** ▶その火事は商店街を焼き尽くした The fire (*completely*) *burned down* the shopping arcade. ／ The shopping arcade was reduced to ashes by the fire.

やきつける 焼き付ける **print** ＋目 (フィルムを); **burn** ＋目 (ＣＤ，ＤＶＤなどを).

やきとり 焼き鳥 *yakitori*

日本紹介 ✉ **焼き鳥は串に刺した鶏肉にたれや塩をつけ，あぶって焼いたものです．安価な居酒屋や屋台で酒を飲むときに最も好まれる料理の一つです** *Yakitori* is skewered chicken dipped in a special sauce or seasoned with salt and then grilled. It is one of the most popular foods that people munch on while drinking at cheap drinking places or street booths.

やきなおし 焼き直し **1【映画・文学作品などの】**(a) **rehash**; an **adaptation**(改作，翻案物) ▶この映画はほとんど彼の旧作の焼き直しだ This film is nothing but *a rehash* of his earlier one(s). ‖ そのテレビシリーズはある小説の焼き直しだ The TV series is *an adaptation* of a novel.

2【食べ物の】 **rebaking**, **rebroiling**(➤ 前者はオーブンで，後者はじか火で).

やきなおす 焼き直す

1【映画・文学作品などを】 **rehash** ＋目; **adapt** ＋目 (➤ 前者には軽蔑的な含みがあることが多い) ▶古い物語を焼き直す *rehash* an old story ‖ 小説を映画に焼き直す *adapt* a novel to a movie.

2【食べ物を】 **rebake** ＋目 (オーブンで); **rebroil** ＋目 (じか火で) ➤ピザ [パン] を焼き直す *rebake* pizza [bread] ‖ ジャガイモを焼き直す *rebroil* potatoes.

やきにく 焼き肉 **broiled** [**grilled**] **meat**; **Korean barbecue**.

やきはた 焼き畑 ‖**焼き畑農業** slash-and-burn farming [agriculture].

やきはらう 焼き払う ▶畑の一部を焼き払う *burn off* part of the field ‖ この内戦で村中の家が焼き払われた In this civil war, all the houses in the village *were set afire and burned down*.

やきぶた 焼き豚 **roast pork**.

やきまし 焼き増し a **copy**(複製); a **print**(印画) ▶この写真，何枚焼き増ししましょうか How many *copies* of this photograph do you want? ‖ その写真を 5 枚焼き増ししてもらった I *had* five *more prints* of the picture *made*.

やきめし 焼き飯 **fried rice**.

やきもき ━動 (…に，…で)**やきもきする fret** 《over》 ▶母はつまらないことでやきもきするところがある My mom tends to *fret over* trivial things. ‖ 我々は救急車が到着するのをやきもきしながら待った We *impatiently* waited for the ambulance to arrive.

やきもち 焼き餅 **jealousy** /dʒéləsi/ (嫉妬) ▶友だちにやきもちを焼く *feel jealousy* toward a friend ‖ 彼女はすぐにやきもちを焼く She *gets jealous* [*shows her jealousy*] easily. (➤ 前者は「嫉妬心を起こす」，後者は「嫉妬から何らかの行動を起こす」).

▶女より男のほうがやきもちが激しいと言う人もいる Some people say *jealousy* is fiercer in men than in women. ‖ 彼女はやきもち焼きの奥さんだ She is a *jealous* wife.

やきもの 焼き物 **1【陶磁器】** **pottery**(陶器); **earthenware**(土器); **porcelain**, **china**(磁器); **ceramics**, **ceramic ware**(陶磁器) ▶マクドナルドさんは日本の焼き物に

強い関心をもっている Mr. MacDonald has a strong interest in Japanese *pottery*.

2【料理】 a **grilled dish**（直火, または間接的に火で焼いた魚・肉などの料理） →焼き魚.

やきゅう 野球 **baseball** ▶男の子たちは公園で**野球**をしていた The boys were playing *baseball* in the park. ‖ 先週の日曜日に法政対中央の**野球の試合**を見にいった We went to see the *baseball game* between Hosei and Chuo last Sunday. ‖ 毎年春と夏に甲子園球場で全国高校**野球大会**が開かれる Every spring and summer, the National Senior High School *Baseball Tournament* is held at Koshien Stadium.

‖**野球場** a ballpark, a stadium, a baseball ground [field] ‖ **野球選手** a baseball player ‖ **野球チーム** a baseball team ‖ **野球部** a baseball team [club] ‖ **野球ファン** a baseball fan ‖ **野球帽** a baseball cap.

—●**注意すべき野球英語**

日本の野球用語には和製語が多い. 英語として意味をなさないものから, 別の意味に受け取られるものまで, さまざまである. 以下にその代表的なものを挙げる. 右側が正しい英語.

ゲッツー	double play
スリーバント	two-strike bunt
タッチ	tag
テキサスヒット	Texas leaguer
デッドボール	hit by a pitch
ナイター	night game
バックネット	backstop
フォアボール	base on balls
ヘッドスライディング	headfirst sliding
ホームスチール	stealing home

やぎゅう 野牛《動物》a **bison** /báisən/, a **buffalo**（➤ 後者は俗称）.

[1]**やきん 夜勤** **night duty**, a **night shift**（➤ duty は医師・警官や公務員に使うことが多い. shift は「交替制の勤務時間」）▶少なくとも週に１回**夜勤**がある I have *night duty* at least once a week. ‖ 今夜は伊東先生が**夜勤**だ Dr. Ito is *on night duty* tonight. ‖ 私は来週はずっと**夜勤**だ I'll be working (on the) *night shift* all next week.

[2]**やきん 冶金** **metallurgy** /métlə:ʳdʒi/.

[1]**やく 役** **1【仕事, 任務】** a **job**（仕事）; a **duty**（職務）; a **position**, a **post**（地位）

▶風呂掃除は私の**役**だ It is my *job* [*duty*] to clean the bathroom. ‖ 生徒会の会計の**役**なんて私には荷が重すぎる Acting as accountant for the student council would be too big *a job* for me. ‖ 彼は社長の**役**を降りた He resigned from his *position* [*post*] as president.

▶浅野さんは通訳の**役**を買って出た Asano volunteered to *serve as* interpreter.（➤ serve as で「…として働く」）‖ 結婚披露宴の司会**役**を（＝司会をするように）頼まれた They asked me to emcee the wedding reception.

2【劇中の】 a **role**（ある俳優に割り当てられた）; a **part**（ある俳優が演じる）

▶加藤さんには裁判官の**役**がぴったりだ Kato is perfect for the *role* of judge. ‖ 私は舞台でキリスト［お父さん］の**役**をやった I played the *part* of Christ [the *role* of a father] on the stage. ‖ 彼女はこの芝居の中で一人二**役**を演じている She plays *two roles* [*a double role*] in this play.

3【「役に立つ[立てる]」の形で】 **be useful** ▶この辞書は熟語を調べるのにとても**役に立つ** This dictionary *is* very *useful* for looking up idioms. ‖ このウェブサイトは私にはとても**役に立つ** This Web site *is* very *useful* to me [is *of* great *use* to me].（➤ カッコ内はやや堅い言い方）‖ このガイドブックはとても**役に立つ** This guidebook *is* really *handy* [really *comes in handy*].（➤ handy は「手ごろな, 便利な」）‖ このお金は飢餓に苦しむ人々を救う**役に立てて**ください Please put this money to *use* to help people threatened with starvation. ‖ 今ではこの地図はほとんど［**全然**］**役に立たない** This map *is of little use* [*of no use*] now. ／This map *is almost* [*completely*] *useless*. ‖ こんな難しい数学なんか勉強して何の**役に立つ**のだろう What *is the use* [*the point*] *of* studying such difficult math?

▶何かお**役に立てる**ことはないでしょうか Is there anything I *can do for* you? ‖ 少しでもあなたのお**役に立てる**といいのですが I hope I can *be of some help to* you.

▶世界平和の促進に少しでも**役に立つ**よう国連で働きたい I'd like to work at the United Nations so that I can *play a role*, however minor, in promoting world peace. →役立つ.

✉ **あなたのお役に立てて幸いです** I'm glad to *be able to help* you. ➤「あなたを手助けできてうれしい」の意. すでに終わったことであれば I'm glad that I was able to help you. か I'm glad to have been able to help you. とする.

✉ **あまりお役に立てず申し訳ありませんでした** I'm sorry I *wasn't* (*of*) much *help* to you.

逆引き熟語 ○○役

◆**悪役** a bad guy, the role of a villain ／**男[女]役** a male- [female-] role player, a male [female] part ／**子役** a child's part [role] ／**司会進行役** a master of ceremonies, an emcee ／**主役** the leading part [role, actor, actress] ／**代役** a substitute, a stand-in, an understudy（あらかじめせりふを覚えておく人）

◆**橋渡し[パイプ]役** a mediator ／**はまり役** the right person for the role ／**引き立て役** a foil, a setoff ／**ホスト役** a host ／**まとめ役** a coordinator（調整役）, an organizer（世話役）／**脇役** a supporting role

[2]**やく 訳** (a) **translation**, (a) **version**（➤「翻訳されたもの」の意ではともに a をつける）▶優れた**訳** (an) excellent *translation* ‖ 私は『源氏物語』を**英訳**で読んだ I read "The Tale of Genji" *in English translation* [*in an English version*]. ／ I read *an English version* of "The Tale of Genji."

[3]**やく 約** **about, around, some; ... or so; approximately** /əprá:ksmətli/

語法 (1)「およそ」の意味では **about** が最も一般的で, **around** はインフォーマルな語. some は50, 100 など端数のない数を指すのに用いる. or so は「…かそこら」の意.
(2) **approximately** はやや堅い語であるが, 書きことば・話しことばの両方でふつうに用いられる（書きことばでは approx. と省略することが多い）.

▶東京から新青森までは新幹線で**約**３時間10分かかる It takes *about* three hours and ten minutes from Tokyo to Shin-Aomori by Shinkansen. ‖ 日本に

は約230種類のチョウがいる There are *some* 230 kinds of butterflies in Japan. ‖ この学校の生徒数は約2000人です This school has an enrollment of *approximately* [*roughly*] two thousand students. (➤ roughly は「大ざっぱに言うと」) ‖ 対話「あなたの家は駅からどのくらい離れていますか」「約1キロです」"How far is your house from the station?" "A kilometer *or so*."

4**やく** 焼く **1【熱で料理する】bake** +(他) (パン・菓子などをオーブンで)；《主に米》**broil** +(他)，《主に英》**grill** +(他) (じか火で，あぶって)；**roast** +(他) (オーブンで蒸して，またはじか火で)；**barbecue** +(他) (肉などを丸ごと) ▶パン[肉]をオーブンで焼く *bake* bread [*roast* meat] in an oven ‖ 魚を強火で焼く *broil* [*grill*] fish over high heat.
▶ベーコンを(油で)カリカリに焼く *fry* bacon until it is crisp ‖ ホットケーキを焼く(＝作る) *make* pancakes ‖ 庭でチキンを焼こう Let's *barbecue* chicken in the yard. ‖ お母さん，パンを2枚焼いて Mom, could you *make* two pieces of *toast* [*toast* two slices of bread]?
▶ 対話「お客さま，ステーキはどのように焼きましょうか」「レアにしてください」"How would you like your steak, sir?" "Rare, please."
2【燃やす】burn +(他) ▶美和は元カレから来た手紙をすべて焼いた Miwa *burned* all the letters from her ex-boyfriend.
▶私たちは大火で家を焼いてしまった Our house *burned down* in a big fire. (➤ burn down は「焼け落ちる，全焼する」).
3【肌を】tan (+(他)) ▶浜辺の熱い陽光の中で肌を焼いた I *tanned myself* in the hot sun at the beach. ‖ 私たちはワイキキで肌を真っ黒に焼いた We *got a deep (sun)tan* at Waikiki.
4【陶器などを】make +(他) ▶焼き物を焼くのは楽しい It's fun to *make* pottery.

5**やく** 妬く **get jealous** 《of》(嫉妬する)；**get envious** 《of》(人の持ち物や成功を羨ましがる) ▶彼女は(私たちが付き合っているから)やいてるんだと思う I think she*'s jealous of* me (because we're seeing each other).

6**やく** 厄 **bad luck**(不運). →厄年，厄払い，厄日.

やぐ 夜具 **bedding**(寝具類).

やくいん 役員 **1【係員】a person in charge** ▶母はPTAの役員に選ばれた My mother was elected to *a position* [*a post*] in the PTA. (➤ ともに「(責任ある)地位」の意).
2【幹部役員】an executive, a director(会社の重役)；an **officer**(団体などの) ▶おじは会社の役員をしている My uncle is on the board of directors. (➤ board of directors は「取締役会」).

やくがい 薬害 **the harmful (side) effects of (a) medicine；damage by agricultural chemicals**(農薬による)
‖薬害エイズ HIV infection due to medical malpractice.

やくがく 薬学 **pharmacy** /fáːʳməsi/
‖薬学部 the school [college] of pharmacy.

やくがら 役柄 **a role**(役)；**a character**(登場人物) ▶メリル・ストリープはマーガレット・サッチャーの役柄になり切ってみせた Meryl Streep inhabited *the role* [*character*] of Margaret Thatcher.

やくご 訳語 an **equivalent**(相当する語) ▶英語の単語を辞書で調べるときは，訳語だけでなく例文も見るように努めなさい When you look up an English word in the dictionary, try to read the example sentence(s) as well as its *Japanese equivalent*(*s*).

やくざ a **(member of) yakuza, the yakuza**(➤ 英語化している；後者は総称) ▶やくざっぽい男たちの一団が店の周りにたむろしている There are a bunch of men who look like *yakuza* [*gangsters*] hanging around the shop.

やくざいし 薬剤師 a **pharmacist**；《主に米》a **druggist**；《主に英》a **chemist**.

やくし 訳詞 **translation of the lyrics of a song**(訳すこと)；**translated lyrics of a song**(訳された詞).

やくしにょらい 薬師如来 ***Yakushi Nyorai*, Bhaisajya Buddha, the Medicine Buddha.**

やくじほう 薬事法 **the Pharmaceutical Affairs Act.**

1**やくしゃ** 役者 an **actor**(男女とも)；an **actress**(女) ▶歌舞伎の役者 a Kabuki *actor* ‖ 役者になる *become an actor* / *go on the stage* ‖ 最後まですっとぼけるとは，彼も役者だね He played possum till the end. He's really *some actor*. (➤ play possum は「知らないふりをする」の意のインフォーマルな表現).
▶《慣用表現》駆け引きでは，部長と社長じゃ役者が違う(＝相手にならない) The manager *is no match for* [*is outclassed by*] the president as far as business tactics are concerned. ‖ これでやっと役者がそろったな Now we *have all the key players*. / *Everyone we need is here*.

2**やくしゃ** 訳者 a **translator.**

やくしゅつ 訳出 **translation 一動 訳出する translate** +(他).

やくしょ 役所 a **government** [**public**] **office** ▶書類のたらい回しはお役所仕事の典型だ Passing documents around from one section to another (needlessly) is a typically *bureaucratic way of doing things* [*typical bureaucracy*]. (➤ bureaucratic /bjʊərəkrǽtɪk/ も日本語の「お役所的な」と同じような文脈で使われる).
‖区役所 a ward office ‖ 市役所 a municipal office；《米また》a city hall，《英また》a town hall.

やくしょく 役職 a **post**(勤務上の地位)；a **managerial** [**managing**] **post**(管理職) ▶山田さんは会社で役職に就いている Mr. Yamada *holds a managerial post* [*holds an administrative position* / *is an executive*] in his company.
‖役職手当 a post-related allowance, an executive allowance (➤ 後者は役付きの場合).

やくしん 躍進 **progress** /práːgrəs/ **一動 躍進する progress** /prəgrés/ **rapidly, make a rapid progress** ▶ことしこそ，わが社の躍進の年にしようと決意しております We are determined to make this year a year of *progress* for our company. ‖ ここ数十年の中国の世界市場への躍進ぶりには目覚ましいものがある China has remarkably expanded its share in the world market in recent decades. (➤「目覚ましくシェアを伸ばした」の意).

やくす 訳す **translate** /trænsleɪt/ (+(他)), **put** +(他) (➤ 後者はインフォーマル)；**interpret**(通訳する) ▶この小説は多くの言語に訳されている This novel *has been translated* into a lot of languages. ‖ この手紙をイタリア語に訳してください Please *translate* [*put*] this letter into Italian. ‖ この英語のセンテンスは日本語に訳すのが難しい This English sentence is hard to *translate* into Japanese.

やくすう 約数 《数学》a **divisor**
‖最大公約数 the greatest common divisor.

やくぜん 薬膳 **medicinal dishes.**

やくそう 薬草 a **medicinal herb.**

やくそく 約束

📖 **訳語メニュー**
実行の約束 →promise **1**
人と会う約束 →appointment **2**
規定 →rule **3**

1【実行の】a **promise**; one's **word**(約束したことば) 一動 **約束する promise**(+目), **make a promise**; **assure** +目(請け合う) ▶約束を守る keep one's *promise* [*word*] ‖市長は約束を破った The mayor broke his *promise*. ‖彼女は親友との約束を破った She broke her *promise* [her *word*] to her closest friend. ‖約束は約束. 守ってよ *A promise is a promise*. You should keep it.

【文型】
…すると約束する
promise to do
…すると人(A)に約束する
promise A **that** S + V

▶私たちは1年後パリで再会する約束をした We *promised to* meet again in Paris in a year. ‖ **対話**「妹の面倒を見るって約束する?」「うん. 約束する」"Will you *promise* (me) *to* take care of your little sister?" "OK. I *promise*." ‖父が来年カナダに行かせてくれると約束してくれた My father *promised* (me) *that* he would send me to Canada next year. ▶彼は約束どおりお土産を買ってきてくれた He bought me a present *as he had promised*. ‖ **対話**「夏休みの旅行は取りやめだ」「パパ, それじゃあ約束が違うよ」"Our trip this summer is off." "But *you promised*, Dad!" (➤「約束したじゃないか」の意) ‖首相は有権者に, 近い将来の新税はないと約束した The prime minister *assured* the voters that there would be no new tax in the near future.

2【面会などの】an **appointment** (特に医者や弁護士などとの予約); an **engagement**(ある時ある場所へ行くという) ▶明日の午後, 仕事上の約束があります I have *a business engagement* tomorrow afternoon. ‖今夜は約束があるから5時きっかりに職場を出なければならない I'*ve got an engagement* [*a date*] this evening, so I'll have to leave work at 5 sharp. ‖ **対話**(会社の受付で)「社長にお会いしたいのですが」「お約束はおありですか」"I'd like to see the president." "*Do you have an appointment*?" ‖ **対話**「何時のお約束でしょうか」「3時です」"May I ask what time your *appointment* is?" "At three."
▶今夜, 由里と7時に会う約束なの. あなたも来る? I'*m meeting* Yuri at seven this evening. Do you want to come (too)?

3【規定】a **rule** ▶私たちの会には会員が守らねばならない約束があります Our group has *rules* which the members are supposed to observe.

4【有望】▶山田営業課長の将来は約束されている. なぜなら父親が社長だからだ Mr. Yamada, the sales department manager, *has a guaranteed future* (in the company) because his father is the company president.

やくたたず 役立たず ▶役立たずの古いコンピュータ a *useless* [*worthless*] old computer ‖この役立たずめ! You *good-for-nothing*!

やくだつ 役立つ **be useful**(それなりの役目を果たす); **be helpful**(助けになる) ▶旅行中はこの案内書がずいぶん役立った This guidebook *was* very *useful* [*helpful*] during the trip. (➤ was の代わりに proved to be でもよい). ▶外国語を学ぶことは外国の人々との意思の疎通に役立つ Learning a foreign language *helps us* (*to*) communicate with foreigners.

やくだてる 役立てる **make use of**; **use** +目(使用する) ▶どうかこのお金を被災者支援に役立ててください Please *make use of* this money to assist the victims of the disaster. ‖原子力は平和のために役立てなければならない We must *use* nuclear power for peaceful purposes. ‖経験を若い世代のために役立てたいと思うお年寄りは多い There are many seniors who want to put their experience to *use to help* younger generations.

やくちゅう 訳注 a **translator's note**.

やくづき 役付き a **person who holds an important post**.

やくづくり 役作り ▶役作りをする study and prepare for a role / learn how to play [interpret / develop] a role.

やくどう 躍動 ▶彼は躍動感あふれる演技で観客を魅了した He captivated the audience with his *dynamic* performance.

やくとく 役得 a **perquisite**,《インフォーマル》a **perk** ▶忘年会幹事の役得で, 私1人だけホテルからお土産をもらった As *a perk* [*an extra benefit*] for being organizer of the year-end party, I alone got a present from the hotel.

やくどし 厄年 ***yakudoshi***
日本紹介 ✉ **厄年は病気や災難に遭うことが多いので注意しなくてはいけないとされる年齢です. 男性は25・42・61歳, 女性は19・33・37歳がこれに当たります** *Yakudoshi* are ages when it is believed you must be careful because you are prone to get sick or have some misfortune. For men, they are 25, 42 and 61, and for women, 19, 33 and 37.

やくにん 役人 a **public** [**civil**] **servant**, a **government employee**, a **public official**, a **government official**(➤ あとになるほど地位が高くなる) ▶彼は役人根性丸出しだった His *bureaucratic* [*officious*] *attitude* was there for all to see. →**公務員**.

やくば 役場 a **village office**(村の); a **town office**(町の) ▶村[町]役場へ行く道を教えてください Can you tell me how to get to the *village* [*town*] *office*?

やくばらい 厄払い an **exorcism** /éksɔːˈsìzəm/ ▶神社で厄払いをしてもらった I *had my bad luck exorcised* at a (Shinto) shrine. / At a (Shinto) shrine, I *had a ceremony performed to get rid of my bad luck*.

やくび 厄日 ▶きょうはとんだ厄日だった. 何もかもがうまくいかなかったよ I had *a terrible day* today. Nothing went right. / Today was *not my day*. Everything went wrong.

やくびょうがみ 疫病神 a **jinx**(縁起の悪い人; →ジンクス);《インフォーマル》a **plague**(やっかいな人) ▶疫病神に取りつかれたようだ I seem to *be jinxed*.

やくひん 薬品 a **drug**(健康によいものとは限らない); a **medicine**(特に内服薬); a **chemical**(化学薬品) ‖薬品会社 a pharmaceutical company(製薬会社).

やくぶそく 役不足 ▶役不足である be *overqualified* [be *too important*] for a job ‖野田氏が連絡係では役不足だ Mr. Noda *is worthy of a better job* than liaison. / Acting as liaison is *too easy a job* for

Mr. Noda.

やくぶつ 薬物 a **drug**, (a) **medicine** ; a **substance**(依存性のある) ▶選手の薬物検査をする test an athlete for *drugs*.

‖**薬物アレルギー** a drug allergy ‖ **薬物乱用** drug [substance] abuse (➤後者はアルコールの乱用も含む) ‖ **薬物療法** medical therapy ‖ **禁止薬物** a banned drug [substance].

1 **やくぶん 約分** 《数学》 **reduction** ━動 **約分する reduce** ＋目 ▶$^3/_9$は$^1/_3$に約分できる Three ninths *can be reduced to* one third.

2 **やくぶん 訳文** a **translated sentence.**

やくほん 訳本 a **translation.**

やくみ 薬味 ***yakumi*** (➤condiment や relish を訳語にあてることがあるが，日本語の「薬味」にぴったりの語はない).

やくめ 役目 a **job**(仕事) ; a **duty**(任務) ▶**役目を果たす** fulfill one's *duty* ‖ 私の**役目**は毎朝ハナを散歩に連れていくことです My *job* is to take Hana for a walk every morning. ‖ 子供が食うに困らないようにするのは親の**役目**だ It's (the) parents' *duty* to make sure their children get the food they need. ‖ この石はテーブルの**役目をする** This stone *serves as* a table. ‖ ビーバーのしっぽは船のかじと同じ**役目**(＝働き)**をする** The tail of a beaver *functions* in the same way as a ship's rudder.

やくよう 薬用の medical(薬効のある) ; **medicated**(薬物を加えた)

‖**薬用植物** a medicinal plant [herb] ‖ **薬用せっけん** medicated soap.

やくよけ 厄除け ▶**厄よけのお守り** a talisman／an amulet／a charm ‖ 災難続きで彼女は神主さんに**厄よけ**(＝おはらい)**をしてもらった** One misfortune followed upon another for her, so she went to a shrine to *have a Shinto priest perform a ceremony to ward off (her) bad luck*.

やぐら 櫓 a **turret**(城の) ; a **tower**(塔) ▶火の見**やぐら** a fire *tower*.

やぐるまそう 矢車草 《植物》 **a cornflower**(矢車菊).

やくわり 役割 a **role**, a **part**(➤前者のほうがふつう) ; (a) **function**(機能) ▶家庭内の**役割分担** the division of *roles* within a family ‖ 中国は今や世界経済において主要な**役割**を担っている Today China plays a key *role* in the global economy. ‖ 太陽は植物の成長に重要な**役割**を果たす The sun plays an important *part* in the growth of plants.

やけ 自棄 ▶失恋しても**やけになるな** Don't *become desperate* [*lose it*] over a disappointment in love. ‖ **やけっぱちになった**男は誰彼の見境なく発砲した The *desperate* man fired the gun at people indiscriminately.

☛ やけくそ, やけに (→見出語)

やけあと 焼け跡 ▶**焼け跡から**親子が死体となって発見された The parents and child of a family were found dead in the *ruins of the fire*.

1 **やけい 夜景** a **night(time) view** [**scene**] ▶香港の**夜景**はとても美しかった The *night*(*time*) *view* of Hong Kong was very beautiful.

2 **やけい 夜警 night watch**(仕事) ; a **night guard**(人).

やけいしにみず 焼け石に水 ▶1万円程度の寄付では**焼け石に水**かもしれないが，私はアフリカの飢餓を救うために寄付を続けたい Maybe donations of 10,000 yen are just *a drop in the bucket*, but I (still) want to keep donating for victims of the famine in Africa. (➤英語は「バケツの中の1滴」の意).

やけおちる 焼け落ちる be burned down, be burned to the ground ▶その寺院は戦火で**焼け落ちた** That temple *was burned down* during the war.

やけくそ ▶いくら探しても就職先が見つからないからといって**やけくそになるな** Don't *get desperate* [*lose hope*] even though you can't find a job after making every effort to find one.

やけこげ 焼け焦げ a **burn**, a **scorch (mark)**(➤後者のほうが軽度) ▶畳についたたばこの**焼け焦げ** *a cigarette burn* [*a scorch mark*] on the tatami mat ‖ 誰がこの敷物に**焼け焦げを作った**のだろう I wonder who *burned a hole* in this rug. (➤burn a hole で「焼いて穴をあける」の意).

やけざけ やけ酒 ▶**やけ酒を飲む** drink out of desperation ; drown one's sorrows(酒で紛らす).

やけしぬ 焼け死ぬ be burned to death ▶昨夜の火事でお年寄りが2人**焼け死んだ** Two elderly people *were burned to death* in the fire last night.

やけだされる 焼け出される ▶その火事で多くの人が**焼け出された** Lots of people *were made* [*were left*] *homeless* by the fire.

やけつく 焼け付く ▶外は**焼け付くように暑い** *It's scorching* outside. ‖ 砂漠の上では太陽が**焼け付くようだ** The sun is usually *torrid* over the desert.

やけど 火傷 a **burn**(火による) ; a **scald** /skɔːld/ (熱湯などによる) ━動 **やけどする get burned** [**scalded**] ; **burn** ＋目 (➤あとに具体的な体の部分をいう)

▶彼はその火事で(ひどい)**やけどをした** He suffered (severe) *burns* in that fire. ‖ 私は[手を]アイロンで**やけどした** I *burned myself* [*my hand*] on the hot iron. ‖ 子供は熱いみそ汁を浴びて**やけどした** My child *got scalded* by the boiling hot miso soup. ‖ 手の**やけど**がひりひりする The *burn* on my hand smarts. ▶《比喩的》彼女と深い仲になると**やけどするぞ** Don't get involved with her unless you want to *get hurt*.／Getting involved with her is *playing with fire*. (➤play with fire は「危険なことをする」の意).

やけに awfully, terribly(➤後者がより強意) ▶きょうは**やけに**暑いね It's *awfully* [*terribly*] hot today, isn't it? ‖ **やけに**うれしそうだけど，何かあったの？ You *sure* look happy. What's happened?

やけのこる 焼け残る escape the fire ▶幸いなことにこの五重の塔は**焼け残った** Fortunately this five-storied pagoda *escaped* [*survived*] *the fire*.

やけのはら 焼け野原 ▶市街地の多くは**焼け野原と化した** Much of the city *was reduced to ashes*.

やけぼっくい 焼け木杭 ▶《慣用表現》あの2人は**焼けぼっくいに火がついた**格好だ *The embers of their old love have flared up again*.

1 **やける 焼ける**

訳語メニュー

燃える →burn **1**
食物が →be done **2**
肌が →get tanned **4**

1【焼失する】burn, be burned ▶あの火事でホテルの一部が焼けた The hotel partially *burned* in that fire. ‖ その寺はすっかり焼けてしまった The temple *was burned down*. ‖ たばこの吸い殻の不始末から２ヘクタールの山林が焼けた Careless disposal of a cigarette butt caused a fire that *destroyed* two hectares of forest. (➤ destroy は「焼失させる」).
2【食物が】be done（出来上がる）▶パンが焼けたよ The bread *is done*. ‖ この魚は焼けてない［焼け過ぎだ］ This fish *is not done* yet [*is overdone*].
▶このチキンはおいしく焼けている This barbecued chicken *is cooked* just right. (➤ cook は「火を通す」の意).
3【高温になる】▶真っ赤に焼けた火箸 *red-hot* metal chopsticks for handling charcoal ‖ きょうは全く焼けるような暑さだ It's *scorching* hot today.
4【太陽で】get tanned, get a tan（きれいに日焼けする）▶海水浴で真っ黒に［真っ赤に］焼けた I *got a good suntan* [*got sunburned*] on the beach. (➤ sunburned はやけどに近い日焼け) ‖ 西日で畳が焼けてしまった The tatami (mat) has *faded* [has *become discolored*] in the afternoon sun.
5【慣用表現】▶４歳の弟は全く世話が焼ける My four-year-old brother *gives* me *a lot of trouble*. ‖ お餅を食べ過ぎて胸が焼けた Eating too much mochi *gave* me *heartburn*. ／I *got heartburn* after eating too much mochi.

[2]**やける 妬ける get jealous** ▶ 対話「きのうはどうして不機嫌だったの？」「きみがほかの男と話をするとぼくはやけるんだよ」"Why were you in a bad mood yesterday?" "Because I *get jealous* when you talk to other guys." ‖ あいつばかりがもてて全くやけるよな He's the one all the girls like. It really *makes* me *jealous*.

やけん 野犬 a **feral dog**.

やご 水蠆 a **larva** [**larvae**] **of a dragonfly**（とんぼの幼虫）.

[1]**やこう 夜行** ▶彼は夜行列車で札幌へ行った He went to Sapporo *by night train* [*on a night train*].
▶フクロウは夜行性の動物だ The owl is a *nocturnal* animal.

[2]**やこう 夜光** ‖夜光虫 a noctiluca /nɑ̀:ktəlú:kə/ ‖ 夜光塗料 luminous paint.

やさい 野菜 a **vegetable**; **greens**（青物）▶新鮮な野菜と果物 fresh fruit(s) and *vegetables*(➤ 英語はこの語順が多い) ‖ トマトは野菜ですか，果物ですか Is a tomato *a vegetable* or a fruit? ‖ 私は裏庭で野菜を育てている I grow *vegetables* [*greens*] in the backyard.
▶私は健康のために毎朝野菜サラダを食べる I eat *salad* every morning for my health. (➤ vegetable salad とする必要はない；レタスやキュウリなど青物野菜のサラダは green salad).
‖野菜ジュース vegetable juice ‖ 温野菜 steamed vegetable ‖ 根(野)菜 a root vegetable ‖ 自家栽培野菜 a home-grown vegetable ‖ 葉(物)野菜 a leafy vegetable ‖ 無農薬野菜 a chemical-free vegetable ‖ 有機野菜 an organic vegetable ‖ 緑黄(色)野菜 (green) vegetables, greens.

「野菜」のいろいろ オクラ okra ／カブ turnip ／カボチャ pumpkin, squash ／カリフラワー cauliflower ／キノコ mushroom ／キャベツ cabbage ／キュウリ cucumber ／クレソン watercress ／サツマイモ sweet potato ／サトイモ taro ／サヤインゲン string bean ／ジャガイモ potato ／ズッキーニ zucchini ／セロリ celery ／大根 daikon (radish) ／タマネギ onion ／トマト tomato ／ナス eggplant ／ニンジン carrot ／ネギ leek, scallion ／白菜 nap(p)a cabbage ／二十日大根 radish ／ピーマン green pepper ／ブロッコリー broccoli ／ホウレンソウ spinach ／豆 pea, bean ／芽キャベツ Brussels sprout ／もやし bean sprouts ／レタス lettuce

やさおとこ 優男 an **effeminate man**（女のような）; a **slight man**（きゃしゃな）.

やさがし 家捜し searching for a house（捜索）; **house-hunting**（家探し，住む家を探すこと）.

やさき 矢先 ▶消防署が警報を出そうとしたやさきの惨事だった The disaster occurred *just as* the fire department *was about to* issue a warning. (➤ be about to do は「ちょうど…しようとしている」). ‖ 出かけようとしたやさきに雷が鳴り出した I *was about to* go out when it started thundering.

[1]**やさしい 優しい** **1【親切で思いやりがある】kind, nice**(➤ 前者はふつう家族などには用いない); **kindhearted**（心が優しい）; **gentle**（温和な，柔和な）; **good**（思いやりがある）; **understanding**（理解がある）; **sweet**（感じのよい）; **tender**（思いやりの深い）; **fond**（愛情深い）; **soft**（態度・言葉などが） ━副 優しく **kindly, gently, softly, sweetly**
▶優しい先生 an *understanding* teacher ‖ 彼は他人には優しく自分には厳しい He is *kind* [*nice*] to others, but strict with himself. ‖ 彼は優しい男だ He is a *nice* guy. (➤ 日本語の「ナイスガイ」とは意味が異なる).
▶奥さんにたまには優しいことばを掛けてあげなさいよ Say *kind* [*tender*] words to your wife once in a while! ‖ 彼は私たちに優しくしてくれる He is *good* to us. ‖ ご両親に優しくね *Be good* [*nice*] to your parents. ‖ プレゼントありがとう．あなたって優しいのね Thank you for the present. How *sweet* of you! (➤ この sweet は女性が多用する).
▶母親は優しい声で赤ん坊に話しかけた The mother talked to the baby in a *gentle* [*soft*] voice. ‖ ロバは優しい目をしている Donkeys have *gentle* [*soft*] eyes. ‖ 彼は彼女に優しいまなざしを向けた He gave her a *fond* look. ‖ 赤ちゃんの髪にブラシを掛けるときは優しくするのよ *Be gentle* when you brush the baby's hair. ‖ 春風が優しく頬をなでていく The spring breeze is *softly* [*gently*] caressing my cheeks.
2【相手を保護する】friendly; **mild**（髪・肌に）▶髪に優しいシャンプー *mild* shampoo ‖ 環境に優しいシャンプー *eco-friendly* shampoo ‖ 自転車は環境に優しい乗り物です A bicycle is *friendly to the environment* [*environmentally friendly* ／*eco-friendly*].

[2]**やさしい 易しい easy**（簡単な）; **simple**（単純な）; **plain**（わかりやすい）▶今回のテストは易しい問題ばかりだった All the questions on the test this time were quite *easy*. ‖ その本は読んでみると易しかった I *found* the book *easy*. ‖ 物事を易しく説明するというのは実はとても難しいことだ To explain things *in simple, clear language* is actually very hard to do.
ことわざ 言うは易く行うは難し It's easier said than done.

やさしさ 優しさ kindness, gentleness, tenderness(➤ 各語の意味については「優しい」を参照).

[1]**やし 椰子**《植物》a **coconut palm**（ココヤシ）; a **date**

palm(ナツメヤシ)
‖ヤシ油 coconut oil.

2やし 香具師 a street stall vendor(大道商人).

やじ 野次 jeering(下品な笑い声・冷やかしなどによる); hooting(はやす, どなるなどの); booing(ブーイングによる) ▶与野党間に激しいやじの応酬があった There were exchanges of heated *jeering* between the government and the opposition parties. ‖藤村が三振すると観衆は盛んにやじを飛ばした When Fujimura was struck out, the spectators wildly *hooted at* [*booed*] him.

やじうま 野次馬 a curious onlooker, a rubbernecker(➤後者は主に車からの) ▶事故現場にやじ馬が集まった *Curious onlookers* [*Rubberneckers*] gathered at the site of the accident.

やしき 屋敷 a mansion, a residence ▶この辺りには立派な屋敷が多い There are a lot of stately *mansions* [*residences*] around here. 《参考》いずれも日本語でいう「マンション」や「レジデンス」とは異なり, 個人の「大邸宅」の意.

やしなう 養う 1【扶養する】support +目 ▶5人家族を養うのは楽ではない It is not easy to *support* [*provide for*] a family of five. ‖きみが大学を卒業するまで私が養って(=面倒を見て)やる I'll *take care of* you until you graduate from college.
2【能力などを】build up; develop +目 (発達させる) ▶スタミナを養う *build up* stamina ‖読解力を養う *develop* one's reading comprehension skills ‖人を見る目を養う *develop* one's ability to judge people [character] ‖ジョギングで体力を養うことができる Jogging helps you *develop* [*build up*] physical strength.

やしゃご 玄孫 a great-great-grandchild; a great-great-grandson(男); a great-great-granddaughter(女).

1やしゅ 野手 《野球》a fielder.

2やしゅ 野趣 rustic charm [atmosphere] ▶野趣あふれる料理 food with *rustic charm* [*flavor*].

やじゅう 野獣 a wild animal, a beast.

やしょく 夜食 a late-night snack ▶母が夜食に焼きそばを作ってくれた My mother fixed me *a late-night snack* of yakisoba.

やじり 矢尻・鏃 an arrowhead.

やじる 野次る jeer +自 (下品な笑い声を発する, 冷やかす); hoot +自 (ブーブーはやしたてる); boo +自 (ブーイングする); heckle +目 (選挙の候補者などを) ▶立候補者が演説している間ずっと1人の男がやじっていた A man *was heckling* the candidate throughout his speech.

やじるし 矢印 an arrow (sign) ▶矢印に従えば出口に出られます Follow the *arrows* and you will find the exit.

やしろ 社 a Shinto shrine.

やじろべえ 弥次郎兵衛 *yajirobee*; a balancing toy(➤説明的な訳).

やしん 野心 (an) ambition ▶若い人が野心をもつのは当然だ It's natural for young people to *have ambitions* [*to be ambitious*]. ‖彼は野心満々だ He's *highly ambitious*.
▶私は野心家が好きです I like *ambitious people*. ‖この絵は伊藤氏の野心作です This picture is Ito's *most ambitious work*.

やす 簎 a fish spear(漁具の「もり」).

やすあがり 安上がり ▶往復切符はふつう片道2枚の料金より安上がりだ A round-trip ticket is usually a bit *cheaper* than two one-way tickets. ‖トマトを1山買ってあとで2家族で分けたほうが安上がり(=経済的)よ It will be *more economical* to buy tomatoes in bulk and then to divide them between the two families. / *We* can *save money* by buying tomatoes in bulk and dividing them between the two families.

やすい 安い cheap, inexpensive, less expensive, low-priced

> 語法 (1) **cheap** には「安っぽい, 粗悪な」の意味があるので, しばしば **inexpensive, less expensive** が好まれる. また, これらの語はそれ自体が「価格・値段が安い」の意を含むので, 価格や値段の意のある語(price, pay, salary, cost, fare など)とともには用いないのがふつう.
> (2)「安い値段」は a low price,「値段が安い」は The price is low. が原則. くだけた言い方では a cheap price, The price is cheap. もあるが, 学習者は避けたほうがよい.

▶安いかばん a *cheap* bag ‖あの店は魚が安い Fish is *cheap* at that store. ‖安いカーペットを探しています I'm looking for an *inexpensive* carpet. ‖あの店は安い That store is *inexpensive*.
▶あのスーパーは値段が安い *Prices are low* at that supermarket. / That supermarket *has good prices*. ‖この家は家賃が安い The rent of this house is *low*. ‖うちの会社は給料が安い Salaries at our company are *low*.
▶そいつは安い! *That's a bargain!* (➤bargain は「安い買い物, 掘り出し物」の意) ‖このハンドバッグが一万円なら安い This handbag *is a good deal* at ten thousand yen.
▶安い物を買う buy a *cheap thing* / buy *cheap stuff*(➤後者は cheap stuff の形で用い,「安い物, 安物」の意) ‖このカメラはとても安かった I got this camera very *cheap*. / I bought this camera *at a* very *low price*. ‖今ではデジタル音楽がネットで安い値で買える Nowadays, we can get digital music *at low prices* online. ‖円高で外車が安くなった Imported cars have become *cheaper* because of the strong yen. ‖もう少し安くしてよ Can you *make* it a little *cheaper*? / Can you *knock* a bit *off the price*? ‖バスで行ったほうが安くつくよ It's *cheaper* to go by bus. ‖ 対話 「これいくら?」「5000円」「もう少し安くならない?」"How much is this?" "Five thousand yen." "*Can't* you *lower the price* a little more? / *Can't* you *give* me a little more *discount*?"

☛ お安い, お安くない (→見出語)

-やすい -易い 1【簡単な】be easy to do ▶書きやすいボールペン a ballpoint pen that writes *well* ‖この自動車は運転しやすい This car *is easy to* drive. ‖安藤課長と一緒だと仕事がしやすい Section chief Ando *is easy to* work with. ‖私はわかりやすい授業を心掛けています I'm trying to teach in a way that is easy to understand [that will allow my students to *understand easily*].
2【快適な】▶履きやすい靴 *comfortable* shoes ‖働きやすい会社 a company where one can work *comfortably* ‖住みやすい家 a *livable* [*liveable*] house / a *comfortable* house *to live in*.
3【…しがち】tend to do ▶thorough は through と

間違われやすい "Thorough" *tends to* be mistaken for "through." ‖ 人間は過ちを犯しやすい Humans *are subject to* error. (➤ be subject to は「…を受けやすい」の意で「…」の部分には名詞が続く) ‖ 彼女はかぜをひきやすい She *is susceptible to* colds. ‖ この年頃の少女たちは感じやすい Girls at this age *are sensitive.*

▶彼は熱しやすく冷めやすい He gets excited *easily* but cools off just as *easily*.

やすうけあい 安請け合い ▶ぼくは知らないよ. 安請け合いしたのはきみじゃないか It's not my problem. You are the one who *undertook the job* (*too*) *lightly*. (➤「仕事を気軽に引き受けた」の意).

やすうり 安売り a (**bargain**) **sale** ▶安売りでスーツを買った I bought a business suit at *a sale*. ‖ 商店街で安売りをやっている They are having *a sale* at the shopping mall. ‖ あの店で冬服の安売りをしている Winter clothes *are on sale* at that store. (➤ on sale は主に《米》で「特売中で」の意. なお for sale は「(家などを)売り出して」の意) ／That store *is selling* winter clothes *at reduced prices* [*at a discount*].

‖安売り店 a discount store [shop].

☛ 大安売り (→見出語)

やすっぽい 安っぽい **cheap**; **tawdry**, **chintzy** /tʃíntsi/ (けばけばしくて安っぽい) ▶安っぽいイヤリング *cheap* [*tawdry*] earrings (➤ tawdry にはしばしば, 下品というニュアンスがある) ‖ 安っぽいソファー a *chintzy* couch ‖ 安っぽい小説 a *cheap* novel ‖ 安っぽい男 [女] a *shallow* man [woman] (➤ shallow は superficial でも可) ‖ そういう品のない言い方をすると人間が安っぽく見えるよ Such a coarse [vulgar] way of speaking will make you look *cheap* (in other people's eyes).

やすね 安値 a **low price** (➤ a low とだけ言うこともある) ▶安値で売る sell *at a low price* ／sell *cheap* (➤後者はインフォーマルな言い方) ‖ その株は最安値をつけた That stock *hit a new low*.

やすぶしん 安普請 ▶安普請の家 a *cheaply-built* [*jerry-built*] house.

やすまる 休まる ▶バッハの音楽を聴くと心が休まる I *feel relaxed* when I listen to Bach. ／Listening to Bach relaxes me. ‖ うちの子が絶えず問題を起こすので気の休まるときがない My son [daughter] is constantly getting into trouble, so I *can't get a moment's peace*.

やすみ 休み

📖 訳語メニュー
休憩 →rest, break **1**
休日 →vacation, day off **2**
欠席 →absence **3**

1【休むこと】 a **rest** (休息); a **break** (仕事などの小休止); (a) **recess** /ríːses/ (休み時間) ▶ちょっと一休みしないか Shall we *take* [*have*] *a rest* for a while? ／Shall we *take* [*have*] *a breather*? (➤ breather は /bríːðəʳ/ と発音) ‖ 授業の間には10分間の休みがある We have a ten-minute *break* [*recess*] between classes. ‖ 彼は休み時間になると急に元気になる He suddenly livens up when *break time* comes. ‖ 休み時間に次の時限の数学の宿題をした I did my math homework for the next period *during recess*.

▶彼は早朝から休みなく働いている He's been working *without a break* since early this morning. ‖ 学校の事務室は12時から1時までは休みだ The school office *is closed* from twelve to one.

2【休暇, 休日】 a **vacation**, a **holiday** (長期の); a **break** (短めの); a **day off** (仕事を休む日); 《英》a **bank holiday** (法定休日; 《米》では日曜以外の銀行休業日) ▶きょうは休みだ I'm *off* today. ／I *don't have work* today. ／《英》Today is *a holiday*. ‖ 11月23日は勤労感謝の日で学校は休みです (＝休校です) November 23 is Labor Thanksgiving Day and we have *no* school. ‖ きょうは銀行は休み (＝休業) だ Banks *are closed* today.

▶あす休みをいただきたいのですが May I *take tomorrow off*? ／May I *have a day off tomorrow*? ‖ 仕事が休みのときはよくカラオケをしています I often do karaoke *when I'm off*. (➤ off from work あるいは off work ともいう) ‖ 1日休みを取って友人の結婚式に出席した I *took a day off* to attend my friend's wedding. ‖ 太田さんは1週間休みを取っています Mr. Ota *is taking a one-week vacation* [《英》*holiday*]. ／Mr. Ota *is taking a week off*.

▶正月休みを利用して苗場へ行く予定だ I'm going to Naeba during *the New Year vacation* [《英》*holidays*].

✉ 休みの日はどんなことしてますか What do you do on *your days off* [*on holidays*]?

3【欠席, 欠勤】 **absence** ▶安西さんは休みです Anzai-san *is absent*. ／Anzai-san *is off*. (➤前者は「欠席」, 後者は「欠勤」) ‖ 石田は本日お休みをいただいております Ms. Ishida *is absent* today. (➤英語では同僚であっても敬称をつけることが多い. ここでは仮に Ms. をつけた) ‖ きのうは流感で休みの人が多かった A lot of people *were absent* yesterday because of the flu. ／A lot of people *were off* yesterday with the flu.

逆引き熟語 ○○休み
正月休み the New Year holidays [vacation] ／夏休み the summer vacation [《英》holidays] ／春休み the spring break [《英》holidays] ／昼休み a lunch break [hour] ／冬休み the winter vacation [《英》holidays] ／盆休み the *Bon* holidays

やすみやすみ 休み休み ▶冗談も休み休み言え That's enough of your jokes! ／Give the jokes a rest, will you? ／Oh, give me a break!

やすむ 休む

1【休憩する】 **rest**, **take a break**; **relax** (くつろぐ) ▶木の下で休む *rest* under a tree ‖ ちょっと休んでコーヒーでも飲もうか How about *taking a break* for coffee or something? ‖ 食事のあとはしばらく休みなさい You should *relax* a while after meals.

▶途中何度も休みながら頂上まで登った We frequently *paused to rest* on the way to the top of the mountain. ‖ 気分が悪かったけどちょっと休んだら直った I had been feeling sick, but *after a short rest* I felt better. ‖ 彼は一度始めると仕上げるまで仕事を休まない Once he starts a job, he doesn't *take* (*time*) *off* until he finishes it. ‖ 気をつけ! 休め! Attention! *At ease!*

2【学校・仕事を】 **be absent** 《from》, **take a day off** ▶インフルエンザにかかって2週間も学校を休んだ I *was absent* [*was away*] *from school* for two weeks with the flu. ‖ 中田は指のけがで試合を休んだ Nakata *was absent* [*was sidelined*] *from* the game because of a finger injury. (➤ sideline は「参加[出

場」できなくする」の意）‖頭痛で**会社を休んだ** I had a headache and *took a day off* (*from work*). (➤「月曜日に休んだ」は took Monday off のようにいう）‖ **対話**「あす休んでもいいですか」「もちろん」"Can I *have* [*take*] *a day off* tomorrow?／I'd like to *take off* tomorrow." "Sure." ‖小川君は**病気で休んだ** Ogawa *was out* [*off*] *sick*. ‖この3日間体調が悪くてジョギングを**休んでいる** I haven't been feeling well for three days, so I'*m taking a break* from jogging.

▶あの店は日曜も**休まずに**営業している The store is open even on Sundays. ‖英語の授業は1回も**休まないで**出ている I *haven't missed* a single English class.／I *have a perfect attendance record* in my English class.

3【**眠る**】**go to bed**（寝る）; **sleep**（眠る） ▶主人はまだ**休んでおります** My husband is still *sleeping*. ‖**お休みのところ起こして**すみません I'm sorry to wake you (up). ‖ **対話**「いつも何時に**お休みになりますか**」「11時です」"What time do you usually *go to bed* [*turn in*]?" "At eleven." ‖ **対話**「ゆうべはよく**お休みになれましたか**」「はい. ぐっすり眠りました」"Did you *sleep* well last night?／Did you *get* [*have*] a good night's *sleep* last night?" "Yes, I slept like a log."

やすめる 休める **rest** ＋㊐ ▶読書で疲れた目を**休める** *rest* one's eyes from reading ‖きみは一晩ゆっくり**体を休める**必要がある You need a good night's *rest*. ‖私はキーボードを打つ**手を休め**, コーヒーを一口飲んだ I *stopped* typing to take a sip of coffee.

やすもの 安物 a **cheap thing**, 《インフォーマル》a **cheapie** 一形 **安物の cheap** ▶そのネクタイは一見して**安物**だとわかった One look at the tie told me that it was *a cheapie*.

▶ **対話**「まあ, すてきな指輪. 高かったでしょう?」「いいえ, **安物**ですよ」"Oh, you're wearing a beautiful ring. It must be expensive." "No, it's (just) a *cheap* ring." (●「めちゃくちゃに安かった」「ただ同然に買った」という感じを出す場合は I got it for next to nothing. のように表現する).

ことわざ **安物買いの銭失い** Buying cheap things is losing your money.／Those who buy cheap things will end up losing money. (➤ 2例とも日本語からの直訳)／Penny-wise and pound-foolish. (➤ 英語のことわざ).

やすやすと 易々と **easily**（簡単に）; **without difficulty**（難なく） ▶彼女はそう**やすやすと**はだまされないよ She can't be deceived so *easily*. ‖泥棒は**やすやすと**金庫室に忍び込んだ The thief broke into the vault *with ease* [*without difficulty*].

やすやど 安宿 a **cheap inn** [**hotel**].

やすらか 安らかな **peaceful** ▶祖父は退職後田舎で**安らかな**毎日を送っている My grandfather has been living *peacefully* in the country since his retirement. ‖《墓碑銘》**安らかに眠れ** R.I.P. (＝ rest in peace).

やすらぎ 安らぎ **peace of mind** ▶**心の安らぎを覚える**のはどんなときですか When do you *feel* (most) *at peace*?

やすらぐ 安らぐ ▶この雄大な自然を眺めていると**心が安らぐ** When I look at this magnificent natural scenery, I *feel at peace* [*calm and peaceful*].

やすり 鑢 a **file**（鋼鉄製の）; **sandpaper**（紙やすり） ▶木に**やすりを掛けて**滑らかにした I *filed* the wood smooth.

やすんじる 安んじる ▶現状に**安んじる** *be content* with the current situation [with things as they are].

1**やせい 野生の** **wild** ▶**野生の馬** a *wild* horse ‖多くの種類の**野生生物**が絶滅寸前だ Many kinds of *wildlife* are on the verge of extinction. ‖山中に捨てられた犬が**野生化した** The dogs abandoned in the mountains *have become* [*have gone*] *wild*.

‖**野生植物** a wild plant ‖**野生動物** a wild animal.

2**やせい 野性** **wild nature** 一形 **野性的な wild** ▶カルメンは**野性的な**女だった Carmen was a *wild* [*an untamed*] woman. ‖おりの中のこのライオンたちは**野性味を失っている** These caged lions have lost most of their *wild* [*fierce*] *nature*.

やせおとろえる 痩せ衰える **become thin and feeble** ▶祖父は長患いですっかり**痩せ衰えてしまった** My grandfather has *become* very *thin and feeble* because of a long illness.

やせがた 痩せ形 ▶**痩せ形の少年** a *skinny* [*lean*] boy.

やせがまん 痩せ我慢 ▶若い人たちは寒いのを**痩せ我慢して**薄着をする Young people dress lightly *pretending they don't mind* the cold. (➤「寒さが気にならないふりをして」の意) ‖メロン食べたいんでしょ? **痩せ我慢しなくていいのよ** You want to eat some melon, don't you? You don't need to *pretend you don't* (*want it*).

やせこける 痩せこける **become haggard** ▶**痩せこけた**頬をした老人 an old person with *haggard* [*hollow*] cheeks ‖病気で彼女は**骨と皮ばかりに痩せこけてしまった** The illness *reduced* her *to skin and bones*.

やせち 痩せ地 **barren** [**sterile**] **land, poor soil**.

やせっぽち 痩せっぽち ▶**痩せっぽちの人** a *skinny* person ‖この**痩せっぽち**! You *bag of bones*!

やせほそる 痩せ細る **become thin** [**emaciated**] ▶彼女は拒食症で**痩せ細っていた** She *was emaciated* due to anorexia. (➤ anorexia は /ænəréksiə/ と発音) ‖彼女は心配で**痩せ細る思いでいる** She is worrying herself to death. (➤ to death は「死ぬほど, とても」の意).

やせる 痩せる

1【**体重が減る**】**lose weight** 一形 **痩せた thin**; **slim, slender**（細身の）; **lean**（引き締まった）

> **語法** (1) 人の痩せた状態を表す語には thin, slim, slender, lean などがある. このうち **thin** が最も一般的な語で, 特に病気をして痩せた状態を表す. **slim** と **slender** はほっそりして格好がいい状態をいい, **lean** は筋肉質の痩せ方を指す.
> (2)「痩せっぽち」に当たるのが **skinny**.

▶**痩せるために**ダイエットを始める go on a diet to *lose weight* ‖私は半年で5キロ**痩せた** I *lost* 5 kilograms in six months. ‖彼は**痩せている** He *is thin* [*slender*／*slim*／*skinny*].

▶あなたは最近**痩せたんじゃないの** You'*ve become slimmer* [*slenderer*] lately, haven't you? (➤ slender は主に女性に用いる) ‖彼のお姉さんは**痩せ気味だが**美人だ His (older) sister is a bit *on the thin side*, but beautiful.

2【**土地が**】**get sterile**（不毛の地になる） 一形 **痩せた poor, sterile** ▶**痩せた土地** *barren* [*sterile*] land／*poor* [*sterile*] soil ‖干ばつで**土地が痩せた** The drought *made* the soil *sterile*. ‖長い間の放牧の繰

り返しで土地が痩せてしまった Repeated grazing over a long period of time *has impoverished* the land. (➤ impoverish は「貧弱にする」).

やせん 野戦 a **land battle**
‖野戦病院 a field hospital.

やそう 野草 (a) **wild grass.**

やそうきょく 夜想曲《音楽》a **nocturne.**

やたい 屋台 a **booth**, a **stand**
日本紹介 ✉ **屋台は道端に止まって,ラーメン・焼き鳥・おでんなどを出す移動式の小さな店です.ふつう小さなカウンターと長椅子がついています**
A *yatai* is a small movable booth by the roadside where such foods as ramen, grilled skewered chicken (*yakitori*) or *oden* (stewed vegetables and fish cake) are served. Usually it is equipped with a small counter and a bench.

やたいぼね 屋台骨 ▶日本の大抵の家庭では夫が一家の経済的な**屋台骨**となっている The husband is the economic *mainstay* of most Japanese families. ‖不良債権がその銀行の**屋台骨を揺るがせた** Bad loans *shook* that bank *to its foundations*.

やたら extremely(極端に); **terribly**(ひどく) ▶きょうは**やたら**と忙しい I'm *extremely* [*terribly*] busy today. ／Work is hectic today. ‖暑いせいで**やたら**と喉が渇く I get *terribly* thirsty in this heat. ／This heat makes me *terribly* thirsty. ‖今月は**やたら**雨の日が多い We've had *so many* [*a lot of*] rainy days this month.

やちょう 野鳥 a **wild bird** ▶富士の裾野には**野鳥**が多い The slopes of Mt. Fuji abound with *wild birds*.
‖**野鳥観察** bird-watching, birding ‖**野鳥観察者** a bird-watcher, a birder ‖**野鳥保護区** a wild bird sanctuary.

やちん 家賃 (**house**) **rent** ▶私は毎月月末に**家賃**を払う I pay the *rent* on this house [room] at the end of every month. ‖月10万円の**家賃**でこの家を借りています We are renting this house for 100,000 yen a month. ‖ 対話「このアパートの**家賃**はいくら?」「月8万円」"What is the *rent* for this apartment? ／How much (*rent*) do you pay for your apartment?" "Eighty thousand yen a month."

やつ 奴 1【人】a **guy**, a **dude**, a **fellow**

> 語法 (1)「やつ」に相当する語には **guy**, **dude**, **chap**, **bloke** などがあるが, chap と bloke は《英・インフォーマル》で多く用いる.
> (2)**fellow** は「やっこさん」というのに近い.
> (3) ほかに, **creep** (嫌なやつ), **jerk** (ばかなやつ), **nerd**(つまらないやつ)などの言い方がある.
> (4) 文脈や話者の顔の表情などで, he, she が「やつ」のニュアンスを持つことも少なくない.

▶あいつはいい**やつ**さ He's a nice *guy*. ‖あいつはハンサムな**やつ**だ He's a handsome *dude*. ‖事故に遭うなんて,かわいそうな**やつ** That poor *fellow* [*chap*] ... he had an accident.
▶**やつ**(=彼)に頼めよ You should ask *him* for help. →やつら.
2【物】one(➤ 前出の名詞の代わり) ▶ 対話「サケは釣れたの?」「こんな大きい**やつ**を逃がしちゃってさ」"Did you catch any salmon?" "I missed *one* this big."

やつあたり 八つ当たりする ▶腹が立つからといって俺に**八つ当たりする**なよ Don't *take your anger out on* me.

やっか 薬科 ‖**薬科大学** a college [school] of pharmacy, a pharmaceutical university.

やっかい 厄介 1【面倒】trouble; a **pain in the neck**(面倒なこと, 悩みの種) 一形
やっかいな troublesome; **difficult**, **tough** (きつい; 前者は後者2つより堅い語) ▶**やっかいなこと**をお願いして申し訳ありません I am sorry to *trouble* [*bother*] you. (➤ ともに「面倒をかける」の意) ‖**ごやっかいをかけて**すみませんでした I'm sorry to have given you so much *trouble*.
▶英文法は私には**やっかい**だ English grammar is *a pain in the neck* for me. ‖彼は**やっかいな**仕事はすべて人に押しつけようとする He tries to foist every *troublesome* [*tough*] job on others. ‖これは**やっかいな**問題だ This is a *difficult* [*thorny*] problem. (➤ thorny は「一筋縄ではいかない」の意) ‖すい臓がんは克服の難しい**やっかいな**がんだ Pancreatic cancer is a *tough* cancer to beat. ‖タクシーに車をぶつけたときは**やっかいなこと**になると思った When I ran into the taxi, I knew I *was in for trouble*. (➤ be in for は「(嫌なことに)巻き込まれる」の意).
▶**やっかいなこと**になってきたぞ(=ごたついてきた) Things *are getting* a little *messy*. ‖**やっかいなこと**になった Now I'*m in a jam* [*in a fix*]. (➤「にっちもさっちも行かない状態」) ‖会社では私のことをまるで**やっかい者**扱いだ They treat me as *a nuisance* at the office. ‖彼の息子は一家の**やっかい者**だ His son is *a trial* to [*the black sheep* of] the family. (➤ trial は「困り者」の意).
2【世話】▶岡山では田島さんの家に**やっかいになった**(=泊まった) In Okayama, I *stayed with* the Tajimas. ‖いつまでも姉のところに**やっかいになっている**わけにもいかない I can't *live with* my (older) sister forever. ‖金のことで人に**やっかいになる**のは嫌だ I hate to *depend on* others for money. (➤「他人を当てにする」の意).

やっかいばらい 厄介払い ▶横柄な課長が東京に転勤になったので**やっかい払い**できたと皆喜んだ When that arrogant manager was transferred out of our office to Tokyo, we were all glad to *be rid of* him. (➤ be rid of は「(悩みの種が)無くなる」の意;「**やっかい払い**ができてせいせいした」は Good riddance. と言う).

やっかみ jealousy ▶彼女はそれを**やっかみ**から言っているだけだ She's saying that out of *jealousy*.

やっかむ get jealous《of》▶彼女は**やっかんで**あんなことを言ったのだ She said such things *out of jealousy*. ‖弟さんのことをちょっと**やっかんでる**んじゃない? *Aren't* you a little *jealous of* your (younger) brother?

やっき 躍起 ▶彼は昇進しようと**躍起になっている** He's *going all out* in the hope of being promoted. (➤ go all out は「必死になる」) ／He *is making an all-out effort for* promotion. ‖その政治家は**躍起に**なって金をもらったことを否定した The politician *vehemently* [*vigorously*／*heatedly*] denied that he had received any money. (➤ vehemently /víːəməntli/ は「熱烈に」の意. あとの2語はそれぞれ「力強く」,「興奮して」の意).

やつぎばや 矢継ぎ早 ▶皆は彼に**矢継ぎ早**に質問を浴びせた They asked him questions *in quick* [*rapid*] *succession*. ／They *shot* [*fired*] questions at him. ／They *bombarded* him with questions.

やっきょう 薬莢 a **shell**, a **cartridge case.**

やっきょく 薬局 a **pharmacy**,《米また》a **drugstore**,《英また》a **chemist's** (**shop**); a **dispensary**(病院の).

ヤッケ a **parka**, an **anorak**.

やつざき 八つ裂き ▶あの殺人犯を八つ裂きにしてやりたい I could just *tear* that murderer *limb from limb*.

やった **Yippee**! /jípi/, **Hooray**! /hʊréɪ/ (➤ 喜び・熱狂などの叫び声) ▶やったあ,(試験の)山が当たった! I *made it* [*Hooray*]! My guess (about the exam problems) was right. ‖ やったね You *made it*. ‖《入試に合格した友だちに》健ちゃん, やったじゃない! Ken, *way to go* [you *did it*]!

やっつけしごと やっつけ仕事 **shoddy** [**sloppy**] **work**; a **slipshod** [**makeshift**] **job**(ずさんな仕事); a **patch-up job**(間に合わせの仕事) ▶これは納期に間に合わせるためのやっつけ仕事だと思う I think this is *a slipshod job* done to meet the deadline.

やっつける **get** +目 (殴る); **beat** +目 (負かす) ▶おい, あいつをやっつけろ! Hey, go *get* him! / Hey, *let* him *have it*! (➤ let ... have it は「…を殴る」) ‖ そのボクサーはアッパーカット一発で相手をやっつけた The boxer *finished* the opponent with a single uppercut. (➤ finish は「片づける」) ‖ 彼は議論で相手をやっつけた He *beat* [*downed*] his opponent in the debate.

やつで 八手《植物》a **Japanese aralia** /əléɪliə/.

やっていく やって行く **get by**, **get along**(暮らしていく) ▶少ない年金でやっていくのは大変だ It is no easy matter to *get by* on a small pension. ‖ 月12万円ではやっていけない I can't *get along* [*live*] on 120, 000 yen a month. ‖ こんな安月給じゃやっていけない I can't *manage* [*get along*] on such a small salary. ‖ 妻の両親とはうまくやっていけると思います I think I *can get along well with* my wife's parents. ‖ あなたの援助が無くてもやっていけるわ I *can do* without your help.

✉ **(転校した友だちに) 早くクラスのみんなとうまくやっていけるといいね** I hope you *fit in* with all your new classmates before long. ➤ fit in は「グループなどに溶け込む」.

やってくる やって来る **come**(来る); **come along**(到着する); **come around**(巡って来る); **show up**(現れる) ▶サンタさんがやって来た! *Here comes* Santa Claus! / Santa Claus *has come*. ‖ 3分と待たないうちにバスがやって来た We had been waiting for less than three minutes when a bus *came along*.
▶またスキーシーズンがやって来た The skiing season *has come* (*around*) again. ‖ 彼女は約束の場所にやって来なかった She didn't *show up* at the meeting place.

やってのける **pull off**(困難なことを) ▶その新人はノーヒットノーランをやってのけた That rookie *pulled off* a no-hit, no-run game.

やってみる **try**, **have** [**take**] **a try** ▶解けるかどうかやってみなさい (*Try and*) *see* if you can solve it. ‖ ものは試し, やってみなさい Sink or swim, *have* [*take*] *a try* at it. ‖ できるまで繰り返しやってみなさい Keep on *trying* until you can do it. ‖ やってみなければ自分の力はわからない You never know what you can do *untill you try*. ‖ やってみもしないでできないなんて言うな Don't say you can't do it *without trying* [*giving* it *a try*]. ‖ その問題を解こうとやってみる *have* [*take*] *a shot at* solving the problem ‖ 結果はどうであれ, やってみることが大切だ No matter what the outcome is, *trying* is the important thing [*trying* is what counts]. ‖ 確かにやってみる価値はある It's certainly worth *a try*.
▶一か八(ばち)かやってみようじゃないか Let's *try our luck*. / Why don't we *take a chance*? (➤ take a chance は「運を試す」).

やってられない ▶ばかばかしくて, もうやってらんないよ This is ridiculous. I *can't do it any longer* [I *have had enough*].

やっと **1【ぎりぎりで】** **barely**(辛うじて); **just**(ぴったりで) ▶ぼくらは和田の二塁打でやっと勝った With Wada's double, we *just barely* won the game. ‖ 月収15万円では食べていくだけでやっとだ I can *barely* live on a monthly income of 150,000 yen. ‖ 午前7時の新大阪行きのぞみ号にやっと間に合った I was *just* in time for the 7 a.m. Nozomi to Shin-Osaka.
2【ようやく】 **finally**(ついに), **at** (**long**) **last**(長い時間をかけてようやく) ▶3度目の挑戦で彼はやっと北大に合格した He was *finally* admitted to Hokkaido University on his third attempt. ‖ やっと課長に昇進しました *At last* I was promoted to section chief. ‖ 俊夫はやっとの思いでちえみに好きだと言った Toshio *finally gathered up his courage* and told Chiemi that he loved her. (➤「勇気を奮い起こした」の意) ‖ 彼は(いろいろ試みて)やっとのことで逃げ出した He *managed to* escape.

やっとこ 鋏 **pincers**, **pinchers**(➤ ともに複数形で) ▶彼はやっとこで鉄板を挟んで炉に入れた He grasped the iron plate with the *pincers* and put it into the furnace. →ペンチ.

やっぱり →やはり.

ヤッホー **Yoo-hoo**! /júːhuː/, **Yo-ho**! /joʊhóʊ/ ▶「ヤッホー」と言うと「ヤッホー」とこだまが返ってきた I *yoo-hooed* and "*Yoo-hoo!*" echoed back. ‖ ヤッホー(=しめた), 午後は休講だ *Yippee*, they've canceled all the afternoon classes!

やつら 奴等 **they** ▶やつらは何者だ Who are *they*? ‖ なんて嫌なやつらだ What a bunch of creeps! (➤ creep は「嫌なやつ」) ‖ 何て悪いやつらだ What a bad *lot*! (➤ a bad lot は主に《英》で, 個人にもグループにもいう).

やつれる 窶れる **get** [**become**] **haggard** ▶病人のやつれた顔 the patient's *haggard* [*gaunt*] face ‖ やつれた表情 a *pinched* look(➤ pinched は「しょうすいした」の意) ‖ 彼の両親は心配のあまりやつれた顔をしていた His parents looked *haggard* from anxiety. / Anxiety made his parents look *haggard*.

やど 宿 an **inn**(旅館); a **hotel**(ホテル) ▶日本式の宿 a Japanese-style *inn* ‖ その夜は山中湖畔に宿を取った I *stayed* [*put up*] *at a hotel* by Lake Yamanaka that night.
▶その男は一夜の宿を探していた The man was looking for *a night's lodging*. (➤ lodging は「泊まる所」).
▶ **対話**「宿は決まったの?」「うん, ヒルトンホテルに予約したよ」"Have you decided (on) *where to stay*?" "Yes. I made a reservation at the Hilton." →民宿.
‖宿賃 a hotel charge [rate].

やといいれる 雇い入れる **hire** +目, **employ** +目. →雇う.

やといにん 雇い人 an **employee**(雇用される人).

やといぬし 雇い主 an **employer**(雇用する人).

[1]**やとう 野党** an **opposition party**(野党の1つ); **the Opposition**(全野党) ▶与党と野党 the ruling party and *the Opposition* ‖ 今回の選挙では野党の中で共産党が伸びた In this election the JCP increased its share among *the opposition parties*. (➤ JCP は

Japanese Communist Party の略).

²**やとう 雇う** **hire** +㊐, **employ** +㊐ (➤ 動作動詞として「雇う」は employ よりも hire を用いるのがふつうで, employ はサラリーマンなどを継続的に雇用する場合, つまり「雇っている」を表すのに用いる. hire はまた, 日雇い[短期]契約者などを雇用する場合, または観光バスなどを賃借りする場合に多く用いる) ; **engage** +㊐ (専門職の力を借りる ; 堅い語) ▶ヘルパー [弁護士] を**雇う** *hire* a caregiver [a lawyer] ‖ その工場はさまざまな技能を持った人々を**雇っている** The factory *employs* people of various skills. ‖ 息子の家庭教師に大学生を**雇った** I *hired* [*engaged*] a college student as a tutor for my son. ‖ 古都の名所巡りをするのに観光バスを**雇った** We *hired* [*chartered*] a sightseeing bus to see the sights of the old capital. (➤ charter は乗り物を「借り切る」).

やどかり 宿借り 《動物》 a **hermit crab**.

やどす 宿す ▶彼女は子を宿している She'*s with child*.

やどちょう 宿帳 a **guest book** (招待客名簿も含む) ; a **hotel register**.

やどなし 宿無し a **homeless person** ; a **tramp** (浮浪者) ▶その火事で多くの人が**宿無し**になった Lots of people *lost their homes* in the fire. ‖ アパートを追い出されて, きょうから**宿無し**だ I was evicted from my apartment, so I'm *on the streets* [I'm *homeless*] from today on.

やどや 宿屋 an **inn** ▶その夜は金沢の**宿屋**に泊まった I put up for the night at *an inn* [*a hotel*] in Kanazawa.

やどりぎ 宿り木 《植物》 **mistletoe** /mísəltoʊ/.

やどる 宿る ▶この日本人形は祖母が生前とても大事にしていたから, 祖母の魂が**宿っている**かもしれない Since my grandmother cherished this Japanese doll while she was alive, perhaps her soul [spirit] *dwells* in it now.

▶妻のおなかには私の子供が**宿っている** My wife *is carrying my child*.

やとわれ 雇われ ▶バーの**雇われ**マダム the female manager [*hired* head hostess] of a bar.

やなぎ 柳 《植物》 a **willow (tree)** ▶土手の**柳**が芽吹き始めた The *willows* on the bank began to come into bud.

ことわざ **柳の下にいつもどじょうが居るとは限らない** You cannot always expect the same good luck. (➤「いつも同じ幸運に恵まれるとは限らない」の意).

‖**しだれ柳** a weeping willow ‖ **猫柳** a pussy willow.

やなみ 家並み a **row of houses** ▶高山では古い**家並み**を保存している In Takayama some *rows of old houses* have been preserved.

やに 脂 **resin** (樹木の) ; **tar** (たばこの) ▶このパイプは**やに**で詰まっている This pipe is stopped up with *tar*.

‖**松やに** pine resin.

やにょうしょう 夜尿症 **bedwetting** (おねしょ) (➤ 医学用語は nocturnal enuresis /ènjərí:sɪs/).

やにわに 矢庭に **abruptly** (不意に) ; **suddenly** (突然).

やぬし 家主 a **landlord** (男), a **landlady** (女) ; a **home owner** (家の持ち主).

やね 屋根 a **roof**, a **housetop** ; a **dome** (丸屋根) ▶赤いタイルの**屋根** a red tile *roof* ‖ 屋根板で**屋根**をふく *roof* a house with shingles (➤ この roof は他動詞) ‖ 赤い**屋根**の家 a house with a red *roof* ‖ わが家の**屋根**は瓦ぶきだ Our house has a tiled *roof*. /Our house is roofed with tiles. ‖ ロシアの教会にはタマネギ形の**屋根**のものがある Some Russian churches have onion-shaped *domes*.

▶《慣用表現》20年間**一つ屋根の下に住み**ながら彼女は夫の考えが全く理解できないと感じた She felt that she couldn't understand her husband at all, even though they had been *living under the same roof* for twenty years.

‖**屋根裏部屋** an attic, a loft, a garret ‖ **屋根職人** a roofer.

やのあさって **three days from today** [**now**] (しあさって) ; **four days from today** [**now**] (あさっての翌々日).

やばい **1【不都合な】** **chancy** (危なっかしい) ▶**やばい**仕事 a *chancy* job ‖ 部屋に入って来たおふくろにたばこを吸っているところを見られたのは実際**やばかった**よ It *was a* real *bad scene* when Mom came in and caught us smoking. (➤ bad scene は「ひどいザマ」の意の俗語) ‖ あいつにそのこと話したの? **やばい**! You told that guy about it? *No way!* [(*That's*) *bad news!*] (➤ bad news は「やっかいなこと」の意の俗語).

2【すごい】 **terrific**, **awesome** /ɔ́:səm/ (すばらしい) ; **cool** (かっこいい) ; **amazing** (びっくりする) ; **great** (すごい) ▶このラーメン, マジ**やばい**よ This ramen tastes really *terrific*.

やはり

1【思ったとおり】 **just as I thought** ▶あの男が**やはり**犯人だった He was the one who did it, *just as I thought*. ‖ 対話「早川さんは退職するんだって」「**やっぱりね**」"I hear Ms. Hayakawa is going to quit (the company)." "*Just as I thought*."

▶ぼくは彼女は来ないだろうと思ったが, **やはり**来なかった I thought she wouldn't come and I was right [that's *just* what happened].

2【依然として】 **still** ; **again** (再び) ▶今回も**やはり**彼女の答えはノーだった She said no (this time) *again*. ‖ きょうも**やっぱり**雨だね It's raining *again* today. ‖ あなたの言うこともわかるけど, **やっぱり**間違ってると思うよ I understand what you're saying, but I *still* think you're wrong.

▶別れたのにあの二人は**やはり**お互いが好きらしい It seems those two *still* love each other, even though they broke up.

3【同じように】 ▶私も**やはり**同じ所を間違えた I made a mistake *exactly* where you did. /I made the *exact* same mistake. ‖ 彼女は看護師で, 彼女の娘も**やはり**看護師だ She is a nurse, *and so* is her daughter.

4【何といっても】 **after all** ▶ああ疲れた. **やっぱり**うちがいちばんね Boy, I'm tired. Home is best *after all*. ‖ 横綱は**やはり**強い The yokozuna is strong *after all*.

5【思い直して】 **on second thought** ▶ディズニーランドへ行こうと思ったが, **やはり**やめることにした I considered going to Disneyland, but *on second thought* I decided not to (go).

やはん 夜半 **midnight** ▶**夜半**過ぎにかなり大きな地震があった There was a pretty strong earthquake a little *after* [*past*] *midnight*.

やばん 野蛮な **barbarous** ▶戦争はどんなによく見ても**野蛮な行為**だ War is *barbarism* at best. ‖ 切腹は外国人には**野蛮な**習慣と思われた Hara-kiri was regarded as a *barbarous* practice by foreigners.

‖**野蛮人** a barbarian.

やひ 野卑な **vulgar** (下品な) ; **coarse** (粗野な) ▶**野卑**なことば *vulgar* language.

やぶ 藪 a **thicket** ; a **bush** (低木の茂み) ▶竹**やぶ** a bamboo *thicket*.

▶《慣用表現》**やぶから棒**に会社を辞めるだなんて, どうしたんだ？ What's gotten into you, saying *out of the blue* you're going to quit your job？(➤「全く突然に」の意の熟語) ‖ 真相はやぶの中だ The truth *remains a mystery*.

‖やぶ医者 a quack (doctor).

やぶか 藪蚊 《虫》a **striped mosquito**.

やぶく 破く **break** ＋目 (破る)；**tear** /teəʳ/ ＋目，**rip** ＋目 (裂く) ⇀破る ▶兄とプロレスごっこをしていてふすまを破いた I *tore* the paper sliding screen while wrestling with my brother. (➤ tore は tear /teəʳ/ の過去形).

やぶける 破ける **tear**；**rip** (裂ける) ▶この封筒は薄くてすぐ破ける This envelope is thin and *tears* easily. ‖ズボンがくぎに引っ掛かって破けた My pants got caught on a nail and *ripped*.

やぶさか 吝か ▶あなたを支持するにやぶさかでないが，1つ条件がある I'*d be glad* [I *don't hesitate* ／I'*m willing*] *to* support you, but on one condition. (● I'm willing to …. はあまり積極性は感じられない言い方で，「支持するのが務めだから」というニュアンスを感じさせる).

やぶさめ 流鏑馬 ***yabusame***；ceremonial archery in which the archer on a running horse shoots arrows successively at three targets (➤ 説明的な訳).

やぶにらみ 藪睨み ▶少年はひどい［少し］やぶにらみだった The boy had a bad [slight] *squint*.

やぶへび 藪蛇 ▶下手な言い訳はかえってやぶへびになるぞ If you make a poor excuse, you'll *be asking for trouble* [you'll *stir up a hornet's nest*]. (➤ stir up a hornet's nest は「(蜂の巣をつついたときのような)面倒を引き起こす」の意).

やぶる 破る

📖 **訳語メニュー**
引き裂く ⇀tear, rip **1**
壊す ⇀break **2**
違反する ⇀break, violate **3**
負かす ⇀beat, defeat **4**
記録を ⇀break **5**

1【引き裂く】 **tear** /teəʳ/ ＋目 (あとにぎざぎざが残るように)；**rip** ＋目 (勢いよく) ▶紙を破る *tear* [*rip*] a piece of paper ‖封筒を破って開ける *tear* [*rip*] an envelope *open* ／*tear* [*rip*] *open* an envelope ‖京子は正彦からの手紙をずたずたに破った Kyoko *tore up* the letter from Masahiko. (➤ tore は tear の過去形) ‖私は日記帳のそのページを破り取った I *tore* the page *out of* my diary.

▶コートをくぎに引っ掛けて破ってしまった I caught my coat on a nail and *ripped* it. ‖サラはプレゼントを受け取ると，包み紙をびりびりに破って箱を開けた When Sarah received the present, she *ripped off* the wrapping paper and opened the box. (➤ 英米では包み紙を勢いよく破ることでプレゼントを受け取った喜びを表現する).

2【壊す】 **break** ＋目 ▶荒れた中学生たちはドアを蹴飛ばして破った Those violent junior high school students kicked the door and *broke* it. ‖ダンプカーが塀を破って飛び込んで来た A dump truck *broke* through the fence.

▶ひなが殻を破って出て来た *Breaking* [*Cracking*] the shell, a chick came out. ／A chick hatched.

▶《比喩的》女性の鋭い悲鳴が夜の静寂を破った A female scream *broke* the silence [quiet] of the night.

3【約束などを】 **break** ＋目；**violate** ＋目 (違反する) ▶校則を破る *break* [*violate*] a school regulation ‖彼はカトリックのおきてを破って破門された He *violated* the rules of the Catholic church and was excommunicated.

▶彼女は校則を破って(＝に反して)髪を染めた She dyed her hair *against* [*in violation of*] (the) school regulations.

4【負かす】 **beat** ＋目 (…に勝つ)；**defeat** ＋目 (…を負かす) ▶日本のバレーボールチームがキューバを破った The Japanese volleyball team *beat* [*defeated*] Cuba.

5【記録を】 **break** ＋目 ▶彼女は陸上100メートルで世界記録を破った She *broke* the world record in the 100-meter dash.

やぶれかぶれ 破れかぶれの **desperate** ▶彼は失恋して破れかぶれになった He *felt desperate* after breaking up with his girlfriend. ／After breaking up with his girlfriend, he *no longer cared what happened to him*. ‖追い詰められて破れかぶれになった男は次々に人を射殺した The *desperate* man, who had been driven into a corner, shot one person after another. ‖もうこうなったら破れかぶれだ Now that things have come to this, *I don't care what happens next*. (➤「次にどうなろうと知ったことじゃない」の意).

[1]やぶれる 破れる

1【裂ける】 **tear** /teəʳ/ (あとにぎざぎざが残るように)；**rip** (勢いよく) ▶この柔道着は破れることはありません This judo uniform will never *tear*. ‖きみ，ズボンの膝が破れてるよ Hey, your pants *are torn* [*are ripped*] in the knees. (➤ torn は tear の過去分詞形) ‖封筒を乱暴に開けたら中の手紙まで破れてしまった I accidentally *ripped* the letter when I tore open the envelope. ‖あいつ，破れた(＝穴のあいた)靴下を履いてるよ He's wearing socks that *have holes* in them.

2【崩れる】 ▶プロ野球選手になりたいという彼の夢は病気のために破れた His hopes of becoming a professional baseball player *were shattered* by his illness.

▶一男はまたしても恋愛に破れた Kazuo *was disappointed* in love again.

[2]やぶれる 敗れる **lose** /luːz/ (試合などで負ける)；**be beaten** (負かされる) ▶ロッテはオリックスに3対2で敗れた The Marines *lost* (*the game*) *to* the Buffaloes 3–2.

▶400メートルリレーでドイツチームはアメリカに小差で敗れた The German team *was beaten* [*was defeated*] by a narrow margin by the American team in the 400-meter relay.

やぶん 夜分 **night** ▶夜分にお邪魔してすみません I am sorry to disturb you *at night*. ／I am sorry to call on you *at this time of night*.

やぼ 野暮 **1【世事に疎い】**

⚠「やぼ」は「世間の習わしや細かい人情などに通じておらず，気が利かないこと［人］」の意で用いるが，これは，日本のようにことばよりも以心伝心，暗黙の了解などが重視される社会ならではの考え方である．ことばによるコミュニケーションが重視される英語社会には，この日本語にぴったりの語はないので，文脈に応じて近い意味を表す語を選ぶこと．

▶そんなこと聞くだけやぼだよ What an *insensitive* [a *boorish*] question！‖あの人がそんなやぼな(＝ばかげた)

ことを言うはずがない He [She] couldn't have said such a *stupid* thing.
2【趣味などが悪い】unrefined ▶やぼな人 a person *of unrefined taste* ／a *dork* ‖ ぼくのおじはやぼだ My uncle is *corny and clumsy*.

やぼう 野望 (an) **ambition** ▶彼は少年の頃大統領になりたいという**野望**を持っていた In his boyhood, his *ambition* was to become (the nation's) president. ‖ その独裁者は隣国を併合しようという**野望**を抱いていた The dictator cherished the *wild dream* of annexing the neighboring country.

やぼったい 野暮ったい unrefined（洗練されていない）; **dowdy** /dáʊdi/（服装などが；女性に関連して用いられることが多い）; **tacky**（悪趣味な）▶**やぼったい**人 an *unrefined* person ‖ その服**やぼったい**ね That outfit's pretty *dowdy*, isn't it ? ‖ 彼はいつも**やぼったい**服を着ている He always wears *tacky* [*unfashionable*] clothes.

やま 山 **1【山】** a **mountain** ; a **hill**（小山）; **Mount ..., Mt. ...**（➤ 山名につける）
▶高い[低い]山 *a* high [low] *mountain* ‖ **山**に登る climb [go up] *a mountain*（➤ climb /klaɪm/ は歩いて登るときで，ロープウェーなどで登るときには使えない）／go *mountain* climbing ‖ **山**から下りる climb [go] down *a mountain* ‖ **山**越えをする cross [go over] *a mountain*.
▶**山**に囲まれた村 a village surrounded by *mountains* ‖ **山**の頂上に赤い屋根が見える I see a red roof at the top of the *mountain*. ‖ 夏休みは海と**山**とどっちがいい? Which would you like better for the summer vacation, going to the *mountains* or going to the seashore ?
▶山梨県は**山が多い** Yamanashi Prefecture is *mountainous*. ‖ 眼下にヒマラヤの**山々**が見えた I saw the Himalayan *peaks* below.（➤ peak は「峰」）‖ 裏手の**山**が崩れて数軒が土砂に埋まった Several houses were buried in earth and rocks when the *hill* behind them collapsed.

あなたの英語はどう響く?
「山」をいつも mountain と訳すと誤解を招く．ふつう mountain はかなり高くて険しい山をいうからである．500メートル程度の山は mountain でなく hill という．したがって mountain climbing や mountaineering は本格的な「登山」であり，休日などの「山歩き」は hiking である．

《解説》「…山」の言い方
(1)固有名詞の「…山，…岳」は Mount またはその略語 Mt. を山の名前の前につける．例えば，鷹取山は Mount [Mt.] Takatori となる．ただし，白山や北岳のように短いものや，山や岳をとると語調が悪くなるものはそのまま Mt. Hakusan, Mt. Kitadake のように表してよい．
(2)「…山脈」は Mountains を固有名詞のあとにつけて the Kiso Mountains, the Rocky Mountains のようにいう．the が必要．

‖**山焼き** mountain burning.
2【積み上げた物，多量】 a **mountain** ; a **heap**（雑然と積み重ねた物）; a **pile**（きちんとまたは雑然と積み重ねた物）; a **stack**（必ずしもきちんとしてはいないが縦に積み重ねたもの）→山ほど．

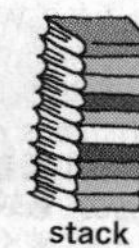

▶宿題の**山** *a mountain of* homework ‖ **山**のようなごみ[借金] *a mountain of* garbage [debts] ‖ 返品の**山** *a stack of* returned merchandise ‖ この道の角はよくごみの**山**になっている There's always *a heap of* trash at this street corner. ‖ 1週間休んだら机の上は書類の**山**になっていた I found papers *piled up in a mountain* on my desk after I took a week off. ‖ きょうは仕事が**山**のようにある I have *a lot of* [*a pile of*] work to do today. ‖ このキュウリは1**山**300円です These cucumbers are 300 yen *per tray* [*box*]. ／These cucumbers are 300 yen *a trayful* [*a boxful*].
▶クリーニング店には洗濯物が**山と積まれていた** There was *a heap of* clothes at the cleaners. ‖ 書店には新刊書が**山と積まれている** There are *mountains of* new books piled up in bookstores.
3【予想】 a **guess** ▶試験の**山**が当たった[外れた] My *guess* about the exam problems was right [wrong]. ‖ 試験で**山を掛ける**（＝一か八(ばち)かやる）のはばかげている It is foolish to *take a hit-or-miss attitude* toward exams.
4【頂点】 a **climax** →山場 ▶おじいさんの病気はここ数日が**山**です The next few days are *critical* for your grandfather. ‖ 対話「お仕事はどう?」「うん，**山は越えた**ね」"How's your work going ?" "Well, I'*m over the hump*."（➤ over the hump は「峠を越して」の意のインフォーマルな言い方）．
☞ **山ほど**（→見出語）

やまあい 山間 ▶**山あい**の村 a village *in the mountains* ‖ **山あい**の集落 *mountain* hamlets ‖ **山あい**を流れる川 a river flowing *through the mountains* ‖ 郡上八幡は**山あい**の町である Gujohachiman is a town *among the mountains*.

ヤマアラシ《動物》a **porcupine** /pɔ́ːʳkjəpaɪn/ →ハリネズミ．

やまあるき 山歩き hiking ; **trekking**（長くて骨の折れる）▶彼は少年時代から**山歩き**が好きだった From his childhood he was fond of *hiking*.

やまい 病 (a) **sickness**, (an) **illness**（病気の状態）; (a) **disease**（病名のある病気）▶**病**を克服する overcome one's *illness* ‖ 胸の**病** (a) chest *disease* ; (a) lung *disease*（肺病）‖ 不治の**病** an incurable *disease* ‖ **病に倒れる** come down with *a disease* ‖ その選手は**病**を押して大会に出場した The athlete took part in the meet in spite of *sickness*. ‖ 恋の**病**にはつける薬がありません There's no cure for *love sickness*.
▶《慣用表現》しっかりしろ．「**病は気から**」って言うじゃないか Cheer up ! As the saying goes, "*Illness starts in the mind*."

やまいも 山芋 a **(Japanese) mountain yam**, a **yamaimo**.

やまおく 山奥 ▶その村は**山奥**にあった The village was (*deep*) *in the mountains*.

やまおとこ 山男 a **mountain-climbing man**, a **mountain climber** /kláɪməʳ/（➤ 後者は女性にも使える）; an **alpinist**（山に登る人；女性にも使える）; a **mountain**

man(山中で生活する男) ▶山男にほれてはいけません Never fall in love with *a mountain-climbing man.*
やまかげ 山陰 the shady side of a mountain.
やまかじ 山火事 a forest fire (on a mountain) ▶山火事はみるみるうちに山全体に広がった The *forest fire* quickly spread across the mountain(s).
やまがり 山狩りをする hunt [shoot] in the mountains.
やまかん 山勘 ▶山勘で答えたら当たった I made *a wild guess* and it was right. ‖ 対話「(答え)どうしてわかったの?」「山勘さ」"How did you know (the answer)?" "Just *a lucky guess.*"
やまくずれ 山崩れ a landslide ▶山崩れで鉄道が不通になった Train service was disrupted [paralyzed] due to *a landslide.*
やまぐに 山国 a mountain [mountainous] country ▶山国の春は遅い Spring comes late in the *mountain country.*
やまごや 山小屋 a mountain hut.
やまざと 山里 a mountain village ▶山里では過疎化が進んでいる *Mountain villages* are becoming depopulated.
やまし 山師 a gambler(相場師); a swindler(詐欺師).
やましい 疚しい feel guilty《about》▶彼女は少しやましく思った She *felt* a little *guilty.* / She *had* a slightly *guilty conscience.* (➤「心にやましいところがある」の意; 反対は have a clear conscience) ‖ あなた, 彼女にうそをついてやましいと思わないの? Don't you *have a guilty conscience* after lying to her? ‖ 私は何もやましい(=恥ずかしい)ことはしていません I have done nothing to *be ashamed of.* / I have a clear conscience since I haven't done anything wrong.
やましさ 疚しさ a sense of guilt ▶助かった者としてのやましさを持つ have survivor's *guilt.*
やまづみ 山積み ▶自動車修理店の庭にはタイヤが山積みになっている There is *a mountain of* tires *piled up* in the auto mechanic's yard.
▶新内閣には立ち向かうべき難問が山積みだ The new Cabinet has *a pile* [*a mountain*] *of* difficult problems to address.
やまでら 山寺 a mountain temple.
やまとことば 大和言葉 *yamatokotoba*; a native Japanese word(日本生まれのことば).
やまとだましい 大和魂 the Yamato [traditional Japanese] spirit.
やまとなでしこ 大和撫子 a Japanese woman with traditional virtues(女性);《植物》a Japanese pink(ナデシコ).
やまとみんぞく 大和民族 the Yamato people, (the) ethnic Japanese.
やまねこ 山猫《動物》a wildcat
‖山猫スト a wildcat strike.
やまのて 山の手 a hilly section(高台); the Bluff(海を見下ろす);《米》uptown(住宅地区) ▶東京の山の手に住む live *uptown* in Tokyo / live in *uptown* Tokyo(➤前者は副詞, 後者は形容詞用法).
‖山手線 the Yamanote [Loop] Line (路線名).
やまのぼり 山登り mountain climbing, mountaineering ▶山登りをする *climb a mountain* / *go mountain climbing.*
やまば 山場 the climax(最高潮); the critical moment [period](危機的瞬間[時期]) ▶ドラマの山場 the *climax* of a drama ‖ このプロジェクトもあと2, 3週間が山場だ In this project the next two or three weeks is *the critical period* [*the busiest period*].
やまはだ 山肌 ▶火事で山肌があらわになってしまった The fire has left (*the face of*) *the mountain* bare.
やまびこ 山彦 an echo /ékoʊ/ ▶やまびこが聞こえる? Can you hear the *echo(es)*?
やまびらき 山開き ▶あすは富士山の山開きです *The climbing season* on Mt. Fuji *officially opens* tomorrow. / Mt. Fuji will *be opened to climbers* from tomorrow.
やまぶき 山吹《植物》a Japanese kerria /kériə/
‖やまぶき色 bright yellow; golden yellow; gold(黄金色).
やまぶし 山伏 a *yamabushi*; a mountain ascetic(➤説明的な訳; ascetic /əsétɪk/ は「苦行者」).
やまほど 山程 ▶あなたに聞きたいことが山ほどある I have *lots of* [*so many*] things to ask you. / I have *a million* questions for you. (➤ a million ... は子供っぽく響く) ‖ きょうは宿題が山ほどある I've got *tons of* homework today.
やまみち 山道 a mountain path [trail / road] ▶山道をたどる follow a *mountain path* ‖ 山道はそこで行き止まりになった *The mountain road* [*trail*] came to a dead end there.
ヤマメ《魚》a masu salmon; a (landlocked) seema.
やまもり 山盛り ▶ご飯を茶わんに山盛りにする *heap* a bowl with rice ‖ ヨーグルトに大さじ山盛り2杯の砂糖を入れなさい Put two *heaping* tablespoonfuls of sugar into the yogurt. (➤「すり切りの」の場合は heaping を level にかえる).
やまやま ▶お会いしたいのはやまやまですが, 当日は先約がありまして I'*d very much like to* [I *really want to*] see you, but unfortunately I have a previous engagement [appointment] on that day.
やまわけ 山分けする divide equally ▶この金は山分けしよう Let's *go halves on* this money. (➤2人で分ける場合) / Let's *split* [*share*] the money *equally.*
▶賞金はみんなで山分けにした We *divided* [*split*] the prize money *equally* among us. ‖ 山分けにしよう Let's *share* them *equally.*
やまんば 山姥 an old mountain witch.
やみ 闇 **1**【暗闇】darkness, the dark ▶闇の中でぼくらは頭をごっつんこした We bumped our heads together in *darkness.*
▶《慣用表現》事件は闇から闇へ葬られた The case was *secretly* dealt with. (➤「こっそりと」の意) / The incident was swept under the rug [the carpet]. (➤ sweep ... under the rug [carpet] は「(恥になることを)隠す」の意).
‖闇夜 a moonless [dark] night.
2【不正】▶闇献金 a donation *made through illegal channels* ‖ S市役所は職員に闇給与を支払った The S City government paid its employees *extra salary illegally.*
‖ヤミ金融 loan-sharking.
やみあがり 病み上がり ▶病み上がりだから無理をするな Don't work too hard since you *have just recovered from your sickness.*
やみいち 闇市 a black market.
やみうち 闇討ち ▶敵にやみ討ちをかける make *a surprise attack* on the enemy *under cover of darkness.*
やみくも 闇雲に haphazardly(無計画に); at random (手当たり次第) ▶サプリメントも闇雲に摂取すればよいとい

うものではありません It's not good for the health to take supplements *haphazardly*.

やみつき 病み付き ▶少年はスマホゲームに**病みつきになっている** The boy *is addicted to* [*is hooked on*] smartphone games. ‖ きみだってツイッターを始めたら**病みつきになる**だろう Once you start using Twitter, you'll *be addicted* [*hooked*].

1**やむ 止む** **stop**; **be over**(終わる); **die down**(風・騒ぎなどが徐々に収まる) ▶雨が**止んだ** It *has stopped* raining. ‖ 突然音楽が**止んで**場面が変わった The music *stopped* suddenly and the scene changed. ‖ 夕立が**止む**までここで雨宿りしよう Let's take shelter here until the shower *passes* [*is over*]. (➤ pass は「過ぎ去る」) ‖ 雨は夜明けに降り始めたが, 昼前に**止んだ** The rain started at dawn but *ended* before noon. ‖ 風は明け方になってやっと**止んだ** The wind finally *died down* at dawn. ‖ 演奏後しばらく拍手が**鳴り止まなかった** The audience *kept clapping* [Applause *continued*] for a while after the performance.

2**やむ 病む** **suffer**《from》 ▶心臓を**病む** *suffer from* a heart disease ‖ つまらんことを**気に病む**な Don't *worry over* trivial things. / Don't *sweat* the small stuff.

ヤムチャ 飲茶 **dim sum**.

やむなく 止む無く ▶天候が悪化したので我々は**やむなく**登頂を断念した The weather got worse, so we *had no choice but* to give up on reaching the summit. →**止むを得ず**.

やむにやまれず 止むに止まれず ▶**やむにやまれず**彼にやめるよう忠告した I *was forced* [*was compelled*] *to* dissuade him.

やむにやまれぬ 止むに止まれぬ ▶**やむにやまれぬ**思い an *uncontrollable* longing ‖ 彼女は**やむにやまれぬ**事情で退学した She quit school due to *unavoidable* circumstances.

やむをえず 止むを得ず **reluctantly**(気の進まぬままに); **against** one's **will**(意志に反して) ▶父親が亡くなって彼は**やむをえず**家業を継いだ He took over the family business *reluctantly* [*against his will*] after his father's death. ‖ 親友の頼みで**やむをえず**その仕事を引き受けた I felt I *had* (*no other choice but*) *to* take on the task because a good friend of mine had asked me to do so. (➤ カッコ内を加えると「…するよりしかたがなかった」の意).

やむをえない 止むを得ない **unavoidable**(避けられない) ▶**やむをえない**事情で会社を辞めた I quit the company owing to *unavoidable* circumstances. ‖ 多少の混乱は**やむをえなかった**(=避けられなかった) A little confusion *couldn't be helped* [*be avoided*]. ‖ それは**やむをえない** It *can't be helped*.

1**やめる 止める** **stop**《doing》,《インフォーマル》**quit** +㊐; **give up**(特に酒・たばこなどを); **refrain**《from doing》(差し控える); **drop** +㊐ (打ち切る)

【文型】
…していることをやめる
stop doing
…するのをやめる
refrain from doing

【解説】
(1)**stop** のあとには doing も to do もくるが意味が違う. これは doing が今まさに動作中のことを表すのに対して to do はこれから起こす動作を表すことから生じる意味の違いである. **stop doing** は, -ing 形からもわかるように,「今している［これまでしていた］ことをやめる」の意. これに対して, stop to do は「立ち止まって［手を休めて］…する」の意になる. 例えば, She stopped chatting. は「彼女はおしゃべりしていたのをやめた」の意だが, She stopped to chat. とすると「彼女は立ち止まっておしゃべりした」(これからおしゃべりしようとしている)の意.
(2)**refrain from** は「したいと思っていることを思いとどまる, 差し控える」の意.

▶泣くのは**やめなさい** *Stop* cry*ing*. ‖ バスケの選手たちは午後 7 時に練習を**やめた** The basketball players *stopped* practic*ing* at 7 p.m. ‖ がみがみ言うのは**やめてよ** *Stop* nagg*ing*. ‖ 歩きたばこは**おやめください** Please *refrain from* smok*ing* while walking.
▶正子, 舌を出すのは**やめなさい**. 悪い癖ですよ *Quit* sticking out your tongue, Masako! It's a nasty habit. ‖ **やめなさいよ** *Stop* it. / *Cut* it *out*. ‖ その話は**もうやめましょう** Let's *drop* the subject. ‖ 今その話は**やめましょう** *Let's not* talk about it now.
▶ギャンブルはなかなか**やめられない** Gambling is*n't easy* [is *hard*] *to give up*. / It's *very difficult* for me *to quit* gambling. ‖ 春男君と付き合うのは**やめなさい** *Don't* go out with Haruo. ‖ きょうは肌寒いからプールに行くのは**やめにしよう** *I think I'd better not* go to the swimming pool because it's a bit chilly today. ‖ あなたが行かないんなら, 私も行くの**やめた** If you don't go, I *won't*, either. ‖《店で買い物をしていて》**やめておきます** *I'll leave it*, thank you. (➤ thank you は省略可).
▶母親は二郎の外出を**やめさせた** Jiro's mother *stopped* him *from* go*ing* out. (➤ stop A (from) doing で「A(人)が…するのをやめさせる」) / Jiro's mother told him not to go out.

直訳の落とし穴「…するのをやめる」
(1)「やめる」は「現在していることをやめる」のと,「行動を起こす前にやめる」のとでは英語が違ってくるので注意が必要. している動作を中止するのは stop doing でよいが, 事前にやめることは not do をはじめ, さまざまな言い方がある. 例えば,「両親はその家を買うのをやめた」は買う前にやめるのだから, (×)stop buying は使えず,「買わないことに決める」と考えて, My parents decided not to buy that house. とする.
(2)電車内でよくあるアナウンスの「車内では携帯電話での通話はおやめください」も (×)Please stop talking on your cellphone on the train. などとしがち. これでは注意された相手は今通話していることになる. 初めからしないで, ということを丁寧に伝えるには refrain from を使って, Please refrain from talking on your cellphone on the train. とする. また,「駆け込み乗車はおやめください」は Please don't rush onto the train. とする. これは駆け込み動作の最中を止める場合と, 初めからやらないで, のどちらの場合にも使える.「控えてください」と考えて, より丁寧な Please refrain from rushing onto the train. としてもよい.

2**やめる 辞める** **resign** (+㊐),《インフォーマル》**quit** (+㊐); **leave**(+㊐)(離れていく); **step down**(公職・重要な地位などを) ▶佐藤さんは任期半ばで市長を**辞めた** Sato *resigned* as mayor in the middle of his term. (➤ resign as で「(役職を)辞任する」) ‖ 父は 3 月で会社を**辞めた** My father *quit* [*retired from*] the company last March. (➤ retire は「定年で辞める」).

▶彼女は病気で仕事を辞めた She *quit* [*left*] her job because of sickness. (➤ 前者には「突然」という含みがある) ‖ 姉は大学をやめた My sister *dropped out of* college. (➤ drop out は「中途退学する」) ‖ 私はサッカー部をやめさせられた I *was told to quit* the soccer team.

✉ **テニス部をやめようかどうしようか悩んでいます** I'm worrying about whether or not I should *quit* [*leave*] the tennis club.

やもたてもたまらず 矢も楯もたまらず ▶彼女は電話を受けると矢も楯もたまらず恋人に会いに出かけた *As soon as* she got a phone call, she *couldn't resist* going to meet her boyfriend.

やもめ a **widow**(女) ; a **widower**(男) ▶彼女は35歳でやもめになった She *lost her husband* [*was widowed*] at the age of thirty-five.

ヤモリ 《動物》 a **gecko** /gékoʊ/.

やや **a little, a (little) bit**(少し) ; **slightly**(僅かに) ▶今では弟のほうが私よりやや背が高い My younger brother is *a little* [*a bit*] taller than I now. ‖ 真佐子はやや太めです Masako is *slightly* plump. ／Masako is on the plump side. (➤ on the ... side は「…気味で」).

▶今月は売り上げがやや伸びた Our sales have increased *slightly* this month. ／Our sales are *somewhat* better this month than last month.

ややこしい **complicated** ▶ややこしい計算は苦手だわ I don't like doing *complicated* calculations. ‖ この小説は筋がややこしい This novel has *a complicated* [*confusing*] plot. ‖ 状況はますますややこしくなってきた The situation has become more *complicated*. ‖ ややこしいことになったなあ I'm *in a bind* [*in a difficult situation*]. (➤ bind は「にっちもさっちもいかない状態」).

ややもすれば 動もすれば ▶今の若者はややもすれば親に頼りがちだ Young people today *are apt* [*liable*] *to* depend on their parents.

やゆ 揶揄する **tease** +目 (からかう) ; **ridicule** +目 (笑い者にする).

-やら **1** 【並べ上げて】 ▶バスに乗り遅れるやら, 雨に遭うやらできょうのハイキングはさんざんだった *What with* missing the bus *and* being caught in the rain, we really had a hard time on today's hike. (➤ 基本形は what with A and (what with) B で「AやらBやらのために」の意だが, 会話ではあとの what with はふつう省略する).

2 【疑問・不確実を示して】 ▶お父さんの朝のジョギング, いつまで続くことやら *I wonder* (*just*) how long Dad will continue his morning jogs. (➤ 強調の just をつけると疑問の気持ちがより明確に出る).

やらかす ▶へまをやらかす *make* a blunder.

やらせ ▶テレビニュースのあの暴力シーンはやらせだった That violent attack scene shown on the TV news was *faked* [*prearranged* ／ *staged*].

やらせる **make ... do**(無理やり) ; **let ... do**(勝手に) ▶彼には好きなようにやらせたほうがいい You should *let* him *do* as he likes.

やられる ▶殴られたって? 誰にやられたんだ? I hear you were beaten up. *Who did it*? ‖ 冷夏で作物はすっかりやられてしまった (＝だめになった) The crops *were ruined* [*seriously damaged*] due to the unusually cool summer. ‖ 満員電車で財布をやられた (＝すられた) I *had* my wallet *picked* in the crowded train.

▶彼は口のうまい営業マンに見事にやられた (＝だまされた) He *was* completely *taken in* by a smooth-talking salesman. ‖ 妻がかぜにやられた (＝倒れた) ので, 私が台所仕事をしています My wife *has come down* with a cold, so I'm the cook.

やり 槍 a **spear**(武器としての) ; a **javelin**(競技用の) ▶人をやりで突く *spear* a person.

‖やり投げ the javelin throw.

やりあう やり合う **argue**(口論する) ▶あの2人, 何をやり合っているの? What *are* those two *arguing about*?

やりがい やり甲斐 ▶今度の仕事は本当にやりがいがある My new job is *really worth doing*. ‖ もっとやりがいのある仕事に就きたい I want a more *challenging* job.

やりかえす やり返す ▶夫が私を罵ったのでやり返した My husband swore at me, so I *swore back* at him.

やりかけ ▶宿題やりかけで, どこへ行くつもり? Where are you going with your homework *half-done* [*unfinished*]?

やりかた やり方 **how to** do ; a **way**(方法) ▶やり方がわかりませんので, 教えてください I don't know *how to do it*. Please tell me. ‖ これから正しいやり方と間違ったやり方をお見せします Now I'll show you the right *way* and then the wrong *way*. ‖ そんなやり方じゃだめだ That *way* won't work. ‖ 私には私のやり方がある I have my own *way* of doing things. ‖ ずるいぞ, そんなやり方は You're a sneak to do things *that way*.

やりきれない やり切れない **1** 【終えられない】 **cannot finish** ▶こんなにたくさんの宿題はきょう中にはやりきれない I *can't finish* this much homework today.

2 【かなわない】 **cannot stand** [**bear**] (耐えられない) ▶道路工事の音がうるさくてやりきれない I *can't stand* [*bear*] the road construction noise. ‖ 暑くてやりきれない The heat *is unbearable*. ／It is *unbearably* hot. ／I *can't stand* [*bear*] the heat. ‖ 夫の身勝手さには全くやりきれない (＝あんまりだ) My husband's selfishness is just *too much* for me (*to bear*).

やりくち やり口 a **way** ▶彼は巧妙なやり口で公金を横領した He found a crafty [a sneaky] *way* to embezzle public funds. (➤ crafty, sneaky はそれぞれ「悪賢い」「こそこそやる」の意で, いずれも皮肉がこもっている).

やりくり やり繰りする **manage**(どうにか行う) ▶母は父の安月給で何とか(家計を)やりくりしている My mother somehow *manages to make ends meet* on my father's small income. (➤ make ends meet は「収支を合わせる」) ‖ 久美子はやりくり上手だ Kumiko *is good at managing* [*juggling*] *the family budget to make ends meet*.

▶ここのところやりくりが大変です It's hard to *make ends meet* these days. ‖ 何とか時間をやりくりしてパーティーに出てくれよ Please *try to find time* to come to the party.

やりこなす ▶その社長は企画・制作から営業まですべて1人でやりこなす The president *deals with* everything from planning to production and sales all by himself.

やりこめる やり込める **argue down**(言い負かす) ▶部長に抗議したが逆にやり込められてしまった I made a protest to our manager, but I *was argued*

や

down. ‖このちびちゃんはよく親をやり込める This little kid often *scores* (*points*) *off* his parents *in arguments*. (➤ score (points) off には「(人を)当意即妙の答えで形なしにする」の含みがある).

やりすぎ やり過ぎ 一動 **やり過ぎる overdo** +目 ; **go too far**(度を越す)

▶彼は何事でもやり過ぎる傾向がある He tends to *overdo* everything. ‖ 対話「彼女，主役をもらおうと監督に高価な贈り物をしているらしいよ」「そりゃ少しやり過ぎだね」"(It) looks like she's sending expensive gifts to the director to win a leading role." "That'*s going* a bit *too far*."

やりすごす やり過ごす let ... go past ▶1台やり過ごせば，すいたバスに乗れますよ *Let* one bus *go past*, and the next one should be less crowded.

やりそこなう やり損なう fail ▶一度やり損なったからといってくよくよするな Don't let one *failure* get you down [discourage you].

やりだま 槍玉 ▶そのウェブサイトは青少年に有害だとしてやり玉に挙がった(＝非難された) That website *came under fire* for being a bad influence on minors.

やりっぱなし やりっ放し ▶彼は何でもやりっぱなしだ He *never puts* things *away*. (➤「後始末をしない」の意) ／He always *leaves* everything *half-done* [*unfinished*]. (➤「中途でやめる」の意).

やりて やり手 a real achiever ; a go-getter, a wheeler-dealer(➤あとの2語はともにインフォーマルな語だが，最後の訳語には非難の響きがある) ▶彼はなかなかのやり手だ He's *a real achiever*. ／He is really capable. ‖ 彼はやり手の青年実業家だ He is a *very capable* young entrepreneur.

やりとげる やり遂げる carry out [**through**] (➤ through のほうが強意) ; **complete** +目 (完成する) ; **accomplish** +目 (うまく成し遂げる ; 堅い語) ▶困難な仕事をやり遂げる *carry out* [*accomplish*] a difficult job ‖ 彼にその計画をやり遂げる能力があるかどうか怪しいものだ It's doubtful that he has the ability to *carry* the plan *out* [*through*]. ‖ 結果はともかく，やり遂げることが何よりも大切だ Nothing is more important than to *complete* the job, whatever the result is. ／It doesn't matter how it turns out ; the important thing is to *see* the job *through* (*to the end*). ‖ 彼が助けてくれたので私たちはその仕事をやり遂げることができた We *got through* that job [*managed to get* that work *done*] because he helped us. (➤ get through は「終える」の意).

やりとり やり取り an exchange(交換) ; **a give-and-take** (ことばの) ▶手紙[贈り物]のやり取り *an exchange* of letters [gifts] ‖ 彼と手紙のやり取りを始めて5年になる It has been five years since I began to *exchange* letters with him. ‖ きょうの会議でおもしろいやり取りがあった At today's meeting there was an interesting *give-and-take* [*exchange* (*of opinions*)].

やりなおし やり直し ▶初めからみんなやり直そう Let's *do* it (*all*) *over again*. ‖ 人生はやり直しが利かない Life cannot *be redone*. ／Life is not a dress rehearsal. (➤「ぶっつけ本番だ」の意).

やりなおす やり直す do ... all over again(もう一度やる) ; **redo** +目 (手直しする) ▶この計算は間違っている. やり直さなくっちゃ These calculations are wrong. I have to *do* them *all over again* [*do* them *once again*]. ‖ 更に完全なものにするためにレポートをやり直した I *redid* my report to make it more complete. ‖ 私たちは結婚生活を一からやり直すつもりです We are determined to *start* our married life *again from scratch*. (➤ from scratch は「最初から」の意のインフォーマルな言い方).

やりにくい be hard to do ▶お母さんがそんな所で見ていると勉強がやりにくいよ It'*s hard to* concentrate on my studying if you stand there watching, Mom. ‖ 課長どうしでいがみ合っているから，私たちはやりにくい(＝困った立場だ) We *are in an awkward position* because those two section chiefs are at loggerheads with each other.

やりぬく やり抜く carry out [**through**] (➤ through のほうが強意) ▶仕事がどんなに困難でも最後までやり抜かなければならない No matter how hard the task may be, we must *carry* it *out* [*through*] to the end.

やりば やり場 ▶やり場のない怒り anger *with no outlet* ‖ 若い女の子がミニスカートをはいていて，目のやり場に困ってしまった The young woman was wearing a miniskirt and I didn't know *where* [*which way*] *to look*.

やる 1【行う】do (+目) →する ▶何やってるの? What *are* you *doing*? ‖ やるだけのことはやった. あとは結果を待つだけだ I *did* my best, and I'm now just waiting for the results. ‖ 彼にこの仕事がやれるだろうか Do you think he *can do* [*handle*] the job? ‖ この計算あしたまでにやっといてくれる? *Could you do* these calculations *for me* by tomorrow?

▶うまくやれよ! *Good luck!* ‖ よくやった *Well done*. (➤やや堅い言い方) ‖ あいつらまたやってるよ. なんでけんかばっかりするんだろう They *are at it again*. Why are they always arguing? (➤ be at it は「(口論・仕事などを)盛んにやる」の意) ‖ やってもみない(＝試みない)うちに諦めてはだめだ Don't give up before you *try*. ‖ その気になればやれないものはない If you put your mind to it, *there's nothing you can't do*. ‖ やればいいんだろう，わかったよ，やるよ You want me to *do* it, right? Okay, okay. I'll *do* it. ‖ 対話「宿題はやった(＝終えた)の?」「まだだよ」"*Have* you *finished* your homework?" "Not yet."

▶みんなでバスケットボールをやろう Let's *play* basketball. ‖ 両親は広島で店をやっています My parents *run* a store in Hiroshima. (➤ run は「経営する」) ‖ あの学校で着付けの速成コースをやっている The school *offers* a crash course in kimono dressing. ‖ あのカラオケ店は朝5時までやっている That karaoke parlor [center] *is open* until 5 a.m. ‖ 今はあまりおもしろそうな映画はやっていない There are no exciting films *showing* [*playing* ／*on*] right now. (➤ on は「上映されて」).

▶やったね! *You did* [*made*] *it*. (➤ make it は「やり遂げる」) ‖ 対話「合格者の中にきみの名前があるよ」「やったあ!」"I found your name in the list of successful applicants." "*Fantastic!* ／I *made it!* ／I *did it!*" (➤ fantastic は「とてもすばらしい」の意のインフォーマルな言い方 ; →やった).

2【与える】give +目 ▶きみにこのヘルメットをやるよ I'll *give* you this helmet. ‖ それはきみにやるよ You can *keep* that. ‖ 毎朝，花に水をやるのを忘れないでね Don't forget to *water* the flowers every morning. ‖ 犬に餌をやるのはきみの仕事だ It's your job to *feed* the dog.

3【移す，行かせる】▶ここに置いてあった手紙，どこへやったんだ Where did you *put* the letter I had left here? ‖ 私は猫が嫌いなの. 早く向こうへやって I hate cats. *Get* it *away* from me. ‖ 浩一を迎えにやるから駅で待ってなさい I'll *send* Koichi *to meet* you at the station, so you wait there. ‖ 子供を大学へやるのは経済的に大変だ It isn't financially easy to *send* our children to college. ／*Sending* a child to college is a big financial burden. (➤ burden は「重荷, 負担」) ‖ 彼女は子供の遊んでいる遊園地の方に目をやった She *looked toward* the playground where children were playing.

4【生活する】 ▶この給料では東京じゃやっていけない You *can't survive* on this salary in Tokyo. ‖ 漫画家としてやっていくのは想像以上に大変だよ You'll find it harder than you imagine to *make a living* as a manga artist［cartoonist］. ‖ きみは一体その仕事をやる気があるのかね？ Do you really *set your mind on doing* the job？ ‖ どう, 元気にやってる？ Hiya, *how are you doing*？ (➤ Hiya は /háɪjə/ と発音).

5【酒を飲む】 ▶このバーで一杯やっていこう Let's *get a drink* at this bar. ‖ 一杯やりに行こう Let's go out *for a drink*.

6【セックスする】 **screw** +目, **lay** +目, **score**《with》(➤ いずれも使用には注意が必要な俗語) ▶で, どうなんだ. 彼女とやったのか？ Well, did you *do it* with her？

7【「…してやる」の形で】 ▶確かに「殺してやる」と言う声を聞いたんです I definitely heard someone say, "I'*ll* kill you." ‖ 犬を散歩に連れていってやらなくちゃ I've got to walk my dog.

やるかたない やる方ない ▶官僚の不正に対し憤まんやる方ないというのが庶民のほとんどだ Most people *feel anger that they don't know how to vent* at the bureaucrats' wrong-doings. (➤ vent は怒りなどを「発散させる」).

やるき やる気 **drive**（積極性）; **enthusiasm**（熱意）; **motivation**（意欲） ▶あいつはやる気が無い He has no *drive*. ‖ もっとやる気を出せよ Have more *drive*. ‖ 彼女はやる気満々だ She's full of *enthusiasm* (for it). ‖ 彼は難癖をつけられてやる気を無くした He lost his *motivation* after being criticized. ‖ きみは一体その仕事をやる気があるのかね？ Have you really *set your mind on doing* the job？ (➤ set one's mind on doing で「…することを熱望する」) ‖ つまらない仕事だと全然やる気が起きない When I'm given a boring job, I *can't get myself motivated*. ‖ 生徒に勉強へのやる気を起こさせることが教師の務めだ It is the duty［job］of teachers to *motivate* their students to work hard. ‖ 私は最近勉強をやる気がしない Lately I haven't *felt like* studying. (➤ feel like doing で「…したい気がする」).

やるせない やる瀬無い **miserable** ▶夢も希望もすべて失って, やるせない毎日だった Since my dreams and hopes had come to nothing, my days were *miserable*［*dreary*］.

やれやれ ▶やれやれ, やっと監督がいなくなったか *Well*, the manager's gone at last！ ‖ やれやれ, 何だこの散らかしようは！ Oh no！ *Good heavens*［*Good grief*］! What a mess！ (➤ 驚き・当惑などを表す) ‖ ようやく計画も動き出してやれやれだ Now that the project has gotten off the ground, we *feel relieved*.

やろう 野郎 ▶パーティーは野郎(＝男)ばかりだった Only *guys* came to the party.
▶あの野郎, この敵(かたき)はとってやるぞ *That rat*, I'll pay him back for this！ (➤ rat は「卑劣なやつ」) ‖ この野郎！ *You idiot*！／*You bastard*！／*Damn you*！‖ ばか野郎 *You fool*！

やわらかい 柔らかい・軟らかい **1【物が硬くない】** **soft**; **tender**（肉や野菜などが食感よく） ▶柔らかいベッド a *soft* bed ‖ この布地は手ざわりが柔らかい This cloth is *soft* to the touch. ‖ フィレミニョンは柔らかくておいしかった The filet mignon was *tender* and tasty. ‖ Bの鉛筆はHの鉛筆より軟らかい The lead of a B pencil is *softer* than that of an H pencil.

2【柔軟である】 **flexible** ▶ホテルの支配人は人当たりが柔らかだ Hotel managers are *affable*［*gentle*］to everyone. ‖ 彼女はエアロビクスをしているから, 体が柔らかい(＝しなやかだ) Since she does aerobics, she has a *supple*［*flexible*］body.
▶この評論家は頭が柔らかい This critic *has a flexible way of thinking*.

3【刺激が少ない】 **mild**; **subtle** /sʌ́t̬l/（淡い, 繊細な） ▶柔らかな春の日ざし *mild* spring sunshine ‖ 柔らかい照明 *soft* lighting［illumination］‖ 柔らかい赤 subtle red.

やわらぐ 和らぐ **ease**（痛みなどが）; **soften** /sɔ́:fən/（表情が）; **relax**（緊張などが）
▶注射してもらったら背中の痛みが和らいだ The pain in my back *eased* (*off*) after the shot. ‖ 事情を説明すると彼の態度は和らいだ When I explained the situation, his attitude *softened*. ‖ 森の中で野鳥のさえずりを聞いて気分が和らいだ I *felt relaxed* when I heard the birds singing in the woods. ／Listening to the birds singing in the woods *soothed* me. ‖ この2, 3日寒さが和らいだ The cold *has let up* the past few days. ‖ 寒さが和らいできた It is getting warmer.

やわらげる 和らげる **ease** +目（痛みなどを）; **alleviate** +目（苦痛・悩み・罰などを一時的または部分的に）; **palliate** +目《医学》（根本治療をせずに痛みを一時的に）; **soften** /sɔ́:fən/ +目（態度・感情などを）; **relax** +目（緊張などを）; **propitiate** /proupíʃieɪt/《フォーマル》+目（神などの怒りを）
▶歯痛を和らげる薬 (a) medicine to *ease*［*alleviate*］a toothache ‖ 骨転移の痛みを和らげる *palliate* pain of bone metastases ‖ モルヒネはがんの激しい痛みを和らげる Morphine *eases* the severe pain of cancer. ‖ 時があなたの悲しみを和らげてくれる Time will *ease*［*lessen*］your grief. ‖ 彼女の優しいことばが彼の気持ち［怒り］を和らげた Her kind words *softened* his heart［anger］. ‖ いけにえをもって神の怒りを和らげる *propitiate* a god with a sacrifice. →和らぐ.

ヤンキー **1【不良】** a **young punk**.
2【アメリカ人】 a **Yankee** /jǽŋki/ (➤ 通例軽蔑的) ‖ ヤンキー気質 Yankee spirit.

やんちゃな **naughty**（わんぱくで言うことを聞かない）; **mischievous**（いたずらな） ▶やんちゃな子供 a *naughty*［*mischievous*］child ‖ あの力士はいかにもやんちゃな顔をしている That sumo wrestler has a *mischievous* look about him.
▶《比喩的》俺も若いときはやんちゃをしたよ I *was bit wild*［*rowdy*／*hard to handle*］when I was young.

ヤンママ a **young punk-looking mother**.

やんや ▶やんやと喝采する applaud *wildly*.

やんわり **mildly**（穏やかに） ▶部長は新入社員の不注意をやんわり注意した The department manager *mildly* cautioned the newly hired employee against being careless. ‖ 申し出をやんわり(＝そつなく)断る turn down a proposal *diplomatically*.

ゆ・ユ

ゆ 湯 1【水に対して】hot water

> **《解説》**日本語では「湯」と「水」は別の語だが，英語には「湯」に当たる1語はない．したがって「湯を沸かす」は「水を熱する」と考える．

▶ぬるい湯 tepid [lukewarm] *water* ‖ 湯を沸かす boil *water* ‖ このお湯，ぬるいよ The *water* isn't hot enough. ‖ 《ホテルで》フロントですか．バスルームのお湯が出ません Is this the front desk? There's no *hot water* in the bathroom. ‖ 《薬服用の指示で》この薬はお湯で飲んでください Please take this medicine *with a warm liquid*. (➤ 決まり文句).

2【風呂】a bath ▶湯につかる soak in *a bath* ‖ パパ，お湯が沸いたわよ The *bath* is ready, Dad. ‖ いいお湯でした I really enjoyed the *bath*. ／I had a nice [an enjoyable] *bath*.

3【温泉】a hot spring；a **spa**(温泉地) ▶湯の町，熱海は有名だ Atami is a famous *hot spring resort*.
‖ **湯あか** scale ‖ **湯の花** hot spring mineral deposits [encrustations].

ゆあがり 湯上がり ▶湯上がりに散歩に出るのは気持ちがいい It's really refreshing to go out for a walk *after a bath*.
‖ **湯上がりタオル** a bath towel.

ゆあつ 油圧の hydraulic(➤ 水圧・油圧の両方に用いる) ‖ **油圧ジャッキ** a hydraulic jack.

ゆいいつ 唯一の only, sole /soul/ (➤ 後者は前者より強意的で堅い語) ▶コウモリは飛ぶことのできる唯一の哺乳類である Bats are the *only* mammals that can fly. ‖ 彼が唯一の財産相続人だった He was the *sole* heir to the fortune.

ゆいごん 遺言 a will, one's **last will and testament** ▶おじは私にこの家を譲ると遺言した My uncle *made (out) a will* leaving this house to me. ／My uncle *willed* me this house. (➤ will A B または will B to A で「遺言でA(人)にB(遺産など)を残す」) ／My uncle left me this house in his will.
▶父の遺言により財産は私どもの間で分配しました We divided our father's property among us *as his will instructed* [*in accordance with his will*].

ゆいしょ 由緒 ▶由緒あるホテル a *vintage* hotel ‖ ロックフェラー上院議員は由緒ある家の出だ Senator Rockefeller is from a *famous* family. ‖ 京都には由緒ある寺が多い In Kyoto, there are a lot of temples *with long (and honorable) histories*.

ゆいのう 結納 *yuino*；betrothal /bɪtróʊðəl/ **gifts**
日本紹介 ✉ **結納は，婚約のしるしに両家や両人の間で贈り物を取り交わすことをいいます．多くの場合，男性が女性に婚約指輪や結納金と呼ばれるお金などを贈り，女性はその半額程度のお返しをします** *Yuino* is the word used to refer to the ceremonial exchange of gifts as a token of engagement between the two families or the two persons involved in a marriage. Most often the man gives the woman an engagement ring in addition to a monetary gift called '*yuinokin*,' and other gifts. The woman gives the man something worth about half as much in return.
▶結納を交わす exchange *yuino* [*betrothal gifts*] (➤ betrothal は「婚約の」).

ゆいぶつ 唯物
‖ **唯物史観** historical materialism ‖ **唯物論** materialism ‖ **唯物論者** a materialist.

1**ゆう 優**《学業成績》**very good**, an **A** ▶数学の成績は「優」だった My math grade was "*very good*." ‖ 私は全優だ I *got straight A's*. **《参考》**英米では一般的には A, B, C, D, F が評価に使われ，「優」に相当するのが A，「良」が B，「可」が C，「一応の可」が D，「不可」が F である．

2**ゆう 結う** ▶近頃は和風に髪を結う人は極めて少ない These days very few women *put up their hair* in traditional Japanese style. (➤ put up one's hair で「(髪を)結う」の意).

ゆうあい 友愛 friendship；《米》**fraternity**(男性間の)；《米》**sorority**(女性間の).

1**ゆうい 優位 an advantage** ▶その都市は8年後のオリンピック誘致で優位に立っている The city has the *advantage* in the bid to host the Olympic Games eight years from now.

2**ゆうい 有為の promising**(有望な)；**talented**(才能のある) ▶前途有為の青年 a youth with a *promising future* ／a young person of *promise*.

ゆういぎ 有意義な meaningful(意味のある)；**instructive**(教育的でためになる)；**worthwhile**(価値のある) ▶誰もが有意義な人生を送りたいと思っている Everybody wants to lead a *meaningful* life. ‖ 有意義なお話，ありがとうございました Thank you very much for your *instructive* talk.
▶この寄付金は何か有意義なことに役立ててください I hope you'll use this donation for something *worthwhile*. ‖ 時間を有意義に(＝有効に)使いなさい Utilize your time *effectively*. ／Try to use your time *to advantage*.

ゆういん 誘因 a cause(原因) ▶過度のストレスが彼の神経衰弱の誘因となった Too much stress was *a cause* of his nervous breakdown. ／Too much stress caused [brought on] his nervous breakdown.

ゆううつ 憂鬱 depression(気がふさいで何もする気にならないこと)；**melancholy** /mélənkɑ̀ːli/ (たったひとりでもの悲しいこと) **一形 憂鬱な depressing**；**gloomy**(陰気な)；**melancholy**(たったひとりでもの悲しい) ▶憂鬱な気分 a *melancholy* mood ‖ 憂鬱な天気が続いている We're having *gloomy* weather. ‖ 憂鬱そうな顔をして，どうしたの? You look *depressed* [look *down in the mouth* ／ look *blue*]. What's the matter? (➤ あとの2者のほうが憂鬱の程度が軽い) ‖ やり残している宿題のことを考えると憂鬱になる I *get depressed* [*feel blue*] when I think of the assignments still left to be done. ‖ **対話**「来週は期末試験だね」「ああ，ユーウツ!」"We have final exams next week." "How *depressing*!"

ゆうえい 遊泳 swimming ▶この海岸では遊泳禁止です *Swimming is not allowed* [*is prohibited*] at this beach. (➤ 掲示の「遊泳禁止」は No Swimming でよい) ‖ 宇宙遊泳をするのが私の夢だ My dream is to *walk in space* [to *do a spacewalk*] someday.

ゆうえき 有益な **useful**(十分に役立つ); **helpful**(助けになる); **instructive**(教育的でためになる); **valuable, invaluable**(価値がある; 後者が強意); **beneficial**(利益を与える)

▶有益なヒント a *useful* hint ‖ 有益な講義 an *instructive* lecture ‖ 彼のアドバイスは有益だった His advice *was helpful* [*beneficial*]. ‖ オーストラリア旅行は有益だった My trip to Australia was very *fruitful*. (➤「実りがあった」の意).

▶この辞書はすべての英語学習者にとって(とても)有益だ This dictionary is *valuable* [*invaluable*] to all students of English. ‖ 夏休みを有益に過ごせとY先生が言った Mr. Y told us to *make the most of* the summer vacation. (➤ make the most of は「…をできる限り有効に使う」).

ゆうえつ 優越 **superiority** 一動 **優越する** **be superior**; **surpass** +目 (…をしのぐ).

ゆうえつかん 優越感 a **superiority complex** ▶日本人の中にはほかのアジア人に対して優越感をもっている人がいる Some Japanese *feel superior to* [*have a superiority complex toward*] other Asians. / Some Japanese think they *are better than* [*superior to*] other Asians.

ゆうえんち 遊園地 an **amusement park**, 《英》a **funfair** ▶遊園地は休日を楽しむ人たちで大変なにぎわいだった The *amusement park* was crowded with holidaymakers.

‖子供遊園地 an amusement park for children.

「遊園地の乗り物」のいろいろ 回転木馬 carousel, merry-go-round / ゴーカート go-kart / ジェットコースター roller coaster / 大観覧車 Ferris wheel / ティーカップ teacups / 電車 train ride / バンパーカー bumper car, Dodgem

ゆうが 優雅 **elegance**(身につけた優美さ); **grace**(天性の優美さ) 一形 **優雅な** **elegant, graceful** 一副 **優雅に** **elegantly, gracefully** ▶あの女優は身のこなしが優雅だ That actress carries herself *elegantly* [*gracefully*].

▶豪華客船で世界一周旅行とは優雅だね Going on an around-the-world trip on a luxury liner? They're *really living it up* [*living the high life*].

ゆうかい 誘拐 **kidnapping, abduction** (➤ 前者が身代金目的に対して, 後者は危害を加えたり逃がさないようにしたりすることに用いる) 一動 **誘拐する** **kidnap** +目, **abduct** +目 ▶先日幼稚園児が身代金目当てに誘拐された The other day, a kindergarten child *was kidnapped* for ransom.

‖誘拐犯 a kidnapper, an abductor.

ゆうがい 有害な **harmful**(害になる); **hazardous** (危険性のある) ▶これらの食品には有害な添加物が入っている These foods contain *harmful* additives. ‖ 喫煙は健康に有害である Smoking is *bad for* [*hazardous to*] your health.

▶アスベストは有害物質だ Asbestos is *a toxic substance*. (➤ toxic は「毒性のある」).

‖有害コンテンツ harmful [offensive] content (on the Internet) ‖ 有害情報 harmful [offensive] information.

ゆうがお 夕顔 《植物》a **moonflower** (ヨルガオ); a **(bottle) gourd**(ヒョウタン).

ゆうかぜ 夕風 an **evening breeze** ▶夏の夕風に当たる feel *a summer evening breeze*.

ゆうがた 夕方 (an) **evening**

> 語法 (1)evening は時に日没近くから床に就くまでの広い時間帯を指すことがある.
> (2)「夕方に」は in the evening だが, 特定の日の夕方には on を使い, *on* the evening of the 25th (25日の夕方に)のようにいう.
> (3)this evening (きょうの夕方), tomorrow evening (あすの夕方)などでは前置詞はつけない.

▶大部分のサラリーマンは朝9時から夕方5時まで働く Most office workers work from nine in the morning to five *in the evening*. (● work nine to five と表現することが多い) ‖ 土曜日の夕方は大抵出掛けています I'm usually out (*on*) *Saturday evenings*. (● 複数形のときは《米》では on を省略する) ‖ きのうの夕方きみの家に寄ったんだよ I dropped by your place *yesterday evening*.

▶夕方にかけて雷雨があるかもしれません We may have a thunderstorm *toward evening* [*in the late afternoon*]. ‖ 夕方のラッシュアワーが始まった The *evening* rush hour has begun. ‖ 夕方になった(＝暗くなってきた)ので家路に就いた We started for home because *it was getting dark*. ‖ 夕方までには帰るわ I'll be home *by evening* [*before dark*]. (➤ 後者は「暗くならないうちに」).

ゆうがとう 誘蛾灯 a **light trap**.

ユーカリ 《植物》a **eucalyptus** /jùːkəlíptəs/ ▶ユーカリの葉はコアラの好物だ *Eucalyptus leaves* are koalas' favorite food.

[1]**ゆうかん 夕刊** an **evening paper**(夕刊新聞); **the evening edition** (朝刊に対して).

[2]**ゆうかん 勇敢な** **courageous, brave**; **gallant**(騎士・武士が) →勇気 ▶燃え盛る火の中に飛び込んで子供を救出するとは実に勇敢な行為だ Jumping into the blazing fire to save the child was truly a *courageous* act. ‖ コサック兵は勇敢さをもって知られた Cossack soldiers were famous for their *bravery*.

[3]**ゆうかん 有閑** ‖有閑階級 the leisured class(es) ‖ 有閑マダム a lady of leisure.

[1]**ゆうき 勇気** **courage** /kə́ːrɪdʒ ‖ kʌ́rɪdʒ/, **bravery** (➤ 前者は精神的な強さに, 後者は行動力に力点がある); **gallantry**(騎士・武士の勇敢さ); **grit**(難局に立ち向かう気骨) 一形 **勇気ある** **courageous, brave** 一動 **勇気づける** **encourage** +目 ▶勇気を出せよ! Have *courage*! / Be brave! ‖ 勇気を出して飛び降りろ *Be brave* and jump! ‖ 我々は国の民主化のために闘った人々の勇気をたたえます We honor the *courage* of the people who fought for the democratization of the country. ‖ 私はあのときお母さんにすべてを打ち明ける勇気がなかった I *didn't have the courage* to tell my mother everything at the time. ‖「嫌だ」と言うにはとても勇気が要ることがある At times, it *takes a lot of courage* to say no. ‖ きみの顔を見たら勇気が湧いてきたよ Seeing you has *given me courage*. / Seeing you has *filled me with courage*. ‖ カウンセラーの三木さんと話すといつも勇気づけられる Whenever I talk to my counselor, Mr. Miki, I *am encouraged*.

▶部長に盾つくとは彼女も勇気があるね It *was courageous* of her to contradict her manager.

[2]**ゆうき 有機の** **organic** ▶このパソコンソフトは5つの主なプログラムが有機的に結ばれている In this computer

software, five main programs are *organically* integrated.

‖有機化学 organic chemistry ‖有機化合物 an organic compound ‖有機栽培 organic farming [cultivation] ‖有機食品 (an) organic food ‖有機水銀 organic mercury ‖有機農業 organic farming [agriculture] ‖有機農産物 organic (farm) produce, organically-grown produce ‖有機発光ダイオード an OLED, an organic light-emitting diode ‖有機肥料 (an) organic fertilizer ‖有機物 organic matter ‖有機野菜 an organic vegetable.

3ゆうき 有期 a **fixed term**

‖有期雇用 fixed-term employment ‖有期雇用契約 a fixed-term employment contract ‖有期雇用者 a fixed-term employee.

1ゆうぎ 遊戯 (a) **play**, a **game** ▶語呂合わせはことばの遊戯だ A pun is *a play* on words. ‖子供は遊戯をするのが好きだ Children like to *play games*. ‖さあ, お遊戯の時間よ It's *play time* (now)!

‖遊戯室 a playroom (子供用の) ; a recreation room (娯楽室) ‖遊戯場 a place of amusement, a playground.

2ゆうぎ 友誼 **friendship**(友情) ; **fellowship**(同志の情).

3ゆうぎ 遊技 ▶遊技施設 a *recreational* facility.

1ゆうきゅう 有給 ▶有給休暇は年に何日もらえますか How many days of *paid vacation* can I get per year? ‖有給休暇は14日取得できます You can have 14 days of *paid leave*. ‖有給休暇を3日取った I took three *days off with pay*. 《参考》超過勤務に対する報酬的な有給休暇で, 残業代の代わりになるものを comp time と呼ぶ.

2ゆうきゅう 遊休の **idle** ‖遊休地 idle land.

ゆうきょう 遊興

‖遊興費 entertainment expense(s).

ゆうぎょせん 遊漁船 a **sportfishing boat**.

ゆうぐ 遊具 **playground equipment**.

ゆうぐう 優遇 ▶人を優遇する *treat* a person *well* ‖当社では経験のある方を優遇いたします Experienced employees *are well paid* at our company. (➤「高給が支払われる」の意) ‖日本の社会では政治家は優遇されている Politicians *receive preferential treatment* in Japanese society. (➤「優先的な扱いを受けている」の意).

ゆうぐれ 夕暮れ **dusk** ; **evening**(夕方) ▶この辺りは夕暮れの景色が殊に良い The view is particularly beautiful around here at *dusk*.

ゆうけい 有形 ▶大学はスポーツ選手の学生に有形無形の援助を与えている The university administration gives *moral and material support* to student athletes. ‖有形資産 tangible assets.

ゆうげきしゅ 遊撃手《野球》a **shortstop**.

1ゆうげん 有限の **limited** ▶地球の資源は有限である (The) Earth's resources *are limited*.

‖有限会社《米》a corporation《略 Corp.》, an incorporated company《略 Co. Inc. または Inc.》,《英》a limited company《略 Ltd. または Limited.》.

2ゆうげん 幽玄 *yugen* ; **subtle profundity** ▶薪能の幽玄な趣 the aesthetic atmosphere of *subtle profundity* of takigi noh play(noh play lit by bonfires).

ゆうげんじっこう 有言実行 ▶彼はまさに有言実行の人だ He's a person who *practices what he preaches* [*walks his talk*].

ゆうけんしゃ 有権者 a **voter**(投票する人) ; an **elector**(選挙人) ; **the electorate** (有権者たち) ▶有権者の意向を見極める discern the intent of *the voter(s)* ‖有権者の皆さま, どうか棄権しないようにお願いします *Voters*, we ask you to go to the polls and exercise your right to vote. ‖彼の政見は有権者たちから広範な支持を得た His political opinions won broad support from *the electorate*.

1ゆうこう 友好 **friendship** 一形 友好的な **friendly** ▶これは両国の友好を回復する絶好の機会だ This is a good chance to restore *friendship* [*friendly relations*] between the two nations. ‖日本はアジア諸国ともっと友好関係を推進すべきだ Japan should further promote *friendly relations* with other Asian countries.

▶現地の人たちは我々に対して友好的[非友好的]だった The local people were *friendly* [*unfriendly*] to us.

‖友好国 a friendly nation ‖友好条約 a treaty of friendship, a friendship treaty.

2ゆうこう 有効な **effective**(効果的な) ; **efficient**(効率的な) ; **valid** (効力のある) ; **good**(通用する) ▶4月1日から有効の新しい時刻表 a new timetable *effective* from April 1 ‖戦争を終結させるための有効な手段を取る take *effective* measures to stop a war ‖時間を有効に使いなさい *Make good use of* your time. / *Use* your time *wisely*. (➤ wisely は「賢く」) ‖石油は有効に使いましょう Let's *use* oil *efficiently* [*without waste*].

▶この運転免許証は5年間有効です This driver's license is *valid* [*good*] for five years. ‖この切符はいつまで有効ですか How long is this ticket *valid* [*good*]? ‖きみの通勤定期は有効期限が切れている Your commuter pass *has* already *expired*.

ゆうごう 融合 **fusion** (溶け合うこと) 一動 融合する **fuse** /fjuːz/ ; **blend** (混ざる) ▶油と水は融合しない Oil and water will not *mix* [*blend*]. ‖東西の文化はコンスタンティノープルで見事に融合された Eastern and Western cultures *have fused* remarkably in Constantinople. ‖太陽は水素原子を融合させてヘリウムを作っている The sun *fuses* hydrogen atoms *into* helium.

‖核融合 nuclear fusion.

ゆうごはん 夕御飯 →夕食.

ユーザー a **user** ▶インターネット [コンピュータ] ユーザー an Internet [a computer] *user* ‖ユーザーに優しいパソコン a *user-friendly* PC ‖ユーザー名とパスワードを入力してください Please enter your *user name* and password.

ゆうざい 有罪の **guilty** /gílti/ ▶彼は有罪か無罪かまだ決まっていない It has not yet been determined whether he is *guilty* or not. ‖裁判官はその被告に有罪を宣告した The judge *convicted* the defendant. / The defendant *was judged guilty*.

ゆうさんかいきゅう 有産階級 **the bourgeois** [**propertied**] **class**.

1ゆうし 有志 a **volunteer** /vɑ̀ːləntíə^r/ (志願者) ▶キャンパスの空き缶を拾う有志の方を募集しています We are looking for *volunteers* to pick up empty cans on campus. ‖ジェリーさん, これは教授会有志からのプレゼントです Jerry, this is something for you from the faculty (members). (この文では特に「有志」を訳出する必要はない).

2ゆうし 融資 **financing**(貸し付けること) ; a **loan**(貸付金) 一動 融資する **finance** +目 ▶新車購入のための融

資をしてもらう get *financing* for a new car ‖ 開発事業に**融資する** *finance* a development project ‖ 資金を**融資する**ことは銀行の主な業務の１つである *Lending money* [*Making loans*] is one of the main services a bank provides. ‖ 当社はM銀行から**融資を受けた** We *borrowed money* [*got a loan*] from M Bank. ‖ T銀行は当社への**融資**を拒否した T Bank refused to *lend* us *money* [*give* us *a loan*].

‖**不正融資** bank fraud, lending fraud.

3**ゆうし 雄姿** a **magnificent** [**majestic**] **figure** ▶ヒマラヤの**雄姿**をこの目で見たい I'd like to see the *majestic* Himalayas with my own eyes.

4**ゆうし 勇士** a **brave soldier**(勇敢な兵士)；a **brave man**(勇者).

5**ゆうし 有史** ▶**有史**以前の時代 the *prehistoric* age ‖ その市の郊外で**有史**以前の人間の頭蓋骨が数個発掘された In a suburb of the city some *prehistoric* human skulls have been excavated.

ゆうじ 有事 ▶**有事**に備える prepare for *an emergency* [*a contingency*].

ゆうしかく 有資格の **qualified**；**licensed**(免許のある)；**eligible**(適格の)

‖**有資格者** a qualified person.

ゆうしきしゃ 有識者 a **knowledgeable** [**well-informed**] **person**；an **expert**(エキスパート) ▶政府は行政改革に関して**有識者**たちの意見を求めた The government sought the advice of *experts* on administrative reform.

ゆうしてっせん 有刺鉄線 **barbed wire** ▶その貯水池は**有刺鉄線**で囲まれている That reservoir is fenced with *barbed wire*.

ゆうしゃ 勇者 a **brave person**, a **person of courage** [**valor**].

1**ゆうしゅう 優秀な** **excellent** ▶**優秀な**生徒 an *excellent* [*a brilliant*] student (➤ brilliant は「才気あふれる」) ‖ わが社は**優秀な**人材を求めています We are looking for *first-rate* men and women to join our company. ‖ 彼は**優秀な成績**で試験に合格した He passed the examination *with a high score*. (➤ 1回の成績の場合).

▶彼女は**優秀な成績**で大学を卒業した She graduated from college *with excellent grades* [*with high marks* / *with honors*]. (➤ 卒業時に特別表彰される優等生を honor student という；→優等) ‖ 日本製品の**優秀さ**は世界的に認められている The *excellence* [*good quality*] of Japanese products is recognized around the world.

‖**優秀賞** a prize for excellence, a merit prize.

☛ **最優秀**(→見出語)

2**ゆうしゅう 憂愁** **melancholy.**

ゆうしゅうのび 有終の美 ▶ペナントレースを制覇した中日は最終戦においてヤクルトを４対１で破り，**有終の美**を飾った The Dragons, winners of the pennant, *capped* the victory by beating the Swallows 4-1 at their final game. (➤ cap は「見事に締めくくる」の意).

ゆうじゅうふだん 優柔不断な **indecisive**, **irresolute** (➤ 後者がより堅い語) ▶彼は**優柔不断な**男だ He is an *indecisive* [*irresolute*] man. ‖ 監督の**優柔不断**が原因で試合に負けた The manager's *indecision* [*indecisiveness*] led to the team's loss.

ゆうしゅつ 湧出 **gush** 一動 **湧出する** **gush** [**spring**] **out** ▶石油の年間**湧出量** *the* annual *output* of oil.

1**ゆうしょう 優勝** a **victory**(勝利)；a **championship**(優勝者の地位) 一動 **優勝する** **win the championship**, **take** [**get**] **first prize** ▶どのチームが**優勝した**の Which team *won the championship*? (➤ won /wʌn/ は win の過去形) ‖ 彼は県の水泳大会で**優勝した** He *took first prize* in the prefectural swim meet. ‖ わが校は合唱コンクールで**優勝した** Our school *won* (*first prize* in) the chorus contest. ‖ 広島と巨人が**優勝**を争っている The Carp and the Giants are competing for the *pennant*. (➤ pennant は「優勝旗」) ‖ **優勝**を懸けて(＝決勝戦で)フランスとブラジルのサッカーチームが戦った The French and Brazilian soccer teams played *in the final match*. ‖ その横綱は今場所も**優勝候補の筆頭**だ The yokozuna is *the odds-on favorite* in this sumo tournament again. (➤ the favorite は「本命」, odds-on は「大いに勝ち目のある」の意).

✉ **優勝おめでとう** Congratulations on *winning the championship*.

‖**優勝カップ** a trophy /tróʊfi/ ‖ **優勝旗** a championship flag, a pennant ‖ **優勝者** a champion, a winner ‖ **優勝チーム** the winning team.

> **逆引き熟語 ○○優勝**
> **逆転優勝** a come-from-behind victory ／**準優勝** the second place；the runner-up(チーム) ／**全勝優勝者** the undefeated champion ／**地区優勝** a division title ／**初優勝** the first victory ／**リーグ優勝** the league title ／**連続優勝** successive [consecutive] victories

2**ゆうしょう 有償** ▶過去の美術展のカタログ，在庫分を**有償**にておわけします Catalogues of past art exhibitions (that we have in stock) are available *for purchase*. ‖ **有償**ですか無償ですか Do we have to *pay* (*for it*) or is it free (of charge)?

ゆうじょう 友情 **friendship** ▶真の**友情**は金では買えない True *friendship* cannot be bought with money. ‖ 2人は固い**友情**で結ばれていた Those two were united by strong *friendship*. ‖ 高校時代には**良い友情が結ばれる**(＝良い友だちができる) You can *find* [*meet*] *good friends* in high school. ‖ 彼は**友情にあつい男**だ He is *a very good friend to have*.

ゆうしょく 夕食 **supper**；**dinner**(ごちそうの出る) ▶**夕食**の時間ですよ It's time for *supper*. ／*Dinner*'s ready. ‖ 早めに**夕食**を済ませておこう Let's have an early *supper*.

ゆうしょくじんしゅ 有色人種 **people of color**, **the colored races** (➤ 後者は最近では差別語と見なされる).

1**ゆうじん 友人** a **friend** ▶**友人**の紹介でマキと知り合った I met Maki through *a friend of mine*. ‖ **友人**の小田君がこの仕事を手伝ってくれた *My friend* Oda [Oda, *a friend of mine*,] helped me with this project.

▶アメリカ留学中に大勢の**友人**ができました I *made* a lot of *friends* while studying in the U.S.

> **直訳の落とし穴「友人ができる」**
> 「私には旅行中にいい［新しい］友人ができた」のつもりで，(×)I got a good [new] friend during the trip. とするのは不自然.「友人ができる」は make a friend と make を使うのがふつうなので，I made a good [new] friend during the trip. とする. 相手をいう場合は I became [made] friends with a young musician.(若いミュージシャンと友人になった)と，複数形 friends になることに注意.

ゆ

²ゆうじん 有人の manned(➤ この語は男性を連想させるので staffed, crewed などで言いかえることもある) ▶火星への有人宇宙船 a *manned* spacecraft going to Mars ‖ 有人宇宙飛行をする make a *manned* space flight.

ゆうすう 有数の distinguished(科学・芸術などの分野で著名な) ; prominent (ぬきんでた) ; leading(主導的な) ; major (ほかより重要な) ▶クラウディオ・アバドは世界でも有数の指揮者だ Claudio Abbado is one of the most *distinguished* [*prominent*] conductors in the world.

⚠「有数の」は「屈指の」「指折りの」と同様に, 特定の形容詞を当てはめるのではなく「one of the ＋形容詞の最上級」で表現されることが多い.

▶(新潟の)長岡高校は日本でも有数の歴史の古い学校だ Nagaoka High School (in Niigata) is *one of the oldest* schools in Japan.

ゆうずう 融通 1【柔軟性】flexibility ▶あいつは融通の利く[利かない]男だ He's *flexible* [*inflexible*]. ‖ 商売で成功するには融通性がなくてはならない To get ahead in business you have to *be flexible* [*adaptable*]. ‖ 彼は融通が利かないために同僚から煙たがられている His co-workers seem to keep away from him because of his *inflexibility* [*stubbornness*].

2【貸し借り】▶おじが20万円融通してくれた My uncle *lent* me [*helped* me *out* with] two hundred thousand yen. ‖ 私たちは僅かの食料を融通し合って(＝分け合って)暮らした We lived *sharing* the little food we had.

‖融通手形 an accommodation bill.

ゆうすずみ 夕涼み ▶夕食後, 土手に出て夕涼みをした After dinner, we went out to the riverbank and *enjoyed the evening cool* [*cooled ourselves in the evening air*].

ユースホステル a (youth) hostel.

¹ゆうせい 優勢 ▶私たちの学校では女の先生のほうが数の上で優勢だ Female teachers *outnumber* male teachers at our school. (➤ outnumber は「数で勝る」) ／At our school, female teachers *predominate over* male teachers (*in number*). ‖ 大方の予想は挑戦者よりチャンピオンのほうが優勢(＝有利)と見ている Most people believe the champion *has the advantage over* the challenger. ／Most people see the champion as *having an edge on* [*over*] the challenger.

▶ここまでは試合は中日が優勢だ So far the Dragons *are leading* [*are in the lead*]. ‖《柔道で》優勢勝ちする score *a yusei gachi* ／win *a yusei* [*superiority*] *decision*(➤ win by superiority ならほかのスポーツにも使える).

²ゆうせい 郵政 postal administration.

³ゆうせい 優性 →顕性.

ゆうぜい 遊説する travel around making political speeches,《米また》stump(+自), go on the stump ▶ジャクソン氏は南部諸州を遊説して回った Mr. Jackson *traveled around* the Southern states *making political speeches*. ／Mr. Jackson *stumped* the Southern states.

‖遊説演説 a political [stump] speech.

ゆうせいおん 有声音《音声学》a voiced sound.

ゆうせいらん 有精卵 a fertile [fertilized] egg.

ゆうせつ 融雪 the melting of snow

‖融雪剤 a snow-melting substance.

¹ゆうせん 優先する give priority《to》▶本学では帰国子女を優先的に入学させています In admitting students, we *give priority to* students who have recently come home from overseas. ‖ 政府は大震災からの復興を最優先させるべきだ The Government should *give top priority to* reconstruction efforts following the great earthquake. ‖ 会社の経営者はとかく利益の追求を社員の福祉に優先させようとする Company managers tend to *consider* pursuit of profit *to be more important than* the welfare of employees [*put* profit-making *before* the welfare of employees]. ‖ 緊急車両には道路通行の際の優先権が与えられている Emergency vehicles have [are given] *priority* on the road. ‖ ここはお年寄りや体の不自由な人のための優先席です This is *priority seating* for the elderly and the physically disabled. ‖ 患者の生命が我々の最優先の関心事でなければならない Our patients' lives must be our *overriding* concern. (➤ overriding は「最も重要な」).

‖優先順位 the order of priority(➤「優先順位をつける」は set priorities).

²ゆうせん 有線

‖有線テレビ cable television ; community antenna television《略 CATV》‖ 有線放送 closed-circuit [cable] broadcasting.

ゆうぜん 悠然と calmly /kɑ́:mli/ ▶彼はいつも悠然としている He always *remains calm*. ‖ 台風の夜も私たちは悠然と夕食を食べた We ate dinner *calmly* [*leisurely*] even on the night of the typhoon.

¹ゆうそう 郵送する mail +目,《英》post +目 ; send … by mail [post] ▶彼に本を郵送する *mail* [*post*] him a book ／*mail* [*post*] a book to him ／*send* a book to him *by mail* [*by post*] ‖ 警察署長の家にナイフが郵送されてきた A knife *was sent by mail* to the police chief's house. ‖ この小包の郵送料はいくらですか What is the *postage* on [for] this parcel?

²ゆうそう 勇壮 ▶勇壮なマーチ a *heroic* [*stirring*] march.

ユーターン a U-turn ▶《掲示》Uターン禁止 No U-turn ‖ Uターンをして戻ることにしよう Let's *make* [*do*] *a U-turn* and go back.

▶《比喩的》大都市の職場を捨てて故郷にUターンする会社員が増えている An increasing number of office workers are quitting their jobs in the big city to *seek employment in their hometowns*. ‖ 彼は東京からのUターン組だ He *came back* after working in Tokyo for a while.

‖Uターンラッシュ the return rush to urban areas (following national holidays).

¹ゆうたい 勇退 ▶彼は後進に道を開くため勇退した He *retired voluntarily* to make way for younger people.

²ゆうたい 幽体 an astral body

‖幽体離脱 astral projection.

ゆうだい 雄大な grand (壮麗な) ; spectacular (壮大な) ; magnificent (堂々として立派な) ▶雄大な景色 *grand* scenery ‖ 私たちはグランドキャニオンの雄大な眺めを楽しんだ We enjoyed the *magnificent* view of the Grand Canyon. ‖ マッキンリー山は雲の上に雄大にそびえている Mount McKinley rises *magnificently* above the clouds.

ゆうたいけん 優待券 a complimentary ticket.

ゆうたいどうぶつ 有袋動物《動物学》a marsupial /mɑːˈsúːpiəl/.

ゆうだち 夕立 a **shower** ▶夕立になりそうだ It looks like *a shower* is coming. ‖ 夕立に遭うといけないから傘を持って行きなさいよ Take an umbrella with you in case you are caught in *a shower*.

ゆうだん 勇断 ▶その博覧会中止の**勇断**を下す make the *drastic decision* to cancel the exposition.

ゆうだんしゃ 有段者 a ***dan*** [**grade**] **holder**, a person with a rank of sho-dan [first dan] or higher (➤説明的な訳).

ゆうち 誘致する **invite** +㊐ ▶市にT自動車の工場を**誘致する** *invite* T Motor Corporation *to build* its factory in the city ‖ 我々はアメリカの大学の分校をこの市に**誘致する**計画だ We plan to *ask* an American university *to open a branch campus* in this city.

ユーチューブ **YouTube** ▶ユーチューブに動画をアップする upload a video to *YouTube*.

ゆうちょう 悠長な **slow**(遅い); **leisurely** (のんびりした) ▶そんな**悠長な**ことを言っている場合ではない There is no time for *leisurely* [*unhurried*] *explanations*.

▶そんなに**悠長に**していていいの? あすは試験でしょ How can you *take it* so *easy*? You're having a test tomorrow, aren't you?

ゆうづき 夕月 an **evening moon**.

ゆうてん 融点 《物理学》a **melting temperature**, **the melting point**.

ゆうとう 優等 **honors** /ɑ́:nəʳz/ (大学の) ▶フレッドはシカゴ大学を**優等**で卒業した Fred graduated from the University of Chicago *with honors*.

> **《解説》** (1)ここでは「優等で」を with honors と訳したが, アメリカの大学では卒業時の成績優秀者を3段階に分けているところも多く, 最高位の成績で卒業することを summa cum laude /sòmə kom láʊdi/, 第2位の成績で卒業することを magna cum laude, 第3位の成績で卒業することを cum laude と呼ぶ(いずれもラテン語). これらを用いる場合, 上の例の with honors の代わりにそこに置くか, graduate と from の間に置けばよい.
> (2)ただし, 日本の「優等生」が, 通例1名(か2名)であるのに対して, アメリカの各位の優秀者は, 一定の成績以上を取っていれば, 何人でも選ばれるので, 日本の優等生とは実質が異なる. →**首席**.

‖**優等賞** an honor (prize [award]) ‖ **優等生** an honor student (特別表彰される;「特待生」の意もある); an outstanding student; a straight-A student (オール5の).

ゆうどう 誘導する **lead** +㊐ (先に立って); **guide** +㊐ (一緒に案内して) ▶火災訓練で客を**誘導する** *lead* [*guide*] the customers in a fire drill ‖ 飛行機は管制塔に**誘導されて**着陸する Planes land *following the instructions* from the control tower. ‖ 子供たちに**誘導尋問**をしないでください Don't ask the children *leading questions*.

‖**誘導弾** a guided missile.

ゆうどく 有毒な **poisonous**, **toxic** ▶このキノコは**有毒**です This mushroom is *poisonous*.

‖**有毒ガス** poisonous gas.

ユートピア an **ideal** [**a wonderful**] **place**; (a) **heaven** (最高にすばらしい場所[状態]); (a) **utopia** /jutóʊpiə/ 《**参考**》英語の utopia という語はトマス・モアの小説 *Utopia* が語源で,「(現実には存在しない)理想郷」を指すが, 比喩的に「理想社会[国家]」「理想的な場所」の意味でも使う. これに対して, 日本語の「ユートピア」は単に「すばらしい場所」の意味で使うことも多い. したがって, 訳例のような別の言い方をするほうが好ましい.

▶**ユートピア**の建設が私たちの夢です The construction of *an ideal world* is our dream. ‖ この高齢者ホームはお年寄りたちの**ユートピア**だ The senior citizens' home is *a heaven* [*is a utopia*] for its elderly residents.

ゆうなぎ 夕凪 an **evening calm**.

ゆうに 優に **well**(十分に) ▶EXILE のコンサートには**優に**1万人を超すファンが詰めかけた *Well over* ten thousand fans went to the EXILE concert. (➤更にくだけた場合 Way over ... ともいう).

ゆうのう 有能な **able**; **capable**(資格・経験があって;堅い語); **competent**(仕事などに要求される能力を持つ); **efficient** (てきぱきやる) ▶**有能な**人 a person *of ability* / a *capable* person ‖ 彼は多くの事件を扱ってきた**有能な**弁護士です He is an *able* [*a competent*] lawyer who has handled many cases. ‖ 西田さんは**有能な**通訳です Miss Nishida is an *skilled* interpreter. ‖ 他社より高い給料を払わなければ**有能な**人材は集まらない You cannot expect *competent* [*capable*] workers to join your company if you don't pay better salaries than other companies.

ゆうばえ 夕映え **the evening glow** ▶古城は**夕映え**に輝いていた The old castle was shining in *the evening glow*.

ゆうはつ 誘発する **induce** +㊐; **trigger** +㊐ (引き金となる) ▶かぜが余病を**誘発する**こともある A cold can *lead to* [*bring on*] complications. ‖ 人工的に排卵を**誘発した**ので5つ子が生まれた The quintuplets were born as the result of artificially *induced* ovulation. ‖ 雪崩を**誘発する** *trigger* an avalanche.

ゆうはん 夕飯 →**夕食**.

ゆうひ 夕日 **the setting sun**(沈む太陽); **the evening sun** (夕方の太陽) ▶**夕日**が部屋にさし込んできた *The evening sun* streamed into the room.

ゆうび 優美 **grace**(体の動きなどが); **elegance**(身につけた上品さ) 一形 **優美な** **graceful**, **elegant** ▶**優美な**物腰 a *graceful* [*refined*] manner ‖ 王妃は**優美な**ドレスを着て現れた The queen appeared in an *elegant* dress.

ゆうびん 郵便

mail, 《英》**post** (➤集合的に「郵便物」を指し, a をつけたり, 複数形にしたりしない) ▶**郵便**が来てるよ There's some *mail* for you. ‖ うちでは**郵便**は大抵11時頃来る The [Our] *mail* is usually delivered to our house (at) around eleven. ‖ きょうはまだ**郵便**が来ていない The *mail* hasn't come yet today. ‖ きょうはずいぶん**郵便**が多い We have had a lot of *mail* today. ‖ きょうは**郵便**が5通来た Today I got five *letters* [five pieces of *mail*]. ‖ 申込書は**郵便**で送ってください Please send the application form *by mail*. / Please mail (in) the application form. ‖ 父は**郵便**(=手紙)を出しに行きました My father went to mail *a letter*. ‖ スイスに**郵便**を出したいんですが何日くらいで届きますか I'd like to send some *mail* to Switzerland. How many days will it take to get there?

‖**郵便受け** 《米》a mailbox, 《英》a letter [post] box 《**参考**》壁やドアなどに設置された投げ込み式のものは《米》では特に mail slot という ‖ **郵便為替** a postal money order ‖ **郵便切手** a postage stamp ‖ **郵便局** a post office ‖ **郵便局長** a postmaster ‖ **郵**

便小包 a parcel ; parcel post(➤集合的) ‖ **郵便制度** a postal system ‖ **郵便貯金** postal savings ‖ **郵便配達** mail [postal] delivery ‖ **郵便配達人** a mail [letter] carrier ‖ **郵便番号** a postal code, 《米また》a zip code, 《英また》a postcode ‖ **郵便物** mail, postal matter(➤ともに集合的) ‖ **郵便振替** (a) postal transfer《参考》イギリスではコンピュータのオンラインシステムによる郵便[銀行]振替を giro /dʒáɪəroʊ/ と呼ぶ ‖ **郵便ポスト**《米》a mailbox, 《英》a pillar box (➤《英》では letter box, postbox をこの意でも用いる) ‖ **郵便料金** postage, postal charges.

逆引き熟語 ○○郵便
宛名不明の郵便 blind mail ／**外国郵便** foreign mail ／**書留郵便** registered mail [post] ／**航空郵便** airmail ／**国際郵便** international mail ／**国内郵便** domestic mail ／**小包郵便** parcel post ／**速達郵便** express mail, special [express] delivery ／**配達証明郵便** certified mail ／**普通郵便** ordinary mail ／**翌日配達郵便** overnight mail ／**料金別納郵便** metered mail ; bulk mail (ダイレクトメールなど大量に送られる同一内容の郵便)

ユーブイ UV(ultraviolet(紫外線の)の略) ▶**UVカット**の化粧品 *UV-protective* [*-blocking*] cosmetics.

ゆ

ユーフォー a **UFO** (➤an unidentified flying object(未確認飛行物体)の略；発音は /jù:efóʊ/ がふつうで /jú:foʊ/ では通じない場合がある).

ゆうふく 裕福な rich, wealthy /wélθi/ (➤後者のほうが堅い語) ; **well-to-do** /wèltədú:/ (金があって社会的地位も高い) ▶ケネディー氏は**裕福な**家に生まれた Mr. Kennedy was born *rich* [was born into a *wealthy* family]. ‖ **裕福な**顧客たち a *wealthy* [*well-heeled*] clientele ‖ 20年前と比べて私たちはずいぶん**裕福になった** We are much *better off* now than (we were) twenty years ago. (➤原級は well off で,「暮らしが楽な」の意).

[1]ゆうべ 夕べ (an) **evening** ▶秋の**夕べ**, 縁側に出て満月を眺めて楽しんだ On an autumn *evening*, I enjoyed the view of the full moon out on the veranda facing the garden.
▶弦楽合奏の**夕べ** a string concert *evening* ／a *soiree* /swɑ:réɪ/ with a string orchestra.

[2]ゆうべ 昨夜 last night, yesterday evening ▶**ゆうべ**は一睡もできなかった I couldn't get a wink of sleep *last night*. ‖ **ゆうべ**はとても楽しかった I had a very good time *yesterday evening*. ‖ **ゆうべから**雨が降り続いている It has been raining *since last night*.

ゆうへい 幽閉 confinement ▶12歳のエドワードは弟のリチャードとともにロンドン塔に**幽閉された** The 12-year-old Edward *was confined* to the Tower of London along with his younger brother Richard.

ゆうべん 雄弁 eloquence /éləkwəns/ **一形 雄弁な eloquent** ▶聴衆は長谷川氏の**雄弁**に深い感銘を受けた The audience was deeply impressed with Mr. Hasegawa's *eloquence*. ‖ パトリック・ヘンリーは**雄弁な**愛国者だった Patrick Henry was an *eloquent* patriot. ‖ この1通の書状は彼がクリスチャンだったことを**雄弁に物語っている** This one letter *testifies* to his Christian faith.

ゆうぼう 有望な promising(前途が有望な) ; **hopeful** (末頼もしい) ▶**有望な**ダンサー a *promising* [*hopeful*] dancer ／a dancer *with a bright future* ‖ その選手の三冠王は**有望だ** That player *has a good chance of* winning the triple crown. ‖ ことしの米作は**有望らしい** It looks like we will have a *good* rice crop this year. ‖ **有望株**を教えてください Could you tell me what *stocks are promising*?

ゆうぼく 遊牧の nomadic /noʊmǽdɪk/ ▶内蒙古(もうこ)には**遊牧生活**を営んでいる人々がいる In Inner Mongolia some people lead *a nomadic life*.
‖**遊牧民** a nomad /nóʊmæd/ ‖ **遊牧民族** a nomadic people [tribe].

ゆうほどう 遊歩道 a **promenade** /prɑ̀:mənéɪd/.

ゆうめい 有名 一形 有名な famous (for, as) ; **well-known**(広く知られた)(➤名詞の前以外は well known がふつう) ; **distinguished**(著名な) ; **notorious** (悪名の高い)

【文型】
A は B [C] で有名である
A **is famous for** B.
A **is famous as** C.

《解説》 for B は「Bによって, Bのことで」でA≠Bの関係にあり, as C は「Cとして」でA＝Cの関係にある. well known などほかの語も同様に for と as を使い分ける.

▶釧路は美しい夕日が**有名です** Kushiro *is famous for* (its) beautiful sunsets. ‖ 軽井沢は避暑地として**有名だ** Karuizawa *is famous* [*is well known*] *as* a summer resort.
▶芭蕉の**有名な**俳句 a *famous* haiku by Basho ‖ **世界的に有名な**俳優 a *world-famous* actor ‖ スイスは山の景色の美しさで**有名である** Switzerland *is renowned for* the beauty of its mountain scenery. (➤renowned は少し改まった語で確固たる知名度や名声を暗示する) ‖ クリストファー・レンは**有名な**建築家だった Christopher Wren *was renowned as* an architect. ／Christopher Wren was a *renowned* architect. ‖ その国はソフトウェアの著作権侵害が多いことで**有名だ** That country *is notorious for* software piracy.
▶木村君は校内でとても**有名です** *Everybody knows* Kimura at our school. ／Kimura *is well known* at our school.《参考》「学内で有名な人気者」のことを《米・インフォーマル》で a big wheel on campus, または男子学生の場合は特に a big man on campus (略して B.M.O.C.)という.
▶私は**有名になりたい** I want to *be famous*. ／I have a desire for *fame*. ‖ 平野さんは処女作で**有名になった** Mr. Hirano *became famous* with his first novel. ‖ 伊藤さんの結婚披露宴には**有名人**が多数招待された A lot of *famous people* [*celebrities*] were invited to Mr. Ito's wedding reception. (➤celebrity /səlébrəṭi/ はタレントや俳優などを含めた「有名人」).
‖**有名校** a prestigious [prestige] school.

ゆうめいむじつ 有名無実 ▶**有名無実な**法律 a law *in name only*.

ユーモア humor /hjú:məʳ/, a **joke** ▶彼は**ユーモア(のセンス)がある** He *has a sense of humor*. ‖ 彼女は**ユーモアを解さない** She *has no sense of humor*. ／She is always serious and *never laughs at jokes*. ‖ おじの話は**ユーモアたっぷりだった**ので, 私たちは笑ってばかりいた My uncle's story was so *funny* we laughed the whole time.
‖**ユーモア作家** a humorist /hjú:mərɪst/, a humorous writer.

危ないカタカナ語✹ ユーモア
1 英語の humor からきているが，wit（機知，ウイット）が理性に訴えるものであるのに対して，humor は感情に訴え，人間的で温かいおかしみを指す語．冗談やしゃれの類いには humor よりも joke が相当する．
2「ユーモラス」も humorous からきているが，funny や amusing を使ったほうがよい場合も多い．

ゆうもうかかん 勇猛果敢な brave ▶**勇猛果敢な**戦士 a *brave* [*fearless*] warrior ‖**勇猛果敢な**武将 a *brave* [*daring*] general ‖**勇猛果敢に**敵を攻める attack the enemy *bravely* [*courageously*].

ゆうもや 夕靄 (an) **evening mist**（薄霧），(an) **evening haze**（かすみ）.

ユーモラス humorous /hjúːmərəs/ ▶山田さんの**ユーモラスな**話しっぷりはよく受けた Ms. Yamada's *humorous* [*amusing*] talk was well received. ‖ペンギンが歩く様子はとても**ユーモラスだ** The way penguins walk is really *funny*.（➤ funny は「おかしい」の意）.

ゆうやけ 夕焼け an **evening glow**; a **sunset**（日没）▶五島で見た**夕焼け**はすばらしかった I saw a fantastic *sunset* in Goto.
‖**夕焼け雲** sunset clouds ‖**夕焼け空** the sky aglow at [after] sunset.

ゆうやみ 夕闇 dusk /dʌsk/ ▶**夕闇**が迫ってきた *The evening dusk* is gathering. ‖**夕闇が迫る頃**彼らは釣りに出かけた They went fishing *at dusk* [*toward evening*].

ゆうゆう 悠々 **1**【慌てないで】▶赤信号になったのにあの老人は**悠々と**通りを渡っている Even though the light has turned red, that old man is *taking his time* to cross the street [is crossing the street *without any sign of hurry*].
▶《慣用表現》上野さんは退職後，**悠々自適の生活をしている** Mr. Ueno has been living *a life of ease* [living *a leisurely* (*and comfortable*) *life*] since he retired from his job.
2【ゆとりある】easily ▶この広間なら50人は**悠々**座れる This hall can seat 50 people *easily*. ‖10時発の電車に**悠々間に合った** I arrived for the ten o'clock train *well ahead of time*.

ゆうよ 猶予 **grace**（支払いなどの）; **delay**（遅れ）; **stay**（刑の執行猶予）▶大家さんは3日間の支払い**猶予を与えてくれた**けど全然お金の当てがない The landlord gave me three days' *grace*, but I still have no idea how to make the rent. ‖**事態はいささかの猶予も許さない**と思う We *have no time to lose* in this situation. ／I'm afraid that the situation *permits of no delay*.
☛ 執行猶予（→見出語）

ゆうよう 有用な **useful** ▶**有用な**機械 a *useful* machine ‖かびには**有用な**ものと，そうでないものとがある Some molds are *useful* and others not.

ユーラシア **Eurasia** /juréɪʒə/.

ゆうらん 遊覧 ‖**遊覧船** a pleasure boat, a cruise boat ‖**遊覧バス** a sightseeing bus ‖**遊覧飛行** a sightseeing flight, a flyover.

[1]**ゆうり 有利な** **advantageous**; **favorable**（都合のいい）; **profitable**（もうかる）▶何かの技能を身につけておくと就職に**有利だ** Having some kind of skill is *an advantage* [is *advantageous*] in job hunting. ‖もっと**有利な条件**でなければ契約はできない We cannot sign the contract unless we are given more *favorable* terms. ‖銀行預金よりこの株に投資したほうが絶対**有利ですよ** It's definitely more *profitable* to invest in this stock than to deposit money in the bank.
▶弁護人は被告人に**有利な**証拠を提出した The lawyer presented evidence *in favor of* the accused. ‖地元での試合は**我々にとって有利だ** It will *be to our advantage* to play the game at home. ‖彼はおじさんが有力な国会議員だから就職のとき**有利だ** He *has an advantage* [*an edge*] in finding a job because his uncle is an influential Dietman.

[2]**ゆうり 遊離** ▶与党の政策が**現実から遊離する**こともある The ruling party's policies can *be unrealistic* at times. ‖あの党の指導者たちは一般大衆から**遊離している**（＝気持ちをつかんでいない）The party leaders *are out of touch with* the general public.

ゆうりすう 有理数《数学》a **rational number**.

ゆうりょ 憂慮 ▶国王の病気は**憂慮すべき状態にある** The king is in *serious* condition. ／The king's illness has reached a *critical* stage. ‖環境破壊は**憂慮に堪えない** I *am deeply concerned* [*anxious*] *about* the destruction of the environment.

[1]**ゆうりょう 有料の** **pay** ▶**有料の**駐車場 a *pay* parking lot ‖《動物園などで》子供も**有料でしょうか** *Is admission charged* for children also?（➤「入場料が課せられますか」の意）‖《飛行機の中で》お酒は**有料ですか** *Do you charge* for alcoholic drinks?
‖**有料テレビ** a pay TV ‖**有料トイレ** a pay toilet ‖**有料道路** a toll road（➤ toll /toul/ は「通行料」）.

[2]**ゆうりょう 優良な** **excellent** ▶サウジアラビアは**品質優良な**石油を産出する Saudi Arabia produces *high quality* oil. ‖息子は**健康優良児**です My son is *a very healthy child*. ／My son is *in excellent health*.

ゆうりょく 有力な **leading**（指導的な，主要な）; **influential**（影響力のある）; **strong**（強力な）; **powerful**（実力のある）▶**有力な**新聞 a *leading* newspaper ‖**有力な**政治家 an *influential* politician ‖**有力チーム** a *strong* team ‖次期党首の**有力候補** a *strong* candidate for party leader in the next election ‖彼の有罪を裏付ける**有力な証拠がある** There is *strong* [*convincing*] evidence to prove that he's guilty.
▶これは事件解決の**有力な**手がかりになりそうだ This should be a *key* [*an important*] clue in solving the case. ‖その歌手は年内に結婚するという見方が**有力だ** People think it *most likely* that the singer will get married by the end of this year.（➤「結婚する可能性が高い」の意）.

ゆうりょくしゃ 有力者 an **influential person**, a **leading figure** ▶田代氏は財界の**有力者だ** Mr. Tashiro *has great influence* [*clout*] in financial circles. ／Mr. Tashiro *is influential* in the business world.

ゆうれい 幽霊 a **ghost** /goust/（亡霊；死人が現れるもの）; a **spirit**（霊；目に見えるものとは限らない）; an **apparition**（異常な現象）;《インフォーマル》a **spook** ▶きみは**幽霊**(の存在)を信じますか Do you believe in *ghosts*? ‖あの家は**幽霊が出る**そうだ People say *a ghost appears* at that house. ／People say the house *is haunted*.
‖**幽霊会社** a ghost [phantom／bogus] company（➤ bogus は「偽の」）‖**幽霊人口** ghost [bogus] population ‖**幽霊船** a phantom ship ‖**幽霊部員** an inactive [a phantom] (club／team) member ‖**幽霊屋敷** a haunted house.

ゆうれつ 優劣 ▶ソフトバンクと日ハムの強さは**優劣つけ難い** It's *hard to say who's stronger*, the Hawks or the Fighters. ‖ 彼らは技量の**優劣を競った** They *competed to outdo each other* (in skill). ／They *competed to see who was the more* skillful. ‖ 日本では人間の**優劣**が出身校で**判断されがちだ** In Japan, there is a tendency for people *to be evaluated* according to which schools they have graduated from. (➤ evaluate は「評価する」).

ユーロ **the euro** (➤ 通貨の呼称) ; a **euro** (➤ 通貨単位) [複 **euros**].

1**ゆうわ 融和** ▶日本は常にほかのアジア諸国との**融和を図るべきだ** Japan should always *try to establish harmonious relationships* [*friendly relations*] with other Asian countries.

2**ゆうわ 宥和** **appeasement** 一動 **宥和する** **appease** +目.

ゆうわく 誘惑 (a) **temptation** ; (a) **seduction** (性的な) 一動 **誘惑する** **tempt** +目 ; **seduce** +目 (性的に) ▶**誘惑**に勝つ [負ける] overcome [give in to] *temptation* ‖ 大都会は**誘惑**が多いから気をつけなさいよ Beware (of) the big city because you'll be exposed to a lot of *temptations* there. ‖ **誘惑に負けない強い心を持ちたい** I'd like to have a strong mind to *resist temptation*. ‖ 甘い物は控えてるんだから, ケーキなんか見せて**誘惑しないでね** I'm cutting down on sweets, so please don't *tempt* me with even the sight of cake. ‖ ドン・ファンは女性を**誘惑する**のがうまかった Don Juan was an expert at *seducing women* [at *seduction*].

1**ゆえん 所以** ▶それが本書を皆さまに推薦する**ゆえんです** *That is* (*the reason*) *why* I recommend this book to you.

2**ゆえん 油煙** **oily smoke.**

ゆか 床 a **floor** ▶**床**の上に500円硬貨が落ちている There's a 500-yen coin on the *floor*. ‖ 講堂の**床**はコンクリート [板] です The auditorium has a concrete [wooden] *floor*. ‖ 体育館の**床面積**はどのくらいですか Could you tell me how large the gym *floor* is ? (➤「床面積」は floor space ともいう).

▶集中豪雨のため約50戸が**床下浸水した** [**床上浸水した**] The *foundations* of about 50 houses *were flooded* [About 50 houses *were flooded above the floors*] due to the torrential downpour. (● foundations は basements でも可).

‖**床運動** floor exercise ‖ **床暖房** floor heating, a floor heating system.

ゆかい 愉快 一形 **愉快な** **fun** ; **delightful** (非常に楽しい) ; **cheerful** (陽気な) ; **enjoyable** (➤ 人には用いない) ▶**愉快な**歌 a *cheerful* song ‖ 私たちはきのう彼女の家で**愉快な**夕べを過ごした We had a *pleasant* [an *enjoyable*] evening at her home yesterday. (➤ pleasant は「楽しくて気分の良くなる」) ‖ サザエさんは時々**愉快な**しくじりをする Sazae-san sometimes makes *amusing* blunders. ‖ 北海道へ行く途中で**愉快な**人と出会った I met a *cheerful* [*delightful*] person on my way to Hokkaido.

▶スケート場では滑ったり転んだりとても**愉快だった** We *had a lot of fun* slipping and falling on our bottoms at the skate rink. ‖ 今晩は大変**愉快だった** I *enjoyed myself* very much this evening. ／This evening *was* very *enjoyable*. ‖ ああ**愉快だ** That is great *fun*, isn't it ? (➤ この fun は「愉快なこと」の意の名詞) ／Oh, this is *great* ! ‖ 一緒に**愉快**にやりましょうよ Let's *have fun*. ‖ ぼくのジョークに父は**愉快そうに笑った** My father laughed *cheerfully* at my joke.

▶えっ, あいつがしくじったって? **そいつは愉快だ** Oh, he blew it ? *I'm glad to hear that*. ‖ 阪神が巨人に勝つのを見るのは**実に愉快だ** It *is really satisfying* to see the Tigers defeat the Giants.

ゆかいた 床板 a **floorboard.**

ゆがく 湯搔く **parboil** /pɑ́ːʳbɔɪl/ +目, **blanch** +目 ▶ホウレンソウを湯がく *parboil* [*blanch*] spinach.

ゆかげん 湯加減 ▶**湯加減**見てもらえるかしら Could you check *how hot the bath is* ? ‖ おばあちゃんが入るお風呂の**湯加減見てきてくれる?** Will you *see to* Grandma's *bath* ? (● see to は「(用件)にきちんと対応する」).

▶ **対話** 「湯加減はいかがですか」「ちょうどいいくらいです」 "How is the bath ?" "It's just right."

ゆかしい 床しい ▶**ゆかしい**人 a *refined and genial* person (➤ genial は「穏やかで気さくな」) ‖ **古式ゆかしい**儀式 a *time-honored* ceremony.

ゆかた 浴衣 a ***yukata***

日本紹介 ✉ **浴衣は夏に着るくつろいだ木綿の着物です. 素肌にじかに着て, 素足にげたを履きます. 花火大会や盆踊りにはうちわを持った浴衣姿の男女がよく見られます** A *yukata* is an informal cotton kimono worn in the summer. People wear one next to their skin and wear *geta* (clogs) on their bare feet. Men and women dressed in *yukata* and carrying round fans are often seen at fireworks displays and *bon* dances.

ゆがみ 歪み a **warp** /wɔːʳp/ (反り) ; (a) **distortion** (ひずみ, ねじれ) ▶**ドアにゆがみができている** The door *is warped*. ‖ CDは音の**ゆがみ**がほとんどないと言ってもよい On CDs, sound *distortion* is (reduced to) virtually zero.

ゆがむ 歪む **be twisted, be distorted** (ねじれる) ; **be warped** /wɔːʳpt/ (反る) ▶**彼女の顔は苦痛でゆがんだ** Her face *was twisted* [*was distorted*] with pain. ‖ 板が乾燥して**ゆがんだ** The board *got* dried and *warped*.

▶《比喩的》家庭にいろいろ問題があって, あの子の性格は**ゆがんでしまった** Numerous problems in his family *warped* his personality. ‖ **性格のゆがんだ**子の扱いはとても難しい It is very hard to deal with *perverse* children.

ゆがめる 歪める **distort** +目 (ねじって自然な形を変える) ; **twist** +目 (ねじる) ▶激しい歯痛にさすがの怪力男も**顔をゆがめた** The violent toothache made even the man of Herculean strength *distort* [*twist*] his face in pain.

▶ダリは絵を描くとき, 対象を**ゆがめる**のを好んだ Dali liked to *distort* the subjects of his pictures when he painted them.

▶《比喩的》**真実をゆがめる** *distort* the truth ‖ ジャーナリストは事実を**ゆがめて**報道してはいけない Journalists must not *distort* (the) facts in reporting news.

ゆかり 縁 ▶中津は福沢諭吉**ゆかりの地**です Nakatsu is known for its *associations* with Fukuzawa Yukichi. (➤「福沢諭吉との連想で知られる」の意).

▶《慣用表現》**縁もゆかりもない人たち**が救いの手を差し伸べてくれた People who were *complete strangers* [who had *no relation what*(*so*)*ever*] *to me* gave me a helping hand.

ゆき 雪 **snow** ; a **snowflake** (ひとひらの) 一動 **雪が降る** **snow** (➤ 主語は it) ▶あ, 雪が降っている

Look, *it's snowing*. ‖ ひどく寒い. 雪が降りそうだ It's bitter cold. It looks like *snow*. ‖ 昨夜はひどく雪が降った *It snowed* heavily last night. ‖ 北海道では冬に雪がたくさん降る In Hokkaido, they *have a lot of snow* in the winter. ／*It snows a lot* in Hokkaido in the winter.

▶雪が舞い始めた Some *snowflakes* began to fall from the sky. ‖ 雪のために首都圏の交通は大混乱した The *snow* threw traffic in the metropolitan area into great confusion. ／Traffic in the metropolitan area was thrown into great confusion *due to the snow*. ‖ 雪やこんこ Snow's falling, plop, plop. (➤ 歌の一節).

▶きょうは時折小雪のちらつく寒い一日だった It was a cold day today with occasional *light snowfall*. ‖ その村は雪に閉じ込められた The village *was snowed in*. ‖ 雪を頂いた伊吹山は見事だ *Snow-capped* Mt. Ibuki is magnificent. ‖ 彼女の肌は雪のように白い Her skin is *snow-white* [is (as) *white as snow*].

▶あなたが私に花束を持って来てくれるなんて珍しいわね. 雪でも降るんじゃないかしら It's quite out of the ordinary for you to bring me a bunch of flowers. *I wonder what'll happen next*. (●「次は何が起きるのかな」と発想する).

✉ **新潟は雪国で冬には一晩で雪が 1 メートルも積もります** Niigata is (in the) *snow country* and as much as a meter of snow accumulates in one night in the winter.

✉ **こちらでは屋根から雪を下ろすのは大切な仕事です** For people here, *shoveling* [*sweeping*] *snow off the roof* is an important task.

✉ **雪が消える春が待ち遠しくてなりません** I can hardly wait for spring when the *snow* disappears.

‖**雪男** an Abominable Snowman, a yeti /jéṭi/ (➤ 前者の Abominable は「忌まわしい」の意. チベット名の yeti が好ましい) ‖ **雪女** a *yukionna* ; a snow woman.

> 「雪」のいろいろ 淡雪 ephemeral snow ／大雪 heavy snow(fall) ／粉雪 powder(y) snow ／小雪 light snow(fall) ／ざらめ雪 corn snow, spring corn ／新雪 fresh [new] snow ／べた雪 slush ／ぼたん雪 snow in large flakes

☛ 大雪, 雪かき (→見出語)

ゆきあかり 雪明かり ▶雪明かりの道を歩いて家に帰る walk home along a *snow-lit* road.

ゆきあたりばったり 行き当たりばったり →いきあたりばったり.

ゆきおれ 雪折れする **break under the weight of snow.**

ゆきおろし 雪下ろし **shoveling** [**sweeping**] **snow off the roof** ▶父を手伝って屋根の雪下ろしをした I helped my father *remove* [*shovel*] *the snow* from the roof.

ゆきかう 行き交う ▶師走の街を行き交う人々はいかにも忙しそうだ At year-end, the streets bustle with people *coming and going* [*going to and fro*].

ゆきかえり 行き帰り →いきかえり.

ゆきがかり 行き掛かり →いきがかり.

ゆきかき 雪搔き **snow shoveling**(除雪) ; a **snow shovel** (道具) ▶道の雪かきをする *remove* [*clear*] *snow from* the road ‖ 父は家の前で雪かきをやっていた My father was *shoveling the snow* from the street in front of the house. ／My father was *clearing* the road *of snow* in front of the house.

ゆきがっせん 雪合戦 a **snowball fight** ▶私たちは校庭で雪合戦をした We *had a snowball fight* in the schoolyard. ‖ 雪合戦をしようよ Let's *throw snowballs*. ／Let's *have a snowball fight*.

ゆきき 行き来 →いきき.

ゆきぐに 雪国 a **snowy country** (雪の多い国) ; **the snow country** (一国内の地域) ▶雪国の春は遅い Spring is late coming in *the snow country*.

ゆきげしき 雪景色 a **snowscape** ▶この絵はシベリアの雪景色を描いたものです This picture shows *a snowscape* [*a snowy scene*] in Siberia. ‖ 野原は一面の雪景色だった The field *was covered* all over *with snow*.

ゆきげしょう 雪化粧 ▶雪化粧をした富士山は神々しいほど美しい *Dusted with snow*, Mount Fuji is breathtakingly beautiful.

ゆきさき 行き先 →いきさき.

ゆきしつ 雪質 **the type of the snow.**

ゆきすぎ 行き過ぎ →いきすぎ.

ゆきずり 行きずり ▶困っていたところを行きずりの人が親切にしてくれた When I was in trouble, *a passerby* helped me out. ‖ 彼女は行きずりの男に恋をした She fell in love with a man *whom she met by chance*.

ゆきぞら 雪空 ▶根室は雪空です *It looks like snow* in Nemuro. (➤「雪になりそうだ」の意).

ゆきだるま 雪達磨 a **snowman** ▶子供たちは外に大きな雪だるまを作った The children made *a* big *snowman* outside.

▶《慣用表現》借金が 5 年の間に雪だるま式に増えた My debts *have snowballed* in the last five years.

ゆきちがい 行き違い →いきちがい.

ゆきつけ 行き付け →いきつけ.

ゆきづまり 行き詰まり →いきづまり.

ゆきづまる 行き詰まる →いきづまる.

ゆきつもどりつ 行きつ戻りつ →いきつもどりつ, 行ったり来たり.

ゆきつり 雪吊り ***yukitsuri*** ; a technique for protecting trees against heavy snow by supporting them with ropes that are stretched from the top of a bamboo pole and attached to the limbs(➤ 説明的な訳).

ゆきどけ 雪解け a **thaw** /θɔː/ ▶北海道の雪解けはいつだろうか I wonder when the *snow will begin to melt* [*thaw*] in Hokkaido. ‖ 雪解け道を単車が突っ走った A motorcycle sped by on the *slushy road*. (➤ slushy は「解けてぬかるんだ」).

ゆきとどく 行き届く →いきとどく.

ゆきどまり 行き止まり →いきどまり.

ゆきまつり 雪祭り a **snow festival.**

ゆきやけ 雪焼けする **get a snow-tan, get snowtanned** (➤ a winter tan という人もいる) ▶国夫はあまりに雪焼けしていたので最初は誰だかわからなかった Kunio *had gotten* [*become*] so *tanned from the snow* that at first I didn't recognize him.

ゆきやなぎ 雪柳《植物》a **Thunberg's meadowsweet.**

ゆきやま 雪山 a **snow(-covered, -capped) mountain.**

ゆきよけ 雪除け a **snow break** [**fence**].

ゆきわたる 行き渡る →いきわたる.

ゆく 行く →いく.

ゆくえ 行方 one's **whereabouts**(居場所) ▶容疑者の行方はまだわかっていない The suspect's *whereabouts* is still unknown. ／We don't yet know *where*

the suspect is. ‖ 警察はいなくなった子供の行方を捜している The police *are looking* [*searching*] *for* the missing child. ‖ 問題の男は昨夜行方をくらました The man in question *disappeared* last night. ‖ 洪水で4人が行方不明だ Four people *are missing* in the flood. ‖ その手紙は行方不明になった The letter *went astray*.
‖行方不明者 a missing person ; the missing (➤集合的).

ゆくさき 行く先 →いきさき.

ゆくすえ 行く末 (a) **future** ▶わが子の行く末が心配です I am anxious about my child's *future*. ‖ 子供たちの行く末を見届けてから死にたい I'd like to make sure of my children's *future* [*what will become of* my children] before I die.

ゆくて 行く手 ▶行く手に山小屋の明かりが見え始めた The lights of the hut could be seen *ahead of us*. ‖ 大きな岩がぼくらの行く手を遮った A big rock *blocked our way*.

ゆくとし 行く年 **the old year** ▶行く年来る年 *the old year* and the new (year).

ゆくゆく 行く行く ▶ゆくゆくは比呂美と結婚したい I would like to marry Hiromi *in the future*. (➤ in the future は「将来」).
▶ゆくゆくは息子に家業を継いでもらいたい I'd like my son to take over [succeed to] our family business *someday*.

ゆげ 湯気 **steam** ▶ラーメンの湯気で眼鏡が曇った The *steam* from the ramen has fogged [clouded] my glasses.
▶湖水から湯気が立っているようだ It looks like *steam* is rising from the lake. ‖ やかんから湯気が立っている The kettle *is steaming*.

ゆけつ 輸血 (a) **blood transfusion** ▶この患者は今すぐ輸血が必要だ This patient needs *a blood transfusion* immediately. ‖ この患者は輸血をしてもらった This patient *received* [*had*] *a blood transfusion*. ‖ 私は自分の血を母に輸血した I *gave* [*donated*] *blood to* my mother.

ゆさぶり 揺さ振り a **shakeup** ; a **jolt**(激しい) ▶ヨーロッパ連合とアメリカは経済制裁を科してイランに揺さぶりをかけた The economic sanctions imposed by the EU and the U.S. *gave* Iran *a jolt* [*jolted* Iran].

ゆさぶる 揺さ振る **shake** +目 ; **jolt** +目 (人・物を激しく) ▶私は木を揺さぶってリンゴを落とした I *shook* apples from the tree.
▶《比喩的》そのスキャンダルは政界を揺さぶった The scandal *rocked* [*jolted*] the political world.
‖揺さぶられっ子症候群 shaken baby syndrome 《略 SBS》.

ゆざまし 湯冷まし **cooled boiled water.**

ゆざめ 湯冷め ▶この温泉はいいぞ. 湯冷めしないよ This hot spring is wonderful. You do*n't feel a chill* [You *stay warm*] after you get out of it.

ゆさゆさ ▶猿が木の枝をゆさゆさ揺すっている A monkey *is shaking* the branches.

ゆしゅつ 輸出 (an) **export** /ékspɔːʳt/, (an) **exportation** (➤前者がより一般的) 一動 **輸出する** **export** /ɪkspɔ́ːʳt/ +目 ▶石油の輸出はサウジアラビアに富をもたらした Oil *exportation* has brought wealth to Saudi Arabia. ‖ 日本では武器の輸出は禁止されている The *export* of weapons is prohibited in Japan. ‖ オーストラリアは原料を日本に輸出している Australia *exports* raw materials to Japan. ‖ ベネズエラは鉄鉱石の輸出国である Venezuela is *an exporter* of iron ore. (「輸出国」は exporting country でもよい. また「輸出する」と考えて exports でもよい) ‖ 日本は輸出志向型の国だ Japan is an *export-oriented* country.
‖輸出額 exports ‖ 輸出港 an export port ‖ 輸出超過 an export surplus ‖ 輸出品 exports, exported goods.

ゆず 柚子 《植物》 a *yuzu* ; a kind of citrus fruit.

ゆすぐ 濯ぐ **rinse** /rɪns/ (+目) →すすぐ ▶口をゆすぐ *rinse* [*wash out*] one's mouth ‖ よくゆすいで洗剤を落としてください *Rinse* well to remove the detergent. ‖ このグラス, さっとゆすいでくれ *Give* this glass *a quick rinse*.

ゆすり 強請 **blackmail**(恐喝) ; **extortion** (脅して金を奪うこと) ; an **extortionist**, a **racketeer**, a **blackmailer** (人) ▶彼はゆすりに遭って100万円を払わされた He *was blackmailed into* paying a million yen.

-ゆずり -譲り ▶彼女は母親譲りのブロンドだ She gets her blonde hair from her mother. ‖ 彼が頭がいいのは父親譲りだ He is smart *like* his father. →親譲り.

ゆずりあい 譲り合い **give-and-take**(互譲) ; (a) **compromise** /kɑ́ːmprəmaɪz/ (妥協) ▶譲り合いの精神 a spirit of *give-and-take*.

ゆずりあう 譲り合う ▶車内で少女とお年寄りが互いに席を譲り合っていた On the train, I saw a girl and an elderly man *offering each other* the same (unoccupied) seat. ‖ 双方とも譲り合う(=妥協する)気持ちはないようだった Neither of them seemed able to *compromise with the other*.

ゆずりうける 譲り受ける **buy** +目 (買う) ; **take over** (引き継ぐ) ▶友だちから車を30万円で譲り受けた I *bought* a car from my friend for 300,000 yen. ‖ 彼は祖父から会社を譲り受けた He *took over* the firm from his grandfather.

ゆずりわたす 譲り渡す **hand over** (権限などを) ; **transfer** +目 (財産などを).

[1]ゆする 揺する **shake** +目 (上下・左右に動かす) ; **rock** +目 (ゆっくりと) ; **swing** +目 (揺り動かす) ▶リンゴの木を揺する *shake* an apple tree ‖ 揺りかごを揺する *rock* a cradle ‖ 男の子は母親を揺すって起こした The boy *shook* his mother awake. ‖ 彼女はその子をハンモックに入れて揺すってやっていた She *was swinging* the child in a hammock. ‖ ぶらんこをそんなに揺すら(=押さ)ないで! 怖いから Don't *push* the swing that hard [high]. It scares me.

[2]ゆする 強請る **blackmail** +目, 《インフォーマル》 **shake down**(恐喝する) ; **extort** +目 (ゆすり取る) ▶暴力団員たちがうちの社長をゆすった The gangsters *blackmailed* our president.
▶驚いた. 銀行員が主婦をゆすって金を取ったんだって What a shock to hear that a bank clerk *extorted* money from a housewife!

ゆずる 譲る

訳語メニュー
与える →give **1**
売る →sell **2**
譲歩する →yield **3**

1【人に渡す】 **give** +目 ; **yield** +目 (権利などを) ▶お年寄りや体の弱い人には席をお譲りください Please *give* (*up*) your seats to the elderly and disabled. ‖ この音楽プレーヤーは佐藤さんから譲ってもらった I *was given* this music player by Mr. Sato. ‖ 彼はその国

会議員に発言権を**譲った** He *yielded* his right to speak to the Diet member. ‖ 彼は息子に財産を**譲った** He *turned* his property *over to* his son. (➤「運用・経営を任せた」) ／He *transferred* his property to his son. (➤ 法律用語).

2【売る】sell ＋目 ▶友人にマンションを**譲った** I *sold* my condo to a friend. ‖ そのビデオカメラ, 要らないなら, (安く) **譲って**よ If you aren't using that camcorder any more, could you *sell* it to me (at a low price)?

✉ (売ります・買います広告で) **中古の iPad 安く譲ります** Used iPad *for sale*. Cheap!

3【譲歩する】yield《to》▶領土問題では日本はロシアに一歩も**譲らない** Japan will never *yield to* Russia on the territorial issue. ‖ 彼はその問題についての議論では一歩も**譲らなかった** He *didn't budge* [*give*] *an inch* on that matter. ‖ 西武とソフトバンクは互いに一歩も**譲らなかった** The Lions and the Hawks both *refused to let* the other *take the lead*. (●「相手にリードを許さなかった」と考える) ▶《慣用表現》**百歩譲って**増税の必要性を認めるにしても, 政府はその前に議員や公務員の給与を思い切って削減してほしい *Even if we make a big concession* and recognize the need for a tax raise, the government should drastically cut the salaries of Diet members and public employees first.

4【あとにする】▶詳しい説明は各論に**譲る** Detailed explanations *will be given* in the following itemized discussions.

[1]**ゆせい 油井** an oil well.

[2]**ゆせい 油性の oil-based**

‖**油性インキ** oil-based [indelible] ink (➤ indelible は「消えない」の意) ‖**油性塗料** oil paint ‖**油性マジック** a permanent marker(➤「水性マジック」は washable marker).

ゆそう 輸送 shipping, transportation 一動 輸送する transport ＋目 ▶トラックは大切な**輸送**手段だ Trucks are an important means of *transportation*. ‖ 大量の木材が船で東南アジアから**輸送されてくる** Great quantities of timber *are transported* by ship from Southeast Asia.

‖**輸送費** transportation costs ‖**陸上[航空／海上]輸送** ground [air／sea] transportation(➤「海上輸送」は marine [maritime] transportation ともいう).

ユタ Utah(アメリカ西部の州; 略 UT, Ut.).

ゆたか 豊か 一形 豊かな rich; affluent (特に社会や環境などが); **abundant** (豊富な) ▶中国は人的資源が**豊かである** China has *abundant* human resources. ‖アフリカは**豊かな**天然資源に恵まれている Africa is *rich* in natural resources. ‖ 我々は**豊かな**社会に住んでいる We live in an *affluent* society. ‖ 彼らは以前より**豊かな暮らしをしている** They *are better off* than before. (➤ be well off で「裕福である」の意).

▶小林さんは**豊かな**音楽的才能に恵まれている Kobayashi is gifted with *abundant* musical talent. ／Kobayashi is a *gifted* musician. ‖ 彼女は**豊かな**胸をしている She has *full* breasts. ‖ 読書は生活を**豊かにする** Reading *enriches* our lives. ‖ 美しい音楽を聴くと心が**豊かになる**ような気がする I feel that listening to beautiful music *cultivates my mind*. ‖ 子供は想像力が**豊かだ** Children *are quite imaginative*. ‖ 人間は物質的な**豊かさ**を手にすると怠ける傾向がある Human beings tend to become lazy once they obtain material *wealth*. ／*Affluence* tends to make people lazy.

ゆだねる 委ねる leave《to》, **entrust**《to》(➤ 後者は堅い語) ▶社長は副社長に経営を**委ねた** The president *left* the management of the company *to* the executive vice president. ‖ 国の政治を一党のみに長期間**委ねる**のはよくない It is not wise to *entrust* the government of a country *to* the same party for a long time.

ユダヤ 一形 ユダヤ(人)の Jewish

‖**ユダヤ教** Judaism ‖**ユダヤ人** a Jew.

ゆだん 油断 carelessness 一動 油断する be careless (不注意である); **be off guard**(警戒を怠っている) ▶**油断**大敵 *Carelessness* is our greatest enemy. ‖ 相手チームはシード校ではないが, **油断する**と負けるぞ Our opponent isn't a seeded (school) team, but if we *are careless*, we'll lose the game. ‖ ゲリラは**油断**につけ込んで政府軍を打ち破った The guerillas *took* the government force *off guard* and routed them. ‖ ちょっと**油断していた**隙にパスポートを盗まれた Someone stole my passport *while I was off guard*. ‖ **油断するな**(＝警戒しろ) *Stay alert*! ／*Be on your guard*! ／*Don't let down your guard*. ‖ あの営業マンは**油断のならない**人物だ(＝信用できない) You *can't trust* that salesman.

▶《慣用表現》あいつは**油断も隙もありゃしない** You *can't be too careful* around him. ／You *can't trust* him *at all*.

ゆたんぽ 湯湯婆 a **foot-warmer** (**with hot water**), a **hot-water bag** [**bottle**].

ゆちゃく 癒着 adhesion(傷口などの) **一動 癒着する adhere**《to》▶《比喩的》保守政党と大企業は**癒着し**やすい Conservative parties tend to *have shady relationships with* big businesses. (➤ shady relationship は「うさんくさい関係」).

ユッカ《植物》a **yucca** /jʌ́kə/.

ゆっくり 1【時間・速度が遅い】slowly ▶**ゆっくり**運転する drive *slowly* ‖ 日本人と違ってタイの人たちは**ゆっくり**歩きます Unlike Japanese, Thais walk *slowly* [*at a leisurely pace*]. ‖ もっと**ゆっくりした**ペースで走ろう Let's jog at a *slower* pace.

2【余裕がある】▶その件は今度**ゆっくり**話し合いましょう Let's talk it over *in detail* next time. ／Let's discuss it (later) when we *have more time*. ‖ **対話**「お手洗いに行ってくるわ」「**ごゆっくり**」"I'm going to the ladies' room." "*Take your time*." ‖ **対話**「そろそろ失礼します」「え, もうお帰り? **ゆっくりしていってください**よ」"I'd better be going." "Oh, so soon? *Don't hurry off*." ／"I have to go now." "Already? *Do stay a bit longer*."

▶**ゆっくり**やろうよ Let's take it *slow*. ‖ 日曜日はいつもより**ゆっくり**起きる On Sundays I get up *later* than usual. ‖ 温泉に**ゆっくり**つかりたいね I'd like to take a *leisurely* [*long*] soak in a hot spring. ‖ 今出れば5時の列車には**ゆっくり**間に合うよ If we leave now, we'll have *plenty of* time to catch the five o'clock train. ‖ 正月休みは家で**ゆっくりする**つもりです I'm going to *take it easy* at home during the New Year holidays. ‖《客に》どうぞ**ゆっくりなさって**(＝くつろいで)ください Please *make yourself at home*. ‖ こんな騒がしい喫茶店では**ゆっくりできない**(＝落ち着けない) I *can't feel relaxed* in such a noisy coffee shop.

ゆったり 一形 ゆったりした loose (緩い); **relaxed** (くつろいだ); **spacious**(内部にスペースがある) ▶**ゆったり**

した着物 a *loose*(*-fitting*) kimono ‖ 内部がゆったりした乗用車 a *spacious* passenger car ‖ 父はソファーにゆったりと腰を掛けて，新聞を読んでいる My father is sitting *comfortably* on the sofa reading a newspaper. ‖ バッハを聴いているとゆったりした気分になる I *feel relaxed* when I listen to Bach.

ゆでたまご 茹で卵 a **boiled egg** ▶ゆで卵の殻をむく shell *a boiled egg* ‖ 私はゆで卵は半熟がいい I like my eggs soft-boiled.

ゆでる 茹でる boil ＋㊐ ▶卵は固くゆでてください Please *boil* my egg hard. ‖ ジャガイモを20分間ゆでなさい *Boil* the potatoes for 20 minutes.

ゆでん 油田 an **oil field.**

ゆどうふ 湯豆腐 ***yudofu***；tofu boiled in *konbu* stock (and served with a soy sauce-based dipping sauce) (➤ 説明的な訳).

ゆどおし 湯通し ▶野菜を湯通しする *blanch* vegetables ‖ カキを湯通しする soak the oysters briefly in boiling-hot water(➤ soak は「(十分に)浸す」).

ゆとり

> **解説** 窮屈でなく余裕があることを「ゆとり」といい，空間だけでなく，時間や気持ちについても用いるが，この日本語に相当する１語の英語はない．英語では場所ならば **room** や **space** (ともに「空間」の意)，時間ならば **time** などを用いて表現する．

ゆ

1【空間・時間の】space, room (空間)；**time** (時間) ▶この部屋にもう１つベッドを置くゆとりはない This room has no *space* for another bed. ‖ うちの車庫には車が３台入るゆとりがある There's enough *room* for three cars in our garage. ‖ 日本の小中学生の生活にはゆとり(＝自由な時間)が少ない Japanese elementary and junior high school students don't have enough *free time*. ‖ 悪いけどきょうはきみに会っている時間的なゆとりがないんだ I'm sorry, but I have no *time* to see you today. ‖ 渋滞があるかもしれないからゆとりをもって早めに出るようにしなさい Be sure to leave early to *allow* (*time*) for possible traffic congestion.

2【経済的な】▶わが家には海外旅行をするゆとりはありません We *can't afford* to travel abroad. ‖ 彼は近頃生活にゆとりが出てきた He seems to *be well off* these days. (➤ be well off は「暮らし向きがよい」；反対は be badly off).

3【気持ちの】▶当時もっとゆとりのある教育が必要だと思われた In those days, people thought we needed a *more relaxed* [*less stressful*] educational system. (● cram-free education としてもよい).

▶両親にもっとゆとりのある(＝安楽な)生活をさせてやりたい I'd like to be able to give my parents a more *comfortable* life.

ユニーク unique /juníːk/ ▶ユニークなコメディアン a *unique* comedian.

▶佐瀬君の考え方は極めてユニークだ Sase's way of thinking *is* quite *unique*.

> **危ないカタカナ語✸ ユニーク**
> 日本語の「ユニーク」は「珍しい」とか「変わった」の意味で用いられるが，英語の unique は「唯一の」「無類の」が第一義．ただし，インフォーマルな英語では「変わった」の意味で用いられることも多い．

ユニオンジャック the Union Jack(イギリスの国旗).

ユニセックス unisex.

ユニセフ UNICEF /júːnɪsef/ (国連児童基金) (➤ United Nations International Children's Emergency Fund の略．現在では United Nations Children's Fund と改称されているが，略称は元のまま).

ユニット a **unit**(構成単位)
‖**ユニット家具** unit furniture ‖ **ユニットキッチン** a sectional kitchen ‖ **ユニット住宅** a prefab(ricated) house ‖ **ユニットバス** a modular bath.

ユニバーサルデザイン universal design.

ユニバーシアード the Universiade(国際学生競技大会)(➤ the World University Games の通称).

ユニフォーム a **uniform** ▶選手たちは全員青いユニフォームを着ていた The players all wore blue *uniforms*. ‖ ユニフォーム姿の少年たちはとてもかわいらしかった The boys looked very cute *in their uniforms*.

ゆにゅう 輸入 (an) **import** /ímpɔːʳt/ (商品の)；**introduction** (文化などの導入) **一動 輸入する import** /ɪmpɔ́ːʳt/ ＋㊐, **introduce** ＋㊐ ▶産業分野では日本は輸入より輸出がはるかに多い In the industrial sector, exports greatly exceed *imports* in Japan. (➤ exports, imports と複数語尾がつくのは「輸出品[額]」,「輸入品[額]」の意) ‖ フランスからワインを輸入する *import* wine from France ‖ 日本はタイから大量の鶏肉を輸入している Japan *imports* a lot of chicken from Thailand. ‖ 古代の日本は大陸の文物を多く輸入した Ancient Japan *imported* [*took in*] many Chinese and Korean cultural products and art works.

▶これはニュージーランドから輸入した品です This is (an *imported* item) from New Zealand. ／This *is imported* from New Zealand. ‖ 今や多くの和食が輸入した原料で作られている Many Japanese traditional foods are now made from *imported* ingredients.

▶流通機構がまずいために輸入品の価格は高い The poor distribution system raises the prices of *imported goods* [*imports*].

‖**輸入課徴金** an import surcharge ‖ **輸入業者** an importer(➤「輸入国」の意にもなる) ‖ **輸入国** an importing country, an importer.

ユネスコ UNESCO (➤ United Nations Educational, Scientific and Cultural Organization の略).

ゆのはな 湯の花 hot spring mineral deposits [**encrustations**].

ゆのみ 湯飲み a **cylindrical (Japanese-style) teacup**；a **yunomi.**

ゆば 湯葉 *yuba*；a **tofu skin,** a **bean curd sheet.**

ゆび 指 1【手や足の】a **finger** (手の指；ただし「親指」だけは thumb という)；a **toe** /toʊ/ (足の) ▶彼は太い[ほっそりした]指をしている He has thick [slender] *fingers*. ‖ リンゴの皮をむいていて指を切った I cut my *finger* while peeling an apple. ‖ 男の子は指を折りながら足し算をやっていた The boy was doing addition *on his fingers*. ‖ 石にぶつけて足の指をけがした I stubbed my foot on the rock and injured my *toes*.

▶子供の頃，指(＝親指)をしゃぶると母に叱られた When I was a child, my mother used to scold me for sucking my *thumb*. ‖ 指を鳴らせる？ Can you snap your *fingers*? (➤ 中指をはじいて音を出すことで，関節をポキポキと鳴らすのは crack your knuckles という) ‖ 人を指でさすのは失礼ですよ It's rude to *point* your *finger at* people.

「「指」のいろいろ **親指** thumb ; big toe (足の) ／**人さし指** index [first] finger, forefinger ／**中指** middle [second] finger ／**薬指** ring [third] finger ／**小指** little [fourth] finger, 《米・インフォーマル》 pinkie, pinky」

‖**指人形** a hand puppet ‖**指ぬき** a thimble /θímbəl/.

2【慣用表現】▶ウォルトン家はアメリカでも5本の指に入るほどの財閥だ The Waltons are *among the five* wealthiest families in America. ‖わが社としてはライバルの躍進ぶりを**指をくわえて見ている**わけにはいかない We can't *sit with our arms folded* while our competitors get all the business. ‖彼女に**指一本でも触れてみろ**. ただじゃおかないぞ If you should *lay a finger on* her, you'll pay for it !

ゆびおり 指折り ▶(自分で)指折り数えてごらん Count *on your fingers*. ‖彼は日本でも**指折りの**人気テレビタレントだ He is *one of the most* popular TV personalities in Japan.

ユビキタス ubiquitous /jubíkwəṭəs/ ▶情報リテラシーとユビキタス・コンピューティングは重要な分野である Information literacy and *ubiquitous* computing are important areas.

ゆびきり 指切り ▶日本の子供は約束するとき**指切りげんまん**をすることがある Japanese children sometimes *link their little fingers* [*pinkies*] to make a promise.

ゆびさき 指先 a **fingertip** ; **the tip of a toe** (足のつま先) ▶私は**指先**をナイフで切った I cut my *fingertip* on a knife. ‖彼女は**指先が器用**だ She is *dexterous* [*clever* ／*deft*] *with her fingers*. (➤ deft は堅い語).

ゆびさす 指差す point 《at, to》 (🏺 at は物自体を, to は方向や離れた物を指すとき) ▶息子はボーイング747を**指さして**「怪獣みたいだ」と言った My son *pointed to* a Boeing 747 and said it was like a monster. ‖人を**指さす**のは失礼だ It's rude to *point at* people. (➤英米では子供にしてはいけないと教えることの1つ. point a finger at は「人を指さして非難する」の意).

ゆびサック 指サック a **finger cot**, a **fingerstall** ; a **thumbstall** (特に親指の).

ゆびずもう 指相撲 finger wrestling.

ゆびづかい 指使い fingering.

ゆびわ 指輪 a **ring** ▶ダイヤ[金]の**指輪** a diamond [gold] *ring* ‖**指輪**をはめる[外す] put on [take off] *a ring* ‖中指に**指輪**をはめる put *a ring* on the middle finger.

▶アメリカ人の男性は**指輪**をはめている人が多い A lot of American men wear *rings*. ‖真理に**婚約指輪**を贈った I gave Mari an *engagement ring*. (🏺 (×) engage ring とはいわない).

ゆぶね 湯船 a **bathtub** ▶**湯船**につかる soak oneself in the *bath*(*tub*) ‖**湯船**から湯があふれていた The hot water was overflowing the *bathtub*.

ゆみ 弓 a **bow** /boʊ/ ; **archery** (弓術) ▶**弓**を引く draw *a bow* ‖バイオリンの**弓**が切れた The *bow* of my violin snapped. ‖父は**弓**の名人です My father is *a good archer*.

ゆみず 湯水 ▶あいつは**湯水のように**賭け事に金を使う He spends money on gambling *like it was water*.

ゆみなり 弓形の curved (カーブした) ; **arched** (アーチ形の) ▶体を**弓なりに**反らせる *arch* one's body *backward*.

ゆみや 弓矢 a **bow and arrows** (弓と矢).

ゆめ 夢 1【睡眠中の夢】 a **dream** 一動 **夢を見る dream, have a dream** ▶きのうは怖い[楽しい]**夢を見た** I *had a* scary [happy] *dream* last night. (🏺 (×) see a dream とはいわない) ‖**夢から覚める** wake up [awake] from a *dream* ‖宝くじに当たった**夢を見た** I *dreamed* [*had a dream*] that I won the lottery. (➤《米》ではつづりは dreamed がふつうだが, 会話では /dremt/ という発音も多い) ‖私は今でも初恋の人の**夢を見る** I still *dream about* my first love.

▶直木賞受賞を知ったときは**夢**ではないかと思いました When I heard that I was to be awarded the Naoki Prize, I thought for sure that I *was dreaming*. ‖あの人にだまされるなんて**夢にも思わなかった** I *never dreamed that* he would deceive me. ‖ホームランを打ったときは**夢のような**気持ちがした Hitting a home run was *like a dream*. ‖まるで**夢を見ているような**気持ちだ I feel as if I *were dreaming* [I *were in a dream*]. ‖**対話**「1等賞が当たりましたよ」「ウッソー! **夢みたい**!」"You've won first prize !" "I can't believe it. *It's like a dream* (*come true*)." (➤最後の文の a dream come true (かなった夢) は一種の慣用句).

✉ **ゆうべあなたの夢を見ました** I *dreamed about* you [I saw you in *a dream*] last night.

2【はかないもの】▶**夢**ばかり追ってないで, もっと真面目に将来のことを考えなさい Stop *chasing after rainbows* and take your future more seriously. ‖ぼくたちは1回戦で敗れて連続優勝は**夢と消えた** When we lost in the first round, our hopes of winning consecutive championships *ended in smoke* [*went down the drain*].

3【望み】 a **dream** ; an **ambition** (野心) ▶途方もない**夢** a wild *dream* ‖見果てぬ**夢** an unfinished *dream* ‖かなわぬ**夢** an impossible *dream* ‖子供時代の**夢をかなえる** fulfill [realize] one's childhood *dream* ‖**夢を追う** pursue one's *dream* ‖プロゴルファーになる**夢が実現した**[**破れた**] My *dream* of becoming a pro golfer came true [was ruined]. ‖ことしも**夢と希望**にあふれた多くの若者が入社した Again this year, many young people full of *hopes and dreams* have joined our company. (➤「夢と希望」は英語ではふつう語順が逆になる).

▶たとえくじけそうになっても, **夢を諦めない**[**追い続ける**]ことが大事だ Even if you get discouraged, it is important (for you) to *never give up* [*pursue* ／ *follow*] *your dream*.

▶**夢をもち**, それを実現するように努めなさい What you should do is *find yourself a dream* and try to make it come true. ‖T大学に合格したんだ. **夢がかなったよ** I got accepted by T University. *My dream has come* [*came*] *true*. ‖彼女と付き合うなんて**夢のまた夢**だなあ I *can't imagine* going (steady) with her, *even in my wildest dreams*. (→夢物語) ‖ふつうのOLになりたいだって? **夢がないなあ** You really want to be an ordinary office worker? How *unimaginative* [*boring*]! (🏺英語では前者のように「想像力がない」と考えるか, 後者のように「退屈な」と考える).

✉ **私の夢は列車でカナダを横断することです** My *dream* is to travel across Canada by train.

ゆめうつつ 夢現 ▶私は小鳥の声を**夢うつつに**聞いていた I was listening to the birdsong *half-dreaming* [*in a trance*].

ゆめごこち 夢心地 ▶奈々子とのデートの日は**夢心地だった** On the day of my date with Nanako, I *felt like I was on cloud nine* [I *felt as if I were* walking on air]. (➤ on cloud nine は「とても幸せな気分である」の意).

ゆめまぼろし 夢幻 a **dream or** a **vision** ▶人生夢幻の如(ごと)くなり Life is like a *dream or a vision*.

ゆめみ 夢見 ▶夢見がよかった［悪かった］I *had* a good [bad] *dream*.

ゆめみる 夢見る dream《of》

> 【文型】
> …することを夢見る
> dream of doing

▶その少年はプロサッカー選手になることを夢見ていた The boy *dreamed of* becoming a pro [professional] soccer player. ／The boy's dream was to become a pro [professional] soccer player.

ゆめものがたり 夢物語 ▶人が空を飛ぶことはかつては夢物語だった For a human to fly in the sky was (considered) *an impossible fancy*. ‖ あんな豪華なマンションに住むなんて, 私たちにとっては夢物語さ To live in a plush condo like that is only *an impossible dream* [*a pipe dream* ／*an empty dream*] for people like us. (➤ pipe dream は「実行不可能な考え」の意).

ゆゆしい 由々しい grave（重大な）; **serious**（深刻な）▶ゆゆしい事態 a *grave* [*serious*] situation ‖ それはゆゆしい問題だ That's a *serious* [*grave*] problem.

ゆ

ゆらい 由来 an **origin**（起源）; a **source**（出どころ）▶この祭りは故事に由来している This festival *has its origin* in a historical event. ‖ 鼻曲山の名はその形に由来している Mt. Hanamagari's name *comes* [*derives*] *from* its shape. (➤ derive は堅い語) ‖ ノースダコタ州のクロキ駅は黒木将軍に由来する(＝ちなんでいる) Kuroki Station in North Dakota *was named after* General Kuroki.

ゆらぐ 揺らぐ ▶母親のことばに若者の決意はひどく揺らいだ The young man's resolve *was* badly *shaken* by his mother's words. (➤ shake は「ぐらつかせる」) ‖ 明子はひさしのプロポーズを受けるべきかどうか心が揺らいだ Akiko *was of two minds about* whether or not she should accept Hisashi's proposal. (🏺「決心がつかなかった」と考えて訳す).

ゆらす 揺らす →揺する.

ゆらめく 揺らめく flicker（ちらちらする）▶ランプの炎が風で揺らめいた The lamp *flickered* in the wind.

ゆらゆら ▶歩くたびにつり橋がゆらゆら揺れた The hanging bridge *swayed* [*swung*] under our feet each time we took a step forward. ‖ 滑走路の上にかげろうがゆらゆら揺れている A heat haze *is shimmering* over the runway.

ゆり 百合《植物》a **lily** ▶花瓶に白いユリが挿してある There is a white *lily* in the vase.
‖鬼ユリ a tiger lily ‖ 鉄砲ユリ a trumpet lily ‖ 山ユリ a *yama-yuri* (➤ 日本固有).

ゆりうごかす 揺り動かす rock ＋㊀ ▶揺りかごを揺り動かす *rock* a cradle ‖ 祖父はロッキングチェアに座って体を揺り動かしていた My grandfather was *rocking* (*himself*) in a rocking chair. ‖ 彼の主張に心を揺り動かされた I *was swayed* by his arguments.

ゆりおこす 揺り起こす shake ... awake ▶私は慌てて彼を揺り起こした I hurriedly *shook* him *awake*.

ゆりかご 揺り籃 a **cradle** ▶赤ん坊が眠るまで揺りかごを揺すった I kept on rocking the *cradle* until the baby fell fast asleep. ‖ その国では揺りかごから墓場まで国民の生活が保障されている In that country, people's livelihoods are guaranteed *from* (*the*) *cradle to* (*the*) *grave*.

ユリカモメ《鳥》a **black-headed gull**.

ユリノキ《植物》a **tulip tree**.

ゆるい 緩い 1【きつくない】loose /luːs/ ; **soft**（柔らかい）▶ちょっと痩せてベルトが緩くなった Since I lost a little weight, my belt has gotten *looser*. ‖ このズボンは腰の回りが緩すぎる These pants *are too loose* around the waist. (➤「きつい」は tight) ‖ このねじは締め方が緩い(＝十分締めていない) You didn't turn this screw tight enough.
▶きのうから赤ん坊のうんちが緩い The baby has been having *watery* [*soft*] stools [having *loose* bowels] since yesterday. ‖ ここは埋め立て地だから地盤が緩い Because this is a reclaimed area, the ground is (quite) *soft*. ‖ 昔あの町では警察の取り締まりが緩かった In that town the police *used to be lax* in enforcing the law.
2【穏やかな】gentle ; **slow**（ゆっくりした）▶緩いカーブ a *gentle* curve ‖ 緩い坂 a *gentle* slope ‖ もっと緩い球を投げてよ Please pitch the ball a little *slower*. ‖ 川は深い所では流れが緩くなる Rivers run [go] *slow* at deep places.

ゆるがす 揺るがす shake ＋㊀ ▶大地を揺るがしながら蒸気機関車がばく進して来た A steam locomotive pulled toward us, *shaking* the earth. ‖ これは世界を揺るがす大事件だ It's an *earthshaking* event.

ゆるがせ 忽せ ▶これはゆるがせにできない問題だ This is a problem we can't *ignore* [*make light of*].

ゆるぎない 揺るぎない ▶彼は会社で揺るぎない地位を築いた He has built (up) a *firm* [*solid*] position in the company. ‖ 彼女の導師に対する信頼は揺るぎないものであった Her belief in the guru was *unshaken*.

ゆるキャラ a **heart-warming cartoon mascot**.

ゆるし 許し permission（許可）; **leave**（特に休暇・外出の）; **forgiveness**（罪を許すこと）▶上司から新しい企画を進める許しを得た I got my boss's *permission* to go ahead with the new project. ‖ 私は秘書に休暇の許しを与えた I gave my secretary *leave* to go on vacation. ‖ 私は彼女に許しを請うた I asked for her *forgiveness*. ／I begged her to forgive me.

ゆるす 許す

1【許可する】allow /əláʊ/《to do》, **permit**《to do》

> 【文型】
> 人(A)が…することを許す
> **permit** A **to** do
> **allow** A **to** do
> **let** A do
>
> 【解説】(1)**permit** は「正式に許可を与える」の意で **allow** よりも形式ばった語. **allow** は「止めたり禁じたりしないで認める. 黙認する」. **let** はいちばんくだけた語で「希望どおりにさせる」の意. →させる.
> (2)**let** のあとは to のない原形がくる.

▶市議会はその住宅区域でのマンションの建設を許さなかった The city council wouldn't *permit* them *to* build condominiums in the residential area. ‖ 永田さんは駐車場に車を止めるのを許してくれた Mr. Nagata *allowed* me *to* park my car in his parking space. ／Mr. Nagata *let* me park my car in his parking space. ‖ 彼に頭を下げて頼むなんて, ぼくのプライドが許さない My *pride won't permit* me *to* bow down and ask him a favor.
▶午前中は患者との面会は許されておりません Visiting

patients in the morning is not *allowed*. ‖ きみたちのクラブ活動には**時間の許す限り**協力するつもりだ I'm going to help you with club activities *as much as time permits* (*me*).

2【容赦する】forgive +目 (人の過失などをとがめずに)；**excuse** 《for》(軽い罪などを)

【文型】
A のことで人(B)を許す
forgive B for A

▶きみの誕生日を忘れたことを**許して**ください Please *forgive* me *for* forgetting your birthday. (● excuse は軽い過ちやエチケット違反などを許すことをいい，家族など親しい人の誕生日を忘れた場合は forgive を用いる) ‖ 彼が私にしたことを私は決して**許さない** I'll never *forgive* him *for* what he did to me.

▶反省しているなら今回は**許してやる** I'll *forgive* you this once if you feel sorry about it. ‖ 今度ミスしたら**許さない**ぞ The next time you slip up, you *won't be excused*. ／If you make another error, I *won't forgive* you.

✉ **お返事が遅れたことをお許しください** Please *forgive* [*pardon*] me for not answering you sooner. ➤ pardon は改まった語／I'm sorry for not answering sooner. ➤ 後者はインフォーマル.

3【認める】▶倉田博士は**自他ともに許す**(＝広く認められた)ドイツ法の権威だ Dr. Kurata is a *generally-accepted* authority on German law. ‖ 病人が手術室に運ばれたときは一刻の猶予も**許されない**(＝一刻も無駄にできない)状態だった When the sick man was carried into the operating room, he was in such a serious condition (that) we didn't have a moment to lose.

4【緊張を緩める】▶古い友人だったのでつい**気を許して**彼に企業秘密を漏らしてしまった He's an old friend of mine, so I carelessly *let my guard down* and told him some of our business secrets. ‖ あんな悪い男とは知らずに彼女は一郎に**体を許して**しまった Not knowing Ichiro was such a bad guy, she *gave herself to* him [*went to bed with* him].

ゆるみ 緩み ▶運転中の**気の緩み**が事故につながる *Carelessness* at the wheel leads to accidents.

ゆるむ 緩む get loose, loosen /lúːsən/ ▶靴のひもがすぐ**緩んで**しまう My shoestrings *get loose* [*loosen*] easily. ‖ ボルトが**緩んで**外れた The bolt *loosened* and came off. ‖ 減税で消費者の財布のひもが少し**緩んだ** Owing to the tax reduction, consumers' purse strings *have loosened* a little. ‖ ねじがだんだん**緩んだ** The screws *worked loose*. (➤ work ... は「次第に動いて…になる」の意).

▶厳しい寒さもこの数日少し**緩んできた** The severe cold *has eased* [*has slackened*] *off* a little over the past several days. ‖ **気が緩む**とかぜをひきやすい You catch a cold easily *when you get too laid back*. (➤ laid back は「気楽に構えた，のんびりした」).

ゆるめる 緩める 1【緩くする】loosen /lúːsən/ +目 (締め具合を) ▶握っている手を**緩める**な Don't *loosen* your grip. ‖ ベルトを**緩めて**，たくさん召し上がれ *Loosen* your belt and eat as much as you want. ▶手綱を**緩める** *slacken off* a rein(➤ 比喩的にも用いる).

2【穏やかにする】relax +目；**slow down** (スピードを) ▶これ以上規律を**緩める**と，寮生の統制がとれなくなる If we *relax* discipline further, we can't expect the dormitory students to be well-behaved. ／If we*'re* any *looser* with the rules, we won't be able to keep the dormitory students in line. ‖ **気を緩めず**に最後まで頑張れ Don't *relax* [*let up*] *your efforts*, and hang in there till the end. ‖ 彼は急に**歩調を緩めた** He suddenly *slowed down* [*slackened*] his pace. ‖ 高速を下りたらスピードを**緩めろ** *Slow down* after you get off an expressway.

ゆるやか 緩やかな gentle (傾斜・流れなどが)；**slow** (速度が)；**gradual** (変化などが) ▶**緩やかな**坂 a *gentle* slope ‖ ミシシッピ川は**緩やかに**流れている The Mississippi flows *slowly* [*gently*]. ‖ 事故の起きた現場は道路が**緩やかに**カーブしている所です The accident occurred on a *gentle* curve. ‖ その変化がとても**緩やか**だったので私たちはそれにほとんど気づかなかった The change was so *gradual* we hardly noticed it.

ゆれ 揺れ motion(動き)；**sway**(動揺)；a **jolt**(突然の激しい上下動) ▶けさの地震，そちらの**揺れ**はどのくらいだった？ *How big* was the earth tremor this morning over there？‖ バスの**揺れ** *the sway* of the bus ‖ 船の**揺れ**で彼女は酔ってしまった *The motion* of the ship made her seasick.

ゆれうごく 揺れ動く ▶**揺れ動く**(＝不安定な)世界情勢 the *unstable* world situation ‖ アシが風に**揺れ動いていた** The reeds *were swaying* in the wind. ‖ 大学院に進むか就職するか，彼女の**心は揺れ動いた** She *wavered* between becoming a graduate student and getting a job.

ゆれる 揺れる 1【振動する】shake (ぐらつく)；**sway**(左右に)；**swing** (つり下げたものがゆらゆらと)；**jolt** (車などがガタンと)；**roll** (船や飛行機が横揺れする)；**pitch** (縦・前後に)；**vibrate** (速く振動する)；**quake** (強く) ▶新幹線の列車が通ると家が**揺れます** When a Shinkansen train passes, our house *shakes*. ‖ 強風に大枝が激しく**揺れている** The branches (of the trees) *are shaking* violently in the strong wind. ‖ その爆発で大地が**揺れた** The explosion *made* the ground *tremble* [*shake*]. ‖ コスモスが秋風に**揺れている** The cosmoses *are swaying* in the autumn breeze.

▶ハンモックが**揺れていた** The hammock *was swinging*. ‖ 電車はカーブで**揺れます**ので，つり皮におつかまりください The train will *jolt* at the curve, so please hang on to the strap. ‖ 船が激しく**揺れた**ので多くの乗客が吐き気を感じた The ship *rolled* so violently (that) many of the passengers felt nauseous. ‖ うちの家は大型トラックが通るたびに全体が**揺れる** Our whole house *vibrates* whenever a heavy truck passes.

2【動揺する】waver ▶彼のプロポーズを受け入れようかどうしようか，彼女の**心は揺れた** She *wavered* between accepting and declining his proposal. ‖ M中学は校内暴力事件で**揺れていた** M Middle School *was jolted* by school violence. ‖ 美術作品の評価をするときは判断の基準が**揺れて**はいけない When you judge works of art, you should not *vary* your standard of evaluation.

ゆわえる 結わえる bind +目 (束ねる)；**tie** +目 (結ぶ) ▶薪(まき)をひもで**結わえる** *bind* firewood with a cord ‖ 彼女は髪をきれいなリボンで**結わえていた** She wore her hair *tied up* with a pretty ribbon.

ゆわかし 湯沸かし a **kettle**, a **teakettle** ▶**湯沸かし**で湯を沸かす boil water in *a kettle*.

‖**ガス湯沸かし器** a gas water heater,《英また》a geyser /gíːzəʳ/.

ユングフラウ the Jungfrau /jʊ́ŋfraʊ/ (➤ スイスにあるアルプス中の高峰).

よ・ヨ

[1]**よ 世** **1【世の中】society**（社会）; **the world**（世間）; **life**（人生）→世の中 ▶きみたちには世のため人のためになる人物（＝社会の有用な一員）になってほしい I hope you will become useful members of *society*. ‖ 世はまさにハイテクの時代だ Today's *world* is one of high [advanced] technology. ‖ この辞書の初版は13年前に世に出た The first edition of this dictionary *was published* 13 years ago. ‖ 彼の作品が世に知られるようになったのは彼の死後のことである His works *became well-known* after his death.

▶《慣用表現》15歳の少年が世をはかなんで自殺した A 15-year-old boy *decided that* (*his*) *life was meaningless* and killed himself. ‖ あの男も世が世なら殿様として威張っていられただろうに The man could have wielded power as a feudal lord *if he had lived in different times*.

▶あんな候補者が当選するようじゃ世も末だね *What is the world coming to* [*It's the end of the world*] when a candidate like him gets elected. ‖ 有為転変は世の習い Vicissitudes are *the way of the world*.

2【現世, 来世】the world ▶滝廉太郎はわずか24歳で世を去った（＝死んだ）Taki Rentaro *died* when he was only 24. ‖ あなたにとってこの世でいちばん大切なものは何ですか What is the most important thing for you *in this world*? ‖ 私はあの世（＝来世）の存在を信じている I believe in *the afterlife* [*the next world* / *the hereafter* / *life after death*]. ‖ あの世とこの世の境には川が流れていると昔から信じられている It has been believed since ancient times that a river flows at the border between *this world and the next*.

[2]**よ 夜** (a) **night** ▶その夜は遅くまで話し合った We talked until late *that night*. ‖ 夜が明けた *The day* [*Dawn*] *broke*. (➤ night を用いないことに注意；日常的には It's morning. とか, Morning has come. という) ‖ あの連中はよく夜が明けるまでパーティーをする Those guys often party *until the day breaks* [*until morning*].

▶夜が更けてきた *Night is wearing on*. / It's *getting late*. ‖ ゆうべは夜が更けるまでトランプをした We played cards *until late* last night. ‖ ぼくらはゆうべガード下で夜を明かした We *spent the whole night* under the railroad bridge.

-よ ⚠ **日本語の「-よ」は念を押したり, 軽く命令や禁止や非難をしたり, 勧誘したりするときなどに用いる助詞であるが, 英語にはこれに対応する語はない.**

▶5時にきっと起こしてよ Be sure to wake me up at five. ‖ 彼の言うことなんか気にするなよ Don't worry about what he says. ‖ ねえ, 教えてよ Tell me, please.

▶さあ, 行こうよ［やろうよ］Now, let's get going [started]. ‖ どうしてそんなばかなことしたんだよ Why did you do a stupid thing like that? ‖ 何だよ, 文句あんのかよ What? You want to say something? *Go ahead*.

よあかし 夜明かしする stay up all night ▶友だちとおしゃべりをしながら夜明かしした I *stayed up all night* chatting with some friends.

よあけ 夜明け dawn /dɔːn/, **daybreak** (➤ 前者は比喩的にも用いられる) ▶夜明けに出発する start *at dawn* ‖ もうじき夜明けだ It's almost *dawn*. ‖ 私たちは夜明け前に釣り場に着いた We arrived at the fishing spot *before daybreak*.

▶新しい時代の夜明け the *dawn* of a new era.

よあそび 夜遊び ▶多くの若者が盛り場で夜遊びしている Many young people *are out on the town for the night*.

[1]**よい 酔い** ▶だんだん酔いが回ってきた I'm *getting drunk*. (➤ほろ酔いの場合は I'm starting to feel a (pleasant) buzz. または I'm feeling a bit tipsy. という) ‖ 財布が無いのに気づいて, いっぺんに酔いがさめた When I found my wallet was gone, I *sobered up* all at once.

▶ゆうべの酔いがまだ後頭部に残っているみたいだ I have a *hangover* from last night. I have a headache in the back of my head. (➤ hangover は「二日酔い」).

[2]**よい 宵 early evening** ▶まだ宵の口だ *It's still early in the evening*. / *The evening* [*night*] *is still young*. (➤ 後者は文語的).

‖**宵の明星** the evening star; Venus (金星).

[3]**よい 良い・善い** **good** →いい ▶牛乳は体によい Milk is *good* for your health. ‖ 彼は彼女によい（＝好ましい）印象を与えた He made a *favorable* impression on her. ‖ よい教師って何だろうと木村先生は自問した Mr. Kimura asked himself what a *good* teacher is. ‖ この辞書は売れ行きがよい This dictionary *is selling well*.

> **【文型】**
> **あなたは…したほうがよい**
> **You should do.**
> **You'd better do.**
> **【解説】**(1)**should** や ought to は「…したほうがいい」という提案から「…すべきだ」という義務まで意味が広い. should は話し手の主観的な意見で, 別の手段を選択する余地がある.
> (2)**had better** はふつう更に意味が強く,「そうしないと困ったことになる」という結果を含意する. しばしば命令調や警告, 強迫にもなるので目上の人には使わないほうがよい. 会話では, くだけて (You) better ともいう.

▶贈り物をもらったら何かお返しをしたほうがよい When [After] you receive a present, *you should* give something in return. ‖ かぜ薬を飲んでたっぷり休んだほうがよい *You'd better* take some cold medicine and get plenty of rest.

> **【文型】**
> **…するのはよい**（＝よいことだ）
> **It's good to do.**
> **…であるのはよい**（＝好都合だ）
> **It's a good thing S + V.**
> **…するのはよい**（＝うれしい）
> **I'm glad to do.**

《解説》 (1)**It's good …** は「よいこと，好ましいことである」の意．あとには to *do* のほかに *doing* や that の文がくる．
(2)**It's a good thing …** は「幸運である，…であって好都合だ」の意．
(3)**I'm glad …** は「…でうれしい」の意．あとには that の文がくることも多い．

▶早寝早起きは健康に**よい** *It's good* for your health *to* keep early hours. ‖ あなたとお会い［お話し］できて**よかった** *It was good* seeing［talking to／to see／to talk to］you.（➤ good のほか nice も用いられる）‖ 有能なスタッフがついて**よかったですね** *It's good to* see *that* you have a capable staff (members). ‖ 傘を持って来て**よかった**ね．雨が降り出したよ *It's a good thing* you brought your umbrella—it's starting to rain. ‖ 試合がテレビで放送されることになって**よかった** *I'm glad* (*to* hear) *that* the match will be televised. ‖ 探し物が見つかって**よかった** *I'm glad* I was able to find what I had been looking for.
▶オートバイ買ったのか，**よかったじゃないか** So you bought a motorcycle. *That's great!*［*Good for you!*］‖ 彼がその事故でけがをしなかったのは**運がよかった** He was *lucky* not to get hurt in the accident. ‖ **よかった**！来週の山田教授の授業は休講だ *Good!* Professor Yamada's lecture will be canceled next week. ‖ ああ，**よかった**．間に合わないかと思った *What a relief*［*Thank goodness*］! I didn't think I'd make it.
▶彼が早まったことを**しなければよいが** I *only hope* he won't do anything rash. ‖ もう出かけても**よいのではないか** You *might* (*just*) *as well* leave now.（➤ might (just) as well do は「…しても悪くない」）．
▶**よかったら**今度の日曜日うちに遊びに来ない？ *If it's convenient for you*, come visit me on Sunday. ‖ 若いうちにもっと**勉強しておけばよかった** *I should have studied*［*I wish I had studied*］more when I was younger.
▶盗み聞きは**よくない** Eavesdropping *is not good*. ‖ 食べ物をそんなに粗末にするのは**よくない** It *is wrong*［*a crime*］to waste so much food.（➤ crime は「ひどい行為，もったいないこと」の意のインフォーマルな語）．
☞ よく，よくなる（→見出語）

よいしょ ▶お年寄りは**よいしょと**(肘掛け)椅子から立ち上がった The elderly man lifted himself *heavily*［heaved himself］from his chair.（➤ heave は「力を入れて持ち上げる」）‖ **よいしょ**，ああ重い *Heave-ho!* It's really heavy.（➤ Heave-ho! はいかりを引き上げるときの掛け声；物を持ち上げるとき英語国民はふつう何も言わない）．
▶ 対話「わあお母さん，その着物似合うじゃない」「**よいしょ**したってお小遣いは値上げしないわよ」"Wow, Mom. That kimono really suits you." "*Your flattering me*［*buttering me up*］won't make me raise your allowance."

よいしれる 酔い痴れる →酔う ▶酒に**酔いしれる** *become heavily intoxicated* with sake ‖ 選手たちは優勝の喜びに**酔いしれた**(＝最高に幸せであった) The players *were euphoric* after winning the championship. ‖ 聴衆は名演奏に**酔いしれた**(＝とりこになった) The audience *was extremely intoxicated*［*was enthralled*］with the superb performance.（➤《主に英》では was ではなく were を用いる）．

よいっぱり 宵っ張り a **night owl** /aʊl/ (人) ▶うちは皆**宵っ張り**です Everyone in my family is *a night owl*. ‖ 兄は**宵っ張りの朝寝坊**だ My (older) brother is always *late to bed and late to get up*.

よいつぶれる 酔い潰れる **get**［**be**］**plastered**（➤ be は状態を指す場合）▶男たちはワインのボトルを数本空けて**酔い潰れた** After emptying several bottles of wine, the men *were plastered*［*were smashed*／*were loaded*］.

よいどめ 酔い止め **medicine to prevent motion**［**car**／**sea**／**air**］**sickness.**

よいどれ 酔いどれ a **drunk**, a **drunkard**. →酔っ払い．

よいのくち 宵の口 ▶まだ**宵の口**だ It's still *early in the evening*.

よいみや 宵宮 a ***yoimiya***; a festival held on the eve of the main festival（➤ 説明的な訳）．

よいん 余韻 a **lingering sound** ▶名鐘と言われるだけあって，この鐘は**余韻**が豊かだ True to its name, this bell has a wonderful *lingering sound*.
▶《比喩的》コンサートの**余韻**を楽しむかのように観客の多くは席を立とうとしなかった Most of the audience lingered in their seats as if they were enjoying the *afterglow* of the concert.（➤ afterglow は「(楽しい思いをしたあとの)名残」）．

[1]**よう 用 1**【用事】**business**; an **errand**（使いの用）▶急ぎの**用** urgent *business* ‖ **用**が済んだらお伺いします I'll visit you as soon as I finish this *errand*. ‖ ちょっと**用**を思い出したので失礼します I've just remembered *something I've got to do*, so I'm leaving now.
▶この古いノートパソコンにはもう**用はない** I *don't need* this old laptop any longer. ‖ きみにはもう**用はない** I *don't need* you any more. ‖ **用もないのに**人の前をうろちょろするな Don't get in my way *for no reason*.／*If you've got nothing to do*, then get out of my way.
▶ 対話「川野君，ちょっと」「何の**用**だい？」"Mr. Kawano!" "Yes, *what is it*?" ‖ 対話「お父さん，何か私に**用**はない？」「今はないよ」"Dad, is there *anything I can do for you*?" "No, not just now." ‖ 《デパートなどで》**ご用を承っておりますでしょうか** Is anyone helping you?／Are you being helped? ‖ 《レストランなどでウエーター・ウエートレスが》**ご用はございませんか** *How's everything?* ‖ 《受付などで》**それでどんなご用でしょうか** And *how may I help you*? →ご用．
▶ちょっと失礼．**用を足し**に行ってきます Excuse me. I've got to *go to*［I've got to *use*］*the restroom*.
2【働き】▶このラジオは**用をなさない**(＝機能しない) This radio *doesn't work*. ‖ 私の祖父は**用がなくなった**電気製品をみんな捨てないで取ってある My grandfather has kept a lot of electrical appliances which are *no longer useful*.
▶イタリア観光旅行ではここにあるフレーズを覚えておけば，結構**用が足ります** If you learn these phrases by heart, they'll *serve you well*［they'll *enable you to make yourself understood*］during your sightseeing trip to Italy.
3【「…用」の形で】▶**家庭用**コピー機 a copier *for home use*［*for family use*］‖ これは**紳士用**ですか？ Is this *for* men?
▶**男性用**［**女性用**］トイレはどこですか Where's the *men's*［*ladies'*］room? ‖ ここは**従業員用**の食堂です This is the *employees'* cafeteria.

[2]**よう 要**
1【大事な点】▶彼女の説明はいつも**簡にして要を得ている** Her explanation is always *brief and to the point*. →要注意，要は．

よ

2【必要】▶精密検査の要 *a need* for a thorough medical checkup ‖その計画は再考の要がある The project *needs* reconsideration.

3【「要-」の形で】▶要介護の年配の女性 an elderly woman who *needs nursing care*.

‖要援護者 a person who needs help(➤「災害時要援護者」全体を言うような場合は people who need help in times of disaster) ‖要保護者 a person in need of welfare assistance.

³よう 酔う 1【酒に】get drunk (酔っ払う) ; get tipsy [high] (ほろ酔い気分になる) ▶父は酔うと歌い出す My father sings when he *gets a little high* [*gets tipsy*]. ‖酔った連中が大きな声でしゃべっている *A group of drunks* are talking loudly. ‖ゆうべはひどく酔ってたね You *were dead drunk* last night. ／You *weren't feeling any pain* last night. ‖西洋人は一般に日本人ほど酒に酔わない Generally speaking, Westerners *don't get drunk* as easily as the Japanese.

2【乗り物に】get sick (to one's stomach) (むかむかする) ▶船[飛行機／車／電車]に酔う *get* sea*sick* [air*sick* ／car*sick* ／train*sick*] ‖私はよくバスに酔う I often *get sick on buses*. ‖すぐ乗り物に酔うので旅行は苦手だ I shy away from traveling since I easily *get motion sickness*.

3【有頂天になる】be euphoric [be intoxicated] 《with》; be spellbound (雰囲気に) ; be heady 《with》(意気揚々として) ▶我々は日本チームの勝利に酔った We *were euphoric with* the Japan team's victory. ‖観客たちはその華麗なショーに酔った The audience *was* [《主に英》*were*] *spellbound* by the spectacular show. ‖その発明家は(自分の)成功に酔っている The inventor *is intoxicated* [*heady*] *with* (his) success.

⁴よう hi(➤ hello よりくだけた語) ; hey (➤ 呼びかけ) ▶よう, 元気かい *Hi* (*there*), how are you? ‖よう, 驚いたな. こんな所で会うなんて *Hey*, what a surprise [*Hey*, imagine] running into you here!

¹-よう 1【意思を示して】▶このサーフボード, きみにあげよう I'*ll* give you this surfboard. ‖今度は私が運転しよう Let me drive next, okay! (➤ この okay は語調を和らげ,「いいね」の意).

2【動作の開始を示して】▶ピッチャーが投げようとしたときランナーは三塁へ走った When the pitcher *was about to* pitch, the runner started for third. (➤ be about to do で「まさに…しようとしている」).

3【勧誘を示して】▶きみの誕生日にはステーキでも食べようよ *Why don't we* have (a) steak or something on [for] your birthday?

☛ -しよう (→見出語)

²-よう -様 →-よう(だ), -ような, -ように.

¹**ようい** 用意 preparation(s) 一動 用意する make preparations 《for》, prepare 《for》, get ready 《for, to do》(➤ この順に用意のための手間や時間が少なくなる) →支度, 準備

> 【文型】
> A のために用意をする
> get ready for A
> prepare for A
> make preparations for A
>
> 《解説》(1)**get ready** は「(すぐ使えるよう, また行動を起こせる状態になるよう)支度をする, 身支度をする」の意で, 日常的なあまり手間のかからないことに多く用いる. be ready は「支度ができている」の意.
>
> (2)**prepare** や **make preparations** は「準備をする」で, 計画を立て, 必要な物をそろえるなど, より手間や時間のかかることに用い, 入念に準備すること自体に力点がある.「…するために用意する」というときは prepare to *do* とする.

▶出発の用意をしよう Let's *get ready for* departure [*to* leave]. ‖彼は万事に用意周到だ He always *prepares thoroughly* [*makes meticulous preparations*] *for* everything he does. ／He never leaves anything to chance. (➤「何事も成り行き任せにはしない」の意).

▶我々はその事業に半額出資する用意がある We*'re prepared to* put up half of the funding *for* the venture. ‖彼らは旅行に行く用意をしていた They *were preparing to* go on a trip. ‖いつでも出発する用意はできています We *are ready to* leave at any time. ‖お父さん, 夕飯の用意ができましたよ Dad, dinner *is ready*. ‖対話「あの学校, 入学金に100万円以上要るらしいよ」「用意してあるわ」"I hear that school's entrance fee is over one million yen." "*I've got it ready*."

▶招待券を用意しておきます I'll *get* a complimentary ticket for you. ‖窓際のテーブルを用意いたしました *We have* a table by the window *ready* for you, sir. ‖位置について, 用意, ドン! On your mark(s)! *Get set!* Go! ／Ready, steady, go!

²ようい 容易な easy 一副 容易に easily, with ease ▶漫画家として食べていくのはきみが考えているほど容易なことではない It is not as *easy* as you think to make a living as a cartoonist. ‖ヒマラヤ登山は容易なことではない Climbing the Himalayas *is no easy matter*.

▶あなたの考えていることは容易に想像がつきます I can guess *easily* [*with ease*] what you have in mind. ‖いいか, 容易に勝てる相手ではないぞ I tell you, they are not *easy* (opponents) *to beat*. ‖コンピュータのおかげで仕事が容易になる Computers *make* our work *easier* [*facilitate* our work].

ようい く 養育する raise +目, bring up (➤ 後者は「育て上げる」に相当) ; foster +目 (実子でない子供を一定期間世話する) ▶子供を養育する *raise* [*bring up* ／*foster*] a child ‖彼女は祖父母に養育された She *was raised* [*was brought up*] by her grandparents. ‖養育費 the expense of bringing up a child; child support (離婚後, 子供を引き取った相手に払う).

¹よういん 要因 a factor(要素) ; a cause(原因) ▶その保険金詐欺事件には複雑な要因が絡んでいた There were complicated *factors* behind the insurance fraud case. ‖ニューヨーク株式市場急落の要因の1つはアメリカ経済の不安定さにあった One of the *causes* of the crash on the New York stock market was the instability of the American economy.

²よういん 要員 ▶代替要員の捕手 a *backup* catcher ‖巨人には代打要員が5人いる The Giants have five *pinch hitters*.

ようえき 溶液 a solution

‖水溶液 a water solution.

ようえん 妖艶な ▶妖艶な美人 a *sensual* [*voluptuous* ／*bewitching*] beauty.

ようが 洋画 a foreign movie [film] (映画) ; a Western [European] painting, an oil painting (油絵) ▶私は邦画より洋画のほうが好きだ I prefer *foreign films*

to Japanese ones.
‖**洋画家** an artist of Western-style painting ; an oil painter (油絵画家).

1**ようかい 妖怪** *yokai* ; a **specter**(超自然的で奇怪な) ; a **monster** (怪物).

2**ようかい 溶解 dissolution** 一動 **溶解する dissolve** /dɪzɑ́:lv/ ▶砂糖は水に溶解する Sugar *dissolves* [*is soluble*] in water.

ようがく 洋楽 Western [**European**] **music.**

ようがし 洋菓子 (a) **cake**(ケーキ) ; **Western-style confectionery** (➤総称).

1**ようかん 羊羹** ***yokan***
日本紹介 ✉ **ようかんは和菓子の一種で，あんに砂糖や寒天などを混ぜて練り固めたものです** *Yokan* is a kind of Japanese sweet, made by kneading a mixture of sweet azuki [bean] paste, sugar and agar-agar.

2**ようかん 洋館** a **Western-style house** [**building**].

ようがん 溶岩・熔岩 lava /lɑ́:və/ ▶その村は噴火口から流出した大量の溶岩に埋まった The village was buried under the mass of *lava* which flowed (out) from the crater. ‖**溶岩流** a lava flow.

1**ようき 容器** a **container** ; a **vessel** (特に液体用の)
‖**ポリ容器** a plastic container ‖**密閉容器** an airtight container.

2**ようき 陽気 1【性格などが明るい】** 一形 **陽気な cheerful** (快活な) ; **fun-loving** (楽しいことが好きな) ; **lively**(曲などが) ▶あいつは陽気な男だ That guy is *cheerful*. ‖彼女は話し好きで陽気だ She is talkative and *fun-loving*. ‖陽気に(＝楽しく)やろうぜ Let's have fun. ／Let's make merry. (➤後者は古風) ‖陽気な音楽を演奏する play *lively* music.
2【気候】weather ▶いい陽気になりましたね This is *lovely weather*, isn't it? ‖いい陽気ですね *Nice* [*Warm*] day, isn't it?

ようぎ 容疑 (a) **suspicion** ▶その男は殺人の容疑で逮捕された He was arrested *on suspicion of* murder. ‖私は窃盗の容疑をかけられた I *was suspected of* theft. ‖彼の容疑は晴れた He *was cleared of suspicion*.
‖**容疑者** a suspect /sʌ́spekt/.

ようきゅう 要求 a **demand** (強い要求 ; 「当然の権利として」という含みがある) ; a **request**(要望) ; a **requirement**(必要条件) 一動 **要求する demand** ＋目 ; **request** ＋目 ; **require** ＋目 (当然必要なこととして)

【文型】
…することを要求する
demand to do
人(A)に物事(B)を要求する
demand B **from** [**of**] A
人(A)は…せよと要求する
demand [**request**] **that** A (**should**) do
《解説》(1)**demand** 人 **to** do は不可.
(2)《米》では通例 should のない原形を用いる.

▶彼女はマネージャーとの面会を要求した She *demanded to* see the manager. ‖エジプト人は政府に民主化を要求した Egyptians *demanded* democratization *from* their government. ‖住民は計画の白紙撤回を要求した The residents *demanded* [*requested*] *that* the project (*should*) be called off. (➤that 以下は受け身になっている).
▶誘拐犯人がジョンソン家に電話を掛け，100万ドルの身代金を要求した The kidnapper called the Johnsons and *demanded* a ransom of one million dollars. ‖私たちは職場における男女平等を要求します We *demand* [*claim the right to*] gender equality in the workplace. (➤claim は「(権利などを)当然のものとして要求する」).
▶彼は私の要求を拒否した He rejected my *demand*. ‖きみたちの要求には応じられない I can't meet [satisfy] your *demand*. ／I can't comply with your *request*. (➤後者は「要望に応える」に近い) ‖当然の[不当な]要求をする make a reasonable [an unreasonable] *demand* ‖日常生活の要求を満たす meet *the requirements* of daily life.
▶同時通訳には強い集中力が要求される(＝必要だ) Simultaneous interpreting *requires* intense [strong] concentration. ‖彼は自分に要求されている以上のことをした He went beyond what *was required* of him.

1**ようぎょ 幼魚 young fish ; fry.**

2**ようぎょ 養魚 fish farming**
‖**養魚場** a fish farm.

ようぎょう 窯業 the ceramics industry.

1**ようきょく 謡曲** a **Noh chant.**

2**ようきょく 陽極 the anode**(➤「陰極」は cathode).

ようぐ 用具 gear, equipment (➤ともに「道具一式」の意の数えられない名詞) ; a **tool**(道具) ▶テニス用具 tennis *equipment* [*gear*] ‖筆記用具をご持参ください Please bring *something to write with* [*writing implements*]. (➤前者は「何か書くもの」の意).
‖**園芸用具** garden tools, gardening equipment.

ようけい 養鶏 chicken [**poultry**] **farming** (養鶏業) ▶私の友人は養鶏をしている A friend of mine *raises chickens*.
‖**養鶏場** a chicken [poultry] farm.

1**ようけん 用件 business** ▶では用件に入りましょう Well, let's get down to *business*. ‖どんなご用件でしょう *What* can I do for you? 《参考》改まった電話の応答では May I ask what this call is in reference to? のように言うこともある.
▶彼女は大した用件のないときでもよく電話をしてくる She often calls me even when she has nothing special *to talk about*.

2**ようけん 要件** a **requirement** ▶応募のためのすべての要件を満たす meet all *the requirements* for application.

1**ようご 用語** a **term, jargon** (➤後者は集合的に「仲間ことば」の意で，軽蔑的) ▶専門[医学／法律]用語 a technical [medical／legal] *term* ‖学生用語 student *jargon* ‖この小冊子はコンピュータ用語を説明している This booklet explains computer *terminology*. (➤terminology は term の集合名詞) ‖この筆者は難解な用語を使い過ぎる This author uses too many difficult *words*.
‖**用語集** a wordbook ; a lexicon (専門的な).

2**ようご 擁護 protection**(保護) ; **support** (支持) 一動 **擁護する protect** ＋目, **support** ＋目 ▶カーター元アメリカ大統領は人権擁護のために努力した Former U.S. President Carter made efforts to *protect* human rights. ‖戦時中言論の自由を擁護しようとした人々が投獄された During the war, those who tried to *protect* the freedom of speech were thrown into prison. ‖彼らはその法案を擁護した They *supported* the bill. ／They *gave* the bill their *support*.

3**ようご 養護 nursing**(看護) ; **care** (世話)
‖**養護学校**[**学級**] a school [class] for physi-

よ

cally and mentally challenged children (➤身体的・知的障害のある児童・生徒を対象とするもので, a school [class] for disabled [handicapped] children と表現するよりも好ましい) ; a school [class] for children in need of protective care (➤心身障害児・不登校児などを対象とするもので, 長期入院中の子供を対象として病院内に設置するような学級・学校なら an in-hospital class [school] for children in need of protective care のように表現すればよい) ‖ **養護教諭** a school nurse (保健室の先生) ‖ **養護施設** a nursing facility ; a children's home (児童の) ‖ **養護老人ホーム** a nursing home for elderly people.

1**ようこう 要項** ▶**募集要項**を取り寄せる send for *an application booklet* [*brochure*].

2**ようこう 要綱** an **outline** (おおまかなポイント) ; a **summary** (短いまとめ) ▶政策**要綱** a policy *outline* ‖ 《書名》『英文法**要綱**』*An Outline* of English Grammar. ⇀要旨.

ようこうろ 溶鉱炉 a **blast furnace.**

ようこそ ▶日本へ**ようこそ** *Welcome* to Japan! ‖ **ようこそ**おいでくださいました I'm very glad you could come. / Thank you so much for coming. / It's very nice of you to come.

1**ようさい 洋裁 dressmaking** ▶**洋裁**を習う learn [take lessons in] *dressmaking* ‖ 母は**洋裁が上手だ** My mother is *a good dressmaker*. / My mother *sews skillfully*. (➤ sew /soʊ/ は「縫う」).
‖ **洋裁学校** a dressmaking school.

2**ようさい 要塞** a **stronghold** ; a **fortress** (通例都市を含む大きな) ; **fortifications** (要塞化された場所)
▶天然の**要塞** a natural *fortress*.

1**ようざい 用材 lumber,** 《英》 **timber** (材木) ; **building materials** (建築資材).

2**ようざい 溶剤** a **solvent.**

ようさん 養蚕 sericulture /sérəkʌltʃəʳ/, **silkworm raising** ‖ **養蚕業** the sericultural industry.

1**ようし 容姿** a **figure** (スタイル) ; **looks** (顔だち) ▶彼女は**容姿が美しい** She has good *looks* and *a* nice *figure*. ‖ **容姿**にはこだわりませんから, 心の優しい人を紹介してください I don't care about *looks*. Just introduce me to a kind-hearted girl. ‖ うちの会社には**容姿端麗な人が多い** Our company has many *good-looking* [*attractive*] people.

2**ようし 用紙** (a) **paper,** a **sheet** (紙) ; a **form** (書式の決まった) ▶**用紙**に記入する fill out *a form* ‖ **試験用紙**を配る pass out *examination* [*test*] *papers*.
‖ **答案用紙** an answer sheet ‖ **投票用紙** a ballot ‖ **申し込み用紙** an application form.

3**ようし 要旨 the gist** /dʒɪst/, **the main points** (要点 ; 前者はやや堅い語) ; a **summary** (概略) ▶あの方の講演の**要旨**を教えてください Can you please give me *the gist* [*the main points*] of his lecture? ‖ この段落の**要旨**を50字以内の日本語にまとめよ *Summarize* this paragraph in 50 Japanese characters or less.

4**ようし 養子** an **adopted child** ▶赤ん坊を**養子**に出す put a baby up for *adoption* ‖ その夫婦は子供がいなかったので男の子を**養子にもらった** Since they had no children of their own, the couple *adopted* a little boy.
‖ **養子縁組** adoption.

5**ようし 陽子** 《物理学》 a **proton.**

1**ようじ 用事 business** (用件) ; an **errand** (使いの用事) ⇀用件 ▶父は急な**用事**で出かけた My father went out on urgent *business*. ‖ 大事な**用事**を忘れるところだった I almost forgot about an important *errand*. ‖ 私に何か**用事**でしょうか Is there something you want to discuss [talk about] with me? (➤「私に話がありますか」の意) ‖ お父さんが**用事があるから**って呼んでるよ Dad *wants* you (*for something*). ‖ 対話 「今晩うちへ来ません?」「ありがとう, でも**用事**がありますから」 "Why don't you come over tonight?" "Thanks, but I have *something* [*things*] *to do* tonight."

2**ようじ 幼児** a **little child,** an **infant** (➤後者は《米》では2歳ぐらいまでの乳幼児を, 《英》では通例7歳未満の幼児を指すことが多い) ; a **toddler** (よちよち歩きの) ▶**幼児**向きの絵本 a picture book for *little children*.
‖ **幼児期** infancy (就学時までの) ; childhood (子供時代) ‖ **幼児教育** preschool education.

3**ようじ 幼時 childhood** (子供時代) ; **infancy** (乳幼児・幼児の時代) ▶この小説は作者の**幼時**の思い出を基にしている This novel is based on the author's memories of his *childhood* [the author's *childhood* memories].

4**ようじ 楊枝** a **toothpick.**

1**ようしき 様式** (a) **style** ; a **pattern** (型) ▶イルカの行動**様式**を研究する study the behavior *patterns* of dolphins ‖ 能や歌舞伎などの古典芸能は極めて洗練された**様式**をもっている Classical performing arts, such as Noh and Kabuki, have quite refined *styles*.
▶現在のアメリカ先住民の**生活様式**は昔のそれとは大きく異なる The *lifestyle* [The *way of living*] of Native Americans is very different now from what it was in the past.
▶**ゴシック様式**の大聖堂 a *Gothic* cathedral ‖ **ビザンチン様式**の教会 a *Byzantine* church.

2**ようしき 洋式 Western style** ▶祖父は**洋式**の生活にまだ慣れていない My grandfather is not (yet) used to *Western-style* living.
‖ **洋式トイレ** a Western-style toilet.

ようしつ 洋室 a **Western-style room.**

ようしゃ 容赦 **1【許すこと】**▶失礼がありましたらご**容赦**ください If I have offended (you) in any way, please *forgive* me.
2【手加減】▶冷酷な殺し屋たちは**情け容赦なく**家族全員を撃ち殺した The cold-blooded killers shot all the family members to death *without mercy* [*mercilessly*]. ‖ 割り当て時間は**容赦なく**過ぎていく The allotted time is passing *inexorably* [*relentlessly*].

ようしゅ 洋酒 Western liquor.

1**ようしょ 洋書** a **foreign** [**Western**] **book**
‖ **洋書店** a foreign-book store.

2**ようしょ 要所** an **important** [a **key** / a **strategic**] **place** (大事な場所) ▶交通の**要所** *the key* [*strategic*] *points* of a transportation network ‖ **要所要所**を警官が固めていた Police officers were posted at *every important place*.

ようじょ 養女 an **adopted daughter** ▶花子は鈴木家の**養女**になった Hanako became the *adopted daughter* of the Suzuki family. / Hanako was adopted into the Suzuki family.

ようしょう 幼少 childhood, infancy ▶モーツァルトは**幼少**の頃に音楽の神童の誉れが高かった Mozart was praised as a musical prodigy *in his childhood* [*as a child*].

1**ようじょう 養生** ▶十分ご**養生**ください I hope you'll *take* extra *good care of yourself*. ‖ どうか焦らずに**養**

生なさってください Just take it easy and *let yourself get better*. ‖ 彼女は退院後自宅で**養生している** She *is recuperating* [*is resting and recovering* (*her health*)] at her home after having been discharged from the hospital. (➤ recuperate /rɪkjúːpəreɪt/ は「(健康などを)回復する」の意).

2**ようじょう 洋上** ‖**洋上大学** a floating college.

1**ようしょく 洋食** **Western food** [**dishes**] ▶**洋食**と和食とどちらが好きですか Which do you prefer, *Western* or Japanese *food* [*dishes*]?
‖**洋食屋** a (Western-style) restaurant.

2**ようしょく 養殖** **cultivation, culture** (➤ 後者がより堅い語); **farming** (養殖場で養殖すること); **raising** (育てること) 一動 **養殖する** **cultivate** +目, **culture** +目, **raise** +目 ▶カキの**養殖** oyster *farming* [*culture*] ‖ カキ[真珠貝]を**養殖する** *cultivate* oysters [pearl oysters] ‖ 浜名湖ではウナギを**養殖している** Eels *are farmed* [*bred*/*raised*] *artificially* at Lake Hamana. ‖ これは**養殖**のフグだ This is *farm*(*-raised*) globefish.
▶私たちの村にマスの**養殖場**がある There is a trout *farm* [*nursery*] in our village. 《参考》魚介類・海藻類の養殖場を aquafarm と呼ぶこともある.
‖**養殖真珠** a cultured pearl.

3**ようしょく 要職** an **important post** ▶私の父は会社で**要職**に就いている My father holds *an important post* in the company.

4**ようしょく 容色** one's **good looks** (美貌) ▶**容色**が衰える lose *one's good looks*.

1**ようじん 用心・要心** **care**; **caution** (警戒), **precaution** (予防策) 一動 **用心する** **take care** (気をつける); **watch out** (危険なものなどに) ▶かぜをひかないよう**用心し**なさい *Be careful* [*Take care*] not to catch (a) cold. ‖ 投手は肩を冷やさないように**用心し**なくてはならない Pitchers should *be careful* to keep their shoulders warm. ‖ **用心**するに越したことはない Better *safe* than sorry.

> 【文型】
> 人・物(A)に用心する
> **be cautious of** [**about**] A
> **beware of** A
>
> 《解説》ともにやや改まった言い方. 「気をつける」くらいの感じならば **be careful** や **watch out** がよい. ➡気をつける.

▶《標語・掛け声》火の**用心** *Beware of fire.*/*Be cautious about fire.*/*Prevent fires.* ‖ 混雑した電車の中では痴漢に**用心してください** *Watch out for* [*Beware of*] molesters on crowded trains. ‖ 彼女は**用心深い**からアパートに2つの鍵を掛ける She *is* so *cautious* that she uses two locks on her apartment (door).

2**ようじん 要人** a **VIP** [複 **VIPs**] (➤ *V*ery *I*mportant *P*erson の略; 発音は /vìːaɪpíː/ でも /vɪp/ でもよいが, 前者のほうが好まれる).

ようじんぼう 用心棒 a **bodyguard** (護衛係); a **bouncer**, 《英また》a **chucker-out** (酒場などの).

ようす 様子 (●「様子」は condition, state (ともに「状態」の意); situation (状況); things (事態) などと訳せるが, 「様子はどうか?」は How ...? や What ... like? で, 「…の様子だ」は look, appear を使って表す)
▶事故の**様子**を話してくれますか Can you tell me *how* the accident occurred? ‖ そちらの**様子はどうですか** *What is it like* over there? ‖ もう少し**様子**を見よう Let's see *how things go* [*how the situation develops*] for a little while. /Let's *wait and see* (for the time being).
▶彼女はひどく疲れている**様子だった** She *looked* [*appeared* (*to be*)] very tired. ‖ あの**様子**では彼らはこの3日間何も食べなかったに違いない *Judging from their appearance*, they must not have eaten for the past three days. ‖ あの男の人は**様子**(=態度)が少し変だ There's something strange about his *behavior*. /He's *acting* a little strangely. ‖ 赤ん坊の**様子**が変よ *Something is wrong with* our baby.
✉ **あなたの学校の様子を知らせてください** Please tell me *what* your school *is like*. ➤「学校がどんなふうか」の意.

1**ようすい 用水** ▶かんがい**用水** irrigation *water* ‖ 防火**用水** fire-fighting *water*/*water* for putting out fire ‖**用水路** an irrigation canal [ditch/channel].

2**ようすい 羊水** 《解剖学》**amniotic** /æ̀mniɑ́ːṭɪk/ **fluid** (➤ amniotic は「羊膜の」).

ようすこう 揚子江 **the Yangtze** /jǽŋsiː/ **River, the Chang Jiang** /tʃǽŋ dʒǽŋ/ (中国中央部を流れる大河; 後者は「長江」の拼音(ぴんいん)つづり).

ようずみ 用済み ▶こちらの雑誌はもうご**用済み**ですか *Are you done* [*Are you finished*] *with* this magazine? ‖ あいつはもう**用済み**だ(=用はない) We *have no more use for* him.

ようする 要する **need** +目, **require** +目 (➤ 後者がより堅い語); **take** +目 (時間やお金などを) ▶基礎研究には多くの時間と労力を**要する** Basic research *requires* a lot of time and labor. ‖ このダムの建設には5年の歳月を**要する** It will *take* five years to build this dam.

ようするに 要するに **in short** (手短に言えば); **to sum up** (結論を言えば) ▶**要するに**あいつは怠け者なのだ *In short* [*In a word*], he is a lazybones [lazy bum]. (➤ in a word は「ひと言で言えば」の意) ‖ (きみたちに言いたいのは) **要するに**しっかりやれということだ *To sum up*, I want you (all) to do your best. (➤ 相手が複数の場合には all をつけることが多い).
▶**要するに**きみが悪いんだ You are to blame *after all*. (➤ after all は「結局」) ‖ **要するに**それは考え方の問題だ *Basically*, it is a question of how you look at it.

1**ようせい 妖精** a **fairy** (昔話の); an **elf** [複 **elves**] (小妖精).

2**ようせい 養成** **training** 一動 **養成する** **train** +目 (人を); **foster** +目, **cultivate** +目 (精神などを; 前者がより堅い語) ▶自主独立の精神を**養成する** *foster* an independent spirit ‖ 道徳心を**養成する** *cultivate* a sense of morality ‖ 本校では技術者を**養成している** Our school *trains* students to be engineers.
▶看護師**養成学校** a nurses *training school* ‖ 歌手[俳優]**養成所** a singing [an acting] *school* (➤ 通例両方を合わせて performing arts school という) ‖ パイロット**養成所** a flight [flying/pilots' *training*] *school* ‖ 翻訳者**養成所** a *training school* for translators.

3**ようせい 要請** (a) **demand** (当然の権利としての要求); (a) **request** (丁寧に頼むこと) 一動 **要請する** **request**, **call for** ▶日本の大学教育は時代の**要請**に応えているだろうか I wonder if Japanese college education meets the *demands* of the times. ‖ 吉田さんの**要請**で参りました I came at Mr. Yoshida's *request*. ‖

彼らは何度も援助を要請した They *made* repeated *requests* for help. ‖ 知事は自衛隊の出動を要請した The governor *requested* [*called for*] the dispatch of the Self-Defense Forces. ／The governor *asked* that the Self-Defense Forces be dispatched.

4**ようせい 陽性** **1【明るい性格】**▶あの子はもともと陽性です That child has *a sunny* [*cheerful*] *disposition*.

2【正反応】一形 陽性の positive ▶エイズ検査が陽性だったらどうしよう What shall I do if my HIV test turns out (to be) *positive*？(➤「陰性の」は negative).

ようせき 容積 capacity(容量)；**volume**（体積）
▶この缶の容積は１リットルです This can has *a capacity* [*a volume*] of one liter. ／The *capacity* of this can is one liter. ‖ この箱の容積はいくらか What is the *capacity* of this box？／How much can this box *contain* [*hold*]？

1**ようせつ 溶接 welding 一動 溶接する weld** +目
▶２枚の金属板を溶接する *weld* two metal plates *together* ‖ 溶接工 a welder.

2**ようせつ 夭折 premature death**（早死に）▶詩人立原道造は夭折した The poet Tachihara Michizo *died before his time* [*died prematurely*].

よ

1**ようそ 要素** an **element**(成分)；a **factor**（要因）
▶健康は幸福の重要な要素だ Health is an essential *element* of happiness. ‖ 先を読む目はビジネスで成功するための不可欠の要素だ Foresight is an indispensable *element* [*factor*] of success in business. ‖ 理解は結婚生活を成功させる最も大切な要素の１つである Understanding is one of the most important *ingredients* of a successful marriage. (➤ ingredient は「材料，原料」の意だが，ここでは比喩的に「構成要素」).

2**ようそ 沃素**《化学》**iodine** /áɪədaɪn/
‖ 放射性ヨウ素 radioactive iodine.

1**ようそう 様相** an **aspect**；(an) **appearance**（外観）
▶その戦争はますますこう着化の様相を呈してきた The war began to take on [assume] the *aspect* of a stalemate. ‖ 台風に見舞われ，町の様相が一変した The typhoon altered the *appearance* of the town.

2**ようそう 洋装** ▶ふだんは洋装のおばだが，その日は和装だった On that day my aunt, who usually dresses in *Western-style clothes*, was wearing a kimono.

-よう(だ) →-ような, -ように **1【類似を示して】be like, look like**（➤ あとに名詞がくる）；**look**（➤ あとに形容詞がくる）；**look as if** [**like**]（まるで…のようだ；あとに節がくる. この look like はインフォーマルな言い方）

【文型】
A, B のように見える
look A ➤ Aは形容詞
look like B ➤ Bは名詞
(まるで)～であるように見える
look as if [like] S + V

解説 **as if** の文の動詞は「実際はそうでないのにまるで～のようだ」という場合には，事実と食い違うことを表して，現在のことならば過去形，過去のことならば過去完了形にする. しかし「実際に～のようだ」というときには現在形も使われる. →もし, まるで.

▶その歌手の家はお城のようだ That singer's house *is* [*looks*] *like* a castle. ‖ この写真の彼女は(まるで)別人のようです This photo does*n't look like* her at all. ‖ その制服を着たら囚人のようだった I *looked* [*felt*] *like* a prisoner in that uniform. (「囚人のように見えた」場合は looked を,「囚人になったように感じた」場合は felt をそれぞれ用いる) ‖ あの絵の女性は生きているようですね The woman in that picture *looks* almost alive, doesn't she？‖ あの２人はまるで兄と妹のようだ Those two *look as if* they *were* brother and sister. (➤ 事実と異なることを表すには as if の節に仮定法を用いる. この文では２人は兄妹ではない) ／Those two *look like* brother and sister. (➤ ２人が兄妹かどうかは不明).

2【推量を示して】seem (to be), look (like), appear

語法 推量を表す場合, **seem** は話し手の主観的判断で「…と思える」, **look** は顔つきや様子から「(実際)…のように見える」, **appear** は少なくとも外見上は「そう見える」場合に用いる. このほか **feel**（…と感じる), **sound**（…のように聞こえる), **taste**（…のような味だ)などを使い分ける.

【文型】
A, B のように思える
seem (to be) A ➤ Aは形容詞・名詞
seem like B ➤ Bは名詞
人(A)が…しているように思える
A seems to do.
It seems that A does.

▶彼は相変わらず頑張っているようだ He *seems* as hard-working as ever. ‖ 彼女は日本美術にとても興味があるようでした She *seemed to be* very interested in Japanese art. ‖ ついきのうのことのようだ *It seems like* only yesterday. ‖ 彼は何か隠しているようだ *It seems that* he's hiding something.
▶彼女はちょっと怒っているようだったよ She *looked* a little upset. ‖ 気分が悪いようだね You *look* sick. ‖ この先でどうやら事故があったようです *It looks like* there has been an accident on the road ahead. ‖ あなたの彼，ほかの女の子と付き合っているようよ *Looks like* your boyfriend is seeing another girl. (➤ 文頭の It が省略された形でインフォーマルな言い方).
▶電話で話したとき彼女は沈んでいるようだった She *sounded* depressed when I talked with her on the phone.
▶どうやらかぜをひいたようだ *I'm afraid* I must have caught (a) cold. (➤ I'm afraid は好ましくないことについて「…と思う」の意).

ようだい 容体・容態 (a) **condition** ▶患者の容体は急に悪化した The *condition* of the patient took a sudden turn for the worse. ‖ 対話「お母さんのご容体はいかがですか」「落ち着いています」"*How is* your mother？" "She is in stable condition."

ようたし 用足し・用達 ▶用足しに立つ leave one's seat to *go to the bathroom*.
▶母は元町まで用足しに行っています My mother *went* to Motomachi *on an errand*. (➤ errand は自分の用事にも使える).

ようだてる 用立てる ▶必要なときにこの金を用立てて(＝使って)ください Please *use* this money when you need it. ‖ 5000円ばかり用立てて(＝貸して)くれないか Would you *lend* me about five thousand yen？‖ 少し用立てていただけませんか Do you think it would be possible to *get a small loan*?

[1]**ようち 用地** a site; land(土地) ▶マンション建設用地 a condominium *site*／a *lot* for building a condominium ‖その不動産会社は団地建設用地を買収した That real estate company bought the *land* for a housing development.

[2]**ようち 幼稚な** childish(子供っぽい) ▶姉は子供たちを相手に幼稚な遊びをやっている My big sister is playing a *childish* game with some little kids.

ようちえん 幼稚園 a kindergarten ▶幼稚園に入る start [enter] *kindergarten* ‖幼稚園の先生 a *kindergarten* teacher (➤「園長」は kindergarten director) ‖うちの子は幼稚園に通っている Our son [daughter] goes to *kindergarten*. (➤この意味では school と同様に a や the をつけない).

‖**幼稚園児** a kindergarten child, a kindergart(e)ner.

《参考》(1)アメリカの kindergarten はその年の8月までに満5歳になる児童が入園資格を持つ. 2～4歳の幼児は preschool に行く. (2)イギリスでは2～5歳の幼児は nursery school や playschool [playgroup] に行く. (3)日本の幼稚園の年少組, 年中組, 年長組はそれぞれ Playgroup 1, Playgroup 2, Playgroup 3, あるいは Primary 1, Primary 2, Primary 3 のように便宜的に区別すればよい.

ようちゅう 幼虫 a larva [複 larvae /lǽːrviː/] ▶青虫はチョウの幼虫である A caterpillar is the *larva* of a butterfly.

ようちゅうい 要注意 ▶彼は要注意だ He's one you'd better *be careful about*. ‖彼は警察から要注意人物と見られている He is on the police's "to be watched" list. ／He's been blacklisted by the police. (➤ blacklist は「要注意人物のリストに載せる」の意;「要注意人物」を a suspicious character という).

ようつい 腰椎 《解剖学》 the lumbar spine.

ようつう 腰痛 lower back pain, a backache (➤後者は「背中の痛み」の意にもなる); lumbago /lʌmbéɪgoʊ/ (➤主に医学用語) ▶私は梅雨どきになると腰痛が出る I get *lower back pain* during the rainy season. ‖腰痛のためきょうは休みます I'd like a day off because of *lower back pain* [because I have *a backache*].

ようてん 要点 the (main) point ▶要点をつかむ[つかみ損なう] get [miss] *the point* ‖授業中は要点だけ書き留めておきなさい During the class write down only the *main* [*important*] *points*. ‖細かいことはいいから要点を言ってくれ Never mind the details—*get to the point*.

ようでんし 陽電子 《物理学》 a positron.

ようと 用途 (a) use /juːs/ ▶鉄は用途が広い Iron has a wide variety of *uses*. ／Iron is used for many different *purposes*.

[1]**ようど 用土** soil for horticulture.

[2]**ようど 用度** ‖**用度課** the supplies section [department] ‖**用度係** a person in charge of supplies ‖**用度品**(office) supplies.

ようとん 養豚 ▶養豚に従事する be engaged in *raising pigs* [*hogs*] ‖彼は養豚場で働いている He works on *a pig* [*hog*] *farm*.

‖**養豚家** a person who raises pigs, a pig farmer.

-ような **1【類似を示して】** like ▶天使のような子 a child *like* an angel ‖強盗は散弾銃のような物を持っていた The robber had something that *looked like* a shotgun. ‖恋ははしかのようなものである. 誰でも一度はかかる Love is *like* measles; we all have to go through it. (➤イギリスの作家ジェロームのことば).

▶その子はまるで大人のような口を利く The child talks *like* an adult. ／The child talks *as if* he were [was] an adult. ‖彼にとって音楽はふつうの人々にとってのことばのようなものであった Music was to him *what* language *was to* ordinary people.

2【種類·具体例を示して】 such (...) as ▶金や銀のような金属 *such* metals *as* gold and silver ／metals *such as* gold and silver ‖ラグビーやサッカーのようなスポーツはこの公園では禁じられている You can't play sports *such as* rugby and soccer in this park. ‖私は彼女のような態度をとる人は好きではない I don't like people who behave *like* her [*the way* she does].

▶親を泣かせるようなことはするな Don't do *anything to* make your parents unhappy. ‖うちの息子は絶対女の子をいじめるような子ではない My son would never pick on little girls. ‖ほとんど毎日予備校通いをしているので夏休みのような気がしない I go to *yobiko* almost every day, so I *don't feel like* it's summer vacation.

3【推量を示して】 ▶ここに居ると家に居るような気がする(＝くつろげる) I *feel* at home here. ‖彼女は熱があるような気がした She *felt* she had a fever. ‖雨が降るような気がしたので彼は傘を持っていった He *had a hunch* that it would rain, so he took along an umbrella. (➤ hunch は「予感」の意).

ようなし 洋梨 a pear /peəʳ/.

-ように **1【様態·状態を示して】** as ▶好きなようにしなさい Do *as* you like. ／Suit yourself. (➤後者は「勝手にしなさい」に近い) ‖ボールは矢のようにまっすぐに飛んだ The ball flew straight *as* [*like*] an arrow. (➤ like はインフォーマルな言い方).

2【目的を示して】 to do, in order to do (➤後者は目的を特に強調する必要がある場合) ▶電車に間に合うように速く走った I ran fast (*in order*) *to* catch the train. ‖交通事故を起こさないように気をつけてね Be careful *not to* cause a traffic accident. ‖ストレッチャーが戸口を通れるように私たちは脇にどいた We stepped aside *to* let the gurney pass through the doorway.

> 【文型】
> A が…するように
> so that A will do
> so as to do
>
> 《解説》(1)「Aが…できるように」の意では can を使って, **so that** A can *do* の形になる. **so as to** *do* はやや堅い言い方.
> (2)「…のために」の意では, 単に to *do* ということが多い.

▶彼がすぐに気づくようにそのメモをここに貼っておこう Let's stick that note here *so* (*that*) he'*ll* notice it easily [*so* (*that*) he can't miss it]. ‖老人は転ばないように注意して歩いた The elderly man walked carefully *so as* not *to* fall down. ‖中村教授はブラックホールについて素人にもわかるように易しく説明してくれた Professor Nakamura explained about black holes *so* simply *that* even a layman *could* understand.

3【結果を示して】 become; come to do ▶彼は物思い

にふけるようになった He *became* pensive. ‖ 私はようやく人生において何が大切なのかを理解するようになった I finally *came to* understand what is (really) important in life.

4【願望や命令を示して】▶お父さんの病気が早くよくなりますように *I hope* my father will get well soon. ‖ 試験に合格できますように！*I hope* I('ll) pass the examination！‖ 祖父母が長生きしますように *May* my grandparents live long！

✉ すばらしい年でありますように *Best wishes for* a wonderful New Year.

▶必ず 9 時前に空港に着くようにしなさい *Make sure* you get to the airport before nine. ‖ これからは，(もっと) 注意するように You'*d better* be (more) careful next time [from now on].

ようにん 容認 approval 一動 容認する approve《of》(よいと認める)；accept ＋目 (適当と認める) ▶知事は原発の稼動再開を容認する発言をした The governor stated that he would *approve* of restarting the nuclear power plant. ‖ 彼の行為を容認できない I *cannot accept* [*tolerate*] his behavior. ‖ 暴力は全く容認できない Violence is totally *unacceptable*.

ようねん 幼年 ▶彼女は幼年時代をニューヨークで過ごした She spent her (*early*) *childhood* [*early days*] in New York.

ようは 要は ▶要は英語で自分の意思が伝えられればいいのです *Basically*, if you can get your meaning across in English, that is good enough.

ようび 曜日 a day of the week ▶ 対話「きょうは何曜日だっけ？」「木曜日よ」"*What day* (*of the week*) is it today？" "Thursday." ‖ きょうは11月28日土曜日です Today is *Saturday*, November 28. ‖ 私は 6 月の第 3 火曜日に健診に行った I went for a medical checkup *on the third Tuesday* in [of] June. ‖ 彼女は 2 月のある日曜日に私を訪ねて来た She visited me *on a Sunday* in February. ‖ それはある雨の水曜日だった It was a rainy *Wednesday*. ‖ 忘年会はこの前の金曜日にあった[今度の金曜日にある] The year-end party was held *last Friday* [will be held *next Friday*]. ‖《別れ際に》月曜日に会おう See you *on Monday*. (➤ 次の月曜日を意味する) ‖ 私たちは日曜日には働かない We don't work (*on*) *Sundays*. (➤on を省くのは主に《米・インフォーマル》) ‖ 25日は何曜日？ *What day* is the 25th？‖ 22日は月曜日？火曜日？Is the 22nd *a Monday or a Tuesday*？‖ あなた，曜日を間違えているんじゃないの？きょうは木曜日よ Haven't you *got the wrong day*？ Today is Thursday.

ようひし 羊皮紙 parchment.

ようひん 用品 goods；a utensil /juténsəl/ (用具) ▶事務用品 office *supplies* (➤ supplies は「必要品」の意) ‖ スポーツ用品売り場はどこですか Where is the sporting *goods* department？

逆引き熟語 ○○用品
家庭用品 household goods／キャンプ用品 camping equipment [gear]／軍用品 military hardware, munitions／自動車用品 auto supplies／事務用品 office supplies／スポーツ用品 sports gear [equipment], sporting goods／生理用品 sanitary items／台所用品 kitchen utensils, kitchenware／日用品 daily necessities [goods]／不用品 a discarded [useless] article／ベビー用品 baby goods [products]／旅行用品 travel goods, traveling gear

ようひんてん 洋品店 a clothing store(衣料品店)；a boutique /buːtíːk/ (ブティック)；《米》a haberdashery /hǽbəˊdæʃəri/,《英》a (men's) outfitter's (紳士物の) 《参考》このほか a men's store [《主に英》shop], a women's store [《主に英》shop] のような言い方もある.

ようふ 養父 an adoptive father(養子縁組みをした)；a foster father (里親).

ようふう 洋風 Western style ▶洋風建築 a *Western-style* building.

ようふく 洋服 Western clothes (和服に対して)；a dress (ドレス)；a suit (スーツ) ▶着物より洋服のほうが活動しやすい You can move more freely in *Western clothes* than in a kimono. ‖ 女の子はお気に入りのピンクの洋服を着ていた The little girl wore her favorite pink *dress*.
‖洋服掛け a coat hanger ‖ 洋服だんす a wardrobe /wɔ́ːˊdroʊb/ ‖ 洋服店《米》a tailor shop,《英》a tailor's (shop) (紳士物の)；《米》a dressmaker shop,《英》a dressmaker's (shop) (婦人物の).

ようぶん 養分 nourishment /nə́ːrɪʃmənt/ ▶植物は土から養分をとる Plants take *nourishment* from the soil.

ようへい 傭兵 a mercenary (soldier).

ようべん 用便 ▶用便を済ます *relieve oneself* ‖ バスに乗る前に用便を済ませておきなさい You should *use* [*go to*] *the restroom* before boarding the bus.

ようぼ 養母 an adoptive mother(養子縁組みをした)；a foster mother (里親).

1**ようほう 用法** use /juːs/；usage (語法) ▶ぼくは敬語の正しい用法(＝使い方)をよく知らない I don't know much about the correct *use* of honorifics [about *how to use* honorifics correctly].

2**ようほう 養蜂** beekeeping, apiculture
‖養蜂家 a beekeeper, an apiarist /éɪpiərɪst/.

1**ようぼう 容貌** looks ▶結婚するなら相手は容貌より気立てだよ You should choose your marriage partner for his [her] temperament [disposition] rather than for his [her] *looks*.

2**ようぼう 要望** (a) request；(a) demand (強い要求) 一動 要望する request, demand ▶客の要望に応える meet [satisfy] customers' *demands* ‖ きみの要望は受け入れられない I can't grant your *request*.／I can't comply with your *wishes*. ‖ 当番組に対するご要望(＝提案)をお寄せください Please send *your suggestions* about our program. (➤ この文で request を使うと音楽の「リクエスト」ととられやすい) ‖ 皆さまのご要望にお応えして私のデビュー曲を歌います I'm singing my debut song *at* [*in response to*] your *request*.

ようま 洋間 a Western-style room ▶わが家には洋間が 3 つある My house has three *Western-style rooms*.

ようみゃく 葉脈《植物学》a leaf vein；veins of a leaf.

ようむいん 用務員《米》a janitor,a custodian,《英》a caretaker.

ようめい 用命 ▶社員旅行のご用命はぜひ当社へどうぞ Please *let us handle* [*take care of*] *the arrangements* for your company trip.

ようもう 羊毛 wool /wʊl/
‖羊毛製品 woolen goods.

ようもうざい 養毛剤 →育毛剤.

1**ようやく 要約** a summary, a summing-up 一動 要約する make a summary《of》, summarize ＋目, sum up

(➤1文，または数語というごく短い要約には sum up を用いる. summarize はそれ以上の内容の多さを暗示する) ▶作者の言おうとしていることを200語程度に要約しなさい *Make* [*Give*] *a summary of* what the author is saying in about 200 words. (➤「日本語で200字程度に」なら in Japanese in about 200 characters).

▶彼女はその新聞記事の内容を1パラグラフに要約した She *summarized* the newspaper article in one paragraph. ‖ キリスト教の教えは「神は愛なり」ということばに要約できる The message of Christianity can be *summed up* as 'God is love.'

2 **ようやく 漸く** **at last**(やっと); **finally** (最後に) ▶遠征隊はようやく頂上に到達した *At last* [*Finally*] the expedition reached the summit. ‖ 大学生活にもようやく(＝次第に)慣れてきました I'm *gradually* getting accustomed to college life.

▶夕方になってようやくその本を読み終えることができた *It wasn't until* that evening that I finished the book. ／I did*n't* finish the book *until* that evening.

ようゆう 溶融 a **meltdown**(原子炉の炉心の) **一動 溶融する melt down.**

ようよう 洋々 ▶前途洋々たる若者 a young person *with a bright future* ‖ 息子さん，T大へ入られたんですって？ 前途洋々ですね Your son got into T University? (That means) *his future will be smooth sailing*! (➤ smooth sailing は「順風満帆」の意).

1 **ようらん 要覧** ▶会社要覧 a company *catalog* ‖ 大学要覧 a college *catalog*. ⇀**便覧.**

2 **ようらん 揺籃** a **cradle**

‖揺らん期 the early developmental stage.

3 **ようらん 洋蘭** a **tropical** [**subtropical**] **orchid.**

ようりつ 擁立 ▶私たちは知事選に鈴木氏を擁立した We (*strongly*) *supported* Mr. Suzuki in the gubernatorial election. (➤ gubernatorial /gùːbəʳnətɔ́ːriəl/ は「(県・州)知事の」の意).

1 **ようりょう 要領** **1**【要点】**the point** ▶彼の説明は要領を得ていた His explanation *was to the point*. ‖ 彼女の言うことはちっとも要領を得ない I *can't see* [*get*] *the point of* what she says.

2【やり方】a [**the**] **knack, the hang** (こつ) ▶一度要領を覚えればあとは簡単だ You'll find it easier once you get *the knack* [*hang*] of it. ‖ もっと要領よく(＝能率よく)やらないと，その仕事は午前中に終わらないよ If you don't work more *efficiently*, you won't get the job done before noon.

▶やつは要領がいい He's *a clever guy*. (➤良い意味でも悪い意味でも使う) ／He's very *shrewd*. (➤常に悪い意味) ‖ 何をやらせても要領の悪いやつだ He can't do anything right.

2 **ようりょう 容量** **capacity** ▶ハードディスクの記憶容量 the *storage capacity* of a hard disk.

ようりょく 揚力 《物理学》**lift.**

ようりょくそ 葉緑素 《生化学》 **chlorophyll** /klɔ́ːrəfɪl/.

ようれい 用例 an **example** (例); an **example sentence** (例文) ▶用例を示す cite [give] *an example*.

ようろういん 養老院 ⇀**老人ホーム.**

ヨーガ ⇀**ヨガ.**

ヨーグルト **yoghurt** /jóʊgəʳt/ (➤ yogurt ともつづる)

‖低脂肪ヨーグルト low-fat yog(h)urt.

ヨーデル a **yodel** ▶ヨーデルで[を]歌う *yodel* ／*sing a yodel*.

ヨード 《化学》**iodine** /áɪədaɪn ‖ -diːn/

‖ヨードチンキ (a) tincture of iodine, iodine.

ヨーヨー a **yo-yo** /jóʊjoʊ/ ▶ヨーヨーをして遊ぶ play with *a yo-yo*.

ヨーロッパ **Europe** /jʊ́ərəp/ **一形 ヨーロッパの European** ▶東[西／北]ヨーロッパ Eastern [Western／Northern] *Europe* ‖ ヨーロッパの国々 *European* countries ‖ ヨーロッパを旅行する travel in *Europe* ‖ ヨーロッパのどこに行って来たの？ *Where* did you travel *in Europe*?

‖ヨーロッパ人 a European ‖ ヨーロッパ大陸 the European Continent ‖ ヨーロッパ連合 the European Union (➤略称は EU).

1 **よか 余暇** **leisure** /líːʒəʳ ‖ léʒə/ (**time**), **free time** ⇀**レジャー** ▶かつて日本人は余暇の過ごし方が下手だと言われた It used to be said that Japanese don't know how to spend their *leisure* [*free time*].

2 **よか 予価** an **expected price** ▶《広告で》2000円(予価) ¥2,000 (*tentative*) (➤ tentative は「仮の」の意).

ヨガ **yoga** /jóʊgə/ ▶ヨガをする practice [do] *yoga*.

よかぜ 夜風 an **evening breeze**(心地よさをイメージさせる語); a **night wind**(冷たさをイメージさせる語).

よかれあしかれ 良[善]かれ悪しかれ ▶よかれあしかれ，来週になれば面接の結果がわかる *For better or worse*, I will know the result of my interview by next week.

よかん 予感 a **premonition**, a **presentiment** (通例悪い予感; 後者はより堅い語); a **feeling** (感じ); a **sign**(兆し); 《インフォーマル》a **hunch** /hʌntʃ/ (直感) ▶春の予感 *a sign* of spring ‖ 飛行機に乗っていて危険なことが起こりそうな予感がした I had *a premonition* [*a presentiment*] of danger while on the plane. ‖ きょうは何かいいことがありそうな予感がする I have *a hunch* [*a feeling*] that something good will happen to me today.

▶夕飯は焼き肉？ そんな予感がしたんだ We're having yakiniku [Korean barbecue] for dinner? That's just what I *expected* [I *had a feeling* that's what we would be having]. ‖ 彼女は何か悪いことが起こりそうな予感がした She *felt that* something bad was going to happen.

よき 予期 **expectation** **一動 予期する expect** ＋㊐, **anticipate** ＋㊐ ▶予期に反して *contrary to one's expectations* ‖ 予期したとおりに彼は現れなかった As I *expected*, he didn't show up. ‖ 息子の予期しない返事に父親は当惑した The father was perplexed by his son's *unexpected* reply.

よぎ 余技 a **hobby** ▶余技で俳句を作る compose [write] haiku as *a hobby*.

よぎない 余儀無い ▶余儀ない事情で大学を休んでしまった Due to *unavoidable* circumstances, I took time off from college. ‖ 私たちは後退を余儀なくされた We *had to* retreat *in disgrace* [*in shame*].

よきにつけあしきにつけ 良[善]きに付け悪しきに付け **for good or** (**for**) **evil** [**bad**].

よきょう 余興 (an) **entertainment** ▶余興に歌を歌う sing (songs) for [by way of] *entertainment*.

よぎり 夜霧 a **night fog** ▶港は夜霧に包まれた The port was veiled in *a night fog*. ／*A night fog* hung over the port.

よぎる 過る ▶不安が突然，心をよぎった A sudden fear *flashed* [*flitted*] through my mind.

よきん 預金 (a) **deposit** **一動 預金する deposit** ＋㊐ ▶預金を引き出す draw out [withdraw] *a deposit* ‖ 私は銀行に500万円の預金がある I have *a deposit* of

よ

five million yen in the bank. ／I have five million yen in my bank account. (➤ bank account は「銀行口座」) ‖ボーナスの3分の1を預金することにしています I always *deposit* a third of my bonus in the bank.

‖**預金通帳** a bankbook, a passbook ‖**たんす預金** under-the-mattress savings, hoarded money ‖**定期預金** a fixed deposit ‖**当座預金**《米》a checking account,《英》a current account ‖**普通預金** a regular savings account.

1 **よく** 欲 (a) **desire**(欲望)；**greed** (貪欲) ▶**欲のない人** a person *free of desires* ／an *unselfish* person ‖**欲の深い人** a *greedy* person ‖**人は皆いろいろな欲を持っている** Everybody has many *desires*. ‖**町長は欲に目がくらんで収賄した** The mayor was blinded by *greed* [*lust for money*] and accepted a bribe.

▶《慣用表現》**彼の打率は悪くないが欲を言えば3割3分は打ってもらいたい** His batting average isn't bad, but *I wish* he would bat .330. ‖**もっと欲を出しなさい** You should *be* more *ambitious*.

▶**子供は知識欲が旺盛だ** Children have a keen *appetite* [*desire*] *for knowledge*. ／Children are thirsty for knowledge. ‖**人の金銭欲には切りがない** There is no limit to human *desire for money*. ‖**彼女は読書欲が旺盛だ** She is an avid reader. (➤ avid /ǽvɪd/ は「貪欲な」) ‖**彼は名誉欲が強い** He has a strong *desire for fame* [*(high) status*].

逆引き熟語 ○○欲
意欲 (an) eagerness ／**禁欲** abstinence, celibacy ／**権力欲** (a) desire [lust] for power ／**食欲** (an) appetite ／**所有欲** possessiveness ／**私利私欲** self-interest ／**情欲** (a) sexual desire, lust ／**性欲** (a) sexual desire, sex drive ／**独占欲** possessiveness ／**貪欲** greed, avarice ／**物欲** (a) materialistic desire

2 **よく** 良く・善く

訳語メニュー
うまく →well **1**
十分 →well, fully **4**
徹底的に →thoroughly **4**
注意深く →carefully **4**
しばしば →often **5**

1【うまく】well ▶**この水彩画はよく描けている** This watercolor is *well* painted. ‖**その帽子，とてもよく似合うね** That hat looks *really* good on you. ／That hat suits you *very well*. (➤ 堅い言い方) ‖ **対話**「**お父さん，英語で満点取ったよ**」「**よくやったね**」"Dad, I got a perfect score on the English test." "*Well done!* ／*Great!* ／*Good* [*Nice*] *job!*" (➤ 答えの最初の2文には That's を，最後の文には You did a を補って言ってもよい) ‖ **対話**「**職場では男女は平等に扱われるべきよ**」「**よく言ったわ．全く同感よ**」"Men and women should be treated equally in the workplace!" "*Well said!* I agree completely."

2【評価・賞賛して】▶**ここに来てるってことがよくわかりましたね** *It's a wonder that* you could find me here. ‖**網走までよくいらっしゃいました** Thank you very much for coming *all the way* to Abashiri. (➤ all the way は「はるばる」) ／How nice of you to have come to Abashiri! ‖**明子はよくできる生徒だ** Akiko is a *very* bright student. (➤ very は形容詞・副詞を強める) ／Akiko always gets good grades.

3【憤慨・非難・疑問視して】▶**あんな歌がよくヒットしたものだ(＝不思議だ)** *It's a wonder* (that) such a song ever became a hit. ‖**俺が短足だなんてよく言うよ．自分はどうなんだ** *What do you mean* I have short legs? What about yours? ‖**あんなひどいこと言われてよく笑っていられるわね** *How can* you take such insults and keep smiling? ‖ **対話**「**彼女はきっと俺が好きなんだ**」「**よく言うよ**」"I'm sure she's in love with me." "*Don't give me that.* ／*Give me a break.*" (➤ 前者は「信じないよ，うそつけ」，後者は「呆れて「冗談でしょう」というニュアンス)．

4【十分】well；**fully** (十分に(は))；**thoroughly** /θʌ́:rouli ‖ θʌ́rəli/ (徹底的に)；**hard** (一生懸命に)；**carefully** (注意して)；**really**(実に) ▶**ゆうべは暑くてよく眠れなかった** It was so hot last night that I couldn't sleep *well*. ‖**周りがうるさくてよく聞こえないんだ** It's so noisy (here) I can't hear you (*well*). ‖**バンコクならよく知っていますよ** I know Bangkok *very well*. ‖**よく降りますね** It's been *really* raining [snowing], hasn't it? (➤ hasn't it は省略可) ‖**よくは知らないけど，彼は国立大を受けるらしいよ** I don't know *for sure*, but I hear he's aiming for a national college.

▶ **対話**「**美術館へはこの道でいいんですか**」「**すみません，私もよくわかりません(＝不確かです)**」"Is this the right way to the art museum?" "I'm sorry. *I'm not sure* myself." ‖**当時，人々は運動の重要性によく気づいていなかった** In those days, people were not *fully* aware [did not *fully* realize] the importance of exercise.

直訳の落とし穴「よく知っている[知らない]」
「よく知っている」「よく知らない」をすぐ know well, not know well としがちだが，これが使える場面は意外に少ない．「山田さんならよく知っている」は I know Mr. Yamada well. でよいが，これは山田さんと親しい付き合いがある，という含みになる．聞き及んだりして，いろいろ(情報として)知っているだけなら，I know a lot about Mr. Yamada. となる．逆に「よく知らない」は I don't know much about Mr. Yamada. という．これを (×) I don't know well about Mr. Yamada. と間違えて言う学習者が多い．また，「何があったかよく知らない」も (×) I don't know well what happened. ではなくて，この場合は for sure (確実に，はっきりと)を用いて，I don't know for sure what happened. という．

▶**よく学び，よく遊べ** Work *hard* and play *hard*. ‖**監督の言うことをよく聞きなさい** Listen to the director *carefully*. ‖**よく(＝念入りに)見ればこの絵が偽物だとわかる** If you look at this picture *closely*, you'll find it is a fake. ‖**転職のことはよく考えてからお返事します** As to my changing jobs, I'll give my reply after *thinking* it *over*. ‖**彼女はお姉さんによく似ている** She looks *a lot* like her (older) sister. ‖ **対話**「**筆箱が無いよ**」「**よく捜したの？**」"I can't find my pencil case." "Did you search for it *thoroughly*?"

▶**人生，よくしたもので，雨の降る日もあれば，晴れる日もある** Life is*n't all that bad*. Some days it rains and some days the sun shines.

5【しばしば】often ▶**渡辺さんはよく学校を休む** Watanabe is *often* absent from school. ‖ 幸枝とはよくバスで一緒になる Sachie and I *often* ride on the same bus. ‖ こんなミスはよくあることだ. 気にするな This kind of mistake is *quite common* [This kind of thing *happens all the time*]. Don't worry about it.

▶(昔から)よくある話さ It's *the same old* story. ‖ 初心者によくあることだが, すぐ高度なテクニックに飛びつこうとする *As is often the case with* beginners, they are eager to go on to more advanced techniques. (➤ as is often the case with は「…によくあることだが」の意) ‖ よくある質問 *frequently asked questions* (➤ FAQ と略す).

▶昔はよく多摩川で泳いだものだ In the old days we *used to* go swimming in the Tama River. (➤ used to は過去の習慣を表す) ‖ おうわさは兄からよく伺っております I've heard *a lot* about you from my (older) brother.

☛ よくなる, よくも (→見出語)

よくあさ 翌朝 the next [following] morning ▶彼女からの速達は翌朝手元に届いた A special delivery letter from her reached me *the next morning*. (➤ 過去を起点に「その次の朝」の意なので the が必要. 現在を起点に「明日の朝」は, the をつけずに tomorrow morning とする).

よくあつ 抑圧 oppression ; suppression (弾圧) 一動 抑圧する oppress +目, suppress +目 ▶長年抑圧されてきた民衆は反乱を起こした After many years of *oppression*, the people revolted. ‖ 独裁者は言論の自由を抑圧した The dictator *suppressed* freedom of speech.

▶その国の経済を抑圧する *strangle* the country's economy (➤ strangle は「…を窒息させる」の意の比喩用法).

よくいえば よく言えば ▶うちのマネージャーはよく言えば慎重だが, 本当のことを言うと煮え切らないということだ *To be nice about it* [*To put it nicely*], you could say our manager is cautious, but the fact is, he's [she's] indecisive. ‖ 彼はよく言えば一匹おおかみ, 悪く言えばはみ出し者だ He's a maverick *at best* and a misfit at worst.

よくげつ 翌月 the next [following] month ▶残金を翌月へ回す carry the balance forward to *the next month*.

よくし 抑止 deterrence 一動 抑止する deter +目 ‖ 核抑止 nuclear deterrence ‖ 核抑止力 a nuclear deterrent.

よくしつ 浴室 a bathroom.

よくじつ 翌日 the next [following] day ▶翌日になって初めて私はその事実を知った It wasn't until *the next* [*following*] *day* that I learned the truth [what had (actually) happened]. ‖ その患者は手術を受けた翌日に死亡した The patient died (*on*) *the day after* the operation.

よくしゅう 翌週 the next [following] week ▶和夫は翌週また遊びに来た *The next week* Kazuo came to see me again. (➤「その次の週」の意なので the が必要).

よくじょう 浴場 a bath, a bathhouse ▶ホテルの自慢はローマ風の大浴場です The hotel boasts a big Roman *bath*.

‖ 公衆浴場 a public bath [bathhouse].

¹よくする 良くする improve +目 (改良する) ▶日本の政治をよくするにはどうすればいいと思いますか What do you think we should do to *improve* Japan's politics?

▶順子おばさんは子供の頃私にとてもよくしてくれた Aunt Junko *was* very *kind to* me when I was a child.

²よくする 浴する ▶自然の恩恵に浴する *enjoy* the blessings of nature ‖ 我々は日常生活においてコンピュータの恩恵に浴している We *enjoy the benefits* of computerization in our daily lives. / Our lives *have benefited greatly from* computerization.

よくせい 抑制 control 一動 抑制する control +目, curb +目 ▶インフレを抑制する *curb* [*control*] inflation ‖ あの男は自分[感情]を抑制することができない He can't *control* himself [his feelings].

よくぞ 善くぞ ▶遠いところをよくぞおいでくださいました Thank you for coming all the way to visit us. (➤ 訳文には特に表れない) ‖ よくぞ言ってくれた *Well* said. / I *appreciate* your saying that. / I (*completely*) agree with what you said.

よくそう 浴槽 a bathtub.

よくて 良くて at best (せいぜい) ▶私の英語の成績はよくてCだ My grade in English will be a C *at best* [*if I'm lucky*]. ‖ ことしのカープはよくて4位だろう The Carp will end up fourth place *at best* this season.

よくとくずく 欲得尽く ▶あの人は何でも欲得ずくだ That man always acts *for personal* [*material*] *gain*. (➤ for 以下は for selfish motives でもよい).

よくなる 良くなる improve ; get well (元気になる) ; look up (景気などが上向きになる) ▶弟は学校の成績がずいぶんよくなった My brother's grades (have) *improved* considerably. ‖ 天気は次第によくなった The weather gradually *improved*. ‖ 患者の容体はとてもよくなった The patient *has gotten* much *better*. ‖ 昔に比べると, 交通事情が格段によくなった Compared to the past, the traffic situation *is* much *better* now. ‖ 景気が再びよくなってきた Business *is looking up* again.

✉《見舞い状で》早くよくなってください I hope you will *get well* soon [you will *be feeling better* soon]. / *Get well* soon. / Hurry up and *get better*. ➤ 最後の例は「急いでよくなれ」の意で, 親しい人への見舞いのことば.

よくねん 翌年 the next [following] year ▶翌年彼はアメリカに留学した *The next year* he went to the United States to study.

よくばり 欲張りな greedy ▶あの人は何て欲張りなんだろう What a *greedy* [*grasping*] person he is!

よくばる 欲張る be greedy ▶そんなに欲張るな Don't be so *greedy*. / Don't try to get so much. / Don't bite off more than you can chew. (➤ 最後の文は「自分の能力以上のことをやろうとするな」の意) ‖ そんなに欲張って食べないの! Don't *make a pig of yourself*! / Don't *eat like a pig*!

よくぼう 欲望 (a) desire ▶飽くなき欲望 (an) insatiable *desire* ‖ 性的欲望 sexual *desire* ‖ 欲望を満たす[抑える] satisfy [suppress] one's *desire*(*s*) ‖ 人間の欲望には限りがない There's no limit to human *desire*. →欲.

よくめ 欲目 ▶親の欲目かもしれないが, 息子には音楽の才能があると思う I *may be biased as his parent*, but I think my son has musical talent. (➤「親の偏った見方かもしれないが」の意).

よくも ▶よくもこの俺に向かってそんなことが言えるな *How dare* you say such a thing to me? (➤ How dare ... ? は「どうして…できるほど生意気なのか」の意) ‖ よくも俺の頼みを断ってくれたな *How could* you turn down my request ? (➤ How could ... ? は「何てことをしてくれたのだ」の意で，相手をとがめる言い方).

[1]よくよう 抑揚 (an) **intonation** ▶抑揚のない話し方 a *monotonous* way of talking ‖ 抑揚に気をつけて次の一節を読んでごらん Read the next paragraph aloud paying attention to *intonation*.

[2]よくよう 浴用 ‖浴用せっけん a bathroom soap ‖ 浴用タオル a bathroom towel.

よくよく ▶きょうはよくよくついてないや This is *really* not my day. ‖ 息子さんが暴力を振るうなんてよくよくのことでしょう There must have been some *compelling* reasons for your son to have resorted to force. (➤ compelling は「やむにやまれぬ」) ‖ 彼女がうちに相談に来るなんてよくよく(＝ひどく)困っていたんだろう She must have been *badly* in need of help when she came to talk with us.

よくよくじつ 翌々日 ▶翌々日彼は手術を受けた He had an operation *two days later*.

よくりゅう 抑留 ▶第二次大戦後多くの日本人兵士がシベリアに抑留された Many Japanese soldiers *were detained* [*were interned*] in Siberia after World War II.

よけい 余計 **1**【余分】一形 余計な **more** (➤ ほかの比較級に変わることもある) 一副 余計に **too much** (量が多過ぎる), **too many**(数が多すぎる) ▶うっかり代金を余計に払ってしまった I carelessly paid *too much* [*overpaid*]. ‖ 店員は1000円余計にお釣りをくれた The clerk gave me back 1,000 yen *too much*. ‖ 我々はほかのチームより余計に練習した We practiced *harder* than other teams.

▶1枚余計にコピーしておいてください Please make one *extra* copy. ‖ あの人に余計なことを言わないでよ Please don't tell him *more than is necessary*. ‖ 彼女はいつもひと言余計なことを言う She always says *one word too many*.

▶ご両親に余計な心配をかけるんじゃないよ Don't *make* your parents *worry unnecessarily*. ‖ 対話「早くいい男を見つけろよ」「余計なお世話よ」"Find a nice man (and get married) soon." "*None of your business*."

2【ますます】**all the more** ▶有害な(ウェブ)サイトを見るなと言われると余計に見たくなる When I'm told not to access harmful websites, I want to access them *all the more* [I get *all the more* curious about them].

よける 除ける **avoid** +目 (避ける) ; **dodge** +目 (さっと身をかわす) ▶前から来た車をよけようとして水たまりに足を突っ込んだ I stepped into a puddle trying to *avoid* an oncoming car. ‖ カラスは男の子の投げた棒切れをうまくよけた The crow *managed to dodge* the stick (that) the boy threw at it.

よけん 予見する **foresee** +目 ▶未来 [結果] を予見する *foresee* the future [an outcome]. →予測.

よげん 予言・預言 a **prediction**(将来起こりそうなことを予測すること) ; **foretelling** (何かが起こる前にそれについて語ること) ; a **prophecy** (➤ 宗教上の「預言」) 一動 予言する **predict** +目, **foretell** +目, **prophesy** /prá:fəsaɪ/ +目 ▶誰も未来のことを正しく予言することはできない No one can accurately *predict* [*foretell*] the future.

‖預言者 a prophet.

よこ 横 **1**【縦に対して】**width** /wɪdθ/, **length**

(解説) 英語では，長方形の短いほうを width (形容詞は wide)，長いほうを length (形容詞は long) といい，正方形では左右を width，上下を length というのが原則. →縦.

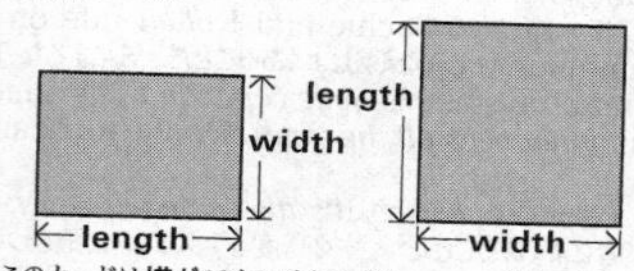

▶このカードは横が13センチある This card is thirteen centimeters *wide* [*in width*]. (➤ 後者は堅い言い方) ‖ 横60センチ縦40センチのベニヤ板をください I'd like a plywood board sixty centimeters *long* and forty centimeters wide [sixty by forty centimeters].

▶ラグビー競技場は縦が160ヤード，横が75ヤードある A rugby playing field is 160 yards long [in length] and 75 yards *wide* [*in width*]. ‖《横長の物の場合》この世界地図は縦が70センチ，横が1メートルある This world map is 70 centimeters high and 100 centimeters *long*. ‖《縦長の物の場合》はがきは縦14.8センチ，横10センチだ A postcard is 14.8 cm tall and 10 cm *wide*. ／A postcard measures 10×14.8 centimeters. (➤ ×は by と読む).

▶横向きの(パソコン)ディスプレー a *landscape* display ‖ 文書を横向きに表示する display a documentation *in landscape orientation* ‖ 写真を横向きに撮る take a *horizontal* shot.

▶狭い道で横に広がって歩いてはいけない Don't walk *spread out* along the narrow street. ‖ ではそちらのベッドに横になってください *Lie down* on the bed, please. ‖ 彼女は私の頼みを聞くと首を横に振った When she heard my request, she *shook her head*. ‖ カニは地面を横に動く Crabs move *sideways* along the ground. ‖ このたんすは横にしないと部屋に入らないぞ We have to turn the chest of drawers *sideways*, or we won't be able to get it into the room.

2【脇，側面】a **side** ▶会社の所在地は箱の横に書いてあります The company's address is written on the *side* of the package. ‖ 私の横へいらっしゃい Come and sit *by me* [*at my side*]. ／Sit *next to me*. ‖ 電気スタンドはソファーの横に置いてください Put the floor lamp *next to* the sofa. ‖ 銀行の横を曲がった所が市役所です *Turn* (*the corner*) at the bank, and you'll come to the city hall. ‖ いいって言うまで横を向いてて Please keep *looking aside* until I say OK. ‖ 授業中に横を向くんじゃない Don't *gaze off* during class.

3【慣用表現】▶兄は家の中では横のものを縦にもしないようなタイプです My brother *won't lift a finger* around the house. (➤ not lift a finger で「何一つしない」) ／My brother is a *real lazybones* [is *really lazy*]. (➤ lazybones は「ものぐさな人」) ‖ 横から口を出すな Don't butt in. ／Don't cut in [butt in] on people's conversations. ／ Mind your own business. (➤ 最後の文は「大きなお世話だ」の意で，非常に強い言い方) ‖ あの男は他人の話にすぐ横から口を挟みたがる He often *butts in* on other people's conversations.

よご 予後 《医学》a **prognosis**(複 **prognoses**) ▶医師は私に予後は良好 [厳しい] と言った My doctor gave me a good [grim] *prognosis*.

よこいっせん 横一線 ▶2頭の馬は横一線に走った The two horses ran *neck and neck* (with each other).

よこいと 横糸 the weft, the woof.
よこうえんしゅう 予行演習 a rehearsal.
よこおよぎ 横泳ぎ sidestroke ▶横泳ぎをする swim the *sidestroke*.
よこがお 横顔 a profile /próʊfaɪl/ ▶小百合は横顔が美しい Sayuri has a beautiful *profile*.
▶《比喩的》学校新聞は新監督の横顔を紹介した The school paper carried *a profile* of the new manager.
よこがき 横書き ▶原稿は横書きでお願いします Please *write* the manuscript *horizontally*.
よこかぜ 横風 a crosswind.
よこぎ 横木 a rail(垣根・柵などの).
よこぎる 横切る cross +㊐ ▶道路を横切るときは左右をよく確かめなさい Carefully look both ways well before you *cross* [*go across*] the street. ‖この駐車場を横切って行こう Let's *cut across* this parking lot. (➤ cut across は「横切って近道する」).
よこく 予告 (a) notice(通知) ; (a) warning(警告) ━ 動 予告する give a notice ▶会社を辞めるときには1か月前に予告しなければならない When you want to quit a company, you have to give a month's *notice*. ‖《カタログなどの表示》価格は予告なしに変更することがあります Prices are subject to change *without* (*prior*) *notice*. ‖何者かが空港に爆破予告の電話を掛けてきた Someone called the airport with *a bomb warning*.
‖予告編 a trailer, a preview (➤ 後者には「試写会」の意もある).
よこぐるま 横車 ▶課長の横車でそのプロジェクトはだめになった The manager's *unreasonable intervention* [*move*] killed the project. (➤「理不尽な干渉[やり方]」の意) ╱The manager *forced his unreasonable idea* (*on us*) and killed the project.
よこじく 横軸 a horizontal axis.
よこしま 邪な evil /íːvəl/, wicked /wíkɪd/ ▶よこしまな心を抱く have *evil* intentions.
よこじま 横縞 horizontal stripes.
よこす 寄越す ▶そのナイフをよこせ. 危ないから *Hand over* that knife. It's dangerous. ‖久しぶりに秋田のいとこが手紙をよこした My cousin in Akita *wrote to* me for the first time in ages. ‖たまには電話くらいよこせよ *Give* me a call once in a while, would you? ‖《電器店への電話で》アンテナの修理に誰かよこしてもらえますか Could you *send* someone *around* to repair the antenna?
よごす 汚す get [make] ... dirty, soil +㊐ ▶その油だらけの手でソファーを汚さないでね Don't *get* the couch *dirty* [*soil* the couch] with those oily hands of yours. ‖洗剤で川を汚さ(＝汚染し)ないようにしましょう Let's not *pollute* the river with detergents.
よこすべり 横滑り a skid(車輪の) ━ 動 横滑りする skid ▶ハンドルを切った瞬間, 車は横滑りした The moment I turned the steering wheel, my car *skidded* [*went into a skid*].
よこずわり 横座りする sit with one's legs folded out to one side ▶母は男性が横座りするのをひどく嫌う My mother detests seeing men *sitting with their legs folded out to one side*.
よこたえる 横たえる lay (down) ▶村人は傷ついた兵士を草の上に横たえた The villager *laid* the wounded soldier on the grass. (➤ laid は lay の過去形) ‖ソファーに身を横たえる *lie down* on the sofa. (→横たわる).
よこだおし 横倒し ▶強い風で私の自転車は横倒しになった The strong wind *flipped* my bicycle *on its side*. ╱The strong wind *blew* my bicycle *over* [*toppled* my bicycle].
▶車は完全に1回転してからゆっくりと横倒しになった The car completely flipped and slowly *toppled over sideways*.
よこたわる 横たわる lie (down) ▶ベッドに横たわる *lie* (*down*) on a bed ‖大木が前方に横たわっている A big log *is lying* ahead of us.
▶《比喩的》我々の前途にはいくつかの難問が横たわっている There are several difficulties *lying* ahead of us. ╱A number of difficulties *lie* before us.
よこちょう 横町 a side street ; an alley (小路) ▶横町の酒場 a bar in *a side street* [*an alley*].
よこづけ 横付け ▶黒塗りのリムジンがホテルの前に横付けになった(＝止まった) A black limo *pulled up* in front of the hotel.
よこっつら 横っ面 ▶もう一度言ってみろ. 横っ面をはり飛ばすぞ If you say that again, I'll *slap* you *on the cheek* [*smack you across the face*]!
よこづな 横綱 a ***yokozuna*** ; a grand champion in sumo wrestling (➤ 説明的な訳) ‖横綱審議委員会 the *Yokozuna* Promotion Council.
よごと 夜毎 every night, night after night ▶被害者は夜毎に悪夢にうなされた The victim was troubled by nightmares *night after night*.
よこどり 横取りする steal +㊐ (盗む) ; snatch +㊐ (ひったくる) ▶雄猫のトラは雌猫ミーの餌をいつも横取りする Our male cat Tora is always *stealing* food *from* our female cat Mi. ‖ハクトウワシはしばしばほかの猛きんが捕まえた魚を横取りする Bald eagles often *snatch away* the catch of other birds of prey.
よこなが 横長の horizontally long ; landscape (用紙・画面などが).
よこながし 横流し ▶密輸品を横流しする *sell* smuggled goods *on the black market* [*through illegal channels*].
よこなぐり 横殴り ▶横殴りの雨の中でバスを待つ wait for the bus in the *driving* [*slanting* ╱ *sideswiping*] *rain* ‖傘を差してはいたが, 横殴りの雨のためぬれてしまった Though I had my umbrella up, I got wet because of the *driving, horizontal rain*.
よこなみ 横波 a side [lateral] wave ;《物理学》a shear [transverse] wave ▶船は横波を受けて転覆した The ship was capsized by *a side* [*lateral*] *wave*.
よこならび 横並び ▶電力各社が電力料金を横並びで値上げした All the electric (power) companies *raised their rates to the same level*.
よこばい 横這い ▶消費者物価指数はここ数か月横ばいだ The consumer price index *has remained stable* for the past several months. ‖人の脳は25歳くらいまで成長し, 20年間くらい横ばいになり, 45歳くらいで衰え始める The human brain continues to grow till about 25. After that it *plateaus* for about 20 years before it starts to decline at about 45. (➤ plateau は「台形状に高止まりする」).
よこはば 横幅 the (horizontal) width ▶横幅30メートル 30 meters *across*.
よこはら 横腹 a side ▶左の横腹が痛い I have a pain in my left *side*.
よこぶえ 横笛 a flute ▶横笛を吹く *play the flute*.
よこぶり 横降り ▶台風の接近に伴って, 雨は横降りになった The approaching typhoon *blew* [*drove*] the rain *sideways*.
よこみち 横道 a side road →脇道 ▶《比喩的》校長

よ

先生の話はよく横道にそれる The principal often *wanders from the subject* [*gets sidetracked*] while talking.

よこむき 横向き ▶横向きの(=横顔の)写真 a photograph *in profile* ‖ 横向きに寝てください Please lie *on* your *side*.

よこめ 横目 a **sidelong** [**sideways**] **glance** ▶彼を横目で見る give him a *sidelong* [*sideways*] glance ‖ 兄はそのグラマーな女性を横目で盗み見た My older brother stole a glance at the busty woman *out of* [*from*] *the corner of his eye*.

よこもじ 横文字 ▶最近, 多くの若者が横文字入りのTシャツを着ている Nowadays many young people wear T-shirts with *phrases in English or other European languages* on them.
▶母は横文字(=欧米語)に弱い My mother knows little about *English and other Western* [*European*] *languages*.

よこやり 横槍 ▶同僚が私の企画に横やりを入れた(=干渉した) My colleague *stuck his nose into* [*interfered in*] my plans. (➤ stuck は stick の過去形).

よこゆれ 横揺れする **roll**(船・飛行機が) ▶船はひどく横揺れした Our ship *rolled* a great deal. ‖ でこぼこ道で車は大きく横揺れした My car *jolted* [*lurched*] *from side to side* on the bumpy road.

よごれ 汚れ **dirt**(泥やほこり) ; **grime** /graɪm/ (すすやあか) ; a **stain** (染み) ; **spots**(点々とついた染み) ▶白いシャツは汚れが目立つ *Dirt* stands out on a white shirt. ‖ このズボンは汚れがひどい These pants *are terribly dirty*. ‖ この汚れは落ちない This *stain* will not come out.
‖汚れ物 dirty things [clothes] ‖ 汚れ役 the role of a socially undesirable character [a social outcast].

よごれる 汚れる **become** [**get**] **dirty** ; **be soiled** (汗などで) ; **be stained** (落ちにくい染みで) 一形 **汚れた** **dirty** ; **polluted** (汚染された) ▶汚れた手 a *dirty* hand ‖ 汚れた空気 *foul* [*polluted*] air ‖ 泥んこで遊ばないで. 服が汚れるでしょ Don't play in the mud. Your clothes will *get dirty*. ‖ 汗で襟や袖口がすぐ汚れる My collars and cuffs soon *get soiled* with sweat. ‖ その海岸はタンカーから流出した重油で真っ黒に汚れている That coast *is stained* pitch black by the heavy oil that leaked out of the tanker. ‖ 工場の煙で空気が汚れている The air *is polluted* by smoke from the factories. ‖ 長椅子が汚れないようにカバーを掛けた I put a cover on the couch *to keep it clean*.

よさ 良さ・善さ a **good point** ; a **merit** (長所) ; a **virtue** (美点) ▶彼にはきみの良さがわからないのだ He can't see your *good points* [your *merits*]. ‖ この絵の良さがわかりますか Can you see *what's good* about this painting? ／Can you appreciate this painting?
▶彼はこれらの外国を訪れて初めて日本の生活スタイルの良さがわかった He did not realize the *virtues* of the Japanese lifestyle until he visited these foreign countries.

よざい 余罪 **other** [**additional**] **crimes** ▶放火で捕まった男は余罪を追及されている The man arrested for arson is being questioned about *additional crimes*.

よざくら 夜桜 ▶夜桜を見るには上野がいちばんよい Ueno is the best place to *enjoy cherry blossoms at night*.

よさそう ▶そろそろ彼が来てもよさそうなものだ He *should* be coming soon. (➤ should は「…するはず」という期待を込めた予測を表す) ／It's about time he got here. (➤ この got は仮定法) ‖ あの連中, 少しくらいこちらのことを考えてくれてもよさそうなものだ They *should* show a little consideration for us. ‖ もうそろそろ雨が降ってもよさそうだが It *should* start to rain any time now.

よさん 予算 a **budget** /bʌ́dʒɪt/ ▶今年度の予算 the *budget* for this fiscal year ‖ 思い切った予算の削減 drastic *budget* cuts ‖ 限られた予算で生活する live *on a limited budget* ‖ 予算案を作成する draw up *a budget* (➤ (×)budget plan とはしない) ‖ このパソコンは予算をだいぶオーバーした This personal computer far exceeded my *budget* [*the amount I had set aside* (*for it*)].
▶ 対話「冷蔵庫を買いたいのですが」「ご予算はどれくらいでしょう」"I'm looking for a new refrigerator." "*What price range*?" (➤「(ご予定の)値段の範囲はどのくらいですか」の意 ; 「予算オーバーです」は It's out of my price range.).
‖予算委員会 a budget committee.

[1]**よし** **all right, OK** ▶よし, わかった *All right* [*OK* ／ *Yes*], I understand. ／*I('ve) got it*. ／*Got it*. ‖ よし, それでは始めよう *Well*, let's get started.

[2]**よし 由** ▶私たちの会社の電話が盗聴されているなんて知る由もなかった We *had no way of* knowing that our company's telephones were being tapped.
✉ **お元気でお過ごしの由, 安心いたしました** I am relieved *to learn* [*hear*] *that* you are getting along well.
✉ **婚約なさった由, おめでとうございます** Congratulations on your engagement. ➤「由」は強いて訳さなくてもよいときがある.

[3]**よし 葦** 《植物》 a **reed**.

よしあし 善し悪し **1**【善悪】▶あなたはもう事のよしあしがわかっていい年なんですよ You are old enough to *know* [*tell*] *right from wrong*.
2【長所と短所】▶家と職場が近いのもよしあしだ Living near your workplace *has both advantages and disadvantages*.

ヨシキリ 《鳥》 a **reed warbler**(➤ オオヨシキリは oriental reed warbler, コヨシキリは black-browed reed warbler).

よじげん 四次元 **four dimensions** ▶この映画は四次元の世界を見せる This movie shows a *four-dimensional* world.

よしず 葦簾 a **reed screen**.

よじのぼる 攀じ登る **climb** (**up**) ; **clamber** (**up**) (手足を使って苦労して) ▶崖をよじ登る *climb up* a cliff ‖ 健二と私は険しい山道をふうふう言いながらよじ登った Kenji and I panted as we *struggled* [*clambered*] *up* the steep mountain path.

よしみ 誼・好 ▶友だちのよしみで, 力を貸してくれよ Please help me (out) *for friendship's sake*. ‖ 同郷のよしみで(=同郷なので)彼に仕事を世話してもらった He found me a job *because* he and I came from the same town.

よしゅう 予習 **preparation** 一動 **予習する** **prepare for a class** [**a lesson**] ▶自宅での予習 home *preparation* ‖ 教科書の予習をする *study* the textbook *beforehand* (➤ (×)prepare the textbook とはいわない) ‖ あすの英語の予習をしておこう I think I'll *prepare for* tomorrow's English *lesson*.

よじょう 余剰の **surplus** /sə́ːʳplʌs/ ▶余剰人員を減ら

す cut *surplus* [*excess*] *workers*.
‖**余剰農産物** surplus farm products [produce], farm surpluses ‖**余剰米** surplus rice.

よじょうはん 四畳半 a small room in the size of four and a half tatami mats(➤ 説明的な訳).

よしよし ▶《相手を褒めて》よしよし！*That's right!*／*Good!*／*Good boy* [*girl*]*!* (➤ 小さい子供に向かって言うほか，ペットなどに向かっても言う) ‖《子供などを慰めて》よしよし，泣かないで *There, there, dear*. Don't cry [Stop crying].

よじれる 捩れる ▶リュックのひもがよじれてるよ Your backpack straps *are twisted*.
▶《慣用表現》**腹の皮がよじれる**ほど笑った I almost *split my sides* laughing.

1 **よしん 予震** →前震.
2 **よしん 余震** an **aftershock** ▶体に感じる余震が３回あった We felt three *aftershocks*. ‖絶え間ない [繰り返す] 余震に住民は不安な一夜を過ごした The residents spent an anxious [a fearful] night due to continuous [repeated] *aftershocks*.
3 **よしん 予診** (a) **preliminary diagnosis** [**examination**].
4 **よしん 予審** (a) **preliminary examination**.
‖**予審請求** a demand for preliminary examination.

よじん 余人 ▶彼女は余人をもって代え難い人物だ She *is not* (*easily*) *replaceable*.／She *is a hard act to follow*.

よす 止す **stop** +目，《インフォーマル》**quit** +目 (やめる)；**give up** (諦める) ▶わめくのはよせ *Stop* shouting. ‖人の陰口をたたくのはよせ *Stop* talking about others behind their backs. ‖乱暴はよせよ *Don't* get violent. ‖もうよしなさい(＝もうたくさんだ) That's enough (of that). ‖危ない橋を渡るのはよしなさい You *had better not* run the risk. ‖**対話**「私，宝くじに当たったの」「冗談はよせよ」"I won the lottery." "*You must be joking.*／*Don't put me on.*" (➤ put ... on は「…をからかう」の意のインフォーマルな言い方で，主に《米》) ‖**対話**「きみはすてきだ」「冗談はよして！」"You look superb." "*Oh, come on.*" (➤ come on は「いいかげんにしてよ」の意で，相手をたしなめるような場合に用いる).

よすてびと 世捨て人 a **recluse** /rɪklúːs/ (➤ 日本語の「出家」の意にもなる)；a **hermit**(宗教的理由による).

よすみ 四隅 **four corners** ▶部屋の四隅 *the four corners* of a room.

よせ 寄席 a *yose* **theater**；《米》a **vaudeville theater**, 《英》a **music hall**
日本紹介 ✉ **寄席は，落語・漫才・手品などを演じる大衆的な劇場です．今ではごく少数しか残っていません** *Yose* is a popular theater where *rakugo* (comic storytelling), *manzai* (comic dialogue) and magic are performed. Only a few of them remain today.

よせあう 寄せ合う ▶１つの傘に肩を寄せ合って歩く walk *shoulder to shoulder* under an umbrella ‖子供たちは体を寄せ合って火の周りに集まった The children *huddled* together around the fire. (➤ huddle は「(暖をとるために)押し合いへし合い集まる」).

よせあつめ 寄せ集め a **jumble** (ごたまぜ)；a **patchwork** (雑多なものの) ▶わがチームは寄せ集めのチームです Ours is a *scratch* [*pickup*] team. ‖廃材の寄せ集めで物置を作った I built a barn with *a jumble* of used lumber. ‖彼の本は他人の意見の寄せ集めだ His book is *a patchwork* of other people's opinions.

よせあつめる 寄せ集める **collect** +目 (収集する)，**put together**
▶自分の論文を寄せ集めて本にした I *put* all my papers *together* into a book. ‖野菜や肉を寄せ集めてごった煮シチューを作った I *threw together* some meat and vegetables and made hotchpotch.

1 **よせい 余生** **the rest of** one's **life** ▶余生はオーストラリアで送りたい I want to spend *the rest of my life* in Australia.
2 **よせい 余勢** ▶連勝の余勢を駆って阪神は巨人に勝った *Emboldened by* their winning streak, the Tigers beat the Giants.

よせえ 寄せ餌 →まき餌.

よせがき 寄せ書き ▶帰国するジョン君のために級友みんなの寄せ書きを贈った We presented John, who is going home, with a card *containing messages from all his classmates*.

よせぎざいく 寄せ木細工 **wooden mosaic work**；**parquetry** /pάːˈkɪtri/ (床の).

よせつけない 寄せ付けない ▶チャンピオンは(強くて)挑戦者を全く寄せつけなかった The champion was so strong (that) *the challenger wasn't even close to being his equal*. ‖あの教授には人を寄せつけない厳しさがある There's a sternness about the professor that *keeps people at a distance* [*at arm's length*].

よせなべ 寄せ鍋 ***yosenabe***；a hotpot dish containing chicken, fish and vegetables cooked in a broth(➤ 説明的な訳).

よせる 寄せる

1【近づける】bring [**move**／**pull**] **close** 《to》 ▶人の耳元に口を寄せる *bring* one's mouth *close to* a person's ear ‖彼は扇風機をそばに寄せた He *brought* [*moved*／*pulled*] the electric fan *near* him. ‖冷蔵庫をもう少し壁に寄せなさい *Move* the refrigerator a bit *closer* to the wall. ‖私は車を道路の端に寄せた I *pulled* (my car) *over to* the side of the road.

2【送る】send in ▶この番組に対する皆さまのご感想をお寄せください Please *send in* your comments on the program.／We'd like to hear your comments on this program. *Please write to us*. ‖共同募金にはたくさんのお金が寄せられた A lot of money *was donated* to the community chest.

3【気持ちを】▶人に信頼を寄せる *place* one's *confidence in* a person ‖兄は彼女にひそかな思いを寄せている My brother *is* secretly *in love with* her. ‖日本の人たちはマラソン選手に金メダルの期待を寄せている Japanese fans *are hoping that* one of their runners will win the gold medal in the marathon. ‖多くの人が誘拐された少女に同情を寄せた Many people *had* [*felt*] *sympathy* for the kidnapped girl.

4【集める】▶この数字を全部寄せて(＝足して)みてください Please *add* all these figures.

よせん 予選 a **preliminary**, a **trial** [**qualifying**] **heat** ▶第一次[最終]予選 the first [final] round of *the preliminary* ‖100メートル予選 a 100-meter dash *preliminary* ‖私たちのチームは地区予選の３回戦で敗れた Our team lost in the third round of *the district preliminaries*.
▶有力選手はすべて予選を通過した All the hopefuls passed *the* (*trial*) *heats*. ‖日本選手はすべて予選落ちした All the Japanese athletes *were eliminated in the heats*.
‖**予選通過者** a qualifier.

よそ 余所 **some other place** ▶(ここではなく)よそで遊びな

さい Play *(at) some other place.* ／Play *somewhere else.* ‖よそ(の店)ではこんなに安くしていないよ You can't get it cheaper *anywhere else.* ／You won't find a cheaper one (than this) *at any other store.* ‖よそはよそ, うちはうちだよ *Let's not be concerned about other people's business.* ‖よその人(＝知らない人)についていってはいけないよ Don't go off with *strangers.*

[1]**よそう 予想** (an) **expectation** (予期); a **guess** (当て推量) **一動 予想する expect, guess; predict** (予測する) →予測 ▶嵐を予想する *expect* a storm ‖予想される5000人の群衆 an *expected* crowd of 5,000 people ‖来年は約2万人の高校生がうちの大学に応募するものと予想される Next year about 20,000 high school students *are expected* to apply to our university. ‖その津波の規模は予想を大きく超えていた The scale of the tsunami far exceeded *our expectations.* ‖待ち合わせ場所に現れた男性は私の予想していた人とは全く違っていた The man who came to the place we had arranged to meet was completely different from how I *expected* he would be. ‖予想どおり, 日本シリーズはホークスが優勝した The Hawks won the Japan Series *as (was) expected.* ‖猛暑による売り上げの落ち込みは予想の範囲内でした The drop in sales due to the extra hot summer was *within expectations* [was *within the expected range* ／was *in line with our forecast*]. ‖家は予想したよりも高く売れた The house was sold for more *than expected.* ‖日本チームは予想以上の活躍をした The Japanese team performed *better than I expected.* (➤ unexpectedly well とすると「予想外の」の意味となり, 活躍を予想していなかったという含みになる).
▶予想外の成功 an *unexpected* success ‖視聴者からは予想外の反響があった We received an *unexpectedly* good response from the audience. ‖こんなに時間と金がかかるとは予想外だった I *never expected* it to take so much time and money.
▶私の予想が当たって[外れて]その馬が勝った My *guess* proved right [wrong] and that horse won. ‖森さんに日本シリーズの(勝敗の)行方を予想してもらいましょう Let's ask Mr. Mori to *predict* the outcomes of the Japan Series games. ‖ゲームの結果は予想がつきません I *can't predict* [I *have no idea*] which team will win the game.
‖予想屋 a tipster (競馬などの).

[2]**よそう 装う** ▶ご飯は自分でよそって食べてね *Help yourself to* the rice. ‖妹がご飯をよそってくれた My (younger) sister *gave* me *a helping* of rice.

よそおい 装い ▶装いを凝らした女性 a *gorgeously-dressed* lady ‖そのブティックは装いも新たに店開きした(＝新装開店した) The boutique reopened *after a complete makeover* [*facelift*]. (➤ makeover と facelift は「模様替え」).

よそおう 装う **1**【着飾る】**be dressed** (服を着ている) ▶華やかに装った美女たち gorgeously-*dressed* beauties.
2【ふりをする】**pretend** ▶彼は重病を装って長期休暇を取った He took many days off, *pretending* to be seriously ill. ‖彼女は平静[無関心]を装った She *tried to appear* calm [indifferent]. ‖正直を装う *put on* a facade of honesty(➤ facade /fəsɑ́ːd/ は「外観, 見せかけ」の意).

よそく 予測 (a) **prediction** (推論や事実に基づく); (a) **projection** (データから割り出した); **foreseeing** (何かが起こることを前もって知ること); a **forecast** (最新の情報に基づく予想) **一動 予測する predict** +㊐, **project** +㊐, **foresee** +㊐, **forecast** +㊐ ▶未来を予測する *predict* [*foresee*] the future ‖来年の売上高を予測する *project* next year's sales figures(➤「来年の売上予測」は sales projections for next year) ‖事故を予測する *foresee* an accident ‖天気を予測する *forecast* the weather ‖来年の経済を予測することは難しい You can't easily *predict* what will happen to the economy next year.

よそごと よそ事 **someone else's problem** (ひと事) ▶その原発事故はよそ事ではない That nuclear power station accident is not (just) *someone else's problem.*

よそみ よそ見する ▶ほら, 車が来ますよ. よそ見をしないで Look! A car's coming this way. *Pay attention!* (➤ Watch where you're going! としてもよい) ‖事故は運転手のよそ見が原因らしい The accident seems to have been caused by the driver's *failure to keep his eye on the road.* (➤「道路を注視していなかったこと」の意).

よそめ よそ目 ▶よそ目にも彼が困っていることは明白だった *Even to a casual observer,* it was obvious that he was suffering hardship.

よそもの よそ者 an **outsider** (部外者); a **stranger** (見知らぬ人) ▶土地の人に溶け込むようにしなければ, いつまでたってもあなたはよそ者よ You'll be forever treated as *an outsider* if you don't try to mix with the local people.

よそゆき よそ行き ▶美知子はよそ行きの服を着て出かけた Michiko went out in her *best clothes.* (➤ in her Sunday best とするのは古風な表現) ‖母が電話でよそ行きことばでしゃべっている My mother is talking more *formally* than usual on the phone.

よそよそしい standoffish,《インフォーマル》**offish; distant** (隔てのある); **cold, cool** (冷たい) ▶パーティーで涼子はなぜかぼくによそよそしかった I don't know why but Ryoko *was cool* [*standoffish*] to me at the party. ‖ガールフレンドが最近ぼくによそよそしくなった Recently, my girlfriend *has grown cold* [*cool*] toward me.

よぞら 夜空 **the night sky** ▶打ち上げ花火が夜空を照らした The fireworks display lit up *the night sky.*

よた 与太 ▶あの男はよたばかり飛ばしている He's always *talking through his hat.* (➤「いいかげんなことを言う」の意) ／He's always *talking nonsense.*
‖よた者 a punk; a hooligan (ごろつき).

よたよた ▶酔っ払いがよたよたしながら近づいて来た A drunk *staggered* toward me.

よだれ 涎 **drool,**《インフォーマル》**slobber** ▶健ちゃん, よだれが出てるよ Ken, you're *slobbering* [*drooling*]. ‖よだれの出そうなケーキだ The cake looks so delicious, it's *making my mouth water* [it's *making me drool*]. (➤ make one's mouth water は「(人に)唾が出るほど食欲をそそらせる」の意. make ... drool はインフォーマルな表現) ／The cake is *mouth-watering.*
‖よだれ掛け a bib,《英また》a feeder.

[1]**よだん 余談** a **digression** /daɪgréʃən/ ▶余談はこれくらいにして本題に戻りましょう So much for the *digression,* let's return [get back] to the subject. ‖余談ですが, あの女優さんは私の高校の2年先輩です *By the way* [*Incidentally*], that actress was two years ahead of me in (my) high school.

[2]**よだん 予断** ▶状況がどう変わるか, 予断を許さない(＝わ

からない) *No one can tell* [*There is no knowing*] how things will go. ‖ 勝敗は予断を許さない(＝予測できない) The outcome of the game is *anybody's guess*.

1**よち 余地** **room**《for》(余裕) ▶この試作品にはまだまだ改善の余地がある There is still a lot of *room for* improvement on this (product's) prototype. ‖ 駐輪場はいっぱいで私の自転車を入れる余地はなかった The lot was so packed there was no *room* [*space*] *for* my bicycle. ‖ やつらの仕業であることは疑いの余地がない They are the culprits. *There is no room for* doubt about that. ／This is undoubtedly their doing. ‖ きみの行為は弁解の余地がない What you did *is inexcusable*.

2**よち 予知** **foresight**(将来を見通すこと) ; (a) **prediction** (予測) **一動 予知する** **foresee** ＋目, **predict** ＋目 ▶地震や噴火の予知は難しい It is hard to *foresee* [*predict*] earthquakes and volcanic eruptions.

よちょう 予兆 a **sign** ▶地滑りの予兆を検知する detect (early) *signs* of a landslide.

よちよち ▶うちの子はよちよち歩きを始めた My baby has begun to *toddle*. (➤ よちよち歩きの子供を toddler という).

よつかど 四つ角 a **crossing**, a **crossroads** ▶まっすぐ行って最初の四つ角を右へ曲がってください Go straight and turn right at the first *crossing* [*crossroads* ／*corner*].

よつぎ 世継ぎ a **successor** (人) ; **succession** (後継) ▶天皇の世継ぎ問題 the imperial *succession* issue.

よっきゅう 欲求 (a) **desire**(欲望) ▶欲求を満たす[抑える] satisfy [suppress] *a desire* ‖ このがん患者たちの生への欲求は強い These cancer patients have a strong *desire* [*will*] to live. (➤ will は「意志」) ‖ その主婦は欲求不満から万引きを重ねた That housewife shoplifted many times *out of frustration* (with life).

よつぎり 四つ切り ▶四つ切りにする *cut into quarters* ‖ 四つ切りの写真 a photo in *a quarter size*.

よつご 四つ子 **quadruplets** /kwɑːdrúːpləts ‖ kwɔ́drʊpləts/, 《インフォーマル》**quads** (➤ その1人は a quadruplet).

よって 因って ▶本件は証拠不十分, よって棄却する This case is based on insufficient evidence. *Therefore* we dismiss it. (➤ 法廷では Case dismissed. と宣言する). →因(よ)る.

よってたかって 寄って集って ▶数人の中学生が寄ってたかってその少年を殴った Several junior high students *ganged up on* the boy and beat him up. ‖ マスコミは寄ってたかって首相のその決断を非難した The media *joined together* to criticize the prime minister's decision.

ヨット a **yacht** /jɑːt/ ; a **sailboat**, 《英また》a **sailing boat** ▶ヨット遊びに行く go *sailing* ‖ 葉山の沖にヨットが点々と浮かんでいる The sea off Hayama is dotted with *sailboats*.

‖**ヨットハーバー** a yacht harbor [basin], a marina ‖ **ヨットレース** a yacht race.

> **危ないカタカナ語✹ ヨット**
> **1** 日本語で「ヨット」というと, ふつうレースやスポーツで用いる小型の帆船を連想するが, 英語の yacht は船室のある遊覧用の豪華船(帆はない)をも指す.
> **2** したがって, 小型の帆船であることをはっきりさせるためには sailboat, sailing boat という必要がある.

よっぱらい 酔っ払い a **drunk** [**drunken**] **person**, 《インフォーマル》a **drunk** ▶OL が酔っ払い男に絡まれていた A woman office worker was harassed by *a drunken man*. ‖ 父は酔っ払い運転で捕まったことがある My father was once caught for *drunk* [*drunken*] *driving*. ／My father was once caught *driving drunk*. (➤「酔っ払い運転手[ドライバー]」を drunk-driver という).

よっぱらう 酔っ払う **get drunk** ▶ぐでんぐでんに酔っ払う *get* dead [blind] *drunk* ／get plastered ‖ ワインで酔っ払った I *got drunk* on wine. ‖ 酔っ払った女性が道路に寝ていた A *drunk*(*en*) woman was lying in the street.

よっぽど 余っ程 →よほど.

よつゆ 夜露 **evening** [**night**] **dew** ▶芝生に座ったらお尻が夜露にぬれた When I sat on the grass, my bottom got wet from the *evening* [*night*] *dew*.

よづり 夜釣り **night fishing** [**angling**] ▶夜釣りに出かける[をする] go [do] *night fishing*.

よつんばい 四つん這い ▶赤ん坊が四つんばいになって立とうとしている The baby *is on all fours* trying to stand up.

よてい 予定

a **plan** (計画) ; a **schedule** /skédʒuːl ‖ ʃédjuːl/ (時間に従った) **一動 予定を立てる** **plan** ＋目, **make plans**《for》(➤ plan は複数形で用いることが多い) ▶旅行の予定を立てる *plan* a trip ‖ 彼女が行くかどうかわからないので旅行の予定が立てられない We can't make our travel *plans* because we aren't sure if she will join us or not. ‖ 母の病気で温泉旅行の予定がだめになった Our *plans* to go to a hot spring fell through due to my mother's illness.

▶台風のため予定していた行事がすべて中止になった All (the) *scheduled* events were called off because of the typhoon. ‖ 開会式では住民参加のマスゲームが予定されている Mass gymnastic exercises with the participation of residents *are planned* for the opening ceremony.

> **【文型】**
> …する予定である《計画・意思》
> **be planning to** do
> **plan to** do
> …する予定である《日程》
> **be scheduled to** do
> 日時(A)に予定されている
> **be scheduled for** A

▶来月沖縄へ行く予定だ I'*m planning* [I *plan*] *to* go to Okinawa next month. (➤ 前者は計画中, 後者はすでに計画しているという意味で用いるのがふつう) ‖ 当機は4時に成田に到着の予定です We'*re scheduled to* arrive at Narita at four o'clock. ‖ 卒業式は3月25日の予定です The graduation ceremony *is scheduled for* March 25.

▶私たちは来月修学旅行で北海道へ行く予定だ We *are going* on a school trip to Hokkaido next month. (➤ この進行形は近い未来の行動を表す) ‖ **対話**「週末のご予定は?」「特に何もありません」“*What are you going to do* this weekend?” “I don't have anything planned.” ‖ 私たちの列車は7時に着く予定だったが雪で遅れた Our train *was due* at seven, but was late because of (the) snow. (➤ due は「(到着の)予定で」の意).

▶道が混んでいて予定の時刻には(＝予定どおりには)着けそうもない Traffic is backed up, so we are not likely to get there *on schedule* [*on time*]. ‖ ショーは予定どおり進行しています The show is proceeding just *as scheduled* [*as planned*].

▶仕事の都合で予定より1日早く帰ることになった I had to leave a day earlier *than planned* because of work. ‖ 開会式はすでに1時間も予定より遅れている The opening ceremony is already one hour *behind schedule*. ‖ **対話**「水曜日はお忙しいですか」「はい，その日は予定がぎっしり詰まっています」"Are you busy on Wednesday ?" "Yes, *I have a tight schedule* on that day. ／I'm *all booked up* (on) that day."

▶ここが新体育館の予定地です This is the *projected site* for the new gymnasium. (➤ planned site は一般的でない) ／This is *the site where we plan to build* a new gymnasium. ‖ **対話**「(出産の)予定日はいつですか」「1月11日です」"*When is* your baby *due* ?" "On January 11."

✉ **東京にいらっしゃる間のご予定を教えてください** Please let me know your *plans* [*schedule*] while in Tokyo.

直訳の落とし穴「予定があるか」
「予定」＝schedule と考えて，「今度の土曜日，何か予定ある？」を (×) Do you have a schedule this Saturday ? などと言っても全く通じない．予定 (＝スケジュール) 全体を聞くのであれば，How's your schedule [What's your schedule like] (for) this Saturday ? ／What's on your schedule [What do you have scheduled] (for) this Saturday ? (土曜日の予定はどうなっている？) などでよいが，最初の日本語は予定 (＝計画) の有り無しを聞いているので，Do you have any plans for this Saturday ? とするか，もっとストレートに暇の有無を聞いて，Are you free this Saturday ? とする．

‖**予定表** a schedule ‖ **出発** [**到着**] **予定時刻** the estimated time of departure [arrival].

よとう 与党 **the ruling party, the governing party** ▶与党はその法案をごり押しした *The ruling party* used its power to push the bill through. ／*The ruling party* railroaded the bill.

よどおし 夜通し **all night long** ▶嵐が夜通し吹き荒れていた The storm raged *all night long* [*throughout the night*].

よどみなく 澱みなく **fluently** ▶英語がよどみなくしゃべれるようになりたい I'd like to learn to speak English *fluently* [*without faltering* ／ *without hesitation*].

よどむ 澱む 一形 **よどんだ** **stagnant** (水などが), **stale** (空気がむっとする) ▶よどんだ水 *standing* water (流れていない)；*stagnant water* (よどんで臭い) ‖ 川の水はふちの辺りでよどんでいる The water *is* [*stands*] *still* at the deep part of the river. ‖ ここは空気がよどんでいる The air *is stale* in here. ‖ よどんだ目をしているね Your eyes look *dull*.

よなおし 世直し **social reform.**

よなか 夜中 ▶夜中に働く work late *at night* ‖ **夜中に** (＝眠っているときに) 歯ぎしりする grind one's teeth *in one's sleep* ‖ **夜中に地震があった** We had [There was] an earthquake *in the middle of the night*. ‖ 私は夜中に何度もトイレに起きた I went to the bathroom several times *during* [*in*] *the night*. ‖ 隣の息子さんは毎晩**夜中の2時か3時まで**勉強している The boy next door studies *till the small* [*wee*] *hours* every night. (➤ the small [wee] hours は夜12時から3時頃までをいう)．

よなが 夜長 ▶秋の夜長は読書にもってこいだ *Long autumn nights* are perfect for reading.

よなき 夜泣き ▶母親は赤ん坊の夜泣きに悩まされている The mother is troubled by her baby's (*frequent*) *crying at night*.

よなべ 夜業 **night work.**

よなれた 世慣れた **worldly-wise**；《インフォーマル》 **streetwise** [**street-smart**] (➤「どんな状況でも生き抜く」というニュアンスの語) ▶あの人は世慣れた人だ He is *a man of the world*. ／He knows much of the world. ‖ あの若者は年の割には**世慣れている** That young man *is worldly-wise* [*has been around*] for his age.

よにげ 夜逃げ ▶あのパン屋の一家は借金取りから逃れるため夜逃げした That baker's family *skipped town by night* [《英》 *did a moonlight flit*] to escape their debt-collectors.

よにも 世にも ▶橋が突然落ちたなんて世にも不思議な話ね The bridge collapsed suddenly ? That's *an extremely strange incident*.

1**よねつ 余熱** **residual heat** ▶エンジンは止まってもしばらく余熱で熱い The engine is hot for some time with *residual* [*lingering*] *heat* after it stops. (➤ residual は「残余の」に近い堅い語)．

2**よねつ 予熱する** **preheat** ＋目 ▶オーブンを180度に予熱しておきます *Preheat* the oven to 180 (degrees) Celsius [350 (degrees) Fahrenheit]. (➤アメリカでは華氏で表すことが多いので注意)．

よねん 余念 ▶若き学究たちは研究に余念がない The young researchers *are completely absorbed* [*engrossed*] *in* their studies.

よねんせい 4年生 a **fourth grader** (小学校の)；a **fourth year college student**, a **college senior** (大学の).

よのなか 世の中 **the world** (世間)；**life** (人生)；an **age** (時代) ⇀世

▶彼女は世の中のことがまだわかっていない She knows nothing of *the world* yet. ‖ 最近は世の中の変化が速すぎてついていけない *The world* is changing so fast these days we can hardly keep up. ‖ **世の中には**さまざまな人がいるものだ There are all kinds of people *in the world* [*out there*]. ／It takes all sorts to make a world. (➤「あらゆる種類の人が集まって世の中を作る」の意の英語のことわざ) ‖ **対話**「コルカタで古い友人に出会ったよ」「**世の中狭いね**」"I met an old friend of mine in Kolkata." "*It's a small world, isn't it ?*"

▶世の中 (＝人生) が嫌になっただけよ I'm sick and tired of *life*, that's all. ‖ 今はスマートフォンの世の中 (＝時代) だけど，私は持っていない This may be the *smartphone age*, but I (still) don't have one.

よは 余波 an **aftereffect, the aftermath** ▶台風19号の余波 *aftereffects* of Typhoon No.19.

▶《比喩的》ニューヨーク株価暴落の余波を受けて東証の株価も暴落した Stock prices on the Tokyo Stock Exchange plummeted *in the aftermath of* the crash on the New York Stock Exchange.

よはく 余白 a **blank space** (空所)；a **margin** (欄外) ▶余白にメモを書く write a note in the *margin* ‖ 以下余白 The remainder left *blank*. ／The remainder of this page is (intentionally) left *blank*. (➤説明的な表現.「以下余白」は英語にはない表現)．

よばわり 呼ばわり ▶彼を無能呼ばわりする *call* him [*accuse* him *of being*] incompetent ‖ 彼をひきょう

者呼ばわりする *brand* him *with* cowardice (➤ brand A with B で「A(人)にB(汚名)のレッテルを貼る」).

よび 予備の spare (代替物として取ってある); reserve (蓄えてある); extra (余分の) ▶予備のタイヤ a *spare* tire ‖ スーツケースの底に少し予備のお金を入れておきなさい Put some *reserve* money at the bottom of your suitcase. ‖ ここに予備の椅子があります Here are some *extra* chairs. ‖ 何の予備知識もなしに能の舞台を見ても楽しめないよ You won't (be able to) enjoy a Noh performance without any *background knowledge* of it. (➤ any を some にすると「ある程度の予備知識がないと」の意になる).
‖予備交渉 a preliminary negotiation ‖ 予備選挙 a preliminary election, 《米》 a primary ‖ 予備調査 a preliminary survey ‖ 予備費 a reserve fund.
☛ 予備軍, 予備校 (→見出語)

よびあつめる 呼び集める call ... together ▶スタッフ全員をすぐ呼び集めてくれ Please *call* [*bring*] all the staffers *together* quickly.

よびおこす 呼び起こす inspire +目 (感情などを); bring back (記憶などを) ▶親切心はしばしば愛情を呼び起こす Kindness often *inspires* love. ‖ その1枚の写真は私の過去の記憶を呼び起こした That one photograph *brought back* [*awakened*] memories of the past. (➤ awaken は「(人)に…を気づかせる」) ‖ その演説は聴衆に大きな感動を呼び起こした That speech deeply *moved* [*elicited* a huge emotional response from] the audience. (➤ elicit は「(反応などを)引き出す」).

よびかけ 呼び掛け an appeal ▶交通遺児基金への呼びかけは大きな成果を収めた The *appeal* for funds to help children who have lost (their) parents in traffic accidents was highly successful.

よびかける 呼び掛ける appeal (訴える); call on (人に協力を求める); call for (要求する); invite (勧める) ▶台風で被害を受けた人々のために援助を呼びかける *appeal* for help for the typhoon victims ‖ 彼は割り箸を使うのをやめようとみんなに呼びかけた He *called on* [*appealed to*] everyone to stop using disposable chopsticks. ‖ 静岡のある画家が初日の出を一緒に描きませんかと呼びかけている A painter in Shizuoka *has invited* people to paint the sunrise on New Year's Day with him.

よびぐん 予備軍 ▶生活習慣病の予備軍がわんさといる There is a huge number of *people who are likely to* get lifestyle (-related) diseases. / There is a huge number of *candidates for* lifestyle(-related) diseases.

よびこう 予備校 a *yobiko*
《参考》 preparatory school を「予備校」に当てる場合もあるが, これはアメリカでは大学進学のための寄宿制の私立校を, イギリスではパブリックスクール進学のための寄宿制の私立校を指す.
日本紹介 ✉ **予備校は高校や大学入試を目指す学生がその準備のために通う特別な学校です. 受験に失敗した者の多くは翌年の受験を目指して勉強するために通います** A *yobiko* is a special school for students who want to study to prepare for senior high school or college entrance exams. Many of those who have failed entrance exams attend a *yobiko* to study in the hope of passing entrance examinations the next year.
▶前田さんは受験に失敗して予備校に行っている Maeda flunked the entrance exams and is now attending a *yobiko*. ‖ 予備校生 a *yobiko* student.

よびごえ 呼び声 a call (遠く離れた人に聞こえるように発する); a cry (大声での) ▶遠くから呼び声がした *A call* [*cry*] came from a distance. / There was *a cry* in the distance.
▶《慣用表現》竹田氏は次期社長の呼び声が高い Many people speak of Mr. Takeda as the best choice for the next president of our company.

よびこみ 呼び込み a barker (人) ▶サーカスの呼び込み a *barker* at a circus.

よびすて 呼び捨て ▶近頃の女子高生は男子生徒を呼び捨てにする High school girls today *call* boys *only by their family names, without adding -kun or -san*.

よびだし 呼び出し a summons /sʌ́mənz/ (警察・裁判所などへの); paging (館内放送での); a ***yobidashi***, a ring announcer (相撲の) ▶警察から呼び出しを受ける receive *a summons* from the police ‖ 太郎の高校時代, 母親は何度も学校から呼び出しを食った When Taro was in high school, his mother *was called* to the school many times.
▶《館内放送で》お呼び出しを申し上げます. 芦屋の山村さま, フロントまでご連絡ください *Paging* Mr. Yamamura from Ashiya. Please contact the front desk. ‖ 呼び出しをお願いしたいのですが I'd like to have someone *paged*. ‖ 私はホテルのロビーで呼び出しを受けた I *was paged* in the hotel lobby.

よびだす 呼び出す call +目; call ... up (電話に); summon +目 (出頭させる); page +目 (ホテルや劇場などで放送を使って) ▶彼女は職員室に呼び出されて欠席が多いことを注意された She *was called* to the teachers' room and warned against missing school too often. ‖ 彼は被告の証人として法廷に呼び出された He *was summoned* to court as a defense witness. ‖ 人をこんな所に呼び出して何の用だ Why did you *call* me *out* to this place? What happened? ‖ マージャンをするのにあと1人足りない. 電話で良明を呼び出そう We need one more person to play mah-jongg. *Let's call* Yoshiaki *and ask* him *to come over*. ‖ 劇場の入り口で姉を呼び出してもらった I *had* my sister *paged* at the theater entrance.

よびたてる 呼び立てる ▶こんな朝早くからお呼び立てして申し訳ありません I am very sorry to have troubled you by *asking* you *to come* this early in the morning.

よびつける 呼び付ける ▶トムは課長に呼びつけられて絞られた Tom *was called before* the section chief and chewed out.

よびとめる 呼び止める call to ... to stop; stop +目 (動きを中止させる); flag +目 (タクシーを) ▶門番が大学生を呼び止めた The gatekeeper *called to the college student to stop*. ‖ 久保田先生が私を廊下で呼び止めた Mr. Kubota *stopped* me in the hallway. ‖ 流しのタクシーを呼び止めた I *hailed* [*flagged*] a cruising taxi.

よびな 呼び名 a name ▶タンポポは地方によっていろいろな呼び名がある Dandelions have different *names* in different regions. ‖「江戸」は東京の古い呼び名だ "Edo" is an old *name* for Tokyo.

よびみず 呼び水 pump priming ▶その値下げが呼び水となって値下げ戦争が起こった The price reduction *triggered* a price war.

よ

よびもどす 呼び戻す call ... back ▶急用で旅先から呼び戻された I *was called back* from my trip on urgent business.

よびもの 呼び物 the (chief) attraction, the highlight, a feature ▶そのサーカスの呼び物は空中ぶらんこだ *The chief attraction* of the circus is its trapeze act. ‖この種の雑誌は有名人のゴシップを呼び物にしている Magazines of this kind *feature* gossip about celebrities. →アトラクション.

よびょう 余病 a complication(➤しばしば複数形で) ▶患者は糖尿病から余病を併発して死んだ The patient died of *complications* from diabetes.

よびよせる 呼び寄せる call over ▶監督は打者を呼び寄せて指示を与えた The manager *called* the batter *over* and gave him instructions. ‖家族をできるだけ早く国元から東京へ呼び寄せたい I'd like to *call* my family from home *to live with me* in Tokyo as soon as possible.

よびりん 呼び鈴 a bell ; a doorbell (玄関の) ▶玄関の呼び鈴が鳴った The *doorbell* rang.

よぶ 呼ぶ

> 📖 訳語メニュー
> 声を掛ける →call 1
> 来いと言う →call, want 2
> 招待する →invite, ask 3
> 呼称する →call 4

1【声を掛ける】 call +目 ▶「江田さん」と誰かが人混みの中から私の名を呼んだ "Mr. Eda !" Somebody in the crowd *called* my name. ‖誰かが助けを呼ぶ声が聞こえた I heard someone *call* [*cry*] for help. ‖名前を呼ばれたら返事をしなさい Answer when your name *is called*. ‖呼べば聞こえる[呼んでも聞こえない]所にいる stay *within* [*out of*] *earshot*.

2【来るように言う】 call +目 ; want +目 (用があって) ▶医者を呼びにやる *send for* a doctor ‖すぐに出ていけ, でないと警察を呼ぶぞ Get out of here right now. Otherwise [If you don't] I'll *call* the police. ‖すぐ救急車を呼んだほうがいい You'd better *call* an ambulance at once. ‖恵理子, お父さんが呼んでいる(=用があると言っている)わよ Eriko, Dad *wants* you. (➤実際に「大声で呼んでいる」ときは Dad is calling you.) ‖彼は秘書を呼んだ He *called for* his secretary. ‖島田君, 職員室で山崎先生が呼んでいるよ Shimada, Ms. Yamazaki *wants* (*to see*) you in the teachers' room. ‖すみませんが安藤さんを電話口に呼んで(=電話に出して)いただけますか Excuse me, but can you please *put* Mr. Ando *on the phone* [*call* Mr. Ando *to the phone*] ? (➤ put の代わりに get を使うと命令的になる).

3【招待する】 invite +目, ask +目 ▶娘の誕生パーティーにはお友だちを10人くらい呼ぼうと思います I think we should *invite* around ten of her friends to our daughter's birthday party. ‖私は彼女の結婚式に呼ばれている I *am invited* [*asked*] to her wedding. ‖そのうち, その新しいお友だちをうちに呼んだら? Why don't you *have* [*ask*] your new friend *over* sometime?(➤have A over で「A(人)を家に呼ぶ」).

4【…と呼ぶ, 称する】 call +目

> 【文型】
> A を B と呼ぶ
> call A B ➤ Bは名詞

▶私の名前は温子.「アッコ」って呼んでください My name's Atsuko. *Just call* me "Akko."

5【呼び起こす】 ▶彼の写楽についての新著は大きな反響を呼んだ(=引き起こした) His new book on Sharaku *caused* a sensation. ‖この提案は今後, 関係者の間でも論議を呼びそうです This proposal is likely to *create* controversy among the people concerned.

よふかし 夜更かしする stay [sit] up late ▶友だちと話し込んでいて, ゆうべは夜更かししてしまった I *stayed* [*sat*] *up late* last night talking with my friends. ‖夜更かしの癖が直らない I can't break my *late night habit* [*habit of keeping late hours*]. (➤ keep late hours は夜更かしが習慣になっている場合の言い方) ‖わが家は皆夜更かしだ Our family are all *night owls*.

よふけ 夜更け ▶夜更けまで町をふらつく prowl the town *till late at night* [*far into the night*] ‖私は夜更けまで勉強した I *burned the midnight oil*. (➤決まった言い方).
▶こんな夜更けにお隣さんは何をトンカンやってるんだろう What on earth is our neighbor hammering on *at this* (*late*) *hour of the night* ?

よぶん 余分の extra /ékstrə/ (追加の) ; spare (予備の) ; excess(過剰な) ; superfluous /supə́ːrfluəs/ (過剰な ; 堅い語) ▶バッグにはいつも余分のハンカチを入れてある I always carry an *extra* [*a spare*] handkerchief in my purse. ‖私には余分なお金も時間もない I have neither money nor time *to spare*. (➤ to spare は「余っている…」の意で, 前の名詞を修飾する) ‖余分な(=必要以上の)物を入れるからスーツケースが重くなるんだよ That suitcase is going to weigh a ton because you are putting *more than you need* in it. (➤ weigh a ton は「(物が)とても重い」の意のインフォーマルな表現).
▶アイスクリーム10個と言ったけど, 1つ余分に買って来て I said ten ice cream cones, but could you get *one more* ? ‖余分な語を削りなさい Cut out *superfluous* words.

よほう 予報 a forecast 一動 **予報する** forecast +目 ▶長期予報 a long-range *forecast* ‖天気を予報する *forecast* the weather ‖きょうは(天気)予報が外れた[当たった] Today's *weather forecast* was off [accurate]. ‖天気予報によると夕方にかけて雪です According to the *weather report*, it will snow [we will have snow] toward evening. / *The weatherperson says* it will snow toward evening.
‖気象予報士 a certificated weather forecaster.

よぼう 予防 (a) prevention(防止) ; protection (保護) 一動 **予防する** prevent +目, protect +目 ▶かぜの予防に何かいい方法はないですか Is there any good way of *preventing* [*staving off*] a cold ? ‖かぜの予防にうがいをしなさい Gargle to *protect yourself against* colds. ‖歯周病は注意すれば予防できる Periodontal disease *can be prevented* if you are careful enough. ‖火災予防週間です. お休み前にもう一度火の元を確かめましょう This is *Fire Prevention* Week. Double-check for fire hazards before you go to bed.
‖予防医学 preventive medicine ‖予防措置 a preventive measure ‖予防薬 a preventive [preventative] medicine.

よぼうせっしゅ 予防接種 (a) vaccination /væksinéiʃən/ (ワクチンの) ▶うちの息子はポリオの予防接種はもう受けた My son has already had *a vaccination* [been vaccinated] *against* polio. ‖インフルエンザ

の予防接種を受けた I've gotten a flu *shot*.（➤ shot は「注射」）.

よぼうせん 予防線 ▶彼らとの争いを避けるために予防線を張る *take every precaution* to avoid disputing with them.

よほど 余程 **1**【ずいぶん】extremely, badly（➤ 後者のほうがインフォーマル）▶中村さんの口ぶりからすると奥さんはよほどの美人なのだろう From the way Nakamura talks, his wife must be *extremely* beautiful. ‖ 彼はよほどその金が必要だったのだろう He *badly* needed the money, I suppose. ‖ 彼はよくカレーライスを食べる. よほど好きなんだろう He eats curry and rice quite often. He must like it *a lot*. ‖ そのくらいの値段で新品が手に入るんなら，修理してもらうより買ったほうがよほどいい If you can get a new one at such a (low) price, it's *much better* buying it than having the old one repaired. ‖ よほどの（＝重大な）ことがない限り，あすの運動会は行われる Tomorrow's athletic meet will be held *unless something serious comes up*.

2【もう少しで】▶私はよほど大学を辞めようかと思った I *came* (*awfully*) *close to* dropping out of college.

よぼよぼ ▶よぼよぼのおじいさん a *doddering* [*feeble and shaky*] old man.

よまつり 夜祭り a night festival.

よまわり 夜回り (a) night patrol ▶夜回りに行く go on *night patrol*.

よみ 読み (an) insight /ínsaɪt/（洞察力）; (a) judgment（判断力）▶読みの深い[浅い]人 a person of deep [shallow] *insight* ‖ その監督は読み（＝判断）が深い[浅い] The manager has good [poor] *judgment*.

▶正確な読みを心がける try to *read* for accuracy ‖ 難しい漢字に読みをつける give *the reading* of a difficult kanji.

よみあげる 読み上げる read out（声を上げて読む）▶官房長官が新内閣の名簿を読み上げた The Chief Cabinet Secretary *read out* the list of the newly-appointed ministers. ‖ 裁判長が判決文を読み上げた The presiding judge *pronounced* the sentence.（➤「判決を下した」の意）.

よみあやまる 読み誤る misread ＋目; mispronounce（誤った発音をする）▶漢字を読み誤る *misread* [*mispronounce*] a kanji ‖ ビジネスの世界では，国際情勢を読み誤ると命取りだ In the business world, *misjudging* [*misreading*] the international situation can be fatal.

よみあわせる 読み合わせる collate the copy with the original by reading aloud.

よみおわる 読み終わる finish reading; read through（読み通す）▶その雑誌を読み終わったら私に貸してください Can you lend me the magazine when you *have* [*are*] *finished reading* it [you *are done with* it / you *are through with* it]?

よみかえす 読み返す read over again ▶手紙を読み返す *read* the letter *over again* ‖ ケアレスミスがないかどうか，答案を読み返した I *reread* my answer sheet to be sure I hadn't made a careless mistake.

よみがえる 蘇る・甦る come to life, revive（生き返る）▶この雨で公園の緑がよみがえったようだ The greenery of the park seems to have been *revived* by the rain. ‖ 写真を見ているうちに，あのときの苦い思い出がよみがえってきた As I looked at the pictures, the bitter memories of those days *came back to me* [*revived within me*].

よみかき 読み書き reading and writing ▶読み書きの能力 *literacy* ‖ ジョンは読み書きができる John is a *literate* person.（➤「（特に文学に関して）教養のある人」の意にもなる）‖ 読み書きが全然できない人もいる Some people cannot *read or write* at all. / Some people are completely illiterate.

よみかた 読み方 a reading; (a) pronunciation（発音）; (an) interpretation（解釈）▶この漢字には何とおりの読み方がありますか How many *readings* does this *kanji* have? ‖ 彼は 'psychiatrist' という単語の読み方がわからなかった He didn't know the *pronunciation* of [*how to pronounce*] the word 'psychiatrist.'

よみきり 読み切り ▶読み切りの小説 a novel [short story] *complete in one issue* (*of a magazine*).

よみごたえ 読み応え ▶この本はとても読み応えがある This book is *rich in content* [is well *worth reading* / is *rewarding*].（➤ 前者は「内容が豊か」，後者の2例は「読む価値がある」の意）.

よみこなす 読み熟す ▶私にはこの哲学書は読みこなせない I find it difficult to *fully understand* [*digest*] this philosophy book.

よみこむ 読み込む read thoroughly（本や資料などを）; scan（スキャンする）▶私はその画像をパソコンに読み込んだ I *scanned* the image to my computer.

よみさし 読み止し ▶読みさしの本 a *half-read* book.

よみすて 読み捨て ▶この種の雑誌は読み捨てにしている I *throw away* magazines like this after a quick read-through.

よみせ 夜店 a stall set up in the evening.

よみち 夜道 ▶夜道の一人歩きは危険だから駅まで車で送っていくよ It's not safe to *walk alone at night*, so I'll drive you to the train station.

よみちがえる 読み違える →読み誤る.

よみで 読みで ▶この本は読みでがある It will *take* you *a while to get through* this book.（➤「読み通すには時間がかかる」の意）.

よみとおす 読み通す read through ▶その小説はとてもおもしろかったので一気に読み通した That novel was so interesting I *read* it *through* in one sitting. ‖ 何か1冊でも英語の本を読み通せば大いに自信がつくよ You will gain a lot of confidence if you manage to *read* an English book *from cover to cover*.

よみとばす 読み飛ばす ▶この本は軽く読み飛ばせる内容だ The content of this book is simple so you can *read through* it *in no time*.

よみとりき 読み取り機 a [an electric] reader; a bar code reader（バーコードの）▶レジ係は私のカードを読み取り機にさっと通した The cashier swiped my card through *the reader*.

よみとる 読み取る read ＋目 ▶人の心を読み取る *read* a person's mind ‖ 升目からはみ出して書かれた数字は機械で読み取ることができません Machines can't *read* figures written outside of the boxes.

✉ あなたの手書きの手紙は読み取るのが難しいです It is difficult for me to *read* your handwriting.

よみなおす 読み直す read again [over].

よみながす 読み流す skim through (a book).

よみのくに 黄泉の国 the land of the dead, Hades /héɪdiːz/（ギリシャ神話の）.

よみびと 読み人・詠み人 a composer（詩歌の）; a writer（作者）《参考》和歌などで作者の名前がわからないときにいう「読み人知らず」は (composer unknown)

または (anonymous) と訳す．特に後者は作者の名前を伏せたい場合にも用いる．

よみふける 読み耽る ▶その少年は漫画を読みふけっている That boy *is absorbed* [*is lost*] *in reading* a comic book.

よみもの 読み物 **reading**；an **article**（新聞・雑誌の記事）；a **book**（本）；**books and magazines**（本と雑誌）▶ためになる[軽い]読み物 good [light] *reading* ‖ これは大人の読み物だ This *stuff* is for adults.（➤ stuff は漠然と「物」の意）．

よみやすい 読み易い ▶（易しくて）読みやすい文章 an *easy-to-read* style ‖ この本は字が大きいので読みやすい This large print makes this book *easy to read*.

[1]**よむ 読む** **1【本などを】read** ＋目；**read through**（読み通す）▶本を読む *read* a book ‖ 私の娘はまだ字が読めない My daughter can't *read* yet. ‖ お母さん，この字（＝漢字）何て読むの？ Mom, how do you *read* this *kanji*? ‖ その小説は世界中で広く読まれている The novel *is* widely *read* throughout the world.（➤ この read /red/ は過去分詞形）‖ その事件のことならいつか雑誌で読んだことがある I once *read* about that incident in a magazine. ‖ 彼はアメリカの現代小説を原書でたくさん読んでいる He *has read* a lot of modern American novels in the original. ‖ この小説を１週間で読むのは不可能だとわかった I found (that) it was impossible to *read through* this novel in a week. ‖ 川口君，その段落を声を出して読んでください Kawaguchi, please *read* the paragraph *aloud*. ‖ マキは彼の手紙を１行１行貪るように読んだ Maki *devoured* every line of his letter.
▶子供の頃は寝る前に母に必ずお話の本を読んでもらっていた When I was a child, my mother always *read* me stories at bedtime. ‖ きょうの夕刊は読むところ（＝読む価値のあるところ）がほとんどない There's not much *worth reading* in today's evening paper. ‖ お坊さんがお経を読んでる間は静かにしなさい You should keep quiet while the priest *recites* the sutra.
▶PC 上に必要なアプリがないのでこのファイルは読めません This file *cannot be read* because the necessary application is not installed [does not exist] on your PC.
‖字の読めない人 an illiterate.
2【見抜く】read ＋目；**see through**（見破る）▶監督は相手チームのサインを読んでいた The manager *read* the opponent team's signal. ‖ チェスでは相手の次の手を読むことが大切だ In chess, it is important to *see through* the opponent's next move. ‖ あのときはどうしても彼女の心が読めなかった I couldn't *tell* what she was thinking [couldn't *read* her mind] at that time.

[2]**よむ 詠む** ▶俳句を詠む *compose* [*write*] a haiku ‖ この俳句は雪景色を詠んだ（＝表現した）ものです This haiku *describes* a snowy landscape. ‖ 短歌を詠むのは祖母の楽しみの１つだ One of my grandmother's hobbies is *composing* tanka (poems).

[1]**よめ 嫁** **1【息子の連れ合い】**a **daughter-in-law**, one's **son's wife**.
2【妻】a **wife**；a **bride**（花嫁）▶彼女ならきっとおまえのいい嫁さんになるぞ I'm sure she'll make you a good *wife*. ‖ 絶対お嫁になんか行かないわ There's no way I'll (ever) get married!

[2]**よめ 夜目** ▶［ことわざ］夜目遠目笠（かさ）の内 Women look beautiful when you get a glimpse of them at night, from a distance or under a (conical) straw hat.

よめい 余命 one's **remaining days** ▶彼女は余命いくばくもない Her *days are numbered*.
‖平均余命 average life expectancy.

よめいり 嫁入り **marriage** ▶名家に嫁入りする *marry into* a good family ‖ 嫁入り前の娘がそんなはしたないまねをしてはいけません An *unmarried* woman shouldn't do such an indecent thing.
‖嫁入り道具 a trousseau /trúːsoʊ/.

よもぎ 蓬《植物》(a) **mugwort**.

よもや ▶よもやあんな相手に敗れようとは思わなかった I *never dreamed that* I would lose to an opponent like that. ‖ よもやあのことを忘れてはいないだろうね *Surely* you haven't forgotten that, have you? ／*Don't tell me* you've forgotten that!

よもやまばなし 四方山話 ▶久しぶりに会ったので私たちはよもやま話に花を咲かせた Since we hadn't met for a long while, we *thoroughly enjoyed talking about all sorts of things*.

よやく 予約

> 訳語メニュー
> ホテルなどの予約 →reservation **1**
> 医者などの予約 →appointment **2**
> 予約購読 →subscription **3**

1【ホテルなどの】a **reservation**,《英また》a **booking** ━動 **予約する reserve** ＋目，**book** ＋目 ▶ホテルは予約してありますか *Have* you *reserved* [*booked*] a room at the hotel?（● 日本語では「ホテルを予約する」と言えるが，英語では「部屋を予約する」と言うことに注意）‖ サボイ（ホテル）に部屋を予約してある I *have a reservation* at the Savoy. ／I *have* a room *reserved* [*booked*] at the Savoy. ‖ そのホテルは予約でいっぱいだった The hotel *was* fully *booked*. ‖ コンサートのチケット予約はこちらの電話番号へどうぞ Please call this number to make *a ticket reservation* for the concert. ‖ 出発の前日に飛行機の予約を確認したほうがいい You should reconfirm your *flight reservation* the day before departure. ‖ すみませんが宿泊の予約を取り消します I'm sorry, but I'd like to cancel my (*hotel*) *reservation*. ‖ 対話（電話で）「京都ホテルですか？５月５日にシングルを予約したいのですが」「あいにくその日は満室でございます」"Is this the Kyoto Hotel? I'd like to *reserve* [*make a reservation for*] a single room for May 5." "I'm sorry. All (of) our rooms are reserved."
‖予約金 a deposit ‖ 予約席 a reserved seat.
2【医者・美容院などの】an **appointment** ━動 **予約する make an appointment** ▶病院［医者／歯医者］の予約 a hospital [doctor's／dental] *appointment* ‖ 医者に２時の予約をした I *made an appointment* with [to see] a doctor for two o'clock.
語法 at two o'clock とすると，「予約をしたとき（予約の電話を掛けたとき）の時刻が２時だった」という意味になる；have an appointment ... のときは at two o'clock で予約時刻を表す．２つ下の訳例を参照 ‖ 美容院に今度の金曜日３時の予約をした I *made an appointment* at the beauty parlor for three next Friday. ‖ 歯医者には２時に予約してある I *have a* two o'clock dental *appointment* [*an appointment* with my dentist at two o'clock].
3【雑誌などの】subscription（予約購読）━動 **予約する subscribe**《to》▶私は『タイム』を予約購読している I *subscribe to* "Time" magazine. ‖ 申し訳ありませ

んが, この家具は一点物で, すでに**予約済み**になっております(＝売れました) We are sorry, but we had only one piece of furniture of this kind, and it's already *sold*.

よゆう 余裕 **1【ゆとり】space, room**（空間的な）; **time**（時間的な）▶私の書斎にはそんな大量の本を置く**余裕はない** My study has no *space* [*room*] for so many books. ‖ 日本の父親の多くは子供と遊ぶ十分な**時間的余裕がない** Many Japanese fathers don't have enough *time* to play with their children. ‖ その問題に対処するだけの**精神的余裕がなかった** I didn't have enough *mental space* to deal with the problem. ‖ 私たちは**余裕をもって**駅に着いた We got to the train station *with time to spare*. ‖ 締め切りが厳しくて**余裕が全くない** The deadline is firm with no *latitude* [*leeway*].

2【経済的な】▶生活に**余裕がない** *have trouble* making ends meet(➤「生活に余裕がある」は live a comfortable life).

> **【文型】**
> **…する余裕がある**
> **can afford to** do
>
> **【解説】** afford は通例否定文・疑問文に用い, 主に「…するだけの経済的ゆとりがある[ない]」の意になるが, ときに時間的なゆとりにも使う. to *do* でなく, 名詞を続けて can afford a new suit (スーツを新調する金がある)のようにいうこともできる.

▶うちにはおまえを大学へやるような**余裕はない** We *can't afford to* send you to college. ‖ 私には外国旅行をする**余裕はない** I *can't afford* an overseas trip. ‖ **対話**「このレストランで食事したいわ」「**そんな余裕はないよ**」 "I'd like to have dinner at this restaurant." "We *can't afford it*."

3【気持ちの】▶土井さんはいつも**余裕しゃくしゃくとしている** Mr. Doi is always *calm and relaxed*.

1**より 縒り** ▶あの２人, 別れたと思ったらすぐに**よりを戻した** Those two *got back together again* soon after they broke up. ‖ きょうは結婚記念日だから, **腕によりを掛けて**ごちそうを作ったわ Today's our wedding anniversary, so I cooked a *special* dinner.

2**より**《一層》**more** ▶この本は**より多くの**人に読んでほしいと思います I hope *more* people will read this book. ‖ 人は常に**より便利な**[**よりよい**]生活を望むものだ People always wish for a *more comfortable* life [a *better* life]. ‖ **より一層やる気のある**生徒たち students *with* (*even*) *greater motivation*.

1**-より** **1【比較の基準を示して】than**

> **【文型】**
> A **よりもっと…**
> **比較級＋ than** A

▶うちでは父のほうが母**より早く**起きる My father gets up earli*er than* my mother (does). ‖ きょうはきのう**より暖かい** It's warm*er* today *than* (it was) yesterday. ‖ 彼は**私より背が高い** He is tall*er than I* [*me*]. (➤ than の次にくる代名詞は前にくる比較相手と同じ格にするのが原則だが, インフォーマルではしばしば目的格がくる) ‖ 甲子園球場は思っていた**よりずっと広かった** Koshien Stadium was much larg*er than* I had thought it would be.
▶私は**ベンツより** BMW のほうが好きだ I like BMWs better *than* Mercedes. ／I prefer BMWs *to* Mercedes. ‖ ぼくはほかの**誰よりも**きみのことを思っているつもりだよ I'm sure I love you *more than* anyone else could. ‖ 海外旅行者の数は**去年より**２割も増えている The number of overseas travelers has increased by as much as twenty percent *over* [*as compared with*] last year. (➤ 後者は「…に比べて」) ‖ 人のこと**より**自分のことを心配しなさい You should worry about yourself *instead of* [*rather than*] other people. ‖ 彼は頭がいいと**言うより**要領がいいんだ He is *not so much* smart *as* efficient.

2【基点を示して】▶点数が60点**より下の**人には再試験をします Those students whose scores are *below* 60 have to take a makeup test. ‖ 仙台**より北**にはまだ行ったことがない I've never been further north *than* Sendai. ‖ 10時**より**首相の記者会見が行われます The Prime Minister's press conference begins *at* 10 o'clock.
✉ **きみが好きだ. 健より** I love you. *From* Ken.

3【以外】except, but (➤ 前者のほうが除外の意味が強い) ▶以前は大島へは船で行く**よりほかなかった** Once there was no way to get to Oshima *except* by ship. ‖ あのときは彼女の頼みを断る**よりほかなかった** At the time I had no choice *but* to refuse her request.

2**-より -寄り** ▶南[北]**寄りの**風 a *southerly* [*northerly*] wind ‖ 飯田橋駅の市ケ谷**寄りの**改札口 the ticket gate *at* [*on*] *the* Ichigaya *side of* Iidabashi Station ‖ 政治的には彼女はいくぶん**左寄りだ** Politically, she *leans* a little *to the left* [is a little *on the left*].

よりあい 寄り合い a **gathering**; a **meeting**(会合); a **get-together**(非公式な集まり).

よりあつまる 寄り集まる get together.

よりかかる 寄り掛かる lean《against, on》▶間仕切りに**寄りかかるな** Don't *lean against* the partition. ‖ 亜矢子はそっと恋人の腕に**寄りかかった** Ayako *leaned on* her boyfriend's arm ever so tenderly.

よりけり ▶高価だからと言って品質がよいとは限らない. ものに**よりけりだ** What's expensive isn't necessarily of good quality. *It depends on* the item.

よりごのみ 選り好み →**えりごのみ**.

よりそう 寄り添う ▶優子と健が**寄り添う**ように歩いていたぞ I saw Yuko and Ken walking *close to each other*. ‖ 私たちは被災者の**気持ちに**できるだけ**寄り添いたい**と思っています We'd like to *stay close to* the disaster victims *in our hearts* and try to understand how they feel as much [long] as possible.

よりつく 寄り付く ▶あそこの息子はぐれて, 近頃はさっぱり**家に寄りつかなく**なった Their son got into bad company and hasn't *come home* recently.
▶その株は4500円で**寄り付いた** The stock *opened* at ¥4,500. (➤「4500 円 で 引 け た」の「引 け る」は close).

よりどころ 拠り所 a **support**, a **stay**（支え; 後者はやや文語的な語); (a) **ground**（根拠）▶多くのマレーシア人にとってイスラム教は精神的な**よりどころだ** Islam is the spiritual *support* of many Malaysians. ‖ 彼女は聖書を心の**よりどころにしている** The Bible is her *spiritual support*.

よりどり 選り取り ▶スラックスが**より取り**２本で5000円です *Any* two pairs of pants for five thousand yen! ‖ **より取り見取り**で100円! *Take your choice* [*pick*] for one hundred yen.

よりによって (●「よりによって」は「たくさんある中で(わ

ざわざ)」の意味だから of all … を使って表す. … には場所ならば places, 人ならば people [men, women など] がくる) ▶誰かがよりによってわが家の玄関先に車を止めていった *Of all the places they could have parked*, they (just) had to park in front of our entrance. ‖ よりによって結婚式の日に大雪が降るなんて It's snowing so heavily, and on my wedding day *of all days*! ／I can't believe that it has to snow on my wedding day! ‖ ルリ子がよりによってあの男を選んだとは驚きだ I'm surprised that Ruriko chose him (out) *of all the men she could have picked*.

よりぬき 選り抜きの select, choice ▶世界各地のより抜きの品 *select* [*choice*] goods from all over the world ‖ 今, その美術館で日本美術のより抜きの作品が展示中だ *The cream* [*very best*] of Japanese art is now on display at the museum. (➤ the cream は「最良のもの」).

よりみち 寄り道する drop in《at, on》(➤ at は「場所」, on は「人」の場合) ▶帰りにもう1か所寄り道する所がある I have one more place to *drop in at* on my way home. (➤ 前の place にかかるので at が必要) ‖ 寄り道しないで早く帰ってらっしゃい Come straight home *without stopping on the way*. ‖ 岡山へ行く途中, 姫路に寄り道をした I *made a stopover* at Himeji on my way to Okayama. (➤ stopover は「途中下車」).

よりめ 寄り目 ▶うちの息子は少し寄り目だ Our son is slightly *cross-eyed*.

よりよい より良い (even) better《than》▶人は誰もより良い生活をしたいと願っている Everybody wants to lead a *better* life. ‖ 当店ではより良い品, より良いサービスを心がけております We're committed to providing '*Better* goods, and *better* service.'

よりょく 余力 ▶余力があれば, こちらの仕事を手伝ってくれないか If you have *the energy* [*strength*] *to spare*, could you help me with this work? (➤ 時間を問題にするのなら energy, strength の代わりに time を用いる).

よりわける 選り分ける →えり分ける.

[1]**よる 夜** (a) night; (an) evening

> **《解説》** night は day, daytime(昼間)に対する語で, 広義では日没から朝太陽が昇るまでをいう. evening は日没から夜9時ぐらいまでで, それ以降人が就寝するくらいまでの時間帯は night を用いる.

▶きのうの夜(に) *last night* (➤ 前置詞は不要) ‖ 今, 日本では昼だが, ニューヨークは夜だ It is day now here in Japan, but it is *night* in New York. ‖ 冬は夜が長い *Nights* are long in wintertime. ‖ 静かな夜だね We're having *a* quiet *night*. (➤ 形容詞があるとその前に a がつく) ‖ 夜にジョギングする人もいる Some people jog *at night* [*in the evening*]. ‖ 夜の間に雪がだいぶ積もった It snowed quite a lot *during the night*. ‖ 夜(＝今夜)電話するよ I'll call you *tonight*. (➤「夜9時に」なら call you at nine tonight) ‖ 彼の乗ったフェリーはあすの夜10時に大島に着く His ferry arrives in Oshima *at ten tomorrow night*.

▶金曜の夜はいつも楽しい We always have fun *on Friday night(s)*. (➤ 特定の日の夜の場合, 前置詞は on になる) ‖ 彼は夜遅く[きのうの夜遅く]到着した He arrived *late at night* [*late last night*]. ‖ 彼は日曜[8月15日]の夜遅く到着した He arrived *late on Sunday night* [*late on the night of August 15*]. ‖ 父は若い頃, よく夜遅くまで勉強したそうです My father says he often studied *late into the night* [*until late at night*] when he was young. ‖ 夜にならないうちにデンバーに着かねばならない We must reach Denver *before dark*. ‖ 夜も更けてきた It's *getting late*. ‖ 予備校生は夜も昼も勉強する *Yobiko* students study *day and night* [*night and day*].

[2]**よる 寄る** **1【近づく】** go [come] near ▶ガスタンクのそばへ寄らないでください Please don't *go near* the gas tank. ‖ ドーベルマンがそばへ寄って来るとさすがに怖い I really get scared when a Doberman *comes near* me. ‖ もっと近くに寄ってよく見てごらん *Come closer* and have a good look at it. ‖ 端の人, 写真に入りませんので内側へ寄ってください You at the far end, please *move* (*in*) a bit *closer*, or you'll be out of the picture. ‖ 車が来るよ. 脇へ寄って A car is coming. *Step aside*. ‖ 救急車が通ります. 脇へ寄ってください Ambulance (passing)! *Move to the side*! [*Pull aside*!] (➤ pull aside は「車を道路脇に寄せる」).

▶《慣用表現》寄る年波には勝てない You can't beat [stop／reverse] *the aging process*. (➤ beat と stop は「止める」, reverse は「逆行させる」).

2【立ち寄る】 stop [drop] by, drop in《at, on》(➤ at は「場所」, on は「人」の場合) ▶学校の帰りにデパートに寄ってきちゃった I *stopped by* the department store on my way home from school. ‖ オーストラリアからの帰りに香港に寄った We *stopped over in* Hong Kong on our way back from Australia. (➤ stop over は「(旅の途中で)立ち寄る, 途中下車する」の意) ‖《呼び込み》さあ, 寄ってらっしゃい. 見てらっしゃい *Step right up*! See for yourself.

✉ **名古屋へいらしたときはうちへ寄ってください** Please *drop by* when you come to Nagoya.

3【集まる】 gather, get together ▶死んだ野牛の周りにハイエナが何匹も寄ってきた Hyenas *gathered* around the dead buffalo. ‖ あした彼の家にみんなが寄ることになっている We *are* all *getting together* at his house tomorrow. (➤ この現在進行形は近い未来の予定を表している).

▶《慣用表現》村人たちは寄ると触るとそのうわさで持ちきりだ The villagers begin to talk about the rumor whenever they *get together*.

[3]**よる 因る・由る・依る・拠る** **1【手段として使う】** by ▶その問題は力によって解決することはできない You cannot settle the issue *by* force. ‖ わが社ではデータはすべてコンピュータによって処理している All data is processed *by* computers at our company.

2【根拠となる】

> **【文型】**
> A **によると〜だ**
> **According to** A, 〜.
> A **shows that** S ＋ V.

▶天気予報によるときょうは雷雨があるそうだ *According to* the weather report, we will have a thunderstorm today. ／ The weather forecast says there will be a thunderstorm today. ‖ ある調査によると子供は平均で1家庭に1.37人だそうだ *A survey shows that* there are 1.37 children per family on (the) average.

▶ 18歳未満の方の入場は法律によって禁止されています Admission of those under eighteen is prohibited *by* law. ‖ わが社は新入社員を学歴によらずに採用する We don't take educational background into consideration in choosing our new employees for this company. (➤「考慮に入れない」の意).

3【原因となる】be due to ▶エチオピアの飢きんは干ばつと内戦によるものだった Starvation in Ethiopia *was due to* the drought and the civil war. ‖ 彼の大けがは自分の不注意によるものだ He was seriously injured *because* he was careless [*due to* his own carelessness]. ‖ ついにがんによる死亡者数が脳卒中を抜いた Deaths *from* cancer have finally surpassed those *caused by* stroke. ‖ この火事は漏電によって起きた3つ目の火事だ This fire is the third one to have *been caused by* a short circuit. ‖ 雨により試合は中止になった The game was canceled *because of* rain. ‖ 彼女の先見の明によって(=のおかげで)我々はその計画を成功させることができた *Thanks to* [*Owing to*] her foresight, we were able to make the project a success.

4【事情による】depend on ▶土地を売るかどうかは買い手の出す条件による It *depends on* the terms of the buyer's offer whether I sell the land or not. ‖ 場合によってはきみに会社を辞めてもらうことになるかもしれない *Depending on the circumstances*, you may have to quit the company. ‖ あすは晴れ時々曇り，所により一時小雨がぱらつくでしょう It will be sunny with occasional cloudiness, and it may rain on and off *depending on the location*. ‖ 親切も時と場合によりけりだよ You should be kind only *when the time and circumstances are right* [*appropriate*]. ‖ 人によって好みは違う Tastes *differ* (*from person to person*).

[4]**よる 縒る twist** +㊐ ▶糸をよってひもを作る *twist* threads into a string.

[5]**よる 選る pick and choose** ▶どれも同じです．よらないでください They're the same. Don't *pick and choose*.

よるがた 夜型 ▶私は夜型です I am *a night person*. ⇀朝型.

よるべ 寄る辺 ▶彼は天涯孤独，寄る辺ない身だ He's alone in the wide world and *has no one to turn to* [*depend on*].

よれよれ ▶彼はよれよれのコートを着ている He's wearing a *shabby* [*worn-out*] coat.

よろい 鎧 armor (➤よろいかぶとの一そろいは a suit of armor という).

よろいど 鎧戸 the shutters, a **louver door**.

よろく 余禄 an **additional profit** [**gain**].

よろける stagger (よろめく) ; **stumble** (つまずく) ▶電車から降りようとしたとき，戸口で押されてよろけた When getting off the train, I was pushed at the door and *staggered*. ‖ 暗闇で何かにぶつかってよろけた I *stumbled* over something in the dark.

よろこばしい 喜ばしい good (良い) ; **happy** (うれしい) ▶喜ばしいニュース *good* news ‖ これは喜ばしい傾向ではない This trend is not very *desirable*. ‖ 今回の根本さんの受賞は喜ばしい限りだ I am very *happy* [*glad*] to hear that Mr. Nemoto won a prize. ／Mr. Nemoto's winning a prize is *delightful* news.

よろこばせる 喜ばせる delight +㊐, **please** +㊐ (➤前者がより強意) ▶私たちは結婚して両親を喜ばせることができました Our marriage *delighted* our parents. ‖ 清はよい成績を持って帰って両親を喜ばせた Kiyoshi brought home a good report card and *pleased* his parents. ‖ うまいこと言ってあまり人を喜ばせるなよ (=お世辞を言うな) Don't *flatter* me so much, please.

よろこび 喜び (a) **joy**, (a) **delight**, **pleasure** ▶モーツァルトの音楽は私に生きる喜びを与えてくれる Mozart's music makes me feel the *joy* of being alive. ‖ この喜びをどう表現してよいかわかりません I don't know how to express my *joy*. ／I can't tell you how happy I am. ‖ 優勝の喜びを皆で分かち合いたい I'd like to share the *joy* of victory with all the members. ‖ 皆さまと本日お会いできたことは，私の大きな喜びとするところです It is my great *pleasure* to see you today. ‖ 人生には喜びもあれば悲しみもある Life is full of *joys* and sorrows.

よろこぶ 喜ぶ

be glad (うれしくなる) ; **be pleased** (気に入る，満足する) ; **be happy** (楽しい気分になる) ; **be delighted** (➤glad または pleased の強意語) ▶彼はその知らせを聞いて喜んだ He *was glad* to hear the news. ‖ 彼女は私の電話をとても喜んでくれた She *was* very *glad* [*pleased*] that I'd called. ‖ 両親は兄の結婚をとても喜んでいる My parents *are* very *pleased with* my (older) brother's marriage. ‖ あなたのお兄さん，私の手紙を受け取って喜んでた？ *Was* your brother *pleased to* get my letter?

> 【文型】
> **(私は)喜んで…する**
> **I'll [I'd] be glad to** do.
>
> 【解説】(1) 相手の頼み事に積極的に応じるときには **I'll be glad to.** を使う. I'd は断定を避けた仮定的な表現で，必ずしも「そうする」ことを表さない. しかし，積極性の度合いは言い方によって示されることも多い.
> (2) 招待に応じるときには，エチケット上多少の遠慮や控えめな気持ちを込めて **I'd be glad to.** や，より積極的に I'd love to. と言う.
> (3) be glad の代わりに be happy も使う.

▶喜んで駅まで車でお送りしますよ *I'll be glad to* give you a ride to the train station. ‖ 対話「ギリシャへ一緒に行きませんか」「喜んで」"Will you go to Greece with me?" "*I'd be glad to.* ／*I'd love to.* ／*With pleasure.*"

▶ 対話「パーティーに出席していただけますか」「はい，喜んで」"Can you attend the party?" "Yes, *I'd be glad to* [*I'd love to*]."

▶ 対話「飲みに行かない？」「喜んで」"Shall we go out for a drink?" "*Sure, why not?*"

▶子供たちの喜ぶ顔が見たい I want to see my kids' *happy faces*. ‖ 産業廃棄物処理施設の建設を喜ばない住民が多い Many residents *are unhappy* [*displeased*] about the construction of a treatment facility for industrial waste. ‖ 学生たちが喜ぶ授業とはどんな授業だろうか I wonder what kind of class students would *enjoy*.

✉ **女のお子さんがお生まれになった由，お喜び申し上げます** *Congratulations* on the birth of your baby girl. ➤「おめでとう」の意.

✉ **喜んでカラオケ大会に参加します** *I'd love* [*I'll be glad*] *to* join the karaoke contest.

よろしい 宜しい 1【許可，承諾】may, can

> 【解説】(1) 先生や上司などに向かって改まった調子で「…してよろしいですか」と尋ねる場合には **May I ...?** を使う. 少しくだけて「…して(も)いいですか」には **Can I ...?** を使う. ⇀いい.

(2) 許可や承認を与える場合の「よろしいですよ」には "Sure.", "O.K.", "All right.", "Good." などが対応するが，これらの表現には日本語の「よろしい」が持つ尊大さはない．したがって下位の者が上位の者に対して用いることもできる．

▶ 対話「このノートパソコンを使ってもよろしいでしょうか」「どうぞ」"*May I* use this laptop ?" "Sure." ‖ 窓を閉めてよろしいでしょうか *Would you mind* if I closed [*Would you mind* my closing] the window ? ‖ 試験中，辞書を見てもよろしい You *can* use a dictionary during the exam. ‖ よろしい，私が代わりにやってあげよう *All right*, I'll do it for you.

2【好み】 ▶よろしかったら，クッキーをどうぞ Please help yourself to some cookies, *if you like*. ‖ どちらでもよろしいですよ Either *will do*. ‖ 対話「コーヒーとお茶とどちらがよろしいですか」「お茶をください」"Which would you *prefer* [*like*], coffee or tea ?" "Tea, please." ‖ 対話「ちょっと紙を１枚もらえませんか」「これでよろしいですか」"Can I have a sheet of paper ?" "Sure. Is this (one) *all right* ?"

3【良い】good ▶このスープはお味がとてもよろしいですね This soup tastes very *good*. ‖ お利口な坊ちゃんでよろしい (＝お幸せ) ですね You must be very *happy* to have such a bright [smart] son.

よろしく 宜しく

《解説》「よろしく」は使用範囲の広いことばで，今後の成り行きにしたがって適宜に何かをすることを相手に頼む場合，こちらの好意を第三者に伝えてもらう場合，今後の交際を相手に頼む場合などに用いるが，その真意は「あなたの判断でうまく事を運んでください」ということである．個人の独立を重んじる英語文化にはない考え方なので，訳例のように場面にふさわしい英語表現を用いる必要がある．

1【挨拶】 ▶小沢と申します．よろしく My name's Ozawa. *Nice to meet you*. (➤くだけた挨拶だが，英語では名字だけを言うのは横柄に響くことが少なくないので，姓名を言うほうがよい) ‖ 初めまして．どうぞよろしく How do you do ? *I'm glad to meet you*. (➤改まった挨拶で，「お会いできてうれしいです」の意)．

▶圭子さんによろしくね *Give* Keiko *my best*. ‖ 母がよろしくと申しておりました My mother joins me in sending you all the best. (➤「母はあなたのご健康を祈ることで私に加わっています」が原義) ‖ 今後ともよろしくお願いします Let's keep [stay] in touch. ／I'm looking forward to working with you. (➤I look forward to... とすると，フォーマル度が上がる) (🗣 (1) 英語にはこれにぴったりの表現はないが，前者の場合のように「これからも連絡を取り合いましょう」と発想したり，後者のように「あなたと一緒に働くことを楽しみにしています」と発想したりするものが日本語の場面的相当表現として存在するので，それらを適宜用いるとよい．(2) 後者は新入社員の挨拶として用いたり，転勤先での挨拶として用いたりすることが多い) ‖ 対話「ご家族の皆さんによろしくお伝えください」「はい，申し伝えます」"*Give my best regards to* your family." "Yes, I will."

あなたの英語はどう響く?

日本人は相手に一度も会ったことがないのに，「ご主人さま[奥さま]によろしく」というような言い方をするが，これを直訳して Please give my best regards to your husband [wife]. とか，くだけて Say hello to your husband [wife] for me. と挨拶するのは，英語では一般的ではない．

✉ お父さまによろしくお伝えください *Please send my best regards to* your father. ➤「お父さまに私からの最良のことばをお伝えください」の意；相手から何かをもらったことで礼を言ってもらいたい場合は Please thank your father for me. のように表現してもよい．

✉ 明けましておめでとうございます．本年もどうぞよろしく Happy New Year ! (I'm) looking forward to seeing you [working with you] again this year. ➤「ことしもまた会えるのを[一緒に仕事をすることを] 楽しみにしています」の意．「ことしはもっと頻繁に会いましょう」の意なら Let's see more of each other this year. ／Let's get together more often this year., レストラン・店などの客への挨拶ならば，We hope that you will continue to patronize our restaurant [store ／shop] this year. (本年も当レストラン[当店]をごひいきください) のように訳せる．

2【相手の裁量に任せて】 ▶《協力を求めて》私は彼によろしくと言った I *asked* him *for* his cooperation. ‖ 《新学期・転校などの際に担任に》娘をどうぞよろしくお願いします I hope my daughter *will do all right*. (🗣 英語では「しっかりやってくれることを望む」と発想する) ‖ 息子を泊めていただけるそうで，どうかよろしくお願いします *Thank you for* letting my son stay with you. ‖ 私は先に帰るからあとはよろしく頼むよ I'm going home, so I'll *leave the rest up to you*. (🗣 英語では「あとのことは任せる」と発想する)．

▶ 対話「冷蔵庫はあすお届けします」「ではよろしく」"We'll deliver the refrigerator to you tomorrow." "*Thank you very much*." (➤「ありがとうございます」と考える)．

3【依頼】 ▶《商取引の文書などで》ご用命のほどよろしくお願い申し上げます *Please* favor us with your business. (🗣 英語にはこの「よろしく」に相当する語がないので，全体を「私どもにお取り引きの恩恵をお与えください」と発想して訳例のようにする)．

よろず 万 ▶よろず相談承ります Please contact us about *any* (*kind of*) *problem you may have* [*encounter*].

よろめく **stagger** ; **reel** (ふらふらと歩く) ; **stumble** (つまずく) ▶お年寄りは立ち上がろうとしてよろめいた The elderly man *staggered* when he tried to stand up. ‖ 向こうから酔っ払いが２人よろめきながらやって来る Two drunks are *reeling* up the road.

よろよろ ▶年老いた犬が前をよろよろと歩いていく There is an old dog *staggering along* down the road ahead of me.

よろん 世論 **public opinion** ▶世論に訴える appeal to *public opinion* ‖ 世論は増税に反対している *Public opinion* is against the tax increase. ‖ 政権にある者はもっと世論に耳を傾けるべきだ Those in power should pay more attention to *public opinion* [*feeling* ／ *sentiment*]. ‖ 国際世論は中国政府のやり方に反対した *International opinion* was against the measures taken by the Chinese government.

‖ **世論調査** a public opinion poll [survey].

よわい 弱い

1【丈夫でない】weak ▶私は胃が弱い I have a *weak* stomach. ／I have poor digestion. (➤後者は「消化力が弱い」の意) ‖ おばあちゃんは体が弱いから外国旅行は無理だ Since grandma *is in delicate health* [*has a weak con-*

stitution], She can't travel abroad. ‖ 子供の頃は体が弱かった When I was a child, I *got sick easily*. (➤「すぐ病気になった」の意) ‖ 意志が弱くてたばこがやめられない I have such *weak* willpower that I can't quit smoking. ‖ 弱い者いじめはするな Don't bully *weak people*. ／Don't pick on *the weak*. (➤「弱い者いじめ」は bullying) ‖ 抽象的な説明ばかりで具体的な例がないと説得力が弱いね An abstract explanation without concrete examples is *not very persuasive*.

2【能力・技術が低い】weak ▶このチームは弱いから楽勝だ This team is so *weak* (that) they'll be a pushover. (➤ pushover は「ちょろい相手」) ‖ 私はじゃんけんが弱い I'*m weak at* janken. ‖ 私は化学はいいんだが, 物理が弱い I'm strong in chemistry, but *weak* in physics. ／I'm good at chemistry, but *bad* at physics. ‖ 英会話は弱いんです(＝上手に話せない) I do*n't* speak English *well*.

3【程度が低い】light ; weak (勢いがない) ▶弱い風が吹いている A *light* wind is blowing. (➤ この意味では weak は不可) ‖ ただいま, 関東地方で弱い地震がありました There was a *slight* [*light*] earthquake in the Kanto district just a moment ago. ‖ 暖房[冷房]を弱くしてくれる? Would you please *turn down* the heater [air conditioner]? ‖ 出火から一夜たって, だいぶ火の勢いが弱くなった After raging all night, the fire had *become* much *weaker* [had *weakened* considerably].

4【抵抗力が低い】 ▶私は酒に弱い(＝すぐ酔う) I *get drunk easily*. ‖ 妻は船[乗り物]に弱い My wife *gets seasick* [*carsick*] *easily*. ‖ 彼女ははやりのダイエットに弱い She *has a weakness for* new diet fads. ／She *is a sucker for* new diet fads. (➤ sucker は「だまされやすい人」) ‖ あの男も母親にだけは弱い Even he *has a soft spot for* his mother. ‖ 犬は一般に寒さよりも暑さに弱い Dogs *are* generally more *easily affected* by heat than cold. ／Dogs *are* more *sensitive* to heat than cold.

よわき 弱気 ▶弱気になるな. いつも当たって砕けろでいかなくっちゃ Don't *be* so *ready to give up*. You'll never get anywhere unless you're ready to go for broke.

よわごし 弱腰 ▶私はわが国の外交官が弱腰だとは思わない I don't think that Japanese diplomats are *weak-kneed*. (➤ 英語では「膝」で表す. なお, 肉体的に「腰が弱い」ときは He has weak knees. という).

よわさ 弱さ weakness ▶彼はしばしば大事なところで意志の弱さを見せてしまう He often shows *weakness of will* when it counts.

よわせる 酔わせる get ... drunk [**tipsy**] ((人)を酒で ; 後者は「ほろ酔いの」) ; **charm** ＋㊐ (うっとりさせる) ; **spellbind** ＋㊐ ((魔法にかけるように)魅了する) ▶彼を酔わせる *get* him *drunk* [*tipsy*] ‖ 演奏は聴衆を酔わせた The performance *charmed* [*spellbound*] the audience.

よわたり 世渡り ▶あの男は世渡りがうまい He *knows how to get on in the world*. ／He is *worldly-wise* [*sophisticated*]. (➤ worldly-wise, sophisticated はともに「世故にたけている」の意).

よわね 弱音 ▶佐藤君はすぐ弱音を吐く Sato is a habitual *whiner* [*complainer*]. (➤ whiner は「泣き事を言う人」) ‖ 頑張れ, 弱音を吐くな Keep it up and *never say die* !

よわび 弱火 a low [**gentle**] **flame** (こんろの) ; **low heat** (電子レンジの) ▶弱火でスープを30分ほど煮詰めます Boil the soup over *a low flame* for about thirty minutes.

よわまる 弱まる weaken ; die down, 《インフォーマル》 **ease up** ▶嵐もだいぶ弱まった The storm *has weakened* [*has subsided*] considerably. (➤ subside は堅い語) ‖ 山火事の勢いはすぐには弱まりそうにない The forest fire seems unlikely to *die down* soon.

よわみ 弱味 a weakness ; a weak point (弱点) ▶人の弱みにつけ込むな Don't take advantage of people's *weakness*. ‖ 相手に弱みを見せるな Don't reveal [show] your *weakness* to your opponent. ‖ 俺はやつの弱みを握っているんだ I *have something on* him.

よわむし 弱虫 a wimp ; a chicken (臆病者) ; **a sissy** (女々しいやつ) ▶この弱虫! You *wimp* ! ／You *chicken* ! ‖ あんな弱虫, ほっとけよ Leave that *wimp* alone.
▶息子は弱虫で, ひとりで遊びにいこうとしない My son is *timid* and can't go out to play by himself. (➤ timid は「臆病な」).

よわめる 弱める weaken ＋㊐ ▶経済力を弱める *weaken* the economy ‖ バックの色を弱める *tone down* the colors in the background ‖ 暖房を弱めてください Could you *turn down* the heater (, please)?

よわよわしい 弱々しい weak (力がない) ; **feeble** (力が欠けている) ; **faint** (かすかな) ▶弱々しい声を出して, どうした? Your voice is so *weak* [*feeble* ／*faint*]. What's happened? ‖ 姉は弱々しく(＝ひ弱に)見えるけど実は剣道をやっている My sister looks *weak*, but actually she does kendo.

よわりめ 弱り目 ▶ [ことわざ] 弱り目にたたり目 Misfortunes never come singly. (➤「不幸は単独では決してやって来ない」の意のことわざ) ／It never rains but it pours. [《米》 When it rains, it pours.] (➤「降れば必ずどしゃ降り」の意のことわざ).

よわる 弱る 1【衰える】become weak ▶目が弱ってきた My eyes have gotten *weak*. ‖ あの若者たちは栄養失調で体が弱っている Those young people *are weak* from malnutrition.

2【困る】 ▶ああ弱った. 500円しか金が無い Oh, no! [Uh-oh.] I have only 500 yen. ‖ 息子には本当に弱ったよ(＝頭痛の種だ) My son is a real *headache*. ‖ 彼女に連絡しようがないの? 弱ったなあ(＝どうしよう) ‖ 彼女に連絡しようがないの? You have no idea how to reach her? *What shall I do?* ‖ 弱ってるんだ. 助けてくれ Please help me. I'*m in trouble*.

よん 四 four ; the fourth (4番目) ▶11月の第4木曜日 *the fourth* Thursday of November.
‖ (小説などの) 4部作 a tetralogy ‖ 4分の1 a fourth ／ a quarter ‖ 4文字語 a four-letter word.

よんこままんが 4コマ漫画 a **four-frame comic strip**.

よんじゅう 四十 forty ▶40代の人 a person *in his* [*her*] *forties* ‖ 父もそろそろ40に手が届きます My father is going to be *forty* before long. ／My dad is pushing *forty*. (➤ くだけた言い方. be pushing は年齢に用いて「…に近づいている」の意).

よんどころない 拠所無い ▶よんどころない用事で出かけなければならない I have to go out on *unavoidable* business.

よんりん 四輪 ‖ 四輪駆動車 a car with four-wheel drive, a four-wheel drive [4 WD] car (➤ car の代わりに vehicle も可).

ら・ラ

-ら -等 (◉ 主に名詞や代名詞につけて複数を表す語であるが，英語にはこれに相当する単独の語はない．したがって，名詞や代名詞の複数形を用いて表す)．
▶少年ら boys ‖ その子供らは自分らが悪かったことを認めた The *children* [*boys and girls*] themselves admitted that *they* were at fault. ‖ 我ら皆古き良き友 *We* are all good old friends. ‖ おまえらの知ったことではない It's none of *your* business.

ラード lard.

ラーメン ramen ‖ ラーメン屋 a ramen shop.

ラーゆ 辣油 *rayu*；(hot) chili oil ▶食べるラー油 *chili oil*, not as a condiment, but as food.

らい- 来- next, the coming ▶娘は来春小学校に入学する My daughter will start school *next spring*. (→来春) ‖ 来学期 the next [coming] term ‖ 来年 next [the coming] year.

-らい -来 ▶祖父は昨年来寝たきりです My grandfather has been bedridden *since* last year. ‖ 野上君にはもう３年来(＝３年間)会っていない I haven't seen Nogami *for three years*. ‖ 新潟では10年来の大雪に見舞われた Niigata was hit by *the heaviest snowfall in ten years* [*in a decade*].

ら

らいい 来意 the purpose of one's visit.

らいう 雷雨 a thunderstorm ▶山中で雷雨に襲われた We were caught in *a thunderstorm* in the mountains.

らいうん 雷雲 a thundercloud ▶多摩地区に雷雲が発生しています *Thunderclouds* are gathering in the Tama district.

ライオン a lion；a lioness(雌) ▶ライオンは百獣の王だ The *lion* is the king of beasts.

らいかん 雷管 a blasting cap, a detonator(爆薬の)；a percussion cap(銃用の).

らいきゃく 来客 a visitor(訪問者)；a guest(招待客)；company(➤ 集合的に)
▶父は来客中ですので少々お待ちください Please wait a moment. My father *has a visitor* now. ‖ 午後は来客がある予定だ I'm having *company* [*guests*] this afternoon.

らいげつ 来月 next month ▶来月のきょう this day *next month* ‖ 兄は来月３日に帰国する予定だ My older brother will be back home on the third of *next month*.

1**らいこう 来校** ▶来週，知事が本校に来校の予定です The governor is scheduled to *visit our school* [*college*] next week. ‖ ご来校をお待ちしております We are looking forward to *your visit to our school*.

2**らいこう 来航** ▶1853年ペリー提督は浦賀に来航した Commodore Perry *arrived by ship* at Uraga in 1853.

らいさん 礼賛 praise /preɪz/ 一動 礼賛する praise ＋目，laud /lɔːd/ ＋目 (➤ 後者は多くは新聞の見出しに用いる) ▶ブルーノ・タウトは桂離宮の美しさを礼賛した Bruno Taut *praised* [*lauded*] the beauty of the Katsura Imperial Villa.

らいしゃ 来社 ▶あす10時にご来社ください *Please come to my office* at ten tomorrow. ‖ ぜひ一度ご来社ください You're welcome to *visit our company*. (➤ 見学などのために訪問するとき).

1**らいしゅう 来週** next week ▶来週ロシアの外相がワシントンを訪問する The Russian foreign minister is going to Washington *next week*. ‖ 来週の土曜日に日本シリーズが始まる The Japan Series will start *next* Saturday [on Saturday *next week* / 《英》on Saturday *next*]. (➤ 発言の時点が週の初めなら next Saturday は「今週の土曜日」の意にもなる) ‖ 来週の今頃は私たちはインドに居ます We'll be in India (at) this time *next week*.

2**らいしゅう 来襲** (an) attack 一動 来襲する attack ＋目 ▶刈り入れ前の田んぼにイナゴの大群が来襲した A great swarm of locusts *attacked* the rice paddies right before the harvest. ‖ 沖縄地方に大型の台風が来襲した A big typhoon *hit* the Okinawa area.

らいしゅん 来春 next spring ▶娘は来春結婚する My daughter is getting married *next spring* [*in the new year*]. (➤ 後者は「来年の正月」の場合).

らいじょう 来場 ▶立会演説会へは多数の来場者があった There was a large *attendance* at [*Many people attended*] the campaign speech meeting. (➤ attendance は集合的に「会合の出席者数」「催しの参加者数」. 施設を訪れる「来場者」は a visitor) ‖ 《呼びかけ》ご来場の皆さま Ladies and Gentlemen.

らいじん 雷神 the thunder god.

ライス rice (➤「ライス」は炊いたご飯(boiled rice)をいうが，英米は米［稲作］文化ではないので，「米」と「ご飯」を区別する単語がない．「ご飯」も，ふつうは単に rice という) ▶ステーキにはライスをお付けしますか Would you like *rice* with your steak?

ライスカレー →カレーライス.

らいせ 来世 life after death；the afterlife(死後の生命，あの世)；the hereafter(後世) ▶多くの日本人は来世の可能性について考えたがらない Many Japanese close their mind to the possibility of *life after death*. (➤ close one's mind to は「…を考えないようにする」) ‖ あなたは来世というものを信じますか Do you believe in *the afterlife*?

ライセンス 《米》a license, 《英》a licence ▶レーサーのライセンスを得る get a racing driver's *license* ‖ 航空機をライセンス生産する *manufacture* aircraft *under license*.

1**ライター** 《点火道具》a (cigarette) lighter ▶このライターつかないぞ This *lighter* doesn't work.
‖ ガスライター a gas lighter ‖ 使い捨てライター a disposable lighter.

2**ライター** 《作家》a writer ▶フリーのライター a freelance *writer* [*journalist*].

ライダー a rider.

ライチ 《植物》a lychee, a litchi.

らいちょう 雷鳥 《鳥》a (rock) ptarmigan /tɑ́ːrmɪɡən/.

らいてん 来店 ▶またのご来店をお待ちしております We hope you will *visit us* again. / Please *come* again. (➤ 後者は「またどうぞ」という決まり文句).

1**ライト** 《灯火》a light ▶お客さん，車のライトがつけっぱなしですよ Sir [Ma'am], your *headlights* are still on. ‖ライト(＝明かり)をつけて[消して]ください Turn on [off] the *light*, please.

²**ライト** 《野球》 **right field, right** (右翼); a **right fielder** (右翼手) ▶鳥谷はライトスタンドにツーランをたたき込んだ Toritani slammed a two-run homer into *the right field stands*.

ライトアップ ▶夏の間, その城はライトアップされている The castle *is illuminated* at night during the summer. (➤「ライトアップ」は和製語).

ライトきゅう ライト級 **the lightweight class** [**division**] ▶ライト級の選手 *a lightweight*.

ライトバン a **light (commercial) van,** 《主に米》 a **minivan.**

ライトブルー **light blue.**

ライトペン 《コンピュータ》 a **light pen.**

ライナー 《野球》 a **liner,** a **line drive** ▶いい当たりのレフトライナー a sharp *liner* to left ‖中村は鋭いライナーのヒットをレフト線に放った Nakamura *lined a* sharp *single* down the left foul line.

らいにち 来日する **come to** [**visit**] **Japan** ▶イタリアの歌劇団が今秋来日する An Italian opera troupe will *come to Japan* this fall. ‖来日中の大統領補佐官は首相と会談した The presidential aide, who is *now visiting Japan*, held talks with the Prime Minister.

らいねん 来年 **next year** ▶来年外相はインドを訪問する The Foreign Minister plans to visit India *next year*. ‖父は来年の５月ドイツへ行く My father is going to Germany *next May* [*in May* (*of*) *next year*]. (➤ 今が１～３月ならば next May は「この５月」) ‖私たち, 来年早々結婚します We're getting married *early next year*.

らいはい 礼拝 →礼拝(れいはい).

ライバル a **rival,** a **competitor** /kəmpétəṭəʳ/ (競争相手) (◎後者が客観的な語であるのに対して, 前者にはしばしば「敵意をもって競争する相手」というニュアンスがある) ▶彼は私の仕事上のライバルだ He and I are business *rivals* [*competitors*]. ‖早稲田(大学)と慶應(大学)は良きライバルですか Are Waseda and Keio (Universities) *good rivals*? ‖あの２校は互いにライバル意識をもっている There is *rivalry* between those two schools.

▶わが社の最大のライバル会社が最近営業を停止した Our biggest *competitor* [*rival*] went out of business recently.

らいびょう 癩病 《医学》 **leprosy** /léprəsi/. →ハンセン病.

らいひん 来賓 a **guest** /gest/ ▶卒業式で来賓が祝辞を述べた *A guest speaker* gave a congratulatory address at the graduation. (◎卒業生の親以外の客であることをはっきりさせるために speaker を入れる).

‖**来賓席** the guests' seats; 《掲示》 For Guests.

ライフ **life** ‖**ライフジャケット** a life jacket [vest] ‖**ライフボート** a lifeboat.

ライブ **live** /laɪv/ ▶来週「ネスト」でライブ(コンサート)をやるからぜひ来てね We're giving *a* (*live*) *concert* [*performance*] at Nest. So be sure to come.

‖**ライブハウス** (→かこみ記事) ‖**ライブ録音** live recording.

> **危ないカタカナ語✸ ライブ**
> **1**「生きている」の意味の形容詞 live /laɪv/ からで, 放送や番組などについて「生の, 実況の」の意味で用いられる.
> **2** 生演奏を聞かせる店のことを「ライブハウス」というが, これは和製語. 英語では生演奏の有無に関係なく, 単に club とか bar というだけである. 特に生演奏があることを説明しなければならないのなら a place with live music などとする.

ライフライン a **lifeline**; **infrastructure** (インフラ) ▶主要なライフラインを確保する secure *the basic* [*key*] *infrastructure*.

ライフル a **rifle** ▶標的に向けてライフルを発射する fire *a rifle* at a target.

ライフワーク one's **lifework,** one's **life's work** ▶遺伝病の研究は彼のライフワークだ Research on hereditary diseases is his *lifework*.

らいほう 来訪 a **visit** 一動 **来訪する** **visit** ＋目 ▶貴国大統領のご来訪をお待ち申し上げております We are looking forward to your President's *visit* to Japan. ‖イタリアのビジネスマンの一行が当社に来訪した A group of Italian businesspeople *visited* our company.

‖**来訪者** a visitor.

ライム 《植物》 a **lime.**

ライむぎ ライ麦 **rye** /raɪ/.

らいめい 雷鳴 a **clap** [a **peal**] **of thunder** ▶ものすごい雷鳴がとどろいて雨が降り出した There was a terrific *clap* [*peal*] *of thunder*, and then it began to pour (down).

ライラック 《植物》 a **lilac** /láɪlək/ (木); **lilac** (花).

らいれき 来歴 ▶芸術作品の来歴 *the provenance* of an artwork (➤ provenance は美術品の「歴代所有者リスト」) ‖伝説的人物の来歴 *the history* of a legend.

ライン a **line**; (a) **standard** (水準) ▶まっすぐなラインを引く draw a straight *line* ‖合格ラインに達したのはクラスの半分だけだった Only half of the class made *the passing mark* [*a passing grade*]. (➤ この文では line は使えない).

‖**ラインダンス** a line dance ‖**ガイドライン** a guideline ‖**スタート[ゴール]ライン** the starting [finish] line ‖**生産ライン** a line of production.

ラインアップ **the lineup** ▶スターティングラインアップが発表された *The starting lineup* was announced.

ラインがわ ライン川 **the Rhine** (スイスに発し, 北上して北海に注ぐ川).

ラウンジ a **lounge** (ホテルや劇場の; 空港などの「ラウンジ」は waiting room ともいう)

‖**ラウンジカー** a club car, a lounge car.

ラウンド a **round** (ゴルフ・ボクシング・ボウリングの) ▶ゴルフをワンラウンドプレーする play *a round* of golf ‖防衛戦でチャンピオンは第２ラウンドでノックアウトされた The defending champion was knocked out in *the second round*.

ラオス **Laos** /lɑ́ːoʊs ‖ laʊs/ ‖**ラオス語** Laotian /leɪóʊʃən ‖ láʊʃən/ ‖**ラオス人** a Laotian.

ラオチュー 老酒 ***laojiu***; **Chinese rice wine.**

らがん 裸眼 **the naked eye** ▶右の視力は裸眼で0.2しかないんだ The eyesight in my right eye is only 0.2 *without glasses*.

らく 楽 **1**【安楽】**comfort** /kʌ́mfəʳt/ (楽な気持ち); **ease** (緊張・心配などがないこと) 一形 **楽な** **comfortable** /kʌ́mfəʳṭəbəl/, **easy** 一副 **楽に** **comfortably** ▶人は誰でも楽な暮らしがしたいと思っている Everybody wants to live *comfortably* [*in comfort*]. ‖家に居るときは楽な格好に限る It's best to dress *casually* at home.

▶《客に向かって》どうぞお楽になさって Please *make yourself comfortable* [*at home*]. ‖ 気を楽にしてやりなさい *Take it easy.* ‖ そんなに力を入れずもっと楽にクラブを振ってごらん Just relax and swing the club more *naturally.* ‖ 鍼(はり)の治療を受けたら体が楽になった The acupuncturist's treatment *made* me *feel better.*

▶取調官にすべてを白状したら気が楽になった(＝ほっとした) I *felt relieved* after I confessed everything to the interrogator. ‖ 50年前よりは暮らしが楽になった We're leading *an easier life* [We're *better off*] than 50 years ago. ／*Life is easier* than it was 50 years ago.

あなたの英語はどう響く?
外国人に「さあ入って！座って楽にしてください」の意味で Come (on) in ! Please sit down and *take it easy.* と言う日本人がいるが，この場合の take it easy は「そう興奮しないで」の意に解釈されるのがふつう.「くつろぐ」には例えば make yourself comfortable [at home] などを使うほうがよい.

2【容易】一形 楽な **easy**；**effortless**(骨の折れない) 一副 楽に **easily, effortlessly**
▶営業の仕事はきみが思っているほど楽じゃないよ A salesperson's job isn't as *easy* as you might imagine. ‖ 満員電車での通勤は楽じゃない Commuting on jam-packed trains *is no picnic.* (➤ この picnic は「楽な仕事」の意のインフォーマルな語. 否定形で用いることが多い) ‖ カウボーイにとって馬に乗るのは楽なことだろう Riding a horse seems *effortless* for a cowboy. ‖ 機械のおかげで農作業は以前より楽になった Machines have made farm work *easier* than before. ‖ こんな問題なら私は楽に解ける I can solve this kind of problem *with ease* [*quite easily*]. ／Solving this kind of problem is *a cinch.* (➤ a cinch は「たやすいこと」).

▶このパソコンは子供でも楽に操作できる This computer is *easy* to operate, even for a child. ‖ 彼は2メートル20のバーを楽にクリアーした He *had no trouble* clearing the bar at 2.20 meters. (➤ have no trouble doing で「難なく…する」).

らくいん 烙印 a **brand** ▶いったん犯罪者のらく印を押されると就職は容易ではない Once you*'re branded* [*labeled*] (as) a criminal, it is difficult to get a job.

らくえん 楽園 (a) **paradise** (➤ しばしば, Ⓤ 扱い. ただし, 形容詞などが付くと Ⓒ 扱いで, a を付ける. 宗教的な「天国」の意では通例 Paradise とする) ▶地上の楽園 *a paradise* on earth ／*an* earthly *paradise* ‖ タヒチは熱帯の楽園だ Tahiti is *a* tropical *paradise.* ‖ この森はまさに小鳥の楽園だ This forest is *a* birds' *paradise.*

らくがき 落書き **graffiti** /grəfíːt̬i/ (公共の場所の)；a **scribble** (ノートなどへのなぐり書き) ▶落書きをする write *graffiti* ／scribble ‖ その公園には落書きがたくさんある There is a lot of *graffiti* in the park. ‖《掲示》落書き禁止 No Writing on the Walls ／No Scribbling.

¹らくご 落後する・落伍する **drop out** 《of》 ▶そのマラソンでは10人のランナーが落後した Ten runners *dropped out of* the marathon.

²らくご 落語 ***rakugo***
日本紹介 ✉ 落語は「おち」をつけて結ぶ滑稽なひとり話芸で，この話芸を職業とする人のことを「落語家」とか「噺(はなし)家」と呼びます A *rakugo* is a comic monologue ending with a skillfully delivered punch line called an '*ochi.*' A professional *rakugo* performer is called a '*rakugo-ka*' or a '*hanashika.*'

らくさ 落差 a **drop**；a **gap**(隔たり) ▶華厳の滝は落差が100メートルある Kegon Falls has *a drop* of 100 meters.

▶《比喩的》夢と現実との落差 *a gap* between one's dreams and reality ‖ 昔は都会と田舎では生活水準に大きな落差があった There used to be a wide *gap* in living standards between urban and rural areas.

らくさつ 落札 a **successful bid**(競り勝ち；bid は競りなどの「付け値」) ▶その古書は50万円で庄司氏が落札した Mr. Shoji *successfully bid* 500,000 yen for the old book. (➤ bid は「入札する」だが, successfully を付けることで「落札する」を表す).
‖落札価格 the highest bid price ‖ 落札者 a successful bidder.

らくじつ 落日 **the sinking sun, the setting sun**(➤「沈む夕日」は後者がふつう) ▶落日の産業 a *declining* industry.

らくしょう 楽勝 an **easy victory** [**win**],《インフォーマル》a **walkover** ▶横綱は大関に楽勝した The yokozuna *beat* the ozeki *easily.* ／The yokozuna *won an easy victory over* the ozeki. ‖ ベイスターズはスワローズに10対3で楽勝した The BayStars *walked over* the Swallows 10–3. (➤ 10–3 は ten-to-three または ten-three と読む).

▶《比喩的》英語のテストは楽勝だったよ The English test was *a breeze* [*a piece of cake* ／*a walk in the park*]. (➤ いずれも「ごく簡単なこと」の意のインフォーマルな言い方).

らくじょう 落城 **the fall of a castle.**

らくせい 落成 **completion** ▶この水族館は来月落成する This aquarium *will be completed* next month. ‖ 新校舎の落成式が昨日行われた Yesterday they *celebrated the completion* of the new school building. (●「完成を祝った」と考える；「落成式」に当たる英語は inauguration だが, この語は「就任式」「開業式」「除幕式」の意味にもなる).

らくせき 落石 a **falling rock** ▶《掲示》落石注意 Watch Out for *Falling Rocks* ‖ この道は落石のため通行できません The road is blocked by *fallen rocks.* (➤ 物理的に通行不可能である事実をいう) ／The road is closed due to *fallen rocks.* (➤ 道路管理者が通行を禁止している場合).

らくせん 落選 ▶彼は前回の市長選挙で落選した He *was defeated* in [He *lost*] the previous mayoral election.

▶私は数点の絵を展覧会に出品したがどれも落選した I entered several paintings in the exhibition, but *none of them was accepted* [*was placed*]. (➤ 後者の be placed は「入選する」の意).

らくだ 《動物》a **camel** ▶ラクダは「砂漠の船」と呼ばれている *Camels* are called 'ships of the desert.'
‖ヒトコブラクダ a dromedary /drάːmədèri/ ‖ フタコブラクダ a Bactrian camel 《参考》ラクダのこぶは hump という.

らくだい 落第 **1【留年】**▶成績不良のため, 大学3年生30人が落第した Thirty college juniors *had to repeat the third year* [*were not promoted to the fourth year*] due to their poor academic records.

▶彼は落第生だ He is *an academic repeater*.
2【不合格】▶彼は全科目に落第した He *failed* [*flunked*] all subjects. ‖その教授はどしどし学生を落第させる That professor *flunks* a lot of students.
▶《比喩的》彼は偉大なプロ野球選手だったが, 監督としては落第(=失敗)だ He was an outstanding pro baseball player, but is *a failure* as a manager.

らくたん 落胆 discouragement ; disappointment (失望) 一動 **落胆する** be discouraged, be disappointed
▶試合に負けたからといって落胆するな Don't *be discouraged* just because you lost a game. ‖彼は失恋して落胆している He *is depressed* [*is downhearted*] since he broke up with his girlfriend.

らくちゃく 落着 ▶その事件はようやく落着した The legal matter *has* finally *been settled*. / The incident *has been resolved*.

らくちょう 落丁 a missing page
‖落丁本 a book with missing pages ; a defective book(欠陥本).

らくてんか 楽天家 an optimist /ά:ptɪmɪst/.

らくてんてき 楽天的 ▶きみは楽天的だね You are *optimistic*. / You are an optimist. ‖私は楽天的な人生観をもっている I have an *optimistic* view of life.

らくのう 酪農 dairy /déəri/ (farming) ▶おじは北海道で酪農をしている My uncle runs *a dairy* (*farm*) in Hokkaido. (➤ dairy (farm) は「酪農場」) / My uncle is a dairy farmer in Hokkaido.
‖酪農 [乳] 製品 dairy products.

らくば 落馬 a fall from a horse 一動 **落馬する** fall from [off] one's horse.

らくばん 落盤 a cave-in ▶坑内で落盤事故が発生した *A cave-in* (*disaster*) occurred in the mine.

ラグビー rugby (football),《インフォーマル》rugger ▶ラグビーをやる play *rugby*.
‖ラグビー選手 a rugby player ‖ラグビーボール a rugby [rugger] ball.

らくよう 落葉 fallen leaves ▶そろそろ落葉の季節だ The trees will shed their leaves before long. / Leaves will be falling from the trees before long.
‖落葉樹 a deciduous tree.

らくらい 落雷 ▶ゴルフをしていた人が落雷に遭った A golfer *was struck by lightning*. (➤ 鳴る雷は thunder で, 落ちる雷(稲妻)は lightning) ‖昨夜関東各地で落雷があった *Lightning struck* [*hit*] in many places in the Kanto region last night.

らくらく 楽々 easily, with ease ▶うちのチームなら楽々優勝できる Our team can win the championship *easily* [*with ease*]. ‖この競技場は5万人を楽々収容できる This stadium can seat 50,000 people *easily*.

ラクロス lacross /ləkrɔ́:s/.

ラケット a racket (テニス・バドミントン・卓球用の) 《参考》卓球のラケットは paddle とも呼ばれる ▶テニスのラケット a tennis *racket*.

ラザニア lasagna /ləzά:njə/ (イタリア料理).

ラジアルタイヤ a radial (tire).

-らしい 1【典型的であることを示して】like ▶そういうことを言うなんていかにも彼女らしいね It's just *like* her to say that. ‖彼女はあまり女優らしくない She *doesn't look* much *like* an actress. ‖(そんな沈んだ顔をして)きみらしくないよ. どうしたの? You'*re not acting like yourself*. What's the matter?
▶彼はいかにもスポーツマンらしいさわやかな青年だった He was a fine and healthy young man, just *as* an athlete *is expected to be*. (➤「運動選手がそうであるよう期待されているように」の意) ‖このクリスマスカードはあまりクリスマスらしくない This Christmas card isn't very *Christmassy*.
▶あの作家はこのところ作品らしい作品を発表していない Recently, that writer hasn't published any *work to speak of*. (➤ to speak of は「取り立てて言うほどの」).
▶トンネルとは後藤にしてはらしからぬミスだ Missing a grounder and letting it go through his legs *isn't like* Goto.
2【推定・推測を示して】

> **語法「…らしい」の言い方**
> (1)推定や推測を表す「…らしい」には **I think** (…だと思う), **look like** (…になりそうだ), **seem** (…だと思われる), **appear** (外見的に…のようだ)などが相当する.
> (2)**I hear** [**I've heard** / **I've been told**] **…** や **They say …, It is said that …** などもこの意味を表すが, これらはいずれも情報源を明らかにしたくないような場合に用いることが多く, 一般的には My father told me(父の話だと…らしい), According to the weather forecast (天気予報によると…らしい), I read in today's *Asahi*(きょうの朝日新聞によると…らしい)などのように具体的に言うことが多い.

▶あの背の高い人が鶴田さんらしい *I think* that tall man is Tsuruta. ‖彼女は私たちを夕食に招いてくれるらしい It *looks like* she's going to invite us to dinner. ‖対話「来週, 田代先生の授業休講なの?」「らしいね」"Is it true that Mr. Tashiro's class next week has been canceled?" "*Looks like it*." ‖あのガードマンが金を盗んだらしい The security guard *seems* to have stolen money. ‖彼女, 私が言ったことをまだ気にしてるらしいんだ She *appears* to be worrying over what I said. ‖私たちのクラスに転校生が来るらしい *I hear that* a transfer student will join our class.
▶天気予報ではあすも雨らしい The weather report *calls for* rain again tomorrow. (➤ call for は「(天気を)予報する」).

ラジウム 《化学》radium /réɪdiəm/
‖ラジウム温泉 a radium spa ‖放射性ラジウム radioactive radium.

ラジエーター a radiator /réɪdieɪṭəʳ/.

ラジオ a radio /réɪdioʊ/ (set) ▶ラジオをつける[切る] turn on [turn off] the *radio* ‖ラジオの音を大きく[小さく]する turn up [down] the *radio* ‖その事故のことはテレビとラジオで知った I learned of the accident *on* TV and *radio*.
▶私はラジオでよくＡＦＮを聴く I often listen to AFN *on the radio*. ‖母はラジオの音楽を聴きながら料理を作る My mother cooks while listening to music *on the radio*. ‖近くの公園で毎朝ラジオ体操をやっている人たちがいる Every morning some people do their *radio exercises* [do their *exercises following the instructions on the radio exercise program*] in the park near my house. ‖私はラジオをNHK-FM に合わせた I tuned in (my *radio*) to NHK-FM.
✉ **私はラジオ講座で英語を勉強しています** I am studying English *by listening to an English*

radio course.

‖ **ラジオ局** a radio station ‖ **ラジオドラマ** a radio play [drama] ‖ **ラジオ番組** a radio program ‖ **カーラジオ** a car radio.

ラジカセ **a radio cassette player**, **a portable radio and cassette player** ;《インフォーマル》**a boom box**(CD ラジカセを含む)

‖ **CD ラジカセ** a portable radio and CD player.

ラジカル **radical**(過激な) ▶あの男はラジカルな思想の持ち主だ He is a man of *radical* ideas.

ラジコン **radio control**(無線操縦) ▶ラジコンの模型ボートを操縦する operate a *radio-controlled* model boat.

らしんばん 羅針盤 **a compass** /kʌ́mpəs/.

ラスク a **rusk**(菓子).

ラスト **the last**(最後) ▶打つのは私がラストだ I'm *the last one* to bat. / I'm *the last* batter. ‖ 映画『タイタニック』のラストシーンにはじんと来た I was deeply moved by *the last scene* of the movie "Titanic."

▶清水はゴールに向かってラストスパートを掛けた Shimizu made *a final spurt* to reach the goal.

ラスベガス **Las Vegas**(アメリカ, ネバダ州のカジノで有名な観光都市).

ラズベリー《植物》a **raspberry** /rǽzbèri ‖ rɑ́:zbəri/ (キイチゴ).

らせん 螺旋 a **spiral**

‖ **らせん階段** a spiral [winding] staircase.

らぞう 裸像 a **nude sculpture** [**statue**].

らたい 裸体 a **naked** /néıkıd/ **body** ; a **nude**(写真・芸術作品の ; 女性を指すことが多い) →**ヌード**.

‖ **裸体画** a nude (picture) ‖ **裸体像** a nude statue.

[1]**らち 埒** ▶その和平交渉はなかなからちが明かない(=うまくいかない) The peace talks *aren't going smoothly*. ‖ 部長相手の賃上げ交渉ではらちが明かない(=成果が得られない) If we negotiate with the general manager, we *won't get anywhere* in our negotiations for a pay raise.

[2]**らち 拉致** **abduction** 一動 **拉致する** **abduct** +目 ▶山口さんは帰宅途中, (何者かに)拉致されたまま行方不明になっています Miss Yamaguchi *was abducted* on her way home, and has not been seen since.

‖ **拉致問題** an abduction [kidnapping] issue.

らっか 落下 a **fall**, a **drop** 一動 **落下する** **fall**, **drop** ▶人工衛星の破片が太平洋上に落下した Satellite fragments *fell* in the Pacific. ‖《掲示》**落下物注意** Danger Overhead.

ラッカー **lacquer** /lǽkəʳ/ 《参考》Japanese lacquer または black lacquer は「漆」で, lacquerware は「漆器」.

らっかさん 落下傘 →**パラシュート**.

らっかせい 落花生 a **peanut**,《英また》a **groundnut**.

[1]**らっかん 楽観する** **be optimistic** /ɑ́:ptımístık/ 《about》 ▶多くの学生たちは将来に対して楽観的だ Most students *are optimistic about* their future. ‖ 経済見通しは楽観を許さない We can't afford to *be optimistic about* the economic outlook.

‖ **楽観主義** optimism /ɑ́:ptımìzəm/ ‖ **楽観主義者** an optimist.

[2]**らっかん 落款** an **artist's signature**.

ラッキー **lucky** ▶満塁ホームランを打てたのは本当にラッキーでした I was really *lucky* to hit a grand slam. ‖ 対話「浅井教授の授業, 休講だって」「ラッキー!」"I hear that Professor Asai's class was canceled." "*How lucky!*" ‖ (占いで) 今週のあなたのラッキーカラーはピンクです Your *lucky color* this week is pink.

‖ (野球の) **ラッキーセブン** the lucky seventh.

らっきゅう 落球する **muff** +目 ▶鈴木は何でもないフライを落球し, 2者の生還を許した Suzuki *muffed* a pop fly, allowing two runners to score.

らっきょう 辣韮 a **shallot bulb**(植物) ; a **pickled shallot**(漬物).

ラック a **rack**

‖ **マガジンラック** a magazine rack.

らっこ 海獺《動物》a **sea otter**.

ラッシュ a **rush**(殺到) ; **the rush hour(s)**, **the rush**(ラッシュアワー) ▶ラッシュを避ける avoid *the rush* (*hour*) ‖ ラッシュ時の新宿駅の混雑ぶりはすごいものだ Shinjuku Station is overcrowded (with people) *during the rush hour*. (朝夕で区別するときは the morning [evening] rush hour とする) ‖ この駅のラッシュアワーは何時頃ですか When are *the rush hours* at this station? (ふつう朝と夕方にあるので複数形になる).

▶建設ラッシュ a construction *rush*(➤ 建設による活況は construction boom).

ラッセル ‖ **ラッセル車** a snowplow /snóʊplaʊ/.

らっぱ 喇叭 a **trumpet** ; a **bugle** /bjú:gəl/ (軍用の) ▶らっぱを吹く blow *a trumpet*.

▶らっぱ飲みはよしなさい Stop *drinking straight from the bottle*.

ラッピング **wrapping** ▶このネクタイを誕生日祝い用にラッピングしてください I'd like this tie *wrapped* as a birthday present.

[1]**ラップ** **plastic wrap**, **Saran Wrap** (➤ 後者は商標名. (plastic) cling wrap ともいう) ▶キャベツをラップで包む *wrap* cabbage *in plastic* [*Saran Wrap*] (➤ plastic は「ビニール」の意).

▶シューマイをチンするときはラップしなきゃだめよ Chinese pork dumplings should *be wrapped in plastic* [*in cling wrap*] before you put them in a microwave (oven).

[2]**ラップ** a **lap** (➤ 英語の lap は競技場の周回コースの1周, 競泳のプールの1往復, スケート競技のリンクの1周などを指す. マラソンの5キロ, 10キロの区切りには用いない) ▶高橋選手はラップ(=ラップタイム)では日本最高記録を上回っています Takahashi's *lap time* was under the Japanese national record.

‖ **ラップタイム** (a) lap time.

[3]**ラップ**《音楽》**rap** (**music**)

‖ **ラップ歌手** a rapper, a rap artist.

ラップトップ(パソコン) a **laptop computer**, a **notebook computer**.

らつわん 辣腕 ▶その社長は会社の再建に辣腕を振るった The company president *showed his great ability* [*his prowess*] in the company's reconstruction. (➤ prowess /práʊəs ‖ -es/ は「並外れた腕前 [能力]」).

‖ **辣腕家** a man [a woman] of uncommon shrewdness, a wheeler-dealer.

ラディッシュ《植物》a **radish**.

ラテン **Latin**(ラテン民族の)

‖ **ラテンアメリカ** Latin America ‖ **ラテン音楽** Latin (American) music ‖ **ラテン語** Latin ‖ **ラテン民族** the Latin peoples.

らでん 螺鈿 *raden* ; a Japanese decorative craft of applying cut linings of mother-of-pearl, ivory, and other shells into the surface of

ら

lacquerware or wood(➤ 説明的な訳).
ラドン 《化学》**radon** /réɪdɑ:n/.
らば 騾馬 《動物》 a **mule**.
ラバー rubber(ゴム)
‖**ラバーソール** a rubber sole.
らふ 裸婦 a **woman in the nude**, a **nude** ▶裸婦をデッサンする sketch *a woman in the nude*.
ラフ rough(乱暴な); **casual** (ふだん着の, 気取らない) ▶ラフなプレー *rough* play ‖ パーティーにはラフな格好で来てください Please come to the party in *casual* wear [clothes]. (➤ この場合 rough は使えない).
▶ティーショットをラフに打ち込む hit a tee shot into *the rough*.
ラブ love ▶日本のテレビにはラブシーンが多すぎる Japanese TV has too many *love* [*sex*] *scenes*.
‖**ラブホテル** a love hotel; a hotel for sexual rendezvous /rɑ́:ndeɪvu:/ ‖**ラブレター** a love letter.
ラプソディー 《音楽》 a **rhapsody**.
ラベル a **label** /léɪbəl/ ▶ラベルを貼る[剝がす] put on [take off] *a label* ‖ 試験管に「毒物」のラベルをちゃんと貼ったかい? Are you sure you put the Poison *label* on the test tube?
‖**警告ラベル** a warning label.
ラベンダー 《植物》 (a) **lavender**.
ラマ a **lama**(ラマ僧)
‖**ラマ教** Tibetan Buddhism.
ラマダン Ramadan /ræ̀mədɑ́:n/ (イスラム教の断食月).
1**ラム rum**(酒).
2**ラム lamb** /læm/ (子羊肉).
ラムネ (a) **soda pop**, (a) **pop** (➤ 説明的には a bottled carbonated soft drink with a glass marble used as a stopper といえる).
ラメ lamé /lɑ:méɪ/ (金糸や銀糸を織り込んだ布).
ラリー a **rally** ▶そのバレーの試合ではラリーの応酬が観客を沸かせた The spectators at the volleyball game were excited by the *repeated rallies*.
‖**サファリラリー** a safari rally.
ラルゴ 《音楽》 **largo** /lɑ́:ʳgoʊ/.
られつ 羅列 (an) **enumeration** /ɪnjù:məréɪʃən/ 一動 **羅列する enumerate** +目 ▶きみのレポートは数字が羅列してあるだけじゃないか Your paper is nothing but *an enumeration* [*a list*] of figures, isn't it?

-られる

> 《解説》(1) 日本語の「-られる」は「-れる」の場合と同様,「受け身・可能・尊敬・自発」を表すのに用いるが, これらを表す1語の英語はない.
> (2)「受け身」の場合は動詞の受動態を用いるが, 英語では同じことを能動態でいうことも多い.
> (3)「可能」の意は「(…することが) できる」と考えて, can, be able to などを用いる.
> (4)「尊敬」については, 英語には日本語の場合のような特別な敬語表現法は少ないので, 一般の動詞表現を用いればよい. →-れる.

1【受け身を示して】▶廊下のごみを拾っていたら, 校長先生に褒められた The principal *praised me* for picking up litter in the hallway. ‖ きょう塾の先生に褒められたよ I *was given a pat on the back* by my *juku* teacher today. (➤ give ... a pat on the back は「…の背中を優しくたたく」が原義) ‖ 汚職をした役人は法律によって厳しく罰せられるべきだ Corrupt officials should *be punished* severely under the law.

2【可能を示して】▶どのくらい潜っていられる? How long *can* you hold your breath underwater? ‖ 少しくらい静かにしていられないのか *Can't* you be quiet even for a short time? ‖ あなたは来られる? Will you *be able to* come? ‖ 大人なんて信じられない I just *can't* trust adults.

3【尊敬を示して】▶先生がこれまでに手がけられた彫刻は何点ほどありますか How many sculptures have you made so far? ‖ お仕事でこちらに来られたのですか? Did you come here on business? (● 2例とも特に尊敬表現を使わない).

4【自然にそうなる状態(自発)を示して】▶そのタオルはぬれているように感じられた The towel *felt* wet. ‖ 模様替えをしたら部屋が広く感じられた Rearranging the room *made* it *feel* bigger. ‖ 朝晩に秋の気配が感じられる A hint of autumn could *be felt* in the morning and evening air.

ラワン lauan /lú:ɑ:n, laʊɑ́:n/ (木材); a **lauan** (木).
1**らん 欄** a **column** /kɑ́:ləm/ (➤ 新聞のコラムニストによる寄稿欄を指すことが多い) ▶家庭欄 a family *page* ‖ スポーツ欄 a sports *page* ‖ 投書欄 the Letters to the Editor *column*.
2**らん 蘭** 《植物》 an **orchid** /ɔ́:ʳkɪd/ ▶ランは花の女王と呼ばれている *Orchids* are called the queen of flowers.
‖**コチョウラン** a phalaenopsis /fæ̀lənɑ́:psɪs/, a moth orchid.
ラン LAN 《コンピュータ》 a **local area network**.
らんおう 卵黄 yolk /joʊk/, **yellow**. →黄身.
らんがい 欄外 the margin ▶欄外の注を参照のこと See the *marginal* note [the note *in the margin*].
《参考》「脚注」は footnote,「(巻末の)後注」は endnote という.
らんかいはつ 乱開発 indiscriminate [**haphazard**] **economic development** (➤ indiscriminate は「見境のない」, haphazard は「行き当たりばったりの」) ▶その珍種の植物は(地域の)乱開発のために絶滅した The rare plants became extinct due to the *indiscriminate* [*haphazard*] *economic development* (of the area).
らんかく 乱獲 indiscriminate hunting [**fishing**] (➤ fishing は魚の場合) ▶乱獲がたたって近海魚の水揚げが減っている The catch of shore fish has been on the decrease due to *indiscriminate fishing*.
らんがく 蘭学 Dutch learning.
1**らんかん 欄干** a **railing** ▶欄干にもたれる[から身を乗り出す] lean against [over] *a railing*.
2**らんかん 卵管** 《解剖学》 a **fallopian tube**.
らんぎり 乱切り ▶ニンジンを乱切りにする *chop* a carrot.
らんきりゅう 乱気流 turbulence, turbulent currents ▶乱気流のせいで飛行機がひどく揺れた Our plane pitched heavily because of *turbulence*.
ランキング ranking ▶あのボクサーはフライ級の世界ランキングの第2位だ That boxer *ranks second* in world flyweight standings.
▶ジョコビッチは世界ランキング1位だ Djokovic *is ranked first in the world*.
ランク (a) **rank** 一動 **ランクする rank** +目 ▶その大学のフットボールチームはAP通信社により第1位にランクされた The university's football team *was ranked* first by the Associated Press. ‖ M大学は女子高生の人気ではランクが高い M University *is ranked high* in popularity among female high school students.

▶当社では年齢による社員のランクづけはしません We don't *rank* employees according to age.

らんこう 乱交 **group sex, an orgy.**

らんざつ 乱雑な **disorderly**; **cluttered**（取り散らかした）; **messy**（ごたごたした, 汚い）▶乱雑な部屋 a *disorderly* room ‖ 竹村先生の机の上はいつも乱雑になっている Mr. Takemura's desk is always *cluttered*. ‖ 私の部屋はいつも乱雑だ My room is always *messy* [*a mess*].

1**らんし 乱視**《医学》**astigmatism** /əstígmətìzəm/ 一形 乱視の **astigmatic** /æ̀stɪɡmǽtɪk/ ▶私は少し乱視だ I'm slightly *astigmatic*.

2**らんし 卵子**《生物学》an **ovum** /óʊvəm/［複 **ova**］▶赤ん坊は精子と卵子が結合してできる The union of a sperm and *an ovum* produces a baby.

ランジェリー **lingerie** /lɑ̀:ndʒəréɪ ‖ lǽndʒəri/（女性用の下着）.

らんしゃ 乱射 **random shooting** ▶覚醒剤中毒の男が通りでピストルを乱射した A drug addict *fired random shots* [*fired* his gun *at random*] on the street.

らんじゅく 爛熟 ▶文化・文政時代, 江戸の町人文化はらん熟期を迎えた The Bunka and Bunsei eras (1804〜1830) *marked the mature period* [*the most flourishing period*] of Edo mercantile culture. ／The Edo (mercantile) culture *grew into maturity* during the Bunka and Bunsei eras.

らんすう 乱数《数学》**random numbers** ▶乱数を生成する generate *random numbers*.
‖乱数表 a random-number table.

らんせい 乱世 **turbulent days** ▶16世紀後半の日本は戦国乱世の時代だった The late sixteenth century was *a period of turbulent war* in Japanese history.

らんせん 乱戦 ▶試合は大乱戦になった The game became *a slugfest* with a lot of runs scored on both sides.（➤ slugfest は「打撃戦」).

らんそう 卵巣《解剖学》an **ovary** /óʊvəri/
‖卵巣ホルモン an ovarian hormone.

らんぞう 乱造する **churn out** ▶安っぽいおもちゃ［小説］を乱造する *churn out* cheap toys [novels] ‖ 1960年代には安い住宅が乱造された Cheap houses *were turned out* [*were thrown up*] *by the thousands* in the 1960's.（➤ turn out は「どんどん作り出す」, throw up は「(家を)急ごしらえする」の意）.

ランダム **random**
‖ランダムサンプリング a random sampling.

ランタン a **lantern**（手さげランプ）.

1**ランチ**《昼食》**lunch** ▶ランチに出かける go out for *lunch* ‖ ランチは大体社食で食べます I usually eat *lunch* at the company cafeteria. ‖ 日替わりランチを注文する order a *daily lunch*.
‖ランチタイム lunchtime ‖ お子さまランチ a child's [children's] meal, a child's [children's] plate.

2**ランチ**《港湾内で使用する舟艇》a **launch**.

らんちきさわぎ 乱痴気騒ぎ a **spree**, an **orgy**（➤後者は乱交パーティーを指す場合がある）▶隣の学生たちはゆうべ乱痴気騒ぎをしていた The students next door were (*really*) *partying* (*loudly*) last night.

ランチョン (a) **luncheon**（➤ lunch より格式ばった語で「午さん会」に当たる）.
‖ランチョンマット a place mat（➤「ランチョンマット」は和製語）.

ランデブー a **rendezvous** /rɑ́:ndeɪvu: ‖ rɔ́ndɪvu:/.

らんとう 乱闘 a **scuffle**（取っ組み合い）一動 乱闘する **scuffle** ▶試合の途中で選手どうしがグラウンド上で乱闘した The players *scuffled* in the field during the game.

らんどく 乱読 ▶彼は小説を手当たり次第に乱読している He *reads* every novel *he can get his hands on* [*that comes his way*].
▶乱読は避けて良書を選びなさい You should not *read* books *at random*. Choose good ones carefully.

ランドセル a **school rucksack** /rʌ́ksæk/［**backpack**／**bag**］▶ランドセルを背負う carry *a school rucksack* on one's back.

ランドリー a **laundry** /lɔ́:ndri/（洗濯する部屋や店）.

ランナー a **runner** ▶長距離ランナー a distance *runner* ‖ マラソンランナー a marathon *runner*. →走者.

らんにゅう 乱入する **burst** [**break**] **into** ▶きのうデモ隊が与党事務所に乱入した Yesterday a group of demonstrators *broke into* the office of the ruling party.

ランニング **running**（走ること）; **jogging**（ジョギング）
‖ランニングシューズ running shoes.

> **危ないカタカナ語✹ ランニング**
> **1** 日本語の「ランニングシャツ」は男性の下着を指すことが多いが, これは英語では sleeveless undershirt, (英また) vest という. 運動選手などが着るランニングシャツは athlete shirt, (athletic) jersey, tank top, (英また) gym /dʒɪm/ [running] vest などという. いずれにしても (×)running shirt は不可.
> **2**「ランニングホームラン」は和製語で, 英語では inside-the-park home run [homer]（球場内ホームラン）という.

ランニングコスト **running costs**（機械の運用コストあるいは運転資金）.

らんちょう 乱丁 ▶この本は乱丁だ The pages of this book *are not in the correct order*.

らんぱく 卵白 an **egg white**.

らんばつ 乱伐 **indiscriminate logging** ▶山林の乱伐が山崩れを引き起こした *Indiscriminate logging* [*Reckless deforestation*] caused the landslide. ／The landslide resulted from *indiscriminate felling* of trees.

らんぱつ 乱発 **overissue** 一動 乱発する **overissue** ＋目 ▶紙幣の乱発 the *overissue* of paper money ‖ 小切手を乱発する *overissue* checks.

らんはんしゃ 乱反射《光学》a **diffuse(d) reflection.**

らんぴ 乱費 ▶政府は税金の乱費を慎むべきだ The government should be careful not to *waste* our taxes [*throw away* our tax money *through careless spending*].

らんぴつ 乱筆 ▶乱筆をお許しください I apologize for my *messy writing*.
✉ **乱筆乱文にて失礼いたします** Please excuse my *poor handwriting* [*sloppy writing*]. ➤ 英米人は手紙であまりこういうことは書かない.

らんぶ 乱舞 **boisterous dancing.**

1**ランプ**《灯火》a **lamp** ▶ランプをつける［消す］light [put out] *a lamp* ‖ ランプの明かりで手紙を書く write a letter by *lamplight*.

2**ランプ**《傾斜路》a **ramp**（➤高速道路に限らない）▶このランプを下りると500メートルほど先にいいレストランがある *Exit at this ramp*, and after about 500 meters there is a good restaurant.

ら

らんぼう 乱暴 violence（暴力）**―形 乱暴な** violent；rough（荒々しい）**―副 乱暴に** violently，roughly ▶乱暴はやめなさい（＝暴力を振るうな）Don't use *violence*. ‖男の子だもの，時には乱暴もするわよ Since he's a boy, he sometimes gets a little *rowdy* [*unruly*]. ▶乱暴なプレーをする play *rough*（➤ rough は roughly よりくだけた副詞）‖乱暴なことばを使ってはいけない Don't use *rough* [*violent*] language. ‖ドライバーの中には乱暴な（＝向こう見ずな）運転をする人がいる Some motorists drive *recklessly*. ‖健二は乱暴にドアを開けた Kenji opened the door *roughly* [*in a rough manner*]. ‖ハードディスクを乱暴に扱うな Don't handle the hard disk *roughly*. ／Be careful with the hard disk.
▶彼は女性に乱暴（＝暴行）をして投獄された He was put in prison for *raping* [*assaulting*] a woman.（→暴行）.

らんま 欄間 a *ranma*；a decorative wooden parcel above fusuma [paper-covered sliding doors]（➤ 説明的な訳）.

らんまん 爛漫 ▶吉野は全山が桜の花に埋もれてまさに春らんまんだ All the mountains at Yoshino are covered with cherry blossoms, and *spring is in full swing*.

らんみゃく 乱脈 ▶小野氏の乱脈な女性関係 Mr. Ono's *chaotic* [*messy*] relations with women ‖H銀行の元経営者たちは乱脈経営の責任を追及された The former directors of H Bank were accused of *poorly planned and haphazard* management.（➤「計画がお粗末で行き当たりばったりの」の意）.

らんよう 乱用 abuse /əbjúːs/（誤った，または過度の使用）；overuse（過度の使用）**―動 乱用する** abuse /əbjúːz/ ＋目，overuse ＋目 ▶職権［権力］乱用 *abuse* of authority [power] ‖薬物の乱用が深刻な社会問題になっている *Substance* [*Drug*] *abuse* has become a serious social problem.（➤ substance abuse はアルコールも含む）.
▶かぜ薬を乱用するな Don't *take too much* [*take an overdose of*] cold medicine. ‖「ニーズ」という単語は日本で乱用されている The word 'needs' *is overused* in Japan.

らんらん 爛々 ▶獲物を狙うヤマネコの目が暗闇の中でらんらんと光っている A wildcat's eyes *are shining* in the darkness as it hunts down its prey.

らんりつ 乱立 ▶駅前通りにはスーパーが乱立している *Too many* supermarkets *are competing* with one another on the street in front of the train station.（●「あまりに多くのスーパーが競い合っている」と考える）‖東京都知事選挙には多数の候補者が乱立した There *were too many* candidates *running* for governor of Tokyo.

り・り

¹り 理 ▶いちばん強い力士が優勝するのは理の当然だ *It is quite natural that* the strongest sumo wrestlers are the ones who win tournaments.

²り 利 (a) profit（利益）；an advantage（利点）；interest（利子）▶何と利にさといやつだ He's *quick to see what is to his advantage*. ／He sure *has an eye on his own interests*.
▶《慣用表現》ホテル東京は地の利を得ている The Hotel Tokyo has the *advantage of a good location*.

リアクション reaction ▶彼のリアクションが大げさだった His *reaction* was exaggerated.

リアス ▶リアス（式）海岸 a *ria* coast（➤ 地理用語で，一般には rugged coastline（ぎざぎざした海岸線）などとしか言わない）.

リアリスト a realist.

リアリズム realism.

リアリティー reality, a sense of reality ▶リアリティーがある *realistic*.

リアル real（真に迫った）；realistic（写実的な）▶ワイエスはリアルな描写で知られている Wyeth is known for his *realistic* depictions.

リアルタイム real time **―形 リアルタイムの** real-time ▶事件をリアルタイムで伝える report an incident *in real time*.

リーク leakage **―動 リークする** leak ＋目 ▶機密情報をマスコミにリークする *leak* confidential information to the media.

リーグ a league ▶セントラル［パシフィック］リーグ the Central [Pacific] *League* ‖阿部は32本塁打で現在リーグのトップだ Abe leads the *league* with 32 home runs now.
‖**リーグ戦** a league game [match]（個々の試合）；the league series（全試合）；a round robin（総当たり戦）‖**メジャーリーグ**（アメリカの）the major leagues.

リーシュ →リード 3.

¹リース a lease（賃貸）▶リース契約を結ぶ sign *a lease* ‖このコピー機はリースです We have this copying machine *on lease*.
‖**リース業者** a leasing company ‖**リース料金** a rental (fee).

²リース a wreath（花輪）.

¹リーダー《指導者》a leader ▶部員たちは島田君にリーダーとして全幅の信頼を置いている The club members put absolute trust in Shimada as their *leader*.（➤ in 以下を in Shimada's leadership としてもよい．leadership は「リーダーとしての資質，指導力」）‖首相には行政改革でリーダーシップを発揮してほしい I hope the Prime Minister will show some *leadership* in administrative reform(s).

²リーダー《読本》a reader.

リーディングヒッター《野球》the leading hitter（その時点での首位打者）；the batting champion（最終的な首位打者）.

¹リード 1【先導すること】 the lead **―動 リードする** lead（＋目）▶産業ロボットの生産では日本は世界をリードしている Japan *leads* the world in the production of industrial robots.
2【勝っていること】 a lead **―動 リードする** lead ＋目 ▶6点のリードを守る hold a six-run *lead* ‖6回を終わって中日は巨人を7対2でリードしている Going into the seventh (inning), the Dragons *lead* the Giants 7-2.

‖リードオフマン a leadoff (batter／man) (➤「１番打者」「(その回の)先頭打者」の両意がある) ‖リードボーカル a lead vocal.

3【犬用の皮ひも】《主に米》a **leash**,《主に英》a **lead** (➤前者は《英》では堅い語) ▶犬をリードにつないでおく keep a dog on *a leash* [*a lead*].

[2]**リード**《音楽》a **reed**

‖リード楽器 a reed instrument.

リーフレット a **leaflet**(１枚刷りの印刷物).

リール a **reel** ▶釣り用のリール a (fishing) *reel* ‖リールにテープを巻く wind tape onto *a reel*.

リウマチ《医学》**rheumatism** /rúːmətìzəm/ ▶季節の変わり目にはよくリウマチが出る I often suffer from *rheumatism* when the seasons change.

‖リウマチ患者 a rheumatic.

りえき 利益 **1【役立つこと】**(a) **benefit** ▶彼は自分の利益になることにのみ熱心だ He is only interested in doing things that *benefit* [*are beneficial to*] him.

▶そんな漫画を読んでも何の利益にもならないよ Reading comic books like that won't *do* you any *good* [won't *benefit* you].

2【利潤】(a) **profit** (経費を差し引いたあとの)；**proceeds** (特別な目的のためにものを売って得た) ▶彼女は投資で大きな利益を上げた She made a large *profit* from her investment. ‖この製品が利益を上げるようになるまでには長い時間がかかった It took a long time for us to *turn a profit* on this product. ‖大学祭の模擬店で20万円の純利益があった The fast-food stall we ran during the campus festival brought us *a net profit* of 200,000 yen. ‖《バザーで》その利益はユニセフに送ろうよ Let's donate the *proceeds* to UNICEF.

▶この商売は利益が大きい This business is *profitable* [*lucrative*].

‖利益幅 a profit margin ‖利益率 a profit rate [ratio].

☛ 不利益 (→見出語)

リエゾン《音声学》a **liaison** /líːəzɑːn ‖ liéɪzn/.

リオデジャネイロ **Rio de Janeiro**(ブラジル南東部の都市).

りか 理科 **science** ▶理科の先生 a *science* teacher ‖私は大学は文科系よりも理科系に進みたい I'd rather study *science* than liberal arts in college [when I go to college].

‖理科室 a science lab [classroom].

りかい 理解 (an) **understanding**, **comprehension** (➤後者は堅い語) ━動 理解する **understand**(＋目), **comprehend** ＋目

▶私の言っていることが理解できますか Do you *understand* what I'm saying? ‖彼女がどうして反対したのか理解できない I can't *understand* why she disagreed. ‖この哲学書は私には理解できない This philosophy book *is beyond my comprehension* [*is impossible* for me *to understand*].

▶その子は素早く文の意味を理解した The child quickly *grasped* the meaning of the sentence. (➤grasp は「意味をつかむ」) ‖この子は理解が早い This boy *grasps things quickly*.／This boy *is quick on the uptake*. ‖彼の意図が全く理解できない I simply can't *figure out* what his intention is. (➤figure out は「理解する」の意のインフォーマルな言い方).

▶仏教 [心理学] に対する深い理解のある人 a person with a deep *understanding* of Buddhism [psychology] ‖きみのお母さんは理解があるね Your mother is *understanding*. (「理解のある母親」なら an understanding mother).

☛ 無理解 (→見出語)

りがい 利害 an **interest** ▶関係者の利害が対立している There is a conflict of *interest* (*s*) among the parties concerned. ‖生産者と消費者の利害が一致することはまれだ Producers seldom share common *interests* with consumers. ‖わが社はその会社と利害関係がある We have *an interest* [*a stake*] in that company.

[1]**りがく 理学** **science**

‖理学博士 a doctor of science(人)；Doctor of Science(称号)《略 D. Sc.》‖理学部 the school [college] of science ‖理学療法 physical therapy ‖理学療法士 a physical therapist.

[2]**りがく 離学** **early school** [**college**] **leaving**(卒業前の)

‖離学者 an early school [college] leaver (➤《英》school leaver は「義務教育年限修了者」の意味での「離学者」) ‖離学(者)率 the drop-out rate, the rate of early school [college] leaving.

りき 利器 a **convenience** ▶スマートフォンは文明の利器である The smartphone is a modern *convenience*.

りきえい 力泳 ▶彼は学校の代表として力泳した He *swam as hard as possible* [*with all his strength*] for his school.

りきがく 力学 **dynamics** /daɪnǽmɪks/

‖熱力学 thermodynamics ‖量子力学 quantum mechanics.

りきさく 力作 a **tour de force** /tʊ̀əʳ də fɔ́ːʳs/；a **masterpiece**(傑作).

りきし 力士 a **sumo wrestler**

‖小兵(こひょう)力士 a small(-statured) sumo wrestler.

りきせつ 力説する **emphasize** /émfəsaɪz/《that》(強調する)；**stress**《that》(重点を置く) ▶私たちの学校の校長先生は勇気の必要性をしばしば力説する Our principal often *emphasizes* [*stresses*] that students need to have courage.

りきそう 力走 ▶アンカーはゴールを目指して力走した The anchorperson *ran as fast as he* [*she*] *could* to the goal.

リキッド **liquid** /líkwɪd/.

りきてん 力点 (an) **emphasis**, **stress** (➤stress のほうが事の重大さ・重要性をより強調する) ▶先生は世界史の勉強に力点を置くようにと言った The teacher told me to *put an emphasis* [*put stress*] *on* studying world history.

りきとう 力投 ▶西田投手は力投したが，打線の援護が無くわがチームは４対１で敗れた Despite Nishida's *fine pitching*, our team lost 4-1 because of poor hitting.

りきむ 力む **strain** (**oneself**) ▶力まずにプレーする perform *without straining* ‖きみは少し力み過ぎだ．もっと楽にしたら？ You are *straining yourself* too much [You *are pushing yourself too hard*]. Take it easy.

▶いくら力んでも，きみの力ではそのバーベルは上がらないよ *No matter how hard you try*, you are not going to be able to lift that barbell.

りきゅう 離宮 a **detached palace** ▶桂離宮 the Katsura *Detached Palace* (➤宮内庁による英語表記は the Katsura Imperial Villa).

リキュール **liqueur** /lɪkɔ́ːʳ ‖ -kjʊ́ə/.

りきりょう 力量 **ability**, **capacity** /kəpǽsəṭi/ (➤両

語は同義でも用いるが，前者がより一般的な語である上，実際に証明できる能力という含みがある）；**skill**（技能的に優れていること）

▶ここは彼女の社長としての力量が問われる場面だ This situation will test her *ability* [*capacity*] as president. ‖ 彼には与えられた任務を果たすだけの力量は無い He *is not capable of accomplishing* the task he's been assigned.

▶その野球チームはことし優勝するだけの力量はあるように思われる It seems that the baseball team has *enough skill* [has *what it takes*] to win the championship this year.

りく 陸 land ▶ウミガメは産卵のため陸に上がる Turtles come on to *land* to lay their eggs. ‖ 陸が見えるぞ *Land* ho！（➤「おおい，陸だぞ」の意；ho は呼びかけの発声）.

▶《慣用表現》雪が２メートルも積もると，その山村は陸の孤島となる When the snow reaches two meters, the mountain village becomes '*a solitary island on land*.'

りくあげ 陸揚げ unloading (a boat) ▶積み荷を陸揚げする *unload* a ship（➤ unload は「(積み荷を)降ろす」）／*remove* cargo *from a ship*.

りくうん 陸運 land [ground] transportation
‖陸運会社 a land transportation company ‖ 陸運局 a Land Transport Bureau ‖ 陸運事務所 a Land Transport Office.

リクエスト a request 一動 リクエストする request ＋㊐, make a request ▶その歌手は聴衆のリクエストで『ダンシング・クイーン』を歌った The singer sang "Dancing Queen" *at the request* of the audience. ‖ (ＤＪが) 次の曲はＦさんのリクエストによりお送りいたします I'll play the next song *by request* from Mr. F. ‖ (ＤＪが) リクエスト曲がございましたら局まで電話でお知らせください Call in your *requests*. ‖《シャンソンバーなどで》何かリクエストはございますか Do you have any *requests*？‖《ＤＪに》クイーンの『ボヘミアン・ラプソディ』をリクエストします I'd like to *request* [*ask you to play*] "Bohemian Rhapsody" by Queen.
‖リクエスト番組 a request program.

りくぐん 陸軍 the army ▶陸軍に入隊する join *the army* ‖ その国は陸軍を増強した The country built up their *army* [*land power*].
‖陸軍将校 an army officer.

りくじょう 陸上 land（陸地）▶カエルは水中だけでなく陸上にもすめる Frogs can live *on land* as well as in the water. ‖ 陸上競技は最も古いオリンピック種目である *Track-and-field competitions* are the oldest events in the Olympic Games.（➤「陸上競技(大)会」は a track meet）‖ 陸上輸送より空輸のほうが速い Air transportation is faster than *land transportation*.
‖陸上自衛隊 the Ground Self-Defense Force ‖ 陸上部 a track(-and-field) team [club].

> 「陸上競技」のいろいろ 円盤投げ discus throw ／競走 dash, run ／競歩 walk ／五種競技 pentathlon ／三段跳び triple jump ／十種競技 decathlon ／障害物競走 steeplechase ／七種競技 heptathlon ／ハードル hurdle ／走り高跳び high jump ／走り幅跳び long [broad] jump ／ハンマー投げ hammer throw ／砲丸投げ shot put ／棒高跳び pole vault ／マラソン marathon ／やり投げ javelin throw ／リレー relay

りくせいどうぶつ 陸生動物《動物学》a land [terrestrial] animal.

りくそう 陸送する transport by [over] land.

りくち 陸地 land ▶陸地は地球表面のおよそ30パーセントである About thirty percent of the surface of the earth is *land*. ／*Land* occupies about 30% of the earth's surface.

りくつ 理屈 1【道理】reason；logic（論理）；a theory（理論）▶なるほど，それも理屈だ（＝もっともだ）You've got a point there. ／What you say *is reasonable*.

▶もう理屈はいい．必要なのは実践だ No more *theory*. What we need is practice. ‖ 経済は経済学の理屈どおりには動かない The economy rarely operates in accordance with economic *theories*.

▶彼は時々理屈に合わないことを言う He sometimes says *unreasonable* things. ‖ きみの主張は理屈に合わない Your argument *is illogical* [*irrational*].（➤ illogical は「論理の筋が通っていない」，irrational は「理性を欠いた，不合理な」）‖ 理屈では（＝頭では）わかったつもりになっていても体が動かない I understand how to do it *in my head* but I can't get my body to follow.

▶《慣用表現》『新世界より』は理屈抜きの名曲だ "From the New World" is *unquestionably* a musical masterpiece.

2【議論】(an) argument ▶勝手な理屈をこねる put forth a self-serving *argument* ‖ 大抵理屈では息子に負ける My son wins *arguments* with me. ／I lose most of *the arguments* I have with my son. ‖ 彼の同僚に言わせると彼は理屈っぽいという The people working with him say that he is *too argumentative*.

りくつづき 陸続き ▶ガラパゴス諸島は大陸と陸続きでなかったために，固有の動植物が進化した Since the Galapagos Islands have *never been connected* to a continent *by land*, flora and fauna unique to the islands have evolved.

リクライニングシート a reclining seat [chair].

リクルーター a recruiter（新人採用担当者）.

リクルート recruitment（人材募集）；looking for a job, job-hunting（就職活動）（➤ 英語の recruit は「新兵」が原義で，比喩的に「新入社員」「(新人を)募集する」の意で用いる）▶大学４年の彼は今リクルートで忙しい Being a university senior, he is busy *looking for a job* now. ‖ 当社は優秀な学生をリクルートしたい Our company wants to *recruit* excellent students.
‖リクルートカット a short haircut suitable for a job interview ‖ リクルートスーツ a job-hunting suit, a conservative navy-blue or gray suit suitable for a job interview.

りくろ 陸路 a land [an overland] route ▶陸路をとる *go by land* ／*take a land route* ／*go overland* ‖ 一行は陸路ローマに着いた The party reached Rome *by land* [*overland*].（➤ 後者は文語的）.

りけい 理系 the science course ▶理系の大学生 a college student *majoring in science* ‖ 理系の大学 a *technical* college [university ／institute].

▶きみは理系向きだね You have (an) aptitude for *science*. ‖ 理系に進むか文系にするかで迷っている I can't decide whether I will major in *science* or humanities.

りけん 利権 rights and interests ▶アメリカはサウジアラビアに石油の利権（＝所有権）を持っている The United States owns oil *interests* in Saudi Arabia. ‖ 政治

り

家の中には利権をあさる人もいる Some politicians are *profit-seekers*.

りこ 利己 ▶1人でも利己的な態度をとる人がいるとチームワークが乱れる If even one person takes a *self-centered* [*selfish*] attitude, our teamwork will suffer.

‖利己主義 egotism /íːgətɪzəm/ ‖利己主義者 an egotist /íːgətɪst/.

[1]**りこう 理工** science and engineering ▶理工系の学生 a university [college] student *majoring in science and engineering* ‖理工学部 the school [college] of *science and engineering*.

[2]**りこう 利口** 一形 利口な bright (頭のよい) ; intelligent (思考力·理解力などが優れている) ; wise (優れた判断力がある) ; smart (機転が利く) ; clever (器用で抜け目がない ; しばしばよくないニュアンスで用いられる) ▶あの子は利口だ That child is *bright* [*smart*]. ‖チンパンジーは利口な動物である Chimpanzees are *intelligent* animals.

▶傘を持って出たのは利口(＝賢明)だったね It was *wise* [*smart*] of you to carry an umbrella with you. ‖彼は利口だから自分の損になるようなことは言わない He's *clever*, so he doesn't say anything to his disadvantage.

▶電車の中ではお利口にしてね *Behave yourself* on the train. (➤「行儀よくしていなさい」の意) ‖お利口さんだから(＝いい子だから)牛乳を取って来てね *Show me what a good boy* [*girl*] *you are* and go get the milk, O.K.?

[3]**りこう 履行** performance 一動 履行する do +目, perform +目, carry out ▶警官としての義務を履行する *do* [*perform*] one's duty as a police officer.

☛ 不履行 (→見出語)

リコーダー a recorder ▶リコーダーを演奏する play the *recorder*.

リコール a recall 一動 リコールする recall +目 ▶市長のリコール運動を組織する organize *a drive for the recall* of the mayor ‖市長は住民投票でリコールされた The mayor *was recalled* [*was removed from office*] by a (public) referendum.

▶製品のリコール a product *recall* ‖トヨタは50万台をリコールすると発表した Toyota announced that it would *recall* half a million cars.

りこん 離婚 (a) divorce 一動 離婚する divorce, get divorced, get a divorce ▶離婚訴訟を起こす file for *divorce* ‖夫と離婚する *divorce* one's husband ‖熟年夫婦の離婚が増えている *Divorce* among older couples is on the increase.

▶彼女は離婚を経験している She went through *a divorce*. (➤「二度の離婚」なら two divorces) ‖一郎と明子は離婚した Ichiro and Akiko *divorced* [*got a divorce*].

‖離婚式 a divorce ceremony ‖離婚者 a divorcé (男性) ; a divorcée (女性) (➤ともに発音は /dɪvɔ̀ːrséɪ/) ‖離婚訴訟 a divorce suit ‖離婚届 a divorce notice ‖協議離婚 a divorce by mutual consent, an uncontested [amicable] divorce.

リサーチ research (➤数えられない名詞) ▶あるテーマでリサーチを行う *do* [*conduct*] *research* on a subject.

リザーブ リザーブする reserve +目, 《主に英》 book +目 ▶ホテルの1室をリザーブする *reserve* [*book*] a room at a hotel / *reserve* [*book*] a hotel room ‖緊急時のために燃料をリザーブしておく *reserve* fuel for emergencies.

りさい 罹災 ▶おじの一家は東日本大震災でり災した My uncle's family *were victims* of the Great East Japan Earthquake.

‖り災者 a (disaster) victim.

リサイクル recycling (再生利用) 一動 リサイクルする recycle +目 ▶空き瓶を回収してリサイクルする collect empty bottles and *recycle* them.

‖リサイクルショップ a recycled-goods store [shop] ; a second-hand store [shop] (中古品店).

リサイタル a recital ▶彼女は昨夜公会堂でピアノリサイタルを開いた Last evening she gave *a piano recital* at the public hall.

りざや 利鞘 《ビジネス》 a profit margin.

りさん 離散する break up (ばらばらになる) ▶会社の倒産で山田家は一家離散してしまった Mr. Yamada's family *broke up* because his company went bankrupt.

りし 利子 interest ▶その公債には6分の利子がつく The public bond bears [carries] six percent *interest*.

▶かつて政府は学生たちに無利子で学費を貸与した The government used to lend students money for school expenses [tuition] *at no interest*.

りじ 理事 a director (団体の) ; a trustee /trʌ̀stíː/, a regent (大学の ; 後者はアメリカの州立大学の場合) ▶この問題は理事会に掛けなければならない We have to present this problem to *the board of directors*.

‖理事長 the chairperson (of the board of directors [trustees / regents]).

りしゅう 履修する take a course 《in, on》 (コースを取る) ▶教員免許を取るには憲法を履修する必要がある In order to get a teaching certificate, you need to *take a course on* the Constitution. ‖学生は卒業には40科目130単位を履修しなければならない Students must *complete* 40 courses and get 130 credits to graduate.

‖履修科目 a subject ‖履修単位 a credit.

りじゅん 利潤 a return ; (a) profit (収益) ▶投資で大きな利潤を上げる get a good *return* on an investment ‖利潤を追求する pursue *profits* ‖利潤の大きな商売 a business which gives large *returns* / a *profitable* business ‖当社は中古車を売り大きな利潤を上げた We made a big *profit* (by) selling used cars.

[1]**りしょく 利殖** moneymaking ▶利殖に株を少々やっています I dabble in stocks to *make* a little *money*.

[2]**りしょく 離職** separation from work [one's job] (➤堅い言い方) ; leaving [quitting] one's job 一動 離職する separate from employment ; leave [quit]

‖離職者 an employee who has quit ; a person who has left his [her] job (➤ left は quit でもよい) ‖離職票 an unemployment slip ‖離職率 a job separation rate ; a job turnover rate (➤後者は, 社員の入れ替わりの率を表す).

りす 栗鼠 《動物》 a squirrel /skwə́ːrəl/ ; a chipmunk (シマリス).

りすう 理数 science and mathematics ▶私は理数系が得意です I'm strong in *science and mathematics*.

リスク (a) risk ▶我々の計画はリスクが大きい Our project involves great *risks*. / Our project is too risky.

▶リスクの大きい投資には手を出すな Stay away from investments that *may involve a lot of risk*. / Don't get involved in *risky* investments.

[1]**リスト** (表) a list ▶買う物をリストアップする *make a*

list of things to buy ／*list* things to buy ‖息子の名前が行方不明者のリストに載っていない My son's name is not on the *list* of the missing persons. ‖警察は極右の人物たちをリストアップした The police have *made a blacklist* of ultra-rightists. ‖あなたのリストから私(の名)を外してください Please take me off your *list*.

危ないカタカナ語✹ リストアップ
必要な品物などを選び出して一覧表を作ることを「リストアップする」というが, list up という英語はない. list を動詞として使うか, make a list of とする.

2**リスト**《手首》a **wrist** /rɪst/ ▶井口選手はリストが強い Iguchi has strong arms. (● 英語では「腕が強い」と表現する).
‖**リストバンド** a wrist band.

リストカット **wrist cutting, wrist slashing**(➤ 後者は「さっと切る」のイメージ) ▶リストカットする *cut* [*slash*] one's *wrist*.

リストラ **restructuring**(再構築) ; **downsizing** (人員削減) ▶父はリストラで子会社へ回された My father was transferred to a subsidiary company under his company's *restructuring plan*. ／My father's company underwent *restructuring*, and he was transferred to a subsidiary company.

直訳の落とし穴「リストラされた」
「彼はリストラされた」や「彼女はリストラに遭った」に(×) He [She] was restructured. などと restructure を用いることはできない. restructure は会社などの組織や制度を「再構築する」ことで, 人には使えない.「解雇する」の lay off を使って, He [She] was layed off (under his [her] company's restructuring plan). のようにする.

リスナー a **listener** ▶ラジオでリスナーに語りかける talk to one's *listeners* on the radio.

リスニング **listening** ▶英語のリスニングテスト an English *listening comprehension test* (➤ listening test はステレオ装置などの「聞こえ方テスト」の意にもなる).
‖**リスニングルーム** a listening room.

リスボン **Lisbon** /lízbən/ (ポルトガルの首都).

リズミカル **rhythmic(al)** /ríðmɪk(əl)/ ▶リズミカルな音楽 *rhythmical* [*rhythmic*] music ‖もっとリズミカルに体を動かしてごらんなさい Try to move your body more *rhythmically*.

リズム (a) **rhythm** /ríðəm/ ▶サンバのリズムに合わせて踊る dance to a samba *rhythm* ‖マイケルは速いリズムで踊りながら歌った Michael sang while dancing to fast *rhythms*.
▶その新人歌手はリズム感がいい That new singer has a good *sense of rhythm*.

りせい 理性 **reason** 一形 **理性の** **rational** /rǽʃənəl/ ▶人間は理性のある動物である Human beings are *rational* animals. ‖私は理性的な男性が好きです I like *calm, rational* men.
▶戦場では人間は理性を失う People *lose control of themselves* [*lose their reason*] in the heat of battle.

リセット ▶パスワードをリセットする *reset* one's password.
▶人生をリセットすることは難しい *Resetting* one's life is difficult.

りそう 理想 an **ideal** /aɪdíːəl/ 一形 **理想の** **ideal** ▶理想を実現する realize one's *ideals* ‖理想と現実の間には大きなギャップがある There is a wide gap between *ideals* and reality. ‖アメリカの政治は理想(の状態)から程遠い American politics is far from *ideal*.
▶スカーレット・オハラが私の理想の女性です Scarlett O'Hara is the woman *of my dreams*. ‖彼女がなかなか結婚しないのは理想が高いせいだ The reason she doesn't get married is that *her expectations for a potential husband* are too high.
▶恋する者はしばしば相手を理想化する People in love often *idealize* the object(s) of their affection. ‖この天気はサーフィンに理想的だ This weather is *ideal* for surfing. ‖ここは大学を建てるには理想的な場所だ This is the *ideal* [*perfect*] site for building a university. ‖きみの考え方は理想主義的すぎる You are too *idealistic*.
‖**理想家** an idealist ‖**理想郷** a utopia (→ユートピア) ‖**理想像** an ideal image.

リゾート a **resort** ▶その島は新しいリゾート地として注目されている That island has recently attracted attention as *a new resort*.
‖**リゾートウエア** resort wear, resort clothing ‖**リゾートホテル** a resort hotel.

りそく 利息 →利子.

リゾット **risotto** /rɪsɔ́:toʊ, rɪzɔ́toʊ/ (イタリア料理).

リターンマッチ a **return match**, a **rematch**.

リタイア リタイアする **retire** ▶鈴木, 8周目でエンジントラブルのためリタイアです In the 8th lap Suzuki *is retiring* from the race because of engine trouble. ‖もう70歳だ. いいかげんリタイアしたいよ I'm now 70 years old. I really feel it's about time for me to *retire*.

りだつ 離脱 (a) **separation** ;《医学》**withdrawal** ; an **opt-out**(脱退) ▶党から離脱する *secede* from the party.
‖**離脱感** a sense of detachment ‖**離脱症候群**《医学》withdrawal syndrome ‖**離脱症状**《医学》a withdrawal symptom(たばこなどをやめたときなどの) ‖**離脱療法**《医学》withdrawal treatment.

リチウム《化学》**lithium** /líθiəm/
‖**リチウムイオン電池** a lithium-ion battery.

りちぎ 律儀な・律義な **honest** /ɑ́:nəst/ (正直な) ; **conscientious** /kɑ̀:nʃiénʃəs/ (良心的な) ▶私の祖父は非常に律儀な働き者だった My grandfather was a very *honest* [*conscientious*] *and hardworking* person. ‖その秘書は上司のために律儀に働いた The secretary worked *dutifully* for her boss.
▶彼女はどうでもいい口約束でも律儀に守る She keeps even unimportant verbal agreements *conscientiously*.

りちてき 理知的な **intellectual** (➤「高度な教養・知性・判断力がある」の意) ▶理知的な人 an *intellectual* person.

りちゃくりく 離着陸 **take off and landing.**

りつ 率 **1**【割合】a **rate** ; an **incidence**(発生率)
▶インドでは人口の増加率が依然として高い The *rate* of population increase is still high in India. ‖この実験は成功率が低い The *success rate* of this experiment is low. ‖税率が上がった[下がった] *Tax rates* were raised [were lowered]. ‖この大学の競争率は20倍だ The *admission rate* of this university is 20 to 1. (➤「入学できる率」の意) ‖がんの発生率は都市部のほうが高い There is a higher *incidence* of cancer in urban areas.

2【損得の割合】▶これは率のいい仕事だ This job *pays well.*

逆引き熟語 ○○率
確率 probability, (a) chance ／**競争率** a competitive rate, an admission rate, the rate of competition ／**経済成長率** an economic growth rate ／**視聴率** audience ratings ／**失業率** an unemployment rate ／**死亡率** a death rate ／**出生率** a birth rate ／**成功率** a success rate ／**生存率** a survival rate ／**税率** a tax rate ／**打率** a batting average ／**犯罪発生率** a crime rate ／**百分率** (a) percentage ／**比率** a ratio ／**割引率** a discount rate

りつあん 立案する **plan** +目（計画する）; **draft** +目（草案を作る）▶法律を立案する *draft* a bill ‖ 父母会は学校の創立5周年記念計画を立案した The P.T.A. *drew up* a plan to celebrate the 5th anniversary of the school's founding.（➤ draw up は「(計画を)練る」）.
‖**立案者** a planner ; an architect /áːʳkɪtekt/（政策などの）; an author（法律などの）.

りっか 立夏 ***rikka*** ; the day that marks the beginning of summer according to the lunar calendar（➤ 説明的な訳）.

りっきゃく 立脚する **be based** 《on》▶彼の体験に立脚した議論には極めて説得力があった His arguments *based on* his own experience were extremely persuasive.

りっきょう 陸橋 《米》 an **overpass**, 《英》 a **flyover** ; a **pedestrian bridge**（歩道橋）.

[1]**りっけん 立件する** **build a case** ▶検察は彼に対して収賄容疑での立件に努めている Prosecutors are trying hard to *build a case* against him on a graft charge.

[2]**りっけん 立憲** ▶日本は立憲君主制の国だ Japan is *a constitutional monarchy.*
‖**立憲政治** constitutional government.

りっこうほ 立候補する 《米》 **run** 《for》, 《英》 **stand** 《for》▶高橋君は生徒会長に立候補した Takahashi *ran for* president of the Student Council. ‖ 三井氏は前回の総選挙で自民党から立候補した Mr. Mitsui *ran* in the last general election on the LDP ticket.（➤ on the ... ticket は「…党の公認で」）‖ 今回の選挙には5人が立候補している Five people *are running* [*are competing*] in the current election.（➤ 後者は「競っている」）.
‖**立候補者** a candidate.

りっしでん 立志伝 a **success story** ▶立志伝中の人物 *a self-made man* [*woman*]（➤ self-made は「たたき上げの」）.

りっしゅう 立秋 ***risshu*** ; the day that marks the beginning of autumn according to the lunar calendar（➤ 説明的な訳）.

りっしゅん 立春 ***risshun*** ; the day that marks the beginning of spring according to the lunar calendar（➤ 説明的な訳）.

りっしょう 立証 **proof** 一動 **立証する** **prove** +目, **give proof** 《of》, **support** +目（裏付ける）; **corroborate** +目（確証する）; **verify** +目（➤ verify は法律用語として用いることが多い）▶自分の無実を立証するのが非常に難しいことがある It's sometimes very difficult to *prove* one's innocence. ‖ あなたは自分のアリバイを立証する証拠を提出しなければならない You must come up with evidence that will *prove* [*support* ／ *corroborate*] your alibi.

りっしょく 立食 a **buffet** /bəféɪ/ ▶立食パーティーを催す give [have] *a buffet party.*

りっしん 立身 ▶立身出世する *succeed* [*get ahead*] *in life*（➤「立身出世」は success in life）‖ 立身出世だけを目指すな Don't be a social climber.（➤ social climber は軽蔑的に「立身出世主義者」の意）.

りっすい 立錐 ▶モーターショー初日は立すいの余地もないほどの混雑ぶりだった The first day of the auto show *was* (*jam-*)*packed with people.*

りっする 律する ▶自分自身を厳しく律する *be critical of oneself* ‖ 彼は自分の基準で人を律する傾向がある He tends to *judge* [*measure*] others by his own standard(s).

りつぜん 慄然 ▶あの優しそうな若者が殺人犯と知って慄然とした *Terror shot through my body* [*My hair stood on end* ／ *I was horrified*] when I learned that the mild-looking young man was a murderer.

りつぞう 立像 a **statue** ▶西郷隆盛の立像 *a statue* of Saigo Takamori.

リッター a **liter** /líːṭəʳ/, 《英》 a **litre** ▶私の車はリッター当たり15キロ走る My car gets 15 kilometers *to the liter.* →リットル.

りったい 立体 a **solid** (**body**) ; a **cube**（立方体）▶立体感のある絵 a picture *with a three-dimensional effect*（➤ three-dimensional は「3次元の」; 3-D と略される）‖ コンピュータグラフィックスを使えば好きな角度から立体的に見ることができる Using computer graphics, you can produce *three-dimensional* images that can be viewed from any angle.
‖**立体交差** a two-level crossing, a grade separation ‖**立体駐車場** a multistory parking garage.

りっちじょうけん 立地条件 **geographical conditions** ▶このレストランは立地条件がいいので, いつも客でいっぱいだ This restaurant *is conveniently located,* so it is always filled with customers.

りっとう 立冬 ***ritto*** ; the day that marks the beginning of winter according to the lunar calendar（➤ 説明的な訳）.

りつどう 律動 **rhythm.**

リットル a **liter** /líːṭəʳ/, 《英》 a **litre** ▶ガソリンはリットルいくらで売られる Gasoline is sold *by the liter.*

りっぱ 立派 **1【優れた, 偉大な】** **fine, splendid**（すばらしい）; **great**（偉大な）; **admirable**（感心な）
▶あの人のお父さんは立派な人だ His father is *a man of fine character* [*a man of integrity*]. ‖ 吉田松陰は立派な教育者だった Yoshida Shoin was a *great* educator. ‖ 息子さんはすっかり立派な青年におなりだこと Your son has become such a *fine* young man. I'm impressed.
▶どの候補者も選挙中は立派なことを言う All the candidates say *admirable* things during the campaign. ‖ 横綱の連続優勝は立派だ It *is splendid* for the yokozuna to have won (the title in) two consecutive tournaments.
2【豪華な, すばらしい】 **magnificent**（壮大な）; **deluxe**（ぜいたくな）; **gorgeous**（豪華な）▶立派な屋敷 a *stately* mansion ‖ 私たちの学校には立派な体育館がある We have a *well-equipped* gymnasium on our campus. ‖ 立派なお住まいですね This is a *gorgeous* [*fabulous*] house.
3【完全な】▶畑中君はキャプテンとして立派に務めた

Hatanaka *did a good job* as captain. ‖ わがチームは強豪を相手に**立派に戦った**(＝善戦した) Our team *put up a good fight against* such a powerful team. ‖ 二十歳といえば**立派な**(＝一人前の)大人じゃないか Once you turn twenty, you are a *full-fledged* adult. ‖ 他人の作品を盗用するのは**立派な**犯罪だ It's a *real* crime to plagiarize other people's works.

りっぷく 立腹する get angry(怒る) ; take offense(気を悪くする) ▶ご**立腹**はもっともですが, まず話を聞いてくださいよ You have every reason to *be angry*, but please listen to me first.

リップクリーム (a) lip balm /líp bɑːm/ ; 《英また》(a) lip salve ; (a) chapstick (➤もと商標名 ChapStick から. lip cream は和製英語)
▶唇がかさかさになったので, **リップクリーム**をつけた My lips got chapped, so I applied some *lip balm* to them.

リップサービス ▶あの政治家は有権者にしょっちゅう**リップサービスしている** That politician is always *flattering* [*sucking up to*] the voters.

直訳の落とし穴「リップサービスする」
「あの政治家は有権者にしょっちゅうリップサービスしている」をそのまま lip service を使って, (×)That politician is always giving lip service to the voters. などとはいわない. lip service は「実行を伴わない口先だけの支持や賛意」で, to のあとにくるのは主に主張や考え方である. 日本語のほうは「その場限りのお世辞やご機嫌取り」という意味であるから, 例文のように flatter (お世辞を言う)または suck up to (ご機嫌取りをする)を使って表現する. さらにくだけた言い方には brown-nose や ass-kiss がある.

リップスティック (a) lipstick. ⇀口紅.

1**りっぽう 立方** ‖**立方センチ** a cubic centimeter [《英》 centimetre] ‖ **立方メートル** a cubic meter [《英》 metre].

2**りっぽう 立法** legislation ━形 **立法の** legislative /lédʒɪsleɪṭɪv/ ▶この法律の**立法**の趣旨は次のとおりです The aims of this *legislation* are as follows. ‖ 国会は**立法機関**である The Diet is *a legislative* [*law-making*] *body*.
‖**立法府** the legislature.

りっぽうたい 立方体 a cube ━形 **立方体の** cubic ▶さいころは**立方体**だ Dice are *cubic*. ／Dice are *cubes*.

りづめ 理詰め ▶彼は**理詰め**でものを言い過ぎる He tries too hard to sound *logical* when he speaks. ‖ 経営者は**理詰め**で労働組合にその条件をのませた The management *reasoned* [*persuaded*] the labor union into accepting the condition.

りつめんず 立面図 an elevation(al) view.

りてきこうい 利敵行為 ▶その機密漏えいは**利敵行為**になる That secret information leak is tantamount to *aiding and abetting the enemy*.

リテラシー literacy ▶メディア**リテラシー**が高い have high *media literacy*.
‖**コンピュータリテラシー** computer literacy ‖ **情報リテラシー** information literacy.

りてん 利点 an advantage(有利な点) ; a benefit (得する点) ▶宇宙飛行では女性は男性に比べていろいろな**利点**があると言われている Women are said to have various *advantages* over men in space travel. ‖ 会員になるとどんな**利点**がありますか What are the *advantages* [*benefits*] of becoming a member? ‖ この車の**利点**は狭い道にも入っていけることです The *advantage* [The (*chief*) *merit* ／The *beauty*] of this car is that you can maneuver it on narrow streets.

1**りとう 離島** an isolated [outlying] island.

2**りとう 離党する** leave [quit ／ desert] a (political) party(➤quit, desert はそれぞれ「突然, 急に」,「見捨てる」のイメージで, 後者は集団での離党や重要人物の離党を連想させる) ▶スキャンダルでその政治家は**離党**に追い込まれた The scandal drove that politician to *leave* [*quit*] *his party*.

リトグラフ a lithograph /líθəgræf/ (石版画).

リトマス ‖**リトマス試験紙** litmus paper.

リニアモーターカー a maglev train (➤linear motor car は和製英語).

りにゅう 離乳 weaning ▶そろそろ赤ん坊の**離乳**を始めています I'm beginning to *wean* my baby little by little. ／I have started my baby on baby food.
▶《比喩的》彼はまだ母親から(精神的に)**離乳していない** He *is* still *tied to his mother's apron strings*. (➤「母親に頭が上がらない, 言いなりになっている」の意).
‖**離乳食** baby food.

リニューアル リニューアルする renovate ＋目 (改修する, 新しくする) ; remodel ＋目 (作り直す, リフォームする) ▶店を**リニューアルする** *renovate* [*remodel*] a store ‖ 台所を**リニューアルする** *remodel* a kitchen.
‖(店舗の) **リニューアルオープン** a (grand) reopening.

りにょう 利尿 《医学》diuresis /daɪjərí:sɪs/ ▶**利尿作用**がある have *a diuretic effect*.

りにん 離任する leave one's post [position].

りねん 理念 an idea (考え) ; a philosophy /fɪlɑ́:səfi/ (主義, 方針) ▶我々は「克己」という教育**理念**に基づいた教育を受けている At our school we are educated under the *philosophy* of self-control [self-discipline].

リネン linen /línɪn/ ‖**リネン製品** linens.

リノリウム linoleum /lɪnóʊliəm/, 《英・インフォーマル》lino /láɪnoʊ/ (床材).

リハーサル (a) rehearsal ━動 **リハーサルする** rehearse (＋目) ▶あすこの劇の最終**リハーサル**をします The *final* [*dress*] *rehearsal* for the play will be held tomorrow.

リバーシブル reversible ▶このジャケット, **リバーシブル**になってるの This jacket *is reversible*.

リバイバル a revival ▶古い映画の**リバイバル** the *revival* of old films ‖ **リバイバルソング**が最近若者に受けている Some *old songs that have recently been revived* are popular among young people. (● (×) revival song という英語はない ; a revived golden oldie なら通じる).
‖**リバイバルブーム** a retro fad.
《参考》日本語では「リバイバル」を専ら映画の再上映とか流行の復活の意味で用いるが, 英語の revival はこれよりはるかに意味が広く,「(経済の)復興, 再生」「意識の回復」「信仰回復運動」などの意味で用いることが多い.

リバウンド rebound ▶ダイエットに失敗して**リバウンドした** My diet failed, and my weight *rebounded* [and I *gained* the weight *back*].

1**りはつ 利発な** bright, intelligent ⇀利口 ▶この子は**利発そうな**顔をしている This boy here *looks intelligent*.

2**りはつ 理髪** haircutting(散髪) ; hairdressing (整髪)
‖**理髪師** a barber(➤客は男性) ; a hairdresser (➤客は男女とも) ‖ **理髪店** 《米》 a barbershop,

り

《英》a barber's (shop).

りはば 利幅 a margin ▶低い利幅 a low *margin*.

リハビリ(テーション) rehabilitation, 《インフォーマル》 rehab /ríːhæb/ ▶身体障害者のリハビリ *rehabilitation* of a disabled person ‖ 脳卒中のリハビリはつらいらしい I hear that *rehabilitation training* for stroke patients is very hard.

‖**リハビリ施設** a rehabilitation center, rehabilitation facilities.

> **危ないカタカナ語✸リハビリ**
> **1** 障害者や病人を社会復帰させるための訓練を「リハビリ」といっているが，これは「リハビリテーション」の日本式省略. rehabilitation は日本語の「リハビリテーション」よりももっと意味が広く，犯罪者や麻薬中毒患者の社会復帰訓練の意味で用いることが多い.
> **2** 日本でいう「リハビリ」の中心は運動・マッサージなどの物理的手段による機能回復訓練であるから，physical therapy(理学療法)という語を使って表すこともできる.

リバプール Liverpool(イングランド北西部の港湾都市).

りはん 離反 ▶その国の停滞した経済が指導者から人心を離反させる原因となった The country's stagnant economy caused the leader to *lose popular support*.

リピーター a repeat customer [buyer] (➤ 文脈によっては repeater でも通じるが，これは主に「留年生」や「再犯者」の意で用い，日本語の「何度も来てくれる客」は上記や repeat guest [visitor] (ホテルや遊園地の)などで表すほうが明確) ▶あの店はリピーターが多い That store [restaurant] has many *repeat customers*.

りびょう 罹病する get [contract] a disease ▶胃がんのり病率 *the incidence* of stomach cancer.

リビング(ダイニング) a living (room), dining room.

リビング(ルーム) a living room ▶このマンションはリビングを広々ととってある This condominium has a large *living room*.

リフォーム リフォームする remake +目, make over (作り直す) ; remodel +目 (改築する) ; renovate +目 (改修する) ; redecorate +目, refurbish +目 (改装する) ▶母は私のワンピースをリフォームして(＝仕立て直して)娘のパジャマを作った My mother *remade* my dress *into* a pair of pajamas for my daughter. ‖ 妻は居間のリフォームを望んでいる My wife wants to *remodel* the living room. / My wife wants to have the living room *remodeled*. (➤「リフォームしてもらう」の意).

‖**リフォームローン** a home improvement loan.

> **直訳の落とし穴「家をリフォームする」**
> (1)カタカナ語のリフォームは「家をリフォームする」「台所をリフォームする」「ドレスをリフォーム［リメイク］する」などと使うが，reform は政治形態や社会制度などを「改革する」ことであって，「改築する」「仕立て直す」という意味はなく，これらに reform を当てることはできない. 改築には remodel (作り替える，改造する)，renovate (改修する，古いものを新しくする)などを当てて，remodel a house [kitchen], renovate a house [kitchen] とする. 壁紙や家具を変える程度の模様替えならば redecorate や refurbish がよい.
> (2)洋服の簡単な仕立て直しは alter a dress とし，「着物をすてきなスカートにリフォーム［リメイク］する」は turn [convert] a kimono into a nice skirt とする.

りふじん 理不尽な unreasonable ▶遺産に50パーセントの税金をかけるのは理不尽というものだ It is *unreasonable* to impose a 50% tax on inheritances.

リフティング juggling, kick ups (➤ lifting はボールを持ち上げたり，蹴り上げたりすることを連想する) ▶彼はリフティングが得意だ He's good at *juggling a ball* (*with his feet*).

リフト a ski lift, a chair lift (➤《英》では lift は主に「エレベーター」の意) ▶リフトを使う use *a* (*ski*) *lift* / go up by *lift*.

リプリント a reprint.

リフレッシュ リフレッシュする feel refreshed, refresh oneself(気分を) ; remodel +目, refurbish +目 (建物を ; →リフォーム) ▶熱いシャワーを浴びてリフレッシュした I *felt refreshed* after taking a hot shower.

リベート a rebate /ríːbeɪt/ (支払い金の一部返却) ; a kickback, a rake-off(不正な) ; a commission (委託に対する手数料) ▶市長は建設業者からリベートを受け取ったといううわさだ It is rumored that the mayor got *a kickback* [*a rake-off*] from a construction company.

> **危ないカタカナ語✸リベート**
> 英語の rebate からきていて，発音は /ríːbeɪt/. また，日本語の「リベート」は「(ひそかにもらう)世話料，手数料」という悪い意味で用いることが多いが，rebate の本来の意味は「(支払い金の一部の)払い戻し」である. 悪い意味の「リベート」に当たるのは kickback や rake-off.

りべつ 離別 (a) separation(縁が切れること) ; a parting (別れること) **一動** (…と)**離別する** be separated 《from》 ▶母とは小さい頃離別したので顔もはっきり覚えていない Since I *was separated from* my mother when I was very little, I can't recall her face clearly.

リベラリスト a liberal (➤ liberalist はあまり用いない).

リベラル liberal ▶彼女はリベラルな考え方の家庭で育ったようだ She seems to have grown up in a *liberal-minded* family.

リベンジ revenge ▶斉藤投手はリベンジに燃えている Pitcher Saito *is full of determination to avenge his team's loss*.

> **直訳の落とし穴「リベンジする」**
> スポーツではしばしば，前回負けたチームに勝つことを「リベンジする」と使うが，これに revenge を当てるのは適当ではない. 英語でもスポーツ記事では大げさに get one's revenge などと用いることがあるが，revenge は恨みや復しゅう心などが籠もった強い語なので，スポーツでいう「雪辱する」に当たる表現としては avenge a loss を用いるのがよい. カタカナ語では往々にして，原語の強いインパクトが失われるので注意が必要である.

りべんせい 利便性 usefulness ; user-friendliness(使いやすさ) ; convenience(便利さ) ▶スマートフォンは利便性に優れている Smartphones *are very useful*.

リポーター a reporter. →レポーター.

リポート →レポート.

リボン a ribbon(髪用，またプリンターなどの) ; a band (帽子の) ; a streamer (飾り用の紙テープのような) ▶彼女の髪はリボンで結わえてあった Her hair was tied with *a ribbon*. (➤「ちょう結びにしたリボン」は a bow (of ribbon) という ; 次例参照).

▶リサは髪にかわいい白いリボンをしていた Lisa had a pretty white *bow* in her hair. ‖ 審査員は胸に赤いリボンをつけていた The judges wore red *ribbons* on their jackets.

リマ Lima（ペルーの首都）.

りまわり 利回り a **yield**；a **return**（利潤）；(an) **interest**（利子）▶この債券は利回りがいい You can get a good *yield* on this bond. ／This bond yields a good *return*. ‖ どの貯蓄が高利回りになりますか Which types of savings yield *high-rate interest*？

リミット a **limit** ▶リミットを超える exceed *the limit*. ‖ タイムリミット a time limit.

リミッター a **limiter** ▶リミッターが働いている *The limiter* is activated.

リムジン a **limousine** /límәzi:n/（空港への送迎バスも含む），《インフォーマル》a **limo**；a **courtesy car**［**van**］（無料送迎車）▶当ホテルとサンフランシスコ国際空港の間にはリムジンサービスがあります There's *limousine service* between our hotel and San Francisco International Airport.

リメーク a **remake** 一動 **リメークする remake** +⽬ →リフォーム ▶その映画はリメーク版だ That movie is a *remake* (version).

りめん 裏面 **the back**；**the reverse side**（反対側）▶自分の絵の裏面に名前を記入すること Write your name on *the back* of your picture. ‖ 裏面に続く《米》*Over*. ／《英》*P.T.O.* （➤ Please turn over. の略）. →裏.

▶《比喩的》私は人生の裏面をいろいろ見てきた I've seen a lot of *the seamy side* of life. ‖ ある有力政治家が裏面工作をしている Some influential politician *is maneuvering* ［*manipulating*］ *behind the scenes*. （➤ maneuver /mәnú:vәʳ/ behind the scenes は「陰で策動する」）.

リモート **remote** ‖ リモート会議 a remote meeting ‖ リモート授業 a remote class ‖ リモートワーク remote working.

リモコン a **remote control**（遠隔操作機）；《インフォーマル》a **zapper**（テレビなどの）▶リモコンでテレビのチャンネルを変える change TV channels with *a remote control*.

リヤカー a **cart**（手押し車；（×）rear car とはしない）.

りゃく 略 an **abbreviation** /әbrì:viéiʃәn/, a **shortened form** ▶ＣＤは compact disc の略である CD is *an abbreviation* ［*a shortened form*］ of 'compact disc.' ‖ N.Y. は New York の略である N.Y. *stands for* New York. （➤ stand for は「…を意味する」）‖ 以下略 The rest *is omitted*.

✉ **この前のお手紙中のＬＯＬって何の略ですか** In your last letter you wrote LOL. What does that *stand for*？ ➤ LOL は laughing out loud（高笑い）の略.

りゃくご 略語 an **abbreviation** ▶「レーザー」も「レーダー」も本来は略語です The words 'laser' and 'radar' are originally *abbreviations*. 《参考》「レーダー」は *r*adio *d*etecting *a*nd *r*angingの頭文字から作ったもの.このような語を正式にはacronym/ǽkrәnım/（頭字語）という.

りゃくじ 略字 a **simplified form of a kanji**.

りゃくしき 略式の informal ▶略式の結婚式 an *informal* wedding ceremony ‖ 祝賀会は略式で行います The celebration will be held *without formality*.

りゃくしょう 略称 an **abbreviation**（一部を省いて短くしたもの）；an **acronym**（各語の頭文字をとったもの）▶NHK は「日本放送協会」の略称だ NHK *is an acronym of* ［*is short for*］ Nippon Hoso Kyokai.

りゃくす 略す **omit** +⽬（省略する）；**abbreviate** /әbrí:vieıt/ +⽬（短縮する）▶敬称は略させていただきます Titles (will be) *omitted*. ‖ 国際通貨基金は略して IMF と呼ばれる The International Monetary Fund is called IMF *for short*.

▶名前は略さずに書いてください Write your name *in full*, please.

りゃくず 略図 a **rough sketch** ［**map**］▶あなたの勤務先の付近の略図を書いてください Draw *a rough map* of the area around your office ［working place］. ‖ きみの家までの略図（＝道順）を書いてくれ Draw *a road map* to your house.

りゃくだつ 略奪 **plunder** /plʌ́ndәʳ/（特に軍隊による）一動 **略奪する plunder** +⽬；**loot** +⽬（物を奪って荒らす）▶侵略軍は村々の略奪を始めた The invading army started *plundering* the villages. ‖ スーパーマーケットが暴徒の略奪に遭った The supermarkets *were looted* by rioters.

‖ 略奪者 a looter, a plunderer.

りゃくれき 略歴 a **brief sketch of** one's **life** ［**career**］, one's **bio** ▶彼は面接で自分の略歴を述べた He gave *a brief sketch of his life* ［*career*］ at the interview.

りゃっき 略記 a **brief account**（簡潔な記述）▶the United Nations（国際連合）をU.N. と略記する（＝略して書く）*abbreviate* United Nations to U.N.

リャマ《動物》a **llama**.

りゆう 理由 (a) **reason**（訳）；(a) **cause**（正当な根拠）；a **pretext** /prí:tekst/（口実）▶やむにやまれぬ［もっともらしい］理由 a compelling ［plausible］ *reason* ‖ 父は健康上の理由でたばこをやめた My father quit smoking for health *reasons*. ‖ 社長が辞職した理由がわからない *The reason* (that) the president resigned isn't clear. ／I can't understand (*the reason*) *why* the president resigned. （➤「私は理解できない」の意；目的語の場合は the reason why では重複表現と考える人もおり，the reason は省略することが多い）‖ なぜ欠席したのか理由を言いなさい Tell me (*the reason*) *why* you were absent.

▶学問に興味を失ったという理由で彼は大学をやめた He dropped out of college *because* he had lost interest in his studies. ‖ 我々の提案は現実性がないという理由（＝根拠）で受け入れられなかった Our proposal was turned down *on the ground(s) that* it was impractical. ‖ 理由はともあれ，うそはよくない Lying is not good *whatever the reason* ［*for whatever reason*］. ‖ 彼女は正当な理由もなく解雇された She was dismissed *without* (*good*) *cause*. （➤ 決まり文句）／She was dismissed *for no valid* ［*good*］ *reason*. ‖ 社長は病気を理由に（＝口実にして）報道陣の前に姿を見せなかった The president didn't appear before the press *on* ［*under*］ *the pretext of* being sick.

りゅう 竜 a *ryu*, a **dragon**.

-りゅう -流 **1**【やり方】a **way**（しかた）；a **style**（様式・型）▶それがアメリカ流のやり方だ That's the American *way* of doing things. ‖ スミス先生は日本流のおじぎをした Mr. Smith bowed (in the) Japanese *style*.

2【流派】a **school** ▶小原流の華道 the Ohara *school* of flower arrangement.

りゅうい 留意する keep [bear] ... in mind(心に留めておく); pay attention to(注意する) ▶初心者の方は以下の点に留意してください Beginners should *bear* these points *in mind*.

りゅういき 流域 a basin /béɪsən/; a valley(大河の) ▶岡崎市は矢作川の流域にある The city of Okazaki is situated in the Yahagi *basin*. ‖ インダス文明はインダス川流域に栄えた The Indus civilization thrived in the Indus *Valley*.

りゅういん 溜飲 ▶その意地悪な部長が支店に飛ばされて我々はりゅう飲を下げた Since that spiteful department head was relegated to a branch office, we *felt quite satisfied* [*felt that we had gotten our revenge*].

りゅうかい 流会 ▶出席者が定員に満たないため教授会は流会になった Due to lack of a quorum, the faculty meeting *was canceled*.

りゅうがく 留学 (●「外国に留学する」「海外に留学する」は go abroad to study [for study], go overseas to study [for study] あるいは study abroad, study overseas のように訳せるが, このように漠然というより study in Egypt (エジプトに留学する) のように具体的な国名を挙げていうほうが好ましい).
▶彼女は韓国のソウル大学に留学して韓国史を研究している She is studying Korean history at Seoul University in South Korea. ‖ 兄はアイルランド留学中にメアリーと結婚した My older brother married Mary *while he was studying in Ireland*.
▶伊藤さんの留学先はテネシー大学だ Ito is studying at the University of Tennessee. ‖ 去年の夏はオックスフォードへ短期留学しました I *went* to Oxford *on a short study program* last summer. ‖ うちの大学にはマレーシアからの[外国人の]留学生がいる We have some Malaysian [foreign] *students* at our college. 《参考》「外国人の留学生」に相当するのは foreign students であるが, foreign にはよそよそしい響きがあるために overseas や international などを代わりに用いる傾向がある.
‖留学生 a student from overseas, an overseas student, a foreign student (ともに外国からの); a student studying overseas(外国へ行っている) ‖ 留学生課 an overseas [a foreign] student adviser(s) office, an international student office.

りゅうかすいそ 硫化水素 《化学》 hydrogen sulfide.

りゅうかん 流感 (the) flu ▶流感にかかる come down with (*the*) *flu* ‖ ことしは悪性の流感がはやっている There's a bad *flu* going around this year.

りゅうき 隆起 (an) upheaval 一動 隆起する upheave ▶その地震の前には地表の隆起が見られた Before the earthquake slight *upheavals* of the ground were seen.

りゅうぎ 流儀 a way; a style (様式, スタイル) ▶おばあちゃんは何事も昔ながらの流儀でやる Grandma does everything the traditional [conventional] *way*. ‖ 俺は俺の流儀でやる I'll do it *my* (*own*) *way* [*as I please*]. (➤ 後者は「自分の好きなように」) ‖ あとでぐずぐず言うのは私の流儀ではない It's not my *style* to complain afterward.

りゅうぐう(じょう) 竜宮(城) the Dragon King's Palace; the Sea God's Palace(海神の城).

りゅうけつ 流血 bloodshed ▶機動隊と抗議する人々との衝突は流血の惨事になった The clash between the riot police and the protesters developed into *a bloody incident* [resulted in *bloodshed*].

りゅうげんひご 流言飛語 a groundless [false] rumor ▶大災害のあとにはとかく流言飛語が飛び交うものだ *All sorts of rumors* fly [go] around after a great disaster.

りゅうこう 流行 (a) fashion, (a) vogue /voʊg/ (➤ 後者は一時的な); a craze, a fad (一時的な; しばしば軽蔑して); a trend (傾向); (a) style (流行の型); an epidemic (病気などの) 一形 流行の fashionable; popular(人気のある) 一動 流行する come into fashion; be in fashion (流行している)
▶この型の靴が今流行している This type of shoe *is in fashion* [*in style*]. ‖ ロングスカートがまた流行し始めたようです It seems that long skirts *have come back in fashion*.
▶なぜ1990年代に社交ダンスが流行していたのか私には全く理解できない The ballroom dancing *craze* of the 1990s was completely incomprehensible to me. ‖ その頃はミニスカートが流行していた Miniskirts *were* then *in vogue*. ‖ 白のネクタイを締めるのがその年に流行した Wearing white ties was the *fad* of the year.
▶この秋の流行は何ですか What'*s in* this fall? (●インフォーマルでは in fashion の代わりに単に in ということが多い. in にアクセントを置く) ‖ 高校生たちの間で幸運を招くおまじないが流行している Good-luck charms *have caught on* with high schoolers. (➤ catch on は「はやる」).
▶その年はベトナム料理が流行した Vietnamese cooking *enjoyed a boom* that year. (➤「ブームになった」の意). →はやる.
▶このスーツはもう流行後れだ This suit is *out of fashion*. ‖ この型のハンドバッグはもう流行後れになった This type of handbag *has gone out of style*. ‖ 彼女は常に最新の流行に後れない(＝流行についていく)ようにしている She tries to keep up with *the latest trends*. ‖ 原宿は最新流行のファッションを身に着けた十代の若者であふれている Harajuku is swarming with teens in *trendy* clothes.
▶若い女性は流行に敏感だ Young women are *fashion-conscious*. ‖ 若者がしばしば流行を作り出す Young people often *set new trends*. ／Young people often *become trendsetters*.
▶コレラの流行を防ぐ prevent *an epidemic* of cholera.
‖流行歌 a popular song ‖ 流行語 a vogue word ‖ 流行作家 a popular writer ‖ 流行性感冒 epidemic influenza.

りゅうこつ 竜骨 a keel (船の).

りゅうさん 硫酸 《化学》 sulfuric acid /sʌlfjʊ̀ərɪk ǽsɪd/ ‖硫酸アンモニウム ammonium sulfate.

りゅうざん 流産 (a) miscarriage 一動 流産する miscarry ▶彼女は妊娠初期に流産した She *had a miscarriage* [She *miscarried*] in the early stage of pregnancy.
▶《比喩的》地下鉄建設計画は予算の裏付けがなく流産に終わった The plan to build a subway *was aborted* [*fell through*] due to a lack of budgetary support.

りゅうし 粒子 《物理学》 a particle
‖ヒッグス粒子 the Higgs boson(➤ 粒子１つは a Higgs boson; boson /bóʊsɑːn/ は素粒子の１種「ボゾン」の意の物理学用語).

りゅうしつ 流失 ▶洪水でその地域の橋がいくつか流失した Several bridges in that area *were washed out* [*were* (*swept*) *away*] by the flood.

りゅうしゅつ 流出 ▶土砂の流出 *a washout* ‖ 科学者の頭脳流出を食い止める halt *the brain drain* of scientists ‖ タンカーから原油が流出した(＝漏れた) Crude oil *leaked* from the tanker. (➤「石油の流出事故」は an oil spill という).

りゅうじょう 粒状の granular ▶粒状の塩 *granular* salt.

1 **りゅうせい 流星** 《天文学》 a **meteor** /míːṭiəʳ/, a **shooting star**
‖ **流星雨** a meteor shower ‖ **流星群** a meteor swarm ‖ **しし座流星群** Leonids.

2 **りゅうせい 隆盛** **prosperity** /prɑːspérəṭi/ ▶柔道部の今日の隆盛は谷選手に負うところが大きい The judo club owes most of its present *prosperity* [*popularity*] to judoka Tani.

りゅうせんけい 流線型の **streamlined** ▶流線型の自動車[列車] a *streamlined* car [train] ‖ サメの体は流線型をしている Sharks have *streamlined* bodies.

りゅうたい 流体 (a) **fluid** /flúːɪd/.
‖ **流体力学** fluid dynamics, hydrodynamics.

りゅうち 留置 **detention** 一動 **留置する** **detain** +目, **keep ... in custody** ▶その旅行者は武器不法所持の疑いで留置された The tourist *was detained* on suspicion of illegal possession of a firearm.
‖ **留置場** a detention house.

りゅうちょう 流暢な **fluent** /flúːənt/ 一副 **流ちょうに** **fluently** ▶流ちょうな英語を話す speak *fluent* English／speak English *fluently* ‖ そのタイ人男性はレポーターの質問に流ちょうな日本語で答えた The Thai man answered the reporter's questions in *fluent* Japanese.

りゅうつう 流通 **distribution**(物の); **circulation**, **currency**(金銭の; 後者はより堅い語) 一動 **流通する** **circulate** ▶新米が流通し始めた New rice has begun to *come on the market* [*to appear in the stores*]. ‖ 日本の流通機構はあまりに複雑だった The Japanese *distribution system* used to be too complicated. ‖ 大阪は一大流通センターだ Osaka is a big *distribution center*.
▶日銀は貨幣の流通高を発表した The Bank of Japan made public the *amount of circulating money* [*money in circulation*].

リュート a **lute**(楽器).

りゅうどう 流動 ▶その患者は流動食をとっている That patient is getting *liquid food* [is on *a liquid diet*]. ‖ 事態は依然流動的だ The situation is still *fluid* [*unstable*].
‖ **流動体** a fluid /flúːɪd/ (気体も含む).

りゅうとうだび 竜頭蛇尾 ▶4月を10勝2敗でスタートしたジャイアンツだが, 竜頭蛇尾でシーズンを終えた The Giants, who started with 10 wins and 2 losses in April, *fizzled out* [*ran out of steam*] toward the end of the season. (➤ それぞれ「尻すぼみになる」「スタミナ切れになる」の意).

りゅうにゅう 流入 **influx** /ínflʌks/; **invasion**(大量の) ▶外国人労働者の流入は一部の先進国でも問題になりつつある The *influx* of foreign workers is becoming a problem in some developed countries.

りゅうにん 留任する **remain in office** ▶外務大臣の留任が決定した It has been decided that the Foreign Minister will *remain in office*.

りゅうねん 留年する **repeat the year** ▶彼は出席日数不足で留年しそうだ He will probably have to *repeat the year* because of his poor attendance. ‖ 単位不足のため留年することになった I have to *stay at this university one more year* to get enough credits for graduation.

りゅうは 流派 a **school** ▶茶道の作法は流派によって大きく異なる Tea ceremony etiquette varies greatly from *school* to *school*.

りゅうひょう 流氷 **drift ice**; a **floe**(大きな塊) ▶オホーツクの海はすっかり流氷に閉ざされた The Sea of Okhotsk was completely bound with *drift ice*.

りゅうほ 留保する **suspend** +目 (承諾・回答などを); **reserve** +目 (権限などを) ▶承諾を留保する *suspend* (one's) consent ‖ 判断を留保する *withhold* judgment.
‖ **留保権限** reserve powers.

りゅうぼく 流木 **driftwood**.

リューマチ →リウマチ.

りゅうよう 流用する **misuse** /mìsjúːz/ +目 (不正に使う); **divert** +目 (転用する) ▶その役人は公金を流用して首になった The government official got fired for *misusing* public money. ‖ 寄付金の一部が私的な目的に流用された Part of the donations *was diverted to* personal purposes.

りゅうりゅう 隆々 ▶筋骨隆々っていうのは今ははやらない *Being brawny* [*Having big muscles*] is not fashionable these days.

りゅうれい 流麗な **flowing**(流れるような); **elegant**(優美な) ▶流麗な筆跡 a *flowing* [an *elegant*] hand.

リュック(サック) a **rucksack** /rʌ́ksæk/, a **knapsack** /nǽpsæk/.

> **危ないカタカナ語✹ リュック(サック)**
> 「リュックサック」はドイツ語の *Rucksack* から日本語になったことばだが, 英語でも rucksack という. また backpack (特にハイキング用)ともいい, アメリカでは knapsack もよく使う.

1 **りよう 利用** **use** /juːs/ 一動 **利用する** **use** /juːz/ +目, **make use of**; **utilize** +目 (➤堅い語)

> 【文型】
> 物(A)を利用する
> **use** A
> **make use of** A
> **take advantage of** A
>
> 《解説》 **use** は「使う」の意の最もふつうの語. **make use of** も同じだが, しばしば make good use of (…を上手に活用する), make the best use of (…を最大限に生かす)のように使われる. **take advantage of** は「(チャンスなどを)自分に都合よく利用する」であるが, 悪い意味で「人の親切・無知につけいる, 乗じる」にも使う.

▶もっと図書館を利用しなさい You should *use* the library more. ／You should *make* more *use of* the library. ‖ 時間をうまく利用するようにしなさい Try to *make good use of* your time. ‖ 合気道は相手の力を利用して技をかける The techniques [*waza*] in aikido allow you to *make use of* your opponent's power.
▶先生は「あらゆる機会を利用しなさい」と言った The teacher said, "*Take advantage of* every opportunity." ‖ 太陽エネルギーは今後ますます利用されるようになるだろう More and more solar energy will *be used* in the future. ‖ この川の水は発電に利用されている The water of this river *is used* [*is utilized*] for

り

power generation.
▶クーポン券を**利用して**ワイシャツを6枚買った I *used* coupons to buy a half dozen new shirts. ‖あの歌手は美貌を**利用して**スターダムにのし上がった That singer shot to stardom by *capitalizing on* her beauty. (➤ capitalize on は「(自分の利点などを)利用する」).
▶今度の連休を**利用して**グアムに行く計画だ We're planning to go to Guam during the coming consecutive holidays. (👄「連休に」の意味だから,「利用」は訳さなくてよい).
▶きみはあいつにただ**利用されただけ**だ You *were* only *used* (by him).
▶《デパートなどで》カードは**利用できますか** Do you *accept* [*take*] (credit) cards? ‖箱根に行ったときは会社の保養所を**利用した**(=に泊まった) We stayed at the company's resort house in Hakone. ‖《機長などが》皆さま, 本日は全日空を**ご利用いただき**ありがとうございます We thank you very much for traveling with ANA today. / Thank you for *choosing* ANA for your trip today. ‖《エレベーターで》**ご利用階数**をお知らせください Which floor (would you like), please? ‖この資料は**利用価値が高い**[**低い**] These materials *are of considerable* [*little*] *practical value*.
‖**利用者** a user.
👉 **再利用** (→見出語)

²りよう 理容 haircutting(散髪); hairdressing (整髪)
‖**理容学校** a barber school ‖**理容師** a barber ‖**理容室**《米》a barbershop,《英》a barber's (shop).

¹りょう 寮《米》a **dormitory** /dɔ́ːʳmətɔ̀ːri/, a **dorm** (➤後者はインフォーマル),《英》a **hall of residence** ▶わが校では全員**寮**に住まなければならない At our school, all students have to live in the *dormitory*.
‖**寮生** a dormitory student,《英》a boarder ‖**寮母** a dorm mother, a housemother, a matron /méɪtrən/ ‖(会社の)**独身寮** a dormitory [an apartment house] for single employees.

²りょう 量 (a) **quantity** (➤ quality (質)に対する語); an **amount**(数量); **volume**(分量)
▶一部の出版社では質より**量優先だ** For some publishing companies *quantity comes before quality*. ‖糖尿病患者は**砂糖の摂取量**を制限しなければならない Diabetics must limit *their sugar consumption* [*the amount of sugar they consume*].
▶コンピュータがダムの水の**量**を制御している The *volume* of water in [behind] the dam is controlled by a computer.
▶給料は大して増えないのに**仕事の量**は増えた Though my pay didn't go up much, my *work load* (certainly) did. (➤ load は「割り当て量」) ‖上越地方は**積雪量が多い** The Joetsu district *has* [*gets*] *heavy snowfall*. / They *have heavy snowfall* in the Joetsu district.

³りょう 良《学業成績》**good, above average**, a **B** ▶私の英語の成績は「**良**」だった My English grade was '*good*.' / I got *a B* in English.

⁴りょう 漁 fishing; **fishery**(大規模な); a **catch**(漁獲量) ▶海へ**漁に出る** go *fishing* in the sea ‖江差はかつてニシン**漁**で栄えた Esashi once thrived on *herring fishery*.
‖**漁期** the fishing season.

⁵りょう 猟 hunting (猟をすること); **shooting** (銃猟); **game**(獲物) ▶カモ**猟**に行く go *wild duck hunting*.

⁶りょう 涼 the cool ▶木陰でしばし**涼をとる** *enjoy the cool* under the shade of a tree for some time.

りょう- 両- ▶**両氏**とも出席していた The *two* people [*Both* men / *Both* women] were present. ‖人質は**両手両足**を縛られ, 猿ぐつわをかまされていた *Both of* the hostage's *hands and legs* were bound up and his mouth gagged.
‖**両脇** both sides.

¹-りょう -料 a **charge**, a **fee** →料金 ▶宿泊[配達]**料** hotel [delivery] *charges* ‖診察**料** a doctor's *fee* ‖原稿**料** a manuscript *fee*《参考》admission(入場料), postage (郵送料)など, 個別の単語を使う場合も多い.
👉 **手数料** (→見出語)

²-りょう -領 (a) **territory** ▶グアムはアメリカ**領**だ Guam is *a territory* of the United States. / Guam is a U.S. *territory*.

³-りょう -両・-輛 ▶ 13**両**編成の列車 a 13-*car* [*carriage*] train / a train made up of 13 *cars* [*carriages*] (➤ made up を composed にしてもよい) ‖前から3**両目の車両** *the third car* from the front.

りょういき 領域 a **field**(仕事・研究などの専門分野); a **domain**(研究・活動などの担当範囲) ▶この研究にはいくつかの学問**領域**にまたがる専門知識が要求される This research requires expertise in several different *fields* (*of study*).
▶プロの(料理人の)台所はかつて男性の**領域**だった The professional kitchen used to be *the domain* of men.

りょういん 両院 both [**the two**] **Houses** (**of the Diet**) ▶その法案は**両院**通過は難しそうだ It seems it will be difficult for that bill to pass *both Houses*.

りょうえん 良縁 a **good match**(良い縁組) ▶太郎は**良縁**に恵まれた Taro made *a good match*. / Taro married the right girl.

りょうおもい 両思い ▶明子と真彦は**両思い**だ Akiko and Masahiko *love each other*.

りょうが 凌駕する surpass /səʳpǽs/ +Ⓐ ▶そのバスケットボールチームは試合ではスピード・技術ともに相手チームを**りょうがした** The basketball team *surpassed* their opponents in both skill and speed in the game.

¹りょうかい 領海 territorial waters
‖**領海侵犯** an intrusion into [a violation of] (a nation's) territorial waters ‖**領海法**《法学》the Territorial Sea Law.

²りょうかい 了解 (an) **understanding**(理解); **consent** (同意); **approval** (承認) 一働 **了解する understand, consent**《to》▶2人の間に暗黙の**了解**があった There was *a tacit understanding* [*consent*] between the two.
▶この件については社長の**了解**をとらなければならない We have to ask for the president's *consent* [*approval*] on this matter. ‖**了解**! *O.K.* / *All right.* / *Got it.* /《無線で》*Roger*.
‖**了解事項** an agreed item.

りょうがえ 両替 exchange(通貨の); **making change** (小額の金銭への) (➤この change は「くずした金, 小銭」) 一働 **両替する exchange** [**change**] **money**(通貨を交換する); **make** [**give**] **change**(金をくずす); **break** [**change**] A **into** B(金(A)をくずして金(B)にする)
▶円をドルに**両替する** *change* yen *into* dollars / *exchange* yen *for* dollars ‖5000円札の**両替**をお願いします *Could you break* this 5,000 yen bill (for me)?

▶500円玉を100円玉に両替してくれますか Could you *break* [*change*] this 500-yen coin *into* 100-yen coins？ ‖コピー機を使いたいので両替をお願いします *Could I have change* for the photocopy machine？ ‖《コンビニなどで》両替のみは致しかねます *We don't make* [*give*] *change without a purchase*. (● (×)We don't exchange money. としない. また, よく見かける掲示の (×)No exchange. では意味が通じず, (×)No exchanges. とすると「商品の交換お断り」の意味となる).

‖両替機 a change machine, a money changer (くずす機械) (➤ 特に小銭両替機を明示する場合は a coin changer) ; a foreign currency exchange machine (通貨交換の) ‖両替所 a money exchange counter [booth], a currency exchange shop.

りょうがわ 両側 both sides ▶隅田川の両側で大勢の人が花火を見物した A large number of people enjoyed the fireworks on *both sides* [on *either side*] of the Sumida River.

りょうかん 量感 ▶量感のある仏像 a *massive* statue of Buddha.

りょうがん 両岸 ▶その川の両岸には桜並木がある There are rows of cherry trees on *both banks of that river*.

1**りょうき 漁期** a fishing season.

2**りょうき 猟期** a hunting [shooting] season.

3**りょうき 猟奇** ▶猟奇的な犯罪 a *bizarre* [*grotesque*] crime.

りょうきょく 両極 the North and South Poles(南北の両極) ; the positive and negative poles(電気の両極) ▶彼らはいつも意見が両極に分かれる They are always *poles apart* in their opinions.

りょうきょくたん 両極端 ▶こう意見が両極端に分かれてしまっては, まとめようがありません With opinions so *polarized*, a satisfactory conclusion is impossible.

りょうきん 料金 charge(s)(請求代金) ; a rate (一定の率に基づいた) ; a fare (交通機関の) ; a fee(謝礼)

▶座席の料金はA席で8000円になります The *charge* for an A-rank seat is 8,000 yen. ‖今, 銭湯の大人[子供]料金はいくらですか What is the *charge* for adults [children] at a public bath now？ ‖ホテル・エドモンドの料金は1泊で200ドルだった The Hotel Edmond *charged* me 200 dollars for one night. ／They *charged* me 200 dollars for an overnight stay at the Hotel Edmond. (➤ いずれの charge も「請求する」の意).

▶ここの1時間当たりの駐車料金は400円です The hourly *rate for parking* [The hourly *parking fee*] here is 400 yen. ／They *charge* 400 yen per hour for parking here. ‖長距離通話料金が値下げになった *Telephone rates* for long-distance calls have been reduced. ‖ニューヨークのタクシーのチップは料金の2割が相場だ When you take a taxi in New York, you're expected to tip the driver 20 percent of the *fare*.

▶航空郵便の料金は北米の場合, 25グラムまで110円です Airmail to North America *costs* 110 yen for letters of 25 grams or less. (➤ cost は「(料金が)かかる」) ‖この手紙を書留にしたいのですが料金はいくらですか I'd like to have this letter registered. How much [What] is the *postage*？ (➤ postage は「郵便料金」) ‖先月のガス料金は1万5000円だった The *gas bill* for last month was 15,000 yen. (➤ bill は「請求書」).

‖料金所 a tollgate ‖料金箱(バスの) a fare box ‖料金表 a list of charges(サービス行為の) ; a price list(売られる品物の).

> **逆引き熟語 ○○料金**
> 大人[子供]料金 the charge for adults [children] ／ガス料金 a gas bill ／サービス料金 a service charge ／深夜料金(タクシーの) an additional fare for late-night passengers ／水道料金 a water bill ／駐車料金 a parking fee [charge] ／通話料金 a telephone charge, a (tele)phone bill ／電気料金 an electricity bill ／特急料金 an express fare ／入場料金 an admission (fee [charge]) ／バス料金 a bus fare ／初乗り料金 base fare ／郵便料金 postage ／割引料金 a discount rate ／割増料金 an extra charge

りょうくう 領空 the (territorial) airspace ▶わが国の領空が昨夜2機の国籍不明機に侵犯された Our (*territorial*) *airspace* was violated by two unidentified aircraft last night.

‖領空侵犯 an intrusion into [a violation of] (a nation's) territorial airspace.

りょうけ 良家 a 'good family' (● 逆の「悪家」があるわけではないので,「いわゆる」の意を表す引用符をつける) ▶良家の子女 sons and daughters *from 'good families'*.

1**りょうけん 猟犬** a hunting dog ; a hound(➤《英》では特にキツネ狩り用) ; a gundog(銃猟犬).

2**りょうけん 了見・料簡** an idea, a thought ▶そんな了見の狭いことでどうするんだ Why be so *narrow-minded*？

りょうこう 良好な good ▶手術後の患者の経過は良好です The patient is making *good* progress after the operation.

▶無線の感度は良好だ Our CB radio has *good* reception. (➤ CB は citizens band の略語) ‖視界良好 The visibility *is good*.

りょうこく 両国 both [the two] countries ▶両国間の友好関係を促進する promote friendly relations between *the two countries* [*nations*] ‖日米両国は不公正貿易慣行解消のため一層の努力をすることで一致している *Japan and the United States* have agreed to make further efforts to eliminate unfair trade practices.

りょうさいけんぼ 良妻賢母 a good wife and wise [virtuous] mother ▶あの女子大では良妻賢母の育成が基本方針になっている That women's college's basic policy is to educate students to become '*good wives and wise mothers*.'

りょうさん 量産 mass production 一動 量産する mass-produce ＋目 ▶当社はソーラーパネルの量産のため, ベトナムに工場を造る計画です We are going to build a factory in Vietnam to *mass-produce* [for the *mass production* of] solar panels.

1**りょうし 量子**《物理学》a quantum /kwá:ntəm/ ‖量子物理学 quantum physics ‖量子力学 quantum mechanics ‖量子論 the quantum theory.

2**りょうし 猟師** a hunter ; a huntsman (男の) ▶猟師はクマをしとめた The *hunter* shot a bear.

3**りょうし 漁師** a fisher ; a fisherman (男の).

りょうじ 領事 a consul /ká:nsəl/ ▶大阪駐在のイギリ

ス領事 the British *Consul* in Osaka.
‖**領事館** a consulate /kɑ́:nsələt/ ‖**総領事** a consul general.

りょうしき 良識 good [common] sense ; sound judgment (健全な判断力) ▶**良識**で判断しなさい Use your *good* [*common*] *sense*.
▶**良識**のある人なら賄賂など受け取らないだろう A *sensible* person should know better than to accept a bribe. →常識.

りょうしつ 良質の high-quality, quality ▶**良質の**チーズ (a) cheese *of good* [*high*] *quality* ／(a) *high-quality* cheese ‖クウェートは**良質の**石油を産する Kuwait produces *high-grade* oil. (➤ 石油には grade を用いる).

りょうしゃ 両者 both sides, both parties ▶**両者**は合意に達した *Both sides* [*parties*] reached an agreement. ‖**両者**に大きな違いはない *The two* aren't much different from each other. ‖裁判所による調停は債権者・債務者の**両者**を満足させた The court's mediation satisfied *both* the creditor *and* the debtor.
▶彼女はその**両者**に話をした She spoke to *both* of them. ／She spoke to them *both*. ‖土俵上で**両者**にらみ合っております *The two* (*sumo*) *wrestlers* are glaring at each other in the ring.

りょうしゅ 領主 a feudal lord.

1**りょうしゅう 領袖** a leader, a head ▶党の**領袖** *the leader* of a political party ／a political *leader* ‖派閥の**領袖** a faction *leader*.

2**りょうしゅう 領収** receipt /rɪsíːt/ 一動 **領収する** receive ＋目 (受け取る)
▶金50000円正(まさ)に**領収**いたしました I *acknowledge receipt* of the sum of ¥50,000. ／*Received* the sum of ¥50,000. (➤ 後者は証書の場合) ‖**領収書**を書いてください Please make out *a receipt*. ‖**領収書**をください May I have *a receipt*? →レシート.
‖**領収者** a receiver (受け取り人) ; a recipient (受領者) ‖**領収済み** Received. ／Paid.

りょうじゅう 猟銃 a hunting rifle ; a shotgun (散弾銃) ▶**猟銃**でシカを撃つ shoot [fire] at a deer with *a shotgun* ／fire *a shotgun* at a deer.

りょうしょう 了承 approval /əprúːvəl/ (承認) ; consent (同意) ; (an) understanding (了解) 一動 (…を) **了承する** approve《of》, consent《to》, understand ▶私は父の**了承**なしに家を売ってしまった I sold our house without the *approval* of my father. ‖私どもの計画をご**了承**くだされば幸いです We would be happy if you would *approve* [*give your approval to*] our project. ‖節電中で照明を減らしております. **どうぞご了承ください** We've reduced the lighting to save electricity. *We ask for your understanding*.

1**りょうしん 両親** one's parents, one's mother and father ▶ご**両親**はお元気ですか How are *your parents*?

2**りょうしん 良心** (a) (good) conscience /kɑ́:nʃəns/ (➤ conscience は厳密には「善悪感, 善悪の判断力」の意なので, good conscience とするほうが明確) 一形 **良心的な** conscientious /kɑ̀:nʃiénʃəs/
▶あいつには**良心**というものがあるのだろうか I wonder if that guy has *a conscience*. ‖きみはきみ自身の**良心**に従うべきだ You should follow your own *conscience*.
▶村人を皆殺しにしたナチス将校は**良心のかしゃく**に悩んだ After annihilating the whole village, the Nazi officer was tormented by *a guilty conscience*. ‖彼女は両親にうそをついていたので**良心がとがめた** She *had a bad* [*guilty*] *conscience* since she had lied to her parents.
▶あの大工さんは**良心的な**仕事をする That carpenter is *conscientious* about his work. (➤「良心的な仕事」の１つをいう場合は a conscientious [an honest] piece of work) ‖もうけ第一主義の不動産屋もいれば, **良心的な**不動産屋もいる Some realtors only care about profit, but others can be quite *honest*. ‖あの店の品はすべて**良心的な値段がついている** Everything [Every item] in that store *is priced fairly* [*has a fair price*]. (➤ is reasonably priced としてもよい.「良心的な店」は trustworthy store).

1**りょうせい 両性** both [the two] sexes ▶**両性**の合意 the consent of *both sexes*.
‖**両性具有者** a hermaphrodite /həːrmǽfrədaɪt/.

2**りょうせい 良性の** 《医学》 benign /bənáɪn/ ▶乳房のしこりは**良性**とわかった The lump in my breast turned out to be *benign*. (➤「悪性の」は malignant /məlígnənt/).

りょうせいるい 両生類 《動物学》 an amphibian /æmfíbiən/.

りょうせん 稜線 a ridge.

りょうたん 両端 both ends (両方の端) ; either end (どちらの端も) ▶ロープの**両端**を結びなさい Tie *the two ends* of the rope together.

1**りょうち 領地** a fief /fiːf/ (封土(ほうど)) ; (a) territory (領土). →領土.

2**りょうち 料地** preserved land
‖**皇室御料地** an imperial estate.

りょうて 両手 both hands ▶**両手**を上げてください Please raise *both of your hands*. ‖観光客たちは**両手**に持ち切れないほどの土産物を買った The tourists bought so many souvenirs that they could hardly carry them in *both hands*.

りょうてい 料亭 a high-class Japanese (members-only) restaurant /réstərənt/ (➤ 一見(いちげん)の客をとらない料亭の場合はカッコ内の語をつける必要がある).

りょうてんびん 両天秤 →天秤.

りょうど 領土 (a) territory ▶戦争に負けて**領土**の一部を失った国は多い Many countries have had to cede part of their *territory* after losing wars.
‖**領土侵犯** an intrusion into [a violation of] (a nation's) territorial sovereignty ‖**北方領土** the Northern Territories.

りょうどうたい 良導体 《物理学》 a good conductor.

りょうどなり 両隣 ▶**両隣**で犬を飼っているので, 鳴き声がうるさくてかなわない *The people who live on both sides of me* [*my house*] have dogs, and their loud barking is just too much to bear.

りょうはんてん 量販店 a big discounter, a giant discount retailer, a mass retailer [merchandiser]
‖**家電量販店** a home appliance and electronics discounter [discount store].

りょうひ 良否 quality (人や物の質のよしあし) ▶品物の**良否**を吟味する check the *quality* of goods ‖きみは物事の**良否**をよく考えずにすぐ結論を出したがる You tend to jump to a conclusion *without weighing the pros and cons*. (➤ pros and cons は「良い面と悪い面」「賛成意見と反対意見」).

りょうびらき 両開き ▶**両開き**のドア *a double door*.

りょうふう 涼風 a cool breeze (風) ; cool air (空気).

りょうぶん 領分 one's territory, one's domain /doʊméɪn/ ▶きみは他人に自分の**領分**を侵されて平気なのか How can you feel at ease when someone infringes on *your territory* [*domain*] ?

1**りょうほう 両方** **both**(➤ 肯定文で); **neither, not ... either**(両方とも[どちらも]…でない) ⇀-も ▶**両方の親が**二人の結婚を望んでいる *The parents of both families* wish (for) the couple to get married. ／*The parents of both families* hope the couple will get married. (● Both parents とすると, 二人にはそれぞれ親が一人でそのどちらも, の意にとれる. また, もし「両方の親が二人の結婚を望んでいない」の場合は The couple's parents do not wish for them to get married. とするか, None of the (couple's) parents wish (for) them to get married. とする) ‖ 父の足は**両方とも**痛んだ *Both* (*of*) my father's legs ached. ／My father's legs *both* ached. (➤ 前者がふつう).

▶彼はスキーもスケートも**両方とも**できる He can *both* ski *and* ice-skate.

▶ (うちの)親は**両方とも**たばこを吸わない *Neither of* our parents smoke(s). (● 形容詞の neither は単数名詞をとるので, (×)Neither parents は不可. また, neither parent は両親とは限らず, 文脈でわかる「別の子の親のどちらも…でない」の意となる) ‖ その2つの方法は**両方とも**うまくいかなかった *Neither of* the two methods worked.

▶その案は**両方とも**気に入っていない I'm *not* satisfied with *either of* those drafts. ‖ フランス語もドイツ語も**両方とも**話せない I can speak *neither* French *nor* German. ／I can*'t* speak *either* French *or* German.

2**りょうほう 療法** a **cure**(完治させる方法); (a) **treatment**(治療法); **therapy** /θérəpi/ (特に薬を使わない) ▶この恐ろしい病気はまだ確かな**療法**がわかっていない A sure *cure* has yet to be found for this dreadful disease.

‖ **安静療法** a rest cure ‖ **音楽** [**ショック**] **療法** music [shock] therapy ‖ **温泉療法** (a) spa treatment ‖ **化学療法** chemotherapy /kìːmoʊθérəpi/ ‖ **食事療法** a dietary /dáɪəteri/ cure ‖ **放射線療法** (a) radiation treatment.

りょうめん 両面 **both sides** [**faces**] ▶用紙の**両面**に印刷する print *both sides* of a sheet of paper(➤「両面印刷」は duplex printing).

▶原子力発電所について議論するときは長所と短所の**両面**を考慮することが必要だ When you discuss nuclear power plants, you should consider *both* the advantages *and* disadvantages.

‖ **両面テープ** double-sided tape.

りょうやく 良薬 (a) **good medicine**

ことわざ **良薬は口に苦し** (A) good medicine is [tastes] bitter.

1**りょうゆう 領有** **possession** 一動 **領有する** **possess** +㊐ ▶植民地を**領有する** *possess* [*take possession of*] a colony.

2**りょうゆう 両雄** **two great men** [**rivals**].

りょうよう 療養 **medical treatment**(治療); **recuperation** /rɪkjùːpəréɪʃən/ (病後の保養) 一動 **療養する** **recuperate** /rɪkjúːpəreɪt/ ▶温泉で**療養**に努める try to *recover one's health* at a hot spring ‖ 彼女は自宅で**療養中**だ She *is recuperating* at home.

‖ **療養所** a rest home (回復期の患者・老人などの); a sanatorium, 《米また》a sanitarium (結核患者の) ‖ **転地療養** health resort therapy(➤「軽井沢に転地療養する」は recuperate [convalesce] in Karuizawa).

りょうり 料理 **1**【**料理すること**】**cooking**; **cookery**(料理法) 一動 **料理する** **cook** (+㊐) (火を通して); **prepare** +㊐ (支度をする) (➤ 日本語の「支度をする」に似て, 下ごしらえから完成して整うまでを指すが, やや手の込んだ料理を指すことが多い)

▶私は学校で**料理**を勉強しています I am studying *cooking* at school. ‖ きみのうちでは誰が**料理する**の? Who *does the cooking* in your home? ／Who *cooks* (*the meals*) in your family? ‖ 母は今, 魚を**料理している** My mother is *cooking* [*preparing*] fish. ‖ 最近は**料理の上手な男性**が多い A lot of men are *good cooks* these days.

▶《比喩的》横綱は新大関をあっさり**料理した**(＝負かした) The yokozuna easily *beat* the wrestler who had just been promoted to Ozeki rank.

2【**料理したもの**】a **dish** (1皿に盛った); **food** (食物); **cuisine** /kwɪzíːn/ (レストランなどの) ▶フランス[中国]**料理** French [Chinese] *cuisine* ／French [Chinese] *food* ‖ きょうの**特別料理** today's *special* ‖ 手の込んだ**料理**を幾皿か整える prepare several elaborate *dishes*.

▶何でもきみの好きな**料理**を頼みなさい Order any *dish* you like. ‖ おいしいお**料理**ね. This *dish* is very tasty. ‖ このレストランはおいしい**料理**を出す They serve good *food* at this restaurant. ／This restaurant serves tasty *food*.

▶ 対話「どんな**料理**がお好きですか」「メキシコ**料理**が好きです」"What kind of *food* do you like?" "I like Mexican *food*."

‖ **料理学校** a cooking [《英また》cookery] school ‖ **料理教室** a cooking class ‖ **料理長** a chef /ʃef/ ‖ **料理人** a cook ‖ **料理番組** a cooking program [show] (➤ 後者は有名料理家が取りしきるショー形式のもの) ‖ **料理法** cookery; a recipe /résəpi/ (個々の料理の); cuisine(ある国・ホテル特有の) ‖ **料理本** a cookbook, a cookery book, a recipe book ‖ **料理屋** a restaurant /réstərənt/ ⇀料亭 ‖ **小料理屋** a small restaurant.

> **逆引き熟語 ○○料理**
> **一品料理** à la carte /àːlɑːkáːʳt/ ／**おすすめ料理** today's special ／**お節料理** *osechi*, New Year's dishes ／**コース料理** a course meal (➤ three-course, five-course など品数を明示するのがふつう) ／**シーフード料理** seafood ／**仕出し料理** catered food ／**付け合わせ料理** a side dish ／**鍋料理** *nabe*, a hot pot

りょうりつ 両立 ▶私の妻は教師と主婦の仕事をうまく**両立させている** My wife *is doing* very well as *both* a school teacher *and* a housewife. ‖ 女性は家庭と仕事を**両立させる**ことはできないという説に私は納得できない I don't accept the idea that women are incapable of *having both* a family *and* a career. ‖ クラブ活動と勉強を**両立させる**のは難しい It is difficult to *keep up both* club activities *and* studies. ‖ 理論と実践とは必ずしも**両立する**とは限らない Theory and practice don't always *go together* [*are* not always *compatible*].

りょうりん 両輪 **two** [**both**] **wheels** ▶車の**両輪** *two* [*both*] *wheels* of a car ‖ PTA と教育委員会が車の**両輪**となっています The PTA and the board of education *work cooperatively* [*hand in hand*]. (➤ 比喩的な意味での「車の両輪」は a cooperative relationship のようにもいう).

りょかく 旅客 a **traveler**(旅行者); a **passenger**(乗

客）▶事故が起きたとき，飛行機には150人の**旅客**が乗っていた When the accident occurred, there were 150 *passengers* on board the plane.
‖**旅客運賃** passenger fares ‖**旅客機** a passenger plane.

りょかん 旅館 a (Japanese-style) hotel /hòutél/；an inn（宿屋）▶温泉地の由緒ある**旅館** a *ryokan* [*Japanese inn*] with a long history in a hot spring (resort) town.

りよく 利欲 greed for money ▶彼は**利欲**に駆られて行動しがちだ He tends to let his *greed for money* get the better of him.

-りょく -力
‖**営業力** the ability to sell ‖（大学の）**就職力** the ability to get jobs for its students ‖**造語力** word-coining ability ‖**友だち力** the ability to make friends ‖**プレゼン力** presentation ability ‖**老人力** the advantages of being old.

りょくおうしょくやさい 緑黄色野菜 green and yellow vegetables.

りょくち 緑地 a green tract of land ▶**緑地**の少ない所には住みたくない I don't want to live in a place where there is little *greenery*.
‖**緑地帯** (a) greenbelt.

りょくちゃ 緑茶 green tea.

りょくないしょう 緑内障《医学》glaucoma /glaʊkóʊmə/ ▶父は右目が**緑内障**になった My father had *glaucoma* in his right eye.

りょけん 旅券 a passport /pǽspɔːʳt/.

り

りょこう 旅行 travel, a trip, a tour, a journey ━**動** **旅行する** travel；take [make] a trip（観光旅行の場合は take が，商用旅行では主に make が使われる）

> **語法** (1)「旅行」の意の最も一般的な語は **travel** だが，この語は foreign [air] travel のように前に修飾語を伴って用いるか，a travel bag [agency] のように形容詞的に用いる以外は，単独の名詞としてはあまり用いない．ただし，動詞としてはよく用いる．
> (2) **trip** は主に短期の旅行，**tour** は周遊旅行を指す．また **journey** は用事・遊びにかかわらず，陸上・海上などの長旅のことをいい，必ずしも出発点に戻らなくてもよい．人生を旅にたとえる場合はこの語が用いられる．

▶4日間の**旅行** a four-day *trip* ‖3週間のヨーロッパ**旅行**に出かける go on a three-week *tour* of Europe ‖趣味は**旅行**です I'm interested in *traveling* [*taking trips*].
▶蔵王へのスキー**旅行**が待ち遠しい I can hardly wait for our *ski trip* to Zao. ‖（高校）2年生が九州**旅行**[九州一周**旅行**]から帰って来た The junior class returned from their *trip* to Kyushu [*trip* around Kyushu].
▶母は今，**旅行に出ております** My mother is *away on a trip* now.
▶**外国旅行をする** *travel abroad* ‖**世界一周旅行をする**のが私の夢です My dream is to *take a trip around the world*. ‖私，ひとりで**旅行する**のはこれが初めてです It's the first time for me to *travel* alone. ／This is my first time to *travel* alone. ‖学生時代には全国各地を**旅行して回った** While in college, I *traveled all over* Japan.
▶ことしの夏，津和野に**旅行した** I *took* [*made* ／*went on*] *a trip* to Tsuwano this summer. ／I *traveled* [*journeyed*] to Tsuwano this summer. ‖夏休みを利用して能登半島を**旅行する**計画です I'm planning to *tour* the Noto Peninsula during (the) summer vacation.
▶**よいご旅行を** *Have a nice* [*good*] *trip*. ／*Bon voyage!*（➤ bon voyage /bɑ̀ːn vwɑɪɑ́ːʒ/ はフランス語から）.
▶ **対話**「インド**旅行**はいかがでしたか」「とても楽しかったです」"How was your *trip* to India?" "It was very enjoyable [a lot of fun]." ‖ **対話**「**海外旅行**をしたことがありますか」「**団体[パック]旅行**でハワイに一度行きました」"Have you ever *traveled overseas*?" "Yes. I once went to Hawaii *on a group trip* [*on a package tour*]."

> **逆引き熟語 ○○旅行**
> **1泊旅行** an overnight trip ／**宇宙旅行** space travel ／**海外旅行** an overseas trip ／**家族旅行** a family trip ／**観光旅行** a sightseeing tour ／**見学旅行** a field trip ／**研修旅行** a study tour ／**国内旅行** a domestic trip, domestic travel ／**視察旅行** an inspection tour ／**修学旅行** a school [an educational] trip ／**新婚旅行** a honeymoon ／**世界一周旅行** a trip around the world ／**徒歩旅行** a walking tour ／**2泊3日の旅行** a three day [three-day two-night] trip ／**バス旅行** a bus trip [tour], bus travel ／**パック旅行** a package tour ／**日帰り旅行** a day trip

‖**旅行案内書** a travel guide, a travel guidebook ‖**旅行案内所** a tourist (information) office, a tourist [travel] bureau ‖**旅行会社[代理店]** a travel agency ‖**旅行かばん** a (traveling) bag, a suitcase ‖**旅行業者** a travel agent ‖**旅行シーズン** the tourist season ‖**旅行者** a traveler, a tourist.

りょしゅう 旅愁 ▶晩秋のヨーロッパで**旅愁**に浸ってみませんか How about experiencing the *sweet melancholy* [*elegiac sadness*] *of travel* in Europe during late autumn?

りょじょう 旅情 ▶列車でゆっくり旅するのも**旅情**があっていいものだ A leisurely train trip really let you *enjoy the traveling mood*.

りょだん 旅団《軍事》a brigade.

りょっか 緑化 greening；tree planting（植樹）▶砂漠の**緑化** desert *greening* ‖大規模な**緑化運動**を展開する stage an extensive *greening* [*tree-planting*] *campaign*.

りょてい 旅程 an itinerary /aɪtínəreri/.

りょひ 旅費 travel(ing) expenses ▶ **対話**「ロンドンまで**旅費**はどのくらいかかるの？」「そうですね，今なら往復20万円くらいでしょうか」"How much does it *cost to travel* [*fly*] to London?" "Well, a round-trip ticket costs about two hundred thousand yen now."

リラ《植物》a lilac（ライラック）.

リラックス リラックスする relax ▶ぼくはきみのアパートに来るととても**リラックス**できるんだ I can really *relax* [*feel at home*] in your apartment. ‖この仕事が終わったら温泉にでも行って**リラックスしたい** Once I get finished with this work, I want to go *relax* at a hot spring.

リリース (a) release ━**動** **リリースする** release +**目**
▶あの演歌歌手のCDが3年ぶりに**リリースされた** That enka singer's first CD in three years *has been released*. ‖私は釣りをすると小魚は必ず**リリースする**

When fishing, I always *release* [*throw back*] the fry.
▶私のモットーは「キャッチ・アンド・リリース」だ My motto is "*Catch-and-Release.*" (➤ catch-and-release は「釣り上げた魚を再び水に放す」こと).

リリーフ 《野球》**relief** (救援) **一動** **リリーフする re-lieve** +目 ▶石井は8回に渡辺のリリーフを仰いだ Ishii *was relieved* in the eighth by Watanabe.
‖**リリーフ投手** a relief pitcher, a reliever, a fireman.

りりく 離陸 (a) **takeoff** **一動** **離陸する take off** ▶離陸の際, シートベルトをバックルで留める buckle one's seatbelt during *takeoff* ‖当機は定刻どおり成田を離陸いたしました Our plane *took off* from Narita Airport on schedule. ‖飛行機は離陸のため滑走路の端に移動した The plane taxied to the end of the runway for *takeoff*.

りりしい 凛々しい ▶りりしい青年 a *noble and high-spirited* young man ‖子供たちは消防士たちのりりしい姿に憧れた The children long to be like the *gallant-looking* firefighters.

りりつ 利率 an **interest rate** ▶預貯金の利率が来月から上がる[下がる] The *interest rate* on savings will be raised [be lowered] starting next month.

リレー a **relay** /ríːleɪ/ (**race**) ▶オリンピックの聖火リレー an Olympic *torch relay* ‖400メートルリレーを走る run a 400-meter *relay*.
▶バケツリレーで火を消した We *passed water in buckets from person to person* to put out the fire.

りれき 履歴 one's **personal history**; one's **career** /kəríəʳ/ (職歴); a **history**, a **log** (コンピュータの作業など); a **record** (活動の) ▶この用紙に履歴を簡単に書いてください Please write down a brief *personal history* on this form.
▶私は彼の履歴をよく知らない I don't know much about his *career*. ‖履歴書を持参してください Please bring your *résumé* [*personal history* / *curriculum vitae*] with you. (➤ résumé /rézəmeɪ/ は《米》で好まれる; curriculum vitae /kərìkjələm víːtaɪ/ は CV と略されることも多い) ‖検索履歴 a search *history*.

りろせいぜん 理路整然 ▶彼の主張は理路整然としている His argument is *well-organized and logical* [*well-reasoned*].

りろん 理論 (a) **theory** /θíːəri/ **一形** **理論(上)の theoretical** /θìːərétɪkəl/
▶物事はそう理論どおりすんなりとはいかない Things don't always go as smoothly as they do in *theory*.
▶理論に実践は必ずしも伴わない *Theory* and practice do not always match. ‖タイムトラベルは理論上は可能らしい It seems that time travel is *theoretically* possible.
‖**理論家** a theoretician, a theorist ‖**理論物理学** theoretical physics ‖**相対性理論** the theory of relativity ‖(物理学の)**標準理論** the Standard Model.

りん 燐 《化学》**phosphorus** /fɑ́ːsfərəs/.

りんか 隣家 **the** [one's] **neighboring house** (家); a **next-door neighbor** (人).

[1]**りんかい 臨海の** **seaside** (海辺の); **coastal** (沿岸の)
‖**臨海学校** a seaside summer school ‖**臨海工業地帯** a coastal industrial zone.

[2]**りんかい 臨界** 《物理学》**criticality** **一形** **臨界の critical** ▶原子炉は臨界に達した The reactor has reached *the critical state*.
‖**臨界事故** a criticality accident.

りんかく 輪郭 **the outline(s)** ▶木炭で山の輪郭をざっとスケッチする sketch a rough *outline* of the mountains with charcoal.
▶《比喩的》事件の輪郭がまだはっきりしない *The outline* of the incident is not clear yet.

りんかんがっこう 林間学校 a **summer school camp**, a **summer school in the woods.**

りんぎ 稟議 *ringi*; a formal method of getting management or executive approval in a Japanese organization (➤ 説明的な訳).
‖**稟議書** a request form to get management approval (➤「稟議書を回す」は circulate a request form).

りんきおうへん 臨機応変 ▶新たな問題が生じたら臨機応変に処理しましょう When a new problem arises, let's *take appropriate measures to deal with the situation* [let's *deal with it flexibly*]. ‖全く用意していなかったので臨機応変にやるしかなかった We were totally unprepared for the situation and had to *play it by ear*. (➤「聞き覚えで演奏する」が原義).

りんぎょう 林業 **forestry** ▶林業がこの地域の主要な産業だ *Forestry* is the principal industry of this region.

[1]**リンク** a (**skating**) **rink** (スケートの) ▶リンクに下りる go down to the *rink*.

[2]**リンク** a **link** (つながり) **一動** **リンクする link** +目, **link** 《to》 ▶そのサイトには関連サイトへのリンクが張ってある That site provides *links* to related ones. ‖私のサイトへはリンク自由です Feel free to *link* my website. / You are free to *put a link* from your website to this.
▶リンクしてくださった場合, お知らせくださればこちらからもリンクさせていただきます If you *link* (*to*) me, let me know, so I can *link* back *to* you. ‖リンク歓迎です We welcome *links* from other websites.
▶リンクされたドキュメント a *linked* document.

リング **1**【指輪】a **ring** ▶エンゲージリング an engagement *ring*.
2【ボクシングなどの】**the ring** ▶まず挑戦者がリングに上がった The challenger was the first to appear in *the ring*.
‖**リングサイド** a ringside.

りんげつ 臨月 ▶妻は臨月に入っている My wife is in her *final* [*ninth*] *month of pregnancy*. (→妊娠).

りんけん 臨検 **an on-the-spot inspection.**

りんご an **apple** (果実); an **apple tree** (木) ▶リンゴが枝もたわわになっている The *apple trees* are heavy with fruit. ‖このリンゴの皮をむいてください Will you please pare this *apple* for me?
▶リンゴのような頬をした子供たちが雪の中で遊んでいる Children with *rosy* [*apple-red*] cheeks are playing in the snow. (➤日本ではリンゴは赤の連想が強いが, 欧米では緑(apple-green)と結び付くことも多い) ‖1日1個のリンゴで医者いらず *An apple a day keeps the doctor away*. (➤英語のことわざ).

りんごく 隣国 a **neighboring country** (➤文脈により, 単に neighbor で表すこともある).

りんさく 輪作 **crop rotation** **一動** **輪作する rotate crops.**

りんさん 燐酸 《化学》**phosphoric acid.**

りんじ 臨時の **temporary** (一時的な); **special, extraordinary** /ɪkstrɔ́ːʳdneri/ (特別の) ▶この措置は臨時のも

のです These are just *temporary* measures. ‖ 臨時国会は7月17日に召集される *An extraordinary session of the Diet* [*An extraordinary Diet session*] will be convened on July 17.

▶私は臨時雇いです I'*m* (*working here as*) *a temp*. (➤ temp は temporary のインフォーマルな言い方) ‖ 本日は17時新宿発の臨時列車があります Today there is *a special train* that leaves Shinjuku Station from 5 p.m.

▶《掲示》臨時休業 Closed ‖ 交通ストが行われたときはあすは臨時休校にします If railroad and bus company workers go on strike, there will be no school tomorrow. (➤ 以上の2例では「臨時」を特に訳す必要はない) ‖ 番組の途中ですが, 臨時ニュースをお伝えします We're sorry to interrupt the program, but we've just received *a newsflash* [*some breaking news*].

‖臨時語(その場限りの) a nonce word ‖ 臨時収入 extra income ‖ 臨時政府 a provisional government ‖ 臨時総会 an extraordinary general meeting ‖ 臨時増刊号 a special issue (of a magazine) ‖ 臨時便 a special flight, an extra flight.

りんしたいけん 臨死体験 a **near-death experience** 《略 NDE》.

りんしつ 隣室 **the next room** ▶隣室のテレビの音にはいらいらする The noise from the TV in *the next room* really gets on my nerves.

りんじゅう 臨終 one's **hour of death**, one's **last moments** ▶ご臨終です I'm sorry to say that he [she] *has passed away*. (➤ pass away は「亡くなる」).

▶渡米中で祖母の臨終に間に合わなかった Since I was away in the United States, I could not be with my grandmother in her *last moments*.

りんしょ 臨書する do calligraphy following another person's work as an example(➤ 説明的な訳).

1**りんしょう 輪唱**《音楽》a **round** ▶3組みに分かれて『かっこう』を輪唱する divide into three groups and *sing a round* of "Cuckoo".

2**りんしょう 臨床の** **clinical**

‖臨床医 a clinician ‖ 臨床医学 clinical medicine ‖ 臨床外科 clinical surgery ‖ 臨床研究 clinical studies [research] ‖ 臨床試験 a clinical trial ‖ 臨床心理学 clinical psychology ‖ 臨床心理学者 a clinical psychologist ‖ 臨床心理士 a clinical psychologist.

りんじょうかん 臨場感 **presence** ▶SACD(スーパーオーディオCD)はすばらしい臨場感で音を再現する SACDs reproduce sound with astonishing *fidelity*. (➤ fidelity は「(原音再生の)忠実度」) / SACDs give astonishingly lifelike sound.

りんじん 隣人 one's **(next-door) neighbor** (🔴 同じ並びのすぐ隣であることをはっきりさせるためには next-door neighbor という) ▶彼は良い隣人です He is a good *neighbor*. ‖ 皆さまの良き隣人になれるよう努めます I'll try my best to be a good *neighbor*. ‖ その大邸宅に誰が住んでいるのか隣人たちも知らない Not even *people in the neighborhood* know who lives in the mansion.

リンス (a) **hair conditioner**(➤ rinse は毛染めに用いる「カラーリンス」の意. また主に動詞で「すすぐ」) ▶髪をリンスする *use conditioner* on one's hair *and rinse* it.

1**りんせき 臨席** ▶卒業式は市長の臨席を仰いで厳かに挙行された The commencement exercises were held solemnly with the mayor *in attendance*.

2**りんせき 隣席** ▶私の隣席の人 a person *sitting next to me*.

りんせつ 隣接する **adjoin** +㊐; **border** +㊐ (➤ 地理的境界を強調する) ▶隣接する国々 *neighboring* [*adjoining*] countries(➤ 後者のほうが接触度が高い) ‖ カナダとアメリカ合衆国は隣接している Canada *adjoins* [*borders* (*on*)] the U.S.

▶私の家は青山墓地に隣接している My house *is next to* Aoyama Cemetery.

リンチ ▶新入部員にリンチを加える *beat up* freshmen members.

> **危ないカタカナ語✹ リンチ**
> **1** 「リンチ」は英語の lynch からきているが, この語は法的手続きによらずに集団で裁いて, 絞首刑などにして殺すことを意味する.
> **2** 日本語でいう「リンチ」は単に暴力的制裁を加えることなので, lynch でなく beat up などの語を用いて表すのがよい.

りんてんき 輪転機 a **rotary press.**

1**りんどう 林道** a **path through a forest**; a **logging road** (木材搬出用の).

2**りんどう 竜胆**《植物》a **gentian** /dʒénʃən/.

りんどく 輪読 ▶数人で集まって『不思議の国のアリス』を輪読した Some of us got together to *take turns reading and discussing* "Alice in Wonderland."

りんね 輪廻 **samsara**(➤ 仏教用語); **the cycle of reincarnation**

‖輪廻転生 transmigration.

リンネル **linen** /línɪn/

‖リンネル製品 linens.

リンパ《生理学》**lymph** /lɪmf/ (液) ▶リンパ節 [腺] が腫れた My *lymph nodes* [*glands*] have swollen up. / I have swollen *lymph nodes* [*glands*].

‖リンパ液 lymph [lymphatic] fluid ‖ リンパ節 a lymph node.

りんばん 輪番で **in rotation** ▶英語科の主任には輪番でなる The English teachers *rotate* as [*take turns* being] chairperson of the English Department.

りんびょう 淋病《医学》**gonorrhea** /gɑ̀ːnəríːə/ ▶りん病にかかる get [contract / catch] *gonorrhea*.

りんぶ 輪舞 a **round dance** 一㊀ **輪舞する** **dance in a circle.**

りんり 倫理 **ethics** /éθɪks/; **morals** (道徳) 一㊁ **倫理の** **ethical** ▶医師の倫理 medical *ethics* ‖ 倫理感のない人 a person with no *sense of ethics* [*morality*] ‖ 贈収賄は政治倫理にもとる Bribery is against *political ethics*.

‖倫理学 ethics.

りんりつ 林立 ▶林立するテレビアンテナ *a forest of* TV antennas ‖ 官庁地区には高層ビルが林立していた The civic center *was crowded with* towering buildings.

1**りんりん 凛々** ▶勇気りんりんたる少年 a *brave*, *high-spirited* boy.

2**りんりん** ▶鈴虫がリンリン鳴いている The crickets are chirping *with a gentle ringing sound*.

る・ル

ルアー a **lure**; **artificial bait**（疑似餌）▶ルアーで釣る fish with *a lure*.
‖**ルアーフィッシング** lure fishing.

1**るい 類** a **kind**, a **sort**（種類）; a **parallel**（匹敵するもの）▶私は肉類は好みません I don't like meat.（「肉を好まない」と考える）‖彼の新しい考えは類のないものだ His new concept has no *parallel*. ／His new concept is without (a) *parallel*. ‖1917年のロシア革命は史上類のない（＝前例のない）出来事であった The Russian Revolution in 1917 was an *unprecedented* event in history. ‖グランドキャニオンのような自然の壮観はほかに類がない *There is no* natural spectacle that *can rival* [that *is as magnificent as*] the Grand Canyon. ／The Grand Canyon is a natural spectacle of *unparalleled* grandeur. → 種類.
ことわざ 類は友を呼ぶ Birds of a feather flock together.（➤「同じ羽を持った鳥は一つ所に集まる」の意）.

2**るい 塁**《野球》a **base** ▶一塁 first *base* ‖塁に出る get on *base* ／reach *first base* ‖走者が2人塁に出ている Two runners *are on base*.
☛ 満塁, 塁審（→見出語）

るいかん 涙管《解剖学》a **tear duct**.

るいぎご 類義語 a **synonym** /sínənɪm/ ▶wealthy は rich の類義語である 'Wealthy' is *a synonym* for 'rich.' ／Wealthy is *synonymous* with rich.

1**るいけい 類型** a **type** ▶発掘された化石は5つの類型に分けられる The excavated fossils can be divided into five *types*.

2**るいけい 累計 the sum** [**cumulative**] **total** ▶累計すると費用は100万円になる The expenses *total* [*amount to* ／*add up to*] one million yen.

るいご 類語 a **synonym** /sínənɪm/
‖**類語辞典** a thesaurus /θɪsɔ́:rəs/.

るいじ 類似 similarity（さまざまな点で性質が）; **resemblance**（格好・顔形の）; an **analogy**（性質・機能の）; a **parallel**（傾向・方向の）; (an) **affinity**（構造, デザインの）
一動 **類似する resemble** ＋目 一形 **類似の similar** ▶歴史上の類似 *a parallel* in history ／a historical *parallel* ‖ブランドものバッグに類似したバッグがたくさん出回っている There are a lot of bags on the market that *are similar to* designer [brand-name] bags.
▶（日本の）かまくらと（イヌイットの）イグルーは形が類似している *Kamakura* and igloos *resemble* each other in shape. ／*Kamakura* and igloos *are similar* [*alike*] in shape. ‖数学と音楽の類似性を指摘する人もいる Some people *draw parallels between* mathematics *and* music.
▶教授はコンピュータのデータ蓄積と脳の記憶蓄積との類似性を指摘した The professor drew *an analogy* between data storage in a computer and memory storage in the brain. ‖両者には類似点が多い There is a great *similarity* between the two. ／The two have many *points in common*.（➤ in common は「共通の」）‖類似品（＝まがい物）にご注意ください Beware of *imitations* [*fakes*].

ルイジアナ Louisiana /luì:ziǽnə/（アメリカ南部の州; 略 LA, La.）.

るいしょ 類書 ▶パソコンの活用法に関する類書は多い There are many *similar books* on how to use PCs.

るいしょう 類焼 ▶彼の家は隣の家の火事で類焼した His house *caught fire from* his neighbor's house as it burned down.
▶3年前の火災では幸いにもわが家は類焼を免れた Fortunately, our house *escaped the fire* three years ago.

るいじょう 累乗《数学》a **power**
‖**累乗根** a (power) root.

るいしん 塁審《野球》a **base umpire** /ʌ́mpaɪəʳ/ ▶三塁塁審 a third *base umpire*.

るいじんえん 類人猿《動物学》an **anthropoid** /ǽnθrəpɔɪd/ (**ape**) ▶ゴリラやチンパンジーやオランウータンは類人猿だ Gorillas, chimpanzees, and orangutans are *anthropoids*.

るいしんかぜい 累進課税《経済学》**progressive** [**graduated**] **taxation**.

るいすい 類推 analogical inference, an **analogy** /ənǽlədʒi/ 一動（…と）**類推する judge**《that》（判断する）; **infer**《that》（事実から推測する）▶前回の選挙の結果から類推すると今回も投票率は50パーセントくらいだろう *Judging* [*Inferring*] *from* the previous election result(s), the voter turnout this time should be about 50 percent.

るいする 類する ▶物理, 化学, その他それに類する科目 physics, chemistry, and *similar* subjects.

るいせき 累積 accumulation 一動 **累積する accumulate** 一形 **累積の cumulative** /kjú:mjələṭɪv/ ▶100億円の累積赤字 *a cumulative deficit* of 10 billion yen.

るいせん 涙腺《解剖学》a **tear** [**lacrimal**] **gland** ▶涙腺が緩む *get* [*become*] *tearful*.

るいれい 類例 a **similar example**; a **parallel**（匹敵するもの）▶類例を挙げてみましょう Let me give you *a similar example*.
▶そのような事件は歴史上に類例がない Such an incident has no *parallel* in history.

ルー (a) **roux** /ru:/（複 **roux** /ru:z/）▶カレーのルー a curry *roux* ／a curry *block*.

ルーキー a **rookie** /róki/（新人）.

ルーズ sloppy（ずさんな）; **careless**（不注意な）▶ルーズな仕事 a *sloppy* [*shoddy* ／*slovenly*] job ‖経営のルーズな病院 a *sloppily*-run hospital ‖彼は時間にルーズだ He's very *careless* about keeping appointments.
‖**ルーズソックス** large baggy socks (that go up to the knee)（➤ loose socks は boot socks とも呼ばれ, 登山靴を履くときに着用するものを指す）.

危ないカタカナ語✸ルーズ
1「ルーズ」は英語の loose からきているが, 英語の発音は /lu:s/ で語尾が濁らないことに注意.
2 loose は「緩い, たるんだ」という意味だが, 主に衣類などに関していう. 道徳的に「だらしない」という意味もあるが，今では古めかしい用法.
3「きちょうめんでない」の意味の「ルーズ」には sloppy,「怠慢な」という意味なら negligent,「不注意な」なら careless,「散らかしっぱなしの」なら untidy を用いる. また「時間にルーズな」は not (very) punctual,「男女関係がルーズな」は promiscuous などという.

ルーズリーフ a **loose-leaf** /lù:slí:f/ **notebook**(ノート)；**loose-leaf paper**(紙).

ルーツ one's **roots**(先祖)；an **origin**(起源) ▶家のルーツを求める search for one's family *roots* ‖ ようかんのルーツは中国にある(＝中国起源だ) *Yokan* (sweet bean jelly) *originated in* China.

[1]ルート《道筋》a **route**, a **way**；a **channel**(物流の) ▶脱出[避難]ルート an escape [an evacuation] *route* ‖ 別ルートで行こう Let's take another *route*. ‖ 名古屋から金沢へ行くにはいくつかのルートがある There are several *routes* [*ways*] to go from Nagoya to Kanazawa.
▶彼らは拳銃を密輸ルートを通して手に入れた They got their guns through illegal *channels*. ／They smuggled in their guns. (➤ smuggle は「密輸する」).

[2]ルート《平方根》a **square root** ▶ルート 3 は1.732である The *square root* of 3 is 1.732.

ループ a **loop**(輪) ‖ **ループタイ** a bolo tie.

ルーブル **1**【ロシアの貨幣単位】a **r(o)uble** (➤《米》では ruble のつづりがふつう).
2【パリの美術館】**the Louvre**.

ルーペ a **magnifying glass**, a **loupe** /lu:p/ 《参考》「ルーペ」はドイツ語の *Lupe*(拡大鏡)から.

ルーマニア **Romania**(ヨーロッパ南東部の国)
‖ **ルーマニア語** Romanian ‖ **ルーマニア人** a Romanian.

ルーム a **room** ▶ルームサービスをお願いします. こちらは123号室です *Room service*, please. [Could you give me *room service*, please ?] This is Room 123.
‖ **ルームクーラー** an air conditioner ‖ **ルームメート** a roommate ‖ **ルームランナー** a treadmill.

ルーメン《光学》a **lumen**(光束の単位；複数形は lumens または lumina).

ルール a **rule**；**the ground rules** (当事者が決めた決まり) ▶交通ルールを守ろう Let's observe the *traffic rules*. ‖ 我々漁師の間にもいくつかのルールがある We fishermen observe a certain number of *ground rules*.
▶サッカーではゴールキーパー以外の選手がボールに手を触れるのはルール違反だ It is *against the rules* for any player except the goalkeeper to handle the ball in soccer.

ルーレット **roulette** /rulét/ ▶ルーレットをする play *roulette*.

ルクス《光学》a **lux** /lʌks/ (照度の単位；複数形も lux).

ルクセンブルク **Luxembourg**(ベルギーの東隣の大公国).

るけい 流刑 **exile** ▶流刑に処する *send* someone *into exile*.
‖ **流刑地** a penal colony [settlement].

るす 留守 一動 **留守をする be not (at) home** (家に居ない)；**be away** (離れている)；**be out** (外出している) ▶その日私は家を留守にしていました I *wasn't home* on that day. ／I *wasn't at home* that day. ‖ しばらく旅行で留守にしますのでよろしくお願いします I'm going to *be away* on a trip for a while. Please take care of things while I'm away.
▶母は買い物に出かけて留守です My mother *is out* shopping.
▶ 対話「ジミーさんはご在宅ですか」「ただいま留守をしております」"Is Jimmy home ?" "No, he *is out* now."
‖ すぐ帰って来るから，2 人で仲よくお留守番しててね Both of you, be good and *stay home*. I'll be right back.
▶私が会社に行っている間，祖母が留守番をしていてくれます My grandmother *looks after things at home* while I'm at work.
▶《比喩的》彼女，手は動いているが心はお留守のようだ Although her hands are moving, her mind seems *far away*.
▶彼女に電話して留守番電話に用件を残した I called her and left my message on the *answering machine*. 《参考》留守番電話の応答のメッセージは，例えば，I'm sorry (that) I can't come to the phone right now, but if you leave a message at the sound of the beep, I'll return your call as soon as possible. または，We're unable to come to the phone right now. If you wish to leave a message, please record after the beep. のようにする.
‖ **留守録** time-shift recording, time-shifting (テレビ番組の).

ルックス **looks** (美貌) ▶ルックスのいい人 a *good-looking* person ／a looker.

るつぼ 坩堝 a **melting pot** ▶アメリカは人種(と文化)のるつぼだ America is *a melting pot* of ethnic groups (and cultures). ‖《慣用表現》球場は興奮のるつぼと化した The ballpark turned into *a scene of feverish excitement*.

るてん 流転 ▶流転の人生を送る lead *a rootless life*.

ルネサンス **the Renaissance** /rènəsá:ns/ ▶ルネサンスの芸術[画家] *Renaissance* art [painters] ‖ ダ・ビンチはイタリア・ルネサンス期の巨人だ Da Vinci is a giant of *the Italian Renaissance*.

ルビ kana that show the readings of kanji (➤ 説明的な訳)；***furigana***.

ルビー (a) **ruby** /rú:bi/ ▶ルビーは 7 月の誕生石だ *The ruby* is [*Rubies* are] the birthstone for July.

るふ 流布 **circulation** 一動 **流布する circulate, spread** ▶この話は当地に広く流布している This story *has spread* [*has circulated*] throughout our region.

ルポ **reportage** /rɪpɔ́:ʳtɪdʒ, rèpɔ:ʳtá:ʒ/ (ルポの手法；フランス語から)；a **report** (記事) 一動 **ルポする report** ▶新宿歌舞伎町のルポ *a report* on Kabukicho in Shinjuku ‖ 本社特派員がテヘランの現状についてルポします Our correspondent will *report* on the present situation in Teheran.
‖ **ルポライター** a reporter.

るりいろ 瑠璃色 **azure** /ǽʒəʳ/ (**blue**) (➤ 日常的には sky blue がふつう).

るる 縷々 **at great length**；**in great detail** ▶るる説明する explain *at great length* [*in great detail*].

るろう 流浪 **wandering** 一動 **流浪する wander** ▶その俳人は妻子を捨てて流浪の旅に出た The haiku poet abandoned his wife and children and embarked on *a life of wandering*.

ルンバ a **rumba** /rʌ́mbə/ ▶ルンバを踊る dance the *rumba*.

るんるん ▶るんるん気分で帰って来たら泥棒に入られていた I came home *in a happy mood* only to find that my house had been broken into.

る

れ・レ

レア rare（肉が生焼けの）▶ 対話「ステーキの焼き具合はどうなさいますか」「レアにしてください」"How would you like your steak?" "*Rare*, please."
‖**レアアース**《化学》(a) rare earth ‖**レアメタル**《化学》a rare metal ‖**レアもの** a rare item, a rarity.

¹**れい** 礼

訳語メニュー
感謝 →thanks **1**
謝礼 →reward **1**
おじぎ →bow **2**
礼儀 →politeness **3**

1【感謝, 謝礼】**thanks**; a **reward**（謝礼金）▶ジョージは私に贈り物の礼を言った George *thanked* me for the gift. ‖私が席を譲ってあげるとおばあさんは丁寧に礼を言って座った The elderly woman expressed her *thanks* politely and sat down when I offered her my seat. ‖犬を見つけてくださった方にはお礼を差し上げます We offer *a reward* to the person who finds our dog. ‖広瀬さんに講演のお礼として5万円差し上げた We presented 50,000 yen to Mr. Hirose as *an honorarium* for his lecture.（➤ honorarium /ɑ̀:nəréəriəm/ は「謝礼金」の意の堅い語）. →お礼.

✉ **息子にホームステイの機会をお与えいただき, お礼のことばもありません** *I don't know how to thank you* for giving my son an opportunity to stay with your family.

2【おじぎ】a **bow** /baʊ/ 一動 **礼をする bow** ▶起立, 礼! Stand up. *Bow!*（➤英米では見られない慣習）‖（軍隊で）気をつけ, 礼! Attention! *Salute!*（➤ salute は「敬礼」）.

3【礼儀正しさ】**politeness** ▶来賓の方々に対して礼を失することのないように Don't *be impolite* to our honored guests.

²**れい** 例 **1**【実例】an **example**（代表的な例）; an **instance**（一例, 個別の例）▶一例を挙げる give *an example* [*an instance*] ‖例をいくつか挙げてみましょう Let me give (you) some *examples*. ‖この事件はコンピュータ犯罪の典型的な例だ This case is a typical *example* of a cybercrime.
▶では例に倣って自分で書いてみなさい Now *follow the example* and try to write something similar yourself.

2【先例】a **precedent** /présɪdənt/ ▶この種の問題が裁判で争われるケースは今まで例がない There is no *precedent* for this kind of case being tried in court. ‖この炭鉱爆発事故ではかつて例がないほどの犠牲者が出た The mine explosion claimed an *unprecedented* number of lives. ‖過去に例がない（ほどの）凶悪犯罪だ It is a crime of *unprecedented* cruelty.

3【事例】a **case** ▶同様の例 a similar *case* ‖こういう例はいくらでもある There are many similar *cases*.

4【いつもの例】▶例によって新郎新婦の友人たちの挨拶が長々と続いた *As is always the case*, the speeches by the friends of the bride and bridegroom dragged on.
▶例の喫茶店で6時に会おうね Meet me at the *usual* coffee shop at six. ‖（バーなどで）例のやつもらおうか Just give me *the usual*. ‖例月の会議を開く We meet *monthly*. ／We hold a *monthly* meeting. ‖例月どおり温泉へ行った I went to a hot spring *as I do every month*.

5【問題になっている】▶例の国会議員のことだけど… About *that* Diet member, …. ‖例の旅行の話だけど, きみは行けそう? Speaking of *that* trip we're planning, do you think you'll be able to come?

☛ 例になく（→見出語）

逆引き熟語 ○○例
慣例 a custom ／**好例** a good example ／**恒例** an established custom ／**実例** an example ／**事例** an example, a case ／**前[先]例** a precedent ／**代表例** a typical example ／**通例** a custom, a rule, a normal practice ／**特例** a special case, an exception ／**判例** a judicial precedent ／**用例** an example

³**れい** 零 (a) **zero** /zíəroʊ/, **nothing** ▶零度 *zero* degrees（➤ 0 のあとの数えられる名詞は通例複数形）‖0.12 *zero* point one two（➤ zero は言わなくてもよい）／point twelve ‖外の気温は零度以下になっているに違いない The temperature outside must be *below zero* (*degrees*). ‖うちの電話番号は302-0070です Our phone number is three-*o*-two *double-o*-seven-*o*.（➤電話番号の0はふつう /oʊ/ と読む）‖我々のチームは5対0で負けた Our team lost the game by five to *zero* [*nothing*].
‖**零歳児** a baby [an infant] less than a year old.

☛ 零時, 零点（→見出語）

⁴**れい** 霊 **the spirit, the soul**（➤後者のほうが宗教的意味合いが強く,「霊魂」に相当）→霊魂
▶この記念碑は国に殉じた人々の霊を祭ったものです This monument is dedicated to *the spirits* [*memory*] of those who gave their lives for their country.
‖**地縛霊** a soul tied to a specific piece of land, an earthbound soul [entity] ‖**背後霊** a guardian spirit behind a person.

レイ a **lei** /leɪ/ ▶少女がぼくの首にレイを掛けてくれた A girl hung *a lei* around my neck.

レイアウト a **layout** ▶部屋のレイアウトを考える think of *a layout* for the room.

れいあんしつ 霊安室 a **morgue**（死体安置所）; a **mortuary (viewing room)**, a **(hospital) chapel of rest**（➤特に病院のものをいう場合は前に hospital をつけるとよい. また厳密に宗教と関係なくても chapel を使える）.

れいえん 霊園 a **cemetery** /sémәteri/ ▶祖父は多磨霊園に葬られている My grandfather is buried in Tama *Cemetery*.

レイオフ a **layoff** 一動 **レイオフする lay off** ▶不景気のため工場労働者の大量レイオフが行われた Many fac-

れ

tory workers *were laid off* due to the recession. ／The recession caused mass *layoffs* of factory workers.

1**れいか 零下** ▶気温が零下になった The temperature has dropped *below zero* [*below the freezing point* ／*below freezing*]. ‖ 今零下20度だ It's 20 degrees *below zero*.

2**れいか 冷夏** a **cool summer** ▶ことしは冷夏になりそうだ It seems as if we are going to have *a cool summer* this year.

れいかい 例会 a **regular meeting** ▶毎月の例会はふつう第２水曜日に開かれます Our *monthly meeting* is usually held on the second Wednesday of every month.

1**れいがい 例外** an **exception** 一形 **例外の exceptional**
▶門限は11時. 例外は認めません The curfew is 11 p.m., and we allow no *exceptions*. ／The curfew is 11 p.m. with no *exceptions*. ‖ 今回のみ例外としよう I'll *make an exception* this once. ‖ ことしの暑さは例外だ(＝例外的に暑い) It is *exceptionally* hot this summer.

2**れいがい 冷害** **cold-weather damage (to crops), damage (to crops) from cold weather**
▶多くの農家で作物が冷害を被った Many farmers suffered *damage to their crops from* the *cold weather*.

れいかん 霊感 (an) **inspiration** ▶霊感がひらめいた I had a sudden *inspiration*. ‖ 古代の日本人は自然から宗教的な霊感を受けることがよくあった The ancient Japanese *were* often religiously *inspired* by nature.
‖霊感商法 fraudulent sales of spiritual charms.

れいき 冷気 a [**the**] **chill** ▶ほてった頰に夜の冷気が心地よかった The *cool night air* felt refreshing on my glowing cheeks.

れいぎ 礼儀 **manners, etiquette** (礼儀作法) ; **courtesy** /kə́ːʳṭəsi/ (礼儀正しさ；丁寧であるだけでなく，相手に対して思いやりがあることを強調する) ▶父は礼儀にうるさい My father is fussy about *manners* [*etiquette*]. ‖ 人に収入額を聞くのは礼儀に反する(＝失礼だ) It is *impolite* to ask other people how much they earn.
▶彼女は礼儀正しい She *has good manners*. ／She is *well-mannered*. ／She is *polite*. ‖ 礼儀正しい青年は見ていて気持ちがいい A *polite* young man is pleasant to see.
▶お客さまの前では礼儀正しくしなさい *Behave properly* in front of our guests.
ことわざ 親しき仲にも礼儀あり Politeness [Courtesy] is important, even between friends. ／Good fences make good neighbors. (➤ 後者は「しっかりした垣根が良き隣人を作る」から「プライバシーは大切にしなさい」の意の英米のことわざ).

れいきゃく 冷却 **cooling** 一動 **冷却する cool** ＋目
▶上田夫人は夫との間にしばらく冷却期間が必要だ Mrs. Ueda and her husband need *a cooling-off period*. ‖冷却装置 a cooling apparatus /æpəræ̀ṭəs/, a cooler.

れいきゅうしゃ 霊柩車 a **hearse** /həːʳs/, a **funeral car**.

れいきん 礼金 ***reikin*, thank-you money**

> 《解説》(1)借家人が家主に礼金を払う習慣は英米では一般的ではないので，「礼金」は日本語のまま *reikin* とするか，thank-you money とする. 説明的には nonrefundable money given to a landlord [landlady] upon renting a house or an apartment (家やアパートを借りるときに家主に支払う戻って来ないお金) のようにいえばよい.
> (2)「権利金」「保証金」に相当する言い方に key money がある. これは家やアパートを借りる際に「key (鍵)」を手渡されることからきている.
> (3)一般に「謝礼」の意では reward,「(習い事の師匠や専門職者に対する)謝礼金」は fee,「(講演者などへの) 謝礼金」は honorarium /ɑ̀ːnəréəriəm/ を用いる.

れいぐう 冷遇 **cold treatment** (冷たい扱い) ; **inhospitality** (もてなしの悪さ) 一動 **冷遇する treat coldly** [**unfavorably**]
▶どういう訳か彼らはそのホテルで冷遇された For some reason, they were given rather *cold treatment* [*a cold reception*] at the hotel. ‖ その会社では年配の社員は冷遇される傾向がある In that company, elderly employees tend to *be treated coldly* [*unfavorably*].

れいけつ 冷血の **cold-blooded** (体温の低い；冷酷な) ; **cold-hearted** (薄情な) ▶あんな冷血漢は見たことがない I've never seen such *a cold-hearted* [*heartless*] *person*.
‖冷血動物 a cold-blooded animal.

れいげん 霊験 ▶ (熊本の)お池さんの水は霊験あらたかだそうだ The water of "Oikesan" spring is said to *have special curative* [*beneficial*] *properties*.

れいこう 励行 ▶私は時間厳守を励行しています I *always make an effort to* be punctual [*make a point of* being punctual].

れいこく 冷酷な **cruel, heartless, cold-blooded**
▶トンボのしっぽをちょん切るなんて，どうしてきみはそんな冷酷なことができるんだい？ How can you do such a *cruel* thing as to cut off a dragonfly's tail ? ‖ 少し冷酷かもしれないが，これもきみのためを思えばこそだ You may think I'm being a little too *cruel* to you, but it's for your own good.

れいこん 霊魂 **the soul, the spirit** ▶きみは霊魂の不滅を信じますか Do you believe in the immortality of *the soul* ?

れいさい 零細な **small** (小さい) ; **small-scale** (小規模の) ▶零細企業 a *small-scale* business [enterprise] ／a *small* business ‖ 私ら零細農家にどうしてそんな重税をかけるのか Why do they impose such a heavy tax on *small farmers* like us ? ‖ 彼は零細な資金で商売を始めた He started his business *with little capital* [*on a shoestring*].

1**れいじ 例示** an **illustration** (説明の補助となる例) ; an **example** (典型例) ▶このマニュアルはよくあるエラーとその対処法が例示されているのでわかりやすい This manual is easy to understand because it *gives examples* of common errors and how to correct them.

2**れいじ 零時** **(twelve o'clock) midnight** (午前０時) ; **twelve noon** (正午) ▶隣のご主人は帰宅がいつも零時過ぎだ The man next door always comes home *past midnight*.

1**れいしょう 冷笑** a **cold smile**, a **sneer** 一動 (…を)**冷笑する sneer** 《at》, **scoff** 《at》 (➤ 前者のほうがばかにする感じがより強い) →笑う
▶彼女は口元に冷笑を浮かべて求婚者を見た She looked at her suitor with *a cold smile* on her lips.
▶彼はあらゆる権威を冷笑する He *sneers* [*scoffs*] *at*

all authority.

[2]**れいしょう 例証** illustration **一動 例証する** illustrate /íləstreɪt/ +目, exemplify +目 ▶この説はいくつかの事実によって**例証する**ことができます I can *illustrate* this theory with several facts.

[1]**れいじょう 令嬢** a daughter ▶あの方は野村氏の(ご)**令嬢**です She is Mr. Nomura's *daughter*. ‖ あちらはどなたの(ご)**令嬢**ですか Who is that *young lady*? ／Whose *daughter* is she?

[2]**れいじょう 礼状** a letter of thanks, 《インフォーマル》a thank-you letter [note] ▶彼女が贈り物をしてくれたので**礼状**を出した I sent her *a letter of thanks* for the present she had sent me. ／I sent her a letter thanking her for the present.

[3]**れいじょう 令状** a warrant ▶容疑者宅から証拠品が出てきたので警察は**逮捕令状**を請求した The police asked for *an arrest warrant* after they found evidence during a search of the suspect's home.
‖**家宅捜索令状** a search warrant.

れいすい 冷水 cold water ▶**冷水**摩擦をする rub oneself with a cold wet towel.

[1]**れいせい 冷静** calmness /kɑ́ːmnəs/ **一形 冷静な** cool; calm(穏やかな) ▶**冷静**を装ってはいたが彼の足は震えていた He pretended to keep *cool* [*calm*], but his legs were trembling. ‖ 突然の火事に母は日頃の**冷静**さを失った My mother lost her usual *calm*(*ness*) when a fire broke out suddenly. ‖ **冷静**になれ *Calm down*. ／*Pull yourself together*.

[2]**れいせい 冷製** ▶**冷製**パスタ *cold* [*chilled*] pasta.

れいせつ 礼節 decorum /dɪkɔ́ːrəm/, good [proper] manners ▶**礼節**を重んじる value *decorum*.
ことわざ 衣食足りて**礼節**を知る Well-fed, well-bred.

れいせん 冷戦 a cold war(➤「東西の冷戦」はしばしば the Cold War) ▶両国[父と母]は**冷戦**状態にある The two countries [My parents] are in a state of *cold war*.

れいぜん 霊前 ▶**霊前**に花を供える offer flowers *to the spirit of a deceased person*.

れいそう 礼装 full [formal] attire(正装) ▶彼は和服の**礼装**で結婚式に来た He came to the wedding in *formal* Japanese *attire*.

れいぞう 冷蔵 cold storage /stɔ́ːrɪdʒ/ **一動 冷蔵する** refrigerate /rɪfrídʒəreɪt/ +目 ▶そのケーキは**冷蔵**しておいてください Please *refrigerate* the cake. ‖《標示》要**冷蔵** Keep refrigerated.
‖**冷蔵庫** a refrigerator, 《インフォーマル》a fridge.

れいぞく 隷属 subordination(従属); enslavement, bondage(奴隷状態) ▶**隷属**的な態度 a *servile* attitude.

れいだい 例題 a sample problem; an exercise(練習問題) ▶**例題**を解く solve the *sample* [*example*] *problems*.

れいたいさい 例大祭 an annual festival (of a Shinto shrine).

れいたん 冷淡な cold《to》(冷たい); cool《to》(冷ややかな); unfriendly《to》(非友好的な); indifferent《to》(無関心な) ▶訪問客に**冷淡**な態度をとる give a visitor a *cool* reception ‖ 真紀子は最近ぼくに**冷淡**だ Makiko has been *cold* [*unfriendly*] to me recently. ‖ ボランティア活動に**冷淡**な人もいる Some people are *indifferent* to [*apathetic* toward] volunteer activities. (➤ apathetic /æ̀pəθétɪk/ は「無感動な」) ‖ 外国人労働者の中には日本の雇用主から**冷淡**な扱いを受けた人たちもいる Some of the foreign laborers *were coldly treated* by their Japanese employers.

れいだんぼう 冷暖房 air conditioning and heating ▶**冷暖房**の無い教室 a classroom without *air conditioning or heating*.

れいちょうるい 霊長類《動物学》a primate /práɪmeɪt/(1種); the primates(総称).

れいてつ 冷徹な cool-headed.

れいてん 零点 (a) zero /zíəroʊ/, 《米・インフォーマル》a goose egg ▶数学で**零点**を取った I got (*a*) *zero* [*a goose egg*] in math. ‖ 6回を終わって両チームとも**零点**だ At the bottom of the sixth, neither team had chalked up any runs. (➤ chalk up は「(得点を)あげる」の意のインフォーマルな言い方).

れいとう 冷凍 freezing, refrigeration **一動 冷凍する** freeze +目, refrigerate /rɪfrídʒəreɪt/ +目 ▶**冷凍**保存する *freeze* ／*preserve by freezing* ‖ 私は肉を買ってその半分を**冷凍**にした I bought some meat and *froze* half of it. (➤ froze は freeze の過去形).
‖**冷凍魚** a frozen fish ‖**冷凍庫** a freezer ‖**冷凍車** a refrigerator car ‖**冷凍食品** frozen food.

れいになく 例になく exceptionally ▶12月だというのに**例になく**暖かい日が続いている We have had a long spell of *exceptionally* warm days [an *exceptionally* long warm spell] this December.

れいねん 例年 an average year ▶ことしの米の収穫は**例年**より多い The rice crop this year is better than in *an average year*. ‖ この夏は**例年**(＝ふだん)より涼しい We've been having a cooler summer this year *than usual*. ‖ ことしの夏は**例年**になく涼しい It has been *unusually* cool this summer. ‖ **例年**(＝毎年)今頃サケが川を上ってくる Salmon come upstream about this time *every year*.

れいのう 霊能 psychic /sáɪkɪk/ ability
‖**霊能者[師]** a psychic; a medium(霊媒).

[1]**れいはい 礼拝** worship /wə́ːrʃɪp/(拝むこと); a church [worship] service(教会での) ▶朝[夕べ]の**礼拝**を行う hold a morning [an evening] *service*.
‖**礼拝堂** a chapel /tʃǽpəl/.

[2]**れいはい 零敗する** fail to score; be shut out.

れいばい 霊媒(師) a (spiritualistic) medium.

れいびょう 霊廟 a mausoleum /mɔ̀ːsəlíːəm/.

レイプ (a) rape **一動 レイプする** rape +目 ▶**レイプ**の被害者 *a rape victim* ‖ 女子大生が夜帰宅途中に**レイプ**された A female college student *was raped* on her way home at night.
‖**レイプ犯** a rapist.

れいふく 礼服 formal wear [attire／dress] ▶参列者は**礼服**着用のこと All the attendants are required to *dress formally*.

れいぶん 例文 an example (sentence), an illustrative sentence ▶instrumental という語の使い方を**例文**で確かめなさい Check the use of the word 'instrumental' in the *example* [*illustrative*] *sentences*.

れいほう 礼砲 a gun salute ▶21発の**礼砲**を放つ fire a *21-gun salute*.

れいぼう 冷房 air conditioning; an air conditioner(装置) ▶この電車は**冷房**が効き過ぎている The *air conditioning* in this train is (on) too strong. ‖ 一日中**冷房**の効いた部屋に居るのは健康によくない It is not good for the health to stay in an *air-conditioned* room all day long. ‖ この電車は**冷房**が

ついていない This train isn't *air-conditioned.*
‖冷房車 an air-conditioned car ‖冷房装置 air-conditioning(設備); an air conditioner(器具).

1れいめい 令名 renown ▶令名の高い学者 a *renowned* scholar.

2れいめい 黎明 the dawn ▶文明の黎明期 *the dawn* of civilization.

れいらく 零落 ▶あの名家はすっかり零落してしまった That famous family *has* really *come down in the world.*

れいれいしい 麗々しい ▶麗々しいスピーチ a *flowery* speech.

レインコート a raincoat,《米また》a slicker,《英また》a mackintosh /mǽkɪntɑːʃ/.

レインシューズ rain shoes, rain boots; overshoes, rubbers(靴の上から履くもの).

レーサー a racer, a racing driver.

レーザー a laser
‖レーザー光線 a laser beam ‖レーザー治療 (a) laser treatment ‖レーザープリンター a laser printer.

レーシック Lasik ▶財前医師はこれまで2000人以上にレーシック手術を行っている Dr. Zaizen has conducted *Lasik* surgery on more than 2,000 people.

レーシングカー a racing car,《米また》a race car.

1レース《競走》a race ▶レースに勝つ[負ける] win [lose] *a race.*
‖自動車レース an auto(mobile)[《英》a motor] race ‖ペナントレース the pennant race ‖ボートレース a boat race, a regatta /rɪgǽṭə/ ‖ヨットレース a yacht race.

2レース《飾り》lace ▶レースのカーテン a *lace* curtain ‖彼女のドレスにはレースの縁飾りがついている Her dress is trimmed with *lace.*
‖レース編み tatting.

レーズン a raisin(干しブドウ) ▶レーズン入りのアイスクリーム (an) ice cream with *raisins* in it.
‖レーズンブレッド raisin bread.

レーダー (a) radar /réɪdɑːʳ/
▶雨雲の分布をレーダーで観測する observe the distribution of rain clouds *by radar* ‖国籍不明の航空機がレーダー網に映った An aircraft of unknown nationality was detected on *a radar screen* [*fence*].
‖レーダーシステム a radar system.

レート a rate ‖為替レート the exchange rate, the rate of exchange.

レーヨン rayon.

レール a rail ▶暑さのためにレールが曲がった The heat warped the *rails.*
▶《比喩的》その計画実現へのレールを敷いたのは前内閣であった The former cabinet *paved the way for* the realization of the project.
‖カーテンレール a curtain rail, a curtain rod.

レーン a lane(車線・ボウリングの) ▶バスレーン a bus *lane.*

レーンジャー a ranger(森林監視員, 自然観察指導員).

レオタード a leotard /líːətɑːʳd/.

レガッタ a regatta /rɪgǽṭə/, a boat race ▶きのう隅田川で早慶レガッタが催された The *regatta* between Waseda University and Keio University was held on the Sumida River yesterday.

-れき -歴 ▶彼はテニス歴20年のベテランだ He is an expert tennis player with twenty years' *experience.* ‖私は運転歴15年です I've been driving for fifteen years. ‖吉田さんには2回の離婚歴がある Mr. Yoshida has had two divorces. / Mr. Yoshida has been divorced twice.

1れきし 歴史 (a) history 一形 歴史上の historical; 歴史的な historic(➤ historic は「歴史的に重要な, 由緒のある」の意) ▶世界の歴史 world *history* / the *history* of the world ‖歴史上の人物 a *historical* figure [personage] ‖歴史的に有名な場所 a *historic* spot ‖歴史的事件 a *historic* [*historical*] event ‖これは歴史的な勝利だ This is a *historic* victory.
▶エジプトは歴史の古い国だ Egypt has a long *history.* ‖それぞれの家族にはそれぞれの歴史がある Each family has its own *history.*
▶東京駅は約100年の歴史がある Tokyo Station has *a history* of about one hundred years. ‖人類の歴史はせいぜい数百万年だが, 魚には4億年の歴史がある Human beings have only been around a few million years or so, but fish have existed for some 400 million years. ‖この寺は8世紀に歴史を遡る This temple *dates back* to the 8th century. (➤ date back は「時代を遡る」) ‖今回の大震災は歴史に残るだろう This great earthquake will *go down in history.*
✉ 私たちの学校はまだ歴史が浅いです Our school does not *have a long history.*
ことわざ 歴史は繰り返す History repeats itself.
‖歴史家 a historian /hɪstɔ́ːriən/ ‖歴史小説 a historical novel ‖歴史地区 a historic district ‖歴史的瞬間 a historic [historical] moment.

2れきし 轢死 ▶昨夜, 線路上で寝込んでいた酔っ払いがれき死した A drunk dozing off on the rails *was* (*run over and*) *killed by a train* last night.

れきせん 歴戦 ▶歴戦のつわもの[勇士] a veteran *of many battles.*

れきぜん 歴然たる obvious, clear(明白な) ▶彼が学生を扇動したことは歴然たる事実である It is an *obvious* [*undeniable*] fact that he incited the students. ‖前回のチャンピオンの優位は誰の目にも歴然としている It is *obvious* [*clear*] to everyone (who knows both boxers) that the defending champion has an edge.

れきだい 歴代 ▶歴代の社長の写真 the photographs of the *past* presidents ‖彼女の記録は歴代3位だ Her record is the third best *ever.* ‖彼は歴代ヘビー級チャンピオンの中でも最強だろう He is probably the most outstanding among all the heavyweight champions *in history.*

れきにん 歴任 ▶新大臣は政府の要職を歴任した The new Minister *has held* [*has filled*] *a succession of* important government posts.

れきねん 暦年 a calendar year.

れきほう 歴訪 ▶首相は秋に中東歴訪を控えている The Prime Minister is to make *a series* [*round*] *of official visits* to Middle East countries this fall.

レギュラー a regular(正選手, レギュラー出演者) ▶彼女はそのテレビ番組にレギュラーで出ている She appears as a *regular* (*guest*) on the TV program. ‖恵子と由美はレギュラーになれるように頑張った Keiko and Yumi tried hard to become *regulars* [*regular members*].
▶レギュラー満タンでお願いします Fill it [her] up with *regular,* please. ‖大抵の車はレギュラーガソリンで走る Most cars run on *regular gas.*

レギンス leggings /légɪŋz/.
レクイエム a requiem(鎮魂ミサ曲).
レクリエーション (a) recreation ▶野外のレクリエーション open-air *recreation* ‖ 私にとってスカイダイビングはとてもよいレクリエーションだ To me, skydiving is a great *pastime* [*form of recreation*].
‖**レクリエーション施設** recreational facilities.
レゲエ reggae /régeɪ/ (ジャマイカ発祥の音楽).
レコーダー a recorder ▶ＩＣレコーダー IC *recorder* (➤ integrated chip recorder のこと) ‖ タイムレコーダー a time *recorder* ‖ テープレコーダー a tape *recorder*.
レコーディング (a) recording ▶エリック・クラプトンは新曲のレコーディングをした Eric Clapton *made a recording* of [*recorded*] his new song.
レコード **1【音盤】** a record /rékəʳd/ ▶レコードを掛ける play *a record*.
‖**レコード会社** a record company ‖ **レコード針** a stylus ‖ **レコードプレーヤー** a record player.
2【記録】 a record ▶レコードを作る[破る] set [break] *a record* ‖ 彼女は自己のレコードを更新した She improved her *record*.
‖**レコードホルダー** a record holder.
1**レザー** 《革》 leather
‖**レザーコート** a leather coat ‖ **レザージャケット** a leather jacket.
2**レザー** 《かみそり》 a razor /réɪzəʳ/ ▶髪をレザーカットしてもらう *have* one's hair *razor-cut*.
‖**レザーカット** a razor (hair)cut.
レジ a checkout counter (スーパーなどの勘定台); a (cash) register /rédʒɪstəʳ/ (金銭登録機); a cashier /kæʃíəʳ/ (レジ係) ▶レジが混んでいる There are long lines at the *checkout counters*. ‖ 絵美はスーパーのレジをしている Emi is working as *a cashier* at a supermarket.
‖**レジ袋** a (supermarket) checkout bag.

> **危ないカタカナ語✹レジ**
> 「レジ」は英語の register からきているが，金銭登録機そのものは cash register という．それを扱う係の人は cashier または checker で，「レジ」の場所は checkout counter という．

レシート a receipt /rɪsíːt/ ▶どんな物でも買ったら必ずレシートをもらうようにしなさい Be sure and get *a receipt* for anything you buy. ‖ レシートをください I'd like *a receipt*, please.
レシーバー a receiver (受話器，受信機；レシーブする人).
レシーブ receiving 一動 **レシーブする** receive +㊐ ▶ボール[サーブ]をレシーブする *receive* a ball [serve].
レジスタンス resistance ▶パルチザンたちはドイツ軍に対して執ようなレジスタンスを行った The Partisans persistently *resisted* the German army.
レシピ a recipe /résəpi/ ▶レシピを見ながらシチューを作る make stew from *a recipe* [while looking at *a recipe*].
レジャー leisure /líːʒəʳ ‖ léʒə/ (余暇); recreation (気晴らし); amusement (楽しみ) ▶働き過ぎの日本人の中にはレジャー(＝暇な時間)の使い方がわからない人もいる Some Japanese workaholics don't know what to do with [how to spend] their *leisure time*.
▶時々私は大島までレジャーに出かける I occasionally go to Oshima for *recreation*. ‖ この夏200万人を超える日本人が海外でレジャー(＝休日)を楽しんだ More than two million Japanese enjoyed *vacations* overseas this summer. ‖ 当店では各種のレジャーウエアを取りそろえております We have [carry] all kinds of *leisure wear*.
‖**レジャー産業** the leisure industry ‖ **レジャーシート** a picnic blanket, an outdoor blanket ‖ **レジャーセンター** a recreation [an amusement] center, 《英》 a leisure centre ‖ **レジャーランド** a recreational area; an amusement park (遊園地).

> **危ないカタカナ語✹レジャー**
> 英語の leisure は「(仕事を離れた)自由時間，余暇」の意．日本語では余暇を利用しての遊びや楽しみのことも「レジャー」といっているが，英語の leisure にはこの意味はない．「遊び」の意味ならば recreation や amusement を使う必要がある．

レジュメ a résumé /rézəmeɪ/ (➤ フランス語から); a summary (要約，概要) ▶論文のレジュメを英語で書く write *a summary* of one's paper in English.
レスキュー rescue
‖**レスキュー隊** a rescue team [squad].
レストラン a restaurant /réstərənt/ ▶私たちはたまに近所のレストランで食事します We occasionally go out to [eat out at] a *restaurant* in our neighborhood.
レスビアン lesbianism /lézbiənìzəm/ (女性間の同性愛); a lesbian /lézbiən/ (同性愛の女性).
レスラー a wrestler
‖**プロレスラー** a pro wrestler.
レスリング wrestling ▶彼はレスリングの試合を見るのが好きだが，彼自身もレスリングが強い He likes watching *wrestling* matches, and he himself is a good wrestler.
レセプション a reception ▶新しい駐日アメリカ大使のためにレセプションが開かれた *A reception* was given [was held] in honor of the new American ambassador to Japan.
レター a letter ‖ **レターオープナー** a letter opener ‖ **レターヘッド** a letterhead.
レタス (a) lettuce /létɪs/ (➤ (1) 植物としてのレタスは Ⓒ 扱い，食品としては Ⓤ 扱い．(2) 日本でいうレタスは iceberg lettuce が近い) ▶レタス１個 a head of *lettuce*. ‖ **サニーレタス** Bibb lettuce.
レタリング lettering.

れつ 列 a line, a row

> **語法** (1)「列」は **line** でも **row** でも表せるが，「順番を待つ行列」の意味では line を用いる(《英》では queue /kjuː/ が一般的)．
> (2) **row** は「横の列」で，特に「(劇場などの)座席の横の列」の意味で用いることが多い．
>
> 
>

▶切符売り場の前に長い人の**列**ができた There was a long *line* [《英》 *queue*] of people in front of the ticket office.
▶若い男がバスを待つ人の**列に割り込んだ** A young man *cut into the line* [《英》 *jumped the queue*] of people waiting for a bus. (➤「列に割り込む人」を line [queue] jumper という).
▶縦**2列**に並びなさい Line up in *two columns*. ‖ 写真は**前列**左から右へ, 京子, ちえみ, 芳恵です The photo shows in *the front row*, from left to right, Kyoko, Chiemi and Yoshie. ‖ 私は(劇場, または教室の) **2列目**に座った I sat in *the second row*. ‖ 子供が数人**列を作った** Several children *lined* [《英》 *queued*] *up*. ‖ **列を離れ**てはいけません Don't *get out of line*. ‖ **列を乱さない**ように Keep *the line* straight. ‖ (モスクワの)赤の広場を兵士たちが**列を組んで**行進した *Ranks* of soldiers marched in Red Square. (➤ rank は「(兵隊の) 横列」; 「縦列」は file という).
✉ **(写真説明で) 3 列目の左から 4 番目が私です** I am the fourth one from the left in *the third row*.

れつあく 劣悪 ▶その作業場は狭いスペースに騒音など, **劣悪**な環境に置かれている The workshop has a *poor* environment, with limited space and noise pollution.

[1]**れっか 劣化する** **deteriorate** ▶デジタルの音楽ファイルはコピーを繰り返しても音質はほとんど**劣化しない** The sound quality of digital music files almost never *deteriorates* even after repeated copying.

[2]**れっか 烈火** ▶大臣は記者からのぶしつけな質問に**烈火のごとく怒り出した** The minister *flew into a rage* [*exploded in anger*] when he was asked a rude question by a reporter.

レッカーしゃ レッカー車 《米》a **tow truck, a wrecker**; 《英》a **breakdown truck** [**lorry**] ▶ここに車を止めると**レッカー車で警察に持っていかれるよ** The police will *tow away* your car if you park it here.

れっき 列記する **list** +目, **make a list.**

れっきとした 歴とした ▶**れっきとした**証拠 *undeniable* [*irrefutable*] evidence (➤ 前者は「否定できない」, 後者は「反ばくできない」の意) ‖ **れっきとした**画家 a painter *in his* [*her*] *own right* ‖ あの警備員はかつては**れっきとした**警察官だった That security guard used to *be respected* [used to *have social status*] as a police officer.

れっきょ 列挙 **enumeration**(数え上げること); **recitation**(一つ一つ順に言うこと) **一動 列挙する** **enumerate** /ɪnjúːməreɪt/ +目; **recite** +目
▶アメリカの歴代大統領名の**列挙** the *enumeration* [*recitation*] of the names of the U.S. Presidents.
▶アジアのすべての国名を**列挙する** *enumerate* [*recite*] the names of all the countries in Asia ‖ K教授はその本の誤訳箇所を**列挙した** Professor K *enumerated* mistranslated words and sentences in the book. / Professor K *listed* wrongly translated words and sentences in the book.

れっきょう 列強 **the great (world) powers.**

レッグウォーマー **leg warmers.**

れっこく 列国 **the countries** [**nations**] **of the world** ▶その会議では**列国**の首脳が一堂に会した Leaders from *nations around the world* gathered under one roof at the meeting.

れっしゃ 列車 a **train**(数車両を連結したもの; 個々の「車両」はアメリカでは car, イギリスでは carriage という)
▶《駅のアナウンス》4 番線に東京行きの**列車**が入ります. 黄色い線より下がってお待ちください *A train* for Tokyo is arriving at Track No. 4. Please stay behind the yellow line. (➤ 欧米ではこのようなアナウンスはふつうはしない) ‖ この**列車**は16両編成です This *train* has sixteen cars.
▶鹿児島まで**列車で**行った I went to Kagoshima *by train*. ‖ 大阪発 **9 時の列車**で行けばお昼には向こうへ着ける You can get there by noon if you take *the 9 o'clock train* from Osaka Station. ‖ 雪のため**列車のダイヤ**が大幅に乱れています *Train schedules* have been disrupted significantly due to (the) snow.

> **逆引き熟語 ○○列車**
> **折り返し列車** a shuttle train / **貨物列車** a freight [《英また》 goods] train / **急行列車** an express (train) / **始発** [**最終**] **列車** the first [last] train / **寝台列車** a sleeper [sleeping] train / **スキー列車** a special train for skiers / **直通列車** a through train / **通過列車** a passing train / **特急列車** a limited [special] express / **上り** [**下り**] **列車** an up [a down] train, an inbound [an outbound] train / **普通列車** a local train / **夜行列車** a night train / **臨時列車** a special train

れっしょう 裂傷 (a) **laceration** /læsəréɪʃən/, a **cut** (➤ 後者はややインフォーマル) ▶彼はガラスの破片で足にひどい**裂傷を負った** His foot *was* [His feet *were*] badly *lacerated* by pieces of glass. ‖ 彼は自動車事故で額に深い[8 センチの]**裂傷**を負った He got a deep *laceration* [an 8-cm *cut*] on his forehead in the car accident.

れっしん 烈震 a **disastrous** [**violent**] **earthquake.**

レッスン a **lesson**(習い事); (a) **practice**(練習) ▶個人**レッスン** a private *lesson* ‖ **レッスン**を(1回)受ける take *a lesson* ‖ 彼女は週2回安田先生についてピアノの**レッスン**を受けている She has [takes] piano *lessons* from Mrs. Yasuda twice a week. ‖ 彼女は幼少期から厳しい**バレエのレッスン**を受けてきた She has taken rigorous *ballet lessons* from early childhood. (➤ hard lesson は「つらい体験で得た教訓」の意がふつう).
▶夕食後, 毎晩 1 時間チェロの**レッスン**をします I have one hour of cello *practice* [I practice the cello for one hour] after supper every night.

[1]**れっせい 劣勢** ▶この試合で早稲田は慶應に対し終始**劣勢だった** In this game Waseda *fought a losing battle* against Keio from beginning to end. (➤「勝ち目のない試合をした」の意).
▶日本代表チームは連続サービスエースで**劣勢をばん回した** The Japanese national team *rallied* [*turned the tables on their opponents* / *turned the game around*] by scoring back-to-back aces. (➤ 順に「盛り返した」,「形勢を逆転させた」,「試合の情勢を好転させた」の意).

[2]**れっせい 劣性の** 《生物学》**recessive** →潜性
‖**劣性遺伝** recessive inheritance [transmission] ‖ **劣性遺伝子** a recessive gene.

れっせき 列席する **attend** +目; **be present at**(出席している)
▶式には有名人が多数**列席した** Many celebrities *attended* [*were present at*] the ceremony. ‖ 列席

者の中に前首相がいた The former prime minister was among *those present.* ‖ その会は列席者が多かった[少なかった] There was a large [poor] *attendance* at the meeting. (➤ attendance は集合的に「出席者」の意).

レッテル a **label** /léɪbəl/ ; a **sticker (label)** (のり付きの)
▶レッテルを貼る put on [stick on] *a label.*
▶《比喩的》その政治家は偽善者のレッテルを貼られた That politician *has been labeled* [*branded*] as a hypocrite.

1**れっとう 列島** an **archipelago** /ɑ̀ːʳkəpéləgoʊ/
▶日本列島は北東から南西に延びている *The Japanese Archipelago* extends northeast to southwest.

2**れっとう 劣等** **inferiority** /ɪnfɪəriɔ́ːrəṭi/ 一形 **劣等の** **inferior** /ɪnfɪ́əriəʳ/ ▶私は時々劣等感に悩まされる I sometimes suffer from *feelings of inferiority.* ‖ 人は訳もなく劣等感をもつことがある People sometimes *feel inferior* to [*have an inferiority complex* toward] others for no apparent reason. (● inferiority complex は心理学で用いるやや専門的な用語；→コンプレックス) ／People sometimes *feel that they are not as good as* others for no good reason.
▶劣等生 *a poor student* (しっかり勉強しない生徒) ／ *a slow learner* (理解力の低い学習者, 覚えの遅い人) ‖ ニュートンもアインシュタインもピカソも劣等生だった Newton, Einstein, and Picasso were all *poor students.*

レッドカード 《サッカー》 a **red card.**

れっぷう 烈風 a **violent** [a **very strong**] **wind,** a **gale**
▶その日は烈風が吹き荒れた A *gale raged* [*blew*] that day.

レディー a **lady** /léɪdi/ ▶「レディーらしくしなさい」が母の口癖だ My mother is always saying, "Act like *a lady.*" ‖ レディーファースト *Ladies first.*

レディーメード **ready-made** ▶レディーメードの洋服 *ready-made* [*ready-to-wear*] clothes.
▶うちは何でもレディーメードで買う We buy everything *ready-made.* ／We buy all our clothes *off-the-rack.*

レトルト a **retort**
‖レトルト食品 a retort [retortable] pouch.

レトロ **retro** ▶その冷蔵庫はレトロな外観だ The refrigerator has a *retro* look.

1**レバー** 《肝臓》 **(a) liver** /lívəʳ/ ▶牛[鶏]のレバー cow [chicken] *liver.*

2**レバー** 《取っ手》 a **lever** /lévəʳ/
▶(車の)変速レバー《米》 a gearshift ／《英》 a gear lever ‖ 中のレバーを引けばドアは手動で開けられます Pull the *lever* (inside) to open the door by hand.

レパートリー a **repertory** /répəʳtɔːri/, a **repertoire** /répəʳtwɑːʳ/ (➤ フランス語から) ▶レパートリーを広げる expand one's *repertory* [*repertoire*] ‖ あのピアニストはレパートリーが広い That pianist has a large [wide] *repertoire.*

レバノン **Lebanon** (地中海東岸, イスラエルの北にある国).

レビュー a **review** (論評) ; a **revue** (娯楽ショー).

レフェリー a **referee** /rèfəríː/ ▶ボクシングの試合のレフェリーを務める *referee* a boxing match.

レフト 《野球》 **left field, left** (左翼) ; a **left fielder** (左翼手).

レプリカ a **replica** (複製品).

レフレックス ‖レフレックスカメラ a reflex camera ‖ レフレックス受信機 a reflex receiver.

レベル a **level** ▶その選手のサッカーはプロのレベルに達していた The player's soccer was at the *level* of a pro [at the pro *level*]. ‖ 今回の絵画の出品作はどれもレベルが高い Every picture in this exhibition shows a high *level* of achievement. ‖ S 大はレベルが高いよ You need *a high level* of academic ability to enter S University. ‖ もっとレベルの低い(＝易しい)大学を受けたら？ How about trying an *easier* college?
▶生徒の数学のレベルアップを図りたい I want to *improve* my students' math ability. ‖ 大学生の国語力はレベルダウン(＝低下)した There *has been a deterioration* [*a decline*] in college students' Japanese ability. (➤ deterioration /dɪtɪəriəréɪʃən/ は「悪化, 低下」).

> **危ないカタカナ語✸ レベルアップ**
> **1** level up という表現はあるが, これは「低い所を埋めて平らにする」の意. 日本語の「レベルアップ」は単に「高める」の意で用いられることが多いので, improve が相当する.
> **2** 同様に level down は「高い所を低くすることによって平らにする」の意で用いられることが多い. 日本語の「レベルダウン」には deteriorate が相当する.

レポーター a **reporter.**

レポート **1【報告書, 記事】** a **report** ▶レポートを書く write *a report* ‖ レポートを提出する file [submit] *a report.*
2【学生の論文】 a **(term) paper** (● この意味では report とはいわない) ▶講義のレポートを書く do [write] *a paper* on lectures.
▶今月15日までにレポートを提出のこと You are required to hand in your *paper* by the 15th of this month.
✉ **夏休みにはレポートを3つ書かねばなりません** I have three *papers* to write during summer vacation.

レモネード 《米》 **lemonade** /lèmənéɪd/, 《英》 **lemon squash** 《参考》《英》では日本で「レモネード」と呼ぶものを lemon squash, 炭酸の入った「レモンスカッシュ」と呼ぶものを lemonade と呼んでいるので注意.

レモン a **lemon** ▶レモンを絞る squeeze *a lemon* ‖ レモンの皮 a *lemon* peel.
‖**レモン絞り器** a lemon squeezer ‖ **レモンジュース** lemon juice ‖ **レモン水** 《米》 lemonade →レモネード ‖ **レモンスカッシュ** 《米》 lemon soda, 《英》 lemonade /lèmənéɪd/ ‖ **レモンティー** tea with (a slice of) lemon (➤ lemon tea はレモンエキスで味付けした紅茶の葉の意).

レリーフ **relief** (手法) ; a **relief** (作品).

-れる →-られる
1【受け身を示して】 ▶郵便配達員が犬にかまれた The postal carrier *was bitten* by a dog. ‖ 冬になるとその山は雪で覆われます The mountain *is* [*becomes*] *covered* with snow in winter. ‖ 何と言われても平気だ I could(n't) care less what they say about me.
▶帰り道で雨に降られた I *was caught* in a shower on the way back home.
▶彼女はパスポートを盗まれた Her passport *was stolen.* ／She *had* her passport *stolen.* (● stolen に強勢を置く ; (×)She was stolen her passport. とはしない).

直訳の落とし穴「…と見なされている」
日本語では受け身形「-れる」「-られる」を使って，主語を示さず，「…と言われている」(It is said that ...)，「…と思われている」(It is thought that ...)，「…と信じられている」(It is believed that ...)などと使いがちであるが，英語ではこういう曖昧な表現は好ましくない．もし，世間一般にそのように受け止められている場合は widely (広く) や generally (一般に) などをつけることが多い．many people を使う場合は by many people とせずに Many (people) think that ... と能動態にするほうが好まれる．したがって，「彼は優秀な研究者と見なされている」もそのまま，He is considered (to be) an excellent researcher. としないで，能動態で誰の見方かをはっきり示して，I [All of his colleagues] consider him (to be) an excellent researcher. あるいは，端的に，He is an excellent researcher. のようにいうほうがよい．「手術を受けるのがその患者のベストな選択肢だと思われる」も (×) It is thought that an operation is his best option. は不自然で，I think that having an operation is his best option. あるいは，Having an operation is (probably) his best option. とする．

2【可能を示して】▶今度の旅行は行かれると思う I think I *can* go on this trip.
3【尊敬を示して】▶この書は先生自身が書かれたものです This calligraphy was done by the master himself. (👄 特に尊敬を表す言い方はないので内容だけを取って英訳する).
4【自然にそうなる状態(自発)を示して】▶この曲を聴くと，きみと一緒に過ごしたあの頃が思い出される When I listen to this piece of music, it reminds me of those days I spent with you. ‖ 彼女は間違っているように思われる It *appears* [*seems*] that she is wrong.

れんあい 恋愛 **love** ▶恋愛は人に生きる喜びを与える *Love* makes people feel the joy of being alive. ‖ 雄二としのぶは恋愛中です Yuji and Shinobu *are in love*. ‖ 私は恋愛をしたことがない I've never *fallen in love*. ‖ ほとんどの若者は見合い結婚よりも恋愛結婚を望む Most young people would prefer *a love marriage* to an arranged marriage. (👄 欧米では結婚といえば恋愛結婚と決まっているから，特に恋愛結婚に当たる英語はないが love marriage で通じる；→見合い).
‖**恋愛小説** a love story.

れんか 廉価な **inexpensive** ▶廉価なデジタルカメラ an *inexpensive* digital camera ‖ このパソコンは廉価で手に入れた I got this computer *at a reasonable price*. (➤ reasonable は「手ごろな」).
‖**廉価版** a popular edition (➤「普及版」の意).

れんが 煉瓦 (a) **brick** ▶れんがの家 a *brick* house ‖ 東京駅はれんが造りだ Tokyo Station is built of *brick*(*s*). (➤ 建築材料としては集合的に用いて，brick とすることが多い).
‖**れんが塀** a brick wall.

れんき 連記 ▶3名連記で投票する *write three names* on a ballot.
‖**連記制** the plural ballot system.

れんきゅう 連休 **(consecutive) holidays** ▶今度の連休はどこかへお出かけですか Are you planning to go somewhere during the coming *holidays*? ‖ 金曜が祭日なので，3連休になる This Friday is a national holiday, so I have *three days off in a row*. (👄「(3日)引き続いて」と考えて in a row を用いる) ／This Friday falls on a national holiday, so I have *a three-day weekend*. (👄「3日間の週末だ」と考える).

レンギョウ《植物》a **forsythia** /fɔːˈsíθiə ‖ -sáɪθ-/.

れんきんじゅつ 錬金術 **alchemy**
‖**錬金術師** an alchemist.

れんげ 蓮華 a **lotus flower**(ハスの花)；(a) **Chinese milk vetch**(レンゲソウ)；a **porcelain spoon**(陶器のスプーン).
‖**蓮華経** the Lotus Sutra.

¹れんけい 連携 **cooperation** ▶我々には PTA との密接な連携が求められています We need to *work in close cooperation with* our PTA.

²れんけい 連係 ▶レフトとショートの見事な連係プレーで走者は本塁寸前タッチアウトとなった *Thank to superb teamwork* [*perfect cooperation*] between the left fielder and the shortstop, the runner was tagged out just in front of the home plate. ‖ わが社では研究部門と営業部門の連係をもっと密にする必要がある Our company needs to *link* the research and sales divisions *more closely* [to *strengthen the connection* between the research and sales divisions].

れんけつ 連結 **coupling** /kʌ́plɪŋ/ **一動 連結する** **couple** +㊐
▶次の金沢駅で前に2両連結いたします At Kanazawa (Station), which is the next stop, two more cars will *be added* [*be coupled* ／*be connected*] to the first car of this train.
‖**連結決算** consolidated financial results (決算上の実績).

れんこ 連呼 ▶選挙カーが候補者の名前を連呼して回っている Campaign cars are driving around *repeatedly yelling* [*calling*] *out* candidates' names.

れんご 連語《文法》a **collocation**.

れんこう 連行 ▶容疑者は警察に連行された The suspect *was taken to the police station*. ／The suspect *was taken into police custody*. (👄 後者は「拘置するために」と考えた場合の訳例).

れんごう 連合 (a) **union** **一動 連合する** **combine**, **unite**(団結する)；**ally** /əláɪ/ (同盟する)
▶この祭りは仙台の商店連合会が後援している This festival is sponsored by Sendai Shopkeepers *Association*.
‖**連合国** allies；the Allies (世界大戦の) ‖ **連合政権** a coalition /kòʊəlíʃən/ government.

れんごく 煉獄《カトリック》**Purgatory**.

れんこん 蓮根 a **lotus root**《参考》欧米にはハスの根を食べる習慣はない.

れんさ 連鎖 ▶大銀行の倒産が連鎖反応を引き起こした The bankruptcy of a big bank has triggered *a chain reaction*.
‖**食物連鎖** the food chain.

れんざ 連座する **be involved**《in》▶大統領の側近がクーデターに連座していたことが判明した It turned out that the aide to the President *was involved in* the coup.

れんさい 連載の **serial** /síəriəl/ **一動 連載する** **serialize** +㊐ ▶性教育に関する記事がその雑誌に連載されている An article on sex education *is now being serialized* in the magazine. ／There's *a column* on sex education in the magazine. (➤ column はあるテーマで，あるいは特定の執筆者が書いて，定期的に載る記事) ‖ この本は遠藤氏が新聞に連載したコラムをま

とめたものだ This book comprises columns by Mr. Endo that *were serialized* in a newspaper. ／This book is a collection of articles by Mr. Endo that originally *appeared serially* in a newspaper.

‖連載漫画 serial comics ‖ 連載物 a serial.

れんさく 連作する plant every year (in the same field).

れんざん 連山 mountains ▶那須連山 Nasu *Mountains*.

レンジ 《米》a gas stove [range], 《英》a gas cooker (ガスレンジ) ; an oven /ʌ́vən/ (オーブン) ▶レンジアップする *heat up in a microwave oven*.

危ないカタカナ語✸ レンジ
1 台所の「レンジ」は《米》では range というが, stove のほうがよりふつう. 《英》では range は古めかしい言い方で, ふつうは cooker という.
2「電子レンジ」は microwave /máɪkrəweɪv/ oven または単に microwave という.

れんじつ 連日 day after day (来る日も来る日も) ; every day (毎日) ▶連日蒸し暑い日が続いている We have had muggy weather *every day*. ／We have been having hot and humid weather *for days on end*. (● 期間を示す複数名詞のあとに「続けて」の意を表す on end を用いるとよい) ‖ 連日の雨で大会関係者は頭を痛めている This *rainy spell* is giving the organizers of the tournament a big headache. (➤ spell は「(天候などの)連続」).

¹れんしゃ 連写 continuous shooting, a continuous shot 一動 **連写する** shoot continuously.

²れんしゃ 連射する shoot in rapid succession.

レンジャー a ranger (森林監視員).

れんしゅう 練習 (a) practice (稽古) ; exercises (練習問題) ; training, 《インフォーマル》a workout (特に運動の) ; (a) drill (指導者のもとでの組織立った訓練) 一動 **練習する** practice, train, drill

▶きょうはサッカーの練習がある Today we have [there is] soccer *practice*. ‖ きのうの水泳の練習はきつかった Yesterday's swim *practice* was hard. ‖ 応援団の練習はこのビルの屋上でやっている Cheerleading *practice* is held on the roof of this building. ‖ 祖父はよく多摩川に巨人軍の練習を見にいったと言う My grandfather says he would often go to see the Giants' *workouts* [*training*] at Tamagawa. ‖ 選手たちは夏休み中は練習に明け暮れています The players have *been practicing day in, day out* during the summer vacation.

▶練習不足で今大会ではいい成績を残せなかった I wasn't able to perform well at this meet due to *lack of practice*.

▶１週間後に初日を控えて俳優たちは練習に励んでいる With a week to go before the premiere, the actors and actresses are *rehearsing* very hard. (➤ rehearse は「劇や演奏会の下稽古をする」の意) ‖ ＣＤ[クリス先生]のあとについて新しい単語と表現の発音を練習しましょう Now let's *practice pronouncing* the new words and expressions after the CD [Chris].

▶私たちはリレーの練習をするために学校に残りました We stayed after school to *train* for the relay. ‖ 小林先生は英語の発音を私たちにみっちり練習させた Mr. Kobayashi *drilled* us thoroughly on English pronunciation. ‖ では各自練習問題を５分間でやりなさい Now do the *exercise*(*s*) yourselves within five minutes.

‖練習曲 an étude /eɪtjúːd/ (➤ フランス語から) ‖ 練習試合 a practice game [match] ‖ 練習所 a training school (訓練所) ; a driving range (ゴルフの) ‖ 練習帳 an exercise book, a workbook.

☞ 猛練習 (⇀見出語)

れんしょ 連署 joint signature 一動 **連署する** jointly sign.

れんしょう 連勝 a winning streak (勝ち続け) ▶ドラゴンズの連勝は11でストップした The Dragons' *winning streak* stopped after 11 games [after the 11th game].

▶ジャイアンツは７連勝した The Giants *won seven consecutive games*. ／The Giants *won seven games in a row*. ／The Giants *won their seventh straight game*.

‖《競馬》連勝複式 a quinella /kiːnélə, kwi-/.

レンズ a lens

‖広角[望遠]レンズ a wide-angle [telephoto] lens ‖ 凸[凹]レンズ a convex [concave] lens.

れんせい 錬成する train +目 ▶人格を錬成する *train* one's character.

れんせん 連戦 ▶連戦連勝する *win game after game* (➤ 試合で) ／*win battle after battle* (➤ 戦争で).

▶オリックスは西武との３連戦を全部ものにした The Buffaloes swept the *three-game series* against the Lions.

れんそう 連想 (an) association 一動 **連想する** associate /əsóʊʃieɪt/ +目

【文型】
A で B を連想する
associate A with B

▶ベーコンという名を聞くと私は同名の哲学者を連想する When I hear the name Bacon, I *associate* it *with* the philosopher [it *reminds* me *of* the philosopher]. (➤ remind A of B で「A(人)に B を思い出させる」) ／I always *associate* the name Bacon *with* the famous philosopher of the same name.

▶これを見てきみは何を連想する？ What does this *remind* you *of*? ／What does this *bring to mind*? ‖「干潟」と聞いて何を連想しますか What *comes to* (*your*) *mind* when you hear the word '*higata* (tideland)'? ‖ この曲は広い海を連想させる This music *makes me think of* a vast sea. ／This music *suggests* a great ocean to me. (➤ suggest は「暗示する」).

▶吉野は詩的連想が豊かな所だ Yoshino is a place rich in poetic *associations*.

‖連想ゲーム a word association game.

れんぞく 連続 (a) succession ; a series (同種のものの) 一形 **連続の** consecutive (切れ目なく続く) ▶３回連続の優勝 three *consecutive* victories ‖ ３日間連続して雨が降った It rained (*for*) *three consecutive days*. ／It rained *for three days in a row* [*in succession*]. (➤ in a row はややインフォーマル) ／It *continued* to rain [The rain *continued*] *for three days*. (● 日常会話では continue を使った言い方が多く用いられる) ‖ その知事は連続４期選ばれた The governor has been elected to his *fourth straight* [*consecutive*] *term*. (➤ ４期目に焦点を当てて序数

詞で表す).
▶地震が連続して伊豆を襲った *A series of* earthquakes hit Izu. (➤a series of ... で「一連の…」) ‖トム・ソーヤーの人生は冒険の連続だった Tom Sawyer's life was *a series of adventures*. ／Tom Sawyer's life was *one adventure after another*.
▶朝の連続テレビドラマを見てますか Do you watch that *TV drama series* in the morning? (➤「連続番組」は serial という) ‖その連続殺人事件のニュースが新聞に出ていた That *serial murder case* was reported in the paper. (➤「連続殺人犯」は serial killer [murderer]) ‖1, 2, 3, 4は連続した番号だ One, two, three, and four are *consecutive* numbers.

れんだ 連打《野球》**consecutive hits** ▶3連打を許す give up [allow] *three consecutive hits* ‖阪神は6回に4連打で3点をあげた The Tigers drove in three runs in the sixth on *a barrage of four hits*. (➤barrage /bərɑ́:ʒ/ は「連発」).

1**れんたい 連帯 solidarity** /sɑ̀:lɪdǽrəṭi/ (団結) 一形 **連帯の joint**(共同の)
▶おいの銀行ローンの連帯保証をする *cosign* (for) my nephew's bank loan ‖働く仲間よ, 連帯して(＝結束して)要求を勝ち取ろう My fellow workers, let's *unite* in our struggle until our demands are met. ‖この事故に対し私どもは連帯責任を取ります We take *collective* [*joint*] *responsibility* for this accident.
‖**連帯保証人** a joint surety /ʃóərəṭi/, a cosigner.

2**れんたい 連隊**《軍事》a **regiment**
‖**連隊旗** the regimental colors ‖**連隊長** a regimental commander.

レンタカー a **rental car**, a **rent-a-car** ▶レンタカーで北海道を一周した I *rented a car* and traveled all around Hokkaido. ‖レンタカーを借りるつもりです I'm going to *rent a car*.

レンタル rental ▶ベビーベッドは買うよりレンタルのほうが(＝借りるほうが)賢明だよ You'd be wiser to *rent* a (baby) crib than to buy one.
‖**レンタルショップ** a rental shop ‖**レンタルビデオ店** a video rental shop (➤語順に注意).

れんたん 練炭・煉炭 a **briquette** /brɪkét/.

れんだん 連弾 a **four-hand(ed) performance (on the piano)**, a **piano duet**
▶ピアノの連弾曲 a piano *piece for four hands* ‖連弾する *play a piano duet* ‖妹と連弾で『ドリー』を弾いた I played "Dolly" on the piano with my (younger) sister.

れんちゅう 連中 guys ▶あの連中は一体何者だろう Who on earth are those *guys*? ‖あの連中はよくこの喫茶店にたむろしている That *gang* [《英》*lot*] often hangs around this coffee shop.

れんとう 連投 ▶田中投手は今夜の試合で3連投となる Pitcher Tanaka will *take the* (*pitcher's*) *mound in the third game in a row* tonight.

れんどう 連動 ▶この測定器はコンピュータに連動していて, 即座にデータがグラフ化されます This measuring instrument, which works *connected to* a computer, can convert the data into a graph on the spot.

レントゲン an **X-ray**(写真および検査) ▶まず骨折はしてないでしょうが, 念のためレントゲンを撮りましょう You probably don't have a broken bone, but let's take *an X-ray* just to be sure. ‖胸のレントゲンを撮ってもらった I got a chest *X-ray*.
‖**レントゲン検査** an X-ray examination.

れんにゅう 練乳 condensed milk (加糖の); **evaporated milk**(無糖の).

1**れんぱ 連破** ▶千葉ロッテが北海道日本ハムを3連破した The Marines *defeated* [*downed*] the Fighters *three times in a row*. ／The Marines *gained three consecutive victories* over the Fighters.

2**れんぱ 連覇** ▶興南高校は2010年, 甲子園の全国高校野球大会で春夏連覇を成し遂げた Konan High School *won the championship* in *both* the Spring *and* Summer National Senior High School Baseball Tournaments at Koshien in 2010.
▶能代工業高校バスケットボール部は全国高校総体で7連覇を成し遂げたことがある The Noshiro Technical High School basketball team once *won seven consecutive championships* in the national inter-high school athletic meet.

れんばい 廉売 a **sale**
‖**廉売合戦** a price war.

れんぱい 連敗 a **losing streak**(負け続け) ▶中日は巨人を3対1で破り, 連敗を4で食い止めた The Dragons broke a four-game *losing streak* by beating the Giants 3–1.
▶千葉ロッテは北海道日本ハムに3連敗した The Marines *have lost three straight games* to the Fighters. (➤straight は「連続した」)

れんぱつ 連発 ▶授業中, 後ろの方で誰かがしゃっくりを連発したので皆が振り返った Everyone in class looked back when someone in the back row *kept* hiccupp*ing*. (➤keep doing は「…し続ける」) ‖記者たちは大臣に質問を連発した(＝浴びせた) The reporters *fired* [*shot*] questions at the Minister.
‖**連発銃** a repeating firearm, a repeater.

れんばん 連番 consecutive numbers ▶宝くじを10枚連番で買った I bought ten lottery tickets with *consecutive numbers*.

1**れんぽう 連邦** a **union**, a **federation**, a **commonwealth** 一形 **連邦の federal**
‖**連邦政府** the federal government ‖(アメリカの)**連邦捜査局** the Federal Bureau of Investigation《略 FBI》‖**英連邦** the Commonwealth (of Nations) ‖**ロシア連邦** the Russian Federation.

2**れんぽう 連峰** a **chain** [**range**] **of mountains** ▶この峠から穂高連峰の雄大な姿を見ることができる You can get a magnificent view of the *peaks of the Hotaka Mountains* [*Range*] from this pass.

れんま 錬磨する hone ＋目 (技能を) ▶技能を錬磨する *hone* one's skill(s).

1**れんめい 連名** ▶我々は市議会に連名で陳情書を提出した We sent in a petition *in our joint names* to the municipal assembly. ／We sent in a *joint* petition to the municipal assembly.

2**れんめい 連盟** a **league**
‖**東京六大学野球連盟** Tokyo Big 6 Baseball League ‖**関西学生野球連盟** Kansai Big 6 Baseball League.

れんや 連夜 consecutive nights ▶私は連夜の残業で疲れ果ててしまった I was exhausted from working overtime *night after night* [*on consecutive nights*]. (➤night after night は「毎晩毎晩」で繰り返しのニュアンスが強い) ‖彼は連夜の徹夜マージャンで体を壊した Playing mah-jongg *all night for days on end* ruined his health.

れ

れんらく 連絡 1【知らせること, つながり】**contact, touch**(➤後者は「接触」の意に基づく比喩的用法) 一動 **連絡する contact** +目, **get in touch with**
▶詳細をお知りになりたい方は最寄りの出張所までご**連絡**ください For further information, please *contact* the nearest branch office. ‖ 社長の所在がわかりませんので**連絡が取れません** I don't know the whereabouts of our (company) president, so I have no way of *contacting* him. ‖ 北海道へいらっしゃったときは**連絡してください** Please *get in touch with* me when you come to Hokkaido. (●「電話で連絡する」なら call me でよい) ‖ 何かありましたらご**連絡します** I'll *get in touch* [*let you know*] if anything should come up. ‖ 別れた妻とは今でも(Eメールで)**連絡を取り合っている** I still *keep in touch with* my ex-wife (through email).
▶不審な者を見かけたら警察に**連絡して**(＝知らせて)ください If you happen to see a suspicious person, please *report* (him [her]) to the police. ‖ その村とは全く**連絡がつかない**(＝通信が途絶えている) *Communication* with that village has been cut off.
▶久保さんがきょうは病気で休むと**電話で連絡してきた** Kubo *called in* sick today. ‖ イタリアに居る娘から長い間**連絡**(＝音信)**がない** I *haven't heard from* my daughter in Italy for a long time. ‖ これが旅行中の**連絡先**です These are my *contact addresses* while on the trip.
▶これが留守中の**連絡先の電話番号**です Here's my *contact number* while I'm away. ‖ あなたの**連絡先**を教えてください Could you tell me *where I can reach you*?
‖**連絡係** a contact person, a liaison (person) ‖ **連絡網** network, networking.
✉ **あなたが日本を去られる日も迫りましたが, これからも連絡を取り合いましょう** You will be leaving Japan soon, but let's *keep* [*stay*] *in touch.*
✉ **日程が決まり次第ご連絡いたします** We will *contact* you as soon as the schedule is decided.
2【乗り物の接続】**a connection** 一動 (…に)**連絡する connect**《with, to》▶この電車は八王子で特急あずさ25号に**連絡します** This train *connects with* [*to*] the limited express *Azusa* 25 at Hachioji.

れんらくせん 連絡船 a **ferry**, a **ferryboat** ▶**連絡船で**その島に渡る go to that island *by ferry*.

れんりつ 連立 ‖**連立内閣**[**政府**] a coalition cabinet [government] ‖ **連立方程式** simultaneous equations.

ろ・ロ

[1]**ろ 炉** a **fireplace**(暖炉); a **hearth**(炉床)
‖**原子炉** a nuclear reactor ‖ **ごみ焼却炉** an incinerator ‖ **溶鉱炉** a blast furnace.

[2]**ろ 櫓** a **scull** /skʌl/, an **oar** ▶舟のろをこぐ *row* a boat.

ロイヤルゼリー royal jelly.

[1]**ろう 労 trouble**(手間); **hard work** (勤勉)
▶司会者は**労をいとわず**(＝面倒がらずに)祝電をすべて紹介した The emcee *took the trouble* to read out all the congratulatory telegrams.
▶社長は彼女の**労**[永年の**労**]に謝意を表した The president thanked her for her *hard work* [long years of *service*].

[2]**ろう 蠟 wax** ▶ろうそくからろうがたれた *Wax* dripped down from the candle.
‖**ろう細工** (a) waxwork ‖ **ろう人形** a wax figure ‖ **ろう人形館** a wax museum, 《英》a waxworks.

[3]**ろう 牢** a **dungeon** /dʌ́ndʒən/ (土ろう, 地下ろう); a **prison** (刑務所, ろう獄).

ろう- 老- old, elderly (●後者は前者を遠回しに言うときによく用いられる) ▶**老夫婦** an *elderly* couple ‖ **老彫刻家** an *old* sculptor.

ろうあ 聾啞の deaf-mute /dèfmjúːt/
‖**ろうあ者** a deaf-mute, a hearing and speech impaired person (➤後者が丁寧な言い方).

ろうえい 漏洩 leaking ▶機密情報の**漏えい**(事件) *a leak* of classified information.

[1]**ろうか 廊下** a **corridor** /kɔ́ːrədəʳ/, 《米また》a **hall(way)**, 《英また》a **passage(way)** ▶音楽室はこの**廊下**の突き当たりです The music room is at the (far) end of this *corridor*. ‖ こら, **廊下を走るんじゃない** Hey, don't run in the *corridor*.
▶授業中にいたずらをしてよく**廊下**に立たされたものです I was often kicked out of class and kept standing in the *hallway* [*hall*] as a punishment for misbehavior.
‖**渡り廊下** a passageway between two buildings, a connecting corridor (学校などの); a breezeway (家とガレージなどの間の屋根つき通路).

[2]**ろうか 老化 aging** /éɪdʒɪŋ/ (老化現象; 《英》では ageing ともつづる) 一動 **老化する age, get** [**grow**] **old** ▶**老化**の兆し a sign of *aging* ‖ **老化**は自然な流れだ *Aging* is a natural process.
▶脳の**老化**は20歳頃から始まると言われている The *aging* of our brains is said to begin as early as twenty (years old).

ろうかい 老獪な cunning, sly.

ろうがい 老害 *rogai*; harm caused by elderly people who stay in positions of authority for too long (➤説明的な訳).

ろうかく 楼閣 a **tower** ▶**空中の楼閣** a *castle in the air* ‖ この計画は**空中の楼閣だ** This plan *is unfeasible* [*unrealistic*].

ろうがっこう 聾学校 a **school for the deaf.**

ろうがん 老眼 farsightedness (due to old age), presbyopia /prèzbióʊpiə/ (➤後者は医学用語)
▶この頃小さな字が読みづらい. **老眼**かな I've been having trouble reading small print lately. I'm afraid I'm getting *farsighted because of my age*. (●ふつうは単に I must be getting old.(年かな)と言う).
‖**老眼鏡** reading glasses (for the elderly).

ろうきゅう 老朽 ▶**老朽化した船** a *decrepit old* ship (➤発音は /dɪkrépɪt/) ‖ 部室のある建物の**老朽化**が著しい The building that houses our clubroom is very *timeworn*.

ろうきょう 老境 (an) **old** [**advanced**] **age**(老年) ▶

老境に入る attain [reach] *an advanced age*.

ろうく 労苦 **pains**(骨折り); **labor**(労力); **trouble**(面倒, 手数). ⇀労.

ろうご 老後 **in** one's **old age**(老齢期・高齢期); **after** one's **retirement**(退職後) ▶老後に備える prepare for one's *old age* [*life after retirement* / *golden years*] (➤ golden years は老後を, 健康で生活を楽しめる年月と捉えたプラスイメージの語) (日本語の「老後」は退職後かなり早い時期(例えば65歳以降)を連想させるが, 英語の old age はもっと進んだ年齢(例えば80歳以降)で体力のかなり衰えた時期を連想させることが多いので,「老後」の意味を考えて訳語を選ぶ必要がある) ‖ 彼は老後の蓄えを失った He lost his *life savings*. (➤「一生かけてためたお金」の訳としても使える) ‖ 老後の安心のために蓄えが十分にある人は少ない Not many people have enough savings to *ensure financial security in their old age* [*after retirement*]. ‖ 老後は田舎へ帰って少し農業をするつもりです I plan to go back to my home(town) and spend time farming [do a little farming] *after my retirement* [*in my old age*].

ディベートルーム「親の老後の面倒は子供が見るべきだ」

ろうこう 老巧 ▶老巧な政治家 an *experienced* [*a seasoned* / *a veteran*] politician.

ろうごく 牢獄 a **prison** ▶ろう獄に入る[入っている] *go to* [*be in*] *prison*.

ろうさい 労災 a **work-related accident**, an **accident on the job**(事故); **workers' compensation insurance**(保険).

ろうさく 労作 **the fruit** [**product**] **of hard work** ⇀力作 ▶本書はM教授の多年の労作である This book is *the fruit of* Professor M's many years of *hard work* [*dedicated effort*].

ろうし 労使 **labor and management, management and work force** ▶我々の会社では労使関係はうまくいっている *Labor-management relations* are pretty good at our company.

ろうじょう 籠城 ▶会津藩は籠城の構えをとった The Aizu Domain prepared itself to *endure a siege*.

ろうしょうかいご 老障介護 an **elderly parent caring for a disabled son** [**daughter**] (➤ 両親の場合なら elderly parents).

ろうじん 老人 an **old man** [**woman**]; the **old** (➤ 総称) 《参考》日本語でも婉曲(えんきょく)語の「お年寄り」を使うことがあるように, 形容詞は old の露骨さを避けて elderly を使う傾向になってきている. 名詞の婉曲語は a senior, a senior citizen [複 seniors, senior citizens]. ⇀高齢, シルバー, 年寄り
▶寝たきりの老人 a bedridden *old man* [*woman*] ‖ 老人をいたわる be kind to *elderly people* ‖ バスの中で老人に席を譲った I gave my seat to *an elderly man* [*woman*] in the bus.
‖老人 [老年] 医学, 老人病学 geriatrics ‖ 老人学 gerontology /dʒèrəntɑ́:lədʒi/ ‖ 老人差別 ag(e)ism ‖ 老人性痴ほう症 senile dementia ‖ 老人病 diseases of old age ‖ 老人ホーム a home for the elderly, a nursing home (➤「特別養護老人ホーム」は a home for elderly people requiring special care).

1**ろうすい 老衰** **the infirmities of old age, weakening due to old age** ▶かつての名優は自宅で老衰のため息を引き取った The one-time great actor *died of old age* at his home.

2**ろうすい 漏水** (a) **leakage of water** ▶地下のどこかで水道管が漏水しているらしい It seems that *water is leaking* somewhere from a pipe underground.

1**ろうする 労する** ▶天野さんは宝くじに当たり, 労せずして大金を手に入れた Mr. Amano won the lottery and got a lot of money *without having to work* (*at all*).

2**ろうする 弄する** ▶策を弄する *use* an underhanded trick(➤ underhanded は「不正の」).

ろうそ 労組 《米》a **labor union**, 《英》a **trade union** ▶労組を作る organize [form] *a labor union*.

ろうそく 蠟燭 a **candle** ▶ろうそくをともす[吹き消す] light [blow out] *a candle* ‖ エイブラハム・リンカーンは昔ろうそくの明かりで勉強した Abraham Lincoln used to study *by candlelight*.
‖ろうそく立て a candlestick ‖ ろうそくの芯 a wick.

ろうたい 老体 ▶師匠はご老体のため最近は外出を控えています Nowadays, the master [teacher] avoids going out because he *is very old* (*and frail*).

ろうでん 漏電 a **short circuit**, an **electric leak** [**leakage**] ▶その火事の原因は漏電だった *A short circuit* [*An electric leak*] caused the fire.

ろうどう 労働 **work, labor**(➤ 後者は「骨の折れる肉体労働」の意味合いが強い) ━ 動 **労働する** **work** ▶強制労働 forced *labor* ‖ 筋肉労働 manual *labor*(➤「手仕事」の意にもなる).
▶長年にわたる戸外での労働で農夫の腕は赤銅色に日焼けしていた Many years of outdoor *labor* had turned the farmer's arms bronze. ‖ この年では深夜労働はきつい *Working late at night* is tough for a person my age.
‖労働委員会 a labor relations commission ‖ 労働運動 a labor movement ‖ 労働基準法 the Labor Standards Law ‖ 労働組合 《米》a labor union, 《英》a trade union ‖ 労働時間 working hours ‖ 労働者 a worker; a laborer(肉体労働者); labor(労働者たち, 労働力) ‖ 労働条件 working conditions ‖ 労働争議 a labor dispute ‖ 労働党 the Labour Party(イギリスの) ‖ 労働保険 worker's insurance ‖ 労働力 the work [labor] force; labor (➤「安い労働力」は cheap labor).

逆引き熟語 ○○労働
1日8時間労働 an eight-hour workday / 家事労働 domestic work / 季節労働 seasonal labor [work] / 時間外労働 overtime work, extra work after business hours / 週40時間労働 (a) forty-hour workweek / 重労働 hard labor / 頭脳労働 intellectual [mental, brain] work / 単純労働 manual labor / 肉体労働 manual [physical] labor / 日雇い労働 day labor / 不法労働 illegal work

ろうどく 朗読 **reading**; (a) **recitation** /rèsɪtéɪʃən/ (詩などの) ━ 動 **朗読する** **read** (**aloud**) +目, **recite** /rɪsáɪt/ +目 ▶授業で『坊っちゃん』を順に一節ずつ朗読した Everybody took turns (at) *reading* passages *aloud* from "Botchan" in class.

ろうにゃくなんにょ 老若男女 **men and women of all ages** ▶元日には大勢の老若男女がこの神社に参詣する Crowds of people, *young and old, men and women*, visit this shrine on New Year's Day.

ろうにん 浪人 a **ronin**(➤ 英語化している)
日本紹介 浪人は封建時代には主君のいない武士をいいましたが, 現代では受験に失敗し, 翌年

に備えて勉強している学生をいいます. 公的に認可された教育機関に所属していないからです In the feudal times a ronin was a samurai without a lord. Today the word refers to students who have failed school entrance exams and are studying to prepare for the next chance in the next year. They are called ronin because they don't belong to any publicly accredited educational institution.
▶敏明はことしの入試に失敗して今浪人中です Toshiaki failed this year's college entrance exams and *is studying to prepare for another chance* [*other chances*] *next year*.
▶私は2年浪人して(＝2度失敗して)希望の大学に入った I got into the university of my choice *after having failed the entrance exams two years in a row*.

ろうねん 老年 old [advanced] age ▶老年とは癒やし得ぬ病のことである *Old age* is an incurable disease. (➤ ローマの哲学者セネカのことば).

ろうば 老婆 an old woman ▶《慣用表現》老婆心ながら, パスポートだけは必ず肌身離さず持ち歩くように I'm telling you *out of kindness* [*out of concern for you*] that you should carry your passport with you at all times.

ろうばい 狼狽 confusion(混乱, 当惑); a fluster(慌てふためき) 一動 **ろうばいする** get confused, become flustered ▶突然の出火に看護師たちはろうばいして廊下を駆け回った At the outbreak of fire the nurses milled around in the corridors *in confusion*. ‖急に何かしゃべってくれと言われて私はろうばいした When I was suddenly asked to make a speech, I *became flustered*.

ロウバイ 臘梅 《植物》a Japanese allspice.

ろうはいぶつ 老廃物 waste products [matter].

ろうひ 浪費 (a) waste 一動 **浪費する** waste ＋目, squander /skwɑ́ːndəʳ/ ＋目
▶つまらないことに金を浪費するな Don't *waste* [*squander*] money on useless things. ‖彼にきみの話をわからせようとするのは時間の浪費だよ It will be *a waste of time* to try to make him understand what you want to say. ‖女房の浪費癖がなかなか直らない My wife won't [can't] get over her *wasteful habits*.
‖**浪費家** a spendthrift, a (big) spender, an extravagant person.

ろうほう 朗報 good [welcome] news ▶ふるさとの母親のもとに初孫誕生の朗報が届いた *Good* [*Welcome*] *news* reached the mother back home that her first grandchild had been born.

ろうむしゃ 労務者 a laborer.

ろうや 牢屋 a prison, a jail. →刑務所.

ろうりょく 労力 labor(労働); effort(ある目的のための努力) ▶古代エジプト人は途方もない労力をつぎ込んでピラミッドを造った Ancient Egyptians put tremendous *labor* [*effort*] into constructing the pyramids.
▶コンピュータは時間と労力を省いてくれる Computers save (us) time and *labor*.
▶この計画を実現させるために, 私は労力を惜しまないつもりだ I'll *spare no effort* [*pains*] to carry out this plan. ／I'll *put all my efforts* into realizing this project.

ろうれい 老齢 (ripe) old age ▶老齢年金で暮らす live on *an old age pension*(➤ その受給者は old age pensioner という).
‖**老齢人口** an aging population. →高齢.

ろうれん 老練な experienced, seasoned(熟練した); expert(専門家の) ▶老練なハンター an *experienced* hunter.

ろうろう 朗々 ▶社長は朗々と詩吟を詠んだ The company president recited a shigin *in a clear, sonorous voice*.

ろうろうかいご 老々介護 elder-to-elder nursing (care); an elderly person taking care of another elderly person(人).

ローカル local ▶その地方にはローカルカラーがまだたっぷり残っている That region still retains an abundance of *local color*.

危ないカタカナ語✹ ローカル
英語の local は「ある特定の土地の, 地元の, 現地の」の意. 国全体から見て「地方の」の意味ではあるが, 都会に対して「田舎の」の意味ではない(この意味は英語では regional という). local news は「その土地の[地元の]ニュース」, local call は「市内通話」の意味である.

‖**ローカル線** a local line ‖**ローカル版** a local edition ‖**ローカル放送** a local broadcast.

ローション (a) lotion ▶アフターシェーブローションをつける apply (*an*) *aftershave lotion*.

ロース 《参考》「ロース」は roast(オーブンで蒸し焼きにする)がなまった和製語. sirloin /sə́ːʳlɔɪn/ や tenderloin などの上質の肉がこれに相当する.
‖**ロースハム** (high-quality) processed ham.

ローストチキン roast chicken.

ローストビーフ roast beef ▶ローストビーフを薄切りにする slice *roast beef*.

ローズマリー 《植物》a rosemary.

ローター a rotor(機械の回転子).

ロータリー 《米》a rotary, a traffic circle, 《英》a roundabout(環状交差点)
‖**ロータリーエンジン** a rotary engine ‖**ロータリークラブ** the Rotary Club.

ローティーン early teens(13～15歳の人); preteens(10～12歳の人) ▶彼はローティーンの女の子に人気がある He is popular among girls *in their early teens*. →ハイティーン.

ローテーション rotation ▶その投手はローテーション入りが早々と決まった It was soon decided that the pitcher would be in the pitching *rotation*. ‖私たちはローテーションで英語科主任を務めている We act as chief of the English department *in rotation*.

ロードアイランド Rhode Island(アメリカ北東部の州; 略RI, R.I.).

ロードゲーム a road game, an away game(➤ 本拠地での試合は home game).

ロードショー a first-run movie 《参考》英語の road show は「(劇・ミュージカルなどの)地方巡回興行」,「(選挙・販売活動などの)地方巡回」の意 ▶私は高校時代に『タイタニック』をロードショーで見た I saw "Titanic" at a first-run movie theater in my high school days.
‖**ロードショー劇場** a first-run movie theater.

ロードマップ a road map(道路地図; 行程表).

ロードレース a road race(個々の); road racing(➤ 競技の総称).

ローヒール ▶ローヒールの靴 shoes *with low heels* ／ *low-heeled* shoes.

ロープ (a) **rope** ▶強盗は被害者をロープで縛って逃げた The burglar tied the victim up with *a rope* and escaped.
ロープウェー a **ropeway**, a **cable car** ▶ロープウェーに乗る ride *a cable car*.
ローマ **Rome**(イタリアの首都)
‖**ローマ数字** a Roman numeral ‖ **ローマ法王** the Pope.
ローマじ ローマ字 ***Romaji*** ; **Roman letters**
▶ヘボン式ローマ字できみの名前を書きなさい Write your name in *the Hepburn system of Romaji*.
《参考》日本語をローマ字で表す場合, 小学校で習う訓令式と古いヘボン式があるが, 地名など日常的には英米人に理解しやすい後者を使うことが多い. し(shi), じ(ji), ち(chi), つ(tsu), ふ(fu), ちゃ(cha), じょ(jo)などと書くほか, p, b, m の前の「ん」は n ではなく m を使うので,「新聞」は *shimbun* となる.
ローラー a **roller**.
ローラースケート **roller-skating**(すること) ; (a **pair of**) **roller skates**(靴) ▶ローラースケートをする *roller-skate*.
ロール a **roll**(巻いたもの, ロールパン) ▶トイレットペーパー 4 ロール入り 1 袋 a pack of four *rolls* of toilet paper.
‖**ロールキャベツ** a cabbage roll ‖ **ロールパン** a roll.
ロールプレイング **role-playing**
‖**ロールプレイングゲーム** a role-playing game.
ローン a **loan** ▶この車は 6 か月のローンで買った I bought this car on a six-month *loan* [*credit plan*].
▶家を買うために大抵の人が銀行ローンに頼っている Most people have to get *a bank loan* [*a mortgage*] in order to buy a house. (➤ mortgage は「住宅ローン」).
▶私は銀行ローンを完済した I paid off my *bank loan*. ‖私は F 銀行の**住宅ローン**で家を建てた I had my house built on *a home loan* [*a mortgage*] from F Bank.
ろか 濾過 **filtering** ; **filtration**(ろ過作用) **一動 ろ過する filter** +㊐ ▶砂と木炭で水をろ過する *filter* water through sand and charcoal.
‖**ろ過器** a filter.
ろかた 路肩 **the shoulder (of a road)** ▶彼はタイヤチェーンを取り付けるため, **路肩**に車を寄せた He pulled over to *the shoulder* (of the road) to put on tire chains.
▶《掲示》**路肩注意** Soft Shoulders.
ろく 六 **six** ; **the sixth**(6 番目) ▶日本の子供たちの多くは 6 歳で小学校に上がる Most Japanese children start (elementary) school at the age of *six*.
ろくおん 録音 (a) **recording** **一動 録音する record** /rɪkɔ́ːʳd/ +㊐
▶野鳥の声を録音する *record* the calls of wild birds ‖ぼくは FM の音楽番組を I C レコーダーで録音した I *made a recording of* [*recorded*] the FM radio music program on an IC recorder. ‖ CD はデジタル**録音**だから音の劣化は問題にならない Since CDs are *recorded digitally*, sound deterioration is negligible. (➤ 名詞の「デジタル録音」は digital recording).
‖**録音機** a recorder ‖ **録音技師** a recording engineer ‖ **録音室** a recording room ‖ **録音テープ** a (magnetic) tape ; a cassette tape(カセットの) ‖ **ライブ** [**スタジオ**] **録音** live [studio] recording.
ろくが 録画 (a) **video(tape) recording** **一動 録画する videotape** +㊐ , **tape** +㊐ ▶『ハムレット』をデジタル録画機で [D V D に] **録画した** I *recorded* "Hamlet" on DVR [DVD]. ‖きのうあの番組を**録画して**おけばよかった I wish I had *recorded* [(*video*) *taped*] the program yesterday.
‖**録画放送** a transcribed program, a broadcast by transcription.
ろくがつ 六月 **June**《略 Jun.》▶ことしの入梅は **6 月** 15日だった The rainy season started on *June* 15 this year.
▶イギリスでは **6 月**が最も気候がよい In Britain the weather is best in *June*.
ろくさんせい 六三制 **the 6 -3 school education system** ; the Japanese system of compulsory education comprising six years of elementary school and three years of junior high school (➤ 説明的な訳).
ろくじゅう 六十 **sixty** ; **the sixtieth**(60番目)
ことわざ **六十の手習い** It is never too late to learn. (➤「学ぶのに遅すぎるということはない」の意).
ろくしょう 緑青 **verdigris** /vɚ́ːʳdəgrɪs/, **copper corrosion**(➤ 前者は専門用語).
ろくすっぽ ▶きょうはろくすっぽ食ってないんだ I'*ve eaten practically nothing* today. ‖あの生徒は私が授業で教えたことをろくすっぽ覚えていない That student remembers *almost nothing* that I taught him [her] in class.
ろくでなし 碌で無し a **good-for-nothing (fellow)**, a **bum**(➤ 後者がよりくだけた語).
▶このろくでなし! You *good-for-nothing* ! ‖両親は私のことをろくでなしだと思っている My parents think of me as *a good-for-nothing* [consider me *a bum*].
ろくでもない 碌でも無い **useless**(役に立たない) ; **worthless**(価値のない) ▶そんなろくでもない物は捨てなさい Throw away such *useless* [*worthless*] things. (➤「ろくでもない物」は 1 語でいえば junk).
ろくな 碌な ▶あいつが電話してくるときはろくなことがない When he calls, it's never *good* news. ‖私が去年作った俳句にはろくなものがない There isn't a *decent* haiku among all those I wrote last year. (➤ decent は「ちゃんとした」の意) ‖今夜はろくな(=見る価値のある)テレビ番組がない Tonight there is nothing *worth watching* on TV.
▶きょうはろくなことがなかった *Everything went wrong* for me today. /It's been a bad day today. (➤ 前者は「ひとつもうまくいかなかった」, 後者は「ついていない日だった」の意. a bad hair day ともいう) ‖あんなやつと付き合うとろくなことはないよ(=困ったことになるよ) If you get mixed up with that guy, you are *asking for trouble*.
ろくに 碌に ▶ 5 年間英語を勉強しているがろくに(=ほとんど)話せない I can *hardly* speak English, though I've been studying it for five years. ‖きょうは朝からろくに食事もしていない I've had *hardly* anything to eat since this morning. ‖ゆうべは気持ちが高ぶってろくに(=十分に)眠れなかった Last night I was s nervous that I couldn't sleep *well*. ‖隣の娘さ 道で会ってもろくに挨拶もしない Our next-door nei bor's daughter does*n't even* [*so much as*] me when we meet on the street. (➤「挨 ない」の意).
ろくねんせい 6 年生 a **sixth grader**.
ログハウス a **log house**.
ろくまく 肋膜《解剖学》**the pleura** /plɔ́r
‖**ろく膜炎** pleurisy /plʊ́ərəsi/.

ろくめんたい 六面体《幾何学》a **hexahedron** /hèksəhíːdrən/.

ろくろ 轆轤 a **pulley**（滑車）; a **potter's wheel**（陶芸用）.

ろくろく 碌々 ▶我々の同僚でろくろく（＝ちゃんと）挨拶もできない人がいる One of the guys we work with can't even greet people *properly*. →ろくに.

ロケ(ーション) a **location**（立地場所）; **location shooting** [**filming**]（映画撮影；location は「ロケ地」の意）▶最高のロケーションにあるホテル a hotel in a prime *location* ‖ 彼らは新作映画のため北海道へロケに行った They *went on location* in Hokkaido for a new film.

1**ロケット**《飛行体》a **rocket** ▶宇宙［月］ロケットを打ち上げる launch *a space* [*moon*] *rocket*.
‖**ロケットエンジン** a rocket engine ‖ **ロケット工学** rocket engineering.

2**ロケット**《装身具》a **locket** ▶彼は恋人の写真の入ったロケットを肌身離さず着けている He always wears *a locket* with his girlfriend's photo in it next to his skin.

ろけん 露見 **exposure, disclosure** 一動 **露見する** **be exposed** ▶彼らは陰謀が露見して捕まった They were arrested when the plot *was exposed* [*came to light*].

ロゴ a **logo** ▶会社のロゴ（マーク） a corporate [company] *logo* ‖ ロゴの刺しゅうがしてある be embroidered with a *logo*.

ろこつ 露骨な **open**（隠し立てのない）; **blatant**（見え透いた）; **explicit**（はっきり見せる）
▶露骨な敵意 *open* hostility ‖ 露骨な嫌がらせ *obvious* [*flagrant*] harassment ‖ 露骨な性描写 *explicit* description of sex ‖ 露骨なポルノ *hard-core* pornography ／*hard* porn ‖ 彼の露骨な人種差別発言に人々は仰天した People were appalled at his *blatantly* racist remark.（➤「露骨な人種差別」は blatant racial discrimination）.
▶彼は露骨にものを言う男だ He *is too outspoken*.／He *speaks too frankly*.／He does*n't mince his words*.
▶返品を頼むと店員は露骨に嫌な顔をした When I asked the salesperson to accept my returned item, he [she] *gave* me *a dirty look*.（➤ give A a dirty look で「A(人)に非難の目を向ける，嫌な顔をする」）.

ロザリオ a **rosary** /róʊzəri/（数珠）▶ロザリオを手にして祈る say the *rosary*.

ロサンゼルス **Los Angeles**（アメリカ，カリフォルニア州の都市）.

ろし 濾紙 **filter paper** ▶コーヒー用のろ紙 a *paper* coffee *filter*.

ろじ 路地 an **alley(way)**（横町）; a **lane**（小道）▶路地裏に住む live in *a back alley* ‖ 家々が狭い路地を挟んで立っている The houses stand separated only by a narrow *lane*.

ロシア **Russia** /rʌ́ʃə/ 一形 **ロシアの** **Russian** /rʌ́ʃən/
‖**ロシア語** Russian ‖ **ロシア人** a Russian ‖ **ロシア料理** (a) Russian food, a Russian dish ‖ **ロシア連邦** the Russian Federation.

ロシアンルーレット **Russian roulette**.

ろじさいばい 露地栽培 **raising (vegetables) outside**.

ろしゅつ 露出 **1**【さらすこと】**exposure** 一動 **露出する** **expose** ＋目 ▶数人の若い女性たちがあそこで肌を露出して日に焼いている Several young women are *exposing* their skin to the sun to get a good suntan over there.
▶この山道には大きな岩がたくさん露出している Many huge rocks *crop out* along this mountain path.
‖ 露出度の大きい水着 a *scanty* bathing suit（➤ scanty は「肌もあらわな」）.
‖**露出狂** an exhibitionist/èksɪbíʃənɪst/, a flasher.
2【露光】an **exposure** ▶この写真は露出オーバー［不足］だ This picture is *overexposed* [is *underexposed*].

ろじょう 路上 ▶路上で遊んではいけません Don't play *in* [*on*] *the street*.
▶《掲示》路上駐車禁止 *Parking on the street* is prohibited.
‖**路上試験** a road test ‖ **路上生活者** a street [homeless] person.

ろしん 炉心 a **(nuclear) reactor core**.

ロス (a) **loss**（損失）; (a) **waste**（浪費）
▶一人一人個別に意見を聞いて決めるのは時間のロスではない To make a decision after listening to each person's opinion is not *a waste of time*. ‖ 5分間のロスタイム 5 minutes *injury time* ／5 minutes *added* [*additional*] *time*（➤最近では日本語でも「アディショナルタイム」という場合が多い）.

ロゼ (a) **rosé** /roʊzéɪ/（ワイン）.

ろせん 路線 **1**【交通の】a **route** /ruːt/, a **line** ▶このバス路線は来月廃止になる This *bus route* [*line*] will be discontinued next month.
‖**路線図** a route map（➤地下鉄の路線図は a subway route map）‖ **路線バス** a route bus.
2【方針】a **line** ▶党の路線に従う follow the party *line*.

ロッカー a **locker** ▶部長はロッカーにゴルフクラブのセットを置いている The manager keeps a set of golf clubs in his *locker*.
‖**ロッカールーム** a locker room. →コインロッカー.

ろっかく 六角《幾何学》a **hexagon**（六角形）一形 **六角の** **hexagonal, six-sided** ▶六角形の建物 a *hexagonal* [*six-sided*] building.

ろっかん 六感 →第六感.

ロッキーさんみゃく ロッキー山脈 **the Rocky Mountains, the Rockies**（北アメリカ大陸西部の大山脈）.

ロッキングチェア a **rocking chair**.

1**ロック**《音楽》**rock (music), rock'n'roll** ▶あの歌手は以前ロックバンドで活躍していた That singer used to be active as a member of *a rock band*.
‖**ロック歌手** a rock singer, a rocker.

2**ロック**《錠》a **lock** 一動 **ロックする** **lock** ＋目 ▶部屋に入ったらドアを必ずロックしなさい After you enter your room, be sure to *lock* the door. ‖ 車の中にキーを入れたままロックしてしまった I *locked* my key(s) in the car.

ロックアウト a **lockout** 一動 **ロックアウトする** **lock out**.

ロッククライミング **rock climbing** ▶ロッククライミングをする *go rock climbing*.

ロックンロール《音楽》**rock'n'roll, rock and roll**.

ろっこつ 肋骨 a **rib**（1本）; **the ribs**（全体）▶息子ははしごから落ちて，ろっ骨を1本折った My son broke *a rib* when he fell off a ladder.

ロッジ a **lodge** ▶私たちは蔵王のスキーロッジで2泊した We spent two nights at *a ski lodge* in Zao.

ろっぽうぜんしょ 六法全書 **the Compendium of Laws**（➤ compendium は「情報を集成した本」）.

ろてい 露呈 ▶その原発の大惨事で政府の危機管理体制の不備が露呈される結果になった The nuclear

ろ

power plant disaster *exposed* the government's lack of crisis management preparation.

ロデオ a **rodeo** /roʊdéɪoʊ, róʊdioʊ/.

1**ろてん 露店** a **roadside stand** [**stall**] (田舎の); a **street stall** [**stand**] (➤ 一般に road は都会の道路をさすことは少ない. 都会の露店をさす場合は roadside ではなく street を使う)

▶縁日には境内に**露店**がたくさん出る A lot of *stands* [*stalls*] are put up in the temple precincts on festival days.

2**ろてん 露天** ‖**露天商** a stand [stall] keeper, a street vendor ‖**露天掘り**《米》strip mining, 《英》opencast mining.

ろてんぶろ 露天風呂 an **open-air bath** ▶満天の星を見ながら**露天風呂**につかる soak in *an open-air bath* while looking up at the stars that fill the sky.

ろとう 路頭 ▶今彼が病気で倒れでもしたら家族は**路頭**に迷う(＝生活に困る)ことになるだろう If he came down with a serious illness now, his family would *find it almost impossible to make a living* [would *be destitute*]. (➤ destitute は「困窮状態の」).

ろば 驢馬《動物》a **donkey**, an **ass**.

ロハス LOHAS (➤ Lifestyles of Health and Sustainability (「健康と地球環境の持続性を重んじるライフスタイル」の頭字語)).

ろばた 炉端 the fireside.

ロビー a **lobby** ▶ホテルの**ロビー** a hotel *lobby* ‖ (空港の)出発**ロビー** a departure *lounge* ‖ 帝国ホテルの**ロビー**で旧友に会った I met with an old friend of mine in the *lobby* of the Imperial Hotel.

ロビイスト a **lobbyist**(政府や議会に圧力をかける人).

ロビング《テニス》**lobbing**; a **lob**(球).

ロブスター《動物》a **lobster**.

ロフト a **loft**(天井裏の収納用空間, 部屋).

ろぶん 露文 Russian literature(文学).

ロボット a **robot** /róʊbɑːt/ ▶精巧な**産業用ロボット** a sophisticated *industrial robot*.

‖**ロボットアーム** a robot arm ‖**ロボット工学** robotics /roʊbɑ́ːṭɪks/ ‖**人型ロボット** a humanoid robot.

ロマン ▶これは**ロマン**の香り高き小説である This is a *romantic* novel [a novel *filled with romance*].

‖**ロマン主義** romanticism /roʊmǽnṭəsɪzəm/ ‖**ロマン派** the romantic school.

ロマンス a **romance** /roʊmǽns/; **love**(愛); a **love affair**(情事) ▶二人の間に**ロマンス**が芽生えた *A romance* began to develop between the two. ‖ 私はもともと**ロマンス**などに縁はない I never have any *romantic experiences*.

‖**ロマンスカー** a deluxe /dəlʌ́ks/ train [coach] ‖**ロマンスグレー(の男)** (a man with) silver gray hair ‖**ロマンス語** a Romance language.

ロマンチスト a **romantic** /roʊmǽnṭɪk/ (夢想家); a **romanticist** /roʊmǽnṭəsɪst/ (ロマン主義者) ▶植村さんは**ロマンチスト**だった Mr. Uemura was *a romantic*.

> **危ないカタカナ語✹ ロマンチスト**
> 「ロマンチスト」は英語では romanticist というが, この語は「ロマン派の芸術家」の意味で使われることが多い. 日本語の「ロマンチスト」は「夢想家」の意味であるから, romantic や dreamy person を用いるのがよいが, これらは文脈によっては軽蔑的な含みをもつ.

ロマンチック romantic /roʊmǽnṭɪk/ ▶藤村は**ロマンチック**な詩人だと思いませんか Don't you think Toson is a *romantic* poet? ‖ 彼女と 2 人で眺めたペナンの夕焼けはとても**ロマンチック**だった Watching the sunset on Penang with my girlfriend was quite *romantic*.

ロム《コンピュータ》(a) **ROM** (➤ Read Only Memory (読み出し専用メモリー)の頭字語).

ろめん 路面 ▶**路面**(＝道路)が凍結しておりますのでタイヤにチェーンを巻いてください The *road* is icy, so please use (tire) chains.

‖**路面電車**《米》a streetcar, 《英》a tram.

ロリコン a **Lolita complex** (➤ この語は日本におけるほど一般的ではない. また, lolicon は和製英語) ▶**ロリコン**の中年男 a middle-aged man with *a Lolita complex*.

ろれつ 呂律 ▶彼は**ろれつ**が回らなくなるほど酔っていた He was so drunk (that) he *couldn't speak clearly*. ／He was so drunk that he *slurred his words*.

ろん 論 a **theory**(理論); an **argument** (議論); an **opinion**(意見) ▶進化**論** the *theory* of evolution ‖ 抽象**論** an abstract *argument* ‖人生**論** one's *view* [*philosophy*] of life ‖ 音楽**論** an *essay* on music.

▶早期教育が是か非か**論**の分かれるところだ *Opinion* is divided as to whether early education is good or bad.

[ことわざ] **論より証拠** Example is better than precept. (➤「手本は教訓に勝る」の意)／The proof of the pudding is in the eating. (➤「プディングの味は食べてみなければわからない」の意).

ろんがい 論外 ▶いくらお祝いだからといって子供に酒を飲ませるなんて**論外**です It may be a festive occasion, but it's *out of the question* to force a child to drink sake. (●「問題外の」と考えて out of the question を用いる).

ろんぎ 論議 (a) **discussion**, (an) **argument** →**議論** ▶今更その問題を**論議**してみても始まらない At this stage, there is no point in *discussing* the matter further.

ろんきゃく 論客 a **controversialist**.

ろんきゅう 論及する discuss +Ⓜ (論じる); **refer to** (言及する)

▶彼は各国のマスコミを論じているが, 発展途上国の状況には**論及していない** Although he deals with mass media in various countries, he never *discusses* [*touches on*] the situation in the developing world.

ろんきょ 論拠 the ground(s) ▶自衛隊が違憲だというきみの**論拠**はどこにあるの? On what *grounds* do you say that the Self-Defense Forces are unconstitutional?

ロングシュート a **long shot**.

ロングスカート a **long skirt**.

ロングセラー a **longtime best seller** (➤ best-seller, bestseller のつづりもある) ▶珍しく哲学書が**ロングセラー**になっている It is unusual for such a philosophy book to become *a longtime best seller* [to sell so well over a long period].

ロングヘア long hair

▶**ロングヘア**の若い女性 a young woman *with long hair*／a young, *long-haired* woman ‖ 早紀ちゃんは**ロングヘア**にしている Saki *wears her hair long*.

ロングラン a **long run** ▶ 9 か月の**ロングラン**をする have *a long run* of nine months.

▶『オペラ座の怪人』はブロードウェーで**ロングラン**を続けた

"The Phantom of the Opera" enjoyed *a long run* on Broadway.

ろんご 論語 **the Analects of Confucius**(➤ analects は「(哲学的)語録」, Confucius は「孔子」).

ろんこうこうしょう 論功行賞 ▶論功行賞をする *award someone for their* (*distinguished*) *service* [*support*].

ろんし 論旨 **the point of an argument ; the drift** (要点) ▶論旨をつかむ get *the point* [catch *the drift*] *of an argument*.

ろんじゅつ 論述 a **discussion** (➤「説明」の意の堅い語) 一動 **論述する** **discuss** +目 ; **set forth** (one's) **opinion** ▶日本の高齢化社会について論述せよ *Discuss* Japan's aging society (in an essay).
‖**論述試験** an essay exam(ination).

ろんしょう 論証 (a) **demonstration** 一動 **論証する** **demonstrate** +目 .

ろんじる 論じる **argue** +目 (相手を説得するために自分の意見を主張する) ; **discuss** +目 (問題解決のために建設的に議論する) ; **talk** 《about》(話し合う) ; **debate** +目 (反対側と賛成側に分かれて討論する) ▶その損害を誰が弁償するのかを論じる *argue* over who should pay for the damage ‖ 私は彼と政治について何時間も論じ合った I *argued* about [*discussed*] politics with him for hours.
▶学園祭で何をやるかをクラスで論じ合った We *had a* class *discussion* about what we should do for the school festival. ‖ 彼は教育について論じた He *talked about* education.

ろんじん 論陣 ▶彼は堂々とその計画反対 [賛成] の論陣を張った He *set forth a strong argument* against [for] the project.

ろんせつ 論説 an **article** (論 文) ; an **editorial** /èdɪtɔ́:riəl/, 《英また》 a **leading article** (社説)
‖**論説委員** 《米》an editorial writer, 《英》a leader writer.

ろんせん 論戦 (an) **argument** ; (a) **dispute**(激しい) ▶両者は教育改革を巡って論戦を交わした The two of them *had an argument* [*a dispute*] over educational reform.

ろんそう 論争 (a) **dispute** /dɪspjú:t/ (しばしば感情的な) ; (a) **controversy** /kɑ́:ntrəvə:ʳsi/ (長期にわたる公の) ; (a) **debate** (公式な議論, 討論) 一動 **論争する** **dispute, argue** ▶論争に巻き込まれる get involved in *a dispute* ‖ 彼らはその土地の所有権を巡って激しく論争した They *had a* violent *dispute* over the ownership of the land.
▶邪馬台国論争がますますおもしろくなってきた The Yamataikoku *controversy* has become more and more interesting.
▶この訴訟は大論争を引き起こした This lawsuit gave rise to [led to] *much controversy*. ‖ その法案を巡って多くの論争があった There has been much *debate* about the bill.

ろんだい 論題 a **theme** [**topic**／**subject**] **for discussion**(➤ for の代わりに of も可).

ろんだん 論壇 ▶華々しく論壇に登場する make a brilliant debut in *intellectual circles*.

ろんちょう 論調 ▶その法律の改正問題では各紙とも論調は控えめだ The various newspapers have made only *muted comments* on the revision of that law.

ろんてん 論点 **the (main) topic, the point at issue** ▶国会での論点が経済から政治の問題に移った *The topic* (*of discussion*) at the Diet session shifted from economic to political questions.

ロンド 《音楽》 a **rondo**.

ロンドン **London** /lʌ́ndən/ (イギリスの首都).

ろんぱ 論破する **refute** +目 ; **argue down** (言い負かす)
▶反対意見を論破する *refute* an opposing opinion ‖ 彼女を論破するのは難しい It is hard to *refute* her [*argue* her *down*].

ろんばく 論駁 **refutation** 一動 **論ばくする** **refute** +目 .

ろんぴょう 論評 (a) **comment** (意見) ; (a) **criticism**, (a) **review** /rɪvjú:/ (批評) 一動 **論評する** **comment** 《on》, **criticize** +目 ▶官房長官は交渉の結果について論評した The Chief Cabinet Secretary *made a comment* [*commented*] *on* the results of the negotiations. ‖ 評論家はその本について好意的な論評をした The critic gave the book a favorable *review*.

ろんぶん 論文 a **treatise** /trí:ţəs ‖ -tɪz/ (専門的・科学的な長い論文) ; a **paper** (研究論文) ; a **thesis** /θí:sɪs/ (博士や修士の), a **dissertation** (学位論文) ; an **essay** (小論文) ▶私はヘミングウェーについての論文を出した I presented *a paper* on Hemingway. ‖ 卒業論文のテーマは決まりましたか Have you decided on the subject of your *graduation paper*?
‖**修士論文** a master's thesis ‖ **小論文** a short essay [paper] ‖ **博士論文** a doctoral dissertation [《英また》 thesis].

ろんぽう 論法 **logic**, a **line** [**method**] **of reasoning** ▶きみの論法でいくと, ほかの人がみんな悪いことをするならば自分もやってかまわないということになる Following your *logic*, it is all right to do something wrong if everyone else does it, too.
‖**三段論法** 《論理学》 a syllogism /sílədʒɪzəm/.

ろんり 論理 **logic** ▶きみの話は論理に飛躍がある There is a leap in your *logic*. ／You've made a leap [jump] in your *logic*. ‖ 彼の推理は論理的だ His reasoning is *logical*.
▶きみの論文には論理的に矛盾がある Your paper is not *logically* consistent. ‖ 非論理的な意見は説得力がない *Illogical* assertions have no persuasive power.
‖**論理学** logic ‖ **論理学者** a logician /loodʒíʃən/.

わ・ワ

[1]わ 輪 **1【円い物】a ring**; **a circle**（円）; **a loop**（ひもなどで作った）; a **wheel**（車輪）▶たばこの煙で輪を作る blow a smoke *ring* ‖ 生徒たちは輪になって座った The schoolchildren sat *in a ring* [*circle*].
▶私はひもで輪を作った I tied the string to make *a loop*.
2【慣用表現】▶道子は姉に輪を掛けてわがままだ Michiko is *even more* self-centered than her (older) sister. ‖ 会話の内容が高尚すぎて, なかなか話の輪に入れなかった The conversation was too deep for me to *join in*.

[2]わ 和 **1【調和】harmony**; **peace**（平穏なこと）; **friendship**（仲がよいこと）▶クラスの和 *harmony* of the class ‖ 人の和を保つ maintain *harmony* [*peace*] among people ‖ 日米間の和 *friendship* between Japan and the U.S.
▶日本の社会は和を尊ぶ Japanese society values (*a sense of*) *harmony*.
▶和を以(もっ)て尊しとなす *Harmony should be valued*. ‖ この国では和を乱す者は爪はじきにされる Those who upset *harmony* in this country are often shunned by other people.
2【合計】the sum, the total →合計 ▶3と4の和は7だ *The sum* of three and four is seven. ／Three plus four equals seven.
3【日本】Japan ▶茶道文化は和の心の典型だ The culture of the tea ceremony typifies *the soul of Japan*.

[1]-わ -羽 ▶1羽のウサギ *one* [*a*] rabbit ‖ 数十羽のスズメが電線に止まっている *Several dozen* sparrows are perching on the electric wire.

[2]-わ -把 ▶ホウレンソウ3把 three *bunches* of spinach.

わあ《感動して》**Oh!**, **Wow** /waʊ/!, **Gee** /dʒiː/! ▶わあ, きれい *Oh!* It's really beautiful! ‖ 対話「ことしの夏休みにはハワイへ行こうか」「わあ, すごいや!」"How about going to Hawaii this summer vacation?" "*Gee*, that would be great!" ‖ わあ, やった! *Great*, we've done it! ‖ わあ, すばらしい! *Wow*, that's nice!

ワーキング ‖ワーキングプア the working poor ‖ ワーキングホリデー a working holiday.

ワークシェアリング **work sharing.**

ワークショップ a **workshop**（研修会; 工房）▶夏期ワークショップに参加する attend a summer *workshop*.

ワークブック a **workbook** ▶ワークブックの練習問題をする do exercises in *a workbook*.

ワースト **worst** ▶ワースト記録 *the worst record* ‖ その年の自殺者数はワースト記録を塗り替えた The number of suicides that year *reached a record high*. (「新記録となる最大の数値に達した」と考える) ‖ あの司会者は嫌いなテレビタレントのワーストテンに入っている That emcee is one of *the ten most disliked* TV personalities.

ワードローブ a **wardrobe** /wɔ́ːʳdroʊb/（洋服だんす, 持ち衣装）.

ワープ **warp.**

ワープロ a **word processor** /prɑ́ːsesəʳ/
‖ワープロソフト a word-processing program, word-processing software.

ワールドカップ **the World Cup** ▶サッカーのワールドカップ・トーナメント *the World Cup* soccer *tournament* ‖ 我々の目標はワールドカップの決勝トーナメントに進むことです Our aim is to advance to *the World Cup* final tournament.

ワールドシリーズ **the World Series**（アメリカ大リーグの）▶その年のワールドシリーズはニューヨーク・ヤンキースが優勝した The New York Yankees won *the World Series* of that year.

わあわあ ▶息子がワーワー泣きながら帰って来た My son came home *bawling* [*blubbering*]. (➤ bawl は「泣きわめく」, blubber は「(主に子供が)わあわあ泣く」) ‖ もう決まったことだ. 今さらワーワー言ってもしょうがない It's been decided. There's no point in *making such a fuss about it*.

ワイオミング **Wyoming** /waɪóʊmɪŋ/（アメリカ北西部の州; 略 WY, Wyo., Wy.）.

ワイキキ **Waikiki** /wáɪkɪkiː/（ハワイ州ホノルル市の海岸）.

わいきょく 歪曲 a **distortion** 一動 わい曲する **distort** ＋㊐ ▶この記事は事実をわい曲して伝えている This article presents *a distorted version* of the facts.

わいざつ 猥雑な **squalid** ▶歌舞伎町には独特のわい雑な雰囲気があった The Kabuki-cho district used to have a uniquely *squalid* atmosphere.

ワイシャツ a **shirt** ▶社員の多くはオフィスではワイシャツ姿で働く Most of our employees work *in their shirts* [*in their shirt sleeves*] while in the office.

> **危ないカタカナ語✹ ワイシャツ**
> 「ワイシャツ」は white shirt がなまったものだが, 英語では単に shirt という. white shirt は「白いワイシャツ」であることを明確にするときに用いる. dress shirt ということもあるが, これは半袖シャツ(short-sleeved shirt)やスポーツシャツ(sport shirt)などと区別したり礼装用のシャツを指したりするときにいう.

わいしょう 矮小の **very small** ▶問題をわい小化する *trivialize* a problem.

ワイじろ Y字路 a **forked road**; a **Y-junction**（Y字交差点）.

[1]わいせい 矮性の **dwarf, undersized**
‖わい性遺伝子 a dwarf gene.

[2]わいせい 矮星《天文学》**a dwarf star.**

わいせつ 猥褻 **obscenity** /əbsénəṭi/（わいせつ物）; **indecency**（下品）一形 わいせつな **obscene, indecent**; **dirty**（淫らな）▶わいせつ画像 an *indecent* image ‖ わいせつな映画 a *dirty* film.
▶インターネットでわいせつ画像を見る look at *smut* on the Internet (➤ smut は pornography よりも軽蔑的な語).
‖わいせつ行為 an obscene act ‖ わいせつ本 an obscene book, a dirty book, a pornographic [smutty] book, porn(ography), smut (➤ porn, pornography は雑誌, 映画なども含む) ‖ 強制わいせ

つ(罪) indecent assault ‖ **公然わいせつ(罪)** indecent exposure.

わいだん 猥談 **dirty** [**smutty**] **talk** ▶連中は集まると決まってわい談を始める That bunch can never get together without telling *dirty* [*smutty* / *raunchy*] *jokes*. (● raunchy は「下がかった, エッチな」; without talking dirty としてもよい).

ワイド **wide** ▶ワイドスクリーン a *wide* screen.
‖**ワイドショー** a long (TV) variety program (➤「ワイドショー」は和製語).

ワイパー **wipers**, 《米また》 **windshield wipers**, 《英また》 **windscreen wipers** ▶ワイパーを動かす turn on the *wipers*.

ワイファイ 《コンピュータ》 **Wi-Fi**
‖**ワイファイ接続** a Wi-Fi connection.

ワイヤー (a) **wire** ‖**ワイヤーブラシ** a wire brush ‖ **ワイヤーロープ** a wire rope.

ワイヤレス **wireless** ▶ワイヤレスマイク a *wireless* microphone.

ワイルドピッチ 《野球》 a **wild pitch** [**throw**] ▶前田の5球目はワイルドピッチとなった Maeda's fifth pitch *went wild*.

わいろ 賄賂 a **bribe**, 《インフォーマル》 a **payoff** (賄賂としての金品); **bribery** (賄賂を贈ったり受け取ったりすること) ▶**賄賂**を贈る offer [give] *a bribe* ‖ **賄賂**を求める solicit *a bribe*.
▶その役人は**賄賂**を受け取ろうとしなかった The official wouldn't take *a bribe*.

わいわい ▶子供たちがわいわい騒いでいる The children are shouting *noisily*. ‖ そうわいわい言うなよ Don't *make* such *a fuss* [*commotion*] *about* it. (●「そう騒ぎ立てるな」と考えて訳す).

ワイン **wine** ▶1杯の赤 [白 / ロゼ] ワイン a glass of red [white / rosé] *wine* ‖ 辛口 [甘口] のワイン dry [sweet] *wine*.
▶ドイツは優れた白ワインを生産する Germany produces excellent *white wines*. (➤ 銘柄を表すときは数えられる名詞扱い).
‖**ワインカラー** wine color ‖ **ワイングラス** a wineglass ‖ **ワインレッド** wine red.

ワインドアップ 《野球》 a **windup** ▶ワインドアップして投げる *wind up* and throw ‖ ノーワインドアップで投げる pitch *without winding up*. →**モーション**.

わえい 和英 ▶**和英**辞典を引く see [use / refer to / consult] *a Japanese-English dictionary* (➤ refer to と consult は堅い言い方) / look up a word in *a Japanese-English dictionary*.

わおん 和音 a **chord** /kɔːʳd/ (音楽の)
‖**三和音** a triad ‖ **主 [属] 和音** a tonic [dominant] chord ‖ **分散和音** an arpeggio.

わか 和歌 ***waka*** **(poetry)**; a ***waka*** **(poem)** (一首の); a form of classic Japanese poetry, consisting of five-, seven-, five-, seven-, and seven-syllabled lines (➤ 説明的な訳).

わが 我が **my**, **our** (➤ このほか, 代名詞の所有格で表す)
▶おばはプードルをわが子のようにかわいがっている My aunt dotes on the poodle like *her* (*own*) *child*. ‖ 私は金メダルの獲得をわが事のように喜んだ I was as delighted by the gold medal *as if I had won it myself*. ‖ わが国は世界有数の経済大国だ *Our country* is one of the leading economic powers of the world. (● 日本について言う場合は Japan でよい).
▶《慣用表現》ぼくは常に「わが道を行く」さ I always *go my own way* [*do things my way*].

▶平家はわが世の春をおう歌した *The world was* the Heike clan's *oyster*. (➤ The world is A's oyster. は「世界は A(人)の思いのままだ」の意).

[1]**わかい 和解** (a) **reconciliation** (再び仲よくさせること); (a) **settlement** (解決); (a) **compromise** (妥協) 一動 (…と)**和解する** **reconcile** 《with》, **reach a settlement** 《with》, **come to terms** 《with》; **settle (out of court)** (➤ out of court は裁判をやめて示談にした場合) ▶彼女はようやく夫と**和解した** She *reconciled with* her husband at long last. (● 当事者が努力して「人(A)と和解する」は reconcile with A だが, 仲介によって和解する場合はしばしば受け身形, be reconciled with A を用いる).
▶長らく絶交していた友人と**和解した** I *reconciled* [*made up* / *made peace*] *with* a friend I had been at odds with for a long time. (● あとの2者は「仲直りした」と考えた場合).
▶彼女は2人の兄弟を**和解させた** She *made peace* between her two brothers. ‖ 裁判所は両者に**和解**を勧告した The court recommended *a settlement* to both parties. / The court urged both parties to *settle* (*out of court*).
▶遺族は2000万円の補償金を受け取ることで会社側と**和解した** The bereaved family *reached a settlement* [*came to terms*] *with* the company on condition they would receive twenty million yen in compensation. ‖ 労働組合は会社側と**和解した** The labor union and management *reached a compromise* [*settled out of court*]. (➤ compromise は「歩み寄り」).

[2]**わかい 若い** **1**【年齢などが】**young** ▶若い男性 a *young* man ‖ 彼は私より5つ若い He is five years *younger than* I. ‖ 若いうちにアメリカに留学したい I want to study in the United States *while young*.
▶若い人たちには若い人たちの考えがある *Young people* have their own ways of thinking. ‖ ああ, もし私が10歳若かったらなあ Oh, I wish I were ten years *younger*!
▶父は年より若く見える My father *looks younger* than his age. / My father *looks young* for his age. (● 後者は「年の割に若い」と考えた場合) ‖ 兄は若くして死んだ My older brother died *young*. ‖ きみんとこのおじいさんは気が若いね Your grandfather *is* still *young at heart*.
▶この会社は2年前に創立された若い会社です This is a *young* company founded two years ago. ‖ 番号の若いほうが古い会員です Members with *smaller* membership ID *numbers* joined the club earlier.
2【未熟な】**immature** /ìmətjʊ́əʳ/ ▶そんなことを考えているようではきみはまだ若いね If that's what you think, you are still *immature*.
▶やつらはまだまだ若い They are still *green* [*greenhorns*]. / Those people are still *wet behind the ears*. (➤ いずれも「青二才だ」の意. →**若造**) / They are still *just kids*.

わがい 我が意 ▶彼女の発言にわが意を得たりと感じた When I heard her comment, I felt *she had said just what I was thinking* [*she had taken the words out of my mouth*].

わかがえり 若返り **rejuvenation** /rɪdʒùːvənéɪʃən/ ▶チームの若返りを図る *plan to rejuvenate* the team ‖ わが校は教員スタッフの若返りを図る必要がある We must consider *hiring young people to lower the*

わ

average age of our teaching staff.

わかがえる 若返る **be rejuvenated** /rɪdʒúːvənèɪtɪd/ ; **look younger**(より若く見える) ▶彼は若い奥さんをもらって若返ったようだ Marrying a young woman seems to *have rejuvenated* him [*have taken years off his age*]. ▶若い女性たちに囲まれて働いているので気持ちが若返る Since I work among young women, I myself *feel young at heart*.

わかぎ 若木 a **sapling**.

わかくさ 若草 **fresh** [**young**] **grass** ‖若草色 bright [grass] green.

わかげ 若気 ▶若気の至りです *Blame it on my youth*. (「私の若さのせいにしてください」と考える) ‖若気の至りでおやじのやり方に一から十まで反発した *Out of youthful arrogance*, I rebelled at everything my father said or did. (「若さゆえの思い上がりで」と考えて訳す).

わかさ 若さ **youth**(若いこと) ; **youthfulness** (若々しさ) ▶若さを保つために水泳をやっています I swim to *stay young*. ‖私の若さの秘密は楽天主義だ The secret of my *youthfulness* is my optimism. ‖彼は30歳の若さで市長になった He became mayor *at the early* [*tender*] *age* of 30. ‖若さは一度限りのもの *You're only young once*. (➤英語の決まった言い方). ▶大事なところで彼の若さ(=未熟さ)が出た His *immaturity* was revealed at the critical moment.

わかさぎ 公魚 《魚》 a **smelt**.

わがし 和菓子 **Japanese confectionery** (➤総称) ; **Japanese-style** [**Japanese traditional**] **sweets**.

わかじに 若死に an **early** [**a premature**] **death** ▶その作家は若死にした That writer *died young*.

わかしらが 若白髪 **premature gray hair** ▶彼は若白髪だ He has *a lot of premature gray* [*white*] *hair*.

わかす 沸かす **1【湯を】boil** +目 (沸騰させる) ; **heat** +目 (熱する) ▶(料理番組などで)まず鍋にお湯を沸かし, 次に麺を入れます First, *boil* water in the pan and then add noodles.

2【熱狂させる】excite +目 ▶そのタイトルマッチは観衆を大いに沸かせた The title match greatly *excited* the spectators.

わかぞう 若造 a **youngster**(若者) ; 《インフォーマル》 a **whippersnapper** (生意気なやつ, 青二才 ; 古風な語) ▶あんな若造にはまだまだ負けられん I'm not about to let myself be beaten by *a kid* like him. ‖当時俺はまだ若造だった Back then, I was (still) *wet behind the ears*. (➤wet behind the ears は「(人が)未熟な, 経験不足の, 世間知らずの」の意 ; 体を洗ったあとの子供が耳の後ろをよく拭かないことに由来).

わかちあう 分かち合う **share** +目 (共用・共有する) ▶山中では少ない食糧を分かち合わねばならなかった We had to *share* what little food we had in the mountains. ‖その老夫婦は50年以上苦楽を分かち合ってきた The elderly couple *have shared* joys and sorrows (with each other) for over fifty years. →分け合う.

わかづくり 若作り ▶彼女若作りだけど, とうに40は越してるよ She is well over forty, though she always *makes herself up to look young* [*dresses young*]. (前者は「化粧が若作り」, 後者は「服装が若作り」と考えて訳す).

わかて 若手 **young people** 一形 若手の **young** ▶若手の実業家 a *young* businessperson ‖テニス界はこのところ若手の伸びが著しい In recent years, *young* tennis *players* have made great strides.

わかどり 若鶏 a **spring chicken** ; a **broiler** (**chicken**) (➤焼き肉用).

わかば 若葉 **young leaves, fresh greenery** ▶上高地は若葉の頃が最高だ Kamikochi is most beautiful in the season of *young leaves* [*fresh greenery*].

わかはげ 若禿げ ▶兄は最近抜け毛が多く, 若はげを心配している My (older) brother has been losing a lot of hair recently, so he's afraid of *going bald prematurely*.

わかふうふ 若夫婦 a **young** (**married**) **couple** ▶老夫婦は引退して, 若夫婦があの旅館を切り盛りしている Since the elderly couple retired, the *young couple* have [has] been running the inn. (➤couple は2人を個々に考える場合は複数扱い, まとまった1組と考える場合は単数扱い).

わがまま 我が儘 **selfishness** 一形 わがままな **selfish** (自分勝手の) ; **spoiled**(甘やかされた) ▶自分のわがままを抑える control one's *selfishness* ‖わがまま言うなよ Don't *think only of yourself*. (「自分のことだけを考えるな」と考えて訳す) ‖一人っ子はよくわがままに育つと言われる It is often said that an only child grows up to be *selfish*. ‖したい放題にさせるとわがままな子になるよ If you let him do as he pleases, he will become a *spoiled* brat. (「甘やかされた悪がきになる」と考えて訳す) ‖あなたのわがままは許しませんよ I won't let you *have your own way*. (「自分の好きなようにする, 身勝手を通す」と考えて have one's own way を用いる).

わがみ 我が身 ▶ 対話 「内山さんが肩たたきされたんだって」「あすはわが身だよ」"I hear Mr. Uchiyama was asked to quit the company." "*It could be my turn tomorrow.* / *My turn may come tomorrow.*" (➤turn は「順番」).

わかみどり 若緑 **fresh green**(色が).

わかむき 若向きの **suitable for young people**.

[1]**わかめ 若布** ***wakame*** (**seaweed**).

[2]**わかめ 若芽** a **sprout** /spraʊt/, a **shoot** (新芽) ; a **bud** (まだ皮に包まれたもの) ▶このところの暖かさで木々の若芽が伸びてきた *Budding leaves* have begun to appear on the trees with the recent warm weather.

わかもの 若者 a **young man** (男), a **young woman** (女) ; **young people, young men and women** (若者たち) ; **the youth** (➤総称)

> **《解説》**(1)「若者たち」を表すふつうの言い方は young people で, the youth を使った the youth of today [the world] (今日 [世界] の若者たち) などは堅い言い方. the youth は Ⓒ 扱いの「(犯罪や暴力事件などに関係した)(10代の)その若者」(男を指す)の意で用いることが多い.
> (2) youth は形容詞的に「若者たちの」の意ではいくつかの表現でよく用いる : youth culture (若者文化), a youth group (若者たちのグループ, 青年グループ), youth sports (青少年スポーツ), a youth center (青少年センター).

▶最近の若者は体格がいい *Young people* today have good physiques. ‖その歌手は若者たちに人気がある That singer is very popular among [with] *young people*.

わがものがお 我が物顔 ▶康夫はおじさんのフェラーリをわが物顔に乗り回している Yasuo drives around in his uncle's Ferrari *as if it belonged to him*. ‖彼はどこへ行ってもわが物顔でふるまう Wherever he goes, he acts *as if he owns the place*. (●「その場所を所有しているかのように」と考える).

わがや 我が家 **our house** [**home**] ; **our family** (家族) ▶わが家は二階建てだ *Our house* has two stories. (➤ My house とすると「ひとり住まい」の印象を与える可能性がある) ‖ わが家はみなプロ野球ファンです Everyone in *our family* is a pro baseball fan. ‖ この掛け軸はわが家の家宝です This hanging scroll is *our family* treasure.

▶わが家に勝る所はない There's no place like home. ／East or west, home is best. (➤ ともに英語のことわざ ; 慣用表現で my や our をつけない) ‖ 狭いながらも楽しいわが家 Although our house is rather small, *our family* is a happy one.

わかやぐ 若やぐ ▶小山さんは若やいだ服装で現れた Mr. Koyama showed up, *dressed like a much younger man*.

わからずや 分からず屋 ▶あのわからず屋(＝頑固者)には困ったものだ That *obstinate* [*stubborn*] *guy* has given us a lot of trouble. ‖ このわからず屋め！ You *numbskull* [*dummy*] ! ／ You're *a pigheaded fool* !

わからない 分からない ▶わからない人だな. さっきから何べん同じことを言わせるんですか *Blockhead!* How many times do I have to say the same thing! (●「愚かな人だなあ」と考えて blockhead を用いるとよい).

わかり 分かり ▶きみはわかりがいいね！ You *catch on quick*(*ly*) ! ‖ この子はわかりが速い[遅い] This child *is quick* [*slow*] *to catch on*. ／He is a quick [slow] learner. ‖ 彼はわかりのいい人だ He's a *sensible* [*reasonable*] man. (●「思慮分別を持った人」または「道理をわきまえた人」と考えて, 用例のような形容詞を用いるとよい).

わかりきった 分かり切った **obvious**, **clear** (明白な) ▶わかり切ったことを聞くなよな Don't ask me such a stupid question (about *something that should be obvious*). ‖ 地元民がこの計画に反対するのは最初からわかり切っていた It was *quite clear* from the beginning that the local residents would oppose this project.

わかりにくい 分かりにくい **be hard to understand** ▶この文章はわかりにくい This passage *is hard to understand* [*is unintelligible*]. ‖ 私たちの先生の字はわかりにくい Our teacher's handwriting *is hard to read*. (●「読みにくい」と考える).

わかりやすい 分かり易い **be easy to understand** ▶この説明はわかりやすい This explanation *is easy to understand*. ‖ この数字を図にしたほうがわかりやすいだろう It would *be easier to understand* if you put these figures into a diagram. ‖ 池上さんは難しい問題をわかりやすく説明してくれる Mr. Ikegami explains difficult issues so clearly that *anyone can easily understand* them. (●「誰にでも理解できるように」と考える) ‖ もっとわかりやすく言ってください Please say it more *plainly* [*simply*]. (●「簡潔に」と考える).

わかる 分かる

> 📖 **訳語メニュー**
> 理解する →understand, see **1**
> 良さがわかる →appreciate **1**
> 知る →find, know **3**
> 気づく →recognize **3**

1【理解する】 **understand** (+目), **get** (+目) (➤ 後者はインフォーマル) ; **see** (+目) (要点などが) ▶私の言っていること[私の質問の意味]がわかりますか Do you *understand* what I am saying [my question] ? ‖ 私はドイツ語はわからない I don't *understand* German. ‖ きみはお母さんがどれだけ心配したかわからないのか Don't you *understand* [*know*] how worried your mother was? ‖ その子はどうしてどなられたのか訳がわからない様子だった The little boy appeared not to *understand* why he was being yelled at. ‖ 対話「きみ, 今の教授の講義はわかったかい」「50パーセントくらいわかりました」"Did you *understand* the professor's lecture?" "I *understood* about fifty percent (of it)."

▶ 対話「結果が気になって落ち着かないんです」「わかる, その気持ち」"I feel restless because I'm very worried about the results." "*I understand the feeling*." ‖ ぼくの言ったこと, わかってもらえた？ Did I *make myself clear*?

▶彼女はそのアメリカ人の言った冗談がわからなかった She didn't *get* [*understand*] the American's joke. ‖ 対話「このボタンで安全装置が作動します」「わかりました」"This button activates the safety device." "*I see.* ／*All right.*" ‖ 彼の言うことは私には何のことかわかりません What he says just doesn't *make sense* to me. ／I can't *understand* what he's trying to say.

▶《議長が発言者に》ご趣旨はわかりました I *get* [*see*] your point.

▶彼には文学がまるでわかっていない He simply doesn't *appreciate* literature. (●「良さがわかる」と考えて appreciate を用いる) ‖ もっとゆっくり頼みます. よくわからないので Slow down, please. I'*m not following you* very well.

▶インターネットのことは全くわからない I *don't know* anything about the Internet. ‖ きみに何がわかる！ What do you know about it?

2【承諾する】 **get** +目 (➤ インフォーマル) ▶今度やったらおまえは首だ. わかったか？ If you do that again, you'll get fired. *Is that understood* [*clear*] ? ‖ 対話「5時までには帰って来るのよ, わかった？」「うん, わかった」"Be sure to be home by five. *Got it?*" "Yeah, *got it*." ‖ 対話「この本を木田さんに送ってくれ」「わかりました」"Send this book (off) to Mr. Kida." "*Yes, sir.* ／*Sure.*" (➤ 前者のほうが丁寧な言い方).

3【知る, 判断する】 **find** +目 (状況などから), **know** +目 (知っている), **tell** +目 (区別する) ; **recognize** +目 (認める, 気づく) ; **realize** +目 (実感する) ▶うちの大学は御茶ノ水駅のそばですからすぐわかります Since our university is located near Ochanomizu Station, you *can find* it *easily* [you *can't miss* it]. ‖ 彼女が看護師だってことがどうしてわかるんだい *How do you know* that she is a nurse? ‖ 字を見ればきちょうめんな人かどうかがわかる You *can tell* whether people are methodical from their writing. (●この場合のように tell は can と一緒に使うことが多い) ‖ 政治の世界ではあす何が起きるかわからない You *can't tell* what will happen tomorrow in the political world.

▶すっかり変わってしまったから, きみだとわからなかったよ I *didn't recognize* you because you have changed so much. ‖ わかってるの？ もう12時過ぎよ Do you *realize* it's past midnight?

4【判明する】 **prove**, **turn out** (➤ 後者はややインフォーマル) ; **find** +目, **find out** (➤ find out は「偶然わかる」

という場合には用いない)

【文型】
A が B だとわかる, A が B であることがわかる
find A B
find that A **is** B / **find out that** A **is** B
A **turns out** (**to be**) B.
➤ B は形容詞・名詞

【解説】(1) **find** A B は「自分で経験してわかる」, または「偶然わかる」.
(2) **find that** A **is** B は「伝聞でわかる場合」にも用いる. 学術的な調査・研究の結果「わかる」にもこの文型を用いる.
(3) **find out** は人に尋ねたり, ものを読んだり, 調べたりという過程を経て情報を得ることをいうので「調べる」や「知る」の意になることも多い. あとに **that** の文だけでなく, wh- の文や about もくる. 後者の前では通例 find でなく, find out を用いる.
(4) **turn out** は「結果として判明する」の意.

▶このキノコは食べても大丈夫と**わかった** I *found* this mushroom safe to eat. (➤ 自分で食べてみた結果) / I('ve) *found out that* this mushroom *is* safe to eat. (➤ 人に聞いたり, 調べたりして) ‖ その女性の死が事故か事件かそのうち警察には**わかる**ことだろう The police should soon *find out* whether the woman's death was caused by accident or by a crime incident. ‖ 隣人がどういう人たちか**わかった** We've *found out* what kind of people our neighbors are.

▶実験の結果, その新薬は有効**であることがわかった** As a result of the experiment, the new drug *was found* to be effective. / The experiment *proved* the effectiveness of the new drug. (後者は「実験で新薬の有効性が証明された」と考えての訳) ‖ その弁護士は信頼できると**わかった** The lawyer *proved* [*turned out*] (*to be*) trustworthy. ‖ 対話「生理ってなあに?」「そのうち**わかる**わよ」"What's a period?" "You'll *find out* soon enough."

▶入試の結果は2月28日に**わかる** The results of the entrance exams *will be announced* on February 28. (「発表される」と考えて訳す) ‖ 犠牲者の正確な数はまだ**わかっておりません** It *is not* yet *known* exactly how many casualties there are. ‖ 対話「(パーティーに)来られる?」「まだ(よく)**わからない**」"Can you make it (to the party)?" "I'*m not* (quite) *sure* yet."

5【理解がある】▶うちの監督は**話がわかる** Our manager *is sensible* [*reasonable*]. (「思慮分別を持っている」「道理をわきまえている」と考える) ‖ 彼は**物のわかる**男だから仕事がしやすい He is pleasant to work with since he's a *reasonable* man. ‖ お母さんは私の気持ちなんてちっとも**わかっていない** My mother never *understands* how I feel.

わかれ 別れ (a) **parting**; (a) **goodbye,** (a) **farewell** (さようなら(ということば); 後者は堅い語) ▶人生にはさまざまな出会いがあり, **別れ**がある Life is full of meetings and *partings*.

▶友との**別れ**は悲しい I feel sad when I have to *part from* a friend. (英語ではこのように動詞で表現することが多い).

☛ **お別れ会** (→見出語)

わかればなし 別れ話 ▶女房が出し抜けに**別れ話**(=離婚話)を持ち出してきた My wife sprang (her desire for) *a divorce* on me.

▶今更**別れ話**なんて嫌よ Don't talk about *splitting up*, please.

わかれみち 分かれ道 a **fork in the road** (枝分かれする道); a **crossroads** (交差する所) ▶《慣用表現》あれが2人の運命の**分かれ道**だった The two were standing at *a* fateful *crossroads* at that time.

わかれめ 分かれ目 ▶ここが勝負の**分かれ目**だ This is *the turning point* in the game. / This is *the tipping point* between victory and defeat. / This is *the critical moment* that will decide whether we win or lose (the game).

[1]**わかれる 別れる** **1**【離れる】**part** 《from》; **say goodbye** ▶伊坂さんとは福岡駅で**別れた** I *parted from* Mr. Isaka at Fukuoka Station.

2【関係を絶つ】**break up** 《with》, **leave** +目 ▶ユミのようなすばらしい女性と**別れる**のはつらい It is painful to *break up with* [*to leave*] a wonderful girl like Yumi.

▶ 対話「きみはまだ近藤と付き合っているのかい」「いいえ, **別れました**」"Are you still going out with Kondo?" "No, we *broke up*." ‖ 小川さんは10年前に奥さんと**別れた**(=離婚した) Mr. Ogawa *got a divorce* [*divorced his wife*] ten years ago.

[2]**わかれる 分かれる** **branch off** (枝分かれする); **divide** (分割する); **split** (分裂する) ▶この道は1マイルほど先で**何本かに分かれている** This road *branches off* about a mile ahead. ‖ オーストラリアは6州に**分かれている** Australia *is divided into* six states. ‖ 憲法を修正すべきかどうかは**意見の分かれるところだ** *Opinion is divided* [*People are divided in opinion*] on whether or not the constitution should be amended.

▶5人ずつのグループに**分かれなさい** *Break up into* groups of five.

わかれわかれ 別れ別れ ▶彼が抜けたあと, クラブのメンバーはやがて**別れ別れ**になった After he quit, the club gradually *fell apart* [the club members gradually *went their separate ways*].

わかわかしい 若々しい **youthful** ▶高校生たちの**若々しい**歌声を聞くのは気持ちがいい Hearing the *youthful* singing voices of high school students gives me pleasure.

▶その画家は80歳を超えているが気持ちはまだ**若々しい** Though the artist is over eighty, he *is* still *young* at heart.

わき 脇 **1**【体の側面と腕の間】▶消防士は子供を**脇**に抱えた The firefighter carried the child *under his arm*.

▶**脇**を締めて竹刀をしっかり持て Keep your *arms* close to your sides and grip your bamboo sword firmly.

2【そば, 端】▶あのたばこ屋さんの**脇**に清涼飲料の自動販売機がある There is a soft drink vending machine *next to* [*beside*] that tobacco shop. ‖ 道子は**脇に寄って**自転車を通した Michiko *stepped aside* [*made way*] *for* a bicycle to pass. (「道を空けた」と考えれば make way が使える) ‖ **脇から口を出す**な Don't *interrupt* [*butt in*]. (➤ butt in はややぞんざい).

‖**脇机** a drawer unit (next to a desk).

3【よそ】▶この問題はしばらくの間, **脇**へ置いておこう Shall we put this issue *aside* for a while?

☛ **わき毛, わきの下** (→見出語)

わきあいあい 和気藹々 ▶試合後, 両チームの選手たち

は和気あいあいと談笑した After the game, the players of both teams had a *friendly* chat.

わきあがる 沸き上がる **spring up** ▶コーチに褒められたとき，私の胸に新たな希望が沸き上がってきた When the coach praised me, I *felt a surge* of renewed hope in my heart. ‖ 四番打者が打席に歩み寄ると球場は沸き上がる歓声に包まれた As the cleanup stepped up to the batter box, *rousing cheers* filled the stadium.

わきおこる 沸き起こる **arise**(発生する，生じる) ▶割れるような喝采が沸き起こった A thunderous applause *arose*.

わきが 腋臭 **underarm odor, body odor** (➤ 後者は体臭も含む) ▶私はわきがが強い I have strong *underarm odor*. ‖わきが止め an underarm deodorant /dióudərənt/.

わきかえる 沸き返る **be excited**《over, about》(興奮する) ▶地元チームの優勝に町全体が沸き返った The whole town *was excited over* [*about*] the home team's winning the championship. ‖ ひとしきりそのテレビドラマの話でクラスが沸き返った For some time the classroom *was buzzing* with talk about the TV drama. (➤ buzz は「ざわざわする」).

わきげ 脇毛・腋毛 **underarm hair, armpit hair** ▶わき毛をそる shave off one's *underarm hair* / shave under one's arms.

わきたつ 沸き立つ ▶両チームの乱闘に場内は沸き立った The scuffle between the two teams *caused a* general *uproar* in the gym.

わきでる 湧き出る **gush out** ▶畑から突然温泉が湧き出た A hot spring suddenly *gushed out* from the field.

わきのした 脇の下・腋の下 **the armpit, the underarm** ▶わきの下をくすぐったら赤ん坊はくちゅくちゅ笑った When I tickled the baby *under his arm* (*s*), he giggled. (➤ 女の子の場合は her, she にする)

わきばら 脇腹 one's **side** ▶そのランナーは脇腹を押さえてしゃがみ込んだ The runner crouched down holding *his side*.

わきまえる 弁える **know** +目 (心得る) ; **distinguish** +目 (区別する) ▶エチケットの基本すらわきまえていない大人が多すぎる Too many adults *don't know* even the basics of good manners. ‖ 彼は善悪をわきまえている He *knows* good *from* evil. / He *can distinguish* [*tell*] right *from* wrong. ‖ 校長先生は物の道理をわきまえた人です Our principal is *a very reasonable man*.

わきみ 脇見 ▶授業中に脇見をするんじゃない *Don't look around* during class. / *Keep your eyes* (*focused*) *on the teacher and the blackboard* during class.
▶トラックの運転手は脇見運転をして前の車に追突した The truck driver *took his eyes off the road* and hit the car in front of him. ‖ 脇見運転をするな *Keep your eyes on the road while you are at the wheel.* 《参考》「脇見運転」は inattentive driving (不注意運転)と訳せるが，英語では上の訳例のように「道路から目を離す」と表現するのがふつう.

わきみず 湧き水 **spring water** ▶湧き水を飲む drink *spring water* / drink from a spring (➤ 後者は直接飲む場合).

わきみち 脇道 a **side road** ; a **by-path**, a **by-road**, a **byway** (➤ いずれも地方の「間道」; あとの 2 語はより堅い語) ▶脇道を行く take *a side road*.
▶《比喩的》すまない，話が脇道にそれてしまったようだね Sorry, I seem to *have wandered from* [*have gotten off*] *the subject*. ➞横道.

わきめ 脇目 ▶脇目も振らずに勉強する *devote oneself to* study ‖ 子供たちが脇目も振らずに粘土で何か作っている The children *are deeply absorbed in* shaping things out of clay. (🏺「すっかり夢中になっている」と考える).

わきやく 脇役 a **supporting role**(役) ; a **supporting actor** [**actress**](人) ▶《比喩的》今回はぼくは脇役に回ることにするよ I'll *take a back seat* this time around. (➤「出しゃばらないでいる」の意).

わぎゅう 和牛 a **wagyu, wagyu cattle**(牛) (➤ 1 頭の場合，雌は a wagyu cow, 雄は a wagyu bull, 若い去勢した雄は a wagyu steer という) ; **wagyu beef** (肉).

わぎり 輪切り ▶パイナップルの輪切り *a round slice* of pineapple ‖ 大根を輪切りにする *cut* a daikon *in round slices*.

1**わく 枠** **1**【囲い】a **frame**(窓や額縁の) ; a **box**(囲み枠) ▶窓ガラスを取り替えるため窓の枠を外した I took off the window *frame* to replace the pane. ‖ 空欄に下の枠の中から適当な語を選んで入れよ Fill in each blank with a suitable word (chosen) from the *box* below.
2【制限】a **limit** ▶親が月々送ってくれる15万円の枠内で生活しなければならない I have to live *within* the 150,000 yen that my parents send me monthly (for living expenses). ‖ 和夫の行動はしばしば良識の枠からはみ出す Kazuo's conduct often *goes beyond the bounds of* good sense.

2**わく 沸く** **1**【沸騰する】**boil** ▶お湯が沸いたらガスを止めてくださいね Please turn off the gas when the water *boils*. ‖ お風呂が沸いた(＝準備ができた)わよ The bath *is ready*. (🏺 この場合，boil は使えない．煮えたぎったお風呂の意味になってしまう).
2【騒ぐ】**get excited** ▶コメディアンの演技に場内が沸いた The audience *roared with laughter* at the comedian's performance. (🏺「大笑いした」と考えて訳す) ‖ 熱戦に観客が沸いた(＝興奮した) The spectators *got excited* over the heated game.

3**わく 湧く** **gush**(吹き出す) ; **spring** (**up**) (湧き出す) ▶対戦相手が前回の優勝チームと聞いて，ファイトが湧いてきた When we learned we were pitted against the defending champion team, fighting spirit *sprang up* within us.

わくぐみ 枠組み a **framework** ; an **outline** (あらまし) ▶自衛隊は憲法の枠組みを越えない範囲で活動すべきだ The Self-Defense Forces should act within the *framework* of the Constitution. ‖ 伊藤氏はそのプロジェクトの枠組みを発表した Mr. Ito announced the *outline* of [the *framework* for] the project. ‖ 早急に支援活動の枠組みを策定する必要がある We need to quickly *establish* [*create*] *a framework for* support activities.

わくせい 惑星 a **planet** ▶地球は太陽系の 3 番目の惑星だ (The) Earth is the third *planet* from the sun.
‖準惑星 a dwarf planet.

> 「惑星」のいろいろ 水星 Mercury / 金星 Venus / 地球 Earth / 火星 Mars / 小惑星 Asteroids / 木星 Jupiter / 土星 Saturn / 天王星 Uranus / 海王星 Neptune / 冥王星 Pluto(準惑星)

ワクチン (a) **vaccine** /væksíːn/ ▶インフルエンザワクチン (a) flu *vaccine* ‖ 子供に小児まひのワクチンを注射しても

らった I had my child *vaccinated* against polio. ‖**ワクチン注射** a vaccination.

わくわく 一動 **わくわくする** be excited, be thrilled ▶**胸がわくわくするような映画** an *exciting* [a *thrilling*] movie ‖**観客はEXILEの登場をわくわくしながら待っている** The audience is waiting for EXILE's appearance on stage *with great excitement* (*and expectation*). (「期待して」と考えて訳す) ‖**あすはニューヨークかと思うと胸がわくわくする** When I think that I'll be in New York tomorrow, I *get really excited*.

✉ **あなたが日本へ来られると聞き，うれしくてわくわくしています** I *am* really *thrilled* to hear you are coming to Japan.

わけ 訳 **1【理由，事情】**(a) reason ▶**佑香が怒っているのには訳がある** Yuka has good *reason* to be angry. (➤ はっきりした1つの理由の場合には a good reason とすることもある) ‖**彼が大学を中退したのにはいろいろ[深い]訳があるらしい** I hear he dropped out of college for various [serious] *reasons*. ‖**どういう訳で練習をサボったのか言ってみろ** Tell me *why* [Explain *why*] you skipped practice. ‖**そういう訳なら許してやろう** If that's the *reason* [*case*], I'll forgive you.

▶**若者たちは時に訳もなく車をぶっ飛ばしたくなるときがあるらしい** It seems that young people sometimes feel like driving their cars recklessly *for no reason at all*.

▶**どうしてこんなばかな間違いをしたのか自分でも訳がわかりません** I *have no idea* [*I don't understand myself*] *why* I made such a stupid mistake.

2【意味，内容】 sense ▶**私はひどく上がってしまって自分で何を言ってるのか訳がわからないくらいだった** I got so nervous I *didn't know* what I was saying. ‖**彼の主張は訳がわからない** His argument *does not make sense*. (「意味をなさない」と考えて訳す) ／His argument *is not clear at all*. ‖**私はこういう古文書を見ても何が何だか訳がわからない** These old documents *make no sense* to me.

▶**その患者は熱に浮かされて時々訳のわからないことをつぶやいたりしている** The patient mumbles *meaningless things* [*nonsense*] in his fever from time to time.

3【当然の帰結】 ▶**彼は中学時代に陸上部にいたんだって？ 道理で足が速い訳だ** Did you say he used to be on the track(-and-field) team in junior high school? Then *it's only natural* that [*it's no wonder* that] he is such a fast runner.

4【「わけがない」の形で】 ▶**練習もしないで上達するわけがない** You *can hardly expect* to improve [get better] without practice. ‖**彼らがぼくたちに勝てるわけがないよ** *There's no way* they can beat us. ‖**そんなことあるわけないよ** That *couldn't* happen [be]. (「…のはずがない」と考えて現在の可能性を表す could の否定を用いて訳す) ‖**彼がナンシーのようなかわいい子を嫌うわけはないさ** *How could* he *possibly* [*ever*] dislike a charming girl like Nancy? ‖**あんなぜいたくな暮らしがいつまでも続くわけがない** He [She／They] *can't continue to* have such an extravagant lifestyle forever.

5【意図，つもり】 ▶**あなたを非難するわけではないが，もう少し筋道を立てて話してください** I *don't mean to* criticize you, but please try to be more logical. ‖**結婚に反対するわけじゃないけれど，少し早すぎると思うの** *It's not that* I object to your marriage, but I think it's a bit too early to get married. (➤ It's (not) that は状況や理由を説明して「…ということ(ではない)」) ‖**先生は生徒が憎くて叱ったわけではない** The teacher did*n't* scold the student *because* she disliked him.

6【「わけにはいかない」の形で】 ▶**それは頂くわけにはまいりません** I *really shouldn't* accept it. ‖ **対話** 「どうしてそんなに遅くまで会社に居るの？」「課長より先に帰るわけにはいかないんだ」"Why do you stay so late at the office?" "I *can't* leave earlier than the manager [leave before the manager does]."

7【部分否定で】

> **語法** 「すべて…というわけではない」の意の部分否定は not every A ... (すべての A が…だというわけではない), not everyone [everything] ... (すべての人[物]が…だというわけではない), not always ... (いつも…というわけではない), not altogether [entirely／all] ... (すっかり…だというわけではない), both of A are not ... (両方の A が…だというわけではない)などの形式を用いる.

▶**どの言語にも敬語があるというわけではない** *Not every* language has honorific words and expressions. ‖**クラスのみんながみんな英語が好きというわけではない** *Not everyone* in my class likes English. ‖**この店の品のどれもが高価だというわけではない** *Not everything* in this shop is expensive. ‖**そのうわさが全部間違っているというわけではない** The rumor is *not altogether* false.

▶**私は先生たち全員を尊敬しているというわけではない** I can*not* say that I respect *all* of the teachers. ‖**学校へはいつも歩いて行くわけではない** I do*n't always* walk to school.

▶**彼女の両親が両方ともＰＴＡの会合に出席したわけではない** *Both* of her parents did*n't* attend the PTA meeting. (➤ Her parents didn't both attend ... も可) ‖**外国へはそれほどよく行くわけではない** I do*n't often* go overseas.

☞ **わけない** (→見出語)

わけあう 分け合う share +目 (分けて，それぞれを持ち分として取る)；divide +目 (分配する) ▶**2人は持っていた食べ物をすべて分け合った** The two *shared* all the food they had. ‖**彼らは利益をみんなで同じように分け合った** They *divided* the profit equally among themselves.

わけあり 訳有り ▶**何か訳ありと見た** I see that *there must be some reason* [*something wrong*].

‖**訳あり商品** goods with some minor defect(s) [problem(s)]；《主に米》irregulars(きず物).

わけいる 分け入る ▶**山奥に分け入る** *push* [*force*] *one's way into* the depth of a mountain (into の代わりに through でもよい).

わけても 別けても especially, particularly. →特に.

わけない 訳無い easy(簡単な) ▶**あいつを負かすなんてわけないよ** It's *easy* [It's *a breeze*／It's *a piece of cake*／It's *a walk in the park*] to beat him. (➤ 言いかえはどれも《米・インフォーマル》で「簡単にできること」の意) ‖**車の運転ができればモーターボートの運転なんてわけないよ** Driving a motorboat is *easy* [*a piece of cake*] if you can drive a car. ／You *should be able to* drive [*have no trouble* driving] a motorboat if you can drive a car. ‖**彼はわけなくその問題を解いた** He solved the problem *without* (*any*) *difficulty*. ／He *had no trouble* solving the problem.

わけへだて 分け隔て ▶先生にはできる子もできない子も分け隔てなく扱ってほしい We want our teachers to treat bright and poor students *without any discrimination* [*impartially*]. (● bright and poor の代わりに brighter and slower でもよい).

わけまえ 分け前 a **share**, 《インフォーマル》 a **cut** ▶共犯者たちは分け前を要求した The accomplices all demanded their *shares*.

わけめ 分け目 《米》 a **part**, 《英》 a **parting** (髪の) ▶ 《床屋で》分け目は右にしてください *Part* it [my hair] on the right, please.

▶1600年, 関ヶ原で天下分け目の戦いが行われた In 1600 *a decisive battle* was fought at Sekigahara.

わける 分ける 1【分割する】**divide** ＋㊐; **separate** ＋㊐ (区分する, 切り離す); **part** ＋㊐ (髪を) ▶ケーキを3つに分ける *divide* a cake into three pieces ‖ 先生はゲームをするためクラスを2つに分けた The teacher *divided* [*split*] the class in [into] two to play a game. ‖ おばあちゃんは洗濯物を白と色物に分けた My grandma *separated* her laundry into white and colored items. ‖ 髪を七三に分けてください Please *part* my hair on one side.

2【かき分ける】▶私たちのパーティーはやぶを分けて進んだ Our party *pushed* [*thrust*] *our way through* the bush. ‖ ヨットは波を分けて進んだ The yacht sailed on, *cutting* [*slicing*] *through* the waves.

3【分類する】**sort** (**out**), **classify** ＋㊐ ▶彼女は卵を大きさによって分けた She *sorted* the eggs according to size. ‖ この雑誌の中から要るものを分けておいてください Could you go through these magazines and *pick out* the ones you need? (➤ pick out は「選び出す」).

4【分配・分割する】**split** ＋㊐ (すぱっと分ける, ときに無理やり分割する); **divide** ＋㊐ (均等に分割する); **share** ＋㊐ (今あるものを分け合う, 共用する); ▶賞金10万円を4人で分けた The four of us *divided* [*split*] the prize money of 100,000 yen among us. ‖ 仕事を分けて早く終わろうよ Let's *divide up* [*split up*] the work and finish it faster. ‖ アイスクリーム, 私にも分けてくれる? Will you *share* the ice cream with me?

5【売る】**sell** ＋㊐ ▶最高級品を特別のご奉仕価格でお分けいたしております We *sell* top-quality goods at bargain prices.

わご 和語 a **native Japanese word**.

わごう 和合 **harmony** ▶夫婦和合 *harmony* [*a harmonious relationship*] between husband and wife.

わこうど 若人 **young people** ▶ことしもまた陸上競技大会に大勢の若人が集まった Many *young people* gathered at the track meet this year, too.

わゴム 輪ゴム a **rubber** [《英また》an **elastic**] **band** ▶鉛筆は輪ゴムで留めておきましょう You should fasten together your pencils *with a rubber band*.

ワゴン a **wagon**; a **van** (箱型のトラック)

> **危ないカタカナ語✹ ワゴン**
> 1 英語の wagon からきた語で, wagon と同様いろいろな意味があるが, 「手押し車」の意味と「ワゴン車」の意味が最もふつう.
> 2 「手押し車」には料理や飲み物を載せて移動する《米》(tea) wagon, 《英》(tea) trolley, trolley-table と, スーパーマーケットなどで使う買い物用の shopping cart がある.
> 3 乗用車としての「ワゴン車」の意味では《米》station wagon, 《英》estate car がふつう. 貨物自動車としての「ワゴン車」の意味では van がふつう.

わこんようさい 和魂洋才 (**the**) **Japanese spirit and Western knowledge**.

わざ 技・業 1【技術・技巧】a **skill**, a **technique** /tekníːk/; a ***waza*** (柔道などの) ▶技を磨く polish [hone] one's *skill*(*s*) ‖ 技を極める perfect one's *skill*(*s*) ‖ 師匠の技を盗む *learn* [*acquire*] *a skill* [*a technique*] *by carefully observing* your teacher / *teach yourself a skill* [*a technique*] *by carefully observing* your teacher perform it and then practicing it secretly.

▶相撲には82種の決め技がある In sumo, there are eighty-two different *waza* [*techniques*] *to defeat one's opponent*. ‖ 《柔道》技あり! *Waza-ari!* (➤英語化している).

2【仕事】a **task** ▶至難の業 *a nearly impossible task* / *the most difficult task* / *a Herculean task* ‖ この壮大な景観はまさに自然のなせる業だ The grandeur of this scenery is truly *Mother Nature's handiwork*.

▶100メートルを10秒未満で走るなんて人間業とは思えない It *seems beyond human power* to run 100 meters in less than 10 seconds.

わさい 和裁 **Japanese dressmaking, kimono-making**.

わざと 態と **on purpose, intentionally, deliberately** (➤後になるほど目的意識が強い表現) ▶彼女はわざと消しゴムを机の下に落とした She let her eraser slip off the desk *on purpose*. ‖ 私は碁で部長にわざと負けてやった I *intentionally* lost to the manager in a game of Go.

わざとらしい 態とらしい **artificial** (作った); **unnatural** (不自然な) ▶わざとらしい話し方 an *unnatural* way of talking ‖ 部長は社長に会ったとたん, わざとらしい微笑を浮かべた When he met the president, the manager gave him an *artificial* smile [*a forced* smile]. ‖ 彼の態度は親切すぎてわざとらしい He is *unnaturally* kind.

わさび 山葵 (a) ***wasabi*** (**horseradish**) (植物); **grated *wasabi*** (おろしわさび) 《参考》horseradish は「セイヨウワサビ」で, すりおろしてローストビーフに添えることが多い.

わざわい 災い・禍 (a) **disaster** (災害); (a) **misfortune** (不運) ▶災いを未然に防ぐ prevent *a disaster* ‖ 災いを転じて福にするよう努力しましょう Let's do our best so that we can turn this *misfortune* into a blessing.

▶ギャンブルが彼の災いの元だった Gambling was his *ruin*. / Gambling was *what ruined* [*destroyed*] *him*.

ことわざ 口は災いの門(かど) The more you open your mouth, the more likely you are to put your foot in it. (➤ put one's foot in it は「へまなことを言う」)

▶天気が災いして見物客は少なかった *Because of* the bad weather, we had only a few visitors. / The bad weather kept visitors away.

わざわざ 態々 ⚠「わざわざ」には「そのことのために特別に」の意と, 「わざと」の意の両義があるが, 英語にはこれらに相当する1語はない. したがって用例のように, 「…するように骨折る」の意の take the trouble to do や「故意に」の意の **deliberately** などを適宜用いる.

1【ふつう以上の骨折りをして】

> **【文型】**
> **わざわざ…する**
> **take the trouble to** do
> **go out of** one's **way to** do
> **わざわざ…しない**
> **not bother to** do

▶《出迎えに出てくれた人に》わざわざお出迎えいただきありがとうございます Thank you for *taking the trouble to* come and meet me. ‖ 宿の主人は私たちをわざわざ駅まで車で送ってくれた The innkeeper *went out of the* [*his* ／*her*] *way to* drive us to the train station. ‖ 誰もわざわざ理由を聞かなかった *Nobody bothered to* ask why.

▶ジョー君がわざわざカナダから会いに来てくれた Joe came *all the way* from Canada to see me. (「はるばる」と考えて訳す) ‖ わざわざご自分で行かれるには及びません *You don't have to* go yourself. ／*There's no need for you to* go. ‖ わざわざ来ていただいてすみません *It's very kind of you* to come. ／*How kind of you* to come.

✉ **私の欲しかった情報をわざわざ見つけてきてくださって感謝します** Thank you for *taking the trouble to* find the information I needed.

2【わざと】▶嫌だと何度も言っているのに夫はわざわざ私の前でたばこを吸うんですよ Even though I've repeatedly told him I don't like it, my husband *deliberately* smokes in front of me.

1**わし 鷲**《鳥》an **eagle** ▶ワシは鳥の王者と言われている The *eagle* is said to be the king of birds.

‖**わし鼻** an aquiline /ǽkwɪlaɪn/ nose ‖ **イヌワシ** a golden eagle ‖ **オオワシ** a Steller's sea eagle ‖ **オジロワシ** a white-tailed eagle ‖ **ハクトウワシ** a bald eagle.

2**わし 和紙** ***washi*** **(paper)**; **Japanese paper.**

わしき 和式の **Japanese-style** ▶和式トイレ *a bathroom* [*restroom*] *with a Japanese-style toilet* (➤ 便器が複数あるときは toilets).

わしつ 和室 a **Japanese-style room** ▶私たちは大抵6畳の和室で寝ます We usually sleep in the six-mat *Japanese-style room*. (家に2部屋以上ある場合は one of the six-mat Japanese-style rooms といえばよい).

わしづかみ 鷲掴み ▶強盗は札束をわしづかみにして逃げた The robber *grabbed* wads of bills and ran away.

わじまぬり 輪島塗 a ***Wajima-nuri***, ***Wajima*** **lacquerware.**

わしゃ 話者 a **speaker.**

わじゅつ 話術 ▶その政治家は話術にたけている The politician *is an eloquent speaker*. (「雄弁である」と考えて訳す).

わしょく 和食 ***washoku***, a **Japanese dish** (日本料理), **Japanese cuisine** (➤ 高級な響きがある); **Japanese food** (日本食) ▶うちの子供たちは洋食より和食のほうが好きだ Our children prefer *Japanese food* to Western food.

▶すき焼きは人気の和食だ Sukiyaki is a popular *Japanese dish*.

ワシントン 1【首都】Washington, D.C. (アメリカの首都; コロンビア特別区 (the District of Columbia) にある).

2【州】(the) Washington (State) (アメリカ北西部の州; 略 WA, Wash.).

わずか 僅か 1【たった】only, just (➤ 後者はややインフォーマルな語) ▶この本は古本屋で僅か300円で買った I bought this book for *only* [*just*] three hundred yen at a secondhand bookstore. ‖ 彼らは結婚して僅か2か月で離婚した They were married for *all of* two months before they divorced. (➤ all of は数量の大きさまたは小ささを強調する).

2【少しの】few (数が); **little** (量が); **slight** (程度が) ▶正解者はごく僅かだった Only *a few* [Very *few*] could give the right answer. ‖ 今月はお小遣いが僅かしか残っていない I have only *a little* pocket money left this month. ‖ 2学期もあと僅か(2, 3日)だ We have *only a couple of days* left before the second term ends.

▶うちと彼女の家は僅かしか離れていない It is only a *short* distance from my house to hers. ‖ 僅かの間ですがパリに住んでいました I lived in Paris, though only (for) a *short* time.

▶彼の身長は2メートルを僅かに超えている He is *a little* over two meters tall. ‖ 馬は耳を僅かに動かしていた The horse was twitching its ears *slightly*. (「かすかに」と考えて訳す) ‖ 入江選手は僅かの差で3位に落ちた Irie slipped to third place by a *narrow* margin.

3【かろうじて】▶火事で家が全焼し, 僅かに物置だけが焼け残った Our house burned down, and *only* the shed was left (untouched).

1**わずらい 患い** an **illness**, a **sickness** ▶長患い *a long illness* [*sickness*].

2**わずらい 煩い** a **worry**, a **trouble.**

1**わずらう 患う** **suffer (from)** ▶昨年生まれて初めての大病を患った Last year I *suffered from* the most serious illness of my life.

2**わずらう 煩う** **worry (about).**

わずらわしい 煩わしい **troublesome** (面倒な); **complicated** (複雑な) ▶近頃親戚付き合いが煩わしくなってきた Recently, I have begun to find it *troublesome* to socialize with my relatives. ‖ 彼女は子供のために弁当を作るのを煩わしく思っている She *considers* making bentos for her children *a hassle*. (「…を面倒なこと(だと考えている)」と考えて hassle を用いるとよい).

▶認可を受けるには多くの煩わしい手続きが必要だ In order to get permission, you have to go through a lot of *complicated* formalities.

わずらわす 煩わす **trouble** +㊐ (困らせたり悩ませたりする); **bother** +㊐ (迷惑をかけて煩わしい思いをさせる) ▶これ以上私を煩わせないでくれよ Please don't *bother* [*trouble*] me any more. ‖ お手を煩わせてすみません I'm sorry for *troubling* [*bothering*] you. ／I'm sorry *to trouble* [*bother*] you. ‖ そんなつまらないことに心を煩わすのはよしなさい Don't *worry about* such a small thing. ／Don't *let* such little things *bother* you.

わすれがたみ 忘れ形見 1【記念の品】a **memento** (形見); a **keepsake** (小さな形見).

2【遺児】a **child born after the death of his or her father** (父親を知らない子); a **child whose father [mother] has died** (父親または母親を亡くした子; 両親の場合は whose parents have died とする) ▶彼は兄の忘れ形見です He is *the son of my late elder brother*.

わすれっぽい 忘れっぽい **forgetful** ▶彼はひどく忘れっぽい He's very *forgetful* (*of things*). ‖ 祖父は年を

わ

取って忘れっぽくなった My grandfather has become *forgetful* [has started *forgetting things*] with age.

ワスレナグサ《植物》a **forget-me-not.**

わすれもの 忘れ物 a **lost article**(遺失物) ▶車内の忘れ物では傘が断然トップだ Umbrellas lead the list of *articles* (most often) *left* on trains by a wide margin. ‖ 何か忘れ物をしたような気がする I feel like I *have forgotten something* [*have left something behind*]. (➤ leave は場所を表す語句とともに使う) ‖ 忘れ物のないように! *Be sure to leave nothing behind you!*

わすれる 忘れる

訳語メニュー
思い出せない →forget **1**
…し忘れる →forget (to do) **2**
置き忘れる →leave, forget **3**

1【思い出せない】forget +目 ▶過ぎたことは忘れよう Let's *forget* the past. / Let bygones be bygones. (➤ 後者は英語のことわざ) ‖ きみのこと, 忘れないよ I'll *never forget* you. / I'll (always) *remember* you. ‖ 数学の公式はもうすっかり忘れてしまった I *forgot* all the mathematical formulas I knew. ‖ その映画は前に見たけど, 筋はすっかり忘れてしまった I saw the movie before, but I'*ve completely forgotten* the story. ‖ **対話**「あの本, 買って来てくれた?」「あっ忘れた」"Did you buy me that book?" "Oh, *I forgot*."

✉ **お誕生日を忘れてしまって本当にごめんなさい** I'm terribly sorry for *forgetting* your birthday.

✉ **滞在中していただいたご親切は決して忘れません** I'*ll never forget* the kindness you showed me during my stay.

【文型】
～ということを忘れる
forget that S + V
➤ that の代わりに, wh- の文もくる
…したことを忘れる
forget doing

《解説》2 の forget to do の to do がまだ行われていないことを表すのに対して, doing はもう起きたことを表す. したがって forget doing は「…したこと(=経験)を忘れる」であるが, 主に否定形で will never forget doing で用いる. 肯定文では **forget that** S + V の文で表すのがふつう.

▶私はその夜, 彼女に会う約束をしていたことをすっかり忘れていた I completely *forgot that* I had promised to meet her that night. (● I forgot having promised her ... ともいえるが, forget doing の形を肯定文に用いるのはふつうではない;「忘れていた」を (×)I was forgetting としない) ‖ 世界には飢えに苦しんでいる人々が大勢存在することを(決して)忘れてはならない You *must not forget* [*must never forget*] *that* there are a lot of starving people in the world. ‖ そのことばは誰が言ったのか忘れた I *forgot* who said that (phrase).

▶けさ薬を飲んだかどうか忘れた I *forgot if* [*whether (or not)*] I took my medicine this morning. ‖ 去年の夏, 初めて彼女とキスをしたことは決して忘れないだろう I *will never forget* kissing my girlfriend for the first time last summer.

▶入学式での校長先生のお話は今でも忘れません I *still remember* the principal's speech at the start-of-school ceremony. (● 英語では「覚えている」と発想するのがふつう) ‖ 手紙を出すつもりだったのにすっかり忘れてしまった I meant to mail the letter, but it completely *slipped my mind*. (●「(物事が)…に忘れられる, 記憶から抜け落ちる」の意の slip one's mind を用いて訳すとよい).

▶昔のガールフレンドのことが忘れられない I *can't forget* my ex-girlfriend. / I *can't get* my ex-girlfriend *out of my mind*. (➤ 後者はインフォーマル) ‖ このことを忘れるな *Keep* [*Bear*] this *in mind*. (➤「心に留めておけ」の意).

2【…し忘れる】forget (to do)

【文型】
…するのを忘れる, …し忘れる
forget to do
忘れずに…しなさい
Don't forget to do
Remember to do

▶宿題を持って来るのを忘れた人は手を挙げなさい Those who *forgot to* bring the assignment, raise your hand. ‖ 彼女は玄関の鍵を掛け忘れたのではないかと心配になり始めた She began to worry that she might *have forgotten to* lock the front door. ‖ おばあちゃんに電話してお礼を言うのを忘れないように *Don't forget to* [*Remember to*] call your grandma and say thank you. (● Remember to do ... は文字どおりには「覚えていて…する」という, 英語ではふつうの言い方; Don't forget to do ... は注意しないと忘れそうな人への言い方).

▶寝る前に忘れずにヒーターを切りなさい *Don't forget to* [*Remember to*] turn off the heater before you go to bed.

▶サッカーの試合を見ていると時間のたつのを忘れる When I am watching a soccer game, I *lose track of the time*.

3【置き忘れる】leave +目, **forget** +目 (● 場所への言及があれば leave を用いるのがふつう; leave は意図的に「置いてくる」の場合もあるが文脈でどちらかわかることが多い) ▶彼女はよく電車の中に傘を忘れる She often *leaves* her umbrella on the train. ‖ 図書館にラケットを忘れてきちゃった I *left* [*forgot*] my racket in the library.

▶その紙袋をどこに忘れてきたのかわからない I have no idea where I *left* the paper bag.

わすれんぼう 忘れん坊 a **forgetful person** ▶忘れん坊だね, きみは What *a forgetful boy* you are! / How *absent-minded* you are!

わせ 早稲の・早生の early ▶わせの稲 *early* rice ‖ わせのリンゴ *early* apples.

[1]**わせい 和声**《音楽》**harmony**
‖和声法 the law of harmony.

[2]**わせい 和製の Japanese** ▶彼女は和製オードリー・ヘップバーンと言われた She was called the *Japanese* Audrey Hepburn. (● the をつける点に注意) / She was referred to as *a Japanese version of* Audrey Hepburn.
‖和製ポップス Japanese pop music.

わせいえいご 和製英語 a **Japanese adaptation of an English word**; **Japanese English**,《インフォーマル》**Japanglish**,《インフォーマル》**Janglish**,《インフォーマル》**Japlish**(日本人英語; 日本でしか通用しない英語風の単語

も，日本人話者特有の英語表現も言う）．

《解説》和製英語について
(1)「テーブルスピーチ」や「(討論会などの)パネラー」を「和製英語」と呼ぶことが多いが，これらはカタカナで書かれている以上，厳密には「日本語」である．それを英語であるかのように table speech, paneler のように書いたり言ったりした場合が和製英語 (Japanese adaptation of an English word) である（ちなみに，両語はそれぞれ after-dinner speech, panelist が本来の英語）．
(2)また，これらの語句を使って，「テーブルスピーチをする［パネラーとしてその討論会に参加する］ように頼まれた」を I was asked to do a table speech [to become a paneler in the discussion]. のように英訳した場合が Japanese English（日本人英語）である．これらは I was asked to make an after-dinner speech [to take part in the discussion as a panelist]. のように言えば英語らしい英語になる．
(3)Japanese English を Japanglish, Janglish, Japlish などと言うこともあるが，これらは軽蔑的な響きを伴うことがある．
(4)日本人の多くが l と r の区別をつけられない点をからかって，和製英語を Engrish と呼ぶ英語圏人もいる．

ワセリン **Vaseline**(➤ 商標)；**petroleum jelly.**

わた 綿 **cotton** ▶ふわふわの綿を詰めた布団 a futon stuffed with fluffy *cotton*.
‖綿入れ a wadded kimono ‖ 綿菓子 《米》 cotton candy, spun sugar, 《英》 candyfloss ‖ 綿雲 cottony clouds ‖ 綿ぼこり fluff.

わだい 話題 a **topic** [**subject**] (**of conversation**) ▶話題の人 the man [woman] *in the news* ‖ このレストランは今話題の店だ This restaurant is *the talk of the town*.
▶話題を変えよう Let's change the *topic* [*subject*]. ‖ 彼は話題が豊富だ He can talk on a variety of *topics*. ‖ その万引き事件は学校中の話題になっていた The shoplifting incident was *the talk* of the school. ‖ 近頃，再生医療がよく話題になる *There is a lot of talk* about regenerative medicine these days.
▶話題はすぐに尽きた We soon ran out of *things to talk about*. ‖ 彼女の話題は彼と映画スターのことばかりだ The only *things she talks about* are her boyfriend and movie stars.

わだかまり 蟠り **bad** [**hard**] **feelings** ▶もう過ぎたことです．今はあなたに何のわだかまりもありません It's something that happened in the past, and I have no *bad* [*hard*] *feelings* against you any more. ‖ 2人の間にはわだかまりがあった The two had some *ill feelings* against each other. ‖ あなたのお話を聞いて心のわだかまりが解けました What you said took *a load* off my mind. (この「わだかまり」は「重荷」と解釈できるので load を用いる).

わだかまる 蟠る ▶彼女の心にはまだ不満がわだかまっているようだ It seems she *is* still *harboring* some dissatisfaction (in her mind). (「(感情などを)心に抱く」の意の harbor を用いるとよい).

わたくし 私 **1**【自分】**I** (主格), **my** (所有格), **me** (目的格)；**mine** (私の物)；**myself**(私自身) ▶わたくしは木村一郎と申します．こちらが私の妻，陽子です *I am* [My name is] Kimura Ichiro, and this is *my* wife Yoko.
2【個人】▶わたくし事になりますが，大宮へ引っ越すことになりました Excuse me for bringing up *a personal subject*, but soon I will be moving to Omiya. ‖ 日本の大学生の約80パーセントは私立の大学へ行っている About eighty percent of Japanese students attend *private* universities.

わたげ 綿毛 ▶タンポポの綿毛 a dandelion *fluff* [*puff*].

[1]**わたし 私** **I**(主格), **my** (所有格), **me** (目的格)；**mine** (私の物)；**myself** (私自身) ▶このセーター，私が自分で編んだのよ *I* knitted this sweater *myself*. ‖ 対話「あなたが使ってるの私の消しゴムよ」「違うわよ．私のよ」"That's *my* eraser you're using!" "No, it's *mine*." ‖ 対話《ノックに》「誰？」「私よ」"Who is it?" "It's *me*."
▶ 対話《電話で》「伸子さんいらっしゃいますか」「私です」"Can I speak to Nobuko?" "*This is she* (*speaking*)." (➤ 電話での応答の場合の決まった言い方；当人が男の場合は she を he にする．ややくだけた言い方では This is Nobuko. という．単に "Speaking." だけでもよい；日本語をそのまま置き換えた，Yes, I am. でも理解されるであろうが，ネイティブは使わない．質問文も Are you Nobuko? とはしない．電話では姿が見えていなくて声だけなので，Is that Nobuko? が正しく，その場合の返事は Yes, it is. となる).
✉ **私の家族は父母と弟と，それに私の４人です** *My* family has four members—my parents, my younger brother, and *myself*. ➤ myself の代わりに me を用いるのはインフォーマルな言い方.
☛ **わたし的** →-的.

[2]**わたし 渡し** **ferry crossing**(渡ること)；a **ferry point**(場所).

わたしたち 私たち **we**(主格), **our**(所有格), **us**(目的格)；**ours**(私たちの物)；**ourselves**(私たち自身) ▶私たちは全力を尽くしたが，試合に負けた Although *we* did *our* best, *we* lost the game. ‖ 私たちはうちの子供たちがいじめにあってほしくありません *We* don't want *our* children to be bullied.

わたしぶね 渡し船・渡し舟 a (**small**) **ferry**, a (**small**) **ferryboat** ▶渡し船で川を渡る cross a river *by ferry*.

わたす 渡す

訳語メニュー
手渡す →hand **1**
与える →give **1**
譲る →give up **2**
運ぶ →carry **3**

1【手渡す】**hand** +㊐；**give** +㊐ (与える) ▶私は確かにあなたに１万円渡しましたよ I'm sure I *handed* you 10,000 yen. (渡しながら，念を押す場合は Here you are. Ten thousand yen. のように言う) ‖ コーチにこのメモを渡して来てくれ Go *give* this note to the coach. ‖ 優勝旗は高木主将に渡された The winner's flag *was given to* captain Takagi. ‖ 次の走者にバトンを渡す *pass* the baton to the next runner.
2【譲る】**give up** ▶あんなやつに部長の椅子を渡すものか I'll never *give up* my position as manager to that guy.
▶この家を他人に渡すなよ Don't *let* this house *go to* anyone else.
3【運ぶ】**ferry** +㊐ ▶昔は舟で旅人を湖の向こう岸へ渡したものだ Travelers used to *be ferried* to the other side of the lake. ／Travelers used to *be*

transported to the other side of the lake *by ferry*.
4【架ける】▶川に橋を渡す *build* a bridge over a river ‖小川に丸太を渡して橋にした We *put* logs *across* the stream to serve as a bridge.

わだち 轍 a **rut**.

わたり 渡り ▶《慣用表現》転職を考えていたので，私はその話に渡りに船と飛びついた I *quickly* jumped at the offer since I had been thinking of changing jobs.
‖渡り廊下 a passageway between two buildings, a connecting corridor（学校などの）; a breezeway（家とガレージなどの間の屋根つき通路）.

わたりあう 渡り合う ▶横綱は大関と土俵上で激しく渡り合った The yokozuna *had a fierce struggle with* the ozeki in the ring.
▶その計画を巡って2人の重役が激しく渡り合った（＝議論した）Two directors *had a* heated *argument* [*crossed swords with* each other fiercely] over the project.

わたりあるく 渡り歩く ▶私はいくつもの職場を渡り歩いてきた I*'ve changed* jobs many times.

わたりぞめ 渡り初め **the first crossing of a new bridge.**

わたりどり 渡り鳥《鳥》a **migratory** /máɪgrətɔːri/ **bird**, a **bird of passage** ▶多くの渡り鳥はいくつかの決まったコースを飛ぶ Most *migratory birds* take one of several fixed routes.

わたる 渡る 1【向こうへ行く】**cross** ＋㊐（横切る）; **go over**《to》（越えて向こうへ行く）▶道路を渡るときは車に気をつけてね Look out for cars when you *cross* the street. ‖本田さん一家はオーストラリアに渡った The Hondas *went* (*over*) *to* Australia (to settle). ‖ドーバー海峡を泳いで渡った日本人もいます There are some Japanese who *have swum* (*across*) the Straits of Dover. ‖浅瀬を渡って向こう岸へ行こう Let's *ford* the stream.（➤ ford は「浅瀬を渡る」の意）.
▶川面を渡る風が心地よい The breeze (that is) *coming from* [*across*] *the river* feels refreshing. ／The breeze *blowing off* [*across* ／ *from* ／ *over*] *the river* feels pleasant.
2【渡来する】**migrate** /máɪgreɪt/《from, to》▶伊豆沼にことしもたくさんの白鳥が渡って来た A lot of swans *migrated to* Izu-numa this year, too. ‖仏教は6世紀に日本に渡って来た Buddhism *came to* [*was brought to*] Japan in the sixth century.
3【暮らしていく】**get along** ▶彼はどこへ行っても世の中をうまく渡っていける男だ He will be able to *get along* wherever he goes. ‖そんな甘い考えじゃ世の中渡っていけないぞ You'll *never make it in this world* with such an easygoing attitude.（●「しっかりやっていく，成功する」と考えて make it を用いて訳すとよい）.
4【人の物になる】**pass**《to》▶軍事機密がスパイを通じてロシアに渡った Classified military information *was given* [*was passed*] *to* Russia by spies. ‖スパイはその情報が敵の手に渡る前に潰した The spy destroyed the information rather than let it *fall into* enemy *hands*. ‖わが家の土地は今では人手に渡ってしまっている Our land now *belongs to someone else*.（●「他人の物だ」と考えて訳す）‖プリントは全員に渡りましたか Has everybody *gotten* a handout?
5【広がる】**extend**（及ぶ）; **stretch**（伸びる）; **spread**（広がる）; **last**（続く）; **span**（またがる）▶この平原は500キロにも渡って広がっている This plain *extends* [*stretches*] *for* 500 kilometers. ‖雨雲が関東平野の広い範囲に渡って広がっています Rain clouds *are spread over* a large area of the Kanto Plains.
▶試合は延々5時間にもわたった The game *lasted* as long as five hours. ‖彼女の学識は広範囲にわたっている Her learning *is extensive*. ‖博士は4半世紀にわたる研究成果をこの本にまとめた The doctor compiled a book of his research findings *covering* a span of twenty-five years.

ワックス **wax** ▶車にワックスを掛ける *wax* a car.

わっしょい ▶ほら，わっしょい，わっしょいっておみこしが来たよ Here comes an *omikoshi* with cries of "*Wasshoi! Wasshoi!*"（➤"ONE-two, ONE-two!" が「ワッショイ！」に近い）.

わっと ▶子供が転んでわっと泣き出した The little child *burst out crying* [*burst into tears*] when he fell (down). ‖本田が得点すると観衆はわっと歓声を上げた The spectators *let out cheers* [The spectators *cheered*] when Honda made a goal.

ワット a **watt**《略 w, W》▶60ワットの電球 a 60-*watt* (light) bulb ‖20ワットの蛍光灯 a 20-*watt* fluorescent lamp.

ワッフル a **waffle**.

ワッペン an **emblem**（記章）; a **sticker**（ステッカー）▶ジャケットにワッペンを縫い付ける sew *an emblem* on one's jacket.

> **危ないカタカナ語✸ ワッペン**
> 「ワッペン」はドイツ語の *Wappen*（紋章）から. 英語では emblem が相当する. 貼り付けるタイプのものは sticker という.

わな 罠 a **trap**（ばね仕掛けの）; a **snare**（輪縄による）▶イノシシにわなを仕掛けた We set *a trap* for wild boars. ‖タヌキがわなに掛かった A *tanuki* was caught in the *trap*.
▶《比喩的》あの男の親切にはわながあるに違いない There must be some *catch* in [to] his kindness.（●「落とし穴」と考えて catch を用いるとよい）‖その候補者は政敵のわなにはまった That candidate fell into his rival's *trap*.

わなげ 輪投げ a **ringtoss**; **quoits** /kɔɪts/（➤単数扱い）▶輪投げをする play *quoits*.

わななく 戦慄く **tremble** ▶彼女は緊張のあまりわなないていた She *was trembling* from nervousness.

わなわな ▶幽霊を見たと言って彼女はわなわなと震えていた She was *shaking all over*, saying she had seen a ghost.（➤ all over は「体じゅう」）‖惨劇を目の当たりにして彼女はわなわなと震えていた Having witnessed a tragedy right before her eyes, she was *shaking like a leaf*.（●英語では「木の葉のように震える」と考える）.

わに 鰐《動物》a **crocodile**（ナイルワニなど）; an **alligator**（ミシシッピーワニなど）▶ワニ皮のベルト a *crocodile* [*an alligator*] belt.

ワニス **varnish**. →ニス.

[1]**わび 詫び** (an) **apology** ▶おわびのしるしに彼から贈り物が届いた He sent me a gift as a token of *apology*. ‖先方が非を認めてわびを入れてきた The other party admitted that they were wrong and offered *an apology* to us. ‖おわびのことばもございません *I really don't know how to apologize*. 《参考》日本はおわびの文化として知られるほど，ささいなことでもすぐわびる姿を日常的に見聞きすることが多い. わびが多用される分，心の籠もらない，型どおりの，薄っぺらなわびも横行する. 英米では，

使用を控える分，わびるときには重大性を認識した，心から発したものになる可能性が高い．

‖**わび状** a letter of apology.

2**わび 侘び** ***wabi***; **rustic simplicity**; simplicity and quietness that typify the essence of the world of haiku or the tea ceremony (➤説明的な訳).

わびしい 侘しい **lonely**(寂しい); **desolate**(孤独で惨めな); **shabby** (みすぼらしい) ▶独りアパートでラーメンをすするなんて**わびしい**もんだよ I feel quite *lonely* when I eat a bowl of ramen all by myself in my apartment. ‖峠に**わびしい**古家がある There stands a *shabby* old house at the mountain pass.

わびる 詫びる **apologize** 《to》 ▶彼女は約束を守らなかったことを**わびた** She *apologized to* me for having broken her promise.

わふう 和風の **Japanese-style** ▶**和風**の家 a *Japanese-style* house／a house *built in the Japanese style* ‖この城下町にはいくつかの**和風庭園**がある This castle town has several *Japanese gardens*.

‖**和風スパゲッティ** soy sauce-flavored spaghetti.

わふく 和服 **Japanese clothes**; a **kimono** (➤英語化している) ▶祐子さんは洋服より**和服**のほうが似合う *A kimono* suits Yuko better than Western clothes.

わぶん 和文 **Japanese**(日本語); a **Japanese sentence** (日本語の文) ▶次の**和文**を英訳せよ Put the following *Japanese* (*sentences*) into English. (● sentences は独立した複数の文の場合．まとまった1節の場合は Japanese passage とする).

わへい 和平 **peace** ▶中東の**和平**が成立するのはいつのことだろうか I wonder when *peace* will be established in the Middle East.

‖**和平案** a peace plan ‖**和平交渉**［**会談**］peace negotiations［talks］.

わほう 話法 《文法》**speech, narration**

‖**間接話法** indirect［reported］speech ‖**直接話法** direct speech.

わぼく 和睦 **reconciliation** /rèkənsìliéiʃən/ (和解); **peace** (講和).

わめい 和名 a **Japanese name** ▶シクラメンの**和名**は2つあって，ブタノマンジュウとカガリビバナだ A cyclamen has two *Japanese names*: Butanomanju and Kagaribibana.

わめく 喚く **shout, yell**(恐ろしいほど大声で何かを言う); **rant and rave** (どなり散らす；rant も rave も同じ意味) ▶酔っ払いたちが通りで何事か**わめいている** Some drunks *are yelling* (*out*) on the street.

わやく 和訳する **put**［**translate**］**... into Japanese**(➤ translate は「翻訳する」) ▶この章を各自で**和訳しなさい** *Put*［*Translate*］this chapter *into Japanese* by yourselves.

わようせっちゅう 和洋折衷 ▶日本人の多くは**和洋折衷**の暮らしをしている The lifestyles of most Japanese are *a combination of Japanese and Western elements*. ／Most Japanese have a *semi-Western* lifestyle. ‖この家は**和洋折衷で造られている** This house is built *half in Japanese and half in Western style*.

わら 藁 (a) **straw** ▶**わらにもすがる**思いでいます Now I feel that I'm (just) *grasping*［*clutching*］*at straws*.

‖**わら人形** a straw figure.

わらい 笑い **laughter**(笑うこと); a **laugh, laughter** (笑い声) (➤ laugh が行為としての「笑い」や「笑い声」であるのに対して，laughter は「どっと沸き起こり，ひとしきり続く(複数の人の)笑い声」); a **smile** (微笑) ▶必死で**笑い**をこらえる try hard to stifle［suppress］*a laugh* ‖彼の答えは聴衆の**笑い**を誘った His answer drew *laughter* from the audience. ‖あのときの彼の慌てぶりを思い出すたびに**笑いが込み上げてくる** I feel like *laughing* whenever I recall how frantic he was at that time. ‖彼女はヒステリックな**笑い方をする** She *laughs* hysterically. ‖きみの**笑い顔**が大好きだ I really like your *smile*.

▶《慣用表現》チームが6連勝して監督は**笑いが止まらない** With his team's six consecutive wins, the manager *is all smiles*. (●「喜色満面だ」と考えて訳すとよい) 《参考》メールやブログなどで「今週は3日連続で学校に遅刻した(笑)」などと書くことがあるが，英語では顔文字(emoticon)で，I was late to school three days in a row this week. :-) とするか，LOL (＝laughing out loud 大笑い)と書くことが多い．

☛ **大笑い，お笑い** (→見出語)

わらいごえ 笑い声 **laughter**, a **laughing voice**, a **laugh** ▶教室に**笑い声**がはじけた The classroom erupted in *laughter*.

わらいごと 笑い事 ▶**笑い事じゃないよ** It's *no laughing matter*. ／It's *no joke*. ‖これは**笑い事で済む**ようなことじゃない This is not a sort of thing that you *can just laugh off*. (●「笑い飛ばす」と考えて laugh off を用いるとよい).

わらいころげる 笑い転げる **laugh** one's **head off** ▶ピエロのおかしなしぐさを見て子供たちは**笑い転げた** My children *laughed their heads off* at the clown's antics.

わらいじょうご 笑い上戸 a **person who laughs a lot** (**when he**［**she**］**drinks**), a **merry drinker** ▶彼女は**笑い上戸**だ(＝よく笑う) She *laughs at anything*. ／It doesn't take much to make her laugh. 《参考》酒が入るとよく笑う人のことを a laughing drunk ということがある．

わらいとばす 笑い飛ばす **laugh off** ▶私の深刻な悩みを父は**笑い飛ばした** My father *laughed off*［*just laughed at*］my serious problem.

わらいばなし 笑い話 a **funny story**(おもしろい話); a **joke** (冗談) ▶**笑い話**では済まされない This is not *something that you can just laugh off*.

わらいもの 笑い物 a **laughingstock** ▶こんな格好で学校へ行ったらクラス中の**笑い物**だよ If I go to school in this outfit, I'll be the *laughingstock* of the whole class. ‖日本人の多くは**笑い物にされる**のを極度に恐れる Most Japanese are extremely afraid of *being laughed at by others*.

わらう 笑う **1【おかしくて，またはうれしくて】laugh** 《at》(声を出して); **smile** 《at》(ほほえむ); **grin** 《at》(歯を見せて笑う) ▶私のジョークにみんなが**笑った** Everybody *laughed at* my joke. ‖靖子がぼくを見てにっこり**笑った** Yasuko *smiled at* me. ‖チャップリンが浅瀬に飛び込むシーンを見て観客は**どっと笑った** The audience *exploded with laughter*［*were rolling in the aisles*］when they saw the scene where Chaplin plunged into shallow water. ‖あんまり**笑って**涙が出ちゃった I *laughed* myself to tears. ／I *laughed* so hard I cried. ‖兄がテレビのどたばた番組を見ながら**おなかを抱えて笑っている** My (older) brother *is* watching a TV comedy show and *splitting his sides*［*rolling on the floor*］*with laughter*.

▶**笑ってごまかすな**．おまえのたくらみはわかってるんだ Don't try to *laugh* it *off*; I know what you're up to. ‖

わ

これは深刻な問題だ. **笑って済ますわけにはいかない** This is a serious problem. It's not something you *can laugh about and dismiss* [*shrug off*].

ことわざ **笑う門(かど)には福来たる** Fortune comes to a cheerful home. (➤ 日本語からの直訳).

> 「笑う」のいろいろ **くすくす笑う** giggle ／(満足そうに)**くっくっと笑う** chuckle ／(魔女などが)**けっけっと笑う** cackle ／**げらげら笑う** roar (with laughter) ／(得意げに)**高笑いする** chortle ／**せせら笑う** sneer ／**にたにた笑う** smirk ／**にっこり笑う** smile ／**歯を見せて笑う** grin (➤ 前者5語は声を出して, 後者4語は声に出さずに笑う表現)

2【ばかにする】laugh (at) ▶授業中, 間違った答えをした人を**笑う**のはよくない It isn't nice to *laugh at* a student for giving the wrong answer in class. ‖ 彼女, 自分が町いちばんの美人だと思ってるのよ. **笑っちゃうわ** She thinks of herself as the most beautiful girl in town. *What a laugh!* ‖ 母はよく言っていた, **人のことを笑ってはいけません, 人と一緒に笑いなさい**と My mom used to say, "*Don't laugh at people, laugh with people.*" ‖ 日本の親はよく子供に「そんなことをすると人に**笑われるよ**」と言う Japanese parents often say to their children, "Everybody will *laugh at* you if you do that."

わらえる 笑える ▶それ, チョー**笑える** That's really *funny*! (➤ 皮肉を込めて「何てばかげたことを」の意でも用いられる) ／That's *hilarious*! (➤ hilarious /hɪléəriəs/ は「腹を抱えて笑うほどおもしろい」の意) ‖ それジョークのつもり？ **笑えないわ** That was supposed to be a joke? I do*n't find* it (*at all*) *funny*. ‖ そのコントのくだらなさが**笑える** The short skit is so silly it's *funny*.

わらじ 草鞋 ***waraji***; (a pair of) **straw sandals**. ⇀二足のわらじ.

わらび 蕨 《植物》 ***warabi***; **edible bracken**.

わらぶき 藁葺き ▶**わらぶきの**屋根 a *thatched* roof.

わらべうた 童歌 a **traditional children's song**, a **nursery rhyme**.

わらわせる 笑わせる **make ... laugh** ▶ピエロはおかしな顔をして観客を**笑わせた** The clown made faces to *make* the audience *laugh*. ‖ 彼は冗談を言って私たちを**笑わせた** He told a joke to *amuse* us. (➤ 笑いより楽しくさせることに重点がある).

▶やつはあれで将来のスター気取りなんだから**笑わせるよ**(＝お笑いだ) *What a laugh* [*a joke*] that he thinks he's a future star!

わり 割 **1【割合】**(a) **rate**; (a) **ratio** /réɪʃoʊ/ (比率) ▶あなたは8時間働いて7200円もらったから, 1時間につき900円の**割だね** Since you were paid 7,200 yen for 8 hours of work, the *rate* for one hour is 900 yen, right? ‖ 宝塚の観客は4対1ほどの**割**で圧倒的に女性が多い In most audiences at the Takarazuka revue, women overwhelmingly outnumber men at *a ratio* of around 4 to 1.

2【10分の1】ten percent /pərsént/ (1割) ▶うちの高校は女生徒は全体の2**割**くらいしかいない Only twenty *percent* of the students in our high school are girls. (➤ 動詞は students に合わせて are となる) ‖ あの店はそのカメラを4**割**引きで売っている That camera is for sale at 40 *percent* off the store's regular price. ／That store sells the camera at a 40 *percent* discount. ‖ その選手の打率は5月25日現在, 3**割**3分6厘だ As of May 25th, the player's batting average is .336. (➤ three hundred thirty six と読む;「3割打者」は a .300 (＝three hundred) hitter という) ‖ **対話** 「この会社に女性は**何割**いますか」「ほぼ8**割**です」"*What percentage of* the employees at this company are women?" "Roughly 80 *percent*." (➤ percentage がふつうだが, くだけた会話では What percent ...? も用いる).

3【「(…の)割に」の形で】▶彼女は年の**割に**若く見える She looks young *for her age*. ‖ このレストランは値段が高い**割に**おいしくない The quality of the food at this restaurant doesn't match the price. (●「質が値段に見合わない」と考えて訳したもの) ‖ 彼は練習に時間をかけている**割に**(＝ことを考慮すると)テニスの腕が上達しない He hasn't made much progress in tennis *considering* how much time he is spending practicing (it).

▶彼女はロンドンに半年間しか行っていなかった**という割には**英語がとても上手だ *Considering the fact that* she was in London (for) only six months, she speaks English quite well.

4【慣用表現】▶音楽家の仕事はきみが考えるほどには**割がよくない** Musicians are *not paid* [*compensated*] as well as you might think. ‖ こんな**割に合わない**仕事はなるべく早くやめたい I'd like to quit this job as soon as possible since it *doesn't pay* (*well*). (➤「**割のいい**仕事」は well-paying [plum] job という) ‖ 自営業者に比べ, 日本のサラリーマンは税制面で**割を食っている** Japanese salaried workers *are getting the short end of the stick* in the tax system, compared to self-employed people.

☛ **割に** (⇀見出語)

わりあい 割合 **1【比率】**(a) **ratio** /réɪʃoʊ/; (a) **rate** (率) ▶アメリカにおける黒人とほかの人種との**割合**は1対7だ The *ratio* of blacks to other races in the U.S. is one to seven. ‖ S市の人口は年に1万人の**割合**で増加している The population of S City is growing at the *rate* of 10,000 a year. ‖ 本校の生徒は**5人に1人の割合**で眼鏡を掛けている *One out of five* students at our school wears glasses.

2【比較的に】comparatively; **relatively** (相対的に); **rather** (ふつう以上に) ▶この辺りは**割合**静かだ This area is *comparatively* [*relatively*] quiet. ‖ 英語の試験は**割合**よくできた I did better on the English test *than I had expected*. (●「予想よりよくできた」と考えて訳す). ⇀**割に**.

わりあて 割り当て (an) **assignment** (仕事などの); (an) **allotment** (金や時間の); a **quota** (割り当て数量) ▶仕事の**割り当て**を決めるから集まってくれ I'm going to make job *assignments*, so please gather round (me). ‖ 車の輸出**割り当て量**が削られた Our auto export *quotas* have been cut.

わりあてる 割り当てる **assign** /əsáɪn/ +⊞ (仕事を); **allot** +⊞ (金や時間を)

> **【文型】**
> 人(A)に仕事(B)を割り当てる
> **assign** A B ／**assign** B **to** A

▶どの刑事にも聞き込みの任務が**割り当てられた** The detectives *were* all *assigned* the task of doing the legwork. ‖ その仕事は彼に**割り当てられた** The job *was assigned to* him.

▶ボーナスから10万円を北海道旅行の費用に**割り当てた** I *allotted* 100,000 yen out of my bonus for my trip to Hokkaido. ‖ 彼女は割り当てられた仕事をやり終えた She has finished her *assigned* [*allotted*] task.

わりいん 割り印 a (Japanese) seal over the edges of two papers [on a perforated line] ▶契約書に割り印を押す *press* [*affix*] *one's seal so that it overlaps two pages* of a contract.

わりかん 割り勘

> ◀解説▶ (1)「割り勘」には自分が飲み食いした分だけを払うケース(各自持ち)と, めいめいが平等に同額を負担するケースとがあるので, 注意が必要. (2) 各自持ちの割り勘を go Dutch ということもあるが, この表現はオランダ人に対して差別的に響くので, 避けたほうがよい.

▶支払いは割り勘にしよう Let's *have separate checks*. (➤各自持ちの場合) ／Let's *split the bill* [*check*]. (➤通例, 各人が均等に負担する場合) ／Let's *go fifty-fifty*. (➤2人の場合).

わりきる 割り切る ▶その問題はもっと割り切って考えるべきだ You should approach the problem *in a* more *practical* [*businesslike*] *manner*. ‖ 仕事と割り切らなければこんな幼稚な手紙の翻訳はできないよ If I didn't *accept it* [*consider it* ／*regard it*] *as part of my job*, I wouldn't be able to translate such a childish letter.

わりきれる 割り切れる 1【分割できる】▶100は4で割り切れる 100 *is divisible* by 4. ／4 *divides* 100. ‖ 7は3で割り切れない 7 *is not divisible* by 3. ‖ 3で割り切れて2で割り切れない数を1つ挙げよ Tell me a number that *can be divided* by 3 and not by 2. →割れる.

2【「割り切れない」の形で】▶あの男が無罪放免とは割り切れない I *can't understand* why he was acquitted. (●「納得できない」と考えて訳す) ‖ 社の業績が良いのに賃上げなしとは割り切れない気持ちだ I'*m not convinced that* there is a good reason why I can't get a raise despite the fact that our company is performing well.

わりこむ 割り込む break into (列に) ; interrupt +⑪, cut in on (人の話に) ▶列に割り込むな Don't *break* [*cut*] *into* the line. ／《英》Don't *jump* the queue. ‖ 大きなトラックが前に割り込もうとしている A big truck is trying to *cut* (*in*) in front of our car.

▶彼女は私たちの話に割り込んできた She *interrupted* us while we were talking. ／She *cut in* [*horned in*] *on* our talk. ／She *butted into* our conversation.

わりざん 割り算 division (➤筆算しながら過程を逐一書き出していく方式を long division (長除法) と呼ぶ) ▶そろばんで割り算をどうやるか知ってますか Do you know how to do *division* on the abacus?

わりだか 割高 ▶日本の航空運賃は諸外国と比べて割高だ Airfares in Japan *are rather high* in comparison with those in other countries. ‖ 小瓶のほうが割高だ The small bottle is *more expensive in terms of the unit price*. (●「単位当たりで考えれば高い」と考える).

わりだす 割り出す calculate +⑪ (計算する) ; figure out (見つけ出す ; インフォーマル) ▶費用が総額いくらになるか割り出してみた I *calculated* how much the total cost would be. ‖ 犯人を割り出すのに声紋は役立つ Voiceprints are useful in *figuring out* who committed a crime.

わりつけ 割り付け a layout ▶写真の割り付け a photo *layout*.

わりつける 割り付ける lay out ▶ページを割り付ける *lay out* a page.

わりと 割と →割に.

わりに 割に quite (かなり ; 《米》では very と同じくらい強意) ; comparatively (比較的に) ; relatively (相対的に) ▶きょうは割に暖かいね It's *relatively* [*pretty*] warm today, isn't it? ‖ その映画は割によかった The movie was *quite* good. ‖ 割に大きな地震だった The earthquake was *comparatively* [*fairly*] big. ‖ この絵は自分でも割によく描けたと思う I did a better job of painting this picture *than I had expected*. (●「予想以上によく描けた」と考えて訳すとよい). →割合, 割.

わりばし 割り箸 *waribashi*

日本紹介 ✉ 割り箸は使い捨ての木や竹の箸です. 簡単に割れるように中央に溝が切ってあります *Waribashi* are disposable chopsticks made of wood or bamboo. The chopsticks have a slit down the middle so that you can easily separate them.

わりびき 割引 (a) discount /dískaʊnt/ ; (a) reduction (減じること) 一動 割引する give a discount, discount /dɪskáʊnt/ ▶スーツを割引で買う buy a suit *at a discount* [*at a reduced price*] ‖ 1000円の割引をする give [make] *a reduction* of 1,000 yen ‖ 当店では全品を3割引きで販売しています We sell all items *at 30 percent off* [*at 30 percent discounts*]. ‖ 現金でのお支払いですと割引があります We'll *give* you *a discount* [*reduce the price*] if you pay (in) cash. ／We *offer a discount* for cash purchases.

▶割引券をどうぞ Here's *a discount ticket* [*coupon*]. ‖ 20名以上ですと団体割引料金になります You can get *a group rate* with twenty persons or more.

‖割引料金 a reduced charge [rate] (➤a discount rate も可).

> **逆引き熟語 ○○割引**
> 会員割引 a member [member's] discount ／学生割引 a student discount ／家族割引 a family discount [rate] ／現金割引 a cash (purchase) discount ／高齢者割引 a discount for senior citizens, a senior (citizen) discount ／障害者割引 a discount for disabled persons ／団体割引 a group discount [reduction] ／特別割引 an extra discount ／平日[休日]割引 a weekday [holiday] discount

わりびく 割り引く discount /dɪskáʊnt/ +⑪ ; reduce +⑪ (減じる) ▶定価から20パーセント割り引く *reduce* the price by twenty percent ‖ あの店は火曜日に行けば10パーセント割り引いてくれる They *discount* all the prices by 10 percent [You can *get a* 10 percent *discount*] on Tuesdays at that store.

▶《比喩的》あいつは何でも自慢する傾向があるから, 話を割り引いて聞いたほうがいい He tends to brag, so you should *take* what he says *with a grain* [*a pinch*] *of salt*. (●英語では「(人の話などを)割り引いて聞く」に対して take with a grain [a pinch] of salt という慣用句を用いる).

わりふり 割り振り an assignment.

わりふる 割り振る assign /əsáɪn/ +⑪ ▶スタッフに仕事を割りふる *assign* jobs to all the staffers ‖ 先生が

生徒たちに部屋を割りふった The teacher *assigned* rooms to his students.

わりまし 割り増しの extra（別途の）; additional（追加の）▶夜10時以降のタクシー料金は２割割り増しになる Taxi fares go up 20% after 10 p.m. ‖ 超過勤務の割り増し賃金はいくらですか How much is *the extra pay* for overtime work?

‖割り増し料金 an extra charge.

わりもどし 割り戻し a refund, a rebate（➤ 前者が一般的）▶税金の割り戻し a tax *refund* [*rebate*] ‖ 出資金の割り戻し *a return* on one's investment（➤ 保険金や出資金の割り戻しには return を用いる）.

わりもどす 割り戻す ▶即時払いの方には１割割り戻します We *offer a* 10% *rebate* for immediate payment.

わりやす 割安 ▶高齢者向けの割安な切符 a *cheap* [an *economy*] ticket for elderly people ‖ 円高で海外旅行が割安になった The strong yen *makes* overseas trips *comparatively cheap* [*inexpensive*]. ‖ まとめて買うと割安になりますよ You can get them *cheaper* by buying in bulk.

1**わる 悪** ▶その歌手はデビュー前は相当のワルだったらしい I hear that singer was quite *a baddie* [*a bad lot*] before his debut.

2わる 割る

📖 訳語メニュー
壊す →break **1**
分割する →divide **2**
縦に裂く →split **3**

1【壊す】break ＋目 ▶コップを割る *break* a glass ‖ ボールをぶつけて隣の家の窓ガラスを割ってしまった I *broke* the window of the next door with a ball. ‖ ウエーターが皿を床に落として割ってしまった The waiter dropped a dish and it *shattered* [*smashed*] on the floor.（➤ shatter と smash は「粉々になる」）‖ ぼくは片手で卵を割ることができる I can *crack* [*break*] eggs in one hand.（➤ crack は「ピシッと割る」）‖ 凍った大地を割って雑草が芽を出した Weeds sprouted, *breaking* the frozen earth.

2【分割する】divide ＋目 ▶ 20を６で割ると３で２余る *Divide* 20 by 6, and you get 3 with 2 left over. ‖ **対話**「40を５で割るといくつ？」「８」"What's forty *divided* by five? ／What's five *into* forty?" "Eight."（➤ 答えは Forty divided by five [Five into forty] is eight. の短縮）／"How many times does five *go into* forty?" "Eight times."（➤ 答えは Five goes into forty eight times. の短縮）‖ 25を３でぴったり割ることはできない 25 cannot *be divided* by 3 evenly. ／3 won't *go into* 25 evenly. ‖ ここの勘定は頭数で割ろう Let's *divide* [*split*] the check between us evenly.（→割り勘）.

▶ホームでつかみ合っている男たちの間に駅員が割って入った A station employee *broke up* the men fighting on the platform.（🏺「中に入って分ける」と考えて break up を用いる）.

3【木材などを】split ＋目; **chop** ＋目（ぶち割る）▶丸太を割って薪を作った I *split* the log into firewood.

4【下回る】▶１ドルは80円を割った The dollar *has depreciated* [*fallen*] below 80 yen.（🏺「80円未満に価値を下げた」と考えて訳す）‖ 今回の投票率は40パーセントを割った（＝未満だった）The voter turnout in this election *was below* 40 percent.

5【薄める】▶ウイスキーを水で割る *mix* [*dilute*] whiskey *with* water ／ *water down* whiskey ‖ 冬にはウイスキーをお湯で割って（＝お湯を加えて）飲むのもいい It's a good idea to *add* some hot water to your whiskey in the winter.

わるあがき 悪足掻き ▶きみの負けだ．悪あがきはよせ You lost. *Give up the fight* [*Don't press the fight*]. ／ *Try to lose graciously*.（🏺最後の例は「潔く敗北を認めろ」と考えた場合の訳）.

わるい 悪い

📖 訳語メニュー
良くない →bad **1**
間違った →wrong **2**
調子・質が悪い →wrong, poor **3**

1【良くない，不正な】bad; **nasty**（意地悪な）; **wrong** ▶悪い知らせ *bad* news ‖ 悪い成績 *bad* grades ‖ 悪い子ね！触っちゃだめって言ったでしょ！You *bad* boy [girl]! I told you not to touch that! ‖ きのうは一日天気が悪かった The weather was *bad* [*nasty*] all day yesterday.（➤ この nasty は「荒れ模様の」）‖ 試験は全く悪かった I *did* really *bad* on my exam (s).（🏺「試験で悪い点を取る」なら get a bad grade on an exam ／do poorly on an exam）‖ この子は行儀が悪い He [She] has *bad manners* [is *ill-mannered*].

▶彼はことばづかいが悪い He uses *bad* language. ／ He has a *foul* [*bad*] mouth. ‖ たばこは健康に悪い Smoking is *harmful* to the health.（🏺「害がある」と考える）‖ ここは俺に任せておけ．悪いようにはしないから Let me take care of everything here. *You won't regret it*.（🏺英語では「きみは後悔しないだろう」と考える）.

▶人のメールを読むのは悪いことだ It is *wrong* to read other people's e-mail. ‖ 悪いことをするとお巡りさんに連れていかれるよ If you *do something really bad* [*wrong*], you'll be taken to the police. ‖ 彼は高校へ入ってから悪くなった He *became delinquent* after getting into high school.（➤ delinquent /dɪlíŋkwənt/ は「非行を行う」）.

2【間違っている】wrong ▶先に手を出したおまえが悪い You *are wrong* [*are to blame*] because you lifted your hand against him first. ‖ 私が悪いんじゃない It's not my *fault*. ／I didn't do anything *wrong*. ‖ クラブの握り方が悪いからうまくボールを打てないんだ You are gripping the club *improperly*. That's why you can't hit the ball well.

▶悪いことは言わないから賭け事には手を染めないほうがいい *I'm advising you for your sake* not to get involved in gambling.

3【調子や質が悪い】wrong（調子が）; **poor**（質が）▶この車，エンジンの調子がどうも悪い Something *is wrong* with the engine (of my car). ‖ きょうは体の具合が悪いので休みます I *don't feel well* today, so I'm taking the day off. ‖ 最近胃の調子が悪い I *have been having stomach trouble* recently. ‖ 私は目が悪い I have *poor* eyesight. ‖ きみ，顔色が悪いね．どこか悪いんじゃないかい？ You *look pale*. *Is anything wrong* [*the matter*]? ‖ テレビばかり見ていると目が悪くなるよ Watching TV all the time *is bad for your eyes* [will *weaken your eyes*]. ‖ そんなに酒を飲むと今に体を悪くするぞ You'll surely *ruin* [*injure*] your health if you drink so much. ‖ 満員電車に揺られていたら気分が悪くなった I *got sick* (*to my stom-*

わ

ach) while being jostled on a crowded train. ‖ 道路工事の期間中は水の出が悪くなることがあります The water supply may *be affected* while road work is in progress. (「悪く作用する，影響を及ぼす」と考えて affect を用いて訳す).
▶あの女優，顔はいいけどスタイルが悪い Though that actress has a pretty face, she has a rather *poor* figure. ‖ ぼくは頭が悪い一親に似たらしい I'm *stupid*—(I) guess I got that from my parents. ‖ 梅雨どきは食べ物がすぐ悪くなる Food *goes bad* [*spoils*] quickly during the rainy season. (➤「悪くなった食べ物」は spoiled food という) ‖ 社長は大学時代，出来が悪かったそうだ I hear our president *did poorly* in college.
4【都合などが】▶午前中は都合が悪いので午後にしてください I *can't make it* [*It's inconvenient for me*] in the morning, so could you change the time to (the) afternoon? ‖ 運の悪いことに授業中スマホをいじっているところを先生に見つかってしまった *Unluckily*, I was caught by my teacher using my smartphone during the class.
5【申し訳ない，失礼だ】 **be sorry**(すまない)；**feel bad**(残念に思う)；**impolite**(礼を欠く) ▶私が悪かった．少し言い過ぎたよ I'*m sorry*. I said too much. ‖ 悪いけど約束があるからお先に *Sorry*, (but) I have to leave now. I have an appointment. ‖ 対話「おい，例のＤＶＤいつまで持ってるんだよ」「悪い悪い，あした返すよ」"Hey, how much longer are you going to keep that DVD?" "*Oh, sorry* about that. I'll return it to you tomorrow." ‖ デートを断って彼女に悪いことをした I *feel bad* about having turned down a date with her. ‖ お返しをしないと悪い(＝失礼)よ It would be *impolite* of you not to give him a gift in return.
▶貸してあげたいけど今金が無いんだ．悪く思わないでくれ I'd really like to lend you some money but I don't have any. *No hard feelings, please*. ‖ 私のことを悪く思わない[悪く取らない]でね Please *don't think badly of* me. ／ Please *don't hold it against* me. (「恨むな」と考えて訳した場合) ／ *Don't get* me *wrong*.
▶悪いわね，いつもお土産を頂いて Oh, I *shouldn't have*—but thank you. You're always bringing me gifts.

わるがき 悪がき a **brat**.

わるがしこい 悪賢い **cunning** /kʌ́nɪŋ/ (こうかつな)；**sly** /slaɪ/,《インフォーマル》**crafty** (ずるい) ▶悪賢いキツネ a *cunning* fox《参考》悪賢いことをキツネにたとえて，(as) cunning as a fox のようにいう．

わるぎ 悪気 ▶ごめん，悪気はなかったんだよ Sorry. I *meant no harm* [I *didn't mean to hurt your feelings*]. (➤ mean は「意図する」の意) ／Sorry. I *didn't do it on purpose* [*intentionally*].

わるくすると 悪くすると ▶悪くすると彼は二度と立ち上がれないかもしれない *If things turn for the worse*, he may not have a chance of making a comeback.

わるくち 悪口 ▶人の悪口を言うな Don't *say bad things about* [*talk bad about* ／ *bad-mouth*] others. (➤ bad-mouth は「悪口を言う」の意のインフォーマルな語) (「悪口を言う」に speak ill of を用いるのは堅い[古めかしい]言い方で「あっこうを言う」に近い) ‖ のび太がきのうきみの悪口を言っていたよ Nobita was *saying some nasty things about* you yesterday. ／Nobita was *bad-mouthing* you yesterday.

わるさ 悪さ **mischief** /místʃɪf/；a **prank** (罪のないいたずら) ▶あの子はしょっちゅう悪さをしている He's always getting into *mischief*. ／ He's always *up to something or other*.

ワルシャワ **Warsaw** /wɔ́ːˈsɔː/ (ポーランドの首都).

わるずれ 悪擦れ ▶あの子，変に悪ずれしているわね He's *a little too wise in the ways of the world*. ／He is too *worldly-wise* [*sophisticated*]. (前者は「世間の実情に少しばかり通じ過ぎている」，後者は「世間を知り過ぎている」と考えた場合).

わるだくみ 悪巧み an **evil** [**nefarious**] **scheme** /skiːm/ (悪計；nefarious /nɪféəriəs/ は「邪悪な」の意の堅い語)；a **trick** (いたずら)；an **insidious scheme** (人をだまそうとする企て) ▶やつらは何か悪だくみをしている They are cooking up some *evil* [*nefarious*] *scheme*.

わるぢえ 悪知恵 ▶弘は悪知恵のよく働く子だ Hiroshi is a *very crafty* boy. ‖ 誰がおまえに悪知恵をつけたんだ? Who *put* you *up to* it? (英語では「A(人)を唆(そそのか)してＢさせる」の意の put A up to B を用いる).

ワルツ a **waltz** /wɔːlts/ ▶ウィンナワルツを踊る dance *a Viennese waltz*.

わるのり 悪乗り ▶彼は悪乗りして同じ手品を３回も続けてやった He *got carried away* and performed the same trick three times in a row. ‖ 悪乗りするなよ．冗談が過ぎるぞ *You're taking it too far*. It's not funny any more.

わるびれずに 悪びれずに **without embarrassment**；**unapologetically** ▶少年は友達のノートから答えをそのまま写したことを悪びれずに認めた The boy admitted *without embarrassment* [*nonchalantly*] that he had copied the answers from his friend's notebook. ‖ 少女は今月は５日学校を休んだと悪びれずに言った The girl said *unapologetically* that she had missed five days of school this month. ‖ 青年は悪びれずに自分の言いたいことを主張した The young man said what he had to say *with no trace of shyness*.

わるびれる 悪びれる ▶家出少女たちの顔には少しも悪びれたところがなかった The runaway girls didn't look *ashamed* [*guilty* ／ *embarrassed*] in the least.

わるふざけ 悪ふざけ a **practical joke** (人を困らすいたずら)；a **prank** (罪のないいたずら) ▶先生に対して悪ふざけをしてはいけない Don't play *practical jokes* on your teacher. ‖ あのテレビタレントは悪ふざけが過ぎる That TV personality *carries his jokes* [*pranks*] *too far*.

わるぶる 悪ぶる ▶山田君，悪ぶってるけど本当はいい人よ Yamada *pretends to be mean* [*nasty*], but he's really a nice guy.

わるもの 悪者 a **bad person** (悪人)；a **baddie** [**baddy**] (悪役) ▶私だけを悪者にしないで Don't *make* me *the baddie*. ／Don't *make a scapegoat of* me. (後者は「身代わりにする」と考えて訳したもの).

わるよい 悪酔い ▶それ以上飲むと悪酔いするよ You'll *feel sick* if you drink more than that. ‖ ワインは飲み過ぎると悪酔いすることがある Too much wine can *make* you *sick*.

われ 我 ▶《慣用表現》我と思わん者は挑戦してみなさい Does anyone here think he can do it? If so, give it a try. ‖ 彼女はやっと我に返った She finally *came to* [*regained consciousness*]. (英語では「意識を取り戻す」と解釈して come to を用いる；to に

強勢を置く）‖ぼんやりしていたら，先生に名前を呼ばれて我に返った The teacher's calling my name *woke* me from my daydream.
▶その話を聞きながら我にもなく泣いてしまった Tears welled up in my eyes *in spite of myself* while I was listening to the story. ‖彼女は悲しみのあまり我を忘れていた She *was beside herself* with grief. ‖近頃の大学生は我も我もと海外旅行に行く College students today are *falling over each other* to go on a trip overseas. (➤ fall over each other は「先を争う」).

われがちに 我勝ちに ▶観客は我勝ちに前の方の席を取ろうとした The spectators *scrambled* [*rushed in*] *for* seats in the front row.
▶ファンたちは我勝ちにサインをもらおうとした The fans *tripped over* [*fell over*] *each other* to get an autograph. ‖買い物客は特売品に我勝ちに飛びついた The shoppers *snapped up* [*fought over*] the bargains.

われかんせず 我関せず ▶このような国家的大災害に当たって我関せずという態度は許されない In the face of this national disaster, an *it's-no-concern-of-mine* attitude can't be tolerated.

われさきに 我先に ▶デパートで火事でも起これば我先に逃げようとする客で大混乱になるのは目に見えている It is obvious that customers will *scramble to escape* in a free-for-all if a fire breaks out in a department store. (➤ free-for-all は「手のつけられない乱闘」) →我勝ちに.

われしらず 我知らず ▶我知らず涙した *Without* (*my*) *realizing it* [*In spite of myself*], tears ran down my face. (➤ in spite of oneself は「抑えきれない」というニュアンスがある).

われながら 我ながら ▶我ながら名案だと思う It's a good idea, *if I do say so myself*. (●「自分で言うのも何だが」と考えた場合) ／*I hate to brag*, but my idea is really good. (●「自慢したくはないが」と考えた場合) ‖こんな間違いをして我ながら(＝自分が)恥ずかしい I feel ashamed of *myself* for having made a mistake like this.

われめ 割れ目 a **crack** (壁・ガラスなどの); a **chasm** /kǽzəm/ (岩などの); a **split** (まっすぐな裂け目) ▶歩道の割れ目からタンポポが顔をのぞかせている Dandelions are peeping out from the *cracks* in the sidewalk. ‖地震のあと，壁にいくつも割れ目ができた Several *cracks* appeared in the wall after the quake.

われもの 割れ物 a **fragile** /frǽdʒəl ‖ -dʒaɪl/ **article** ▶割れ物だから気をつけて It's *fragile*, so be careful. ‖《表示》割れ物注意 Fragile. Handle with Care.

われる 割れる 1【壊れる】**break**; **crack** (ひびが入る); **shatter, smash** (粉々になる；前者のほうがより細かい割れ方を連想させる) ▶貴重な陶器の花瓶を落としたら割れた The precious pottery vase *broke* when I dropped it. ‖地震で窓ガラス数枚がビシッと割れた Several windowpanes *cracked* when the earthquake hit.
▶グラスが手から床に滑り落ちて割れた The glass slipped from my hand and *shattered* [*smashed*] on the floor. ‖ガラスは割れやすい Glass *breaks easily*. ／Glass *is fragile*. ／Glass *is easily broken*. (● Glass is easy to break. は「割るのは簡単」の意なので注意).
▶《慣用表現》ゲイツ氏が演壇に立つと割れるような拍手が起こった When Mr. Gates took the podium, *thunderous applause* arose. ‖頭が割れるように痛い I *have a terrible* [*splitting*] *headache*.
2【分裂する】**divide, split** ▶原子力発電の問題で世論が割れた The nuclear power generation issue *divided* public opinion.
▶過激派がいくつもの派に割れた The radicals *split* into many factions.
3【割り算で割り切れる】**be divided, be divisible** ▶100は25で割れる One hundred *can be divided* by twenty-five. ／100 *is divisible* by 25.
4【判明する】▶ようやく被害者の身元が割れた We finally *know who* the victim *is*. ／We've *identified* the victim at last.

われわれ 我々 **we** ▶我々にも言い分がある *We* want to have our say too.
▶我々日本人はいつもせかせかしている (*We*) *Japanese* are always in a hurry.

> **あなたの英語はどう響く?**
> 「我々日本人は」の直訳 We Japanese は，ともすると排他的に響く. We か Japanese (people) かのいずれかで十分である.

[1]わん 湾 a **bay**, a **gulf** (➤ 後者のほうが大きい) ▶ペルシャ湾 the Persian *Gulf* ‖メキシコ湾 the *Gulf* of Mexico ‖東京湾に橋を架ける build a bridge across *Tokyo Bay* [*the Bay of Tokyo*] (➤ 前者の言い方では a や the はつけない).

[2]わん 椀 a (**wooden**) **bowl**.

[3]わん ▶犬がワンと鳴いた The dog *barked*. ‖《犬に》ワン! *Speak!*

わんがん 湾岸 a **bayside**
‖湾岸戦争 the Gulf War ‖湾岸地帯 a bayside area.

わんきょく 湾曲 a **curve**, (a) **curvature** (➤ 後者は堅い語) 一動 湾曲する **curve** ▶川はZ市の周りを湾曲して流れている The river *curves* [*makes a loop*] around Z City.

ワンぎり ワン切り (a) **one-ring call** [**fraud**] ▶ワン切りはもううんざりだよ I'm sick of *one-ring calls*.

わんさ ▶好天に誘われて上野の山に人がわんさと繰り出した Thanks to the fine weather, *great numbers of people* turned out in Ueno Park.

ワンサイド **one-sided, lopsided** ▶ワンサイドゲーム a *one-sided* game.

わんしょう 腕章 an **armband** ▶腕章を着ける wear *an armband*.

ワンダーフォーゲル ‖ワンダーフォーゲルクラブ a hiking club (➤「ワンダーフォーゲル」はドイツ語の *Wandervogel* (渡り鳥)から).

ワンタッチ ▶冷房と暖房の切り替えがワンタッチでできます You can switch from cooling to heating and vice versa *with one touch of your finger*.

ワンタン 餛飩・雲呑 a **wonton**, a **wantan**.

わんぱく 腕白な **naughty** /nɔ́:ṭi/ (聞き分けがない), **mischievous** /místʃɪvəs/ (いたずら好きな) ▶男の子のわんぱくはしかたがない Boys can't help being *naughty*. ／Boys will be boys. (➤ 後者は「男の子はどこまでも男の子だ；いたずらはしかたがない」の意のことわざ).

ワンパターン ▶彼のやることはいつもワンパターンだ Everything he does *follows the same old pattern*. ‖きみの発想はワンパターンだ Your ideas *are all the same*. ／You always come up with *the same* (*kind of*) ideas. ／Your ideas *are predictable*. ‖あの教授の講義はワンパターンで実に退屈だ That pro-

わ

fessor's lectures are incredibly boring because he teaches *the same way all the time.* ‖ あの教授の講義はワンパターンで実に退屈だ That professor's lectures are boring to tears because he teaches *the same way all the time.* ‖ きみの服装はワンパターンだね All your clothes *look alike.* ‖ 生活がワンパターンになっている I'*ve gotten into a rut.* (➤ rut の原義は「車輪の通った跡」).

> **危ないカタカナ語✸ ワンパターン**
> one pattern では「1つの型」の意味にしかならない. 日本語は「いつも同じやり方」の意味だから,「ワンパターンだ」は follow the same (old) pattern とするか, stereotyped(型にはまった)などの語を使って表す.

ワンピース a (**one-piece**) **dress** 《参考》one-piece は形容詞で a one-piece swimsuit (ワンピースの水着)のように使う. 服の場合は a one-piece dress または単に a dress という.

ワンポイント ▶**ワンポイントアドバイス** *a tip* ‖ 日曜日には水泳のインストラクターが希望者に**ワンポイントレッスン**をしてくれる A swimming instructor gives *brief* [*one-point* / *single-point*] *lessons* on Sundays to those who wish for one.

ワンボックスカー a **minivan** 《参考》「ワンボックスカー」は和製語だが, 自動車好きの外国人には one-box car で通じることも多い.

ワンマン an **autocrat**(独裁者) ▶吉田茂は典型的な**ワンマン政治家**だった Yoshida Shigeru was a typical *autocratic politician.* ‖ 佐田氏がその会社の**ワンマン社長**だ Mr. Sada is *the autocratic president* of the company.

▶エルトン・ジョンの**ワンマンショー**はすばらしかった *The one-man show* [*solo concert*] by Elton John was splendid.

‖**ワンマンバス** (→かこみ記事).

> **危ないカタカナ語✸ ワンマン**
> **1** 英語にも one-man という形容詞はあるが, これは「ひとりで行う」という意味であって, 日本語のような「独裁的な」の意味はない. したがって「ワンマン社長」は autocratic(独裁的な)などを使って表す必要がある.
> **2**「ワンマンショー」は男性なら one-man show でよいが, 女性なら one-woman show となる. 最近では性差のない solo show [concert] という言い方もされる.
> **3**「ワンマンバス」は, イギリスでは車掌のいるバスと区別して one-man bus というが, アメリカでは運転手だけのバスがふつうなので, 特にワンマンであることをいいたいときは one-man operated bus, driver-operated bus などと説明する必要がある.

わんりょく 腕力 **physical strength**(体力) ; **force, violence** (暴力) ▶**腕力**では息子にかなわない I'm no match for my son in *physical strength.* / My son is stronger than I am. ‖ 彼は**腕力**で妹からおもちゃを奪った He took the toy from his (younger) sister *by force.* (●「力ずくで」と考えて by force を用いるとよい) / He wrested the toy from his (younger) sister. ‖ 子供はすぐ**腕力**(=暴力)に訴えがちだ Children are quick to resort to *violence.*

ワンルーム ‖**ワンルームマンション** a one-room apartment [《英》 flat], a studio (《米》 apartment, 《英》 flat) 《参考》《米》では an efficiency (apartment) と呼ぶこともある.

わんわん 1【犬の鳴き声】bowwow /bàʊwáʊ/ (➤ 幼児が犬を指す「わんわん」も bowwow) ▶誰か玄関先に居るのかな? 犬が**ワンワン**ほえてるよ The dog is *barking.* I wonder if there is someone at the door.
2【大声で泣く様】▶恋人と仲たがいした夜, ひとりになって彼女は**わんわん泣いた** She *cried her heart out* [*cried bitterly*] the night she broke up with her boyfriend and was left alone.

わ

を・ヲ

-を 1【行為の対象を示して】

> **《解説》「…を〜する」の言い方**
> 「…を〜する」という場合, 英語では次のようになる. すなわち, 他動詞のあとではそのまま名詞を続ける. 自動詞の場合は, あとに前置詞をつけ, 例えば look at ... (…を見る), look for ... (…をさがす), look up to ... (…を尊敬する)のようにする. いずれの場合も, 名詞は形は変わらないが, 代名詞は目的格(me, him, it など)にする.

▶彼女はぼくを愛している She loves me. ‖ 父は自分で車を修理した My father fixed the car by himself. ‖ 彼女は5人の子供を育てた She raised five children.

▶彼女は友達を数人誕生パーティーに招待した She invited several of her friends to her birthday party. ‖ 洗濯物を干しておいてね Please hang out the laundry.

▶私は仕事をさがしています I'm looking for a job. ‖ あの人を見て! Look at him. / Look at that man. ‖ 泥棒に預金通帳を盗まれた I had my bankbook stolen by a burglar. ‖ おまえの彼女を泣かせるなよ Don't make your girlfriend cry.

2【移動する場所を示して】▶車で旧道を走る drive *on* [*along*] an old road ‖ 橋の下を行く船 a boat going *under* a bridge ‖ 青山を歩いていたら野中君にばったり会った While walking *in* Aoyama, I ran into Nonaka. ‖ この間, 空を飛ぶ夢を見たよ The other day I had a dream in which I was flying. ‖ 早春の飛鳥路を一人で旅してみたい I'd like to travel *around* the Asuka area in early spring all by myself.

3【出発点・経過点を示して】▶列車は今, 青森駅を出たところだ The train has just left Aomori Station. ‖ 我々は御殿場を経由して山中湖へ行った We went to Lake Yamanaka *via* [*passing through*] Gotenba.

▶皆さま, 当機はただ今, 国際日付変更線を通過しました Passengers, we have just crossed the international date line.

付　録　目　次

SA 和英・ライティング基礎講座

編集主幹＝山岸勝榮（明海大学名誉教授）

英語表現のための基本文型利用法

◉英語表現のための基本文型を覚えよう

日本で生まれ育った私たちは、生まれながらにして日本語を聞き、話す環境、あるいは日本語を理解し、それに反応する環境に身を置いています。したがって、日本語の基本文型については、それらを無意識のうちに習得してしまいます。しかし、外国語としての英語は、ほとんどの人にとって、日常性が希薄ですし、それだけに意識的に努力し、練習を積まなければ、十分に習得することはできません。具体的には、英語を日常的に用いる環境に身を置いたり、そのような環境を作り出したりして、意識的に活用し、十分に慣れなければなりません。

以下に示すのは、網羅的なものではありませんが、平素、私が初級者に英語を教える際に使用する平叙文の主だった文例で、英語で何かを説明する際に必須と思われるものです。便宜上、大まかに文型としてまとめてあります。日本語で言えば、「～は…です」「～は…の意味です［…を意味します］」「～は…をするときに使うもの［語］です」などに相当します。日本人学習者が、英語で自分の意思や伝達内容をきちんと伝えられるようになるには、まずこのような基本文型を十分に使いこなせるようになっている必要があります。最初に簡単な文例を、あとに文型を記載します。

1　（文例）　A cat is an animal.（猫は動物です）
A package is an object with something in it.
（包みは中に物を入れたものです）
（文型）　～ is ＋ 名詞（＋句）

2　（文例）　Ice is something cold and hard.
（氷は冷たく、固いものです）
(A) dessert is something sweet to eat.
（デザートは甘い食べ物です）
（文型）　～ is something ＋ 形容詞（＋ to不定詞）

3 (文例) A can is something to hold things in.
(缶は物を入れておくものです)
A cage is something to keep an animal or a bird in.
(おり［かご］は動物や小鳥を入れて飼っておくものです)
(文型) ～ is something ＋ to不定詞＋名詞＋前置詞

4 (文例) A chair is something to sit on. It has four legs and a back.
(いすは座るものです。脚が４本と背があります)
(文型) ～ is something ＋ to不定詞（＋前置詞）

5 (文例) A balloon is a thing (that) you blow air into.
(風船は空気を吹き込むものです)
A cap is something (that) you wear on top of your head to cover it.
(帽子は頭をおおうようにかぶるものです)
(文型) ～ is a thing［something］＋(that)節

6 (文例) An airplane is a thing that can fly in the air.
(飛行機は空を飛ぶことができるものです)
A law is something that tells people what they can do and cannot do.
(法律はしていいことと、いけないことを教えるものです)
(文型) ～ is a thing［something］＋ that節

7 (文例) Day is the time when it is light outside.
(昼は外が明るい時間です)
Peace is a time when there is no fighting.
(平和は争いのないときです)
(文型) ～ is the time［a time］＋ when節

8 (文例) A center is a place that is in the middle of something.
(中心は物の中ほどにある場所です)
(文型) ～ is a place ＋ that節

9 (文例) A house is a place to live.
(家は生活する場所です)
(文型) ～ is a place ＋ to不定詞

10 (文例) A factory is (a place) where things are made.
(工場は物が作られる場所です)
(文型) ～ is (a place)＋ where節

11 (文例) A camera is a thing used to take pictures.
(カメラは写真を撮るのに使うものです)
A bag is something used to hold things.
(袋は物を入れておくのに使うものです)
(文型) ～ is a thing［something］used ＋ to不定詞

12　(文例)　Few is a word used to show that there are not many of something.
(fewという単語は数が多くないときに使います)
(文型)　～ is a word used ＋ to不定詞＋ that節

13　(文例)　Because is a word you use when you tell why something has happened or is happening.
(becauseという単語はなぜそういうことが起きたか、または起きているかを言うときに使います)
(文型)　～ is a word you use ＋ when節

14　(文例)　A barber is someone who cuts and shampoos your hair.
(理髪師は髪を刈ったり、洗ったりする人です)
(文型)　～ is someone［a person］＋ who節

15　(文例)　Zero means nothing［none].
(ゼロは何もない［全然ない］を意味します)
(文型)　～ means ＋名詞［形容詞、etc.］

16　(文例)　To live means to have life.
(「生きる」とは生命があることです)
To shine means to send or give out light.
(「輝く」とは光を発することです)
(文型)　～ means ＋名詞句

17　(文例)　Dark means that something is not light.
(「暗い」とは明るくないことを意味します)
To start means that you begin to do something.
(「始める」とは何かをやり出すことを意味します)
(文型)　～ means ＋ that節

18　(文例)　When something is cheap, it means (that) it does not cost a lot of money.
(何かが安いというのは、お金があまりかからないという意味です)
When something is beautiful, it is very pretty to look at.
(何かが美しいというのは、見た目がとてもきれいだということです)
(文型)　When something is ＋形容詞, (it means (that)) it is ～.

19　(文例)　When something worries you, it means (that) it makes you feel unhappy about something.
(何かで心配というのは、そのために不安な気持ちでいることです)
(文型)　When something＋ 動詞 ～, it means ＋ (that)節 … .

20　(文例)　When you behave, you are being good.
(お行儀よくしているのは、いい子のときです)
When you ask a question, you want to know something.
(質問するのは、知りたいことがあるときです)

（文型） When you＋動詞（＋名詞, etc.）, you ＋動詞 ～.

21 （文例） If you are happy, it means (that) you feel very good about something.
（うれしいというのは、あることでとても気分がいいという意味です）
If something is soft, it means (that) it is not hard or firm and changes shape easily when you touch it.
（何かがやわらかいというのは、固くしっかりしていなくて、さわると簡単に変形するという意味です）
（文型） If you are［something is］＋形容詞, it means ＋(that)節.

英語圏の子供たちは、このような文型を１つ１つ早い時期に無意識のうちに習得していきます。当然、日本人学習者にとってもきわめて有益なもので、これらの文型を活用できるようになれば、何かを定義することがかなり楽な作業になるでしょう。ちなみに、私はかつて、英語学習を始めて１年半ほどの、ある日本人の少女に、bicycle（自転車）、bird（鳥）、clock（時計）、coffee（コーヒー）、restaurant（レストラン）の５つの名詞を定義してもらったことがあります。

① What is a bicycle?
② What is a bird?
③ What is a clock?
④ What is coffee?
⑤ What is a restaurant?

その少女はこれらを次のように定義しました。

① It is a thing you ride on.（乗って走るものです［文型**5**］）
② It is an animal with wings.（羽のある動物です［文型**1**］）
③ It is a thing that tells the time.（時刻を教えてくれるものです［文型**6**］）
④ It is something to drink. It is brown.（飲み物で茶色をしています［文型**4**］）
⑤ It is a place to eat.（食事をする場所です［文型**9**］）

このように、基本文型を用いて簡単に定義する練習を積んでいれば、身の回りのたいていの事物は平易な英語で表現できます。そして、それらを英語ライティング力の基盤作りに活用することができます。あとは語彙(ごい)力です。参考までに言えば、英単語の頻度上位語100語で日常の言語活動の７割近くが、500語で８割以上が、1000語で９割近くが表現できるといわれています。そして、なんと3000語の語彙を駆使できればほとんどのことは言えたり書けたりするという調査結果もあります。実際、それだけの語彙があれば、英語圏で発行されている学習用英英辞典を使いこなすこともさほど困難なことではありません。

第2講

モデル・パラグラフの利用法

◉モデル・パラグラフで練習しよう

「英作文は英借文だ」と言った人がいます。私自身の過去を振り返っても、それは真実だと思います。平易な英語で書かれた文章を多く読み、その中で出合った、これと思う表現をできるだけ多く暗記する努力をし、折あるごとにそれらを使ってきました。

そのような「英借文」行為の中で、もっとも有効だったのが、モデル・パラグラフの利用でした。これは例えば、My Day（私の１日）、My Family（私の家族）、My Dream（私の夢）、My Best Friend（私のいちばんの仲よし）といったような、身近な話題を取り上げて、200〜300語程度を使用し、パラグラフも４、５個程度から成る比較的短い、モデルとなる英文のことです。日本人英語の問題点を熟知しているような英語母語話者が書いた高校用副読本・大学用教科書などでよく見かけるタイプのものです。

例えば、My Day（私の１日）と題した次のようなモデル・パラグラフがあったとします。

I live in Shinagawa, Tokyo. I live in a unit on the 8th floor of a high-rise apartment complex with my family. My apartment has a living room, a kitchen-cum-dining area and four other rooms. I go to a private girls' senior high school in Kawasaki.

I usually get up at 6:45 and go to the bathroom to wash my face and brush my teeth. I usually have two slices of toast and a glass of orange juice for breakfast; sometimes I have rice and misoshiru. By 7:45 I am ready to go to school by train.

I usually get to school around 8:50. My favorite subject is World History. I like Japanese History as well. Each period is fifty minutes long. There is a ten-minute break between classes. During the break many students buy something to drink from vending machines in the school cafeteria. School is over at 3:30.

After school I practice tennis. I am a member of the tennis club. All our school club activities are very popular and some of the sports clubs have produced professional players. I usually go home by train at 5:30; sometimes at 6:00.

When I get home, I usually check e-mail from my friends overseas and after that I help my mother prepare dinner. After dinner I study for two hours and watch some TV or search for information on the Internet. I take a bath before going to bed at around 11:00.

私は東京の品川に住んでいます。高層団地の８階で、家族といっしょです。アパートは４LDKです。川崎にある私立の女子高に通っています。

ふつうは６時45分に起きて、バスルームで顔を洗い、歯をみがきます。朝食はふつう、トースト２枚とオレンジジュースで済ませますが、ときにはご飯とみそ汁を食べます。７時45分までには電車で通学の準備をします。

学校にはふつうは８時50分ごろ着きます。私のいちばん好きな科目は世界史です。日本史も好きです。１時限は50分で、授業と授業の間に10分の休み時間があります。休み時間には学校の食堂にある自動販売機で飲み物を買う生徒が多くいます。学校は3時半に終わります。

放課後、私はテニスの練習をします。テニスクラブの部員になっているのです。私が通う学校はどのクラブ活動もとても盛んで、クラブの中にはプロの選手を送り出しているところもあります。ふつうは5時半の電車で帰宅しますが、ときには6時になることもあります。

帰宅するとたいていは、海外の友だちから来るメールを確認してから、母の夕食の手伝いをします。夕食が終わると、2時間勉強して、少しテレビを見たり、インターネットで情報を探したりします。11時ごろ、寝る前にふろに入ります。

このモデル・パラグラフの内容が全ての人に当てはまるわけがなく、一日の生活パターンは個人個人、みな異なります。とりわけ下線部を施した箇所は個人差が反映すると思いますので、そこを自分の場合に当てはめて、声に出して読んだり、目で追ったりしながら、英語表現の練習をしていけば、まとまったパラグラフで英語を書いたり、話したりすることに、少しずつ慣れていくはずです。

私は高校1年生のころから、そのようにして少しずつ、内容的にまとまりのある英文を書く練習をしてきました。みなさんもぜひ試してみてください。

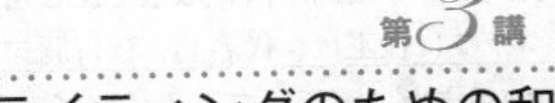

第3講 ライティングのための和英辞典の利用法

◉ライティングと和英辞典の1つの利用法

私たちの毎日の言語活動には、過去に言ったことも書いたこともないような表現や文がいくらでも出てきます。つまり、人間の言語表現生成能力は無限だということです。この事実を知れば、本辞典のような学習辞典規模のものが収録しうる情報量には自ずと限界があるということも納得できるでしょう。

したがって、学習レベルが上がれば上がるほど、複雑な日本語表現を英語に直す際の補助的手段としての学習和英辞典に不満が感じられるという人が出てくるでしょう。しかし、私たちの日常的な事柄に関する限り、本辞典規模のものでたいていは間に合うと思います。間に合わない場合には、後述する言い換え法（paraphrasing）を導入すれば、不足の部分は少なからず埋められるはずです。

1．求める用例や参考になる情報が収録されている場合

前述したように、日常的に用いる日本語の語句や表現に関する情報は、本辞典規模のものでもだいたいは調べられると思います。具体例として、第2講で使用したモデル・パラグラフの冒頭の4文を再録してみましょう。

私は東京の品川に住んでいます。高層団地の8階で、家族といっしょです。アパートは4 LDKです。川崎にある私立の女子高に通っています。

①「私は東京の品川に住んでいます。」
→これを英訳するための情報は、本辞典の「住む」の項に、応用のきく例文の形で何例か見つかります。

②「高層団地の8階で、家族といっしょです。」
→この場合の「高層団地の8階」の訳出に必要な情報も本辞典の「団地」の項に収録されています。

③「アパートは4LDKです。」
→この場合の「4LDK」については見出語の「LDK」を引けば、そのまま利用できる表現が収録されています。

④「川崎にある私立の女子高に通っています。」
→この場合は「私立」「女子校」「高校」「通う」などを見れば、参考になる用例が収録してあります。

上記程度の日本語に相当する英文は、いちいち辞書を引かなくても書けるようになりたいものですが、ここでは和英辞典を活用するという前提に立っていますから、①から④までの例を英訳するための用例や情報の収集のしかたに触れました。

本辞典を利用すれば、上掲の4文の英訳に利用できる用例や情報は全て探し当てることができます。あとは、1文1文の英文を作り、それをパラグラフに仕上げ、代名詞、移行語句［表現］(第4講II 3参照)、事実、例証、比較・対照などを巧みに使用または実行して、各パラグラフを内容的・論理的にリンクさせ、全体的に一貫性を持ったものに発展させていけばよいのです。

2. 求める用例や参考になる情報が収録されていない場合

本辞典規模の和英辞典では、求める用例や参考になる情報が収録されていない場合が多々あります。前記したように、人間が生成する文の数はまさに無限ですから、あらゆる表現が載った辞典というものはありません。

そこで、本辞典規模のものを最大限に活用する方法を考えなければなりません。その有効な方法の1つが、別のことばを使って表現し直す言い換え法 (**paraphrasing**) です。

例えば、

例1) 彼は父親似だ。

これを和英辞典を使って英訳しようとする場合、たいていの人は「〜似」に注目して、その見出語を探そうとするでしょう。本辞典には幸い「-似」の見出語があるので、そこの記述を参考にすればよいのですが、もしこの見出語がなかった場合、何とかして参考になる情報を探さなければなりません。このときに有効なのが上記の「言い換え法」です。「彼は父親似だ」とは「彼は父(親)に似ている」と言い換えられますから、早速「似る」を引いてみます。すると、「彼は父親によく似ている He looks very (much) like his father./ He is very (much) like his father.」という用例文が見つかります。次に、「よく」という語が不要ですから、それに対応するvery (much) を削除します。答えは He looks like his father.またはHe is like his father.となります。ただし、この2つは意味あいが違います。最初に訳語を示してあるところに説明があるように、似ているのが外見だけなら前者の言い方になります。

例2）親と違い、彼女はとても長身だ。

この場合であれば、「親と違い」を「親に似ず」、「長身」を「背が高い」と言い換えて、「似る」か「背」のいずれかの見出語の下に、例題の「親と違い、彼女はとても長身だ」を英訳する手がかりになるものを探します。本辞典には、「似る」に、「親に似ず、彼女はとても背が高い　Unlike her parents, she is very tall.」という例文が収録されていますから、それをそのまま利用できます。この段階で正解を得ましたので、「背」の項目参照は省略します。また、「親と違い」を「親と違って」と考え、「違う」の項で類例を探してもいいでしょう。

例3）十中八九ぼくたちのチームが優勝する。

「十中八九」を「まずまちがいなく」または「九分九厘」と言い換えて、各見出語を引きます。すると、前者の「まず」の項には「まずまちがいなく」に関連した用例としては、「わたしの勘にまずまちがいはありません I'm almost［pretty］sure my hunch is right.」が収録されており、「九分九厘」の項には「九分九厘私たちのチームの優勝だ Ten to one, our team will win the victory. / In all likelihood, our team will win the championship.」が収録されていますので、後者をそのまま利用すればよいことになります。

例4）こちらに来られることがあれば寄ってください。

「来られることがあれば」の「あれば」に注目して、「こちらにおいでの際は寄ってください」と言い換え、「際」の項を見ます。するとそこには、「お近くへおいでの際はぜひお立ち寄りください Be sure to visit us when you are in our area.」のような文例が示してありますから、それを利用します。数例を示しただけですが、言い換え法の有効性については理解できたことと思います。この方法を実践することにより、英語学習者は学習和英辞典の活用法のみならず、日本語の表現法も補強することができます。

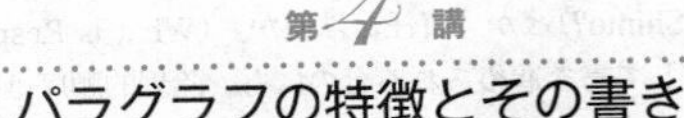

第4講　パラグラフの特徴とその書き方

Ⅰ．文章を書く２つの目的

私たちは目的があって文章を書きます。１つは、特定の相手に特定の情報を伝達するためです。友人・知人などに送るメールや、学校・会社などで提出するレポートがそのよい例です。インターネット・テレビ・雑誌・新聞などの報道は不特定多数を相手にしていますが、それらの人々を当該媒体の視聴者・読者と考えれば、やはり特定の人々を相手にしていると考えてよいことになります。２つめは、読者を想定せずに、あくまでも自己表現を目的とする場合です。例えば、日記や回想録がこれに属します。後日、それらが不特定多数の人々の目に触れることになれば、それはそれで一定の情報伝達力を有することになりますが、最初から読者を想定して書かれるわけではありません。その点で、文学作品も後者に属するといえます。なぜなら、文学作品は虚構の世界であるのがふつうですし、作家自身の精神世界を自己表現あるいは独白していると考えられるからです。

私たちが書く文章が、そのいずれのタイプに属するものであっても、書いた意図や真意が読み手や、後日再読する自分自身に正しく理解できるものでなければ、その文章は「よい文章」とは呼べません。すなわち、「記述の展開が整然としていて、文脈がよく通ること」という条件を満たしている必要があります。

以下に、それを具体化しながら、よい文章、具体的には「よい英文ライティング」を実現するための基本的な事柄を学んでいきましょう。

Ⅱ．記述の展開が整然としていて、文脈がよく通ること

1．文章の内容の配列

私たちは日常、他人の話や、他人が書いたものについて、「何が言いたいのかよくわからない」とか「支離滅裂だ」などと言うことがあります。これは、ふつうは、その話や書いたものの展開に一貫性が欠けていることを意味します。それとは反対に、話や書いたものが論理的に展開し、わかりやすい場合をさして「理路整然としている」と言います。私たちが求める文章の形はもちろん後者です。

そのような理路整然とした文章を書くためには、私たちは

① 論理的順序［議論や推論の筋道］を大事にする、
② 時間的・空間的順序を大事にする、

この2つを厳守する習慣を身につけておかなければなりません。

①に沿って書かれるものの例としては新聞記事を挙げることができます。新聞記事は最重要事項を書き出し部分に持ってきて、読者の関心をつかもうとします。そのあとで、論理的に話を展開していきます。レポートや論文などもこの順序に沿って書かれるのがふつうです。読み手に書き手の意図を正確に把握してもらうためです。この書き方は重要性の順序に従ったもので、逆ピラミッド型の書き方と呼ぶこともあります。

「日本人と県民性」(Japanese and their Prefectural Characteristics)とか「アメリカ人と階級意識」(Americans and their Class Consciousness)といった例に見るように、分類を行いつつ書き進めるものや、「神道とは何か」(What is Shinto?)とか「責任とは何か」(What is Responsibility?)といった例に見るように、全体の定義をめざして書き進められるものにも、論理的順序は重要です。

また、自分がよく知っている物事、言い換えれば、既知の物事から、未知の物事に、あるいはその逆に、未知の物事から、既知の物事へと説明するという方法、すなわち理解度の順序に従った書き進め方も、やはり論理的でなければなりません。

①に属する文章の組み立て方には、一般論や真理から具体例へ、またはその逆に具体例から一般論や真理へという順序で書き進めるものもあります。

②の例として、例えば、「昭和高等学校80年の歩み」(Showa Senior High School and Its 80-year History）とか「私の半生」(Looking Back on My Earlier Life）といったような題名で書く学校史や自分史が挙げられますが、これらの場合、文章の内容の配列は時間的順序に従って行うのがふつうです。例えば、第2講の「モデル・パラグラフ」の例文として用いたMy Day（私の1日）も一日を時間的順序に従って書いています。ただし、「昭和高等学校80年の歩み」を書いている中で、校庭や職員室の描写をする場合には、空間的順序によって文章を組み立てていきます。すなわち、描写対象を外周から内周、あるいはその逆に、内周から外周に向かって並列的に記述していきます。

2. パラグラフと主題文

前出のいずれのスタイルで文章を書くにせよ、日本人英語学習者にとって重要なものはパラグラフです。これは段落とも節とも呼ばれ、(長い) 文章における内容上の切れ目のことです。きちんとした英文を書くためには、パラグラフの本質を理解し、それを巧みに構築する練習をしなければなりません。

1つのパラグラフには通例1つの**主題文 (topic sentence)** があります。そして主題文はそのパラグラフに記述されている全内容を凝縮したものでなければなりません。通例と言ったのは、それが文として明りょうになっておらず、後述するように、段落全体が暗示している場合もありうるからです。1つのパラグラフには、「主題文」だけでなく、それを補ったり、発展させたりする**副題文 (sub-topic sentence)** があることも少なくありませんが、これは必須のものではありません。

主題文は、中心的概念を早く提示し、読み手の興味をそそる可能性が高いという点で、パラグラフの導入部 (最初か2番目) に置くのが効果的ですが、前述したことを分析し、結論し、総括するという点で、末尾に置くのも同じく効果的です。ときに、パラグラフの中間に置くこともあり、これは末尾の場合同様、細かい事例から一般的結論を導き出すという形でアイディアを展開させていく場合に便利な置き方です。なお、導入部に置いた主題文によって示した中心的概念を強調するために、パラグラフの末尾で、別の表現でもう一度その概念を繰り返すこともあります。

英語の具体的な文章で見てみましょう。パラグラフの先頭が、英語の場合には2文字分スペースが取って [indentして] あるのに対して、日本語の場合には1文字分を引っ込めて書かれていることに注意してください(英語の場合は、ふつうは2文字分から5文字分程度のスペースを取ることが多いようですが、個人差もあり、一定していません。最初のパラグラフの先頭にはスペースを置かない人もいます)。

・例文 1

The movement of words between Britain and the United States is mostly eastward; every year, more and more words that were once exclusively American are found in the spoken and written language of Britain. Half a century or so ago, the use in Britain of such words as "guy" or "campus" would stamp one unmistakably as an American or a Canadian. Today, however, these words have been completely naturalized in Britain.

英米間の単語の移動は主に東向きである。毎年、かつてはもっぱらアメリカ英語であった語が以前にもましてイギリスの話しことばや書きことばに見出される。半世紀かそこら昔、イギリスで "guy" とか "campus" といった語を用いれば、まちがいなく、アメリカ人あるいはカナダ人の刻印を押されたものである。ところが、今日では、これらの語は完全にイギリスに順化している。

このパラグラフの「主題文」は冒頭の1文です。セミコロン (;) に続く第2文を「副題文」ととらえることも可能です。Half a century or so agoで始まる第3文は事実によって、また、第4文は副詞の however(しかしながら)を用いて対比を示すことによって、中心的概念を発展させています。

(例文1) を次のように書いたとします。

・例文２

Half a century or so ago, the use in Britain of such words as "guy" or "campus" would stamp one unmistakably as an American or a Canadian; these words were uncommon in British English.

Today, however, they have been completely naturalized in Britain; every year, more and more words that were once exclusively American are found in the spoken and written language of Britain. The movement of words between Britain and the United States is mostly eastward.

半世紀かそこら昔、イギリスで"guy"とか"campus"といった語を用いれば、まちがいなく、アメリカ人だカナダ人だと刻印を押されたものである。これらの語はイギリスではふつうではなかったからだ。

ところが、今日では、これらの語は完全にイギリスに順化しており、毎年、かつてはもっぱらアメリカ英語であった語が以前にもまして多くイギリスの話しことばや書きことばに見出される。英米間の単語の移動は主に東向きである。

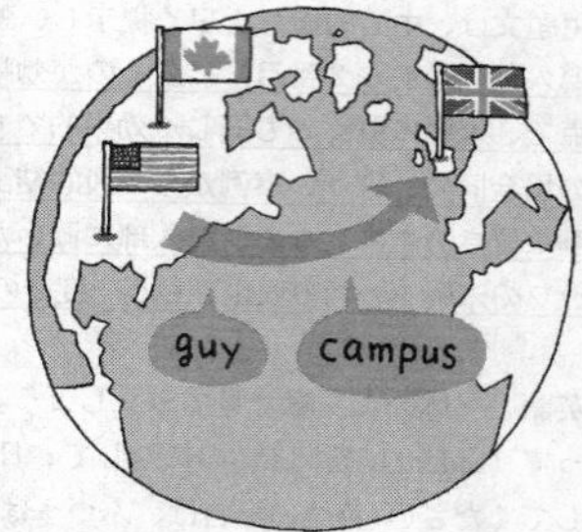

上の（例文２）の場合、（例文１）で文頭にあったThe movement of words between Britain and the United States is mostly eastward.（英米間の単語の移動は主に東向きである。）という主題文が文末に来ています。主題文をここに置くことによって、前述したことを総括しており、（例文１）に次いで、効果的です。

３．移行語句と移行表現

１つの文やパラグラフが次の文やパラグラフに明確かつ論理的につながるようにする場合に用いる語句を移行語句とか移行表現と呼びます。上の例（例文１、例文２）では"however"でしたが、対比を表す移行語句には、ほかにいろいろあります。なお、厳密にいえば、（例文１）、（例文２）の「セミコロン（；）」は後続節が直前の節と密接に結び付いていることを意味していますので、移行語句［表現］の一種と考えられます。次に、移行語句［表現］の代表的なものを列挙してみましょう。

〈役割〉	〈主な表現〉
換言	in other words（換言すれば）；namely（すなわち）
強化	anyway（とにかく）；at any rate（少なくとも）；indeed（たしかに）；in any case（いずれにせよ）；in fact（実のところ）；regardless（とにかく）；still（それでも、やはり）
結果、効果	accordingly（したがって、よって）；as a result（結果として）；consequently（その結果）；hence（このゆえに、だからして）；in［as a］consequence（その結果、成り行きとして；悪い結果を連想させる）；in that［this］case（その［この］場合は）；in the end（最後に、結局）；therefore（それゆえに）；thus（ゆえに、かくて）

結論	finally（最後に；完結を強調する）；in conclusion＝to conclude（終わりに臨んで）；in short（手短に言えば、つまり）；in summary＝to summarize（要約すれば）；lastly（最後に；順序の終わりをいう）
言及	as for［to］（～について言えば）；as regards＝regarding（～に関しては）；speaking of（～のことだが）；talking of（～の話だが）；with［in］ regard to（～に関しては）
強調、補強	actually（実際に、ほんとうに）；as a matter of fact（いや実際、それどころか）；indeed（ほんとうに、たしかに）；in fact（いや実は）
コメント	oddly（enough）（奇妙なことに；enoughは意外性が強いとき）；maybe（あるいは、ひょっとして）；perhaps（あるいは、ひょっとして）；strangely（enough）（不思議なことに）；surely（たしかに）；wisely（賢明にも）
時、発生順	after（～したあとで）；as soon as（～するとすぐに）；before（～する前に）；earlier（前に、以前）；first［second, third, etc.］（第１に［第２に、第３に］）；later（(時間的に見て)あとで）；meanwhile（その間に）；next（次に）；now（さて、ところで）；soon（まもなく）；then（それから、その次に）；while（～しているうち［間］に）
修正	instead（代わりとして）；on the contrary（実際はその反対で）；(or) rather（もっと正確に言えば）
条件	but for（～なしでは）；on（the）condition that（～という条件で）；unless（～でなければ）
対比	although（～だけれども）；but（だが、しかし）；even if（たとえ～だとしても）；however（しかしながら）；by［in］ contrast（対照的に）；meanwhile（一方、ところで）；nevertheless（それにもかかわらず）；on the other（hand）（他方）；rather（むしろ）；though（～だけれども）；while（～である一方）
選択	at the same time（同時に）；or（else）（さもないと）；in all other ways（ほかの全ての点で）；otherwise（ほかの点では）
比較、類例	by［in］ comparison（比較して）；in the same way（同様に）；likewise（～もまた、それに加えて）；similarly（同様に）
方法	in that［this］ way（その［この］ように）
付言・追加	all the more（なおさら、かえって）；also（また）；besides（そのうえ）；but then（しかしながら）；furthermore（そのうえ、おまけに）；in addition（さらに）；in addition to（～に加えて）；moreover（そのうえ）；too（～もまた）；thereby（それによって）；what is more（おまけに）
目的、理由	in order that（～するためには）；in order to（～するために）；so（that）（～するように）
要約	all things considered（全てを考え合わせれば）；in short（簡単に言えば、要するに）；in summary（要約すれば、要するに）；that is（to say）（すなわち）；i.e.（すなわち）
理由	as（～だから、～なので）；because（なぜなら）；for（というのは）；for this［that］ reason（この［その］理由から）；since（～なので）
例証	for example［instance］（例えば）；e.g.（例えば）；in particular（とりわけ）；specifically（具体的に(は)）

以上のように分類した多数の語句が移行語句とか移行表現と呼ばれるもので、それらの語句によって各パラグラフが論理付けられ連結されて、より大きな文章の集団を構成していきます。

１つのパラグラフには１つのトピック（**one paragraph, one topic**）」ということも鉄則です。したがって、上に示したパラグラフ（例文１または例文２）の中に、「日本語に及ぼすアメリカ英語の影響」

(the influence of American English upon Japanese) というようなトピックを混在させることはできません。前出の２例の場合、いずれも「英米間の単語の移動」(the movement of words between Britain and the United States) ということでトピックはまとまっているからです。

そこで、例えば、下の（例文３）に示すような文章であれば、トピックは重ならないうえ、論理的な思考順序にも従った自然な流れのものになります。

・例文３

It is clear that the influence of American English upon British English is partly due to America's position in commerce, economics, finance, politics, films, and TV programs, and partly due to the increased communication between the two countries in the last and present centuries.

明らかなことは、イギリス英語に及ぼすアメリカ英語の影響がある程度は商業・経済・財政・政治・映画・テレビ番組におけるアメリカの立場によるものであり、またある程度は前世紀から今世紀にかけて両国間に増大したコミュニケーションによるものだということである。

このように、「１つのパラグラフには１つのトピック」の原則を守りつつ、１つのパラグラフから次のパラグラフへ、またその次のパラグラフへと、トピックを展開させていきます。

※

もう１つ忘れてはならないのは、パラグラフ間の連続性ということです。換言すれば、各パラグラフは内容的にリンクしている必要があります。こうして全体的に一貫性を持ったもの一具体的には章からエッセイ、さらには本一に発展させていきます。この一貫性を保つために、代名詞、移行語句［表現］、事実、例証、比較・対照などを巧みに使用しつつ、パラグラフを展開させていかなければなりません。

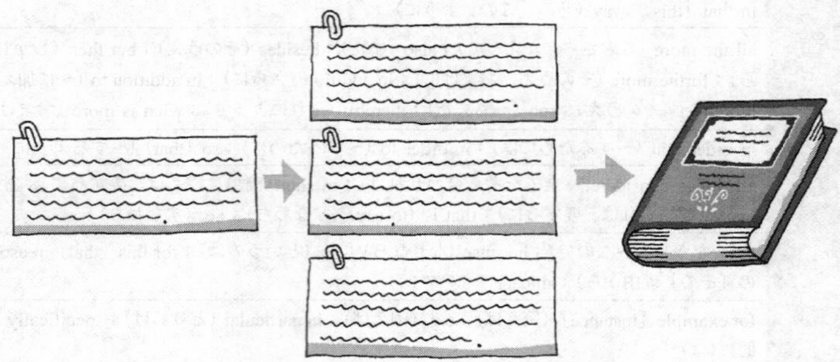

4．中心テーマ

パラグラフを構成する場合の主題文の重要性については、前記したとおりですが、パラグラフによってはそれが明りょうになっておらず、むしろ中心テーマ（**main topic**）だけが全体の背景を成している場合があります。例えば、次の英文を見てください。

・例文 4

I frequently have the following questions asked by non-Japanese teachers. Why do Japanese university students sit in back rows in classrooms — why not sit in front where they can hear and see better? Why do they sit in a group, boys in a boys' group and girls in a girls' group— why not sit in a mixed way? Why do they avoid eye contact with their teacher in class— why not look the teacher in the eye and keep eye contact with him or her? Why don't they ask questions during class? Japanese students often look very unfriendly, uncooperative, and sometimes even dishonest.

Some of my non-Japanese colleagues have also asked me these questions. I can understand how they feel, how much they are frustrated, and how unhappy they are with those Japanese students. Most teachers from overseas have trouble getting Japanese university students to sit in front rows, to look them straight in the eye, and to speak up. When they found out that it is almost impossible for them to make Japanese classes be active or positive and to help them to be more responsive or cooperative, they end up being frustrated with the Japanese students' response.

私は外国人の先生から次のような質問を頻繁に受けます。日本人大学生は教室ではどうして、後ろの列に座るのですかーどうして、よく聞こえ、よく見える前の席に座らないのですか。彼らはどうして、男子は男子同士、女子は女子同士、固まって座るのですかーどうして、混ざり合って座らないのですか。彼らはどうして、授業中に教師とのアイコンタクトを避けるのですかーどうして、教師の目をまっすぐに見て、アイコンタクトを取らないのですか。彼らはどうして、授業中に質問をしないのですか。日本人学生はとても非友好的で、非協力的に思えるときが多く、不正直に思えることさえあります。

私の外国人の同僚の一部にも、こうした質問を私にした人がいます。彼らが、そうした日本人学生たちに、どんな感情を持ち、どれほどフラストレーションを感じ、どれほど不満に思っているかを理解することはできます。海外からやって来たたいていの教師たちは、日本人学生たちに前の列に座らせたり、まっすぐに目を見させたり、発言させたりすることに苦労します。彼らが、日本人のクラスを活発で積極的なものにしたり、反応よく協力的なものにしたりすることが不可能に近いと知ったとき、彼らは結果的に日本人学生たちの態度にフラストレーションを感じてしまうのです。

この英文は大きく２つのパラグラフから成っていますが、それらには主題文も副題文もありません。しかし、これらの文章から「(日本の大学における)外国人教師の不満」(Foreign Teachers' Dissatisfactions (in Japanese Universities))、「(日本人学生に関する)外国人教師の疑問」(Foreign Teachers' Questions (about Japanese Students))といった中心テーマの存在を察知することが可能です。「異文化における教育の問題点」(Educational Problems in Different Cultures) というようなテーマだと考えることもできるでしょう。どのテーマがもっとも好ましいかは、その２つのパラグラフの発展の仕方と密接に関わりを持ちます。

主題文（および副題文）を持ったパラグラフであっても、中心テーマだけのパラグラフであっても、各パラグラフ間には内容的、テーマ的に一貫性がなければなりません。したがって、上記の２パラグラフに、次のようなパラグラフを追加して文章を続けるのは好ましくありません。

・例文５

I have found that native English teachers who have been successful at teaching Japanese students share certain characteristics. For instance, they are very skillful at encouraging Japanese students to speak up in class, study their lessons and pride themselves on their own language and culture. They tell Japanese students, for example, that foreigners don't come to Japan to learn about Chaucer, Shakespeare, or Hemingway; they come here because they want to know about Izumi Shikibu, Natsume Soseki or Mori Ogai; they come to see new things, visit places they can't see or visit in their own country, so Japanese students should study more about Japan and show them as many wonderful things as possible; English is a useful language to carry out that task now or in the future.

私が気づいたことは、日本人学生を対象とした教育に成功しているネイティブの英語教師たちには、ある共通した特徴があるということです。例えば、彼らは授業中、学生たちに発言させたり、学科を学ばせたり、自分たちの言語や文化に誇りを持たせたりすることがとても巧みなのです。例えば、彼らが日本人学生たちに言うのは、外国人が日本を訪れるのは、チョーサーやシェークスピアやヘミングウェーを学ぶためではなく、和泉式部や夏目漱石や森鷗外について知りたいからであり、自分たちの国では見たり訪ねたりすることのできない新しいものや場所を見たり訪ねたりするためである。したがって、日本の学生諸君は日本についてもっと知るべきであり、多くのすばらしいものを外国人に見せるべきである。英語は現在あるいは将来、その目的を達成するには有用な言語である、ということです。

このパラグラフの場合、これ自体は「（外国人教師による）日本人学生にやる気を起こさせる法」（(Foreign Teachers') Way of Motivating Japanese Students）と呼べる中心テーマを持っていますが、（例文４）の２パラグラフに直結させるには一貫性を欠いています。これを次のようなパラグラフに換えるとどうなるでしょうか。

・例文６

However, no matter how often non-Japanese teachers try to encourage Japanese students to sit in front rows, and to speak up and be heard if they want to learn to speak English, they will sit in back rows and remain silent or unresponsive in classrooms. And no matter how earnestly non-Japanese teachers say that by maintaining eye contact a person can convey "sincerity" (unfortunately the Japanese counterpart of the word is used in a different connotation) and thereby create a friendly atmosphere in classrooms, the Japanese students may well remain silent and hesitate to sit in front rows or look the teacher straight in the eye.

しかし、外国人教師たちがどれほど日本人学生たちに、前列に座るようにと勧めて、英語を話せるようになりたいのなら口を開いて発言を聞いてもらわなければならないと言ったとしても、彼らは教室では後列に座り、あいかわらず沈黙を保つか無反応でいるかだろう。そして、外国人教師たちがどれほど一生懸命に、人はアイコンタクトを取ることによって"誠実さ"(不幸なことに、日本語としてのこの語は英語のそれとは異なった含みで用いられる)を伝えることができ、教室では友好的な雰囲気をつくり出すことが可能だと説いても、日本人学生たちはおそらく沈黙を保ち、前列に座ることや教師の目をまっすぐに見ることを躊躇(ちゅうちょ)するだろう。

上掲のパラグラフは、(例文４) の２パラグラフと内容的にも論理的にも連動しています。このようなパラグラフを後続させて、

・例文７

Not a few foreign teachers, however, have excellent rapport with their Japanese students.

しかし、日本人学生たちとすばらしい心の通わせ合いをしている外国人教師は少なくない。

というような１文のパラグラフを置き、そのあとで、好ましくないとした (例文５) のようなパラグラフを続けるのであれば、先行する (例文４) における２パラグラフとそのパラグラフとの間の一貫性を保つことができます。

Ⅲパラグラフと思考の流れの型

１．主張→理由→結果→まとめ

日本語は、最後まで聞いたり読んだりしなければ、話し手や書き手の論旨を理解できないということが多々あります。換言すれば、日本人は、最初は遠回しに話を始めて、次第に核心に向かい、もっとも重要な事柄を最後に述べるという思考方法を自分たちの傾向として持っています。スピードと平易なことばづかいとわかりやすさとが要求されるインターネットの時代に、さすがにそういった悠長な思考方法に反省が加えられるようになってきていますが、日常的には日本人の心に今も根強く生きているものだと思います。

これに対して、英語では、主張は、できるだけパラグラフの導入部に置き、そのまま最後まで説明していくという形が好まれます。また、論を進めていく際、論点を直線的に述べていくタイプや、枝分かれ式に複数に分けていくタイプや、円を描くように進めていくタイプなど、何種類かありますが、もっとも一般的で英語的なのが主題文もしくは主張を直線的に解説・説明してパラグラフを構成する方法です。本講では、直線的なパラグラフの場合を中心に見ていきます。

次の文章を見てください。英語圏に住んで、近所の犬の飼い主にその犬のことで苦情を述べるという想定です (敬称の付け方など、周辺的な形式についての詳細は本講では省略します)。

付録

・例文８

I am really sorry to have to appear unneighborly, but I must ask you to do something about your dog. Yesterday it came into my front garden and did a great deal of damage. It ruined quite a number of plants and spoiled the appearance of the flower bed.

Trusting that you will see to it that I am put to no further trouble,

I remain,

署　名

ご近所ですので申し上げにくいのですが、お宅の犬の件でお願いがございます。昨日、私どもの前庭に入って来て、そこを台無しにしてしまいました。たくさんの植物をだめにしましたし、花壇を見るも無残にしました。

今後このようなことが起きないよう、よろしくお取り計らいください。

このパラグラフをさらに細かく見ていくと、次のような流れになっていることに気づきます。

（1）　主張（assertion）：
I am really sorry to have to appear unneighborly, but I must ask you to do something about your dog.

（2）　理由（reason）：
Yesterday it came into my front garden and did a great deal of damage.

（3）　結果（result）：
It ruined quite a number of plants and spoiled the appearance of the flower bed.

（4）　まとめ（conclusion）：
Trusting that you will see to it that I am put to no further trouble,
(Trusting that you will ～は「あなたが～してくださることを確信しつつ」という意味の結びの表現ですが、古風または改まっていると感じられるために、最近ではI hope that you'll ～.とかWill you please ～? とかの言い方が好まれるようになってきています。)

2．導入→本体→まとめ

今度は、アメリカの大学院に留学を考えている自分の学生のために日本人教師が書いた推薦状という想定です。

・例文９

I have been asked to write a letter of recommendation for Ms. Koyuki Kamakura, who is applying to enter your graduate program.

I have known Koyuki for about two years. Koyuki was a very well motivated and able student in my undergraduate lecture courses on Contrastive Linguistics, from April 2019 to January 2020, and my Second Language Acquisition Theory class, from April 2020 to January 2021. These courses were taught entirely in English and Koyuki was more than able to handle the spoken and written language demands of the courses. Her English skills are excellent and I think her to be a capable, hard working and determined student, and I have every confidence that she will do very well in your program.

If I can be of further assistance to you in profiling Koyuki, please contact me at the above address.

本推薦状を貴大学院に入学希望の鎌倉小雪さんの依頼により書いております。

小雪さんとは２年近くのお付き合いですが、私の学部の講義科目のうち、2019年４月から2020年１月までの対照言語学、および2020年４月から2021年１月までの第二言語習得論に出席したきわめて学習意欲旺盛な優秀な学生です。これらの科目は完全に英語だけで行われますが、小雪さんは授業に要求される話しことば・書きことばをきわめて巧みに駆使することができました。英語能力に優れており、有能かつ熱心な意志のしっかりした学生ですので、貴大学院においても大いに成果を上げるものと確信いたします。

小雪さんの人となりにつきほかに私でお伝えできることがございましたら、上記の住所にご連絡ください。

この文章の流れは次のようになっていると考えることができます。

（1） 導入 (introduction)―手紙を書く理由 (reason for writing)…１番目のパラグラフ

I have been asked to write a letter of recommendation for Ms. Koyuki Kamakura, who is applying to enter your graduate program.

（2） 本体(body)―詳細(details)

I have known Koyuki for about two years.から始まる２番目のパラグラフ

（3） まとめ(conclusion)・・・３番目のパラグラフ

If I can be of further assistance to you in profiling Koyuki, please contact me at the above address.

すなわち、

① 導入部分で、まず自分の立場を明確にし、

② 本体部分で、必要事項を書き、

③ まとめの部分で、必要な場合の連絡先［問い合わせ先］に言及する、

というような流れです。

この例を見ても、英語のパラグラフではしっかりとした論理展開がなされていることがわかるでしょう。もちろん、常にこの論理展開で文章が書かれるというわけではありませんが、簡単な依頼書・自由作文・レポートなどを書く際にも、大いに役立ちますから、このような文章の書き方に平素から慣れておくとよいでしょう。

別の例で見てみましょう。今度は、外国人講師X氏に新年度の聴講許可を求める大学生のメールという想定です。上記のステップにしたがってパラグラフを書いていくと、例えば、次のようになります。

① I was a student in your British and American History class last year.
（私は昨年先生の英・米国史のクラスに出席した学生です。）

② I really enjoyed the class and learned many things from it. I would be grateful if you would give me permission to attend your class this year as an auditor.

（先生のクラスはほんとうに楽しく、そこから多くのことを学びました。つきましては本年も聴講生として先生のクラスに出席させていただければ幸いです。）

③ I look forward to hearing from you.
（ご返事をお待ちしております。）

以上をまとめれば、次のようなパラグラフになります。

・例文 10

I was a student in your British and American History class last year. I really enjoyed the class and learned many things from it. I would be grateful if you would give me permission to attend your class this year as an auditor. I look forward to hearing from you.

もう１例見てみましょう。今度は、入学試験合格を祝ってくれた外国の友人を、自宅で行うお祝いの会に招待するメールという想定です。

① 導入部分で、友人に対して、まず自分の現時点での気持ちを書き、
② 本体部分で、自分の家で開くお祝いの会にその友人を誘い、
③ まとめの部分で、相手の出席を願う。

というように書き進めます。そうして書いたのが次の文です。

① Thank you for your letter of congratulation on my entrance exam results. I was very pleased to hear from you. The results were a great relief.
（私の入学試験の結果を祝ってくれてありがとう。手紙をもらってとても喜んでいます。結果にほんとうにほっとしました。）

② We are having a celebration party on Saturday, March 3 and we will be pleased if you can come. The party starts at 6.
（３月３日の土曜日に私の家でお祝いの会を開きますので、来てもらえるとうれしいのですが。会は６時からです。）

③ I do hope that you will be able to come.
（来てもらえることを祈っています。）

というように書き進めることができます。以上をまとめれば、次のようなパラグラフになります。

・例文 11

Thank you for your letter of congratulation on my entrance exam results. I was very pleased to hear from you. The results were a great relief. We are having a celebration party on Saturday, March 3 and we will be pleased if you can come. The party starts at 6.

I do hope that you will be able to come.

終わりに

本講では、英語表現のための基本文型の利用法、モデル・パラグラフの利用法、ライティングのための和英辞典の利用法、パラグラフの特徴とその書き方の4点に焦点を当てて、解説を行ってきました。

「英語を書く」ということは、ノートであれば「紙」の上で、パソコンであればキーボードを使ってその「画面」の上で、「英語で話をしている」ことにほかなりません。きちんと筋道を立てて、わかりやすい英語で話をする習慣を身につけておけば、あとはその英語を用いてノートやパソコンの画面上で、「英語で話をすればよい」のです。

本辞典では、堅い日本語には堅い英語を、くだけた日本語にはくだけた英語を当てるという配慮をしています。したがって、自らの話す日本語を頼りに、本辞典の見出語を引くことが可能です。

英語学習者にとっての理想は、和英辞典を使わなくても、最初からわかりやすい英語を書けることです。しかし、それは容易には実現できないことですし、最近の和英辞典はよくできて、使いやすくなっていますから、それを利用しない手はありません。できるだけ頻繁に辞書を引き、よく読み、自分に必要な用例文を可能なだけ多く身につけ、それらを実際に使ってみるうちに、パラグラフを構築することも、それをまとまった長さの文章にすることも、さほど難しいことではないと感じられるようになるでしょう。結局は、慣れることがいちばんです。

最後に、日本語と英語とは背景を成す文化が異なります。したがって、似たような表現でありながら、両者間には意味やニュアンスの点で大きな違いが存在することもあります。本辞典では「解説」「語法」「あなたの英語はどう響く？」など、さまざまなコラムを設けて、英語学習に必要と思われる情報を紹介していますので、折あるごとにそれらのコラムを精読し、英語を話したり書いたりするときの役に立ててください。

辞書を
よく引き
よく読み
実際に
使う

ディベートルーム
debate room

ディベートとは

「ディベート」とは何らかのテーマについての，特に公式の場で行う議論や討論のことです。また，ディベートスキルを身につけるための「**教育ディベート**」の意味でも使われ日本ではたいていこちらの意味で用いられています。教育ディベートでは，与えられた**論題**（motion）について，**肯定側**（affirmative side）と**否定側**（negative side）に分かれて議論を交わし，どちらがより論理的に相手を説得することができたかを競います。

ディベートではおもに公共性のあるテーマが論題として取り上げられ，個人的な感情ではなく，客観的な事実や資料に基づいて相手側を説き伏せます。自分が個人的にどちら側の意見に賛成であるか否かにかかわらず，参加者は振り分けられた側の立場で議論を展開していきます。

ディベートは物事を論理的に考え，1つの事柄を様々な角度から見る力を養ってくれるとともに，学校での英語教育においても重要な役割を果たすものと思われます。ディベートの英語教育における効果としては，英語でディベートを行うことで総合的な英語力を高められることと，自分の意見を公式の場でも臆せずに伝えるスキルを培えることなどがあげられます。特に後者は，これから国際社会に出て行く学生にとっては欠かせないスキルであり，英語力とディベートスキルを身につけることで，英語でのコミュニケーション能力が一層高まるものと思われます。

ディベートは実際にはどのようなかたちで行われるのでしょうか。ディベートは言わば「**競技**」ですので，一定の**フォーマット**（format）に基づいて進行します。以下が，フォーマットの一例です。

ディベートのフォーマット例

❶肯定側立論（affirmative opening speech） → **❷否定側立論**（negative opening speech）
→ **❸否定側反駁**（negative rebuttal） → **❹肯定側反駁**（affirmative rebuttal）
→ **❺肯定側まとめ**（affirmative closing speech） → **❻否定側まとめ**（negative closing speech）

※それぞれの側の立論のあとに，質疑（cross examination）が入る場合もあります。
また，反駁は2～3回繰り返し行うのがふつうです。

この辞書では，ディベートで取り上げられる可能性の高い17のテーマを論題として取り上げ，肯定側の意見・否定側の意見を一対として日英対訳で紹介しています。限られたスペースの都合上，上記のようなフォーマットでの正式なディベートを載せることはできませんが，実際のディベートで出てきそうな具体的な意見を，わかりやすい言葉で掲載してあります。ディベートで具体的にどのような論拠を述べればいいのかを知っていただくと同時に，実際のディベートを行うときのフレーズのサンプル，あるいは論理の組み立ての見本として，役立てていただければと思います。

なお，p. 1721から「**発信の時事英語**」として，「ディベートルーム」掲載英文から自分で意見を述べる際に使える語句を**本文掲載語句**としてまとめ，本文中には出てこないけれども活用度の高い語句を**関連語句**としてまとめてありますので，そちらも参考にしてください。

目 次

付録

► 論 題 **1**_motion 1

高校生は積極的にアルバイトをすべきだ。

High school students should be encouraged to have part-time jobs.

	► 肯定側 _affirmative side		► 否定側 _negative side
1	実社会に出る前に実際の仕事を体験することはとても有益です。高校生は積極的にアルバイトをすべきです。 **It's beneficial to experience working before going out into the world so high school students should be encouraged to have part-time jobs.**	→	生徒がアルバイトをすると，学業に専念できなくなります。 **If students have part-time jobs, they will not be able to concentrate on their studies.**
2	学校での勉強がすべてではありません。アルバイトは，生徒が責任感や勤勉の大切さを学ぶのにも役立ちます。 **Studying in the classroom is not everything. Having a part-time job can help students learn about responsibility and hard work.**	→	生徒は，アルバイトなどせずとも，勉強や日常生活から，責任感や勤勉の大切さを学ぶことができます。 **Even without working part-time, students can learn about responsibility and hard work by studying and from everyday life.**
3	アルバイトで学んだことが，実際の仕事でさまざまな役に立ちます。 **What students learn from their part-time jobs will be useful when they enter the workforce.**	→	もし生徒が学業に専念しなければ，自分に適した仕事につくために必要な知識を身につけることができません。 **If students don't concentrate on their studies, they won't have the knowledge required to find suitable jobs.**
4	アルバイトをすることで，親から自立した自分自身の視点で物事を考えられるようになります。 **Having a part-time job will help students (to) become more independent from their parents and (to) think for themselves.**	→	高校生は自立するには若すぎますし，自分自身で考える習慣はアルバイトをせずとも身につけることができます。 **High school students are not old enough to be independent, and they can learn to think for themselves even without a part-time job.**
5	生徒は，アルバイトをしながらでも勉強する時間が十分にあります。 **Students have plenty of time to work part-time and also do their schoolwork.**	→	生徒がアルバイトをすれば，友だちを作る時間もなくなってしまいます。友だちを作ることも高校生活の重要な一部です。 **If students work part-time, they will not have any time to make friends. Making friends is also an important part of high school life.**
6	アルバイトをしている生徒のほうが，自分が将来何をしたいのかがしっかりとわかっています。 **Students who work part-time have a better understanding about what they want to do in the future.**	→	アルバイトの仕事は正社員とは別物ですから，職業の選択には役立ちません。 **Part-time jobs are not the same as full-time jobs, so working part-time won't help you (to) choose a career.**

► 論題 2 _motion 2

安楽死は人間の正当な権利である。

People have a legitimate right to euthanasia.

► 肯定側 _affirmative side		► 否定側 _negative side
1 人間には，みずからの決断で死を選ぶ権利があると思います。治療の施しようのない末期症状の患者には，安楽死という選択肢が与えられるべきです。 People have the right to make the choice to die. We should offer the choice of euthanasia for terminally ill patients for whom nothing can be done.	→	死を選ぶことを社会的に認めることは，生命の軽視につながります。安楽死を人間の権利と認めるのは，とても危険なことです。 Allowing people to choose death shows a disregard for human life. Saying that euthanasia is a human right is very dangerous.
2 安楽死を望む末期患者は，耐えがたい痛みと闘っています。死以外に痛みを和らげる方法がない以上，痛みから解放されたいという意志は尊重されていいはずです。 Patients who desire euthanasia suffer from unbearable pain. If there is no other way to relieve the pain except death, then their desire to be released from the pain should be respected.	→	安楽死が認められれば，患者の意志によらない安楽死が起きる可能性があります。医師や家族による殺人も起こりかねないのです。 If euthanasia is permitted, euthanasia that is not voluntary may occur. It is even possible that murder by a doctor or family members might take place.
3 患者の意志であることを明確にできるよう，認定の条件を厳しくしておくことで，患者の意志によらない安楽死は防げます。 By setting strict conditions for approval of euthanasia so that it is clear that the choice is based on the patients' own will, euthanasia that is not voluntary can be prevented.	→	安楽死の認定制度など作るべきではありません。そもそも，人の生死に対して認定や許可を出すなど，倫理的にも認めうることではありません。 We shouldn't legalize euthanasia. In the first place, it is not ethical to issue approval or permission concerning whether someone will live or die.
4 安楽死という選択肢があることが，患者に安心感を与え，残された時間を希望を持って過ごすことにつながります。 The option of euthanasia gives patients a sense of security and helps them (to) spend the rest of their lives with hope.	→	そうではありません。家族に迷惑をかけないためにも安楽死を選んだほうがいいのではないかという重圧が，患者の精神的苦痛を増大させるのです。 That is not true. Patients will be under more pressure to choose euthanasia so as not to burden their families. This will only increase the patients' mental pain.
5 現実的な問題として，末期患者の介護は体力的にも精神的にも経済的にも大変な負担です。安楽死は，この負担の軽減につながります。 As a practical problem, caring for terminally ill patients is a tremendous burden physically, mentally and economically. Euthanasia will help (to) lighten this burden.	→	安楽死を望む患者は，死期を目前にしている場合がほとんどです。安楽死の選択は，それほど経済的負担とはかかわりをもたないことなのです。 In most cases, the days are numbered for patients hoping for euthanasia. Therefore, choosing euthanasia has little to do with the economic burden.

注：「安楽死」は，広義では「尊厳死（Death with Dignity）」（＝本人の意志で必要以上の延命治療を辞退すること）も含むが，ここではほとんどの国で違法とされている，狭義での「安楽死」（＝耐え難い痛みで苦しむ末期患者を投薬などによって死に至らしめること）について議論していると想定している。狭義での安楽死は，オランダやベルギーなど，一部の国や地域で合法化されており，議論を呼んでいる。

► 論題3 _motion 3

手紙よりEメールや携帯メールのほうがすぐれたコミュニケーション手段だ。

Email(s) and text messages are better communication tools than letters.

► 肯定側 _affirmative side

1 Eメールや携帯メールはパソコンや携帯電話があれば，思いたったときにすぐに相手に送ることができる便利なコミュニケーション手段です。

Email(s) and text messages are convenient communication tools because you can send them immediately whenever you want as long as you have a computer or a cellphone.

► 否定側 _negative side

→ 人といっしょにいるときにも，携帯電話のEメールに没頭している人が多く，コミュニケーションを阻害していると思います。

Many people are focused on text messaging with their cellphones even when they are with other people, and so you can say that it actually hinders communication.

2 Eメールや携帯メールは手軽に送れるので，遠方に住んでいる家族や友人ともまめに連絡が取れます。

You can send email(s) and text messages easily and keep in touch with family or friends living a long way off.

→ 手間をかけて書かれた手紙のほうがEメールや携帯メールより心がこもっていますから，もらったほうもよりうれしい気持ちになります。

Handwritten letters that take a long time to write include more feeling than email(s) and text messages. They make the recipient happier.

3 Eメールや携帯メールは手紙と違い，郵便事故や紛失・盗難のおそれがありません。

Letters are sometimes undelivered, lost or stolen, but you don't have to worry about this with email(s) or text messages.

→ Eメールや携帯メールには，ウイルスメールや迷惑メールを受け取る恐れがありますし，誤送信の可能性もあります。

You might receive viruses or spam in email(s) or text messages, and you might even send an email or text message to the wrong address.

4 Eメールや携帯メールは，漢字変換や消去が簡単にできるので，短時間で文章が書け，とても効率的です。

Email(s) and text messages are efficient because you can write a message in a short time by converting kana to kanji and deleting words easily.

→ Eメールや携帯メールでは，自分で漢字を書かないので，メールが普及するにつれて，日本人の漢字能力は衰えていくでしょう。

With email(s) or text messages, people don't write kanji by themselves, so the ability of Japanese to write kanji will decline as email and text messaging become more common.

5 同じ文面を複数の相手に伝えたいとき，Eメールや携帯メールなら一度にたくさんの人に送信できます。

When you want to tell the same thing to more than one person, you can send the same email or text message to many people at a time.

→ そのような事務的な作業はコミュニケーションとは呼べません。あいさつや報告でも，一人一人に向けてのことばを付け加えて書くべきです。

Such impersonal tasks cannot be called communication. You should add a personal message, even a greeting or a piece of news, for each person you write to.

6 手紙を送ると大げさになるようなことでも，Eメールや携帯メールなら気軽に書けます。感謝の気持ちを手短に伝えたり，ちょっとした相談事をしたりするのにも便利です。

By using email(s) and text messages, you can casually write what might sound serious in letters. Email(s) and text messages are convenient when you want to convey your thanks briefly or consult with someone about something minor.

→ 本来なら手紙や電話で伝えるべき内容でも，Eメールや携帯メールで送るようになってきています。メールへの依存は，日本人の文章によるコミュニケーション能力を低下させています。

People are starting to use email and text messaging for messages that normally should be expressed via letter or phone. Dependence on email and text messaging is harming the communication abilities of Japanese.

►論題4 _motion 4

インターネットは無制限に普及されるべきではない。

The Internet shouldn't be promoted without any restrictions.

►肯定側 _affirmative side

1 インターネットは無制限に普及されるべきではありません。例えば，インターネットの掲示板では，無数のデマやひぼう中傷が飛び交っているからです。

The Internet shouldn't be promoted without any restrictions. One reason is that discussion boards are filled with false rumors and slanderous comments.

►否定側 _negative side

→ インターネットは個人が自由に情報を発信し，意見を交換できる，これまでにない貴重なメディアです。ネット上の情報が有益か無益かは，受け手の側で判断すればいいのです。

The Internet is a valuable new medium where individuals can freely provide information and exchange opinions. Users can judge whether the information on the Net is useful or not by themselves.

2 インターネット上には，未成年者に有害なサイトが氾濫しています。こうしたサイトには，規制や罰則を加えるべきです。

Websites harmful to minors are rampant on the Net. We should place restrictions and penalize such websites.

→ 未成年者にとって有害だという理由でサイトに規制をかければ，大人には問題のないサイトからも言論の自由を奪うことになります。有害なサイトから未成年者を守るのは，親が行うべきことです。

If we place restrictions on websites because they are harmful to young people, we are infringing freedom of speech on websites that are acceptable for adults. Parents should protect children from these websites.

3 インターネットでは便利に買い物ができる反面，クレジットカードの番号を含む個人情報を業者に送信しなければならず，セキュリティーの問題が不安です。

While on the one hand you can shop conveniently on the Internet, you also have to send private information, including credit card numbers, to the seller, and this has increased concerns about security.

→ セキュリティーの問題は，インターネットに限ったことではありません。実際の店舗においても，クレジットカード情報の盗難は多発しています。

Security problems don't occur only on the Net. Credit card information is often stolen at brick-and-mortar stores.

4 インターネットの急速な普及により，サイト登録時に得られる個人情報の漏えいが深刻な問題になってきています。

With the rapid expansion of the Internet, the leaking of personal information obtained when users register at websites has become a serious problem.

→ 個人情報の管理は，人為的な漏えいの回避策も含め，より徹底されてきています。

Management of personal information, including measures to prevent intentional leaking, is becoming more and more thorough.

5 インターネットでは情報がデジタル化されているため，著作物のコピーがいとも簡単に行われてしまします。

You can easily make copies of copyrighted materials because information is digitalized on the Internet.

→ デジタルであってもなくても，著作物の複製は著作権法に違反します。コピーされやすいからといって，インターネットに規制を加えるのは不適切です。

Making copies of copyrighted materials is a violation of the copyright law, whether the copies are digital or not. Placing restrictions on the Internet to stop this is inappropriate.

► 論 題 5 _motion 5

英語の教育は小学生から始めるべきである。

Elementary school-age children should be taught English.

	► 肯 定 側 _affirmative side		► 否 定 側 _negative side
1	日本人の多くは，中学・高校の６年間英語を勉強しても英語が習得できていないと言われます。より早期からの英語教育が必要です。 **Many Japanese have not acquired English skills even after studying it for six years in junior high school and high school. Earlier English language education is needed.**	→	日本人が，必ずしも英語ができないとは思いません。TOEICの平均点の低さがよく指摘されますが，日本では英語に対してさほど真剣でない人もこうしたテストを受けることが多いことも一因です。 **I don't think that Japanese are necessarily poor at English. The low average scores on the TOEIC test is often pointed out, but one of the reasons for this is that many Japanese who take the test are not so serious about English.**
2	英語は中学から始めるよりも，物事をより自然に吸収できる小学生のころから始めたほうが効果的に身につきます。 **Children can learn English more effectively if they start in elementary school when they can easily absorb things, rather than in junior high school.**	→	中学から始めれば十分です。学校の英語教育だけでバイリンガルになるわけではありませんから，小学生のうちはしっかりとした国語の力を身につけるべきです。 **Starting in junior high school is early enough. It's impossible to become bilingual only by going to English classes, so children should study their own language in elementary school.**
3	帰国子女は幼いころから英語に触れているケースが多く，その中には日本語同様に英語を話す人も少なからずいます。 **Many returnees from overseas are exposed to English from an early age, and quite a few speak English as fluently as they do Japanese.**	→	帰国子女でも，日ごろから英語に接する環境にいないと徐々に英語が話せなくなります。 **Even returnees gradually forget English if they are not regularly exposed to it.**
4	小学校で英語を勉強することは，異なる文化を持つ人々を理解することにつながり，国際社会を生きていくうえでの必要な資質をはぐくみます。 **Studying English in elementary school helps students understand people of different cultures and helps them develop the qualities needed to live in a global society.**	→	英語を習得することと国際理解は，同じではありません。国際理解のためには，英語にとらわれず，幅広く日本や世界のことを学ぶことが大切です。 **Learning English and international understanding are not the same thing. For international understanding, it is important to acquire extensive knowledge of Japan and the world.**
5	ALT（外国語指導助手）などの指導を通じて，小学校のころからネイティブの発音に触れることは子供の英語教育にとって重要なことです。 **It is important for children to be exposed to the pronunciation of native speakers through such methods as instruction by ALTs (assistant language teachers) while still in elementary school.**	→	全国のすべての小学校に，優秀なネイティブの英語指導者を派遣することは，人員や予算面で不可能です。 **Putting good native English teachers in all the elementary schools in Japan is impossible considering the number of teachers and the budget required.**
6	小学校の英語では，英語の歌やゲームを使った授業が行われていますが，これは子供たちにとって楽しいものです。 **Songs and games are used to teach English in elementary school, and this is fun for children.**	→	学力低下が叫ばれる現在，従来の教科に加えて外国語を覚えることは，子供たちの大きな負担となります。 **At this time when academic ability is in decline, learning a foreign language in addition to existing subjects is a big burden.**

►論題 6 _motion 6

外来語は積極的に日本語に採り入れるべきである。

We should actively make use of loanwords in Japanese.

►肯定側 _affirmative side

1 外来語は日本にない物事や概念を言い表すのにとても便利なので，どんどん採り入れるべきです。

We should actively make use of loanwords because they are very convenient for expressing things and concepts that we do not have in Japan.

►否定側 _negative side

→ 外来語は，お年寄りなど，外来語になじみのない層にとってはコミュニケーションを阻害するものにもなりえます。何でもかんでもむやみに採り入れるべきではありません。

Loanwords could be an obstacle to communication for people who are not familiar with them, such as the elderly. We shouldn't make unrestrained use of loanwords.

2 国際化が進展している現在，世界共通語とも言えるボキャブラリー（語い）も少なくありません。例えば，「インターネット」をわざわざ日本語に訳すことに何か意味があるでしょうか？

Now that internationalization is progressing, many words are recognized as part of a common global vocabulary. What is the point of translating "Internet" into Japanese?

→ 年齢層や職業，個人の興味によって，外来語の定着度合いは大きく異なります。だれに対しても同じように外来語を使うのには賛成できません。

The level of understanding of loanwords differs greatly by age group, profession and personal interest. It doesn't make sense to use loanwords when communicating with everyone.

3 外来語は，日本語にぴったりと合う表現がないからこそ使われます。無理に日本語に置き換えることで，言いたいニュアンスとずれてくる場合もあると思います。

Loanwords are used because there are no Japanese words with exactly the same meaning. Therefore, if you replace loanwords with Japanese expressions, you may change the nuance of what you want to say.

→ それは，ある程度外来語になじみのある人の発想です。だいたいのことを日本語で表現してくれたほうがありがたいと思う人はたくさんいます。

That is how someone who is somewhat familiar with loanwords tends to think. Many people feel it would be more helpful to have the approximate meaning explained in Japanese.

4 外来語の普及のおかげで，英語をあまり勉強したことがない人でも，ある程度外国人と意思の疎通ができるようになっています。

The current popularity of loanwords helps those who have not studied English very much to communicate with foreigners to some extent.

→ 外来語の中には和製英語や，「ウイルス」「アレルギー」のように英語の発音と大きく異なるものもあり，日本人の英語力の向上に悪影響を与えています。

Some loanwords are actually Japanese-English words, or the pronunciation is very different from the original such as "uirusu" (virus) and "arerugi" (allergy). These words cause problems for Japanese learning English.

5 外来語には，語いが増えることで日本語をより豊かにしているという側面もあります。

One more aspect is that loanwords enrich the Japanese language by expanding its vocabulary.

→ 外来語に頼ることは，母語である日本語の表現力を弱めてしまいます。

Dependence on loanwords weakens our ability to express ourselves in Japanese, our native language.

►論題 7 _motion 7

生徒の携帯電話の使用はよくない。

Students should be discouraged from using cellphones.

►肯定側 _affirmative side

►否定側 _negative side

1 携帯電話を学校で使うと，使っている人だけでなく，ほかの生徒の勉強の邪魔にもなります。
Using cellphones at school distracts not only the users but also other students from their studies.

→ まじめな生徒は，他人の迷惑にならないように，授業中はたいてい携帯電話の電源を切ります。
Serious students turn off their cellphones during class so that they won't disturb others.

2 携帯電話を使っている者の多くに，電話料金がかさんで，親の大きな負担になっているケースが見受けられます。
Cellphone users often run up big bills, and in some cases it is an economic burden on their parents.

→ 支払いを増やさないためには携帯電話を効率よく使うことが必要なので，生徒たちは携帯電話を持つことで，お金を節約する方法を学ぶことができるのです。
Having cellphones can help students learn how to save money because they have to use them efficiently in order to keep their cellphone bills from increasing.

3 携帯電話を使っている生徒が犯罪に巻き込まれるケースも発生していて，大きな社会問題になっています。
There are some cellphone-related crimes involving students. This is a serious social problem.

→ 子供に携帯電話を持たせることで，両親は子供の居場所や無事を常に確認できるのです。
Cellphones are helpful because they let parents check where their children are and make sure that they're safe.

4 携帯電話のユーザーにはたくさんのバーチャルフレンドがいますが，彼らにとって，現実に友だちを作るのは難しいのです。
Cellphone users have a lot of virtual friends, but it's difficult for them to make real friends.

→ 自信をもって言えることは，携帯電話を使えば，内気な生徒でも実社会でたくさんの友だちを作ることができるということです。
I'm sure even a shy student can make a lot of real friends by using a cellphone.

5 生徒は公共のマナーが十分身についていないので，携帯電話を持つとまわりの人に迷惑をかけます。
Students haven't learned how to behave politely in public, so they could disturb others if they have cellphones.

→ マナーが身についていない人は，携帯電話を持たなくても迷惑をかけます。携帯電話を持つことで，公共のマナーを学ぶこともできます。
Those who lack good manners will disturb others even if they don't have cellphones. They can learn good manners by having cellphones.

►論題 8 _motion 8

高速道路はもっと増やすべきだ。

There should be more expressways.

	►肯定側 _affirmative side		►否定側 _negative side
1	日本の道路は渋滞が多いのが問題の1つですが，高速道路を増やすことで渋滞が緩和されます。 **One problem with roads in Japan is the frequent traffic jams. More expressways will make traffic jams less serious.**	→	高速道路を増やせば，さらに乗用車の利用が増え，結果的に渋滞が激化する可能性もあります。バスや飛行機など，公共の乗り物がより利用しやすくなるような対策のほうをとるべきです。 **If more expressways are built, there's a possibility that more people will use cars, resulting in worse traffic jams. We should instead take measure to make public transportation, including buses and planes, more convenient.**
2	高速道路が増えると，交通の便がよくなるので地方の経済が活性化します。 **Building more expressways will make public transportation more convenient and this will revitalize regional economies.**	→	逆です。交通の便がよくなると，これまで以上に都市部への人口流出が激化するので，地方の過疎化が一段と進行します。 **On the contrary, convenient transportation will accelerate the population outflow into cities, and thus speed up the depopulation of rural areas.**
3	高速道路は自動車の専用道路なので，歩行者などを巻き込んだ交通事故が減少します。 **Traffic accidents involving pedestrians and others will decrease because expressways are exclusively for vehicles.**	→	高速道路での交通事故は，全体のほんの一握りにすぎません。不注意なドライバーが減らない限り，事故が減ることはないのです。 **Traffic accidents on expressways are just a small part of the total number of traffic accidents. Unless drivers are more careful, the number of traffic accidents won't decline.**
4	従来よりも物流がスムーズになり，日本の産業や経済のさらなる発展につながります。 **The distribution system will function more smoothly and this will help to develop Japanese industries and the economy.**	→	物流の効率化のためには，よりスピーディーで大規模な共同輸送が可能な，空港や港湾のインフラ整備を進めるべきです。 **In order to improve distribution efficiency, we should develop infrastructure, including airports and ports to make faster large-scale joint distribution possible.**
5	高速道路の増加により，日帰り旅行などが盛んになり，観光産業も発達します。 **If there are more expressways, day trips and other forms of travel will become more common, helping to develop the tourist industry.**	→	森林を伐採し，高速道路をつくることは自然破壊につながります。また，高速道路沿いの地域には，新たに排気ガスや騒音などの環境汚染も発生します。 **Cutting down trees to construct expressways will destroy nature. The environment along the expressways will also be disrupted by exhaust and noise.**

►論題9 _motion 9

死刑は絶対に必要である。

Capital punishment is absolutely necessary.

	►肯定側 _affirmative side		►否定側 _negative side
1	死刑がなければ，家族を殺された遺族の怒りは行き場がありません。被害者の立場から，死刑は絶対に必要です。 **Without capital punishment, the families of murder victims will not be able to get over their anger. From the perspective of the victims and their families, capital punishment is absolutely necessary.**	→	遺族の報復感情は当然ですが，殺人の罪が重いのは人の命が尊いからです。その尊い命を奪う死刑も，生命を軽視する殺人と変わりありません。 **It is natural for the victims' families to want revenge, but murder is a serious crime because human life is precious. Capital punishment also takes human life, and in that sense it also shows disregard for human life.**
2	罪のない尊い命を奪うのと，その尊い命を奪った人間を死刑にするのとは意味が違います。 **Taking the life of an innocent victim and putting to death the person who took that life are different.**	→	命の大切さは，人によって優劣があってはならないものです。たとえ死刑が合法であるとしても，人の命を奪う行為であることに違いはないのです。 **One life is never superior or inferior to another. Even if capital punishment is legal, it is still the taking of a human life.**
3	死刑には犯罪を抑止する効果があります。極刑がなくなることによって，殺人が増える可能性があります。 **Capital punishment can act as a deterrent against crime. Abolishing capital punishment could lead to an increase in the murder rate.**	→	犯罪者は死刑の有無によって，罪を犯したり，思いとどまったりするわけではありません。死刑を廃止した国々でも，死刑に犯罪抑止力があるとは証明されていません。 **Criminals do not decide to commit or not commit a crime based on the absence or presence of capital punishment. The deterrent effect of capital punishment has not been proven in countries where capital punishment has been abolished.**
4	重い罪に重い罰を与えるのは当然です。残虐非道な犯罪者を法律で保護するというのはおかしな話です。 **Heavy punishment should be given in cases of serious crimes. Legal protection of cruel criminals doesn't make sense.**	→	犯罪者にも人権はあります。えん罪などの可能性もあるので，極刑以外の重い罰で解決すべきです。 **Criminals also have human rights. They should be given heavy sentences other than capital punishment because there's the possibility of a false conviction.**
5	殺人犯が釈放後に野放しになってしまっては，市民は安心して生活を送ることができません。 **If murderers are left free after they are released, citizens will not feel secure.**	→	懲役刑には犯罪者を更生させる目的もあります。また，仮釈放のない絶対的終身刑を導入すれば，その心配はありません。 **One purpose of imprisonment is to reform criminals. Introducing a life sentence without parole will solve the security problem.**

▶論題 10 _motion 10

電子辞書は紙の辞書に勝っている。

Electronic dictionaries are superior to paper-based ones.

▶肯定側 _affirmative side

1 電子辞書は軽量です。紙の辞書は１冊でも重く，多数持ち歩くことは困難ですが，電子辞書なら可能です。
Electronic dictionaries are light. Even one paper-based dictionary is heavy, and so it's hard to carry around several at a time, but this is easy with electronic dictionaries.

▶否定側 _negative side

→ 持ち歩くのが困難なほどの数の辞書を携帯する場面は多くありません。携帯するためだけに買うには，電子辞書は割高です。
There are not many situations where you have to carry so many dictionaries that it's difficult. It is economically inefficient to buy an electronic dictionary just because it's easier to carry around.

2 電子辞書は，収録辞書数のわりに値段が安いのが特徴です。すべての辞書を紙の辞書でそろえるには，もっと多額のお金がかかります。
One of the characteristics of electronic dictionaries is that they are inexpensive considering the number of dictionaries they contain. It would cost much more to buy all of them in their paper-based versions.

→ 電子辞書には自分には必要のない辞書もたくさん入っています。自分にとってほんとうに必要な辞書だけを持っていれば十分です。
Electronic dictionaries contain a lot of dictionaries that you probably don't need. It is enough to have just the ones you really do need.

3 電子辞書では，英英辞典で調べた語義中の単語をそのまま英和辞典で調べ直すなど，辞書と辞書を飛び越えた検索もでき，非常に便利です。
With an electronic dictionary, you can look at a word in an English-English dictionary and then look up the word and its definition in an English-Japanese dictionary. This jump function is very convenient for users.

→ 電子辞書では，複数の辞書を使っても１つの画面でしか見ることができません。紙の辞書を並べて見比べるほうが，すんなりと頭に入ってきます。
With an electronic dictionary, you only have one screen even if there are several dictionaries. You can learn better if you open two or more paper-based dictionaries and compare them.

4 紙の辞書でページを繰りながら単語を調べるより，電子辞書のキーボードで入力するほうがすばやく知りたい単語にアクセスできます。
Compared with turning the pages to find a word in a paper-based dictionary, it's quicker to look up a word using the keyboard of an electronic dictionary.

→ 電子辞書のキーボードは，サイズが小さく操作しづらいものです。またキー操作も辞書ごとに異なり，覚えるだけでも大変な苦労です。紙の辞書ならそんなことはありません。
The keyboard of an electronic dictionary is small and difficult to operate. Also, different models have different keyboards, and so just learning how to operate the keyboard is difficult. You don't have this problem with paper-based dictionaries.

5 電子辞書には苦手な単語を登録できるなど，さまざまな学習支援（ヘルプ）の機能があります。
Electronic dictionaries have a variety of helpful functions such as the registration of hard-to-remember words.

→ 好きなように手書きでメモをしたり，パラパラと見たりできるので，紙の辞書のほうが学習効果が高いと言えます。
You can write your own notes in paper dictionaries and you can flip through them, so it's easier to learn using paper dictionaries.

►論題 11 _motion 11

生徒には制服が必要である。

Students should be required to wear school uniforms.

►肯定側 _affirmative side		►否定側 _negative side
1 制服の着用は社会に出てからの規律を守る勉強にもなるので，生徒にとって大切です。 **Wearing school uniforms is important for students, because it helps them learn to observe the rules of society after they go out into the world.**	→	規律を覚えることは制服を着なくてもできます。むしろ外国から見ると，画一的な教育を想起させ，マイナスイメージを持たれる可能性もあります。 **You don't have to wear school uniforms to learn to observe rules. Actually, school uniforms symbolize the standardized education system and may give a negative image to people from other countries.**
2 私服の学校だと毎日のように着替えを用意しなければならず，洋服にかかるお金はばかになりません。 **If students wear ordinary clothes at school, they will have to buy a lot of new clothes to change almost every day, and this could be quite expensive.**	→	制服があっても，ふだん着としての私服も必要なのですから，両者の出費にそれほど大きな差はありません。 **You need ordinary clothes even if you have to wear school uniforms, so the cost would not be much different.**
3 私服の場合，毎日着ていくものを選ぶのが大変です。ファッションにばかり気を取られ学業がおろそかになる生徒も出てきます。 **It would be a lot of trouble to choose what to wear every day with ordinary clothes. Some students might worry a lot about fashions and pay little attention to their studies.**	→	毎日同じ制服を着るのは，衛生上問題があります。また，私服は自由に選べるので，制服のように夏暑くて冬寒いといったことも避けられます。 **Wearing the same school uniform every day is not sanitary. Also, you can choose ordinary clothes freely, so you can keep cool in summer and warm in winter.**
4 私服と制服の両方が可能な学校もありますが，そのような学校では，生徒はたいてい制服を着ることを選んでいます。 **Some schools allow both school uniforms and ordinary clothes, and students in such schools mostly choose to wear school uniforms.**	→	私服を着て仲間外れになるのがこわいから，制服を選択する生徒が多いのだと思います。全員を私服着用にしなければ，結局，制服着用を義務づけているのと同じことです。 **They probably choose school uniforms because they're afraid of being excluded. Unless schools require students to wear only ordinary clothes, it's the same as requiring them to wear only school uniforms.**
5 私服では，服装によって，クラスメートにからかわれたり，いじめられたりすることがよくあります。だれもが同じ制服を着れば，そのような心配はありません。 **With ordinary clothes, some students get teased or bullied because of what they wear. This is not a problem when all students wear the same clothes.**	→	日本人の没個性が言われて久しい時代にあって，全生徒が同じ制服を着ることは時代に逆行しています。 **For a long time it's been said that the Japanese lack individuality, so making students wear the same school uniform is going against the trend of the times.**
6 制服はどこの学校の生徒かを判別するよい目印になります。タバコを吸う生徒がいても，校内に部外者が入ってきても，すぐに判別できます。 **School uniforms make it easy to recognize what school a student attends. Students who smoke can easily be spotted, and outsiders who enter the school can easily be detected.**	→	制服が引き出す集団意識は，しばしば学校の違う生徒間での対立や争いを招きます。 **Group consciousness evoked by school uniforms often causes friction or conflict between students from different schools.**

► 論題 **12** _motion 12

地球温暖化は人類の発展上やむをえない。

Global warming is unavoidable for human development.

	► 肯定側 _affirmative side		► 否定側 _negative side
1	地球温暖化の原因になっている石炭・石油などの化石燃料は，現代生活に必要不可欠な基盤です。生活を犠牲にしてまで地球温暖化を阻止すべきではありません。 **Fossil fuels such as coal and oil, which cause global warming, are indispensable parts of our society's infrastructure. We shouldn't stop global warming by sacrificing our standard of living.**	→	温暖化を放置しておくと，海面の上昇や異常気象，農作物の収穫高や漁獲量に悪い影響を及ぼすなど，人類の生活や生命さえも脅かす深刻な危機が起こります。 **If we ignore global warming, serious crises affecting our lifestyles and life itself will occur, such as rises in the sea level, abnormal weather conditions and negative effects on crop yields and fish catches.**
2	発電や自動車には化石燃料が使われていますが，現代生活において電気や自動車のない生活は考えられません。 **Fossil fuels are used for electricity and in vehicles, and it's impossible to think about how we would live without them.**	→	太陽光・水力・天然ガスなどの資源を主要エネルギーとして使う方向へシフトしていく必要があります。車に頼りすぎないなど，環境に優しい生活にも心がけなければなりません。 **We need to gradually shift our main energy sources to solar energy, hydrogen or natural gas. We should also try to achieve a more environmentally friendly lifestyle by, for example, not depending too much on cars.**
3	代替エネルギーはコストが高価で，従来のエネルギーに取って代わるのは現実的には不可能です。 **Alternative energy sources are expensive, and it is not realistic to use them to replace current sources of energy.**	→	世界規模で積極的に普及に取り組めば，代替エネルギーのコストは下がります。 **We can reduce the cost of alternative sources of energy by working to expand their use worldwide.**
4	温暖化防止策として二酸化炭素の排出量に規制がかかると，企業や工場の活動が阻害され，経済の発展に大きな損失を与えます。 **If CO_2 emissions are reduced to prevent global warming, the activities of companies and factories will be impeded. This will be very harmful to economic development.**	→	今の経済を守るために，子，孫の世代に起こりうる深刻な危機に対応しないのは，人類の発展にとって大きな過ちです。 **Failing to deal with this serious crisis that could impact our children and grandchildren just to protect the current economy would be a serious mistake for human development.**
5	二酸化炭素が温暖化の原因だという科学的根拠にも，不完全な部分があるという指摘があります。むやみに規制を進めるべきではありません。 **Some people point out that the scientific proof that CO_2 causes global warming is incomplete. We shouldn't blindly implement restrictions.**	→	人類の長い歴史のうち，ここ100年ほどで二酸化炭素濃度と平均気温が同じように上昇しているという事実に間違いはありません。すぐに対策を練り，少しでも進行を遅らせるべきです。 **When looking at the long history of humanity, never before have CO_2 levels and average temperatures risen at the same time as they have over the last 100 years. We need to take immediate action and slow down the warming as much as possible.**

►論題 13 _motion 13

都会はいなかよりも住みやすい。

Cities are better to live in than the countryside.

►肯定側 _affirmative side		►否定側 _negative side
1 都会は公共交通機関が発達していて，コンビニや店もたくさんあるので，生活しやすい環境にあると言えます。 **Public transportation is highly developed and there are lots of convenience stores and other shops in cities, so it can be said that cities are desirable places to live.**	→	生活が便利な分，都会はどこに行ってもあわただしく，満員電車や渋滞は日常茶飯事です。一方，いなかではのんびりとしたゆとりのある生活を送れます。 **Although cities might be more convenient, it's crowded everywhere you go. Crowded trains and traffic jams are everyday scenes in cities. By contrast, you can have a slow and relaxing life in the countryside.**
2 いなかには医療施設が少なく，夜間に急病になったときや事故を起こしたときの受け入れ体制に不安があります。 **Because there are few medical facilities in the countryside, you'll be worried about emergency services if you suddenly get sick or injured in the middle of the night.**	→	都会は人口が多い分，夜間でも病人やけが人の数が多いため，急患でもすぐに診てもらえない可能性があります。 **Many people become sick or are injured in cities even in the middle of the night because of the large population, and so you cannot always get emergency medical attention.**
3 都会はビジネスチャンスにも富んでいるため，好きな仕事につける機会が多く，また転職もしやすいのが魅力です。 **One of the advantages of cities is that there are plenty of business opportunities, and it is easier to find a job you like or to change jobs.**	→	今はインターネットなどの普及で，いなかにいても好きな仕事を選ぶことが可能です。また，都会での労働はストレスが多く，過労死の可能性もより高いのです。 **Wide use of the Internet makes it possible to choose a job you want even if you live in the countryside. Also, working in a city is stressful and the possibility of dying from overwork is higher.**
4 都会にはレベルの高い学校や，設備の整った教育施設がたくさんあるので，子供の教育により適しています。 **Cities are better for children because there are many quality schools and good educational facilities.**	→	学校だけが教育の場ではありません。いなかは自然が豊富なので，子どもは自然から多くのことを学びながら，のびのびとした健康的な生活が送れます。 **Schools are not the only place for education. The countryside abounds with nature and children can learn much from nature and live a healthy life with little stress.**
5 都会では自分のペースで自由に生活ができますが，いなかには古いしきたりが残っていたり，近所付き合いがめんどうだったりします。 **You can live carefree at your own pace in cities, but in the countryside there are sometimes old traditions and dealing with neighbors may be a nuisance.**	→	都会ではあまり近所付き合いがなく，助け合いの精神が希薄です。近くに不審者がいてもわからないことが多く，犯罪発生率もいなかとは比較になりません。 **People are not very neighborly in cities and they have little desire to help each other. You probably won't know if there is a suspicious individual in your neighborhood, and the crime rate in cities is beyond comparison with that in the countryside.**

►論題 14 _motion 14

漢画は子供に悪影響を与えている。
Comics have a bad influence on children.

►肯定側 _affirmative side		►否定側 _negative side
1 漫画の中には，暴力的な描写や性的な描写などを含むものが多く，子供の教育上問題があります。 Many comics contain violent or sexual material and have a negative effect on children's development.	→	大半の子供は漫画と現実の世界の違いを認識しています。それを認識できないのは，家庭でのしつけや学校での教育に問題があるからです。 Most children recognize the difference between comics and the real world. If they can't, there's a problem with their training at home and education at school.
2 電車の中など，公共の場で大人が成人向けの漫画を読んでいると，子供の目に入ります。 If adults read adult comics in public places such as trains, they can be seen by children.	→	大人が読んで楽しめる漫画も日本の文化の１つです。それを子供に見せないようにするのは，大人の責任です。 Comics that entertain adults are a part of Japanese culture. Adults are responsible for keeping them out of the sight of children.
3 漫画は活字離れを助長しています。漫画ばかり読んでいては，言葉や表現から状況を思い描く想像力を養えません。 Comics discourage people from reading. If you read nothing but comics, you lose the ability to imagine situations from words and expressions.	→	それは単に小説離れの問題です。漫画にも活字はありますし，むしろ活字と絵をいっしょに見ることで，活字の意味を理解する手助けになる場合もあります。 It's only a matter of people not reading novels as much as they used to. Comics have sentences, and looking at both the sentences and pictures can help you to understand the meaning of the words.
4 漫画ばかり読んでいて，学校の勉強がおろそかになるというのは珍しい話ではありません。漫画は子供たちの学習を阻害していると言えます。 It's not uncommon for children to read comics most of the time and pay little attention to their studies. It can be said that comics hinder children's learning.	→	子供たちは，漫画があるがために勉強をしないわけではありません。漫画を通じてさまざまな知識を得たり，感性を養ったりもできます。 It's not true that children don't study because of comics. By reading comics, children can gain a lot of knowledge and emotional enrichment.
5 漫画は，小説などに比べて内容が低俗で，教育的ではありません。 Compared with novels and other books, comics are vulgar and not educational.	→	漫画の中にも歴史を扱ったものなど，勉強になるものはたくさんあります。日本の漫画は，世界にも誇れるほど成熟した文化だと思います。 There are comics that are educational such as those that deal with historical topics. Comics are a part of a mature culture that Japanese can be proud of.
6 最近では，子供が深夜に漫画喫茶で長時間過ごす例もあります。暴力的な漫画をまねた少年犯罪も発生しています。 It has recently been reported that many children spend many hours in *manga kissa* ［comic cafés］ late at night. There have also been many crimes by juveniles imitating the violence in comic books.	→	子供を取り巻く環境については，子供が意識を高めるとともに，行政など大人の真剣な取り組みが必要です。 Adults, especially those in administrative positions, have to deal seriously with the social environment of children, and the morals of children also have to be improved.

►論題 15 _motion 15

親の老後のめんどうは子どもが見るべきだ。

Children should take care of their elderly parents.

►肯定側 _affirmative side

1 日本では，親の扶養は子供の義務であることが民法で定められています。親の老後のめんどうは子供が見るべきです。

Under Japanese civil law, children have a duty to support their parents. Children should take care of their parents when they get old.

►否定側 _negative side

→ 個人の権利や自立が尊重される現代においては，子供も親も自立した個人として生き方を自由に選択できるよう，親の扶養義務制度は見直されるべきです。

The rights of the individual and independence are respected today, so the law should be reconsidered so that both children and parents can freely choose how to live as independent individuals.

2 親が年を取れば，経済的にも身体的にも不自由になってきます。家族である子供がめんどうを見なくて，いったいだれが見るのでしょうか。

When parents get old, they usually suffer economic and physical hardships. If their children won't take care of them, who will?

→ 親も，子供に頼らずに安心して生活ができるよう，福祉制度や福祉施設を充実させる必要があります。

Welfare systems and facilities should be enhanced so that people can live with peace of mind without depending on their children.

3 日本では，子供に老後のめんどうを見てもらいたいと思っている親がまだまだたくさんいるのが実情です。

It's a fact that there are still many parents in Japan who want their children to look after them.

→ さまざまな事情で子供が親のめんどうを見られないケースも多いのです。子供にも自分の自由に生きていく権利はあります。

There are many cases where children can't look after their parents because of various circumstances. Children also have a right to live life freely.

4 親も子供に頼らずに自立するという概念は欧米的な個人主義に基づくものであり，日本の風土には合いません。

The idea of parents being independent from their children is based on Western individualism, and doesn't fit in with Japanese culture.

→ 最近は，老後を夫婦で悠々自適に過ごしたいという志向をもつ夫婦が増えてきています。この傾向は今後もますます大きくなるでしょう。

Recently, more couples want to live in comfort after they get old. This tendency will continue to grow in the future.

5 倒れたり，寝たきりになったりしたときに，介護を他人に任せるのはつらいものです。自分の子供に世話をしてもらいたいと思うのが，親として自然な心情ではないでしょうか。

It's painful to have someone other than a family member take care of you when you are sick or bedridden. It seems natural for parents to want their children to take care of them.

→ 実際に親族が寝たきりになると，つきっきりで介護をするのは並たいていのことではありません。だれもがプロに介護を任せられるように，制度全般を見直すことが重要です。

It's no easy matter to pay constant attention to a bedridden family member. It's important to redesign the entire system so that anyone can receive the services of a professional caregiver.

►論題 16 _motion 16

公共交通機関に優先席は必要である。
We need priority seats on public transportation.

►肯定側 _affirmative side

1 優先席があることで，体が不自由な人やお年寄り，それに妊娠している女性など座席を必要としている人に，席をゆずりやすくなります。
The existence of priority seats helps passengers offer seats to those who really need them, including the disabled, seniors and pregnant women.

→ ►否定側 _negative side
たとえ優先席がなくとも，成熟した社会では，乗客全員が座席を必要としている人には進んでゆずるものですから，公共交通機関に優先席は必要ありません。
In a mature society, all passengers are expected to readily offer their seats to those who need a seat, even if there are no priority seats. Therefore, we don't need priority seats on public transportation.

2 このところ社会的マナーが衰退しているといわれます。信じがたいほどのひどい行いや利己的で他者への思いやりを欠いた振る舞いが，今では目立つようになりました。乗客の善意を常に信じることはできないため，優先席は必要です。
Recently, social manners have been declining in some places. Incredibly bad manners and selfish, inconsiderate behavior are now conspicuous. We cannot always trust in passengers' goodwill. And that is why priority seating is necessary.

→ 優先席は廃止すべきです。こうした座席があることで，それ以外の普通の座席はゆずる必要がないと考えるようになってしまうかもしれません。
Priority seats should be abolished. The existence of those seats makes people think that they don't have to offer regular seats to those who need them.

3 体が不自由な人やお年寄り，それに妊娠している女性などでも，ラッシュアワーに電車やバスを利用しなくてはいけない人がいます。そうした場合，この混雑した車内で無事に過ごすためにも，公共交通機関に優先席は必要です。
Some disabled people, seniors and pregnant women have to take a train or bus even in rush hours. Such being the case, we need priority seats to assure their safety on crowded trains or buses.

→ 多くの人は優先席にはふつう座りません。ラッシュアワーの混雑した車内に優先席があると，だれも座らない優先席が無駄になり，車内がさらに混雑してしまいます。
Generally, most people don't sit in priority seats, so unoccupied priority seats on trains or buses may be wasted during rush hours and trains or buses may become even more crowded.

4 高齢化が進む社会では，車の運転をやめるお年寄りが増加しています。ですから，優先席制度を維持しさらに充実したものにして，運転ができなくなった高齢者を支えていくべきでしょう。
In an aging society, the number of seniors who give up driving a car is increasing. Therefore, we should keep the priority seating system and make it more effective to support seniors who no longer drive.

→ 常に高齢者が優先されることを不公平だと思う若い人が出てくるかもしれません。社会的な公平性を保証するためにも，優先席制度は廃止するべきです。
Some young people may feel that it is unfair that seniors always have priority over young people. To assure social fairness, we should abolish priority seating system.

5 健康に見えても実際は優先席を必要としている人もいます。そのように，本当に座席を必要とする人が簡単に空席を見つけられるようにするために，優先席を確保しておかなくてはいけません。
Some people look healthy but actually need priority seats. We ought to keep priority seats for those who need them so that they can easily find empty seats.

→ 自分は若くて健康だと思っているのに優先席を勧められて不快に思ったり，優先されることに申し訳なさを感じたりする人もいるので，必ずしも優先席が常に必要だとはいえません。
We don't always need priority seats since some seniors get upset when they are offered priority seats although they think they are young and healthy, or they feel guilty for being prioritized.

►論題17 _motion 17

80歳以上の高齢者は運転をやめるべきだ。

Seniors 80 or older should give up driving.

►肯定側 _affirmative side

►否定側 _negative side

1 ほとんどの80歳以上の高齢者は視力が衰えています。特に夜は，黒っぽい服装の歩行者をはっきり認識できなくなるので，明るい照明がない道路での運転はとても危険です。

Most seniors 80 years or older have diminished eyesight. Driving on roads without bright lighting at night is very dangerous because it is hard for them to clearly recognize pedestrians who are wearing dark clothes.

→ 最近の車のライトはとても明るくなっています。さらに，歩行者を感知する歩行者検知システムが事故を回避する助けになります。

These days, headlights are far brighter than before. Moreover, pedestrian detection systems, which improve drivers' recognition of pedestrians, help senior drivers to avoid causing accidents.

2 高齢者は，刻々と変化する交通状況に対する認識，反応に時間がかかるようになります。そのため事故を起こす確率も上がります。

People 80 years or older need more time to recognize or respond properly to traffic conditions that change from moment to moment. That leads to a higher probability of causing an accident.

→ AI技術の進歩により，自動運転車がいっそう実用化される時代になってきています。自動運転車は，そういった高齢者の認知スピードの問題への解決になるでしょう。

With the progress of AI technology, self-driving vehicles are being put to more practical use. This will be the solution to the recognition speed problems that seniors 80 and older experience.

3 軽度の認知症は，本人も周りも気づかないうちに進行している場合があります。そのような状態の高齢者の運転は，悲劇的な事故に結びつく可能性があります。

If an 80-or-older senior has mild dementia, it may not be easily recognized by himself/herself and the people around him/her. Driving in such a condition can lead to a tragic accident.

→ 運転をすることで，80歳以上の高齢者は社会で強い責任感を担う構成員だとの自覚ができます。また，運転は認知症対策に役立つとも考えられます。

Driving a car makes senior drivers who are 80 or older feel they are members of society with a strong sense of responsibility. Also, driving a car may prevent them from getting senile.

4 地域によっては，高齢者は無料で公共交通機関を利用できます。また，事故を起こしたときの補償金のことを考えれば，タクシーを利用するほうが安くなるかもしれません。

In some cities, seniors can use public transportation for free. And if you think about the compensation money that must be paid to the victims if he or she causes a traffic accident, it may be much cheaper to use taxis.

→ 田舎に住んでいると，公共交通機関は十分発達していないし，タクシーの数も多くはありません。車なしではとても不便で，快適な生活ができなくなります。

If they live in a rural area, public transportation is not fully developed and there are not many taxis. Without a car, life is very inconvenient and people cannot live comfortably.

5 75歳以上の人が受けなければならない，運転免許更新の際の認知機能検査に合格しても，事故を起こした例もあります。やはり，一定の年齢，例えば８0歳で運転はできなくすべきです。

There are cases of senior drivers who have caused traffic accidents even though they have passed the mandatory cognitive ability test as part of the 75-or-older senior driver's license renewal process. So they should give up driving a car at a fixed age, for example 80.

→ 認知機能や運動神経には個人差があります。認知機能検査をもっと精密なものにして，高齢者でも優良な成績のドライバーには運転を続けさせるべきです。一律に決めるのはいけません。

Cognitive ability and reflexes differ from person to person. We should make the cognitive test more precise and allow good drivers to drive even though they are of advanced age. It is not good to decide when drivers should give up driving on a uniform basis.

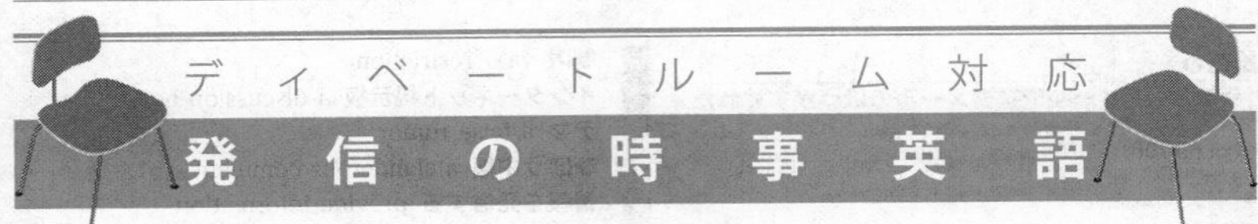

ディベートルーム対応 発信の時事英語

論題1

高校生は積極的にアルバイトをすべきだ。
(→p.1704)

◉本文掲載語句

アルバイト a part-time job
奨励する encourage
有益な beneficial
仕事を体験する experience working
学業に専念する concentrate on one's studies
勤勉 hard work, diligence
役に立つ useful
適した仕事 a suitable job
知識 knowledge
自立した independent
自分自身で考える think for oneself
十分な時間 plenty of time
アルバイトをする work part-time, have a part-time job
友だちをつくる make friends
高校生活 high school life
重要な一部 an important part
(常勤の) 仕事 a full-time job
職業 a career; a profession

◉関連語句

求人情報サイト a job search website
求職者 a job seeker
雇用契約 a job contract
仕事上の差別 on-the-job discrimination
就職難 difficulty in finding employment; a job drought
職業訓練 job training
バイト代 wages from a part-time job
アルバイト禁止 ban on part-time work
時給 an hourly wage, hourly pay
インターンシップ制度 an internship program
新聞配達 newspaper delivery
ウエーター a waiter
ウエートレス a waitress
給仕 food server, table server (男女の区別なく使える)
雇う employ, hire
解雇する dismiss, lay off
労働時間 working hours
深夜労働 late-night work, night shift
残業 overtime work
収入 (an) income
お小遣い an allowance
小銭を稼ぐ earn pocket money

論題2

安楽死は人間の正当な権利である。
(→p.1705)

◉本文掲載語句

安楽死 euthanasia
正当な権利 a legitimate right
末期症状患者 a terminally ill patient
生命の軽視 disregard for human life
耐えがたい痛み unbearable pain
尊重する respect
容認する, 認める permit
自由意志による voluntary
殺人 murder, manslaughter; killing
自分自身の意志 one's own will
認定 approval
厳しい条件 a strict condition
法的に認める legalize
安心感 a sense of security
余生 (残された時間) the rest of one's life
精神的苦痛 mental pain

◉関連語句

選択肢 an option
医師による自殺ほう助 physician-assisted suicide
自殺ほう助する aid and abet a suicide
看護師 a nurse
治療 a treatment
看病 nursing
死期 one's end [death]
尊厳死 death with dignity
脳死 brain death
筋肉し緩剤 a muscle relaxant
医療行為 a medical procedure
外科医 a surgeon
内科医 an internist, a physician
死を宣告する tell someone they are going to die
尊厳死を守るための遺書 a living will

論題3

手紙よりEメールや携帯メールのほうがすぐれたコミュニケーション手段だ。
(→p.1706)

◉本文掲載語句

手紙 a letter
Eメール email, an email; a text message (携帯電話の)
コミュニケーション手段 a communication tool
パソコン a (personal) computer
携帯電話 a cellphone
携帯メールに没頭する be focused on text messaging, be absorbed in text messaging
手軽に送る send ... easily
遠方に住む live a long way off [away]
連絡を取り合う keep in touch with
手書きの手紙 a handwritten letter
受取人 a recipient
ウイルス(メール) a virus
迷惑メール spam
メールを誤送信する send an email to a wrong address
効率の良い efficient
普及する become common [popular]
事務的な作業 an impersonal task, a mundane task
相談する consult, talk to
コミュニケーション能力 communication ability [skills]

◉関連語句

携帯メール依存症 texting addiction
携帯メール依存症である be addicted to texting
電報 a telegram
郵便局 a post office
メールアドレス one's e-mail address
メル友 an email pal
添付ファイル an attached file
国際郵便 international mail
切手 a (postage) stamp
便せん letter paper
封筒 an envelope
転送する forward
匿名で anonymously, on an anonymous basis
音声メール a voice message
受信メール an incoming message

論題4

インターネットは無制限に普及されるべきではない。
(→p.1707)

◉本文掲載語句

インターネット the Internet
制限 (a) restriction
インターネット掲示板 a discussion board
デマ a false rumor
ひぼう中傷 a slanderous comment
情報を発信する provide information
意見を交換する exchange opinions [ideas]
貴重なメディア a valuable medium
ネット上の情報 information on the Net
(インターネット)サイト a website
未成年者に有害なサイト a website harmful to minors
ネット上に氾濫している be rampant on the Net
サイトに規制を設ける place restrictions on websites
言論の自由 freedom of speech
クレジットカード番号 a credit card number
個人情報 private [personal] information
セキュリティー(安全性) security
急速な普及 rapid expansion [spread]
人為的な漏えい intentional leaking
著作物をコピーする make copies of copyrighted materials

◉関連語句

罰則 a penalty
アナログ回線 an analog circuit
ブロードバンド時代 the broadband era
ノート型パソコン a laptop [notebook] computer
デスクトップ型パソコン a desktop computer
インターネットに接続する connect to the Internet
回避策 preventative measures
知的財産 intellectual property
海賊版ソフト pirated software
衛星通信 satellite communications
インターネット詐欺 an Internet scam [fraud]
インターネット端末 an Internet terminal
インターネットの常時接続 constant Internet access
情報のデジタル化 the digitization of information
著作権法に違反する violate the copyright law

論題5

英語の教育は小学生から始めるべきである。
(→p.1708)

◉本文掲載語句

小学校 an elementary school
英語教育 English language education
習得する acquire, learn
平均点 an average score
指摘する point out

テストを受ける take a test
吸収する absorb
効果的に effectively
バイリンガル bilingual
国語 one's own language (自国語); Japanese (日本語)
帰国子女 a returnee from overseas, a child [student] who has recently returned from overseas
英語に触れる be exposed to English
異文化 different cultures
国際社会 global [international] society
資質をはぐくむ develop the qualities; develop one's talents [abilities], develop one's qualifications
国際理解 international understanding
ネイティブの発音 the pronunciation of native speakers
低下して in decline
外国語 a foreign language

◉関連語句

学力 scholastic [academic] ability
学歴 one's educational [academic] background
国際交流 international exchange
なまりがある have an accent
英語力 English proficiency, English language ability [skill]
英語の検定試験 an English proficiency test
教科書英語 textbook English
課外授業 an extra class, an extracurricular lesson
第二言語 a second language
英文法 English grammar
ヒアリング listening comprehension
英文学 English literature
言葉の壁 a language barrier
公用語 an official language
万国共通言語 a universal language
英語を話す環境 an English speaking environment
ジェスチャー body [non-verbal] language
片言の英語 broken English
ゆとり教育 pressure-free [cram-free] education, more relaxed [flexible] education
教育方針 (an)educational policy
教育費 education expenses
中学生 a junior high school student
高校生 a (senior)high school student
アメリカに留学する go to the U.S. to study, study in the U.S.

論題6

外来語は積極的に日本語に採り入れるべきである。
(→p.1709)

◉本文掲載語句

外来語 a loanword, a borrowed word
概念を言い表す express a concept
阻害するもの an obstacle
むやみな使用 unrestrained use, overuse
国際化 internationalization, globalization
日本語に訳す translate into Japanese
年齢層 an age group
定着度合い the level of understanding
置き換える replace
だいたいの意味 an approximate meaning
和製英語 a Japanese-English word, a Japanese adaptation of an English word
豊かにする enrich
(自己)表現力 one's ability to express oneself, one's expressive ability

◉関連語句

ローマ字 Romaji, Roman letters
表記法 notation
造語 a coined word
(習慣などが)定着する take root
言い換える paraphrase, rephrase
語いを増やす develop [expand] one's vocabulary
注釈をつける add [include] a note [an explanatory note]
頭文字 an initial
頭字語 an acronym
略語 an abbreviation
少数言語 a minority language
文化の多様性 cultural diversity
専門用語 a technical term [word]
固有名詞 a proper noun
使いすぎる overuse
ことばづかい one's way of speaking, one's language, wording
英語が氾濫する be inundated [flooded] by English
弊害 a negative [bad] effect
誤用 wrong usage
概念 a concept; an idea (考え方)
微妙な違い a subtle difference

論題7

生徒の携帯電話の使用はよくない。
(→p.1710)

◉本文掲載語句

(人の) 注意をそらす distract someone
授業中に during [in] class
携帯の電源を切る turn off one's cellphone
経済的負担 an economic burden
節約する save money, economize
犯罪に巻き込まれる be involved in a crime
携帯電話絡みの犯罪 a cellphone-related crime
社会問題 a social problem
確認する make sure, check, verify
迷惑をかける disturb

◉関連語句

(個人の) 電話代 a telephone bill
電話代の支払い a telephone bill payment
多額の電話料金を支払う spend a lot of money paying for one's phone
番号表示 a number display
履歴 a calls-received record [history]
学生割引 a student discount
毎月の基本使用料 a basic monthly charge [fee]
電話をかける call, make [place] a call
内蔵カメラ a built-in camera
プリペイド式携帯電話 a prepaid cellphone
携帯で連絡をとる contact someone on a cellphone
(人の) 位置を探知する detect the location of someone
マナー manners
加入者 a subscriber, a user
携帯電話のケース a cellphone case
機種 a model
盗聴する bug [tap] a telephone
携帯電話番号 a cellphone number
表示画面 a display (screen)
携帯電話サイト a mobile-web site
公衆電話 a payphone, a public phone
受信する receive a call (電話), receive an e-mail [a text message] (メール)

論題8

高速道路はもっと増やすべきだ。
(→p.1711)

◉本文掲載語句

高速道路 an expressway
渋滞を緩和する make traffic jams less serious
乗用車 a car
公共の交通機関 public transportation, mass transit
地方経済 a regional [local] economy
経済を活性化する revitalize the economy
人口流出 population outflow
加速する accelerate
地方 a rural area
過疎化 depopulation
交通事故 a traffic accident
物流 distribution, a distribution system
日本の産業 Japanese industries
効率化する improve efficiency
共同輸送 joint distribution
インフラ整備する develop infrastructure
日帰り旅行 a day trip
観光産業 the tourist [travel] industry
自然破壊する destroy nature
排気ガス exhaust, exhaust emissions [gas(es)]
騒音 noise

◉関連語句

利用率 the rate of utilization
交通渋滞 traffic congestion, a traffic jam
交通の便がいい be conveniently located
交通網 a transportation network
高速道路料金 a expressway toll
道路交通法 a road traffic law
道路工事 road construction
交通整理 traffic control [regulation]
スピード違反 a speeding violation, speeding
郊外 the suburbs
交差点 an intersection, a crossing
道路公団 a public highway corporation
道路税 a road tax
ETC (ノンストップ自動料金支払いシステム) an electronic toll collection system

論題9

死刑は絶対に必要である。
(→p.1712)

◉本文掲載語句

死刑 capital punishment, the death penalty
遺族 the victim's families
報復 revenge
重罪 a serious crime [offence], a felony
人命 (a) human life
犯罪の抑止力 a deterrent against crime
死刑の有無 the absence or presence of capital punishment
重い罰 a heavy [severe] punishment
残虐な cruel
犯罪者 a criminal
法律での保護 legal protectin
人権 human rights
えん罪 a false conviction [charge]
殺人者 a murderer
釈放する release (on parole)

一般市民 (ordinary) citizens [people], the general population
懲役刑 imprisonment
更生させる reform
仮釈放 parole
◉関連語句
死刑判決 a death sentence
有罪判決 a guilty verdict, a guilty ruling [judgment]
無罪判決 a not guilty verdict
無実の innocent
被害者 a victim, a sufferer
廃止する abolish
控訴を退ける dismiss an appeal
上告する appeal (to a higher court)
刑務所 a prison
家庭裁判所 a family court, a domestic relations court
最高裁判所 the Supreme Court
裁判 (a) judgment(審判;判決), a trial (公判)
裁判官 a judge, a justice
傍聴人 a spectator
死刑執行人 an executioner
死刑囚 a condemned criminal, a criminal on death row
無期懲役を課せられる get a life sentence
原告 a plaintiff
被告 a defendant
検察官 a prosecutor

論題10

電子辞書は紙の辞書に勝っている。
(→p.1713)

◉本文掲載語句
電子辞書 an electronic dictionary
軽量な light
紙の辞書 a paper(-based) dictionary
重い heavy
持ち歩く carry around
割高な economically inefficient, expensive, costly
安価な inexpensive, cheap
特徴 characteristics, features
英英辞典 an English-English dictionary
単語を調べる look up a word
英和辞典 an English-Japanese dictionary
ページをめくる turn (the) pages
キーボード a keyboard
さまざまな機能 a variety of functions
パラパラめくる flip through, browse
◉関連語句
寸法 the dimensions
重さ weight
場所を取る take up space
新しい単語を登録する register a new word
使い勝手の悪い inconvenient
音声機能 a voice function
電卓機能 a calculator function
スペルチェック機能 a spell-check function
特色 a key feature, an outstanding characteristic
品質 quality
最新の辞書 an up-to-date dictionary
アルファベット順 alphabetical order
辞書を引く use [consult/look up a word in] a dictionary
辞書に載っている be listed in a dictionary
ユーザー辞書 a custom [user] dictionary
索引 an index
和英辞典 a Japanese-English dictionary
類義語辞典 a thesaurus

論題11

生徒には制服が必要である。
(→p.1714)

◉本文掲載語句
制服 a school uniform, a uniform
規律を守る observe [obey] (the) rules
画一的な教育 a standardized education system, uniform education
マイナスイメージ a negative image
象徴する symbolize
私服 ordinary clothes
面倒 trouble
衛生的な sanitary
自由に freely
仲間外れにされる be excluded, be left out
着用を義務づける require (students) to wear
からかわれる get teased
いじめる bully
個性がない (没個性) lack individuality
時代に逆行する go against the trend of the times
部外者 an outsider
集団意識 group consciousness
他校生 a student from a different school
生徒同士の争い a conflict between students
◉関連語句
校則 school regulations
授業に出席する attend a class
ファッションセンス fashion sense
不経済な uneconomical

セーラー服 a sailor-style school uniform
校則違反 a violation of school regulations
学生帽 a school cap
軍国主義 militarism
茶髪 dyed [bleached] brown hair
長髪 long hair
学生寮 a dormitory
体操服 gym clothes [wear]
真面目な生徒 a hard-working [serious] student
不良の delinquent

論題12

地球温暖化は人類の発展上やむをえない。
(→p.1715)

◉本文掲載語句

地球温暖化 global warming
やむをえない unavoidable
石炭 coal
石油 oil, petroleum
化石燃料 (a) fossil fuel
必要不可欠な indispensable
基盤 the infrastructure
犠牲にする sacrifice
深刻な危機 a serious crisis; a threat (脅威)
海面の上昇 a rise in (the) sea level, a sea level rise
異常気象 abnormal weather
天然ガス natural gas
代替エネルギー an alternative energy source
取って代わる replace
世界規模に worldwide
二酸化炭素の排出 CO_2 emissions
科学的根拠 scientific proof
人類の歴史 the history of humanity
平均気温 the average temperature
過去100年間 the last 100 years

◉関連語句

防止策 preventative measures
温暖化ガス a heat-trapping gas, a greenhouse gas
京都会議, 温暖化防止会議 the Kyoto Conference, COP3
京都議定書 the Kyoto Protocol
参加国 a participating country
温室効果 the greenhouse effect
削減目標 a reduction target
二酸化炭素濃度 the CO_2 concentration
オゾン層 the ozone layer
フロンガス chlorofluorocarbon, CFC (gases)
国連環境開発会議 the U. N. Conference on Environment and Development (UNCED)
気候変動 a climate change
一次エネルギー a primary energy source
省エネ energy conservation

論題13

都会はいなかよりも住みやすい。
(→p.1716)

◉本文掲載語句

都会 a city, an urban area
いなか the countryside, the country
コンビニ a convenience store
望ましい場所 a desirable place
満員電車 a crowded train
日常的な光景 an everyday scene
のんびりとしたゆとりのある生活 a slow and relaxing life
医療施設 medical facilities
救急(医療)サービス emergency (medical) services
ビジネスチャンス a business opportunity
転職する change jobs
都会の利点 an advantage of cities [living in a city]
ストレスの多い stressful
過労死する die from overwork, work oneself to death
古いしきたり an old tradition, an outdated custom [practice]
不審者 a suspicious individual
犯罪発生率 the crime rate
比較にならない beyond comparison

◉関連語句

賃貸マンション a rental apartment
一戸建て住宅 a (single) house
農村 a farming village
漁村 a fishing village
第一次産業 a primary industry
競争社会 a competitive society
希薄な人間関係 poor personal relationships
人口密度 population density
地域社会 a local community
生活習慣 lifestyle habits
物価 prices
生活費 living expenses
生活水準 the standard of living, living standards
地方自治体 a local government

論題14

漫画は子どもに悪影響を与えている。
(→p.1717)

◉本文掲載語句

漫画 a comic (book); an animated film, anime, a cartoon (アニメ)
悪影響 a bad influence, a negative effect
暴力的な violent
(内容を)含む contain
違いを認識する recognize a [the] difference
家庭でのしつけ training at home
学校での教育 education at school
小説 a novel
阻害する hinder, obstruct
低俗な vulgar
教育的な educational
成熟した文化 a mature culture
模倣する imitate, mimic

◉関連語句

日本のアニメ anime, Japanimation, Japanese cartoons
原作 the original
漫画家 a cartoonist, a comic artist, an anime artist
フィクション fiction
過激な extreme
性描写 sexual depiction [content]
誘発する induce, cause, bring about
娯楽 (an) entertainment
少女漫画 a comic book for girls, a girls' comic book
恋愛もの a love story
創造性 creativity
名作 a masterpiece, a fine work
漫画雑誌 a comic magazine
週刊[月刊]誌 a weekly [monthly] magazine
連載漫画 a serial comic
ギャグ漫画 a gag comic
漫画文化 comic [anime] culture
風刺漫画 a caricature
大衆文化 pop culture
主人公 the main character
漫画ブーム a manga boom
ストーリー展開 a storyline
長編アニメ映画賞(アカデミー賞) Best Animated Feature Film
夜更かしする stay up late
活字離れの傾向 a tendency of people not to read books and newspapers

論題15

親の老後のめんどうは子どもが見るべきだ。
(→p.1718)

◉本文掲載語句

老後 when [after] someone gets old, in one's old age
めんどうを見る look after, take care of
義務 a duty
民法 civil law
個人の権利 the rights of the individual
尊重する respect
自立した個人 an independent individual
頼る depend on
施設 a facility
さまざまな事情 various circumstances
自由に生きる live life freely
個人主義 individualism
悠々自適の生活を送る live in comfort, take life easy
寝たきりになる be bedridden
介護者 a caregiver
制度全般を見直す redesign [review] the entire system

◉関連語句

高齢者 the elderly, an elderly person
老人ホーム a home for the elderly [aged], a nursing home
老人性認知症 senile dementia
社会保障制度 a social security system
社会福祉 social welfare
介護保険料 the premium of nursing care insurance
在宅介護 home (nursing) care
老後の楽しみ enjoyment in one's old age
デイサービス(通いの介護サービス) daycare service
車いす a wheelchair
年金 a pension
親に仕送りをする send money to one's parent(s)
二世帯住宅 a two-generation home
定年退職 age-limit retirement, retirement age
高齢化社会 an aging society
老後の蓄え one's life savings
経済支援 economic assistance
核家族 a nuclear family
平均寿命 the average life span [life expectancy]

論題16

公共交通機関に優先席は必要である。
(→p.1719)

◉本文掲載語句

優先席 a priority seat
乗客 a passenger
席をゆずる offer a seat
体が不自由な人 a disabled
お年寄り a senior
妊娠している女性 a pregnant woman
成熟した社会 a mature society
公共交通機関 public transportation
社会的マナー social manners
廃止する abolish
ラッシュアワー rush hours
混雑した電車 crowded trains
高齢化社会 an aging society
運転をやめる give up driving a car
高齢者を支える support seniors
不快に思う get upset
若くて健康な young and healthy
申し訳なさを感じる feel guilty

◉関連語句

超高齢化社会 a super aging society
現役世代 working generations
公共交通機関 a public transportation system
車いす a wheelchair
車いす対応車両 a wheelchair-accessible vehicle [car]
車いす席 a wheelchair seating/wheelchair spaces
車いす対応トイレ a wheelchair-compatible toilet / a wheelchair-accessible toilet
福祉車両 a vehicle for disabled people
罰金 a fine
ためらう hesitate
寝たふり pretend to be sleeping
促す encourage
席を譲る offer [give up] one's seat
車両 a vehicle
電車の車両 car
けが人 an injured person
病人 a sick person
乳幼児連れの人 man/woman with a baby, a man/woman with a baby
思いやり consideration, thoughtfulness

論題17

80歳以上の高齢者は運転をやめるべきだ。
(→p.1720)

◉本文掲載語句

視力が衰える diminish eyesight
歩行者 pedestrian
はっきり認識する clearly recognize
歩行者検知システム pedestrian detection systems
事故を回避する avoid causing accidents
刻々と変化する change from moment to moment
交通状況に対する認識, 反応 recognize or respond properly to traffic conditions
事故を起こす確率が上がる lead to a higher probability of causing an accident
AI技術 AI technology
自動運転車 self-driving vehicles
…の解決法 a solution to...
軽度認知症 mild dementia
悲劇的な事故 a tragic accident
強い責任感 strong sense of responsibility
無料で for free
補償金 compensation money
田舎 a rural area
不便な inconvenient
快適に生活する live comfortably
認知機能検査 cognitive ability test
運動神経 reflexes
一律に on a uniform basis

◉関連語句

運転免許自主返納 voluntarily giving up one's driver's license
先進運転支援システム advanced driver assistance system (ADAS)
交通事故死亡者数 the number of deaths caused by traffic accidents
免許取り消し revocation of one's driver's license
医師による検査 an examination by a doctor
誤発進防止 preventing an unintended start
ブレーキとアクセルの踏み間違え mistake the brake pedal for the gas pedal
強制的な免許返上 give up one's driver's license against his/her will
運転する権利 the right to drive
記憶力 memory
判断力 decision making ability, decisiveness
高齢者講習 a safe driving class for seniors
信号無視 ignoring traffic lights
逆走 wrong-way driving, driving on the wrong side of the road/street
歩道へ突っ込む drive onto a sidewalk
交通違反 breaking traffic rules

■会社役職名■　（日・英・米で組織形態が異なり、会社によっても名称はさまざま）

日本		アメリカ	イギリス
会長	chairperson	chairperson	chairperson（実質上の社長）
社長	president	president　または chief executive officer	managing director
副社長	executive vice president	executive vice president	●常勤で、執行責任がある取締役は chief executive と呼ばれ、会長が兼任することが多い ●役員会構成員は非常勤の社外重役（outside director）であることが多い
専務	senior managing director	senior vice president	
常務	executive managing director		
部長	general manager	vice president または　manager	director　または general manager
課長	section chief		manager
係長	subsection chief	manager	

●このほか、部長代理、課長代理、課長補佐、主任については各項参照

■大学役職名■　（同一国でも大学によって名称が異なることがある）

日本		アメリカ	イギリス
総長または学長	president	presidentまたはchancellor（後者は一部の大規模大学分校の）	chancellor（総長）は名誉職で、vice-chancellor（副総長）が実質的な総長. provostは各college の責任者（学寮長、学長）で、principal, wardenなどと呼ぶところもある
学部長	dean	dean	（deanは一部の大学で学生監、学生部長）
(正)教授	(full) professor	(full) professor	(full) professor（日本・アメリカより人数が少なく地位が高い）
准教授	associate professor	associate professor	reader

●日本の「助教」（国立大系に多い）や「専任講師」（私立大系に多い）は assistant professor や《英》senior lecturerを用いるとよい
●このほか、理事(長)、名誉教授、客員教授、客員研究員、(専任)講師、助手については各項参照

Eメール・手紙例文索引

本文の中で用例として出したEメール・手紙文のうち，主なものを内容別に分類してまとめた．英文は［⇀○○］の見出語に出ている．ペンパルとの文通や，外国の友人にEメールや手紙を書くときなどに大いに活用していただきたい．なお，本文でコラム扱いにした「日本紹介」の英文については，巻頭の索引を参照のこと．

1 愛と友情

✉ 菜々子より愛を込めて ［⇀愛］
✉ あなたを心から愛しています ［⇀愛する］
✉ いつもあなたのことを思っています ［⇀思う］
✉ あれからずっとあなたのことばかり考えています ［⇀ずっと］
✉ 一日中あなたのことばかり考えています ［⇀-ばかり］
✉ 明けても暮れても思うはきみのことばかりだよ ［⇀明けても暮れても］
✉ ぼくは一生きみを愛し，大切にします ［⇀一生］
✉ もうすぐあなたにお会いできると考えただけで胸がわくわくします ［⇀考える］
✉ あなたに会った瞬間，私はそれが恋だとわかりました ［⇀恋］
✉ あなたが恋しくて食事も喉を通りません ［⇀食事］
✉ 思い切って言います．実はずっと前からあなたのことが好きでした ［⇀好き］
✉ お手紙ありがとう．毎日首を長くして待っていました ［⇀手紙］
✉ 私と友だちになっていただけませんか ［⇀友だち］
✉ 早くあなたにお会いしたいです ［⇀早い］
✉ チョコレートを贈ります．バレンタインデーに愛を込めて ［⇀バレンタイン(デー)］
✉ あなたからのお手紙を待ち焦がれています ［⇀待ち焦がれる］
✉ もし私が鳥だったらすぐにでもあなたのもとへ飛んでいくのに ［⇀もし］
✉ ゆうべあなたの夢を見ました ［⇀夢］
✉ きみが好きだ．健より ［⇀-より］
✉ あなたのことを教えてください ［⇀あなた］
✉ 私たちって共通点が多いですね ［⇀共通］
✉ 私たちは(運命の)赤い糸で結ばれているんですね ［⇀赤い］
✉ あなたと再会できてとてもうれしく思いました ［⇀再会］
✉ あなたの励ましのことばが身にしみてうれしかったわ．ありがとう ［⇀しみる］
✉ いつかあなたの国に行きたいと思っています ［⇀行く］
✉ 私の写真を同封します．あなたの写真を送ってくれますか ［⇀送る］
✉ 私たちの友情が両国をつなぐ懸け橋となりますように ［⇀懸け橋］
✉ 文通だけでなくぜひ一度お会いしたいですね ［⇀ぜひ］
✉ あなたが日本へ来られると聞き，うれしくてわくわくしています ［⇀わくわく］
✉ きみとはもうこれ以上付き合えなくなりました．さようなら ［⇀付き合う］

2 手紙の決まり文句

✉ しばらくお会いしていませんが，お元気ですか ［⇀会う］
✉ すっかりご無沙汰しておりますが，お元気でしょうか ［⇀すっかり］
✉ いかがお過ごしでしょうか．お元気のことと存じます ［⇀過ごす］
✉ いかがお過ごしですか ［⇀いかが］
✉ その後いかがお過ごしですか ［⇀その後］
✉ ご機嫌いかがですか ［⇀ご機嫌］
✉ 早速お返事いただきありがとう ［⇀早速］
✉ またお便りいただいてうれしかったです ［⇀うれしい］
✉ 初めてお便りします ［⇀便り］
✉ 私と文通していただけませんか ［⇀文通］
✉ 実は外国の人と文通するのはこれが初めてです ［⇀初めて］
✉ 文通［メール］を通じてお友だちになれたらどんなにすてきでしょう ［⇀友だち］

3 グリーティングカード

4 自己紹介

✉ 家族の動画を送ります. 私の右でギターを弾いている人が兄の圭介です [→右]
✉ 私の夢は列車でカナダを横断することです [→夢]
✉ 私はラジオ講座で英語を勉強しています [→ラジオ]
✉ 3列目の左から4番目が私です [→列]

5 学校生活

✉ 新しい学校はいかがですか [→いかが]
✉ 私の学校は私立で, 女子校です [→学校]
✉ 日本の公立学校は週5日制です [→週]
✉ 日本では新学期は4月に始まります [→新学期]
✉ 日本では3月が卒業の月です [→卒業]
✉ 私たちの学校は周りに緑地帯がある美しい町にあります [→地帯]
✉ あなたの学校生活について教えてください [→学校]
✉ 今, テニスクラブの合宿で蓼科に来ています [→合宿]
✉ 私たちの学校では髪を染めることは禁止されています [→禁止]
✉ 夏休みも終わりに近づいて来ました [→近づく]
✉ オーストラリアのティーンエージャーの生活ってどんなふうなんですか [→どんな]
✉ 昼休みは友だちとおしゃべりをして過ごします [→昼休み]
✉ 演劇部の部活のある日は帰りは8時ごろになります [→部活]
✉ 私たちの学校には厳しい服装規定があります [→服装]
✉ 私たちの冬休みは12月21日に始まります [→冬休み]
✉ 来週学校で文化祭があります. 今その準備で大忙しです [→文化祭]
✉ 文化祭では私たちのクラスはホットドッグの模擬店をやりました [→文化祭]
✉ 10月に英語の弁論大会があります [→弁論]
✉ 休みの日はどんなことしてますか [→休み]
✉ 早くクラスのみんなとうまくやっていけるといいね [→やっていく]
✉ テニス部をやめようかどうしようか悩んでいます [→やめる]
✉ あなたの学校の様子を知らせてください [→様子]
✉ 日本史は私の好きな科目の1つです. あなたはどんな科目が好きですか [→科目]
✉ 夏休みは宿題が山ほどあります [→宿題]
✉ 優等で卒業なさったなんてすごいですね [→卒業]
✉ 私は今卒論を書くために図書館にせっせと通っています [→卒論]
✉ 大学に進学しようかどうかまだ迷っています [→迷う]
✉ あなたはどこの大学を目指していますか. 私は東大です [→目指す]
✉ 夏休みにはレポートを3つ書かねばなりません [→レポート]

6 趣味・関心

✉ アメリカ人のペンパルを1人紹介してください [→ペンパル]
✉ 宇宙探査に関心のある人, 英語で文通しませんか. 性別・年齢は問いません [→文通]
✉ あなたの国のポップミュージックについて教えてください [→教える]
✉ あなたと私は趣味が共通してますね [→共通]
✉ あなたはどんなことに興味がありますか [→興味]
✉ どういう訳で日本に興味をもつようになられたのですか [→興味]
✉ アメリカではどんな職業が大学生に人気がありますか [→職業]
✉ きみのEメールのアドレスを知らせてください [→知らせる]
✉ あなたの国では今どんなファッションがはやっていますか [→はやる]
✉ これらは私の作った英語の俳句です. あなたの批評をお聞かせください [→批評]
✉ 私は大のビートルズファンです [→ファン]
✉ ロックの歴史の本ありがとう. これこそ私の欲しかった物です [→欲しい]
✉ あなたは何かボランティア活動をしていますか [→ボランティア]

7 日本事情

✉ 日本は周囲を海に囲まれた国です [→囲む]
✉ 日本の秋は木々が紅葉し, 食欲が増し, 私のいちばん好きな季節です [→秋]
✉ 四季の区別がはっきりしているので, ぼくは日本の気候が気に入っています [→気候]
✉ 京都の山々は美しく紅葉する頃が見頃です [→紅葉]
✉ 日本の国土の約67パーセントは山地で, 多くは森林に覆われています [→国土]
✉ 日本は地震国です. あなたは地震というものを経験したことがありますか [→地震]
✉ 日本でいちばん高い山は富士山です [→日本]
✉ 元日には大勢の日本人が (新年の健康や幸福を願って) 神社や寺院にお参りに行きます [→元日]
✉ 多くの日本人は正月に神社へ行って商売繁盛と家内安全を祈ります [→神社]
✉ 相撲は日本の国技で, 野球, サッカー, ゴルフとともに最も人気のあるスポーツの1つです [→国技]
✉ ご存じかもしれませんが, 日本では鶴と亀は長寿を象徴する生き物です [→ご存じ]
✉ 金沢は城下町として有名です [→城下町]
✉ きょうは冬至です. 日本ではこの日にゆず湯に入り, かぼちゃを食べる習慣があります [→冬至]
✉ 夏の夕方, 日本各地で花火大会が開かれます [→日本]
✉ 同封の写真は日本の代表的な食べ物を写したものです. いちばん左が「すし」, その右が「うどん」です [→左]

私たちは玄関で必ず靴を脱ぎます [→必ず]
日本人は家の中では靴を履きません [→靴]
日本では人を訪問するときに手土産を持参するのが慣例です [→慣例]
日本人は米を主食としています [→米]
日本では生徒は6月1日に(夏服に)衣替えをします [→衣]
日本は島国なので魚は日本人にとって大切なたんぱく源となっています [→魚]
日本には人に会って挨拶するときにおじぎをする習慣があります [→習慣]
日本の人口は1億2500万人以上です [→日本]
日本の人口はあなたの国の人口の約10倍です [→倍]
日本ではバレンタインデーに女の子が男の子にチョコレートを贈る習慣があります [→バレンタイン(デー)]

8 お祝い

ご卒業を心からお祝い申し上げます [→祝う]
卒業祝いにネクタイをお送りします [→送る]
ご昇進おめでとうございます. 今後のますますのご活躍をお祈りいたします [→活躍]
あなたの社会人としての新しい門出をお祝いいたします [→門出]
ご就職おめでとうございます. 私は就職活動を始めたところです [→就職]
後ればせながらお誕生日おめでとうございます [→後ればせながら]
ささやかですが, 誕生日のプレゼントをお送りしますのでお受け取りください [→誕生日]
ご新築おめでとう. 新築祝いとして日本の版画をお送りします [→新築]
ご結婚のお知らせをいただき大変うれしく思いました. お二人の末永いお幸せを心よりお祈りいたします［末永くお幸せにお暮らしください］ [→末永い]
スタンフォード大学に入学されるとのこと, おめでとう! [→入学]
ご結婚おめでとう! プレゼントとして日本の湯のみ一式を送ります [→プレゼント]
婚約なさった由, おめでとうございます [→由]
お子さんのお誕生おめでとうございます [→誕生]
女のお子さんがお生まれになった由, お喜び申し上げます [→喜ぶ]

9 お礼

いろいろお世話になりました [→いろいろ]
いろいろお骨折りいただきありがとうございます [→骨折り]
いろいろお力添えいただき感謝いたします [→感謝]
あなたのご親切は片ときも忘れません [→片とき]
ご親切には心から感謝しております [→心から]
私の感謝の気持ちはことばでは言い表せません [→ことば]
ロンドン滞在中はいろいろとお世話になりました. ご厚意に深く感謝いたします [→厚意]
そちらに滞在中はいろいろご親切にしていただき, ありがとうございました [→滞在]
在米中はひとかたならぬお世話になり, ありがとうございました [→ひとかたならぬ]
お心尽くしの贈り物をいただき厚くお礼申し上げます [→厚い]
ネクタイをお送りくださってありがとう [→送る]
お礼のしるしにちくわをお送りしました. ほんの気持ちばかりですが, お受け取りください [→気持ち]
お心尽くしの品をお送りいただき, 厚くお礼申し上げます [→心尽くし]
結構なお品(＝プレゼント)をありがとうございました [→品]
感謝のしるしに私が編んだテーブルセンターをお送りします [→しるし]
あなたからのプレゼント大切にします [→大切]
すてきなプレゼントをお送りいただきありがとうございます [→プレゼント]
お忙しいところ, 街を案内してくださいましてありがとうございました [→忙しい]
いろいろありがとう. トロントからたくさんの楽しい思い出を持ち帰りました [→思い出]
先日はごちそうになりどうもありがとうございました [→ごちそう]
先日はご丁寧に駅まで車でお送りいただき, ありがとうございました [→丁寧]
この間はすてきな夜をありがとう [→すてき]
きれいな絵はがきを送っていただきありがとう [→はがき]
あなたのお手紙は大きな励ましとなりました [→励まし]
昨夜のディナーがどんなに楽しかったかひと言お礼を申し上げたくて筆をとりました [→ひと言]
あなたの温かいおもてなしのおかげでとても思い出深い旅になりました [→もてなし]

10 おわび

ご無沙汰してしまってごめんなさい [→ご無沙汰]
お便りが遅くなってごめんなさい [→ごめん]
お返事が遅くなってすみません [→遅い]
お返事が遅れたことをお許しください [→許す]
あなたにひどいことを言ってしまって後悔しています. ごめんなさい [→後悔]
ご招待いただきましたが, あいにく伺うことができません [→あいにく]
せっかくのお招きをお受けできず, 心苦しく思っています [→心苦しい]
残念ながらあなたのご要望にはお応えできません [→こたえる]
申し訳ありませんが, 寄付のご依頼はお断りさせていただきます [→断る]
謹んでおわび申し上げます [→謹んで]
あまりお役に立てず申し訳ありませんでした [→役]
お誕生日を忘れてしまって本当にごめんなさい

[→忘れる]

11 お見舞い・お悔やみ

✉ どうか早くよくなってください [→どうか]

✉ 焦らずにゆっくり休養なさってください [→焦る]

✉ みどりさん，早く元気になってください―クラス一同より [→一同]

✉ おばあさまが回復に向かっていらっしゃると伺い，うれしく思います [→伺う]

✉ １日も早いご回復をお祈りしております [→回復]

✉ お加減が悪いとはお気の毒です [→加減]

✉ このところ気候が変わりやすいので体には十分気をつけてください [→気候]

✉ 体調を崩されているとのこと，心配しています．ゆっくり休んで早く元気になってください [→元気]

✉ お母さまが重病と伺いました．ご心配のこととご推察申し上げます [→推察]

✉ ご病気だそうですね．早く元気になられるのを願っております [→病気]

✉ ご病気とのこと，お見舞い申し上げます [→見舞い]

✉ お父さまが癌(がん)とうかがい，心からお見舞い申し上げます [→見舞い]

✉ ハリケーンとはとんだ災難でしたね．心からお見舞いを申し上げます [→見舞い]

✉ お父さまご逝去の由，誠にご愁傷さまに存じます．謹んでお悔やみ申し上げます [→お悔やみ]

✉ 奥さまを亡くされ，どれほどお寂しいことかお察しいたします [→察する]

✉ お父さまが亡くなられてどんなにかお力落としのことと存じます [→力]

✉ 謹んでお父上のご逝去をお悔やみ申し上げます [→謹んで]

✉ 取り急ぎお見舞い［お悔やみ］申し上げます [→取り急ぎ]

✉ 残されたご家族の皆さまに何と申し上げてよいかわかりません [→残す]

✉ お父上ご逝去の報に接し，悲しみに堪えません [→報]

✉ お母さまのご冥福をお祈りいたします [→冥福]

12 案内・連絡

✉ きたる６月３日土曜日の結婚式にぜひご出席くださいますようお願いいたします [→きたる]

✉ 令和３年11月23日，娘昌子の結婚式にご参列くださいますようご案内申し上げます [→案内]

✉ 披露宴へのご招待ありがとうございます．喜んで出席させていただきます [→出席]

✉ うれしいことに息子は無事に大学入試に合格しました [→うれしい]

✉ 私はやっと健康を取り戻しました．どうか心配しないでください [→心配]

✉ ご上京の折にはぜひお立ち寄りください [→折]

✉ 私は６月に孝夫と結婚します．彼は高校時代からの恋人なんです [→恋人]

✉ 心ばかりの品ですが，どうぞお納めください [→心ばかり]

✉ 私儀，この度名古屋支店に転勤いたしましたので，お知らせ申し上げます [→知らせる]

✉ 転職をして新しいスタートを切る決心をしました [→スタート]

✉ 私儀３月31日をもってXY銀行を退職いたしました [→退職]

✉ 飛行機は８日，午後４時15分にロサンゼルス空港に着く予定です．あなたに会えるのを楽しみにしています [→楽しみ]

✉ ニューヨークへ行ったついでに留学中の娘に会いたいと思っています [→ついで]

✉ ヒースロー空港には15時30分に到着の予定です．お会いするのを楽しみにしています [→到着]

✉ このたび表記の場所に転居いたしました [→表記]

✉ 先月ワンルームマンションに引っ越しました．遊びに来てね [→引っ越す]

✉ ５月10日までにお返事ください [→返事]

✉ パーティーにはなるべく多くのお友だちをお連れください．多ければ多いほど楽しいですから [→ほど]

✉ パーティーへお招きにあずかりありがとうございます．喜んで出席させていただきます [→招き]

13 ホームステイ・留学

✉ ホームステイ中はいろいろとお世話になりました [→世話]

✉ 歓待してくださったことにお礼のことばもないほどです [→歓待]

✉ 皆さまは最高のホストファミリーでした．ありがとうございました [→ホストファミリー]

✉ ご両親さまにくれぐれもよろしくお伝えください [→くれぐれも]

✉ あなたの焼いてくれたチェリーパイはとてもおいしかったです．マーブルケーキもおいしかったです [→おいしい]

✉ ご一緒に過ごした楽しい日々をよく思い出します [→思い出す]

✉ 日本にいらっしゃったときはいつでもわが家で歓迎しますよ [→歓迎]

✉ ぜひ日本へいらっしゃってください．大歓迎します [→歓迎]

✉ 日本に来られたらぜひわが家にお泊まりください [→ぜひ]

✉ うちでホストファミリーをやってみたいと思っています [→ホストファミリー]

✉ あなたがアメリカへ帰られたので，家中が寂しがっています [→寂しがる]

✉ ご多忙中大変申し訳ありませんが，空港まで迎えに来ていただけないでしょうか [→多忙]

✉ 空港まで出迎えをお願いします．私は目印に赤い野球帽をかぶっています [→目印]

✉ セントラルパーク駅には７時30分に到着の予定です．迎えに来ていただけるとありがたいのですが [→迎える]

✉ 空港まで見送りに来てくださってどうもありがとう [→見送り]

✉ 息子にホームステイの機会をお与えいただき，お礼のことばもありません [→礼]

✉ 3年間あなたとメールの交換をしたことがとても役立ちました．おかげさまで留学のための奨学金の試験に合格することができました [→おかげ]

✉ 貴校の交換留学生計画についての情報をお送りいただきたく，よろしくお願い申し上げます [→お願い]

✉ 貴財団の奨学金を頂き，誠に光栄に存じます [→光栄]

✉ ウィルソン教授に紹介状を書いていただけないでしょうか [→紹介]

✉ 私の教え子の田中小百合さんを紹介させていただきます [→紹介]

14 ビジネス

✉ 貴社におかれましてはますますご清栄のこととお喜び申し上げます [→清栄]

✉ 貴社の商品についての詳細を知りたいので，カタログをお送りください [→詳細]

✉ 貴社の春のカタログ13号より下記の3点の品を注文します [→注文]

✉ 貴社の時計のカタログを1部お送りください [→カタログ]

✉ 貴社のますますのご発展とご繁栄をお祈りします [→ますます]

✉ 今後ともご愛顧のほどよろしくお願い申し上げます [→愛顧]

✉ 今後ともいっそうご指導ご鞭撻くださいますようお願い申し上げます [→鞭撻]

✉ 初めての仕事で行き届きませんが，全力で頑張りますのでよろしくお願いいたします [→行き届く]

✉ 郵送料込みで3450円お送りください [→込み]

✉ 早速ご返事を賜りありがとうございました [→早速]

✉ ご送金いただきありがとうございました [→送金]

✉ 3月18日付けのお手紙ありがとうございました [→-付け]

✉ 4月1，2日パリに出張します．宿泊の手配をお願いします [→手配]

✉ お支払いいただいた代金の領収証を同封いたしましたのでご査収ください [→同封]

✉ 先月注文した下記の品がまだ届きません [→届く]

✉ ご注文の品は一両日中に宅配便で発送します [→発送]

✉ デニムのジャケットを注文しましたが，間違った商品が送られてきました [→間違う]

✉ 送られてきたジーンズはサイズが違っていましたので返品いたします [→返品]

15 季節のあいさつ

✉ 日ごとに寒さが募るこの頃ですが，お変わりありませんか [→寒さ]

✉ 寒さも日ごとに薄らいできましたね [→薄らぐ]

✉ 風薫る5月となりました [→かおる]

✉ 青葉の目にしみる候となりましたが，お変わりありませんか [→青葉]

✉ 11月も中旬となり，どことなく冬の気配が感じられます [→気配]

✉ この2，3日初夏を思わせるような陽気です [→初夏]

✉ 朝夕めっきり涼しくなりました [→涼しい]

✉ 今，日本は春たけなわです．庭には花が咲き誇っています [→たけなわ]

✉ こちらでは桜の花がぼつぼつ咲き始めました [→ぼつぼつ]

✉ 残暑厳しき折からお変わりありませんか [→残暑]

✉ こちらは連日の猛暑でうだっています．そちらはどうですか [→猛暑]

16 その他

✉ 日本の印象はいかがでしたか [→印象]

✉ 衛兵交替の絵はがきありがとう [→絵はがき]

✉ 送っていただいた写真を見ながらこの手紙を書いています [→書く]

✉ あなたがくださった人形はメキシコ旅行の良い記念です [→記念]

✉ 家族の近況をお知らせしましょう [→近況]

✉ 今バルセロナに来ています．きょうは市内見物をしました [→来る]

✉ 夏休みにお会いできるのを心待ちにしています [→心待ち]

✉ あなたのチームが優勝を逃したのは残念でしたね [→残念]

✉ 日本にいらっしゃったときは，いくつかの史跡をご案内したいと思います [→史跡]

✉ 一度失敗したからといってくよくよしないで，この次頑張ってください [→失敗]

✉ 日本では今インフルエンザがはやっていますが，そちらではどうですか [→どう]

✉ 日本においでのときは，ぜひわが家にも泊まってください [→日本]

✉ 早いものでヨーロッパから帰ってまもなく1年になります [→早い]

✉ 祝いの品を別便で送ります [→別便]

✉ 何か日本から送ってほしい物があったら，おっしゃってくださいね [→欲しい]

✉ あなたの学校にはいじめはありますか [→いじめ]

✉ 3月10日までに到着の時間を知らせてください [→-まで]

✉ 子供が小学校へ行き始めたので昼間は身軽になりました [→身軽]

✉ 英語で自分の思っていることをわかってもらうのは難しいですね [→難しい]

✉ 東京にいらっしゃる間のご予定を教えてください [→予定]

✉ 名古屋へいらしたときはうちへ寄ってください [→寄る]

スクール英語・用語用例集

高校生活でよく使われる用語とその用例を「あいうえお」順にまとめた. 日本語見出しのあとに訳語を示し, そのあとに質問文や説明文などの用例を出してある. 学校でALTと会話をするときに役立つものばかりなので, 大いに活用してほしい.

赤点 a failing grade [mark/score], an F (落第点, 欠点)	私は英作文の授業で赤点を取りました ➡I received a failing grade in English composition.
アクセント an accent, a stress	英語のアクセントはどれくらい大切なのですか ➡How important is accent in English? どの音節にアクセントを置けばいいのですか ➡On which syllable should I place the accent?
アルバイト a part-time job (仕事); a part-time worker (人)	カナダではアルバイトをして大学を出る学生がけっこういるそうですね ➡I hear in Canada quite a few students work part-time through college.
暗唱 recitation	英語の暗唱のこつを教えてください ➡Could you give us some pointers for English recitation?
委員 a member of a committee	佐藤先生はいくつかの委員会の委員をしています ➡Ms. Sato is a member of several committees.
委員会 a committee(機関); a committee meeting (会議)	あす委員会があるそうです ➡I hear a committee meeting will be held tomorrow.
一夜漬け overnight cramming (勉強の)	歴史の試験はいつも一夜漬けです ➡I always cram overnight for history exams.
イントネーション intonation	この英文を正しいイントネーションで読んでいただけませんか ➡Would you read this English sentence with the correct intonation?
裏口入学 a backdoor admission, an admission fraud	先生の国でも大学に裏口入学するような生徒はいますか ➡Are there any students who get into college by[through] the back door in your country?
英才教育 special education for gifted children	英才教育は必要だとお考えですか ➡Do you think special education for gifted children is necessary?
遠足 an outing, a school excursion, a field trip	来週の遠足が待ち遠しい ➡I can't wait for the (school) excursion next week.
落ちこぼれ a dropout	クラスの落ちこぼれにはなりたくありません ➡I don't want to fall behind the rest of the class.
音節 a syllable	単語を音節に分けるルールを教えていただけませんか ➡Could you teach us the rules for dividing words into syllables?
カウンセラー室 a counseling room, a counselor's office	最近カウンセラー室を訪れる生徒がますます増えているそうです ➡I hear that more and more students have been visiting the counselor's office recently.
課外活動 extracurricular activities	アメリカで最も高校生に人気のある課外活動は何ですか ➡What's the most popular extracurricular activity among high school students in the United States?

課外授業 an extracurricular class[lesson], an after-school class[lesson]
先生の国ではどんな課外授業が行われているのですか
➡What extracurricular classes [lessons] are given in your country?

化学実験室 a chemistry lab(oratory)
化学実験室はさまざまの薬品が入り交じったにおいがします
➡The chemistry laboratory smells of a mixture of various chemicals.

係 a student in charge（担当者）; a charge（担当）
私は今度の文化祭の係に選ばれました
➡I was elected as a student in charge of the (coming) school festival.

画一的教育 uniform education, a standardized education system
画一的教育にはどのような弊害がありうるとお考えですか
➡What harmful[bad] effects can result from uniform[standardized] education?

学生時代 one's school days
何か高校生時代の思い出を聞かせていただけませんか
➡Could you tell us about your high school days?

学生証 a student ID card
学生証を見せないと図書館が利用できません
➡You can't use the library without showing your student ID card.

学生生活 school life
私はもう少し長く学生生活を楽しみたい
➡I'd like to enjoy my school life a little longer.

学生割引 a student discount
アメリカにも学生割引があるのですか
➡Do you have student discounts in the United States?

学年主任 the head of homeroom teachers
鈴木先生が高校1年の学年主任です
➡Mr. Suzuki is the head of the tenth grade homeroom teachers.

学年末試験[考査] a final (examination)
学年末試験ではいい点が取れるよう精一杯がんばります
➡I'll do my best to get high scores on the finals.

学力 scholastic[academic] ability
最近は社会問題にもなるほどまでに生徒の学力が低下してきています
➡The recent decline in students' scholastic[academic] ability has become a social problem.

学歴 one's educational[academic] background
学歴社会についてはどのように思われますか
➡What do you think of a society where[in which] educational background counts a lot(in deciding social position)?

課題 an assignment, homework（宿題）; a subject（題目）
夏休みの課題を予定されていますか
➡Are you planning to give us homework to do over summer vacation?

学級委員(長) a class representative; a homeroom leader（委員長）
きっと私が学級委員に選ばれると思います
➡I'm quite confident of (my) being elected a class representative.

学級担任 a homeroom teacher, a class teacher
だれが新しい学級担任になるのか興味津々です
➡I'm really interested in who our new homeroom teacher will be.

学級日誌 a class journal, a daily record of class activities
私はきのう学級日誌をつけ忘れました
➡I forgot to write in the class journal yesterday.

学級閉鎖 temporary closing[suspension] of a class
インフルエンザで2クラスが学級閉鎖になりました
➡Two classes were suspended temporarily due to the influenza.

家庭科室 a home economics room
私たちはときどき家庭科室で実際に料理します
➡Sometimes we actually cook in the home economics room.

願書 an application
TOEICの願書の受付はいつからですか
➡When will applications for the TOEIC test start being accepted?

付録

カンニング cheating, cribbing	英語のテストでカンニングをしたので罰を受けました ➡I was punished for cheating on the English exam.
慣用句 an idiom	英会話では慣用句を使うことが多いのですか ➡Do you often use idioms when you speak in English?
聞き取り listening	英語の聞き取りがうまくなるにはどうしたらいいですか ➡How can I improve my listening ability in English?
期末試験［考査］ an end-of(-the)-term exam(ination), a final (exam), a term exam	英語の期末試験は失敗するわけにはいきません ➡I can't fail the English final exam[the English final].
決まり文句 a set phrase [expression]	英語の決まり文句をいくつか教えていただけませんか ➡Could you teach us some English set phrases?
休学 a leave of absence (from school)	1年間休学したいのですが ➡I'd like to have one-year leave of absence from school.
休憩時間 a break, (a) recess	アメリカの高校生はどのように休憩時間を過ごしますか ➡How do high school students spend their recess in the United States?
休講 (a) class cancellation	次の授業は休講になるのですか ➡Are you going to cancel your next class?
教育 (an) education（学校の）; (an) upbringing（家庭でのしつけ）	日本の英語教育をどう思われますか ➡What do you think of[about] the English language education in Japan? 生涯教育は今後ますます大切になると思います ➡I think lifelong education will become increasingly important in the future.
教育改革 (an) educational reform	教育改革があまりはかどっていないのはなぜでしょうね ➡I wonder why educational reform has made little progress (so far).
教育費 educational [school] expenses, cost of education	教育費がかかるのを嘆く母親は多いです ➡Many mothers complain[moan] about (the) high educational expenses.
教員 a teacher	父は高校の英語教員です ➡My father is a high school English teacher.
教科 a subject（科目）	どの教科に興味がありますか ➡What subjects are you interested in?
教科担当 a subject teacher; a specialist teacher（特殊技能の）	山田先生が音楽の教科担当です ➡Ms. Yamada is our music teacher.
教務 school [educational] affairs	教務係の先生がだれなのかは知りません ➡I don't know who is in charge of educational affairs.
欠席日数 the number of absences	私の場合,実は欠席日数がかなり多いんです ➡In my case, I have been absent for quite a few days.
健康診断 a physical checkup [examination]	先生の国でも生徒は定期的に健康診断を受けるのですか ➡Do students get regular physical checkups in your country as well?
研修 study（研究）; training（訓練）	いつかロンドンに英語の研修に行きたいと思っています ➡I hope to go to London to study English someday.
研修旅行 a study tour	来月には研修旅行でシドニーへ行くことになっています ➡We are going to go to Sydney on a study tour next month.
検定 official approval, authorization（認定）; a test（検査）	アメリカでも教科書の検定は行われていますか ➡Do textbooks have to get official approval[authorization] in the United States?

検定試験 a licensing examination, a proficiency test
日本語能力検定試験は難しかったですか
➡Was the Japanese proficiency test difficult[hard]?

合格 a pass, (a) success
私の英語力で英検２級に合格できますか
➡Is my English ability sufficient to pass Eiken Grade 2?

合格点 a passing grade [mark/score]
英語の合格点は何点ですか
➡What's the passing score in English?

講師 a lecturer, an instructor
我が校には常勤講師と非常勤講師がいます
➡Some instructors teach full-time and others (teach) part-time at our school.

講習 a course; a class（クラス）
英語の夏期講習を受けたほうがいいですか
➡Should I take a summer course in English?

校則 school regulations, the school code
校則は守らなければなりません
➡Everyone must follow school regulations.

校内暴力 school violence
校内暴力を防ぐにはどうすればよいとお考えですか
➡How do you think we can prevent school violence?

購買部 a school store
レポート用紙は購買部で買えますか
➡Can I get a writing pad at the school store?

語順 word order
この文の語順は合っていますか
➡Is the word order of this sentence correct[all right]?

再試験 a makeup (exam), (a) reexamination
あした英語の再試験を受けなければなりません
➡I have to take a makeup (exam) in English tomorrow.

採点 grading, marking
これは採点ミスではないでしょうか
➡I'm afraid this is a mistake in grading.

参考書 a reference book; a study-aid (book)（学習用の）
何か英作文に役立つ学習参考書があればほしいのですが
➡I'd like to get a useful study-aid for English composition. Can you suggest[recommend] any?

資格 qualification(s)（資格）; a license（免許）; a certificate（免状）; requirement(s)（必要条件）
ALT（外国語指導助手）になるにはどんな資格がいるんですか
➡What qualifications do you need to become an ALT?
姉は英検１級の資格を持っています
➡My sister has a first level certificate of Eiken Grade 1.

資格試験 a qualifying exam(ination)
イギリスでは奨学生の資格試験は難しいですか
➡Are qualifying exams for scholarships difficult[hard] in Britain?

始業式 the opening ceremony
カナダの学校には始業式がありますか
➡Do you have opening ceremonies at Canadian schools?

自習 self-study, self-teaching
自習の時間は何をすればいいのですか
➡What are we supposed to do during (self-)study hours?

辞書 a dictionary
英作文に役立つ辞書をご存じありませんか
➡Do you (happen to) know any dictionaries that are helpful for English composition?
辞書の上手な使い方を教えてください
➡Could you tell us how to use a dictionary effectively?

視聴覚室 an audio-visual room
視聴覚室には最新の設備が整っています
➡Our audio-visual room is provided with the latest equipment.

実技 a practical skill/ gymnastic exercises（体育の）
実技にはあまり自信がありません
➡I'm not so confident about my practical skills.

実技試験 a skill test[exam]
ピアノの実技試験はかなりうまくいきました
➡I did rather well on the skill test of piano performance.

しつけ discipline	先生は学校でのしつけは厳しいほうがよいと思われますか ➡Do you think it's better that discipline at school be strict?
実行委員会 an executive committee	実行委員会のメンバーに選ばれました ➡I was elected as a member of the executive committee.
実習 practice, (practical) training	私たちはときどき家庭科の授業で調理実習をします ➡We sometimes have practical training in cooking in home economics class.
実習室 a practice[training] room	新しい実習室はとても作業するのに快適です ➡Our new practice room is very comfortable to work in.
質問 a question	質問してもいいですか ➡May I ask you a question? 質問の意味が(あまり)よくわからなかったのですが ➡I'm afraid I couldn't understand your question (very) well.
実力試験[考査] a proficiency exam(ination)	あすの実力試験では必ず英語の実力を発揮してみせます ➡I promise to demonstrate my English ability in the proficiency exam tomorrow.
志望校 one's choice school, a school of one's choice	現役で志望校(大学)に入りたいと思っています ➡I'd like to enter the university of my choice directly upon graduation.
事務室 an (administration) office	必要な書類をもらいに事務室に行って来ました ➡I've been to the office to get the necessary papers[documents].
締め切り a deadline, a due date	このレポートの締め切りはいつですか ➡When is the deadline for this report?
終業式 a closing ceremony (held on the last day of the school term)	アメリカの学校では終業式を行いますか ➡Do you hold closing ceremonies at American schools?
習熟度 the degree of advancement [mastery]	習熟度別のクラス分けをどう思われますか ➡What do you think of the division of classes according to the degree of advancement?
就職 finding a job[occupation], finding employment	カナダの高校では就職の世話をしてくれますか ➡Do high schools in Canada give assistance in finding employment?
授業 a class, a lesson	アメリカの学校生活についての授業はとても楽しかったです ➡We've enjoyed your class on American school life very much.
授業参観日 a parent's open [visiting] day	あすは保護者参観があるそうです ➡I hear the students' parents will sit in on[observe] classes tomorrow.
宿題 homework, an assignment	いつまでに宿題を提出すればいいのですか ➡When is the deadline for the assignment?
受験 taking an (entrance) examination	英語の受験勉強はどうすればいいか教えてください ➡Please tell us how we should prepare for the English entrance exams.
出席日数 the number of days of attendance, the required attendance	出席日数が足りなくなりそうです ➡I don't think I will satisfy the attendance requirement.
出席簿 a roll (book), an attendance book	私がきょうの出席簿の係です ➡I'm in charge of the roll book today.
(教師用の)準備室 a teachers' preparation room	この準備室は少し狭いので生徒全員は入り切りません ➡This preparation room is a bit small, so not all the students fit in.

職員室 a teachers' room, a staffroom, a faculty room
生徒の多くが職員室に呼ばれるとどきどきするようです
➡Most students appear to feel uneasy when they are called to the staffroom.

書類選考 screen records, school record screening
まずは書類選考をパスしなければなりません
➡First of all, you have to pass a school record screening.

進級 (a) promotion
単位不足で進級できない生徒がいます
➡Some students cannot be promoted to the next grade due to a lack of credits.

進度 progress
授業の進度が速過ぎてついていけません
➡I'm afraid the class is progressing too fast for me to keep up.
中間考査までに各クラスの授業の進度をそろえておかなければなりません
➡Every class must cover the same material by midterm exam.

進路指導 (career) guidance counseling
２人の先生が進路指導にあたっています
➡Two teachers provide career guidance counseling.

推薦入学 admission by [on] recommendation
推薦入学の欠点はどこにあると思われますか
➡What do you think are the shortcomings of admission on recommendation?

正解 a correct [right] answer
この問題の正解を教えてくださいませんか
➡Could you tell me the correct answer to this question?

生活指導 guidance about school life; civic guidance (教育上の)
中には頻繁に生活指導を必要とする生徒もいるのではないかと思います
➡I think some students often need guidance about school life [school regulations].

成績 a score, a mark, a grade, a result
奨学金をもらうにはどの程度の成績が必要ですか
➡What kind of grades do I need to win a scholarship?
ここのところ英語の成績があまり芳しくないのです
➡I'm afraid my English grades [scores] are not very good these days.

成績表 a report card
高校の成績表について日本とアメリカとの違いは何ですか
➡What are the differences between Japan and the States regarding high school report cards?

生徒会 a student council (自治会); a students' meeting (総会)
生徒会の運営は生徒の自主性に任せてもらいたいと思います
➡The administration of the student council should be left to the students.

生徒会長 the president of a student council
私は生徒会長の選挙に出るつもりです
➡I'm going to run for president of the student council.

生徒指導 student guidance
ときには厳しい生徒指導も必要なのではないでしょうか
➡I think that strict student guidance is sometimes necessary.

生徒数 the number of students; (an) enrollment (在籍者数)
このところ高校の生徒数が徐々に減る傾向にあります
➡Recently there has been a gradual decrease in the number of high school students.

生徒手帳 a student handbook, a student ID
カナダの高校生も生徒手帳を持っているのですか
➡Do high school students have [carry] student handbooks in Canada?

席次 ranking [standing] (成績の); seating order (席順)
クラスでの席次を知りたいのですが
➡I'd like to know my class ranking [how I rank in my class].

選挙 (an) election
彼女は選挙で学級委員に選ばれました
➡She was chosen as a class representative by election.

選挙管理委員 a student in charge of school elections (学校の)
私は今度の選挙の選挙管理委員の１人です
➡I'm among the students in charge of the next (school) election.

選択科目 an elective (subject)
どの教科が選択科目になるのですか
➡What subjects are elective?

選抜試験 a screening test, a selective exam(ination)	あすの選抜試験には必ず合格してみせます ➡I'm sure I'll pass[succeed in] the screening test tomorrow.
専門 a specialty, a major (専攻科目)	大学での専門は何でしたか ➡What was your major at college[the university]?
専門科目[教科] a special subject; a major field (of study) (専門分野)	カナダの大学では一般に専門科目で何単位取る必要がありますか ➡How many credits are students generally required to earn in their major field at Canadian universities?
早退 early[earlier] leaving	気分がすぐれないので早退してもいいですか ➡I'm not feeling well. May I leave class[school] early?
相談 a talk, consultation	授業のあとでちょっとご相談したいことがあるのですが ➡I have something to talk to you about after class.
卒業式 graduation[commencement] exercises, (a) graduation [commencement]	アメリカでの卒業式はどのようなものですか ➡ What's graduation in the U.S. like?
卒業証書 a diploma, a certificate of graduation	卒業証書は一人一人に手渡しされるそうです ➡I hear that diplomas are handed out to each student.
体育祭 an athletic meet [festival], a field day, a sports day	オーストラリアの高校でも体育祭を行いますか ➡Do you have athletic meets at Australian high schools?
退学 leaving[quitting] school, (a) withdrawal from school	家庭の事情で退学する生徒が何人かいます ➡Some students leave school (before graduation) for family reasons.
退学処分 expulsion from school	万引きで退学処分になった生徒もいます ➡Some students were expelled from school for shoplifting.
体験学習 experiential learning, learning by [through] experience, hands-on learning	先生の国ではどんな体験学習に人気がありますか ➡What kind of experiential[hands-on] learning is popular in your country?
体罰 corporal punishment	体罰は日本の学校では認められていません ➡Corporal punishment is not allowed in Japanese schools.
代返 answering the roll (call) for[in place of] others	だれか代返してくれないかなあと思います ➡I hope someone will answer the roll call for me.
単位 a credit (学科の)	アメリカの大学ではふつう卒業するのに何単位必要ですか ➡How many credits do I need to graduate from an American university? この科目は何単位もらえますか ➡How many credits do I get for this subject?
短縮授業 a shortened school hour	きょうは40分の短縮授業になるそうです ➡I hear each period will be shortened to 40 minutes today.
男女共学 coeducation	生徒数の全般的な減少により男女共学の学校が増えています ➡The number of coeducational schools is increasing due to the overall decrease in the number of students.
遅刻 tardiness, lateness	私はめったに学校に遅刻したことがありません ➡I've seldom been late for school.
知能指数 an intelligence quotient (IQ)	高い知能指数は賢さと同意ではありません ➡Having a high IQ[intelligence quotient] doesn't mean that someone is smart[should not be equated with being smart].
中間試験[考査] a midterm exam(ination)	英語の中間試験はいつですか ➡When are we going to have the midterm(exam) in English?

中高一貫教育 unified[integrated] education from junior through senior high school	**生徒にとっては中高一貫教育が望ましいと考える先生もいます** ➡Some teachers think that unified [integrated] education from junior to senior high school is desirable.
中(途)退(学)者 a (school) dropout	**中退者の増加が深刻な問題になっています** ➡The increase in school dropouts has become a serious problem.
長(期)欠(席) a long absence	**長欠する生徒が徐々に増えてきました** ➡The number of students who take a long absence from school[who are absent from school for a long time] has gradually increased.
朝礼 a morning assembly [meeting]	**朝礼はオーストラリアの学校でもふつうのことですか** ➡Is a morning assembly a common practice at schools in Australia?
追試(験) a makeup (exam), a supplementary examination	**できれば英語の追試は避けたいと思っているのですが** ➡I hope I won't have to take a makeup in English.
通信教育 a correspondence course	**通信教育で大学卒業資格を得るのは大変でしょうか** ➡Is it difficult [hard] to get a college degree by taking correspondence courses?
詰め込み cramming (教育の)	**詰め込み勉強では英語は上達しないと思います** ➡I don't think we can improve our English (ability) by cramming.
停学 (a) suspension from school	**3日間の停学処分になった生徒が何人かいます** ➡Some students were suspended from school for three days.
定期試験[考査] a regular [periodic] exam(ination)	**アメリカの高校でも定期試験がありますか** ➡Do they have periodic tests in American high schools as well?
提出期限 a deadline; a due date (締め切り日)	**提出期限を延ばしていただけませんか** ➡Could you postpone[put off] the deadline?
テスト範囲 a range of a test[an exam]	**テスト範囲はどこからどこまでですか** ➡What does the test cover?
点呼 a roll call	**朝何時に点呼をとるおつもりですか** ➡What time in the morning are you going to take attendance[have roll call]?
転校 (a) transfer to another school, (a) change of one's school	**私は子どものころ何度も転校を余儀なくされました** ➡I was compelled to change schools many times when I was a child.
転校生 a transfer student	**今度の転校生は帰国子女です** ➡The new transfer student has recently returned from overseas.
添削 (a) correction	**私の英作文を添削していただけませんか** ➡Could you correct my English composition?
点数 a score; a grade [mark] (試験の)	**試験に合格するには何点とればいいのですか** ➡What score do I need to get to pass the exam?
答案用紙 an answer sheet	**答案用紙は裏返しにするのですか** ➡Should I turn over my answer sheet?
同級生 a classmate	**彼は高校の同級生でした** ➡He and I were classmates in high school[were high school classmates].
登校拒否 (a) refusal to attend [go to] school, school truancy	**このごろ生徒はさまざまな理由で登校拒否をします** ➡Students refuse to attend[go to] school for various reasons these days.

同窓生 a schoolmate; a fellow student
ときどきは同窓生にメールします
➡I sometimes e-mail[send e-mails to] my schoolmates.

当番 one's duty (任務); one's turn (順番)
きょうの当番は私です ➡I'm on duty today.
教室の掃除は生徒が当番でやります
➡Students take turns cleaning their classroom.

特殊学級 a special class
障害児のための特殊学級を担当されたことがおありですか
➡Have you ever been in charge of a special class for disabled children?

難易度 degree of difficulty
それらの問題を難易度で分けていただけませんか
➡Could you classify these questions according to their difficulty?

日直 day duty (任務); a student in charge of day duty (担当者)
私は今度の金曜日が日直です
➡I'm on day duty this (coming) Friday.

入学式 an entrance[enrollment] ceremony
先生の国でも入学式は行われますか
➡Do you hold entrance ceremonies in your country?

入(学)試(験) an entrance exam(ination)
だれもが大学入試に備えて猛勉強中です
➡Everybody is studying hard to prepare for the university entrance exams.

抜き打ち試験 a pop quiz, a surprise test
私たちの英語の先生はしょっちゅう抜き打ち試験をします
➡Our English teacher gives us pop quizzes very often.

能力別クラス編成 tracking, ability grouping
能力別クラス編成の利点はどこにあるとお考えですか
➡What do you think are the advantages[good points] of arranging classes according to ability?

発音 pronunciation
イギリス英語とアメリカ英語の発音の主な違いは何ですか
➡What are the main differences in pronunciation between British English and American English?

早引け early[earlier] leaving
頭が痛いので早引けしてもいいですか
➡Could I go home early? I have a headache.

範囲 a range, an area, limits
試験は主にどの範囲が出るのですか
➡What areas will be covered in the exam mainly?

美術(教)室 an art room
私はよく美術室でデッサンの練習をします
➡I often practice drawing[making] sketches in the art room.

筆記試験 a written exam[examination]
英語の筆記試験にはけっこう自信があります
➡I'm quite confident about written exams in English.

筆記体 cursive, script
先生が筆記体で書くと読みにくいのですが
➡I'm afraid your cursive writing is rather hard[difficult] to read.

必修科目 a required[compulsory] subject
英語が必修科目でなかったらいいのになあと思うことがあります
➡I sometimes wish English weren't[wasn't] a compulsory[required] subject.

評定 rating, (an) evaluation
さまざまな角度からの人物評定が望ましいと思います
➡I think it's desirable to evaluate a person from different angles.

風紀委員 a student in charge of discipline (学校の)
今度の風紀委員はみんなにすごく口うるさく注意します
➡The new student in charge of discipline persistently nags at the other students.

復学 (a) return to school
私はまもなく復学できると思います
➡I'll be able to return[go back] to school soon[before long].

復習 (a) review, revision
あとで復習したいのできょうの授業のポイントを教えてもらえますか
➡Could you tell us key points of today's class so that we can review them later?

服装規定 a dress code
先生の国の学校には厳しい服装規定がありますか
➡Do schools in your country have strict dress codes?

不正入学 dishonest[unfair] admission(s), backdoor admission(s)
不正入学は恥ずべき行為だと思います
➡I think that backdoor admission (to college) is a disgraceful [shameful] practice.

普通科目[教科] an ordinary [a general] subject
オーストラリアの高校でも普通科目と専門科目が区別されていますか
➡Do you make a distinction between ordinary subjects and special subjects in Australian high schools?

プリント a printed sheet; a handout（授業などで配る）
プリントは全部で何枚ありますか
➡How many handouts are we supposed to have?

文科系 (the) humanities（人文科学）
自分には文科系が向いているように思います
➡It seems that majoring in one of the humanities would suit me.

文化祭 a school festival
カナダの高校でも文化祭を行いますか
➡Do you hold school festivals in Canadian high schools?

文型 a sentence pattern
この文は第何文型ですか
➡Which sentence pattern does this sentence fall into?

平均点 an average score [mark]
今度の英語の平均点は何点でしたか
➡What was the average score for English this time?

平常点 a mark for one's classwork
成績に平常点は加味されますか
➡Does our classwork[class participation] affect our grades?

偏差値 *hensachi*, a T-score, a standard score
偏差値教育をどう思われますか
➡What do you think of education strongly based on T-scores?

ホームルーム a homeroom (class), a homeroom (hour)
今度のホームルームでは修学旅行について話し合います
➡We're going to discuss the school trip in the next homeroom (hour).

補欠入学 admission [entrance] to fill a vacancy
アメリカでは大学への補欠入学はよくあることですか
➡Is admission to a university to fill a vacancy common in the States?

保健室 a (school) nurse's room[office], a sickroom
私は気分が悪くて保健室で休みました
➡I felt sick and took a rest in the (school) nurse's room.

補講 a supplementary lecture, a make-up class
いつ補講がありますか
➡When are we going to have a make-up (class)?

補習 a supplementary class[lesson]
英語の補習を受けたいと思っています
➡I'd like to take[attend] a supplementary class[lesson] in English.

丸暗記 rote-learning, rote memorization[learning]（学習の）
英語の上達に丸暗記が役立つこともあると思います
➡I think that rote memorization sometimes helps our English (ability) improve.

○×式テスト a true-false test
私たちの英語の先生は，授業で毎回短い○×式テストを出します
➡Our English teacher gives us a short true-false test in every class.

満点 a perfect score, full marks
今度の英語のテストでは満点を取る自信があります
➡I'm confident of getting a perfect score on the next English test.

無期停学 (a) suspension from school for an indefinite period
彼は無期停学処分を受けました
➡He was suspended from school for an indefinite period (of time).

面接試験 an interview; an oral examination（口頭試問）
就職の面接試験ではどんなことに注意しなければいけませんか
➡What things should I pay attention to[be careful about] in a job interview?

申し込み an application（応募）; a reservation（予約）; an order（注文）	**英検の申し込みの期限はいつまでですか** ➡When is the application deadline for the Eiken test?
申込書 an application; an application form（用紙）	**奨学金の申込書の提出期限はいつですか** ➡When is the deadline for submitting an application for the scholarship?
模擬店 a refreshment stand[booth]	**うちのクラスはたこ焼きの模擬店を出すつもりです** ➡Our class is planning to open[run] a refreshment stand of *takoyaki*.
模（擬）試（験） a practice exam(ination), a mock exam	**今度の英語の模試では何としても満点を取ってみせます** ➡No matter what it takes, I'll get a perfect score in the next English practice exam.
問題 a question, a problem	**英語のテストに出そうな問題を教えていただけませんか** ➡Could you tell us some questions likely to come up on the English test?
問題用紙 a question sheet	**問題用紙を持って帰ってもいいですか** ➡May I take the question sheet home?
野外活動 outdoor activities	**カナダの高校ではどのような野外活動が盛んですか** ➡What outdoor activities are popular at Canadian high schools?
ゆとりのある教育 more relaxed[flexible] education (policy), depressu-rized education	**ゆとりのある教育の意義が生徒に正しく理解されているとお考えですか** ➡Do you think students correctly understand the meaning of the more relaxed[flexible] education policy?
養護教諭 a school nurse	**養護教諭の仕事はほんとうに大変だなと思います** ➡I think the job of a school nurse is really hard[tough].
予習 preparation	**先生の授業にはどのような予習をしておけばいいですか** ➡How should I prepare for your class?
予備校 a *yobiko*, a college prep school, a cram(ming) school	**オーストラリアにも（日本の）予備校（のようなもの）がありますか** ➡Do you have college prep schools in Australia?
落第 (a) failure	**なんとか英語は落第しないようにがんばります** ➡I'll study hard so that I don't fail[flunk] English.
理科系 (the) sciences	**どちらかというと大学は理科系に進みたいと思っています** ➡I'd rather pursue a (college) degree in the sciences.
履修 completion (of a course)	**少なくとも30科目は履修したいと思っています** ➡I'd like to take at least 30 courses.
留学 studying overseas [abroad]	**イギリスの大学に留学するにはどうすればいいのですか** ➡What should I do to study at a British university?
留年 repeating a year	**アメリカの高校では留年する生徒が多いですか** ➡Do many students have to repeat a year in American high schools?
履歴書 a résumé, one's personal history	**履歴書を持参したほうがいいでしょうか** ➡Should I bring my résumé with me?
レポート a (term) paper（学生の論文）; a report（報告書，記事）	**あすには必ずレポートを提出します** ➡I promise to hand in my paper tomorrow.
浪人 a ronin	**どうしても浪人したくはありません** ➡I want to go to college directly after high school (without being a ronin).

協力：大阪市立生野工業高校英語科

数・数式の英語表現

ここでは，年月日や時間，年齢などを伝える基本表現から，数学で使われる計算式や割合など，数に関する英語表現をまとめてあります．英語の表記は読み方を示すために１語１語スペルアウトしてあります．

1　西暦・年月日

・1964年
nineteen sixty-four
・2000年
two thousand
・2021年
two thousand twenty-one / twenty twenty-one
・2022年８月３日
《米》8/3/2022
August (the) third, twenty twenty-two
《英》3/8/2022
(the) third (of) August, twenty twenty-two
・私は1999年３月23日に生まれました．
I was born on March (the) twenty-third, nineteen ninety-nine.
・私は平成６年に生まれました．
I was born in the sixth year of the Heisei era. / I was born in Heisei six.
・賞味期限：2022年２月12日
Best before: Feb. 12, 2022 [Feb. (the) twelfth, two thousand twenty-two]

2　世紀

・21世紀は日本では2001年に始まりましたが，2000年からだとする国もあります．
The twenty-first century started in two thousand and one in Japan, but in some countries it started in two thousand.
・それは紀元前２世紀に建てられました．
It was built in the second century B.C.
（B.C. は before Christ の略）
・これらの絵は12世紀に描かれたものです．
These pictures were painted in the twelfth century.

3　年齢

・18歳以上の市民に選挙権があります．
Every citizen aged eighteen or over has the right to vote.
・18歳未満入場お断り（映画など）．
No One Under Eighteen Admitted.
・12歳以下の子どもは入場無料です．
Admission is free for children aged 12 and under.
・日本人の４人に１人は65歳以上です．
One in four Japanese people is over sixty-five years old.
（厳密には over sixty-five は「66歳以上」となる）

4　時刻・時間

・午前０時
midnight / twelve midnight
・正午
noon / twelve noon
・午前６時15分です．
It's six fifteen a.m. / It's fifteen[a quarter] past [after] six in the morning.
・午後２時30分です．
It's two thirty p.m. / It's half past two in the afternoon.
・午後８時50分です．
It's eight fifty p.m. / It's ten to nine in the evening.
・彼は100メートルを９秒95で走りました．
He ran one hundred meters in nine point nine five seconds.
・ローマ行き624便は午前11時07分に29番ゲートより出発します．
Flight six two four to Rome will depart from gate twenty-nine at eleven oh seven a.m.

5　お金

・私は１セント硬貨を５枚，10セントを３枚，25セントを２枚持っています．
I have five pennies, three dimes and two quarters.
・それは12ドル98セントです．
That will be twelve (dollars and) ninety-eight (cents).
（dollars，cents はよく省略される）
・それは５ユーロ25セントです．
That will be five (euros and) twenty-five (cents).
（euros，cents はよく省略される）
・１ドルは現在110円です．
One dollar is currently valued at one hundred ten yen.

付録

6　得点

・得点
point, goal（サッカー）, run（野球）
・私たちのチームが３対０で勝ちました.
Our team won (by a score of) three to nothing.
・私たちは２点差で勝っています［負けています］.
We are two points [goals, runs] ahead [behind].
・彼らのチームは７回表［裏］に５点を取りました.
Their team scored five runs in the top [bottom] of the seventh inning.

7　人口・大きい数

・日本の人口は約１億2500万（125,000,000）人です.
The population of Japan is about one hundred and twenty-five million.
・東京の人口は約1400万（14,000,000）人です.
Tokyo Metropolis has a population of about fourteen million.
・世界の人口はもうすぐ80億（8,000,000,000）に届くでしょう.
The world's population will reach 8 billion soon.
・日本の2020年の輸出総額は641億ドルでした.
Japan exports totaled sixty-four point one billion dollars in two thousand twenty.

8　順位

・私は100m走で１位［２位］になりました.
I won[took] the first [second] place in a one-hundred-meter race.
・私はそのマラソンレースで優勝しました.
I won the marathon race.
・私はコンテストで４位になりました.
I won the fourth in the contest.
・私は後ろから２番で終わりました.
I finished second to last.

9　順番・番号

・私はクラスで５番です.
I am (the) fifth in the class.
・私はその写真の左から３番目です.
I'm the third from the left in the picture.
・私の席は15列目です.
My seat is in the fifteenth row.
・36ページの円グラフ２を見てください.
Look at pie chart two on page thirty-six.
・彼は今日, 38号ホームランを打ちました.
He hit his thirty-eighth home run today.

10　等級

・これは一級河川です.
This is a class A river.
・２級の試験に合格すれば２級の証明書がもらえます.
If you pass the second level exam, you'll get a level two certificate.
・彼は一流［二流］の詩人です.
He is a first-rate [second-rate] poet.

11　回数

・１回/２回/３回/何回も
once / twice / three times / many times
・２・３回
two or three times / a few [a couple of] times
・あなたはハワイに何回行きましたか.
　－５回です.
How many times have you been to Hawaii?
　－ (I've been there) Five times.
・結婚20周年を祝いました.
We celebrated our twentieth wedding anniversary.

12　比較・倍数

・２倍
twice / two times / double
・３倍
three times / triple
・…倍
… times
・100億の100倍は１兆です.
One hundred times ten billion is one trillion.
・あの力士の体重は私の３倍あります.
That sumo wrestler weighs three times as much as I do.
・イギリスの人口は日本の約半分です.
The population of the UK is half as large as that of Japan.
・私は新しい仕事に就いて, 給料が３倍になりました.
I got a new job and my salary tripled.

13　割合・配分

・この大学の競争率は７倍です.
The admission rate of this university is seven to one.
・AとBを４対１の割合で混ぜなさい.
Mix A and B at a ratio four to one.
・人体の70％は水です.
Seventy percent of the human body is water.
・それを３割引きで買いました.
I got it at a thirty percent discount.

・その会社は年間30%成長しています. That company is growing at thirty percent per year.

・勝負は五分五分です.
The chances of winning are even. / You have a fifty-fifty chance of winning.

・12：9＝4：3
Twelve is to nine as four is to three.

・半分ずつにしよう. Let's share it equally.

14 分数・小数・累乗・根

★$\frac{1}{2}$, $\frac{1}{4}$以外は, 分子を基数, 分母を序数にする.

・$\frac{1}{2}$
a half

・$\frac{1}{4}$
a quarter

・$\frac{3}{4}$
three quarters / three fourths

・$\frac{1}{3}$
one[a] third

・$\frac{2}{3}$
two thirds

★分子と分母の数が大きいときは,「分子 over 分母」で表す. その場合, 分子, 分母ともに基数.

・$\frac{29}{33}$ twenty-nine over thirty-three

★帯分数

$2\frac{2}{3}$ two and two thirds

★小数点は point と読み, 小数点以下は順に数を並べる.

・12.345
twelve point three four five

★2乗は square, 3乗は cube, 4乗は the fourth (power)

・3^2
three squared / the square of three

・3^3
three cubed / the cube of three

・3^4
three to the fourth power

★2乗根は the square [second] root, 3乗根は the cube [third] root, n乗根は the nth root

・$\sqrt{5}$
the square root of five

・$\sqrt[3]{3}$
the cube root of three

・$1\frac{3}{4}$は1.75と同じです.
One and three quarters is the same as one point seven five.

・4の平方根は2と−2です.
The square roots of four are two and minus two.

15 平均

・15, 18, 20, 21の平均は18.5です.
The average of fifteen, eighteen, twenty and twenty-one is eighteen point five.

・先月の平均気温は25度でした.
The average temperature last month was twenty-five degrees Celsius.

・このテストの平均点は60点です.
The average score of this test is sixty.

16 合計

・合計で15万（150,000）円になります.
That comes to one hundred (and) fifty thousand yen. / That totals one hundred (and) fifty thousand yen.

・合計1万（10,000）人が集まりました.
A total of ten thousand people gathered there.

17 長さ（身長・高さ・距離）

★長さの単位
1 inch＝約2.54 centimeters
1 foot (feet)＝12 inches＝約30.48 centimeters
1 yard＝3 feet＝91.44 centimeters
1 mile＝1,760 yards＝約1,609 meters

・私の身長は173センチ［5フィート8インチ］です.
I am one hundred (and) seventy-three centimeters [five eight [five feet eight inches]] tall.

・富士山は3776メートルです.
Mt. Fuji is three thousand seven hundred (and) seventy-six meters high.

・フルマラソンは42.195キロメートルです.
A full marathon is forty-two point one nine five kilometers long.

18 面積

1 are＝100 m^2(square meters)
1 hectare＝100 ares＝10,000 m^2
1 acre＝約40 ares＝約4,046.7 m^2

・一辺が1mの正方形の面積は1m^2です.
A square with sides of one meter has an area of one square meter.
・日本の面積は約37万8000平方キロメートルです.
The area of Japan is about three hundred seventy-eight thousand square kilometers.
・その農地は30ヘクタールほどです.
The farmland is about thirty hectares.

19 体積

1 milliliter (mL)＝1 cubic centimeter (cc)
1 deciliter (dL)＝100 milliliters
1 liter (L)＝1000 milliliters
1 kiloliter (kL)＝1000 liters
1 pint＝《米》約0.47 liters, ＝《英》約0.57 liters
1 gallon＝《米》3.785 liters, ＝《英》4.546 liters
1 barrel＝《米で石油の場合》42 gallons＝約159 liters
1 m^3＝1 cubic meter＝1,000,000 cc

・このペットボトルは500ミリリットル入りです.
This plastic bottle holds five hundred milliliters.
・サウジアラビアは1日1200万バレルの石油を生産している.
Saudi Arabia produces twelve million barrels of oil per day.

20 体重・重さ

1 mg＝1 milligram
1 g＝1 gram＝1,000 milligrams
1 kg＝1 kilogram＝1,000 grams
1 t＝1 ton＝1,000 kilograms
1 oz.＝1 ounce＝28.35 grams
1 lb.＝1 pound＝16 ounces＝453.6 grams

・このスーツケースの重さは20ポンドです.
This suitcase weighs twenty pounds.
・私の体重は60キロです.
I weigh sixty kilograms.
・このトラックの最大積載量は25トンです.
This truck has a maximum load capacity of twenty-five tons.

21 速度

・その車は時速60キロで走っています.
The car is going sixty kilometers per hour.
・彼は時速100マイルの速球を投げます. He throws one hundred miles per hour fastball.
・音は秒速約340メートルです.
Sound travels at a speed of about three hundred and forty meters per second. / The speed of sound is about three hundred and forty meters per second.

22 温度

・この部屋の温度は26度で, 外は零下10度です.
The temperature in this room is twenty-six degrees Celsius and it's minus ten degrees [ten degrees below zero] outside.
・華氏では100度は摂氏約38度です.
One hundred degrees Fahrenheit is about thirty-eight degrees Celsius.

23 角度・緯度・経度

・角度90度は直角です.
An angle that measures ninety degrees is a right angle.
・三角形の内角の和は180度です.
The sum of the internal angles of a triangle is one hundred eighty degrees.
・その市は東経135度, 北緯35度に位置しています.
The city is located at one hundred thirty-five degrees east longitude[135° E] and thirty-five degrees north latitude[35° N].

24 加減乗除

・$2+3=5$
Two plus three is [equals] five. / Two and three makes five.

・$\frac{2}{3}+\frac{3}{5}=1\frac{4}{15}$
Two thirds plus three fifths is one and four fifteenths.

・$8-6=2$
Eight minus six is [equals] two. / Six from eight is two.

・$\frac{1}{3}-\frac{1}{2}=-\frac{1}{6}$
One third minus one half is negative one sixth.

・$4\times 6=24$
Four multiplied by six is twenty-four.

・$2.1\times 1.1=2.31$
Two point one multiplied by one point one is two point three one.

・$8\div 4=2$
Eight divided by four is two.

・$20 \div 3 = 6\ \text{r}\ 2$ [6 rem 2,　6あまり2]
Twenty divided by three is six with a remainder of two.

・$\dfrac{4 \times (2+7)}{6} = 6$
Multiplying the sum of two and seven by four, and dividing the result by six is six.

25 等式・不等式

・$A = B$
A equals B. / A is equal to B.

・$A \neq B$
A is not equal to B. / A differs from B.

・$A > B$
A is greater than B.

・$A < B$
A is less than B.

・$A \geqq B$
A is greater or equal to B.

・$x^2 + 2x - 2 > 1$
x squared plus two x minus two is greater than one.

26 関数・方程式・幾何

・$y = 2x + 3$
y equals two x plus three.

・$2x^2 + 3x + 4 = 0$
Two x squared plus three x plus four equals zero.

・$x = \dfrac{-b \pm \sqrt{b^2 - 4ac}}{2a}$
x equals negative b plus or minus the square root of b squared minus four ac all over two a.

・$a^2 = b^2 + c^2$
a squared equals b squared plus c squared.

・$(a+b)^2 = a^2 + 2ab + b^2$
The quantity of a plus b squared equals a squared plus two ab plus b squared.

・$x = a^3 + \dfrac{2}{(a^4 - 1)^2}$
x equals a cubed plus two over the quantity of a to the fourth power minus one, squared.

・$p(x) = \sum_{k=0}^{n} a_k x^k$
The polynomial function p of x equals the sum from k equals zero to n of a sub k times x to the k.

・$\sin(A+B) = \sin A \cos B + \cos A \sin B$
Sine of the quantity A plus B equals sine A cosine B plus cosine A sine B.

・$\cos(A+B) = \cos A \cos B - \sin A \sin B$
Cosine of the quantity A plus B equals cosine A cosine B minus sine A sine B.

・$\tan(A+B) = \dfrac{\tan A + \tan B}{1 - \tan A \tan B}$
Tangent of the quantity A plus B equals tangent A plus tangent B all over the quantity one minus tangent A tangent B.

・$\sin^2\theta + \cos^2\theta = 1$
Sine squared (of) theta plus cosine squared (of) theta equals one.

・$a^{-n} = \dfrac{1}{a^n}$
a to the negative n equals one over a to the n.

・$\sum_{k=1}^{n} 1 = n$
The sum from k equals one to n of one equals n.

27 順列・組み合わせ

・${}_nP_r = \dfrac{n!}{(n-r)!}$
The number of permutations of n total elements taken r selected elements at a time equals factorial n divided by factorial of the quantity n minus r.

・${}_nC_r = {}_nC_{n-r}$
The combination of n taken r equals the combinations of n taken n minus r. (Of the n total number of elements, ${}_nC_r$ means the number of possible combinations with r number of selections from the set n. This is then equal to the number of combinations of 'n-r' elements within the set n.)

・${}_nC_r = \dfrac{n!}{r!(n-r)!}$
The combinations of n taken r at a time equals n factorial divided by r factorial times n minus r factorial.

・$(a+b)^n = \sum_{r=0}^{n} {}_nC_r a^{n-r} b^r$
The quantity a plus b to the n equals the sum from r equals zero to n of the number of combinations of n elements taken r at a time times a to the power of the quantity n minus r, times b to the r.

28 微分・積分

・$f(x) = \lim_{h \to 0} \frac{f(x+h) - f(x)}{h}$

f prime of *x* equals the limit, as *h* tends to zero, of *f* of the quantity *x* plus *h*, minus *f* of *x* over *h*.

・$F(x) = \int f(x)\,dx + C$

Antiderivative *F* of *x* equals the integral of *f* of *x* times *dx* plus a constant *C*.

・$\int_a^b f(x)\,dx \equiv \lim_{n \to \infty} \sum_{k=0}^{n-1} f\left(a + k\frac{b-a}{n}\right) \frac{b-a}{n}$

The integral from *a* to *b* of *f* of *x d x* is defined to be the limit as *n* tends to infinity of the sum from *k* equals zero to *n* minus one of the function *a* plus *k* times the quantity *b* minus *a*, over *n*, times the quantity *b* minus *a*, over *n*.

・$\frac{d}{dx}\int_a^x f(z)\,dz = f(x)$

The derivative of the integral from *a* to *x* of the function *f* of *z d z* equals *f* of *x*.

・$F(x)$をxで微分しなさい.

Differentiate *F* prime of *x* with respect to *x*.

29 対数

・$\log x$

$\log x$ / log of *x*

・$\log_2 x$

log of *x* to the base two

・$\log x^n = n \log x$

log of *x* to the *n*th power equals *n* times log of *x*

30 ベクトル・行列

・$\vec{v} = \overrightarrow{PQ}$

The vector *v* equals the vector PQ.

・$\overrightarrow{PQ} = \overrightarrow{OQ} - \overrightarrow{OP}$

The vector PQ equals the vector OQ minus the vector OP.

・$|\vec{v}|$はベクトルvの長さを表す.

The norm of *v* denotes the length of the vector *v*.

・単位ベクトルの大きさは1である.

The magnitude of a unit vector is one.

・$\vec{v} = \begin{pmatrix} v_1 \\ v_2 \\ v_3 \end{pmatrix}$

The vector *v* equals the three by one matrix *v* sub one, *v* sub two, and *v* sub three.

31 確率・統計

・$0 \leqq P(A) \leqq 1$

The probability of the event *A* takes values between zero and one, including 0 and 1.

・$P(A^c) = 1 - P(A)$

The probability of the complement of *A* equals one minus the probability of *A*.

32 集合

・$a \in A$（要素aは集合Aに属する）

The element *a* is a member of set *A*. / *a* is in *A*. /*A* contains *a*.

・$A = \phi$（Aは空集合である）

A equals the empty set.

・$C = A \cap B$

C equals the intersection of *A* and *B*.

・$N = \{n | {}^\forall n \text{ natural number}\}$

The symbol *N* represents the set of all natural numbers.

・$A \times B \equiv \{(a, b | {}^\forall a \in A, {}^\forall b \in B\}$

The Cartesian product (cross product) of *A* and *B* is defined to be the set of all ordered pairs, (*a*, *b*) for any *a* in *A* and any *b* in *B*.

・$\prod_{k=1}^{n} A_k$

The Cartesian product from *k* equals one to *n* of *A* sub *k*.

世界の国名・首都名

193の国連加盟国を50音順に一覧してある(2012年現在). 配列順序は次のようになっている. 国名(日本語)/国名(英語)/発音/①形容詞形と～人[語]/②～人(形容詞形と異なる場合)/③首都名(英語と日本語)/補注➤

ア行

アイスランド　Iceland /áɪslənd/ ①Icelandic ②Icelander ③Reykjavik (レイキャビク)

アイルランド　Ireland /áɪəˈlənd/ ①Irish ③Dublin (ダブリン) ➤アイルランドの成人男性[女性]はIrishman[Irishwoman]ともいう.

アゼルバイジャン　Azerbaijan /àːzəˈbaɪdʒáːn/ ①Azerbaijani ③Baku (バクー)

アフガニスタン　Afghanistan /æfgǽnəstæn/ ①Afghan ③Kabul (カブール)

アメリカ合衆国　the United States of America (USA) /əmérɪkə/ ① American ③ Washington, D.C. (ワシントンD.C.) ➤the U.S.やthe U.S.A. と省略形を用いることが多い. America, the States(合衆国)ともいう.

アラブ首長国連邦　the United Arab Emirates (UAE) /ærəb émərəts/ ① Emirati ③ Abu Dhabi (アブダビ)

アルジェリア　Algeria /ældʒíəriə/ ①Algerian ③Algiers (アルジェ)

アルゼンチン　Argentina /àːˈdʒəntíːnə/ ① Argentine ②Argentinian ③Buenos Aires (ブエノスアイレス)

アルバニア　Albania /ælbéɪniə/ ①Albanian ③Tirana (ティラナ)

アルメニア　Armenia /ɑːˈmíːniə/ ①Armenian ③Yerevan (エレバン)

アンゴラ　Angola /æŋgóʊlə/ ① Angolan ③Luanda (ルアンダ)

アンティグア・バーブーダ　Antigua and Barbuda /æntíːgə ən bɑːˈbjúːdə/ ① Antiguan ③ St. John's (セントジョンズ)

アンドラ　Andorra /ændɔ́ːrə/ ①Andorran ③Andorra la Vella (アンドララベリャ)

イエメン　Yemen /jémən/ ①Yemeni ③Sanaa (サヌア)

イギリス　Britain /brítn/ ①British ③London (ロンドン) ➤正式名:the United Kingdom of Great Britain and Northern Ireland(グレートブリテンおよび北部アイルランド連合).

イスラエル　Israel /ízriəl/ ①Israeli ③Jerusalem (エルサレム) ➤国際的には未承認.

イタリア　Italy /ítəli/ ①Italian ③Rome (ローマ)

イラク　Iraq /ɪráːk/ ①Iraqi ③Baghdad (バグダッド)

イラン　Iran /ɪráːn/ ①Iranian ③Tehran (テヘラン)

インド　India /índiə/ ①Indian ③New Delhi (ニューデリー)

インドネシア　Indonesia /ìndəníːʒə/ ①Indonesian ③Jakarta (ジャカルタ)

ウガンダ　Uganda /jugǽndə/ ① Ugandan ③Kampala (カンパラ)

ウクライナ　Ukraine /jukréɪn/ ①Ukrainian ③Kiev (キエフ)

ウズベキスタン　Uzbekistan /ʊzbékɪstæn/ ①Uzbek ③Tashkent (タシケント)

ウルグアイ　Uruguay /jʊ́ərəgwaɪ/ ①Uruguayan ③Montevideo (モンテビデオ)

エクアドル　Ecuador /ékwədɔːˈ/ ①Ecuadorian または Ecuadorean ③Quito (キト)

エジプト　Egypt /íːdʒɪpt/ ①Egyptian ③Cairo (カイロ)

エストニア　Estonia /estóʊniə/ ①Estonian ③Tallinn (タリン)

エスワティニ　Eswatini /eswatíni/ ①Eswatini ③Mbabane (ムババーネ)

エチオピア　Ethiopia /ìːθióʊpiə/ ①Ethiopian ③Addis Ababa (アディスアベバ)

エリトリア　Eritrea /erìtréɪə/ ①Eritrean ③Asmara (アスマラ)

エルサルバドル　El Salvador /el sǽlvədɔːˈ/ ①Salvadoran, Salvadorian ③San Salvador (サンサルバドル)

オーストラリア　Australia /ɔːstréɪljə/ ① Australian ③Canberra (キャンベラ)

オーストリア　Austria /ɔ́ːstriə/ ①Austrian ③Vienna (ウィーン)

オマーン　Oman /oʊmáːn/ ①Omani ③Muscat (マスカット)

オランダ　the Netherlands /néðəˈləndz/ ①Dutch ② Dutchman[Dutchwoman] ③Amsterdam (アムステルダム) ➤別名:Holland

カ行

ガーナ　Ghana /gáːnə/ ①Ghanaian ③Accra (アクラ)

カーボベルデ　Cape Verde /kèɪp vɜ́ːˈd/ ①Cape Verdean ③Praia (プライア)

ガイアナ　Guyana /gaɪáːnə/ ① Guyanese ③Georgetown (ジョージタウン)

カザフスタン　Kazakhstan /kæ̀zækstáːn/ ①Kazakh ③Nur-Sultan (ヌルスルタン)

カタール　Qatar /káːtɑːˈ/ ①Qatari ③Doha (ドーハ)

カナダ　Canada /kǽnədə/ ① Canadian ③ Ottawa (オタワ)

ガボン　Gabon /gəbóʊn/ ① Gabonese ③ Libreville (リーブルビル)

カメルーン Cameroon /kæ̀mərúːn/ ①Cameroonian ③Yaoundé (ヤウンデ)

韓国 South Korea /sàʊθ kəríːə/ ①South Korean ③Seoul (ソウル) ➤正式名: the Republic of Korea(大韓民国).

ガンビア Gambia /gǽmbiə/ ①Gambian ③Banjul (バンジュール)

カンボジア Cambodia /kæmbóʊdiə/ ①Cambodian ③Phnom Penh (プノンペン)

北朝鮮 North Korea /nɔ̀ːʳθ kəríːə/ ①North Korean ③Pyongyang (ピョンヤン) ➤正式名: the Democratic People's Republic of Korea (朝鮮民主主義人民共和国).

北マケドニア North Macedonia /nɔ̀ːʳθ mæ̀sɪdóʊniə/ ①North Macedonian ③Skopje (スコピエ)

ギニア Guinea /gíni/ ①Guinean ③Conakry (コナクリ)

ギニアビサウ Guinea-Bissau /gìnibɪsáʊ/ ①Guinea-Bissauan ③Bissau (ビサウ)

キプロス Cyprus /sáɪprəs/ ①Cypriot ③Nicosia (ニコシア)

キューバ Cuba /kjúːbə/ ①Cuban ③Havana (ハバナ)

ギリシャ Greece /griːs/ ①Greek ③Athens (アテネ)

キリバス Kiribati /kìːrɪbáːti/ ①Kiribati ③Tarawa (タラワ)

キルギス Kyrgyz /kìrgɪs/ ①Kyrgyz ③Bishkek (ビシュケク)

グアテマラ Guatemala /gwɑ̀ːṭəmáːlə/ ①Guatemalan ③Guatemala City (グアテマラシティー)

クウェート Kuwait /kuwéɪt/ ①Kuwaiti ③Kuwait City (クウェートシティー)

グレナダ Grenada /grənéɪdə/ ①Grenadian ③St. George's (セントジョージズ)

クロアチア Croatia /kroʊéɪʃə/ ①Croatian ②Croat ③Zagreb (ザグレブ)

ケニア Kenya /kénjə/ ①Kenyan ③Nairobi (ナイロビ)

コートジボアール Côte d'Ivoire /kòʊt diːvwáːʳ/ ①Ivorian ③Yamoussoukro (ヤムスクロ)

コスタリカ Costa Rica /kòʊstə ríːkə/ ①Costa Rican ③San José (サンホセ)

コモロ the Comoros /káːməroʊz/ ①Comoran ③Moroni (モロニ)

コロンビア Colombia /kəlʌ́mbiə/ ①Colombian ③Bogotá (ボゴタ)

コンゴ共和国 Congo /káːŋgoʊ/ ①Congolese ③Brazzaville (ブラザビル)

コンゴ民主共和国 the Democratic Republic of the Congo /dèməkræṭɪk rɪ̀pʌblɪk əv ðə káːŋgoʊ/ ①Congolese ③Kinshasa (キンシャサ)

サ行

サウジアラビア Saudi Arabia /sàʊdi əréɪbiə/ ①Saudi Arabian ③Riyadh (リヤド)

サモア Samoa /səmóʊə/ ①Samoan ③Apia (アピア)

サントメ・プリンシペ São Tomé and Principe /sàʊ təméɪ ən prínsɪpeɪ/ ①São Tomean ③São Tomé (サントメ)

ザンビア Zambia /zǽmbiə/ ①Zambian ③Lusaka (ルサカ)

サンマリノ San Marino /sæn məríːnoʊ/ ①San Marinese ③San Marino (サンマリノ)

シエラレオネ Sierra Leone /siérə lióʊn/ ①Sierra Leonean ③Freetown (フリータウン)

ジブチ Djibouti /dʒɪbúːti/ ①Djiboutian ③Djibouti (ジブチ)

ジャマイカ Jamaica /dʒəméɪkə/ ①Jamaican ③Kingston (キングストン)

ジョージア Georgia /dʒɔ́ːʳdʒə/ ①Georgian ③Tbilisi (トビリシ)

シリア Syria /síriə/ ①Syrian ③Damascus (ダマスカス)

シンガポール Singapore /síŋgəpɔːʳ/ ①Singaporean ③Singapore (シンガポール)

ジンバブウェ Zimbabwe /zɪmbáːbwi/ ①Zimbabwean ③Harare (ハラレ)

スイス Switzerland /swítsəʳlənd/ ①Swiss ③Bern(e) (ベルン)

スウェーデン Sweden /swíːdn/ ①Swedish ②Swede ③Stockholm (ストックホルム)

スーダン Sudan /su(ː)dǽn/ ①Sudanese ③Khartoum (ハルツーム)

スペイン Spain /speɪn/ ①Spanish ②Spaniard ③Madrid (マドリード)

スリナム Surinam(e) /sʊ̀ərənáːm/ ①Surinamese ③Paramaribo (パラマリボ)

スリランカ Sri Lanka /sriː láːŋkə/ ①Sri Lankan ③Sri Jayawardenapura Kotte (スリジャヤワルダナプラコッテ) ➤旧Ceylon.

スロバキア Slovakia /sloʊvǽkiə/ ①Slovak, Slovakian ③Bratislava (ブラチスラバ)

スロベニア Slovenia /sloʊvíːniə/ ①Slovene, Slovenian ③Ljubljana (リュブリャナ)

セーシェル Seychelles /sèɪʃélz/ ①Seychellois ③Victoria (ビクトリア)

赤道ギニア Equatorial Guinea /ìːkwətɔ́ːriəl gíni/ ①Equatorial Guinean ③Malabo (マラボ)

セネガル Senegal /sènɪgɔ́ːl/ ①Senegalese ③Dakar (ダカール)

セルビア Serbia /sə́ːʳbiə/ ①Serbian ②Serb/ ③Belgrade (ベオグラード)

セントキッツネビス Saint Kitts and Nevis /seɪnt kìts ən níːvɪs/ ①Kittitian, Nevisian ③Basseterre (バステール) ➤Saint Christopher and Nevisともいう.

セントビンセント及びグレナディーン諸島 Saint Vincent and the Grenadines /seɪnt vínsənt ən ðə grènədíːnz/ ①Vincentian ③Kingstown (キングズタウン)

セントルシア Saint Lucia /seɪnt lúːsiə/ ①Saint Lucian ③Castries (カストリーズ)

ソマリア Somalia /səmáːliə/ ①Somali ③Mogadishu (モガディシュ)

ソロモン諸島 the Solomon Islands /sáːləmən àɪləndz/ ①Solomon Islander ③Honiara (ホニアラ)

タ行

タイ Thailand /táɪlænd/ ①Thai /taɪ/ ③Bangkok（バンコク）
タジキスタン Tajikistan /tɑːdʒíːkɪstɑ̀ːn/ ①Tajik ③Dushanbe（ドゥシャンベ）
タンザニア Tanzania /tænzəníːə/ ①Tanzanian ③Dodoma（ドドマ）
チェコ the Czech Republic /tʃèk rɪpʌ́blɪk/ ①Czech ③Prague（プラハ）
チャド Chad /tʃæd/ ①Chadian ③N'Djamena（ンジャメナ）
中央アフリカ the Central African Republic /sèntrəl æfrɪkən rɪpʌ́blɪk/ ①Central African ③Bangui（バンギ）
中国 China /tʃáɪnə/ ①Chinese/tʃàɪníːz/ ③Beijing [Peking]（北京）➤正式名: the People's Republic of China（中華人民共和国）
＊日本人にはなじみのある都市名ではあるが，英語表記と発音に注意しなければならない主な都市: 広東（省） Guangdong/gwɑ̀ːŋdóŋ/ (province) / 桂林 Guilin/gwèɪlín// 広州 Guangzhou/gwɑ̀ːŋdʒóʊ// 四川（省） Sichuan/sìtʃwɑ́ːn/ (province) / 上海 Shanghai/ʃæŋháɪ// 重慶 Chongqing/tʃùŋkíŋ// 西安 Xi'an/ʃiːɑ́ːn// 蘇州 Suzhou/sùːdʒóʊ// 大連 Dalian/dɑ̀ːliǽn// 天津 Tianjin/tiɑːndʒín// 南京 Nanjing/nɑːndʒíŋ/
チュニジア Tunisia /tjuníːʒə/ ①Tunisian ③Tunis（チュニス）
チリ Chile /tʃíli/ ①Chilean ③Santiago（サンティアゴ）
ツバル Tuvalu /tuvɑ́ːluː/ ①Tuvaluan ③Funafuti（フナフティ）
デンマーク Denmark /dénmɑːʳk/ ①Danish /déɪnɪʃ/ ②Dane ③Copenhagen（コペンハーゲン）
ドイツ Germany /dʒə́ːʳməni/ ①German ③Berlin（ベルリン）
トーゴ Togo /tóʊgoʊ/ ①Togolese ③Lomé（ロメ）
ドミニカ Dominica /dɑ̀ːmɪníːkə/ ①Dominican ③Roseau（ロゾー）
ドミニカ共和国 the Dominican Republic /dəmìnɪkən rɪpʌ́blɪk/ ①Dominican /dɑːmɪníːkən/ ③Santo Domingo（サントドミンゴ）
トリニダード・トバコ Trinidad and Tobago /trìnɪdæd ən təbéɪgoʊ/ ①Trinidadian ③Port of Spain（ポートオブスペイン）
トルクメニスタン Türkmenistan /tə̀ːʳkmenɪstǽn/ ①Turkmenian ②Turkman ③Ashgabat [Ashkhabad]（アシガバート）
トルコ Turkey /tə́ːʳki/ ①Turkish ②Turk ③Ankara（アンカラ）
トンガ Tonga /tɑ́ːŋgə/ ①Tongan ③Nuku'alofa（ヌクアロファ）

ナ行

ナイジェリア Nigeria /naɪdʒíəriə/ ①Nigerian ③Abuja（アブジャ）
ナウル Nauru /nərúː/ ①Nauruan ③Yaren（ヤレン）
ナミビア Namibia /nəmíbiə/ ①Namibian ③Windhoek（ウィントフック）
ニカラグア Nicaragua /nìkərɑ́ːgwə/ ①Nicaraguan ③Managua（マナグア）
ニジェール Niger /náɪdʒəʳ/ ①Nigerien ③Niamey（ニアメ）
日本 Japan /dʒəpǽn/ ①Japanese ③Tokyo（東京）
ニュージーランド New Zealand /njùː zíːlənd/ ①New Zealand ②New Zealander ③Wellington（ウェリントン）
ネパール Nepal /nəpɔ́ːl/ ①Nepalese ③Kat(h)mandu（カトマンズ）
ノルウェー Norway /nɔ́ːʳweɪ/ ①Norwegian ③Oslo（オスロ）

ハ行

バーレーン Bahrain /bɑːréɪn/ ①Bahraini ③Manama（マナーマ）
ハイチ Haiti /héɪṭi/ ①Haitian ③Port-au-Prince（ポルトープランス）
パキスタン Pakistan /pǽkɪstæn/ ①Pakistani ③Islamabad（イスラマバード）
パナマ Panama /pǽnəmɑː/ ①Panamanian ③Panama City（パナマシティ）
バヌアツ Vanuatu /vænuɑ́ːtuː/ ①Vanuatuan ③Port Vila（ポートビラ）
バハマ Bahamas /bəhɑ́ːməz/ ①Bahamian ③Nassau（ナッソー）
パプアニューギニア Papua New Guinea /pæpuə njùː gíni/ ①Papua New Guinean ③Port Moresby（ポートモレスビー）
パラオ Palau /pəláʊ/ ①Palauan ③Melekeok（マルキョク）
パラグアイ Paraguay /pǽrəgwaɪ/ ①Paraguayan ③Asuncion（アスンシオン）
バルバドス Barbados /bɑːbéɪdoʊs/ ①Barbadian ③Bridgetown（ブリッジタウン）
ハンガリー Hungary /hʌ́ŋgəri/ ①Hungarian ③Budapest（ブダペスト）
バングラデシュ Bangladesh /bæŋglədéʃ/ ①Bangladeshi ③Dhaka（ダッカ）
東ティモール East Timor /ìːst tíːmɔːʳ/ ①East Timorese ③Dili（ディリ）
フィジー Fiji /fíːdʒiː/ ①Fijian ③Suva（スバ）
フィリピン the Philippines /fíləpiːnz/ ①Philippine ②Filipino ③Manila（マニラ）
フィンランド Finland /fínlənd/ ①Finnish ②Finn ③Helsinki（ヘルシンキ）
ブータン Bhutan /bùːtɑ́ːn/ ①Bhutanese ③Thimphu（ティンプー）
ブラジル Brazil /brəzíl/ ①Brazilian ③Brasília（ブラジリア）

フランス France /fræns/ ①French ③Paris（パリ）➤フランスの成人男性[女性]はFrenchman[Frenchwoman]ともいう.

ブルガリア Bulgaria /bʌlgéəriə/ ①Bulgarian ③Sofia（ソフィア）

ブルキナファソ Burkina Faso /bəʳkì:nə fá:soʊ/ ①Burkinabe ③Ouagadougou（ワガドゥグ）

ブルネイ Brunei /brú:naɪ/ ①Bruneian ③Bandar Seri Begawan（バンダルスリブガワン）

ブルンジ Burundi /bʊrʊ́ndi/ ①Burundian ③Bujumbura（ブジュンブラ）

ベトナム Viet Nam /vì:etná:m/ ①Vietnamese ③Hanoi（ハノイ）

ベナン Benin /bení:n/ ①Beninese ③Porto Novo（ポルトノボ）

ベネズエラ Venezuela /vènəzwéɪlə/ ①Venezuelan ③Caracas（カラカス）

ベラルーシ Belarus /bèlərú:s/ ①Belorussian ③Minsk（ミンスク）

ベリーズ Belize /bɪlí:z/ ①Belizean ③Belmopan（ベルモパン）

ペルー Peru /pərú:/ ①Peruvian ③Lima（リマ）

ベルギー Belgium /béldʒəm/ ①Belgian ③Brussels（ブリュッセル）

ポーランド Poland /póʊlənd/ ①Polish ②Pole ③Warsaw（ワルシャワ）

ボスニア・ヘルツェゴビナ Bosnia and Herzegovina /bá:zniə ən hə:ʳtsəgəví:nə/ ①Bosnian ③Sarajevo（サラエボ）

ボツワナ Botswana /bɑ:tswá:nə/ ①Botswanan または Tswana ③Gaborone（ハボローネ）

ボリビア Bolivia /bəlíviə/ ①Bolivian ③La Paz（ラパス）

ポルトガル Portugal /pɔ́:ʳtʃəgəl/ ①Portuguese ③Lisbon（リスボン）

ホンジュラス Honduras /hɑ:ndjʊ́ərəs/ ①Honduran ③Tegucigalpa（テグシガルパ）

マ行

マーシャル諸島 the Marshall Islands /mà:ʳʃəl áɪləndz/ ①Marshallese ②Marshall Islander ③Majuro（マジュロ）

マダガスカル Madagascar /mædəgæskəʳ/ ①Malagasy ③Antananarivo（アンタナナリボ）

マラウィ Malawi /məlá:wi/ ①Malawian ③Lilongwe（リロングウェ）

マリ Mali /má:li/ ①Malian ③Bamako（バマコ）

マルタ Malta /mɔ́:ltə/ ①Maltese ③Valletta（バレッタ）

マレーシア Malaysia /məléɪʒə/ ①Malaysian ③Kuala Lumpur（クアラルンプール）

ミクロネシア連邦 Micronesia /màɪkrəní:ʒə/ ①Micronesian ③Palikir（パリキール）

南アフリカ South Africa /sàʊθ æfrɪkə/ ①South African ③Pretoria（プレトリア）

南スーダン South Sudan /sàʊθ sudæn/ ①South Sudanese ③Juba（ジュバ）

ミャンマー Myanmar /mjá:nmɑ:ʳ/ ①Myanmarese ③Naypyidaw（ネーピードー）

メキシコ Mexico /méksɪkòʊ/ ①Mexican ③Mexico City（メキシコシティー）

モーリシャス Mauritius /mɔ:ríʃəs/ ①Mauritian ③Port Louis（ポートルイス）

モーリタニア Mauritania /mɔ̀:rətéɪniə/ ①Mauritanian ③Nouakchott（ヌアクショット）

モザンビーク Mozambique /mòʊzəmbí:k/ ①Mozambican ③Maputo（マプト）

モナコ Monaco /má:nəkoʊ/ ①Monacan, Monegasque ③Monaco（モナコ）

モルディブ the Maldives /mɔ́:ldaɪvz/ ①Maldivian ③Malé（マレ）

モルドバ Moldova /mɑ:ldóʊvə/ ①Moldovan ③Chisinau（キシニョフ）

モロッコ Morocco /mərá:koʊ/ ①Moroccan ③Rabat（ラバト）

モンゴル Mongolia /mɑ:ŋgóʊliə/ ①Mongolian ③Ulan Bator（ウランバートル）➤モンゴル人[語]はMongolともいう.

モンテネグロ Montenegro /mà:ntɪní:groʊ/ ①Montenegrin ③Podgorica（ポドゴリツァ）

ヤ行

ヨルダン Jordan /dʒɔ́:ʳdn/ ①Jordanian ③Amman（アンマン）

ラ行

ラオス Laos /lá:oʊs/ ①Laotian ③Vientiane（ビエンチャン）

ラトビア Latvia /lǽtviə/ ①Latvian ③Riga（リガ）

リトアニア Lithuania /lìθuéɪniə/ ①Lithuanian ③Vilnius（ビリニュス）

リビア Libya /líbiə/ ①Libyan ③Tripoli（トリポリ）

リヒテンシュタイン Liechtenstein /líktənstaɪn/ ①Liechtenstein ②Liechtensteiner ③Vaduz（ファドーツ）

リベリア Liberia /laɪbíəriə/ ①Liberian ③Monrovia（モンロビア）

ルーマニア Romania /roʊméɪniə/ ①Romanian ③Bucharest（ブカレスト）

ルクセンブルク Luxembourg /lʌ́ksəmbə̀:ʳg/ ①Luxembourgian ②Luxembourger ③Luxembourg（ルクセンブルク）

ルワンダ Rwanda /ruá:ndə/ ①Rwandan ③Kigali（キガリ）

レソト Lesotho /ləsóʊtoʊ/ ①Sotho ②Mosotho ③Maseru（マセル）

レバノン Lebanon /lébənən/ ①Lebanese ③Beirut（ベイルート）

ロシア Russia /rʌ́ʃə/ ①Russian ③Moscow（モスクワ）➤Russian Federation（ロシア連邦）をさす.

世界の人名

歴史上の人物から，現在各分野で活躍している著名人まで，英米人を中心に選んだ．生没年のないものは生存中の人物である（2021年現在）．

ア

アーチャー, ジェフリー　Jeffrey Archer（イギリスの小説家）
アービング, ジョン　John Irving（アメリカの小説家）
アームストロング船長　Neil A. Armstrong（アメリカの宇宙飛行士；人類で初めて月面に着陸；1930-2012）
アイアコッカ, リー　Lee Iacocca（アメリカの実業家；自動車メーカー，クライスラーを再興した；1924-2019）
アイゼンハワー, ドワイト　Dwight D. Eisenhower（アメリカの第34代大統領；愛称 Ike；1890-1969）
アインシュタイン, アルバート　Albert Einstein（ドイツからアメリカへ帰化した理論物理学者；1879-1955）
アウン・サン・スー・チー　Aung San Suu Kyi（ミャンマーの民主化運動の指導者）
アップダイク, ジョン　John Updike（アメリカの小説家；1932-2009）
アラファト, ヤセール　Yasser Arafat（PLO[パレスチナ解放機構]議長；1929-2004）
アリ, モハメド　Muhammad Ali（アメリカのヘビー級ボクサー；1981年引退；1942-2016）
アリストテレス　Aristotle（古代ギリシャの哲学者；384-322 B. C.）
アルキメデス　Archimedes（古代ギリシャの数学者，物理学者；287?-212 B. C.）
アルフレッド大王　Alfred the Great（古代イギリスの王；849-899）
アレキサンダー大王　Alexander the Great（マケドニア王；356-323 B. C.）
アンデルセン, ハンス　Hans Christian Andersen（デンマークの童話作家；1805-75）

イ

イェーツ, W. B.　William Butler Yeats（アイルランドの詩人，劇作家；1865-1939）
イソップ　Aesop（古代ギリシャの寓話作家；620?-560? B. C.）
イプセン, ヘンリック　Henrik Ibsen（ノルウェーの劇作家，詩人；1828-1906）

ウ

ウィリアムズ, ジョン　John Williams（アメリカの映画音楽作曲家）
ウィリアムズ, テネシー　Tennessee Williams（アメリカの劇作家；1911-83）
ウェブスター, ノア　Noah Webster（アメリカの辞書編さん家；1758-1843）
ウェルズ, オーソン　Orson Welles（アメリカの映画俳優，映画監督，演出家；1915-85）
ウォーホール, アンディ　Andy Warhol（アメリカの画家，映画監督；1928-87）

エ

エジソン, トマス　Thomas Alva Edison（アメリカの発明家；1847-1931）
エバンス, ビル　Bill Evans（アメリカのジャズピアニスト；1929-80）
エラリー・クイーン　Ellery Queen（アメリカの2人の推理作家，またその作品に登場する探偵の名；本名は Frederic Dannay (1905-82) と Manfred B. Lee (1905-71)で，2人はいとこどうし）
エリオット, T. S.　Thomas Stearns Eliot（イギリスの詩人，評論家；1888-1965）
エリザベス女王　Queen Elizabeth II（イギリス女王）；Queen Elizabeth I（イギリス女王；在位1558-1603）
エル・グレコ　El Greco（スペインの宗教画家；名は「ギリシャ人」の意の通称；1541-1614）
エンデ, ミヒャエル　Michael Ende（ドイツの児童文学作家；1929-95）

オ

オーウェル, ジョージ　George Orwell（イギリスの作家．本名 Eric A. Blair；1903-50）
オースティン, ジェーン　Jane Austen（イギリスの小説家；1775-1817）
オー・ヘンリー　O. Henry（アメリカの短編作家．本名 William Sydney Porter；1862-1910）
オールコット　Louisa May Alcott（アメリカの作家；1832-88）
オバマ, バラク　Barack Hussein Obama, Jr.（アメリカ第44代大統領）
オリビエ, ローレンス　Sir Laurence Olivier（イギリスの俳優，監督；1907-89）

カ

ガーシュイン, ジョージ　George Gershwin（アメリカの作曲家；1898-1937）
カーター, ジミー　Jimmy Carter（アメリカ第39代大統領；本名 James Earl Carter, Jr.）
カーネギー, アンドリュー　Andrew Carnegie（アメリ

カの鉄鋼王，慈善家；1835–1919）
カーネル・サンダース Colonel Sanders（ケンタッキー・フライド・チキン創業者；Colonel は「大佐」の意；1890–1980）
ガウディ, アントニオ Antonio Gaudi（スペインの建築家.「カーサ ミラ」「聖家族教会」で有名；1852–1926）
ガガーリン, ユーリ Yuri A. Gagarin（ロシアの宇宙飛行士. 人類で最初に宇宙を飛んだ；1934–68）
カサノバ Giovanni Jacopo Casanova（イタリアの作家；「女たらし」の代名詞；1725–98）
カザルス, パブロ Pablo Casals（スペインのチェリスト，指揮者；1876–1973）
カザン, エリア Elia Kazan（アメリカの俳優，演出家，映画監督；1909–2003）
カストロ, フィデル Fidel Castro（キューバの政治家，革命家. 元国家評議会議長（首相に相当）；1926–2016）
カフカ, フランツ Franz Kafka（チェコ生まれ，オーストリアの作家；1883–1924）
カポーティ, トルーマン Truman Capote（アメリカの作家；1924–84）
カポネ, アル Al Capone（アメリカのギャングの首領；1899–1947）
ガマ, バスコ・ダ Vasco da Gama（ポルトガルの航海者；1469?–1524）
カミュ, アルベール Albert Camus（フランスの作家；1913–60）
カラヤン, ヘルベルト・フォン Herbert von Karajan（オーストリアの指揮者；1908–89）
ガリレオ・ガリレイ Galileo Galilei（イタリアの天文学者，物理学者；1564–1642）
ガルシア・マルケス Gabriel Garcia Marquez（コロンビアの作家；1927–2014）
ガンジー, マハトマ Mahatma Gandhi（インドの宗教指導者，社会改革家；Mahatma は「偉大なる魂」の意；1869–1948）
カンディンスキー, ワシリー Wassily Kandinsky（ロシアの抽象画家；1866–1944）
カント, イマヌエル Immanuel Kant（ドイツの哲学者；1724–1804）

キ

キーシン, エフゲニー Evgeny Kissin（ロシアのピアニスト）
キーツ, ジョン John Keats（イギリスの詩人；1795–1821）
キッシンジャー, ヘンリー Henry Alfred Kissinger（アメリカの政治学者，政治家）
キム・イルソン（金日成） Kim Il Sung（北朝鮮の元最高指導者；1912–94）
キム・ジョンイル（金正日） Kim Jong Il（北朝鮮の前最高指導者；1941–2011）
キム・ジョンウン（金正恩） Kim Jong-Eun（北朝鮮の最高指導者）
キャパ, ロバート Robert Capa（ハンガリー生まれの報道写真家；1913–54）
キャメロン, ジェームズ James Cameron（アメリカの映画監督）
キャロル, ルイス Lewis Carroll（イギリスの童話作家. 本名 Charles Lutwidge Dodgson；1832–98）
キューブリック, スタンリー Stanley Kubrick（アメリカの映画監督；1928–99）
キュリー, マリー Marie Curie（ポーランド生まれ，フランスの化学・物理学者；1867–1934）
キリスト, イエス Jesus Christ（キリスト教の宗祖；4? B. C.–29? A. D.）
キング, スティーブン Stephen King（アメリカの怪奇小説家）
キング, マーティン・ルーサー Martin Luther King, Jr.（アメリカの牧師，黒人の公民権獲得運動の指導者；暗殺された；1929–68）

ク

クーベルタン Pierre de Coubertin（フランスの教育家；近代オリンピック提唱者；1863–1937）
クック, ジェームズ James Cook（オーストラリアや南洋諸島を探検したイギリスの航海者；1728–79）
クビライカン Kublai Khan（中国，元の皇帝；1215–94）
クライスラー, フリッツ Fritz Kreisler（オーストリア生まれのバイオリニスト；1875–1962）
グリーグ, エドバルド Edvard Grieg（ノルウェーの作曲家；1843–1907）
グリーン, グレアム Graham Greene（イギリスの小説家；1904–91）
クリスティ, アガサ Agatha Christie（イギリスの推理作家；1890–1976）
グリム兄弟 the Brothers Grimm（ドイツの民間伝承研究家，言語学者；『グリム童話』を著す；兄 Jacob（1785–1863），弟 Wilhelm （1786–1859））
クリントン, ビル Bill Clinton（アメリカ第42代大統領；本名は William Jefferson Clinton）
クレオパトラ Cleopatra（古代エジプトの女王；69?–30 B. C.）
クロケット, デービー Davy Crockett（本名 David Crockett；アメリカ西部開拓時代の政治家で，伝説的英雄；1786–1836）
クロムウェル, オリバー Oliver Cromwell（イギリスの政治家. 清教徒革命の指導者；1599–1658）

ケ

ゲイツ, ビル Bill Gates（アメリカの実業家；マイクロソフト社共同創業者；本名 William H. Gates）
ゲーテ Johann Wolfgang von Goethe（ドイツの詩人，劇作家，小説家；1749–1832）
ケネディ, ジョン・F John Fitzgerald Kennedy（アメリカ第35代大統領；1917–63）
ケラー, ヘレン Helen Keller（アメリカの社会運動家；1880–1968）
玄宗 Xuanzong（中国，唐の皇帝；685–762）

コ

孔子 Confucius（中国，春秋時代の思想家. 儒教の開祖；中国名 K'ung Futzu；551–479 B. C.）

ゴーギャン, ポール Paul Gauguin（フランスの画家；1848-1903）
コクトー, ジャン Jean Cocteau（フランスの作家, 詩人；1889-1963）
ゴダール, ジャン・リュック Jean-Luc Godard（フランスの映画監督）
ゴッホ, ビンセント・バン Vincent van Gogh（オランダの画家；1853-90）
コッポラ, フランシス・フォード Francis Ford Coppola（アメリカの映画監督）
コペルニクス Nicolaus Copernicus（ポーランドの天文学者；1473-1543）
ゴヤ, フランシスコ Francisco José de Goya y Lucientes（スペインの画家；1746-1828）
ゴルバチョフ, ミハイル Mikhail Sergeevich Gorbachev（旧ソ連の大統領；愛称 Gorby）
コロンブス, クリストファー Christopher Columbus（イタリアの航海者；1451?-1506）

サ

サイモン, ニール Neil Simon（アメリカの劇作家；1927-2018）
ザッカーバーグ, マーク Mark Zuckerberg（アメリカの実業家, Facebookを開設）
サッチャー, マーガレット Margaret H. Thatcher（イギリスの政治家；1925-2013）
サティ, エリック Erik Satie（フランスの作曲家；1866-1925）
サド, マルキ・ド Marquis de Sade（フランスの作家. Marquis は「侯爵」; 1740-1814）
サハロフ, アンドレイ Andrei Sakharov（ロシアの核物理学者；1921-89）
ザビエル, 聖フランシスコ Saint Francis Xavier（スペインの宣教師；1506-52）
サリンジャー, J. D. Jerome David Salinger（アメリカの小説家；1919-2010）
サルトル, ジャン・ポール Jean-Paul Sartre（フランスの哲学者, 劇作家, 小説家；1905-80）
サン・テグジュペリ Antoine de Saint-Exupéry（フランスの作家, 飛行家；1900-44）
サン・ローラン, イブ Yves Saint-Laurent（フランスのファッションデザイナー；1936-2008）

シ

シーザー, ガイウス・ジュリアス Gaius Julius Caesar（古代ローマの政治家, 将軍；100?-44 B. C.）
シートン Ernest Thompson Seton（イギリス生まれ, アメリカの動物物語作家, 博物学者；1860-1946）
シーボルト Philipp Franz von Siebold（ドイツの医学者, 博物学者；1796-1866）
シェークスピア, ウィリアム William Shakespeare（イギリスの劇作家, 詩人；1564-1616）
ジェームズ, ヘンリー Henry James（アメリカ生まれ, イギリスの小説家；1843-1916）
ジェロニモ Geronimo（ネイティブ・アメリカンのアパッチ族の首長；1829-1909）
始皇帝 Shi Huangdi, Shih Huangti（中国, 秦(しん)の皇帝；259-210 B. C.）
ジバンシー Hubert de Givenchy（フランスのファッションデザイナー；1927-2018）
シベリウス, ヤン Jean Sibelius（フィンランドの作曲家；1865-1957）
釈迦(しゃか) Sakyamuni（仏陀(ぶつだ)の別称；563?-483 B. C.）
シャガール, マルク Marc Chagall（ロシア生まれ, フランスの画家；1887-1985）
シャネル, ガブリエル Gabrielle Chanel（フランスのファッションデザイナー；愛称 Coco；1883-1971）
ジャンヌ・ダルク Joan of Arc（百年戦争でフランス軍を率いイギリス軍を破って救世主と仰がれた少女. フランス名は Jeanne d'Arc；1412-31）
習近平 Xi Jinping（中国共産党総書記）
シューベルト, フランツ Franz Schubert（オーストリアの作曲家；1797-1828）
シューマン, ローベルト Robert Schumann（ドイツの作曲家；1810-56）
シュトラウス, ヨハン Johann Strauss（オーストリアの作曲家. 同名の父(1804-49)と子(1825-99)がいるが, 子が「ワルツ王」として有名）
シュトラウス, リヒャルト Richard Strauss（ドイツの作曲家；1864-1949）
シュバイツァー, アルベルト Albert Schweitzer（フランスの医者, 音楽家；1875-1965）
シュリーマン, ハインリヒ Heinrich Schliemann（ドイツの考古学者. トロイとミケーネの遺跡を発掘；1822-90）
シュルツ, チャールズ Charles Schultz（スヌーピーで有名なアメリカの漫画家；1922-2000）
ジョイス, ジェームズ James Joyce（アイルランドの小説家, 詩人；1882-1941）
ショスタコービッチ, ドミトリ Dmitrii Shostakovich（ロシアの作曲家；1906-75）
ショパン, フレデリック Frédéric François Chopin（ポーランド生まれ, フランスの作曲家, ピアニスト；1810-49）
ジョブズ, スティーブ Steve Jobs（アメリカの企業家, アップルコンピュータ社を創立；1955-2011）
シンガー, アイザック Isaac Bashevis Singer（ポーランド生まれ, アメリカの作家；1904-91）
ジンギスカン Genghis Khan（モンゴル帝国の祖；1162-1227）

ス

スウィフト, ジョナサン Jonathan Swift（アイルランド生まれ, イギリスの作家；1667-1745）
スコット, ウォルター Sir Walter Scott（スコットランドの作家, 詩人；1771-1832）
スコット, リドリー Sir Ridley Scott（イギリス生まれ, アメリカの映画監督）
スターリン Joseph V. Stalin（ロシアの政治家；1879-1953）
スタインベック, ジョン John Steinbeck（アメリカの小説家；1902-68）
スタンダール Stendhal（フランスの小説家. 本名 Marie Henri Beyle；1783-1842）
ストーン, オリバー Oliver Stone（アメリカの映画監督）
ストラビンスキー, イーゴリ Igor Stravinsky（ロシア

生まれ，アメリカの作曲家；1882-1971）
スピルバーグ，スティーブン　Steven Spielberg（アメリカの映画監督）
スメタナ，ベドルジハ　Bedřich Smetana（ボヘミアの作曲家；1824-84）

セ

セザンヌ，ポール　Paul Cézanne（フランスの画家；1839-1906）
セルバンテス　Miguel de Cervantes（Saavedra）（スペインの作家；1547-1616）
センダック，モーリス　Maurice Sendak（アメリカの絵本作家，イラストレーター；1928-2012）

ソ

荘子　Zhuangzi，Chuang-tzu（中国，戦国時代の思想家；生没年不詳）
ソクラテス　Socrates（古代ギリシャの哲学者；470?-399 B. C.）
ソルジェニツィン，アレクサンドル　Alexandr Isaevich Solzhenitsyn（ロシアの作家；1918-2008）
ソロー，ヘンリー・デビッド　Henry David Thoreau（アメリカの思想家；1817-62）
ソロモン王　King Solomon（古代イスラエルの王；生没年不詳）
孫文　Sun Wen，Sun Wên，Sun Yat-sen（中国の政治家，革命家；1866-1925）

タ

ダーウィン，チャールズ　Charles Darwin（イギリスの博物学者，進化論者；1809-82）
ターナー，J. M. W.　Joseph Mallord William Turner（イギリスの風景画家；印象派の先駆者の一人；1775-1851）
ダイアナ妃　Princess Diana（イギリスのチャールズ元皇太子妃；パリで自動車事故死；1961-97）
タウト，ブルーノ　Bruno Taut（ドイツの建築家；1880-1938）
ダライ・ラマ　the Dalai Lama（チベット仏教の最高指導者）
タランティーノ，クウェンティン　Quentin Tarantino（アメリカの映画監督）
ダリ，サルバドール　Salvador Dali（スペインの画家；1904-89）
ダンカン，イサドラ　Isadora Duncan（アメリカのダンサー．自由な動きを取り入れてモダンバレエを創始した；1878-1927）
ダンテ　Dante Alighieri（イタリアの詩人；1265-1321）

チ

チェーホフ，アントン　Anton Pavlovich Chek(h)ov（ロシアの作家，劇作家；1860-1904）
チェ・ゲバラ　Che Guevara（キューバの革命指導者；1928-67）
チャーチル，ウィンストン　Sir Winston Churchill（イギリスの政治家，著述家；1874-1965）
チャールズ皇太子　Prince Charles（イギリス皇太子．正式な称号は the Prince of Wales）
チャイコフスキー，ピョートル　Pyotr（Peter）Ilich Tchaikovsky（ロシアの作曲家；1840-93）
チョーサー，ジェフリー　Geoffrey Chaucer（イギリスの詩人；1340?-1400）
チョムスキー，ノーム　Noam Chomsky（アメリカの言語学者．変形生成文法を創始）

ツ

ツタンカーメン　Tutankhamen（古代エジプトの王；生没年不詳）
ツルゲーネフ，イワン　Ivan Sergeevich Turgenev（ロシアの小説家；1818-83）

テ

ディキンソン，エミリー　Emily Dickinson（アメリカの詩人；1830-86）
ディケンズ，チャールズ　Charles Dickens（イギリスの小説家；1812-70）
ディズニー，ウォルト　Walt Disney（アメリカの漫画家，映画製作者；ミッキー・マウスやドナルド・ダックを生み，ディズニーランドを作った；1901-66）
ディラン，ボブ　Bob Dylan（アメリカのフォークとロックのシンガーソングライター；本名 Robert Allen Zimmerman）
デービー・クロケット　→クロケット
デカルト，ルネ　René Descartes（フランスの哲学者，数学者；1596-1650）
デフォー，ダニエル　Daniel Defoe（イギリスの小説家，ジャーナリスト；1660-1731）
デュマ，アレクサンドル　Alexandre Dumas（フランスの小説家，劇作家；親子で，父は Dumas père（デュマ・ペール；1802-70），子は Dumas fils（デュマ・フィス；1824-95）と呼び分ける）
テレサ　→マザー・テレサ

ト

ドイル，コナン　Sir Arthur Conan Doyle（イギリスの探偵小説家；シャーロック・ホームズの生みの親；1859-1930）
トインビー，アーノルド　Arnold J. Toynbee（イギリスの歴史家；1889-1975）
トウェイン，マーク　Mark Twain（アメリカの作家．本名 Samuel Langhorne Clemens；1835-1910）
トールキン，ジョン　John R. R. Tolkien（イギリスのファンタジー作家；1892-1973）
ドガ，エドガー　Edgar Degas（フランスの画家；1834-1917）
ドゴール，シャルル　Charles de Gaulle（フランスの将軍，大統領；1890-1970）
トスカニーニ，アルトゥーロ　Arturo Toscanini（イタリアの指揮者；1867-1957）
ドストエフスキー，フョードル　Fyodor Mikhailovich Dostoevski（ロシアの小説家；Dostoyevskyとも表記する；1821-81）
ドビュッシー，クロード　Claude Debussy（フランスの

作曲家；1862–1918）
杜甫(とほ) Du Fu, Tu Fu（中国，唐代の詩人；712–770）
ドボルザーク，アントニン Antonín Dvořák（ボヘミアの作曲家；1841–1904）
ドラクロワ，ウジーヌ Eugène Delacroix（フランスの画家；1798–1863）
トランプ，ドナルド Donald Trump（アメリカ第45代大統領）
トリュフォー，フランソワ François Truffaut（フランスの映画監督；1932–84）
トルストイ，レフ Lev Nikolaevich Tolstoy（ロシアの作家；1828–1910）

ナ

ナイチンゲール，フローレンス Florence Nightingale（イギリスの看護師；1820–1910）
ナポレオン・ボナパルト Napoléon Bonaparte（フランスの皇帝；1769–1821）

ニ

ニーチェ，フリードリヒ Friedrich Wilhelm Nietzsche（ドイツの哲学者；1844–1900）
ニクソン，リチャード Richard Nixon（アメリカ第37代大統領；1913–94）
ニュートン，アイザック Sir Isaac Newton（イギリスの物理学者，数学者；1642–1727）

ネ

ネール Jawaharlal Nehru（インドの政治家；1889–1964）
ネルソン，ホレイショ Horatio Nelson（イギリスの提督；1758–1805）
ネロ Nero（ローマ皇帝で暴君；37–68 A. D.）

ノ

ノーベル，アルフレッド Alfred Bernhard Nobel（スウェーデンの化学者，実業家；1833–96）
ノストラダムス Nostradamus（フランスの予言者，医師，占星術師；1503–66）

ハ

ハーディ，トマス Thomas Hardy（イギリスの詩人，小説家；1840–1928）
ハーン，ラフカディオ Lafcadio Hearn（イギリスから日本に帰化した作家；日本名，小泉八雲；1850–1904）
バーンスタイン，レナード Leonard Bernstein（アメリカの指揮者，作曲家；1918–90）
バイデン，ジョー Jo Biden（アメリカ第46代大統領）
ハイドン (Franz) Joseph Haydn（オーストリアの作曲家；1732–1809）
ハイネ，ハインリヒ Heinrich Heine（ドイツの詩人；1797–1856）
バイロン George Gordon Byron（イギリスの詩人；1788–1824）
パウロ Saint Paul（キリスト教の伝道者）
パスカル，ブレーズ Blaise Pascal（フランスの数学者，哲学者；1623–62）
パスツール，ルイ Louis Pasteur（フランスの細菌学者；1822–95）
バック，パール Pearl Buck（アメリカの作家；1892–1973）
バッハ，ヨハン・セバスチャン Johann Sebastian Bach（ドイツの作曲家，オルガニスト；1685–1750）
パバロッティ，ルチアーノ Luciano Pavarotti（イタリアのテノール歌手；1935–2007）
バルザック，オノレ・ド Honoré de Balzac（フランスの小説家；1799–1850）
バルトーク，ベラ Béla Bartók（ハンガリーの作曲家；1881–1945）
ハレー，エドモンド Edmund Halley（イギリスの天文学者；1656–1742）
バレンボイム，ダニエル Daniel Barenboim（アルゼンチン生まれの指揮者，ピアニスト）
バン・ダイク Sir Anthony Van Dyck（フランドルの画家；1599–1641）

ヒ

ピアフ，エディット Edith Piaf（フランスのシャンソン歌手；Piaf は「すずめ」の意のフランス俗語．本名 Edith G. Gassion；1915–63）
ピカソ，パブロ Pablo Picasso（フランスで活躍したスペインの画家，彫刻家；1881–1973）
ビクトリア女王 Queen Victoria（イギリスの女王；1819–1901）
ビスコンティ，ルキノ Luchino Visconti（イタリアの映画監督；1906–76）
ビゼー，ジョルジュ Georges Bizet（フランスの作曲家；1838–75）
ピタゴラス Pythagoras（古代ギリシャの哲学者，数学者；580?–500? B. C.）
ヒッチコック，アルフレッド Sir Alfred Hitchcock（イギリスの映画監督；1899–1980）
ヒトラー，アドルフ Adolf Hitler（ドイツの総統；1889–1945）
ビバルディ，アントニオ Antonio Vivaldi（イタリアの作曲家；1678–1741）
ヒラリー，エドモンド Sir Edmund Percival Hillary（ニュージーランドの登山家，探検家；1919–2008）
ビリー・ザ・キッド Billy the Kid（アメリカの西部開拓時代の無法者．本名は William H. Bonney；1859–81）

フ

ファーブル，アンリ Jean-Henri Fabre（フランスの昆虫学者；1823–1915）
フィッツジェラルド，F. スコット F. Scott Fitzgerald（アメリカの作家；1896–1940）
プーシキン，アレクサンドル Aleksandr Sergeevich Pushkin（ロシアの詩人，小説家；1799–1837）
プーチン，ウラジミール Vladimir V. Putin（ロシアの

大統領）
フェリーニ，フェデリコ　Federico Fellini（イタリアの映画監督；1920–93）
フォークナー，ウィリアム　William Faulkner（アメリカの小説家；1897–1962）
フォード，ジョン　John Ford（アメリカの映画監督；1895–1973）
フォード，ヘンリー　Henry Ford（アメリカの実業家，自動車王；1863–1947）
フォスター，スティーブン　Stephen Collins Foster（アメリカの作詞作曲家；1826–64）
ブッシュ，ジョージ　George W. Bush（アメリカ第43代大統領）；George H. W. Bush（アメリカ第41代大統領；1924–2018）
プッチーニ，ジャコモ　Giacomo Puccini（イタリアのオペラ作曲家；1858–1924）
ブラームス，ヨハネス　Johannes Brahms（ドイツの作曲家；1833–97）
ブラッドベリ，レイ　Ray Douglas Bradbury（アメリカの SF 作家；本名 Raymond Douglas Bradbury；1920–2012）
プラトン　Plato（古代ギリシャの哲学者；427?–347? B. C.）
フランク，アンネ　Anne Frank（『アンネの日記』を残したドイツ生まれのユダヤ人の少女；1929–45）
フランクリン，ベンジャミン　Benjamin Franklin（アメリカの政治家，発明家；1706–90）
フランシスコ　Francis（アルゼンチン出身のローマ教皇）
ブリューゲル，ピーター　Pieter Brueghel（フランドルの画家；1525?–69）
プルースト，マルセル　Marcel Proust（フランスの小説家；1871–1922）
ブルータス，マーカス　Marcus Junius Brutus（ローマの政治家．シーザー暗殺の首謀者；85?–42 B. C.）
ブルーナ，ディック　Dick Bruna（オランダの絵本作家；1927–2017）
ブルックナー，アントン　Anton Bruckner（オーストリアの作曲家，オルガニスト；1824–96）
フルトベングラー，ウィルヘルム　Wilhelm Furtwängler（ドイツの指揮者；1886–1954）
ブレイク，ウィリアム　William Blake（イギリスの詩人，画家；1757–1827）
フロイト，ジークムント　Sigmund Freud（オーストリアの精神医学者；1856–1939）
プロコフィエフ，セルゲイ　Sergei Sergeevich Prokofiev（ロシアの作曲家；1891–1953）
ブロンテ，エミリー　Emily Brontë（イギリスの小説家；1818–48）
ブロンテ，シャーロット　Charlotte Brontë（イギリスの小説家．エミリーの姉；1816–55）

へ

ヘーゲル　Georg Wilhelm Friedrich Hegel（ドイツの哲学者；1770–1831）
ベーコン，フランシス　Francis Bacon（イギリスの哲学者，政治家；1561–1626）
ベートーベン，ルートビヒ・ファン　Ludwig van Beethoven（ドイツの作曲家；1770–1827）
ヘッセ，ヘルマン　Hermann Hesse（ドイツの詩人，小説家；1877–1962）
ベッソン，リュック　Luc Besson（フランスの映画監督）
ヘミングウェー，アーネスト　Ernest Hemingway（アメリカの小説家；1899–1961）
ベラスケス　Diego Rodríguez de Silva y Velázquez（スペインの画家；1599–1660）
ペリー　Matthew Calbraith Perry（アメリカの海軍提督；1794–1858）
ヘリング，キース　Keith Haring（アメリカの画家；1958–90）
ベル，アレキサンダー・グラハム　Alexander Graham Bell（スコットランド生まれ，アメリカの電話発明者；1847–1922）
ベルイマン，イングマル　Ingmar Bergman（スウェーデンの映画監督；1918–2007）
ベルディ，ジュゼッペ　Giuseppe Verdi（イタリアのオペラ作曲家；1813–1901）
ベルヌ，ジュール　Jules Verne（フランスの科学冒険小説家；1828–1905）
ベルリオーズ，エクトール　Hector Berlioz（フランスの作曲家；1803–69）
ペロー，シャルル　Charles Perrault（フランスの詩人，童話作家；1628–1703）
ヘンデル　George Frederic Handel（ドイツ生まれで，イギリスで活躍した作曲家；1685–1759）

ホ

ホイットマン，ウォルト　Walt Whitman（アメリカの詩人；1819–92）
ポー，エドガー・アラン　Edgar Allan Poe（アメリカの作家，詩人；1809–49）
ホーキング，スティーブン　Stephen W. Hawking（イギリスの理論物理学者，宇宙物理学者；1942–2018）
ボーボワール，シモーヌ・ド　Simone de Beauvoir（フランスの作家，評論家；1908–86）
ボッカチオ，ジョバンニ　Giovanni Boccaccio（イタリアの作家；1313–75）
ポター，ビアトリクス　Beatrix Potter（イギリスの絵本作家；1866–1943）
ホメロス　Homer（古代ギリシャの詩人）
ボルヘス　Jorge Luis Borges（アルゼンチンの作家，詩人；1899–1986）
ホロビッツ，ウラジミール　Vladimir Horowitz（ロシア生まれ，アメリカのピアニスト；1904–89）

マ

マータイ，ワンガリ　Wangari Maathai（ケニアの女性環境保護活動家；1940–2011）
マーラー，グスタフ　Gustav Mahler（オーストリアの作曲家，指揮者；1860–1911）
マキアベリ，ニッコロ　Niccolò Machiavelli（イタリアの外交家，政治思想家；1469–1527）
マザー・テレサ　Mother Teresa（インドの修道女；1910–97）
マゼラン，フェルディナンド　Ferdinand Magellan（ポルトガルの航海者；1480?–1521）

マタイ Saint Matthew（イエスの12使徒の１人）
マチス, アンリ Henri Matisse（フランスの画家；1869-1954）
マネ, エドワール Édouard Manet（フランスの画家；1832-83）
マラドーナ, ディエゴ Diego Maradona（アルゼンチンのサッカー選手；1960-2020）
マリア Mary（聖母マリア. 別称 the Virgin Mary, Saint Mary）
マリー・アントワネット Marie Antoinette（フランス王ルイ16世の妃；1755-93）
マルクス, カール Karl Marx（ドイツの経済学者, 社会主義者；1818-83）
マルコ・ポーロ Marco Polo（イタリアの旅行家；1254-1324）
マン, トーマス Thomas Mann（ドイツの作家；1875-1955）
マンシーニ, ヘンリー Henry Mancini（アメリカの映画音楽作曲家；1924-94）

ミ

ミケランジェロ Michelangelo Buonarroti（イタリアの画家, 彫刻家, 建築家；1475-1564）
ミラー, アーサー Arthur Miller（アメリカの劇作家；1915-2005）
ミラー, ヘンリー Henry Miller（アメリカの作家；1891-1980）
ミルトン, ジョン John Milton（イギリスの詩人；1608-74）
ミルン, A. A. Alan Alexander Milne（イギリスの作家, 詩人, 児童文学者；1882-1956）
ミレー, ジャン・フランソワ Jean Franois Millet（フランスの画家；1814-75）
ミロ, ホワン Joan Miró（スペインの画家；1893-1983）

ム

ムーア, ヘンリー Henry Moore（イギリスの彫刻家；1898-1986）
ムーア, マイケル Michael Moore（アメリカのジャーナリスト, 映画監督）
ムソルグスキー Modest Petrovich Mussorgsky（ロシアの作曲家；1839-81）
ムハンマド Muhammad（イスラム教の開祖. アラブの預言者；Mohammedともいう；570?-632）

メ

メータ, ズビン Zubin Mehta（インド生まれの指揮者）
メーテルリンク, モーリス Maurice Maeterlinck（ベルギーの劇作家, 詩人；1862-1949）
メニューイン, ユーディ Sir Yehudi Menuhin（アメリカのバイオリニスト；1916-99）
メンデル, グレゴール Gregor Johann Mendel（オーストリアの植物学者；1822-84）
メンデルスゾーン, フェリックス Felix Mendelssohn-Bartholdy（ドイツの作曲家；1809-47）

モ

モア, トマス Sir Thomas More（イギリスの政治家, 人文学者, 著作家；1478-1535）
孟子（もうし） Mengzi, Mencius（中国, 戦国時代の思想家；372?-289? B. C.）
毛沢東 Mao Zedong, Mao Tse-tung（中国の政治家, 共産党指導者；1893-1976）
モーゼ Moses（古代ヘブライの預言者）
モーツァルト, ウォルフガング・アマデウス Wolfgang Amadeus Mozart（オーストリアの作曲家；1756-91）
モーパッサン, ギー・ド Guy de Maupassant（フランスの作家；1850-93）
モーム, サマセット William Somerset Maugham（イギリスの小説家, 劇作家；1874-1965）
モディリアーニ, アメデオ Amedeo Modigliani（イタリアの画家；1884-1920）
モネ, クロード Claude Monet（フランスの画家；1840-1926）
モリスン, トニ Toni Morrison（アメリカの小説家；1931-2019）

ユ

ユークリッド Euclid（古代ギリシャの数学者）
ユーゴー, ビクトル Victor Hugo（フランスの作家, 詩人, 劇作家；1802-85）
ユダ Judas (Iscariot)（イエスの12使徒の１人で裏切者）
ユトリロ, モーリス Maurice Utrillo（フランスの画家；1883-1955）
ユング, カール Carl Gustav Jung（スイスの心理学者, 精神医学者；1875-1961）

ヨ

楊貴妃（ようきひ） Yang Guifei, Yang Kuifei（中国, 唐の玄宗帝の妃；719-756）
ヨー・ヨー・マ Yo-Yo Ma（フランス生まれ, アメリカのチェリスト）
ヨハネ Saint John（イエスの12使徒の１人）

ラ

ライト兄弟 the Wright Brothers（アメリカの飛行機製作者. 兄は Wilbur (1867-1912), 弟は Orville (1871-1948)）
ラガーフェルド, カール Karl Lagerfeld（ドイツ生まれのファッションデザイナー；1933-2019）
ラファエロ Raphael（イタリアの画家, 建築家. イタリア名 Raffaello Santi；1483-1520）
ラフマニノフ, セルゲイ Sergei Vasilyevich Rachmaninoff（ロシアの作曲家, ピアニスト；1873-1943）
ラベル, モーリス Maurice Ravel（フランスの作曲家；1875-1937）
ランボー, アルチュール Arthur Rimbaud（フランスの詩人；1854-91）

リ

リスト, フランツ　Franz Liszt（ハンガリーの作曲家, ピアニスト；1811-86）
リヒター, カール　Karl Richter（ドイツの指揮者, オルガン奏者；1926-81）
リビングストン, デビッド　David Livingstone（スコットランド生まれのアフリカ探検家；1813-73）
リルケ, ライナー・マリア　Rainer Maria Rilke（ドイツの詩人；1875-1926）
リンカーン, アブラハム　Abraham Lincoln（アメリカ第16代大統領；1809-65）
リンドバーグ, チャールズ　Charles A. Lindbergh（アメリカの飛行家. 1927年大西洋単独無着陸飛行に成功して英雄となる；1902-74）

ル

ルイ14世　Louis XIV（フランス王；「太陽王」の名で知られる；1638-1715）
ルーカス, ジョージ　George Lucas（アメリカの映画監督, 製作者）
ルース, ベーブ　Babe Ruth（アメリカ大リーグの強打者；Babe（赤ん坊）はあだ名で, 本名は George Herman Ruth；1895-1948）
ルーズベルト, セオドア　Theodore Roosevelt（アメリカ第26代大統領；1858-1919）
ルーズベルト, フランクリン　Franklin Delano Roosevelt（アメリカ第32代大統領；1882-1945）
ルービンスタイン, アルチュール　Arthur Rubinstein（ポーランド生まれ, アメリカのピアニスト；1887-1982）
ルーベンス, ペーター　Sir Peter Paul Rubens（フランドルの画家；1577-1640）
ルオー, ジョルジュ　Georges Rouault（フランスの画家；1871-1958）
ルソー, ジャン・ジャック　Jean Jacques Rousseau（スイス生まれ, フランスの思想家, 文学者；1712-78）
ルター, マルティン　Martin Luther（ドイツの宗教改革者；1483-1546）
ルノワール, オーギュスト　Pierre-Auguste Renoir（フランスの画家；1841-1919）

レ

レーガン, ロナルド　Ronald Wilson Reagan（アメリカ第40代大統領；1911-2004）
レーニン, ウラジミール　Vladimir Ilyich Lenin（ロシアの革命家；1870-1924）
レオナルド・ダ・ビンチ　Leonardo da Vinci（イタリアの画家, 彫刻家, 建築家, 科学者；1452-1519）
レバイン, ジェームズ　James Levine（アメリカの指揮者）
レンブラント　Rembrandt Harmensz van Rijn（オランダの画家；1606-69）

ロ

ロイド・ウェバー, アンドリュー　Andrew Lloyd Webber（イギリスのミュージカル作曲家）
老子　Lao-tsu, Lao-tzu（中国, 春秋時代の思想家；604?-531? B. C.）
ロートレック, トゥールーズ　Henri de Toulouse-Lautrec（フランスの画家；1864-1901）
ローランサン, マリー　Marie Laurencin（フランスの画家；1883-1956）
ローリング, J. K.　J. K. Rowling（イギリスの小説家；本名 Joanne Kathleen Rowling）
ローレン, ラルフ　Ralph Lauren（アメリカのファッションデザイナー）
ローレンツ, コンラート　Konrad Lorenz（オーストリアの動物行動学者；1903-89）
ロジャーズ, リチャード　Richard Rodgers（アメリカのミュージカル作曲家；1902-79）
ロダン, オーギュスト　Auguste Rodin（フランスの彫刻家；1840-1917）
ロックウェル, ノーマン　Norman Rockwell（アメリカの画家；1894-1978）
ロックフェラー, ジョン・D　John Davison Rockefeller（アメリカの資本家, 石油王；1839-1937）
ロッシーニ, ジョアッキーノ　Gioacchino Rossini（イタリアのオペラ作曲家；1792-1868）
ロラン, ロマン　Romain Rolland（フランスの作家；1866-1944）
ロレンス, D. H.　David Herbert Lawrence（イギリスの小説家, 詩人；1885-1930）
ロレンス, T. E.　Thomas Edward Lawrence（イギリスの考古学者, 軍人；通称 Lawrence of Arabia；1888-1935）

ワ

ワーグナー, リヒャルト　Richard Wagner（ドイツの楽劇作曲家；1813-83）
ワーズワース, ウィリアム　William Wordsworth（イギリスの詩人；1770-1850）
ワイアット・アープ　Wyatt Earp（アメリカの保安官で射撃の名手；1848-1929）
ワイエス, アンドリュー　Andrew Wyeth（アメリカの画家；1917-2009）
ワイダ, アンジェイ　Andrzej Wajda（ポーランドの映画監督；1926-2016）
ワイラー, ウィリアム　William Wyler（アメリカの映画監督；1902-81）
ワイルダー, ビリー　Billy Wilder（アメリカの映画監督；1906-2002）
ワイルダー, ローラ・インガルス　Laura Ingalls Wilder（アメリカの児童文学作家；1867-1957）
ワイルド, オスカー　Oscar Wilde（アイルランドの作家；1854-1900）
ワシントン, ジョージ　George Washington（アメリカ初代大統領；1732-99）
ワルター, ブルーノ　Bruno Walter（ドイツ生まれ, アメリカの指揮者；1876-1962）

英米人のファーストネーム

英米人の主なファーストネーム(姓ではなく名)の正式名と愛称を「アイウエオ」順に示した. 赤字は愛称を示す. そのあとの(<……)はその正式名を示す. ただし, 愛称を正式名としている人もいる.

ア 行

アーサー **Artur**(男) ; 《愛称》Art, Artie
アート **Art**(男)(<Arthur)
アーニー **Ernie**(男)(<Ernest)
アーネスト **Ernest**(男) ; 《愛称》Ern, Ernie
アーノルド **Arnold**(男) ; 《愛称》Arnie
アービング **Irving**(男)
アーロン **Aaron**(男)
アイザック **Isaac**(男) ; 《愛称》Ike
アイリーン **Irene, Eileen**(女)
アガサ **Agatha**(女) ; 《愛称》Aggie
アギー **Aggie**(女)(<Agnes, Agatha)
アグネス **Agnes**(女) ; 《愛称》Aggie
アシュレー **Ashley, Ashleigh**(男/女)
アダム **Adam**(男)
アディー **Addie, Addy**(女)(<Adeline, Adelaide)
アニー **Annie**(女)(<Ann(e), Anna)
アニータ **Anita**(女)
アビー **Abbie, Abb(e)y**(女)(<Abigail)
アビゲイル **Abigail**(女) ; 《愛称》Abbie, Abb(e)y
アブラハム **Abraham**(男) ; 《愛称》Abe
アマンダ **Amanda**(女) ; 《愛称》Manda, Mandy
アメリア **Amelia**(女)
アラン **Alan, Allan**(男) ; 《愛称》Al
アリス **Alice**(女) ; 《愛称》Allie, Ellie
アリスン **Alison, Allison**(女) ; 《愛称》Allie, Elsie
アル **Al**(男)(<Albert, Alfred)
アルバート **Albert**(男) ; 《愛称》Al, Bert
アルフィー **Alfie**(男)(<Alfred)
アルフレッド **Alfred**(男) ; 《愛称》Al, Alfie, Fred
アレクサンダー **Alexander**(男) ; 《愛称》Alec, Aleck, Alex, Sandy
アレクサンドラ **Alexandra**(女) ; 《愛称》Sandra, Sandie, Alex
アレック(ス) **Alec, Aleck, Alex**(男/女)(<Alexander/Alexandra)
アレン **Allen**(男)
アン **Ann, Anne**(女) ; 《愛称》Annie, Nancy
アンジェラ **Angela**(女) ; 《愛称》Angie
アンディー **Andy, Andie**(男/女)(<Andrew/Andrea)
アントーニア **Antonia**(女) ; 《愛称》Toni, Tony
アントニー **Anthony, Antony**(男) ; 《愛称》Tony
アンドリュー **Andrew**(男) ; 《愛称》Andy
アンドレア **Andrea**(女) ; 《愛称》Andie, Andy
イアン **Ian**(男)
イーサン **Ethan**(男)
イーデス **Edith**(女) ; 《愛称》Edie
イザベラ **Isabella**(女) ; 《愛称》Bella
イザベル **Isabel, Isabelle**(女) ; 《愛称》Bel
イブ **Eve**(女) ; 《愛称》Evie
イライジャ **Elijah**(男)
ウィリアム **William**(男) ; 《愛称》Bill, Billy, Will, Willy
ウィル **Will**(男)(<William)
ウェイン **Wayne**(男)
ウェンディー **Wendy**(女)
ウォールター **Walter**(男) ; 《愛称》Walt, Wat, Wally
ウォールト **Walt**(男)(<Walter)
ウォーレン **Warren**(男)
エイヴァ **Ava**(女)
エイブ **Abe**(男)(<Abraham)
エイミー **Amy**(女)
エド **Ed**(男)(<Edgar, Edward, Edwin)
エドウィン **Edwin**(男) ; 《愛称》Ed, Eddie, Ned
エドガー **Edgar**(男) ; 《愛称》Ed, Eddie, Ned
エドワード **Edward**(男) ; 《愛称》Ed, Eddie, Ned, Ted, Teddy
エバ **Eva, Eve**(女) ; 《愛称》Evie
エブリン **Evelyn**(男/女)
エマ **Emma**(女) ; 《愛称》Em, Emmie
エミー **Emmie, Emmy**(女)(<Emily, Emma)
エミリー **Emily, Emilie**(女) ; 《愛称》Emmie, Emmy
エリー **Ellie**(女)(<Eleanor, Alice, Helen)
エリカ **Erica**(女)
エリザベス **Elizabeth**(女) ; 《愛称》Bess, Bessie, Beth, Betty, Eliza, Lisa, Liz, Lizzie, Liza
エリック **Eric**(男)
エレノア **Eleanor, Elinor**(女) ; 《愛称》Elle, Ellie, Nell, Nellie
エレン **Ellen**(女) ; 《愛称》Ellie, Nellie
オードリー **Audrey**(女)
オスカー **Oscar**(男)
オリバー **Oliver**(男) ; 《愛称》Ollie
オリビア **Olivia**(女)

カ 行

カーチス **Curtis**(男)
ガートルード **Gertrude**(女)；《愛称》Gert, Gertie, Trudy
カール **Carl, Karl**(男)(<Charles)
カレン **Karen**(女)
キース **Keith**(男)
キット **Kit**(男)(<Christopher)
キティー **Kitty**(女)(<Katherine, Catherine)
キム **Kim**(女／男)(<Kimberly／Kimberley)
キャサリン **Catherine, Katherine, Catharine, Kathryn**(女)；《愛称》Cathie, Cathy, Kathy, Kate, Kay, Kitty
キャシー **Cathie, Cathy, Kathy**(女)(<Catherine)
キャスリーン **Kathleen**(女)；《愛称》Kate, Kathy, Kay
キャリー **Carrie**(女)(<Caroline)
キャロライン **Caroline, Carolyn**(女)；《愛称》Caro, Carrie
キャロル **Carol(l), Carroll**(男)；**Carol(e)**(女)
ギルバート **Gilbert**(男)；《愛称》Bert, Gib
キンバリー **Kimberly, Kimberley**(女／男)；《愛称》Kim
クインシー **Quincy**(男)
グラハム **Graham**(男)
クリス **Chris**(男／女)(<Christopher／Christina, Christine)
クリスティー **Christie**(女／男)(<Christine／Christopher)
クリスティーナ **Christina**(女)；《愛称》Chris, Tina
クリスティ(ー)ン **Christine, Kristin**(女)；《愛称》Chris, Christie, Tina
クリストファー **Christopher**(男)；《愛称》Chris, Kit, Christie
クリフ **Cliff**(男)(<Clifford)
クリフォード **Clifford**(男)；《愛称》Cliff
クレア **Claire, Clare**(女)
クレーグ **Craig**(男)
グレース **Grace**(女)；《愛称》Gracie
グレゴリー **Gregory**(男)；《愛称》Greg
グレッグ **Greg, Gregg**(男)(<Gregory, Gregor)
グレン **Glen**(男)；**Glenn**(男／女)
ケイ **Kay**(女)(<Katherine)
ケイシー **Casey**(男)
ケイト **Kate**(女)(<Katherine, Kathleen, Catherine)
ゲイル **Gail, Gale**(女)
ゲーリー **Gary, Garry**(男)；《愛称》Gaz
ケネス **Kenneth**(男)；《愛称》Ken, Kenny
ケビン **Kevin**(男)
ケン **Ken**(男)(<Kenneth)
ケント **Kent**(男)
コーネリア **Cornelia**(女)；《愛称》Cory
コーリー **Corey, Cory**(男)
コニー **Connie**(女)(<Constance)
コリーン **Colleen**(女)
コリン **Colin**(男)

サ 行

サイ **Si**(男)(<Simon)
サイモン **Simon**(男)；《愛称》Si
サイラス **Silas**(男)
サマンサ **Samantha**(女)
サミュエル **Samuel**(男)；《愛称》Sam, Sammy
サム **Sam**(男)(<Samuel)
サラ **Sarah, Sara**(女)；《愛称》Sally, Sadie
サリー **Sally, Sallie**(女)(<Sarah)
サンディー **Sandy, Sandie**(男／女)(<Alexander／Alexandra)
サンドラ **Sandra**(女)(<Alexandra)
ジーニー **Jeanie, Jeannie**(女)(<Jean)
シーラ **Sheila**(女)
[1]ジーン **Gene**(男)(<Eugene)
[2]ジーン **Jean, Jeanne**(女)；《愛称》Jeanie, Jeannie
ジェイコブ **Jacob**(男)；《愛称》Jake
ジェイソン **Jason**(男)
ジェイムズ **James**(男)；《愛称》Jim, Jimmy
ジェイン **Jane**(女)；《愛称》Janet, Jenny
ジェシー **Jessie**(男／女)(<Jesse／Jessica)
ジェシカ **Jessica**(女)；《愛称》Jessie, Jess
ジェス **Jesse**(男)；《愛称》Jessie, Jess
ジェニー **Jenny, Jennie, Jenni**(女)(<Jane, Jennifer)
ジェニファー **Jennifer**(女)；《愛称》Jen, Jenny, Jenni, Jenna
ジェフ **Jeff, Geoff**(男)(<Jeffrey, Geoffrey)
ジェフリー **Jeffrey, Geoffrey**(男)；《愛称》Jeff, Geoff
ジェラルディーン **Geraldine**(女)；《愛称》Gerry, Jerry
ジェラルド **Gerald**(男)；《愛称》Gerry, Jerry
シェリー **Sherry**(女)(<Shirley)
ジェリー **Gerry, Jerry**(男／女)(<Gerald, Gerard, Jeremy／Geraldine)
シェリル **Cheryl, Sheryl**(女)；《愛称》Cher
ジェレミー **Jeremy**(男)；《愛称》Jerry
シド **Sid**(男／女)(<Sidney)
シドニー **Sidney, Sydney**(男／女)；《愛称》Sid
ジニー **Ginny**(女)(<Virginia)
ジム **Jim**(男)(<James)
シャーリー **Shirley**(女)；《愛称》Sherry, Shirl
シャーロット **Charlotte**(女)；《愛称》Lotte, Lottie, Lola, Lotta, Charlie
ジャクリーン **Jacqueline**(女)；《愛称》Jackie, Jacqui
ジャスティーナ **Justina**(女)；《愛称》Tina
ジャスティン **Justin**(男)
ジャッキー **Jackie, Jacky**(女／男)(<Jacqueline／Jack)
ジャック **Jack**(男)(<John)
ジャニス **Janice**(女)
ジャネット **Janet**(女)
シャノン **Shannon**(女)
シャロン **Sharon**(女)
ジュディー **Judy, Judie**(女)(<Judith)
ジュディス **Judith**(女)；《愛称》Judy, Jody
ジュリア **Julia**(女)；《愛称》Jill, Julie
ジュリアン **Julian, Julien**(男)
ジュリー **Julie**(女)(<Julia)

ジョアン，ジョアンナ　Joanne，Joanna(女)；《愛称》Jo
ジョイス　Joyce(女／男)
ジョエル　Joel(男)；《愛称》Joe, Joey
[1]ジョー　**Joe**(男)(<Joel, Joseph)
[2]ジョー　**Jo**(女)(<Joanne, Joanna, Josephine)
ジョーイ　**Joey**(男)(<Joel, Joseph)
ジョージ　George(男)；《愛称》Georgie, Geordie
ジョーゼフ　Joseph(男)；《愛称》Joe, Joey
ショーン　Sean(男)
ジョーン　Joan(女)
ジョシュア　Joshua(男)；《愛称》Josh
ジョディー　**Jodie，Jody**(女)(<Judith)
ジョナサン　Jonathan(男)
ジョニー　**Johnny，Johnnie**(男)(<John)
ジョン　John(男)；《愛称》Johnny, Jack
ジル　**Jill**(女)(<Julia, Juliana)
シルビア　Silvia，Sylvia(女)；《愛称》Silvie
シルビー　**Silvie**(女)(<Silvia)
シンシア　Cynthia(女)；《愛称》Cindy, Cindi
ジンジャー　**Ginger**(女)(<Virginia)
シンディー　**Cindy**(女)(<Cynthia)
スー　**Sue**(女)(<Susan, Susannah)
スーザン　Susan(女)；《愛称》Sue, Susie
スージー　**Susie**(女)(<Susan, Susanna, Susannah)
スコット　Scott(男)
スザンナ　Susanna，Susannah(女)；《愛称》Sue, Susie
スタンリー　Stanley(男)；《愛称》Stan
スチーブン→スティーブン
スチュアート　Stuart，Stewart(男)；《愛称》Stu, Stew
スティーブ　**Steve**(男)(<Steven, Stephen)
スティーブン　Steven，Stephen(男)；《愛称》Steve, Stevie
ステイシー　Stacey，Stacy(女／男)
ステファニー　Stephanie(女)；《愛称》Steff, Stevie
ストゥー　**Stu，Stew**(男)(<Stuart, Stewart)
セイディー　**Sadie**(女)(<Sarah)
セオドア　Theodore(男)；《愛称》Ted, Teddy, Theo, Terry
セシール　Cecile(女)
セシル　Cecil(男)
ゾーイ　Zoe(女)
ソフィア　Sophia(女)；《愛称》Sophie
ソフィー　**Sophie**(女)(<Sophia)

タ 行

ダイ　**Di**(女)(<Diana, Diane)
ダイアナ　Diana(女)；《愛称》Di, Dee
ダイアン　Diane(女)；《愛称》Di
ダグ　**Doug**(男)(<Douglas)
ダグラス　Douglas(男)；《愛称》Doug
ダスティン　Dustin(男)
ダニー　**Danny**(男)(<Daniel)
ダニエール　Danielle(女)
ダニエル　Daniel(男)；《愛称》Dan, Danny
ダレル　Darrel(l)，Darryl(男)
ダレン　Darren，Darron(男)
ダン　**Dan**(男)(<Daniel)
チャーリー　**Charley，Charlie**(男／女)(<Charles／Charlotte)
チャールズ　Charles(男)；《愛称》Charley, Charlie, Chuck, Chaz
チャック　**Chuck**(男)(<Charles)
ディーン　Dean，Deane，Dene(男)
ディック　**Dick**(男)(<Richard)
ティナ　**Tina**(女)(<Christina, Christine, Justina)
デイビー　**Davy，Davie**(男)(<David)
デイブ　**Dave**(男)(<David)
ティム　**Tim**(男)(<Timothy)
ティモシー　Timothy(男)；《愛称》Tim, Timmy
ティルダ　**Tilda**(女)(<Mathilda, Matilda)
テオ　**Theo**(男)(<Theodore)
テス　**Tess**(女)(<Theresa, Teresa)
テッド　**Ted**(男)(<Edward, Theodore)
デニー　**Denny**(男)(<Dennis)
デニーズ　Denise(女)
デニス　Dennis，Denis(男)；《愛称》Den, Denny
デビー　**Debbie，Debby**(女)(<Deborah)
デビッド　David(男)；《愛称》Dave, Davey, Davy, Davie
デボラ　Deborah，Debora，Debra(女)；《愛称》Deb(s), Debbie
デューク　Duke(男)
テリー　**Terry**(男)(<Theodore, Terence)；**Terry，Terri**(女)(<Theresa, Teresa)
デリック　Derek，Derrick(男)
テレサ　Theresa，Teresa(女)；《愛称》Tess, Terry, Terri
テレンス　Terence，Terrence(男)；《愛称》Terry
ト(ー)マス　Thomas(男)；《愛称》Tom, Tommy
ドーラ　**Dora**(女)(<Dorothy, Doris)
ドナ　Donna(女)
ドナルド　Donald(男)；《愛称》Don, Donny
トニー　**Tony**(男)(<Anthony)；**Toni，Tony**(女)(<Antonia)
トム　**Tom**(男)(<Thomas)
ドリー　**Dolly**(女)(<Dorothy)
ドリーン　Doreen，Dorene(女)
ドリス　Doris(女)；《愛称》Dolly, Dora
トレイシー　Tracey，Tracy(女／男)
ドロシー　Dorothy(女)；《愛称》Doll, Dolly, Dora, Dot, Dottie
ドン　**Don**(男)(<Donald)

ナ 行

ナイジェル　Nigel(男)
ナオミ　Naomi(女)
ナサニエル　Nathaniel，Nathaneal(男)；《愛称》Nat
ナタリー　Natalie，Nathalie(女)；《愛称》Nat,

Nattie
ナット　Nat(男／女)(<Nathaniel, Nathan／Natalie)
ナンシー　Nancy(女)(<Ann(e), Anna)
ニーナ　Nina(女)
ニール　Neil, Neal(男)
ニコール　Nicole(女)；《愛称》Nicky, Nikki
ニコラス　Nicholas, Nicolas(男)；《愛称》Nick, Nicky, Nicol
ニコル　Nicol(男)(<Nicholas)
ニッキー　Nicky(男／女)(<Nicholas, Nicol／Nicole, Nicola)
ニック　Nick(男)(<Nicholas)
ネーサン　Nathan(男)；《愛称》Nat
ネッド　Ned(男)(<Edward, Edwin, Edgar, Edmond)
ネリー　Nellie, Nelly(女)(<Helen, Eleanor, Ellen)
ノア　Noah(男)
ノエル　Noel(男／女)；Noelle(女)
ノーマ　Norma(女)
ノーマン　Norman(男)；《愛称》Norm

ハ行

バーサ　Bertha(女)；《愛称》Bertie, Berty, Bert
バージニア　Virginia(女)；《愛称》Ginny, Ginger, Virg
バート　Bert, Burt(男)(<Albert, Gilbert, Herbert, Hubert, Robert, Bertram)
バーナード　Bernard(男)；《愛称》Berney, Bern
バーニー　Bernie(男)(<Bernard)
ハーパー　Harper(女)
ハーバート　Herbert(男)；《愛称》Herb, Bert, Berty
バーバラ　Barbara(女)；《愛称》Bab, Babs, Barby, Barbie, Barb
ハービー　Harvey(男)；《愛称》Harve
バービー　Barby, Barbie(女)(<Barbara)
ハーブ　Herb(男)(<Herbert)；Harve(男)(<Harvey)
パール　Pearl(女)
パット　Pat(男／女)(<Patrick／Patricia)
ハティー　Hatty, Hattie(女)(<Harriet(te))
パティー　Pattie, Patty(女)(<Patricia)
パトリシア　Patricia(女)；《愛称》Pat, Pattie, Paddy, Tricia
パトリック　Patrick, Patric(男)；《愛称》Pat, Paddy
バブ(ズ)　Bab, Babs(女)(<Barbara)
パメラ　Pamela(女)；《愛称》Pam
ハリー　Harry(男)(<Henry, Harold)
バリー　Barry(男)
ハリエット　Harriet(te), Harriot(女)；《愛称》Hattie, Hatty
ハル　Hal(男)(<Harold, Henry)
バレリー　Valerie, Valery(女)
ハロルド　Harold(男)；《愛称》Hal, Harry
ハンク　Hank(男)(<Henry)
ピーター　Peter(男)；《愛称》Pete
ピート　Pete(男)(<Peter)
ビクター　Victor(男)；《愛称》Vic, Vick
ビクトリア　Victoria(女)；《愛称》Vickie, Vicky, Vikki
ビッキー　Vickie, Vicky, Vikki(女)(<Victoria)
ビック　Vic, Vick(男)(<Victor)
ビバリー　Beverley, Beverly(女)
ヒュー　Hugh(男)
ヒラリー　Hilary(男)；Hillary, Hilary(女)
ビル　Bill(男)(<William)
ヒルダ　Hilda(女)
ビンセント　Vincent(男)；《愛称》Vin, Vince
ファニー　Fannie, Fanny(女)(<Frances)
フィリップ　Philip, Phillip(男)；《愛称》Phil
フィル　Phil(男)(<Philip)
フェリックス　Felix(男)
ブライアン　Brian, Bryan(男)
ブラッド　Brad(男)(<Bradley, Bradford)
ブラッドレー　Bradley(男)；《愛称》Brad
フラニー　Frannie(女)(<Frances)
フラン　Fran(女／男)(<Frances／Francis)
フランク　Frank(男)(<Francis)
フランクリン　Franklin(男)
[1]フランシス　Frances(女)；《愛称》Fannie, Fran, Frannie
[2]フランシス　Francis(男)；《愛称》Frank, Franky, Fran
ブランディ　Brandy(女)
ブランドン　Brandon(男)
プリシラ　Priscilla(女)；《愛称》Prissie
ブルース　Bruce(男)
フレッド　Fred(男)(<Frederick, Alfred)
フレデリック　Frederick(男)；《愛称》Fred, Freddy
フロー　Flo(女)(<Florence)
フローレンス　Florence(女)；《愛称》Flo, Florrie, Flossie
ヘイリー　Hayley, Haylee, Hailey(女)
ペギー　Peggy(女)(<Margaret)
ヘザー　Heather(女)
ベス　Bess, Beth(女)(<Elizabeth)
ベッキー　Becky(女)(<Rebecca)
ベティー　Betty, Bettie(女)(<Elizabeth)
ベラ　Bella(女)(<Isabella, Isabel, Arabel)
ヘレン　Helen(女)；《愛称》Ellie, Nellie
ベン　Ben(男)(<Benjamin)
ベンジャミン　Benjamin(男)；《愛称》Ben, Benny, Benjie
ヘンリー　Henry(男)；《愛称》Harry, Hank, Hal
ヘンリエッタ　Henrietta(女)；《愛称》Etta
ポーラ　Paula(女)
ポール　Paul(男)
ホセ　José(男)
ボビー　Bobby, Bobbie, Bobbi(男／女)(<Robert／Roberta)
ボブ　Bob(男)(<Robert)

マ行

マーカス **Marcus**(男)
マーガレット **Margaret**(女)；《愛称》Maggie, Meg, Peggy, Peg, Margot, Marge
マーク **Mark**(男)
マーサ **Martha**(女)；《愛称》Marty, Mat, Mattie, Pat
マーチン **Martin**(男)；《愛称》Marty
マーティー **Marty**(男／女)(<Martin／Martha)
マービン **Marvin, Mervin**(男)
マイク **Mike**(男)(<Michael)
マイケル **Michael**(男)；《愛称》Mick, Micky, Mike, Mitch
マイロ **Milo**(男)
マギー **Maggie**(女)(<Margaret)
マクシミリアン **Maximilian**(男)；《愛称》Max
マシュー **Matthew, Mathew**(男)；《愛称》Matt, Matty
マチルダ **Mathilda, Matilda**(女)；《愛称》Mat, Mattie, Tilda
マック **Mack, Mac**(男)
マックス **Max**(男)(<Maximilian, Maxwell)
マット **Matt**(男)(<Matthew)；**Mat**(女)(<Mathilda, Martha)
マテオ **Mateo**(男)
マライア **Maria(h)**(女)
マリア **Maria**(女)
マリー **Marie**(女)
マリリン **Marilyn, Marylyn(ne)**(女)
マルカム **Malcolm**(男)
マンディー **Mandy**(女)(<Amanda)
ミア **Mia**(女)
ミシェル **Michelle, Michele**(女)
ミッキー **Mickey, Micky**(男)(<Michael)
メアリー **Mary**(女)；《愛称》Molly, Polly
メイ **May**(女)
メイソン **Mason**(男)
メグ **Meg**(女)(<Margaret)
メラニー **Melanie**(女)；《愛称》Mel
メリッサ **Melissa**(女)
モー **Mo**(女／男)(<Maureen／Maurice, Morris)
モ(ー)リス **Maurice, Morris**(男)；《愛称》Mo
モニカ **Monica, Monique**(女)
モリー **Molly**(女)(<Mary)
モリーン **Maureen**(女)
モンゴメリー **Montgomery**(男)

ヤ行

ユージン **Eugene**(男)；《愛称》Gene

ラ行

ライアン **Ryan**(男／女)
ライザ **Liza, Lisa**(女)(<Elizabeth)
ライナス **Linus**(男)
ラリー **Larry**(男)(<Lawrence)
ラルフ **Ralph**(男)
ランディー **Randy**(男)(<Randolph)
ランドル **Randall**(男)
ランドルフ **Randolph**(男)；《愛称》Randy
リアム **Liam**(男)
リー **Lee, Leigh**(男／女)
リサ **Lisa**(女)(<Elizabeth)
リズ **Liz**(女)(<Elizabeth)
リチャード **Richard**(男)；《愛称》Rich, Rick, Ricky, Dick
リック **Rick**(男)(<Richard)
リン **Lynn**(男)；**Lynn(e)**(女)
リンジー **Lindsey, Lindsay, Linsey**(女／男)
リンダ **Linda, Lynda**(女)；《愛称》Lindy
ルイ **Louis**(男)；《愛称》Lou
ルイーズ **Louise**(女)；《愛称》Lou, Lu
ルイス **Lewis**(男)；《愛称》Lew
ルー **Lou, Lew**(男)(<Louis, Lewis)；**Lou, Lu**(女)(<Louise)
ルーカス **Lucas**(男)
ルーク **Luke**(男)
ルーシー **Lucy, Luci**(女)；《愛称》Lucille
ルナ **Luna**(女)
レイ **Ray**(男)(<Raymond)；**Rae, Ray(e)**(女)(<Rachel)
レイチェル **Rachel**(女)；《愛称》Rae, Ray(e)
レイモンド **Raymond, Raymund**(男)；《愛称》Ray
レジー **Reggy**(男)(<Reginald)
レジナルド **Reginald**(男)；《愛称》Reg, Reggy
レズ **Les**(男／女)(<Leslie, Lester)
レズリー **Leslie**(男)；**Lesley**(女)；《愛称》Les
レナード **Leonard**(男)；《愛称》Len, Lenny
レベッカ **Rebecca**(女)；《愛称》Becca, Back, Becky
ロイ **Roy**(男)
ローガン **Logan**(男)
ローズ **Rose**(女)；《愛称》Rosie
ローズマリー **Rosemary**(女)；《愛称》Rosie
ローラ **Laura**(女)；《愛称》Laurie, Lolly
ローリー **Laurie**(男／女)(<Laurence／Laura)
ローレンス **Lawrence, Laurence**(男)；《愛称》Larry, Laurie
ロザリン **Rosalyn**(女)(<Rosalind)
ロザリンド **Rosalind**(女)；《愛称》Ros, Rosalyn
ロジャー **Roger**(男)
ロッティー **Lottie, Lotty**(女)(<Charlotte)
ロッド **Rod**(男)(<Rodney, Roderick)
ロドニー **Rodney**(男)；《愛称》Rod, Roddy
ロナルド **Ronald**(男)；《愛称》Ron, Ronny
ロバータ **Roberta**(女)；《愛称》Bobbie
ロバート **Robert**(男)；《愛称》Bob, Bobby, Robin, Rob, Bert, Berty
ロビン **Robin**(男／女)(<Robert)
ロブ **Rob**(男)(<Robert)
ロリ **Lorrie, Lori**(女)(<Lorraine)
ロレーン **Lorraine**(女)；《愛称》Lorrie, Lori
ロン **Ron**(男)(<Ronald)

不規則動詞変化表

原形	過去形	過去分詞形	-ing 形	意味
abide	abided, abode	abided, abode	abiding	我慢する，住む
alight	alighted, alit	alighted, alit	alighting	降りる
arise	arose	arisen	arising	発生する
awake	**awoke,** awaked	**awoken,** awaked	**awaking**	**目が覚める**
backslide	backslid	backslid, backslidden	backsliding	逆戻りする
be (am; is; are)	**was; were**	**been**	**being**	**…である**
bear	**bore**	**borne, born**	**bearing**	**運ぶ，生む**
beat	**beat**	**beaten, beat**	**beating**	**打つ**
become	**became**	**become**	**becoming**	**…になる**
befall	befell	befallen	befalling	降りかかる
begin	**began**	**begun**	**beginning**	**始まる**
behold	beheld	beheld	beholding	見る
bend	**bent**	**bent**	**bending**	**曲げる**
bereave	bereaved, bereft	bereaved, bereft	bereaving	奪う
beseech	besought, beseeched	besought, beseeched	beseeching	嘆願する
beset	beset	beset	besetting	包囲する
bespeak	bespoke	bespoken	bespeaking	示す
bestrew	bestrewed	bestrewed, bestrewn	bestrewing	まき散らす
bestride	bestrode, bestrid	bestridden, bestrid	bestriding	またがる
bet	**bet, betted**	**bet, betted**	**betting**	**かける**
bid	bid; bade	bid; bidden	bidding	値をつける;述べる
bide	bode, bided	bided	biding	待つ
bind	**bound**	**bound**	**binding**	**縛る**
bite	**bit**	**bitten**	**biting**	**かむ**
bleed	**bled**	**bled**	**bleeding**	**出血する**
bless	**blessed,** blest	**blessed,** blest	**blessing**	**祝福する**
blow	**blew**	**blown**	**blowing**	**吹く**
break	**broke**	**broken**	**breaking**	**こわす**
breed	bred	bred	breeding	繁殖する［させる］
bring	**brought**	**brought**	**bringing**	**持って来る**
broadcast	**broadcast,** broadcasted	**broadcast,** broadcasted	**broadcasting**	**放送する**
browbeat	browbeat	browbeaten	browbeating	おどしつける
build	**built**	**built**	**building**	**建てる**
burn	**burned, burnt**	**burned, burnt**	**burning**	**焼く**
burst	**burst**	**burst**	**bursting**	**破裂する**
bust	busted, bust	busted, bust	busting	破裂させる
buy	**bought**	**bought**	**buying**	**買う**
cast	**cast**	**cast**	**casting**	**投げる**
catch	**caught**	**caught**	**catching**	**捕まえる**
chide	chided, chid	chided, chidden, chid	chiding	小言を言う
choose	**chose**	**chosen**	**choosing**	**選ぶ**
cleave	cleaved, cleft, clove	cleaved, cleft, cloven	cleaving	切り裂く
cling	**clung**	**clung**	**clinging**	**くっつく**
come	**came**	**come**	**coming**	**来る**
cost	**cost**	**cost**	**costing**	**(金額を)要する**
creep	**crept**	**crept**	**creeping**	**はう**

原　形	過去形	過去分詞形	-ing 形	意　味
cut	cut	cut	cutting	切る
deal	dealt	dealt	dealing	分配する
dig	dug	dug	digging	掘る
dive	dived, dove	dived	diving	水に飛び込む
do (does)	did	done	doing	する
draw	drew	drawn	drawing	引く
dream	dreamed, dreamt	dreamed, dreamt	dreaming	夢を見る
drink	drank	drunk	drinking	飲む
drive	drove	driven	driving	追い立てる，運転する
dwell	dwelt, dwelled	dwelt, dwelled	dwelling	住む
eat	ate	eaten	eating	食べる
fall	fell	fallen	falling	落ちる
feed	fed	fed	feeding	食物を与える
feel	felt	felt	feeling	触る，感じる
fight	fought	fought	fighting	戦う
find	found	found	finding	見つける
fit	fitted, fit	fitted, fit	fitting	ぴったり合う
flee	fled	fled	fleeing	逃げる
fling	flung	flung	flinging	投げる
fly	flew	flown	flying	飛ぶ
forbear	forbore	forborne	forbearing	差し控える
forbid	forbade, forbad	forbidden	forbidding	禁じる
forecast	forecast, forecasted	forecast, forecasted	forecasting	予報する
foresee	foresaw	foreseen	foreseeing	予測する
foretell	foretold	foretold	foretelling	予告する
forget	forgot	forgotten, forgot	forgetting	忘れる
forgive	forgave	forgiven	forgiving	許す
forgo	forwent	forgone	forgoing	なしで済ませる
forsake	forsook	forsaken	forsaking	見捨てる
forswear	forswore	forsworn	forswearing	誓ってやめる
freeze	froze	frozen	freezing	凍る
gainsay	gainsaid	gainsaid	gainsaying	否定する
geld	gelded, gelt	gelded, gelt	gelding	去勢する
get	got	gotten, got	getting	得る
gild	gilded, gilt	gilded, gilt	gilding	金ぱくをかぶせる
gird	girded, girt	girded, girt	girding	締める
give	gave	given	giving	与える
go	went	gone	going	行く
grind	ground	ground	grinding	粉にひく
grow	grew	grown	growing	成長する
hang	hung; hanged	hung; hanged	hanging	掛ける；絞首刑にする
have (has)	had	had	having	持っている
hear	heard	heard	hearing	聞こえる
heave	heaved; hove	heaved; hove	heaving	上げる；巻き上げる
hew	hewed	hewed, hewn	hewing	たたき切る
hide	hid	hidden, hid	hiding	隠す
hit	hit	hit	hitting	打つ
hold	held	held	holding	手に持つ
hurt	hurt	hurt	hurting	けがをさせる
inlay	inlaid	inlaid	inlaying	はめ込む
input	inputted, input	inputted, input	inputting	入力する
inset	insetted, inset	insetted, inset	insetting	差し込む
interbreed	interbred	interbred	interbreeding	異種交配させる
keep	kept	kept	keeping	持ち続ける
kneel	knelt, kneeled	knelt, kneeled	kneeling	ひざまずく

原　形	過去形	過去分詞形	-ing 形	意　味
knit	**knitted, knit**	**knitted, knit**	**knitting**	**編む**
know	**knew**	**known**	**knowing**	**知っている**
lay	**laid**	**laid**	**laying**	**横たえる**
lead	**led**	**led**	**leading**	**導く**
lean	**leaned,** leant	**leaned,** leant	**leaning**	**もたれる**
leap	**leapt, leaped**	**leapt, leaped**	**leaping**	**跳ぶ**
learn	**learned,** learnt	**learned,** learnt	**learning**	**習い覚える**
leave	**left**	**left**	**leaving**	**去る**
lend	**lent**	**lent**	**lending**	**貸す**
let	**let**	**let**	**letting**	**…させる**
lie	**lay**	**lain**	**lying**	**横たわる**
light	**lit, lighted**	**lit, lighted**	**lighting**	**火をつける**
lose	**lost**	**lost**	**losing**	**失う**
make	**made**	**made**	**making**	**作る**
mean	**meant**	**meant**	**meaning**	**意味する**
meet	**met**	**met**	**meeting**	**会う**
miscast	miscast	miscast	miscasting	不適当な役に割り当てる
mislay	mislaid	mislaid	mislaying	置き忘れる
mislead	misled	misled	misleading	誤った方向に導く
misread	misread	misread	misreading	読み違える
misspell	misspelled, misspelt	misspelled, misspelt	misspelling	つづりをまちがう
mistake	**mistook**	**mistaken**	**mistaking**	**まちがえる**
misunderstand	misunderstood	misunderstood	misunderstand-ing	誤解する
mow	mowed	mowed, mown	mowing	刈る
offset	offset	offset	offsetting	相殺する
outgrow	outgrew	outgrown	outgrowing	より大きくなる
output	outputted, output	outputted, output	outputting	出力する
overbear	overbore	overborne	overbearing	威圧する
overcome	**overcame**	**overcome**	**overcoming**	**打ち負かす**
overdo	overdid	overdone	overdoing	しすぎる
overdraw	overdrew	overdrawn	overdrawing	過振(かぶり)する
overeat	overate	overeaten	overeating	食べすぎる
overhang	overhung	overhung	overhanging	上に張り出す
overhear	overheard	overheard	overhearing	偶然に聞く
overlay	overlaid	overlaid	overlaying	おおう
overlie	overlay	overlain	overlying	上に横たわる
overpay	overpaid	overpaid	overpaying	よけいに払う
override	overrode	overridden	overriding	無視する
overrun	overran	overrun	overrunning	はびこる
oversee	oversaw	overseen	overseeing	監督する
overshoot	overshot	overshot	overshooting	(的を)通り越す
oversleep	overslept	overslept	oversleeping	寝過ごす
overtake	overtook	overtaken	overtaking	追いつく
overthrow	overthrew	overthrown	overthrowing	ひっくり返す
partake	partook	partaken	partaking	ともにする
pay	**paid**	**paid**	**paying**	**支払う**
plead	pleaded, pled	pleaded, pled	pleading	弁護する
prepay	prepaid	prepaid	prepaying	先払いする
proofread	proofread	proofread	proofreading	校正をする
prove	**proved**	**proved, proven**	**proving**	**証明する**
put	**put**	**put**	**putting**	**置く**
quit	quit, quitted	quit, quitted	quitting	やめる
read /ri:d/	**read** /red/	**read** /red/	**reading**	**読む**
rebind	rebound	rebound	rebinding	製本し直す
rebuild	rebuilt	rebuilt	rebuilding	再建する
rehear	reheard	reheard	rehearing	再び聞く
relay	relaid	relaid	relaying	再び置く
remake	remade	remade	remaking	作り直す

原　形	過去形	過去分詞形	-ing 形	意　味
rend	rent	rent	rending	引き裂く
repay	repaid	repaid	repaying	払い戻す
rerun	reran	rerun	rerunning	再上映する
reset	reset	reset	resetting	セットし直す
retake	retook	retaken	retaking	取り戻す
retell	retold	retold	retelling	再び話す
rethink	rethought	rethought	rethinking	再考する
rewind	rewound	rewound	rewinding	巻き戻す
rewrite	rewrote	rewritten	rewriting	書き直す
rid	**rid, ridded**	**rid, ridded**	**ridding**	取り除く
ride	**rode**	**ridden**	**riding**	乗る
ring	**rang**	**rung**	**ringing**	鳴る
rise	**rose**	**risen**	**rising**	昇る；上がる
run	**ran**	**run**	**running**	走る
saw	sawed	sawed, sawn	sawing	のこぎりでひく
say	**said**	**said**	**saying**	言う
see	**saw**	**seen**	**seeing**	見る
seek	**sought**	**sought**	**seeking**	求める
sell	**sold**	**sold**	**selling**	売る
send	**sent**	**sent**	**sending**	送る
set	**set**	**set**	**setting**	置く
sew	**sewed**	**sewn, sewed**	**sewing**	縫う
shake	**shook**	**shaken**	**shaking**	振る
shave	**shaved**	**shaved,** shaven	**shaving**	(ひげを)そる
shear	sheared	sheared, shorn	shearing	(毛を)刈る
shed	**shed**	**shed**	**shedding**	(血・涙を)流す
shine	**shined; shone**	**shined; shone**	**shining**	輝く；みがく
shoe	shod, shoed	shod, shoed	shoeing	靴をはかせる
shoot	**shot**	**shot**	**shooting**	撃つ
show	**showed**	**shown**	**showing**	見せる
shrink	shrank, shrunk	shrunk, shrunken	shrinking	縮む
shut	**shut**	**shut**	**shutting**	閉める，閉じる
sing	**sang**	**sung**	**singing**	歌う
sink	**sank, sunk**	**sunk,** sunken	**sinking**	沈む
sit	**sat**	**sat**	**sitting**	座っている
slay	slew	slain	slaying	殺す
sleep	**slept**	**slept**	**sleeping**	眠る
slide	**slid**	**slid**	**sliding**	滑る
sling	slung	slung	slinging	投げる
slink	slunk	slunk	slinking	こそこそ歩く
slit	slit	slit	slitting	切り開く
smell	**smelled, smelt**	**smelled, smelt**	**smelling**	においをかぐ
smite	smote	smitten	smiting	強打する
sneak	sneaked, snuck	sneaked, snuck	sneaking	こそこそ動く
sow	sowed	sown, sowed	sowing	(種を)まく
speak	**spoke**	**spoken**	**speaking**	話す
speed	**sped, speeded**	**sped, speeded**	**speeding**	促進する，スピードを上げる
spell	**spelled, spelt**	**spelled, spelt**	**spelling**	つづる
spend	**spent**	**spent**	**spending**	(金を)使う
spill	**spilled, spilt**	**spilled, spilt**	**spilling**	(液体を)こぼす
spin	**spun**	**spun**	**spinning**	紡ぐ
spit	**spat, spit**	**spat, spit**	**spitting**	つばを吐く
split	**split**	**split**	**splitting**	割る
spoil	**spoiled, spoilt**	**spoiled, spoilt**	**spoiling**	台なしにする
spread	**spread**	**spread**	**spreading**	広げる
spring	**sprang, sprung**	**sprung**	**springing**	跳ぶ
stand	**stood**	**stood**	**standing**	立っている

原　　形	過去形	過去分詞形	-ing 形	意　　味
stave	staved, stove	staved, stove	staving	穴をあける
steal	stole	stolen	stealing	盗む
stick	stuck	stuck	sticking	突き刺す
sting	stung	stung	stinging	刺す
stink	stank, stunk	stunk	stinking	悪臭を出す
strew	strewed	strewed, strewn	strewing	まき散らす
stride	strode	stridden	striding	大またに歩く
strike	struck	struck, stricken	striking	打つ
string	strung	strung	stringing	糸に通す
strive	strove, strived	striven, strived	striving	努力する
sublet	sublet	sublet	subletting	また貸しする
swear	swore	sworn	swearing	誓う
sweat	sweated, sweat	sweated, sweat	sweating	汗をかく
sweep	swept	swept	sweeping	掃く
swell	swelled	swelled, swollen	swelling	ふくらむ
swim	swam	swum	swimming	泳ぐ
swing	swung	swung	swinging	揺り動かす
take	took	taken	taking	手に取る
teach	taught	taught	teaching	教える
tear	tore	torn	tearing	裂く
tell	told	told	telling	話す
think	thought	thought	thinking	考える
thrive	thrived, throve	thrived, thriven	thriving	繁栄する
throw	threw	thrown	throwing	投げる
thrust	thrust	thrust	thrusting	強く押す
tread	trod	trodden, trod	treading	踏む
unbend	unbent	unbent	unbending	まっすぐにする
unbind	unbound	unbound	unbinding	縛りを解く
undergo	underwent	undergone	undergoing	(苦難を)経験する
underlie	underlay	underlain	underlying	下にある
undersell	undersold	undersold	underselling	より安く売る
undershoot	undershot	undershot	undershooting	到達できない
understand	understood	understood	understanding	理解する
undertake	undertook	undertaken	undertaking	引き受ける
underwrite	underwrote	underwritten	underwriting	保険をつける
undo	undid	undone	undoing	ほどく, はずす
unwind	unwound	unwound	unwinding	巻き戻す
uphold	upheld	upheld	upholding	支える
upset	upset	upset	upsetting	動揺させる
wake	woke, waked	woken, waked, woke	waking	目を覚ます
waylay	waylaid	waylaid	waylaying	待ち伏せする
wear	wore	worn	wearing	着ている
weave	wove ; weaved	woven, wove; weaved	weaving	織る ; ジグザグに進む
wed	wed, wedded	wed, wedded	wedding	結婚する
weep	wept	wept	weeping	泣く
wet	wet, wetted	wet, wetted	wetting	ぬらす
whip	whipped, whipt	whipped, whipt	whipping	むちを当てる
win	won	won	winning	勝つ
wind	wound	wound	winding	巻く
withdraw	withdrew	withdrawn	withdrawing	引っ込める
withhold	withheld	withheld	withholding	保留する
withstand	withstood	withstood	withstanding	抵抗する
work	worked; wrought	worked; wrought	working	働く ; 作り出す
wring	wrung	wrung	wringing	しぼる
write	wrote	written	writing	書く

SA

THE
SUPER ANCHOR
JAPANESE-ENGLISH
DICTIONARY
FOURTH EDITION

スーパー・アンカー和英辞典
第4版

2000年1月12日　初版発行
2021年12月28日　第4版第1刷発行

編者主幹　山岸勝榮
発行人　代田雪絵
編集人　松田こずえ
発行所　株式会社学研プラス
〒141-8415 東京都品川区西五反田2-11-8

印刷所　共同印刷株式会社
製本所　株式会社難波製本
製函所　森紙販売株式会社

●この本に関する各種お問い合わせ先
本の内容については、下記サイトのお問い合わせフォームよりお願いします。
https://gakken-plus.co.jp/contact/
在庫については…販売部
Tel 03-6431-1199
不良品(落丁、乱丁)については…学研業務センター
Tel 0570-000577　〒354-0045 埼玉県入間郡三芳町上富279-1
●上記以外のお問い合わせは
Tel 0570-056-710(学研グループ総合案内)

学研の書籍・雑誌についての新刊情報・詳細情報は、下記をご覧ください。
学研出版サイト https://hon.gakken.jp/

表紙　大比良工業株式会社

英文Eメールの書き方

Eメールには，独自のルールがいくつかあり，内容や相手によって気をつける点も手紙とは多少異なる．ここでは，簡単な用件を伝えるためのメールを取り上げた．

❶件名

あとで件名だけ見たときにも中身が類推できるように，具体的に書く．“Hello”や“Thank you”といった一般的すぎる件名は避ける．

❷あいさつことば

メールでは省略してしまってもよい．

❸本文

- 事務的な内容の場合は，用件を簡潔に書く．
- 段落が変わるところでは1行空ける．
- September 18などのように日付を言うときは，月名をアルファベットでつづる．
- 他人のメールを引用するときは，内容，文体を変えずに使う．
- 特殊な文字は文字化けする可能性があるので使わない．

❹署名

名前・メールアドレス・住所・電話番号などを必要に応じて入れる．海外に出す場合は，電話番号に国番号を入れる．

宛先 garybeck@fujihigh.ac.jp

件名 practice date change ——❶

Dear Mr. Beck, ——❷

This is Ueno Yuki, the leader of the English Drama Club at Fuji High School. Thank you for helping us with our practice last Friday.

We said that our next practice would be on September 18. However we found out that three of our members couldn't make it. Therefore we'd like to change it to either September 17 or 19. Which date is better for you?

I would appreciate it if you would reply to me about this matter before September 12.

Thank you, ——❸

Ueno Yuki
E-MAIL : yukko@surfrider.ne.jp
ADDRESS : 1-2-3 Satsuki-dai, Setagaya-ku, Tokyo,
150-4567 JAPAN
PHONE : +81-(0)3-4567-8910 ——❹

訳 ❶練習日の変更 ❷ベック先生へ
❸富士高校英語劇クラブ部長の上野由希です．先週の金曜日は練習を見てくださってありがとうございました．
次の練習は9月18日とお伝えしましたが，メンバーの3人がそれには参加できないことがわかりました．そこで9月17日か19日に変えたいと思います．先生のご都合はどちらがよろしいですか．
この件について9月12日までにお返事いただければ幸いです．
どうもありがとうございました．

Eメールをもっと楽しく簡潔に!

Eメールでは，楽しくするためのスマイリー(顔文字)や，簡潔にするための略語が多用される．

スマイリー (英文は横向き，和文は縦向きに見る)

意味	英文	和文
にっこり	:-)	(^_^)
大喜び	8->	＼(^O^)／
悲しい，情けない	:-(	(;_;)
びっくり	:-o	(*_*)

略語

AAMOF＝As A Matter Of Fact …実を言うと
AKA＝Also Known As …～としても知られる
BTW＝By The Way …ところで
CU＝See You …またね
FAQ＝Frequently Asked Questions …よく尋ねられる質問
IC＝I See …わかりました
LOL＝Laughing Out Loud …大笑いだ
TIA＝Thanks In Advance …よろしく
TNX/TX＝Thanks …ありがとう